T5-BBV-428

Who's Who in the Midwest

Biographical Titles Currently Published by Marquis Who's Who

Who's Who in America

  Who's Who in America supplements:

    Who's Who in America Birthdate Index

    Who's Who in America Classroom Project Book

    Who's Who in America College Alumni Directory

    Who's Who in America Index:

      Geographic Index, Professional Area Index

Who Was Who in America

  Historical Volume (1607-1896)

  Volume I (1897-1942)

  Volume II (1943-1950)

  Volume III (1951-1960)

  Volume IV (1961-1968)

  Volume V (1969-1973)

  Volume VI (1974-1976)

  Volume VII (1977-1981)

  Volume VIII (1982-1985)

  Index Volume (1607-1985)

Who Was Who in American History—Arts and Letters

Who Was Who in American History—The Military

Who Was Who in American History—Science and Technology

Who's Who in the World

Who's Who in the East

Who's Who in the Midwest

Who's Who in the South and Southwest

Who's Who in the West

Who's Who in American Law

Who's Who of American Women

Who's Who in Finance and Industry

Who's Who in Frontiers of Science and Technology

Who's Who in Religion

World Who's Who in Science

Directory of Women in Marquis Who's Who Publications

Index to Who's Who Books

Directory of Medical Specialists

Marquis Who's Who Directory of Online Professionals

Marquis Who's Who Directory of Computer Graphics

Marquis Who's Who in Cancer: Professionals and Facilities

Marquis Who's Who in Rehabilitation: Professionals and Facilities

Marquis International Who's Who in Optical Science and Engineering

Who's Who
in the Midwest®

Including Illinois, Indiana, Iowa, Kansas, Michigan,
Minnesota, Missouri, Nebraska, North Dakota, Ohio,
South Dakota, and Wisconsin; and in Canada, Manitoba
and western Ontario

20th edition
1986-1987

MARQUIS
Who'sWho

Marquis Who's Who, Inc.
200 East Ohio Street
Chicago, Illinois 60611 U.S.A.

Copyright © 1985 Marquis Who's Who Incorporated. All rights reserved. No part of this publication may be reproduced, stored in a retrieval system or transmitted in any form or by any means, mechanical, electronic, photocopying, recording or otherwise without the prior written permission of the publisher. For information, address Marquis Who's Who Incorporated, 200 East Ohio Street, Chicago, Illinois 60611.

Library of Congress Catalog Card Number 50-289
International Standard Book Number 0-8379-0720-9
Product Code Number 030407

Distributed in Europe by
Thompson, Henry Limited
London Road
Sunningdale, Berks
SL5 OEP, England

Distributed in Asia by
United Publishers Services Ltd.
Kenkyu-Sha Bldg.
9, Kanda Surugadai 2-Chome
Chiyoda-Ku, Tokyo, Japan

Manufactured in the United States of America

Table of Contents

Preface

The twentieth edition of *Who's Who in the Midwest* represents our most recent effort to provide biographical information on men and women of distinction whose influence is concentrated in the midwestern sector of North America. Such individuals are of decided reference interest locally and, to an increasing degree, nationally.

The volume contains more than 17,000 names from the midwestern region of the United States including Illinois, Indiana, Iowa, Kansas, Michigan, Minnesota, Missouri, Nebraska, North Dakota, Ohio, South Dakota, and Wisconsin in the United States and the provinces of Manitoba and western Ontario in Canada. The twentieth edition offers up-to-the-minute coverage of a broad range of Midwesterners based on position or individual achievement.

The persons sketched in this volume represent virtually every important field of endeavor. Included are executives and officials in government, business, education, religion, the press, civic affairs, the arts, cultural affairs, law, and other fields. This edition also includes significant contributors in such fields as contemporary art, music, and science.

Most biographees have furnished their own data, thus assuring a high degree of accuracy. In some cases where individuals failed to supply information, Marquis staff members compiled the data through independent research. Such sketches are denoted by an asterisk. Brief key information is provided in the sketches of selected individuals, new to this edition, who did not submit data. Cross-references to current information in *Who's Who in America* appear for others. As in previous editions, biographees were given the opportunity to review prepublication proofs of their sketches to make sure they were correct.

The question is often asked, "How do people get into a Who's Who volume?" Name selection is based on one fundamental principle: reference value. Biographees of *Who's Who in the Midwest* can be classified in two basic categories: (1) Persons who are of regional reference importance to colleagues, librarians, researchers, scholars, the press, historians, biographers, participants in business and civic affairs, and others with specific or general inquiry needs; (2) Individuals of national reference interest who are also of such regional or local importance that their inclusion in the book is essential.

Marquis Who's Who editors exercise the utmost care in preparing each biographical sketch for publication. Occasionally, however, errors do occur. Users of this directory are requested to draw the attention of the publisher to any errors found so that corrections can be made in a later edition.

Board of Advisors

Marquis Who's Who gratefully acknowledges the following distinguished individuals who have made themselves available for review, evaluation, and general comment with regard to the publication of the twentieth edition of *Who's Who in the Midwest*. The advisors have enhanced the reference value of this edition by the nomination of outstanding individuals for inclusion. However, the Board of Advisors—either collectively or individually—is in no way responsible for the final selection of names appearing in this volume, nor does the Board of Advisors bear responsibility for the accuracy or comprehensiveness of the biographical information or other material contained herein.

Steven C. Beering
President
Purdue University

Gwendolyn Brooks
Poet

Thomas J. Clifford
President
The University of North Dakota

George A. Drake
President
Grinnell College

Horace B. Edwards
Chairman, President and
 Chief Executive Officer
ARCO Pipe Line Company

Reverend Theodore M. Hesburgh, C.S.C.
President
University of Notre Dame

Roger H. Hull
President
Beloit College

Helmut Jahn
President and Chief Executive
 Officer
Murphy/Jahn

Lester B. Knight
Chairman and Chief Executive
 Officer
Lester B. Knight & Associates, Inc.

Martin A. Massengale
Chancellor
University of Nebraska-Lincoln

Gregory Mosher
Director
The New Theatre Company

Reverend John P. Raynor, S.J.
President
Marquette University

Norman Ross
Senior Vice President
The First National Bank
 of Chicago

Irving Shain
Chancellor
University of Wisconsin-Madison

Richard H. Stanley
President
Stanley Consultants, Inc.

Charles E. Stoltz
President and Chief Executive
 Officer
Dubuque Packing Company

Maria Tallchief
Artistic Director
Chicago City Ballet

Evan H. Turner
Director
The Cleveland Museum of Art

Barbara S. Uehling
Chancellor
University of Missouri-Columbia

Marc F. Wilson
Director
The Nelson-Atkins Museum of Art

Board of Nominators

Marquis Who's Who gratefully acknowledges the following distinguished nominators for their assistance with regard to the publication of the twentieth edition of *Who's Who in the Midwest*. They have enhanced the reference value of this edition by the recommendation of outstanding individuals from the respective states or local areas of the nominators. However, the Board of Nominators—either collectively or individually—is in no way responsible for the final selection of names appearing in this volume, nor does the Board of Nominators bear responsibility for the accuracy or comprehensiveness of the biographical information or other material contained herein.

Rodney F. Benson
President
Ann Arbor Area Chamber
  of Commerce
Ann Arbor, Michigan

Robert W. Brennan
President
Greater Madison Chamber
  of Commerce
Madison, Wisconsin

William H. Bryant
President
Greater Cleveland Growth
  Association
Cleveland, Ohio

Richard G. Clark
President and Chief Executive
  Officer
The Greater Fort Wayne Chamber
  of Commerce
Fort Wayne, Indiana

Jan J. Jakiel
President
South Bend/Mishawaka Area
  Chamber of Commerce, Inc.
South Bend, Indiana

Jim Jordan
Executive Vice President
Lansing Regional Chamber
  of Commerce
Lansing, Michigan

David L. May
President
Independence Chamber
  of Commerce
Independence, Missouri

Andrew J. Mooney
President
Greater Des Moines Chamber
  of Commerce Federation
Des Moines, Iowa

James M. O'Flynn
President
St. Louis Regional Commerce
  and Growth Association
St. Louis, Missouri

Frank E. Smith
President
Greater Detroit Chamber
  of Commerce
Detroit, Michigan

Larry J. Waller
President
Cedar Rapids/Marion Area
  Chamber of Commerce
Cedar Rapids, Iowa

John P. Williams, Jr.
President
Greater Cincinnati Chamber
  of Commerce
Cincinnati, Ohio

Standards of Admission

The foremost consideration in selecting biographees for *Who's Who in the Midwest* is the extent of an individual's reference interest. Such reference interest is judged on either of two factors: (1) the position of responsibility held, or (2) the level of significant achievement attained.

Admissions based on the factor of position include:

Members of the U.S. Congress

Federal judges

Governors of states covered by this volume

Premiers of Canadian provinces covered by this volume

State attorneys general

Judges of state and territorial courts of highest appellate jurisdiction

Mayors of major cities

Heads of major universities and colleges

Heads of leading philanthropic, educational, cultural, and scientific institutions and associations

Chief ecclesiastics of the principal religious denominations

Principal officers of national and international businesses

Others chosen because of incumbency or membership

Admission for individual achievement is based on objective qualitative criteria. To be selected, a person must have attained conspicuous achievement. The biographee may scarcely be known in the local community but may be recognized in some field of endeavor for noteworthy accomplishment.

Key to Information

❶ BURKE, GEORGE ALLEN, ❷ toy manufacturing company executive; **❸** b. Highland Park, Ill., Mar. 23, 1926; **❹** s. Miles Benjamin and Thelma (Allen) B.; **❺** m. Leota Gruber, Jan. 28, 1946; **❻** children: Evangeline Marie Burke Rossett, Joseph Paul, Harvey Edwin. **❼** B.S., Northwestern U., 1949. **❽** With Millington Toy Mfg. Co., Peoria, Ill., 1950—, sales mgr., 1955-56, v.p., 1960-69, pres., 1969-76, chmn. bd., 1976—, also dir.; dir. Peoria Title and Trust Co.; lectr. Peoria Community Coll., 1967-68. **❾** Contbr. articles to bus. publs. **❿** Active Boy Scouts Am.; bd. govs. Lincolnwood Home for the Aged; sec. Ill. Gov.'s Commn. on Pub. Safety, 1972-76; mem. Peoria Heights Bd. Edn., 1956-58. **⓫** Served USNR, 1943-45; PTO. **⓬** Decorated Purple Heart; recipient Silver Beaver award Boy Scouts Am., 1967. **⓭** Mem. AIM, NAM, Beta Theta Pi. **⓮** Democrat. **⓯** Presbyterian. **⓰** Clubs: Chgo. Athletic, Peoria Lake Country. **⓱** Lodges: Masons, Shriners. **⓲** Avocations: sailing, golf. **⓳** Home: 903 Spring Dr Peoria Heights IL 61613 **⓴** Office: 1912 Main St Peoria IL 61606

KEY

- **❶** Name
- **❷** Occupation
- **❸** Vital statistics
- **❹** Parents
- **❺** Marriage
- **❻** Children
- **❼** Education
- **❽** Career
- **❾** Writings and special achievements
- **❿** Civic and political activities
- **⓫** Military record
- **⓬** Awards
- **⓭** Professional and association memberships
- **⓮** Political affiliation
- **⓯** Religion
- **⓰** Clubs
- **⓱** Lodges
- **⓲** Avocations
- **⓳** Home address
- **⓴** Office address

Table of Abbreviations

The following abbreviations and symbols are frequently used in this book.

*An asterisk following a sketch indicates that it was researched by the Marquis Who's Who editorial staff and has not been verified by the biographee.

A.A. Associate in Arts
AAAL American Academy of Arts and Letters
AAAS American Association for the Advancement of Science
AAHPER Alliance for Health, Physical Education and Recreation
AAU Amateur Athletic Union
AAUP American Association of University Professors
AAUW American Association of University Women
A.B. Arts, Bachelor of
AB Alberta
ABA American Bar Association
ABC American Broadcasting Company
AC Air Corps
acad. academy, academic
acct. accountant
accg. accounting
ACDA Arms Control and Disarmament Agency
ACLU American Civil Liberties Union
ACP American College of Physicians
ACS American College of Surgeons
ADA American Dental Association
a.d.c. aide-de-camp
adj. adjunct. adjutant
adj. gen. adjutant general
adm. admiral
adminstr. administrator
adminstrn. administration
adminstrv. administrative
ADP Automatic Data Processing
adv. advocate, advisory
advt. advertising
A.E. Agricultural Engineer (for degrees only)
A.E. and P. Ambassador Extraordinary and Plenipotentiary
AEC Atomic Energy Commission
aero. aeronautical, aeronautic
aerodyn. aerodynamic
AFB Air Force Base
AFL-CIO American Federation of Labor and Congress of Industrial Organizations
AFTRA American Federation TV and Radio Artists
agr. agriculture
agrl. agricultural
agt. agent
AGVA American Guild of Variety Artists
agy. agency
A&I Agricultural and Industrial
AIA American Institute of Architects

AIAA American Institute of Aeronautics and Astronautics
AID Agency for International Development
AIEE American Institute of Electrical Engineers
AIM American Institute of Management
AIME American Institute of Mining, Metallurgy, and Petroleum Engineers
AK Alaska
AL Alabama
ALA American Library Association
Ala. Alabama
alt. alternate
Alta. Alberta
A&M Agricultural and Mechanical
A.M. Arts, Master of
Am. American, America
AMA American Medical Association
A.M.E. African Methodist Episcopal
Amtrak National Railroad Passenger Corporation
AMVETS American Veterans of World War II, Korea, Vietnam
anat. anatomical
ann. annual
ANTA American National Theatre and Academy
anthrop. anthropological
AP Associated Press
APO Army Post Office
Apr. April
apptd. appointed
apt. apartment
AR Arkansas
ARC American Red Cross
archeol. archeological
archtl. architectural
Ariz. Arizona
Ark. Arkansas
ArtsD. Arts, Doctor of
arty. artillery
ASCAP American Society of Composers, Authors and Publishers
ASCE American Society of Civil Engineers
ASHRAE American Society of Heating, Refrigeration, and Air Conditioning Engineers
ASME American Society of Mechanical Engineers
assn. association
assoc. associate
asst. assistant
ASTM American Society for Testing and Materials
astron. astronomical
astrophys. astrophysical
ATSC Air Technical Service Command
AT&T American Telephone & Telegraph Company

atty. attorney
AUS Army of the United States
Aug. August
aux. auxiliary
Ave. Avenue
AVMA American Veterinary Medical Association
AZ Arizona

B. Bachelor
b. born
B.A. Bachelor of Arts
B.Agr. Bachelor of Agriculture
Balt. Baltimore
Bapt. Baptist
B. Arch. Bachelor of Architecture
B.A.S. Bachelor of Agricultural Science
B.B.A. Bachelor of Business Administration
BBC British Broadcasting Corporation
B.C., BC British Columbia
B.C.E. Bachelor of Civil Engineering
B. Chir. Bachelor of Surgery
B.C.L. Bachelor of Civil Law
B.C.S. Bachelor of Commercial Science
B.D. Bachelor of Divinity
bd. board
B.E. Bachelor of Education
B.E.E. Bachelor of Electrical Engineering
B.F.A. Bachelor of Fine Arts
bibl. biblical
bibliog. bibliographical
biog. biographical
biol. biological
B.J. Bachelor of Journalism
Bklyn. Brooklyn
B.L. Bachelor of Letters
bldg. building
B.L.S. Bachelor of Library Science
Blvd. Boulevard
bn. battalion
B.&O.R.R. Baltimore & Ohio Railroad
bot. botanical
B.P.E. Bachelor of Physical Education
br. branch
B.R.E. Bachelor of Religious Education
brig. gen. brigadier general
Brit. British, Britannica
Bros. Brothers
B.S. Bachelor of Science
B.S.A. Bachelor of Agricultural Science
B.S.D. Bachelor of Didactic Science
B.S.T. Bachelor of Sacred Theology
B.Th. Bachelor of Theology
bull. bulletin
bur. bureau
bus. business
B.W.I. British West Indies

CA California

CAA Civil Aeronautics Administration
CAB Civil Aeronautics Board
Calif. California
C.Am. Central America
Can. Canada, Canadian
CAP Civil Air Patrol
capt. captain
CARE Cooperative American Relief
  Everywhere
Cath. Catholic
cav. cavalry
CBC Canadian Broadcasting Company
CBI China, Burma, India Theatre of
  Operations
CBS Columbia Broadcasting System
CCC Commodity Credit Corporation
CCNY City College of New York
CCU Cardiac Care Unit
CD Civil Defense
C.E. Corps of Engineers, Civil Engineers
  (in firm's name only or for degree)
cen. central (To be used for court
  system only)
CENTO Central Treaty Organization
CERN European Organization of Nuclear
  Research
cert. certificate, certification, certified
CETA Comprehensive Employment
  Training Act
CFL Canadian Football League
ch. church
Ch.D. Doctor of Chemistry
chem. chemical
Chem.E. Chemical Engineer
Chgo. Chicago
chirurg. chirurgical
chmn. chairman
chpt. chapter
CIA Central Intelligence Agency
CIC Counter Intelligence Corps
Cin. Cincinnati
cir. circuit
Cleve. Cleveland
climatol. climatological
clin. clinical
clk. clerk
C.L.U. Chartered Life Underwriter
C.M. Master in Surgery
C.&N.W.Ry. Chicago & Northwestern
  Railway
CO Colorado
Co. Company
COF Catholic Order of Foresters
C. of C. Chamber of Commerce
col. colonel
coll. college
Colo. Colorado
com. committee
comd. commanded
comdg. commanding
comdr. commander

comdt. commandant
commd. commissioned
comml. commercial
commn. commission
commr. commissioner
condr. conductor
Conf. Conference
Congl. Congregational, Congressional
Conglist. Congregationalist
Conn. Connecticut
cons. consultant, consulting
consol. consolidated
constl. constitutional
constn. constitution
constrn. construction
contbd. contributed
contbg. contributing
contbn. contribution
contbr. contributor
Conv. Convention
coop. cooperative
CORDS Civil Operations and
  Revolutionary Development Support
CORE Congress of Racial Equality
corp. corporation, corporate
corr. correspondent, corresponding,
  correspondence
C.&O.Ry. Chesapeake & Ohio Railway
C.P.A. Certified Public Accountant
C.P.C.U. Chartered Property and Casualty
  Underwriter
C.P.H. Certificate of Public Health
cpl. corporal
CPR Cardio-Pulmonary Resuscitation
C.P.Ry. Canadian Pacific Railway
C.S. Christian Science
C.S.B. Bachelor of Christian Science
CSC Civil Service Commission
C.S.D. Doctor of Christian Science
CT Connecticut
ct. court
crt. center
CWS Chemical Warfare Service
C.Z. Canal Zone

d. daughter
D. Doctor
D.Agr. Doctor of Agriculture
DAR Daughters of the American
  Revolution
dau. daughter
DAV Disabled American Veterans
D.C.,DC District of Columbia
D.C.L. Doctor of Civil Law
D.C.S. Doctor of Commercial Science
D.D. Doctor of Divinity
D.D.S. Doctor of Dental Surgery
DE Delaware
dec. deceased
Dec. December
def. defense
Del. Delaware

del. delegate, delegation
Dem. Democrat, Democratic
D.Eng. Doctor of Engineering
denom. denomination, denominational
dep. deputy
dept. department
dermatol. dermatological
desc. descendant
devel. development, developmental
D.F.A. Doctor of Fine Arts
D.F.C. Distinguished Flying Cross
D.H.L. Doctor of Hebrew Literature
dir. director
dist. district
distbg. distributing
distbn. distribution
distbr. distributor
disting. distinguished
div. division, divinity, divorce
D.Litt. Doctor of Literature
D.M.D. Doctor of Medical Dentistry
D.M.S. Doctor of Medical Science
D.O. Doctor of Osteopathy
D.P.H. Diploma in Public Health
D.R. Daughters of the Revolution
Dr. Drive, Doctor
D.R.E. Doctor of Religious Education
Dr.P.H. Doctor of Public Health, Doctor
  of Public Hygiene
D.S.C. Distinguished Service Cross
D.Sc. Doctor of Science
D.S.M. Distinguished Service Medal
D.S.T. Doctor of Sacred Theology
D.T.M. Doctor of Tropical Medicine
D.V.M. Doctor of Veterinary Medicine
D.V.S. Doctor of Veterinary Surgery

E. East
ea. eastern (use for court system only)
E. and P. Extraordinary and Plenipotentiary
Eccles. Ecclesiastical
ecol. ecological
econ. economic
ECOSOC Economic and Social Council
  (of the UN)
E.D. Doctor of Engineering
ed. educated
Ed.B. Bachelor of Education
Ed.D. Doctor of Education
edit. edition
Ed.M. Master of Education
edn. education
ednl. educational
EDP electronic data processing
Ed.S. Specialist in Education
E.E. Electrical Engineer (degree only)
E.E. and M.P. Envoy Extraordinary and
  Minister Plenipotentiary
EEC European Economic Community
EEG Electroencephalogram
EEO Equal Employment Opportunity

EEOC Equal Employment Opportunity Commission
EKG Electrocardiogram
E.Ger. German Democratic Republic
elec. electrical
electrochem. electrochemical
electrophys. electrophysical
elem. elementary
E.M. Engineer of Mines
ency. encyclopedia
Eng. England
engr. engineer
engring. engineering
entomol. entomological
environ. environmental
EPA Environmental Protection Agency
epidemiol. epidemiological
Episc. Episcopalian
ERA Equal Rights Amendment
ERDA Energy Research and Development Administration
ESEA Elementary and Secondary Education Act
ESL English as Second Language
ESSA Environmental Science Services Administration
ethnol. ethnological
ETO European Theatre of Operations
Evang. Evangelical
exam. examination, examining
exec. executive
exhbn. exhibition
expdn. expedition
expn. exposition
expt. experiment
exptl. experimental

F.A. Field Artillery
FAA Federal Aviation Administration
FAO Food and Agriculture Organization (of the UN)
FBI Federal Bureau of Investigation
FCA Farm Credit Administration
FCC Federal Communication Commission
FCDA Federal Civil Defense Administration
FDA Food and Drug Administration
FDIA Federal Deposit Insurance Administration
FDIC Federal Deposit Insurance Corporation
F.E. Forest Engineer
FEA Federal Energy Administration
Feb. February
fed. federal
fedn. federation
FERC Federal Energy Regulatory Commission
fgn. foreign
FHA Federal Housing Administration
fin. financial, finance
FL Florida

Fla. Florida
FMC Federal Maritime Commission
FOA Foreign Operations Administration
found. foundation
FPC Federal Power Commission
FPO Fleet Post Office
frat. fraternity
FRS Federal Reserve System
FSA Federal Security Agency
Ft. Fort
FTC Federal Trade Commission

G-1 (or other number) Division of General Staff
Ga., GA Georgia
GAO General Accounting Office
gastroent. gastroenterological
GATT General Agreement of Tariff and Trades
gen. general
geneal. genealogical
geod. geodetic
geog. geographic, geographical
geol. geological
geophys. geophysical
gerontol. gerontological
G.H.Q. General Headquarters
G.N. Ry. Great Northern Railway
gov. governor
govt. government
govtl. governmental
GPO Governmental Printing Office
grad. graduate, graduated
GSA General Services Administration
Gt. Great
GU Guam
gynecol. gynecological

hdqrs. headquarters
HEW Department of Health, Education and Welfare
H.H.D. Doctor of Humanities
HHFA Housing and Home Finance Agency
HHS Department of Health and Human Services
HI Hawaii
hist. historical, historic
H.M. Master of Humanics
homeo. homeopathic
hon. honorary, honorable
Ho. of Dels. House of Delegates
Ho. of Reps. House of Representatives
hort. horticultural
hosp. hospital
HUD Department of Housing and Urban Development
Hwy. Highway
hydrog. hydrographic

IA Iowa
IAEA International Atomic Energy Agency

IBM International Business Machines Corporation
IBRD International Bank for Reconstruction and Development
ICA International Cooperation Administration
ICC Interstate Commerce Commission
ICU Intensive Care Unit
ID Idaho
IEEE Institute of Electrical and Electronics Engineers
IFC International Finance Corporation
IGY International Geophysical Year
IL Illinois
Ill. Illinois
illus. illustrated
ILO International Labor Organization
IMF International Monetary Fund
IN Indiana
Inc. Incorporated
ind. independent
Ind. Indiana
Indpls. Indianapolis
indsl. industrial
inf. infantry
info. information
ins. insurance
insp. inspector
insp. gen. inspector general
inst. institute
instl. institutional
instn. institution
instr. instructor
instrn. instruction
intern. international
intro. introduction
IRE Institute of Radio Engineers
IRS Internal Revenue Service
ITT International Telephone & Telegraph Corporation

JAG Judge Advocate General
JAGC Judge Advocate General Corps
Jan. January
Jaycees Junior Chamber of Commerce
J.B. Jurum Baccolaureus
J.C.B. Juris Canoni Baccalaureus
J.C.D. Juris Canonici Doctor, Juris Civilis Doctor
J.C.L. Juris Canonici Licentiatus
J.D. Juris Doctor
j.g. junior grade
jour. journal
jr. junior
J.S.D. Juris Scientiae Doctor
J.U.D. Juris Utriusque Doctor
jud. judicial

Kans. Kansas
K.C. Knights of Columbus
K.P. Knights of Pythias
KS Kansas

K.T. Knight Templar
Ky., KY Kentucky

La., LA Louisiana
lab. laboratory
lang. language
laryngol. laryngological
LB Labrador
lectr. lecturer
legis. legislation, legislative
L.H.D. Doctor of Humane Letters
L.I. Long Island
lic. licensed, license
L.I.R.R. Long Island Railroad
lit. literary, literature
Litt.B. Bachelor of Letters
Litt.D. Doctor of Letters
LL.B. Bachelor of Laws
LL.D. Doctor of Laws
LL.M. Master of Laws
Ln. Lane
L.&N.R.R. Louisville & Nashville Railroad
L.S. Library Science (in degree)
lt. lieutenant
Ltd. Limited
Luth. Lutheran
LWV League of Women Voters

m. married
M. Master
M.A. Master of Arts
MA Massachusetts
mag. magazine
M.Agr. Master of Agriculture
maj. major
Man. Manitoba
Mar. March
M.Arch. Master in Architecture
Mass. Massachusetts
math. mathematics, mathematical
MATS Military Air Transport Service
M.B. Bachelor of Medicine
MB Manitoba
M.B.A. Master of Business Administration
MBS Mutual Broadcasting System
M.C. Medical Corps
M.C.E. Master of Civil Engineering
mcht. merchant
mcpl. municipal
M.C.S. Master of Commercial Science
M.D. Doctor of Medicine
Md, MD Maryland
M.Dip. Master in Diplomacy
mdse. merchandise
M.D.V. Doctor of Veterinary Medicine
M.E. Mechanical Engineer (degree only)
ME Maine
M.E.Ch. Methodist Episcopal Church
mech. mechanical
M.Ed. Master of Education
med. medical

M.E.E. Master of Electrical Engineering
mem. member
meml. memorial
merc. mercantile
met. metropolitan
metall. metallurgical
Met.E. Metallurgical Engineer
meteorol. meteorological
Meth. Methodist
Mex. Mexico
M.F. Master of Forestry
M.F.A. Master of Fine Arts
mfg. manufacturing
mfr. manufacturer
mgmt. management
mgr. manager
M.H.A. Master of Hospital Administration
M.I. Military Intelligence
MI Michigan
Mich. Michigan
micros. microscopic, microscopical
mid. middle (use for Court System only)
mil. military
Milw. Milwaukee
mineral. mineralogical
Minn. Minnesota
Miss. Mississippi
MIT Massachusetts Institute of Technology
mktg. marketing
M.L. Master of Laws
MLA Modern Language Association
M.L.D. Magister Legnum Diplomatic
M.Litt. Master of Literature
M.L.S. Master of Library Science
M.M.E. Master of Mechanical Engineering
MN Minnesota
mng. managing
Mo., MO Missouri
moblzn. mobilization
Mont. Montana
M.P. Member of Parliament
M.P.E. Master of Physical Education
M.P.H. Master of Public Health
M.P.L. Master of Patent Law
Mpls. Minneapolis
M.R.E. Master of Religious Education
M.S. Master of Science
MS, Ms. Mississippi
M.Sc. Master of Science
M.S.F. Master of Science of Forestry
M.S.T. Master of Sacred Theology
M.S.W. Master of Social Work
MT Montana
Mt. Mount
MTO Mediterranean Theatre of Operations
mus. museum, musical
Mus.B. Bachelor of Music
Mus.D. Doctor of Music
Mus.M. Master of Music
mut. mutual
mycol. mycological

N. North
NAACP National Association for the Advancement of Colored People
NACA National Advisory Committee for Aeronautics
NAD National Academy of Design
N.Am. North America
NAM National Association of Manufacturers
NAPA National Association of Performing Artists
NAREB National Association of Real Estate Boards
NARS National Archives and Record Service
NASA National Aeronautics and Space Administration
nat. national
NATO North Atlantic Treaty Organization
NATOUSA North African Theatre of Operations
nav. navigation
N.B., NB New Brunswick
NBC National Broadcasting Company
N.C., NC North Carolina
NCCJ National Conference of Christians and Jews
N.D., ND North Dakota
NDEA National Defense Education Act
NE Nebraska
NE Northeast
NEA National Education Association
Nebr. Nebraska
NEH National Endowment for Humanities
neurol. neurological
Nev. Nevada
NF Newfoundland
NFL National Football League
Nfld. Newfoundland
N.G. National Guard
N.H. NH New Hampshire
NHL National Hockey League
NIH National Institutes of Health
NIMH National Institute of Mental Health
N.J., NJ New Jersey
NLRB National Labor Relations Board
NM New Mexico
N.Mex. New Mexico
No. Northern
NOAA National Oceanographic and Atmospheric Administration
NORAD North America Air Defense
NOW National Organization for Women
Nov. November
N.P.Ry. Northern Pacific Railway
nr. near
NRC National Research Council
N.S., NS Nova Scotia
NSC National Security Council
NSF National Science Foundation
N.T. New Testament
NT Northwest Territories
numis. numismatic

NV Nevada
NW Northwest
N.W.T. Northwest Territories
N.Y., NY New York
N.Y.C. New York City
NYU New York University
N.Z. New Zealand

OAS Organization of American States
ob-gyn obstetrics-gynecology
obs. observatory
obstet. obstetrical
O.D. Doctor of Optometry
OECD Organization of European
  Cooperation and Development
OEEC Organization of European
  Economic Cooperation
OEO Office of Economic Opportunity
ofcl. official
OH Ohio
OK Oklahoma
Okla. Oklahoma
ON Ontario
Ont. Ontario
ophthal. ophthalmological
ops. operations
OR Oregon
orch. orchestra
Oreg. Oregon
orgn. organization
ornithol. ornithological
OSHA Occupational Safety and Health
  Administration
OSRD Office of Scientific Research and
  Development
OSS Office of Strategic Services
osteo. osteopathic
otol. otological
otolaryn. otolaryngological

Pa., PA Pennsylvania
P.A. Professional Association
paleontol. paleontological
path. pathological
P.C. Professional Corporation
PE Prince Edward Island
P.E.I. Prince Edward Island (text only)
PEN Poets, Playwrights, Editors, Essayists
  and Novelists (international association)
penol. penological
P.E.O. women's organization (full name
  not disclosed)
pfc. private first class
PHA Public Housing Administration
pharm. pharmaceutical
Pharm.D. Doctor of Pharmacy
Pharm. M. Master of Pharmacy
Ph.B. Bachelor of Philosophy
Ph.D. Doctor of Philosophy
Phila. Philadelphia
philharm. philharmonic
philol. philological

philos. philosophical
photog. photographic
phys. physical
physiol. physiological
Pitts. Pittsburgh
Pkwy. Parkway
Pl. Place
P.&L.E.R.R. Pittsburgh & Lake Erie
  Railroad
P.O. Post Office
PO Box Post Office Box
polit. political
poly. polytechnic, polytechnical
PQ Province of Quebec
P.R., PR Puerto Rico
prep. preparatory
pres. president
Presbyn. Presbyterian
presdl. presidential
prin. principal
proc. proceedings
prod. produced (play production)
prodn. production
prof. professor
profl. professional
prog. progressive
propr. proprietor
pros. atty. prosecuting attorney
pro tem pro tempore
PSRO Professional Services Review
  Organization
psychiat. psychiatric
psychol. psychological
PTA Parent-Teachers Association
ptnr. partner
PTO Pacific Theatre of Operations,
  Parent Teacher Organization
pub. publisher, publishing, published
pub. public
publ. publication
pvt. private

quar. quarterly
q.m. quartermaster
Q.M.C. Quartermaster Corps.
Que. Quebec

radiol. radiological
RAF Royal Air Force
RCA Radio Corporation of America
RCAF Royal Canadian Air Force
RD Rural Delivery
Rd. Road
REA Rural Electrification Administration
rec. recording
ref. reformed
regt. regiment
regtl. regimental
rehab. rehabilitation
rep. representative
Rep. Republican
Res. Reserve

ret. retired
rev. review, revised
RFC Reconstruction Finance Corporation
RFD Rural Free Delivery
rhinol. rhinological
R.I., RI Rhode Island
R.N. Registered Nurse
roentgenol. roentgenological
ROTC Reserve Officers Training Corps
R.R. Railroad
Ry. Railway

s. son
S. South
SAC Strategic Air Command
SALT Strategic Arms Limitation Talks
S.Am. South America
san. sanitary
SAR Sons of the American Revolution
Sask. Saskatchewan
savs. savings
S.B. Bachelor of Science
SBA Small Business Administration
S.C., SC South Carolina
SCAP Supreme Command Allies Pacific
Sc.B. Bachelor of Science
S.C.D. Doctor of Commercial Science
Sc.D. Doctor of Science
sch. school
sci. science, scientific
SCLC Southern Christian Leadership
  Conference
SCV Sons of Confederate Veterans
S.D., SD South Dakota
SE Southeast
SEATO Southeast Asia Treaty
  Organization
sec. secretary
SEC Securities and Exchange Commission
sect. section
seismol. seismological
sem. seminary
s.g. senior grade
sgt. sergeant
SHAEF Supreme Headquarters Allied
  Expeditionary Forces
SHAPE Supreme Headquarters Allied
  Powers in Europe
S.I. Staten Island
S.J. Society of Jesus (Jesuit)
S.J.D. Scientiae Juridicae Doctor
SK Saskatchewan
S.M. Master of Science
So. Southern
soc. society
sociol. sociological
S.P. Co. Southern Pacific Company
spl. special
splty. specialty
Sq. Square
sr. senior
S.R. Sons of the Revolution

SS Steamship
SSS Selective Service System
St. Saint, Street
sta. station
stats. statistics
statis. statistical
S.T.B. Bachelor of Sacred Theology
stblzn. stabilization
S.T.D. Doctor of Sacred Theology
subs. subsidiary
SUNY State University of New York
supr. supervisor
supt. superintendent
surg. surgical
SW Southwest

TAPPI Technical Association of Pulp
  and Paper Industry
Tb Tuberculosis
tchr. teacher
tech. technical, technology
technol. technological
Tel.&Tel. Telephone & Telegraph
temp. temporary
Tenn. Tennessee
Ter. Territory
Terr. Terrace
Tex. Texas
Th.D. Doctor of Theology
theol. theological
Th.M. Master of Theology
TN Tennessee
tng. training
topog. topographical
trans. transaction, transferred
transl. translation, translated
transp. transportation
treas. treasurer
TV television
TVA Tennessee Valley Authority
twp. township
TX Texas
typog. typographical

U. University
UAW United Auto Workers
UCLA University of California
  at Los Angeles
UDC United Daughters of the Confederacy
U.K. United Kingdom
UN United Nations
UNESCO United Nations Educational,
  Scientific and Cultural Organization
UNICEF United Nations International
  Children's Emergency Fund
univ. university
UNRRA United Nations Relief and
  Rehabilitation Administration
UPI United Press International
U.P.R.R. United Pacific Railroad
urol. urological
U.S. United States

U.S.A. United States of America
USAAF United States Army Air Force
USAF United States Air Force
USAFR United States Air Force Reserve
USAR United States Army Reserve
USCG United States Coast Guard
USCGR United States Coast Guard
  Reserve
USES United States Employment Service
USIA United States Information Agency
USMC United States Marine Corps
USMCR United States Marine Corps
  Reserve
USN United States Navy
USNG United States National Guard
USNR United States Naval Reserve
USO United Service Organizations
USPHS United States Public Health
  Service
USS United States Ship
USSR Union of the Soviet Socialist
  Republics
USV United States Volunteers
UT Utah

VA Veterans' Administration
Va., VA Virginia
vet. veteran, veterinary
VFW Veterans of Foreign Wars
V.I., VI Virgin Islands
vice pres. vice president
vis. visiting
VISTA Volunteers in Service to America
VITA Volunteers in Technical Service
vocat. vocational
vol. volunteer, volume
v.p. vice president
vs. versus
Vt., VT Vermont

W. West
WA Washington (state)
WAC Women's Army Corps
Wash. Washington (state)
WAVES Women's Reserve, U.S. Naval
  Reserve
WCTU Women's Christian Temperance
  Union
we. western (use for court system only)
W. Ger. Germany, Federal Republic of
WHO World Health Organization
WI, Wis. Wisconsin
W.I. West Indies
WSB Wage Stabilization Board
WV West Virginia
W.Va. West Virginia
WY Wyoming
Wyo. Wyoming

YK Yukon Territory (for address)
YMCA Young Men's Christian Association
YMHA Young Men's Hebrew Association

YM & YWHA Young Men's and Young
  Women's Hebrew Association
Y.T. Yukon Territory
YWCA Young Women's Christian
  Association
yr. year

zool. zoological

Alphabetical Practices

Names are arranged alphabetically according to the surnames, and under identical surnames according to the first given name. If both surname and first given name are identical, names are arranged alphabetically according to the second given name. Where full names are identical, they are arranged in order of age—with the elder listed first.

Surnames beginning with De, Des, Du, however capitalized or spaced, are recorded with the prefix preceding the surname and arranged alphabetically, under the letter D.

Surnames beginning with Mac and Mc are arranged alphabetically under M.

Surnames beginning with Saint or St. appear after names that would begin Sains, and are arranged according to the second part of the name, e.g., St. Clair before Saint Dennis.

Surnames beginning with Van, Von, or von are arranged alphabetically under the letter V.

Compound hyphenated surnames are arranged according to the first member of the compound. Compound unhyphenated surnames are treated as hyphenated names.

Parentheses used in connection with a name indicate which part of the full name is usually deleted in common usage. Hence Abbott, W(illiam) Lewis indicates that the usual form of the given name is W. Lewis. In such a case, the parentheses are ignored in alphabetizing. However if the name is recorded Abbott, (William) Lewis, signifying that the entire name William is not commonly used, the alphabetizing would be arranged as though the name were Abbott, Lewis.

Who's Who in the Midwest

AACH, ROY LEE, mechanical engineer; b. St. Louis, Sept. 16, 1928; s. Harold and Pauline (Levy) A.; m. Celeste Eileen Molos, May 31, 1949 (dec. Aug. 1970); children—Robyn, Randall, Karen; m. Beverly Beatrice Wade, Mar. 4, 1978. B.S. in Mech. Engring., Washington U., St. Louis, 1947. Registered profl. engr., Mo., 19 other states. Engr. Albert Rich Co., St. Louis, 1956-58, Smith, Zurheide, Hanlon & Levy, Inc., St. Louis, 1958-60; Cons. ptnr. Wilson & Aach, St. Louis, 1960-65; pres. chief exec. officer Roy L. Aach & Assocs., Inc., St. Louis, 1965-78; exec. v.p. Kromm, Rikimaru & Johansen, Inc., St. Louis, 1978—, also dir. Author newspaper feature, 1970. Pres. Lutheran Village Ch., St. Louis, 1983—; bd. dirs. Cold Water Cemetery, St. Louis, 1979—. Mem. Mo. Cons. Engrs. Council, Mo. Soc. Profl. Engrs., Nat. Soc. Profl. Engrs., ASHRAE. Replican. Clubs: University, Engineers (St. Louis). Lodges: Polar Star Masons (32d degree), Shriners. Avocations: piano, model railroading, watching sports. Office: Kromm Rikimaru Johansen Inc 112 S Hanley St Clayton MO 63105

AADALEN, DAVID KEVIN, lawyer; b. Hamilton, Calif., Dec. 23, 1953; s. Arlie Vernon and Irma Jean (Willig) A.; m. Rhonda Kay Kramer, May 29, 1976; children—Luke David, Amy Johanna. Student U. Kans., 1971; B.A., Washburn U., 1975, J.D., 1979. Bar: Kans. 1980, U.S. Dist. Ct. Kans. 1980. Sole practice, Topeka, 1980—. Deacon Topeka Bible Ch., 1981—. Named Outstanding Young Man Am., U.S. Jaycees, 1982. Mem. Kans. Bar Assn., Topeka Bar Assn. (probate com.), Christian Legal Soc. Republican. Home: 1031 Parkview Topeka KS 66604 Office: 1108 First Nat Bank Tower Topeka KS 66603

AANERUD, MELVIN BERNARD, government agency administrator; b. Spring Lake Park, Minn., Jan. 7, 1943; s. Bernard Melvin and Margaret Agnes (Beck) A.; B.A., U. Minn., 1964; m. Kathleen Dipprey, Aug. 19, 1978; children—Adam Curtis, Eric Christopher. Prodn. analyst Honeywell, Inc., New Brighton, Minn., 1966-68; plant mgr. Ault, Inc., Mpls., 1968-71; gen. mgr. Mille Lacs Reservation Bus. Enterprise, Vineland, Minn., 1971-74; bus. devel. specialist SBA, Mpls., 1974-78; asst. dist. dir. SBA, Mpls., 1978-80, dep. dist. dir., 1980—. Pres., Columbia Hts. Charter Commn., 1971-82; chmn. Minn. Minority Bus. Opportunity Com. 1976-79. Served with Signal Corps, AUS, 1964-66. Recipient Gold Key Man award Minn. Jaycees, 1971, 76, Silver Key, 1973; Columbia Heights Disting. Service award, 1970, Columbia Hgts. Outstanding Civil Servant award, 1970; named One of 10 Outstanding Young Minnesotans, 1978. Mem. Minn. (dir. Minn. Jaycee Found. 1976-82), Columbia Heights (nat. U.S. dir. 1972-73) jaycees, U. Minn. Alumni Assn. Mem. Democratic Farm Labor party. Home: 15041 Fillmore NE Ham Lake MN 55304 Office: 100 N 6th St Butler Square Minneapolis MN 55402

ABADINSKY, HOWARD, criminal justice educator, inspector; b. N.Y.C., July 12, 1941; s. Benjamin and Ann (Kestenbaum) A.; m. Donna Rose Berman, June 24, 1967; children—Alisa Michele, Sandi Hether. B.A., Queens Coll., 1963; M.S.W., Fordham U., 1970; Ph.D., NYU, 1983. Parole officer N.Y. State Div. Parole, N.Y.C., 1964-71, sr. parole officer, 1972-78; asst. prof. criminal justice Western Carolina U., Cullowhee, 1978-81; assoc. prof., St. Xavier Coll., Chgo., 1981—; inspector Sheriff's Office, Cook County, Ill., 1982—. Author: Probation and Parole: Theory and Practice, 1977; Social Service in Criminal Justice, 1978; Organized Crime, 1981; The Mafia in America: An Oral History, 1981; The Criminal Elite: Professional and Organized Crime, 1983; Discretionary Justice: An Introduction to the Use of Discretion in Criminal Justice, 1984; Organized Crime: Second Edition, 1985. Pres. Dist. 28 Sch. Bd., Queens, N.Y., 1970-75, Mem. Am. Soc. Criminology, Acad. Criminal Justice Scis., Am. Sociol. Assn., Nat. Sheriffs' Assn., Internat. Assn. for Study of Organized Crime (founder 1984). Jewish. Home: 433 W Briar Pl Chicago IL 60657 Office: St Xavier Coll 3700 W 103rd St Chicago IL 60655

ABATE, JOSEPH MATTHEW, credit union executive; b. Marsala, Italy, Oct. 16, 1922; came to U.S., 1931, naturalized, 1931; s. Antonio and Vincenza (Perniciaro) A.; m. Maria Puccio, Jan. 3, 1948. B. Mech. Engring., U. Detroit, 1948; postgrad. Wayne State U., 1949-60; spl. student U. Rome, 1944, U. Vienna, Austria, 1945. Draftsman, designer Ford Motor Co., Highland Park, Mich., 1940-43; air conditioning engr. S.J. O'Brien Sales, N.Y.C., 1946-48; mfg. engr. Westinghouse Electric Corp., Pitts., 1948-49; engring. mgr. Parke-Davis & Co., Detroit, 1949-67; pres., chief exec. officer Parda Fed. Credit Union, Rochester, Mich., 1967—; prin. owner, chief exec. officer Small Bus. Consultants, Northville, Mich., 1961-67. Contbr. articles to profl. jours. Served with M.I., U.S. Army, 1942-46, ETO. Recipient Profl. Contbn. award Soc. Safety Engrs., Detroit, 1960, Detroit Safety Council, 1960. Mem. Engring. Soc. Detroit, Credit Union Exec. Soc., Fin. Mgmt. Assn. (charter), Mich. Credit Union League (chmn. McFarland chpt. 1972—). Office: Parda Fed Credit Union PO Box 5010 Rochester MI 48308

ABBASI, TARIQ AFZAL, psychiatrist, educator; b. Hyderabad, India, Aug. 13, 1946; came to U.S., 1976, naturalized, 1983; s. Shujaat Ali and Salma Khatoon (Siddiqui) A.; m. Kashifa Khatoon, Nov. 10, 1972; children—Sameena, Omar, Osman. B.S., Madrasa-I-Aliya, Hyderabad, 1964; M.B.B.S., Osmania Med. Coll., Hyderabad, 1970; Diploma in Psychol. Medicine, St. John's Hosp., U. Sheffield (Eng.), 1976. Diplomate Am. Bd. Psychiatry and Neurology; diplomate in psychiatry Royal Coll. Physicians of Eng. Sr. house officer St. John's Hosp., Lincoln, Eng., 1972-73, registrar, 1973-76; resident in psychiatry Rutgers Med. Sch., Piscataway, N.J., 1976-79, chief resident, 1979, dir. adult in-patient services Community Mental Health Ctr., Rutgers Med. Sch., also asst. prof. psychiatry, 1979-82; staff psychiatrist Northville Regional Psychiat. Hosp. (Mich.), 1982-83, sect. dir., 1983—; cons. psychiatrist Rahway State Prison (N.J.), 1979-82; clin. instr. psychiatry Wayne State U. Med. Sch., Detroit. Mem. Am. Psychiat. Assn., Mich. Psychiat. Soc. Office: Northville Regional Psychiat Hosp 41001 Seven Mile Rd Northville MI 48167 also Personal Dynamics Ctr 22646 Michigan Ave Dearborn MI 48124

ABBASY, IFTIKHARUL H., surgeon; b. Pakistan, Oct. 28, 1935; s. Ikramul Haque and Mumtaz Begum; came to U.S., 1964, naturalized, 1970; M.B., B.S., Dow Med. Coll., Karachi, Pakistan, 1961; m. Karen Gaye Hampton, Feb. 14, 1969; 1 dau., Shameem Ara. Intern, Civil Hosp., Karachi, Pakistan, 1961-62, St. Olaves Hosp., London, 1962-63; resident in surgery E. Ham Meml. Hosp., London, 1963, Michael Reese Hosp., Chgo., 1965-69; practice medicine specializing in gen. surgery and peripheral vascular surgery, Villa Park, Ill., 1969—; mem. staff Meml. Hosp., Elmhurst, Ill., McHenry (Ill.) Hosp., Good Samaritan Hosp., Downers Grove, Ill., Harvard (Ill.) Community Hosp. Diplomate Am. Bd. Surgery. Fellow A.C.S., Internat. Coll. Surgeons, Royal Coll. Surgeons Can.; mem. AMA (Physicians's Recognition award 1974-77). Home: 905 Burroak Ct Oak Brook IL 60521 Office: 10 E Central Blvd Villa Park IL 60181

ABBATE, RUTH RUDYS, librarian; b. Chgo., June 2, 1930; d. Joseph F. and Anna (Serbenta) Rudys; B.A., U. Chgo., 1950; M.A. in L.S., Rosary Grad. Sch. Library Sci., 1972; children—Keith A. Krisciunas, Kevin L. Krisciunas, Kenneth M. Krisciunas; stepchildren—Anita L. Abbate, Vincent A. Abbate. Tchr. elementary sch. Westmont, Ill., 1961-63; librarian Dist. 105 pub. schs., La Grange, Ill., 1972—, tchr. gifted students Dist. 105, 1979-81, 82-84, coordinator gifted program, 1981-82. Mem. ALA, Ill. Library Assn., Nat., Ill. Edn. assns., AAUW, Dist. 105 Tchrs. Assn. (pres. 1983—). Roman Catholic. Home: 5800 Doe Circle Westmont IL 60559 Office: 1001 Spring Ave La Grange IL 60525

ABBENE, MICHAEL THEODORE, JR., information systems executive; b. N.Y.C., May 9, 1948; s. Michael Theodore and Rita (Ring) A.; m. Patricia Ann Maloney, Apr. 28, 1973. B.S. in Indsl. Engring., Northwestern U., 1970; M.B.A. in Fin. So. Ill. U., 1980. Cert. systems profl. Systems analyst GTE Automatic Electric Co., Northlake, Ill., 1970-73, coordinator data adminstrn., 1974-76; data mgmt. specialist Monsanto Co., St. Louis, 1976-77, project mgr., 1978-81, info. systems mgr., 1982—. Advisor Jr. Achievement, Chgo., 1973-76, Jr. Achievement of Miss. Valley, St. Louis, 1976—. Mem. Assn. Systems Mgmt., Jaycees. Roman Catholic. Avocations: photography, reading. Home: 9 Springlake Ct Ballwin MO 63011 Office: Monsanto Co 800 N Lindbergh St Saint Louis MO 63167

ABBOTT, DAVID CHARLES, school superintendent; b. Picton, Ont., Can., Oct. 8, 1939; came to U.S., 1961, naturalized, 1981; s. Lawrence John and Stella Mae (Welsh) A. B.R.E., Wycliffe Coll., 1966; M.A., Eastern Mich. U., 1968; Ph.D., Ohio State U., 1977. Ordained to ministry, Assemblies of God, 1963; minister Emmanuel Tabernacle, Vancouver, B.C., 1961-62, Oak Park (Mich.) Christian Tabernacle, 1963-68; head tchr. Buckeye Boys Ranch, Grove City, Ohio, 1969-72; prin. Georgesville Sch., Grove City, 1972-74; inservice edn. specialist Southwestern City Schs., Grove City, 1974-78; asst. supt. Maumee (Ohio) City Schs., 1978-82, supt., 1982—; vis. prof. Ohio State U., 1977-78. Mem. Placement Council, U. Toledo, 1979-82; chmn. State Supt.'s Adv. Com. for Gifted and Talented, 1982-85; cons. edn. standards Bowling Green State U., 1982-83, Ohio Dept. Edn., 1980-83. Mem. Assn. for Supervision and Curriculum Devel., Ohio Assn. for Supervision and Curriculum Devel., Consortium of Gifted Children Edn. Coordinators, Nat. Assn. Gifted Children, Ohio Assn. Gifted Children, Buckeye Assn. Sch. Adminstrs., Am. Assn. Sch. Adminstrs., Northwestern Ohio Assn. Suprs. and Curriculum Devel., Phi Delta Kappa. Club: Rotary. Contbr. articles to profl. jours. Home: 2817 River Rd Maumee OH 43537 Office: 2345 Detroit Ave Maumee OH 43537

ABBOTT, DAVID HENRY, manufacturing company executive; b. Milton, Ky., July 6, 1936; s. Carl and Rachael (Miles) A.; B.S., U. Ky., 1960, M.B.A., 1961; m. Joan Shefchik, Aug. 14, 1976; children—Kristine, Gina, Beth, Linsey. With Ford Motor Co., Louisville, also Mpls., Dearborn, Mich., 1961-69; div. controller J.I. Case Co., Racine, Wis., 1970-73, gen. mgr. service parts supply, 1973-75, v.p., 1975-81, v.p./gen. mgr. constrn. equipment div., 1975-77, v.p./gen. mgr. Drott div., 1977-79, exec. v.p. worldwide constrn., 1979-81; pres., chief operating officer Portec Inc., Oakbrook, Ill., 1981—, also dir.; dir. Oak Brook Bank. Mem. Constrn. Industry Mfrs. Assn. (dir. 1979-81, 82—). Republican. Mem. Christian Ch. Home: 41 Steeple Ridge Ct Oakbrook IL 60521 Office: 300 Windsor Dr Oakbrook IL 60521

ABBOTT, DONALD FRANKLIN, mfg. co. exec.; b. Sidney, Ohio, Nov. 23, 1941; s. Carl J. and Grace (Davidson) A.; student U. Richmond, 1959-60, Edison State U., 1978; children—Gregg, Ric. With Sidney Oliver Store (IH Trucks), Sidney, 1960-62; machine tool rebuilder Sidney Machine Service, Inc., Sidney, 1962-76, pres., owner, 1977—. Mem. Nat. Tooling and Machining Assn., Dayton Tooling and Machining Assn., Sidney-Shelby County C. of C., Am. Motorcycle Assn. Republican. Baptist. Club: Moose. Home: 13000 CR 25A Anna OH 45302 Office: PO Box 198 Sidney OH 45365

ABBOTT, JAMES WILLIE, educator; b. Bloodland, Mo., Dec. 29, 1933; s. Mons E. and Stella (Anderson) A.; A.B., Drury Coll., Springfield, Mo., 1956; M.A., U. Mo., 1959; Litt.D. (hon.), Concordia Tchrs. Coll., Seward, Nebr., 1980. Secondary sch. tchr., Lebanon, Mo., 1956-59; asst. dir. lab. schs., instrs. edn. U. Mo., Columbia, 1959-66; dir. Kans. Coop. Urban Tchr. Edn. Program, 1968—, Kans. Urban Edn. Ctr., Kansas City, Kans. Youth Trust; condr. Workshops. Mem. Am. Assn. Tchr. Educators, Am. Soc. Curriculum Devel., Phi Delta Kappa. Roman Catholic. Author articles in field. Home: 6375 W 49th St Mission KS 66202

ABBOUD, CHRISTOPHER WILLIAM, state senator; b. Omaha, Aug. 29, 1956; s. Fred Abboud and Bonny Burgess. B.A., Creighton U., 1978; J.D., U. Nebr., 1982. Mem. Nebr. Senate, 1983—. Mem. German-Am. Soc., ABA, Nebr. Bar Assn., Ralston Area C. of C., Phi Alpha Theta, Sigma Alpha Epsilon. Republican. Lodge: Rotary. Office: State Capitol Lincoln NE 68509

ABDNOR, JAMES, senator; b. Kennebec, S.D., Feb. 13, 1923; s. Samuel J. and Mary (Wehby) A. B.A. in Bus. Adminstrn., U. Nebr., 1945. Tchr., coach, Presho, S.D., 1946-48, farmer, rancher, Kennebec, 1945—; mem. 93d-96th Congresses from S.D.; U.S. senator, 1981—; Chmn. S.D. Young Republicans, 1953-55; mem. S.D. Senate, 1956-69, pres. pro-tem, 1967-68; lt. gov. S.D., 1969-70. Served with AUS. Mem. Kennebec Jr. C. of C. (past pres.), Am. Legion, S.D. Wheat Producers, S.D. Stockgrowers, S.D. Farmers Union, S.D. Farm Bur., Isaak Walton League, Sigma Chi. Clubs: Masons, Elks. Home: Kennebec SD 57544 Office: 309 Hart Senate Office Bldg Washington DC 20510

ABDULLAH, SAMELLA B. E. P., psychotherapist, educator; b. Chgo., Mar. 9, 1934; d. Samuel Richard and Addie Loraine (Jordan) Berry; B.S., Howard U., 1955, M.S.W. (NIMH grad. stipendee), 1959; Ph.D. in Psychology, Heed U., Fla., 1978; divorced; children—Tracey, Makola Mjasiri, Ghanima Kibibi. Legal aid social worker United Charities Chgo., 1962-64; instr. med. social work Northwestern U. Med. Sch. Clinic, Chgo., 1964-67; dir. social work Near North Children's Center, Chgo., 1967-69; coordinator children adolescent services Englewood Mental Health Center, Chgo., 1972-75; dir. Woodlawn Mental Health Center, Chgo., 1975-77; pvt. practice psychotherapy, Chgo., 1979—; community prof. Governor's State U., Park Forest, Ill.; lectr. Jane Addams Coll. Social Work U. Ill., Chgo.; instr. Central YMCA Community Coll., Chgo.; cons. Mau-Glo Sch. Mentally Retarded, Chgo.; mem. Chgo. City-Wide Community Health Bd.; mem. Ill. Mental Health Planning Bd., 1968-69. Certified social worker, Ill. Mem. Assn. Black Psychologists, League Black Women, Howard U. Alumni Assn., Chgo. Assn. Commerce and Industry, Am. Assn. Group Pschotherapists. Home: 7204 S Paxton Ave Chicago IL 60649 Office: 111 N Wabash Ave Suite 1104 Chicago IL 60602

ABEL, BRUCE ALAN, transit company executive; b. Montclair, N.J., Jan. 17, 1954; s. Frederick Roland and Edmee (Augsburger) A.; m. Patricia Adams Powell, Aug. 27, 1982. B.A. in Econs., Wake Forest U., 1975; M.B.A. in Mktg., U. N.C., 1980. Transp. planner City-County planning Bd., Winston-Salem, N.C., 1975-77; dir. mktg. Winston-Salem Transit Authority, 1977-81; dir. mktg.-planning Am. Transit Corp., St Louis, 1981—. Mem. Carolina St. Scene Organizing Com., Winston-Salem, 1979, 80. Mem. Am. Pub. Transit Assn. (mem. mktg. steering com. 1977—, chmn. mktg. program devel. subcom. 1981—), Am. Planning Assn. Avocations: Photography, tennis, outdoor activities. Office: Am Transit Corp 120 S Central Ave Suite 1500 Saint Louis MO 63105

ABEL, DONALD WILLIAM, club administrator; b. Milw., Feb. 11, 1936; s. William Frank and Edna Clara (Schuette) A.; m. Rosemary Therese Crimmins; children—Jeffrey James, Theresa Clare, Veronica Katherine. B.A., Mich. State U., 1959. Gen. mgr. Seven Seas, Inc., Hartland, Wis., 1961-66; asst. gen. mgr. Mpls. Athletic Club, 1967-69; gen. mgr. Wayzata Country Club, Minn., 1969-78, Interlachen Country Club, Edina, Minn., 1978—. Columnist The Interlocutor, 1978—. Pres. sch. bd. and parish council Our Lady of Lake Cath. Ch., Mound, Minn., 1973-75, 76-78; gen. chmn. Mound's Incredible Festival, 1979—; pres. Mound Westonka A.F.S. Club, 1983, 84. Served with USN, 1959-61. Recipient plaques of appreciation Our Lady of Lake Cath. Ch. Bd. Edn., 1975, Wayzata County Club Bd. Govs., 1978; Our Lady of Lake Cath. Ch. Parish Council, 1978. Mem. Club Mgrs. Assn. Am. (sec.-treas. 1979, v.p. 1980, pres. 1981). Republican. Club: Edina Rotary (chmn. fellowship com. 1981-83). Avocations: tennis, jogging, gardening, down-hill skiing. Office: Interlachen Country Club 6200 Interlachen Blvd Edina MN 55436

ABEL HOROWITZ, MICHELLE SUSAN, advertising agency executive; b. Detroit, Mar. 31, 1950; d. Martin Louis and Phyllis (Berkowitz) A.; m. H. Jay Abel Horowitz, July 11, 1976; 1 son, Jordan Michael. Student Goucher Coll., 1967-70; B.A. in Econs., U. Mich., 1971; postgrad. in econs. U. Calif.-San Diego, 1973; M.A. in Econs., U. Detroit, 1974-76. Planning group supr. Hill Holliday Connors, Cosmopolus, Mass., 1976-78; econ. analyst Data Resources, Boston, 1978-79; v.p., media dir. Barkley & Evergreen, Southfield, Mich., 1979-80; v.p., dir. mktg. and media Yaffe/Berline, Southfield, Mich., 1980-82; v.p., dir. client services, corp. treas., dir. Berline Group, Birmingham, Mich., 1982—; instr. Oakland U., Rochester, Mich., 1982; trustee, chairperson mktg. com. Harbinger Dance Co., Farmington, Mich., 1983—. Named Advt. Woman of Yr., Women's Ad Club Detroit, 1982. Mem. Adcraft Club Detroit, Women in Communications. Democrat. Jewish. Office: Berline Group 6735 Telegraph Birmingham MI 48010

ABELOV, STEPHEN LAWRENCE, manufacturing company executive; b. N.Y.C., Apr. 1, 1923; s. Saul S. and Ethel (Esterman) A.; B.S., NYU, 1945, M.B.A., 1950; m. Phyllis S. Lichtenson, Nov. 18, 1945; children—Patricia C. (Mrs. Marvin Demoff), Gary M. Asst. div. mgr. Nat. Silver Co., N.Y., 1945; sales rep. Angelica Uniform Co., N.Y., 1945-50; asst. sales mgr., 1950-56, western regional mgr., Los Angeles, 1956-66, v.p. Angelica Uniform Co. of Calif., 1958-66, nat. v.p. sales, 1966-72, v.p. Angelica Corp. 1968— group v.p. mktg., 1972-80, exec. v.p., chief mktg. officer Angelica Uniform Group, 1980—; vis. lectr. mktg. NYU Grad. Sch. Bus. Adminstrn. Vice comdr. Am. Legion; mem. vocational adv. bd. VA.; adv. bd. Woodcraft Rangers; bd. dirs. Univ. Temple. Mem. Am. Assn. Contamination Control (dir.), Am. Soc. for Advancement Mgmt. (chpt. pres.), Am. Mktg. Assn., Health Industries Assn. Am. (dir.), Inst. Environ. Scis., various trade assns., St. Louis Council on World Affairs, NYU Alumni Assn., Phi Epsilon Pi (treas.). Mem. B'nai B'rith (past pres.). Clubs: Men's (exec. v.p.); Town Hall, NYU, Aqua Sierra Sportsmen, Clayton. Contbr. articles to profl. jours. Home: 9821 Log Cabin Ct Ladue MO 63124 Office: 700 Rosedale Ave Saint Louis MO 63112

ABERNATHY, MAX ROLAND, pharmaceutical company executive; b. St. Louis, Nov. 15, 1931; med. technician diploma, Gradwohl Sch. Lab. Technique, St. Louis, 1956; student Stowe Tchrs. Coll., St. Louis; m. Georgia M. Taylor; 9 children. Mem. staff Washington U. Hosps., 1956-68, chief med. technologist Outpatient Clinic and Barnes Hosp. Labs., 1961-68; instr. clin. and lab. medicine Washington U. Med. Sch., 1964-68; clin. systems sales rep., then asso. research scientist tech. services lab. Ames div. Miles Labs. Inc., Elkhart, Ind., 1968-74, various positions, 1974-77, sr. project mgr. blood chemistry systems, growth and devel., 1977-78, sr. tech. tng. specialist, 1978, mgr. tech. tng., 1978-83, mgr. tech. services and tng. internat., 1983, supr. customer services, 1983-84, pub. relations prodn. corp., 1984—. Past pres. Elkhart County NAACP, producer Outreach radio show. Recipient Best Tech. Paper award Internat. Soc. Clin. Lab. Technologists, 1966; Gov.'s award Volunteerism. Mem. Am. Soc. Med. Technologists, Nat. Soc. Histotech. (charter), Ind. Soc. Med. Technologists, Internat. Soc. Clin. Lab. Technologists, Alumni Assn. Gradwohl Sch. (past pres.; Honor Soc. Key 1965). Home: 19 Sunrise Dr Elkhart IN 46517 Office: Miles Labs Inc PO Box 40 Elkhart IN 46515

ABINGTON, EUGENE BRYANT, management consultant; b. Chgo., Aug. 5, 1937; s. Homer Oregon and Petronia Christine (Bryant) A.; B.S., Roosevelt U., 1977, M.S., 1981; m. Michelle Stevens, Jan. 30, 1979; children by previous marriage—Tarra, Carla, Brian, Kimberly. Investigator, Chgo. Police Force, 1964—; chmn. bd. Abington Enterprises, Inc., Chgo., 1978—; pres. AEI Mgmt. & Cons. Co., 1979—; pres. Char-Gene, Ltd., 1982—. Owner, founder Ida B. Wells Barnett Mus., 1981—; pres. Near South Coalition Community Orgns., 1983—, A Growing Concern, 1984—. Democrat. Methodist. Office: 3624 S Martin Luther King Dr Chicago IL 60653

ABLAHAT, NEWTON ANDRE, business consultant; b. Chgo.; s. Haidow and Katie (Samuels) A.; B.S., Northwestern U., 1937; postgrad. U. Chgo., 1940, U. Colo., 1943, Johns Hopkins U., 1953-55, Syracuse U., 1961, Am. U., 1965-67; m. Ella May Cason, June 14, 1947; 1 son, Roger Haydon. Mgr. mdse. research, mgr. credit research Spiegel, Inc., Chgo., 1938-41, mgr. market research, 1946-47, dir. policy, 1948-50; economist WPB, Washington, 1941-42; econ. intelligence officer, Yenan, China, 1943-45; exporter Trans World Assos., 1947; cons. Bur. Labor Stats., Washington, 1950-53; analyst ORO, Johns Hopkins U., 1953-56; head ops. research Gen. Electric Co., Phila., 1956-58; cons. Haskins & Sells, Chgo., 1958; cons. Gen. Electric Co., Syracuse, Europe and Washington, 1959-67; v.p. corp. planning dept. Investors Diversified Services, Inc., Mpls., 1967-80; pres. The Stratcon Group Inc., Mpls., 1980—; bus. cons. to fgn. firms; past cons. U.S. Dept. Transp.; dir. New Beginning Funds, Sherlock's Book Home. Bd. dirs. Suburban Community Services. Served with USNR, 1943; CBI. Mem. Council Ind. Profl. Cons. (dir.), Am. Finance Assn., Nat. Assn. Bus. Economists, Ops. Research Soc., Inst. Mgmt. Scis., N.Am. Soc. Corp. Planners, Assn. Corp. Growth. Home: 5200 Chantrey Rd Edina MN 55436 Office: 7600 Parklawn Ave Suite 257 Minneapolis MN 55435

ABLER, JOYCE LESCELIUS, systems analyst; b. Owosso, Mich., Oct. 13, 1941; d. Toivo Joseph and Agdrina I. (Tidemann) Lescelius; B.S., Central Mich. U., 1963, M.B.A., 1973. Acct., Dow Chem. Co., Midland, Mich., 1963-64, Sterling Nat. Industries, Milw., 1965; with Molson's Breweries Ont., Ltd. (Can.), 1965-67, B.F. Goodrich Can. Ltd., Kitchener, Ont., 1967-71; systems analyst Central Mich. U., Mt. Pleasant, 1971—; faculty Northwood Inst., Midland, Mich., 1976-78, Central Mich. U., 1978—; sec.-treas. Data Basic Inc., 1980-81. Mem. computer adv. com. Mt. Pleasant High Sch., 1976-79; treas. ch. council Zion Luth. Ch., Mt. Pleasant, 1977—. Mem. Data Processing Mgmt. Assn. (sec. 1972-78, v.p. 1978, pres. 1979, newsletter editor 1980-84), Alpha Sigma Alpha (province dir. 1976—, collegiate sorority advisor 1971-80, dir. 1980-83, scholarship chmn. 1982-84). Home: 1018 Main St Mount Pleasant MI 48858 Office: 10 Foust Hall Central Mich Univ Mount Pleasant MI 48859

ABLER, WILLIAM LEWIS, paleopsychologist; b. Chgo., Dec. 6, 1943; s. Julius and Elizabeth (Engelman) A. B.A., U. Pa., 1966, M.A., 1968, Ph.D., 1971. Postdoctoral fellow Stanford U., Calif., 1971-74; asst. prof. Ill. Inst. Tech., Chgo., 1974-81; paleopsychology researcher, Chgo., 1981—. Author: Shop Tactics, 1973. Contbg. author: Scientfic Illustration: A Guide for the Beginning Artist. Contbr. articles to sci. jours. Patentee in field. Mem. Linguistic Soc. Am., Acoustical Soc. Am., Entomol. Soc. Am. Home: 3350 S Michigan Ave Chicago IL 60616

ABNEE, A. VICTOR, trade association executive; b. Lexington, Ky., June 12, 1923; s. A. Victor and Sarah I. (Brogle) A.; m. Doris Heuck, Dec. 28, 1946; children—Janice Abnee Williams, A. Victor III. B.A., U. Cin., 1948; student U. Ala., 1943-44. Mgr. sales and sales promotion U.S. Gypsum, Chgo., 1948-60, gen. advt. mgr., 1960-63; exec. v.p. Gypsum Assn., Evanston, Ill., 1964-83, pres., 1984—. Bd. dirs. Les Cheneaux Islands Assn., Mich., 1984—. Served to capt. C.E., U.S. Army, 1943-46; PTO. Named Man of Yr., Assn. Wall and Ceiling Industry, 1978; Alumnus of Yr., U. Cin., 1967. Mem. NAM (council), Am. Soc. Assn. Execs., Assn. Econ. Council, Sigma Chi. Clubs: University (pres. 1981-83) (Chgo.); Les Cheneaux Yacht (bd. dirs. 1982—) (Mich.); University (pres. 1984—) (Evanston); Foundation (pres. 1984—), Adventurers (Chgo.); Gyro International. Lodges: Masons, Shriners. Home: 707 Elm St Winnetka IL 60093 Office: Gypsum Assn 1603 Orrington Ave Evanston IL 60201

ABNEY, CHARLOTTE MAXINE, school counselor, librarian; b. Courtois, Mo., May 9, 1936; d. Grayfer Leo and Isla (Evans) A.; student (Valedictorian scholar, Delta Kappa Gamma scholar) Flat River Jr. Coll., 1953-54; B.S. in

Edn. cum laude, SW Mo. State U., 1962, M.S. in Guidance and Counseling, 1970. Mgr., Abneys' Restaurant, Caledonia, Mo., 1954-55; tchr. Grandview R-II Sch., Ware, Mo., 1955-60; tchr., librarian Bismarck (Mo.) R-V Sch., 1960-67, 1969-74, counselor, librarian, 1974—; lectr. edn. and child devel.; tchr. rep. Bd. Edn., 1972-75; cons. to Mo. Dept. Edn. Certified tchr., sch. psychol. examiner, counselor, librarian. Mem. Am. Assn. Counseling and Devel., Am. Sch. Counselors Assn., Mo. Sch. Counselor Assn., Southeast Mo. Sch. Counselor Assn. Southeast Mo. Dept. Sch. Librarians, St. Francois County Edn. Assn. (sec. 1965-66), Mo. Assn. Sch. Librarians, Bismarck R-V Community, Mo. State tchrs. assns. Methodist. Home: Box 707 Bismarck MO 63624 Office: Campus Dr Bismarck MO 63624

ABOOD, CALILLE SAM, lawyer; b. Lansing, Mich., May 15, 1931; s. Salim Nasaar and Nebeha (Fawaz) A.; m. Maryalice Abood, Aug. 4, 1962; children—Thomas, Christopher, Richard, Maureen, Mary. B.A., Sacred Heart Sem., 1955; J.D., Detroit Coll. Law, 1961. Research asst. Mich. Supreme Ct., Lansing; v.p., sr. ptnr. Abood, Abood & Rheaume, Lansing, 1961—; cons., gen. counsel Diocese of Lansing; vol. Pro Bono Law Services, Lansing. Chmn. Greater Lansing Food Bank Com., 1983; bd. dirs. Greater Lansing Food Alliance; past pres. Greater Lansing Safety Council; bd. dirs., mem. fin. com. St. Vincents Home, Lansing. Served to cpl. U.S. Army, 1956-58. Recipient Disting. Citizen award Red Cross, Lansing, 1983; Citizen of Year award Mich. chpt. Social Workers Am., 1983, Disting. Service award Mich. Assn. Professions, 1983; Carnation award Tri County Vols., Carnation Co., Lansing State Jour., 1984. Mem. Ingham County Bar Assn., Assn. Trial Lawyers Am., Mich. Atty. Discipline Bd., Sierra Club. Democrat. Roman Catholic. Home: 4424 Wagonwheel Lansing MI 48917 Office: Abood Abood & Rheaume 117 E Allegan Lansing MI 48933

ABOULAFIA, ELIE DAVID, vascular surgeon; b. Jerusalem, Israel, June 16, 1928; came to U.S., 1953, naturalized, 1958; s. David and Mathilda (Yeshaya) Aboulafia; B.Sc., U. Geneva, 1949, M.D., 1953; M.Sc., Tufts U., 1960; m. Eileen Helman, May 2, 1965; children—Diane, David, Albert. Intern, Michael Reese Hosp., Chgo., 1953-54; resident surgery Bellevue Med. Center, N.Y.C., 1954-56; resident surgery, fellow vascular surgery Tufts-New Eng. Med. Center, Boston, 1958-61; practice medicine specializing in vascular surgery, Southfield, Mich., 1961—; dir. surg. edn. Highland Park (Mich.) Gen. Hosp., 1974-76; clin. asso. prof. vascular surgery Mich. State U., 1977—. Served with USN, 1956-58. Diplomate Am. Bd. Surgery. Fellow Soc. Clin. Vascular Surgery, Internat. Coll. Surgeons. Mass. Heart Assn.; mem. Maimonides Med. Soc. (past pres.), Southeastern Mich. Surg. Soc. (pres.), Sigma Xi. Editorial asso. Internat. Surgery, 1978—. Home: 27501 W Fourteen Mile Rd Farmington Hills MI 48018 Office: 17000 W Eight Mile Rd Southfield MI 48075

ABOWD, JOHN MARON, econometrics and industrial relations educator; b. Ann Arbor, Mich., Dec. 22, 1951; s. Richard George and Sara Theresa (Boulus) A.; m. Janet Mary Cullen, Aug. 25, 1979; 1 child, Katherine. A.B., U. Notre Dame, 1973; A.M., U. Chgo., 1975, Ph.D., 1977. Instr., asst. prof. Princeton U., N.J., 1976-79; asst. prof. U. Chgo., 1979-82, assoc. prof. econometrics and indsl. relations, 1982—; research assoc. London Sch. Econs., 1979, Nat. Opinion Research Ctr., Chgo., 1979—, Nat. Bur. Econ. Research, Cambridge, Mass., 1983—. Author: Managing Higher Education, 1981. Contbr. articles to profl. jours. Mem. Am. Econ. Assn., Econometric Soc., Am. Statis. Assn., Indsl. Relations Research Assn. Office: U Chgo Grad Sch Bus 1101 E 58th St Chicago IL 60637

ABRAHAM, BETTE HAVENS, strategic planner; b. Meriden, Conn., June 19, 1946; d. John Joseph and Abina Dorothy (Walsh) Havens; B.A. with honors, Lake Erie Coll., 1968; M.A., U. N.D., 1970; postgrad. M.B.A. program U. Minn., 1981; m. Alden A. Abraham, Aug. 29, 1970. Tchr., Chgo. Sch. for Retarded, 1971; supr. psychology dept. London Meml. Hosp., Chgo., 1971-75; pvt. practice psychotherapy, Chgo., 1975-77, Mpls., 1977—; cons. Paul Cekan, M.D., 1975-77, Anil Godbole, M.D., 1976-77; assoc. Transculture Center for Human Relations, 1974-76, Chgo. Med. Sch. Faculty, 1974-76, Ill. Psychol. Assn., 1974-77; group psychotherapist Abbott Northwestern Hosp., Mpls., 1977-78; family therapist Exodus, St. Paul, 1978; reach coordinator Mental Health Assn. Minn., 1979; fin. analyst Pillsbury Corp., 1981-82; sr. strategic planner First Bank Mpls., 1982-84; v.p. mktg. and strategic planning Glengarry Co., 1984—. Mem. N. Am. Soc. Corporate Planning (chmn. alumni adv. council, v.p. programs), Alumnae Soc. U. Minn. (bd. dirs.), U. Chgo. Library Soc., ACLU, Common Cause, Center for Study of Democratic Instns. Minn. Zool. Gardens, Mpls. Inst. Art, Minn. Hist. Soc., Smithsonian Instn., Sci. Mus. Minn., M.B.A. Assn. Home: 3526 W 28th St Minneapolis MN 55416 Office: Glengarry Co 1450 Energy Park Dr Saint Paul MN 55108

ABRAHAM, IVO LUC, research, statistics and computing educator; b. Antwerp, Belgium, July 24, 1957; came to U.S., 1979; s. Jean-Paul Abraham and Emma Vorlat; m. Laurie Sue Haan, Dec. 24, 1981. B.S., Cath. U. Leuven (Belgium), 1979; M.S., U. Mich., 1982, Ph D., 1984. Clin. intern Washtenaw Community Mental Health Services, Ann Arbor, Mich., 1979-81; research fellow U. Mich., 1981-82; clin. instr. mental health, 1980-84; asst. prof. Case Western Res. U., Cleve., 1984—; pres. Abraham & Assocs., Ann Arbor, 1982-84, Health Scis. Devel. Corp., Cleve., 1984—. Contbr. articles to profl. jours. Grantee in field. Mem. Am Nurses Assn., Am. Statis. Assn., AAAS, Am. Orthopsychiat. Assn., AAUP, Am. Psychol. Assn., Greater Cleve. Nurses Assn. Avocations: microcomputing, international travel, skiing, sailing. Home: 3175 Ludlow Rd Shaker Heights OH 44120 Office: Case Western Res Univ 2121 Abington Rd Cleveland OH 44106

ABRAHAM, ROBERT WILLIAM, controller; b. Chgo., Apr. 29, 1933; s. William H. and Martha (Goura) A.; B.S. in Mgmt., U. Ill., 1963; M.B.A., Governors State U., 1983; m. Louise Marie Spellar, Jan. 28, 1935; children—Robert, Charles. Cost estimator market research Chgo. Bridge & Iron Co., 1957-59; plant acct. Joslyn Mfg. Co., Chgo., 1959-66; cost acct. Velsicol Chem. Co., Chgo., 1966-67; gen. acct. Freeman Coal Co., Chgo., 1967-68; sr. acct. Solo Cup Co., Chgo., 1968-72; cost acctg. mgr. Am. Lock Co., Crete, Ill., 1972-75, controller, 1975—. Sec., Annunciata Baseball League, Chgo., 1969-73. Served with U.S. Army, 1953-55. Roman Catholic. Club: Lions (treas. East Side). Home: 10729 Ave E Chicago IL 60617 Office: 3400 W Exchange Rd Crete IL 60417

ABRAHAM, SAMUEL THARMALETH, clergyman, psychologist; b. Nagpur, India, Sept. 30, 1948; came to U.S., 1972; s. Tharmaleth M. and Mary T. A.; m. Melodee S. Larson, June 22, 1974; children—Isaac T., Matthew T. M.S., N.D. State U., 1976; M.Div., N.Am. Baptist Sem., Sioux Falls, S.D., 1978; Ed.D., U. S.D., 1981. Lic. psychologist, S.D. Ordained to ministry Baptist Ch., 1974; psychologist Psychol. Counseling Ctr., Vermillion, S.D., 1980—; pastor Faith Fellowship Ch., Vermillion, 1981—; pres., Founder Faith Bible Tng. Ctr., Vermillion, 1983—. Mem. S.D. Psychol. Assn., Am. Psychol. Assn., Am. Personnel and Guidance Assn., S.D. Mental Health Assn., Full Gospel Bus. Men's Assn., Word of Faith Assn., Phi Delta Kappa. Office: PO Box 411 Vermillion SD 57069

ABRAHAMSON, SHIRLEY SCHLANGER, justice Wisconsin Supreme Ct.; b. N.Y.C., Dec. 17, 1933; d. Leo and Ceil (Sauerteig) Schlanger; A.B., N.Y. U., 1953; J.D., Ind. U., 1956; S.J.D., U. Wis., 1962; m. Seymour Abrahamson, Aug. 1953; 1 son, Daniel Nathan. Asst. dir. Legis. Drafting Research Fund, Columbia U. Law Sch., 1957-60; admitted to Wis. bar, 1962; mem. firm Lafollette, Sinykin, Anderson & Abrahamson, Madison, Wis., 1962-76; justice Supreme Ct. Wis., Madison, 1976—; prof. U. Wis. Law Sch., from 1966; mem. Wis. Bd. Bar Commrs.; mem. Madison Mayor's Adv. Com., 1968-70; mem. Wis. Gov.'s Study Com. on Jud. Orgn., 1970-72; mem. adv. bd. Nat. Inst. Justice, U.S. Dept. Justice, 1980-82. Bd. dirs. LWV, Madison, 1963-65; bd. dirs. Wis. Civil Liberties Union, 1968-72, chmn. Capital Area chpt., 1969; bd. visitors Ind. U. Law Sch., from 1972. Mem. ABA (council sect. legal edn. and admissions to bar from 1976), Wis. Bar Assn., Dane County Bar Assn., 7th Cir. Bar Assn., Nat. Assn. Women Judges, Am. Law Inst. (council 1985—), Order of Coif, Phi Beta Kappa. Editor: Constitutions of the United States (National and State), 2 vols., 1962. Office: Supreme Ct of Wis State Capitol Madison WI 53702*

ABRAIRA, CARLOS, physician; b. Buenos Aires, Argentina, Mar. 25, 1936; came to U.S., 1963, naturalized, 1976; s. Jose B. and Maria (Cela) A.; m. Rosa Saffier, July 11, 1963; children—Daniel, Irene. Bacchalaureate, U. Buenos Aires, 1953, M.D., 1962. Diplomate Am. Bd. Internal Medicine. Intern, Mercy Hosp., Chgo., 1963-64; resident Mt. Sinai Hosp., Chgo., 1964-66; fellow in medicine Northwestern U. Hosp., Evanston, Ill., 1966-67; fellow in endocrinology Michael Reese Hosp., Chgo., 1967-69, attending physician-medicine, 1969-70; asst. prof. medicine U. Ill. Abraham Lincoln Sch., Chgo., 1970-78, assoc. prof. medicine, 1978-83; assoc. prof. medicine Loyola U., Chgo., 1984—; chief endocrinology Hines VA Hosp. (Ill.), 1972—; lectr. Cook County Grad. Sch. Medicine, Chgo., 1975-77; coordinator diabetes program Chgo. Med. Soc. Midwest Clin. Conf., 1980-83. Editor: How to Be Your Own Diabetes Manager, 1983. Contbr. articles to profl. jours. Grantee Allstate Found., 1966, VA, 1981, UpJohn Co., 1983, Sugar Assn., 1983. Fellow ACP; mem. Am. Diabetes Assn., Am. Soc. Clin. Nutrition, Am. Inst. Nutrition, Am. Fedn. Clin. Research (sr.), Endocrine Soc. Office: Hines VA Hosp 111C-12E 5th and Roosevelt Rd Hines IL 60141

ABRAMS, ALAN EDWIN, journalist, author; b. Detroit, Feb. 19, 1941; s. Harry J. and Mildred (Volod) A.; student public schs., Detroit. Pub. relations dir. Motown Record Corp., Detroit, 1959-66; Pub. relations dir. Gale Research Co., Detroit, 1974-76, editor journalism projects, 1976-81; contbg. editor Contemporary Authors, Detroit, 1976-81; book reviewer, spl. feature writer, paperback columnist The Windsor, (Ont., Can.) Star, 1980—; book reviewer Newsday, L.I., N.Y., 1980—; free-lance journalist, 1981—; spl. writer Detroit Free Press, 1983—, Globe and Mail, Toronto, Ont., Balt. Jewish Times, 1984—, 1984—, Balt. Jewish Times, 1983—, Jewish News, Detroit, 1983—; contbr. to various publs.; appraiser rare books and autographs, IRS, 1978-79; author: Special Treatment: The Untold Story of Thousands of Jews in Hitler's Third Reich, 1985; Why Windsor? An Anecdotal History of the Jews of Windsor and Essex County, 1981; Journalist Biographies Master Index, 1979; Media Personnel Guide, 1979; The Fourth Estate: Gale 1980 Literary Date Book. Recipient award of merit U.S. Dept. Labor, 1969; writing grantee Ont. Arts Council, 1980, 81, 82; award Western Ont. Newspaper Assn., 1984. Mem. Essex County Hist. Soc. Clubs: Detroit Press, Algonquin. Jewish. Office: 4308 W Highland Rd Milford MI 48042

ABRAMS, MARLENE RAE, lawyer; b. Albany, N.Y., May 16, 1949; d. Hyman and Charlotte (Rosenblum) A. B.S. summa cum laude, Boston U., 1971; J.D., Georgetown U., 1974. Bar: Ill. 1974, U.S. Dist. Ct. (no. dist.) Ill., 1974. Assoc. Isham, Lincoln & Beale, Chgo., 1974-77; asst. regional atty. Dept. Health and Human Services, Chgo., 1977—. Mem. cabinet Young Leadership div. Anti-Defamation League; jr. governing bd. Chgo. Symphony Orch.; mem. friends com. Hubbard St. Dance Co., Alliance of Art Inst. Recipient Spl. Citation for Exemplary Service Pub. Health Service Adminstrs., 1984. Mem. Beta Gamma Sigma. Office: 300 S Wacker Dr Suite 1800 Chicago IL 60606

ABRAMS, PERRY CHARLES, systems designer; b. Chgo., Apr. 9, 1943; s. Morris Dwin and Edythe (Krasney) A.; m. Barbara Helen Einstein, July 9, 1967; 1 child, Jolane. B.S., U. Ill.-Urbana, 1964, M.S., 1967; student Northwestern U., Evanston, Ill., 1967-68. Jr. programmer Harris Trust, Chgo., 1964-65; sr. programmer Benefit Trust Life, Chgo., 1968-74; data processing mgr. J. D. Marshall Internat. Inc., Skokie, Ill., 1974-84; system designer Advanced System Applications, Bloomingdale, Ill., 1984-85; systems cons. CNA Ins. Co., Chgo., 1985—; instr. Northwestern U., 1978; cons. programmer Wells Lamont Corp., Niles, Ill., 1982—. Mem. Assn. Computer Machinery. Avocations: Photography, coin collecting, stock market analyses. Home: 10100 Peach Pkwy Skokie IL 60076

ABRAMS, RICHARD BRILL, lawyer; b. Mpls., Nov. 2, 1931; s. Joseph E. and Nettie (Brill) A.; m. Myrna Carole Noodelman, Dec. 5, 1965; children—Jennifer, Adam. B.B.A., U. Minn., 1958, B.S.L., 1958, J.D., 1958. Bar: Minn. 1958, U.S. Ct. Appeals (8th cir.) 1981, U.S. Dist. Ct. Minn. 1981, Wis. 1983. Sole practice, Mpls., 1958-64; pres. Abrams & Spector, P.A., Mpls., 1964—; ad hoc prof. labor edn. U. Minn. Bd. dirs. Mpls. United Way, Multiple Sclerosis Soc. Minn.; v.p. Courage Ctr., 1977-83, bd. dirs., 1977—. Served with U.S. Army, 1955-57. Recipient Disting. and Devoted Service award Human Rights Com., Mpls. Central Labor Union Council, 1975; Meritorious Service award Minn. Rehab. Assn., 1978; Disting. Service award Courage Ctr., 1983. Mem. ABA, Minn. State Bar Assn., Wis. State Bar Assn., Assn. Trial Lawyers Am., Minn. Trial Lawyers Assn. Office: Abrams Spector PA 6800 France Ave S Suite 435 Minneapolis MN 55435

ABRAMS, SYLVIA FLECK, religious educator; b. Buffalo, Apr. 5, 1942; d. Abraham and Ann (Hanf) Fleck; m. Ronald M. Abrams, June 30, 1963; children—Ruth, Sharon. B.A. magna cum laude, Western Res. U., 1963, M.A., 1964, now postgrad.; B.H.L., Cleve. Coll. Jewish Studies, 1976, M.H.L., 1983; postgrad. U. Haifa, 1975, Yad Va Shem Summer Inst., Hebrew U., 1983. Hebrew tchr. The Temple, 1959-77, Hebrew coordinator, 1973-77; tchr. Beachwood High Sch., 1964-66; tchr. Hebrew and social studies Agnon Sch., Cleve., 1975-77, social studies resource tchr., 1976-77; edn1. dir. Temple Emanu El, Cleve., 1977—; chmn. ednl. dirs. council Cleve. Bd. Jewish Edn., 1982—. Recipient Elbert J. Benton award Western Res. U., 1963; Fred and Rose Rosenwasser Bible award Coll. Jewish Studies, 1974; Emmanuel Gamoran Meml. Curriculum award Nat. Assn. Temple Educator, 1978; Samuel Lipson Meml. award Coll. Jewish Studies, 1981 Bingham fellow Case Western Res. U., 1984-85. Mem. Nat. Assn. Temple Educators (bd. dirs. 1984—), Assn. Supervision and Curriculum Devel., Nat. Council Jewish Edn., Coalition for Alternative in Jewish Edn., Union Am. Hebrew Congregations (Israel curriculum task force), Cleve. Bur. Jewish Edn. (chmn. ednl. dirs. council 1982), Phi Beta Kappa. Jewish. Club: Hadassah (life). Editor: You and Your Schools, 1972. Office: 2200 S Green Rd Cleveland OH 44121

ABRAMSON, HERBERT FRANCIS, superintendent schools; b. Chgo., Dec. 16, 1930; s. Maurice P. and Rose (Harris) A.; B.S., Ind. U., 1953; M.Ed., Loyola U., 1961; postgrad. Roosevelt, Purdue, Ind. univs.; m. Sylvia Linde, June 29, 1958; children—Marcia Beth, Jacquelyn, Rachel. Tchr. pub. secondary schs., Lake Ridge, 1955—, prin. Calumet Jr. High Sch., Lake Ridge Sch. System, 1961-69; prin. Lake Jr. High Sch., 1969-74; supt. Lake Ridge Schs., Gary, 1974—; mem. State Supt. Schs. Adv. Com., 1978—, Ind. Planning Com. for Adult and Community Edn., 1979. Prin. Temple Israel Religious Sch., Gary; dir. Gary Sch. Employee Fed. Credit Union; mem. adv. council Urban League N.W. Ind.; mem. President's Roundtable, Meth. Hosp. Served with AUS, 1953-55; bd. dirs. N.W. Ind. Jewish Welfare Fedn.; bd. dirs. Temple Israel, Gary, 1971-72, pres. 1973-75; cons. Hebrew Acad. N.W. Ind. Mem. Am. Fedn. Tchrs. (past pres. No. 662), Nat. Assn. Secondary Sch. Prins., Lake County Jr. and Sr. High Prins. Assn., Ind. Assn. Pub. Sch. Supts. (state policies and resolutions com.), Ind. Assn. Sch. Bus. Ofcls., N.W. Ind. Pub. Sch. Study Council (pres. 1982-83), Am. Assn. Sch. Adminstrs., ACLU. Mem. B'nai B'rith. Contbr. articles to profl. jours. Home: 7210 Polk St Merrillville IN 46410 Office: 6111 W Ridge Rd Gary IN 46408

ABRELL, RONALD LANE, educator; b. Coal City, Ind., Mar. 14, 1934; s. Osce W. and Pauline A. A.; B.S., Ind. State U., 1959, M.S., 1962; Ed.D., Mont. State U., 1972; m. JoAnn Barnhizer, Mar. 31, 1963; 1 son, Lane. Tchr. social scis. Shelbyville (Ind.) High Sch., 1959-62, Broad Ripple High Sch., Inspls., 1962-67, North Putnam Sch. Corp., Bainbridge, Ind., 1967-68; coordinator student teaching in Chgo., Western Ill. U., Macomb, Ill., 1968-73; prof. edn. Coll. Edn., Macomb, 1973—, dir. student teaching, chmn. ednl. field experiences, 1973-81, asst. to dean, 1981-83; pres. Am. Nat. Bus. Hall of Fame, 1983—. Served with U.S. Army, 1953-55. Mem. Ill. Assn. Tchr. Educators (pres. 1978-79, chmn. legis. com. 1977-78, 79-80), Am. Assn. Sch. Adminstrs., Assn. Supervision and Curriculum Devel., Horace Mann League, N. Am. Soc. Tng. and Devel., Am. Mgmt. Assn., Am. Assn. Community and Jr. Colls., Assn. Tchr. Educators, World Future Soc., Phi Delta Kappa. Democrat. Club: Elks. Author: Strictly for Student Teachers, 1973; contbr. articles to profl. jours. Office: Coll of Education Western Ill Univ Macomb IL 61455

ABROMSON, MARIAN FLEMING (MRS. JAMES J. ABROMSON), civic leader; b. Portland, Ind., Sept. 18, 1907; d. James R. and Jennie (Adair) Fleming; student DePauw U., 1926; m. James J. Abromson, July 15, 1933; 1 dau., Suzanne Fleming Abromson Joiner. Dir. Ft. Wayne Jour.-Gazette. Chmn. vol. blood service program ARC, Portland, 1947-83; pres. Jay County Bd. Pub. Welfare, Portland, 1964-80; sec. Earlham Coll. Parents Assn., Richmond, Ind., 1957-58; mem. Jay County Com. Aging, 1951-59; Jay County rep. to NE Ind. Dist. Com. Aging, 1959-60; bd. dirs. Jay County Mental Health Assn., 1958-78; pres. Jay County ARC; mem. Jay County Hosp. Aux.; chmn. Adopt-a-Patient Program, 1961-73; mem. Ind. Mental Health Bd., 1971—; v.p. bd. Ind. Cultural, Ednl. and Fine Arts Found., Ft. Wayne, 1973—; mem. com. Jay County Hosp. Meml. Trust, 1978—; pres. Jay County chpt. ARC, 1983—; bd. dirs. Portland Found., Ft. Wayne Jour.-Gazette Found., 1985—; mem. facility planning com. Jay County Arts Council; del. Democratic Nat. Conv., 1964. Recipient Achievement Service Award, Jay County, 1960; named Woman of Yr., Jay County Bus. and Profl. Women's Club, 1978. Mem. DAR, Daus. Am. Colonists, Delta Theta Tau, Alpha Chi Omega. Presbyterian (deaconess 1960-68, trustee ch. 1969-72). Clubs: Portland Country; Summit (Ft. Wayne). Home: 301 W Race St Portland IN 47371

ABU-ABSI, SAMIR, English and linguistics educator; b. Hasbaya, Lebanon, Apr. 4, 1938; came to U.S. 1964, naturalized, 1973; s. Milhem and Salimeh (Zaghir) A; m. Lucy M. Ogg, Aug. 16, 1968; children—Ramsey, Michael, Nicholas, Daniel, Laura. B.A., Am. U. Beirut, 1963; M.A., Ind. U., 1966, Ph.D., 1972. Instr., U. Toledo, Ohio, 1968-72, asst. prof., 1972-76, assoc. prof. 1976—, dir. linguistics program, 1972—; vis. asst. prof. Am. U. Beirut, 1972-73. Author: Basic Chad Arabic. Contbr. articles to profl. jours. Mem. Linguistic Soc. Am., Am. Assn. Tchrs. Arabic. Office: U Toledo Toledo OH 43606

ABUHL, JEANNE MARIE, real estate salesperson; b. Des Moines, May 13, 1946; d. Albert James and Marjorie Jeanette (Larson) A.; student Moody Bible Inst., 1966, local community colls. Exec. sec. to v.p. Scripture Press Found., Glen Ellyn, Ill., 1967-73; asst. to nat. field dir. Youth for Christ/USA, Wheaton, Ill., 1973-75; office mgr. Youth for Christ Internat., Geneva, Switzerland, 1975-78; dir. adminstrv. services Follett Coll. Stores, Elmhurst, Ill., 1978-83; mgr. client services McKay-Doerschuk & Co., Wheaton, Ill., 1983-84; sales assoc. Baird & Warner, Wheaton, 1984—; cons. Performax Systems. Bd. dirs. campign bd. Fox Valley Youth for Christ, 1981-82. Mem. Nat. Assn. Female Execs. Republican. Evangelical. Club: Zonta. Home: 118 S Erie St Wheaton IL 60187 Office: 400 W Roosevelt Rd Wheaton IL 60187

ACCETTOLA, PAUL EDWARD, lawyer; b. N.Y.C., Nov. 7, 1947; s. Albert Bernard and Rose Marie (Galasso) A.; m. Julia Shaw Holmes, July 21, 1971 (div. 1981); children—Alison and Andrew; m. Judith Ann Kirker, Oct. 9, 1982. B.A., Drew U., 1970; J.D., U. of Toledo, 1975. Bar: Ohio, U.S. Dist. Ct. (no. dist.) Ohio. Staff atty. Toledo Pub. Defenders Office (Ohio), 1975—; ptnr. Herschel, Kuhnle & Accettola, Toledo, 1975—; vis. lectr. U. of Toledo Coll. of Law, 1980—. Mem. exec. bd. Toledo Ct. Dianostic and Treatment Ctr., Toledo, 1983—. Served with U.S. Army, 1970-72. Mem. Ohio Bar Assn., Toledo Bar Assn. (chmn. physician atty. com. 1982—). Democrat. Roman Catholic. Avocations: Woodworking; scuba diving. Office: Herschel Kuhnle & Accettola 830 Spitzer Bldg Toledo OH 43604

ACCURSO, MICHAEL F., data processing analyst; b. Chgo., Sept. 13, 1945; s. Paul J. and Nancy M. (Covelli) A.; m. Carol J. Roemer, June 15, 1968 (div. Jan. 1984); children—Kelly Ann, Scott Kim. B.A. in English, St. Mary's Coll., Winona, Minn., 1967; M.B.A., St. Thomas Coll., St. Paul, 1979. Systems analyst Continental Bank, Chgo., 1970-73; sr. programmer/analyst Fingerhut Corp., Minnetonka, Minn., 1973-74; systems mgr. White Farm Equipment, Hopkins, Minn., 1974-79; dir. systems Nat. Car Rental, Mpls., 1979—. Served to capt. USMC, 1967-70. Mem. Assn. Systems Mgmt. Avocations: golf; jogging; reading. Home: 8537 Xenium Ln Maple Grove MN 55369 Office: Nat Car Rental 7700 France Ave S Minneapolis MN 55435

ACHENBACH, JAN DREWES, engineering scientist, educator; b. Leeuwarden, Netherlands, Aug. 20, 1935; came to U.S., 1959; s. Johannes and Elizabeth (Schipper) A.; m. Marcia Graham Fee, July 15, 1961. M.S., Technische Hogeschool, Delft, Netherlands, 1959; Ph.D., Stanford U., 1962. Preceptor, Columbia U., 1962-63; asst. prof. civil engring. Northwestern U., 1963-66, assoc. prof., 1966-69, prof. civil engring., 1969-81, Walter P. Murphy prof. civil engring. and applied math., 1981—; vis. assoc. prof. U. Calif.-LaJolla, 1969; vis. prof. Tech. U. Delft, 1970-71; cons. Argonne (Ill.) Nat. Lab., 1975-81, Lawrence Livermore Lab., Calif., 1982—, Electric Power Research Inst., Calif., 1982—. Author: Wave Propagation in Elastic Solids, 1973; Ray Methods for Waves in Elastic Solids, 1982. Contbr. articles to tech. jours. Editor-in-chief internat. jour.: Wave Motion, 1979—. Recipient numerous research grants. Fellow ASME, Am. Acad. Mechanics; mem. Am. Soc. Engring. Edn. (recipient Curtis W. McGraw Research award 1975), Am. Geophys. Union, Acoustical Soc. Am., Nat. Acad. Engring. Home: 574 Ingleside Park Evanston IL 60201 Office: Northwestern Univ 2145 N Sheridan Rd Evanston IL 60201

ACHILLES, CHARLES ALBERT, association executive; b. Berwyn, Ill., Sept. 29, 1946; s. Charles Laddie and Mildred Antonette (Volmut) A.; B.S. in Chemistry, No. Ill. U., 1968; M.B.A., Loyola U., Chgo., 1972; m. Sharon Lee Lullo, May 23, 1970; children—Amber Lee, Brylan Charles. Tchr., Woodridge (Ill.) Sch. System, 1968-69, asst. prin., 1969-72; dir. membership services Inst. Real Estate Mgmt., Chgo., 1972-76, staff v.p. membership services and communications, 1976-81, staff v.p. legis. and spl. services, 1981—. Active Community Affairs Com., 1977-79; pres. Oakwood Community Assn., 1978, bd. dirs., 1979; bd. dirs. Oakwood Homeowners Assn., 1979, v.p., 1981, pres., 1982-83; active Community Party of Westmont, 1978, 80, 82 Mem. Am. Mktg. Assn., Am. Soc. Assn. Execs., Community Assns. Inst., Am. Statis. Assn., Nat. Housing Conf. (dir.), Nat. Inst. Bldg. Scis., Assn. MBA Execs., Cavaliers, Phi Eta Sigma. Congregationalist. Clubs: 71; Downtown; Capitol Hill. Home: 5900 Oakwood Dr Apt 3C Lisle IL 60532 Office: 430 N Michigan Ave Chicago IL 60611

ACHTEMEIER, GARY LYNN, atmospheric scientist; b. Wichita, Kans., Mar. 1, 1943; s. Walter John and Phyllis (Norman) A.; B.S., Fla. State U., 1965, M.S., 1969, Ph.D., 1972; m. (Mildred) Sue Dicus, June 15, 1968; children—Cheryl Ann, Scott Alan. NRC grantee Nat. Severe Storms Lab., Norman, Okla., 1972-73; asso. research scientist Ill. State Water Survey, Champaign, 1973-1982; profl. research scientist, 1982 vis. asso. prof. Lab. for Atmospheric Research, U. Ill., 1981; cons. Nat. Forest Expt. Sta., Macon, Ga., 1975—; cons. U. Ill. M.B.A. Program; proposal reviewer NSF, 1976—. Publicity chmn. Full Gospel Businessmen's Fellowship Internat. Rally, 1979, rally co-chmn., 1981, 83, v.p. Champaign-Urbana chpt., 1982-83, pres., 1984—. NSF grantee, 1976-77; NASA grantee, 1982—. Mem. Am. Meteorol. Soc. (com. on severe storms 1980-81), AAAS, Sigma Xi, Chi Epsilon Pi. Republican. Club: Kiwanis. Contbr. articles in field to profl. jours.; tech. paper reviewer for three jours., 1976—. Office: Water Resources Bldg 605 E Springfield St PO Box 5050 Champaign IL 61820

ACHTERMAN, JAMES WILLIAM, management consultant; b. Cin., May 27, 1945; s. Hubert Lewis and Alberta (Moore) A.; B.B.A., U. Cin., 1968; m. Janet C. Gibbs; children—Nicole Lee, Jeffrey Scott. Mgmt. analyst City of Cin., 1968-70; budget dir. Hamilton County Ohio, Cin., 1970-72, asst. county adminstr., 1972-74; controller Cin. Public Schs., 1974-76; mng. cons. Ernst & Whinney, Cin., 1976-77, mgr. services to local govt., 1977-82; sr. mgr. services to local govt. for State of Ohio, Peat, Marwick, Mitchell & Co., 1982—, also dir. mgmt. cons. office, Columbus. Chmn. found. com. United Negro Coll. Fund, 1979-81; councilman City of Wyoming, Ohio, 1979-84; chmn. adv. com. on state acctg. policy State of Ohio. Mem. Ohio-Ky.-Ind. Regional Council Govts. (trustee 1971-74, 81-84), Internat. City Mgmt. Assn., Mcpl. Finance Officers Assn., Ohio Mcpl. Finance Officers Assn. Office: Peat Marwick Mitchell & Co 2 Nationwide Plaza Columbus OH 43215

ACKERMAN, EMERY ELWOOD, organization executive; b. Granite City, Ill., Aug. 9, 1948; s. Elwood Leigh and Evelyn Astrid (Olson) A.; B.S. in Psychology, U. Ill., 1973; postgrad. So. Ill. U., 1975-78. Research asst. So. Ill. U., Carbondale, 1975-76, teaching asst., 1976-78; programmer McDonnell Douglas Automation Co., St. Louis, 1979-81, programmer analyst, 1981-83; program. dir. St. Louis Mensa, 1980, vice chmn., 1981, pres., 1981—. Mem. Pi Mu Epsilon. Club: Intertel. Address: 3032 Buxton Ave Granite City IL 62040

ACKERMAN, LOUISE MAGAW, writer; b. Topeka, July 9, 1904; d. William Glenn and Anna Mary (Shaler) Magaw; B.S., Kans. State U., 1926; M.A., U. Nebr., 1942; m. Grant Albert Ackerman, Dec. 27, 1926; children—Edward Shaler, Anita Louise. Free lance writer, 1930—. Mem. Lincoln Community Arts Council. Mem. Nat. Soc. Daus. Colonial Wars (nat. pres. 1977-80), DAR (past v.p. gen.), Americans of Armorial Ancestry (sec. 1976-82), Nat. Huguenot Soc. (2d v.p. 1977-83), Nebr. Writers Guild (v.p. 1980-81, past sec.-treas.), Nat. League Am. Pen Women, Lincoln C. of C., Phi Kappa Phi. Republican. Club: Nat. Writers. Lodge: Order Eastern Star. Home: Eastmont Towers III Apt 428 6335 O St Lincoln NE 68510

ACKERMAN, MARY ALICE, college administrator; b. Lincoln, Nebr., Dec. 27, 1947; d. James Nils and Jean Caroline (Doty) A.; 1 child, Nils Peter. B.A. in English, Macalester Coll., 1970. Admissions counselor Macalester Coll., St.

Paul, 1970-73, assoc. dir. admissions, 1973-75, dir. admissions, 1975-79, dean of students, 1979—; corp. bd. mem. Am. Coll. Testing Corp., Iowa City, 1979-85; dir. Am. Coll. Personnel Assn., Washington, 1980—; reader Truman Scholarship Com., Ednl. Testing Service, Princeton, N.J., 1985; mem./trainer Higher Edn. Mgmt. Inst., 1981. Bd. dirs. St. Paul Camp Fire Council, 1984—, St. Paul's Childhood Ctr., 1983—. Recipient leadership award YWCA St. Paul, 1983. Mem. Am. Assn. Higher Edn., Nat. Assn. Student Personnel Adminstrs., Nat. Assn. Women Deans, Adminstrs. and Counselors. Congregationalist. Club: P.E.O. (Lincoln). Avocations: cooking; cabin; reading. Office: Macalester College 1600 Grand Ave Saint Paul MN 55105

ACKERMAN, ORA RAY, hospital administrator; b. Mapleton, Minn., Jan. 13, 1931; s. Minnie (Quam) Haney; m. Barbara Elizabeth Singley, Mar. 25, 1951; children—Bruce, David, Cindy. B.S. with distinction, U. Minn., 1953, M.Edn. in Hosp. Recreation, 1955; student Ind. U., 1961-63. Dir. recreation Seton Inst., Balt., 1955-56, Central State Hosp., Indpls., 1956-57; coordinator activity therapy Evansville State Hosp., Ind., 1957-63; dir. edn. and activity therapy Ind. Dept. Mental Health, Indpls., 1963-66; supt. Ft. Wayne State Hosp. and Tng. Ctr., Ind., 1966—; dir. Opportunities, Inc., Fort Wayne, Anthony Wayne Rehab. Ctr., Fort. Wayne. Fellow Am. Assn. on Mental Deficiency. Avocations: golf, flying, scuba diving. Home: 802 Northwood Blvd Fort Wayne IN 46805 Office: Fort Wayne State Hosp and Training Center 4900 St Joe Rd Fort Wayne IN 46815

ACKERMANN, GRETCHEN LOUISE, editor, public relations executive; b. Mt. Clemens, Mich., Sept. 29, 1929; d. Harold F. and Norah Medora (Aldrich) Reinhardt; student Albion Coll., 1947-48; B.S., Mich. State U., 1951; m. Ralph C. Ackermann, Mar. 14, 1953 (dec.); children—Brian, Bradley, Jeffrey. Society editor South Macomb News, 1951-53, research writer City of Dearborn (Mich.), 1953-55; reporter, women's editor Dearborn Times-Herald, 1968-70; religious editor, Lifestyles editor, Dearborn Press & Guide, 1970-82, Lifestyles editor, 1982—; ptnr. Ackermann-Melanyn Assocs., pub. relations, 1982—. Pres., Dearborn Community Arts Council, 1977-79; mem. Mich. Gov.'s Council of Arts, Arts Promotion Adv. Panel; sec. Dearborn Mayor's Telecommunications Commn., 1980—. Recipient editorial awards Mich. Health Council, Mich. Press. Assn. Mem. Women in Communication, Dearborn Writer's Guild. Pub. Relations Soc. Am., Dearborn C. of C., Woman's Nat. Farm and Garden Assn. Presbyterian. Home: 246 S York St Dearborn MI 48124 Office: 15340 Michigan St Dearborn MI 48126

ACKERSON, CHARLES STANLEY, clergyman, social worker; b. St. Louis, June 19, 1935; s. Charles Albert and Glenda Mae (Brown) A.; m. Carol Jean Stehlick, Aug. 18, 1957; children—Debra Lynn, Charles Mark, Heather Sue. A.B., William Jewell Coll., 1957; M.Div., Colgate Rochester Div. Sch., 1961. Ordained to ministry Baptist Ch., 1961. Pastor, Glens Falls (N.Y.) Friends Meeting, 1961-65; assoc. pastor Delmar Bapt. Ch., St. Louis, 1965-68; resource dir. Block Partnership, St. Louis, 1968-71; group home dir. North Side YMCA, St. Louis, 1971-72; group home supr. St. Louis Juvenile Ct., 1973-74; program dir. Youth Opportunities Unltd., casework supr. St. Louis County Juvenile Ct., 1974-83; human resource specialist St. Louis County Dept. Human Resources, 1985—; instr. adminstrn. of justice Mo. Bapt. Coll., St. Louis, 1980—; mem. ordination council area V, Great Rivers region Am. Bapt. Chs. U.S.A., 1982-84; chmn. youth focus group Interfaith Partnership Met. St. Louis, 1985—. Chmn. group home com. Mo. Council on Criminal Justice, 1973-75; chmn. cts. and instns. subcom. Juvenile Delinquency Task Force for Gov. Mo. Action Plan for Pub. Safety, 1976. Mem. Nat. Council Juvenile and Family Ct. Judges, Mo. Juvenile Justice Assn. (v.p., chmn. tng. com.), Cairn Terrier Assn. Am., Three Rivers Kennel Club of Mo. (pres.), Mo. Conservation Fedn., Nat. Rifle Assn., Nat. Muzzle Loading Rifle Assn., Trappers of Starved Rock, Lambda Chi Alpha. Democrat. Baptist. Home: 1221 Havenhurst St Manchester MO 63011

ACKERSON, LAIRD DOUGLAS, optometrist; b. Ridley Park, Pa., June 11, 1956; s. Herbert D. and Rosemary (Kraus) A.; m. Jacqueline Ann Fallon, Sept. 8, 1979; children—Natalie Fallon, Kenneth Herbert William. B.S., Ohio State U., 1978, O.D., 1982. Lic. optometrist, Ohio. Practice optometry, Hilliard, Ohio, 1982—; co-owner, mgr. Sportsoptic, Hilliard, 1982—; lectr. Hilliard High Sch., 1983—. Bd. dirs. Hilliard Athletic Boosters, 1983—; coach Hilliard Baseball Assn., 1975—; vision screener Hilliard Community Ctr., 1982—. Mem. Am. Optometric Assn., Ohio Optometric Assn., Am. Optometric Assn. (sports vision sect.), Hilliard C. of C., Ohio State U. Alumni Assn. Republican. Lutheran. Lodges: Lions (bd. dirs. 1983—), Optimist. Home and Office: 4939 Cemetery Rd Hilliard OH 43026

ACKMANN, DAVID ALAN, data processing consultant; b. St. Louis, Nov. 19, 1948; s. Florenze Alfred and Anna Elizabeth (Ray) A.; m. Kathleen Marie Vander Kraats, Oct. 21, 1972; children—Abigail Suzanne, Alan Robert. B.S.M.E., U. Mo.-Rolla, 1972, M.S. in Computer Sci., 1982. Programmer, analyst McDonnell Douglas Co., St. Louis, 1972-79; pres. ISSCO Graphics Users Group, 1985; cons. Monsanto Co., St. Louis, 1979—; speaker World Computer Graphics Assn., Berlin, 1983, 84. Contbr. articles to profl. jours. Mem. Assn. Computing Machinery, Nat. Computer Graphics Assn. (state officer 1983). Avocations: choral music; woodworking. Office: Monsanto Co 800 N Lindbergh Blvd Saint Louis MO 63167

ACOSTA, JULIO BERNARD, obstetrician, gynecologist; b. Loreto, Peru, S. Am., July 29, 1927; came to U.S., 1955, naturalized, 1960; s. Miguel and Flor Maria (Solis) A.; M.D., St. Marcos U. (Peru), 1955; m. Mary Jane Aedinvice, Aug. 30, 1974; children—Raul, Luis-Miguel, Patricia, Silvia, Douglas, Jill. Intern, St. Alexis Hosp., Cleve., 1955-56; resident St. Alexis Hosp., 1956-57, St. Ann Hosp., Cleve., 1957-59; practice medicine specializing in obstetrics and gynecology, Livonia, Mich., 1964—; chief of staff Plymouth Gen. Hosp., Detroit, 1970-73, chief gynecologic sect., 1974—; med. dir. Northland Family Planning Clinic, Southfield, Mich., 1976—; active staff Grace-Harper Hosp., Detroit, 1973—, St. Mary Hosp., Livonia, 1964—. Served to capt., M.C., USAR, 1959-62. Diplomate Am. Bd. Obstetrics and Gynecology. Fellow Am. Coll. Obstetricians and Gynecologists, Am. Fertility Soc., Am. Soc. for Colposcopy and Cervical Pathology, Am. Soc. Abdominal Surgeons, Internat. Coll. Surgeons, Am. Coll. Internat. Physicians, Mich. Obstetrical-Gynecological Soc.; mem. S.E. Mich. Surg. Soc., Peruvian-Am. Med. Soc. Detroit Tennis and Squash. Contbr. articles to profl. jours. Home: 5280 Inkster Rd Bloomfield Hills MI 48013 Office: 27634 Five Mile Rd Livonia MI 48134

ACS, IMRE ZOLTAN, archival librarian; b. Bacsalmas, Hungary, Feb. 20, 1916; came to U.S., 1952; s. Jozsef Zoltan and Jolan (Szabo) A.; m. Klara I. Szemeredy, May 30, 1946; children—Zoltan, Klara, Csilla. LL.B., Royal Hungarian Francis Joseph U., 1940, Ph.D., 1943. Freelance journalist, Villach, Austria, and Cleve., 1945-75; archival librarian Cuyahoga County Archives, Cleve., 1975—. Author: Michael Kovats de Fabricy 1980. Contbr. articles to profl. jours. Recipient Hungarian Mil. Order: Vitez/Hungarian Medal of Honor. Mem. Arpad Acad. Democrat. Roman Catholic. Office: PO Box 20093 Shaker Heights Station Cleveland OH 44120

ACUFF, CHARLES DAVIS, data processing executive; b. Louisiana, Mo., Aug. 25, 1934; s. Davis Halliburton Acuff and Anna Mae (McGahen) McCuskey; m. Shirley Ann Vincent, Dec. 18, 1954; children—Suzanne Rose, Charles Davis, Jr. B.S., N.E. Mo. State U., Kirksville, 1956, M.A., 1961. Cert. tchr., Mo. Systems analyst Ford Motor Co., Dearborn, Mich., 1966-67; supr. adminstrn. program MCAUTO, St. Louis, 1967-69; dir. EDP, Peabody Coal Co., St. Louis, 1969-80; data processing cons., instr. St. Charles pub. schs., Mo., 1980-81; systems coordination mgr. Emerson Electric, St. Louis, 1982-83, mgr. computer services, 1983—; adj. prof. Lindenwood Coll., St. Charles, 1977—. Asst. cubmaster St. Louis Area council Boy Scouts Am., St. Charles, 1976-77, troop chmn., 1978. Served with U.S. Army, 1956-58. Mem. Inst. Cert. Systems Profls. (cert.), Assn. Systems Mgmt., Data Processing Mgmt. Assn. Methodist. Club: Spanish Lake Quadrils (Mo.). Avocations: bridge, gardening, square dancing. Home: 2420 Westminster Dr Saint Charles MO 63301 Office: Emercons Electric E & S Div 8100 W Florissant St Saint Louis MO 63136

ADAIR, BRUCE JAMES, publishing company official; b. Phila., Apr. 19, 1947; s. Francis and Marion Frances (Kosek) A.; B.A. in Sociology, Eastern Coll., St. David's, Pa., 1969; M.A. in Religious Edn., Eastern Baptist Theol. Sem., Phila., 1971; m. Linda Kushman, Oct. 15, 1982: children—Kenneth, Kristina Marie, Amy Lynne. Asst. pastor Jacobstown (N.J.) Bapt. Ch., 1966-67; dir. youth Upper Merion (Pa.) Bapt. Ch., 1967-68; minister edn. United Presbyn. Ch. of Manoa, Havertown, Pa., 1969-74; instr. phys. edn., head varsity soccer coach Eastern Coll., 1969-73; field cons., then asst. curriculum product mgr. David C. Cook Pub. Co., Elgin, Ill., 1974-76, curriculum product mgr., 1976-79, curriculum market mgr., 1979-82, curriculum mktg. dir., 1982—. Recipient Good Citizenship award Phila. Union League, 1968; named Christian Educator of Year, Phila. Sunday Sch. Assn., 1973. Office: 850 N Grove St Elgin IL 60120

ADAIR, CHARLES VALLOYD, physician; b. Lorain, Ohio, Apr. 20, 1923; s. Waite and Ella Jane (Robertson) A.; A.B., Hobart Coll., Geneva, N.Y., 1944; M.D., Western Res. U., 1947; m. Constance Dean, Apr. 1, 1944; children—Allen V., Richard D. Intern, then asst. resident in medicine Rochester (N.Y.) Gen. Hosp., 1947-49; fellow in medicine Univ. Hosps., Syracuse, N.Y., 1949-51; practice medicine specializing in internal medicine, Mansfield, Ohio, 1953—; mem. staffs Mansfield Gen. Hosp., Peoples Hosp., Richland Neuropsychiat. Hosp.; mem. Mansfield City Bd. Health; trustee, past pres. Mansfield Meml. Homes. Served to capt. AUS, 1943-46, 51-53. Diplomate Am. Bd. Internal Medicine. Fellow A.C.P.; mem. Am. Soc. Internal Medicine, Am., Ohio med. assns., Richland County Med. Soc. Republican. Congregationalist. Clubs: Our, Westbrook Country, University. Home: 1010 Woodland Rd Mansfield OH 44907 Office: 480 Glessner Ave Mansfield OH 44903

ADAM, PAUL JAMES, mech. engr.; b. Kansas City, Mo., Oct. 26, 1934; s. Paul James and Adrienne (Zimmerman) A.; B.S. in Mech. Engring., U. Kans., 1956; m. Barbara Ann Mills, Dec. 18, 1956; children—Paul James III, Blair Dodderidge II, Matthew Mills. Mech. engr. Black & Veatch, Cons. Engrs., Kansas City, Mo., 1956, 59-74, partner, asst. head Power div., 1975-78, exec. partner, head Power div., 1978—; dir. First Continental Bank & Trust Co. Mem. Greater Univ. Fund Adv. Bd., U. Kans., 1964-66; mem. engring. adv. bd. U. Kans., 1982—. Served to 1st lt., USAF, 1956-59. Registered profl. engr., 14 states. Mem. Nat., Mo. socs. profl. engrs., ASME, Am. Nuclear Soc., Atomic Indsl. Forum, Tau Beta Pi, Sigma Tau, Pi Tau Sigma, Omicron Delta Kappa, Alpha Tau Omega. Episcopalian. Clubs: Mission Hills Country, Saddle and Sirloin. Office: 1500 Meadow Lake Pkwy Kansas City MO 64114

ADAMS, ALLAN WILFRED, business consultant, lawyer; b. Beloit, Wis., Aug. 23, 1910; s. Harry Wilfred and Prudence Mary (Bennett) A.; A.B., Harvard Coll., 1932; LL.B., U. Wis., 1935; m. Charlotte Amy Ray, Nov. 26, 1936; children—Allan Wilfred, Prudence B., Polly H., John B. Admitted to Wis. bar, 1935; partner firm Adams & Adams, Beloit, Wis., 1935-61; of counsel firm Hansen, Eggers, Berres & Kelley, Beloit, 1961—; pres. Adams Corp., Beloit, 1946-62; sec. Flakall Corp., Beloit, 1945-61; pres. Dell Foods, Beloit, 1957-61; pres. Adams Internat. div. Beatrice Foods Co., Beloit, 1962-75, cons., 1975-79; corp. sec., gen. counsel Regal-Beloit Corp., 1979-82; dir. Regal Beloit Corp., 1955-81, corp. sec., 1979-82. Pres., Beloit YMCA, 1955-64, dir., 1950-72; dir. Wis. Taxpayers Alliance, 1963—; bd. dirs. Beloit ARC, 1958-70, United Givers, 1978-83, Greater Beloit Steering Com., 1978-81; with OPA-Rent Div., 1942-45; mem. Young Pres. Orgn., 1949-59. Paul Harris Rotary fellow, 1978. Fellow Am. Coll. Probate Counsel, Am. Bar Found., Wis. Bar Found.; mem. Rock County Bar Assn. (pres. 1946), Am., Wis. bar assns. Republican. Congregationalist. Clubs: Rotary, Beloit Country, Madison, Elks, Wis. 49ers. Home: 1628 Emerson St Beloit WI 53511 Office: 419 Pleasant St Beloit WI 53511

ADAMS, ANDREW JAMES, foreign language educator; b. Aurora, Ill., May 8, 1944; s. Arthur G. and Sara J. Adams. B.A., Monmouth Coll., 1966; M.A., Ind. U., 1968, Ph.D., 1975. Teaching assoc. Ind. U., Bloomington, 1967-70; prof. classics North Central Coll., Naperville, Ill., 1970—. Writer newspaper column The Word on Words, 1984—. Mem. Ill. Classical Conf. Office: North Central Coll 30 N Brainard St Naperville IL 60566

ADAMS, ANNIE JENE, educator, consultant; b. Hopkinsville, Ky., Feb. 25, 1947; d. Robert Fulton and Jeanette Juanita (Johnson) Pollard; m. Elijah Harold Adams, Apr. 13, 1968; children—Angela, Norman. M.A. in Recreation Therapy, Wayne State U., 1981, Cert. Ed. S., 1984, doctoral candidate, 1985—. Cert. tchr., Mich. Tchr. adult edn. Hazel Park, Mich., 1974-75, St. Mary Magdalen, Hazel Park, Mich., 1974-75; tchr. spl. edn. Washington Careers Ctr. Detroit Bd. Edn., 1977—; host radio show Women of Power. Mem. Assn. Supervision and Curriculum Devel., Detroit Fedn. Tchrs., NAACP, Phi Delta Kappa. Home: 6433 Sheridan Ave Detroit MI 48213 Office: Washington Careers Ctr 13000 Dequindre St Detroit MI 48212

ADAMS, ARLIE, manufacturing company executive; b. Louisa, Ky., Oct. 22, 1935; s. George and Effie Josephine (Davis) A.; m. Peggy Jo Branham, Sept. 1, 1956; children—Arlie, James Richard. Mgr. systems Galion Mfg. div. Dresser Industries (Ohio), 1983—. Mem. Hilliard (Ohio) Planning and Zoning Commn., 1978-83. Mem. Am. Prodn. and Inventory Control Soc. Home: 988 N Biddle Rd Galion OH 44833 Office: 352 South St Galion OH 44833

ADAMS, BERTRAND, retired physician, electro-acupuncture researcher; b. Webster City, Iowa, Nov. 29, 1907; s. James Edward and Hilda Marie (Sonerholm) A.; m. Mary Elizabeth Beymer, Dec. 20, 1956. B.A., U. Iowa, 1932; D.O., Des Moines Still Coll., 1943; diploma Fed. Sch. Comml. Design, Mpls., 1930. Intern Detroit Osteo. Hosp., 1943-44; practice medicine specializing in cranial therapy, Ames, Iowa, 1944—; researcher high-frequency electro-acupuncture. Contbr. articles to profl. jours. Recipient Dubuque Mural award Art in Fed. Bldgs., 1936. Mem. Internat. Acad. Preventive Medicine (founding mem.), Town and Coll. Toastmasters, Ames Area Amateur Astronomers. Avocation: gardening. Address: 1013 Adams St Ames IA 50010

ADAMS, BRADLEY HASSAN, civil engineer; b. Rochester, Pa., Mar. 16, 1953; s. Elee James and Alease Rebekah A.; m. Mary Ann Kennedy, May 25, 1954; children—Bradley Kennedy, Brenda Renee. B.S. in Civil Engring., Ohio U., 1976; postgrad. Cleve. State U., 1981-82. Registered profl. engr., Ohio. Engr. Factory Mut., Cleve., 1976-78; safety insp. for fire and explosions, constrn. project engr. Polytech Inc., Cleve., 1978—; engring. cons. for bridge rating and demolition. Mem. ASCE. Home: 2449 Channing Rd University Heights OH 44118 Office: 1744 Payne Ave Cleveland OH 44114

ADAMS, CHARLES HENRY, animal scientist, emeritus educator; b. Burdick, Kans., Nov. 7, 1918; s. Henry Lory and Bertha Frances (Westbrook) A.; m. Eula Mae Peters, Apr. 29, 1943. B.S., Kans. State U., 1941, M.S., 1942; Ph.D., Mich. State U., 1964. Instr., Kans. State U., Manhattan, 1946-47; asst. prof. U. Nebr., Lincoln, 1947-64, assoc. prof., 1964-70, prof. animal sci., 1970-84, prof. emeritus, 1984—, asst. dean Coll. Agr., 1973-84. Served to 1st lt. AUS, 1943-46. Recipient Disting. Teaching awards Gamma Sigma Delta, 1969, U. Nebr., 1971, Am. Meat Sci. Assn., 1969, Am. Soc. Animal Sci., 1972. Fellow Am. Soc. Animal Sci.; mem. Am. Meat Sci. Assn., Inst. Food Technologists, AAAS, Nebr. Acad. Sci., Sigma Xi, Gamma Sigma Delta, Alpha Zeta. Republican. Mem. Christian Ch. (Disciples of Christ). Lodge: Rotary. Contbr. articles in field to profl. jours. Home: 7101 Colby St Lincoln NE 68505

ADAMS, DALE RUSSELL, antique automobile restoration shop executive; b. Victorville, Calif., Apr. 6, 1952; s. Roger William and Marjorie Ann (Hull) A.; m. Joanne Eleanor Engholm, Aug. 21, 1971; children—Nathaniel Conrad, Jeremy Michael. Student Oral Roberts U., 1970-71. Technician, Auburn Cord Duesenberg Co., Broken Arrow, Okla., 1972-76; owner, operator Dale Adams Enterprises, Northfield, Ohio, 1976—, Northfield Forming, 1980—. Patentee in field. Elder, Northfield Presbyterian Ch. Recipient Pres.'s Cup, Antique Automobile Club of Am., 1981, 82, James Melton Cup, 1983, AACA Cup, 1984, awards for best profl. restoration of yr. Vet. Motor Car Club of Am., 1981, Classic Car Club of Am., 1983. Mem. Antique Automobile Club of Am., Classic Car Club of Am. Republican. Club: Val Halla Athletic. Avocations: racquetball; model trains. Home and Office: 145 W Aurora Rd Northfield OH 44067

ADAMS, DON KARL, veterinarian; b. Wayne, Ohio, Nov. 5, 1924; s. Gryadon S. and Florence (Dicken) A.; m. Caroline Lucas, Dec. 19, 1948; children—Deborah Lynne Adams Lilly, Elaine Ruth Adams Moore, Anne, Grace Dicken Adams Wenzke, John Lucas. D.V.M., Ohio State U., 1953. Gen. practice vet. medicine, Montpelier, Ohio, 1954—. Vice pres., then pres. Montpelier Exempted Village Bd. Edn., 1962-66, 70, 74, 78, 83, 84, Four County Joint Vocat. Sch. Bd., 1965-75; pres. Montpelier Indsl. Devel. Com., 1984-85. Mem. N.W. Ohio Sch. Bd. Assn. (pres. 1966-77), Ohio Sch. Bd. Assn. (mem. policy and legis. com. 1969-73), William County Hist. Soc. (pres. 1978-79, chmn. bldg. com. 1980-83). Republican. Methodist. Address: 413 W Water St Montpelier OH 43543

ADAMS, EDMUND JOHN, lawyer; b. Lansing, Mich., June 6, 1938; s. John Edmund and Helen Kathryn (Pavlick) A.; m. Mary Louise Riegler, Aug. 11, 1962. B.A., Xavier U., 1960; LL.B., U. Notre Dame, 1963. Bar: Ohio 1963. Assoc. Paxton & Seasongood, Cin., 1965-70; assoc. Frost & Jacobs, 1970-71, ptnr., 1971—. Author: Founding Families of Loretto, 1983. Trustee, Southwest Ohio Regional Transit Authority, 1980—; chmn. Cin. Sister City Program, 1984—; mem. Hamilton County Republican Exec. Com., 1982—. Served to 1st lt. U.S. Army, 1963-65. Mem. ABA, Ohio Bar Assn., Cin. Bar Assn. Roman Catholic. Club: Cin. Tennis. Home: 1346 Park Ridge Place Cincinnati OH 45208 Office: Frost & Jacobs 2500 Central Trust Ctr Cincinnati OH 45202

ADAMS, EENA J. CARLISLE, dietitian, educator; b. Mt. Hope, Kans.; d. Alfred George and Nora Agnes (Kissick) Carlisle; B.S. in Home Econs., Kans. State U., 1939; M.S. in Foods and Nutrition, 1970; student Ohio U., 1954-61; m. Lawrence D. Adams, Dec. 11, 1940: children—Karen Jean Adams McCarthy, Maureen Janet Adams Mitchell. Tchr., Leonardville, Kans., 1939-40, Jan's Pvt. Sch., Front Royal, Va., 1949-52, Forestdale Sch., McCracken County, Ky., 1952-53, Jackson (Ohio) County and City Schs., 1953-68, Head Start, Jackson, 1965-68; grad. teaching asst. Kans. State U., Manhattan, 1969-70; asst. prof. home econs. Wayne (Nebr.) State Coll., 1970-76; asst. prof. home econs. and dietetics Morehead (Ky.) State U., 1976-82, coordinator energy mgmt. asst. program, 1979-80; cons. dietitian, 1982—. Mem. Front Royal (Va.) Recreation Council. Delta Kappa Gamma Annie Webb Blanton scholar, 1968. Mem. Am. Dietetic Assn. (registered dietitian), Nutrition Today Soc., Soc. Nutrition Edn., Am. Home Econs. Assn., Inst. Food Tech., W.Va.-Ohio-Ky. Dietetic Assn., Ohio Dietetic Assn., Ky. Dietetic Assn., Ohio Edn. Assn., Chi Omega, Delta Kappa Gamma (pres.), Alpha Lambda Delta. Home: Ka-Mel Farms Beaver OH 45613 also Crique Side Apt 4 Morehead KY 40351 Office: Crique Side Apt 4 Morehead KY 40351

ADAMS, GENE, editor; b. Springfield, Mo., Nov. 3, 1923; s. Charles H. and Marguerite (Kibbe) A.; B.A., Northwestern U., 1950; m. LaVergne Kanara, Apr. 4, 1945; 1 dau., Bonnie Jean. Pub., Midwestern Baker also Chgo. Retail Baker, Chgo., 1950-53; editor, pub. Mobile Homes & Mobile Living, 1953-58; editor Splty. Salesman, Chgo., 1958-67; editor Modern Garden Center, Barrington, Ill., 1967-68; editorial dir. Selling Sporting Goods, Chgo., 1968-72; editor-in-chief Ground Water Age, Elmhurst, Ill., 1972-77; editorial dir. Scott Periodicals, 1977-80; editor Metal Bldg. Rev., Des Plaines, Ill., 1980—. Publ. cons.; graphic and package designer; tchr. ceramics. Active Boy Scouts Am. Served with USN, 1941-45. Mem. Am. Soc. Bus. Press Editors (pres., dir.), Soc. Publ. Designers. Roman Catholic. Club: Chgo. Press. Home: 810 Manchester St Westchester IL 60153 Office: 1800 Oakton St Des Plaines IL 60018

ADAMS, HAROLD FRANCIS, lawyer; b. Beaver, Ohio, July 8, 1900; s. Lewis W. and Arma F. (Halterman) A.; m. Ada Margaret Gregg, Dec. 4, 1929; children—John Marshall, Robert Gregg. A.B., Ohio State U., 1922, LL.B., 1926. Bar: Ohio 1926. Ptnr. Cowan & Adams, Columbus, Ohio, 1927—; mem. Ohio Bar Exam. Com., Columbus, 1937-42, chmn., 1942. Author: Workmen's Compensation, 1929; Trial and Appellate Practice in Ohio, 1934; Appellate Practice in Ohio, 1953. Trustee Columbus Pub. Library, 1958-74. Served with U.S. Army, World War I. Mem. ABA, Ohio State Bar Assn., Columbus Bar Assn., Lawyers Club Columbus Ohio, Am. Legion. Club: Downtown Sertoma (past pres.) Lodge: Masons (33 degree). Home: 3555 Chowning Ct Columbus OH 43220 Office: Cowan & Adams 3131 W Broad St Columbus OH 43204

ADAMS, HERBERT RICHARDS, publishing executive, clergyman; b. Phila., Apr. 19, 1932; s. Leander Hampton and Helen Marguerite (Richards) A.; m. Carol Anne Levine, Aug. 27, 1956; children—Ashley Ward, Joshua, Lee Hampton, Rachel Ellis; m. 2d, Mary Ryan, Aug. 20, 1977. A.B., Colby Coll., 1954; Ed.D., Harvard U., 1972; student Harvard Divinity Sch., 1955-56, Kent State U., 1957, Boston U., 1963. Ordained to ministry Congregationalist Ch., 1952, Unitarian Universalist Assn., 1968; minister Fairfield and Pine Point, Maine, 1950-56, Chelsea, Mass., 1962-66; Lexington, Mass., 1967-75, Wilmette, Ill., 1978—; editor Allyn and Bacon, Boston, 1959-62; sr. editor Ginn and Co., Boston, 1962-68; v.p. mktg. Visual Learning Corp., Cambridge, Mass., 1968-71; dir. Sci. Research Assocs. subs. IBM, Chgo., 1975-83; v.p. Laidlaw Bros., River Forest, Ill., 1983-84, pres., 1984—; tchr. Greenville (Pa.) High Sch., 1956-58, Euclid (Ohio) High Sch., 1958-59, Lexington (Mass.) High Sch., 1968-69, Harvard Grad. Sch. Edn., 1971-72. Sponsor The Hunger Project. Recipient Coe Found. award DePauw U., 1958. Mem. Soc. Scholarly Publishing, Assn. Supervision and Curriculum Devel., Chgo. Book Clinic, Nat. Council Tchrs. English, SANE, ACLU. Club: Harvard of Chgo. Author: Poetry on Film, 1970; Project Listening, 1975; Listening Your Way to Management Success, 1983; contbr. numerous articles to profl. jours. Home: 2679 Stewart Ave Evanston IL 60201 Office: Thatcher and Madison Sts River Forest IL 60305

ADAMS, J(JOHN) ROBERT, air force officer; b. Provo, Utah, Mar. 7, 1948; s. John Hortt and Betty Lou Jean (Ellis) A.; m. Mary Lucinda Allen, Nov. 26, 1969; children—Jennifer, John Dareld, Matthew Robert, Emily, Samuel David, Rebecca. B.S. in Acctg., Brigham Young U., 1972; M.S. in Systems mgmt., U. So. Calif., 1982. Commd. 2d lt. U.S. Air Force, 1972, advanced through grades to maj., 1984; with research and devel. program evaluation dept. systems command, Wright-Patterson AFB, Ohio, 1972-75; chief mgmt. and budget USAF Europe, Hahn AB, Fed. Republic Germany, 1975-78; chief budget Tactical Air Command, George AFB, Calif., 1978-80; chief cost and mgmt. analysis SAC, Malmstrom AFB, Mont., 1980-82; chief budget Pacific Air Force, Osan AB, Korea, 1983; exec. officer Hdqrs SAC, Offutt AFB, Nebr., 1984—. Scouting coordinator Boy Scouts Am., Omaha, 1984—; lay minister Ch. of Jesus Christ of Latterday Saints, various locations, 1967—. Recipient Eagle Scout award Boy Scouts Am., 1963, awards from U.S. Air Force. Mem. Air Force Assn. (life), Am. Soc. Mil. Comptrollers (founder chpt.). Home: 2621 Ellsworth Ave Omaha NE 68123

ADAMS, JOEL CEDRIC, real estate executive; b. Chgo., Sept. 29, 1931; s. Joel Cedric and Georgia Francis (Moon) A.; m. Janet Kathryn Giles, Aug. 19, 1961 (dec. Feb. 1980); children—Jeffrey Joel, Jennifer Kim; m. Barbara Ann Wilson, Aug. 28, 1982; 1 stepson, Thomas William. Diploma Wright Jr. Coll., Chgo., 1952; B.S., DePaul U., 1959. With Motorola Inc., 1955-77, materials exec., U.S., Europe, Asia, 1968-75; broker First United/Rich Port, Realtors, Wheaton and Glen Ellyn, Ill., 1978—. Mem. U. Ill. Grant and Aids Program, 1984-85. Served with U.S. Army, 1952-54. Mem. DuPage Bd. Realtors (realtors polit. action com. 1983—; named Realtor Assoc. of Yr. 1985), Nat. Assn. Realtors (Gold Pres. Club 1980-84), Ill. Assn. Realtors (bd. dirs.), Ill. Bowling Assn. (bd. dirs. 1983—), Chgo. Met. Bowling Assn. (v.p. 1965—). Republican. Lutheran. Home: 769 Glenbard Glen Ellyn IL 60137 Office: First United Rich Port Realtors 605 E Roosevelt Rd Wheaton IL 60187

ADAMS, JOHN CARTER, accounting firm executive; b. Bismark, N.D., Apr. 20, 1919; s. John Bennett and Olive Hazel (Procter) A.; student Wilson Jr. Coll., 1946, Walton Sch. Commerce, Chgo., 1947-48, LaSalle U., 1954-55; C.P.A., U. Ill., 1956; children—John, Judith Fitzgerald, Paul, William; m. Harriet N. Hall, May 1, 1976. With John E. Burke & Co., 1946-48, Gen. Motors Corp., 1948-51; with Wynn M. Wagner & Co. (now Wagner Sim & Co.), pub. accts., Chgo., 1951-79, partner, 1956-79; ptnr. Lester Witten & Co., C.P.A.s Chgo., 1979-82; pres. John C. Adams & Co. P.C., 1982—; v.p. Naperville (Ill.) Elderly Homes, Inc., 1972-75, pres., 1975-76, also dir.; partner Mill Ogden Venture, Mill St. Properties. Served with USAAF, 1942-46. C.P.A., Ill. Mem. Am. Inst. C.P.A.s, Ill. Soc. C.P.A.s. Club: Union League (vice chmn; mem. fin. com.) (Chgo.). Home: 1001 Belaire Ct Naperville IL 60540 Office: 604 N Washington Naperville IL 60540

ADAMS, JOHN DAVID VESSOT, manufacturing company executive; b. Ottawa, Ont., Can., Jan. 7, 1934; s. Albert Oliver and Estelle Priscilla (Vessot) A.; m. Dorothy Marion Blyth, June 27, 1959; children—Nancy, Joel, Louis. Student Carleton U., 1950-51; B.Eng., McGill U., 1955; M.B.A., U. Western Ont., 1958. Registered profl. engr., Ont. Project engr. Abitibi Paper Co., Toronto, Ont., 1962-63, Cockshutt Farm Equipment Co. Ltd., Brantford, Ont., 1958-62, Can. Industries Ltd., Kingston, Ont., 1955-58; mgr. fin. analysis and planning Rio Tinto Zinc Group, London, 1963-66; mgr. adminstrn. and planning Can. Gypsum Co. Ltd., Toronto, 1966-72; mgr. logistics and fin. Massey Ferguson Co. Ltd., Toronto, 1972-79; pres. Can. Spool & Bobbin Co. Ltd., Walkerton, Ont., 1979—; dir. Knechtel Furniture Ltd. Mem. Assn. Profl. Engrs. Province Ont. Mem. United Ch. of Can. Clubs: Walkerton Golf and Curling, Rotary. Home: 386 14th Ave Hanover ON N4N 2Y1 Canada Office: 604 Durham Walkerton ON N0G 2V0 Canada

ADAMS, JOHN RODGER, hydrologist; b. Milw., Apr. 15, 1937; s. John Henry and Frances Agnes (Rodger) A.; m. Barbara Ruth Froehlich, July 28, 1962; children—Catherine Marie, Robert Rodger. B.C.E., Marquette U., 1959; M.C.E., Mich. State U., 1961, Ph.D., 1966. Asst. prof. Lehigh U., Bethlehem, Pa., 1965-70; research hydrologist Ill. State Water Survey, Champaign, 1970—. Coop. Grad. fellow NSF, 1962. Mem. ASCE (sec., treas. sect. 1973-75, div. news corr. 1981-85), Am. Geophys. Union, Upper Mississippi River Research Consortium. Roman Catholic. Avocations: camping, model railroading. Home: 406 W Nevada St Urbana IL 61801 Office: Illinois Water Survey 2204 Griffith Dr Champaign IL 61820

ADAMS, KENNETH LEROY, systems programmer, consultant; b. Springfield, Ohio, Mar. 6, 1947; s. Cedric Errol and Judith Mary (Brown) A. B.S. in Chemistry, Purdue U., 1969, M.S. in Computer Sci., 1978. Grad. asst. computing systems dept. Purdue U., West Lafayette, Ind., 1969-70; cons., programmer Planit Project, NSF, IRCN Project, 1969-71, SuperComputer Access, 1981—. Contbr. articles to profl. jours. Past vice pres. and pres. Greater Lafayette Aquarium Soc., 1970s; mem. Southside Neighborhood Improvement Coalition, Lafayette, 1982—. Mem. Am. Chem. Soc., Assn. Computing Machinery, Human Factors Soc., Ind. State Beekeepers Assn. Democrat. Quaker. Club: U.S. Sidecar. Home: 1019 Wabash Ave Lafayette IN 47905 Office: Purdue U Computing Ctr Math Sci G-148 West Lafayette IN 47907

ADAMS, LESLIE, composer; b. Cleve., 1932; B.Mus., Oberlin (Ohio) Coll., 1955; M.A., Calif. State U., Long Beach, 1967; Ph.D., Ohio State U., 1973. Mem. faculty Kans. U., 1970-78; composer-in-residence Karamu House, Cleve., 1979-81, Cleve. Music Sch. Settlement, 1981—; Rockefeller Found. fellow, Bellagio, Italy, summer 1979; fellow Yaddo, Saratoga Springs, N.Y., summer 1980, winter 1984; del. Gt. Lakes Assembly for Future Performing Arts, 1980; composer: A Kiss in Xanadu (ballet), 1954, 73; Piano Concerto, 1974; Ode to Life for Orch. (performed by Buffalo Philharm. 1983) 1979; Symphony No. 1, 1980; Dunbar Songs (commd. by Ohio Chamber Orch), 1982; Blake (opera), 1985; also works for piano, horn, cello, brass ensemble, chorus. Winner nat. choral composition competition Christian Arts, 1974; Mem. Am. Composers Alliance, Am. Choral Dirs. Assn., Am. Music Center, Pi Kappa Lambda, Phi Delta Kappa, Phi Mu Alpha Sinfonia, Phi Kappa Phi. Contbr. to profl. jours. Address: 9409 Kempton Ave Cleveland OH 44108

ADAMS, PAUL, company executive, consultant; b. Elyria, Ohio, Aug. 19, 1955; s. Paul and Pauline (Bougioukle) A.; m. Beth Sutter, Oct. 13, 1979. B.B.A., Cleve. State U., 1982. Sales engr. Meriam Instrument, Cleve., 1976-78; tech. rep. Gibson Homans Co., Cleve., 1978-83; nat. mktg. mgr. Fred Wilson Co., Lathrup Village, Mich., 1983; pres., founder R-Tech Co., Elyria, Ohio, 1983—; pvt. practice cons. comml. roof systems. Active Nat. Honor Soc. com., Elyria High Sch., 1973. Mem. Sales and Mktg. Execs. of Cleve., Greater Cleve. Growth Assn. Republican. Home: 732 University Elyria OH 44035 Office: R-Tech Co PO Box 1045 Elyria OH 44036

ADAMS, RICHARD EDWARD, manufacturing exec.; b. Sullivan, Mo., June 25, 1936; s. Woodrow Carl and Helen Elizabeth A.; student public schs., Normandy, Mo.; m. Janet Marie Vie, Apr. 23, 1955; children—Paul Matthew, Dawn Kathleen, Mark Edward. Salesman, Bevo Realty Co., St. Louis, 1955-61; archtl. draftsman Saul Dien-Architect, Olivette, Mo., 1961-63; prefabrication draftsman County Lumber Co., Hazelwood, Mo., 1963-64; mgr. engring. dept. So. Cross Lumber Co., Hazelwood, 1964-72, prodn. mgr., 1972-75; gen. mgr., sales mgr. Chromalloy Bldg. Products, Hazelwood, 1975-81; v.p., dir. U.S. ops. Gainsborough Hardware Industries, Inc., Chesterfield, Mo., 1981—; archtl. and design cons. Committeeman, Boy Scouts Am., 1975-78, cubmaster, 1976-77; co-chmn. United Way, 1973-78. Recipient Homer award St. Louis Home Builders Assn., 1969, Product Presentation award, 1977, Product Mgmt. award, 1978. Mem. Hoo-Hoo Internat., Compass Orgn. (founder). Roman Catholic. Home: Normandie 2366 Greenberry Hill Ln Chesterfield MO 63017 Office: PO Box 569 Chesterfield MO 63017

ADAMS, ROBERT HENRY, art dealer, appraiser; b. Chgo., Aug. 7, 1955; s. Frederic Eli and Jane (Johanson) A.; m. Sandra Michels, Apr. 26, 1981; 1 child, Samuel. B.A. in Philosophy, Franconia Coll., 1973. Pres. Robert Henry Adams Rare Books, Chgo., 1976—; cons. in graphic arts Leslie Hindman Auctioneers, Chgo., 1982—; appraiser Arthur Bailes and Assoc., Chgo., 1983—. Mem. band Sport of Kings; recs. include: Parade, 1984, On a Tall Bldg., 1983, Sing Mary Sing, 1984, Air Moves by Slowly, 1982. Episcopalian. Address: PO Box 11131 Chicago IL 60611

ADAMS, ROBERT MCLEAN, technology services executive; b. Hibbing, Minn., Aug. 4, 1922; s. John William and Julia (Straub) A.; m. Carol Margaret Johnson, Sept. 4, 1943; children—Margaret, William, Carl, John. A.A.S., Blackburn Coll., 1941; B.S. in Chem. Engring., U. Ill., 1943, M.S. in Chem. Engring., 1944, Ph.D. in Chem. Engring., 1950; D.S. (hon.), Blackburn Coll., 1971. Chemist, chem. engr. 3M, St. Paul, 1949-52, mktg. and sales, St. Paul and Ridgefield, N.J., 1952-56, sales mgr., 1956-58, tech. dir. chem. and internat. div., 1958-68, gen. mgr. new bus. ventures div., 1968-69, v.p. research and devel., 1969-81, sr. v.p. tech. services, 1981—; trustee Dunwoody Indsl. Inst., Mpls., 1981—; dir. 3M, Toro Co., Mpls., Graco, Inc., Mpls., Eastern Heights State Bank, St. Paul, Woodbury, Minn. Trustee Carleton Coll., Northfield, Minn., 1980—, Sci. Mus. Minn., St. Paul, 1974-81; chmn. Internat. Sci. and Engring. Fair, St. Paul Civic Ctr., 1980; mem. China Initiative on Tech. Steering Com., Washington, 1984—; mem. exec. com. Minn. Pvt. Coll. Fund, 1972-80. Served with USNR, 1944-46. Mem. Indsl. Research Inst. (alt. rep. 1969—), Minn. Acad. Sci. Republican. Presbyterian. Club: White Bear Lake Yacht (commodore 1984—). Home: 5 Field Ridge Rd White Bear Lake MN 55110 Office: 3M Center Saint Paul MN 55144

ADAMS, THOMAS JOSEPH, food company executive; real estate developer; b. Portsmouth, Ohio, Sept. 2, 1923; s. Allen Willard and Clara Audry (Jones) A.; m. Andree Claudine Jaccard, Sept. 9, 1946; children—Christelle Claire Frost, Paul Allen Patrick Stephen. B.A., Ohio State U., 1949. With Ideal Bakery, Inc., Jackson, Ohio, 1946-72, Tops Cleaners, Inc., Chillicothe, Ohio, 1953-73; owner, operator Adams Baking Co., Portsmouth, Ohio, 1973-78; with Phoenix Pies, Inc., Portsmouth, 1973-85; pres., owner Adams Holdings, Inc., Portsmouth, 1978—. Served with U.S. Army, 1943-45, ETO. Recipient Golden Shovel award State of Ohio House Reps., 1985. Mem. Ohio Bakers Assn. (bd. dirs. 1976). Republican. Club: Columbus Athletic. Lodges: Rotary (Portsmouth); Masons. Avocations: reading; swimming; walking. Home: 1223 Offnere St Portsmouth OH 45662 Office: Adams Holdings Inc PO Box 1481 Portsmouth OH 45662

ADAMS, TIMOTHY RAYMOND, human resource specialist; b. Chgo., July 23, 1951; s. Roy and Norine (Hendrickson) A.; B.S. in Psychology, Loyola U., Chgo., 1973, M.S. in Indsl. Relations, 1977. Employment counselor West Personnel Service, Oak Brook, Ill., 1973-74; personnel asst., human resource rep. Helene Curtis Industries, Inc., Chgo., 1974-78, 78-79; exec. recruiter Ill. Dept. Personnel, Springfield, 1979-80; manpower coordinator Ill. Dept. Mental Health, Chgo., 1980; mgr. personnel resources Chgo. Bd. Options Exchange, 1980-83, mgr. employee relations, 1983-85, mgr. staff devel., 1985—; mem. bus. occupation adv. bd. Dawson Skill Center, Chgo. City Colls., 1975-79; guest lectr. personnel Loyola U., 1976-78. Chmn. 1st aid com. West Cook County dist. Mid-Am. chpt. ARC, 1978-79, 81-82, chmn. dist. bd., 1983—, supr. disaster services, 1980—, instr. 1st aid, 1969—, instr. CPR, 1975—. Recipient service awards ARC, 1974, 79, 81, 83, 84. Mem. Am. Soc. Personnel Adminstrs., Am. Soc. Tng. and Devel., Soc. Personnel Adminstrs. Greater Chgo. (bd. dirs. 1983-84). Office: Chgo Bd Options Exchange La Salle at Van Buren Chicago IL 60605

ADAMS, WILLIAM C., manufacturing company executive; b. Reynoldsville, Pa., 1923. B.S., UCLA, 1950. With Fed.-Mogul Corp., Southfield, Mich., 1950—, various positions Arrowhead Products div., 1950-60, gen. mgr. microtech. div., 1960-65, gen. mgr. Arrowhead Products div., 1965-68, gen. mgr. Nat. Seal div., 1968-71, group mgr. rubber and plastics group, 1971, group mgr. gen. products group, 1972, v.p., group exec. mfg. group, 1973-76, exec. v.p., 1976, pres., chief operating officer, also mem. exec. coms., dir., 1977—. Served with AUS, 1943-46. Mem. NAM (dir.). Office: Federal-Mogul PO Box 1966 Detroit MI 48235*

ADAMS, WILLIAM RICHARD, zooarcheologist; b. Bloomington, Ind., Feb. 21, 1923; s. William Baker and Mildred Florence (Dingle) A.; A.B., Ind. U., 1945, M.A., 1949, S.O.P.A., 1980; m. Connie Marie Christie, Oct. 20, 1968; children—William H., James E., Richard B., Margaret E., Scott C., Teresa M. Archeologist, Ind. Hist. Bur., 1945-47; instr., embalmer Sch. Medicine, Ind. U., Bloomington, 1947-49; ethnozoologist Central Miss. Valley Archaeol. Expdn., St. Louis, 1949; field archaeologist Royal Ont. Museum, 1955-56; dir. Ind. Ethnozoological Lab., Bloomington, 1947—; curator Ind. U. Museums, Bloomington, 1949—, instr. ethnozoology, 1956—; pres., chmn. bd. Bloomington Nat. Bank, 1973-80. Mem. Soc. Am. Archaeology, Southwestern Archaeol. Assn., Wilderness Soc., Sierra Club, Audubon Soc., Ind. Hist. Soc., Ind. Acad. Sci., Monroe County Aux. Police. Republican. Clubs: Trowel and Brush, Elks, Ind. Police League, Ind. Chiefs Police. Office: 407 Rawles Hall Bloomington IN 47401

ADAMSON, GARY MILTON, airline executive; b. Wichita, Kans., Sept. 25, 1936; s. Milton Mathews and Lila Marie (Evans) A.; m. Bernice Beilman, Sept. 13, 1958; children—Chris, Mary, John, Andrea. Salesman Drug Distbn. Inc., Topeka, 1962-65; pres. Air Midwest, Wichita, 1965—; dir. Boatmen's Bank, Kansas City, Mo., 1984—, ARINC, Washington, 1984—. Served with U.S. Army, 1954-57. Recipient Kansan of Yr. award Topeka Capital Jour., 1983. Mem. Regional Airline Assn. (dir. 1975-76, 83—), Assn. Local Transport Airlines (chmn. 1983—). Republican. Roman Catholic. Clubs: Rotary; Arkansas City Country (dir.). Avocations: sailing; golfing. Home: #3 Fairway Ln Arkansas City KS 67005 Office: Air Midwest Inc PO Box 7724 Wichita KS 67277

ADAMSON, HAROLD WOOD, clinical engineer; b. Washington, Sept. 24, 1945; s. James Henry and Mary Frances (Hamilton) A.; m. Carla Sue Surig; 1 child, Robert William. B.S. in Bioengring., Rose-Hulman Inst. Tech., 1971; M.S., Washington U., 1973. Registered profl. engr., Kans. Dir. clin. engring. Wesley Med. Ctr., Wichita, Kans., 1973—. Served with USN, 1963-66. Mem. Am. Soc. Hosp. Engring., Nat. Fire Protection Assn. Democrat. Methodist. Contbr. articles to profl. jours. Office: Wesley Med Ctr 550 N Hillside Wichita KS 67214

ADAMSON, JAMES CANTWELL, automotive engring. co. exec.; b. Kenosha, Wis., May 21, 1935; s. Harry Richard and Esther Taaffe (Cantwell) A.; B.E.E., Marquette U., Milw., 1959; m. Rita Marie Ruffolo, June 24, 1961; children—Michael, Paula, Gregory, Patrick, Margaret, Catherine (dec.). With Am. Motors Corp., Kenosha, 1959—, sr. product devel. engr., 1967-75, resident engr., 1975—. Served with AUS, 1954-56. Mem. Soc. Automotive Engrs., Wis. Hist. Soc., Kenosha County Hist. Soc., Nat. Rifle Assn., Wis. Sportsman's Assn., Triangle frat. Roman Catholic. Clubs: Shamrock, Elks, Southport Gun. Home: 1518 Harmony Dr Racine WI 53402 Office: 5626 25th Ave Kenosha WI 53140

ADAMSON, THOMAS CHARLES, JR., aerospace engineering educator, consultant; b. Cicero, Ill., Mar. 24, 1924; s. Thomas Charles and Helen Emily (Koubek) A.; m. Susan Elizabeth Huncilman, Sept. 16, 1949; children—Thomas Charles III, William Andros, Laura Elizabeth. B.S., Purdue U., 1949; M.S., Calif. Inst. Tech., 1950, Ph.D., 1954. Research engr. Jet Propulsion Lab., Pasadena, Calif., 1952-54; assoc. research engr. U. Mich., Ann Arbor, 1954-56, asst. prof., 1956-57, assoc. prof., 1957-61, prof., 1961—, chmn. dept. aerospace engring., 1983—. Editor: (with M.F. Platzer) Transonic Flow Problems in Turbo Machinery, 1977. Contbr. articles to profl. jours. Served with U.S. Army, 1943-46, ETO. Guggenheim fellow, 1950-51. Fellow AIAA; mem. Combustion Inst., Sigma Xi. Episcopalian. Home: 667 Worthington Pl Ann Arbor MI 48103 Office: U Mich Dept Aerospace Engring 2508 Patterson Pl Ann Arbor MI 48109

ADAN, ADELBERTO JOSE, hospital administrator; b. Camaguey, Cuba, Aug. 21, 1951; came to U.S. 1965, naturalized 1976; s. Adelberto and Bertha (Cepeda) A.; m. Nancy Sue Shepard, June 2, 1979. B.A., Grand Valley State Colls., 1974; M.B.A., Central Mich. U., 1980. Health care worker Health Delivery, Inc., Saginaw, Mich., 1971-76; adminstrv. asst./div. mgr. Midland Hosp. Ctr. (Mich.), 1977-79, asst. v.p. support services, 1979-82, asst. v.p. profl. services, 1982—. Ex-officio mem. bd. dirs. Ernie Wallace Meml. Blood Bank. Republican. Roman Catholic. Home: 1800 Sylvan Ln Midland MI 48640 Office: Midland Hosp Ctr 4005 Orchard Dr Midland MI 48640

ADDINGTON, CHESTER LUTHER, education educator; b. Winchester, Ind., Nov. 6, 1922; s. Willard Clayton and Velma Fern (Coats) A.; m. Dorothy Frances Armistead, June 16, 1945; children—Paul Luther, John Charles, Patricia Ann Addington Johnson. B.S. in Edn., Ball State U., 1952, M.A. in Edn., 1954; Ed.D., Ind. U., 1961. Cert. secondary tchr., Ga., Ind. Tchr. indsl. arts Murphy High Sch., Atlanta, 1952-55; prin. Penn-Knox Pub. Schs., Pennville, Ind., 1955-59; instr. Ind. U., Bloomington, 1959-60; supr. math. Ind. State Dept. Pub. Instrn., Indpls., 1960-61; prof., chmn. dept. edn. Otterbein Coll., Westerville, Ohio, 1961—; resident dir. Ashland-Otterbein Grad. Program Edn., Westerville, 1978-83. Served with USN, 1943-46. Mem. Am. Assn. Colls. Tchr. Edn., Ohio Assn. Colls. Tchr. Edn., Ohio Assn. Pvt. Colls. Tchr. Edn. (pres. 1980-83). Republican. Methodist. Avocations: Woodworking, travel. Home: 310 Illinois Ave Westerville OH 43081 Office: Otterbein Coll Dept Edn Westerville OH 43081

ADDINGTON, JAMES EDWARD, anthropologist; b. Detroit, Mar. 1, 1947; s. Jack Elwood and Virginia Lucille (Tucker) A.; B.S., Western Mich. U., 1969, M.A., 1972; A.B.D., Ohio State U., 1975; m. Nancy Louise Salchow, Sept. 6, 1969; children—Timothy Finley, Peter Henry. Instr., Ohio State U., Columbus, 1972-75; sr. research asso. Ohio State Mus., Columbus, 1972—; field archaeologist W. Va. Geol. Survey, 1974; cultural resource sect. head Ohio Dept. Transp., Columbus, 1975—; cons. archaeologist Ohio Cultural Resource Cons., Columbus, 1976—; cultural resource cons. Active, Indian Guides, YMCA, Columbus, 1977—. Recipient Cert. of Appreciation, Columbus Public Schs., 1974, Kiwanis, 1978-79, Ohio Transp. Engrs. Assn., 1977, 79; commendation Columbus Police Dept., 1983; Historic Preservation Survey grantee, 1978-79. Mem. Ohio Archaeol. Council (treas., dir. 1978—), Nat. Trust for Historic Preservation, Am. Assn. State and Local History, Northeast Anthrop. Assn., Eastern States Archaeol. Fedn., Soc. Hist. Archaeology, Soc. Indsl. Archaeology, Nat. Hist. Soc., Ohio Hist. Soc., Soc. Am. Archaeology, Central State Anthropol. Assn., Sigma Xi, Alpha Phi Omega. Contbr. articles in field to profl. jours. Home: 2590 Dibblee Ave Columbus OH 43204 Office: Ohio Dept Transp Bur Environ Services 25 S Front St Columbus OH 43215

ADDISON, BYRON KENT, fine arts educator, artist; b. St. Louis, July 12, 1937; s. Myron Francis and Violet Georgia (Main) A.; m. Sharon Lee Spanholtz, June 19, 1959; children—Kendall W., Angela D. B.F.A., Washington U., 1959; M.A., U. Notre Dame, 1960. Instr. U. Coll. of Washington U., St. Louis, 1961-63; prof. Maryville Coll., St. Louis, 1961—. One man shows include: Norton's Art Gallery, St. Louis, 1960, 61, Michael Thomas Gallery, Los Angeles, 1962, Maxwell Gallery, San Francisco, 1963, 68, 70, 74, Sculptors Gallery, St. Louis, 1964, 66, 67, Frederick Anthon Gallery, Beverly Hills, Calif., 1965, Mark Anthony Gallery, New Orleans, 1967, Forsyth Gallery, St. Louis, 1969, Maryville Coll., St. Louis, 1968, 70, 74, 83; exhibited in group shows: Birmingham Mus. Art, 1981, Visual Arts Gallery, 1982, Riverside Art Ctr., 1982, Pensacola Mus. of Art, 1982, Oklahoma City House Gallery, 1982, 83, N.Y. Community Arts Ctr., 1983, St. Louis Gallery 210, 1983, Wichita Art Mus., 1984, Mo. Dept. of Art William Woods Coll., 1984, Pitts. Ctr. for the Arts., 1984., George Walter Vincent Smith Art Mus., Springfield, Mass., 1984, Grossmount Coll. Art Gallery, El Cajon, Calif., 1984, Foothills Art Ctr., Golden, Colo., 1984; sculpture commd. for pvt. collectors, chs., colls. Mem., chaplain The Gideons Internat., St. Louis. Recipient First prize Okla. Watercolor Assn. 9th Nat. Exhbn. of Water Color, 1983, Atlanta Artists Club award, Ga. Watercolor Soc. 5th Ann. Exhbn., Valdosta State Coll., 1984, Peggy Buntin Ann. Watercolor prize, Watercolor and Pastel Exhbn., St. Louis Artists' Guild, 1984, Fred Wehrle Ann. Meml. prize Portrait Exhbn., St. Louis Artists' Guild, 1984, and various other awards; Secor scholar, Washington U., 1958-59; grad. scholar, U. Notre Dame, 1959-60; John T. Milliken Travel scholar, 1962; Pillsbury Chair of Fine Arts award Maryville Coll., 1973—. Mem. St. Louis Artists' Guild, So. Watercolor Soc., Midwest Watercolor Soc., Watercolor Soc. Ala., Ga. Watercolor Soc. Mem. Assembly of God Ch. Office: Maryville Coll 13550 Conway Rd Saint Louis MO 63141

ADDUCCI, ANTHONY JOSEPH, venture capitalist; b. Chgo., Aug. 14, 1937; s. Alexander James and Valeria (Vigna) A.; B.A. in Physics, St. Mary's Coll., Winona, Minn., 1959; postgrad. Ill. Inst. Tech., 1960-64, U. Minn., 1965-72; m. Sandra R. Gordon, Nov. 14, 1965; children—Michael Anthony, Brian Alexander, Alicia Ann. Assoc. engr. Jensen Mfg. Co., Chgo., 1960-61; devel. engr. IT&T Kellogg Communications Systems, Chgo., 1961-64; logic design engr. Univac div. Sperry Rand Corp., St. Paul, 1964-66; mgr. sales adminstrn. Medtronic, Inc., Mpls., 1966-72; founder, exec. v.p., dir. Cardiac Pacemakers, Inc., St. Paul, 1972-81; owner, pres. Tech. Enterprises, St. Paul, 1981—; chmn. bd. Check Technology Corp., Dimensional Medicine Corp.; dir. Med. Graphics Corp., Deltec Systems, Inc. Trustee St. Mary's Coll.; mem. Republican Nat. Com.; chmn. bd. Adducci Family Found.; bd. dirs. St. Paul Chamber Orch. Served with USNR, 1954-62. Decorated Knight Order Holy Sepulchre (Vatican). Mem. IEEE. Contbr. articles to profl. jours.; patentee in field. Office: 3585 N Lexington Ave Saint Paul MN 55112

ADDUCCI, JOSEPH EDWARD, obstetrician, gynecologist; b. Chgo., Dec. 1, 1934; s. Dominee Edward and Harriet Evelyn (Kneppreth) A.; B.S., U. Ill., 1955; M.D., Loyola U., Chgo., 1959; m. Mary Ann Tietje, 1958; children—Christopher, Gregory, Steven, Jessica, Tobias. Intern, Cook County Hosp., Chgo., 1959-60; resident in ob-gyn. Mt. Carmel Hosp., Detroit, 1960-64; practice medicine specializing in obstetrics and gynecology Williston, N.D., 1966—; clin. prof. U. N.D. Med. Sch., 1973—. Mem. N.D. Bd. Med. Examiners, 1974—, past chmn.; project dir. Tri County Family Planning Service; past pres. Tri County Health Planning Council. Mem. Williams County Welfare Bd., 1966—; bd. dirs., treas. Blue Shield of N.D. Served with M.C., U.S. Army, 1964-66. Diplomate Am. Bd. Ob-Gyn, Nat. Bd. Med. Examiners. Fellow Am. Soc. Abdominal Surgeons, A.C.S., Am. Coll. Obstetrics and Gynecologists (sect. chmn. N.D.), Internat. Coll. Surgeons (regent 1972-74), Am. Fertility Soc., Am. Assn. Internat. Lamaze Soc., Am. Soc. Gynecol. Laparoscopists, N.D. Obstetricians and Gynecologists Soc. (pres. 1966, 76); mem. Am. Soc. for Colposcopy and Colpomicroscopy, Am. Soc. Cryosurgery, Am. Soc. Contemporary Medicine and Surgery, Am. Assn. Profl. Ob-Gyn., Pan Am. Med. Assn. Lodge: Elks. Contbr. articles to profl. jours. Home: 1717 Main St Williston ND 58801 Office: Med Center Williston ND 58801

ADDY, ALVA LEROY, mechanical engineer; b. Dallas, S.D., Mar. 29, 1936; s. Alva Isaac and Nellie Amelia (Brumbaugh) A.; B.S., S.D. Sch. Mines and Tech., 1958; M.S., U. Cin., 1960; Ph.D., U. Ill., 1963; m. Sandra Ruth Turney, June 8, 1958. Engr., Gen. Electric Co., Lancaster, Calif. and Cin., 1958-60; prof. mech. engring. U. Ill., Urbana, 1963—, dir. mech. engring. lab., 1965—, asso. head mech. engring. dept., 1980—; aerodynamics cons. U.S. Army Missile Command, Redstone Arsenal, Ala., summers 1965—; cons. U.S. Army Research Office, 1964—; cons. in high-speed fluid dynamics to indsl. firms, 1963—; vis. research prof. U.S. Army, 1976; lectr. Von Karman Inst. Fluid Dynamics, Brussels, 1968, 75, 76. Fellow AIAA (assoc.), ASME; mem. Soc. Engring. Edn., Sigma Xi, Pi Tau Sigma, Sigma Tau. Home: 1706 Golfview Dr Urbana IL 61801 Office: 208 Mech Engring Lab U Ill Urbana IL 61801

ADEGBILE, GIDEON SUNDAY ADEBISI, physician; b. Iree, Nigeria, May 18, 1941; s. John Bimpe and Sarah Oyefunke (Awoyemi) A.; came to U.S., 1962, naturalized, 1974; B.S. cum laude, Va. Union U., 1966; M.D., Meharry Med. Coll., 1971; m. Doris Mae Goodman, June 10, 1966; children—Lisa Aderonke, Titilayo Angel, Babalola Oluwole. Intern, Good Samaritan Hosp., Dayton, Ohio, 1971-72; emergency physician PEG, Inc., Dayton, 1972-75; community health physician Drexel Health Center, Dayton, 1972-73; practice medicine specializing in family medicine Dayton, 1973—; asst. prof. Wright State U. Sch. Medicine, 1975-78, assoc. clin. prof., 1978—, chmn. Horizon in Medicine program, 1977—; med. dir. Christel Manor Nursing Home, 1973-80, 82—; part-time physician City of Dayton, 1973—; mem. adv. bd. Miami Valley Child Devel. Center, Inc., 1979—; chmn. longterm care com. Profl. Standard Rev. Orgn., 1978-80, bd. dirs., 1980-84; chmn. quality assurance program St. Elizabeth Med. Center, 1980—. Chmn. bd. Dayton Contemporary Dance Co., 1977-79; mem. bd. Good Samaritan Mental Health Center, 1979-85. Recipient cert. of appreciation Christel Manor Nursing Home, 1977. Mem. AMA, Ohio State Med. Assn., Nat. Med. Assn. (ho. of dels. 1980—), Montgomery County Med. Soc. (trustee 1978), Gem. City Med., Dental and Pharm. Soc. (pres. 1977-80, chmn. Horizon in Medicine program 1977—), Am. Coll. Emergency Physicians, NAACP, Alpha Phi Alpha. Democrat. Baptist. Clubs: Tennis Racket, Optimists. Research on drug abuse. Home: 1617 Burbank Dr Dayton OH 45406 Office: 4001 Free Pike Dayton OH 45416

ADEKUNLE, EDITH LOWERY, education specialist; b. Greenville, Ala., Oct. 24, 1948; d. Ed and Daisy (Hall) Lowery; m. Adeniyi Adekunle, June 23, 1973 (div.); 1 son, Michael. B.S., Ohio State U., 1967, M.A., 1972; Ed.S., U. Toledo, 1977. TV producer, tech. dir., personality Sta. WGTE-TV, Toledo, 1971-73; asst. dir. devel. edn. U. Toledo, 1974-77; prin. edn. officer Grad. Tchr's. Coll., Lagos, Nigeria, 1977-78; health educator pub. relations Cordelia Martin Ctr., Toledo, 1978-80; project mgr., ednl. software designer Control Data Corp., Toledo, 1980-82; founder, cons. Ednl. Services Ltd., Toledo, 1983—; cons. Ctr. for Contemporary Medicine, Detroit, 1982. Presentor NAB Youth Task Force, Toledo, 1980—; edn. facilitator Am. Cancer Soc., Toledo, 1978-80; contest judge Nat. Forensics League, Toledo, 1978—; bd. dirs. Health Planning Council NW Ohio, Toledo, 1978-83; mem. planning com. Health Clinics Internat., Toledo, 1977; bd. trustees Girl Scouts U.S.A., Toledo, 1978—, Women Involved in Toledo, 1980-83. Recipient Woman of Yr. award Greater Harvest Baptist Ch., Toledo, 1973. Mem. Performax Systems Internat. (cons. 1983—), Toledo Press Club, Nat. Thespian Soc., Alpha Kappa Alpha, Pi Lambda Theta, Bus. and Profl. Women's Club. Club: Connecting Point (Toledo).

ADELMAN, CHARLES MARTIN, archaeologist, art historian, educator; b. Bklyn., Sept. 7, 1942; s. Abraham and Lillian (Entes) A.; B.A., Bklyn. Coll., 1965; Ph.D., U. Chgo., 1975, U. Gothenburg, Sweden, 1976. Adj. asst. prof. art and archeology Bklyn. Coll., 1977-83; asst. prof. art U. No. Iowa, Cedar Falls, 1983-85, assoc. prof., 1985—; cons. in field. Ford. Found. archeol. trainee Iran, 1969-70; U. Chgo. Edward L. Ryerson travelling fellow, Greece, Cyprus, 1969-70; Fulbright fellow, Sweden Am. Found. fellow, Kress Found. Fellow, all Sweden, 1971-72; U. Gothenburg fellow, 1972-74; Swedish Research Council scholar, 1977, 83, 84, 85; Fulbright fellow, 1985. Mem. Archaeol. Inst. Am., Coll. Arts Assn., Am. Schs. Oriental Research, N.Y. Oriental Club. Contbr. articles to profl. jours. Home: 727 Maplewood Dr Apt 204 Cedar Falls IA 50613 Office: Dept Art No Iowa Cedar Falls IA 50614

ADELMAN, ERNEST ZANVILLE, lawyer, corporate executive; b. Kansas City, Mo., Jan. 3, 1939; s. Joseph and Sophia (Greenberg) A.; A.B., U. Kans., 1961, J.D., 1965; postgrad Washington U., St. Louis, 1961-62; A.M., Webster U., 1977; m. Barbara Ellen Boley, June 13, 1970; 1 son, James Stephen. Bar: Mo. 1965, U.S. Supreme Ct. 1970. Unit mgr. Southwestern Bell Tel. Co., Kansas City, Mo., 1966-68, supr. ops., 1969-72, dist. mgr., Moberly, Mo., 1972-73, adminstr. earning studies, St. Louis, 1975-78, asst. v.p., 1983—; fin. supr. AT&T, N.Y.C., 1973-75, mgr. banking relations, 1978-79, dir. state regulatory matters, 1979-83. Served to brig. gen. Air N.G., 1963—, to capt. USAF, 1968-69. Mem. ABA, Assn. Evolutionary Econs., Am. Econ. Assn., Phi Beta Kappa. Democrat. Unitarian. Office: One Bell Ctr St Louis MO 63101 also State Def Bldg Topeka KS 66601

ADELMAN, RAPHAEL MARTIN, physician, hospital administrator; b. Plainfield, N.J., May 4, 1915; s. Samuel and Betty (Taich) A.; D.D.S., U. Pa., 1939; M.Sc., Northwestern U., 1940; B.M., Chgo. Med. Sch., 1943, M.D., 1944; m. Doris L. Brundza, Jan. 15, 1983; children—Karen Rae, Robert John, Doreen. Intern Norwegian-Am. Hosp., Chgo., 1943-44; assoc. in surgery Chgo. Med. Sch., 1945-50; assoc. in plastic surgery to Dr. A.M. Brown, Chgo., 1946-50; gen. practice medicine, Wauconda, Ill., 1950—; chief of staff St. Therese Hosp., 1963—, chief exec. com., 1965, asst. adminstr., med. dir., 1965—, v.p. med. affairs, 1973, dir., 1974—, also dir. med. edn.; chief sect. ear nose throat Victory Meml. Hosp., Waukegan, 1963, 65-66; clin. asst. prof. family medicine U. Health Scis./Chgo. Med. Sch., 1979—; med. dir. Am. Hosp. Supply Corp.; cons. physician Coll. Lake County Health Services Trust; physician cons. utilization rev. Region V. HEW, 1973-75, cons. quality and standards, 1975; physician cons. Lake County Bd. Health, 1974-76; cons. continuing med. edn. Downey VA Hosp., 1974-76; authorized agt. for Lake County, Ill. Dept. Pub. Health, 1974-76; FAA sr. examiner, 1973—; mem. Am. Bd. Quality Assurance and Utilization Rev. Physicians, 1978—; mem. Ancillary Services Rev., Crescent Counties for Med. Care, 1979—. Mem. exec. com. Lake County chpt. Am. Cancer Soc., 1963—; pres. Wauconda High Sch. Bd. Edn., 1954-60; mem. Wauconda Grade Sch. Bd. Edn., 1952-60; chmn. health and safety N.W. Dist., North Suburban council Boy Scouts Am., 1964-65, vice. chmn. N.W. dist. North Shore council, 1967, 75, mem. exec. com. Northeastern Ill. council; mem. Lake County Health Services Com., 1969—; mem. profl. adv. com. United Community Services Planning Div., 1969—; mem. exec. com., exec. bd. Evanston-North Shore Area Council, 1969; mem.

mgmt. com. Lake County Mental Health Clinic, 1967-69; mem. budget and fin. com., 1968-69; group chmn. Regional Conf. on Health Care Costs, Health, Edn. and Welfare, Cleve., 1968; del. Hosp. Planning Council Chgo., 1967-69; chmn. subcom. Ill. Hosp. Licensing Bd. Com., 1969; pres. 1968-69 class U. Ala. Health Service Adminstrs. Devel. Program; chmn. Lake County (Ill.) Health Services Planning Council, Inc.; mem. regional com. Hosp. Admission Surveillance Program, State of Ill., 1972-77; mem. Lake County Drug Commn., 1972-73; mem. Lake County Bd. Health, 1973-77; chmn. orgn. and search com. for exec. dir. Lake County Health Dept.; mem. com. on search for dean univ. health scis. Chgo. Med. Sch., 1975; mem. Lake County Coroner's Adv. Commn., 1977; mem. adv. council health edn. programs Coll. Lake County, 1970-77; bd. dirs. Blumberg Blood Bank; bd. dirs. St. Therese Nurse Scholarship Fund, 1962, Lake County Health Planning Council, 1969-72. Fellow Am. Pub. Health Assn. (life mem., community health edn. accreditation panel 1975-76), AAAS, Chgo. Inst. Medicine, Royal Soc. Health, Am. Acad. Med. Adminstrs., Soc. Acad. Achievement (life), Am. Coll. Hosp. Adminstrs.; mem. Am. Acad. Family Practice, Ill. Acad. Family Practice (state del. 1960-63, dir.), Lake County Acad. Family Practice (past pres.), AMA, ADA, Assn. Mil. Surgeons U.S. (life mem.), Ill. Hosp. Assn. (ad hoc com. emergency radio network 1969, state com. safety 1972-77), Ill. Soc. Med. Research, Ill. Med. Soc. (com. physician-hosp. relationship 1974-75), Am. Acad. Dental Radiology, Am. Acad. Family Practice (del. 1974—), Ill. Pub. Health Assn. (exec. council 1976-78), Assn. Hosp. Med. Assn. (resources com. 1976-78), Ill. Found. Med. Care (utilization rev. ednl. accreditation program com. 1973-75, ad hoc com. utilization rev. 1973-75), Am. Coll. Preventive Medicine, Am. Soc. Law and Medicine, Chgo. Acad. Legal Medicine, Ill. Hosp. Attys., Am. Legion (life mem.), Sigma Xi, Alpha Omega, Phi Lambda Kappa. Home: PO Box 488 Round Lake IL 60073 Office: St Therese Hosp Waukegan IL 60085

ADELMAN, STEVEN A., chemistry educator; b. Chgo., July 4, 1945; s. Hyman and Sarah (Leavitt) A.; m. Barbara Ruth Stolberg, May 12, 1974. B.S., Ill. Inst. Tech., 1967; M.A., Harvard U., 1968, Ph.D., 1972. Research assoc. MIT, Cambridge, Mass., 1972-74, U. Chgo., 1974-75; asst. prof. Purdue U., West Lafayette, Ind., 1975-77, assoc. prof., 1977-82, prof. chemistry, 1982—; cons. Exxon Research Co., Linden, N.J., 1980, Los Alamos Lab., 1984—. Contbr. chpts. to books, articles to profl. jours. Vol., U.S. Peace Corps, Turkey, 1969-70. Fellow Alfred P. Sloan Found., 1976-78, John Simon Guggenheim Found., 1982-83; grantee NSF, Am. Chem. Soc., 1975-84. Mem. Am. Chem. Soc., Am. Phys. Soc., AAAS. Avocations: reading; backpacking; jogging. Home: 2827 Wilshire St West Lafayette IN 47906 Office: Dept Chemistry Purdue Univ West Lafayette IN 47907

ADELSON, EDWARD, physicist, musician; b. Bklyn., Aug. 19, 1934; s. Barnet and Sarah (Strongin) A.; m. Juliane A.W. Riedel, Aug. 5, 1961 (div. June, 1982); B.A., N.Y.U., 1956; student (Woodrow Wilson fellow), Eastman Sch. of Music, 1956-57 M.Sc., Ohio State U., 1965, Ph.D., 1974. Prin. physicist Battelle Mem. Inst., Columbus, Ohio, 1957-71; lectr. Ohio State U., Columbus, 1974—. Organist, choirmaster St. Alban's Episcopal Ch., Bexley, Ohio. Mem. Am. Phys. Soc., Am. Assn. Physics Tchrs., Am. Guild Organists, Phi Beta Kappa, Sigma Pi Sigma. Contbr. numerous articles to various profl. jours. Home: 6384 Falkirk Pl Columbus OH 43229 Office: Smith Lab Ohio State Univ Columbus OH 43210

ADELSTEIN, LINDY M., lawyer; b. Cleve., Feb. 24, 1934; s. Adolph M. and Rickie (Berger) A.; m. Harriet P. Hepner, June 12, 1960; children—Terri, Steven, Brian. B.A., Adelbert Coll., Western Res. U., 1955; J.D., Ohio No. U., 1958. Bar: Ohio 1958. Ptnr. Adelstein & Adelstein, Cleve., 1967—; advisor-selective service U.S. Govt., Cleve., 1967—; prof. law Lakeland Community Coll., Mentor, Ohio, 1971—; pres., chief exec. Printing Industries, Cleve., 1980-81. Recipient cert. Appreciation Printing Industries Assn. of No. Ohio, Inc., 1981, cert. Appreciation Pres. of U.S.A., 1972, numerous photo awards. Mem. Cleve. Bar Assn., Cuyahoga Bar Assn., Ohio State Bar Assn. Lodge: Mason. Avocation: photography. Home: 24118 E Baintree Beachwood OH 44122 Office: Adelstein & Adelstein Co L P A 925 Euclid Ave Suite 758 Cleveland OH 44114

ADELT, JAMES MICHAEL, finance company administrator; b. Chgo., Aug. 30, 1953; s. Joseph Walter and Geneviere Rose (Tokarski) A.; m. Phyllis Ann Morton, Aug. 16, 1975. Student, U. Ill., 1971-73, 73-74. Sr. computer operator U. Ill.-Chgo., 1975-77; project mgr. Household Finance Corp., Prospect Heights, Ill., 1977—. Mem. Assn. of Inst. for Cert. of Computer Profls., Chgo. Area Info. Mgmt. System Users Group. Avocation: Fine woodworking. Office: Household Finance Corp 2700 Sanders Rd Prospect Heights IL 60070

ADIARTE, ARTHUR LARDIZABAL, biophysicist; b. San Nicolas, Philippines, Oct. 27, 1943; s. Filomeno Adiarte and Maria Lardizabal; B.S., U. Philippines, 1963; Ph.D., U. Pitts., 1972; m. Rosario Guerrero, May 6, 1972; children—Alexander, Eric. Instr. physics, math. U. Philippines, 1963-66; research fellow U. Regensburg (W. Ger.), 1972-75; research specialist U. Minn., Mpls., 1975-77; research scientist, Minn. Energy Agy., St. Paul, 1977-84; research scientist, supr. Minn. Dept. Energy and Econ. Devel., 1984—. Fulbright Hays travel grantee, 1966-72; Alexander von Humboldt research fellow, W. Ger., 1973-74. Mem. N.Y. Acad. Scis., AAAS, Sigma Xi. Home: 743 Parkview Ave St Paul MN 55117 Office: 980 Am Center Bldg 150 E Kellogg Blvd St Paul MN 55101

ADKINS, TIMOTHY ARTHUR, educator; b. Newark, Ohio, May 28, 1945; s. Philip and Thelma A.; A.A., Lorain County Community Coll., 1971; B.S., Ohio State U., 1972; M.Ed., Kent State U., 1978, Ed.S., 1979; postgrad. Bowling Green State U., 1980, Mt. St. Joseph, 1980, Lesley Coll., 1980, U. South Fla., 1984. Tchr. history, Lorain (Ohio) City Schs., 1972-73; tchr., coordinator occupational work experience Elyria (Ohio) Schs., 1973-75; component coordinator career edn. Parma (Ohio) City Schs., 1978-80, occupational work adjustment coordinator, 1975—; adj. prof. Grad. Sch. Edn., Coll. Mt. St. Joseph, 1980—. Served with USAF, 1965-69; Vietnam. Mem. Am. Vocat. Assn., Ohio Vocat. Assn., NEA, Ohio Edn. Assn., N.E. Ohio Edn. Assn., Parma Edn. Assn., Career Edn. Assn., Ohio Parent Tchrs. Assn., Ohio State Alumni Assn., Kent State U. Alumni Assn. Republican. Methodist. Home: 454 Georgia Ave Elyria OH 44035 Office: Parma City Schools 6726 Ridge Rd Parma OH 44130

ADKISSON, GEORGE BILLY JOE, sales consultant, public speaker; b. Rushville, Ill., June 29, 1918; s. Aaron Arthur and Clara A. (Ritchey) A.; student pub. schs.; 1 dau., Karen Nanette Adkisson Bloomfield. Space salesman, classified mgr. Macomb (Ill.) Daily Jour., 1936-41; gen. sales mgr. Stas. KBUR and KBUR-FM, Burlington, Iowa, 1941-47; gen. mgr. Stas. KOKX and KOKX-FM, Keokuk, Iowa, 1947-51; sales and pub. relations depts. Stas. KSTP and KSTP-FM, Mpls., 1951-53; asst. sales mgr. Midwest div. Peters-Griffin-Woodward, Inc., Chgo., 1953-63; cons., Chgo., 1963-67; sales and radio sta. relations depts. H-R Reps., Chgo., 1967-69; gen. sales mgr. Stas. KFRE and KFRE-FM, Fresno, Calif., 1969-71, Stas. KGNC and KGNC-FM, Amarillo, Tex., 1971-72; nat. sales mgr. Sta. WSPA-TV, Spartanburg, S.C., 1972-73; sales cons. to numerous newspaper and radio stas., 1973-77; sales, credit and collections depts. Indsl. Supply div. Ace Hardware, Elk Grove Village, Ill., 1977-82; sales cons., pub. speaker, seminar lectr., Itasca, Ill., 1982—. Founder Burlington Oral Deaf Assistance Corp., 1945. Served with USNR, 1943-44. Ky. col., 1955; named outstanding rep. for radio and TV in Midwest, 1960; recipient Col. of Yr. and Hall of Fame awards Peters-Griffin Woodward, 1961; recipient more than 200 sales records and recognitions. Mem. Internat. Platform Assn., Am. Bus. Club (pres. 1946), Itasca C. of C., Am. Legion (past dist. liason officer), DAV, Alpha Delta Sigma. Mem. Christian Ch. Clubs: Masons, Shriners, K.T., Elks. Author: Basics of Selling Successfully; Blessed Happiness; Bonfire of Life; God Held My Hand; My Dream; Today; My Perfect Mate; Symphony of Life; The Price of Living Alone; contbr. articles on hunting and fishing to periodicals. Office: PO Box 59 Itasca IL 60143

ADLER, DAVID LEO, pathologist; b. N.Y.C., Sept. 5, 1913; s. Herman and Rose (Herskovitz) A.; A.B., Ind. U., 1934, M.D., 1938; m. Mary Jane Sanders, June 27, 1939; children—David W., Philip I, Douglas R. Intern, St. Elizabeth Hosp., Dayton, Ohio, 1938-39; instr. in pathology, Sch. Medicine, U. Tex., Galveston, 1939-40, Sch. Medicine, NYU, N.Y.C., 1946-47; dir. lab. Bartholomew County Hosp., Columbus, Ind., 1947-74; dir. lab. Columbus Med. Lab., 1976-84. Dir. ARC, 1950-70; pres. Ind. State Bd. Health, 1960-64; pres. Negro Scholarship Found., 1960-61. Served with M.C. U.S. Army, 1941-46. Recipient commendations, Ind. Gov., Ind. Bd. Health, ARC. Mem. Ind. State, Bartholomew County Med. Socs., Coll. Am. Pathologists, Am. Soc. Clin. Pathologists. Contbr. articles to profl. mags. Home: 4224 N Riverside Dr Columbus IN 47203

ADLER, GERSON, business executive; b. Berlin, Germany, Oct. 2, 1927; s. Max and Rosy (Lange) A.; came to U.S., 1939, naturalized, 1945; student CCNY, 1946-56, Western Res. U., 1954-63, Rabbinical Coll. Telshe, 1950-51; m. Naomi Samuel, Aug. 1, 1950; children—Don, Samson, Nathan, Eli, Hillel, Ezra, Zahava Sarah. Owner, operator Eagle Day Camp, N.Y.C., 1948-50; dir. Hebrew Acad. Cleve., 1951-61; inventory controller Am. Greetings Corp., Cleve., 1961-62, dir. audits, 1962-65, asst. v.p., 1965-68, v.p. audit and research, 1968-71; exec. v.p. Courtland Group and affiliated cos., 1971-74; pres., dir. Courtland Communications Corp., 1971-74; exec. v.p. Andover Crest & Co., Inc., Courtland Capital Corp., Courtland Hosp. Systems Corp., 1971-74; mgmt. cons. Gerson Adler and Assocs., Cleveland Heights, Ohio, 1974-78; sr. v.p., dir. Waxman Industries, Inc., Cleve., 1978-83; sr. v.p., treas. Continental Alloy Steel Corp., Solon, Ohio, 1983—; lectr. Am. Mgmt. Assn., 1970; cons. audit standards U.S. Gen. Accounting Office, 1970-72. Bd. dirs. Bur. Jewish Edn. Mem. Ohio Sch. Survey Commn., 1966-67; chmn. com. legislative auditor, State of Ohio, 1970-72; pres. Agudath Israel Orgn., 1961-72; chmn. bd. Rabbinical Coll. Telshe; bd. dirs. Citizens for Ednl. Freedom, Hebrew Acad. Cleve., 1952—. Mem. Inst. Internal Auditors (pres. 1967, internat. v.p. 1977-79). Address: 3595 Severn Rd Cleveland Heights OH 44118

ADLER, MILTON LEON, psychologist; b. Bronx, N.Y., June 11, 1926; s. Siegmund and Josephine (Eppsteiner) A.; B.S., Rutgers U., 1951; M.S., City U. N.Y., 1952; postgrad. N.Y. U., 1952-53; Ph.D., U. Ill., 1963; m. Margrit Klein, Mar. 5, 1948; children—Sandra Ellen, Mark Lawrence. Psychiat. case worker N.J. Neuropsychiat. Inst., Blauenberg, 1953; clin. psychology intern, staff psychologist Manteno (Ill.) State Hosp., 1953-57; regional psychologist Ill. Inst. Juvenile Research, Champaign, 1957-66; sr. psychologist, clin. supr., subregion dir. Herman M. Adler Children's Center, Champaign, 1966-74; cons. psychologist Frederic Chusid and Co., Chgo., 1963-64; lectr. psychology Ill. State U., Normal, 1974-75; instr. psychology Parkland Coll., Champaign, Ill., 1979-80; pvt. practice clin., counseling, cons. psychology, Urbana, Ill., 1965—; presenter growth in groups seminars and workshops on personal growth and interpersonal relationships. Served with USAAF, 1944-47. Registered psychologist, Ill. Fellow Am. Group Psychotherapy Assn. (dir. 1974-76, instr. tng. inst., mem. inst. com.); mem. Internat. Group Psychotherapy Assn., Ill. Assn. Maternal and Child Health (dir. bd. dirs. 1975-83, v.p. 1980-81, pres-elect 1981-82 pres. 1982-83, workshop, seminar presenter), Champaign-Urbana State Employees Assn. (past v.p., pres.), Ill. Group Psychotherapy Soc. (workshop presenter, council rep., awards of distinction 1977, 83, v.p., pres.-elect 1980-81, pres. 1982), Am. Psychol. Assn. (divs. psychotherapy, ind. practice, cons., community, humanistic and family psychology), Am. Soc. Psychologists in Pvt. Practice, Acad. of Psychologists in Marital and Family Therapy, Nat. Assn. Sch. Psychologists, Am. Assn. for Counseling and Devel., Am. Assn. Mental Health Counselors, Ill. Psychol. Assn. (clin. sect.), Ill. Acad. Criminology, Ill. Assn. for Counseling and Devel., Ill. Assn. Mental Health Counselors, Am. Acad. Psychotherapists, Saab Club Am., N. Am. Hunting Club, Phi Delta Kappa. Democrat. Unitarian-Universalist. Contbr. workshops/seminars for community groups on anxiety, risk-taking/and interpersonal relationships, and personal growth, workshops on group psychotherapy to profl. insts. Home: 1507 W University Ave Champaign IL 61821 Office: 404 W Green St Urbana IL 61801

ADLER, RICHARD EDWIN, sporting goods company executive; b. Cleve., Aug. 23, 1932; s. Rube and Mae (Miller) A.; m. Adele Lois Simon, June 23, 1956; children—Mark, Julie. B.A., Case-Western Res. U., 1954; postgrad. John Carroll U., 1957-58. Sec.-treas. Rube Adler Sporting Goods, Cleve., 1960-76; pres. Adler Sporting Goods, Cleve., 1976—, Beachwood, Ohio, 1979—; owner, mgr. Adler Sporting Goods Warehouse & Lettering, Cleve., 1980—. Mem. Beachwood (Ohio) Bd. Edn.; v.p. bd. dirs. Lakewood (Ohio) YMCA, 1964-71; bd. advisors LWV; bd. dirs. Hillcrest YMCA, 1978-82. Served to cpl. U.S. Army, 1955-57. Named Lakewood Man of Yr., 1971. Mem. Nat. Sporting Goods Assn., Greater Cleve. Growth Bd., Lakewood C. of C. (pres. 1970). Democrat. Jewish. Home: 24100 E Groveland St Beachwood OH 44122 Office: 222 Alpha Park Mayfield Heights OH 44143 also 26300 Cedar Rd Beachwood OH

ADLER, SEYMOUR JACK, social services administrator; b. Chgo., Oct. 22, 1930; s. Michael L. and Sarah (Pasnick) A.; B.S., Northwestern U., 1952; M.A., U. Chgo., 1958; m. Barbara Fingold, Mar. 24, 1958; children—Susan Lynn, Karen Sandra, Michelle Lauren. Caseworker, Cook County Dept. Pub. Aid, Chgo., 1955; juvenile officer Cook County Sheriff's Office, 1955-56; U.S. probation-parole officer U.S. Dist. Ct., Chgo., 1958-68; exec. dir. Youth Guidance, Chgo., 1968-73; dir. court services Juvenile ct. Cook County, Chgo., 1973-75; exec. dir. Methodist Youth Services, Chgo., 1975—. Mem. Ill. Law Enforcement Commn., 1969-72; instr. corrections program Chgo. State U., 1972-75; instr. Harper Coll., 1977, St. Joseph's Coll., 1978. Bd. dirs. Child Care Assn. Ill., 1979—. Served to 1st lt. USMCR, 1952-55. Recipient Morris J. Wexler award Ill. Acad. Criminology, 1975, Meritorious Service award Chgo. City Colls., 1968. Mem. Ill. Acad. Criminology (pres. 1972), Nat. Assn. Social Workers (del. Assembly 1977, 79, 81, chmn. Chgo. dist. 1978-80, chmn. group for action planning childrens services 1980—, Disting. Service award Criminal Justice Council 1978), Ill. Probation, Parole and Correctional Assn., Internat. Half-way House Assn. (Ill. dir.), Alpha Kappa Delta, Tau Delta Phi. Contbr. articles to profl. jours. Home: 2524 Happy Hollow Rd Glenview IL 60025 Office: 542 S Dearborn St Chicago IL 60605

ADMAVE, RICHARD JOSEPH, industrial engineer; b. Chgo., Mar. 20, 1934; s. Joseph Paul and Cecil Sarah (Bass) A.; m. Erma Jean Stansberry, Sept. 1, 1956; children—Karen, Patricia. Student pub. schs., Chgo. Machinist, radio insp. Zenith Radio Corp., Sioux City, Iowa, 1956-57, time study engr., 1957-63, sr. indsl. engr., 1963-66, mgr. prodn. engring., 1966-71, mgr. facilities, 1972-73, mgr. safety, ing. and security, 1973-74, mgr. plant engring., 1974-78; mgr. indsl. engring. CMI Load King div., Elk Point, S.D., 57025. Served with USAF, 1952-56. Republican. Lutheran. Home: 405 S Ridge Dr South Sioux City NE 68776 Office: Rose and Elm Sts Box 427 Elk Point SD 57025

ADOLPH, HAROLD PAUL, surgeon, missionary; b. Luan, Shansi, China, Dec. 11, 1932 (parents Am. citizens); s. Paul Earnest and Vivian Antoinette (Mac Dougal) A.; m. Bonnie Jo Adelsman, Aug. 19, 1955; children—David Harold, Carolyn Joy. B.S., Wheaton Coll., 1954; M.D., U. Pa., 1958. Diplomate Am. Bd. Gen. Surgery. Intern, surg. resident Gorgas Hosp., Balboa Heights, Republic of Panama, 1958-62; surg. preceptor Charles A. Cannon Jr. Meml. Hosp., Banner Elk, N.C., 1962-64; missionary surgeon Sudan Interior Mission, Soddo, Ethiopia, 1966-75; surgeon Central DuPage Hosp., Winfield, Ill., 1975—, chief surgery, 1983-84. Author: God's Prescription for Health, 1986. Served as lt. comdr. USN, 1964-66. Fellow ACS, Internat. Coll. Surgeons; mem. AMA, Christian Med. Soc. (pres. Chgo. chpt. 1979—, nat. trustee, sec.-treas. 1976-80), Am. Soc. Abdominal Surgeons. Republican. Mem. Evangelical Ch. Avocation: overseas surgical itineraries. Office: Du Page Profl Bldg ON 150 Winfield Rd Winfield IL 60190

ADOLPHE, ETHEL SAWYER, college adminstr.; b. Malvina, Miss., July 9, 1940; d. Barney and Mary Sawyer; m. Max Gerard Adolphe, Apr. 4, 1974 (div. 1982); 1 son, Karim Gerard. B.A., Tougaloo Coll., 1962; M.A., Washington U., St. Louis, 1967; postgrad. Lindenwood Coll., 1981—. Instr. sociology Haverford (Pa.) Coll., 1968-69, Temple U., Phila., 1969-71; faculty St. Louis Community Coll. at Forest Park Campus, 1971—, assoc. dean bus. and social scis., 1978—. Treas. Nina Place Redevel. Corp., 1980—. Mem. Mo. Sociol. Assn. Club: St. Louis World Trade. Home: 5931 Kingsbury St Saint Louis MO 63112

ADOLPHSON, DAVID WILLIAM, bank executive; b. Omaha, June 20, 1945; s. Evert William and Elsie Loretta (Brewer) A.; m. Priscilla Esther Trubeck, Sept. 20, 1969. B.A., Monmouth Coll., 1967; M.B.A., Northwestern U., 1977. Systems engr. IBM, Moline, Ill., 1967-70; mfg. systems mgr. Internat. Harvester Co., Chgo., 1970-81; quality assurance mgr. Harris Bank, Chgo., 1981—. Contbr. articles to profl. jours. Violinist, Elmhurst Symphony Orch., Ill.; class agt. Monmouth Coll. Alumni Fund. Mem. Guide Internat. (project team 81-84), Blue Key, Tau Kappa Epsilon, Phi Eta Mu. Republican. Presbyterian. Clubs: Medinah Country (Ill.); Monmouth Loop Assocs. (Chgo.). Avocations: fine arts; joinery; organic gardening; walking; angling. Home: 138 E Madison Villa Park IL 60181 Office: Harris Trust and Savs Bank PO Box 755 Chicago IL 60690

ADRIAN, BARBARA ANN, data processing executive; b. Burlington, Iowa, July 3, 1955; d. Ellsworth Walter and Evelyn Louise (Beian) A.; m. Ronald Lee Limkemann, Sept. 9, 1976 (div. June 15, 1979); 1 child, Brandon James. A.A., Southeastern Iowa Community Coll., 1977; B.A. Magna cum laude, Iowa Wesleyan Coll., Mt. Pleasant, 1981; student St. Ambrose Coll., Davenport, Iowa, 1984—. Data processing supr. Champion Products, Burlington, Iowa, 1973-76; programmer analyst Winegard Co., Burlington, 1976-79; data processing mgr. Southeastern Community Coll., W. Burlington, 1981-85; fin. dir., bus. mgr. Burlington Alcohol and Drug Dependency Services, 1985—. Mem. Assn Systems Mgmt., Common IBM User Group, NOW. Democrat. Lutheran. Home: 2111 S 3d St Burlington IA 52601

ADRIAN, PATRICIA LEE GRIMSHAW, association executive; b. Reliance, S.D., July 20, 1938; d. Walter George and Dorthy Veronica (Zastrow) Grimshaw; student Sinte Gleska U., 1973; m. Robert Earl Adrian, Oct. 12, 1957; children—James Robert, Thomas Edward, Kevin Patrick, David Duane. Sec., Cherry Todd Electric, 1956-57; tchr. White River (S.D.) Ind. Sch. Dist., 1970-71; dir. S.D. Beef Industry Council, 1970-73, pres., 1972-73, exec. v.p., 1973—; exec. sec., lobbyist S.D. Livestock Assn., part-time 1977—; dir. Nat. Livestock and Meat Bd., vice chmn. Beef Industry Council, 1984—, chmn. program budget com., 1984—; dir. agrl. devel. State of S.D., 1982-83; mem. steering com. Animal and Range Scis. Found., S.D. State U., 1984-85. Gov.'s rep. to nutrition symposium Old West Regional Commn., 1979-80; mem. Indsl. Devel. Comm. State of S.D., 1979-82; mem. S.D. Agrl. Mktg. Commn., 1980-82; S.D. rep. Dist. Export Council, U.S. Dept. Commerce, 1981-82; mem. S.D. State Devel. Commn., 1983—, S.D. Bd. Indsl. and Agrl. Devel., 1982-83. Recipient Disting. Service award S.D. Stockgrowers Assn., 1974, S.D. State U., 1976. Mem. Nat. Fedn. Press Women, Am. Soc. Assn. Execs., Nat. Cattlemen's Assn., S.D. Livestock Assn., Am. Agri-Women, U.S. Meat Export Fedn. (dir. 1980—), S.D. Press Women's Assn., S.D. CowBelles (pres.). Republican. Roman Catholic. Home: Star Route Box 222 White River SD 57579 Office: 110 W Capitol St Pierre SD 57501

ADRIANOPOLI, BARBARA CATHERINE, librarian; b. Ft. Dodge, Iowa, Jan. 27, 1943; d. Daniel Joseph and Mary Dolores (Coleman) Hogan; m. Carl David Adrianopoli, June 28, 1968; children—Carlin, Laurie. B.S., Mundeline Coll., 1966; M.L.S., Rosary Coll., 1975. Tchr., Father Bertrand High Sch., Memphis, 1966-68; caseworker Dept. Pub. Aid Chgo., 1968; tchr. North Chicago Jr. High Sch. (Ill.), 1968-70, Austin Middle Sch., Chgo., 1970-73; librarian Barrington Pub. Library (Ill.), 1976-79, Schaumburg Twp. Pub. Library (Ill.), 1979—; adv. com. Suburban AudioVisual N. Suburban/Suburban Library Systems, LaGrange, Ill., 1981-84, NEH grants for N. Suburban Library System, Wheeling, Ill., 1981-86. Contbr. articles to jours. Mem. Com. Schaumburg Twp. Disabled, 1981—; pres. Lakeview Pub. Sch. PTA, Hoffman Estates, Ill., 1983-84; mem. Sch. Dist. 54-Citizens Adv. Com., Schaumburg, 1983—; advisor Boy Scout Am. handicapped badge, Schaumburg Twp., 1981—. N. Suburban Library System grantee, 1983. Mem. ALA, Ill. Library Assn., Library Assn. No. Ill. (v.p. 1981-84), NOW, Am. Film Inst., Common Cause. Democrat. Roman Catholic. Home: 1105 Kingsdale Rd Hoffman Estates IL 60194 Office: Schaumburg Twp Pub Library 21 W Library Ln Schaumburg IL 60194

ADSIT, GORDON EDWIN, city official, educator; b. Lansing, Mich., Apr. 3, 1930; s. Guy Everett and Matilda (Montanye) A.; m. Patricia Lavey, Feb. 3, 1951; children—Constance L., Douglas G., Judith K., Susanne M. A.S. in Fire Sci. Tech., Lansing Community Coll., 1972; postgrad. Mich. State U. With fire fighting div. Lansing (Mich.) Fire Dept., 1953-64, insp. II, 1964-65, insp. IV, 1965-72, fire marshal, 1972-83; chief charter Twp. of Lansing, 1983—; mem. faculty Lansing Community Coll.; tech. adv. arson assistance program U.S. Fire Adminstrn.; cons. ins. cos., architects, gen. contractors, real estate cos.; speaker at confs., seminars. With U.S. Army, 1948-50, USAR, 1950-56. Named Insp. of Yr. Mich. Fire Inspector Soc., 1980. Mem. Nat. Fire Protection Assn., Fire Marshal's Assn. N.Am., Am. Soc. Safety Engrs., Internat. Assn. Arson Investigators, Mich. Fire Insps. Soc., Lansing Safety Council, Internat. Assn. Fire Chiefs, Mich. Fire Chiefs Assn. Roman Catholic. Lodge: Elks. Home: 1600 Boston Blvd Lansing MI 48910 Office: 3301 W Michigan Ave Lansing MI 48917

AEH, RICHARD KENT, telecommunications executive; b. Jackson, Ohio, Aug. 3, 1939; s. Richard Clayton and Julia (Bryan) A.; m. Sandra Leigh Magruder, June 28, 1969; children—Jennifer Kristin, Allison Leslie, Meridith Courtney. B.S. in Bus. Adminstrn., Ohio State U., 1966. Dist. mgr. systems devel. AT&T Communications, Cin., 1966—; mem. adv. council Miami U. Sch. Applied Sci., Oxford, Ohio, 1982—. Vol. mgmt. cons. Community Chest, Cin., 1979—; trustee Housing for Older Ams., 1984—, Better Housing League, Cin., 1982-83, Lower River Nursing Assn., Cin., 1980-83; mem. Citizens Adv. Com. on Cable TV, Cin., 1979. Served with U.S. Army, 1959-62. Recipient Community Service award Community Chest and United Appeal, 1985. Mem. Assn. for Systems Mgmt. (v.p. 1984-85, chpt. pres. 1985—, mem. internat. pub. policy com.). Republican. Episcopalian. Avocations: running, camping. Home: 7059 Royalgreen Dr Cincinnati OH 45244 Office: AT&T Communications 221 E 4th St 11th St Atrium II Cincinnati OH 45202

AERY, SHAILA ROSALIE, state educational administrator; b. Tulsa, Dec. 4, 1938; d. Silas Cleveland and Billie (Brewer) A. B.S., U. Okla., 1964; M.S., Okla. State U., 1972, Ed.D., 1975. Spl. asst., chancellor Okla. Regents for Higher Edn., Oklahoma City, 1977; spl. asst., chancellor U. Mo., Columbia, 1978-80, asst. provost acad. affairs, 1980-81; dep. commr. higher edn. State of Mo., Jefferson City, 1981, commr., 1982—; dir. Mo. Higher Edn. Loan Authority, St. Louis, 1982—; commr. Edn. Commn. of the States, Denver, 1983—; mem. exec. bd. State Higher Edn. Offices, Denver, 1983—. Contbr. articles to profl. jours. Mem. AAUW. Democrat. Episcopalian. Office: Higher Edn Coordinating Bd 600 Monroe St Jefferson City MO 65101

AFFOLTER, LEROY MARION, optometrist; b. Mankato, Minn., Aug. 12, 1932; s. John E. and Josephine (Huss) A.; m. Carol J. Rohlin, June 6, 1954; 1 child, Sheri. B.S., Mankato State U., 1954; O.D., Ill. Coll. Optometry, 1958. Gen. practice optometry, Marshall, Minn., 1958—. Chmn. Marshall Planning Commn., 1973-79; pres. Christ Evang. Luth. Ch., Marshall, 1969-72, treas., 1982-84. Mem. Am. Optometric Assn., Minn. Optometric Assn., Jaycees (pres. 1965). Republican. Home: 302 Jean Ave Marshall MN 56258 Office: 121 N 3d St Marshall MN 56258

AGGARWAL, SHIV KUMAR, business executive; b. New Delhi; s. Ishwari Prasad and Bhagwati Devi A.; came to U.S., 1956, naturalized, 1975; B.A., U. Delhi, 1953; M.S.W., U. Baroda, India, 1955; M.B.A., U. Mo., 1957. Pres., Imperial Cycle & Motor Co., Bombay, India, 1959-62; dir. neighborhood services East End Neighborhood House, Cleve., 1962-67; founder, exec. dir. Collinwood Community Services Center, Cleve., 1967-80; pres. Century Bus. Systems, Cleve., 1980-82, Macon Internat. Inc., Cleve., 1982-85, Profl. Weight Control Systems, Inc., 1985—. Mem. Gerontol. Soc., India Assn. Greater Cleve. Home: 2595 Hickory Ln Cleveland OH 44124 Office: 2496 Dysart Rd Cleveland OH 44118

AGIN, GARY PAUL, physics educator, researcher; b. Kansas City, Mo., Dec. 22, 1940; s. George Franklin and Minnie Irene (Holt) A. B.S. in Engring. Physics, U. Kans., 1963; M.S. in Physics, Kans. State U., 1967, Ph.D. in Physics, 1968. Asst. prof. physics Mich. Technol. U., Houghton, 1968—; presenter numerous papers in nuclear physics at profl. meetings. Mem. AAAS, Am. Assn. Physics Tchrs., Am. Phys. Soc., Mensa, Tau Beta Pi, Sigma Pi Sigma (councillor Zone 8 Soc. Physics Students 1982—), Sigma Xi. Home: 717 Cedar Bluff Dr Houghton MI 49931 Office: Dept Physics Mich Technol U Houghton MI 49931

AGIN, JAMES EUGENE, health care company executive; b. Salina, Kans., Feb. 16, 1943; s. Harold F. and Agnes E. (Curry) A.; m. Sally Sue White, May 15, 1972; children—Robert A., Scott C. B.S. in Bus., Fort Hays State U., 1970, M.B.A., 1971. Dist. sales mgr. Frito-Lay, Inc., Indpls., 1971-72; exec. asst. Kans. Med. Soc., Topeka, 1972-74; exec. dir. Kans. Found. Med. Care, Topeka, 1974-82; v.p. Health Care Plus, Inc., Wichita, Kans., 1983-84; dir. planning, radiology and nuclear medicine, P.A., Topeka, Kans., 1985; chief exec. officer Physicians Health Plan of Kans., Topeka, 1985—; adj. instr. Coll. Health Sci. Wichita State U., 1979-82; speaker confs. Mem. Topeka Police Chief's Com. Police-Community Relations, 1972; mem. exec. staff Kans. Med. Polit. Action Com., Topeka, 1972-74; mem. Christ the King Fund Dr. Com., Topeka, 1983. Served with USMC, 1963-66. Fort Hays State U. fellow, 1970-71; recipient Cert. of Commendation, Kans. Found. Med. Care, Topeka, 1982; Resolution of Commendation, Kans. Med. Soc., 1982; Exec. Dir. Testimonial award Am. Assn. Profl. Standards Rev. Orgns., 1979. Mem. Am. Assn. Med. Soc. Execs., Am. Assn. Profl. Standards Rev. Orgns., Am. Mgmt. Assn., Am. Legion. Republican. Roman Catholic. Lodge: Elks. Office: Physicians Health Plan of Kans Capitol Towers 400 SW 8th St Topeka KS 66603

AGIN, MICHAEL LAWRENCE, science education educator; b. Chgo., Dec. 12, 1933; s. Lawrence Eugene and Mary Lucille (Yergovich) A.; m. Fran Jackson, June 6, 1960 (div. July 1981); children—Michael, Frank J., Carolyn T. B.S., Beloit Coll., 1958; M.A., Loyola U., 1963; Ph.D., U. Wis. Madison, 1970. Tchr. chemistry Riverside Brookfield High Sch., Ill., 1959-68; research fellow. U. Wis.-Madison, 1968-70; prof. Mich. Tech. U., Houghton, 1970—. Author: Teaching Science Via Social Historical Approach, 1971. Editor: School Science/Math, 1978. Bd. dirs., v.p., Houghton-Portage Schs., Houghton, Mich., 1976—, POLAR Community Schs., Houghton, 1978—. Mem. Assn. Media-Based Continued Edn. for Engrs. (bd. dirs.). Avocation: mineral collecting. Home: Route 1 Box 145 Chassell MI 49916 Office: Div Edn and Pub Services Mich Tech U Houghton MI 49931

AGNEW, NETTIE LOU, nurse, administrator; b. Jasper, Mo., Jan. 23, 1948; d. Andrew J. and Mary Marie (Burton) Butler; m. Edwin John Agnew, Oct. 23, 1973; 1 dau., Rhian Mallorie. Diploma Burge Sch. Nursing, 1969; B.S. magna cum laude, Drury Coll., 1970; M.S., No. Ill. U., 1977. Staff nurse Cox. Med. Ctr., Springfield, Mo., 1969-70; staff nurse U.S. Air Force, Mather AFB, Calif., 1970-71, aero-med. staging nurse Scott AFB, Ill., 1971-73, Flight Nurse Sch., Brooks AFB, Tex., 1972; vis. nurse St. Clair County Vis. Nurse Assn., East St. Louis, Ill., 1973-75; staff nurse North Kansas City (Mo.) Meml. Hosp., 1975, clin. nurse specialist, 1978-79, dir. nursing, v.p. nursing, v.p. clin. services, 1979—; instr. Research Med. Ctr. Sch. Nursing, Kansas City, Mo., 1975-76. Mem. adv. council St. Mary Coll. Sch. Nursing, Leavenworth, Kans., 1981—; bd. advisors dept. nursing William Jewell Coll. 1983. Served with USAF, 1969-73. Mem. Dirs. Nursing Greater Kansas City Area Hosp. Assn., Mo. Assn. Nursing Services Adminstrs., Am. Assn. Nurse Execs., Am. Nurses Assn. (cert.), Sigma Theta Tau. Club: Soroptimist. Office: North Kansas City Meml Hosp 2800 Hospital Dr North Kansas City MO 64116

AGRUSS, NEIL STUART, physician; b. Chgo., June 2, 1939; s. Meyer and Frances (Spector) A.; B.S., U. Ill., 1960, M.D., 1963; m. Teresa Marie Stafford; children—David, Lauren, Michael, Joshua, Susan Intern, U. Ill. Hosp., Chgo., 1963-64, resident in internal medicine, 1964-65, 67-68; fellow in cardiology, Cin. Gen. Hosp., 1968-70, dir. coronary care unit, 1971-74, dir. echocardiography lab., 1972-74; dir. cardiac diagnostic labs., Central DuPage Hosp., Winfield, Ill., 1974—; asst. prof. medicine, U. Cin., 1970-74, Rush Med. Coll., 1976—. Chmn. coronary care com. Heart Assn. DuPage County, 1974-76; active Congregation Beth Shalom, Naperville, Ill. Served to capt. M.C. U.S. Army, 1965-67. Diplomate Am. Bd. Internal Medicine. Fellow ACP, Am. Coll. Cardiology, Am. Coll. Chest Physicians, Council Clin. Cardiology, Am. Heart Assn.; mem. AMA, DuPage County, Ill. State Med. Socs., Am. Fedn. Clin. Research, Chgo. Heart Assn. Author and co-author publs. in field. Office: 454 Pennsylvania Ave Glen Ellyn IL 60137

AHERN, CINDY FRANCIS, optometrist; b. Lancaster, Ohio, June 7, 1956; d. Ross and Stella (Dwyer) Francis; m. John Kevin Ahern, Sept. 1, 1979. B.S., Ohio State U., 1978, O.D., 1982. Gen. practice optometry, Urbana, Ohio, 1982—; clin. instr. Ohio State U., Columbus, 1983-84. Mem. Miami Valley Soc. Optometrists (sec. 1984-85, 2d v.p. 1985-86), Ohio Optometric Assn., Am. Optometric Assn. Urbana C. of C. (bd. dirs.). Club: Soroptomist (Urbana). Avocations: history of art; sewing; golfing. Home: 268 Nova Dr Urbana OH 43078 Office: 128 Miami St Urbana OH 43078

AHERN, WILLIAM BREWSTER, biology educator; b. McPherson, Kans., June 27, 1941; s. Alvin A. and Helen A. (Green) A.; m. Sharon Irene Ray, Apr. 13, 1963; children—Todd Alan, Eric William. A.A., Central Coll., 1961; B.S., Emporia State U., 1963; M.S., Kans. U., 1967; D.A., U. No. Colo., 1975. Cert. secondary edn. tchr. Grade sch. tchr. Lyon County Schs., Emporia, Kans., 1963-65; biology tchr. Greenville Coll., Ill., 1966—, head dept. biology, 1977—; cons. Kingsbury Park Dist. Nature Preserve, Greenville, 1978, 1980; mem. faculty adv. council Ausauble Trains Environ. Inst., Mancelona, Mich., 1981—. Editor student manual Pre-Medicine, 1983. Mem. Am. Inst. Biol. Scis., Am. Soc. Parasitologists, Nat. Assn. Advisors for Health Professions, Central Assn. Advisors for Health Professions, Sigma Xi. Republican. Free Methodist. Avocations: camping; raising bonsai trees. Home: 819 N Locust Greenville IL 62246 Office: Dept Biology Greenville Coll Greenville IL 62246

AHMAD, BUSHARAT, ophthalmologist; b. Ferozepur, Pakistan, Oct. 22, 1931; came to U.S., 1964, naturalized, 1977; s. Sardar and Anwati Begum (Anwari) Ali; m. Adeeba Bashir, Feb. 3, 1968; children—Samra, Umber. F.S.C., U. Karachi, W. Pakistan, 1948, M.D., 1956; D.O., U. London, 1962. Diplomat Am. Bd. Ophthalmology. House Surgeon ophthalmology Jinnah Central Hosp., Karachi, W. Pakistan, 1956-57, research ophthalmologist, 1970; med. officer Govt. Hosp., W. Pakistan, 1957-59; rotating intern St. Josephs Gen. Hosp., Port Arthur, Ont., Can., 1959-60; clin. asst. Moorfields Eye Hosp., London, 1960-61; sr. house surgeon Royal Eye Hosp., Manchester, Eng., 1961; house officer St. Elizabeth Hosp., Covington, Ky., 1962-63; resident neurosurgery and plastic surgery Vancouver Gen. Hosp., B.C., Can., 1963-64; resident ophthalmology St. Louis U. Hosp., 1964-66; research fellow Retina Found., Boston, fellow ophthalmology cornea service Mass. Eye and Ear Infirmary, Boston, 1967-69; instr. ophthalmology Dow Med. Coll., Karachi, 1969-70; opthalmic surgeon Civil Hosp., Karachi, 1969-70; practice ophthalmology, Marquette, Mich., 1971—; asst. clin. prof. ophthalmology Mich. State U., East Lansing, 1979—. Contbr. articles to profl. jours. Named Man of Yr., Kiwanis Internat. Marquette chpt., 1984. Fellow Internat. Coll. Surgeons, Soc. Eye Surgeons, ACS, Internat. Acad. Cosmetic Surgery, Am. Acad. Ophthalmology and Otolaryngology, Royal Soc. Medicine; mem. Contact Lens Soc. Ophthalmologists, Assn. Research Ophthalmology, Am. Assn. Ophthalmologists, AMA, Mich. State Med. Soc., Marquette-Alger County Med. Soc. (chmn. pub. relations and fin. com. 1972-84, pres. 1975-76, Upper Peninsula Med. Soc. (pres. 1974-76), North Central Region Eye Bank Assn. Am. (pres. 1975-77, 1981-82), Eye Bank Assn. Am. (pres. elect 1982-83, pres. 1984—), Aero-Space Med. Assocs., Flying Physicians Assn., Am. Assn. Tissue Banks, Am. Council Transplantation (chmn. pub. edn. com. 1984—), Marquette Area C. of C. (pres. 1981-82). Republican. Islam. Lodge: Rotary (pres. Marquette chpt. 1977-78, youth exchange officer Marquette West 1984—). Avocations: photography; travel. Office: Marquette Med Dental Ctr Suite 105 1414 W Fair Ave Marquette MI 49855

AHMANN, DAVID LAWRENCE, physician, educator; b. St. Cloud, Minn., May 21, 1933; s. Norbert T. and Clotilda (Hall) A.; m. Rosemary Morrisey, Dec. 29, 1957; children—David, Mary, Mark, Carla, Gregory, Christopher. B.S., Marquette U., Milw., 1954, M.D., 1958. Diplomate Am. Bd. Internal Medicine. Intern, Walter Reed Army Hosp., Washington, 1958-59; resident Mayo Grad. Sch. Medicine, Mayo Found., Rochester, Minn., 1962-65; instr. Mayo Med. Sch., Mayo Clinic, Rochester, Minn., 1968-72, asst. prof., 1972-75, assoc. prof., 1975-77, prof., 1977—, chmn. div. med. oncology, 1972—; dep. dir. Mayo Clinic Cancer Ctr., Rochester, 1980—. Contbr. articles to profl. publs. Mem. Zumbro Valley Med. Soc. (pres. 1975), Am. Assn. Clin. Oncology, Am. Soc. Clin. Oncology (sec.-treas. 1982-84). Home: 6830 Buckthorn NW Rochester MN 55901 Office: Mayo Clinic 200 1st St SW Rochester MN 55902

AHONEN, CLIFFORD JOHN, marketing cons.; b. Ironwood, Mich., Mar. 1, 1934; s. Telfield John and Helen Tina (Kuula) A.; B.B.A., U. Wis., 1959; M.B.A., Roosevelt U., 1963; postgrad. U. Chgo., 1964-65; Ph.D., Calif. Western U., 1980; m. Patricia Ann Doyle, Aug. 20, 1961; children—Helen, Allan, Michael, Mark. Sales engr. Richards-Wilcox Mfg. Co., Aurora, Ill., 1959-61; marketing specialist Link-Belt Co., Chgo., 1961-64; dir. long range planning Joy Mfg. Co., Michigan City, Ind., 1964-69; v.p. mktg. strategy Starcraft Co., Goshen, Ind., 1969-72; exec. v.p. Marketing Cons., Inc., Elkhart, Ind., 1972—, also dir.; faculty Goshen (Ind.) Coll., 1971-74, Southwestern Mich. Coll., Dowagiac, 1974—, Ind. U., 1975—. Chmn. Cherokee dist. Boy Scouts Am., 1975-77. Served with U.S. Army, 1955-57. Mem. Am. Mktg. Assn. (chpt. pres. 1973), Am. Statis. Assn. Republican. Roman Catholic. Club: Sales and Advt. Home: 250 S Main St Goshen IN 46526 Office: 339 Communicana Bldg Elkhart IN 46514

AHR, PAUL ROBERT, state government administrator; b. Irvington, N.J., Jan. 4, 1945; s. Wilbur Frederick and Marcella Elizabeth (Brady) A.; m. Kathryn Danielle Cramer; children by previous marriage—Thomas Brady, Andrew Travers. A.B., U. Notre Dame, 1966; Ph.D., Cath. U. Am., 1971; M.P.A., U. So. Calif., 1977. Postdoctoral fellow Harvard Med. Sch., Boston, 1972-73; dir. children's program Va. Dept. Mental Health and Mental Retardation, Richmond, 1973-74, dir. program analysis planning, 1974-75, asst. commr., 1975-79; dir. Mo. Dept. Mental Health, Jefferson City, 1979—; lectr. U. Mo. Sch. Health Related Professions, Columbia, 1980, clin. assoc. prof. U. Mo. Sch. Medicine, 1980—; clin. assoc. prof. dept. psychiatry U. Mo., Kansas City, 1980—; assoc. clin. prof. St. Louis U. Sch. Medicine, 1982—. Served with USN, 1969-72. NIMH fellow, 1972-73, Vocat. Rehab. Adminstrn. fellow, 1966-69. Fellow Am. Coll. Mental Health Adminstrs.; mem. Nat. Assn. State Mental Health Program Dirs. (pres. 1984—), Am. Psychol. Assn., Am. Soc. Pub. Adminstrn. Roman Catholic. Office: Mo Dept Mental Health 2002 Missouri Blvd Jefferson City MO 65101

AHSENS, ROBERT JOHN, III, lawyer; b. San Juan, P.R., Dec. 23, 1949; s. Robert John II and Doris (Sonebraker) A.; m. Michel Leslee Beil, June 10, 1972 (div. 1983); 1 child, Robert John IV. B.A., Westminster Coll., 1972; J.D., U. Mo., 1979. Bar: Mo. 1980, U.S. Dist. Ct. (we. dist.) Mo. 1980. Law clk. Mo. Ct. Appeals, Kansas City, 1979-80; assoc. Carson, Monacco et al, Jefferson City, Mo., 1980-81; asst. pros. atty. Cole County, Jefferson City, 1982—. Asst. editor, contbr.: Missouri Prosecutors Trial Casebook, 1983. Mem. campaign com. Jefferson City United Way, 1983; bd. advisors Area Drug Abuse Council, 1983. Served to capt. U.S. Army, 1972-77. Mem. Mo. Assn. Pros. Attys. (legis. com. 1983—), Mo. Bar Assn. (criminal law com. 1983—), Nat. Dist. Attys. Assn., Jefferson City C. of C. (property com. 1981). Methodist. Lodge: Rotary. Office: Cole County Courthouse Suite 400 Jefferson City MO 65101

AIKEN, ROGER GEORGE, energy systems research analyst; b. Feilding, N. Z., Jan. 12, 1933; s. Henry George and Muriel Christine; came to U.S., 1973; B.Sc., U. Canterbury, Christchurch, N.Z., 1954, B.E. with honours, 1956, M.E. with distinction, 1958; postgrad. in mech. engring., U. Minn., 1973-83; m. Susan Graham Hamilton, July 14, 1962 (div. 1980); children—Andrew Graham, David George; m. 2d, Connie Lynn Haugen, Feb. 19, 1983. Sci. officer physics and engring. labs., Dept. Sci. and Indsl. Research, Lower Hutt, N.Z., 1958-59; devel. engr. Collier and Beale Ltd., Wellington, N.Z., 1959-61; sr. sci. staff Hirst Research Centre, Brit. Gen. Electric Co., Wembley, England, 1961-65; mem. sci. staff Bell No. Research, Ottawa, Ont., Can., 1965-67; temporary engr. transmission dept. N.Z. Post Office, Wellington, 1968; research scientist, engr. Communications Research Centre, Canadian Fed. Dept. Communications, Ottawa, Ont., 1968-73; research fellow Center for Studies of Phys. Environment, Inst. Tech., U. Minn., Mpls., 1974-76; energy research analyst research div. Minn. Energy Agy., St. Paul, 1976-78; research fellow Underground Space Center, U. Minn., Mpls., 1978-79, Bio Energy Coordinating Office, 1980, instr. energy, honors program Coll. Liberal Arts, 1982-83; prin. energy systems analyst Synergistic Design and Engring., Mpls., 1981-82; bldg. mgmt. systems analyst Honeywell, Inc., Mpls., 1982-83; tng. supr. MTS Systems Corp., Mpls., 1984—. Coordinator, Future Lifestyle Planners Program, U. Minn. YMCA, 1978-80. Mem. Instn. Elec. Engrs. (U.K.), IEEE, Biomass Energy Inst. (Can.), AIAA, Internat. Solar Energy Soc., Minn. Solar Energy Assn. (chmn. policy com. 1978-79, treas. 1984—), Twin Cities Energy Engrs., Phi Kappa Phi. Presbyterian. Clubs: U. Minn., YMCA. Contbr. articles to profl. jours. and meetings. Home: 1589 Hollywood Ct Saint Paul MN 55108

AIKEN, THOMAS DAVID, food company official; b. Texas City, Tex., Dec. 29, 1953; s. Robert Lawrence and Helen Lee (Beard) A.; B.S., U. Ill., 1976, M.S., 1977; student Moscow State U., 1974, Leningrad State U., 1974; postgrad. in bus. adminstrn., Washington U., St. Louis, 1982—. Nutritionist, Animal Nutrition, Inc., Belleville, Ill., 1978-79; asst. mgr. mktg. services Ralston Purina Co., St. Louis, 1979-80, tech. sales rep. for indsl. sales protein div., 1980-82, mgr. nat. accounts, 1982—. Mem. Inst. Food Technologists, Am. Mktg. Assn., Alpha Kappa Lambda. Home: 7018 Forsyth Saint Louis MO 63105 Office: Checkerboard Sq Saint Louis MO 63164

AILSLIEGER, ROSS EDWARD, aircraft company human factors engineer, flight instructor; b. Hays, Kans., Sept. 24, 1937; s. Herbert George and Mary May (Pizinger) A.; m. Sharon Marie Shue, June 12, 1965; children—Paul Edward, Kristafer Ross, Alex Mathew. A.B. in Psychology, Ft. Hays State U., 1964, M.S. in Exptl. Psychology, 1965. Cert. flight instr., FAA. Human factors engr. N.Am. Rockwell, Los Angeles, 1966-68; human factors and maintainability lead engr. Spartan Missile program McDonnell-Douglas Astronautics Co., Huntington Beach, Calif., 1968-76; sr. human factors engr. AH-64 attack helicopter program Hughes Helicopters, Culver City, Calif., 1976-77; supr. human factors engring., and flight simulation Boeing Mil. Airplane Co., Wichita, Kans., 1977—; cons. aircraft cockpit design requirements. Served with U.S. Army, 1955-59. Mem. Aircraft Owners and Pilots Assn., Tri-Service Aircrew Sta. Standardization Panel, Exptl. Aircraft Assn. Republican. Lutheran. Club: University (Wichita). Patentee in field. Home: 303 Wheatland Pl Wichita KS 67235 Office: Boeing Mil Airplane Co PO Box 7730 Wichita KS 67277

AINSWORTH, BARBARA ARLENE, curriculum coordinator, writer; b. Buffalo, N.Y., Aug. 8, 1935; d. Stanley R. and Barbara M. (Price) Fund; B.A., U. Md., 1962, Ed.M., 1967, Ph.D., 1974; m. Peter D. Ainsworth, May 11, 1962; (dec. 1975); children—Peter David II, John, Mary; m. David H. Trautman, Dec. 29, 1978. Tchr. elem. public schs. Sch. Dist. 50, Washington, Ill., 1960-61; tchr. Prince George's County (Md.) Public Schs., 1962-74, study skills specialist, 1970-72; instr. off-campus div. Coll. Edn., American U., Washington, 1973; grad. asst. Coll. Edn., U. Md., College Park, 1973-74; project editor, writer and cons. Educational Challenges, Inc., Alexandria, Va., 1972-80; project coordinator ednl. programs for sr. citizens Iowa Lakes Community Coll., Estherville, Iowa, 1975, instr. sociology, 1975; asst. prof. geography Buena Vista Coll., Storm Lake, Iowa, 1975-76, dir. student teaching, 1975-76; ednl. servies cons. Arrowhead Area Edn. Agy. 5, Fort Dodge, Iowa, 1976-78; free-lance cons. and edn. writer, 1978-82; curriculum coordinator Escuela Americana, 1982—; instr. Marshalltown (Iowa) Community Coll., 1978-81, Universidad Americana, 1982—. Mem. Spirit Lake (Iowa) Bicentennial Com., 1975. Mem. Assn. Supervision and Curriculum Devel., Phi Delta Kappa (historian Iowa chpt. 1977-78). Democrat. Unitarian. Author: Macmillan Social Studies Series, 1978; Education Through Travel, 1979; Handbook of Ideas for Curriculum Improvement, 1981; Reflections of Yesterday, 1981; English to Use, 1983; BASIC for Beginners, 1985; producer cassette learning packages, film strips, 1975—; editor Basic Ideas, 1980-82. Home: 3102 W Lincoln Way Marshalltown IA 50158 Office: Escuela Americana Apartado (01) 35 San Salvador El Salvador

AIREY, CHRISTIAN G., clergyman; b. Port-au-Prince, Haiti, W.I., Sept. 14, 1938; came to U.S., 1963; s. George and Luciana (Antonio) A.; m. Marnelle Pluviose, June 27, 1981; children—Chrisner, Emmanuel Pluviose, Marnelle-Anastasie. B.A., Va. Union U., 1967; M.Div., Howard U., 1970; Th.M., Harvard U., 1972; Ph.D., U. Paris, 1974. Ordained minister Lutheran Ch. French lab. dir. Howard U., Washington, 1968-70; pastor Zion Luth. Ch., Bklyn., 1974-78, St. Stephen Luth. Ch., Chgo., 1978—; refugee resettlement program dir. Luth. Child and Family Services, Chgo., 1980-82; exec. dir. Haitian Christian Alliance for Progress, Chgo., 1979—. Democrat. Home and Office: 8500 S Maryland Ave Chicago IL 60619

AKEHURST, F(RANK) RONALD P(OWELL), French educator; b. Stoke-on-Trent, Eng., Apr. 29, 1938; came to U.S., 1962; s. Frank and Emma (Powell) A.; m. Judith Marion Hougland, Dec. 30, 1964; children—Mary Kathleen, Colin David. B.A., Oxford U., 1962; Ph.D., U. Colo., 1967. Teaching asst. U. Colo., Boulder, 1962-65; asst. prof. French, U. Rochester (N.Y.), 1965-68; asst. prof. U. Minn., Mpls., 1968-70, assoc. prof., 1970-82, prof., 1982—; cons. La. Bd. Regents, Baton Rouge, 1982; dir., chmn. bd. advisers Univ. Research Consortium, Mpls., 1982—. Served with RAF, 1956-58. Mem. Medieval Acad. Am., Internat. Courtly Lit. Soc. (v.p. Am. br. 1983—). Home: 6800 Park View Ln Eden Prairie MN 55344 Office: U Minn Dept French and Italian 200 Folwell Hall Minneapolis MN 55455

AKEMANN, DAVID ROY, lawyer; b. Elgin, Ill., Oct. 31, 1951; s. Theodore H. and Lois (Marr) A.; m. Vickie C. Skala, Aug. 5, 1978; children—Carrie, Julie. B.S., Brigham Young U., 1972; J.D., Lewis U., 1978. Bar: Ill. 1978, U.S. Dist. Ct. (no. dist.) Ill. 1978, U.S. Ct. Appeals (7th cir.) 1979, U.S. Supreme Ct. 1981. Clk. States Atty. Office, Kane County, Geneva, Ill., 1977-78; asst. states atty., 1978-79, chief civil div., 1979—; sole practice, Elgin, 1978—; ptnr. Gov. Services Enterprises, Elgin, 1985—; labor cons. Ill. States Attys. Appellate Service Commn. Author booklet in field. Precinct committeeman Elgin Twp. Republican Central Com., 1980, 82, 84. Recipient Am. Jurisprudence Constn. Law award Lawyers Coop. Pub. Co., 1978. Mem. ABA, Ill. Bar Assn., Kane County Bar Assn., Ill. Pub. Employers Labor Relations Assn. (prin.). Methodist. Office: 63 Douglas Ave #204 Elgin IL 60120

AKER, FRANK, political science consultant; b. South Bend, Ind., Feb. 17, 1946; s. Frank and Golda Mae (Hudson) A.; B.A., Ind. U., 1970, M.A., 1971; D.M.D., U. Louisville, 1975; M.A. in Hosp. Adminstrn., Webster Coll., 1981; grad. Marine Corps Staff and Command Coll., 1983. Commd. ensign U.S. Navy, 1975, advanced through grades to lt. comdr., 1979; resident Naval Regional Med. Center, Gt. Lakes, Ill., 1975-76; dental officer Naval Mobile Constrn. Bn. 40, Port Hueneme, Calif., 1976-79; chief facilities support Naval Dental Research Inst., Great Lakes, Ill., 1979-82; with USMC Command and Staff Coll., 1982-83; with Dept. Def., 1983-85. Served with USNR, 1985—. Fellow Acad. Gen. Dentistry; mem. ADA, Ky. Dental Assn., Louisville Dental Soc., Acad. Gen. Dentistry, Assn. Mil. Surgeons U.S., Am. Security Council, U.S. Naval Inst., Am. Def. Preparedness Assn., Council for Nat. Policy, Marine Corps Assn., Assn. U.S. Army, Air Force Assn., U.S. Armor Assn., Delta Sigma Delta, Beta Delta, Omicron Delta Kappa, Kappa Sigma. Ky. Col. Author: Hammer of God: 1973 Yom Kippur War, 1977; The Inflammatory Reaction, 1980; October 1973: The Arab-Israeli War, 1985; Breaking the Stranglehold: The Liberation of Grenada, 1984; Jan Zizka and the Hussite Wars, 1985. Inflammatory Reaction, 1980. Home: Bldg 1-H NDRI Great Lakes IL 60088

AKIN, CAVIT, biotechnologist, research scientist; b. Nigde, Turkey, Feb. 28, 1931; came to U.S., 1957; s. Ahmet and Fatma Kenan (Yuceeren) A.; m. Ingeborg Katharina Tange, Feb. 24, 1978; children—Deniz Leyla, Suzan Sema, Tulin Selma, Aylin Neva. M.S.Chem.E., U. Ankara, 1954; M.S. in Food Tech., U. Ill., 1959, Ph.D., 1961; postdoctoral U. Mass., 1962. Research scientist Sugar Research Inst., Turkey, 1956-57; sr. bioengr. Falstaff Research Lab., St. Louis, 1962-67; sr. research engr. Am. Oil Co., Whiting, Ind., 1967-70; sr. research engr. Standard Oil Co., Naperville, Ill., 1971-73, research assoc., supr. biotech. research, 1979—; research supr. Amoco Chems., Naperville, Ill., 1973-77; mgr. foods exploratory research Amoco Foods, Naperville, 1978-79. Served to lt. Signal Corps, Turkish Armed Forces, 1955-56. Fulbright scholar U. Ill., 1957-61. Mem. Am. Chem. Soc., Am. Soc. Microbiology, Soc. Indsl. Microbiologists, Inst. Food Technologists, AAAS. Moslem. Patentee in field; contbr. articles to profl. jours. Home: 1462 Inverrary Dr Naperville IL 60540 Office: Amoco Research Ctr Naperville IL 60566

AKIN, PHILLIP GLENN, coin laundry franchising executive; b. Waterloo, Iowa, Feb. 20, 1962; s. Philip D. and Claudia E. (Christensen) A.; m. Lisa Jean Peterson, May 30, 1981. B.S., Iowa State U., 1985. Owner, pres. Rand L. Automatic Service, Ames, Iowa, 1980—, Akin Enterprises, Ames, 1982—; pres. Duds 'n Suds Francorp., Ames, 1984—; officer Sara Corp., Ames, 1985—. Mem. Coin Laundry Assn., Internat. Franchise Assn. Republican. Lutheran. Avocations: swimming, boating, motorcycle riding. Office: Duds 'n Suds Francorp PO Box B Welch Station Ames IA 50010

AKINKUNLE, AMBROSE ADETUNJI, economics educator; b. Lagos, Nigeria, Aug. 15, 1938; children—Adedeji, Adebayo. B.A. in Pub. Adminstrn., U. London, Eng., 1962; B.S. in Econs., U. Wisc.-Eau Claire, 1967; M.A. in Economics, No. Ill. U., 1970. Account dept. London City Council, England, 1960-62; acct. G.M. Gest & Inspiration, Toronto, Ont. Can., 1967-69; assoc. prof. econs. City Colls. of Chgo., 1970—, chmn. dept. social scis. Olive-Harvey Coll., Chgo., 1982—; dir. Coll. and U. Credit Union, Chgo., 1980—; del. Cook County Coll. Tchrs. Union, Chgo., 1978—, Ill. Fedn. Tchrs., Chgo., 1978—. Named Hon. Profl. Mem., Helenic Profl. Assn., 1982. Mem. Acad. Polit. Sci., Acad. Polit. and Social Sci., Omicron Delta Epsilon. Democrat. Episcopalian. Avocations: soccer, bicycling, reading. Office: Olive-Harvey Coll 10001 S Woodlawn Ave Chicago IL 60628

AKINS, DAVID WAYNE, mortician; b. Somerville, N.J., Oct. 20, 1955; s. Willie Lee and Allean (Black) A. B.S. in Criminal Justice, Trenton State Coll., 1976; M.A., U. Detroit, 1979; mortuary sci. cert. Wayne State U., 1981. Community adv. Trenton (N.J.) State Coll., 1974-76; investigator Office of Public Defender, New Brunswick, N.J., 1977; residence hall dir. U. Detroit, 1977-78, residence area coordinator, 1978-79; mortician Barksdale Funeral Homes, Detroit, 1979—. Participant, Community Devel. Workshop, Detroit, 1978; trustee Hartford Meml. Bapt. Ch.; vice chmn. bd. dirs. Hartford Agape House. Recipient Minority Exec. Council Outstanding Service award, 1976; W.E.B. Dubois award, 1977. Mem. Nat. Funeral Dirs. and Morticians Assn., Mich. Select Morticians Assn., Mich. Funeral Dirs. Assn. Lodge: Masons. Address: 17170 Meyers #10 Detroit MI 48235

AKINS, WILLIAM JOHN, security and investigation agency executive; b. Rockford, Ill., Apr. 26, 1947; s. Donald Leroy and Marion Elizabeth (Drohan) A.; student Rock Valley Jr. Coll., Rockford, 1968; m. Lynn Ann Black, May 25, 1973; children—Erin Elizabeth, Kelly Jane. Cert. protection profl. Asst. mgr. Karl Schoening & Sons, Rockford, 1968-70; controller Colonial Builders, Rockford, 1970-71, Fairview Builders, Rockford, 1971; spl. projects cons. Pinkerton's, Inc., Oak Park, Ill., 1971-81; stockholder, dir. public relations and bus. devel. Argus Agy. Inc., Chgo., 1981—; chief exec. officer COMSEC Inc., Chgo.; pres. Midwest Indsl. Emergency Planning Group; dir. Unit Systems, Addison, Ill. Served with USAR, 1966-72. Cert. protection profl. Mem. ABA Assocs., Am. Soc. Indsl. Security (editor newsletter 1979-80, (chpt. chmn. 1984), Am. Fedn. Police, Ill. Security Conf. Republican. Roman Catholic. Home: 4053 Prairie Schiller Park IL 60176 Office: Argus Agy Inc 25 E Washington Suite 939 Chicago IL 60602 also COMSEC Inc 8600 W Bryn Mawr Suite 200 N Chicago IL 60631

AKTARY, SUSAN THYGERSON, counselor, educator, writer; b. Detroit, Dec. 1, 1946; d. William Robert and Dorothy Estelle (Tremaine) Thygerson; 1 child, David Alexander. B.A. with distinction, Oakland U., 1967; M.A., U. Mich., 1969; M.Ed., Wayne State U., 1975; M.A., Central Mich. U., 1983; Ph.D. candidate Wayne State U., 1984—. Cert. secondary tchr., Mich. Tchr. Rochester and West Bloomfield, pub. high schs., Mich., 1967-68; prof. Inst. Estudios Norteamericanos, Barcelona, Spain, 1968-70; counselor Mich. Employment Security Commn., Detroit, 1970-73; account exec. Bell Telephone, Detroit and Houston, 1974-78; dir., instr. Sweeney Hall, Central Mich. U., Mt. Pleasant, 1979-83; counselor, cons., journalist, Royal Oak, Mich., 1983—. Actor, dir. various theatrical prodns. Contbr. articles to profl. jours. Pres. Parents Without Ptnrs., Mt. Pleasant, 1983; fundraiser Detroit Area council Boy Scouts Am., Royal Oak, 1984. U.S. Dept. Edn. fellow, 1984. Mem. Am. Assn. Counseling and Devel., Sigma Delta Pi. Congregationalist. Avocations: Writing music; playing guitar and piano; swimming; singing, dancing, acting.

ALATZA, GEORGE E(LIAS), product development designer, artist, photographer; b. Anderson, Ind., Oct. 31, 1925; s. Elias P. and Mildred E. (Dilts) A.; m. Judith Anne Nooney, Apr. 29, 1950; children—Marianne, Michael, Jayne, Andrew. Student in Fine and Comml. Art, Ft. Wayne Art Sch., 1943-44, Cin. Acad., 1946-47, Am. Acad., 1947-49. Instr. New Orleans Acad. Art, 1949-51; designer New Orleans Pub. Service, 1951-53; art dir. Lahr Advt. Co., Indpls., 1953-56, Gen. Color Cards Co., Ft. Wayne, Ind., 1956-79; product designer Colwell Gen. Inc., Ft. Wayne, 1979—; dir. Color Mktg. Group, Washington, 1976—. Served with USAF, 1944-45. Mem. Ft. Wayne C. of C. Episcopalian. Avocations: calligraphy; woodworking; recording; crossword puzzles. Home: 1127 Oakdale Dr Fort Wayne IN 46807 Office: Colwell Gen Inc 200 6th St Fort Wayne IN 46807

ALBANESE, MICHELE OTTOLINO, optometrist; b. Oak Park, Ill., June 1, 1956; d. Michael Joseph and Ines Rosalie (Grolla) O.; m. Lee Alan Albanese, June 7, 1980. B.S., Loyola U.-Chgo., 1978; O.D., Ill. Coll. of Optometry, 1982. Optometric asst. to Dr. Edgar Fox, Des Plaines, Ill., 1981-82; eye clinic coordinator Infant Welfare Soc., Chgo., 1982-84; gen. practice optometry, Cicero, Ill., 1983-84; regional ops. mgr., Midwest dir. recruiting Dr. James Ellis & Assocs., Chgo., 1984—; cons. optometrist Eyeland Optical, Chgo., 1983-84; clin. instr. Ill. Coll. Optometry, Chgo., 1984. Mem. Am. Optometric Assn., Am. Pub. Health Assn. Roman Catholic. Home: 2555 N Montclare St Chicago IL 60634 Office: Eyexam 2000 9450 Skokie Blvd Skokie IL 60077

ALBANESE, VINCENT MICHAEL, chemist, marketing executive; b. Bridgeport, Conn., Dec. 22, 1948; s. Emilio John and Mary Antoinette (Sciole) A.; m. Marlene Louise Paluzzi, July 15, 1973; children—Erica Mary, Joseph William. B.S. in Chemistry, Manhattan Coll., 1970; M.S., Villanova U., 1973. Research chemist GAF Inc., Joliet, Ill., 1973-75; assoc. chemist Nalco Chem.

Co., Oak Brook, Ill., 1975-77, chemist, 1977-79, product specialist, 1979-80, product mgr., 1980-84, account mgr., 1984—. Patentee in field. Contbr. articles to profl. jours. Served wtih Air N.G., 1970-76. Mem. Air Pollution Control Assn. Roman Catholic. Clubs: Four Lakes, Meadows (Lisle). Avocations: running; tennis; golfing; audiophile, reading. Office: 6216 W 66th Pl Chicago IL 60638

ALBANO, GRACE ALMA, pharmacist; b. Cleve., Mar. 14, 1944; d. Theodore H. and Gertrude A. (Boehne) Hoelzel; m. Michael Albano, Aug. 13, 1966; children—Christine, Sarah. B.S., U. Mo.-Kansas City, 1967. Registered pharmacist, Mo., Kans. Intern, Kans. U. Med. Ctr., Kansas City, 1963-65; staff pharmacist Menorah Med. Ctr., Kansas City, Mo., 1967-70, Children's Mercy Hosp., Kansas City, Mo., 1974—. Bd. dirs. U. Mo.-Kansas City Pharmacy Found., 1982—; pres. Am. Field Service, Independence, Mo., 1978; mem. curriculum adv. com. Lee's Summit Sch. Dist., 1980—. Mem. Mo. Soc. Hosp. Pharmacists, Greater Kansas City Soc. Hosp. Pharmacists, U. Mo.-Kansas City Alumni Assn. (sec. to bd. dirs.), U. Mo.-Kansas City Pharmacy Sch. Alumni Assn. (acting pres. 1984), Kappa Epsilon (past pres.), Rho Chi, Chi Omega (1st v.p. 1970-72). Democrat. Lutheran. Club: Lakewood Garden (Lee's Summit). Avocations: tennis; roses; piano.

ALBAZZAZ, FAIQ JABER, physician, researcher, educator; b. Baghdad, Iraq, July 1, 1939; s. Jaber Mehdi and Fadela (Hassoun) AlBazzaz Ismail; m. Paulette Ann Dodds, Nov. 15, 1969; children—Alexandra Nesreen, Michael Basheer, Brian Senan. M.B., Ch.B., U. Baghdad, 1962. Diplomate Am. Bd. Internal Medicine, Am. Bd. Pulmonary Diseases. Intern, Teaching Hosp., Mosul, Iraq, 1965-66; resident in medicine U. Miss. Med. Ctr., 1966-68, Mpls. VA Hosp.-U. Minn. Hosp., 1968-69; pulmonary fellow Mass. Gen. Hosp.-Harvard Med. Sch., Boston, 1969-71; asst. prof. medicine U. Ill.-Chgo., 1971-78, assoc. prof., 1978—; dir. pulmonary lab. VA Westside Med. Ctr., Chgo., 1971—, chief respiratory and critical care sect., 1977—. Contbr. articles to profl. jours. Fellow ACP, Am. Coll. Chest Physicians; mem. Am. Physiol. Soc., Am. Thoracic Soc. Avocation: photography. Home: 6733 Plymouth St Downers Grove IL 60516 Office: VA 820 S Damen Ave Chicago IL 60612

ALBECK, STAN (CHARLES STANLEY ALBECK), professional basketball coach. Head coach Chgo. Bulls, Profl. Basketball Team, Chgo., 1985—. Office: Chicago Bulls 333 N Michigan Ave Suite 1325 Chicago IL 60601*

AL-BEIRUTI, MUHAMMAD SAID, pathologist; b. Damascus, Syria, 1947; came to U.S., 1973; M.D., Damascus U., 1973; m. Basima Dabbas, Nov. 18, 1975; children—Amru, Eiyass, Abdul Rahman. Intern, Marymount Hosp., Cleve., 1973-74; resident in pathology St. Alexis Hosp., Cleve., 1974-78; fellow in hematopathology Henry Ford Hosp., Detroit, 1978-79; pathologist Lapeer County Gen. Hosp., Lapeer, Mich., 1979—. Diplomate Am. Bd. Pathology. Fellow Am. Soc. Clin. Pathologists, Coll. Am. Pathologists; mem. Assn. Clin. Scientists, Mich. Soc. Pathologists. Office: 1375 N Main St Lapeer MI 48446

ALBERDING, CHARLES HOWARD, petroleum, hotel exec.; b. Cleyville, N.Y., Mar. 5, 1901; s. Charles and Doris (Roberts) A.; E.E., Cornell U., 1923; m. Bethine Wolverton, May 2, 1930; children—Beth Ann, Mary Katherine, Melissa Linda, Lab. asst., draftsman, operator Producers & Refiners Corp., Parco, Wyo., 1923-25; engr., cracking plant supt. Imperial Refineries, Ardmore Okla., also Eldorado, Ark., 1925-27; head fgn. operating dept. Universal Oil Products Co., London, Eng., Ploesti, Roumania, Rangoon, Burma, Venice, Italy, 1927-33, head operating, service depts., Chgo. hdqrs., 1933-42; pres., dir. Paradise Inn, Inc., Jokake Inn, Inc., Vinoy Park Hotel Co., Holiday Hotel Corp., Alsonett Hotels, Sabine Irrigation Co., Sabine Canal Co., Tides Hotel Corp., Harmony Oil Corp., London Square Corp., Petroleum Spltys., Lincoln Lodge Corp., Peabody Hotel Corp., Memphis, Hermitage Hotel Co., Nashville, Royal Palms Inn, Inc., Torrey Pines Inn, La Jolla, Calif., Charleston First Corp. Petroleum cons. WPB, 1942-43; dist. dir. petroleum refining Petroleum Adminstrn. for War, 1943-45. Mem. Scorpion. Republican. Conglist. Clubs: Valley (Phoenix); Kenilworth, Cornell (Chgo.); Sunset Country, Bath (St. Petersburg, Fla.); Tides Country (pres., dir.). Home: 99 Tudor Pl Kenilworth IL 60043 Office: 9 E Huron Chicago IL 60611

ALBERG, LINDA KAY SCHREMPP, college administrator; b. Mpls., July 31, 1951; d. Gerald E. and Dolores (Schindler) Schrempp; m. Thomas L. Alberg, Sept. 22, 1978. B.A., U. Minn., 1973; M.A. in Counseling, Mankato State U., 1977. Complex dir. Mankato State U., Minn., 1974-77; dir. student life Augsburg Coll., Mpls., 1977—; tchr. Roseville Community Edn., Minn., 1978-82; trainer St. John's Hosp., St. Paul; grants reader U.S. Dept. Edn., 1979, 84. Mem. Minn. Coll. Personnel Assn. (del.-at-large 1980-82, chpt. pres. 1983-84), Am. Assn. Counseling and Devel., Am. Coll. Personnel Assn. Roman Catholic. Avocations: tennis; skiing; racquetball; reading; travel. Home: 4715 Mackubin Shoreview MN 55126 Office: Augsburg College 731 21st Ave S Minneapolis MN 55454

ALBERG, WALTER SCOTT, consulting geologist; b. Topeka, May 24, 1956; s. Walter Clemens and Marilyn Gladies (Johnson) A.; m. Marilyn Ann Ronnau, Apr. 16, 1977; children—Seth Scott, Lucas Michael, Lindsay Ann. B.S. in Earth Sci., Emporia State U., 1979. Geologist, State of Kans., Lawrence, 1979-81; staff geologist Tex. Energies, Inc., Pratt, Kans., 1981-83, ops. geologists, 1983-84, cons., 1984—; cons. geologist in pvt. practice, Pratt, 1984—; cons. Tex. Energies, Inc., Pratt, D & D Prodns., Inc., Pratt, 1984—. Mem. Kans. Geol. Soc., Am. Assn. Petroleum Geologists, Assn. Engring. Geologists (assoc.), Soc. Petroleum Engrs. (jr.). Republican. Avocations: golf; hunting; swimming. Address: 205 Champa Pratt KS 67124

ALBERICI, GABRIEL J., construction company executive. With J.S. Alberici Constrn. Co., Inc., St. Louis, chmn. bd.; chmn. bd. Alberici Denver Inc., Gunther-Nash Mining Constrn. Co., St. Louis, J.D. Hudson Constrn. Co., Greenville, N.C., Gen. Installation, Inc., St. Louis, Chase Electric Co., St. Louis. Past pres. Mo. Safety Council; bd. dirs. St. Louis Regional Indsl. Devel. Corp.; mem. St. Louis Mayor's Apprenticeship adv. com.; commr. St. Louis Airport Commn. Recipient 1967 City of Hope award, St Paul Man of the Year, 1982, 10 year Chmn. award Constrn. Advancement Found., St. Louis Area Constrn. Industry 1974 Man of the Year award, Achievement award, Engrs. Club of St. Louis, others. Mem. Assoc. Gen. Contractors Am. (nat. bd. dirs.), Cons. Constructors Council Am., Assoc. Gen. Contractors of St. Louis (past pres., trustee Teamster Pensio and Welfare fund.). Clubs: St. Louis Engrs., Mo. Athletic, Glen Echo Country (pres, dir.). Lodge: Knights of Holy Sepulcher. Address: J S Alberici Constrn Co Inc 2150 Kienlen Ave Saint Louis MO 63121

ALBERS, LOIS HELEN, nurse; b. Peotone, Ill., Oct. 30, 1926; d. Carl John and Florence Magdalene (Pries) Schneeweis; R.N., St. Luke's Hosp., 1948; B.S., St. Francis Coll., 1978; m. John Albers, Feb. 14, 1948; children—Steven John, Linda Susan. With Westlake Community Hosp., Melrose Park, Ill., 1948—, dir. nursing services, 1968-76, adminstrv. coordinator for health programming services, 1976—. Mem. Presbyn.-St. Luke's Alumni Assn. Republican. Lutheran. Home: 465 Fairview Ave Elmhurst IL 60126 Office: 1225 Superior St Melrose Park IL 60160

ALBERS, MICHAEL WILLIAM, manufacturing company executive, pilot; b. Celina, Ohio, June 24, 1947; s. Cletus Joseph and Irene Julian (Wenning) A.; m. Eileen Josephine Frilling, Dec. 28, 1968; children—Michelle, Melissa, Michael. Student Toledo U., 1970-71, Parson's Coll., 1965-66. Draftsman Richmond Mfg. Co., Ashland, Ohio, 1971-73, service mgr., 1973-78, sales mgr., 1978—, co. chief pilot, 1971—; designated pilot examiner FAA, Cleve., 1980—. Served with U.S. Army, 1966-70. Decorated D.F.C., Air medal with 34 clusters, Army Commendation medal, Vietnamese Cross of Gallantry. Mem. Nat. Utility Contractors Assn., So. Gas Assn., Am. Legion. Republican. Roman Catholic. Club: Ashland Country. Lodge: Elks. Avocation: fishing. Home: 1475 County Rd 1575 Rural Route 6 Ashland OH 44805 Office: Richmond Mfg Co US 42 N PO Box 188 Ashland OH 44805

ALBERS, WALTER ANTHONY, JR., automobile company official; b. McKeesport, Pa., July 19, 1930; s. Walter Anthony and Mary D. (Roberts) A.; m. Nancy Ann Rock, Aug. 2, 1952 (dec. June 1966); m. Betty Grace McKinley, June 24, 1967; children—Patricia, Jodie, Kevin, Gaylen, Kurt. B.S., Wayne State U., 1952, M.S., 1954, Ph.D., 1960. Mem. tech. staff Bell Labs., Allentown, Pa., 1954-57, Bendix Corp., Southfield, Mich., 1957-62; research group leader Gen. Motors Research Labs., Warren, Mich., 1962-72, head societal analysis, 1973—; research assoc. Wayne State U., 1958-59; instr. Lawrence Inst. Tech., Southfield, 1960-61. Editor: Physics of Opto-Electronics, 1970; Societal Risk Assessment, 1980. Patentee semicondr. treatments. Contbr. articles to profl. jours. Bd. dirs. Men's Dist. Golf Assn. Detroit, 1982—; bd. govs. Golf Assn. Mich., 1984—. Mem. Am. Phys. Soc., Soc. Risk Assessment, Am. Mgmt. Assns., AAAS, Sigma Xi. Club: Farmington Hills Country (pres. 1978-79) (Mich.). Avocations: golf; tennis. Home: 2068 S Hammond Lake Dr West Bloomfield MI 48033 Office: Gen Motors Research Labs Warren MI 48090

ALBERT, JANICE MARY, broadcasting company executive; b. Quincy, Ill., Dec. 6, 1952; d. Robert A. and Juletta W. (Peters) Mast. B.S., Quincy Coll., 1975; A.A., John Wood Community Coll., 1979; M.B.A., Western Ill. U., 1981. Data base adminstr. Harris Corp., 1980-82, supr., 1982-84, mgr. fin., mktg. systems Harris Broadcast Group, Quincy, 1984—; pres. Harris Internal Users Group, 1981-82. Mem. Assn. Systems Mgmt., Cullinet Midwest User Group. Office: Harris Broadcast Group PO Box 4290 Quincy IL 62305

ALBERT, JANYCE LOUISE, banker; b. Toledo, July 27, 1932; d. Howard C. and Glenola Mae (Masters) Blessing; m. John R. Albert, Aug. 7, 1954; children—John R., James H. Student Ohio Wesleyan U., 1949-51; B.A., Mich. State U., 1953; M.S., Iowa State U., 1980. Asst. personnel mgr./tng. supr. Sears, Roebuck & Co., Toledo, 1953-56; tchr. adult edn. Tenafly Pub. Schs. (N.J.), 1966-70; personnel officer, tng. officer, tng. and edn. mgr. Iowa Dept. Transp., Ames, 1974-77; coll. recruiting coordinator Rockwell Internat., Cedar Rapids, Iowa, 1977-79, engring. adminstrn. mgr., 1979-80; employee relations and job evaluation analyst Phillips Petroleum Co., Bartlesville, Okla., 1980-81; v.p., dir. personnel Republic Bancorp, Tulsa, 1981-83; v.p. and dir. human resources First Nat. Bank, Rockford, Ill., 1983—. Bd. dirs. United Way of Ames, 1976-77; publicity chmn. Tenafly 300th Ann. Celebration, 1969; bd. deacons Presbyterian Ch., Ames, 1972-75; mem. adv. council Rockford YWCA, bd. dirs., 1986; mem. bravo council Rockford Dance Co. Pres.'s scholar, 1951-53; named Outstanding Student scholar, 1951-53. Mem. Rockford Network (pres. 1986), Rockford C. of C., Rockford Personnel Assn., Am. Soc. Personnel Adminstrn., Employee Benefits Assn. No. Ill., Rockford Symphony Guild, Rockford Council Affordable Health, P.E.O., Sigma Epsilon, Alpha Gamma Delta, Phi Kappa Phi. Home: 5587 Thunderidge Dr Rockford IL 61107 Office: 401 E State St Rockford IL 61101

ALBERT, WILLIAM CHESTER, ophthalmologist; b. Boston, June 22, 1943; s. Harry and Dorothy (Silverman) A.; m. Toby Renee Rutman, June 27, 1965; children—Evan, Gabrielle Alan. B.A., Columbia U., 1965; M.D., Case Western Res. U., 1968. Diplomate Am. Bd. Ophthalmology. Intern Michael Reese Hosp., Chgo., 1969-70; resident in ophthalmology Manhattan Eye, Ear and Throat Hosp., N.Y.C., 1972-75; attending ophthalmologist William Beaumont Hosp., Royal Oak, Mich., 1976—, Sinai Hosp. of Detroit, 1976—, Mt. Carmel Mercy Hosp., Detroit, 1977—, Harper-Grace Hosp., Detroit, 1977—; clin. instr. Harvard U. Sch. Medicine, Boston, 1975-76; clin. asst. prof. ophthalmology Kresge Eye Inst., Wayne State U. Sch. Medicine, Detroit, 1977—; clin. assoc. prof. ophthalmology Mich. State U. Coll. Human Medicine, Lansing, 1978—. Served as lt. comdr. USPHS, 1970-72. Research fellow NIH, 1970-72, Bausch and Lomb fellow, 1975, Cornea and External Desease fellow Harvard U., 1975-76, Heed Found. fellow, 1976. Fellow Am. Acad. Ophthalmology, ACS; mem. Mich. Ophthal. Soc. (chm. eye bank com. 1977—), AMA, Oakland County Med. Soc., Castroviejo Soc., Midwest Soc. Corneal Surgeons, Mich. State Med. Soc., Am. Soc. Contemporary Ophthalmology, Am. Intra-ocular Implant Soc., Assn. Research in Vision and Ophthalmology, Soc. Heed Fellows. Avocations: sailing; opera; symphony; literature. Home: 28145 Tavistock Trail Southfield MI 48034 Office: 29275 Northwestern Hwy # 100 Southfield MI 48034

ALBERTI, CHARLES EDWARD, hospital planning and fund raising executive; b. Chgo., July 14, 1945; s. Joseph J. and Gwen G. (Doering) A.; m. Valerie J. Vaughan, Aug. 14, 1970; children—Leo Charlton, Christina Nicole. B.F.A., Sch. Art Inst. Chgo., 1969; M.Ed., Loyola U., Chgo., 1971, Ph.D., 1975. Cert. tchr., adminstr., Ill. Lectr., Loyola U., Chgo.; tchr., asst. prin. Oak Forest (Ill.) High Sch., 1969-74; asst. prof. Ill. Benedictine Coll., 1975-76; assoc. prof., chmn. grad. and undergrad. edn. Lewis U., Lockport, Ill., 1976-80; adj. asst. prof. bus. Webster U., McConnell AFB, 1981; dir. planning and devel. Coordinated Services Sisters of St. Joseph Health Care Orgn., Wichita, Kans., 1981-84; dir. devel. Alexian Bros. Med. Ctr., Elk Grove Village, Ill., 1984—. Arthur J. Schmitt scholar Loyola U., 1974-75. Mem. Soc. for Hosp. Planning, Nat. Assn. Hosp. Devel., Nat. Soc. Fund Raising Execs. (pres. 1982-84; cert. fund raising executive), Phi Delta Kappa (past pres.), Roman Catholic. Author: Money Makers: A Systematic Approach to Special Events Fund Raising, 1982; contbr. articles to profl. jours. Home: 613 N Walnut Schaumburg IL 60194 Office: 800 W Biesterfield Elk Grove Village IL 60007

ALBERTS, JOHN HARRY, JR., insurance broker; b. Chgo., Apr. 21, 1950; s. John H. and Monette T. A.; B.A., Knox Coll., 1972; m. Judith C. Zabinski, Sept. 10, 1972; 1 dau., Kathryn Ruth. With Wm. H. Thompson & Co., Chgo., 1972—, sec., treas., 1976—, sr. v.p., 1983—; pres. Pullman Agy., Inc., 1982—. Vice pres. Crestwood (Ill.) Pub. Library Dist., 1976-78. C.P.C.U. Mem. Chgo. Bd. Underwriters (regional v.p. 1979-82, exec. v.p. 1982-83, pres. 1983-84, chmn. task force on agts. assistance 1979-80, chmn. steering com. 1979-80, presdl. citation 1982-83), Ind. Ins. Agents Ill. (regional v.p. 1979-82; Presdl. citation 1982), Ind. Ins Agents Am., ACLU, Am. Soc. C.P.C.U.s. Clubs: Union League, LaSalle Street (bd. govs. 1982-84) (Chgo.). Office: 11422 S Western Ave Chicago IL 60643

ALBERTS, MARION EDWARD, physician; b. Hastings, Nebr., Mar. 14, 1923; s. Eddie and Mary Margaret (Hilbers) A.; B.A., U. Neb., 1944, M.D., 1948; m. Jeannette McDaniel, Dec. 25, 1944; children—Kathryn, Brian, Deborah, Timothy. Intern, Iowa Methodist Hosp., Des Moines, 1948-49; resident in pediatrics Raymond Blank Hosp. Children, Des Moines, 1949-50, 52-53; practice medicine specializing in pediatrics, Des Moines, 1953—; chief pediatrics Mercy Hosp., 1958-78; mem. med. staff Iowa Luth. Hosp., Iowa Meth. Hosp., Broadlawns Polk County Hosp.; instr. clin. pediatrics Coll. Osteo. Medicine and Surgery, 1970-82. Pres. Polk County Tb and Respiratory Diseases Assn., 1965, 66, 70. Served to comdr. USNR, 1943-45, 50-52. Recipient Whitaker Interstate Teaching award Interstate Postgrad. Med. Assn., 1980; Service award Sisters of Mercy, 1978. Licenciate, Am. Bd. Pediatrics. Fellow Am. Acad. Pediatrics, Internat. Coll. Pediatrics; mem. AMA (recognition awards 1969-85), Iowa Med. Soc. (sci. editor jour.). Republican. Presbyterian (elder). Club: Masons. Sci. editor Iowa Medicine; 1971—. Contbr. articles to profl. jours. Home: 5104 Ashworth Rd West Des Moines IA 50265 Office: 1071 5th Ave Des Moines IA 50314

ALBIN, JOHN SANFORD, farmer; b. Newman, Ill., Oct. 28, 1928; s. Leonard Bruce and Grace Nettie (Herrington) A.; B.S. with honors, U. Ill., 1950; m. Marjorie Ann Martin, Sept. 10, 1949; children—Perry S., David A. Farmer, Newman, 1951—; operator Albin Farm; pres. Albi Pork Farm, Inc., Plants Pals Inc.; chmn. bd. Longview State Bank (Ill.). Pres., Newman Community Unit 303 Sch. Bd., 1958-66; trustee Parkland Coll., Champaign, Ill., 1968-85, v.p., 1977-85. Recipient Ill. 4H Alumni award, 1968, Master Farmer award Prairie Farmer mag., 1970, award of merit U. Ill. Coll. Agr. Alumni Assn., 1977. Mem. Am. Shropshire Registry Assn. (pres. 1962-65), Ill. Farm Bus. Farm Mgrs. Assn. (pres. 1968-83), E. Central Farm Bus. Farm Mgrs. Assn. (pres. 1965-72), Douglas County Farm Bur. (dir. 1968-85), Top Farmers Assn. Am., Farm House, Alpha Zeta. Republican. Clubs: Villa Grove Country, Masons. Address: PO Box 377 Newman IL 61942

ALBINGER, PAUL ERNEST, JR., banker, fire chief: b. Port Washington, Wis., Nov. 7, 1952; s. Paul Ernest and Helen Rose (Link) A.; m. Sandra Lee Pearl Jacoby, July 15, 1978; children—Marcia Lee, Carrie Ann. Fireman Saukville Fire Dept., Wis., 1970-79; chief, 1979—; gen. Laborer Sprague Electric Co., Grafton, Wis., 1971; material handler Freeman Chem. Corp., Saukville, 1971-74; asst. v.p. 1st Nat. Bank, Saukville, 1974—. Contbr. articles to profl. mags. Pres. Friends of Saukville Fire Dept., Wis., 1983-84; bd. dirs. United Way Port Washington- Saukville, Wis., 1975-78. Named Wis. State Firefighter of Yr., 1979; Flag Day Post Man of Yr., 1980, 81. Mem. Wis. State Fire Chiefs Assn. (chmn. 1979-83), Wis. State Fireman's Assn., Ozaukee County Assn. Fire Depts. (sec., treas. 1975-82, v.p. 1982-84, pres. 1984—), Vocat./Tech. Adult Edn. (fire service instr. 1981—), Wis. Soc. Fire Service Instrs., Ozaukee County Bankers Assn., Am. Inst. Banking, Ozaukee Assn. Fire Dept., Saukville C. of C. (bd. dirs. 1975-84, treas. 1983-84), Badger Fireman's Assn. Roman Catholic. Club: Big Bros. and Sisters (Ozaukee County, Wis.) (dir. 1976-78). Lodge: Moose. Avocation: basketball; automobiles; reading. Home: 114 Niesen Dr Saukville WI 53080 Office: Saukville Fire Dept 100 S Main St Saukville WI 53080

ALBRECHT, EDWARD DANIEL, metals manufacturing company executive; b. Kewanee, Ill., Feb. 11, 1937; s. Edward Albert and Mary Jane (Horner) A.; B.S. in Metall. Engring., U. Ariz., 1959, M.S., 1961, Ph.D., 1964, Metal. Engr. (hon.), 1973; m. Mignon Y. Buehler, Jan. 1, 1973; children—Renata E., Deborah J., Paul R. Research metallurgist, U. Calif. Los Alamos Lab., 1959-61; sr. physicist, project mgr. U. Calif. Lawrence Radiation Lab., Livermore, 1964-71; pres. Metall. Innovations Inc., Pleasanton, Calif., 1969-71; gen. mgr. Buehler Ltd. & Adolph I. Buehler, Inc., Lake Bluff, Ill., 1972, v.p., gen. mgr., 1973-76, chmn., pres., 1976, also dir.; pres. bd. dirs. Buehler-Met AG Basel, Switzerland, 1983—; pres. Mowlem Tech. Inc., Lake Bluff, 1984—; dir. Mowlem Tech. Ltd., London, 1984—; chmn. bd. Soiltest, Inc., Evanston, Ill., 1984—, CPN Corp., Pacheco, Calif., 1984—; dir. Tech Met Canada Ltd., Toronto, Ont., Banner Sci. Ltd., Coventry, Eng. Bd. dirs. Danville (Calif.) Homeowners Inc., treas., 1966-68; trustee Lake Forest Acad. - Ferry Hall Prep Sch., 1977-81; mem. nat. adv. bd. Heard Mus. Anthropology, Phoenix, 1980—; trustee Millicent Rogers Mus., Taos, N.Mex., 1982—, chmn. devel. com., 1983—. NDEA fellow, 1959-62. Fellow Am. Soc. Metals (chmn. Tucson 1961), Royal Micros. Soc. Eng.; mem. Internat. Metallographic Soc. (pres. 1973-75, dir. 1975-81 chmn. gen. tech. meeting San Francisco 1969, Chgo. 1972, Brighton, Eng., 1980), Deutsche Gesellschaft für Metallkunde, Sigma Gamm Epsilon, Delta Upsilon. Clubs: Chicago, Onwentsia, Desert Highlands. Contbr. articles to profl. jours. Patentee in field. Office: PO Box 1 Lake Bluff IL 60044

ALBRECHT, FRANK WAYNE, data processor; b. Bloomington, Ill., May 30, 1936; s. Frank Peter and Ellen May (Middlekauff) A.; A.A. in Computer Sci., Lincoln Land Community Coll., Springfield, Ill., 1972; m. Patsy Ann Florence, Jan. 13, 1958; children—Michelle Rae, Traci Lynn. Computer operator Franklin Life Ins. Co., Springfield, 1957-61; with State of Ill., 1961—, mgr. data preparation ops. Dept. Public Aid, 1979-83, mgr. prodn. ops., 1983—; adv. bd. Capitol Area Vocat. Tng. Center, Springfield. Mem. Sangamon County Sheriff's Patrol, 1968-80, Springfield/Sangamon County CD Group, 1968-80. Served with USN, 1954-57; Korea. Cert. in data mgmt., 1983. Mem. Data Entry Mgmt. Assn., Optical Character Reader Users Assn., Ill. Welfare Assn. Roman Catholic. Club: Moose. Office: 100 S Grand Ave E Springfield IL 62704

ALBRECHT, MICHAEL, JR., mgmt. cons.; b. Mediasch, Rumania, Mar. 30, 1940; s. Michael and Elsa (Heihn) A.; came to U.S., 1956, naturalized, 1962; B.S., Ill. State U., 1963; M.B.A., Mich. State U., 1978; m. Kathleen Kay Koerner, Sept. 2, 1961; children—Steven Michael, David Phillip. Asst., Ill. State U., 1963-64; tchr. Aurora (Ill.) Public Schs., 1964-66; quality control engr. Chgo. Aerial Industries, Barrington, Ill., 1966-67; mktg. rep. IBM, Chgo., 1967-74, instr. Customer Exec. Edn. Center, Poughkeepsie, N.Y., 1974-75; asst. to vice chmn. Am. Natural Resources, Detroit, 1975-77; dir. info. systems Mich. Consol. Gas Co., Detroit, 1977-79, exec. dir. corp. info. services, 1978-80; mgmt. cons. M. Albrecht, Jr. & Assos., Inc., Grosse Pointe, Mich., 1980—; cons. corp. planning. Mem. Am. Gas Assn., Advanced Mgmt. Program Club, AAU, Pi Gamma Mu. Office: 12 Lakeside Ct Grosse Pointe MI 48230

ALBRECHT, ROBERT JOHN, banker; b. Sacramento, Dec. 30, 1945; s. John Jacob and Virginnia Ann (Klein) A.; m. Cynthia Patricia Koper, June 14, 1969; children—Sarah Marie, Samuel John. Student Valley City State Coll. (N.D.), 1964-65; student U. N.D., 1965-66, B.S. in Bus. Adminstrn., 1972; post-grad. Stonier Sch. Banking, Rutgers U., 1982-84. Personal banker Red River Nat. Bank, Grand Forks, N.D., 1972-76; v.p. sales Chex Systems, Bloomington, Minn., 1976-77; mng. officer Iowa Des Moines Bank, 1977-79; corp. credit mgr. Quarry Supply Inc., Des Moines, 1979-80; pres., chief exec. officer Custer County Bank, Custer, S.D., 1980—. Bd. dirs. Custer Hosp. Assn., 1981-82. Served with USMC, 1966-69. Mem. Buster C. of C. (Businessman of Yr. 1983, Bus. of Yr. 1983), Amvets (fin. officer 1979-80), Marine League (comdt. Des Moines 1979-80). Republican. Roman Catholic. Lodges: KC, Rotary. Club: Custer Golf Assn. Office: Custer County Bank 648 Mount Rushmore Rd Custer SD 57730

ALBRIGHT, DONALD HENRY, pharmacist; b. Omaha, July 8, 1930; s. Henry Howard and Clare Marie (Holub) A.; m. Maxine Joyce Thedens, Jan. 25, 1953; children—Linda, Cheryl, Paul. B.S. in Pharmacy, Creighton U., 1953. Registered pharmacist. Pharmacist Sprague Pharmacy, Omaha, 1955-62, prin., pharmacist, 1962—; mem. Bur. Examining Bds. Pharmacy, State of Nebr., 1972—. Chmn. Benson Bus. Improvement Dist., Omaha, 1978—. Served to 1st lt. U.S. Army, 1953-55. Recipient Hon. Pharmacy Lic. Ark. Bd. Pharmacy, 1984; Preceptor of Yr. award U. Neb., 1976; Alumni Merit award Creighton U., 1981; named to Alumni Hall of Fame Benson High Sch., 1980. Mem. Nat. Assn. Bds. Pharmacy (adv. com. on exams.), Omaha Pharmacists Assn. (Pharmacist of Yr.), Nebr. Pharmacists Assn. (pres. 1971-72), Nat. Assn. Retail Druggists. Republican. Lutheran. Office: Sprague's Benson Pharmacy 6103 Maple St Omaha NE 68104

ALBRIGHT, HAROLD KIRBY, lawyer; b. Detroit, July 18, 1955; s. Harold Charles and Evelyn Anne (Harris) A.; m. Gina Kay Maida, Aug. 20, 1977 (div. Nov. 1983). B.A., Mich. State U., 1977; J.D. cum laude, Thomas M. Cooley Law Sch., 1980. Bar: Mich. 1981, U.S. Dist. Ct. (we. dist.) Mich. 1981. Law clk. Mich. Dist. Ct., Howell, Mich., 1978-80; assoc. Hubbard, Fox, Thomas, White & Bengtson, P.C., Lansing, Mich., 1980—; vis. judge Thomas M. Cooley Law Sch. trial practice classes, 1983—. Mem. ABA, Assn. Trial Lawyers Am., Ingham County Bar Assn. (exec. com. young lawyers sect. 1983-84). Office: Hubbard Fox Thomas White & Bengtson PC 500 Mich Nat Tower Lansing MI 48933

ALBRIGHT, JUSTIN W., lawyer; b. Lisbon, Iowa, Oct. 14, 1908; B.S.C., U. Iowa, 1931, J.D., 1933; m. Mildred Carlton, 1935; 1 son, Carlton J. Admitted to Iowa bar, 1933; now mem. firm Simmons, Perrine, Albright & Ellwood, Cedar Rapids. Served with AUS, World War II. Mem. Am., Iowa, Linn County bar assns., Cedar Rapids C. of C., Phi Delta Phi. Mason (Shriner), Rotarian. Clubs: Cedar Rapids Country, Pickwick (Cedar Rapids). Editor Iowa Law Rev., 1932-33. Office: 12th Floor Mchts Nat Bank Bldg Cedar Rapids IA 52401

ALBRIGHT, TOWNSEND SHAUL, investment banker; b. Anderson, Ind., May 1, 1942; s. Townsend S. and Maxine Aree (Zimmerman) A.; m. Eileen Therese Argent, Aug. 30, 1968; children—Megan Eileen, Alexandra Michele. B.A., Wabash Coll., 1964; M.B.A., U. Mich., 1966. With Mead Corp., Cin. and Chgo., 1966-69; mcpl. bond underwriter No. Trust Co., Chgo., 1969-71; v.p. Channer Newman Securities Co., Chgo., 1971-80; v.p., treas., dir., Croake Roberts, Inc., Chgo., 1980—. Bd. dirs., mem. adv. council Urban Gateways, Chgo., 1976—; v.p., bd. dirs. Wilmette Jaycees, 1979-80. Served with USAR, 1966-72. Mem. Mcpl. Bond Club Chgo., Chgo. Assn. Wabash Men, U. Mich. Alumni Assn. Presbyterian. Clubs: Economic (Chgo.); Wilmette Sailing Assn. (dir.-treas. 1980-81), Michigan Shores (Wilmette, Ill.). Home: 2019 Beechwood Ave Wilmette IL 60091 Office: Croake Roberts Inc 135 S LaSalle St Chicago IL 60603

ALBY, JAMES FRANCIS PAUL, priest, educator; b. Milw., July 16, 1936; s. Francis Joseph and Sarah Sophie (Hansen) A.; B.A., Gallaudet Coll., 1963, M.S. in Edn., 1964; M.Div., Va. Theol. Sem., 1971; m. Jan Lorraine Peplinski, Aug. 2, 1980; 1 child. Ordained priest Episcopal Ch., 1971; priest to the deaf St. James Mission of the Deaf, Milw., 1971-76; priest assoc. St. Peter's Ch., West Allis, Wis., 1972-83; asst. to rector Ministry of the Deaf, St. James Parish, Milw., 1983—; tchr. high sch. hearing impaired Milw. Pub. Schs., 1972—; priest assoc. Holy House of Our Lady of Walsingham, Norfolk, Eng., 1984—; instr. interpreting for deaf U. Wis., Milw., 1975-77; sr. high sch. boys dorm supr.-counselor St. John's Sch. for the Deaf, St. Francis, Wis., 1971-72; tchr. lang. of signs Milw. Area Tech. Coll., 1974-75; mem. adv. com. continuing edn. deaf adults, Milw., 1976-84, mem. adv. com. on edn. hearing impaired Milw. Pub. Schs., 1977—; mem. sect. 504 com. Southeastern Wis. Disabilities Coalition, 1979-81, mem. adult edn. adv. com. Milw. Hearing Soc., 1976-83. Contbr. articles to profl. jours. Mem. Nashotah House Sem. Alumni Assn. (assoc.), Gallaudet Coll. Alumni Assn., Alpha Sigma Pi. Lodges: Lions (charter pres.), Lioness (liaison 1980-84). Office: St James Episcopal Ch 833 W Wisconsin Ave Milwaukee WI 53233

ALDAG, JEROME MARVIN, mechanical engineer, executive; b. Sheboygan, Wis., Nov. 19, 1929; s. Marvin Otto and Daisy B. (Jackson) A.; m. Sally Lou Lahnke, May 4, 1956 (dec. 1969); children—David, Heidi, Timothy, Jessica; m. Patricia Jean Schmidt, July 11, 1970. Student Wis. Engring. Sch., 1950-52. Registered profl. engr., Wis. Engr., Aldag Sheet Metal Works Inc., Sheboygan, 1954-60, engr. in charge, 1960-68, pres., 1968—; pres. Aldag Engring. Cons.,

Sheboygan, 1974—. Served with USNR, 1949-56. Mem. ASHRAE, Nat. Soc. Profl. Engrs., Air Pollution Bd. Republican. Lutheran. Club: Sheboygan Country, Yacht. Lodges: Elks, Kiwanis. Avocations: skiing, sailing, hunting. Home: 645 Greentree Rd Kohler WI 53044 Office: Aldag Sheet Metal Works Inc 3509 S Business Dr Sheboygan WI 53081

ALDEN, DALE, psychologist; b. McLeansboro, Ill., Apr. 25, 1936; s. William and Dora J. (Field) A. m. Elaine (Fiorentino), Sept. 1, 1974; children—John Wesley, James Dale. B.S., So. Ill. U., 1961, M.S., 1965; Ph.D., U. Pitts., 1970. Registered psychologist, Ill. Lectr., psychologist U. Pitts., 1965-69; vis. prof. U. Iowa, Iowa City, 1971; sr. research scientist U. Ark., Fayetteville, 1971-73; assoc. prof. So. Ill. U., Carbondale, 1976-78; pvt. practice psychology Alden Assocs., Anna, Ill., 1977—. Mem. Am. Psychol. Assn., Soc. Behavioral Medicine. Episcopalian. Clubs: Rotary, VFW, Scottish Rite, Shriner. Office: Alden Assocs 515 E Vienna St PO Box 666 Anna IL 62906

ALDEN, DON EDWARD, food company executive; b. Long Beach, Calif., Oct. 29, 1937; s. John James and Nathell (Larson) A.; B.S., Okla. State U., 1962; cert., honor grad. Inst. for Mgmt., Ill. Benedictine Coll., 1971; m. Sandra Jean Horn, July 6, 1963; children—Laura Marie, John Vincent. With Swift & Co., Oak Brook, Ill., 1963—, ind. investigator in research, 1963-71, div. head vegetable protein research, 1971-76, research mgr. new product devel., 1978-80, grocery product devel., 1980-84; dir. research Alberto-Culver, 1984—. Served with M.C., U.S. Army, 1960-66. Mem. Inst. for Mgmt. (v.p. bd. dirs. 1979-81, pres. 1982), Am. Assn. Cereal Chemists, Internat. Food Technologists, Peanut Butter Mfrs. Assn. Democrat. Roman Catholic. Developer texturized vegetable protein, 1971; patentee flavor-free undenatured legume seeds, 1976, vegetable oil extraction, 1980, process for prodn. of flavored protein foods, 1971. Home: 3143 Everglade St Woodridge IL 60517 Office: 2525 Armitage Ave Melrose Park IL 60160

ALDEN, JOHN ROYAL, electrical engineer; b. Ft. Wayne, Ind., Sept. 24, 1942; s. John W. and Marion Alice (Straub) A.; m. Leanne Barbara Emmons, June 22, 1968; children—John Whiting, Ann Elise. B.S.E.E., U. Calif.-Davis, 1964; M.B.A., Pa. U., 1972. Engr. processing Procter & Gamble Paper Products, Tunkhannock, Pa., 1972-74, chem. engr., 1975-77, research and devel. engr., Cin., 1977-79, sect. leader, 1980—. Pres. Unitarian Universalist Ch., Cin., 1981. Served to lt. USNR, 1964-70. Home: 789 Carini Ln Cincinnati OH 45218 Office: Procter & Gamble 6100 Center Hill Rd Cincinnati OH 45224

ALDER, ALTHEA ALICE, marketing service agency executive; b. Wilmore, Kans., Jan. 4, 1933; d. Lloyd Lewis and Margaret Mae (Baldwin) A.; student Ft. Hays State U., 1952-55. Owner, operator 2 beauty shops, 1961-67; quality control mgr., supr. women Solo Cup Co., 1967-70; v.p. purchasing, prodn. and premiums William A. Robinson, Inc., Northbrook, Ill., 1970-79; pres. A-three Services Agy., Ltd., Lake Forest, Ill., 1979—, Lake Forest Tng. Salon, Ltd., 1979-80. Served with W.A.C., AUS, 1951-53, 55-61; Korea. Decorated Army Commendation medal. Mem. Am. Legion. Clubs: Eastern Star, The Exec. Female. Home: 24400 N Hwy 45 Mundelein IL 60060 Office: 249 W Holbrook Dr Wheeling IL 60090

ALDERSON, THOMAS LEE, osteopathic physician; b. Chgo., Feb. 19, 1952; s. Leland Burdette and Fermy Adrianne (Skoniecki) A.; m. Joyce Elaine Peterson, Apr. 1, 1978; 1 dau., Courtney Lynn. B.S., Western Ill. U., 1973; D.O., Chgo. Coll. Osteo. Medicine, 1977. Intern, Chgo. Osteo. Med. Ctr., 1977-78; resident in ob-gyn, 1978-82; research fellow in reproductive endocrinology Michael Reese Hosp. and Med. Ctr., Chgo., 1982-84; asst. prof. ob-gyn Chgo. Osteo. Med. Ctr., 1982—. Mem. Am. Osteo. Assn., Ill. Assn. Osteo. Physicians and Surgeons, Am. Coll. Osteo. Obstetricians and Gynecologists, Am. Fertility Soc., Am. Soc. Colposcopy and Cervical Pathology. Office: Michael Reese Hosp and Med Ctr 2900 S Ellis St Chicago IL 60616

ALDIS, HENRY, obstetrician, gynecologist; b. Basim, Berar, India, Nov. 3, 1913; s. Steadman and Ethel Rebecca (Fry) A. (parents Am. citizens); A.B., U. Kans., 1938, M.D., 1941; m. Margaret Elizabeth Warner, June 24, 1941; children—John Warner, Henry Weeks, William Leggett, David Fry. Intern, City Hosp., Winston-Salem, N.C., 1941-42; resident, Gorgas Hosp., C.Z., 1942-43, asst. resident in surgery U. Kans., 1943-44, asst. resident in ob-gyn., Balt. City Hosps., 1954-56, chief resident in ob-gyn., 1956-57; asso. Walter Sheeley, M.D., Shepherdstown, W.Va., 1946-52; gen. practice medicine, Ft. Scott, Kans., 1952-54; practice medicine specializing in ob-gyn., Ft. Scott, 1957—; mem. staff Newman-Young Clinic, Mercy Hosp., Ft. Scott, Bourbon County. Served with AUS, 1944-46; ETO; served to col. M.C. Kans. N.G., 1956-73. Diplomate Am. Bd. Ob-Gyn (also recert.). Mem. AMA, Bourbon County Med. Soc., Kansas City Gynecol. Soc. Republican. Methodist. Home: 501 S Main St Fort Scott KS 66701 Office: Newman-Young Clinic Fort Scott KS 66701

ALDRICH, ANN, See *Who's Who in America,* 43rd edition.

ALDRICH, MARILYN JEAN, pharmacist; b. Akron, Ohio, July 2, 1955; d. Robert L. and Sarah C. (Moulton) Minkler; m. Warren Charles Aldrich, Sept. 8, 1984. B.S. in Pharmacy, Drake U., 1977. Registered pharmacist, Iowa. Switchboard operator Sta. KCCI-TV, Des Moines, 1972-75; pharmacy clk. Target, Des Moines, 1975-76; pharmacy intern Hammer Pharmacy, Des Moines, 1976-77; pharmacist Easter's, Creston, Iowa, 1977; pharmacist/asst. mgr. Dahl's Foods, Inc., West Des Moines, Iowa, 1977—. State of Iowa scholar, 1973; Drake U. Presdl. scholar, 1973; U.S. Govt. grantee, 1973, 74. Mem. Iowa Pharmacists Assn., Polk County Pharmacists Assn. (sec. 1981-82), Chi Omega Alumni. Republican. Presbyterian. Avocations: reading; sewing; knitting; racquetball; swimming. Home: 1414 68th St Des Moines IA 50311 Office: Dahl's Pharmacy 1208 Prospect St West Des Moines IA 50265

ALDRICH, MAX THOMPSON, JR., optometrist; b. Nevada, Mo., Aug. 2, 1941; s. Max T. Sr. and Helen E.; m. Ann J. Freeman; children—Todd, Kristin, Kara. A.A., San Angelo Coll., 1962; O.D., Southern Coll. of Optometry, 1965. Practice medicine specializing in optometry, St. Joseph, Mo., 1965—. Mem. Mo. Optometric Assn. (pres. 1980-81, Optometrist of the Year award 1983), Jaycees. Lodges: Masons, Lions. Office: Tom Aldrich OD 110 S 7th St Saint Joseph MO 64501

ALDRICH, STEPHANIE RAE HEGEDUS, chemist; b. Akron, Ohio, June 26, 1944; d. Stephen Paul and Fannie Alberta (Beck) Hegedus; student Purdue U., South Bend (Ind.) Campus, evenings 1972-74; grad. Varian Inst. Chromotography, 1981; children—Todd Clifton, Robert LeRoy. Charge nurse LaGrange Nursing Home, Ind., 1972-73; tchr. reality therapy, activities dir. Rehab. Center, Michigan City, Ind. 1973-75; metallurgy, sand control apprentice Josam Mfg. Co., Michigan City, 1978-79; with Manley Bros. div. Brit. Indsl. Sands, Ltd., Chesterton, Ind., 1979—, mgr. quality control, research and devel. labs., 1980-82, analytical chemist, 1982—. Mem. AAAS, Nat. Assn. Female Execs. Democrat. Lutheran. Contbr. poetry to various publs. Home: 1215 Earl Rd Michigan City IN 46360 Office: Manley Bros 128 S 15th St Chesterton IN 46304

ALDRIDGE, ALEXANDRA, educator; b. Chgo., July 23, 1940; B.A. in Sociology (asst.), Millikin U., 1961; M.A. in English, Northwestern U., 1963; Ph.D. in Comparative Lit. (fellow 1967-68), U. Mich., 1978. Instr. English, Wayne State U., Detroit, 1968-72; lectr. Am. culture U. Mich., 1975, lectr. humanities, 1980, lectr. humanities/engring., 1975-81; assoc. prof., dir. grad. studies in tech. Eastern Mich. U., Ypsilanti, 1982—, also chair design com. Corp. Tng. Ctr.; lectr. univs. throughout Europe; writer, cons. Westdeutscher Rundfunk, 1972-73; cons. Ctr. 20th Century Studies, U. Wis., Milw., Kent State Univ. Press, others. Hon. degree Instituto Politechnico National de Mex., 1981; Eastern Mich. U. grantee, 1985, recipient Dean's award, 1983-84. Mem. Soc. Utopian Studies, World Future Soc., N.Am. Soc. Corp. Planning (v.p. chpt., chpt. bd. dirs. 1984-85), Soc. History of Tech., Mich. Tech. Council. Co-editor: Alternative Futures quar., 1978—; editor issue Extrapolation, 1977; contbr. articles to scholarly jours. Author: The Scientific World View in Dystopia, 1984. Home: 1548 Broadway Ann Arbor MI 48105 Office: Sill Hall Coll Tech Eastern Mich U Ypsilanti MI 48197

ALDRIDGE, MARY HELEN, business educator; b. Evansville, Ind., Jan. 17, 1923; d. Walter James and Helen Amanda (Sanders) Blue; m. James F. Aldridge, July 26, 1949. M.A., U. Evansville (Ind.), 1970. Registered vocat. bus. and office edn. tchr., Ind. Vocat. bus. tchr. Chrisney (Ind.) High Sch., 1944-74; vocat. bus. tchr. Heritage Hills High Sch., Lincoln City, Ind., 1974—. Mem. Ind. Bus. Edn. Assn., Ind. Vocat. Assn., Nat. Bus. Assn., Office Edn. Assn., Delta Kappa Gamma. Methodist. Home: PO Box 315 Santa Claus IN 47579

ALEMAN, MINDY R., advertising and public relations executive, freelance writer; b. N.Y.C., Nov. 23, 1950; d. Lionel Luskin and Jocelyn (Cohen) L.; m. Gary Aleman, Aug. 27, 1983. B.A., U. Akron, 1972, M.A., 1975. Instr. speech U. Akron, 1973-83; car salesperson Dave Towell Cadillac, Akron, 1977-79, mgr. fin. and ins., 1979; account exec., pub. relations dir. Loos, Edwards & Sexauer, Akron, 1980-82; mktg. services coordinator Century Products, Stow, Ohio, 1982-83; mgr. advt., pub. relations Century Products, Gerber Furniture Group, Stow, 1983—. Author: (play) Danny's Choice, 1972. Mem. Am. Mktg. Assn., Pub. Relations Soc. Am., Akron Advt. Club (various awards 1983-85), Akron Women's Network, Sales and Mktg. Execs. of Cleve. Office: Century Products Inc 1366 Commerce Dr Stow OH 44224

ALEMAN, NARCISO L., lawyer; b. Edcouch, Tex., Nov. 25, 1946; s. Don Alfredo Y. and Dona Teresa (Limas) A.; m. Rita Mary Hagen, June 4, 1983; children by previous marriage—Maria Guadalupe Taina M., Estanislado Luis G. Student Colo. State U., 1965-67; M.A.T., Antioch Grad. Sch., 1971; J.D., U. Wis., 1983, postgrad., 1979—. Bar: Wis. 1983. Mem. faculty U. Utah, Salt Lake City, 1976; career counselor SER-Jobs for Program, Milw., 1976; adminstrv. asst. IV DILHR, Madison, Wis., 1977; mem. faculty U. Wis.-Madison, 1978-80; sole practice, Milw., 1983—; econ. devel. cons. La Raza Unida, Inc., Jefferson, Wis., 1978—; personnel deve. specialist Comunidad de Amigos, Sheboygan, Wis., 1979—; researcher Esperanza Unida, Inc., Milw., 1976—; planner cons. Latin Am. Union, Milw., 1976—. Treas., Social Devel. Commn. Milw., 1976-79; 2d v.p. Wis. Council on Mibrant Labor, 1979, mem. council, 1978-80. Recipient award for Edn., S. Clara Muhammad Prep., 1979; Nat. Hispanic scholar, 1983. Mem. Wis. Bar Assn., Milw. Bar Assn., Wis. Hispanic Lawyers Assn. Democrat. Club: Latino Law Students (pres. Madison 1981-82). Home: 2566A S Howell Ave Milwaukee WI 53207 Office: 3741 W National Ave Milwaukee WI 53215

ALEXANDER, BARBARA LEAH SHAPIRO, psychiatric social worker; b. St. Louis, May 6, 1943; d. Harold Albert and Dorothy Miriam (Leifer) Shapiro; B.Mus. Edn., Washington U., St. Louis, 1964; postgrad. U. Ill., 1964-66; M.S.W., Smith Coll., 1970; postgrad. Inst. Psychoanalysis, Chgo., 1971-73, Child Therapy Program, 1976-80; certified therapist Sex Dysfunction Clinic, Loyola U., Chgo., 1975; m. Richard E. Alexander. Research asst., NIMH grantee Smith Coll., 1968-70; probation officer Juvenile Ct. Cook County, Chgo., 1966-68, 70; therapist Madden Mental Health Center, Hines, Ill., 1970-72; supr., therapist, field instr. U. Chgo., U. Ill. Grad. Schs. Social Work, also Pritzker Children's Hosp., Chgo., 1972—; therapist, cons., also pvt. practice, 1973—; instr. tng. and advanced tng. Effectiveness Tng. Assos., Chgo., 1974; instr. psychology Northeastern U., Chgo., 1975; intern Divorce Conciliation Service, Circuit Ct. Cook County, 1976-77. Bd. dirs. North Am. Found., Grant Park Concerts Soc. Recipient Sterling Achievement award Mu Phi Epsilon, 1964. Certified social worker, Ill. Mem. Acad. Certified Social Workers, Nat. Assn. Social Workers, Ill. Soc. Clin. Social Work (dir., chmn. services to mems. com., dir. Pvt. Practitioners' Referral Service), Am. Assn. Marriage and Family Therapy, Assn. Child Psychotherapists, Am. Assn. Sex Educators and Counselors, Amateur Chamber Music Players Assn., Jewish Geneal. Soc., Smith Coll. Alumni Assn. (dir.). Democrat. Jewish. Contbr. to profl. publns. Home: 179 E Lake Shore Dr Chicago IL 60611 Office: 919 N Michigan Ave #3012 Chicago IL 60611

ALEXANDER, CHARLES RICHARD, JR., financial planning and analysis administrator; b. Fremont, Nebr., July 14, 1955; s. Charles Richard Sr. and Shirley (Madden) A. B.S., B.A., Creighton U., Omaha, 1977. Acct., Rockwell Internat., Cedar Rapids, Iowa, 1977-80, fin. analyst, mgr. fin. planning and analysis, 1982—. Vol. United Way, Cedar Rapids, 1980—. Mem. Nat. Assn. Accts. (v.p., bd. dirs. 1977—, pres. 1985-86, named Mem. Yr., 1978-79), Rockwell Mgmt. Club. Republican. Roman Catholic. Avocations: skiing, softball, basketball, camping, volleyball, bowling. Office: Rockwell Internat 400 Collins Rd NE Cedar Rapids IA 52498

ALEXANDER, CHARLES WILLIAM, psychologist, consultant; b. Zanesville, Ohio, Feb. 13, 1951; s. Charles and Doris (Paxson) A.; B.S., Denison U., 1973; M.A., Bowling Green State U., 1975, Ph.D., 1978. Psychol. intern Southwestern Med. Sch., Dallas, 1977-78; asst. prof. psychology Wichita (Kans.) State U., 1978-83; pvt. practice clin. psychology, Wichita, 1979—; cons. Roots & Wings Foster Care Project, Mental Health Assn. Sedgewick County, also residential mental retardation and psychiat. facilities. Mem. Am. Psychol. Assn., Soc. Behavioral Medicine, Soc. Psychophysiol. Research, Mental Health Assn. Sedgewick County, Southwestern Psychol. Assn., Wichita Psychol. Assn. Author: (with Richard and Muriel Saunders) The Small Home Handbook: A Kansas Guide to Develop, Fund, and Operate Small Residential Facilities for the DD Adult. Home: 2323 N Woodlawn #433 Wichita KS 67220 Office: 2525 E Central Wichita KS 67214

ALEXANDER, CHRISTINE ELLEN, educator; b. Ashland, Ohio, Jan. 19, 1936; d. Myron Lee and Beulah (Grafton) Hootman; student Ohio State U., 1954-55, William Jewell Coll., 1959-64; B.S., Okla. State U., 1966, M.S., 1969; postgrad. Miami U., Oxford, Ohio, 1978-80; m. William S. Alexander, Dec. 21, 1974; children by previous marriage—Laura Lynn Smith Phillips, Mathis Andrew Smith, Rachael Elaine Smith. Dental asst., receptionist, Springfield, Ohio, 1956; clk.-typist Wittenberg U., Springfield, 1957; tech. math. and sci., Perkins, Okla., 1968-69; tchr. home econs. Dayton (Ohio) City Schs., 1969-74, coordinator/tchr. Family Life Program, 1973—; mem. Ohio Council United Services for Effective Parenting. Mem. Am. Vocat. Assn., Ohio Vocat. Assn., Dayton Sch. Mgmt. Assn., Omicron Nu. Home: 3525 Dandridge Ave Dayton OH 45407

ALEXANDER, COLLIN HERBERT, consulting company executive; b. Carsonville, Mich., Dec. 27, 1916; s. George Herbert and Emma Louise (Strong) A.; m. Mary Elizabeth Horrall (dec.); m. 2d, Suzanne Revier, Dec. 28, 1977; children—Graham, Carolyn, Nancy, Katherine, Alice, Jonathan, Robert. B.S., Alma Coll., 1937; postgrad. MIT, 1937-39. With Kimberly Clark Co., Niagara Falls, N.Y., 1940-41, Bausch & Lomb Optical Co., Rochester, N.Y., 1941-51, Minn. Mining & Mfg. Co., St. Paul, 1951-70; pres. Tech. Enterprises Co., St. Paul, 1970—. Mem. Am. Optical Soc., Am. Chem. Soc., Am. Phys. Soc., Am. Vacuum Soc. Republican. Presbyterian. Club: St. Paul. Patentee. Office: Box 8022 Saint Paul MN 55113

ALEXANDER, DAVID LOUIS, marketing specialist; b. Chgo., Nov. 8, 1944; s. Isadore E. and Alice M. (Cohen) A.; m. Clare Leanne Nesler, June 26, 1971; 1 child, Elise Michele. B.S. in Math., U. Ill.-Urbana, 1967; M.B.A. with honors, U. Chgo., 1981; M.B.A. with distinction, U. Leuven, Belgium, 1981. Project leader Am. Hosp. Assn., Chgo., 1972-76; mgr. fin. systems Bankers Life & Casualty Co., Chgo., 1977-80; internat. bus. exchange rep. U. Leuven, Belgium, 1980-81; gen. mgr. Network Mktg. Internat., Evanston, Ill., 1981—; cons. Netherlands Consulate, Chgo., 1984-85. Active Big Bros., Evanston, 1974-80. Mem. Soc. Nuclear Medicine, Midwest Soc. Profl. Cons. (bd. dirs. 1984-85). Avocations: music; tennis; sailing. Home: 2006 Brummel St Evanston IL 60202 Office: Network Mktg Internat 1723 Howard St Evanston IL 60202

ALEXANDER, DON HERMAN, chemical company executive; b. Amsterdam, Netherlands, July 11, 1938; came to U.S., 1964, naturalized, 1974; s. Titus Herman and Helena Johanna (Simons) Buitenhuis; B.B.A., Nijenrode N.O.-I.B., Breukelan, Netherlands, 1961; B.B.A., Washburn U., 1962; m. Sharon A. Hampton, Nov. 10, 1962 (div. 1984); children—Karen Ann, Matthew Vincent. Project planner Royal Dutch Shell, Zwolle, Netherlands, 1962-64; office mgr. Koch Industries, Inc., Wichita, Kans., 1964-66; exec. v.p. Commerce Bank Kansas City (Mo.), 1966-82; pres. Perkins Industries, Inc., Overland Park, Kans., 1982—. Hon. consol for Netherlands, Kansas City, Mo.; bd. dirs., treas. Internat. Relations Council, Kansas City; fundraiser Jr. Achievement, Kansas City, Hist. Found., Kansas City. Served with M.C. Dutch Army, 1957-59. Rotary scholar, 1961-62. Mem. Adhesive and Sealant Council, NAM. Republican. Unitarian. Club: Univ. (Kansas City). Home: 8747 Rosewood Dr Prairie Village KS 66207 Office: 6405 Metcalf Ave Suite 422 Overland Park KS 66202

ALEXANDER, ERNEST ROBERT, urban planning educator, consultant; b. Dresden, Germany, Dec. 11, 1933; came to U.S., 1969, naturalized; s. Fritz Ludwig and Malvina (Mund) A.; m. Shulamith Stock, Mar. 6, 1960; children—Michael, Dana. B.Arch., U.Cape Town, S. Africa, 1954; M. City Planning, U. Calif.-Berkeley, 1971, Ph.D. in City and Regional Planning, 1974. Head research teams Inst. Planning and Devel., Tel-Aviv, 1965-69; vis. prof. U. Wis.-Milw., 1972-73, assoc. prof., 1973—, chmn. dept. urban planning, 1981—; cons. in field, 1972—. Author: Approaches to Planning, 1985. Contbr. articles to profl. jours. Mem. Design Rev. Bd., Village of Shorewood, 1983—. Lady Davis fellow, 1977-78, Neaman fellow, 1979-80; Fulbright grantee, 1984. Mem. Am. Planning Assn. (exec. com. Wis. chpt. 1984—), AAUP (exec. com. U. Wis.-Milw. chpt. 1982-85). Avocations: reading; swimming; cross-country skiing. Home: 2216 E Stratford Ct Shorewood WI 53211 Office: U Wis Dept Urban Planning PO Box 413 Milwaukee WI 53201

ALEXANDER, HENRY LEE, manufacturing engineer; b. Ashland, Ky., Mar. 6, 1949; s. Henry Thomas and Thelma (Jones) A.; m. Jean Ann Shirey, June 9, 1973; children—Heather Lee, Christopher Vernon, Jason Henry. A.A. in Applied Sci., Lorain County (Ohio) Community Coll., 1974; student Terra Tech. Coll., 1982—. Apprentice tool and die maker MTD Products, Willard, Ohio, 1967-71, journeyman, 1971-74, supr. quality control, 1974-76, supr. tool and die dept., 1976-85; mfg. engr. Die and Stamping div. Weiss Industries, 1985—; quality control instr., adv. com. quality control Terra Tech. Coll. Adv. com. mfg. tech. Firelands br. Bowling Green State U. (Ohio). Served to 2d lt. Ohio N.G., 1971-77. Recipient Am. Spirit Honor medal Citizens Com. Armed Forces, 1971. Sr. mem. Soc. Mfg. Engrs. Baptist. Home: 1367 Snyder Rd Norwalk OH 44857

ALEXANDER, JOANN SAYRE, nurse, educator; b. Evansville, Ind., Dec. 24, 1934; s. Joseph Sayres and Evelyn Catherine (Schmitt) Coughlin; B.S. in Nursing, St. Louis U., 1956; M.S. in Nursing, U. Evansville, 1976; m. James Edward Alexander, Oct. 11, 1958; children—James Edward, Laurie Ann, Mary E., Jan R. Asst. head nurse Marion (Ill.) VA Hosp., 1956-57; staff nurse Firmin Desloge Hosp., St. Louis, 1957-58; staff nurse Herrin (Ill.) Hosp., 1963-64; staff nurse Byron (Ill.) Clinic, 1966-67; sch. nurse Vanderburgh Sch. Corp., Evansville, Ind., 1968-69; asst. prof. nursing U. Evansville, 1973—; inservice edn. program cons. Welborn Hosp., Evansville; reviewer Ind. Continuing Edn. for Nursing, 1978-79. Tchr., Confraternity of Christian Doctrine, 1973-77, Service award, 1977; active Women's Service Guild, 1968-72; nursing del. Ind. State Conv., 1977, 79. Mem. Am. Nurses Assn., Ind. Nurses Assn., Dist. #4 Nurses Assn. (chmn. nomination com.), Nat. League Nursing, Ind. Citizens League for Nursing, Bus. and Profl. Women's Club (treas. 1958), Beta Sigma Phi. Clubs: Holy Rosary Women's; Horseshoe Bend. Home: 5801 Monroe Ave Evansville IN 47715 Office: Box 329 Evansville IN 47702

ALEXANDER, JOHN J., chemistry educator; b. Indpls., Apr. 13, 1940; s. John Gregory and Inez Helene (Snedaker) A. A.B. summa cum laude, Columbia U., 1962, M.A., 1963, Ph.D., 1967. Postdoctoral fellow Ohio State U., Columbus, 1967-69, research assoc. 1977-78, 85-86; asst. prof. chemistry U.Cin., 1969-73, assoc. prof., 1973-79, prof., 1979—, faculty fellow, 1972-74. Mem. Clifton Town Meeting. Woodrow Wilson fellow; NSF fellow Columbia U., 1963-66, faculty fellow, 1966; Petroleum Research Fund grantee, 1970-73; Research Corp. grantee, 1970-77; NSF grantee, 1972-74, 79-81. Mem. Am. Chem. Soc. (past chmn., trustee), Phi Beta Kappa, Sigma Xi, Phi Lambda Upsilon. Democrat. Co-Author: (with M.J. Steffel) Chemistry in the Laboratory, 1976; (with B.E. Douglas, D.H. McDaniel) Concepts and Models of Inorganic Chemistry, 1983, Problems in Inorganic Chemistry, 1983; contbr. chpts. to books and articles to profl. jours. Home: 3446 Whitfield Ave Cincinnati OH 45220 Office: Dept Chemistry U Cin Cincinnati OH 45221-0172

ALEXANDER, JOHN MOFFETT, lawyer; b. East Cleveland, Ohio, Aug. 19, 1945; s. Homer Caleb and Mariam Moffett (Tritt) A.; m. Nancy Ellen Stewart; children—Mathew, Bethany, Kelly. B.A., Ohio State U., 1967; J.D., Case Western Res. U., 1970. Sr. law clk. U.S. Dist. Ct., Cleve., 1970-71; assoc. Greenfield & Malitz, Cleve., 1971-73, Weiner, Orkin & Abbate, Shaker Heights, Ohio, 1973-75; sr. ptnr. John M. Alexander & Assocs., Cleve., 1975—; cons. D.C. Filter and Chem., Inc., Sandusky, Ohio, 1979—, Preform Sealants, Inc., Cleve., 1980—, King's Path Condominium Assn., Olmstead, Ohio, 1981—; fin. cons. Seaway Gas and Petroleum Co., Cleve., 1983—; dir. Manning, Inc., Twinsburg, Ohio, North Coast Adhesives, Inc., Cleve. Officer S. Euclid-Lyndhurst Jaycees, Ohio, 1976-81. Mem. Greater Cleve. Bar Assn., Ohio State Bar Assn., Fed. Bar Assn., Chagrin Falls C. of C. Club: Chagrin Valley, Athletic. Avocations: landscaping; interior design; tennis; literature. Home: 5237 Maple Springs Chagrin Falls OH 44022 Office: John M Alexander & Assocs 800 Engrs Bldg Cleveland OH 44114

ALEXANDER, J(OSEPH) EDWARD, def. industry co. exec.; b. Eugene, Oreg., Mar. 17, 1948; s. Joseph Edward and Opal Marie (Robison) A.; B.S. in Mech. Engring., Oreg. State U., 1970; M.S. in Mech. Engring., Carnegie-Mellon U., 1973; m. Judith Elaine Koharik, July 26, 1980. Mech. design engr. Westinghouse Corp.-Bettis Atomic Power Lab., Pitts., 1970-75, Bettis resident mgr. at FMC Corp., 1976-78; mil. mktg. engr. No. Ordnance div. FMC Corp., Mpls., 1978-79, mgr. concepts devel., 1979—. Registered profl. engr., Pa. Mem. Am. Def. Preparedness Assn., Phi Kappa Phi, Tau Beta Pi, Pi Tau Sigma, Sigma Tau, Phi Eta Sigma. Home: 2633 Natchez Ave S Minneapolis MN 55416 Office: No Ordnance Div FMC Corp 4800 E River Rd Minneapolis MN 55421

ALEXANDER, LEN, theatrical producer, manager; b. Ware, Mass., Mar. 20, 1947; s. Leonard Robert Jr. and Evelyn Virginia (Rutledge) A. B.F.A., Carnegie-Mellon U., 1969. Gen. mgr. New York Pro Musica, N.Y.C., 1969-71; mng. dir. Playhouse in the Park, Phila., 1971-73; program dir. Phila. Bicentennial Corp., 1973-76; gen. mgr. Shubert Orgn., Chgo., 1977-83; mng. dir. Ind. Repertory Theatre, Indpls., 1983—; v.p. League of Chgo. Theatres, 1981-83; producer, ptnr. The Alkan Co., Chgo., 1980; cons. Mem. Walker Urban Life Ctr., Indpls., 1984. Producer: musical play Ladies In Waiting, 1982. Theatre panelist Ind. Arts Commn., Indpls., 1983-85; mem. Mayor's Cultural Adv. Panel, Indpls., 1983-85; dir. Chgo. Theatre Festival, 1979. Recipient 1st prize, environ. sculpture competition Three Rivers Arts Festival, Pitts., 1968. Mem. Indpls. Cultural Consortium (pres. 1984-85), Assn. Theatrical Press Agts. and Mgrs. (Midwestern rep. 1978-85). Office: Indiana Repertory Theatre Inc 140 W Washington St Indianapolis IN 46204

ALEXANDER, MACK ALFRED, engineer; b. Hartwell, Ga., May 5, 1916; s. John Wesly and Daisy (Rucker) A.; m. Creola, July 26, 1936; children—Delores, Juanita. Tech. cert. Cleve. Community Coll. Lic. engr., Ohio. Laborer, Aluminum Co. Am., Cleve., 1949-50; stationary engr. City of Cleve., 1950-78; operating engr. Brentwood Hosp., Warrensville, Ohio, 1968-80; instr. Westside Sch. Engring., Cleve., 1977-79; examiner steam engrs. State of Ohio, 1979—. Chmn., Concerned Citizens Com. Warrensville Twp., 1980. Mem. Nat. Assn. Power Engrs., Am. Nuclear Soc. Club: Benedict (pres. 1981—) (Cleve.). Home: 20741 Patterson Pkwy Warrensville Township OH 44122

ALEXANDER, NORMAN E., chemical executive; b. N.Y.C., 1914; m. Marjorie Wulf; four children. A.B., Columbia U., 1934. LL.B., 1936. Chmn. bd., chief exec. officer Sun Chem. Corp., N.Y.C., 1957—; chmn. bd. Chromalloy Am. Corp., St. Louis, 1980—, chief exec. officer, 1982—, pres., 1985—; dir. Kidde & Co., Inc.; Past chmn. bd. trustees N.Y. Med. Coll./Flower-Fifth Ave. Hosps.; trustee Rockefeller U. Council. Mem. NAM (trustee), Conf. Bd., Chief Execs. Forum (dir.). Address: Chromalloy Am Corp 120 S Central Ave Saint Louis MO 63105

ALEXANDER, ROBERT HARWOOD, oil company executive; b. Detroit, Nov. 5, 1928; s. Robert Zimmerman and Mary (Harwood) A.; m. Frances Standish Hake, Dec. 22, 1953; children—Lisa Webber, Charles Hake, Robert Harwood. A.B., Princeton U., 1951; M.A., U. Tex., 1956. Geologist, Humble Oil & Refining Co., Amarillo, Tex., 1955-64; cons. geologist, Columbus, Ohio, 1964-75; geologist, pres. Pominex, Inc., Columbus, 1975—; mem. oil and gas bd. rev. Ohio Dept. Natural Resources, 1979—. Served as lt. (j.g.) USCG, 1951-53. Mem. Am. Assn. Petroleum Geologists, Am. Inst. Profl. Geologists (cert.), Ohio Geol. Soc. (pres. 1969-70). Republican. Episcopalian. Clubs: Columbus Country, Columbus Petroleum (pres. 1972-73). Avocations: golf, sailing. Office: Pominex Inc 6660 Doubletree Ave Columbus OH 43229

ALEXANDER, ROBERTA SUE, history educator; b. N.Y.C., Mar. 19, 1943; d. Bernard Milton and Dorothy (Linn) Cohn; m. John Kurt Alexander, 1966 (div. Sept. 1972); m. Ronald Burett Fost, May 7, 1977. B.A., UCLA, 1964; M.A., U. Chgo., 1966, Ph.D., 1974. Instr., Roosevelt U., Chgo., 1967-68; assoc. prof., chmn. dept. U. Dayton, Ohio, 1969—; mem. editorial bd. Cin. Hist. Soc., 1973—. Author: North Carolina Faces the Freedmen: Race Relations During Presidential Reconstruction, 1985. Recipient Summer stipend NEH, Washington, 1975; fellow in residence NEH, 1976-77, fellow Inst. for Legal Studies,

NEH, 1982, summer research fellow U. Dayton, 1972, 74, 76, 80. Mem. Am. Hist. Assn., Orgn. Am. Historians, Am. Soc. Legal History, So. Hist. Assn., Mortar Board, Phi Beta Kappa, Phi Alpha Theta. Club: Am. Contract Bridge Assn. (life master 1983). Avocations: bridge; golf. Home: 72 Twin Lakes Dr Fairfield OH 45014 Office: U Dayton Dept History Dayton OH 45469

ALEXANDER, WILLIAM MICHAEL, lawyer; b. Omaha, June 10, 1942; s. Michael Edward and Marie Francie (Roesing) A.; B.A., Creighton U., 1966, J.D., 1972; m. Mary Catherine Wiehl, July 28, 1968 (div. May 1983); children—Mark Michael, Beth Catherine, Megan Marie; m. 2d Patricia Orwig Kluver, Jan. 2, 1984. Admitted to Iowa bar, 1972, Nebr. bar, 1972; analyst, underwriter Mutual of Omaha, 1966-69; mem. firm George T. Qualley, Sioux City, Iowa, 1972-75, William M. Alexander, Laurens, Iowa, 1976-81. Mem. Laurens C. of C., Am., Iowa, Nebr. bar assns., Delta Theta Phi. Republican. Roman Catholic. Clubs: Lions, Laurens Country, K.C. Home: 122 E Main St Laurens IA 50554 Office: 123 3d St N Laurens IA 50554

ALEXANDER, WILMA JEAN, business education educator, records management/information processing consultant; b. Columbus, Kans., May 25, 1938; d. Glen Burton and Wilma Mae (Jenner) Heavin; m. Leslie Wayne Alexander, Dec. 20, 1958; 1 child, Glenella Jean. B.S., Pittsburg State U., 1959, M.S., 1967; Ed.D., Okla. State U., 1973. Tchr. English, Baxter Springs High Sch., Kans., 1959-61; tchr. bus., English, Pineville High Sch., Mo., 1961-63, Netawaka High Sch., Kans., 1963-64; tchr. bus. Hillsboro High Sch., Mo., 1964-68; faculty Ill. State U., Normal, 1970—, prof. bus. edn., 1978—, chmn. dept. bus. edn. and adminstrv. services, 1983—; project dir. Dept. Adult Vocat. and Tech. Edn., Ill. State Bd. Edn., Springfield, 1975-83; cons. Pekin Ins. Co., Ill., 1984—. Author: (workbook, study guide) Introduction to Business, 1976, 79; Office Automation, 1985. Editor: Business Education into the Eighties, 1980-84. Mem. Assn. Records Mgrs. and Adminstrs. (pres. 1976-79), Office Systems Research Assn., Nat. Bus. Edn. Assn., Ill. Bus. Edn. Assn. (bd. dirs.), Data Processing Mgmt. Assn. Avocation: piano. Home: Route 1 Box 109 Towanda IL 61776 Office: Dept Bus Edn and Adminstrv Services 327 Williams Hall Ill State Univ Normal IL 61761

ALEXEJUN, ROBERT JOHN, optometrist; b. Green Bay, Wis., June 6, 1948; s. Albert John and Mary Helen (Juranek) A.; m. Mary Jeanne DeYoung, Sept. 4, 1971; children—Christa Nicole, Brooke Erin, Bryan David. Student U. Wis.-Madison, 1966-69; O.D., Ohio State U., 1973. Optometrist, Optometric Ctr., Wausau, Wis., 1973—. Mem. Am. Optometric Assn., Wis. Optometric Assn., Wis. Valley Optometric Soc. Roman Catholic. Club: Wausau Noon Optimists (v.p. 1983-84). Avocations: cross country ski racing, flatwater canoe racing. Home: 510 E Lakeshore Dr Wausau WI 54401 Office: Optometric Center 120 S First Ave Wausau WI 54401

ALEXIS, MARCUS, economics educator; b. N.Y.C., Feb. 26, 1932; B.A., Bklyn. Coll., 1953; M.A. (Univ. scholar, Hinman fellow), Mich. State U., 1954; Ph.D. (Univ. fellow), U. Minn., 1959; m.; 3 children. Instr. econs. U. Minn., 1954-57; asst. prof. econs. and mktg. Macalester Coll., 1957-60; asso. prof. mktg. DePaul U., 1960-62; asso. prof. to prof. bus. adminstrn. U. Rochester, 1962-70; prof. econs. Northwestern U., Evanston, Ill., 1970—, chmn. dept., 1976-79, 82—; mem. ICC, 1979-80, vice chmn., 1981, acting chmn., 1981; vis. prof. U. Calif. at Berkeley, 1969-71; vis. scholar, Ford Found. fellow Grad. Sch. Bus. Harvard, 1961-62; vis. asso. prof. U. Minn., 1962, 65. Trustee, chmn. fin. and endowment com. Roycemore Sch.; trustee Macalester Coll. Recipient Outstanding Achievement award U. Minn., 1981, scholar award Carib-bean-Am. Intercultural Orgn., 1981. Mem. Am. Econ. Assn. (mem. com. to increase supply of minority economists 1971-74, mem. com. on honors and awards 1972—, chmn. com. status of minorities in the profession 1974—, dir. summer program in econs. for minority students 1974-79, mem. nominating com. 1981-82, adv. com. to U.S. Census 1983), Am. Mktg. Assn. (dir. 1968-70), Nat. Econ. Assn. (steering com. 1976—, Samuel Z. Westerfield Disting. Achievement award 1979), Caucus Black Economists (chmn. 1969-71, mem. steering com. 1969-73, 76—). Office: Econs Dept Northwestern U Evanston IL 60201*

ALF, JOHN JAMES, chem. co. exec.; b. Aurora, Ill., May 7, 1936; s. Frank Peter and Anne Mary (Urlaub) A.; B.S., St. Mary's Coll., Winona, Minn., 1958; M.B.A., U. Mich., Ann Arbor, 1966; m. Marianne E. Schmidt, Jan. 24, 1959; children—Christine, Julie, Elizabeth, Eric. Chemist, Chemetron Corp., Rockhill Labs., Newport, Tenn., 1960-63, sr. chemist N.W. Chem. div., Detroit, 1963-65; mgr. adminstrv. services Vulcan Labs., Inc., Pontiac, Mich., 1965-68; v.p. ops. water mgmt. div. Clow Corp., Pontiac, 1968—. Mem. Am. Chem. Soc., Mensa. Home: 35306 Lancashire Ct Livonia MI 48152 Office: 408 Auburn Ave Pontiac MI 48058

ALFIDI, RALPH JOSEPH, radiologist; b. Rome, Apr. 20, 1932; came to U.S., 1933, naturalized, 1937; s. Luca and Angeline (Panella) A.; M. Rose Esther Senesac, Sept. 3, 1956; children—Sue, Lisa, Christine, Catherine, Mary, John. A.B. Ripon Coll., 1955; M.D., Marquette U., 1959. Diplomate Am. Bd. Radiology. Staff mem. radiology Cleve. Clinic, Ohio, 1965-78; head dept. of radiology hosp., 1968-78; prof., chmn. dept. radiology Case Western U. Sch. Medicine, 1978—; dir. dept. radiology Univ. Hosps. of Cleve., Ohio, 1978—dir. Cuyahoga Savs. & Loan; cons. in field. Contbr. articles to profl. jours. Served to capt. USAR, 1963-65. Fellow Am. Cancer Soc.; mem. Radiol. Soc. N.Am., Am. Roentgen Ray Soc., Soc. Computed Body Tomography, AMA, Ohio State Med. Soc., Am. Heart Assn. Clubs: Hillbrook, Chagrin Valley Racquet, Kirtland Country. Home: 247 Coy Ln Chagrin Falls OH 44022 Office: Dept Radiology Room B-006 MacDonald House 2074 Abington Rd Cleveland OH 44106

ALFRED, KARL SVERRE, orthopedic surgeon; b. Stavanger, Norway, July 10, 1917; s. Alfred Bjarne Abrahamsen Floen and Thora Garpestad; student U. Va., 1935-38; M.D., L.I. Coll. Medicine, 1942; m. Amalia Leona Bombach, July 26, 1951; children—Patricia (Mrs. Dennis Alleman), Richard Lincoln, Peter Karl. Intern, Mountainside Hosp., Montclair, N.J., 1942-43; resident orthopedics Univ. Hosps., Cleve., 1947-50; practice medicine specializing in orthopedic surgery, Cleve., 1950—; chief orthopedic surgery St. Vincent Charity Hosp., Cleve., 1955-81, orthopedic surgery dir. emeritus, 1981—, chief of staff, 1971-75; assoc. staff Euclid Gen. Hosp., Cleve.; courtesy staff Univ., St. Luke's hosps., Cleve., Geauga Community Hosp., Chardon, O.; orthopedic cons. Norfolk & Western R.R.; affiliate tchr. orthopedics Bunts Edn. Inst., Cleve. Clinic Found. Trustee St. Vincent Charity Hosp., Cleve. Served with M.C., USNR, 1943-47. Episcopalian. Mason, Rotarian. Contbr. articles to profl. jours. Home: 20 Brandywood Dr Pepper Pike OH 44124 Office: 2475 E 22d St Cleveland OH 44115

ALI, MIR MASOOM, educator; b. Bangladesh, Feb. 1, 1937; s. Mir Muazzam and Azifa Khatoon (Chowdhury) A.; came to U.S., 1969; B.Sc. with honors, U. Dacca, 1956, M.Sc., 1957; M.Sc., U. Toronto, 1967, Ph.D., 1969; m. Firoza Chowdhury, June 25, 1959; children—Naheed, Fahima, Farah, Mir Ishtiaque. Research officer Ministry of Food and Agriculture, Ministry of Commerce, Central Pub. Service Commn., Govt. of Pakistan, 1958-66; teaching asst. U. Toronto (Ont., Can.), 1966-69; asst. prof. math. scis. Ball State U., Muncie, Ind., 1969-74, assoc. prof., 1974-78, prof., 1978—; vis. prof. U. Dhaka, 1983-84, Jahangirnagar U., 1983-84; vis. spl. lectr. U. Windsor (Can.), 1972-73; cons., researcher. Grantee Ball State U., 1974-85, Ind. Com. for Humanities, 1976-77. Recipient Outstanding Researcher award Ball State U., 1984-85. Fellow Royal Statis. Soc. London; mem. Am. Statis. Assn., Inst. Math. Statistics, Am. Math. Soc., AAAS. Moslem. Mem. editorial bd., overseas coordinator Jour. Statis. Research; mem. editorial bd. Aligarh Jour. Stats., Jour. Statis. Studies; mem. exec. editorial bd. South Asian Population Dilemma; cons. editor Daktar; contbr. articles to profl. jours. Home: 3003 Riverside Ave Muncie IN 47304 Office: Ball State U Dept Math Scis Muncie IN 47306

ALIBER, JAMES A., bank executive. Chmn., chief exec. officer, dir. First Fed. of Mich., Detroit. Office: First Federal of Michigan 1001 Woodward Detroit MI 48226*

ALICH, AGNES AMELIA, chemistry educator, nun; b. Loman, Minn., June 10, 1932; d. John James and Delvina Rosalie (St. Lawrence) A. B.S., Marquette U., 1960, M.S., 1961; Ph.D., Northwestern U., 1971. Instr. sci. Cathedral High Sch., Duluth, Minn., 1954-57, Gerard High Sch., Phoenix, Ariz., 1964-67; prof. chemistry Coll. St. Scholastica, Duluth, 1961-64, 67—. Contbr. articles to profl. jours. Mem. symphony chorus, Duluth, 1967—. Grantee NSF, 1976, 81, Miller Dwan Med. Found., 1978-80, Duluth Clinic Edn. and Research Found., 1981-83; nominee Catalyst award Chem. Mfg. Assn., 1985. Mem. Am. Chem. Soc. (chmn. Lake Superior Sect. 1977-79), Chem. Soc. London, Sigma Xi, Iota Sigma Pi. Democrat. Home: 1200 Kenwood St Duluth MN 55811 Office: College St Scholastica Duluth MN 55811

ALIG, FRANK DOUGLAS STALNAKER, construction company executive; b. Indpls., Oct. 10, 1921; s. Clarence Schirmer and Marjory (Stalnaker) A.; student Mich. U., 1939-41; B.S., Purdue U., 1948; m. Ann Bobbs, Oct. 22, 1949; children—Douglas, Helen, Barbara. Project engr. Ind. State Hwy. Commn., Indpls., 1948; pres. Alig-Stark Constrn. Co., Inc., 1949-57, Frank S. Alig, Inc., 1957—; chmn. bd. Concrete Structures Corp., Indpls.; v.p., dir. Bo-Wit Products Corp., Edinburg, Ind.; pres. dir. Home Stove Realty Co.; pres, dir. Home Land Investment Co., Inc. Served with AUS, 1943-46. Registered profl. engr., Ind. Mem. U.S., Ind. socs. profl. engrs., Prestressed Concrete Producers Ind. (pres.), Indpls. C. of C. Republican. Presbyn. (deacon). Clubs: Woodstock, Dramatic, Lambs (Indpls.). Home: 8080 N Pennsylvania St Indianapolis IN 46240 Office: 4849 W 96th St Indianapolis IN 46268

AL-JADDA, SOUHEIL, surgeon; b. Souwera, Iraq, June 27, 1946; came to U.S., 1971; s. Muhammad Aadel and Souheila (Dassouki) Al-J.; M.D., Damascus (Syria) U., 1971; m. Sahar Dassouki, Aug. 5, 1971; children—Souheila, Aadel, Omar. Intern, Fairview Gen. Hosp., Cleve., 1971-72, surg. resident, 1972-76; practice medicine, specializing in gen. surgery, Norwalk, Ohio, 1976—; staff Fisher Titus Meml. Hosp., Norwalk, 1976—. Diplomate Am. Bd. Surgery. Fellow A.C.S., Internat. Coll. Surgeons; mem. AMA, Ohio Med. Assn., Huron County Med. Soc. Home: 115 Sycamore Dr Norwalk OH 44857 Office: 34 Executive Dr Norwalk OH 44857

ALKIRE, BETTY JO, artist, marketing consultant; b. Kansas City, Mo., June 20, 1942; d. Robert Emmitt and Gladys Faye (Craigg) Sharp; m. Daniel Wayne Hedrick, Nov. 15, 1958 (div.); children—Diane Laurie, Lisa Kay, Brett, Darin, Julie; m. William Edgar Alkire, Sept. 23, 1975. Tchr. art Independence Adult Edn., Mo., 1967—; portrait artist Silver Dollar City Nat. Crafts Festival, 1971—; owner, operator portrait artist's concession Kansas City Worlds of Fun, 1972—; tchr. pvt. art classes, 1970—; tchr., lectr. mktg. art U. Mo. Extension Program, 1982—; cons. mktg. and life-planning for artists. Contbr. articles in field to various mags. Bd. dirs. Mid-Coast Pub. Radio Project, Kansas City, 1980-83. Mem. Mo. Arts Council, Table Rock Art Guild, Independent Profl. Artists Assn. (pres. 1980—). Methodist. Clubs: Rockaway Beach Ladies, Rockaway Beach Booster (Mo.). Avocations: art; history. Home: Historic Taneywood Rockaway Beach MO 65740

ALKJAERSIG, NORMA KIRSTINE, biochemist, educator; b. Ikast, Denmark, Dec. 25, 1921; came to U.S., 1951, naturalized, 1961; d. Christen and Laura (Christensen) A.; m. Anthony P. Fletcher, June 25, 1961. M.S. in Chem. Engring., Polytech. Inst., Copenhagen, Denmark, 1949; Ph.D. in Biochemistry, U. Copenhagen, 1965. Research assoc. Biol. Inst. Carlsbery Found., Copenhagen, 1949-51, Wayne State U., Detroit, 1951-54; research assoc. Washington U., St. Louis, 1954-57, research asst. prof., 1957-61, research assoc. prof., 1961—. Contbr. articles to profl. jours. Mem. Physiol. Soc., Central Soc. Clin. Research, Internat. Soc. Thrombosis and Hemostasis, Internat. Soc. Hematology. Home: 30 Oak Bend Ct Saint Louis MO 63124 Office: VA Med Ctr Jefferson Barracks Saint Louis MO 63125

ALLABEN, ROBERT DEWITT, surgeon; b. Grand Rapids, Mich., Sept. 26, 1930; s. Fred Roland and Joanna Jo (Dewitt) A.; m. Ruth Elaine Six, Aug. 29, 1952; children—Elizabeth Ann, Janet Louise, Bruce Atwood. B.S. in Zoology, U. Mich., 1952; M.D., Wayne State U., 1956. Diplomate Am. Bd. Surgery. Intern, Woman's Hosp., Detroit, 1956-57; gen. surgery resident Harper Hosp., Detroit, 1957-61, chief sect. gen. surgery, 1968-72, vice chief dept. surgery, 1971-77, 79—; dir. transplantation Mt. Carmel Hosp., Detroit, 1975-79; vice chief-of-staff Harper-Grace Hosps., Detroit, 1981—; assoc. prof. surgery Wayne State U. Sch. Medicine, Detroit, 1979—; dir. Organ Procurement Agy. Mich., Ann Arbor, 1974—. Contbr. articles to profl. publs. Pres. Village of Quakertown (Mich.), 1971-73. Fellow ACS (sec. Mich. chpt. 1983—); mem. Transplantation Soc. Mich. (bd. dirs. 1974—), Mich. Soc. Gen. Surgeons (bd. dirs. 1978—), AMA (del. 1980—), Midwest Surgery Assn. (pres. 1980), Soc. Surgery Alimentary Tract, Collegium Internationale Chirurgiae Digestivae, Pan-Pacific Surg. Assn., Am. Soc. Transplant Surgeons, Western Surg. Soc., Detroit Acad. Surgery (pres. 1983), Detroit Acad. Medicine, Detroit Surg. Assn. (pres. 1982). Home: 33000 Biddestone Ln Farmington Hills MI 48018 Office: Harper-Grace Hosps Dept Surgery 3990 John R St Detroit MI 48201

ALLASTER, GEORGE GREGORY, building and hardware company executive; b. London, Ont., Can., Apr. 24, 1938; came to U.S., 1975; s. Harold J. and Ruth A. A.; m. Gail Ann Vanstone, Nov. 26, 1960; children—Gregory, George, Jr., Sean. B.A., U. B.C., 1964. Gen. sales mgr. 3 M Co., London, Ont., 1958-72; dir. mktg. Leigh Products Co., London, 1972-75; v.p. mktg. Williams Products Co., Elkhart, Ind., 1975-76, pres., 1976-80; pres. Midlakes, Inc., Elkhart, 1980—; pres. dir. A.B.H. Bldg. Products Inc.; House and Home Products Inc.; dir. Fed Paks Inc., London. Served with RCAF, 1953-56. Republican. Roman Catholic. Clubs: Elcona Country, Sunningdale Country, KC. Home: 3104 Crabtree Ln Elkhart IN 46514 Office: Midlakes Inc 215 E Jackson Blvd Elkhart IN 46516

ALLEGRETTI, JOSEPH NICHOLAS, retail drug company executive; b. Chgo., Oct. 28, 1937; s. Carlo and Adeline (Truppa) A.; m. Annette Mae Davis, Oct. 3, 1959; children—Carl, Paul, James. B.S. in Pharmacy, Butler U., 1959. Registered pharmacist. Pharmacist Ribordy Pharmacy, Gary, Ind., 1959-61; mgr., pharmacist Portage Prof. Pharmacy, Ind., 1961-72; mgr., pharmacist Ribordy Drugs Co., Valparaiso, Ind., 1972-73, exec., corp. office, 1973—. Pres. Sts. Peter and Paul Sch. Bd., Merrillville, 1980-81, Junedale Little League, Gary, 1975-76; mem. Andrean Found., Merrillville; bd. dirs. Respite Care Services for Handicapped. Mem. Lake County Pharmacy Assn. (pres. 1967-68, treas. 1964-66), Ind. Pharmacy Assn., Northwest Ind. Bus. Group Health, Butler U. Pres. Club, Phi Delta Chi. Democrat. Roman Catholic. Lodges: Elks, Italian Benevolent Soc. Avocations: Sports, racquetball. Home: 2800 W 55th Ave Merrillville IN 46410 Office: Ribordy Drugs Inc PO Box 432 730 W US Hwy 30 Valparaiso IN 46410

ALLEN, ALTON PATRICK, business administration educator; b. Alma, Mich., May 1, 1950; s. Alton Junior and Marion Lucille (Keisser) A.; m. Martha Sue Harris, June 2, 1973. A.B. in Psychology, Olivet Nazarene Coll., 1973; M.A. in Liberal Arts, So. Meth. U., 1978; M.S. in Mgmt., Bethany Nazarene Coll., 1980; postgrad. U. Okla., 1981—. Asst. v.p. Commerce Bank of Blue Hills, Kansas City, Mo., 1973-76; asst. dean students Mid-Am. Nazarene Coll., Olathe, Kans., 1976-78; Title III coordinator Bethany Nazarene Coll., Okla., 1978-82; chmn. div. bus. Friends U., Wichita, Kans., 1982—; external evaluator and cons. Bethany Nazarene Coll., 1982—. Mem. Am. Mgmt. Assn., Acad. Mgmt., Am. Assn. Higher Edn., Wichita C. of C. (instr. leadership 2000, 1984). Mem. Ch. of Nazarene. Avocations: collecting etchings; golfing. Home: 9004 Harvest Ln Wichita KS 67212 Office: Friends U 2100 University Wichita KS 67213

ALLEN, BELLE, management consultant, communications company executive, b. Chgo.; d. Isaac and Clara (Friedman) A. Ed., U. Chgo. Cons. v.p., treas., dir. William Karp Cons. Co., Inc., Chgo., 1961-79, chmn. bd., pres., treas., 1979—; pres. Belle Allen Communications, 1961—; v.p., treas., dir. Cultural Arts Surveys Inc., Chgo., 1965-79; cons., dir. Am. Diversified Research Corp., Chgo., 1967-70; v.p., sec. dir. Mgmt. Performance Systems, Inc., 1976-77; cons. City Club Chgo., 1962-65, Ill. Commn. on Tech Progress, 1965-67. Editor, contbr. Operations Research and the Management of Mental Health Systems, 1968; editor The Bulletin, 1981; editor, contbr. articles to profl. jours. Mem. Ill. Gov.'s Grievance Panel for State Employees, 1979—, Ill. Dept. Transp. Grievance Panel, 1985—; mem. adv. governing bd. Ill. Coalition on Employment of Women, 1980—; spl. program advisor Pres.'s Project Partnership, 1980—. Recipient Outstanding Service award United Cerebral Palsy Assn., Chgo., 1954, 55, Communications Program award The White House, 1961; Am. Bicentennial Research Inst. award Library of Human Resources, 1973, Cert. of Appreciation, Ill. Dept. Human Rights, 1985. Mem. Affirmative Action Assn. (bd. dirs. 1981—, chmn. membership and program coms., 1981—, pres., 1983—), Fashion Group (bd. dirs. 1981-83, chmn. Retrospective View of An Historical Decade 1960-70), Indsl. Relations Research Assn. (bd. dirs. chmn. personnel placement com. 1960-61), AAAS, NOW, Sarah Siddons Soc., Soc. Personnel Adminstrs., Womens Equity Action League, Nat. Assn. Inter-Group Relations Ofcls. (nat. conf. program 1959), Publicity Club of Chgo. (chmn. inter-city relations com. 1960-61, Disting. Service award 1968). Club: Chgo. Press (chmn. women's activities 1969-71). Office: 111 E Chestnut St Chicago IL 60611

ALLEN, BEM PRICE, JR., psychology educator; b. Vincennes, Ind., June 4, 1940; s. Bem Price and Margaret (Price) A.; m. Paula Margaret Stratton; children—Margaret Elizabeth, Kathleen Suzanne, Bem Price. B.S., U. Houston, 1963, M.A., 1966, Ph.D., 1969. Prof. Western Ill. U., Macomb, 1968—. Neighborhood coordinator Am. Cancer Soc.; active ERA. NIMH grantee, 1970. Mem. Am. Psychol. Assn., Midwestern Psychol. Assn., Psychology and Law Soc., Psychonomic Soc., Sigma Xi (local Researcher of Yr. award 1976), Sigma Nu. Author: Social Behavior, 1978; Adjective Generation Technique, 1983; also articles. Home: 499 S Madison St Macomb IL 61455 Office: Western Ill U Psychology Dept Macomb IL 61455

ALLEN, C. EUGENE, college dean, agriculture educator; b. Burley, Idaho, Jan. 25, 1939; s. Charles W. and Elsie P. (Fowler) A.; m. Connie J. Block, June 19, 1960; children—Kerry J., Tamara S. B.S. in Agr., U. Idaho, 1961; M.S., U. Wis.-Madison, 1963, Ph.D., 1965. Postdoctoral fellow NSF, Sydney, Australia, 1966-67; asst. prof. U. Minn., St. Paul, 1967-69, assoc. prof., 1969-72, prof., 1972—, dean, coll. agr., 1984—; cons. in field. Contbr. articles to profl. jours. Recipient Morse-Amoco All-Univ. Outstanding Teaching award U. Minn., 1984; Disting. Tchr. award U. Minn. Coll. Agr., 1984. Mem. Am. Soc. Animal Sci. (Meat Sci. Research award 1977), Am. Inst. Nutrition, Inst. Food. Tech., Am. Meat Sci. Assn. (Disting. Meats Research award 1980). Avocations: photography; skiing; bowling; outdoor sports; reading. Office: 277 Coffey Hall Coll of Agr U Minn Saint Paul MN 55108

ALLEN, CHARLES RICHARD, financial exec.; b. Cleve., Mar. 10, 1926; s. Charles Ross and Jennie (Harmon) A.; student Occidental Coll., 1942-43; B.S., UCLA, 1945; m. Marion Elizabeth Taylor, Aug. 17, 1946; children—Kathleen Allen Templin, Jeanne Allen Duffy, Kenneth. Acctg. supr. N.Am. Aviation, Inc., Los Angeles, 1946-55; div. controller TRW, Inc., Los Angeles, 1955-61, dir. finance, 1961-64, asso. controller, Cleve., 1964-66, controller, 1966-67, v.p., 1967-77, exec. v.p., 1977—, chief financial officer, 1967—, also dir.; adv. New Court Partners, N.Y.C. Trustee John Carroll U. Served with USNR, 1943-46. Mem. Financial Execs. Inst., Am. Finance Assn., Greater Cleve. Growth Assn., Inst. of Dirs. (London). Clubs: Shaker Heights Country, Union, Pepper Pike (Cleve.); Wall Street (N.Y.C.). Office: TRW Inc 1900 Richmond Rd Cleveland OH 44124

ALLEN, CONSTANCE JANE, lawyer; b. Grand Rapids, Mich., Feb. 19, 1954; d. James Pershing and Emily (Just) A. B.A., Kalamazoo Coll., 1976; J.D., Wayne State U., 1979. Bars: Mich. 1979, U.S. Dist. Ct. (ea. dist.) Mich. 1979, Ill. 1980, U.S. Ct. Appeals (9th cir.) 1982, U.S. Tax Ct. 1983. Assoc. Colista, Green & Adams, Detroit, 1979-82, Colista, Urso & Green, Detroit, 1982-83, Colista & Urso, Detroit, 1983—. Cooperating atty. ACLU, Detroit, 1984. Mem. Women Lawyers Assn. (program. chmn. Wayne sect. 1982-83, recording sec. 1983-84, regional dir. 1984-85). Roman Catholic. Office: Colista and Urso 407 E Fort St 5th Floor Detroit MI 48226

ALLEN, DANIEL LEE, computer management firm executive; b. Zanesville, Ohio, Sept. 14, 1955; s. Loren D. and Ruth Ann (Biery) A.; m. Linda C. Koehler, June 4, 1983; 1 child, Timothy D. B.S.B.A., Bowling Green State U., 1977; postgrad. studies in computer mgmt., acctg., Franklin U., 1983—. Savs. officer State Savs. Bank, Columbus, Ohio, 1981-83; computer programmer CoDaSci, Columbus, 1983—. Served to capt. U.S. Army, 1977-81; Korea; now capt. Ohio Army N.G. Army ROTC scholar Bowling Green State U., 1975; Franklin U. upperclass scholar, 1984. Decorated Meritorious Service medal, 1981. Mem. Assn. for Systems Mgmt. (treas. Franklin U. chpt. 1984—), Sigma Nu (v.p., pres. Bowling Green chpt. 1973-77). Mem. United Ch. of Christ. Avocations: golf; softball; fishing. Home: 3780 Rutledge Dr Hilliard OH 43026 Office: CoDaSci 6800 Lauffer Columbus OH 43229

ALLEN, DELMAS JAMES, anatomist; b. Hartsville, S.C., Aug. 13, 1937; s. James Paul and Sara (Segars) A.; B.S. in Biology, Am. U. of Beirut, Lebanon, 1965, M.S., 1967; postgrad. Med. Coll. Ga., 1968; cert. in Radiation Sci., Colo. State U., 1969; Ph.D., U. N.D., 1974; m. Sarah Bahous, July 5, 1958; children—Carolyn, James, Susan. Teaching fellow dept. biology Am. U. Beirut, 1965-67; instr. dept. biology Clarke Coll., Dubuque, Iowa, 1968-69, asst. prof., 1969-72, chmn. dept. biology, 1969-72; grad. teaching fellow and research asst. U. N.D., Grand Forks, 1972-74; asst. prof. dept. anatomy U. South Ala., Mobile, 1974-75; asst. prof. dept. anatomy Med. Coll. Ohio, Toledo, 1975-77, assoc. prof., 1977-82, prof., 1982—; asst. dean Grad. Sch., 1979—; vis. prof., Brazil, 1980, Ryad U. Sch. Medicine, Saudi Arabia, 1981. Recipient A. Rodger Denison award N.D. Acad. Sci., 1973; Ala. Heart Assn. grantee, 1974-75, Am. Cancer Soc. grantee, 1977, Am. Heart Assn. grantee, 1977-80; geriatrics-gerontology grantee, 1980-81; recipient Golden Apple award for Excellence in Teaching, Med. Coll. Ohio, 1977, 78, 79, 80, 82; research award Brazilian Acad. Sci., 1980, Northwestern Ohio Electron Microscopic Soc., 1980; Faculty Recognition award Med. Coll. Ohio, 1983. Fellow Ohio Acad. Sci. (membership chmn. med. sci. sect. 1977-78, v.p. med. sect. 1978-79); mem. Soc. for Neurosci., Am. Assn. Anatomists, So. Soc. Anatomists, Am. Soc. Cell Biology, Midwest Assn. Anatomists, Pan Am. Soc. Anatomy, N.Y. Acad. Scis., Am. Heart Assn., European Brain and Behavior Soc. (hon. mem.), Brit. Brain Research Assn. (hon. mem.), Sigma Xi (Thesis Excellence award 1967, Award of Merit 1974, pres. Med. Coll. Ohio club 1978-79). Contbr. articles on neuroanatomy and electron microscopy to sci. jours.; editor: Three-Dimensional Microanatomy; contbr. chpts. in field to various textbooks; co-author neurosci. text. Home: 2243 Robinwood St Toledo OH 43620 Office: Dept Anatomy Med Coll Ohio C S 10008 Toledo OH 43699

ALLEN, DONALD RAY, physician; b. Evansville, Ind., Dec. 6, 1932; s. William Delmar and Mildred Adelaide (Ashworth) A.; A.B. cum laude, U. Evansville, 1957; M.D., Ind. U., 1960. Intern, Marion County Gen. Hosp., Indpls., 1960-61; resident VA Hosp., Louisville, 1963, St. Louis City Hosp., 1964, Washington U. Barnes Hosp., St. Louis, 1965; practice medicine specializing in family practice, Evansville. Diplomate Am. Bd. Family Practice. Fellow Am. Acad. Family Physicians; mem. AMA, Ind. Med. Assn., Vanderburgh County Med. Soc., Alpha Omega Alpha, Phi Chi. Office: VA Outpatient Clinic Evansville IN 47708

ALLEN, ERNIE ALBERT, JR., chemical company executive; b. Decatur, Ill., Jan. 16, 1950; s. Ernie Albert and Luise Hefner A.; B.S. in Fin.-Acctg., So. Ill. U., Carbondale, 1972; m. Lynda Ishee, Dec. 1, 1972; children—Christina, Carla, Eric. Jr. acct. Kaiser Agrl. Chems., Inc., Sullivan, Ill., 1972-76, acct. supr. III, 1976-77, regional acctg. mgr., 1978, regional controller, 1978-85, adminstrv. mgr., 1985—. Bd. dirs. United Way Moultrie County, 1980—; pres. citizens adv. council Sullivan High Sch., 1983-84. Mem. So. Ill. U. Alumni Assn., Beta Alpha Psi. Democrat. Methodist. Clubs: Am. Business (v.p. 1979-80, pres.-elect 1980-81, pres. 1981-82), Sno-n-Go Snowmobile. Home: 19 Corey Ave Sullivan IL 61951 Office: Kaiser Agrl Chems Inc 101 W Jefferson St Sullivan IL 61951

ALLEN, EUGENE, JR., mfg. co. exec.; b. Chgo., Nov. 7, 1937; s. Eugene and Pearl (Smith) A.; B.S., Ill. Inst. Tech., 1970; M.B.A., U. Chgo., 1976; m. Ledell Fields, Apr. 16, 1961; children—Sheryl, Karla, Nicole, Eugene M. Chemist, formulator and paint technologist Sherwin-Williams Co., 1963-67; materials engr. Libby, McNeill & Libby, 1967-69; prodn. supr., div. sales mgr. Avon Products Inc., 1969-74; exec. trainee, ops. mgr. Jewel Cos. Inc., Chgo., 1974-75; v.p. mktg. and sales Valeer Industries Inc., Mundelein, Ill., 1975-76; sr. v.p., dir. mktg. and sales HUB States Corp., Indpls., 1976-79; pres., chief operating officer Clinitemp, Inc., Indpls., 1979-81; pres., chief exec. officer Aquamint Labs., Inc., Indpls., 1981—. Pres., Stoney Island Heights Civic Assn., Chgo., 1968-70; bd. dirs. Ivy Hill Civic Assn., Arlington Heights, Ill., 1972-76, Youth for Christ, Indpls.; adv. bd. Lawrence Twp. Sch. Dist., Ind., 1977-78; mem. Dist. Export Council for Ind., 1979—. Served with U.S. Army, 1961-63. Recipient Paint Technologist award Nat. Paint Industry Ednl. Bur., 1966. Club: Exec. Program (U. Chgo.). Home: 7527 N Cape Cod Ln Indianapolis IN 46250 Office: 6256 La Pas Trail Indianapolis IN 46268

ALLEN, FLORENCE BROTHERTON, cosmetic company executive; b. Detroit, Apr. 19, 1918; d. Norton T. and Mary (Kleinow) Brotherton; B. in Design, U. Mich., 1940; postgrad. Chgo. Sch. Design, 1940-41, Eastern Mich. U., 1969-70; m. Arthur W. Allen, Dec. 27, 1940 (dec.); children—Arthur W., David, Barbara (dec.). Asst., Archtl. and Design Library, U. Mich., Ann Arbor, 1969-71; beauty cons. Mary Kay Cosmetics, Ann Arbor, 1971-73, sales dir. mktg. mgmt., 1973-74, sr. sales dir., 1974—; paintings shown at U. Mich.

Sch. Architecture, 1970. Recipient Cadillac car award Mary Kay Cosmetics, 1977, 79, 82; named to $250,000 Club, 1980. Mem. U. Mich. Alumni Assn., Internat. Assn. Sales and Mktg. Execs., Ann Arbor C. of C., Women Painters, Washtenaw County Med. Aux. (v.p. 1970), St. Joseph Mercy Hosp. Aux. (co-founder 1946-47). Founders Soc. Detroit Inst. of Arts, Friends of the Mus. Ann Arbor, Kappa Kappa Gamma. Republican. Presbyterian. Clubs: Women's City, Faculty Women's. Address: 895 Greenhills Dr Ann Arbor MI 48105

ALLEN, GEORGE WHITAKER, physician, educator; b. Milledgeville, Ga., Feb. 8, 1928; s. Henry Dawson and Caroline (Reynolds) A.; m. Lis Margaret Jensen, Oct. 1, 1951 (div. 1973); 1 son, John Whitaker; m. 2d., Janice Alene Mandabach, Apr. 26, 1980. A.B., Harvard U., 1948; M.D., Columbia U., 1952. Diplomate Am. Bd. Otolaryngology. Intern, Presbyn. Hosp., N.Y.C., 1952-53; Jr. asst. resident in otolaryngology U. Chgo. Clinics, 1955-56, sr. asst. resident, 1956-57, resident, 1957-58, NIH spl. trainee, 1958-59; instr. dept. otolaryngology Northwestern U. Med. Sch., Chgo., 1959-60, asst. prof., 1961-64, assoc. prof., 1964—, dir. teaching and research, 1959-63, acting chmn. dept. otolaryngology, 1964-67; sole practice otolaryngology, Chgo., 1967—; attending physician Northwestern Meml. Hosp., Chgo., 1959—; attending physician in surgery Children's Meml. Hosp., Chgo., 1979—; attending physician Henrotin Hosp., Chgo., 1981—; vis. prof. U. Colo. Med. Sch., 1965; vis. prof. Emory U. Med. Sch., 1967; cons. Nat. Ctr. for Devices and Radiol. Health, FDA, 1983—. Served to 1st lt. M.C., U.S. Army, 1953-55. Recipient research award Am. Acad. Otolaryngology, 1960. Mem. AMA, Ill. Med. Soc., Chgo. Med. Soc., Chgo. Laryngological and Otological Soc., ACS, Pan Am. Med. Assn., Triological Soc., Inst. Medicine Chgo., Am. Acad. Facial Plastic and Reconstructive Surgery, Am. Council of Otolaryngology, Nu Sigma Nu, Alpha Omega Alpha, Sigma Xi. Republican. Methodist. Club: Carlton (Chgo.). Contbr. articles to med. jours.; mem. editorial bd. Archives of Otolaryngology, 1960-69; co-author: (movie) Carcinoma of the Tonsil, 1960. Office: 150 E Huron St Suite 801 Chicago IL 60611

ALLEN, GERALD CAMPBELL FORREST, management consulting company executive; b. Boston, Nov. 1, 1923; s. Charles Francis and Sarah Ann (Campbell) A.; m. Anne Elisabeth Conrad, May 23, 1944; children—Katherine Sarah Anne, Ethan William John Campbell, Elisabeth Amy Martha Joan. Student Harvard U., 1945-49, U. Chgo., 1950-52. Ordained to Ministry Unitarian Ch., 1978. Ency. editor Consol. Book Pub., Chgo., 1952-54; advt. exec. Chgo. Tribune, 1954-59; pres. Gerald Allen Co., Chgo., 1960-66; v.p. Klau-Van Pietersom-Dunlap, Inc., Milw., 1967-71; v.p., dir. Unidex Pub. Co. Inc., Milw., 1971-80; chmn., chief exec. officer Allen Mgmt. Group, Inc., Milw., 1980—; pres. Psychologists in Advt., Chgo., 1965; instr. mktg. U. Wis., 1967-68; v.p., dir. Benchmark Mfg. Co., Inc., Milw. Mem. Ad Hoc Low Income Energy Task Force, State of Wis.; mem. Energy Crisis Planning Com., City of Wis. Served with Royal Arty., 1944-45, ETO. Fellow Royal Hort. Soc.; mem. Am. Mktg. Assn., Am. Statis. Assn., AAAS, Am. Econ. Assn. Republican. Clubs: Harvard of Wis., Harvard of Chgo. Home: 712 Knapp Milwaukee WI 53202 Office: Allen Mgmt Group Inc 700 Knapp Milwaukee WI 53202

ALLEN, HAROLD LEROY, biology educator, dean, researcher; b. Bloomington, Ill., Nov. 8, 1940; s. Ferrell Wilbur and Leota Zella (Fisher) A.; m. Carin Maria Lindblad, June 4, 1966; children—Morgan Stewart, Jayson Clark. B.S. in Natural Sci., Redlands U., 1962; F.K. in Natural Sci., Uppsala U., Sweden, 1966; M.S. in Botany and Plant Pathology, Mich. State U., 1967, Ph.D. in Botany and Plant Pathology, 1969. Asst. prof. biol. scis. Dartmouth Coll., Hanover, N.H., 1970-74; dir. environ. scis. program Nat. Commn. Water Quality, Washington, 1974-76; asst. dean grad. sch., prof. biology U. Toledo, 1976-78, acting dean, dir. research, 1978-79, dean grad. sch., 1979—; research project dir. NSF, 1972-74, Smithsonian Instn., 1972-84; cons., 1974-76. Contbr. articles to profl jours. Council mem. Youth Services Coordinating Council, 1977-82; trustee arts Commn. Greater Toledo, 1984—. Recipient Research Devel. award Smithsonian Inst., 1971, 1977; fellow Swedish-Am. Found., 1962-63, 1964; recipient numerous grants for research. Mem. Am. Soc. Limnology and Oceanography, Ecol. Soc. Am., Freshwater Biol. Assn., Internat. Assn. Theoretical and Applied Limnology, Assn. Aquatic Vascular Plant Biologists, Ohio Acad. Scis., Sigma Xi. Democrat. Protestant. Avocation; restoration of antique automobiles. Office: The Grad Sch U Toledo 2801 Bancroft St Toledo OH 43606

ALLEN, HENRY SERMONES, JR., lawyer; b. Bronxville, N.Y., Aug. 26, 1947; s. Henry S. and Cecelia Marie (Chartrand) A.; A.B. magna cum laude, Washington U., St. Louis, 1969; M.P.A., Cornell U., 1973, J.D., 1974; m. Louann Beckman, June 25, 1976; children—David Beckman, Amy Louise. Adminstrv. resident Montefiore Hosp. and Med. Center, Bronx, N.Y., 1971; research trainee Nat. Center Health Services Research, HEW, 1974-75; admitted to Ill. bar, 1974; adj. asst. prof. hosp. law Ithaca (N.Y.) Coll., 1974-75; lectr., adj. asst. prof. health services adminstrn. and law Sangamon State U., Springfield, Ill., 1975-82; adj. asst. prof. hosp. law Coll. of St. Francis, Joliet, Ill., 1980-81; asso. firm Vedder, Price, Kaufman & Kammholz, Chgo., 1975-79; ind. practice law, health care cons., Chgo. and Springfield, 1979-81; partner firm Allen & Reed, Chgo., 1981—; lectr. in field. Bd. dirs. Dr. Deepak K. Merchant Found. HUD fellow, 1969-71. Mem. Am. Soc. Hosp. Attys., Am. Acad. Hosp. Attys., Ill. Soc. Hosp. Attys., Nat. Health Lawyers Assn., Phi Beta Kappa, Omicron Delta Epsilon. Club: Cornell U. of Chgo. Home: 10421 S Longwood Dr Chicago IL 60643 Office: 208 S LaSalle St Suite 1873 Chicago IL 60603

ALLEN, HERBERT JOSEPH, social worker; b. Jersey City, May 19, 1922; s. Benjamin James and Jeanetta Gladys (Casey) A.; B.S. in Edn., U. Cin., 1946; M.S. in Social Work, Case Western Res. U., 1948; m. Gwen Cann, July 26, 1949 (div.); 1 dau., Deborah Allen Kane. Dir. social work dept. Barney Children's Med. Center, Dayton, Ohio, 1967; supr. Family and Children's Service, Dayton, 1968; dir. social work dept. Good Samaritan Hosp., Dayton, 1968; field service asso. prof., dir. social work dept. Cin. Gen. Hosp.-U. Cin. Med. Center, 1970—; adj. asst. prof. Thomas More Coll., Ft. Mitchell, Ky., 1978; field service asso. prof. Coll. Community Services, U. Cin., 1979; adj. asso. prof., dir. dept. social work U. Cin. Pres., Central Community Health Bd. Catchment Area 11, 1976, Mt. Auburn Health Center, 1977; lectr. Am. Hosp. Assn., Soc. for Dirs. Hosp. Social Work Depts. Served with U.S. Army, 1942-46. Named Cin. Social Worker of Year, Social Service Assn. Greater Cin., 1952, Nat. Assn. Black Social Workers, 1973; award Pride mag., Cin., 1979. Mem. Soc. Dirs. Hosp. Social Work Depts., Am. Hosp. Assn. (dir. 1975-77, v.p. personal membership com. 1984-85), Soc. Hosp. Social Work Dirs. (pres.-elect 1982), Ohio Hosp. Assn. (pres. 1982-83), Kappa Alpha Psi. Democrat. Roman Catholic. Home: 144 Dorsey St Cincinnati OH 45210 Office: Univ Hosp U Cin Med Center 234 Goodman St Cincinnati OH 45229

ALLEN, JAMES ALVIN, SR., safety supervisor; b. Camp Hill, Ala., Apr. 9, 1934; s. Forest and Alva (Vines) A.; m. Audrey Burris, Apr. 13, 1958; children—James Alvin, Tamra Denise. B.S., Tuskegee Inst., 1958; M.Ed., S.C. State Coll., 1969; M.B.A., Western Mich. U., 1980. Tech. specialist Uniroyal, Inc., 1967-68, quality control supr., 1968-69, acting supt. texturizing, 1968-69; asst. plant supt. Coca-Cola U.S.A., 1970-74; processing shift supr. infant formula Ross Labs/Abbott Labs., Sturgis, Mich., 1974-81, safety supr., 1981—. Bd. dirs. St. Joseph County Substance Abuse Council, 1982—; trustee Sturgis (Mich.) Bd. Edn. Served to capt. inf., U.S. Army, 1959-65. Mem. Am. Soc. Safety Engrs., Am. Chem. Soc., Internat. Platform Assn., Assn. MBA Execs. Republican. Mem. African Methodist Ch. Clubs: Nat. Exchange, Masons. Home: 316 S Clay St PO Box 372 Sturgis MI 49091 Office: 700 W Lafayette St Sturgis MI 49091

ALLEN, JAMES CURTIS, manufacturing company executive; b. Winston, Mo., June 7, 1922; s. Vernon and Carrie Belle (Palmer) A.; grad. Chillicothe Bus. Coll., (Mo.), 1942, Internat. Corr. Schs., 1946; m. Juanita G. Kennedy, Dec. 4, 1944; children—Daryl C., Karen A., Marti L., Jimmie, Randy. Accountant, Nat. Bellas Hess, Kansas City, Mo., 1946-48; controller Lawn-Boy div. Outboard Marine Corp., Lamar, Mo., 1948-63; sec.-treas. EFCO Corp., Monett, Mo., 1963-66; co-owner, sec-treas. F.M. Thorpe Mfg. Co., Lamar, Mo., 1966-84; pres. Allen Investments, 1984—; dir. Barton County State Bank. Pres., United Fund, 1970-71; pres. Community Betterment, 1968-70; dist. chmn. Sowemco council Boy Scouts Am., 1964-66, Arrowhead council, 1972 Big 3 dist., 1982-83, v.p. Mo-Kans Area council, 1975-79; mem. Lamar Sch. Bd., 1969-71; mem. Lamar Park Bd., 1955—, pres., 1973-84. Served with USNR, 1942-45. Recipient Outstanding Leadership award Mo. Municipal League, 1971; Distinguished Service award Kiwanis Club Monett, Mo., 1965; Leadership award Mo. Community Betterment, 1970; Golden Sun Silver Beaver, Order Arrow awards Boy Scouts Am. chpt. farmer award Future Farmers Am., 1979; Boss of Yr. award Am. Bus. Womens Assn., 1980. Mem. Lamar C. of C. (Person of Yr. 1981), Mo. C. of C. Methodist (chmn. bd. 1971, del. conf. 1968-71, treas. 1966—, supt. 1955-63). Mason (Shriner), Rotarian (pres. 1971-72, Man of Yr. award 1979, Paul Harris award), Kiwanian (pres. 1968). Home: 400 W 1st St Lamar MO 64759 Office: 1801 Gulf St Lamar MO 64759

ALLEN, J(OHN) MICHAEL, dentist; b. Aurora, Nebr., Jan. 21, 1951; s. John Martin and Pamela Mary (Tudor) A.; m. Glenda Lee Herron, Aug. 19, 1973. D.D.S., U. Nebr., 1976. Gen. practice dentistry Aurora Dental Clinic, P.C., 1976—. Mem. council Federated Ch. of Aurora, 1977-83, chmn., 1979-82; mem. Aurora Planning Commn., 1980—, chmn., 1982-83; chmn. drug abuse com. Nebr. dist. Optimists Internat. Mem. Central Nebr. Dental Soc. (pres. 1985—), Nebr. Dental Assn. (del. 1979—, polit. action com. 1981—), ADA, Am. Soc. Dentistry for Children, Econ. Assn. Health Profls., U.S. Tennis Assn., Am. Assn. Functional Orthodontists, Am. Profl. Practice Assn., Aircraft Owners and Pilots Assn. Republican. Mem. United Ch. of Christ. Club: Optimists (pres. Aurora 1982-83, lt. gov. Nebr. 1983-84). Office: 1219 N St Aurora NE 68818

ALLEN, JOHN TREVETT, JR., lawyer; b. Evanston, Ill., Apr. 9, 1939; s. John Trevett and Eleanor Rose (Hatfield) A.; m. Marguerite DeHuszar, Jan. 18, 1969; children—John Trevett, Samuel DeHuszar. A.B., Williams Coll., 1961; LL.B., Harvard U., 1964; postgrad. Central U. Ecuador, Quito, 1964-65. Bar: Ill. 1964. Assoc., Goodrich, Dalton, Little & Riquelme, Mexico City, 1962, Graham, James & Rolph, San Francisco, 1963; assoc. MacLeish, Spray, Price & Underwood, Chgo., 1963-71, ptnr., 1973-80; gen. atty. U.S. Gypsum Co., Chgo., 1971-73; ptnr. McBride, Baker & Coles, Chgo., 1980—. Alderman City of Evanston, 1977-81; governing mem. Orchestral Assn. Chgo., 1980—; pres. Internat. Bus. Council MidAm., 1982—; vice chmn. Ill. Export Council, 1984—. Fulbright scholar, 1964-65. Mem. ABA, Ill. Bar Assn., Chgo. Bar Assn., Vermilion County Bar Assn., Legal Club Chgo., Law Club Chgo. Republican. Presbyterian. Clubs: Union League, Mid Day (Chgo.). Office: Three 1st National Plaza Suite 3800 Chicago IL 60602

ALLEN, JULIUS OLU, alcoholism and mental health counselor; b. Cape Coast, Ghana, Feb. 6, 1930; came to U.S., 1962, naturalized, 1970; s. James Akerele and Dorcas Ade (Ejide) Ale; B.A. with high honors, Lewis U., Lockport, Ill., 1975; diploma Chgo. Counseling Center, 1978; M.A., Internat. U., 1979; m. Prudence Addy, Jan. 20, 1957; children—Coni, Moumi, Rotimi, Sonya, Aku. Lic. ins. broker, 1965-75; counselor, dir. drug abuse and prevention program Garfield Counseling Center, Chgo., 1977—; counselor Northwestern Meml. Hosp., 1977-80, Volta House Corp., 1980-83, Spiegel Inc., 1983—; vol. Peoples Community Outreach Mission. Recipient Citizen's award Chgo. Police Dept., 1978. Mem. Am. Assn. Mental Deficiency, Center Counseling and Psychotherapy, Afro-Am. Corrections Officers Movement (pres.). Mormon. Club: Human Growth Book; editor Shegun 1975. Research on mentally health persons, better prison systems. Home: 4028 S King Dr Chicago IL 60653

ALLEN, LAURENCE GEORGE, real estate appraiser; b. Idaho Falls, Idaho, May 17, 1950; s. George Henry and Lois L. (Fisher) A.; m. Charmaine Sanders, May 30, 1971 (div. 1975); m. Susan Marie Connor, Apr. 1, 1977; 1 child, Jeremy. B.A. cum laude with honors, Linfield Coll., 1972; M.B.A., U. Mich., 1982. Lic. real estate broker/appraiser, Mich. Real estate appraiser Dean Appraisal Co., Detroit, 1973—, v.p., 1980—. Contbr. articles to Appraisal Jour., 1976-83, articles to Right of Way Mag. (Outstanding Article award 1984), 1984. Dir. Oakland County Republican Precinct, 1981-82. Mem. Am. Inst. Real Estate Appraisers (sec. Mich. chpt. 1984), Am. Soc. Appraisers (pres. Detroit chpt. 1981-82), Inst. Chartered Fin. Analysts. Methodist. Lodges: Shriners, Masons. Avocation: owner and operator Macrobiotics Activity Ctr. of Mich., a nonprofit nutritional ednl. orgn. Home: 2300 W Maple Rd Birmingham MI 48009 Office: Dean Appraisal Co 1019 Haynes Birmingham MI 48008

ALLEN, LOIS ARLENE HEIGHT (MRS. JAMES PIERPONT ALLEN), musician; b. Kenton, Ohio, Sept. 2, 1932; d. Robert Harold and Frances (Sims) Height; B.S., Ohio State U., 1954, M.A., 1958; m. James Pierpont Allen, June 14, 1953; children—Daniel Pierpont, Carole Elizabeth. Tchr. jr. and sr. high music, Upper Arlington High Sch., Columbus, O., 1954-56; high sch. music supr., Westerville, Ohio, 1956-67; tchr. music Ohio State U. Sch., 1957-59; pvt. tchr. music, Columbus, 1960—; exec. dir. Battelle Scholars Program Trust Fund, 1983—; ch. organist, choir dir. Mountview Bapt. Ch., Upper Arlington, Ohio, 1960-77; ednl. radio interviewer WOSU, 1970, 71, 72. Mem. Project Hope, Central Ohio, 1967-73; mem. sustaining bd. Maryhaven House for Alcoholic Women, 1969-73, 1st v.p.; mem. women's bd. Columbus Symphony, 1965-79, chmn. youth council, 1965-68, pres.-elect women's assn., 1973, pres., 1974-76; chmn. juried art competition Central Ohio Arts Festival, 1969, 70, chmn. fine and applied arts, 1971, gen. chmn. of festival, 1972; area chmn. United Appeals Franklin County, 1966-68, Heart drive, 1968-85; pres. Ohio State U. Soc. Friends Sch. Music, 1977-78; trustee Columbus Symphony Orch., 1973-81, Opera/Columbus, 1981-85; mem. vol. council Am. Symphony Orch. League, 1981—, v.p., 1983-84; organist, choir dir. North Congregational Ch., 1979-85; area leader Republican party, 1966-68; mem. Mayor's Award Council Com., 1981-84. Mem. Am. Guild Organists, Choristers Guild Am., Fedn. Am. Bapt. Musicians, Center Sci. and Industry, Ohio State Hist. Soc., Ohio Orgn. Orchs. (treas. 1976-79, sec. 1979—), Nat. Trust U.S.A., Tau Beta Sigma, Delta Omicron, Kappa Delta (Central Ohio Woman of Yr. 1970). Mem. Order Eastern Star, White Shrine of Jerusalem. Clubs: Ohio State U. Alumnae of Franklin County (pres. 1962-64, 71-72). Home: 3355 Somerford Rd Columbus OH 43221

ALLEN, MARGERY ANNE, social service agency executive; b. Medford, Wis., Nov. 20, 1938; d. Joseph James and Johanna (Lewandowski) Kalmon; m. Richard G. Allen, Feb. 7, 1959; children—Christine, Jessica, Natalie. Student Layton Art Sch., 1956-57, Winona State U., 1976-80. Co-owner, mgr. Snoop Shop, Rochville, Md., 1972-76; exec. dir. SEMCO, Rochester, Minn., 1977-80, Channel One, Inc., 1980—. Mem. Mayors Adv. Com. on Hunger, 1984—; mem. Senator Boschwitz Adv. Com. on Aging, Mpls., 1983—; trainer of trainers State of Minn., 1985—. Mem. Minn. Gerontol. Soc. Avocations: painting; reading; cooking; travel. Office: Channel One Inc 525 6th Ave NW Rochester MN 55901

ALLEN, MARION CARROLL, clergyman; b. Spartanburg, S.C., Dec. 12, 1914; s. Albert Mayfield and Caroline May (Rogers) A.; B.A., Furman U., 1937; M.Div., Yale, 1940; M.A., Kans. U., 1960; m. Eleanor Earl Burt, July 31, 1943; children—Marian, Burt, Robert, Louise. Ordained to ministry Am. Bapt. Conv., 1940, received into United Ch. of Christ; pastor Bapt. chs., Bristol, Conn., 1940-47, Beaufort, S.C., 1947-50, Clemson, S.C., 1950-56, Lawrence, Kans., 1956-76; pastor First Congregational Ch., Topeka, 1976, Central Congregational Ch., 1977-80, Pilgrim Congregational Ch., Wichita, Kans., 1980—; instr. religion Clemson U., 1951-56, instr. homiletics Central Sem., Kansas City, Kans., 1959-61, English, Kans. U., 1958, 76—. Bd. dirs. YMCA, U. Kans., 1956-60; v.p. Lawrence Friends of Music, 1968-75; sec. adv. bd. Kans. Sch. Religion, 1970-76. Mem. Topeka Ministerial Alliance, Lawrence Ministerial Alliancce, Topeka Council Chs., Consultation of Cooperating Chs. Kans., Kans. Okla. Conf. United Ch. of Christ. Clubs: Masons. Author: A Voice Not Our Own, 1963. Editor: The Springs of Learning, 1969. Editor: Serving in the Armed Forces, monthly 1972-74. Home: 3508 Riverview Rd Lawrence KS 66044

ALLEN, MICHAEL WAKEFIELD, educational psychologist; b. Hampton, Iowa, June 6, 1946; s. Eugene Richard and Wilma Mary (Wakefield) A.; B.A., Cornell Coll., 1968; M.A., Ohio State U., 1969, Ph.D., 1971; m. Mary Ann Hoel, Oct. 23, 1976; 1 son, Christopher Wakefield. Dir. research and devel. in computer assisted instrn. Ohio State U., 1970-73; sr. cons. advanced ednl. systems Control Data Corp., Mpls., 1974-78, prin. cons., 1979-80, exec. dir. advanced ednl. systems research and devel., 1980—; mem. faculty dept. curriculum and instructional systems U. Minn., 1981—; pres. Authorware, Inc., 1985—. Mem. Assn. for Devel. of Computer-Based Instructional Systems (pres. 1980-83), Am. Ednl. Research Assn., Am. Assn. Artificial Intelligence, Assn. for Intelligence Stimulation and Behavior Modeling. Methodist. Founding editor Jour. Computer Based Instrn., 1975-79, mem. editorial rev. bd., 1980—. Home: 8621 Pine Hill Rd Bloomington MN 55438 Office: Control Data Corp HQ S05J Box O Minneapolis MN 55440

ALLEN, MILTON NICHOLAS, computer company executive; b. N.Y.C., Apr. 15, 1927; s. Nicholas Demetrius and Adele (Fortune) A.; m. Barbara Scarlett, Feb. 21, 1954 (div. Dec. 1981); children—Peter M., Thomas H., Jane S.; m. Liesa Bing, May 1, 1982. Student Princeton U., 1944-45; B.S., U.S. Naval Acad., 1949; postgrad. Trinity Coll., 1955. Asst. to chmn. Conn. Gen. Life Ins. Co., Hartford, 1954-60; cons. Robert Heller & Assocs., Cleve., 1960-64; asst. to pres. Sherwin Williams Co., Cleve., 1964-69; pres. Milton Allen & Assocs., Cleve., 1969—; dir. Actron Mfg. Co., Cleve., Aga Gas Inc., Cleve., Day Glo Color Corp., Cleve., DeSantis Coatings, Inc., Cleve., Progressive Corp., Cleve., Mueller Electric, Cleve., Women's Fed. Savs. Bank, Cleve. Trustee, Ctr. Venture Devel., Cleve., 1983—, Cleve. Playhouse, 1984—, treas. Laurel Sch., Cleve., 1976-84. Served to lt. USN, 1949-54. Republican. Episcopalian. Clubs: Union, Lakeside Yacht (Cleve.). Avocations: sailing, piano playing. Home: 1801 E 12th St Cleveland OH 44114 Office: 1717 E 9th St Cleveland OH 44114

ALLEN, RICHARD BLOSE, lawyer, editor; b. Aledo, Ill., May 10, 1919; s. James Albert and Claire (Smith) A.; B.S., U. Ill., 1941, J.D., 1947; m. Marion Treloar, Aug. 27, 1949; children—Penelope, Jennifer, Leslie Jean. Admitted to Ill. bar, 1947; staff editor Am. Bar Assn. Jour., 1947-48, 63-66, exec. editor, 1966-70, editor, 1970—, editor, pub., 1983—; pvt. practice law, Aledo, 1949-57; gen. counsel Ill. State Bar Assn., 1957-63. Served from pvt. to maj. Q.M.C., AUS, 1941-46. Mem. Am., Ill. (mem. assembly 1972-74), Chgo. bar assns., Am. Law Inst., Selden Soc., Scribes, Sigma Delta Chi, Kappa Tau Alpha, Phi Delta Phi, Alpha Tau Omega. Clubs: Law (Chgo.); Cosmos (Washington); Mich. Shores (Wilmette). Home: 702 Illinois Rd Wilmette IL 60091 Office: 750 N Lake Shore Dr Chicago IL 60611

ALLEN, ROBERT SHAW, chemical engineer; b. Providence, Nov. 12, 1931; s. Ray Spencer and Madeline (Shaw) A.; B.S. in Chem. Engring., Worcester Poly. Inst., 1956; m. Norma Elaine Porter, Nov. 8, 1958; children—Trudi Lynn, Ronald Shaw. With Am. Cyanamid Co., 1956-59; with Dewey & Almy Chem. div. W.R. Grace Co., 1959-62, Monroe Mfg. Co., 1962-67; Neutron Produ- cts, Inc., 1967-68, Continental Oil Co., 1968-72, Allen-Herzog Asso., Framingham, Mass., 1972-73, World-Wide Constrn. Services, Inc., Wichita, Kans., 1973-76; prin. Allen Assos., engrs. and consultants, Wichita, 1976—. Chmn., Sedgwick County Republican Central Com., 1977-82. Served with U.S. Army, 1953-55. Mem. Am. Inst. Chem. Engrs., Instrument Soc. Am., Nat. Soc. Profl. Engrs., Kans. Engring. Soc., Wichita Soc. Profl. Engrs., Wichita Area C. of C. Home: 5400 E 21st St #102 Wichita KS 67208 Office: 250 N Rock Rd Suite 350 Wichita KS 67206

ALLEN, ROBERT W., molecular biologist; b. Tulsa, Okla., Feb. 21, 1950; s. William E. and Rose Ann (McClain) A.; m. Marcia Ann Waul, Mar. 27, 1970. B.S. in Zoology, U. Tulsa, 1972; Ph.D. in Cell Biology, Purdue U., 1977. Postdoctoral fellow Scripps Clinic and Research Found., LaJolla, Calif., 1977-80; asst. clin. prof. molecular biology St. Louis U. Med. Sch., St. Louis, 1980—; asst. sci. dir. ARC, St. Louis, 1980—; cons. Office of Tech. Assessment, Washington, 1984—. Contbr. sci. articles to profl. jours. Am. Cancer Soc. grantee, 1977-79, ARC grantee, 1983—. Mem. Am. Soc. Hematology, AAAS, N.Y. Acad. Sci. Home: 709 Landscape Ave Saint Louis MO 63119 Office: Am Red Cross 4050 Lindell Blvd Saint Louis MO 63108

ALLEN, SUSAN JOHNSON, lawyer; b. Nassawadox, Va., Nov. 16, 1952; d. Littleton Wales and Nancy Nottingham (Taylor) Johnson; m. Douglas Willis Allen, Oct. 15, 1977. B.A. in Polit. Sci., Miami U., 1974; J.D., DePaul U., 1978. Bar: Ill. 1978, U.S. Dist. Ct. (no. dist.) Ill. 1979, U.S. Ct. Appeals (7th cir.) 1980. Assoc., Marvin N. Benn & Assocs., Chgo., 1978-81; atty. A.C. Nielsen Co., Northbrook, Ill., 1981—. Mem. ABA, U.S. Trademark Assn., Ill. State Bar Assn., Chgo. Bar Assn. (chmn. small firms com. 1980—), Am. Cancer Soc., Phi Alpha Delta. Mem. United Ch. of Christ. Office: A C Nielsen Co Nielsen Plaza Northbrook IL 60062

ALLEN, VERNON EUGENE, retired marketing executive; b. Cleve., Dec. 24, 1919; s. Vernon L. and Beatrice (Figgins) A.; student pub. schs., Cleve.; m. Florence Wilma Stanard, Mar. 5, 1942; children—Vernon William, Carol Jean Allen Holmes, Gregory, Holly L. Allen May. Machine operator, Tinnerman Products Inc., Cleve., 1938-42; devel. engr. Eaton Corp., Cleve., 1946-47, sales supr., 1947-70, sales mgr., 1970-72, div. mktg. mgr., 1972-80, dir. community affairs, 1980-82. Capt. of Ohio Hwy. Patrol Aux., 1968-70; chmn. bd. Hospice Found., Inc.; mem. Ret. Execs. Adv. Panel. Served with C.E., U.S. Army, 1940-46; PTO, ETO. Decorated Bronze star. Mem. Eaton Soc. Inventors, Am. Arbitration Assn., Internat. Platform Assn., Suncoast C. of C., Am. Legion, VFW. Republican. Clubs: Wedgewood Country, Countryside Country. Home: 2736 Timberline Ct Clearwater FL 33519

ALLEN, WARREN GEORGE, college administrator, dean; b. Deering, N.D., Oct. 10, 1921; s. Fred L. and Clara (Holo) A.; m. Marjorie H. Thorpe, Aug. 24, 1952; children—Fred, Joellen. B.A., Minot State Coll., 1943; M.S., U. N.D., 1952, Ph.D., 1957; D.H.L. (hon.), Sioux Empire Coll., 1966. Sch. adminstr. Deering and Antler Pub. Schs., N.D., 1946-51; secondary sch. educator Richmond Pub. Schs., Calif., 1951-57; chmn. div. edn. psychology Minot State Coll., N.D., 1957-84, v.p., 1984—; mem. tchrs. profl. practice commn. State of N.D., 1981-84; mem. com. Nat. Council Accreditation Tchr. Edn., Washington, 1973—. Mem. N.D. State Legislature, Bismarck, 1969. Served to maj. M.C., U.S. Army, 1943-46. Republican. Presbyterian. Home: 30 Robinwood Estates Minot ND 58701 Office: Minot State Coll Minot ND 58701

ALLEN, WARREN WILLIAM, JR., brick co. exec.; b. St. Louis, Jan. 2, 1924; s. Warren William and Edith (Eilers) A.; student Purdue U., 1942-43; B.S. in Chem. Engring., Wash. U., 1948; m. Ruth Reddish, June 11, 1949; children—William Reddish, Margaret, John Warren. Sales engr. Presstite Engr. Co., 1948-51; with Hydraulic Press Brick Co., St. Louis, 1951—, sales engr., Cleve., 1951-52, sales mgr., Cleve., 1952-55, mgr. Haydite div., 1955-63, v.p., St. Louis, 1963-67, pres., Cleve., 1967—, also dir.; dir. St. Louis Steel Casting Inc. Dir. Expanded Shale Clay and Slate Inst. Served with AUS, 1943-46. Mem. Am. Ceramic Soc., Am. Concrete Inst., ASTM, Alpha Chi Sigma, Phi Delta Theta. Home: 1690 E Shore Dr Martinsville IN 46151 Office: PO Box 7 Brooklyn IN 46111

ALLEN, WILLIAM CECIL, physician; b. La Belle, Mo., Sept. 8, 1919; s. William H. and Viola O. (Holt) A.; A.B., U. Nebr., 1947, M.D., 1951; M.P.H., Johns Hopkins U., 1960; m. Madge Marie Gebhardt, Dec. 25, 1943; children—William Walter, Linda Diane Allen Deardeuff, Robert Lee, Leah Denise Allen Rogers. Intern, Bishop Clarkson Meml. Hosp., Omaha, 1952; practice medicine specializing in family practice, Glasgow, Mo., 1952-59, specializing in preventive medicine, 1960—; dir. sect. chronic diseases Mo. div. health, Jefferson City, 1960-65; asst. med. dir. U. Mo. Med. Center, Columbia, 1965-75, assoc. coordinator Mo. Regional Med. Program, 1968-73, coordinator health programs, 1969—, clin. asst. prof. community health and med. practice, 1962-65, asst. prof. community health and med. practice, 1965-69, assoc. prof. dept. community health and med. practice, 1969-75, prof., 1975-76, prof. dept. family and community medicine, 1976—; cons. Mo. Regional Med. Program, 1966-76, Norfolk (Va.) Area Med. Sch. Authority, 1965-66; mem. governing body Area II Health Systems Agy., 1977—, mem. coordinating com., 1977—; founding dir. Mid-Mo. PSRO Corp., 1974-75, dir., 1976—. Mem. Gov.'s Adv. Council for Comprehensive Health Planning, 1970-73; trustee, sec. U. Mo. Med. Sch. Found., 1976—. Served with USMC, 1943-46. Diplomate Am. Bd. Preventive Medicine, Am. Bd. Family Practice. Fellow Am. Coll. Preventive Medicine, Am. Acad. Family Physicians, Royal Soc. Health; mem. Mo. Acad. Family Physicians (dir. 1956-59, publs. com. 1962—, edn. and sci. assembly com. 1975, v.p. 1983, pres. 1985), Mo. Med. Assn. (mem. com. on med. edn. and hosps. 1967-70, chmn. com. vol. health agys. 1972-79), Howard County Med. Soc. (pres. 1958-59), Boone County Med. Soc. (pres. 1974-75), Am. Diabetes Assn. (pres. 1978, dir. 1974-77), Mo. Diabetes Assn. (pres. 1972-73), Soc. Tchrs. Family Medicine (mem. com. on constn. and by-laws com. 1971-74), AMA, Mo. Public Health Assn., Mo. Heart Assn. (dir. 1971—, sec. 1979, v.p. 1980, pres.-elect 1982, pres. 1984). Methodist. Club: Optimist. Contbr. articles to profl. jours. Home: 508 W Briarwood Columbia MO 65203 Office: M144A Medical Center Univ Missouri Columbia MO 65212

ALLIE, MICHAEL DUANE, computer services company manager, consultant; b. Dearborn, Mich., Feb. 14, 1954; s. Mike and Dorothy Mae (Cadry) A.; m. Louise Henriette Pinvidic, Apr. 24, 1976; children—Cheryl Ann, Alan Michael. B.S. in Bus. Adminstrn., Detroit Coll. Bus., 1975; M.B.A., U. Mich., 1981. Computer programmer Bundy Tubing Co., Warren, Mich., 1974-76; project leader Chevrolet div. Gen. Motors Corp., Warren, 1976-80, 1981-84; cons. Ernst & Whinney, Detroit, 1980-81; mgr. Electronic Data System, Troy,

Mich., 1985—; adv. DCB Curricula Adv. Com., Dearborn, 1982—. Mem. Assn. Systems Mgmt. (chmn. program com. 1984-85). Avocation: photography.

ALLISON, BRENDA DENISE, benefits administrator; b. Macomb, Ill., Mar. 3, 1953; d. George M. and Anna Ruth (McGaughey) A. B.S., Western Ill. U., 1976, postgrad., 1977-83; cert. Harvard Bus. Sch., 1981. Dir. field services, pub. relations dir. Two Rivers Council Girl Scouts, Quincy, Ill., 1977-82; apprentice pharmacist Jack Stites Pharmacy, Macomb, Ill., 1976-77; program/camp services dir. Shining Trail Council Girl Scouts, Burlington, Iowa, 1975-77; apprentice pharmacist Christy Apothecary Shop, Pekin, Ill., 1972-74; pub. relations cons., farm mgr., Macomb, Ill., 1983-84; asst. adminstr. Central Laborers Pension, Annuity and Welfare Funds, 1984—. Mem. WIBC Child Advocacy Interagy. Council; past pres. Parents Anonymous; bd. dirs. Girl Scouts U.S.A. Recipient Cert. of Honor, Girl Scouts, 1977, Appreciation Pin, 1977; Cert. Recognition, Mayor of Macomb, 1981, 82; Ill. state scholar, 1972-76. Mem. Assn. Girl Scout Exec. Staff, Am. Camping Assn., Am. Mgmt. Assn., Pub. Relations Soc., Internat. Platform Assn., Farm Bur., Am. Polled Herefords, Am. Quarter Horse Assn., Home Extension, Social Welfare Assn., Ill. Quarter Horse Assn. Republican. Clubs: Rushville Saddle (sec., treas.); Lamoine Trails Saddle (Macomb). Home: 6 E Gardendale Jacksonville IL 62650 Office: PO Box 1246 Jacksonville IL 62650

ALLISON, DEBRA HUST, systems analyst, university official; b. Cin., Feb. 10, 1951; d. Elmer George and Laverne Marie (Guckiean) Hust; B.A. (Howard White award 1973), Miami U., Oxford, Ohio, 1973, M.S., 1983; m. Christopher E. Allison, Sept. 3, 1977. Congl. intern, 1972-73; congl. aide, 1973-75; systems analyst Miami U., 1975-83, mgr. Info. Ctr., 1983—; project officer SHARE, Inc. Info Ctr. Project, 1982—. Mem. Miami U. IBM Personal Computer Users Group (founder, pres.), Nat. Fedn. Bus. and Profl. Women (named Young Career Woman, Oxford chpt. 1979), Oxford C. of C. (charter), Phi Kappa Phi. Republican. Presbyterian. Club: Order Eastern Star. Home: 7 Quail Ridge Dr Oxford OH 45056 Office: 137 Hoyt Miami U Oxford OH 45056

ALLISON, JAMES RALPH, lawyer; b. Salineville, Ohio, Feb. 14, 1930; s. Samuel D. and Lois M. (Willis) A.; m. Eleanor Kathryn Nealis, May 2, 1959; children—James Bradley, Matthew Samuel, Jonathan Alexander, Ann Elizabeth. B.A., Maryville Coll., Tenn., 1952; J.D., U. Chgo., 1955. Bar: Ohio 1955. Sole practice, East Palestine, Ohio, 1957—; mem. Cohen & Allison, 1957-74, Allison & Blasdall, 1974—; city solicitor East Palestine, 1970-74. Chmn. bd. dirs. Union Comml. & Savs. Bank, East Palestine. Pres. East Palestine Sch. Dist. Bd. Edn., 1965-71. Bd. dirs. Columbiana County Mental Health Assn., Columbiana County Mental Health Clinic, 1975-78; mem. alumni bd. Maryville Coll., 1967-72; councilman City of East Palestine, 1974-80. Served with CIC, U.S. Army, 1955-57. Mem. ABA, Ohio Bar Assn., Columbiana County Bar Assn. (sec.-treas.). Presbyterian. Lodge: Rotary (dist. gov. 1967-70, dist. sec.-treas. 1972—). Home: 569 Sugar Camp Dr East Palestine OH 44413 Office: 25 E Rebecca St East Palestine OH East Palestine OH 44413

ALLISON, LOUIS DEE, pharmacist; b. Columbus, Nebr., July 23, 1936; s. Louis Frank and Wilma Mae (Buchholtz) A.; m. Marvis Jeanne Blatchford, June 7, 1964; children—Michelle Mae, Robert Louis. B.A. in Edn. and Bus., Wayne State Tchrs. Coll., 1959; B.S. in Pharmacy, U. Nebr., 1963; A.A. in Real Estate, Northeast Tech. Community Coll., 1980. Registered pharmacist, Nebr., Iowa; lic. real estate broker, Nebr. Pharmacist Jessup Rexall Drug Store, Nebraska City, Nebr., 1963-65, Daniel Rexall Drug Store, Fremont, Nebr., 1965-71, Nobel Rexall Drug Store, Holdrege, Nebr., 1971-72, North Bend Drug Store, Nebr., 1972-77, Westgate Pharmacy, Norfolk, Nebr., 1977-79; pharmacist, land mgr., Norfolk, 1979—. Recipient Scholastic Achievement award Norfolk Rotary Club, 1980. Mem. Nat. Assn. Retail Druggists. Democrat. Presbyterian. Lodges: Masons, Eastern Star (worthy patron). Avocations: fishing; bowling.

ALLISON, RICHARD DRING, government official; b. Murphysboro, Ill., Sept. 21, 1944; s. Reuel Dring and Ruby Francis (Jungewaelter) A.; student So. Ill. U., 1973-78, Belleville Area Coll., 1974-78; m. Beverly Lindsey, Oct. 17, 1968; children—Billy Wayne, Jay Dean. Land surveyor R.M. Harrison Co., St. Louis, 1967-70; license examiner Office Sec. of State, Sparta, Ill., 1970-75; corrections clk. Menard (Ill.) Correctional Center, 1975-84, coorectional counselor, 1984—. Chmn. Bicentennial Wagon Train, Chester, Ill., 1976; coordinator Randolph County Reagan-Bush Campaign. Served with U.S. Army, 1965-67. Mem. Ill. Jaycees (John H. Armbruster award 1978, Outstanding Local V.P. 1977-78), Chester Jaycees (pres. 1978-79, mem. internat. senate 1979—), Am. Legion (sr. vice comdr. 1982-83, comdr. 1983-84, vice comdr. 1984-85), VFW (life). Republican. Roman Catholic. Clubs: KC, Elks. Home: 1735 Swanwick St Chester IL 62233 Office: Menard Correctional Center Menard IL 62259

ALLISON, THEODORE CHRISTIAN, pharmacist; b. Duluth, Minn., Nov. 14, 1950; s. Richard Curtis and Joyce Theresa (Horn) A.; m. Sharon Elizabeth Donlan, Dec. 7, 1974; children—Colleen Marie, David Donlan. B.S. in Pharmacy, U. Minn., 1973; cert. OTC Sch., Cin. 1983. Registered pharmacist, Minn., Wis. Pharmacist, Racine, Wis., 1973-74, White Bear Lake, Minn., 1974-77; pharmacist, asst. mgr. Thrifty Drug Store Inc., Hasting, Minn., 1977-79, pharmacist mgr., Rochester, Minn., 1979-81, Red Wing, Minn., 1981—; cons. Red Wing Group Home, Minn., 1984—. Republican. Roman Catholic. Lodge: Kiwanis. Avocations: Cross country skiing, hunting, fishing. Home: Rural Route 4 Box 117 Red Wing MN 55066 Office: Snyder Drug Store 417 Potter St Red Wing MN 55066

ALLMAN, MARION KALLENBACH, educational administrator; b. Milw., Nov. 2, 1934; d. Fritz and Anna (Miller) Kallenbach; m. Glenn William Allman, July 7, 1952; children—Sharon, Chris. Student, U. Cin., 1958-62; student Layton Art Sch., 1953; Cert., Al Gable Art Sch., 1964. Art dir., ptnr. CDI Studios, Cin., 1964-73; mgr. art dept. Freedman Advt., Cin., 1973-76; owner, dir. ACA Coll. Design div. Acad. Communicative Art, Inc., Cin., 1976—. Charter mem. Internat. Council Design Schs., Chgo., 1983—. Designer Jeanie, 1974. Mem. Art Dirs. Club Cin., Cin. Indsl. Advertisers (program v.p. 1977), Advt. Club Cin., Sierra Club. Office: Acad Communicative Art 2528 Kemper Lane Cincinnati OH 45206

ALLMARAS, ALICE ANN, superintendent of schools; b. New Rockford, N.D., Aug. 21, 1927; d. Hugh C. and Anna (Roffler) O'Connor; m. Jacob William Allmaras, June 27, 1950; 1 child, Jean. B.S., Valley City State U., 1964; M.S., Moorhead U., 1972. Tchr., St. Catherine's Sch., Valley City, N.D., 1964-68; instr. Valley City State U., 1968-73; supt. schs. Eddy County, New Rockford, 1973—. Mem. N.D. Assn. Sch. Adminstrs., N.D. Assn. County Supts. Roman Catholic. Avocation: traveling. Home: 314 Central Ave New Rockford ND 58356 Office: Eddy County Courthouse New Rockford ND 58356

ALLOTTA, JOSEPH JOHN, lawyer; b. Rochester, N.Y., May 1, 1947; s. Sam J. and Sarah L. (Cerrito) A.; m. Elizabeth Dingwall, July 17, 1971; children—John Joseph, Leslie Denise, Jeffrey James. B.A., Am. U., 1969; J.D., Case Western Reserve U., 1972. Bar: Ohio 1972. Law clk. to presiding justice U.S. Dist. Ct. (no. dist.) Ohio, 1972-74; assoc. Gallon, Kalniz & Iorio, 1974-79; sr. ptnr. Allotta, Singer & Farley, Toledo, 1979—; instr. U. Toledo, 1975-76. Dem. precinct committeeman Sylvania Twp., 1983—. Served with U.S. Army, 1969-75. Mem. Internat. Boilermakers (hon.), Ohio State Bar Assn. (labor law sect.), ABA (employment law sect.). Dem. Episcopalian. Club: Health. Lodge: Howard Johnson. Avocations: Logging; tennis; racquetball. Home: 6127 Cross Trails Rd Sylvania Twp OH 43560 Office: Allotta Singer & Farley 3450 W Central Ave Suite 366 Toledo OH 43606

ALLRED, LAWRENCE ERVIN, cell biologist; b. Matewan, W.Va., June 9, 1946; s. William Ervin and Dorothy L. (Rutherford) Steiner; m. Barbara J. Bors-Koefoed, Nov. 7, 1970; children—Aaron W., Brenna K. B.S., U. Houston, 1968; M.S., U. Tex.-Houston, 1970, Ph.D., 1973. Research assoc. U. Colo., Boulder, 1973-78; clin. asst. prof. Ohio State U., Columbus, 1978—, adj. assoc. prof. U. Wis.-Kenosha, 1980—, clin. assoc. prof. Med. Coll. Wis., Milw., 1984—; sr. scientist S.C. Johnson & Son Inc., Racine, Wis., 1980—. Contbr. articles to profl. jours. Mem. Am. Soc. Cell Biology, Skin Pharmacology Soc., Tissue Culture Assn., Genetic Toxicology Assn., Soc. Toxicology (assoc.). Office: SC Johnson & Son 1525 Howe St Racine WI 53403

ALMEN, LOWELL GORDON, editor; b. Grafton, N.D., Sept. 25, 1941; s. Paul Orville and Helen Eunice (Johnson) A.; m. Sally Arlyn Clark, Aug. 14, 1965; children—Paul Simon, Cassandra Gabrielle. B.A., Concordia Coll., Moorhead, Minn., 1963; M.Div., Luther Theol. Sem., St. Paul, 1967; Litt.D., Capital U., 1981. Ordained to ministry Lutheran Ch., 1967. Pastor St. Peter's Luth. Ch., Dresser, Wis., 1967-69; assoc. campus pastor, dir. communications Concordia Coll., Moorhead, 1969-74; mng. editor Luth. Standard ofcl. publ. Am. Luth. Ch., Mpls., 1974-78, editor, 1979—. Editor: World Religions and Christian Mission, 1967, Our Neighbor's Faith, 1968. Recipient Disting. Alumnus award Concordia Coll., 1982; Bush Found. grantee, 1972. Mem. Assoc. Ch. Press, Evangel. Press Assn. Club: Minn. Press. Office: Luth Standard 426 S 5th St Box 1209 Minneapolis MN 55440

ALMICH, BRUCE PATRICK, government agency administrator; b. Cheyenne, Wyo., Jan. 25, 1950; s. Vernon E. and Gertrude J. A.; B.S.E. with high honors (Outstanding Undergrad. Research award 1972), Princeton U., 1972; M.B.A., U. Cin., 1974; M.S. in E.E., Stanford U., 1975; M.P.H., Harvard U., 1982. Research engr. USPHS/NIH, Cin., 1972-74; owner Nassau Systems Computer Systems Consulting, Cin., 1972—; group leader Distributed Computer Devel. Group EPA, Cin., 1977-80, chief systems analysis, 1980—; adj. prof. engring. U. Cin. Recipient EPA Bronze medal, 1979. Mem. IEEE, Assn. Computing Machinery, Sigma Xi (recipient book award 1972). Contbr. articles in field to profl. jours. Office: 26 W Saint Clair St Cincinnati OH 45268

ALMONY, ROBERT ALLEN, JR., librarian; b. Charleston, W.Va., Oct. 14, 1945; s. Robert A. and Margaret E. (Morrison) A.; A.A., Grossmont Coll., 1965; B.A., San Diego State U., 1968; M.L.S., U. Calif., Berkeley, 1977; m. Carol Krzeminski, May 6, 1972; children—Robert Allen III, Michael Anthony, Chandra Rene, Rachel Elizabeth. Sr. clk. Humanities Library, San Diego Univ. Library, 1965-68; accountant Calif. Tchrs. Fin. Services, Inc., Orange County, 1968-70, v.p., gen. mgr., 1971-76; reference librarian Oberlin (Ohio) Coll. Library, 1977-79; asst. dir. U. Mo. Ellis Library, Columbia, 1979—; owner Robert Almony and Assocs., tax and fin. planning, 1979—, USA Today Distbn., Columbia, 1984—. Treas. L.S.A. Bahais, Columbia. Mem. ALA, Mo. Library Assn. Contbr. articles to profl. jours. Home: 301 Rothwell Dr Columbia MO 65201 Office: University of Missouri 104 Ellis Library 9th & Lowry Columbia MO 65201

ALONGI, JOHN RICHARD, government official, consultant, inventor; b. St. Louis, Jan. 1, 1927; s. Guy and Rosalie (Finazzo) A.; m. Betty Ann Kremer, Oct. 14, 1962; children—Guy William III, Rosalie, John R. II. Student Washington U., St. Louis, 1946-47. Pres. Alongi Enterprises, Du Quoin, Ill., 1952-79, Mid-Am. Mine & Tool, Du Quoin, 1955-85; sec.-treas. Pin-Set Internat., Du Quoin, 1955-80; nat. mixer cons. Coca-Cola USA, Atlanta, 1964-66; exec. legis. aide U.S. Congressman Kenneth J. Gray (Ill.), Washington, 1985—; dir. Du Quoin State Bank; cons. Sandvic Mine & Tool, Mountain Top, Pa., 1978-80, Smith Mine & Tool, Mentor, Ohio, 1980-83; dir. Du Quoin State Bank, 1984-85; exec. dir. Econ. Devel. Council, 1985—. Patentee in field. Bd. dirs. Boys Club Am., Du Quoin, 1972-82; pres. Du Quoin Bus. Assn., 1969-70; chmn. So. Ill. Indsl. Commn., Du Quoin, 1970-78, So. Ill. Tourism Commn., Du Quoin, 1978-85. Served to cpl. U.S. Army, 1950-52, Korea. Decorated Korean Combat medal, 1952; recipient Congl. Citation, 1952. Mem. Nat. Inventors Assn., Nat. Pizza Assn., Nat. Beverage and Soft-Drink Assn., Nat. Restaurant Assn., Am. Legion, V.F.W., Du Quoin Bus. Assn. (pres. 1969-70). Roman Catholic. Lodge: K.C. Home: 350 E Main DuQuoin IL 62832 Office: Alongi Enterprises PO Box 344 Du Quoin IL 62832

ALONSO, LOU JOHNSON, counseling and educational psychology educator; b. Mason, Mich.; d. James Reginald and Mabel Elizabeth (Reid) Johnson; B.A., Mich. State U., 1947, M.A., 1950, postgrad., 1951-54; m. Noah Alonso, Dec. 17, 1948; 1 son, Jose Gregory II (dec.). Speech pathologist Flint (Mich.) Pub. Schs., 1947-48; tchr., then asst. prin. Mich. Sch. for Blind, Lansing, 1949-56; prof. spl. edn., coordinator programs preparing personnel for visually handicapped and deaf-blind pupils, dir. Gt. Lakes Region Spl. Edn. Instl. Materials Center, Mich. State U., East Lansing, 1959-80; cons. Office Spl. Edn., U.S. Dept. Edn.; mem. adv. bd. numerous agy.; co-owner Riggers' Den, 1978—, Yankee Art Co., 1975—. Mem. Council for Exceptional Children, Am. Assn. Workers for the Blind, Assn. Educators Visually Handicapped, Mich. Restaurant Assn., Delta Zeta. Author books, research reports, numerous articles, brochures and instrnl. media. Home: PO Box 1562 East Lansing MI 48823 Office: 331 Erickson Hall Michigan State U East Lansing MI 48824

ALPER, ALLEN MYRON, carbide manufacturing company executive; b. N.Y.C., Oct. 23, 1932; s. Joseph and Pauline (Frohlich) A.; B.S., Bklyn. Coll., 1954; Ph.D., Columbia (Univ. fellow, Dyckman Inst. Scholar, Univ. pres.'s scholar), 1957; m. Barbara Marshall, Dec. 20, 1959; children—Allen Myron, Andrew Marshall. Sr. mineralogist Corning Glass Works (N.Y.), 1957-59, research mineralogist, 1959-62, mgr. ceramic research, also sr. research asso., 1962-69; with GET Sylvania Inc., Towanda, Pa., 1969—, chief engr., 1971-72, dir. research and engring., 1972—, 75, dir. research and engring., mgr. aperture mask prodn., 1975-78, mgr. ops., 1978-80; pres. GTE Walmet, 1980— mem. ad hoc. advisory com on phase equilibria data ctr. Nat. Bur. Standards and Am. Ceramic Soc., 1983—. Mem. Pa. Gov.'s Adv. Panel on Materials, 1971—; mem. materials lab. adv. bd. Pa. State U., 1979—. Recipient Disting. Achievement award Bklyn. Coll., 1983; grantee N.M. Bur. Mines, 1954-57. Fellow Am. Ceramic Soc., Geol. Soc. Am., Am. Inst. Chemists; mem. British Ceramic Soc., Am. Soc. Metals, Geophy. Union, Am. Chem. Soc., Internat. Platform Assn., Sigma Xi. Presbyterian. Mason. Clubs: Explorers, Towanda Country, Great Oaks Country. Patentee in field. Contbr. to profl. jours. Editor: Phase Diagrams: Materials Science and Technology, 4 vols., 1976; High Temperature Oxides, 4 parts, 1970-71. Editorial bd. High Temperature Sci. jour., 1969—, High Temperature Chemistry, 1973—, Materials Handbook, 1974—; editor Materials Sci. and Tech. Series, Acad. Press, 1972—. Contbr. articles to profl. jours. Home: 880 Great Oaks Blvd Rochester MI 48063 Office: GTE Walmet Royal Oak MI 48068

ALPERS, DAVID HERSHEL, medical educator, biomedical scientist; b. Phila., May 9, 1935; s. Bernard Jacob and Lillian (Sher) A.; children—Ann, Ruth, Barbara; m. Melanie Ann Goldman, Aug. 12, 1977. B.A., Harvard U., 1956, M.D., 1960. Diplomate Am. Bd. Internal Medicine. Intern, resident Mass Gen. Hosp., Boston, 1960-62; asst. prof. medicine Harvard U., Boston, 1965-69, Washington U. Sch. Medicine, St. Louis, 1969-71, assoc. prof. medicine, 1971-73, prof. medicine, 1973—. Author: Manual of Nutritional Therapeutics, 1983. Contbr. articles to med. jours. Served to Surgeon USPHS, 1960-62. Mem. Am. Soc. Biol. Chemists, Am. Soc. Clin. Investigation (assoc. editor jour. 1977-82), Assn. Am. Physicians, Am. Gastroent. Assn. (chmn. tng. and edn. com. 1977-82). Avocation: chamber music; cello. Office: GT Div Washington U Sch of Medicine 660 S Euclid St Saint Louis MO 63110

ALSAKER, ROBERT ALLAN, performing arts executive, theater administrator; b. Winston-Salem, N.C., Aug. 22, 1945; s. Allan Kallan and Nora Mildred (Hjelmeseth) A.; m. Carole Lynda Woodcock, Apr. 18, 1969; B.A., Bradley U., 1968. Indsl. engr. Zenith Radio Corp., Chgo., 1968-70; product mgr. reverse osmosis systems Culligan Internat., Northbrook, Ill., 1970-80; exec. dir., gen. mgr. Auditorium Theatre Council, Chgo., 1981—. Author: Chicago Symphony Orchestra Notes, 1971, Theodore Thomas Exhibit, 1976, Frederick Stock Exhibit, 1977, Sir Georg Solti Exhibit, 1980. Active Archestral Assn. Chgo. Symphony Orch., 1969—, Ill. Arts Alliance, Chgo., 1983—, Chgo. Council Fgn. Relations, 1984—. Mem. Internat. Soc. Performing Arts Adminstrs. (bd. dirs.), Chgo. Council Fine Arts, League Chgo. Theaters. Republican. Lutheran. Club: Norwegian of Chgo. (chmn. bd. dirs. 1976-83). Lodge: Sons of Norway (pres. 1978-81). Avocations: foreign policy; sailing. Home: 1050 Cherry St Winnetka IL 60093 Office: Auditorium Theatre Council 70 E Congress Pkwy Chicago IL 60605

ALSOP, DONALD DOUGLAS, See *Who's Who in America,* 43rd edition.

ALSTON, HARRY LUTHER, JR., business consultant; b. Atlanta, Aug. 7, 1953; s. Harry L. and E. Clarice (Jones) A.; 1 child, Harry L. B.Indsl. Adminstrn., Gen. Motors Inst., 1977; M.B.A., Ind. U., 1980. Dist. sales mgr. Gen. Motors Parts Div., Flint, Mich., 1977-78; account exec. Ill. Bell Telephone Co., Chgo., 1980-82, Am. Bell/A.I.S., Chgo., 1982-83; relocation coordinator AT&T Info. Systems, Chgo., 1983; account exec. Designology, Inc., Indpls., 1978-84; staff cons. Inland Steel Co., Chgo., 1984—; pub.'s rep. Avenues mag., Indpls., 1980-83; dir. Minority Career Conf., Indpls., 1979-81; assoc. cons. Designology, Inc., 1980—; vis. prof. Black Exec. Exchange Program, Nat. Urban League, 1983. Mem. Chgo. support com. Trans Africa. Consortium for Grad. Study in Mgmt. fellow, 1978. Mem. Black Profl. Resources and Devel. Assn. (treas. 1982-84, editor 1982—, pres. 1985—), Assn. M.B.A. Execs., Ind. U. Alumni Assn., Nat. Black MBA Assn., G.M.I. Alumni Assn.; Alpha Phi Alpha (charter mem., state sec. 1974-75, chpt. sec. 1973-76). Avocations: reading; graphic arts; theatre. Home: 2015 Roosevelt Pl Gary IN 46404 Office: Inland Steel Co 30 W Monroe St Chicago IL 60603

ALT, ROBERT NICHOLAS, JR., lawyer, wire company executive; b. Grand Rapids, Mich., Dec. 30, 1942; s. Robert Nicholas and Catherine Rita (McInerney) A.; m. Mary Houseman, Sept. 11, 1963 (div. 1969); children—Andrew E., Margaret R.; m. Lucinda Dewey, Dec. 29, 1977; 1 dau., Emily Catherine. Bar: Calif. 1978, Mich. 1979, U.S. dist. ct. (we. dist.) Mich. 1979. Assoc. Lascher & Wilner, Ventura, Calif., 1978-79, Hillman, Baxter & Hammond, Grand Rapids, 1979-80, Baxter & Hammond, Grand Rapids, 1980-84; founding ptnr. Bremer, Wade, Nelson & Alt, Grand Rapids, 1984—; mem. litigation sect. Mich. State Bar; mem. adv. com. Mich. State Bar Jour., 1983—; chmn. bd., sec. McInerney Spring and Wire Co., Grand Rapids, 1984—, chief exec. officer, 1985—. Co-editor column: Litigation Strategies, 1984—. Chmn. City of Grand Rapids Urban Homestead Commn., 1982-84; mem. lay adv. bd. Cath. Info. Ctr., 1984—. Recipient 2 1st prizes Mich. Newspaper Assn., 1968; editor-in-chief U. Detroit Law Rev., 1977-78; presdl. scholar U. Detroit, 1977-78; Clarence M. Burton scholar Burton Found., 1977-78; named to honor roll Best Am. Short Stories, Houghton-Mifflin Pub. Co., 1971. Mem. ABA, Mich. Bar Assn., Calif. Bar Assn., Grand Rapids Bar Assn. (co-chmn. Law Day 1981), Mich. Def. Trial Lawyers. Roman Catholic. Home: 2815 E Fulton Grand Rapids MI 49506 Office: Bremer Wade Nelson & Alt 190 Monroe NW 5th Floor Grand Rapids MI 49503 also 655 Godfrey SW Grand Rapids MI 49503

ALTAN, TAYLAN, mechanical engineer; b. Trabzon, Turkey, Feb. 12, 1938; s. Seref and Sadife (Baysal) A.; came to U.S., 1963, naturalized, 1970; diploma in mfg. engring. Tech. U. Hannover (W.Ger.), 1962; M.S. in Mech. Engring., U. Calif., Berkeley, 1964, Ph.D., 1966; m. Susan Borah, July 18, 1964; children—Peri, Aylin. Research asst. U. Calif., Berkeley, 1963-66; research scientist DuPont de Nemours Co., Wilmington, Del., 1966-68; sr. research scientist Battelle Inst., Columbus, Ohio, 1968-73, sr. research leader Battelle Columbus Labs., 1973—; adj. prof. indsl. engring. Ohio State U.; cons. in field to U.S. and fgn. cos. Fellow Am. Soc. Metals; mem. ASME (chmn. div. prodn. engring. 1977), Soc. Mfg. Engrs., Internat. Prodn. Engring. Research Instn. Author: (with F.W. Boulger and J.R. Becker) Forging Equipment, Materials and Practices, 1973; (with S.I. Oh and H. Gegel) Metal Forming—Fundamentals and Applications; contbr. numerous articles to nat., internat. tech. jours.; asso. editor Jour. Mech. Working Tech., 1976. Home: 1380 Sherbrooke Pl Columbus OH 43209 Office: Battelle Labs 505 King Ave Columbus OH 43201

ALTEMUS, JAMES ROY, farm bureau official; b. West Frankfort, Ill., Jan. 12, 1946; s. Harold and Grace Marie (Chick) A.; B.S. in Edn., Ill. State U., 1969; m. Allida Frisch, Feb. 4, 1967; children—Sarah, Emily. Info. services mgr. Ill. Farm Bur., Bloomington, 1969-73, dir. public relations, 1973-78, dir. public info., 1978—; communications cons. Am. Coll. Testing, Nat. Inst. Fin. Aid. Mem. Dist. 87 Sch. Adv. Com., 1978-79; bd. dirs. Central Ill. Jr. Achievement, 1977-79; bd. dirs. McLean County ARC, 1977-81, 1st v.p., 1979, chmn. bd., 1980-81. Served with Chem. Corps, USAR, 1969-75. Mem. Public Relations Soc. Am. (accredited; chpt. pres. 1981, dist. sec. 1982, treas. 1983, dist. chmn. 1985), Bloomington-Normal Advt., Mktg. and Pub. Relations Assn. (pres. 1984). Home: 319 Hillside Ln Bloomington IL 61701 Office: 1701 Towanda Ave Bloomington IL 61701

ALTER, JOHN, otolaryngologist, educator; b. Hoffgastein, Austria, Feb. 6, 1946; came to U.S., 1948; s. Irving Israel and Clara Klara (Scotchinsky) A.; m. Denise Mary Webber, Apr. 17, 1982; children—Andrea Leah, Geoffrey Ian. B.S., Wayne State U., 1967; D.O., Des Moines Coll. Osteo. Medicine and Surgery, 1971. Intern, Botsford Hosp., Farmington, Mich., 1971-72; resident in surgery Providence Hosp., Southfield, Mich., 1972-73; resident in otolaryngology Wayne State U., Detroit, 1973-76; practice medicine specializing in otolaryngology and facial cosmetic surgery, Pontiac, Mich., 1976—, West Bloomfield, Mich., 1981—; clin. instr. Wayne State U. Med. Ctr., also local hosps.; past chmn. dept. otolaryngology and ophthalmology Pontiac (Mich.) Gen. Hosp. Mem. Simon Weisenthal Found., Zionist Orgn. Am., Zero Population Growth, Nat. Abortion Rights League, Sierra Club (West Bloomfield, Mich.). Fellow Am. Acad. Otolaryngology, Am. Facial Plastic and Reconstructive Soc.; mem. Am. Osteo. Assn., Oakland County Osteo. Assn., Mich. Osteo. Assn. Physicians and Surgeons, Mich. Otolaryn. Soc. Democrat. Jewish. Office: 7001 Orchard Lake Rd West Bloomfield MI 48033

ALTER, JOSEPH DINSMORE, physician, educator; b. Lawrence, Kans., Apr. 19, 1923; s. David Emmet and Martha (Payne) A.; M.D., Hahnemann Med. Coll., 1950; M.P.H., U. Calif.-Berkeley, 1961; m. Marian Elizabeth Wengert, May 31, 1946 (div. Feb. 1981); children—Robert Emmet, Janet Lynn; m. Joyce Ellen Willis, Apr. 10, 1981; 1 son, Joseph Leslie. Intern, Huntington Meml. Hosp., Pasadena, Calif., 1950-51; mem. med. staff Group Health Coop. Puget Sound (Wash.), 1951-60, chmn. family practice dept., 1956-57; field dir. Houses for Korea, Coordinated Community Devel. Project, 1953-54; lectr. med. care adminstrn. Sch. Pub. Health, U. Calif., Berkeley, 1961-62; lectr. Sch. Hygiene and Pub. Health, Johns Hopkins U., Balt., 1962-65, asst. prof., 1965-67, dep. dir. rural health research projects, dept. internat. health Sch. Hygiene and Pub. Health, Narangwal Village, Punjab, India, 1962-67, asst. prof. dept. internat. health Sch. Hygiene and Pub. Health, Balt., 1965-68; assoc. prof., field prof. community medicine, dept. community medicine Coll. Medicine, U. Ky. Med. Center, 1968-70; med. dir. Pilot City Health Center, Cin., 1970-73, HealthCare of Louisville, 1973-75; chief domiciliary med. service VA Center, Dayton, Ohio, 1975-77, assoc. chief staff for extended care, 1977; prof., chmn. dept. community medicine Wright State U. Sch. Medicine, 1977—. Chmn. Dayton regional exec. com., mem. nat. bd. Am. Friends Service Com., 1977-78; pres. bd. trustees Sr. Citizens Ctr. of Greater Dayton; trustee Quaker Heights, Waynesville, Ohio. Recipient Physician's Recognition award AMA, 1976, 79, 82; diplomate Am. Bd. Preventive Medicine. Mem. Am. Pub. Health Assn., AMA, Am. Acad. Family Physicians, Am. Coll. Preventive Medicine, Gerontol. Soc., Aerospace Med. Assn., Ohio, Montgomery County med. assns. Quaker. Author: Narrowing Our Medical Care Gap, 1972; (with others) The Health Center Doctor in India, 1967, Doctors for the Villages, 1976; Life After Fifty-Your Guide to Health and Happiness, 1983; contbr. articles to profl. jours. Home: 6607 Morrow Dr Dayton OH 45415 Office: Dept Community Medicine Wright State U Sch Medicine Box 927 Dayton OH 45401

ALTERMAN, IRWIN MICHAEL, lawyer; b. Vineland, N.J., Mar. 4, 1941; s. Joseph and Rose A.; m. Susan Simon, Aug. 6, 1972; 1 child, Owen. A.B., Princeton U., 1962; LL.B., Columbia U., 1965. Bar: N.Y., 1966, Mich. 1967. Law clk. U.S. Dist. Ct. (ea. dist.) Mich., 1965-67; assoc. firm Kaye, Scholer, Fierman, Hays & Handler, N.Y.C., 1967-70; assoc. Hyman, Gurwin, Nachman, Friedman & Winkelman, Southfield, Mich., 1970-74, ptnr., 1974—; lectr. Inst. Continuing Legal Edn., Ann Arbor, Mich. Founding editor: Mich. Antitrust, 1975—; editor: Mich. Antitrust Digest. Contbr. articles to profl. jours. Mem. nat. young leadership cabinet United Jewish Appeal, 1978-79, mem. nat. exec. com., 1980; v.p. Adat Shalom Synagogue, Farmington Hills, Mich. Mem. Am. Law Inst., ABA, Assn. Bar City N.Y., State Bar Mich. (past chmn. com. on plain English, past chmn. antitrust sect.), Detroit Bar Assn. Club: Princeton (past pres. Mich.). Home: 6065 Worlington Birmingham MI 48010 Office: 17117 W Nine Mile Rd Suite 1600 Southfield MI 48075

ALTHEIMER, ALAN MILTON, messenger company executive; b. Chgo., July 25, 1940; s. Milton Louis and Rena (Cohen) A.; student Drake U., 1959-61; children—Amy, Marcy. Pres., Altheimer & Baer, Inc., Chgo., 1968-80; pres. v.p. Fast Messenger Service, Inc., Chgo., 1976-83; v.p. Cannonball Inc., Chgo., 1983—. Chmn. Chgo. dist., disaster services ARC, 1980-83; vice chmn. Mid-Am. Disaster Services, ARC, 1983-85; bd. dirs. Midwest Epilepsy Center, 1980-82. Mem. Ill. Messenger Service Assn. Home: 3200 N Lake Shore Dr Chicago IL 60657 Office: Cannonball Inc 400 N Orleans St Chicago IL 60610

ALTIERE, EUGENE THOMAS, periodontist, educator; b. Youngstown, Ohio, Nov. 29, 1945; s. James Nicholas and Constance Ann (Balestra) A.; m. Joan Carol Moreira, Feb. 3, 1968; children—Anthony Eugene, Nicholas Eugene. D.D.S., Ohio State U., 1974; M.S., Mayo Grad. Sch., 1978, cert. periodontics, 1978. Periodontist, Duluth, Minn., 1978—; asst. prof. periodontics U. Minn.-Duluth, 1979—. Mem. dist. exec. council Lake Superior council

Boy Scouts Am., 1965-70; mem. choir St. Michael's Ch., Duluth, 1978—. Recipient Callahan prize Ohio State U., 1974. Mem. Am. Acad. Periodontology (Balent Orban award 1978), Midwest Soc. Periodontology (exec. council 1983—), Minn. Assn. Periodontists (pres. 1984—), ADA, Minn. Dental Assn. (chmn. state membership com. 1984—), Northeastern Dist. Dental Soc. (sec.-treas. 1984—). Republican. Roman Catholic. Clubs: Pope and Young. Lodge: K.C. Avocations: bow hunting; fishing; camping; photography; music. Home: 4329 Peabody Ln Duluth MN 55804 Office: 712 Medical Arts Bldg Duluth MN 55802

ALTMAN, HARVEY JAY, psychobiologist, researcher; b. Bklyn., June 28, 1949; s. David and Audrey Sydell (Garfield) A.; m. Barbara Nan Hefter, June 12, 1974; children—Jill Robyn, Paul Todd, Stefanie Nicole. B.S. in Biology, N.Y. Inst. Tech., 1973; postgrad. in Biology, L.I. U., 1976; postgrad. in Psychobiology, NYU, 1976—. Researcher dept. neurology Sch. Medicine, NYU, N.Y.C., 1976-77, supr., research asst. div. behavioral neurology, 1977-79, research asst. dept. neurology, 1979-80; instr. Mercy Coll., Dobbs Ferry, N.Y., 1979-80; dir. animal facilities dept. behavioral animal research Lafayette Clinic, Detroit, 1980—. Contbr. articles to profl. publs. Mem. adv. bd. Alzheimer's Disease and Related Disorders Assn., Birmingham, 1984. A.H. Robins Co. grantee, 1984—; Wayne State U. Sch. Medicine grantee 1983-84, 82-83, 84-85; Nat. Inst. Aging grantee, 1983, NIH/Nat. Inst. Aging grantee, 1982—. Mem. AAAS, Soc. for Neurosci., Gerontol. Soc. Am., N.Y. Acad. Scis. Republican. Office: Lafayette Clinic Dept Behavioral Animal Research 951 E Lafayette Detroit MI 48207

ALTMAN, JOSEPH, biological sciences educator, researcher; b. Budapest, Hungary, Oct. 7, 1925; came to U.S., 1955; s. Samuel and Honor (Teitelbaum) A.; m. Shirley Ann Bayer, Dec. 8, 1973; 1 child, Magda. Ph.D., NYU, 1959. Asst. prof. NYU, N.Y.C., 1960-61; assoc. prof. MIT, Cambridge, 1962-68; prof. dept. biol. scis. Purdue U., West Lafayette, Ind., 1968—, dir. devel. neurobiology tng. program, 1968-75; mem. neurology study sect. NIH, 1972-76, 81. Author: Organic Foundation of Animal Behavior, 1966; Development of Spinal Cord, 1984. Editor: Experimental Brain Research, 1975-83. Recipient research awards, NIH, 1962—, NSF, 1970—. Mem. Soc. Neurosci., Internat. Soc. for Devel. Psychobiology (pres.). Avocations: philosophy; psychology. Home: 231 Spring Valley Ln West Lafayette IN 47906 Office: Dept Biol Scis Lilly Hall Purdue U West Lafayette IN 47907

ALTMAN, MILTON HUBERT, retired lawyer; b. Mpls., July 18, 1917; s. Harry Edmund and Lee (Cohen) A.; B.S., U. Minn., 1938, LL.B., 1947; m. Helen Horwitz, May 21, 1942; children—Neil, Robert, James. Admitted to Minn. bar, 1947; ptnr. Altman, Weiss & Bearmon, St. Paul, 1947-85. Mem. gov's adv. com. on Constl. Revision, 1950, on Gift and Inheritance Tax Regulations, 1961-65; chmn. atty. gen.'s adv. com. on Consumer Protection, 1961-65. Spl. atty. for Minn. Bd. Med. Examiners, 1963-75; spl. atty. for U. Minn., 1963-75; dir. SPH Hotel Co. Mem. nat. emergency com. Nat. Council on Crime and Delinquency, 1967-69; mem. Minn.-Wis. small bus. adv. council SBA, 1968-70; mem., v.p. Citizens Council on Delinquency and Crime, 1968-76; bd. dirs. Correctional Service Minn., 1968-76; mem. Lawyers Com. for Civil Rights Under Law, 1965-67; mem. U.S. Dist. Judge Nominating Commn., 1979. Chmn. Minn. Lawyers for Johnson and Humphrey, 1968. Bd. dirs. St. Paul Jewish Fund and Council, 1966-69, Minn. Soc. Crippled Children and Adults. Mem. Am., Minn. (chmn. tax sect. 1960-62), Ramsey County (exec. council 1968-71) bar assns., Am. Arbitration Assn. (nat. panel arbitrators), Fgn. Policy Assn. (nat. council 1969), U. Minn. Law Sch. Alumni Assn. (dir. 1967-70), UN Assn. (nat. legacies com. 1967), Am. Law Inst. Clubs: Minn. (dir. 1975-78); St. Paul Athletic. Author: Estate Planning, 1966. Home: 2353 Youngman Ave Saint Paul MN 55116 Office: Degree of Honor Bldg St Paul MN 55101

ALTMAN, MIMI ANGSTER, contracting company executive; b. Chgo., Jan. 13, 1935; d. Herbert Charles and Marian Agnes (McGrath) Angster; m. Robert S. Altman, Jan. 31, 1970; 1 dau., Marian Catherine. Mus.B., DePauw U., 1957. Lic. real estate broker, Ill.; cert. piano tuner. Owner, mgr. secretarial service, Joliet, Ill., 1966-67; legal sec. various firms, Waukegan, Ill.; adminstrv. asst. to pres. Lake Forest Sch. Mgmt., Ill., 1982-84; sec.-treas. Altman Air Conditioning & Heating, Inc., Highland Park, Ill. Mem. Mu Phi Epsilon (nat. exec. sec.-treas, 1977-82 pres. North Shore chpt.), Kappa Kappa Gamma. Republican. Presbyterian. Lodges: Women of Rotary, Zonta Internat. (local and dist. officer). Avocation: travel. Office: Mu Phi Epsilon Nat Exec Office 833 Laurel Ave Highland Park IL 60035

ALTMAN, ROBERT LEE, internist, consultant, educator; b. Grand Rapids, Minn., Oct. 2, 1935; s. Harry Edwin and Dagne Geraldine (Andersen) A.; m. Ann Louise McDowell, June 28, 1958 (div. May 1974); children—John David, Peter Alan, Andrew Robert, Thomas Robert, Robert Lee (dec.); m. Lynda Lee Milbery, June 12, 1974; children—Robyn Lee, Erika Lee, Melissa Lee, Michael David (dec.). B.S. in Chemistry, Westminster Coll., 1957; M.D., George Washington U., 1961. Diplomate Am. Bd. Internal Medicine. Intern Mpls. Gen. Hosp., 1961-62; fellow in internal medicine Mayo Clinic, Rochester, Minn., 1965-67, in pulmonary disease, 1967-69, NIH tng. grantee in pulmonary physiology, 1967-68; practice medicine specializing in internal medicine and pulmonary disease, Honolulu, 1969-70, St. Paul, 1970—; mem. staff Ramsey County Hosp., St. Paul, United Hosp.; pres. Drs. Altman, Guiton, and Arensen, M.D. P.A.; assoc. prof. clin. medicine U. Minn.; pres. Peguot Properties, 1979—; participant People to People Ambassador Program, Peoples Republic of China, 1982. Mem. exec. com. Indianhead dist. Boy Scouts Am.; youth chmn. Salem Lutheran Ch., West St. Paul, Minn., 1979, v.p., 1980, pres., 1981, chmn. stewardship, 1982, dist. del. Am. Luth. Ch., 1982; pres. Somerset PTA, West St. Paul, 1981-82; v.p. Ramsey County (Minn.) Lung Assn., 1971-74, dir. emphysema clinic, 1971-76. Served to lt. M.C., USN, 1958-65. NIH fellow, 1967-68. Fellow Am. Coll. Chest Physicians; mem. Am. Thoracic Soc., Ramsey County Med. Soc., AMA, Minn. State Med. Soc., Minn. Thoracic Soc., Am. Soc. Internal Medicine, Sigma Xi. Republican. Clubs: Pool and Yacht, Lillydale Tennis (Lillydale, Minn.). Lodge: Rotary (St. Paul). Contbr. articles to profl. jours. Home: 1000 Winston Circle Mendota Heights MN 55118 Office: Doctors Profl Bldg 280 N Smith St Suite 708 Saint Paul MN 55102

ALTON, ANN LESLIE, lawyer; b. Pipestone, Minn., Sept. 10, 1945; d. Howard Robert, Jr. and Camilla Ann (DeMong) Alton; B.A., Smith Coll., 1967; J.D., U. Minn., 1970; m. Gerald Russell Freeman, Sr.; 1 son, Matthew Alton Freeman (dec.). Bar: Minn. 1970, U.S. Dist. Ct. Minn. 1972, U.S. Supreme Ct. 1981. Asst. county atty., Hennepin County, Mpls., 1970—, felony prosecutor, criminal div., 1970-75, acting chief citizen protection div., 1975-76, chief citizen protection/econ. crime div., 1976—; instr. Hamline U. Law Sch., St. Paul, 1973-76; adj. prof. law William Mitchell Coll. Law, St. Paul, 1977—; adj. prof. U. Minn. Law Sch., 1978—; lectr. in field, 1970—; vice chmn. bd. dirs. Minn. Program on Victims of Sexual Assault, 1974-76; bd. dirs. Physician's Health Plan, Health Maintenance Orgn., 1976-80, exec. com. 1977-80; mem. legal drug abuse subcom. Gov. Minn. Adv. Com. Drug Abuse, 1972; bd. visitors U. Minn. Law Sch., 1979—; mem. child abuse project coordinating com. Hennepin County Med. Soc., 1982—, chmn. corp., labor, ins. subcom. 1982. Mem. Am., Minn., Hennepin County (ethics com. 1973-76, criminal law com. 1973—, vice chmn. 1979-80, unauthorized practice law com. 1977-78, individual rights and responsibilities com. 1977-78) bar assns., Nat. Dist. Attys. Assn., Minn. County Attys. Assn., Minn. Trial Lawyers Assn., Am. Judicature Soc., Minn. Women Lawyers, U. Minn. Law Sch. Alumni Assn. (dir. 1979—). Author articles, pamphlet, manual. Home: 2105 Xanthus Ln Plymouth MN 55447 Office: 2000 Hennepin County Govt Center Minneapolis MN 55487

ALTUGLU, SHENOL M., engineering company executive, consultant; b. Karsiyaka, Izmir, Turkey; came to U.S. 1959, naturalized 1968; s. Hamit and Naciye Altuglu; m. Susana Piedra, July 25, 1964; children—Yasemin, Aylin, Lisa. B.S. in Chem. Engring., Purdue U., 1964; M.S., U.Iowa, 1965; Ph.D., U. Akron, 1971. Process engr. PPG Industries, Barberton, Ohio, 1965-69, sr. supr., engr., 1971-76, plant tech. supt., 1976-83; researcher, asst. tchr. U. Akron, Ohio, 1969-71; exec. v.p. APEL Assocs., Akron, Ohio, 1983—; dir. Blue Isle Holding Co., Hong Kong; cons. Intrachem Chem. Co., Manila, 1983—. Patentee in field. PPG Industries fellow, 1971. Mem. Am. Inst. Chem. Engrs., Sigma Xi, Pi Mu Epsilon. Avocations: Tennis, downhill skiing, jogging, swimming. Home: 455 Circle Dr Doylestown OH 44230

ALTVATER, PHILIP C., JR., marketing executive; b. Upland, Pa., Jan. 16, 1945; s. Philip C. and Elsie C. (Moore) A.; B.A., Pa. State U., 1966. Sales rep. Westvaco Corp., N.Y.C., 1969-73, Oxford Paper Co., Chgo., 1974; product mgr. Hobart McIntosh Paper Co., Elk Grove, Ill., 1975-76; dist. mktg. mgr. Consol. Papers, Inc., Chgo., 1976—. Served with U.S. Army, 1967-69. Home: 21W 754 Huntington Rd Glen Ellyn IL 60137 Office: 200 W Madison St Chicago IL 60606

ALVAREZ, RONALD, hospital administrator, consultant; b. Columbus, Ohio, Aug. 25, 1944; s. Ralph and Mildred Ann (Stout) A.; m. Linda Kay Williams, Aug. 27, 1966; children—Ronda Lynn, Brenda Lee. B.S. in Bus. Adminstrn., Ohio State U., 1967; M.B.A., Xavier U., Cin., 1978. Inventory control mgr. Borden Inc./Columbus Coated (Ohio), 1969-73, Lunkenheimer Value/Condec Corp., Cin., 1973-74; prodn. and inventory control mgr. Sybron/Liebel-Flarsheim, Cin., 1974-77; v.p. Jewish Hosp. Cin., 1977—, also cons. material mgmt.; instr. master's program and continuing edn. Xavier U.; frequent seminar speaker. Served to 1st lt. U.S. Army, 1967-69; Vietnam. Decorated Bronze Star, Mem. Am. Prodn. and Inventory Control Soc., Internat. Material Mgmt. Soc., Health Care Materiel Mgmt. Soc. (pres. Cin. chpt. 1983-84, internat. dir. 1983-85, cert. profl. in health care mgmt.; Health Care Materiel Mgr. of Yr. award 1983), Ohio State U. Alumni Assn., Alpha Kappa Psi (life). Lutheran. Contbr. numerous articles to profl. jours. Office: 3200 Burnet Ave Cincinnati OH 45229

ALVINO, SYLVIA MARIE, reading educator, educational company executive, consultant; b. Chicago Heights, Ill., Oct. 17, 1948; d. John Joseph and Diana (Urbinati) A. B.A. in English, Loyola U., Chgo., 1970, M.Ed. in Reading, 1977. Reading specialist Project Upward Bound, Loyola U., Chgo., 1972—; v.p. fin., cons. Assocs. for Career Devel., Inc., Chgo., 1980—, The Phoenix Group, Inc., Chgo., 1982—; mgr. high sch. Renaissance program Chgo. Bd. Edn., 1984—. Recipient plaques Rush Med. Ctr., 1982, Loyola U. Upward Bound Program, 1982, Calumet High Sch., 1978. Mem. Mid-Am. Equal Ednl. Opportunity Program Personnel, Assn. Supervision and Curriculum Devel.; Ind. Voters Ill., Ill. Guidance and Personnel Assn., Internat. Reading Assn., Nat. Council Tchrs. of English, Phi Delta Kappa, Phi Chi Theta (officer Beta Psi chpt.). Roman Catholic. Author: (with others) Tutorial Supervisor's Manual, 1977; Cable TV Training Manual, 1981; editor Vineyard, 1971-73. Home: 915 W Margate Terr Chicago IL 60640 Office: Loyola U Project Upward Bound 1041 W Loyola Ave Chicago IL 60626 also 6101 N Sheridan Rd Chicago IL 60660

ALWIN, LEROY VINCENT, JR., mechanical engineer; b. Mpls., Sept. 23, 1931; s. LeRoy Vincent and Norma Constance (Hartmuth) A.; B.M.E., U. Minn., 1958; m. Barbara June Hecker, Sept. 23, 1972; children—Elizabeth Ann, Anthony Jay; stepchildren—Pamela Jeanne Bohach, Joel Edward Bohach. Engring. designer, asst. "Linac Project", Dept. Physics, U. Minn., Mpls., 1953-58; weather observer, forecaster, USN, Coco Solo, Canal Zone, 1954-56; design mech. engr. Temperature Control Div., Honeywell, Inc., Mpls., 1958-71; cons. mech. engr., pres. Park Engring., Mpls., 1971-83; pres., owner Alwin Engring., Inc., Mound, Minn., 1983—; v.p. Scantec, Inc., heating cons., St. Paul, 1984—; propr. Sugar Wood Farm, Mound, Minn., 1959—. Chmn., N. Am. Maple Syrup Council, 1975-77; chmn. Mound, Minn. Park Commn., 1968-71. Served with USNR, 1954-56. Registered profl. engr., Minn., Wis., Iowa, S.D., Mich., N.D., Ga., La. Mem. ASME, Am. Meteorol. Soc. Republican. Club: Engrs. Patentee in field; contbr. articles to profl. jours. Home: Robin Ln Mound MN 55364 Office: Robin Ln Mound MN 55364

AMACHER, DONALD LAVERNE, construction company executive; b. Green County, Wis., Sept. 25, 1941; s. Sindolf Juan and Helen Elizabeth (Disch) A.; m. Donna Jean Waefler, Nov. 22, 1959; children—Debra Marie, Delinda Kay. Asst. mgr. Fullerton Lumber Co., Monroe, Wis., 1965-69; counter salesman Fish Bldg Supply, Monroe, 1969-70; mgr. Hiland Homes, Inc., Monroe, 1970-75; mgr. Amwood Homes, Inc., Brodhead, Wis., 1975-76; pres., owner Home-Craft Constrn. Inc., Monroe, 1976—; owner, mgr. Don Amacher Realty, Monroe, 1973—. Mem. U.S. C. of C., Green Country Bd. Realtors (pres. 1982-84), Nat. Assn. Realtors. Mem. Ch. of Christ. Club: Marshall Bluff Bowhunters. Home: Route 2 Monroe WI 53566 Office: 1818 1st St Monroe WI 53566

AMARILIO, JOSEPH DANIEL, lawyer; b. Tel Aviv, Feb. 21, 1952; came to U.S., 1958, naturalized, 1963; s. Daniel Amarilio and Rosa (Stoyanova) Amarilio Hart; m. Deborah Lynn Pierce, June 25, 1978; 1 son, Jonathan Benjamin. Student Ill. State U., 1971-72; B.A., Northwestern U., 1975; J.D., John Marshall Law Sch., 1979. Bar: Ill. 1979, U.S. Dist. Ct. (no. dist.) Ill. 1979. Research asst. dept. polit. sci. Northwestern U., Evanston, Ill., 1974; assoc. McKenna, Storer, Rowe, White & Farrug, Chgo., 1979-82, Jack Ring, Ltd., Chgo., 1982-84; sole practice, Chgo., 1984—; of counsel Law Offices of Stephen M. Waters, Chgo., 1984—. Editor John Marshall Law Jour., 1978 (Citation of Excellence 1978). Lawyer, Legal Clinic for Disabled, Inc., Chgo., 1984. Mem. ABA, Assn. Trial Lawyers Am., Ill. State Bar Assn., Chgo. Bar Assn. Office: 150 N Wacker Dr Suite 1060 Chicago IL 60606

AMARO, JOHN ANTHONY, chiropractic physician; b. Kansas City, Mo., Apr. 1, 1947; s. Carl and Virginia (Belmonte) A.; D. Chiropractic, Cleve. Chiropractic Coll., 1970; postgrad. in bionutrition Columbia Coll., 1977; cert.in acupuncture N.Y. Chiropractic Coll., 1973, Waseda Acupuncture Coll., Tokyo, 1974, Tex. Chiropractic Coll., 1984; D. Acupuncture, Chinese Medicine and Acupuncture Assn. Can. Pvt. practice chiropractic N.E. Chiropractic Center, Kansas City, Mo., 1971-75, Metcalf Chiropractic Offices, P.A., Overland Park, Kans., 1975—; prof. acupuncture postgrad. div. Tex. Chiropractic Coll.; fgn. cons. Chinese Med. Inst. Trustee, Nat. Council on Alcoholism. Served with 135th Hosp. Corps, AUS, 1970-73. Fellow Am. Council Applied Clin. Nutrition; mem. Acupuncture Soc. Am. (v.p. 1974—), Mo. Acupuncture Soc. (pres. 1975—), Am., Kans., Mo., Ky. chiropractic assns., Internat. Acad. Clin Acupuncture (cert., pres.), London and County Soc. Physiologists; Editorial bd. Am. Chiropractic Mag. Developer Am. style non-invasive acupuncture needle. Home: 12 Wycklow St Overland Park KS 66207 Office: 7203 Metcalf Ave Overland Park KS 66204

AMARY, ISSAM BAHJAT, adminstrv. recreation therapist; b. Jerusalem, July 11, 1942; s. Bahjat Kamel and Essaf (El-Khiami) El-Amary; came to U.S., 1962, naturalized, 1972; B.S., Mo. Valley Coll., 1968; M.S., Central Mo. State U., 1974; m. Wilma Jeanne Blinn, Aug. 20, 1967; children—Jason Issam, Jarred Jamal, Dax Tallal. Recreation therapist, dir. activity therapy Marshall (Mo.) State Sch. Hosp., 1969-75, unit dir., 1975—; exec. dir. Mo. Spl. Olympics, 1970-72, chmn. bd. dirs., 1970-73; founding mem. Betterment of Youth Program. Recipient Viki award in dramatic arts. Mem. Nat. Park and Recreation Assn., Nat. Therapeutic Recreation Soc. Clubs: Optimist (dir.), Masons. Author: Creative Recreation for the Mentally Retarded, 1974; A Taste of Lebanon, 1975; Effective Meal Planning and Food Preparation for the Mentally Retarded-Developmentally Disabled, 1979; The Rights of the Mentally Retarded-Developmentally Disabled to Treatment and Education, 1980; Social Awareness, Hygiene, and Sex Education for the Mentally Retarded-Developmentally Disabled, 1980. Home: 711 Plaza Dr Marshall MO 65340 Office: Marshall State School Hospital E Slater St Marshall MO 65340

AMBELANG, JOEL RAYMOND, social worker; b. Milw., Aug. 23, 1939; s. Raymond Frank and Clara Ottilie (Alft) A.; student Concordia Coll., Milw., 1953-59; B.S., Concordia Sr. Coll., Ft. Wayne, Ind., 1961; M.S. in Community Devel., U. Mo., 1971; m. Lois Jean Yarbrough, Aug. 15, 1964; children—Joel Mark, Kimi Lee, Elizabeth Jean. Chief officer juvenile ct. 11th Jud. Circuit Mo., St. Charles, 1968-74, dir. juvenile ct. services, 1974-76; dir., owner Counseling and Clin. Services, St. Charles, 1976-80; exec. dir. Luth. Family Services N.W. Ind., Inc., Merrillville, 1980—; field instr., part-time asst. prof. dept. social work Valparaiso (Ind.) U., 1981—; instr. sociology and adminstrn. of justice evening coll. Lindenwood Colls., St. Charles, 1975-80; co-founder Youth in Need, Inc., 1973, bd. dirs., 1974-78, pres., 1976-78; cons. Mo. Council on Criminal Justice, Juvenile Tech. Adv. Com., 1973-75; cons., tng. chmn. Mo. Juvenile Justice Assn., 1972-74; mem. St. Charles County Child Welfare Adv. Bd., St. Charles County Child Abuse Task Force; mem. U.S. Cycling Fedn.; chmn. Nat. Bicycle Safety Program, 1979-80. Recipient awards Nat. Dist. Attys. Assn., 1974, Nat. Council Juvenile Ct. Judges, 1979, Juvenile Ct. Services Adminstrn. Nat. Coll. Juvenile Justice, 1971; cert. advanced alcoholism counselor Mo. Dept. Mental Health. Mem. Acad. Cert. Social Workers, Nat. Council Juvenile and Family Ct. Judges, St. Charles Community Council (award 1978), Nat. Assn. Social Workers, Legal Services Eastern Mo. (adv. com.). Lutheran. Originator, host program Lean On Me, sta. KCLC-FM, 1973-80; participant seminars in field; designer, author courses of study in field. Home: 2606 Sears St Valparaiso IN 46383 Office: Merrillville Rd Suite 1 Merrillville IN 46410

AMBRE, JOHN JOSEPH, physician, toxicologist, clinical pharmacologist, researcher; b. Aurora, Ill., Sept. 14, 1937; s. Frederick Mathias and Cecelia Angela (Petit) A.; m. Anita Marie Sievert, Nov. 3, 1962; children—Susan, Peter, Denise, Matthew. B.S., Notre Dame U., 1959; M.D., Loyola U., Chgo., 1963; Ph.D. in Pharmacology, U. Iowa, 1972. Fellow Mayo Clinic, Rochester, Minn., 1966-68; asst. prof. medicine U. Iowa, Iowa City, 1972-75, assoc. prof., 1975-78; med. dir. CBT Labs., Highland Park, Ill., 1978—; assoc. prof. medicine Northwestern U. Med. Sch., 1980—; cons. MetPath Labs., Teterboro, N.J., Abbott Labs., North Chicago, Time, Inc., Chgo. Served as capt. U.S. Army, 1964-66. Mem. Am. Fedn. Clin. Research, Am. Soc. Pharmacology and Exptl. Therapeutics. Democrat. Author: Drug Assay, 1983; chpt. textbook; mem. editorial bd. Jour. Analytical Toxicology; contbr. articles to profl. jours. Home: 1210 Walden Ln Deerfield IL 60015 Office: 303 E Superior St Room 209 Chicago IL 60611

AMBROSE, FRANK PETER, manufacturing company official; b. Chgo., Dec. 28, 1945; s. Anthony and Anna A.; m. Joanne Marie Martino, Sept. 1, 1971; children—Julie Marie, Frank Peter, Jr. B.B.A., Coll. Santa Fe, 1968; M.B.A., Roosevelt U., Chgo., 1974. With customer service/shipping dept. Rego Co., Chgo., 1968; with Zenith Radio Corp., Chgo., 1968-76, supr. mfg. product planning prodn. planning dept., 1974-76; with Wilson Jones Co., Chgo., 1976-83, dir. mfg., 1980-83; mgr. mfg. ops. Gen. Loose Leaf Co., Chgo., 1983—. Tchr. mktg. and mgmt. Coll. of DuPage, 1975-83. Counselor, Jr. Achievement, Chgo.; officer Norridge Youth Assn. Mem. Am. Prodn. and Inventory Control Soc., Tau Kappa Epsilon. Served with U.S. Army, 1969-75. Contbr. in field. Home: 730 E View St Lombard IL 60148 Office: 209 S Jefferson St Chicago IL 60608

AMBROSE, JERE BRITTON, engineer, inventor, automobile industry products mfg. co. exec.; b. Detroit, Mar. 6, 1939; s. Richard Wright and Mary (Van Allsburg) A.; B.S., Trinity U., 1961; m. Norma Jean Nicol, Sept. 8, 1961; children—Joe, Nicole, Richard. Sales engr. No. Fibre Products Co., Holland, Mich., 1961-64, sales mgr., Birmingham, Mich., 1964-66, v.p., 1966-73, exec. v.p., 1973-79, pres., 1979—; pres. So. Fibre Products Co., Thomson, Ga.; dir. 1st Mich. Bank, Zealand, 1980—. Served with U.S. Army, 1962. Recipient Ray S. Erlandson award. Republican. Presbyterian. Patentee in field. Home: 4301 Gulfshore Blvd N Apt 303 Naples FL 33490

AMBROSE, TOMMY W., research exec.; b. Jerome, Idaho, Oct. 14, 1926; s. Fines M. and Avice (Barnes) A.; B.S. in Chem. Engring., U. Idaho, 1950, M.S., 1951, Ph.D. (hon.), 1981; Ph.D., Oreg. State U., 1957; m. Shirley Ball, June 23, 1951; children—Leslie Ann, Julie Lynn, Pamela Lee. With Gen. Electric Co., Richland, Wash., 1951-54, 57-60, supr., 1960-63, mgr. process and reactor devel., 1963-65, mgr. research and engring., 1965; mgr. research and engring. Douglas United Nuclear, Richland, 1965-69; asst. dir. Battelle Meml. Inst., Seattle, 1969-71, exec. dir. Research Center, 1971-75, mgr. W. Jefferson Nuclear Facility, Columbus, Ohio, 1975, dir. research, Richland, 1975, dir. Battelle-N.W. Div., 1975-79, v.p., corp. dir. multicomponent ops., Columbus, 1979—. Mem. engring. adv. bd. U. Idaho, Moscow, 1975—; mem. vis. com. Sch. Engring., U. Wash., Seattle, 1974—; exec. com. bd. trustees Columbus Symphony Orch., 1981—. Served with USN, 1944-46. Registered profl. engr., Ohio, Wash. Mem. Am. Inst. Chem. Engrs., Am. Nuclear Soc., Sigma Xi, Phi Lambda Upsilon. Home: 530 Plymouth St Worthington OH 43085 Office: 505 King Ave Columbus OH 43201

AMBROSE, WILLIAM HAYDN, college administrator, minister; b. Ammanford, Wales, Nov. 20, 1922; came to U.S., 1929, naturalized, 1940; s. William and Jane Ann (Evans) A.; m. Jane Post, July 13, 1946 (dec. 1969); children—Diana, Nancy; m. Ione Bailey, Mar. 5, 1971; children—Brian, Ross. B.A., Eastern Coll., 1945; B.Th., Eastern Baptist Sem., 1945; B.D., Lancaster UCC Sem., 1950; M.A., Western Mich. U., 1970; D.D. (hon.) ABC Sem. of West, 1963. Ordained to ministry Baptist Ch., 1945. Pastor Am. Bapt. Chs., U.S.A., various locations, 1945-56; univ. chaplain U. Ill., Champaign, 1956-62; nat. staff Am. Bapt. Chs., U.S.A., Valley Forge, Pa., 1962-67; adminstr. Kalamazoo Coll., Mich., 1967-82, v.p., 1982—; pres. Am. Bapt. Ch. Commn. on Ministry, Midwest, 1982—. Author: The Church and University, 1968. Mem. Am. Bapt. Pub. Relations Assn. (pres. 1970-75), Am. Assn. Higher Edn., Council for Advancement and Support of Edn. Democrat. Lodge: Rotary. Avocations: gardening; photography. Home: 1523 Edington Kalamazoo MI 49002 Office: Kalamazoo Coll 1200 Academy Kalamazoo MI 49007

AMBROSIUS, G. RICHARD, marketing company executive; b. Huron, S.D., Apr. 25, 1946; s. George Norman and Lillian Fern (McGaughey) A.; children—Jennifer Joanne, Matthew Logan; m. Karen Anne Derr, Sept. 8, 1984. B.A., U.S.D., 1968, M.A., 1975. Asst. city mgr. City of Vermillion, S.D., 1973-74; ct. service officer Woodbury County, Sioux City, Iowa, 1974-75; security supr. Iowa Beef Processor, South Sioux City, Nebr., 1975-76; exec. dir. Iowa Lakes Area Agy. on Aging, Spencer, Iowa, 1976-83; owner, pres. Phoenix Systems, Inc., Sioux Falls, S.D., 1983—. Author: Marketing Is Not A Four Letter Word, 1983. U.S. Adminstrn. on Aging grantee, 1982, 84. Mem. Nat. Council on Aging, Mid-Am. Congress on Aging, Western Gerontol. Soc., Sioux Falls C. of C. Republican. Methodist. Home: 1901 S Main Ave Sioux Falls SD 57105 Office: Phoenix Systems Inc 601 S Minnesota Ave Suite L102 Sioux Falls SD 57104

AMBROZIAK, SHIRLEY ANN, communication specialist; b. Saginaw, Mich., July 8, 1953; d. John Joseph and Stella Mary (Wasik) A.; B.A. with honors, Mich. State U., 1975; M.A. (grantee), Purdue U., 1977. Speech instr. Purdue U., West Lafayette, Ind., 1975-77, Hammond, Ind., 1977-78; journalism instr. West Side High Sch., Gary, Ind., 1977-78; dir. communications Northwestern U. Transp. Center, Evanston, Ill., 1978, asst. dir., 1978-83; account exec. Arthur Andersen & Co., St. Charles, Ill., 1983—; speech instr. Northeastern Ill. U., 1979-80. Bd. dirs. Cook County Am. Cancer Soc., 1977-79; chmn. Gov's. Commn. on Higher Edn. Student Adv. Com., East Lansing, Mich., 1973-75. Mem. Women's Transp. Assn. (chmn. seminar and Chgo. program 1980-81). Internat. Assn. Bus. Communications, Women in Communications (co-chmn. job placement 1980-82), Transp. Research Forum, Speech Communication Assn. Am., Purdue Alumni Assn. Author: Organizational Communication, 1974; Human Communications, 1975; (with L. Stewart) The Relationship Between Adherence to Traditional Sex Roles and Communication Apprehension, 1976; (with Leon N. Moses) Corporate Planning under Deregulation: The Case of the Airline, 1980; (with Robert P. Neuschel) Managing Effectively under Deregulation, 1981; contbr. articles to profl. jours. and newspapers. Home: 107-C N 15th St Saint Charles IL 60174 Office: 1405 N 5th Ave Saint Charles IL 60174

AMDAHL, DOUGLAS KENNETH, state supreme ct. justice; b. Mabel, Minn., Jan. 23, 1919; s. Olean Knute and Beulah Beth (Franklin) A.; B.B.A., U. Minn., 1946; J.D. summa cum laude, William Mitchell Coll. Law, St. Paul, 1951; m. Phyllis J. Lampland, Apr. 14, 1949; children—Faith Ann, Charles Olean. Admitted to Minn. bar, 1951; pvt. practice, Mpls., 1951-55; asst. county atty. Hennepin County, 1955-61; mcpl. judge City of Mpls., 1961-62; dist. ct. judge, Hennepin County, 1962-80; justice Minn. Supreme Ct., 1980—, chief justice, 1981—; instr. law and judges schs. Served with USAAF, 1942-45. Mem. Am. Bar Assn., Minn. Bar Assn. Lutheran. Office: 230 State Capitol Blvd St Paul MN 55155

AMERINE, JOHN RICHARD, sales executive, consultant; b. Chgo., Mar. 2, 1944; s. Orron W. and Cecelia Eve (Marso) A.; m. Josella Antoinette Palopoli, Mar. 23, 1973; 1 dau., Lauren Beth. Student Amundsen Coll., 1965-66, North Park Coll., 1967-68. Prin., Ramer Sales, Inc., Park Ridge, Ill., 1973-77; mktg. rep. Formica Corp., Cin., 1977-80; account exec. Southland Paint Co., Gainesville, Tex., 1980-82; regional sales mgr. Leigh Products Corp., Miami, Fla., 1982-83; sales mgr. W.E. Kautenberg Co., Freeport, Ill., 1983—; prin. Brickton Assocs., Park Ridge, Ill., 1975—. Mem. Park Ridge Citizens Patrol. Author: Training and Information Manual, 1980. Alderman, City of Park Ridge, 1983. Named Ill. Citizen of Yr., Ill. Crime Prevention Officers Assn., 1979. Roman Catholic. Home: 1921 Walnut St Park Ridge IL 60068

AMES, GEORGE RONALD, insurance data processing executive; b. Washington, Dec. 9, 1939; s. George Franklin and Elizabeth L. (Martin) A.; m. Cherie Ann Cernik, Feb. 14, 1983; children by previous marriage—Jennifer Ann, Elizabeth Louise. B.S. in Aerospace Engring. with high honors, U. Md., 1969; M.S. in Indsl. Adminstrn., Purdue U., 1970. With Arthur Andersen &

Co., Chgo., 1970-72, Omaha, 1972-76, mgmt. cons. specializing in mgmt. info. systems; exec. v.p. computer data services Mut. of Omaha and United of Omaha ins. cos., 1976—. Served to sgt. USAF, 1962-67. Mem. Assn. for Systems Mgmt. (pres. Omaha chpt. 1972-77), Tau Beta Pi (nat. officer 1969-77), Sigma Gamma Tau, Phi Kappa Phi, Omicron Delta Kappa. Home: 16609 Hilo Circle Omaha NE 68128 Office: Mut of Omaha Mut of Omaha Plaza Omaha NE 68175

AMES, THOMAS TREES, steel company executive; b. New Kensington, Pa., Mar. 12, 1924; s. Francis Edward and Mary Agnes (Trees) A.; m. Rena June Connor, July 19, 1946; children—James Connor, Howard Francis. Student Va. Poly. Inst., Blacksburg, 1946-49. With Aluminum Co. of Am., New Kensington, Pa., 1949-56; plant mgr. Gen. Electric Co., New Kensington, 1956-66; mgr. ops. conduit div. Jones & Laughlin Steel Corp., Niles, Ohio, 1966-75, works mgr., Hennepin, Ill., 1975—. Bd. dirs. Citizens Gen. Hosp., New Kensington, 1963-66, YMCA, New Kensington, 1963-66. Served with USAAF, 1942-45. Mem. Assn. Iron and Steel Engrs., C. of C. Clubs: Elks, Bureau Valley Country. Office: PO Box 325 Hennepin IL 61327

AMFT, ROBERT ERNEST, artist, designer, photographer; b. Chgo., Dec. 7, 1916; s. Fred and Elizabeth (Koopman) A.; children—Peter, Sally, Robert J., Mark. Student, Art Inst. of Chgo. One man shows include Morris Gallery, N.Y., 1957-59, Panoras Gallery, N.Y., 1963, Old Town Art Ctr., 1961, 62, 64, Cliff Dwellers, 1964, St. Xavier's Coll., 1967, 68, Med. Ctr. U. Ill., 1968, Welna Gallery, Chgo., 1970, Junior Mus., Art Inst., Chgo., 1970, Art Inst. Chgo. Rental/Sales Gallery, 1978, Western Ill. U., 1979, Hammer & Hammer Gallery, Chgo., 1981, Joy Horwich Gallery, Chgo., 1981, Countryside Art Ctr., Arlington Heights, 1982; exhibited in group shows at Chgo. Artist Guild Show, 1955, Art U.S.A., N.Y., 19 Tacoma Wash. Mus., 1965, Chgo. Vicinity Show, 1975, Painting & Sculpture Today, Indpls., 1978. Avocations: Photography; sculpture; fishing. Home and Office: 7340 N Ridge Chicago IL 60645

AMICK, SHIRLEY MARILYN, marketing services executive; b. Armour, S.D., Dec. 4, 1925; d. Robert and Bertha Breen; sudent pub. schs. Eastern and Madison, S.D.; children—Sally, Matthew, James, Terry, Darlene. Supr. credit card acquisitions A.J. Wood Corp., Milw., 1968—. Mem. Internat. Traders Guild, Internat. Entrepreneurs Assn., Consumer Credit Assn. Jehovah's Witness. Home: 2927 S Logan Ave Milwaukee WI 53207 Office: A J Wood Corp 405 E Lincoln Ave Milwaukee WI 53207

AMIDON, PAUL CHARLES, pub. co. exec.; b. St. Paul, July 23, 1932; s. Paul Samuel and Eleanor Ruth (Simons) A.; B.A., U. Minn., 1954; m. Patricia Jean Winjum, May 7, 1960; children—Karen, Michael, Susan. Bus. mgr. Paul S. Amidon & Assos., Inc., St. Paul, 1956-66, pres., 1966—. Served with AUS, 1954-56. Home: 1582 Hillcrest Ave Saint Paul MN 55116 Office: 1966 Benson Ave Saint Paul MN 55116

AMIDON, WILLIAM DOUGLAS, retail executive; b. Ashtabula, Ohio, Mar. 23, 1954; s. Douglas B. and Velma J. Amidon; student Kent State U., 1973; B.B.A., U. Toledo, 1976; m. Nancy Ann Kingston, Aug. 26, 1978. With Ashtabula Office Equipment Inc., 1970—, salesman, 1977-78, v.p., 1978—. Mem. Am. Fedn. Musicians. Club: Exchange (past pres.). Home: 3231 Plymouth Ridge Rd Ashtabula OH 44004 Office: 5402 Main Ave Ashtabula OH 44004

AMIGONI, ALBERT RONALD, lawyer; b. Cleve., Oct. 19, 1950; s. Albert A. and V. Marie (Pavlic) A.; m. Patricia C. Berlan, Aug. 30, 1980; 1 child, Christine Marie. B.A., John Carroll U., 1972; J.D., Cleve. State U., 1975. Bar: Ohio 1975, U.S. Dist. Ct. (no. dist.) Ohio 1977, U.S. Supreme Ct. 1983. Sole practice, Cleve., 1975—; dir. Am. Mut. Life Assn., Cleve. Recipient Services as Guardian Ad Litem award Bd. County Commrs. Juvenile Ct., Cuyahoga County, 1980. Mem. Ohio State Bar Assn., Cuyahoga County Bar Assn. Roman Catholic. Club: Euclid Kiwanis (dir. 1984-85). Avocations: fishing, gardening.

AMIRJAHED, ABDOLREZA KASRA, pharmacist, educator; b. Tehran, Iran, Dec. 15, 1940; s. Mohammad Ali and Khadijeh Kutchak (Bananshahi) A.; came to U.S., 1958; B.S., Am. U. Beirut, 1965; M.S., U. Ill. at Med. Center, Chgo., 1969, Ph.D., 1972. Instr. pharmacy U. Ill. at Med. Center, Chgo., 1969-72, resident in pharmacy research and devel. hosp., 1972; asst. prof. pharmacy U. Toledo, 1972-77, assoc. prof., 1977—. Am. Field Service scholar, 1958-59, AID scholar, 1960-65. Mem. Am. Pharm. Assn., Am. Assn. Colls. Pharmacy, Acad. Pharm. Scis., Internat. Transactional Analysis Assn., Sigma Xi, Phi Kappa Phi, Rho Chi. Office: Coll Pharmacy U Toledo 2801 W Bancroft Ave Toledo OH 43606

AMIS, ROBERT WALTER, equipment leasing executive, consultant; b. Canton, Ohio, Feb. 24, 1923; s. Everett Lynes and Mary (Orme) A.; m. Lucille Hamer, Oct. 20, 1949; children—Robert Walter, Allan W. B.A. Southwestern U. (now Rhodes Coll.), 1948. Asst. dir. Nat. Cotton Council, Memphis, 1948-54; v.p. Advance Machine Co., Spring Park, Minn., 1954-78; pres. World Floor Machine Co., Mpls., 1966-74; mng. dir. Advance Internat., Luxembourg, 1977-78; sr. v.p. Advance Machine Co., Spring Park, Minn., 1978—; pres. Advance Acceptance Corp., Spring Park, 1973—; dir. Advance Machine Co., 1957-74, Dyersburg (Tenn.) Fabrics, Inc., 1967—, First Bank of the Lakes, Navarre, Minn., 1970—. Elder Presbyn. Ch., Memphis and Edina, Minn., 1960—. Served to lt. (j.g.) USN, 1943-46; PTO. Mem. Southwestern Alumni Assn. (pres. 1950). Republican. Presbyterian. Clubs: Minikahda (Mpls.); Mill Reef (Antigua, W.I.). Home: 5720 View Ln Edina MN 55436 Office: Advance Acceptance Corp PO Box 888 Spring Park MN 55384

AMLADI, PRASAD GANESH, health care consulting executive, researcher; b. Mudhol, India, Sept. 12, 1941; came to U.S., 1967, naturalized, 1968; s. Ganesh L. and Sundari G. Amladi; m. Chitra G. Panje, Dec. 20, 1970; children—Amita, Amol. B.Tech. with honors, Indian Inst. Tech., Bombay, 1963; M.S., Stanford U., 1968; M.B.A. with high distinction U. Mich., 1975. Sr. research engr. Ford Motor Co., Dearborn, Mich., 1968-75; mgr. strategic planning Mich. Consol. Gas Co., Detroit, 1975-78; mgr. planning services The Resources Group, Bloomfield Hills, Mich., 1978-80; project mgr., sr. cons. Mediflex Systems Corp., Bloomfield Hills, 1980-85; mgr. strategic planning services Mersco Corp., Bloomfield Hills, 1985—. Author numerous research papers. Mem. Inst. Indsl. Engrs. (sr.), N.Am. Soc. Corp. Planning, Economic Club Detroit, Beta Gamma Sigma. Office: 2750 N Woodward Ave Bloomfield Hills MI 48013

AMMAR, RAYMOND GEORGE, physicist, educator; b. Kingston, Jamaica, July 15, 1932; s. Elias George and Nellie (Khaleel) A.; came to U.S., 1961, naturalized, 1965; A.B., Harvard U., 1953; Ph.D., U. Chgo., 1959; m. Carroll Ikerd, June 17, 1961; children—Elizabeth, Robert, David. Research asso. Enrico Fermi Inst., U. Chgo., 1959-60; asst. prof. physics Northwestern U., Evanston, Ill., 1960-64, asso. prof., 1964-69; prof. physics U. Kans., Lawrence, 1969—; cons. Argonne (Ill.) Nat. Lab., 1965-69, vis. scientist, 1971-72; project dir. NSF grant for research in high energy physics, 1962—. Fellow Am. Phys. Soc.; mem. AAUP. Contbr. articles to physics jours. Home: 1651 Hillcrest Rd Lawrence KS 66044 Office: Dept Physics U Kans Lawrence KS 66045

AMMER, WILLIAM, common pleas judge; b. Circleville, Ohio, May 21, 1919; s. Moses S. and Mary (Schallas) A.; B.S. in Bus. Adminstrn., Ohio State U., 1941, J.D., 1946. Admitted to Ohio bar, 1947; atty., examiner Ohio Indsl. Commn. Columbus, 1947-51; asst. atty. gen. State of Ohio, Columbus, 1951-52; practiced in Circleville, 1953-57, pros. atty. Pickaway County, Circleville, 1953-57, common pleas judge, 1957—; asst. city solicitor Circleville, 1955-57. Past pres. Pickaway County ARC, Am. Cancer Soc. Served with inf., AUS, 1942-46. Mem. Am., Ohio (chmn. criminal law com. 1964-67), Pickaway County (pres. 1955-56) bar assns., Ohio Common Pleas Judges Assn. (pres. 1968). Methodist. Mason (K.T., Shriner), Kiwanian (Ohio dist. chmn., past lt. gov.). Home: 141 Pleasant St Circleville OH 43113 Office: Courthouse Circleville OH 43113

AMMERMAN, JAY NEIL, bar association data processing executive; b. Richmond, Ind., Aug. 21, 1945; s. Francis Andrew and Pollyanna (Kitchel) A.; B.S. in Mathematics, U. Chgo., 1967, M.B.A. in Fin., 1977; M.S. in Mathematics (NSF fellow), Northwestern U., 1968; m. Paula Jean Lorig, Dec. 19, 1969; 1 son, Jason Lorig. Sr. programmer Vapor Corp., Chgo., 1969, systems analyst, 1970, sr. systems analyst, 1970-72, asst. mgr. systems and programming, 1972-75; mgr. systems and programming Am. Bar Assn., Chgo., 1975-77, asst. dir. data processing, 1977-81, dir. data processing, 1981—. Chmn. supervisory com. Hyde Park Co-op Credit Union; sec. 5227 S. Blackstone Corp.; treas. The Manor Condominium Assn. Mem. GUIDE, (assn. for large scale IBM computer users), Sigma Xi, Beta Gamma Sigma. Home: 5222 S Blackstone Ave Chicago IL 60615 Office: 750 N Lake Shore Dr Chicago IL 60611

AMMON, HELMUT VOLKER, gastroenterologist, educator, researcher; b. Duisburg, Federal Republic Germany, Dec. 20, 1937; came to U.S., 1964; s. Christian and Charlotte Elisabeth (Franke) A.; m. Sandra Stiger Ferry, Aug. 7, 1972; children—Kristin, Peter, Christopher. Cand. Med., Ludwig Maximilians U., Munich, Federal Republic Germany, 1959, M.D., 1963. Diplomate Am. Bd. Internal Medicine, Am. Bd. Gastroenterology. Surg. intern St. Barbara Krankenhaus Hosp. Schwandorf, Federal Republic Germany, 1963; med. intern Krankenhaus Schwabing, Munich, 1963-64; rotating intern St. Vincent Hosp. Worcester, Mass., 1964-65; med. resident Woman's Med. Coll., Phila., 1965-66, Mayo Clin., Rochester, Minn., 1966-68; fellow in gastroenterology, 1971-73; asst. prof. Med. Coll. Wis., Milw., 1973-77, assoc. prof., 1977-82, prof. medicine, 1982—; chief gastroenterology sect. VA Med. Ctr., Milw., 1976—, asst. chief, med. service, 1980—. Contbr. articles and book chpts. to profl. lit. Served to maj. M.C. U.S. Army, 1968-70. Govt. Bavaria scholar, Munich, 1957-63. Mem. Am. Assn. for Study Liver Diseases, Am. Gastroenterol. Assn., Am. Soc. for Gastrointestinal Endoscopy, Am. Fedn. for Clin. Research, Central Soc. for Clin. Research, Milw. Gastroenterol. Soc. (pres. 1983-84). Lutheran. Office: VA Med Ctr 5000 W National Ave Milwaukee WI 53193

AMMONS, EDSEL ALBERT, bishop; b. Chgo., Feb. 17, 1924; s. Albert Clifton and Lila Kay (Sherrod) A.; B.A., Roosevelt U., 1948; B.D., Garrett Theol. Sem., 1956; D.Min., Chgo. Theol. Sem., 1975; D.D. (hon.), Westmar Coll., 1975; m. June Billingsley, Aug. 18, 1951; children—Marilyn, Edsel, Carol, Kenneth, Carlton, Lila. Social case worker Dept. Welfare Cook County, Chgo., 1951-56; ordained to ministry Meth. Ch., 1949; pastor Whitfield Meth. Ch., Chgo., 1957-60, Ingleside-Whitfield Meth. Ch., Chgo., 1960-63; dist. dir. urban work Rockford dist. No. Ill. Conf. United Meth. Ch., 1963-66, council staff ann. conf. No. Ill. Conf., 1966-68; urban ch. cons., prof. ch. and soc., dir. basic degree studies Garrett Evang. Theol. Sem., Evanston, Ill., 1968-76; bishop United Meth. Ch., Mich. area, 1976-84; bishop United Meth. Ch., West Ohio area, Columbus, 1984—; exec. dir. Ednl. and Cultural Inst. Black clergy, Chgo., 1972-73. Vice pres. Chatham-Avalon Community Council, Chgo., 1958-61; pres. W. Avalon Community Council, Chgo., 1959-60. Served with U.S. Army, 1943-46. Mem. Alpha Phi Alpha. Office: 471 E Broad St Suite 1106 Columbus OH 43215

AMOS, EUNICE CARRIE, home economist, educator; b. Litchfield, Minn., Jan. 20, 1936; d. Arnold and Irene (Martine) Paulson; B.S., U. Minn., 1958; M.S., Mankato State U., 1982; m. Marlin Amos, July 19, 1959; 1 son, Paul. Instr. home econs. Lake Crystal (Minn.) Pub. Schs., 1958-64, dept. head adult evening sch., 1958-64; free-lance work with home econs. occupations and edn., 1964-67; tchr. and supr. home health aides Nicollet County (Minn.) Pub. Health Nursing Service, 1967-68; tchr. and coordinator home econs. Mankato (Minn.) Area Vocat. Tech. Inst., North Mankato, 1968-75; instr. home econs., dept. lead tchr. St. Peter (Minn.) Pub. Schs., 1975—, instr. adult tailoring, tutor teenage program for pregnant girls, 1975—, mem. supt.'s adv. council, 1976-78; guest instr. Minn. State Dept. Edn., 1970, 71; mem. Minn. Dept. Vocat. Edn. Evaluation and North Central Assn. Schs. and Colls. teams, 1979-81. Judge, 4-H County Fairs, Minn., 1965-67; sec. exec. bd. St. Peter Play Group for Children, 1967-69; active Cub Scouts, Boy Scouts Am., 1969-70; bd. dirs. Citizens Scholarship Found., Community Edn. Adv. Council, St. Peter-Kasota area, Minn., 1977-80. Mem. NEA, Minn. Edn. Assn., St. Peter Edn. Assn., Am. Home Econs. Assn., Minn. Home Econs. Assn., Am. Vocat. Assn., Minn. Vocat. Assn., Minn. Home Economists in Edn., Minn., Lake Crystal High Sch., St. Peter High Sch. assns. future homemakers Am. (hon. mem.), Gustavus Adolphus Coll. Library Assos., Phi Upsilon Omicron. Lutheran. Club: Order Eastern Star (St. Peter, Minn.). Contbr. articles on home econs. to profl. publs. Home: 323 S 7th St Saint Peter MN 56082 Office: Lincoln Dr Saint Peter MN 56082

AMPEL, LEON LOUIS, anesthesiologist; b. Kansas City, Mo., Oct. 29, 1936; s. Joseph and Eva (Resnick) A.; B.A. in Chemistry, U. Mo., 1958, M.D., 1962; m. Jane Lee Isador, June 21, 1959; children—Jill, Ross, Jackie. Intern, Evanston (Ill.) Hosp., 1962-63, resident in anesthesiology, 1965-67, attending anesthesiologist, 1967-74, sr. attending anesthesiologist, 1974—; head dept. anesthesiology Glenbrook Hosp., Glenview, Ill., 1977—; asst. prof. clin. anesthesiology Northwestern U. Active Northbrook (Ill.) Sch. Caucus, 1975-76. Served to lt., M.C., USN, 1963-65. Diplomate Am. Bd. Anesthesiology. Fellow Am. Coll. Anesthesiologists; mem. AMA, Ill. Med. Assn., Chgo. Med. Assn., N. Suburban Med. Soc. (pres., 1974), Am. Soc. Anesthesiology, Ill. Soc. Anesthesiology, Chgo. Soc. Anesthesiology. Clubs: Old Willow, U.S. Lawn Tennis Assn., Chgo. Dist. Tennis Assn. (v.p., dir. 1976—). Contbr. articles to pubis. Home: 2701 Oak St Northbrook IL 60062 Office: 2100 Pfingsten St Glenview IL 60025

AMRHEIN, JEROME BRADFORD, pharmacist; b. Cape Girardeau, Mo., June 18, 1952; s. Jerome Francis and Patricia Jo (Schwartz) A.; m. Rebecca Jo McCommack, Dec. 27, 1974; children—Pamela Elaine, Sarah Denise, B.S. in Pharmacy, St. Louis Coll., 1977. Chief pharmacist Amrhein Pharmacy, Scott City, Mo., 1977—; Lay adv. Bi-State Home Health, Cape Girardeau, 1983—; councilman Scott City, 1984. Mem. Cape County Pharm. Assn., Mo. Pharm. Assn. Roman Catholic. Lodge: K.C. Home: 921 7th St Scott City MO 63780 Office: Amrhein Pharmacy Inc 601 Second St East Scott City MO 63780

AMROMIN, GEORGE DAVID, pathologist, educator; b. Gomel, USSR, Feb. 27, 1919; came to U.S., 1923, naturalized, 1929; s. David Rachmiel and Fannie (Simonoff) Amromin; m. Elaine Barbara Sabath, June 13, 1942; children—Joel, Richard, Barbara, Steven, James. B.S., Northwestern U., 1940, M.D., 1943. Diplomate Am. Bd. Pathology. Intern Michael Reese Hosp., Chgo., 1943, resident in pathology, 1946-48, asst. pathologist, 1949, asst. dir., assoc. pathologist, 1954-56; rotating gen. resident Edgewater Hosp., Chgo., 1944; practice medicine specializing in pathology, Tulare, Calif., 1950-54; clin. instr. U. Ill. Med. Sch., Chgo., 1954-56; chmn. dept. pathology City of Hope Nat. Med. Ctr., Duarte, Calif., 1956-71, chmn. dept. neuropathology and research pathology, 1971-76, mem. hon. staff, cons. neuropathologist, 1976-77, pathologist emeritus, 1976—; asst. prof. pathology Loma Linda U., Calif., 1958-70, clin. prof., 1970-77; prof. pathology U. Mo., Columbia, 1977-84, emeritus, 1984—. Author: The Pathology of Leukemia, 1968. Contbr. articles to profl. jours., chpts. to books. Pathologist, Project Hope, Ecuador, South Am., 1963, 64. Neuropathology research fellow Nat. Inst. Neurologic Diseases and Blindness, Belleview Hosp., N.Y.C., 1968. Fellow ACS, Coll. Am. Pathologists (emeritus), Am. Soc. Clin. Pathologists (emeritus); mem. Boone County Med. Soc., Mo. State Med. Soc., AMA, Am. Assn. Neuropathologists, Sigma Xi, Alpha Omega Alpha. Jewish. Avocation: painting. Home: 104 Defoe Ct Columbia MO 65203

AMSTUTZ, HAROLD EMERSON, veterinary medicine educator, consultant; b. Barrsmill, Ohio, June 21, 1919; s. Nelson David and Viola Emma (Schnitzer) A.; m. Mabelle Josephine Bower, June 26, 1949; children—Suzanne Marie, Cynthia Louise, Patricia Lynn, David Bruce. B.S. in Agr., Ohio State U., 1942, D.V.M., 1945. Diplomate Am. Coll. Vet. Internal Medicine. Pvt. vet. practice, Orrville, Ohio, 1946-47; from instr. to prof. Ohio State Vet. Coll., Columbus, 1947-61; head dept. clinic-sch. vet. medicine Purdue U., West Lafayette, Ind., 1961-75, prof. Sch. Vet. Medicine, 1975—; cons. Ind. Mich. Electric Co., Ft. Wayne, 1972—, Pub. Service Ind., Plainfield, 1972—. Editor: Bovine Medicine and Surgery, 1980; bd. editors: Merck Veterinary Manual, 1985; contbr. articles to profl. jours. Served with U.S. Army, 1945-46. Recipient Distng. Alumnus award Ohio State U. Coll. Vet. Medicine, 1974. Mem. AVMA (del. nat. conv. 1970—; Borden award 1977), World Assn. Buiatrics (pres. 1972-84), Am. Assn. Bovine Practitioners (exec. sec.-treas. 1966—), Am. Assn. Vet. Clinicians (pres. 1962-64), Gamma Sigma Delta (award of merit 1983), Omega Tau Sigma (Nat. Gamma award 1981). Republican. Lutheran. Avocation: tennis. Home: 112 Mohican Ct West Lafayette IN 47906 Office: Purdue U Lynn Hall West Lafayette IN 47907

AMUNDSON-EASTER, NANCY ELLEN ANDERSON, occupational therapist; b. Monroe, Wis., Oct. 10, 1936; d. Wallace Lowell and Martha Elizabeth (Burmaster) Anderson; student Kalamazoo Coll., 1954-55; B.S., U. Minn., 1958, postgrad., 1973—; m. Elmo Erickson, May 12, 1957 (dec. 1976); children—Jeffrey Alan, Darcy Lynn; m. 2d, Loren Amundson, 1971 (div. 1974); m. 3d, Douglas King Easter, Aug. 8, 1979. Therapist out-patient rehab. Mpls. Curative Workshop, 1960, outpatient therapy supr., 1961-62, 67-69; cons. Mpls. Nursing Homes, 1965-66; therapist Met. Med. Center, Mpls., 1970; cons. retarded children Didlake Sch., Manassas, Va., 1970-71; propr. Hand Some Things, Mpls., 1974-75; research coordinator Impact Inc., 1975-76; vol. learning disabilities Mpls. Sch. System, 1972—; occupational therapy dir. Sunset Nursing Home, Park Rapids, Minn., 1977-81; occupational therapy chairperson Cambridge (Minn.) State Hosp., 1981-83; partner Easterwoods, 1977—. Vol., Vols. Am., 1972-73; leader 4-H, 1973-74; active Boy Scouts Am. Registered occupational therapist. Mem. Am., Minn. occupational therapy assns., Minn. Civil Liberties Union, Children's Home Soc. Minn., Delta Zeta. Democrat. Presbyterian. Home: Rt 3 Box 832 Cambridge MN 55008 Office: Easterwoods Box 1592 Lake George MN 56458

ANBAR, DAN, statistician, educator; b. Haifa, Israel, June 11, 1939; came to U.S., 1967, naturalized, 1979; s. Samuel Berenstein and Beba (Gerenburg) Minsky; m. Sybille Wolf, Oct. 23, 1975; children—Amanda, Rinat, Samuel. B.Sc., Hebrew U., Jerusalem, 1964, M.Sc., 1968; Ph.D., U. Calif.-Berkeley, 1971. Lectr. Princeton U. (N.J.), 1971, Tel-Aviv U. (Israel), 1972-75; asst. prof. stats. Case Western Res. U., Cleve., 1975-79, Mt. Sinai Med. Sch., N.Y.C., 1980-82; sr. statistician Abbott Labs., North Chicago, Ill., 1982—; adj. prof. Northwestern U., Evanston, Ill., 1984—. Editor spl. issue Communications in Statistics, 1984. Contbr. articles to sci. jours. NSF grantee, 1984. Mem. Biometric Soc., Am. Statis. Assn. (pres.-elect local chpt. 1984—). Office: Abbott Labs D-431 North Chicago IL 60064

ANCELL, ROBERT M., publisher; b. Phoenix, Oct. 16, 1942; s. Robert M. and Alice (Lovett) A.; m. Janet C. Neuber, Dec. 21, 1966 (div. 1984); children—Kevin, Kristin; m. Christine Marie Miller, Mar. 30, 1985. Sr. sales representative Xerox Corp., Albuquerque, 1972-78; gen. sales mgr. Sta. KRDO-TV, Colorado Springs, Colo., 1978-79; publisher Titsch Pub., Denver, 1979-82; publ. dir. Denver Bus. Mag., 1982-83; advt. mgr. U.S. Naval Res. (active duty), New Orleans, 1984-85; publisher Endless Vacation Pubs., Indpls., 1985—; cons. Media Masters, Denver, 1983-84. Contbr. articles to mags., profl. jours., newspapers, 1960—. Served to lt. comdr. USNR, 1984-85. Recipient First Place award N.Mex. Broadcasters, 1970; First Place award UPI, 1970, Pres. Club award Xerox Corp., 1973, 75, 76. Mem. Reserve Officers Assn. of U.S. (tng. officer 1980-81, Cert. of Appreciation 1981), U.S. Naval. Inst., Pub. Relations Soc. U.S., Air Force Assn., Manuscript Soc. Republican. Presbyterian. Avocations: flying (pvt. pilot); bicycling; bridge; writing; photography. Office: Endless Vacation Pubs Inc 9333 N Meridian St Indianapolis IN 46260

ANDERL, STEPHEN, clergyman; b. Chippewa Falls, Wis., July 13, 1910; s. Henry A. and Katherine (Schneider) A.; B.A. magna cum laude St. John's U., 1932, M.Div., 1974; postgrad. Catholic U. Am., 1940; Ph.D., World U., 1982; D.D., Partasarathy Acad., Madras, India, 1984. Ordained priest Roman Catholic Ch., 1936; curate in Wisconsin Rapids, Wis., 1936-37; chaplain Villa St. Joseph, LaCrosse, Wis., 1942-49; pastor in Spring Valley, Wis., 1949-52, Hewitt, Wis., 1952-53, Assumption Parish, Durand, Wis., 1953-82; tchr., guidance counselor, vice prin. Aquinas High Sch., La Crosse, Wis., 1937-49. Censor books, clergy examiner, vicar gen. for religious Diocese of La Crosse, 1951-66; vicar forane Durand Deanery, 1953-82; diocesan chaplain Boy Scouts Am., Girl Scouts U.S.A., 1936-49; chaplain XII World Jamboree Boy Scouts, 1967, Nat. Jamboree Boy Scouts Am., 1969, 73; mem. Diocesan Clergy Personnel Bd., 1970-74; exec. sec. Cath. Youth Orgn., Diocese of La Crosse, 1938-49; diocesan dir. Sodality, 1938-49; cons. Central Commn. of Diocese of LaCrosse for Implementation of Vatican Council. Mem. exec. com. Chippewa Valley council Boy Scouts Am., mem. nat. Cath. com. on scouting, 1974—, vice chmn. diocesan Cath. com. on scouting; housing commr., La Crosse, 1948-49; mem. Gov.'s Com. on Children and Youth, 1957-63; adviser Wis. Youth Com., 1960—; mem. State Comprehensive Mental Health and Retardation Planning Com., Durand Community Council; dir. West Central Wis. Community Action Agy., OEO; bd. dirs. La Crosse Diocesan Bd. Edn., La Crosse Diocesan Cath. Social Agy., Inc., Silver Waters council Girl Scouts U.S.A.; founder, dir. West Central Wis. Community Action Agy. Created domestic prelate with title of right reverend msgr. by Pope John XXIII, 1962; recipient Silver Beaver award Boy Scouts Am., 1968; St. George award, 1969; St. Ann. award Girl Scouts U.S., 1980, citation West Cap, 1975. Mem. Wis. Geneol. Soc., Am. Acad. Religion, Wis. Acad. Arts, Sci. and Letters, Am. Numis. Soc., Collectors of Religion on Stamps, Christian Writers Assn. Lodge: K.C. (4th degree; chaplain Durand council 1953-82, John F. Kennedy council 1984—, faithful friar Pope John XXIII gen. assembly 1960-82, Bishop Sheen assembly 1984—). Author: Technique. of the Catholic Action Cell, 1942; Papal Teaching on Catholic Action, 1946; The Religious and Catholic Action, 1947; Catholic Action, a Responsibility of the School, 1948; Parish of the Assumption, Life and Times of the Mystical Christ in Durand, 1960. Contbr. articles to religious mags. and jours. Address: Ramsgate II Apt 309 2214 Peters Dr Eau Claire WI 54701

ANDERS, LESLIE, history educator; b. Admire, Kans., Jan. 22, 1922; s. Ray Leslie and Bertie Mae (Hasson) A.; A.B., Coll. Emporia, 1949; A.M. (Allen Cook White, Jr. fellow), U. Mo., 1950, Ph.D., 1954; m. Mardellya Mary Soles, Oct. 17, 1942; children—Geraldine (Mrs. Robert C. Hunt), Charlotte (Mrs. Alexander Wilson). Historian, Office of Chief of Engrs., Dept. Army, Balt., 1951-55; faculty history Central Mo. State U., Warrensburg, 1955—, prof., 1963—. Hon. commr. Mo. Am. Revolutionary Bicentennial Commn., 1974. Served with AUS, 1940-45. Recipient Merit award Am. Assn. for State and Local History, 1976. Mem. Am. Mil. Inst., State Hist. Soc. Mo., Sons of Union Vets. of Civil War, Scabbard and Blade, Phi Kappa Phi. Republican. Presbyn. Author: The Ledo Road, 1965; The Eighteenth Missouri, 1968; Education for Service, 1971; The Twenty-First Missouri, 1975; Gentle Knight, 1985. Home: 318 Goodrich Dr Warrensburg MO 64093

ANDERS, MICHEAL FRED, vocal music educator; b. Kountze, Tex., Nov. 20, 1954; s. Fred and Mae Bertie (Basar) A. B.S. in Vocal Music Edn. with highest honors, Lamar U., Beaumont, Tex., 1976, M.M. in Music Lit. and Vocal Performance, 1979. Instr. music Port Arthur (Tex.) Ind. Sch. Dist., 1977; instr. choral and vocal music, music coordinator Silsbee (Tex.) Ind. Sch. Dist., 1977-81; minister of music Calvary Baptist Ch., Beaumont, 1981; prin. roles Beaumont Civic Opera, 1974-81; dir. choral activities, asst. prof. music Findlay (Ohio) Coll., 1981—; choir dir. First Christian Ch., Findlay, 1983—; vocal recitalist. Mem. Interfaith Choral Soc., 1977-81, v.p., 1980-81, bd. dirs., 1978-81; mem. Beaumont Jr. Forum LUV Follies, 1977-81, Silsbee Bicentennial Musical Prodn. Co., 1976, Heidelburg Summer Theatre, 1983. Lamar U. Summer Opera Workshop, 1974-82, others. Recipient Cert. of Recognition for disting. achievement by a graduating senior Lamar U., 1976. Mem. Tex. Music Educators Assn., Tex. Classroom Tchrs. Assn. Am. Choral Dirs. Assn., So. Bapt. Ch. Music Conf., Phi Eta Sigma, Phi Kappa Phi. Appeared in My Fair Lady, 1776, Funny Girl, Kismet, George M, Once Upon a Mattress, The Most Happy Fellow, Trial by Jury, Fiddler on the Roof, Gianni Schicchi, Cavalleria Rusticana, Madama Butterfly, Der Zigeunerbaron, La Traviata, La Fille du Regiment, Amahl and the Night Visitors; also solo appearances in maj. choral works; producer Amahl and the Night Visitors; producer, mus. dir. No, No, Nanette, The Sound of Music. Home: 400 S West St Findlay OH 45840 Office: Findlay Coll 1000 N Main St Findlay OH 45840

ANDERSEN, DALE VERLYNNE, state agricultural director; b. Platte, S.D., Mar. 2, 1917; s. Frank and Mae (Prouty) A.; m. Evelyn Francis DuBois, June 18, 1940; children—David Dale, Calvin Frank, Roberta Gayle. B.A., Dakota Weslyan U.-Mitchell, S.D. Ptnr. Andersen Fur Farm; mgr. Mitchell Packing Co., mgr. Andersen Farms; state rep. 17th Dist., S.D.; state dir. Fed. Reserve Dist., Agrl. Stabilization and Conservation Service, Huron, S.D. Mem. Republican Party Com.; mem. bd. dirs. Crippled Children's Hosp., Sioux Falls, S.D.; mem. bd. dirs. Davison County Farm Bur. Recipient Disting. Service award Dakota Weslyan, 1979. Methodist. Clubs: Masons, Shriners, Elks. Office: Huron SD 57350

ANDERSEN, ELMER LEE, adhesive manufacturing company executive; b. Chgo., June 17, 1909; m. Eleanor Johnson; children—Anthony, Julian, Emily. Grad., Sch. Bus. Adminstrn., U. Minn., 1931. Chmn. H.B. Fuller Co., St. Paul, 1974—; pres. Princeton Pub. Inc. (Minn.), 1976—, ECM Pubs. Inc., Princeton, 1981—. Bd. dirs. U. Minn. Found., Minn. 4-H Found.; chmn. Alliss Ednl. Found.; mem. exec. council Minn. Hist. Soc.; bd. dirs. Voyageurs Nat. Park Assn.; pres. Charles A. Lindbergh Fund; chmn. Commn. on Future of Post-secondary Edn. in Minn. Mem. Am. Antiquarian Soc. Lutheran. Clubs:

Grolier, University (N.Y.C.); Minneapolis. Home: 1483 Bussard Ct Arden Hills MN 55112 Office: 800 Rosedale Towers Roseville MN 55113

ANDERSEN, HAROLD WAYNE, newspaper publisher; b. Omaha, July 30, 1923; s. Andrew B. and Grace (Russell) A.; B.S. in Edn., U. Nebr., 1945, L.H.D. (hon.), 1975, L.H.D. (hon.), Dana Coll., Blair, Nebr., 1983, Doane Coll., Crete, Nebr., 1984; m. Marian Louise Battey, Apr. 19, 1952; children—David, Nancy. Reporter, Lincoln (Nebr.) Star, 1945-46; with Omaha World-Herald, 1946—, pres., 1966-85, chmn., chief exec. officer, 1985—; dir. AP, chmn. AP Fgn. Ops. Com.; dir. Raleigh (N.C.) News & Observer; chmn. World Press Freedom Com.; past chmn. Fed. Res. Bank, Kansas City (Mo.). Pres. United Arts Omaha; trustee U. Nebr. Found., Midwest Research Com.; trustee, past pres. Jr. Achievement Omaha; chmn. Nebr. selection com. Rhodes Scholarship; bd. dirs. Omaha Zoo Found.; chmn. Nebr. Game and Parks Found. Recipient Disting. Journalist award U. Nebr. chpt. Kappa Tau Alpha, 1972, Americanism citation Henry Monsky lodge B'nai B'rith, 1972, Nebr. Builder award U. Nebr., Lincoln, 1976; Nat. Soc. Park Resources award for excellence, 1984; named to Vikings of Distinction Hall of Fame, North High Sch., Omaha, 1983. Mem. Am. Newspapers Pubs. Assn. (past chmn., dir.), Newspaper Advt. Bur. (bd. dirs.), Internat. Fedn. Newspapers Pubs. (past pres.), Nebr. Press Assn. (Master Editor-Pub. award 1979), Council Fgn. Relations, Omaha C. of C. (dir.), Phi Beta Kappa, Phi Gamma Delta. Republican. Presbyterian. Home: 6545 Prairie Ave Omaha NE 68132 Office: Omaha World-Herald World-Herald Sq Omaha NE 68102

ANDERSEN, HARRY EDWARD, oil equipment co. exec.; b. Omaha, Apr. 25, 1906; s. John Anton and Caroline (Ebbensgaard) A.; student pub. schs. and spl. courses, including Ohio State U., 1957, U. Okla., 1959; Ph.D. in Bus. Adminstrn. (hon.), Colo. State Christian Coll., 1972; m. Alma Theora Vawter, June 12, 1931; children—Jeanenne Dee (Mrs. Gaylord Fernstrom) and Maureen Lee (Mrs. Roger Podany) (twins), John Harry. Founder N.W. Service Sta. Equipment Co., Mpls., 1934, pres., treas., 1956—; owner Joint Ops. Co., real estate mgmt.; dir. Franklin Nat. Bank, Mpls. Spl. dep. sheriff Hennepin County, 1951—; hon. fire chief of Mpls., 1951—; pres. Washington Lake Improvement Assn., 1955. Mem. Shrine Directors Assn. (N.W. gov.), Nat. Assn. Oil Equipment Jobbers (pres. 1957-58, dir. 1954-56), C. of C., Upper Midwest Oil Mans Club. Lutheran. Mason (32deg., K.T., Shriner), Jester. Clubs: Viking (pres.), Engineers, Toastmasters, Minneapolis Athletic, Golden Valley Golf, Le Mirador Country (Lake Geneva, Switzerland). Home: 2766 W River Pkwy Minneapolis MN 55406 Office: 2520 Nicollet Ave Minneapolis MN 55404

ANDERSEN, JOHN MICHAEL, optometrist; b. Superior, Nebr., Jan. 15, 1947; s. Floyd H. and Sara Jo (Shipman) Z.; children—London, Jonnie. O.D., So. Coll. Optometry, 1970. Diplomate Nat. Bd. Examiners in Optometry. Gen. practice optometry, Superior and Mankato, Kans., 1972—, Omaha, 1981-83, York, Nebr., 1984—; cons. Internat. Contact Lens, Omaha. Pres. Superior Flyers, 1983, Superior Alumni, 1979. Served as capt. U.S. Army, 1970-72. Mem. Am. Optometric Assn., Nebr. Optometric Assn., Heart of Am. Contact Lens Congress, Am. Legion, Danish Brotherhood. Methodist. Lodges: Kiwanis (pres. 1976, Outstanding Kiwanian of Superior award 1977), Elks (chmn. Nebr. youth activities 1979-81, best nat. program award 1981, dist. dept. grand exalted ruler Nebr., 1981-82, 3d v.p. Nebr. 1984), Eagles. Home: 5730 Prescott Ave Lincoln NE Office: 314 Central Superior NE 68978

ANDERSEN, JUDITH MARIE, pharmacist, educator, consultant; b. Des Moines, Apr. 1, 1953; d. Robert Lee and Dolores Bethine (Madsen) A.; m. Romualdas Mickevicius, Nov. 11, 1978; 1 child, Kristina Marie. B.S. in Pharmacy, Creighton U., 1976; Pharm.D., U. Minn., 1978. Registered pharmacist, Iowa, Nebr., Minn. Asst. prof. Creighton U., Omaha, 1978-85; cons. pharmacist Omaha Devel. Ctr., 1981—; clin. pharmacist St. Joseph Ctr. for Mental Health, Omaha, 1980—, Omaha Psychiat. Assocs., 1983—. Author (with others) MICRODID (drug interaction detection computer program), 1981. Contbr. (with others) articles to profl. jours. Mem. Nebr. Democratic Party; bd. dirs. Nebr. Council Continuing Pharmacy Edn. Grantee Upjohn, 1983. Mem. Am. Coll. Clin. Pharmacy (assoc.), Am. Soc. Hosp. Pharmacists, Nebr. Pharmacists Assn. (mem. polit. action com. 1980—), Greater Omaha Pharmacists Assn. (bd. dirs. 1981—), Rho Chi, Lambda Kappa Sigma (chpt. advisor 1978—). Lutheran. Club: Midwest Investors (Omaha). Lodges: Danish Brotherhood, Danish Sisterhood. Home: 3660 S 44th Ave Omaha NE 68105

ANDERSEN, LEONARD CHRISTIAN, former state legislator, real estate investor; b. Waukegan, Ill., May 30, 1911; s. Lauritz Frederick and Meta Marie (Jacobsen) A.; B.A., Huron (S.D.) Coll., 1933; M.A., U. S.D., 1937; m. Charlotte O. Ritland, June 30, 1937; children—Karen (Mrs. Fred Schneider), Paul R., Charlene (Mrs. Kurt Olsson), Mark Luther. Tchr., Onida (S.D.) High Sch., 1934-35; dir. bus. tng. Waldorf Coll., Forest City, Iowa, 1935-39; ins. salesman, 1939-41; tchr. econs., current history Morningside Coll., Sioux City, Iowa, 1941-43; engaged in ins. and real estate, Sioux City, 1943-76; mem. Iowa Ho. of Reps. from Woodbury County, 1961-64, 66-71; mem. Iowa Senate from 26th Dist., 1972-76, chmn. rules and adminstrn. com. Mem. Iowa Commn. on Aging; mem. Sioux City Housing Appeals Bd., past mem. Siouxland Council on Alcoholism; bd. regents Augustana Coll., Sioux Falls, S.D., 12 yrs., now mem. Augustana Fellows; chmn. Morningside Lutheran Ch. Mem. UN Assn. (past pres. Siouxland chpt.), Siouxland Rental Assn. (pres. 1984), Sioux City C. of C., United Comml. Travelers. Republican. Lodges: Masons, Lions. Home: 712 S Glass St Sioux City IA 51106 Office: 712 S Glass St Sioux City IA 51106

ANDERSEN, R. CLIFTON, business educator, dean; b. Chgo., Apr. 8, 1933; s. Rudolph T. and Myrtle (Lloyd) A.; m. Carolyn Marie Johnstone, Dec. 28, 1955; children—Lynn Elizabeth, Kathleen Mary. B.S., Ind. U., 1955, M.B.A., 1958, D.B.A., 1960. Asst. prof., then assoc. prof. U. Tex., Austin, 1963-67; chmn. dept. mktg. So. Ill. U., Carbondale, 1967-72, prof., 1972-76, 84—, assoc. dean, 1976-81, 83-84, acting dean, 1981-83. Editor: Marketing Insights, 1963, 68, 74; Distribution Systems, 1972. Contbr. articles to profl. and acad. jours. Served with U.S. Army, 1955-57. Ford Found. fellow, 1958-60. Mem. Am. Mktg. Assn., Alpha Kappa Psi. Republican. Episcopalian. Avocations: Travel, reading. Home: 1604 Taylor Dr Carbondale IL 62901 Office: So Ill U Dept Mktg Coll Bus Carbondale IL 62901

ANDERSON, ALAN DALE, geologist; b. Canton, Ohio, Sept. 23, 1951; s. Dale Leroy and Iris Marcette (Kurtz) A.; m. Kathy Starrett, Sept. 23, 1974; children—Zachary John, Molly Dale, Kate Elizabeth. Student Adrian Coll., Mich., 1969; B.S. in Geology, U. Akron, 1974. Jr. Geologist Nuclear Dynamics, Moorcroft, Wyo., 1974-75; geologist Appalachian Exploration, Canton, Ohio, 1975-77, exploration mgr., drilling supt., 1977-81; v.p. E.O. Gregory Enterprises, Uniontown, Ohio, 1981-83, pres., Canton, 1983—; pres. Cumberland Exploration, Canton, 1981—. Mem. Am. Assn. Petroleum Geologists, Ohio Oil and Gas Assn., Ohio Geol. Soc., Am. Assn. Petroleum Geologists (cert.). Republican. Avocations: fishing, hunting. Home: 5832 Linder Circle North Canton OH 44721 Office: E O Gregory Enterprises and Cumberland Exploration Inc 1201 30th St Canton OH 44709

ANDERSON, ARTHUR RODNEY, vocat. educator; b. Oak Park, Ill., Feb. 14, 1930; s. Arthur J. and Hilda Marie (Fauske) A.; B.S., So. Ill. U., 1981, M.S., 1983; m. Marjorie Raglin, June 23, 1965. Carpenter, Wade Constrn. Co., Itasca, Ill., 1962-72, foreman, 1962-65, supt., 1965-72; tchr. bldg. trades Lockport (Ill.) Twp. High Sch., 1972—, developer vocat. bldg. trades course; lectr. secondary edn. workshops, 1968—. Recipient Outstanding Service award James McKinnon Smith chpt. Nat. Honor Soc., 1975; citation for outstanding contbn. to vocat. edn. studies So. Ill. U., 1981. Mem. Am. Vocat. Assn., Ill. Vocat. Assn., Ill. Indsl. Edn. Assn. (pres. Roundtable 4, 1983-84), United Brotherhood of Carpenters and Joiners (pres. local 558, Elmhurst, Ill. 1967-76), Iota Lambda Sigma. Lutheran. Club: Sons of Norway. Home: 603 S Dunton Ave Arlington Heights IL 60005 Office: Lockport Twp High School 12th and Jefferson Sts Lockport IL 60441

ANDERSON, AUSTIN GOTHARD, educator, lawyer; b. Calumet, Minn., June 30, 1931; s. Hugo Gothard and Turna Marie (Johnson) A.; B.A., U. Minn., 1954, J.D., 1958; m. Catherine Antoinette Spellacy, Jan. 2, 1954; children—Todd, Susan, Timothy, Linda, Mark. Bar: Minn. 1958, Ill. 1962, Mich. 1974. Mem. firm Spellacy, Spellacy, Lano & Anderson, Marble, Minn., 1958-62; dir. Ill. Inst. Continuing Legal Edn., Springfield, 1962-64; dir. dept. continuing legal edn. U. Minn., Mpls., 1964-70, assoc. dean gen. extension div., 1968-70; adminstrv. ptnr. firm Dorsey, Marquart, Windhorst, West & Halladay, Mpls., 1970-73; assoc. dir. Nat. Center for State Cts., St. Paul, 1973-74; dir. inst. continuing legal edn., U. Mich., Ann Arbor, 1973—; adj. faculty U. Minn., 1974, Wayne State U., 1974-75, William Mitchell Coll. Law, 1973-74; project dir. Select Com. on Judiciary State of Minn., 1974-76; chmn. City of Bloomington (Minn.) Park and Recreation Adv. Commn., 1970-72; pres. bd. King Sch. Parent-Tchr. Orgn., 1977-78; sec. bd. dirs. Ann Arbor Amateur Hockey Assn., 1979—; mem. citizens recreation adv. com. Ann Arbor Pub. Schs., 1982—; mem. parks adv. com. City of Ann Arbor, 1983-84; mem. adv. com. Ferris State Coll. Served with USN, 1950-51. Fellow Am. Bar Found.; mem. Assn. Legal Adminstrs. (pres. 1969-70), Am. (chmn. sect. econs. of law practice 1981-82), Mich., Ill., Minn., Washtenaw County bar assns., Am. Mgmt. Assn., Assn. Continuing Legal Edn. Adminstrs. Co-editor, contbg. author: Lawyer's Handbook, 1975; cons. editor: Webster's Legal Secretaries Handbook, 1981; contbr. chpt. to book. Home: 3617 Larchmont Dr Ann Arbor MI 48105 Office: 432 Hutchins Hall Ann Arbor MI 48109

ANDERSON, BARRY STANLEY, health care executive; b. Atlanta, Sept. 6, 1942; s. Rex and Virginia A.; m. Katherine Krupp, Dec. 26, 1966 (div. 1973); 1 child, Jon Robert; m. Patricia Ann O'Neil, May 25, 1974; 1 child, Russell Barry. A.A., Foothill Coll., 1968; B.A., San Francisco State U., 1976; M.B.A., U. N.D., 1984. Vice pres. Ventilation Assocs., Inc., Houston, 1971-74; program dir. Inst. Med. Studies, Berkeley, Calif., 1976-78; program dir. Sch. Respiratory Therapy, St. Alexius Med. Ctr., Bismarck, N.D., 1978-84, dir. edn., 1984—; pres. Creative Marketing, Inc., Bismarck, 1982—; asst. prof. Mary Coll., 1982—. Author: (with D. Quesinberry) Blood Gas Interpretations, 1974; mem. editorial adv. bd. Respiratory Therapy; contbr. articles to profl. jours. Mem. Am. Mktg. Assn., Am. Mgmt. Assn., Am. Assn. Respiratory Therapy, Am. Assn. Respiratory Care, Dakota Soc. Respiratory Care, Dakota Soc. Respiratory Therapy, Am. Hosp. Assn., U. N.D. Alumni Assn. Lodge: Elks. Avocations: computer programming; writing; reading; lecturing. Office: St Alexius Med Ctr 900 E Broadway Bismarck ND 58501

ANDERSON, BOB, state legislator, business executive; b. Wadena, Minn., Jan. 16, 1932; s. Alfred Emmanuel and Frances Agnes (Hassler) A.; m. Janet Lynn Hemquist, Aug. 3, 1967. B.B.A., U. Miami, 1959. Small businessman, Minn., 1954—; mem. Minn. Ho. of Reps., 1976—, mem. appropriations com. mem. exec. com.; Nat. Conf. State Legislatures; vice chmn. Minn. Legis. Commn. on Waste Mgmt. Past pres. Viking-Land, U.S.A., Explorers Highroad Found., Ottertail Lake Property Owners Assn.; mem. Minn. Fuel Alcohol Assn., Fergus Falls N.G. Citizens Com.; mem. chem. dependency adv. com. Fergus Falls State Hosp. Served with U.S. Army, 1952-54. Decorated D.S.M. Named Hon. Citizen, City of Winnipeg; recipient Highroad Explorer award, Hon. Viking award. Mem. Minn. Meat Processors Assn. (past pres.), Otter Trail County Hist. Soc., Am. Legion, VFW. Republican. Clubs: Bal Moral Golf, Fergus Falls Fish and Game, Pelican River Sportsmen, St. Paul Athletic. Lodges: Elks, Masons, Shriners.

ANDERSON, CLARENCE AXEL FREDERICK, retired mechanical engineer; b. Muskegon, Mich., Dec. 14, 1909; s. Axel Robert and Anna Victoria (Wikman) A.; student Muskegon Jr. Coll., 1929, Internat. Corr. Schs., 1934; m. Frances K. Swem, Apr. 9, 1934; children—Robert Curtis, Clarelyn Christine Anderson Schmelling, Stanley Herbert. With Shaw-Walker Co., Muskegon, Mich., 1928-78, mech. engr., 1940-65, project engr., 1965-70, chief engr., 1970-78; ret., 1978. Mem. Christian edn. bd. Forest Park Covenant Ch., 1959-61, 67-73, usher, 1953—, trustee, 1985—, co-chmn. Jackson Hill Oldtimers Reunion, 1982, 83. Mem. Nat. Rifle Assn. Club: Holland (Mich.) Beagle (pres. 1966-68, 70-73, 75—). Home: 5757 E Sternberg Rd Fruitport MI 49415

ANDERSON, CLAUDIA SMITH, lawyer; b. Peoria, Ill., Mar. 21, 1953; d. Lester Berry and June Edda (Kopal) Smith; m. Curtis A. Anderson, Aug. 26, 1972. Student Stephens Coll., 1971-72; B.S. in Elem. Edn., Rockford Coll., 1976; J.D. cum laude, Gonzaga U., 1979. Bar: Ill. 1979, U.S. dist. ct. (cen. dist.) Ill. 1980. Assoc. Acton, Acton, Meyer & Smith, Danville, Ill., 1979-83; ptnr. Acton, Meyer, Smith, Miller & Anderson, Danville, 1984—. Apptd. mem. Danville Plan Commn., 1984—; bd. dirs. YWCA, Danville, 1984—. Recipient Am. Jurisprudence award, 1979. Mem. Ill. Bar Assn., Vermilion County Bar Assn. (pub. relations chmn. 1984—), Assn. Trial Lawyers Am., Ill. Trial Lawyers Assn., Danville C. of C. (bd. dirs. 1984—), DAR. Republican. Roman Catholic. Club: Executive (pres. Danville 1981-82). Office: Acton Meyer Smith Miller & Anderson 11 E North St Danville IL 61832

ANDERSON, DANITA RUTH, minister; b. Chgo., Nov. 5, 1956; d. Walter and Doris E. (Terrell) A. B.S.B.A., Chgo. State U., 1978; M.Div., Gammon Theol. Sem., Atlanta, 1983. Ordained deacon United Methodist Ch., 1983, elder, 1985. Ch. sec. Grace-Calvary Ch., Chgo., 1976-78; parish sec. Ingleside-Whitfield Meth. Ch., Chgo., 1978-79; computer programmer trainee Sears, Roebuck & Co., Chgo., 1979-80; ch. sec. Gorham United Meth. Ch., Chgo., 1980; asst. pastor Cascade United Meth. C., Atlanta, 1980-83; assoc. minister St. Mark Ch., Chgo., 1983—. Former mem. NAACP, Atlanta Assn. Black Journalists; sec. Black Methodists for Ch. Renewal, Chgo., 1979. Bd. Global Ministries Crusade scholar, 1981-83; Women's Div. United Meth. Ch. grantee, 1982; recipient Joseph W. Queen award Gammon Sem., 1982, James and Emma Todd award, 1983. Mem. Black Chgo. United Meth. Clergy Orgn., Chgo. Black Methodists for Ch. Renewal (corr. sec. 1984). Home: 8959 S Euclid Ave Chicago IL 60617 Office: 8441 S Saint Lawrence Chicago IL 60619

ANDERSON, DAVID CARL, graphic designer; b. Rockford, Ill., Oct. 27, 1941; s. Carl Gustav and Frances Caroline (Rydholm) A.; m. Jane Ravlin, Oct. 31, 1964 (div.); 1 child, Justin Ravlin; m. Gay Lynn Pearson, May 29, 1983. B.S., Ill. Inst. Tech., Inst. of Design, 1963. Designer, Sta. WTTW-TV, Chgo., 1963-64, Unimark Internat., Chgo. 1965-67, RVI Corp., Chgo., 1967-70; prin. David Anderson Design, Chgo., 1970—. Designer trademarks, brochures, exhibits for various midwest corps. Exhibitor: Ill. Inst. Tech. Alumni Exhibit, Chgo., 1976. Bd. dirs. Unity Temple Restoration Found., Oak Park, Ill., 1981—, The Frank Lloyd Wright Home and Studio Found., Oak Park, 1982—. Included in Fifty Years of Graphic Design in Chicago: 1927-1977, The Soc. Typographic Arts, Chgo., 1978. Mem. Twenty-Seven Chgo. Designers, Soc. Typographic Arts, Am. Inst. Graphic Arts. Office: David Anderson Design 333 N Michigan Ave Chicago IL 60601

ANDERSON, DAVID DANIEL, educator; b. Lorain, Ohio, June 8, 1924; s. David and Nora Marie (Foster) A.; B.S., Bowling Green State U., 1951, M.A., 1952; Ph.D., Mich. State U., 1960; m. Patricia Ann Rittenhour, Feb. 1, 1953. From instr. to prof. dept. Am. thought and lang. Mich. State U., East Lansing, 1957—, editor U. Coll. Quar., 1971-80; Fulbright prof. U. Karachi, Pakistan, 1963-64; lectr. Hungarian Acad., 1984; Am. del. to Internat. Fedn. Modern Langs., and Lit., 1969-84, Internat. Congress Orientalists, 1971-79; lectr. Am. Mus., Bath, Eng., 1980. Served with USN, 1942-45, AUS, 1952-53. Decorated Silver Star, Purple Heart; recipient Disting. Alumnus award Bowling Green State U., 1976; Disting. Faculty award Mich. State U., 1974. Mem. AAUP, Popular Culture Assn., Modern Lang Assn., Soc. Study Midwestern Lit. (founder, exec. sec.; pres. 1971-73; disting. service award 1982), Assn. Gen. and Liberal Edn. Author: Sherwood Anderson, 1968 (Book Manuscript award 1961); Louis Bromfield, 1964; Critical Studies in American Literature, 1964; Sherwood Anderson's Winesburg, Ohio, 1967; Brand Whitlock, 1968; Abraham Lincoln, 1970; Suggestions for the Instructor, 1971; Robert Ingersoll, 1972; Woodrow Wilson 1978; Ignatius Donnelly, 1980; William Jennings Bryan, 1981; editor: The Black Experience, 1969; The Literary Works of Abraham Lincoln, 1970; Sunshine and Smoke: American Writers and the American Environment, 1971; (with others) The Dark and Tangled Path, 1971; MidAmerica I, 1974, II, 1975, III, 1976, IV, 1977, V, 1978, VI, 1979, VII, 1980, VIII, 1981, IX, 1982, X, 1983, XI, 1984; Sherwood Anderson: Dimensions of his Literary Art, 1976; Sherwood Anderson: The Writer at His Craft, 1979; Critical Essays on Sherwood Anderson, 1981; Michigan: A State Anthology, 1983; editor Midwestern Miscellany, SSML Newsletter. Home: 6555 Lansdown Dr Dimondale MI 48821 Office: Dept Am Thought and Lang Mich State U East Lansing MI 48824

ANDERSON, DEBRA JEAN, science educator; b. Pipestone, Minn., Mar. 22, 1951; d. Darwin Gene and Delilah Mae (Mohlmann) A. B.S., Mankato State U., 1973, M.S., 1979; Ed.D., U. No. Colo., 1983. Cert. tchr., Minn. Sci. tchr. Moundsview, Minn., 1973-75, Hopkins, Minn., 1975-76, Gillette, Wyo., 1976-78; grad. asst. geography/curriculum, instr. Mankato State U., 1978-80, instr. chemistry, 1982-83; upward bound sci. cons., 1979-82; field cons. profl. field experience U. No. Colo., Greeley, 1980-81; sci. tchr./coach Amboy-Good Thunder High Sch., Amboy, Minn., 1981-82; asst. prof. edn. Northland Coll., Ashland, Wis., 1983—; Co-sponsor Women in Sci. Orgn. Mem. Nat. Sci. Tchrs. Assn., Wis. Assn. Tchr. Educators, Minn. Assn. Tchr. Educators, Bus. and Profl. Women's Club, Phi Delta Kappa. Democrat. Lutheran. Lodge: Moose. Home: Route 8 Box 162 Mankato MN 56001 Office: Box 595 Northland Ashland WI 54806

ANDERSON, DENNIS KEITH, molecular biologist, computer scientist; b. Moorhead, Minn., Mar. 21, 1956; s. Alvin Eugene and Eileen Catherine (Wilkinson) A. B.S. with scholastic honors, N.D. State U., 1978; M.S., Kans. State U., 1981. Research assoc. Molecular Genetics, Inc., Minnetonka, Minn., 1981, mgr. support services, 1981-83, dir. data mgmt. and info. systems, 1983—. Recipient Cora M. Downs award Mo. Valley chpt., 1980. Presdl. fellow Am. Soc. Microbiology, 1977. Mem. N.Y. Acad. Scis., Minn. Acad. Scis., Sigma Xi, Phi Kappa Phi. Lutheran. Office: 10320 Bren Rd E Minnetonka MN 55343

ANDERSON, DONALD GEORGE, marketing educator; b. Burlington, Iowa, Oct. 11, 1930; s. George Hamilton and Esther Susan (McCaleb) A.; m. Beulah Esther Fargo, June 6, 1959; children—David A., Susan R. B.S.C., U. Iowa, 1956, M.A., 1967, Ph.D., 1962. Instr. U. S.D., Vermillion, 1957-59, U. Iowa, Iowa City, 1959-61; asst. prof. U. N.D., Grand Forks, 1961-62, prof. mktg., 1963—; asst. prof. U. South Fla., Tampa, 1962-63. Contbr. articles to profl. jours. Pres. Full Gospel Businessmen chpt., Grand Forks, 1977-78, sec., 1983—; bd. dirs. Valley Advt./Mktg. Club, Grand Forks, 1979-82. Served with USN, 1951-54. Recipient B.C. Gamble Disting. Teaching award U. N.D., 1979; Cert. of Appreciation, Distributive Edn. Clubs Am., 1969; Kiplinger Found. fellow, 1977. Mem. So. Mktg. Assn., Southwestern Mktg. Assn., Am. Mktg. Assn., Small Bus. Inst., Delta Sigma Pi, Beta Gamma Sigma. Methodist. Avocations: photography; tropical fish. Home: 2910 Clover Dr Grand Forks ND 58201 Office: Mktg Dept University Station Grand Forks ND 58202-8163

ANDERSON, DORRINE ANN PETERSEN (MRS. HAROLD EDWARD ANDERSON), librarian; b. Ishpeming, Mich., Feb. 24, 1923; d. Herbert Nathaniel and Dorothy (Eman) Petersen; B.S. with distinction, No. Mich. U., 1944; postgrad. Northwestern U., summer 1945, U. Wash., summer 1967, U. Mich. Extension, 1958-65; M.S. in L.S., Western Mich. U., 1970; m. Harold Edward Anderson, Aug. 23, 1947; children—Brian Peter, Kent Harold, Bruce Herbert, Timothy Jon. Tchr. English jr. high sch., Eaton Rapids, Mich., 1944-45; tchr. English, speech Arlington Heights (Ill.) High Sch., 1945-48; tchr. English high sch., Nahma, Mich., 1948-49, 54-61, Gladstone, Mich., 1961-62; librarian Gladstone Sch. and Pub. Library, 1962-70; dir. library services Gladstone Area Pub. Schs., 1971—, Bicentennial coordinator, 1975-76; mem. planning com. Upper Peninsula Region Library Cooperation, 1982—; rep.-at-large Mich. Citizens for Libraries. Acting dir. Mid-Peninsula Library Fedn., 1965-66; chmn. Region 21 Media Advisory Council, 1972—; chmn. adv. com. Regional Ednl. Materials Center 21, 1973—; regional del. Mich. White House Conf. on Libraries and Info. Services, 1979. Pres., Delta County League Woman Voters, 1970-72; mem. human resources subcom. Upper Peninsula Com. for Area Progress, 1964—; mem. com. for library devel. Upper Peninsula, chmn. Delta County Library Bd., 1967-76; mem. region 17, Polit. Action Team, 1968-70; history chmn. Gladstone City Centennial Com., 1982—. County del. Delta County Democratic Com., 1968; trustee Library of Mich., 1984—. Named Tchr. of Year, Region 17 (Mich.), 1969. Mem. NEA, Mich. Edn. Assn. (pres. region 17 council 1967-68, chmn. Upper Peninsula dels. to rep. assembly 1966-68), ALA, Mich. Library Assn., Internat. Reading Assn., Mich. Assn. Media in Edn. (state Library Week chmn. 1973-74; recipient leadership award 1977), Mich. Assn. Sch. Library Suprs., Upper Peninsula Reading Conf. (program chmn. Leadership award planning com. 1981), AAUW, Assn. Ednl. Communications and Tech., Kappa Delta Pi, Phi Epsilon, Beta Phi Mu, Delta Kappa Gamma (recipient citation for seminars in mgmt. for women 1977, v.p., program chmn. Beta Sigma chpt. 1980-82). Home: 1723 Montana Ave Gladstone MI 49837 Office: Gladstone Area Sch and Pub Library Gladstone MI 49837

ANDERSON, DOUGLAS R., communications company executive; b. McMinville, Oreg., Sept. 22, 1951; s. Harland A. and Mary Theresa (Bernards) A.; m. Sharon G. Striplin, Dec. 17, 1971 (div. 1976); 1 child, Chad Douglas. A.S.D.P., A.A.S.S., Linn Benton Community Coll., Albany, Oreg., 1972; B.S.C.S., Oregon State U., 1975; postgrad. Intel U., 1978, Milw. Tech. Coll., 1981. Cert. systems profl. Data processing facilities planner Intel Corp., Portland, Oreg., 1978-79; v.p. ops. Inter Active Graphics Inc., Milw., 1979-81; dir. data processing Cattle Mktg. Info. Service, Englewood, Colo., 1982-83; dir. software devel. North West Telephone Co., Tomah, Wis., 1983—; cons. D.R. Anderson, 1980—. Mem. U.S. Congl. Adv. Bd., Washington, 1984. Mem. Am. Mgmt. Assn., Assn. Systems Mgmt., Data Processing Mgmt. Assn., Local Users Group Digital Equipment Corp Soc. (chmn). Republican. Roman Catholic. Home: 1619 Kilbourn Ave Tomah WI 54660 Office: North West Telephone Co 306 Arthur Tomah WI 54660

ANDERSON, EDGAR LANOLAN, JR., computer company official; b. Harvey, Ill., Sept. 26, 1950; s. Edgar LaNolan and Charlotte Jean (King) A.; m. Pamela Regina (div. Jan. 1975); 1 son, Edgar LaMont. B.S. in Engring., U.S. Mil. Acad., 1972; M. Mgmt., Yale U., 1981. Project engr. Dow Chem. Corp., Anderson, S.C., 1975-76; personnel cons. Cummins Engine Co, Jamestown, N.Y., 1976-79; sr. personnel rep. Hewlett-Packard Co., Cleve., 1981—. Served to 1st lt. U.S. Army, 1972-75. Mem. Ill. High Sch. Athletic Assn. All State football team, 1967, All State wrestling team, 1967-68, Nat. Honor Soc., 1967-68. Democrat. Home: 11884 The Bluffs Strongsville OH 44136

ANDERSON, EDWARD FRANCIS, anesthesiologist; b. Phila., Aug. 1, 1943; s. John Marcus and Lillian May (Carroll) A.; m. Candice Jo Sundvold, July 3, 1971. B.A., Notre Dame U., 1965, B.S. in Mech. Engring., 1966; M.D., Georgetown U., 1970. Diplomate Nat. Bd. Med. Examiners, Am. Bd. Anesthesiology. Intern, Naval Hosp., Great Lakes, Ill., 1970-71; resident in anesthesiology Nat. Naval Med. Ctr., Bethesda, Md., 1971-73, fellow critical care, 1973-74; anesthesiologist Naval Regional Med Ctr., Great Lakes, 1974-77, asst. chief anesthesiology dept., 1974-77; anesthesiologist Sioux Valley Hosp. (S.D.), 1978—; cons. Royal C. Johnson Vets. Hosp., Sioux Falls, 1978—; med. dir. Pain Control Clinic, Sioux Valley Hosp., 1984—; lectr. in field. Contbr. articles to profl. jours. Profl. edn. chmn. Am. Cancer Soc., Sioux Falls, 1984—; mem. Am. Heart Assn., Sioux Falls, 1984—. Served to lt. comdr. USN, 1969-77. Fellow Am. Coll. Anesthesiologists, Am. Coll. Chest Physicians; mem. Am. Soc. Anesthesiologists, Internat. Anesthesia Research Soc., Am. Soc. Regional Anesthesia, Soc. Cardiovascular Anesthesiologists, Soc. Critical Care Medicine, AMA. Democrat. Lutheran. Avocations: gradening, farming, reading, antiques. Home: RR 2 Box 12A Brandon SD 57005 Office: Anesthesia Physicians Ltd 1201 S Euclid St Sioux Falls SD 57105

ANDERSON, EDWIN R., city official; b. Hickson, N.D., June 7, 1920; m. LaVern Weisser, Oct. 12, 1947; children—Pam Anderson Phillips, Frank, Bill, Susan. A.A. in Police Sci., Minot State Coll., 1978, B.S. in Police Sci., 1979; B.S., N.D. State U., 1978. With Fargo Police Dept., N.D., 1946—, patrolman, 1946-49, sgt., 1949-51, lt., 1951-53, capt., 1953-64, asst. chief of police, 1964-66, chief, 1966—; pres. North Central Crime Conf., N.D.; mem. Red River Valley Peace Officer Assn., N.D. rep. to bd. trustees Midstates Organized Crime Info. Ctr., Springfield, Mo., 1980-85; chmn. Nat. Com. State Assns. Chiefs of Police; mem., past pres. Fargo Safety Council. Served with U.S. Army, 1942-46; PTO. Mem. N.D. Peace Officers Assn. (pres. 1978), N.D. Police Chiefs (past pres.), Internat. Assn. Chiefs of Police (numerous coms.). Lutheran. Lodge: Masons. Office: Fargo Police Dept Box 150 200-N 3d St Fargo ND 58107

ANDERSON, ERIC ANTHONY, city manager; b. New Orleans, June 2, 1946; s. Eric Albert and Edna (Barrie) A.; B.A., Syracuse U., 1967; M.P.A., SUNY, Albany, 1968; M.A., Maxwell Sch., Syracuse U., 1970; m. Linda Jane Briefstein, June 22, 1967; children—Eric Scott, Stacy Alissa. Adminstrv. intern City of Phoenix, 1970-71; asst. dir. Research and Devel. Center, Internat. City Mgmt. Assn., Washington, 1971-73; asst. town mgr. Town of Windsor (Conn.), 1973-78; town mgr. Munster (Ind.), 1978-83; city mgr. Eau Claire (Wis.), 1984—. Bd. mgrs. Windsor-Bloomfield YMCA, 1976-78; adv. council Urban League N.W. Ind., 1979. Nat. Endowment for Humanities fellow, 1977. Mem. Ind. Mcpl. Mgmt. Assn. (pres. 1979-80), Conn. City Mgmt. Assn. (treas. 1977-78), Internat. City Mgmt. Assn., Nat. League of Cities, (community and econ. devel. policy com. 1984), League of Wis. Municipalities (com. on fin. and taxation 1984). Club: Rotary. Home: 9129 Birch Ave Munster IN 46321 Office: 805 Ridge Rd Munster IN 46321

ANDERSON, ERIC EDWARD, psychologist, consultant; b. Mpls., Jan. 24, 1951; s. Charles Eric and Elizabeth (Engstrand) A.; B.A. summa cum laude,

U. Minn., 1973; M.A. in Theology, Fuller Sem., 1977, Ph.D. in Clin. Psychology, 1978; m. Florence Kaye, June 18, 1978; children—Cara Elizabeth, Evan Travis. Asst. prof. Sch. Public Health U. Minn., Mpls., 1979-83, coordinator tng. in aging, 1979-83; dir. profl. services Kiel Clinic, Mpls. and St. Paul, 1979-84; group v.p. Kiel Profl. Services, Inc., St. Paul, 1983-84, pres., 1984—; cons. on aging, govt. task forces; cons. Wilder Found., St. Paul, Ebenezer Soc., Mpls. Lic. cons. psychologist, Minn. Mem. Am. Psychol. Assn., Gerontol. Soc. Am., Minn. Psychol. Assn., Assn. Health Service Providers in Psychology, Phi Beta Kappa. Lodge: Rotary. Contbr. articles to profl. jours. Office: Kiel Clinic 7550 France Ave S Edina MN 55435

ANDERSON, EUGENE I., See *Who's Who in America,* 43rd edition.

ANDERSON, EUGENE WALTER, JR., public relations executive; b. Chgo., Oct. 9, 1935; s. Eugene Walter and Alice Roberta (Crosby) A.; m. Judith Anne Dunkle, Nov. 15, 1958; children—Eugene W. III, Eric L. B.S. in Metall. Engring., Carnegie-Mellon U., 1958; post-grad. Indsl. Coll. of Armed Forces, Washington, 1960. Advt. mgr. Elliott div. Carrier Corp., Jeannette, Pa., 1958-60; account exec. Marsteller Inc., Pitts., 1960; account exec. Burson-Marsteller, Pitts., 1960-62, account supr., 1962-66, v.p., client services mgr., 1966-71, gen. mgr., 1971-72, dir., London, 1972-76, group mgr., Chgo., 1976-80; dir. pub. affairs and advt. Amsted Industries Inc., Chgo., 1980—. Mem. pub. relations adv. com. Chgo. Heart Assn., 1981—; DuPage (Ill.) County chmn. U. Ill. Dad's Assn., 1980—. Served to 1st lt. U.S. Army, 1958-59. Mem. Chgo. Pub. Relations Clinic (pres. 1984-85), Machinery and Allied Products Inst. (pub. affairs council), Pub. Affairs Council, Pub. Relations Soc. Am., Ry. Progress Inst. (chmn. pub. relations com. 1983—). Republican. Episcopalian. Clubs: Econ. of Chgo., Tavern. Office: 3700 Prudential Plaza Chicago IL 60601

ANDERSON, FRANCES SWEM, nuclear medical technologist; b. Grand Rapids, Mich., Nov. 27, 1913; d. Frank Oscar and Carrie (Strang) Swem; student Muskegon Sch. Bus., 1959-60; cert. Muskegon Community Coll., 1964; m. Clarence A.F. Anderson, Apr. 9, 1934; children—Robert Curtis, Clarelyn Christine (Mrs. Roger L. Schmelling), Stanley Herbert. X-ray file clk., film librarian Hackley Hosp., Muskegon, Mich., 1957-59; student refresher course in nuclear med. tech. Chgo. Soc. Nuclear Med. Techs., 1966; radioisotope technologist and sec. Hackley Hosp., 1959-65; nuclear med. technologist Butler Meml. Hosp., Muskegon Heights, Mich., 1966-70, Mercy Hosp., Muskegon, 1970-79; ret., 1979. Mem. Muskegon Civic A Capella choir, 1932-39; mem. Mother-Tch. Singers, PTA, Muskegon, 1941-48, treas. 1944-48; with Muskegon Civic Opera Assn., 1950-51. Soc. Nuclear Medicine Cert. nuclear medicine technologist Soc. Nuclear Medicine. Mem. Am. Registry Radiologic Technologists. Mem. Forest Park Covenant Ch. (mem. choir 1953-79, 83—, choir sec. 1963-69, Sunday sch. tchr. 1954-75, supt. Sunday sch. 1975-78, treas. Sunday sch. 1981—, chmn. master planning council, coordinator centennial com. to 1981, ch. sec. 1982-84). Home: 5757 E Sternberg Rd Fruitport MI 49415

ANDERSON, GARY LEE, utility company executive; b. Harlan, Iowa, Feb. 3, 1946; s. Lake Nels and Helen Margaret Anderson; A.B., Creighton U., Omaha, 1969; M.P.A., U. Nebr., 1975; m. Jeanne Kwapiszeski, Oct. 15, 1977; children—Gary Lee, John Nicholas. Supr., Panganerix, Omaha, 1969-71; asst. adminstr. Doctors' Hosp., Omaha, 1971-73; mem. research team Social Security Adminstrn., Omaha, 1974; dir. Nebr. Dept. Public Instns., Lincoln, 1975-80; systems analyst Mut. of Omaha, Omaha, 1980-84, No. Natural Gas, Omaha, 1984—. Home: 6006 N 109 Plaza Omaha NE 68164

ANDERSON, GEORGE ELI, engineering executive; b. Mpls., Mar. 24, 1946; s. Clifford Hawkins and Katharine (Irving) A.; m. Barbara Jean Kredit, Mar. 31, 1973; 2 children. B.S. in Mech. Engring., Stanford U., 1969. Draftsman, Crown Iron Works Co., Mpls., 1969-70, engr., 1970-72, project mgr., 1972-75, chief engr., 1975-84, v.p. engring., 1984—, sec., 1974—, dir., 1979—; dir. Crown Holdings, Inc. Contbr. articles to profl. jours. Inventor in field. Adult tchr. Redeemer Covenant Ch., Bklyn. Park, Minn., 1977—; del. Rep. County Conv., 1984; trustee Redeemer Covenant Ch., 1978-80. Recipient Cert. of Merit Nat. Merit Scholarship program, 1964, others. Mem. ASME, Nat. Soc. Profl. Engrs., Minn. Soc. Profl. Engrs., Am. Oilseed Chemists Soc., Internat. Oil Mill Supts. Assn., Nat. Fire Protection Assn. Republican. Avocations: Classic autos.; computers; comparative religions. Office: Crown Iron Works Co PO Box 1364 Minneapolis MN 55440

ANDERSON, GEORGE LEE (SPARKY), professional baseball team manager; b. Bridgewater, S.D., Feb. 22, 1934. Player, Phila. Phillies, from 1959; mgr. Cin. Reds, 1970-78, Detroit Tigers, 1979—. Winner Nat. League championship, 1970, 72, 75, 76, World Series, 1984; mgr. Nat. League All Star Team, 1971, 73, 76, 77; named Nat. League Mgr. of Year, 1972. Address: Detroit Tigers Tiger Stadium Detroit MI 48216*

ANDERSON, GERALDINE LOUISE, clinical laboratory scientist; b. Mpls., July 7, 1941; d. George M. and Viola Julia-Mary (Abel) Havrilla; B.S., U. Minn., 1963; m. Henry Clifford Anderson, May 21, 1966; children—Bruce Henry, Julie Lynne. Med. technologist Swedish Hosp., Mpls., 1963-68; hematology supr. Glenwood Hills Hosp. lab., Golden Valley, Minn., 1968-70; asso. scientist dept. pediatrics U. Minn. Hosps., Mpls., 1970-74; instr. health occupations and med. lab. asst. Suburban Hennepin County Area Vocat. Tech. Center, Brooklyn Park, Minn., 1974-81, St. Paul Tech. Vocat. Inst., 1978—; research med. technologist Miller Hosp., St. Paul, 1975-78; research asso. Children's and United Hosps., St. Paul, 1979—; mem. health occupations adv. com. Hennepin Tech. Centers, 1975—, chairperson, 1978-79; mem. hematology slide edn. rev. bd. Am. Soc. Hematology, 1976—. Mem. Med. Lab. Tech. Polit. Action Com., 1978—; resource person lab. careers Robbinsdale Sch. Dist., Minn., 1970-79; mem. Luth. Chaplaincy Aux. of Mpls., 1978-80; del. Crest View Home Assn., 1981—; mem. sci. and math. subcom. Minn. High Tech. Council. Recipient service awards and honors Omicron Sigma. Mem. Minn. Soc. Med. Tech. (sec. 1969-71), Am. Soc. Med. Tech. (del. to ann. meetings 1972—, chmn. hematology sci. assembly 1977-79, nomination com. 1979-81, bd. dirs. 1985-88), Twin City Soc. Med. Technologists, Twin Cities Hosp. Assn. (speakers bur. 1968-70), Assn. Women in Sci., World Future Soc., AAAS, AAUW, Minn. Med. Tech. Alumni, Am. Soc. Hematology, Soc. Analytical Cytology, Nat. Assn. Female Execs., Sigma Delta Epsilon (corr. sec. Xi chpt. 1980-82, pres. 1982-84), Alpha Mu Tau Lutheran. Contbr. articles to profl. publs. Office: United Hosps Inc Burnham-Harris Cancer Research Lab 333 Smith Ave N Saint Paul MN 55102

ANDERSON, GLENDA GALE, technical manager; b. Turlock, Calif., June 28, 1957; d. Glenn Walter Anderson and Jacqueline Ann (Elliott) Aitken. B.S. in Indsl. Engring., Stanford U., 1979; M.B.A., Harvard U., 1983. Applications engr. Packard Electric, Warren, Ohio, 1979-80, methods engr., 1980-81; asst. to controller CFS Continental, Chgo., 1982; asst. to v.p., engr. Travenol Labs., Round Lake, Ill., 1983-84, molded product control mgr., 1984-85, internat. bus. mgr., 1985—; research assoc. Harvard Bus. Sch., Boston, 1983. Pres. Hawaii State Achiever's Assn., Honolulu, 1974; adviser Jr. Achievement, Warren, Ohio, 1980; v.p. Women Student Assn., Harvard Bus. Sch., 1983. Jr. Achievement scholar, 1981-83. Mem. Stanford Alumni Assn., Harvard Alumni Assn. Democrat. Avocation: travel. Home: 619 Buckingham Libertyville IL 60048 Office: Travenol Labs Inc Route 120 and Wilson Rd Round Lake IL 60073

ANDERSON, HAROLD EDWARD, dermatologist; b. Battle Creek, Mich., Dec. 1, 1913; s. Olaf Andrew and Ethel Margaret (Stephan) Andersen; B.S., Battle Creek Coll., 1937; M.D., Loma Linda (Calif.) U., 1940; M.S., Wayne State U., Detroit, 1943; m. Mary Vivian Spomer, June 12, 1939; children—Robert, Nancy, Kent. Intern Henry Ford Hosp., Detroit, 1939-40; resident in dermatology Wayne State U., Detroit, 1940-43; practice medicine specializing in dermatology, Long Beach, Calif., 1943-50, Battle Creek, 1950—; mem. staff Leila Y. Post Montgomery Hosp., Community Hosp., Battle Creek Sanitarium Hosp.; cons. VA Hosp., Battle Creek; instr. Loma Linda U. Med. Sch., 1943-50. Diplomate Am. Bd. Dermatology. Mem. Am. Acad. Dermatology, AMA, Mich. Dermatol. Soc., Mich., Calhoun County med. socs., Mich., Central states dermatol. socs. Contbr. med. jours. Home: 951 Riverside Dr Battle Creek MI 49015 Office: 131 E Columbia Ave Battle Creek MI 49015

ANDERSON, HAROLD JAMES, forest products company executives; b. Green Bay, Wis., Sept. 4, 1928; s. John Elmer and Irene Emily (Cormier) A.; m. Patricia Margaret Basten, July 8, 1950; children—Mark, Therese, Debra, Tricia, John, Christopher. Student U. Wis., 1948-49; B.S. in Chemistry, St. Norberts Coll., 1952. Scientist, Marathon Corp., Rothschild, Wis., 1952-57; sr. scientist Am. Can. Co., Neenah, Wis., 1957-63, group leader, 1963-68, supr., 1968-72, mgr., 1972-74, mgr. new product tech., 1974-75, product mgr., Green Bay, 1975-79; assoc. dir. paperboard process devel. James River Corp., Neenah, Wis., 1979-83, dir. paperboard devel., 1983—. Served with U.S. Army, 1946-48. Mem. TAPPI. Baptist. Home: 1334 Westwood Ct Neenah WI 54956 Office: 1915 Marathon Ave Neenah Tech Ctr Neenah WI 54956

ANDERSON, HARRY DUANE, educator; b. Clarinda, Iowa, Apr. 7, 1927; s. Harry E. and Thelma A.; B.A., Central Wash. U., 1951; postgrad Drake U., U. S.D., U. No. Iowa; M.A., Clayton U., 1978; m. Marilyn Sue Miller, Nov. 20, 1965; children—Harry L., Edi R., Melissa W., Melissa L., Melanie M., Samuel A. Tchr., coach Central Decatur High Sch., Leon, Iowa, 1951-59, Oelwein (Iowa) Community High Sch., 1959-62, Cedar Falls (Iowa) Community High Sch., 1962—. Served with USAR, 1954-57. Recipient Outstanding Contbn. to Amateur Boxing award Iowa Sec. of State, 1975, Cedar Falls Jaycees Youth award, 1974. Mem. Iowa Edn. Assn., NEA, Nat. Assn. Curriculum Devel., Nat. Assn. Amateur Boxing Coaches, Iowa Football Coaches Assn., Iowa Track Coaches Assn., Cedar Falls Edn. Assn. Democrat. Episcopalian. Home: 1419 State St Cedar Falls IA 50613 Office: 10th and Division Sts Cedar Falls IA 50613

ANDERSON, HOWARD DOUGLAS, health association administrator; b. Lumpkin, Ga., Feb. 28, 1936; s. James M. and Lila M. (Glenn) A.; B.A., Morehouse Coll., 1968; m. Louise Clapp, Sept. 13, 1958; 1 son, Howard D.; m. 2d, Susan Benson, Oct. 10, 1975; stepchildren—Deborah, Robert Taylor. Postal clk., 1958-66; sales rep. Merck Sharp & Dohme, Chgo., 1969-70; staff writer U. Chgo. Office Pub. Info., 1970-72; exec. dir. Midwest Assn. Sickle Cell Anemia, Chgo., 1972-82, pres., 1982—. Former bd. dirs. Chgo. Regional Blood Program; former mem. citizens adv. council U. Chgo. Sickle Cell Center, U. Ill. Sickle Cell Center; mem. adv. council Chgo. State U. Coll. Nursing, 1983—. Served with U.S. Army, 1958-60. Mem. Nat. Assn. Sickle Cell Disease (founder). Home: 2231 E 67th St Chicago IL 60649 Office: 36 S Wabash Ave Suite 1113 Chicago IL 60603

ANDERSON, JAMES HARRY, utility engineer; b. Mpls., Aug. 30, 1927; s. Harry Aden and Leilah Betty (Anderson) A.; B. Civil Engring., U. Minn., 1952; m. Marilyn Louise Graaf, Sept. 7, 1951; children—Christine, Richard, Mark, Susan. Cadet engr. Mpls. Gas Co., 1952-54, engr., 1954-56, coordinator suburban div. main and service, 1956-58, asst. chief engr., 1958-68, chief design engr., 1968-72; chief design engr. Minn. Gas Co., Mpls., 1972-76, chief engr., 1977-80, mgr. operating services, 1980-82, mgr. Mpls. region ops., 1982—; mem. utility com. Nat. Transp. Research Bd.; lectr. in field. Chmn. Mpls.-St. Paul Met. Utilities Coordinating Com., 1973-80; planning commr. City of Bloomington, 1962-68, city councilman, 1971-75. Chmn. bd. dirs. South Hennepin County Human Service Council. Served with AUS, 1945-47; PTO. Registered profl. engr., Minn., Iowa, S.D., Nebr. Mem. Minn. Pub. Works Assn. (dir. 1966-72), Am. Gas Assn. (chmn. com. distbn. design 1968-69, chmn. com. system protection 1980, gas industry rep. to Am. Pub. Works Assn. 1975-80, operating sect. award of merit 1964, Silver award of merit 1982), Midwest Gas Assn., Nat., Minn. socs. profl. engrs., Mpls. Engrs. Club (pres. 1966, Engr. of Year award 1976), Internat. Right-of-Way Assn. (pres. Tri State chpt. 1979, internat. liaison com.), Bloomington (Minn.) C. of C. (pres. 1970), ASCE. Contbr. articles to trade mags. Home: 1400 E 100th St Bloomington MN 55420 Office: Minnagasco Inc 700 Linden Ave Minneapolis MN 55403

ANDERSON, JERRY WILLIAM, JR., electronics co. exec.; b. Stow, Mass., Jan. 14, 1926; s. Jerry William and Heda Charlotte (Petersen) A.; B.S. in Physics, U. Cin., 1949, Ph.D. in Econs., 1976; M.B.A., Xavier U., 1959; m. Joan Hukill Balyeat, Sept. 13, 1947; children—Katheleen, Diane. Research and test project engr. meteorol. equipment, Wright-Patterson AFB, Ohio, 1949-53; project engr., electronics div. AVCO Corp., Cin., 1953-70, program mgr., 1970-73; program mgr. Cin. Electronics Corp. (successor to electronics div. AVCO Corp.), 1973-78; pres. Anderson Industries Unltd., 1978; chmn. dept. mgmt. and mgmt. info. services Xavier U., 1980—; lectr. No. Ky. U., 1977-78; tech. adviser Cin. Tech. Coll., 1971—. Served with USNR, 1943-46. Mem. Madeira (Ohio) City Planning Commn., 1962—; founder, pres. Grassroots, Inc., 1964; active United Appeal, Heart Fund, Multiple Sclerosis Fund; co-founder, tech. Presbyterian Ch., Cin., 1964. Named Man of Year, City of Madeira, 1964. Mem. Assn. Energy Engrs. (charter), Soc. Non-Destructive Testing, Nat. Wood Carvers Assn., Am. Legion (past comdr.), Acad. Mgmt., Madeira Civic Assn. (past v.p.), Omicron Delta Epsilon. Republican. Contbr. articles on lasers, infrared detection equipment, air pollution to govt. publs. and profl. jours. Home and office: 7208 Sycamorehill Ln Cincinnati OH 45243

ANDERSON, JOEL MARK, engineering company executive; b. Bronx, N.Y., July 31, 1947; s. Samuel I. and Mildred G. A.; B.S. in Physics, Carnegie-Mellon U., 1969, B.S. in Psychology, 1969; m. Rita M. Meinert, Sept. 27, 1969; children—Michael D., Jason R., Melisa R. Engr., Westinghouse Electric Corp., Balt., 1969-71, Phila., 1971-74; sr. engr. Bechtel Corp., Ann Arbor, Mich., 1974-78, engring. supr., 1978-81, engring. mgr., 1981—; cons. on alt. methods of power generation. NSF grantee, 1968. Mem. IEEE, ISA. Inventor gas turbine controls, alt. methods power generation, nuclear and fossil power plant computer simulation. Office: PO Box 1000 Ann Arbor MI 48106

ANDERSON, JOHN BALFOUR, safety engineer; b. Cleve., Dec. 1, 1931; s. John Balfour and Gertrude Alberta (Bellamy) A.; m. Monda Lee Shipman, Aug. 4, 1956; children—Cynthia, David. B.A. in Mgmt., Baldwin-Wallace Coll., 1959. Safety trainee Republic Steel Corp., Cleve., 1956, fire marshall Cleve. dist., 1957-62, corp. safety engr., 1962-67, sr. safety engr., 1967-74, asst. dir. for safety, 1974—; chmn. pattern for progress com. Ohio Div. Safety and Hygiene, Columbus, 1972-73. Author numerous safety booklets; developed customized safety audits for steel and mfg. plants and coal mines, 1971. Chmn. ch. bldg. com. Evangelical Friends Ch., North Olmsted, Ohio, 1979. Served with USN, 1951-54. Mem. Nat. Safety Council (gen. chmn. metals sect. indsl. div. 1972-73, dir. 1979-84, chmn. indsl. div. 1982-83; Cameron award 1972-73, Disting. Service to Safety award 1983; hon. life mem. indsl. div. 1983—), Soc. Ohio Safety Engrs. (pres. 1972-73), Am. Soc. Safety Engrs. (profl.), Nat. Fire Protection Assn., Am. Iron and Steel Inst. Republican. Home: 22150 MacBeth Ave Fairview OH 44126 Office: Republic Steel Corp PO Box 6778 Room 217-R Cleveland OH 44101

ANDERSON, JOHN ROBERT, educator, mathematician; b. Stromsburg, Nebr., Aug. 1, 1928; s. Norris Merton and Violet Charlotte (Stromberg) A.; student Midland Coll., 1945-46; A.A., Luther Jr. Coll., 1949; B.S., U. Nebr., Lincoln, 1951, M.A. in Mathematics, 1954; Ph.D., Purdue U., 1970; m. Bertha Margery Nore, Aug. 27, 1950; children—Eric Jon, Mary Lynn. Tchr. mathematics and coach, Bloomfield (Nebr.) High Sch., 1951-52; control systems analyst, Allison Div. Gen. Motors Corp., Indpls., 1954-60; prof. math. Depauw U., Greencastle, Ind., 1960, asst. dean, dir. grad. studies, 1973-76, dir. grad. studies, 1976-84, chmn. dept. math. and computer sci., 1984—; resident dir. W. European Studies Program, W. Ger., France, Mediterranean Studies program, Athens, 1982; dir. NSF Coop. Coll. Sch. Sci. Inst., 1969-70, instr. NSF summer inst., 1972; bd. dirs. Law Focused Edn., Indpls., 1975—, Ind. Regional Mathematics Consortium, 1977—; mem. Commn. on Instns. Higher Edn., North Central Assn., 1974-78. Bd. dirs. br. No. 8657 Lutheran Brotherhood. Served with U.S. Army, 1946-48. U. Nebr. regents scholar, 1945-46; Danforth Teacher fellow, 1963-64; NSF sci. faculty fellow, 1964-65; Lilly Found. edn. grantee, summers 1961, 62, 63. Mem. Math. Assn. Am., Nat. Council Teachers of Mathematics, AAHE, Sigma Xi, Pi Mu Epsilon, Kappa Delta Pi, Beta Sigma Psi. Club: Rotary Internat. (sec., 1976-77., v.p. 1977-78, pres. 1978-79). Home: 1560 Bloomington St Greencastle IN 46135

ANDERSON, JON M., lawyer; b. Rio Grande, Ohio, Jan. 10, 1937; s. Harry Rudolph and Carrie Viola (Magee) A.; m. Deborah Melton, June 1, 1961; children—Jon Gordon, Greta. A.B., Ohio U., 1958; J.D., Harvard U., 1961. Bar: Ohio. Law clk. Hon. Kingsley A. Taft, Ohio Supreme Ct., Columbus, 1961-62; assoc. Wright, Harlor, Morris & Arnold, Columbus, 1962-67, ptnr., 1967-76; ptnr. Porter, Wright, Morris & Arthur, Columbus, 1977—; adj. prof. law Ohio State U. Law Sch., Columbus, 1977—; bar examiner State of Ohio, 1971-76, chmn., 1975-76; lectr. tax and estate planning insts. Trustee Berea Coll, Ky., 1976—, Buckeye Boys' Ranch, Columbus, 1984—, Pro Musica Chamber Orch., Columbus, 1979—, Opera Columbus, 1985—, 1st Congl. Ch., Columbus, 1980-84. Mem. ABA, Ohio State Bar Assn., Columbus Bar Assn. Democrat. Club: University (Columbus). Avocations: Music; art; textiles; literature. Office: Porter Wright Morris & Arthur Huntington Ctr Columbus OH 43215

ANDERSON, KARL PAUL, chemist; b. Fergus Falls, Minn., Jan. 10, 1934; s. Paul R. and Irma I. Anderson; B.Sc., Ohio State U., 1958; postgrad. (scholar) U. Göttingen (W.Ger.), 1956; m. Ruby M. Porter, Sept. 7, 1958; children—Ronald Richard, Karen Lynn. Devel. chemist Hanna Chem. Coatings Co., Columbus, Ohio, 1959-65, group leader metal deco. dept., 1965-67, coil coating dept, 1967-69, dir. coil coating div., 1971-81, tech. dir. Atech. chem. coatings, 1981-84, dir. product devel. Atech. chem. coatings, 1984—; group leader coil coating lab. Lilly Indsl. Coatings, Indpls., 1969-70; v.p. Karencraft, Inc., Columbus, 1975—; dir. Corboard, Inc. Asst. scoutmaster Central Ohio council Boy Scouts Am., Columbus, 1969—; head coach N. Columbus Girls Baseball, 1977-79, Univ. Boys Assn., Boys Basketball, 1974-75. Recipient Order of Arrow, Boy Scouts Am., 1976. Mem. Nat. Coil Coaters Assn., Cin. Dayton Indpls. Columbus Soc., Fedn. Socs. Coatings Tech., Nat. Flyers Assn., Scioto Model A Ford Club, North Columbus Ski Club, Buckeye Glider Club, Flying Farmers, Sigma Pi (sec., trustee), Phi Eta Sigma (treas.). Methodist. Clubs: Masons, Shriners. Contbr. articles to profl. jours. Home: 612 E Como Ave Columbus OH 43202 Office: 199 S Saint Clair St Toledo OH 43602

ANDERSON, KARL STEPHEN, newspaper executive; b. Chgo., Nov. 10, 1933; s. Karl William and Eleanore (Grell) A.; B.S. in Editorial Journalism, U. Ill., 1955; m. Saralee Hegland, Nov. 5, 1977; children by previous marriage—Matthew, Douglas, Eric. Successively advt. mgr., asst. to pub., plant mgr. Pioneer Press, Oak Park and St. Charles, Ill., 1955-71; asst. to pub., then pub. Crescent Newspapers, Downers Grove, Ill., 1971-73; assoc. pub. and editor Chronicle Pub. Co., St. Charles, 1973-80; assoc. pub. Chgo. Daily Law Bull., 1981—. Bd. govs. Hotel Baker Sr. Living Center, Kane County Republican Central Com.; trustee Chi Psi Ednl. Trust; mem. legis. com. Chgo. Crime Commn.; bd. overseers Ctr. for Freedom of Info. Studies, Loyola U.; mem. fair trial free press com. Ill. State Bar. Recipient C.V. Amenoff award dept. journalism No. Ill. U., 1976. Mem. Ill. Press Assn. (Will Loomis award 1977, 80), Nat. Newspaper Assn., No. Ill. Newspaper Assn., Soc. Profl. Journalists-Sigma Delta Chi, Chi Psi. Clubs: Headline (pres. elect), Chgo. Press. Home: 3180 N Lake Shore Dr Unit 14-D Chicago IL 60657 Office: 415 N State St Chicago IL 60610

ANDERSON, KENNETH OSCAR, film company executive; b. Rembrandt, Ia., Dec. 23, 1917; s. Oscar Frank and Ethel Mae (Anderson) A.; student Wheaton Coll., 1936-37, 45-51, Northwestern U., 1947-48; m. Doris Ilene Jones, Nov. 16, 1938; children—Naoma (Mrs. Larry Clark), Margaret (Mrs. T. Landon Mauzy), Donn, Lane, Max, Ken D., Melody. Editor, Campus Life Mag., Wheaton, Ill., 1945-51; with Gospel Films, Muskegon, Mich., 1949-61, exec. producer, 1949-61; pres. Ken Anderson Films, Winona Lake, Ind., 1963—; dir. Master Investments Corp., Warsaw, Ind.; dir. Internat. Films, London, 1969-72, Reach & Teach, London; vis. instr. Haggai Inst., Singapore, 1974—; vis. lectr. St. Xavier's Coll., Bombay, 1979. Mem. pres.'s com. Grace Coll., Winona Lake, 1972—; adv. com. League for the Handicapped, Walworth, Wis., 1965—; bd. dirs. Youth Haven Ranch, Rives Junction, Mich., Crusade Evangelism, London, Ont., Can. Named Evang. Press Assn. Writer of Year, 1962; Nat. Evang. Film Found. award as Dir. of Year, 1970. Mem. Gidions Internat. Presbyterian (elder 1963—). Author: Himalyan Heartbeat, 1966; Stains on Glass Windows, 1969; Adjustable Halo, 1969; Satan's Angels, 1975; (with Tony Mockus) I'm Learning from Protestants How to be a Better Catholic, 1975; producer, dir. film of book Pilgrim's Progress, 1977, film Christiana, 1978, Some Through the Fire (Uganda), 1980, Hudson Taylor, 1981; dir. Mud, Sweat and Cheers, 1984; Fanny Crosby, 1984. Home: 720 North Lake St Warsaw IN 46580 Office: PO Box 618 Winona Lake IN 46590

ANDERSON, KIM EDWARD, manufacturing company executive; b. Okarche, Okla., Nov. 6, 1950; s. Kermit E. and Zeta F. (Crawford) A.; m. Rebecca Cogwell, May 29, 1976; children—Kristin Lain, Courtney Lynn. B.S., East Central U., Ada, Okla., 1972; M.S., Okla. U., 1973, postgrad., 1985—. Engr. Okla. Health Dept., Ada, 1971-72; indsl. hygienist Johnson Space Ctr., NASA, Houston, 1973-74; supervisory indsl. hygienist U.S. Dept. Labor, Little Rock, 1974-78; corp. dir. environ. and occupational safety and health A.O. Smith Corp., Milw., 1978—; asst. prof. U. Ark., Little Rock and Fayetteville, U. Central Ark., 1976—. Author: Fundamentals of Industrial Toxicology, 1981. Contbr. articles to profl. jours. Chmn. indsl. environ. com. Ark. Fedn. Water and Air Users, 1979-81, chmn. hazardous waste com., 1983-85, chmn. annual meeting, 1983—, bd. dirs., v.p., 1983—; mem. clean air com. Am. Lung Assn., Little Rock, 1980—; mem. workers compensation com. Ark. State C. of C., Little Rock, 1983—, chmn. right to know com. USPHS grantee, 1972-73, EPA grantee, 1980-82; Okla. Frontiers Sci. scholar, 1972-73; recipient Environ. award Merit Okla. Health Dept., 1973, Skylab Achievement award Johnson Space Ctr., 1973; named Ark. Safety Profl. of Yr., 1984, Region IV Safety Profl. of Yr. (Ark., Mo., Okla., Kans., Nebr., Iowa), 1984, Nat. Safety Profl. of Yr., 1984-85. Mem. Am. Soc. Safety Engrs. (pres. Ark. chpt. 1982-83, v.p. 1981-82, sec.-treas. Gulf Coast sect. 1973), Am. Indsl Hygiene Assn. (pres. Ark. sect. 1979, toxicology com. 1978-81, workroom environ. exposure level com. 1979-81), Am. Welding Soc. (co-chmn safety and health com. 1980-81). Republican. Methodist. Avocations: athletics. Office: A O Smith Corp PO Box 23974 Milwaukee WI 53223

ANDERSON, LELA GERALDINE, association executive; b. Leeper, Mo., Aug. 7, 1917; d. Walter Nathan and Letha May (Powers) Asberry; student pub. schs.; m. Carl Albin Anderson, Oct. 7, 1962. Bookkeeper, asst. sales mgr. Double L Style Shop, Piedmont, Mo., 1937-40; teller, bookkeeper, instr. of tellers 1st Nat. Bank of Waukegan (Ill.), 1943-55, 1st Fed. Savs. & Loan Assn., Waukegan, 1955-60; librarian, head circulation dept. Waukegan Pub. Library, 1960-62; asst. state dir. Am. Assn. Ret. Persons, 1984—. Bd. dirs., treas. Lake County Community Concerts Assn., Inc., 1953—. Mem. Am. Theatre Organ Soc., Chgo. Area Theatre Organ Enthusiasts, Land of Lincoln Organ Soc., Dairyland Organ Soc. in Wis., Nat. Hist. Soc., U.S. Capitol Hist. Soc., Lake County Women Vols., Am. Assn. Ret. Persons (com. mem.). Baptist. Clubs: Order of Eastern Star (past worthy matron); Gurnee Women's (1st v.p. 1965); Christian Women's of Lake County (com. mem.). Home: 933 N Greenleaf St Gurnee IL 60031

ANDERSON, LINDA JEAN FULLER, manufacturing company executive; b. Chgo., Sept. 24, 1948; d. Otmar and Delores (Newman) Fuller; student No. Ill. U., 1966-68; m. John Richard Anderson, Mar. 20, 1971. Budget dir. Leo Burnett Inc., Chgo., 1968-70; controller Leaf-Donruss div. Leaf, Inc., Chgo., 1970—. Mem. Am. Mgmt. Assn., Ill. Mfrs. Assn. Lutheran. Office: 1155 N Cicero Ave Chicago IL 60651

ANDERSON, LOIS MARILYN, psychologist; b. Cambridge, Minn., Mar. 19, 1934; d. Oliver Ferdinand and Marjorie Constance (Strait) Ledin; m. Malcolm Charles Anderson, July 9, 1960; 1 son, Andrew. B.S., Gustavus Adolphus Coll., 1956; Ph.D., U. Minn., 1969. Intern counseling Student Counseling Bur., Univ. Hosps. dept. of phys. medicine and rehab. U. Minn., 1959-60; research fellow Indsl. Relations Center, U. Minn., 1960-65; research psychologist InterStudy, Mpls., 1969-73; state program mgmt. coordinator Minn. Dept. Adminstrn., St. Paul, 1973-77, projects coordinator Mgmt. Analysis div., 1977-79; staff psychologist Minn. State Services for the Blind, St. Paul, 1979-81, dir. psychol. services, 1981—. Governing mem. YMCA of Met. Mpls., 1971-79; bd. mgmt. Northwest (Mpls.) YMCA, 1970-76; bd. dirs., chmn. Camden Community Theater, 1981-83; lectr. U. Minn. Grad. Schs. of Pub. Affairs and Social Work, 1975, 76; mem. Twin City Met. Council Advisory com. on Waste Mgmt. and Water Quality, 1976-78. Mem. Am. Psychol. Assn., Minn. Psychol. Assn., Am. Assn. for Counseling and Devel., Minn. Assn. for Counseling and Devel., Psi Chi, Pi Lamdba Theta. Recipient Annual Research award, Am. Rehab. Counseling Assn., 1965. Author: (with others) AFDC Employment and Referral Guidelines, 1973; Impact of Welfare Reform on the Elderly Poor, 1973; Medicaid Cost Containment and Long Term Care, 1976. Home: 4400 Victory Ave Minneapolis MN 55412 Office: 1745 University Ave Saint Paul MN 55104

ANDERSON, LOYAL EDWARD, oil jobber, farmer; b. Hugoton, Kans., Aug. 24, 1931; s. Webb Huitt and Lucille Caroline (Flummerfelt) A.; student Mt. Carmel (Ill.) public schs.; m. Mary Ann Baumgart, June 24, 1953; children—Ray, Randy, Ricky, Rose Ann. Pres., Anderson Bros. Oil Co., Mt. Carmel, 1953—; farmer, 1974—; dir. Security Bank & Trust Co. Bd. dirs. Ill. Jaycees, 1953-56; 4-H leader, 1953—; pres. 4-H Youth Found., 1970—; bd. dirs. Wabash County Retarded Children, 1975, Fair Bd., 1954—; pres. Extension Council, 1973—, St. Mary Sch. Bd., 1970-76. Served with USAF, 1950-53. Recipient Community Service award Phillips Petroleum Co., 1975. Mem. Nat. Fedn. Ind. Bus., Am. Legion, Mt. Carmel C. of C. (dir. 1974).

Roman Catholic. Clubs: K.C., Elks, Moose. Home: Rural Route 1 Mount Carmel IL 62863 Office: 909 W 9th St Mount Carmel IL 62863

ANDERSON, LUANN MARIE, advertising executive; b. Chgo., Jan. 6, 1958; d. Ronald Jacob and Patricia Agnes (Hoglund) Ringenberg; m. Christopher Anderson, Apr. 27, 1985. B.S., Ill. State U., 1980. Word processing supr. Foote, Cone & Belding, Chgo., 1980, word processing mgr., 1981-83, mgr. adminstrv. services, 1983—. Mem. Assn. Info. Systems Profls. Roman Catholic. Avocations: golf; skiing; reading; religious education teacher. Office: Foote Cone & Belding 401 N Michigan Chicago IL 60611

ANDERSON, MARIAN MARGARET, county extension agent; b. Osage, Iowa, Aug. 15, 1946; d. Leo and Stella Marie (Heimermann) Smith; A.A., Austin Jr. Coll., 1966; B.S., Iowa State U., 1968; m. Arthur E. Anderson, Sept. 6, 1975. County extension agt., Big Stone County, Ortonville, Minn. Bd. dirs. United Fund, 1978-79, Emergency Food Shelf, 1983—. Mem. Minn. Assn. Extension Agts. (officer), Nat. Assn. Extension Home Economists. Am. Home Econs. Assn., Epsilon Sigma Phi. Roman Catholic. Home: Rt 2 Box 100 Ortonville MN 56278 Office: 342 NW 2d St Ortonville MN 56278

ANDERSON, MARLIN DEAN, animal health product development administrator; b. Stanton, Iowa, Nov. 30, 1934; s. Anton D. and Ruby A. L. (Peterson) A.; m. Asyneth J. Conway, June 8, 1968; 1 child, Scott D. B.S., Iowa State U., 1959, M.S., 1962, Ph.D., 1964. Cert. animal scientist. Sect. head swine research Hess & Clark, Ashland, Ohio, 1965-76; coordinator clin. research Diamond Shamrock Co., Cleve., 1977-82; mgr. spl. product devel. S.D.S. Biotech Corp., Painesville, Ohio, 1983—. Contbr. articles to profl. jours. Served with U.S. Army, 1954-56. Mem. Am. Soc. Animal Sci. Republican. Lutheran. Avocation: gardening. Home: 1575 State Route 511 R D 6 Ashland OH 44805 Office: SDS Biotech Corp 7528 Auburn Rd Painesville OH 44077

ANDERSON, MARY ANN, hospital nursing administrator, nurse; b. Sparta, Wis., Nov. 22, 1939; d. Harold C. and Laura R. (DeWitt) Woolley; m. James A. Anderson, Aug. 26, 1960; children—Sandra, Julianne, Mark, Janine. Diploma St. Francis Sch. Nursing, LaCrosse, Wis., 1960; student Viterbo Coll., 1962-65, U. Wis.-LaCrosse, 1972-82, Milton Coll./Mt. Senario Coll., 1982-84. R.N., Wis. Staff nurse St. Francis Hosp., LaCrosse, Wis., 1961-63, LaCrosse Lutheran Hosp., 1963-72; head nurse emergency dept. LaCrosse Luth. Hosp., 1972-76, nursing coordinator, 1976-84, assoc. dir. nursing, 1984—; nat. LaCrosse sexual assault area counselor coordinator; chmn. LaCrosse County Emergency Med. Services, bd. dirs. Western Wis. Emergency Med. Services Inc. Mem. Western Wis. Emergency Dept. Nurses Assn. (past pres.), Nat. Emergency Dept. Nurses Assn. (cert.), Wis. Council Emergency Dept. Nurses Assn. (pres.), Am. Trauma Soc. (Wis. chpt.), Am. Heart Assn. (Wis. chpt.) Roman Catholic. Contbr. chpt. to book. Home: 508 11th Ave N Onalaska WI 54650 Office: La Crosse Lutheran Hosp 1910 South Ave LaCrosse WI 54601

ANDERSON, MARY LOU, educator; b. Mt. Pleasant, Iowa, Aug. 29, 1949; d. Carl Marion and Hazel Lucile (Mitchell) A. B.S. in Edn., Northeast Mo. State U., 1971, M.S. in Elem. Guidance, 1974. Lic. elem. tchr., Mo. Elem. tchr. Waynesville pub. schs., Mo., 1971-73, Hannibal pub. schs., Mo., 1973-79, Bel Ridge Elem. Sch., St. Louis, 1979—; ERA cons. ERAmerica, Washington, 1980-81, NEA, Washington, 1980-82; LEAST discipline cons. Mo. NEA, 1981—, state conf. workshop leader, 1979-83; co-founder, chmn. Mo. NEA Women's Caucus, 1975-78. Pres. Mo. ERA Coalition, 1980-82; pres. Polit. Action Com. St. Louis Women's Polit. Caucus, 1984-85; campaign worker Mo. Democratic Orgn., 1982—. Mem. NEA, Mo. NEA (Lorna Bottger Polit. Action award 1982), St. Louis Suburban Tchrs. Assn., Normandy Tchrs. Assn., NOW, ACLU, Phi Delta Kappa. Mem. United Ch. of Christ. Avocations: playing piano; aerobics; reading; plays and movies. Home: 4497 Pershing St Apt 107 Saint Louis MO 63108 Office: Bel Ridge Elem Sch 8930 Boston Ave Saint Louis MO 63121

ANDERSON, MARY VIRGINIA, actuary; b. Washington, Apr. 14, 1941; d. Bascom Slemp and Mary Ellen (Long) Damron. A.A., Nat. Bus. Coll., Roanoke, Va., 1960. Bookkeeper Alexander Grant & Co., Roanoke, 1960-61; math. aid NASA, Hampton, Va., 1962-64; statis. clk. Blue Cross Blue Shield, Indpls., 1967-74, asst. actuary, 1974-75, actuary, 1975-78, sr. actuary, 1978-80, asst. corp. actuary, 1980—. Vol. City Ctr., Indpls., 1984. Fellow Soc. Actuaries; mem. Am. Acad. Actuaries, Indpls. Actuaries (chmn. membership com. 1984-85), Am. Statis. Assn. (chpt. treas. 1982). Republican. Episcopalian. Avocations: hiking, bicycling, reading. Office: Blue Cross Blue Shield 120 W Market St Indianapolis IN 46204

ANDERSON, MAX ELLIOT, television film production company executive; b. St. Charles, Ill., Nov. 3, 1946; s. Kenneth O. and Doris I. (Jones) A.; B.A. in Psychology, Grace Coll., 1973; m. Claudia Lynd, Aug. 17, 1968; children—James Brightman, Sarah Lynd. Cinematographer, Ken Anderson Films, Winona Lake, Ind., 1966-78; partner Q Media Group, Rockford, Ill., 1978-82, assoc. producer TV, films, 1978—, also cinematographer, since 1963—, advt. exec., 1965—; pres. Philip Lasz Gallery, 1973—, The Market Place; ptnr. Thunderbolt Prodns.; producer nat. TV spots for True Valu Hardware, 1985; nat. distbr. inspirational home video cassettes, 1985—. Assoc. producer Gospel at the Symphony, 1979. Mem. Summerwood Amphitheater com., Rockford, 1980—. Served with U.S. Army, 1971-73. Recipient Best Cinematography award Christian Film Distbrs. Assn., 1978. Mem. Christian Film Distributor Assn., Internat. Christian Video Assn., Christian Booksellers Assn. Republican. Mem. Evang. Free Ch. Home: 4112 Marsh Ave Rockford IL 61111 Office: 4112 Marsh Ave Rockford IL 61111

ANDERSON, PAUL STEWART, lawyer; b. Chgo., Aug. 19, 1952; s. Robert Garfield and Ruth Helen (Hjorth) A.; m. Linda Joy Quinn, Sept. 29, 1984. B.A., Wake Forest U., 1974; J.D., Ill. Inst. Tech.-Chgo. Kent Law Sch., 1978; cert. in European Programs (hon.), U. Pacific, Sacramento and Salzburg, Austria, 1978. Bars: Ill. 1979, U.S. Dist. Ct. (no. dist.) Ill. 1979, U.S. Ct. Appeals (7th cir.) 1979, (D.C. cir.) 1979, U.S. Ct. Internat. Trade 1979. Intern Mannheimer & Zetterlof, Gothenburg, Sweden, 1978; assoc. Barnes, Richardson & Colburn, Chgo., 1979-81; ptnr. Sonnenberg, Anderson & O'Donnell, Chgo., 1981—; Supporting mem. Union League Boys' Club, Chgo., 1984. Mem. ABA, Ill. State Bar Assn., Chgo. Bar Assn. (customs law com. 1981—), Mid-Am. Swedish Trade Assn. (bd. dirs. 1982—), Norwegian-Am. C. of C. (v.p. 1984), Methodist. Clubs: Can. of Chgo. (bd. dirs. 1984—), Union League. Office: Sonnenberg Anderson & O'Donnell One N LaSalle St Chicago IL 60602

ANDERSON, PHYLLIS REINHOLD, management consultant, engineer; b. Denver, July 29, 1936; d. Floyd Reinhold and Minerva Eva (Needham) A.; Metall. Engr., Colo. Sch. Mines, 1962; M.B.A., U. Chgo., 1968; children—Kristin Elizabeth, Michele Ann. Mill metallurgist, supr. U.S. Steel Corp., 1962-66; research and devel. sr. metallurgist, supr., planner Continental Can Co., 1966-73; mgr. corp. planning B. F. Goodrich Co., 1973-76; regional assoc. Strategic Planning Inst., Cambridge, Mass., 1975-76; project mgr. corp. planning, sales engring., then project mgr. corp. devel. Signode Corp., Glenview, Ill., 1976-80; mgmt. cons., 1974—; pres., prin. cons. Corp. Devel. Assocs., Inc., mgmt. cons. in strategic planning, mktg., product and systems devel., CAD/CAM/CAE, Oak Brook, Ill., 1980—; assoc. Strategic Planning Inst., 1982—; initial exec. com., chmn. membership com. Strategic Planning Inst., 1975-76; dir. Quest Assos. Mgmt. and Quality Consultants; instr. bus. analysis methods. Active psychiat. support services, career counseling women's groups and individuals. Recipient leadership award Chgo. YWCA, 1977. Mem. Am. Soc. Metals, Soc. Women Engrs., Am. Mktg. Assn., N.Y. Acad. Scis., Women in Mgmt., Nat. Assn. Women Bus. Owners, AAAS, Mensa. Clubs: Executives of Chgo., Whitehall. Author: Corporate Strategic Planning: An Integrated Approach, 1981. Home: 2201 S Highland Ave Lombard IL 60148 Office: PO Box 946 Oak Brook IL 60521

ANDERSON, RAYMOND VERNON, political science educator; b. Newfolden, Minn., Oct. 6, 1922; s. Pearnel J. and Tillie A. (Ostmoe) A.; m. Zora Ellen Houkom, June 2, 1953; children—Denise, Barbara, Gregory. B.S., Moorhead State U., 1946; M.A., U. Minn., 1949, Ph.D., 1962. Prin., Aneta High Sch., N.D., 1947-48; instr. Gustavus Adolphus Coll., St. Peter, Minn., 1949; asst. prof. Mayville State Coll., N.D., 1951-61; asst. prof. Western Ill. U., Macomb, 1961-63; prof. polit. sci. U. Wis.-River Falls, 1963—. Contbg. editor: Dictionary of Political Science, 1964. Mem. Pierce County Bd. Suprs., 1974-85; pres. Wis. Assoc. County Extension Coms., Inc., 1979-84; mem. Nat. Extension Adv. Council, 1980—; pres., bd. dis. Western Wis. Health Systems Agy., 1979-80. Mem. NEA, Wis. Polit. Sci. Assn., Midwest Polit. Sci. Assn., Am. Polit. Sci. Assn., AAUP (chpt. pres. 1968-70). Democrat. Lutheran. Club: River Falls Country. Avocations: golf; canoeing; gardening; fishing; bridge. Home: 410 S 5th St River Falls WI 54022 Office: U Wis River Falls WI 54022

ANDERSON, RICHARD AUGUST, mechanical engineer; b. Rockford, Ill., Aug. 7, 1923; s. Richard E. and Fanny D. (Johnson) A.; m. Lois May Korff, Nov. 10, 1945; children—Richard E., Terry L., Kenneth L., Jane M. A.A., Rockford Coll., 1949. Cert. mfg. engr. Designer, Whitcomb Diesel Locomotive Co., Rochelle, Ill., 1949-50; tool designer Mechanics Universal Joint, Borg Warner Corp., 1950-51, 53-56; chief engr. and designer Redin Corp., 1956-64, v.p. sales and engring, 1978-84; chief engr. Rockford Automation, 1964-67; mgr. sales White Sundstrand Machine Tool Co., Rockford, 1967-78; mgr. product devel. and sales Bourn & Koch Machine Tool Co., Rockford, 1984—. Served to capt. U.S. Army, 1941-53, PTO, Korea; N.G., 1939-64. Republican. Avocations: model airplanes; fishing and golf; swimming; electronics; computers. Home: 3111 Dartmouth Dr Rockford IL 61108 Office: Bourn & Koch Machine Tool Co 2500 Kishwaukee St Rockford IL 61108

ANDERSON, RICHARD HODGSON, sales executive; b. Fergus Falls, Minn., Apr. 22, 1937; s. Paul Raymond and Irma Ione A.; B.A., Ohio State U. Columbus, 1959; children—Jeffrey Allen, Diana Lynne. Pub. Relations, Western Electric Co., 1959-64; Div. mgr. Universal Guaranty Life Ins. Co., Dayton, Ohio, 1964-66; mktg. asso. IBM, Dayton, 1966-69; v.p. Champion Service Corp., Cleve., 1969-72; mgmt. cons. Mgmt. Horizons Data Systems, Columbus, Ohio, 1972-79; pres. R.H. Anderson and Assocs., Columbus, 1980-81; dist. mgr. MCI, Columbus, 1980—. Chmn., Gettysburg (Ohio) Neighborhood Sch. Coordination Com., 1978-79; active Columbus Symphony Orch. Recipient Disting. Sales award Profl. Sales Assocs., 1978, Dale Carnegie Sales award, 1966, Nat. Assn. Life Cos., highest award for outstanding performance, 1966, top sales award, 1965; named Regional Sales Mgr. of Year MCI, 1984. Republican. Methodist. Author: Executive Associates Guide to Successful Selling, 1965. Office: MCI 180 E Broad St Suite 1402 Columbus OH 43215

ANDERSON, ROBERT CHARLES, writer, magazine editor; b. Sault Ste. Marie, Mich., May 22, 1930; s. James Orville and Nesta Grace (Cottle) A.; student Mich. Coll. Mining and Tech., 1954-55; B.A. (Winthrop Burr Chamberlain scholar), U. Mich., 1957; postgrad. Chgo.-Kent Coll. Law, 1969-70; m. Frances Theresa Merimee, July 25, 1952; children—James Russell, Helen Christine Anderson Doepel. Reporter, Evening News, Sault Ste. Marie, 1954-55, Ypsilanti (Mich.) Press, 1957; circulation worker Ann Arbor (Mich.) News, 1956; reporter, TV columnist, mag. editor Chgo. Tribune, 1957-72; mng. editor Oui mag., Chgo., 1972-75; free-lance writer, editor Profl. Photographer, Chgo., 1976-78; editor Success mag., Chgo., 1978-84, editor-at-large, 1984—; editorial cons., author PMA Books div. W. Clement Stone PMA Communications, Inc.; lectr. to writers groups, tchr. workshops. Mem. Winnetka (Ill.) Caucus Selection Com., 1968; leader, merit badge counselor Boy Scouts Am. Served with U.S. Army, 1948-52; Korea. Mem. Am. Soc. Journalists and Authors, Midwest Writers (co-chmn.), Kappa Tau Alpha, Phi Eta Sigma. Republican. Unitarian. Author: (with Ray Kroc) Grinding It Out: The Making of McDonald's, 1977; contbr. numerous articles to various mags. Office: 401 N Wabash Ave Suite 530 Chicago IL 60611

ANDERSON, ROBERT HUNTER, data processing and data communications consultant; b. Duluth, Minn., Sept. 17, 1941; s. Herbert Andrew and Mildred May (Hunter) A.; student public schs., Duluth; m. Nancy Jeanne Overland, May 23, 1970; children—Christina Jeanne, John Robert. Programmer, Litton Industries, Duluth, 1967-69; programmer/analyst Paper Calmenson & Co., St. Paul, 1970-71, State of Minn., St. Paul, 1971-74, Apache Corp., Mpls., 1974-76; EDP auditor Coopers & Lybrand, Mpls., 1976-78; data communications cons. AT&T, Mpls., 1978-85; tech. cons. Contel Info. Systems, 1985—. Served with Minn. Air N.G., 1963-69. Address: 9033 Kell Ave S Bloomington MN 55437

ANDERSON, ROBERT JACK, film director; educator; b. Duluth, Minn., Apr. 20, 1953; s. Robert Jr. and Betty Jane (Rutter) A.; m. Lorna Anne Wiley, Feb. 29, 1984. B.A., Univ. N.Mex., 1975; M.A., Univ. San Diego, 1977; Ph.D., Univ. Wis., Madison, 1983. Asst. prof. Wash. State U., Pullman, 1981-83; film dir. Prehistoric Prodns., Sarasota, Fla., 1984; v.p., lectr. Sarasota Film Soc., 1983-85. Dir. films: Unaffected, 1980, Military Division, 1981, Viet Harlan, 1982; co-dir. film Press Kit, 1984. Mem. Soc. Cinema Studies, Univ. Film and Video Assn., Am. Ind. Film and Video. Democrat. Avocations: reading non-fiction. Home: 4329 W 8th St Duluth MN 55807 Office: Prehistoric Prodns 280 Golden Gate Point Sarasota FL 33577

ANDERSON, ROBERT LAWRENCE, electrical engineering technology educator; b. Lebanon, Ind., Oct. 14, 1918; s. Stanley Martin and Elizabeth May (James) A.; m. Grace Louise Main, Jan. 9, 1944; children—Neil Robert, Suellen Louise Anderson Stookey, Paul Martin, Glenna Jean Anderson Beshears. B.S. in Elec. Engring., Rose Poly. Inst., 1942; postgrad. U. Pitts., 1944, Purdue U., 1950, 53-54, Northwestern U., 1955-57. Registered profl. engr., Ind. Test engr. Westinghouse Electric Corp., East Pittsburgh, Pa., 1942-45; service engr. Gen. Electric Corp., Chgo., 1946-47; faculty Purdue U.-Calumet, Hammond, Ind., 1947—, prof. elec. engring. tech., 1966—. Served with U.S. Army, 1945-46. Mem. Am. Soc. Engring. Edn., IEEE (life). Mem. Christian Ch. Lodge: Masons. Office: Purdue U Calumet Room P-202 2233 171st St Hammond IN 46323

ANDERSON, ROBERT LEROY, educator; b. Wadena, Minn., Nov. 22, 1940; s. Eddie Irvin and Elsie Amelia (Winter) A.; B.S., U. Minn., 1966, in bus. mgmt., 1974. County extension dir. U. Minn., Walker, 1970-71; vets. farm mgmt. instr. Little Falls (Minn.) Community Schs., 1971-74, Area Vo-Tech. Inst., Staples, Minn., 1974-76; adult farm bus. mgmt. instr. Woodland Coop. Center, Staples, 1976—; mgmt. cons. Served with U.S. Army, 1962-64. Mem. NEA, Minn. Edn. Assn., Nat. Agrl. Edn. Instrs. Assn., Minn. Agrl. Educators Assn., Nat. Hort. Therapy Assn. Home: PO Box 281 Rural Route 2 Staples MN 56479 Office: Woodland Coop Center Clarissa MN 56440

ANDERSON, ROBERT MARSHALL, clergyman; b. S.I., N.Y., Dec. 18, 1933; s. Arthur Harold and Hazel (Schneider) A.; m. Mary Artemis Evans, Aug. 24, 1960; children—Martha, Elizabeth, Catherine, Thomas. B.A., Colgate U., 1955; S.T.B., Berkeley Div. Sch., 1961; D.D. (hon.), Seabury Western Sem., 1978, Berkeley Div. Sch. Yale U., 1977. Ordained priest Episcopal Ch., 1962; curate St. John's Ch., Stamford, Conn., 1961-63, vicar, 1963-67; priest in charge Middle Haddan, Conn., 1963-67, rector, 1967-68; assoc. rector St. John's Ch., Stamford, 1968-72; dean St. Mark's Cathedral, Salt Lake City, 1972-78; bishop Episcopal Diocese Minn., Mpls., 1978—. Served with AUS. Danforth fellow, 1959-60. Mem. Berkeley Alumni Assn. (pres. 1972-76). Democrat. Clubs: Mpls., Minikahda. Office: 309 Clifton Ave Minneapolis MN 55403

ANDERSON, ROBERT THEODORE, lieutenant governor, educator; b. Marshalltown, Iowa, Mar. 8, 1945; s. Robert T. and Ida M. (Halverson) A.; m. Elsie M. Ulland, June 10, 1967; 1 son, Robert Elias. B.A. in Journalism and Edn., U. Iowa, 1967, M.A. in Journalism, 1972. Cert. secondary tchr., Iowa. High sch. journalism tchr., 1967-76; mem. Iowa Ho. of Reps., 1974-82, asst. majority leader, 1977-78, asst. minority leader, 1979-82; lt. gov. State of Iowa, Des Moines, 1983—; assoc. Wilson O'Brien Grant & Ginre, Newton, Iowa, 1981-82. Democrat. Methodist. Club: Optimist (pres. 1981-82) (Newton, Iowa). Home: Route 2 Newton IA 50208 Office: State House Des Moines IA 50319*

ANDERSON, ROBERT WILLIAM, manufacturing company salesman; b. Mpls., Aug. 25, 1929; s. William Everett and Marion Robb Muir (Denham) A.; m. Melrose Louise Moloy, May 27, 1950; children—Lee William, Scott Robert. Student U. Minn., 1948. Salesman, GAF Corp., Mpls., 1953—. Chmn. Sch. Bd., Alexandria, Minn., 1977-80, 83-85. Recipient Pres.'s Club award GAF Corp., 1974, 83. Republican. Baptist. Club: Toastmasters (dist. gov. 1972). Lodge: Kiwanis. Avocations: reading; golf; hunting; cross country skiing. Home: 803 S Darling Dr PO Box 758 Alexandria MN 56308 Office: GAF Corp 50 Lowry Ave N Minneapolis MN 55411

ANDERSON, RUSSELL DWAYNE, educational consultant, former superintendent schools; b. Hendricks, Minn., Aug. 23, 1920; s. Inest Robert and Florence Clara (Olson) A.; student Mankato State Tchrs. Coll., 1938-39; B.A., Gustavus Adolphus Coll., 1942; M.A., U. Minn., 1951, Ed.S., 1957, Ph.D., 1968; m. Genevieve Dolores Quam, May 2, 1943; children—Constance, Steven, Kathleen, Rebecca, Mark. Sci. tchr., coach Balaton High Sch., 1942, Hoffman High Sch., 1946; prin. Cottonwood High Sch., 1946-47; rep. Prudential Ins. Co., Blue Earth, Minn., 1947-48; prin. Delavan High Sch., 1948-51, Park Rapids High Sch., 1951-54, Two Harbors High Sch., 1954-58; asst. supt. schs., West Saint Paul, Minn., 1958-67, supt. schs., 1967-82; univ. and seminar instr. and cons. Active Bay Lake Improvement Assn. Served to lt. (s.g.), USNR, 1943-46; PTO. Recipient Outstanding Sch. Adminstrs. award Dakota County, 1979, Adminstrn. Day Recognition plaque Minn. State Fair, 1979. Mem. NEA, Minn. Edn. Assn., Dakota County Area Supts. Assn. (pres. 1980-81), Nat. Acad. Sch. Execs. (Devel. award 1975), Minn. Assn. Sch. Adminstrs. (pres.'s service plaque 1977), Minn. Assn. Sch. Adminstrs. (pres. 1976-77), Sch. Adminstrs. Minn. (pres. 1976-77), Am. Legion. Lutheran. Clubs: Kiwanis, Rotary. Home: 11 E Emerson Ave West Saint Paul MN 55118

ANDERSON, RUTH NATHAN, syndicated columnist, TV news host, writer, recording artist; b. N.Y.C., Jan. 28, 1934; d. Solomon and Anna (Cornick) Gans; student N.Y. U., George Washington U., evenings 1952-56; m. Arthur Aksel Anderson, Jr., Sept. 11, 1971; stepchildren—Jack Anderson, Barbara Anderson, Terri Anderson. Newsletter editor Washington Post, 1952-53; chief med. writer, press officer Nat. Multiple Sclerosis Soc., N.Y.C., 1953-55; feature editor Crusade for Freedom, Radio Free Europe, N.Y.C., 1955-58; editor jr. TV dept. TV Revue, N.Y.C., 1958-61; feature-series reporter N.Am. Newspaper Alliance, Women's News Service, N.Y.C., 1961-69; writer, originator Doctor's Grapevine column Nat. Features Syndicate, Chgo., 1969-73; author-owner syndicated column VIP Med. Grapevine, Round Lake, Ill., 1973—; feature news corr. Waukegan (Ill.) News-Sun, 1977-82; writer, host Celebrity Health News, Cablenet TV, Chgo. feature writer Scripps-Howard News Service, Chgo.; Chgo. contbg. editor Music City Entertainer; tchr. journalism, creative writing, speech arts Fla. State Bd. Adult Edn., 1968-69; lectr. writing seminars for faculty U. Ill. at Chgo. Circle Campus, 1970-80. Trustee, v.p. bd. Round Lake Pub. Library, 1977—; Right-to-Read vol. tutor jr. high schs., Round Lake, 1977—; singer ARC entertainment com. Bedside Network, 1974—. Mem. Chgo. Women in Broadcasting, Am. Med. Writers Assn., Lake County Assn. Journalists, Nat. Assn. for Female Execs., Chgo. Unltd., Press Vets. Assn., Internat. Platform Assn., Future Physicians Am. (hon.). Clubs: Chgo. Press, Chgo. Advt. Author booklet: How You Can Be a Part of Your United Nations, 1959; contbg. writer Woman's World mag.; contbr. articles to various mags. including Parents, Pageant, Mademoiselle, Science Digest, Reader's Digest, TV Guide, TV Radio Mirror, This Week, Am. Weekly, Am. Home, others; features on U.S. presidents in archives of Hoover, Truman, Eisenhower, Kennedy and Johnson presdl. libraries. Rec. artist mus. comedy songs, pop for Am. Sound label. Home: 161 Nasa Circle Round Lake IL 60073

ANDERSON, SANDRA WILLIAMS, optometrist, educator; b. Columbus, Ohio, May 5, 1958; d. Frederick Ted and Margaret Ann (Carr) W.; m. Paul Raymond Anderson, Dec. 19, 1981. Student U. Evansville, 1976-78; O.D., Ohio State U., 1982. Lic. optometrist, Ohio. Dep. auditor Franklin County, Columbus, 1976-81; gen. practice optometry, Columbus, 1982—; clin. instr. visual therapy Ohio State U., Columbus, 1982—; vision specialist Columbus Achievement Ctr., 1982-84; vision cons. Hilliard City Schs., Ohio, 1982—. Optometry chmn. Franklin County United Way, 1984; mem. choir First Community Ch., Columbus, 1982—. Mem. Am. Optometric Assn., Ohio Optometric Assn., Central Ohio Assn. for Children with Learning Disabilities, Am. Legion Aux., Ohio State U. Alumni Assn. (gov. 1983—), Beta Sigma Kappa (Silver medal 1982). Republican. Lodges: White Shrine of Jerusalem, Amaranth.

ANDERSON, SHARON ROE, university administrator; b. Trona, Calif., Nov. 3, 1944; d. Lawrence A. and Kathryn L. Roe; B.A., St. Olaf Coll., 1966; m. Roger Hartley Anderson, Aug. 28, 1965; 1 son, Colby Pierce. Asst. dir. vol. services Mt. Sinai Hosp., 1984—. dir. inner city field services Greater Mpls. council Girl Scouts U.S.A., 1966-70; adminstr. and registrar Edina (Minn.) Montessori Schs., 1973-76; research specialist Hubert H. Humphrey Inst. Public Affairs, U. Minn., 1976-78, asst. to dir. 1977-80, adminstr., 1980-82, assoc. to dir., 1982-85, assoc. dir., 1985—. Mem. com. on aging United Way Mpls., 1980—, mem. allocations com., 1982—, mem. evaluation com., 1985—; mem. Minn. Bd. on Aging, 1973-81; chmn. task force Minn. Long Term Care State Plan, 1981—; mem. sch. bd. Edina Montessori Sch., 1973-74; pres. Minn. unit bd. Am. Contract Bridge League, 1981—; trustee Sci. Mus. Minn., 1981—; bd. dirs. Chrysalis, 1984. Home: 5701 Bryant Ave S Minneapolis MN 55418 Office: 909 Social Sciences Bldg 267 19th Ave S Minneapolis MN 55455

ANDERSON, STEPHEN JOEL, engineer, manufacturing company executive; b. Des Moines, Feb. 9, 1953; s. Noel Merrill and Mary Mabel A.; m Jacqueline Rae Fagen, July 26, 1975; children—Matthew Joel, Joel Justin. B.S.C.E., Iowa State U., 1975. Engr., Black and Veatch, Kansas City, Mo., 1975-76; engr., gen. mgr., pres. Merrill Mfg. Co., Storm Lake, Iowa, 1976—, also dir. Patentee yard hydrant. Mem. Nat. Water Well Assn., Iowa Assn. Bus. and Industry (minuteman 1982). Republican. Methodist. Home: 132 Mallard Ave Box 1214 Storm Lake IA 50588 Office: Merrill Mfg Co 315 Flindt Dr Storm Lake IA 50588

ANDERSON, STEPHEN THOMAS, medical diagnostic testing systems manufacturing company executive; b. Duluth, Minn., Mar. 8, 1947; s. Elmer M. and Linnea (Eklund) A.; m. Catherine A. Middleton, Dec. 5, 1970; children—Amy, Carver. B.S. in Elec. Engring., U. Minn., 1970. Sci. programmer Sperry Univac Corp., 1970-73; system sales engr. Honeywell, Inc., 1973-75; sales engr. Tektronix, Inc., St. Paul, 1975-77; dist. sales mgr. Computervision Corp., St. Paul, 1977-79; pres. Med. Graphics Corp., St. Paul, 1979—. Patentee respiratory analyzer system, cardio-pulmonary exercise stress system, numerical data display method. Mem. Am. Mgmt. Assn. Home: 14253 St Croix Trail N Stillwater MN 55082 Office: Medical Graphics Corp 501 W County Rd E Saint Paul MN 55112

ANDERSON, THODORE EDMUND, chemical company executive, researcher; b. Dallas, Nov. 27, 1929; s. Theodore Edmund and Agnes Amelia (Hagman) A.; m. Phyllis Jane Beacom, Sept. 8, 1956; children—Mary, Joan. Student Augustana Coll., 1948-49; B.S., U. Mich., 1953; M.S., Mich. State U., 1958, Ph.D., 1963. Research chemist Union Carbide, Pitts., 1958-59; research sect. head Dow Chem. Co., Midland, Mich., 1963-69; quality control devel. mgr. Miles Labs., Elkhart, Ind., 1969-76, quality assurance dir., 1976-79; research mgr. Badische Anilin & Soda Fabrik Co., Diversey-Wyandotte Corp., Wyandotte, Mich., 1979—. Inventor in field. Vice pres. St. Thomas Lutheran Ch., 1983-84; fund raiser Republican Party, East Lansing, Mich., 1960. Served with U.S. Army, 1954-55. Recipient Sigma Xi Research award, 1963; Pickle Packers Assn. grantee, 1959-61. Mem. Am. Chem. Soc., U. Mich. Alumni Assn. (pres. Midland chpt. 1966-67). Club: Grosse Ile Yacht. Lodges: Masons, Rotary. Avocations: tennis; downhill skiing; boating; music; reading. Home: 8534 Manchester Rd Grosse Ile MI 48138 Office: Diversey-Wyandotte Corp 1532 Biddle Ave Wyandotte MI 48192

ANDERSON, THOMAS WINLOW, college administrator; b. Moline, Ill., Aug. 19, 1943; s. Winlow Carlson and Gladys Virginia (Lindquist) A.; m. Pamela Ray Wells, Aug. 23, 1964; children—Thomas Jr., Cara. B.A., Iowa Wesleyan Coll., 1965; M.A., Mich. State U., 1970; J.D., U. Dayton, 1979. Bar: Ohio 1980. Admissions counselor Iowa Wesleyan Coll., Mt. Pleasant, 1965-66; asst. dean Albion Coll., Mich., 1966-70; asst. dean U. Dayton, Ohio 1970-77; dean students Case Western Res. U., Cleve., 1977-81, v.p., 1981—. Contbr. articles to profl. jours. Adv. bd. Ctr. Profl. Ethics, Cleve., 1981—; class mem. Leadership Cleve., 1983; commn. mem. Fedn. Community Planning, Cleve., 1985. Mem. Bar Assn. Cleve., Am. Assn. Higher Edn., Council Advancement and Support Edn. Methodist. Clubs: Univ., Playhouse. Avocation: racquetball. Home: 3798 Washington Blvd University Heights OH 44118 Office: Case Western Res U 2040 Adelbert Rd Cleveland OH 44106

ANDERSON, VIDYA LAURA KATE, therapist; b. Washington, Mar. 7, 1946; d. Lawrence Joseph and Frances MacRae Viernstein; m. Robert C. Anderson, June 10, 1972; children—Colleen Marie, Crystal Elizabeth. B.A., Queens Coll., 1968; M.A., Wake Forest U., 1970. Researcher, Child Research Project, N.C. Meml. Hosp., N.C., 1970-71; staff psychologist Opportunity Village, Assn. Retarded Citizens, Las Vegas, Nev., 1972-73; psychol. cons. So. Nev. Mental Retardation Center, Las Vegas, 1974-75; sch. psychologist Clark Country Sch. Dist., Las Vegas, 1975-76; pvt. practice therapy Bourbonnais Family Inst. (Ill.), 1978—; coordinator, pres. Am. Meditation Soc., 1982—; exec. asst. to Hon. Gururaj Ananda Yogi of S. Africa, 1980—. Dana scholar Queens Coll., 1967-68; Wake Forest U. fellow, 1968-70. Mem. Am. Psychol. Assn. Republican. Methodist. Home: 1371 Plum Creek Dr Bourbonnais IL 60914 Office: PO Box 244 Bourbonnais IL 60914

ANDOLSHEK, RICHARD ANDERS, retail executive; b. Crosby, Minn., Mar. 13, 1952; s. Albin Henery and Alice Louise (Arvidson) A.; student U. Minn., 1970-73; children—Kimberly, Albin, Daren. Owner, operator Crosslake IGA Grocery Store (Minn.), 1973—, Dick's Package Liquor Store, Crosslake, 1973—, Andy's Restaurant, Crosslake, 1973—; v.p. Country Printing Enterprises Inc., Pequot Lakes, Minn., 1977-80, LAR, Inc., night club and restaurant, Crosslake, 1977-82; pres. Jonable Inc., chain restaurant, Crosslake, 1979—, Richard-Curtis, Inc., Pequot Lakes, 1980—, Brann and Assos., Inc., Brainerd, Minn., 1981—, Chadco of Duluth, Inc., 1982—, No. Food King, 1982—, R-C Mktg. & Leasing, Inc., 1982—; chmn. bd. Sport Shacks, Inc., 1982—, Lakes Broadcasting Corp., Inc., 1984—. Mem. Crosslake Planning and Zoning Commn., 1973-74, Region 5 Devel. Commn., 1975-77; mem. Minn. Outdoor Recreation Commn., 1978; mem. Ind. Sch. Dist. 186 Bd. Edn., Pequot Lakes, Minn., 1975—, chmn., 1977. Named Minn. Liquor Retailer of Yr., Midwest Beverage Jour., 1977. Mem. Minn. Food Retailers, Minn. Liquor Retailers (pres. 1978-80), Midwestern States Fedn. Beverage Licensees (adv. bd.), Nat. License Beverage Assn. (sec., bd. dirs.), Crosslake C. of C., Nat. Fedn. Small Bus. Club: Elks. Office: Box 358 Pequot Lakes MN 56472

ANDORFER, DONALD EDWIN, advt. co. artist; b. Clinton, Ia., Jan. 1, 1912; s. Arthur and Mildred Susan (Cram) A.; student Wis. State Coll., 1930-32, Art Inst. Chgo., 1946-47; m. Loretta Adeline Kuhnke, Dec. 24, 1935; children—Donald, Sylvia (Mrs. Gerry Schwindt), Joseph, Virginia (dec.). Free lance artist, Grand Rapids, Mich., 1936-50; artist So. States Coop., Richmond, Va., 1950-60; free lance artist, illustrator, South Bend, Ind., 1960-63; artist Fletcher & Assos., Advt. Inc., St. Joseph, Mo., 1963-67; artist in residence North Mo. area Mo. State Council of Arts; represented in permanent collection at Mo. State Hist. Soc.; commd. to paint mural of Callaway County history, Fulton, Mo., 1978; pvt. instr. in art; propr. Rural Am. Art Gallery, St. Joseph, Mo.; mem. Grand Central Galleries, N.Y.C. Bd. dirs. Albrecht Gallery, 1966-69; founder mem. Mo. Citizens for Arts, St. Louis. Recipient numerous ribbons and trophies in art exhbns.; named one of best artists of Am., Wis. Hist. Soc., 1981. Mem. Internat. Soc. Artists, Soc. N. Am. Artists, Greater Kansas City Art Assn., Clinton (Iowa) Art Assn. Methodist (ofcl. bd. 1964-67). Illustrator: Nation of Might, 1942. Home: Rural Route 3 Saint Joseph MO 64505

ANDRACHIK, GARY STEVE, lawyer; b. Cleve., Apr. 26, 1947; s. Steve and Elizabeth (Magyar) A.; m. Marie J. Ruth, July 3, 1971; 1 child Keith. B.A., Boston Coll., 1969; J.D., Case Western Res. U., 1972. Bar: Ohio 1972. Trial atty. Cuyahoga County Pros. Atty.'s Office, Ohio, 1973-81; atty. Continental Ins. Co., Cleve., 1981-83; ptnr. Reid, Johnson, Downes, Andrachik & Webster, Cleve., 1983—. Mem. Ohio State Bar Assn. Democrat. Roman Catholic. Avocations: golf; racquetball; fishing; hiking. Home: 3645 Glenbar St Fairview Park OH 44126

ANDRAE, ROLLA PHELPS, historical site administrator; b. Robertsville, Mo., Mar. 13, 1905; s. Alexander Andrae and Mary (Helm) Smith; m. Gertrude Mae Palmer, Sept. 1, 1934; 1 child, Randall Dean. Factory worker Ford Motor Co., St. Louis, 1925-28; constrn. worker, Washington, 1928-39; real estate sales, farmer, Franklin County, Mo., 1949-67; judge Franklin County Ct., 1965-66; pres., curator Daniel Boone Home, Defiance, Mo., 1967—. Democrat. Lodges: Elks, Shriners. Home: Route 1 Box 236 Defiance MO 63341 Office: Daniel Boone Home Defiance MO 63341

ANDRE, ELLEN CAROL, business educator; b. Parkston, S.D., Jan. 17, 1945; d. Leonard David and Fern Carol (Fox) Hanson; m. William Elmer Andre, June 27, 1969; children—Marcus William, Erica Ellen. B.S. in Edn., U. S.D.-Springfield, 1967; M.A. in Adult and Higher Edn., U. S.D.-Vermillion, 1980. Permanent profl. cert. edn., Iowa. Tchr., Akron (Iowa) Community High Sch., 1967-69; sec. Pacific Ordnance and Electronics Co., Long Beach, Calif., 1969-70; tchr. Andes Central High Sch., Lake Andes, S.D., 1970-74; adminstrv. asst. Fed. Land Bank Assn., Sioux City, Iowa, 1974-76; instr. Bus. and Office Occupations div. Western Iowa Tech. Community Coll., Sioux City, 1976—, advisor Office Edn. Assn., 1978-83. Mobile dep. registrar for Woodbury County, Iowa, 1982; Americanism chmn. VFW Aux., 1970-74; mem., treas. Sioux City Civic New Comers, 1974-77; mem., sec. parent adv. com. Nodland Elem. Sch., Sioux City, 1981-82, 84-86. Mem. Profl. Secs. Internat., Iowa Vocat. Assn., NEA, Iowa State Edn. Assn., Am. Vocat. Assn., Western Iowa Tech. Community Coll. Edn. Assn. (sec., treas.). Democrat. Lutheran. Developer Competency Based Instructional Learning Materials, 1978-80.

ANDRÉ, WILLIAM VINCENT, computer room design exec.; b. Chgo., Feb. 4, 1937; s. Kenneth B. and Margret E. (Wood) A.; M.E., Ill. Inst. Tech., 1960; m. Patricia A. Karl, Apr. 26, 1957; children—Peter J., Mary R., Laurie M., William Vincent. Design engr. C.F. Murphy Architects & Engrs., Chgo., 1957-69; constrn. rep. J.C. Penney Co., Inc., Rolling Meadows, Ill., 1971-75; project mgr. Michael Reese Med. Center, Chgo., 1975; mgr. engring. Brunswick Corp., Skokie, Ill., 1975-76; mgr. ops. Dayton Hudson Corp., Mpls., 1976-80; owner W.V. André Co., computer room design, 1980—; lectr. energy conservation. Mem. Am. Soc. Hosp. Engrs., Am. Soc. San. Engrs., Am. Soc. Plumbing Engrs., ASHRAE, Cons. Inst. Roman Catholic. Clubs: Holy Name Soc. (sec. 1971-72), Newman Boys (counselor 1970-71), K.C. (4 deg.). Author: Energy Conservation Thru Preventative Maintenance, 1976. Office: 5013 Dominick Spur Minnetonka MN 55343

ANDREADIS, KLEON CONSTANTINE, school administrator; b. Bklyn., Jan. 2, 1952; s. Constantine and Catherine (Vafiadou) A.; m. Alexandra Roxanne Natsios, June 21, 1982. B.A. in Psychology, SUNY-Albany, 1974; M.A. in Psychology, New Sch. Social Research, 1977; M.Ed. in Ednl. Adminstrn., Columbia U., 1979, postgrad. in edn., 1979—. Cert. supt. schs., N.Y., Ohio. Tchr. sci. Dalton Sch., N.Y.C., 1974-77, math/sci. coordinator, 1977-79, asst. to headmaster, 1979-80; headmaster Cathedral Sch., N.Y.C., 1980-81; prin. Malvern Elem. Sch., Shaker Heights (Ohio) City Sch. Dist., 1982—. Mem. Assn. Supervision and Curriculum Devel., Nat. Assn. Elem. Sch. Prins., Ohio Assn. Elem. Sch. Adminstrs., Council Basic Edn., Shaker Hist. Soc., Phi Delta Kappa. Home: 3290 Warrensville Center Rd Shaker Heights OH 44122 Office: 19910 Malvern Rd Shaker Heights OH 44122

ANDREADIS, NICHOLAS ANDREW, cardiologist; b. Canton, Ohio, Sept. 27, 1948; s. Nicholas Harry and Nina (Rossetti) A.; B.A., Kent State U., 1969; M.D., Creighton U., 1974; m. Barbara Ann Kirkwood, July 4, 1970; children—Tiffany, Peter, Phillip. Intern, Creighton U. and Affiliated Hosps., Omaha, 1974-75, resident and cardiology fellow, 1975-78; practice medicine specializing in cardiovascular diseases, Fed. Way and Auburn, Wash., 1978-84; past mem. staff, dir. non-invasive cardiac lab. Auburn Gen. Hosp., also past mem. exec. com., sec. treas.; staff cardiovascular and gastroenterology research div. Upjohn Co., Kalamazoo, Mich., 1984—; mem. staff Tacoma Gen. Hosp. Recipient Disting. Citizen award State Wash., 1983. Fellow Am. Coll. Cardiology; mem. AMA (physicians recognition award 1978-83), Mich. Heart Assn., Am. Soc. Echocardiography, Am. Soc. for Clin. Pharmacology and Therapeutics, Am. Heart Assn. (council on clin. cardiology, council on high blood research), ACP. Home: 8480 Valleywood Ln Kalamazoo MI 49002 Office: Upjohn Co 7000 Portage Rd Kalamazoo MI 49001

ANDREAS, BRUCE FREDERICK, pathologist; b. Cleve., May 10, 1925; s. Frederick William and Edna Louise (Buehler) A.; A.B., Heidelberg Coll., 1949; M.D., Ohio State U., 1953; m. Jean Bobbitt, Aug. 28, 1954; children—Karen, Frederick, Patricia, Jonathan; m. 2d, Marie Greder Nimietz, July 4, 1976. Intern, Miami Valley Hosp., Dayton, Ohio, 1953-54, resident in pathology, 1954-58; pathologist, dir. lab., Geauga Community Hosp., Chardon, Ohio, 1959—, chief of staff, 1969-70; pres. Geauga Lab. Services, Inc.; regional dir. Ohio Peer Rev. Orgn., Inc. Charter mem., trustee Met. Health Planning Corp. N.E. Ohio, 1967-76; del. Am. Cancer Soc., 1966-68; v.p. Geauga County Bd. Health, 1966-69; mem. adv. council N.E. Ohio ARC Blood Center, 1966—; mem. adv. bd. med. lab. technologists program Lakeland Community Coll., 1975—; mem. Geauga County Health Adv. Council, 1969-73, pres., 1973; bd. dirs. Geauga County Mental Health Clinic, 1966-69; cons. pathologist to Geauga County coroner, 1962—; bd. dirs., charter mem. Geauga Emergency Med. Services, Inc., 1965-72; field liaison asso. Commn. on Cancer, A.C.S., 1981. Served with U.S. Army, 1943-46. Decorated Bronze Star with two oak leaf clusters. Diplomate Am. Bd. Pathology. Fellow Coll. Am. Pathologists (lab. insp. accreditation program 1976—), Am. Soc. Clin. Pathologists, Am. Coll. Utilization Rev. Physicians; mem. AMA, Ohio Soc. Pathologists, Cleve. Soc. Pathologists (pres. 1971), Ohio Med. Assn. (del.), Geauga County Med. Soc. (pres. 1966), Cleve. Acad. Medicine. Home: 11296 Brookside Rd Chardon OH 44024 Office: Geauga Community Hosp Box 249 Chardon OH 44024

ANDREAS, DWAYNE O(RVILLE), business executive; b. Worthington, Minn., Mar. 4, 1918; s. Reuben P. and Lydia (Stoltz) A.; student Wheaton (Ill.) Coll., 1935-36; m. Bertha Benedict, 1938 (div.); 1 dau., Sandra Ann McMurtrie; m. 2d, Dorothy Inez Snyder, Dec. 21, 1947; children—Terry Lynn Bevis Herbert Burns, Michael D. Vice pres., dir. Honeymead Products Co., Cedar Rapids, Iowa, 1936-46; v.p. Cargill, Inc., Mpls., 1946-52; chmn. bd., chief exec. officer Honeymead Products Co. (now Nat. City Bancorp.), Mankato, Minn., 1952-72; chmn. bd., chief exec. officer Archer-Daniels-Midland Co., Decatur, Ill., 1970—; pres. Seaview Hotel Corp., 1958—; Lone Star Industries, Greenwich, Conn. Nat. dir. Boys Club of Am.; trustee Hoover Inst. on War, Revolution and Peace; mem. Trilateral Commn.; chmn. U.S.-USSR Trade and Econ. Council, 1984; mem. Pres.'s Gen. Adv. Com. Fgn. Assistance Programs, 1965-68, Pres.'s Adv. Council on Mgmt. Improvement, 1969-73, Pres.'s Task Force on Internat. Pvt. Enterprise, 1983—. Pres., Andreas Found.; trustee U.S. Naval Acad. Found. Mem. Fgn. Policy Assn. N.Y. (dir.), Econ. Club of N.Y. (vice chmn.). Clubs: Union League (Chgo.); Minneapolis, Minikahda (Mpls.); Indian Creek Country (Miami Beach, Fla.); Links, Knickerbocker, Friars, Econ. (vice-chmn.) (N.Y.C.); Blind Brook (Port Chester, N.Y.). Office: Archer Daniels Midland Co Box 1470 Decatur IL 62525

ANDREASEN, GEORGE FREDRICK, dentist, educator; b. Fremont, Nebr., Feb. 16, 1934; s. George T. and Laura Mae (Hynek) A.; B.S. (Regents scholar), U. Nebr., 1959, D.D.S., 1963, M.S. (NIH fellow), 1963; children—Susan, Robin. Research fellow Worcester Coll., Oxford, Eng., 1960-61; asst. prof. orthodontics U. Iowa Coll. Dentistry, Iowa City, 1963-67, asso. prof., acting head dept. orthodontics, 1967, asso. prof., head dept., 1968, prof., head dept. orthodontics, 1968—; practice dentistry, Iowa City, 1963—. Cons. to various dental corps. on dental materials. Named hon. adm. Nebr. Navy, 1972; U. Nebr. Alumnus Master, 1974. Fellow Am. Coll. Dentists, Royal Soc. Health (Eng.); mem. Am. Assn. Orthodontists (chmn. sci. com. 1971-72, nat. com. on research 1976-79, pres. 1980), Iowa Orthodontic Soc. (pres. 1972-73), Am., Iowa dental assns., Univ. Dist. Dental Assn., Iowa Alumni Assn. (life), U. Iowa Med. Center (life), Am. Oxonion, Phalanx Blue Print Key, Sigma Xi, Pi Tau Sigma. Omicron Kappa Upsilon, Delta Tau Delta, Xi Psi Phi. Club: Athletic (Iowa City). Contbr. articles to profl. jours. Patentee in field. Home: 1104 Penkridge Dr Iowa City IA 52240 Office: Room S221 DSB U Iowa Iowa City IA 52240

ANDREJEVICH, MILAN, historian; b. Gary, Ind., Oct. 23, 1953; s. Ivan and Eva (Steidel) A.; B.A., Ind. U. N.W., 1975; postgrad., U. Pitts., 1975-76; Fulbright-Hays (IIE), Yugoslav Govt. grantee U. Belgrade, 1976-77; M.A., U. Chgo., 1978; m. Marcia June Nedoff, May 17, 1975; 1 dau., Lydia Marie. Grad. asst. history dept. U. Ill., Chgo., 1978-79, asst. instr., 1979—, coordinator/lectr. Honor's program, 1981-82, research asso. Summer Research Lab. on Slavic Studies, 1981; instr. Coll. St. Francis, Joliet, Ill., 1980. Fulbright-Hays grantee (U.S. Dept. Edn.), Yugoslavia, 1983—. Mem. Am. Assn. Advancement Slavic Studies, Am. Assn. S.E. European Studies, N.Am. Soc. Serbian Studies, Fulbright Alumni Assn., Yugoslav-Am. Students Assn. (pres. 1980). Contbr. articles to profl. jours. Home: 3900 Willow St Hobart IN 46342 Office: Dept History Box 4348 U Ill Chicago IL 60680

ANDREOLI, CHARLES ANTHONY, designer, sculptor; b. Kenosha, Wis., Aug. 26, 1928; s. Ralph and Jenny Andreoli; student Am. Acad. Art, 1946-48, DePaul U., 1948-49; student of Alexandre Zlatoff-Mierski, 1947-51; m. Mary Celebre, Nov. 28, 1953. Portrait painter, 1949—; interior designer DaPrato Studio, Chgo., 1954-56, J. Cotey Co., Chgo.; free lance designer to home furnishing trade, including Hillenbrand Industries (Ind.), Sandel Lamps, Chgo., Fuggiti Studios, Chgo., U.S. Industries Lamp div., Chgo., L.C.A. Lamp div., (Ky.), Erie Glass Co., Chgo.; lamp design cons. Prestige Lamp div. McGraw Edison Co., Chgo.; important works include Mayan Room Restaurant, Rockefeller Centre, sculptured arches Emerald Door Restaurant, New Orleans; created Andreoli Porcelaine Sculptures Ltd. Edition. Address: 1340 N Astor St Chicago IL 60610

ANDRES, CARL WESLEY, insurance agent; b. Belleville, Ill., Jan. 5, 1935; s. Edwin F. and Marella M. (McElroy) A.; m. L. Frances Andres, June 13, 1968 (div. Aug. 1983); 1 child, Carl W. Underwriting mgr. Ill. Nat. Ins. Co., Springfield, 1972-73; owner, operator Downstate Ins. Agency, Harrisburg, Ill., 1974—. Served with USAF, 1954-57. Mem. Harrisburg C. of C. (pres. 1982). Baptist. Lodges: Rotary (pres. 1981), Lions (pres. 1984-85). Office: Downstate Insurance Agency PO Box 411 15 E Poplar Harrisburg IL 62946

ANDRES, RONALD PAUL, engineering educator; b. Chgo., Jan. 9, 1938; s. Harold William and Amanda (Breuhaus) A.; m. Jean Elwood; July 15, 1961; children—Douglas, Jennifer, Mark. B.S. in Chem. Engring., Northwestern U., 1959; Ph.D. in Chem. Engring., Princeton U., 1962. Asst. prof. chem. engring. Princeton U., 1962-66, assoc. prof., 1968-72, prof., 1972-81; prof., head. dept. chem. engring. Purdue U., West Lafayette, Ind., 1981—. Mem. AAAS, Am. Soc. Engring. Edn., Am. Chem. Soc., Am. Inst. Chem. Engrs., Sigma Xi. Home: 119 Sunset Ln West Lafayette IN 47906 Office: Purdue U Sch Chem Engring West Lafayette IN 47907

ANDRES, WILLIAM ALFRED, retail chain executive; b. Fayette, Iowa, Aug. 9, 1926; s. Alfred G. and Eva Levetta (Eide) A.; B.A., Upper Iowa U., Fayette, 1948, D.B.A. (hon.), 1977; M.A., U. Pitts., 1949; m. Betty Ruth Follett, June 4, 1947; children—Robert A., Charles W., Richard W. With Dayton Hudson Corp., Mpls., 1958—, exec. v.p. retail ops., 1971-74, pres., 1974—, chief exec. officer, 1976—, chmn., 1977—, also dir.; dir. EXXON Corp., 1st Bank Systems, Inc., Internat. Multifoods, The St. Paul Cos., Scott Paper Co.; chmn. Retail Industry Trade Action Coalition. Bd. dirs. United Way, Mpls., 1975—. Served to 2d lt. U.S. Army, 1944-46. Clubs: Minneapolis. Office: 777 Nicollet Mall Minneapolis MN 55402

ANDREW, ROBERT HARRY, agronomist; b. Platteville, Wis., Aug. 2, 1916; s. Harry Roscoe and Lu (Howery) A.; B.A., U. Wis., Madison, 1938; Ph.D., 1942; m. Nancy H. Wright, Apr. 15, 1944; children—Stephen, Elizabeth, Sarah, Martha, Charles. Agronomist Wis. Expt. Sta., 1942-46; asst. prof. agronomy U. Wis., Madison, 1946-52, asso. prof., 1952-58, prof., 1958—; vis. Fulbright lectr. U. Wageningen (Netherlands), 1953-54. Fellow Am. Soc. Agronomy; mem. Crop Sci. Soc. Am., Sigma Xi, Phi Sigma, Gamma Sigma Delta, Phi Beta Kappa, Gamma Alpha. Methodist. Contbr. articles to profl. jours. Home: 3809 Hillcrest Dr Madison WI 53705 Office: Dept Agronomy U Wis Madison WI 53706

ANDREWS, CHARLES EDWARD, physician, medical center administrator; b. Stratford, Okla., Jan. 22, 1925; s. Guy Eldrige and Esther Elenor (Smith) A.; m. Evelyn Hevesy, Aug. 18, 1946 (dec. Apr. 1982); children—Evelyn E., Mary; m. Theresa Paoletti, Nov. 24, 1982. Student NYU, 1943-45; M.D., Boston U., 1949. Diplomate Am. Bd. Internal Medicine, Nat. Bd. Med. Examiners. Intern, U. Kans. Med. Ctr., 1949-50, resident, 1953-55; resident VA Hosp., Wichita, Kans., 1950-51; gen. practice medicine, 1955—; instr., assoc. medicine, asst. prof. medicine U. Kans.-Kansas City, 1955-61; assoc. prof., prof. medicine W.Va. U. Med. Ctr., Morgantown, 1961-63, 1963-68, provost health scis., 1968-77, v.p. health scis., 1978-81, acting dir., 1967-68; chancellor U. Nebr. Med. Ctr., Omaha, 1983—. Served to capt. M.C., USAF, 1951-53. Fellow Am. Coll. Chest Physicians, ACP; mem. Central Soc. Clin. Research, Am. Thoracic Soc. Office: Univ Nebraska Med Ctr 42d & Dewey Ave Omaha NE 68105

ANDREWS, DONALD LOUIS, banker; b. Indpls., Nov. 20, 1939; s. Louis Paul and Winifred Agnes (Boyer) A.; m. Karen Ann Teipen, Aug. 2, 1964 (div. Nov. 1979); children—Paul Louis, Julie Michele, Krista Lynn; m. Linda Kay Hinshaw, Oct. 3 1980. B.B.A., Ind. Central Coll., 1961. Mem. consumer lending dept. Indpls. Morris Plan, 1961-65; mem. consumer lending dept. Mchts. Bank, Indpls., 1965-83, dir. consumer mktg., 1983—; cons., speaker, 1981—. Republican. Presbyterian. Lodge: Lions (v.p.). Avocations: fishing, coaching youth, spectator sports. Home: 2345 E Banta Rd Indianapolis IN 46227 Office: Mchts Nat Bank One Merchants Plaza Indianapolis IN 46255

ANDREWS, KENNETH D., agricultural educator, military historian, professional auctioneer; b. Casper, Wyo., Sept. 14, 1932; s. Harry D. and Agnes O. (Farris) A.; m. Georgia R. Hayden, Aug. 16, 1962; 1 dau., M. Arlene. B.S. in Gen. Agr. and Plant Sci., U. Wyo., 1969, M.S. in Agrl. Edn., 1976. Cert. educator, Nebr.; cert. vocat. educator, Colo. Teaching asst. U. Wyo., Laramie, 1973-74; classroom tchr. Sch. Dist. R-6, Otis, Colo., 1975-76, Sch. Dist. 31, Mitchell, Nebr., 1976—; adj. faculty Nebr. Western Coll. Agr., Scottsbluff. Mem. Nat. Vocat. Agr. Tchrs. Assn., Am. Vocat. Assn., State Assn. Vocat., Nat. Auctioneers Assn., Alpha Zeta, Phi Delta Kappa. Club: Masons. Home: 1403 1/4 14th Mitchell NE 69357 Office: Mitchell High Sch Mitchell NE 69357

ANDREWS, LARRY HOWARD, data processing company executive; b. St. Peter, Minn., Mar. 28, 1942; s. Howard L. and Anna Mae (Bartak) A.; B.A. in Math. cum laude, Doane Coll., 1965; m. Virginia Faye Rannie, Aug. 4, 1962; children—Kurt, Mark; m. 2d, Carolyn Sue Molnar, July 29, 1978; children—Christina, Emily Lori, Todd. Instr. math. Dist. 66 Schs., Omaha, 1965-66; computer systems analyst and programmer Western Electric Co., Omaha, 1966-69; data processing mgr. UNICO, Bellevue, Nebr., 1969-70; pres. ALR Computer Services, Omaha, 1970-77, ALR Systems and Software, Inc., 1977—; treas., dir. K-Kal Products Inc., 1976—. Pres., Meadows Community Assn., 1981, bd. dirs., 1981-82. Cert. in data processing, systems profl. Mem. Assn. Computer Machinery, Data Processing Mgrs. Assn., Omaha C. of C. Republican. Methodist. Clubs: Sertoma. Home: 7104 S 140th Ave Omaha NE 68138 Office: 10334 Ellison Circle Omaha NE 68134

ANDREWS, MARK, senator; b. Fargo, N.D., May 19, 1926; s. Mark and Lillian (Hoyler) A.; B.S., N.D. State U., 1949, hon. doctorate, 1978; m. Mary Willming, June 28, 1949; children—Mark III, Sarah Jane, Karen Louise. Farmer, Mapleton, N.D., 1949—; mem. 88th-92d Congresses from 1st. Dist. N.D., 93d-96th Congresses, at-large N.D.; mem. U.S. Senate from N.D., 1981—; mem. Congl. Environ. Study Conf.; ofcl. del. FAO Conf., Rome, 1975; founding mem. Congl. Rural Caucus. Mem. Rep. Nat. Com. for N.D.; Named hon. Am. farmer Future Farmers Am., 1976; recipient Disting. Service award Nat. Rural Electric Assn., 1983. Mem. Rep. Nat. Farm Council, N.D. Young Republicans (past chmn.), Farm Bur., Am. Legion, N.D. Stockmen's Assn., N.D. Crop Improvement Assn. (pres.) Greater N.D. Assn., Northwest Farm Mgrs., N.D. Water Users Assn., Nat. Reclamation Assn. (chmn. land limitations com.). Episcopalian. Office: SH-724 Hart Senate Office Bldg Washington DC 20510*

ANDREWS, SUNNY, social work educator, university administrator; b. Alwaye, Kerala, India, Nov. 4, 1935; came to U.S., 1957; s. Chacko P. and Kanda (Mathai) A.; m. Sara-Kovoor, May 13, 1963; children—Susan, Jacob. A.B., Lincoln U., 1961; M.S.W., U. Pa., 1961; M.P.H., Johns Hopkins U., 1969, D. Pub. Health, 1973. Spl. project group worker St. Martha's Settlement House, Phila., 1961-62; social scientist Rural Health Research Projects, Narangwal, Punjab, India, 1963-67; research asst. Johns Hopkins U., Balt., 1970-73; dir. social work, asst. prof. Meyer Children's Rehab. Inst., Omaha, 1973-78; assoc. prof. Sch. Social Work, U. Nebr., Omaha, 1978-81, dir., prof., 1981—; vis. prof., research cons. U. City of Manila, 1985. Author: (with others) Doctors for the Villages: Study of Rural Internships in Seven Indian Medical Colleges, 1976. Mem. adv. bd. Vol. Bur., United Way, Omaha, 1976—; pres. India Assn. Omaha, 1979. Named Hon. Faculty Affiliate, Mt. Marty Coll., Yankton, S.D., 1976-77. Mem. Am. Pub. Health Assn. (governing council 1976-79, chmn.-elect social work sect. 1985), Nat. Assn. Social Workers, Council Social Work Edn., Nat. Council Deans and Dirs. Grad. Schs. of Social Work. Clubs: Lehigh Country (Fla.); Bella Vista Country (Bentonville, Ark.). Avocations: tennis; jogging; philately. Home: 16706 Martha Circle Omaha NE 68130 Office: Sch Social Work U Nebr 60th and Dodge Sts Omaha NE 68182

ANDREWS, WILLIAM HENRY, hospital administrator; b. Wellston, Mo., Oct. 16, 1919; s. William H. and Viola (Williams) A.; B.S. in Edn., Lincoln U., 1941; M.H.A., Washington U., 1954; m. Mildred E. Joyce, Aug. 7, 1943; children—William H., Brenda J. Asst. adminstr. Homer G. Phillips Hosp., 1941-52; adminstr. People's Hosp., 1954-55, George W. Hubbard Hosp., Meharry Med. Coll., 1955-59; adminstr. Forest City Hosp., 1959-64; asst. dir. Cleve. Met. Gen. Hosp., later dep. dir., dir., 1969—, sr. v.p., 1981—; adminstr. Kaiser Permanente Med. Center, Cleve., 1981-84; sr. staff assoc. Kaiser Permanente Med. Ctr., Cleve., 1984—. Mem. faculty health services adminstrn. Grad. Sch. Ohio State U.; mem. council Nat. Inst. Arthritis and Metabolic Diseases, 1968-71; mem. physicians clin. asst. adv. com. Cuyahoga Community Coll.; mem. personnel adv. com. and Social Service clearing house com. Cleve. Fedn. for Community Planning. Mem. Catholic Interracial Council, Cleve. Arthritis Found. Trustee Cleve. Hemophilia Found., Hough Norwood Family Health Care Program. Commonwealth Fund fellow, 1952. Life fellow Am. Coll. Hosp. Adminstrs. (examiner); mem. Wash. U. Alumni Assn. (treas.), Nat. Assn. Health Services Execs (2d v.p.), Ohio Hosp. Assn. (shared services com. and social work adv. panel), Am. Hosp. Assn. (life), Greater Cleve. Hosp. Assn. (exec. com., blood bank com., house staff com.), Kappa Alpha Psi. Club: Rotary. Home: 2960 Ripley Rd Cleveland OH 44120 Office: Bond Ct Blvd 1300 E 9th St Cleveland OH 44120

ANDROLI, ROY GEORGE, accounting educator; b. Kasota, Minn., Nov. 13, 1939; s. George A. and Elizabeth Rosalia (Weaver) A.; m. Celestine Mary Hall, Dec. 26, 1981; 1 son, Troy. B.A. in Bus., Winona State U., 1969; M.S., Bemidji State U., 1980. Auditor Holiday, Mpls., 1969-72; acctg. instr. Sch. Dist. 181, Brainerd, Minn., 1972—; bus. cons. Mem. Nat. Acctg. Assn. Roman Catholic.

ANDRZEJEWSKI, THOMAS STANLEY, journalist, lecturer; b. Cleve., Oct. 19, 1945; s. Stanley Vincent and Cecilia Helen (Ciechanowicz) A.; m. Leslie Kay, Sept. 9, 1973; 1 child, David Aaron. Student Cuyahoga Community Coll., 1963-65; B.A., Cleve. State U., 1968. Copy boy The Plain Dealer, Cleve., 1963-66, news reporter, 1966-75, writer, columnist urban affairs, 1975—; dir. Cleve. Newspaper Guild Local 1. Served with U.S. Army, 1968-70, Vietnam. Decorated Bronze Star; named best series writer Ohio A.P., 1980; recipient Spl. Media award Nat. Assn. Criminal Def. Lawyers, 1979; Silver Gavel, ABA, 1979. Avocation: running. Office: 1801 Superior Ave Cleveland OH 44114

ANGE, CONSTANCE ELIZABETH, psychiatrist; b. Plymouth, N.C., Sept. 24, 1949; d. Mack West and Irma (Perry) A.; m. Richard Jay Fryman, Sept. 9, 1978. D.O., Chgo. Coll. Osteo. Medicine, 1974. Intern, Grandview Hosp., Dayton, Ohio, 1974-75; resident U. Cin., 1977-79, fellow in child psychiatry, 1979-81; gen. practice family medicine, Springboro, Ohio, 1975-77; practice adult and child psychiatry, Dayton, Ohio, 1981—; faculty Ohio U., Athens, 1982-83; cons. Contbr. articles to profl. jours. Robert Wood Johnson scholar, 1973. Mem. Am. Osteo. Assn., Ohio Osteo. Assn., Am. Coll. Neuropsychiatry, Am. Psychiat. Assn., Am. Acad. Child Psychiatry, Sigma Sigma Phi. Avocations: reading; horticulture. Home: 901 McBurney Lebanon OH 45036 Office: 1410 Talbott Tower 131 N Ludlow Dayton OH 45402

ANGELINE, JOHN FREDERICK, management consultant; b. Somerville, Mass., Sept. 29, 1929; s. Jack L. and Edith (Ciavatti) A.; B.S., Northeastern U., 1952, M.B.A., 1963; m. Doris Helen L'Heureux, Nov. 9, 1957; children—Karen E., Rachel A., Andrea M. Mgmt. cons. Arthur D. Little Inc., Cambridge, Mass., 1952-77; v.p. research and devel. grocery products Quaker Oats Co., 1979-80; prin. Technomic Consultants, Chgo., 1980-84. Mem. various town coms. and commns. Topsfield, Mass., 1963-76. Served with U.S. Army, 1954-62. Mem. Inst. Food Technologists, Am. Chem. Soc., N.Y. Acad. Sci., Phi Tau Sigma. Republican. Patentee prodn. odorless carbon. Contbr. articles to profl. jours. Home: 496 Thomas Dr North Barrington IL 60010

ANGELL, MADELINE (MRS. KENNETH F. JOHNSON), writer; b. Devils Lake, N.D., Jan. 6, 1919; d. Bernard Oscar and Evelyn May (Smith) Angell; student Stephens Coll., 1936-37; B.S., U. Minn., 1940; m. Kenneth Frederick Johnson, Aug. 31, 1940; children—Mark Frederick, Randall David. Works include: 120 Questions and Answers about Birds, 1973; America's Best Loved Wild Animals, 1975; The Fantastic Variety of Marine Animals, 1976; Red Wing, Minnesota, Saga of a River Town, 1977; Snakes and Frogs and Turtles and Such, 1979; (with Mary Cavaness Miller) Joseph Woods Hancock: The Life and Times of a Minnesota Pioneer, 1980; A Field Guide to Berries and Berrylike Fruits, 1981; contbr. articles to publs. including Parents' Mag., Better Homes and Gardens, Sci. World. Mem. Mayor's Citizens Com. for Red Wing Tng. Sch., co-chmn., 1970-72. Recipient McKnight Found. Humanities award for novel, 1966, Blue Flame Ecology Salute, 1974. Mem. AAUW (co-pres. 1956-58), Audubon Soc., Goodhue County Hist. Soc., Minn. Hist. Soc., Authors Guild, Alpha Chi Omega, Phi Upsilon Omicron, Omicron Nu (pres. 1939-40). Lutheran. Home and office: Route 4 Cardinal Dr Red Wing MN 55066

ANGLE, ANN ZEHNER, pharmacist; b. Evansville, Ind., July 10, 1951; d. Darwin Berl and Julia Ellyn (Hudelson) Zehner; m. Richard Allen Angle, July 14, 1974. B.S. in Pharmacy, Purdue U., 1974. Registered pharmacist, Ind., Va.,

N.C. Staff pharmacist Braeburn Pharmacy, Salem, Va., 1974, Edmonds Pharmacy, Greensboro, N.C., 1975, Rite-Aid Pharmacies, Greensboro, 1975, Scottie Pharmacy, Kernersville, N.C., 1976-78, West Side Pharmacy, Bowling Green, Ohio, 1978-80; pharmacist, mgr., owner Lucas Pharmacy, Inc., Rensselaer, Ind., 1980—. Pres. Am. Cancer Soc., Jasper County Unit, Rensselaer, 1982-84, treas., 1984—. Named Young Career Woman, Rensselaer Bus. and Profl. Women's Club, 1981. Mem. Acad. Pharmacy N.C. Pharmacists, Am. Pharm. Assn., Ind. Pharmacists Assn. (employers com. 1981—), Am. Bus. Women's Assn. (pres. 1984-85, Woman of Yr. 1984), Kappa Epsilon (nat. pres. 1977-81, nat. adviser 1981—), Alpha Gamma Delta (province dir.-alumnae 1983—, Arc of Epsilon Pi 1979, Arc of Epsilon with Diamond 1985), Psi Iota Xi (v.p. 1983-84, treas. 1984—). Club: United Methodist Women. Home: RD 3 Sherwood Forest Rensselaer IN 47978 Office: Lucas Pharmacy Inc 114 S Van Rensselaer St Rensselaer IN 47978

ANGLE, MARGARET SUSAN, lawyer; b. Lincoln, Nebr., Feb. 20, 1948; d. John Charles and Catherine (Sellers) A.; B.A. with distinction in Polit. Sci., U. Wis., Madison, 1970, M.A. in Scandinavian Studies (scholarship, (NDEA fellow), 1972, J.D. cum laude, 1976. Bar: Wis. 1977, Minn. 1978. Law clk., Madison, Mpls., Chgo., 1974-76; law clk. U.S. Dist. Ct., Mpls., 1977-78; mem. firm Faegre & Bensen, Mpls., 1978-84; sr. atty. Nat. Car Rental Systems, Inc., Mpls., 1984—. Mem. ABA, Minn. Bar Assn., Wis. Bar Assn., Hennepin County Bar Assn., ACRA; Order of Coif. ACRA. Note and comment editor U. Wis. Law Rev.; contbr. articles to profl. publs. Home: 210 W Grant St No 221 Minneapolis MN 55403 Office: 7700 France Ave S Minneapolis MN 55435

ANGSTROM, JAMES ALBERT, health systems company executive, consultant; b. Boston, Oct. 27, 1922; s. Walter Edward and Helen Jane (Sheehan) A.; m. Valerie Mae Witt, May 21, 1982; children—Nancy Jane, James Walter. Grad. Morgan Park High Sch., Chgo. Mgr. various laundry, dry cleaning cos. Chgo., 1945-71; dir. fabric service Northwestern Meml. Hosp., Chgo., 1971-74; dir. linen services Evangelical Health Systems Corp., Oak Brook, Ill., 1974—; cons. Bellhaven Nursing Home, Chgo., 1978-82, Camelot Nursing Home, Westmont, Ill., 1982-84, Cambridge Court Nursing Home, Charleston, Ill., 1984—. Served with U.S. Army, 1943-45, ETO. Mem. Nat. Assn. Institutional Laundry Mgrs. (v.p. 1978, bd. dirs. 1979; named Laundry Mgr. of Yr. Ill. chpt. 1977), Internat. Fabricare Inst., Internat. Assn. Hosp. Textile Mgrs. Lodge: Masons. Avocations: traveling, camping, reading. Office: Evangelical Hospitals Corp 2025 Windsor Dr Oak Brook IL 60521

ANGUS, ROBERT BELL, sales and engineering executive; b. Chgo., June 21, 1925; s. William Muir and Jemima (Menzies) A.; m. Mary Catherine O'Malley, June 2, 1951; children—Robert, William, John, James, Kevin, Scott. B.S., DePaul U., 1974; postgrad. Moraine Valley Coll., 1982-84. Office mgr. Silverman & Wexler, Chgo., 1954-64; sales rep. Addressograph Multigraph, Chgo., 1964-66, Prehler, Chgo., 1966-85; sec.-treas. Ramag, Inc., Posen, Ill., 1985—. Served with USN, 1942-46, PTO. Mem. Am. Legion. Roman Catholic. Home: 9212 S Harding Ave Evergreen Park IL 60642 Office: Ramag Inc 2450 W 147th St Posen IL 60469

ANICHINI, MARIO, artist, sculptor; b. Lucca, Italy, Sept. 26, 1941; s. Tarcisio Socrate and Clementina (Paladini) A.; came to U.S., 1955, naturalized, 1963; student public schs., Chgo.; m. Mary Dolores Bernardini, Nov. 26, 1961; children—Mary Ellen, Mario Peter. One-man show: Kenosha (Wis.) Public Mus., 1975; exhibited at Artists/USA, 1977-80, Palm Beach Art Galleries, New Orleans, 1983-84; represented in permanent collections: Kenosha Public Museum, Salem (Wis.) Consol. Grade Sch., 1st Nat. Bank of Antioch (Ill.); numerous pvt. collections; paintings include: Stone Age, 1973, Evolution, 1973, 20th Century, 1974, Paul Revere, 1975, Agony and Ecstasy, 1976, Self Portrait, 1977, Spirit of St. Louis, 1978, Perception of Dimension, 1980, Eleven O'Clock in the Afternoon, 1980, transfer of Energy, 1981. Recipient Gold medal Accademia Italia, 1980. Address: 12319 233d Ave Trevor WI 53179

ANKENY, DEWALT H., JR., bank executive. Pres., chief operating officer, dir. First Bank System, Inc., Mpls. Office: First Bank System Inc 1200 First Bank Place East Minneaplis MN 55402*

ANNETT, BRUCE JAMES, JR., college official; b. Pontiac, Mich., May 3, 1952; s. Bruce James and Frances Ann (Bach) A. B.A., Albion Coll., 1974. Admissions counselor, publ. coordinator DePauw U., Greencastle, Ind., 1974-76; dir. coll. relations and alumni services Lawrence Inst. Tech., Southfield, Mich., 1976—; chmn. publ. com. Engring. Soc. Detroit, 1984—. Editor, designer LIT Magazine, 1977—. Bd. dirs. Oakland County Pioneer and Hist. Soc., Pontiac, Mich., 1981—. Recipient numerous awards Nat. Sch. Pub. Relations Assn. Mem. Econs. Club Detroit, Internat. Assn. Bus. Communicators. Presbyterian. Avocations: woodworking, auto restoration. Home: 1034 Northlawn Ave Birmingham MI 48009 Office: Lawrence Inst Tech 21000 W Ten Mile Rd Southfield MI 48075

ANNETT, RICHARD BROOKS, marketing executive; b. Bethlehem, Pa., Dec. 2, 1947; s. Edward and Mary (Luch) A.; m. Cynthia Perin Annett, Nov. 24, 1973; children—Julie Brooks, Lindsay Brooks. Grad. Marietta Coll., 1970. Sales supr. Stouffer Foods, Boston, 1973-74, area sales mgr., Hartford, Conn., 1974-75, regional sales mgr., Boston, 1975-78, asst. plant mgr., Solon, Ohio, 1978-80, plant mgr., 1980-82, mktg. mgr. Lean Cuisine, 1982—. Named Outstanding Young Alumnus, Marietta Coll., 1983. Home: 2096 Edgeview Dr Hudson OH 44236 Office: Stouffer Foods Corp 5750 Harper Rd Solon OH 44139

ANNO, JAMES NELSON, scientist, educator; b. Niles, Ohio, Feb. 6, 1934; s. James Nelson and Opal Mae (Gentry) A.; m. Janet Winkel, June 12, 1955; children—James David, Sara Jennifer, Jefferson Nelson. B.S., Ohio State U., 1955, M.S., 1961, Ph.D., 1965. Technician, Battelle Meml. Inst., Columbus, Ohio, 1953-55, supr. research reactor, 1955-60, asst. chief applied nuclear physics div., 1960-65, asst. chief lubrication mechanics div., 1965-67, chief lubrication mechanics div., 1967-70; asso. prof. nuclear engring. U. Cin., 1970-73, prof., 1973—; pres. Research Dynamics Inc., 1977—. Recipient Civic award Columbus Jr. C. of C., 1961; honored by Sat. Evening Post, 1961. Mem. Am. Phys. Soc., Am. Nuclear Soc., Phi Beta Kappa, Sigma Pi Sigma. Club: Masons. Author: Encyclopedia of Draw Poker, 1973; (with J.A. Walowit) Modern Development in Lubrication Mechanics, 1975; Wave Mechanics for Engineers, 1976; Mechanics of Liquid Jets, 1977; Notes on Radiation Effects on Materials, 1984. Contbr. articles to profl. jours. Home: 5882 Ropes Dr Cincinnati OH 45244 Office: 509 Old Chemistry Bldg Cincinnati OH 45221

ANNUNZIO, FRANK, congressman; b. Chgo., Jan. 12, 1915; B.S., M.Ed., DePaul U.; m. Angeline Alesia, Dec. 28, 1935; children—Jacqueline Annunzio Lato, Linda Annunzio O'Donnell, Susan Annunzio Tynan. Asst. supr. Nat. Def. Tng. Program Austin Evening Sch., Chgo.; legis. and ednl. dir. United Steelworkers of Am., Chgo.: mem. 89th-99th Congresses from 11th Dist. Ill., chmn. ho. adminstrn. com., chmn. subcom. consumer affairs and coinage banking, fin. and urban affairs com. Dir. Ill. Dept. Labor; mem. adv. com. on Unemployment Compensation; mem. adv. com. to Ill. Indsl. Commn. on Health, Safety; mem. adv. bd. Cook County (Ill.) Health and Survey; chmn. Community Services Com.; mem. Chgo. Commn. on Human Relations. Gen. chmn. Villa Scalabrini Devel. Fund; v.p., lay adv. bd. Villa Scalabrini Italian Old People's Home. Mem. Catholic Youth Orgn. Clubs: KC (4th deg.), Club: City (Chgo.). Office: 2303 Rayburn Bldg Washington DC 20515

ANSARI, MOHAMMAD MOHSUNULLAH, mechanical engineer, lead design engineer; b. Ghazipur, India, Jan. 2, 1947; came to U.S., 1973, naturalized, 1979; s. Mohammad Mohibullah and Wasia Begum (Shafi) A.; m. Afroz Mirza, Oct. 17, 1975; children—Azmat, Faraz, Uzma. B.S.M.E., Karachi U., Pakistan, 1969; M.S. in Indsl. Engring., Ill. Inst. Tech., 1978. Registered profl. engr., Ill., Ohio. Asst. mgr. Pakistan Machine Tools, Karachi, 1970-73; mech. designer Mid Am. Engring., Chgo., 1973-76; design engr. Phillips Mfg. Co., Chgo., 1976-77; engring. designer Lester B. Knight Inc., Chgo., 1977-78; mech. engr. TVA, Knoxville, 1980-81; lead design engr. Sargent & Lundy Engrs., Chgo., 1978—. Mem. Nat. Geog. Soc., Washington, 1983-84. Mem. ASHRAE, ASME (chmn. membership devel. com. Fox Valley sect. 1983-84, sec. 1984-85; membership devel. award 1984). Democrat. Islam. Avocations: gardening, reading, travel and sight-seeing. Home: 655 Niagra Dr Bolingbrook IL 60439 Office: Sargent & Lundy Engrs 55 E Monroe St Chicago IL 60603

ANSARI, MOHAMMED RAFIULLAH, surgeon; b. Gokaram, Andhra Pradesh, India, Oct. 10, 1935; came to U.S., 1967, naturalized, 1977; s. Mohammed Mahboob Ali and Abbas (Bibi) A.; m. Raoof Yasmin, June 2, 1962; 1 child, Farrah Yasmin. B.S., Osmania U., India, 1957, M.B. B.S., 1962. Asst. surgeon Dist. Hosp., Karimnagar, India, 1963-67; intern St. Luke Hosp., St. Paul, 1967-68; resident Henry Ford Hosp., Detroit, 1968-73, staff surgeon, 1973—; clin. instr. surgery U. Mich., Detroit, 1976-80, clin. asst. prof., 1980—. Recipient Roy D. McClure Surg. award Henry Ford Hosp.-McClure Surg. Soc., 1971. Mem. AMA, Mich. State Med. Soc., ACS, Acad. Surgery of Detroit, Midwest Surg. Assn. Republican. Muslim. Home: 3016 Westman Ct Bloomfield Hills MI 48013 Office: 2799 W Grand Blvd Detroit MI 48202

ANSBERRY, WILLIAM FRANCIS, political science educator; b. North Vernon, Ind., July 18, 1926; s. Michael Charles and Mary Elizabeth (Freking) A.; m. Ruth Elizabeth Baynes, Apr. 17, 1954; children—Michael, Ann, William, Patricia. Student, U. Notre Dame, 1944; Miami U., Oxford, Ohio, 1960-63; B.S., Ball State U., 1947, M.A., 1951; Ph.D., U. Cin., 1968. Educator, N. Vernon High Sch., Ind., 1951-56, Lowell High Sch., Ind., 1956-57, North Coll. Hill High Sch., Ohio, 1957-67; faculty SE Mo. State U., Cape Girardeau, 1967—, prof. polit. sci., 1967—. Author: Arms Control and Disarmament, 1970. Vice chmn. bd. dirs. Sheltered Workshop, Cape Girardeau, 1975—; pres. Notre Dame Sch. Bd., Cape Girardeau, 1976-78; chmn. bd. dirs. Cape Girardeau County Assn., Retarded Citizens, 1981—. Taft fellow U. Cin., 1962. Mem. So. Polit.-Sci. Assn., Acad. Polit. Sci. Roman Catholic. Lodge: K.C. (navigator 1977-80). Office: SE Mo State Univ Cape Girardeau MO 63701

ANSELL, MIRIAM NAOMI, sales executive; b. Winkler, Man., Can., May 18, 1940; came to U.S., 1977; d. Jacob P. and Helen (Giesebrecht) Winters; m. Gene L. Ansell, July 15, 1967 (div. Oct. 1980). B.Sc., U. Man., 1961, B.Ed., 1964: C.L.U., Am. Coll., Bryn Mawr, Pa., 1984, Chartered Fin. Cons., 1985. Tchr. English, dept. head Man. Sch. System, Winnipeg, 1961-77; ins. salesman N.Y. Life, Omaha, 1978-81, sales mgr., 1982-84, assoc. gen. mgr., 1985—. Recipient Agy. Builder award N.Y. Life, 1982; named Agt. of Yr., N.Y. Life, Nebr. Office, 1978. Mem. Women's Life Underwriters Council. Club: Free Enterprise Women's Exchange (Omaha) (Pres. 1982-84). Avocation: travel. Home: 12727 W Dodge Rd Apt 247B Omaha NE 68154 Office: NY Life 11704 W Center Rd Omaha NE 68144

ANSELMO, JEROME JAMES, insurance executive; b. St. Louis, Aug. 2, 1945; s. James Jerome and Theresa (Simeone) A.; m. Mary Ellen Mitchell, Mar. 29, 1969; children—Julie, Lori, Brian. B.S., Rockhurst Coll., 1967; postgrad. St. Mary's U., San Antonio, Rockhurst Coll. Tchr., St. Louis Pub. Schs., 1967-68, Kansas City Pub. Schs. (Mo.), 1968-69; life ins. agt. Nat. Assn. Life Underwriters, Kansas City, Mo., 1973—. Contbr. articles on ins. to profl. jours. Bd. dirs. Leukemia Soc., Kansas City, 1975-79; alumni bd. dirs. Rockhurst Coll., Kansas City, 1976. Recipient Joint Service Accomodation medal, San Antonio, 1972; recipient Nat. Sales Achievement award, Nat. Quality award. Mem. Million Dollar Round Table, Gen. Agts. and Mgrs. Assn., Nat. Assn. Securities Dealers. Roman Catholic. Home: 901 W 121st St Kansas City MO 64145 Office: Anselmo Fin Services 8400 W 110th Suite 600 Overland Park KS 66210

ANSETT, JOHN FREDERICK (JACK), book wholesaler; b. Cornwell Heights, Pa., Sept. 26, 1921; s. Russell L. and Dorothy Martha (Bockius) A.; B.A., Valparaiso U., 1948; postgrad. Northwestern U., 1950-51, Mich. State U., 1968; m. Lois Helen Grote, Nov. 14, 1948; children—John Frederick, Timothy G., Karen L., Kathleen B. With Internat. Packers Ltd., Chgo., 1948-51; treas. Internat. Packers Can. Ltd., Toronto, Ont., 1951-56, pres., 1956-59; dir. mktg. Armour & Co., Ltd. (U.K.), London, 1959-62; pres. Book House, Inc., Jonesville, Mich., 1962-83, chmn. bd., 1984—. Served with USAAF, 1942-45; ETO. Mem. ALA, Am. Booksellers Assn. Republican. Lutheran. Home: 105 N Walnut St Jonesville MI 49250 Office: 208 W Chicago St Jonesville MI 49250

ANSHUTZ, WILLIAM MAURICE, radiologist; b. Somerton, Ohio, Sept. 16, 1917; s. Harvey and Atrella (Tomlinson) A.; A.B., Ohio State U., 1942; M.D., 1948; m. Betty Millisor, Sept. 10, 1944; children—Wendy Lee, Cathy Jo. Intern Lima (Ohio) Meml. Hosp., 1949; resident in radiology Henry Ford Hosp., Detroit, 1956-59; gen. practice medicine, Ohio, 1953-56; practice medicine specializing in radiology, Ind., 1959-64; mem. staffs St. Francis Hosp., Beech Grove, Ind., 1959-61; radiologist Meth. Hosp., Indpls., 1961-69, Witham Meml. Hosp., Lebanon, Ind., 1959-61, 70-83, Clinton County Hosp., Frankfort, Ind., 1969-79. Served with U.S. Army, 1942-44; USAF, 1951-53. Decorated Bronze Star. Mem. AMA, Radiol. Soc. N.Am., Am. Coll. Radiology, Ind. Roentgen Soc. Republican. Methodist. Home and office: 6340 Breamore Rd Indianapolis IN 46220

ANSTETT, ANDRUE JOHN, Canadian government official; b. Gronigen, Netherlands, June 25, 1946; came to Can., Oct. 13, 1946; s. Rueben John and Cornelia Alida (Wynia) A.; m. Phylis Nancy Kathleen Budgell, June 7, 1980; children—Joshua Bevan Andrue, Kaleigh Meighan. B.A., U. Waterloo, 1969, postgrad., 1969-70. Dep. clk., Province of Man., Winnipeg, Can., 1973-79; dep. chief electoral officer, project supr. Stats. Can., Winnipeg, 1980-81; minister mcpl. affairs, govt. house leader Govt. of Man., Winnipeg, 1981—; mem. Legis. Assembly for Springfield, 1981—. Mem. Springfield Recreation Commn., Oakbank, Man., 1978-80; treas. Hazelridge Arena Com., 1980-82. Fellow Province of Ont., Waterloo, 1969-70, U. Waterloo, 1969-70. Mem. Can. Assn. Clks.-at-the-Table. Club: Hazelridge Community (bd. dirs. 1976-81). Home: Box 23 Hazelridge MB R0E 0Y0 Canada Office: Govt Man 330 Legis Bldg Winnipeg MB R3C 0V8 Canada

ANTHOLINE, WILLIAM ERNST, research chemist, spectroscopist; b. Milw., July 1, 1943; s. Robert E. Gertrude M. (Jacobsen) A.; m. Lynn M. Kangas; children—William Jr., Thomas, Michael. B.S., U. Wis., 1965; Ph.D., Iowa State U., 1971; postdoctoral, fellow Med. Coll. Wis., Milw., 1972-76. Asst. prof. dept. radiology Med. Coll. Wis., 1976—; adj. prof. chemistry U. Wis.-Milw., 1978—. Contbr. chpt. to book, articles to profl. jours. Mem. Am. Chem. Soc., Phi Lambda Upsilon. Office: Med Coll Wis Nat Biomed ESR Ctr 8701 Watertown Plank Rd Milwaukee WI 53226

ANTHONY, YVONNE ELIZABETH, hospital administrator; b. Phila., Oct. 31, 1951; d. Charles and Consolacion (Terrado) Speller; m. Walter Anthony, Jr., June 28, 1980; 1 son, Jeffrey Todd. B.A., Macalester Coll., 1973; M.H.A., U. Minn., 1978; postgrad. U. Mich., 1983—. Sales rep. Drackett Products subs. Bristol-Meyers Corp., St. Paul/Mpls., 1973-75; adminstrv. resident U. Mich. Hosps., Ann Arbor, 1977-78, asst. to assoc. dir. for ops., 1978-79, group ops. adminstr. med. units, 1979-81, asst. adminstr., 1981—; consultant in field, 1982. Macalester Coll. scholar, 1969-73. Mem. Am. Pub. Health Assn., Am. Hosp. Assn., Am. Coll. Hosp. Adminstrs. Office: Main Hosp Adminstrn U Mich Hosps 1405 E Ann St Ann Arbor MI 48104

ANTHONY-PEREZ, BOBBIE MURPHY, psychology educator, researcher, consultant; b. Macon, Ga., Nov. 15, 1923; d. Solomon Richard and Maude Alice (Lockett) Cotton; m. William Anthony, Aug. 22, 1959 (dec.); 1 dau., Freida; m. 2d, Andrew Silviano Perez, June 20, 1979. B.S., DePaul U., 1953, M.S., 1954; M.S., U. Ill., 1959; Ph.D., U. Chgo., 1967; M.A., DePaul, 1975. Tchr. Chgo. Pub. Schs., 1954-68; math. cons. U. Chgo., 1965; prof. Chgo. State U., 1968—; psychol. cons. Chgo. Pub. Schs., 1971-72; ednl. cons. Urban Affairs Inst., Howard U., Washington, 1978; coordinator Higher Edn. Careers Counseling Campus Ministry, Ingleside Whitfield Parish. Vice-pres. Community Affairs Chatham Bus. Assn.; bus. relations chmn. Chatham Avalon Park Community Council; bd. dirs. United Meth. Found., U. Chgo., Community Mental Health Council, Inc. NSF fellow, 1957, 1958-59; recipient numerous awards religious, civic and ednl. instns. and assns. Mem. Am. Psychol. Assn., Internat. Assn. Applied Psychology, Internat. Assn. Ednl. and Vocat. Guidance, Assn. Black Psychologists, Chgo. Psychol. Assn., Nat. Council Tchrs. Math., Am. Ednl. Research Assn., Midwest Ednl. Research Assn., Am. Soc. Clin. Hypnosis, Midwestern Psychol. Assn. Methodist. Contbr. numerous articles to profl. jours. Office: Psychology Dept 9500 S King Dr Chicago IL 60628

ANTIEL, MARK SCOTT, biostatistical consultant, human physiologist; b. Duluth, Minn., Nov. 13, 1956; s. Raymond and Charlotte (Johnson) A.; m. Julia Ann Meteer, Aug. 25, 1979; children—Ryan, Meteer. B.A. in Biology, Coll. St. Scholastic, 1979; M.S. Biology, U. Toledo, 1983; M.S. in Preventive Medicine, U. Iowa, 1984. Research asst. Coll. St. Scholastica, Duluth, 1976-79; research asst. U. Toledo, Ohio, 1979-80, teaching asst., 1980-81; statis. cons. U. Iowa, Iowa City, 1981-84; biostatistician Kimberly-Clark Corp., Neenah, Wis., 1984—. Mem. Am. Statis. Assn., Biometric Soc., AAAS. Office: Kimberly-Clark Corp 2100 W Winchester Rd Neenah WI 54956

ANTOLINO, DEBRA ANN, interior designer; b. Cleve., Apr. 28, 1955; d. Thomas Paul and Antoninette Cecilia (Pusateri) Daquila; m. Dominick A. Antolino, Jr., Aug. 5, 1980. B.A., Kent State U., 1980. Interior design asst. Thomas J. Holzheimer & Assocs., Chagrin Falls, Ohio, 1978-80; interior designer Designers East Inc., Beachwood, Ohio, 1980-82, Bonhard Interiors, Shaker Heights, Ohio, 1982—. Co-chmn. exec. com. Cleve. Ballet Council, 1985—. Mem. Am. Soc. Interior Designers (assoc.). Roman Catholic. Avocations: reading; aerobic exercise. Home: 18716 Newell Rd Shaker Heights OH 44122 Office: Bonhard Interiors 20710 Chagrin Blvd Shaker Heights OH 44122

ANTONACCI, ANTHONY EUGENE, beer corporation engineer; b. Sept. 21, 1949; s. Salvatore Natali and Odile Estella (Stanton) A.; m. Sherry Lee Kessler, Mar. 6, 1971; children—Don Warren, Lance Anthony. Student U.S. Air Force Acad., 1968-69; Assoc. in Sci., Forest Park Coll., St. Louis, 1971. Lic. stationary engr. Asst. supr. data processing ops. First Nat. Bank, St. Louis, 1969-71; engr. Installation and Service Engring. (Mech. and Nuclear) div. Gen. Electric Corp., St. Louis, 1971-76; engr. Anheuser-Busch Corp., St. Louis, 1976—; software author. Trustee, treas. Antonette Hills Trusteeship, Affton, Mo., 1976-80. Recipient Spl. Performance awards Gen. Electric Co., 1972, 74. Mem. Brewers and Maltsters Local 6 (del. 1982, 83), Nat. Aerospace Edn. Council. Republican. Roman Catholic. Avocations: classic auto restoration; music (trumpet). Home: 8971 Antonette Hills Saint Louis MO 63123 Office: Anheuser-Busch Corp 1 Busch Pl Saint Louis MO 63118

ANTONACCIO, MICHAEL JOHN, pharmaceutical company executive; b. Yonkers, N.Y., Mar. 6, 1943; s. Mario and Frances (Renda) A.; m. Jeanne Borman, June 20, 1970; 1 child, Nicholas; m. Patricia Ann McDevitt, July 8, 1978. B.S. in Pharmacy, Duquesne U., 1966; Ph.D. in Pharmacology, U. Mich., 1970. Sr. scientist I, Geigy Pharms., 1970-72, sr. scientist II, 1972-73, sr. staff scientist, 1973-75, mgr. cardiovascular pharmacology, 1975-77; dir. pharmacology Squibb Inst. Med. Research, 1977-81; v.p. new drug discovery Schering Corp., 1981-83, chmn. cardiovascular project team, 1982-83; v.p. cardiovascular research and devel. Bristol-Myers Co., 1983—. Editor: Cardiovascular Pharmacology, 1977; mem. editorial bd. Clin. and Exptl. Hypertension, 1980—, Neuropharmacology, 1981—, Drug Devel. Research, 1981—, Blood Vessels, 1981—; editor: Cardiovascular Pharmacology, 2d edit., 1984. Contbr. articles to profl. jours. Patentee in field. Recipient Harry Goldblatt award Am. Heart Assn., 1981; N.Y. State Regents scholar, 1961. Fellow Council High Blood Pressure, Council on Circulation of Am. Heart Assn.; mem. Am. Pharmacology Assn., AAAS, Am. Heart Assn., Am. Soc. Pharmacology and Exptl. Therapeutics (subcom. on pharmacology in industry), Soc. Neurosci., Internat. Soc. Hypertension, Internat. Soc. Heart Research, InterAm. Soc. Hypertension, Internat. Soc. Immunopharmacology, N.Y. Acad. Sci., Phila. Physiol. Soc., Rho Chi. Home: 915 Sycamore Lake Dr Evansville IN 47712 Office: Bristol-Myers Co 2404 Pennsylvania Ave Evansville IN 47721

ANTONIC, JAMES PAUL, internat. mktg. cons.; b. Milw., Mar. 29, 1943; s. George Paul and Betti Ware (Littler) A.; B.S. in Metallurgy, U. Wis., 1964; M.B.A., Boston U., 1976; m. Irene Robson, Dec. 26, 1970; 1 child, Glenn. Owner JPA Supply and Warehouse Co., Milw., 1966-68; product mgr., market mgr. Delta Oil Products, Milw., 1968-74; v.p. internat. ops., Brussels, 1974-76; pres. Internat. Market Devel. Group, Barrington, Ill., 1976—; exec. v.p. J & M, Ltd., Okazaki, Japan; lectr. Cast Metals Inst., Am. Mgmt. Assn., various colls. Served with U.S. Army, 1964-66. Mem. Licensing Execs. Soc., Internat. Trade Club Chgo. Episcopalian. Home: 97 Surrey Ln W Barrington Hills IL 60010 Office: PO Box 751 Barrington IL 60010

ANURAS, SINN, gastroenterologist; b. Bangkok, Thailand, Apr. 6, 1941; s. Tiang and Ratana (Suppipat) A.; came to U.S., 1967; M.D., Chulalongkorn U., Thailand, 1966; m. Jitra Suppamongkol, Aug. 8, 1969; children—Julia, Sandy. Intern, Resurrection Hosp., Chgo., 1967; resident in internal medicine VA Hosp., Long Beach, Calif., 1968-70; asst. prof. medicine U. Iowa, Iowa City, 1974-80, assoc. prof., 1980—. Diplomate Am. Bd. Internal Medicine. Fellow A.C.P.; mem. Am. Gastroenterol. Assn. Buddhist. Research on intestinal motility, clin. liver disease. Home: 55 Arbury Dr Iowa City IA 52240 Office: University of Iowa Iowa City IA 52242

ANYAETO, ATHANASIUS ANYAHURUNWA, educator, accountant; b. Ihitte-Ngor, Nigeria, June 2, 1939; came to U.S., 1979, permanent resident, 1984; s. Patrick Ugo and Mgbakwo (Ibeto) Anyaeto; m. Angelina Anyanwu, Dec. 4, 1960 (div. 1983); children—Callistus, Emmanuel, Ernest, Doris; m. Karen Gess, Aug. 24, 1984. B.Sc., U. London, 1972; M.B.A., Lincoln U., 1979, M.Ed., 1981; D.B.A., Nova U., 1984. Chief instr. State Schs. Mgmt. Bd., Owerri, Nigeria, 1970-77, dep. chief fin. officer, 1977-78; acct. Lincoln U., Jefferson City, Mo., 1980-84. Contbr. articles to profl. jours. Organizer YMCA, Owerri, 1977. Served as maj. Biafran Army, 1968-70. Fellow Inst. Adminstrv. Acctg.; mem. Acad. Mgmt.; assoc. mem. Nigerian Inst. Mgmt., Brit. Inst. Mgmt., Assn. Cost and Exec. Accts. Avocations: freelance journalism; tennis; soccer; travelling. Home: 3005 Country Club Dr Jefferson City MO 65101 Office: Lincoln U 820 Chestnut St Jefferson City MO 65101

APA, ALBERT ALEX, association executive; b. Chgo., June 5, 1921; s. Michael and Rose (Tenuta) A.; student schools Chgo.; m. Betty J. Jones, Nov. 6, 1949; 1 dau., Candice Sue Apa Kvitek. Supr. Stewart Warner Corp., 1939-42; sgt. Chgo. Police Dept., 1947-79; exec. dir. Ill. Local Govtl. Law Enforcement Officers Tng. Bd., Springfield, 1979—; chmn. Police of Ill., 1975-78. Pres., Chgo. Police Pension Protective Assn., 1967-78, trustee, 1978-79; mem. Gov.'s Arson Adv. Bd. Served with U.S. Army, 1942-46. Decorated Bronze Star with 3 oak leaf clusters, Purple Heart. Named Man of Year, Chgo. Patrolmen's Assn., 1973; recipient achievement award Ill. Fraternal Order of Police, 1978, Ill. Sheriff's Assn., 1980. Mem. Ill. Police Assn., Internat. Assn. Chiefs of Police, Nat. Assn. State Dirs. of Law Enforcement Tng. (pres.), Am. Soc. Tng. and Devel. Roman Catholic. Clubs: Fraternal Order of Police, Exchange of Springfield. Author: Handbook on Pensions, 1964; contbr. legis. articles to Ill. Police Jour. Office: 524 S 2d St Suite 400 Springfield IL 62706

APKE, DAMIAN JOSEPH, hospital executive, general contractor; b. Effingham, Ill., Nov. 22, 1940; s. Bernard Joseph and Beatrice Sarah (Richards) A.; m. Linda Kay Apke, Aug. 7, 1976; children by previous marriage—Stacie Lynn, Stefan Bernard, Stephanie Nicole. B.S. in Bus. Adminstn., U. Ill. Br. mgr. Household Fin. Co., Chgo., 1963-67; project dir. Standard Bus. Research, Chgo., 1967-70; pres. Anton & Damian, Inc., Morton, Ill., 1971-79; v.p. mktg., planning and engring. Burlington (Iowa) Med. Ctr., 1979—; cons. in field. Served with U.S. Army, 1959-62. Mem. Am. Hosp. Assn., Health Mgmt. Systems Soc., Hosp. Planning Soc., Internat. Accts. Soc., VFW. Republican Lodge: Moose. Home: 4 Val Halla Dr Burlington IA 52601 Office: 602 N 3d St Burlington IA 52601

APPELSON, WALLACE BERTRAND, college administrator; b. Bklyn., June 9, 1930; B.S., N.Y.U., 1951, M.A., 1952; Ed.D., Columbia U., 1959. Chief X-ray technician Samaritan Hosp., Bklyn., 1951-52; tchr. art White Plains (N.Y.) public schs., 1954-57; research asst. Inst. Adminstrv. Research, Columbia U., 1957-58; asst. prof. ednl. adminstrn. Rutgers U., 1958-60; coordinator terminal program N.J. State Dept. Higher Edn., 1960-65; dean acad. affairs Bucks County Community Coll., Newtown, Pa., 1965-70; pres. Atlantic Community Coll., Mays Landing, N.J., 1970-73; dean faculty LaGuardia Community Coll. CUNY, 1973-76; pres. Truman Coll., Chgo., 1976—. Pres. bd. dirs. North Bus. and Indsl. Council Chgo.; bd. dirs. Ravenswood Hosp. Med. Center, Chgo., Uptown Chgo. Commn. Served with U.S. Army, 1952-54. Mem. Am. Assn. Sch. Adminstrs., Am. Assn. Higher Edn., Am. Assn. Community and Jr. Colls., Uptown C. of C. (bd. dirs.), Phi Delta Kappa, Kappa Delta Pi. Editor: Associated Public School System Yearbook, 1958; Toward Higher Education Newsletter, N.J. Div. Higher Education, 1960-65; contbr. articles to profl. jours. Office: 1145 W Wilson Ave Chicago IL 60640

APPLEBERRY, JAMES BRUCE, university president; b. Waverly, Mo., Feb. 22, 1938; s. Earnest and Bertha Viola (Lane) A.; m. Patricia Ann Trent, June 5, 1960; children—John Mark, Timothy David. B.S., Central Mo. State U., 1960, M.S., 1963, Edn. Specialist, 1967; Ph.D., Okla. State U., 1969. Tchr. music Knob Noster pub. schs., Mo., 1960-62, prin., 1962-64; asst. dir. field services Central Mo. State U., Independence, 1964-68; mem. faculty ednl. adminstrn. and higher edn. Okla. State U., Stillwater, 1968-74, assoc. prof., 1971-75, prof., 1975, chmn. dept., 1975; prof. adminstrn., founds. and higher edn., dir. planning U. Kans., Lawrence, 1975-77, asst. to chancellor, 1977; pres. Pittsburg State U., Kans., 1977-83; pres. No. Mich. U., Marquette, 1983—. Chmn. commn. on leadership devel. Am. Council Edn. Mem. Am. Assn. State Colls. and Univs. (policy and purposes com.), Am. Assn. Higher Edn., Am. Ednl. Research Assn., Nat. Edn. Adminstrn., Nat. Conf. Professors of Ednl. Adminstrn., Pi Delta Kappa, Phi Kappa Phi, Kappa Delta Pi, Phi Sigma Phi, Kappa Mu Epsilon, Alpha Kappa Psi. Baptist. Avocation: Civic activities. Home: 1240/1440 Center St Marquette MI 49855 Office: No Mich U Marquette MI 49855

APPLEBY, LESLIE VERE, architect; b. Wichita, Kans., Feb. 17, 1931; s. Vere Griffith and Marie Margaret (McCoy) A.; student Wichita State U., 1949-50; B.Arch., Kans. State U., 1958; children—Vickie Lee Appleby Jones, Bryan Kent, Stephen L. Thyault, Linda G. Maroney; m. 2d, Louise A. Giersch, June 25, 1976. Architect William R. Brown, Ponca City, Okla., 1958-63; architect, mng. partner Shaver & Co., Salina, Kans., 1963-71; architect, sr. partner Appleby & Marsh, Wichita, Emporia, and Salina, 1971—; pres. Lamco Co., Salina, 1972—, 215 Group, Salina, 1974—. Pres. Okla. Jr. Miss Inc., Ponca City, 1961-63. Registered architect Kans., Okla., Mo., Iowa, S.D., Nebr., Tex., Tenn., Nat. Council Archtl. Registration Bds. Mem. AIA (corp.), Kans. State U. Alumni Assn., Salina C. of C. Episcopalian. Elk. Club: Salina Country. Home: 647 Rockview Rd Salina KS 67401 Office: 112 N Santa Fe St Salina KS 67401 also 1215 Franklin Wichita KS 67203

APPLEGATE, DOUGLAS, congressman; b. Steubenville, Ohio, Mar. 27, 1928; grad. high sch.; m. Betty Jean Engstrom, 1950; children—Kirk, David. Engaged in real estate bus.; mem. Ohio Ho. of Reps., 1961-69, Ohio Senate, 1969-77; mem. 95th-98th Congresses from 18th Ohio Dist. Mem. Steubenville Community Club, Catholic Community Center, Polish Nat. Alliance. Democrat. Presbyterian. Club: Polish Athletic. Lodges: Elks, Eagles. Office: Room 435 2464 Rayburn House Office Bldg Washington DC 20515

APPLEGATE, SARA JOAN, insurance executive; b. Knoxville, Tenn., Aug. 2, 1938; d. Kenneth C. and Elizabeth Winsor (Snead) A.; B.S. in Bus. Adminstrn., Ohio U., 1960; postgrad. U. Cin., 1962. With Hartford Ins. Group, 1960-82, property and package underwriting mgr., Cleve., 1974-77, asst. gen. mgr., Milw., 1977-82; v.p. U.S. Counseling Services, Inc., Milw., 1982—; tchr. profl. courses. Active Cystic Fibrosis Assn., Jerry Lewis Telethon. Mem. C.P.C.U. Soc. (past pres. Milw. chpt.), Ins. Women Milw. (past pres.; named Ins. Woman of Yr. 1980), Am. Mgmt. Soc., Nat. Assn. Ins. Women. Home: 4912F S 19th St Milwaukee WI 53221 Office: 120 Bishops Way Brookfield WI 53008

APPOLD, JAMES MARTIN, baking company executive; b. Saginaw, Mich., Apr. 10, 1939; s. Martin J. and Louise S. Appold; B.S., Gen. Motors Inst., 1962; M.B.A., U. Toledo, 1977; M.S. in Indsl. Engring., 1978; m. Patricia J. Kirchner, Aug. 20, 1960; children—Jonn, Karen, Melinda, Caitlin, Andrew. Engr., maintenance foreman, maintenance dept. Chevrolet Saginaw (Mich.) Grey Iron, 1957-66; sales engr. Honeywell, Inc., Saginaw, 1966-68; plant supt./engring. mgr. A T. Ferrell & Co., Saginaw, 1968-75; mgr. tech. services The Andersons, Maumee, Ohio, 1975—; v.p. gen. mgr. Consol. Biscuit Co., McComb, Ohio. Mem. Am. Soc. Agrl. Engrs., Biscuit and Cracker Mfrs. Assn., Am. Inst. Plant Engrs., Air Pollution Control Assn., Internat. Maintenance Inst., Nat. Grain and Feed Assn. Home: 2049 Scottwood Ave Toledo OH 43620 Office: PO Box 847 McComb OH 45858

AQUILA, AUGUST JOSEPH, professional services marketing executive, marketing educator; b. Chgo., Mar. 15, 1944; s. Louis and Rose (DelMonaco) A.; m. Emily Haliziw, Nov. 12, 1966; 1 child, Kate Haliziw. B.A., DePaul U., 1966, M.B.A., 1979; M.A., Ind. U., 1970, Ph.D., 1973; B.A. (hon.) Inst. Hispanic Culture, Madrid, Spain, 1966. Asst. prof. Williams Coll., Williamstown, Mass., 1972-75; dir. devel. DePaul U., Chgo., 1975-79; dir. mktg., Coopers & Lybrand, Chgo., 1979-83, Friedman Eisenstein, C.P.A.s, 1983—; translator Roper Pub. Research Center, Williamstown, Ma., 1973-74; lectr. DePaul U. Coll. Commerce, Chgo., 1980—. Author: Alonso De Ercilla, 1975. Contbr. articles to profl. jours. Mem. Young Execs. Club, Chgo., 1980—, Execs. Club Chgo., 1982—; bd. dirs. Lyric Opera Chgo., 1983—; chmn. Our Lady Mt. Carmel Sch. Bd., Chgo., 1984—. Fulbright fellow, 1966; NDEA fellow Ind. U., 1967-70; NDFL fellow Ind. U., 1970-72, Humanities fellow Williams Coll., 1972, 1973. Mem. Am. Mktg. Assn., Am. Assn. Tchrs. Spanish and Portuguese, Fulbright Alumni Assn. Roman Catholic. Club: Downtown Court. Avocations: sailing; jogging; philately. Home: 336 W Wellington #2501 Chicago IL 60657 Office: Friedman Eisenstein Raemer & Schwartz 401 N Michigan Ave #2600 Chicago IL 60611

AQUINO, ROSITA NG, physician; b. Subic, Zambales, Philippines, Apr. 8, 1940; d. Pio and Heng Fong (Kuan) Aquino; came to U.S., 1968, naturalized, 1980; M.D., Far Eastern U., 1966; m. Alexander Wu, Nov. 15, 1975; children—Sabrina Han-Rine, Clarissa Han-Yin. Intern, Niagara Falls (N.Y.) Meml. Med. Center, 1968; resident, St. Joseph Mercy Hosp., U. Mich. Med. Center, Ann Arbor, Mich.; dir. Maternal Infant Care project, Crittenton Gen. Hosp., Detroit, 1973-74, Henry Ford Hosp., Detroit, 1974-79; practice medicine specializing in obstetrics and gynecology, Canton, Mich., 1979—; mem. staff St. Mary's Hosp., Livonia, Mich. Diplomate Am. Bd. Obstetrics and Gynecology. Fellow Am. Coll. Obstetricians and Gynecologists; mem. AMA, Mich. Med. Soc., N.Y. State Med. Soc., Mich. Obstetrics and Gynecol. Soc., Wayne County Med. Soc. Roman Catholic. Home: 63 Hillview Dr Norwich NY 13815 Office: Route 23 East Norwich NY 13815

ARAC, JONATHAN, English educator; b. N.Y.C., Apr. 4, 1945; s. Benjamin and Evelyn (Charm) A.; A.B., Harvard Coll., 1967, M.A., 1968, Ph.D., 1974. Jr. fellow Soc. Fellows, Harvard U., 1970-73; asst. prof. English, Princeton U., 1973-79; vis. assoc. prof. English and comparative lit. Columbia U., 1981-82; assoc. prof. English, U. Ill.-Chgo., 1979—, assoc. dir. Inst. for Humanities, 1983-84. Author: Commissioned Spirits, 1979; editor The Yale Critics: Deconstruction in America, 1983; asst. editor Boundary 2: A Journal of Postmodern Literature and Culture, 1979—. Am. Council Learned Socs. fellow, 1978-79. Mem. Soc. Critical Exchange (dir. 1983—), Modern Lang. Assn. (exec. com. div. comparative studies in romanticism and 19th century 1984—), English Inst. Offi · Dept English U Ill Box 4348 Chicago IL 60680

ARAI, HAROLD YUTAKA, orthodontist; b. Los Angeles, Feb. 1, 1936; s. Akira B. and Joan Fusako (Fujisawa) A.; B.A., Ohio Wesleyan U., 1957; D.D.S., Loyola U., 1961, M.S., 1966; m. Irene Shigihara, Aug. 27, 1961; children—David Andrew, Shaunna Lynn. Pvt. practice orthodontics, Park Ridge, Ill., 1967—; Lectr. Loyola U., 1966-73, 77, Ind. U., 1975, Emory U., 1975, La. State U., 1977. Pres., U. Chgo. Jarabak Orthodontic Found., 1975-76; v.p. Denver Orthodontic Summer Seminar, 1974, pres., 1975-76; lectr. Fox River Valley Dental Soc. meeting, Greater Miami Midwinter Dental meeting, 1977, Mid-Atlantic Soc. Orthodontists, 1978, Pacific Coast Soc. Orthodontists, 1978, Rocky Mountain Provocative Discussion Seminar, 1979, Cleve. Soc. Orthodontists, 1979, Colo. Orthodontic Assn., 1979. Served to capt. USAF, 1961-63. Mem. ADA (orthodontic chmn. sci. sessions 1974—), Japanese Civic Assn., Am. Assn. Orthodontics (clinician, chmn. round table programs 1979 meeting), Eastern Orthodontic Study Club, Midwestern Orthodontic Soc., Japanese Orthodontic Soc., Mexican Orthodontic Soc., Southwestern Soc. Orthodontists, Japanese Citizens League, Blue Key, Alpha Sigma Phi, Omicron Delta Kappa, Omicron Kappa Upsilon, Delta Sigma Delta. Author: Welcome to the World of Orthodontics, 1973. Home: 2026 Abbotsford Dr Inverness IL 60010 Office: 101 S Washington Park Ridge IL 60068

ARAKAWA, KASUMI, physician, educator; b. Toyohashi, Japan, Feb. 19, 1926; s. Masumi and Fayuko (Hattori) A.; M.D., Tokyo Med. Coll., 1953; m. June Hope Takahara, Aug. 27, 1956; children—Jane Riet, Kenneth Luke, Amy Kathryn. Came to U.S., 1954, naturalized, 1963. Intern Iowa Methodist Hosp., Des Moines, 1954-56; resident U. Kans. Med. Center, Kansas City, 1956-58; practice medicine specializing in anesthesiology; Kansas City, Kans., 1958—; instr. anesthesiology U. Kans. Med. Center, Kansas City, 1961-64, asst. prof., 1964-71, asso. prof., 1971-77, prof., 1977—, chmn. dept. anesthesiology, 1977—; clin. asso. prof. U. Mo.-Kansas City Sch. Dentistry, 1973—. Bd. dirs. Kansas City Health Care, Inc. Fulbrig' scholar, 1954. Recipient Outstanding Faculty award Student AMA, 197' Diplomate Am. Bd. Anesthesiology. Fellow Am. Coll. Anesthesiolog, mem. Asso. Univ. Anesthesiologists (sec.-treas. 1969—), Acad. Anesthesiology, Japan-Am. Soc. Midwest (v.p. 1965, 71). Home: 7917 El Monte St Shawnee Mission KS 66208 Office: Univ Med Center 39 Rainbow St Kansas City KS 66103

ARASMITH, NEIL HARVEY, state senator, insurance agent; b. Jewell, Kans., Feb. 23, 1930; s. James H. and Jessie M. (Fields) A.; B.A., U. Kans., 1951; m. Donna Schindler, July 1, 1951; children—David, Jeffrey, Susan, Timothy. Adjustor, Mason Investment Co., Salina, Kans., 1951-54, br. mgr., Garden City, Kans., 1954, Philipsburg, Kans., 1955-68; with Interstate Securities, Philipsburg, 1968-77; ins. agt. Central Nat. Life Ins. Co., Phillipsburg, 1977—; mem. Kans. State Senate, 1972—. Past chmn. bd. Phillips County Hosp., Phillipsburg Community Found. Served in USAF, 1951. Mem. C. of C. (past dir.). Republican. Methodist. Clubs: Elks, Masons, Shriners. Address: Phillipsburg KS 67661

ARATA, JUSTIN EUGENE, surgeon; b. Mishawaka, Ind., Oct. 31, 1921; s. Alphonsus P. and Mary (Schroeder) A.; m. Mary Welsch, Feb. 1944; children—Catherine, Nancy, Michael, Patrick, James, Mary, John. A.B., Ind. U., 1942, M.D., 1944. Diplomate Am. Bd. Surgery. Intern U.S. Naval Hosp., Oakland, Calif., 1945-47; resident St. Joseph Hosp., Ft. Wayne, Ind., 1947, Mayo Clinic 1948-52; practice medicine specializing in surgery, Ft. Wayne, 1956—; chmn. bd. G.C.I., Inc., Ft. Wayne, 1974—; pres. Arata Med. Group, Ft. Wayne, 1980—; assoc. clin. prof. surgery Ind. U., Ft. Wayne, 1978—. Contbr. articles to profl. jours. Mem. Sch. Bd., Bishop Dwenger Sch., Ft. Wayne, 1983—. Served to lt. (j.g.), USN, 1944-46; capt. USAF, 1953-54. Mem. AMA, Am. Bariatric Soc., ACS. Roman Catholic. Home: 224 W Ludwig Fort Wayne IN 46825 Office: 3301 Lake St Fort Wayne IN 46805

ARAVOSIS, GEORGE DEMETRIOS, manufacturing company executive, engineer; b. Chgo., May 27, 1929; s. Demetrios Peter and Bessie (Polychronopoulos) A.; m. Mary A. Dalianis, Apr. 12, 1953; children—Kathryn, Valerie, George, John. B.S. in Mech. Engring., Ill. Inst. Tech., 1951. Test engr. Bendix Corp., South Bend, Ind., 1951-52; product engr. Ford Motor Co., Chgo., 1952-54; asst. chief engr. Allis Chalmers Mfg. Co., Harvey, Ill., 1956-63; v.p. mktg., sales planning Internat. Harvester Co., Chgo., 1963—; dir. Deerbrook State Bank, Northbrook, Ill. Bd. dirs. Hellenic Found., 1972—, pres., 1976-80. Served with U.S. Army, 1954-56. Mem. Soc. Automotive Engrs. (bd. dirs. 1982—, Cert. Appreciation, 1972). Avocation: photography. Home: 222 Elm Park Elmhurst IL 60126 Office: Internat Harvester Co 401 N Michigan Ave Chicago IL 60611

ARBAUGH, ROBERT BRUCE, data processing executive; b. Charleston, W.Va., Dec. 31, 1948; a. William Harry and Peggy Jane (Pitts) A.; B.S. in Elec. Engring., Milw. Sch. Engring., 1971; postgrad. (Asso. Western Univs. fellow) U. Ariz., 1971-73. With PolySystems, Inc., Chgo., 1973—, dir. data center, 1974—, v.p. ops., 1978—. Mem. IEEE, Am. Nuclear Soc., Am. Theater Organ Soc. Episcopalian. Office: 400 55 E Jackson Blvd Chicago IL 60604

ARBUCKLE, PHILIP WAYNE, travel company executive; b. West Memphis, Ark., Feb. 9, 1954; s. Wayne C. and Betty Jo (Atkins) A. B.B.A., Mid-Am. Nazarene Coll., 1976; M.A., North Am. Sch. of Travel, 1979. Asst. to pres. Medco Inc., Overland Park, Kans., 1976-80; v.p. ops. Group Travel Service Ltd., Overland Park, 1980—; cons. travel Ozark Council of Govs., Jefferson City, Mo., 1983-84, Internat. Congress of Radiology, Kans. City, Kans., 1983—. Author: Paris for Little or Nothing, 1972. Mem. community development City of Olathe, Kans. 1982-83; mem. bi-centennial com. County of Johnson, Kansas, 1976. Mem. Am. Mgmt. Assn., Olathe C. of C. (community affairs com. 1983-84), Olathe Hist. Soc. Republican. Mem. Nazarene Ch. Club: Kans. City Friends of Art (Mo.). Avocations: computers; genealogy; archaeology. Office: Group Travel Service Ltd 6340 Glenwood St Overland Park KS 66202

ARCHAMBAULT, RENE FRANCIS, business executive, surgeon, educator; b. Barre, Vt., Oct. 31, 1911; s. Francois Xavier and Antonia (Pauze) A.; B.A., U. Montreal, 1930; M.D., Creighton U., 1936; M.Sc., U. Pa., 1940; m. Marilyn Miehls, Oct. 13, 1950; children—George, Susan, Rene, Mary Ann. Intern, Mercy Hosp., Council Bluffs, Iowa, 1936-37; resident Sacred Heart Hosp., Allentown, Pa., 1938-40; practice medicine specializing in surgery, Barre, 1940-41, Wayne, Mich., 1951—; adminstr. Nankin Hosp., Wayne, 1951—; formerly assoc. prof. anatomy Wayne State U., Detroit. Del., Mich. Republican Conv., 1968. Served to maj. AUS, 1941-46. Diplomate Am. Bd. Surgery. Mem. Pan Am. Med. Assn., Am. Acad. Med. Adminstrs. (regional v.p. 1967). Contbr. articles to profl. jours. Home: 35550 Michigan Ave Wayne MI 48184 Office: 35550 Michigan St Wayne MI 48184

ARCHBOLD, THOMAS JOHN, trust farm exec.; b. Fargo, N.D., July 10, 1947; s. Francis John and Eileen Mary (Fridgen) A.; B.S., N.D. State U., 1969, M.S., 1972; m. Sharon Joan Daub, June 22, 1968; children—Jason Thomas, Kristin Leigh, Kerry Lynn. Research asst. N.D. State U., Fargo, 1969-72; asst. Burleigh County agt. Extension Service, U.S. Dept. Agr., Bismarck, N.D., 1972-73, Ransom County extension agt., Lisbon, 1973-75; farm mgr. 1st Bank of N.D., N.A., Fargo, 1975—; v.p. 1st Trust Co. of N.D. Sec., Ransom County Crop and Livestock Improvement Assn., 1973-75; dir. Extension Staff Devel. Adv. Com., 1974-75; sec. Ransom County Soil Conservation Dist., 1973-75, Ransom County Twp. Officers Assn., 1973-75; bd. dirs. Ransom County Fair Bd., 1973-75. Named Man of Year, Lisbon Jr. C. of C., 1974. Mem. Am. Soc. Farm Mgrs. and Rural Appraisers (pres. N.D. chpt. 1979-80), N.W. Farm Mgrs., N.D. Acad. Sci., Lisbon Jr. C. of C. (dir. 1975), Sigma Chi. Roman Catholic. Clubs: Agassiz, Fargo Elks, K.C. Home: 93 23d Ave N Fargo ND 58102 Office: 1st Trust Co of ND Fargo ND 58102

ARCHER, BERNARD THOMAS, radiologist; b. Rock Island, Ill., Dec. 8, 1935; s. Marcus Matthew and Janet Christita (Rank) A.; student St. Ambrose Coll., 1953-56; M.D., U. Iowa, 1960; m. Doreen Mary Smith, Aug. 26, 1961; children—Martha, Amy, Christopher, Stephen, Megan, Matthew. Intern, Milw. County Gen. Hosp., 1960-61; resident Univ. Hosps. Cleve., 1963-66, fellow in radiology, 1966-67; practice medicine specializing in radiology, 1967—; pres. Huron Rd. Radiologists, Cleve., 1970—; dir. dept. radiology Huron Road Hosp., East Cleveland, Ohio, 1970-85; asst. clin. prof. Case Western Res. U., 1977—. Served with USAF, 1961-63. Certified Am. Bd. Radiology. Mem. AMA, Ohio Med. Assn., Acad. Medicine Cleve., Radiol. Soc. N. Am., Am. Col. Radiology, Ohio State, Cleve. Radiol. Socs. Roman Catholic. Home: 1009 Hillcreek Ln Gates Mills OH 44040 Office: 13951 Terrace Rd Cleveland OH 44112

ARCHER, JOHN THOMAS, optometrist; b. Bellevue, Ohio, Nov. 12, 1949; s. Richard Thomas and Jean (Greenslade) A.; m. Deborah Lynn Johnson, Sept. 15, 1973; children—Jeffrey Thomas, David Thomas. Student Wittenberg U., 1968-71; B.S., Ohio State U., 1973; O.D., 1975. Lic. optometrist, cert. splty. topical ocular pharm. agts. Ptnr. Drs. Beattie & Archer, Inc., Bowling Green, Ohio, 1975—. Mem. adv. bd. Wood Ln. Industries, 1977-83; trustee The Link, 1979-82. Mem. Toledo Area Optometric Soc. (pres. 1982-83, 83-84), Ohio Optometric Assn. (chmn. com. 1980), Am. Optometric Assn., Vision League of Ohio (bd. dirs. 1977-79), Better Vision Inst., Ohio State U. Coll. Optometry Alumni Assn., Bowling Green C. of C. (trustee 1978-80), Epsilon Psi Epsilon. Clubs: Bowling Green Country, Falcon. Lodges: Elk, Kiwanis (pres. 1982-83). Avocations: sports; coin collecting. Home: 605 Crestview Dr Bowling Green OH 43402 Office: 1022 N Prospect Dr PO Box 74 Bowling Green OH 43402

ARCHER, MARTHA JANE, psychologist; b. Cambridge, Ohio, Nov. 30, 1933; d. Ralph Herbert and Edith Sarah (Lemmon) Heller; m. Robert Dale Archer, Sept. 26, 1953; children—Robert, Gregory, Richard. M.Ed., Kent State U., 1969. Lic. psychologist, Ohio. Coordinator inpatient adolescent program Fallsview Psychiat. Hosp., Cuyahoga Falls, Ohio, 1970-72; counselor Hawthornden State Hosp., Northfield, Ohio, 1972; counselor-coordinator Residential Intervention Ctr.-YWCA, Akron, Ohio, 1973-74; dir. rehab. treatment Portage County (Ohio) Juvenile Ct., 1974-76; family counseling psychologist Portage Family Counseling and Mental Health Ctr., Ravenna, Ohio, 1976-78; pvt. practice psychology, Ravenna, 1978—; cons. Portage County Juvenile Ct. HEW grantee, 1968. Mem. Am. Psychol. Assn., Ohio Psychol. Assn., Acad. for Edn. and Research in Profl. Psychology (trustee 1982—, treas. 1981—). Home: 1102 Ledgeview Rd Macedonia OH 44056 Office: 830 W Main St Ravenna OH 44266

ARCHER, WESLEY LEA, chemist; b. Marietta, Ohio, Feb. 20, 1927; s. Daniel Wesley and Thelma A. (Marsh) A.; B.A., Kalamazoo Coll., 1950; Ph.D., Ind. U., 1953; m. Mary Susan Walker, May 29, 1971; 1 child, James Wesley. Research chemist Irwin Neisler Co., Decatur, Ill., 1953-56; research asso. Dow Chem. Co., Midland, Mich., 1956—. Served with USNR, 1945-46. Contbr. articles to profl. jours. Patentee in field. Home: 1117 Scott St Midland MI 48640 Office: Dow Center 2020 Midland MI 48640

ARCILA, MARILYN WALSH, corporation executive; b. Bklyn., June 13, 1948; d. James Joseph and Wanda Josephine (Zelenski) Walsh; student U. Otaawa, 1977-79; children—Therese-Marie, Elizabeth-Marie. Mem. staff purchasing dept. Simmonds Precision Co., N.Y.C., 1967-68; exec. sec. Bronson Imports, N.Y.C., 1968-75; reporter Ottawa Jour. and Emporium Echo, 1975-77; chief acct. Arcila and Assocs., N.Y.C., 1973-75; pres., gen. mgr. Mich. Etching Inc., Grand Rapids 1979-84; pres. Electroluminescent Displays Technology, Inc., 1983-85, El Diaelectrics. Dir. Confraternity of Christian Doctrine, Okla. and Pa. Roman Catholic Ch.; mayor, Borough of Driftwood, Cameron County, Pa., 1976; adviser N.Y. State Assembly, 1974. Mem. Nat. Assn. Female Execs., Nat. Fedn. Ind. Bus., Soc. Automotive Engs. (subcom. 1979—), Soc. Mfg. Engrs., Am. Soc. Women Accts. Republican. Office: PO Box 261 Ada MI 49301

ARD, SOLOMON JOHN, fire chief; b. Houston, Tex., Oct. 16, 1937; s. Solomon William and Olivia Mildred (Dean) A.; m. Anita Lavern Dawson, June 21, 1959; children—De-Etta, Monica, Angel, Mickey. B.S., Ind. U., Northwest, 1980; A.S., Ivy Tech. Coll., 1985. Master firefighter East Chicago Fire Dept., Ind., 1961-67, chauffeur, 1967-68, capt., 1968-80, fire chief, 1980—. Served with USAF, 1956-60, Can. Recipient Fireman of Yr. award Am. Legion, 1983, Fireman of Yr., Exchange Club, 1982, Hon. Student, Ind. U., 1977, 79, 80, Pub. Service, Cesare Battiste Lodge, 1982. Mem. East Chicago Mayor's Task Force, Lake County Arson Task Force (exec. bd. dirs.), Ind. Fire Chief's Assn. (exec. bd. dirs.), Ind. Assn. Bldg. Offices, Internat. Fire Chiefs Assn., Northwest Ind. Fire Chiefs Assn. (bd. dirs. 1982-83), Ind. Firefighters Assn. Democrat. Roman Catholic. Clubs: Ind. Alumni, East Chicagoans, Exchange. Avocations: golf; guitar. Home: 3815 Euclid Ave East Chicago IN 46312 Office: East Chicago Ind Fire Dept 3903 Indianapolis Blvd East Chicago IN 46312

ARDUSSI, WALLACE PHILIP, business executive; b. Detroit, Feb. 28, 1934; s. Wallace F. and Faith (Farmer) A.; B.S., U. Mich., 1958; m. Ann Covell, July 26, 1958; children—Suzanne, John, Elizabeth, Deborah. Sales engr. Variety Stamping Corp., Cleve., 1961-62, sales mgr., 1962-64, corporate sec., dir., 1964-69; prodn. mgr. The Auer Register Co., Cleve., 1964-65, mktg. mgr., 1965-66, corporate sec., 1964-69, dir., 1966—; br. mgr. Transport Pool, 1969-70, br. mgr. Rentco div. Fruehauf Corp., 1970-72, nat. accounts mgr., 1973-80; leasing mgr. Indsl. Truck div. Allis Chalmers Corp., Matteson, Ill., 1980-83; pres. Auer Register Co., Cleve., 1983—. Served to 1st lt. USAF, 1958-61. Mem. Cleve. Engring. Soc., Soc. Mfg. Engrs., Am. Mgmt. Assn., Chi Phi. Presbyterian (deacon 1968-71, elder). Rotarian (dir. 1967-70, 75-80, pres. 1979-80). Home: 19029 Schlather Ln Rocky River OH 44116 Office: 6600 Clement Ave Cleveland OH 44105

ARENA, NICK FRANK, telephone company executive; b. Parma, Ohio, June 20, 1939; s. Anthony and Rose (Pugliano) A.; m. Sandra Carol Iafelice, Sept. 15, 1962; children—Anthony, Nick, Michael. M.E., Cleve. State U., 1962; M.B.A., Case Western Res. U., 1969. Registered profl. engr., Ohio. Assoc. project engr. Cleve. Electric Ill. Co., 1962-70; mkt. research analyst Acme-Cleve. Corp., 1970-71; dir. corp. planning Midland-Ross Corp., Cleve., 1971-76; mgr. corp. planning AM Internatl., Shaker Heights, Ohio, 1976-78; asst. v.p. fin. planning ALLTEL Corp., Hudson, Ohio, 1978—. Mem. planning task force local sch. bd., Brecksville, Ohio, 1979; trustee Homeowners Assn., Brecksville, 1978-81; coach Pony League baseball team, Brecksville, 1980-81. Mem. Planning Execs. Inst., Risk and Ins. Mgmt. Soc. Republican. Roman Catholic. Avocation: Golf. Home: 10237 Log Cabin Ct Brecksville OH 44141 Office: ALLTEL Corp 100 Executive Pkwy Hudson OH 44236

ARENDS, DAVID ANTHONY, accountant, consultant, business executive, farmer; b. Marshalltown, Iowa, Nov. 26, 1939; s. Jesse E. and Phyllis J. (Pace) A.; m. Linda E. Templeton, Sept. 20, 1967 (div. Mar. 1983). B.A. in History, Elmhurst Coll., 1965; LL.B., Blackstone Sch. Law, Chgo., 1969. Enrolled agt., U.S. Treasury Dept.; pub. acct., Iowa. Asst. corp. controller Coleman Cable & Wire Co., Broadview, Ill., 1971-72; chief corp. acctg. Wieboldt Stores, Inc., Chgo., 1972-73; corp. controller Foremost-McKesson, Skokie, Ill., 1979-84; acct., tax cons. Toledo, Iowa, 1984—; exec. officer China Trade Inc., Toledo, 1977—. Del. Democratic State Conv., 1980. Served to maj. U.S. Army, 1960-63; USAR, 1963—. Mem. Am. Assn. Astronautics, Assn. Old Crows. Democrat. Lutheran. Club: Baker Street Irregulars (Chgo.). Lodges: Masons, Shriners. Avocations: video collecting; pulp magazines; high tech.

ARENDS, JUDITH LEE, executive recruiting executive; b. Sheboygan, Wis., Aug. 23, 1948; d. Henry J. and Verda N. (Kopetsky) Otten; m. Gene C. Arends, Oct. 9, 1965; children—Gregg, Douglas. B.S. in Bus., Marion Coll., Wis., 1973. Owner/tchr., Wonderland Nursery Sch., Plymouth, Wis., 1973-75; owner/operator Added Touch Plants, Plymouth, 1977-78; adult edn. tchr. Lakeshore Tech., Cleveland, Wis., 1982-84; sales/mktg. mgr. Lakeside Cablevision, Sheboygan, Wis., 1982-83; pres./owner Mgmt. Recruiters of Fond du Lac, Wis., 1983—; career cons. Charter mem., founder chpt. Big Sisters Sheboygan, 1977-82. Mem. Data Processing Mgmt. Assn., Univac Sci. Exchange. Avocation: photography. Office: 824-A S Main St Fond du Lac WI 54935

ARENTZ, ANDREW ALBERT, holding company executive; b. Chgo., May 12, 1928; s. Andrew A. and Ruth J. (Gulbransen) A.; B.S.C.E., Ill. Inst. Tech., 1950; J.D., John Marshall Law Sch., 1960; m. Lillian Regina Ivanovsky, Sept. 1, 1950; children—Andrew Anton, Alethea Ruth, Paul David. Supr. ops. research AMF, Niles, Ill., 1959-62; assoc. dir. advanced transp. planning Gen. Am. Transp. Corp., Chgo., 1963-66, asst. to v.p. corp. planning, 1966-68; pres., chief exec. officer GARD, Inc., Niles, 1968-77; dir. planning and devel. GATX Corp., Chgo., 1977-83, spl. asst. to v.p. fin., 1983-84, dir. personnel research and benefits planning, 1984—. Bd. dirs. Chgo. Bot. Garden, 1979-82, Luth. Sch. Theology, Chgo., 1972-78; trustee Village of Riverwoods, 1969-73. Served with AUS, 1952-54. Mem. Planning Execs. Inst., N.Am. Planning Soc., Midwest Planning Assn. Lutheran. Home: 333 Juneberry Rd Riverwoods IL 60015 Office: 120 S Riverside Plaza Chicago IL 60606

ARENZ, A. JOHN, lawyer; b. Dubuque, Iowa, Dec. 16, 1952; s. James T. and Mary Margaret (Malin) A.; m. Cynthia Ann Howell; children—Allison Mae, James Howell. A.B. magna cum laude, Marquette U., 1975; J.D., Georgetown U., 1978. Bars: Iowa 1978, U.S. Dist. Ct. (no. and so. dists.) Iowa 1978, U.S. Tax Ct. 1978, U.S. Ct. Claims 1978, U.S. Supreme Ct. 1983. Assoc. O'Connor, Thomas, Hammer, Bertch & Norby, Dubuque, 1978-84; prin. O'Connor & Thomas, P.C., Dubuque, 1984—. Mem. bd. edn. St. Catherine's Ch., Iowa. Mem. Dubuque County Bar Assn., Iowa Bar Assn., ABA, Assn. Trial Lawyers Iowa, Assn. Trial Lawyers Am., Phi Beta Kappa, Phi Alpha Theta, Phi Beta Gamma (bd. editors The Tax Lawyer). Home: Rural Route 1 Box 71 La Motte IA 52054 Office: O'Connor & Thomas PC 200 Dubuque Bldg Dubuque IA 52001

AREY, LEO BETRAM, clin. psychologist; b. Richfield, N.C., June 19, 1913; s. Nathan Green and Nina (Trexler) A.; m. Jennie Lind Mitchell, Dec. 31, 1941; A.B., Lenoir Rhyne Coll., 1935; Ph.D., U. Chgo., 1952. Registered psychologist, Ill., 1964; diplomate Am. Bd. Profl. Psychology. Psychology intern VA Hosp., Hines, Ill., 1947-51, staff clin. psychologist, 1952-61, research psychologist, 1962-66, asst. chief, psychology service, supervisory psychologist, psychiatry service, 1966-80, pvt. practice, 1981—. Mem. Am., Midwest, Ill. psychol. assns., Assn. Psychophysiol. Study Sleep, Am. Acad. Psychotherapists, Assn. Advancement Psychology, Sigma Xi. Contbr. to psychol. jours. and book. Home: 5532 South Shore Dr Chicago IL 60637

AREY, RICHARD EVERETT, hotel executive; b. Shelby, N.C., June 4, 1927, s. William Griffin and Catherine (Roberts) A.; m. Anice Miller, Sept. 2, 1950; 1 child, Ann Rochelle Arey Mason. Student Davidson Coll., 1944-45, Mcht. Marine Acad., 1945-46; cert. hotel adminstrn., Ech. Inst. of Am. Hotel and Motel Assn. From mgmt. trainee to dept. head Robert E. Lee Hotel, Winston-Salem, N.C., 1950-58; gen. mgr. Washington Duke Hotel, Durham, N.C., 1958-60; v.p., gen. mgr. Jack Tar Hotel, Durham, 1960-70, Hilton Plaza Inns, Kansas City, Mo., 1970—; treas. N.C. Travel Council, 1960-61; Pres. Durham Mchts. Assn., 1968; mem. faculty dept. food and lodging Penn Valley Coll.; commr. Planned Indsl. Expansion Authority, Kansas City, Mo.; bd. dirs. Kansas City Tourist and Conv. Bur., Country Club Plaza Assn. Served as midshipman USNR and USMC, 1945-46. Recipient Rocamora award N.C., 1967, Salut Au Restaurateur award Fla. State U., 1967. Mem. Hotel Sales Mgrs. Assn., Am. Soc. Travel Agts., Am. Hotel Motel Career Devel. Assn., Hotel Motel Greeters Assn., Hotel and Motel Assn. Greater Kansas City, (pres. 1977), Mo. Restaurant Assn. (pres. Kansas City chpt. 1978, Kansas City Restaurateur of Yr. 1983), N.C. Hotel Motel Assn. (pres.), N.C. Restaurant

Assn. (pres. 1966), So. Innkeepers Assn. (v.p. 1962), Am. Hotel Motel Assn. (bd. dirs. 1960-70). Presbyterian. Office: Hilton Plaza Inns 45th and Main Kansas City MO 64111

ARINDAENG, GENE REMITIRA, physician; b. Naga City, Philippines, July 20, 1929; came to U.S., 1960; s. Eulogio and Prudencia (Rametira) A.; m. Katherine Ann Wachowiak, Apr. 24, 1965; children—Geno, Mario. M.D., Far Eastern U., 1957. Asst. prof. Far Eastern U. Coll. Medicine, 1957-60; intern, St. Elizabeth Hosp., Elizabeth, N.J., 1960-61; chief resident Princeton Hosp. (N.J.), 1961-63; gen. practice medicine, Pontiac, Mich., 1982—; practice internal medicine Met. Hosp., Detroit, 1963-67, chief emergency dept., 1967-82, dir. personnel health service, 1965-82; part-time emergency physician Pontiac Gen. Hosp. Mem. Philippine Med. Assn. in Am. (past pres.), Far Eastern U. Alumni Assn. in Am., Am. Coll. Emergency Physicians (cert.), Oakland County Med. Assn., Mich. Med. Assn. Republican. Home: 1456 Lochridge St Bloomfield Hills MI 48013 Office: 2153 Orchard Lake Rd Pontiac MI 48013

ARKFELD, DONALD LEO, ophthalmologist; b. Portsmouth, Iowa, Aug. 31, 1947; s. Vincent Joseph and Anna Marie (Schmitz) A. B.S., Creighton U., 1969; D. Medicine University Med. Ctr., 1973. Intern Univ. Hosp. Omaha, 1973-74; resident in ophthalmology University Meds. Center, Omaha, 1973-76; fellow Bascom Palmer Eye Inst., Miami, Fla., 1978; practice medicine specializing in ophthalmology, Omaha, 1979; ophthalmologist Gifford, Eagle, Arkfeld, Omaha, 1979—; dir. Lions Eye Found., Omaha, Commn. Low Vision, Omaha. Contbr. articles to med. jour. Served to lt. USN, 1976-78. Mem. Alpha Omega Soc. Republican. Roman Catholic.

ARKING, LUCILLE MUSSER, nurse epidemiologist; b. Centre County, Pa., Jan. 26, 1936; d. Boyd Albert and Marion Anna (Merryman) Musser; m. Robert Arking, May 8, 1959; children—Henry David, Jonathan Jacob. R.N., Episcopal Sch. Nursing, 1958; B.S.N., U. Pa., 1968; postgrad. Wayne State U., 1979—. Psychiat. research nurse Boston City Hosp., 1958; hosp. supr. Phila. Psychiat. Ctr., 1959-61; pub. health nurse Community Nursing Service, Phila., 1961-64; dir. nursing Green Acres Nursing Ctr., Phila., 1966-67; head nurse U. Va., Charlottesville, 1967-68; asst. dir. nursing U. Ky., Lexington, 1968-70; asst. dir. nursing edn. Rio Hondo Hosp., Downey, Calif., 1973-75; dir. nursing Bellwood Hosp., Bellflower, Calif., 1974-75; nurse epidemiologist Henry Ford Hosp., Detroit, 1975-84, dir. hosp. epidemiology, 1984—; instr. Santa Ana Coll., 1971-73; lectr. drug abuse Fountain Valley, Calif., 1970-75. Co-founder Parents and Friends Learning Disabilities Orgn., 1968-70; den leader Cub Scouts, Fountain Valley, Calif. 1968-75; mem. Wellness Networks, Detroit, 1983—. Women's Club of Centre County scholar, 1954-58; grantee Community Nursing Service Ednl., 1963-64; USPHS nursing trainee, 1965. Mem. Am. Nurse's Assn., Mich. Nurse's Assn., Am. Pub. Health Assn. (mem. epidemiology sect. 1975—), Assn. Practitioners of Infection Control, Mich. Infection Control Soc., Nat. League of Nursing. Contbr. articles to profl. jours. Home: 4705 Stoddard Troy MI 48098 Office: Dept Hosp Epidemiology Henry Ford Hosp 2799 W Grand Blvd Detroit MI 48202

ARKING, ROBERT, geneticist, gerontologist, educator; b. Bklyn., July 1, 1936; s. Henry and Mollie (Levinson) A.; B.S., Dickinson Coll., 1958; Ph.D., Temple U., 1967; m. Lucille Mae Musser, May 8, 1959; children—Henry David, Jonathan Jacob. Sci. tchr. Phila. Public Schs., 1959-61; asst. prof. zoology U. Ky., Lexington, 1968-70; research biologist Center for Pathology, U. Calif., Irvine, 1970-75; asst. prof. biology Wayne State U., Detroit, 1975-81, assoc. prof. 1981—. NSF fellow, 1964-66, NIH fellow, 1967-68; NIH and NSF grantee, 1970—. Mem. AAAS, Am. Soc. Zoologists, Genetics Soc. Am., Soc. for Developmental Biology, Sigma Xi. Contbr. articles to profl. jours. Office: Wayne State University Dept Biological Sciences Detroit MI 48202

ARLINGHAUS, EDWARD JAMES, health administration educator; b. Cin., Jan. 6, 1925; s. Edward A. and Irene (Custer) A.; B.B.A., U. Cin., 1948, Ph.D., 1981; M.B.A., Xavier U., 1958, M.Ed., 1971, M.S., 1973; m. Ilse Denninger, Aug. 10, 1974; 1 dau., Toni Gail. Dir. personnel tng. Mabley & Carew Co., Cin., 1948-51; sales researcher John Shillito Co., Cin., 1951-53; personnel devel. specialist Gen. Elec. Co., Cin., 1953-57; dir. personnel, pub. relations and security Jewish Hosp. of Cin., 1957-66; dir. grad. program in hosp. and health adminstrn. Xavier U., Cin., 1966—; mem. health care sect. Cath. Conf. Ohio; sec. bd. trustees Providence Hosp., 1968-77, St. Francis Hosp., 1968-75, St. Mary's Hosp., 1968-72 (all Cin.); trustee Epp Meml. Hosp., 1983—, Otterbeni Homes, 1981—; chmn. health manpower com. CORVA, Cin., 1970-75; mem. Ohio Bd. Examiners Nursing Home Adminstrs., 1974-76. Served with AUS, 1943-45; col. Res. (ret.). Fellow Royal Soc. Health; Am. Coll. Hosp. Adminstrs., Am. Acad. Med. Adminstrs.; mem. Assn. Mental Health Adminstrs., Cath. Hosp. Assn., Am. Public Health Assn., Scarbard and Blade, Phi Delta Kappa. Home: 8060 Indian Hill Rd Cincinnati OH 45243 Office: Xavier University Cincinnati OH 45207

ARLOOK, THEODORE DAVID, dermatologist; b. Boston, Mar. 12, 1910; s. Louis and Rebecca (Sakansky) A.; B.S., U. Ind. Sch. Medicine, 1932, M.D., 1934; postgrad. dermatology U. So. Calif., 1946-47. Intern, Luth. Meml. Hosp., Chgo., 1934-35; resident in dermatology Indpls. Gen. Hosp., 1947-49; practice medicine specializing in dermatology, Elkhart, Ind., 1950—; mem. staff Elkhart Gen. Hosp.; asso. mem. dermatology dept. Wishard Meml. Hosp., Indpls. Pres., Temple Israel, Elkhart, 1963-64; pres. B'nai B'rith, 1955. Served to capt. M.C. AUS, 1941-46; PTO. Diplomate Am. Bd. Dermatology. Mem. AMA, Am. Acad. Dermatology, Elkhart County Med. Soc. (pres. 1967), Noah Worcester Dermatol. Soc. Contbr. articles to med. jours. Office: 912 W Franklin St Elkhart IN 46516

ARMACOST, ROBERT LEO, management educator, former coast guard officer, educator; b. Balt., July 17, 1942; s. Leo Mathias and Margaret Virginia (Ruth) A.; m. Susan Marie Danesi, Jan. 16, 1965; children—Robert Leo, Andrew Paul, Kathleen Erin. B.S. with honors, U.S. Coast Guard Acad., 1964; M.S., U.S. Naval Postgrad. Sch., 1970; D.Sc. in Ops. Research, George Washington U., 1976. Engring. officer USCG Cutter Mendota, Wilmington, N.C., 1964-66; ops. officer USCGC Cook Inlet, Portland, Maine, 1966-68; ops. research analyst, ops. planning staff USCG Hdqrs., Washington, 1970-75; planning officer, aids to navigation div., 1976-78; comdr. Coast Guard Group, Milw., 1978-81; comdg. officer USCG Marine Safety Office, Milw., 1981-84, capt. of port, 1981-84, officer in charge of marine inspection, 1981-84; ret., 1984; instr. computer sci. Milw. Area Tech. Coll., 1982-83; asst. prof. mgmt. sci. Marquette U., Milw., 1984—. First v.p. Md. Right to Life, 1976-78; active Wis. Marine Hist. Soc., Manitowoc Maritime Mus., Little League, Glendale, Wis. Recipient USCG commendation award, 1972, 74, 78, 81, 84; named Outstanding Civic Vol., Bowie, Md., 1976; nat. finalist White House fellow, 1977-78. Mem. Ops. Research Soc. Am. (mem. com. 1983-84), Math. Programming Soc., Inst. Mgmt. Sci., Am. Assn. of Budget and Program Analysts, Soc. for Indsl. and Applied Math. Roman Catholic. Contbr. articles to profl. jours. Home: 7012 N Bethmaur Ln Glendale WI 53209 Office: Marquette Univ Coll Bus Adminstrn Milwaukee MI 53233

ARMAGOST, ELSA GAFVERT, computer industry communications consultant; b. Duluth, Minn., Jan. 26, 1917; d. Axel Justus and Martina Emelia (Magnuson) Gafvert; grad. with honors Duluth Jr. Coll., 1936; B.J., U. Minn., 1938; postgrad. in public relations, bus. mgmt., computer tech., 1965-81; Ph.D. (hon.) in Computer Communication Cons. Sci., Internat. U. Found.; m. Byron William Armagost, Dec. 8, 1945; children—David Byron, Laura Martina. Freelance editor, Duluth, 1939-42; procedure editor and analyst U.S. Steel, Duluth, 1942-45; fashion advt. staff Dayton Co., Mpls., 1945-48; systems applications and documentation mgr. Control Data Corp., Mpls., 1969-74, promotion specialist, mktg. editor, 1974-76, corp. staff coordinator info. on edn., 1976-78; instr. communications, publ. specialist, 1978-79, communication cons. peripheral products group, 1979-83; communications consultant, 1983—. Mem. steering com. U.S. Senatorial Bus. Adv. Bd.; bd. dirs. LWV, Pitts.; v.p. Sewickley Valley Hosp. Aux., Sewickley Valley Mental Health Council; dir. publicity Sacred Arts Expo, World Affairs Council radio program, Pitts., 1962-68; mem. U.S. Congl. Adv. Bd., 1985. Recipient Communications award Toastmasters Club, 1984. Mem. Process Mgmt. Inst. (adv. bd. 1984), AAUW (1st v.p. Venezuela), Minn. Press Club, Internat. Platform Assn., Friends of Mpls. Inst. Art. Club: Woman's of Mpls. Home and Office: 9500 Collegeview Rd Bloomington MN 55437

ARMITAGE, CHARLES FLOYD, educator; b. Peoria, Ill., Aug. 22, 1937; s. Floyd B. and Regina M. (Dougherty) A.; children—Amy, Angelie, Patrick. B.S., Western Ill. U., 1959, M.S., 1962; Ed.S., Central Mich. U., 1967; Ed.D., Ill. State U., 1971. Lic. pvt. pilot, motorcycle safety instr. Asst. coach, instr. Western Ill. U., Macomb, 1959-61; head football coach, tchr., Allegan, Mich., 1961-66; asst. coach, instr. Central Mich. U., Mt. Pleasant, 1966-67; asst. to v.p. Ill. State U., Normal, 1967-69; sr. high sch. prin. Tri-Valley, Downs, Ill., 1969-70; fed. project dir. Ill Bd. Higher Edn., Springfield, 1970-71; field supr. Ill. Office Edn., State Bd. Edn., Springfield, 1971—. Candidate for mayor, Town of Normal, 1976; mem. McLean County Bd., 1984—; umpire Amateur Softball Assn. Mott Found. scholar, 1966-67; named Area Football Coach of Yr., Kalamazoo Gazette, 1965. Mem. Am. Assn. Sch. Adminstrs., AAHPER, AAUP, Western Ill. U. Alumni Assn. (pres. 1975-77), Nat. Rifle Assn. (cert. police firearms instr.), Phi Delta Kappa. Roman Catholic. Lodge: Elks. Home: 400 N Cottage Ave Normal IL 61761 Office: 100 N 1st St Springfield IL 62777

ARMITAGE, THOMPSON SHAW, JR., consulting engineer; b. Mpls., Apr. 17, 1925; s. Thompson Shaw and Lenora A. (Larson) A. B.C.E., U. Minn., 1950. Registered profl. engr., Tex. Asst. engr. Iowa State Conservation Commn., Des Moines, 1950-51; field insp. E.I. Dupont de Nemours & Co., Inc., Wilmington, Del., 1951-54; cost engr. Arrowhead Constructors, Mpls., 1954-55; cost engr., estimator Holmes & Narver, Inc., Los Angeles, 1955-56; cost engr. McKee-Raymond de Cuba, N.Y.C., 1956-58; office engr. Sevdrup & Parcel Internat. Inc., St. Louis, 1958-60; specification engr. Rulph M. Parsons, Los Angeles, 1960-62; with Lyon Assocs., Inc., engring. cons., Balt., 1962—, sr. v.p., 1980—. Served with USN, 1943-46. Fellow ASCE, Indian Soc. Engrs.; mem. Constrn. Specification Inst., Am. Assn. Cost Engrs., Internat. Soc. Appraisors. Home: 4820 W 39th St Minneapolis MN 55416

ARMON, JOSEPH JOHN, lawyer; b. Cleve., May 4, 1950; s. Joseph Constantine and Angela Josephine (Verhovnik) A. B.A. in Psychology, Case Western Res. U., 1973; J.D., Toledo U., 1976. Bar: Ohio, U.S. Dist. Ct. (no. dist.) Ohio, U.S. Dist. Ct. (so. dist.) Ohio, U.S. Ct. Appeals (6th cir.). Founder, prin. firm Joseph J. Armon, Esq., Cleve., 1976—. Pres. Perry Home Owners Assn., Cleve., 1977-78; candidate for City Council, Cleve., 1977. Mem. Ohio State Bar Assn., Cuyahoga County Bar Assn., Greater Cleve. Bar Assn. Roman Catholic. Home: 24455 Barrett Rd Olmsted Township OH 44138 Office: Suite 905 526 Superior Ave NE Cleveland OH 44114

ARMONDO, ANGELO ANTHONY, army officer, hospital administrator; b. Chgo., Nov. 16, 1948; s. Michael Louis and Janet Therese (Piemonte) A.; m. Linda Lee Dickson, Dec. 30, 1967; children—Michael R., Andrew A., Jena T. B.A., Ind. U., 1970; M.H.A., Baylor U., 1982. Commd. 2d lt. U.S. Army, 1970, advanced through grades to maj., 1981; inventory mgr. U.S. Army Med. Materiel Agy., Pacific, Ryuku Islands, Japan, 1971-72; comdr. Hdqrs. Detachment, U.S. Army Med. Materiel Agy., Pacific, Ryukyu Islands, 1972-73; chief logistics div. U.S. Army Hosp., Fort Benjamin Harrison, Indpls., 1974-77; chief supply and service br. 41st Combat Support Hosp., Fort Sam Houston, 1978-80; adminstrv. resident U.S. Army Hosp., Fort Knox, Ky., 1981-82; chief logistics div. U.S. Army Hosp., Bremerhaven Fed. Republic Germany, 1982—, acting insp. gen., 1983—. Active Trans Atlantic council Boy Scouts Am., 1983—; mem. U.S. Army Norddeutschland Mil. Community Chaplain's Fund Council, 1983—. Hoosier scholar, 1966-70. Mem. Assn. U.S. Army, Am. Coll. Hosp. Adminstrs., Phi Epsilon Pi, Phi Eta Sigma. Roman Catholic. Club: Bremerhaven Officers and Civilians. Home: 14 Adolf Butenandt Strasse Bremerhaven 2850 Fed Republic Germany Office: US Army MEDDAC APO New York NY 09069

ARMSTRONG, CURTIS E., marketing representative; b. Martins Ferry, Ohio, Sept. 8, 1946; s. Ralph Edward and Eileen Virginia (Brown) A.; student West Liberty (W.Va.) State Tchrs. Coll., 1964-66, Franklin U., 1970-71; m. Judy Kay Shutt, June 9, 1979. Employment mgr. Grossman & Sons, Inc., Columbus, Ohio, 1976-77; state coordinator handicapped services safety and hygiene div. Indsl. Commn. Ohio, Columbus, 1977-79, dir. public relations rehab. div., 1979-81, acting dir. rehab. div., 1981-82; mktg. rep. P.M. Computer Services, 1982—. pres. dir. Time, Inc., Columbus, 1979—; adviser Ohio Gov.'s Com. for Employment Handicapped, Nat. Center Research in Vocat. Edn., Ohio State U., rep. President's Com. on Employment Handicapped, Washington, 1977-78; pres., co-founder Handi-Capable, Inc., 1980—; pres. Central Ohio Employability Awareness Council, 1976-78. Mem. Nat. Assn. Accts., Am. Soc. Personnel Adminstrn., Press Club of Ohio. Rec. artist Gateway Records, 1962-70. Home: 1054 S James Rd Columbus OH 43227

ARMSTRONG, HART REID, minister, editor, publisher; b. St. Louis, May 11, 1912; s. Hart Champlin and Zora Lillian (Reid) A.; m. Iona Rhoda Mehl, Feb. 21, 1932; 1 son, Hart Reed. Grad. Life Bible Coll., 1931; A.B., Christian Temples U., 1936; Litt.D., Geneva Theol. Coll., 1967; D.D. (hon.) Central Sch. Religion, Surrey, Eng., 1972; Th.M., Central Christian Coll., 1968, Th.D., 1970; Ph.D. in Religion, Berean Christian Coll., 1980. Ordained to ministry Assembly of God, 1932; pastor, 1932-34; dean Bible Standard Coll., Eugene, Oreg., 1935-40; missionary, Indonesia, 1941-42; editor Open Bible Pubs., Des Moines, 1944-46, Gospel Pub. House, Springfield, Mo., 1947-53, Gospel Light Pubs., Glendale, Calif., 1954; crusade adminstr. Oral Roberts Assn., Tulsa, 1955-62; exec. dir. Assembly Homes, Inc., Glenwood, Minn., 1963-66; pres. Defenders Christian Faith, Kansas City, Mo., 1967-80; founder, pres., editor Christian Communications, Inc., Wichita, Kans., 1981—; editor Communicare mag. Fellow London Royal Soc. Arts; mem. Nat. Sunday Sch. Assn., Pope County Hist. Soc., Sigma Delta Chi. Lodge: Rotary (past charter pres. Glenwood, Minn.). Author: To Those Who Are Left, 1950; You Should Know, 1951; The Rebel, 1967; The Beast, 1967; How Do I Pray, 1968; All Things for Life, 1969; What Will Happen to the United States, 1969; Impossible Events of Bible Prophecy, 1979; All You Need to Know about Bible Prophecy, 1980; Thoughts at Three Score and Ten, 1981; The A-B-C of Last Day Events, 1982. Home: 6436 N Hillside Ave Wichita KS 67219 Office: 6450 N Hillside Ave Wichita KS 67219

ARMSTRONG, JOHN BENJAMIN, lawyer; b. Cin., Apr. 20, 1947; s. Charles B. and Ruth H. (Biehl) A.; m. Robin S. Smith, Mar. 21, 1970; children—John Philip, Charles B., Margaret K. B.S., U. Cin., 1970, J.D., 1973. Bar: Ohio 1973. Assoc. Jones, Hammel & Avery, Cin., 1973-78; ptnr. Higgs, Ritter & Armstrong, Cin., 1978-80; head litigation sect. Schwartz, Manes & Ruby, Cin., 1981—; gen. counsel Crocker Fels Co., Cin., 1974—, Chester Labs., Cin., 1974—; solicitor City Silverton, Ohio, 1977-83. Mem. Cin. Bar Assn., ABA. Episcopalian. Club: Camargo (Indian Hill, Ohio). Home: 1 Swallowfield Terrace Park OH 45174 Office: Schwartz Manes & Ruby Co 36 E 4th St Cincinnati OH 45202

ARMSTRONG, NAOMI YOUNG, retired educator; b. Dermott, Ark., Oct. 17, 1918; d. Allen Wesley and Sarah Elizabeth (Fluker) Young; B.S., Northwestern U., 1961; L.H.D. (hon.), U. Libre, Karachi, Pakistan, 1974; Ph.D. (hon.), World U., Tucson, 1979; D.LiH. (hon.), Universal Orthodox Coll., Iperu-Remo, Ogun State, Nigeria, 1980; Litt.D. (hon.) World Acad. Arts and Culture, Taipei, Taiwan, 1981; m. Joe Leslie Armstrong, July 17, 1938; 1 dau., Betty-Jo Armstrong Dunbar. Actress, Skyloft Players, also Center Aisle Players, Chgo., 1945-59; silk dress operator Rue-Ann Originals, Chgo., 1947-55; clk. Bur. Pub. Debt, 1955-56, IRS, 1956-59; caseworker Cook County Dept. Pub. Aid, Chgo., 1961-62; tchr. Chgo. pub. schs., 1962-83, creative writing instr., 1975-77, instr. Social Center, 1965-67; dramatic instr. Crerar Meml. Presbyn. Ch., Chgo., 1972; real estate salesman Century 21 Maner, 1978—. Mem. exec. bd., membership chmn. Northwestern U. Young Alumni Council, 1971-72; trustee World U., 1973-74. Recipient Hon. Gold diploma, spl. award 3d World Congress Poets, 1976; named Internat. Woman of 1975, United Poets Laureate Internat. others; lic. real estate salesman. Mem. United Poets Laureate Internat. (exec. bd.), Internat. Platform Assn. (life; bd. govs.; 3d Preview winner 1976), World Poets Resource Center, Poetry Soc. London, Centro Studi e Scambi Internat., Intercontinental Biog. Assn. (life), World Poetry Soc., NAACP (life, chpt. chmn. edn. com. 1983), Sigma Gamma Rho. Author: A Child's Easter, 1971; Expression I, 1973; Expression III, 1976; Naomi's Two Line Sillies (A Guide for Living) Expression IV, 1985. Address: 9257 S Burnside Ave Chicago IL 60619

ARMSTRONG, RUTH MILDRED, educator; b. Moulmein, Burma, Aug. 22, 1924; d. Gustaf Adolph and Edna Blanche (Grandin) Sword; parents U.S. citizens; B.A., William Jewell Coll., 1945; postgrad. Northwestern U., 1946, Nat. Coll. Edn., 1960, U. Iowa, 1970; m. Walter Armstrong, Aug. 16, 1975; children from previous marriage—Nancy Ruth Berggren, James Otto Tinzmann. Instr. North Park Jr. Coll., Chgo., 1948-50; tchr. pub. schs., Morton Grove, Ill., 1958-62; instr. psychology Judson Coll., Elgin, Ill., 1964-66; counselor Warrenville (Ill.) Clinic, 1966-68; asst. prof. psychology North Park Coll., Chgo., 1966-78, asso. prof., 1978—; cons. Oak Therapeutic Sch., Chgo., 1972-73. Mem. Niles Township Bd. Spl. Edn., Sch. Bd. Dist. 67, Morton Grove, Ill., 1963-66. Mem. Internat. Council Edn. for Teaching, Am. Assn. Higher Edn., AAAS, AAUP, AAUW, Ill. Assn. Tchr. Educators. Baptist. Contbr. articles to profl. jours. Home: 1746 Good Park Ridge IL 60068 Office: North Park Coll 5125 N Spaulding Chicago IL 60625

ARMSTRONG, THEODORE MORELOCK, corporate executive; b. St. Louis, July 22, 1939; s. Theodore Roosevelt and Vassar Fambrough (Morelock) A.; B.A., Yale, 1961; LL.B., Duke, 1964; m. Carol Mercer Robert, Sept. 7, 1963; children—Evelyn Anne, Robert Theodore. Admitted to Mo. bar, 1964; with Mississippi River Transmission Corp. and affiliated Cos., St. Louis, 1964—, corp. sec. Mo. Pacific Corp., 1971-75; corp. sec. River Cement Co., 1968-75; asst. v.p. Mississippi River Transmission Corp., 1974-75; v.p. Gas Supply, 1975-79, exec. v.p., 1979-83, pres., chief exec. officer, 1983—, dir., 1982—; dir. United Mo. Bank of St. Louis. Mem. Am., Met. St. Louis bar assns., Mo. Bar, So. Gas Assn. (dir. 1984—), Tenn. Soc. St. Louis, Phi Alpha Delta. Republican. Presbyterian (deacon). Clubs: Bellerive, St. Louis, Yale (St. Louis); Yale (N.Y.C.). Home: 43 Countryside Ln Saint Louis MO 63131 Office: 9900 Clayton Rd Saint Louis MO 63124

ARMSTRONG, THOMAS PEYTON, educator; b. Atchison, Kans., Nov. 24, 1941; s. Floyd Draper and Mary Elizabeth (Wohlgemuth) A.; m. Jeanette Carol Fry, June 9, 1962; children—Elizabeth, Stuart. B.S., U. Kans., 1962; M.S., U. Iowa, 1964, Ph.D., 1966. Asst. prof. dept. physics and astronomy U. Kans., Lawrence, 1968-70, assoc. prof., 1970-73, prof., 1973—. Contbr. articles to profl. jours. Recipient Higuchi Research award U. Kans., 1983. Mem. Am. Geophys. Union, Am. Phys. Soc., AAAS. Home: 3217 W 9th Lawrence KS 66044 Office: U Kans Dept Physics and Astronomy Lawrence KS 66045

ARMSTRONG, WILLIAM JOHN, dentist; b. Benton Harbor, Mich., Dec. 6, 1924; s. Fred George and Barbara Ann (Schairer) A.; m. Dolores H. Domke; children—William J., Gail E., Thomas F. A.S., Benton Harbor Jr. Coll., 1948; D.D.S., U. Mich., 1952, M.S. in Dentistry, 1975. Lic. dentist, Mich. Gen. dentist, Ypsilanti, Benton Harbor, and Coloma, Mich., 1952—; clin. asst. prof. U. Mich. Dental Sch., Ann Arbor, 1972-75. Mem. ADA. Republican. Avocations: cabinetry; skiing; jogging; hunting; fishing. Home: 1915 N Valleyview St Joseph MI 49085 Office: 213 N Paw Paw PO Box 7 Coloma MI 49038

ARN, KENNETH DALE, city official, physician; b. Dayton, Ohio, July 19, 1921; s. Elmer R. and Minna Marie (Wannagat) A.; B.A., Miami U., Oxford, Ohio, 1943; M.D., U. Mich., 1946; m. Vivien Rose Fontini, Sept. 24, 1966; children—Christine H. Hulme, Laura P. Hafstad, Kevin D., Kimmel R. Intern, Miami Valley Hosp., Dayton, Ohio, 1947-48; resident in pathology U. Mich., 1948-49, fellow in renal research, 1949-50; fellow in internal medicine Cleve. Clinic, 1950-52; practice medicine specializing in internal medicine, public health and vocat. rehab., 1952—; commr. of health City of Oakwood (Ohio), 1953—; assoc. clin. prof. medicine Wright State U., 1975—; mem. staffs Kettering Med. Center, Dayton, Miami Valley Hosp; adj. assoc. prof. edn. Wright State U.; field med. cons. Bur. Vocat. Rehab., 1958—, Bur. Services to Blind, 1975—; med. dir. Ohio Rehab. Services Commn., 1979—; mem. Pres's. Com. on Employment of Handicapped, 1971—; chmn. med. adv. com. Goodwill Industries, 1960-75; mem., chmn. lay adv. com. vocat. edn. Dayton Public Schs., 1973-82; exec. com. Gov.'s Com. on Employment Handicapped; bd. dirs. Vis. Nurses Assn. of Greater Dayton; chmn. profl. adv. com. to Combined Gen. Health Dist. Montgomery County. Named City of Dayton's Outstanding Young Man, Dayton Jr. C. of C., 1957; 1 of 5 Outstanding Young Men of State, Ohio Jr. C. of C., 1958; Physician of Year, Pres's. Com. on Employment of Handicapped, 1971; Bishop's medal for meritorious service Miami U., 1972. Mem. Am., Ohio State (del. 1955-65) med. assns., Montgomery County (Ohio) Med. Soc. (chmn. com. on diabetic detection 1955-65, chmn. polio com. 1954-58), Nat. Rehab. Assn., Am. Diabetes Assn., Am. Profl. Practice Assn., Am. Heart Assn., Am., Ohio public health assns., Aerospace Med. Assn., Nu Sigma Nu, Sigma Chi. Lutheran. Clubs: Dayton Country, Kiwanis, Royal Order Jesters, Masons (33 deg. Scottish Rite, Shriners (past potentate Antioch Shrine), K.T., Order Police, Fraternal Order Police. Home: 167 Lookout Dr Dayton OH 45409 Office: 55 Park Ave Dayton OH 45419

ARNDT, CORWIN VERNELL, educational administrator; b. Lake City, Iowa, Sept. 16, 1936; s. Chriss F. and Elva M. (Ralph) A.; m. Susan E. Fickes, Aug. 6, 1972; children—Michelle Lee, Matthew David. B.S., Peru State Coll., 1958; M.S. in Edn., U. Nebr., 1965. Cert. tchr., admin., Nebr. Sci. tchr. Fullerton Pub. Sch., Nebr., 1962-65; prin. Pleasanton Pub. Sch., Nebr., 1965-68, Oshkosh High Sch., Nebr., 1968-71, Nelson Pub. Schs., 1971-74; supt. schs. Maxwell Pub. Schs., 1974-80; county supt. schs. Garden County, Oshkosh, 1982—. Mem. Nebr. Council Sch. Admins., Nebr. Assn. County Supts., Beta Beta Beta. Republican. Lutheran. Lodge: Masons. (past-master 1983, sec. 1984—). Avocations: Amateur radio; fishing; hunting; stamps; coins. Home: Box 178 Oshkosh NE 69154 Office: Box 488 Oshkosh NE 69154

ARNDT, ROBERT GORDON, educator, psychologist; b. Flint, Mich., Apr. 29, 1938; s. Gordon and Charlotte A.; B.S., Carroll Coll., Waukesha, Wis., 1961; M.S., Bradley U., 1962; m. Judith Ann Nissley, June 26, 1965; children—Nicole M., Dean R. In-patient dir. alcoholism unit Singer Zone Center, Rockford, Ill., 1966-68; chief psychologist Stephenson County (Ill.) Mental Health, Freeport, Ill., 1968-74; dir. adult clinic Saginaw County (Mich.) Mental Health, 1974-77; adminstr. Planning for Living, Bay City, Mich., 1977-78; coordinator developmental disability asso. degree Delta Coll., University Center, Mich., 1978—, asst. prof. dept. psychology, 1979—; chmn. spl. edn. com. Saginaw Twp. Sch. Parent Adv. Com., 1982-83; pres. Saginaw County Inter. Agy. Coordinating Com., 1977-79; cons. Saginaw Valley Rehab. Center. Mem. adult edn. com. First Congregational Ch., Saginaw, 1975—; mgr. Little League, 1977-80. Served to lt. (j.g.) USN, 1963-66. Ill. State fellow, 1968-76; cert. psychologist, Ill.; lic. psychologist, Mich. Mem. Am. Psychol. Assn. Psychol. Assn., Mich. Psychol. Assn., Mid-Mich. Psychol. Assn. (past pres.). Author tng. manual. Home: 2905 Reppuhn St Saginaw MI 48603 Office: Delta College University Center MI 48710

ARNDT, ROGER EDWARD ANTHONY, educator; b. N.Y.C., May 25, 1935; s. Ernest Otto Paul and Olive (Walters) A.; children—Larysa, Tanya. B.C.E., CCNY, 1960; M.S., MIT, 1962, Ph.D., 1967. Sr. research engr. Lockheed Calif. Co., Burbank, 1963-64; NASA fellow, MIT, 1964-67; mech. engr. Littleton Research, Mass., 1965; asst. prof. Pa. State U., State College, 1967-71, assoc. prof., 1971-77; dir., prof. St. Anthony Falls Hydraulic Lab., Mpls., 1977—; cons. in field. Contbr. articles to jours., chpts. to books. Mem. Com. for Mpls. Hydropower Mus., 1979. Recipient Lorenz G. Straub award U. Minn., 1968, George Taylor Teaching award, 1978; Outstanding Faculty award AIAA, 1971-74; 1st Theodor Ranov Disting. lectr. SUNY-Buffalo, 1978. Fellow ASME; assoc. fellow; AIAA; mem. Acoustical Soc. Am., ASCE, Internat. Assn. for Hydraulic Research, Am. Water Resources Assn., Sigma Xi. Club: Twin City Cloud 7. Avocations: Fying, canoeing; hiking; camping. Home: 1820 N Ham Lake Dr Anoka MN 55304 Office: Saint Anthony Falls Hydraulic Lab Mississippi River at 3rd St Minneapolis MN 55414

ARNDT, RONALD FRED, dentist; b. Cleve., Nov. 23, 1946; s. Max and Edna Ruth (Schmahl) A.; m. Patricia Helen Conway; children—Ashley Lynn, Brianne Conway. B.A., Ohio State U., 1969, D.D.S., 1973; M.B.A., Baldwin-Wallace U., 1983. Gen. practice dentistry, North Ridgeville, Ohio, 1973—. Mem. Health Adv. Com., North Ridgeville, 1979—. Recipient Outstanding Young Man award North Ridgeville Jaycees, 1976. Fellow Acad. of Gen. Dentistry; mem. Am. Dental Assn., Am. Mgmt. Assn., Ohio Dental Assn., Lorain County Dental Soc., North Ridgeville C. of C. Protestant. Lodge: Kiwanis (pres. 1979, 81-83). Avocations: racquetball; reading; computers; scuba diving. Home: 5338 Case Rd North Ridgeville OH 44039 Office: 33650 Center Ridge Rd North Ridgeville OH 44039

ARNELL, PAULA ANN YOUNGBERG, pathologist; b. Moline, Ill., Nov. 25, 1938; d. Paul Phillip and Mabel Eleanor (Arnell) Youngberg; B.A. summa cum laude, Augustana Coll., 1960; M.D., U. Iowa, 1964; m. Richard Anthony Arnell, June 28, 1969; children—Carla Ann, Paula Marie, Paul Anthony. Intern, St. Lukes-Mercy Hosp., Cedar Rapids, Iowa, 1964-65; resident pathology U. Iowa, Iowa City, 1965-68; chief resident State U. Iowa Hosp., Iowa City, 1968-69; pathologist, dir. labs. Luth. Hosp., Moline, Ill., 1970—; mem. staffs Moline Pub. Hosp., Franciscan Hosp., Rock Island, Ill. Sec., Rock Island County Blood Bank, 1972-73, v.p., 1973-74; cons. Rock Island Tb Center, 1970-72; profl. del. Am. Cancer Soc., 1971-73; tchr. Luth. Hosp. Sch. Inhalation Therapy, Sch. Nursing, 1970—; med. dir. Royal Neighbors of Am.

Ins. Co., Rock Island; asso dir. Met. Med. Lab., Moline, Quad-Cities Pathologists Group Sch. of Med. Tech.; dir. 7th Street Realty Co. Pres. Rock Island County Cancer Soc., 1970-78; mem. alumni bd. Augustana Coll., Rock Island, 1972-75, bd. dirs., 1976-83, chmn. bd. dirs., 1977-83; sec. med. sect. Nat. Fraternal Congress, 1976—; bd. dirs. Mississippi Valley Regional Blood Bank, 1973—, Ill. div. Am. Cancer Soc., 1980—. Fellow Coll. Am. Pathologists (insp.), Am. Soc. Clin. Pathologists; cons. pathologist, ICON, 1981—; mem. Internat. Acad. Pathologists, Am. Assn. Cytologists, Am. Assn. Blood Banks, Am. Assn. Clin. Scientists, Am. Womans Med. Assn., AMA, Iowa Ill. med. socs., Ill. Pathologists Asso., Rock Island County Hist. Soc., Phi Beta Kappa, Beta Beta Beta. Home: 3904 7th Ave Rock Island IL 61201 Office: Luth Hosp 501 10th Ave Moline IL 61265

ARNELL, RICHARD ANTHONY, radiologist, nuclear medicine physician; b. Chgo., Aug. 21, 1938; s. Tony Frank and Mary Martha (Oberman) Yaki; B.A. (Younker Achievement scholar), Grinnell Coll., 1960; M.D., U. Iowa, 1964; m. Paula Ann Youngberg, June 28, 1964; children—Carla Ann, Paula Marie, Paul Anthony. Intern, Mercy and St. Luke's hosps., Cedar Rapids, Iowa, 1964-65; resident in radiology and nuclear medicine U. Iowa Hosps., 1965-68; practice medicine specializing in radiology and nuclear medicine, Moline, Ill., 1968—; mem. Moline Radiology Assos., 1968—, v.p., 1970-78, sec., 1978—, trustee pension and profit plan, 1979—; mem. staff Luth. Hosp., Moline, dir. continuing med. edn. program for physicians, 1979—, bd. dirs., 1977-83; mem. staff Moline Pub. Hosp., Hammond-Henry Dist. Ill., Geneseo, Ill.; trustee Midstate Found. for Med. Care, 1975-79, exec. com., 1976-79; v.p. Quad City HMO Health Plan, 1979; clin. lectr. U. Iowa, 1980—. Supt. Sunday Ch. Sch. St. John's Luth. Ch., Rock Island, Ill., 1974-79, mem. ch. cabinet, 1975-76; del. Chs. United of Scott and Rock Island counties, Ill., 1977; mem. nat. exec. com. Augustana Coll., Rock Island, Ill., 1977-81; bd. dirs. Luth. Hosp. Found., 1981-84, pres., 1982-84; bd. dirs. Quad Cities Health Care Resources, Inc., 1984—; chmn. Luth. Health Care Found., 1984—. Recipient David Theophillus trophy for outstanding athlete Grinnell Coll., 1960; diplomate Am. Bd. Radiology, Am. Bd. Nuclear Medicine. Mem. Am. Coll. Radiology, Ill. Radiol. Soc., Am. Coll. Nuclear Medicine, Soc. Nuclear Medicine, AMA, Ill. (ho. of dels. 1974-79), Rock Island County (exec. com. 1974-79, peer-rev. com. 1975-79), Iowa-Ill. Central (pres.-elect 1977, pres. 1978) med. socs., Central Ill. Med. Assn. (v.p. 1977, pres. 1978), Ind. Physicians Assn. Western Ill. (dir. 1984—, v.p. 1985), World Med. Assn., Tri-City Med. Jour. Club (sec.-treas. 1972-77), Am. Coll. Med. Imaging. Club: Short Hills Country. Home: 3904 7th Ave Rock Island IL 61201 Office: 1505 7th St Moline IL 61265

ARNESEN, PAUL MUSAUS, orthopedic surgeon, educator; b. Bklyn., Feb. 12, 1923; s. Sigurd J. and Martha Marie (Musaus) A.; m. Dorothy May, June 22, 1946; children—Paul Roholt, Glenn David, Marilyn Ruth, Phillip Bruce. B.A., NYU, 1943, M.D., 1947. Diplomate Am. Bd. Orthopedic Surgery. Intern, Bethesda Hosp., St. Paul, 1947-48; resident Columbia Hosp., Milw., 1951-55, Children's Hosp., Milw., 1953-54; practice medicine specializing in orthopedic surgery, Fond du Lac, Wis., 1955-58, Orthopedics and Fracture Clinic, Mankato, 1974-76, P.M. Arnesen, M.D., P.A., Mankato, 1976—; asst. prof. U. Minn. Med. Sch., Mpls., 1958-64; clin. asst. prof., 1964—. Campaign mgr. Arnulf Ueland for State Senate, Mankato. Served to lt. cdr. USNR, 1943-45, 49-51. Fellow Am. Acad. Orthopedic Surgeons. Republican. Lutheran. Home and Office: 75 Teton Ln Mankato MN 56001

ARNETT, GREGORY KIM, civil engineer; b. Peoria, Ill., Oct. 3, 1954; s. Paul Dee and Eula Mae (Leuthold) A.; m. Sandra Jean Branan, May 22, 1976. B.S. in Civil Engring., Bradley U., Peoria, Ill., 1976. Registered profl. engr., Ill. Civil Engr., Freeman United Coal Mining Co., Canton, Ill., 1976—. Mem. Nat. Soc. Profl. Engrs., Ill. Soc. Profl. Engrs. Home: 1430 E Sycamore St Canton IL 61520 Office: PO Box 570 Canton IL 61520

ARNETT, JERRY BUTLER, systems study engineer; b. Pike County, Ohio, July 19, 1938; s. Lucian Clinton and Marjorie Gray (Dunkle) A.; m. Sharon Lee Hossler, Aug. 11, 1962; children—Katherine Marie, David Scott. B.S., Ohio U., 1960, M.S., 1963; Ph.D., N.Mex. State U., 1967. Research engr. N.Am. Aviation, Los Angeles, 1962-64; sr. engr. Gen. Dynamics Co., Ft. Worth, 1967-71, San Diego, 1971-73; staff scientist Technology Inc., Dayton, Ohio, 1973-76; radar engr. BOM Services Co., Dayton, 1976-77; systems study engr. U.S. Air Force, Wright-Patterson AFB, Ohio, 1977—. Contbr. numerous articles to profl. publs. Mem. Air Force Assn., Sigma Xi, Sigma Pi Sigma. Home: 3491 Clar Von Dr Beavercreek OH 45430 Office: Aeronautical Systems Div Wright Patterson AFB OH 45433

ARNEY, MARCIA SHARI, consultant pharmacist; b. Bethany, Mo., May 11, 1951; d. Trevlyn P. and Charlene Harrison; m. William Propst Arney, Aug. 4, 1970; children—Carolyn Gay, David Harrison. Student William Jewell Coll., 1969-70; B.A. cum laude, Graceland Coll., 1973; B.S. in Pharmacy, Drake U., 1980. Registered pharmacist, Iowa, Mo. Pharmacy intern Drug Mart Pharmacy, West Des Moines, Iowa, 1979; relief pharmacist Medicine Store, Ankeny, Iowa, 1981; pres. Pharmacy Research and Cons., Inc., Norwalk, Iowa, 1981—. Fellow Am. Soc. Cons. Pharmacists; mem. Iowa Pharmacists Assn., Am. Pharm. Assn., Republican. Club: Bethany Country (Mo.). Lodges: Order of Eastern Star, Rainbow Girls. Home and Office: Pharmacy Research and Cons Inc 1200 N Cherry Pkwy Norwalk IA 50211

ARNOLD, CHARLES PARKER, telephone company executive; b. Salem, Nebr., Apr. 23, 1933; s. L.G. and Dollie E. (Schultz) A.; student U. Mich., 1969; m. Janet Ellen Hook, Mar. 8, 1958; children—John Charles, Andrew Parker. Garage serviceman Lincoln Telephone Co. (Nebr.), 1950-51, frameman, 1951-52, combinationman, 1956-57, comml. rep., 1957, service engr., 1957-62, area sales supr., 1962-65, sales supr., 1965-66, field comml. supr., 1966-67, gen. comml. supt., 1967-73, 2d v.p. comml., 1973-76, v.p. customer services, 1976-82, sr. v.p., 1982—. Bd. dirs. Better Bus. Bur., 1968-71; bd. dirs. Better Lincoln Com., 1965-71, pres., 1965; mem. exec. bd. Cornhusker council Boy Scouts Am., 1964-76, pres., 1966, v.p., 1967, 68; adv. bd. Salvation Army, 1981-83; bd. dirs. Community Emergency Shop, 1963-72, Contact Center, Inc., 1980-84; pres. Lincoln Center Assn., 1980, dir., 1977-85; Lancaster County chmn. Nebr. Heart Assn., 1969. Served with USN, 1952-56. Named Lincoln's Young Man of Yr., Lincoln Jaycees, 1964. Mem. Frank H. Woods Telephone Pioneer Assn., U.S. Ind. Telephone Assn. (chmn. comml. subcom. 1979-82, mem. customer services com. 1981, mktg. and news service com. 1985-86), Nebr. Telephone Assn. (pres. 1972-73, dir. 1970-73), Am. Legion, Lincoln C. of C. (dir. 1961-62, 71-74, 81-83). Republican. Clubs: Hillcrest Country, Lincoln U., Nebraska, Masons, Shriners, Rotary (pres. 1977-78). Home: 1620 Brent Blvd Lincoln NE 68506 Office: 1440 M St Lincoln NE 68508

ARNOLD, DEAN EDWARD, anthropology educator; b. Sioux Falls, S.D., Aug. 2, 1942; s. Eldon Earl and Reva Iola (Marquette) A.; m. June Ann Trottier, June 22, 1968; children—Michelle Rene, Andrea Celeste. B.A. in Anthropology, Wheaton Coll., 1964; M.A. in Anthropology, U. Ill., 1967, Ph.D., 1970. Asst. prof. anthropology Pa. State U., University Park, 1969-72; Fulbright lectr., vis. prof. anthropology Universidad Nacional San Antonio Abad del Cuzco, Cuzco, Peru, 1972-73; asst. prof. Wheaton Coll. (Ill.), 1973-77, assoc. prof., 1977-82, prof., 1982—; vis. fellow Clave Hall, Cambridge U., Eng., 1985. Nat. Def. Fgn. Lang. fellow, 1966-69; Fulbright research fellow, Yucatan, Mex., 1984. Fellow AAAS; mem. Am. Anthrop. Assn., Soc. Am. Archaeology, Ill. Archaeol. Survey, Chgo. Anthrop. Soc. (sec. 1975-77), Inst. Andean Studies, Soc. Med. Anthropology, Fulbright Alumni Assn., Sigma Xi. Democrat. Presbyterian. Author: Ceramic Theory and Cultural Process, 1985. Contbr. numerous articles to profl. jours. Office: Dept Sociology-Anthropology Wheaton Coll Wheaton IL 60187

ARNOLD, DUANE, JR., utility company official; b. Cedar Rapids, Iowa, Apr. 24, 1950; s. Duane and Henrietta (Dows) A.; A.A., Wentworth Mil. Acad., 1970; B.A., Coe Coll., 1971; postgrad. U. Mich., 1981; m. Mary Colleen Geraghty, Aug. 28, 1971; children—Duane Joseph, Mary Brigid, Stephen Richard and Kevin Sutherland (twins). With Iowa Electric Light & Power Co., Cedar Rapids, 1970—, supt. transp., 1977-81, dir. purchasing, stores and transp., 1981—; dir. Dows Real Estate Co., Dows Farms Inc., Dows Manifi Dairys. First aid chmn. local chpt., bd. dirs. ARC, 1976—, Cerebral Palsy, Linn County Emergency Bd., 1976—; dep. sheriff Linn County Sheriff's Office, 1972—; bd. dirs. Cedar Rapids Symphony. Mem. Soc. Automotive Engrs. (governing bd.), Nat. Assn. Fleet Adminstrs., Edison Electric Inst. (dir.), Jaycees, C. of C., Sports Car Club Am., Porsche Club Am., Am. Biog. Inst. Research Assn. Republican. Presbyterian. Office: Iowa Electric Light & Power Co 200 1st St Cedar Rapids IA 52401 Home: 530 Knollwood Dr SE Cedar Rapids IA 52403

ARNOLD, LEONARD CHARLES, physician, lawyer; b. Chgo., Aug. 26, 1921; s. Charles L. and Bessie (Schmigelsky) A.; B.S., Northwestern U., 1943, M.B., Chgo. Med. Sch., 1946, M.D., 1947; LL.B., John Marshall Law Sch., 1965, J.D., 1970; m. Janet Lorraine Bloom, Apr. 11, 1943 (div. Dec. 1961); children—Larry I. and Gary R. (twins), Bruce R., Leslie M.; m. Jeannette G. Zini, Nov. 14, 1962 (dec. July 1971); m. Dawn J. Cheskes Fennema, Apr. 13, 1973; children—Bradley Todd Cheskes, Chad Douglas. Intern Edgewater Hosp., Chgo., 1946-47; gen. practice medicine, Chgo., 1947—; mem. attending staff Edgewater Hosp.; admitted to Ill. bar, 1965; practice law, Chgo., 1968—; instr. medico-legal seminar DePaul U. Coll. of Law; lectr. medico-legal subjects John Marshall Coll. Law, Chgo. Med. Sch. Served as capt. M.C., AUS, 1952-54. Recipient Disting. Alumni award John Marshall Coll. Law. Fellow Am. Coll. Legal Medicine, Am. Acad. Family Practice (charter); mem. Chgo. Acad. Law and Medicine (co-founder), Acad. Psychosomatic Medicine, Ill. Bar Assn., Chgo. Bar Assn., Tau Delta Phi. Co-editor: Med. Trial Technique Quarterly. Home: 1055 Starr Rd Winnetka IL 60093 Med Office: 5701 N Ashland Ave Chicago IL 60660 Legal Office: 20 N Clark St Chicago IL 60602

ARNOLD, LYNN ELLIS, metallurgical engineer; b. Cin., Nov. 17, 1934; s. Leslie Lee and Emma R. (Betscher) A.; Metall. Engr., U. Cin., 1957; M.S. in Mech. Engring., U. Ill., 1959. Grad. asst. U. Ill., Urbana, 1957-59; with Xtek, Inc., Cin., 1959—, sales mgr., mgr. tech. service, 1984—. Served with USAF, 1958-59. Registered profl. engr., Ohio. Fellow Am. Soc. Metals (past pres. Cin. chpt., mem. tech. div. bd., 1981-84; Wm. H. Eisenman Meml. award 1979), AAAS; mem. Nat. (past chmn. indsl. div., past v.p.), Ohio (past pres. Cin. chpt., Young Engr. award 1965) socs. profl. engrs., ASME (past pres. Cin. sect., past pres. Ohio council), Soc. Mfg. Engrs. (past pres. Cin. chpt.), Cin. Tech. and Sci. Socs. Council (past pres.; Community Service award 1979), Engring. Soc. Cin. (past pres.), Cin. Mgmt. Assn. (past pres.), Cin. Editors Assn. (past pres.), Tool Steel Mgmt. Club (past pres.), U. Cin. Engring. Alumni Assn. (past pres.; Disting. Alumnus award 1979), SAR (past pres. Cin. chpt.), Audubon Soc. Ohio (past pres.), Ohio Audubon Council (past pres.), Am. Gear Mfg. Assn. (chmn. metallurgy and materials com.), AIME (roll tech. com.), Tau Beta Pi, Alpha Sigma Mu, Alpha Phi Omega, Pi Delta Epsilon, Alpha Chi Sigma. Republican. Methodist. Author articles in field. Home: 5154 Montgomery Rd Cincinnati OH 45212 Office: 11451 Reading Rd Cincinnati OH 45241

ARNOLD, MARY ANN, mathematical statistician; b. Louisville, Dec. 8, 1938; d. Stanley A. Gatewood and Mary Elizabeth (Church) G.; m. Gabriel Thomas Arnold, July 2, 1960; 1 child, Gabriel T., II. A.B., Spalding Coll., 1960. Math. statistician Bur. of Census, Jeffersonville, Ind., 1967—. Mem. Am. Statis. Assn., Internat. Assn. of Survey Statisticians, Am. Soc. Quality Control. Roman Catholic. Avocation: walking. Home: Route 2 Box 204 Georgetown IN 47122 Office: Bur of Census 1201 E 10th St Jeffersonville IN 47132

ARNOLD, ROBERT LLOYD, art educator, artist; b. Buffalo, June 28, 1940; s. J. Lloyd and Elsie (Klepzig) A.; m. Carole W. Walters, July 29, 1973; 1 child, Leah. B.S., SUNY-Buffalo, 1966; M.S., Fla. State U., 1968; Ed.D., Ind. U., 1972. Asst. prof. Ohio State U., Columbus, 1970-76, assoc. prof., 1976—. One-man shows include Ohio State U., 1979, Ashland Coll., 1979, Bowling Green State U., 1980. Pres. Columbus Art League, 1979-80, bd. govs., 1981-82. Recipient Lester C. Bush Meml. award, Columbus Mus. of Art, 1974, Drawing award Dollar Savings, Columbus, 1977, Painting award Columbus Mus. of Art, 1979. Mem. Nat. Art Edn. Assn., Ohio Art Edn. Assn. Home: 383 Canyon Dr N Columbus OH 43214 Office: Dept of Art Edn 128 N Oval Mall Columbus OH 43210

ARNOLD, ROSA NELL, medical records administrator; b. Lometa, Tex., Mar. 3, 1931; d. Barney and Veris Alba (Miller) Trammell; m. Charles A. Davis, June 23, 1950; children—Lisa Merle Curtis, Leslie Ann; m. 2d, Bob L. Arnold, Aug. 21, 1971. Student Colo. State U., 1948-50, U. San Francisco, 1969, Sch. Med. Record Adminstrn. Hillcrest Med. Ctr., 1969-70, Mo. So. State Coll., 1971—. Br. librarian Marin County Free Library, Point Reyes, Calif., 1967-69; cons. med. record services Bradshaw Meml. Hosp., Miami, Okla., 1977-79; dir. med. records St. John's Regional Med. Ctr., Joplin, Mo., 1970-82, quality assurance dir., 1982—. Mem. Nat. Assn. Quality Assurance Profls., Mo. Assn. Quality Assurance Profls., Am. Med. Record Assn., Mo. Med. Record Assn. (pres. 1978-79), St. John's Hundred Club, Ozark Orators, Toastmasters Internat. Editor: The Missouri Courier, publ. of Mo. Med. Record Assn., 1975-77. Home: RD 1 Box 8 Seneca MO 64865 Office: 2727 McClelland Blvd Joplin MO 64801

ARNOLD, THOMAS BURTON, physician; b. Mpls., May 29, 1939; s. Duma Carroll and Ann (Whelan) A.; m. Janet Onstad, June 16, 1957 (div. 1977); children—Pamela, Thomas, Virginia Ann. B.A., Dartmouth Coll., 1951; M.D., U. Pa., 1955. Diplomate Am. Bd. Internal Medicine. Rotating intern U. Chgo. Clinics, 1955-56; fellow in internal medicine Mayo Found., Rochester, Minn., 1960-63; practice medicine specializing in internal medicine, Mpls., 1970-77, Edina, Minn., 1977—; mem. staffs Abbott Hosp., Northwestern Hosp., Fairview Hosp., Southdale Hosp.; regional med. dir. Standard Oil Co. Ind., Chgo., 1966—; sr. aviation med. examiner FAA, 1963—; asst. prof. medicine U. Minn., Mpls., 1970—. Served to capt. USAF, 1956-59. Fellow ACP; mem. AMA, Minn. Med. Assn., Hennepin County Med. Soc. Republican. Advocation: gardening. Office: Thomas Arnold & Assocs 681 Southdale Med Bldg 6545 France Ave S Edina MN 55435

ARNOLD, WILLIAM LEE, lawyer; b. Cleve., Oct. 7, 1952; s. William Glosser and Elsie S. (Meyers) A.; m. Ann Louise Clark, Dec. 2, 1978. B.A., Bowling Green State U., 1974; J.D., Cleve. State U., 1977. Bar: Ohio 1977, U.S. Dist. Ct. (no. dist.) Ohio 1977. Asst. gen. counsel Developers Diversified Ltd., Moreland Hills, Ohio, 1977-79, First Union Real Estate Investments Co., 1983—; leasing atty. Jacobs, Visconsi & Jacobs Co., Westlake, Ohio, 1979-83. Mem. Greater Cleve. Bar Assn., Ohio State Bar Assn. Republican (exec. com.). Avocations: travel; reading; listening to short wave radio. Home: 5830 Blair Dr Highland Heights OH 44143 Office: First Union Real Estate Investments Suite 1900 55 Public Sq Cleveland OH 44113

ARNOLDT, ROBERT PATRICK, international banking analyst; b. Chgo., Oct. 16, 1944; s. Frederick Werner and Margaret (O'Callaghan) A.; A.A., Chgo. City Coll., 1970; B.A. in History, Elmhurst (Ill.) Coll., 1973; M.A. in History, Northeastern Ill. U., 1979; m. Patricia Ellen Ruh, Dec. 27, 1970; children—Robert Kevin Patrick, James Matthew Patrick, Kathleen Patricia Maureen, Thomas Michael Patrick, Brian Joseph Patrick. Dist. exec. Boy Scouts Am., Oak Park, Ill., 1970-71; supr. trust dept. Continental Ill. Nat. Bank, Chgo., 1972-77, analyst internat. banking dept., 1977-84, sr. internat. analyst econ. research dept., 1985—; mil. historian and writer, 1975—. Served with U.S. Army, 1965-68. Decorated Bronze Star medal, Air medal, Combat Infantryman's badge. Home: 1134 S Scoville Ave Oak Park IL 60304 Office: 231 S LaSalle St Chicago IL 60693

ARNOLDY, JAMES PETER, hospital facilities manager; b. Rollingstone, Minn., Aug. 18, 1928; s. Theo M. and Margaret O. (Maus) A.; ed. high sch.; m. Johanna Gullickson, Jan. 15, 1954; children—Gilbert, Mary Ann, Jane. Operating engr. Owatonna (Minn.) State Sch., 1956-61; supt. maintenance St. Elizabeth Hosp., Wabasha, Minn., from 1961, now facilities mgr.; tchr. steam engring. course vocat. sch., Winona, Minn., 3 yrs.; lectr. in field. Mem. Wabasha City Council, 1976-78, 83—. Served with U.S. Army, 1951-53; Korea. Mem. Nat. Assn. Power Engrs. (pres.'s award 1977, trustee Minn. assn., dir. Minn. assn. 1981—, merit award 1971), So. Minn. Hosp. Engrs. (pres.'s award 1979), Am. Soc. Hosp. Engring., Am. Legion, VFW. Roman Catholic. Home: 124 E Grant Blvd Wabasha MN 55981 Office: St Elizabeth Hosp 1200 5th Grant Blvd W Wabasha MN 55981

ARNSDORF, MORTON FRANK, medical educator, cardiology researcher; b. Chgo., Ill., Aug. 7, 1940; s. Selmar N. and Irmgard Clara (Steinman) A. B.A. magna cum laude, Harvard U., 1962; M.D., Columbia U., 1966. Diplomate Am. Bd. Internal Medicine. Intern, U. Chgo. Hosps., 1966-67, resident in medicine, 1967-69; fellow in cardiology Columbia-Presbyn. Hosp., N.Y.C., 1969-71; asst. prof. U. Chgo., 1973-78, assoc. prof., 1978-83, prof. medicine, 1983—, chief, sect. cardiology, 1981—; mem. pharmacology study sect. NIH. Author numerous publs. in clin. cardiology, cardiac arrhythmias, cellular electrophysiology. Served to maj. M.C., USAF, 1971-73. Recipient Research Career Devel. award NIH, 1976-81; NIH grantee, 1974—; Chgo. Heart Assn. grantee, 1976-78. Fellow Am. Coll. Cardiology; mem. Am. Heart Assn. (bd. dirs. 1981-83, chmn. exec. com. basic sci. council 1981-83, mem. exec. com. 1977-83, council affairs com. 1981-83, steering com. 1982—), Chgo. Heart Assn. (bd. govs. 1983—), Central Soc. for Clin. Research (councillor 1983-85), Am. Fedn. Clin. Research, AMA, Assn. Univ. Cardiologists, Chgo. Med. Soc., Ill. Med. Soc. Club: Quadrangle (Chgo.).

ARNZEN, JAMES JACOB, construction company executive; b. Leopold, Mo., Mar. 21, 1935; s. William Joseph and Julia Joanna (VanDeven) A.; m. Charlene Doris Struwe, Apr. 26, 1958; 1 child, Alicia Marie. Student pub. schs., Leopold, Mo. Carpenter, Joseph H. Vaterott, Florissant, Mo., 1953-58, 60-62; Riverside Home Builders, Cape Girardeau, Mo., 1962-66; pres., owner James Arnzen Constrn. Co., 1966—. Served with U.S. Army, 1958-60. Mem. Nat. Assn. Home Builders, Home Builders Assn. Mo. (v.p. 1984—), Southeast Mo. Home Builders Assn. (pres. 1984—), Cape Girardeau C. of C. Republican. Roman Catholic. Lodge: Optimist (pres. 1985—). Avocations: flying; golf. Home: James Arnzen Constrn Co Route 2 Box 517D Cape Girardeau MO 63701

ARON, ROBERT HENRY, geography educator; b. Los Angeles, Dec. 24, 1941; s. Herbert L. and Lore (Gunzburger) A.; m. I-Ming, Wang, Mar. 27, 1973; 1 child Rebecca Ann. A.A. in Geography, Santa Monica U., 1963; B.A., UCLA, 1965; M.A., Calif. State Coll.-Long Beach, 1970; Ph.D., Oreg. State U., 1975. Instr. dept. geography E. Los Angeles Jr. Coll., 1970-71; teaching asst. Oreg. State U., Corvallis, 1972-73; instr. Calif. State Coll.-Dominguez Hills, 1975; lectr. Calif. State U.-Northridge, 1975-76; asst. prof., then assoc. prof. Central Mich. U., Mt. Pleasant, 1976-84, prof., 1984—; vis. prof. dept. atmospheric physics Nat. Central U., China, 1983-84. Contbr. articles to profl. jours. Mem. Am. Meterol. Soc., Air Pollution Assn., Assn. Am. Geographers. Home: 1507 Briarwood Mount Pleasant MI 48858 Office: Central Mich U Mount Pleasant MI 48858

ARONOWITZ, JACK LEON, biotechnology and diagnostic manufacturing company executive, consultant; b. Bklyn., Feb. 29, 1940; s. Harry and Evelyn (Kaftal) A.; m. Jeanette T. Sofia, Nov. 9, 1983; children—Eric Scott, Francine Marie. B.S., Poly. Inst. Bklyn., 1960, M.S., 1962, Pres. Hall Labs, Plainview, N.Y., 1960-67; v.p. Internat. Hosp. Supply Corp., N.Y.C., 1967-68; dir. labs. Sigma Chem. Co., St. Louis, 1968-70; v.p., tech. dir. Reliable Chem. Co., St. Louis, 1970-74; pres., tech. dir. Leon Industries Inc., St. Charles, Mo., 1974-83; pres., chief exec. officer Technimed Corp., St. Charles, 1983—; instr. analytical chemistry C.W. Post U., Greenvale, N.Y., 1964-65; panel mem., lectr. Tissue Culture Soc., Lake Placid, N.Y., 1978-80; lectr. clin. and biochem. procedures, 1972-80. Author: (with others) Growth Requirements of Vertebrate Cells in Vitro, 1982. Patentee multi purpose mixer, 1960. Scoutmaster St. Louis Boy Scouts Am., 1974, 77. Mem. Empire State Soc. Med. Tech., Am. Assn. Exfoliative Cytologists, Am. Assn. Clin. Chemists, Am. Chem. Soc., Registry Med. Technologists Internat. Republican. Jewish. Club: Bellerose Rod and Gun. Avocations: pilot; outdoor sports; hunting; fishing.

ARONSON, DAVID EMMERT, clinical psychologist, consulting psychologist; b. Syracuse, N.Y., May 2, 1953; s. Manuel and Ruth (Hammer) A.; m. Dee A. Emmert, July 19, 1980; 1 child, Benjamin Owen Emmert-Aronson. B.A., SUNY-Buffalo, 1975; M.A., Kent State U., 1977, Ph.D., 1980. Lic. psychologist, Ohio, N.J. Intern in psychology Albany (N.Y.) Med. Coll., 1978-79; asst. dir. Kent State U. psychology clinic, 1979-80; clin. psychologist Alliance Mental Health Clinic (Ohio), 1980-82; adj. asst. prof. psychology Kent State U., 1980—; cons. psychologist Massillon (Ohio) State Hosp., 1981-85, dir. psychology, 1985—; pvt. practice psychology, Cuyahoga Falls, Ohio, 1981—; psychologist supr. Child and Adolescent Service Center, Canton, Ohio, 1982—. Mem. Am. Psychol. Assn., Midwest Psychol. Assn., Eastern Psychol. Assn., Ohio Psychol. Assn., N.J. Psychol. Assn., State Assn. Psychologists and Psychology Assts., Contbr. articles to profl. jours. Home: 2524 Balmoral Dr Akron OH 44313

ARORA, GULSHAN K. (JIM), stair treads and walkway products manufacturing executive; b. India, Jan. 2, 1941; came to U.S., 1967, naturalized, 1974; s. Ganesh Das and Vidya Wati (Gulati) A.; B.S. in Mech. Engring., U. Jammu and Kashimir, 1965; M.S. in Indsl. Engring., Wayne State U., Detroit, 1968, M.B.A., 1973; m. Urmil Jeirath, Feb. 22, 1970; children—Poonam, Geeta. Indsl. engr. Ford Motor Co., Dearborn, Mich., 1968-75; mgr. cost analysis Premier Indsl. Corp., Wooster, Ohio, 1975-77; mem. corp. staff Figgie Internat. Inc., Willoughby, Ohio, 1977-78; mgr. mfg. engring. Flow Control div. Rockwell Internat. Corp., Barberton, Ohio, 1978-80; pres., chief exec. officer, dir. Wooster Products Inc., 1980—. Mem. Am. Prodn. and Inventory Control Soc. Office: 1000 Spruce St Wooster OH 44691

ARRATHOON, LEIGH ADELAIDE, medievalist, editor; b. N.Y.C., Nov. 30, 1942; d. Henry and Peggy Adelaide (Weed) A.; m. Raymond Arrathoon, June 10, 1967. Cours de Vacances at U. de Genève, Lausanne, Lille at Boulogne, 1961-63; A.B. in French and Spanish, Hunter Coll., 1963; M.A. in French, Stanford U., 1966, M.A. in Spanish, 1968; M.A. in Medieval French Lit., Princeton U., 1975, Ph.D., 1975. With UN Secretariat, N.Y.C., 1963-64; tchr. Spanish and French, Convent of Sacred Heart, Menlo Park, Calif., 1966-67; asst. prof. Spanish, Rider Coll., Trenton, N.J., 1970-71; pub. editor-in-chief Solaris Press, Troy, Idaho, 1975-80, Rochester, Mich., 1980—. Scholar, Centre d'Art Dramatique, 1957. Mem. MLA, Medieval Acad. Am., Courtly Lit. Soc., Sigma Delta Pi, Alpha Gamma Delta. Editor and contbr. The Craft of Fiction: Essays in Medieval Poetics, 1984; editor, translator The Lady of Vergi, 1984; Chaucer and the Craft of Fiction, 1985; contbr. articles and book revs. to profl. jours. Office: PO Box 1009 Rochester MI 48063

ARRATHOON, RAYMOND, physicist; b. Teheran, Iran, Sept. 26, 1942; came to U.S., 1945, naturalized, 1951; s. Tigran and Siran (Shanizarian) A.; m. Leigh Adelaide, June 10, 1967. B.S. (Nat. Merit scholar, Regents scholar), Cornell U., 1964; M.S., Calif. Inst. Tech., 1965; Ph.D. (NSF trainee), Stanford U., 1969. Assoc. mem. tech. staff Bell Telephone Labs., Murray Hill, N.J., 1966; mem. tech. staff, 1969-71; vis. research physicist Princeton U. Plasma Physics Lab. (N.J.), 1971-73; sr. research officer Clarendon Lab. dept. physics Oxford (Eng.) U., 1973-74; chmn. bd. Deuterium Mfg. facility Solaris Ltd., Troy, Idaho, 1974-80; physicist Energy Conversion Devices, Troy, Mich., 1980; assoc. chmn., assoc. prof. dept. elec. and computer engring. Wayne State U., Detroit, 1981—; head sci. div. Solaris Press, Rochester, Mich., 1977—. Mem. Am. Phys. Soc., Optical Soc. Am., IEEE, Sigma Xi. Congregationalist. Club: West Side Tennis (Forest Hills, N.Y.). Author: Advances in Lasers, 1974; contbr. chpts. to books, articles to profl. jours.; patentee in field. Office: PO Box 1009 Rochester MI 48063

ARRINGTON, DOROTHY M. CHRISTIAN, dietitian; b. Birmingham, Ala., July 25, 1929; d. Noah and Maggie Louise (Cook) Christian; B.S. (scholar), Tuskegee Inst., 1950; m. W.C. Arrington, Apr. 25, 1950; children—Kathleen Yvonne, William Curtis, Maragret Elaine, Christopher Jay. Dietary technician Michael Reese Hosp., Chgo., 1952-53; library clk. Chgo. Public Library, 1959-61; lunchroom mgr. Chgo. Bd. Edn., 1961-62; dietitian-mgr. St. Peter Lutheran Sch., 1962-64; adminstrv. dietitian Mercy Hosp., Chgo., 1965-77, nutritionist Mercy Hosp. Diagnostic and Treatment Center, 1977—, nutritionist Calorie Anonymous; clin. instr. U. Ill.-Chgo. Mem. parent-tchr. leagues St. Peter Luth. Sch., 1957-76, Luther High Sch. S., 1964-74, Morgan Park High Sch., 1974-76; mem. fund raising com. Whitney Young High Sch. Band Booster Club, 1977-79; active Beverly Area Planning Assn., 1974—. Mem. Am. Dietetics Assn., Ill. Dietetics Assn., Chgo. Dietetic Assn., Dietitians in Gen. Clin. Practice, Diabetes Educators of Chgo Area. Democrat. Lutheran. Club: Tuskegee Inst. Alumni. Office: Mercy Hosp Diagnostic and Treatment Center Stevenson Expressway at King Dr Chicago IL 60616

ARRIVEE, SALLY D., librarian; b. Chgo., Sept. 26, 1949; d. Charles Louis and Dorothy Jane (Mendenhall) A. B.A., Western Mich. U., 1971, M.L.S., 1972. Head children's services Portage Pub. Library (Mich.), 1971-80; dir. Riverview Pub. Library (Mich.), 1980-82; dir. Mitchell Pub. Library, Hillsdale, Mich., 1982—. Mem. City Mgrs. Cable Commn., 1983—. Mem. ALA, Mich. Library Assn. Roman Catholic. Office: Mitchell Pub Library 22 N Manning Hillsdale MI 49242

ARSENOVIC, ALEXANDAR ILIJA, physician; b. Beograd, Yugoslavia, Dec. 19, 1928; came to U.S., 1969, naturalized, 1975; s. Ilija P. and Ann J. (Muk) A.; M.D., U. Belgrade, 1953; m. Vukosava Dokovic; children—Ilija, Nanka. Intern, U. Beograde, 1954-55; ednl. asst. Acad. Sci. Serbia, Inst. Med. Research, 1954, 55; practice medicine specializing in internal medicine, Belgrade, 1955-59; chief lab., Belgrade, Yugoslavia, 1961-68; resident in family practice Edgewater Hosp., Chgo., 1969-70; chief internal medicine dept. Downtown Hosp., Kansas City Med. Center, 1978-80; internist VA Hosp., Topeka, 1980—. Diplomate Am. Bd. Family Practice, Am. Bd. Quality Assurance. Mem. AMA (awards 1974, 78), Am. Geriatrics Soc., N.Y. Acad. Scis., Am. Coll. Utilization Physicians. Methodist. Author: Viral Cause of Cancer, 1956. Office: Room 145B 2200 Gage Blvd Topeka KS 66622

ARSLAN, ORHAN ENAYET OMAR, anatomist, veterinary scientist; b. Kirkuk, Iraq, May 15, 1951; came to U.S., 1981; s. Enayet Omar and Zubeydeh (Ahmed) A. B.V.M.S., D.V.M., U. Baghdad (Iraq), 1973; Ph.D., Hacettepe U., Ankara, Turkey, 1979. Postdoctoral fellow Med. Sch., 1981-82; asst. anatomy Hacettepe U., Ankara, Turkey, 1975-79, instr., 1979-81; asst. prof. Nat. Coll. Chiropractic, Lombard, Ill., 1982—. Mem. Found. for Advancement Edn. in Scis., AVMA. Home: 1115 Lorraine Rd Apt 139 Wheaton IL 60187 Office: Nat Coll Chiropractic 200 E Roosevelt Rd Lombard IL 60148

ARTER, TERRENCE JOHN, computer consultant; b. Aurora, Ill., Aug. 21, 1946; s. Clark Melvin and Rita (Frieders) A. A.A., in Computer Sci., Highland Community Coll. (Kans.), 1972; B.A. in Behavior Sci., Nat. Coll. Edn., Evanston, Ill., 1980. Programmer, analyst Bankers Life and Casualty Co., Chgo., 1972-73; lead programmer, analyst Time-Life Publs., Chgo., 1973-75; supr. Blue Cross/Blue Shield, Chgo., 1975-81; project mgr. Cognos, Evanston, 1981—. Served with U.S. Army, 1968-72. Mem. Assn. Systems Mgmt., Ind. Computer Cons. Assn., Assn. Inst. Cert. Computer Professionals. Avocations: Micro computers, outdoor sports. Home: 5812 N Magnolia Ave Chicago IL 60660 Office: Cognos 722 Brown Ave Evanston IL 60202

ARTHAUD, JOHN BRADLEY, pathologist; b. Wheeling, Mo., May 7, 1939; s. Lawrence Frank and Charlotte Ruth (White) A.; m. Elizabeth Burton, Oct. 3, 1966 (div. 1975); children—Victoria, Catherine, Gwyneth; m. Saleme Rose Michael, Nov. 18, 1977. A.B., U. Mo., 1960, M.D., 1965; M.S., U. Tex. Health Sci. Ctr., 1975. Diplomate Am. Bd. Pathology. Asst. pathologist Peter B. Brigham Hosp., Boston, 1971-72; asst. prof. U. Tex. Med. Sch., Houston, 1972-77; assoc. prof. U. Mo. Med. Sch., Columbia, 1977-79; pathologist Lab. Clin. Medicine, Sioux Falls, S.D., 1979-80, Pathology Profl. Services, Columbia, 1980—. Author: The Emile Arthaud Family Genealogy, 1968. Contbr. articles to profl. jours. and chpt. to book. Served to maj. USPHS, 1968-70. Fellow Am. Soc. Clin. Pathologists, Coll. Am. Pathologists; mem. AMA, Phi Beta Kappa, Alpha Omega Alpha. Avocation: genealogy. Home: 3201 Woodkirk Dr Columbia MO 65203 Office: Pathology Profl Services 2703 Clark Ln Columbia MO 65202

ARTHUR, BARBARA JOHNS, medical technologist; b. Feb. 19, 1925; d. Tony and Warda Johns; m. William J. Arthur, Sept. 5, 1948 (dec. 1958); children—Douglas Reed, Rex Rene, Chad A., Janet Susan. B.S., U. Pitts., 1948. Cert. med. technologist. Resident, St. Luke's Hosp. Sch. Med. Tech., 1950-51; med. technologist offices of H. P. Boughnou, M.D., and Philip Byers, M.D., 1952; supr. clin. chemistry St. Mary's Hosp. Lab., 1953-55; supr. clin. chemistry, routine metabolites, U. Kans. Med. Ctr., Kansas City, 1959—, instr. routine chemistry med. technologists. Mem. Am. Soc. Clin. Pathologists. Republican. Episcopalian. Home: 5532 Aberdeen Fairway KS 66205 Office: 39th and Rainbow Sts Kansas City KS 66103

ARTHUR, JAMES WILLIAM, constrn., fin., devel. co. exec.; b. Akron, Ohio, Jan. 29, 1940; s. William L. and Ethel H. A.; B.A., Kent State U., 1963; m. Nancy L. Sage, June 28, 1964; children—William, Walter, Jennifer. Broker, Merrill Lynch Pierce Fenner & Smith, Akron, 1964-71; owner, pres. Arthur Constrn. Co., Kent, Ohio, 1971-73; pres. Trans Ohio Land Corp., Kent, 1972—; pres. Mahoning River Valley Corp., Kent, 1978—. Mem. Village Council, Sugar Bush Knolls, 1981—. Served with U.S. Army, 1957. Home: 1515 Lake Martin Dr Kent OH 44240 Office: 1640 Franklin Ave Kent OH 44240

ARTINIAN, HARRY LEOPOLD MARTINUS, automotive executive; b. Amsterdam, The Netherlands, Apr. 26, 1951; came to Can., 1951; s. Harry Richard and Hendrika (Baars) A.; 1 child, Ashley Theresa Rose. B.S., Brock U., St. Catharines, Ont., Can., 1973; M.B.A., U. Windsor, Ont., 1975. Profit and cost analyst Chrysler Corp., Windsor, Ont., 1976-78; supr. profit analysis Ford Motor Co., Windsor, 1978-84, statistician, Dearborn, Mich., 1984—; cons. transp., retail industries; instr. U. Windsor, 1974-85. Advisor, strategist Progressive Conservative Party, Windsor, Toronto, Ottawa, 1984; mem. Planning and Adv. Com., Windsor, 1985, Windsor in 80's Com., 1984, Provincial Council, Windsor, 1984-85. Mem. Am. Soc. Quality Control, Am. Statis. Assn. Armenian Orthodox. Avocations: reading; bowling; golf. Home: 350 Elliott St E Apt 709 Windsor ON N9A 6Y7 Office: Ford Motor Co World Hdqrs Room 524 Dearborn MI 48121

ARTS, DAVID J., real estate company executive, accountant; b. Carroll, Iowa, June 21, 1947; s. L. David and Margaret N. Arts; B.A., Loras Coll., Dubuque, Iowa, 1969; C.P.A., U. Ill., 1974; m. L. Elizabeth Kennedy, Sept. 7, 1968; children—Peter J., Katherine L., Margaret K. Staff acct. Deloitte Haskins & Sells, C.P.A.s, Chgo., 1969-71; controller, asst. treas. Budget Rent A Car Corp., Chgo., 1971-78; v.p. fin. Century 21 Real Estate Corp. No. Ill., Chgo., 1978—; cons. Phoenix Systems; pvt. practice acctg., Western Springs, Ill., 1977—. Treas., St. John's Theatre Guild, 1971-78. C.P.A., Ill. Mem. Am. Inst. C.P.A.s, Ill. Soc. C.P.A.s. Office: 9501 W Devon Ave Rosemont IL 60018

ARTZT, EDWIN LEWIS, consumer products company executive; b. N.Y.C., Apr. 15, 1930; s. William and Ida A.; B.J., U. Oreg., 1951; m. Ruth Nadine Martin, May 12, 1950; children—Wendy Anne, Karen Susan, William M., Laura Grace, Elizabeth Louise. Account exec. Glasser Gailey Advt. Agy., Los Angeles, 1952-53; with Procter & Gamble Co., Cin., 1953—, brand mgr. advt. dept., 1956-58, asso. brand promotion mgr., 1958-60, brand promotion mgr., 1960, 62-65, copy mgr., 1960-62, advt. mgr. paper products div., 1965-68, mgr. products food div., 1968-69, v.p., 1969, v.p., acting mgr. coffee div., 1970, v.p., group exec., 1970-75, dir., 1972-75, 80—, group v.p. Europe, Belgium, 1975-80, exec. v.p. internat., 1980-84, pres. internat., vice chmn. bd., 1984—. Past chmn. residential div. United Appeal; past chmn. Public Library Capital Funds campaign; past dist. chmn. Capital Fund Rasing dr. Boy Scouts Am., past leadership tng. chmn.; past chmn. advt. com. Sch. Tax Levy, County Govt. Issue; past trustee Kansas City Philharmonic, Nutrition Found., Boys' Clubs Greater Cin.; past bd. dirs. Kansas City Lyric Theater; past bd. govs. Kansas City Art Inst. Mem. Am. C. of C. Belgium (v.p.), Conf. Bd. Europe (adv. council), Internat. C. of C. (exec. com. U.S. council), Nat. Fgn. Trade Council. Clubs: Queen City, Cin. Country, Comml., Camargo (Cin.). Office: Procter & Gamble Co PO Box 599 Cincinnati OH 45201

ARVEDON, RICHARD DAVID, lawyer; b. N.Y.C., Dec. 11, 1947; s. Kenneth Ronald and Dorothy (Davidson) A. B.A., U. Mass., 1976; J.D., Northeastern U., 1980. Bar: Mass. 1980, Ky. 1982, U.S. Dist. Ct. (we. dist.) Ky. 1982. Sr. pub. advocate Dept. Pub. Advocacy Ky., 1981—. Home: 418 Shelby St Frankfort KY 40601 Office: Dept Pub Advocacy State Office Bldg Annex Frankfort KY 40601

ARVIN, CHARLES STANFORD, librarian; b. Loogootee, Ind., Apr. 17, 1931; s. Leland Stanford and Mary Hope (Armstrong) A.; A.B., Wayne State U., 1953, postgrad., 1956-57; M.A. in Library Sci., U. Mich. 1960. Asst. divisional Librarian U. Mich. Natural Sci. Library, 1960-62; head reference Genesee County Library, Flint, Mich., 1962-67, 77-83, head central services, 1967-77, head acquisitions, 1983—. Served with AUS, 1953-56. Mem. ALA, Mich. Library Assn., Mich., Ind., Genesee County hist. socs., ACLU. Club: Flint Library. Editor: Flint Geneal. Quar., 1981—. Home: 702 W Oliver St Owosso MI 48867 Office: 4195 W Pasadena St Flint MI 48504

ARZOUMANIDIS, GREGORY G., chemist; b. Thessaloniki, Greece, Aug. 16, 1936; came to U.S., 1964, naturalized, 1976; s. Gerasimos and Sophia A.; B.S.-M.S. in Chemistry, U. Thessaloniki, Greece, 1959; Ph.D. in Inorganic Chemistry, U. Stuttgart (Germany), 1964; M.B.A., U. Conn., 1979; m. Anastasia Anastasopoulos, Jan. 2, 1966; children—Sophia, Alexis. Research asso. M.I.T., Cambridge, 1964-66; research chemist Monsanto, Everett, Mass., 1966-69; sr. research chemist Am. Cyanamid Co., Stamford, Conn., 1969-72, Stauffer Chem. Co., Dobbs Ferry, N.Y., 1972-79, Amoco Chems. Corp., Naperville, Ill., 1979—. Served to 2d lt. Greek Army, 1959-61. Recipient acad. award, Govt. of W. Ger., 1963. Mem. Am. Chem. Soc., Sigma Xi. Greek Orthodox. Inventor comml. catalysts for polypropylene plastics, new processes; U.S. and fgn. patentee; contbr. articles to sci. jours. Home: 7 S 610 Carriage Way Naperville IL 60540 Office: PO Box 400 Naperville IL 60566

ASBJORNSON, HELEN E. (LONGSTRETH), real estate investment company executive; b. N.Y.C., Dec. 8, 1935; d. Clyde Marion and Elizabeth (Rudolph) Longstreth; B.A., State U. Iowa, 1957, J.D., 1959, postgrad., 1960; M.Ed., Mont. State Coll., 1961; postgrad. U. Minn., 1961-62; m. Norman H. Asbjornson, March 1963; children—Elizabeth Erica, Scott Marion. Mem. bus. adminstrn. staff Northwestern Bell Telephone Co., Omaha, 1959-60; bus. adminstrn. mgr. Diversified Equities, Mpls., 1961; research asst. U. Nebr., 1962; instr. Elkhorn (Nebr.) public schs., 1963-64. Vol. worker Children's Hosp.; active Omaha Symphony Guild, Women's Assn. of Joslyn Art Mus., Omaha Civic Music Assn. Mem. Am. Council Christian Ch., Amvets Aux., C. of C., Am. Legion Aux., State U. Iowa Alumni Assn., AAUW (legis. chmn.), Soc. Liberal Arts, Nat. Vocat. Guidance Assn., Inc., Am. Personnel and Guidance Assn., Inc., Nat. socs. profl. engrs. auxs., Omaha Montessori Soc., Neb. Hist. Soc., Airplane Owners' and Pilots' Assns., Am. Citizens' Forum, Mont. Guidance Assn., DAR (bd. dirs.), Mensa (highest group, Intertel), NOW, Minn. Fencing Assn., Les Amis du Vin, Bacchus Wine Soc., Psi Chi, Kappa Beta Pi (pres. chpt. 1957-58, del. Province conv. 1958). Republican. Protestant. Address: 6442 Margaret's Ln Edina MN 55435

ASBURY, JEAN ANN, hospital executive; b. Charleston, W.Va., Nov. 11, 1947; d. Arnold Crawford and Selma Clara (Bek) A. B.A., Coll. of Wooster, 1969; student Bowling Green State U., 1976—. Editor, mktg. asst. Toledo Trust Co., 1969-71; campaign asst. for fund devel. campaign Ketchum, Inc., Toledo, 1971; grants asst. St. Vincent Med. Center, Toledo, 1971-73; dir. public relations St. Charles Hosp., Oregon, Ohio, 1973-84, mem. adv. bd., 1973-84; mgr. pub. relations for health-related subs. corps. Sisters of Mercy Health System, North, 1982-84; dir. mktg. communications Hillcrest Med. Ctr., 1984—. Pres., Northwest Ohio Regional Alcoholism Council, 1979-81; dist. capt. Am. Cancer Soc. Fund Drive, 1976-80; bd. dirs. First Call for Help, United Way agy., 1980—, pres. bd., 1981—; mem. Northwestern Ohio chpt. Arthritis Found., 1983—. Mem. Hosp. Council Northwest Ohio (chmn. public relations dirs. com. 1976), St. Charles Hosp. Aux., Public Relations Soc. Am., LWV, Ohio Hosp. Assn. (public relations com. 1976-77, 79-80), Am. Soc. Hosp. Public Relations, Ohio Soc. Hosp. Public Relations (charter), Okla. Hosp. Assn., Pub. Relations Soc., Press Club Toledo, Ohio Assn. Hosp. Devel., Am. Mgmt. Assn., AAUW. Presbyterian. Club: Zonta (asst. sec.-treas. 1977-78, sec. 1979-80). Contbr. articles to profl. publs. (Toledo). Home: 1222 E 21st St Tulsa OK 74114 Office: Hillcrest Med Ctr 1120 S Utica Tulsa OK 74104

ASCHER, JAMES JOHN, pharmaceutical executive; b. Kansas City, Mo., Oct. 2, 1928; s. Bordner Fredrick and Helen (Barron) A.; student Bergen Jr. Coll., 1947-48, U. Kans., 1946-47, 49-51; m. Mary Ellen Robitsch, Feb. 27, 1954; children—Jill Denise, James John, Christopher Bordner. Rep., B.F. Ascher & Co., Inc., Memphis, 1954-55, asst. to pres., Kansas City, Mo., 1956-57, v.p., 1958-64, pres., 1965—. Bd. dirs. Childrens Cardiac Center, 1964-70, pres., 1968-70; mem. central governing bd. Children's Mercy Hosp., 1968-80; bd. dirs. Jr. Achievement of Middle Am., 1970—, pres., 1973-76, chmn., 1979-81; edn. chmn. Young Pres.'s Orgn. 6th Internat. Univ. for Pres., Athens, 1975. Served to 1st. lt. inf., U.S. Army, 1951-53; Korea. Decorated Bronze Star, Combat Infantryman's Badge. Mem. Pharm. Mfrs. Assn., Drug, Chem. and Allied Trades Assn., World Bus. Council, Proprietary Assn., Chief Execs. Orgn., Midwest Pharm. Advt. Club, Sales and Advt. Execs. Club, Am. Mgmt. Assn. (pres.'s assn.), Kansas City C. of C., VFW, Delta Chi. Clubs: Lotos, N.Y. Athletic; Kansas City; Mercury; Indian Hills Country (Prairie Village, Kans.); Rotary. Home: 6706 Glenwood Shawnee Mission KS 66204 Office: 15501 W 109th St Lenexa KS 66219

ASCHOM, DONALD F., university administrator; b. LaCrosse, Wis., Mar. 24, 1928; s. George C. and Edna D. Aschom; B.A. in Bus. Adminstrn., Luther Coll., Decorah, Iowa, 1950; postgrad. Northwestern U., Mich. State U.: children—Kenneth, Gail, Janet. High sch. tchr., Sanborn, Iowa, 1952-53; asst. to dir. tng. Traffic Inst., Northwestern, 1953-56; mem. adminstrv. staff Mich. State U., 1956-64, dir. civil def. tng. contract, 1964-65, assoc. dir. ins. program, 1965-66, dir. ins. program, 1966—. Served with AUS, 1950-52. Mem. Nat. Univ. Extension Assn. Republican. Presbyterian. Clubs: Univ. (Mich. State U.), Masons. Home: 2740 Still Valley Dr East Lansing MI 48823 Office: 2 Kellogg Center Mich State Univ East Lansing MI 48824

ASGAR, KAMAL, dentistry educator, consultant; b. Tabriz, Iran, Aug. 28, 1922; s. Salmon and Rogheye Asgarzadeh; m. Safieh Seyedi, Sept. 4, 1948; children—Alexander, Andrew. B.A. in Chemistry, Tech. Coll. Tehran, 1945; M.S., U. Mich., 1948, B.S. in Chem. Engring., 1950, Ph.D., 1959. Paint chemist, Tehran, 1945-46; research asst. U. Mich., Ann Arbor, 1949-56, research assoc., asst. prof., 1956-62, assoc. prof., 1962-66, prof. dentistry, 1966—; cons. U.S. Army, U.S. Navy. Recipient Gibbon award U. Mich., 1963, 70, 80, Hollenback Meml. prize Acad. Operative Dentistry, 1984. Fellow Internat. Coll. Dentistry; mem. Internat. Assn. Dental Research (Souder award 1970), Am. Electron Probe Assn., Am. Soc. Metals, Fedn. Dentaire Internationale. Contbr. articles to sci. jours.; patentee in field. Home: 2240 Belmont St Ann Arbor MI 48104 Office: School of Dentistry University of Michigan Ann Arbor MI 48109

ASH, GALEN LOWELL, police officer, security consultant; b. Bowling Green, Ohio, Feb. 16, 1939; s. Ernest M. and Opel (Kidwell) A.; m. Carol J. Orwig, May 5, 1979; children—Kim, Pam, Marcia, Tom. Student Owens Tech. Coll., Bowling Green State U., U. Va.-Quantico, Ohio State U. Coll. Engring. Chief of police City Police Bowling Green, 1961—; security cons. Continental Distbg. Co., Findlay, Ohio, 1978—, C.W.C. Cos., Findlay, 1978—, Great Scot, Findlay, 1978—, Community Markets, Marysville, Ohio, 1978—; adj. asst. prof. criminal justice Bowling Green State U. Contbr. articles to profl. jours. Chmn., Bowling Green Traffic Commn., 1978—; v.p. Wood County Council on Alcoholism (Ohio), 1978—; nat. chmn. law enforcement com. Nat. Safety Council, 1982-84. Recipient Community Service award C. of C. Bowling Green, 1976, 77, 78; award citation 112th Gen. Assembly Ohio, 1978; Service Above Self award Rotary Club, 1976; named Bus. Assoc. of Yr., Am. Bus. Women's Assn., 1980. Mem. Fraternal Order of Police (v.p. 1965-66), Am. Criminal Justice Assn., Internat. Assn. Chiefs of Police, Ohio Assn. Chiefs of Police (exec. com. 1982—, v.p. 1984-85), Nat. FBI Acad. Assocs., Ohio Crime Prevention Assn. Lutheran. Club: Falcon (Bowling Green). Home: 719 Rosalind Dr Bowling Green OH 43402 Office: Bowling Green Police Div 175 W Wooster St Bowling Green OH 43402

ASH, JAMES BOYD, marketing consultant; b. Haverford, Pa., Feb. 10, 1927; s. Harrison Boyd and Wilda Jane (North) A.; B.S., U. Pa., 1949; M.S., Northwestern U., 1951; m. Iris Gaillard Pond, Mar. 14, 1953; children—Margaret Susan Ash Watkins, Jeffrey Boyd. Mag., newspaper editor, Phila., Lancaster, Coatesville, Pa., 1949-52; asst. mgr. pub. relations Lukens Steel Co., Coatesville, 1952-59; mgr. pub. relations. advt. Borg-Warner Corp., Chgo., 1959-66; dir. pub. info. Perkins & Will Partnership, Chgo., 1966-68; v.p. Crown Center subs. Hallmark Cards, Kansas City, Mo., 1968-69; owner, operator James B. Ash Mktg. Counsel and Service, Shawnee Mission, Kans., 1969—; cons., lectr. in field. Served with inf. and Transp. Corps, U.S. Army, 1945-47; PTO. Mem. Sigma Delta Chi. Methodist. Contbr. articles to profl. archtl., engring., bus. Schs., Soc. Behavioral Medicine, Inst. Advancement Health. 1969—. Home: 2620 W Balmoral Chicago IL 60625 Office: Northwestern U Dental Sch 311 Chicago Ave Chicago IL 60611

ASHBACH, DAVID LAURENCE, internist, nephrologist; b. Chgo., Nov. 17, 1942; s. Sol Henry and Lila Mae A.; A.B., Knox Coll., 1964; M.S., Case Western Reserve U., 1969, M.D., 1970; m. Arlene Rosenthal Nov. 28, 1963; children—Barbara, Deborah, Robert. Intern, Presbyterian-St. Luke's Hosp., Chgo., 1970-71, resident, 1971-73, fellow in nephrology, 1973-75; practice medicine specializing in nephrology, Hammond, Ind., 1975—; mem. staffs St. Margaret's Hosp., Hammond, Ind., Presbyterian-St. Luke's Hosp., Chgo., Meth. Hosp., Gary, Ind., St. Anthony's Hosp., Crown Point, Ind.; instr. Rush Med. Coll.; asst. clin. prof. medicine Ind. U.; asst. prof. health sci. Purdue U. Diplomate Am. Bd. Internal Medicine. Mem. A.C.P., Am. Internat. socs. nephrology. Jewish. Home: 20457 Ithica St Olympia Fields IL 60461 Office: 5500 Hohman Ave Hammond IN 46320

ASHBY, JOHN FORSYTHE, bishop; b. Tulsa, Mar. 26, 1929; s. Thomas Albert and Margaret (Mote) A.; m. Mary Carver, Aug. 12, 1954; children—Anne Carver Ashby Jones, Elizabeth Ashby McBride. B.A., Okla. State U., 1952; M.Div., Episcopal Theol. Sem. of Southwest, Augsin, Tex., 1955, D.D., 1981; postgrad. U. Cambridge (Eng.), 1966-67. Ordained to ministry Episcopal Ch., as deacon, 1955, as priest, 1955. Vicar St. John's Ch., Durant, Okla., 1955-59, St. Peter's Ch., Coalgate, Okla., 1955-59; rector St. Luke's Ch., Ada, Okla., 1959-81; bishop Episcopal Diocese of Western Kans., Salina, 1981—. Chmn. bd. St. John's Mil. Sch., Salina; bd. dirs. St. Francis Boys Homes, Salina. Served to lt. col., chaplain Okla. N.G., 1959-81. James Mills fellow U. Cambridge, 1966-67. Office: PO Box 1383 Salina KS 67402

ASHBY, ROBERT SAMUEL, lawyer; b. Crawfordsville, Ind., July 9, 1916; s. William Wallace and Nellie Ward (Graybill) A.; m. Susan Gatch, June 4, 1949; children—Jean G., Willis G. A.B. with highest honors, Ind. U., 1938; LL.B., Harvard U., 1941. Bar: Ind. 1941, N.Y. 1942. Assoc. Carter, Ledyard & Milburn, N.Y.C., 1941-42; ptnr. Barnes, Hickam, Pantzer & Boyd, Indpls., 1946-81; ptnr. Barnes & Thornburg, Indpls., 1981—; dir. Ind. Nat. Corp., Danner's Inc., other corps. Chmn. Indpls. Mus. Art. Served to lt. comdr. USNR, 1942-46. Mem. ABA, Ind. State Bar Assn., Assn. Bar N.Y. Republican. Congregationalist. Club: Univ. (Meridan Hills, Ind.). Contbr. articles to profl. jours. Home: 7248 N Pennsylvania St Indianapolis IN 46240 Office: 1313 Merchants Bank Bldg Indianapolis IN 46204

ASHBY, WILLARD EDWIN, optometrist; b. Pittsburg, Tex., Jan. 18, 1946; s. Oran Donnaly and Eva Istaline (Bunn) A.; m. Rebecca Ann Keel, Dec. 31, 1966. B.S., Southern Coll. Optometry, 1969, O.D., 1969. Diplomate Am. Bd. Optometry. Staff doctor So. Coll. Optometry, Memphis, Tenn., 1969; practice optometry Longview, Tex., 1970; chief optometry U.S. Air Force bases at McConnell, Kans., Eielson AFB, Alaska, Davis-Montran, Ariz., 1971-80; chief optometry, area eye care coordinator USPHS Indian Health Service, Red Lake, Minn., 1980—. Contbr. articles to Jour. of Safari Club Internat., 1975-76. Served as comdr. USPHS, 1971—. Mem. Commissioned Officers Assn. USPHS, Commissioned Officers Optometric Soc., Nat. Rifle Assn. (life), Sigma Alpha Sigma. Baptist. Club: N. Am. Hunting. Avocations: bow hunting (only person to have taken a white rhino with bow and arrow, Oct. 1984); competitive rifleman; hunter. Home: Rural Route 1 Box 139A Puposky MN 56667 Office: UPHS Indian Hosp Red Lake MN 56671

ASHCRAFT, LAURIE CRAGG, marketing executive; b. Washington, May 28, 1945; d. Richard Edwards and Dorothy (Shawhan) Cragg; B.A., Northwestern U., 1967; m. C. Brian Pendleton, May 20, 1972 (div.); m. 2d, W. Dale Ashcraft, Sept. 3, 1977. Psychol. research analyst Allstate Ins. Co., Northbrook, Ill., 1968-70; project supr. Marsteller, Inc., Chgo., 1970-74; mktg. research mgr. corporate mktg. research dept. Internat. Harvester, Chgo., 1974-76; assoc. dir. mktg. research Libby, McNeill & Libby, Chgo., 1976-78; project mgr. mktg. research S.C. Johnson & Son (Johnson Wax), Racine, Wis., 1978-80; mktg. research mgr. Minnetonka Inc. (Minn.), 1980-82; mgr. Custom Research Inc., 1982—; guest lectr. market research various univs. and assns. Research collaborator: The Coming Matriarchy, 1981. Mem. Am. Mktg. Assn. (chmn. career conf. 1976, pres. chpt. 1986—), Jr. League, Nat. Orgn. Women, Alliance Francaise, Alpha Delta Pi. Club: Woman's Athletic (Chgo.). Office: Custom Research Inc 625 N Michigan Ave Chicago IL 60611

ASHCROFT, JOHN DAVID, governor of Missouri b. Chgo., May 9, 1942; s. J. Robert and Grace Pauline (Larson) A.; m. Janet Elise Roede, Dec. 23, 1967; children—Martha, Jay, Andrew. B.A. in History cum laude, Yale U., 1964; J.D., U. Chgo., 1967. Bar: Mo. Assoc. prof. bus. law S.W. Mo. State U., Springfield, 1968-72; auditor State of Mo., Jefferson City, 1973-75, asst. atty. gen., 1975-76, atty. gen., 1976-85, governor State of Mo., 1985—. Bd. dirs. Greene County chpt. ARC, Sunshine Children's Home, Greater Ozarks chpt. Cystic Fibrosis Found. Mem. ABA, Mo. Bar Assn., Cole County Bar Assn., Nat. Assn. Attys. Gen. Republican. Mem. Assembly of God Ch. Author (with wife), College Law for Business, It's the Law; co-rec. artist albums Truth, In the Spirit of Liberty. Office: Office Governor PO Box 720 Jefferson City MO 65102*

ASHFORD, LARRY WAYNE, structural engineer, consultant; b. Waco, Tex., Sept. 19, 1949; s. Sheldon Earl and Ruby Lee (Webb) A.; m. Nancy Jane Simon, June 15, 1974; 1 child, Ashley Jayne. B.S. in Mech. Engring., Okla. State U., 1972; M.S. in Engring. Mechanics, U. Mo.-Rolla, 1980. Registered profl. engr., Mo. Lead engr. McDonnell Aircraft Co., St. Louis, 1972—; cons. engr. Recipient Outstanding award engring. U.S. Army Advanced Material Concepts Agy., Alexandria, Va., 1972. Avocations: racquetball; snow skiing; water skiing. Home: 14633 Gravelle Ln Florissant MO 63034 Office: McDonnell Aircraft Co PO Box 516 Saint Louis MO 63105

ASHHURST, ANNA WAYNE, educator; b. Phila., Jan. 5, 1933; d. Astley Paston Cooper and Anne Pauline (Campbell) Ashhurst; A.B., Vassar Coll., 1954; M.A., Middlebury Coll., 1956; Ph.D., U. Pitts., 1967; m. Ronald G. Gerber, July 22, 1978. English tchr. Internat. Inst. Spain, Madrid, 1954-56; asst. prof. Juniata Coll., Huntingdon, Pa., 1961-63; asst. prof. Spanish dept. Franklin and Marshall Coll., Lancaster, Pa., 1968-74, acting chmn. Spanish dept., 1972, convenor, fgn. lang. council, 1972-74; asso. prof. dept. modern fgn. langs. U. Mo., St. Louis, 1974-78. Mem. Welcome Wagon Wagon of Lancaster, Pa., 1968-70, 71-74. Fulbright-Hays grantee, Colombia, S.Am., summer 1963; Ford Humanities fellow, summer 1970; Mellon fellow, 1970-71. Mem. Internat. Inst. in Spain, Instituto Internacional de Literatura Iberoamericana, Am. Assn. Tchrs. Spanish and Portuguese, Women's Equity Action League (pres. Mo. div. 1975-76). Author: La literatura hispano-americana en la crítica española, 1980. Home: 2105 Barcelona Dr Florissant MO 63033

ASHLAND, EMELYNE IDA ANDREA, educator; b. Chgo., Oct. 29, 1910; d. Gustav A. and Ida Frances (Alex) A.; B.S., U. Chgo., 1931, S.M., 1933; postgrad. U. Calif. at Berkeley, 1939, U. Colo., 1940. Silhouette artist Century of Progress World's Fair, Chgo., 1933; trade mark artist Colgate-Palmolive Peet Co., Chgo., 1933-34; artist non-verbal Test I.J.R., 1934; med. social worker Unemployment Relief Services, Chgo., 1934-35; tchr. Sterling Twp. (Ill.) High Sch., 1936-37, Chgo. Pub. High Schs., 1937-76; adv., chmn. sci. dept. Gage Park High Sch., 1939-48, Morgan Park High Sch., 1948-54, Senn High Sch., 1954-76; pioneer in traffic safety edn., 1948-51; evaluator sci. materials representing Chgo. South Side schs., 1948-51. Recipient certificate of appreciation Lake County Health Dept., 1976. Mem. Chgo. Tchrs. Union (charter), Soc. Circumnavigators (mem. Marco Polo club). Baptist. Researcher tomato canker incitant: Aplanobactor Michiganese; author (with Tsu-kiang Yen) Devel. of Flower and Fruit of Myrica Rubra, pub. China, 1950. Home: 773 Marion Ave Highland Park IL 60035-5123

ASHLEY, JAMES PHILLIP, educational administrator; b. Michigantown, Ind., July 31, 1933; s. Jesse Orville and Margaret Susan (Frawley) A.; B.S., Ind. U., 1955, M.S., 1960; postgrad. U. Ill., 1958, U. Colo., 1964, Notre Dame U., 1965; Ph.D., U. Tex., 1967. Tchr., South Bend (Ind.) schs., 1958-62, sci. supr., 1962-65; dir. sci. publications, exec. editor, nat. sci. cons. Ginn and Co., Lexington, Mass., 1966-78; curriculum cons. South Bend Community Sch. Corp., 1979-80, dir. spl. edn. programs, 1980-84, dir. planning and research, 1984—; instr. St. Mary's Coll., 1961—; cons. in field. Bd. dirs. Tb Assn. of St. Joseph County, 1964; community ambassador Experiment in Internat. Living, Poland, 1962. Served with USAF, 1955-57. Recipient Council for Elem. Sci. Disting. Service award, 1971; Danforth Found. scholar, 1951. Mem. Nat. Sci. Tchrs. Assn., Council for Elem. Sci. Internat., Assn. Supervision and Curriculum Devel., Nat. Council Tchrs. Math., Nat. Council Social Studies, Council Exceptional Children, Phi Delta Kappa. Roman Catholic. Club: Am. Contract Bridge League. Contbr. articles in field. Home: 2025 Waterview Ct South Bend IN 46637 Office: 635 S Main St South Bend IN 46601

ASHLEY, MICHAEL ALLAN, psychologist; b. Union City, Ind., Feb. 5, 1949; s. Raymond Wilson and Phyllis Aleen (Easter) A.; m. Linda Diane Moore, July 9, 1983. M.A. in Math., Ball State U., 1970, M.A. in Counseling Psychology, 1976, Ph.D., 1979. Vol., Peace Corps, Botswana, Africa, 1971-72; residence hall dir., instr. Ball State U., Muncie, Ind., 1972-75; cons. Aquarius House, Fed. Drug Intervention Center, Muncie, 1975-78; research and evaluation specialist Center for Mental Health, Anderson, Ind., 1977-78; psychologist Grant-Blackford Mental Health Center, Marion, Ind., 1979—; assoc. prof. sociology Marion Coll., 1980—; assoc. prof. counseling psychology Ball State U., 1983—; mem. Ind. State Geriatrics Com., 1979-83; coordinator sub-grant Ind. Manpower Tng. Grant, 1982-83. Bd. dirs. Grant County Am. Cancer Soc. Recipient cert. of performance Am. Coll. Personnel Assn., 1974, Ind. State Scholarship award, 1967-70. Mem. Am. Psychol. Assn., Am. Group Psychotherapy Assn. Democrat. Home: PO Box 203 Swayzee IN 46986 Office: 505 Wabash Ave Marion IN 46952

ASHWORTH, RONALD BROUGHTON, accountant; b. San Francisco, Apr. 19, 1945; s. Robert William and Tracy Marie (Parks) A.; m. Carol Lynn Heaps, Oct. 2, 1970; 1 dau., Christina Ann. B.B.A., U. Mo.-Columbia, 1967, M.A., 1968. C.P.A., Mo., N.C., Ill., La. With Peat Marwick Mitchell & Co. 1968—, ptnr., 1975—, in charge St. Louis Office health care practice, 1975-77, nat. dir. health care practice, 1978—, Chgo., 1979—. Bd. dirs. Chgo. Lung Assn., Mid-Am. chpt. ARC. Recipient Haskins and Sells award, 1967; Fin. Execs. Inst. award, 1967; Alpha Kappa Psi scholar, 1967. Mem. Healthcare Fin. Mgmt. Assn., Am. Inst. C.P.A.s, Fedn. Am. Hosps. Am. Hosp. Assn., Ill. Soc. C.P.A.s. Clubs: Tavern, Medinah Country, Country Club of Mo. Office: 303 E Wacker Dr Chicago IL 60601

ASIK, JOSEPH RICHARD, staff engineer; b. Lorain, Ohio, Aug. 8, 1937; s. Joseph and Helen (Chonka) A.; m. Grace Nayper, Aug. 29, 1959; children—Jeffrey, Wendy, Charles. B.S. in Physics, Case Inst. Tech., 1959; M.S. in Physics, U. Ill., 1961, Ph.D. in Physics, 1966. With IBM Research, Yorktown Hgts., N.Y., 1966-69; staff engr. Ford Motor Research, Dearborn, Mich., 1969—; lectr. Lawrence Inst. Southfield, Mich., 1978—. Contbr. articles to encys. and profl. jours. Patentee automotive ignition system and engine controls. Mem. IEEE (sr.), Am. Phys. Soc., Soc. Automotive Engrs. Avocations: Personal computers; amateur radio; ballroom dancing. Office: Ford Motor Co E2166 SRLB Box 2053 Dearborn MI 48121

ASKEN, EVIE (YVONNE WARNER), architect; b. Kans. City, Kans., Oct. 27, 1936; d. Floyd B. Warner and Frances (Kalinich) W.; m. Eugene J. Asken, Apr. 10, 1960; children—Gregory, Linda, Richard. B.Arch., Kans. State U. 1959. Registered architect, Mich. Architect, Tower/Pinkster Architects, Kalamazoo, 1970-75, Evie Asken Architect, AIA, Kalamazoo, 1975-78, sta. WBDC Inc., Kalamazoo, 1978-80, Kingscott Assos., Inc., Kalamazoo, 1980—; cons. Mem. Kalamazoo Econ. Devel. Corp., treas 1979-81; mem. Kalamazoo County Overall Econ. Expansion, Portage City Planners Commn., 1977-80, Kalamazoo 2000 Com., 1982, Downtown Devel. Authority Com. on Arcadia Creek, 1982; chmn. Michael Fleck campaign for rep., 1980; mem. Kalamazoo Area Network, Adrian Coll. Parents Council. Mem. AIA (pres. task force affirmative action, pres. Western Mich. chpt. 1976-77), Mich. Soc. Architects (dir. 1978-82, sec. 1978-80, pres. 1981), Mich. Council Soc. and Profl. Assn., LWV, Kalamazoo C. of C. (dir. 1978-82, pres. Portage div. 1981, 82). Office: PO Box 671 Kalamazoo MI 49005

ASMAN, ROBERT JOSEPH, lawyer; b. St. Louis, Feb. 7, 1924; s. Robert J. and Anna M. (Spaeth) A.; student Holy Cross Coll., 1941-43; A.B., Cath. U. Am., 1948; LL.B., Georgetown U., 1951; m. Mary Elizabeth Kane, Sept. 8, 1948; children—Kathryn Anne, Robert Joseph III, Peter Kane, Teresa Elizabeth, Suzanne Marie, Elizabeth Jane. Admitted to D.C. bar, 1952, Ohio bar, 1961; asso. firm Cummings, Truitt & Reeves, Washington, 1956; trial atty. anti-trust div. Dept. Justice, 1952-53; asst. U.S. atty. D.C., 1953-60; counsel flight propulsion lab. dept. Gen. Electric Co., 1960-63, v.p., sec., gen. counsel Pneumo Dynamics Corp., Cleve., 1963-70; pres., chief exec. officer Ohio State Bar Assn. Automated Research, Cleve.; mem. firm Van Aken, Bond, Withers, Asman & Smith, Cleve. Mem. Bd. Zoning Appeals, Cleveland Heights, Ohio; mem. Ohio Mental Health and Mental Retardation Adv. Council, 1972—, mem. com. Met. Health Planning Corp.; mem. Cuyahoga County Community Mental Health and Retardation Bd., 1972—. Pres. Hill House, Cleve., 1964; trustee Cleve. Mental Health Assn., 1966-68, St. John's Coll., Hill House. Served with AUS, 1943-45; ETO. Decorated Bronze Star. Mem. Am., Fed., D.C., Ohio bar assns., Greater Cleve. Growth Assn., Phi Delta Phi. Clubs: Clevelander, Union, Rowfant Skating (Cleve.). Home: 2676 Berkshire Rd Cleveland Heights OH 44106 Office: 1519 Nat City Bank Bldg Cleveland OH 44114

ASPEN, MARVIN EDWARD, See Who's Who in America, 43rd edition.

ASPER, BERNICE VICTORIA, newspaper editor; b. Luck, Wis., Apr. 1, 1920; d. Harry Lars and Christine Marie (Hilseth) Johansen; student Mpls. Bus. Coll., 1939; m. Verdie S. Asper, Dec. 23, 1942 (dec.); 1 dau., Vickie Sharon. Bookkeeper, news editor, proofreader Enterprise-Herald, Luck, 1943-44; cashier, sec. Thorp Fin. Corp., Frederic, Wis., 1948-53; bookkeeper Rudell Motor Co., 1953-59, Frederic Telephone Co., 1959-63; editor Inter-County Leader, Frederic, 1963—, also columnist Midweek Musings, As Per Bernice, also editorial writer. Sec., Frederic Citizens Adv. Com., 1970—; bd. dirs. Western Wis. Health Systems Agy., 1976—, Frederic Devel. Corp., 1979—, Frederic Mcpl. Hosp.; pres. Polk County Health Forum, 1979; supt. St. Peters Lutheran Sunday Sch., 1947-77, treas. St. Peter's Luth. Ch. Named Frederic Citizen of Yr., 1980. Author: 75 Years in Frederic, 1976. Home: 302 N Wisconsin Ave Frederic WI 54837 Office: 303 N Wisconsin Ave Frederic WI 54837

ASPHAHANI, AZIZ IBRAHIM, research and development director, researcher; b. Beirut, Lebanon, Sept. 16, 1947; came to U.S., 1970; s. Ibrahim Mehdi and Nazek Sanya (Sudki) A.; m. Wendy Jane Barron, Oct. 3, 1973; children—Fareid, Aaron, Joseph. M.P.C. in Chemistry, U. Paris, 1966; Math. speciales, Lycee Janson de Sailly, Paris, 1967; diploma in Phys. Engring., Ecole Centrale, Paris, 1968-70; Ph.D. in Materials Sci., MIT, 1975. Corrosion engr. Cabot Corp., Kokomo, Ind., 1975-77, group leader, 1978-80, dir. tech., 1983—; chmn. subcom. 8 Metal Properties Council, N.Y.C., 1983-85, TMS sub program Offshore Tech. Conf., Dallas, 1983-85. Patentee new alloys; author papers in field. Mem. Electrochem. Soc., ASTM, Welding Research Council, Nat. Assn. Corrosion Engrs. (com. mem. 1982—), Am. Soc. for Metals. Republican. Club: Kokomo Country. Avocations: reading; history; tennis; skiing; handball. Office: Cabot Corp 1020 W Park Ave Kokomo IN 46901

ASPIN, LES(LIE), congressman; b. Milw., July 21, 1938; B.A. summa cum laude, Yale, 1960; M.A., Oxford U. (Eng.), 1962; Ph.D. in Econs., Mass. Inst. Tech., 1965. Asst. prof. econs. Marquette U., Milw., 1969-70; mem. 92d-99th Congresses from 1st Dist. Wis., chmn. subcom. on mil. personnel and compensation; mem. House Armed Services, Budget, Govt. Ops. coms. Served from 2d lt. to capt. AUS, 1966-68. Mem. Phi Beta Kappa. Office: 442 Cannon House Office Bldg Washington DC 20515*

ASPLIN, EDWARD WILLIAM, packaging company executive; b. Mpls., June 25, 1922; s. John E. and Alma (Carlbom) A.; B.B.A., U. Minn., 1943; postgrad. U. Mich., 1947-48, Wayne State, 1949-50, Rutgers U. Sch. Banking, 1957-59; m. Eleanor Young Rodgers, Oct. 20, 1951; children—Sarah L., William R., Lynn E. Cost accountant Nat. Bank Detroit, 1947-50; asst. v.p. adminstrn. Northwest Bancorp., Mpls., 1950-59; v.p. mktg. Northwestern Nat. Bank, Mpls., 1959-67; chmn., chief adminstrv. officer Bemis Co., Inc., Mpls., 1967—, also dir.; dir. Milacron Inc., DeLuxe Check Printers, Inc. Adviser Opportunity Workshop, Inc. Served with USNR, 1943-46. Mem. NAM. Clubs: Minikahda, Minneapolis; University (N.Y.C.). Office: 800 Northstar Center Minneapolis MN 55402

ASRAR, GHASSEM, soil physicist, civil engineer; b. Shiraz, Iran, Oct. 12, 1951; came to U.S., 1976; s. Naser and Masoomeh Asrar (Takesh) A.; B.Sc., U. Shiraz, 1974; M.S., Mich. State U., 1978, 80, Ph.D. (Sage Found. fellow), 1981. Research aide U. Shiraz, 1970-74, lab. instr. 1974; agr. extension specialist, Isfahan, Iran, 1975-76; grad. research asst. Mich. State U., East Lansing, 1976-81; research assoc. Kans. State U. Manhattan, 1981-85, asst. prof., 1985—. Mem. Am. Soc. Agronomy, Soil Sci. Soc. Am., Internat. Soil Sci. Soc., Am. Meteorol. Soc., Am. Geophys. Union, AAAS. Republican. Moslem. Contbr. articles to tech. publs. Home: 1218 Pomeroy #12 Manhattan KS 66502 Office: Kans State U Manhattan KS 66506

ASSELIN, PAUL JOSEPH, interior designer; b. Bay City, Mich., July 20, 1953; s. Francis John and Alice (Lanouette) A. Cert. Kendall Sch. Design, Grand Rapids, 1977. Prin., Free Lance Design Assocs., Grand Rapids, Mich., 1977-78; sr. designer Contract Interiors, Grand Rapids, 1978-81; sr. designer Custer Office Environments, Grand Rapids, 1981-83; instr. Kendall Sch. Design, Grand Rapids, 1983—; prin. P. Asselin & Assocs., Grand Rapids, Mich., 1983—. Mem. Am. Soc. Interior Designers (v.p. chpt. 1982-83, v.p. Mich. 1983—). Roman Catholic. Office: P Asselin & Assocs 50 Louis St NW Suite 150 Grand Rapids MI 49503

ASSUE, CLARE MELBA, psychiatrist; b. N.Y.C., Dec. 27, 1922; d. Charles Alexander and Ada Syrena (Taylor) A.; m. Frank Meukler Brown, Aug. 24, 1956 (dec. Dec. 7, 1984); children—Thea Robin, Laurie Elizabeth, Charles Assue Brown. A.B., Hunter Coll., 1949; M.D., Howard U., 1954. Diplomate

Am. Bd. Psychiatry and Neurology. Intern, Brookdale Hosp. Ctr., Bklyn., 1954-55; resident Larue Carter Hosp., Indpls., 1955-56, St. Elizabeth's Hosp., Washington, 1956-58; staff psychiatrist Larue Carter Hosp., Indpls., 1958—, chief male service, 1960-77, dir. special study ward, 1963-65, dir. med. edn., 1977—, supt. med. dir., 1982—; prof. psychiatry Ind. U. Sch. Medicine, 1972—, dir. psychiat. residency tng., 1979—; cons. Midtown Community Mental Health Ctr., Wishard Hosp., Indpls., 1969—. Co-author: Examination of Personality, 1972. Mem. Am. Psyciat. Assn., Am. Assn. Dirs. Psychiat. Residency Tng., Ind. Psychiat. Soc. Episcopalian. Office: Larue D Carter Meml Hosp 1315 W 10th St Indianapolis IN 46202

ASTON, KENNETH PRESTON, JR., real estate salesman and investments; b. St. Louis, Mar. 29, 1959; s. Kenneth Preston and Carol Audrey (Dependahl) A.; m. Lori Ann Shikany, Apr. 17, 1982; 1 child, Andrea Roxanne. A.B. in Polit. Sci., U. Mo., 1981. Mgr., cons. Oliver Realty Inc., St. Louis, 1981-82; apt./investment salesman Coldwell Banker Comml. Real Estate, St. Louis, 1982—; pres. Aston & Aston Properties, St. Louis, 1982—. Fund raiser Dream Factory, Inc., St. Louis, 1983-84. Recipient awards apt. investment salesperson Coldwell Banker, North Central Region U.S.A., 1983, 84. Mem. Phi Delta Theta. Republican. Mem. United Ch. of Christ. Clubs: Jaycees (pres. Chesterfield 1985—), Toastmasters. Avocations: wrestling; golf. Home: 1112 Edward Terr Saint Louis MO 63117 Office: Coldwell Banker 222 S Central Ave 1104 Saint Louis MO 63105

ASTRUP, JENS LEO, civil engineer; b. Plentywood, Mont., Sept. 21, 1934; s. Jens Legend and Dagmar (Jensen) A.; m. Susanne Elizabeth Laime, Nov. 25, 1967; children—Moriah Ann, Jens Aaron. B.S. in Agrl. Engring., N.D. State U., 1956; M.B.A., Keller Grad. Sch. Mgmt., 1983. Registered patent agt., Ill.; registered profl. engr., Ill. Civil engr. City of Chgo. Dept. Urban Renewal, 1964-65, Harza Engring. Co., Chgo., 1965-69; city engr. City of Williston, N.D., 1969-70; civil and resident engr. Bauer Engring., Inc., Chgo., 1970-71; civil and structural sr. engr. Brown and Root Inc., Chgo., 1971-82; project engr. Lester B. Knight & Assocs., Chgo., 1983—. Recipient Outstanding Young Adult award Augustana Luth. Ch., Washington, 1960; People-to-People trip to China, 1982. Mem. Nat. Soc. Profl. Engrs., Ill. Soc. Profl. Engrs. (state v.p. 1979-80, chmn. state activities com. 1976-77, chpt. 1977-78), ASCE, Am. Soc. Agrl. Engrs. Lutheran. Home: 21 W 604 Monticello Glen Ellyn IL 60137

ATAM-ALIBECKOFF, GALIB-BEY, sponge company executive; b. Paris, Jan. 1, 1923; came to U.S., 1967; s. Abbas-Bey and Reana (Vekiloff) A.; m. Nadezda Vicentic, Oct. 20, 1959; children—Dominique, Tamara. B.S., Sorbonne U., Paris, 1944. Chief chemist Royonhil, Llo-Lleo, Chile, 1949-57; project mgr. VonKohorn Internat., Egypt, India, Yugoslavia, 1957-66, Chemtex Inc., Alexandria, Egypt, 1966-67; v.p. Nylonge, Cleve., 1967-78; exec. v.p. Sponge Inc., Cleve., 1978—. Patentee in field. Served to sgt. French Army, 1944-46. Mem. Am. Chem. Soc., Tech. Assn. Pulp and Paper Industry. Home: 19541 Frazier Dr Rocky River OH 44116 Office: Sponge Inc 1294 W 70th Cleveland OH 44102

ATEN, ROSEMARY, physical education educator, administrator; b. Browning, Ill., Nov. 13, 1935; d. Keith Howard and Helen Rose (Gee) A.; M.S., Western Ill. U., 1957; M.A., U. Wyo., 1960; Ph.D., U. Wis., 1970. Asst. prof. U. Idaho, Moscow, 1960-66; teaching assoc. U. Wis., Madison, 1966-70; prof. Western Ill. U., Macomb, 1970-81, dept. chmn. 1981—; assessment cons. Ill. State Bd. Edn., 1984—. Author: Systematic Evaluation of Teaching Improvement Program, 1978. Editor: Softball Guide, 1966-68. Pres., co-organizer Macomb Health-Phys. Fitness Council, 1983—. Mem. Am. Alliance for Health, Phys. Edn., Recreation and Dance, Ill. Assn. Health, Physical Educ. and Recreation (v.p., dist. service award 1979), Am. Assn. Higher Edn., Phi Delta Kappa. Republican. Methodist. Avocations: golf; travel; reading. Home: 519 Meadow Dr Macomb IL 61455 Office: Western Ill Univ Macomb IL 61455

ATHA, ALAN JON, psychologist, management consultant; b. Bellefontaine, Ohio, Sept. 15, 1941; s. LaVerne Crane and Elizabeth Laura (Taylor) A.; m. Gail Roselyn Ofte, June 7, 1964; children—Timothy Alan, Kjersten Elizabeth. B.A. in Psychology, Taylor U., 1963; M.A. in Psychometrics, Ind. State U., 1964, Ph.D. in Clin. Psychology, 1967. Cert. psychologist, Ill.; Ind. Dir. clin. services Northwest Edn. Ctr., Valparaiso, Ind., 1967-70; sr. cons. Rohrer, Hibler & Replogle Cons., Chgo., 1970-80; pres. Alan J. Atha & Assocs., mgmt. cons., Valparaiso, 1980—; pres. Ctr. for Life Change; personal, marital counselor. Mem. Republican Presdl. Task Force. Mem. Am. Psychol. Assn. Lutheran. Author: Interviewing for Understanding, 1980. Home: 3012 Campbell St Valparaiso IN 46383 Office: Alan J Atha & Assocs Inc 3012 Campbell St Valparaiso IN 46383

ATHANS, MICHAEL JAMES, psychologist; b. N.Y.C., Jan. 9, 1953; s. Michael and Christine (Georgalas) A.; B.A., St. John's U., 1975; M.A., Columbia U., 1976, M.Ed., 1977; Ph.D., Mich. State U., 1982. Intern, Inst. Psychiat. and Psychosomatic Research and Tng., Michael Reese Hosp. and Med. Ctr., Chgo. and Orthogenic Sch., U. Chgo.; child psychologist Luth. Gen. Hosp. Mem. Am. Psychol. Assn.

ATHERTON, PATRICIA ANN, special education educator, consultant; b. Blue Island, Ill., July 26, 1932; d. Otho Kelly and Jeanette (Whisenant) McFarland; m. Charles Daniel Atherton, Jr., Oct. 25, 1963; children—Leo Henry, Christopher Andrew, Jeanette Marie. B.S. in Ednl. Psychology, Loyola U., 1954, M.A. in Spl. Edn., 1973, Ph.D. in Counseling Psychology, 1983. Cert. tchr., Ill.; registered art therapist, Ill. Various teaching positions in spl. edn., Chgo. and Highland Park, Ill., 1954-76; ednl. specialist Chgo. State U., dept. spl. edn., 1976—; dept. chmn., 1978-76; coordinator faculty devel. programs; cons. Lake County Head Start Programs, Lake County Ill., Ednl. Facilities Lab., N.Y.C., Gifted Edn. Program, Norfolk, Va. Recipient Leadership award Loyola U., 1954; Outstanding Educator award Council for Exceptional Children, Chpt. 57, 1977. Mem. Chgo. Assn. for Children with Learning Disabilities (profl. adv. bd.), Council for Exceptional Children, Ill. Art Therapy Assn. (founder 1974), Higher Edn. Adv. Council in Ill., Marion Adult Tng. Ctr. (adv. bd.), Central Community Mental Health Orgn. (adv. bd.) Author: The Value of Creative Art for Learning Disabilities, 1977; Analysis of Parent-Teacher Communication, 1978. Founded Creative Children's Arts, a private sch. for gifted and handicapped children, 1973.

ATHREYA, KRISHNA BALASUNDARAM, mathematics and statistics educator; b. Madras, India, Dec. 12, 1939; came to U.S., 1963; s. Ananthanarayanan Balasundaram and Narayani (Baradway) A.; m. Uma Mani, June 6, 1968 (dec. 1975); children—Kartik, Dwijavanti; m. 2d, Krishna Siddhanta, Jan. 19, 1979; 1 child, Jayadev. B.A. with honors, Loyola Coll. (India), 1959; postgrad. Indian Statis. Inst., Calcutta, 1959-61; Ph.D. in Math., Stanford U., 1967. Asst. prof. U. Wis.-Madison, 1969-70, assoc. prof., 1970-71; prof. Indian Inst. Sci., Bangalore, 1972-79, Iowa State U., Ames, 1980—. Co-author: Branching Processes, 1972. Contbr. articles in probability and stats. to profl. jours. Fulbright scholar Stanford U., 1963-67. Fellow Indian Acad. Scis., Inst. Math. Stats. U.S.A. Avocation: classical Indian music. Office: Iowa State U Depts Stats and Math Ames IA 50011

ATKINS, CHARLES GILMORE, medical school administrator; b. Stambaugh, Mich., July 4, 1939; s. Howard B. and Bernice M. (Gilmore) A.; m. Kay Roberta Bueschen, Dec. 28, 1958 (div. 1983); children—Robert Howard, Karla Marie, James Charles. B.A., Albion Coll., 1961; postgrad. Med. Sch., U. Mich., 1960-62; M.S., Eastern Mich. U., 1963; Ph.D., N.C. State U., 1969. Instr. Com Coll., 1963-66; lectr. genetics Cornell Coll., Mt. Vernon, Iowa, 1964-65; NIH predoctoral genetics trainee N.C. State U., Raleigh, 1966-69; asst. prof. microbiology Ohio U., Athens 1969-74, assoc. prof., 1974—; dir. Appalachian life sci. coll. tng. program, 1972-74, dir. willed body program, 1976-77, assoc. dean for basic scis., 1976—, del. to state-level Ohio faculty senate, 1970-73; cons. in field. Elder 1st Presbyn. Ch., Athens, 1971—; scoutmaster Boy Scouts Am., 1972-82, dist. and council commr., 1978—. Served to maj. USAR, 1981—. Dist. Award of Merit, Boy Scouts Am., 1976; Silver Wreath award, Nat. Eagle Scout Assn., 1981; Alfred E. Noyes scholar, 1957-60. Mem. Genetics Soc. Am., AAAS, Assn. Am. Med. Colls., Am. Soc. Microbiology, Ohio Acad. Sci., Nat. Eagle Scout Assn., Order of the Arrow, Sigma Xi. Lodge: Rotary. Contbr. articles to profl. jours. Home: 6 Riverview Dr Athens OH 45701 Office: 226 Irvine Hall Ohio Univ Athens OH 45701

ATKINS, JAMES ALBERT, food services administration consultant; b. Washington, Apr. 24, 1945; s. James Earl and Dorothy (Mix) A.; A.A. in Applied Sci., Ferris State Coll., 1966; student health care mgmt. program U.

Ill., 1978-79; m. Joan Marie Pierce, Nov. 7, 1976; children—James Norman, Katherine Marie, Michael William. Food service mgr., Fred Harvey Restaurants, Chgo., 1966-69; food and beverage mgr. Quality Motels, Jackson, Mich., 1969-70, St. Louis, 1970; food service mgr. Venture Stores, Ann Mo., 1971; asst. dir. food services St. Francis Hosp., Evanston, Ill., 1971-72; gen. mgr. Food Mgmt. Assos., Glen Ellyn, Ill., 1973; asso. dir. of food services St Annes Hosp., Chgo., 1973-79, St. Elizabeth's Hosp., Chgo., 1979-82; dir. food and nutrition services U. Chgo. Med. Center, 1979-82; instr. (part-time) in food service curriculum Coll. of Du Page, Glen Ellyn, Ill., 1976—, adv. coll. food service curriculum, 1979—; chmn. food service com. Ancilla Domini Health Services, 1977-79; cons. food services, 1975—; pres. Atkins & Assos., 1976—; instr. restaurant mgmt. tng. program Triton Jr. Coll., 1978—; coll. curriculum adv. U. Ill., 1979—; lectr., key speaker at food service and mgmt. seminars, 1978—; chmn. Tri-State Conv. for Health Care Food Service, 1979; seminar leader food service tng. programs. Served with USN, 1967-68; Vietnam. Recipient cert. of recognition Evanston Sch. System and Chgo. Food Service Mktg. Club, 1973; designated disting. healthcare food service adminstr. Mem. Internat. Food Service Execs. Assn. (1st v.p.), Am. Soc. for Hosp. Food Service Adminstrs. (past pres.), Am. Hosp. Assn. Assn. Catering Execs. Clubs Am. Roman Catholic. Club: Lion. Home and Office: 1019 Carol St Downers Grove IL 60516

ATKINS, THOMAS LEE, human resources development specialist; b. Chgo., Dec. 4, 1921; s. Samuel Merritt and Alphonsine Marie (La Londe) A.; B.A., U. Notre Dame, 1943; postgrad. Cath. U. Am., 1947-51; m. Marylin E. Bowman, Dec. 19, 1966; children—Elizabeth Ann, Catherine Marie. Ordained priest, Roman Cath. Ch., 1951; asst. pastor Saginaw (Mich.) Sts. Peter & Paul Ch., 1951-54, St. Helen Ch., Saginaw, 1954-58; chaplain VA Hosp., Saginaw, 1954-58, USNR Tng. Ctr., Bay City, Mich., 1958-64; pastor Sebewaing (Mich.) St. Mary's Nativity Ch., 1958-63; tng. specialist Bur. Personnel Services, Mich. Employment Security Commn., 1974—. Bd. dirs. Saginaw Valley Indian Assn., 1972—, pres., 1981—. Served with USNR, 1943-46. Mem. Social Workers Roundtable (pres. 1969-74). Portrait editor, Notre Dame DOME, 1942; lit. editor Sacred Heart Gothic, 1946-47. Home: 4695 Kingswood Dr Okemos MI 48864 Office: 7310 Woodward St Detroit MI 48202

ATKINSON, ARTHUR JOHN, JR., clinical pharmacologist, educator; b. Chgo., Mar. 22, 1938; s. Arthur John and Inez (Hill) A.; A.B. in Chemistry, Harvard U., 1959; M.D., Cornell U., 1963. Intern and asst. resident in medicine Mass. Gen. Hosp., Boston, 1963-65, chief resident and Howard Carroll fellow in medicine Passavant Meml. Hosp., Chgo., instr. in medicine Northwestern U., Chgo., 1967-68; fellow in clin. pharmacology U. Cin., 1968-69, asst. prof. pharmacology, 1969; vis. scientist dept. toxicology Karolinska Inst., Stockholm, Sweden, 1970; asst. prof. medicine and pharmacology Northwestern U., Chgo., 1970-73, assoc. prof., 1973-76, prof., 1976—. Served with NIH, USPHS, 1965-67. Recipient Faculty Devel. award in clin. pharmacology Pharm. Mfrs. Assn., 1970-72; Burroughs Wellcome scholar in clin. pharmacology, 1972-77. Fellow ACP; mem. Am. Fedn. Clin. Research, Central Soc. Clin. Research, Am. Soc. for Clin. Investigation, Am. Soc. Pharmacology and Exptl. Therapeutics, Am. Soc. Clin. Pharmacology and Therapeutics (Rawls Palmer award 1983), Chgo. Soc. Internal Medicine, Alpha Omega Alpha. Club: Chgo. Yacht. Mem. editorial bd. jours. Rational Drug Therapy, 1972-83, Clin. Pharmacology and Therapeutics, 1973—, Pharm. Revs., 1977—, Therapeutic Drug Monitoring, 1979—. Home: 175 E Delaware Pl Chicago IL 60611 Office: 303 E Superior St Chicago IL 60611

ATKINSON, JERRY ALLEN, lawyer; b. Marion, Ind., Oct. 9, 1941; s. Roy Raymond and Hester Delene (Nelson) A.; m. Vari Scudi, Apr. 6, 1968. B.S., Ball State U., 1963; postgrad. Butler U., 1964-65; J.D., Ind. U., 1969. Bar: Ind. 1969, U.S. Dist. Ct. (so. dist.) Ind. 1969, U.S. Ct. Appeals (7th cir.) 1969. Law clk. to presiding justice U.S. Dist. Ct., So. Dist., Ind., 1969-70; dep. pros. atty. 1st Judicial Dist. Ind., 1971—; ptnr. Hayes & Atkinson, Evansville, Ind., 1971-78; sr. ptnr. Atkinson, Welborn & Bohleber, Evansville, 1979—. Mem. ABA, Ind. State Bar Assn., Evansville Bar Assn. Trial Lawyers Am. Club: Columbia (Indpls.); Petroleum (Evansville); Nu Plaza Yacht. Lodge: Masons, Shriners, Scottish Rite. Office: Atkinson Welborn & Bohleber 112 NW 7th St Evansville IN 47708

ATKINSON, LARRY GORDON, newspaper publisher and editor; b. Mobridge, S.D., Jan. 2, 1951; s. Gordon Faye and Marilyn Joan (Carlson) A.; m. Roberta Rae Gedstad, June 4, 1972; children—Corey, Amy, Lisa. B.S., S.D. State U., 1973; M.A., Ball State U., 1978; cert. Am. Press Inst., 1982. Editor Prairie Pioneer, Pollock, S.D., 1979-81; asst. publisher, mng. editor Mobridge Tribune, 1981—. Pres. Oake Area Arts Council, Mobridge, 1983-84; publicity chmn. Mobridge Community Fund, 1982-83; state chmn. S.D. Teenage Republicans, 1968; appt. bd. dirs. S.D. Tourism, 1985-88. Recipient numerous awards S.D. Better Newspaper Contest, Nat. Newspaper Assn. Mem. Soc. Profl. Journalists, Nat. Newspaper Assn., S.D. Press Assn. (mem. newspapers in edn. com. 1985—), Mobridge C. of C. (pres. 1984), Jaycees. Lutheran. Lodge: Moose. Avocations: photography; collecting photographica. Home: 1301 Sunset Ave Mobridge SD 57601 Office: Mobridge Tribune 111 3rd St West Mobridge SD 57601

ATREYA, SUSHIL KUMAR, science educator, researcher; b. Ajmer, India, Apr. 15, 1946; came to U.S., naturalized, 1975; s. Harvansh Lal and Kailash Vati (Sharma) A.; m. Evelyn M. Bruckner, Dec. 31, 1970; 1 dau., Chloé E. Sc.B., U. Rajasthan, India, 1963, M.Sc., 1965; M.S., Yale U., 1968; Ph.D., U. Mich., 1973. Research assoc. physics U. Pitts., 1973-74; asst. to assoc. research scientist Space Physics Research Lab., U. Mich., Ann Arbor, 1974-78, asst. prof., 1978-81, assoc. prof. atmospheric sci., 1981—; prof. associé U. Paris, 1984-85; mem. sci. teams Voyager, Galileo and Space Lab I Projects; prin. guest investigator Copernicus Orbiting Astron. Observatory; guest investigator Internat. Ultraviolet Explorer Satellite; mem. sci. working groups NASA and Jet Propulsion Lab. Recipient NASA award for exceptional sci. contbns. Voyager Project, 1981, Group Achievement award for Voyager Ultraviolet Spectrometer Sci. Team, 1981. Mem. Am. Geophys. Union, AAAS, Am. Astron. Soc. Contbr. numerous articles to books and profl. jours. Office: Dept Atmospheric and Oceanic Sci Space Research Bldg 2455 Hayward U Mich Ann Arbor MI 48109

ATTEBERRY, WILLIAM DUANE, manufacturing company executive; b. Decatur, Ill., 1920. Grad. bus. engring. U. So. Calif., 1943. With Western lead Products Co., 1946-51; with Eagle-Picher Industries Inc., Cin., 1952-85, v.p., 1963-65, exec. v.p. and group exec., 1965-66, pres., then chmn. bd., pres. 1967-78, now chmn. bd., chief exec. officer, dir., ret.; dir. Empire Dist. Electric Co., Fifth Third Bancorp, Kroger Co., Vulcan Materials Co., Xtek; also adv. dir. First Nat. Bank, Joplin, Mo. Trustee Ohio No U.; chmn. bd. Bethesda Hosps., Cin.; assoc. dir. Greater Cin. Found. Office: Eagle-Picher Industries Inc 580 Walnut St PO Box 779 Cincinnati OH 45201

ATTIA, SABRY M., state official; b. Damanhour, Egypt, Apr. 25, 1927; s. Hassan and Galila A. (El-Sayed) A.; came to U.S., 1970, naturalized, 1975; B.S.W., Cairo Sch. Social Work, 1956; M.S.W., Wayne State U., 1973, now doctoral candidate; M.Public Adminstrn. U. Detroit, 1979; m. Serria Moustafa Rashid, June 9, 1951; children—Mervat, Mona, Madiha, Mayssa. Social planning cons. The Egyptian Govt., 1961-70; instr. social work Cairo Sch. Social Work, 1958-61; cons. Egyptian Nat. Planning Com., 1961-70; unit mgr. Henry Ford Hosp., Detroit, 1970-72; program dir. Catholic Youth Orgn., Detroit, 1972; med. social worker Hutzel Hosp., Detroit, 1973-75; welfare services supr. Wayne County Dept. Social Services, State of Mich., Detroit, 1975-78, program specialist, central adminstr., 1979-81; dist. dir. N.E. Med. Dist., 1981—; pvt. practice social work, St. Clair Shores, Mich.; dir. Profl. Counseling Services, P.C., Grosse Pointe; dir. The Council Social Agys., Cairo. Recipient Exceptional Achievement award CASE, 1981; cert. social worker, Mich. Mem. Nat. Assn. Social Workers, Acad. Cert. Social Workers, Am. Hosp. Assn., Mich. Unit Mgmt. Assn., Brit. Council Social Workers, Egyptian Assn. Social Workers, Wayne State U. Social Work Alumni assn. (pres.). Home: 19777 E Ida Ln Grosse Pointe Woods MI 48236 Office: 14060 Maddelin Detroit MI 48205 also 23915 E Jefferson St Saint Clair Shores MI 48080

ATTIX, FRANK HERBERT, medical physics educator; b. Portland, Oreg., Apr. 2, 1925; s. Ulysses Sheldon and Alma Katherine (Michelsen) A.; m. Evelyn Louise Van Scoy, Apr. 19, 1946 (div. 1958); m. Shirley Adeline Lohr, Jan. 24, 1959; children—Shelley Anne, Richard Haven. A.B., U. Calif.-Berkeley, 1949; M.S., U. Md., 1953. Physicist NIH, Bethesda, Md., 1949-50, Nat. Bur. Standards, Washington, 1950-57, Am. Car and Foundry, Washington, 1957-58, Naval Research Lab., Washington, 1958-76; prof. med. physics U.

Wis.-Madison, 1976—. Author, editor: (3 vol. treatise) Radiation Dosimetry, 1966-69. Editor: Topics in Radiation Dosimetry, 1972. Contbr. articles to profl. publs. Patentee in field. Served to lt. USN, 1943-46. Recipient Applied Sci. award Research Soc. Am., 1969. Mem. Am. Assn. Physicists in Medicine (bd. dirs. 1978-80), Health Physics Soc. (bd. dirs. 1968-71), Am. Phys. Soc., August Derleth Soc. (treas. 1980). Avocations: hiking, camping. Home: 3333 Westview Ln Madison WI 53713 Office: U Wis 1300 University Ave Madison WI 53706

ATWATER, H. BREWSTER, JR., food products company executive; b. Mpls., 1931; A.B., Princeton U., 1952; M.B.A., Stanford U., 1954; married. With McCullough Corp., 1954-58; with Gen. Mills, Inc., Mpls., 1958—, v.p. consumer foods group, 1969-70, exec. v.p., 1970-76, chief operating officer, 1976-77, pres., chief operating officer, 1977-81, pres., chief exec. officer, 1981-82, chmn., chief exec. officer, 1982—, also dir.; dir. Northwestern Nat. Life Ins. Co., Northwest Bancorp, Donaldson Co. Inc., New Ct. Pvt. Equity Fund, Inc., Norwest Corp., Honeywell Inc. Trustee, MacAlester Coll., Princeton U., Walker Art Center, Mpls.; mem. adv. council Stanford U. Grad. Sch. Bus. Served to lt. (j.g.) USNR, 1955-58. Office: Gen Mills Inc 9200 Wayzata Blvd Minneapolis MN 55440*

ATWATER, JAMES D., university dean; b. Westfield, Mass., Oct. 25, 1928; m. Patricia A., 1955; 6 children. B.A., Yale U., 1950. Editorial trainee Time mag., Washington, 1953-54, staff corr., 1954-57, writer, 1957-62; writer Saturday Evening Post, 1962-65, sr. editor, 1965-68; spl. asst. Pres. Nixon, 1969-70; London corr. Reader's Digest, 1971-73; writer nat. affairs sect. Time mag., 1973-77, sr. editor, 1977-83, sr. journalist-in-residence Duke U., 1981; Presdl. fellow Aspen Inst. Humanistic Studies, 1982; dean U. Mo. Sch. Journalism, Columbia, 1983—. Author: Timebomb, 1977; co-author: Physical Fitness, 1969; Out From Under. Served with USAF, 1950-53. Office: 100 Neff Hall U Mo Columbia MO 65211

ATWELL, WILLIAM ALAN, food scientist; b. Balt., Aug. 26, 1951; s. William Joseph and Delore Bernice (Bachman) A.; m. Janine Marie Elizabeth Andersone, Aug. 11, 1973; children—Tabitha, Stephanie. B.S., SUNY-Oswego, 1973, M.S., 1976; Ph.D., Kans. State U., 1979. Research scientist Pillsbury Co., Mpls., 1979—; cons. Magnolia Labs., Pascagoula, Miss., 1977-78. Contbr. articles to profl. jours. N.Y. State Regents scholar, 1969-73. Mem. Am. Assn. Cereal Chemists (assoc. editor jour. 1984—), Phi Lamda Upsilon. Democrat. Presbyterian. Avocations: piano; guitar; singing; songwriting; racquetball. Office: Pillsbury Co Research and Devel 311 2d St SE Minneapolis MN 55414

ATWOOD, H(ARRY) MASON, educator; b. Marshfield, Wis., Oct. 19, 1916; s. Henry Harrison and Anna Rosetta (Mason) A.; B.S., U. Wis.-Stevens Point, 1940, M.S., Madison, 1953, Ph.D., 1958; m. Opal Thompson Tellman, June 5, 1959; children—Carol Tellman Clark, Diane Tellman Baker, Peggy Tellman Davis, Amy Doris. Tchr., Florence (Wis.) High Sch., 1941-42; instr. chemistry U. Wis., Racine, Milw., Green Bay, Wausau, Marinette, 1946-55, grad. asst., Madison, 1955-57; asst. prof. adult edn. Ind. U., 1957-71; prof. adult and community edn. Ball State U., Muncie, Ind., 1971-83, prof. emeritus, dir. Inst. Gerontology, 1973-76, dir. emeritus, 1976—; mem. Ind. Health Facility Adminstrs. Bd. Registration and Edn., 1976—; cons. in field. Mem. homes for aging div. Ind. Health Facilities Council, 1964-82; bd. dirs. Delaware County (Ind.) Council on Aging, 1973-80. Served with AUS, 1942-46. Mem. Gerontol. Soc., Assn. Gerontology in Higher Edn., Am. Assn. Adult and Continuing Edn., Ind. Assn. Adult and Continuing Edn. Episcopalian. Clubs: Exchange, Elks. Book rev. editor Adult Leadership, 1973-77, Lifelong Learning: The Adult Years, 1977-78, The AGHE Newsletter, 1978-81; contbr. chpts. to books and articles to profl. jours. Home: 220 Alden Rd Muncie IN 47304

AUCLAIR, MICHAEL CURTIS, software company executive; b. Waukeesha, Wis., Oct. 14, 1949; s. Donald Francis and Adelia Mae (Nichols) A.; m. Delores Marleen Becwar, June 13, 1970; children—Craig Daniel, Steven Francis. Grad. Capital Radio Engring. Inst., 1973. Electronics technician Tektronix, Inc., St. Paul, 1977-79; dir., mgr. Biomed. Research Assn., St. Paul, 1979-82; pres., co-founder Profl. Data Mgmt. Systems, Inc., River Falls, Wis., 1982—; computer cons. Circuit rep. Luth. Ch. Extension Fund, 1982—. Served with U.S. Army, 1968-77. Mem. Wis. Sheriff's and Dep. Sheriff's Assn. Democrat. Lutheran. Office: 7100 France Ave S Minneapolis MN 55435

AUERBACH, MARSHALL JAY, lawyer; b. Chgo., Sept. 5, 1932; s. Samuel M. and Sadie (Miller) A.; student U. Ill.; J.D., John Marshall Law Sch., 1955; m. Carole Landsberg, July 3, 1960; children—Keith Alan, Michael Ward. Admitted to Ill. bar, 1955; pvt. practice law, Evanston, Ill., 1955-72; partner in charge matrimonial law sect., law firm Jenner & Block, Chgo., 1972-80; mem. firm Marshall J. Auerbach & Assocs., Ltd., Chgo., 1980—; mem. faculty Ill. Inst. for Continuing Legal Edn. Fellow Am. Acad. Matrimonial Lawyers; mem. Ill. State (chmn. family law sect. 1971-72), Am. (vice-chmn. family law sect. com. for liaison with tax sect. 1974-76) bar assns. Author Ill. Marriage and Dissolution of Marriage Act, enacted into law, 1977; (with Albert E. Jenner, Jr.) Historical and Practice Notes to Illinois Marriage and Dissolution of Marriage Act, 1980, also ann. supplements; contbr. chpts. to Family Law, Vol. 2. Home: 2314 Orrington Ave Evanston IL 60201 Office: 180 N LaSalle Chicago IL 60601

AUGSPURGER, RICHARD EDWIN, pastoral psychotherapist, executive director, editor; b. Trenton, N.J., Sept. 10, 1943; s. Edwin Arthur and Mary Ailene (Ballinger) A.; m. Joanne Elaine Baumann, Aug. 14, 1966; children—Luke, Brett. B.S., Ohio State U., 1966; M.Div., Garrett Theol. Sem., 1972; Ph.D., Northwestern U., 1976. Diplomate Am. Assn. Pastoral Counselors. Assoc. chief of party Internat. Voluntary Services, Laos, 1966-69; teaching asst. Garrett Theol. Sem., Evanston, Ill., 1977; dir. pastoral counseling and research Va. Inst. Pastoral Care, Richmond, 1978-80; exec. dir. Inst. Living Pastoral Counseling Ctr., Winnetka, Ill., 1980—. Instr., Kendall Coll., 1976-78; cons. various hosps. and orgns., 1977—. Task force chmn. Ministry with Families, Winnetka Congregational Ch. All-Am. Lacrosse player, 1965. Mem. Nat. Alliance Family Life, Joint Council on Research. Mem. United Ch. of Christ. Editor Abstracts of Research in Pastoral Care and Counseling, 1978-80; book rev. editor Jour. Supervision and Tng. in Ministry. Office: 690 Oak St Winnetka IL 60093

AUGUSTIN, ANN SUTHERLAND, author, realtor; b. Evergreen Park, Ill., Aug. 11, 1934; d. Donald A. and Helen E. (Dorsey) Sutherland; student Iowa State U., 1951-53; m. Edward J. Augustin Jr., Jan. 8, 1955 (div. 1974); children—Edward J. III, Kathryn, Donald J., Suzanne. Exec. sec. Standard Register Co., Chgo., 1953-55; tchr. adult edn. Maine Twp. Sch., Park Ridge, Ill., 1961-68; now realtor Century 21, Arlington Heights, Ill., monthly columnist regional Century 21 newsletter; free lance writer. Republican. Roman Catholic. Author: Help! I Want to Remodel My Home, 1975; contbr. articles to Reader's Digest, MacFadden-Bartell, Playboy, Chgo. Daily News, Chgo. Tribune, Mt. Prospect Herald, others. Home: 1100 Randville Dr Palatine IL 60667 Office: 1635 N Arlington Hts Rd Arlington Heights IL 60004

AUGUSTIN, CARROLL DARWIN, hardware store exec.; b. Lorain, Ohio, June 6, 1933; s. Arthur Conrad and Edith (Rollason) A.; B.S. in Edn., Miami U., Oxford, Ohio, 1956, M.Ed., 1958; m. Penelope Gifford Tiedjens, Sept. 17, 1955; children—Leslie Gifford, Tracy Carroll, Lindsay Victoria. Tchr., Roosevelt Jr. High Sch., Hamilton, Ohio, 1956-59, Garfield High Sch., Hamilton, 1959-63; dir. adult and vocat. edn., supr. indsl. arts Hamilton Bd. Edn., 1963-66; supr. Miami U. Acad. Center, Hamilton, 1963-67; coordinator fed. study on drop-outs Greater Miami Conf. Schs., 1967; dir. vocat. edn. Butler County (Ohio) Schs., Hamilton, 1968-78; owner Augustin's True Value Hardware Store, Greenwich, Ohio, 1978—. Bd. dirs. Am. Cancer Soc., Hamilton, 1963-65, chmn. edn. com., 1964—; chmn. membership com. Hamilton YMCA, 1966, div. chmn. fund drive, 1970, chmn. gen. fund drive, 1971; bd. mgmt. Hamilton West YMCA, 1971—, chmn., 1974-75. Nat. Def. grad. fellow, 1966-67; recipient Outstanding Layman award YMCA, 1971. Mem. Hamilton Classroom Tchrs. Assn. (pres. 1962-63), Hamilton Assn. trade and industry (chmn. com. 1964), Miami-Hamilton Alumni Assn. (mem. control bd. 1963), Sigma Phi Epsilon, Epsilon Pi Tau, Kappa Phi Kappa, Phi Delta Kappa. Presbyterian. Lodges: Greenwich Rotary (pres. 1983); Kiwanis (pres. 1971). Home: Rural Route 2 PO Box 122B New London OH 44851 Office: Augustin's True Value Hardware Store 14 Main St Greenwich OH 44837

AUGUSTINE, CARY GEORGE, judge; b. Washington, Mo., Oct. 21, 1954; s. Edwin Charles and Genevaa B. (Means) A.; m. Rosemary Helen Rieken, Jan. 8, 1977. B.S. in Criminal Justice, Central Mo. State U., 1975; J.D., U. Mo.-Kans. City, 1978. Bar: Mo. 1978, U.S. Dist. Ct. (we. dist.) Mo. 1978. Asst. atty. gen. Office Atty. Gen. Mo., Jefferson City, 1978-81; assoc. judge Mo. Cir. Ct., Fulton, 1981—. Republican. Office: Courthouse 5th and Market Fulton MO 65251

AUGUSTINE, EUGENE JAMES, sales executive; b. Wausau, Wis., Oct. 27, 1944; s. Adam John and Fern Mary (Simolke) A.; m. Jane Squires, Dec. 27, 1967; children—Elizabeth, Douglas, Jennifer. B.S. in Biology, U. Tex., 1970. Salesman, Wyeth Labs., Ft. Worth, 1970-73, Fison's Corp., 1973-75; sales mgr. EMC, Walled Lake, Mich., 1975-77, Olsonite Corp., Detroit, 1977-80, Gott Corp., Winfield, Kans., 1980—; cons. sales, West Bloomfield, Mich., 1978-80, Arkansas City, Kans., 1981-83. Served with USN, 1962-65. Mem. Canadian Sporting Goods Assn. Republican. Roman Catholic. Lodges: KC, Eagles. Home: RR3 Box 322-5 Arkansas City KS 67005 Office: Gott Corp 1616 Wheat Rd Winfield KS 67156

AUGUSTINE, JACK HERSCHEL, college dean; b. Meadville, Pa., Mar. 6, 1933; s. P.H. and Astrid (Holmquist) A.; m. Ramona Ferguson, June 23, 1956; children—Robert Jack, Sheril Lynn, Steven Mark. A.B., Taylor U., 1955, B.D., Gordon Div. Sch., 1959; M.A., Mich. State U., 1964; M.S., U. R.I., 1972. Coach baseball, football Gordon Coll., Wenham, Mass., 1956-57; dir. athletics, coach Berkshire Christian Coll., Lenox, Mass., 1957-62, Barrington Coll., R.I., 1962-74; dean students, coach basketball Aurora Coll., Ill., 1974—. Bd. dirs. Barrington YMCA, 1970-74, Dept. Recreation Town of Barrington, 1971-74, Wayside Cross Rescue Mission, Aurora, 1979—. Mem. Chicagoland Deans Assn., Assn. Christians Student Devel., Ill. High Sch. Ofcls. Assn. Republican. Baptist. Lodge: Lions (pres. 1985—). Avocations: referee high school and college football and baseball games. Home: 1348 Park Manor Aurora IL 60506 Office: Aurora Coll 347 Gladstone Ave Aurora IL 60506

AUKAMP, MERLE LOUIS, hosp. adminstr.; b. St. Peter, Ill., Nov. 16, 1932; s. George H. and Lela M. (Niehaus) A.; B.S. in Phys. Edn., U. Ill., 1957; M.H.A., Washington U., St. Louis, 1968; m. Joyce H. Metter, Nov. 16, 1957; children—Regina, Donna, Craig. Coach, tchr. Armstrong (Ill.) Twp. High Sch., 1957-58; recreational dir. Barnes Hosp. Med. Ctr., St. Louis, 1958-67; mem. adminstrv. staff Meml. Hosp., Belleville, Ill., 1967-72, asso. dir., 1971-72; adminstr. Jane Lamb Meml. Hosp., Clinton, Iowa, 1972-75, Alton (Ill.) Meml. Hosp., 1975-82, Marion (Ill.) Meml. Hosp., 1982—; preceptor health care adminstrn. U. Minn., 1976-78, Washington U., St. Louis, 1983—; mem. health adv. council Clinton Community Coll.; mem. part-time faculty Belleville Area Coll.; bd. dirs. Madison County Cancer Soc., Upper Madison County Heart Assn. Served with AUS, 1953-55. Mem. Am. Coll. Hosp. Adminstrs., Am. Hosp. Assn., Am. Assn. Hosp. Planning, Am. Protestant Hosp. Assn., Ill. Hosp. Assn. (regional pres. 1978-79), Southwestern Ill. Hosp. Assn., Greater Alton C. of C. (dir.). Lutheran. Club: Rotary. Office: Marion Meml Hosp 917 W Main St Marion IL 62959

AUKSEL, MILDRED ISABEL, art company executive; b. East Chicago, Ind., Mar. 11, 1941; d. John Joseph and Isabel Bernadette (Bucsanyi) Arndt; m. Joseph Edward Auksel, Apr. 21, 1961; children—Dawn, Jolene, Johnna, Jo Lynne, Joseph. Student pub. schs., Hammond, Ind. Co-founder CI Internat., Inc., Hobart, Ind., 1973, now pres.; dir. EGO Enterprises, Inc., AIC, Inc.; dir., pres. Charters, Inc. Roman Catholic. Home: 414 E Burdick Rd Chesterton IN 46304 Office: 101 E 3d St Hobart IN 46342 also 1520-1A W Mineral Rd Tempe AZ 85283

AULABAUGH, NORMAN RICHARD, manufacturing company executive; b. Geneva, Ill., Oct. 29, 1944; s. Norman Lee and Vivian (Savatson) A.; B.S. in Mgmt., No. Ill. U., 1966, M.B.A. in Mgmt., 1968; m. Carol Grace Topel, June 6, 1970. Systems analyst Parker Pen Co., Janesville, Wis., 1972-77, system and programming mgr., 1978-79, then dir. mgmt. info., 1980-85; mgr. materials/mfg. SSI Techs., Janesville, 1985—. Public Expenditure Survey County Budget review chmn., 1978-80. Served with USN, 1968-72. Mem. Assn. for System Mgmt. (pres. Madison chpt.). Republican. Home: Rural Route 4 Janesville WI 53545 Office: PO Box 5002 Janesville WI 53547

AULD, FRANK, psychologist; b. Denver, Aug. 9, 1923; s. Benjamin Franklin and Marion Leland (Evans) A.; m. Elinor James, June 29, 1946; children—Mary, Robert, Margaret. A.B., Drew U., 1946; M.A., Yale, 1948, Ph.D., 1950. Certified psychologist Mich., Conn., Ontario. Instr. psychology Yale, 1950-52, asst. prof., 1952-59; asso. prof. Wayne State U., 1959-61, dir. clin. psychology training program, 1960-66, prof. psychology, 1961-67; prof. U. Detroit, 1967-70, dir. psychol. clinic, 1967-69; prof. psychology U. Windsor, Ontario, Canada, 1970—. Chmn. Dearborn (Mich.) Community Council, 1962; mem. advisory com. on college work Episcopal Diocese Mich., 1962-71; cons. in field. Recipient Alumni Achievement award, Drew U., 1965. Fellow Am. Psychol. Assn. (mem. com. on evaluation 1961-66); mem. Can., Mich. psychol. assns. Can. Assn. Univ. Tchrs., Soc. for Psychotherapy Research, Ont. Psychol. Assn. (mem. Edn. and tng. bd. 1976—), Conn. State Psychol. Soc., (pres. 1958), Sigma Xi. Club: Economic (Detroit). Author: Steps in Psychotherapy, 1953; Scoring Human Motives, 1959; contbr. articles to profl. jours. Home: 1340 Pierce St Birmingham MI 48009 Office: Dept Psychology U Windsor Windsor ON N9B 3P4 Canada

AULT, THOMAS JEFFERSON, III, manufacturing company executive, manufacturing consultant; b. Portland, Ind., June 23, 1911; s. Ross Earl and Olga (Sattler) A.; Assoc. in Sci., Cumnock Coll., 1932; B.A. in Econs., UCLA, 1934; student Los Angeles Stock Exchange Inst., 1930-32; cert. Am. Mgmt. Assn. m. Mary C. Carr, June 30, 1938; 1 child, Brian Carr. Mgmt. trainee, buyer, Borg-Warner Corp., Chgo., 1937-41, asst. purchasing agt., 1941-51, dir. purchasing, 1951-53, v.p. and asst. gen. mgr. Detroit gear div., 1953-54, pres., 1954-56, pres., gen. mgr. Long mfg. div., Detroit, 1956-58; pres., chief exec. officer Saco-Lowell Shops, Boston, 1958-60, also dir.; pres., gen. mgr. The Budd Co., Detroit, 1960-64, dir. automotive div. Can., Mexico, Argentina, 1960-64; v.p. McCord Corp., Detroit, 1965-68, dir., 1965-70; pres., chief exec. officer Avis Indsl. Corp., Madison Heights, Mich., 1968-70, also dir.; pres., gen. mgr. Flyer Industries Ltd., Winnipeg, Man., Can., 1970-73, chmn. bd., 1972-76, chief exec. officer, 1970-76; chmn. bd., chief exec. officer Saunders Aircraft Corp. Ltd., Gimii, Man., Can., 1972-73; chief exec. officer Superior Kendrick Bearings, Inc., Detroit, 1974-75, also dir.; chief exec. officer Washington Heat Transfer, Inc., Polo, Ill., 1976-79, also dir.; exec. v.p. Duffy Tool and Stamping Corp., Muncie, 1979—, also sr. exec. in residence lectr. and exec. in residence Ball State U. Coll. Bus., Muncie, Ind., 1980—; cons. to mgmt. Arthur D. Little Consulting, Inc., 1959—. Bd. dirs. United Found. of Southeastern Mich., 1961-64, ARC, Detroit, 1961-64, Jr. Achievement of Southeastern Mich., 1960-63, Employers Assn. of Detroit, 1955-58, Boston Mus. Sci., 1958-60, Mass. Meml. Hosp., 1958-60; bd. dir. Muncie Ind. Transit System, 1981—, chmn., 1983—. Served to capt. U.S. Army, 1941-45. Recipient Purchasing Progress award Purchasing News, 1953, Outstanding Service award Jr. Achievement of Detroit, 1963, named to Automotive Hall of Fame, Coll. Bus. Prof. of Yr. Ball State Univ., 1983, All Univ. We-ness award Student Leadership Devel. Bd. Ball State Univ., 1984. Mem. President's Profl. Assn., Engring. Soc. Detroit, NAM, Mich. Mfrs. Assn., Soc. for Advancement Mgmt., Nat. Safety Council, Acad. of Mgmt., Am. Inst. Mgmt., Nat. Assn. Purchasing Mgmt., Am. Textile Machinery Assn., Automotive Parts Mfg. Assn., Farm Equipment Assn., Am. Ordinance Assn., Am. Soc. for Metals, Soc. Mfg. Engrs. (robotics internat.), Am. Prodn. and Inventory Control Soc., Am. Soc. Quality Control, U.S. C. of C., Air Conditioning and Refrigeration Inst., Econ. Club of Detroit (dir. 1961-64), Ind. Hist. Soc., Am. Security Council, Sigma Nu, Sigma Iota Epsilon, Delta Sigma Pi, Beta Gamma Sigma. Clubs: Elks, Masons, Shriners, Country of Detroit, University; La Coquille (Palm Beach); Delaware Country, Muncie (Muncie); Columbia (Indpls.), Rotary (Muncie). Contbr. articles on material control, long range planning and mgmt. to indsl. pubs. Home: 4501 N Wheeling St Apt 3-102 Muncie IN 47304 Office: Dept of Mgmt Science Coll of Bus Ball State Univ Muncie IN 47306

AUMAN, GARY WILLIAM, lawyer; b. Reading Pa., Jan. 18, 1947; s. William Henry and Dorothy V. (Seidel) A.; m. Rachel Mary Reiner, June 22, 1968; children—Meg Elizabeth. B.E.E., U. Louisville, 1969; J.D., Ohio State U., 1976. Bar: Ohio 1976. Assoc. Smith & Schnacke, Dayton, Ohio, 1976-81, ptnr., 1982—. Served to capt. USAF, 1969-73. Mem. Dayton Bar Assn., Ohio State Bar Assn., ABA, Southwest Ohio Self Insured Assn. Republican. Methodist. Club: Dayton Racquet. Avocation: study of American history. Office: Smith & Schnacke PO Box 1817 Dayton OH 45401

AUMULLER, JEAN MARIE, educator; b. N.Y.C., Dec. 6, 1929; d. John Gerald and Emily Anne (Walsh) Higgins; m. Richard W. Aumuller, Feb. 13, 1954 (dec.); children—Karen, David, Richard (dec.). B.A. cum laude, D'Youville Coll., Buffalo, 1951; M.A. in Humanities, Ohio State U., 1978. Cert. tchr. English and history, Ohio. Editor Comet Press, N.Y.C., 1951-54; tchr. Dublin (Ohio) public schs., 1965—, chmn. English Dept. K-12. Jennings scholar, 1975, 79; named Ohio Most Creative Tchr., Findlay (Ohio) Coll., 1978. Mem. Nat. Council Tchrs. English, Ohio Conf. Tchrs. English and Language Arts, Internat. Soc. Gen. Semantics, Assn. Supervision and Curriculum Devel., Phi Delta Kappa, Kappa Gamma Pi. Republican. Contbr. articles to profl. jours.

AURELIO, ROGER LOUIS, pneumatic nailing and stapling company executive; b. Chgo., May 3, 1947; s. Joseph John and Dorothy May (Fanaselle) A.; m. Paulette Marie Kraj, Nov. 16, 1968; children—Joseph, Heather, Roger Louis, Michael. Cert. Bogan Jr. Coll., 1968. Salesman Duo Fast Corp., 1967-75; founder, pres. New Supplies Co. Inc., Orland Park, Ill., 1975—. Club: Riviera Country. Home: 10541 S Lockwood St Oak Lawn IL 60453 Office: PO Box 240 Orland Park IL 60462

AUSNEHMER, JOHN EDWARD, lawyer; b. Youngstown, Ohio, June 26, 1954; s. John Louis and Patricia Jean (Liguore) A.; m. Margaret Mary Kane, Oct. 17, 1981; 1 child, Jill Ellen. B.S., Ohio State U., 1976; J.D., U. Dayton, 1980. Bar: Ohio 1980, U.S. Dist. Ct. (no. dist.) Ohio 1981, U.S. Supreme Ct. 1984, U.S. Ct. Appeals (6th cir.) 1984. Law clerk Ohio Atty. Gen., Columbus, 1978; assoc. Dickson Law Office, Petersburg, Ohio, 1979—; sole practice, Youngstown, Ohio, 1984—. Mem. Am. Trial Lawyers Assn., Ohio Acad. Trial Lawyers, ABA, Ohio State Bar Assn., Mahoning County Bar Assn., Columbiana County Bar Assn., Phi Alpha Delta. Democrat. Roman Catholic. Club: Mahoning Valley Soccer (rep. 1982-84). Home: 310 Ewing Rd Youngstown OH 44512 Office: 14 Boardman-Poland Rd Youngstown OH 44512

AUSTIN, DOROTHY WITTE, journalist; b. Necedah, Wis., Aug. 22, 1918; d. Emil Alfred and Marie (Wake) Witte; B.A. cum laude in Journalism, Marquette U., 1940; m. Harry Russell Austin, Oct. 3, 1953; children—Richard Kirk, Stephen Russell, Christopher. With Cath. Herald Citizen, 1940-43; staff asst. ARC, Africa and Italy, 1943-45; advt. copy chief Gimbels, Milw., 1945-50; reporter Milw. Jour., 1950-67; asst. and asso. dir. Summerfest, 1967-69; reporter, feature writer Milw. Sentinel, 1970—; public speaker. Former pres. Women's Overseas Service League, Milw.; former bd. dirs. Milw. County Hist. Soc. Recipient Women in Action award, U. Wis., Milw., 1964, award for women's interest features, Milw. Press Club, 1963, award for features, Wis. Press Women, 1976, staff award for excellence in reporting, Milw. Sentinel, 1977, Headliner award Southeastern Wis. chpt. Women in Communications, 1979, Faith and Humanities award, Nat. Council Jewish Women, Milw., 1979; Women of Yr., Milw. chpt. NOW, 1983; Journalistic Achievement award Wis. Women's Network, 1983. Mem. Wis. Press Women (past pres.), Washington Press Club, Milw. Press Club (past sec.), Kappa Tau Alpha, Gamma Pi Epsilon. Unitarian. Home: 5858 N Lake Dr Milwaukee WI 53217 Office: 918 N 4th St Milwaukee WI 53201

AUSTIN, JACK KENNETH, banker; b. Anderson, Mo., Sept. 28, 1923; s. Chester Andrew and Edna Sue (Eddins) A.; B.S., U. Denver, 1952, postgrad., 1953; m. Vivian Lenore Bell, July 21, 1966; children—Kathleen, Mary Ann, Debra. Escrow officer, office mgr., acct. Titles Inc., 1954-58; asst. trust officer Am. Nat. Bank, Denver, 1958-65; asst. account adminstr. 1st Nat. Bank, Denver, 1965-69; trust officer Bank of Commerce, Sheridan, Wyo., 1969-73; v.p., trust officer Wyo. Nat. Bank, Casper, 1973-75; v.p., trust officer Central Trust & Savs. Bank, Geneseo, Ill., 1975—; cons. estate planning, taxation. Served with AUS, 1943-46; ETO. Mem. Quad City Estate Planning Council, Rock Island County Assn. Life Underwriters, Am. Bankers Assn., Henry County Bankers Assn., Henry County Bar Assn. Republican. Conglist. Clubs: Elks, Lions, Kiwanis. Home: 26 Geneseo Hills Geneseo IL 61254 Office: 101 N State St Geneseo IL 61254

AUSTIN, KENNETH RALPH, insurance company executive; b. Keosauqua, Iowa, Mar. 15, 1920; s. James Clayton and Nancy Matilda (Landreth) A.; m. LaVerne Eleanor Turin, May 9, 1942; children—Marilyn Austin Rumelhart, Alan Karl. B.C.S., Drake U., 1941; M.S., U. Iowa, 1942; D.H.L. (hon.), Buena Vista Coll., 1980. With Equitable Life of Iowa, 1947—, agy. v.p., Des Moines, 1960-64, v.p., controller, 1964-66, exec. v.p., 1966-69, pres., 1969-81, chmn., 1981-85, vice chmn., 1985—, pres. Equitable of Iowa Cos., 1977-85; pres. DDM Devel. Corp., Des Moines, 1984—. Chmn., Greater Des Moines Com., 1981, Iowa Coll. Found., 1973-75, United Campaign Central Iowa, 1980; pres.-elect, United Way Central Iowa; many others. Served to lt. comdr. USN, 1942-45. Fellow Life Mgmt. Inst. Republican. Methodist. Club: Des Moines. Office: Equitable Ia Cos 604 Locust St Des Moines IA 50306

AUSTIN, MICHAEL HERSCHEL, lawyer; b. nr. Water Valley, Miss., Nov. 7, 1896; s. Michael Green and Willie C. (Roberson) A.; student U. Miss., 1915-18, LL.B., 1922; postgrad. Akron U., 1919; postgrad. Ohio State U., 1919-21, J.D., 1923; m. Esther Catherine Seebach, Nov. 26, 1920 (dec.); m. 2d, Mary Inez Harpst. Tchr. pub. elementary sch., Miss., 1914-15; admitted to Miss. bar 1922, Ohio bar, 1924, since practiced in Columbus, Ohio; partner firm Pfeiffer and Austin, 1927-30. Franklin County atty. Farmers Home Adminstrn., 1963-70. Mem. chmn.'s council Franklin County Democratic Com., mem. Ohio Dem. Party. Fellow of Harry Truman Library; hon. fellow Truman Library Inst. Served with U.S. Army World War I. Recipient Cross of Honor, UDC, 1944, award for service to Am. Legion and vets. Am. Legion, Lancaster, Ohio, 1969; Golden Circle Certificate Ohio State U. Assn.; named mem. Exec. and Profl. Hall of Fame. Mem. Internat. Platform Assn., Am. Bar Assn. (estate gift tax sect.), Ohio (50 Yrs. Practice award), Columbus (probate ct. com., 50 Yrs. Practice award) bar assns., Am. Judicature Soc., Columbus Real Estate Bd. (asso.). Ohio State U. Alumni Assn., Columbus Area C. of C., Am. Legion (post comdr. 1944-45, county comdr. 1953-54, dist. comdr. 1955-56, state treas. 1958-59, Big Four Vets. Council 1956-57, pres. Past Comdrs. Club 1960-61, judge adv. 12th dist. Ohio, 1967, 68, 69, 75-76, named 12th. dist. Outstanding Legionnaire). Phi Alpha Delta. Mason. Clubs: Columbus Lawyers (past sec.), Franklin County Democratic. Home and Office: 47 Richards Rd Columbus OH 43214

AUSTIN, ORLO BLAINE, educational administrator; b. Fillmore County, Minn., Apr. 12, 1940; s. Gilbert Austin and Ethel Beneeta (Scheevel) Sears; m. Cheryl Winnis Peterson, Aug. 9, 1964; children—Peter, Ingrid. B.A., Mankato State U. (Minn.), 1963; M.A., U. Minn., 1972, Ph.D., 1977; postgrad. Harvard U., 1984. Tchr. Pub. High Sch., Sleepy Eye, Minn., 1963-64; counselor Youth Opportunity Ctr., Mpls., 1964-65; counselor U. Minn., Mpls., 1965-72, asst. dir. student fin. aid, 1972-81; dir. student fin. aid U. Ill., Champaign, 1981—; mem. fin. aid adv. com. Minn. Higher Edn. Coordinating Bd., St. Paul, 1978-81; mem. Midwest Adv. Council, Am. Coll. Testing, Iowa City, Iowa, 1980-83, mem. nat. adv. council, 1983-84. Jr. League coordinator Good Shepherd Lutheran Ch., Champaign, Ill., 1983—; coach Champaign Park Bd., 1983-84; bd. dirs. Children's Home and Aid Soc., Champaign, 1984-85. Mem. Midwest Assn. Student Fin. Aid Adminstrs. (pres. 1985—), Am. Assn. Counseling and Devel., Am. Coll. Personnel Assn., Ill. Assn. Student Fin. Aid Assn. Avocations: Jogging; spectator sports. Home: 2504 Nottingham Dr Champaign IL 61821 Office: U Ill 420 Fred H Turner Student Services Bldg 610 E John St Champaign IL 61820

AUSTIN, RICHARD HENRY, state official; b. Ala., May 6, 1913; s. Richard H. and Lelia (Hill) A.: B.S., Detroit Inst. Tech., 1937; LL.D., Detroit Coll. Bus., 1971; LL.D., Detroit Inst. Tech., 1979, Mich. State U., 1985; m. Ida B. Dawson, Aug. 19, 1939; 1 dau., Hazel. Practice as pub. accountant, Detroit, 1941-71; auditor Wayne County, Mich., 1967-70; sec. of state State of Mich., Lansing, 1971—. Del. Mich. Constl. Conv., 1961-62. Bd. dirs. Harper-Grace Hosp., Detroit, Detroit United Found., Detroit YMCA, Oakland Housing, Inc. Mem. Am. Inst. C.P.A.'s, Mich. Assn. C.P.A.'s (Distinguished Achievement award 1972). Democrat. Office: Treasury Bldg Lansing MI 48918

AUSTIN-LETT, GENELLE, educator; b. Chgo.; d. Howard Joseph and Evelyn Gene (Reynolds) Blomquist. B.A., U. Ill., Chgo., 1969; M.A., No. Ill. U., 1972. Teaching and research asst. No. Ill. U., 1970-71; TV prodn. asst. Nat. Coll. Edn. High Sch. Workshop, 1972; prof. mass media and critical consumer Principia Coll., summer 1975; reviewer in interpersonal communication, media and behavioral scis. Houghton Mifflin, Harper & Row, William C. Brown, and Wadsworth Pub., 1972—, also asso. prof. speech communication and media Ill. Central Coll., East Peoria, 1971-79; editorial cons. Concordia Pub. House,

1978-82; program dir. Clayton (Mo.) U., 1978-82; tchr. English, Principia Upper Sch., 1983—; asst. prof. communications Meramec Community Coll.; coordinator performing arts multimedia presentations, publicity and recruitment; lectr. media consumerism, psychopolitics and advt.; instr. communications, cons. crisis intervention Fed. Police Tng., 1974-75. Group leader Community Devel. Council, 1974; organizer 9th Ward Teenage Republicans, Chgo., 1963, coordinator, 1967-69; adviser to Ill. Central Coll. Young Reps., 1971-75; clk., dir. exec. bd., chmn. bd. 1st Ch. of Christ, Scientist, Peoria; nat. advisory bd. Am. Security Council; mem. Rep. Nat. Com. Recipient Honors Day recognition U. Ill., 1968, hon. mention Nat. Arts and Letters playwriting contest, 1972; lic. life ins. agt., Mo. Mem. Ill. Speech and Theatre Assn., Speech Communication Assn., Central States Speech Assn., Internat. Data Speak. Clubs: U.S. Senatorial, Bible Investigation, Racquet. Author: (with others) Instructor's Manual for Mass Communication and Human Interaction, 1977; (with Jan Sprague) Talk to Yourself, 1976; contbr. articles to Christian Sci. periodicals.

AUSTINSON, CARLYLE PALMER, banker, city ofcl.; b. Fillmore, N.D., Oct. 10, 1914; s. Austin K. and Louise (Sterry) A.; student State Sch. Sci., Wahpeton, N.D., 1940; m. Helen Sylvia Rauk, 1941; children—Sharon Sylvia, Kent Carlyle. Asst. cashier First Internat. Bank, Esmond, N.D., 1941-43; cashier Farmers State Bank, Leeds, N.D., 1945-50; cashier Northwood State Bank (N.D.), 1950—, v.p., 1970-75, exec. v.p., 1975-79, chief exec. officer, 1977—, pres., 1979—, dir. 1958—. Alderman, City of Northwood, 1952-56, mayor, 1958—; bd. dirs. Northwood Deaconess Hosp. and Home Assn., pres., 1961—; mem. nat. adv. council Nat. Fedn. Ind. Bus.; mem. corp. United Hosp., Grand Forks, N.D. Served from pvt. to sgt., U.S. Army, 1943-45. Mem. Am. Bankers Assn. (governing council 1981, 82, state v.p. 1983), N.D. Bankers Assn. (pres. N.E. dist. 1955, chmn. bank mgmt. com. 1957, chmn. Northeast dist. Centennial Commn. 1963, chmn. pub. relations 1964, mem. legis. com. 1972, 1st v.p. 1975, pres. 1976), League N.D. Municipalities (regional v.p. 1958, pres. 1961), Am. Legion (comdr. post 92, 1967). Republican. Lutheran. Lodges: Elks, Masons. Office: Northwood State Bank Northwood ND 58267

AUXIER, PETER MERRILL, electronic component salesman; b. Chgo., June 15, 1958; s. William Charles and Evangeline (Williams) A.; m. Lori Jo Trumpy, July 31, 1982. B.S.B.A., U. Wis.-La Crosse, 1980. Salesman, Guardian Electric Co., Chgo., 1980-82, NEP Electronics Inc., New Berlin, Wis., 1982—. Mem. Jr. C. of C. (Muskego, Wis.). Lodge: Eagles. Home: W170 S6804 Timber Ct Muskego WI 53150 Office: NEP Electronics Inc 2604-06 S 162d St New Berlin WI 53151

AVEDISIAN, ARMEN G., corporate executive, investor; b. Chgo., Oct. 28, 1926; s. Karekin Der and Kardovil (Ignatius) A.; B.S., U. Ill., 1949; m. Dorothy D. Donian, Nov. 22, 1952; children—Guy A., Vann A., Donna A. Civil engr. Standard Paving Co., Chgo., 1949; constrn. supt. Gallagher Asphalt Corp., Thornton, Ill., 1950-55; v.p., dir. Am. Asphalt Paving Co., Chgo., 1956-64; chmn. bd., pres. Lincoln Stone Quarry, Inc., Joliet, Ill., 1964—, Avedisian Industries, Inc., Hillside, Ill., 1964—; chmn. bd. Delta Constrn. Corp., Joliet, 1968—, Swenson, Inc., Joliet, 1970—, Midstate Stone Corp., Gillespie, Ill., 1970—; chmn. bd., chief exec. officer Hillside (Ill.) Stone Corp., 1969—, Avedisian Co., 1978—; chmn. bd., chief exec. officer Geneva Capital Corp., Lake Geneva, Wis.; chmn. bd., Citizens Nat. Bank, Geneva. Dir. pres.'s com. Lyric Opera, Chgo., 1968—, dir. Easter Seal Soc.; mem. classical art acquisitions com. Art Inst. Chgo., 1961—; apptd. by Pres. Reagan to Statue of Liberty/Ellis Island Centennial Com., 1982; trustee Avery Coonley Sch. (chmn. European Tour Com.), Chgo. Symphony Orch., 1978—, Glenwood (Ill.) Sch. for Boys, Max McGraw Wildlife Found.; v.p. Geneva Lake Water Safety Patrol; mem. exec. bd. Boy Scouts Am., 1978—; gen. com. La Societe des Bains de Herde Monte Carlo World Backgammon championship. Served with AUS, 1944-45. Mem. Nat. Limestone Inst. (chmn. bd. 1971—), Midwest Crushed Limestone Inst. (pres. 1966-67), Nat. Crushed Stone Inst. (bd. govs. 1972—), Ill. Rd. Builders Assn. (dir., treas. 1963), Am., Western socs. civil engrs., Ill. Assn. Aggregate Producers (dir., pres. 1968), Sigma Nu. Clubs: Casino, Chicago, Racquet (Chgo.); Butler Nat. Golf (gov. 1978—) (Oak Brook, Ill.); Dunham Woods Riding (Wayne, Ill.); Casa de Campo Golf (Dominican Republic); Palm Beach Polo and Country (Fla.); Lake Geneva (Wis.) Country. Patentee impermeable ecol. shale barrier in U.S., Can., U.K., France, West Germany. Home: Hinsdale IL Office: PO Box 68 Hinsdale IL 60521 also 401 Broad St Lake Geneva WI 53147

AVEDON, BRUCE, insurance consultant; b. Atlantic City, Dec. 31, 1928; s. N. Jay and Rosalie Ann (Sholtz) A.; B.S., Yale U., 1950; m. Shirlee Florence Young, May 19, 1951; children—Linda Michele, Bruce Frederick. Vice pres. Sholtz Ins. Agy., Inc., Miami, Fla., 1950-51; various positions to dir. planning State Mut. Life Assurance Co. Am., Worcester, Mass., 1953-69, also sec. Am. Variable Annuity Life Assurance Co., Worcester, 1967-69; v.p. equity products Ohio Nat. Life Ins. Co., Cin., 1969-83, also v.p., dir. O.N. Equity Sales Co., Cin, 1973-83; pres., dir. Ohio Nat. Fund, Inc., 1978-83; ins./investment products cons. to fin. services industry, 1983—. Served to lt. AUS, 1951-53; maj. Finance Corps Res. ret. Mem. Investment Co. Inst. (pension com.), Life Office Mgmt. Assn. (equity products and annuity com.), Nat. Assn. Securities Dealers (qualifications com. 1982—), Res. Officers Assn., Mil. Order World Wars. Republican. Methodist. Clubs: Yale (Cin.), Masons, Order Eastern Star. Home: 6601 Hitching Post Ln Cincinnati OH 45230 Office: PO Box 30324 Cincinnati OH 45230

AVEDON, LINDA MICHELE, charitable organization executive; b. Worcester, Mass., Sept. 27, 1954; d. Bruce and Shirlee (Young) A.; B.S., Ohio U., 1976, M.A., 1978. Intern, Office of U.S. Senator Robert Taft, Jr. of Ohio, Cin., summers 1973, 74, 75; asst. to fin. dir. 76 Taft for Senate Com., Cin., 1976; grad. asst. Devel./Alumni Office, Ohio U., Athens, 1977; fin. dir. Aronoff for Congress com., Cin., 1978; sr. campaign-communications assoc. United Appeal, Cin., 1979-83; exec. dir. United Way Wayne County, Richmond, Ind., 1984—; cons. polit. fund raising. Mem. student govt. reorgn. task force, Ohio U., 1975-76, jud. reorgn. task force, 1975-76, center program bd., 1975-76; campaign staff worker Pres. Nixon, Pres. Ford, Senator Robert Taft Jr., Ohio Senator Stanley J. Aronoff, county commr. Robert Taft II, Senator Howard Baker, Pres. Reagan campaigns; mem. Hamilton County Rep. Policy Com.; mem. adv. com. Sta. WECI-FM, vice chmn., 1985. Mem. Nat. Soc. Fund Raising Execs., Greater Cin. Soc. Fund Raising Execs., Women In Communications (treas. Cin. chpt. 1980-81), Richmond Area C. of C. (all-Am. city com. 1985), Hamilton County Young Reps. (v.p. 1982, pres. 1983), Hamilton County Rep. Women (dir. 1982), Ohio League Young Rep. Clubs (vice chmn. 1975-76), Ohio U. Alumni Assn. (sec. 1980-83), Sigma Sigma Sigma. Republican. Club: Altrusa (Richmond). Home: 135 S 3d St Richmond IN 47374 Office: 42 S 9th St Richmond IN 47374

AVELLONE, FRANCIS PAUL, actuarial and pension consulting firm exec.; b. St. Louis, Mar. 5, 1926; s. Salvatore Carmelo and Mary Amanda (Gingrich) A.; B.B.A., Miami U., 1947; M.B.A., Roosevelt U., 1964; m. Elizabeth Therese Byrne, Apr. 26, 1947; children—Mary Eichmann, Richard, William, Francis, Thomas, Anne. Joined U.S. Navy, 1943, commd. ensign, 1945, advanced through grades to comdr.; ret., 1966; with Louis Behr Orgn., Inc., Chgo., 1966—, exec. vice-pres., 1972-76, pres., 1976—. Mem. Am. Acad. Actuaries, Am. Soc. Chartered Life Underwriters, Am. Soc. Pension Actuaries, Am. Legion, Navy League. Roman Catholic. Rotarian. Home: 650 Green Bay Rd Lake Bluff IL 60044 Office: 401 N Michigan Ave Chicago IL 60611

AVENI, ANTHONY JOSEPH, lawyer, educator; b. Cleve., Aug. 1, 1938; s. Vincent James and Antoinette Elizabeth (Finelli) A.; m. Marie-Terese Sweeney, Aug. 22, 1964; children—Karen Marie, James Vincent, Laura Ann. B.S.C.E., U. Notre Dame, 1961; M.S.C.E., Stanford U., 1962; J.D., Cleve.-Marshall Law Sch., 1966. Bar: Ohio 1966, U.S. Dist. Ct. (no. dist.) Ohio 1969. Ptnr., Sweeney & Aveni, Painesville, Ohio, 1966-75; assoc. Milburn, Cannon, Stern & Aveni, Painesville, 1975-80, Cannon, Stern, Aveni & Krivok, Painesville, 1980—; instr. real estate law Lakeland Community Coll., Mentor, Ohio, 1970—; mcpl. law dir. City of Mento-on-the-Lake, 1983—; bd. atty. Lake County Bd. Realtors, Mentor, 1982—. Bd. dirs. Western Res. Counseling Service, Painesville, 1968—; chmn., prof. div. United Way Lake County, 1978; county chmn. March of Dimes, Cleve., 1973. Mem. Lake County Bar Assn., Ohio State Bar Assn. (bd. govs., real property sect.). Democrat. Roman Catholic. Club: Laker Anchor (Mentor) (pres. 1979) Gyro-Western Res. (Painesville) (pres. 1973-74), Madison Country. Lodge: K.C. Avocations: Golf; fishing. Home: 28 Fairfield Rd Painesville OH 44077 Office: Cannon Stern Aveni & Krivok Co L P A 41 E Erie St Painesville OH 44077

AVERILL, FRANCES EDWINA CRANE, hospital official; b. Saginaw, Mich., Nov. 27, 1923; d. Benjamin Franklin Alonzo and Ethel (Dustin) Crane; student public schs., Saginaw; m. Donald Lewis Averill, Nov. 28, 1942 (dec. May 1978); children—Carole Averill Hernandez, Kathleen Averill Easterling, Donald Edwin, Colleen Averill Avery. Central supply aide Saginaw Gen. Hosp., 1958-65, central supply supr., 1965-76, dir. central sterile dept., 1976—. Mem. Internat. Assn. Hosp. Central Service Mgmt., Am. Soc. Hosp. Central Service Personnel, Mich. Soc. Hosp. Central Service Personnel, Mid Mich. Central Service Assn. Methodist. Home: 1512 Durand St Saginaw MI 48602 Office: Saginaw Gen Hosp 1447 N Harrison St Saginaw MI 48602

AVERS, JOHN MICHAEL, hospital administrator; lawyer; b. Adrian, Mich., Oct. 22, 1951; s. Maurice E. and Kathryn L. (Underwood) A.; m. Susan A. Stageman, Aug. 18, 1973 (div. Sept. 1975); m. Patricia L. Parsons, June 24, 1978. A.B., Augustana Coll., Ill., 1973; J.D., U. Toledo, 1977. Bar: Ohio 1978. Sole practice law, Toledo, 1978-80; adminstrv. dir. Riverside Hosp., Toledo, 1980-82, mktg. mgr., 1982-84; contract mgr. St. Vincent Med. Ctr., Toledo, 1984—; exec. dir. Addison Community Hosp., Mich., 1984—. Mem. ABA, Ohio Bar Assn., Soc. Ohio Hosp. Attys., Am. Mktg. Assn., Toledo Bar Assn., Am. Soc. Law and Medicine, Mich. Hosp. Assn., Am. Hosp. Assn. Avocations: golf; sailing; tennis. Office: Addison Community Hosp 421 N Steer St Addison MI 49220

AVERY, ARTHUR CHESTER, hotel, restaurant and institutional management educator, food service consultant; b. New London, Conn., May 4, 1915; s. Arthur Chester and Lillian (Hedges) A.; m. Ethel Meurer, Aug. 24, 1940 (div. 1961); children—Arthur Rollin, Carol Margaret, Paul Felix; m. Nanette DuShane Robertson, June 10, 1961. B.S., Mass. State Coll., 1938; M.S., U. Mass., 1947; Ph.D., U. Mo., 1969; cert. bus. adminstrn. Rutgers U., 1958. Food technologist, U. Mass., Amherst, 1945-47; fishery products technologist Philippine Fisheries Program, Manila, 1947-50; dir. Food Sci. and Engring. div. US Navy, Bayonne, N.J., 1950-66; instr. instl. mgmt. U. Mo., Columbia, 1967-69; prof. restaurant, hotel, and instl. mgmt. Purdue U., West Lafayette, Ind., 1969—; foodservice cons. Avery & Avery, West Lafayette, Ind., 1967—; trustee Nat. Sanitation Found., Ann Arbor, Mich., 1980—; adv.-cons. Army Natick Labs., Mass. 1970-82. Author: Cosmopolitan Fish Cookery for the Phillippines, 1949; Food Preservation for the Philippines, 1950; Modern Guide to Foodservice Equipment, 1980. Contbr. articles to profl. jours. Pres. N.J. Assn. Retarded Children, 1968-69; trainer Union council Boy Scouts Am., Roselle, N.J., 1951-57. Served to maj. U.S. Army, 1940-46, ETO. Recipient Mary Matthews award Consumer and Family Scis. Sch., Purdue U., 1980. Fellow Soc. Adv. Food Service (pres. 1960-61); mem. Inst. Food Technologists, Foodservice Cons. Internat. Soc. (pres. 1970-71), Council Hotel, Restaurant and Instl. Edn. (dir. 1969-70, Howard B. Meek award for outstanding educator 1978). Republican. Episcopalian. Avocations: sports; reading; writing. Office: Purdue U 153 Stone Hall West Lafayette IN 47907

AVERY, WILLIAM PAUL, political scientist, educator; b. Erwin, N.C., Feb. 7, 1942; s. Sherrill William and Vida (Parker) A.; B.S., U. Tenn., Knoxville, 1968, M.A., 1971; Ph.D., Tulane U., 1975; children—Paul Kevin, Amanda Kay. Instr. polit. sci. Tulane U., New Orleans, 1972-74; asst. prof. polit. sci. U. Nebr., Lincoln, 1974-78, assoc. prof., 1978-83, prof., 1983—, vice chmn. dept. polit. sci., 1977-79; vis. prof. Warsaw U., Poland, 1980-81. Nebr. chmn. Com. of Ams. for Canal Treaties, 1978; U. Nebr. coordinating com. United Way, 1979; mem. state steering com. Common Cause Nebr., 1984—; exec. com. Lancaster County Democratic Party, 1984—; bd. dirs. Nebraskans for Peace, 1985—. Served with USAF, 1960-64. U.S. Office Edn. grantee, 1976-78. Mem. Am. Polit. Sci. Assn., Internat. Studies Assn., Peace Sci. Soc., Midwest Polit. Sci. Assn., So. Polit. Sci. Assn., Latin Am. Studies Assn., Midwest Assn. Latin Am. Studies. Editor: The Process of Rural Transformations, 1979; Rural Change and Public Policy, 1980; America in a Changing World Political Economy, 1982; contbr. articles to profl. jours. Home: 1925 E St Lincoln NE 68510 Office: Dept Polit Sci U Nebr Lincoln NE 68588

AVINS, LAURENCE RICHARD, ophthalmologist; b. N.Y.C., Mar. 13, 1946 s. Jack Avins and Ellen (Stern) Sharfstein; m. Carol Flannery, July 30, 1973; children—Sara, Jennifer. A.B., Amherst Coll., 1967; M.D., Cornell U., 1971. Diplomate Am. Bd. Internal Medicine, Am. Bd. Ophthalmology. Resident in internal medicine U. Rochester, N.Y., 1971-73; research assoc. USPHS, 1973-75; resident in ophthalmology Yale U., New Haven, 1975-76, Washington U., St. Louis, 1976-78; fellow in vitreoretinal surgery, U. Calif.-San Francisco, 1978-79; practice medicine specializing in vitreoretinal surgery, St. Louis, 1979—; clin. asst. prof. ophthalmology St. Louis U. Sch. Medicine, 1979—. Contbr. articles to profl. jours. Fellow Am. Acad. Ophthalmology; mem. Vitreous Soc. Home: 10 Carrswold Clayton MO 63105 Office: Retina and Vitreous Consultants Inc 1034 S Brentwood St Saint Louis MO 63117

AVIOLI, LOUIS VINCENT, physician, educator; b. Coatsville, Pa., Apr. 13, 1931; s. Louis and Edith (Croce) A.; m. Joan Truax, June 25, 1955; children—Richard C., Michael F., Edith A., Judith L., Gregory C. B.A. magna cum laude, Princeton U., 1953; M.D., Yale U., 1957. Intern, N.C. Meml. Hosp., Chapel Hill, 1957-58, asst. resident, 1958-59; clin. assoc. Nat. Cancer Inst., NIH, Bethesda, Md., 1959-61; instr. medicine N.J. Coll. Medicine, Jersey City, 1961-62, asst. prof., 1962-66, dir. research isotope lab., clin. research ctr., 1961-66, asst. sci. dir., 1961-65, chmn. radioisotope com., 1964-66; attending physician Jersey City Med. Ctr., 1962-66; asst. prof. medicine Washington U. Sch. Medicine, St. Louis, 1966-68, Shoenberg prof. medicine and oral biology, 1970—, prof. oral biology and medicine, 1977—, dir. div. bone and mineral metabolism, 1975—; attending physician Jewish Hosp. St. Louis, 1966—, Barnes Hosp., St. Louis, 1966—, St. Louis Children's Hosp., 1966—; mem. arthritis and metabolic diseases program NIH, Bethesda, 1966-71, chmn., 1969-71; perceptor dept. community medicine St. Louis U. Sch. Medicine, 1975—; mem. adv. panel endocrinology U.S. Pharmacopeia and the Nat. Formulary, 1976—; adviser Nat. Health and Med. Research Council, Australia, 1981—; bd. dirs. Internat. Conf. Calcium Regulating Hormones Inc., 1981—; vis. prof. medicine U. Siena (Italy), 1972, U. Caracas (Venezuela), 1974; vis. Alpha Omega Alpha prof. medicine Med. Coll. Ga., Augusta, 1974; vis. prof. medicine U. Capetown (South Africa), 1975; cons. Chinese Ministry Health, People's Republic of China. Recipient Andre Lichwitz Internat. prize, 1979. Fellow AAAS; mem. Soc. Exptl. Biology and Medicine, Am. Soc. Bone and Mineral Metabolism (founder, pres. 1979-80), Am. Inst. Biol. Scis. (space sci. com. 1983—), Radiation Research Soc., Am. Nuclear Soc., N.Y. Acad. Scis., AMA, Am. Fedn. Clin. Research, Am. Soc. Cell Biology, Endocrine Soc. (council), Orthopaedic Research Soc., Am. Physiol. Soc., Am. Soc. Clin. Investigation, Nat. Acad. Scis. (mem. space sci. bd. NRC 1972—), Acad. Sci. St. Louis (trustee 1981-83), St. Louis Soc. Internal Medicine, Royal Soc. Medicine (Eng.), Alpha Omega Alpha (lectr. 1973). Editor-in-chief Calcified Tissue Internat., 1978—. Contbr. chpts. to books and articles to profl. jours. Office: Jewish Hosp St Louis 216 S Kingshighway Saint Louis MO 63110

AVNET, ALLAN, construction company owner, engineering consultant; b. Detroit, June 16, 1939; m. Jane Ann Simpson, Mar. 12, 1977; children—Jeff Wayne, Jay Robert. B.S. M.E., Am. Western U., 1972. Pvt. practice cons. mech. engr. Boardman, Ohio, 1970-77; mech. engr. BASF Video Corp., Fountain Valley, Calif., 1977-80, Gen. Monitors, Costa Mesa, Calif., 1980-82; prin. mech. engr. MAI/Basic Four, Tustin, Calif., 1982-84; owner Tri-County Diecor Built, Salem, Ohio, 1984—; cons. engr. Trans Com, Costa Mesa, 1980. Mem. ASME, Soc. Plastic Engrs. Jewish. Club: Outspoken Wheelmen. Avocation: Photography. Home: 11615 Beaver Creek Rd Salem OH 44460

AWAD, GEORGE S., radiologic technologist, educator; b. Alexandria, Egypt, Mar. 5, 1948; came to U.S., 1973; s. Sobhi and Ester A.; m. Catherine Haddad, Aug. 31, 1973; children—Rachelle, Christina, George Meena. A.S. in Radiology, Triton Coll., 1979. Cert. radiologic technologist. Staff technologist Alexian Bros. Med. Ctr., Elk Grove, Ill., 1977-80; ednl. dir. Northwest Community Hosp., Arlington Heights, Ill., 1981—; asst. instr. Triton Coll., River Grove, Ill., 1979-81. Mem. Am. Soc. Radiologic Tech., Ill. Soc. Radiologic Tech., Assn. Univ. Radiologic Technologists. Avocations: flying; stamp and coin collecting. Home: 105 Forest Park Ln Hoffman Estates IL 60194 Office: Northwest Community Hosp 800 W Central Rd Arlington Heights IL 60005

AWAIS, GEORGE MUSA, obstetrician, gynecologist; b. Ajloun, Jordan, Dec. 15, 1929; s. Musa and Meha (Koury) A.; A.B., Hope Coll., 1955; M.D., U. Toronto, 1960; m. Nabila Rizk, June 24, 1970. Intern, U. Toronto Hosps., Ont., Can., 1960-61, resident in obstetrics and gynecology, 1961-64, chief resident, 1965; chief resident Harlem Hosp., Columbia U., N.Y.C., 1966; asst. obstetrician and gynecologist, Cleve. Met. Gen. Hosp., 1967, asso., 1969; instr. obstetrics and gynecology Case Western Res. U., Cleve., 1967-70, asst. obstetrician and gynecologist MacDonald House, 1970, asst. prof., 1970, asst. clin. prof. dept. reproductive biology, 1971, asst. obstetrician and gynecologist Univ. Hosps., 1971; staff dept. gynecology, Cleve. Clinic Found., 1971—; chmn. dept. obstetrics and gynecology King Faisal Specialist Hosp. and Research Center, Riyadh, 1975-76; cons. panel mem. Internat. Corr. Soc. Obstetricians and Gynecologists, 1971. Diplomate Am. Bd. Obstetrics and Gynecology. Fellow A.C.S., Am. Coll. Obstetricians and Gynecologists, Royal Coll. Surgeons Can.; mem. AMA, AAAS, Acad. Medicine of Cleve., Am. Infertility Soc. Contbr. articles to publs. in field, papers, reports to confs., TV appearances, Saudi Arabia. Office: Dept Gynecology Cleveland Clinic Cleveland OH 44106

AWL, CHARLOTTE JANE, nursing educator; b. St. Louis, Apr. 28, 1935; d. Herbert Vincent and Elizabeth Edwards (White) Pate; diploma Presbyn. Hosp. Sch. Nursing, Phila., 1956; student U. Pa., 1957-58; B.S. with distinction in Gen. Nursing, U. Ind., 1960, M.S. in Nursing Edn., 1961; postgrad. (Ada Belle Clark Welsh scholar), Ill. State U., 1978—; cert. CPR instr.; m. Richard Allen Awl, Sept. 2, 1962; children—Deborah Jane, David Allen, Stephen Scott. Team leader Presbyn. Hosp., Phila., 1956-57, head nurse women's surg. ward, 1957-58; staff nurse Bloomington (Ind.) Hosp., part-time 1958-60; pvt. duty nurse Robert Long Hosp., Indpls., spring 1960, Nursing Service Bur. Dist. 5, Ind. State Nurses Assn., Indpls., summer 1962; instr. med.-surg. nursing De Pauw U. Sch. Nursing, Greencastle and Indpls., 1961-63; instr. Meth. Med. Center Sch. Nursing, Peoria, Ill., 1963-64, part-time staff nurse Meth. Med. Center of Ill., 1964-66; cons. dept nursing Bradley U., Peoria, 1966-67, asst. prof., 1967-74, asso. prof., 1974—, assoc. chmn. dept. nursing, 1972-78, assoc. dir. div. nursing, 1978—. Mem. AAUP, Am. Nurses Assn., Nat. League Nursing, Assn. Operating Room Nurses, Council on Grad. Edn. for Adminstrn. in Nursing, AAUW, Sigma Theta Tau, Pi Lambda Theta, Kappa Delta Pi, Phi Kappa Phi. Presbyterian. Office: Div Nursing Bradley U Peoria IL 61625

AWOTUA-EFEBO, EBI BIODOMOYE, training consultant; b. Lagos, Nigeria, Oct. 16, 1951; s. Lucky Awotua and Matilda Enemi (Dufegha) E.; children—Otari, Karina, Otonye. B.Sc., Kent State U., 1974; M.A., Wayne State U., 1977, Ph.D. (grad./profl. scholar 1979-80), 1981. Tchr. high sch. Govt. Boys Secondary Sch., Nigeria, 1972; instr. dept. geology Wayne State U., 1975-77, instr. program area of instructional tech., 1978-81; sr. instructional technologist Burroughs Corp., Detroit, 1981—; prin. Efebo Assocs., Detroit, 1980—; cons. instructional design and implementation, mgmt. tng., field engring. tng. Active, Campus Crusade for Christ. Recipient award of merit for outstanding leadership as pres. Orgn. Nigerian Citizens in Am., 1978-79, 1980. Mem. Nat. Soc. Performance and Instrn., Assn. Ednl. and Tng. Tech., Assn. Ednl. and Communication Tech., Inst. Tng. and Devel. (Eng.), NAACP, Urban League. Democrat. Episcopalian. Clubs: Renaissance, Calvary Squadron. Contbr. articles to profl. jours. Home: 4688 St Antoine St Apt 102 Detroit MI 48201 Office: Burroughs Corp Suite 1414 Fisher Bldg 1 Burroughs Pl Detroit MI 48232

AXELROD, BARRY, air force officer; b. Willimantic, Conn., Mar. 23, 1949; s. Samuel and Esther (Steinberg) A.; B.S. in Acctg., U. Conn., 1972; m. Paula J. DesSureault, Aug. 5, 1979. Commd. in USAF, 1972, advanced through grades to maj., 1984; mem. missile combat crew Malmstrom AFB, Mont., 1972-76, jr. officer counsel, v.p., 1973-75; airborne missile ops. comdr. Ellsworth AFB, S.D., 1976-80; airborne launch control system evaluator and emergency war order instr. airborne command post SAC, Offutt AFB, Nebr., 1980-81, chief airborne launch control system tng. sect., 1981-83, hdqrs. ICBM code controller SAC, 1983-85; asst. ops. officer 741 Strategic Missile Squadron 91 Strategic Missile Wing, Minot AFB, N.D., 1985—. Mem. Vol. Fire Dept. S.D., 1978—. Mem. Rapid City Jaycees, Big Bros. Assn., Am. Legion. Jewish.

AXELROD, BARRY LEON, real estate financier; b. N.Y.C., Apr. 25, 1947; s. John and Frances Virginia (Cohen) A.; m. Holly Beth Golding, July 19, 1970; children—Rebecca Elyse, Jessica Gayle. B.A., No. Mich. U., 1969; M.A., Northeastern Ill. U., 1970. Producer, dir. New Trier Twp. Instructional TV, Winnetka, Ill., 1969-71; mortgage analyst Heitman Mortgage Co., Chgo., 1971-74; loan officer S.B. Cohen & Co., Chgo., 1974-75; asst. v.p. Banco Mortgage Co., Chgo., 1975-79; v.p. Cohen Fin. Corp., Chgo., 1979-83; pres. Golding Axelrod & Co., Chgo., 1983—. Sportcaster, football, basketball and hockey, high sch. and colls. Chgo. area, 1981—. Bd. dirs. Young Men's Jewish Council, Chgo., 1972-79, v.p. 1979; mem. Jr. Real Estate Bd. Chgo., pres. 1978. Mem. Internat. Council Shopping Ctrs., Assn. Ind. Real Estate Brokers, Aircraft Owners and Pilots Assn., No. Mich. U. Alumni Assn. (co-chmn. Chgo. chpt.). Office: Golding Axelrod & Co 4001 W Devon Ave Chicago IL 60646

AXELROD, LEONARD, management consultant; b. Boston, Oct. 27, 1950; s. Morris and Doris S. Axelrod. B.A., Ind. U., 1972; M.P.A., U. So. Calif., 1974; J.D., Hamline U., 1982. Asst. dir. Ind. Jud. Ctr., Sch. Law, Ind. U., Indpls., 1974-76; cons. Booz, Allen & Hamilton, Washington, 1976-77; staff assoc. Nat. Ctr. State Cts., St. Paul, 1977-82; ptnr. Ct. Mgmt. Cons., Mpls., 1982—; ptnr. Friedman, Farrar & Axelrod, Mpls., 1984—; cons. Ctr. Jury Studies, Vienna, Va., 1979-82, Calif. Atty. Gen., 1972-73, Control Data Bus. Advisers, Mpls., 1982—; mem. presdl. search com. Hamline U., 1980-81. Author: North Dakota Bench Book, 1982; contbr. articles to profl. jours.; assoc. editor Law Rev. Digest, 1982. Mem. exec. bd. Am. Jewish Com., Mpls.-St. Paul, 1980; reporter Minn. Citizen Conf. on Cts., 1980. Samuel Miller scholar, 1981. Mem. ABA, Am. Soc. Pub. Adminstrn., So. Calif. Soc. Public Adminstrn., Am. Judicature Soc., Booz, Allen & Hamilton Alumni (pres. Minn. 1980), Brandeis Soc. (exec. dir. Mpls. 1980), U. So. Calif. Midwest Alumni (exec. bd. Chgo. 1974), Phi Alpha Alpha. Republican. Jewish. Home: 2051 Loop Station Minneapolis MN 55402 Office: Friedman Farrar & Axelrod Inc 400 Marquette Ave Suite 560 Minneapolis MN 55401

AXELSON, JOSEPH ALLEN, professional basketball executive; b. Peoria, Ill., Dec. 25, 1927; s. Joseph Victor and Florence (Ealen) Massey A.; m. Malcolm Rae Smith, Oct. 7, 1950; children—David Allen, Mark Stephen, Linda Rae. B.S., Northwestern U., 1949. Sports info. dir. Ga. So. Coll., Statesboro, 1954-55, Furman U., Greenville, S.C., 1956; pub. relations dir. Ga. So. Coll., Statesboro, 1957-60, Nat. Assn. Intercollegiate Athletics, Kansas City, Mo., 1961-62; tournament dir. Bowling Proprs. Assn. Am., Park Ridge, Ill., 1963-64; asst. exec. sec. Nat. Assn. Intercollegiate Athletics, Kansas City, 1965-68; exec. v.p., gen. mgr. Cin. Royals Profl. Basketball Team, 1969-72; mgr. Cin. Gardens, 1970-72; pres., gen. mgr. Kansas City Kings Profl. Basketball Team, 1972-79, pres., gen. mgr., 1982—; v.p. ops. NBA, N.Y.C., 1979-82, chmn. competition and rules com., 1975-79. Served to capt. Signal Corps, U.S. Army, 1949-54. Named Nat. Basketball Exec. of Yr., Sporting News St. Louis, 1973; recipient Ann. Dirs. award Downtown, Inc., Kansas City, 1979. Mem. Naismith Basketball Hall of Fame (exec. com., 2d v.p.), Phi Kappa Psi. Republican. Presbyterian. Lodge: Rotary (Kansas City). Office: Kansas City Kings 1800 Genessee St Kansas City MO 64102

AXFORD, ROY ARTHUR, educator; b. Detroit, Aug. 26, 1928; s. Morgan and Charlotte (Donaldson) A.; B.A., Williams Coll., 1952; B.S., Mass. Inst. Tech., 1952, M.S., 1955, Sc.D., 1958; m. Anne-Sofie Langfeldt Rasmussen, Apr. 1, 1954; children—Roy Arthur, Elizabeth Carole, Trevor Craig. Supr. theoretical physics group Atomics Internat., Canoga Park, Calif., 1958-60; asso. prof. nuclear engring. Tex. A. and M. U., 1960-62, prof., 1962-63; asso. prof. nuclear engring. Northwestern U., 1963-66; asso. prof. U. Ill. at Urbana, 1966-68, prof., 1968—; cons. Los Alamos Sci. Lab., 1963—. Recipient cert. recognition for excellence in undergrad. teaching U. Ill., 1979, 81; Everitt award for teaching excellence, 1985; MIT sustaining fellow, 1984. Vice-chmn. Mass. Inst. Tech. Alumni Fund Drive, 1970-72, chmn., 1973-75. Mem. Am. Nuclear Soc., ASME, Am. Inst. Aeros. and Astronautics, SAR (sec.-treas. Piankeshaw chpt. 1975-81, v.p. chpt. 1982-83, pres. 1984—), Sigma Xi, Tau Beta Pi, Phi Kappa Phi. Home: 2017 S Cottage Grove Urbana IL 61801

AYDELOTTE, MARGARET BEESLEY, research biochemist, biochemistry educator; b. London, Eng., June 1, 1934; d. William Cameron and Mary Ann (Womersley) Walker; m. James Ernest Aydelotte, Sept. 16, 1961; children—John Mark, Marian Ruth, Allison Rachel. B.A., Cambridge U., 1956, M.A., 1960, Ph.D., 1961. Demonstrator, physiology Cambridge U., Eng., 1959-63; assoc. prof. biology Tarkio Coll., Mo., 1963-68; asst. prof. anatomy, U. Iowa, Iowa City, 1971-75; assoc. prof. biology Franklin Coll., Ind., 1975-78; asst. prof. anatomy Ind. U., Bloomington, 1978-81; asst. prof. biochemistry Rush Med. Coll., Chgo., 1981—. Contbr. articles to various publs. Research scholar Med. Research Council, U.K., 1956-59; Postdoctoral fellow NIH, 1971. Mem.

AAAS, Am. Assn. Anatomists, Orthopaedic Research Soc., Am. Soc. Cell Biology. Presbyterian. Office: Rush Med Coll 1753 W Congress Pkwy Chicago IL 60612

AYERS, LEONA WESTON, pathologist, physician, educator; b. Garner, N.C., Jan. 14, 1940; d. William Albert and Ida Bertha (Bell) Weston; B.S., Duke, 1962, M.D., 1967; m. James Cordon Ayers, Aug. 1, 1965; children—Ashley Albert, Alan Andrew. Intern, Duke U. Med. Center, Durham, N.C., 1967-68, resident in pathology, 1968-69; resident in pathology Univ. Hosps., Columbus, Ohio, 1969-71; individual practice medicine, specializing in pathology Columbus, Ohio, 1970—; dir. div. clin. microbiology Univ. Hosp., Columbus, 1970—; attending staff, 1971—; asst. prof. allied health professions Ohio State U., Columbus, 1974-78, pathology, 1971-77, assoc. prof. pathology, 1977—, allied health professions, 1978—; cons. in field. Diplomate Am. Bd. Pathology. Fellow Am. Soc. Clin. Pathologists (commn. on continuing edn. faculty, cons. nat. com. on affiliate and assoc. affairs; chmn. council microbiology), Coll. Am. Pathologists (mem. microbiology resource com.). Contbr. articles to profl. publs.; mem. editorial bd. Am. Jour. Clin. Pathology. Home: 3870 Lyon Dr Columbus OH 43220 Office: 410 W 10th Ave Columbus OH 43210

AYERS, RICHARD WAYNE, electrical manufacturing company official; b. Atlanta, Aug. 23, 1945; s. Harold Richard and Martha Elizabeth (Vaughan) A.; B.B.A., Ga. State Coll., 1967; M.B.A., Ind. U., 1969; m. Nancy Katherine Martin, Aug. 9, 1969. Specialist mktg. communications research Gen. Electric Co., Schenectady, 1969-70, copywriter Lamp div., Cleve., 1970-73, supr., distbr. advt. and sales promotion, 1973-75, supr. comml. and indsl. promotional programs Gen. Electric Lighting Bus. Group, 1975-79, mgr. comml. and indsl. market distbr. and promotional programs, 1979—; lectr. in field. Recipient Best Indsl. Promotion award Advt. Age, 1974, Premium Showcase award Nat. Premium Sales Execs., 1975, 76, Gold Key award Nat. Premium Mfrs. Reps., 1976, 77, Golden Key Communicators award Factory mag., 1976; Leader award Direct Mktg. Assn., 1983. Dir.-at-large Ga. Young Reps., 1966-67. Mem. Blue Key, Delta Sigma Pi, Beta Gamma Sigma. Home: 25801 Lake Shore Blvd Apt 86 Euclid OH 44132 Office: Nela Park Bldg 308 Cleveland OH 44112

AYLSWORTH, ROBERT REED, lawyer; b. Evansville, Ind., Oct. 24, 1953; s. Robert Earl and Loraine L. (Simmons) A.; m. Carolyn Sue Cundiff, Mar. 6, 1976; children—Beth Anne, Benjamin Reed. B.S., Ind. State U.-Evansville, 1976; J.D. magna cum laude, Ind. U.-Indpls., 1979. Bar: Ind. 1979, U.S. Dist. Ct. (so. dist.) Ind. 1979. Assoc. Phillips and Long, Boonville, Ind., 1979-82; dep. pros. atty. Warrick County-2d Jud. Cir. Ind., Boonville, 1980—; sole practice, Boonville, 1982—. Mem., v.p. Bd. Health of Warrick County, Boonville, 1980—; bd. dirs. Boonville Jr. Football League, 1982-83. Mem. ABA, Ind. State Bar Assn., Warrick County Bar Assn. (pres. 1983). Democrat. Home: 824 S 4th St Boonville IN 47601 Office: PO Box 461 316 S 2nd St Boonville IN 47601

AYNES, RICHARD LEE, lawyer, educator; b. Dayton, Ohio, June 12, 1949; s. Carl D. and B. Louise (Burton) A.; m. Kathleen H. Szokan, Aug. 20, 1971; 1 child, Jennifer Elizabeth. B.S., Miami U., Oxford, Ohio, 1971; J.D., Cleve.-Marshall Coll. Law, Cleve. State U., 1974. Bar: Ohio 1975, U.S. Supreme Ct. 1979; cert. tchr., Ohio. Intern, atty. Cleve. Legal Aid, 1974-75; law clk. 8th Dist. Ohio Ct. Appeals, Cleve., 1975-76; mem. faculty U. Akron Sch. Law, Ohio, 1976-84, assoc. dean, 1984—. Vice pres., trustee Western Res. Legal Services, Medina, Summit and Portage Counties, Ohio, 1982—. Fellow U. Akron, 1980. Mem. ABA (amicus com. criminal justice sect. 1982—, cons. victims com. 1982-83, reporter spl. com. on evaluation jud. performance 1983-84). Democrat. Office: U Akron Sch Law Akron OH 44325

AYRES, DAVID SMITH, b. Boston, June 14, 1939; s. Kenneth N. and Madeline (Smith) A.; m. Kathleen Nelson, Feb. 6, 1965. B.A., Williams Coll., Williamstown, Mass., 1961; M.A., U. Calif.-Berkeley, 1963, Ph.D., 1968. Postdoctoral fellow Lawrence Berkeley Lab., Calif., 1968-69; postdoctoral fellow Argonne Nat. Lab., Ill., 1969-71, asst. physicist, 1971-75, physicist, 1975-84, sr. physicist, 1984—; vol. Peace Corps, U. Nigeria, Enugu, 1963-64. Contbr. articles to profl. publs. Fellow Am. Phys. Soc.; mem. AAAS. Office: Argonne Nat Lab Bldg 362-HEP Argonne IL 60439

AYRES, PAUL JULIUS, insurance company executive; b. Lansing, Mich., Jan. 15, 1936; s. Julius S. and Rosalie M. (Ruonavaara) A.; A.A., Mich. State U., 1959; m. Ann M. Edwards, Feb. 22, 1958; children—Robert P., Sandra A., Cheryl L. Mgr. accident and health dept. H.T. Chadwell & Assos., Lansing, 1959-62; group rep. Blue Cross of Mich., Ann Arbor, 1962-65, acting mgr., 1964-65; v.p. Mich. Service Corp., Lansing, 1965-67, sr. v.p., 1967-69, exec. sr. v.p., 1969-71, dir., 1965-71; sec., treas., dir. Electronic Homes, Inc., Okemos, Mich., 1966-69; gen. mgr. Robb-Co, Okemos, 1969—; pres. Paul Ayres and Assos., Okemos, 1972—, Mich. Programmers Ins. Agy., Inc., Okemos, 1974—; owner, pres. Mich. Service Corp. Inc., Okemos, 1981-83. Maj., M.I., Air N.G. Mem. Lansing Life Underwriters, Mich. Assn. Life Underwriters (chmn. health com. 1982—), Mich. Employers Assn. (pres. 1969—), N.G. Assn., Am. Legion. Republican. Club: Eagles. Contbr. articles on ins. to various mags. Office: 1749 Hamilton Rd Okemos MI 48864

AYRES, ROBERT FRANKLIN, superintendent schools; b. nr. Warren, Ind., Apr. 29, 1925; s. James Madison and Dora Evelyn (Lucas) A.; B.S., Butler U., 1949, M.S., 1952; postgrad. Purdue U., 1958-62; m. Helen Denton, Mar. 7, 1947; children—James Michael, Robert William, John David, Christopher Allen, Carolyn Ann. Tchr., Orchard Country Day Sch., Indpls., 1948-50; tchr., dean of boys Frankfort High Sch. (Ind.), 1950-59, prin., 1959-65; asst. supt. schs. Huntington County, Ind., 1965-70; supt. schs. Rensselaer Sch. System, 1970-75; supt. Community Schs. Frankfort, 1975—; instr. Huntington Coll., 1967-70; lectr. Butler U.; dir. Citizen's Savs. and Loan. Exec. bd. Anthony Wayne council Boy Scouts Am.; bd. dirs. Huntington Coll. Found., Rensselaer chpt. Red Cross, Big Bros. Am., Retarded Children's Assn.; mem. Clinton County Area Plan Commn., 1976-78; v.p. and campaign drive chmn. Clinton County United Way. Served to lt. AUS, 1943-46. Nat. Defense Edn. Act fellow, 1960; St. Joseph's Coll. fellow, 1974. Mem. Ind. Assn. Pub. Sch. Supts., N.E.A., Am. Legion, V.F.W., Ind. Schoomen's Club, Am. Assn. Sch. Adminstrs., Clinton County C. of C. (dir. 1977—), Phi Delta Kappa, Lambda Chi Alpha, Tau Kappa Alpha, Alpha Phi Omega. Methodist. Optimist (pres. 1970), Rotarian, Lion. Home: 709 Williams Rd Frankfort IN 46041 Office: 50 S Maish Rd Frankfort IN 46041

AYRES, RUSSELL WILLIAM, JR., construction equipment company executive; b. Utica, N.Y., Mar. 8, 1926; s. Russell William and Helen A. (Gates) A.; m. Rebecca Thatcher, June 30, 1948; children—Russel William III, Carolyn, Stephen, Nancy. B.S.E.E., Yale U., 1948; M.E., U. Mich., 1946; postgrad. Harvard Bus. Sch., 1965. Mktg. mgr. Gen. Electric Co., 1948-61; corporate dir. strategic planning Westinghouse Air Brake Co., 1962-63; v.p., gen. mgr. Westinghouse Air Brake div. Am. Standard, 1963-70; pres., chief exec. officer Mosler Safe Co., Hamilton, Ohio, 1971-78; sr. v.p. corp. ops. J.I. Case Co., Racine, Wis., 1978-82, sr. v.p., gen. mgr. service parts supply div., 1982—. Vice chmn. bd. dirs. profl. affairs com. St. Lukes Hosp., Racine; v.p. fin. Racine Area United Way. Served with USN, 1943-46. Republican. Episcopalian. Club: Racine Country (Wis.). Office: 700 State St Racine WI 53404

AZAR, MIGUEL M., medical center administrator, pathologist; b. Cordoba, Argentina, Oct. 21, 1936; came to U.S., 1960, naturalized, 1970; s. Mariana (Rodriguez) A.; m. Silvia Herrera, Apr. 2, 1960; children—Silvia, Miguel, Victor, Pablo, Sandra, Daniel. B.A., Colegio Nat. Dean Funes, Argentina, 1954; M.D., Cordoba U., 1958; Ph.D. in Exptl. Pathology, U. Tenn., 1965. Diplomate Am. Bd. Pathology. Dir. blood bank U. Minn., Mpls., 1969-70; chief clin. lab, VA Med. Ctr., Mpls., 1970-75; dir. Pathology Grad. Edn., U. Minn., Mpls., 1973-75, dir. lab. med. edn., 1973-77; chief lab. services VA Med. Ctr., Mpls., 1975—; med. co-dir. St. Paul Vocat. Sch., St. Paul, 1984—; faculty adv. Latino med. students U. Minn., 1982—. Editor: Advanced Cell Biology, 1982, Monographs in Cell Biology, 1984. Assoc. editor Survey in Immunological Research, 1981—, Survey in Pathology, 1981—. Contbr. articles to profl. jours. Producer Momento Deportivo, 1976, Minn. Latino Media-Hispanic Perspective Sta. KUXL, 1976. Served with Argentine Army, 1953-54. Fellow NIH; grantee VA. Mem. Am. Assn. Immunology, Am. Soc. Pathology, Central Soc. Clin. Research. Roman Catholic. Avocations: ham radio, soccer. Office: VA Med Ctr 34th St and 48th Ave S Minneapolis MN 55417

AZARNOFF, DANIEL LESTER, pharmaceutical company executive; b. Bklyn., Aug. 4, 1926; s. Samuel J. and Kate (Asarnow) A.; m. Joanne Stokes, Dec. 26, 1951; children—Rachel, Richard, Martin. B.S., Rutgers U., 1947, M.S., 1948; M.D., U. Kans., 1955. Asst. instr. anatomy U. Kans. Med. Sch., 1949-50, research fellow, 1950-52, intern, 1955-56, resident Nat. Heart Inst., 1956-58, asst. prof. medicine, 1962-64, assoc. prof., 1964-68, dir. clin. pharmacology study unit, 1964-68, assoc. prof. pharmacology, 1965-68, prof. medicine and pharmacology, 1968, dir. Clin. Pharmacology-Toxicology Ctr., 1967-78, Disting. prof. medicine and pharmacology, 1973-78; spl. trainee Nat. Inst. Neurol. Diseases and Blindness, Washington U. Sch. Medicine, St. Louis, 1958-60; asst. prof. medicine St. Louis U. Sch. Medicine, 1960-62; vis. scientist Fulbright scholar Karolinska Inst., Stockholm, Sweden, 1968; sr. v.p. worldwide research and devel. G.D. Searle & Co., Chgo., 1978; pres. Searle Research and Devel., Skokie, Ill., 1979—; prof. pathology, clin. prof. pharmacology Northwestern U. Med. Sch., 1978—; lectr. U. Chgo., 1979; cons. various govtl. agys.; bd. dirs. Lorex Pharm. Co. Editor: Devel. of Drug Interactions, 1974-77; Yearbook of Drug Therapy, 1977-79; series editor: Monographs in Clin. Pharmacology, 1977—; mem. editorial and adv. bds. various profl. jours. Served with U.S. Army, 1945-46. Recipient Ginsburg award in phys. diagnosis U. Kans. Med. Ctr., 1953, Outstanding Intern award, 1956, Ciba award for gerontol. research, 1958, Rectors medal U. Helsinki, 1968; John and Mary R. Markle scholar, 1962, Burroughs Wellcome scholar, 1964; William N. Creasy vis. prof. Med. Coll. Va., 1975; Bruce Hall Meml. lectr. St. Vincents Hosp., Sydney, 1976; 7th Sir Henry Hallett Dale lectr. Johns Hopkins U. Med. Sch., 1978. Fellow ACP, N.Y. Acad. Scis.; mem. Am. Soc. Clin. Nutrition, Am. Nutrition Inst., Am. Soc. Pharmacology and Exptl. Therapeutics (chmn. clin. pharmacology div. 1969-71, exec. com. 1966-73, 78—, del. 1975-78, 80, bd. publ. trustees), Am. Soc. Clin. Pharmacology and Therapeutics, Am. Fedn. Clin. Research, Brit. Pharmacol. Soc., AMA (vice chmn. council on drugs 1971-72, editorial bd. Jour.), Central Soc. Clin. Research, Royal Soc. Promotion Health, Inst. Medicine of Nat. Acad. Scis., Soc. Exptl. Biology and Medicine (councillor 1976—), Internat. Union Pharmacologists (sec. clin. pharmacology sect. 1975—, internat. adv. com. Paris Congress 1978), Sigma Xi. Home: 1030 Lake Shore Blvd Evanston IL 60202 Office: 4901 Searle Pkwy Skokie IL 60077

BAALMANN, RICHARD FENTON, retail hardware executive; b. St. Louis, Oct. 30, 1935; s. Roderick Oliver and Melba (Bertholdt) B.; student St. Louis U., 1953-57; m. Kathleen Felke, June 12, 1957; children—Richard Fenton, Mary Kathleen, Margaret Grace, Anne Patricia. Vice pres. Mars Enders, Inc., retail hardware, St. Louis, 1956-68, pres., 1968-79; pres. Hardware Center, Inc., retail hardware, St. Louis, 1956-79, Markat, Inc., St. Louis, 1970-79, Bramm, Inc., 1979—. Past pres., chmn. bd. trustees Nat. Cystic Fibrosis Research Found.; chmn. St. Louis chpt. Jesuit Program for Living and Learning, nat. chmn., 1979-83; mem. Mo. Air Conservation Commn., 1980-83; bd. commrs. Bi-State Devel. Agy., 1982—, chmn., 1982-83; bd. dirs. East-West Gateway Coordinating Council, Glennon Children's Hosp., 1985—. Served as 1st lt. USAF, 1958-59. Mem. Brentwood C. of C. (pres. 1966), St. Louis Regional Commerce and Growth Assn., Advt. Club St. Louis, Delta Sigma Pi. Club: Rotary (pres. 1972). Home: 458 Bambury Way Saint Louis MO 63131 Office: 11767 Manchester Saint Louis MO 63131

BABA, MARIETTA LYNN, university official, b. Flint, Mich., Nov. 9, 1949; d. David and Lillian (Joseph) Baba; m. David Smokler, Feb. 14, 1977 (div. 1982); 1 dau., Alexia Baba Smokler. B.A. with highest distinction, Wayne State U., 1971, M.A. in Anthropology, 1973, Ph.D. in Phys. Anthropology, 1975. Asst. prof. sci. and tech. Wayne State U., Detroit, Mich., 1975-80, assoc. prof., 1980—, assoc. prof. anthropology, 1980—, spl. asst. to pres., 1980-82, econ. devel. officer, 1982-83, asst. provost, 1983—; founder, corp. officer Applied Research Teams Mich., Inc., Detroit, Intelligent Techs., Inc., Detroit; evolution researcher Wayne State U., 1975-82; lectr. nat. and internat. symposia, profl. conferences. Contbr. numerous papers and abstracts to profl. jours, tech. publs. Bd. dirs. City-Univ. Consortium, Detroit, 1980-83; v.p. Neighborhood Service Orgn., Detroit, 1980-85; mem. State Research Fund Feasibility Rev. Panel, 1982-85; active Leadership Detroit Class IV, 1982-83; dir. Mich. Tech. Council (SE div.), 1984-85. Job Partnership Tng. Act grantee, 1981-85; NSF grantee, 1982, 84-85. Mem. Am. Anthrop. Assn., Nat. Assn. Practice Anthropology (pres-elect), Soc. Applied Anthropology, Phi Beta Kappa, Sigma Xi. Office: Wayne State U 1050 Mackenzie Hall Detroit MI 48202

BABAI, MASSOOD REZA, psychiatrist; b. Zahedan, Iran, Jan. 27, 1939; s. Gholam Reza and Fatomeh G. B.; came to U.S., 1968; M.D., U. Tehran, 1965; m. Simin Soltanzadeh, May 6, 1963; children—Mojgan, Sarah, Dora. Pvt. practice medicine, Tehran, 1965-66; intern Misericordia Hosp., N.Y.C., 1968-69; resident Rollman Psychiat. Inst., Cin., 1969-72; pvt. practice medicine, specializing in psychiatry, Cuyahoga Falls, Ohio, 1973—; dir. ambulatory services Fallsview Psychiat. Hosp., 1972-74, dir. med. edn., 1974-77; dir., div. psychiatry St. Thomas Hosp., Akron, Ohio, 1976—; tchr. interns and residents St. Thomas Hosp., Fallsview Psychiat. Hosp. Med. Sch.; asso. prof. psychiatry N.E. Ohio U. Coll. Medicine. Served as 2d lt., Health Corps, Iranian Imperial Army, 1966-68. Diplomate Am. Bd. Psychiatry and Neurology. Mem. Am. Psychiat. Assn., Ohio Psychiat. Assn. Translator from English to Persian, Applied Physiology, 1965. Office: 275 Graham Rd Suite 8 Cuyahoga Falls OH 44223

BABAR, RAZA ALI, industrial engineer, educator; b. Shujabad, Punjab, Pakistan, May 29, 1947; came to U.S., 1972, naturalized, 1978; s. Syed Mohammad Ali Shah and Syeda Hafeeza (Gilani) Bukhari; m. Sufia K. Durrett, July 23, 1974 (div. 1983); children—Azra Yasmeen, Imran Ali, Amenah Ali; m. Syeda Afshan Gilani, Aug. 23, 1983; 1 child: Abdullah Ali. B.S. in Mining Engring., U. Engring. and Tech., Lahore, Pakistan, 1969; M.S. in Indsl. Engring., Wayne State U., 1978; postgrad Detroit Coll. Law, 1982. Engr., planner Bukhari Elec. Concern, Multan, Pakistan, 1969-70; mgr. mining operations Felezzate Yazd Co., Iran, 1970-72; salesman Great Books, Inc., Chgo., 1972-73; field underwriter N.Y. Life Insurance Co., 1972-73; indsl. engr. Ellis/Naeyaert Assocs., Inc., Warren, Mich., 1973-74; grad. asst. dept. indsl. engring. and ops. research Wayne State U., Detroit, 1974-75; prin. engr., work leader project services div. Generation Constrn. Dept., Detroit Edison Co., 1975-79; tech. advisor Ministry of Prodn., Govt. Pakistan, Islamabad, 1979-80; chmn. dept. bus. adminstrn. Zakariya U., Multan, Pakistan, 1980-82; prin. engr. project controls Enrico Fermi 2 Detroit Edison Co., 1981-82, supr. Fermi 2 rate case task force, 1982-84, spl. projects engr. planning, 1984—. Author research papers. Founder Fedn. Engring. Assns. Pakistan, 1969; pres. acad. staff assn. Zakariya U., Pakistan, 1980-81; pres. Pakistan Cultural Group, Detroit, 1975-76; bd. dirs. Detroit Islamic Library, 1976-77. Recipient Pride of Performance medal Engring. U., Pakistan, 1967; Acad. Merit scholar Detroit Coll. Law, 1982. Mem. Am. Mgmt. Assn., Am. Mgmt. Assn. Internat., Econ. Club Detroit, Am. Inst. Indsl. Engrs., Am. Assn. Cost Engrs., Engring. Soc. Detroit, ESD Profl. Activities Council, Pakistan Engring. Congress, Pakistan Inst. Mining Engrs., ABA (student chpt.), Am. Assn. of MBA Execs. Republican. Islam. Home: 2310 Coolidge Apt 105 Troy MI 48084 Office: 2000 Second Ave Detroit MI 48226

BABB, E. MAURLEA, marriage and family therapist; b. Newtown, Ind., June 22, 1927; d. B. Dewey C. and Bessie Arlotta (Fine) Scannel; m. Russell W. Babb, Feb. 9, 1947; children—A. Sue, Joyce A., Janet I. Student DePauw U., 1945-47; B.M.E., Am. Conservatory, 1949; M.S.E., No. Ill. U., 1964, Ed.D., 1984. Supr., tchr. Midlothian (Ill.) Pub. Schs., 1950-58; tchr. Dist. 41, Glen Ellyn, Ill., 1958-61; counselor Geneva (Ill.) High Sch., 1961-63, Glenbard West High Sch., Glen Ellyn, 1964-77; owner, dir. Chrysallis Ctr. for individual and family devel., Wheaton, Ill., 1977—; cons., lectr. on family dynamics to hosps., schs.; cons. agys. for handicapped; pub. family simulation game, a teaching tool. Chmn., Milton Twp. Com. on Youth, 1970-78; mem. task force Drug Abuse Community Action Team, 1978; mem. staff-parish relations com., United Methodist Ch., Glen Ellyn. Mem. AAUW, Am. Orthopsychiatric Assn., Am. Assn. Marriage and Family Therapists (approved supr.), Nat. Council Family Relations, Ill. Assn. Marriage and Family Therapists, Ill. Council Family Relations.

BABB, MICHAEL PAUL, engineering magazine editor; b. Logansport, Ind., May 17, 1944; s. Paul G. and Eleanor Ruth (Berg) B.; m. Sharon Jean Spence, Dec. 8, 1973; children—Sara, Melissa. B.S. in Physics, Ind. U., 1967. Teaching asst. U. Nebr., Lincoln, 1967-68; programmer Atomic Energy of Can., Pinawa, Man., 1968-70; tchr. high sch., jr. coll., Shawinigan, Que., Can., 1971-78; mgr. engring. services Nuclear Data, Schaumburg, Ill., 1979-85; assoc. editor Control Engring. Mag., Barrington, Ill., 1985—. NSF research fellow, 1966; U. Nebr. Grad. Sch. teaching asst., 1968. Mem. Am. Phys. soc., Soc. Tech. Communications, IEEE., Ind. U. Alumni Assn. Home: 322 Lovell St Elgin IL 60120 Office: Control Engring Mag 1301 S Grove Ave Barrington IL 60120

BABBINI, VICTOR LAWRENCE, educational administrator, educator; b. Wilkes-Barre, Pa., Mar. 4, 1942; s. I. and Clara B.; B.A., West Liberty State Coll., 1966; M.S., Eastern Ill. U., 1972; M.S. in Adminstrn., Niagara U., 1980. Dir. instrumental music Richmond, Ohio, 1966-69; music cons./specialist South Orange-Maplewood, N.J., 1969-71; music editor, staff writer-critic N.J. Music and Arts Mag. of Metro N.Y.C., 1970-72; prof. humanities, dir. fine and performing arts Medaille Coll., Buffalo, 1976—, admissions adv. counsel to pres., faculty curriculum com. for v.p. of acad. affairs, 1977-79, trustee council student affairs, 1978—, trustee com. for Non-Traditional Edn.; evaluator North Central Assn. of Schs. and Colls.; curriculum cons. Lorain County Office Edn., Ohio, since 1983—, cons. in edn. adminstrn; chmn. All-City Music, Niagara Falls, N.Y.; N.Y. State humanities resource cons. Mem. Music Critics Assn. Am., Ohio Art Educators Assn., Nat. Assn. Schs. Music, Music Educators Nat. Conf., Coll. Band Dirs., Nat. Assn., Nat. Assn. Coll. Wind and Percussion Instrs., Ohio Music Educators Assn., Assn. for Supervision and Curriculum Devel., Jr. C. of C., Phi Delta Kappa. Contbr. article to profl. jours.; author: N.Y. state pioneer B.S. program in arts mgmt. Home: 139 Shakespeare Ln Avon OH 44011

BABBITT, DONALD PATRICK, radiologist; b. Oshkosh, Wis., Aug. 24, 1922; s. James Sylvester and Loretta Gertrude (Sensenbrenner) B.; student U. Wis., River Falls, 1939-42; M.D., Med. Coll. Wis., 1946; m. Elizabeth May Gerhard, Apr. 28, 1945 (dec. Nov. 1971); children—Patrick, Ann, James; m. 2d Jill Ann Sieg, Jan. 29, 1975. Intern, Meth. Hosp., Indpls., 1946-47; resident Milw. Hosp. and Milw. Ch Hosp., 1949-52; practice medicine specializing in radiology, Milw.; mem. staff Milw. Children's Hosp., 1952—, chief radiology, 1964-82; mem. staff Milwaukee County Gen. Hosp., 1964—; cons. St. Mary's Hosp., Milw., 1968-76, attending staff, 1982—; instr. radiology Med. Coll. Wis., 1958, asso. prof. radiology, 1964-70, clin. prof., 1970—, clin. prof. pediatrics, 1979—; asso. clin. prof. radiology U. Wis. Center Health Scis., Madison, 1968-70, clin. prof., 1970—. Served as capt. M.C., AUS, 1947-49; ETO. Named Tchr. of Yr., Milw. Children's Hosp. Dept. Pediatrics, 1980; diplomate Am. Bd. Radiology. Fellow Am. Coll. Radiology (medallion in nuclear medicine 1959), Am. Acad. Pediatrics; mem. Am. Roentgen Ray Soc., European Soc. Pediatric Radiology, Soc. Pediatric Radiology, Radiol. Soc. N. Am., Wis. Radiol. Soc. (pres. 1976), State Wis. Med. Soc., Milw. Surg. Soc. (pres. 1978), Milw. Roentgen Ray Soc. (pres. 1975-77), Milwaukee County Med. Soc. (pres. 1974), Milw. Acad. Medicine 1973), Milw. Pediatric Soc., AMA, Med. Coll. Wis. Alumni Assn., Boy Scouts Am. (century mem.), Alpha Omega Alpha, Phi Chi. Roman Catholic. Clubs: Flying Physicians; Rotary (Milw.). Contbr. numerous articles to profl. jours. Home: 2701 E Beverly Rd Milwaukee WI 53211 Office: 2353 N Lake Shore Dr Milwaukee WI 53211

BABBO, JOSEPH THOMAS, rehab. counselor, social work therapist; b. Chgo., Jan. 24, 1932; s. Angelo and Anna Maria (Cereso) B.; student Loras Coll., 1956-58; Ph.B., Belmont Abbey Coll., 1963; M.S., Ill. Inst. Tech., 1973, postgrad., 1975—; m. Mary Josephine Hamrock, Oct. 29, 1967; children—Angelo Joseph, Mary Immaculata, Martin Francis, Thomas John, Annamaria, Giovanna Carmella. Rehab. counselor Ill. Dept. Rehab. Services, Chgo., 1964—; marriage and family counselor and therapist; union rep., steward AFSCME Local 2000, 1971—, collective bargaining com., 1975—; counselor rep. Dept. Vocat. Rehab. Visitor chmn. Christian Outreach, ch. lecter, Extraordinary Minister of Holy Communion, Ch. commentator; mem. N.W. Neighborhood Fedn. Served with USN, 1951-55; Korea. Cert. rehab. counselor; cert. social worker. Mem. Nat. Rehab. Assn., Ill. Rehab. Assn., Nat. Rehab. Counselor Assn., Ill. Rehab. Counselor Assn., Am. Psychol. Assn. (asso.), N.W. Neighborhood Fedn. Roman Catholic. Club: Good Counsel High Sch. Fathers. Home: 2910 N Meade Ave Chicago IL 60634 Office: 5015 W Lawrence Ave Chicago IL 60630

BABBUSH, CHARLES AARON, oral and maxillofacial surgeon; b. Detroit, Mar. 12, 1938; s. Sol and Jean (Aichenbaum) B.; m. Sandra Ellen August, July 2, 1961; children—Jill, Jeffrey, Amy, David. D.D.S., U. Detroit, 1962, M. of Dental Sci., Boston U., 1972. Diplomate Am. Bd. Surgery. Intern, Boston U. Sch. Medicine; resident in oral surgery Mt. Sinai Hosp., Cleve., 1963-65, now sr. vis. oral surgeon; guest lectr., cons. Nat. Taiwan Def. Med. Center Dental Sch., Taipei, 1966-67; cons., vis. surgeon VA Hosp. Chinese Nationalist Army, Taipei, 1966-67; sr. clin. instr. anesthesia and oral surgery dept. Case Western Res. Sch. Dentistry, Cleve., 1968-72; asst. prof. anesthesia and oral surgery, 1972—; guest lectr. Jane Addams Dental Assts. Program, Cleve., 1970—, Cuyahoga Community Coll. Dental Hygiene Program, Cleve., 1974; practice dentistry specializing in oral and maxillofacial surgery, Beachwood, Ohio, 1981—; chief, dept. oral and maxillofacial surgery Hillcrest Hosp., Cleve., 1972—; sr. vis. oral cons. oral surgery Kaiser Community Found., Cleve.; asst. editor Jour. of Oral Implantology, 1976; lectr., condr. seminars various colls., univs., hosps., profl. meetings. Author: Surgical Atlas of Implant Techniques, 1980; contbr. numerous articles in field to profl. jours. Served to lt. Dental Corp., USN, 1965-68. Recipient cert. of recognition NASA, 1979; Winthrop Co. grantee, 1964; E. R. Squibb Co. grantee, 1964, 65, 68; Mt. Sinai Hosp. Cleve. grantee, 1970; Oratronics Inc. grantee, 1970; Federated Steel Inc. of Cleve. grantee, 1974; Vitredent Corp. grantee, 1974; NASA grantee, 1976. Fellow Am. Dental Soc. Anesthesiology, Am. Coll. Dentists, Internat. Coll. Dentists; mem. ADA, Ohio Dental Assn. (program chmn. ann. meeting 1974-75), Cleve. Dental Soc. (bd. dirs. 1970, 76-78, chmn. ann. meeting 1972, chmn. program com. 1973-74, mem. council dental care programs 1972—, mem. jud. council 1976, 78, asst. sec. 1976-78), Am. Soc. Oral Surgeons, Great Lakes Soc. Oral Surgeons, Am. Acad. Implant Dentistry (chmn. research and edn. com. 1972, v.p. central states sect. 1974, pres.-elect central states sect. 1976, gen. chmn. annual meeting 1976, v.p. 1976, pres.-elect 1977, pres. 1978), Internat. Coll. Oral Implants, Cleve. Soc. Oral Surgeons (chmn. ins. com. 1972), Ohio Soc. Oral Surgeons, Taiwan Med. Assn. (hon.), Nat. Italian Implant Assn. (hon.), Japan Acad. Implant Dentistry (hon.), Danish Soc. Implant Dentistry (hon.), Alpha Omega (treas. Cleve. chpt. 1971). Jewish. Office: 26900 Cedar Rd Beachwood OH 44122

BABCOCK, JAMES ARTHUR, educational administrator; b. Greencastle, Ind., June 19, 1937; s. Arthur A. and Ruth E. (Claxton) B.; m. Dorothy Wesemann, June 8, 1958; children—Timothy, Jonathan, Amy. B.A., Western Ky. U., 1960; M.S., Ind. U., 1967; Ed.S., 1976. Tchr., Paoli Community Schs., Ind., 1963-66, counselor, 1967-79; sch. adminstr., 1970—, prin. Jr.-Sr. High Sch., 1974—; admissions dir. Northwood Inst., West Baden, Ind., 1969-70; area dir. Ind. Div. Student Activities, 1983—. Bd. dirs. So. Hills Mental Health Ctr., Jasper, Ind., 1970-74. Served to 1st lt. arty. U.S. Army, 1960-63. NDEA fellow, 1966-67. Mem. Nat. Assn. Secondary Sch. Prins., Ind. Secondary Sch. Adminstrs. Republican. Mem. Ch. of Christ. Avocation: coin collecting. Home: PO Box 49 Paoli IN 47454 Office: 501 Elm St Paoli IN 47454

BABCOCK, MICHAEL WARD, economics educator; b. Bloomington, Ill., Dec. 10, 1944; s. Bruce W. and Virginia (Neeson) B.; B.S. in B.A., Drake U., 1967; M.A. in Econs., U. Ill., 1971, Ph.D. in Econs., 1973; m. Virginia Lee Brooks, Aug. 4, 1973; children—John, Karen. Teaching asst. U. Ill., Urbana, 1968, 71, research asst., 1972; prof. econs. Kans. State U., Manhattan, 1972—. Served with U.S. Army, 1969-71. Fed. R.R. Adminstrn. grantee, 1976-78; U.S. Army C.E. grantee, 1978-79; U.S. Dept. Agr. grantee, 1978-79, 80-82, 84-85. Mem. Am. Assn. Agrl. Economists, Missouri Valley Econ. Assn., Mid-Continent Regional Sci. Assn., So. Regional Sci. Assn., Kans. Econ. Assn., Transp. Research Forum, Beta Gamma Sigma, Omicron Delta Epsilon. Club: Optimist. Contbr. articles to profl. jours. Home: 720 Harris St Manhattan KS 66502 Office: Econ Dept Kan State Univ Manhattan KS 66506

BABCOCK, PATRICIA ANN, nurse; b. Shelbyville, Ind., Oct. 31, 1934; d. Laurence H. and Reba D. (Conway) Underwood; B.S. in Nursing, Ball State U., Muncie, Ind., 1957, M.A., 1975, Ed.D. (fellow), 1980; m. Robert A. Babcock, Mar. 30, 1958; children—Brett Alan, Richard Scott, Laura Ann. Office nurse, Muncie, 1957-60; staff nurse Porter Meml. Hosp., Valparaiso, Ind., 1961; head nurse St. Joseph Hosp., Logansport, Ind., 1963-65; sch. nurse, Gary, Ind., 1967-76; asso. prof. nursing Purdue U. North Central Campus, Westville, Ind., 1976—, chairperson; cons. in field. Mem. AAUW (br. pres.), Am. Nurses Assn., AAUP, (chpt. pres.), Nat. Assn. Female Execs., Concern for Dying, Ind. State Nurses Assn. (dist. pres.), Hospice of Porter County, Compassionate Friends, Ind. Assn. Health Educators, Nat. League Nursing, Ind. League Nursing, Ind. Assn. Univ. Profs., Eta Sigma Gamma, Sigma Theta Tau, Phi Delta Theta, Sigma Kappa. Republican. Methodist. Home: 115

Washington Ave Chesterton IN 46304 Office: Purdue U North Central Campus Westville IN 46391

BABCOCK, RICHARD DEAN, children's services executive; b. Labette City, Kans., June 9, 1942; s. Marvin Dean and Mary Conception (Yanez) B.; B.A., U. Kans., 1964; M.S., Central Mo. State U., 1971; m. Teresa Ann Olson, Dec. 13, 1972; children—Kelley, Dominick, Deidre, Chelsea, Luke, Patrick. Treatment program adminstr. Glenwood (Iowa) State 1976-77; social worker Parsons (Kans.) State Hosp. & Tng. Center, 1966-68; dir. Neighborhood Youth Corp. project, Ottawa, Kans., 1968; speech and lang. cons. Project Head Start, Springfield, Mo., 1969; speech therapist Mansfield (Mo.) public schs., 1970; dir. speech and hearing services Joplin (Mo.) Regional Center for Mental Retardation/Devel. Disabilities; unit dir. Marshall (Mo.) State Hosp. and Sch., 1974-75; dir. treatment programs, asst. ctr. dir. Springfield Regional Ctr. for Mental Retardation/Devel. Disabilities, 1977-80; adminstr. Springfield Children's Home, 1980—; speech and hearing cons. U.S. Med. Center for Fed. Prisoners, Springfield, 1971; mem. Child Welfare Adv. Council. Mem. Greene County (Mo.) Child Protection team, 1978-79; mem. Greene County Child Advocacy Council bd., 1979-80, 83-84, mental health rep., 1979—, sec. exec. com. 1979-81; liaison Greene County Multidisciplinary/Child Protection team, 1979-80; mem. Greene County Assn. for Retarded Citizens, 1978-79; Spl. Olympics volunteer, 1969-84. Served with USNR, 1961-64. United Cerebral Palsy Found. grad. scholar, 1970; Mental Health Grad. fellow, 1970-71; Spl. Olympics Appreciation award, 1971-79; Certificate of Clin. Competency in Speech Pathology, Am. Speech and Hearing Assn., 1972. Mem. Mo. Tchrs. Assn. (assembly del. 1969-70), Mo. Speech and Hearing Assn., Mo. Child Care Assn. (pres.-elect), In Child's Interest (dir., officer 1981—), Phi Kappa Theta. Democrat. Roman Catholic. Club: Ozark Mt. Ridgerunners Running. Lodges: Kiwanis, Optimists. Contbr. articles to profl. jours. Home: Route 20 Box 2097-6 Springfield MO 65803 Office: 1212 W Lombard St Springfield MO 65806

BABCOCK, ROBERT ALLEN, construction company executive; b. Indpls., May 4, 1935; s. William Harvey and Beatrice Opal (Durst) B.; student Butler U., 1953-54; m. Virginia Ann Richardson, Sept. 2, 1955; children—Patricia Ann, Debra Sue. With William H. Babcock & Son, Indpls., 1954-70; owner Robert A. Babcock, Gen. Contractor, Indpls., 1970-77; pres. Babcock Constrn., Inc., Indpls., 1977—. Pres., Wayne Twp. Screening Caucus, 1970, pres. Danville Band Parents, 1972; trustee Danville United Methodist Ch., 1980-84, chmn. adminstrv. council, 1983—. Mem. Better Bus. Bur. Republican. Methodist. Clubs: Masons, Shriners, Scottish Rite, Indpls. Country. Home: Rural Route 6 Box 174 Danville IN 46122 Office: 951 Western Dr Indianapolis IN 46241

BABCOCK, WILLIAM LOTHROP, lawyer; b. Mpls., Jan. 24, 1950; s. William Carlyle and Mary Margaret (McCall) B. A.B., Harvard U., 1973; J.D., Hastings Law Sch., 1980. Bar: Minn., 1980. Tennis profl., 1973-77; assoc. Oppenheimer, Wolff, Foster, Shepard & Donnelly, Mpls., 1980—. Pres., bd. dirs. Youth Futures, 1980—; mem. Downtown Council Mpls., 1980—. Served with USMCR, 1970-72. Mem. ABA, Minn. State Bar Assn., U.S. Profl. Tennis Assn., Northwest Tennis Assn. (bd. dirs. 1982—). Presbyterian. Club: Greenway Athletic. Office: Oppenheimer Wolff Foster Shepard & Donnelly 4824 IDS Ctr Minneapolis MN 55402

BABLER, JAMES CARL, lawyer; b. Antigo, Wis. Oct. 13, 1955; s. Carl Leo and Barbara Ruth (Hoppe) B. B.A., U. Wis., 1976, J.D., 1979. Bar: Wis. 1979, U.S. Dist. Ct. (we. dist.) Wis. 1979. Asst. dist. atty Barron County, Barron, Wis., 1979-80; asst. dist. atty. Polk County, Balsam Lake, Wis., 1980-83; dist. atty. Barron County, 1983—; instr. Wis. Indianhead Tech. Inst., Rice Lake, Wis., 1981—. Mem. Wis. Dist. Attys. Assn., Wis. Law Enforcement Officers Assn. Democrat. United Methodist. Home: 266 W Monroe St Barron WI 54812 Office: Barron County Dist Attys Office 237 Courthouse Barron WI 54812

BABLES, MARILYN MARIE, laboratory technician; b. Kans., Nov. 21, 1954; d. Leon B.; A.A., Kansas City (Kans.) Community Coll., 1976; B.A. in Biology, Park Coll., 1978. Quality control lab. technician Bayvet Labs., Shawnee Mission, Kans., 1979; microbiology lab. technician Bd. Pub. Utilities, Kansas City, Kans., 1979—; pres., founder Bables Investment Properties. Mem. Kan Valley Med. Soc., Am. Water Works Assn., Nat. Assn. Female Execs., Women in Bus. (pres. 1980—), Urban League, AAUW, Internat. Fedn. Univ. Women, Internat. Platform Assn., Smithsonian Assocs., Friends of Park Coll. Library. Republican. Mem. Christian Ch. (Disciples of Christ). Home: 1968 N 32d St Kansas City KS Office: 3601 N 12th Kansas City KS 66104

BABU, SURESH PANDURANGAM, chemical engineer; b. Secunderabad, India, July 15, 1941; came to U.S., 1965, naturalized, 1978; s. Pandurangam, Namala and Sarojini Devi (Varada) Naidu; m. Rosy Bommadevara, Mar. 26, 1970. B.S. in Chem. Engring., Osmania U., Hyderabad, 1958-62; M.S. in Chem. Engring., Indian Inst. Tech., Kharagpur, India, 1963; Ph.D. in Gas Engring., Ill. Inst. Tech., 1971. Sr. research fellow C.S.I.R., India, Hyderabad, 1963-65; asst. prof. W.Va. U., Morgantown, 1971-73; from chem. engr. to assoc. dir. process devel. Inst. Gas Tech., Chgo., 1973-84, assoc. dir. coal and biomass conversion and utilization, 1984—; vis. research assoc. East-West Ctr., Honolulu, 1980, 82; tech. expert UNIDO, Vienna, Austria, 1981, Asian Inst. Tech., Bangkok, Thailand, 1982, UNOP, Hyderabad, India, 1985. Editor: Trace Elements in Fuel, 1975. Patentee in field. Mem. Assn. Insians in Am., Assn. Scientists of Indian Origin (founder), Am. Inst. Chem. Engrs., Am. Chem. Soc. Hindu. Avocations: travel; reading; music. Home: 8303 Regency Ct Willow Springs IL 60480 Office: Inst Gas Technology 3424 S State St Chicago IL 60616

BACCUS, ANITA LOUISE, health clinic executive; b. Tulsa, Nov. 13, 1945; d. James Benjamin and Mary (Griffin) B.; 1 child, Michael McKay Baccus-Williams. B.S., Okla. State U., 1968; Ph.D., Meharry Med. Coll., 1977. Med. scientist Moton Comprehensive Health Ctr., Tulsa, 1969-71; cyto-technician Meharry Med. Coll., Nashville, 1971-77; postdoctoral fellow Atlanta U., 1977-79; research assoc. Emory U., Atlanta, 1979; asst. prof. dept. biology Clark Coll., Atlanta, 1979-80; exec. dir. Southside Community Clinic, Mpls., 1980—. Mem. Communith Clinic Consortium (pres. 1982), Black Women's Health Orgn., Alpha Kappa Alpha. Democrat. Episcopalian. Club: Jack & Jill Am. (Mpls.) (parlimentarian). Avocations: down hill skiing; needlecrafts; piano. Home: 7412 W 22d St #105 Saint Louis Park MN 55426 Office: Southside Community Clinic Inc 4243 4th Ave S Minneapolis MN 55409

BACH, JAMES WILLIAM, educational administrator; b. Stevens Point, Wis., Apr. 2, 1948; s. Vernon R. and Edna G. (Fredrickson) B.; m. Margaret Elizabeth Mitchell, June 12, 1971; children—Jessica, Mitchell, Justin. B.S., U. Wis-Eau Claire, 1970; M.S., U. Wis.-Superior, 1975. Tchr., Kimberly Pub. Schs., Wis., 1970-74; prin. Southern Door Schs., Brussels, Wis., 1974-75, West De Pere Pub. Schs., Wis., 1975—. Pres., West De Pere PTO, 1982. Mem. Assn. Wis. Sch. Adminstrs., De Pere Jaycees (pres. 1979). Democrat. Roman Catholic. Avocations: woodworking; tennis; golf; reading; fixing cars. Home: 235 Colleen Ln De Pere WI 54115 Office: 1155 Westwood St De Pere WI 54115

BACH, LAWRENCE CHRISTOPHER, music educator; b. Pitts., Jan. 24, 1954; s. Kenneth Eugene and Louise (Mento) B.; m. Jerilyn Ann Sorbo, July 28, 1979. B.S. in Music, W. Va. Wesleyan U., 1976; Mus.M., U. Minn., 1986. Music minister Christian Life Ch., Trafford, Pa., 1976-79, music minister, assoc. pastor, 1979-81; instr. music North Central Bible Coll., Mpls., 1981-83, asst. prof., chmn. music dept., 1984—; clinician, condr. Zondervan Family Bookstores, Pitts., 1978-80. Mem. Am. Choral Dirs. Assn., Phi Mu Alpha, Omicron Delta Kappa, Alpha Psi Omego. Republican. Mem. Assembly of God. Avocations: racquetball; golf; reading; travel. Home: 1766 Forssa Way Eagan MN 15122 Office: North Central Bible Coll Dept Music 910 Elliot Ave Minneapolis MN 55404

BACH, STEVE CRAWFORD, lawyer; b. Jackson, Ky., Jan. 31, 1921; s. Bruce Grannis and Evelyn (Crawford) B.; A.B., Ind. U., 1943, J.D., 1948; postgrad. Eastern studies U. Mich., 1944, Nat. Trial Judges Coll., 1966, U. Minn. Juvenile Inst., 1967; m. Rosemary Husted, Sept. 6, 1947; children—John Crittenden, Greta Christine. Bar: Ky., Ind. 1948. Atty., Bach & Bach, Jackson, 1948-51; investigator U.S. CSC, Indpls., 1951-54; individual practice law, Mt. Vernon, Ind., 1954-65; judge 11th. Jud. Circuit, Mt. Vernon, 1965-82; spl. overseas rep. Nat. Council Juvenile and Family Ct. Judges; moderator Ind. Conf. Crime and Delinquency, Indpls., 1968; tchr. seminar on juvenile delinquency Ind. Trial Judges Assn., 1969, del. Internat. Youth Magistrates Conf., Geneva, 1970, Oxford, Eng., 1974, Can., 1977; faculty adviser Criminal Law Inst., Nat. Trial Judges Coll., 1973; treas. Ind. Council Juvenile Ct. Judges, 1975, v.p., 1976, pres., 1978-79, mem. juvenile study com., 1976; bd. dirs. Jud. Conf., Ind. Jud. Center; faculty adv. Nat. Jud. Coll., 1978; mem. faculty Seminar for Inst. for New Judges, State of Ind., 1979. Pres., Greater Mt. Vernon Assn., 1958-59; bd. dirs. Regional Mental Health Planning Commn., Criminal Justice Planning Commn. 8th Region Ind., Evansville, Ind.; mem. Juvenile Justice div. Ind. Jud. Study Commn.; mem. Ind. Gov.'s Juvenile Justice Delinquency Prevention Adv. Bd., 1976-82. Served with intelligence Signal Corps, AUS, 1943-46. Mem. Nat. Council Juvenile Ct. Judges, Am. Legion, Ind. Soc. Chgo., Ind. Bar Assn. (del.), Ind. Judges Assn. (bd. mgrs. 1966-71), Sigma Delta Kappa, Delta Tau Delta. Democrat. Methodist. Mason (Shriner), Kiwanian, Elk. Home: 512 Walnut St Mount Vernon IN 47620 Office: 203 E 4th St Mount Vernon IN 47620

BACHER, ROSA W., optometrist; b. Chgo., Dec. 7, 1928; d. Franz Xaver and Rosa (Suess) Wieshuber; m. Joseph Thomas Bacher, May 1, 1954; children—Rosanna Voss, Mary Cardwell, Joseph Jr., Elizabeth Thompsen, Ellen. O.D., Ill. Coll. Optometry, 1951. Cert. optometrist, Ill. Optometrist Herbert Solomon, Chgo., 1972-75; practice medicine specializing in optometry, Park Ridge, Ill., 1975-83; pres. S. Pk. Vision Care Ctr. Inc., Park Ridge; 1983—; lectr. Triton Coll., 1973-74. Mem. Park Ridge C. of C., Am. Optometric Assn., Ill. Optometric Assn., West Suburban Soc., North Suburban Soc., Am. Interprofl. Assn. (sec. 1970-75, v.p. 1976-77, founding mem.), Nat. Eye Research Found., Optometric Extension Program. Republican. Roman Catholic. Club: Pk. Ridge Women Entrepeneurs (founder 1981, treas. 1985). Avocations: hiking; golf; travel; cooking; reading. Office: South Pk Vision Care Ctr Inc 703 Devon Ave Park Ridge IL 60068

BACHMAN, NEAL KENYON, librarian; b. Iowa City, Aug. 10, 1950; s. Neal and Phyllis Jean (Mattes) B.; B.Mus. in Edn., U. Nebr., 1972, M.Ed., 1978. Tchr. instrumental and vocal music Osceola (Nebr.) Schs., 1972-73; band dir. Elkhorn (Nebr.) Public Schs., 1973-75; retail salesman Musicland, Lincoln, Nebr., 1975-76; media specialist Malcolm (Nebr.) Public Schs., 1978-83; librarian Clarinda (Iowa) High Sch., 1983-85, Eisenhower Sch., Fort Leavenworth Unified Schs., Kans., 1985—; vis. instr. U. Nebr.-Lincoln, 1982. Recipient Malcolm Parent-Tchr. Orgn. cert. of recognition, 1981. Mem. Malcolm Edn. Assn. (pres. 1980-81), Assn. for Ednl. Communications and Tech., Nebr. Alumni Band (charter), Kans. Ednl. Media Assn., Nebr. Ednl. Media Assn. (dir. 1982-83), Phi Delta Kappa. Mem. Reorganized Ch. of Jesus Christ of Latter-day Saints. Contbr. articles to profl. jours. Home: 410 Sheridan St Leavenworth KS 66048 Office: Unified Sch Dist 207 Fort Leavenworth KS 66027

BACHMANN, FREDERICK MELVIN, sales director; b. Madison, Wis., July 1, 1940; s. Melvin N. and Mayre (Nichols) B.; m. Mary Louise Vaughan, Dec. 16, 1961; children—Kevin, Stuart, Renee. Student U. Wis.-Madison, 1958-61. C.L.U. Ins. agt. Penn Mut. Life, Madison, 1962-77; gen. agt. Nat. Life of Vt., Madison, Wis., 1977-81; regional sales dir. Empire Gen. Life, Monona, Wis., 1981—. Mem. C.L.U. Soc., Life Underwriters Assn., Mgrs. Assn. Republican. Mem. Moravin Ch. Club: Rotary (bd. dirs.). Lodge: Masons. Home: 1090 Shorewood Hills Rd Lake Mills WI 53551 Office: 802 W Broadway Suite 300 Monona WI 53719

BACHMANN, WILLIAM VINCENT, combustion engine cons.; b. Bozen, S. Tyrol, Italy, Apr. 8, 1913; s. Johann and Franziska (Demetz) B.; student engring. Koenigliche Staatsgewerbeschule, 1929-30, pvt. study art and graphics, 1931-34; m. Diane Thomson, Jan. 3, 1977; children by former marriages—George, Francisca, Vincent. With Massey Ferguson Co., Toronto, Ont., Can., 1953-56; with Dilworth Ewbanks, cons. Can. Air Research Project, Toronto, 1956-58; body A engr. Chrysler Corp., Highland Park, Mich., 1958-70; test engr. cons. Volkswagen Mfg. Corp. Am., Warren, Mich., 1977-78; pres. Bachmann Fire Ring Engine Research Co., St. Clair Shores, Mich., 1979—. Mem. Engring. Soc. Detroit, United Inventors and Scientists Am., Am. Def. Preparedness Assn. Patentee internal combustion engines. Address: 22517 Ten Mile Rd Saint Clair Shores MI 48080

BACK, ROBERT WYATT, institutional investment company executive; b. Omaha, Dec. 22, 1936; s. Albert Edward and Edith (Elliott) B.; m. Linaya Gail Hahn, Aug. 30, 1964; children—Christopher Frederick, Gregory Franklin. B.A., Trinity Coll., 1958; M.A., Yale U., 1959; postgrad. London U., 1959-60, Harvard U., 1960-61. Investment adv. acct. mgr. Brown Bros. Harriman & Co., Chgo., 1972-74; asst. v.p., investment analyst Harris Trust & Savs. Bank, 1974-82; v.p., instl. equity analyst Prescott Ball & Turben, 1982-83; v.p., sr. investment analyst Blunt, Ellis & Loewi, Inc., 1983-84; v.p. instl. equity sales Rodman & Renshaw, Inc., 1984—. Contbr. articles to profl. jours. Corp. mem. Scholarships for Ill. Residents, Inc., 1969—; mem. planning com. Fin. Analysts Fedn. Conv., 1984—; del. Assn. Yale Alumni, 1983-85. Served to capt. USAF, 1958-64. Club: Yale (bd. dirs. 1983-85). Home: 942 Twisted Oak Ln Buffalo Grove IL 60090 Office: Rodman & Renshaw Inc 120 S LaSalle St Chicago IL 60090

BACKER, DONALD JOSEPH, hosp. adminstr.; b. St. Louis, Dec. 23, 1931; s. Joseph A. and Mable A. (Moore) B.; B.S. in Psychology, St. Louis U., 1957, M.B.A., 1961; m. Irene J. Kustra, Oct. 18, 1958; children—Michele, Mark, Eric, Paul. Dir. indsl. relations Granite City (Ill.) Steel, 1962-70; dir. indsl. relations Gen. Steel Industries, Granite City, 1970-72; dir. employee relations Jewish Hosp. of St. Louis, 1972-74; v.p. human resources Christian Hosp. Northeast-Northwest, St. Louis, 1974—; lectr., cons. in field. Pres. St. Casimir Sch. Bd., St. Louis; Served with U.S. Army, 1953-55. Mem. Florissant Valley C. of C. (pres. 1980-81), Mo. Hosp. Assn., Hosp. Personnel Mgrs. of Greater St. Louis, Hosp. Assn. Greater St. Louis, Indsl. Relations Assn. Greater St. Louis (pres. 1969-70), East Side Indsl. Relations Assn. (pres. 1967-68). Club: Rotary (exec. com. 1983) (Ferguson, Mo.). Coll. Placement Assn. Office: 11133 Dunn Rd Saint Louis MO 63136

BACKES, ORLIN WILLIAM, lawyer; b. Glenburn, N.D., May 11, 1935; s. Leonard P. and Irene G.(Keller) B.; m. Millie Jensen, Oct. 15, 1958; children—Brent, Jon, Mary, Paul. B.S., Minot State Coll., 1958; J.D., U. N.D., 1963. Bar: N.D. Faculty Max Pub. Sch., N.D., 1958-60; ptnr. McGee Law Firm, Minot N.D., 1963—; dir. First Western Bank, Minot. Mem. N.D. Real Estate Commn., 1978—; pres. 4 Dam Ltd. Flood Control Orgn., Minot, 1970—; pres. bd. dirs. Bishop Ryan High Sch., Minot, 1971; pres., bd. regents Minot State Coll., 1981. Recipient Golden award Minot State Coll., 1984. Mem. Order of Coif, Minot C. of C. (pres. 1974). Democrat. Roman Catholic. Lodge: Eagles (pres. 1969), Elks, Lions (pres. 1974), K.C. (state advocate 1965-70). Avocations: tennis, skiing. Home: 2425 Brookside Dr Minot ND 58701 Office: McGee Law Firm Norwest Bank Bldg Minot ND 58701

BACKYS, DONALD JEROME, systems engineer; b. Waukegan, Ill., July 12, 1944; s. Jerome P. and Frances L. (Grobelch) B.; B.S.E.E., Mlw. Sch. Engring., 1967; M.B.A., Keller Grad. Sch. Mgmt., 1984. Registered profl. engr., Ill., Wis. Project engr. Collins Radio Co., Cedar Rapids, Iowa, 1967-69; devel. engr. Motorola, Inc., Schaumburg, Ill., 1969-72, mfg. engr., 1972-74, system design engr., 1974-77, system engring. group leader 1977—; electronics instr. Oakton Community Coll., Des Plaines, Ill., 1974-76, 80-81; cons. Hoffman Estates Zoning Bd., Ill., 1975. Mem. indsl. adv. com. Milw. Sch. Engring., 1975-81. Recipient Outstanding Alumnus award Milw. Sch. Engring., 1982. Mem. Milw. Sch. Engring. Alumni Assn. Republican. Roman Catholic. Avocations: flying; amateur radio; racquetball. Home: 3930 N Firestone Dr Hoffman Estates IL 60195 Office: Motorola 1309 E Algonquin Rd Schaumburg IL 60196

BACON, BRETT KERMIT, lawyer; b. Perry, Iowa, Aug. 8, 1947; s. Royden S. and Aldeen A. (Zuker) B.; m. Peggy Darlene Smith, July 30, 1972; children—Jeffrey Brett, Scott Michael. B.A., U. Dubuque, 1969; J.D., Northwestern U., 1972. Bar: Ohio 1972, U.S. Ct. Appeals (6th cir.) 1972, U.S. Supreme Ct. 1980. Assoc., Thompson, Hine & Flory, Cleve., 1972-80, ptnr., 1980—; speaker in field. Author: Computer Law, 1982, 1984. Vice-pres. profl. sect. United Way, Cleve., 1982—; pres. Shaker Heights Youth Ctr., Inc., Ohio, 1984—. Mem. Bar Assn. Greater Cleve. (chmn. 1983—). Home: 2924 Manchester Rd Shaker Heights OH 44122 Office: Thompson Hine & Flory 1100 Nat City Bank Bldg Cleveland OH 44114

BACON, GEORGE EDGAR, pediatrician, educator; b. N.Y.C., Apr. 13, 1932; s. Edgar and Margaret Priscilla (Anderson) B.; B.A., Wesleyan U., 1953; M.D., Duke U., 1957; M.S. in Pharmacology, U. Mich., 1967; m. Grace Elizabeth Graham, June 30, 1956; children—Nancy, George, John. Intern in pediatrics Duke Hosp., Durham, N.C., 1957-58; resident in pediatrics Columbia-Presbyn. Med. Center, N.Y.C., 1961-63; instr. U. Mich., Ann Arbor, 1963, asst. prof., 1968, asso. prof., 1971, prof. pediatrics, 1974—, chief pediatric endocrinology service, dept. pediatrics, 1970-83; dir. house officer programs, dept. pediatrics, 1982—, assoc. chmn. dept. pediatrics, 1983—; coordinator profl. services C.S. Mott Children's Hosp., 1973-83, mem. exec. com. for clin. affairs, 1975-76, 77-79, asso. vice chmn. med. staff, 1978-79; chmn. exec. com. C.S. Mott Children's, Women's, Holden hosps., Ann Arbor, 1973-82; mem. Senate Assembly, U. Mich., 1978-80; vice chmn. dir.'s adv. council Univ. Hosp., Ann Arbor, 1981-82. Served to capt., U.S. Army, 1958-61. Diplomate Am. Bd. Pediatrics, subsplty. Bd. Pediatric Endocrinology. Fellow Am. Acad. Pediatrics (treas. Mich. chpt. 1983—); mem. Am. Pediatric Soc., Soc. Pediatric Research (emeritus), Endocrine Soc., Lawson Wilkins Pediatric Endocrine Soc., Am. Diabetes Assn. (bd. dirs. Mich. affiliate 1984—). Republican. Author: A Practical Approach to Pediatric Endocrinology, 1975, 2nd edit. 1982; contbr. articles to med. jours. Home: 3911 Waldenwood Ann Arbor MI 48105 Office: Dept Pediatrics U Mich Ann Arbor MI 48109

BACON, WILLIAM THOMPSON, JR., investment company executive; b. Chgo., Feb. 6, 1923; s. William Thompson and Martha (Smith) B.; grad. Phillips Acad., 1941; B.A., Yale, 1945; m. Margaret Hoyt, Apr. 18, 1942; children—William Thompson III, Catherine (Mrs. Von Stroh), Hoyt Wells, J. Knight, Christopher S. Asst. cashier First Nat. Bank of Chgo., 1946-55; partner Bacon, Whipple & Co., Chgo., 1956-82, assoc., 1982—; dir. Walbro Corp., Safecard Services, Inc., Trappers Loop, Inc.; hon. dir. Stifel Fin. Corp. Trustee Hadley Sch. for Blind, Winnetka, Ill., Fountain Valley Sch., Colorado Springs, Colo. Served with AUS, 1943-44. Mem. Elihu, Delta Kappa Epsilon. Republican. Episcopalian. Clubs: Yale (pres. 1962-63), Chicago, University (Chgo.); Onwentsia (Lake Forest, Ill.); Shoreacres (Lake Bluff, Ill.); Old Elm (Ft. Sheridan, Ill.); Indian Hill (Winnetka, Ill.); Yale (N.Y.C.); Gulfstream Golf (Delray Beach, Fla.). Home: 184 Winthrop Ln Lake Forest IL 60045 Office: 135 S LaSalle St Chicago IL 60603

BADAL, DANIEL WALTER, psychiatrist; b. Lowellville, Ohio, Aug. 22, 1912; s. Samuel S. and Angelina (Jessen) B.; m. Julia Lovina Cover, June 1939; children—Petrina Badal Gardner, Julia Badal Graf, Peter C.; m. 2d Eleanor Bosworth Spitler, Sept. 5, 1969. A.B., Adelbert Coll., Case Western Res. U., 1934, M.D., 1937. Resident in medicine, neurology and psychiatry Peter Bent Brigham Hosp., Mass. Gen. Hosp. and Boston City Hosps., 1937-41; fellow in psychiatry and neurology Harvard U., Boston, 1937-41; asst. prof. psychiatry Washington U., St. Louis, 1945; faculty Sch. Medicine, Case Western Res. U., Cleve., 1946—, assoc. clin. prof. emeritus psychiatry, 1983—; faculty Cleve. Psychoanalytic Inst., Cleve., 1975—; pvt. practice psychiatry and psychoanalysis, 1955—. NRC Office Sci. Research and Devel. fellow, 1941-45. Fellow Internat. Psychoanalytic Assn. (life), Am. Psychiat. Assn.; mem. Ohio Med. Assn., Assn. Research in Nervous and Mental Diseases, Cleve. Soc. Neurology and Psychiatry, Acad. Medicine of Cleve., AMA, Am. Psychoanalytic Assn., Phila. Assn. Psychoanalysis, Cleve. Psychoanalytic Soc. (pres. 1963), Internat. Contbr. articles to profl. jours. Home: 2257 Woodmere Dr Cleveland Heights OH 44106 Office: 11328 Euclid Ave Cleveland OH 44106

BADEER, HENRY SARKIS, physician, educator; b. Mersine, Turkey, Jan. 31, 1915; s. Sarkis and Persape Hagop (Koundakjian) B.; came to U.S., 1965, naturalized, 1971; M.D., Am. U., Beirut, Lebanon, 1938; m. Mariam Mihran Kassarjian, July 12, 1948; children—Gilbert H., Daniel H. Gen. practice medicine, Beirut, 1940-51; asst. instr. Am. U. Sch. Medicine, Beirut, 1938-45, adj. prof., 1945-51, asso. prof., 1951-62, prof. physiology, 1962-65, acting chmn. dept., 1951-56, chmn., 1956-65; research fellow Harvard U. Med. Sch., Boston, 1948-49; prof. physiology Creighton U. Med. Sch., Omaha, 1967—, acting chmn. dept., 1971-72; vis. prof. U. Iowa, Iowa City, 1957-58, Downstate Med. Center, Bklyn., 1965-67; mem. med. com. Azounieh Sanatorium, Beirut, 1961-65; mem. research com. Nebr. Heart Assn., 1967-70. Recipient Golden Apple award Students of AMA, 1975; Rockefeller fellow., 1948-49; grantee med. research com., Am. U. Beirut, 1956-65. Mem. AAAS, Internat. Soc. Heart Research, Am. Physiol. Soc., Alpha Omega Alpha. Author textbook; contbr. chpts. to books, articles to profl. jours. Home: 2808 S 99th Ave Omaha NE 68124 Office: Creighton U Med Sch 2500 Calif St Omaha NE 68178

BADER, JOAN LARSON, dentist; b. Dayton, Ohio, June 29, 1942; d. Harold A. and M. Barbara (Gwyther) Larson; m. Robert Smith Bader. B.A. in Biology, U. Nebr.-Omaha, 1964; Ph.D. in Zoology, U. Ill.-Urbana, 1971; D.D.S., Case Western Res. U., 1978. Asst. prof. biology Kenyon Coll., Gambier, Ohio, 1971-74; dentist VA Hosp., Kansas City, Mo., 1978-79; practice dentistry, St. Louis, 1979-83, Topeka, 1983—. NDEA fellow, 1968-70; AAUW fellow, 1977-78. Fellow Omicron Kappa Upsilon; mem. ADA, Kans. Dental Assn., Topeka Dist. Dental Soc. Home: 2925 SE 61st St Berryton KS 66409 Office: 2715 SW 29th St Topeka KS 66614

BADER, KENNETH LEROY, association executive; b. Carroll, Ohio; s. Clara M. (Walter) B.; m. Linda Mary Silbaugh, Sept. 17, 1955; children—Bradley, Brent. B.Sc., Ohio State U., 1956, M.Sc., 1957, Ph.D., 1960. Prof. agronomy Ohio State U., 1960-72, asst. dean coll. agr., 1963-67, dean students, 1968-72; vice chancellor U. Nebr., Lincoln, 1972-76; chief exec. officer Am. Soybean Assn., St. Louis, 1976—. Mem. Pres.'s Export Council, 1979—, U.S. Trade Policy Com., 1979—. Am. Council on Edn. Acad. Adminstrn. fellow. Mem. Am. Soc. Agronomy, Sigma Xi. Contbr. articles to profl. jours. Office: 777 Craig Rd Saint Louis MO 63141

BADRA, ROBERT GEORGE, educator; b. Lansing, Mich., Dec. 8, 1933; s. Razouk Anthony and Anna (Paul) B.; m. Maria Teresa Beer, Oct. 25, 1968 (div. 1973); m. 2d, Kristen Lillie Stuckey, Dec. 30, 1977; 1 dau., Rachal Jennifer. B.A., Sacred Heart Sem., 1957; M.A., Western Mich. U., 1968; M.Div., St. John's Provincial Sem., 1985. Ordained priest Roman Catholic Ch., 1961. Faculty Kalamazoo Valley Community Coll., 1968—, prof. philosophy, religion and humanities, 1968—; adj. prof. Nazareth Coll., 1985—. Bd. dirs. Kalamazoo Council for the Humanities, 1983—. Mem. NEA, Inst. World Order. Democrat. Author: Meditations for Spiritual Misfits, 1983; columnist Western Mich. Cath., Grand Rapids, 1983—. Office: Kalamazoo Valley Community College 6767 West O Ave Kalamazoo MI 49009

BADTRAM, GENE ALLAN, veterinarian, consultant; b. Davenport, Iowa, Dec. 22, 1955; s. Henry and Mildred (Leumock) B. B.S. in Animal Sci., Iowa State U., 1978, D.V.M., 1982. Intern U. Sask., Saskatoon, 1982-83; gen. practice vet. medicine Dairyland Animal Health Inc., Weyauwega, Wis., 1983-84, Vet. Services, Randolph, Wis., 1984—. Mem. AVMA, Iowa Vet. Med. Assn., Wis. Vet. Med. Assn., Vet. Med. Assn. of Northeast Wis., Am. Assn. Bovine Practitioners, Phi Kappa Phi, Phi Zeta, Gamma Sigma Delta. Home: 104 Grove St Apt 3 Randolph WI 53956 Office: Vet Services 326 S High St Randolph WI 53956

BAECHLE, THOMAS RAYMOND, physical education educator; b. Cin., Nov. 2, 1943; s. Walter Emil Schmidt and Elnora (Rose) Schmidt; m. Susan Jean Parks, May 31, 1969; children—Todd Emil, Clark Alan. B.S., Eastern Ky. U., 1966; M. Ed., U. Nebr., 1969; Ed. D., U. S.D., 1976. Phys. edn. tchr. U. Nebr., Lincoln, 1967-69; phys. edn. tchr. Briar Cliff Coll., Sioux City, Iowa, 1969-71, chmn. phys. edn., 1971-77; phys. edn. tchr. Creighton U., Omaha, 1977-78, chmn. dept. phys. edn., 1978—. Contbr. articles to profl jours. and mags. Coordinator Jump Rope For Heart, Am. Heart Assn., Omaha, 1980-81. Recipient award Gov's. Council on Phys. Fitness and Sports, 1976, Appreciation award Spl. Olympics, 1983-84. Mem. AAHPERD (coaching cert. com. 1985, outstanding service award 1983), Nat. Assn. Phys. Edn. in Higher Edn. (nomination com. 1983), Nat. Strength and Conditioning Assn. (bd. dirs. 1978—assoc. editor 1979—, dir. cert. 1981—, pres. 1983-85, coach of the year region IV, 1981, 82, 83, nat. coach of yr. 1984), Nebr. Assn. Health, Phys. Edn., Recreation and Dance (pres. 1984-85, Outstanding Service award 1983), Central Assn. Health, Phys. Edn., Recreation and Dance (v.p. sports 1985), Am. Coll. Sports Medicine, Sigma Delta Phi, Phi Epsilon Kappa. Mem. United Ch. of Christ. Avocations: fishing, woodworking. Home: 11118 U St Omaha NE 68137 Office: Creighton Univ 2500 California St Omaha NE 68178

BAER, DAVID, JR., lawyer; b. Belleville, Ill., Sept. 24, 1905; s. David and Sunshine (Lieber) B.; LL.B., Washington U., 1928; m. Mary Lynne Cockrell Sweet, Apr. 18, 1938 (dec.); m. 2d, Jane Caulfield, Sept. 11, 1982. Ptnr. Lashly, Caruthers, Baer & Hamel, St. Louis; dir. Lindell Trust Co.; former pres., dir. Mo.-Lincoln Trust Co.; former dir. Scullin Steel Co., St. Louis. Former mem. St. Louis Boy Scout Endowment Fund Com. Served as sgt. AUS, 1943-45.

Mem. Estate Planning Council St. Louis (past pres., dir.), Am., Mo., St. Louis (past chmn. group ins. com.) bar assns., Washington U. Law Alumni Assn., Jr. (life), Ill. Jr. (past pres.), U.S. Jr. (senator) chambers commerce. Mason, De Molay (past master councilor, sr. mem.; mem. Legion of Honor). Clubs: Mo. Athletic, University. Home: 625 S Skinker Blvd Saint Louis MO 63105 Office: 714 Locust St Saint Louis MO 63101

BAER, JULIE ANNE, assistant to city administrator; b. Charleston, W.Va., Sept. 5, 1955; d. Ben Kayser and Eleanor Weil (Hirsch) Baer. B.S. in Home Econs., U. Mo.-Columbia, 1977; M.P.A., U. Mo.-Kansas City, 1981. Archtl. designer Butcher Block Co., Kansas City, Mo., 1977-79; claims supr. Mut. Benefit Life Ins., Kansas City, Mo., 1979-81; intern City of Kansas City, 1981; asst. to city adminstr. City of Leawood, Kans., 1981—. Vol. Menorah Med. Ctr., Kansas City, Mo., Jewish Fedn., Kansas City, Mo., Folly Theater, Friends of Art (Nelson/Atkins Art Mus.), Kansas City, Mo. Mem. Internat. City Mgrs. Assn., Internat. Personnel Mgrs. Assn., Am. Soc. Pub. Adminstrs., Mid-Am. Regional Council Personnel Commn. (chmn.), U. Mo. Sch. Bus. and Pub. Adminstrn. Alumni Assn. (bd. dirs. 1983—).

BAER, LISA PELTER, counselor, health director; b. St. Louis, May 19, 1952. Student U. Mo., 1970-73; B.A. in Psychology, U. Mo.-Kansas City, 1976, M.A. in Psychology, 1981. Counselor Comprehensive Health Assocs., Overland Park, Kans., 1979-80, research, counseling coordinator, 1980-81, exec. dir., 1981—; instr. dept. ob-gyn U. Mo.-Kansas City, 1980-81; a planner and developer The Woman's Place, Columbia, Mo. Recipient Martha Jane Starr Endowment award Women's Council U. Mo., 1980. Mem. Nat. Assn. Female Execs., Nat. Abortion Fedn., NOW, Union Concerned Scientists. Contbr. articles to publs.

BAER, TIMOTHY, statistician, quality consultant; b. Elgin, Ill., Aug. 22, 1952; s. Harold George and Jean Catherine (Daniels) Moore B.; m. Kerry Suzanne Lemmerman, Oct. 2, 1976. B.S. in Math., Bethany Nazarene Coll., 1974; M.S. in Applied Stats., Purdue U., 1976. Statistician, Union Carbide-Nuclear Div., Oak Ridge, 1976-80, stats. sect. head, 1980-83, quality dept. staff statistician Coatings Service, Indpls., 1983—. Mem. Am. Soc. Quality Control, Am. Statis. Assn. Republican. Presbyterian. Avocations: golf; softball; basketball. Home: 7002 N College Ave Indianapolis IN 46220 Office: Union Carbide Coatings Service 1500 Polco Indianapolis IN 46222

BAER, ZENAS, lawyer; b. Fordville, N.D., Nov. 11, 1951; s. Allan and Edna (Brubacher) B. B.A. in Polit. Sci. and German, U. Minn., 1976; J.D., Hamline U., 1980. Bar: Minn. 1980, U.S. Dist. Ct. Minn. 1980. Mng. ptnr. Wefald & Baer, Hawley, Minn., 1980—; dir. Baers Poultry Ranch, Lake Park, Minn. Councilman City of Hawley, 1981—. Alt. service as consciencious objector, 1969-72. Recipient 2 awards for excellence Lawyers Coop., Bancroft-Whitney, 1979. Mem. ABA, Assn. Trial Lawyers Am., Minn. Trial Lawyers Assn., Minn. Bar Assn., Clay County Bar Assn., Hawley C. of C. Home: 420 8th St Hawley MN 56549 Office: Wefald & Baer 222 6th St Hawley MN 56549

BAERMANN, DONNA LEE, insurance analyst; b. Carroll, Iowa, Apr. 28, 1939; d. Omer H. and Awanda Lucille (Mathison) Roth; m. Edwin Ralph Baermann, Jr., July 8, 1961; children—Beth, Bryan, Cynthia. B.S., Mt. Mercy Coll., 1973; student Iowa State U.-Ames, 1957-61. Cert. profl. ins. woman; fellow Life Mgmt. Inst. Ins. agt. Lutheran Mut. Ins. Co., Cedar Rapids, Iowa, 1973; home economist Iowa-Ill. Gas & Electric Co., Cedar Rapids, Iowa, 1973-77; supr. premium collection Life Investors Ins. Co., Cedar Rapids, 1978-83, methods-procedures analyst, 1983—, mem. telecommunications study group com. 1982-83, mem. productivity task force, 1984—. Mem. Nat. Assn. Ins. Women, Nat. Mgmt. Assn. (bd. dirs. Cedar Rapids chpt.), DAR, Chi Omega. Republican. Presbyterian. Home: 220 Carnaby Dr NE Cedar Rapids IA 52402 Office: 4333 Edgewood Rd NE Cedar Rapids IA 52499

BAETZ, ALBERT LEWIS, research and analytical chemist; b. Cleve., Dec. 25, 1938; s. Ralph George and Helen (Hite) B.; m. Ann Theresa Webb, Nov. 20, 1965 (div. 1983); 1 child, Brad. B.S., Purdue U., 1961; M.S., Iowa State U., 1963, Ph.D., 1966. Research chemist Nat. Animal Disease Ctr., Ames, Iowa, 1966—. Editor: Diet and Resistance to Disease, 1981. Mem. Am. Chem. Soc., AAAS. Club: Ames Tennis (pres. 1972-74). Avocations: tennis, square dancing. Home: 105 O'Neil Dr Ames IA 50010 Office: Nat Animal Disease Ctr PO Box 70 Ames IA 50010

BAETZHOLD, HOWARD GEORGE, educator; b. Buffalo, Jan. 1, 1923; s. Howard Kuster and Harriet Laura (Hofheins) B.; student Brown U., 1940-43, MIT, 1943-44; A.B. magna cum laude, Brown U., 1944, M.A., 1948; Ph.D., U. Wis., 1953; m. Nancy Millard Cheesman, Aug. 5, 1950; children—Howard King, Barbara Millard. Asst. dir. Vets. Coll., Brown U., Providence, 1947-48, dir., 1948-49, admissions officer, 1948-50; teaching asst. U. Wis.-Madison, 1950-51, asst. to assoc. dean Coll. Letters and Sci., 1951-53; asst. prof. English, Butler U., Indpls., 1953-57, assoc. prof., 1957-67, prof. English, 1967—, head dept., 1981—, Rebecca Clifton Reade prof., 1981—, vis. prof. U. Del., summer 1963. Served to 1st lt. AC, AUS, 1943-46. Butler U. faculty fellow, 1957-58, 69-70; Am. Philos. Soc. grantee, 1958; Am. Council Learned Socs. grantee, 1967. Mem. AAUP (v.p. state conf. 1955), MLA, Am. Studies Assn. (nat. council 1974-76), Midwest MLA, Ohio-Ind. Am. Studies Assn. (pres. 1967-68), Nat. Council Tchrs. of English, Ind. Coll. English Assn., Ind. Tchrs. of Writing, Indpls. Lit. Club, Indpls. Com. Internat. Visitors, Indpls. Opera Guild, Art Assn. Indpls., Butler U. Odd Topics Soc., Delta Upsilon. Author: Mark Twain and John Bull: The British Connection, 1970. Contbr. articles to profl. publs. Home: 6723 Riverview Dr Indianapolis IN 46220

BAGBY, MARVIN ORVILLE, chemist; b. Macomb, Ill., Sept. 27, 1932; s. Byron Orville and Geneva Floriene (Filbert) B.; B.S., Western Ill. U., 1957, M.S., 1957; m. Mary Jean Jennings, Aug. 31, 1957; children—Gary Lee, Gordon Eugene. With No. Regional Research Center, U.S. Dept. Agr., Peoria, Ill., 1957—, research leader fibrous products research unit, 1974-80, mgr. No. Agrl. Energy Center, 1980—, also research leader hydrocarbon plants and biomass research unit. Served with AUS, 1953-55. Mem. Am. Chem. Soc., AAAS, TAPPI, Am. Oil Chemists Soc. Methodist. Contbr. articles to profl. jours. Home: 209 S Louisiana St Morton IL 61550 Office: 1815 N University St Peoria IL 61604

BAGLEY, CHARLES VAN, pharmacist; b. Elwood, Ind., June 11, 1937; s. Frank and Geraldine Beatrice (Havens) B.; m. Gay Rumple, June 15, 1958; children—Charles Bret, Velvet Michele, Jason Christopher. B.S., Butler U., 1959. Pharmacist owner Charles Drugs, South Whitley, Ind., 1960-65; pharmacist Whitley County Hosp., Columbia City, Ind., 1964-65, Haag Drug, Indpls., 1965-68, Woods Drugs, 1968-73; owner pharmacist Criterion Pharmacy, Inc., Indpls., 1973—, Heather Glen Pharmacy, Indpls. 1984—. Scoutmaster Cross Roads of Am. council Boy Scouts Am., 1973—. Named Scouter of Yr., Boy Scouts Am., 1979, Firecrafter, 1976; recipient Wood Badge, 1978, Order of Arrow, 1977, Boy Scouts Am. Mem. Ind. Pharm. Assn., Kappa Psi, Rho Chi. Lodge: Masons. Avocations: gem hunter; faceting; birding; photo wild flowers; nature lore. Home: 16 Roundhill Ct Danville IN 46122

BAGLEY, RONALD LAIRD, air force officer, flight test engineer; b. Indiana, Pa., May 31, 1947; s. Ronald Dale and Sarah (Macpherson) B.; m. Ellen Louise Isaksen, June 26, 1971; children—Ross Andrew, Melissa Anne. B.S., MIT, 1969, M.S., 1971; Ph.D., Air Force Inst. Tech., 1979; postgrad. Air Command and Staff Coll., Maxwell, AFB, Ala., 1983—. Commd. 2d lt. U.S. Air Force, 1971, advanced through grades to maj., 1982; instr. U.S. Air Force Acad., 1979-80, asst. prof., 1980-82, assoc. prof., 1982-83, lab. dir. civil engring. and engring. mechanics lab., 1981-83; cons. in field. Decorated Air Force Commendation medal with oak leaf cluster, Air Force Meritorious Service medal. Mem. ASME. Presbyterian. Contbr. articles to profl. jours.

BAHLE, DOUGLAS MICHAEL, educational adminstrator; b. Sioux City, Iowa, Apr. 9, 1945; s. Wilfred Walter and Elizabeth Ann (McCullough) B.; m. Judith Ann Dempsey, May 31, 1969; children—Angela Marie, John Douglas, Mark John. B.S., Omaha U., 1968; M.S., U. Nebr.-Omaha, 1972; Edn. Specialist, U. Nebr.-Lincoln, 1973, D.Edn., 1974. Tchr. Omaha Pub. Schs., 1969-72, asst. prin., 1972-73, prin., 1973—; instr. Creighton U., Omaha, 1976—. Lector St. Philip Neri Ch., Omaha, 1980-84, extra-ordinary minister of the eucharist, 1983-84. Mem. Nat. Assn. Secondary Sch. Prins., Omaha Sch. Adminstrs. Assn. (pres. 1978), Phi Delta Kappa. Democrat. Roman Catholic. Lodge: Kiwanis. Avocations: Reading; gardening; coaching. Home: 8726 N 52d Ave Omaha NE 68152 Office: Norris Jr High Sch 2235 S 46th St Omaha NE 68106

BAHN, ROBERT CARLTON, physician, educator; b. Newark, N.Y., July 24, 1925; s. Arlington M. and Helen E. (Houck) B.; m. Miriam Bahn, July 30, 1949; children—David, Rebecca, Mark, Curtis. M.D., U. Buffalo, 1947; Ph.D., U. Minn., 1953. Cert. Am. Bd. Anatomic Pathology, Clin. Pathology, Neuropathology. Intern, resident E.J. Meyer Meml. Hosp., Buffalo, 1947-49; resident in pathology Mayo Found., Rochester, Minn., 1950-54, cons., 1957, instr. pathology, 1957, prof., 1957—, mem., chmn. Mayo Clinic Computer Commn., 1963-75, Mayo Med. Sch. Curriculum Com., 1978—, Mayo Med. Sch. Edn. Com., 1982—; USPHS surgeon NIH, Bethesda, Md., 1955-56; founder Creative Assocs. Contbr. chpts. to books, articles to profl. jours. Bass trombonist Rochester Mcpl. Band, 1970—. Recipient Alumni Research award Mayo Found., 1954; Heinrich Leonard award U. Buffalo Med. Sch., 1947; NIH research grantee co-investigator. Mem. Am. Physiol. Soc. (research group for pathology edn.), Am. Assn. Pathologists and Bacteriologists, Inter Acad. Pathology, Endocrine Soc., Am. Assn. Neuropathologists, Am. Heart Assn. (council on basic scis.). Presbyterian. Clubs: Notochord Band (Rochester, Minn.); Chatfield Brass Band (Minn.). Advocations: Music; swimming. Home: 1650 11th Ave NE Rochester MN 55904 Office:# Mayo Clinic 200-1st St SW Rochester MN 55905

BAHNFLETH, DONALD ROBERT, engineering and architectural company executive, consultant; b. West Chicago, Ill., July 16, 1927; s. William Oscar Bahnfleth and Charlotte Isabel (Hartman) Bahnfleth Larson; m. Joan Harbelis, July 1, 1951; children—William Parry, Matthew David, Andrew John. B.S. in Mech. Engring., U. Ill., 1952, M.S. in Mech. Engring., 1956. Registered profl. engr., Ill., Ohio, Ky., N.Y., Ala., Va., Ind., Vt. Research asst. prof., U. Ill., Urbana, 1955-60; editor Heating, Piping and Air Conditioning, Chgo., 1960-70, editorial dir., 1970-71; exec. v.p. Z.B.A., Inc., Cin., 1976-84, pres., 1984—. Contbr. author books, various other publs. Contbr. articles to profl. jours. Adv. bd. Nat. Acad. Sci., 1958-71; chmn. congregation and council Immanuel Luth. Ch., 1969-70; treas. St. Paul Luth. Village, Inc., 1972-76; bd. elders St. Paul Luth. Ch., 1977-80, chmn. new mission com., 1977—. Served with USN, 1945-48. Named Outstanding Alumnus dept. mech. engring. U. Ill., 1985. Fellow ASHRAE (chmn. various coms., pres. 1985-86); mem. Air Pollution Control Assn., Nat. Soc. Profl. Engrs., U. Ill. Mech. and Indsl. Engring. Alumni Assn. (pres. bd. dirs. 1970-71), Cin. C. of C., Sigma Xi. Republican. Lodge: Rotary. Avocations: photography, hiking, fishing, golf. Home: 7466 Glenover Dr Cincinnati OH 45236 Office: ZBA Inc 23 E 7th St Cincinnati OH 45202

BAHNSEN, RONALD RUSSELL, hospital official; b. Rockford, Ill., Dec. 2, 1947; s. Wesley and Marjorie E. Bahnsen; B.Pharmacy, Drake U., 1970; M.B.A., U. Ill.; m. Karen Marie Amundson, Dec. 28, 1968; 1 son, Jeffrey. Mgr., Suprex Drug Store, Peoria, Ill., 1970-71; pharmacy mgr. Venture Dept. Store, Peoria, 1971-73; asst. dir. pharmacy Pekin (Ill.) Meml. Hosp., 1973-77, dir. pharmacy, 1977—, ops. coordinator, 1983—; mem. part-time staff Ill. Central Coll., East Peoria, 1977—. Mem. Am. Pharm. Assn., Ill. Pharm. Assn., Ill. Council Hosp. Pharmacists (v.p., dir. legal and pub. affairs), Am. Soc. Hosp. Pharmacists (ho. of dels.), Am. Soc. Parenteral and Nutrition, Assn. M.B.A. Execs., Sigma Iota Epsilon. Republican. Roman Catholic. Club: K.C. Home: 13 Oak Hill Pekin IL 61554 Office: Pekin Meml Hosp Court and 14th Sts Pekin IL 61554

BAHR, DONALD WALTER, chemical engineer; b. Chgo., Dec. 13, 1927; s. Walter James and Justine Antonia (Schwegler) B.; m. Mary Estelle Zieverink, Oct. 15, 1960; children—Donald Walter Jr., Susan Mary. B.S. in Chem. Engring., U. Ill., 1949; M.S. in Chem. Engring., Ill. Inst. Tech., 1951, M.S. in Gas Tech., 1951. Registered profl. engr., Ohio. Aero. research scientist Lewis Flight Propulsion Lab., Cleve. 1951-54; chem. engr. Gen. Electric Co., Cin., 1956-62, engring. mgr., Phila., 1962-68, Cin., 1968—; vice chmn. jet engine fuels panel U.S. NASA Lewis Research Ctr., Cleve., 1973-76. Contbr. articles to profl. jours. Patentee in field. Served to 1st lt. USAF, 1954-56. Recipient Outstanding Engring. Achievements award Gen. Electric Co., 1982. Mem. ASME (combustion and fuels com. 1975—), AIAA (Outstanding Achievement award air breathing propulsion, 1983), Combustion Inst., Aerospace Industries Assn. (chmn. aircraft engine emissions com. 1971—). Republican. Roman Catholic. Club: Kenwood Swim (Cin.). Avocations: gardening; photography. Home: 6576 Branford Ct Cincinnati OH 45236 Office: Gen Electric Co Mail Drop K-64 Cincinnati OH 45215

BAHR, PATRICIA ALICE, occupational coordinator; b. Euclid, Ohio, Mar. 4, 1956; d. Joseph Edward and Alice Alberta (Skebe) Graben; m. David Lee Bahr, Sept. 8, 1978. A.A. in Applied Bus., Bowling Green State U. (Ohio), 1978, B.S. in Edn., 1978, M.Ed., 1985. Cert. techr. bus. With sales and modeling depts. Halles Dept. Store, Cleve., 1974-76; sec. Citizens Fed. Savs. and Loan Co., Cleve., 1975-77; tutor, home instr. North Ridgeville City Schs. (Ohio), 1979—; shorthand instr. City of North Ridgeville Adult Edn., 1981, 83; intern English dept. Bowling Green State U., summers 1983—; instr. high sch. bus. North Ridgeville City Schs., 1978-85, occupational work experience coordinator, 1985—, head girls volleyball coach, 1978-85, asst. athletic dir., 1983—. Judge Voice of Democracy contest VFW North Ridgeville, 1979—. Recipient Civic Commendation, City of North Ridgeville, 1983; Commendation-coaching, North Ridgeville City Schs., 1982. Mem. North Ridgeville Edn. Assn. (rec. sec. 1980—, corr. sec. 1979—), Ohio Edn. Assn., NEA, Ohio Bus. Edn. Assn., Nat. Bus. Edn. Assn., Lorain County Guidance Assn. Chi Omega. Republican. Roman Catholic. Clubs: North Ridgeville Athletic Boosters, Slovenian Women's Union. Home: 25151 Brookpark Rd #1207 North Olmsted OH 44070 Office: North Ridgeville High Sch 7000 Pitts Blvd North Ridgeville OH 44039

BAIA, ARLENE VIVIAN SKJEVELAND, nursing educator; b. Duluth, Minn., Aug. 15, 1922; d. Theodore Owen and Pearl Ruby (Thompson) Skjeveland; B.S. in Nursing Edn., U. Minn., 1945; M.S. in Edn., Iowa State U., 1973; children—Barbara Baia Thompson, Gloria Bonnie (dec.). Instr., U. Minn. Sch. Nursing, Mpls., 1945-46; asso. dir. edn. Naeve Hosp. Sch. Nursing, Albert Lea, Minn., 1954-60; instr. St. Joseph Sch. Nursing, Mason City, Iowa, 1960-62, Meth. Kahler Sch. Nursing, Rochester, Minn., 1962-68; instr. nursing North Iowa Area Community Coll., Mason City, 1968-79, chmn. health related div., 1979—. Recipient certificate for distinguished teaching in nursing Rochester C. of C., 1964; Edith Ruppert award, 1982. Mem. Am. (council advanced practitioners in med.-surg. nursing), Iowa (chmn. rev. panel for continuing edn. 1972-76) nurses assns., P.E.O., Delta Kappa Gamma. Republican. Congregationalist. Club: Order Eastern Star. Contbg. author: Child and Family: Concepts in Nursing Practice. Home: 417 S Tennessee Pl Apt 6 Mason City IA 50401 Office: 500 College Dr Mason City IA 50401

BAIC, DUSAN, experimental morphologist, electron microscopist; b. Zagreb, Yugoslavia, Feb. 11, 1918; came to U.S., 1961, naturalized, 1972; s. Aleksandar and Ivanka (Malcic) B.; m. Branka Janjic, Oct. 10, 1955. M.D., U. Zagreb, 1952. Asst. prof. Med. Sch., U. Zagreb, 1953-61; postdoctoral trainee dept. anatomy U. Chgo., 1961-63; vis. scientist dept. zoology U. Mich., 1963-64, lectr. div. biol. scis., 1967-83, assoc. prof., 1983—, coordinator electron microscopy facility, 1967—; lectr. Inst. for Exptl. Medicine and Surgery, U. Montreal, 1964-67. U. Mich. Horace H. Rackham Sch. Grad. Studies grantee, 1971; recipient Spl. award U. Mich. Coll. Lit., Sci. and Arts, 1972. Mem. Electron Microscopy Soc. Am., N.Y. Acad. Scis., Mich. Electron Microscopy Forum. Republican. Mem. Serbian Eastern Orthodox Ch. Club: U. Mich. Sci. Research. Contbr. articles to profl. jours. Home: 803 Sycamore Pl Ann Arbor MI 48104 Office: Div Biol Scis U Mich Ann Arbor MI 48109

BAIKERIKAR, KAMALAKAR GHANASHYAM, chemist; b. Halge, India, Apr. 5, 1941; came to U.S., 1971, naturalized, 1975; s. Ghanashyam Ramachandra and Gulabi Dattatray (Revankar) B.; B.S., Karnatak U., 1963, M.S., 1965; Ph.D., Indian Inst. Tech., 1970; m. Vijaya Vernekar, May 25, 1970; 1 child, Kiran. Research fellow Indian Inst. Tech., Bombay, 1965-71; U.S. AEC postdoctoral fellow Ames Lab., Iowa State U., 1971-75, asst. chemist Ames Lab., U.S. Dept. Energy, 1975-80, asso. chemist, 1980—. Mem. Am. Chem. Soc., Electrochem. Soc., Sigma Xi. Hindu. Contbr. articles to profl. jours. Home: 1456 Breckinridge Ames IA 50010 Office: 108 O & L Ames Lab Iowa State Univ Ames IA 50011

BAILEY, ANNELL DEANNE, accountant; b. Kansas City, Mo., Aug. 31, 1943; d. Ward Norman and Vida Fae (Votaw) Gibson; B.A. summa cum laude, Mo. Valley Coll., 1966; M.B.A., U. Mo., Kansas City, 1978; m. Willard Lance McGowan, May 28, 1965 (div. 1970); 1 dau., Cherlyn Deanna; m. 2d, Robert Edson Bailey, Dec. 4, 1971. Editor, Hallmark Cards, Inc., Kansas City, Mo., 1967-75; acct. Wolkow & Calys, C.P.A.s, Fairway, Kans., 1977-79, Craven Wooldridge & Dooley, C.P.A.s, Kansas City, Mo., 1979-80, Aubrey E. Richardson, C.P.A., Kansas City, Mo., 1980-82; mgr. revenue acctg. Jefferson Lines, Inc., Joplin, Mo., 1982-84, acctg. mgr., Mpls., 1984—. Bd. dirs. Jr. Women's Philharm. Assn., 1972-79. C.P.A., Mo. Mem. Nat. Assn. Accts., Am. Inst. C.P.A.s, Beta Alpha Psi. Presbyterian. Home: 5521 10th Ave S Minneapolis MN 55417 Office: 1206 Currie Ave PO Box 978 Minneapolis MN 55440

BAILEY, BONNIE SUZANNA, social service agency administrator; b. South Bend, Ind., Aug. 19, 1939; d. Marshall Irving and Winifred Marie (Hoyt) Hewitt; m. Robert Elwood Bailey, Jr., June 9, 1962 (div. June 1977); children—Laura, Lisa, Robert, Samuel. Tchr., South Bend Community Sch. Corp., 1960-61, Penn-Harris-Madison Sch. Corp., Mishawaka, Ind., 1961-64; probation officer Juvenile Ct., South Bend, 1976-77; counselor Family and Children's Ctr., Mishawaka, 1977-79, dir. devel. service, 1979—. Mem. Women in Communications (Instl. Promotion award 1984), South Bend-Mishawaka C. of C. (leadership selection chmn. 1981—), Pi Beta Phi. Republican. Presbyterian. Avocations: soccer; jogging; antiques; collectibles. Office: Family and Children's Ctr 1411 Lincoln Way W Mishawaka IN 46544-1690

BAILEY, DARREL EVANS, new products marketing company executive; b. Kansas City, Mo., Sept. 23, 1952; s. Lane E. and Anna L. (Norman) B.; m. Valerie Ann Wesseling, July 19, 1975; children—Sarah, Julie, Katie, Daniel. B.E.E., Wash. U.-St. Louis, 1975, M.B.A., 1975. Asst. product mgr. Hallmark Cards, Kansas City, Mo., 1975-79; sr. product mgr. Consol. Foods, 1979-82, Con Agra, St. Louis, 1982—. Southwestern Bell scholar, 1970-74; Boatman's Bank scholar, 1974-75. Evangelical. Advocations: Hiking; racquetball; antique collecting; biblical history. Home: 231 Orrick Lane Saint Louis MO 63122

BAILEY, DAVID JOSEPH, pharmacist; b. Painesville, Ohio, Sept. 20, 1955; s. David Eugene and Dolores Marion (Jopko) B.; m. Loretta Jane Hess, Mar. 7, 1981; 1 dau., Rebecca. B.S., U. Cin., 1978. Asst. mgr. pharmacy Cunningham Drugs, Cleve., 1978-79; mgr. pharmacy Chapeldale Pharmacy, Madison, Ohio, 1979—; cons. pharmacist Northea. Ohio Gen. Hosp., Madison, 1979—. Mem. Brithright of Lake County, 1983, Madison Citizens League, Medic Alert Internat., 1978—; vol. Medic Alert, 1982-84. Mem. Nat. Assn. Retail Druggists, Ohio State Pharm. Assn., Northeastern Ohio Acad. Pharmacy (sec. 1979, pres.-elect 1980, pres. 1981; Presdl. award 1981). Democrat. Roman Catholic. Home: 2246 Chaucer Way Madison OH 44057

BAILEY, GLORIA JEANNE, interior designer, consultant; b. Columbus, Ohio, Aug. 31, 1947; d. James Ronald Harmony and Eleanor Jeannette (Crane) H.; m. Theodore Fowler, Dec. 17, 1966 (div.); 1 dau., Koreen Victoria; m. 2d, Lloyd Stephen Bailey, Oct. 27, 1979; 1 stepdau., Jennifer Lynn. Student Patricia Stevens Inst., 1965-66, Bowling Green State U., 1967-69, Columbus Coll. Art and Design, 1973-75. Designer, Harry L. Morgan Co., Columbus, 1973-77; sales mgr. Liston Co., Columbus, 1977-80; dir. design Continental Office, Columbus, 1980-83; design cons. Gloria Bailey, Columbus, 1983—. Active Peace Makers, 1983, Parents Without Partners, 1978. Mem. Inst. Bus. Designers (v.p. Ohio regional chpt. program 1981-83, membership 1979-81), Bus. and Profl. Women. Presbyterian. Home: 159 E Schrock Rd Westerville OH 43081 Office: 3636 N High St Columbus OH 43214

BAILEY, GWENDOLYN LEE MANNING, educator; b. Dayton, Ohio, Sept. 1, 1930; d. Edgar William and Thelma Evelyn (Doughman) Vahle; B.S. in Edn., U. Dayton, 1963, M.S. in Edn., 1969; m. Charles Sydney Bailey, Aug. 3, 1949; 1 son, Bruce Eugene. Tchr., Northridge Morrison Elementary Sch., Dayton, 1960-63; tchr. Beavercreek Fairbrook Elementary Sch., Beavercreek, Ohio, 1963-70, counselor Beavercreek High Sch., 1970—, dir. guidance, 1984—. Co-chmn. United Appeal. Recipient Counselor of Yr. award AHEAD, 1980. Mem. Am., Ohio, Miami Valley personnel and guidance assns., NEA, Ohio, Western Ohio edn. assns., Nat. Assn. Coll. Admissions Counselors, Ohio Assn. Coll. Admission Counselors, Ohio High Sch. Drill Team Assn. (v.p., state dir.), Half-Time U.S.A., Ohio Sch. Counselors Assn., Beavercreek Classroom Tchrs. Assn. Home: 3159 Cymar Dr Beavercreek OH 45430 Office: 2940 Dayton-Xenia Rd Beavercreek OH 45385

BAILEY, JAMES DAVID, former school district public relations official, writer, consultant; b. Menomonie, Wis., Sept. 3, 1922; s. Paul E. and Ruth (Chickering) B.; B.S., U. Wis., Stout, 1948; M.A., U. Denver, 1950; postgrad. U. Colo., 1962; m. Barbara Jean Swanson, Sept. 18, 1981; children by previous marriage—Dianne Bailey Zemichael, Andrea Bailey Hartwig, Jerri Pederson, Jan Rohleik, Joan Johnson, Jill White. Printing instr. Keating Jr. High Sch., Pueblo, Colo., 1948-49; instr. communications U. Denver, 1949-50; sales mgr./newscaster/announcer various radio stas., 1950-56; mgr. Northfield (Minn.) C. of C., 1956-64; free lance public relations cons., Northfield, Mpls., 1964-66; public relations/advt. asst. F&M Savings Bank, Mpls., 1966-69; owner James Bailey & Assocs., Public Relations/Advt. Agy., Mpls., 1969-72; dir. coll. relations St. Norbert Coll., Green Bay/DePere, Wis., 1972-73; public relations officer Wis. Indianhead Vocat.-Tech. Adult Edn. Dist., Shell Lake, 1973-83; freelance writer, consultant. Mem. Shell Lake planning commn., 1974-81; bd. dirs. UN of Minn., 1969-72; mem. N.G. Citizens Com., Northfield, Minn., 1963-66; safety council chmn. Red Wing, Minn., 1953-56. Recipient cert. of appreciation Shell Lake Bicentennial Com., 1976, Stout U. Found., 1975; commendation cert. Shell Lake, Wis., 1976. Mem. Public Relations Soc. Am., Wis. Newspaper Assn., Nat. Assn. Vocat. Tech. Communicators, Nat. Council for Community Relations, Shell Lake C. of C., Am. Legion (comdr. 1947-48). Republican. Clubs: Minn. Press, Lions (dist. gov. 1981-82, chmn. Wis. council govs. 1982-83), Masons Shriners. Contbr. articles to profl. jours. Newsletter editor Minn. Press Club, 1970-72, UN Assn. of Minn., 1971-72; editor Minn. Farm Bur. Tabloid, 1964-65; newspaper columnist. Home: Route 2 Box 13 Shell Lake WI 54871

BAILEY, JOHN CHARLES, economic development organization executive; b. Osage, Iowa, Feb. 27, 1930; s. Roy Lynn and Dorothy Rachel (Bucknam) B.; m. Shirley Ann Senn, July 30, 1950; 1 child, Carolyn Kay. Student, U. Iowa, 1947-50. Dist. mgr. C. of C. of U.S., N.Y.C., 1964-66, div. mgr., Mpls., 1966-77, regional mgr., Dallas, 1977-81; pres. C. of C., Mpls., 1981-83; dir. Iowa Devel. Commn., Des Moines, 1983—. Mayor City of Minnetonka, Minn., 1973-77; chmn. bd. Pub. Affairs Leadership Mgmt., 1976-77. Served with USAF, 1951-53. Named Outstanding Young Man, U.S. Jaycees, 1956, 59. Mem. Am. C. of C. Execs. (cert., sec-treas. 1981-82). Congregationalist. Lodge: Masons. Office: Iowa Devel Commn 600 E Court Ave Des Moines IA 50309

BAILEY, KAREL LYNNE, physical education educator, coach; b. Pontiac, Mich., Nov. 14, 1952; d. Jack Thomas and Ruth Edna (Ingamells) McCulloch; m. Tony Lee Bailey, Apr. 5, 1979; 1 dau., Meghan Marie. B.S., Western Mich. U., 1974, M.A., 1982. Tchr., coach North Muskegon Pub. Schs. (Mich.), 1975—. Author paper in field, 1979. Instr. North Muskegon Recreation Dept., 1983. Named Coach of Yr. Mich. Interscholastic Track Coaches Assn., Lansing, 1980, 79, 77; Dist. Coach of Yr., Nat. High Sch. Coaches Assn., 1984. Mem. Mich. Interscholastic Track Coaches Assn., Mich. High Sch. Coaches Assn. (coach of yr. 1980), Southwest Mich. Field Hockey Assn. Office: North Muskegon High Sch 1507 Mills Ave North Muskegon MI 49445

BAILEY, MAX EDWARD, optometrist; b. Richmond, Ind., Mar. 2, 1954; s. James Earl and Joan Francis (Spalding) B.; m. Eva Lynn Tischuk, Aug. 19, 1972; children—Travis, Aaron. B.S. in Optometry, Ind. U., 1976; O.D. with honors, 1978. Gen. practice optometry Barnhart, Logan & Bailey, Richmond, Ind., 1978—. Sec. United Way of Wayne County, Richmond, 1984; v.p. Richmond Symphony Orch., 1983-84, bd. dirs., 1982-83; radio disk jockey on local pub. radio sta. Recipient Irvin M. Borish award Am. Optometric Found., 1978, Bausch and Lomb Outstanding Achievement award, 1978. Mem. Whitewater Valley Optometric Soc. (pres. 1982-83), Ind. Optometric Assn., Am. Optometric Assn. Presbyterian. Avocations: running; gardening, music. Home: 316 Thornwood Ct Richmond IN 47374 Office: Drs Barnhart Logan & Bailey 2519 E Main St Richmond IN 47374

BAILEY, NANCY MARTIN, university dean; b. Chgo., July 26, 1944; d. Ross J. and Marian Allen (Shepard) M.; m. Richard Ryan Malmgren; 1 child, Ryan Martin; m. Leslie Francis Bailey; 1 child, Stuart Martin. B.A., U. Wis., 1967; M.A., U. Ill., 1981, Ph.D., 1985. Specialist, botanist U. Wis.-Madison, 1967-72; English tchr. U. Ill. Univ. High Sch., Urbana, 1977-80; placement dir. Sch. Life Sci. U. Ill., Urbana, 1980-85, asst. dean, 1985—. Contbr. articles to profl. jours.

Chmn. Urbana park dist. adv. com. 1982-83. Recipient Excellence in Profl. Writing award Midwest Coll. Placement Assn., 1981. Mem. Am. Ednl. Research Assn., Philosophy of Edn. Soc., Phi Kappa Phi, Kappa Delta Pi, Alpha Chi Omega, Phi Delta Kappa. Club: Thirty (Urbana). Avocation: photography; fishing; flute playing. Office: 390 Morrill Hall U Ill Sch Life Sci 505 S Goodwin St Urbana IL 61801

BAILEY, NAOMA JUNE, nurse; b. Toledo, July 7, 1923; d. Theo W. and Eunice Lucy (Crown) Harris; L.P.N., Northwestern Ohio Practical Nurse Sch., 1965; A.D.S., Cuyahoga Coll., 1969, R.N., 1969; B.Ed., U. Toledo, 1976, M.Ed., 1981; m. James Arthur Bailey, Sept. 14, 1946; children—Mark Bruce, Paul Kim. Nurse, Maumee Valley Hosp., 1969-71; clin. instr. practical nurses at Mercy Hosp. for Toledo Bd. Edn., 1971-79, coordinator, 1979-80, supr. Practical Sch. Nursing, 1981—; public relations speaker. Vol. counselor Crisis Rescue Service, 1979-80; vol. Republican Party, 1973. Served with WAVES, USNR, 1941-43. Mem. Buckeye State Nurses Orgn., Ohio Orgn. Practical Nurse Educators, Vocat. Edn. Assn., Ohio Nurses Assn., Am. Bus. Women's Assn., Lic. Practical Nurses Orgn. (cons. bd.). Home: 64 Walnut Hills Walbridge OH 43465 Office: 144 Blum St Toledo OH 43602

BAILEY, PORTIA ANDREA, author, producer; b. Chgo., Aug. 5, 1945; d. A. Leon and Portia H. (Thomas) B. Student Lawrence U., 1961-64, Lake Forest Coll., 1965-66, MacMasters U., 1967-75, Peters/Long creative writing seminars, 1971-74, language, communications, dance and music tng., 1951-70, 77-78. Dir., producer Carey Temple theatrical prodns., 1958; tech. dir., producer Thomas Meml. Theatre, Chgo., 1962-65; lit. translator from and into German, 1969-75; guest lectr. German seminar, Lawrence U., 1971; lighting designer, tech. dir. touring Prosenium Players, 1971-73; guest dir., theatre prodn. cons.; developer exptl. designers research project Linguistic Cultural Communication Devel. Corp., 1972-74, music copyist, 1978; cons., demonstrator Skinner Sch. Gifted Program, 1974-78; co-producer Gil Helmsley's God Is My Lighting Designer, U.S. Inst. Theatre Tech. Midwest sect., 1978; producer, propr. Andrea Bailey Enterprises, 1979-82; producer Black Ind. Cinema, U.S.A. Film Festival, 1981. Editor Midwest Report, 1978-82. Author: (book) Christophe, One Amoung Giants; (plays) The Greatest of These, 1970, 84, (an adapted transl.) Iphigenia In Tauris, Part I, 1983, Depth of the Shadow, 1963. Author monographs including The Black Lifestyle and Period of Training, 1974, Communicators Coming into Being, 1974, Our Concept of God and Man, 1984, From Dream to Dream, 1985. Author: (TV scripts) 9 program series America—Our Ideal, Our Reality, 1983, 22 program series America—Our Ideal, Our Reality, 1984. Author of literal transls. Recipient First prize Dist. Twenty Sci. Fair, 1961. Mem. Am. Soc. Theatre Research Internat., Am. Fedn. TV and Radio Artists, U.S. Inst. Theatre Tech. (vice chmn. Midwest sect. 1981-82). Methodist. Avocations: embroidery; fine arts photography. Office: PO Box 49279 Chicago IL 60649

BAILEY, THOMAS LEE, musician, physical plant administrator; b. Birmingham, Ala., June 2, 1932; s. Tom and Lola E. (Gilmer) B.; children—Miriam, Ronald and Donald (twins). A.A., Cuyahoga Community Coll., 1974; B.A., Cleve. State U., 1977. Ordained minister of music Nat. Baptist Congress of Christian Edn., 1972. Profl. singer; with Fame, Inc., Cleve., 1959-62; social worker House of Correction, City of Cleve., 1972-74; minister of music St. John Bapt. Ch., Cleve., 1972—; supr. phys. plant services Cleve. State U., 1974—; singing waiter, Fla., 1956-59. Clk., St. John Missionary Bapt. Ch., 1972-83, trustee, 1974—; mem. Inspirational Choir Cleve.; dir. Wilson Jubilee of Cleve., 1981—. Recipient awards St. John Ch., Phi Beta Sigma; honored on 50th birthday by New Bethel Bapt. Ch., Birmingham, 1982. Mem. Calvary Hill Dist. Assn., Future Farmers Am., Phi Beta Sigma (chpt. sec. 1977-80, chaplain 1977-78). Democrat. Home: 1627 Pontiac Ave Cleveland OH 44112 Office: 2300 E 100th St Cleveland OH 44106

BAILEY, WENDELL, state government official. Treas., State of Mo., Jefferson City. Office: Office of the Treasurer PO Box 210 Jefferson City MO 65102*

BAILEY, WILLIAM ARTHUR, electronics company executive; b. Mpls., Nov. 16, 1945; s. Walter George and Bernice Evelen (Okerlund) B.; m. Karen Lee Hafdal, Sept. 10, 1966; children—Kristin, Teresa. Student St. Cloud State Coll., 1963-65, U. Minn., 1965-67. Supr. prodn. control Univac/Sperry, St. Paul, 1965-70; mktg. adminstr. Data 100 Corp., Edina, Minn., 1970-73, 76-79; ops. mgr. Systematics, St. Paul, 1974-76; materials mgr. Audiotronics, Minnetonka, Minn., 1980-83; materials mgr. Interconics-IMC, Hopkins, Minn., 1983—. Bd. dirs. Atheltic Booster Assn., Columbia Heights, Minn., 1981-83; sec. City Charter Commn., Columbia Heights, 1985; mem. Hockey Assn., Columbia Heights, 1985—; mem. sports program Group W CAble, Columbia Heights, 1984-85. Republican. Roman Catholic. Clubs: Athletic Boosters (bd. dirs. 1981-83), Hockey Assn. Avocations: sports broadcasting; fishing; golf; electronics.

BAILEY, WILSON PEASE, pediatrician; b. Waverly, N.Y., Sept. 1, 1929; s. Percival Dee and Ella Marie (Wilson) B.; B.A., Alfred U., 1952; Dr. Osteopathy, Kirksville (Mo.) Coll. Osteo. Medicine, 1959; M.D. (Mead Johnson fellow), Calif. Coll. Medicine, 1962; m. Barbara Ann Miller, Apr. 5, 1958; children—Wilson Pease, John, Valerie, Bruce. Intern, Kirksville Osteo. Hosp., 1959-60, resident, 1960-62, chmn. dept. pediatrics Kirksville Coll. Medicine and Surgery, 1962-68, med. dir. children and youth program, 1966-68, asso. prof., 1965—; practice medicine specializing in pediatrics, Kirksville, 1968—; mem. staff attending pediatric Grim Smith Hosp., Kirksville, chief of staff, 1970-73: cons. OEO programs, rural pediatrics; lectr. N.E. Mo. U., 1962-72. Mem. Sch. Bd. Dist. III, 1972-73, pres., 1972-75; chmn. Head Start Bd., 1966-70. Served to col. M.C., AUS, 1952-55. Diplomate Coll. Osteo. Pediatricians. Mem. Mo. Assn. Osteo. Physicians, Am. Coll. Osteo. Pediatricians, N.E. Mo. Osteo. Physicians, Am. Osteo. Assn. Mason. Club: Kirksville Country. Contbr. articles to profl. jours. Home: RD 3 Kirksville MO 63501 Office: 2905 N Baltimore St Kirksville MO 63501

BAILLIEUL, THOMAS ALEXANDER, geologist; b. Westfield, Mass., Dec. 17, 1949; s. Paul Brouard and Geneva Jeanette (Gillam) B.; m. Deborah L. Stevens, July 29, 1972; children—Alexander Bain, Benjamin Pierce. B.A., U. Mass., 1971, M.S., 1976. Mineralogist Botswana Geol. Survey, Lobatse, 1971-73; teaching asst. U. Mass., Amherst, 1974-76; mineral curator Amherst Coll., 1975-76; geologist Falconbridge Exploration, Francistown, Botswana, 1976-77; prin. investigator Bendix Field Engring., Pitts., 1977-81; geologist U.S. Dept. Energy, Columbus, Ohio, 1981—. Author folios in uranium assessment in eastern and western U.S., 1979-81. Contbr. articles to profl. jours. Recipient Superior Performance awards U.S. Dept. Energy, 1983, 84. Mem. Geol. Soc. Am., AAAS, Ohio Acad. Sci. Home: 2582 Glen Echo Dr Columbus OH 43202 Office: US Dept Energy 505 King Ave Columbus OH 43201

BAILLON, AUSTIN JOHN, real estate exec.; b. Duluth, Minn., June 22, 1927; s. Austin L. and Marie M. (McDonald) B.; B.A., U. Minn., 1950; B.S., St. Paul Coll. Law, 1952, LL.B., 1954; J.D., William Mitchell Coll. Law, 1969; m. Caroline Myers, Aug. 16, 1958; children—Caroline M., Paul A., Peter M., Catherine G., Alexandra R., Frances E. Claims examiner Minn. Mut. Life Ins. Co., St. Paul, 1950-52, claims mgr., 1952-54, atty. legal dept., 1954-55; sales mgr., appraiser F. M. and E. V. Dolan, Realtors and Appraisers, St. Paul, 1955-56; pres. Baillon Co., Realtors, Real Estate Brokerage and Investment, St. Paul, 1956—; founder, pres. St. Paul Title Ins. Co. subs. St. Paul Cos., Inc., 1963-67; founder Baillon Mortgage Corp., 1964, Bailon Agy., Inc., 1963. Bd. dirs. Minn. Landmarks, 1971-74. Served with USCG, 1945-46; with U.S. Army Res., 1951-54. Mem. Soc. Real Estate Appraisers (past sec.-treas., dir.), Am., Minn. State, Ramsey County bar assns., St. Paul Bd. Realtors (past treas., dir.), St. Paul Bldg. Owners and Mgrs. Assn., Chi Psi, Delta Theta Phi. Clubs: Minn. (dir. 1970-73), Athletic (St. Paul); K.C.; Somerset Country; Biltmore Hunting. Office: 60 W 4th St Saint Paul MN 55102

BAINES, HAROLD DOUGLASS, professional baseball player. Outfielder Chgo. White sox. Office: Chgo White Sox Comiskey Park Chicago IL 60616*

BAINTER, JACK JEFFRIES, technical institute official; b. Jennings, Kans., Sept. 20, 1931; s. Corral William and Nellie Kathleen (Randall) B.; m. Diane Flanigan, Mar. 14, 1967; children—Stephen F., Marcia Bainter Kirkpatrick, David J., Jason J., Jeffrey C. B.G.E., U. Omaha, 1964; M.S., U. So. Calif., 1968; Ed. D., Ind. U., 1974. Lic. real estate broker, Ind. Commd. U.S. Air Force, 1958, advanced through grades to maj., 1968; ret., 1971; chmn. div. gen. and tech. studies Ind. U. S.E.-New Albany, 1974-75; dean of instrn. Barton County Community Coll., Great Bend, Kans., 1975-76; program officer for acad. affairs Ind. Commn. for Higher Edn., Indpls., 1976-78; dir. instrn. Ind. Vocat. Tech. Coll., Muncie, 1978-81; v.p., dean Ind. Vocat. Tech. Coll.-S.W., Evansville, 1981-83; dir. ITT Tech. Inst., Ft. Wayne, Ind., 1983-85; nat. dir. edn. resident div. ITT Ednl. Services, Inc., Indpls., 1985—; cons. in field. Decorated Bronze Star, Meritorious Service medal, Air medal with oak leaf cluster. Mem. Ind. Vocat. Assn. (life mem.; Outstanding Service award 1982), Am. Vocat. Assn. (life), Kans. Vocat. Assn. (life), Ind. Post-Secondary Vocat. Edn. Assn. (pres. 1981-82), Ind. Council Vocat. Adminstrs. Methodist. Lodges: Elks, Masons, Order Eastern Star. Office: PO Box 68888 Indianapolis IN 46268

BAIOCCHI, DONALD PAUL, management consultant; b. Chgo., Feb. 8, 1939; s. Francis and Esther Marie (Betti) B.; m. Judith Angela Albin, Sept. 1, 1969; children—Francis, Cara, Michael, Donald. B.B.A., Northwestern U., Evanston, Ill., 1966; postgrad. Law Sch. Notre Dame U., 1967; M.B.A., DePaul U., Chgo., 1971. C.P.A., Ill. Systems analyst Exchange Nat. Bank, Chgo., 1961-64; staff auditor Arthur Andersen & Co., Chgo., 1966-67; 2d v.p. The No. Trust Co., Chgo., 1967-73; mgr. bus. devel. Quaker Oats Co., Chgo., 1973-75; sr. v.p. Heidrick and Struggles, Chgo., 1975-81; pres. Baiocchi, Ryan Assocs. Ltd., Chgo., 1981-85; ptnr. Heidrick and Struggles, Chgo., 1985—. Served with USAF, 1957-60; Japan. Mem. Am. Inst. C.P.A.s, Ill. C.P.A. Soc., Fin. Exec. Inst. Home: 1101 Ashland St Wilmette IL 60091 Office: Heidrick and Struggles 125 S Wacker Dr Suite 2800 Chicago IL 60606

BAIRD, DOUGLAS GORDON, law educator; b. Phila., July 10, 1953; s. Henry Welles and Eleanora (Gordon) B. B.A., Yale U., 1975; J.D., Stanford U., 1979. Law clk. U.S. Ct. Appeals (9th cir.), 1979, 80; asst. prof. law U. Chgo., 1980-83, prof. law, assoc. dean, 1984—. Author: (with others) Security Interests in Personal Property, 1984. Mem. Order of Coif. Home: 5825 S Dorchester Chicago IL 60637 Office: Univ Chgo Law Sch 1111 E 60th St Chicago IL 60637

BAIRD, GEORGE HENRY, educational association administrator; b. Rushville, Ill., Sept. 24, 1922; s. George H. and Rose (Cook) B.; B.E., Western Ill. U., 1943; M.A., U. Wyo., 1949; Ed.D., Columbia, 1954; m. Karole V. Litchfield, May 14, 1944; 1 dau., Cheryl Sue Baird Ramsey. Tchr., coach, Alexis, Ill., 1946-47, Dwight, Ill., 1947-48; asst. supt. elementary schs., Worland, Wyo., 1948-53; dir. research spl. services and guidance Shaker Heights, Ohio, 1954-59; exec. dir. Ednl. Research Council of Am., Cleve., 1959-66, pres., exec. dir., 1966—; chmn. bd. Ramsey-Baird Enterprises. Ednl. cons. Jr. Achievement of Greater Cleve.; mem. regional interviewing com. U.S. Internat. Ednl. Exchange Program. Mem. steering com. Cleve. Energy Center. Served with Inf., AUS, 1944-46. Recipient Disting. Alumnae award Western Ill. U.; Melville Dewey gold medal internat. award for contbn. to edn. in Am. Mem. Greater Cleve. Growth Assn., Am. Assn. Sch. Adminstrs., Phi Delta Kappa, Kappa Delta Pi. Clubs: Union, Rotary Masons (33d degree), Shriners. Home: 2200 Devonshire Dr Cleveland Heights OH 44106 Office: Rockefeller Bldg Cleveland OH 44113

BAIRD, JAMES NICHOLSON, JR., obstetrician-gynecologist; b. N.Y.C., Feb. 29, 1940; s. James Nicholson and Jean (Sanford) B.; B.S., Ohio State U., 1962, M.D. cum laude (Dean's award), 1966; m. Veronica De Prisco, Aug. 25, 1962; children—Lisa Nicholson, James Nicholson III. Intern, Riverside Methodist Hosp., Columbus, Ohio, 1966-67, resident in obstetrics and gynecology, 1968-71; practice medicine specializing in ob-gyn, Columbus, 1971—; mem. staff Riverside Meth. Hosp., chmn. dept. ob-gyn, 1979-81, pres. med. and dental staff, 1983-84; mem. staff Ohio State U. Hosp.; asst. clin. prof. Ohio State U. Coll. Medicine. Bd. dirs. Columbus Zool. Gardens, Columbus Sch. Girls, Franklin County Conservatory; bd. dirs., treas. U.S. Health Corp. Diplomate Am. Bd. Obstetrics and Gynecology. Mem. AMA, Central Assn. Ob-Gyn, Am. Coll. Ob-Gyn, Columbus Gynecol. and Obstetric Soc. (treas. 1975, sec. 1976, pres. 1978), Internat. Soc. Aquatic Medicine, Acad. Medicine of Franklin County, Ohio State Med. Assn., Order of Hippocrates, Alpha Omega Alpha, Phi Gamma Delta (pres. bd. dirs. 1971-73). Republican. Roman Catholic. Clubs: Rotary (bd. dirs.), City (bd. dirs.), Columbus, Scioto Country, Pres.'s of Ohio State U. Home: 4700 Old Ravine Ct Columbus OH 43220 Office: 3545 Olentangy River Rd Columbus OH 43214

BAIRD, JOHN EDWARD, JR., management consultant; b. Portland, Oreg., July 6, 1948; s. John Edward and Eleanor Grace Baird; B.A., Calif. State U., Hayward, 1969; Ph.D., Ind. U., 1972. Asst. prof. U. N.D., 1973-74, U. Mich., 1974-78; corp. mgr. communication and opinion research Travenol Labs., Inc., Deerfield, Ill., 1978-79; mgmt. cons. Modern Mgmt. Methods, Inc., Bannockburn, Ill., 1980-83; chmn. Baird, De Groot & Assocs., Inc., Redwood City, Calif., 1983—; cons. editor for various publishers; lectr. and guest prof. communications. U. Mich. research grantee, 1976. Mem. Am. Mgmt. Assn., Speech Communications Assn., Improvement Inst., Central States Speech Communication Assn., Am. Bus. Communication Assn. Author: Workbook for Effective Speaking, 1974; The Dynamics of Organizational Communication, 1977; Communication, 1977; Speaking by Objectives, 1980; Effective Employment Interviewing, 1982; Quality Circles, 1983; contbr. articles to profl. jours. and trade mags. Home: 905 Vose Dr Gurnee IL 60031 Office: Baird De Groot & Assocs Inc 489 Seaport Ct Redwood City CA 94063

BAIRD, LAURA LEE, lawyer; b. Gaylord, Mich., Oct. 1, 1952; d. Boyd Cantrell and Nancy Lee (Tingley) B.; m. Duane Seastrom, July 17, 1975 (div. 1979); m. George Zulakis, Jan. 1, 1980; children—Michael Boyd, Nicholas Lee. B.S., Western Mich. U., 1975; J.D. with honors, Thomas Cooley Law Sch., 1979. Bar: Mich. 1979. Mem. faculty Colegio Internat., Valencia, Venezuela, 1974-75; assoc. Family Law Clinic, 1979-80; ptnr. Baird & Zulakis, Lansing, 1980—; atty. United Cerebral Palsy of Lansing, 1983—; speaker on family law YWCA, Lansing, 1983—. Com. mem. Lansing Sch. Preprimary Study, 1983; bd. dirs. United Cerebral Palsy Assn., Lansing, 1982-84; mem. parents adv. bd. Resurrection Day Care Ctr., Lansing, 1984. Mem. Mich. Trial Lawyers, Woman Lawyers, Ingham County Bar Assn. Democrat. Club: YMCA-Oakpark (Lansing). Office: Baird and Zulakis 115 W Allegan Suite 810 Lansing MI 48933

BAIRD, MICHAEL JEFFERSON, chemical engineer; b. New Orleans, Oct. 21, 1939; s. Albert Jerry and Helen Mary (Cooper) B.; m. Gayle Ann Amlie, Dec. 16, 1967; children—David, Debbie, Dan, DeAnna. B.S. in Chem. Engring., Tex. A&M U., 1963, Ph.D. in Phys. Chemistry, 1971; M.S. in Chem. Engring., U. Pitts., 1979. Chem. engr. U.S. Bur. Mines, Mpls., 1971-74, U.S. Dept. Energy, Pitts., 1974-79; sr. research chemist Ashland Oil, Ky., 1979-80; research chem. engr. Amoco Oil Research and Devel., Naperville, Ill., 1980—; instr. chem. engring. Ill. Inst. Tech., Chgo., 1981, U. Ill.-Chgo., 1982-84. Patentee in field. Mem. Am. Chem. Soc., Catalysis Club Chgo. (program chmn. 1982-83, pres. 1983-84). Avocations: Polish dancing; drummer. Office: Amoco Oil Research and Devel PO Box 400 Naperville IL 60566

BAIRD, NOLAN HARRINGTON, JR., investment counsel; b. N.Y.C., Aug. 2, 1936; s. Nolan H. and Freida (Wittmann) B.; m. Nancy Ellen Moore, Sept. 6, 1958; children—Gregory W., Bonnie S., Nolan H. III. B.A., Yale U., 1958; M.B.A., Harvard U., 1960. Chartered investment counsel. Assoc. Stein Roe & Farnham, Chgo., 1960-66, ptnr., 1966—; dir. SteinRoe Govt. Reserves Fund, Universe Fund, Tax-Exempt Bond Fund, Cash Reserves Fund, Bond Fund, Total Return Fund, Tax-Exempt Money Fund, Discovery Fund, High Yield Mcpls. Fund. Pres. United Way Suburban Chgo., 1976-77, bd. dirs., 1974-76; trustee Crusade of Mercy, Chgo., 1974-78, bd. dirs., 1974—. Clubs: Metropolitan, Tower, River (Chgo.). Avocation: underwater photography. Office: Stein Roe & Farnham One S Wacker Dr Chicago IL 60606

BAIRD, ROBERT DAHLEN, religions scholar, educator; b. Phila., June 29, 1933; s. Jesse Dahlen and Clara (Sonntag) B.; B.A., Houghton Coll., 1954; B.D., Fuller Theol. Sem., 1957; S.T.M., So. Meth. U., 1959; Ph.D., U. Iowa, 1964; m. Patty Jo Lutz, Dec. 18, 1954; children—Linda Sue, Stephen Robert, David Bryan, Janna Ann. Instr. philosophy and religion U. Omaha, 1962-65; fellow Asian religions Soc. for Religion in Higher Edn., 1965-66; asst. prof. religion U. Iowa, Iowa City, 1966-69, assoc. prof., 1969-74, prof., 1974—, acting dir. Sch. Religion, spring 1985; vis. prof. religious studies Grinnell Coll. (Iowa), 1983; faculty fellow Am. Inst. Asian Studies, India, 1972. Mem. Am. Acad. Religion, Assn. Asian Studies. Democrat. Presbyterian. Contbr. articles in field to profl. jours.; author: Category Formation and the History of Religions, 1971; (with W. Richard Comstock, et al) Religion and Man: An Introduction, 1971; Indian and Far Eastern Religious Traditions, 1972; editor and contbr. Methodological Issues in Religious Studies, 1975; Religion in Modern India, 1981; book rev. editor Jour. of Am. Acad. Religion, 1979-84. Home: 3733 Rohret Rd Iowa City IA 52240 Office: School of Religion University of Iowa Iowa City IA 52242

BAIRD, ROBERT LEADLEY, police chief; b. Waukesha, Wis., Aug. 15, 1929; s. Robert L. and Daisey (Beales) B.; m. Fran Ward, May 5, 1951; children—Marty Lynn, Robert L. III, Thomas W. B.A., Governors State U., 1981; grad. FBI Nat. Acad., U.S. Army Command and Gen. Staff Coll. Dep. sheriff Waukesha County Sheriff Dept., Wis., 1953-62, sgt., 1962-64, lt., 1964-65, sheriff, 1965-72; chief of police City of Elgin (Ill.), 1972—; lectr. Traffic Inst. Northwestern U., Evanston, Ill., 1967—. Pres. Greater Waukesha United Fund, 1969; bd. dirs. Greater Elgin United Way, 1984—, Greater Elgin YMCA, 1984—, Community Concern Alcohol/Drugs, 1981—. Served to lt. col. U.S. Army, 1947-75. Recipient Citation award Wis. Legislature, 1972, Meritorious Service medal. Mem. Wis. Council Criminal Justice, FBI Acad. Grads., Wis. Sheriffs Assn. (treas. 1966-67), Waukesha Dep. Sheriff Assn. (pres 1960-61), Nat. Sheriffs Assn., Ill. Chiefs Assn. (dir. 1979—), Internat. Chiefs of Police. Republican. Episcopalian. Lodge: Masons. Avocations: jogging; golf; skiing. Home: 905 Ruth Dr Elgin IL 60120 Office: Police Dept Headquarters 150 Dexter Ct Elgin IL 60120

BAIRD, WILLIAM MCKENZIE, chemical carcinogenesis researcher, biochemistry educator; b. Phila., Mar. 23, 1944; s. William Henry Jr. and Edna (McKenzie) B.; m. Elizabeth A. Myers, June 21, 1969; children—Heather Jean, Elizabeth Joanne, Scott William. B.S. in Chemistry, Lehigh U., 1966; Ph.D. in Oncology, U. Wis., 1971. Postdoctoral fellow Inst. Cancer Research, London, 1971-73; from asst. to assoc. prof. biochemistry Wistar Inst., Phila., 1973-80; assoc. prof. medicinal chemistry Purdue U., West Lafayette, Ind., 1980-82, prof., 1982—; faculty participant cancer ctr., biochemistry program Purdue U., 1980—. Contbr. articles to profl. jours. Grantee NCI, 1984. Mem. Am. Assn. Cancer Research, Am. Soc. Biol. Chemists, Genetic Toxicology Assn., Am. Chem. Soc., AAAS. Office: Purdue Univ Dept Medicinal Chemistry Sch Pharmacy West Lafayette IN 47907

BAKEN, ROBERT EDWARD, electrical engineer; b. Oak Park, Ill., Feb. 2, 1930; s. Edward Albert and Katherine C. (Schlegal) B.; student DePaul U., 1947-49; B.S., Ill. Inst. Tech., 1958; m. Barbara Marie Marik, Aug. 2, 1975; 1 son, Matthew Robert. Draftsman Chgo. Park Dist., 1950-51, Commonwealth Edison, Chgo., 1953-55; with Dept. Pub. Works, City of Chgo., 1955-68, civil engr., 1958-68; with Dept. Water and Sewers, City of Chgo., 1968—, asst. engr. water distbn., 1975-78, engr. water distbn., 1978—. Served with U.S. Army, 1951-53. Mem. ASCE, Western Soc. Engrs. (trustee), Am. Water Works Assn., Am. Public Works Assn., Art Inst. Chgo. Roman Catholic. Clubs: Elmhurst Country; Union League (Chgo.). Home: 8629 W Leland Ave Chicago IL 60656 Office: 1000 E Ohio St Chicago IL 60611

BAKER, ALFRED STANLEY, II, computer scientist; b. Hopewell, Va., Oct. 27, 1947; s. Alfred Stanley and Koma Jo (Johnson) B.; B.A. in Math., Ill. Inst. Tech., 1970; m. Janet Marie Borowski, Feb. 15, 1969; children—Jennifer, Nathan. System software designer STAT-TAB, Chgo., 1968-71; supr. system software devel. Standard Oil Co. Ind., 1971-79; v.p., programming dir. Datamension Corp. (formerly Image Producers, Inc.), Northbrook, Ill., 1979—; speaker, cons. in field. Mem. Nat. Space Inst. Baptist. Columnist for magazines; author: TRS-80 Programs and Applications for the Color Computer; also games for Apple, TRS-80 and Atari. Home: 2327 S Westminster St Wheaton IL 60187 Office: 615 Academy Dr Northbrook IL 60062

BAKER, BARNET, civil engineer; b. Boston, Oct. 7, 1898; s. Joseph and Sarah (Bloch) B.; B.S. in Civil Engring., Case Inst. Tech., 1922; m. Florence Kleinman, July 25, 1923; children—Saul Phillip, Melvin. Plant engr. Columbia Chem. Co., Barberton, Ohio, 1922-23; asst. civil engr. City of East Liverpool (Ohio), 1923-24; mem. engring. staff City Cleve., 1924-69, asst. civil engr., sr. asst. civil engr., civil engr., 1924-63, chief civil engr., 1963-69. Mem. social agy. com. Jewish Welfare Fedn. Cleve., 1948-57. Bd. dirs. Ind. Montefiore Shelter Home, pres., 1952-54. Zone warden, Cuyahoga County, Ohio, World War II. Registered profl. engr., surveyor, Ohio. Fellow ASCE (life); mem. Cleve. (charter, life), Ohio, Nat. socs. profl. engrs., Am. Pub. Works Assn. (life). Clubs: Masons (32 degree), Shriners (pres. sr. club 1974-75). Home: 1422 SOM Center Rd PO Box 24566 Mayfield Heights OH 44124

BAKER, BETTY LOUISE, mathematician, educator; b. Chgo., Oct. 17, 1937; d. Russell James and Lucille Juanita (Timmons) B.: B.E., Chgo. State U., 1961, M.A., 1964; Ph.D., Northwestern U., 1971. Tchr. math. Harper High Sch., Chgo., 1961-70; tchr. math. Hubbard High Sch., Chgo., 1970—, also chmn. dept.; part-time instr. Moraine Valley Community Coll., 1982-83, 84—. Cultural arts chmn. Hubbard Parents-Tchrs.-Student Assn., 1974-76, lst v.p., program chmn., 1977-79, 82-84, pres., 1979-81; organist Hope Lutheran Ch., 1963—. Univ. fellow, 1969-70; cert. tchr. high sch. and elem. grades 3-8 math., Ill. Mem. Nat., Ill. councils tchrs. of math., Math. Assn. Am., Chgo. Tchrs. Union, Nat. Council Parents and Tchrs. (life), Sch. Sci. and Math. Assn., Assn. for Supervision and Curriculum Devel., Am. Guild of Organists, Luth. Collegiate Assn., Kappa Mu Epsilon, Rho Sigma Tau, Mu Alpha Theta (sponsor), Kappa Delta Pi, Pi Lambda Theta, Phi Delta Kappa. Club: Walther League Hiking. Contbr. articles to profl. jours. Home: 3214 W 85th St Chicago IL 60652 Office: 6200 S Hamlin St Chicago IL 60629

BAKER, CARL THOMAS, veterinarian; b. Belle Vernon, Pa., Oct. 4, 1933; s. Thomas Wesley and Katie Marie (Kennedy) B.; m. Barbara Lee Sanders, Sept. 5, 1957; children—Carla Jane, Sandra Lee Baker Rice, Charles Thomas, Donna Jo. B.S. in Agr., W.Va. U., 1959; D.V.M., Ohio State U., 1963. Lab. tech. South Africa Iron and Steel Corp., Vanderbijk, 1950-51; veterinarian Huntington Dog and Cat Hosp. (W.Va.), 1963-65, Washington Blvd. Vet. Clinic, Pitts., 1965-67; owner, mgr. Chesapeake Vet. Clinic (Ohio), 1967—. Active Lawrence County Humane Soc.; mem. Chesapeake Sch. Bd., 1972-79, pres., 1977-79; mem. Bd. Commrs. Lawrence County, 1979—, pres., 1980-83. Served with U.S. Army, 1952-55; Korea. Mem. AVMA, Ohio Vet. Med. Assn. Lodges: Lions, Masons. Home and office: Route 3 Box 216 Chesapeake OH 45619

BAKER, CARVER LOWELL, architect, urban planner; b. Bird Island, Minn., Nov. 26, 1918; s. James Bradford and Matilda Katherine (Putzier) B.; m. Lucille Hall, Dec. 26, 1945. Student Sch. Architecture, U. Minn. Inst. Tech., 1939-42; B.Arch., U. Wash., 1947. Registered architect, Wash., Calif., Tex., Wis., Minn.; cert. Nat. Council Archtl. Registration Bds. Chief architect Wash. State Parks and Recreation Commn., 1951-53; supervising architect Seattle City Parks, 1953; prin. Carver L. Baker, AIA & Assocs., Palos Verdes Estates, Calif., 1953-65; architect Gt. Lakes Properties & Assoc. Cos., Palos Verdes and Rolling Hills, Calif., 1953-71, on assignment to plan and develop new city of Vilamoura, Lisbon, Portugal, 1965-70; sole practice architecture, Mpls., St. Paul, Prescott, Wis.; cons. architect Urban Planning Internat. Served with USAAF, 1941-45. Mem. AIA, Tau Sigma Delta. Republican. Methodist. Address: 1089 Monroe St S Prescott WI 54021

BAKER, CLARENCE ALBERT, SR., structural steel constrn. co. exec.; b. Kansas City, Kans., July 2, 1919; s. Earl Retting and Nancy Jefferson (Price) B.; student Kans. U., 1939-40, Finley Engring. Coll., 1937-39, Ohio State U., 1967, 69; m. Marjorie Ellen Yoakum, Mar. 19, 1959 (dec. Feb. 1981); children—Clarence Albert, Jorgeann (Mrs. Harry L. Hiebert); stepchildren—Robert Beale, Barbara Anne Stegner (Mrs. Robert T. Kenney II); m. Katherine V. Cochran, Nov. 6, 1982. With Kansas City (Kan.) Structural Steel Co., 1937—, shop supt., 1959-68, v.p., plant mgr., 1968-73, v.p. plant ops., 1973-77, v.p. engring., 1977—, also dir. Curriculum adv. Kansas City (Mo.) Met. Jr. Coll., 1971-72, Kansas City Vocat. Tech. Sch., 1973—. Committeeman, Republican Party, 1970-72; chmn. City of Mission (Kans.) Rep. Party, 1970-72; councilman, City of Merriam, Kans., 1957-59. Adv. bd. Wentworth Mil. Acad. Served with USNR, 1944-46. Mem. ASTM, Am. Welding Soc. (pres. 1970-71, chmn. 1970, code com. 1976—), Kans. Engring. Soc., Kansas City C. of C. Mason. Home: 6635 Milhaven Dr Mission KS 66202 Office: 21st and Metropolitan Sts Kansas City KS 66106

BAKER, CLORA MAE, educator; b. Bedford, Ind., Jan. 21, 1948; d. Howard Perry and Bethel (Newlin) B.; B.S., Ball State U., 1970, M.A.E., 1971. Sec. to dir. human performance lab. Ball State U., Muncie, Ind., 1967-70; bus. tchr. Carmel (Ind.) High Sch., 1970—; instr. evening div. Ind. U./Purdue U., Indpls., 1979. Mem. Internat. Word Processing Assn. (educator's adv. council 1979-81), Ind. Vocat. Assn., Am. Vocat. Assn., NEA, Ind. Tchrs. Assn., Nat. Bus. Edn. Assn., Delta Pi Epsilon (nat. council rep. 1978—), Am. Bus. Women's Assn. (named Woman of Yr., Hamilton chpt. 1980). Mem. Christian

Ch. Home: 2486 Chaseway Ct Indianapolis IN 46268 Office: 520 E Main St Carmel IN 46032

BAKER, DALE B., chemical company executive; b. Bucyrus, Ohio, Sept. 19, 1920. B.S. in Chem. Engring., Ohio State U., 1942; postgrad. Rutgers U., 1942-43; M.Sc., Ohio State U., 1948. Chemist, supr. E.I. duPont de Nemours & Co., 1942-46; asst. editor Chem. Abstracts Service, Columbus, Ohio, 1946-50, assoc. editor, 1951-57, assoc. dir., 1958, dir., 1958—; acting mgr. Am. Chem. Soc., Columbus, 1972, chief operating officer, 1980, dep. exec. dir., 1983—; cons. Battelle Meml. Inst., Columbus Labs., 1962-75; trustee Ctr. Sci. and Industry, 1982—. Mem. adv. bd. Central Ohio Council Internat. Visitors, 1958-66; mem. interim bd. Tech. and Productivity Ctr., Ohio, 1982—; mem. pastor-parish relations com. North Broadway United Methodist Ch., 1968-72. Named Tech. Man of Yr., Columbus Tech. Council, 1968. Mem. Internat. Council Sci. Unions Abstracting Bd. (exec. sec. 1983—), Internat. Union Pure and Applied Chemistry; mem. Orgn. Econ. Cooperation and Devel., UNESCO, AAAS, Am. Chem. Soc. (Patterson-Crane award 1979, 25 Year Service award 1971), Am. Inst. Chem. Engrs., Am. Inst. Physics, Am. Mgmt. Assn., Am. Soc. Info. Sci. (pres. 1975), Am. Nat. Standards Inst., Nat. Acad. Scis., Nat. Acad. Engring., Nat. Fed. Sci. Abstracting and Indexing Services (pres. 1962-63, treas. 1970-72; Miles G. Conrad award 1974), Columbus Area C. of C., Ohio Acad. Sci., Ohio C. of C., Ohio State U. Research Found., Tech. Info. Exchange and Innovation Network, Ohio State U. Alumni Assn., Sigma Xi. Clubs: Ohio State U. Faculty, Torch. Lodge: Rotary. Office: Chem Abstracts Service PO Box 3012 Columbus OH 43210

BAKER, DONALD EUGENE, librarian; b. Winamac, Ind., Oct. 8, 1945; s. Willard Jared and Beulah Belle (Taylor) B.; A.B., Ind. U., 1966, A.M., 1968, M.Library Sci., 1976; Asst. editor Indiana Mag. of History, Bloomington, 1972-74; head librarian Willard Library of Evansville (Ind.), 1976—. Former pres. Evansville Arts and Edn. Council; mem. Evansville Museum History Com. Served with USAF, 1968-72. Mem. Vanderburgh County Hist. Soc., Tri State Genealogical Soc. (dir. ex officio), Four Rivers Area Library Services Authority (past pres.), Soc. Indiana Archivists, Midwest Archives Conf., Ind. Library Assn. (pres. dist. VII 1983-84), ALA, Adminstrs. Large Pub. Libraries in Ind. Episcopalian. Lodge: Downtown Kiwanis (sec. Evansville). Picture editor: At the Bend of the River, A Pictorial History of Evansville, 1982. Home: 219 Oak St Evansville IN 47713 Office: Willard Library 21 1st Ave Evansville IN 47710

BAKER, EARL CUBA, JR., water well contracting company executive; b. Mattoon, Ill., Jan. 19, 1920; s. Earl Cuba and Hester Hedwig (Wolf) B.; m. Evelyn Maxine Oakley, July 12, 1943; children—Stephen (dec.), Linda, Charles, Marla. Student pub. schs., Sigel, Ill.; lic. water well contractor, Ill. Driller asst. E.C. Baker & Sons (Inc. 1965), Sigel, 1933-42, head driller, site mgr., 1942-65, pres., chmn. bd., 1965—. Active Boy Scouts Am., 1953-62; instl. rep. Westside PTA. Served with U.S. Army, 1942-45. Decorated Bronze Star (3); recipient Achievement award Govt. of Can., 1942. Mem. Nat. Water Well Assn., So. Ill. Water Works and Sewage Treatment Operators Assn. (hon.), Internat. Union Operating Engrs. (Chgo. local), Am. Legion, VFW. Baptist. Field researcher in devel. of hydrofracturing and acidizing treatments for water wells.

BAKER, ELMER EARL, English educator; b. West Fork, Ark., May 20, 1927; s. Garrett Hobart and Martha Isabelle (Hann) B.; children—Carl Earl, Kathleen Baker Wheeler. B.S., Abilene Christian Coll., 1949; M.L.S., East Tex. State U., 1956, M.S., 1968. Tchr. Bethany Sch., Balko, Okla., 1948-49; adminstr. Boles Home Sch., Quinlan, Tex., 1949-57, 59-66; library dir. York Coll., Nebr., 1975-59, English prof., 1966—; cons. Area Writer's Guild, York, 1984—. Bd. dirs. York Pub. Library, 1983—. Served with USN, 1944-46. Recipient Tchr. of Achievement award York Coll., 1980. Mem. Nat. Council Tchrs. English, Midwest Council Tchrs. English, Nebr. Library Assn., Nebr. Hist. Assn. Republican. Mem. Ch. of Christ. Club: York Geneology. Avocations: travel, reading, music, gardening. Home: 808 Elmer Ave York NE 68467 Office: York Coll York NE 68467

BAKER, GARY EDWARD, real estate and small business investment company executive; b. Detroit, Apr. 15, 1955; s. Wayne Eugene and Dorothy Jean (Wolfe) B. B.A. in Speech Communications, U. Mich., 1976, B.A. in Polit. Sci., 1976, postgrad., 1982—. Agy. unit mgr. Fidelity Union Life, Ann Arbor, Mich., 1976-80; pres. Century Systems, Inc., Livonia, Mich., 1983—, Baker Investment Group, Ann Arbor, 1980—; ptnr. Baker Mgmt. Co., Ann Arbor, 1977—. Mem. citizen's adv. com. Community Devel. Block Grant, Ann Arbor, 1975-77; games chmn. Mich. Theater Benefit Com., Ann Arbor, 1983—; mem. Mayor's Task Force on Affordable Housing, Ann Arbor, 1984—, Founder's Soc. Detroit Inst. Art, 1984—. Mem. Mich. Tech. Council, Growth Capital Found., Mensa, U. Mich. Alumni Assn., Ann Arbor Area C. of C. (chmn. small bus. council, adv. council innovation ctr. 1984—, occupancy com. 1984—, seed capital com. 1985), Real Estate Alumni of Mich. (life). Republican. Methodist. Clubs: U. Mich. Pres.'s (Ann Arbor); Whitmore Lake Water Ski (Mich.) (chmn. publicity). Home: 1010 Belmont Ann Arbor MI 48104 Office: Baker Investment Group 201 E Liberty St Ann Arbor MI 48104

BAKER, GARY EUGENE, environmental engineer; b. Greenville, Ohio, Apr. 28, 1951; s. Paul Richard and Thelma L. (Hollinger) B.; m. Irene Frances Stolz, Mar. 25, 1972; children—Christopher, Laurie, Jeffrey. B.S., Miami U., Oxford, Ohio, 1973, M. Environ. Sci., 1977; M.S., U. Cin., 1978. Tchr. Lebanon City Schs., Ohio, 1973-76; project mgr. Pedco Environ., Inc., Cin., 1977—. Mem. ASME (assoc.). Office: Pedco Environ Inc 11499 Chester Rd Cincinnati OH 45246

BAKER, GEORGE SEVERT, materials educator; b. Chgo., Aug. 2, 1927; s. Benard and Mildred (Meacham) B.; m. Shari Dawn Jennings, May 22, 1959; children—Gail, Geoffrey. B.S. in Physics, Purdue U., 1950; M.S. in Physics, U. Ill., 1951, Ph.D., 1956. Assoc. prof. U. Utah, Salt Lake City, 1957-63; tech. specialist Aerojet Gen., Sacramento, 1963-67; prof. U. Wis., Milw., 1967—, prof., chmn. dept. materials sci., 1978—. Contbr. articles to profl. jours. Served with U.S. Army, 1945-47. Mem. Am. Soc. Metals, Am. Soc. Engring. Edn. Avocation: Philately. Home: 8065 N Mohawk Milwaukee WI 53217 Office: Materials Dept Univ Wis Milwaukee WI 53201

BAKER, HAROLD ALBERT, See *Who's Who in America,* 43rd edition.

BAKER, HELEN, lawyer; b. Cleve., May 6, 1922; d. Harry and Belle (Speiser) Manheim; m. Marvin Baker, Nov. 10, 1944 (div. 1973); children—Jon, Scott, Lauren. B.S. cum laude, Northwestern U., 1943; J.D. summa cum laude, Cleve. State U., 1977. Bar: Ohio 1979, U.S. Dist. Ct. (no. dist.) Ohio 1979. Staff children's rights project ACLU of Ohio Found., Inc., Cleve., 1977-78; staff counsel ACLU of Greater Cleve. Found., 1979-80, dir. children's rights advocacy project, 1980-81; cons., adv. ACLU, others, 1982—. Contbr. to books, articles to profl. jours. Active politics, civil rights, anti-war movement, nuclear freeze movement, others. Recipient Wall St. Jour. award, 1978; Civil Libertarian award ACLU of Ohio, 1981; Civil Libertarian of Yr. award ACLU of Greater Cleve. Mem. Ohio Bar Assn., ABA, Assn. Trial Lawyers Am., Nat. Lawyers Guild. Home: 440 Addison Ave Elmhurst IL 60126

BAKER, JAMES ALLAN, banker; b. Dayton, Ohio, Mar. 4, 1942; s. Wilbur and Lucille (Heck) B.; B.S. in Bus. Adminstrn. (Wall St. Jour. Student Achievement award 1964), Bowling Green (Ohio) State U., 1964; M.B.A., Ind. U., 1966; m. B. Lyn Wallace, Aug. 25, 1962; 3 children. With City Nat. Bank, Columbus, Ohio, 1966-75, banking officer, 1971-75; pres., chief exec. officer Bank One Mansfield (Ohio), 1975-82; pres. Bank One Eastern Ohio, Youngstown, 1982—. Chmn., Mansfield United Fund dr., 1976, chmn. allocation com., 1976-82; mem. exec. com. Youngstown United Way, 1983—; mem. govt. relations com. United Way of Am., chmn. 1985 drive; chmn. steering com. Leadership Youngstown; mem. exec. com. Youngstown Community Corp.; trustee Mansfield Art Center, 1980, Youngstown Hosp. Assn., Youngstown Symphony Soc.; bd. dirs., pres. Richland County Growth Corp., 1975-82; bd. dirs., treas. Area Indsl. Growth, 1975-82, Mansfield Growth Corp., 1977-82; pres. Mansfield United Community Service, 1978. Named Boss of Yr., Mansfield Jr. C. of C., 1977. Mem. Am. Banking Assn., Banking Adminstrn. Inst., Young Pres. Orgn. (chmn. 1983, internat. bd. dirs., fin. com.), Ohio Bankers Assn., Ohio Citizens Council (pres. 1981-83). Republican. Episcopalian. Clubs: Youngstown Country, Youngstown. Office: 6 Federal Plaza W Youngstown OH 44503

BAKER, JAMES DONALD, religious educator, minister; b. Brownbranch, Mo., Nov. 7, 1930; s. John C. and Riffie (Ashwell) B.; m. Pat A. Hoffmeister, June 22, 1952; children—Pamela Bultmann, Dana Harrigan, Beth Grabowski. A.A.A.S., S.W. Bapt. Coll., 1950; A.B., William Jewell Coll., 1953; B.D., Central Bapt. Theol. Sem., 1957, M.Div., 1968; Th.D., New Orleans Bapt. Theol. Sem., 1970. Pub. relations dir. S.W. Bapt. Coll., Bolivar, Mo., 1957-66; pub. relations asst. New Orleans Bapt. Theol. Sem., 1967-70; pastor Bapt. chs., Ark., La., Mo., 1967-76; dir. in-service tng. S.W. Bapt. U., Bolivar, 1976—, acting dean Redford Sch. Theology, 1983—. Author: Mr. Baptist Hour, 1974. Editor: SWBC Newsletter, 1957-66. Contbr. articles to profl. jours. Bd. dirs. ARC, Bolivar, 1963-65. Recipient Life Beautiful award, S.W. Bapt. Coll., 1950. Mem. Assn. Bapt. Tchrs. Religion, In-Service Guidance Conf. (sec.), Redford Curators (founding chmn. 1964-65), C. of C. Lodge: Kiwanis. Avocations: Woodworking; canoeing; antique autos; fishing; hunting. Office: Southwest Bapt Univ Bolivar MO 65613

BAKER, JAMES EDWARD SPROUL, lawyer; b. Evanston, Ill., May 23, 1912; s. John Clark and Hester (Sproul) B.; A.B., Northwestern U., 1933, J.D., 1936; m. Eleanor Lee Dodgson, Oct. 2, 1937 (dec. Sept. 1972); children—John Lee, Edward Graham. Admitted to Ill. bar, 1936, to practice U.S. Supreme Ct., 1957; practiced in Chgo., 1936—; assoc. firm Sidley & Austin and predecessor firms, Chgo., 1936-47, ptnr., 1948-81, of counsel, 1981—; lectr. Northwestern U. Sch. Law, Chgo., 1951-52; mem. Am. team Anglo-Am. Legal Exchange, 1980. Nat. chmn. Stanford Parents Com., 1970-75; bd. visitors Stanford Law Sch., 1976-84. Served to comdr. USNR, 1941-46. Fellow Am. Coll. Trial Lawyers (regent 1974-81, sec. 1977-79, pres. 1979-80); mem. ABA, Ill., Bar Assn., Chgo. Bar Assn., Bar Assn. 7th Fed. Circuit, Soc. Trial Lawyers Ill., Northwestern U. Law Alumni Assn. (past pres.), John Henry Wigmore Club (past pres.), John Evans Club of Northwestern U. (chmn. 1983—), Order of Coif, Phi Lambda Upsilon, Sigma Nu. Republican. Methodist. Clubs: University, Midday, Legal, Law (pres. 1983-84) (Chgo.); Westmoreland Country (Wilmette, Ill.). Home: 1300 N Lake Shore Dr Chicago IL 60610 Office: 1 First Nat Plaza Chicago IL 60603

BAKER, JAMES KENDRICK, specialty metals company executive; b. Wabash, Ind., Dec. 21, 1931; s. Donald Dale and Edith (Swain) B.; m. Beverly Baker, Apr. 11, 1959; children—Betsy Ann, Dirk Emerson, Hugh Kendrick. A.B., DePauw U., 1953; M.B.A., Harvard U., 1958. Regional sales mgr. Arvinyl div. Arvin Industries, Inc., Columbus, Ind., 1958-60, gen. mgr. div., 1960-66, v.p., gen. mgr. div., 1966-68, exec. v.p., dir., 1968-81, pres., dir., 1981—; dir. Columbus Bank & Trust Co., Ind. Nat. Corp., Indpls. Bd. dirs. Associated Colls. Ind., DePauw U.; pres. Columbus Found. for Youth, 1965, United Way of Bartholomew County, 1979; pres. Vinyl-Metal Laminators Inst. div. Soc. Plastics Industry, 1963-64, dir., 1960—; vice chmn. Ind. Republican Conv., 1966. Served with AUS, 1953-55. Named Outstanding Boss, C. of C., 1965; recipient Disting. Service award Ind. Jaycees, 1966. Mem. Columbus C. of C. (dir.). Clubs: DePauw Univ. Alumni (pres. 1974), Harrison Lake Country. Lodge: Rotary. Office: Arvin Industries 1531 E 13th St Columbus IN 47201

BAKER, JOHN STEVENSON (MICHAEL DYREGROV), author, collector, donor; b. Mpls., June 18, 1931; s. Everette Barrette and Ione May (Kadletz) B.; B.A. cum laude, Pomona Coll., Claremont Colls., 1953; M.D., U. Calif. at Berkeley and San Francisco, 1957. Writer, 1958—; book cataloger Walker Art Center, Mpls., 1958-59; editor, writer neurol. research articles L.E. Phillips Psychobiol. Research Fund, Mpls., 1960-61. Recipient Disting. Service award Minn. State Hort. Soc., 1976; Cert. of Appreciation U.S. Nat. Arboretum, 1978. Mem. Nu Sigma Nu. Contbr. articles and poetry to various publs. in Eng. and U.S.; author 59 pub. poems, 16 short essays and 8 sets of aphorisms. Donor numerous varieties of native plants to Minn. Landscape Arboretum and U.S. Nat. Arboretum, papers of LeRoi Jones and Hart Crane to Yale U., Brahms recs. to Bennington Coll., many others. Office: PO Box 16007 Minneapolis MN 55416

BAKER, KATHLEEN ELLEN, food products executive; b. Victoria, Tex., Oct. 22, 1956; d. Ralph Lanier and Barbara Elaine (Carroll) B. B.S. in Food Sci., Pa. State U., 1978. Food chemist Tony's Pizza/Schwan's Sales, Salina, Kans., 1979-84, assoc. standards mgr., 1984—. Singles leader Trinity Lutheran Ch., Salina, 1985. Mem. Inst. Food Technologists, Am. Soc. Quality Control, Kappa Kappa Gamma. Avocations: aerobics; biking; tennis. Office: Schwan's Sales Enterprises 3019 Scanlan Rd Salina KS 67401

BAKER, KENTON LEE, financial executive; b. Layton, Utah, Feb. 25, 1951; s. John Age and Clara Jean (Simkins) B.; m. Cheryl Jean Bigelow, Dec. 6, 1973; children—Jennifer Kay, Elizabeth, Callie Jo, Kenton Lee. B.S. in Acctg., Brigham Young U., 1975. C.P.A., Minn. Acct. Ernst & Whinney, Mpls., 1979-84; corp. controller Conklin Co. Inc., Mpls., 1984—. Cons. Am. Lung Assn., 1982-83; bishopric counselor Mormon Ch., Mpls., 1983—. Served to capt. U.S. Army, 1975-79. Mem. Am. Inst. C.P.A.s, Minn. Soc. C.P.A.s, Brigham Young U. Mgmt. Soc. (bd. dirs. 1983—), Nat. Assn. Accts. Avocation: marathon running. Office: Conklin Co Inc 4660 W 77th St Edina MN 55435

BAKER, MARILYN KAY, nurse, educator; b. Rochester, Minn., Feb. 24, 1952; d. Thomas Hubert and Mary Lucille (Keefe) Baker. A.A. in Nursing, Rochester State Jr. Coll., 1972; B.S.N., U. Dubuque, 1978. R.N., Minn. Ind. coll. health service nurse U. Dubuque, 1976-80, community health nursing instr., 1978-80; staff nurse Rochester Methodist Hosp. (Minn.), 1972-73, staff nurse CCU, 1973-75, asst. head nurse and acting head nurse cardiovascular unit, 1975-76; staff nurse Madonna Towers, Rochester, 1980; substitute instr., cons.-instr. (part-time) Rochester Area Vocat. Tech. Inst., 1980-81; staff nurse St. Mary's Hosp., Rochester, 1981-82, asst. head nurse rehab., 1982—; instr. nursing Rochester Community Coll., (part-time), 1981-82. Co-chmn. Olmsted County Citizens Concerned for Life, Rochester, 1983—; profl. vol. Am. Cancer Soc. Dubuque, 1978-80. Mem. Minn. Nurses Assn. (nurse practice com. 1980—). Mem. Democratic Farm Labor Party. Roman Catholic. Home: Rt 3 PO Box 168A Rochester MN 55904

BAKER, ROBERT RUSSELL, osteopathic physician; b. Tahlequah, Okla., Oct. 8, 1950; s. Robert Lincoln and Tommie Sue (Russell) B.; m. Julie Ann Love, July 21, 1984; 1 child, Amy Renee. B.S. Northwestern Okla. State U., 1972; D.O., U. Health Scis., 1978. Diplomate Nat. Bd. Med. Examiners. Intern, Osteo. Hosp., Wichita, Kans., 1978-79, dir. emergency medicine, clin. instr., 1980-81, now med. staff; owner, operator family med. ctr. Arkansas City, Kans., 1981—; staff Meml. Hosp., Arkansas City, Riverside Hosp., Wichita; FAA med. examiner; owner, operator Shidler Clinic (Okla.), 1982—; co-owner, operator GWM Co.; med. dir. Cowley County Emergency Med. Services. Mem. Arkansas City Devel. Corp.; bd. dirs. Cowley County Developmental Services, Inc. Mem. Kans. Med. Soc., Kans. Osteo. Assn., Am. Osteo Assn., Cowley County Med. Soc., South Central Kans. Osteo Assn., Aerospace Med. Assn., Nat. Assn. Disability Evaluating Physicians, Arkansas City C. of C., Nat. Jaycees. Republican. Lodge: Masons. Home: Rt 1 Box 714 Arkansas City KS 67005 Office: 2508 Edgemont Dr Suite 5 Arkansas City KS 67005

BAKER, SAUL PHILLIP, geriatrician, cardiologist, internist; b. Cleve., Dec. 7, 1924; s. Barnet and Florence (Kleinman) B.; B.S. in Physics, Case Inst. Tech., 1945; postgrad. Western Res. U., 1946-47; M.Sc. in Physiology, Ohio State U., 1949, M.D., 1953, Ph.D. in Physiology 1957; J.D., Case Western Res. U., 1981. Intern, Cleve. Met. Gen. Hosp., 1953-54; sr. asst. surgeon gerontology br. Nat. Heart Inst., NIH, 1954-56, now Gerontology Research Center, Nat. Inst. Aging; asst. vis. staff physician dept. medicine Balt. City Hosps. and Johns Hopkins Hosp., Balt., 1954-56; sr. asst. resident in internal medicine U. Chgo. Hosps., 1956-57; asst. prof. internal medicine Chgo. Med. Sch., 1957-62; asso. prof. internal medicine Cook County Hosp. Grad. Sch. Medicine, Chgo., 1958-62; assoc. attending physician dept. medicine Cook County Hosp., 1957-62; practice medicine specializing in geriatrics, cardiology, internal medicine, Cleve., 1962-70, 72—; head dept. geriatrics St. Vincent Charity Hosp., Cleve. 1964-67; cons. internal medicine and cardiology Bur. Disability Determination, Old-Age and Survivors Ins., Social Security Adminstrn., 1963—; cons. internal medicine City of Cleve., 1964—; medicare med. cons. Gen. Am. Life Ins. Co., St. Louis, 1970-71; cons. internal medicine and cardiology Ohio Bur. Worker's Compensation, 1964—; cons. cardiovascular disease FAA, 1973—; cons. internal medicine and cardiology State of Ohio, 1974—. Mem. sci. council Am. Heart Assn. Northeastern Ohio affiliate; former mem. adv. com. sr. adult div. Jewish Community Center Cleve.; mem. vis. com. bd. overseers Case Inst. Tech.; former mem. com. older people Fedn. Community Planning Cleve. Fellow Am. Coll. Cardiology, AAAS, Gerontol. Soc. Am. (former regent for Ohio), Am. Geriatrics Soc., Cleve. Med. Library Assn.; mem. Am. Physiol. Soc., Am., Ohio med. assns., N.Y. Acad. Scis., Chgo. Soc. Internal Medicine, Am. Fedn. Clin. Research, Soc. Exptl. Biology and Medicine, Diabetes Assn. Greater Cleveland (profl. sect.), Am. Heart Assn. (fellow council arteriosclerosis), Nat. Assn. Disability Examiners, Nat. Rehab. Assn., Am. Pub. Health Assn., Assn. Am. Med. Coll., Acad. Medicine Cleve., Internat. Soc. Cardiology (council epidemiology and prevention), Am. Soc. Law and Medicine, Sigma Xi, Phi Delta Epsilon, Sigma Alpha Mu (past pres. Cleve. alumni). Mason (32 deg. Shriner). Club: Cleveland Clinical (past sec.). Contbr. articles to profl. sci. jours. Home: 200 Chatham Way Mayfield Heights OH 44124 Office: 6803 Mayfield Rd Mayfield Heights OH 44124 Mailing Address: PO Box 24246 Mayfield Heights OH 44124

BAKER, STEVEN LEE, banker, farm management consultant; b. Quincy, Ill., Nov. 20, 1959; s. C. Richard and Venita E. (Schafer) B.; m. Mae Marie Anderson, May 30, 1981. B.S., U. Ill.; M.B.A., So. Ill. U., Edwardsville. Research assoc. agrl. econs. dept. U. Ill., Champaign, 1979-81; assoc. editor Century Communications Inc., Skokie, Ill., 1980; credit analyst 6th Dist. Bank for Coop., St. Louis, Mo., 1981-83; loan rep., 1982-84; sr. loan rep. St. Louis Farm Credit Banks, 1984—; pvt. practice farm mgmt. cons., St. Louis. Contbg. author, editor: Farmland, 1981. Editor articles for mag. Ill. Bankers Assn. scholar, 1981; U. Ill. Hunter acad. scholar, 1981. Mem. Nat. Soc. Accts. for Coops., Am. Mgmt. Assn., Gamma Sigma Delta, Alpha Lambda Delta, Alpha Zeta. Republican. Methodist. Avocations: music; softball; hunting; cooking. Office: Saint Louis Bank for Cooperatives 1415 Olive St Saint Louis MO 63166

BAKER, THERESE LOUISE, sociology educator; b. Mpls., June 20, 1939; s. Lloyd L. and Gussie G. (Miller) Elzas; m. Keith Michael Baker, Oct. 25, 1961; children—Julian Charles, Felix James. B.A., Cornell U., 1961; Ph.D., U. Chgo., 1973. Secondary sch. tchr. Rosa Bassett Sch., London, 1962-64, Gresham High Sch., Portland, Oreg., 1964-65; instr. sociology U. Ill., Chgo., 1969-71; asst. prof. DePaul U., Chgo., from 1971, now assoc. prof. and chmn. dept. sociology; dir. Chgo. Area Studies Ctr., DePaul U., 1983—. Author: Doing Social Research (in press). Contbr. articles to profl. jours. Research grantee NIMH, 1977-78; research contractee Nat. Inst. Child Health and Devel., 1979-81. Mem. Am. Sociol. Assn., Midwest Sociol. Soc. (state dir. 1982-84), Sociologists for Women in Soc. Avocations: jogging; collecting plates. Home: 5540 S Kimbark Chicago IL 60637 Office: DePaul U 2323 N Seminary St Chicago IL 60614

BAKER, (VIRGINIA) EVE WOOD, bookstore owner; b. Elwood, Ind., Dec. 24, 1943; d. Warren Willard and Clara Bell (Johnson) Wood; m. Everett Earl Baker, June 11, 1966; 1 child, Julie Elizabeth. B.A., Purdue U., 1966. Cert. tchr., Fla. Tchr. Merritt Island Schs., Fla., 1966-67; English tchr. Satellite Beach High Sch., Fla., 1967-68; social worker Tex. Dept. Welfare, Dallas, 1970-72; ednl. dir. Happiness House, Dallas, 1972-73; owner, pres. Eve's Books, Wyoming, Mich., 1976—. Mem. 101st Airborne Assn. (life assoc. mem.), Vietnam War Newsletter Assn. (life), Nat. Rifle Assn. (endowment mem.) Ohio Gun Collectors (life), Mich. Antique Arms Assn. (life), Grand Valley Corvette Assn. (sec. 1981-83). Republican. Methodist. Avocations: reading, book collecting, needlecraft, writing. Home and Office: 10509 Brandywine Dr Fort Wayne IN 46825

BAKEWELL, STANLEY ELLSWORTH, personnel consultant; b. Eagle Bend, Minn., Apr. 10, 1920; s. Benjamin Levis and Eva Mary (Macaulay) B.; B.S. in Fgn. Service, Georgetown U., 1947-49; B.S. in Edn. and Animal Industry, U. Minn., 1943. Econ. asst., vice consul U.S. Fgn. Service, Am. embassy, Mexico City, Mexico, 1949-52; sr. market analyst Kimberly Clark Corp., Neenah, Wis., 1952-60; mgr. market research Forest Products div. Owens-Ill. Glass Co., Toledo, 1960-64; project dir. indsl. research Elrick & Lavidge, Chgo., 1964-66; pres., gen. mgr. Bryant & Bakewell Marketing Services div. Bryant Assos., Chgo., after 1967, now exec. v.p. Trustee Bakewell Investment Trust. Served to lt. (j.g.) USNR, 1944-46. Mem. Chgo. Symphony Soc., Am. Mktg. Assn., Am. Iris Soc., Chgo. Council Fgn. Relations, Alpha Gamma Rho. Republican. Episcopalian. Clubs: Chgo. Athletic Assn., Whitehall, Georgetown (Chgo.); Mason, Shriner, K.T. Author: Bakewell History-Genealogy, Part I, 1980, Part II, 1983. Home: 411 Hickory St Joliet IL 60435 Office: Bryant Assos John Hancock Center 875 N Michigan Ave Chicago IL 60611

BAKIEROWSKI, WACLAW, political activist, Polish government in exile official; b. Jekaterynburg, Russia, Dec. 9, 1915; came to U.S., 1952; naturalized, 1957; s. Kazimierz and Lidja (Popow) B.; m. Lisaweta Albrecht, Feb. 1, 1950; 1 son, Waclaw K. Law student, Poland until World War II; D. Diplomacy (hon.). With Polish Underground, 1939-44, participant Warsaw Insurrection, 1944; POW, Germany, 1944-45; tchr., Germany, 1945-46; Polish unit transport officer, Germany, 1946-52; ins. agt. N.Y. Life Ins. Co., N.Y.C., Chgo., 1953-74; work instr. Workshop for Retarded, Dixon, Ill., 1974-76; dep. prime minister, minister fgn. affairs, minister fin. Polish Govt. in Exile, 1976—; brig. gen. Polish Forces. Mem. Republican Presdl. Task Force; senator Internat. Parliament for Safety and Peace. Author numerous newspaper articles. Decorated Virtuti Mil., Order White Eagle, Great Cordon of Polonia Restituta, Cross of Valour, Golden Cross of Merit with swords, Roman Catholic. Lodges: Knights of Temple of Jerusalem, Knights of Malta, others. Address: A-6372 140th Ave Holland MI 49423

BAKIRCI, ONEL, metal stamping company executive; b. Izmir, Turkey, Dec. 10, 1939; came to U.S., 1962; d. Ibrahim and Zeynep (Salk) B. B.S., Am. Internat. Coll., 1965; M.A., Sangamon State U., 1972. Asst. to chmn. dept. pediatrics So. Ill. U. Med. Sch., Springfield, 1972-75; gen. mgr. Sonotone Corp., Elmsford, N.Y., 1975-78; gen. mgr. Burgess Inc., Freeport, Ill., 1978-81; v.p., gen. mgr. Barrett Mfg. Co., Chgo., 1981—. Mem. Assn. Commerce and Industry, Am. Hardware Mfrs. Assn., Splty. Tools and Fasteners Distbrs. Assn., Mfrs. Agts. Nat. Assn. (assoc.), Nat. Assn. Elec. Distbrs. (assoc.). Office: Barrett Mfg Co 4124 W Parker Ave Chicago IL 60639

BAKKE, CANDACE ANN, state official; b. Sioux City, Iowa, Dec. 5, 1949; d. John V. and LaVetta L. (Stark) Collins; 1 child, Kathleen. B.A., U. Iowa, 1972. Adminstrv. officer Office Operating Authority, Iowa Dept Transp., Des Moines, 1974-79, asst. dir., 1977-79, dir., 1979-83, dir. pub. transit div., 1983—, chmn. Day Care Task Force, 1984-85; Mem. Iowa Pub. Transp. Assn. Am. Pub. Transp. Assn., Am. Assn. Motor Vehicle Adminstrs. (chmn. vehicle reciprocity com. 1981-83), Nat. Assn. Transp. Alts. (chmn. legis. com. 1984—). Roman Catholic. Office: Iowa Dept Transp Pub Transit Div 5268 N W 2d Ave Des Moines IA 50313

BAKKE, GILBERT BENJAMIN, construction company executive, mechanical engineer; b. Milw., Sept. 13, 1937; s. Martin A. and Lydia Mary (Wittenberger) B.; B.S. in Mech. Engring., U. Wis., 1961; m. Lorraine Frenz, Aug. 11, 1961; children—Lila, Laura, James, Rebekah. Chief engr., Alby Mfg. Co., Waterford, Wis., 1961-63; design engr. Nomad Equipment, Milw., 1963; design engr. Rex Chainbelt, Milw., 1963-68; mgr. Bakke Electric Co., Waterford, 1968-73, propr., pres., 1973—; propr., pres. Aber Cutters Co., Waterford, 1976—. Chmn. Waterford Fire and Police Commn., 1976-80; mem. Waterford Sch. Bd., 1972-80; trustee Village of Waterford, 1983—. Registered profl. engr., Wis. Mem. Am. Soc. for Metals, Tri-County Contractors Assn. (dir. 1974—, pres. 1983). Lutheran. Club: Lions (pres. 1976). Home: 646 E Main St Waterford WI 53185 Office: 818 W Bakke Ave Waterford WI 53185

BAKKEN, EARL E., medical instruments manufacturing company executive. Founder, sr. chmn. Medtronic Inc., Mpls. Office: Medtronic Inc 3055 Old Hwy Eight PO Box 1453 Minneapolis MN 55440*

BALACEK, THOMAS VINCENT, corporation executive, engineer, management consultant; b. N.Y.C., Sept. 24, 1937; s. Theodore Vincent and Margaret Alice (Tuohy) B.; student Acad. Aeros., 1956-60; m. Joyce Eldeene Iden, Nov. 19, 1960 (dec. May 5, 1978); children—Thomas Vincent, Valerie Anne, William Theodore, Paul Frederick. Started as engr. Executone, Inc., N.Y.C., 1958-60, U.S. Testing Co., Inc., Hoboken, N.J., 1961; sales engr. Nuclear-Chgo. subs. Siemens Med. Systems, Inc., Des Plaines, Ill., 1961-65, regional mgr., 1966-67, sales mgr., 1968, advt. mgr., 1969; v.p. sales and mktg. Telemed Corp. div. Becton-Dickinson, Hoffman Estates, Ill., 1969-76; founder, pres., chief exec. officer Cardiassist Corp. div. Intermedics, Inc., Hoffman Estates, Ill., 1976-82; pres. Highview Corp., 1982—; prin. Technology Mktg. Group, Ltd., Des Plaines, Ill., 1984-85. Home: 506 N River Rd Fox River Grove IL 60021 Office: 401 Highview Dr Fox River Grove IL 60021

BALACHANDRAN, BALA V., accounting systems educator; b. Pudukkottai, India, July 5, 1937; came to U.S., 1967, naturalized , 1977; s. Venrataraman and Jambagam (Venkataraman) Aiyar; m. Dandapani Vasantha, Mar. 25, 1964; children—Sid, Dave. B.S. with honors, Annamalai U., India, 1959, M.Sc., M.A., 1962; M.S.E., U. Dayton, 1968; M.S.I.A., Carnegie Mellon U., 1972, Ph.D., 1973. C.P.A., Ill. Asst. prof. stats. Annamalai U., India, 1959-65; asst. prof. indsl. engring. U. Dayton, 1969-73; assoc. prof. mgmt. decision scis. Northwestern U., Evanston, Ill., 1973-79, chmn. dept. acctg. and info. scis., 1979-83, J.L. Kellogg disting. prof. Sch. Bus., 1983—; pres. Mgmt. Decision Assocs., Northbrook, Ill., 1974—; cons. and lectr. in field. Contbr. chpts. to books, articles to profl. jours. U.S. Air Force scholar, 1967-68; William L. Mellon fellow, 1971-73, Arthur Anderson faculty fellow, 1978. Mem. Ops. Research Soc. Am. (Nicholson 1st prize Ph.D. 1973), Inst. Mgmt. Sci. (sr.), Am. Inst. Indsl. Engring., Beta Sigma Gamma. Hindu. Clubs: YMCA (Northbrook, Ill.); Touhy Tennis (Chgo.). Avocations: tennis, photography. Home: 3269 Prestwick Ln Northbrook IL 60062 Office: Acctg & Info Systems Dept Leverone Hall 2001 Sheridan Rd Evanston IL 60201

BALAGOT, REUBEN CASTILLO, anesthesiologist; b. Manila, Philippines, July 28, 1920; s. Pedro G. and Ambrosia (Castillo) B.; B.S., U. Philippines, 1941, M.D., 1944; came to U.S., 1949, naturalized, 1955; m. Lourdes Ramirez, July 10, 1946; children—Joseph, Edgar, Victoria (Mrs. Peter Hermann), Ophelia (Mrs. James Julien). Intern, Philippine Gen. Hosp., Manila, 1943-44; resident U. Ill., Chgo., 1949-50, research fellow, 1951, clin. instr., 1952-54, asst. prof., 1954-56, asso. prof., 1956-60, prof., 1960—, chmn. dept., 1969-71; chmn. Chgo. Med. Sch., Downey, Ill., 1971—; chmn. div. anesthesiology Grant Hosp., 1957, Ill. Masonic Hosp., 1966-67; pres. St. Lukes Hosp., 1967-71, Hines (Ill.) VA Hosp., 1971-75; chmn. dept. anesthesiology Cook County Hosp., Chgo., 1981—. Served with AUS, 1944-46. Named Disting. Physician of Year, Philippine Med. Assn., 1968; Outstanding Filipino Overseas in Med. Research award Philippine Govt., 1977. Diplomate Am. Bd. Anesthesiology. Fellow Am. Fedn. Clin. Research; mem. AMA, A.C.S., AAUP, AAAS, N.Y. Acad. Sci., Ill., Chgo. med. socs., Am. Soc. Anesthesiologists, Ill. Soc. for Med. Research, Am. Writers Research, Am. Assn. for Med. Instrumentation, Sigma Xi. Contbr. articles to profl. jours. Home: 4246 Hazel St Chicago IL 60613 Office: 1825 W Harrison St Chicago IL 60612

BALAGURA, SAUL, neurosurgeon; b. Cali, Colombia, Jan. 11, 1943; s. Itco and Sara (Zieghelboim) B.; M.D., U. Calle (Colombia), 1964; M.A., Princeton U., 1966, Ph.D., 1967; m. Ursula Lowy, Aug. 15, 1964. Intern, Univ. Hosp., Cali, Colombia, 1963-64; resident in gen. surgery SUNY Downtate Med. Ctr., Bklyn., 1974-76, Albert Einstein Sch. Medicine, N.Y.C., 1976-80; asst prof. biopsychology U. Chgo., 1967-71; assoc. prof. bio-psychology U. Mass., Amherst, 1971-74; asst. prof. neurosurgery and anatomy Emory U., Atlanta, 1980-81; attending neurosurgeon Watson Clinic, Lakeland, Fla., 1981-82; neurosurgeon Carle Clinic, Urbana, Ill., 1983—. Fellow Am. Psychol. Assn.; mem. AMA, Soc. Neurosci, Physiol. Soc., Am. Bd. Neurol. Surgery. Jewish. Author: Hunger: A Biopsychological Analysis, 1973; contbr. articles to profl. jours. Office: Carle Clinic 602 W University Ave Urbana IL 61801

BALASA, RICHARD WAYNE, pathologist, educator; b. Chgo., Feb. 11, 1946; s. Frank John and Lucille Eleanor (Holsman) B.; B.A. cum laude, Yale U., 1968; M.D., St. Louis U., 1973. Research fellow pathology Rush-Presbyn.-St. Luke's Med. Center, Chgo., 1968-69; research assoc. Inst. Molecular Virology, St. Louis U. Med. Sch., 1969-72; acting intern dept. pathology Peter Bent Brigham Hosp., Boston, 1972-73; sr. asst. surgeon USPHS, resident in anatomic pathology Lab. Pathology, Nat. Cancer Inst., 1973-75; fellow surg. pathology, then resident in lab. medicine, then fellow chem. pathology, dept. lab. medicine and pathology, U. Minn. Med. Sch., Mpls., 1975-78; pathologist, dir. dept. clin. biochemistry Lutheran Gen. Hosp., Park Ridge, Ill., 1978—; clin. asst. prof. U. Ill. Coll. Medicine, Chgo., 1978—. Diplomate Nat. Bd. Med. Examiners, Am. Bd. Pathology. Mem. Am. Soc. Clin. Pathologists, Coll. Am. Pathologists, Ill. Soc. Pathologists, Chgo. Pathology Soc. Clubs: Berzelius (Yale U.); Elizabethan (New Haven); Yale (Chgo.). Home: 2959 N Mason Ave Chicago IL 60634 Office: 1775 Dempster St Park Ridge IL 60068

BALASH, MICHAEL C., gasket company official; b. Cin., Feb. 14, 1946; s. Clarence and Ida Helen (Dears) B.; m. Tay Ann Sharpe, Apr. 19, 1969; children—Peter Michael, Cameron Lloyd. Student Toledo U., 1967-68, Bowling Green State U., 1968-69. Purchasing agt. Am. Gage & Mfg. Co., Wauseon, Ohio, 1964-70; purchasing mgr. Fayette Tubular Co. (Ohio), 1970-73; prodn. control supr. Gould Corp., Napoleon, Ohio, 1973-76; materials mgr. Globe-Weis, Wauseon, 1976-81, McCord Gasket Corp., Wauseon, 1981—; mem. purchasing council ExcelloCorp., Troy, Mich., 1983, 84-85. Bd. dirs. Fulton County YMCA, Wauseon, 1982-84. Served with USMC, 1966-72. Recipient Spotlight On Packaging Performance award Package Engring. Mag., 1981. Mem. Am. Prodn. and Inventory Control Soc. (reviewer 1980). Republican. Home: 449 Mashall St Wauseon OH 43567 Office: McCord Gasket Corp/Excello Corp Sycamore and Potter Sts Wauseon OH 43567

BALAZS, BILL (BELA) ANTAL, mechanical engineer; b. Miercurea-Ciuc, Romania, June 13, 1933; s. Andras and Emilia (Sallo) B.; came to U.S., 1957, naturalized, 1962; B.S., U. Budapest (Hungary), 1955; diploma tool die engring. Acme Tech. Inst., Cleve., 1963; A.P.M., John Carroll U., 1976; m. Vivienne Miskey, Apr. 1, 1960; 1 dau., Corrinne. Instr. tool die engring., machine design, indsl. electronics, Acme Tech. Inst., 1960-65; design engr., heating, ventilating, Morrison Product Inc., Cleve., 1963-65; project engr. Reuter-Stokes, Inc., Cleve., 1965-70, engring. project mgr., 1970-73, engring. mgr., chief engr., 1973—. Pres., Transylvania Hungarian League, 1960—. Registered profl. engr., U.S.A., Can.; cert. cost engring. engr., mfg. mgmt. engr., plant engring. engr. Mem. Am. Inst. Indsl. Engrs., Instrument Soc. Am., Soc. Mfg. Engrs., ASME, Am. Nuclear Soc., Nat., Ohio socs. profl. engrs. Designer nuclear radiation detectors and multi-sensor environ. radiation monitoring systems. Home: 7500 Woodlake Dr Walton Hills OH 44146 Office: 8499 Darrow Rd Twinsburg OH 44087

BALÁZS, LOUIS ATTILA PETER, physicist, educator; b. Tsing-tao, China, July 31, 1937; came to U.S., 1956, naturalized, 1961; s. Istvan and Nina (Shuisky) B.; m. Beth Ann Winebrenner, May 27, 1984. B.A., U. Calif., Berkeley, 1959, Ph.D., 1962. Mem. Sch. Math., Inst. Advanced Study, Princeton, N.J., 1962-63; research fellow Calif. Inst. Tech., Pasadena, 1963-64; vis. prof. Tata Inst. Fundamental Research, Bombay, India, 1964-65; asst. prof. UCLA, 1965-70; assoc. prof. Purdue U., West Lafayette, Ind., 1970-78, prof. physics, 1978—. Contbr. articles to profl. jours. Pres. Centennial Neighborhood Assn., Lafayette; active Bread for World, Washington. Alfred P. Sloan fellow, 1967-69. Fellow Am. Phys. Soc.; mem. AAUP, Phi Beta Kappa, Sigma Xi. Democrat. Roman Catholic. Avocations: drawing; sketching. Office: Purdue U Physics Dept West Lafayette IN 47907

BALBACH, DANIEL ROSSWELL, orthodontist; b. Grand Rapids, Mich., Jan. 17, 1938; s. William Rosswell and Clarice J. (Lybart) B.; A.S., Grand Rapids Jr. Coll., Grand Rapids, 1957; D.D.S., U. Mich., Ann Arbor, 1961, M.S. in Orthodontia, 1965; m. Barbara Jean Sands, June 21, 1968; children—Jane Anne, John Daniel. Clin. instr. U. Mich., 1961-62, asst. prof., 1965-69; research asso. Center Human Growth and Devel., U. Mich., 1969-71; spl. lectr. Case Western Res. U., Cleve., 1972-75; lectr. U. Western Ont., 1973—, also pvt. practice specializing in orthodontia, Ann Arbor, 1965—; mem. human subject review com. U. Mich. Sch. Dentistry; mem. research team Found. Orthodontic Research. Sect. leader United Fund, St. Joseph Hosp. Bldg. Fund. Mem. Am., Mich. dental assns., Washtenaw Dist. Dental Soc. (past pres.), Mich. Orthodontic Alumni (pres., sec.-treas.), Am. Soc. Dentistry for Children, Am. Assn. Orthodontics, Great Lakes Soc. Orthodontics, Mich. Soc. Orthodontists (bd. dirs.), Mich. Assn. Professions (bd. dirs.), Phi Kappa Phi, Omicron Kappa Upsilon. Republican. Baptist. Clubs: Ann Arbor Rotary (pres.), U. Mich. of Ann Arbor (sec., treas., pres.). Home: 3989 Penberton St Ann Arbor MI 48105 Office: 1303 Packard St Ann Arbor MI 48104

BALDRIDGE, RICHARD STANLEY, agronomist; b. Cherry Fork, Ohio, Dec. 8, 1934; s. William Robert and Laura Lucille (Hamilton) B.; B.S., Ohio State U., 1957; m. Betty Jo Tilden, May 18, 1963; children—Brian Keith, Jane Tilden. Insp., Ohio Seed Improvement Assn., Columbus, 1957-58; agronomist Landmark Co-op, Winchester, Ohio, 1959-62; agronomist Texaco, Columbus, Cranberry, N.J., 1963-66; agronomist Sohio Chem. Co., Lima, Ohio, 1966-67; sales mgr. Kenworthy Seed Co., 1967-69; agronomist Occidental Chem. Co., Houston, 1969-73; pres. Baldridge Seed Co., Cherry Fork, Ohio, 1973—; cons. Chem-Lawn. Pres., Adams County Republican Club, 1980—; vice chmn. Adams County Republican Exec. Com., 1980-81, chmn., 1982-83; mem. Adams County Bd. Elections, 1982—; pres. Adams County Hist. Soc., 1976-78. Cert. profl. agronomist Am. Registry Cert. Profls. in Agronomy, Crops and Soils. Mem. Am. Soc. Agronomy, Ohio Seed Improvement Assn., Ohio Grain, Feed and Fertilizer Assn., Ohio Soil Improvement Soc. (past pres.), Ohio Turfgrass Found. (past treas.), Aircraft Owners and Pilots Assn., Adams County Pilots Assn. Presbyterian, Clubs: Masons, Scottish Rite. Address: PO Box 82 Cherry Fork OH 45618

BALDWIN, BRAD ALAN, osteopathic physician, educator; b. Albuquerque, May 21, 1954; s. Donald and Georgia Marie Baldwin; m. Diane Kay Baldwin, Sept. 18, 1955; 1 child, Sarah Beth. B.S., U. N.D., 1976; D.O., Coll. Osteo. Medicine, Kirkville, Mo., 1981. Intern, Kirkville Osteo. Hosp., 1981-82; resident in surgery Des Moines Gen. Hosp., 1982-85; faculty surgery Coll. Osteo. Medicine and Surgery, Des Moines, 1985—. Contbr. articles to profl. jours. Mem. Am. Osteo. Assn., Iowa Soc. Osteo. Physicians and Surgeons. Republican. Mem. Ch. of the Nazarene. Home: 496 Sherrylynn Blvd Des Moines IA 50317 Office: 603 E 12th St Des Moines IA 50307

BALDWIN, ELDON DEAN, agricultural economics educator, grain marketing consultant; b. Ashley, Ohio, Sept. 23, 1939; s. John Wesley and Inez Catherine (Reeley) B.; m. Judith Carolyn Fogel, Feb. 22, 1964; children—Jeffrey, Amy. B.S., Ohio State U., 1963; M.S., U. Ill., 1967, Ph.D., 1970. Agrl. statistician Bur. Census, Washington, 1963-65; research assoc. U. Ill., Champaign, 1965-69; asst. prof. Eastern Ill. U., Charles, 1969-70, Miami U., Oxford, Ohio, 1970-74; assoc. prof. agrl. econs. Ohio State U., Columbus, 1974—; dir. electronic mktg. hog accelerated mktg. system project, 1978-81; cons. grain cos., 1976—. Webelos leader Cub Scouts Am., 1976-77, master, 1976-78, instl. rep. Boy Scouts Am., 1978-79, master, 1979-80. Anderson Grain Co. grantee, 1976, U.S. Dept. Agr. grantee, 1978-81. Mem. Am. Agrl. Econs. Assn., North Central Agrl. Econs. Assn., So. Regional Grain Mktg. Research Coms. (chmn.), Gamma Sigma Delta. Presbyterian. Contbr. articles, papers in field to profl. lit. Developer slaughter hog electronic market. Home: 4324 Hollandia Ct Westerville OH 43081 Office: Dept Agrl Econs Ohio State U 2120 Fyffe Rd Columbus OH 43210

BALDWIN, GEORGE KOEHLER, department stores company executive; b. Cedar Rapids, Iowa, Nov. 17, 1919; s. Nathan and Ada Lillian (Koehler) B. B.B.A., State U. Iowa, 1942. Office mgr., mgr. Wapsie Valley Creamery, Cedar Rapids, 1946-60; treas., head payroll, accounts payable, sales audit depts. Armstrong's, Inc., Cedar Rapids, 1960—, also dir.; treas. Armstrong's of Dubuque (Iowa), 1982—, also dir.; also theatre organist. Mem. Cedar Rapids Performing Arts Commn.; bd. dirs. Cedar Rapids Community Concert Assn. Served with U.S. Army, 1942-46. Decorated Bronze Star medal; named hon. Ky. col. Mem. Cedar Rapids Consumer Credit Assn. (pres. 1968-69), Am. Theatre Organ Soc. (dir., treas. Cedar Rapids chpt.), Am. Legion. Methodist. Lodges: Rotary, Masons, Shriners (past pres. uniformed units). Home: 1017 F Ave NW Cedar Rapids IA 52405 Office: 3d Ave and 3d St SE Cedar Rapids IA 52401

BALDWIN, GERT A., computer system company executive; b. Oberstdorf, Germany, Mar. 26, 1937; came to U.S., May 1956, naturalized, 1966; d. Joseph and Annie (Wegscheider) Mayer; m. Frank J. Baldwin, May 14, 1959; children—Edwin, Buckley. Diploma in Commerce and Industry, Lindau Sch. Commerce and Industry, Germany, 1957; diploma in acctg. LaSalle Extension U., 1966; B.S. in Computer Sci. and Acctg., Roosevelt U., 1974, M.S. in Info. Systems, 1982. Mktg. trainee Garden Supply Co., Lindau, Germany, 1952-55; mktg. and retail clk. Garden Supply House, Munich, Germany, 1955-56; internal auditor clk. Morgan Dept. Store, Toronto, Ont., Can., 1967-69; auditor, acct. Weltman & Gallant, C.P.A.s, St. Louis, 1966-69; sr. auditor Lipschultz, Levin & Gray, C.P.A.s, Skokie, Ill., 1970-79; dir. systems implementation, pres. G. Baldwin & Assocs., Ltd., Schaumburg, Ill., 1979—; instr. in systems analysis DePaul U., Chgo., 1982—; instr. in EDP, Nat. Coll. Edn., 1984—. Mem. Inst. Mgmt. Cons. (cert.), North Shore Assn. Commerce and Industry (small bus. com. 1983—), Assn. Systems Mgmt. (treas. Chgo. chpt. 1984-85, v.p. 1985-86). Avocations: tennis; skiing; boating; stained glass; gardening; travel. Home: 84 N Inverway Inverness IL 60067 Office: G Baldwin & Assocs 1821 Walden Office Sq 4th Floor Schaumburg IL 60195

BALDWIN, KEITH IVAN, educational administrator, basketball coach; b. Indianola, Ill., Mar. 11, 1939; s. Kenneth I. and Helen M. (Gardner) B.; m. Pamela S. Burke, Aug. 14, 1970; 1 son, Keith Shaylan. B.E., Eastern Ill. U., 1962; M.S. in Ednl. Adminstrn., Ill. State U., 1974. Coach, athletic dir. Ridgefarm Schs., Ill., 1962-65, Rossville Schs., Ill., 1965-70; coach, athletic dir., prin. Watseka Community High Sch., Ill., 1970—; state basketball chmn. Ill. Prairie State Games, Champaign, 1984, 85; TV commentator Ill. State High Sch. Basketball Tournament, Champaign, 1981, 82, 83. Mem. Ill. Basketball Coach's Assn. (pres. 1983—, pub. newsletter 1970—), Ill. Prins. Assn. Republican. Mem. Ch. of Christ. Avocations: travel; raquetball; investing; coins. Home: 629 S 3rd St Watseka IL 60970 Office: Watseka Community High Sch 138 Belmont Ave Watseka IL 60970

BALDWIN, LLOYD DEANS, management consultant, computer software company executive; b. Logan, Utah, Feb. 15, 1936; s. Kelvin Alma and Helen Ann (Deans) B.; student pub. schs., Bountiful, Utah; m. Arlene Ruth Simonis, Oct. 17, 1960; children—Rebecca Ann, Danna Lynn, David Alma, Stefanie Janine, Karina Louise, Emaline Sarah, Carl Nathaniel, Brian Lloyd. Engr., Sperry Engring Co., 1958; missionary Ch. of Jesus Christ Latter-day Saints, 1959-60; engr. IBM, 1960, tech. and mgmt. positions, San Jose, Calif., 1961-69, regional mgr., 1968-69; asst. to v.p. mktg. Info. Storage Systems, Cupertino, Calif., 1969-71; dir. ops. Cincom Systems, Cin., 1971-75; pres. Lloyd Baldwin & Assos., Cin., 1975-76; v.p. Pansophic Systems Inc., Oak Brook, Ill., 1976-78; pres. SDA Products Inc., N.Y.C., 1978-80; dir. ops. Interactive Info. Systems, Inc., Cin., 1980-83, exec. dir. product and market devel. and data decisions, 1983-85; prin. LB Assocs., Cin., 1975—. Trustee, Deaconess Hosp., Cin., 1974. Served with USN, 1954-58. Mem. Software Industry Assn. (dir. 1970-77, pres. 1975-76), Computer Industry Assn., Am. Mgmt. Assn. Lodge: Rotary. Home: 6790 N Clippinger Cincinnati OH 45243 Office: 6790 N Clippinger Dr Cincinnati OH 45243

BALDWIN, MICHAEL REID, school principal; b. Concordia, Kans., Oct. 4, 1950; s. Henry Wilson and Virgie Marie (Reid) B.; m. Sandra Rae Tennant, June 4, 1977; children—Lucas Reid, Aaron Michael. A.A. in Edn., Cloud County Jr. Coll., 1970; B.A. in Elem. Edn., Wesleyan Coll., Salina, Kans., 1972; M.S. in Sch. Adminstrn., Ft. Hays State U., 1980. Cert. elem. and secondary tchr. Tchr., coach Unified Sch. Dist. 310, Langdon, Kans., 1972-76, Unified Sch. Dist. 428, Great Bend, Kans., 1976-80; prin., tchr. Unified Sch. Dist. 496, Rozel, Kans., 1980-82, Unified Sch. Dist. 408, Marion, Kans., 1982—. Asst. scoutmaster, Boy Scouts Am., Turon, Kans., 1975-76. Fellowship Coll. Athletes staff fellow, 1970. Mem. United Sch. Adminstrs., Kans. Assn. Elem. Sch. Prins., Phi Delta Kappa. Roman Catholic. Lodge: Lions. Avocations: hunting; fishing; baseball card collecting; golf; tennis. Home: 130 S Freeborn St Marion KS 66861

BALDWIN, SUSAN OLIN, lawyer; b. Battle Creek, Mich., Sept. 1, 1954; d. Thomas Franklin and Gloria Joan (Skidmore) Olin; m. James Patric Baldwin, Sept. 15, 1979. B.A., Miami U., Ohio, 1976; J.D., U. Cin., 1979. Bar: Ohio 1979, Mich. 1984. Assoc. editor Am. Legal Pub. Co., Cin., 1979-80; corp. atty. Hosp. Care Corp., Cin., 1980-84; legal counsel Peak Health Plan, Cin., 1984; assoc. Cook Pringle Simonsen & Goetz, P.C., Birmingham, Mich., 1984—. Contbr. articles to profl. jours. Pres. Hunter's Green Homeowner's Assn., Independence, Ky., 1982-83; charter mem. Young Republicans, Ashland, Ohio, 1972. Mem. ABA, Ohio State Bar Assn., Mich. Bar Assn., Alpha Lambda Delta, Phi Alpha Delta. Club: Am Businesswomen's Assn. (v.p. 1980-81, editor 1980). Office: 1400 N Woodward Ave Suite 101 Birmingham MI 48011

BALDWIN, TIMOTHY WAYNE, marketing executive; b. Akron, Ohio, Mar. 14, 1946; s. Frank B. and Margaret H. (Herrington) B.; m. Kathy J. Trego, July 8, 1982; children—Veronica, Mark, Darren. B.S. in Orgn. Sci., Case Inst. Tech., 1968; postgrad. U. So. Calif., 1969, San Jose State Coll., 1972. Indsl. salesman ALCOA, Los Angeles, 1968-71; region sales mgr. Johnson & Johnson, Denver, 1971-77; zone sales mgr. Hills Bros. Coffee, San Francisco, 1977-78; sr. product mgr. Borden Inc., Columbus, Ohio, 1978-83; dir. mktg. Benco Pet Foods, Inc., Zanesville, Ohio, 1983-84; mktg. dir. Shopsmith, Inc., Dayton, Ohio, 1984—. Vice pres. English Gardens Condominiums, Westerville, Ohio, 1982-83. Republican. Methodist. Club: Toastmasters (sec. San Jose 1972-73). Avocations: tennis, golf, volleyball, racquetball, skiing. Office: Shopsmith Inc 6640 Poe Ave Dayton OH 45414

BALENT, ARTHUR DAVID, process control and automation company executive; b. Pitts., Oct. 27, 1941; s. David Anthony and Margaret Ann (Hann) B.; m. Susan Ann Daly, Sept. 14, 1968; children—David, Jamison. B.S., Ind. Inst. Tech., 1967; M.S., Fla. Inst. Tech., 1970. Sales engr. Sq. D., Davenport, Iowa, 1970-73; sr. sales engr. Allis Chalmers, Cin., 1973-74, Lear Siegler, Cin., 1974; account mgr. LFE Corp., 1974-77; region mgr. Fife Corp., 1977-84; region mgr. Robin Process Mgmt. Systems Corp., 1984—. Served with USN, 1959-62. Mem. TAPPI, Cin. C. of C. Republican. Roman Catholic. Avocations: Reading; water sports. Home: 5752 Lindenwood Lane Fairfield OH 45014

BALESTER, VIVIAN SHELTON, law librarian, lawyer, legal research consultant; b. Pine Bluff, Ark., Dec. 10, 1931; d. Marvin W. and Mary Lena (Burke) Shelton; m. James Beverly Standerfer, Aug. 1, 1951 (dec. 1952); 1 son, Walter Eric; m. 2d, Raymond James Balester, Oct. 19, 1956; children—Carla Maria, Mark Shelton. B.A. cum laude, Vanderbilt U., 1955; M.S.L.S., Case Western Res. U., 1972, J.D., 1975. Bar: Ohio 1975, U.S. Dist. Ct. (no. dist.) Ohio 1975. Ind. bibliographic and legal research cons., Cleve., Washington, Nashville, 1959—; head law librarian Squire, Sanders & Dempsey, Cleve., 1975—; Ohio del. White House Conf. Libraries/Information Services, 1979; speaker Law Librarians Nat. Conf., 1978, 80, 82; mem. adv. com. on profl. ethics Case Western Res. U., 1982—. Lay reader St. Alban's Episcopal Ch., 1978—, mem. vestry, 1977-79, 84—, warden, 1979, 84; mem. council Diocese of Ohio, 1980-82, chmn. racial justice com., 1980—, chmn. nominating com., 1982, del. Nat. Confs. on Faith Pub. Policy, Racism, 1982; dep. gen. Conv. of Episcopal Ch. in U.S., 1985; mem. Women's Polit. Caucus, 1978—; founder and co-chmn. Greater Cleve. Ann. Martin Luther King Celebration, 1980—; mem. County Commrs. adv. com. on handicapped, 1980-84; chmn. adolescent health coalition Fedn. Community Planning, 1979-81, mem. health concerns commn., 1981—; regional chmn. alumni edn. Vanderbilt U., 1982-83; mem. community adv. com. Cleve. Orch., 1983—; bd. dirs. Hospice Council No. Ohio, 1979-81, vol. atty., 1982—; bd. dirs. Interch. Council Greater Cleve., 1978-84; mem. Ohio Com. Nat. Security, 1983; bd. dirs. WomenSpace, 1979-83. Recipient Outstanding Community Service award Fedn. Community Planning, 1980, Woman of Profl. Excellence award YWCA, 1983; Cleve. Mayor's award for volunteerism, 1984; Nat. Endowment for Humanities fellow, 1980. Mem. ABA, Bar Assn. Greater Cleve. (Merit Service award 1979) Am. Assn. Law Libraries, Am. Soc. Info. Sci. (chmn. law sect. 1978). Democrat. Home: 2460 Edgehill Rd Cleveland Heights OH 44106 Office: Squire Sanders & Dempsey 1800 Huntington Bldg Cleveland OH 44115

BALESTRINO, MARCIA ANN, computer programming executive; b. Youngstown, Ohio, July 2, 1949; d. Anthony F. and Virginia M. (DePaul) B. Student Ohio State U., 1966-68; B.A., Youngstown State U., 1970, M.B.A., 1984. Cert. data processor. Programmer, Ohio Edison Co., Akron, 1970-73, programmer-analyst, 1972-73; systems engr. Logics Corp., Cleve., 1973-75; programmer analyst St. Elizabeth Hosp. Med. Ctr., Youngstown, 1975-79, systems programmer, 1979-81, systems and programming mgr., 1981—; trustee, cons. YWCA, Youngstown, 1984—, Home Owner's Warranty, Washington, 1984. Mem. Assn. for Systems Mgmt. (treas. Steel Valley chpt. 1981-83, v.p. 1983-85, awards chmn. 1979-81), Youngstown State U. Alumni Assn., Williamson Soc., Phi Kappa Phi. Republican. Roman Catholic. Avocations: skiing; aerobics; travel; concerts. Home: 2445 E Rancho Dr Phoenix AZ 85016 Office: St Elizabeth Hospital Med Ctr 1044 Belmont Ave Youngstown OH 44501-1790

BALFOUR, HENRY HALLOWELL, JR., pediatrician, virologist, clinical pathologist, educator; b. Jersey City, Feb. 9, 1940; s. Henry Hallowell and Dorothy Kathryn Dietze B.; A.B. with honors, Princeton, 1962; M.D., Columbia, 1966; m. Carol Lenore Pries, Sept. 23, 1967; children—Henry Hallowell III, Anne Lenore, Caroline Dorothy. Intern, U. Minn. Hosps., Mpls., 1966-67; resident pediatrics Babies Hosp., Columbia-Presbyn. Med. Center, N.Y.C., 1967-68; asst. prof. lab. medicine, pathology, pediatrics U. Minn., 1972-75, asso. prof., 1975-79, prof., 1979—, dir. sect. virology, 1972—, dir. div. clin. microbiology, 1974—; cons. clin. virology VA Hosp., Mpls., 1973—. Served to capt. M.C., USAF, 1968-70. NIH grantee, 1974—. Diplomate Am. Bd. Pediatrics. Fellow Am. Acad. Pediatrics, Infectious Disease Soc. Am.; mem. Am. Fedn. Clin. Research, Am. Soc. Microbiology, Soc. Exptl. Biology and Medicine, Northwestern Pediatric Soc., Soc. Pediatric Research, Central Soc. Clin. Research, Acad. Clin. Lab. Physicians and Scientists. Author: (with Ralph C. Heussner) Herpes Diseases and Your Health, 1984; contbr. clin. and research articles to med. books and jours.; reviewer numerous med. jours. and agys.; invited speaker nat. and internat. med. confs. Home: 6820 Harold Ave N Minneapolis MN 55427 Office: Box 437 Mayo U Minn Health Scis Center Minneapolis MN 55455

BALINSKY, DORIS, research biochemist, biochemistry educator; b. Frankfurt, Germany, Dec. 3, 1934; came to U.S., 1975; d. Robert Emil and Else Leonora Rosa (Machol) Goldschmidt; d. John Boris Balinsky, Mar. 29, 1958 (dec. 1983); children—Andrew Paul, Martin George. B.Sc., U. Witwatersrand, Johannesburg, S. Africa, 1955, B.Sc. with honors, 1956; Ph.D., U. London, 1959. Biochemist, later head enzyme research unit S. African Inst. for Med. Research, Johannesburg, 1960-76; adj. prof. biochemistry Iowa State U., Ames, 1976—. Contbr. articles to sci. jours., chpts. to books. NIH grantee, 1978-81, 81-85; AAUW postdoctoral fellow, 1968, 75. Mem. Am. Soc. Biol. Chemists, Am. Assn. Cancer Research, S. African Soc. Biochemistry, S. African Soc. Exptl. Biology (past sec.-treas.). Avocations: swimming, hiking, travelling, music. Office: Dept Biochemistry Iowa State U Ames IA 50011

BALISTRERI, JERRY PAUL, industrial arts administrator, educator; b. Beloit Wis., Nov. 22, 1952; s. Vito Jerome and Virginia Marie (Parrinello) Bari. B.S., U. Wis.-Stout, 1974, M.S., 1977; M.Ed., S.D. State U., 1980, postgrad., 1982—. Cert. high sch. tchr., prin., supt., Wis. Tchr. indsl. arts Thorp (Wis.) High Sch., 1974-76, S.D. State U., Brookings, 1977-79; prin. Wauzeka (Wis.) Pub. Schs., 1979-81; state supr. indsl. arts N.D. State Bd. for Vocat. Edn., Bismarck, 1981—; cons. in field. Mem. Big Bros. of Am., Thorp, 1974-76. Named hon. citizen State of S.D. Mem. Wis. Indsl. Edn. Assn., Am. Indsl. Arts Assn., Am. Vocat. Assn., Am. Council on Indsl. Arts Tchr. Edn., Nat. Assn. Secondary Sch. Prins., N.D. Indsl. Arts Assn., N.D. Vocat. Assn., Am. Council Indsl. Arts Suprs., Jaycees. Phi Delta Kappa, Phi Kappa Phi, Epsilon Pi Tau. U.S. Office of Edn. grantee, 1977—. Roman Catholic. Home: 500 Wachter Ave Bismarck ND 58501 Office: 15th Floor State Capital Bismarck ND 58505

BALL, BEVERLY HODGES, association executive, author; b. Meridian, Miss., Dec. 27, 1927; d. Bryant Bevil and Nola Mae (Williams) Hodges; m. Armand B. Ball, Jr., Sept. 15, 1957; children—Kathryn Lynn, Robin Armand. B.A., Blue Mountain Coll., 1948; M.R.E., Southwestern Bapt. Theol. Sem., 1957. Program dir. YMCA Camp Widjiwagan, St. Paul, 1970-74; exec. sec. Sch. Bus., Ind. U., Bloomington, 1976-77; publs. supr. Am. Camping Assn., Martinsville, Ind., 1977—, dir. instrs., outdoors living skills program. Vol. dir. tng. St. Croix Valley council Girl Scouts U.S.A., St. Paul, 1970-74, Tulip Trace council, Bloomington, 1974-76. Recipient Gold award St. Croix Valley council Girl Scouts U.S.A., 1974, cert. of appreciation Tulip Trace council, 1974-76; cons. Nat. Girl Scout Tng. Summit, 1975. Presbyterian. Co-author: Basic Camp Management, 1979. Home: 2812 Fawkes Way Bloomington IN 47401 Office: Am Camping Assn Bradford Woods Martinsville IN 46151

BALL, CHESTER EDWIN, editor, consultant; b. Seth, W.Va., Aug. 19, 1921; s. Roman Harry and Hattie (White) B.; A.B., Marshall U., 1942; M.A., Ohio State U., 1947; m. Betty June Hively, Dec. 29, 1945; children—Beth Elaine (Mrs. John Michael Watkins), Harry Stuart, Chester Edwin. Stringer, Charleston (W.Va.) Daily Mail, 1936-40; reporter, copy editor Huntington (W.Va.) Pub. Co., 1945, 47-48; assoc. pub. Wolf Pub. Co., Cin., 1953-55; instr. journalism Marshall Coll., Huntington, W.Va., 1947-51; asst. prof. journalism Ohio State U., Columbus, 1951-56, publs. editor Engring. Expt. Sta., 1956-63; tech. editor, dir. reprographics Ohio State U. Research Found., Columbus, 1963-81, editorial cons. Ednl. Resources Info. Ctr., 1981—. Mem. Hilliard (Ohio) Charter Commn., 1958-63, vice-chmn., 1958, sec., 1960-61, 62-63; treas. Hilliard chpt. Am. Field Service, 1974-76, pres., 1976-77; mem. Scioto Darby Bd. Edn., Hilliard, 1962-78; bd. dirs. Franklin County Epilepsy Assn., 1976-82, treas., 1978-80, pres., 1980-81. Served with AUS, 1942-45; col. Res. (ret.). Decorated Silver Star, Bronze Star medal with one oak leaf cluster, Purple Heart with two oak leaf clusters. Mem. In-Plant Printing Mgmt. Assn. (pres. 1971, cert. graphics communication mgr.), Res. Officers Assn. (sec.-treas., pres.

Huntington, W.Va. 1948-50), U.S. Army 5th Div. Soc. (pres. 1984-85), Columbus Zoo Docent Assn. (parliamentarian 1985). Republican. Methodist (mem. bd. ushers 1956—). Club: Hilliard Kiwanis (pres. 1983-84). Home: 6174 Sunny Vale Dr Columbus OH 43228

BALL, CLIFFORD NEIL, greeting card co. exec.; b. Olathe, Kans., Jan. 20, 1928; s. Loren Gordon and Edythe Virginia (Woolery) B.; B.S. in Bus., U. Kans., 1950; m. Jo Ann Boyer, June 4, 1948; children—Neila Jo, Malissa, Twila Sue, Mark, Daniel. Merchandiser, Hallmark Card Co., Kansas City, Mo., 1950-53, mdse. control mgr., 1954-64, dir. product promotions, 1965-68, planning mgr., 1969-70, dir. product mgmt. services, 1971-72, sr. product mgr., 1973-78, group product mgr., 1978-80, corp. dir. fixture line mgmt. and visual merchandising, 1981-82, dir. retail environment, 1982-84, dir. prodn. control, 1984—. Chmn. bd. trustees, ruling elder First United Presbyn. Ch., Olathe, 1970-82; pres. Olathe Interchurch Alliance, 1971; v.p. Olathe Arts Council, 1978-79; chmn. ministerial relations crisis com. Kansas City Union Presbytery, 1979—. Served with USN, 1945-46. Recipient Family of Builders award Kans. Kiwanis Found., 1976. Democrat. Home: 605 Edgemere Dr Olathe KS 66061 Office: 25th and McGee Sts Kansas City MO 64141

BALL, DAVID WARD, lawyer; b. Morristown, N.J., Oct. 21, 1952; s. William David and Janice Marie (Ward) B.; m. Carol Diane Clyde, Sept. 16, 1978. B.A., Miami U., Oxford, Ohio, 1974; J.D., Loyola U., Chgo., 1979. Bar: Idaho, U.S. Dist. Ct. Idaho, U.S. Ct. Appeals (9th cir.) 1980. Dep. pros. atty. Ada County Pros. Atty.'s Office, Boise, Idaho, 1980-83; city atty. City of Pocatello, Idaho, 1983—. Active Nat. Ski Patrol, Boise, 1980-83; mem. adv. bd. Salvation Army, Pocatello, 1984—. Mem. Idaho State Bar, Assn., 6th Dist. Bar Assn., Nat Inst. Mcpl. Law Officers, Idaho City Attys. Assn. (chmn. depository com.). Methodist. Home: 223 S Lincoln Pocatello ID 83204 Office: City of Pocatello 902 E Sherman Pocatello ID 83201

BALL, DIANE ALTMAN, librarian; b. Chattanooga, Sept. 4, 1932; d. William A. and Louise (Kendrick) Altman; B.S. in Edn., Miami U., Oxford, Ohio, 1968; M.Ed., Wright State U., Dayton, Ohio, 1977; m. Richard E. Ball, Oct. 10, 1953; children—David Allen, Anne Louise. Children's librarian Miamisburg (Ohio) Public Library, 1952-53; librarian W. Carrollton (Ohio) Jr.-Sr. High Sch., 1958-60; substitute tchr. Miamisburg, W. Carrollton and Oakwood City sch. dists., 1964-68; media specialist Oakwood Jr.-Sr. High Sch., Dayton, 1968—; adj. instr. Wright State U.; mem. various assessment and evaluation teams for state and pvt. agys.; vice-chmn. Ohio Multitype Interlibrary Cooperation Com., 1975-81; co-founder Southwestern Ohio Young Adult Materials Rev. Group; Mem. Ohio Assn. Sch. Librarians (dir. Western dist. 1971-73, state pres. 1975-76), Oakwood Tchrs. Assn. (com. chmn. 1973-74, 78—), Ednl. Media Council Ohio, NEA, Ohio, Western Ohio edn. assns., ALA, Am. Assn. Sch. Librarians (mem. standards com. 1976—, mem. exec. com. 1981; rep. to rev. com. Am. U. Press Services 1977—, chmn. AUPS 1982, chmn. Unit II, 1981-85; regional dir. 1978-81, rep. exec. com. 1982-83, 2nd v.p. 1984-85), Ohio Ednl. Library Media Assn. (1st past pres., co-chmn. consol. project, award of merit 1983), Delta Kappa Gamma. Contbr. profl. publs. Home: 2410 Fairmont Ave Dayton OH 45419 Office: 1200 Far Hills Ave Dayton OH 45419

BALL, JOANN FLYNN, company communication executive; b. Athens, Ala., Nov. 2, 1946; d. Marvin Elgar and Ruby Elizabeth (Johnson) Flynn; m. John C. Vandemark, Aug. 28, 1965 (div. 1972); 1 child, Lyle E.; m. Ronald E. Ball, Sept. 11, 1977; children—Stephen, Stacey. B.S., Auburn U., 1971, M.A., 1974; postgrad. Purdue U. Instr. Purdue U., West Lafayette, Ind., 1974-76; mgr. mgmt. devel. Am. Mgmt. Services, Denver, 1976-77; mgr. human resources TRW Ross Gear div., Lafayette, Ind., 1978-81; mgr. orgn. com. TRW Co. Staff, Cleve., 1981-84; mgr. communication and orgn. devel. TRW Aircraft Components Group, Cleve., 1984—. Author: Interpersonal Communication, 1976; Small Group Communication, 1976; producer film: Walking the Line (Bronze Quill award 1983), 1982. Counselor, trainer Lafayette Crisis Ctr., 1974-80. Mem. Orgn. Devel. Network, Internat. Communication Assn., Phi Kappa Phi, Kappa Delta Pi. Avocations: skiing; needlework; pottery. Office: TRW Aircraft Components Group 23555 Euclid Ave Cleveland OH 44117

BALL, LOUIS ALVIN, insurance company executive; b. Kansas City, Mo., Oct. 25, 1921; s. George Rhodom and Frances Mariam (Beals) B.; B.A. in Bus. Adminstrn., Kans. State U., 1947; m. Norma Jane Laudenberger, Jan. 17, 1947. Asst. purchasing agt. Kansas City (Mo.) br. Ford Motor Co., 1942-46; with Farm Bur. Mut. Ins. Co., Inc., Manhattan, Kans., 1947—, claims underwriting mgr., 1956-61, systems and procedures mgr., 1961—, asst. sec., 1977-81, corp. sec., 1981—. Mem. Nat. Assn. Ind. Insurers, Conf. Casualty Cos., Assn. Systems Mgmt. (Internat. Merit award 1971, Internat. Achievement award 1978, Kansas City chpt. Merit award 1970, Kansas City chpt. Diamond Merit award 1977, chmn. ann. conf. 1982). Club: Manhattan Country. Home: 1101 Pioneer Ln Manhattan KS 66502 Office: 2321 Anderson Ave Manhattan KS 66502

BALL, ROY ORVILLE, engineer, educator; b. Washington, Oct. 24, 1945; s. Rura O. and Dorothy R. (Toynton) B.; m. Jacqueline Sue Childress, Apr. 4, 1970; children—Christian, David. B.S. in Civil Engring., U. Fla., 1967; M.S. in Environ. Engring., U. Tex., 1972; Ph.D., U. Del., 1976. Registered profl. engr., Del., Minn., Iowa, Ill. Facilities engr. U.S. Armor Ctr., Fort Knox, Ky., 1967-69; IBM, Fishkill, N.Y., 1970-71; environ. engr. DuPont, Newark, Del., 1972-77; asst. prof. engring. U. Tenn., Knoxville, 1978-80; mgr. process design Roy F. Weston, West Chester, Pa., 1980-81; prin. ERM, Chgo., 1981—; adj. faculty mem. Villanova U (Pa.), 1980, Drexel U., Phila., 1980. Co-author: Engineers Guide to Hazardous Waste Management, 1985. Contbr. articles to profl. publs. Served to 1st lt. U.S. Army, 1968-69. Davis fellow, 1975-77. Mem. Am. Inst. Chem. Engrs., Air Pollution Control Assn., Water Pollution Control Fedn. Republican. Avocations: piano; chess. Home: 1130 Knollwood Deerfield IL 60015 Office: ERM-N Central Inc 835 Sterling Ave Palatine IL 60067

BALL, TRAVIS, JR., ednl. adminstr.; b. Newport, Tenn., July 13, 1942; s. Travis and Ruth Annette (Duyck) B.; B.A., Carson Newman Coll., 1964; M.A., Purdue U., 1966. Instr., then asst. prof. English, Ill. Wesleyan U., Bloomington, 1966-69; vis. prof. English edn. Millikin U., 1969; asst. headmaster, chmn. English dept. Brewster Acad., Wolfeboro, N.H., 1969-72; dir. admissions, asst. to headmaster Park Tudor Sch., Indpls., 1972—; pres. Travis Ball & Assos., 1980—; mem. commn. on curriculum and grad. requirements Ind. Dept. Public Instrn., 1974-76; mem. adv. council Ednl. Records Bur. Mem. Indiana Non-Public Edn. Assn. (treas., dir.), Independent Schs. Assn. Central States (conf. chmn.), Nat. Council Tchrs. English, Assn. Supervision and Curriculum Devel., Council Advancement and Support Edn. (adv. com. on ind. schs.), Nat. Assn. Ind. Schs., Sigma Tau Delta, Pi Kappa Delta, Phi Delta Kappa. Baptist. Editor, Tchrs. Service Com. Newsletter for English Tchrs., 1977-82; dept. editor English Jour., 1976-82; editor/pub. Contact: Newsletter for Admissions Mgmt., 1980—. Home: 2625 N Meridian St Indianapolis IN 46208 Office: 7200 N College Ave Indianapolis IN 46240

BALL, WILLIAM JAMES, physician; b. Charleston, S.C., Apr. 16, 1910; s. Elias and Mary (Cain) B.; B.S., U. of South, 1930; M.D., Med. Coll. S.C., 1934; m. Doris Hallowell Mason, July 9, 1938. Intern, Roper Hosp., Charleston, 1934-35; resident dept. pediatrics U. Chgo. Clinics, 1935-37; instr. pediatrics Med. Coll. S.C., 1938-42; practice medicine specializing in pediatrics, Charleston, 1938-42, Aurora, Ill., 1951-70; physician student Health Service No. Ill. U., 1970-72; mem. staff Copley Meml., St. Joseph Mercy hosps.; pediatrician N.W. Clinic, Minot, N.D., 1946-51; asso. prof. Sch. Nursing, No. Ill. U., 1971-72. Mem. Bd. Health, Aurora, Ill., 1958-62; pediatrician, div. services for crippled children U. Ill., 1952—; pediatric cons. sch. dists. 129 and 131, Aurora, 1972—, DeKalb County Spl. Edn. Assn., 1972-81, Sch. Assn. Spl. Edn. Dupage County, 1980-83. Mooseheart, Ill., 1970-83, Northwestern Ill. Assn. Handicapped Children; med. cons. Aurora Easter Seal Rehab. Center; pres. Kane County sub-area council Health Systems Agy., Kane, Lake, McHenry Counties, 1977-78, sec., 1978-79. Served as capt. M.C., AUS, 1942-46; col. Res., ret. Diplomate Am. Bd. Pediatrics. Fellow Royal Soc. Health, Am. Acad. Pediatrics; mem. AMA, Kane County Med. Soc. (pres. 1962), Am. Heart Assn., Am. Sch. Health Assn., Am. Cancer Soc., Easter Seal Soc., Phi Beta Kappa, Phi Chi, Pi Kappa Phi. Republican. Rotarian. Club: Union League (Aurora). Address: 433 S Commonwealth Ave Aurora IL 60506

BALL, WILLIAM LEE, operations specialist in marketing; b. Elkhorn, Wis., Aug. 25, 1959; s. William Lee and Pauline Lucy (Anderson) B. B.S., No. Ill. U., 1981, M.A., 1984. Counselor, No. Ill. U., DeKalb, 1981-82; cons. Gen. Employment Enterprises, Chgo., 1982-83; dir. grad. placement DeVry Inst. Tech., Chgo., 1983-84; ops. specialist Gen. Employment Enterprises, Chgo., 1984—; speaker Niles Twp. Sch. Dist., Ill., 1983; disc jockey Sta. WKDI, 1981. Author: Job Search Handbook, 1983. Editor: Career Logic Mag., 1983. Chmn. bd. dirs. Talkline/Kidsline Inc., Elk Grove Village, Ill., 1984; vice chmn. Family Care Services Northwest Bd., Mt. Prospect, Ill., 1984; mem. Planning Commn., Rolling Meadows, Ill., 1983-84; asst. dist. commr. N.W. Suburban council Boy Scouts Am., 1983-84. Mem. Assn. Field Service Mgrs., Am. Soc. Personnel Adminstrs., Midwest Coll. Placement Assn., Coll. Placement Council, Data Processing Mgmt. Assn. Democrat. Lutheran. Club: Drama (pres. 1984) (Rolling Meadows). Home: 4738 Arbor Dr 213 Rolling Meadows IL 60008 Office: Gen Employment Enterprises 150 S Wacker Dr Chicago IL 60606

BALLANCE, LYLE LEON, supervisor of assessments, real estate appraiser; b. Vernon Ill., Apr. 24, 1925; s. Robert and Susan Irene (Oates) B.; m. Mary Josephine Lincicum, Nov. 14, 1948; children—Lyle Leon, Arlen Dale. Student Kaskaskia Coll., 1974. Cert. assessing officer, rev. appraiser, sr. appraiser, Ill. Farmer, Vernon, 1925-74; clk. Pope (Ill.) Twp., supr., 1961-66; oil assessor Fayette County, 1967-69; supr. of assessments, Vandalia Ill., 1971—, real estate salesman, appraiser, 1974—, oil and gas lease landman, 1970—. Served to staff sgt. U.S. Army, 1945-46. Mem. Internat. Assn. Assessing Officers, Am. Assn. Cert. Appraisers, Nat. Assn. Review Appraisers. Republican. Methodist. Clubs: Am. Legion, VFW, Masons, Eastern Star, Masons, K.T., York Rite. Home: 1305 W Madison St Vandalia IL 62471 Office: 221 S 7th St Vandalia IL 62471

BALLANTYNE, DOROTHY DUNNING, museum worker, retired educator; b. Aetna, Ind., Mar. 17, 1910; d. Harry Leland and Ella L. (Larson) Dunning; m. Donald Bock Ballantyne (dec. June, 1973); children—Elin Christianson, Dorothy Eastwood, Brianne Lowery, Alexander. Student Ind U. Newspaper editor Hobart Gazette, Ind., 1929-32; clk. Home Owners Loan Fed. Govt., Hammond, Ind., 1932; dep. auditor Lake County, Crown Point, Ind., 1932-36; sub. tchr. Hobart Schs., Ind., 1954-65, spl. edn. tchr., 1965-72; vol. dir. Hobart Hist. Soc. Mus., Ind., 1970—. Contbr. articles to profl. jour. Author pamphlets Hobart Hist. Soc. Mem. adv. com. Hobart Sch. Bd., 1980—, Hobart PTA. Recipient Disting. Service award West Hobart Civic Club, 1970; named one of 12 most valuable women in country Trade Winds, Lake County, Ind., 1978. Mem. Ind. Hist. Soc., Hobart Hist. Soc. (pres. 1970-76), Mensa, Hobart Jaycees (Laura Bracken Woman of yr. award 1968), LWV (pres.). Lodge: Order Eastern Star (worthy matron 1938, dist. dep. 1940). Home: 121 South Ash St Hobart IN 46342 Office: Hobart Hist Soc Mus Box 24 Hobart IN 46342

BALLARD, DOROTHY MAE, labor union representative, consultant; b. Kansas City, Mo., Dec. 8, 1916; d. Frank and Eva (Powell) Cann; widowed; 12 children. Ed. in Labor Edn., Norman Coll. Machinist, N. Am. Aviation, 1942-46; assemblyline worker Gen. Motors Co., Kansas City, Mo., 1953-55, instr, in electronics; labor rep. local 31 United Auto Workers, Kansas City; now cons.; lectr. in labor edn. and prison reform, 1974-85; organizer seminars, Operation PUSH convs., Kansas City, also workshops for women; leader petition drives for women's rights and labor reform. Mem. Black Awareness Program, Lansing, Mo.; co-founder, pres. Greater Kansas City Minority Women's Coalition for Human Rights; pres. Met. United Citizens for Prison Reform and Assistance; adv. bd. Mid-Am. Regional Council, Jackson County Jail Com., Council on Crimes and Delinquency, Creative Enterprises, New Directions Ctr., Mo. Probation and Parole Bd., Salvation Army Task Force, Job Partnership Tng. Programs; past bd. dirs. Ann Skinner Women's Fellowship, Am. Bapt. Ch.; affirmative action chmn. Greater Kansas City Women's Polit. Caucus; mem. platform com. Mo. Democratic Party, 1978-80. Recipient numerous community service awards including Women's award U.S. Sec. Labor, Woman of Yr. award United Auto Workers, Jefferson award. Mem. Nat. Assn. Colored Women, Negro Bus. and Profl. Women (Woman of Yr. Central chpt. 1979), Coalition Labor Union Women (past chpt. pres., nat. exec. bd., chmn. women's history week 1985), Assn. Blacks in Criminal Justice, Nat. Alliance Bus. (task force), Mo. Leadership Assn., Urban League of Greater Kansas City. Address: 13517 Lowell St Grandview MO 64030

BALLARD, JOSEPH GRANT, photographer, photog. co. exec.; b. Greenville, N.C., Nov. 29, 1928; s. Charlie Edgar and Mary Velma (Keel) B.; B.S., Calif. Western U., 1976, M.B.A., 1978; grad. Woodward Sch. of Photography, 1949, Modern Sch. of Photography, N.Y.C., 1950; Ph.D. (hon.), Pacific Coll., 1976; D.D. (hon.), Christian Bible Coll., 1982, Ala. Bible Coll., 1982; H.H.D., Covington Theol. Sem., 1982; m. Sherry Rae Hall, May 2, 1961; children—Joseph Grant, Don, Patricia, Mike, Ron, Jeffrey Grant, Warren Scott, Vikki Kristine. Exec. v.p. Goldcraft Studios, Cin., 1951-61; pres. Photoland, Inc., Cleve., 1961-71, Nelson's Photography, Inc., Cleve., 1972—; cons. in mktg., promotions, budget controls and fund raising to various bus. firms and orgns., 1975—. Mem. Bicentennial Commn., Cleve., 1975; pres. Recreation Advisory Bd., North Olmsted, Ohio, 1977—; lay Baptist minister; mem. The Chapel in Berea, ordained deacon, 1981, chmn. of deacons, 1981; chmn. com. Child Evangelism Fellowship, Cleve., 1977-79; trustee Child Evangelism Fellowship, Warrenton, Md. Served with USAAF, 1945-47. Recipient numerous awards for portrait photography, 1953—; Joseph G. Ballard Day proclaimed in honor by mayor of Cleve., April 4, 1975. Mem. Profl. Photographers of Am. Assn., Wedding Photographers of Am. Assn., Ohio Assn. Chiefs of Police, Fraternal Order of Police, Cleveland Ad Club, Ohio Profl. Photography Assn. Home: 5612 Allandale Dr North Olmsted OH 44070 Office: 41 Colonial Arcade Cleveland OH 44115

BALLARD, LYNN ANITA, pediatrics dentist; b. Chgo., Aug. 19, 1948; d. Fred. S. and Thelma (King) B.; 1 child, Fritz. B.S. in Biology, Ky. State Coll., 1970; D.M.D., U. Ky., 1974; M.S., U. Mich., 1976. Asst. prof. U. Chgo. Zoller Dental Clin., 1977-81; clin. assoc., 1982—; mem. attending staff pediatric dentistry Michael Reese Hosp., Chgo., 1981—; practice dentistry specializing in pediatrics, Chgo., 1976—. Mem. Am. Soc. Dentistry For Children, Am. Dental Assn., Am. Acad. Pediatric Dentistry, Chgo. Dental Soc., Ill. State Dental Soc. Office: 1525 E 55th St Suite 703 Chicago IL 60615

BALLAS, ZUHAIR KHAMIS, physician; b. Beirut, Lebanon, Oct. 14, 1950; came to U.S., 1974; s. Khamis Mahmoud and Ellen (Kallenbach) B. B.S., Am. U. Beirut, 1970, M.D., 1974. Diplomate Am. Bd. Internal Medicine, Allergy/Clin. Immunology Bd. Resident Rugers Med. Sch., N.J., 1974-75, Thomas Jefferson U., Phila., 1975-76; fellow in allergy Johns Hopkins U., Balt., 1976-78; assoc., sr. fellow Fred Hutchinson Cancer Research, U. Wash., 1978-80; asst. prof. U. Iowa Coll. Medicine, Iowa City, 1980—; staff physician allergy div. VA Med. Ctr., Iowa City, 1980—. Contbr. articles to profl. jours. Recipient Research Assoc. Career award, VA, 1981-84, Clin. Investigator Career award, 1984—; grantee VA, 1980-81, 81—, NIH, 1982—, Am. Heart Assn., 1984—. Fellow Am. Acad. Allergy, ACP; mem. N.Y. Acad. Sci., Am. Assn. Immunology, Am. Fedn. Clin. Research. Office: Univ Iowa Hosps and Clinics Iowa City IA 52442

BALLENGER, WILLIAM SYLVESTER, III, state racing commissioner, writer; b. Flint, Mich., Mar. 28, 1941; s. William S. amd Marie E. (Daley) B.; m. Virginia Lee (Bunny) Woodard, June 20, 1964; children—Josephine, William Sylvester V. A.B., Princeton U., 1962; M.P.A., Harvard U., 1977. Mem. Mich. Ho. of Reps., 1969-70; mem. Mich. Senate, 1971-74, chmn. agrl., consumer affairs, health and social services coms., mem. standing com. on edn. and taxation and vets. affairs; dep. asst. sec. for legislation, asst. to sec. spl. projects HEW, 1975-77; mem. Mich. Organized Crime Commn., 1980-81; gov.'s ofcl. liaison with U.S. Consumer Product Safety Commn., 1977-81; chmn. Mich. Gov.'s Consumer Protection and Regulatory Cabinet, 1977-81; dir. Mich. Dept. Licensing and Regulation, 1977-81; sec. 3d Congl. Dist. Republican Com., 1983-85; racing commr. State of Mich., Plymouth, 1982—; vis. adj. prof. Lymann Briggs and Justin Morrill Colls., Mich. State U.; vis. adj. prof. pub. adminstrn. program Western Mich. U. Contbr. articles on horseracing to Hoofbeats mag. Chmn. campaign state employees div. Capital area United Way, 1979-80, cancer drive, 1981. Recipient Disting. Service award Mich. Agrl. Conf., 1972; named 1 of 5 Outstanding Young Men of Mich., Mich. Jaycees, 1974. Mem. SAR, Alpha Zeta. Presbyterian. Club: Princeton of Mich. (treas.). Home: PO Box 30017 101 S Pine St Lansing MI 48909 Office: Mich Office Racing Commr 485 S Main St Plymouth MI 48170

BALLER, ROBERT STUART, ophthalmologist; b. Lincoln, Nebr., Apr. 26, 1936. B.A., U. Ill., 1957, B.S., 1959, M.D., 1961. Diplomate Am. Bd. Ophthalmology and Otolaryngology. Intern, U. Iowa, Iowa City, 1961-62, resident in ophthalmology, 1962-65; practice medicine specializing in ophthalmology, Normal, Ill., 1966—; clin. assoc. U. Ill. Coll. Medicine, 1973-85; mem. staff Mennonite Hosp., Bloomington, Ill., Brokaw Hosp., Normal, St. Joseph's Hosp., Bloomington; lectr. in field. Contbr. articles to profl. publs. Med. adviser Planned Parenthood, Bloomington-Normal, 1975-76; mem. adminstrv. bd. Calvary Methodist Ch., Bloomington-Normal, 1975-76; mem. adv. bd. Children and Family Services, Bloomington-Normal, 1976-79. Served to lt. comdr. USN, 1966-68. Fellow ACS; mem. Am. Acad. Ophthalmology and Otolaryngology, Ill. Assn. Ophthalmology (pres. 1976), Ill. Soc. Ophthalmology and Otolaryngology, Ophthalmic Photographer's Soc., Internat. Eye Found., AMA, David Kelman Research Found., Pan-Am. Assn. Ophthalmology, Am. Intraocular Implant Soc., Royal Soc. Medicine (affiliate mem.), Keratorefractive Soc., Hawaiian Eye Found. (treas. 1983-85), Alpha Kappa Kappa, Omega Beta Pi. Home: 24 Country Club Pl Bloomington IL 61701 Office: 108 Boeykens Pl Normal IL 61761

BALLIN, ANDREW RICHARD, oral and maxillofacial surgeon; b. Mpls., Aug. 24, 1948; s. Henry M. and Natalie (Mahoff) B.; m. Sharon Ann Haller, Oct. 22, 1983. B.A., U. Minn., 1971, B.S., 1971, D.D.S., 1973. Diplomate Am. Bd. Oral and Maxillofacial Surgery. Intern U. Wash., Seattle, 1973-74; resident U. Minn., Mpls., 1974-77; practice dentistry specializing in oral and maxillofacial surgery, Duluth, Minn., 1977-80, Mpls., 1980—; staff mem. Fairview Hosp., Abbott-Northwestern Hosp., Met. Med. Ctr. Staff mem. Union Gospel Mission Clinic, St. Paul, 1971—; den leader, asst. cubmaster Viking council Boy Scouts Am., 1984—. Recipient Am. Acad. Oral Pathology award, 1973; fellow in cytogenetics U. Minn., 1971, 72. Mem. Minn. Dental Assn., Mpls. Dist. Dental Soc., Am. Dental Assn., Minn. Soc. Oral and Maxillofacial Surgeons, Twin City Oral Surgery Study Club, Nat. Dental Honor Soc., U. Minn. Alumni Assn., Omicron Kappa Upsilon. Republican. Russian Orthodox. Office: 1531 Med Arts Bldg 825 Nicollet Mall Minneapolis MN 55402

BALLOU, WILLIAM EUGENE, retail executive; b. Lake Preston, S.D., Jan. 7, 1941; s. Charles Sprague and Myrtle Henrietta (Mydland) B.; m. Ila Ann Boilesen, July 16, 1948; children—Carmin Dee, Aaron Andrew, Isaac Nathan. Student Luth. Bible Sem., 1963-64, Ind. Luth. Sem., 1967-68. Dept. head Billy Graham Assn., Mpls., 1963-68; sales rep. Wm. Eerdman Pub., Grand Rapids, Mich., 1968-70; office mgr. Word of Life Inc., Schroon Lake, Nebr., 1970-73; pres., mgr. The Solid Rock Inc., Kearney, Nebr., 1973—; bd. dirs. Retail Merchants Assn., Lincoln, Nebr., 1980—; bd. dirs., 2nd v.p. Christian Booksellers Assn. Internat., Colorado Springs, Colo., 1982—. Bd. dirs. Citadel Bible Coll., Ozark, Ark., 1980—; chmn. Buffalo County Republican Party, Nebr., 1980-82, Downtown Improvement Bd., Kearney, 1984—. Recipient Bookselling award Tyndale House Pub., 1979. Mem. Kearney C. of C. (bd. dirs. 1981-83). Republican. Mem. Evangelical Ch. Club: Gideon Internat. Lodge: Rotary. Avocation: yo-yoer. Office: The Solid Rock Inc 2010 Central Ave Kearney NE 68847

BALM, DARLINE DAWN MILLER, marketing promotion coordinator; b. Marshall, Minn., Dec. 16, 1933; d. Russell Neil and Laura Esther (Seiler) M.; m. Thomas Ree Balm, Apr. 15, 1954 (div. Dec. 1981); children—Stephen Paul, Jonathon Mark, Brian Scott, Michelle Dawn. B.A., Westmar Coll., 1954; M.A., U. North Iowa, 1968; postgrad., State U. Iowa, 1977-79. Cert. tchr., Iowa. Tchr. Pub. Sch., Lisle, Ill., 1954-55, Allamakee High Sch., Lansing, Iowa, 1961-63, Dysart-Geneseo Sch., Dysart, Iowa, 1964-69; English instr. Westmar Coll., LeMars, Iowa, 1970-76; sec. Wesley Found., Iowa City, 1978-79; promotion adminstr. Control-o-fax- Corp., Waterloo, Iowa, 1980-81, promotion coordinator, 1981—. Pres. LWV, Black Hawk-Bremer Counties, 1983-85; vice chmn. Dist. Council on Ministries United Meth. Ch., Waterloo, 1984—; chmn. nominating com. Council on Ministries United Meth. Ch., Iowa conf., 1984—. Mem. AAUW. Democrat. Avocations: reading; piano; biking; travel; theater. Home: 209 Pearl St Cedar Falls IA 50613 Office: Control-o-fax Corp 3070 W Airline Hwy Waterloo IA 50704

BALMER, ROBERT THEODORE, mechanical engineering educator, researcher; b. Chelsea, Mich., Nov. 26, 1938; s. Homer Theodore and Elsie Amelia (Horne) B.; m. Mary Anne Sorensen, Nov. 4, 1961; children—Christine Anne, Robert Lance, Theodore Austin. B.S.E. in Mech. Engring., U. Mich., 1961, M.S.E. in Mech. Engring., 1963, B.S.E. in Engring Math., 1964; Sc.D. in Mech. Engring., U. Va., 1968. Registered profl. engr., Wis. Engr. Bettis Atomic Power Lab., Pitts., 1961-62; research engr. E.I. duPont, Waynesboro, Va., 1964-68; asst. prof. U. Wis.-Milw., 1969-72, assoc. prof. mech. engring., 1972-79, prof. mech. engring., 1979—, engring. research coordinator, 1984—; vis. prof. NATO, U. Naples, Italy, 1968-69. Contbr. articles on mech. engring. to profl. jours. Patentee chem. to mech. energy converter, 1973. Com. mem. Lakefront Festival of Arts, Milw., 1983. Recipient Teetor award Soc. Automotive Engrs., 1961, Eminent Engr. award Tau Beta Pi, 1981; numerous research grants NSF and Nat. Inst. Aging; 1970—. Mem. Am. Soc. Engring. Edn., Soc. Rheology, AAAS, Sigma Xi. Methodist. Avocation: history of Am. tech.

BALSBAUGH, EDWARD ULMONT, JR., entomology educator; b. Harrisburg, Pa., Jan. 12, 1933; s. Edward U. Sr. and Margaret Irene (Haas) B.; m. Karen Elaine Hofer, July 7, 1968; children—Julie Ann, Daniel Edward. B.S. in Biology, Lebanon Valley Coll., 1955; M.S. in Entomology, Pa. State U., 1961; Ph.D. in Entomology, Auburn U., 1966. Entomologist, Pa. Dept. Agrl., Harrisburg, 1958-62; from asst. prof. to assoc. prof. S.D. State U., Brookings, 1965-76; assoc. prof. entomology N.D. State U., Fargo, N.D., 1976-83, prof., 1983—; cons. in field. Author: Genealogy, History, 1983. Contbr. articles to profl. jours. Served with U.S. Army, 1955-57. Mem. Coleopterists' Soc., Kans. Entomology Soc., Entomology Soc. Am., N.D. Acad. Sci., Sigma Xi (pres. 1974-75), Gamma Sigma Delta (pres. 1972-73), Beta Beta Beta. Republican. Methodist. Club: Edgewood Men's (Fargo) (sec.-treas. 1979-80). Lodge: Kiwanis (chmn. 1984—). Avocations: golf; travel; painting. Home: 3208 N Elm St Fargo ND 58102 Office: N D State U Dept Entomology Fargo ND 58103

BALTES, KENNETH GEORGE, consultant; b. Melrose, Minn., Sept. 6, 1942; s. Ralph H. and Mae Rose (Primus) B.; m. Nancy Mashie, Aug. 21, 1965 (div. 1975); children—Christopher, Jennifer; m. Dorothy Ann Elion, July 30, 1977; children—Rebecca, Jesse. B.S.B., U. Minn., 1968, M.A. in Ednl. Adminstrn., 1975, Ph.D. in Ednl. Adminstrn., 1977. Asst. dir. adminstrn. U. Minn., Mpls., 1975-77, asst. to chief fin. officer, 1977-78; asst. prof. Coll. St. Thomas, St. Paul, 1979-80; v.p. Munsingwear, Mpls., 1981-82; pres. Baltes/Elion Inc., St. Paul, 1975—; cons. Minn. Opera Co., st.Paul, 1982-85, Micro Technology Edn. Ctrs., Mpls., 1983-84. Treas., Town House Villages of Arden Hills, St. Paul, 1982—; mem. fin. com. Newman Ctr., U. Minn., 1972-76; mem. coordinating com. St. Paul Campus Ministries, 1971-75; bd. dirs. Minn. Opera Co., St. Paul, 1985—. Served with USN, 1960-63. Mem. Assn. Computing Machinery. Club: Greenway Athletic (Mpls.). Avocations: painting wildlife; drawing; skiing; hunting; fishing. Home: 9 Ironwood Ln North Oaks MN 55110

BALTHASER, LINDA IRENE, university administrator; b. Kokomo, Ind., Feb. 25, 1939; d. Earl Isaac and Evelyn Pauline (Troyer) Showalter; B.S. magna cum laude, Ind. Central U., 1961; M.S., Ind. U., 1962; m. Kenneth James Balthaser, June 1, 1963. Tchr. bus. edn. Southport High Sch., Indpls., 1962-63; sec., adminstrv. sec. Office of Pres., Ind. U., Bloomington, 1963-66; with Ind. U.-Purdue U., Fort Wayne, Ind., 1969—, asst. to dean Arts and Letters, 1970—, founding co-dir. Weekend Coll., 1979-80. Bd. dirs. Associated Chs. Fort Wayne, 1980. Ind. Conf. N. Evang. United Brethren Ch. scholar, 1957-61. Mem. Fort Wayne-Allen County Hist. Assn., Embassy Theatre Found., Fort Wayne Mus. Art, Historic Fort Wayne, Fort Wayne Zool. Soc., Nat. Assn. Women Deans, Adminstrs. and Counselors, Am. Assn. Univ. Adminstrs., Internat. Platform Assn., AAUW, Delta Pi Epsilon, Phi Alpha Epsilon, Alpha Chi, Mensa. Mem. United Ch. of Christ. Club: Univ. Women's (pres. 1968-69). Home: 2917 Hazelwood Ave Fort Wayne IN 46805 Office: 2101 Coliseum Blvd E Fort Wayne IN 46805

BALTHROPE, JACQUELINE MOREHEAD, educator, author, administrator, consultant; b. Phila.; d. Jack Walton and Minnie Jessie (Martin) Morehead; B.S. in Edn., Central State U., Wilberforce, Ohio, 1949; M.A. in Edn., Case Western Res. U., 1959; m. Robert Granville Balthrope, Sr.; children—Robert Granville, Yvonne Gertrude, Robin Bernice. Elem. master tchr. Cleve. Bd. Edn., 1950-65, leadership devel. tchr., 1965-69, asst. prin. elem. sch., 1969-77, prin. elem. sch., 1977-80; ednl. cons., 1980—. Recipient numerous civic, ednl. religious and social rewards. Mem. AAUW, Cleve. Council Adminstrs. and Suprs., Elem. Sch. Prins., Internat. Reading Assn., Phi Delta Kappa Frat., Delta Kappa Gamma, Alpha Kappa Mu, Zeta Sigma Pi, Pi Lambda Theta, Alpha Kappa Alpha, Phi Delta Kappa, Eta Phi Beta, Gamma Phi Delta (vol., tutor). Methodist. Clubs: Top Ladies of Distinction (local founder, past pres.), Jr. League, Sen Mer Rek, Zen Mer Rekh. Author: African Boy Comes to

America, 1960, sequal, 1960. Contbr. articles to profl. jours., mags., newspapers. Address: 16220 Delrey Ave Cleveland OH 44128

BALTIS, WALTER STANLEY, property management executive; b. Poland, Sept. 19, 1904; s. Matthew and Amelia (Adaszkiewicz) Baltruszajtis; brought to U.S., 1910, naturalized, 1932; student parochial sch., Chgo.; m. Marie Rita Nexdlik, June 22, 1929; children—Phyllis (Mrs. L. James Paul), Joan (Mrs. Joan Lindstrom), Bonnie (Mrs. Robert N. Hutchison), Rita (Mrs. Ralph E. Sheese, Jr.). Sales mgr. Cicero Motor Sales (Ill.), 1926-30; owner Arrow Motor Sales, 1930-35; mgr. Stastny Builders, Berwyn, Ill., 1936-41; pres. Baltis Built Homes, Inc., Westchester, Ill., 1941—, First Fed. Savs. and Loan Assn. of Westchester, 1953-60. Trustee Met. San. Dist. of Greater Chgo., 1958-64, pres. credit union, 1960-62. Mem. Cermak Rd. Business men's Assn. (pres. 1932-34). Democrat. Roman Catholic. Elk. Club: Golf (Riverside, Ill.). Home: 306 Downing Rd Riverside IL 60546 Office: 10529 Cermak Rd Westchester IL 60153

BALTZ, SYLVIA ANN, educator; b. Mobile County, Ala., Feb. 10, 1938; d. Lawrence Monroe and Rosa Mae (Havard) Clayton; m. Howard Burl Baltz, June 23, 1967; children—Debra, Geoffrey, Jami. B.S., U. So. Miss., 1959, M.S., 1960. Instr. Tyler (Tex.) Jr. Coll., 1960-62, U. Tex., Austin, 1962-68; assoc. prof. bus. edn., coordinator dept. St. Louis Community Coll. at Forest Park, St. Louis, 1969—. Mem. Nat. Bus. Edn. Assn., North Central Bus. Edn. Assn., Mo. Bus. Edn. Assn., Am. Vocat. Assn., Mo. Vocat. Assn., St. Louis Bus. Educators Assn., Assn. Info. Systems Profls. (dir.), Profl. Secs. Internat. (assoc., exec. adv. bd.). Mem. United Ch. of Christ.

BALZEKAS, STANLEY ROBERT, JR., automobile dealership executive, museum administrator; b. Chgo., Oct. 8, 1924; s. Stanley Robert and Emily (Gregorow) B.; m. Irene E. Radvilas, June 10, 1953 (dec. 1976); children—Stanley Robert III, Robert A., Carole Rene. B.A., DePaul U., 1950, M.A., 1951. Pres., owner Balzekas Motor Sales, Inc., Chgo., 1945—; owner operator Archer Advt., Chgo., 1976—; pres. Balzekas Mus. Lithuanian Culture, Chgo., 1966—. Bd. dirs. Ill. Art Alliance, NCCJ, Ill. Consultation Ethnicity in Edn., 1975, Ukrainian Inst. Modern Art, 1984—; commr. Commn. Human Relations, 1978; mem. City of Chgo. Bd. Health; sec. bd. dirs. Chgo. Pub. Library, 1970-82. Served as staff sgt. U.S. Army, 1943-45, ETO. Decorated Bronze Star. Mem. Ill. Library Assn., Stephan A. Douglas Assn. Club: Literary (Chgo.). Avocations: armor; antiques. Office: Balzekas Motor Sales Inc 4030 Archer Ave Chicago IL 60632

BAMBAKIDIS, GUST, physics educator; b. Akron, Ohio, June 22, 1936; s. Nicholas and Joy (Moskou) B.; m. Elli Montiadou, Apr. 24, 1968; children—Nicholas, Steven, Evan. B.Sc., U. Akron, 1958; M.Sc., Case Inst. Tech., 1963, Ph.D., 1966. Research physicist NASA-Lewis Research Ctr., Cleve., 1966-74; research assoc. Observatoire de Paris, Meudon, France, 1974-75; assoc. scientist NASA-Ames Research Ctr., Moffett Field, Calif., 1975-76; prof. physics Wright State U., Dayton, Ohio, 1977—; dir. NATO Advanced Study Inst., Rhodes, Greece, summer 1980. Editor: Metal Hydrides, 1981. Contbr. articles to profl. jours. Faculty research participant U.S. Air Force, 1982; sr. postdoctoral research assoc. NRC, 1983—. Mem. Am. Phys. Soc., AAAS, N.Y. Acad. Sci., Phys. Soc. Greece, Internat. Assn. Hydrogen Energy. Greek Orthodox. Lodge: Order of Ahepa. Office: Physics Dept Wright State U Dayton OH 45435

BAMBERGER, DAVID, opera executive; b. Albany, N.Y., Oct. 14, 1940; s. Bernard J. and Ethel K. Bamberger; m. Carola Beral, June 8, 1965; 1 son, Steven B. B.A., Swarthmore Coll., 1962; (postgrad. U. Paris (France), 1961, Yale U., 1963. Mem. directing staff N.Y.C. Opera, 1966-70; guest dir. Nat. Opera Chile, 1970, Cin. Opera, 1968, Augusta Opera (Ga.), 1970—, Pitts. Opera, 1971, 76, 81, Columbus Opera (Ohio); gen. mgr., artistic dir. Cleve. Opera, 1976—; artistic dir. Toledo Opera Assn., 1983-85. Bd. dirs. Opera Am. Author Jewish history textbooks; contbr. articles to Opera News. Office: Cleve Opera 1438 Euclid Ave Cleveland OH 44115

BAMBERGER, GEORGE, professional baseball executive. Mgr. Milw. Brewers. Office: Milw Brewers Milwaukee County Stadium Milwaukee WI 53214*

BANACH, ART JOHN, graphic art exec.; b. Chgo., May 22, 1931; s. Vincent and Anna (Zajac) B.; grad. Art. Inst. of Chgo., 1955; pupil painting studies Mrs. Melin, Chgo.; m. Loretta A. Nolan, Oct. 15, 1966; children—Heather Anne, Lynnea Joan. Owner, dir. Art J. Banach Studios, 1949—, cartoon syndicate for newspapers, house organs and advt. functions, 1954—, owned and operated advt. agy., 1954-56, feature news and picture syndicate, distbn. U.S. and fgn. countries. Dir. Speculators S Fund. Recipient award 1st Easter Seal contest Ill. Assn. Crippled, Inc., 1949. Chgo. Pub. Sch. Art Soc. Scholar. Mem. Artist's Guild Chgo., Am Mgmt. Assn., Chgo. Assn. of Commerce and Industry, Chgo. Federated Advt. Club, Am. Mktg. Assn., Internat. Platform Assn., Chgo. Advt. Club, Chgo. Soc. Communicating Arts. Clubs: Columbia Yacht, Advertising Executives; Art Directors (Chgo.). Address: 1076 Leahy Circle E Des Plaines IL 60016

BANAS, EMIL MIKE, physicist, educator; b. East Chicago, Ind., Dec. 5, 1921; s. John J. and Rose M. (Valcicak) B.; ed. Ill. Benedictine Coll., 1940-43; B.A. (U.S. Rubber fellow), U. Notre Dame, 1954, Ph.D., 1955; m. Margaret Fagyas, Oct. 9, 1948; children—Mary K., Barbara A. Instr. math. and physics Ill. Benedictine Coll., Lisle, 1946-48, adj. faculty mem., 1971-82, trustee, 1959-61; with Civil Service, State of Ind., Hammond, 1948-50; lectr. physics Purdue U., Hammond, 1955-60; staff research physicist Amoco Corp., Naperville, Ill., 1955-82; cons., 1983—. Served with USNR, 1943-46. Mem. Ill. Benedictine Coll. Alumni Assn. (dir. hon., named alumnus of yr., 1965, pres. 1959-60), Sigma Pi Sigma. Roman Catholic. Clubs: Soc. of Procopians. Contbr. articles to sci. jours. Home: 8 Huntington Circle W Naperville IL 60540

BANAS, STANLEY ROBERT, manufacturing company executive; b. Chgo., May 3, 1927; s. Stanley John and Agnes Pearl (Wilczewski) B.; m. Dorothy Helen Skaja, Sept. 11, 1954. children—Veronica, Stanley John, Andrea, Michael Francis, James, Mary Agnes. B.S. in Mech. Engring., Purdue U., 1950. Salesman, Stanley Spring Co., Chgo., 1950-53, v.p., 1953-54, pres., 1954—; dir. Gladstone Norwood Bank. Bd. dirs. Regina High Sch., Wilmette, Ill. Served with USCG, 1945-46. Mem. Spring Mfrs. Inst. (pres. 1974-76; Spring award 1974, 76), ASME. Roman Catholic. Club: Ridgemoor Country (pres. 1979—). Lodge: KC. Home: 430 Chapel Hill Ln Northfield IL 60093 Office: Stanley Spring & Stamping Corp 5050 W Foster Ave Chicago IL 60630

BANAS, THOMAS PAUL, public affairs executive; b. Detroit, Apr. 15, 1937; s. Ted J. and Pearl (Danilowicz) B.; Ph.B., U. of Detroit, 1958; M.B.A., Wayne State U., 1964; m. Carolyn Ann Burch, May 23, 1958; children—Scott, Amy, Polly. Gen. tech. aide City of Detroit, 1958-60; market research asst. Micromatic Hone Corp., Detroit, 1960; copywriter Ruben Advt., Detroit, 1960-61; promotion writer The Detroit News, 1961-63; publicity mgr. Sta. WWJ AM-FM-TV, 1963-67; sr. writer G. & D Communications Inc., Detroit, 1967; asst. promotion mgr., Sta. WWJ AM-FM-TV, 1967-73, community relations dir., 1973-76; sr. v.p., P/R Asso., Inc., Detroit, 1976-78; exec. dir. Am. Lung Assn. S.E. Mich., Detroit, 1978—. Instr. Highland Park Coll., 1968-70, U. of Detroit, 1970. Bd. dirs. Royal Oak Boys' Club, 1974—; bd. exec. com. Southeastern Mich. chpt. ARC, 1973-79; mem. exec. bd. Met. Detroit chpt. Nat. Found. March of Dimes, 1976-79, Comprehensive Health Planning Council S.E. Mich., 1973—, Oakland County Mental Health Bd., 1976-82, Pleasant Ridge City Commn., 1973-77; del. S.E. Mich. Council Govts., 1973-77, Council on Regional Devel., 1973-81, Council on Environ. Strategy, 1973—; coordinator Internat. Freedom Festival, 1977. Recipient Mich. Vol. Leadership award, 1972, Spl. Tribute Mich. Ho. Reps., 1973. Mem. Pub. Relations Soc. of Am., Am. Soc. Laws and Medicine, Am. Mgmt. Assn. Assn. Execs. Met. Clubs: Detroit Press, Economic, Adcraft (Detroit). Home: 9 Wellesley Ave Pleasant Ridge MI 48069 Office: 28 W Adams St Detroit MI 48226

BANASIK, ROBERT CASMER, nursing home administrator, educator; b. Detroit, Dec. 8, 1942; s. Casmer John and Lucille Nathalie (Siperek) B.; B.S. in Mech. Engring., Wayne State U., 1965; M.S. in Indsl. Engring., Tex. Tech. Coll., 1967; M.B.A., Ohio State U., 1973, Ph.D., 1974; m. Jacqueline Mae Miller, Aug. 28, 1965; (div. 1985); children—Robert John, Marcus Alan, Jason Andrew; m. Barbara Jean Willows, Oct. 12, 1985. Mgmt. systems engr. Riverside Methodist Hosp., Columbus, Ohio, 1970, 71; owner, mgmt. systems cons. Banasik Assos., Columbus, 1972—; dir. mgmt. systems engring. Grant Hosp., Columbus, 1973-78; owner, mgr. RMJ Investment Enterprises, Columbus, 1975-85; pres. Omnilife Systems, Inc., Columbus, 1979—, RMJ Mgmt., Inc., 1983-85. Bryant Health Ctr., Inc., Ironton, Ohio, 1983—, Equity Mgmt., 1985—; owner Omnivend, 1985—; adminstr. Patterson Health Center, Columbus, 1980—; asst. prof. Capital U. Grad. Sch. Adminstrn., Columbus, 1973-79, assoc. prof., 1979—; dir. Asset Data Systems, Columbus. Pres. bd. dirs. United Cerebral Palsy Franklin County, 1979-80; mem. founding bd. Support Resources, Inc., 1978-85; bd. dirs. Transp. Resources, Inc., 1979-80. Registered profl. engr., Ohio; lic. nursing home adminstr., Ohio. Mem. Am. Hosp. Assn., Nat. Soc. Profl. Engrs. (dir. Franklin County chpt. 1976-77), Ohio Soc. Profl. Engrs., Am. Inst. Decision Scis., Am. Coll. Health Care Adminstrs., Sigma Xi, Beta Gamma Sigma, Alpha Pi Mu, Phi Kappa Phi, Alpha Kappa Psi. Republican. Lutheran. Editor: Tropics in Hospital Material Management, 1978-84; contbr. articles to profl. jours. Office: 1207 N High St Suite 300 Columbus OH 43201

BANDA, ARPAD FREDERIC, finance and economics educator; b. N.Y.C., June 16, 1928; s. John and Terecia (Varga) B.; B.S. in Social Scis., City Coll. N.Y., 1950; M.B.A., N.Y. U., 1956, Ph.D., 1964, C.F.A., 1977. Instr. econs. Milw.-Downer Coll., 1959-61, Upsala Coll., 1961-62; asst. prof. econs., fin. U. Hartford (Conn.), 1963-66, asso. prof., 1966-68, chmn. dept., 1966-67; assoc. prof. fin. U. Akron (O.), 1968-71, prof., 1971—, head dept., 1970-73, 77-78; pres. C.P. Banda & Co. Inc., registered investment advisors, 1981—. Chief elder Synod of Free Hungarian Reformed Ch., 1983—; elder Free Hungarian Reformed Ch. Akron; pres. Hungarian Found., Inc.; v.p. Lorantffy Care Ctr., Inc.; bd. dirs. Am. Hungarian Fedn., 1977-79, 83—. Mem. Fin. Mgmt. Assn. (coordinating editor jour. 1970-75), Am., Ohio (pres. 1972-73), Eastern (dir. 1975-78) fin. assns. Home: 2299 Winter Pkwy Apt 295 Cuyahoga Falls OH 44221 Office: 302 E Buchtel Ave Akron OH 44325

BANDT, CARL LEE, periodontist; b. Wisconsin Rapids, Wis., Mar. 22, 1938; s. Lawrence E. and Ethel Marie (Schultz) B.; m. Mary Virginia Rice, June 22, 1963; children—Laura Maria, Mary Louise, Daniel Michael, Matthew Phillip. Student, U. Wis.-Madison, 1956-57; B.S., U. Minn., 1960, D.D.S., 1962, M.S.D., 1966, M.S., 1968. Instr. U. Minn., Mpls., 1966-68, assoc. prof., 1968-74, prof. dentistry, chmn. dept., 1978—. Contbr. articles to profl. pubs. Named Prof. of Yr., U. Minn. Sch. Dentistry, 1972; recipient periodontal research awards. Fellow Internat. Coll. Dentists, Am. Coll. Dentists; mem. ADA, Am. Acad. Periodontology, Internat. Assn. Dental Research. Office: U Minn Dept Periodontology 515 Delaware St SE Minneapolis MN 55455

BANDY, IRENE GESA, state education ofcl.; b. Montgomery, W.Va., Aug. 30, 1940; d. Ernest and Gesa (Koehne) Wolff; B.S.Ed., Ohio U., 1962; M.A., Eastern Ky. U., 1967; Ph.D., Ohio State U., 1979; 1 son, Nicholas. Tchr., pub. schs., Gainesville, Fla., 1962-64, Cin., 1964-65; guidance supr. Eastern Ky. U., Richmond, 1967-68; counselor, jr. high sch., Napoleon, Ohio, 1968-73; cons. Ohio Div. Guidance and Testing, Columbus, 1973-76, asst. dir., 1977-79, exec. dir. adminstrn., 1980-82, asst. supt., 1982—. Mem. Am. Personnel and Guidance Assn., (chmn. Midwest region 1977-79, dir. 1979-82), Assn. Counselor Educators and Suprs. (co editor Newsletter 1976-77), Am. Sch. Counselors Assn., Am. Assn. Sch. Adminstrs., Buckeye Assn. Sch. Adminstrs., Phi Delta Kappa (pres. Ohio State U. chpt. 1981-82). Home: 6678 Willow Grove Ln Dublin OH 43017 Office: 65 Front St S Room 808 Columbus OH 43215

BANE, KEITH JAMES, manufacturing executive, lawyer; b. Chgo., May 20, 1939; s. Joseph Kenneth and Frances Carol (Wachewicz) B.; m. Kathleen Margaret Coffey, Dec. 15, 1962; children—Kimberly Ann, Kristen Marie, Karayn Lynn. B.S., Bradley U., 1961; J.D., Northwestern U.-Ill., 1968. Bar: Ill. 1968, U.S. Dist. Ct. (no. dist.) Ill. 1968. Ptnr. Kirkland & Ellis, Chgo., 1968-73; v.p. Motorola, Inc., Schaumburg, Ill., 1973—; dir. Western Acadia, Chgo., 1970-76. Mem. planning commn. City of Rolling Meadows, Ill., 1972-76; trustee Bradley U., Peoria, Ill., 1983—. Served to lt. USN, 1962-65. Decorated U.S. Navy Commendation medal, 1964. Roman Catholic.

BANERJEE, SAMARENDRANATH, orthopaedic surgeon; b. Calcutta, India, July 12, 1932; s. Haridhone and Nihar Bala (Mukherjee) B.; M.B. B.S., R.G. Kar Med. Coll., Calcutta, 1957; postgrad. U. Edinburgh, 1965-66; m. Hima Ganguly, Mar. 1977; 1 son, Rabindranath. Intern R.G. Kar Med. Coll., 1956-58; resident in surgery Bklyn. Jewish Hosp. Med. Center, 1958-60, Brookdale Med. Center, Bklyn., 1960-61, Jersey City Med. Center, 1961-63; research fellow Hosp. for Sick Children, U. Toronto (Ont., Can.), 1968-69; practice medicine specializing in orthopedics, Sault Ste. Marie, Ont.; past pres. med. staff, chmn. exec. com. Gen. Hosp., Sault Ste. Marie, chief dept. surgery, mem. med. adv. com., 1980—; cons. orthopaedic surgeon Gen. Hosp., Plummer Meml. Hosp., Crippled Children Center, Ministry Nat. Health and Welfare, Dept. Vets. Adminstrn.; civilian orthopaedic surgeon to 44th Div. Armed Forces Base Hosp., Kaduna, Nigeria, 1969. Trustee Gen. Hosp., Sault Ste. Marie, 1975-76. Miss Betsy Burton Meml. fellow, 1963-64. Fellow Royal Coll. Surgeons Can., A.C.S., Royal Coll. Surgeons Edinburgh; mem. Can. Orthopaedic Assn., Ont. Orthopaedic Assn., Can. Med. Assn. Home: 50 Alworth Pl Sault Sainte Marie ON P6B 5W5 Canada Office: 125-955 Queen St East Sault Sainte Marie ON Canada

BANEY, JAMES RANDALL, insurance company executive; b. Columbus, Ohio, July 16, 1950; s. Ralph James and Vonna Louise (Webb) B.; m. Jonda Lynn Steinhauser, Aug. 6, 1977; children—Kristin Patricia, Stephen Randall. B.S., Ohio State U., 1972; M.B.A., U. Dayton, 1978. Securities analyst Heritage Securities, Inc., Columbus, 1972-77; sr. securities portfolio mgr. Nationwide Mut. Ins. Co., Columbus, 1977—. Deacon, elder Central Coll. Presbyn. Ch., U.S.A., Westerville, Ohio, 1967. Fellow, Fin. Analysts Fedn. (Columbus Soc.). Home: 108 Daniel Dr Westerville OH 43081 Office: Nationwide Mutual Ins Co One Nationwide Plaza Investments 33T Columbus OH 43216

BANGERT, CHARLES JEFFRIES, computer graphics administrator; b. Fargo, N.D., Aug. 6, 1938; s. Harold Wallace and Mary Kathryn (Jeffries) B.; m. Colette Stuebe, June 9, 1959. B.A., U. N.D., 1961; student Harvard Coll., 1955-59, Chgo. Art Inst., 1959; postgrad U. Kans., 1965-70. With Computing Ctr. U. Kans., Lawrence, 1965—, applications cons., 1978-79, supr. graphics, 1979—. Author: (with William Diedrich) Articulation Learning, 1980; contbr. articles to profl. jours. Mem. Assn. Computing Machinery, Am. Statis. Assn., IEEE Computer Soc. Episcopalian. Home: 721 Tennesse Lawrence KS 66044 Office: Acad Computing Services U Kans Lawrence KS 66045

BANKER, CAROL ANN GOTTSCHALK, medical technologist; b. Milw., Jan. 16, 1935; d. Earl Irving and Bernice Marcella (Spehn) Gottschalk; m. Donald James Banker, May 28, 1966; children—John C., Aaron P. B.A., Alverno Coll., 1957; M.S., U. Wis.-Milw., 1974. Cert. clin. lab. scientist Nat. Certifying Agy. for Med. Lab. Personnel. Supr. chemistry lab. St. Mary's Hosp., Milw., 1958-64, St. Luke's Hosp., 1964-68; supr. research and devel. St. Luke's Hosp., Milw., 1968-70, project coordinator, 1970-80, quality control coordinator, 1980—; guest lectr. U. Wis.-Milw. Sch. Med. Tech., 1982-83; liaison rep. Am. Soc. Quality Control, biomed. div. to Am. Soc. Med. Technologists, 1976-80; also workshop facilitator. Discussion leader Project Understanding, 1970; mem. sch. bd. St. Gregory the Great Christian Parochial Sch., 1978—, chmn. bd., 1981-83, v.p., 1985-86. Mem. Am. Soc. Med. Technologists, Am. Soc. Quality Control, Wis. Soc. Med. Technologists, Alverno Coll. Alumnae Assn. (v.p. 1961-63, bd. dirs. 1963-65), Am. Assn. Lab. Animal Sci. (assoc. organizer met. Milw. br. 1970, sec. 1970, treas. 1971-72) U. Wis. Alumnae Assn. Author papers in field. Office: 2900 W Oklahoma Ave Milwaukee WI 53215

BANKERT, GARY LOUIS, language arts educator, radio consultant; b. Sandusky, Ohio, May 15, 1944; s. Louis Frank and Dorthy Marie (Majors) B.; m. Carolee Stamper, June 16, 1968; 1 dau., Alexandra. B.F.A., U. Cin., 1966; M.A., Bowling Green State U., 1982. Pub. relations dir. Sta. WCET-TV, Cin., 1963-65; sta. mgr. WFIB Radio, Cin., 1965-66; advt. rep. Sandusky (Ohio) Register, 1966-69; language arts educator Berlin-Milan Schs., Berlin Heights, Ohio, 1969—, athletic dir., 1981—; chmn. Ohio's Search for Consensus, Huron, 1973-74; co-ordinator Ohio's Excellence for Edn., Columbus, 1982-83; lectr. Bowling Green (Ohio) State U., 1982-83. Author: Effects of In-School Peer Tutoring, 1983. Mem. adv. bd. Salvation Army, Erie County, Ohio, 1970-83; pres. Emmanuel United Ch. of Christ, Sandusky, Ohio, 1983. Named Man of Yr., Rho Tau Delta, 1966. Mem. NEA, Ohio Edn. Assn., Ohio Assn. Athletic Dirs., Berlin-Milan Tchrs. Assn. (pres. 1969-83). Republican. Lodge: Lions (festival chmn. 1973) (Huron). Home: RD 1 Valley View Dr Berling Heights OH 44814 Office: Berlin Milan Schs Main St Berlin Heights OH 44814

BANKIT, PAUL, educator; b. Milw., June 16, 1929; s. Joseph and Sally Josephine B.; student engring., U. Wis., 1946-50; B.G.E., U. Nebr., 1960; M.B.A., Mich. State U., 1966, Ph.D., 1972; m. Esther Lilly Halversen, July 8, 1950; children—Eric J., Paula A.; m. Judith Beale Watson, Aug. 9, 1980. Commd. 2d lt., U.S. Army, 1952, advanced through grades to col., 1978; armor unit comdr., Ft. Hood, Tex., 1954-57; aviation officer, Germany, 1957-59; instr. Ft. Rucker, Ala., 1959-60, test pilot, 1961-64; combat pilot, Vietnam, 1966-67; div. chief Combat Devels. Command, Ft. Eustis, Va., 1967-70; comdr. Transp. Engring. Agy., Washington, 1973-76; ret., 1978; prof. mgmt. sci. Mich. State U., East Lansing, 1978-83; chmn. bd., chief exec. officer Midwestern Airlines Inc., Lansing, Mich.; pres. Protec Research, Lansing. Decorated Legion of Merit, Bronze Star, Air Medals; named lectr. of year Army Logistics Mgmt. Center, 1974; recipient achievement award Boy Scouts Am., 1968. Mem. Ops. Research Soc. Am., Am. Mktg. Assn., Acad. Mgmt., Am. Mgmt. Assn. Republican. Lutheran. Club: Masons. Author: Logistics Systems Design, 1972; Logistics Systems Analysis, 1975. Home: 2587 Woodhill Dr Okemos MI 48864 Office: Frandor Sq Suite 105 Lansing MI 48912

BANKS, BEVERLY ANN, former restaurant executive; b. Hammond, Ind., May 26, 1933; d. Dewey Earl and Inez Irene (Clark) Rodkey; student public schs., St. Francisville, Ill.; children—Elizabeth, Gail. Co-owner St. Joe Drive In, St. Joseph, Mo., from 1965; owner, pres., gen. mgr. Henry's Restaurants, including Pyramid Drive In Inc., St. Joseph, 1971-83, Spar Investments Inc., St. Joseph, 1971-83, B.E.V. Foods, Inc., St. Joseph, 1978-83. Named Mrs. Missouri, 1965. Mem. Mo. Restaurant Assn., Nat. Restaurant Assn., St. Joseph C. of C. (diplomat). Methodist. Home and Office: 8 Dunn Dr Saint Joseph MO 64506

BANKS, JAMES DAVID, financial planning consultant; b. Boonville, Mo., Sept. 22, 1951; s. Leon F. and Phyllis J. (Linsey) B.; B.S., U. Mo., 1973; postgrad. Lincoln U., 1975; m. Eileen Biesemeyer, Jan. 8, 1972; children—John David, Daleen Michelle. Asst. cashier First Nat. Bank of Callaway County, Fulton, Mo., 1973-76; securities salesman NIS Fin. Services, Kansas City, Mo., 1976—; group mgr. Ozark Nat. Life Ins. Co., Kansas City, Mo., 1977-78, dist. mgr. for Central Mo., 1979—. Fulton chmn. Jerry Lewis Telethon, 1975. Mem. Fulton Jr. C. of C. (treas. 1974), Nat. Assn. Life Underwriters. Lutheran. Address: 2611 Luan Ct Columbia MO 65203

BANKS, MARTHA JOAN, sampling specialist, consultant; b. Fort Wayne, Ind., Feb. 20, 1947; s. Paul M. and Madelyn I. (Weseman) B. A.B., Manchester Coll., 1969; M.A., U. Chgo., 1984. Math. statistician U.S. Bur. Census, Washington, 1969-73; sampling dir. Nat. Opinion Research Ctr., Chgo., 1973-75; sampling specialist Ctr. for Health Adminstrn. Studies, Chgo., 1975-82; sampling dir. Ctr. for Health Adminstrn. Studies, Chgo., 1982—; election cons. Columbia Broadcasting System, N.Y.C., 1972; cons., Chgo., 1976—. Mem. Am. Statis. Assn., Am. Sociol. Assn.

BANKS, PHILLIP LEE CHRISTOPHER, biometrician; b. Dayton, Ohio, Apr. 26, 1957; s. William Wallace and Sandra Lee (Newsock) Montgomery; m. Christine Elaine Rogers, June 18, 1983. B.S. in Psychology, Ohio State U., 1980, M.S. in Preventive Medicine, 1983. Grad. asst. biostatistician dept. preventive medicine Ohio State U., Columbus, 1981-82; biometrician Kali-Duphar Labs., Inc., Worthington, Ohio, 1982—. Contbr. research papers to profl. jours. Mem. exec. com. Ohio Spl. Olympics, Columbus, 1981. Stadium scholar Ohio State U., 1979. Fellow Royal Statis. Soc.; mem. Am. Statis. Assn. (project team assoc. biopharm. sect. 1984—), Bernoulli Soc., Biometrics Soc., Soc. for Clin. Trials. Democrat. Roman Catholic. Avocations: languages, zymurgy. Office: Kali-Duphar Labs Inc 200 Old Wilson Bridge Rd Worthington OH 43085

BANKS, WILLIAM DRESSEL, publishing executive, book retailer, educator; b. St. Louis, May 3, 1938; s. W. Jack and Louis (Dressel) B.; m. Susan B. Bay, Aug. 19, 1961; children—Kevin, Steve. Grad. Webster High, Webster Groves, Mo., 1956. Student Coll. of Wooster, 1956-57; B.S., Washington U., St. Louis, 1960, B.A., 1960. Salesman, H. J. Heinz, St. Louis, 1960-62; agt. Gen. Am. Life, St. Louis, 1962-70; pres. Impact Books, Inc., Kirkwood, Mo., 1971—; owner, mgr. Successful Life Bookstore, Kirkwood, 1971—; tchr. New Wine Ministries, Kirkwood, 1971—, president, 1973—. Author: Alive Again!, 1977; Ministering to Abortion's Aftermath, 1982. Editor numerous books on religion. Recipient Man of Yr. award Kirkwood C. of C., 1982. Republican. Office: Impact Books Inc 137 W Jefferson Ave Kirkwood MO 63122

BANNER, JOHN GEORGE, lawyer, lecturer; b. Chgo., Feb. 22, 1951; m. Julie Benthaus, June 30, 1979. B.S. in Fin. with honors, U. Ill., 1973; student U. Stirling, Scotland, 1973-74; J.D., Georgetown U., 1977. Bar: Ill. 1977, D.C. 1979, Ohio 1980. Staff asst. U.S. Congress Banking Com., Washington, 1974-77; atty.-advisor Interstate Commerce Commn., 1977-79; corp. legal counsel Ace Doran Hauling & Rigging Co., Cin., 1979—; lectr. bus. law U. Cin., 1980—. Republican precinct exec. Hamilton County Central Com., 1984—. Rotary Found. fellow, 1973-74; Legisl. scholar Ill. Gen. Assembly, 1970-73; recipient Outstanding Sr. award U. Ill., 1973. Mem. Assn. Transp. Practitioners (pres. Ohio Valley chpt. 1984—), ABA, Ohio State Bar Assn., Cin. Bar Assn., Cin. Hist. Soc., U.S. Capitol Hist. Soc. Rep. Roman Catholic. Club: Clifton Meadows. Avocations: Piano; photography. Home: 3470 Whitfield Ave Cincinnati OH 45220 Office: Ace Doran Hauling & Rigging Co 1601 Blue Rock St Cincinnati OH 45223

BANNES, LORENZ THEODORE, construction company executive; b. St. Louis, Oct. 24, 1935; s. Lawrence Anthony and Louise Clair (Vollet) B.; B.S. in Civil Engring., St. Louis U., 1957; m. Janet Ann Bruening, Aug. 10, 1957; children—Stephen W., Michael F., Timothy L. From project engr. to exec. v.p. Gamble Constrn. Co. Inc., St. Louis, 1960-69, pres., 1969-72; founder, pres. Bannes-Shaughnessy, Inc., St. Louis, 1972-77, chmn. bd., 1977—; dir., v.p. St. Louis Constrn. Manpower Corp., 1977—. Tchr. civil engring. dept. St. Louis U., 1969—; tchr. contracting and concrete methods U. Mo. Extension Center, 1970—; tchr. constrn. mgmt. Grad. Engring. Center, U. Mo., St. Louis, 1968—, Sch. Architecture, Washington U., St. Louis, 1974—; lectr. So. Ill. U., Edwardsville, 1982; tchr. Nat. Assn. Women in Constrn., 1973. Mem. adv. com. in civil engring. Florissant Valley Community Coll.; mem. adv. com. constrn. tech. Jefferson Coll. Chmn. trustees Aspenhof, 1973; adv. bd. Little Sisters of Poor, 1975—; nat. bd. Living and Learning, Jesuit edn. program for disadvantaged; mem. Human Rights Commn., Archdiocese of St. Louis, 1980—; chmn. bd. trustees Christian Bros. Coll. High Sch., St. Louis, 1980—. Served with USAF, 1957-60. Recipient Alumni Merit award St. Louis U., 1972; named Man of Yr., Exec. Club of St. Louis U., 1978; named to Hall of Fame, Christian Bros. Coll. High Sch., 1981. Mem. Nat. Soc. Profl. Engrs. (recipient Young Engr. of Year award 1971), Mo. Soc. Profl. Engrs. (chmn. Y.E. com.), Concrete Council of St. Louis (pres. 1972-73, Distinguished Service award 1973), Assoc. Gen. Contractors Am. (Nat. Build/Am. award 1973), Assoc. Gen. Contractors St. Louis (Chmn. of Year 1973), ASCE (nat. com. constrn. research 1973-74), Am. Soc. Concrete Constructors (nat. bd. dirs. 1982—), Young Presidents Orgn., Engrs. Club St. Louis (dir. 1975), Nat. Assn. Women in Constrn. (hon., Disting. service award 1974), Xe Chi Epsilon (chpt. hon. mem. 1980). Home: 1345 Cragwold Rd Kirkwood MO 63122 Office: 6780 Southwest Ave Saint Louis MO 63143

BANNISTER, MARGARET ALICE TRIMBLE, ednl. adminstr.; b. Oklahoma City, Dec. 15, 1924; d. Clyde Waldrop and Mary Melissa (Murray) Trimble; B.A. in Journalism, U. Okla., 1945; teaching cert. U. Mo., St. Louis, 1969, postgrad. extension, 1970-71; postgrad. U. Wash., 1973; m. Lawrence R. Bannister, Jan. 18, 1947 (div. 1968); children—Karen, Barbara Jean, Sally Ann. Reporter, Alva (Okla.) Review-Courier, 1945-46, Clinton (Okla.) Daily News, 1946-47; pub. relations asst. U. Okla., Norman, 1947-51; editorial asst. Consol.-Vultee Aircraft Corp., Ft. Worth, 1951-53; coordinator community relations Berkeley (Mo.) Sch. Dist. (merged with and name changed to Ferguson Sch. Dist. R-2 1975), 1968-72, dir. community relations, 1973-81; pub. relations dir. YWCA Met. St. Louis, 1984—. Mem. Women in Communications (v.p. St. Louis chpt. 1983-84), Nat. Sch. Public Relations Assn. (officer Greater St. Louis chpt. 1969-71, 73-74), Soroptimists Internat. (charter mem. N. St. Louis County chpt.). Methodist (past mem. bd. stewards, youth council). Office: 1015 Locust Suite 310 St Louis MO 63101

BANSAL, AJAY KUMAR, construction engineer; b. Ambala, India, Jan. 26, 1941; came to U.S., 1969, naturalized, 1976; s. Amrit Lal and Leela Bansal; m.

Veena Gupta; children—Manisha, Anurag. I.Sc. in Sci., Calcutta U. (India), 1958; B.Sc. in Elec. Engring., Banaras Inst. Engring., India, 1963; M.S. in Indsl. Mgmt., Dehli U., India, 1969; M.S. in Indsl. and Systems Engring., Ohio U., 1971. Project mgr. High Voltage Systems, Toledo, Ohio, 1971-82; pres. Unicustom Inc., Cin., 1982—. Home: 6685 Timberwood Dr Westchester OH 45069 Office: Unicustom Inc 3263 Homewardway Fairfield OH 45014

BANSE, TIMOTHY PAUL, consultant, author; b. Clinton, Iowa, Oct. 12, 1951; s. Robert Louis and Helen Leone B.; B.A. in Journalism, U. Iowa, 1981; m. Dianne Marie Larsen; children—Christopher Patrick, Jessica Marie. Pres., Banse and Kelso Assocs., Iowa City, 1979—; author articles in mags. including Mechanix Illustrated, Timex/Sinclair User, Personal Computer World (U.K.), MicroComputing, Boating, Pick-Up, Van; contbg. editor Motor Boating and Sailing; monthly columnist Tim Banse's Engine Room. Served with M.I., Spl. Forces, U.S. Army, 1969-72. Recipient Wilbur Petersen award U. Iowa Sch. Journalism, 1975, James W. Blackburn award, 1975. Mem. Am. Defense Preparedness Assn., Washington Ind. Writers Group, Writers Guild Am., Author's Guild, Authors League Am. Author: Home Applications and Games for Atari Computer, The Atari Book of Secrets. Home: 3512 N 2d St Clinton IA 52732 Office: PO Box 5535 Coralville IA 52241

BANSEN, NORMAN C., English and Danish educator; b. Ferndale, Calif., Nov. 26, 1920; s. Peter H. and Anne M (Andersen) B. B.A., Dana Coll., 1947; M.A., U. Minn., 1954; H.H.D. (hon.), Luther Coll., 1982. Dir. pub. relations Dana Coll., Blair, Nebr., 1947-49, from instr. to prof. English and Danish, 1953—; vis. assoc. prof. Scandinavian, U. Calif.-Berkeley, 1964. Contbr. articles to profl. jours. Pres. Dana chpt. Am.-Scandinavian Found., Blair, 1954-77; bd. dirs. Danish Immigrant Mus., Elk Horn, Iowa, 1981—. Served to capt. U.S. Army, 1942-46. Decorated knight Order of Dannebrog. Mem. Soc. Advancement Scandinavian Study. Democrat. Club: Danish Brotherhood (Blair). Avocations: gardening, philately, travel. Home: 2960 College Dr Blair NE 68008 Office: Dana Coll Blair NE 68008

BANSER, ROBERT FRANK, JR., newspaper editor; b. Chgo., Aug. 20, 1946; s. Robert Frank and Alice Rita (Proctor) B.; student Chgo. City Coll., 1965-67; B.S., No. Ill. U., 1969; M.A., 1972; m. Lucille Ann Collins, Nov. 7, 1976; children—Robert Ernest, Christopher James, Mary Louise. News reporter Paddock Publs., Arlington Heights, Ill., 1968; adminstrv. intern, City of Elgin, Ill., 1969-71; gen. assignment news reporter Star-Tribune, Publs., Chicago Hts., Ill., 1971-76, assoc. editor, 1976—. Bd. dirs. United Way of Chicago Hts. Mem. Internat. City Mgmt. Assn., Soc. Profl. Journalists, Chgo. Headline Club, Sigma Delta Chi, No. Ill. U. Alumni Club, Jaycees. Roman Catholic. Home: 1346 Campbell Ave Chicago Heights IL 60411 Office: 1526 Otto Blvd Chicago Heights IL 60411

BANTA, FRANK G., German language educator; b. Franklin, Ind., May 31, 1918; s. Frank and Caroline (Graham) B. A.B., Ind. U., 1939; M.A., U. Md., 1941; Ph.D., U. Berne, Switzerland, 1951. Instr., U. Md., College Park, 1941-44; mil. govt. officer State Dept., Germany, 1946-49; prof. U. Ill., Urbana, 1951-64; prof. German, Ind. U., Bloomington, 1964—. Contbr. articles to profl. jours. Served with U.S. Army, 1945-46. Mem. Am. Assn. Tchrs. German (v.p. 1971-73), MLA, Linguistic Soc., Indogermanische Gesellschaft. Home: 1400 Longwood Dr Bloomington IN 47401 Office: Germanic Lang Ind U Bloomington IN 47405

BANTA, MERLE HENRY, sales and service company executive, civil engineer; b. East St. Louis, Ill., Dec. 11, 1932; s. Albert Merle and Vivian Mae (Brown) B.; m. June M. Mueller, June 17, 1955; children—Brenda June Banta Williams, Berton Merle, Bradford Charles. B.S., Washington U., St. Louis, 1954; M.S., Iowa State U., 1955; M.B.A., Harvard U., 1961. Registered profl. engr. Cons., McKinsey & Co., Los Angeles, 1961-64; chmn., pres., chief exec. officer The Leisure Group, Los Angeles, 1964-84, Pacific Homes, Los Angeles, 1981-84, Am. Internat. Inc., Chgo., 1984—; dir. Mark Controls Corp. Trustee, Pasadena Poly. Sch., Calif., 1977—; overseer, sec. Huntington Library, 1969—. Served to lt. USN, 1955-59. Baker scholar Harvard Bus. Sch., 1961; recipient Daniel Mead award ASCE, 1955. Republican. Presbyterian. Clubs: Calif., Jonathon (Los Angeles); Econ. (Chgo.). Office: AM Internat Inc 333 W Wacker Dr Suite 900 Chicago IL 60606-1265

BANTLI, HEINRICH, scientist; b. Zurich, Switzerland, Apr. 13, 1943; came to U.S., June 1967; s. Heinrich Jakob and Louise (Kaser) B.; m. Billie Patricia Boal, July 15, 1967. B.S., U. Calif.-Berkeley, 1969, Ph.D., 1973. Instr. U. Calif.-Berkeley, 1972-73; instr. U. Minn., Mpls., 1973-74, asst. prof., 1973-78; sr. scientist SM-Bioscis. Lab., St. Paul, 1979-80, mgr., 1980-84, lab. mgr., 1984—. Contbr. articles on cerebellum, motor function to profl. jours. NIH fellow, grantee. Mem. Am. Physiol. Soc., Phi Beta Kappa. Avocations: horseback riding, skiing. Home: 13565 116th St N Stillwater MN 55082 Office: 3M Biosciences Lab Bldg 270-2A-08 Saint Paul MN 55144-1000

BANTON, JAMES FOWLER, manufacturing company executive; b. Chgo., May 29, 1937; s. Fowler Boyton and Margaret Collin (Gilruth) B.; B.S. in Acctg., U. Ill., Champaign, 1959; M.S. in Engring., Ill. Inst. Tech., 1963; m. Susan Mary Abendroth, Sept. 1, 1966; children—James Andrew, Pembrook Collin and Bridget Gilruth (twins). Mgr. project control Automatic Elec. Co. subs. Gen. Telephone & Electronics, Northlake, Ill., 1961-64, program dir. ops. analysis, 1964-68; cons. mgr. Rexnord, Inc., Milw., 1968-79; v.p. ops. Agro Indsl. Group, Blount, Inc., Montgomery, Ala., 1979-81; pres. George A. Rolfes Co., West Des Moines, Iowa, 1981—; dir. G.A. Rolfes Co., Rolfes Internat., Rolfes Can., LBI/Farmrite, Rolfes Agro S.A. de C.V.; lectr. U. Wis., 1966-72; guest lectr. Harvard U., 1973-76. Mem. Brookfield (Wis.) Parks and Recreation Commn., 1975-79, chmn., 1977-79; alderman Fourth Dist., Brookfield, 1978-79. Served with Army N.G., 1955-63. Mem. Inst. Mgmt. Scis. (chmn. Milw. chpt. 1965-66; nat. v.p. meetings 1977), Ops. Research Soc. Am. (chmn. chpt. 1965-66, nat. publs. com. 1966-73, nat. meetings com. 1968-77, chmn. 1973-76, chmn. joint nat. meetings com. 1973-75, chmn. 43d nat. meeting). Clubs: Des Moines, Bohemian, Wakonda Country. Contbr. articles to profl. jours. Home: 3511 St Johns Rd Des Moines IA 50312 Office: 939 Office Park Rd Suite 120 West Des Moines IA 50265

BANTZ, ORVILLE LINCOLN, JR., information systems executive; b. Dayton, Ohio, Sept. 15, 1943; s. Orville Lincoln and Glenna (Beck) B.; m. Susan Kay Becher; children—Jason, Jennifer. B.S. in Math., Manchester Coll., 1966; M.B.A., U. Dayton, 1983. Math. tchr. Northmont local schs. Englewood, Ohio, 1966-69; programmer N.C.R. Corp., Dayton, 1969-75, systems analyst, 1975-77, cons. analyst, 1977-83, mgr. info. mgmt., 1983—. Elder Slifers Presbyterian Ch., Farmersville, Ohio, 1978—; mem. sch. bd. Valley View local schs., Germantown, Ohio, 1983—. Mem. Toastmasters Internat. (pres. 1982-83 C.T.M. award 1983). Republican. Lodge: Rotary. Avocations: golf, gardening. Home: 1788 Preble County Line Rd Farmersville OH 45325 Office: NCR Corp 1700 S Patterson Blvd Dayton OH 45479

BANVILLE, EDMUND JOSEPH, III, educational administrator; b. Cleve., Mar. 28, 1948; s. Edmund Joseph and Leocadia Patricia (Dremel) B.; m. Judith Cain, Aug. 22, 1970; 1 child, Melissa Anne. B.S. in Edn., Ohio U., Athens, 1970, M.Ed., 1972. Cert. Ohio Dept. Edn. Elem. tchr. mentally retarded students Nelsonville (Ohio)-York City Schs., 1970-72; work-study coordinator mentally retarded students Whithall (Ohio) City Schs., 1972-74; high sch. tchr. mentally retarded students Lancaster (Ohio) City Schs., 1974-75; supr. programs for educable mentally retarded Fairfield County Schs., Lancaster, 1975-78, dir. spl. projects, 1978-84, asst. county supt., 1985—; lectr. spl. edn. adminstrn. Pres. bd. trustees Fairfield Industries, Inc., 1978—; chmn. edn. com. Fairfield Assn. Disabled Citizens, 1981-82. Recipient Exceptional Adminstr. of Yr. award Hocking Valley Council Exceptional Children, 1978. Mem. Council for Exceptional Children, Assn. for Supervision and Curriculum Devel., Buckeye Assn. Sch. Adminstrs., Ohio Assn. Pupil Personnel Adminstrs., Mensa. Home: 1194 N Columbus St Lancaster OH 43130 Office: 216 E Main St Hall of Justice Lancaster OH 43130

BANZHAF, CAROL ROTTIER, civic worker; b. Beaver Dam, Mich., Sept. 16, 1923; d. John A. and Marguerite (Mueller) Rottier; student Calvin Coll., 1942-43; A.B., Kalamazoo Coll., 1946; postgrad. Long Beach State Coll., 1954; M.A., Stetson U., 1959; m. Roger A. Goodspeed, 1946; children—Linn Marie, Carol Rottier; m. 2d, Henry F. Banzhaf, Aug. 6, 1965. Service rep. Mich. Bell Telephone Co., Grand Rapids, 1946; receptionist Littles' Studio, Palm Beach, Fla., 1947; tchr. kindergarten Cosa Mesa Union Schs., Calif., 1953-55; directress St. James' Day Sch., Ormond Beach, Fla., 1955-60; dean of girls, tchr. English, Milw. U. Sch., 1960-65; tchr. adult edn. Milw. Area Tech. Coll., 1973-75. Bd. dirs. Vol. Services of Greater Milw., 1963-66, Episcopal Campus Rectory, Milw., 1964-72, Women of St. Mark's Episcopal Ch., 1967-73, St. John's Home, Milw., 1976—, Dept. of Missions, Episcopal Diocese, 1978; bd. dirs. Women of St. Simon the Fisherman, Port Washington, Wis., 1973—, chmn., 1974-76; bd. dirs. St. John's Home and Tower, 1981, v.p., 1983—; vol. Lit. Services Wis.; mem. Milw. Children's Hosp. Aux.; pres. St. John's Home Aux. and Assn. Mem. Nat. Women Deans and Counselors, Am. Personnel and Guidance Assn., Herb Soc. Am. Episcopalian. Club: Women's of Wis. Home: Rural Route 1 5236 Sandy Beach S Belgium WI 53004

BAPTIST, ERROL CHRISTOPHER, pediatrician, educator; b. Colombo, Sri Lanka, Feb. 24, 1945; came to U.S., 1974; s. Egerton Cuthbert and Hyacinth Margaret (Colomb) B.; M.B.,B.S., Faculty of Medicine, U. Ceylon, 1969; m. Christine Rosemary Francke, Aug. 7, 1976; children—Lauren Marianne, Erik Christopher. Intern, Colombo Gen. Hosp. and Children's Hosp., Colombo, Sri Lanka, 1969-70; resident house officer Dist. Hosp., Gampola, Sri Lanka, 1970-71; resident house officer Base Hosp., Kegalle, Sri Lanka, 1971-74; family practitioner, Marawila, Sri Lanka, 1974; resident physician in pediatrics Coll. Medicine and Dentistry N.J., Newark, 1975-77; practice medicine specializing in pediatrics, Rockford, Ill., 1977—; asst. prof. pediatrics U. Ill. Coll. Medicine, Rockford, 1977—. Recipient Raymond B. Allen Instructorship award U. Ill., 1979, 80; diplomate Am. Bd. Pediatrics. Mem. Am. Acad. Pediatrics, So. Med. Assn. Roman Catholic. Home: 10696 Whispering Pines Way Rockford IL 61111 Office: 461 N Mulford Rd Rockford IL 61107

BAPTIST, JEREMY EDUARD, allergist; b. Chgo., Mar. 22, 1940; s. Arthur Henry and Margaret Jane (Beck) B.; m. Sylvia Evelyn Bonin, July 21, 1962; children—Sarah, Margaret, Catherine. B.S. in Physics, U. Chgo., 1960, Ph.D. in Biophysics (USPHS predoctoral fellow), 1966; M.D., U. Mo., Kansas City, 1978. Asst. prof. radiation biophysics U. Kans., 1966-73; claims authorizer Social Security Adminstrn., 1974-75; intern in medicine Northwestern U., 1978-79; allergist Speer Allergy Clinic, Shawnee Mission, Kans., 1979—, v.p., 1985—. Co-author: Handbook of Clinical Allergy, 1982; contbr. to Britannica Yearbook of Science and the Future, 1973, 74; mem. editorial bd. Topics in Allergy and Clinical Immunology, 1982-83. Brown-Hazen grantee, 1970. Mem. So. Med. Assn., AMA, Am. Coll. Allergists, Kans. Med. Soc., Johnson County Med. Soc., AAAS, N.Y. Acad. Scis., Am. Assn. Clin. Immunology and Allergy, Internat. Corr. Soc. Allergists (asst. editor Allergy Letters 1984-85, assoc. editor 1985—), Internat. Assn. Aerobiology, Sigma Xi. Mem. Reorganized Ch. of Jesus Christ of Latter-day Saints. Home: 3501 W 92d St Leawood KS 66206 Office: 5811 Outlook Dr Shawnee Mission KS 66202

BAPTIST, SYLVIA EVELYN, data service company executive, consultant; b. Chgo., Feb. 15, 1944; d. Clarence Walter and Evelyn Alphild (Fagerberg) Bonin; m. Jeremy Eduard Baptist, July 21, 1962; children—Sarah, Margaret, Catherine. Student Mich. State U., 1961-62; B.S., Roosevelt U., 1965. Instr. IBM, Chgo., 1965-66, systems engr., Topeka, Kans., 1966-67; tchr. computer sci. Lawrence High Sch., Kans., 1968; pres. Multiple Data Services, Leawood, Kans., 1983—; cons. in field. Alumni Disting. scholar Mich. State U., 1961-62, Internat. Ladies' Garment Workers Union scholar Roosevelt U, 1964-65. Lodge: Vasa. Avocations: Scandinavian dancing; cooking; writing. Office: Multiple Data Services 3501 W 92nd St Leawood KS 66206

BARACH, PHILIP G., shoe company executive; b. Boston, 1930. Grad. Boston U., 1951; student Harvard Grad. Sch. Bus. Adminstrn., 1955. Pres., chmn. bd. U.S. Shoe Corp., Cin., 1972—; dir. Fifth Third Union Trust Co. Trustee Country Day Sch. Office: US Shoe Corp One Eastwood Dr Cincinnati OH 45227*

BARAK, ANDREW PAUL, otorhinolaryngologist; b. Detroit, Dec. 12, 1952; s. Morrey Aaron and Shirley Lillian (Spoon) B.; m. Bethany Ann Heitzner, June 1, 1980; children—Sean Adam, Lindsey Danielle. B.S., Wayne State U., 1974; D.O., Kirksville Coll. Medicine, 1978. Intern Garden City Osteo. Hosp., 1978-79; resident Met. Hosp., 1979-82, resident trainer, 1985—; practice medicine specializing in otorhinolaryngology, 1984—. Contbr. articles to profl. jours. Mem. Am. Osteo. Assn., Am. Osteo. Bd. Ophthalmology and Otorhinolaryngology, Mich. Osteo. Physicians and Surgeons, Kent County Osteo. Physicians and Surgeons. Democrat. Jewish. Lodge: Centennial. Avocations: baseball, hockey, golf.

BARAK, GREGG, criminology educator; b. Los Angeles; s. Walter B. and Lillian (Korman) B.; m. Charlotte Pagni, June 12, 1976. A.B. in Criminology, U. Calif.-Berkeley, 1970, M. Criminology, 1971, D. Criminology, 1974. Asst. prof. sociology Edinboro U. of Pa., 1974-75; asst. prof. criminal justice U. Nev., Los Vegas, 1975-77; lectr. criminology, law enforcement, sociology U. Md., European div., 1978-79; policy analyst Office Justice Planning and Evaluation, Portland, Oreg., 1979-80; prof. sociology and criminal justice Aurora U., Ill., 1980—. Author: In Defense of Whom?, 1980. Contbr. articles to profl. jours. Assoc. editor Crime and Social Justice, 1982—. Pres., Interfaith Food Pantry, Inc., Aurora, 1984—; mem. Aurora Twp. Com. on Youth, 1984—; adv. council Fox Valley Release Ctr., 1983—. Mem. Am. Sociol. Assn., Am. Soc. Criminology, Acad. Criminal Justice Sci. Avocations: racketball; tennis. Home: 446 Fifth St Aurora IL 60506 Office: Aurora U 347 S Gladstone Aurora IL 60506

BARANOWSKI, FRANK JOHN, JR., school administrator, educator; b. Chgo. Apr. 12, 1950; s. Frank John, Sr., and Vilma Marie (Toth) B. B.A. in History and Political Sci., U. Scranton (Pa.), 1976; language cert. Jagiellonian U., Cracow, Poland, 1975; edn. cert. Madonna Coll., Livonia, Mich., 1981 state of Mich., 1981; M.A. in History, Oakland U. Rochester, Mich., 1985; M.Religious Edn., Sts. Cyril and Methodius Sem., 1984. Public relations cons., Scranton, Pa., 1973-76; agt. Equitable Life Ins. Co. Am., 1976-77; public relations cons., Arlington, Va., 1977-78; tchr. St. Michael's Sch., Tunkhannock, Pa., 1978-79; tchr. St. Mary's Preparatory Sch., Orchard Lake, Mich., 1979-82, dean, 1982-85; prin. Our Lady of Lakes High Sch., Waterford, Mich., 1985—. Recipient Outstanding Advisor in Nation award Nat. Teen-Age Republicans, Manassas, Va., 1976, 81; Jaycees Outstanding Young Men in Am. award, 1976, 80, 81. Mem. Nat. Assn. Student Activity Advisors, Nat. Council for the Social Studies, Nat. Assn. Secondary Sch. Prins., Mich. Assn. Secondary Sch. Prins., Cath. Edn. Assn., Mich. Council for Social Studies. Republican. Roman Catholic. Author: (monographs) Lackawanna County Home Rule Charter, 1975; Casimir Pulaski, 1976; In Congress Assembled, 1982. Home: 14248 Glastonbury St Detroit MI 48219 Office: 5495 Dixie Hwy Waterford MI 48095

BARANY, JAMES WALTER, industrial engineering educator; b. South Bend, Ind., Aug. 24, 1930; s. Emery Peter and Rose Anne (Kovacsics) B.; m. Judith Ann Flanigan, Aug. 6, 1960 (div. 1982); 1 dau., Cynthia. B.S.I.E., Notre Dame U., 1953; M.S.I.E., Purdue U., 1958, Ph.D., 1961. Prodn. worker Studebaker-Packard Corp., 1949-52; prodn. liaison engr. Bendix Aviation Corp., 1955-56; mem. faculty Sch. Indsl. Engring., Purdue U., West Lafayette, Ind., 1958—, now prof., assoc. head indsl. engring.; cons. Taiwan Productivity Ctr., Western Electric, Gleason Gear Works, Am. Oil Co., Timken Co. Served with U.S. Army, 1954-55. Recipient best counselor award Purdue U., 1978, best engring. tchr. award, 1983; NSF and Eastern Seal Found. research grantee, 1961, 63, 64, 65. Mem. Inst. Indsl. Engring. (Fellows award 1982), Am. Soc. Engring. Edn., Methods Time Measurement Research Assn., Human Factors Soc., Order of Engr., Sigma Xi. Alpha Pi Mu. Home: 101 Andrew Pl Apt 201 West Lafayette IN 47906 Office: Indsl Engring Purdue U West Lafayette IN 47907

BARBARA, PAUL FRANK, chemistry educator; b. Jamaica, N.Y., Apr. 23, 1953; s. Dominic and Virginia (Bambara) B.; B.A., Hofstra U., 1974; Ph.D., Brown U., 1978. Postdoctoral assoc. Bell Labs., Murray Hill, N.J., 1978-80; asst. prof. Univ. Minn., Mpls., 1980—. Recipient Presdl. Young Investigator award NSF, 1984-89; Alfred P. Sloan fellow Sloan Found., 1983-85. Mem. Am. Phys. Soc., Am. Chem. Soc., AAAS, Optical Soc. Am. Office: Univ Minn Dept Chemistry 207 Pleasant St SE Minneapolis MN 55455

BARBER, DAVID RAYMOND, radio-television talk show host, motivational speaker; b. Flint, Mich., Apr. 25, 1955; s. Raymond Wallace and Catherine (Davelich) B. A.A., Mott Coll. postgrad., Central Mich. U.; B.S., Saginaw Valley State Coll. Disc Jockey Sta. WTRX, Flint, Mich., 1973-82; talk show host Sta. WTAC, Flint, 1982—, Sta. WEYI-TV, Flint, 1984—; cons. in field. Bd. dirs. Big Brothers, Flint, 1983—. Named Salesman of Yr., Sales and Mktg. Execs., 1980, 82. Roman Catholic. Clubs: Univ., Atlas Golf. Avocations: flying; golf; entertaining. Home: 2114 Barth St Flint MI 48504 Office: Sta WTAC PO Box 600 Flint MI 48501

BARBER, KENT EDWARD, investment executive; b. Wichita, Kans., Sept. 4, 1942; s. Glenn Howard and Genevieve Lenore (Jones) B.; m. Imelda Jane Wahl, Mar. 6, 1965; children—Gregory, Kimberly. B.S., Evangel Coll., 1964; cert. in fin. planning Coll. Fin. Planning, 1983. With Hallmark Cards, Kansas City, Mo., 1965-74; v.p., gen. mgr. Tempo Inc., Kansas City, 1974-80; MAS fin. planner Busby Keller & Co., 1980-82; v.p. Innovative Fin. Services, Shawnee Mission, Kans., 1982-85; pres. Christian Fin. Mgmt., Shawnee Mission, 1985—. Bd. dirs. Central Assembly of God Ch., Raytown, Mo., 1981—. Served with USAR, 1965-70. Mem. Internat. Assn. Fin. Planning, Inst. Cert. Fin. Planners. Republican. Lodge: Rotary. Office: 8500 W 63d St 121 Shawnee Mission KS 66202

BARBER, TENA IRENE, nursing educator; b. Wichita, Kans., Aug. 16, 1944; d. Gloyd Varian and Lucy (Higgins) Vogle; m. Richard Rollin Barber, Aug. 8, 1964; children—Todd Jerard, Lea Jdene. R.N., St. Francis Sch. of Nursing, 1965; B.A., Kans. Newman Coll, 1972; M.A., Kans. State U., 1974; M. in nursing, Wichita State U., 1979. Registered nurse, Kans. Staff nurse St. Francis Hosp., Wichita, Kans., 1965-67; instr. St. Francis Sch. of Nursing, Wichita, 1967-80; nursing service educator St. Joseph Hosp., Wichita, 1980-81; asst. prof. St. Mary Plains Coll., Wichita, 1981-82, assoc. prof., coordinator Assoc. Degree Nursing program, 1982—; adv. bd. Wichita Area Vocat.-Tech. Lic. Practical Nursing Sch. Mem. Am. Nurses Assn. (bd. dirs. dist. 6, 1985—), Nat. League for Nursing. Democrat. Roman Catholic. Avocations: writing fiction; sewing; reading.

BARBER, THOMAS LEROY, beverage company executive; b. Joliet, Ill., Jan. 27, 1944; s. John Gaylord and Marcella Jane (Black) B.; B.S. in Indsl. Mgmt., So. Ill. U., 1967; m. Marsha Eileen Hursey, June 15, 1968; 1 son, Brett. Tng. specialist Olin Corp., East Alton, Ill., 1968-71; tng. supr. Seven-Up Co., St. Louis, 1971-77; mgr. sales tng. Beverage Mgmt. Inc., Columbus, Ohio, 1977-80, dir. tng., 1980-83; supr. sales tng. Seven-Up Co., St. Louis, 1983—, mgr. sales and bottler tng., 1984—; instr. Florissant Valley Jr. Coll., 1975-76; mem. vocat. adv. com. Alton High Sch. Ordained elder Presbyterian Ch. Mem. Am. Soc. Tng. and Devel., Nat. Assn. Watch and Clock Collectors, Phi Mu Alpha, Iota Lambda Sigma. Office: Seven-Up Co 121 S Meramec Saint Louis MO 63105

BARBER, TIMOTHY ALLEN, air force noncommissioned officer, translator; b. Framingham, Mass., June 23, 1960; s. Donald Edmund and Marjorie Louise (Johnston) B.; m. Silvania Brandao de Andrade, Sept. 14, 1985. Cert. in law enforcement City Colls. Chgo., 1980; diploma U.S. Air Force Command Non-commd. Officer's Acad., 1984. Enlisted U.S. Air Force, 1977, advanced through grades to staff sgt., 1982; aircraft guard, alarm response team leader Fairchild AFB, Wash., 1978-79; security response team leader Zaragoza AFB, Spain, 1979-81, security controller, 1981-83, security controller and desk sgt., 1983-84, translator Spanish and Portuguese, 1979-84; alert fire team leader, Minot AFB, N.D., 1984—, site security supr., 1985—, trainer, 1981—, dormitory council mem., 1985—, fin. mgmt. adviser, 1985—. Youth soccer coach, honor guard, hostage negotiator, bailiff, Zaragoza AFB, 1980-84. Mem. Air Force Assn. Republican. Mem. Pentecostal Ch. Avocations: jogging; soccer; foreign languages. Home: 12 Buchanan St Minot AFB ND 58704

BARBOLINI, ROBERT R., chem. engr.; b. N.Y.C., May 30, 1938; s. Renato J. and Dorothy L. (Curry) B.; B.S., Mass. Inst. Tech., 1959; M.Engring., Yale U., 1962; M.B.A., U. Chgo., 1973; m. Betty M. Halford, Sept. 11, 1976. Chem. engr. Union Carbide Corp., Tonawanda, N.Y., 1959-60; project mgr. Process Plants Corp., N.Y.C., 1961-68; asst. chief engr. Met. San. Dist. Greater Chgo., 1968—. Registered profl. engr., Conn., Ill., N.Y. Mem. Water Pollution Control Fedn., Air Pollution Control Assn., Am. Pub. Works Assn. Home: 2500 Lakeview Ave Chicago IL 60614 Office: 100 E Erie St Chicago IL 60611

BARBOSA, JOSE JOAQUIM, physician, researcher; b. Oporto, Portugal, Oct. 1, 1933; came to U.S., 1972; s. Jose C. and Mary Barbosa; m. Georgiana Smet, June 24, 1965 (dec. 1968); 1 child, Manny. M.D., Oporto Med. Sch., 1958; M.Sc., U. Minn., 1968. Intern St. Raphael Hosp., New Haven, Conn.; resident Albany Med. Coll., N.Y.; asst. prof. U. Minn., Mpls., 1972-78; assoc. prof. medicine, 1978—. Contbr. articles to profl. jours. on diabetes genetics and complications. Home: Box 716 Mayo Meml Bldg Minneapolis MN 55455 Office: U Minn Dept Medicine Minneapolis MN 55455

BARBOSA, RAYMOND, lawyer; b. Long Island City, N.Y., Oct. 2, 1954; s. Atilano and Patria (Olivarez) B.; m. Judith M. Price, Jan. 30, 1982. B.S., Fordham U., 1976; M.B.A., NYU, 1979, J.D., 1979, LL.M., 1981. Bar: N.Y. 1980, Ill. 1980, U.S. Dist. Ct. (so. and ea. dists.) N.Y. 1980, U.S. Dist. Ct. (no. dist.) Ill. 1980, U.S. Tax Ct. 1980. Auditor Ernst & Whinney, N.Y.C., 1976; tax acct. Deloitte Haskins & Sells, N.Y.C., 1978-79; tax atty. Winston & Strawn, Chgo., 1980-84; atty. Seki & Jarvis, Chgo., 1984—; lectr. Chgo.-Kent Sch. Law, Ill. Inst. Tech., Chgo., 1983—. Mem. Chgo. Bar Assn., Ill. State Bar Assn., ABA, Cook County Bar Assn., N.Y. State Bar Assn. Democrat. Roman Catholic. Home: 1227 N Kenilworth Oak Park IL 60302 Office: Seki & Jarvis 3 First Nat Plaza Chicago IL 60602

BARBU, ROBERT CORNELL, educational administrator; b. Cleve., Apr. ll, 1937; s. Cornelius Alexander and Flora Jane (Siegler) B.; B.S., Ohio State U., 1959; M.Ed., Kent State U., 1972; m. Janice Marilyn Jacobs, Nov. 28, 1960; children—Scott, Terrance, Troy. Engring. drawing instr. West Tech. High Sch., Cleve., 1960-65; instr. electronics Westlake (Ohio) High Sch., 1965-70; AV-ITV dir. Westlake City Schs., 1970-83; instr. indsl. robotics Lorain County Community Coll., 1984—; v.p. Profl. Computer Services, Inc., Avon Lake, Ohio, 1971, Guidelines, Inc., Fairview Park, Ohio, 1975. Chmn. audio-visual com. Greater Cleve. Sch. Supts. Group Purchasing Council, 1976-77, 80-81; chmn. Avon Lake Cable Adv. Com., 1982-83; recreation dir. City of Avon Lake, 1974-75. Mem. Assn. Ednl. Communication Tech., Ohio Ednl. Library Media Assn. (dist. dir. 1978-80), NEA, Ohio Edn. Assn., Northeastern Ohio Tchrs. Assn., Ohio Indsl. Arts Assn., Westlake Tchrs. Assn., Nat. Ski Patrol System, Boy Scouts Am. Writer, producer, host instrnl. TV series Choose It, 1974. Home: 32699 Carriage Ln Avon Lake OH 44012 Office: 27830 Hilliard Rd Westlake OH 44145

BARCELONA, MICHAEL JOSEPH, aquatic chemist, state official; b. Chgo., Aug. 20, 1949; married; 3 children. B.A. in Chemistry, St. Mary's Coll., Winona, Minn., 1971; M.S. in Inorganic Chemistry, Northeastern U., 1974; Ph.D. in Marine Chemistry/Chem. Oceanography, U. P.R., 1977. Nat. Inst. Environ. Health postdoctoral research fellow Calif. Inst. Tech., Pasadena, 1977-79; sect. head, assoc. chemist aquatic chemistry sect., water survey div. Ill. Dept. Energy and Natural Resources, Champaign, 1979—. Mem. Champaign Park Dist. Adult Band. EPA grantee, 1979-85; Dept. Interior Office Water Research and Tech. grantee, 1980, 81; Ill. Dept. Energy and Natural Resources grantee, 1982. Mem. Am. Chem. Soc., Am. Soc. Limnology and Oceanography, Nat. Water Well Assn. (div. ground water scientists and engrs.), Sigma Xi. Contbr. articles on chem. aspects of environ. problems to profl. publs.; research on groundwater contamination as a result of hazardous waste management activities. Office: 2204 W Griffith Champaign IL 61820

BARCH, JAMES JOHN, educational administrator; b. Manistee, Mich., July 28, 1939; s. Barch Edward Raymond and Myrtle Etta (Anderson) B.; B.S., Central Mich. U., 1965, M.A., 1968; m. Joan Beverly Carr, Aug. 9, 1969; children—James Preston, Jon Craig, Julie Kristin. Tchr. public schs., Bay City, Mich., 1968-69; tchr. public schs., Okemos, Mich., 1969-75, bldg. adminstr., 1976—; v.p. Beyond Aerobics Inc., 1982-83. Pres., Lakeside Village Homeowners Assn., 1973-75; counselor Boy Scouts Am., 1981—; mem. council of elders Peoples' Ch. of East Lansing (Mich.). Served with U.S. Army, 1965-67. Decorated Bronze Star, Purple Heart with oak leaf cluster. Mem. Assn. Supervision and Curriculum Devel., Nat. Assn. Middle Sch. Educators, Nat. Assn. Secondary Sch. Prins., Mich. Assn. Middle Sch. Educators, Mich. Assn. Secondary Sch. Prins., Nat. Geographic Soc., Smithsonian Assocs., VFW. Republican. Presbyterian. Lodge: Optimists. Home: 2766 Still Valley Ct East Lansing MI 48823 Office: 4406 Okemos Rd Okemos MI 48864

BARCIA, JAMES A., state senator; b. Bay City, Mich., Feb. 25, 1952. Student Saginaw Valley State Coll., 1974. Staff asst. to U.S. Senator Philip Hart, 1971; community service coordinator Mich. Community Blood Ctr., Bay City, 1974-75; adminstrv. asst. to State Representative Donald Albosta, 1975-76; mem. Ho. of Reps. from 101st Mich. Dist., 1977-82, mem. edn. com., 1977-82, mem. joint legis. sub-com. higher edn., 1979-82, chmn. pub. works com., 1979-82; majority whip, 1979-82; mem. Mich. Senate, 1983—; vice chmn. agrl. and forestry com., mem. Senate state affairs com., vets. and transp. com., edn.

com., 1983—; asst. minority whip, 1983—; mem. UAW Local 688, 1970-71, Saginaw Valley Coll. Bd. Control, 1973-74. Active Mus. of Great Lakes, Bay City YMCA. Recipient Disting. Service award Saginaw Valley State Coll. Alumni Assn., 1977, Outstanding Community Service award B.A.S.I.S. Corp., 1978, Mich. Jaycees Top Five I.M.P.A.C.T. award, 1979, Spanish Speaking Council Community Involvement award, 1979, Chicano-Latino Substance Abuse Program award, 1979; elected to Bay City Central Hall of Fame, 1981. Mem. Bay Area C. of C., Mich. United Conservation Clubs, VFW Nat. Home (life), Nat. Rifle Assn., Mich. Assn. Osteopathic Physicians and Surgeons (hon. lay mem.), Bay City Jaycees (Disting. Service award 1982). Lodges: Elks, Eagles. Home: 4027 Dover Ln Bay City MI 48706

BARCKHOFF, JACK RONALD, welding company executive, consultant; b. Columbus, Ohio, May 31, 1928; s. Felix Carl B. and Bernadine Mary (Tate) Wilson; m. Joan Mary Reinhart, Mar. 22, 1963 (div. 1975); 1 child, Jodi Ann; m. Gloria Jean Snydal, Nov. 24, 1979. Student in engring. and mktg. Ohio State U., 1953. Registered profl. engr., Calif. Dist. mgr. Lincoln Electric Co., Mpls., 1956-76; pres. Barckhoff & Assocs., Inc., Excelsior, Minn., 1976—; welding mgt. cons., 1976—. Contbr. articles to publs. Served to capt. U.S. Army, 1953-55. Mem. Am. Soc. Metals, Council Profl. Cons., Cons. Engrs. Council, Cons. Engrs. Council Am. (Honor award 1984), Am. Welding Soc. (chmn. 1977, Dist. Meritorious award 1978), Soc. Mfg. Engrs., Metal Fabrication Assn., Am. Inst. Steel Constrn. Lutheran. Avocations: Biking; walking; gardening. Office: Barckhoff & Assocs Inc 1255 W 78th St Excelsior MN 55331

BARCLAY, ALLAN GENE, psychologist, educator; b. Masonville, Iowa, Dec. 22, 1930; s. Otho R. and Marian (Lee) B.; student U. Louisville, 1949-50; A.B. cum laude, U. Tulsa, 1955; postgrad. U. Iowa, 1955-56; Ph.D., Washington U., St. Louis, 1960; children—Lisa, Allan. Clin. psychologist Mental Hygiene Clinic, VA Regional Office, St. Louis, 1959-60; faculty St. Louis U., 1960—, prof. psychology, 1965—, assoc. univ. research adminstr., 1968-72, dir. program in developmental psychology, 1965—, dir. Sch. Medicine Child Devel. Clinic, 1972—; chief psychologist dept. pediatrics Cardinal Glennon Meml. Hosp. for Children, St. Louis, 1960—, asso. dean acad. affairs Sch. of Profl. Psychology, Wright State U., Dayton, Ohio, 1979—. Cons. to hosps., govt. agys.; spl. adviser Pres.'s Com. on Mental Retardation; councilor Joint Commn. on Hosps., Accreditation Council on Facilities for Mentally Retarded. Bd. dirs., pres., mem. adv. com. New Hope Found. St. Louis, 1977-79. Served with AUS, 1948-52. Grantee USPHS, 1961-79, U.S. Children's Bur., 1960-68, Joseph P. Kennedy, Jr. Found., 1965, Children's Research Found., 1965, Office Econ. Opportunity, 1965-68, Social Rehab. Service, 1972—; Am. Psychol. Found., 1980; diplomate Am. Bd. Examiners in Profl. Psychology; mem. Nat. Register Health Service Providers in Psychology. Fellow Am. Assn. on Mental Deficiency; Soc. for Rorschach Research and Projective Techniques, Mo. Psychol. Assn., Internat. Council Psychologists (past pres.); mem. Am. Psychol. Assn. (fellow div. clin. psychology, fellow div. developmental psychology, chmn. bd. profl. affairs, sec.-treas., past pres. div. clin. psychology, past pres. div. mental retardation), Ill. Psychol. Assn., Mo. Psychol. Assn., Ohio Psychol. Assn., AAAS, AAUP, Am. Assn. Mental Deficiency, So. Soc. Philosophy and Psychology, Soc. Research in Child Devel. Inter-Am. Soc. Psychology, Internat. Council Psychologists (past pres.), Am. Pub. Health Assn., AMA, Sword and Key, Sigma Xi, Pi Gamma Mu, Psi Chi (nat. pres.), Phi Gamma Kappa. Editor: Jour. Profl. Psychology; contbr. articles to publs. Home: 100 Devonhurst Kettering OH 45429

BARCO, MARTIN THOMAS, SR., dentist; b. Tallahassee, Fla., Jan. 28, 1919; s. Thomas Ford and Frieda Charolette (Furcht) B.; m. Helen Juanita Louise Clark, July 6, 1941; children—Martin Thomas II, Clark Tobias. D.D.S., Ind. U., 1940; postgrad. Ohio State U., 1947-48, Ind. U., 1943, U. Pa., 1943, U. Ky., 1964. Intern and resident Indpls. City Hosp., 1940-41; gen. practice dentistry and oral surgery, Winamac, Ind., 1946—; mem. staff Starke Meml. Hosp., 1950-63, Pulaski Meml. Hosp., 1963-85. Chmn. fund raising and bldg. com. Community Swimming Pool, Winamac; active Three Rivers council Boy Scouts of Am.; life bd. dirs. Ind. affiliate Am. Heart Assn., chmn. 1972-74, also del., mem. numerous coms.; trustee, Sunday sch. tchr., lay leader, mem. numerous coms. 1st United Meth. Ch., Served to maj. U.S. Army, 1941-46. Recipient Silver Beaver award Boy Scouts Am. Mem. ADA, Ind. Dental Assn., Wabash Valley Dental Assn. (pres. 1966-67), Ind. U. Alumni Assn., Winamac C. of C. (Man of Yr. 1985), Theta Chi. Republican. Club: Dad's (pres. 1970). Lodges: Kiwanis (bd. dirs., pres., chmn. boys and girls com.), Elks, Masons. Home: 115 Shady Ln Winamac IN 46996 Office: 115 E Pearl St Winamac IN 46996

BARCUS, CHAUNCEY HAROLD, architect, educator; b. Farmersville, Ill., Sept. 9, 1921; s. Chauncey Hobart and Edna Rose (Smith) B.; B.S. in Archtl. Engring., U. Ill., 1947, M.S. in Architecture, 1948; m. Georganne Coon, Dec. 28, 1946; children—Harold Lloyd, David Alan. Grad. asst. U. Ill., 1948; draftsman, archtl. supt. U. Ill. Architect's Office, Urbana, Ill., 1949; architect assoc. Small, Wertz, Barcus & Swift, Architects and Engrs., Oxford, Ohio, 1950-78; prof. architecture Miami U., Oxford, Ohio, 1950—; works include library, dining hall, dormitories for Western Coll., Oxford, city recreation bldg., swimming pool and bathhouse, fire sta., Oxford, Delta Zeta Nat. Hdqrs. and Mus., several comml. bldgs., chs., frat. houses and residences; cons. architect in energy-efficient bldg. design and solar heating. Served with USN, 1941-45; PTO. Registered architect, Ill., Ohio. Mem. AIA, Assn. Collegiate Schs. Architecture, Illuminating Engring. Soc., Architects Soc. Ohio, ASHRAE, Internat. Solar Energy Soc. Clubs: Oxford Country; Fairfield Glade (Tenn.) Community. Home: 5176 Westgate Dr Oxford OH 45056 Office: Dept Architecture Miami U Oxford OH 45056

BARCUS, GILBERT MARTIN, marketing executive; b. N.Y.C., Sept. 20, 1937; s. Leon A. and Dorothy (Brownstein) B.; m. Sondra Etttin, May 6, 1961; children—David A., Ruth A. B.S., NYU, 1959; M.B.A., L.I. U., 1969. Stock broker Ernst & Co., N.Y.C., 1962-65; sales mgr. McNeil Labs., Ft. Washington, Pa., 1965-75; mktg. mgr. U.S.A. Devices, Ltd., New Brunswick, N.J., 1976-77; dir. product mgmt. Stimtech. Inc., Mpls., 1978; dir. product mgmt. Critikon/AMR, Tampa, Fla., 1979-80; v.p. mktg. Electro-Biology, Inc., Fairfield, N.J., 1980-82; exec. dir. mktg. Medtronic/Med. Data Systems, Ann Arbor, Mich., 1982—; assoc. adj. prof. bus. dept. CUNY; lectr. dept. bus. Brookdale Coll. Chmn. Marlboro (N.J.) Bd. Fire Commrs., 1976-82. Clubs: Holland Orchards Country; NYU. (N.Y.C.). Home: 3725 Tremont Ln Ann Arbor MI 48105 Office: 2311 Green Rd Ann Arbor MI 48105

BARCUS, ROBERT GENE, association executive; b. Monticello, Ind., Oct. 22, 1937; s. Harold Eugene and Marjorie Irene (Dilling) B.; B.P.E. (Alumni scholar 1957), Purdue U., 1959; M.A., Ball State U., 1963; postgrad. Ind. U., summer 1966; supts. license Butler U., 1967; m. Mary Evelyn Shull, Aug. 9, 1959; children—Jennifer Sue, Debra Lynn. Tchr., coach Wabash (Ind.) Jr. High Sch., 1959-63; tchr. Wabash High Sch., 1963-64; tchr., coach North Central High Sch., Indpls., 1964-65; salary cons. Ind. Tchrs. Assn., Indpls., 1965-67, asst. dir. research, 1967-68, dir. spl. services, 1968-70, exec. asst., 1971-72, adminstrv. asst., 1972-73, asst. exec. dir. spl. services and tchr. rights, 1973-82; asst. exec. dir. adminstrn., personnel and governance, 1982-85, asst. exec. dir. labor relations and adminstrn., 1985—. Mem. NEA, Wabash City (past pres.), Washington Twp. (past pres.) tchrs. assns., Kappa Delta Pi, Pi Delta Kappa. Mem. Ch. of the Brethren (clk. 1966-74, chmn. 1979-83). Clubs: Indpls. Press, Columbia, Ind. Schoolmen's. Home: 2230 Brewster Rd Indianapolis IN 46260 Office: 150 W Market St Indianapolis IN 46204

BARDACH, JANUSZ, plastic surgeon, educator; b. Odessa, Russia, July 28, 1919; came to U.S., 1972; s. Mark and Ottylia (Neuding) B.; Physician, Moscow Med.-Stomatological Inst., 1950, M.D., 1953; 1 dau., Ewa. Resident, Moscow Med.-Stomatological Inst., 1950-54; dept. head, asso. prof. dept. maxillofacial surgery Lodz (Poland) Med. Acad. (Coll. Medicine), 1954-59, docent, 1959-62, prof., 1962-72, dept. head, prof. dept. plastic surgery, 1971-72, asso. dean Coll. Medicine, 1967-71, dir. center for congential facial deformities, 1962-72; vis. prof. dept. otolaryngology and maxillofacial surgery U. Iowa, Iowa City, 1972-73, prof. dept. otolaryngology-head and neck surgery, 1973—, prof. plastic surgery, dept. surgery Univ. Iowa Hosps. and Clinics, 1977—, chmn. div. plastic and reconstructive surgery of head and neck, 1973—; vis. prof. dept. plastic surgery Univs. Pekin, Kanton, Shanghai, Tientsin and Kuondiou, China, 1966, Oxford U., Eng., 1968, Haccettepe U., Ankara, U. Istanbul, Turkey, 1971; fellow in gen. plastic surgery, Prague, 1954, Oxford, Eng., 1962. Recipient highest sci. award Ministry of Health, Poland, 1966, 68, Town Council of Lodz, 1970, third prize for clin. research in otolaryngology Am. Assn. Ophthalmology and Otolaryngology, 1977; fed. grantee Maxillofacial Growth Project, 1973-75, 76—. Mem. Internat. Soc. Plastic Surgeons, Brit. Assn. Plastic Surgery, Royal Soc. Medicine (sect. plastic surgery), Internat. Soc. Maxillofacial Surgery, Am. Soc. Plastic and Reconstructive Surgeons (asso.), Turkish Soc. Plastic and Reconstructive Surgery (hon.), AMA, Johnson County Med. Assn., Am. Cleft Palate Assn., Am. Acad. Facial Plastic and Reconstructive Surgery. Club: Rotary Internat. Author six books; contbr. 100 research articles to sci. publs. in English, Polish, Czech, Russian, French and German. Home: 328 Highland Dr Iowa City IA 52240 Office: Dept of Otolaryngology—Head and Neck Surgery U Iowa Hospitals Iowa City IA 52242

BARDAWIL, WADI ANTONIO, pathologist; b. Hualahuises, Mex., May 13, 1921; came to U.S., 1950; s. Haical and Angela B.; m. Cosette Gannam, Dec. 7, 1947; children—Antonio, Ronald, Lawrence, Angela, Carol, Nancy. M.D., Nat. Autonomous U. of Mex., 1946. Diplomate Am. Bd. Pathology. Practice medicine, 1947-49; asst. in pathology Hosp. for Nutritional Disease, Gen. Hosp., Mexico City, 1949-50; resident in pathology, sr. resident Mary Fletcher Hosp., Burlington, Vt., also instr. pathology U. Vt., 1950-52; fellow in pathology Boston Lying-In Hosp. and Free Hosp. for Women, Boston, 1952-54; asst., instr., research assoc. dept. pathology Harvard Med. Sch., Boston, 1952-59; asst. in pathology Peter Bent Brigham Hosp., Boston, 1954-56; asst. prof. pathology dept. ob-gyn Tufts U., 1957-59, asst. prof. pathology, 1957-62, assoc. prof., 1959-66, assoc. prof. pathology, 1962-71, prof., 1966-73, prof. pathology, 1971-73; prof., chmn. dept. pathology Creighton U., Omaha, 1973-76; dir. labs. Creighton Meml. St. Joseph Hosp., Omaha, 1973-76; prof. pathology U. Ill.-Chgo., 1977—, prof. pathology dept. ob-gyn, 1979—, assoc. head dept. pathology, 1980-83; cons. Omaha VA Hosp., 1974-77; lectr. pathology Boston U., 1965-68; cons. pathologist Boston City Hosp., and Mallory Inst., Boston, 1965-68; dir. dept. pathology and med. research St. Margaret's Hosp., Dorchester, Mass., 1957-73; lectr. pathology U. Mass., 1971-73. Fellow Coll. Am. Pathologists; mem. Am. Soc. Exptl. Pathology, Mass. Med. Soc., Boston Obstet. Soc., Am. Assn. Pathologists and Bacteriologists, Internat. Acad. Pathology, Sociedad Latino Americana de Pathologia. Roman Catholic. Contbr. articles to profl. jours. Home: 5400 S Hyde Park Blvd Apt C5 Chicago IL 60615 Office: 1853 W Polk St Room 410 Chicago IL 60612

BARDEEN, JOHN, physicist, educator; b. Madison, Wis., May 23, 1908; s. Charles Russell and Althea (Harmer) B.; B.S., U. Wis., 1928, M.S., 1929; Ph.D., Princeton, 1936; D.Sc. (hon.), Union Coll., 1955, U. Wis., 1960; m. Jane Maxwell, July 18, 1938; children—James Maxwell, William Allen, Elizabeth Ann (Mrs. Greytak). Geophysicist Gulf Research & Devel. Corp., Pitts., 1930-33; asst. prof. physics U. Minn., 1938-41; with Naval Ordnance Lab., Washington, 1941-45; research physicist Bell Telephone Labs., Murray Hill, N.J., 1945-51; prof. physics and elec. engring. U. Ill., Urbana, 1951-75, emeritus, 1975—. Mem. Pres.'s Sci. Adv. Com., 1959-62. Recipient Ballantine medal Franklin Inst., 1952; John Scott medal, Phila., 1955; Fritz London award, 1962; Vincent Bendix award, 1964; Nat. Medal Sci., 1966; Michelson-Morley award Case Western Res. U., 1968; co-recipient Nobel prize in physics, 1956, 72; Presdl. Medal of Freedom, 1977; Washington award, 1983. Fellow Am. Phys. Soc. (pres. 1968-69, Buckley prize 1954); mem. Am. Acad. Arts and Sci., Am. Philos. Soc., Nat. Acad. Sci. Nat. Acad. Engring. (Founders award 1984). Home: 55 Greencroft Champaign IL 61820

BARDIS, PANOS DEMETRIOS, sociologist, author, poet, editor; b. Lefcohorion, Arcadia, Greece; m. Donna Jean; children—Byron Galen, Jason Dante. B.A. magna cum laude, Bethany (W.Va.) Coll., 1950; M.A., Notre Dame U., 1953; Ph.D., Purdue U., 1955. Prof. sociology, editor Social Sci., U. Toledo, 1959-81; editor Internat. Social Sci. Rev., 1982—, Internat. Jour. World Peace, 1983—; cons. Nat. Assn. Standard Med. Vocabulary, 1963—; Am. rep. Internat. Congress Social Scis., Barcelona, Spain, 1965, 66, 71; participant Conf. International de Sociologie des Religions, Rome, 1969, Strasbourg, 1977, Venice, 1979, London, 1983, Louvain, 1985, Internat. Sci. Congress, Athens, Greece, 1973, 77, Internat. Conf. on Love and Attraction, Swansea, Wales, 1977, Nat. Council on Family Relations, Toronto, Can., 1973, Ohio Acad. Scis., 1975; participant numerous other internat. confs. on peace, sci., philosophy and religion, 1976—. Sec.-treas. World Student Relief, Athens, 1947-48; chmn. crime reduction com. Commn. for Community Devel., Toledo, 1967-68; trustee Marriage Mus., N.Y.C. Fellow AAAS, Am. Sociol. Assn., Institut Internat. de Sociologie (chmn. membership com. 1970—, coordinator for U.S.A. 1974—, participants confs. Rome 1969, Montreal, 1972, Caracas, 1972, Uppsala, 1978, Lisbon, 1980, Mexico City, 1982), Internat. Inst. Arts and Letters (life), World Acad. Scholars; mem. AAUP, Am. Soc. Neo-Hellenic Studies (bd. advisers), Democritos, Group for Study Sociolinguistics, Inst. for Mediterranean Affairs (adv. council), Internat. Sci. Commn. on Family, Internat. Sociol. Assn. (Am. rep., Evian, France 1966, Rome 1969, Varna, Bulgaria 1970, Algiers 1972, Toronto 1974, Uppsala 1978), North Central Sociol. Assn., Modern Greek Soc., Nat. Acad. Econs. and Polit. Sci. (dir.), Nat., Ohio councils on family relations, Nat. Soc. Lit. and Arts, Nat. Writers Club, N.Y. Acad. Scis., Nat. Soc. Published Poets, Sigma Xi, Alpha Kappa Delta, Phi Kappa Phi, Pi Gamma Mu, Kappa Delta Pi. Recipient award for outstanding achievement in edn. Bethany Coll., 1975, Outstanding Teaching award Toledo U., 1975; winner Internat. Lachian Poetry competition, 1981; Kulikowski spl. award in poetry, 1981. Author: Studies in Marriage and the Family, 1975, 78; History of the Family, 1975; The Family in Changing Civilizations, 1967, 69; Ivan and Artemis (novel), 1957; The Future of the Greek Language in the United States, 1976; Encyclopedia of Campus Unrest, 1971; translator On Balances (Archimedes), 1980; co-editor, contbr.: The Family in Asia, 1978, 79; History of Thanatology, 1981; Poetry Americas 1982; Atlas of Human Reproductive Anatomy Illustrated by the Author, 1983; Evolution of the Family in the West, 1983; Global Marriage and Family Customs, 1983; Nine Oriental Muses, 1983; Dictionary of Quotations in Sociology, 1985; also articles in profl. jours., poetry. Editor, assoc. editor or book rev. editor 35 nat. and internat. jours. Composer songs for mandolin: Byron Ballad, 1972; Carnival Dance, 1972; The Gypsy Dreamer, 1973; Jeu de Jason, 1973; Lamentation, 1973; Merlin's Magic, 1973; Minerva Melody, 1973; The Nereid of the North, 1973; Threnody, 1974; Verlaine's Chanson d'Automne, 1974; The Pines of Olympia, 1975; Echoes of Arcadia, 1975; The Dance of the Neutrino, 1975; Multis cum Lacrimis, 1976; Legend of Love, 1978; Death of a Nymph, 1978; The Sorceress of Saturn, 1979; Death of Aphrodite's Dove, 1979; Artemis in the Moonlight, 1979; Cypress Ghosts, 1981; Atalanta's Golden Apples, 1984. Office: U Toledo Toledo OH 43606

BAREN, JOHN BENNETT, psychiatric social worker; b. San Francisco, July 25, 1944; s. Morton Paul and Juliet (Luton) B.; B.A., U. San Francisco, 1966; M.S.W., Calif. State U., Sacramento, 1968; 1 son, Robert John. Psychiat. social worker Bur. Social Work, Sacramento, 1968-70; dir. East Area Community Mental Health Center, div. mental health U. Calif. Davis/Sacramento Med. Center, 1970-77; clin. asst. prof. psychiatry U. Calif. Med. Sch., Davis, 1972-77; pvt. practice psychotherapy, 1968—; exec. dir. Montgomery County (Ohio) Mental Health Bd., Dayton, also clin. asso. prof. psychiatry Wright State U. Med. Sch., 1977—. Mem. Freedom of Choice Coalition, Miami Valley, 1978—. Recipient cert. appreciation Calif. Policewomen's Assn., 1974, Mental Health Assn. Miami Valley, 1979. Mem. Nat. Assn. Social Workers, Acad. Cert. Social Workers, Nat. Assn. Mental Health Adminstrs., Wright State U. Acad. Medicine. Home: 265 Springbrook Blvd Dayton OH 45405 Office: 11 W Monument St Suite #213 Dayton OH 45402

BARES, WILLIAM G., petroleum products manufacturing company executive; b. 1941. B.S. in Chem. Engring., Purdue U., 1963; M.B.A., Case Western Res. U., 1969. With Lubrizol Corp., 1963—, Wickliffe, Ohio, process devel. engr., 1963-67, group leader pilot plant, 1967-71, asst. dept. head, 1971, dept. head, 1972-78, asst. to pres., 1978, v.p., 1978-80, exec. v.p., dir., 1980-82, pres., 1982—. Office: Lubrizol Corp 29400 Lakeland Blvd Wickliffe OH 44092*

BARGER, VERNON DUANE, physicist, physics educator; b. Ourllsville, Pa., June 5, 1938; s. Joseph F. and Olive (McCall) B.; m. Annetta McLeod, 1967; children—Victor A., Amy J., Andrew V. B.S., Pa. State U., 1960, Ph.D., 1963. Research assoc. U. Wis.-Madison, 1963-65, from asst. prof. to assoc. prof. physics, 1965-68, prof., 1968-83, J.H. Van Vleck prof., 1983—, dir. Inst. Elem. Particle Research, 1984—; vis. prof. U. Hawaii, 1970, 79, 82, U. Durham, 1983, 84 vis. scientist CERN, 1972, Rutherford Lab., 1972. Author: (with others) Phenomenological Theories of High Energy Scattering, 1969; Classical Mechanics, 1973. Pa. State U. alumni fellow, 1974; Guggenheim fellow, 1972. Fellow Am. Phys. Soc.; mem. Phi Kappa Phi, Tau Beta Pi. Methodist. Lodge: Masons. Home: 5711 River Road Waunakee WI 53597 Office: U Wis Dept Physics Madison WI 53706

BARKER, DANIEL THOMAS, JR., manufacturing company executive; b. Appleton, Wis., Apr. 9, 1954; s. Daniel James and Nancy Louise (Stadler) B.; m. Dawn Gay Fritz, Mar. 5, 1977; children—Rachel, Adam, Ruth. A.A. in Metal Fabrication and Welding, Fox Valley Tech. Inst., Appleton, Wis., 1973; A.A., U. Wis.-Fox Valley, Menasha, 1978; B.S. in Econs., U. Wis., Oshkosh, 1981. Assembly supr. Pierce Mfg., Appleton, Wis., 1981-83, plant supt., 1983—. Mem. Delta Omicron Epsilon. Roman Catholic. Home: 804 Tayco St Menasha WI 54952 Office: Pierce Mfg 2600 American Dr PO Box 2017 Appleton WI 54911

BARKER, HUGH ALTON, electric utility company executive. Chmn., chief exec. officer Public Service Co. of Ind. Inc., Plainfield, Ind., also dir. Office: Pub Service Co Ind Inc 1000 E Main St Plainfield IN 46168*

BARKER, JOSEPH ALAN, lawyer; b. Buchanan, Mich., Mar. 25, 1953; s. Lemuel Deward and Freida (Czepregi) B. B.A., Mich. State U., 1975; J.D., magna cum laude, 1978, U. Detroit. Bar: Mich. 1978. Law clk. Mich. Supreme Ct., Lansing, 1978-79; atty. NLRB, Detroit, 1979—. Symposium editor Jour. Urban Law, U. Detroit Law Sch., 1977-78. Mem. State Bar Mich. (labor law sect.), Frank L. Murphy Honor Soc. Home: 1300 Lafayette St E Apt 706 Detroit MI 48207

BARKER, KEITH RENE, investment banker; b. Elkhart, Ind., July 28, 1928; s. Clifford C. and Edith (Hausmna) B.; A.B., Wabash Coll, 1950; M.B.A., Ind. U., 1952; children by previous marriage—Bruce C., Lynn K.; m. Elizabeth S. Arrington, Nov. 24, 1965; 1 dau., Jennifer Scott. Sales rep. Fulton, Reid & Co., Inc., Ft. Wayne, Ind., 1951-55, office, 1955-59, asst. v.p., 1960, v.p., 1960, dir., 1961, asst. sales mgr., 1963, sales mgr., 1964, dir. Ind. ops.; sr. v.p. Fulton, Reid & Co., 1966-75; pres., chief exec. officer Fulton, Reid & Staples, Inc., 1975-77; ptnr. William C. Roney & Co., 1977-79; exec. com. Cascade Industries, Inc.; assoc. A.G. Edwards & Sons, Inc., 1984—; dir. Fulton, Reid & Staples, Inc., Craft House Corp., Nobility Homes, Inc. Pres. Historic Ft. Wayne, Inc.; cons. to Mus. Historic Ft. Wayne; mem. Smithsonian Assocs.; bd. dirs. Ft. Wayne YMCA, 1963-64. Served to lt. USNR, 1952-55. Recipient Achievement certificate Inst. Investment Banking, U. Pa., 1959. Mem. Ft. Wayne Hist. Soc. (v.p.), Alliance Française, VFW (past comdr.), Co. Mil. Historians, Cleve. Grays, Am. Soc. Arms Collectors, Phi Beta Kappa. Episcopalian. Mason. Clubs: Beaver Creek Hunt, Cleve. Athletic. Home: 351 Cranston Dr Berea OH 44017 Office: 1965 E 6th St Cleveland OH 44114

BARKER, LAWRENCE EDWARD, pastor; b. Marion, Ind., Aug. 13, 1938; s. Ray H. and Ruth E. (Lloyd) B.; m. Sarah Elizabeth Heavilin, June 24, 1962; children—Bartholomew E., Daniel L. A.B., Earlham Coll., 1960, M.A. in Religion, 1963. Pastor, Friends Meeting, W. Milton, Ohio, 1959-65, assoc. pastor, 1965-67, pastor, 1967-84, trustee Friends Extension Corp., Richmond, Ind., 1981, Wilmington Yearly Meeting (Ohio), 1982—; v.p. Quality Quaker Mgmt. Inc, Wilmington, 1978. Mem. City Planning Commn. Wilmington, 1976—, Bd. Zoning Appeals Wilmington, 1981—; chmn. Clinton County Bd. Mental Retardation, 1967-82. Mem. Wilmington Area Ministrial Assn. Democrat. Contbr. articles to profl. jours. Lodge: Rotary. Home: 1334 Ridge Rd Wilmington OH 45177

BARKER, NANCY LEPARD, educator; b. Owosso, Mich., Jan. 22, 1936; d. Cecil L. and Mary Elizabeth (Stuart) Lepard; B.S., U. Mich. 1957; m. Richard William Barker, Nov. 18, 1972; children—Mary Georgia Cline Harker, Mark Lepard Cline, Melissa Bess Cline, John Charles Cline, Daniel, Richard, Helen Grace, James, Wiley. Instr., U. Mich. Med. Center, Polio Rehab. Center and Burn Units of Hosp. Sch., Ann Arbor, 1958-61; v.p. Med-educator, Chgo., 1967-69; dir. Careers for Women, Northwood Inst., Midland, Mich., 1971-74, dir. spl. services and asst. to chmn., 1974-76, v.p., 1976—. State advisor Mich. Child Study Assn., 1972—; chmn. Midland Art Council, 1964-66; bd. dirs. Midland Center for the Arts, 1971-77, Midland Symphony League; past chmn. Matrix Midland Festival; bd. dirs. Family & Children's Services. Named Mich. Outstanding Young Woman in Community Service, Jr. C. of C., 1967; Disting. Woman, Northwood Inst., 1970. Mem. Nat. Council Women of U.S. (pres. 1982-84, bd. dirs.), Nat. Home Fashions League (pres. Mich. chpt. 1979-81), Mich. Women's Studies Assn. (founding com.), Fashion Group, Career Women's Forum, Phi Gamma Nu, Delta Delta Delta, Phi Beta Kappa, Phi Kappa Phi, Alpha Lambda Delta, Phi Lambda Theta. Republican. Episcopalian. Clubs: Zonta, Contemporary Review, Midland County Lawyers Wives. Co-author: Wendy Well and Bill Better series of books, 1970; series of books for hospitalized children; mem. editorial bd. Woman's Life mag., 1981—. Home: 209 Revere Midland MI 48640 Office: Northwood Inst Midland MI 48640

BARKER, ROBERT OSBORNE, assn. exec.; b. Cleve., June 13, 1938; s. Cecil E. and Barbara O. (Osborne) B.; student Henry Ford Community Coll., 1950; B.A. in Communication Arts and Sci., Mich. State U., 1954; student LaSalle U. Law Sch., 1966-68; m. Sharon Ann; children—Debra, Stephen Robert, Dawn, Michael, Colleen. With public relations dept. Ford Motor Co., Dearborn, Mich., 1953; mgr. Kaiser Aluminum Co., Chgo., 1956-58; advt. adminstrv. mgr. Bastian Blessing Co., Chgo., 1958-59; mgr. Sun Co., Detroit, 1959-71, Goodyear Tire & Rubber Co., Detroit, 1971-72; pub. relations dir. NAM, Southfield, Mich., 1972—, registered lobbyist, 1978—. Twp. trustee, Findlay, Ohio, 1962; mem. vestry Episcopal Ch., 1981; precinct del. Mich. Republican Conv.; bd. dirs. Dearborn Civic Theater, 1980-84; City Beautiful commr. emeritus, chmn. bus. com., 1970-84; res. police officer, Dearborn, 1968—. Served with USNR, 1954-56. Mem. Assn. Execs. Met. Detroit, Pub. Relations Soc. Am., Mich. State U. Alumni (past pres.). Clubs: Elks; Rotary; Masons (master); Shriners (dir. pub. relations 1984). Home: 201 N York Blvd Dearborn MI 48128 Office: 801 Northland Towers West Southfield MI 48075

BARKER, WALTER LEE, thoracic surgeon; b. Chgo., Sept. 9, 1928; s. Samuel Robert, M.D., and Esther (Meyerovitz) B.; A.B. cum laude, Harvard U., 1949, M.D., 1953; m. Betty Ruth Wood, Apr. 4, 1967. Intern, resident in gen. and thoracic surgery Cook County Hosp. and Presbyn. St. Luke's Med. Center and affiliated hosps., Chgo., 1953-62; practice medicine specializing in thoracic surgery, Chgo., 1962—; asso. clin. prof. surgery U. Ill.; head sect. thoracic surgery Cook County Hosp.; chmn. dept. surgery St. Joseph Hosp., Chgo. Served with M.C., USNR, 1955-57. Diplomate Am. Bd. Surgery, Am. Bd. Thoracic Surgery. Fellow Am. Coll. Chest Physicians, A.C.S.; mem. Am. Assn. Thoracic Surgery, AMA, Boylston, Chgo., Ill. med. socs., Chest Club, Chgo., Ill., Central surg. socs., Inst. Medicine, Soc. Thoracic Surgeons (founding mem.), Sigma Xi. Author: The Post Operative Chest, 1977. Contbr. articles profl. jours. Research on tuberculosis, pleural infections, lung cancer. Home: 2912 N Commonwealth Ave Chicago IL 60657 Office: 2800 N Sheridan Rd Room 604 Chicago IL 60657

BARKIN, BEN, public relations consultant; b. Milw., June 4, 1915; s. Adolph and Rose Dora (Schumann) B.; student pub. schs.; m. Shirley Hinda Axel, Oct. 19, 1941; 1 son, Coleman. Nat. field dir. Jr. B'nai B'rith, 1937-41; cons. war finance dept. U.S. Treasury Dept., 1941-45; pub. relations cons. Ben Barkin & Asso., 1945-52; chmn. Barkin, Herman, Solochek & Paulsen, Inc. and predecessor firm, Milw., N.Y.C., pub. relations counsel, 1952—; partner, dir. Milw. Brewers Baseball Club, Inc., 1970—. Bd. dirs., v.p., mem. exec. com. Mt. Sinai Med. Center, also chmn. corp. program; pres. Mt. Sinai Med. Center Found.; trustee Milw. Boys Club; chmn. bd. trustees Athletes for Youth, Inc.; corp. mem. Milw. Children's Hosp., Columbia Hosp., United Way; mem. mgmt. adv. com. Milw. Urban League, We-Milwaukeeans, Greater Milw. Com.; bd. dirs. Nat. Com. against Discrimination in Housing, Inc., Mus. African Art, Washington; mem. civil rights exec. com. Anti-Defamation League; past mem. music adv. panel orch. sect. Nat. Endowment for Arts; bd. dirs. Am. Council for the Arts, 1983. Named man of yr., Milw., 1945; recipient Knight of Bohemia award Milw. Press Club, 1978, Headliner of Year award, 1983. Mem. Pub. Relations Soc. Am. (Paul Lund award 1978, Dorothy Thomas Black award Wis. chpt. 1983), NCCJ. Mem. B'nai B'rith (nat. chmn. youth commn. 1966-68). Home: 1610 N Prospect Ave Milwaukee WI 53202 Office: 777 E Wisconsin Ave Milwaukee WI 53202

BARKLEY, OWEN HERBERT, photographer; b. Muskegon Heights, Mich., Aug. 9, 1922; s. Kirk Delmont and Mabel Eva (Fowler) B.; student U.S. Navy Photo Sch., 1943, Nat. Camera Repair Sch., 1968; m. Karen Ann Gray, Nov. 13, 1965; children—Matthew Scott, Russell Dean, Jeffrey Wade. Served to chief photographer, USN, 1943-64; mem. photog. sales-service dept. Crescent Camera & Lithography Supply Corp., Kalamazoo, 1965-66; indsl. photographer Clark Equipment Co., Battle Creek, Mich., 1966-80; co-owner K & O Photography, Inc.; works exhibited nat. conv. Profl. Photographers Am., 1975,

79, featured in mag. article, 1976, 80. Pres. Village of Climax, Mich., 1976—; leader Kalamazoo County 4-H Club, 1978—. Mem. Profl. Photographers Am., Profl. Photographers Mich. Soc. Photog. Technologists, Am. Legion. Mason (pres. temple bd. assn. 1974); mem. Order Eastern Star (past patron), Order Eagles, Rotary. Home: 126 N Main St Climax MI 49034 Office: 126 N Main St Climax MI 49034

BARKLEY, RUSSELL ALLAN, neuropsychologist; b. Newburgh, N.Y., Dec. 27, 1949; s. Donald S. and Mildred M. (Terbush) B.; A.A. summa cum laude, Wayne Community Coll., N.C., 1972; B.A. summa cum laude with honors in Psychology, U. N.C., 1973; M.A. in Clin. Psychology, Bowling Green State U., 1975, Ph.D., 1977; m. Patricia Marie Gann, Mar. 15, 1969. Predoctoral intern dept. med. psychology Child Devel. and Rehab. Center, U. Oreg. Med. Sch., Portland, 1976-77; asso. prof. dept. neurology and psychiatry Med. Coll. of Wis., Milw., 1977—; child neuropsychologist Milw. Children's Hosp., 1977—; exec. dir. Willow Glen adv. bd. Willow Glen Acad. for Autistic and Psychotic Children, 1979—. Served with USAF, 1968-72; Vietnam. NSF research grantee, 1974, 76; Med. Coll. Wis. grantee, 1978; NIMH research grantee, 1979; lic. psychologist, Wis. Mem. Am. Psychol. Assn., Midwestern Psychol. Assn., Wis. Psychol. Assn., Milw. County Psychol. Assn., Assn. for Advancement of Behavior Therapy, Soc. Pediatric Psychology, Sigma Xi. Author book on hyperactive children; contbr. numerous articles and revs. on child psychology to sci. jours., chpts. to books. Office: Neuropsychology Sect Med Coll Wis 9001 Watertown Plank Rd Wauwatosa WI 53226 Home: 2837 N 77th St Milwaukee WI 53222

BARKMAN, RICHARD LEE, school principal; b. Argos, Ind., Jan. 24, 1938; s. Herman Everett and Shirley Yvonne (Simpson) B.; m. Sally Jo Brown, Aug. 24, 1958; children—Steven, Michael, Lori. B.S., Ball State Tchrs. Coll., 1960, M.S., 1964. Tchr., coach McKenney-Harrison Sch., Auburn, Ind., 1960-67; tchr., coach McIntosh Sch., Auburn, 1967-70; asst. prin. Huntertown Sch., Ind., 1970-72; asst. prin. athletic dir. DeKalb Jr. High Sch., Waterloo, Ind., 1972-79; prin. DeKalb Middle Sch., Waterloo, 1979—; sch. evaluator North Central Accreditation, Bloomington, Ind., 1981—. Mem. Ind. Secondary Sch. Adminstrs. Republican. Lutheran. Lodge: Rotary. Home: 2913 CR52 Auburn IN 46706 Office: DeKalb Middle Sch 3338 CR 427 Waterloo IN 46793

BARLAND, THOMAS HOWARD, judge; b. San Francisco, Mar. 3, 1930; s. George C. and Lois M. Barland; m. Ann Marie Carlson, May 10, 1964; 1 stepchild, David. B.A. in Econs., U. Wis.-Madison, 1951, LL.B., 1956. Bar: Wis. 1956. Ptnr. Ramsdell, King, Carroll & Barland, Eau Claire, Wis., 1957-67; county judge Eau Claire, 1967-76; circuit judge 28th jud. circuit, Eau Claire, 1976-78, Eau Claire County, 1978—; rep. Wis. Assembly, Madison, 1961-67; instr. Wis. Jud. Coll., Madison, 1970—. Author: (with others) (handbook) Wisconsin Rules of Evidence, 1982. Bd. curators Wis. State Hist. Soc., 1962—, pres. 1967-70; v.p. Wis. History Found., 1984—. Named An Outstanding Young Man in Wis., Jaycees, 1963. Mem. ABA, Am. Judicature Soc. Presbyterian. Avocations: gardening, history, music, art, flying. Home: 1617 Drummond St Eau Claire WI 54701 Office: Courthouse Circuit Ct Br 1 Oxford St Eau Claire WI 54703

BARLOW, ALICE MARTHA, gemologist, appraiser; b. Appleton, Wis., Aug. 30, 1953; d. F. John and Dorthy (Marx) B. B.A. in Art History, U. Wis., 1976, M.L.S., 1977; grad. gemologist Gemological Inst. Am., 1978; grad. with distinction Gemological Assn. Gt. Britain, 1984. Registered jeweler; cert. gemologist. Librarian, U. Wis., Madison, 1977-78; mgr., gemologist Earth Resources, Appleton, Wis., 1980-82, gen. mgr., gemologist (2 stores), 1983—; v.p., dir. Sanco Inc., Appleton, 1983—; lectr. and cons. in field. Visual tech. asst. Excellence brochure, 1984. Fellow Gemological Assn. of Gt. Britain; mem. Assn. Women Gemologists (Diamond in the Rough award 1985), Gemological Inst. Am. Alumni Assn., Am. Gem Soc., Accredited Gemologists Assn. Club: Bus. and Profl. Women's Assn. (Appleton). Avocations: antiquarian book collector; flower gardening; sailing; reading. Office: Earth Resources 2000 S Memorial Dr Appleton WI 54915

BARLOW, JOHN LESLIE ROBERT, physician; b. Skipton, Yorkshire, Eng., May 6, 1926; came to U.S., 1966; s. John and Louise Baker (Pollok) B.; m. Janice Barlow; children—Louise Claire, Donal Patrick, Mary Teresa, Margaret Anne, Catherine Jayne Maria. B.A., Cambridge U., 1947, M.B., B.Chir., 1950. Resident in gen. medicine, gen. surgery, ob-gyn. South West Eng., 1950-56; practice medicine South West Eng., 1956-66; with internat. div. Abbott Labs., North Chicago, 1966-77, med. dir., 1974-77; dir. clin. research Merrell Dow Pharms., Cin., 1976—. Mem. Brit. Med. Assn., Drug Info. Assn. Office: Merrell Dow Pharmaceuticals 2110 Galbraith Rd Cincinnati OH 45215

BARLOW, ROBERT LEWIS, II, lawyer; b. Indpls., Jan. 20, 1949; s. William Price and Mary Ann (Stewart) B.; m. Michele Ann Fondiller, July 18, 1970; children—Colene Rene, Robert Lewis III. B.S., Ball State U., 1972; J.D., Mercer U., 1980. Bar: Ga. 1980, Ind. 1980, U.S. Dist. Ct. (so. dist.) Ind. 1980. Ptnr. Cooper, Cox, Jacobs, Reed & Barlow, Madison, Ind., 1980—. Pres., dir. Jefferson County United Way, Madison, 1985-86; pres. Jefferson-Switzerland Assn. for Retarded Citizens, Madison, 1984-86. Mem. ABA, Ind. State Bar. Assn., Jefferson County Bar Assn. Roman Catholic. Lodges: Rotary (treas. Madison 1985-86), K.C., Elks. Home: 505 W Main St Madison IN 47250 Office: Cooper Cox et al 1315 Clifty Dr PO Box 736 Madison IN 47250

BARMORE, FRANK EDWARD, physics educator; b. Manhattan, Kans., June 20, 1938; s. Mark Alfred and Elizabeth (Jenkins) B.; m. Irene Elizabeth Wilcox, Jan. 21, 1967; children—Nathaniel, Christopher. B.S. with honors, Wash. State U., 1960; M.S., U. Wis.-Madison, 1963, Ph.D., 1973. Asst. prof. natural sci. Milton Coll., Wis., 1970-73; asst. prof. physics Middle East Tech. U., Ankara, Turkey, 1974-76; research assoc. physics U. Calgary, Alta., Can., 1976-77; project scientist physics York U., Toronto, Ont., Can., 1977-78; asst. prof. physics U. Wis.-La Crosse, 1978—. Contbr. articles to profl. publs. Mem. AAAS, Am. Geophys. Union, Am. Assn. Physics Tchrs., Optical Soc. Am., Soc. Archtl. Historians, Sigma Xi, Phi Beta Kappa. Home: 1623 Main St La Crosse WI 54601 Office: U Wis Physics Dept Cowley Hall La Crosse WI 54601

BARNA, CARMELA JOY, pharmacist, administrator; b. Broken Bow, Nebr., Apr. 15, 1958; d. William Victor and Roberta Lela (Morris) Dunn; m. Michael Frank Barna, Apr. 9, 1983; stepchildren—Christopher, James, Jason. Pharm.D., U. Nebr., 1981. Registered pharmacist, Iowa, Nebr. Staff pharmacist Fountain Square Pharmacy, Red Oak, Iowa, 1981-82; dir. pharmacy Montgomery County Meml. Hosp., Red Oak, 1983—; cons. Good Samaritan Nursing Home, Vista Gardens Nursing Home. Mem. Iowa Soc. Hosp. Pharmacists, Am. Soc. Hosp. Pharmacists, Iowa Pharmacists Assn., Am. Pharm. Assn. Republican. Avocations: Volleyball, running. Home: 2006 Eastern Ave Red Oak IA 51566 Office: Montgomery County Meml Hosp 1201 Highland Ave Red Oak IA 51566

BARNA, JOSEPH VINCENT, computer company official; b. Cleve., Aug. 26, 1955; s. Joseph and Marge Mary (Thurn) B.; m. Carmen Ortiz, Aug. 12, 1984. B.A. in Mass Media and Interpersonal Communications, Cleve. State U., 1977. Sales rep. Xerox Corp., Cleve., 1978-79, sr. sales rep., 1979-80, mktg. exec., 1980-81, sr. mktg. exec., 1981-83, account mgr., 1983-84, maj. account sales mgr., 1984—. Mem. Xerox Community Involvement Programs, Cleve., 1979-82; mem. Upper Prospect Planning Assn., Cleve., 1974-75. Recipient N.Y. Gold Keys, Nat. Scholastic Art Competition, 1970; MacDonough Counselor award Sigma Phi Epsilon, 1980. Mem. Sales and Mktg. Execs. Cleve., Sigma Phi Epsilon Alumni (pres. Cleve. 1983—). Democrat. Roman Catholic. Home: 2240 Carabel Lakewood OH 44107 Office: Xerox Corp 1100 Superior Ave Cleveland OH 44114

BARNARD, ELEANOR BETTY, public relations executive; b. Chgo., Aug. 16, 1912; d. Harry S. and Lona Ruth (Brill) Spivak; Ph.B., U. Chgo., 1933, postgrad., 1936; m. Morton John Barnard, Aug. 16, 1936; 1 son, James W. Pres. Elbar Assocs., public relations and advt., Winnetka, Ill., 1974—; vol., fundraiser law-related edn., 1974—; bd. dirs. Chgo. project Constl. Rights Found.; mem. bd. sch. St. Law Project Loyola U. Law Sch., Chgo.; mem. standing com. Law-Related Edn. for Public, Ill. State Bar Assn.; mem. Ill. Commn. Edn. Law and Justice; mem. Youth Edn. for Citizenship Adv. Commn., ABA, 1983—; mem. steering com. Ill. Pub./Pvt. Partnership Conf. on Law-Related Edn., 1984. Mem. LWV (asso. editor county bull. 1972-74), Am. Lawyers Aux. (bd. dirs. 1973-84), Sigma Delta Tau. Author articles, pamphlets in field; contbg. author: Building Bridges to the Law, 1981. Address: 228 Woodlawn Ave Winnetka IL 60093

BARNARD, KATHLEEN RAINWATER, educator; b. Wayne City, Ill., Dec. 28, 1927; d. Roy and Nina (Edmison) Rainwater; B.S., So. Ill. U., 1949, M.S., 1953; postgrad. Ind. U., 1953; Ph.D., U. Tex., 1959; m. Donald L. Barnard, Aug. 17, 1947 (div. Mar. 1973); children—Kimberly, Jill. Tchr. pub. high sch., Wayne City, Ill., 1946-51; faculty asst., lectr. Vocat. Tech. Inst., So. Ill. U., Carbondale, 1951-53; lectr. bus. edn. Northwestern U., Chgo., 1953-55; chmn. dept. bus. adminstrn. San Antonio Coll., 1955-60; chmn. dept. bus. edn. DePaul U., Chgo., 1960-62; chmn. dept. bus. Loop Coll., City Colls. Chgo., 1962-67, prof., 1968—, exec. sec., bd. dirs. credit union, 1975-78; cons., evaluator Ill. Program for Gifted Children, State Demonstrator Center, Oak Park (Ill.) Pub. Schs.; cons. First Nat. Bank Chgo., 1974; ednl. cons. Ency. Brit., 1969. Cons. edn. and tng. div. Continental Ill. Nat. Bank & Trust Co., Chgo., 1967, Victor Corp., 1965—; cons. IBM, Inc., summer 1968. Mem. North Central Bus. Edn. Assn., Nat. Bus. Edn. Assn., Chgo. Assn. Commerce and Industry, Delta Kappa Gamma, Pi Omega Pi, Alpha Delta Pi (sponsor), Sigma Phi (sponsor), Delta Pi Epsilon (pres. Alpha Theta chpt. 1958). Contbg. author: College Typewriting, 1960; Business Correspondence, 1962. Home: 920 Courtland Ave Park Ridge IL 60068 Office: 64 E Lake St Chicago IL 60601

BARNARD, LYNN ROGER, insurance executive; b. Montivideo, Minn., June 19, 1947; s. Clarence E. and Doris V. (Tischer) B.; m. Amber D. Keim, July 22, 1967 (div. 1975); children—Brian L., Scott M.; m. Susan Link, Mar. 21, 1975; children—Eric D., Grant P. Student life ins. underwriting, South Bend, Ind., 1968-73. With Prudential Ins. Co., Elkhart, Ind., 1968-75; pres. Barnard & Assocs., Elkhart, 1975—. Recipient awards Prudential, 1971, 72, 73; mem. Millionaires Club Midwestern United Life, 1979. Mem. Nat. Assn. Life Underwriters (nat. quality award 1975, nat. sales achievement award 1977), Profl. Ins. Agts. Assn., Life Ins. Leaders Club (life). Republican. Lutheran. Lodge: Elks. Home: 56812 Pearl Ann Dr Elkhart IN 46516 Office: Barnard & Assos 724 W Bristol PO Box 2206 Elkhart IN 46515

BARNARD, WILLIAM GROVER, III, manufacturing company executive, consultant; b. Keokuk, Iowa, Sept. 29, 1935; s. William Grover and Ruth Mona (Pellett) B.; children—Jennifer Ann, Elizabeth Claire, William Grover IV. B.A., Bowling Green State U., 1957, postgrad., 1957-59. Certified quality engr.; certified reliability engr. Russian linguist U.S. Army, 1959-62; gen. mgr., sec. treas. Vita-Mix Corp., Cleve., 1962—, also dir. Mem. Friends of the Library, Olmsted Falls, Ohio. Served with U.S. Army, 1959-62, ETO. Mem. Am. Soc. Quality Control (chmn. Cleve. sect. 1984-85), Am. Statis. Assn., AAAS, Am. Prodn. and Inventory Control Soc. Lutheran. Clubs: Sierra, Nat. Wildlife Fedn., IQ LISP Users Group. Lodge: Masons. Avocations: outdoors; camping. Home: 8811 Usher Rd Olmsted Township OH 44138 Office: Vita-Mix Corp 8615 Usher Rd Cleveland OH 44138

BARNES, BILL LLOYD, clergyman, seminary official; b. Kansas City, Mo., July 16, 1926; s. William Lloyd and Augusta (Moore) B.; B.A., Drake U., 1948; M.Div., Christian Theol. Sem., 1952; M.S., Butler U., 1957; m. Shirley Nadine Malone, Oct. 9, 1945; children—Judith Diane (Mrs. Robert Stall), Janis Caryl (Mrs. Kent Barnard). Student minister in Kellogg, Iowa, 1946-48, Indpls., 1948-52; ordained to ministry Christian Ch. (Disciples of Christ), 1947; minister in St. Louis, 1952-60; dir. devel. Christian Theol. Sem., Indpls., 1960-67, v.p. devel., 1967—. Mem. home and state missions planning council Disciples of Christ 1956-60; sec. Mo. Disciples State Conv., 1954; evangelism rep. St. Louis Met. Ch. Fedn., 1956; pres. St. Louis Ministers, 1957, Disciple Ministers, 1959; substitute tchr. TV program Lessons for Living, Sta. WTTV, Indpls., 1962-65; ministerial enlistment chmn. St. Louis Counseling Center, 1959; mem. Indpls. Ch. Fedn. New Direction Com., 1973, 74. Mem. bd. higher edn. Disciples of Christ, 1961-79, chmn. Ind. inter agy. com., 1971-75, chmn. askings commn., 1972-73, mem. theol. commn. Div. Higher Edn., 1979—; chmn. time/place com. Indiana Christian Church Conv., 1964-66. Community relations representative YMCA, St. Louis, 1955; institutional rep. Boy Scouts Am., St. Louis, 1955-60; mem. Indpls. Urban Forum Series Com., 1969-70. Served with USAAF, 1945. A Seminarian of Year Sermon contest winner Pulpit mag., 1951, 52; recipient Distinguished Alumnus award Christian Theol. Sem., 1975. Mem. Sem. Mgmt. Assn. (pres. 1972-74), Hoosier Power Squadron (chaplain 1971—), Theta Phi. Kiwanian. Clubs: Riviera, Indpls. Athletic. Contbr. articles and Sunday Sch. lessons to religious publs. Home: 411 Braeside South Dr Indianapolis IN 46260 Office: 1000 W 42d St Indianapolis IN 46208

BARNES, BRUCE ERNEST, mktg. exec.; b. Lowville, N.Y., June 16, 1949; s. Earle Ernest and Marion L. (Sunderhaft) B.; B.S., Syracuse U., 1972; M.B.A., Fairleigh Dickinson U., 1974; m. Candyce A. Boutin, Oct. 25, 1980. Sales rep. N.Y. area Warner-Lambert Co., Morris Plains, N.J., 1972-74; mktg. staff asst. Colgate Palmolive, Internat. div., N.Y.C., 1974-75, internat. product mgr. Household Products div., 1975-78; product mgr. new products Swift & Co., Chgo., 1978-79, sales planning merchandising mgr., 1979, product mgr. C.P.D. div., 1979, product mgr. Strongheart Pet Products, new products Derby Foods, 1979-81; gen. mgr. Skilcraft div. Monogram Models Inc., Morton Grove, Ill., 1981—. Co-chmn. Syracuse U. ann. fund raising, 1975. Club: Syracuse U. Alumni. Home: 555 W Cornelia Chicago IL 60657 Office: 8601 Waukegan Rd Morton Grove IL 60053

BARNES, BRUCE FRANCIS, cons. engr.; b. Evanston, Ill., Nov. 18, 1926; s. Bruce Francis and Ruth Evelyn (Achuff) B.; B.M.E., Washington U., St. Louis, 1949; m. Gwendolyn Lou Gnaegy, Feb. 17, 1951; children—Sharon Anne Barnes Koch, Steven Bruce. With Fairbanks Morse Engine div. Colt Industries, Beloit, Wis., 1949-68, area sales mgr. St. Louis, 1960-68; asso. Warren & Van Praag, Inc., St. Louis, 1969-72; pres., gen. mgr. Barnes, Henry, Meisenheimer & Gende, Inc., St. Louis, 1972—. Mem. adminstrv. bd. Webster Hills United Meth. Ch., 1968—. Served with USAF, 1944-45. Recipient Order of the Arrow, Boy Scouts Am., 1967. Mem. Nat., Mo. socs. profl. engrs., ASME, Engrs. Club St. Louis. Clubs: Pachyderm, Mo. Athletic. Home: 1503 Azalea Dr Webster Groves MO 63119 Office: 4658 Gravois Ave Saint Louis MO 63116

BARNES, FRANCIS MERRIMAN, III, state legislator, lawyer; b. St. Louis, July 19, 1918; s. Francis M. and Carlotta (Kimlin) B.; A.B., U. Mo., 1941; LL.B., Washington U., 1948; m. Mary Shore Johnson, Oct. 16, 1948; children—Elizabeth J., Francis Merriman, Barbara Anne. Admitted to Mo. bar, 1947; asst. city counselor City of St. Louis, 1948-49; atty. Southwestern Bell Telephone Co., St. Louis, 1949-51, Gaylord Container Corp., St. Louis, 1951-59; sr. v.p. Crown Zellerbach Corp., San Francisco, 1959-73; state rep. State of Mo., Jefferson City, 1977—. Mem. Gov. Reagan's Com. to Reform Tax Laws, 1968-69; bd. dirs. St. Louis YMCA, 1975—; trustee St. Louis Art Mus., 1976-79; trustee Mo. Hist. Soc., 1978—, pres., 1983—. Served with U.S. Army, 1941-46. Mem. St. Louis Bar Assn., Mo. Bar Assn. Republican. Presbyterian. Editor, Kirkwood (Mo.) Hist. Rev., 1980-84. Home: 217 S Woodlawn Ave Kirkwood MO 63122 Office: 101 State Capitol Jefferson City MO 65101

BARNES, JAMES RICHARD, county official, retired rancher; b. Reeds Spring, Mo., Nov. 2, 1921; s. George Alvis and Bessie Armenta (Blair) B.; m. Faye Margaret Norris, July 6, 1940; 1 dau., Barbara Anne Doucey. Grad. numerous law enforcement seminars. Sheriff Stone County, Galena, Mo., 1965-85; rancher, Galena, 1946-85, now ret. Mem., v.p. Law Enforcement Council, Springfield, Mo., 1970-80; mem. com. Farm and Home Orgn., Galena, 1960-64; past pres. Reeds Spring Sch. Bd.; former mem. County Sch. Bd., Galena, Galena County Rd. Commn.; chmn. Agrl. Stabilization Corp., Galena. Served with U.S. Army, 1944-46, CBI. Mem. Mo. Sheriff Orgn., Peace Officers Assn., VFW. Republican. Lodges: Lions, Masons. Avocation: ranching. Home and Office: Route 3 Box 19 Galena MO 65656

BARNES, JOANNE, computer company executive; b. Iowa, Jan. 28, 1939; d. Ellis and Ruth (Deardorff) Abuhl; children—Daniel, Linda, Kathryn. B.A., San Jose State U., 1972; M.B.A., Coll. St. Thomas, 1977. Dir. Coop. Bus. Ventures, Control Data Corp., Mpls., 1980-83, Microcomputer Services, 1983—; dir. Medctrs. Health Plan, St. Louis Park, Minn. Mem. Assn. Women in Computing. Avocations: reading, running, other outdoor activities. Office: Control Data Corp 304 N Dale St Saint Paul MN 55103

BARNES, JOHN JAMES INGALLS, business executive; b. Detroit, July 4, 1936; s. Russell Curtis and Ruth Constance (Ingalls) B.; A.B. in Econs., Harvard U., 1958; 1 son, Andrew Harrison. Trainee, Ford div. Ford Motor Co., 1961-63; research analyst, copywriter J. Walter Thompson, Detroit, 1963-65; copywriter Gray & Kilgore Advt., 1965-67; sr. copywriter, creative supr. Young & Rubicam Advt., Atlanta and Detroit, 1967-70; creative dir. Detroit News, 1970-74; gen. adminstrv. asst., mgr. advt. and sales promotion, mktg. staff mgr. Mich. Bell Yellow Pages, Detroit, from 1974, later mgr. direct mktg.; now mgr. new ventures Mich. and Ill. divs. Ameritech Pub.; cons. ARAMCO, Dhahran, Saudi Arabia, 1984; v.p., mktg. dir. AT&T Internat., Bangkok, Thailand, 1985—. Mem. Friends of Modern Art, Founders Soc. of Detroit Inst. Arts. Episcopalian. Club: Cranbrook Indoor Tennis. Home: 159 Marlborough Dr Bloomfield Hills MI 48013 Office: 882 Oakman Detroit MI 48238

BARNES, KAREN KAY, lawyer; b. Independence, Iowa, June 22, 1950; s. Walter William and Vashti (Greenlee) Sessler; m. James Alan Barnes, Feb. 12, 1972; 1 child, Timothy Matthew. B.A., Valparaiso U., 1971; J.D., DePaul U., 1978, LL.M. in Taxation, 1980. Bar: Ill. 1978, U.S. Dist. Ct. (no. dist.) Ill. 1978. Ptnr. McDermott, Will & Emery, Chgo., 1978—. Contbr. case note to DePaul Law Rev., 1976, note and comment editor DePaul Law Rev., 1976-77. Mem. ABA, Ill. State Bar Assn., Chgo. Bar Assn., Midwest Pension Conf., Women in Employee Benefits. Mem. Christian Ch. Club: River (Chgo.). Home: 705 Crescent Ct Glen Ellyn IL 60137 Office: McDermott Will & Emery 111 W Monroe St Chicago IL 60603

BARNES, LOIS SANDVEN, government official; b. York, N.D., June 8, 1921; d. Kittle Bernhard and Elvira (Trandum) Sandven; B.A., Concordia Coll., Moorhead, Minn., 1943; M.A. in Public Adminstrn. (HEW grantee), U. Minn., 1970. Bookkeeper various cos., Washington and Rugby, N.D., 1946-56; claims rep. Social Security Adminstrn., Minot, N.D., 1956-68, claims rep., Devils Lake, N.D., 1973—; intern Ramsey County (Minn.) Dept. Welfare, 1969, Minn. State Dept. Welfare, St. Paul, 1969, aging program OEO, Washington, 1970. Mem. AAUW, Am. Acad. Polit. and Social Sci., Smithsonian Assocs., Nature Conservancy, Am. Assn. Ret. Persons, Nat. Assn. Ret. Fed. Employees, Beta Sigma Phi. Republican. Lutheran. Clubs: Sons of Norway, 400 of Concordia Coll., 1200 of N.D. Home: Box 349 Leeds ND 58346

BARNES, MICHAEL DENNIS, coal mining co. exec.; b. San Antonio, Tex., Jan. 26, 1948; s. William David and Mildred Boatner (Crosley) B.; B.S. in Mech. Engring., Mont. State U., 1972; A. in Mechanics and Welding, No. Mont. Coll., 1969; m. Carol Ann Faller, June 17, 1972; children—Shaina, Ian, Rachel. Mechanic, partsman, engr. Long Constrn. Co., Colstrip, Mont., 1972-77; master mechanic Arch Minerals Corp., Hanna, Wyo., 1977-78; dragline erection engr., constrn. supt. N.Am. Coal Co., Bismarck, N.D., 1978-80, shop ops. mgr., 1981-83, maintenance mgr., 1984—. Den leader, com. chmn. Big Sky council Boy Scouts Am., 1972-77; vol. fireman City of Colstrip, 1973-77. Mem. Assn. Emergency Care Technicians, Nat. Registry Emergency Med. Technicians. Roman Catholic. Clubs: Elks, Lions. Home: 1201 Sunrise Dr Hazen ND 58545 Office: Kirkwood Office Towers North American Coal Bismarck ND 58501

BARNES, RICHARD LEE, law educator; b. Willcox, Ariz., Dec. 14, 1954; s. Hoyt Calvin Barnes and Marie Ardith (Turner) Barnes Chester; m. Kathleen Joyce Dornan, Apr. 1, 1980; 1 child, Robert Clayton. B.A., U. Ariz., 1976, J.D., 1979; LL.M., Northwestern U., 1983. Bars: Ariz. 1979, U.S. Dist. Ct. Ariz. 1979; U.S. Ct. Appeals (9th cir.) 1981. Law intern subcom. on judicial improvement U.S. Senate, Washington, 1978; law clk. to judge Ariz. Ct. Appeals, Tucson, 1979-80; assoc. DeConcini, McDonald, Brammer, Yetwin & Lacy, Tucson, 1980-82; asst. prof. Sch. Law, U. S.D., Vermillion, 1983—; vis. assoc. prof. J. Reuben Clark law sch. Brigham Young U., 1985—. Contbr. articles to profl. jours. Democrat. Methodist. Home: 320 S University Vermillion SD 57069 Office: Univ SD Sch Law 414 E Clark St Vermillion SD 57069

BARNES, ROBERT PAUL, college official; b. Minot, N.D., Jan. 16, 1934; s. Richard Neil and Erna Margaret (Broeckel) B.; m. Pamela Kay Frantz, Mar. 13, 1976; children—Claire Margaret, Elizabeth Renee. B.A., U. Wash., 1956; M.A., U. Colo., 1963; Ph.D., U. So. Calif., 1967. Tchr. public schs., Calif., Ill., 1960-62; lectr. U. Pacific, 1966; asst. prof. history Western State Coll., Gunnison, Colo., 1966-67; Purdue U., 1967-68; assoc. prof. Central Wash. U., 1968-72; acad. dean N.W. Mo. State U., 1972-75, ednl. cons. and devel. officer, 1975-80; v.p. Rockmont Coll., Denver, 1980-82; v.p. Westmar Coll., LeMars, Iowa, 1982-84; sr. devel. officer Ohio State U., Columbus, 1984—; mem. Fulbright Selection Com., 1977—. Served with U.S. Army, 1957-58. Contbr. articles to profl. jours. U. So. Calif. scholar, 1967; faculty research grantee Central Wash. U., 1970-71. Mem. Am. Hist. Assn., Am. Assn. Higher Edn., Conf. Brit. Studies, Faith and History, Assn. Instl. Devel. Officers, Western Social Sci. Assn., Phi Alpha Theta. Republican. Mem. Christian Ch. Home: 6407 Shelton Ct Dublin OH 43017

BARNES, RONALD LEIGH, electronic research and devel. co. exec., elec. engr.; b. Winfield, Kans., June 8, 1940; s. Kirby Paul and Mary (Doramus) B.; B.S. in Physics, Wichita State U., 1963, M.E.E., 1968, M.S. in Physics; m. Geraldine Carver, Mar. 21, 1958; children—Kim, Mike, Cherie. Elec. design engr. Beech Research & Devel. Co., Boulder, Colo., 1963-64; asso. engr. The Boeing Co., Wichita, Kans., 1964-65; dir. research and devel. Albright Neucleonics, Inc., Wichita, 1965-66; sr. electronic system engr. Beech Aircraft Corp., Wichita, 1966-69, data engr., 1969-70, value engr., 1970-72; founder Barnes Devel. Co., Wichita, 1969, pres., 1969—; electro-optics staff engr. The Boeing Co., Wichita, 1975-76; project engr. Kustom Electronics, 1976-77, Gates-Lear Jet, 1977-79; pres. Prozone Corp., 1979—; project engr. for optical storage devel. NCR Corp., 1979—. Vice chmn. Wichita Water Festival, 1969. Registered profl. engr., Kans. Mem. IEEE, Am. Phys. Soc. Republican. Methodist. Club: Tall Grass Country. Address: 1350 Fieldcrest Wichita KS 67209

BARNETT, BEATRICE ANN, educational administrator; b. Okeana, Ohio, July 10, 1942; d. Earl Don and Helen Louise (Handy) Loos; B.S., Youngstown State U., 1964; M.Ed., Ohio U., 1978, postgrad., 1979-81; m. David Barnett, Aug. 6, 1966 (div. Nov. 1984); children—Brian, Beth. Tchr., West Branch Local Sch. Dist., Beloit, Ohio, 1964-67, Jefferson Local Sch. Dist., Gahanna, Ohio, 1968-70, Teays Valley Local Sch. Dist., Ashville, Ohio, 1974-79, Groveport (Ohio) Madison Local Sch., 1979-80; asst. prin. Groveport Freshman Sch., 1980-81, Groveport Madison High Sch., 1981-83, Groveport Middle Sch., 1983—; cons. individualized instrn. workshop. Mem. steering com. Ohio U. Mem. Assn. Supervision and Curriculum Devel., Nat. Assn. Secondary Sch. Prins., Ohio Assn. Secondary Sch. Adminstrs. (mem. com. 1984-85), Ohio U. Coll. Edn. Soc. Alumni and Friends (founding mem.), Phi Delta Kappa. Club: Order Eastern Star (worthy matron 1979). Home: 9698 State Route 752 Ashville OH 43103 Office: 4400 Glendening Dr Groveport OH 43125

BARNETT, DON BLAIR, plumbing contractor; b. Mt. Vernon, Ohio, Oct. 21, 1921; s. Homer V. and Bessie (Skeels) B.; student public schs., LaRue, Ohio; m. Virginia V. Ireland, June 24, 1943; children—James, Faye. Maintenance and supervision positions Perfection Steel Body Co., Galion, Ohio, 1942-44; owner, operator Barnett Plumbing and Hearing, Galion, 1948—. Active, Jehovah's Witness Ch., supr. installation and maintenance, nat. and internat. convs., 1950—. Mem. Galion Plumbing Contractors Assn., Christian Labor Union Assn. Home and Office: 127 Wilson Ave Galion OH 44833

BARNETT, JAMES MCKOWN, ophthalmologist; b. Milw., Sept. 9, 1935; s. Clifford Edward and Kathryn Eleanor (McKown) B.; m. Winifred Anne Hampton, Aug. 1, 1958 (dec. 1977); children—Catherine Anne, Stephen Hampton; m. Mary Martha Miles, June 9, 1979. B.A., Ohio Wesleyan U., 1957; M.D., U. of Mich.-Ann Arbor, 1961, M.Sc., 1970. Diplomate Am. Bd. of Ophthalmology. Intern U. Mich. Med. Ctr., Ann Arbor, 1961-62, resident, 1968-71; gen. practice of medicine, Muskegon, Mich., 1962-66; ophthalmologist, Muskegon, 1971—. Served as capt., U.S. Army, 1966-68. Mem. AMA, Mich. State Med. Soc., Muskegon County Med. Soc. (treas. 1973-75). Club: History (Muskegon). Lodge: Elks. Avocations: Skeet shooting; hunting. Home: 410 E Circle Dr North Muskegon MI 49445 Office: James M Barnett MD 1560 E Sherman Suite 315 Muskegon MI 49444

BARNETT, MARGARET EDWINA, nephrologist, researcher; b. Ft. Benning, Ga., July 28, 1949; d. Eddie Lee and Margaret Thomas (Herndon) Barnett. B.S. magna cum laude with distinction in Zoology, Ohio State U., 1969; M.D., Johns Hopkins U., 1973; Ph.D. in Anatomy, Case Western Res. U., 1984. Intern, Greater Balt. Med. Center, Towson, Md., 1973-74; med. resident Cleve. Clinic Ednl. Found., 1974-75, Univ. Hosps. Cleve., 1975-76; nephrology fellow, 1976-78, med. teaching fellow, 1978-84; nephrology rounding physician Community Dialysis Ctr., Cleve. and Mentor, Ohio, 1978-83; research assoc. Case Western Res. U., Cleve., 1978-79, 83-84;

physician emergency medicine Huron Regional Urgent Care Ctrs., Inc., Cleve., 1983-84; preceptor renal correlation conf., Case Western Res. Sch. Medicine, 1980-81, lectr. anatomy and histology 1979-83; asst. prof. medicine/nephrology Milton S. Hershey Med. Ctr. Penn. State Univ., Hershey, 1984—. Scholar Gen. Motors, Leo Yassinoff, Alpha Epsilon Delta, Beanie Drake, Am. Heart Assn., 1977; recipient NIH-Nat. Research Service award, 1979-82; Ohio div. Am. Heart Assn. grantee, 1980-81; Ohio Kidney Found. grantee, 1977-78; Pres.'s Scholarship award, 1967-69; AMA Physician Recognition award, 1984-87. Mem. Nat. Assn. Residents and Interns, John Hopkins Med. and Surg. Soc., AMA (physician research evaluation panel 1981-83), Nat. Kidney Found., World Tae Kwon Do Fedn., Seoul, Korea, AAAS, MENSA, Am. Film Inst., Phi Beta Kappa, Alpha Epsilon Delta, Alpha Kappa Alpha. Democrat. Baptist.

BARNETT, MARILYN, advertising agency executive; b. Detroit, June 10, 1934; d. Henry and Kate (Boesky) Schiff; B.A., Wayne State U., 1953; children—Rhona, Ken. Supr. broadcast prodn. Northgate Advt. Agy., Detroit, 1968-73; founder, part-owner, pres. Mars Advt. Co., Southfield, Mich., 1973—. Mem. AFTRA (dir. 1959-67), Screen Actors Guild, Adcraft. Women's Adcraft. Office: 24209 Northwestern Hwy Southfield MI 48075 also 1584-A Cross Roads of World 6671 Sunset Blvd Hollywood CA 90028

BARNETT, RALPH LIPSEY, mechanical engineer; b. Chgo., July 15, 1933; B.C.E., Ill. Inst. Tech., 1955, M.S. in Mechanics, 1958; married; 2 children. Asso. research engr. structural mechanics Armour Research Found., Chgo., 1955-60; evening instr. civil engring. Ill. Inst. Tech.; structural research engr. research and devel. dept. Stanray Corp., Chgo., 1960-62; sr. research engr., group leader Ill. Inst. Tech. Research Inst., Chgo., 1962-68; evening instr. mech. and aerospace engring. Ill. Inst. Tech., 1967-69, mem. faculty full time, 1969—, prof. mech. and aerospace engring., 1969—; dir. research and devel., dir. rubber lab., dir. indsl. chemistry lab. Felt Products Mfg. Co., Skokie, Ill., 1968-69; chmn. bd. Triodyne, Inc., cons. engr., Niles, Ill., 1972—, Alliance Tool Co., Maywood, Ill., 1984—. Chmn. bd. Inst. Advanced Safety Studies, Niles, 1984—. CECO Steel Co. scholar, 1953; Armour Research Found. research fellow, 1955. Mem. Am. Acad. Mechanics, ASCE (Collingwood prize 1960, Prize paper Chgo. sect. 1962), ASME, Am. Concrete Inst., Am. Soc. Safety Engrs., Nat. Safety Council, Graphic Arts Tech. Found., Am. Soc. Metals, Am. Nat. Standards Inst., Am. Soc. Engring. Edn., AAUP, Sigma Xi, Chi Epsilon, Pi Tau Sigma, Tau Beta Pi. Author papers, chpts. in books. Address: 2721 Alison Ln Wilmette IL 60091

BARNETT, ROBERT FULTON, JR., radiologist; b. Pitts., Feb. 7, 1929; s. Robert Fulton and Mary Elizabeth (Henry) B.; A.B., Princeton U., 1946-50; M.D., U. Pa., 1954; m. Elizabeth Sherwood McConnel, June 21, 1952; children—Katherine, Robert, William, James. Intern, Henry Ford Hoso., Detroit, 1954-55; communicable disease officer Los Angeles County (Calif.) Health Dept., 1957-58; resident in radiology U. Mich., Ann Arbor, 1958-61; practice medicine specializing in radiology, Grayling, Mich., 1961-69, Cadillac, Mich., 1961—; clin. instr. radiology, U. Mich., 1960-61; cons. in field; dir. radiology, nuclear medicine Mercy Hosp., Cadillac; cons. med. arts. group, Cadillac; dir. 1st Nat. Bank of Evart (Mich.), West Mich. Fin. Corp., Cadillac State Bank. Served with M.C., USN, 1955-57. Diplomate Am. Bd. Radiology. Mem. AMA, Mich. State, Wexford-Missaukee County (sec. 1963-64, pres. 1964-65) med. secs., W. Mich., Mich. radiol. secs., Am. Coll. Radiology, F.J. Hodges Radiology Soc., Phi Beta Kappa. Republican. Presbyterian. Home: 1000 Stimson St Cadillac MI 49601 Office: Mercy Hosp Cadillac MI 49601

BARNETT, WALLACE H., music educator, composer; b. Evansville, Ind., May 23, 1916; s. Charles H. and Dorothy W. (Blair) B.; m. Mary Lois Armor, Apr. 20, 1924; children—Paul Christopher, Kerry Daniel. B.S., U. Evansville, 1946; M.A. in Music Edn., Millikin U.; postgrad. U. So. Calif., U. Maine. Tchr. instrumental music, music cons. Decatur (Ill.) Pub. Schs., 1948-72; assoc. prof. Millikin U., Decatur, 1972—, head of percussion dept., dir. univ./sch. relations Coll. Fine Arts, 1983—; cons. J.C. Deagan Inc. Bd. dirs. Decatur Mcpl. Band. Mem. Piano Technicians Guild, Am. Fedn. Musicians, ASCAP, Music Educators Nat. Conf., Phi Mu Alpha (Alpha Orpheus award for lasting contbn. to music in Am.) Presbyterian. Composer numerous works. Home: 1737 Burning Tree Dr Decatur IL 62521 Office: 1184 W Main Decatur IL 62522

BARNETT, WILLIAM A., lawyer; b. Chgo., Oct. 13, 1916; s. Leo James and Anita (Olsen) B.; LL.B., Loyola U., Chgo., 1941; m. Evelyn Yates, June 23, 1945; children—William, Mary Leone (Mrs. John J. Fahey), Therese, Kathleen (Mrs. William D. Norwood). Admitted to Ill. bar, 1941; with U.S. IRS, 1948-54, atty. chief counsel's office, Chgo., 1948-52, dist. counsel penal div., Detroit, 1952-54; chief tax atty. U.S. Atty's Office, Chgo., 1955-60; practitioner before the 6th Circuit Court of Appeals, since 1954, 7th Circuit Ct. Appeals, since 1955, U.S. Supreme Ct., since 1959. Fellow Internat. Acad. Trial Lawyers; mem. Am., Fed., Ill. and 7th Circuit bar assns., Am. Judicature Soc., Nat. Assn. Criminal Def. Lawyers, Ill. Trial Lawyers Assn. Home: 1448 Norwood St Chicago IL 60660 Office: 135 S LaSalle St Chicago IL 60603

BARNETTE, HARRIETTE LOUISE AMOS (MRS. LEWIS FREDERICK BARNETTE), bookseller; b. Chgo., July 20, 1912; d. Gilbert Bitters and Harriette Louise (Medicus) Amos; student Western Mich. U., 1930-32; m. Lewis Frederick Barnette, Aug. 10, 1942; 1 son, William Amos (dec.). Owner Barnette's Books, specializing in antiquarian Americana, South Bend, Ind., 1962—. Mem. Am. Printing History Assn., Bibliog. Soc. Am., Assocs. John Carter Brown Library, Ind. Hist. Soc. Address: 22727 Adams Rd South Bend IN 46628

BARNEY, DUANE LOWELL, scientist, consultant; b. Topeka, Kans., Aug. 3, 1928; s. James Earl and Irene (Franz) B.; m. Virginia Beulah Eddy, June 30, 1950; children—Linda Elizabeth, Mary Virginia. B.S. in Chemistry with honors, Kans. State U., 1950; M.S., Johns Hopkins U., 1951, Ph.D., 1953. Research chemist Gen. Electric Co., Gainesville, Fla., 1953-66, mgr. battery tech. lab., 1966-68, mgr. engring., 1968-72, battery sect., 1972-74, gen. mgr. home laundry engring. dept., 1974-78; assoc. dir. chem. tech. div. Argonne Nat. Lab., Ill., 1978—. DuPont fellow, 1952-53. Mem. Am. Chem. Soc., Electrochem. Soc., AAAS, Phi Kappa PHi, Sigma Xi. Republican. Presbyterian. Contbr. articles in field.

BARNHART, GENE, lawyer; b. Pineville, W. Va., Dec. 22, 1928; s. Forrest H. and Margaret (Harshman) B.; student W.Va. U., 1946-48; student Coll. Steubenville, 1949-50; J.D., U. Cin., 1953; m. Shirley L. Dunn, Jan. 28, 1952; children—Sheryl Lynne (Mrs. John Dickey), Deborah Lee (Mrs. Kim Orians), Taffie Elise, Pamela Carole, Margaret Melanie. Admitted to Ohio bar, 1953; counsel clothing br. Armed Services Procurement Agy., Washington, Phila., 1953-55; assoc. Black, McCuskey, Souers & Arbaugh, Canton, Ohio, 1955-60, ptnr., 1961—; gen. counsel First Fed. Savs. and Loan Assn. of Canton; lectr. Ohio Legal Center Inst., Ohio Bar Assn., Am. Inst. Banking. Mem. Jackson Local Bd. Edn., 1966-74, pres., 1970; mem. Jackson Twp. Bd. Zoning Appeals, 1964—, chmn., 1978—; vice-chmn. Jackson Zoning Ordinance Revision Com.; past pres. Council of Chs. of Central Stark County; past pres. Family Counseling Services Central Stark County; com. chmn. Congressional Action Com., Greater Canton Chamber; trustee Canton Preservation Soc., Interfaith Campus Ministry Kent State-Stark Regional Campus. Served with USNR, 1948-49. Recipient Disting. Service award Jackson Twp. Jaycees, 1981; Community award Jackson-Belden C. of C., 1982. Mem. ABA, Stark County (grievance, disputed fee, voluntary pro bono coms.), Ohio State (legal edn. com., com. legal specialization), bar assns., Order of Coif, Phi Alpha Delta. Mem. Calvary Chapel (elder, choir). Home: 2805 Coventry Ln NW Canton OH 44708 Office: 1200 Harter Bank Bldg Canton OH 44702

BARNO, DOUGLAS SANDEN, manufacturing company executive; b. Berea, Ohio, Aug. 27, 1941; s. Peter Sanden and Janet Campbell B.; B.A., Ohio Wesleyan U., 1963; postgrad. U. Toledo, 1964; children—David Douglas, Christopher Sanden, Mark Andrew; m. Lynn Byers Barno; children—Benton Fair, Amy Beecher, George Byers Kauffman. Sr. buyer corp. purchasing Owens-Corning Fiberglas Corp., 1964-66, resident residential constrn. mgr., Columbus, Ohio, 1967-68, indsl. sales mgr., Grand Rapids, Mich., 1969-70, resident mgr., Kansas City, Mo., 1970-71, mgr. market devel., Toledo, Ohio, 1972-77, div. gen. mgr. Stebbins Engring. and Mfg. div., Baton Rouge, 1978-79, group mgr. new corp. ventures, Owens-Corning Fiberglass Tech. Center, Granville, Ohio, 1979-81, project mgr. African-Nigerian ventures, Toledo, 1981—; gen. mgr. Fiberglas Nigeria, Ltd., Lagos., 1983-84; mgr. market devel. Owens-Corning Fiberglas Corp., Toledo; pres. DSB Assos., importers Oriental rugs, Granville, Ohio, 1981—; dir. Atlantic Export Grain Corp. Composer, performer sacred/secular music. Mem. Citizens Criminal Justice Adv. Bd.; chmn. Licking County Jail Com.; mem. choir Centenary United Methodist Ch. Mem. NTDRA, ARA, Soc. Plastics Industry, ASTM, Internat. Platform Assn., Nigerian-Am. C. of C., Am. Bus./Indsl. Bd. Republican. Home: 2300 Lancaster Rd NW Granville OH 43023 Office: Fiberglas Tower Toledo OH 43659

BARNOSKY, ANDREW ROY, osteopathic physician; b. Trenton, Mich., July 6, 1951; s. Godfrey Charles and Dorothy Marie (Candela) B.; m. Barbara Jean Kahn, June 30, 1974; children—Adrienne Ruth, Adam Ross. B.Sc., N.E. Mo. State U., 1974; student Eastern Mich. U., 1969-73; D.O., Kirskville Coll. Osteo. Medicine, 1978. Intern, Riverside Osteo. Hosp., Trenton, 1978-79; staff physician dept. emergency medicine Seaway Hosp., Trenton, 1981—; dir. emergency dept., 1983—, chief of staff, 1985—; mem. staff Riverside Osteo. Hosp., Heritage Hosp., Taylor, Mich.; gen. practice Profl. Center Clinic, P.C., Taylor, 1979-82; emergency medicine staff Seaway Hosp., 1982—, chmn. dept. family practice, 1983. Mem. Am. Coll. Emergency Physicians, Am. Coll. Gen. Practitioners, Am. Osteo. Assn., Mich. Assn. Osteo. Physician and Surgeons, Wayne County Osteo. Assn. Home: 2906 Riverside Dr Trenton MI 48182 Office: 5450 Fort St Trenton MI 48183

BARNUM, CAROL LEE, lawyer; b. Columbus, Ohio, June 8, 1951; d. Frank Lon Jr. and Dorothy Helen (Gross) B. B.A. cum laude, Ohio State U., 1973, post-grad., 1973-74, J.D., 1977. Bar: Ohio 1977. Staff atty. Buckeye Internat. Inc., Columbus, Ohio, 1977-80; Worthington Industries, Inc., Columbus, 1980-83, Carpenter Tech. Corp., Reading, Pa., 1984. Mem. Columbus Bar Assn., Ohio State Bar Assn., ABA, Phi Beta Kappa. Home: 1608 Sandy Side Dr Worthington OH 43085

BARNUM, TERRY MARTIN, manufacturing company executive; b. Canandaigua, N.Y., June 4, 1948; s. Frederik Martin and Shirley (Holden) B.; B.A., Adrian Coll., 1969; M.Div., Garrett Theol. Sem., 1972; M.A.L.S., Rosary Grad. Sch. Library Sci., River Forest, Ill., 1973; Ed.D., No. Ill. U., 1979; m. Sally Carolyn Justis, June 4, 1969. Media technician/studio mgr. Oakton Community Coll., Morton Grove, Ill., 1973-74; dir. instructional media Coll. Podiatric Medicine, Chgo., 1974-76; designer edn. and tng. AM Internat., Schaumburg, Ill., 1979-81, mgr. tng. eval., 1981-82; corporate mgr. tech. tng. Container Corp. Am., Chgo., 1982—. Mem. Assn. Edn. Communications and Tech., Am. Soc. Tng. and Devel., Ill. Tng. and Devel. Assn., No. Ill. Media Assn. Home: 1234 Dewey Ave Evanston IL 60202 Office: One First Nat Plaza Chicago IL 60603

BAROCCI, NANCY, food company and restaurant executive; b. Janesville, Wis., Feb. 17, 1940; d. Raymond Stone and Thelma Winefred (Evans) Brussat; m. Robert Louis Barocci, Aug. 22, 1964; children—Robert Louis, Candace. B.A., U. Wis., 1962. Cert. tchr. Tchr. history and English, Lincoln Hall Sch., Lincolnwood, Ill., 1962-64, Lexington, Mass., 1965-66; owner operator gourmet food and wine shops, restaurant and bar Convito Italiano, Wilmette, Ill., 1980—, Chgo., 1984—. Author brochures in field. Recipient Vinarius awards, Italian Enoteca, Milan, 1983. Mem. Les Dames D'Escoffier. Office: Convito Italiano 11 E Chestnut Chicago IL 60611

BARON, JEFFREY, pharmacologist, educator; b. Bklyn., July 10, 1942; s. Harry Leo and Terry (Goldstein) B.; m. Judith Carol Rothberg, June 27, 1965; children—Stephanie Ann, Leslie Beth, Melissa Leigh. B.S. in Pharmacy, U. Conn., 1965; Ph.D. in Pharmacology, U. Mich., 1969. Research fellow in biochemistry U. Tex. Southwestern Med. Sch., Dallas, 1969-71, research asst. prof. biochemistry, 1971-72, research asst. prof. pharmacology, 1971-72; asst. prof. pharmacology U. Iowa, Iowa City, 1972-75, assoc. prof. pharmacology, 1975-80, prof. pharmacology, 1980—; mem. chem. pathology study sect. NIH, Bethesda, Md., 1983—, tech. review panel Nebr. Cancer and Smoking Disease Research program, Lincoln, 1984. Contbr. articles to sci. jours. and chpts. to scholarly texts. Predoctoral fellow in pharmacology USPHS-NIH, 1965-69; grantee NIH, 1973—; recipient Research Career Devel. award NIH, 1975-80. Mem. Am. Soc. Pharmacology and Exptl. Therapeutics, Am. Soc. Biol. Chemists, Am. Assn. Cancer Research, Soc. Toxicology, Internat. Soc. Study of Xenobiotics. Avocations: photography, sports, fishing. Office: U Iowa 2-230 Bowen Sci Bldg Iowa City IA 52242

BARONE, PAUL LOUIS, retired hospital administrator, physician; b. Paterson, N.J., Oct. 11, 1902; s. Joseph and Jennie (Iozia) B.; B.S., Alfred U., 1926; M.D., Royal U., Naples, Italy, 1936; m. Martha Watkins, Jan. 20, 1940; children—Joe A., Jean Ann. Intern, St. Joseph (Mo.) Hosp., 1937, resident, 1938-39; practice medicine, specializing in psychiatry, Nevada, Mo., 1939-83; staff physician Mo. State Hosp., 1939-83, asst. supt., 1943-48, supt., 1948-70, 72-83; clin. dir. Nevada (Mo.) State Hosp., 1970-72, 75-76, supt., 1972-75, 76-83. Fellow Am. Geriatric Soc., Am. Psychiat. Assn. (life mem., certified mental hosp. adminstr.); mem. AMA, West Central Mo. Counties Med. Assn., Mo. Med. Assn., Mid Continent Psychiat. Assn. (life), Mo. Internat. Physicians, Western Mo. Psychiat. Assn. (counselor, past pres.). Clubs: Elks, Rotary. Home: 716 S Main St Nevada MO 64772

BARR, JOAN HARRIS, career counselor; b. N.Y.C., July 30, 1925; d. William Eber and Rachel Augusta (Sheffield) Harris; B.A., Ohio Wesleyan U., 1947; M.Ed., Kent State U., 1976, Ed.S., 1978; m. Wayne Arthur Barr, 1949 (div. 1969); children—Jacqueline and Jeffrey (twins). Sec. to v.p. Internat. B.F. Goodrich, 1949-54; sec. to headmaster Old Trail Sch., Bath, Ohio, 1969-73; sec. to v.p. pub. affairs Kent State U., 1973-74; aftercare counselor Portage Family Counseling and Mental Health Services, Ravenna, Ohio, 1976-77; asso. Cons. for Orgnl. and Personal Effectiveness, Inc., Kent, 1976-82; pvt. practice career counseling, 1976—; psychiat. social worker, vocat. counselor Western Res. Psychiat. Habilitation Center, 1977-82. Mem. Am. Assn. for Counseling and Devel., Ohio Personnel and Guidance Assn., Nat. Vocat. Guidance Assn., Am. Mental Health Counselors Assn., Ohio Mental Health Counselors Assn., Kappa Kappa Gamma, Gertrude Sandford Doll Club. Home and office: 3575 Darrow Rd Stow OH 44224

BARR, JOHN BALDWIN, research scientist; b. Niagara Falls, N.Y., Nov. 8, 1932; s. Lorne Haworth and Myra (Alvera) B.; m. Patricia Jane Kromer, Sept. 18, 1954; children—Mark Kromer, John Robert, Kathryn Jean, Karen Patricia. B.A., U. Buffalo, 1954; M.S., U. Mich., 1956; Ph.D., Pa. State U., 1961. Research chemist Corning Glass Works (N.Y.), 1961-62; sr. research chemist Union Carbide Corp., Parma, Ohio, 1962-71, research scientist, 1971-82, sr. research scientist, 1982—. Shell Oil Co. fellow, 1959. Mem. Am. Chem. Soc., Am. Carbon Soc., N.Am. Thermal Analysis Soc., Sigma Xi, Phi Lambda Upsilon. Republican. Episcopalian. Contbr. articles to profl. jours.; patentee in field. Office: 12900 Snow Rd Parma OH 44130

BARR, JOHN MONTE, lawyer; b. Mt. Clemens, Mich., Jan. 1, 1935; s. Merle James and Wilhelmina Marie (Monte) B.; student Mexico City Coll., 1955; B.A., Mich. State U., 1956; J.D., U. Mich., 1959; m. Marlene Joy Bielenberg, Dec. 17, 1954; children—John Monte, Karl Alexander, Elizabeth Marie. Admitted to Mich. bar, 1959, since practiced in Ypsilanti; mem. firm Ellis B. Freatman, Jr., 1959-61; partner, chief trial atty. Freatman, Barr, Anhut & Moir and predecessor firm, 1961-63; pres. Barr, Anhut, Sacks, P.C., 1963—; city atty. City of Ypsilanti, 1981. Lectr. bus. law Eastern Mich. U., 1968-70. Pres., Ypsilanti Family Service, 1967; mem. Ypsilanti Public Housing Com., 1980-84; sr. adviser Explorer law post Portage Trail council Boy Scouts Am., 1969-71, commr. Potawatomi dist., 1973-74, commr. Washtenong dist., 1974-75, dist. committeeman, 1984; bd. dirs. Mich. Mcpl. League Legal Def. Fund. Served with AUS, 1959-60. Mem. State Bar Mich. (grievance bd. 1969—, state rep. assembly 1977-82), Am., Ypsilanti, Washtenaw County (pres. 1975-76) bar assns., Am., Mich. trial lawyers assns., Mich. Mcpl. Attys. Assn. (bd. dirs.), U.S. (instr. piloting, seamanship, sail), Ann Arbor (comdr. 1972-73) power squadrons. Lutheran. Clubs: Ypsilanti Breakfast Optimist (v.p. 1965), Washtenaw Country. Contbr. articles to boating mags. Home: 1200 Whittier Rd Ypsilanti MI 48197 Office: 105 Pearl St Ypsilanti MI 48197

BARR, LONSON LEE, physician, surgeon; b. Waterloo, Iowa, Nov. 4, 1938; s. Nathan Lucas and Jean R. (Borland) B.; m. Martha McGavic, Dec. 22, 1961 (div. May 1978); children—John Hunter, Joel Borland; m. Mary Moran, Apr. 12, 1980; children—Mary Katherine, Margaret Moran. B.S., U. Iowa, 1962; D.O., Kans. City Coll. Osteo. Medicine, 1966. Diplomate Am. Coll. Osteo. Surgeons. Intern, Detroit Osteo. Hosp., 1966-67, resident in gen. surgery, 1967-70; postdoctoral fellow U. Mich., Ann Arbor, 1970-71; asst. prof. surgery Kans. City Coll. Osteo. Medicine, Mo., 1971-75, Mich. State U., Lansing, 1975—. Author sci. papers. Pres.-elect Am. Cancer Soc. Mich. Div., Lansing, 1984-85; v.p. Grand Rapids Symphony Orch., 1984—. Fellow Am. Coll. Osteo. Surgeons; mem. Am. Bd. Examiners (diplomate). Mem. Congregational Ch. Club: Penninsular (Grand Rapids). Avocations: music; art. Office: The Breton Med Group PC 1801 Breton Grand Rapids MI 49506

BARR, RODERICK WOOD, communications exec.; b. Oak Park, Ill., Jan. 2, 1931; s. Charles Lee and Aileen (Wood) B.; B.A., Northwestern U., 1952; m. Barbara Bates, July 12, 1952; children—Carolee, Daniel, Diane, Roderick. Sales rep. U.S. Gypsum Co., Chgo., 1955-59, Union Carbide Corp., Chgo., 1959-68; founder, pres. Applied Facsimile Communications Inc., Cin., 1968—, Fleetline Permit Service Inc., Cin., 1974—, Tel-Graphic Products Inc., Cin., 1976—, Fleetline Transp. Service Inc., 1979—; dir. Am. Facsimile Systems Inc. Served with U.S. Army, 1952-54. Roman Catholic. Clubs: Union League (Chgo.); University, Kenwood Country. (Cin.). Home: 7260 Drake Rd Cincinnati OH 45243

BARR, ROGER LEROY, court officer; b. St. Louis, May 18, 1946; s. Clarence and Vivian (Earney) B.; m. Linda Hogue, 1965 (div. 1971); m. Jill Sigler; children—Brian, Heather. Student Tarkio Coll., Mo., 1983—; cert. Ohio Atty. Gen. Police Acad., 1971; grad. Traffic Accident Sch., Northwestern U., 1971, Dept. Justice Drug Enforcement Sch., 1973. Officer, Amherst Police Dept., Ohio, 1971-74; narcotic officer Lorain County, Ohio, 1974-76; chief of police Salem Police Dept., Mo., 1976-78; chief juvenile officer 42d Cir. Ct. of Mo., Salem, 1978—. Bd. dirs. Airport Bd., Salem, 1983—; mem. Region 17 Mental Health Adv. Bd., 1983—. Served to sgt. USAF, 1964-68, Vietnam. Named Outstanding Young Law Enforcement Officer, Salem Jaycees, 1978; named one of Outstanding Young Men Am., U.S. Jaycees, 1979. Mem. Mo. Juvenile Justice Assn. (regional v.p.), Fraternal Order Police (v.p. Lodge 122). Democrat. Methodist. Lodge: Optimists (pres.). Office: 42d Cir Ct of Mo Salem MO 65560

BARR, ROY RASSMANN, lawyer; b. Chgo., Sept. 28, 1901; s. Alfred Eugene and Pauline (Rassmann) B.; student Northwestern U., 1918-20; Ph.B., U. Chgo., 1923; J.D., John Marshall Law Sch., Chgo., 1924; m. Katharine Roberts, Sept. 9, 1924 (dec. Sept. 1981); children—Robert Roy (dec.), Barbara Ann (Mrs. Robert E. Newlin), Alfred Eugene II. Admitted to Ill. bar, 1924; in law office of father, 1924, practiced law as Barr & Barr, 1924-26, then Barr, Barr & Corcoran; now individual practice, Chgo. Mem. Am., Ill. State (sr. counselor), Chgo., West Suburban bar assns., Am. Judicature Soc., Phi Sigma Soc., Delta Sigma Phi. Congregationalist. Clubs: Masons, Interfraternity Chgo. Home: 320 Wisconsin Ave Oak Park IL 60302 Office: 53 W Jackson Blvd Chicago IL 60604

BARRALE, ISIDORE CHARLES, optometrist; b. St. Louis, Oct. 29, 1923; s. John Joseph and Jennie (Bruno) B.; m. Josephine Margaret Morreale, Feb. 3, 1951; children—Joseph, Vincent. Student Harris Tchrs. Coll., 1946-48; O.D., Chgo. Coll. Optometry, 1951. Gen. practice optometry, 1951—; optometrist, St. Louis U. Firmin Desloge Eye Clinic, 1951-63, Washington U. McMillan Hosp. Eye Clinic, St. Louis, 1955-58, Cardinal Glennon Hosp. for Children Eye Clinic, St. Louis, 1960-67, Mt. St. Rose Hosp., St. Louis, 1966-68. Mem. St. Louis Air Pollution Bd.; mem. planning com. St. Louis City Hosps.; mem. exec. bd. dirs. Dismas House. Served with U.S. Army, 1943-47. Mem. Italian Cultural Soc., Profl. Bus. Men Club UNICO (past pres.). Roman Catholic. Clubs: Cherokee Lions, Cherokee Bus. Men Assn., St. Louis Variety. Home: 140 Trailsweet Chesterfield MO 63017 Office: 2735 Cherokee St Louis MO 63118

BARRATT, WILLIAM RUGGLES, management and research consultant; b. Palo Alto, Calif., Aug. 21, 1950; s. Raymond William and Helen (Ruggles) B.; m. Leslie Burke, Dec. 30, 1973; 1 child, Elissa Burke Barratt. A.B., Beloit Coll., 1972; M.S., Miami U., 1973; Ph.D., U. Iowa-Iowa City, 1983. Area coordinator Northwest Mo. State U., 1974-76; research asst. U. Iowa-Iowa City, 1977-81; mgmt. cons. Hamilton Ctr., Terre Haute, Ind., 1982-83; dir. Applied Research, Terre Haute, 1983—. Contbr. articles to profl. jours. Pres. bd. dirs. Planned Parenthood of Wabash Valley, 1985. Mem. Am. Coll. Personnel Assn., Assn. Humanistic Psychology, Assn. Psychol. Type. Unitarian-Universalist. Home: 1511 S 4th St Terre Haute IN 47802

BARRE, CHARLES HOWARD, refining company executive; b. Mooringsport, La., Aug. 8, 1922; s. Aubertin Hypolite and Edna Josephine (Brouillette) B.; m. France Lorraine McLain, Mar. 18, 1944 (dec. Aug. 1978); children—Herby C., John B.; m. Mary Wiseley, Smithson, June 1, 1980. B.S., La. State U., 1943; postgrad. in advanced mgmt. Harvard U., 1965. With Plymouth Oil Co., Texas City, Tex., (acquired by Marathon Oil Co. 1962), 1946, chief chemist, 1948-55, coordinator mfg., 1955-58, plant mgr., 1958-65, mgr. spl. product sales, Findlay, Ohio, 1965-67, mng. dir. Deutsche Marathon Petroleum GmbH, Munich, W. Ger., 1967-71, v.p. refining Marathon Oil Co., Findlay, 1971-82, co. dir., 1977—, chmn. supervisory bd. Deutsche Marathon GmbH, 1977—; dir. Compania Iberica Refinadora de Petroleos, S.A., Madrid, 1977-83; dir. Marathon Petroleum Co., 1982—, v.p. refining, 1982—; pres. Marathon Oil Found., 1977—; dir. Citizens Savs. and Loan Assn., Tiffin, Ohio. Chmn. bd. dirs. San Francisco Plantation Found., Garyville, La., 1976—. Recipient Verdienstorden, State of Bavaria, W.Ger., 1982. Mem. Nat. Petroleum Refiners Assn. (dir. 1972—, v.p. 1975-78), Am. Petroleum Inst. (cert. of appreciation 1979, gen. com. div. refining 1971—, vice chmn. 1975-76, chmn. 1977-78). Lodge: Lions (pres. Texas City 1951-52). Office: 539 S Main St Findlay OH 45840

BARRETT, BERNADINE EVELYN, internal auditor; b. Chgo., Nov. 5, 1944; d. John and Josephine (Overaa) Scheid; m. James John Barrett, Feb. 22, 1964; children—Charles F., Christine A. A.A. in Bus. Admin., Thornton Community Coll., 1978; B.Sc. in Acctg., DePaul U., 1980. C.P.A., Ill. File clerk Kemper Ins., Chgo., 1962-63; actuarial clerk Crop-Hail Ins. Actuarial, Chgo., 1963-64; cashier Bargain Town USA, Calumet City, Ill., 1970-71; payroll clerk Scot Lad Foods, Inc., Lansing, Ill., 1972-77; assoc. acct. Standard Oil Ind., Chgo., 1980-81; internal auditor Ill. Bell Telephone Co., Chgo., 1981—. Co-founder Ill. Right to Life Com. South Suburban Chpt., Calumet City, Ill., 1971, sec., treas., Midlothian, Ill., 1972; cheerleader coach St. Victor Grammar Sch., Calumet City, Ill., 1974-75. Mem. Ill. C.P.A. Soc., Beta Alpha Psi. Roman Catholic. Avocations: Golf; scuba diving; tennis. Office: Ill Bell Telephone Co 225 W Randolph St HQ15B Chicago IL 60606

BARRETT, CHARLES MARION, physician, insurance company executive; b. Cin., Mar. 10, 1913; s. Charles Francis and May (Ryan) B.; A.B., Xavier U., 1934; LL.D. (hon.), 1974; M.D., U. Cin., 1938; m. May Belle Finn, Apr. 27, 1942; children—Angela Barrett Eynon, Charles, John, Michael, Marian Barrett Leibold, William. Assoc. med. dir. Western-So. Life Ins. Co., Cin., 1942, med. dir., 1951-73, exec. v.p., 1965-73, pres., 1973-84, chmn., chief exec. officer, 1984—, also dir.; chmn. bd. Columbus Mut. Life Ins. Co., 1982—, chief exec. officer, 1984—; prof. depts. surgery and radiology U. Cin. Coll. Medicine, 1957-74, prof. emeritus, 1974—; dir. Eagle Savs. Assn., Eagle-Picher Industries, Inc. Bd. dirs. Our Lady of Mercy Hosp., U. Cin.; chmn. bd. trustees U. Cin., 1977; mem. Ohio Bd. Regents, 1970-73; mem. Bethesda Hosp. and Deaconess Assn. Recipient Taft medal U. Cin., 1973; Spl. award Ohio Radiol. Soc., 1974; All-Am. award Sports Illus., 1958; Nat. Jewish Hosp. award, 1975; Daniel Drake award, 1985. Fellow Am. Coll. Radiology; mem. AMA, Life Ins. Assn. Am., Greater Cin. C. of C. (chmn. bd. 1985-86), Alpha Omega Alpha. Office: Western-So Life Ins Co 400 Broadway Cincinnati OH 45202*

BARRETT, EDWARD DUANE, dentist, microbiologist; b. Detroit, July 1, 1925; s. Thomas Joseph and Thelma Louise (Johnson) B.; student Marquette U., 1944-45; B.S., U. Detroit, 1947, M.S., 1949, D.D.S., 1954; postgrad. Wayne State U., 1949-50; m. Evelyn Thelma Trammell, Sept. 2, 1950; children—Heather, Mary Patricia, Theresa, Edward D., Margaret. Microbiologist, Wayne State U., Detroit, 1948-50; practice dentistry, Auburn Heights, Mich., 1955-85; mem. microbiology faculty U. Detroit Dental Sch., 1950-57, grad. div., 1965-70, dir. continuing edn., 1977—. Pres. Auburn Heights Boys Club, 1960-66; Active Pontiac (Mich.) United Fund, 1963-65. Bd. mgrs. Rochester (Mich.) YMCA, 1971-77, chmn., 1973-75. Served with USNR, 1944-46. Fellow Internat. Coll. Dentists, Acad. Dentistry International, Acad. Gen. Dentistry (master, pres. Mich. 1976-78, nat. dir. 1979-85, v.p. 1985-86), Am. Coll. Dentists; mem. Am. Acad. Oral Medicine, U. Detroit Dental Alumni Assn. (dir.), Oakland County Dental Soc. (pres. 1969-70), Am. Dental Assn. (ho. of dels. 1981—), Mich. Dental Assn. (trustee 1981—), Pierre Fauchard Acad., Detroit Dental Clinic Club, Eastern Conf. Dental Continuing Educators (pres. 1982-83), Am. Legion, Alpha Sigma Nu, Psi Omega. Roman Catholic. K.C., Elk. Club: Auburn Heights Lions (pres. 1960-61). Author: (with Mattman,

Barrett) Laboratory Experiments in Nursing Microbiology, 1952; (with Mattman, Barrett) Laboratory Experiments in Medical Microbiology, 1956; (with Mattman, Barrett, Rossmore) Exercises in Introductory Microbiology, 1958. Contbr. articles to sci. and profl. jours. Home: 220 Rochdale St Rochester MI 48063

BARRETT, ELWIN MARTIN, social work educator; b. Berkeley, Calif., May 21, 1935; s. Mark and Elaine (Martin) B. B.A., U. Calif.-Berkeley, 1957, M.S.W., 1959; D.Social Work, U. So. Calif., 1974. Lic. specialist clin. social worker, Kans. Sr. clin. social worker VA Neuropsychiat. Hosp., Pitts., 1961-67; asst. prof. social work U. Wash., Seattle, 1967-71; asst. prof., dir. social work Wichita State U., Kans., 1974—; ednl. cons. Council on Social Work Edn., Washington, 1983—; mem. Kans. Bd. Social Work Examiners, 1978-80; pres. Kans. Council on Social Work Edn., 1978-79; mem., chmn. social work com. Kans. Behavioral Scis. Regulatory Bd., 1980-82. NIMH fellow, 1972. Mem. Am. Assn. State Social Work Bds. (pres. 1983-84; Disting. Service award 1984). Home: 1020 N Harding St Wichita KS 67208 Office: Dept Sociology and Social Work Wichita State U Wichita KS 67208

BARRETT, JAMES THOMAS, immunologist, microbiologist, educator; b. Centerville, Iowa, May 20, 1927; s. Alfred Wesley and Mary Marjorie (Taylor) B.; m. Nancy Ann Tabor, June 17, 1949 (div. 1967); children—Sara, Robert; m. Barbro Anna-Lill Nilsson, July 31, 1967; children—Annika, Nina. B.A., State U. Iowa, 1950, M.S., 1951, Ph.D., 1953; M.D. (hon.), U. Republica Sch. Medicine, Uruguay, 1984. Asst. prof. microbiology U. Ark. Sch. Medicine, Little Rock, 1953-57; asst. prof. U. Mo. Sch. Medicine, Columbia, 1957-59, assoc. prof., 1959-67, prof. microbiology, 1967—; exchange prof. U.S. Acad. of Sci., Romania, 1971; vis. prof. NSF, Lagos, Nigeria, 1979; vis. scholar Fulbright-Hays Act, Montevideo, Uruguay, 1984. Author: Basic Immunology and Its Medical Application, 1978; Textbook of Immunology, 1983. Served with USN, 1945-46, Fogarty Sr. fellow NIH, Munich, Germany, 1977-78. Mem. Am. Assn. Immunologists, Am. Soc. Microbiology, Sigma Xi. Home: 901 Westport Dr Columbia MO 65203 Office: Dept Microbiology Sch Medicine U Mo Columbia MO 65212

BARRETT, JOHN ANTHONY, trauma surgeon; b. Cork, Ireland, Apr. 17, 1945; came to U.S., 1971; s. Richard and Rita (O'Keefe) B.; m. Kathleen M. Curzon; children—Julia, Dominic. M.B., B.Ch., B.A.O., Nat. U., Ireland, 1963-69, M.Ch., 1975. Ainsworth research fellow, Cork, 1973-74; research fellow Tulane U., New Orleans, 1973-75; attending surgeon Cook County Hosp., Chgo., 1980-82, dir. trauma unit, 1982—; asst. prof. surgery U. Ill.-Chgo., 1980—. Contbr. chpt. to book, articles to med. jours. Chmn. Ill. Coalition for Safety Belt Use, 1984. Fellow Royal Coll. Surgeons Ireland, ACS (sec.-treas. Chgo. com. on trauma); mem. AAAS, Assn. for Acad. Surgery, Am. Trauma Soc. (bd. govs. Ill. div.), Am. Soc. Law and Medicine. Home: 1256 Westgate Terr Chicago IL 60607 Office: Trauma Office M7 Cook County Hosp 1835 W Harrison St Chicago IL 60612

BARRETT, MICHAEL ARTHUR, financial management executive; b. Forest Hills, N.Y., Apr. 8, 1938; s. Arthur Joseph and Alice Parker (Murphy) B.; m. Margaret Ann Scheuerle, July 24, 1965; children—Michael, Timothy, Kathleen. B.A., U. Notre Dame, 1960. Asst. v.p. Channing Co. Inc., Houston, 1962-68, Kemper Fin. Services, Chgo., 1969-80, v.p., 1981—. Author: (manual) Mutual Fund Transfer Agent Processing, 1970; editor newsletter Cash Lines, 1983. Served with U.S. Army, 1960-62. Recipient Outstanding Contbn. and Service award Kemper Fin. Services, Chgo., 1982. Mem. Nat. Investment Co. Service Assn., Nat. Assn. Securities Dealers (registered prin.). Republican. Roman Catholic. Club: U. Notre Dame Alumni (Chgo.). Home: 5 S 661 Mockingbird Ct Naperville IL 60540

BARRETT, PHILLIP HESTON, lawyer; b. Detroit, May 7, 1943; s. Richard Hamilton and Jeanne Marcille (Webb) B.; m. Nancy Rose Samson, June 23, 1967 (div. 1979); children—Jeffrey Adam, Douglas Austin; m. Karen Lee Hock, Jan. 10, 1981; 1 child, Andrew Hamilton. B.S., Ohio State U., 1965, J.D., 1968. Bar: Ohio 1968, D.C. 1983. Mem. firm Porter, Stanley, Platt & Arthur, Columbus, Ohio, 1970-74; ptnr. Porter, Wright, Morris & Arthur, 1974—; dir. The Klingbeil Co., Reporter Pub. Co., Mgmt. Group, Inc. Chmn. planning com. United Way of Franklin County, Inc., 1982—, trustee, 1985—. Served to capt. Signal Corps, U.S. Army, 1968-70. Mem. ABA, Ohio Bar Assn., D.C. Bar Assn., Columbus Bar Assn., Ohio State U. Pres.'s Club. Clubs: Scioto Country, Athletic. Home: 1809 Upper Chelsea Columbus OH 43212 Office: Porter Wright Morris & Arthur 37 W Broad St Columbus OH 43215

BARRETT, SONJA SUE, university dean, physical education educator; b. Danville, Ill., May 21, 1938; d. Martin G. and Emma H. Switzer; m. Richard W. Barrett, Aug. 27, 1960; 1 child, Amanda Jane. B.S., Purdue U., 1960, M.S., 1965; postgrad. Ind. U., 1972. Tchr. Eagle Twp. Schs., Zionsville, Ind., 1960-62, Washington Twp. Schs., Indpls., 1962-66; prof. Normal Coll. Am. Gymnastic Union, Indpls., 1968-72; prof. dept. phys. edn. Ind. U.-Purdue U., Indpls., 1972—, assoc. dean Sch. Phys. Edn., 1977—; assoc. instr. ind. study Sch. Continuing Studies, Ind. U., Bloomington, 1975—. Author: Study for Organization of Health Education, 1975. Awards chmn. swimming and modern pentathlon Nat. Sports Festival, Indpls., 1982; mem. Central coordinating com. United Cerebral Palsy Sports Games, Indpls., 1981-84; mem. exec. com. team aerobics AAU-Ind., Indpls., 1984. Mem. AAHPERD, Ind. Assn. Health, Phys. Edn., Recreation and Dance (pres. elect 1984), Delta Psi Kappa, Phi Epsilon Kappa, Delta Kappa Gamma. Avocations: bridge; collecting clowns; travel. Office: Sch Phys Edn Ind U Purdue U 901 W New York St Indianapolis IN 46223

BARRETT, THOMAS DAVID, municipal official; b. Newton, Kans., Nov. 21, 1949; s. Benjamin F. and Ella Mae (Hopkins) B.; m. Vickie Sue Mosler; children—Eric David, Ryan Thomas. B.S., Pittsburg State U., Kans., 1977, M.S., 1978, Ed.S., 1979. Cert. law enforcement officer, Kans. Dispatcher, Topeka Police Dept., Kans., 1969-71, patrol officer, 1971-72, tactical officer, 1973-76; evening dir. Labette Community Coll., Parsons, Kans., 1978-79, dir. criminal justice dept., 1977-81; chief of police Parsons Police Dept., 1981—; mem. Kans. Law Enforcement Tng. Commn., 1984—; mem. exec. bd. Labette County Domestic Violence Assn., Parsons, 1982—, Youth Crisis Shelter, 1980—. Recipient Crime Prevention award Southeast Kans. Planning Com., 1979; named to Who's Who in Am. Law Enforcement, Am. Police Acad., 1984; named one of Outstanding Young Men of Am., U.S. Jaycees, 1979, 84. Mem. Kans. Chiefs of Police Assn. (exec. bd. 1983—), Internat. Chiefs of Police Assn. (bd. dirs., edn. and tng. com. 1984—), Kans. Intelligence Assn., Nat. Assn. Chiefs of Police, Kans. Criminal Justice Educator's Assn. (exec. bd. 1978-80). Republican. Lodge: Rotary. Avocations: painting; swimming; travel. Home: Box 54 Parsons KS 67357 Office: 1819 1/2 Parsons Police Dept 1819 1/2 Washington St Parsons KS 67357

BARRETT, TOM HANS, See *Who's Who in America,* 43rd edition.

BARRIGER, JOHN WALKER, IV, railroad executive; b. St. Louis, Aug. 3, 1927; s. John Walker and Elizabeth Chambers (Thatcher) B.; B.S., MIT, 1949; C.T., Yale U., 1950; m. Evelyn Dobson, Dec. 29, 1955; children—John Walker V, Catherine Brundige. With Santa Fe Ry., 1950-68, 70-83, supt. transp., 1965-68, mgr. staff studies and planning, Chgo., 1970-77, asst. v.p. fin., 1977-79, asst. to pres., 1979-83; dir. spl. services Santa Fe So. Pacific Corp., 1983—; mgr. transp. controls div. Sylvania Info. Systems, Waltham, Mass., 1968-70; mem. vis. com. dept. civil engring. M.I.T., 1972-75; chmn. MIT Mgmt. Conf., Chgo., 1974. Trustee, Village of Kenilworth (Ill.), 1978-85, chmn. sts., sanitation and public works; trustee North Suburban Mass Transit Dist., 1985—, John W. Barriger III R.R. Library, St. Louis; bd. dirs. St. Louis Merc. Library. Served with USN, 1946. Recipient Bronze Beaver award MIT, 1975, Employee Campaign Chmn. of Yr. award United Way/Crusade of Mercy, 1979. Mem. Am. Assn. R.R. Supts. (dir. 1958-68), Am. Ry. Engring. Assn., Ry. Planning Officers Assn. (chmn. 1971-76), Transp. Research Bd., Transp. Research Forum, Western Ry. Club (pres. 1979-80), Newcomen Soc., MIT Alumni Assn. (dir. 1968-72), Delta Kappa Epsilon. Republican. Roman Catholic. Clubs: Econ. Chgo. Exec. Chgo., MIT Chgo. (pres. 1972-73), Kenilworth, Mich. Shores, Union League Chgo. Home: 155 Melrose Ave Kenilworth IL 60043 Office: 224 S Michigan Ave Chicago IL 60604

BARRON, FRANCIS HAROLD, educator, broadcast adminstr.; b. Edna, Tex., Apr. 15, 1933; s. Francis Henry and Rosalie (Norcross) B.; B.F.A. in Radio-TV (Sta. KTRH scholar), U. Houston, 1955; M.S. in Edn., Butler U., 1973; grad. basic personnel mgmt. course CSC, 1978, effective exec. course U.S. Army, 1977; postgrad. U. S.C., 1981; m. Gloria J. Bolz, Apr. 20, 1963; 1 dau., Tracy Lynn. Engr., Sta. KTRK-TV, Houston, 1955-56; prodn. mgr. Sta. KETC-TV, St. Louis, 1956-60, Sta. KTVI-TV, St. Louis, 1960-64, Sta. WISH-TV, Indpls., 1966-67; dir. spl. events Sta. WFBM-TV, Indpls., 1964-66; chief instructional TV div. dept. radio-TV, Def. Info. Sch., Ft. Benjamin Harrison, Ind., 1967—; assoc. prof. radio-TV dept. Butler U., 1966—. Recipient letter of commendation White House, 1966, 11 Outstanding Ratings, Dept. Army, 1967-81. Mem. Internat. TV Assn., Soc. Broadcast Engrs., Radio TV News Dirs. Assn., Nat. Assn. Ednl. Broadcasters, Nat. Acad. TV Arts and Scis. (charter), Soc. Motion Picture and TV Engrs., Broadcast Edn. Assn., Armed Forces Communications and Electronics Assn., Aircraft Owners and Pilots Assn., Soc. Profl. Journalists, Phi Delta Kappa. Methodist. Clubs: Officers, Flying, Press. Producer: Missouri Constitution, 1956 (Ohio State Outstanding Ednl. TV award 1956). Home: 10187 Orchard Park W Indianapolis IN 46280 Office: Def Info Sch Fort Benjamin Harrison IN 46216

BARRON, HOWARD ROBERT, lawyer; b. Chgo., Feb. 17, 1930; s. Irving P. and Ada (Astrahan) B.; Ph.B., U. Chgo., 1948; B.A., Stanford U., 1950; LL.B., Yale, 1953; m. Marjorie Ruth Shapira, Aug. 12, 1953; children—Ellen Jean, Laurie Ann. Admitted to Ill. bar, 1953; assoc. Jenner & Block and predecessor firms, Chgo., 1957-64, partner, 1964—. Regional rep. Ill., exec. com. Yale Law Sch. Assn., 1971-77; chmn. Chgo. maj. gifts com. Yale Law Sch. Sesquicentennial Campaign. Mem. bd. edn. Lake County Sch. Dist. 107, Highland Park, Ill., 1964-71, pres., 1969-71; chmn. com. on interdistrict cooperation Lake County Sch. Dists. 106-113, 1967-68; pres. Lake County Sch. Bd. Assn., 1970-71; mem. Bd. Edn. Lake County High Sch. Dist. 113, 1973-77. Served to lt. (j.g.) USNR, 1953-57. Mem. ABA (chmn. labor subcom. corp. counsel com. litigation sect. 1983—), Fed., Chgo. (grievance com. 1965-73), Ill. (chmn. antitrust sect. 1968-69), bar assns., Yale Law Sch. Assn. Ill. (pres. 1962), Yale Law Sch. Assn. (v.p. 1978-80). Clubs: Legal, Law, Cliff Dwellers, Standard (Chgo.). Contbr. articles to profl. jours. and books. Home: 433 Ravine Dr Highland Park IL 60035 Office: One IBM Plaza Chicago IL 60611

BARRON, ILONA ELEANOR, reading teacher, cons.; b. Mass, Mich., Sept. 19, 1929; cert. in elem. teaching No. Mich. U., 1951; B.S. in Elementary Edn., Central Mich. U., Mt. Pleasant, 1961; M.A. in Edn., U. Mich., Ann Arbor, 1966; postgrad. Mich. State U., East Lansing; m. George Barron; 1 son, Fred. Tchr. elem. schs., 1952-67; Title I dir. Saginaw (Mich.) Twp. Community Schs., 1967-68, reading cons., 1971—; elementary internal cons. Mich. State U., 1968-71; elementary reading cons. Saginaw Twp. Public Schs., 1972—. Mem. NEA, Mich., Saginaw Twp. Edn. Assns., Saginaw Area Reading Council. Specialist in reading, methods of teaching developmental reading skills and enrichment. Home: 4891 Hillcrest Dr Saginaw MI 48603 Office: Plainfield Elementary Sch 2775 Shattuck Rd Saginaw MI 48601

BARRON, PAMELA GURSKY, marketing specialist; b. N.Y.C., Apr. 23, 1943; d. Aaron Harry and Ruth (Bernstein) G.; student Cornell U., 1959-62; B.A., CCNY, 1963; M.A., Kent State U., 1968, postgrad., 1974; children—Matthew, Seth, Leila. Social worker Canton (Ohio) Welfare Dept., 1964-66; caseworker Info. and Referral Service, 1973-78; founder, exec. dir. Pyramid, Inc., Canton, 1976-79; dir. mktg. services ABS div. Diebold, Inc., North Canton, 1979-82, mgr. media ops., 1982-84, mktg. mgr. media, 1984—; tchr., cons. Kickoff chmn. United Way, 1975-77; media programmer Canton City Schs., 1975-77; program adminstr. Goodwill Industries, 1974-76; bd. dirs. Canton Hometown Affirmative Action Plan, Planned Parenthood; mem. exec. com., chmn. employment com. Canton-Stark-Wayne CETA Adv. Council. Mem. Nat. Personnel and Guidance Assn., Am. Mgmt. Assn., North Central Sociol. Assn., Pi Gamma Mu. Jewish. Clubs: Hadassah (pres. 1974-76), Jr. League. Office: Diebold Inc 5995 Mayfair Rd North Canton OH 47720

BARRON, RANDALL DEWAYNE, telephone company executive; b. Wichita, Kans., Oct. 25, 1929; s. Hawk Loy and Ada Irene (Blakeman) B.; m. Oct. 18, 1953; children—Steven Ray, Elizabeth Ann Barron Papageorge. B.A. in Indsl. Psychology, Wichita State U., 1951; postgrad. Advanced Mgmt. Program, Harvard U., 1970. With Southwestern Bell Telephone Co., 1948-63, 64—, plant supr., Houston, 1964-65, div. plant supt., Tulsa, 1965-67, St. Louis, 1967-69, gen. plant mgr., St. Louis, 1969-72, asst. v.p., gen. mgr., Houston, 1972-73, v.p. staff, St. Louis, 1973-77, v.p. customer services, 1977, v.p., gen. mgr., 1977-78, v.p. customer services (residences and bus.), 1979-81, v.p. Mo. ops., 1981-82, v.p. Mo., 1982-84, pres. Mo. div., 1984—; acct. AT&T, N.Y.C., 1963-64; dir. Commerce Banchares, Inc., Kansas City, Mo., Commerce Bank, St. Louis, 1982-84, Landmark Bank, Creve Coeur, Mo., 1978-82. Pres. Methodist Men's Club, St. Louis, 1972; pres. Manchester United Meth. Ch., St. Louis, 1972, chmn. bd., trustee, 1976-78; bd. dirs. Downtown YMCA, St. Louis, 1976, Girl Scouts U.S.A., St. Louis, 1976, CONTACT, St. Louis, 1974-81, St. Louis Area Constrn. Users' Council, 1978-81, Conv. Plaza Redevel. Corp., St. Louis, 1978—, St. Louis Arts and Edn. Council Greater St. Louis, 1984—; bd. dirs., Downtown St. Louis, Inc., 1981—, mem. chancellor's council U. Mo.-St. Louis, 1981—; bd. dirs., mem. exec. com. United Way, St. Louis, 1981—, Jr. Achievement, St. Louis, 1981—, Hawthorn Found., Jefferson City, Mo., 1984—. Named Man of Yr., Manchester United Meth. Ch., 1981, Disting. Citizen of Yr., Mathews-Dicky Boy's Club, St. Louis, 1985. Mem. Mo. C. of C. (bd. dirs., exec. com. 1979—), St. Louis Regional Commerce and Growth Assn. (bd. dirs. 1982—). Avocations: golf; fishing; woodworking; hunting. Office: Southwestern Bell Telephone Co 100 N Tucker St Room 1118 Saint Louis MO 63101

BARROQUILLO, JIMMIE LEE, educational administrator; b. LaGrange County, Ind., Feb. 2, 1941; s. Servando Pedro and Jessie Pauline (Koon) B. B.S., Ind. U., 1963; M.S., 1969. Tchr., Lakeland Sch. Corp., Wolcottville, Ind., 1963; vol. U.S. Peace Corps, Brazil, 1964-65; art dir. Lance Litho Corp., Chgo., 1969-70; v.p. Kitzrow Co., Chgo., 1971-75; adminstr. Kennedy-King Coll., City Colls. Chgo., 1976—, asst. dean adult continuing edn., 1981—; sr. cons. Ednl. Mgmt. Assocs. & Cons., Inc., Park Forest, Ill., 1980—. Leader, 4H, 1974; sec., founding trustee Chgo./Cook County 4-H Found., 1976—; mem. adv. council U. Ill./USDA Agr. Extension Service, 1974-79. 81—; U.S. del. 4-H, Philippines, 1963; Recipient Outstanding Nat. 4-H Alumni award, 1978; recipient Merit award Youth Motivation com. Chgo. Assn. Commerce and Industry, 1980—. Mem. Ind. U. Alumni Assn. (life), Ind. U. Found., Nat. Coll. Placement Council, Newberry Library Assocs., Nat. Geneal. Soc., Artists Guild Chgo., Smithsonian Instn. Assocs., Field Mus. Natural History, Tau Kappa Epsilon, Theta Alpha Phi, Phi Theta Kappa (hon.). Recipient Design award Champion Paper, 1975 Home: Rural Route 1 Wolcottville IN 46795

BARROW, CHARLES HERBERT, banker; b. Evanston, Ill., July 23, 1930; s. Franklin and Ardis (Mozingo) B.; A.B., Princeton U., 1952; M.B.A., U. Chgo., 1956; m. Patricia Wandelt, Dec. 27, 1952; children—Paula, Carla, Barbara. With No. Trust Co., Chgo., 1952—, v.p., 1962-68, sr. v.p., 1968-74, exec. v.p., 1974-78, sr. exec. v.p., 1978-81, pres., 1981—, also dir. Bd. dirs. Planned Parenthood Assn., Chgo., 1965-81, pres., 1972-73; bd. dirs. Rehab. Inst. Chgo., chmn., 1982-83. Mem. Chgo. Assn. Commerce and Industry (bd. dirs.). Presbyterian. Clubs: Chicago, University, Commonwealth, Bond, Economic, Commercial, Bankers (pres. 1979-80) (Chgo.); Glen View; Michigan Shores (Wilmette, Ill.). Office: 50 S LaSalle St Chicago IL 60675

BARROW, CHARLES WALLACE, JR., architect; b. San Antonio, July 8, 1946; s. Charles Wallace and Sugie (Williams) B.; 1 son, Hunter Denson. B.Arch., U. Tex., 1969. Sr. cons. Bolt, Beranek & Newman, Inc., N.Y.C., 1969-71, Chgo., 1971-76; prin. cons., treas. R. Lawrence Kirkegaard & Assocs., Inc., Chgo., 1976—. Mem. Howard Brown Soc., 1982—. Mem. AIA, ASHRAE, Am. Theatre Assn., U.S. Inst. Theatre Tech. Democrat.

BARRY, JAMES P(OTVIN), writer, editor, association executive; b. Alton, Ill., Oct. 23, 1918; s. Paul Augustine and Elder (Potvin) B.; m. Anne Elizabeth Jackson, Apr. 16, 1966; B.A. cum laude, Ohio State U., 1940. Commd. 2d. lt. Arty., U.S. Army, 1940, advanced through grades to col., 1953; served ETO, 1944-46; adviser to Turkish Army, 1951-53; detailed Army Gen. Staff, Washington, 1953-56; ret., 1966; adminstr. Capital U., Columbus, Ohio, 1967-71; freelance writer, editor, Columbus, 1971-77; dir. Ohioana Library Assn., 1977—; editor Ohioana Quar., 1977—; sr. editor Inland Seas, 1984—; photographer, exhbn. and book illustrator, 1968—. Recipient award Am. Soc. State and Local History, 1974, nonfiction history award Soc. Midland Authors, 1982. Mem. Gt. Lakes, Marine, Ohio hist. socs., World Ship Soc., Phi Beta Kappa. Clubs: Royal Can. Yacht; Columbus Country, University (Columbus). Author: Georgian Bay: The Sixth Great Lake, 1968, rev. edit., 1978; The Battle of Lake Erie, 1970; Bloody Kansas, 1972; The Noble Experiment, 1972; The Fate of the Lakes, 1972; The Louisiana Purchase, 1973; Henry Ford and Mass Production, 1973; Ships of the Great Lakes (Dolphin Book Club selection), 1973; The Berlin Olympics, 1975; The Great Lakes: A First Book, 1976; Wrecks and Rescues of the Great Lakes (Dolphin Book Club selection), 1981; also booklet on Lake Erie for Ohio EPA, 1980; also mag. and jour. articles. Home: 353 Fairway Blvd Columbus OH 43213 also Thunder Beach PO Penetanguishene ON Canada Office: 1105 Ohio Depts Bldg 65 S Front St Columbus OH 43215

BARRY, THOMAS HUBERT, pub. co. exec.; b. Phillips, Wis., Mar. 18, 1918; s. John Sumner and Helen (Maloney) B.; student U. Notre Dame, 1936-38; B.A., Marquette U., 1941; m. Rosemary Klein, July 8, 1944 (dec. May 1983); children—Kathleen Barry Ingram, Patricia Barry Turriff, Mary Beth Barry O'Donnell, Julie Barry Carden. Western mgr., welding engr. McGraw Hill Pub. Co., Chgo., 1947-53; Western mgr. Iron Age, Chilton Co., Chgo., 1953-66; Western mgr. Control Engring., Tech. Pub. (a Dun and Bradstreet Co.), Chgo., 1966-69, sales mgr., N.Y.C., 1969-72, asso. pub., Chgo., 1972-76, pub., Barrington, Ill., 1977—. Bd. dirs. Boys' Hope. Served with USMC, 1941-47. Decorated Bronze Star, Purple Heart. Mem. Nat. Indsl. Advertisers Assn., Assn. Indsl. Advertisers (dir. Chgo. chpt. 1963-65), Bus.-Profl. Advt. Assn., Indsl. Mktg. Club St. Louis, Rockford Advt. Club, Marine Corps Res. Officers Assn., 1st Marine Div. Assn. (officer, dir. 1954—, pres. 1979—). Roman Catholic. Clubs: KC, Notre Dame of Chgo., Marquette U. Chgo., Holy Name Soc. Home: 611 Carriage Hill Dr Glenview IL 60025 Office: 1301 S Grove Ave Barrington IL 60010

BARSEVICK, LOUIS CHARLES, lawyer; b. Chgo., Aug. 25, 1947 s. Louis Charles and Alvina Ruth Anna (Petschinsky) B.; m. Elizabeth Jean Casey, June 10, 1972; 1 son, Steven Barrett. B.A., Western Mich. U., 1969; M.S., No. Ill. U., 1973; J.D., DePaul U., 1983. Bar: Ill. 1983. Tchr. English, coach Thornton Fractional N. High Sch., Calumet City, Ill., 1970-74, guidance counselor, coach, 1975-80; assoc. Steven M. Levin & Assocs., Chgo., 1983; sole practice, Chgo., 1983—. Mem. Chgo. Bar Assn., Ill. Bar Assn., ABA, Southwest Bar Assn. Home: 2630 W 103d Pl Chicago IL 60655 Office: 11103 S Whipple Chicago IL 60655

BARSHES, WARREN BARRY, corporate compensation official; b. Chgo., July 14, 1943; s. John and Anne (Jonases) B.; B.A. in Psychology, DePaul U., 1965, M.A. in Psychology, 1967; M.S. in Indsl. Relations, Loyola U., 1975; m. Laraine Chorvat, Aug. 10, 1969; children—David Warren, Neal Ryan, Krista Hope. With Wm. Wrigley Jr. Co., Chgo., 1969—, personnel mgr., 1977-81, corp. compensation mgr., 1981—; instr. psychology, personnel mgmt. Moraine Valley Community Coll., Palos Hills, Ill., 1974-82. Pres. Palos Gardens Civic Assn., 1985. Served to lt. 1st, U.S. Army, 1967-69. Mem. Am. Compensation Assn., Ill. Psychol. Assn., Indsl. Relations Assn. Chgo. (past dir., sec.), Vietnam Vets. of Am. Office: 410 N Michigan Ave Chicago IL 60611

BARSUK, SIDNEY ALAN, hospital fund raising executive; b. Batavia, N.Y., June 22, 1941; s. Max and Nellie (Greenberg) B.; m. Maxene Frances Soloway, Aug. 19, 1967; children—Peter Scott, Jeffrey Howard. B.S., Rochester Inst. Tech., 1969, M.B.A., 1971. Acting devel. dir. Rochester (N.Y.) Inst. Tech., 1969-72, spl. asst. to v.p., 1971-72; dir. devel. Upper Iowa Coll., Fayette, 1972-73; regional devel. officer Northwood Inst., Midland, Mich., 1973-75; asst. v.p. devel. Jackson Park Hosp., Chgo., 1975-80, v.p. resource devel., 1980—. Chmn., Citizens Referendum Com., Homewood, Ill., 1980; mem. Homewood Sch. Dist. 153 Bd., 1980—; chmn. South Shore Revitalization Ctr., Chgo., 1980; vice-chmn. Rosenblum Boys Club, Chgo., 1980-84, chmn., 1984—. Named Outstanding Young Person, Chgo.-Southend Jaycees, Chgo., 1977. Mem. Nat. Soc. Fund Raising Execs. (dir., mem. exec. com. 1977-82), Nat. Assn. Hosp. Devel. (legislative chmn. 1983), South Shore C. of C. (pres. 1978, 79). Republican. Jewish. Home: 18612 Carpenter St Homewood IL 60430

BART, WILLIAM MARVIN, psychologist; b. Chgo., Nov. 29, 1943; s. Joseph Marvin and Madelynne Joanne (Stroik) B.; B.S., Loyola U., Chgo., 1965; A.M., U. Chgo., 1967, Ph.D., 1969. Asst. prof. ednl. psychology U. Minn., Mpls., 1969-72, asso. prof. ednl. psychology, 1972-80, prof., 1980—. Fulbright-Hays Research scholar, W. Ger., 1974-75. Mem. Am. Psychol. Assn., Am. Ednl. Research Assn., Soc. Research in Child Devel., Jean Piaget Soc. Contbr. articles to Jour. Math. Psychology, Jour. Ednl. Psychology. Home: 890 22nd Ave SE Minneapolis MN 55414 Office: 330 Burton Hall U Minn Minneapolis MN 55455

BARTEK, GORDON LUKE, radiologist; b. Valpraiso, Nebr., Dec. 27, 1925; s. Luke Victor and Sylvia (Bonner) B.; m. Ruth Evelyn Rowley, Sept. 10, 1949; children—John, David, James. B.Sc., U. Nebr., 1948, M.D., 1949. Diplomate Am. Bd. Radiology. Intern Bishop Clarksen Hosp., Omaha, 1949-50; resident in medicine Henry Ford Hosp., Detroit, 1952-53, resident in radiology, 1953-56; staff radiologist Ferguson Hosp., Grand Rapids, Mich., 1956-76, Holland City Hosp., Mich., 1956-76, Logan Hosp., Utah, 1976-78, St. Lawrence Hosp., Lansing, Mich., 1978—; dir. Accord Ins. Co., Cayman Islands, 1983—. Served to lt. USN, 1949-52. Fellow Am. Coll. Radiology; mem. Mich. Radiology Practice Assn. (bd. dirs. 1984—, chmn. western Mich. sect. 1970-71), Am. Coll. Radiology (councilor 1972-76). Republican. Roman Catholic. Club: Manhattan Tennis (pres.). Avocations: flying; photography; skiing; snorkling. Home: 1536 Stanlake Dr East Lansing MI 48823

BARTEL, FRED FRANK, consulting engineer; b. Milw., Nov. 4, 1917; s. Fred F. and Alma O. (Koppelmeyer) B.; B.S. in Civil Engring., U. Wis., 1940; M.S. (Stanton Walker research fellow), U. Md., 1942; m. Ann E. Staudacher, Oct. 23, 1943; children—Betty Jo, Susan, Mary Jo, Robert. Engring. aid Wis. Highway Dept., 1936-40; asst. dir. engring. Nat. Ready Mixed Concrete Assn., Silver Spring, Md., 1942-49; chief engr., sales mgr. Tews Lime and Cement Co., Milw., 1949-75, pres., chief exec. officer, 1975-83; cons. engr. on concrete and concrete aggregates, 1983—; trustee in bankruptcy 4X Corp., Neenah, Wis., 1985. Served to capt. USAAF, 1942-46. Fellow ASCE; mem. ASTM, Am. Concrete Inst., Nat. Ready Mixed Concrete Assn. (chmn. bd. dirs. 1979, hon. bd. dirs. 1984—), Wis. Ready Mixed Concrete Assn. (pres. 1969), Builders Exchange of Milw. (pres. 1966-67). Republican. Roman Catholic. Clubs: Rotary, West Bend Country, Wisconsin. Author book sect. in three editions; contbr. articles to tech. publs. Home and Office: 5421 N Shoreland Ave Milwaukee WI 53217

BARTELS, KENNETH ERVIN, educational administrator; b. Elmhurst, Ill., Aug. 24, 1948; s. Harvey Herman and Violet Clara (Mueller) B.; m. Claire Marie Zimmerman, Apr. 17, 1971; 1 child, Amy Beth. B.A., Carthage Coll., 1970. Devel. assoc. Carthage Coll., Kenosha, Wis., 1974-76; assoc. dir. devel., dir. planned giving Marquette U., Milw., 1977-81; dir. of devel. and pub. relations Elmhurst Coll., Ill., 1981—. Mem. com. Cable TV for City of Elmhurst, 1984—. Served with USN, 1971-74. Mem. Council for the Advancement and Support of Edn., Nat. Soc. of Fund Raising Execs., Ill. Coll. Relations Council, Carthage Coll. Nat. Alumni Council Bd., Sigma Tau Delta, Phi Alpha Theta, Blue Key. Republican. Lutheran. Lodge: Rotary (dir. 1983—). Avocations: collecting stained glass windows; creative writing. Home: 794 Linden Ave Elmhurst IL 60126 Office: Elmhurst Coll 190 Prospect Ave Elmhurst IL 60126

BARTH, CHARLES JOHN, art educator; b. Chgo., Nov. 27, 1942; s. Chester Edward and Adeline Evelyn (Pozdolski) B.; m. Ellen Jane Yankura, June 25, 1966; children—Paul, Courtney. B.E., Chgo. Tchrs. Coll., 1963; M.S., Ill. Inst. Tech., 1966; Ed.D., Ill. State U., 1978. Art instr. J.F. Kennedy High Sch., Chgo., 1965-69, Lincoln U., Jefferson City, Mo., 1969-72; faculty Mount Mercy Coll., Cedar Rapids, Iowa, 1972—, prof. art, 1983—. Author, artist: Che-ca-gou, 1966. Mem. Am. Color Print Soc., Print Club. Roman Catholic. Avocation: traveling. Home: 1137 Elmhurst Dr NE Cedar Rapids IA 52402 Office: Mount Mercy Coll 1330 Elmhurst Dr NE Cedar Rapids IA 52402

BARTHELMAS, NED KELTON, stock broker; b. Circleville, Ohio, Oct. 22, 1927; s. Arthur and Mary Bernice (Riffel) B.; B.S. in Bus. Adminstrn., Ohio State U., 1950; m. Marjorie Jane Livezey, May 23, 1953; children—Brooke Ann, Richard Thomas. Stock broker Ohio Co., Columbus, 1953-58; pres. First Columbus Corp., investment bankers, 1958—; pres. dir. Ohio Fin. Corp., Columbus, 1960—, United Capital Corp; dir. Nat. Foods, 1st Columbus Realty Corp., Franklin Nat. Corp., Lancaster Colony Corp., 1st Nat. Equity Corp., Union Nat. Corp., Midwest Nat. Corp., Midwest Equity Corp., Court Realty Co., Medex Inc., Liebert Corp.; chmn., trustee Am. Guardian Fin.; trustee Republic Fin. Trust (all Columbus); former full mem. N.Y. Stock Exchange, Midwest Stock Exchange. Served with Adj. Gen.'s Dept., AUS, 1945-47. Mem. Nat. Assn. Securities Dealers (past vice chmn. dist. bd. govs.),

Nat. Stock Traders Assn., Securities Industry Assn., Nat. Investment Bankers Assn. (pres. 1973), Ohio Investment Dealers (pres. 1973), Columbus Jr. C. of C. (pres. 1956), Ohio Jr. C. of C. (trustee 1957-58), Columbus Area C. of C. (dir. 1956; named an outstanding young man of Columbus, 1962), Am. Mgmt. Assn. (pres.'s council), Young Pres. Orgn. (pres. 1971), Newcomen Soc., Phi Delta Theta. Clubs: Executives, Stock and Bond, Columbus Athletic, Columbus, Scioto Country (Columbus); Crystal Downs Country (Frankfort, Mich.). Home: 1000 Urlin Ave Columbus OH 43212 Office: 1241 Dublin Rd Columbus OH 43215

BARTHOLD, CLEMENTINE B., judge; b. Odessa, Russia, Jan. 11, 1921; came to U.S., 1925; d. Joseph Anton and Magdalene (Richter) Schwan; m. Edward Brendel Barthold, July 5, 1941 (dec.); children—Judith Anne Barthold DeSimone, John Edward; m. Joel L. Stokes, Jr., Feb. 7, 1981. Student Aberdeen Bus. Coll., 1940; B.G.S., Ind. U. Southeast, 1978; J.D., Ind. U.-Indpls., 1980. Bar: Ind. 1980, U.S. Dist. Ct. (so. dist.) Ind., 1980. Sec. and asst. to mgr. Clark County C. of C. (Ind.), 1959-60; chief probation officer Clark Circuit Ct. and Superior Cts., Jeffersonville, 1960-72; research cons. Pub. Action Correctional Effort, Clark and Floyd Counties, 1972-75; instl. parole officer Ind. Women's Prison, Indpls., 1975-80; atty. State of Ind., 1980-83; judge Clark Superior Ct. No. 1, Jeffersonville, 1983—. Active in developing and implementing juvenile delinquency prevention and alternative programs, group counseling for juvenile delinquents and restitution programs. Treas. Ladies Elks Aux., Jeffersonville. Recipient Good Govt. award Jeffersonville Jaycees, 1966, also Good Citizenship award, 1967; Outstanding Community Service award Social Concerns League, Jeffersonville, 1966. Mem. ABA, Ind. Bar Assn., Clark County Bar Assn., Ind. Correctional Assn. (pres. 1971, Disting. Service award 1967), Ind. Judges Assn., Nat. Assn. Women Judges (Disting. Leadership award), LWV, Bus. and Profl. Women's Club (award). Democrat. Roman Catholic. Home: 948 E 7th St Jeffersonville IN 47130 Office: Clark Superior Ct No 1 500 E Court Ave Jeffersonville IN 47130

BARTHOLOW, ROGER DALE, manufacturing company official; b. Huron, S.D., Dec. 5, 1933; s. Cecil Duane and Della Elizabeth (Jeske) B.; m. Llewellyn Kiene, Aug. 12, 1961; children—Peter, Elizabeth, Matthew. Student U. S.D., 1951-53, 1956-58; B.S. in History, Ind. U., 1964. Personnel mgr. Sheraton Hotel Corp., Chgo., 1959-61; indsl. relations cons. Internat. Harvester, Indpls., 1961-65, indsl. relations mgr., Shadyside, Ohio, 1965-67, San Leandro, Calif., 1967-75, mgr. human resources, Ft. Wayne, Ind., 1975—. Moderator, Ann. Bus. Conf., Purdue U.-Ind. U., Ind. U.-Fort Wayne; v.p. Northeast Bus. Group on Health, 1981—; chmn. industry adv. council Opportunity Industrialization Ctr., 1979—; chmn. mktg. and program com. St. Joseph Hosp., 1978—. Served with U.S. Army, 1954-55. Mem. Ind. Personnel Assn., Personnel Club Wheeling, W.Va., No. Calif. Personnel Assn., Jaycees Indpls. Democrat. Episcopalian. Lodge: Masons. Home: 7634 Hermitage Pl Fort Wayne IN 46815 Office: 2701 S Coliseum Blvd Fort Wayne IN 46803

BARTKO, GREGORY, lawyer; b. Trenton, N.J., Aug. 12, 1953; s. Joseph and Jacquelyn (Pullen) B.; m. Mary Beth Churilo, Sept. 4, 1976. B.S., Central Mich. U., 1975; J.D., Detroit Coll. Law, 1979. Bar: Mich. 1979, U.S. Ct. Appeals (26 cir.) 1979. Ptnr. Jason, Kowalski, Poch & Bartko, Alpena, Rogers City, Mich., 1979—; pres. Presque Isle County Econ. Devel. Corp., Rogers City, 1982—. Chmn. lawyers' fundraising Alpena County United Way, 1984. Mem. ABA, Assn. Trial Lawyers Am., Mich. Trial Lawyers Assn., Mich. Bar Assn. Lodge: Lions (v.p. 1983-84). Home: 14978 US 23 North Alpena MI 49707 Office: Jason Kowalski Poch & Bartko 416 North Third St Rogers City MI 49779

BARTLETT, BUD (BYRON ALLAN), TV executive; b. Las Vegas, Nev., Feb. 14, 1940; s. Byron Edwin and Yvonne (Lodwick) B.; B.A. in Radio-TV, Ariz. State U., 1963; M.A. in Radio-TV-Film, U. Denver, 1967. Producer Sta. KAET-TV, Phoenix, 1963-65; producer, instr. So. Ill. U. Broadcasting Service, stas. WSIU-TV, WUSI-TV, WSIU Radio, Carbondale, 1966-71; instructional TV specialist TV sect. Ill. State Bd. Edn., Springfield, 1971—; pres. Springfield Ednl. Communications Assn., 1977-78, producer, writer 39 public TV programs and ednl. films including; A Tale of Two Builders, Number Please and Sifting the Sands of Time, 1963—; co-producer: Survival in Auschwitz. Served with U.S. Army, 1963. Mem. Nat. Assn. Ednl. Broadcasters, Nat. Writers Club; contbr. articles to profl. jours. Author: By Wave and Wire, 1974. Home: 520 S 2d St Apt 1102 Springfield IL 62701 Office: 100 N 1st St Springfield IL 62777

BARTLETT, PETER GREENOUGH, engineering company executive; b. Manchester, N.H., Apr. 22, 1930; s. Richard Cilley and Dorothy (Pillsbury) B.; Ph.B., Northwestern U., 1955; m. Jeanne Eddes, July 8, 1954 (dec. 1980); children—Peter G., Marta, Lauren, Karla, Richard E.; m. Kathleen Organ, Aug. 25, 1984. Engr., Westinghouse Electric Co., Balt., 1955-58; mgr. mil. communications Motorola, Inc., Chgo., 1958-60; pres. Bartlett Labs., Inc., Indpls., 1960-63; assoc. prof. elec. enging. U. S.C., Columbia, 1963-64; dir. research Eagle Signal Co., Davenport, Iowa, 1964-67; div. mgr. Struthers-Dunn, Inc., Bettendorf, Iowa, 1967-74; pres. Automation Systems, Inc., Eldridge, Iowa, 1974, also dir. Mem. IEEE. Republican. Presbyterian. Patentee in field. Home: 2336 E 11th St Davenport IA 52803 Office: Lancer Park Eldridge IA 52748

BARTLETT, ROBIN LYNN, educator; b. Muncie, Ind., Nov. 16, 1947; d. Charles Daniel and Marcella Gretchen (Frazier) B.; A.B., Western Coll. Women, 1969; M.A., Mich. State U., 1972, Ph.D., 1974. Reserach asst., summer intern Fed. Res. Bd. Govs., Washington, 1970-72; faculty Denison U., Granville, Ohio, 1974—, prof. econs., 1979—. Mem. NOW, Am. Econ. Assn. (com. on status of women in econs. profession), Western Econ. Assn., Eastern Econ. Assn., So. Econ. Assn. Author: (with Christine E. Amsler) How To Manage Economic News, 1981; contbr. articles to profl. jours. Home: 116 E College Granville OH 43023 Office: Denison U Dept Econs Granville OH 43023

BARTLETT, ROGER DANFORTH, engineering executive; b. Brentwood, Mo., Dec. 19, 1949; s. Robert Danforth and Margaret Elizabeth (Gruber) B.; m. Cynthia A. Adkins, July 1, 1978; children—Rex Danforth, Ryan Andrew, Megan Leigh. B.S. in E.E., Bradley U., Peoria, Ill., 1971. Engr., Revomat, Parkville, Mo., 1971-72; div. engr. Am. Multi-Cinema, Inc., Kansas City, Mo., 1972-75, project mgr., 1975-78, assoc. dir. corp. enging., 1978-82, dir. corp. enging., 1982-85; dir. constrn. Commonwealth Theatres, Inc., 1985—. Mem. IEEE, Constrn. Specifications Inst., Nat. Fire Protection Assn. Home: 8701 W 72d St Merriam KS 66204 Office: Commonwealth Theatres Inc 215 W 18th St Kansas City MO 64108

BARTLETT, VIRGIL LOUIS, emeritus teacher educator; b. Roswell, N.Mex., Mar. 20, 1916; s. Brant Louis and Elsie Mert (Allee) B.; B.A., Andrews U., 1944; M.A., Tex. Christian U., 1947; Ed.D. (fellow), Ball State U., 1970; m. Frances Irene May, July 3, 1939; children—Verlyne May, Sandra Ann. Book and Bible house mgr. Texico Conf. of Seventh Day Adventists, 1944-45; head bus. adminstrn. dept. Southwestern Jr. Coll., Keene, Tex., 1945-48; prin. Union Springs (N.Y.) Acad., 1948-51; bus. mgr. Philippine Union Coll., Manila, 1951-52; pres. Mountain View Coll., Malaybalay, Philippines, 1952-55; ordained to ministry Seventh-day Adventist Ch., 1956; ednl. supt., treas. Far Eastern Island Mission, Agana, Guam, 1955-56; prin. Sheyenne River Acad., Harvey, N.D., 1956-59; prin. Ind. Acad., Cicero, 1959-68; ch. pastor, Muncie, Ind., 1968-69; coordinator tchr. edn., dir. student tchrs. Andrews U., Berrien Springs, Mich., 1970-83, prof. emeritus, 1983—. Mem. Phi Delta Kappa. Republican. Club: Lions (pres.). Home: 2719 Willo Dr Berrien Springs MI 49103 Office: Bell Hall Andrews U Berrien Springs MI 49104

BARTLETTE, DONALD LLOYD, social worker, counselor, educator, consultant, public speaker, lay minister; b. Walhalla, N.D., Dec. 17, 1939; s. Abraham Bruno and Lily Alice (Houle) B.; Ph.B., U. N.D., 1962; M.A., N.D. State U., 1966; Ph.D., C.P.U., 1981; m. Julie Gay Poer, Feb. 1, 1969; children—Lisa Maaca, Joanna Leigh, Andrea Gay, Marisa Anne, Laura Bethany, Sara Elizabeth, Seth VanAdams. Camp worker, program dir. Camp Grassick, N.D., 1957-62; Unit supr., counselor Cambridge State Sch. and Hosp., 1963-64; group worker Children's Village, Fargo, N.D., 1964-65; supr. Meth. Children's Village, Detroit, 1966-68; program dir. Mich. Children's Inst., Ann Arbor, 1968-70; exec., program dir. Madison County (Ind.) Assn. for Retarded, 1970-71; dir. program and social work services Outreach Community Center, Mpls., 1972-73; exec. dir. Minn. Epilepsy League, St. Paul, 1974-75; pvt. cons. in retardation, 1972-75; coordinator spl. services, adviser Human Rights Commn. City of Bloomington (Minn.), 1975-78; assoc. pastor, dir. social services Am. Indian Evang. Ch., Mpls., 1978-79; dir. social services Stark County (Ohio) Bd. Mental Retardation, 1979-80; field work instr. Sch. Social Work, U. Minn., Augsburg Coll., Mpls., 1972-73; off-campus tchr. in retardation and social work Anderson Coll., 1970-71; adj. faculty Univ. Without Walls, U. Minn., 1972-73. Founder Bartlette Scholarship award U. N.D., 1971-75; pres. Nat. Minority Affairs Coalition, 1977-78, sec., 1976-77; mem. Met. Developmental Disabilities Task Force, 1975; chmn. Pub. Info. Coalition Project on Developmental Disabilities, 1974-75; vol. mem. Pres.'s, Minn. Gov.'s coms. on employment handicapped; task force minority affairs Pres.'s Com. Mental Retardation. Bd. dirs. N.W. Hennepin Human Services Council, 1975-76; bd. dirs., chmn. poverty com. Anoka County Assn. for Retarded, 1974-79; bd. dirs. Family and Childrens Services of Greater Mpls., Stark County Mental Health Bd., Citizen Advocacy Program of Stork County; cons. People First of Stark County; adv. Indian children Council for Exceptional Children; patron and com. mem. Lake Center Christian Sch., Hartville, Ohio; trustee Cuyahoga Valley Christian Acad., 1985—; mem. adv. bd. Mentor, Inc., Ohio; speaker Assn. Christian Schs. Internat.; founder travel ministry, 1974—. Fellow Acad. Ednl. Disciplines; mem. Am. Acad. Mental Retardation, Nat. Assn. Christian Social Workers, Nat. Assn. Retarded Citizens (dir., chmn. com. on poverty and mental retardation 1973-74), Internat. Platform Assn., Assn. Am. Indian Social Workers, Soc. for Protection Unborn through Nutrition (life mem.), Reading Reform Found., Am. Coalition Citizens with Disabilities, Focus on Family, Internat. Inst. for Christian Sch. Tchrs., Christian Home Educators Ohio, Phi Delta Kappa, Kappa Delta Pi. Club: 200. Author presentation: Macaroni at Midnight; film participant Believing for the Best in You, 1985. Home: 2602 Ocelot NE North Canton OH 44721

BARTLEY, DIANA ESTHER RIVERA, educator; b. N.Y.C., May 18, 1940; d. Manuel Peláez Rivera and Lila Esther Camacho; cert. in French, U. Fribourg (Switzerland), 1960; B.A., Rosemont Coll., 1961; cert. in Italian, U. Florence, 1962; M.A., Middlebury Coll., 1963; A.M., Stanford U., 1964, Ph.D., 1970; research scholar U. Leningrad (USSR), Hertzen Pedagogical Inst., Leningrad, 1967-68, U. Moscow and First Moscow State Pedagogical Inst. Fgn. Langs., 1968, U. Helsinki, 1967; 1 son. Tchr., USIA Bi-Nat. Center, Madrid, 1961-62; tchr. French and Spanish, Fairfield (Conn.) Sch. Dist., 1963, Palo Alto (Calif.) Unified Sch. Dist., 1964-66; research asst. Ctr. R&D in Teaching, Stanford U., 1966-69; instr. dept. Spanish and Portuguese, U. Wis.-Milw., 1969-70, asst. prof. dept. curriculum and instrn., 1970-73, asso. prof., 1973-78, 80—, fed. project dir., 1970-78; cons., lectr. in field; mem. nat. rev. panels U.S. Office Edn. and U.S. Dept. Edn., 1975, 77, 80, 81, 82, 83, 84, 85; mem. scholar diplomat seminar U.S. Dept. State, 1981. Bd. dirs. Florentine Opera Aux., Milw., 1973-76, Literacy Services of Wis., 1974-76, Centro del Nino, Inc., Milw., 1982-84; past mem. Jr. League, Milw.; mem. bd. Mequon PTA, 1981-83; other civic activities USIA visitor to Bulgaria, 1979. Fulbright Hays Sr. Fellow U. Warsaw (Poland), 1978-80, Ministry, Edn., Sofia, Bulgaria, 1980. Mem. Am. Council Teaching Fgn. Langs., Am. Assn. Tchrs. French, Am. Assn. Tchrs. Spanish and Portuguese, MLA, Nat. Assn. Bilingual Edn., Am. Ednl. Research Assn., AAUW, TESOL, Wis. TESOL Assn., Fulbright Alumni Assn. Author numerous books and monographs, including: The Latin Child Goes Forth, Bilingual Early Education Experience Based Lessons, 1975; The Adult Basic Education TESOL Handbooks, 1979; contbr. numerous articles to profl. jours. Third place Helen H. Heffernan scholar, 1966. Office: Dept Curriculum Sch Edn U Wis PO Box 413 Milwaukee WI 53201

BARTMAN, HERBERT MARVIN, electrical engineer; b. Sheboygan, Wis., May 26, 1923; s. John and Lena (Frei) Pluskat; B.S. in Elec. Engring., U. Wis., 1950; postgrad. Ohio State U. 1964-72; M.S. in Engring. Mgmt., U. Dayton, 1979; m. Alma A. Glanert, Sept. 3, 1949; children—Douglas M., Debra A., Margarett L. Project scientist communications lab. Wright Patterson AFB, Ohio, 1951-61, sr. project engr. Air Force avionics lab., 1961-70, prin. electronic engr., avionics lab., 1970-79, Air Force aero. lab., 1980-85; fed. annuitant, 1985—; lectr. Sinclair Community Coll., 1985—. Asst. scoutmaster, instl. rep. Miami Valley Council Boy Scouts Am., 1962-72; mem. bd. evangelism Concordia Evang. Luth. Ch., 1980-82, chmn. Bd. Christian Edn., 1982—. Served with AUS, 1943-46, USAF, 1950-51. Mem. IEEE Engring. Mgmt. Soc., Air Force Assn., Sigma Xi. Asso. editor IEEE Electromagnetic Compatibility Transactions, 1971-83. Home: 5303 Middlebury Rd Dayton OH 45432

BARTOLOME, FRANCISCO MABALAY, food technologist; b. Manila, P.I., Nov. 6, 1939; s. Fruto Feliciano and Emiliana (Mabalay) B.; came to U.S., 1965; B.S. in Chem. Engring., U. Philippines, 1962; M.S., Purdue U., 1968, Ph.D., 1971; m. Dr. Linda Gutierrez, Sept. 3, 1966. Product devel. mgr., packaging engr. Procter & Gamble, Manila, 1962-65; group leader product devel. Hunt-Wesson Foods, Inc., Fullerton, Calif., 1971-75; dir. research and devel. Golden Dipt Co., Millstadt, Ill., 1975-77; mgr. tech. devel. Pillsbury Co., Mpls., 1977-82; pres. Am. Best Computers, Mpls., 1983—; instr. chem. enging. Manuel L. Quezon U., Manila, 1965-65; research asst. Purdue U., 1966-71. Recipient Dee Chuan grant, 1962. Mem. Inst. Food Technologists, Am. Assn. Cereal Chemists, Phi Tau Sigma. Home: 6501 Vernon Ave S Edina MN 55436 Office: 525 7th St S Minneapolis MN 55415

BARTOLOMEI, MARGARET MARY, community education director, nursing consultant; b. Detroit, Nov. 28, 1933; d. Fred and Mary Dolores (Bonaudo) Colombo; m. Peter Bartolomei, Aug. 18, 1956 (div.); children—Frederick, Edward. B.S. in Nursing, Mercy Coll. Detroit, 1955; M.S. in Edn., U. Mich., 1978, Ph.D. in Edn., 1984. R.N., Mich. Mem. faculty Mercy Sch. Nursing, Detroit, 1955-57; charge nurse St. John Hosp., Detroit, 1958-64; mem. faculty St. Joseph Sch. Practical Nursing, Mt. Clemens, Mich., 1967-70; inservice coordinator Harrison Community Hosp., Mt. Clemens, 1970-73; nursing cons. Qualicare Nursing Center, Detroit, 1973—; tchr., coordinator Fraser (Mich.) High Sch., 1973—; program asst. leadership devel. program in adminstrn. of vocat. tech. edn. U. Mich., 1979-80; cert. instr. Competency Based Edn.; secondary chairperson for health occupations Macomb Occupational Articulation project; mem. task force on health occupations Mich. Vocat.-Tech. Edn. Service. Recipient John Trytten award; named Mich. Vocat. Tchr. of Yr., Mich. Vocat. Tchr. of Excellence. Mem. Am. Vocat. Assn., Am. Vocat. Edn. Personnel Devel. Assn., Council Vocat. Edn., Fraser Edn. Assn., Macomb Oakland Coordinators Assn., Mich. Edn. Assn., Mich. Health Occupations Educators (past pres.), Mich. Occupational Edn. Assn. (sec. 1978—), Mich. Vocat. Coordinators Assn., Mich. Vocat. Curriculum Leaders, Nat. Assn. Health Occupations Tchrs., Phi Delta Kappa, Iota Lambda Sigma. Democrat. Roman Catholic. Club: Prosperity (pres. women's aux.) (Detroit). Co-author: Tuned-in Teaching, 1977. Home: 19442 Rockport Dr Roseville MI 48066 Office: 34270 Garfield Rd Fraser MI 48026

BARTON, COLLEEN MARIE, insurance underwriter; b. Des Moines, Jan. 13, 1944; d. Robert Irwin and Harriett Hester (Judkins) B. Student Drake U., 1973-74, Grandview Coll., 1964-66. Casualty clk. Continental Western Ins. Co., Des Moines, 1966-76, truck underwriter, 1976-83, personal lines underwriter, 1983—. Mem. Ins. Women of Des Moines, Inc. Republican. Baptist. Lodge: Order Eastern Star. Home: 3701 E 38th St Des Moines IA 50317 Office: Continental Western Ins Co 11201 Douglas St Des Moines IA 50315

BARTON, KENNETH ALLEN, biologist; b. Columbia, Mo., Jan. 30, 1951; s. Donald Wilbur and Virginia (Winston) B.; m. Jacqueline Ethel Starr, June 9, 1973 (div. 1979). B.S., Bucknell U., 1973; Ph.D., Purdue U., 1977. Postdoctoral fellow Cornell U., Ithaca, N.Y., 1978-80, Washington U., St. Louis, 1980-82; scientist Cetus Madison Corp., Middleton, Wis., 1982-84; project leader Agracetus, Middleton, 1984—; reviewer panel competetive research grants office USDA, 1984-85. Contbr. articles to profl. jours. Patentee in field. Martin Found. fellow Cornell U., 1977-80; Monsanto fellow, 1980-81; NIH fellow, 1981-82. Mem. Internat. Soc. Plant Molecular Biologists. Avocations: sailing, skiing, gourmet cooking, wines. Home: 1718 Aurora St Middleton WI 53562 Office: Agracetus 8520 University Green Middleton WI 53562

BARTON, ROBERT, bakery company executive; b. Bklyn., Aug. 20, 1936; s. Martin Arthur and Veronica Julia (Keenan) B.; A.A.S., Bklyn. Coll., 1961; B.B.A., St. Francis Coll., 1965; m. Ann C. Whelan, Nov. 12, 1960; children—Robert, Timothy, Jonathan, Brenda. Purchasing agt. Ebingers, Bklyn., 1960-69; commodity analyst Quality Bakers, N.Y.C., 1969; dir. purchasing Sunshine Biscuit Co. div. Am. Brands Corp., N.Y.C., 1969-73; v.p. Am. Bakeries Co., Chgo., 1973—. Served with USMC, 1957-59. Mem. Am. Soc. Bakery Engrs., Am. Bakers Assn., Am. Inst. Baking, Chicago Bakers Club (pres. 1978-82). Club: Met (N.Y.C.). Home: 1531 N King George Ct Palatine IL 60067 Office: Am Bakeries Co 10 S Riverside Plaza Chicago IL 60606

BARTTER, KENNETH LEE, telephone company executive; b. Toledo, Oct. 8, 1932; s. Clarence A. and Hazel D. (Watson) B.; B.A., Ohio State U., 1958, M.A., 1961; m. Loretta J. Hurst, June 27, 1953; children—Sheryl Lea Higgins, Kathleen Ann Meginness, Barbara Lee Wilson, Carolyn J. Prodn. mgr. Sta. WOSU-TV, Columbus, Ohio, 1957-60; mgmt. trainee Gen. Telephone Co. of Ohio, Marion, 1960-62, div. public relations rep., 1962-65, gen. office public relations rep., 1965-67, community relations mgr., 1967—; pres. Bartter & Assocs.; frequent public speaker; speech cons. Mem. exec. bd. Harding Area council Boy Scouts Am., 1968—; bd. dirs. Jr. Achievement of Dover-New Philadelphia, Inc., 1963-65; vice chmn. planning and steering com. for proposed Tuscarawas County Joint Vocat. Sch., 1965; vice chmn. Marion Repeater com., 1979; mem. Marion Econ. Council; trustee Ohio Council Econ. Edn., 1981—. Served with USN, 1951-55. Named Lion of the Yr., Marion Lions, 1974. Mem. Laser Inst. Am., Ind. Telephone Pioneer Assn. (dir. 1978—), Am. Radio Relay League, Nat. Soc. to Prevent Blindness, Marion Area C. of C., Alpha Epsilon Rho. Republican. Presbyterian. Clubs: Marion Amateur Radio, Marion Racquet, Central Ohio Radio, Masons, Shriners, Lions (pres. 1978-79, zone chmn.). Home: 1196 Yorkshire Dr Marion OH 43302 Office: 100 Executive Dr Marion OH 43302

BARTUNEK, JOSEPH WENCESLAUS, lawyer; b. Cleve., Feb. 16, 1924; s. Otto Joseph and Anna Barbara (Hlavin) B.; m. Pauline Frances Evans, Jan. 15, 1945; children—Kenneth J., Rod, Deborah Hees, Donna Kissner. B.S., Case Western Reserve U., 1948; L.L.B., Cleveland-Marshall Coll., 1955. Sole practice, Cleve., 1955-64; probate judge Ohio courts, Cleve., 1964-70; of counsel Ginsberg, Guren & Merritt, Cleve., 1970-75; ptnr. Bartunek, Garofoli & Hill, Cleve., 1975—; trustee Cleve. State U., 1964-77, chmn. 1975-76. State senator Ohio Gov., Columbus, 1949-58, 59-64; county chmn. Democratic Party, Cleve., 1971-72. Served with U.S. Army, 1943-46. Cleve. State U. Law Library named in his honor. Recipient Alumni Disting. Service award Cleve. State U., 1973, Outstanding Alumnus award Cleveland-Marshall Alumni Assn. Mem. ABA, Am. Judicature Soc., Ohio Bar Assn. Assn. Trial Lawyers Am., Bar Assn. Greater Cleve. Democrat. Roman Catholic. Clubs: Hermit, Athletic (Cleve.) Office: Bartunek Garofoli & Hill 950 Bond Court Bldg 1300 E Ninth St Cleveland OH 44114

BASAVARAJA, HIRE MATADA, anesthesiologist; b. Bellary, India, Aug. 30, 1944; came to U.S. 1975, naturalized, 1981; s. Gurusanthiah and Nagamma (Nagamma) Hirematada; m. Ratna Basappa, Mar. 11, 1974; 1 child, Vinay. B.S. Veerasaiva Coll., Karnataka, India, 1963; M.D., Mysore Med. Coll., Karnataka, 1969. Diplomate Am. Anesthesiology Bd. Intern Fairview Gen. Hosp., Cleve., 1975-76; resident in anesthesiology Huron Rd. Hosp./Cleve. Clinic, 1976-77, Univ. Hosps. of Cleve., 1977-78; lectr. in anatomy Mysore Med. Coll., 1970-75; anesthesiologist Ball Mem. Hosp., Muncie, Ind., 1978—. Mem. Am. Soc. of Anesthesiology. AMA, Ind. State Med. Assn. Home: 4109 Squire Muncie IN 47304

BASCO, MAXIMINO PLATON, physician, diagnostic radiologist; b. Batangas City, Philippines, Nov. 29, 1945; came to U.S., 1971, naturalized, 1973; s. Eusebio Alcantara and Purificacion Laurel (Platon) B.; m. Evelyn Carpena Ganaden, May 20, 1971; children—Michael, Maria Theresa, Martelino, Marvin. B.S., U. Santo Tomas, 1965, M.D., 1970. Diplomate Am. Bd. Radiology. Intern U.S. Naval Hosp., Zambales, 1969-70; resident physician Philippine Gen. Hosp., Manila, 1970-71; intern Columbus Cuneo Med. Ctr., Chgo., 1971-72; resident physician Northwestern U., 1972-75; attending physician Holy Cross Hosp., Chgo., 1975—, staff radiologist, 1975—, sect. chief C.T. Lab, cons., chmn. radiol. equipment procurement com., radiol. standardization com., emergency room radiology staff. Mem. AMA, Ill. Med. Assn., Chgo. Med. Soc., Am. Coll. Radiology, Radiol. Soc. N.Am., Am. Coll. Nuclear Medicine, Philippine Med. Assn. Chgo. (past pres.), U. Santo Tomas Med. Alumni Assn. of Midwest (past pres.). Roman Catholic. Office: 2701 W 68th St Chicago IL 60629

BASFORD, JAMES O., corrugated manufacturing company executive; b. Akron, Ohio, Apr. 17, 1931; s. Hazel M. (Fernsner) Basford; m. Mary Eleanor Hagemeyer, Mar. 16, 1957; children—Jeffrey James, Gregory Robert, Lisa Jean. Student Kent State U., 1949-51, 55-58. Asst. sales mgr. San Hygene Furniture, Akron, 1957-59; gen. sales mgr. Adjusta Post Mfg. Co., Akron, 1959-61; area sales mgr. Crown Zellerbach Corp., Columbus, Ohio, 1961-74; v.p. Buckeye Container Corp., Wooster, Ohio, 1974-78, pres., chief exec. officer, 1978—, also dir.; dir. Peoples Fed. Savs. Bank, Wooster. Served to staff sgt. USAF, 1951-54, Korea. Mem. Wooster C. of C. (bd. dirs. 1975-78). Republican. Lutheran. Lodge: Rotary (bd. dirs. 1976-79). Avocations: golf; skiing; tennis. Home: 1580 Arthur Dr Wooster OH 44691 Office: Buckeye Corrugated Inc PO Box 16 Wooster OH 44691

BASHA, ANWER, research chemist, educator; b. Vellore, India, Mar. 14, 1947; s. Qader and Khairun Nisa (sharif) B.; m. Fatima Zehra Ghias, Aug. 5, 1977; children—Umaer, Anwer. Ph.D. Karachi U., Pakistan, 1975. Research officer Pakistan Council Sci. and Indsl. Research, Karachi, 1968-75; research fellow Fordham U., N.Y.C., 1976-78; research assoc. MIT, Cambridge, 1978-81, U. Ill., Urbana, 1981—. Internat. Found. Sci. grantee, Sweden, 1976. Mem. Am. Chem. Soc., Sigma Xi, Phi Lambda Epsilon. Patentee anticancer drug. Author: Biosynthesis of Indole Alkaloids, 1983; contbr. articles to profl. jours. Home: 232 Bayshore Dr Lake Bluff IL 60044 Office: U Ill 361 Roger Adams Lab Urbana IL 61801

BASHAW, DONALD EUGENE, county agency superintendent; b. Columbus, Ohio, March 16, 1948; s. Donald E. and Hazel M. (Walter) B.; m. Kathleen L. Baldwin; children—Kerrie, Corey, Andrew, Stephanie. B.S. Kent State U., 1969, M.Ed., 1971, Ed. S., 1972. Cert. supt. and qualified mental retardation profl. Tchr. Portage County Bd. of Mental Retardation and Developmental Disabilities, Ravenna, Ohio, 1970-71, dir., 1972-73; supt. Richland County Bd. of Mental Retardation and Developmental Disabilities, Mansfield, Ohio, 1973—; partner-owner Woodcarver Designs, Mansfield, 1980—; cons.-surveyor Commn. on Accreditation of Rehab. Facilities, Tucson, 1985—; contract cons. U.S. Dept. Edn. Author: I Am Me, 1976, Self Management Development, 1979. Mem. Profl. Assn. for Retardation (pres. 1979-82), Am. Mgmt. Assns., Am. Assn. on Mental Deficiency, Nat. Rehab. Assn., Nat. Assn. Residential Operators. Democrat. Avocations: swimming; golf; reading; gardening. Home: 2559 Crider Rd Rt 11 Mansfield OH 44903 Office: Richland County Bd of MR/DD Richland Newhope Adminstrn Bldg 314 Clevland Ave Mansfield OH 44903

BASHIAN, AUDREY JOAN, school psychologist; b. Cleve., Sept. 4, 1932; d. Otto Herman and Hermine Johanna (Wlotzko) Schwarzmann; m. Charles Bashian, Jan. 25, 1958; children—Alison Hermine, Jack Otto. B.S., Northwestern U., 1954; M.A., Cleve. State U., 1973. Psychologist, East Cleveland (Ohio) City Schs., 1972-79; dir. children's services Northeast Community Mental Health Center, Cleve., 1979-80; sch. psychologist PSI Assocs., Cuyahoga Falls, Ohio, 1980—. Mem. Nat. Assn. Sch. Psychologists, Am. Psychol. Assn., Ohio Sch. Psychologists Assn., Cleve. Assn. Sch. Psychologists. Baptist. Home: 6355 Huntington Dr Solon OH 44139

BASILE, FRANK MICHEL, property management company executive; b. New Orleans, Oct. 6, 1939; s. Vincent Charles and Ursula Mary (Sendker) B.; B.B.A., Tulane U., 1961; children—Jeffrey, Jason. With Ford Motor Co., 1963-75, gen. field mgr., Indpls., 1971-75; pres. Charisma Publs., Inc., Indpls., 1977—; v.p. Gene Glick Mgmt. Corp., Indpls., 1975—; pres. Indpls. Free U., 1982-83; internat. bd. dirs. Parents Without Partners, 1977-78; bd. dirs. Ind. Better Bus. Bur. Cert. property mgr.; cert. Speaking profl. Mem. Nat. Apt. Assn. (v.p. 1980), Nat. Assn. Home Builders, Inst. Real Estate Mgmt. (nat. faculty), Nat. Speakers Assn. (pres. Ind. chpt.), Apt. Assn. Ind. (pres. 1979), Indpls. Sales and Mktg. Execs. (pres. 1981-82), Beta Gamma Sigma. Club: Woodland Springs. Author: Come Fly With Me, 1978; Back to Basics with Basile, 1978; Management Company Reporting Structure, 1978; Beyond The Basics, 1980; Professional Multihousing Management, 1981; Flying to your Success, 1983; also articles; Contbg. editor mgmt. Indpls. Bus. Jour.; columnist Ind. Bus. Mag. Office: 9102 N Meridian St Indianapolis IN 46260

BASILE, ROBERT MANLIUS, geographer, soil scientist, emeritus educator; b. Youngstown, Ohio, Mar. 12, 1916; s. Giustino G. and Minnie H. (Bailey) B.; B.S., Washington and Lee U., 1938; M.S., Mich. State U., 1940; Ph.D., Ohio State U., 1953; m. Anne Judson Webb, May 23, 1945; children—Elizabeth Anne (dec.), L. Lorraine Allison, Karen L. Nofziger. Instr., Northwestern State Coll., Alva, Okla., 1940-42; soil scientist Bur. Reclamation, Huron, S.D., 1947-48, 1950; instr. geography Ohio State Univ., Columbus, 1953-56, asst.

prof., 1956-62, assoc. prof., 1962-68, prof., 1968-69; prof. geography U. Toledo, 1969-81, prof. emeritus, 1981—; vis. prof. Ohio U., summer 1952, U. Winnipeg, summer 1960, San Jose State U., summer 1966, U. S.C., summer 1967, U. Wyo., summer 1981. Served with USN, 1942-45. NATO grantee, 1966; Nat. Resources Inst. grantee, 1966-67. Mem. Assn. Am. Geographers, Soil Sci. Soc. Am., AAAS, Assn. Ohio Pedologists, Smithsonian Instn., Wilderness Soc., Phi Kappa Phi, Gamma Theta Upsilon. Author: A Geography of Soils, 1972; editor: Selected Readings in the Geography of Soils, 1980; illustrator textbook Ohio: The Buckeye State; contbr. articles to profl. jours. Home: 5929 Angleview Ct Sylvania OH 43560 Office: Univ of Toledo Bancroft St Toledo OH 43606

BASKIN, JOHN ROLAND, lawyer; b. Cleve., Dec. 23, 1916; s. Roland A. and Frances M. (Schwoerer) B.; A.B. magna cum laude, Western Res. U., 1938, LL.B., 1940; m. Madeline Stricker, Feb. 26, 1949 (dec. 1965); d., Barbara Anne; m. 2d, Betty Anne Meyer, May 12, 1967. Admitted to Ohio bar, 1940, FCC, 1949, U.S. Supreme Ct., 1955; practiced in Cleve., 1940—, asso. mem. firm Baker & Hostetler, 1941-54, partner, 1954—. Spl. agt. AUS CIC, U.S. Atomic Bomb project, 1942-46, CIC officer, Armed Forces Spl. Weapons project, 1951-52. Mem. Am., Ohio, Cleve. bar assns., Order of the Coif, Phi Beta Kappa, Delta Tau Delta, Delta Theta Phi, Court of Nisi Prius. Republican. Episcopalian. Clubs: Union, Mayfield Country (Cleve.). Home: 2679 Ashley Rd Shaker Heights OH 44122 also Buttonwood Bay Key Largo FL 33037 also East Chop Martha's Vineyard MA 02557 Office: 3200 National City Center Cleveland OH 44114

BASKIN, LAWRENCE MARVIN, school superintendent; b. Rochester, N.Y., May 27, 1947; s. Paul and Ruth (Freedman) B.; m. Barbara Sue Baskin; children—Lindsay Michelle, Jaime Lynn, Traci Cheryl. B.S., Bradley U., 1970; M.Ed., Loyola U. Chgo., 1973; Ed.D., 1984. Tchr., Sch. Dist. 63, Niles, Ill., 1970-73; asst. prin. Sch. Dist. #21, Wheeling, Ill., 1973-77, prin. elementary sch., 1977-79; prin. jr. high sch. Sch. Dist. #70, Libertyville, Ill., 1979-81, asst. supt. schs., 1981-86, supt., 1986—. Mem. Nat. Assn. Elementary Sch. Prins., Assn. for Supervision and Curriculum Devel., Ill. Prins. Assn., Ill. Assn. Supervision and Curriculum Devel., Phi Delta Kappa. Jewish. Home: 4129 Ridge Ave Arlington Heights IL 60004 Office: 1441 W Lake St Libertyville IL 60048

BASOLO, FRED, chemistry educator; b. Coello, Ill., Feb. 11, 1920; s. John and Catherine (Marino) B.; m. Mary P. Nutley, June 14, 1947; children—Mary-Catherine, Fred, Margrete Ann, Elizabeth. B.Ed., So. Ill. Normal U., 1940; M.S., U. Ill., 1942, Ph.D., 1943. Research chemist Rohm & Haas, 1943-46; instr. Northwestern U., Evanston, Ill., 1946-49, asst. prof., 1949-52, assoc. prof., 1952-58, prof. chemistry, 1958-80, Morrison prof. chemistry, 1980—, chmn. dept. chemistry, 1969-72; lectr., cons. in field. Recipient Bailar medal, 1972, So. Ill. Alumni Achievement award, 1974, Dwyer medal, 1976, James Flack Norris award for outstanding achievement in teaching chemistry, 1981; Guggenheim fellow, 1954-55; sr. NSF fellow, 1962; NATO sr. scientist fellow, Italy, 1981. Fellow AAAS, Japanese Soc. for Promotion of Sci.; mem. Italian Chem. Soc. (hon.), Am. Chem. Soc. (dir., award for research in inorganic chemistry, 1964, award for disting. service in inorganic chemistry 1975, pres. 1983), Nat. Acad. Scis., Am. Acad. Arts and Scis., Chem. Soc. London, Sigma Xi, Kappa Delta Phi, Phi Lambda Upsilon, Alpha Chi Sigma. Author: (with R.G. Pearson) Mechanisms of Inorganic Reactions, 1958, 67; (with R.C. Johnson) Coordination Chemistry, 1964; asst. editor Jour. Am. Chem. Soc., 1961-64; assoc. editor Chem. Rev., 1960-65, Inorganica Chemica Acta, 1967—, Inorganic Chemica Acta Letters, 1977—; mem. editorial adv. bd. Advances in Chemistry Series, Accounts in Chem. Research, many others; co-editor: Inorganic Syntheses, Vol. XVI, 1976; Catalysis, 1973; Transition Metal Chemistry, 2 vols., 1973, 77; contbr. over 250 articles to profl. jours. Address: Northwestern Univ Dept Chemistry Evanston IL 60201

BASS, DERWIN HARTLEY, architect, developer; b. Midland, Mich., Feb. 23, 1946; s. Shailer Linwood and Elisabeth (Alberti) B.; m. Katherine Ruth Malzahn, Aug. 31, 1968; 1 child, Melissa Marie Malzahn-Bass. B. Arch., U. Minn., 1971; A.A. in Archtl. Tech., Delta Coll., 1967. Registered architect, Mich. Archtl. designer Kellogg & Kiefer Architects, Kalamazoo, 1971-73; project architect Kingscott Assoc., Inc., Kalamazoo, 1973-77; architect, planner, prin. Environ. Social Planners, Kalamazoo, 1977-79; project architect Alden B. Dow Assoc., Inc., Midland, Mich., 1979-81; dir. mktg. and devel. Dow-Howell-Gilmore Assoc., Midland, 1981—; dir. mktg. plan Orgn. & Effort; real estate devel. Chmn. Midland Hist. Adv. Commn., 1979-85; mem. Kalamazoo County Met. Planning Commn., chmn., 1974-79; mem. Rotary Internat. study team to Argentina, spring 1982. Mem. AIA (Design Award, 1975), Mich. Soc. Architects, Soc. Mktg. Profl. Services, Mich. Indsl. Developers Assoc. Presbyterian. Architect/designer numerous schools. Home: 4406 Hampshire St Midland MI 48640 Office: 315 Post St Midland MI 48640

BASS, HAROLD EUGENE, communications company executive; b. Neosho, Mo., July 30, 1940; s. Harold Virgil and Mildred Lucille (Charelton) B. m. Virginia Lea Bass, Sept. 27, 1958; children—David Eugene, Carolyn Sue, Robert Lee, Ronald Dean. A.A., West Valley Jr. Coll., 1971. Frameman to chief equipment man Pacific Telephone Co., Santa Clara, Calif., 1968-79; switching equipment technician, supr. network services Southwestern Bell Telephone, Sedalia, Mo., 1979-84, Marshall, Mo., 1984—. Pres., Pettis County unit Am. Cancer Soc., 1979-83, v.p., 1984, chmn. pub. edn. com. Pettis County unit, 1981-83, dir. pub. edn. dist. 5, 1982-84, bd. dirs.-at-large Mo. div., 1983-84, chmn. div. pub. edn., exec. com. Mo. div., 1984-85; bd. dirs. United Way, Jr. Achievement; chmn. human rights commn. City of Sedalia. Served with USN, 1958-68. Mem. Naval Enlisted Res. Assn. Republican. Baptist. Club: Noonday Optimist. Lodge: Masons. Home: 1001 Douglas Ln Sedalia MO 65301 Office: 220 E 5th St Sedalia MO 65301

BASS, JOHN F., state senator; b. St. Louis, July 18, 1926; s. Dee and Alma (Brown) B.; m. Frieda Whitmore, Mar. 20, 1946; 1 child, Jill Triplett. B.B.A., Lincoln U., 1959; M.A., Washington U., St. Louis, 1962, also postgrad. Comptroller, City of St. Louis, 1973-77; mem. St. Louis Bd. Aldermen, 1978-79; dir. Mo. Dept. Transp., 1979-81; mem. Mo. State Senate, 1981—. Mem. rules com. Democratic Nat. Conv., 1980; sec.-treas. Nat. Black Caucus of Local Elected Ofcls., 1975-77; del. Democratic Nat. Conv., 1976, 84; mem. adv. council St. Louis Mcpl. Employment Pension Bd., St. Louis Agy. on Tng. and Employment, St. Louis Pub. Schs. Vocat. Tech. Edn.; mem. adv. bd. Mathews-Dickey Boys Club; social human resources advisor Cardinal Ritter. Bd. dirs. Mo. Mcpl. League, St. Louis Police Pension Bd.; trustee Parson Blewett Found. Served with USNR, 1944-46. Mem. NAACP, St. Louis Ambassadors, Urban League, Mcpl. Fin. Officers. Assn., Am. Legion, Lincoln Univ. Found. Democrat. Roman Catholic. Clubs: Royal Vagabonds, Anniversary. Office: Room 220 State Capitol Jefferson City MO 65101

BASS, LARRY JUNIOR, clinical psychologist, educator; b. Granby, Mo., Aug. 2, 1944; s. Harold Virgil and Mildred Lucille (Charlton) B.; B.S., U. Mo., 1966, M.S. (NDEA fellow), 1967; Ph.D., Washington U., St. Louis, 1972; m. Meredith Aenone Copeland, Aug. 17, 1968; children—Mark, Darren, Adam. Research asst. Washington U., 1967-68, staff psychologist Child Guidance Clinic, 1970; intern Mt. Zion Med. Center, San Francisco, 1968-69; clin. psychologist Jewish Hosp., St. Louis, 1971-75; assoc. prof. Evangel Coll., Springfield, Mo., 1975-84; pvt. practice clin. psychology, Springfield, 1975-84; dir. Montclair Psychol. Ctr., Inc., 1984—. Mem. Am. Psychol. Assn., Mo. Psychol. Assn. (chmn. com.), Mo. State Com. Psychologists (chmn. 1983-85), Phi Delta Kappa. Home: 936 E Manchester St Springfield MO 65807 Office: 3050 S National Suite 104 Springfield MO 65804

BASS, MITCHELL H(IRSCH), mortgage broker; b. Chgo., May 12, 1935; s. Saul Z. and Juliet C. (Cohn) B.; m. Marlene Stein, June 30, 1957; children—Leonard E., Deborah P., Naomi R. B.S. in Fin., U. Ill., 1957; M.B.A., U. Chgo., 1972. Asst. cashier Fox Lake State Bank (Ill.), 1958—; exec. v.p. Unity Savs., Norridge, Ill., 1981—; pres. Bass Fin. Corp., Chgo., 1981—; pres., chmn. bd. Midwest Mortgage Co. Inc., Chgo., 1983—. Chmn. Chgo. Norridge Crusade of Mercy; active Weitzman Inst., Rehovot, Israel; bd. dirs. North Suburban Jewish Community Ctr., Highland Park, Ill. Jewish. Office: 206 Honeysuckle Dr Northbrook IL 60062

BASSETT, KEITH T., metallurgist; b. Leicester, Eng., Apr. 28, 1933; came to U.S., 1974; s. Joseph William and Lillian May (Wightman) B.; B.Sc. in Applied Sci., U. Durham (Eng.), 1954; m. Doris Nicholson, May 14, 1955; children—Martyn John, Peter Richard, Joanne Elizabeth. Metallurgist, Fairey Aviation, Hayes, Eng., 1954-56; mgr. extraction metallurgy Henry Wiggin & Co., Hereford, Eng., 1956-60; sales metallurgist Park Gate Iron & Steel Co., Rotherham, Eng., 1960-62; vacuum degassing service metallurgist English Steel Corp., Sheffield, Eng., 1962-65; sr. service metallurgist Atlas Steels Co., Welland, Ont., Can., 1965-74; mgr. metallurgy Danly Machine Corp., Cicero, Ill., 1974-84; mgr. quality assurance Sci. Metal Treating, Des Plaines, Ill., 1984—; seminar lectr.; lectr. Coll. of DuPage; Metals Engring. Inst. course instr., 1969—, nat. chmn., 1981-83. Chmn. Hamilton and Dist. Cricket League, 1968-74, Ont. Cricket Assn., 1972-74; nat. rep. Can. Cricket Assn., 1973-74. Mem. Am. Welding Soc. (nat. subcom. chmn. 1975—), Am. Soc. Metals (nat. com. 1978-83, chmn. nat. com. 1981-83, vice-chmn. 1983-84, chpt. chmn. 1982-83, nat. com. vice-chmn. 1983—; Outstanding Chpt. Mem. 1982-83). Office: 2100 S Laramie Ave Cicero IL 60650

BASSETT, MARIAN KAY, telephone company executive; b. Dayton, O., May 19, 1945; d. Harry Richard and Lucy Bell (Hetzler) Weikert; B.S., Manchester Coll., 1967; M.S. in Bus. Adminstrn. St. Francis Coll., 1981; m. Ronald William Bassett, June 1, 1974; 1 stepson, Patrick Obrien. Tchr., Concord Community Schs., Elkhart, Ind., 1967-68; mgmt. trainee Gen. Telephone Co. Ind., Fort Wayne, 1968-69, chief operator, 1969-71, coordinator results and budgets, 1972-77; market research adminstr. GTE Services Corp., Stamford, Conn., 1977-79, market research adminstr., No. region, Indpls., 1979-81; gen. operator service mgr. GTE Ind./Mich., Ft. Wayne, Ind., 1981-82; service mgr. operator services GTE Midwestern Telephone Ops., Ft. Wayne, 1982—. Nat. Assn. Female Execs., Inc. Republican. Club: Rathkamp Matchcover Soc. Office: GTE Ind 8001 W Jefferson Blvd Fort Wayne IN 46801

BASSETT, PAUL MERRITT, educator; b. Lima, Ohio, May 28, 1935; s. Paul Gardner and Ruth Abbott (Wiess) B.; B.A., Olivet Nazarene Coll., 1957; B.D., Duke U. Div. Sch., 1960; postgrad. Ohio State U., 1960-62; Ph.D., Duke U., 1967; m. Pearl Ann Householter, Aug. 8, 1958; children—Emilie Ruth, Paul Stephan, Anita Suzanne. Tchr., Southeastern High Sch., Ross County, Ohio, 1961-62; asso. prof. Greek and history Trevecca Nazarene Coll., Nashville, 1965-66; asst. prof. religious studies W. Va. U., Morgantown, 1966-69; asso. prof. history of Christianity, Nazarene Theol. Sem., Kansas City, Mo., 1969-76, prof., 1976—, dir. Master of Div. program, 1981—, dir. Mex. Extension program, 1981—; vis. prof. Point Loma Coll., San Diego, 1969-72, Seminario Nazareno Centroamericana, San Jose, Costa Rica, 1972-76; lectr. U. Mo., Kansas City, others. Rockefeller fellow in religion, 1964-65; Assn. of Theol. Schs. in U.S. and Can. grantee, 1976-77. Mem. Am. Soc. Ch. History, Am. Hist. Assn., Am. Cath. Hist. Soc., Mediaeval Acad. Am., Acad. Religion, Soc. Bibl. Lit., Wesleyan Theol. Soc. (pres. elect 1980-81, pres. 1981-82), Kansas City Soc. for Theol. Studies (sec.-treas. 1981—), Am. Acad. of Research Historians in Medieval Spain. Mem. Ch. of the Nazarene. Author: Keep the Wonder, 1979; contbr. articles to profl. jours. Home: 9930 Linden Ln Overland Park KS 66207 Office: 1700 E Meyer Blvd Kansas City MO 64131

BASTIAN, LAWRENCE JACOB, talent agent; b. Chgo., July 11, 1930; s. Lawrence J. and Charlotte J. (Templeton) B.; m. Dianne L. Holmberg, Jan. 16, 1965; children—Michelle, Nicolle, Danielle. Student U. Ill., 1952. Mem. staff William Morris Agy., Chgo., 1954-55, 60-67; agt. Ziv TV Co., Cin., 1956-59, M.C.A., Chgo., 1959-60; owner, mgr., agt. Larry Bastian Agy., Riverwoods, Ill. 1967—. Served with U.S. Army, 1952-54. Home and Office: 2580 Crestwood Ln Riverwoods IL 60015

BASTILLA, ROBERT FRANCIS, banker; b. Elmira, N.Y., Feb. 2, 1927; s. Francis John and Marjorie Flora (Hoag) B.; m. Shirley Jean Hug, June 7, 1947; children—Robert Michael, Nancy Ann Bastilla Rusick. Owner, operator Bastilla Egg Co., Highland, Ill., 1959-67; sales mgr., broadcaster Sta. WIN-U, Highland, 1967-68; newsman, broadcaster Sta. WRTH, Cottage Hills and Woodriver, Ill., 1968-69; dir. public relations 1st Nat. Bank of Highland, 1969-81, asst. v.p., dir. pub. relations, 1981—. Alderman, City of Highland, 1957-63; mem. exec. bd. Cahokia Mound council Boy Scouts Am., 1970-75, 79—, dist. chmn., 1979-81, 84—; bus. chmn. Highland Cancer Crusade, 1980-84; pres. Madison County Fair Assn., 1973-79; mem. and sec. Planning Commn., City of Highland, 1979-83; exec. bd. Faith Countryside Homes, 1980-84. Served with USN, 1945-46. Recipient Outstanding Civic Leader award Highland Jaycees, 1979, dist. award of merit Kickapoo dist. Cahokia Mound council Boy Scouts Am., 1982, Silver Beaver award, 1985. Mem. Ill./Mo. Mktg. Assn. (past pres.), Bank Mktg. Assn., Am. Inst. Banking, Highland C. of C., Highland Pistol and Rifle Assn., Hevetta Sharpshooters Soc., VFW. Clubs: Lions (past pres., zone chmn. 1981-82, dep. dist. gov. 1982-83); Lion of Yr. 1981, Membership Growth award 1983, zone chmn. 1984-85), Toastmasters (past pres.). Home: 521 Dophin Dr E Highland IL 62249 Office: 1000 Broadway PO Box 10 Highland IL 62249

BATCHELDER, ANNE STUART, former publisher, political party official; b. Lake Forest, Ill., Jan. 11, 1920; d. Robert Douglas and Harriet (McClure) Stuart; student Lake Forest Coll., 1941-43; m. Clifton Brooks Batchelder, May 26, 1945; children—Edward, Anne Stuart, Mary Clifton, Lucia Brooks. Clubmobile driver ARC, Eng., Belgium, France, Holland and Germany, 1943-45; pub., editor Douglas County Gazette, 1970-75; dir. Omaha Nat. Bank; dir., treas. U.S. Checkbook Com. Mem. Republican Central Com. Nebr., 1955-62, 70-83, vice chmn. Central Com., 1959-64, chmn., 1975-79, mem. fin. com., 1957-64; chmn. women's sect. Douglas County Rep. Finance Com., 1955, vice chmn. com., 1958-60; v.p. Omaha Woman's Rep. Club, 1957-58, pres., 1959-60; alternate del. Nat. Conv., 1956, 72, del., 1980; mem. Rep. Nat. Com. for Nebr., 1964-70; asst. chmn. Douglas County Rep. Central Com., 1971-74; 1st v.p. Nebr. Fedn. Rep. Women, 1971-72, pres., 1972-74; chmn. Nebr. Rep. Com., 1975-79; chmn. ways and means com. Nat. Fedn. Rep. Women; mem. Nebr. State Bldg. Commn.; Rep. candidate for lt. gov., 1974. Sr. v.p. Nebr. Founders Day, 1958; past trustee Brownell Hall, Vis. Nurse Assn.; trustee Hastings Coll., Nebr. Meth. Hosp. Found.; pres. Nebr. chpt. Freedoms Found. at Valley Forge. Mem. Mayflower Soc., Colonial Dames, P.E.O., Nat. League Pen Women. Presbyterian (elder). Clubs: Omaha Country, Omaha. Home: 6875 State St Omaha NE 68152

BATE, CHARLES THOMAS, lawyer; b. Muncie, Ind., Nov. 14, 1932; s. Thomas Elwood and Vina Florence (Jackson) B.; A.B., Butler U., 1955, postgrad., 1955-56; student Christian Theol. Sem., Indpls., 1956-57; J.D., Ind. U., 1962; m. Barbara Kay Dailey, June 17, 1955; children—Charles Thomas, Gregory Andrew, Jeffrey Scott. Admitted to Ind. bar, 1962; staff adjuster State Automobile Ins. Assn., Indpls., 1953-57, claim supr., 1958-59, office mgr., 1960-61, casualty claim mgr., 1961-62, atty., 1962-63; mem. firm Smith & Yarling, Indpls., 1963-67; sr. partner Soshnick, Bate & Harrold, Shelbyville, Ind., 1967—; city atty., Shelbyville, 1981—. Dir., v.p., gen. counsel Discovery Life Ins. Co., Indpls., 1966-70. Bd. dirs. Nat. Pensions Bd. of Ch. of God, 1970-74; trustee Warner Pacific Coll., Portland, Oreg., 1977-79, Anderson (Ind.) Coll., 1982—. Recipient Merit award Ind. Jud. Council, 1962, Outstanding Student award Ind. U. Law Week, 1962. Fellow Ind. Bar Found.; mem. ABA, Ind. (ho. of dels. 1978-80), Indpls., Shelby County (pres. 1979) bar assns., Ind. Mcpl. Lawyers Assn., Am. Judicature Soc., Am. Arbitration Assn. (panel arbitrators), Am., Ind. (dir. 1979—), Tex. trial lawyers assns., Pa. Trial Lawyers Assn., Am. Bd. Trial Advocates. Republican. Mem. Ch. of God (dir. Glendale Ch. of God Inc. 1958-80, lay speaker 1962—, sec. nat. by-laws com. 1968-72). Club: Shelbyville Elks. Home: Box 26 Shelbyville IN 46176 Office: 24 W Broadway Shelbyville IN 46176

BATES, GARY DEAN, engineering corporation executive; b. Covington, Ky., May 10, 1941; s. Harold V. and Anna J. (Crupper) B.; student Anderson (Ind.) Coll., 1959-61; B.S. in Civil Engring., U. Ky., 1964, M.S., 1967; postgrad. U. Cin., 1977-79; postgrad. in real estate Cin. Tech. Coll., 1978-79; m. Joyce Ann Wiedemer, Nov. 14, 1964; children—Cynthia Lynne, Christopher Scott. Design engr. Ky. Dept. Highways, Lexington, 1963-67; project engr. Exxon Corp., Linden, N.J., 1967-69; project mgr. Skilken-Roslovic Design-Build, Inc., Columbus, Ohio, 1969-71; asst. ops. mgr. Miller-Valentine Constrn. Co., Dayton, Ohio, 1971-72; constrn. mgr. Jackson's Realty and Builder's, Indpls., 1972-74; v.p. Fisher-Deyore Constrn. Co., Cin., 1974-75; v.p., dir. tech. services KZF, Inc., Cin., 1975-81; bus. mgr. indsl. cons. SDRC, Inc., Milford, Ohio, 1981—; instr. constrn. mgmt. program U. Cin., 1975-82. Tutor minority children Urban League program, Columbus, 1970-71; v.p. Woodlands Homeowners Assn., Carmel, Ind., 1973-74; mem. Leadership Cin.; mem. Anderson Twp. Planning and Zoning Commn. Cert. fallout shelter analyst U.S. Dept. Def.; registered profl. engr., Ohio, Ky., Ind.; lic. real estate agt., Ohio. Mem. ASCE (exec. com. engring. mgmt. div.), Lambda Chi Alpha Alumni. Republican. Methodist. Home: 730 Birney Ln Cincinnati OH 45230 Office: 2000 Eastman Dr Milford OH 45150

BATES, JAMES EDWARD, trade association executive; b. Elkhart, Ind., Aug. 6, 1921; s. Roy E. and Margret (Lynn) B. B.S., N. Central Coll., 1943; M.B.A., Harvard Bus. Sch., 1961. Cert. assn. exec. With Finnell System, Inc., Elkhart, 1946-68, v.p., dir.; account exec. Proven Mgmt., Inc., Evanston, Ill., 1969-75; pres. Jebinc Mgmt. Services, Arlington Heights Ill., 1975—. Mem. Am. Soc. Assns. Execs., Chgo. Soc. Assn. Execs., Inst. Assn. Mgmt. Cos. U.S. C. of C. Club: Masons. Home: 1717 Crystal Ln Mount Prospect IL 60056

BATES, MARK WELDON, university administrator; b. Bloomington, Ill., Aug. 14, 1934; s. Ralph Elbert and Margaret (Weldon) B.; student U. Ill., 1952-54; B.S. in Journalism, Northwestern U., 1956; m. Janet Alice Fjellberg, Jan. 5, 1957; children—Michael John, Scott Weldon, Anne Elizabeth. Personnel asst. Washington Nat. Ins. Co., Evanston, Ill. 1957-58; asst. dir. devel. Northwestern U., Evanston, 1958-61; dir. devel. Ill. Inst. Tech., Chgo., 1961-67, v.p. instl. devel., 1968-72, v.p. planning and devel., 1975-79, v.p., exec. sec. to bd. trustees, 1979-83; v.p. instl. advancement Coll. of St. Francis, Joliet, Ill., 1983-85; asst. vice chancellor Washington U., St. Louis, 1985—; exec. v.p. Am. Fund for Dental Health, Chgo., 1973-75; dir. PSI Inc. Trustee Union League Boys Club; governing mem. Ill. Tech. Coll.; bd. dirs. Simon Found. Served with AUS, 1957. Mem. Nat. Soc. Fund Raisers, Chgo. Soc. for Fund Raising Execs. (pres. 1972-73), Union League Club. Clubs: Economic, Chicago Press; Michigan Shores; Wilmette. Home: 54 York Dr Saint Louis MO 63144 Office: 6510 Ellenwood Saint Louis MO 63105

BATES, NORMAN JAMES, manufacturing engineer, mechanical technologies educator; b. Bay City, Mich., Jan. 28, 1952; s. Norman R. and Theresa Mary (Carbary) B. B.S.E. in Aerospace, U. Mich., 1974. Coordinator numerical control Wilson Machine, Saginaw, Mich., 1978—; instr. mech. techs. Delta Coll., University Center, Mich., 1980—; mgr. numerical control programming Am. Hoist & Derrick, Bay City, 1976-78; dir. StarPak Energy Systems, Novi, Mich., 1976—. Author: SPIDAR (Solar Powered Ion Driven Asteroid Belt Research), 1974; chpt. preface Metalworking, 1982. Sr. mem. Soc. Mfg. Engrs. Roman Catholic. Avocations: botanist; hang gliding; ultralight pilot; cross country skiing. Home: 1500 S Mackinaw Kawkawlin MI 48631 Office: Wilson Machine Div 400 Florence St Saginaw MI 48602

BATESON, KATHLEEN PANDAK, advertising executive; b. Warren, Ohio, Oct. 17, 1947; d. John Michael and Angeline June (Simoni) Pandak; B.F.A. magna cum laude, Seton Hill Coll., 1969. Cert. tchr., Pa. Dir. pub. relations Casto Devel., Columbus, Ohio, 1973-75; mktg. mgr. Hallmark Dev. Ltd., Victoria, B.C., 1975-76; advt. mgr. St. Clair Paint, Toronto, Ont., 1976-78; broadcast advt. mgr. Am. Hardware, Butler, Pa., 1978-82; v.p., dir. client service Saffer, Cravit & Freedman, Chgo., 1982-83; v.p. retail div. W.B. Doner & Co., Southfield, Mich., 1983—; lectr. Retail Advt. Conf., Chgo., 1981-83; cons. Philines Inc., Chardon, Ohio, 1982-84; chmn. Direct Mktg. Group, Butler, 1981-82; mem. Mgmt. Adv. Com., Butler, 1982; art dir., set designer St. Vincent Theater, 1969-73. Bd. dirs. Hemlocks Assn., Allison Park, Pa., 1982. Mem. Retail Advt. Conf., Dir. Mail Mktg. Assn., Am. Women in Radio & TV, Adcrafter Assn., Seton Hill Alumnae Assn. Republican. Roman Catholic.

BATESON, KENDRICK NORMAN, marketing and sales executive; b. Pontiac, Mich., Sept. 11, 1942; s. Norman Eric and Alice Lydia (Davies) B.; m. Julienne Argentine, Aug. 1, 1964; children—Norman, Kendrick, Brian, Elizabeth. B.S. in Bus., Ind. U., 1967. Salesman, Westvaco, Chgo., 1967-69; advt. mgr. Graver Tank, East Chicago, Ind., 1969-71; market research mgr. Hilti, Inc., Stamford, Conn., 1971-77; pres. Market Data Services, Waukesna, Wis., 1977—; mktg. mgr. Enerpac, Butler, Wis., 1977-83; v.p. sales Norson Industries, Culver, Ind., 1971—; mktg. and sales mgr. Power-Packer Div. Allied Power, New Berlin, Wis., 1983—. Mem. Am. Mktg. Assn., Sales and Mktg. Execs. Assn. Methodist. Club: Merrill Hills Country. Home: S40 W27290 Stonegate Rd Waukesha WI 53186 Office: Power-Packer Div Applied Power 16901 W Glendale St New Berlin WI 53151

BATT, NICK, lawyer; b. Defiance, Ohio, May 6, 1952; s. Dan and Zenith (Dreher) B. B.S., Purdue U., 1972; J.D., U. Toledo, 1976. Bar: Ohio 1976. Asst. prosecutor Lucas County, Toledo, 1976-80, civil div. chief, 1980-83; village attorney, Village of Holland, Ohio, 1980—; law dir. City of Oregon, Ohio, 1984—. Mem. Maumee Valley Girl Scout Council, Toledo, 1977-80; bd. mem. Bd. Community Relations, Toledo, 1975-76; mem. Lucas County Democratic Exec. Com., 1981-83. Named One of Toledo's Outstanding Young Men, Toledo Jaycee's, 1979. Mem. Toledo Bar Assn., Ohio Bar Assn., ABA, Ohio Council of Sch. Bd. Attorneys, Ohio Mcpl. Attorneys Assn. Democrat. Roman Catholic. Club: Toledo. Lodge: K.C. Office: Batt & Zychowicz 405 N Huron St Suite A Toledo OH 43604

BATTEN, MICHAEL ELLSWORTH, manufacturing executive; b. Racine, Wis., Apr. 14, 1940; s. John Henry and Katherine (Vernet) B.; m. Gloria Strickland, July 6, 1963; children—John, Elizabeth, Louise, Timothy. B.A., Yale U., 1964; M.B.A., Harvard U., 1970. Account exec. Ted Bates & Co., N.Y.C., 1964-68; asst. sec. Twin Disc, Inc., Racine, Wis., 1970-71, sec. and asst. treas., 1971-75, v.p. and sec., 1975-76, exec. v.p., 1976-83, pres. and chief exec. officer, 1983—; dir. Briggs & Stratton Corp., First Wis. Corp., Universal Foods Corp., Wehr Corp., Milw., Walker Forge, Inc., Racine. Trustee Prairie Sch., Racine, 1974—; bd. dirs. Jr. Achievement; exec. com. Pub. Expenditure Survey Wis. Mem. Machinery and Allied Products Inst., Soc. Automotive Engrs., Farm and Indsl. Equipment Inst., Racine Area Mfrs. and Commerce (dir.). Republican. Clubs: University, Milwaukee. Home: 3419 Michigan Blvd Racine WI 53402 Office: Twin Disc Inc 1328 Racine St Racine WI 53403

BATTERSBY, JAMES LYONS, JR., English educator; b. Pawtucket, R.I., Aug. 24, 1936; s. James Lyons and Hazel Irene (Deuel) B.; m. Beverly Ann McClure, Aug. 24, 1957 (div. 1980); 1 dau., Julie Ann. B.S. magna cum laude, U. Vt., 1961; M.A., Cornell U., 1962, Ph.D., 1965. Asst. prof. U. Calif.-Berkeley, 1965-70; assoc. prof. English, Ohio State U., Columbus, 1970-82, prof., 1982—. Cons., Ohio State U. Press, U. Ky. Press, U. Calif. Press, Prentice-Hall, McGraw Hill. Served with U.S. Army, 1954-57. Woodrow Wilson fellow, 1961-62, 64-65; Samuel S. Fels fellow, 1964-65; U. Calif. Summer Faculty fellow, 1966, Humanities Research fellow, 1969. Mem. MLA, Am. Soc. 18th Century Studies, Midwest Soc. 18th Century Studies. Democrat. Author: Typical Folly: Evaluating Student Performance in Higher Education, 1973; Rational Praise and Natural Lamentation: Johnson, Lycidas and Principles of Criticism, 1980; Elder Olson: An Annotated Bibliography, 1983; contbr. articles to profl. jours. Home: 472 Clinton Heights Ave Columbus OH 43202 Office: 164 W 17th Ave Dept English Ohio State U Columbus OH 43210

BATTEY, CHARLES W., telecommunications corporation executive; b. 1932; married. B.B.A., U. Nebr., 1954. With Continental Ill. Nat. Bank & Trust Co., Chgo., 1954-70; pres. Commerce Bank of Kansas City, 1970-73; sr. v.p. corp. relations United Telecommunications, Inc., Kansas City, Mo., 1973-75, sr. v.p. staff, 1975-77, exec. v.p., 1977-79, exec. v.p. fin. and adminstrn., chief fin. officer, 1979-81, then pres., chief operating officer, vice chmn., chief fin. officer, 1985—, dir.; dir. First Nat. Bank Kansas City, Kans.-Nebr. Natural Gas Co. Bd. dirs. Kansas City Crime Commn., Midwest Research Inst., United Community Services Council on Edn.; pres. Kansas City Public TV. Office: United Telecommunications Inc PO Box 11315 Kansas City MO 64112*

BATTISTI, FRANK JOSEPH, federal judge; b. Youngstown, Ohio, Oct. 4, 1922; s. Eugene and Jennie (Dalesandro) B.; B.A., Ohio U., 1947; LL.B., Harvard U., 1950. Admitted to Ohio bar, 1950; asst. atty gen. Ohio, 1950; atty. Admitted to Ohio bar, 1950; asst. atty gen. Ohio, 1950; atty. adviser C.E., U.S. Army, 1951-52; 1st asst. dir. law, Youngstown, 1954-59; judge Common Pleas Ct., Mahoning County, Ohio, 1959-61; U.S. judge No. Dist. Ohio, Cleve., 1961-69, chief judge, 1969—. Served with C.E., U.S. Army, 1943-45; ETO. Mem. ABA, Mahoning County, Cleve. bar assns., Am. Judicature Soc. Roman Catholic. Office: 302 US Courthouse Cleveland OH 44114*

BATTISTO, JACK RICHARD, immunologist, researcher; b. Niagara Falls, N.Y., Sept. 13, 1922; s. Pat and Mary (Astorino) B.; m. Lillian Mangone; children—Scott Anthony, Jeth Richard. B.S., Cornell U., 1949; M.S., U. Mich., 1950, Ph.D., 1953. Fellow NIH, Rockefeller Inst., 1953-55, vis. investigator, 1953-55; asst. prof. U. Ark. Sch. Medicine, Little Rock, 1955-57; asst. prof. Albert Einstein Coll. Medicine, Bronx, N.Y., 1957-61, assoc. prof., 1961-67, prof., 1967-74; mem. staff research div. Cleve. Clinic Found., 1974—, dir. dept. immunology, 1974-82. Exec. editor Jour. Immunological Methods, 1971-78, Immunopharmacology, 1978—. Editor: (with J.W. Streilein) Immunoaspects of the Spleen, 1976, (with H. Claman and D. Scott) Ann. N.Y. Acad. Sci., 1982.

Pres. Westchester Toastmasters, New Rochelle, N.Y., 1968. Served with USAF, 1943-46, PTO. Fellow F.G. Navy Research, U. Mich., 1952-53; sr. research fellow Population Council, Inc., Weizmann Inst. Sci., 1963-64. Mem. Am. Assn. Immunologists, Am. Soc. Microbiology, N.Y. Acad. Scis., Transplantation Soc., Harvey Soc., Reticuloendothelial Soc. Home: 2505 Milford Rd University Heights OH 44118 Office: Cleveland Clinic Found 9500 Euclid Ave Cleveland OH 44106

BATTON, CALVERT VORWERK, appliance co. exec.; b. Cuyahoga Falls, Ohio, June 29, 1926; s. Ramsey T. and Mildred B. (Vorwerk) B.; student Bowling Green U., 1946; B.S. in Bus. Adminstrn., Kent State U., 1950, postgrad. Grad. Bus. Sch., 1960-63; m. Edith Sayre Jones, May 18, 1957; children—Susan, Sally, Pamela. With Hoover Co., Canton, Ohio, 1951—, auditor, 1951-53, mgr. br. office, 1953-56, mgr. field accounting, 1956-58, gen. office mgr., 1958-61, asst. budget mgr., 1961-62, mgr. adminstrv. services, 1962-64, asst. v.p., 1964-65, adminstrv. v.p., 1965-75, v.p. adminstrn., 1975—; adv. bd. dirs. Diebold Research, Inc. Bd. dirs. United Way, Canton, Canton Cultural Center, Bowling Green U. Found.; bd. dirs., v.p. Kent U. Found. Served with AUS, 1944-45. Mem. Adminstrv. Mgmt. Soc., Nat. Assn. Accountants, Am. Mgmt. Assn., Sigma Delta Epsilon. Republican. Presbyn. Home: 30 Auburn Ave SE North Canton OH 44709 Office: PO Box 2200 North Canton OH 44720

BATTS, WARREN LEIGHTON, manufacturing company executive; b. Norfolk, Va., Sept. 4, 1932; s. John Leighton and Allie Belle (Johnson) B.; B.E.E., Ga. Inst. Tech., 1961; M.B.A., Harvard U., 1963; m. Eloise Pitts, Dec. 24, 1957; 1 dau., Terri Allison. With Kendall County, Charlotte, N.C., 1963-64; exec. v.p. Fashion Devel. Co., Santa Paula, Calif., 1964-66; dir. mfg. Olga Co., Van Nuys, Calif., 1964-66; v.p. Douglas Williams Assos., N.Y.C., 1966-67; founder Triangle Corp., Orangeburg, S.C., 1967, pres., chief exec. officer, 1967-71; v.p. Mead Corp., Dayton, Ohio, 1971-73, pres., 1973-80, chief exec. officer, 1978-80; pres., dir. Dart Industries Inc., Los Angeles, 1980—; pres., chief operating officer Dart & Kraft, Inc., Northbrook, Ill., 1981—. Trustee Am. Enterprise Inst., Com. for Econ. Devel., Ga. Tech. Found., Art Inst. Chgo. Author: (with others) Creative Collective Bargaining, 1964. Office: Dart & Kraft Inc 2211 Sanders Rd Northbrook IL 60062

BAUDER, GARY LEE, accounting co. exec.; b. Sturgis, Mich., Nov. 28, 1949; s. Ray Orlo, Jr. and Grace Marguerite (Haney) B.; A.A., Glen Oaks Community Coll., 1970; certificate in jr. accounting, State Tech. Inst. and Rehab. Center, 1974. Supervisory trainee Arch Workshop, Inc., Sturgis, 1969-71; mgr. B & F Tax & Accounting Service Corp., Sturgis, 1974-76, pres., dir., 1976—; dir., instr. income tax div. B & F Tax Tng. Inst.; instr. personal income taxes Sturgis Pub. Sch. Sec.-treas. Glen Oaks Community Coll. Circle K, 1968-70; notary pub. Mich.; treas. St. Joseph County (Mich.) Young Democrats, 1968-70; precinct del. St. Joseph County Dem. Party, 1970. Recipient Outstanding Service awards Mich. Assn. Distributive Edn. Clubs Am., 1970, Glen Oaks Community Coll. Boosters, 1970; named Officer of Year, Distributive Edn. Clubs Am., 1970-71. Mem. Distributive Edn. Clubs Am., Glen Oaks Community Coll. alumni assns., Sturgis C. of C., Sturgis Jaycees, Am. Mgmt. Assn., Nat. Small Bus. Assn., St. Joseph County Wheelchair Sports Boosters Assn., Internat. Platform Assn., Nat. Audubon Soc., Smithsonian Assos. Methodist. Office: 221 Susan St Sturgis MI 49091

BAUDER, KENNETH F., association executive; b. Chgo., Sept. 26, 1946; s. Frederick William and Myrtle Emma (Zenke) B.; B.S., So. Ill. U., 1969, M.A., 1971. Founder with E.R. Homewood, The Ontario Press, Chgo., 1971-74, dir., 1972—; dir. Lambda Books; dir. pub. relations Am. Bar Endowment, Chgo., 1974-75; freelance photographer, journalist, 1975-77; dir. publs. Shoe Service Inst. Am., Chgo., 1977-80, asst. treas., 1977-80. Tchr., Model Cities program, Chgo., 1972-74; bd. dirs. Our Children Found., Chgo., 1980-81; corp. fundraiser Ill. chpt. Nat. Kidney Found. Mem. Chgo. Soc. Assn. Execs. (vice chmn. coll. and univ. relations com. 1978-79), Am. Assn. Assn. Execs., MLA, Am. Pub. Works Assn. (dir. publs. 1980—, mem. communications com. 1982-83). Office: 1313 E 60th Chicago Il 60637*

BAUER, ARMAND, soil scientist, researcher; b. Zeeland, N.D., Nov. 29, 1924; s. Edward and Maria Magdalena (Walz) B.; m. Elaine June Levi, Mar. 25, 1949; children—Candice, Debra, Sydney, Andrew. A.S., N.D. Sch. Forestry, 1948; B.S., N.D. State U., 1950, M.S., 1955; Ph.D., Colo. State U., 1963. Profl. soil classifier. Asst. prof. N.D. Agrl. Exptl. Sta., Fargo, 1955-65, assoc. prof., 1965-69, prof., 1969-76; soil scientist Agrl. Research Service U.S. Dept. Agr., Mandan, N.D., 1976—; reclamation research coordinator N.D. Agrl. Exptl. Sta., 1974-76. Author papers (Best Paper award 1977); translator: Russian-German Settlements in the United States, 1974; editor: Heritage Rev. (quar. publ. Germans from Russia Heritage Soc.). Served with USN, 1944-46. Nat. Def. Ednl. fellow, 1961-63. Fellow Soil Conservation Soc. Am. (Profl. award 1983); mem. Am. Soc. Agronomy, Soil Sci. Soc. Am., Council Agrl. Sci. Tech., Sigma Xi, Phi Kappa Phi, Alpha Zeta. Lutheran. Club: Germans from Russia Heritage Soc. (Bismarck). Home: 1814 N 20th St Bismarck ND 58501 Office: USDA Agrl Research Service Box 459 Mandan ND 58554

BAUER, CARL THOMAS, lawyer; b. Springfield, Mass., Dec. 23, 1945; s. Edmond S. and Jean L. (Benney) B.; m. Patti Jane Hawkins, Aug. 1, 1975. A.B., Colgate U., 1967; J.D., Wash. U., 1980. Bar: Mo., 1980. Counsel, St. Louis Blues Hockey Club, 1981-83; atty. Ralston Purina Co., St. Louis, 1980—; asst. gen. counsel, sec. Continental Baking Co., 1985—. Served as lt. comdr. USN, 1968-78. Decorated D.F.C., Air Medal (14), others. Mem. ABA, Mo. Bar Assn., Met. St. Louis Bar Assn., Colgate U. Alumni Club of St. Louis.

BAUER, DALE ROBERT, publisher; b. Evanston, Ill., June 10, 1928; s. Valentine H. and Luti E. (Jacobson) B.; m. Sheila Gregory, Feb. 1955 (div. Aug. 1982); children—Richard Gregory, Courtney Anne. B.S. in Econs., U. Pa., 1954. Pub. Med. World News, N.Y.C., 1966-72; group pub., v.p. McGraw-Hill, Inc., N.Y.C., 1972-76; pres. Billboard Pub. Co., N.Y.C., 1976-78, Standard Rate & Data Service, Wilmette, Ill., 1978—; group v.p. Macmillan, Inc., N.Y.C., 1981—; dir. Am. Bus. Press, N.Y.C., 1984—, Dati e Tariffe Pubblicitarie, Tarif Media, Medios Publicitarios. Served to lt. (j.g.) USNR, 1946-52, Korea. Republican. Episcopalian. Club: University (N.Y.C.). Avocation: boating. Office: 3004 Glenview Rd Wilmette IL 60091

BAUER, DORIS ADELE, charitable organization executive; b. Chgo., June 24, 1933; d. Henry and Adele N. (Johnson) Matson; m. Arthur Henry Bauer, Nov. 24, 1956; children—Carl, Timothy, Elizabeth. A.A., North Park Coll., 1953; B.S. in Edn., Chgo. Tchrs. Coll., 1955. Elem. sch. tchr., Chgo., 1955-66; exec. dir. Lydia Home Assn., Chgo., 1976—; sec.-treas. Benevolent Council, Mpls., 1980-84; pres. Chgo. Have-A-Heart Charity, 1975-77, com. chair, 1967-75; rep. Ill. Commn. on Children, 1977-84. Pres., Hoffman Sch. PTA, Glenview, Ill., 1974-76; supt. Evangelical Free Ch. Sunday Sch., Glenview, 1974-76; bd. dirs. Phantom Ranch— Jr. High Girls' Camp, Wis., 1971-75, Camp Willabay, 1958-59. Named Citizen of Week, Sta. WCLR, 1981. Mem. Child Care Assn. Ill. (conf. com. 1984), Group for Active Plan for Children's Services. Republican. Avocations: cross-country skiing; swimming; traveling. Home: 1954 Robin Crest Ln Glenview IL 60025 Office: Lydia Home Assn 4300 W Irving Park Rd Chicago IL 60641

BAUER, EDWARD ALPHONSE, electrical contractor; b. Waite Park, Minn., Aug. 6, 1942; s. Michael Frank and Olive Ann (Lardy) B.; grad. jr. acct. Drews Bus. Coll., St. Cloud, 1961; elec. grad. Dunwoody Indsl. Sch., Mpls., 1967; A.A., St. Cloud State Coll., 1969; m. Carol Ann Lobb, July 8, 1967; children—Steven J., Gwen Marie, John Edward. Owner, pres. Bauer Inc., elec. contractors, Waite Park, Minn., 1969—; sec., v.p. JAB, Inc., 1975-82. Chief, Waite Park Fire Dept., 1980—; scoutmaster Boy Scouts Am., 1979-84. Served with USNR, 1961-62; Res. ret. Decorated Naval Meritorious Service medal, Nat. Def. medal; others. Mem. Nat. Assn. Bus. and Ednl. Radio, U.S. C. of C., Minn. Elec. Assn., Waite Park C. of C., Am. Legion. Republican. Roman Catholic. Clubs: Boosters, Rifle (Waite Park). Lodges: Eagles, Moose. Home: 149 7th Ave N Waite Park MN 56387 Office: 522 3d St N Waite Park MN 56387

BAUER, ELIZABETH HALE WORMAN, human services exec.; b. Mpls., Dec. 28, 1937; d. James R. and Virginia H. (Murty) Worman; B.A., Mt. Holyoke Coll., 1959; M.A., Ohio State U., 1975; postgrad. U. Minn., 1959, Wayne State U., 1978, Mich. State U., 1978; m. George Bittner Bauer, Sept. 12, 1959; children—Anna Stuart, Robert Bittner, Virginia Hale, Edward Russell. Speech therapist Morris County Easter Seal Rehab. Center, Morristown, N.J., 1959-60; travel coordinator AFS Internat., N.Y.C., 1960-63; speech therapist St. Barnabas Home, Gibsonia, Pa., 1967-71; tchr. St. Peter's Child Devel. Center, Sewickley, Pa., 1971-72; tchr. cons. spl. edn., Pontiac, Mich., 1975-78; dir. tng. Plymouth Center for Human Devel., Northville, Mich., 1978-80; adminstr. community placement Mich. Dept. Mental Health, Met. Region, 1980-81; exec. dir. Mich. Protection and Advocacy Service for Developmentally Disabled Citizens, Inc., Lansing, 1981—; cons. devel. disabilities tech. assistance system U. N.C., 1974-75; mem. adv. bd. Georgetown U. Child Devel. Center, 1978—. Founder, Montessori in Arlington, Upper Arlington, Ohio, 1973; bd. dirs. Franklin County (Ohio) Assn. Retarded Citizens, 1973-75, Ohio Assn. Retarded Citizens, 1975; bd. dirs. Southfield Youth Symphony Orch., pres., 1978-79; bd. dirs. Epilepsy Center Mich., Detroit, 1975-80, pres., 1978-80; bd. dirs. Mich. Acad. Dentistry for Handicapped, 1983—; trustee St. Mark's Day Sch., Jackson Heights, N.Y., 1962-67; trustee internat. scholarships Am. Field Service, 1971-73, bd. dirs., 1973—. Named Outstanding Tchr. Sch. Dist. City of Pontiac, 1978. Mem. Council for Exceptional Children, Epilepsy Found. Am., Assn. Persons with Severe Handicaps, Am. Assn. on Mental Deficiency, Nat. Assn. for Retarded Citizens, Mich. Assn. for Retarded Children, Mt. Holyoke Coll. Alumnae Assn. Episcopalian. Club: Zonta Internat. Contbr. articles to profl. publs. Home: 1355 Lake Park Birmingham MI 48009 Office: 313 S Washington Sq Lansing MI 48933

BAUER, ELIZABETH ROSE, medical record administrator; b. Spalding, Nebr., Aug. 19, 1947; d. Laurence J. and Josephine A. (Glaser) Bauer. B.S. in Med. Record Adminstrn., Coll. St. Mary, Omaha, 1969. Registered record adminstr. Am. Med. Record Assn. Med. records dir. St. Francis Med. Ctr., Grand Island, Nebr., 1969—; cons., lectr. in field; mem. adv. com secretarial courses Central Nebr. Tech. Community Coll., 1978—. Bd. dirs. Hall County chpt. Nebr. affiliate Am. Heart Assn., v.p., campaign chmn., 1984, now pres. Hall County chpt. Mem. Am. Med. Record Assn. (Nebr. del. 1978), Nebr. Med. Record Assn. (pres. 1978-79), Region IV Nebr. Med. Record Assn. (chmn. nominating com. 1977), Grand Island Bus. & Profl. Women's Luncheon Club. Democrat. Roman Catholic.

BAUER, EUGENE ANDREW, dermatologist, educator; b. Mattoon, Ill., June 17, 1942; s. Eugene C. and Madge L. (Armer) B.; m. Gloria Anne Hehman, Feb. 19, 1966; children—Marc A., Christine A., J. Michael, Amanda F. B.S., Northwestern U., 1963, M.D., 1967. Diplomate Am. Bd. Dermatology, Nat. Bd. Med. Examiners. Intern, Barnes Hosp., St. Louis, 1967-68; resident, fellow div. dermatology Washington U. Med. Ctr., 1968-70; instr. Washington U., St. Louis, 1971-72, asst. prof. dermatology, 1974-78, assoc. prof., 1978-82, prof., 1982—. Contbr. numerous articles to profl. jours. Served to lt. comdr. USNR, 1972-74. Fellow Am. Acad. Dermatology; mem. Am. Fedn. Clin. Research, Am. Soc. Clin. Investigation, Am. Dermatol. Assn., Soc. Investigative Dermatology (bd. dirs. 1981—, assoc. editor Jour. Investigative Dermatology 1982—), Central Soc. Clin. Research. Office: Washington U Sch Medicine Div Dermatology St Louis MO 63110

BAUER, FREDERICK CHARLES, JR., physician, pathologist; b. Champaign, Ill., Jan. 19, 1918; s. Frederick Charles and Louise (Garrett) B.; m. Margaret Vaniman, June 21, 1941; children—Richard Charles, Peter Frederick. B.S., in Chemistry, U. Ill., 1939; M.D., Harvard U., 1943; M.S. in Pathology, U. Chgo., 1945, Ph.D. in Pathology, 1949. Diplomate Am. Bd. Pathology, Nat. Bd. Med. Examiners. Chief lab. U.S. Army. and Vet. Hosp., Northport, N.Y., 1945-47; Seymour-Coman fellow in pathology U. Chgo., 1947-49, asst. prof. pathology, 1951-59; clin. assoc. prof. pathology U. Ill., Chgo., 1959—; attending med. staff St. Lukes and Presbyn. St. Lukes Hosps., Chgo., 1950-60; dir. dept. pathology Silver Cross Hosp., Joliet, Ill., 1960-79, chief of staff, 1968-69, dir. Sch. Med. Tech., 1961-79. Contbr. articles to profl. jours. Trustee Coll. St. Francis, Joliet, 1974-79; pres. Am. Cancer Soc., Joliet, 1978-79. Fellow Am. Soc. Clin. Pathologists, ACP, Inst. Medicine Chgo.; mem. Internat. Acad. Pathologists, AMA. Clubs: Chgo. Yacht; Sturgeon Bay Yacht. Lodge: Rotary. Home: PO Box 173 Sturgeon Bay WI 54235

BAUER, KURT WALTER, civil engineer; b. Milw., Aug. 25, 1929; B.S. in Civil Engring., Marquette U., 1951; M.S., U. Wis., 1955, Ph.D., 1961. Registered profl. engr., registered land surveyor, Wis. City planner City of South Milwaukee, Wis., 1953-55; instr. civil engring. U. Wis., Madison, 1955-56, Ford Found. research fellow, 1960-61; assoc. civil engr. H.C. Webster & Son, Milw., 1956-59; chief current planning City of Madison, 1959-60; dir. Southeastern Wis. Regional Planning Commn., Waukesha, 1961—. Contbr. articles to profl. jours. Served to lt. col. USAF, 1953—. Fellow ASCE; mem. Am. Inst. Cert. Planners, Am. Congress on Surveying and Mapping, Am. Pub. Works Assn., Inst. Mcpl. Engring., Transp. Research Bd., Sci. Adv. Bd., Internat. Joint Commn. on Gt. Lakes. Lutheran. Office: Southeastern Wis Regional Planning Commn 916 N East Ave Waukesha WI 53186

BAUER, NANCY MCNAMARA, TV and radio network executive; b. Madison, Wis., Mar. 17, 1929; d. Richard Hughes and Lucy Jane (Whitaker) Marshall; B.A., U. Wis., 1950, M.S., 1963; m. J.B. McNamara, Dec. 29, 1952 (div. Mar. 1962); children—Margaret Ann, William Patrick; m. 2d, Helmut Robert Bauer, Mar. 10, 1974. Elem. tchr., Madison, 1963-66; specialist ednl. communications U. Wis., Madison, 1966-71, asst. prof., 1971-72; dir. educative services Ednl. Communications Bd., Wis. Ednl. TV and Radio Networks, Madison, 1972—; dir. Central Ednl. Network, 1973-80, 83—, exec. com., 1973-74, chmn. Instructional TV Council, 1977-79; adv. bd. Instructional TV Coop., 1972-75, exec. com., 1976-77; mem. instrnl. radio adv. com. Nat. Public Radio, 1979—; mem. instructional TV adv. com. Public Broadcasting System, 1978-79, service com., 1980-83; mem ITV Study com. Corp. for Pub. Broadcasting, 1983—. Ford Found. scholar, 1961-63; recipient Ohio State award, 1975, ABA Gavel award, 1975, Am. Legion Golden Mike award, 1976. Mem. Nat. Assn. Ednl. Broadcasters. Producer, writer numerous instructional series, as nationally distributed Patterns in Arithmetic and Looking Out Is In, TV, 1967, Inquiry: The Justice Thing, radio, 1973. Home: 127 Kensington Dr Madison WI 53704 Office: 732 N Midvale Blvd Madison WI 53705

BAUER, WILLIAM JOSEPH, See *Who's Who in America,* 43rd edition.

BAUGH, MARYMARGARET MAGDALEN OSADCHY, nurse; b. Minot, N.D., Aug. 1, 1928; d. Nazar and Mary (Paul) Osadchy; B.S. in Nursing, Jamestown Coll., 1971; M.S. in Edn. and Adminstrn., N.D. State U., 1979; postgrad. Minn. State U., Moorhead, 1978—; m. Donald P. Baugh, May 13, 1950; children—Deborah, Seemann, Patrick, MaryBeth, Michael. With N.D. State Hosp., Jamestown, 1961—, staff devel. dir., 1974—; nurse ARC, 1959—. Registered nurse, N.D. Mem. Am., N.D. nurses assns., Am. Soc. Health Edn. Tng. (pres. N.D. 1977-78), AAUW (treas., historian, publicity Jamestown 1975-79). Roman Catholic. Home: 1103 1st Ave N Jamestown ND 58401 Office: Staff Devel Dept ND State Hosp Jamestown ND 58401

BAUGHIN, JUDITH ANN, French educator; b. June 5, 1938; d. John R. and Virginia (Clark) Hahn; m. William A. Baughin, Mar. 2, 1962. B.A., U. Cin., 1959, B.S. in Edn., 1960, Ed.M., 1964, M.A. in French, 1969. Asst. prof. Raymond Walters Coll., U. Cin., 1972-78, assoc. prof. French, 1978—. Contbr. articles to profl. jours. Mem. Ohio Modern Lang. Tchrs. Assn. (v.p. 1982-83, pres. 1983-84,), Am. Assn. Tchrs. of French, Am. Council on Teaching Fgn. Langs., Central States Conf. on Teaching Fgn. Langs. (adv. bd.), Pi Delta Phi, Alpha Lambda Delta. Avocation: Travel in France. Office: Raymond Walters Coll U Cin 9555 Plainfield St Cincinnati OH 45236

BAUGHMAN, GEORGE WASHINGTON, III, university official, fin. cons.; b. Pitts., July 7, 1937; s. George W. and Cecile M. (Lytel) B.; B.S. in Psychology, Ohio State U., 1959, M.B.A., 1961, postgrad., 1961-63; 1 dau., Lynn. Pres., Advanced Research Assos., Worthington, Ohio, 1960—; asst. instr. fin. Ohio State U., Columbus, 1961-63, research asso., office of controller, 1964-66, dir. data processing, 1966-68, 70-72, dir. adminstrv. research, 1966-72, asso. to acad. v.p., 1968-70, exec. dir. univ. budget, 1970-72, dir. spl. projects, office of pres., 1972—; chmn. bd. Hosp. Audiences, Inc., 1974—. Founding bd. dirs. Coll. and U. Machine Records Conf., 1971-73; bd. dirs. Uniplan Environ. Groups, Inc., 1970-73, chmn., 1971-73; chmn. Franklin County (Ohio) Republican Demographics and Voter Analysis Com., 1975-80; bd. dirs. Cedar Hill Assn., 1980—, Alarm Ctr. Internat., 1984—, Inventors Council Ohio, 1984—; mem. Ohio State Dental Bd., 1980—; mem. Gov.'s Export Council, 1982-83; mem. Gov.'s Tech. Task Force, 1982-83; treas. Tech. Info. Exchange and Info. Network, 1983—. Am. Council on Edn. grantee, 1976-77; Nat. Assn. Coll. and Univ. Bus. Officers grantee, 1977-79; NSF grantee, 1980—; Reisman fellow, 1962. Mem. Assn. Instl. Research, Instl. Research Council of Eleven, Coll. and Univ. Systems Exchange, AAAS, Tech. Info. Exchange and Innovation Network (treas.), Phi Alpha Kappa, Delta Tau Delta. Republican. Presbyterian. Author: (with D.H. Baker) Writing to People, 1963; (with R.W. Brady) University Program Budgeting, 1968, Administrative Data Processing, 1975; contbr. articles to profl. publs. Home: 833 Lakeshore Dr Worthington OH 43085 Office: 190 N Oval Mall Columbus OH 43210

BAUGHMAN, MELVIN JAY, extension forester; b. Tiffin, Ohio, Jan. 13, 1948; s. Melvin Dean and Betty Jane (Dietsch) B.; m. Susan Sarah Spalding, Feb. 12, 1977. B.S., Mich. State U., 1970, M.S., 1971; Ph.D., U. Minn., 1982. Research asst. Mich. State U., East Lansing, 1970-71; area extension forester Kans. State U., Chanute, Garden City, Kans., 1971-78; research asst. U. Minn., St. Paul, 1978-81; extension forestry specialist Pa. State U., State College, 1981-82; program leader renewable resources U. Minn., St. Paul, 1982—; project leader nat. recreation trail, 1977-78. Contbr. articles on forest land valuation and taxes to profl. jours. Explorer post advisor Sante Fe Trail council Boy Scouts Am., 1972-74; pres. Kans. Trails Council, Chanute, 1977, Kans. Canoe Assn., Chanute, 1977. Served with U.S. Army, 1966-72. Recipient Mil. Achievement award Burr, Patterson & Auld Co., Lansing, Mich., 1972; grantee Ruffed Grouse Soc., St. Paul, 1983, Grad. Sch. U. Minn., St. Paul, 1984. Mem. Soc. Am. Foresters, Kans. Trails Council (hon.), Epsilon Sigma Phi, Alpha Zeta, Xi Sigma Pi (v.p. 1980-81). Republican. Mem. United Ch. of Christ. Avocations: Fishing; hunting; canoeing; back packing; reading mystery novels. Home: 1506 Simpson St Saint Paul MN 55108 Office: U Minn 1530 N Cleveland Ave Saint Paul MN 55108

BAUGHN, MICHAEL LYNN, educator, mayor; b. Colby, Kans., Apr. 30, 1948; s. James Leslie and Wilma Jean (Burkhead) B.; A.B., Asbury Coll., 1970; M.S., Ft. Hays Kans. State U., 1976. Tchr., Brewster (Kans.) Unified Sch. Dist., 1970-76, instr. secondary social studies, 1970-81, prin., 1976-81; curator Butterfield Trail Mus., 1966-73, elem. supr., 1973-76. Dep. sheriff Thomas County, 1970-81, 82—, Logan County, 1970—, dir. Brewster Civil Def., 1971-79; city marshal, Brewster, 1970-74; mem. Brewster City Council, 1974-79, pres., 1979, mayor, 1979—; owner, operator Brewster IGA Store, 1981-85; pres., Butterfield Trail Assn., 1974—; chmn. Hi-Plains History Commn., 1971-73, dir. pub. relations, 1973-79; vol. rural fireman, 1975-85; vol. city fireman, 1980-85; mem. CAP, 1981—; precinct committeeman Republican Party, 1974—; mem. Thomas County Rep. Central Com., 1974—, sec.-treas., 1980—; justice of peace, 1972-74; mem. Selective Service Local Bd. 31, 1983—; mem. adv. bd. Ret. Sr. Vol. Program, 1978-81; mem. Thomas County Council on Aging, 1979-82; mem. adult edn. adv. bd. Colby Community Coll., 1975-82; mem. adminstrv. bd. Brewster United Meth. Ch., 1976-79; treas. Thomas County Centennial Com., 1983—. Mem. Northwestern Plains Am. Revolution Bicentennial Park Assn. (pres. 1974-77, treas. 1981—), Western Plains Arts Council (sec. 1973-74), Nat. Assn. Secondary Sch. Prins. (chpt. sec. 1981), Kans. Hist. Soc. (dir. 1979-82), Phi Delta Kappa (chpt. sec.). Clubs: Masons (past master), Shriners, Lions (pres. 1975, gov. dist. 17NW 1979). Home: PO Box 216 Brewster KS 67732 Office: 225 N Court Colby KS 67701

BAUKOL, RONALD OLIVER, company executive; b. Chgo., Aug. 11, 1937; s. Oliver Peter and Clara Marie (Haugstad) B.; m. Gay Lynn Gollan, Aug. 29, 1959; children—David, Andrew, Kathlyn. B.S. in Chem. Engring., Iowa State U., 1959; M.S. in Chem. Engring., MIT, 1960. Engr., group leader Procter & Gamble, Cin., 1960-66; dir. regional offices EPA, Washington, 1971-72; White House fellow, Washington, 1970-71; dept. mgr. dental, new enterprises, diagnostic depts. Minn. Mining & Mfg. Co., St. Paul, 1974—, v.p. and gen. mgr. Riker Labs., 1982—. Chmn. bd. ARC St. Paul, 1979-81, dir. regional blood com., 1972-84; co-chmn. Operation Succeed, Minn. Ind. Republican Party, St. Paul, 1977-78. Named Outstanding Young Alumnus, Iowa State U., 1969. Methodist. Avocation: Tennis. Home: 1725 Park Ave Mahtomedi MN 55115 Office: 3M Co 3M Center Saint Paul MN 55144

BAULDRICK, WALTER RYLAND, SR., human resources executive; b. Winston Salem, N.C., Oct. 10, 1946; s. Cleveland P. and Rachel (Allen) Cheek; m. Patricia Ann White, June 8, 1968; children—Walter, Shani, Rahmad. B.S. in Civil Engring., S.C. State Coll., 1968; M.Div., McCormick Theol. Sem., 1981. Design engr. Process div. UOP, Des Plaines, Ill., 1968-72, sr. engr., 1972-79, mgr. employee relations, 1979-82, dir. employee relations, 1982—. Bd. dirs. NAACP, DuPage County, Ill., 1982; mem. Maywood Human Relations Commn., Ill., 1970-76; mem. African Episcopalian Ministerial Alliance, Chgo., 1981—. Mem. Am. Soc. Personnel Adminstrn., Tech. Human Relations Mgrs. Assn., Alpha Phi Alpha. Office: Signal Research Ctr Inc 50 E Algonquin Rd Box 5016 Des Plaines IL 60017

BAUM, DAVID ROY, research psychologist; b. Kings County, N.Y., Feb. 13, 1946; s. John Harold and Sylvia (Adler) B.; B.S., U. Pitts., 1967; M.A., SUNY, Stony Brook, 1969; Ph.D., U. Mich., 1977. Sr. prin. research scientist Honeywell Systems and Research Center, Mpls., 1977-85, staff scientist, 1985—, innovator human factors internship program, 1978-83; cons. to flying tng. div. Air Force Human Resources Lab. and NRC Judge, 31st Ann. Sci. and Engring. Fair, St. Paul, 1980. Served with USAF, 1969-73. Mem. Human Factors Soc., Am. Psychol. Assn., AAAS, N.Y. Acad. Scis. Contbr. articles to profl. jours. Office: Honeywell SRC MN17-2318 2600 Ridgway Pkwy Minneapolis MN 55413

BAUM, H. JAMES, retailing executive; b. Morris, Ill., Mar. 20, 1938; s. George Humphrey and Iona (Grey) B.; m. Carol Topping, Nov. 4, 1961. B.A., Dartmouth Coll., 1961. City planner Boston Redevel. Authority, 1961; v.p. Baum's Inc., Morris, 1963—; dir. Grundy County Nat. Bank, Morris. Pres. Morris Community High Sch. Bd. Edn., 1984, Morris Community Hosp., 1975-79; chmn. Morris Planning Commn., 1965-68; v.p. Rainbow council Boy Scouts Am., 1974; elder First Presbyn. Ch., Morris, 1980—. Served with U.S. Army, 1961-63. Republican. Club: Morris Country (v.p. 1973-74). Avocations: Reading, outdoor landscaping, sailing. Home: 718 Briar Ln Morris IL 60450 Office: Baum's Inc 221 Liberty St Morris IL 60450

BAUM, M(ARY) CAROLYN, occupational therapist; b. Chgo., Mar. 26, 1943; d. Gibson Henry and Nelle (Curry) Manville; B.S., U. Kans., 1966; M.A., Webster Coll., 1979; 1 dau., Kirstin Carol. Staff occupational therapist U. Kans. Med. Center, 1966-67; staff occupational therapist Research Med. Center, Kansas City, Mo., 1967, dir. occupational therapy, 1967-73, dir. phys. medicine and rehab., 1973-76; dir. occupational therapy, clin. services Washington U. Sch. Medicine, St. Louis, 1976—, asst. research prof. neurology; allied health rep. AMA Health Policy Agenda for Am. People. Coordinator St. Louis Ind. Living Council, 1980-81; mem. nominating com. Greater Kansas City Health Systems Agy.; vice-chmn. Village Ch. Accessibility Task Force, 1974-76. Named Employee of Yr., Research Hosp., 1974, Kans. Occupational Therapist of Year, 1975. Fellow Am. Occupational Therapy Assn. (chmn. standards and ethics commn. 1973-77, nat. v.p. 1978-82, pres. 1982-83, Eleanor Clarke Slagel Lectureship award 1980, award of Merit 1984); mem. Mo. Occupational Therapy Assn., Mo. Assn. Rehab. Facilities (chmn.). Contbg. author: Occupational Therapy, 1978, 83; contbr. articles to profl. jours. Office: Dept Occupational Therapy Washington U Sch Medicine 509 S Euclid St Saint Louis MO 63110

BAUMAN, DAVID WILLIAM, hospital administrator; b. Flandreau, S.D., Sept. 19, 1952; s. Bill William and Dorothy Jean B.; m. Mary Frances Ellis, July 8, 1972 (div. Jan. 1983); 1 son, Christopher D.; m. Caryn Lee Balaban, May 1983; 1 child, Stefanie Anne. A.D. in Nursing Dakota Wesleyan U., Mitchell, S.D., 1977; B.S. in Health Service Adminstrn., U. Nebr.-Omaha, 1978; postgrad. U. Minn. Adminstrv. asst. U. Nebr. Med. Ctr., Omaha, 1977-79; assoc. adminstr. Gentry County Meml. Hosp., Albany, Mo., 1979-80; chief exec. officer Horton Community Hosp. (Kans.), 1980—, bd. dirs., 1980-82; chief exec. office Horton Health Found., 1981—, sec./treas. bd. dirs., 1981—. Chmn. Horton Airport Adv. Com., 1982-83. Served with USN and USMC, 1971-75. Mem. Kans. Assn. Young Health Care Execs. (pres. elect 1983), Health Care Fin. Mgmt. Assn., Am. Hosp. Assn., Kans. Hosp. Assn. (com. on small and rural hosps. 1982—), Horton C. of C. (pres. 1981-83), VFW. Clubs: Terrace (Kansas City, Kans.); Horton Country. Lodges: Elks, K.C. Home: Rural Route 4 308 River Rd Warrensburg MO 64093 Office: 240 W 18th St Horton KS 66439

BAUMAN, GEORGE DUNCAN, retired publisher; b. Humboldt, Iowa, Apr. 12, 1912; s. Peter William and Mae (Duncan) B.; student Loyola U., Chgo., 1930-35; J.D., Washington U., St. Louis, 1948; Litt.D. (hon.), Central Methodist Coll.; LL.D. (hon.), Maryville Coll.; L.H.D. (hon.), Mo. Valley Coll.; L.H.D. (hon.), St. Louis Rabbinical Coll., 1981; m. Nora Kathleen Kelly, May 21, 1938. Reporter, Chgo. Herald Examiner, 1931-39; archtl. rep. Pratt

& Lambert, Inc., St. Louis, 1939-43; with St. Louis Globe-Democrat, 1943-84, personnel mgr., 1951-59, bus. mgr., 1959-67, pub., 1967-84; dir. City Bank St. Louis. Bd. dirs. Boys Clubs Am., 1969-84, St. Louis YMCA, 1967-72, St. Louis City Welfare Commn., 1967-70, Better Bus. Bur., 1968-72, St. Louis Mcpl. Theatre Assn., 1968—, St. Louis Symphony Soc., 1968—, Arts and Edn. Council, 1972-83; mem. lay adv. bd. St. Vincent's Hosp., 1952-75, pres., 1957-58; mem. voting membership bd. Blue Shield, 1968-77; mem. nat. citizens adv. com. Assn. Am. Med. Colls., 1975—; mem. lay adv. bd. DePaul Community Health Center, 1975—; adv. bd. St. Louis Med. Soc., 1976-78; mem. exec. bd. St. Louis council Boy Scouts Am., 1967—, mem. pres.'s council St. Louis U., 1968—; bd. visitors Mo. Mil. Acad., 1970-84; mem. adv. bd. Newman Chapel, 1964—, pres., 1968—; bd. dirs. Policemen and Firemen Fund St. Louis, 1959—, sec., 1963-69, pres., 1969-70; bd. dirs. Herbert Hoover Boys Club, St. Louis, 1966—, pres., 1968, 76, 78; bd. dirs. United Way Greater St. Louis, 1964—, mem. exec. com., 1964-79, v.p., 1968-71; chmn. exec. com. and regional adv. com. Bi-State Regional Med. Program, 1968-75; mem. subdist. commn. St. Louis Zool. Park, 1982—; bd. dirs. Health and Welfare Council Met. St. Louis, 1960-70, pres., 1965-67; chmn. Mo. Com. Employer Support of Guard and Res., 1981—; mem. exec. com. Nat. Com. for Employer Support of the Guard and Res., 1983—; chmn. Regional Justice Info. Service, 1984—; sec. Bd. Election Commrs., St. Louis, 1957-61; bd. dirs. Catholic Charities, 1967-81, pres., 1969-70; bd. dirs. Child Center Our Lady of Grace, 1965-80, pres., 1965-68; bd. dirs. Jr. Achievement Mississippi Valley, 1953-74, v.p., 1968, pres., 1978-80, nat. bd. dirs., 1979-84; mem. Conv. and Visitors Bur. Greater St. Louis, 1968-77, v.p., 1974, pres., 1975-76; bd. dirs. Dismas House, 1964-73, pres., 1968; bd. dirs. Human Life Found., 1973-81, Downtown St. Louis, Inc., 1977-83, Civic Progress, 1984—; trustee Mo. Baptist Hosp., 1970—, exec. com., 1974—, treas., 1978-79, asst. sec., 1979-80, sec., 1980-81, vice chmn., 1981—; trustee Jefferson Nat. Expansion Meml. Assn., 1968—, Mo. Public Expenditure Survey, 1968—, Freedoms Found. at Valley Forge, 1968-75, David Ranken Jr. Tech. Inst., 1969—, Nat. Jewish Hosp. and Research Center, 1970-84, Govtl. Research Inst., 1968—, Laclede Sch. Law, 1981—. Decorated knight of Malta; recipient Disting. Alumnus citation Washington U., 1972, Bus. Leader of Year award Religious Heritage Am., 1973, citation Loyola U. Alumni Assn., 1973; Silver Beaver award Boy Scouts Am., 1978; Silver Crown award St. Louis Rabbinical Coll., 1983; Disting. Pub. Service medal Dept. Def., 1983; Disting. Communal Service award B'nai B'rith, 1983; named to Loyola U. Athletic Hall of Fame, 1976; Right Arm of St. Louis award St. Louis Regional Commerce and Growth Assn., 1980. Mem. Newspaper Personnel Relations Assn. (past pres.), Mo. (dir. 1969-74), St. Louis (exec. com. 1969-73, dir. 1969-73) chambers commerce, Mo. Acad. Squires, Bar Assn. St. Louis, ABA, Mo. Bar Assn., Advt. Club St. Louis (gov. 1972-75). Clubs: Bogey (pres. 1980, 81), Mo. Athletic, St. Louis, Round Table, Media (dir. 1968—) (St. Louis).

BAUMANN, JAMES LEROY, state environmental board chairman; b. Columbus, Ohio, May 2, 1931; s. Herman E. and Catherine (Haley) B.; m. E. Ann Dougherty, Nov. 19, 1955; children—H. Matthew, Margaret Mathues, James E., David M., Lisa M., Stephen R. B.A., Coll. St. Charles Borromeo, Columbus, 1953. Lic. plumbing and heating contractor; lic. real estate broker. Gen. mgr., ptnr. Baumann Bros. Inc., Columbus, 1960-76; pres. Lockhurst, Inc., Columbus, 1977-83; broker James L. Baumann Realty, Columbus, 1976—; councilman City of Columbus, 1965-69; mem. Ohio Ho. of Reps., 1971-78; mem. Ohio Environ. Bd. Rev., Columbus, 1979—, chmn., 1984—; bd. dirs. Ohio Alliance for Environ. Edn., 1984—. Chmn., Ohio Retirement Study Commn., 1975-78; chmn. Cath. Social Service Agy., Columbus, 1967-68. Mem. Columbus Area C. of C., Greater Columbus Area Bd. Realtors. Democrat. Roman Catholic. Avocations: boating; fishing; politics. Home: 1434 Lonsdale Rd Columbus OH 43232 Office: Ohio Environ Bd Rev 250 E Town St Columbus OH 43215

BAUMEISTER, CARL F., retired physician; b. Dolliver, Iowa, May 15, 1907; s. Charles F. and Lida Bard (Moore) B.; B.S.; Chicago U., 1930; M.D., Iowa U., 1933; m. Eleanor Hoskins, Apr. 19, 1930; children—Richard. Physician in internal med., Ind. U. Hosps., 1933-36, Louisville U. Hosps., 1936-37, Council Bluffs Clinic, 1937-43, Berwyn (Ill.) Surburban Med. Center, from 1943; mem. staff MacNeal Meml. Hosp., Berwyn; instr. internal medicine U. Ill., 1943-50, clin. asst. prof., 1950-71, 73-82, ret., 1982; clin. asst. prof. medicine Stritch Sch. Medicine Loyola U., Maywood, Ill., 1971-73; med. staff Loyola U. Hosp., 1971-73. Fellow Inst. of Medicine Chgo.; member AMA, Am. Heart Assn., Assn. Am. Med. Colls., Am. Med. Writers Assn., Am. Diabetes Assn., S.A.R., N.Y. Acad. Sci. Mason. Contbr. articles to med. jours. Abstract editor on med. education Excerpta Medica of Amsterdam. Author: Computer Diagnosis of the Acute Surgical Abdomen. Research diagnosis and treatment new type vascular headache. Home: 120 S Delaplaine Rd Riverside IL 60546

BAUMEISTER, ELEANOR H. (MRS. CARL F. BAUMEISTER), club woman; b. Lake Linden, Mich., Oct. 2, 1909; d. Thomas and Sarah (Madigan) Hoskins; B.; Music Edn., U. Minn., 1930; m. Carl Frederick Baumeister, Apr. 8, 1929; 1 son, Richard. Co-founder, advt. mgr. The Corn Belt Livestock Feeder trade mag., 1948-51. Publicity dir. Patron's Council, Riverside-Brookfield High Sch., 1951-53; pres. MacNeal Meml. Hosp. Women's Auxiliary, 1956, mem. adv. bd., 1957. Bd. dirs. Riverside Pub. Library, 1961-71, pres., 1967-71; dir. Ill. P.E.O. Home, Knoxville, 1956-58, fin. adviser, 1958-63; vice chmn. bd. dirs. Southwest Suburban chpt. Am. Cancer Soc., 1968-69, chmn. bd. dirs. Central Suburban unit, 1969-71, sec.-treas. Central Suburban unit, 1972-84; sect. Dist. 208 Caucus; mem. citizens adv. bd. Morton Coll. Sch. Nursing, 1972—. Mem. Gen. Fedn. Women's Clubs, P.E.O. (pres. Riverside 1955-56, 60-61, Ill. corr. sec., 1956-57, rec. sec. 1957-58). Republican. Presbyterian. Clubs: Chgo. Farmers, Riverside Woman's (pres. 1954-56, chmn. auditing com. 1963). Home: 120 S Delaplaine Rd Riverside IL 60546

BAUMER, BEVERLY BELLE, journalist; b. Hays, Kans., Sept. 23, 1926; d. Charles Arthur and Mayme Mae (Lord) B.; B.S., William Allen White Sch. Journalism, U. Kans., 1948. Summer intern reporter Hutchinson (Kans.) News, 1946-47; continuity writer, women's program dir. Sta. KWBW, Hutchinson, 1948-49; dist. editor Salina (Kans.) Jours., 1950-57; commd. writer State of Kans. Centennial Year, 1961; contbg. author: Ford Times, Kansas City Star, Wichita (Kans.) Eagle, Ojibway Publs., Billboard, Modern Jeweler, Floor Covering Weekly, other bus. mags., 1962-69; owner and mgr. apts., Hutchinson, 1970—; broadcaster Reading Radio Room, Sta. KHCC-FM, Hutchinson, 1982—; info. officer, maj. Kans. Wing Hdqrs. CAP, 1969-72. Mem. Republican Presdl. Task Force. Recipient Human Interest Photo award Nat. Press Women, 1956; News Photo award AP, 1952. Mem. Fellows Menninger Found., Suffolk County Hist. Soc., Nat. Fedn. Press Women, Kans. Press Women, Am. Soc. Profl. and Exec. Women, Am. Film Inst., Nat. Soc. Magna Charta Dames, Nat. Soc. Daus. Founders and Patriots Am., Nat. Soc. Daus. Am. Colonists, Kans. Soc. Daus. Am. Colonists (organizing regent Dr. Thomas Lord chpt., state chmn. insignia com.), Nat. Soc. Sons and Daus. Pilgrims (elder Kans. br.), D.A.R., Ben Franklin Soc. (nat. adv. bd.), Daus. Colonial Wars, Order Descs. Colonial Physicians and Chirurgiens, Colonial Dames 17th Century (chaplain, charter mem. Henry Woodhouse chpt.), Plantagenet Soc., Internat. Platform Soc., U. Kans. Alumni Assn., Nat. Geneal. Soc. Author book of poems, 1941; editor: A Simple Bedside Book for People Who Are Kinda, Sorta Interested in Genealogy, 1983. Home and Office: 204 Curtis St Hutchinson KS 67502

BAUMGARDNER, RUSSELL HOWARD, See *Who's Who in America,* 43rd edition.

BAUMGARDT, BILLY RAY, university official, agriculturist; b. Lafayette, Ind., Jan. 17, 1933; s. Raymond P. and Mildred L. (Cordray) B.; m. D. Elaine Blain, June 8, 1952; children—Pamela K. Baumgardt Farley, Teresa Jo Baumgardt Adolfsen, Donald Ray. B.S. in Agr., Purdue U., 1955, M.S., 1956; Ph.D., Rutgers U., 1959. From asst. to assoc. prof. U. Wis.-Madison, 1959-67; prof. animal nutrition Pa. State U., University Park, 1967-70, head dept. dairy and animal sci., 1970-79, assoc. dir. agrl. expt. sta., 1979-80; dir. agrl. research Purdue U., West Lafayette, Ind., 1980—, assoc. dean, 1980—. Contbr. chpts. to books, articles to sci. jours. Recipient Wilkinson award Pa. State U., 1979. Fellow AAAS; mem. Am. Dairy Sci. Assn. (Nutrition Research award 1966; pres. 1984-85), Am. Inst. Nutrition, Am. Soc. Animal Sci., Sigma Xi. Lodge: Rotary. Home: 812 Lazy Ln Lafayette IN 47904 Office: Purdue U West Lafayette IN 47907

BAUMGARTNER, ALDEN (FREDERICK), JR., transportation and distribution executive; b. Chgo., Nov. 29, 1930; s. Alden F. and Anne R. (Sehocke) B.; A.A., Wilson Jr. Coll., 1947-49; B.A., Roosevelt U., 1949-51; Asso., Coll. Advanced Traffic, 1956-57; m. Rosalie O'Connor, Nov. 13, 1954; children—Diane, Iris, Melissa, Kevin. Dist. mgr. Spector Freight Systems Co., St. Louis, 1961-63; regional mgr. To FC div. Fruehauf Co., Chgo., 1970-76, Acme Fast Freight, 1978-79; v.p. Transp. Cons., Chgo., 1978—; mem. faculty Coll. Advanced Traffic. Mem. com. Ind. Voters Mo. and Ill. Served with USNR, 1945-50; Transp. Corps USAR, 1955-59; flotilla comdr. USCG Aux. Mem. Am. Soc. Traffic, Delta Nu Alpha (pres. St. Louis chpt. 1969-70). Roman Catholic. Clubs: St. Louis Transp., Chgo. Transp., Masons, Shriners. Office:16224 Prince Dr South Holland IL 60473

BAUMGARTNER, RICHARD MARK, insurance executive, investment consultant; b. Mpls., Feb. 11, 1958; s. Benedict Fredrick and Darlene Margaret (Peterson) B. B.A. cum laude, Coll. St. Thomas, 1980. Cert. ins. counselor. Sales rep., mgmt. staff IPS Incorporated, St. Paul, 1980—; pres., chief exec. officer T-Bone, Inc., Wayzata, Minn., 1984—. Mem. Profl. Ins. Agents Assn., Soc. Cert. Ins. Counselors. Republican. Roman Catholic. Lodges: Elks, K.C. Avocations: outdoor sports; fishing; skiing. Home: 9937 Morris Rd Bloomington MN 55437 Office: IPS Inc 1450 Energy Park Dr St Paul MN 55108

BAUMGARTNER, WILLIAM HANS, JR., lawyer; b. Chgo., July 24, 1955; s. William H. and Charlotte Burnette (Lange) B. B.A., U. Chgo., 1976; J.D. magna cum laude, Harvard U., 1979. Bar: Ill. 1979, U.S. Dist. Ct. (no. dist.) Ill. 1979. Assoc. Sidley & Austin, Chgo., 1979—. Mem. ABA, Chgo. Bar Assn., Phi Beta Kappa. Office: Sidley & Austin One First Nat Plaza Chicago IL 60603

BAUMHART, RAYMOND CHARLES, clergyman, university president; b. Chgo., Dec. 22, 1923; s. Emil and Florence (Weidner) B. B.S., Northwestern U., 1945; Ph.L., Loyola U., 1952, S.T.L., 1958; M.B.A., Harvard U., 1953, D.B.A., 1963, LL.D. (hon.) Ill. Coll., D.H.L. (hon.) Scholl Coll. Joined Jesuit Order, 1946; ordained to ministry Roman Catholic Ch., 1957; asst. prof. mgmt. Loyola U., Chgo., 1962-64, dean Sch. Bus. Adminstrn., 1964-66, exec. v.p. acting v.p. Med. Ctr., 1968-70, pres., 1970—; dir. Jewel Cos., Inc., 1973-84, Continental Ill. Corp., 1976-85. Served to lt. (j.g.) USNR, 1944-46. Fellow John W. Hill, 1961-62, Cambridge Ctr. for Social Studies, 1966-68. Recipient Rale medal Boston Coll.; Order of Cavalier, Italy. Mem. Assn. Jesuit Colls. and Univs., Fedn. Ind. Ill. Colls. and Univs.; chmn. Com. for Chgo. Catholic Hosp. Collaboration. Clubs: Comml., Econ., Mid-Am. (Chgo.). Author: An Honest Profit, 1968; (with Thomas Garrett) Cases in Business Ethics, 1968; (with Thomas McMahon) The Brewer-Wholesaler Relationship, 1969. Home: 6525 N Sheridan Rd Chicago IL 60626 Office: 820 N Michigan Ave Chicago IL 60611

BAUR, ANDREW N., banker; b. Apr. 25, 1944. A.B., Washington & Lee U.; M.B.A., U. Ga. Mgmt. trainee First Nat. Bank of Atlanta, 1967-70; comml. banking officer Mercantile Trust Co. N.Am., 1970-74; pres. Commerce Bank of St. Louis, chmn. bd., pres.; chmn., chief exec. officer County Bank of St. Louis and pres., chief operating officer County Tower Corp., 1978-84; chmn. bd., chief exec. officer Southwest Bank and Miss. Valley Investment Co., St. Louis, 1984—; pres., dir. Tree Ct. Indsl. Devel., Inc. Bd. dirs. Webster Coll., Municipal Theatre Assn. St. Louis, Arts and Edn. Council, Mo. Pub. Expenditure Survey, Jr. Achievement, Boy Scouts Am. Address: Southwest Bank of Saint Louis 2301 S Kingshighway Saint Louis MO 63139

BAUR, EDWARD T., real estate developer; b. St. Louis, July 8, 1946; married, 3 children. A.B. in Econs., U. N.C., 1968. With Baur Properties, St. Louis, 1971—, pres. Trustee St. Louis Country Day Sch., Ronald Beasley Sch.; mem. St. Louis Children's Hosp. Devel. bd., St. Louis County Tech. Adv. Commn.; bd. dirs. Mid-County YMCA, St. Louis; pres. Hawthorne Found. Address: 700 Office-Jarkway PO Box 27389 Saint Louis MO 63141

BAURER, JOAN RUTH, investment company executive, financial consultant; b. N.Y.C., July 10, 1934; d. Jack Maurice and Elsie Frank (Galkin) Lawson; B.A., Queens Coll., 1955; postgrad. Hunter Coll., 1955-57, Fresno State Coll., 1966-67; postgrad. in fin. Calif. State Coll., Bakersfield, 1973-76; m. Martin E. Baurer, Sept. 23, 1953 (div. May 1979); children—Benjamin Zachary, Valery Suzanne. Tchr. home econs., Astoria, N.Y., 1957-59, New Rochelle, N.Y., 1958-60; tchr. gen. sci., Liverpool, N.Y., 1960; account exec. Internat. Securities Co., Bakersfield, 1975-77, Blunt, Ellis & Loewi Co., Inc., Waukegan, Ill., 1977-79; with All Am. Mgmt., Des Plaines, Ill., 1979-83; br. mgr., registered rep. Integrated Resources Equity Corp., Denver, 1984—; pres. Joan Baurer & Co., Inc., registered investment advisors. Vol. dir. menu planning Guild House, restaurant for benefit Child Guidance Clinic, Bakersfield, 1964-66; pres., bd. dirs. McHenry County Estate Planning Council. Mem. Internat. Assn. Fin. Planners. Clubs: Women's Network (Crystal Lake); Ski. Office: 610 Crystal Point Dr Suite 1400 Crystal Lake IL 60014

BAUSCHARD, RICHARD BACH, architect; b. N.Y.C., July 11, 1944; s. Fred George and Harriett (Durlin) B.; m. Jane M. O'Brien, July 2, 1966; 1 dau., Laura. B.A., Syracuse U., 1967, B.Arch., 1968; M.Arch., U. Pa., 1969. Project designer Van Dijk, Johnson & Partners-Architects, Cleve., 1971-75, assoc. design, 1976-78, assoc. partner, dir. mktg., 1979-81, partner, dir. mktg., 1982—; adj. lectr. Case Western Res. U., 1973-78; architecture lectr. Cleve. Area Arts Council, Cleve. State U., 1979-85. Vol., United Way campaign, 1975-79, team leader, 1980-83, group leader, 1984—. Served to lt. (j.g.) USN, 1969-71. Recipient medal N.Y. State Soc. Architects, 1968, Sch. medal AIA, 1968. Mem. AIA (exec. com. Cleve. chpt. 1980—, treas. 1982-83, pres. 1985—), Soc. Mktg. Profl. Services, Architects Soc. Ohio (bd. mem. 1980), Psi Upsilon. Clubs: Union League (Chgo.); Skating, Athletic (Cleve.). Home: 3256 Chalfant Rd Shaker Heights OH 44120 Office: 1 Erieview Plaza Suite 300 Cleveland OH 44114

BAVASI, PETER, professional baseball executive. Pres., chief operating officer Cleve. Indians. Office: Cleve Indians Cleveland Stadium Cleveland OH 44114*

BAXTER, JOSEPH DIEDRICH, dentist; b. New Albany, Ind., Sept. 11, 1937; s. James William, Jr. and Beatrice (Diedrich) B.; A.B., Ind. U., 1959, D.M.D., U. Louisville, 1969; m. Carroll Jane Bell, Dec. 23, 1972. Practice dentistry, New Albany, 1969—. Bd. dirs. Floyd County (Ind.) Econ. Opportunity Corp., 1971-76. Served with AUS, 1960-61. Mem. Floyd County Dental Soc. (pres. 1972-74), Am. Dental Assn., Phi Gamma Delta. Republican. Methodist. Home: 36 Bellewood Dr New Albany IN 47150 Office: Professional Arts Bldg New Albany IN 47150

BAXTER, JOSEPH MERLIN, county official, farmer; b. Grant County, Wis., Aug. 25, 1918; s. Charles P. and Josephine (Peebles) B.; m. Dorothy Adeline Ross, Apr. 22, 1944; children—Mary Ann, Charles. B.A., Madison Bus. Coll., 1939. Cert. bridge insp. Acct., Oscar Mayer Co., Madison, Wis., 1939-40; farmer, Cuba City, Wis., 1940-42, Darlington, Wis., 1947-68; mem. LaFayette (Wis.) County Bd., 1955-68; chmn. Town of Darlington, 1955-68; hwy. commr. LaFayette County, 1968—; land appraiser; mem. State of Wis. Roads Standards Com. Served to lt. (j.g.) USN, 1942-46. Recipient award U.S. Office of Emergency Preparedness, 1970. Mem. Am. Road Builders Assn., Am. Legion, VFW. Roman Catholic. Lodge: K.C. Home: Route 1 Darlington WI 53530 Office: Box 100 Darlington WI 53530

BAYGENTS, ANNA MARY, educator; b. Poplar Bluff, Mo., July 13, 1926; d. George Francis and Bertha Louise (Franck) AuBuchon; student U. N.C., 1956, U. Mo., 1972, S.E. Mo. U., 1973-74; A.A., Three Rivers Community Coll., 1984; m. Roy Emerson Baygents, May 11, 1968 (dec. 1978); 1 son, Ralph George (dec.); step-children—Steven Warren, Edris Marie, Roy Emerson, William Michael, Jeffrey Thomas, Timothy Gregory, Patricia Joy. Lab. technician, chairside asst., secretarial asst. to dentist, 1944-68; bookkeeper Baygents Holiday Inn Texaco, Poplar Bluff, 1968-78; instr. dental assisting Three Rivers Community Coll., Poplar Bluff, part-time 1972-76, full time 1976—; owner, bus. mgr., bookkeeper Baygents Mobil Service Co., Poplar Bluff, 1978-83. Sec., Butler County United Fund Bd., 1960-61, chmn. budget com., 1959-61; chmn. reunion com. Poplar Bluff High Sch. Class of 1944, 1969, 74, 79, 84; active Butler County Assn. for Retarded Children, 1974—, pres., 1981-82, v.p., 1983; troop com. chmn. Boy Scouts Am., Girl Scouts U.S.A., 1979-82; mem. parish council Sacred Heart Ch., 1984—; organizing bd., sec., treas. Willhaven Residential Complex, Inc. Mem. Am. Dental Assts. Assn. (life, treas. 1963-68, Achievement award 1967), Mo. Dental Assts. Assn. (life, pres. 1956-57, Cooperation award 1974, Achievement award 1976), S.E. Mo. Dental Assts. Soc. (life), Am. Vocat. Assn., Mo. Vocat. Assn., Mo. Dental Assisting Educators (v.p. 1984—), Mo. State Tchrs. Assn., Mo. Assn. Community and Jr. Colls., Butler County Geneal. Soc. (1st v.p. 1980-83), DAR (treas. Poplar Bluff chpt. 1980-81, chaplain 1983), Butler County (Mo.) Hist. Soc. Democrat. Roman Catholic. Contbr. articles to profl. jours. Home: 725 Kinzer St PO Box 506 Poplar Bluff MO 63901 Office: Three Rivers Community Coll Three Rivers Blvd Poplar Bluff MO 63901

BAYLESS, LAWRENCE GRANT, artist; machinery company executive; b. Crawfordsville, Ind., May 19, 1935; s. Lloyd Richard and Geneice (Patton) B.; B.F.A., Bradley U., 1957; m. Joyce Ann Stribling, June 23, 1957; children—Robert, Michael, John, Ann, Mark, Amy, Joe. Artist, Squires Advt. Agy., Springfield, Ill., 1957-59, Greeley Advt., Springfield, 1959-60; artist, designer Mueller Co., Decatur, Ill., 1960-65; art dir. Evan and Assoc., Springfield, 1965-70; head designer Bur. of Design, Public Hearing Services, State of Ill., Springfield, 1970; acting supr. program design, artist edn. center Fiat-Allis, Springfield, 1970-74, supr. multi-media graphics, world-wide publs., 1974—; judge Macon County Art Exhibit, 1964, 67, 71, 73, Town and Country Art Exhibit, U. Ill., 1971; tchr. Bement Art Club. Bd. dirs. Aid to Retarded Citizens, 1968-70; bd. dirs. Lincolnland Pony Baseball, 1972, 73, v.p., 1974-83, coach, 1974-85; mem. com. Boy Scouts Am., 1969-79; bd. dirs. Petersburg Jr. Baseball, 1973-85; coach Thorobred Baseball, 1978, 80-82; coach Little League, 1966-70, Flag football, 1969-71; pres. Lincolnwood Pony League, 1983-84; trustee Methodist Ch.; bd. dirs. Porta Athletic Booster Club, 1974-81, pres., 1975, 79; bd. dirs. Lake Petersburg Assn., 1981-82; field dir. Div. I North Zone Pony Baseball Inc., 1981-85. Served with U.S. Army, 1958, 61-62. Recipient art edn. award State of Ill., 1957; award of merit State of Ind. Art Award, 1953. Mem. Advt. and Pub. Relations Club Springfield, Sangamon County Referees Assn., Internat. Graphics Inc. (charter), Nat. Audio-Visual Inst., Am. Amateur Baseball Congress, Bradley U. Alumni Assn., Sigma Phi Epsilon Alumni. Republican. Club: Elks. Home: Rural Route 1 424 Hemlock St Petersburg IL 62675 Office: Fiat-Allis 3000 S 6th St Springfield IL 62710

BAYMILLER, LYNDA DOERN, social worker; b. Milw., July 6, 1943; d. Ronald Oliver and Marian Elizabeth (Doern) B.; B.A., U. Wis., 1965, M.S.W., 1969; student U. Hawaii, 1962, Mich. State U., 1965. Peace Corps vol., Chile, 1965-67; social worker Luth. Social Services of Wis. and Upper Mich., Milw., 1969-77, contract social worker, 1978-79; dist. supr. Children's Service Soc. Wis., Kenosha, 1977-78; social work supr. Sauk County Dept. Social Services, Baraboo, Wis., 1979—. Bd. dirs. Zoo Pride, Zool. Soc. Milw. County, 1975-77, Sauk County Mental Health Assn., 1979—; mem. Harmony chpt. Sweet Adelines, West Allis, Wis., 1970-75, pres. chpt., 1971; pres. bd. dirs. Growing Place Day Care Center, Kenosha, 1977-78; mem. Baraboo (Wis.) Centennial Com., 1982. Mem. Nat. Assn. Social Workers, Acad. Cert. Social Workers, Wis. Social Services Assn., AAUW (br. sec. 1982-84), U. Wis. Alumni Assn. (life mem.), Am. Legion Aux., DAR, Nat. Soc. Magna Charta Dames, Eddy Family Assn. (life mem.), Nat. Soc. Ancient and Hon. Arty. Co. of Mass., Morris Pratt Inst., Sauk County Hist. Soc., Internat. Crane Found. (patron), Daus. Colonial Wars, Zool. Soc. Milwaukee County (life), Am. Bus. Women's Assn., Friends of Baraboo Zoo, Alpha Xi Delta. Lodges: Order Eastern Star, Ladies Aux. of Fraternal Order Eagles. Author: (with Clara Amelia Hess) Now-Won, A Collection of Feeling (poetry and prose), 1973. Home: 332 4th Ave Baraboo WI 53913

BAYS, KARL DEAN, hospital supply company executive; b. Loyall, Ky., Dec. 23, 1933; s. James K. and Myrtle (Criscillis) B.; B.S., Eastern Ky. U., 1955, LL.D. (hon.), 1977; M.B.A., Ind. U., 1958; D.C.S. (hon.), Union Coll. (Ky.), 1971; m. Billie Joan White, June 4, 1955; children—Robert D., Karla. With Am. Hosp. Supply Corp., 1958—, pres., dir., 1970, chief exec. officer, 1971—, chmn. bd., 1974—; dir. Amoco Corp., Delta Air Lines, Inc., No. Trust Corp., The No. Trust Co. Trustee emeritus Duke U.; trustee Northwestern U.; life mem. bd. dirs. Lake Forest Hosp. Served with USMCR, 1955-57. Recipient Trojan M.B.A. Achievement award U. So. Calif., 1972; Horatio Alger award, 1979; Disting. Alumni Service award Ind. U., 1977; named Outstanding Alumnus Eastern Ky. U., 1973; Mktg. Man of Year Sales & Mktg. Execs. Assn. Chgo., 1977; Outstanding Chief Exec. Officer in hosp. and health-care supplies industry Financial World, 1975, 81, 82, 85; Outstanding Chief Exec. Officer in hosp. supply industry Wall St. Transcript, 1980, 84. Clubs: Execs., Econ., Comml., Mid-Am., Chicago (Chgo.); Glen View, Old Elm, Onwentsia. Office: One Am Plaza Evanston IL 60201

BAZIK, EDNA FRANCES, mathematician, educator; b. Streator, Ill., Dec. 26, 1946; d. Andrew and Anna Frances (Vagasky) B.; B.S.Ed., Ill. State U, 1969; postgrad. Hamilton Coll., summer 1971, Augustana Coll., summer 1973; M.Ed., U. Ill., 1972; Ph.D., So. Ill. U., 1976, gen. adminstrv. cert., 1980. Tchr. math. Northlawn Jr. High Sch., Streator, 1969-74; instr. math. edn. So. Ill. U., 1974-76; asst. prof. math. Concordia Coll., 1976-78; asst. prof. math. Ill. State U., Normal, 1978—; inservice presentations, workshops for tchrs.; cons. to sch. dists. NSF grantee, 1980—. Mem. AAUP, Assn. Tchr. Educators, Ill. Assn. Tchr. Educators, Nat. Council Tchrs. Math., Ill. Council Tchrs. Math. (governing bd., dir. coll. and univ. level), Math. Assn. Am., Nat. Council Suprs. Math., NEA, Ill. Edn. Assn., Sch. Sci. and Math. Assn., U.S. Metric Assn., Am. Ednl. Research Assn., Assn. Supervision and Curriculum Devel., Ill. Assn. Supervision and Curriculum Devel., Assn. Childhood Edn. Internat., Council Exceptional Children, Research Council Diagnostic and Prescriptive Math., Kappa Delta Pi, Phi Delta Kappa (pres. Ill. State U. chpt. 1982-83), Pi Mu Epsilon, Phi Kappa Phi. Republican. Lutheran. Co-author: Elementary Mathematical Methods, 1978; Mind Over Math, 1980; Teaching Mathematics to Children with Special Needs, 1983; Step-by-Step: Addition, 1984; Step-by-Step: Subtraction, 1984; Step-by-Step: Multiplication, 1984; Step-by-Step: Division, 1984. Home: 202 Riss Dr Normal IL 61761 Office: Math Dept Ill State U Normal IL 61761

BEACH, OSCAR HARDING, JR., statistician; b. Cottekill, N.Y., Feb. 5, 1929; s. Oscar H. and Edna Mae (Pine) B.; B.S., Syracuse U., 1954, M.B.A., 1961; m. Mary Louise Nisbet, Sept. 1, 1951; 1 dau., Nancy Woodburn. Field rep. Travelers Ins. Co., Conn., Cleve., 1954-58, group supr., Cleve., 1958; sr. research asst. Fed. Res. Bank, Cleve., 1959-61, asst. economist, 1961-63, asso. economist, 1963, statistician, 1963-65, asst. cashier, 1965-71, asst. v.p., 1971—. Served with U.S. Army, 1946-49. Mem. Am. Statis. Assn. Office: Fed Res Bank PO Box 6387 Cleveland OH 44101

BEACHELL, EILEEN JEANETTE, statistician; b. Newark, Del., Oct. 24, 1953; d. Harold Charles and Georgianna Katherine (Sorm) B. B.A., U. Del., 1975; M.S., Fla. State U., 1976. Product design engr. Ford Motor Co. Heavy Truck Div., Dearborn, Mich., 1976-84; statis. methods engr. Ford Motor Co. Transmission and Chassis Div., Livonia, Mich., 1984—. Mem. Am. Statis. Assn. Avocations: sailing; gardening.

BEACHLER, KENNETH CLARKE, univ. adminstr.; b. Battle Creek, Mich., Oct. 11, 1935; s. Hubert Waldo and Nina Kathryn (Eitelbuss) B.; B.A. with high honors, Mich. State U., 1963. Profl. actor and singer, Chgo., 1955-57; radio announcer WKAR-AM/FM, East Lansing, Mich., 1959-62, WSWM-FM, East Lansing, 1962-64; music program dir. WKAR-FM, East Lansing, 1964-70; dir. lecture-concert series Mich. State U., East Lansing, 1971-81, dir. Wharton Ctr. for Performing Arts, 1981—. Host weekly radio program Arts Billboard, 1972—. Bd. dirs. Lansing Symphony Orch., 1971-73, 78-82, Okemos Barn Theatre, 1970-71, Opera Co. Greater Lansing, 1978-79, Pashami Dancers, 1976—. Served with AUS, 1957-59; to comdr. USNR. Named Best Actor, Okemos Barn Theatre, 1974, Best Dir., 1969, 71, 76, 80, 81; recipient Mich. Gov.'s Minuteman award, 1983; Mich. State U. Bd. Trustees tuition scholar, 1960, Hinman Broadcasting scholar, 1961-63. Mem. Internat. Soc. Performing Arts Adminstrs. (dir. 1974-77), Assn. Coll., Univ. and Community Arts Adminstrs., Naval Res. Assn. (life). Mem. United Ch. of Christ. Lodge: Rotary (bd. dirs. 1985). Club: University of Mich. State U. (dir. 1978-82, v.p. 1980-82). Home: 1450 Hitching Post Rd East Lansing MI 48823 Office: Mich State U East Lansing MI 48824

BEACHUM, LOCK PATTERSON, educational administrator; b. Florence, Ala., Oct. 2, 1934; s. Lock T. and Nellie E. B.; m. Janice Lucille Womack, July 15, 1967; children—Lock Patterson, Jenise Darcel. B.S., Fayetteville U., 1961; M.S., Youngstown State Coll., 1972; Ph.D., Kent State U. Elem. sch. tchr., Ga., Ala., Ohio, 1961-71; asst. prin. North High Sch., Youngstown, Ohio, 1971-80, prin., 1980; prin. East High Sch., Youngstown, 1980—; cons. Ohio Dept. Edn., Columbus. Contbr. articles to profl. jours. Bd. dirs. Youngstown Community Action Council; bd. dirs. Youngstown Assn. Sch. Adminstrs., pres., 1985-86; bd. dirs. McGuffey Youth Ctr., pres. 1981-83; mem. Leadership Youngstown Council; pres. Youngstown Urban League, 1981-85; mem. Youngstown City Council, 1986—; chmn. Children Service Bd., 1984. Served with U.S. Army, 1953-56. Recipient Man of Yr. award United Vets. Council, 1983, Profl. award

Nat. Assn. Negro Bus. and Profl. Women, 1983, Community Service award Democrat Old Timers Com., 1983, Community Service award VFW 1984, Acad. Excellence award Northside Oldtimers Com., 1984. Mem. Omega Psi Phi. Democrat. Methodist. Avocation: golf. Office: East High Sch 1544 East High Youngstown OH 44505

BEAGLE, PETER FRANCIS JUDE, lawyer; b. Schenectady, N.Y., May 14, 1949; s. Kenneth Earl and Mary Jacqulin (Wall) B.; m. Janice Rae Wick, Dec. 27, 1969; children—Jennifer Wick, Peter Francis Jude Jr. A.A., Hudson Valley Coll., 1974; B.A., Union Coll., 1975; J.D., Capital U., 1978. Bar: Ohio 1978. Assoc. Jughes & Morgan, Newark, Ohio, 1978-79; faculty Central Ohio Tech. U., Newark, 1978-79; sole practice, Columbus, Ohio, 1983—. Sustaining mem. Boy Scouts Am., Columbus, 1984; active Fraternal Order of Police, Columbus, 1984, Retain Judge Wonnell Com., Columbus, 1984, Charity Newsies, Columbus, 1984. Served to capt. USAF, 1979-83. Recipient Outstanding Oral Argument award Capital U., 1975-76; Harter Scholarship award, 1977; Assoc. Justice/Moot Ct. award, 1977-78. Mem. Assn. Trial Lawyers Am., Ohio Bar Assn., ABA, Columbus Bar Assn., Order of Barristers, Delta Theta Phi. Republican. Roman Catholic. Home: 47 S Roosevelt Ave Columbus OH 43209

BEAL, BERT LEONARD, JR., elec. engr.; b. Birmingham, Ala., June 19, 1911; s. Bert Leonard and Catherine (Marks) B.; B.S., Washington U., St. Louis, 1934; m. Josephine Watkins, Feb. 24, 1943; 1 son, Albert G. Asst. mine mgr. So. Coal, Coke & Mining, Belleville, Ill., 1935-36; engr. Carrier Corp., Newark, 1936-37; asst. foreman, foreman tng. supr., engr., asst. gen. mech. supt. St. Joe Minerals Corp., Bonne Terre, Mo. 1937-54. gen. mech. supt., 1954-66, dir. engring., 1966-75; pres. Beal Enterprises, engring. cons. and agribus., 1975—. Active in civic affairs. Trustee Presbyterian Children's Home, bd. chmn., 1973. Served from lt. to lt. col. AUS, 1941-46. Registered profl. engr. Mem. Soc. Mining Engrs., Rivermines Engrs. Club (sec. 1951, v.p. 1952, pres. 1953), St. Francis County Hist. Soc. (pres. 1964), Am. Legion. Presbyterian (deacon, elder). Rotarian (sec. 1955, dir. 1972). Home and Office: 615 W Columbia St Farmington MO 63640

BEAL, LARRY JOHN, production engineer; b. Jackson, Mich., Oct. 13, 1956; s. John Preston and Marilyn Birdell (Kendall) B.; m. Margaret Ellen Fear Apr. 22, 1978; children—Brandon John, Alison Nicole. B.S. in Mech. Engring., Rose-Hilman Inst., 1978. Registered profl. engr., Ind. Test engr. Central Ill. Pub. Service Co., Hutsonville, 1978-80; engr. Pub. Service Co. of Ind., Gibson County, 1980-82, prodn. engr., 1982—. Bd. dirs. Ind. chpt. Cystic Fibrosis Found., also county br. coordinator; mem. adminstrv. bd. United Methodist Ch. Mem. ASME, Nat. Soc. Profl. Engrs. Lodge: Kiwanis (Fort Branch, Ind.). Avocations: golf; tennis; softball. Home: 102 E Oak St Fort Branch IN 47648 Office: Pub Service Co of Ind PO Box 1009 Mount Carmel IL 62863

BEAL, PHILIP E., college dean; married; 2 children. A.B., Cornell Coll., 1957; M.A., Northwestern U., 1961; Ph.D., U. Oreg., 1965. Dean of men Pacific Luth. U., 1968-72, dean for student life, 1972-73, faculty grad. program in student personnel, 1968-78, v.p., dean student life, 1973-78; vis. scholar Nat. Ctr. Higher Edn. Mgmt. Systems, 1978-79; dean students Saginaw Valley State Coll., Mich., 1979—; cons. pub. and pvt. instns. Contbr. articles to profl. jours. Mem. Nat. Assn. Student Personnel Adminstrs. (v.p. region v 1976-77), N.W. Coll. Personnel Assn. (exec. com. 1967-68, treas. 1970-72), Am. Coll. Personnel Assn., Am. Coll. and Univ. Housing Officers (regional com. host, chmn. 1971), Mich. Coll. Personnel Assn. Home: 1050 Sauk Ln Saginaw MI 48603 Office: Saginaw Valley State Coll University Center MI 48710

BEALE, HELEN RUBY, insurance company official; b. Michigamme, Mich., Mar. 29, 1922; d. Edwin Martin and Katherine Mae (Rahilly) Stensrud; m. Roland Earl Beale, June 19, 1944 (dec.); children—John Robert, Ann Marie Beale Trachtenberg, James Edward. Student Mich. State U., St. Catherine's Coll. Cert. adminstrv. mgr. Owner Beale Funeral Home, Michigamme, 1943-60; asst. to pres. Ind. Mgmt. Cons., Madison, Wis., 1966-73; sec. Sch. Dist. Office, Oregon, Wis., 1974-76; adminstrv. asst. Modern Kitchen Supply, Madison, 1976-81; agy. adminstrv. asst. Bankers Life, Madison, 1981—. Mem. Nat. Tax Limitation Com., 1984-85; state advisor U.S. Congl. adv. bd. Am. Security Council Found., Washington, 1983-85. Mem. Adminstrv. Mgmt. Soc. (pres. 1981-82, Am. Mgmt. Assn., Nat. Assn. Female Execs. Madison Deanery (v.p. 1982-84, regents 1981-85). Roman Catholic.

BEALL, KAREN FRIEDMANN, graphic arts specialist; b. Washington, Apr. 15, 1938; d. Herbert and Karen Juul (Vejlo) Friedmann; m. John N. Beall, Oct. 17, 1969; children—4 stepsons; m. Dale K. Haworth, Dec. 31, 1983. B.A., Am. U., 1959, postgrad., 1961-62; postgrad. Johns Hopkins U., 1965-66. Specialist fine prints Library of Congress, Washington, 1964-68, curator fine prints, 1968-82; research assoc. Carleton Coll., Northfield, Minn., 1983—; freelance curator. Author: Cries and Itinerant Trades, 1975 (50 Bks of Yr award, Germany, 1975). Compiler: American Prints in the Library of Congress, 1970. Author (catalog) Contemporary Czechoslovakian Prints, 1979. Contbr. articles to profl. jours. Grantee Am. Philos. Soc., 1966, 82; recipient Outstanding Service award Nat. Gallery Art, 1962. Mem. Print Council Am., Coll. Art Assn., Nat. Council on Edn. in Ceramic Arts, Minn. Ind. Scholars Forum. Club: Am. Travelar (Falls Church, Va.) (trip dir. 1974-79, bd. dirs. 1977-79). Office: Carleton Coll Northfield MN 55057

BEALL, MELISSA LOUISE CHRISTENSEN, English and speech educator, consultant; b. Pilger, Nebr., June 4, 1944; d. Emil Peter and Olga Elizabeth (Hansen) Christensen; m. Hugh Fulton Beall, Mar. 13, 1971. B.S., U. Nebr., 1967, M.A. (Ak-Sar-Ben tchr. scholar), 1971, Ph.D., 1982; fellow Northwestern U., 1978. Tchr. English, speech and drama Raymond Central pub. schs., Agnew, Nebr., 1967-71; instr. speech U. Nebr., Lincoln, 1971-74; 1981, 82 (summer); tchr. English, speech and debate Lincoln S.E. High Sch., 1974—, dir. forensics, 1979—; communication cons. U.S. V.I. Dept. Edn., 1980-81; mem. implementation team Target: Communications Skills Program, in-service team leader, 1982-83; dir. Lincoln Pub. Schs. Repertory Theatre Co., 1975-77; mem. Helping Tchr. Cadre, Lincoln Pub. Schs., 1982-83; asst. prof. U. N.D., U. Nebr.; speech cons. Campaign worker Kerrey for Gov., 1982. Named Outstanding Young High Sch. Tchr. Speech, Nebr. Speech Communication Assn., 1974; recipient John Thurber Disting. Teaching award Nebr. Speech Communication Assn., 1981. Mem. Central States Speech Assn., Nebr. Speech Communication Assn. (exec. sec.), Speech Communication Assn., Nebr. Council Tchrs. English, Nat. Council Tchrs. English, Nebr. Assn. of Gifted, Am. Forensic Assn., Phi Delta Kappa, Delta Kappa Gamma. Democrat. Lutheran. Writer, editor communication skills curriculum guide; contbr. articles to profl. jours.; mem. numerous editorial rev. bds. Home: 3802 S 37th St Lincoln NE 68506 Office: Lincoln Southeast High Sch 2930 S 37th St Lincoln NE 68506

BEALS, KENNETH LLOYD, social worker; b. St. Louis County, Mo., Feb. 19, 1935; s. Arthur Loyd and Edna (Dollar) B.; B.S., Washington U., St. Louis, 1961, M.S.W., 1967; postgrad. S.W. Baptist Sem., 1961-62; m. Frances Kay Stricklin, Apr. 18, 1959; children—Michael Lloyd, Rebecca Kay. Cartographer, negative engraver Aero Chart Plant, U.S. Air Force, St. Louis, 1954-61; caseworker Mo. Bapt. Children's Home, St. Louis, 1962-65; protective service caseworker Child and Family Service, State of Ill., East St. Louis, 1965-68; acting dir. Hoyleton (Ill.) Children's Home, 1968-69; dir. residential care Child and Family Service, Muskegon, Mich., 1969-75; exec. dir. Brookview, Inc., Fenton, Mich., 1975-79; supr. Central Bapt. Family Service, Effingham, Ill., 1979-81; adminstr. New Hope Living and Learning Center, Waterloo, Ill., 1981-83; dir. social services St. Mary's Hosp., Centralia, Ill., 1983—; pvt. practice, 1981—; mem. faculty Mich. Assn. Child Agys., 1972-74. Ordained to Gospel ministry So. Bapt. Conv., 1963; Explorer leader Boy Scouts Am., 1976-79; recipient 30 Yr. Vet. Scouter award, 1974. Mem. Nat. Assn. Social Workers, Ill. Child Care Assn., Acad. Certified Social Workers. Home: 615 N Market St Waterloo IL 62298 Office: 400 Pleasant Centralia IL 62801

BEAM, CLARENCE ARLEN, federal judge; b. Stapleton, Nebr., Jan. 14, 1930; s. Clarence Wilson and Cecile Mary (Harvey) B.; m. Betty Lou Fletcher, July 22, 1951; children—Randal, James, Thomas, Bradley, Gregory. B.S., U. Nebr., 1951, J.D., 1965. Bar: Nebr. 1965. Feature writer Nebr. Farmer Mag., Lincoln, 1951; with sales dept. Steckley Seed Co., Mt. Sterling, Ill., 1954-58, advt. mgr., Lincoln, 1958-63; mem. Knudsen, Berkheimer, Beam, et al., Lincoln, 1965-82; judge U.S. Dist. Ct., Omaha, 1982—; mem. Com. on Inquiry 3d Judicial Dist. Nebr., 1974-82, Conf. of Commrs. on Uniform State Laws, 1980—, Nebr. chmn. 1980-82. Mem. City Charter Revision Commn., Lincoln, 1964-68; chmn. Nebr. State Young Republicans, 1960-62; mem. Nebr. State Rep. Central Com., 1970-78. Served to capt. U.S. Army, 1951-53; Korea. Roscoe Pound scholar, 1964; U. Nebr. Regents scholar, 1947. Mem. ABA, Nebr. State Bar Assn. Republican. Presbyterian. Lodges: Kiwanis, Masons. Office: U S Dist Ct 215 N 17th St Omaha NE 68101

BEAM, NORMAN LEWIS, educator; b. Golden, Miss., Sept. 18, 1939; s. Noel D. and Lovie (Humphrey) B.; m. Ima Marlin, May 18, 1963; children—John, Sally. B.S., Florence State U., 1968; M.Ed., Western Md. Coll., 1972; Ed.D., Ball State U., 1983. Foreman, Blue Bell, Inc., Greensboro, N.C., 1963-65; with Reynolds Metals Co., Listerhill, Ala., 1965-68; tchr. Franklin County Schs., Russellville, Ala., 1968-69; tchr. Ala. Sch. for the Deaf, Talladega, 1969-73; tchr. Ind. Sch. for the Deaf, Indpls., 1973-78, supervising tchr., 1978-80, curriculum projects dir., affirmative action expediter, chmn. comprehensive system of personnel devel. com., 1980—, middle sch. supervising tchr., 1983—; cons. in field; conductor workshops in field. Served to capt. Army N.G., 1962-68. Ball State U. doctoral fellow, 1977-78. Mem. Conv. of Am. Instrs. of Deaf, Conf. of Ednl. Adminstrs. Serving the Deaf, Assn. for Supervision and Curriculum Devel., Ind. Auctioneers Assn., Phi Delta Kappa. Presbyterian. Office: 1200 E 42d St Indianapolis IN 46205

BEAN, DAVID KEITH, osteopathic physician, surgeon; b. Moberly, Mo., Jan. 22, 1948; s. Pollard and Lavonne (Conway), B.; m. Judith Ann Orlet, Apr. 24, 1976; 1 child, Emily Louise B.S., Northeast Mo. State U., 1970; D.O., Kirksville Coll. Osteo. Medicine, 1974. Cert. Am. Osteo. Bd. Gen. Practice, 1982. Intern, then resident in internal medicine Normandy Osteo. Hosps., St. Louis, 1974-77; practice medicine Ellisville Family Medicine, Inc., Mo., 1977—; chmn. dept. gen. practice, Normandy Osteo. Hosps., St. Louis, v.p., St. Louis Assn. Osteo. Physicians and Surgeons. Bd. dirs. Normandy Osteo. Med. Ctr. St. Louis and Normandy Osteo. Hosps., 1984—. Mem. Am. Osteo. Assn., Mo. Assn. Osteo. Physicians and Surgeons (chmn. pub. relations com. 1983-84, Presidents award 1983), St. Louis Assn. Osteo. Physicians and Surgeons (v.p. 1979—), West St. Louis County C. of C. Republican. Baptist. Avocations: music; piano. Home: 3751 Sawmill Rd Pacific MO 63069 Office: Ellisville Family Medicine Inc 53 Clarkson Rd Ellisville MO 63011

BEAN, JERRY JOE, lawyer; b. Lebanon, Ind., Apr. 19, 1954; s. Russell Lowell and Mary Ethel (Jett) B.; m. Cheryl Lynn Smith, May 29, 1976; 1 child, Angela. B.A., Wabash Coll., 1976; D. Jurisprudence, Ind. U., 1979; Bars: U.S. Dist. Ct. (so. and no. dists.) Ind. 1979, 81. Exec. dir. Legal Aid Corp., Lafayette, Ind., 1979-80; dep. prosecuting atty. IV-D, Tippecanoe County Prosecutors Office, Lafayette, 1980-81, county ct., 1981-83, felony intake, 1983-84, chief dep. prosecutor, 1984—. Mem. ABA, Assn. Trial Lawyers Am., Ind. State Bar Assn., Tippecanoe County Bar Assn. Republican. Methodist. Lodge: Arman, Fraternal Order of Police (hon.). Office: Tippecanoe County Prosecutor's Office Court House Lafayette In 47901

BEAN, MARVIN DAY, clergyman; b. Tampa, Fla., Sept. 8, 1921; s. Marvin Day and Lillian (Howell) B.; A.B., Fla. So. Coll., 1946, M.S. in Social Work, Vanderbilt U., 1948; postgrad. Ohio State U., 1951-52, Northwestern U., 1950; B.D., Garrett Theol. Sem., 1950; children—Bethany Louise, Thomas Holmes, Carol Sue. Ordained to ministry Methodist Ch., 1950; pastor, Lena Vista, Fla., 1946; asso. pastor San Marcos Meth. Ch., Tampa, 1947; pastor Cedar Lake (Ind.) Meth. Ch., 1948-50, Shepard Meth. Ch., Columbus, Ohio, 1951-68, Stonybrook Meth. Ch., Gahanna, Ohio, 1960-65, Obetz (Ohio) Meth. Ch., 1968-73, Neil Ave. Ch., Columbus, 1973-79, St. Andrew Ch., Columbus, 1979—. Asst. to exec. sec. Meth. Union in Ch. Extension, Columbus, 1965-74; v.p. com. info. and pub. relations Ohio Conf. Meth. Ch., 1964-68, vice chmn. health and welfare ministries, 1968-72, chmn. urban life com. Bd. Missions, 1968-70, asso. sec. Bd. Missions, 1968-72, chmn. Services to Children and Youth, 1962-72; chmn. research Ohio Area Study on Aging, Ohio area Meth. Ch., 1959-64; sec. Columbus dist. conf. Meth. Ch., 1960-68; chmn. sch. religion Columbus area Council Chs., 1953; trustee Meth. Retirement Ctr. Central Ohio, Columbus; trustee United Meth. Children's Home, Worthington, Ohio, 1973-74; chmn. bd. trustees Neil Ave. Found., 1973-79; sec. W. Ohio Commn. Archives and History. Served with AUS, 1943-46. Recipient Wolfley Found. recognition award for inner city work, 1961. Mem. Columbus Meth. Ministerial Assn. (pres. 1960-61), Ohio Council Chs. (rep. com. strategy and planning 1965-68). Nat. Assn. Social Workers, Acad. Cert. Social Workers. Author: A Guide to United Methodist Building, 1973; You Are on the District Board, 1974; Unto the Least of These, 1981; contbr. articles to profl. jours. Home: 122 W Henderson Rd Columbus OH 43214 Office: 1033 High St Worthington OH 43085

BEAR, CAROL JANE, nursing educator; b. Columbia, Mo., Jan. 3, 1934; d. Herbert Hadley and Mary Oneeda (McMaster) Dickson; m. Ronald Stephen Miller, Dec. 21, 1956; 1 son, Stephen; m. 2d, Karl Richard Bear, Sept. 14, 1962; children—Lisa, Richard, Leslie. B.S. in Nursing, U.Mo.-Columbia, 1956, M.Ed., 1979; postgrad. So.Ill.-Edwardsville U. Registered nurse, Mo.; cert. tech. tchr., Mo. Nurse Boone County Hosp., Columbia, 1956-57, 59, Skaggs Meml. Hosp., Branson, Mo., 1957, 59, Burge Hosp., Springfield, Mo., 1957-58; office nurse, Columbia, 1960; supr. cardiac lab U.Mo., Columbia, 1960-62, charge nurse, 1960-62; night supr. Christian Hosp. N.W., Florissant, Mo., 1968-69; nurse Depaul Hosp., St. Louis, 1973-79, instr., 1962-64, 69-72; nurse Christian Old People's Home, St. Louis, 1979-80; instr. Mo. Baptist Hosp. Sch. Nursing, St. Louis, 1966; instr. Jewish Hosp. Sch. Nursing, St. Louis, 1966-67; assoc. prof. nursing St. Louis Community Coll., Florissant, 1973—; cons. and lectr. in field. Mem. Ferguson (Mo.) Citizens Com., 1976—. Mem. Am. Nurses Assn., Mo. Perinatal Assn., Nat. Perinatal Assn., Midwest Congress on Aging, U. Mo. Alumni (rep. 1956—), Nat. Assn. Health Occupations Tchrs. (v.p. Region 3), Mo. Vocat. Assn., Am. Vocat. Assn., NEA, Am. Primrose Assn., Mo. Bot. Garden Friends Soc., Beta Sigma Phi. Democrat. Presbyterian (elder 1985—). Clubs: DeMolay Mothers, St. Louis Zoo Assn. Author and developer of edn. programs in nursing. Home: 108 Fenwick Dr Saint Louis MO 63135 Office: 3400 Pershall Rd Ferguson MO 63135

BEAR, ROBERT J., trucking company executive. Pres., chief operating officer, United Van Lines, Inc., Fenton, Mo. Office: United Van Lines Inc One United Dr Fenton MO 63026*

BEAR, SHARON LOUISE, broadcasting company official; b. Dover, Ohio, June 28, 1946; d. Byron Williams and Dicie Edna (Willis) B.; B.A., Malone Coll., 1968; M.A., Bowling Green State U., 1970. Communication disorders cons., Akron, 1970-82; instr. mass media communications U. Akron, 1981; cons. Group Travel Sales and Incentive Travel Cons., Akron, 1977-82; promotions dir. Sta. WHLO, Susquehanna Broadcasting Co., Akron, 1982-84; local sales mgr., 1984—. Mem. Women in Communication. Clubs: Akron Woman's City, Jr. League of Akron. Office: 2650 W Market St Akron OH 44313

BEARD, (BARBARA) SUE, communications consultant; b. Logansport, Ind., Nov. 24, 1940; d. James Orma and Gertrude Lucille (Williams) Handy; B.A., Franklin Coll., 1962; M.A., Butler U., 1971; m. John A. Beard, Aug. 26, 1961; children—Kent A., Tracy Lynne. English tchr. Indpls. Public Schs., 1967-70; lectr. Ind. U., Ind. Central U. and Ind. Vocat. Tech. Coll., 1971-79; dir. extended services Ind. Vocat. Tech. Coll., Indpls., 1979-82; cons. English composition; communications seminar and workshop leader. Mem. Lawrence Twp. Sch. Bd. Candidate Selection Com.; dist. chmn. fundraising for ednl. TV, 1971. Mem. Ind. Bus. Communicators, Am. Bus. Communicators, Women in Communications, Ind. Vocat. Assn., Am. Soc. Tng. and Devel., Delta Delta Delta. Club: Women's Dept. (pres. 1974-76). Author: The Counselor's Handbook, 1976. Home: 7222 Brompton Ct Indianapolis IN 46250

BEARD, BOBBY JO, petroleum geologist; b. Cushing, Okla., Feb. 1, 1958; s. Bobby Gene and JoAnn (Culp) B. Student Barton County Coll., Great Bend, Kans., 1976-77; B.S. in Geology, Fort Hays State U., 1980. Summer trainee ARCO Oil and Gas Co., Covington, Okla., 1976-80, Great Bend, Kans., 1980; staff geologist Roxanna Corp., Great Bend, 1981-83; pres. Bobby J. Beard Inc., Great Bend, 1983—; cons. petroleum geologist, Kans., Okla., Colo., 1980—. Mem. Am. Assn. Petroleum Geologists, Kans. Geol. Soc., Am. Petroleum Inst. (central Kans. chpt. 1980—), Great Bend Jaycees, Sigma Tau Gamma. Republican. Baptist. Avocation: Hunting; fishing; waterskiing; snowskiing. Home: 1324 Warner Circle Great Bend KS 67530 Office: PO Box 1910 1622 Main Great Bend KS 67530

BEARD, RALPH ALEXIS, financial executive, lawyer; b. Youngstown, Ohio, Aug. 30, 1947; s. Ralph A. and Lenore C. (Chambers) Bates; m. Antoinette L. Lucarelli, May 5, 1971; 1 child, Luke. B.A., Youngstown State U., 1971; J.D., Ohio State U., 1974. Bar: Ohio 1975. V.P. Mahoning Bank, Youngstown, 1975-83, Creative Fin. Services, Inc., Youngstown, 1983—. Chmn. planning council United Way, Youngstown, 1984; pres. Send a Kid to Camp, Youngstown, 1983. Mem. Mahoning County Bar Assn., Mahoning and Shenango Valley Estate Planning Council. Democrat. Home: 59 Skyline Ave Candield OH 44406 Office: 5211 Mahoning Ave Youngstown OH 44515

BEARDSLEE, KENNETH ROBERT, college administrator; b. Owosso, Mich., Jan. 7, 1925; s. Robert Vanderveer and Fern Lavern (Hoag) B.; m. Estella Jane Cleveland, Aug. 17, 1950; children—Janice Kay, Linda Jean, Kendra Elaine, Paul Kenneth. A.A., Spring Arbor Jr. Coll., 1948; B.S., Western Mich. U., 1950; M.S. in Bus. Edn., U. Mich., 1951. Instr. bus. Spring Arbor Coll., Mich., 1951-54, v.p. bus. affairs, 1954—. Contbr. articles to profl. jours. Pres. Western Sch. Dist. Bd. Edn., Jackson County, 1960—; com. chmn. Jackson County Republican Party, 1966—; county chmn. Reagan Campaign Com., Jackson County, 1980, 84; Jackson rep. 2d Congl. Dist. Exec. Com., Ann Arbor, Mich., 1982—; del. Nat. Rep. Conv., 1980, 84. Recipient Haskell and Mary Nichols Service award Jackson County Reps., 1982; LeRoy Lowell Service award Spring Arbor Coll., 1983; 22 Yr. Service award Mich. Sch. Bd. Assn., 1983. Mem. Nat. Assn. Coll. and Univ. Bus. Officers, Mich. Assn. Sch. Bds., Assn. Bus. Adminstrs. Christian Colls. (bd. dirs. 1960—, chmn. ins. liaison com. 1970—). Republican. Methodist. Avocations: gardening; genealogy. Office: Spring Arbor Coll 106 E Main Spring Arbor MI 49283

BEARE, GENE KERWIN, business executive; b. Chester, Ill., July 14, 1915; s. Nicholas Eugene and Minnie Cole (St. Vrain) B.; B.S. in Mech. Engring., Washington U., 1937; M.B.A., Harvard, 1939; m. Doris Margaret Alt, Dec. 11, 1943 (dec.); children—Gail Kathryn, Joanne St. Vrain; m. 2d, Patricia Pfau Cade, Sept. 12, 1964. With Automatic Electric Co., Chgo., 1939-58, successively asst. to v.p. and gen. mgr., asst. to pres., mgr. internat. affiliated cos., gen. comml. mgr., 1939-54, v.p. prodn., 1954-58, dir., 1956-61; pres., dir. Automatic Electric Internat., Inc., 1958-61; chmn., dir. Automatic Electric (Can.), Ltd., Automatic Electric Sales (Can.), Ltd., 1958-61; pres., dir. Sylvania Internat., 1959-60; pres. Gen. Telephone & Electronics Internat., Inc., 1960-61, dir., 1960-72, also dir. numerous subsidiaries in Colombia, Mexico, Venezuela, Argentina, Switzerland, Panama, Brazil, Belgium, Can., Italy; pres. Sylvania Electric Products, Inc., 1961-69, dir., 1961-72; exec. v.p. mfg., dir. Gen. Telephone & Electronics Corp., 1969-72; exec. v.p., dir. Gen. Dynamics Corp., St. Louis, 1972-77; pres. Gen. Dynamics Comml. Products Co., 1972-77; chmn. Asbestos Corp. Ltd., 1974-77; dir. Arkwright-Boston Mut. Ins. Co., Westvaco Corp., Emerson Electric Co., Stromberg Carlson Corp., 1972-77, Canadair Ltd., 1972-75, St. Joe Minerals Corp., Am. Maize-Products Corp., Datapoint Corp., Nooney Realty Trust, Inc. Served from ensign to lt. USNR, 1942-45. Registered profl. engr., Ill. Mem. Pan Am. Soc., Nat. Elec. Mfrs. Assn. (bd. govs. 1963-72, v.p. 1964, pres. 1965-66), Armed Forces Communications and Electronics Assn., Nat. Security Indsl. Assn. (trustee 1969-72). Clubs: Wee Burn (gov. 1963-68) (Darien, Conn.); Union League, Economic (N.Y.C.); St. Louis; Old Warson (Ladue, Mo.). Home: 801 S Skinker Blvd Saint Louis MO 63105 Office: Pierre Laclede Center 7701 Forsyth Blvd Suite 545 Saint Louis MO 63105

BEART, ROBERT WOODWARD, lawyer, consultant; b. Chgo., Nov. 13, 1917; s. Ralph Woodward and Florence (Olson) B.; m. Helen E. Wamsley, Oct. 25, 1942; children—Robert Woodward Jr., Beth J. Beart Drost. A.B., Augustana Coll., 1939; J.D., Chgo. Kent Coll. Law, 1947; M.P.L., John Marshall Law Sch., 1950; AMP 33, Harvard U., 1957. Bars: Ill. 1947, U.S. Dist. Ct. (no. dist.) Ill. 1950, U.S. Supreme Ct. 1969. Sr. v.p., dir. Ill. Tool Works Inc., Chgo., 1936-80, cons. 1980—; chmn. bd. dirs. Luth. Mutual Life Ins. Co., Waverly, Iowa; vice chmn. bd. Ill. Inst. Tech., Chgo., Inst. Gas Tech., Chgo. Patentee in fastener industry. Mem. sch. bd. Sch. Dist. 207, Park Ridge, Ill., 1967-70. Served to maj. USAC, 1942-46, Decorated Commendation medal, 6 Bronze Stars. Mem. Chgo. Bar Assn. (coms.), Licensing Exec. Soc. (life). Republican. Lutheran. Club: Union League. Home: 759 Sussex Corner Ln Prospect Heights IL 60070 Office: Ill Tool Works Inc 8501 W Higgins Rd Chicago IL 60631

BEARY, RODNEY PAUL, consulting company executive; b. Phila., May 9, 1944; s. Louis A. and Natalie M. (Deck) B.; m. Mary Carter Ford, Apr. 8, 1967; children—Todd, Matthew, Susannah. B.A. in Sociology, Pa. State U., 1966; M.S. with honors in Indsl. Relations, Loyola U., Chgo. 1981. Personnel rep. Radio Corp. Am., Camden, N.J., 1967-68; personnel adminstrn. rep. Fibre Industries div. Celanese Corp., Shelby, N.C., 1968-70; regional personnel mgr. Standard Brands Inc., Kensington, Ga., 197074; labor relations mgr. Weyerhaeuser Co. Inc., Chgo., 1974-80; indsl. relations mgr. North Am. Car Co., Chgo., 1980-81; sr. cons. John Sheridan Assocs., Chgo., 1981-83; owner, operator The Beary Consulting Group, Naperville, Ill., 1983—; dir. Paper Ind. Mgmt. Assn. Tng.-Inst.; chmn. bd. Amerchee Investment Corp., 1974; instr. George Williams Coll., Downers Grove, Ill., also Inst. Indsl. Relations, Loyola U., Chgo. Chmn. Opportunities Industrialization Ctr. for Eastern N.C., 1975; active Republican Nat. Com. Mem. Am. Soc. Personnel Adminstrs. Club: Penn State Alumni. Nat. quadruple skulls champion, 1964-65. Address: 903 River Oak Dr Naperville IL 60565

BEASLEY, KENNETH LOWELL, university administrator, research administrator; b. Bedford, Ind., Sept. 16, 1930; s. Glen M. and Estella (Walls) B.; m. Betsy Turner, Nov. 22, 1953; children—Jonathan, Christopher, Timothy, Thomas. B.A., Wabash Coll., 1952; M.A.T., Harvard U., 1953; Ph.D., Northwestern U., 1962. Assoc. dean grad sch. No. Ill. U., DeKalb, 1966-72, asst. to pres., 1972—; asst. to chancellor UCLA, 1969-70; asst. to pres. Am. Council Edn., Washington, 1979-80; exec. dir. Central States U., DeKalb, 1972—; advisor research mgmt. NSF, Washington, 1973-74, Antarctic Research Rev., 1974; mem. commn. manpower and edn. Phi Delta Kappa, Bloomington, Ind., 1963-67. Author: The Administration of Sponsored Programs, 1982. Scout dir. Two Rivers council Boy Scouts Am., 1973-74; chmn. Task Force Governance Schs., Ill., 1972-74, govs. adv. com. Block Grants, 1982—. Served to cpl. U.S. Army, 1953-55. Recipient Excellence in Research Adminstrn. award Soc. Research Adminstrs. 1978. Grantee NSF 1972-75, U.S. Office Edn. 1966-67. Mem. DeKalb C. of C. (v.p. 1982—), Council Advancement and Support Edn., Soc. Research Adminstrs. (pres. 1971-72), Nat. Council U. Research Adminstrs. (regional pres. 1971-72). Avocations: skiing, camping. Home: 127 W Sunset DeKalb IL 60115 Office: No Ill U Office of Pres DeKalb IL 60115

BEASLEY, RANDALL LIONEL, agricultural engineer; b. Witt, Ill., July 15, 1925; s. Arthur Edwin and Mildred (Mitchell) B.; m. Virginia Gladys Rackett, June 4, 1947; children—Beth Ann Beasley Watson, Sue Ellyn Beasley Meyer, Nancy Jeanne Beasley Levin. Student Blackburn Coll., 1944-45; B.S. in Agrl. Engring., U. Ill., 1948; postgrad. Lake Land Coll., 1966, 72, 82. Cert. Class A water treatment plant operator, Ill. Agrl. engr. Coles-Moultrie Electrical Coop., Mattoon, Ill., 1948—; dir. Clear Water Service Corp., Mattoon. Served with USN, 1943-44. Recipient 25 Yr. award Ill. 4-H Clubs, 1976. Mem. Mattoon Assn. Commerce, Charleston Area C. of C., Ill. Citizen's Edn. Council, Internat. Assn. Elec. Inspectors (25 Yr. award 1978), Ill. Farm Electrification Council (25 Yr. award 1983), DAV, Am. Legion. Methodist. Lodges: Lions, Masons. Home: Route 3 Box 240 Mattoon IL 61938 Office: PO Box 709 Mattoon IL 61938

BEASLEY, WALLACE ROLAND, petrochemical company executive; b. Archer City, Tex., Apr. 9, 1936; s. Wallace David and Ella Louetta B.; m. Jean Ann Puddy, Aug. 24, 1957; children—Shelley, June, Lori, Rebecca. B.S., Tex. A&M U., 1958; student advanced mgmt. program Harvard U., 1977. Mgr. bus. ctr. Arco Polymers, Phila., 1978-80; exec. v.p. ops. No. Petrochem. Co., Omaha, 1980-81, pres., 1982—. Bd. dirs. Omaha Symphony. Served with AUS, 1959. Mem. Am. Chem. Soc., Am. Inst. Chem. Engrs., Soc. Plastics Engrs. Office: 2 Central Park Plaza Omaha NE 68102

BEATON, IAN WILSON, advertising agency executive; b. Sydney, N.S., Can., Mar. 10, 1924; s. William Murray and Margaret (MacKenzie) B.; came to U.S., 1924, naturalized, 1945; B.S., Northwestern U., 1950; m. Carol Jean Lindner, Dec. 30, 1950; children—Lynda (Mrs. David Bence), Scot. Merchandising mgr. AC Spark Plug Div., Gen. Motors Corp., 1950-56; copywriter Leo Burnett Co. Mich. Inc. (formerly D. P. Brother & Co.), 1956-58, account exec., 1958-61, v.p., gen. account exec., 1961-66, v.p., adminstrn., personnel, 1966-70, v.p., account supr., 1970-74; v.p., sr. account supr. Campbell-Ewald Co., Detroit, from 1975, now sr. v.p., group mgmt. supr., Warren, Mich. Served with AUS, 1943-45; PTO. Mem. Detroit Advt. Assn., Pi Kappa Alpha. Presbyterian. Clubs: Detroit Adcraft, Great Oaks Country, Recess. Home: 1200

Oakwood Ct Rochester MI 48063 Office: Campbell Ewald Bldg Warren MI 48093

BEATTIE, RICHARD LEWIS, motivational consultant, programmer; b. Flint, Mich., Nov. 22, 1955; s. Lewis Joseph and Deanna Joy (Ledger) B. Student Wayne State U., Long Beach City Coll. Customer service mgr. Hasbach Co., Carson, Calif., 1977-79; sr. programmer Numerical Machining Co., Inc., Rochester, Mich., 1979—; dir., corp. sec. Numerica, Inc., Rochester, 1980—; pres. Creative Thoughtware, Pontiac, Mich., 1983—; dir. Numerica, Inc., 1980—. Mem. student clergy Met. Community Ch., Detroit, 1983—; dir. Excel of the Lakes, 1980-83; mem. Mich. Orgn. for Human Rights, Detroit, 1982—, Human Right Campaign Fund, Washington, 1981—, Gay Rights Nat. Lobby, Washington, 1981—, Assn. Suburban People, Detroit, 1981—. Recipient Vol. award Project S.T.A.R.T., 1977; Leadership award, Boys Club of Pontiac (Mich.), 1967. Mem. Am. Entrepreneurs Assn. Home: 89 Dwight St Pontiac MI 48053 Office: Creative Thoughtware 89 Dwight St Pontiac MI 48053

BEATTY, JOHN DUNTON, jewelry store executive, newspaper columnist; b. Brookings, S.D., Dec. 1, 1914; s. Edgar Harvey and Mary Ruth (Dunton) B.; m. Glenna Opal Johnson, Oct. 2, 1941; children—Jo Anne, David Edgar. B.A., S.D. State U. Want ad mgr. Daily Huronite, Huron, S.D., 1937-39; advt. salesman Pioneer Directory, St. Paul, 1939-41; news editor Brookings Register, 1941-45; pub. Redfield Press, Redfield, S.D., 1945-48; jeweler Beatty's Jewelry, Brookings, 1948—; instr. news editing, advt. S.D. State U., Brookings, 1949-50. Writer newspaper column Pokings, 1971—. Sec., Brookings Indsl. Devel. Corp., 1951; founder, sec. Area Progress, Brookings, 1958; treas. Brookings Sch. Bd., 1943-44; trustee Sioux Falls Coll., S.D., 1947; moderator First Bapt. Ch., Brookings, 1960-63; pres. United Fund Bd., Brookings, 1980; bd. dirs. Brookings County Red Cross, Minn-Ia-Kota council Girl Scouts U.S. Recipient Outstanding Service awards Brookings Jr. C. of C., 1950, Brookings C. of C., 1958, Good Shepherd award Nat. Bapt. Scouting Orgn., 1983, 30 Yr. award Sioux council Boy Scouts Am., 1982. Republican. Lodge: Rotary. Avocation: reading. Home: 1735 Garden Sq Brookings SD 57006 Office: Beatty's Jewelry 322 Main Ave Brookings SD 57006

BEATTY, MARION LEE, lawyer; b. Vinton, Iowa, Apr. 24, 1953; s. Charles Edward and Marcella Ann (Robbins) B.; m. Peggy Jo Hall, Apr. 15, 1976; children—Benjamin Wade, Laura Ann. B.A., Luther Coll., 1975; J.D., U. Iowa, 1977. Bar: Iowa, U.S. Dist. Ct. (no. and so. dists.) Iowa. Practiced in Decorah, Iowa; ptnr. firm Miller, Pearson, Gloe, Burns, Beatty & Cowie, P.C., Decorah. Bd. dirs. Porter House Mus., Decorah, 1978-84; mem. ch. council Decorah Luth. Ch., 1980-82; mem. Decorah Republican Central Com.; Winneshiek County chmn. for re-election Congressman Tom Tauke, 2 terms, for re-election Congressman Cooper Evans, 1982-84; past pres. Winneshiek County Hist. Soc., Decorah; mem. Congressman Tauke's Acad. Selection com. 2d dist. Iowa, 4 yrs.; gen. gifts chmn. Fund for Luther, Luther Coll., Decorah, 1983-84; mem. legal adv. bd. Area Agy. on Aging, N.E. Iowa Tech. Inst., 1982-84. Recipient Regional Key Man award Iowa Jaycees, 1981. Mem. Iowa Bar Assn., Winneshiek County Bar Assn. (pres. 1979), Docorah C. of C. (sec.-treas. 1981, v.p. 1982, pres. 1983), Decorah Jaycees (dir. 1980, Outstanding Dir. award 1978), Young Lawyers Assn. Iowa (various coms. 1977—), Winneshiek County Hosp. Found. (pres. bd. dirs. 1984-85). Republican. Lutheran. Club: Silvercrest Golf and Country (v.p. 1982, pres. 1983). Lodge: Elks. Home: 1303 Panorama Dr Decorah IA 52101 Office: Miller Pearson Gloe Burns Beatty & Cowie PC 301 W Broadway Box 28 Decorah IA 52101

BEATTY, ROBERT ALFRED, surgeon; b. Colchester, Vt., May 7, 1936; s. George Lewis and Leila Margaret (Ebright) B.; B.A., U. Oreg., 1959, B.S., 1960, M.D., 1961; m. Frances Calomeni, Aug. 24, 1963; children—Bradford, Roxanna. Intern, U. Ill. Research and Edn. Hosp., Chgo., 1961-62; resident neurosurgery U. Ill., 1962-66; practice neurosurgery, Hinsdale, Ill., 1967—; mem. staff Hinsdale San., Community Meml. Hosp., LaGrange, Ill., Meml. Hosp., Elmhurst, Ill., U. Ill. Hosp., Chgo., Good Samaritan Hosp., Downers Grove, Ill.; clin. assoc. prof. neurosurgery U. Ill., 1967—; adviser Marion Joy Rehab. Center, Wheaton, Ill., 1969-72. Served to capt. M.C., AUS, 1968. Research fellow St. George's Med. Sch., London, 1966-67. Diplomate Am. Bd. Neurol. Surgery. Mem. AMA, Ill. Med. Soc., Dupage County Med. Soc., Am. Assn. Neurol. Surgeons, A.C.S., Congress Neurol. Surgeons, Soc. Brit. Neurol. Surgeons, Internat. Microsurg. Soc., English Speaking Union, SAR, Phi Beta Kappa, Phi Beta Pi, Phi Kappa Psi. Republican. Clubs: Les Nomades, Butterfield Country. Contbr. articles to profl. jours.; research on intracranial aneurysms, lumbar discs. Office: 40 S Clay St Hinsdale IL 60521

BEATTY, WILLIAM LOUIS, See *Who's Who in America*, 43rd edition.

BEATY, JAMES RALPH, clergyman; b. Evansville, Ind., May 16, 1929; s. James Clifford and Amanda Ann (Apgar) B.; m. Emma Jean Galloway, June 13, 1950; children—Ralph Norman, James Robert, Ann Lynn, Jerri Elizabeth, William Clifford. B.A., Franklin Coll. Ind., 1951, D.D., 1979. M.Div., So. Bapt. Theol. Sem., 1954; D.D., Judson Coll., 1970. Ordained to ministry Am. Baptist Chs. U.S.A., 1952. Asst. to pastor 1st Bapt. Ch., Evansville, 1948; pastor Exeter Ave. Bapt. Ch., Indpls., 1949-52, Veale Creek Bapt. Ch., Washington, Ind., 1952-54, 1st Bapt. Ch., Salem, Ind., 1954-57; field counselor Div. World Mission Support, Am. Bapt. Conv., 1958-66; exec. minister Indpls. Bapt. Assn., 1966-67; regional minister Am. Bapt. Chs. of the Great Rivers Region, 1977—. Mem. alumni council Franklin Coll., 1960-70; mem. Ch. Fedn. Greater Indpls., 1966-67; mem. Ill. Conf. Chs., 1977—, Mo. Council of Chs., 1977—; bd. dirs. Shurtleff Fund, 1977—; trustee No. Bapt. Theol. Sem., 1977—, Franklin Coll., 1982—, Judson Coll., 1971; mem. Midwest commn. on ministry Am. Bapt. Conv., 1966—, mem. Regional Exec. Ministers Council, 1966—, mem. Gen. Staff Council, 1972—. Recipient citations Christian Higher Edn. Challenge, Am. Bapt. Conv., 1960, Franklin Coll. Alumni Council, 1971, Ch. Fedn. Greater Indpls., 1975, Ind. Bapt. Conv., 1976, Indpls. Bapt. Assn., 1977; Alumni of Yr. citation So. Bapt. Theol. Sem., 1981; Certificate of Appreciation, World Mission Campaign of Am. Bapt. Conv., 1968. Mem. Lambda Chi Alpha. Address: Box 3786 Springfield IL 62708

BEATY, RICHARD THOMAS, orthopedic surgeon; b. Chgo., Apr. 4, 1947; s. Frank Joseph and Maerose C. (Byrne) B.; m. Helen Ann Vlachos, July 7, 1973; children—Ryan, Dana, Megan. B.A., Ill. Wesleyan U., 1969; D.O., Chgo. Coll. Osteo. Medicine, 1975. Am. Osteo. Bd. Orthopedic Surgery. Intern. Chgo. Osteo. Med. Center, 1975-76, resident, 1976-80; staff physician Davenport Osteo. Hosp., Iowa, 1980-84, Palos Community Hosp., Palos Heights, Ill., 1984—; dir. Blackhawk Epilepsy Assn., Rock Island, Ill., 1981-83, Miss. Valley Physicians Assn., Davenport, 1981-84; team physician Quad City Cubs, Davenport, 1981-84, Augustanna Coll. Basketball Team, Rock Island, 1981-83; mem. adv. bd. Medic Emergency Med. Services, Davenport, 1982-84, Arthritic Swim Program Adult Edn. Davenport Sch. System, 1980-81. Recipient Cert. Appreciation Black Hawk Epilepsy Assn., 1983, Service award Quad City Health Plan HMO, 1984. Mem. Am. Osteo. Assn. (diplomate nat. bd. examiners 1976), Am. Osteo. Acad. Orthopedic Surgeons, Ill. Assn. Osteo. Physicians and Surgeions, Chgo. Med. Soc., Ill. State Med. Soc. Avocations: fishing; hunting; coaching, biddy basketball; antique cars. Office: College Drive Clinic SC 6450 W College Dr Palos Heights IL 60463

BEAUBIEN, ELAINE ESTERVIG, business educator, human relations consultant; b. Madison, Wis., Oct. 27, 1949; d. Raymond Knute and Hazel (Shultis) Estervig; m. Kenneth Charles Beaubien, Aug. 2, 1975. B.S., Wis. State U.-Platteville, 1971; M.B.A., U. Wis., 1975. Dept. mgr. J.C. Penney Co., Madison, 1971-74; instr., chmn. dept. econs. Detroit Coll. Bus., 1975-76; instr. bus., econs. Mercy Coll. of Detroit, 1976-78; lectr. mgmt. dept. U. Wis.-Whitewater, 1978-81; assoc. prof., chmn. dept. bus. Edgewood Coll., Madison, 1981—; cons. in human relations, 1978—; tng. coordinator, owner Mgmt. Tng. Seminars, 1980—; speaker, seminar leader on women in mgmt., 1980—. Mgmt. mem. Adv. Com. for Cert. Profl. Secs. Cert., 1982—. Recipient Outstanding Alumnus award Wis. State U.-Platteville, 1973, Appreciation cert. Madison Met. Distributive Edn. Assn., 1973; named An Outstanding Young Woman of Am., Gen. Fedn. Women's Clubs, 1982. Evjue scholar, 1970. Mem. Wis. Profl. Speakers Assn., Internat. Bus. Assn., Nat. Assn. Female Execs. Methodist. Lodge: Order Eastern Star (trustee 1979-82). Home: Route 1 Box 66-E Waterloo WI 53594 Office: Edgewood Coll 855 Woodrow St Madison WI 53711

BEAUCHAMP, DON WENDELL, petroleum geologist; b. Guide Rock, Nebr., Oct. 10, 1936; s. Howard Scott and Erma Lorene (Miner) B.; m. Billy Ray Brown, May 15, 1959 (div. 1975); children—Toni R., Jeffrey S., Brian Craig; m. Linda Sue Peterson, July 24, 1976; step children—Troy Bailey, Brenda Bailey. B.S. in Geology, Wichita State U., 1959. Exploration geologist Walters Drilling Co., Wichita, Kans., 1959-71; v.p. Berexco Inc., Wichita, 1971—, exploration mgr. Beren Corp., Wichita, 1971—, exploration mgr. Okmar Oil Co., Wichita, 1971—. Mem. Am. Assn. Petroleum Geologists (alt. del. midwestern sect.) Kans. Geol. Soc. (bd. dirs. 1970-72, pres. 1985—), Petroleum Club Wichita (1st v.p. 1978-79). Republican. Methodist. Clubs: Nat. Red Setter Field Trial (pres. 1978-80), Kans. Field Trial Assn. (pres. 1982-84), Kans. Red Setter Field Trial (pres. 1976-79). Avocations: hunting; field trailing; skiing; tennis; golf. Home: RR 1 Box 118 Cheny KS 67025

BEAULIEU, RONALD PATRICK, educator; b. Indpls., Mar. 15, 1949; s. Peter Calice and Charlotte Genevieve Beaulieu; B.S., Purdue U., 1972; M.B.A., Ind. U., 1975, D.B.A., 1976; m. Kathleen Michele; 1 dau., Allison Kathleen. Asso. instr., Ind. U., Bloomington, 1973-76; asst. prof. mgmt. U. Notre Dame (Ind.), 1976-79. Central Mich. U., Mt. Pleasant, 1979—. Mem. Am. Psychol. Assn., Am. Inst. Decision Scis., Acad. Mgmt., Am. Soc. Personnel Adminstrn., Beta Gamma Sigma, Sigma Iota Epsilon. Home: 515 N Kinney Mount Pleasant MI 48858 Office: Central Michigan U Sch Bus Mount Pleasant MI 48859

BEBOUT, BRADLEY CAREY, lawyer; b. Convoy, Ohio, Oct. 8, 1950; s. Eugene Harold and Carol C. (Carey) B.; m. Carol Anne Hall, Aug. 2, 1975; 1 child, Stephen Eugene. B.A., Bowling Green State U., 1972; J.D., Ohio No. U., 1979. Bars: Ohio 1980, U.S. Dist. Ct. (no. dist.) Ohio 1980. Vol. Peace Corps, Washington, 1972; market auditor Market Facts, Fort Wayne, Ind., 1972-73; claims rep. Crawford & Co., Cleve., 1973-77; ptnr. Hall & Bebout, Marion, Ohio, 1980—; ct. referee Juvenile Ct. for Marion County. Sec. bd. dirs. Marion Goodwill Industries, 1983-86; treas. bd. dirs. Handicap Awareness Assn., Marion; pres., bd. dirs. Marionaires; mem. Spl. Wish Found. Mem. Marion County Bar Assn., Ohio State Bar Assn., ABA, Assn. Trial Lawyers Am., Marion C. of C. (bd. dirs. 1985), Willis Soc., Phi Kappa Phi. Lodge: Kiwanis (bd. dirs. 1982-84). Home: 637 Girard Ave Marion OH 43302 Office: Hall and Bebout 125 S Main St Marion OH 43302

BECHER, MARILYN JUDITH, medical consultation services executive; b. Appleton, Wis., May 28, 1941; d. Alvin O. and Ethel M. (Braun) Adrian; Diploma Madison (Wis.) Gen. Hosp. Sch. Nursing, 1962; student U. Wis.-Madison, 1962-63; B.S. in Nursing, Alverno Coll., 1980; postgrad. Cardinal Stritch Coll., Milw. R.N., Wis. Staff nurse Univ. Hosps., Madison, 1962-63; staff nurse Theda Clark Regional Med. Ctr., Neenah, Wis., 1963-65, asst head nurse ob-gyn, 1965-68, head nurse orthopedic, neurology unit, 1968-70, head nurse med.-surg., pediatrics, 1970-71, head nurse psychiatry, 1971-80, dir. nurses, 1980-81, v.p. nursing adminstr., 1981-85; program mgr. rehab. program; lectr. in field. Bd. dirs. Rehab. House, Neenah, 1973-76; v.p. Winnebago County Health Resource Bd., 1978-81, pres., 1981-82; mem. Alverno Coll. Pres. Task Force, 1980; bd. dirs. Rynderson Foster Home, Appleton, Wis., 1983; mem. Nursing Interaction Group, Winnebago County, 1981—. Mem. Am. Nurses Assn. (cert. nursing adminstr.), Wis. Nurses Assn., Appleton Dist. Nurses Assn., Wis. League Nursing, Nat. League Nursing, Am. Orthopsychiat. Assn., Wis. Assn. Nursing Adminstrs., Am. Assn. Rehab. Nurses, Alverno Coll. Alumni Assn. Home: 824 Zemlock Ave Neenah WI 54956 Office: Med Cons Services 824 Zemlode Ave Neenah WI 54956

BECHTOL, LAUREN LEONHARDT, JR., jewelry company executive; b. Bryan, Ohio, Apr. 15, 1951; s. Lauren Leonhardt and Ann Margaret (Schuck) B.; m. Christine Ann King, Sept. 10, 1977; children—Jeremy Lauren, Kaitlyn Christine. B.S. in Geology, Kent State U., 1973; cert. diamond grader, cert. colored stones identifier Gemological Inst. Am., 1980, 84; cert. advanced goldsmithing, repair Queen City Seminars, E.J. Swigart Co., Cin., 1981. Jewelry clk., buyer Schuck Jewelers, Bryan, 1973-76, jeweler, goldsmith, 1976—, diamond appraiser, 1980—, co-owner, 1983—, gemstone appraiser, 1984—; appraiser, local ins. cos., 1980—. Bd. dirs., bd. pub. affairs, city utilities Bryan, 1973-83, chmn., 1976, 79, 82. Colored Gemstone Identification scholar Gemological Inst. Am., 1981. Mem. Gemological Assn. Gt. Britain, Alumni Assn. of Kent State U., Gemmological Inst. Am., Wilderness Soc., Sierra Club. Republican. Roman Catholic. Avocations: gemstone research; jewelry design; camping; bicycle touring. Office: Schuck Jewelers 120 S Lynn St Bryan OH 43506

BECK, DAVID ALLAN, lawyer; b. Cleve., Nov. 29, 1944; s. Henry Louis and Miriam Doris (Lockwood) B. B.S., Ohio State U., 1970; M.A., U Iowa, 1971; J.D., Cleve. Marshall Law Sch., 1981. Bar: Ohio 1982, U.S. Ct. Appeals (6th cir.) 1982, U.S. Dist. Ct. (no. dist.) Ohio 1982. Asst. prof. history Kirkwood Community Coll., Cedar Rapids, Iowa, 1971-74; chief steward AFSCME, Iowa City, 1976-78; sole practice law, Cleve., 1982—. Instr. Creative Learning Inst., Cleve., 1984—. Editor: Cleve. Law Rev., 1980-81. Mem. ABA, Assn. Trial Lawyers Am., Ohio Bar Assn., Bar Assn. Greater Cleve., Cuyahoga County Bar Assn., Citizens League Greater Cleve., Ohio State Alumni Assn. Lodge: Lions. Home: 271 Vivian Dr Berea OH 44017

BECK, DENNIS JAMES, steel company executive; b. Pitts., Oct. 31, 1946; s. Robert Joseph and Virginia Agnes (Mahoney) B.; m. Elaine Kocak, June 27, 1970; children—Hadley, Sara, Quentin, Hilary. B.S., Pa. State U., 1968; M.B.A., U. Pitts., 1974. Foreman area Jones & Laughlin Steel Co., Aliquippa, Pa., 1972-74, gen. foreman, 1974-79; asst. mgr. plant MacSteel Div., Jackson, Mich., 1979-80, mgr., 1980-82, gen. mgr., 1982—. Mem. Jackson Area Mfrs. Assn. (bd. dirs. 1982—), AIME (Iron and Steel Soc.). Roman Catholic. Avocations: running, tennis. Home: 3615 Sassafras Dr Jackson MI 49201 Office: MacSteel Div 3100 Brooklyn Rd Jackson MI 49203

BECK, EVELYN TORTON, literature and women's studies educator; b. Vienna, Austria, Jan. 18, 1933; d. Max Moses and Irma (Lichtman) Torton; came to U.S., 1940; m. Anatole Beck, Apr. 10, 1954 (div.); children—Nina Rachel, Micah Daniel. B.A., Bklyn. Coll., 1954; M.A., Yale U., 1955; Ph.D., U. Wis., 1969. Vis. lectr. U. Md., College Park, 1971-72; asst. prof. U. Wis., Madison, 1972-76, assoc. prof. comparative lit., German and women's studies, 1976-83, prof., 1983—; Jane Watson Irwin prof. comparative lit. Hamilton Coll., Clinton, N.Y., 1982-83; mem. editorial bd. Monatshefte, 1978—. Mem. Di Vilde Chayes, 1981—. Recipient hon. mention Florence Howe Essay award, 1975; Am. Council Learned Socs. grantee, 1971-72; Nat. Endowment for Humanities grantee, 1973, sr. fellow, 1983-84. Mem. MLA (commn. on status of women), Nat. Women's Studies Assn., Women in German Assn., Midwest MLA (pres. 1981-82). Author: Kafka and the Yiddish Theater: Its Impact on His Work, 1971; (with Jost Hermand) Interpretive Synthesis: The Task of Literary Scholarship, 1975; (with J. Sherman) The Prism of Sex: Essays in the Sociology of Knowledge, 1979; Nice Jewish Girls: A Lesbian Anthology, 1982. Office: 958 Van Hise Hall U Wis Madison WI 53706

BECK, JAMES HAYES, lawyer; b. Canton, Ohio, Aug. 29, 1935; s. Harry W. and Helen E. B.; m. Monika Feld, June 12, 1965; children—Barbara E., James R. A.B., Wittenberg U., 1956; LL.B., U. Va., 1959, J.D., 1970. Bar: Ohio 1959, U.S. Dist. Ct. (no. dist.) Ohio 1960, U.S. Supreme Ct. 1971. Sole practice, Cleve., 1959-63; jr. ptnr. Leanza, Longano, Farino & Mendelson, Cleve., 1963-66; assoc. Nadler & Nadler, Youngstown, Ohio, 1966-73, Beck & Tyrrell, Canfield, Ohio, 1973-83; sr. ptnr. Beck & Vaughn, Canfield, 1984—; instr. real estate law Youngstown State U., 1972. Precinct committeeman, ward leader, Bay Village, Ohio, 1962-66, Canfield, Ohio, 1976-78; v.p. Canfield Civic Assn., 1972-74; mem. stewardship and fin. coms. Lord of Life Lutheran Ch.; sec. SMR Residents' Council, Inc.; comdr., Youngstown Power Squadron, 1985—. Mem. Am. Arbitration Assn. (panel of arbitrators and regional adv. council 1969—), ABA (sect. on econs. of law practice 1978—), ACLU (legal com. Youngstown chpt. 1966—), Assn. Trial Lawyers Am., Commercial Law League Am., Ohio State Bar Assn. (unauthorized practice of law com. 1978—, profl. econs. com. 1980—), Mahoning County Bar Assn. (chmn. profl. econs. com. 1979-82, chmn. unauthorized practice of law com. 1976-79, grievance com. 1983-84, ins. com. 1984-85), Beta Theta Pi, Phi Alpha Theta, Pi Sigma Alpha, Tau Kappa Alpha. Clubs: Ashtabula Yacht; Point Yacht. Lodge: Lions. Avocations: tennis; bridge; boating. Home: 265 Saw Mill Run Rd Canfield OH 44406 Office: Beck & Vaughn Olde Courthouse Bldg Canfield OH 44406

BECK, JAMES WELTON, educational administrator; b. Oconto, Nebr., Feb. 15, 1936; s. Donald William and Mary Loretta (Bolliger) B.; m. Roberta Ann Evans, April 4, 1959; children—Mike, Michelle, Jeff, Doug, Todd, Jackie, Bob. B.S., Kearney State U., 1960, M.S., 1966. Prin. Greeley High Sch., Nebr., 1960—, county supt. Greeley County Schs., 1966—. Served with US Army, 1955-58. Mem. Nebr. Council Sch. Administrn., Am. Legion. Republican. Roman Catholic. Lodges: KC, Elks. Home: Box 250 Greeley NE 68842

BECK, JANET GAY, association executive; b. Rochester, Pa., Nov. 14, 1956; d. John Frederick and Bonita Kathleen (Reed) B. B.A. in Music cum laude, Wittenberg U., 1978. Asst. mgr. Springfield Symphony Orch., Ohio, 1977-79, gen. mgr., 1981-83; asst. to exec. dir. Ohio Theater Alliance, Springfield, 1980-81; tech. dir. Springfield Summer Arts Festival, 1980; gen. mgr. Saginaw Symphony Assn., Mich., 1983—. Mem. Am. Symphony Orch. League, Mich. Orch. Assn. (bd. dirs. 1984—), Concerned Citizens for Arts in Mich., Jr. League Saginaw, Met. Orch. Mgrs. Assn. Republican. Presbyterian. Home: 6181 Fox Glen Dr Apt 252 Saginaw MI 48603 Office: Saginaw Symphony Assn PO Box 415 Saginaw MI 48606

BECK, JOHN MATTHEW, educator; b. Rogoznig, Austria, Apr. 10, 1913; s. Matthias and Antoinette (Bukowski) B.; came to U.S., 1914, naturalized, 1942; B.S., Ind. State Coll. (Pa.), 1936; M.A., U. Chgo., 1947, Ph.D., 1953; m. Frances Josephine Mottey, Aug. 23, 1941. Tchr., Clymer (Pa.) High Sch., 1937-41; instr. history and philosophy of edn. De Paul U., 1948-53; instr. Chgo. State College, 1953-56, chmn. dept. edn., 1959-60, asst. dean, prof. edn., 1960-66, dean coll., 1966-67; dir. Chgo. Tchr. Corps, 1967—; exec. dir. Chgo. Consortium Colls. and Univs., 1968—; prof. urban tchr. edn. Govs. State U., 1972—; cons. U.S. Office of Edn., 1968—. Mem. Ill. State Advisory Com. on Guidance, 1963—, Citizens Schs. Com., Chgo., 1953—; chmn. curriculum adv. com. Ednl. Facilities Center, Chgo., 1971—; exec. bd. Cook County OEO, 1971—; adv. com. interstate interinstnl. cooperation Ill. Bd. Higher Edn., 1972—; mem. Chgo. Mayor's Adv. Commn. Sch. Bd. Nominations, 1975, Mayor's Adv. Council on Aging, 1976—, Exec. Service Corps. of Chgo., 1983—, Mayor Washington's Task Force on Edn., 1983. Bd. govs. Chgo. City Club, 1961—, v.p., 1962-63, 64-65; mem. Exec. Service Corps of Chgo., 1983—. Served with AUS, 1941-46. Decorated Bronze Star. Recipient W. Germany grant, 1972. Fellow AAAS, Philosophy of Edn. Soc.; mem. Am. Hist. Assn., Am. Edn. Research Assn., Ill. Edn. Assn. (pres. Chgo. div. 1960-62). Co-author: Extending Reading Skills, 1976. Editor: Chgo. Sch. Jour., 1964-65; co-editor: Teaching the Culturally Disadvantaged Child, 1966; contbr. articles to profl. jours. and encys. Home: 5832 Stony Island Ave Chicago IL 60637 Office: 95th and King Dr Suite 204 Chicago IL 60628

BECK, JOSEPH GEORGE, musician, educator; b. Youngstown, Ohio, Feb. 19, 1935; s. George B. and Anna (Eveland) B.; student Youngstown U., 1953-56; Mus.B., Westminster Choir Coll., 1956-59; M.A., Kent State U., 1966; Ed.D., St. Louis U., 1979; m. Sara Louise Ramser, Nov. 17, 1962. Mem., soloist Westminster Choir, Princeton, N.J., 1958-59; pvt. vocal tchr., Youngstown, 1959-62; minister of music, Lowell Ch., Canton, Ohio, 1962-64; instr. music, dir. glee clubs Kent State U., 1964-69; minister music, Main St. Meth. Ch., Akron, 1966-69; vocal dir. Kent State Summer Theater, Kent, Ohio, 1966-68; vocal cons. Kent State U. Theater and Speech Therapy depts.; vis. instr. music dir. chapel choir, voice instr. Mt. Union Coll., Alliance, Ohio, 1968-69; asst. prof., dir. choral activities Webster Coll., St. Louis, 1969-72; mus. dir., cons. dept. theater arts, 1970-72; mus. dir. Repertory Theatre, 1969-70; asst. prof., dir. choral and vocal activities St. Louis U., 1973-78, musical dir. theater dept., 1974-77; asst. prof. Metro Coll., St. Louis U., 1978-80; dir. community relations Spl. Sch. Dist. St. Louis County, 1981-83; pres. JGB Prodns., Inc., St. Louis, 1983—; artist-in-residence, adj. prof. music Maryville Coll., St. Louis, 1981—; vis. lectr., vocal cons. St. Louis U. Med. Ctr., 1978—; cons. in edn. and fine arts Warner Amex Cable of St. Louis, 1980-81; master class student John Finley Williamson, choral and voice, 1954-63, Roger Wagner, choral, 1970, Robert Shaw, choral, 1972; producer, musical dir. film O That We Were There, 1979. Served with AUS, 1960-61. Recipient local Emmy award, 1982. Mem. Am. Choral Dirs. Assn. (chmn. local arrangements com. for nat. conv. 1975), AAUP, Assn. Choral Condrs., Nat. Assn. Tchrs. Singing, Music Educators Nat. Conf. Phi Mu Alpha Sinfonia, Alpha Psi Omega. Book reviewer, choral reviewer for Am. Music Teacher mag., 1966-72; contbr. to The Choral Jour., 1976—. Home: 520 Edgar Ct Saint Louis MO 63119

BECK, KENNETH DAVID, lawyer; b. Columbus, Ohio, June 29, 1932; s. Norman E. and Helen (Bender) B.; m. Frances Latcomb, Apr. 26, 1969; children—John, Norman, Joseph. B.S., Ohio State U., 1954, J.D., 1964. Bar: Ohio 1965; C.P.A., Ohio. Acct. Lybrand, Ross Bros. & Montgomery, Columbus, 1956-62; investment officer Ohio Tchrs. Retirement System, Columbus, 1964-66; ptnr. Vorys, Sater, Seymour & Pease, Columbus, 1966—; dir. Credit Life Ins. Cos., Springfield, Ohio. Served to lt. AUS, 1954-56. Mem. ABA. Home: One Sweetbriar Ln Westerville OH 43081 Office: Vorys Sater Seymour & Pease 52 E Gay St Columbus OH 43215

BECK, LOUIS GEORGE, medical supply company executive; b. Bklyn., May 31, 1946; s. Louis and Carmen Mildred (De Rosa) B.; A.A., Temple U., 1969; B.S. in Med. Tech., Cleve. State U., 1971; m. Mary Catherine Manley, Aug. 10, 1974; children—Kelly Ann, Christopher Louis, Michael Joseph. Med. technician Episcopal Hosp., Phila., 1967-69; dir. purchasing Healthco-Schuemann-Jones Co., Cleve., 1969-72; mfrs. rep. Christiansen & Barber Assoc., Chgo., 1972-76; pres. Corpsman Med. Supply Co., Lodi, Ohio, 1976—, Louis Beck & Assocs., Inc. Served with USN, 1964-67; Vietnam. Decorated Air medal with 3 oak leaf clusters, D.F.C., Purple Heart with 2 oak leaf clusters, Bronze Star, Navy Cross, Silver Star, Navy Commendation medal, Vietnamese Cross of Gallantry, Vietnamese Army Service medal, others; cert. med. lab. technologist, blood bank technologist, notary public. Mem. Am. Legion, VFW, DAV, Combat Vets. Assn., Mil. Order Purple Heart, Amvets. Republican. Roman Catholic. Club: Medina Kiwanis. Home: 8721 Chippewa Rd Chatham OH 44254 Office: PO Box 179 Lodi OH 44254

BECK, ROBERT KNOWLTON, retired newspaper publisher; b. Centerville, Iowa, July 17, 1915; s. Jesse McFall and Edna (Needham) B.; B.A., Iowa Wesleyan Coll., 1937, LL.D. (hon.), 1977; m. Charlotte V. Allen, June 24, 1939; children—Thomas Allen, Barbara (Mrs. Phil Climie), Martha Bryant. Editor-pub. Daily Iowegian and Citizen, Centerville, Iowa, 1943-83; asso. pub. Weekly Corydon Times-Republican, 1967-78; partner Daily Blade-Tribune, Oceanside, Calif., 1943-54, asso. pub. semi-weekly newspaper Glendora, Charter Oak, Azusa, 1958-65; chmn. bd. dirs. Centerville Nat. Bank, 1968-76; pres. Centerville Broadcasting Co., 1948-54; dir. Hawkeye Bancorp., Iowa Blue Cross. Mem. Iowa Ho. of Reps., 1953-54; mem. Iowa Hwy. Commn., 1955-59; commr. Iowa Devel. Commn., 1969-77. Bd. trustees Iowa Wesleyan Coll., 1962-81; trustee Hoover Library Assn., 1975—. Recipient 1st place in Iowa for editorial writing excellence, 1954; newspaper classed 1st in Ia. cities 12000 population or less, 1951, 53, 60, 2d place, 55, 57, 58; recipient Des Moines Press and Radio Bent Cane award, 1960; Ia. Master-Editor Pub. award, 1963, Iowa Daily Press Community Service award, 1963, 83. Mem. Iowa Press Assn. (past pres.), C. of C. (past pres.), Iowa Good Roads Assn. (pres. 1963-65, chmn. bd. 1966-74), Sigma Delta Chi. Methodist (del. jurisdictional conf. 1952 and 1964). Mason, Elk, Lion (past pres.). Clubs: Centerville Country (past pres.); Rathbun Lake Assn. (pres.); Lincoln of Iowa (pres. 1979-81). Home: Golfview Addition R3 Centerville IA 52544 Office: 105-7 N Main St Centerville IA 52544

BECK, ROGER FREDERICK, manufacturing company official; b. Saginaw, Mich., Dec. 22, 1939; s. Carl Conrad and Rose Elmira (Owen) B.; m. Jean Lynne Hillier, June 1, 1963; children—James Roger, Edward Frederick. A.A., Bay City (Mich.) Jr. Coll., 1959; B.A., Mich. State U., 1961; postgrad. U. Mich., 1981—. Various positions purchasing dept. Dow Corning Corp., Midland, Mich., 1963-73, design mgr., 1974-82, mgr. real estate and space planning, 1982—; lectr. various univs., profl. groups, including Am. Mgmt. Assn.; design curriculum advisor Delta Coll., Northwood Inst., Central Mich. U. Contbr. articles to profl. jours. Trustee Swan Valley (Mich.) Sch. Dist., 1983—; advisor Explorer div. Lake Huron council Boy Scouts Am. Served with U.S. Army, 1961-63. Recipient Design award Office Adminstrn. and Automation mag., 1983. Mem. Office Landscape Users Group, Nat. Facility Mgmt. Assn., Nat. Assn. Corp. Real Estate Execs. Republican. Episcopalian. Club: Swan Valley Sports Boosters. Home: 7706 Madeline St Saginaw MI 48603 Office: PO Box 1767 Dow Corning Corp Midland MI 48640

BECKER, BENJAMIN MAX, lawyer; b. Chgo., Feb. 3, 1909; s. Max and Etta Becker; J.D., DePaul U., 1933; m. Jean Merin, Dec. 25, 1930; children—David M., Merle Lynn. Admitted to Ill. bar, 1935; since practiced in Chgo.; partner firm Warden & Becker, 1935-42; asso. mem. firm Levinson Becker Peebles & Swiren, 1942-47; sr. partner firm Becker & Savin, 1947-72; counsel firm Antonow & Fink, Chgo., 1973—. Dir. DePaul Inst. Fed. Taxation, 1952, 53. Mem. Chgo. City Council, 1947-55. Bd. dirs. Chgo. chpt. UN Assn. Recipient distinguished service award Chgo. Life Ins. Underwriters Assn., 1970, several civic awards. Mem. Am., Ill., Chgo. bar assns., Internat. Soc. Law, Decalogue Soc. Author: (with Edward Warden) Illinois Lawyer's Manual (2 vols.) 1939, (with Bernard Savin and David M. Becker), ann. supplements, 1948—; (with

David M. Becker) Simplified Estate Planning, 1965, (with BenPoth, 1982; (with Bernard Savin and David M. Becker) Legal Checklists (3 vols.), 1966, ann. supplements, 1984; Is the United Nations Dead, 1969; (with Fred A. Tillman) The Family Owned Business, 1975, 2d edit., 1978; contbr. numerous articles to profl. jours. Home: 1771 W Mission Hills Rd Northbrook IL Office: 111 E Wacker Dr Chicago IL 60601

BECKER, BETTIE GERALDINE, artist; b. Peoria, Ill., Sept. 22, 1918; d. Harry Seymour and Magdalene Matilda (Hiller) Becker; B.F.A. cum laude, U. Ill., Urbana, 1940; postgrad. Art Inst. Chgo., 1942-45, Art Student's League, 1946, Ill. Inst. tech., 1948; m. Lionel William Wathall, Nov. 10, 1945; children—Heather Lynn (dec.), Jeffrey Lee. Dept. artist Liberty Mut. Ins. Co., Chgo., 1941-43; with Palenskie-Young Studio, 1943-46; free lance illustrator N.Y. Times, Chgo. Tribune, Saturday Rev. Lit., 1948-50; co-owner, operator Pangaea Gallery/Studio, Fish Creek, Wis.; pvt. tutor, tchr. studio classes. Exhibited one-man show Crossroads Gallery, Art Inst. Chgo., 1973; exhibited group shows including Critics' Choice show Art Rental Sales Gallery Art Inst. Chgo., 1972, Evanston-North Shore exhbns., 1964, 65, Chgo. Soc. Artists, 1967, 71, Union League, 1967, 72, Women in Art, Appleton (Wis.) Gallery Art; represented in permanent collection Witte Meml. Mus., San Antonio; executed mural (with F. Wiater) Talbot Lab. U. Ill., Urbana, 1940. Active Campfire Girls, Chgo., 1968, 70; art chmn., mem. exec. bd. local PTA, 1959-60; active various art festivals, 1967—. Recipient Newcomb award U. Ill., 1940. Mem. Chgo. Soc. Artists (rec. sec. 1968-77), Internat. Platform Assn., Accademia d' Europa, Soc. Illustrators, Wis. Arts Council, Northeast Wis. Arts Council (dir.), Alumni Assn. Art Inst. Chgo., Accademia d'Europa, Internat. Platform Assn. Republican. Mem. Unity Ch. Contbr. articles, illustrations to mags. and newspapers. Home: 3992 Juddville Rd Fish Creek WI 54212

BECKER, BRUCE CARL, II, medical educator, family physician; b. Chgo., Sept. 8, 1948; s. Carl Max and Lillian (Podzamsky) B. B.S. in Aero. and Astron. Engring., U. Ill., 1970; M.S.M.E., Colo. State U., 1972; postgrad. Wright State U., 1973-74; M.D., Chgo. Med. Sch., 1978; M.S. in Health Services Adminstrn., Coll. St. Francis, Joliet, Ill., 1984. Diplomate Am. Bd. Family Practice. Resident in surgery U. N.C.-Chapel Hill, 1978-79, in family practice St. Mary of Nazareth Hosp. Ctr., Chgo., 1979-81; clin. instr. Chgo. Med. Sch., 1982, affiliate instr., 1982-83, asst. prof., vice chmn. dept. family medicine, 1983—; asst. dir. med. edn. St. Mary of Nazareth Hosp. Ctr., Chgo., 1981-82, dir. family practice residency, 1983—, chief Family Practice Ctr., 1983—, chmn. dept. family practice, 1985—, med. dir. Home Health Service, 1985—, med. dir. HMO-Ill., 1985—. Served to capt., USAF, 1970-75. Recipient Literary Key award St. Mary of Nazareth Hosp. Ctr., 1981, 85. Fellow Am. Acad. Family Physicians; mem. Ill. Acad. Family Physicians, Soc. Tchrs. of Family Medicine, Assn. Am. Med. Colls., Alliance Continuing Med. Edn., Am. Coll. Hosp. Adminstrs., AMA, Ill. Med. Assn., Chgo. Med. Soc., Phi Delta Epsilon. Lutheran.

BECKER, DAVID BRUCE, data processing company executive; b. Indpls., Nov. 8, 1953; s. Alton Arthur and Minnie Ann (Pierce) B.; m. Bonita Ann Linxwiler, May 30, 1980 (div. Oct. 1983); 1 son, Jason Edward. B.A., DePauw U., 1975. Br. mgr. Gen. Electric, Indpls., 1975-76, Credit Corp., South Bend, Ind., 1976-78; sr. cons. Ind. Credit Union League, Indpls., 1979-81; pres., founder Re Member Data processing, Indpls., 1981—; pres., dir. Compass, Inc., Indpls., 1982—, Becker & Assocs., Inc., Indpls., 1982—, Checks, Inc., Indpls., 1983—; dir. L. Scott Corp., Indpls., Muskies Inc. Mem. Indpls. C. of C. Home: 9030 Mud Creek Rd Indianapolis IN 46256 Office: Re Member Data Processing Services Inc 8455 Keystone Crossing Indianapolis IN 46240

BECKER, DAVID NORBERT, insurance company executive; b. St. Louis, July 18, 1945; s. William Paul and Estelle Katherine (Meyer) B.; B.S. cum laude, St. Louis U., 1967, Ph.D. (fellow), 1973; M.A. (fellow) Washington U., St. Louis, 1969, A.S.A., 1977, F.S.A., 1979; m. JoAnn Elizabeth Clark, June 7, 1969. Instr. John Burroughs Sch., Ladue, Mo., 1969-70; instr. math. St. Louis U., 1970-73; asst. prof. math St. Francis Coll., Fort Wayne, Ind., 1973-75; actuarial cons. Lincoln Nat. Life Ins. Co., Ft. Wayne, 1975-79, asst. actuary, 1979-80, dir. group/ind. products, 1980-81; asst. v.p., dir. fin. planning and analysis, reins. div. Lincoln Nat. Corp., 1982-83, asst. v.p., individual life actuary individual products div., 1983-85, 2d v.p., 1985—. Fellow Soc. Actuaries; mem. Am. Math. Soc., Math. Assn. Am., Pi Mu Epsilon. Contbr. articles to profl. jours. Home: 2208 Forest Glade Fort Wayne IN 46825 Office: 1401 S Harrison St Fort Wayne IN 46801

BECKER, DENNIS JEROME, medical benefits company executive; b. St. Johns, Mich., June 8, 1947; s. Aloysious Benedict and Florence (Thelen) B.; m. Carole Elizabeth Emmons, June 20, 1969; children—Amy, Jeff, David. B.A., Mich. State U., 1969, M.A., 1971; M.P.H., U. Mich., 1972. Dir. hosp. bed need project State of Mich., 1974-76; cons. health planning, Lansing, 1976-77; supr. employee ins. Ford Motor Co., Dearborn, Mich., 1977-83; v.p. customer services Medstat Systems Inc., Ann Arbor, 1983—. Pack leader Cub Scouts, Boy Scouts Am., Ann Arbor, 1983—. Mem. Comprehensive Health Planning Council S.E. Mich. (bd. dirs., exec. com. 1979-83), Midwest Bus. Group on Health (bd. dirs. 1981-83). Home: 2907 Logan Ct Ann Arbor MI 48104 Office: Medstat Systems Inc Eisenhower St Ann Arbor MI 48104

BECKER, H. PHILLIP, investment advisor; b. Waukegan, Ill., Oct. 12, 1943; s. David and Mildred B.; B.S., U. Pa., 1965; J.D., U. Ill., 1968; m. Ellen Kuneck, Nov. 23, 1969; children—Dana Leslie, Jaime Lynn, Casey Erin. Admitted to Ill. bar, 1968; investment counselor Gofen & Glossberg, Chgo., 1968-71; founder, v.p. Cable Corp. Am., Chgo., 1971-73; v.p., dir. fin. Capital Resources Fin. Advisors, Chgo., 1973-75; pres. HPB Trading Systems, Chgo., 1980—; chmn. Chronometrics Inc., Chgo., 1980—; pres. Becker Williams and Co., 1983—; commentator Ask An Expert, WCIU-TV, Chgo., 1983—. Mem. fin. com. Chgo. Bd. Options Exchange, 1975-82; bd. dirs. Organic Theater Co. Mem. Chgo. Bd. Trade, Chgo. Merc. Exchange, Security Traders Assn. Chgo., Nat. Futures Assn. (arbitration com.), Chgo. Bar Assn. (past mem.), ABA, Chgo. Bd. Options Exchange. Fin. editor Young Lawyers Jour. Chgo. Bar Assn., 1971-73. Office: 327 S La Salle St Chicago IL 60604

BECKER, MARK MATTHEW, school administrator; b. Burt, Iowa, May 5, 1934; s. Mathew and Justine (Bormann) B.; m. Mary Jo Schmidt, July 15, 1961; children—Susan Marie, Colleen Marie. A.A., St. Lawrence Coll., 1954; B.A., Loras Coll., 1956; M.A., U. Colo., 1966; postgrad., Loras Coll., 1965-70. Cert. tchr. Counselor, coach Turkey Valley High Sch., Jackson Junction, Iowa, 1963-64; counselor Brodhead High Sch., Wis., 1964-65; counselor, dean Dubuque High Schs., Iowa, 1965-73; prin. Greene Jr./Sr. High Sch., Iowa, 1973-80, Westwood Jr./Sr. High Sch., Sloan, Iowa, 1980—. Served to Sp-4 U.S. Army, 1956-62. Mem. Ednl. Adminstrn. Iowa (charter mem.), Nat. Assn. Secondary Prins., NEA (life), Am. Assn. Sch. Curriculum, Iowa Assn. Sch. Curriculum. Democrat. Roman Catholic. Club: Greene Country (pres. 1973-80). Avocations: woodworking, photography. Home: Box 355 Sloan IA 51055 Office: Westwood Jr Sr High Sch 2016th St Sloan IA 51055

BECKER, NORMAN OTTO, surgeon; b. Fond du Lac, Wis., Jan. 16, 1918; s. John H. and Otillia A. (Graf) B.; B.A., U. Wis., 1940, M.D., 1943; m. Mildred Murdoch, June 20, 1943; children—Mary Gail, James Murdoch, Julia Brown, Constance Marjorie. Intern, resident, chief resident in surgery Cleve. Met. Hosp., 1943-49; surgeon Asso. Physicians, Fond du Lac, 1949—; asst. clin. prof. surgery U. Wis. Bd. dirs. Med. Coll. Wis.; dir. 1st Wis. Nat. Bank, Fond du Lac. Chmn. bd dirs., mem. exec com. U. Wis. Found., 1983—; pres. Citizens Council of U. Wis. Center. Served with USNR, 1944-46; PTO. Diplomate Am. Bd. Surgery. Fellow A.C.S. (bd. govs.); mem. Wis., Fond du Lac County med. socs., AMA, U. Wis. Alumni Assn. (past pres., Distinguished Service award 1976), Wis. Surg. Soc. (past pres.). Lutheran. Club: Fond du Lac Rotary (past pres.). Home: 1022 Mary Hill Park Fond du Lac WI 54935 Office: 505 E Division St Fond du Lac WI 54935

BECKER, RICHARD HARMAN, wholesale hardware executive; b. Evansville, Ind., July 26, 1940; s. Richard Fenneman and Daisy Elizabeth (Harman) B.; m. Sally Ann Newhouse, Aug. 4, 1974 (div.); children—Ann Sweeny, John Harman. B.E.S. in Indls. Engring., Johns Hopkins U., 1962. With Ohio Valley Hardware Co., Inc., Evansville, 1965-77, pres., dir., 1977—; chmn. bd., dir. Davidson-Amos, Inc., Evansville, 1979—; dir. Complete Lumber Ky., Inc. Served to capt. AUS, 1963-64. Mem. Soc. Am. Mil. Engrs., Evansville C. of C. Club: Evansville Country. Lodge: Rotary. Home: Rural Route 8 Browning Rd Evansville IN 47711 Office: Ohio Valley Hardware Co Inc 1300 Pennsylvania Ave Evansville IN 47708

BECKER, TIMOTHY TODD, lawyer; b. Cresco, Iowa, Oct. 19, 1953; s. Herbert Barton and Elizabeth Jane (Liewer) B.; m. Mary Jane Koehn, June 1, 1975; children—Lisa Ann, Justin Todd. B.A. with high distinction, U. Iowa, 1976, J.D. with honors, 1980. Bar: Iowa 1980, U.S. Dist. Ct. (no. and so. dists.) Iowa 1980, U.S. Ct. Appeals (8th cir.) 1980, U.S. Dist. Ct. (cen. dist.) Ill. 1984; diplomate Ct. Practice Inst. Mem. Tom Riley Law Firm, P.C., Cedar Rapids, Iowa, 1980—. Mem. Iowa State Bar Assn., Assn. Trial Lawyers Am., Linn County Bar Assn., Phi Beta Kappa. Lutheran. Home: 430 Fairway Terr SE Cedar Rapids IA 52403 Office: Tom Riley Law Firm PC 4040 First Ave NE Cedar Rapids IA 52402

BECKER, VELMA ELIZABETH, association executive; b. Cin., Aug. 3, 1930; d. Jacob and R. Ellen (Culbertson) B. B.S., U. Cin., 1964. Exec. sec. Am. Leather Chemists Assn., Cin., 1950—. Mem. Westwood Civic Assn., Ohio, 1984. Mem. Am. Leather Chemists Assn. (hon., O'Flaherty award 1980), Pilot Club Cin. (rec. sec. 1984—), Mu Omega Beta (good cheer chmn. Cin. 1984-85). Avocations: Swimming, tennis and reading. Office: Am Leather Chemists Assn care Campus Station 14 Cincinnati OH 45221

BECKER, WILLIAM DENNIS, health administrator; b. St. Louis County, Mo., Oct. 23, 1931; s. Robert James and Virginia Hazel (Windmoeller) B.; B.S., U. Mo., 1953; postgrad. So. Ill. U., Edwardsville, 1974—; m. Mary Ann Hanson, Sept. 27, 1952; children—Katherine Ann, William David. Mdse. mgr., asst. mgr. sales Brown Shoe Co., St. Louis, 1953-68; mgr. contract service A.S. Aloe Co., St. Louis, 1968-69; adminstrv. officer health planning Alliance for Regional Community Health, Inc., St. Louis, 1969-73, dep. dir., 1973-76; exec. dir. Mo. Area V Health Systems Agency, Poplar Bluff, 1976-82; exec. dir. Community Health Ctr., Hillsboro, Mo., 1982-84; adminstr. Olsten Health Care, Clayton, Mo., 1985—; pres. B&D Gun Shop, Inc., owner The Shoe Box. Pres. Clayton (Mo.) Brownbilt Credit Union, 1964-68; bd. dirs. greater St. Louis Family Planning Council; active YMCA. Served as officer USAF, 1953-55; Korea. Mem. Am. Health Planning Assn., Mo. Public Health Assn. Mem. United Ch. Christ. Lion. Home: 36 Lake Wood Dr Hillsboro MO 63050 Office: 225 S Meramec Clayton MO 63105

BECKER, WILLIAM HENRY, federal judge; b. Brookhaven, Miss., Aug. 26, 1909; s. William Henry and Verna (Lilly) B.; m. Geneva Moreton, June 9, 1932; children—Frances Becker Mills, Patricia (Mrs. Richard H. Hawkins), Nancy (Mrs. G. Lemuel Hewes), Geneva Becker Jacks, William Henry III; student La. State U., 1927-28; LL.B., U. Mo., 1932. Bar: Miss. 1930, Mo. 1932, U.S. Supreme Ct. 1937. Assoc. firm Clark & Becker, Columbia, Mo., 1932-36; mem. firm, 1936-44, 46-61; spl. counsel Mo. Ins. Dept., 1936-44; counsel to gov. on Kansas City criminal investigation, 1938-39; spl. asst. to dir. Econ. Stablzn., Office of War Moblzn. and Reconversion, Washington, 1945-46; chmn. Mo. Supreme Ct. Com. to draft Mo. Rules of Civil Procedure, 1952-59; spl. commr. Mo. Supreme Ct., 1954-58; judge U.S. Dist. Ct., Western Dist. Mo., Kansas City, 1961—, chief judge, 1965-77, sr. judge, 1977—; judge Temporary Emergency Ct. Appeals U.S., 1977—; mem. com. on operation of jury system U.S. Jud. Conf., 1966-68, chmn. sub-com. to draft Jury Selection and Service Act of 1968, 1966-67, mem. coordinating com. for multiple litigation, 1962-68, vice chmn., 1967-68; mem. Jud. Panel on Multi-dist. Litigation, U.S. Jud. Conf., 1968-77; faculty Fed. Jud. Center Seminars and Workshops for U.S. Dist. Judges, 1968—. Served as lt. (j.g.) USN, 1944-45, Res., 1945-52. Decorated Navy commendation medal, Philippines Liberation Ribbon, Bronze Star; recipient Charles E. Whittaker award. Fellow Am. Bar Found., Am. Coll. Trial Lawyers, Am. Coll. Probate Counsel; mem. Am. Judicature Soc., Lawyers Assn. Kansas City, Am., Fed., Mo., Kansas City bar assns., Order of Coif. Bd. editors Manual for Complex Litigation, 1968—, chmn., 1977-81. Office: 741 US Courthouse 811 Grand Ave Kansas City MO 64106

BECKER, WILLIAM KOHL, engr.; b. St. Louis, June 13, 1927; s. William C. and Bessie (Kohl) B.; m. Lois Matthews, Feb. 4, 1951; 1 dau., Joan. B.S., Washington U., 1949; M.S., U. Ill., 1951. Registered profl. engr., Iowa, Mo., Minn., Nebr., Ohio, Pa., Tex., and others. Structural engr. Convair Aircraft Inc., Ft. Worth, 1953-55, William C. E. Becker, St. Louis, 1955-70; pres. Becker, Becker and Pannell, Inc., St. Louis, 1970—. Bd. govs. Washington U., 1975—, chmn. alumni annual giving fund Sch. of Engring. and Applied Sci., 1975—. Mem. ASCE, Am. Concrete Inst., Nat., Mo. socs. profl. engrs., Am. Consulting Engrs. Council, Mo. Athletic Club, Rotary, William Greenleaf Eliot Soc., Theta Xi, Sigma Xi. Office: 411 N 7th St Saint Louis MO 63101

BECKERLE, PAUL MICHAEL, alderman, manufacturers' representative; b. St. Louis, July 16, 1956; s. John Francis and Marjorie Carol (McNabb) B. B.S., U. Mo.-St. Louis, 1977, M.Adminstrn. (fellow), 1979. Criminal case analyst FBI, Washington, 1979-82; mfr.'s rep. Dakotah Inc. and Karpel Co., St. Louis, 1982—; mem. St. Louis Bd. Aldermen, 1985—; profl. model. Mem. Teens Encounter Christ, St. Louis, 1975—; mem. St. Louis City Council. Democrat. Roman Catholic. Home: 4443 Dewey St Saint Louis MO 63116 Office: 4901 Pernod Ave Saint Louis MO 63139

BECKETT, DARRELL CHRIS, insurance company executive; b. Moweaqua, Ill., Aug. 17, 1942; s. George C. and Mercedes (Mouche) B.; m. Carolyn Kay Cutler, Jan. 19, 1961; children—Carmine, Kari, Chris, Kendra. Student U. Ill. 1960-61. Cert. gen. agt. Chief draftsman Radson Engring., Macon, Ill., 1961-63; co-owner, v.p. cosmetology schs., Decatur and Taylorville, Ill., 1966-71; salesman to regional mgr. Standard Life & Accident Ins. Co., 1971-75; gen. agt., regional dir. Pioneer Life of Ill., Rockford, 1975—; chmn. bd. D.C. Beckett & Co., Am. Interstate Mktg. Corp., Taylorville, 1977—; pres., chief exec. officer Pan Am. Mktg. Assocs., Inc., Taylorville, 1979—. Chm. bd. Evangelical Free Ch., Taylorville; sponsor, coach YMCA soccer teams. Named to Millionaire Club, Standard Life Ins. Co., 1972, 73, 74, Agt. of Yr., 1974; recipient Pres.'s Millionaire Roundtable award Pioneer Life Ins. Co. of Ill., 1975-79, cert. of appreciation, 1983, Pres'. Council award, 1976-83. Mem. Nat. Assn. Life Underwriters. Lodges: Kiwanis, Masons (32 degree), Shriners. Office: Pan Am Mktg Assocs 900 Springfield Rd Taylorville IL 62568

BECKETT, GRACE, economics educator emerita; b. Smithfield, Ohio, Oct. 7, 1912; d. Roy M. and Mary (Hammond) Beckett; A.B., Oberlin Coll., 1934, A.M., 1935; Ph.D., Ohio State U., 1939. Music supr. Pub. Schs., Kelleys Island, Ohio, 1935-36; grad asst. econs. Ohio State U., 1936-39; assoc. prof. econs. and music Ind. Central Coll., 1939-41: with U. Ill., 1941—, asst. prof. econs., 1945-51, assoc. prof. econs., 1951-73, assoc. prof. emerita, 1973—. Mem. Am., Midwest econ. assns., Music Educators Nat. Conf., Ill. Music Educators Assn., Econ. History Assn., Am. Finance Assn., Am. Hist. Assn., AAAS, N.Y. Acad. Scis., Ohio Acad. History, Winchester-Frederick County (Va.) Hist. Soc., Ohio, Md. geneal. socs., Ill. Music Tchrs. Assn., Music Tchrs. Nat Assn., Interlochen Alumni Assn. (life), Oberlin Friends of Art, Nat. Sch. Orch. Assn., Krannert Art Mus. Assocs. (U. Ill.), Ohio State U. Alumni Assn., Nat. Honor Soc., Mary Ball Washington Mus. and Library, Met. Mus. Art (N.Y.C.) (nat. asso.), Alpha Lambda Delta (hon.), Phi Beta Kappa, Pi Lambda Theta, Phi Chi Theta (hon.). Methodist. Club: University of Ill. Women's. Author: Reciprocal Trade Agreements Program, 1941, 72; contbr. profl. pubs. Address: PO Box 386 Urbana IL 61801

BECKETT, THEODORE CORNWALL, lawyer; b. Heidelberg, Fed. Republic of Germany, Nov. 21, 1952 (parents Am. Citizens); s. Theodore Charles and Daysie Margaret (Cornwall) B.; m. Patricia Anne McKelvy, June 18, 1983. B.A., U. Mo., 1975, J.D., 1978. Bar: Mo. 1978, U.S. Dist. Ct. (we. dist.) Mo. 1978. Ptnr. Beckett & Steinkamp, Kansas City, Mo., 1978—. Mem. ABA, Mo. Bar Assn., Kansas City Bar Assn., Mo. Assn. Trial Attys., Assn. Trial Lawyers Am., Beta Theta Pi. Democrat. Presbyterian. Clubs: Kansas City, Carriage. Office: Beckett & Steinkamp PO Box 13425 Kansas City MO 64199

BECKMANN, BETH PEARSALL, educational administrator; b. Elgin, Ill., Oct. 19, 1950; d. Burton Sawyer and Ruth (Helm) Pearsall; m. William Edward Beckmann, Aug. 11, 1973; 1 dau., Jennifer. B.A., Northwestern U., 1972; M.Ed., Loyola U., Chgo., 1979. Cert. tchr., prin., Ill. Math. tchr. Elgin (Ill.) Acad., 1972-76, head middle sch., 1976-80, asst. to headmaster, 1981-82, asst. headmaster, 1982—. Publicity chmn. Elgin Jr. Service Bd., 1982-83, mem., 1980—; bd. dirs. Big Bros. Fox River Valley (Ill.), 1982—, chmn. program and agy. services com., 1983-84. Named Outstanding Secondary Tchr. Am., 1974; recipient faculty service award Elgin Acad., 1982. Mem. Nat. Council Tchrs. Math., Ill. Council Tchrs. of Math., Assn. Supervision and Curriculum Devel., Phi Delta Kappa. Lutheran. Office: Elgin Acad 350 Park St Elgin IL 60120

BECKSTEDT, JOHN EDGAR, truck equipment company executive; b. Milw., May 12, 1947; s. Carl A. and Ada (Kelley) B.; B.A., Wis. State U., 1971; postgrad. John Marshall Law Sch., 1971-73; m. Linda Nienow, June 12, 1971; children—John Edgar, Robert Christopher. Law clk. firm Walsh, Case and Coale Assos., Chgo., 1971-73; mgr. sales and leasing Royal Truck & Trailer Co., Chgo., 1974-80; v.p. Seng Truck Leasing Co., Bensenville, Ill., 1980—; dir. H.P. Transfer Co., Seng Warehouse & Distbn. Co. Sec. Wilmette (Ill.) Council for Comml. Renewal, 1976-77; co-chmn. Wilmette Fourth of July Commn., 1976, 77, 78; precinct capt. Republican Party, Wilmette, 1975—; plan commr. for Wilmette, 1980—; bd. dirs. Wilmette United Way, 1979—. Named Outstanding Young Man Am., Jaycees, 1978. Mem. Chgo. C. of C., Ill. Trucking Assn., Traffic Club Chgo., Truck Rental and Leasing Assn. Am., Wilmette Jaycees (external v.p. 1976-77, 78-79), U.S. Yacht Racing Union, Nat. Handball Assn. Am., Whitewater Alumni Assn., Phi Alpha Delta, Phi Sigma Epsilon (chpt. v.p. 1968-69). Roman Catholic. Home: 2501 Thornwood Rd Wilmette IL 60091 Office: Heart Truck & Trailer Sales 600 N Thomas Dr Bensenville IL 60106

BECKWITH, SANDRA SHANK, judge; b. Norfolk, Va., Dec. 4, 1943; d. Charles L. and Loraine M. (Sterneberg) Shank; m. Thomas R. Ammann, Mar. 3, 1979. B.A., U. Cin., 1965, J.D., 1968. Bar: Ohio 1968, Ind. 1976, Fla. 1979, U.S. Supreme Ct. 1973, U.S. Dist. Ct. (Ohio) 1971, U.S. Dist. Ct. (so. dist.) Ind. 1976. Sole practice, 1968-77; judge Hamilton County Mcpl. Ct., 1977-79, 82—; sole practice, 1979-81. Trustee U. Cin. Law Coll. Alumni; mem. evaluation com. Cin. Community Chest; chmn. Large Agencies Task Force. Recipient Betty Kuhn Meml. prize, 1968. Mem. Lawyers Club Cin., Women Lawyers Club, Nat. Assn. Women Judges, Am. Judges Assn., LWV, Nat. Women's Polit. Caucus. Methodist. Clubs: Bus. and Profl. Women, Altrusa, Hamilton County Rep., Hamilton County Rep. Women's, Green Twp. Rep. Office: 222 E Central Pkwy Cincinnati OH 45202

BEDELL, BERKLEY WARREN, congressman. b. Lake, Iowa, March 5, 1921; student Iowa State U., 1940-42; m. Elinor Healy, 1943; children—Kenneth, Tom, Jeanne. Mem. 94th-99th Congresses from 6th Iowa Dist.; pres. Dickinson County Meml. Hosp. Assn., 1964-66. Assoc. lay leader Iowa Conf., United Meth. Ch., 1971-74. Served as 1st lt. USAF, 1942-45. Named Nation's Small Businessman of Yr., 1964. Methodist. Lodges: Kiwanis, Masons. Club: Izaak Walton League. Office: US House of Representatives 2459 Rayburn Washington DC 20515*

BEDELL, RALPH CLAIRON, psychologist, educator; b. Hale, Mo., June 4, 1904; s. Charles E. and Jennie (Eaton) B.; B.S. in Edn., Central Mo. State U., 1926; A.M., U. Mo., 1929, Ph.D., 1932; m. Stella Virginia Bales, Aug. 19, 1929 (dec. 1968); m. Ann Barclay Sorency, Dec. 21, 1968 (dec. 1975); m. Myra Jervey Hoyle, Feb. 14, 1976. Tchr., Hale Pub. Schs., 1922-24; tchr. sci. and math. S.W. High Sch., Kansas City, Mo., 1926-30, 32-33; asst. prof. ednl. psychology N.E. Mo. State U., 1933-34, prof. ednl. psychology, 1934-37, dir. Bur. Guidance, 1934-37; dean, faculty and student personnel Central Mo. State U., 1937-38; freshman counselor, dir. reading labs., asso. prof. ednl. psychology and measurements U. Nebr., 1938-46, prof., 1946-50; chmn. dept., prof. psychology and edn. Sch. Social Scis. and Pub. Affairs, Am. U., Washington, 1950-52; dir. program planning and review br. internat. div. U.S. Office Edn., HEW, 1952-55; sec.-gen. South Pacific Commn. Noumea, New Caledonia, 1955-58; dir. counseling and guidance insts. br. U.S. Office of Edn., Washington, 1958-66; prof. edn., dir. nat. edn. studies U. Mo.-Columbia, 1967 prof. emeritus, 1974—, research asso. Center for Ednl. Improvement, 1974-75; cons. on faculty devel. Lincoln U. of Mo., 1976-77; mem. study group to Surinam, 1954; adviser U.S. delegation UN, 1953, 62, U.S. delegation Caribbean Commn., and West Indian Conf., 1952, 53; cons. Stephens Coll., Columbia, 1974, U.S. Office Edn., 1974; chmn. tech. com. access and retention for master planning Mo. Coordinating Bd. Higher Edn., 1976-78; edn. cons. Prince of Songkla U., Pattani, Thailand, 1980, 84. Vice pres., trustee Sigma Tau Gamma Found., 1972-74; dean Sigma Tau Gamma Leadership Inst., 1973. Served as comdr. USNR, 1942-46. Named Honored Alumnus, Central Mo. State U., 1971, Disting. Alumnus, 1983; Top Tau, Sigma Tau Gamma, 1970, named to Soc. of the 17, 1980; pres. Wilson C. Morris Fellowship, 1984-86; recipient Outstanding Contbn. cert. Assn. for Counselor Edn. and Supervision, 1967, award for outstanding contbn. to profession, 1984; Award of Merit, Mo. Assn. Sch. Librarians, 1971; U. Mo.-Columbia Alumni Assn. citation for outstanding achievement and meritorious service in edn., 1979; Disting. Achievement award Sigma Tau Gamma, 1985. Diplomate Am. Bd. Profl. Psychology. Fellow Am. Psychol. Assn. (Disting. Sr. Counseling Psychologist award 1985), Royal Soc. Health; mem. NEA (life), Nat. Soc. for Study Edn. (life), Mil. Order of World Wars (perpetual), Am. Assn. Counseling and Devel. (life), Internat. Soc. Polit. Psychology, Am. Assn. for Higher Edn., N.Y. Acad. Scis., Mo. State Tchrs. Assn., Mo. Guidance Assn. (award of merit 1971), Mo. Assn. Counseling and Devel. (life), Mo. Coll. Personnel Assn. (profl. award 1982), Kappa Delta Pi, Phi Kappa Phi, Phi Delta Kappa (life). Clubs: Explorers (life fellow) (N.Y.C.); Army and Navy (Washington). Author several books in field; also textbooks and standardized achievement exams., articles profl. publs. Home: 106 S Ann St Columbia MO 65201

BEDROSIAN, CLARK DEXTER, mgmt. service co. exec.; b. Seattle, May 11, 1924; s. Celak Der and Arshaluis (Atmadjian) B.; A.B., DePauw U., Greencastle, Ind., 1948; postgrad. Northwestern U., 1949-50; m. Rosemary Carlson, July 5, 1958; children—Lisa Bennett, Marc Der. Mdse. buyer Spiegel, Inc., Chgo., 1948-50; with store mgmt. then mdse. buyer Sears, Roebuck & Co., Chgo., 1950-61; with Service Master Industries Inc., Downers Grove, Ill., 1961—, pres. Health Care div. Midwest, 1976-77, group v.p. franchise group, 1978, pres. materials mgmt. div. health care, 1979—; lectr. in field. Pres. 50th Ward Young Republican Orgn., Chgo., 1951-52; exec. com. Rep. Nat. Com., 1953-55; chmn. chmns. council Chgo. Jr. C. of C., 1954-55; mem. sch. bd. Dist. 30, Northbrook, Ill., 1963-66. Served with USNR, 1943-46. Mem. Am. Mgmt. Assn., Am. Hosp. Assn. Presbyterian.

BEDWELL, TOMMY JOE, mechanical engineer; b. Linton, Ind., June 17, 1939; s. Harry Clifford and Mary Teressa (White) B.; B.M.E., Rose Poly. Inst., 1961; m. Freda Faye Speedy, June 16, 1961; 1 dau., Cathy Lynne. Engr., Ind. Pub. Service Co., summer 1960; test engr. truck div. Internat. Harvester, Ft. Wayne, Ind., 1961-64, rotational trainee, 1964-65, devel. engr. research div., 1965-68, sr. devel. engr., 1968-75; staff engr. piston design and devel. Bohn Aluminum and Brass Co. div. Gulf and Western Industries, Inc., South Haven, Mich., 1975—; asst. chief engr. piston design and devel. Bohn Aluminum & Brass Co., 1979-80, chief engr. piston design and devel., 1980-82, chief engr. and v.p. Research and Engring. Ctr., Engine and Foundry Div., 1982—. Registered profl. engr., Ind. Mem. Soc. Automotive Engrs., Am. Soc. for Metals. Republican. Mem. Christian Ch. Club: Masons. Home: 739 Seawatch Rd Holland MI 49423 Office: Gulf and Western Mgf Co Engine and Foundry Div 1310 Kalamazoo St South Haven MI 49090

BEECH, GARY DEAN, army officer, civil engineer; b. Parsons, Kans., Apr. 15, 1937; s. John Raymond and Bernice Louise (Jones) B.; m. Nadine Louise Pedlar, Sept. 2, 1962; children—Cynthia Ann, Mark Douglas. B.S., U.S. Mil. Acad., 1959; M.S. in Civil Engring., U. Ill., 1970. Registered profl. engr., Va. Commd. 2d lt. U.S. Army, 1959, advanced through grades to col., 1980; resident engr. C.E., U.S. Army, Saudi Arabia, 1968-69, area engr., West Point, N.Y., 1971-74, constrn. bn. comdr., Korea, 1975-76, dir. tng., Ft. Leonard Wood, Mo., 1979-82, dist. engr., St. Louis, 1982—; mem. exec. bd. Fed. Exec. Bd., St. Louis. Mem. Sci. and Tech. Com., St. Louis Regional Commerce and Growth Assn., 1982; chmn. Greater St. Louis Combined Fed. Campaign, 1984. Decorated D.F.C., Bronze Star, Air medal. Mem. Soc. Am. Mil. Engrs. (pres. 1984—), ASCE, Am. Def. Preparedness Assn. (bd. dirs. St. Louis 1982—), Assn. U.S. Army. Lodges: Rotary, Masons. Avocations: tennis, hunting, woodworking. Home: 426 Glan Tai Dr Manchester MO 63011 Office: US Army Engr Dist St Louis 210 Tucker Blvd North Saint Louis MO 63101

BEECHER, REXINE ELLEN, civic worker; b. Eldora, Iowa, Aug. 16, 1915; d. Vernon Richard and Gladys Metha (Bateson) Wardman; student U. No. Iowa, 1936-37; B.A., State U. of Iowa, 1939; m. Loyd Giff Beecher, June 15, 1939; 1 dau., Ellen Beth Beecher Feldick. Legal sec. Bateson & Ryan, attys., Eldora, Iowa, 1932, 33-35; asst. bus. mgr. College Eye Newspaper, Cedar Falls, Iowa, 1936-37; sec. econs. dept. Iowa State U., Ames, 1961-62; tchr. English, Union (Iowa) Sch., 1962-63; librarian Union Pub. Library, 1967-69; nat. promoter Children Am. Revolution. Mem. DAR (state registrar 1976-78), DAR State Officers Club, Daus. Colonial Wars, Farm Bur., Iowa Lassies (25-yr. mem. honoree 1981). Republican. Author hist. brochures, books and genealogies. Home: Rural Route 1 Union IA 50258

BEECKMAN, RICHARD LEE, insurance agency executive, consultant, educator; b. San Francisco, June 29, 1943; s. Albert Oscar and Virginia Lee (Paul) B.; m. Phyllis Ann Chandler, Apr. 19, 1974; children—Megan Elizabeth, Michael Albert, Brian George, Carol Ann, James Paul. Student Wayne State U., 1962-72; Assoc. in Risk Mgmt., Ins. Inst., Malvern, 1976; C.P.C.U., Am. Inst., Malvern, Pa., 1977. With Variable Annuity Life Co., Detroit, 1966-70; mktg., claims, EDP, mgmt. positions State Mut. Ins. Co. and subs. Citizens Ins. Co., various cities, 1970-80; prin., owner, v.p. Blanchet, Weadock & Co., Saginaw, Mich., 1980—; part-time faculty Wayne State U./U. Mich., 1978-81, Delta Coll., Saginaw, 1981—, coordinator ins. studies, 1981—; part-time faculty Lawrence Inst., Southfield, Mich., 1984—; seminar instr. Mich. Assn. C.P.A.s, 1979—, Ind. Assn. C.P.A.s, 1984—, Lawrence Inst., 1984, 85; seminar leader Mich. State U. Mgmt. Cons. Program, 1983—. Author: How to Read Financial Statements for the Producer, other seminar instrn. material. Bd. dirs. Saginaw YMCA, 1984—, bus. chmn., 1982-83, gen. chmn., 1984-85. Served with USNR, 1963-65. Mem. Am. Soc. C.P.C.U.s (sec. Northeastern Mich. chpt. 1982-83, v.p., 1983-84, pres. 1984-85, ednl. chmn. 1982—), Mich. Assn. Cons. Avocations: reading; chess; running; triathlon bicycling; karate. Home: 4865 Cactus Dr Saginaw MI 48603 Office: Blanchet Weadock & Co 1711 Court St Saginaw MI 48602

BEEKMAN, STANLEY, podiatrist; b. Bklyn., Aug. 27, 1951; s. David and Sylvia M. (Armel) B.; B.S., CCNY, 1972; D.P.M., N.Y. Coll. Podiatric Medicine, 1976; m. Marion Della Kiefer, June 4, 1978; 1 dau., Amy. Asso. prof. Cleve. Foot Clinic, 1978—; pvt. practice podiatry, Cleve., 1978—; asso. prof. sports medicine Ohio Coll. Podiatric Medicine, 1980—; staff St. John-West Shore Hosp.; cons. podiatry to Cleve. Indians, North Coast Bobsled Team. Recipient award of excellence in orthopedics, 1978; diplomate Am. Bd. Podiatric Orthopedics, Am. Bd. Podiatric Surgery. Fellow Am. Acad. Podiatric Sports Medicine; mem. Am. Coll. Sports Medicine, Can. Podiatric Sports Medicine Acad., Am. Podiatry Assn., Ohio Podiatry Assn., N.E. Ohio Acad., Am. Soc. Biomechanics, Am. Coll. Podopediatrics, Am. Med. Joggers Assn. Democrat. Jewish. Club: Cleve. West Road Runners. Home: 13601 Saint James Ave Cleveland OH 44135 Office: 2500 Clark Ave Cleveland OH 44109

BEEM, JOHN KELLY, mathematician, educator; b. Detroit, Jan. 24, 1942; s. William Richard and June Ellen (Kelly) B.; A.B. in Math., U. So. Calif., 1963, M.A. in Math. (NSF fellow), 1965, Ph.D. in Math. (NSF fellow), 1968; m. Eloise Masako Yamamoto, Mar. 24, 1964; 1 son, Thomas Kelly. Asst. prof. math. U. Mo., Columbia, 1968-71, assoc. prof., 1971-79, prof., 1979—. Co-author: Doubly Time like Surfaces; Global Lorentzian Geometry; contbr. articles to profl. jours. Mem. Math. Assn. Am., Am. Math. Soc., Phi Beta Kappa. Home: 1906 Garden Dr Columbia MO 65202

BEEMAN, DANIEL EUGENE, human resources executive; b. Kansas City, Mo., Mar. 29, 1942; s. Eugene A. and Doris M. (White) B.; m. Carol F. Wise, Oct. 14, 1978. B.A. in Edn., U. South Fla., 1971; Ph.D. in Design and Mgmt. Postsecondary Edn. Systems, Fla. State U., 1978. Dir. student services U. South Fla., St. Petersburg, 1972-75; jud. officer Fla. State U., 1975-76; mgmt. analyst State of Fla., 1976-78; exec. dir. Phi Mu Alpha Sinfonia, Evansville, Ind., 1978-83; v.p. human resources Lewis Bakeries, Inc., Evansville, 1983—. Pres., bd. dirs. Evansville Arts and Edn. Council. Served with USAF, 1964-68. Recipient U. South Fla. Outstanding Sr. award, 1971, Omicron Delta Kappa Meritorious Service award, 1976. Mem. Am. Soc. Tng. and Devel., Nat. Assn. Student Personnel Adminstrs., Am. Personnel Assn., Am. Mgmt. Assn., Profl. Frat. Assn. (pres.), Omicron Delta Kappa (nat. v.p.). Methodist. Contbr. articles to profl. jours. Office: 500 N Fulton Evansville IN 47710

BEEMSTER, JOSEPH ROBERT, manufacturing company executive; b. Chgo., Nov. 11, 1941; s. Joseph Z. and Emily (Dehaus) B.; B.A., DePaul U., 1962; postgrad. Ill. Inst. Tech., 1976, 77, U. Minn., 1979, 80; m. Judith L. Scheffers, Sept. 7, 1963; children—David, Susan. Mfg. mgr. Johnson & Johnson, Chgo., 1967-71, mgr. safety and security, 1971-78; corporate dir. safety and health GNB, Inc., St. Paul, 1978—. Author: Safe Work Practices for Workers Exposed to Lead; producer videotapes. Chmn., Bolingbrook (Ill.) Human Relations Commn., 1971-77. Mem. Am. Soc. Safety Engrs., Am. Indsl. Hygiene Assn. Home: 6908 W 83d St Bloomington MN 55438 Office: PO Box 43140 Saint Paul MN 55164

BEENENGA, KENNETH GENE, educational administrator; b. Spring Valley, Ill., May 19, 1941; s. John H. and Evelyn L. (Signer) B.; m. Evelyn J. Bell, Jan. 25, 1963; children—Christy, Lisa, Liana. B.S., Ill. State U., 1961, M.S. in Ednl. Adminstrn., 1964. Cert. tchr., ednl. adminstr. Tchr. Community Dist. 16, Paxton, Ill., 1966-72; indsl. cons. Ill. State Bd. Edn., Springfield, 1972-78; coordinator placement Capitol Area Vocat. Ctr., Springfield, 1978-83; dir. bus. indsl. ctr. Lincoln Land Community Coll., Springfield, 1983—; lectr. in field. Advisor Sangamon Cass Consortium Youth Council, 1978—; asst. supt. Jr. Livestock div. Ill. State Fair; elder Chatham Christian Ch.; advisor Lewis Meml. Christian Village, 1978—. Mem. Ill. Indsl. Coop. Edn. Assn., Am. Soc. Profl. Engrs. (cert.), C. of C., Iota Lambda Sigma. Avocations: sailing, hunting, target shooting, cabinet making. Home: Rural Route 1 New Berlin IL 62670 Office: Lincoln Land Community Coll Shepard Rd Springfield IL 62706

BEER, BARRETT LYNN, historian, educator; b. Goshen, Ind., July 4, 1936; s. Peter J. and Mabel M. Beer; B.A., DePauw U., 1958; M.A., U. Cin., 1959; Ph.D., Northwestern U., 1965; m. Jill Parker, July 31, 1965; children—Peter, Caroline. Instr. history Kent (Ohio) State U., 1962-65, asso. prof., 1968-76, prof., 1976—; asst. prof. U. N.Mex., Albuquerque, 1965-68, asst. dean Coll. Arts and Scis., 1966-68; Fulbright prof. U. Tromso (Norway), 1983. Am. Philos. Soc. grantee, 1966; Am. Council Learned Socs. grantee, 1973. Mem. Am. Hist. Assn., Conf. on Brit. Studies, Ohio Acad. History, Phi Beta Kappa (charter mem. Nu of Ohio). Episcopalian. Author: Northumberland: The Political Career of John Dudley, Earl of Warwick and Duke of Northumberland, 1973; Rebellion and Riot: Popular Disorder in England during the Reign of Edward VI, 1982; editor: (with S.M. Jack) The Letters of William, Lord Paget of Beaudesert, 1547-1563, 1974. Home: 445 Dansel St Kent OH 44240 Office: Dept History Kent State U Kent OH 44242

BEER, RICHARD LAMBERT, law librarian, educator; b. Detroit, Sept. 14, 1930; s. William John and Dora (Lambert) B.; m. Jean O., June 29, 1957; 1 dau., Laurie Ann. B.A., U. Mich., 1957; M.L.S., Wayne State U., 1971. Dir., Adams-Pratt Oakland County Law Library, Pontiac, Mich., 1960—; mem. faculty legal asst. program Oakland U., Rochester, Mich., 1973—; exec. dir. Oakland Law Library Found., Pontiac, 1981—; law library cons., 1968—; mem. budget and fin. com. Mich. Library Consortium, 1984—. Author: Michigan Legal Literature, 1973; Access to American, 1976; (with M.S. Merzon) Legal Research and Writing, 1979. Chmn., Twp. Planning Commn., Lake Orion, Mich., 1964-78; sr. warden St. Mary's Episcopal Ch. vestry, Lake Orion, 1970, lay reader, 1973—; bd. dirs. Pontiac-Oakland Symphony Orch., Pontiac, 1982—. Named Lion of Yr., Lions Club, Lake Orion, Mich., 1962; recipient Meritorious Service award Waterford Orgn. Retarded Children, 1966; Outstanding Service award Oakland County Bar Assn., 1977. Mem. Am. Assn. Law Libraries (treas. 1983-86), Ohio Regional Assn. Law Libraries (pres. 1977-78), Mich. Assn. Law Libraries (exec. bd. 1980-81), Mich. Library Assn. Episcopalian. Office: Adams-Pratt Oakland County Law Library 1200 N Telegraph Rd Pontiac MI 48053

BEERING, STEVEN CLAUS, university administrator; b. Berlin, Fed. Republic Germany, Aug. 20, 1932; s. Steven and Alice (Friedrichs) B.; m. Catherine Jane Pickering, Dec. 27, 1956; children—Peter, David, John. B.S., U. Pitts., 1954, M.D., 1958; Sc.D., Ind. Central U., 1983, U. Evansville, 1984. Asst. dean Ind. U. Sch. Medicine, Indpls., 1969-70, assoc. dean, 1970-74, dean, 1974-83; dir. Ind. U. Med. Ctr., Indpls., 1974-83; pres. Purdue U., W. Lafayette, Ind., 1983—; cons. in field. Contbr. articles to profl. jours. Served with Medical Corps, USAF, 1957-69. Steven C. Beering professorship in medicine Ind. U. Sch. Medicine, 1983; Convocation medal Am. Coll. Cardiology, 1983; Disting. Med. Alumnus award U. Pitts., 1983. Mem. Nat. Acad. Scis., Inst. Medicine, Assn. Am. Med. Colls. Avocations: music; photography; reading; travel. Home: 575 McCormick Rd West Lafayette IN 47906 Office: Purdue Univ West Lafayette IN 47907

BEERMANN, ALLEN JAY, lawyer, state official; b. Sioux City, Iowa, Jan. 14, 1940; s. Albert and Amanda (Schoenrock) B.; B.A., Midland Luth. Coll., 1962; J.D., Creighton U., 1965; m. Linda Dierking, May 23, 1971; children—Matthew Allen, John William. Radio announcer KHUB, Fremont, Nebr., 1960-62; admitted to Nebr. bar, 1965; adminstrv. asst. to sec. state State of Nebr., Nebr., Lincoln, 1965-67, dep. sec. state, legal counsel, 1967-71, sec. state, 1971—; mem. adv. panel Fed. Election Commn.; guest lectr. Taft Inst. Mem. exec. bd. Cornhusker council Boy Scouts Am., 1969—, Tabitha Devel. Corp., Lincoln; bd. dirs. Nebraskaland Found., Immanuel Med. Center, Omaha, People to People Internat.; mem. bd.-at-large Lincoln Found. Recipient Disting. Service plaque Omaha Legal Aid Soc., 1965, Outstanding Young Man award Lincoln Jaycees, Nebr. Jaycees; Silver Beaver award Boy Scouts Am., 1979, Alumni Achievement award Midland Luth. Coll.; Meritorious Service award N.G. Mem. Am., Nebr. bar assns., Nebr. Press Assn., Nat. Assn. Secs. State (pres. 1976-77, Meritorious Service medallion 1977), Am. Judicature Soc., Nat. Honor Soc., Am. Legion, Newcomen Soc. N.Am., Nebr. Jaycees (hon. life), Pi Kappa Delta, Phi Alpha Delta, Kappa Phi. Lutheran. Elk. Contbg. editor Neb. State Govt., 1966—. Avocations: racquetball, jetskiing. Office: Suite 2300 State Capitol Bldg Lincoln NE 68509

BEERY, DWIGHT BEECHER, physics educator; b. Troy, Ohio, Dec. 5, 1937; s. Beecher and Mary Lucile (Berkebile) B.; m. Helen Hideko Tanigawa, June 3, 1962; children—Lynn Marie, James Beecher, Stephanie Joy. B.A., Manchester Coll., 1959; M.S., U. Ind., 1962; Ph.D., Mich. State U., 1969. AEC fellow U. Calif., Berkeley, 1959-60; teaching asst. U. Ind., Bloomington, 1960-62; instr. physics Manchester Coll., North Manchester, Ind., 1962-64, asst. prof., 1969-71, assoc. prof., 1971-79, prof., 1979—, assoc. acad. dean, 1984—; teaching assoc. Mich. State U., East Lansing, 1964-65, research assoc., 1965-69. Contbr. articles to profl. jours. Bd. dirs., sec. Am. Com.-World Friendship Ctr., 1980—. Mem. Am. Assn. Physics Tchrs., Am. Phys. Soc., Ind. Acad. Scis., Sigma Pi Sigma, Mu Pi Epsilon. Mem. Ch. of the Brethren. Club: Manchester Table Tennis (sec., treas. 1979—). Avocations: piano; travel. Home: 901 S Orchard Dr North Manchester IN 46962 Office: Manchester Coll Physics Dept North Manchester IN 46962

BEERY, KENNETH EUGENE, food scientist; b. Lancaster, Ohio, Apr. 30, 1943; s. Robert David and Lucille Ester (Scholl) B.; B.S., Ohio State U., 1965; Ph.D., Pa. State U., 1970; m. Marci Annear, Aug. 22, 1965; children—Kevin, Kendra, Kelli, Kyle. With U.S. Dept. Agr., Berkeley, Calif., 1972-75, Union Carbide Corp., Chgo., 1975-76; dir. research Archer Daniels Midland Co., Decatur, Ill., 1976-84, Central Soya Co., Ft. Wayne, Ind., 1984—. Served with U.S. Army, 1970-72. Recipient Honored Grad. Student award Am. Oil Chemists Soc., 1969. Mem. Inst. Food Technologists (chmn. Iowa sect. 1978-79), AAAS, Am. Meat Sci. Assn., Am. Soc. Animal Sci., Am. Mgmt. Assn., Am. Assn. Cereal Chemists, Research Soc. Am., Sigma Xi, Alpha Gamma Sigma, Gamma Sigma Delta, Alpha Zeta, Phi Tau Sigma. Editorial adv. bd. Food Tech. mag., 1975-78; contbr. articles profl. jours. Office: PO Box 1400 Fort Wayne IN 46801

BEETS, F. LEE, insurance company executive; b. Paola, Kans., Apr. 2, 1922; s. William Francis and Nellie (Bryan) B.; B.B.A., Tulane U., 1945; postgrad. Harvard U., 1945, evening sch. U. Kansas City, Rockhurst Coll.; m. Dorothy Loraine Shelton, June 20, 1945; children—Randall Lee, Pamela Lee. Sr. accountant Lunsford Barnes & Co., Kansas City, Mo., 1946-49; v.p., gen. mgr. Viking Refrigerators, 1949-53; v.p., sec.-treas. Equipment Finance Co., 1949-53; exec. v.p., treas., gen. mgr. T.H. Mastin & Co., Consol. Underwriters, Mo. Gen. Ins. Co., Plan-O-Pay, Inc., Mid-Am. Data Co., B O L Assos., Inc., 1953-69; founder, chmn. bd., chief exec. officer Fin. Guardian Group, Inc., and subs., 1969-84; now pres. CIMCO, Inc., ins. cons. firm. Served with USNR, 1942-45. C.P.A., Mo. Mem. Mo. Soc. C.P.A.'s, Am. Inst. C.P.A.'s, Soc. C.P.C.U.'s, Pi Kappa Alpha, Sigma Tau Gamma, Phi Mu Alpha Sinfonia. Home: 16 Le Mans Ct Prairie Village KS 66208

BEHLING, CHARLES FREDERICK, psychology educator; b. St. George, S.C., Sept. 8, 1940; s. John Henry and Floy (Owings) B.; B.A., U. S.C., 1962, M.A., 1964; M.A., Vanderbilt U., 1966, Ph.D., 1969; 1 son, John Charles. Asst. dean of students U. S.C., Columbia, 1962-63; asst. state news editor The State Newspaper, Columbia, S.C., 1963-64; asst. prof. psychology Lake Forest (Ill.) Coll., 1968-74, assoc. prof., 1974-77, prof., 1977—, chmn. dept. psychology, 1977-84; pvt. practice psychotherapy, Lake Bluff, Ill., 1970—. Mem. long-range planning com. Lake Bluff Bd. Edn. Named Outstanding Prof., Underground Guide to Colls.; Outstanding Tchr., Lake Forest Coll., 1981; NASA fellow. Mem. Am. Psychol Assn., Soc. Psychol. Study of Social Issues, Assn. Humanistic Psychology, AAUP, ACLU, U. S.C. Alumni Assn., Psi Chi, Sigma Delta Chi. Democrat. Contbr. articles to profl. jours. Home: 116 E Prospect St Lake Bluff IL 60044 Office: Lake Forest Coll Dept Psychology Lake Forest IL 60045

BEHLMANN, F. LEE, aerospace company executive; b. Florissant, Mo., Apr. 24, 1922; s. John H. and Mary A. (Gettemeier) B.; m. Eileen R. Healy, Dec. 31, 1944; 1 child, Sheila. B.S., DePaul U., 1951. Engring adminstr. to mgr. McDonnell Aircraft Co., St. Louis, 1951-68; dir. engring adminstn. and chmn. performance measurement systems McDonnell Douglas Astronautics, St. Louis, 1968-78, dir. bus. systems and computer applications, 1978-84, dir. info. resource mgmt. and systems, facilities, 1984—. chmn., pres. Florissant Tire Center, 1963-84; dir., v.p. Behlmann GMC Trucks, Florissant, 1971—; pres. Behlmann Investments, Florissant, 1970—. Chmn., Friends of Scouting, Boy Scouts Am., St. Louis; gen. chmn. Florissant 200th Anniversary Celebration, 1985-86. Mem. Am. Legion, Am. Mgmt. Assn., AIAA, Am. Inst. Indsl. Engrs., Air Force Assn. Home: 1410 St Louis St Florissant MO 63033 Office: PO Box 516 Saint Louis MO 63166

BEHNKE, RICHARD THOMAS, tool and die company owner; b. Chgo., Feb. 8, 1934; s. Harry John and Beatrice Ulma (Choitz) B.; m. Arlene Virginia Alberts, July 13, 1957; children—Barbara, Tom, Lorraine, Mike, Richard, Amy, Joe, Cathleen, Ray, Jill. Student Wright Jr. Coll., 1952-53. Tool and die maker Hill Engring., Villa Park, Ill., 1953-71, Chgo. area, 1971-78; owner Behnke Tool & Die, Wheeling, Ill., 1978—. Pres. John Hersey High Sch. Booster Club, Arlington Heights, Ill., 1983-85. Served with USN, 1956-58. Roman Catholic. Clubs: St. Emily Bowling League (Mount Prospect, Ill.) (pres. 1961-62); Hill Engring. Golf League (Melrose Park, Ill.) (sec. 1967-68). Home: 404 Owen Ct Prospect Heights IL 60070 Office: Behnke Tool & Die 505 Harvester Ct Wheeling IL 60090

BEHNKE, WILLIAM DAVID, biochemistry educator; b. Pasadena, Calif., Jan. 15, 1941; s. William and Elizabeth (Williamson) B.; m. Carolyn Goodwin, Aug. 25, 1962. A.B., U. Calif.-Berkeley, 1963; Ph.D., U. Wash., 1968. Postdoctoral, fellow Harvard Med. Sch., Boston, Mass., 1968-71, research assoc., 1971-72; asst. prof. chemistry U. S.C., 1972-74; asst. prof. biol. chemistry U. Cin., 1974-79, assoc. prof., 1979—, dir. biophysics lab., 1974—. NIH grantee, 1979—; recipient award Phi Beta Kappa, 1963. Mem. Am. Soc. Biol. Chemists, Biophys. Soc., N.Y. Acad. Sci. Democrat. Episcopalian. Club: Literary. Contbr. articles to profl. jours. Home: 688 Riddle Rd #100 K Cincinnati OH 45220 Office: 231 Bethesda Ave Suite 3259 Cincinnati OH 45267

BEHRENS, GREGORY ROBERT, pharmacist; b. Quincy, Ill., Oct. 29, 1947; s. Robert C. and Mary M. (Johnson) B.; m. Ann Kathleen Sorenson, Aug. 1, 1970; children—Paul, Kristin, Peter. B.S. in Pharmacy, U. Ill.-Chgo., 1970; cert. tchr. Western Ill. U., 1974; M.Health Services Adminstrn., Sangamon State U., Springfield, Ill., 1983. Registered pharmacist, Ill.; cert. secondary tchr., Ill. Pharmacist, Osco Drug Co., Champaign, Ill., 1970-71, Brown Drug Co., Quincy, Ill., 1971-74, St. Mary Hosp., Quincy, 1974-82; dir. pharmacy services Blessing Hosp., Quincy, 1982—. Mem. Quincy Sch. Dist. #172 Bd. Edn. Mem. Am. Soc. Hosp. Pharmacists. Republican. Methodist. Home: 2928 Cabot Rd Quincy IL 62301 Office: 1005 Broadway Quincy IL 62301

BEHRENS, KENNETH CHARLES, wholesale importing and distributing company executive; b. St. Louis, Mar. 19, 1942; s. Miller Louis and Theresa Mary Behrens; B.S., Southeast Mo. State U., 1967; m. Patricia Ann Eckstrand, 1965; children—Cheryl Ann, Brian Charles. Acct. Coopers & Lybrand, St. Louis, 1967-70, Alexander Grant & Co., 1970-75; chief fin. officer Tacony Corp., 1975, sr. v.p. fin., 1976—. Trustee, Employees Pension Plan and Employees Profit Sharing Plan, bd. dirs., 1984—. Served with U.S. Army, 1961. Recipient Most Outstanding Performance award Alexander Grant & Co., 1974; C.P.A., Mo. Mem. Nat. Assn. Accts., Am. Inst. C.P.A.s, Mo. Soc. C.P.A.s, Sigma Chi. Home: 6830 Ravenscroft Dr Saint Louis MO 63123 Office: Tacony Corp 4421 Ridgewood Ave Saint Louis MO 63116

BEHRING, DANIEL WILLIAM, college administrator, psychologist; b. Sheboygan, Wis., Jan. 9, 1940; s. Melvin William and Frieda (Ostwald) B.; m. Nancy Jean Steeno, July 28, 1962; children—Deanna, Shelley, Tanya, Jonathan. B.A., Ripon Coll., 1962; M.A., Ohio U., 1964, Ph.D., 1969. Teaching fellow Ohio U., Athens, 1965-66, acting instr., 1966; asst. instr. So. Ill. U., Edwardsville, 1968-71; dean students, asst. prof. Monmouth Coll., Ill., 1971-76; assoc. prof., v.p. Alma Coll., Mich., 1976—; cons. colls., high schs., mental health orgns. Contbr. articles to profl. jours. Bd. dirs. Hoogerland Meml. Workshop, St. Louis, 1977—; reviewer United Way, Alma, 1983, 84. Served to capt. U.S. Army, 1966-68. Kellogg Found. grantee, 1976-80; U.S. Office Edn. grantee, 1977, 78, 79. Mem. Am. Psychol. Assn., Am. Assn. Higher Edn., Am. Assn. Counseling and Devel., Nat. Assn. Student Personnel Adminstrs., Sigma Xi, Sigma Chi (Grand Consul Merit award 1984). Club: Rotary (pres. 1983-84). Avocations: numismatics; Studebaker automobiles; model trains; science; sailing. Home: 5769 N Luce Rd Alma MI 48801 Office: Alma Coll 616 W Superior Alma MI 48801

BEHRINGER, SAMUEL JOSEPH, JR., lawyer; b. Detroit, Oct. 6, 1948; s. Samuel Joseph and Evania Theresa (Cherry) B.; m. Linda Suzanne Gross, Sept. 7, 1979; 1 child, Kathryn Elizabeth. B.S. in Labor and Indsl. Relations, Mich. State U., 1970; J.D., U. Detroit, 1973. Bar: Mich. 1974, U.S. Dist. Ct. (eastern dist.) Mich. 1974, U.S. Ct. Claims 1975, U.S. Tax Ct. 1975, U.S. Ct. Appeals (6th circuit) 1974, U.S. Supreme Ct. 1980. Asst. U.S. atty. Eastern Dist. Mich., Detroit, 1974-80; group v.p., gen. counsel Mich. Nat. Bank Detroit, 1980-83; ptnr. Simpson & Moran, Birmingham, Mich., 1983—. Recipient Merit commendations U.S. Dept. Justice, 1977, 78; Spl. Commendation Outstanding Service U.S. Atty. Gen., 1979. Mem. ABA, Fed. Bar Assn. (chmn. chpt. host com. of nat. conv. Detroit, 1985, mem. exec. bd. Detroit chpt. 1979-81), State Bar Mich. (chmn. young lawyers sect. 6th circuit admission ceremony 1975-83), Detroit Bar Assn., Comml. Law League Am., Am. Corp. Counsel Assn., Am. Trial Lawyers Assn., Phi Kappa Tau, Gamma Eta Gamma. Contbr. legal articles to profl. publs. Home: 333 McKinley Ave Grosse Pointe Farms MI 48236 Office: Simpson & Moran 5th Floor North 555 S Woodward Birmingham MI 48011

BEIDEMAN, RONALD PAUL, chiropractor, college dean; b. Norristown, Pa., Mar. 22, 1926; s. Jonas Paul and Bertha May (Cane) B.; student Temple U., 1948; D. Chiropractic, Nat. Coll. Chiropractic, Chgo., 1952; postgrad. Wheaton Coll.; B.A., Lewis U., 1976; m. Lorraine Marian Barrett, Aug. 19, 1950 (dec.); children—Ronald Paul, J. Kirk; m. 2d, Peggy Ann Bartlett, May 31, 1980. Dir. dept. diagnosis Nat. Coll. Chiropractic, Chgo., 1952-66, registrar, 1966-78, dean admissions and records, 1973—; exam. physician Chgo. Gen. Health Service, 1954-65; lectr. in field; pvt. practice chiropractic Chgo., 1954—; mem. nat. profl. standards rev. council, Health Care Financing Adminstrn., HHS, 1982; prof. Nat.-Lincoln Sch. Postgrad. Edn., 1964—; accrediting evaluator Council on Chiropractic Edn., 1978—, mem. task force panels on admissions Commn. on Accreditation, 1980, 84-86; accrediting evaluator Western Assn. Schs. and Colls., 1985. Served with USAAF, 1944-46. Fellow Internat. Coll. Chiropractors (faculty); mem. Nat. Coll. Chiropractic (corp. sec. 1972—), Nat. Bd. Chiropractic Examiners (chmn. test com. 1967-69), Ill., Chgo. chiropractic socs., Am. Chiropractic Assn. (vet. affairs com. 1979-81), Am. Legion (post comdr. 1957-58), Am., Ill. assns. Collegiate Registrars and Admissions Officers, Ill. Assn. Student Financial Aid Adminstrs., Nat. Assn. Coll. Admissions Counselors, Sigma Phi Kappa, Lambda Phi Delta. Contbr. articles to profl. publs. Office: 200 E Roosevelt Rd Lombard IL 60148

BEIDLER, DONALD BERNARD, Base Dental Surgeon, Air Force officer; b. Bryn Mawr, Pa., Aug. 19, 1939; s. Charles Bernard and Nellie Belle (Hepfer) B.; m. Sandra Jean Margetson, Mar. 21, 1964; children—Kristina, Susan, David. B.S., U. Wis.-Madison, 1962; D.M.D., U. Pa., 1966. Commd. Capt. U.S. Air Force, 1966, advanced through grades to Col. 1982; Asst. Base Dental Surgeon USAF Hosp., CCK AFB, Republic of China, 1968-69, USAF Hosp., Myrtle Beach AFB, S.C., 1970-73; Base Dental Surgeon USAF Hosp., Zaragoza AB, Spain, 1973-76; Chmn. Dept. Gen. Dentistry USAF Med. Ctr., Wright-Patterson AFB, Ohio, 1976-82; dental resident Eglin Regional Hosp., USAF, Eglin AFB, Fla., 1982-83; Base Dental Surgeon USAF Hosp., Grand Forks, N.D., 1983—. Vestryman, Lay Reader, Chalice Bearer Episcopal Ch., decorated Air Force Commendation Medal and Air Force Meritorius Service Medal Fellow and Master of Acad. of Gen. Dentistry; mem. Amer. Dental Assoc., Acad. Operative Dentistry, Assn. Mil. Surgeons U.S., ADA. Lodges: Elks, Lions, Masons, Scottish Rite, Shriners. Avocations: golf, stamps, travel, reading. Home: 3722 Simon View Ct Grand Forks ND 58201 Office: USAF Hosp Grand Forks (SGD) AFB ND 58205

BEILMAN, MARK EMIL, architect; b. Nebraska City, Nebr., Feb. 23, 1935; s. Ewald A. and Rose (Sand) B.; B.Arch., U. Nebr., 1966; m. Marlene Maria Freeman, May 11, 1957; children—Eric M., Kurt W., Mark E. Draftsman, Walter, Dorwin, Teague & Assos., Denver, 1957-58; estimator M.W. Anderson Constrn. Co., Lincoln, Nebr., 1966-67; draftsman John J. Flad & Assos., Madison, Wis., 1967-68; designer Daverman & Assos., Madison, Wis., 1968-69; asst. project mgr. State of Wis., Madison, 1970-77, roofing specialist, 1977-81; propr. Mark E. Beilman, Architect, Roofing Cons., 1981—. Served with USAF, 1954-57. Mem. Badger Bonsai Soc. Republican. Roman Catholic. Clubs: Waunona Way Assn., Lake Monona Sailing. Inventor Adjus-to-Fit bicycle handlebar adjuster. Home and office: 2702 Waunona Way Madison WI 53713

BEIN, LINDA H., book and gift shop owner; b. Evanston, Ill., Nov. 30, 1940; d. Robert Clark and Maybelle Elizabeth (Pick) Hill; m. William Carl Bein, June 20, 1969. B.S., Northwestern U., 1962. Tchr. Denver Pub. Schs., 1962-64, Albuquerque Pub. Schs., 1964-65, Greenfield Pub. Schs., Wis., 1966-71; owner, mgr. The Bookworm, Boulder Junction, Wis., 1979—. Chmn. bd. dirs. Sta. WXPR, Rhinelander, Wis. Bd. dirs. Boulder Junction Pub. Library, 1980—. sec. Wis. project loon watch Sigurd Olson Environ. Inst. Northland Coll., Ashland; Mem. Am. Booksellers Assn. Republican. Avocations: Reading; skiing; classical music. Home: PO Box 417 Boulder Junction WI 54512 Office: The Bookworm PO Box 343 Boulder Junction WI 54512

BEINFELD, MARGERY COHEN, neurobiology educator; b. Washington, Oct. 21, 1945; d. Robert Abraham and Mabel (Blake) Cohen; m. Solon Beinfeld, June 1970; children—Benjamin Ezra, Molly Toba. B.A., Washington U., St. Louis, 1968, Ph.D., 1973. Postdoctoral fellow St. Louis U., 1973-75, Washington U., St. Louis, 1975-79; staff fellow NIAMDD, NIH, Bethesda, Md., 1979-81; asst. prof. St. Louis U. Med. Sch., 1981-85, assoc. prof., 1985—. Contbr. chpts. to books, articles to profl. jours. NIH grantee, 1976-79, 81—. Mem. AAAS. Democrat. Jewish. Avocations: gardening; camping; hiking; biking. Office: 1402 S Grand Blvd Saint Louis MO 63104

BEIS, SARA JANE, laboratory executive, pharmacist; b. Akron, Ohio, Aug. 25, 1954; d. George Andrew and Buena Marie (Greer) B. B.S. in Pharmacy, U. Mich., 1977. Registered pharmacist, Ohio. Pharmacy intern Akron Gen. Med. Ctr., 1973-76; staff pharmacist Ohio State U., Columbus, 1977-80; clin. pharmacist VA, Columbus and Columbia, S.C., 1980-82; sales rep. Smith Kline & French Labs., Phila., 1983—; clin. instr. Coll. Pharmacy, Ohio State U., 1978-81, U. S.C., Columbia, 1981-82. Patentee pill packaging. Vol. Children's Hosp., Columbus, 1983. Recipient dist. achievement award Smith Kline & French Labs., Inc., 1985. Mem. Am. Soc. Hosp. Pharmacists, Akron Area Soc. Hosp. Pharmacists, U. Mich. Alumni Assn. (life), Pi Beta Phi. Republican. Roman Catholic. Avocations: Photography, physical fitness, swimming, golf, football. Home: 2556 Durand Rd Akron OH 44313

BEITO, GEORGE ANTHONY, banker; b. Thief River Falls, Minn., Jan. 11, 1933; s. George A. and Anne J. (Strande) B.; B.A., St. Olaf Coll., Northfield, Minn., 1955; grad. Rural Banking Sch., 1968; m. Gretchen Urnes, June 29, 1957; children—David A., Kathryn A., Laura E. Asst. cashier No. State Bank, Gonvick, Minn., 1958-60, pres., chmn. bd., 1965—, v.p., No. State Bank, Thief River Falls, 1960-65, pres., chmn. bd., 1965—; pres., chmn. bd. Security State Bank, Oklee, Minn., 1st Nat. Bank, McIntosh, Minn., Marshall County State Bank, Newfolden, Minn.; treas. Valley Home, Thief River Falls. Treas. Northland Community Coll. Found.; treas. Jobs Inc., Thief River Falls; v.p. Hartz Found. Served to lt. USNR, 1955-58. Named outstanding young man of Thief River Falls, 1962. Mem. Am. Bankers Assn. (governing council 1978-79; EDP council 1983—), Minn. Bankers Assn. (mem. council 1970-73, pres. 1977-78), Thief River Falls C. of C. (pres. 1963). Clubs: Rotary, Elks, Eagles. Home: 2211 Nelson Dr Thief River Falls MN 56701 Office: 201 E 3d St Thief River Falls MN 56701

BEJA, MORRIS, English literature educator; b. N.Y.C., July 18, 1935; s. Joseph and Eleanor (Cohen) B.; m. Nancy Friedman, Nov. 27, 1957;

children—Andrew Lloyd, Eleni Rachel. B.A., CCNY, 1957; M.A., Columbia U., 1958; Ph.D., Cornell U., 1963. From instr. to prof. English, Ohio State U., Columbus, 1961—, chmn. dept., 1983—; vis prof. U. Thessaloniki, Greece, 1965-66, Univ. Coll. Dublin, 1972-73. Author: Epiphany in the Modern Novel, 1971; Film and Literature, 1979. Editor: Samuel Beckett's Humanistic Perspectives, 1983; James Joyce's Dubliners and Portrait of the Artist, 1973; 3 other books. Served with USAR, 1958-63. Guggenheim fellow, 1972-73; Fulbright lectr., 1965-66, 72-73; recipient Disting. Teaching award Ohio State U. 1982. Mem. James Joyce Found. (pres. 1982—), Virginia Woolf Soc. (trustee 1976—), MLA, Am. Com. Irish Studies. Jewish. Avocations: photography; travel; cycling. Home: 79 Richards Rd Columbus OH 43214 Office: Ohio State U 164 W 17th Ave Columbus OH 43210

BEKKUM, OWEN D, gas company executive; b. Westby, Wis., Mar. 2, 1924; s. Alfred T. and Huldah (Storbakken) B.; B.B.A., U. Wis., 1950; postgrad. Northwestern U.; m. Dorothy A. Jobs, Aug. 26, 1950. With Arthur Andersen & Co., 1951-57, Hertz Corp., 1957-62; with No. Ill. Gas Co., 1963—, mgr. tech. acctg., 1964-66, asst. comptroller, 1966-68, comptroller, 1968-70, adminstrv. v.p., 1970-73, exec. v.p., 1973-76, pres., 1976—, chief exec. officer, 1981—, also dir.; dir. NICOR Inc. and all NI-Gas subs., New Eng. Energy Co., Andrew Corp. Bd. dirs. Protestant Found. Greater Chgo., 1975—, PACE Inst., 1977-83, Gas Research Inst. Served with AUS, 1943-46. C.P.A., Wis., Ill. Mem. Am. Mgmt. Assn., Am. Gas Assn. (dir. 1978—), Inst. Gas Tech. (trustee 1978-82), Gas Research Inst. (dir. 1982—). Clubs: Commercial, Mid-Day, Economic (Chgo.). Home: 46 Royal Vale Dr Oak Brook IL 60521 Office: PO Box 190 Aurora IL 60507

BELAYNEH, GETACHEW, commerce and economics educator; b. Nazareth, Choire, Shewa, June 25, 1937; came to U.S., 1958, naturalized, 1980; s. Belayneh and Lickyellesh (Afferu) Tegegn; m. Julia Rose Mavline, Sept. 12, 1970 (div. 1976); 1 dau., Brhane. B.B.A., Central State U., 1963; M.S. in Mktg., So. Ill. U., 1965; Ph.D. in Econs., U. Utah, 1971. Prof. econs. Talladega Coll., Ala., 1970-72; prof., head dept. econs. Central State U., Wilberforce, Ohio, 1972—; cons. Export Mgmt. Co., Columbus, Ohio, 1974-79; pres. Internat. Mktg. Inc., Fairborn, Ohio, 1975-80. Mem. Ohio Econ. Edn., Columbus, 1974, World Trade Council, Dayton, 1981; trustee Ohio Council on Econ. Edn., 1978-82. Recipient award for consumers econ. edn. curriculum devel. Ohio Dept. Edn., 1979. Mem. Am. Econ. Assn., Am. Mktg. Assn., Nat. Econ. Assn. Republican. Coptic Christian. Avocations: tennis; swimming; creative writing. Home: 251 W Dayton-Y-S-RD Fairborn OH 45324 Office: Central State U Dept Econs Wilberforce OH 45384

BELCASTRO, FRANK PATRICK, psychology educator; b. Pitts., Oct. 16, 1928; s. Samuel and Sarah (Mosca) B.; m. Joan Margaret Gallant, July 20, 1969; 1 child, Sarah Marie. B.A., U. Pitts., 1950, M.Ed., 1951, Ph.D., 1961. Cert. tchr., Pa., Mass. Tchr. math. Burrell Sch. Dist., Pa., 1953-65; asst. prof. edn. Merrimack Coll., North Andover, Mass., 1965-69; assoc. prof. edn. U. San Diego, 1969-72; assoc. prof. edn. and psychology Merrimack Coll., 1972-76; prof. edn. and psychology U. Dubuque, Iowa, 1976—, dir. placement office, 1965-69, chmn. dept., 1970-72, chmn. dept. spl. edn., 1977-78. Contbr. articles to profl. jours. Bd. dirs. Iowa Talented and Gifted; v.p. Parents and Friends of Talented and Gifted. NSF grantee, 1959, 61, 62; Paul Witty Found. fellow, 1979. Mem. NEA, Pa. Edn. Assn., Iowa Higher Edn. Assn., Sch. Sci. and Math. Assn., Nat. Council Tchrs. of Math., Phi Delta Kappa, Kappa Delta Pi. Roman Catholic. Home: 3690 Keystone Dr Dubuque IA 52001 Office: U Dubuque 2000 University Ave Dubuque IA 52001

BELCZYK, HATTIE, artist; b. Lorain, Ohio, July 30, 1920; d. Victoria Losiewicz. Student Lorain Bus. Coll. Exhbns. include Pa. Soc. Watercolor Painters, 1981, Ky. Watercolor Soc., 1981, 82, Baycrafters, 1981, Vermilion Boat Club, 1981, 82, 83, Lorain County Rotary Art Exhbn., 1981, Community Coll. Ann. Art Exhbn., 1981, 82, 83, Ann. Hispanic Arts and Crafts Show, 1981, 82, Houchins Ctr., Bowling Green, Ky., 1981, Indpls. Art League Teaching Ctr. and Gallery, 1981, Clara M. Eagle Gallery, Murray (Ky.) State U., 1981, Terrance Gallery, Palenville, Ky., 1981, Celebration Women and Arts, Stocker Ctr., 1981, 82, 83, Gt. Lakes Regional Art Exhbn., 1982, 1st Ann. Avon Lake Art Exhbn., 1983, also at colls. and univs.; represented in permanent collections: Baycrafters, Bay Village, Ohio, Lorri's Gallery, Vermilion, Ohio, DecHorizons, Sandusky, Ohio. Mem. Am. Watercolor Soc. (assoc.), Midwest Watercolor Soc., Ky. Watercolor Soc., Ohio Watercolor Soc., Pa. Soc. Watercolor Painters (silver medal 1981), Ga. Watercolor Soc. Home and studio: 3704 Amherst Ave Lorain OH 44052

BELDING, ESER UZUN, management educator; b. Sivas, Turkey, Mar. 23, 1951; came to U.S., 1975; d. Irfan and Hayriye Uzun; B.A., U. Istanbul (Turkey), 1974; M.A., U. Mich., 1977, Ph.D. in Organizational Psychology, 1979. Lectr., mem. research staff dept. psychology and Sch. Bus. Adminstrn., U. Istanbul, 1973-75; teaching asst., coordinator dept. psychology U. Mich., Ann Arbor, 1975-77, research assoc. Inst. for Social Research, 1976-79; health services research scientist VA Med. Center, Ann Arbor, 1979-80; research investigator Inst. Social Research; 1980-81; adj. prof. organizational scis. Wayne State U., Detroit, 1982; asst. prof. mgmt. U. Mich.-Flint, 1982—. Mem. Acad. Mgmt. Assn., Soc. for Gen. Systems Research, Internat. Council Psychologists, Internat. Assn. Applied Psychology. Contbr. articles to profl. jours. Home: 7270 Parkwood Dr Fenton MI 48430 Office: Sch Mgmt U Mich Flint MI 48503

BELKNAP, ELMER CLINTON, retired medical social worker; b. Gordon, Nebr., Dec. 24, 1905; s. Elmer Curtis and Kitty Luella (Moss) B.; B.A., Simpson Coll., 1929; M.A., U. Chgo., 1937; m. Mildred Pearl Breniman, May 23, 1932 (dec. June 1978); children—Rowan Curtis, Dean Edward; m. 2d, Mildred Shook Robson, June 7, 1979. Asso. boys' work sec. YMCA, Sioux City, Iowa, 1930-31; jr. boys clubs and handicraft dir. U. Chgo. Settlement House, 1932-33; sr. case worker Cook County Bur. Pub. Welfare, Chgo., 1933-34; dir. Hall County Emergency Relief and Pub. Assistance Adminstrn., Grand Island, Nebr., 1934-44; Nebr. field rep. Nat. Found. Infantile Paralysis, N.Y.C. and Lincoln, Nebr., 1944-65; with Nebr. State Dept. Pub. Welfare, Lincoln, 1965—, dir., 1967-68, med. social work cons., 1969-76; mem. Nebr. Crippled Children Adv. Com., Lincoln, 1947-55, Nebr. Health Planning Com., 1947-52, Nebr. Comprehensive Health Planning Adv. Council, 1967-69. Bd. dirs. Lancaster County chpt. Nat. Found.-March of Dimes, 1965-69. Recipient Distinguished Service citation Nat. Found.-March of Dimes, N.Y.C., 1964. Mem. Am. (nat. bd. dirs. 1968-69), Nebr. (pres. 1937-38) pub. welfare assns., Nebr. Pub. Health Assn. (state sec. 1955-56), Nat. Rehab. Assn. (state dir. 1961-64), Nebr. State Hist. Soc., New Eng. Historic and Geneal. Soc., Pi Kappa Delta. Methodist (chmn. com. edn. 1955-56). Author: A Belknap Genealogy, 1974; A Moss Genealogy, 1977; Nebraska and the Fight Against Polio, 1944-1965, 1982. Home: 2019 Harwood St Lincoln NE 68502

BELL, ALBERT LEO, lawyer; b. Columbus, Ohio, May 22, 1930; s. Jerome E. and Elizabeth Mary (Murphy) B.; m. Jean M. DiFino, Aug. 22, 1959; children—Albert, Kathleen, Paul. B.A. in Journalism, Ohio State U., 1956, J.D., 1958. Bar: Ohio, 1959. Ptnr. Walter & Bell, Columbus, Ohio, 1959-64, McGuire & Bell, Columbus, 1965-71; referee Franklin County Probate Ct., Columbus, 1964-65; counsel Ohio State Bar Assn., Columbus, 1971—. Contbr. articles to profl. jours. Served as sgt. U.S. Army, 1948-52. Mem. ABA, Ohio State Bar Assn., Columbus Bar Assn., Nat. Organ. Bar Counsel (pres. 1975-76), Forest Park Civic Assn., Am. Legion. Club: Columbus Power Squadron. Home: 1743 Sandalwood Pl Columbus OH 43229 Office: Ohio State Bar Assn 33 W 11th Ave Columbus OH 43201

BELL, ALLEN ANDREW, JR., lawyer; b. Paris, Ill., June 23, 1951; s. Allen Andrew and Mary Elizabeth (Charley) B.; m. Carol Anne Larson, June 15, 1974; children—Sara Elizabeth, Emily Anne. B.A., DePauw U., 1973; J.D. cum laude, Ind. U.-Indpls., 1980. Bar: Ill. 1980, Ind. 1980, U.S. Dist. Ct. (so. dist.) Ind. 1980, U.S. Dist. Ct. (cen. dist.) Ill. 1980. Underwriter Am. States Ins. Co., Indpls., 1973-80; assoc. Dillavou Overaker Asher & Smith, Paris, Ill., 1980-85; ptnr. Ruff, Garst & Bell, Paris, 1985—; pub. defender Edgar County, Ill., 1982-84, Clark County, Ill., 1982-84. Mem. ABA, Ill. State Bar Assn., Ind. State Bar Assn., Edgar County Bar Assn. (pres. 1982-83). Republican. Lodges: Kiwanis (treas. local club 1981-83), Masons (sr. warden local lodge 1985). Home: 802 Shaw Ave Paris IL 61944 Office: Ruff Garst & Bell 150 E Wood St Paris IL 61944

BELL, CARL COMPTON, psychiatrist, researcher, consultant, martial artist; b. Chgo., Oct. 28, 1947; s. William Yancy and Pearl Louise (Debnam) B.; m. Joanne Scott, Jan. 1, 1969 (div. Apr. 1971); 1 dau., Cristin Carol; m. Dora Dixie, Dec. 1984. B.S. in Biology, U. Ill.-Chgo., 1967; M.D., Meharry Med. Coll., 1971. Diplomate Am. Bd. Psychiatry and Neurology (examiner). Intern, Ill. State Psychiat. Inst., Chgo., 1971-72, resident, 1972-74, pvt. practice medicine specializing in psychiatry, Chgo., 1974—; dir. psychiat. emergency services Jackson Park Hosp., Chgo., 1976-77, assoc. dir. div. behavioral and psychodynamic medicine, 1979-82, mem. staff, 1972—; staff psychiatrist Human Correctional and Services Inst., Chgo., 1977-78, Chgo. Bd. Edn., 1977-79, Chatham Avalon Mental Health Ctr., Chgo., 1977-79; staff psychiatrist Community Mental Health Council, Chgo., 1977-79, med. dir., 1983—; assoc. prof. clin. psychiatry U. Ill., 1983—; cons. Mem. profl. adv. panel Mental Health Assn. Greater Chgo., 1983—; bd. dirs. Nat. Commn. on Correctional Health Care, 1983—; tchr. martial arts, 1973—. Producer, creator animation Book Worm, 1984. Served to lt. comdr. USN, 1974-76. Recipient plaque in recognition and appreciation Chatham-Avalon Mental Health Ctr., 1979; plaque in gratitude and appreciation Div. Behavioral Medicine, 1982; Scholastic Achievement award Chgo. chpt. Nat. Assn. Black Social Workers, 1980; Goldberger fellow, 1969; Dr. Martin Luther King, Jr. fellow, 1970-71; Am. Psychiat. Assn. Falk fellow, 1972-73. Mem. Am. Psychiat. Assn. (task force-delivery psychiat. services to poverty areas 1972-73), Nat. Med. Assn. (local chmn. sect. on neurology and psychiatry 1983 conv.), conv., nat. chmn. sect. on psychiatry and behavioral scis. 1985-86), Black Psychiatrists Am. (editor Bottom Line newsletter 1977-82, v.p. 1980-82), Cook County Physicians Assn., Prairie State Physicians, Ill. Psychiat. Soc., Soc., Underwater Explorers Soc., Shorei Goju Karate Soc. (5th degree Black Belt), Martial Arts Karate Assn., Alpha Omega Alpha. Contbr. chpts., numerous articles to profl. publs. Office: Jackson Park Hosp 7531 Stony Island Chicago IL 60649 also Community Mental Health Council 1001 E 87th St Chicago IL 60619

BELL, CHARLES EDWARD, psychologist; b. Galveston, Tex., Feb. 7, 1936; s. Ben Franklin and Johnnie Odet (Rush) B.; B.S., U. Houston, 1962, M.A., 1965; Ed.D., N. Tex. State U., 1977; m. Marvell Marie Mossom, Dec. 20, 1968; children—Charles Butler, Beverly Ann, Laurie Marvell. Asst. prof. Ouachita Bapt. U., Arkadelphia, Ark., 1967-69; staff psychologist Benton (Ark.) State Hosp., 1968-71; staff psychologist Vernon (Tex.) Project for Drug Dependent Youth, 1973-74; staff psychologist S.E. Kans. Mental Health Center, Humboldt, 1974-78; dir. S.E. Kans. Mental Health Assos., Chanute; staff psychologist Ozark Ctr., Neosho, Mo., 1982—; vis. prof. Vernon Regional Jr. Coll., 1974, Henderson State Coll., 1967-68; teaching fellow U. Houston, 1963-67, N. Tex. State U., 1972-73. Chmn. bd. dirs. Circle B Boys Ranch, Inc.; mem. council, mayor pro tem, Neosho. Mem. AAUP, Am., Southwestern psychol. assns., Phi Chi, Phi Delta Kappa. Republican. Mem. Assembly of God Ch. Clubs: Rotary, Kiwanis, Elks. Author: Transactional Analysis for Classroom Teachers, 1977; A Comparison of Three Techniques for Teaching Oral Hygiene, 1978. Home: 1510 Oakridge Dr Neosho MO 64850 Office: 214 N Washington Neosho MO 64850

BELL, CHARLES EUGENE, JR., industrial engineer; b. N.Y.C., Dec. 13, 1932; s. Charles Edward and Constance Elizabeth (Verbelia) B.; B. Engring., Johns Hopkins U., 1954, M.S. in Engring., 1959; m. Doris R. Clifton, Jan. 14, 1967; 1 son, Scott Charles Bell. Indsl. engr. Signode Corp., Balt., 1957-61, asst. to plant mgr., 1961-63, plant engr., 1963-64, div. indsl. engr., Glenview, Ill., 1964-69, asst. to div. mgr., 1969-76, engring. mgr., 1976—; host committeeman Internat. Indsl. Engring. Conf., Chgo., 1984. Served with U.S. Army, 1955-57. Registered profl. engr., Calif. Mem. Am. Inst. Indsl. Engrs. (pres. 1981), Indsl. Mgmt. Club Central Md. (pres. 1964), Nat. Soc. Profl. Engrs., Ill. Soc. Profl. Engrs. Republican. Roman Catholic. Home: 4350 W Lake Ave Glencoe IL 60025 Office: 3650 W Lake Ave Glenview IL 60025

BELL, DAVID CURTIS, manufacturing company executive; b. St. Paul, Nov. 5, 1953; s. Dwain Curtis and Aurel Lorna (Waknitz) B.; B.A. summa cum laude with honors, Concordia Coll., 1975; postgrad. Am. U., 1973. Prodn. asst. Pako Photo, Mpls., 1975; sales rep. Pako Corp., Chgo. and eastern Wis., 1976-79; venture plant sales mgr. Pako Corp., Mpls., 1979-83; mktg. dir. system sales Multi-Arc Vacuum Systems, Inc., St. Paul, 1983—; dir. Bell Mfg. & Services, Inc., Mpls. Mem. North Side Jaycees (officer 1976-78), New Hope Jaycees (pres. 1981-82). Republican. Lutheran. Club: C-400, Kiwanis (Mpls.). Office: 261 E 5th St Saint Paul MN 55101

BELL, DELORIS WILEY, physician; b. Solomon, Kans., Sept. 30, 1942; d. Harry A. and Mildren H. (Watt) Wiley; children—Leslie and John. B.A., Kans. Wesleyan U., 1964; M.D., U. Kans., 1968. Diplomate Am. Bd. Ophthalmology. Intern St. Luke's Hosp., Kansas City, Mo., 1968-69; resident U. Kans. Med. Ctr., Kansas City, 1969-72; practice medicine specializing in ophthalmology, Overland Park, Kans., 1973—. Mem. AMA, Kans. Med. Soc. (pres. sect. ophthalmology 1985—), Am. Acad. Ophthalmology, Kansas City Soc. Ophthalmology and Otolaryngology (sec. 1984). Avocations: photography; travel. Office: 4601 W 109th St Suite 116 Overland Park KS 66211

BELL, DENIS MICHAEL, financial consultant; b. Bismarck, N.D., May 1, 1951; s. Theodore, Jr. and Joyce Lillian (Hanson) B.; student public schs. Pres., Am. Venture Resources Inc., entrepreneur cons., Brooklyn Park, Minn., 1979—. Mem. Internat. Entrepreneurs Assn. Lutheran. Home and Office: 709 5th St NE Little Falls MN 56345

BELL, DENNIS ARTHUR, lawyer; b. Chgo., July 5, 1934; s. Samuel Arthur and Frances (Gordon) B.; m. Judith Gail Young, Nov. 6, 1977. B.S. in Accountancy, U. Ill., 1955; J.D., DePaul U., 1961. Bar: U.S. Supreme Ct., 1964. C.P.A., Ill., 1956. C.P.A. Peat, Marwick Mitchell, Chgo., 1957-62; staff acct., atty. SEC, Washington, 1957-62; capital devel. officer U.S. AID, Ankara, Turkey, 1966-68; pvt. cons., Chgo., 1968-70; group controller Nat. Student Mktg. Corp., Chgo., 1970-72; dir. corp. fin. dept. and house counsel Rothschild Securities Corp., Chgo., 1973-74; corp. sec., assoc. gen. counsel Midwest Stock Exchange, 1974-79; pres. Dennis A. Bell & Assocs. Ltd., Chgo., 1979—; dir., sec., treas. Joy Internat. Corp., 1977—, Lyric Internat. Corp., Chgo. and Hong Kong, 1983—. Bd. dirs. Mental Health Assn., Chgo. Clarence Darrow Community Ctr. Served with USAR, 1957-62. Mem. ABA, Fed. Bar Assn., Ill. Bar Assn., Ill. C.P.A. Soc., Am. Soc. Corp. Secs. Democrat. Jewish. Club: Attic (Chgo.); International (Chgo.). Home: 1325 N State Pkwy 10F Chicago IL 60610 Office: Three First Nat Plaza 3410 Chicago IL 60602

BELL, JOHN MCMORRIS, title insurance company executive; b. Wichita, Kans., Dec. 1, 1930; s. Orville Allen and Mildred Frances (Baer) B.; B.S. in Bus. Adminstrn., Mo. U., 1952; m. Charlotte Ann Hatcher, Aug. 30, 1952; children—John Mitchell, Holly Susan, Jeffrey Logan. Exec. v.p. Security Abstract & Title Co., Inc., Wichita, 1954—; exec. officer Abstractors Bd. Examiners, Mo.; pres. Wesley Retirement Communities Inc. Chmn. Wichita's 100th Birthday, 1970, Wichita Bicentennial Commn., 1976; pres. Historic Wichita, 1977, Wichita Symyphony, 1977-78, 82; chmn. Republican Gov.'s Conf., 1975; mem. exec. com. Wichita Crime Commn., 1982—, Wichita State U. Endowment Com., bd. dirs. Jr. Achievement, Kans. Food Bank, 1983—, Epilepsy Kans. Inc., 1983—; mem. City Council, Eastborough, Kans. Served to 1st lt. USAF, 1952-54. Named Salesman of Yr. for Kans., Sales and Mktg. Execs., 1974; One of Top 15 Leaders in Community, Wichita Eagle, 1977; recipient Recognition award Wichita Arts Council, 1984. Mem. Am. Land Title Assn. (bd. govs. 1982—), Kans. Land Title Assn. (pres. 1968, exec. officer 1981—), Nat. Assn. Home Builders, Nat. Assn. Realtors, Wichita Execs. Assn. (pres. 1960), Wichita Area C. of C. (pres. 1972-73). Episcopalian. Lodges: Masons, Shriners, Kiwanis (chpt. pres. 1977). Home: 21 Hillcrest St Wichita KS 67208 Office: 434 N. Main St Wichita KS 67202

BELL, JOHN RICHARD, dentist; b. Peoria, Ill., May 18, 1922; s. Ross G. and Frances A. (Seiler) B.; D.D.S., Washington U., St. Louis, 1946; m. Norma Jean Oltmann, June 1979. Gen. practice dentistry, Peoria, Ill., 1946—; mem. hosp. staff St. Francis Hosp., Peoria, Ill. 1953—. Dental cons. Aetna Life & Casualty Co. Bd. dirs., past treas. Peoria County chpt. Am. Cancer Soc. Served to lt. comdr. USNR, 1954-56. Mem. Am. Dental Assn., Ill., Peoria Dist. (treas. 1963-65, pres. 1965-66) dental socs., Sigma Chi, Delta Sigma Delta. Republican. Roman Catholic. Home: 25 Oriole Ln Pekin IL 61554 Office: 1133 N North St Peoria IL 61606

BELL, NICHOLAS MONTGOMERY, II, public relations executive; b. St. Louis, May 5, 1921; s. Richard E. and Marjorie Peper (Bell) Hinrichs. Grad. Phillips Acad., 1936; A.B., Knox Coll., 1941; postgrad. Northwestern U., 1941-42. Pub. relations and fund raising counsel, Chgo., 1947-51; founder, chmn. Nicholas M. Bell II & Assocs., Chgo., 1952—. Served as commd. officer AUS, 1942-46; ETO. Mem. Pub. Relations Soc. Am., Chgo. Assn. Commerce and Industry (govt. affairs com. 1968—, ednl. com. 1968—, pub. relations com. 1968—), VFW (comdr. 1953), Sigma Nu. Episcopalian. Clubs: Lions; Minnesota (St. Paul). Office: PO Box 1427 Chicago IL 60690

BELL, ROBERT PAUL, university president; b. Charlottesville, Ind., Sept. 28, 1918; s. Paul H. and Emma Adaline (Overman) B.; B.S., Ball State Tchrs. Coll., Muncie, Ind., 1940; M.C.S., Ind. U., 1942, Ed.D., 1952; m. Margaret Cora Strattan, Apr. 3, 1942; children—Paul Strattan, Barbara Ann. Tchr. bus. Pendleton (Ind.) High Sch., 1940-41; grad. asst. Sch. Bus., Ind. U., 1941-42, instr. U.S. Naval Tng. Sch., 1942-44; instr. Lab. Sch., Sch. Edn., Ind. U., 1944-47; mem. faculty Ball State U., Muncie, 1947—, prof. head dept. bus. 1954-61, prof. bus. edn., dean div. fine and applied arts, 1961-65, dean Coll. Bus., 1964-73, v.p. bus. affairs, treas., 1972-81, univ. pres., 1981-84. Dir. Muncie Fed. Savs. & Loan Assn. Div. chmn. Muncie United Fund, 1962-63. Bd. dirs. Delaware County Soc. Crippled, 1963—, United Way, 1973—. Mem. Nat. Bus. Tchrs. Assn. (1st v.p. 1960), N. Central (pres. 1963), Nat. (bd. dirs. 1963) bus. edn. assns., Future Bus. Leaders Am. (Ind. adviser 1954-61), N.E.A., Ind. Tchrs. Assn., Nat. Thrift Com., Blue Key, Delta Pi Epsilon, Pi Omega Pi, Sigma Tau Gamma, Beta Gamma Sigma, Sigma Iota Epsilon. Clubs: Rotary (hon.), Exchange (pres. Muncie 1962-63). Author: Instructional Materials in Accounting, 1948; Instructional Materials in Typewriting, 1963, 2d edit., 1972; also articles. Editor Ball State Commerce Jour., 1954—. Home: 3200 W Beechwood Muncie IN 47304

BELL, ROGER EUGENE, marketing representative, educator; b. Kansas City, Mo., July 12, 1939; s. Iran Morris and Evelyn Flora (Kresin) B.; m. Patricia Louise Francis, June 11, 1961; children—Michael Eugene, Michelle Annette. B.A. in Bus. Adminstrn., Park Coll., Parkville, Mo., 1978; M.A. in Bus. Mgmt., Central Mich. U., 1979. With Burroughs Corp., 1962-75; mktg. rep. Sycor Inc., Kansas City, Mo., 1975-78; br. mgr. Anderson Jacobson Inc., Kansas City, Mo., 1978-80; mktg. rep. NCR Comten, Kansas City, Mo., 1980—. Prof. bus. adminstrn., mgmt. Park Coll., 1980. Mem. Park Bd. City of Lenexa (Kans.), 1983, damage assessment supr. Office of Emergency Preparedness, 1967. Served with USAF, 1957-62. Mem. Data Processing Mgmt. Assn., Sigma Iota Epsilon, Osborne Computer Users Group. Republican. Baptist. Home: 8914 Rene St Lenexa KS 66215 Office: 1601 Broadway Kansas City MO 64108

BELL, ROUZEBERRY, dentist; b. Pitts., July 13, 1934; s. Rouzeberry and Velma (Pratt) B.; children—Cheryl Lynn, Karen Diane; m. Alice McGhee, Aug. 20, 1966; 1 child, Jeffrey Sanford. B.S. in Pharmacy, U. Pitts., 1959; D.D.S., Howard U., 1970. Staff pharmacist U. Hosp. of Cleve., 1959-66, Washington Hosp. Ctr., 1966-70; staff dentist Hough Norwood Family Care Ctr., 1971-76; anesthesiology fellow St. Lukes Hosp., 1971; dental intern St. Lukes Hosp., 1970-71; gen. practice dentistry, Cleveland Heights, Ohio, 1973—; dental dir. K.W. Clement Family Health Care Ctr. Mem. Big Bros., Washington, 1966-70, Cleve., 1972-77. Served with USN, 1952-55. Mem. Forest City Dental Soc., Am. Soc. Dentistry for Children, Cleve. Dental Soc., Nat. Dental Assn., Ohio Dental Assn., Buckeye State Dental Assn., Am. Soc. Hosp. Pharmacists. Democrat. Avocations: photography; sports; record collecting. Home: 3687 Townley Rd Shaker Heights OH 44122 Office: 5 Severence Circle 413 Cleveland Heights OH 44118

BELL, SAM H., judge. U.S. Dist. judge Sixth Cir., No. Ohio, 1982—. Office: US Dist Ct 228 US Courthouse Public Square and Superior Ave Cleveland OH 44114*

BELL, THOMAS MICHAEL, home building corporation executive, realty executive; b. Marietta, Ohio, Sept. 5, 1954; s. Grosvenor Story and Louise (Crew) B. Student Ohio U., Ohio State U. Owner, mgr. Bell Properties, Columbus, Ohio, 1975—; pres. Bell Homes, Inc., Columbus, 1976—; dir. Bel-Per Properties, 1981—, Olentangy Builders, Columbus, 1979—, Columbus First Realty, 1981—; guest lectr. Coll. Bus. Adminstrn., Miami U., Ohio, various profl. groups. Mem. Building Industry Assn. Central Ohio, Columbus Bd. Realtors. Republican. Presbyterian. Home: 7691 Southwick Dr Dublin OH 43017 Office: Bell Homes Inc 1050 Freeway Dr N Suite 301 Columbus OH 43229

BELLA, DANTINA CARMEN QUARTAROLI, consultant; b. Providence, May 11, 1922; d. Bernardo and Jennie (Zinno) Quartaroli; B.A., Bryant Coll.; M.A., Alfred U., 1952, M.S. in Adminstrn., U. Notre Dame, 1973; postgrad. U. Mich., 1977; m. Salvatore J. Bella, Dec. 30, 1946; children—Theresa, Joseph, Jennifer. Rehab. counselor R.I. Dept. Edn., 1942-46; admissions counselor Coll. Bus. Adminstrn., Boston U., 1946-49; asst. to dean Coll. of Ceramics, Alfred (N.Y.) U., 1949-53; dir. pupil personnel services, asst. prin. Marian High Sch., Mishawaka, Ind., 1968-74; registrar, admissions officer Ind. Vocat. Tech. Coll., South Bend, 1974-76; resident counselor, dir. Forever Learning Inst., Harvest House, South Bend, 1977-84; cons. Potentials for Greying Ams., Notre Dame, Ind., 1984—. textbook cons. South Bend Community Sch. Corp., 1974-77; lectr., workshop coordinator, 1974-80. Bd. dirs. Cath. Social Service Center, 1968—, Women Career Center, 1974; pres. South Bend Commn. on Status of Women, 1975-78. Mem. Am. Assn. Counseling Devel., AAUW, Beta Gamma Sigma. Democrat. Roman Catholic. Author, also producer TV series Pub. Broadcasting System; Better Understanding of Self Through Literature, 1978; Mothers of the Depression, 1979. Home: 1029 Clermont Dr South Bend IN 46617 Office: Potentials for Greying Ams PO Box 505 Notre Dame IN 46556

BELLAFIORE, JOSEPH ANTHONY, dentist, consultant; b. Kansas City, Mo., Dec. 7, 1947; s. Anthony John and Rose Marie (Marrone) B.; m. Cathleen Jo Badami; children—Christina, Toni Jo, Jo Ann. D.D.S., U. Mo., 1974. Gen. practice dentistry, Kansas City, 1974-80; pres., dir., adminstr. dental corps., Kans., Mo.; cons., dir. Innovated Products Corp., Kansas City, 1979—; founder, pres. Innovative Dental Services, Inc., Kansas City, 1985—; cons. for health welfare groups, Kans., Mo., 1982—. Inventor med. device. Dentist for dental screening Kansas City Health Fair; guest speaker local schs. Kansas City. Mem. ADA, Mo. Dental Assn., Kans. Dental Assn., Greater Kansas City Dental Soc. (trustee 1979-81), Fifth Dist. Dental Soc., U. Mo. Kansas City Alumni Assn., Kansas City Convention and Visitors Bur. Roman Catholic. Clubs: Mid-Century Dental Study (Kansas City) (program chmn. 1980-81, sec., treas. 1981-82, v.p. 1982-83, pres. 1983-84), Fifth Dist. Dental Study Club (Johnson County). Avocations: golf; music; travel; private piloting. Office: 10346 State Line Rd Leawood KS 66206

BELLAH, KENNETH DAVID, lawyer; b. Joliet, Ill., Aug. 17, 1955; s. Virgil and Joyce (Allen) B.; m. Lori Ann Piazza, Nov. 26, 1983. B.A., Augustana Coll., 1977; J.D., Chgo. Kent Coll. Law, Ill. Inst. Tech., 1980. Bar: Ill. 1980, U.S. Dist. Ct. (no. dist.) Ill. 1980, U.S. Ct. Appeals (7th cir.) 1980. Assoc. Matthias & Matthias, Chgo., 1980-83; ptnr. Matthias & Bellah, Chgo., 1983—. Mem. Chgo. Bar Assn., Ill. State Bar Assn. Republican. Methodist. Club: Union League of Chgo. Office: Matthias & Bellah 230 W Monroe St Suite 2220 Chicago IL 60606

BELLAIRS, HERBERT JACK, medical social worker, educator; b. Rochester, Mich., Jan. 2, 1941; s. Herbert Henry and Lottie Pearl (Evans) B.; m. Kathleen Sue Ernsberger, June 9, 1962; children—Colleen, Peggy Ann, Rebecca. B.R.E., Grand Rapids Bapt. Coll., 1963; M.S.W., Wayne State U., 1972. Cert. Registry of Clin. Social Workers. Asst. to pastor, 1st Bapt. Ch., Rochester, 1964-66; child care worker Pontiac State Hosp. (Mich.), 1967-70, instl. social worker, 1967-70; clin. social work supr. Clinton Valley Ctr., Pontiac, 1970-74; dir. social services Bapt. Children's Agy., St. Louis, Mich., 1974-76; dir. social services Meml. Hosp., South Bend, Ind., 1976-83; assoc. instr. Bethel Coll., Mishawaka, Ind., 1977—; pvt. practice in counseling, 1977—. Bd. advisers Compassionate Friends of St. Joseph County, Hospice of St. Joseph County, Kelley Home Health Services; bd. dirs. Child Abuse and Neglect Coordination. Recipient Green Derby award Kelley Home Health Services, 1979. Mem. Nat. Assn. Social Workers, Acad. Cert. Social Workers, Ind. Soc. Hosp. Social Work Dirs. (bd. dirs., sec.), Nat. Soc. Hosp. Social Workers, Ind. Hosp. Assn. Am. Hosp. Assn. Democrat. Mem. Evangelical Ch. Author weekly column, Reflections, Mishawaka Enterprise. Home: 3834 E 10th St Mishawaka IN 46544 Office: Memorial Hosp 615 N Michigan St South Bend IN 46601

BELLAMY, JOHN, JR., recording co. exec.; b. Chgo., Dec. 15, 1948; s. John Prather and Viola (Miles) P.; student Malcolm X Coll., 1969-72; m. Shannon Vernon, Dec. 23, 1967; children—Angela, Latasha. Driver salesman Capitol Laundry, 1965-67; letter carrier U.S. Postal Service, Chgo., 1969-75; pres. Source Records, Chgo., 1974—; Artistic Communications, Inc., 1982—; pres., chmn. bd. dirs. Black Arts Celebration, Inc., Chgo., 1975—; adminstrv. asst. Soc. Writers and Editors Am., 1974-75. Adv. bd. Pro and Con Screening Bd., 1977—; bd. dirs. Chgo. Soc. Writers and Editors, 1975-76; 6th Annual Conf. Steering Com. Ill. Commn. on Human Relations, 1979; bd. dirs., exec. com. League Chgo. Theatres, 1981; mem. hypertension subcom. City of Chgo. Health Systems Agy., 1981; coordinator Dick Gregory Run Against Hunger, 1974-76; panelist Nat. Coll. of Edn., 1979; judge Alpha Kappa Internat. Year of the Child, 1979; Ill. caucus treas. Nat. Assn. Community Based Orgns., 1980-81; del. 11th World Festival Youth and Students, Cuba, 1978; active NAACP, Operation PUSH, So. Christian Leadership Conf.; interim bd. dirs. Ill. Arts Alliance, 1981; chmn. Community Cable Com., 1981; mem. adv. com. Chgo. Public Library Cultural Ctr., 1981—. Served with U.S. Army, 1967-69; Vietnam. Decorated Purple Heart; recipient Image award Fred Hampton Scholarship Fund, 1967, Inspiration of Youth Community Achievement award, 1976, Community Spotlight award Sta. WVON, 1980, Gov.'s award for Arts, 1981. Mem. Lowrey Nickerson Edn. Advancement Inst. Producer Slow Motion Suicide (by Mavis Staples), 1980, Ascension, female vocal group, 1980, 81, First World Symphony, 1980, 81, film/video documentary Dick Gregory Run Against Hunger, 1974, 76; producer, mgr. musical group Grand Slam, 1983, music video producer, 1983; talent coordinator, producer TV spl. Celebration of Life: A Tribute to Martin Luther King Jr. Office: 39 S LaSalle St Suite 825 Chicago IL 60603

BELLAS, ROBERT CALDWELL, JR., venture capitalist; b. Miami, Fla., Mar. 23, 1942; s. Robert Caldwell and Audrey (Conner) B.; B.S., U.S. Naval Acad., 1966; M.B.A., Stanford U., 1973; m. Terrye Lynn Armstrong, July 1, 1967; children—Tamsinn, Erika. Vice pres. mktg. EMI Therapy Systems, Inc., Sunnyvale, Calif., 1973-78; dir. mktg. Acurex Corp., Mountain View, Calif., 1978-80; gen. mgr. Crystal and Electronic Products div. Harshaw/Gulf Oil Co., Solon, Ohio, 1980-83; gen. ptnr. Morgenthaler Venture Ptnrs., Cleve., 1983—. Served to lt. USN, 1966-71; Vietnam. Mem. Stanford U. Alumni Assn., U.S. Naval Acad. Alumni Assn. Republican. Home: Woodstock Rd Gates Mills OH 44040 Office: 700 Nat City Bank Bldg Cleveland OH 44114

BELLETIRE, MICHAEL ANDREW, government official; b. Chgo., Apr. 25, 1946; s. John Frank and Dorothy Elizabeth (Curtis) B.; m. Ann Elizabeth Brainard, Jan. 2, 1970; children—James, Joshua, Elizabeth. B.S., Ill. Inst. Tech., 1969; M.S., Northwestern U., 1977. Supr. project mgmt. City of Chgo. Com. Urban Opportunities, 1970-72; research asst. Sch. Mgmt. Northwestern U., Evanston, Ill., 1972-74; asst. dir. Gov.'s Office of Manpower, Springfield, Ill., 1974-77; ops. chief Ill. Dept. Pub. Aid, Springfield, 1977-82; asst. to dep. gov. State of Ill., Springfield, 1982-83; dir. Ill. Dept. Mental Health and Devel. Disabilities, Springfield, 1983—; mem. manpower council City of Chgo. Manpower Dept., 1978-82; mem. employment and training council Ill. Dept. Commerce and Community Affairs, Springfield, 1978-81. Vice pres. Edgewater Community Council, Chgo., 1972-74; elected mem. Springfield Bd. Edn., 1977-80; commr. Springfield Human Rights Authority, 1979-82; v.p. Springfield Theatre Guild, 1980—; mem. Model Cities North Area Council, Chgo., 1971-73. Northwestern U. Urban Affairs Ctr. fellow, 1974. Mem. Nat. Assn. State Mental Health Dirs. (com. chmn. 1984). Presbyterian. Avocation: sporting activities. Home: 1933 S Glenwood St Springfield IL 62704 Office: Ill Dept Mental Health 401 Stratton Bldg Springfield IL 62706

BELLON, ERROL MANFRED, radiologist, educator, researcher; b. Beaufort West, South Africa, May 13, 1938; s. Michael and Roslyn (Sklaar) B.; m. Eveline Morgenstern, Apr. 5, 1962; children—Steven F., Richard J., Jennifer R. M.D., U. Cape Town (South Africa), 1961. Diplomate Am. Bd. Radiology. Intern Groote Schuur Hosp., Cape Town, 1962; resident in radiology Mpilo Central Hosp., Bulawayo, Rhodesia, 1963; resident in radiology Univ. Hosps. Cleve., 1964-67, asst. radiologist, 1967—; chief radiology service VA Hosp., Cleve., 1968-73; assoc. dir. dept. radiology Cuyahoga County Hosp., Cleve., 1973-76, dir. dept. radiology, 1976—; asst. prof. radiology Case Western Res. U., Cleve., 1968-73, assoc. prof., 1973-82, prof., 1982—; surveyor AMA Joint Rev. Com. on Edn. in Radiologic Tech., 1975—. James Picker Found. scholar, 1967-69. Fellow Am. Coll. Radiology; mem. Radiol. Soc. N.Am., Soc. Photo-Optical Instrumentation Engrs., Assn. Univ. Radiologists, Am. Roentgen Ray Soc., Am. Acad. Med. Dirs. Author: Radiologic Interpretation of ERCP: A Clinical Atlas, 1983 also sci. papers. Office: Dept Radiology 3395 Scranton Rd Cleveland OH 44109

BELLO-REUSS, ELSA NOEMI, physician, educator; b. Buenos Aires, Argentina, May 1, 1939; d. Jose F. and Julia M. (Hiriart) Bello; came to U.S., 1972; B.S., Assn. (kidney council), Chile, 1957, M.D., 1964; m. Luis Reuss, Apr. 15, 1965; children—Luis F., Alejandro E. Intern J.J. Aguirre Hosp., Chile, 1963-64; resident in internal medicine U. Chile, Santiago, 1964-66; practice medicine specializing in nephrology Santiago, Chile, 1967-72; Internat. NIH fellow U. N.C., Chapel Hill, 1972-74; vis. asst. prof. physiology U. N.C., Chapel Hill, 1974-75; Louis Welt fellow U. N.C.-Duke U. Med. Center, 1975-76; asst. prof. medicine and physiology Washington U. Sch. of Medicine, St. Louis, 1976—, Jewish Hosp. of St. Louis, 1976—. Mem. Internat., Am. socs. nephrology, Am. Fedn. Clin. Research, N.Y. Acad. Scis., AAAS, Am. Heart Assn. (Kidney Council), Am. Physiol. Soc. Contbr. articles on nephrology and physiology to med. jours.; also chpt. in splty. book. Office: 660 S Euclid Ave Box 8101 Saint Louis MO 63110

BELLOS, MICHAEL BRUCE, sales representative; b. Chgo., June 9, 1954; s. Allen Sheldon and Rena (Taich) B. B.S. in Broadcasting, U. Wis.-Oshkosh, 1976. Broadcast engr. Sta. WGN Radio and TV, Chgo., 1976-77; diamond salesman I. Starck Co., Chgo., 1977-78; nat. watch salesman G.K.G. Inc., Skokie, Ill., 1978—; spokesman for G.K.G. Midwest Product Knowledge Seminar, Chgo., 1984—. Recipient $1,000,000 Sales Achievement award Seiko Time Corp., 1980, 81, 82, 83, $2,000,000 Sales Achievement award Seiko Time Corp., 1984. Mem. Chgo. Salesman Alliance, Golden Roosters. Jewish. Avocations: sailboat racing; water and snow skiing; martial arts. Home: 224 Charles Pl Wilmette IL 60091

BELLOW, SAUL, writer; b. Lachine, Que., Can., June 10, 1915; s. Abraham and Liza (Gordon) B.; student U. Chgo., 1933-35; B.S., Northwestern U., 1937, Litt.D., 1962; hon. degrees Bard Coll., 1962, Harvard U., 1972, Yale U., 1972, McGill U., 1973, Brandeis U., 1974, Hebrew Union Coll.-Jewish Inst. Religion, 1976, Trinity Coll., Dublin, 1976; m. Alexandra Bagdasar; children—Gregory, Adam, Daniel. Tchr., Pestalozzi-Froebel Tchrs. Coll., Chgo., 1938-42; mem. editorial dept. Ency. Britannica, Chgo., 1943-46; faculty mem. Bard Coll., N.Y., 1953-54; faculty Princeton U., N.Y. U., U. Minn.; faculty English dept. U. Chgo., 1963—, mem. Com. on Social Thought, 1963—, chmn., 1970-76, now Raymond W. and Martha Hilpert Gruner Disting. Service prof.; Jefferson lectr. Nat. Endowment Humanities Decorated Croix de Chevalier des Arts et Lettres (France); recipient Nat. Inst. Arts and letters award, 1952; Nat. Book Award in Fiction for The Adventures of Augie March, 1954, Herzog, 1965, Mr. Sammier's Planet, 1970; Friends of Lit. Fiction award, 1960; Internat. Lit. prize, 1965; Communicator of Year award, U. Chgo., 1971; Soc. Midland Authors Fiction award, 1976; Nobel Prize for lit., 1976; O'Henry prize for short Story A Silver Dish, Guggenheim fellow, 1955-56; Ford Found. grantee, 1959-61. Mem. Am. Acad. Arts and Scis. Author: Dangling Man, 1944; The Victim, 1947; Best Stories of 1950; The Adventures of Augie March, 1953; Seize The Day, 1956; Henderson The Rain King, 1959; Herzog, 1964; (Internat. Lit. prize 1965, James L. Dow award, 1964); Mosby's Memoirs and Other Stories, 1968; Mr. Sammier's Planet, 1969; Technology and the Frontiers of Knowledge, 1974; Humboldt's Gift, 1975 (Pulitzer Prize 1976); To Jerusalem and Back: A Personal Account, 1976; The Dean's December, 1982; contbr. fiction to nat. mags. and lit. quars. Address: care Com on Social Thought U Chicago 1126 E 59th St Chicago IL 60637

BELLOWS, GLEN LEE, consulting engineer; b. Spencer, Iowa, Jan. 9, 1937; s. Glen LeVern and Virginia Irene (Adams) B.; B.S. in M.E., U. Ill., 1959; m. Sylvia Ruth Dean, June 11, 1959; children—Alice, Ann (dec.), Kevin, Peter. Mech. engr. Brown, Manthei, Davis & Mullins, Champaign, Ill., 1959-65; prin., pres. Buchanan, Bellows & Assocs., Ltd., Bloomington, Ill., 1966—; tchr. seminar Am. Mgmt. Assn., 1974. Bd. dirs. McLean County Occupational Devel. Center, 1969-78, treas., 1972-73, 75-78; vice chmn. Bloomington Bldg. Code Rev. Bd., 1972—; mem. Bloomington Heating and Cooling Bd., 1969-73, Normal (Ill.) Heating and Cooling Bd., 1973—, chmn., 1979—. Registered profl. engr., Ill. Mem. ASHRAE, Constrn. Specifications Inst., Nat., Ill. socs. profl. engrs., Ill. C. of C., Nat. Fire Protection Assn., Delta Sigma Omicron (Harold Sharper service award 1959). Republican. Mormon (ward bishop 1977-84, welfare services region agt. 1984—). Home: 210 Foster Dr Normal IL 61761 Office: 1509 N Clinton Blvd Bloomington IL 61701

BELLOWS, RANDALL TRUEBLOOD, ophthalmologist; b. Chgo., June 1, 1946; s. John D. and Mary Frances (Trueblood) B. B.S., Northwestern U., 1968, M.D., 1971. Intern, Los Angeles County-U. So. Calif., 1972; resident U. Fla., Gainesville, 1972-75; practice medicine specializing in eye surgery and diseases, Chgo., 1975—; assoc. dir. Am. Soc. Contemporary Medicine, Surgery and Ophthalmology, 1975—; chmn., head dept. surgery Henrotin Hosp., 1981-83; cons. Chgo. Bd. Edn. Editor Glaucoma Jour., Annals of Ophthalmology, Jour. Ocular Therapy and Surgery, Comprehensive Therapy. Contbr. articles to profl. jours., chpts. to textbooks. Recipient cert. of competence in ophthalmic practice. Mem. AMA (recognition award 1981, 82, 83), Am. Soc. Contemporary Ophthalmology, Am. Soc. Contemporary Medicine and Surgery, AAAS, Am. Acad. Ophthalmology, Am. Intraocular Implant Soc., Chgo. Med. Soc., Ill. Med. Soc., Chgo. Inst. Medicine, Chgo. Ophthmol. Soc., Pan-Am. Assn. Ophthalmology, Internat. Glaucoma Congress, Internat. Assn. Ocular Surgeons. Office: 211 E Chicago Ave 1044 Chicago IL 60611

BELLUSCHI, ANTHONY C., architect; b. Portland, Oreg., Aug. 2, 1941; s. Pietro and Helen (Hemila) B.; m. Helen Risom, June 25, 1966 (div. 1975); children—Pietro Antonio, Catharine Camilla. B.Arch., R.I. Sch. Design, 1966. Lic. architect, N.Y., Mass., R.I., Vt., Calif., N.J., Oreg., Ill., Fla., Ga. Draftsman, Ernest Kump Assocs., San Francisco, 1964; designer Zimmer-Gunsel-Frasca, Portland, Oreg., 1965; assoc. Jung, Brannen Assocs., Boston, 1968-73; prin., treas. Belluschi, Daskalakis Inc., Boston, 1973-77; sr. v.p. Charles Kober Assocs., Los Angeles, 1977-84; mng. ptnr. Kober, Belluschi Assocs., Chgo., 1984—; pres. Anthony Belluschi Assocs. Inc., 1984—; exec. com. Archtl. Fabric Structures Inst., Chgo., 1983—; archtl. cons. U.S. Peace Corps, El Salvador, 1966-68. Recipient First Prize, Sculpture Contest, RKO & Reden Agy., Boston, 1973; Award of Merit, Mass. Commn. Housing, 1975; Alumni of Yr. award, R.I. Sch. Design, 1982-83. Mem. AIA, Urban Land Inst., Internat. Council Shopping Ctrs., R.I. Sch. Design Alumni Assn. (chmn., founder, pres. Avocations: Photography; stamps, coins; automobiles, skiing. Home: 50 E Bellevue Pl #405 Chicago IL 60611 Office: Kober/Belluschi Assocs Architects & Planners 30 W Monroe St Suite 500 Chicago IL 60603

BELLUZZI, MICHAEL JOSEPH, computer systems consultant, educator; b. Chgo., July 30, 1950; s. Louis Joseph and Mary Ellyn (Martinucci) B. B.A., Elmhurst Coll., 1974, B.S., 1978; M.B.A., DePaul U., 1982. Prin. Michael J. Belluzzi & Assocs., Computer System Cons., Northlake, Ill., 1974—; asst. prof. computer sci. DeVry Inst. of Tech., Chgo., 1981-82; asst. prof. data processing William Rainey Harper Coll., Palatine, Ill., 1982-84; lectr. computer sci. Roosevelt U., Chgo., 1983—; adj. prof. math. Elmhurst Coll., Ill., 1983-84; adj. prof. computer literacy Columbia Coll., Chgo., 1985—. Mem. Assn. Systems Mgmt. (sec. Chgo. chpt. 1984, editor 1984), Data Processing Mgmt. Assn., Ind. Computer Cons. Assn., Epsilon Delta Pi, Phi Theta Kappa, Psi Chi, Pi Gammu Mu, Delta Mu Delta, Alpha Kappa Lambda, Beta Gamma Sigma. Roman Catholic. Avocations: numismatics; bibliophily; weight-lifting. Office: Michael J Belluzzi & Assocs Computer Systems Cons PO Box 2087 Northlake IL 60164

BELMONTE, STEVEN JOSEPH, hotel chain executive; b. Oak Park, Ill., Aug. 25, 1952; s. Silvio J. and Vilma (Giannini) B.; B.A. in Hotel Mgmt., Wright Coll., Chgo., 1974; student Holiday Inn U., Memphis, 1974; B.M. in Innkeeping, Harper Coll., Rolling Meadows, Ill., 1981; 1 son, Gino Anthony. With Hyatt Hotels, Inc., 1971; dir. sales Holiday Inns, Chgo., 1974-78, gen. mgr., O'Hare Airport Holiday Inn, regional dir., Schiller Park, Ill., 1978—; speaker Ill. Budget for Tourism, 1978-81. Bd. advisors Wright Jr. Coll.; mem. Joint Civic Com. Italian Ams.; co-chmn. Citizens for Percy, 1984; active fund raiser for various charities and retirement homes. Recipient citation Italo-Am. War Vets. U.S., 1980. Mem. Am. Soc. Travel Agts., Hotel Sales Mgmt. Assn., Soc. Mng. Execs., Justinian Soc. Lawyers, Am. Automobile Assn., Schiller Park C. of C., Chgo. Innkeepers Assn. (v.p. 1979-81). Home and office: 3801 N Manheim Rd Schiller Park IL 60176

BELONGIA, CLAY O., banking executive; b. Oconto Falls, Wis., July 24, 1948; s. David and Stella (Venne) B.; m. Carolyn M., Aug. 9, 1969; children—Mark, Jennifer. B.A. in Bus. Adminstrn. and Econs., U. Wis.-Platteville, 1970; grad. Nat. Comml. Lending Grad. Sch., 1981. With Maywood-Proviso State Bank (Ill.), now v.p. loans, dir. Mem. Villa Park Zoning Bd.; pres. N. Terrace Park Homeowners Assn. Mem. Tau Kappa Epsilon. Office: 411 Madison St Maywood IL 60153

BELOTE, GLENDA ANN, university administrator, b. Detroit, Dec. 1, 1938; d. Richard Tyler and Virginia Mae (Carpenter) B.; B.A. Western Mich. U., 1960; M.A., Mich. State U., 1969, Ph.D., 1973. Tchr. English, history San Diego City Schs., 1960-62; tchr. English, Pontiac, Mich., 1963-66; residence hall staff Mich. State U., 1966-69, grad. assoc., 1971-72; dir. residence life Grand Valley State Coll., Allendale, Mich., 1969-71, dir. counseling and testing, 1972-73; dir. counseling, state devel. Southwest State Coll., Marshall, Mich., 1973-75; asst. dir. Counseling Ctr., Ohio State U., Columbus, 1975-79, assoc. dir. residence and dining halls, 1979—. Mem. Am. Coll. Personnel Assn., Nat. Assn. Women Deans, Adminstrs. Counselors, Am. Assn. Counseling and Devel., Phi Delta Kappa. Clubs: University Golf, Zonta, Leatherlips Yacht (Columbus). Avocations: sailing; golf. Home: 2458 Edgevale Rd Upper Arlington OH 43221

BELSARE, JAYANT VISHNU, physician; b. Sinnar, India, Dec. 19, 1938; s. Vishnu Govind and Triveni Vishnu (Khaladkar) B.; came to U.S., 1967; M.B., B.S., U. Poona, 1963; M.S., 1966; children—Shubhada, Geeta Nandini. Intern, CPR Hosp., Kolhapur, India, 1962; resident in gen. surgery Sassoon Hosps., Poona, 1963-64, in anesthesia, 1964-65, in orthopedics, 1965; jr. lectr. B.J. Med. Coll., Poona, 1965-66; hon. surgeon Talegaon Gen. Hosp. (India), 1966-67; resident surgery Watts Hosp., Durham, N.C., 1967-69, Johnston Willis Hosp., Richmond, Va., 1969-71; preceptee surgery Surg. Asso., Mason City, Iowa, 1971-72; pvt. practice surgery, Clarinda, Iowa, 1972-73, Mt. Pleasant, Iowa, 1973—; mem. staff Henry County Health Center, Mt. Pleasant, Burlington (Iowa) Med. Center; med. adviser Henry County Cancer Soc. Diplomate Am. Bd. Surgery. Fellow Royal Coll. Surgeons Can.; mem. ACS, Iowa, Henry County med. socs., AMA, Iowa Acad. Surgery, Mt. Pleasant C. of C. Home: 612 N Lincoln Mount Pleasant IA 52641 Office: 114 E Monroe St Mount Pleasant IA 52641

BELTER, EDGAR WILLIAM, clergyman, addiction clinic administrator; b. Guttenberg, Iowa, Jan. 6, 1929; s. Robert Rudolf and Erna Dora (Teegan) B.; B.A., Carthage Coll., 1948, D.D., 1969; M.Div., N.W. Lutheran Theol. Sem., 1951; m. Deloris Ann Koenig, July 10, 1954; children—Timothy William, Christine Ann. Ordained to ministry Lutheran Ch., 1951; pastor Peace Luth. Ch., Steelville, Ill., 1951-57; asst. to pres. Wartburg Synod, United Luth. Ch. in Am., 1958, 59; sr. pastor Emmanuel Luth. Ch., Racine, Wis., 1959-69; pres., exec. dir. A-Center, Racine, 1969—; dir. Carthage Addiction Inst., 1969—; chmn. legis. com. Alcohol/Drug Problems Assn. N.Am., 1972—, bd. dirs., chmn. bd. mgrs., council of agys., 1977—; chmn. Gov.'s Task Force Alcohol-Drug Ins., 1970-76, Nat. Invitational Policy Forum on Alcohol/Drugs, 1982—; cons. Nat. Inst. Drug Abuse, S.C. Commn. on Alcohol and Drugs, Wis. Bur. Alcohol and Other Drug Abuse; mem. program rev. com. S.E. Wis. Health Systems Agy.; mem. alcohol/drug adv. com. Mission in N. Am. div. Luth. Ch. Am., 1977-78; dir. Wis.-Upper Mich. Synod, Luth. Ch. Am., Strength for Mission Campaign, 1977-78. Pres. Racine County Mental Health Assn., 1969-72; v.p. Wis. Mental Health Assn., 1972-74. Mem. Alcohol/Drug Problems Assn. N. Am. (treas. 1980—), Wis. Alcohol Drug Treatment Providers Assn. (pres. 1982—), Racine Mfg. and Employers Assn. (dir.). Home: 6520 Hoods Creek Rd Franksville WI 53126 Office: A-Center 2000 Domanik Dr Racine WI 53404

BELTON, JOHN THOMAS, lawyer; b. Yonkers, N.Y., Feb. 24, 1947; s. Harry James and Anne Marie (Kupko) B.; m. Linda Susanne Cheugh, Jan. 6, 1973; 1 child, Joseph Timothy. B.A., Ohio State U., 1972; postgrad. in bus. adminstrn. 1972-73; J.D., Ohio No. U., 1976. Bar: Ohio 1977. Sole practice, Columbus, Ohio, 1976-83; ptnr. Belton, Goldwin & Cheugh, Columbus, 1983—; arbitrator Franklin County Ct. Common Pleas, 1983—; dir. Weeks-Finneran Inc. Republican precinct chmn., 1983; v.p. Far Northwest Coalition, 1984; mem. ch. council St. Peter's Parish, 1984—. Served with USAF, 1968-71. Mem. Dublin Jr. C. of C., ABA, Columbus Bar Assn. (com. chmn. 1976—), U.S. Dist. Ct. Fed. Bar, Ohio Bar Assn., Assn. Trial Lawyers Am., Order of Barristers, Omicron Delta Kappa, Phi Alpha Delta (justice 1975). Clubs: The Pres., Ohio State Alumni, Republican Glee. Republican. Roman Catholic. Lodge: K.C. Avocations: reading; chess; golf; racquetball; recreational activities. Home: 2510 Slateshire Dr Dublin OH 43017 Office: Belton Golowin & Cheugh 2066 W Henderson Rd Columbus OH 43220

BELTZ, CHARLES ROBERT, engineer; b. Pitts., Feb. 23, 1913; s. Charles Fred and Ester (Johnston) B.; student Greenbrier Mil. Sch., 1930-33; M.E., Cornell U., 1934; B.S. in Aero. Engring., U. Pitts., 1937; m. Amy Margaret Ferguson, Oct. 23, 1935; children—Charles R., A.M. Bonnie (Mrs. Hatch), Homer F., William T., Carol E. (Mrs. Marks), M. Joy (Mrs. O'Keefe). Engr. Crane Co., 1937-39; design engr. Stout Skycraft Corp., 1939-43; project engr. Cycle-Weld Labs., 1943-44; project engr., mgr. Fairchild E & A Corp., Roosevelt Field, 1944-46; corp. engr. Chrysler Corp., 1946-47; pres. Beltz Engring. Labs., 1950—. Mem. Nat. Aero. Assn. Am. Heating, Refrigerating and Air Conditioning Engrs. (contbg. author), Engring. Soc. Detroit, Detroit Hist. Soc., Internat. Plastic Aircraft Soc., Air Force Assn. Clubs: Aero (dir.), Economic, Curling (Detroit); Grosse Pointe Yacht; Lost Lake Woods. Author: Ice Skating; Skating Weather or Not: ABC's Air-conditioning; Roatable Aircraft. Address: 500 Lakeland Ave Grosse Pointe MI 48230

BELZER, FOLKERT OENE, surgeon; b. Soerabaja, Indonesia, Oct. 5, 1930; s. Peter and Jacoba H. (Gorter) B.; came to U.S., 1951, naturalized, 1956; A.B., Colby Coll., Waterville, Maine, 1953; M.A., Boston U., 1954, M.D., 1958; m. Aug. 4, 1956; children—Ingrid J., John B., G. Eric, Paul O. Intern, Grace-New Haven Hosp., 1958-59, asst. resident, 1960-62; chief resident U. Oreg. Med. Sch., 1962-63, instr. surgery, 1963-64; asst. research surgeon U. Calif. Med. Center, San Francisco, 1964, asst. prof. surgery, 1966-69, asst. prof. ambulatory and community medicine, 1966-69, asst. chief Transplant Service, 1967-69, co-chief, 1969-72, chief, 1972-74, asso. prof. surgery, 1969-72, asso. prof. ambulatory and community medicine, 1969-72, prof. surgery, 1972-74, dir. Exptl. Surgery Labs., 1973-74; sr. lectr. Guys Hosp., London, Eng., 1964-66; prof., chmn. dept. surgery U. Wis., Madison, 1974—, A.R. Curreri prof. surgery, 1982—. Recipient Samuel Harvey award as outstanding resident, 1960. Diplomate Am. Bd. Surgery. Mem. A.C.S., Am., Calif. med. assns., Am. (pres. 1975), Calif. (pres. 1970-72) socs. transplant surgeons, Am., Central surg. assns., Calif. Acad. Medicine, Halsted Soc., Howard C. Naffziger, Madison, Pacific Coast, San Francisco (chmn. program com. 1973-74), Wis. surg. socs., Nat. Kidney Found. (vice chmn. com. on dialysis and transplantation 1974-76), Société Internationale de Chirurgie, Soc. Vascular Surgery, Soc. Surg. Chairmen, Soc. U. Surgeons, Surg. Biology Club III, Transplantation Soc., Whipple Soc. Republican. Contbr. articles to med. jours. Developed method and machine for human kidney preservation. Home: 6105 S Highlands Dr Madison WI 53705 Office: U Wis Center for Health Scis 600 N Highland Ave Madison WI 53706

BELZER, JEFFREY A., lawyer, automobile dealer and developer; b. Mpls., Sept. 8, 1941; s. Meyer S. and Kathleen (Bardin) B.; B.A., St. Cloud State U., 1963; J.D., Drake U., 1968; children—Steven, Michael, Anna, Jeffrey. Admitted to Minn. bar, 1968, U.S. Dist. Ct. bar., 1969; mem. firm Henretta, Muirhead, McGinty, Ltd., Mpls., 1968-71; pres., sr. atty. Belzer & Brenner Ltd., Mpls., 1971-80; pres., dir. Walesch Devel. Co., Mpls., 1969—, Walsch Estates, Inc., Mpls., 1971—, Jeff Belzer's Todd Chevrolet Inc., Lakeville, Minn., 1980—. Mem. Am., Hennepin County, Minn. bar assns., Phi Alpha Delta. Staff: Drake Law Rev., 1966-67. Office: PO Box 965 Hwy 50 and Cedar Ave Lakeville MN 55044

BENBOW, DONALD WALLACE, mathematics educator; b. Clear Lake, Iowa, June 26, 1936; s. Robert Benjiman and Ruth Louise (Maxfield) B.; m. Martha Jane Johnson, Nov. 15, 1958; children—Mark Wayne, Pamela Sue, Timothy Jon, Elizabeth Anne. B.S. in Math., Iowa State U., 1959; M.S. in Math., Mich. State U., 1966. Profl. teaching cert. State Iowa. Tchr. math. Marshalltown High Sch., Iowa, 1959-66; instr. dept. math. and engring. Marshalltown Community Coll., Iowa, 1966—. Served to 2d lt. U.S. Army, 1960. Mem. Am. Assn. Engring. Educators, Soc. Mfg. Engrs. Home: 909 S 8th Ave Marshalltown IA 50158 Office: Marshalltown Community Coll 3700 S Center St Marshalltown IA 50158

BENCHIK, EDWARD JOHN (JACK), city official, safety engineer, columnist; b. Logansport, Ind., May 25, 1938; s. Edward Andre and Betty Jane (Bowen) B.; m. Rosemary Cecelia Boughal, July 4, 1964; children—Edward Patrick, Jacquelyn Rosemary, Marilyn Cecelia. B.S. in Geology, U. Notre Dame, 1959, postgrad. in law, 1972-73; M.S. in Engring., L.I. U., 1971. Registered instr. Nat. Safety Council. Geologist, NASA Apollo Project, Grumman Aerospace Corp., 1968-71; engring. mgr. Facilities Devel. Corp., 1971-72; mem. staff U. Notre Dame, South Bend, Ind., 1972-73; safety engr. Travelers Ins. Co., Cleve., 1973-77; cons. Safety Engring. Resources, Inc., South Bend, 1977-80; safety dir., risk mgr. City of South Bend (Ind.), 1980—; philatelic writer Cleve. Press, 1975-80. Treas. Mayor's Citizen Traffic Commn. Served with C.E., U.S. Army, 1960-68; maj. Res. and N.G. Recipient Zone Chmn. award Greater Cleve. council Boy Scouts Am., 1976; Apollo Achievement award NASA, 1969; named hon. Ky. Col. Mem. Am. Soc. Safety Engrs. (past pres. Michiana sect.), U. Notre Dame Band Alumni Assn. (pres.), South Bend C. of C. (chmn. safety sect. 1977-79, Nat. Eagle Scout Assn.). Clubs: Elks, Collectors. Editor: The Czechoslovak Specialist, 1969-71. Home: 2104 Rockne Dr South Bend IN 46617 Office: City of South Bend County City Bldg South Bend IN 46601

BENCIN, EDWARD STEVEN, fire department chief; b. Cleve., Nov. 7, 1945; s. Edward Joseph and Mary Frances (Parillo) B.; m. Karen Anne Schikowski, June 21, 1969; children—Amanda Jeanne, Stephanie Lynn. A.A., Cuyahoga Community Coll., 1969. Mgr. Pick-n-Pay, Cleve., 1962-68, Stop-n-Shop, Cleve., 1968-73; fire chief City of Highland Heights, Ohio, 1973—. Coordinator Greater Cleve. council Boy Scouts Am., 1983-84. Mem. Internat. Fire Chiefs Assn., Ohio Fire Chiefs Assn., N.E. Ohio Fire Chiefs Assn., Nat. Fire Protection Assn., N.E. Ohio Fire Prevention Assn. Club: North Coast Investment. Home: 943 Rose Blvd Highland Heights OH 44143 Office: City of Highland Heights 5827 Highland Rd Highland Heights OH 44143

BENCKENDORF, DAVID ALAN, lawyer; b. Peoria, Ill., Nov. 29, 1956; s. Glenn Eldon and Norma Jean (Wilson) B.; m. Sandra Bowers, Nov. 29, 1980; children—Rynell Jean, Alexander Brehm. B.S. cum laude, Bradley U., 1977; J.D., U. Ill., 1981. Bar: Ill. 1981, U.S. Dist. Ct. (cen. dist.) Ill. 1981. Ptnr. Benckendorf & Benckendorf, Peoria, 1981—. Mem. land use adv. com. Tri-County Planning Commn., East Peoria, Ill., 1982—; bd. dirs. League Women Voters Peoria, 1982-83, Peoria Civic Opera Co., 1985—; pres. Tazewell County Young Reps., 1985; Mem. Ill. State Bar Assn., Peoria County Bar Assn. Republican. Methodist. Office: Benckendorf & Benckendorf 101 NE Randolph Peoria IL 61606

BENDEL, WILLIAM LOUIS, JR., physician; b. Monroe, La., Mar. 1, 1921; s. William Louis and Marie (Gariepy) B.; B.S., Tulane U., 1941, M.D., 1944; Ph.D. in microbiology, Baylor U., 1966; m. Margaret Rose Butler, Feb. 18, 1944 (dec. Jan. 1970); children—Susan Marie, Jan Ann; m. 2d, Kathleen Doris Mabley, Apr. 16, 1971. Intern, Charity Hosp., New Orleans, 1944, resident gen. surgery, 1949-52, resident thoracic surgery, 1952; resident gen. surgery Mt. Carmel Mercy Hosp., Detroit, 1947-48; surgery teaching fellow Tulane U., New Orleans, 1948-49; gen. practice medicine, Monroe, 1953-58; resident pathology Baylor U. Med. Center, Dallas, 1959-63; dir. labs. Unity Hosp., Mpls. Served from 1st lt. to capt., M.C., AUS, 1945-46. Diplomate in anatomic pathology and clin. pathology Am. Bd. Pathology, Am. Bd. Med. Microbiology. Mem. AMA, Minn., Hennepin County med. assns., Holy Name Soc., Alpha Kappa Kappa, Kappa Sigma. Republican. Roman Catholic. Club: K.C. (4 deg.). Contbr. numerous articles to med. jours. Home: 14501 Atrium Way Apt 223 Minnetonka MN 55345 Office: Unity Hosp Fridley MN 55432

BENDER, CARL AUGUST, mfg. co. safety and security ofcl.; b. Belleville, Ill., Mar. 27, 1929; s. August Carl and Mattie Elizabeth (DeTienne) B.; A.A. in Engring., Belleville Twp. Jr. Coll., 1950; A.S. in Police Sci., Belleville Area Coll., 1975; B.S. in Bus. Adminstrn., So. Ill. U., Edwardsville, 1978, postgrad., 1979—; m. Olga Eloise Jennings, Jan. 10, 1954; children—Nancy Lee, Janet Lee, Gary Carl, Donald Allen. Patrolman, Belleville Police Dept., 1950-51; served as enlisted man U.S. Air Force, 1951-52, commd. 2d lt., 1952, advanced through grades to lt. col., 1969; served as navigator, bombardier, radar observer, squadron comdr., provost marshal, dir. security and law enforcement, chief of police Travis AFB, Calif., 1968-71, base defense officer Tan Son Nhut AB, Saigon, Vietnam, 1968, ret., 1971; mgr. safety and security Monsanto Co. World Hdqrs., St. Louis, 1971—; instr. Tarkio Coll. Extension, St. Louis, 1980; guest speaker, participant seminars. First aid instr. ARC, 1973—; CPR instr. Am. Heart Assn., 1974—; active Kaskaskia council Boy Scouts Am., 1941-51, 71-75, staff and camp dir., 1946-50, Eagle Scout, Lodge Chief Order of Arrow. Decorated Silver Star, Bronze Star, Air Medal with oak leaf clusters, Purple Heart. Mem. Am. Soc. Indsl. Security (cert. protection profl., chpt. chmn., pub.

monthly newsletter St. Louis Chpt. 1972—), Profl. Investigators Council Greater St. Louis, Internat. Assn. Chiefs of Police, Mo. Peace Officers Assn., Law Enforcement Ofcls. of St. Louis County, Ill. Sheriff Assn. Mem. United Church of Christ. Club: Toastmasters (officer, area speech contest winner 1963). Author Security Survey, St. Louis Metropolitan Area, 1978. Office: 800 N Lindbergh Blvd Saint Louis MO 63166

BENDER, CARL MARTIN, physics educator; b. Bklyn., Jan. 18, 1943; s. Alfred and Rose (Suberman) B.; m. Jessica Dee Waldbaum, June 18, 1966; children—Michael Anthony, Daniel Eric. A.B, Cornell U., 1964; A.M., Harvard U., 1965, Ph.D., 1969. Mem. Inst. Advanced Study, Princeton, 1969-70; asst. prof MIT, Cambridge, 1970-73, assoc. prof., 1973-77; prof. Washington U., St. Louis, 1977—; research assoc. Imperial Coll., London, 1974; cons. Los Alamos Nat. Lab., 1979—. Mem. editorial bd. Jour. Math. Physics, 1980—, Advances in Applied Math, 1980—; author: Advanced Mathematical Methods for Scientists and Engineers, 1978. Contbr. articles to profl. jours. Fellow NSF, 1964-69, Woodrow Wilson Found., 1964-65, Sloan Found. 1973-77. Mem. Am. Phys. Soc. Home: 509 Warren Ave University City MO 63130 Office: Dept Physics Washington U St Louis MO 63130

BENDER, CLIFFORD EARL, civil engineer, geotechnical consultant; b. Jamestown, N.Y., May 23, 1935; s. Clifford Lewis and Florence Adeline (Stanton) B.; student Allegheny Coll., 1953-55; B.C.E., Syracuse U., 1962; m. Hildegarde Elsa Groseclose, Aug. 21, 1955; children—William Stanton, Clifford Earl, Jennifer Smiley, Amy Lynette. Project engr. Linde div. Union Carbide Corp., Tonawanda, N.Y., 1963-64, design engr., 1964-66, estimator and cost control, 1966-69; estimator, design engr. Turzillo Contracting Co., Richfield, Ohio, 1969-77, chief engr., chief estimator, 1977-83; geotech. cons., 1983—; instr. math. Erie County Tech. Inst.; soils cons. Registered profl. engr., N.Y., Ohio, Minn., Ga., Tex., Fla. Mem. ASCE, Nat. Soc. Profl. Engrs., Ohio Soc. Profl. Engrs. Episcopalian. Home and Office: 1378 Wilbur Rd Medina OH 44256

BENDER, EILEEN TEPER, humanities educator; b. Madison, Wis., Dec. 1, 1935; d. Samuel and Sonia (Roitblat) T.; m. Harvey Alan Bender, June 16, 1956; children—Leslie, Samuel, Philip. B.S.J. with distinction, Northwestern U., 1956; Ph.D. in English, U. Notre Dame, 1977. Editor, photographer, adv. mgr., free-lance writer, book reviewer, Chgo., South Bend, Ind., Pasadena, 1956-66; lectr. English lit. and writing Ind. U.-South Bend, 1966-70; asst. instr. Yale U., New Haven, 1973-74; asst. chmn. div. arts and scis. Ind. U., 1978-80; asst. prof. English, U. Notre Dame (Ind.), 1980-84; lectr. English, St. Mary's Coll., Notre Dame, 1984—; exec. dir. Community Edn. Roundtable, 1985—; cons. Danforth Found., Newcombe Fellowship, Rhodes Scholarship. Vice chmn. exec. com. Ind. Com. for Humanities, 1978—; pres. St. Joseph County Library Bd., 1980-82; trustee South Bend Bd. Schs., 1978-82; advisor Michiana Arts and Scis. Council, 1980—. Kent fellow, 1968; Danforth Found. fellow, 1968; NEH summer grantee, 1983; Ind. Commn. on Higher Edn. grantee, 1977-78. Mem. Soc. for Values in Higher Edn., MLA, Nat. Conf. Tchrs. English, Ind. Congress on Edn., LWV. Democrat. Jewish. Editor Yarns, 1956-58, Cable Newsletter, 1976-77, Cable Access Guide, 1979; editorial bd. Soundings; contbr. articles to profl. jours. Home: 1512 Belmont Ave South Bend IN 46615 Office: 313 Madeleva Hall Notre Dame IN 46556

BENDER, ROBERT EDWARD, educator; b. Marion, Ohio, Nov. 7, 1952; s. Walter John and Leona Lucille (Slob) B.; m. Sue Ann Stahr, Dec. 18, 1982. B.S., Ohio State U., 1974, M.S., 1981. With Quality Farm & Fleet, Inc., Marion, Ohio, 1974-76; former Walter J. Bender Farm, Prospect, Ohio, 1974—; sales agt. Bender Ins. Agy., Prospect, 1973—; instr. agrl. edn. River Valley High Sch., Marion, Ohio, 1976—; condr. workshops in field. Adminstrv. bd. Prospect St. United Meth. Ch., 1974—; adviser Future Farmers Am., 1976—. Named Dist. 6 Outstanding Young Vocat.-Agrl. Tchr., 1980-81, Outstanding Tchr. Dist. 3, 1982, Outstanding Young Vocat.-Agr. Tchr., State of Ohio, 1982, others. Mem. Ohio Vocat. Agr. Tchrs. Assn., Nat. Vocat. Agr. Tchrs. Assn., Ohio Vocat. Assn., Am. Vocat. Assn., River Valley Tchrs. Assn., Central Ohio Tchrs. Assn., Marion County Edn. Assn., Ohio Pork Improvement Assn., Marion County Pork Improvement Assn., Farm Bur., Prodn. Credit Assn., Prospect Farmer's Exchange, Am. Soybean Assn., Ohio State U. Alumni Assn., Ohio State U. AES Alumni Assn. Clubs: Ohio Yorkshire, Am. Yorkshire, Moose. Office: 1267 Columbus-Sandusky Rd Marion OH 43302

BENEDICT, GARY CLARENCE, educational administrator; b. Valley City, N.D., Oct. 22, 1938; s. Clarence Augustus and Mary Rae (Spink) B.; m. Carmen Jean Schreiner, May 29, 1965; children—Andrew Scott, Anne Kathleen. B.E., Wis. State U., 1964; M.S., U. Wis., 1968; Ed.D., Marquette U., 1978. Tchr., New Berlin (Wis.) Pub. Schs., 1960-67; supt. Merton (Wis.) Joint Sch. Dist. 9, 1967-75; dir. curriculum and instrn. Mukwonago (Wis.) Sch. Dist., 1975-84; adminstrv. asst. curriculum Shorewood Sch. Dist., 1984—; adj. instr. Lakeland Coll., Sheboygan, Wis., 19-. Mem. state adminstrv. com. Democratic Party, 1983; active Mental Health Assn. Waukesha County. Charles F. Kettering Found. fellow, 1981-85. Mem. Am. Assn. Sch. Adminstrs., Nat. Assn. Supervision and Curriculum Devel., Wis. Sch. Pub. Relations Assn. (sec.), Wis. Assn. Supervision and Curriculum Devel., Wis. Assn. Tchr. Educators, Phi Delta Kappa. Contbr. articles in field to profl. jours. Home: 21388 Oakcrest Dr New Berlin WI 53151 Office: 1701 E Capitol Dr Shorewood WI 53211

BENEDICT, JOHN ANTHONY, social worker; b. Pittsburg, Kans., June 27, 1943; s. Frances Loriene B.; B.A. in English Lit., St. Meinrad Coll., 1965; M.S. in Counselor Edn., Kans. State Coll., Pittsburg, 1975; m. Marcia Kathleen McCullough, Nov. 22, 1974; 1 stepdau., Amber Peterson; 1 adopted dau., Crystal Kerry. Family social service worker Parsons (Kans.) area office Kans. Social and Rehab. Services, 1965-66, social worker, family services, 1968-69, income maintenance worker, 1969-71, Work Incentive Program social service worker, 1971-77, social worker II, protective service work, youth, 1977-84, social service supr., Fredonia, Kans., 1984—; parenting edn. instr. S.T.E.P. Vice pres. Labette County Cancer Soc., 1969, 70, pres., 1971, 72; mem. Parsons Youth Council, 1969—; mem. community action bd. Labette County Mental Health, 1969, 73; mem. SRS Consortium on Youth; mem. Labette County Coalition on Parenting Edn. Served in U.S. Army, 1966-68. Mem. Nat. Com. Prevention of Child Abuse. Roman Catholic. Home: 223 S 15th St Box 326 Fredonia KS 66736 Office: SRS Office Box 516 Fredonia KS 66736

BENEDICT, RONALD LOUIS, lawyer; b. Cin., Feb. 22, 1942; s. Harold Lloyd and Thelma (Bryant) B.; m. Carol Joyce Worthington, Sept. 9, 1961 (div. Sept. 1980); children—Karen Elizabeth Benedict Sterwerf, Jennifer Lynn; m. Deborah Ann Taggart, Aug. 14, 1982. B.A. in Polit. Sci., U. Cin., 1964; J.D., Salmon P. Chase Coll., 1968. Bar: Ohio 1968, U.S. Supreme Ct. 1985. Methods analyst Western-So. Life Ins. Co., Cin., 1964-69; atty. Ohio Nat. Life Ins. Co., Cin., 1969-71, sr. atty., 1971-73, asst. gen. counsel, 1973-80, assoc. counsel, 1980—; sec., dir. Ohio Nat. Fund, Inc., Cin., 1973—; sec. Ohio Nat. Investment Mgmt. Co., Cin., 1971—, Ohio Nat. Equity Sales Co., Cin., 1971—. Author, lectr.: (treatise and course) Trial and Execution of Jesus, 1978; Pseudochristian Cults, 1977. Pres. Young Democrats, U. Cin., 1964; arbitrator Ct. Common Pleas, Hamilton County, Ohio, 1973—; mem. and counsel Tri-State Billy Graham Crusade Com., Cin., 1977. Recipient cert. Adult Christian Edn. Found., 1977; Life Office Mgmt. Inst. fellow, 1971. Mem. ABA, Ohio State Bar Assn. (corp. counsel com.), Cin. Bar Assn. (securities law com.), Assn. Life Ins. Counsel (securities law com.), Investment Co. Inst. (SEC rules com.), Alpha Tau Omega. Democrat. Presbyterian. Avocations: theology; Bible teaching; church leadership; outdoor activities. Home: 7029 Gaines Rd Cincinnati OH 45247 Office: Ohio Nat Life Ins Co PO Box 237 Cincinnati OH 45201

BENEKE, MILDRED (MILLIE) STONG, civic worker, city ofcl., author; b. Prairie City, Iowa; d. Rueben Ira and Lillian (Garber) Stong; student Wash. U., 1942-43; off-campus student U. Minn., Mankato State Coll., 1951-67; m. Arnold W. Beneke, Aug. 10, 1939; children—Bruce Arnold, Paula Rae, Bradford Kent, Cynthia Jane, Lisa Patrice. Exec. sec. chmn. Vol. Services, ARC, St. Paul, 1940-41; v.p. Pi House, St. Paul, 1972—; founder, bd. dirs. chmn. Project Interaction Boutique, Minn. Correctional Instn. for Women, Shakopee, 1971—, supervising vol., 1970—. Bd. dirs. Mpls. Children's Theatre Co. Republican chairwoman McLeod County (Minn.), 1969-73; mem. Rep. Minn. Platform com., 1970; bd. dirs. Buffalo Creek Players, 1975—, v.p., 1980-82; mem. Rep. Feminist Caucus; alderman Glencoe City Council, 1974-80. Glencoe elderly housing named Millie Beneke Manor, 1977. Mem. Dramatists Guild, Glencoe Bus. and Profl. Women (Woman of Yr. 1975). Lutheran. Author: (play) The Garage Sale, 1978; Politics Unusual, 1979; (play) The Househusband and the Working Wife, 1982. Home: 330 Scout Hill Dr Glenview Woods Glencoe MN 55336

BENES, CHARLES JAMES, banker; b. Cleve., May 22, 1904; s. James and Mary (Poskecil) B.; student Dyke Coll. Bus., 1919-20; m. Rose AnnaBelle Jankovsky, July 20, 1950; children—Charles J. Sec., treas. First Fed. Savs. & Loan Assn., Cleve., 1933-78, also dir.; dir. First Fin. Services and Devel. Corp., Cleve., 1st Fed. Savs. Bank. Commr. zoning and planning City of Pepper Pike, Ohio, 1956-69. Mem. Am. Savs. and Loan Inst. (pres. Northeast Ohio chpt. 1951-52). Clubs: Masons (32 deg.), (Shriners; Mentor (Ohio) Yachting; Shaker Heights Country. Home: 29026 Gates Mills Blvd Pepper Pike OH 44124 Office: Park Centre 1255 Superior St Cleveland OH 44114

BENES, SUSAN CARLETON, neuro-ophthalmologist; b. Cleve., Jan. 2, 1948; d. Edward Fulton and Rita Elyse (True) Carleton; m. James Davie Benes, Dec. 27, 1969; children—Jennifer, David, Olivia. B.S., U. Mich., 1970, cert. tchr., 1969; M.D., Med. Coll. Pa., 1975. Diplomate Am. Bd. Ophthalmology. Resident in internal medicine Lankenau Hosp., Phila., 1975-76; resident in ophthalmology Wills Eye Hosp., Phila., 1976-79, fellow in neuro-ophthalmology, 1979-80, staff physician Wills Eye and Grad. Hosp., 1980-81; lectr. in neuro-ophthalmology Kenyatta U., Nairobi, Kenya, 1980; asst. prof. neuro-ophthalmology Ohio State U., Columbus, 1981—; practice medicine specializing in neuro-ophthalmology, Columbus, 1981—. Contbr. chpts. to books. Mem. mission council First Community Ch., Columbus, 1982—; leader Camp Fire Girls, Columbus, 1983—. Recipient Outstanding Grad. award Upjohn Co., 1975. Fellow Am. Acad. Ophthalmology; mem. AMA, Ohio State Med. Med. Soc., Franklin Med. Soc., Alpha Omega Alpha, Kappa Kappa Gamma.

BENFER, DAVID WILLIAM, hospital administrator; b. Toledo, Ohio, May 28, 1946; s. Wilson L. and Marjorie (Baringer) B.; m. Mary Struner, Sept. 5, 1970; children—Emily, Matthew, Andrew. B.A., Wittenberg U., 1968; M.B.A. in Hosp. Adminstrn., Xavier U., 1970. Chief exec. officer, asst. adminstrn., Med. Coll. Ohio Hosp., Toledo, 1971-76, exec. dir., 1976-81; exec. dir., chief exec. officer Bon Secours Hosp., Grosse Point, Mich., 1982-84; exec. dir. chief operating officer Henry Ford Hosp., Detroit, 1985—; chief exec. officer, bd. dirs. Sisters Bon Secours Mich., Grosse Point, 1982-84, Sisters Bon Secours Hosp., 1982-84, Sisters Bon Secours Nursing Care Ctr., St. Clair Shores, Mich., 1982-84, Bon Secours Pharmacy and Health Services, Inc., Grosse Point, 1984-85. Co-author: Issues in Health Care Management, 1982. Contbr. to book: Sisters of Bon Secours Centennial, 1982. Trustee, Family Services Detroit and Wayne County, Detroit, 1982—; mem. fin. com. Grosse Point Acad., 1982—. Recipient Commendation, 114th Ohio Gen. Assembly, 1981. Fellow Am. Coll. Hosp. Adminstrs. (Robert S. Hudgens award 1982); mem. Am. Hosp. Assn., Mich. Hosp. Assn. Roman Catholic. Club: Lochmoor (Grosse Point Woods, Mich.). Lodge: Rotary. Avocations: Jogging, golf. Office: Henry Ford Hosp 2799 W Grand Blvd Detroit MI 48202

BENFORD, ARTHUR EUGENE, plastics engr.; b. Benton Harbor, Mich., July 21, 1931; s. George Everet and Gladys Irene (Hendrix) B.; student Lake Mich. Coll., 1951, U. Mich., 1952; B.S. in Polymer Chemistry, Western Mich. U., 1957; m. Bernice Irene Kowerdlick, June 29, 1952; children—Lauri Beth, Brice Allen, Blair Ashley. Research materials engr. Whirlpool Research Labs., St. Joseph, Mich., 1956-60, mgr. materials research dept., 1960-72; mgr. plastics research and applications Whirlpool Refrigeration Group, Evansville, Ind., 1972-74, sr. product engr., 1974—. Chmn. Parks Dept., St. Joseph Twp., Mich., 1965-72; mem. Republican County Commn., 1965-72. Served with U.S. Army, 1952-55. Cert. mfg. engr. Mem. Research Soc. Am., Soc. Plastics Engrs., Sigma Xi. Lutheran. Patentee, contbr. articles to various publs. Home: Rural Route 7 Box 216B Evansville IN 47712 Office: US 41 North Evansville IN 47727

BENFORD, BENJAMIN J., II, educator, coach, school administrator; b. Wayne County, Mich., Jan. 31, 1949; s. Zack B. and Desiree L. (Bradley) B.; m. Andrea D. White, Sept. 3, 1968; children—Monique D., Benjamin J. III. B.A., Olivet Coll., 1970; M.A., Oakland U., 1975. Tchr., coach River Rouge (Mich.) Sch. Dist., 1970—, adminstrv. asst., head football coach, recreation dir. Pres. Tri City Democrats; exec. bd. 16th Dist. Dem. Orgn.; mem. NAACP. Recipient Martin Luther King award Olivet Coll., 1968; named to Olivet Coll. Hall of Fame. Mem. Mich. Assn. Supervision and Curriculum Devel., Detroit Bus. and Civic League. Baptist. Lodge: River Rouge Optimist (pres.). Office: 340 Frazier River Rouge MI 48218

BENIA, cosmetologist. Grad. So. Ill. U., Pivot Point Hair Design Sch., Chgo., Fran and Leo's Sch. of Beauty Culture, Chgo. Former instr. So. Ill. U., Lydia Adams Sch. Cosmetology, Chgo., Mr. Maurice's Beauty Coll., Chgo., Waukesha City Terminal Inst., Wis., U. S.C., Columbia, Naval Salon, Great Lakes, Ill.; lectr. in field. Pres. Benia De La Coiffures, Internat., Inc., Chgo. Recipient numerous awards; frequent participant in cosmetology trade shows, contests; judge in many competitions. Office: Benia De La Coiffures Internat Inc 108 N State St Chicago IL 60602

BENISHEK, BETTY LOU, insurance company executive; b. Chgo., Sept. 2, 1931; d. Forrest Bryan and Ruth Warner (Shaw) Brunner; cert. advanced safety Nat. Safety Council, 1973; cert. audiometric technician Ear, Nose and Throat Assos. of Wausau, 1973; student U. Wis., Am. Welding Soc., Harvard U., tech. insts.; m. Albert William Benishek, June 28, 1952; children—Michael A., Lori G. Nurses aide delivery room, technician Meml. Hosp., Manitowoc, Wis., 1956-71; safety technician Aluminum Splty. Co., Manitowoc, 1971-72; safety and health adminstr. Armira Corp., Sheboygan, Wis., 1972-77; safety dir. Universal Foundry Co., Oshkosh, Wis., 1977-80; risk control cons. Comml. Union Ins. Cos., Milw., 1980-84; sr. tech. rep. Home Ins. Co., Milw., 1984—. First aid and CPR instr. ARC. Mem. Nat. Safety Council (exec. com.), Wis. Council Safety (exec. com.), No. Wis. Foundry Safety Assn. (founder 1978), Oshkosh Indsl. Safety Council (v.p. 1980), Am. Soc. Safety Engrs. (assoc. safety profl.; sec. 1982-84, v.p., pres. elect 1984, pres. 1985-86; Pres.'s Club 1982-83), Northeastern Wis. Am. Foundrymens Soc., Am. Indsl. Hygiene Assn., Mgmt. Club (sec.). Lutheran. Contbr. articles to Leather Industry Trade Jour. Home: 4442 Just Ct Manitowoc WI 54220 Office: 235 N Executive Dr Brookfield WI 53005

BENJAMIN, GARY DUANE, clergyman, fire chief; b. Garnett, Kans., Mar. 29, 1941; s. Ralph Eugene and Iva Pauline (Bailey) B.; m. Linda Sue Brown, July 30, 1959; 1 son, Stanley Eugene. B.Th., Ozark Bible Coll., 1964. Ordained to ministry Christian Ch., 1964; cert. arson investigator, Kans. Minister, Christ's Ch., Urich, Mo., 1960-62, Filley Christian Ch., El Dorado Springs, Mo., 1962-64, Ch. of Christ, Rockwell City, Iowa, 1964-69; Chaplain coordinator Iowa Women's Reformatory, Rockwell City, 1967; minister Wall Street Christian Ch. and Mound City Federated Ch., Mound City, Kans., 1970—; funeral dir. Farris-Feuerborn Meml. Chapel, Garnett, 1984—; fire chief City of Garnett, 1981—; civil defense dir. Anderson County (Kans.), 1982—, rural fire coordinator, 1982—. Adminstr. Anderson County Planning Commn., 1982—. Recipient Regional Speak Up award Kans. Jaycees, 1972. Mem. Anderson County Firefighters Relief Assn. (sec.-treas. 1984—). Avocations: camping, snow skiing, photography. Home: 315 Orange St Garnett KS 66032 Office: Fire Dept 131 W 5th St Garnett KS 66032

BENJAMIN, HARRISON RUSSELL, computer engineer; b. Hastings, Minn., July 7, 1934; s. Harry Murtice and Florence Elizabeth (Severson) B.; m. Patti Cox, July 16, 1960; children—David, Lisa. B.S. in Engring. with distinction, U. Minn., 1956, postgrad., 1958. Instr., U. Minn. Inst. Tech., 1957-58; electromech. engr. Gen. Mills electronics div., Mpls., 1958-61; engr. mgr. Control Data Corp., Mpls., 1961-68, dir. engring., 1969-71, gen. mgr. terminal devel. div., 1972-75, gen. mgr. small computer devel. div., 1976, gen. mgr. data systems devel., 1977-80, gen. mgr. microcomputer services, 1981—; dir. Inc. U.S.A., N.Y.C., Connectype, Mpls. Mem. Com. for Effective Crime Control. Recipient Honor Student award U. Minn. Mem. Territorial Pioneers Assn. Minn., Hort. Soc. (Minn.), Internat. Wood Collectors Soc., Nat. Rifle Assn., Model T Collectors Assn., Minn. Hist. Soc., Dakota County Hist. Soc., Sci. Mus. Minn., Aircraft Owners and Pilots Assn., Minn. Conservation Fedn., Tau Beta Pi. Home: 4805 Eriks Blvd Eagan MN 55122 Office: 8100 34th Ave S Minneapolis MN 55440

BENJAMIN, NEAL B. H., civil engineer; b. Santa Cruz, Calif., Oct. 24, 1934; s. Charles Hugh and Mildred Emily (Neal) B.; B.S., U.S. Coast Guard Acad., 1956; B.C.E., Rensselaer Poly. Inst., 1962; M.S.C.E., Stanford U., 1967, Ph.D., 1969; m. Mary Louise Schroeder, July 6, 1963; children—Charles Edward, Julia Anne, Kathryn Mary. Served in U.S. Coast Guard, 1956-66; research asst. Stanford U., 1967-69; asst. prof. civil engring. U. Mo.-Columbia, 1969-72, asso. prof., 1972-75, prof., 1975—, coordinator Grad. Program in Constrn. Engring. and Mgmt. Registered profl. engr., Mo. Fellow ASCE (chmn. com. on estimating and cost control 1975-78, exec. com. constrn. div. 1978-82, chmn. 1980-82); mem. Am. Council Constrn. Edn. (trustee), Am. Arbitration Assn. (panel constrn. arbitrators), Nat., Mo. socs. profl. engrs., Project Mgmt. Inst. Roman Catholic. Contbr. articles in constrn.-mgmt. to profl. jours. Home: 1108 S Glenwood Columbia MO 65203 Office: 1039 Engring Bldg U Mo Columbia MO 65211

BENNER, BLAIR RICHARD, metallurgist; b. Braddock, Pa., Mar. 29, 1947; s. Earle and Dorothy Loraine (Chandler) B.; m. Irma Jewel Smith, Dec. 21, 1974; children—Elizabeth, Richard, Robert. B.S., Pa. State U., 1969; M.S., Stanford U., 1970. Jr. metallurgist N.M. Bur. Mines, Socorro, 1971-73; metallurgist Deepsea Ventures, Glouchester, Va., 1973-76; research engr. U.S. Steel, Coleraine, Minn., 1976-80, sr. research engr., 1980—. Contbr. articles to various publs. Mem. AIME. Office: US Steel Research PO Box 188 Colerraine MN 55722

BENNETT, AMELIA SABINO, pharmacist, editor; b. Columbus, Ohio, Sept. 24, 1947; d. Joseph Richard and Helen Virginia (Vellani) Sabino; m. Donald Leroy Bennett, Aug. 10, 1973; children—Mark, Christine, Jenny. B.S. in Pharmacy, Ohio State U., 1970. Registered pharmacist, Ohio. Pharmacy intern, Sabino Pharmacy, Columbus, 1965-67; Ohio State U. Hosps., Columbus, 1967-70; staff pharmacist Grant Hosp., Columbus, 1970-75; pharmacist, editor Acad. Pharmacy Central Ohio, Ohio State Pharm. Assn., Ohio Soc. Hosp. Pharmacists, Columbus, 1977—. Contbr. reviews to profl. publs. Vol. blood pressure screening St. Anthony Ch., Columbus, 1979—; capt. Central Ohio Heart Fund, Columbus, 1980; speaker poison prevention to local schs., 1980—. Mem. Central Ohio Soc. Hosp. Pharmacists (pres. 1977-78, service award 1982), Ohio State U. Coll. Pharmacy Alumni Assn. (Hosp. Pharmacist of Yr. 1975), Am. Pharm. Assn. (mem. various coms. 1973-77), Am. Soc. Hosp. Pharmacists, Ohio State Pharm. Assn., Ohio Soc. Hosp. Pharmacists, Acad. Pharmacy Central Ohio. Avocations: knitting, reading, baking. Home: 5120 Northtowne Blvd Columbus OH 43229

BENNETT, DAVID ALLEN, geologist; b. Strasburg, Ohio, Feb. 4, 1942; s. Chester Arthur and Ruby Donnan (Davis) B.; m. Rosann Jannet Roberts, Mar. 19, 1966; children—Lesia Donnan, Danell Rose. B.S. in Geology, Kent State U., 1967; B.S. in Fin., Ariz. State U., 1974. Cert. profl. geol. scientist, profl. geologist. Engr. trainee Anaconda, Butte, Mont., 1967-68, smelte-supr. Potrerillos, Chile, 1968-69; mine engr. Phelps Dodge, Bisbee, Ariz., 1969-71; engr., systems analyst Magma Copper Co., San Manuel, Ariz., 1973-78; systems analyst R&F Coal Co., Cadiz, Ohio, 1978-81, geologist, 1981—. Mem. Soc. Mining Engrs., Am. Inst. Profl. Geologists, Geol. Soc. Am., Am. Assn. Petroleum Geologists. Club: Tornado. Lodge: Elks. Home: 1103 Weinsz Dr Dover OH 44622 Office: R&F Coal Co 538 N Main St Cadiz OH 43907

BENNETT, EARLE, advt. exec.; b. Fort Ritner, Ind., Jan. 12, 1910; s. Seibert Everett Newton and Myrtle B.; student Monmouth Coll., 1933-37. Monmouth editor Rock Island (Ill.) Argus, 1935-48; with Galesburg (Ill.) Register-Mail, 1948-52; newscaster WGIL, Galesburg, 1948-52; mem. Agrl. Stabilization Com., 1953-67; dir. advt. The Times Record, Aledo, Ill., 1967—. Mem. Ill. Devel. Council, 1940-48. Mem. Aledo Area C. of C. (sec.), Ill. Press Assn., Christian Scientist. Clubs: Lions, Exchange, Pres., Warren County (Ill.) Young Republican Club, 1934-38. Freelance writer including contbns. to Prairie Farmer, Reader's Digest, Western Stories, Graphic Arts, trade jours. Home: Gerlaw IL 61435 Office: 113 S College Ave Aledo IL 61231

BENNETT, FOSTER CLYDE, die casting consultant; b. Wilmette, Ill., Oct. 14, 1914; s. Stacy Clyde and Laurine T. (Foster) B.; m. Mary Lou MacPhail, Jan. 12, 1940; children—Donald, William, Tom, Jim, George, Elizabeth, Karen. B.S. in Engring. Physics, U. Ill., 1936; M.S., Calif. Inst. Tech., 1937. Research engr. to asso. scientist Dow Chem. Co., 1937-72; sr. researcher Battelle Meml. Inst., 1972-81; pres. Die Casting Cons., Inc., Columbus, Ohio, 1981—. Recipient Doehler award Am. Die Casting Inst., 1964; Soc. of Die Casting Engrs. Disting. Life Membership award, 1979; Award of Merit, Am. Foundrymen's Soc., 1962. Mem. Soc. Die Casting Engrs. Republican. Patentee in field; contbr. articles to profl. jours.

BENNETT, FRANCIS WILLIAM, agricultural engineer, consultant; b. Pomona, Kans., Dec. 25, 1926; s. John William and Lena Serelda (Wells) B.; m. Eloise Ruth Hanson, Aug. 15, 1953; children—Gregory Stephen, Randall Wiliam, Roderick Paul, Stanley Harold. Student Ottawa U., 1947-50; B.S., Kans. State U., 1952, M.S., 1963. With sales and product application dept. Caterpillar Tractor Co., Peoria, Ill., 1952-57; career officer U.S. AID, India, Sudan, Sri Lanka, 1957-61; asst. prof., adminstr. W.Va. U., Soroti, Uganda, 1964-66; program dir. agrl. engring. Battelle Meml. Inst., Columbus, Ohio, 1966-68; agrl. engring. advisor U. Tenn., Bangalore, India, 1969-71; program dir. Midwest Research Inst., Kansas City, Mo., 1972-75; program ops. cons. U.S. AID, Nairobi, Kenya, 1975-78; mgmt. and devel. cons. Engring. Cons. Inc., Denver, and Bangkok, Thailand, 1978; program design cons. Pacific Cons., Inc., Nairobi, 1979; div. mgr. W.G. Jaques Co., Des Moines, 1979-82; trade cons. Avanti Internat., Inc., Houston, 1982-83; pres., owner Export Trading Link, Inc., Williamsburg, Kans., 1983—. Contbr. articles to profl. jours. Patentee in field. Served with USN, 1946-47, PTO. Mem. Am. Soc. Agrl. Engrs. (numerous coms.). Club: Williamsburg Wildlife. Methodist. Lodges: Masons, Lions. Home: PO Box 99 Williamsburg KS 66095 Office: Export Trading Link Inc PO Box 5 Williamsburg KS 66095

BENNETT, JOYCE ARLENE, librarian, educator; b. Madison, Wis., Mar. 25, 1944; d. Ralph Eugene and Florence Marie (Cramer) B.; B.A. in Liberal Arts (scholar), Bradley U., 1966; M.S. in L.S., U. Ill., 1971. Library asst. research library Caterpillar Tractor Co., Peoria, Ill., 1966-67; reference librarian, instr. library tech. Ill. Central Coll., East Peoria, 1967-73; asst. prof. Sangamon State U., Springfield, Ill., 1973-80, assoc. prof., 1980—; convenor Council II, Ill. Clearinghouse for Acad. Library Instrn., 1978; presentor 7th Ann. Conf. Acad. Library Instrn., 1977, Nat. Women's Studies Assn., 1983, others; participant Gt. Lakes Women's Studies Summer Inst., 1981. Democratic precinct Committeewoman, 1982—. Pres., Springfield chpt. NOW, 1978-79. Ill. state scholar, 1962-66; recipient Am. Legion citizenship award, 1962; cert. of recognition Ill. Bicentennial Commn., 1974; invited Susan B. Anthony luncheon, 1978, 79. Mem. ALA, Ill. Library Assn. (presentor 1984) Ill. Assn. Coll. and Research Libraries (bibliog. instrn. com.), Am. Fedn. Tchrs., AAUW (chmn. standing com. on women Springfield br., mem. com. on women Ill. state div.), Nat. Women's Studies Assn., Springfield Art Assn., Nat. Trust Historic Preservation, Beta Phi Mu. Reviewer Library Jour., Am. Reference Books Ann. Contbr. article in field to publ. Home: 2226 Concord Ct Springfield IL 62704 Office: Sangamon State University Library Springfield IL 62708

BENNETT, MARGARET BOOKER, psychotherapist; b. Spartanburg, S.C., June 15, 1923; d. Paschal and Ovie (Grey) Booker. B.S., N.C. A&T State U., 1944; M.S.W., U. Mich., 1947; Ph.D., Wayne State U., 1980. Cert. marriage counselor, social worker, Mich.; cert. Mich. Acad. Cert. Social Workers. Caseworker, field instr. Family Service Soc. Met. Detroit, 1947-52; caseworker, field instr., casework supr. Wayne County Consultation Center, 1952-60; caseworker, casework supr., field instr. psychiat. social service Wayne County Gen. Hosp., 1960-62, dir. med. social service, 1976-77; psychotherapist, field instr., asst. dir. Wayne County Mental Health Clinic, 1962-76; treatment cons. Project Paradigm, 1978-83, also pvt. practice psychotherapy, 1965—; psychotherapist, pres. Booker Bennett & Assocs., Detroit, 1980—; founder Consultation Ctr., Ecorse, Mich., 1961; lectr. U. Mich., 1975-76, 1969-74; instr. Immanuel Lutheran Coll., 1944-45. Bd. dirs. Crossroads, 1980—; exec. council Episcopal Diocese of Mich., 1974-77, 80—, exec. com., 1982—; governing bd. Cathedral Ch. St. Paul, Detroit, 1971-74, 76-77, 79-82, v.p. governing bd., 1977; bd. dirs. Cathedral Terr., 1982—. Fellow Am. Orthopsychiat. Assn.; mem. Mich. Assn. Marriage and Family Therapy, Am. Assn. Marriage and Family Therapy, Mich. Assn. Clin. Social Workers, Nat. Assn. Social Workers, Council Social Work Edn., U. Mich. Women (dir. 1983—), Wayne State U. Alumni Assn. (dir. 1982—), Phi Delta Kappa, Alpha Kappa Alpha. Democrat. Anglican. Co-author: The Handbook of Psychodynamic Therapy; contbr. articles to profl. jours. Home and Office: 1971 Glynn Ct Detroit MI 48206

BENNETT, OLGA, lawyer; b. Viroqua, Wis., May 5, 1908; d. John Henry and Olga (Omundson) Bennett; B.A., U. Wis., 1928, LL.B., 1935. Asst. cashier

Farmers Bank, Viroqua, 1929-32; admitted to Wis. bar, 1935; practiced in Viroqua, 1941-70; law clk. to justice Wis. Supreme Ct., Madison, 1936-41; partner firm Bennett & Bennett, 1941-56; individual practice, 1956-70; city atty. City of Viroqua, 1946-48; county judge Vernon County, Viroqua, 1970-76; individual practice law, Viroqua, 1976—; mem. Lower West Central Criminal Justice Planning Council, 1972-77, Vernon County Hwy. Safety Commn. Mem. Vernon County Bar Assn., State Bar Wis., Nat. Coll. State Judiciary, Vernon County Hist. Soc., Benchers, Kappa Beta Pi. Republican. Lutheran. Home: 322 N Dunlap Ave Viroqua WI 54665 Office: 210 N Main St Viroqua WI 54665

BENNETT, RICHARD CARL, social worker; b. Eau Claire, Wis., July 25, 1933; s. Ira Anthony and Marion Rhoda (Johnson) B.; B.A., Hamline U., St. Paul, 1955; M.S., George Williams Coll., 1957; M.S. (Lou Hougttellian fellow, Am. Lutheran Ch. fellow), U. Chgo., 1962; postgrad. Loyola U., Chgo., Roosevelt U., Chgo., Forest Inst., Chgo., Coll. Fin. Planning, Denver; grad. in computer sci. Nat. Radio Inst.; m. Patricia Ann Work, Oct. 27, 1972; children—Matthew, Elizabeth, Kimberly, Timothy. Caseworker, Rock County Welfare Dept., Janesville, Wis., 1957-61; area dir. Luth. Family Service Oreg., Eugene, 1962-67; exec. dir. Family Service Travelers Aid, Fort Worth, 1967-70; mgr. agy. ops. Tarrant County United Way, Fort Worth, 1970-73; exec. dir. Luth. Family Service N.W. Ind., Merrillville, 1973-80; exec. v.p. Listening Inc., 1979—; exec. dir. Family Service Assn. Porter County, 1982—; host TV show Life's Dimensions; cons. internat. bd. Parents without Partners; cons. numerous social agys. Served with U.S. Army, 1958-62. Mem. Nat. Assn. Social Workers (dir. Ind. chpt.), Acad. Cert. Social Workers, Assn. Marriage and Family Therapists. Author divorce mgmt. materials and newspaper column, profl. manuals; pub. Step Parent News, 1979—; editor: The Business of Social Work, 1983-84. Home and office: 8716 Pine St Gary IN 46403

BENNETT, ROBERT THOMAS, lawyer, accountant; b. Columbus, Ohio, Feb. 8, 1939; s. Francis Edmund and Mary Catherine (Weiland) B.; B.S., Ohio State U., 1960; J.D., Cleve. Marshall Law Sch., 1967; m. Ruth Ann Dooley, May 30, 1959; children—Robert Thomas, Rose Marie. Admitted to Ohio bar, 1967; C.P.A., Ernst and Ernst, Cleve., 1960-63; with tax assessing dept. Cuyahoga County (Ohio) Auditor's Office, Cleve., 1963-70; mem. firm Bartunek, Bennett, Garofoli and Hill, Cleve., 1975-79; mem. firm Bennett & Klonowski, Cleve., 1979-83; mem. firm Bennett & Harbarger, Cleve., 1983—; mem. bd. Cuyahoga County Port Authority, 1974-80. Exec. vice chmn. Cuyahoga County Rep. orgn. Republican. Roman Catholic. Clubs: Cleve. Athletic, Clevelander, Citizens League, Communicators of Cleve.; Capitol Hill (Washington). Contbr. articles to profl. publs. Home: 4800 Valley Pkwy Fairview Park OH 44126 Office: 800 Standard Bldg 1370 Ontario St Cleveland OH 44113

BENNETT, THOMAS ERIC, home equipment company executive, materials management consultant; b. Ft. Wayne, Ind., Aug. 19, 1958; s. Edward Young Jr. and Esther (Christiansen) B.; m. Susan M. Glasscock, Oct. 21, 1978. A.S. in Mktg., Ind. U.-Ft. Wayne, 1978. Prodn. scheduler Sheller-Globe Co., Grabill, Ind., 1978-79; prodn. control mgr. Ft. Wayne Truck Parts Co., Ind., 1979-82; buyer Wayne Home Equipment div. Scott Fetzer Co., Ft. Wayne, 1982-84, sr. buyer, 1984—; cons. materials mgmt. Mem. Nat. Assn. Purchasing Mgrs., New Haven Jaycees (internal v.p. 1978). Methodist. Lodge: Lions (sec. 1985). Avocations: photography; golf; working out. Home: 1134 Hartzell St New Haven IN 46774 Office: Wayne Home Equipment 801 Glasgow Ave Fort Wayne IN 46803

BENNETT-KASTOR, TINA, linguist; b. La Mesa, Calif., Feb. 8, 1954; d. Clayton Leon and Patricia Jean (Howard) Bennett; B.F.A., Calif. Inst. Arts, 1973; M.A., U. So. Calif., 1976, Ph.D., 1978; m. Frank Sullivan Kastor, Oct. 28, 1979; children—Kristina Rebecca, Patrick Bennett. Teaching asst. linguistics dept. U. So. Calif., 1975-78, research asst., 1975-76; research asso., co-dir. research John Tracy Clinic, Los Angeles, 1977; research cons. R. M. Lencione, U. Calif. Rehab. Center, Los Angeles, 1977; asst. prof. English and linguistics Wichita (Kans.) State U., 1978—. Recipient Wichita State U. research award, 1979-80, 81-82, 85-86. Mem. AAAS, Linguistic Soc. Am., MLA, Am. Speech-Lang.-Hearing Assn., N.Y. Acad. Scis. Episcopalian. Author books; contbr. articles to profl. publs. Home: 115 N Fountain Wichita KS 67208 Office: Dept English Wichita State Univ Wichita KS 67208

BENNINGTON, MARCY MARIE, school psychologist; b. South Bend, Ind., Feb. 1, 1949; d. John William and Constance Dorothy (Weingartner) Truemper; m. Mark Ian Bennington, Sept. 7, 1968. A.B., Ind. U., 1971; M.Ed., U. Mo., 1976; Ph.D., St. Louis U., 1981. Adminstrv. asst. Psychol. Service Center, St. Louis, 1974-75; personnel asst. Orchard Corp. Am., St. Louis, 1975-77; teaching asst., instr. child psychology St. Louis U., 1978; sch. psychology intern Pattonville Sch. Dist., Maryland Heights, Mo., 1978-79; diagnostician/evaluation coordinator Wentzville (Mo.) R-4 Sch. Dist., 1979-80, dir. spl. edn., 1980-85. Mem. Nat. Assn. Sch. Psychologists, Am. Psychol. Assn., Am. Assn. for Counseling and Devel., Council for Exceptional Children, Phi Beta Kappa. Home: 3017 Silver Lake Blvd Silver Village OH 44224

BENNINGTON, ROGER EUGENE, lawyer; b. Highland County, Ohio, June 24, 1934; s. Ralph P. and Delorice (Dudley) B.; m. Judith L. Hosler, Aug. 3, 1963; children—Jeffrey R., Kevin G. B.S., Ohio State U., 1959, J.D., 1964. Bar: Ohio 1964, U.S. Dist. Ct. (so. dist.) Ohio 1965. Tchr., Columbus Schs., Ohio, 1959-61; sole practice, Circleville, Ohio, 1964—; asst. pros. atty. Pickaway County, Ohio, 1966-68. Bd. dirs. Pickaway County Pub. Library, 1965-70, pres., 1969-70; trustee Circleville United Meth. Ch., 1968-69. Mem. Circleville C. of C. (dir. 1966-69), Pickaway County Law Library Assn. (pres.), Pickaway County Bar Assn. (pres.), Ohio State Bar Assn., ABA. Methodist. Clubs: Sertoma (pres.), Pickaway Country (dir.). Avocations: Little League baseball; basketball. Home: 650 Ridgewood Dr Box 682 Circleville OH 43113 Office: 149 W Franklin St Circleville OH 43113

BENNINK, DUANE EARL, association executive; b. Guthrie County, Iowa, July 21, 1935; s. Lawrence D. and Cora M. Bennink; B.S., Iowa State U., 1959; m. Marlene V. Clark, Aug. 24, 1958; children—Karen C., Kathleen J., David D. Vocat. agr. instr. Marathon (Iowa) Consol. Schs., 1959-63; asst. dir. Iowa Soil Conservation Com., Des Moines, 1963-68; cons. N.W. Iowa Farm Bus. Assn., Sheldon, 1968-79; state coordinator Iowa Farm Bus. Assns., Ames, 1979—. Mem. Iowa Soc. Farm Mgrs. and Rural Appraisers, Am. Soc. Farm Mgrs. and Rural Appraisers, Iowa Consultants Assn. (pres. 1975-77), Nat. Assn. Farm Bus. Analysis Specialists (pres. 1979-80), Iowa State U. Alumni Assn. Methodist. Home: 126 Britson Circle Roland IA 50236 Office: Iowa Farm Bus Assns 226 SE 16th St Ames IA 50010

BENOIT, ALLEN DOUGLAS, educational administrator; b. Chgo., Dec. 5, 1944; s. Allen Raymond and Dorothy Lucille (Outland) B.; m. Lynnette Clare Marshall, Sept. 11, 1965; children—Collette Clare, Nannette Jolie, Juliette Cherie. B.S. in Edn., No. Ill. U., 1962-66; M.A., San Jose State U., 1972; adminstrv. cert. U. Wis.-Milw., 1974-76. Tchr. Castro Valley Schs., Calif., 1966-68, Hayward Area Schs., Calif., 1968-72, Waterford High Sch., Wis., 1972-76; arts adminstr. Milwaukee County War Meml. Corp., Milw., 1976-78; prin. Palmyra-Eagle High Sch., Wis., 1978—. Pres. Lakeland Players, Elkhorn, Wis., 1982; v.p. Artreach Milw., 1976-78; dir. Wis. Dance Council, Madison, 1977. Mem. Nat. Assn. Secondary Sch. Prins., Assn. Supervision and Curriculum Devel., Assn. Wis. Sch. Adminstrs. (dir. 1982-84, recognition award 1984). Avocations: theatre; camping; tennis. Home: Route 2 Box 129 Palmyra WI 53156 Office: Palmyra Eagle High Sch 123 Burr Oak St Palmyra WI 53156

BENSHOFF, DIXIE LEE, psychologist; b. Ravenna, Ohio, Apr. 11, 1950; d. Roy Orrison and Pauline (Gatewood) B.; B.A., Hiram Coll., 1972; postgrad. Cambridge (Eng.) U., 1970, 73; M.Ed., Kent State U., 1973, Ph.D., 1977. Counselor, Hiram (Ohio) Coll., 1973; counselor, counseling and group resources center Kent (Ohio) State U., 1973-74, asst. to sch. counseling program for counseling and personnel services edn. dept., 1974-75; asst. dir. Portage County Mental Health Bd., Kent, 1975-78; psychologist, outpatient dir. Kevin Coleman Mental Health Center, Kent, 1978-81; instr. clin. psychology/family medicine Coll. Medicine, Northeastern Ohio U., 1979—; pres. Portage County Council Health and Social Agys., 1980; dir. aftercare and transitional services Western Res. Human Services, Akron, Ohio, 1981—; allied health profl. Akron City Hosp. Diplomate in profl. counseling Internat. Acad. Profl. Counseling and Psychotherapy; lic. psychologist, Ohio; cert. allied health profl.; listed Nat. Registry Health Services Providers in Psychology. Mem. Am. Psychol. Assn., Ohio Psychol. Assn., Assn. Orthopsychiatry, Am. Assn. Marriage and Family Therapists (clin.), Ohio Women in Psychology, Portage Exec. Women's Network, Ohio State Assn. Psychologists, Kappa Delta Pi. Contbr. articles in field to profl. jours. Home: 231 Beecher Ave Ravenna OH 44266 Office: Western Reserve Human Services 377 S Portage Path Akron OH 44320 also 1640 Franklin Ave Suite 202 Kent OH 44240

BENSHOOF, PAUL THOMAS, lawyer; b. Detroit Lakes, Minn., Oct. 13, 1951; s. Byron Lee and Helen E. B.; m. Jody Marie Grefsrud, Sept. 19, 1981; 1 child, Galen. B.A., Carleton Coll., 1974; J.D., U. Minn., 1978. Bar: Minn. 1978, Calif. 1980. Ptnr. Smith, Carpenter & Benshoof, Bemidji, Minn., 1978—. Pres. Beltrami Humane Soc., Bemidji, 1980; youth dir. United Methodist Ch., Bemidji, 1982—. Mem. Minn. Trial Lawyers Assn., Assn. Trial Lawyers Am., ABA, Minn. State Bar Assn., Bemidji C. of C. (dir. 1982-85). Mem. Democratic-Farmer-Labor Party. Club: Bemidji Kennel (pres. 1980). Home: 1110 Bemidji Ave Bemidji MN 56601 Office: Smith Carpenter & Benshoof 115 5th St Bemidji MN 56601

BENSON, DENNIS KEITH, research consultant b. Dayton, Ohio, Dec. 20, 1946; s. Charles Prue and Virginia Elizabeth (Zindorf) B.; B.A., Miami U., 1969; M.A. (fellow), Ohio State U., 1972, Ph.D. (fellow), 1976; m. Rose Anne Fredericks, Aug. 30, 1969; 1 son, Kristopher Elliott. Simulation dir. behavioral scis. lab., Ohio State U., Columbus, 1969-73, survey research dir., 1972-73, dep. dir., 1971-73, project dir. Coll. Social Work, 1977; assoc. dir. Benchmark program Acad. for Contemporary Problems, Columbus, 1973-74, dir., 1974-75; v.p., treas. C. C. DeJon, Ltd., Columbus, 1976-78; project dir. Capital U., Columbus, 1977-78; pres., chmn. bd. dirs. Appropriate Solutions, Inc., 1978—; conf. evaluator Am. Soc. Pub. Adminstrn., 1980-81; speaker, cons. in field. Bd. trustees, corr. sec. N.W. Civic Assn., 1972-73; state issues coordinator Ohio Carter Campaign Staff, 1976; mem., chmn. com. Central Ohio Bicentennial Commn., 1975-76. Fellow, Acad. for Contemporary Problems, 1974-75, Nat. Security Edn. Seminar, 1972. Mem. Am. Assn. for Pub. Opinion Research, U.S. Capital Hist. Soc., Columbus Bus. Devel. Club (past pres.), Columbus Area C. of C. (edn. and tng. com. 1981-82). Republican. Mem. Am. Bapt. Ch. Author: A Guide to Survey Research Terms, 1975; Social Area Analysis and State Social Policy Management, 1976; A Needs Assessment Survival Kit, 1978; Voluntary Service: A Study of Potential, 1979. Contbg. author: Simulation and Games, 1972, 73; pub. The Columbus Report, TECHnology NETwork; contbr. articles to profl. jours. Home: 94 W Hubbard Ave Columbus OH 43215 Office: 1357 W Lane Ave Suite 207 Columbus OH 43221

BENSON, DONALD DUANE, farmer; b. Hurley, S.D., Nov. 3, 1933; s. Allen Wilburt and Mary Friedrica (Eckstein) B.; m. Dolores Marie Wood, Sept. 2, 1956; children—James, Jacqueline, Judith. Owner, farmer, Hurley, S.D., 1956—. Pres. Zion Lutheran Ch. Council, Hurley, 1969-84; chmn. Hurley Sch. Bd. Edn., 1978-84; co.-chmn. Hurley Centennial Com., 1983; chmn. 4-H Hog Show Turner County Fair, Parker, S.D., 1975-80. Recipient Pzizer Internat. award Pzizer Internat. and S.D. Pork Producers, 1980, Pork for State award S.D. State U., 1976; named Master Pork Producer, S.D. Livestock Export Orgn., 1968. Mem. Nat. Pork Producer Council (mem. identification task force 1983—, exec. bd. dirs. 1970-72, Pork All Am. award 1970), S.D. Pork Council (performance testing com. 1980-84), Nat. Livestock Meat Bd. (bd. dirs. 1983—), Nat. SPF Accrediting Agy. (nat. dir. 1978-82), Am. Yorkshire Club, Hampshire/Duroc Swine Registry, Am. Legion. Republican. Lutheran. Avocations: painting; drawing; woodworking; hunting. Home: RD 1 Box 74-A Hurley SD 57036

BENSON, DONALD E., bottling company executive; b. 1930. B.B.A., U. Minn., 1955. With Arthur Andersen & Co., C.P.A.s, 1955-68; with MEI Corp. Mpls., 1968—, sr. v.p., 1970-77, pres., chief exec. officer, dir., 1977—. Service with U.S. Army, 1951-53. Office: MEI Corp 800 Marquette Nat Bank Bldg 40 S 6th St Minneapolis MN 55402

BENSON, DOROTHY ANN DURICK (MRS. ROBERT BRONAUGH BENSON), psychologist, business exec.; b. Grand Forks, N.D.; d. William James and Grace (Johnson) Durick; B.S. with distinction, U. N.Mex., 1950; M.A. in Psychology, U. Minn., 1952; m. Robert Bronaugh Benson, May 8, 1954. Research asst. psychology dept., U. Minn., 1950-52; instr., counselor Student Counseling Service, Kans. State Coll., 1952-54; psychometrist, counselor Stephens Coll., 1957-58; officer Benson Bldg. Materials, Inc., Columbia, Mo., 1958—; partner of Koti Krafts from Finland. Active mem. League of Women Voters, Columbia, 1955—, bd. dirs., 1955-61, pres., 1958-59; mem. exec. bd. U. Mo. YWCA, 1962-64. Mem. Phi Kappa Phi, Psi Chi, Phi Sigma. Home: PO Box 3 Columbia MO 65205 Office: Benson Bldg Materials Inc 710 Business Loop 70 W PO Box 3 Columbia MO 65205

BENSON, GEORGE LEONARD, telecommunications corporation executive; b. Seattle, Sept. 20, 1934; s. George and Gertrude (Rolph) B.; m. Kyleen Susan Gordon, Sept. 22, 1962; children—William, Barbara, Stephen, Kristin, Shanon, Pamela. B.A. in Bus., U. Wash., 1959. Sales rep. Bus. Systems, Inc., Los Angeles, 1959-64, sales mgr., 1964-66; mgr. Pacific div. NCR, San Francisco, Calif., 1966-69; br. mgr., Rochester, Minn., 1969-74, dist. dir., Milw., 1974-78; pres. Telecom North, Inc., Little Chute, Wis., 1979—. Served to sgt. U.S. Army, 1953-55. Mem. No. Wis. Telecom Assn. Republican. Methodist. Avocations: sports; reading; travel. Lodge: Rotary. Home: 6781 Pheasant Run Rd Hartford WI 53027 Office: Telecom N Inc 2301 Kelbe Dr Little Chute WI 54140

BENSON, KATHERINE ALICE, psychology educator; b. Mpls., June 12, 1949; d. Gerald Philip and Gladys Irene (Berg) B.; m. James Lyman Staebler, Aug. 8, 1981. B.S. summa cum laude, U. Minn., 1972; M.S., U. Mass.-Amherst, 1976, Ph.D., 1979. Instr. psychology U. Mass., Amherst, 1977-78; asst. prof. U. Minn., Morris, 1978—. Precinct chmn. Ward 1 Stevens County Democratic-Farmer-Labor Party, 1982—. Grantee Council on Liberal Edn., 1980, U. Minn. Grad. Sch., 1981-83; U. Minn. Grad. Sch. fellow, 1983; Bush Found. sabbatical fellow, 1985-86. Mem. Minn. Women Psychologists, AAAS, Am. Psychol. Assn., Soc. Research in Child Devel., Nat. Women's Studies Assn., NOW (Minn. chpt. adv. bd. 1983-84), Bus. & Profl. Women. Unitarian-Universalist. Contbr. articles to profl. jours. Office: Div Social Sci Univ Minn Morris MN 56267

BENSON, LAWRENCE EDWARD, ins. co. exec.; b. Mpls., July 31, 1916; s. Linus Edward and Hilma Agnita (Olausson) B.; student Bethel Coll., 1936-37; B.S., U. Minn., 1939; m. Phyllis Elaine Newman, Aug. 23, 1941; children—Laurel, Natalie, Lois, Philip, Kjersti. Underwriter, Employers of Wausau, Mpls., 1940-48; underwriting mgr. Federated Mut. Ins. Co., Owatonna, Minn., 1948-50; underwriting mgr. Mut. Service Ins. Co., St. Paul, 1950-56, dir. underwriting, 1956-61, dir. casualty actuarial dept., 1961-72, v.p. personnel, 1972-76, v.p. casualty, 1976—; dir., chmn. Minn. Ins. Guaranty Fund, Minn. FAIR Plan. Bd. mgmt. YMCA, Mpls., 1955-72, chmn., 1964-66; bd. regents Bethel Coll. and Sem., St. Paul, 1959-64, treas., 1960-62, vice chmn., 1962-64, mem. bd. President's Assos., 1967—; mem. Minn. Central Republican Com., 1966-69; bd. dirs. United Way, St. Paul, 1973-80. Served with U.S. Army, 1942-46. Recipient service award YMCA, 1963, Bethel Coll. and Sem., 1965, Minn. Central Rep. Com., 1966, also various PTA's; cert. Life Office Mgmt. Assn. Mem. Soc. C.P.C.U.'s (cert.), Am. Acad. Actuaries (cert.), Am. Swedish Inst. Republican. Baptist. Club: Midland Hills Country. Contbr. to ins. publs.

BENSON, PAUL, federal judge; b. Verona, N.D., June 1, 1918; s. Edwin C. and Annie (Peterson) B.; B.S.C., U. N.D., 1942; LL.B., George Washington U., 1949; m. Dec. 29, 1942; children—Santal E. Manos, Polly Benson Diem, Amy, Laurel L., Peter. Admitted to N.D. bar; adminstrv. asst. to Senator Milton R. Young, 1946-49; assoc. H.B. Spiller and Cavalier, 1949-50; mem. firm Shaft, Benson, Shaft and McConn, 1950-71; atty. gen. State of N.D., 1954-55; now chief judge U.S. Dist. Ct., Dist. N.D., Fargo. Tchr. U. N.D. Chmn. Grand Forks County chpt. ARC, 1954-55. Served with USNR, 1942-46. Mem. ABA, Am. Judicature Soc., State Bar Assn. N.D., Am. Legion, V.F.W. Lutheran (pres. congregation Grand Forks 1959). Lodges: Masons, Shriners, Elks. Office: 340 Federal Bldg PO Box 3164 US Courthouse Fargo ND 58102*

BENSON, ROBERT HENRY, patent lawyer, biotechnology patent program administrator; b. Chgo., Dec. 15, 1942; s. Henry E. and Mary Ann (Larsen) B.; m. Charlotte Ann Moser, May 21, 1977; 1 child, Jonathan N. B.S., U. Fla., 1967, Ph.D., 1972; J.D., U. Houston, 1980. Bars: U.S. Patent Office 1981, Va. 1982, Ill. 1984. Asst. prof. biochemistry U. Tex. Med. Sch., Houston, 1973-80; assoc. Oblon, Fisher, Spivak, McClelland and Maier, P.C., Arlington, Va., 1981-82; dir. biotech. patent program G. D. Searle & Co., Skokie, Ill., 1982—; adj. faculty Northwestern U., Evanston, Ill., 1983—. Contbr. articles on biochemistry to profl. jours. Research grantee NIH, 1974-77. Mem. Am. Soc. Microbiology, Am. Intellectual Property Law Assn., Chgo. Patent Law Assn., ABA, Va. Bar Assn., Ill. Bar Assn. Home: 723 Monticello Pl Evanston IL 60201 Office: G D Searle & Co Box 1045 Skokie IL 60076

BENSON, RODNEY FREDRICK, chamber of commerce executive; b. Sheldon, Iowa, Jan. 3, 1938; s. Fredrick William and Myrtle (Steen) B.; m. Kay Harlean Halden, Oct. 26, 1963 (div. 1982); children—Darcy, Lisa, Heather, Tricia; m. Carol Roberts, Mar. 5, 1983. B.A., U. Colo., 1961. Cert. chamber exec. Exec. v.p. S. St. Paul C. of C., 1966-67; dist. mgr. U.S. C. of C., Jacksonville, Fla., 1968-69; pres. Kalamazoo County C. of C., Mich., 1970-74, pres. Boulder C. of C., Colo., 1975-80; project mgr. City Venture Corp., Mpls., 1980-81; pres. Ann Arbor Area C. of C., Mich., 1982—; dir. Mich. Tech. Council, Ann Arbor, Mich., 1982—; dir., treas. Tech. Internat. Council, Ann Arbor, 1983—, Washenaw Devel. Council, Ann Arbor, 1983—. Trustee Kalamazoo Valley Community Coll., Mich., 1971-74; regent U.S. C. of C. Insts., Washington, 1973-78; dir. Ann Arbor Summer Festival, 1984—. Served with U.S. Army, 1960-61. Mem. Am. C. of C. Execs., Colo. C. of C. Execs. (pres. 1978), Mich. C. of C. Execs. (pres. 1973-74, bd. dir. 1984—). Republican. Avocations: boating; cooking. Office: Ann Arbor Area C of C 207 E Washington Ann Arbor MI 48104

BENSON, WARREN STEN, seminary administrator, religion educator; b. Chgo., Aug. 23, 1929; s. Sten Walter and Evalyn Gladys (Arneson) B.; m. Lenore Evelyn Ellis, Aug. 22, 1953; children—Scott Warren, Bruce Ellis. B.A., Northwestern Coll., Roseville, Minn., 1952; Th.M., Dallas Theol. Sem., 1956; M.R.E., Southwestern Bapt. Theol. Sem., 1957; Ph.D., Loyola U., Chgo., 1975. Asst. prof. Christian edn. Trinity Evang. Div. Sch., Deerfield, Ill., 1970-74, prof. Christian edn., assoc. dean, 1978, prof., acting dean, 1979, v.p. acad. adminstrn., prof. Christian edn., 1980—; assoc. prof. Christian edn., Dallas Theol. Sem., 1974-78; minister edn. Winnetka Bible Ch., Ill., 1957-62; minister youth and edn. First Covenant Ch., Mpls., 1962-65, minister edn. Lake Ave. Congl. Ch., Pasadena, Calif., 1965-69; central regional dir. Gospel Light Pubs., Ventura, Calif., 1969-72. Author: (with others) Christian Education: Its History and Philosophy, 1983. Editor: (with others) Youth Education in the Church, 1978. Mem. Evang. Theol. Soc., Nat. Assn. Profs. Christian Edn., Religious Edn. Assn., Midwest History of Edn. Soc., Assn. Profs. and Researchers in Religious Edn., Am. Assn. Higher Edn. Republican. Mem. Evang. Free Ch. Am. Avocations: reading; golf. Home: 714 Arthur Ct Libertyville IL 60048 Office: Trinity Evang Div Sch 2056 Half Day Rd Deerfield IL 60015

BENSONHAUER, KAREN LYNN, librarian, lay worker; b. Hammond, Ind., Sept. 29, 1948; d. Ishmael James and Ivory (Pigg) Rose; m. William Jonathon Seum, June 23, 1973 (div. Aug. 1978); m. Robert W. Bensonhauer, Aug. 26, 1985. B.A., Morehead State U., 1970. Cert. tchr. English and library sci., Ohio. Librarian, Circleville High Sch., Ohio, 1971—. Bd. dirs. Good Shepherd United Methodist Ch., Circleville, 1985—, mem. library com., 1984—, youth leader, 1984—, tchr. jr. high Sunday sch., 1984—; pres. Am. Cancer Soc., Circleville, 1983-84, sec., 1982-83. Mem. Circleville Edn. Assn. (pres. 1983—), Ohio Edn. Assn., NEA, Ohio Ednl. Library Media Assn., ALA, Assn. Sch. Librarians. Democrat. Avocations: reading; crafts; computers. Home: 114 Seyfert Ave Circleville OH 43113 Office: Circleville High Sch 380 Clark Dr Circleville OH 43113

BENT, ALAN EDWARD, political science educator, administrator; b. Shanghai, China, June 22, 1939; s. Walter J. and Tamara (Rocklin) B.; m. Dawn Bickler, Aug. 13, 1977. B.S., San Francisco State U., 1963; M.A. in Internat. Relations, U. So. Calif., 1968; M.A. in Govt., Claremont Grad. Sch., 1970, Ph.D. in Govt., 1971; M.B.A., Xavier U., 1985. Instr. polit. sci. Chapman Coll., 1969-70; research assoc. Claremont Grad. Sch., 1970-71; asst. prof. polit. sci., dir. grad. program pub. adminstrn., assoc. dir. Inst. Govtl. Studies and Research, Memphis State U., 1971-74; assoc. prof., chmn. dept. pub. adminstrn. Sch. Mgmt., Calif. State U.-Dominguez Hills, 1974-77; head polit. sci. dept. U. Cin., 1977-81, prof., 1977-81, 82—, dir. grad. program pub. adminstrn., 1982-83, dir. grad. studies, 1985—; prof., dean Coll. Arts and Scis., U. No. Colo., Greeley, 1981-82; cons. in field. Served to capt. USAF, 1964-69; Vietnam. Sr. faculty fellow Nat. Assn. Schs. of Pub. Affairs and Adminstrn., 1981-82. Mem. AAUP, Am. Polit. Sci. Assn., Am. Soc. Pub. Adminstrn. Author: Escape from Anarchy: A Strategy for Urban Survival, 1972; The Politics of Law Enforcement: Conflict and Power in Urban Communities, 1974; (with others) Police, Criminal Justice and the Community, 1976, Collective Bargaining in the Public Sector: Labor-Management Relations and Public Policy, 1978; editor: (with others) Urban Administration: Management, Politics and Change, 1976; mem. editorial bd. Rev. Pub. Personnel Adminstrn., 1980—; contbr. articles to profl. jours. Home: 537 Howell Ave Cincinnati OH 45220 Office: Dept Polit Sci 1017 Crosley Tower U Cincinnati Cincinnati OH 45221

BENTLAGE, RICHARD AUGUST, educator; b. Indpls., June 26, 1936; s. Kurt Fred and Marie (Rossi) B.; grad. summa cum laude Elkhart U., 1955; pre-med. student Ind. U., 1955-58; m. Betty Lynn Thompson, Sept. 6, 1980. Adminstrv. asst. disaster relief ARC, Indpls., 1955-56; X-ray technologist radiol./nuclear St. Vincent's Hosp., Indpls., 1956-57; med./X-ray technologist and dept. head Morgan Health Center, Indpls., 1957-58; med. research technologist, med./surg. staff VA Hosp., Indpls., 1958-61; med. technologist, med. staff White County Meml. Hosp., Monticello, Ind., 1961-64, lab. supr., dept. head, 1964-75; exec. dir. Youth Service Bur. White County, Monticello, 1976-80, coordinator child protection service team, 1978-80; profl. research assoc. dept. pathology Purdue U., 1980—; cons. microbiologist Ind. Bd. Health; cons., lectr. in field. Mem. adv. bd. Planned Parenthood. Served in USNR, 1953-61. Mem. Am. Med. Technologists, Am., Ind. socs. med. technologists, Nat. Assn. Prevention Profls., Am. Personnel and Guidance Assn., Ind. Youth Services Assn., Confrat. Christian Doctrine (cert. instr.), Pi Rho Zeta (life). Home: 124 W Stadium West Lafayette IN 47906 Office: Purdue U Botany and Plant Pathology Lilly Life Sci Bldg West Lafayette IN 47907

BENTLEY, JAMES HERBERT, electrical engineer; b. Portland, Oreg., May 23, 1935; s. Robert Athy and Helen Louise (Niles) B.; B.S. in Elec. Engring., Mich. Tech. U., 1957; M.S. in Elec. Engring. (Hughes Fellow), U. So. Calif., 1959; m. Elizabeth Anne Willard, Aug. 19, 1958; children—Mary Katherine, John Robert. Elec. engr. Hughes Aircraft Co., Los Angeles, 1957-59, Philco Corp., Palo Alto, Calif., 1960-64, Bendix Corp., Washington, 1964-65, Univac, St. Paul, 1965-68, Honeywell, Inc., Mpls., 1968-76, 3M Co., St. Paul, 1976-79, Magnetic Peripherals, Inc., Mpls., 1979; dir. Ecology Enterprises, Inc.; adj. prof. elec. engring. U. Minn., Mpls. Mem. Edina Planning Commn.; past chmn. Edina Environ. Quality Commn., 1975-76. Recipient Mayor's commendation award City of Edina, 1976; registered profl. engr., Minn. Mem. Nat., Minn. socs. profl. engrs., Tau Beta Pi, Eta Kappa Nu. Presbyterian. Home: 5120 Grove St Edina MN 55436 Office: 7801 Computer Ave Minneapolis MN 55435

BENTLEY, JANICE BABB, librarian, retired; b. Phila., Jan. 13, 1933; d. John William and Janice (Whittier) Babb; A.B., U. Ill., 1954, M.S., 1956; Dir. dept. information Nat. Assn. of Real Estate Bds., Chgo., 1956-63; librarian CNA Financial Corp., Chgo., 1963-76, firm Mayer, Brown & Platt, Chgo., 1976-85. Mem. Am. Assn. Law Librarians, Chgo. Assn. Law Libraries (pres. 1978-79), Spl. Libraries Assn. (chmn. housing bldg. and planning sect. 1962-63, chmn. social sci. div. 1965-66, pres. Ill. chpt. 1967-68, chmn. ins. div. 1974-75). Illiniweks (chmn. Chgo. 1959). Author: (with Beverly F. Dordick) Real Estate Information Sources, 1963, Real Estate Appraisal Bibliography, 1965. Home: 1825 N Lincoln Plaza Chicago IL 60614

BENTLEY, LAUREL PALESTINE, motel and restaurant exec.; b. Oran, Iowa, Aug. 26, 1917; s. Burton Fay and Mollie Mary (Williams) B.; B.S.C., U. Iowa, 1938; spl. course Iowa State U., 1941; m. Phyllis Marie Lichty, Aug. 9, 1950; children—P. Dawn Bentley Pollitt, Philip Laurel. Sec., B.F. Bentley-Gilt Edge Creamery Co., Plainfield, Iowa, 1938-44; sales trainee Standard Oil Co., Mason City, Iowa, 1946-47; sales rep. to sales mgr. Louden Machinery Co., Fairfield, Iowa, 1947-60; regional mgr. bldgs. and equipment Honeggers & Co., Fairbury, Ill., 1961-63; mfrs. rep., 1963-72; owner, operator Dream Motel, Fairfield, 1972—, Stever House Restaurant, Fairfield, 1976—. Active Boy Scouts Am.; precinct caucus chmn. Jefferson County Republican Party, 1980; fin. chmn. Jefferson County Rep. Central Com., 1980. Served with USNR, 1945-46. Mem. Barn Equipment Assn. (v.p. 1960), Iowa Hotel and Motel Assn. (pres. 1978-79, 79-80, chmn. bd. 1980-81), Am. Hotel and Motel Assn. Clubs: Elks, Masons. Home and Office: Dream Motel Hwy 34W Fairfield IA 52556

BENTLEY, LYNDA ELLEN, sewage service administrator; b. Green Bay, Wis., Apr. 18, 1945; d. Gordon Noel and Marie Ellen (Bergholz) B. B.S. in Biology, U. Wis., 1969. Cert. wastewater operator, Wis. Lab. technician water pollution research and devel. grant, Green Bay, 1968-69; lab. technician Green Bay Met. Sewerage Dist., 1969-76, lab. supr., 1976-80, quality control mgr., 1980—; vice chmn. Wis. Wastewater Works Operators Clarifier Operators (Lake Michigan dist.), Madison, 1981-82. Co-editor Wis. Wastewater Works Operators, 1980—. Advisor ednl. research and devel., Green Bay, 1977-80; plant chmn. United Way, Brown County, Wis., 1984. Mem. Wis. Lab. Assn., Am. Chem. Soc., Water Pollution Control Fedn., Nat. Wildlife Fedn. Lutheran. Avocations: miniature dollhouse builder; creative stitching, fishing; swimming. Home: 1226 Elmore St Green Bay WI 54303 Office: Met Sewerage Dist 2231 N Quincy St Green Bay WI 54301

BENTLEY, THOMAS HORTON, III, construction company executive; b. Milw., Aug. 3, 1946; s. Thomas Horton and Virginia M. (Zivney) B.; B.S. in Bus. Adminstrn., Bucknell U., 1969; m. Sally Lynne Ross, Oct. 9, 1971; children—Todd, Lauren, Kimberly. Sec.-treas. Bentley & Son, Inc., Milw., 1970-83, pres., 1983—, also dir., export mgr., export boxing div., 1969—; pres., owner Bentley Corp. Wis., 1983—; bd. dirs., chmn. legis. com. Associated Gen. Contractors, Milw. chpt., 1972—, Allied Constrn. Employers Asso., 1974—; chmn. Nat. A.G.C. Legis. Network, Wis., 1974—; vice chmn. City of Milw. Bd. of Standards and Appeals. Bd. dirs. Bel Canto Chorus Milw., 1983-84. Mem. Builders Exchange, Asso. Gen. Contractors, Allied Constrn. Employers Assn. Lutheran. Clubs: Town Tennis, Wis., Sons of Bosses Internat. (pres. Milw. chpt. 1979-81), Milw. North Shore Racquet, Milw. Rotary. Office: 3031 W Mill Rd Milwaukee WI 53209

BENTLEY, WOODROW ALTON, music educator, composer; b. Lynden, Wash., Sept. 11, 1914; s. Charles Henry and Eva (Kenoyer) B.; m. Marjory Katherine Thompson, Jan. 20, 1946 (div. May 1954); m. 2d, Mary Virginia Schmitz, Aug. 19, 1961. Studied piano with Kenneth E. Heun, 1935-41; B.Mus., Sherwood Music Sch., 1950; M.Mus., Northwestern U., 1951; M.A., Columbia U., 1961. Pvt. piano tchr., dance orch. leader, Bellingham, Wash., 1944-46; asst. theory dept. Sherwood Music Sch., Chgo., 1946-50, tchr. piano and theory, 1952-59; tchr. piano Joliet (Ill.) Conservatory Music, 1952-56; tchr. piano and theory Wilbur Wright Coll., Chgo. City Colls., 1952-79; pvt. tchr. piano Fine Arts Bldg., Chgo., 1961-69; propr. Arcturus Music Co., Chgo., 1976—; assoc. prof. Wilbur Wright Coll., Chgo., 1969-75, prof., 1975-79. Mem. Am. Soc. Composers, Authors and Pubs., Am. Fedn. Musicians, Ill. Community Coll. Annuitants Assn., Meridian High Sch. Alumni Assn., Pi Kappa Lambda. Democrat. Clubs: Northwestern, Apollo Mus., Chgo. Hist. Soc. (Chgo.); Northwestern Music Alumni (Evanston, Ill.); Germania. Composer: Two Rhythm Pieces for Piano, 1959; Centennial Hymn for Central Church of Chicago, 1975; Bicentennial Hymn, 1976; also short songs and piano pieces. Home: 2400 Lakeview Ave Chicago IL 60614 Office: 53 W Jackson Blvd Room 928 Chicago IL 60604

BENTON, HUGH ARTHUR, international ventures executive; b. Charlottesville, Va., Oct. 25, 1929; s. Arthur Ferguson and Marion (Duncan) B.; m. Nancy Nubbard, Oct. 6, 1956; children—Anne Arthur, Margaret Hubbard. Student, U. Rochester, 1947-48; B.S., U.S. Naval Acad., 1952. With U.S. Navy Nuclear Submarine Program, 1952-79; dep. to chief of personnel U.S. Navy, Washington, 1979-81; ret. as rear adm., 1981; mgr. adminstrn. and quality assurance Babcock & Wilcox Fossil Power Div., Barberton, Ohio, 1981-82, mgr. operating equipment services, 1982-83; mgr. ventures and licensing Babcock & Wilcox Internat., Barberton, 1983—; mng. dir. PT Babcock & Wilcox Indonesia, Jakarta and Batam Island, 1984—. Gov. Barberton Citizens Hosp. Devel. Fund, 1982—; bd. dirs. Jr. Achievement of Akron Area, Inc., Ohio, 1982—, Akron-Canton Council Navy League, 1984—, Ohio Ballet, 1982-83. Mem. U.S. Naval Alumni Assn. Episcopalian. Club: Navy Flying. Lodge: Rotary. Avocations: skiing, tennis, aerobics, flying light planes. Home: 2070 Ridgewood Rd Akron OH 44313 Office: Babcock & Wilcox Internat 20 S Van Buren Ave Barberton OH 44203

BENTON, PHYLLIS LORETTA, educational administrator; b. Omaha, July 2, 1918; d. William Carl and Kathryn Maude (Coiner) Wilson; student Christian Coll., Columbia, Mo., 1935-36, U. So. Calif., 1937-38; B.E., Drake U., 1940; M.A., U. Nebr., 1961, Ed.D., 1965; m. Dudley Benton Conner, Feb. 2, 1941 (dec. Nov. 1967); children—Ellen Kay Conner Leonard, Phillip Douglas; m. Robert E. Benton, Jan. 2, 1980; stepchildren—Robert K., Harry E. Tchr. sr. high sch., Des Moines, 1939-41; tchr. English and speech, Silver City, Iowa, 1945-47; substitute tchr. sr. high schs., several states, 1941-45; teletype operator Western Union, Los Angeles, 1942-43, Standard Oil Co., 1943; worker family hatchery, feed store Malvern, Iowa, 1930-35, 45-57; sr. high tchr., jr. high sch. counselor, community counselor Omaha Pub. Schs., 1957-82; lectr. adult night sch. Past adv. Rainbow Girls, Boy Scouts Am., Girl Scouts U.S.A. Mem. Greater Omaha C. of C. (pres. women's div. 1976), Pilot Internat. (gov. dist. 12 1976), Nebr. State, Omaha edn. assns., Council for Exceptional Children, AAUW, NEA, Omaha Pub. Schs. Adminstrs. Assn., Am. Legion Aux., Omaha Interclub Council (dir. 1971-72), County Improvement Club, PEO, Kappa Alpha Theta. Republican. Methodist. Clubs: Pilot Omaha pres. 1970-72), Order of Eastern Star (worthy matron 1957). Home: 12519 William Omaha NE 68144 also Route 1 Tabor IA 51653

BENTON, ROBERT DEAN, state school superintendent; b. Guthrie Center, Iowa, July 22, 1929; s. John H. and Luella M. (Rawlings) B.; B.A., U. No. Iowa, 1951, M.A., 1956, Ed.D., U. No. Colo., 1961; m. Rachel Swanson, July 29, 1951; children—Camille, John, Scott. Tchr., Ruthven, Iowa, 1953-56, Mason City, Iowa, 1956-58; dir. public info., coordinator secondary edn., Rapid City, S.D., 1958-61, asst. supt. in charge instrn., 1961-66; supt. schs., Council Bluffs, Iowa, 1966-72; state commr. public instrn. State of Iowa, Des Moines, 1972—; part-time journalism tchr. summer sessions Colo. State Coll., 1959-61; mem. Iowa Adv. Council for Vocat. Edn., 1970-72; mem. Commn. on Fed. Paperwork, 1975-77; mem. adv. council on nutrition U.S. Dept. Agr., 1975-78; mem. Fed. Edn. Data Acquisition Council, 1979-81. Hon. chmn., mem. founding com. Friends of Music Community Concert Series, 1967; bd. dirs. Chanticleer Community Theater, 1968-72, Christian Home, 1968-72. Served with USMC, 1951-53. Named Boss of yr., Jaycees, Council Bluffs, 1970; Outstanding Young Man of yr., Jr. C. of C., Rapid City, 1965. Mem. NEA, Council of Chief State Sch. Officers (pres. 1981), C. of C., Phi Delta Kappa, Theta Alpha Phi. Methodist. Rotarian. Office: Grimes Office Bldg Des Moines IA 50319*

BENTON, ROBERT LEON, banker; b. Chgo., Dec. 26, 1951; s. Francis and Margaret Ruth (Smith) Kantor; m. Janette Diane Harrison, Mar. 11, 1978. Bookeeper, Merrill Lynch, Chgo., 1971-73; mgr. ops. La Salle Nat. Bank, Chgo., 1973-76; credit mgr. Skil Corp., Chgo., 1976-79; ops. officer Am. Nat. Bank, Chgo., 1979-83; asst. v.p. Exchange Nat. Bank, Chgo., 1983—. Lodges: Masons, K.T. (commdr. Siloam Chgo. Commandery 1984—). Home: 9946 W Irving Park Rd Schiller Park IL 60176 Office: Exchange Nat Bank 120 S La Salle St Chicago IL 60690

BENTON, TERRY LEE, engineer; b. Grinnell, Iowa, Aug. 11, 1949; s. Emery Guy and Ethel Mae (Weidendorf) B.; m. Patricia Ann Middleton, June 17, 1967; children—Wendy Elizabeth, Mary Anne. B.S. in Aerospace Engring., Iowa State U., 1972. Registered profl. engr. Mo. Assoc. engr. structural devel. McDonnell-Douglas, St. Louis, 1972-73, engr. fatigue and fracture, 1973-75, sr. engr. product strength, 1975-81, lead engr. structural tech., 1981-82; mgr. applied tech./engring. Nat. Water Lift, Kalamazoo, Mich., 1982—. Patentee in field of control systems. Mem. AIAA, Kalamazoo C. of C. Lutheran. Club: Toastmasters. Avocations: tennis; golf; hunting; fishing. Home: 8497 Warbler Kalamazoo MI 49002 Office: Nat Water Lift 2200 Palmer Kalamazoo MI 49001

BENTON-BORGHI, BEATRICE HOPE, educational consultant; b. San Antonio, Nov. 7, 1946; d. Donald Francis and Beatrice Hope (Peche) Benton; A.B. in Chemistry, North Adams State Coll., 1968; M.Secondary Edn., Boston U., 1972; m. Peter T. Borghi, Aug. 12, 1980; children—Kathryn Benton Borghi, Sarah Benton Borghi. Tchr. chemistry Cathedral High Sch., Springfield, Mass., 1968-69; tchr. sci. and history Munich (W.Ger.) Am. High Sch., 1969-70; tchr. English, Tokyo, Japan, 1970-71; tchr. chemistry and sci. Marlborough (Mass.) High Sch., 1971-80; project dir., adminstr. ESEA, Marlborough Pub. Schs., 1976-77; project dir., proposal writer Title III, Title IX, U.S. Dept. Edn., 1975-76, 76-77; evaluation team New Eng. Assn. Schs. and Colls., 1974, 78; mem. regional dept. edn. com., 1977-78; ednl. cons., lectr., 1978—. Energy conservation rep. Marlborough's Overall Econ. Devel. Com., 1976; chmn. Marlborough's Energy Conservation Task Force, 1975; dir. Walk for Mankind, 1972; sec. Group Action for Marlborough Environment, 1975-76; bd. dirs. Girls Club, Marlborough, 1979; pres. Sisters, Inc., 1979-83. Mem. Parents of Exceptional Children, Council for Exceptional Children. Club: St. Agatha's Women's. Home and office: 2449 Edington Rd Columbus OH 43221

BENTZEL, CHARLES HOWARD, financial executive; b. Balt., July 30, 1928; s. Reece Emory and Idel Burton; B.A., U. Balt., 1952, B.S., 1962; D.Comml. Sci., London Inst. Applied Research, 1973; m. Wandalee Baer, July 27, 1947; children—Brent, Alan, Leslie. Vice pres., chief fin. officer Roblin Industries, Inc., N.Y.C., 1968-69; v.p., dir. fin., controller ITT and subs., N.Y.C. and abroad, 1969-76; v.p., chief fin. officer Trane Co., Wis., 1976-79, Iscott, Trinidad, 1980-82; pres., chief exec. officer Serverance Ref. Lab., San Antonio, 1982-84, also dir.; pres., chief exec. officer Foam Cutting Engrs., Inc., Addison, Ill., also mem. bd. dirs.; dir. Data Terminals Corp. Bd. dirs. YMCA, Wis., 1976-79. Mem. Internat. Assn. Fin. Execs. Insts. (dir.), Brazilian Fin. Execs. Inst. (hon., life mem.), Fin. Execs. Inst., Am. Acctg. Assn., Nat. Assn. Accts., Internat. Treas. Assn. Republican. Clubs: N.Y. Athletic, Marco Polo, Fair Oaks Golf and Country, Plaza; Masons (Md., Argentina, Brazil). Contbg. author: The Modern Accountants Handbook, 1973. Home: 25632 Drake Rd Barrington IL 60010

BENZ, JOHN DOUGLAS, architect; b. Sheffield, Iowa, May 7, 1937; s. Lester G. and Marguerite (Held) B.; m. Diana J. Baker, Dec. 21, 1959; children—Philip Andrew, Mary Elizabeth. B.Arch., Iowa State U., 1962. Registered architect, Iowa, Colo., Calif., Nebr., N.Mex., Fla., Ala., Wis. Architect, Durrant Group, Dubuque, Iowa, 1961-66; prin. Hansen Lind Meyer, Iowa City, 1966—. Archtl. works include: Iowa City Pub. Library, 1982, Green Hills, Ames, Iowa, 1985, Harrogate Community, Lakewood, N.J., 1984, Rose Med. Ctr., Denver, 1985. Mem. AIA, Soc. of Mktg. Profl. Services, Am. Assn. Homes for Aged, Soc. Am. Mil. Engrs., Am. Assn. Hosp. Planning. Republican. Methodist. Clubs: Order of Knoll (Iowa State U., Ames); Univ. Iowa Presidents, Univ. Athletic (Iowa City). Lodge: Rotary. Home: Route 6 Iowa City IA 52240 Office: Hansen Lind Mayer Drawer 310 Iowa City IA 52244

BENZICK, WILLIAM JOSEPH, food service management company executive; b. Le Center, Minn., Jan. 10, 1941; s. Alphonse Cornelius and Johanna Sophia (Malinski) B.; m. Mary Ellen Anderson, Feb. 23, 1963 (div. Apr. 1981); children—John William, Amy (dec.); m. 2d, Linda Rue Benzick, Apr. 22, 1981. Regional food dir. Canteen Corp., Mpls., 1970-73, area food dir., Chgo., 1973-75; pres. Best, Inc., St. Paul, 1975—. Bd. dirs. Sheriffs Youth Programs, Austin, Minn., 1982-83, Ramsey County Sheriffs Sch. Safety Patrol, St. Paul, 1982-83; mem. Council for Econ. Devel., St. Paul. Named Minn. Small Businessman, SBA, 1983. Lodge: Lions (St. Paul). Home: 4137 Brigadoon Dr Shoreview MN 55112 Office: 563 Payne Ave Saint Paul MN 55101

BENZON, HONORIO TABAL, anesthesiologist; b. Ilocos Sur, Philippines, Sept. 12, 1946; came to U.S., 1972, s. Alejo Gonzales and Concepcion Tacto (Tabal) B.; B.S., Far Eastern U., Manila, 1966, M.D., 1971; m. Julieta Palpal-latoc, May 30, 1970; children—Barbara Hazel, Hubert Anthony. Intern, Overlook Hosp., Summit, N.J., 1972-73; resident in anesthesia U. Cin. Med. Center, 1973-75, Northwestern U. affiliated hosps., 1975-76; practice medicine specializing in anesthesiology, Chgo., 1976—; assoc. dept. anesthesia Northwestern U. Med. Sch., 1976-80, asst. prof., 1980—; assoc. staff Northwestern Meml. Hosp., 1976-82, attending staff, 1982—; assoc. dir. Pain Clinic dept. anesthesia, attending staff VA Lakeside Hosp., 1976—; cons. staff Rehab. Inst. Chgo. Diplomate Am. Bd. Anesthesiology. Fellow Am. Coll. Anesthesiologists; mem. AMA, Am. Soc. Anesthesiologists, Internat. Anesthesia Research Soc., Am. Soc. Regional Anesthesia. Roman Catholic. Contbr. numerous articles to med. jours., chpts. to books. Home: 1150 White Mountain Dr Northbrook IL 60062 Office: 303 E Chicago Ave Chicago IL 60611

BERA, ANIL KUMAR, economics educator; b. Midnapore, Bengal, India, Feb. 28, 1955; s. Hari P. and Bimala B. B.S. with honors, Calcutta U. (India), 1975; M.Stats., Indian Statis. Inst., 1977; Ph.D., Australian Nat. U., 1982. Jr. research fellow Indian Statis. Inst., New Delhi, 1977-79; research fellow CORE, Universite Catholique de Louvain, Louvain-La-Neuve, Belgium, 1982-83; asst. prof. econs. U. Ill., Champaign, 1983—. Contbr. articles on estimating and testing of econometric models to profl. jours. Mem. Am. Econ. Assn., Am. Statis. Assn., Econometric Soc., Internat. Inst. Forecasters; jr. fellow Royal Statis. Soc. Avocations: sports, literature, travel. Office: Dept Economics Univ Illinois 1206 S 6th St Champaign IL 61820

BERAN, JAN EMIL, lawyer, real estate broker; b. Schuyler, Nebr., Feb. 21, 1954; s. Emil J. and H. Nadine (Cerny) B.; m. Donna L.; 1 dau., Sarah. A.A., Platte Coll., 1974; B.A., U. Nebr., 1978, J.D., 1983. Bar: Nebr. 1983. Parts salesman Kracl Implement Co., Schuyler, 1974-76; real estate salesman Nebr. Real Estate Co., Lincoln, Nebr., 1977-79; retail sales asst. mgr. Baker Hardware Co., Lincoln, 1979-81; sole practice, Lincoln, 1983—. Author U. Nebr. Coll. Law Alumni Survey, 1983. Mem. ABA, Nebr. Bar Assn. Republican. Office: 734 Stuart Bldg Lincoln NE 68508

BERARD, MARJORIE NELSON, health care administration consultant; b. Chippewa Falls, Wis., Aug. 15, 1918; d. Eli William and Emily (Picotte) Nelson; B.A., Coll. St. Benedict, 1940; M.S. in Social Work, St. Louis U., 1942; m. Celse A. Berard, Oct. 5, 1943; children—Sister Maryann, Michele Berard Reardon, Suzanne Berard Parks, Celse A., Renee, Elise, Jeanne. Social worker, dept. of children Cath. Charities of St. Louis, 1941-69; psychiat. social worker, community mental health clinic St. Louis State Hosp., also outpatient clinic St. Francis Mercy Hosp., 1966-74; founder, exec. dir. Profl. Counseling Center, Inc., New Haven, Mo., 1972-78; founder, adminstr. Profl. Home Health Services, Inc., New Haven, 1974-85; cons. med. social work to community orgns. Recipient Univ. Alumni Merit award St. Louis U. Sch. Social Service, 1984; Disting. Alumna award Coll. of St. Benedict. Mo. Div. Health grantee, 1974. Mem. Acad. Cert. Social Workers, Nat. Assn. Social Workers (named Social Worker of Yr., Mo. chpt. 1981), Mo. Assn. Social Workers (Social Worker of Yr. award 1981), Nat. Assn. Home Health Agys., Mo. Assn. Home Health Agys., Soc. Hosp. Social Work Dirs. Am. Hosp. Assn., Soc. Hosp. Social Work Dirs. Mo. Hosp. Assn. Roman Catholic. Home: 1508 1st Pkwy Washington MO 63090

BERDAHL, CLARENCE ARTHUR, educator; b. Baltic, S.D., June 14, 1890; s. Anders J. and Karen (Otterness) B.; A.B., St. Olaf Coll. 1914, LL.D., 1958; A.M., U. S.D., 1917, LL.D., 1961; Ph.D. (fellow), U. Ill., 1920; m. Evelyn Tripp, June 9, 1926. Cik. archives div. War Dept., Washington, 1914-15; asst. in periodicals div. Library of Congress, 1916; instr. polit. sci. U. Ill., 1920-22, asso., 1922-25, asst. prof., 1925-29, asso. prof., 1929-30, prof., 1930-61, prof. emeritus dept. polit sci., 1961—, chmn. div. social scis., 1935-39, chmn. dept. polit. sci., 1942-48; tchr. summers U. Tex., 1920, Tulane U., 1921, Ohio State U., 1923, U. Colo., 1928, Syracuse U., 1929, Columbia U., 1934, Stanford U., 1950; lectr. L'Institut Universitaire de Hautes Etudes Internationales, Geneva, 1932; vis. prof. govt. So. Ill. U., 1958-67; vis. prof. polit. sci. U. Del., 1965; chmn. bd. editors Ill. Studies in Social Scis., 1941-52; cons. U.S. Dept. State 1942-45; on London staff Office Strategic Services, 1944; mem. Internat. Secretariat, UN Conf., San Francisco, 1945; adv. com. on fgn. relations Dept. State, 1957-64, chmn., 1963-64, cons. hist. office, summer 1961; mem. exec. com. Commn. To Study Orgn. of Peace, 1953—; mem. European Conf. Tchrs. Internat. Law and Relations, Carnegie Endowment for Internat. Peace, summer 1926. Served in inf. U.S. Army, 1918. Social Sci. Research Council grantee for study abroad, 1931-32. Mem. Am. Polit. Sci. Assn. (exec. council 1932-35, 3d v.p. 1939, 2d v.p. 1944), Norwegian-Am. Hist. Assn., Am. Soc. Pub. Adminstrn. (council 1944-47), Ill. Hist. Soc., Midwest Polit. Sci. Assn. (pres. 1957-58), Am. Soc. Internat. Law (exec. council 1939-42, 43-46, 52-54), Fgn. Policy Assn., Soc. Advancement of Scandinavian Study, Geneva Research Center (adv. com. 1932-36), Conf. Tchrs. Internat. Law and Related Subjects (exec. com. 1933-42, 47-50), Internat. Studies Assn. (adv. com. 1965-69), Phi Beta Kappa (book award com. Ralph Waldo Emerson award 1966-68). Clubs: Univ., Cosmos (Washington). Author or co-author books including: War Powers of the Executive in the United States, 1921; The Policy of the United States with Respect to the League of Nations, 1932; Aspects of American Government, 1950; Toward a More Responsible Two-Party System, 1950; Presidential Nominating Politics, 1952; also articles. Home: Clark-Lindsey Village 101 W Windsor Rd Apt 4105 Urbana IL 61801

BERE, JAMES FREDERICK, manufacturing company executive; b. Chgo., July 25, 1922; s. Lambert Sr. and Madeline (Van Tatenhove) B.; student Calvin Coll., 1940-42; B.S., Northwestern U., 1946, M.B.A., 1950; m. Barbara Van Dellen, June 27, 1947; children—Robert Paul, James Frederick, David Lambert, Lynn Barbara, Becky Ann. With Clearing Machine Corp. div. U.S. Industries, Inc., 1946-53, gen. mgr. Clearing Machine Corp., 1953-56, gen. mgr. Axelson Mfg. Co. div., 1956, pres., 1957-61; pres., gen. mgr. Borg & Beck div. Borg-Warner Corp., Chgo., 1961-64, group v.p. 1964-66, exec. v.p. automotive, 1966-68, pres. corp., 1968-75, chief exec. officer, 1972—, chmn. bd., 1975—; dir. Abbott Labs., North Chicago, Continental Ill. Nat. Bank & Trust Co. of Chgo., Continental Ill. Corp. Served as lt. AUS, 1943-45. Mem. Am. Mgmt. Assn., Alpha Tau Omega. Office: Borg-Warner Corp 200 S Michigan Ave Chicago IL 60604

BERENBERG, DANNY BOB, restaurateur; b. Mpls., Sept. 10, 1944; s. Morris and Theresa Clara B.; m. Christina Ann Thompson, Sept. 10, 1977; children—Jake Robert, Jena Thompson. B.A., U. Minn., 1966; J.D., 1970. Bar: Minn. 1970, U.S. Supreme Ct. 1976. Mem. firm Schermer, Schwappach, Borkon & Ramstead, Mpls., 1970-75; mgr. Lincoln Dels Restaurants, Bloomington, Minn., 1975-77, sr. exec., 1981—; vice chmn. Lincoln Baking Co., 1981—, Lincoln Dels Inc., 1981—. Founder Kaiser Roll Found. and Kaiser Roll, wheelcair and able-bodied race; bd. dirs. Bloomington Hospitality Assn.; founder S.W. Hospitality Assn.; founder, pres., bd. dirs. 494 Ministry, 1982—; mem. Minn. Conv. Facility Commn., 1984—, Minn. Internat. Trade Commn., 1984—. Served to 1st lt. AUS, 1968. Named Bloomington Man of Yr., Bloomington mag. 1982, Small Bus. of Yr. award, 1982; recipient Teamsters Law Enforcement Recognition award, 1982, merit award Minn. N.G., 1982; Omar Bonderud-Human Rights award City of Bloomington, 1983, Minn. Human Rights award, 1985. Mem. Conv. Bur. (dir.), Minn. Restaurant Assn., Hennepin County Bar Assn., Minn. Bar Assn., Norwegian Home Guard Friends (founder). Jewish.

BERENDSEN, JAMES RICHARD, lawyer; b. Cleve., Aug. 26, 1942; m. Patricia A. Macklin, Apr. 20, 1974; children—Elaine, Elizabeth. B.B.A., Ohio U., 1964; J.D., Capital U., 1971. Bar: Ohio 1971. Atty., Columbia Gas Distbn. Cos., Columbus, Ohio, 1976—. Served with USMCR, 1965-71. Mem. ABA, Ohio Bar Assn., Columbus Bar Assn. Roman Catholic. Office: Columbia Gas Distbn Cos PO Box 117 Columbus OH 43216

BERETVAS, ANDREW FRANCIS, physicist; b. Los Angeles, Sept. 11, 1939; s. Andor and Helen M. (Sellei) B.; B.S., U. Chgo., 1960, M.S., 1962, Ph.D., 1968. Research asst. Fermi Inst., U. Chgo., 1963-67; asst. prof. physics State U. N.Y., Buffalo, 1968-74; computer cons. U. Chgo., 1974-75; research asso. high energy physics Northwestern U., Evanston, Ill., 1975-76, Argonne (Ill.) Nat. Lab., 1976-77, Fermi Nat. Lab., 1977-78, Rutgers U., 1978—. Mem. Am. Phys. Soc. Address: 6101 N Sheridan Rd Chicago IL 60660

BEREUTER, DOUGLAS KENT, congressman; b. York, Nebr., Oct. 6, 1939; s. Rupert and Evelyn B.; B.A., U. Nebr., 1961; M.C.P., Harvard U., 1966, M.P.A., 1973; postgrad. Eagleton Inst. Politics, 1975; m. Louise Anna Meyer, 1962; children—Eric David, Kirk Daniel. Residential and comml. devel. cons.; div. dir. Nebr. Dept. Econ. Devel., 1967-68; dir. Nebr. Office Planning and Programming, 1969-71; mem. Nebr. Legislature, 1974-78; mem. 96th-99th congresses from 1st Dist. Nebr. Trustee, Nebr. Wesleyan U. Served to 2d lt. U.S. Army, 1963-65. Mem. Nebr. Crime Commn., 1969-71. Mem. Am. Planning Assn., Alumni Assn. John F. Kennedy Sch. Govt. of Harvard U. (exec. council), Phi Beta Kappa. Republican. Office: 2446 Rayburn House Office Bldg Washington DC 20515

BEREVESKOS, SPIRO, patent lawyer; b. Athens, Greece, Mar. 2, 1956; came to U.S., 1956, naturalized, 1961; s. George and Dimitra (Schismenos) B.; m. Sandra Meck, Jan. 4, 1982. B.S. with distinction in Indsl. Engring., Purdue U., 1977; J.D. cum laude, Ind. U., 1981. Bar: Ind. 1981, U.S. Dist. Ct. (so. and no. dists.) Ind. 1981, U.S. Ct. Appeals (D.C. cir.). Ptnr. Woodard, Weikart, Emhardt & Naughton, Indpls., 1981—. Mem. ABA, Assn. Trial Lawyers Am., Ind. Bar Assn., Indpls. Bar Assn. Office: Woodard Weikart Emhardt & Naughton One Indiana Sq Suite 2600 Indianapolis IN 46204

BERG, B(LAINE) RICHARD, association executive; b. Los Angeles, Dec. 21, 1932; s. Henry Clemenson and Winifred Chisholm (Carr) B.; m. Jean Stewart, Apr. 7, 1956; children—Scott Richard, Gregory Stewart. B.A., Calif. State U.-Fresno, 1954; M.S., Boston U., 1957; Ph.D., St. Louis U., 1972. Newspaper reporter Bakersfield Californian and Fresno (Calif.) Bee, 1953-54; dir. pub. relations Crippled Children's Soc. Los Angeles County, 1957-60; dir. pub. info. Occidental Coll., Los Angeles, 1960-63; dir. pub. relations George Washington U., Washington, 1963-65; dir. pub. info. Smithsonian Instn., Washington, 1965-67; v.p. Lindenwood Coll., St. Charles, Mo., 1967-78, Brilliant Builders, Inc., Brentwood, Mo., 1978-80; sr. v.p. communications United Way of Greater St. Louis, 1980—. Bd. dirs. UN Assn. Greater St. Louis, Indsl. Devel. Corp., St. Charles County; mem. coordinating council Presbytery of Giddings-Lovejoy; chmn. Arts and Letters Commn. University City (Mo.). Served with U.S. Army, 1954-56. Mem. Pub. Relations Soc. Am. Club: Nat. Press (Washington). Home: 7103 Waterman Ave University City MO 63130 Office: United Way Greater St Louis 915 Olive St Saint Louis MO 63101

BERG, EVELYNNE MARIE, geography educator; b. Chgo.; d. Clarence Martin and Mildred (Strnad) B.; B.S. with honors, U. Ill., 1954; M.A., Northwestern U., 1959. Geography editor Am. Peoples Ency., Chgo., 1955-57; social studies tchr. Hammond (Ind.) Tech.-Vocat. High Sch., 1958-59; geography tchr. Carl Schurz High Sch., Chgo., 1960-66; faculty geography Morton Coll., Cicero, Ill., 1966—. Asst. leader Cicero council Girl Scouts U.S.A., 1951-53; mem. Greater Chgo. Citizenship Council. Fulbright scholar, Brazil, 1964; NSF scholar, 1963, 65, 71-72; NDEA fellow, 1968-69; fellow Faculty Inst. S. and S.E. Asia, 1980; NEH scholar DePaul U., 1984; recipient award Ill. Geog. Soc., 1977. Fellow Nat. Council Geog. Edn. (state coordinator 1973-74, exec. bd. 1973-77); mem. Nat., Ill. (sec.-treas. 1968-69, sec. 1969-70, v.p. 1970-71, pres. 1971-72), De Paul U., Chgo. (exec. bd. 1980-84, sec. 1984—) geog. socs., Am. Overseas Educators (sec. Ill. chpt. 1974-76, v.p. chpt. 1977-78), AAUW (Chgo. br. rec. sec. 1963-65), Assn. Am. Geographers, Ill., Chgo. acads. sci., AAAS (scholar 1973-74), Nat. Assn. Geology Tchrs., Ill. Council Social Studies, Ill. Community Coll. Faculty Assn. (v.p. membership and del. affairs 1982-84), Sierra Club, Sigma Xi, Gamma Theta Upsilon, Delta Kappa Gamma. Clubs: Order Eastern Star, Bus. and Profl. Women's (acting pres. 1980-81). Contbr. to profl. jours. Home: 3924 N Pioneer Ave Chicago IL 60634 Office: Morton Coll 3801 S Central Ave Cicero IL 60650

BERG, ROBERT STURE, data base administrator; b. Chgo., May 15, 1948; s. Sture John and Josephine Marie (Pitrowski) B.; student U. Ill., Chgo., 1966-68; B.S., U. Ky., 1970. Programmer, U.S. Air Force, Wright Patterson AFB, Ohio, 1970-73, computer specialist, 1973-75; computer specialist VA Hosp., Hines, Ill., 1976; systems analyst Ill. Bell Tel. Co., Chgo., 1976-79; sr. analyst/cons. Gould Inc., Rolling Meadows, Ill., 1979-80; data base adminstr., staff analyst/software support Ill. Bell Telephone Co., Chgo., 1980—. Mem. William Ferris Chorale, Chgo., 1982-85, Grant Park Symphony, Chgo., 1983. Home: 1436 W Thome Ave Apt 1D Chicago IL 60660 Office: 10 S Canal St 3d Floor Chicago IL 60606

BERG, SHERWOOD OLMAN, emeritus university president; b. Hendrum, Minn., May 17, 1919; s. Joseph O. and Ida E. (Tommerdahl) B.; B.S., S.D. State Univ., 1947; M.S., Cornell U., 1948; Ph.D., U. Minn., 1951; m. Elizabeth A. Hall, Aug. 12, 1944; children—Mary E., Bradley J. Head, Berg Hatchery, Hendrum, 1936-40; undergrad. research asst. agrl. econs. S.D. State U., 1940-43; instr. Sch. Agr., Brookings, S.D., 1946-47; research asst. agrl. econs. Cornell U., 1947-48, U. Minn., 1948-51; U.S. agrl. attache, Yugoslavia, 1951-54, Denmark and Norway, 1954-57; prof., head dept. agrl. econs. U. Minn., 1957-63, dean Inst. Agr., 1963-73; resident dir. MUCIA-Indonesian Higher Agrl. Edn. project, 1973-75; pres. S.D. State U., Brookings, 1975-84, emeritus pres., 1984—; dir. George A. Hormel & Co., Farmhand, Inc., Nat. Bank of S.D., Brookings Internat. Life Ins. Co., Brookings; cons. econ. research service, mem. econs. research adv. com. U.S. Dept. Agr., 1960-68; personnel cons. ICA; cons. AID, 1977-81. Vice chmn., dir. Experience, Inc., 1963-77; bd. dirs. North Star Research and Devel. Inst., 1963-73, State Capitol Credit Union, 1965-67. Chmn. Nat. Adv. Commn. Food and Fiber, 1965-67; bd. dirs., vice chmn. Minn. Council Econ. Edn., 1962-73; bd. dirs. Westminster Found. Minn., 1962-68; mem. Pres.'s Commn. Income Maintenance Programs, 1968-70; overseer Jamestown (N.D.) Coll.; bd. dirs. Voyageurs Nat. Park Assn., 1965-73; trustee Farm Found., 1967-77, U. Mid.-Am., from 1977; mem. adv. panel U.S. Army ROTC, 1976-79; mem. critical choices steering com. Upper Midwest Council, from 1976; chmn. joint com. agrl. devel. Bd. Internat.

Food and Agrl. Devel., 1977-79; v.p. Nat. Collegiate Athletic Assn. Council, 1977-80. Served with AUS, 1943-46; ETO; col. Res. Decorated Bronze Star, Combat Inf. badge, Army Commendation ribbon, Meritorious Service medal; recipient Superior Service award Dept. Agr., 1956; Distinguished Alumni award S.D. State U., 1972; Superior Service award Minn. Agrigrowth Council, 1973; Outstanding Achievement award U. Minn. Bd. Regents, 1980, others. Danforth Found. fellow, 1942; Caleb Dorr research fellow U. Minn., 1948, Greater Univ. grad. fellow, 1949; Kellogg Found. Travel fellow, 1958. Mem. Agrl. History Soc., AAUP, Am. Econ. Assn., Am. Farm Econ. Assn., Am.-Scandinavian Found., Assn. U.S. Army, Internat. Assn. Agrl. Economists (U.S. council), Atlantic Community Council U.S. (sponsor 1963-67), St. Paul-Mpls. Com. on Fgn. Relations, Res. Officers Assn., U. Minn. Sci. Club, Alpha Gamma Rho, Alpha Zeta, Gamma Sigma Delta, Pi Gamma Mu, Phi Kappa Phi. Presbyn. Rotarian. Club: Cosmos. Contbr. articles to bulls., profl. jours. Office: Wenona Hall SD State U Brookings SD 57007

BERG, STANTON ONEAL, insurance company executive; firearms and ballistics cons.; b. Barron, Wis., June 14, 1928; s. Thomas C. and Ellen Florence (Nedland) Silbaugh; student U. Wis., 1949-50; LL.B., LaSalle Extension U., 1951; postgrad. U. Minn., 1960-69; qualified as ct. expert witness in ballistics various cts.; m. June K. Rolstad, Aug. 16, 1952; children—David M., Daniel L., Susan E., Julie L. Claim rep. State Farm Ins. Co., Mpls., Hibbing and Duluth, Minn., 1952-57, claim supt., 1957-66, divisional claim supt., 1966-70; firearms cons., Mpls., 1961—; regional mgr. State Farm Fire and Casualty Co., St. Paul, 1970-84; bd. dirs. Am. Bd. Forensic Firearm and Tool Mark Examiners, 1980—; instr. home firearms safety, Mpls.; cons. to Sporting Arms and Ammunition Mfrs. Inst.; internat. lectr. on forensic ballistics. Adv. bd. Milton Helpern Internat. Center for Forensic Scis., 1975—; mem. bd. cons. Inst. Applied Sci., Chgo.; cons. for re-exam. of ballistics evidence in Sirhan case Superior Ct. Los Angeles, 1975; chmn. internat. symposiums on forensic ballistics, Edinburgh, Scotland, 1972, Zurich, 1975, Bergen, Norway, 1981. Served with CIC, AUS, 1948-52. Fellow Am. Acad. Forensic Sci.; mem. Assn. of Firearm and Tool Mark Examiners (exec. council 1970-71, Distinguished Mem. and Key Man award 1972, spl. honors award 1976, nat. peer group on cert. of firearms examiners 1978—), Forensic Sci. Soc., Soc., Internat. Assn. Forensic Scis., Internat. Assn. for Identification (mem. firearms subcom. of sci. and practice com. 1961-74), Am. Ordnance Assn., Nat. Rifle Assn., Minn. Weapons, Internat. Cartridge collectors assns. Contbg. editor Am. Rifleman mag., 1973-84; mem. editorial bd. Internat. Microform Jour. Legal Medicine and Forensic Sciences, 1979—, Jour. Forensic Medicine and Pathology, 1979—; contbr. articles on firearms and forensic ballistics to profl. publs. Address: 6025 Gardena Ln NE Minneapolis MN 55432

BERG, STEVEN WAYNE, lawyer; b. White Hall, Ill., July 16, 1952; s. Gerald Wayne and Shirley Jean (Schroeder) B.; m. Inez Goodzey, Nov. 11, 1978; 1 child, Abra Leigh Goodzey. A.B., U. Ill., 1974; J.D., So. Ill. U., 1978. Bars: Ill. 1978, U.S. Dist. Ct. (cen. dist.) Ill. 1979. Asst. corp. counsel City of Springfield, Ill., 1978-79; ptnr. Calandrino, Logan & Berg, P.C., Springfield, 1979-85; sole practice, Springfield, 1985—. Mem. Am. Soc. Law and Medicine, Ill. State Bar Assn., Sangamon County Bar Assn., Worker's Compensation Section. Home: 1932 Noble Ave Springfield IL 62704 Office: 1307 S 7th St PO Box 2418 Springfield IL 62705

BERG, THOMAS RICHARD, educator; b. Sioux City, Iowa, Jan. 6, 1947; s. Orvis A. and Joan (Huber) B.; m. Sandra Lea McIntosh, June 19, 1976; 1 son, Jason Thomas. B.F.A., S.D. U., 1970; M.S., Iowa State U., 1974. Instr. journalism St. Bonaventure (N.Y.) U., 1974-77; instr. mass communication U. Tex., El Paso, 1977-82; asst. prof. journalism and mass communication Creighton U., Omaha, 1982—. Mem. Assn. for Edn. Journalism and Mass Communication, Broadcast Edn. Assn. (bd. dirs. dist. IV), Sigma Delta Chi. Club: Omaha Press. Office: Creighton University 203B Communication Arts Omaha NE 68178

BERGACKER, JAMES BRIAN, construction company executive; b. Marion, Wis., July 7, 1937; s. Wynand Jacob and Grace Adeline (Watke) B.; m. Julieann Crook, June 26, 1960; children—David Brian, Melissa Jean. B.S., Mich. Coll. Mining and Tech., 1959. Registered profl. engr., Wis.; lic. real estate broker; cert. water and sewage treatment plant operator. Engr., Wis. Hwy. Commn., Rhinelander, 1960-63; field engr. Mathy Constrn. Co., LaCrosse, Wis., 1963-67; dir. public works, city engr. City of Oconto Falls (Wis.), 1967-74; pres. Am. Asphalt of Wis., Wausau, 1974-76; exec. v.p. D.L. Gasser Constrn. Inc., Lake Delton, Wis., 1976—. Gov. apptd. mem. Regionalism Task Force Wis., 1967-70, Wis. Health Planning Council, 1970-73. Pres. bd. dirs. Community Meml. Hosp., 1972-73; elder 1st Presbyn. Ch. Wausau, 1982-84, pres. bd. trustees. Office: Am Asphalt of Wis 1803 W Stewart Ave Wausau WI 54401

BERGAN, JOSEPH ANTHONY, surgeon; b. South Bend, Ind., Mar. 30, 1920; s. William N. and Ellen (Hagerty) B.; m. Marvada Ann French, May 16, 1953; children—Bridget, Joseph, Patrick, Mary, Susan, Thomas, James, George, Peter. B.S., U. Notre Dame, 1942; M.D., Loyola U., 1945. Diplomate Am. Bd. Surgery. Chief surgery St. Anthony Hosp., Michigan City, Ind., 1967-69, 1974-76, pres. staff, 1969-70; practice medicine specializing in surgery Michigan City, 1949—. Served to capt. U.S. Army, M.C., 1946-48. Fellow Internat. Coll. Surgeons, Pan Pacific Surg. Assn., Am. Geriatric Soc.; mem. AMA, Ind. State Med. Assn. Roman Catholic. Clubs: Serra (pres. 1959-60), Notre Dame (pres. 1957-58) (Michigan City). Home: 422 Marquette Trail Michigan City IN 46360 Office: 217 W Homer St Michigan City IN 46360

BERGAN, JUDSON JAY, optometrist; b. Watertown, S.D., Nov. 27, 1949; s. Carl F. and Pearl Jeannette (Haanstad) B.; m. Jean Katherine Nelson, July 28, 1973; children—David and Michael. B.A. in Music, Augustana Coll., 1972; O.D., U. of Houston, 1980. Doctor of optometry Madison Vision Clinic, Madison, S.D., 1980—. Served with U.S. Army, 1972-74. Mem. Optometric Soc. (chmn. se. dist. 1983-84), Am. Optometric Assn., Beta Sigma Kappa. Republican. Methodist. Lodges: Kiwanis (bd. mem. 1984—), Elks (scholarship chmn. 1983—). Avocations: Choral director; chess; golf. Home: 1420 NE 3rd St Madison SD 57042 Office: Madison Vision Clinic 103 S Egan Madison SD 57042

BERGEN, THOMAS JOSEPH, lawyer, nursing homes exec., assn. exec.; b. Prairie du Chien, Wis., Feb. 7, 1913; s. Thomas Joseph and Emma Marilla (Grelle) B.; student U. Wis., 1930-32; J.D., Marquette U., 1937, postgrad., 1937-38; m. Jean Loraine Bowler, May 29, 1941 (dec. Aug. 1972); children—Kathleen Bergen McElwee, Eileen Bergen Bednarz, Patricia Bergen Buss, Thomas Joseph, Patrick Joseph, John Joseph. Admitted to Wis. bar, 1937, U.S. Supreme Ct. bar, 1972; practiced in Milw., 1937—; exec. sec. Wis. Assn. Nursing Homes, 1957-71; legal counsel, exec. dir. Am. Coll. Nursing Home Adminstrs., Milw., 1967-68; sec., dir. Bayside Nursing Home, Milw., 1967—; pres., dir. N.W. Med. Centers, Inc., also Northland Med. Centers, Inc. (both Milw.), 1968—; treas., exec. dir. Nat. Geriatrics Soc., Milw., 1971—; pres. bd. dirs. Senator Joseph R. McCarthy Ednl. Found., Inc., 1982—; mem. program planning com. Nat. Conf. on Aging, also del. to conf., 1974; panel speaker Nat. Justice Found. conv., 1974. Bd. dirs., treas. Nat. Geriatrics Ednl. Soc., 1971—; bd. dirs., pres. Wis. Justice Found., 1971—. Served with AUS, 1943, 44. Recipient Merit award Wis. Assn. Nursing Homes, 1962, Outstanding Leadership award Nat. Geriatrics Soc., 1976. Mem. Am., Wis., Milw. (pres., exec. dir.) bar assns., Real Estate Profls. Assn. (pres. 1974—), Am. Med. Writers Assn., Delta Theta Phi, Delta Sigma Rho. Roman Catholic. Editor: Silver Threads, Wis. Assn. Nursing Homes publ., 1963-71, News Letter, Am. Coll. Nursing Home Adminstrs., 1967-68, Views and News, Nat. Geriatrics Soc., 1971—; editorial bd. Educational Gerontology, 1973-85; contbr. articles to nursing home publs. Home: 10324 W Vienna Ave Wauwatosa WI 53222 Office: 212 W Wisconsin Ave Milwaukee WI 53203

BERGER, EDMOND LOUIS, theoretical physicist; b. Salem, Mass., Dec. 5, 1939; s. Edmond Antonio and Ethel Mary (Brown) B.; m. Susan Katherine Teffner, Sept. 5, 1964; children—Bruce, Catherine, Stephen. B.S., MIT, 1961; Ph.D., Princeton U., 1965. Asst. prof. dept. physics Dartmouth Coll., Hanover, N.H., 1965-68; research assoc. Lawrence Berkeley Lab., U. Calif.-Berkeley, 1968-69; physicist Argonne (Ill.) Nat. Lab., 1969-72, sr. theoretical physicist, theory group leader high energy physics div., 1974—; staff scientist CERN, Geneva, 1972-74, 83-84; vis. prof. Stanford U., 1978-79; mem. physics adv. com. Fermilab, 1980-84. NSF fellow, 1961-65. Fellow Am. Phys. Soc. (exec. com.). Contbr. articles to profl. jours. Home: 5711 Dearborn Pkwy Downers Grove IL 60516 Office: High Energy Physics Div Argonne Natl Lab Argonne IL 60439

BERGER, KENNETH WALTER, audiologist; b. Evansville, Ind., Mar. 22, 1924; s. Walter P. and Ida (Block) B.; B.A., U. Evansville, 1948; M.A., Ind. State U., 1949; Ph.D., So. Ill. U., Carbondale, 1962; m. Barbara Jane Steadman, Aug. 31, 1946; children—Robert W., Kenna J., Laura M., Karen S. Speech and hearing therapist pub. schs., Carmi, Ill., 1955-61; dir. audiology Kent State U., (Ohio), 1962—, prof., 1967—. Served to capt. U.S. Army, 1943-46, USAF, 1951-55. Fellow Am. Speech and Hearing Assn., Am. Audiology Soc., Acoustical Soc. Am. Author: Speechreading: Principles and Methods, 1971; The Hearing Aid: Its Operation and Development, 1974. Home: 647 Longmere Dr Kent OH 44240 Office: Speech and Hearing Clinic Kent State Univ Kent OH 44242

BERGER, KURT WILHELM, fin. counselor; b. Frankfurt, Germany, Mar. 10, 1912; came to U.S., 1937, naturalized, 1943; s. Walter W. and Bea (Wendel) B.; Ph.D. in Econs., U. Frankfurt, 1936; m. Gudrun M. Wolf, Aug. 24, 1959; 1 dau., Gisela P. Market analyst Merck, Darmstadt & N.J., 1936-37; treas. Express Freight Lines, Inc., Milw., 1943-67; v.p., treas. E.F.L. Motors, Inc., Milw., 1945-67, Transport Services, Inc., Milw., 1945-67; exec. v.p. Nat. Life Ins. Co., Frankfurt, 1968-70; pvt. practice counseling internat. fin. and investments, Koenigstein, W.Ger., 1969-70; ind. mgmt. cons., fin. counselor, 1970—. Mem. Wis. N.G., 1947-49. Mem. Nat. Acctg. and Fin. Council (past v.p., pres., chmn.), Am. Trucking Assn., Motor Carrier Accts. Soc. (past pres.), Personnel Evaluation Inst. (past pres.). Unitarian. Contbr. articles to profl. jours. Home: 4540 N Ardmore Ave Shorewood WI 53211

BERGER, MILES LEE, land economist; b. Chgo., Aug. 9, 1930; s. Albert E. and Dorothy (Ginsberg) B.; student Brown U., 1948-50; m. Sally Eileen Diamond, Aug. 27, 1955; children—Albert E., Elizabeth Ann. Engaged in real estate appraisal, research and devel., econs. fields, 1950—; mng. chmn. bd. Berger Fin. Services Corp., Chgo., 1950—; chmn. bd. Mid-Am. Appraisal & Research Corp., Chgo., 1959-80) also dir.; chmn. bd. Real Estate Services Corp., 1969—; vice chmn. bd., trustee Heitman Fin. Services Ltd., 1970—; prin. econ. cons. Columbia Nat. Bank, Chgo., 1965—; dir. Evans Inc.; trustee Heitman Mortgage Investors. Commr., chmn. Chgo. Plan Commn., 1980—; cons. city Chgo. on Ill. Central Air Rights, 1967—; trustee Latin Sch. Chgo., 1967-73, treas., 1953-55, bd. dirs. Latin Sch. Found.; bd. dirs. Albert E. Berger Found. Mem. Am. Inst. Real Estate Appraisers, Soc. Real Estate Appraisers, Soc. Real Estate Counselors, Am. Right-of-Way Assn., Nat. Assn. Housing and Redevel. Ofcls., Nat. Tax Assn., Internat. Assn. Assessing Officers, Lambda Alpha. Jewish (trustee synagogue). Home: Chicago IL 60610 Office: 180 N LaSalle St Chicago IL 60601

BERGER, PAUL HAROLD, insurance executive; b. Cleve., Oct. 14, 1924; s. Ted. Ross and Helen (Hirsh) B.; student Tex. A and M. Coll., 1942-43; So. Methodist U., 1946-47, U. Chgo., 1947-51; M.A. in Social Scis., U. Chgo., 1956; m. Phillis Ottem, July 31, 1954; children—Jessica E., Avery Ross. Adminstrv. asst. to Alderman Robert E. Merriam, 1949-51; sales rep. Mich. Steel Supply, Chgo., 1951-53, Abbot Screw & Bolt Co., Chgo., 1953-54; campaign staff Merriam for Mayor Com., 1954-55; ins. broker, Chgo., 1955—; chmn. bd., pres Hyde Park Fed. Savs. & Loan Assn., Chgo., 1961-82; pres. Alfred Adler Inst., 1984—. Dist. chmn. Boy Scouts Am., 1968-69; treas. Mid South Side Health Planning Orgn., 1969-72, Gateway Houses Found., Inc., 1969-74; bd. dirs. SE Chgo. Commn., 1963—, Woodlawn Hosp., Hyde Park-Kenwood Community Conf., 1964-67; bd. dirs., treas. First Unitarian Soc. Chgo., treas., 1963-64; bd. dirs. Mary McDowell Settlement, 1957-64, v.p., 1960-61; bd. dirs. Chgo. Renewal Efforts Service Corp., 1973-81, chmn., 1976-81; bd. dirs., pres. Hyde Park-Kenwood Devel. Corp., 1974—; bd. dirs. Met. Fair and Expn. Authority, 1975-80, vice chmn. bd., 1978-80; bd. dirs. Community Services and Research Corp., 1975-80. Served with AUS, 1943-46. Life mem. Million Dollar Round Table. Clubs: Economic, Quadrangle (Chgo.). Home: 5816 S Blackstone Ave Chicago IL 60637 Office: 5250 S Lake Park Ave Chicago IL 60615

BERGER, SANFORD JASON, lawyer, securities dealer, real estate broker; b. Cleve., June 29, 1926; s. Sam and Ida (Solomon) B.; m. Bertine Mae Benjamin, Aug. 6, 1950 (div. Dec. 1977); children—Bradley Alan, Bonnie Jean. B.A., Western Res. U., 1950, J.D., 1952. Bar: Ohio 1952, U.S. Supreme Ct. 1979. Field examiner Ohio Dept. Taxation, Cleve., 1952; sole practice, Cleve., 1952—; real estate cons., Cleve., 1960—; investment cons., Cleve., 1970—. Contbr. author: Family Evaluation in Child Custody Litigation, 1982. Copyright 10 songs, 1977. Candidate police judge, East Cleve., 1955, Bd. Edn., Beachwood, Ohio, 1963, mayor, Beachwood, 1967, judge ct. common pleas, Cuyahoga County, Ohio, 1984. Served with USMMCC, 1944-45; PTO. Recipient cert. Appreciation Phi Alpha Delta, 1969. Mem. Ohio State Bar Assn. (family law com.). Republican. Jewish. Lodge: B'nai B'rith (editor 1968-70). Avocations: poet; lyricist; legal writer; drag racer; scuba diving. Home: 6809 Mayfield Rd Apt 972 Mayfield Heights OH 44124 Office: Berger and Fertel 1836 Euclid Ave #305 Cleveland OH 44115

BERGER, STEVEN HARRY, psychiatrist, educator; b. Grand Rapids, Mich., Jan. 14, 1947. Student Mich. State U., 1965-68; M.D., U. Mich., 1972. Diplomate Am. Bd. Psychiatry and Neurology. Intern, then resident in psychiatry Michael Reese Hosp., Chgo., 1972-75; practice medicine specializing in psychiatry, Chgo., 1975-79, Grand Rapids, 1979—; mem. staff Forest View Psychiat. Hosp., Grand Rapids, chief of staff, 1983-84; dir. Kent Oaks Hosp., 1985—; courtesy staff Blodgett Hosp., Grand Rapids, Butterworth Hosp., Grand Rapids Osteo. Hospital; chief geriatric psychiatry program Michael Reese Hosp., Chgo., 1976-78; clin. asst. prof. psychiatry Mich. State U. Coll. of Human Medicine, 1979—. Mem. AMA, Am. Psychiat. Assn., Am. Acad. Psychiatry and Law, Am. Coll. Forensic Psychiatry, Am. Acad. Forensic Scis., Western Mich. Psychiat. Soc., Mich. State Psychiat. Soc., Kent County Med. Soc., Mich. State Med. Soc. Office: 4500 Cascade Rd Suite 201 Grand Rapids MI 49506-3685

BERGERE, CARLETON MALLORY, contractor; b. Brookline, Mass., Apr. 4, 1919; s. Jason J. and Anna Lillian B.; student Burdett Bus. Coll., 1938, Babsons Sch. Bus., 1940; m. Jean J. Pach, Oct. 1, 1950. Self-employed contractor, Chgo., 1949-57; pres. Permanent Bldg. Supply Co., Inc., Chgo., 1957-62, Gt. No. Bldg. Products, Inc., Chgo., 1962-67, C.M. Bergere Co., Inc., Chgo., 1967—. Served with USN, 1944. Named Man of Yr., Profl. Remodelers Assn. Greater Chgo., 1978. Mem. Profl. Remodelers Assn.(dir., past treas., v.p., sec.), Chgo. Assn. Commerce and Industry (chmn. contractor/supplier relations com.), Nat. Assn. Remodeling Industry (indsl. devel. com.), No. Ill. Home Builders Assn., Better Bus. Bur. Met. Chgo., Industry Trade Practice Com. on Home Improvement (chmn.), Nat. Panel Consumer Arbitrators. Club: Exec. (Chgo.). Address: 175 E Delaware Pl Chicago IL 60611

BERGFALK, JAMES ROBERT, management consulting and investment company executive; b. Chgo., May 16, 1945; s. Robert Edward and Gertrude Ann (Gavitt) B.; m. S. Jan Hodgson, Jan. 1, 1977; children—Lara, Brian, Jeffrey. B.S. in Bus. Adminstrn., Rockhurst Coll., 1967; M.Pub. Adminstrn., U. Mo.-Kansas City, 1971. Dir., Jackson County Dept. Health, Welfare and Corrections, Kansas City, Mo., 1971-77; dep. dir. Mo. Dept. Social Services, Jefferson City, 1977-78; regional dir. U.S. Dept. HHS, Kansas City, 1978-81; mgr. health services Midwest Research Inst., Kansas City, 1981-82; pres. First Diversified Investment Services, Kansas City, 1982—; mem. Kans. State Banking Bd.; polit. cons. Bd. dirs. Heartland Econ. Devel. Council, DeLaSalle Edn. Ctr. Recipient Nat. Project award Nat. Assn. Counties, 1974, 75, 76; meritorious service award Jackson County Legislature, 1977; achievement award HEW, 1980. Contbr. chpts. to books, articles to profl. jours. Home: 3907 W 68th Terr Prairie Village KS 66208 Office: First Diversified Investment Services 3535 Broadway Kansas City MO 64111

BERGH, GLORIA JEAN, public relations manager; b. Monticello, Minn., Jan. 26, 1941; d. Merle Durb and Frieda Marie (Zum Brunnen) Sutherland; B.S., U. Minn., 1963; m. Owe Martin Gerhard Bergh, Nov. 14, 1964; children—David Martin, Lisa Marie. Staff writer pub. relations dept. Green Giant Co., LeSueur, Minn., 1964-65; manuscript copy editor C.V. Mosby Co., St. Louis, 1965-71; copywriter, continuity dir. Sta. WQAD-TV, Moline, Ill., 1973; dir. pub. relations Miss. Valley Girl Scout Council, Bettendorf, Iowa, 1974-81; mgr. pub. relations Modern Woodmen Am., Rock Island, Ill., 1981—. Communications chmn. 1983 campaign United Way Quad Cities; bd. dirs. Alternatives for Older Adults, Inc., Moline, Ill., 1984-85; v.p communications Nat. Fraternal Congress Am. Mem. Davenport C. of C. (pub. relations com., chmn. publs. subcom. 1978), Bettendorf C. of C. (civic affairs and edn. com. 1978-79), Pub. Relations Soc. Am. (charter mem. Quad-Cities/Iowa Ill. chpt., pres. 1981, sec.-treas. 1980, publicity chmn. 1978-79). Home: 20 Century Oaks Ct Bettendorf IA 52722 Office: Mississippi River at 17th St Rock Island IL 61201

BERGHOFF, PAUL HENRY, lawyer; b. Chgo., Aug. 25, 1956; s. John Colerick Sr. and Doris Margaret (Anderson) B.; m. Kathryn Elaine Thompson, May 30, 1981. B.A. cum laude in Chemistry, Lawrence U., 1978; J.D. cum laude, U. Mich., 1981. Bars: Ill. 1981, U.S. Dist. Ct. (no. dist.) Ill. 1981, U.S. Ct. Appeals (fed. cir.) 1983. Assoc. Allegretti, Newitt, Witcoff & McAndrews, Ltd., Chgo., 1981—. Mem. ABA, Ill. Bar Assn., Chgo. Bar Assn., Patent Law Assn. Chgo. Mem. United Ch. of Christ. Office: Allegretti Newitt Witcoff & McAndrews 125 S Wacker Dr Chicago IL 60606

BERGIA, ROGER MERLE, educational administrator; b. Peoria, Ill., Nov. 26, 1937; s. Merle Frederick and Doris Ann (Markham) B.; B.A., Eureka Coll., 1960; M.A., Bradley U., 1967, postgrad., 1968—; m. Valerie Jean Lane, Oct. 16, 1960; children—Lori, Amy, Beth. Tchr., coach Jr. High Sch., Peoria Heights Sch., 1960-65; prin., Kelly Ave. Grade Sch., Peoria Heights, Ill, 1965-74; supt. Peoria Heights Schs., 1974—. Mem. exec. com. W.D. Boyce council Boy Scouts Am. Named Sch. Adminstr. of Yr., Ill. Bd. Edn., 1981-82. Mem. Phi Delta Kappa, Lambda Chi Alpha. Republican. Presbyterian. Home: 6723 N Gem Ct Peoria IL 61614 Office: 1316 E Kelly Ave Peoria Heights IL 61614

BERGLUND, ROBERTA LEOLA, educator; b. Freeport, Ill., May 20, 1944; d. Ralph LeRoy and Maxine (Lynch) Hanson; B.S., Ill. State U., 1965; M.S. Ed., No. Ill. U., 1978, postgrad., 1978—; m. David Lee Berglund, June 18, 1966. Tchr. elem. sch. Flanagan, Ill., 1965-69; reading specialist Dixon (Ill.) Public Schs., 1969—, dir. Title I program, 1977-84; instr. Northern Ill. Univ., 1984-85. Mem. Ill. Reading Council (corr. sec. 1981-82), Sauk Valley Reading Council (pres. 1977-78), Ill. Reading Council (dir. 1977-78, 81-83, 84-85, chmn. parents and reading 1982-83, chmn. publs. 1984-85, assoc. editor Jour. 1984—), Internat. Reading Assn., No. Ill. Reading Council, Assn. Supervision and Curriculum Devel., Nat. Reading Conf., NEA, Ill. Edn. Assn., Dixon Tchrs. Assn., Nat. Council Tchrs. English, Lang. Experience Approach Spl. Interest Council (v.p. 1983-84, pres. 1984-85), PEO, Delta Kappa Gamma. Unitarian. Editor, Reading Unlimited newsletter, 1980-82, Ill. Reading Communicator, 1981-82; contbr. articles to profl. jours. Home: Rural Route 6 White Oak Estates Dixon IL 61021 Office: 415 S Hennepin Ave Dixon IL 61021

BERGMAN, GREG ALAN, social worker; b. Lorain, Ohio, Feb. 12, 1951; s. Ivan Russell and Marjorie Ann (Yalman) B.; B.A., Ohio State U., Columbus, 1973; M.S.W., U. Nebr., 1975; m. Katherine Holaday, June 24, 1979. Asst. dir., acting dir. social services Dr. Sher Nursing Home, Omaha, 1975-77; social service worker Richard Young Hosp., Omaha, 1974-75; program dir. Social Settlement Assn. Omaha, 1978-80; social service worker Harry S. Truman Meml. Vets. Hosp., Columbia, Mo., 1980—. Mem. Columbia Community Band, 1982—, No One in Particular Comedy Troupe, 1983—, Catfish Night Club Band, 1983—; mem. Columbia Diamond Council, 1982—, v.p., 1984. Lic. nursing home adminstr., Nebr., Mo. Mem. Acad. Cert. Social Workers, Nat. Assn. Social Workers (state dir. 1978-79, regional chmn. 1978-79), Nebr. Welfare Assn. (regional dir. 1979-80). Author statistics textbook. Home: 2513 Willowbrook Ct Columbia MO 65202 Office: 800 Stadium Rd Columbia MO 65201

BERGMAN, JANET LOUISE, flutist, educator; b. St. Louis, June 15, 1920; d. Isadore and Rose (Seidenberg) Marx; student pub. schs., St. Louis; student John F. Kiburz, Laurent Torno; m. Albert Solomon Bergman, June 15, 1947; children—Shelley, Gary Evan, Dana Lynn. Mem. St. Louis Woman's Symphony, 1937-38, St. Louis Opera Co., 1942, St. Louis Symphony, 1943-47; first flutist St. Louis Little Symphony, 1943-47, soloist, 1943-47; flutist Oklahoma City Symphony, 1944-45, soloist, 1944-45; flutist New Orleans Symphony and Opera Co., 1945-47, Chgo. Women's Sinfonietta, 1948, Civic Orch. of Chgo., 1948, Chgo. Park Band Concerts, 1947—, Chgo. Chamber Orch., 1954-58, Lyric Opera Orch., Chgo., 1964-71; 1st flutist, soloist City Symphony Chgo., 1963—, Aeolian Woodwind Ensemble, Chgo., 1965—; prof. flute Chgo. Conservatory Coll., 1968-78, Northeastern Ill. U., Chgo., 1978—, Am. Conservaory of Music, Chgo., 1978-81; mem. music faculty Niles E. and Niles W. high schs., 1964—, New Trier E. and W. high schs., 1977—; founder, condr. Flute Sinfonietta, 1975—; condr. Chgo. Flute Ensemble, 1980—; soloist Artist Assocs., 1976-77; adjudicator Ill. High Sch. Solo Assn., 1973-79, Flute Concourse, U. Que., Montreal, 1974, 77, 84. Recipient music award Chgo. Pub. Library Cultural Ctr., 1980; 20 Yr. Service award City Symphony Chgo., 1983. Mem. Chgo., St. Louis fedns. musicians, Nat. Flute Assn., Soloist Artists Assn. Chgo., Nat. Health Fedn. (sec. Chgo. chpt. 1975-76, speaker 1976-77, sec. 1978—), Chgo. Flute Soc. (founder, pres. 1977—), Soc. Am. Musicians. Author: Do's and Don'ts of Flute Playing, 1967. Home: 1817 G W Hood St Chicago IL 60660

BERGMAN, LAWRENCE ALAN, engineering educator; b. N.Y.C., Oct. 14, 1944; s. Henry and Sylvia (Kirsch) B.; m. Jane Howell, May 14, 1969; 1 child, Sarah Michelle. B.S.M.E., Stevens Inst. Tech., 1966; M.S.C.E., Case Western Res. U., 1978, Ph.D., 1980. Devel. engr. TRW, Inc., Cleve., 1966-68; tech. staff Lord Corp., Erie, Pa., 1968-75; asst. prof. U. Ill.-Urbana, 1979-85, assoc. prof., 1985—; cons. to industry. Contbr. articles to profl. jours. Patentee in field (4). Mem. ASCE (award 1983), AIAA, Am. Acad. Mechanics, Tau Beta Pi. Office: U Ill Aero and Astronautical Engring Dept 104 S Mathews Ave Urbana IL 61801

BERGMAN, ROBERT SCRIBNER, toy co. exec.; b. Aurora, Ill., Nov. 23, 1934; s. Ross M. and Mary O. (Ochsenschlager) B.; B.S., Ill. Inst. Tech., 1956; postgrad., Stanford U., 1956-58; m. Patricia LeBaron, June 10, 1956; children—David C., Lynne M., Joseph R. With Hughes Aircraft Co., Culver City, Calif., 1956, Gen. Electric Co., Palo Alto, Calif., 1957, Sylvania, Mountain View, Calif., 1958-61; with Processed Plastic, Montgomery, Ill., 1961—, pres., 1969—; pres. Bergman Mfg. & Trading, Montgomery, 1962—; v.p. Moldrite Plastic and Engring., Montgomery, 1962—, Moldrite Tool and Die, Addison, Ill., 1965—; treas. Intertoy, Montgomery, 1977—, Graphic Label Co., Montgomery, Ill., 1977—. Mem. Am. Phys. Soc., Toy Mfrs. Am. (dir. 1981-85). Republican. Mem. Ch. of Christ. Club: Elks. Home: 1330 Monona Ave Aurora IL 60506 Office: 1001 Aucutt Rd Montgomery IL 60538

BERGMAN, ROY THOMAS, surgeon; b. Cassopolis, Mich., Dec. 20, 1935; s. Roy Edwin and Lois (Townsend) B.; B.S. with high honors, Mich. State U., 1957, D.V.M. with high honors, 1959; M.D., Northwestern U., 1964; m. Sally Jo Proshwitz, June 28, 1958; children—Roy T., Amy Lynn, Samara Edlyn. Rotating intern Evanston (Ill.) Hosp. Assn., 1964-65, resident in gen. surgery, 1967-71; Am. Cancer Soc. clin. fellow in oncological surgery Northwestern U., Chgo., 1970-71; practice medicine specializing in gen. surgery and oncology, Escanaba, Mich., 1972; mem. staff St. Francis Hosp., Escanaba, 1972—, chmn. tumor bd., 1972—, also chief of staff, chief of surgery; instr. surgery U. So. Calif. Med. Center, Los Angeles, 1972-73; assoc. prof. surgery Mich. State U. Coll. Human Medicine, East Lansing, 1974—, also surg. coordinator Upper Peninsula med. edn. program; attending physician Nat. Sports Festival, Colorado Springs, 1978, 79, Syracuse, N.Y., 1981, U.S. Olymic Com., Pan Am. Games, P.R., 1979, Summer Games, Russia, 1980, Summer Games, Los Angeles, 1984; head physician U.S. Olympic Com., Caracas, Venezuela, 1983; polyclinic U.S. Olympic Com. Winter Games, Lake Placid, N.Y., 1980; attending physician U.S. Olympic Men's Rowing Team, Germany, 1981; mem. Council on Sports Medicine, U.S. Olympic Com., 1985—. Served to capt. M.C., U.S. Army, 1965-67. Named to Mich. Upper Peninsula Sports Hall of Fame. Diplomate Am. Bd. Surgery. Fellow A.C.S. (local chmn. com. trauma, chmn. com. on applicants Mich. Dist. 4), Alpha Omega Alpha. Office: Doctors Park Escanaba MI 49829

BERGMAN, SIGRID ELIZABETH, hosp. services adminstr.; b. Lafayette, Ind., June 20, 1940; d. Philip A. and Josephine Elizabeth (Miller) Henderson; B.A., U. Nebr., 1963, M.A., 1970; m. Edward T. Bergman, June 9, 1962; children—Kimberly Kay, Lucinda Sue. Pediatric counselor Nat. Jewish Hosp., Denver, 1962-63; home services rep. Cengas, Lincoln, Nebr., 1963-65; guidance counselor St. Elizabeth Sch. Nursing, Lincoln, 1966-70; dir. social services St. Elizabeth Community Health Center, Lincoln, 1970—; guest lectr. social work and vocat. rehab. U. Nebr. Bd. dirs. Lancaster County Unit Am. Cancer Soc., 1975-78; mem. adv. bd. Tabitha Home Health Care, 1975-81, sec. 1975-76; mem. Cath. Social Services Bd., 1977-79; mem. adv. bd. Lincoln Youth Symphony, 1977-82, projects chmn., 1978-79, sec., 1979-80, pres., 1980-81. Mem. Soc. for Hosp. Social Work Dirs. of Am. Hosp. Assn., Nebr. Soc. Hosp. Social Work Dirs. (pres. 1981-82), Zeta Tau Alpha. Democrat. Presbyterian.

Club: Alpha Chi Omega Mothers (co-chmn. 1981-82). Home: 1109 Lancaster Ln Lincoln NE 68505 Office: St Elizabeth Community Center 555 S 70th St Lincoln NE 68510

BERGMANN, BERNARD MAURICE, III, sleep research scientist, psychiatry educator; b. Buffalo, Jan. 6, 1947; s. Bernard M. and Lena Bergmann; m. Linda Ann Shell, Aug. 2, 1969; 1 son, Bernard M. IV. B.S.M.E., Syracuse U., 1968, M.S.M.E., 1972; M.S., U. Chgo., 1978, Ph.D., 1980. Chief research technician sleep research lab U. Chgo., 1974-80, research assoc., 1980—, assoc. lab. dir., 1985—, asst. prof. dept. psychiatry, 1980—. Mem. Sleep Research Soc., Chgo. Art Inst., Chgo. Lyric Opera Guild, Smithsonian Instn. Office: U Chgo Sleep Research Lab 5743 S Drexel Ave Chicago IL 60637

BERGQUIST, BARRY DARRIL, importing company executive; b. Cloquet, Minn., Oct. 18, 1945; s. Richard Emil and Margaret (Bengston) B.; B.A. in Bus. Adminstrn., U. Minn., Duluth, 1968; m. Vivian Elizabeth Cook, Nov. 30, 1974. Salesman, mgr. Cades Ltd., Elk Grove, Ill., 1971; dist. mgr. Mass. food equipment div. McGraw Edison Co., 1973; sales mgr., then v.p. Bergquist Imports, Inc., Cloquet, 1977—, pres., owner, 1980—; dir. Cloquet Devel. Corp., 1981-83. Vice chmn., chmn. fin. com. 8th Congl. Dist. Republican Party, 1979-81, dist. chmn., 1981-83; chmn. Carlton County Rep. Party, 1976-81; trustee Cloquet Library Bd., 1979—; bd. dirs. Cloquet chpt. Am. Cancer Soc., 1980—. Served with USAR, 1968-70. Club: Cloquet Kiwanis (pres.). Home: 318 Ave D Cloquet MN 55720 Office: 1412 Hwy 33 S Cloquet MN 55720

BERGSMARK, EDWIN MARTIN, bank and trust company executive; b. July 14, 1941; married; 2 children. B.B.A. in Acctg., U. Cin., 1964; postgrad., U. Colo., 1965; J.D., U. Toledo, 1972; postdoctoral U. Wis., 1975. Bar: Ohio 1972, U.S. Dist. Ct. (no. dist.) Ohio 1973, U.S. Tax Ct. 1975, U.S. Ct. Customs and Patent Appeals 1975, U.S. Supreme Ct. 1975. Exec. v.p., bd. dirs. Toledo Trust Co., 1970—; pres., chief exec. officer, dir. SeaGate Community Devel. Corp.; pres., chief exec. officer Seagate Small Bus. Investment Corp.; dir. Advanced RC, Inc., Computer Corp. Am. Chmn. Sta. WGTE-TV and Radio, Toledo, Ohio; vice chmn. Toledo/Lucas County Conv. and Visitors Bur., Inc.; bd. v.p., mem. exec. com. Toledo Zool. Soc., 1984—; trustee Toledo Area Regional Transit Authority, Flower Hosp. and Crestview Ctr; chmn. spl. corp. and individual gifts div. United Way; mem. Mayor's Task Force on Downtown Devel.; bd. dirs., exec. com. Toledo Community and Cultural Arts Ctr., Inc. Served with U.S. Army, 1964-66; Vietnam. Mem. Toledo Bar Assn. (chmn. endowment com.), Ohio Bankers Assn. (past state chmn., fed. and state regulatory com.). Clubs: Sylvania Country (bd. dirs., sec.), Toledo, Golf (Columbus). Lodge: Rotary Internat. (Ohio Commodore), Masons (32d degree), Shriners. Avocation: pilot. Home: 4544 Crossfield Rd Toledo OH 43623

BERGSTRESSER, MELVIN HUBERT, retail executive; b. Frobischer, Sask., Can., June 16, 1932; s. Waldemar and Selma (Kolke) B.; student in Bus. Mgmt., U. Man., 1967-70; student in Theology, N. Am. Bapt. Coll., Edmonton, 1950-52; m. Doreen Laura, June 26, 1954; children—Wayne, Arden, Heather, Kevin. With Gambles Can., Winnipeg, Man., 1956-82, buyer major appliances, sporting goods, asst. mgr. sales promotion and advt., group mgr. sporting goods div., 1979-82; pres., owner Creative Family Living Assn., 1969—, Parking Lot Marking Services, 1975—, Distinctive Products, 1975—, Melberg Enterprises Ltd., 1982—, Barbecues Parts and Service Village Ltd., 1983—; lectr. family living seminars. Bd. dirs. N.Am. Bapt. Coll., 1967-79; chmn. Man. Bapt. Assn., 1975-78; moderator Grant Park Bapt. Ch., 1972-78, Sunday Sch. tchr., 1959—, capt. Christian Service Brigade Boys, 1964-82. Home: 16 Glengarry Dr Winnipeg MB R3T 2J6 Canada

BERGSTROM, BETTY HOWARD, association executive; b. Chgo., Mar. 15, 1931; d. Seward Haise and Agnes Eleanor (Uek) Guinter; B.S. in Speech, Northwestern U., 1952, postgrad., 1983; postgrad U. Nev., Reno, 1974; m. Robert William Bergstrom, Apr. 21, 1979; children—Bryan Scott, Cheryl Lee, Jeffrey Alan, Mark Robert, Philip Alan. Dir. sales promotion and pub. relations WLS-AM, Chgo., 1952-56; account exec. E.H. Brown Advt. Agy., Chgo., 1956-59; v.p. Richard Crabb Assocs., Chgo., 1959-61; pres., owner Howard Assocs., Calif. and Chgo., 1961-76; v.p. Chgo. Hort. Soc., 1976—. Del., Ill. Constl. Conv., 1969-70, mem. com. legis. reform, 1973-74, cts. and justice com., 1971-74; apptd. mem. Ill. Hist. Library Bd., 1970, Ill. Bd. Edn., 1971-74. AAUW fellowship grant named in her honor; recipient Communicator of Yr. award Women in Communication, 1983. Mem. Nat. Soc. Fund Raising Execs. (cert. fund raising executive, bd. dirs. 1983-85, sec. 1985), Am. Assn. Bot. Garden and Arboreta, Garden Writers Am., AAUW, Northwestern U. Alumni, U. So. Calif. Alumni Assn., LWV. Mem. Glenview Community Ch. Editorial bd. Garden Mag., 1977—; editor Garden Talk, 1976—; contbr. articles on fund devel., horticulture, edn. advt. and agr. to profl. jours.; editor Ill. AAUW Jour., 1966-67. Office: PO Box 400 Glencoe IL 60022

BERGSTROM, RICHARD NORMAN, civil engineer; b. Chgo., Dec. 11, 1921; s. Carl William and Ellen Amanda Victoria (Anderson) B.; B.S. in C.E., Ill. Inst. Tech., 1942, M.S., 1952; m. Patricia Ann Chessman, Apr. 19, 1947; children—George Norman, James Donald. Laura Ann, Martha Jean. Design engr. Carnegie Ill. Steel Corp.. Gary. Ind., 1942; structural engr. Sargent & Lundy, Engrs., Chgo., 1946-56, asso.. 1956, partner, 1966-82, mgr. tech. services dept., 1977-82. Mem. nuclear standards mgmt. bd. Am. Nat. Standards Insf., 1975-80. Stated clk. Presbyn. Ch. of Barrington (Ill.); bd. dirs. Presbyn. Home, Evanston, Ill. Served to lt., USNR, 1942-46. Decorated Purple Heart. Registered profl. engr., Ariz., Ark., Calif., Colo., Ill., Ind., Iowa, Kans., Ky., La., Mich., N.Y., Ohio, Okla., S.C., Tenn., Tex., Wis. Fellow ASCE, Am. Cons. Engrs. Council; mem. Am. Nuclear Soc., ASME, Am. Concrete Inst., Am. Inst. Steel Constrn., Western Soc. Engrs., Ill. Cons. Engrs. Council (dir.). Presbyn. Clubs: Union League, Barrington Hills Country, Desert Forest Golf, Meadow. Contbr. articles in field to profl. jours. Home: 274 Leeds Dr Barrington Hills IL 60010 Office: 55 E Monroe St Chicago IL 60603

BERGSTROM, ROBERT CARLTON, geologist; b. Highland Park, Ill., Aug. 20, 1925; s. Carl Hilding and Ethel Rose (Hill) B.; B.S., Northwestern U., 1950, M.S., 1954; postgrad. U. Chgo., 1960-61, 67-69; m. Virginia Mae Jensen, June 7, 1952; children—Gary Carlton, Bradley James, Neil Reid. Tchr., Morton High Sch., Cicero, Ill., 1950-53; instr. Morton Coll., Cicero, 1953-63, asso. dean for admissions and records, 1964-74, prof. geology and geography, 1974-84, prof. emeritus, 1984—. Active, Boys Scouts Am. Served with U.S. Army, 1944-46. NSF fellow, 1960-61. Mem. Ill. State Acad. Sci., Nat. Assn. Geology Tchrs., Soc. Vertebrate Paleontology, Great Lakes Planetarium Assn., Sigma Xi. Luthern. Home: Park Ridge IL 60068

BERGSTROM, ROBERT WILLIAM, lawyer; b. Chgo., Nov. 8, 1918; s. C. William and Ellen B. (Anderson) B.; LL.B., Chgo. Kent Coll. Law, 1940, J.D., 1970; M.B.A., U. Chgo., 1947; m. Betty Howard; children—Mark Robert, Philip Alan, Bryan Scott, Cheryl Lee, Jeffrey Alan. Admitted to Ill. bar, 1940, U.S. Supreme Ct. bar, 1950; practiced law in Chgo., 1940—; partner firm Bergstrom, Davis & Teeple, and predecessors, 1951—. Chmn., Glenview (Ill.) Village Caucus, 1961; bd. dirs. Ill. Com. for Constl. Conv., 1969; founding chmn. Com. for Legis. Reform, 1972-75, counsel, 1976-80; founder statewide Com. on Cts. and Justice, exec. com., 1971—. Served to lt. USNR, 1942-46. Named Chicagoan of Year in Law and Judiciary, Chgo. Jaycees, 1969. Mem. Am. Bar Assn. (co-editor antitrust devels. 1965-68), Ill. Bar Assn. (exec. council anti-trust sect. 1967), Chgo. Bar Assn. (sec. 1969-71, editor Chgo. Bar Record 1971-72), Chgo. Assn. Commerce and Industry. Clubs: Execs., Union League (pres. 1971-72, Disting. Public Service award 1981). Author: The Law of Competition in Illinois, 1962; also numerous articles on antitrust law, constl. law, and econs. Office: Bergstrom Davis & Teeple 39 S La Salle St Chicago IL 60603

BERGT, GREGORY PAUL, chemist, consultant; b. West Point, Nebr., Nov. 20, 1948; s. Lowell Duane and Elaine Angela (Schula) B.; m. Diann Helen Stigge, May 6, 1972; children—Matthew, Lisa, Troy. B.S., Nebr. Wesleyan U., 1971; postgrad. U. Minn., 1974. Chemist, Wendt Labs., Belle Plaine, Minn., 1971-77, dir. sci. and regulatory affairs, 1978—; cons. VA Hosp., Mpls., 1977. Patentee in field. Pres., St. John's Lutheran Ch., Belle Plaine, Minn., 1981; sponsoring liason Boy Scouts Am., Belle Plaine, 1980-84; county del. Republican party, Scott County, Minn., 1982. Recipient award Chemistry Tng. Program, NSF, 1967. Mem. Animal Health Inst., Parenteral Drug Assn., Am. Dairy Sci. Assn., Am. Chem. Soc., Am. Inst. Chemists, Am. Fedn. Ind. Pharm. Mfrs. (sec.-treas., dir. 1979—). Republican. Lutheran. Clubs: Tiger Booster (pres. 1973-75), Rotary (pres. 1984-85) (Belle Plaine, Minn.). Home: 200 Oakwood Circle Belle Plaine MN 56011 Office: Wendt Labs Inc 100 Nancy Dr Belle Plaine MN 56011

BERK, BURTON BENJAMIN, optometrist; b. Cleve., Jan. 31, 1930; s. Benjamin C. and Ruth S. (Hirsohn) B.; B.S. in Optometry, Ohio State U., 1953, O.D., 1977; m. Margery A. Rocco, June 17, 1951; children—Deborah L., Bruce C., Michael S., Lawrence R. Practice optometry, Columbus, Ohio, 1953—. Instr. optometry Ohio State U., 1967—. Dir. Corporate Futures, Rochester, N.Y.; sec. Ohio Profl. Investment Corp., 1968—. Pres. Ohio State Bd. Optometry, 1972—. Mem. Nat. Eye Research Found., Optometric Extension Found., Inc., Ohio Vision Service, Better Vision Inst., Vision League of Ohio. Fellow Am. Acad. Optometry; mem. Central Ohio, Ohio, Am. optometric assns., Internat. Orthokeratology Assn., Am. Optometric Found., Phi Sigma Delta. Republican. Clubs: B'nai B'rith, Whitehall Lions, Presidents of Ohio State U. Home: 2775 Brentwood Rd Columbus OH 43209 Office: 5180 E Main St Columbus OH 43213

BERKEBILE, DALE EUGENE, orthopedic surgeon; b. Chgo., Feb. 18, 1935; s. Dale Eugene and Elizabeth Jane (Cook) B.; A.B., DePauw U., 1957; M.S., U. Ind., 1958, M.D., 1962; m. Mary Carroll Jordan, Aug. 25, 1957; children—Charles Jordan, Mary Susan, Sarah Elizabeth. Intern, U. Wis. Hosps., Madison, 1962-63, resident in orthopedic surgery, 1964-66, 68-69; resident in gen. surgery St. Joseph Hosp., Marshfield, Wis., 1963-64; practice medicine specializing in orthopedic surgery, Rapid City, S.D., 1969—; orthopedic surgeon staff Rapid City Regional Hosps., Ft. Meade (S.D.) VA Hosp., 1969—. Served with M.C., U.S. Army, 1966-68. Diplomate Am. Bd. Orthopedic Surgeons. Fellow A.C.S., Am. Acad. Orthopedic Surgeons (bd. councilors). Methodist. Home: 1717 West Blvd Rapid City SD 57701 Office: 725 Meade St Rapid City SD 57701

BERKLEY, RICHARD L., mayor; grad. Harvard U. Sec., treas. Tension Envelope Corp., Kansas City, Mo.; mem. City Council Kansas City (Mo.), mayor, 1979—. Chmn. Jackson County (Mo.) Republican Com. Office: Office of Mayor City Hall 414 E 12th Kansas City MO 64106*

BERKMAN, ARNOLD STEPHEN, clin. psychologist; b. N.Y.C., Sept. 2, 1942; s. Henry and Marion (Lampert) B.; A.B., Oberlin Coll., 1964; M.S., U. Pitts., 1966, Ph.D., 1969; m. Claire Fleet, Apr. 27, 1975; children—Eric, Joshua, Janna. Fellow in clin. psychology U. Chgo. Pritzker Sch. Medicine, Chgo., 1968-69; asst. prof. Counseling Center, Mich. State U., East Lansing, 1969-73, asso. prof., 1973-74; asso. prof. dept. psychiatry, 1974—. UPSHS trainee, 1964-67. Mem. Mich. Psychol. Assn. (v.p. profl. affairs 1978-79, pres. elect 1981, pres. 1982), Am. Psychol. Assn. Jewish. Home: 4780 Arapaho Trail Okemos MI 48864 Office: 1812 Mich Nat Tower Lansing MI 48933

BERLAND, THEODORE, author; b. Chgo., Mar. 26, 1929; s. Samuel and Lena (Siegel) B.; B.S. in Journalism, U. Ill., 1950; A.M. in Sociology, U. Chgo., 1972; postgrad. Bowling Green (Ohio) State U.; m. Cynthia Rich, Dec. 23, 1956; children—Leslie Myra, Elizabeth Ann, David Rueben. Gen. assignment reporter, wire editor Champaign-Urbana (Ill.) Courier, 1950-51; sci. writer Michael Reese Hosp., Chgo., 1955-56, 66-84, Rush-Presbyn.-St. Luke's Med. Ctr., Chgo., 1984—; sci. writer, editor Research Reports, U. Chgo. public relations office, 1956-59; free lance writer, Chgo., 1959—; fgn. corr. Chgo.'s American, Algiers, 1962, Chgo. Daily News, Antarctica, 1963, AMA News, Rotarian Mag., Caribbean, 1965; cons. EPA, 1971-73; instr. sci. writing Medill Sch. Journalism, Northwestern U., 1973, 75; instr. nutrition Columbia Coll., Chgo., 1977-80, chmn. dept. journalism, 1980-82; vis. asst. prof. journalism Bowling Green State U., 1979-80; lectr. in mass. communication U. Wis., Milw., 1980-81; assoc. prof. communications Grand Valley State Coll., Allendale, Mich., 1982—. Pres., North Town Community Council, 1970-73, also Citizens Against Noise; pres. dist. 2 edn. council Chgo. Bd. Edn., 1972-73; v.p. Bernard Horwich Jewish Community Center, 1970-75, pres., 1975-77; pres. Jewish Community Council West Rogers Park, 1975-76; bd. dirs. Ind. Voters Ill., 1974-75, Citizens Schs. Com., 1974-75. Served to 1st lt. USAF, 1951-55. Recipient Journalism award Am. Osteo. Assn., 1963; certificate of Recognition med. journalism awards contests AMA, 1964, 66; 8th prize U.S. sect. Internat. Honeywell/Asahi Pentax Photo Contest, 1965; Med. Journalism award Ill. Med. Soc., 1967; Sci. Writers award ADA, 1968, 69; Distinguished Service in Journalism award Am. Optometric Assn., 1973; Distinguished Achievement in Med. Writing award Chgo. chpt. Am. Med. Writers Assn., 1973; Beth Fonda award for excellence in Med. feature writing, 1975, 78. Fellow Am. Med. Writers Assn. (pres. 1981-82); mem. Headline Club Chgo. (treas. 1972-73), Authors Guild, Nat. Assn. Sci. Writers (life mem.), Soc. Midland Authors (pres. 1975-78, treas. 1978-79), Soc. Profl. Journalists. Author: The Scientific Life, 1962; (with Alfred E. Seyler) Your Children's Teeth, 1968; The Fight for Quiet, 1970; (with Mitchell Spellberg) Living with Your Ulcer, 1971; (with Robert Addison) Living with Your Bad Back, 1972; (with Gordon Snider) Living with Your Bronchitis and Emphysema, 1972; (with Richard Perritt) Living with Your Eye Operation, 1973; Rating the Diets, 1974, rev. edits., 1975-86; (with Leslie Sandlow and Richard Shapiro) Living with Your Colitis and Hemorrhoids and Related Disorders, 1976; (with Frank Z. Warren) Acupuncture Diet, 1976; The Fitness Fact Book, 1980, 81; (with Henry A. Jordan) After the Diet . . . Then What?, 1980, The Doctor's Calories-Plus Diet, 1981; (with L. Fischer-Pap) Living With Your Allergies and Asthma, 1983; The Dieter's Almanac, 1984; Fitness for Life, 1985; contbg. author: Stimulus, 1960; Perspectives on Living, 1962; Compact Handbook of College Composition (Maynard J. Brennan), 1964; A Treasury of Tips for Writers, 1965; Great Ideas Today, 1966; World Book Year Book, 1970; Crisis of Survival, 1970; Writing the Magazine Article, 1971; Readings in Health, 1972; The Endangered Environment (Ashley Montagu), 1974; Current Thinking and Writing, 1976; Together, 1977; The Complete Diet Guide for Runners and Other Athletes, 1978; TV Today, 1981; editor: The Medical Importance of Wine; contbr. over 200 articles to major mags. and jours.; author column The Thin Man, Chgo. Sun-Times, 1978-80, also numerous newspapers through Field News Service, United Feature Syndicate and Enterprise Sci. Service; author documentary movies. Office: PO Box 59170 Chicago IL 60659

BERLEY, ALFRED GARRETT, dentist, consultant; b. Chgo., June 11, 1947; s. Alfred Garrett and Doris Jean (Burroughs) B.; m. Kathleen Mary Cronin; children—Kara, Erin, Daniel. B.S., Loyola U.-Chgo., 1969; D.D.S., Loyola U.-Maywood, Ill., 1973. Gen. practice dentistry, Oakbrook Terrace, Ill., 1973—; clin. instr. Loyola Dental Sch., Maywood, 1974—; cons. dental malpractice St. Paul Ins. Co. and pvt. law firms, Chgo., 1980—, cranio-facial pain Hinsdale Hosp., Ill., 1984—; instr. U.S. Dental Inst., Chgo., 1982—; conductor seminars on treatment of temperomandibular joint dysfunction and cranio-facial pain throughout U.S. and Can. Mem. A.D.A., Ill. Dental Soc., Chgo. Dental Soc., Acad. Stress and Chronic Disease, Am. Acad. Gnathological Orthopedics, Am. Equilibration Soc., Acad. Functional Prosthodontics, Am. Prosthodontic Soc., Am. Assn. Functional Orthodontics. Roman Catholic. Avocations: horseback riding and jumping; hunting; fishing; polo. Home: 33330 Saratoga Ave Downers Grove IL 60615 Office: One S 132 Summit Oakbrook Terrace IL 60181

BERLIN, CHARLES MELVIN, manufacturers' agent; b. Charleston, Ill., Nov. 11, 1932; s. Gilbert Melvin and Aleta Mildred (Halsey) B.; m. Shirley Ann Zimmerman, Aug. 23, 1952; children—Bradley, Ross, Rick, Beth. B.A., U. Ill., 1954. Salesman, Howell Co., St. Charles, Ill., 1957-60; mfrs. agt. Dixie Furniture Co., Lexington, N.C., 1960—. Served to 1st lt. U.S. Army, 1955-57. Mem. Home Furnishing Reps. Mich. (pres. 1971). Republican. Lutheran. Home and Office: 4592 Wagon Wheel Dr Birmingham MI 48010

BERLING, JOHN GEORGE, university dean; b. Melrose, Minn., June 26, 1934; m. Patricia Ann Ehlen, Feb. 23, 1957. B.S. in Bus. Edn., St. Cloud State U., 1957; M.L.S., Wayne State U., 1967; Ph.D. in Ednl. Adminstrn., U. Nebr., 1975. Tchr. Holdingford Pub. Schs., Minn., 1957-62; tchr./librarian Staples High Sch., Minn., 1962-68; dir. resource ctr. Apollo High Sch., St. Cloud, Minn., 1969-75; reference librarian St. Cloud State U., 1968-69, dean learning resources ctr., dir. ctr. for info. media, 1975—; cons. Control Data Corp., St. Paul, 1975, Cambridge Pub. Schs., Minn., 1976, Kearney State U., Nebr., 1977, St. Mary's U., San Antonio, 1977. Producer video tape: Video Censorship: A Dilemma in Our Schools, 1979. Mem. St. Cloud Cable Commn., 1984—; bd. dirs. Central Minn. Edn. Research and Devel. Council, 1985; mem. adv. Central Minn. Ednl. Coop. Service Unit, 1985. Experienced Tchr. fellow Wayne State U., 1966-67; NDEA scholar, 1965. Mem. NEA, Minn. Edn. Assn., Minn. Ednl. Media Orgn., Assn. for Ednl. Communication and Tech. (accreditation com. 1985), Assn. for Coll. and Research Library, ALA. Home: 3011 20th St S Saint Cloud MN 53601 Office: Learning Resources Services & Ctr for Info Media St Cloud State U Saint Cloud MN 56301

BERMAN, ARTHUR LEONARD, state senator; b. Chgo., May 4, 1935; s. Morris and Jean (Glast) B.; B.S. in Commerce and Law, U. Ill., 1956; J.D., Northwestern U., 1958; children—Adam, Marcy. Admitted to Ill. bar, 1958, since practiced in Chgo.; mem. firm White, White & Berman, Chartered, 1958-74, Maragos, Richter, Berman, Russell & White, Chartered, 1974-81, Chatz, Berman, Maragos, Haber & Fagel, 1981-82, Berman, Fagel, Haber, Maragos & Abrams, 1982—; spl. atty. Bur. Liquidations, Ill. Dept. Ins., 1962-67; spl. asst. atty. gen. Ill., 1967-68; mem. Ill. Ho. of Reps., 1969-76, Ill. Senate, 1976—. Adviser dist. edn. council Chgo. Bd. Edn. Bd. dirs. Zionist Orgn. Chgo.; mem. Rogers Park, Edgewater, Northtown communtiy councils. Pres., 50th Ward Young Democrats, 1956-60; v.p. Cook County Young Dems., 1956-60, 50th Ward Regular Dem. Orgn., 1955—; exec. bd. Dem. Party, Evanston, Ill., 1973—. Bd. dirs. Bernard Horwich Jewish Community Center, North Town Community Council; bd. govs. State of Israel Bonds. Mem. Am., Ill., Chgo. (bd. mgrs. 1976-77) bar assns., Decalogue Soc. Lawyers, Am. Trial Lawyers Assn., John Howard Assn., Common Cause, Northwestern U., U. Ill. alumni assns., Phi Epsilon Pi, Tau Epsilon Rho. Home: 5855 N Sheridan Rd Chicago IL 60660

BERMAN, AUBREY, tax consultant; b. Chgo., May 23, 1925; s. William and Ethel (Frankel) B.; B.S., U. Ill., 1948; m. Dorothy Lee Kolodny, Dec. 20, 1949; m. 2d, Penni Maller, July 31, 1977; 1 dau., Wendy. With IRS, 1949-79, internal revenue agt., Chgo., 1949-58, supervising spl. agt., 1966-70, criminal investigator, 1958-79; self-employed tax cons., security cons., Wilmette, Ill., 1979—. Served with AUS, 1943-46. Mem. U.S. Treasury Agts. Assn., Fed. Criminal Investigators Assn. Democrat. Jewish. Address: 2443 Cardinal Ln Wilmette IL 60091

BERMAN, DANIEL JUDAH, insurance broker; b. Chgo., Feb. 17, 1949; s. Barry Leonard and Judith Bloom (Mendelsohn) B.; m. Phyllis Ann Strauss, Dec. 27, 1969 (div. Sept. 1979); children—Emily Nanette, Joshua Strauss, Benjamin Strauss. B.A., Northwestern U., 1970; J.D., DePaul U., 1983. Bar: Ill. 1983, U.S. Dist. Ct. (no. dist.) Ill. 1983; C.P.C.U.; C.L.U. Account exec. Donchin-Hecht & Co., Chgo., 1970-78, Near North Ins. Agy., Chgo., 1978-81, Schwartz Bros. Agy., Chgo., 1981; ind. ins. broker, Chgo., 1981—. Bd. dirs., pres. Sheridan Point Condominium Assn., Chgo., 1979-84. Mem. Soc. C.P.C.U.s, Soc. C.L.U.s. Jewish. Home: 6325 N Sheridan Rd Chicago IL 60660 Office: 20 N Wacker Dr Chicago IL 60606

BERMAN, FRED JEAN, art educator; b. Milw., Nov. 3, 1926; s. Ezra and Frances (Heyman) B.; m. Joy Gross, Sept. 3, 1949 (div. Apr. 1966); children—Joseph Ezra, Jonathan Gerrit. B.S., Milw. State Tchrs. Coll., 1948; M.S., U. Wis., 1949. Instr., Layton Sch. Art, Milw., 1949-60; prof. art U. Wis., Milw., 1960—; exchange lectr. Reading U., Eng., 1966-67. One-man shows: Camden Arts Ctr., London, 1983, U. Reading, Crescent Arts Ctr., Scarborough, Eng., 1984; group shows include: Art Inst. Chgo., Corcoran Gallery Art, Washington; Library of Congress, McRoberts and Tunnard Gallery, London, Mus. Fine Arts, Boston, Pa. Acad. Art, Phila., Royal Acad. Art, London, San Francisco Mus. Art, Venice Biennale, Italy, Va. Mus. Fine Arts, Richmond, Whitney Mus. Am. Art, N.Y.C.; work reproduced in: Art Digest, Art Scene, Art, Sat. Rev., Search and Self-Discovery (book), Inst. Contemporary Art Bull., London, Young Am. of Whitney Mus. Am. Art; numerous pub. and pvt. collections. Recipient 30 awards for art including Joseph Eisendrath award Art Inst. Chgo., 1950, awards Milw. Art Inst., 1947, 49, 51, 52, 53, 56, Wis. Salon of Art, U. Wis., 1951, 53, 67, 2 awards 4th Biennial of Paintings and Prints Walker Art Ctr., Mpls., 1954; Amoco Disting. Teaching award U. Wis.-Milw., 1985. Home: 3133 N Marietta Ave Milwaukee WI 53211 Office: Art Dept Univ Wis Milwaukee WI 53211

BERMAN, HERBERT MARTIN, lawyer, arbitrator, mediator; b. Louisville, Mar. 22, 1936; s. Robert J. and Freda (Baer) B.; B.A., Ind. U., 1958; LL.B., U. Louisville, 1961; m. Sondra Ann Ignatow, Dec. 21, 1958; children—Michael, Frances, Jennifer. Admitted to Ky. bar, 1961, Ill. bar, 1971; asso. firm Shaikun & Helmann, Louisville, 1961-62; field atty. NLRB, Cin., 1962-63; asst. gen. counsel Internat. Brewery Workers Union, Cin., 1963-68; labor relations counselor Brunswick Corp., Chgo., 1968-70; asso. firm Lederer, Fox & Grove, Chgo., 1970-73; partner firm Arnold & Kadjan, Chgo., 1973-76; pres., partner firm Berman & Landrum Ltd., Chgo., 1976-79; prin. firm Herbert M. Berman & Assos., Ltd., Chgo., 1979—; mem. panel labor arbitrators Fed. Mediation and Conciliation Service. Mem. Am. Arbitration Assn. (panel), ABA, Soc. Profls. in Dispute Resolution. Home: 244 Willow Ave Deerfield IL 60015 Office: PO Box 350 Deerfield IL

BERMAN, HOWARD JAMES, assn. exec.; b. Chgo., Feb. 23, 1945; s. Sidney and Mildred B.; B.S. magna cum laude in Fin., U. Ill., 1967; M.H.A., U. Mich., 1969; m. Marilyn Millstone, June 1968; children—Seth, Lindsay. With Commr.'s Office, N.Y.C. Dept. Hosps., 1968-69; asst. prof. hosp. adminstrn. U. Mich., 1970-71; v.p. medicare ops. Blue Cross Assn., Chgo., 1971-77; v.p. charge corp. planning, product devel., data processing and research Am. Hosp. Assn., Chgo., 1977-79; group v.p. Health Services Program Group, Am. Hosp. Assn., 1979—; pres. Hosp. Research and Ednl. Trust, 1984—; lectr. U. Chgo., 1971—; adv. bd. Coop. Info. Center Hosp. Mgmt. Studies, 1972—; Fellow Am. Coll. Hosp. Adminstrs. Exec. editor Health Services Research; editorial bd. Inquiry, Topics in Hosp. Fin. Mgmt.; author and editor publs. in field. Home: 340 Carlisle Ave Deerfield IL 60015 Office: 840 N Lake Shore Dr Chicago IL 60611

BERMAN, RONALD CHARLES, accountant; b. Chgo., July 7, 1949; s. Joseph and Helen (Neiderman) B. B.S. with highest honors, U. Ill., 1971, J.D. with honors, 1974. Bar: Ill. 1974, Wis. 1976; C.P.A., Wis. Tax staff Alexander Grant & Co., Chgo., 1974-76, tax supr., Madison, Wis., 1976-78, tax mgr., 1978-81; ptnr. tax dept. Alexander Grant & Co., Madison, 1981—. Scoutmaster Boy Scouts Am., Middleton, Wis., 1978—; fin. chmn. Mohawk Dist. Four Lakes council Boy Scouts Am., Madison, 1981—, endowment fund chmn., 1984. Recipient Bronze Tablet, U. Ill., 1971. Mem. Wis. Soc. C.P.A.s, State Bar of Wis., Ill. Bar Assn., Order of Coif, Alpha Phi Omega, Phi Kappa Phi, Phi Alpha Delta. Lodge: Optimist. Avocations: photography; philatelÿ; camping. Home: 3906 Rolling Hill Dr Middleton WI 53562 Office: Alexander Grant & Co 2 E Gilman PO Box 8100 Madison WI 53708

BERNARD, BURTON CHARLES, lawyer; b. St. Louis, Oct. 19, 1926; s. Adolph and Anne (Koplovitz) B.; A.B., Washington U., 1947; LL.B., Harvard U., 1950. Staff mem. Ill. Commerce Commn., Chgo., 1950-51; practice in Granite City and Edwardsville, Ill., also St. Louis, 1951—; asst. states atty. Madison County (Ill.), 1957-66. Pres. Jewish Fedn. So. Ill., 1970-72; trustee Jefferson Nat. Meml. Assn.; bd. dirs. Tri-City Regional Port Dist., 1975-78, Opera Theatre of St. Louis, 1983—. Served with AUS, 1945-46. Mem. Madison County Bar Assn. (chmn. pub. relations com. 1963-64), Madison County Hist. Soc. (dir., past pres.), Am. Legion, Am., Ill., Mo., St. Louis, Tri-City, Chgo. bar assns., Ill. Hist. Soc. (dir. 1960-63), Am. Jewish Hist. Soc. (exec. council 1970-73), Phi Beta Kappa. Democrat. Contbr. articles to legal jours. Office: Bernard Davidson 3600 Nameoki Rd Granite City IL also Marquette Bldg Saint Louis MO

BERNARDI, JAMES EDWARD, retail liquor merchant; b. Highland Park, Ill., July 26, 1946; s. Irving D. and Nell D. (Dimonit) B.; m. Michelle DiCarlo, June 12, 1976; children—Jamie Elizabeth, Michael James. B.A., North Park Coll., 1969. Tchr., coach Carmel High Sch., Mundelein, Ill., 1969-75; gen. mgr. Foremost Liquors, Mundelein, 1976—. Mem. Com. Bus. Devel. Commn., Mundelein, ARC, Mundelein. Mem. Ill. High Sch. Assn. (ofcl. 1969—). Roman Catholic. Avocations: officiating football; and basketball; golf. Home: 849 Braemar Mundelein IL 60060 Office: Foremost Liquors 425 Townline Rd Mundelein IL 60060

BERNARDI, RICHARD LOUIS, college administrator; b. LaSalle, Ill., Aug. 7, 1937; s. Adam and Lois Ann (Grivetti) B.; m. Shirley Ann Wenzel, Aug. 26, 1957; children—Brent and Stacy. A.A., LaSalle-Polu Ogelsby Coll., 1957; B.S., Northern Ill. U., 1959; M.A., Colo. State Coll., 1960. Cert. tchr., Calif. Assoc. prof. Rock Valley Coll., Rockford, Ill., 1967-73, dir. admission and records, 1973-77, dean of liberal arts and scis., 1977—; chmn. community coll. transfer co-ordinators Ill. Coll. Transfer Co-ordinators, Rockford, 1984—. Mem. adv. com. Rockford Park Dist., 1978-84. Mem. Community Coll. Humanities Assn., (pres. 1982-84, service award 1984). Club: Northern Ill. Tennis Assn. (pres.

1982-86). Lodge: Rotary. Home: 6101 Cranbrook Lane Rockford IL 61111 Office: Rock Valley Coll 3301 N Mulford Rd Rockford IL 61111

BERNARDIN, JOSEPH LOUIS CARDINAL, archbishop; b. Columbia, S.C., Apr. 2, 1928; s. Joseph and Maria M. (Simion) B.; A.B. in Philosophy, St. Mary's Sem., Balt., 1948; M.Ed., Cath. U. Am., 1952. Ordained priest Roman Catholic Ch., 1952; asst. pastor Diocese of Charleston (S.C.), 1952-54, vice chancellor, 1954-56, chancellor, 1956-66, vicar gen., 1962-66, diocesan consultor, 1962-66, adminstr., 1964-65; aux. bishop Atlanta, 1966-68; pastor Christ the King Cathedral, 1966-68; sec., mem. exec. com. Nat. Conf. Cath. Bishops-U.S. Cath. Conf., gen. sec., 1968-72, pres., 1974-77; archbishop of Cin., 1972-82, archbishop of Chicago, 1982—, elevated to Sacre Coll. of Cardinals, 1983. Mem. Sacred Congregation Bishops, 1973-78; del., mem. permanent council World Synod of Bishops, 1974, 77—; mem. Pontifical Commn. Social Communications, Rome, 1970-72. Mem. adv. council Am. Revolution Bicentennial, 1975, Pres.'s Adv. Com. Refugees, 1975. Mem. Nat. Cath. Edn. Assn. (chmn. bd. dirs. 1978-79). Address: 1555 N State Pkwy Chicago IL 60610*

BERNAUER, NORMAN LANG, advertising executive; b. Pitts., Apr. 19, 1926; s. Norman Leo and Frieda Dorothy (Allmendinger) B.; A.A., Graceland Coll., 1949; B.A., U. Wis., Madison, 1951; cert. TV prodn. Sch. Radio and TV Technic, N.Y.C., 1952; m. Barbara Jean Hands, Sept. 26, 1953; children—Allise Jean, Richard Martin. With Ford Found., WOI-TV, Ames, Iowa, 1952; with Sta. WDAF-TV, Kansas City, Mo., 1952-66; pres. Ber-Raye Prodns. Co., Kansas City, Mo., 1966-68; v.p. Raveill Farley Advt., Independence, Mo., 1968-74; exec. v.p. Everett, Brandt & Bernauer, Inc., Independence, Mo., 1974—. Mem. Kansas City Mayor's Task Force on Airport Commn., 1977-82; chmn. Citizens Com. for Eastern Jackson County Airport, 1978; bd. dirs. Restoration Trail Found.; ordained minister Reorganized Ch. Jesus Christ Latter-day Saints, pastor, 1954-61, 82, mem. Stake High Council, 1963—. Served with U.S. Army, 1944-46. Mem. Kansas City Advt. Fin. Club, Advt. Agencies for Action, FIMA (public relations and public affairs com. 1981-82). Club: Kiwanis. Home: 427 W 70th St Kansas City MO 64113 Office: 314 W 24 Hwy Independence MO 64050

BERNDT, DAVID JOHN, psychologist; b. Elgin, Ill., July 14, 1950; s. Melvin John and Edith W. B.; B.S. summa cum laude, Coll. of Charleston, 1977; M.A., Loyola U., Chgo., 1979, Ph.D. (NIMH fellow, Doyle fellow), 1981; m. Sheila MacDonald, Mar. 7, 1978. Mental health asst. Charleston (S.C.) County Hosp., 1976-77; intern Michael Reese Hosp. and Med. Center, Chgo., 1979-80, staff psychologist, 1981-84, asst. dir. psychology, 1984—; exec. dir. Affect, Behavior and Cognition Faculty, Ctr. Psychoanalytic Study. research assoc., asst. prof. dept. psychiatry U. Chgo. Mem. Assn. Advancement Psychology, Eastern Psychol. Assn., Am. Psychol. Assn., Soc. Personality Assessment. Contbr. articles to profl. jours., chpts. to books. Home: 1831 N Hudson St Unit B Chicago IL 60614

BERNDT, JOAN GASSAWAY, music educator; b. Toledo, May 4, 1936; D. Henry Griffith and Florence Louise (Schwyn) G.; m. William C. Berndt, Aug. 18, 1962; 1 son, Ronald W. B.Mus., U. Mich., 1958, M.Mus., 1962. Dir. orch. Birmingham (Mich.) pub. schs., 1958-64; instrumental music tchr. Rochester (Mich.) Community Schs., 1972-73; dir. orch. Ferndale (Mich.) City Schs., 1979-80, 83—; lectr. music dept. Oakland U., Rochester, Mich., 1973-79; condr. Troy (Mich.) Community Orch., 1982—; pvt. music tchr.; clinician; performer. Recipient Oreon E. Scott Humanities award U. Mich., 1958; James Babcock scholar, 1958. Mem. Mich. Sch. Band and Orch. Assn. (adjudicator), Phi Beta Kappa, Sigma Alpha Iota, Phi Kappa Phi, Pi Kappa Lambda. Republican. Lutheran. Club: Birmingham Musicale. Author: Preliminary Tone Studies for the Beginning Oboist, 1981; Sneaky Sight-Reading Studies, 1981, vol. 2, 1983; The Oboist's Full Range Scales, 1981.

BERNEIS, KENNETH STANLEY, physician, educator; b. Bloomington, Ind., Dec. 25, 1951; s. Hans Ludwig and Regina (Fischhoff) B.; m. Karen Lou Sachs, Nov. 23, 1975; children—Erica, Erin, Ellen, Elaina. B.S., U. Mich., 1973, M.D., 1977. Diplomate Am. Bd. Family Practice. Intern-resident Bronson Hosp., and Borgess Med. Ctr., 1977-80; practice family medicine, Ostego, Mich., 1980—; pres., owner Ostego Family Physicians, P.C., 1981—; clin. instr. Mich. State U., 1980—; preceptor Southwestern Mich. Area Health Edn. Ctr., 1980—; chief of staff Pipp Community Hosp., 1982-85, vice-chief of staff, 1985—, chief ob-gyn, 1985—, chief pharmacy and therapeutics, 1984—; chief quality assurance Mirnet Research Network, 1984—. Mem. Am. Acad. Family Physicians, AMA, Nat. Rifle Assn. Home: 131 N Sunset St Plainwell MI 49080 Office: 900 Dix St Otsego MI 49078 also 1576 Main St Martin MI 49070

BERNETT, THEODORE BYRON, management consultant; b. Chgo., Aug. 30, 1924; s. Joseph and Julia (Gorski) B.; B.S. in M.E., U. Ill., 1950; student bus. adminstrn., U. Wis., Milw., 1953-54; m. Helen Brower, Apr. 23, 1949; children—Richard, Michael, James. Julie, Amy. founder T.B. Bernett & Assos., Kenosha, Wis., 1980—. Served with USNR, 1943-46. Mem. ASME. Home: 6622 59th Ave Kenosha WI 53142

BERNING, DANIEL ROBERT, lawyer; b. Ft. Wayne, Ind., Mar. 4, 1952; s. Henry Fred and Dorothy Marie (Daniel) B.; m. Patricia Leah Stawicki, June 3, 1978; children—Jennifer Kaye, Gregory Patrick. B.A., Wabash Coll., 1974; J.D., Valparaiso Sch. Law, 1977. Bar: Ind. 1977. Investigator, Porter County Prosecutor's Office, Valparaiso, Ind., 1977-78, dep. prosecutor, 1978-79, chief dep., 1979-82, pros. atty., 1982—. Recipient Law Enforcement award Optimist Club of the Dunes, 1982; Porter County Law Enforcement Man of Yr. award, 1984. Mem. Porter County Bar Assn., Nat. Dist. Attys. Assn. Republican. Lutheran. Avocations: Golf, racquetball, tennis, volleyball, softball. Home: 301 Madison Valparaiso IN 46383 Office: Prosecutors Office Courthouse Lincolnway Valparaiso IN 46383

BERNS, PAMELA KARI, artist, publisher; b. Sturgeon Bay, Wis., Sept. 4, 1947; d. Robert Matthew and Judith (Sigurdson) B., B.A., Lawrence U., 1969; M.F.A. U. Wis.-Madison, 1971. Owner, mgr. Sta. Gallery, Ephraim, Wis., 1968-69; pub., editor Chgo. Single Mag., Chgo., 1984—. One woman show includes Francis Hardy Gallery Ephraim, Wis., 1976; exhibited in group shows at New Horizons, Chgo., 1975, Watercolor Wis., Racine, 1972-82 (awarded 2nd prize 1976, 1982); represented in permanent collections State of Ill. Ctr., Bergstrom-Mahler Art Ctr., Kemper Ins. Cos. Graphic designer Ill. Arts Alliance, Chgo., 1984, Yates for Congress Com., Chgo. 1983, Lakeview Mental Health Council, Chgo., 1982; poster design Peninsula Arts Assn., Fish Creek, Wis., 1980. Recipient V.I.P. in her Community award NOW, 1977. Mem. Wis. Watercolor Soc., Wis. Painters and Sculptors Assn., Chgo. Artists Coalition (art dir. 1980—). Avocations: piano; painting. Home: 447 Oakdale St Chicago IL 60657

BERNSTEIN, CHARLES BERNARD, lawyer; b. Chgo., June 24, 1941; s. Norman and Adele (Shore) B.; A.B., U. Chgo., 1962; J.D., DePaul U., 1965; m. Roberta Luba Lesner, Aug. 7, 1968; children—Edward Charles, Louis Charles, Henry Jacob. Admitted to Ill. bar, 1965, U.S. Supreme Ct. bar, 1972; asso. firm Axelrod, Goodman & Steiner, Chgo., 1966-67, Max & Herman Chill, Chgo., 1967-74, Bellows & Assos., Chgo., 1974-81, Marvin Sacks Ltd., Chgo., 1981; individual practice law, 1981—; basketball press dir. U. Chgo., 1967-74. Vice pres. Congregation Rodfei Zedek, 1979, bd. dirs., 1978—. Recipient Am. Jurisprudence award, 1963; citation meritorious service Dist. Grand Lodge 6 B'nai B'rith, 1969; My Brothers Keeper award Am. Jewish Congress, 1977. Mem. Chgo., Ill. State bar assns., Chgo. Jewish Hist. Soc. (treas. 1977-79, v.p. 1979-82, dir. 1977—), Chgo. Pops Orch. Assn. (treas., exec. com. 1975-81), Am. Jewish Hist. Soc., Art Inst. of Chgo., Chgo. Hist. Soc., Jewish Geneal. Soc. (dir. 1977—), Nu Beta Epsilon. Club: B'nai B'rith. Contbr. articles to profl. jours. and mags. Home: 5400 S Hyde Park Blvd Apt 10-C Chicago IL 60615 Office: 120 W Madison St Chicago IL 60602

BERNSTEIN, HARVEY JAY, computer specialist; b. Detroit, Apr. 16, 1945; s. Morris and Bernice (Rothman) B.; student U. Toledo, 1963-65: A.S., Cuyahoga Community Coll., 1974; B.S. magna cum laude, Dyke Coll., 1977; M.B.A., Case Western Res. U., 1984; Sec. of Navy Fin. Mgmt. fellow Weatherhead Sch. Mgmt., Case Western Res. U., 1980-83; m. Irene Harriet Hoffman, Jan. 21, 1968; children—Bradley J., Matthew A. Fiscal acctg. asst. Navy Fin. Center, Cleve., 1971-72, fiscal acct. officer, 1972-73, mil. pay regulation specialist, 1973-79, fin. systems specialist, 1979-82, computer programmer analyst, 1982-84, supervisory computer specialist, dir. resource allocation and evaluation Consol. Data Ctr., 1984—; instr. John Carroll U., 1978-82, Cuyahoga Community Coll., 1977—, Dyke Coll., 1984-85. Served with USN, 1965-71. Recipient Career Service award Cleve. Fed. Exec. Bd., 1978; lic. real estate broker. Mem. Am. Soc. Mil. Comptrollers (pres. Cleve. chpt. 1976-77), Cleve. Area Bd. Realtors, Am. Contract Bridge League, Mensa. Jewish. Home: University Heights OH 44118 Office: US Navy Finance Center Cleveland OH 44199

BERNSTEIN, JESSE AARON, human resource executive; b. Bklyn., Apr. 17, 1948; s. Morris David and Norma Mildred (Sprung) B.; m. Lenore Harriet Orenstein; children—Zachary Jacob, Mara Devorah. B.A., SUNY-New Paltz, 1968; M.S.W., U. Mich., 1970. Social worker Washtenaw County, Ann Arbor, Mich., 1970-73; pres. Western Wayne Counseling Assocs., Mich., 1973-80, Employee Assistance Assocs., Ann Arbor, Mich., 1981—. Pres. Westland C. of C., 1977-78; mem. Blue Cross-Blue Shield Mental Health Adv. Com., 1977—. Mem. Assn. Labor Mgmt. Adminstrs. and Cons. on Alcoholism (pres. Greater Detroit chpt. 1985-86), Nat. Assn. Social Workers, U. Mich. Sch. Social Work Alumni Assn. (bd. dirs. 1983—). Jewish. Home: 3552 Frederick Ann Arbor MI 48105 Office: Employee Assistance Assocs 1250 Eisenhower Pl Ann Arbor MI 48104

BERNSTEIN, LEA HOPE, lawyer; b. Chgo., Apr. 4, 1937; d. Boris and Rose (Tenenbaum) Kummel; m. Herbert A. Blum; children—Merle S., Barry K., Howard E.; m. 2d, Robert Bernstein, Feb. 11, 1971 (div.). B.S. in Commerce, DePaul U., 1976, J.D., 1980. C.P.A., Ill. Bar: Ill. 1980. Paralegal D'Ancona and Pflaum, Chgo., 1971-77; C.P.A. Fields and Fields, Chgo., 1977; controller Taico Design Products, Chgo., 1977-78; C.P.A. Bernstein and Bank, Lincolnwood, Ill., 1978-80; mem. Levenfeld, Eisenberg, Janger, Glassberg & Lippitz, Chgo., 1980-82; prin. Lea Hope Bernstein & Assocs., Chgo., 1983—. Bell and Howell scholar, 1975. Mem. ABA, Chgo. Bar Assn. (probate practice com. 1982—), Chgo. Soc. Women C.P.A.s, Am. Inst. C.P.A.s, Ill. C.P.A. Soc. Home: 8512 N Harding Skokie IL 60076 Office: Lea Hope Bernstein & Assocs 175 N Franklin St Chicago IL 60606

BERNSTEIN, MALCOLM ALBERT, ins. agt.; b. Cin., Feb. 18, 1933; s. Herbert B. and Mildred (Abrohams) B.; B.S., U. Pa., 1954; m. Ann Maxine Berkman, Nov. 24, 1960; children—Sarah Elizabeth, Alexander Isaac Joshua. With Isaacs & Bernstein Inc., Cin., 1954-69; v.p. Frederick Rauh & Co., Cin., 1969-82; owner M.A. Bernstein & Co., Cin., 1982—; pub. Music & Matter mag., 1958-59; pres. Dimension Cin. mag., 1963-65. Bd. dirs. Cin. Jewish Community Relations Council, 1958—, pres., 1980-82; bd. dirs. Jewish Family Service, 1965-79, Assn. Home Care Agencies, 1976-79; bd. dirs. Easy Riders, 1975—, pres., 1977-79. CPCU. Mem. Queen City Assn. (dir. 1968-69), Soc. CPCU. Jewish. Club: Losantiville Country. Home: 59 Oliver Rd Cincinnati OH 45215 Office: 1055 Saint Paul Pl Cincinnati OH 45202

BERNSTEIN, MARTIN STUART, mktg./advt. cons.; b. Omaha, June 5, 1932; s. David B. and Eva (Cohn) B.; B.B.A., U. Tex., 1956; A.B., Del Mar Coll., 1956; postgrad. Harvard U., 1967; m. Martha Gumaer, Sept. 2, 1960; 1 son, Michael David. Advt. dir. U.S. Shoe Corp., Cin., 1962-67; v.p. McManus, John & Adams Advt., Bloomfield Hills, Mich., 1967-68; sr. v.p. Campbell-Ewald Co., Detroit, 1968-72; pres. Sportstats/MCA, Inc., N.Y.C., Universal City, Calif., 1972-75; pres. Mktg. Services Bur., Inc., Southfield, Mich., 1975—. Bd. dirs. Motion Picture Hall of Fame, Los Angeles, 1973-78. Recipient Sec. of Commerce citation for aiding U.S. export sales, 1980. Mem. Am. Mktg. Assn., Am. Footwear Industries Assn. Clubs: Detroit Adcraft, Cin. Advt., N.Y. World Trade, Friars of N.Y., Friars of Calif., Masons. Home: 1560 Brentwood Dr Troy MI 48098 Office: 30555 Southfield Rd Suite 340 Southfield MI 48076

BERNSTEIN, MURRAY M., social worker; b. Milw., July 3, 1938; s. Louis and Rae (Kurzer) B.; B.S., U. Wis., Milw., 1966, M.S.W., 1970; Ph.D., Eastern Nebr. Christian Coll., 1973; m. Nancy Siegel, Jan. 26, 1964; children—David J., Sarah Lynn. Program dir. Milw. Boys Club, 1964-68; social work psychologist VA Hosp., Woods, Wis., 1974—; asst. prof. dept. psychiatry Med. Coll. Wis.; pvt. cons.; dir. Inst. Directive Therapy; cons. therapist Assn. Research and Enlightenment (Edgar Cayce Found.) del., lectr. People to People program, China, 1982. Pres. Temple Anshe Emeth, Milw., 1979-80. Served with USAF, 1956-60; to capt. M.C., U.S. Army, 1970-74. Cert. Acad. Cert. Social Workers. Mem. Am. Group Psychotherapy Assn., Nat. Assn. Social Workers, Internat. Transactional Analysis Assn. Developer directive therapy method of psycho-social approach to psychotherapy. Home: 8615 W Petersik St Milwaukee WI 53224 Office: Woods Veterans Administration Hospital Woods WI 53193

BERNSTEIN, ROBERT LEE, dentist; b. Massillon, Ohio, Feb. 11, 1933; s. Theodore and Dorothy Marie (Huff) B.; m. Ruth Anne Baker, Dec. 19, 1957; children—Jeffrey Kent, Bradley James. B.A., Case Western Res. U., 1956, D.D.S., 1961. Pvt. practice dentistry, Massillon, 1961—. Fellow Acad. Gen. Dentistry, Am. Soc. Dentistry for Children, Acad. Dentistry Internat.; mem. ADA, Stark County Dental Soc. (peer rev. com. 1981), Massillon Dental Soc. (pres. 1975-77). Republican. Episcopalian. Avocations: pottery; woodworking; electronics; boating; swimming. Office: 215 Erie St N Massillon OH 44646

BERNSTEIN, SUSAN, development and fundraising executive; b. Chgo., May 17, 1938; d. Herman and Frances (Dobkin) Powell; m. Phillip Bernstein, Sept. 4, 1957; children—Kenneth, Robert, Michael. B.A. in Human Services, Northeastern Ill. U., Chgo., 1978. Real estate assoc. Martin-Marbry, Inc., Skokie, Ill., 1971—; exec. dir. B'nai B'rith Women, Land of Lakes Region, Skokie, 1978-83; dir. resource devel. Travelers and Immigrants Aid, Chgo., 1984—; fundraising cons. Internat. Women's Ctr. Founder Nat. Forum for Women, Woodstock, Ill., pres., dir., 1980-83; bd. dirs., treas. Y-Me Breast Cancer Program, Chgo., 1984-85; lic. foster parent Kids in Need, Chgo. Named Citizen of Yr., Lerner Life newspapers, Chgo., 1980. Mem. Nat. Soc. Fundraising Execs. (Chgo. chpt.), Women in Devel. Professions, NOW. Democrat. Jewish. Home: 8414 Kedvale St Skokie IL 60076 Office: Travelers and Immigrants Aid 327 S LaSalle St Suite 1500 Chicago IL 60604

BERNTHAL, HAROLD GEORGE, health care company executive. Vice chmn., dir. Am. Hosp. Supply Corp., Evanston, Ill. Office: Am Hosp Supply Corp One American Plaza Evanston IL 60201*

BERNTSON, STANLEY MARSHALL, savings and loan association executive; b. Chgo., Aug. 5, 1907; s. Bernard E. and Margurite (Nelson) B.; evening student Northwestern U., 1925-27; m. Lillian Adelaine Johnson, Oct. 14, 1933; children—Gail Lynda, Grant Morgan. Acct., George Reinberg Co., Chgo., 1927-35, George May & Co., 1935-36; exec. sec. Derby Laundry, 1936-40; chmn. bd. Fidelity Fed. Savs., Chgo., 1940—; v.p. Mars Realty Co., 1945—; exec. sec. Samuel Olson Mfg. Co., 1943-56. Bd. dirs. Elmhurst YMCA; chmn. bd. Kids Alive, Internat.; trustee Trinity Sem.; bd. dirs. Lydia Children's Home. Mem. Nat. League Insured Assns. (legis. com.), Ill. Savs. and Loan League (legis. com.), Cook County Council Insured Savs. Assn. (pres.), C. of C. (dir.). Mem. Evang. Free Ch. Am. Club: Kiwanis (dir.). Home: Elmhurst IL 60126 Office: 5455 W Belmont Ave Chicago IL 60641

BERNZEN, AVRIL MARIE CLARK, microbiologist; b. Quincy, Ill., Jan. 26, 1924; d. Wallace Edward and Marie A. (Recker) Heberling; B.S., Quincy Coll., 1945; voice grad. Quincy Conservatory Music; piano grad. Notre Dame Conservatory Music; student St. John Hosp. Sch. of Med. Tech., 1946-47; m. George W. Bernzen; 1 dau., Joan Marie Clark Queen. Microbiologist, St. John's Mercy Hosp., St. Louis, 1948-52; med. technologist St. Frances Hosp. Lab., Peoria, Ill., 1956-58; lectr. in microbiology Quincy Coll., 1966-70; adminstrv. technologist, ednl. dir. St. Mary Hosp., Quincy, 1959-78, program/ednl. dir., 1978—. Pres. Altrusa Club, 1974-76; bd. govs. for Dogwood Festival, C. of C., 1975-77; bd. dirs. Quincy Soc. Fine Arts, United Way, 1978—, v.p. allocations, 1982-84, sec., 1984-85, also chmn. pub. relations; bd. dirs. Quincy Community Little Theatre, Quincy Art Club, ESA World Center Found., Am. Cancer Soc.; bd. dirs. Quincy Mus. Natural History and Art, pres., 1983-85. Named Outstanding Woman of Ill., ESA Orgn., 1968; Outstanding Woman of Quincy, 1970; Outstanding Alumnus, Biology Dept. of Quincy Coll., 1980. Mem. Am. Soc. Med. Tech.; Am. Soc. Clinical Pathologists, Internat. Platform Assn., Midwest Assn. for Ednl. Resource Sharing (pres. 1981-83). Epsilon Sigma Alpha (Outstanding Mem. award 1977). Republican. Roman Catholic. Clubs: Elks Aux., Spring Lake Country, Altrusa (Outstanding Mem. 1978-79). Home: 2236 Vermont St Quincy IL 62301 Office: 1415 Vermont St Quincy IL 62301

BEROUNSKY, JOSEPH FRANK, electronics engineer; b. Omaha, Mar. 2, 1930; s. Joseph John and Mary (Kracl) B.; m. Mary Francis Taylor, Apr. 8, 1947; children—Joseph John, Mary Catherne (Mrs. John Whitney), Chris Alan. Radio technician Gen. Communications Co., Inc., Omaha, 1961-66, service mgr., 1966-73, systems engr., 1973-80; sales engr. Omaha Communications Systems Ltd., 1980—. Mem. Ak Sar Ben Radio Club (v.p., pres. (1962-63), Quarter Century Wireless Assn. Lodge: Eagles. Home: 9010 Valley St Omaha NE 68124 Office: 8833 J St Omaha NE 68127

BERREY, ROBERT WILSON, III, lawyer, judge; b. Kansas City, Mo., Dec. 6, 1929; s. Robert Wilson and Elizabeth (Hudson) B.; A.B., William Jewell Coll., 1950; M.A., U. S.D., 1952; LL.B., Kansas City U., 1955; LL.M., U. Mo. at Kansas City, 1972; grad. Trial Judges Coll., U. Nev., 1972; m. Katharine Rollins Wilcoxson, Sept. 5, 1950; children—Robert Wilson IV, Mary Jane, John Lind. Admitted to Mo. bar, 1955, Kans. bar, 1955, since practiced in Kansas City; asso. mem. firm Shugert and Thomson, 1955-56, Clark, Krings & Bredehoft, 1956-57, 1957-61, Terry and Welton, 1961-62; judge 4th Dist. Magistrate Ct., Jackson County, Mo., 1962-79; asso. cir. judge 16th Jud. Cir. Ct., Jackson County, Mo., 1979-81, cir. judge, 1981-83, mem. mgmt.-exec. com., 1979-83; judge Mo. Ct. Appeals-Western Dist., Kansas City, 1983—; mem. Supreme Ct. Com. to Draft Rules and Procedures for Mo.'s Small Claims Ct., 1976, 77. Vol. legal cons. Psychiat. Receiving Center. Del. Atlantic Council Young Polit. Leaders, Oxford, Eng., 1965; Kansas City rep. to President's National Conference on Crime Control; del.-at-large White House Conf. Aging, 1972; former pack chmn. Cub Scouts Am.; counselor, com. mem. Boy Scouts Am., sponsor Eagle Scouts; vice chmn. water fowl com. Mo. Conservation Fedn., 1968-69, chmn. water fowl com., 1971-73; v.p. Cook PTA, 1967-68; mem. cts. and judiciary com. Mo. bar, 1969-73; mem. Midwest region adv. com. Nat. Park Service, 1973-78, chmn., 1973-78; mem. Mo. State Judicial Planning Commn., 1977; bd. dirs., founder Kansas City Open Space Found., 1976. Regional dir. Young Rep. Nat. Fedn., 1957-59, gen. counsel, 1959-61, nat. vice-chmn.; chmn. Mo. Young Rep. Fedn., 1960, nat. committeeman, 1959-60, 61-64; Mo. alternate at large Republican Nat. Conv., 1960, asst. gen. counsel, 1964, del. state and dist. convs., 1960, 64, 68. Bd. dirs. Naturalization Council, Kansas City, pres., 1973—; trustee Kansas City Mus., 1972-73, Hyman Brand Hebrew Acad., 1983—; hon. life dir. Rockhurst Coll. Mem. Mo. Bar (Disting. Service award 1973, agr. law com., com. council 1980-81), Kansas City Bar Assn., Urban League (exec. com., dir.), S.A.R., Kansas City Mus. Natural Sci. Soc. (charter), Tex. Longhorn Breeders Assn. (life), Mo. Longhorn Breeders Assn. (life), Alpha Phi Omega, Delta Theta Phi, Pi Gamma Mu, Tau Kappa Epsilon. Mem. Christian Ch. Mason, mem. DeMolay Legion Honor. Clubs: Ward Parkway Country (dir. 1968-69); Leawood Country; Kansas City; Waldo Optimist (v.p. 1967-68); Capitol Hill (Washington); Ducks Unltd. (state com. 1981—). Home: 1235 W 58th St Kansas City MO 64113 also summer Route 2 Battle Lake MN Office: Mo Ct Appeals Bldg 1300 Oak St Kansas City MO 64106

BERRY, BARBARA JUNE, educator; b. Chgo., Apr. 19, 1933; d. James Rufus and Anna Lee (Bramlett) Green; m. Lewis Vernor Berry, Jr., June 30, 1956; children—Lewis, Anne Frances. B.E., Chgo. Tchrs. Coll., 1954; cert. Inst. Psychoanalysis, 1971; M.S.Ed. in Spl. Edn., Chgo. State U., 1976. Tchr. intermediate grades Brownell Sch., 1959-65, Deneen Elem. Sch., 1959-65; tchr. intermediate grades Frank L. Gillespie Sch., Chgo., 1966-74, tchr. moderate/-severe learning disabilities resource, 1974—; instr. Chgo. State U., 1982; condr. workshops. Recipient cert. Spl. Edn. Tchrs. Orgn., 1974. Mem. Chgo. Assn. Children and Adults with Learning Disabilities, Council Exceptional Children, Spl. Edn. Tchrs. Orgn. Episcopalian. Home: 9848 S Calumet Ave Chicago IL 60628

BERRY, CHARLES LEONARD, fin. exec.; b. Granite City, Ill., Sept. 21, 1940; s. P. Louis and Freida (Feltman) B.; B.S., St. Louis U., 1961, M.S., 1972; m. Lynn S. Moore, Oct. 28, 1967; children—Charles Leonard, Catherine, Christopher. With Eastman Kodak Stores, Inc., 1961-70, acct., St. Louis, 1961-63, credit mgr., 1963-66, office supr., San Diego, 1966-70; hosp. controller St. Louis U. Med. Center, 1970-75, adminstrv. controller, 1975-76; asso. controller Normandy Osteo. Hosps., St. Louis, 1977-79; asst. prof. Webster Coll., St. Louis, 1979-80; v.p. fin. McKendree Coll., Lebanon, Ill., 1980—; adj. faculty Maryville Coll., 1975—, Webster Coll., 1974—. Mem. Hosp. Fin. Mgmt. Assn., Alpha Kappa Psi. Home: 280 N Lindbergh Blvd Saint Louis MO 63141 Office: 701 College Rd Lebanon IL 62254

BERRY, DIANE ELIZABETH, lawyer; b. Cleve., Aug. 16, 1950; d. Richard Louis and Rosalyn Ann (Cironi) B.; m. Kevin Leslie Tucker, Aug. 4, 1973 (div. 1980). B.A., Denison U., 1972; postgrad. Coll. Law U. Toledo, 1972-73; J.D., Franklin Pierce Law Ctr., Concord, N.H., 1976; postgrad. in bus. adminstrn., U. Mich., 1985—. Bar: Ohio 1976, U.S. Dist. Ct. (no. dist.) Ohio 1976, U.S. Ct. Appeals (6th cir.) 1984. Legal aide N.H. Gov.'s Com. on Pub. Edn., Concord, 1973-74; legal research asst. N.H. Edn. Voucher Project, Concord, 1974-75; law clk. Perkins & Brock, Concord, 1975-76; assoc. Fuller & Henry, Toledo, 1976-81, ptnr., 1981—; mem. Lucas County Juvenile Ct. Citizen Rev. Bd., 1982—. Bd. trustees Family and Child Abuse Prevention Ctr., Toledo, 1984-85; mem. pub. info. com. Lucas County Unit Am. Cancer Soc., Toledo, 1983—. Honoree Tribute to Women and Industry, Toledo, 1984. Mem. ABA (antitrust sect., litigation sect., young lawyers div. anti-trust com., chmn. complex litigation subcom. 1981-83, exec. com. 1982-83), Ohio State Bar Assn. (anti-trust sect.), Toledo Bar Assn. Clubs: Toledo Country. Office: Fuller & Henry 1200 Edison Plaza PO Box 2088 Toledo OH 43603

BERRY, EDWIN C., business executive, television moderator, civic leader; LL.D., Western Mich. U., 1973; L.H.D., Chgo. State U., 1973; LL.D., Northwestern U., 1975; m. Betsy Gordon Bell; children—Joseph, Melanie Fraser; foster children—Myron Wahls, Charles Carter, Westina Mathews. With Nat. Urban League in Pitts., Portland, Chgo. for 33 yrs.; spl. asst. to pres., urban affairs officer, corp. cons. Johnson Products Co., Chgo., 1970—; treas., adminstrv. officer George E. Johnson Found., George E. Johnson Ednl. Fund. Moderator People to People program WGN-TV, Chgo. Mem. fund raising com. Chgo. Urban League, Chgo. Community Fund, Leadership Council for Met. Open Communities, Woodlawn Devel. Corp., Chgo. United, Chgo. Alliance Businessmen, Nat. Com. against Discrimination in Housing; chmn. Harold Washington for Mayor campaign; chmn. Mayor Washington's Transition Team, Chgo. Recipient John F. Kennedy award Catholic Interracial Council; Citation of Honor Stateway Mother's Soc.; Citation for outstanding service and leadership in black community The Woodlawn Orgn.; Golden Oil Can award Chgo. Econ. Devel. Corp.; named Chicagoan of the Year Chgo. Jr. Assn. Commerce and Industry; Man of Year Ada S. McKinley House; Laureate Lincoln Acad. Mem. UN Assn. of U.S.A. (chmn. Ralph Bunche awards panel). Mem. editorial bd. The Chicago Reporter. Office: Johnson's Products Co 8522 S Lafayette Ave Chicago IL 60620

BERRY, JAMES LEE, scientist, educator; b. Ashland, Ohio, Mar. 17, 1945; s. Lemoine Saviers and Doris Evelyn (Burlingham) B.; m. Barbara Christine Gum, June 18, 1970; children—Thomas Michael, Jennet Susan, Jessica Ann, Christian James. B.S., Ashland Coll., 1967; M.S., Cleve. State U., 1975. Grad. tchng. asst. Kent State U., Ohio, 1967-68; research technologist Cleve. Clinic Fdn., 1974-80; research scientist Cleve. Research Inst., 1981—; instr. Lorain County Community Coll., Elyria, Ohio, 1981—. Contbr. articles to profl. jours. Served with U.S. Army, 1968-70. Recipient, Grad. Assistantship award Kent State U., 1967. Mem. Soc. Biomaterials, Orthopedic Research Soc. Republican. Methodist. Avocation: gardening. Office: Cleve Research Inst 2351 E 22d St Cleveland OH 44115

BERRY, JAN VANCE, lawyer; b. Ames, Iowa, Mar. 14, 1951; s. Burl V. and Helen I. (Messer) B. B.A., Drake U., 1973, J.D., 1977. Bar: Iowa 1978, U.S. Dist. Ct. (so. dist.) Iowa 1978, U.S. Ct. Appeals (8th cir.) 1978. Asst. Polk County Atty., Polk County Attys. Office, Des Moines, 1978-81; ptnr. Handley, Berry & Eisenhauer, Ankeny, Iowa, 1981-85, Handley & Berry, Ankeny, 1985—. Mem. Iowa State Bar Assn. Club: Ankeny Golf and Country. Office: Handley & Berry 110 SE Grant St Suite 205 Ankeny IA 50021

BERRY, JANET PATRICIA, educator; b. Columbus, Ohio, Feb. 12, 1923; d. Maurice Denver and Mary (Funk) B.; B.S., Ohio State U., 1944, postgrad., 1945, 60, 73-76; postgrad. Otterbein Coll., 1960-61; M.A., Ohio State U., 1978; m. Escalus E. Elliott, Jr., Apr. 1944 (div. May 1962); 1 son, Escalus E. III; m. Edward J. Hannon, Jan. 7, 1966 (div. June 1980). Instr. dept. fine arts Ohio State U., 1945-46; art supr., tchr. Gahanna (Ohio) Public Schs., 1960-61; mem. art guide com. Franklin County Bd. Edn., 1960-61; exec. sec. Columbus Town Meeting Assn., producer-dir. Columbus Town Meeting Forum, 1963-72; promotions, personnel devel. and field services div. Nat. Center for Research in Vocat. Edn., Ohio State U., 1972-77, 80—. Pres. bd. trustees West Side and

Ohio Av. Day Care Centers Assn., 1958-60; gen. chmn. Twigs of Children's Hosp., 1955-57. Recipient cert. of merit Franklin County Bd. Edn., 1961. Mem. Pi Lambda Theta, Delta Phi Delta, Kappa Kappa Gamma. Home: 4355 Latin Ln Columbus OH 43220 Office: 1960 Kenny Rd Columbus OH 43210

BERRY, JOHN WILLIAM, III, manufacturing company executive; b. Toledo, Nov. 13, 1945; s. John William and Ruth Louise (Braham) B.; m. Cynthia Lee, June 30, 1979. B. in Indsl. Engring., Ga. Tech. U., 1968; postgrad. Ohio State U., 1969-70, Bowling Green State U., 1963. Sr. prodn. engr. PPG Industries, Pitts., 1968-74; prodn. supt. Guardian Industries, Detroit, 1974-76; dir. ops. Toledo Plate Glass Co., 1976-78; dir. mfg. systems Asist Corp., Detroit, 1978-82, Fruehauf Corp., Detroit, 1982—. Advisor, bd. dirs. Jr. Achievement of Am., Mt. Vernon, Ohio, 1974. Recipient Pres.'s Club award Ga. Tech. U., 1967. Mem. Am. Prodn. and Inventory Control (cert.), Delta Sigma Phi (pres. 1967). Republican. Methodist. Lodge: Elks. (Mt. Vernon; leading knight 1972-73). Home: 24293 El Marco Farmington Hills MI 48018 Office: Fruehauf Corp 10900 Harper Detroit MI 48213

BERRY, LUCILLE MARIE, educator; b. Nameoki, Ill., June 2, 1936; d. P. Louis and Frieda Catherine (Feltman) Berry; B.S., St. Louis U., 1958, M.S. in Commerce, 1963. Supr. cashiers St. Louis U., 1958-64, supr. grants and contracts, 1964-66, chief funds accountant, 1966-71; fin. asst. to provincial treas. Religious of the Sacred Heart, 1971-74, provincial treas., 1974-75; controller Maryville Coll., St. Louis, 1975-76, dir. bus. and fin., 1976-79, adj. instr., 1972-76, adj. asst. prof., 1976-79, asso. prof., 1979—, chmn. mgmt. div., 1979—. Mem. Am. Soc. Women Accountants, Am. Assn. Accountants, Mo. Assn. Accounting Educators, Midwest Bus. Adminstrs. Assn., Pi Lambda Theta. Home: 2100 Richmond Ave Granite City IL 62040 Office: 13550 Conway Rd St Louis MO 63141

BERRY, MARJORIE LOUISE, children's services librarian; b. Hammond, Ind., June 6, 1951; d. Joseph Edward and Thora Elizabeth (Hill) B. B.A. in Sociology, Ind. U., 1973, M.L.S., 1980. Cert. librarian. Br. head Hammond Pub. Library, 1973-76; br. head, children's librarian Lake County Pub. Library, Merrillville, Ind., 1976-78, children's librarian, 1980-83; children's services librarian John McIntire Pub. Library, Zanesville, Ohio, 1983-84; head central children's services Lake County Pub. Library, Merrillville, Ind., 1984—. Mem. adv. bd. dirs. Early Childhood Ednl. Instrs., Zanesville, 1983—. Mem. Children's Lit. Assn., Am. Library Assn., Children's Reading Roundtable, Ind. Library Assn., Nat. Assn. Edn. of Young Children. Republican. Methodist. Lodge: Order of Eastern Star.

BERRY, MICHAEL J., bank executive. Pres., dir. First of Am. Bank-Detroit, N.A., Detroit; v.p. First of Am. Bank Corp., Detroit (parent company). Office: First of Am Bank-Detroit NA 645 Griswold Detroit MI 48226*

BERRY, PAMELA LYNN, physician; b. Detroit, June 26, 1954; d. Harold White and Molean Antoinette (Mole) B.; m. Van Calvin Momon, Jr., May 19, 1979. B.S. in Physiology, Eastern Mich. U., 1975; M.D., Wayne State U., 1979. Diplomate Nat. Bd. Med. Examiners. Intern Henry Ford Hosp., Detroit, 1979-80, resident in pediatrics, 1980-82, chief resident in pediatrics, 1982; physician fellow in adolescent medicine Children's Hosp., Cin., 1982-83; staff physician Children's Med. Ctr., Dayton, Ohio, 1983—; asst. clin. prof. Wright State U. Sch. Medicine, 1985—. Fellow Am. Acad. Pediatrics; mem. Soc. Adolescent Medicine, Western Ohio Med. Soc., Am. Profl. Practice Assn. Democrat. Lutheran. Home: 98 E Vanlake Dr Vandalia OH 45377 Office: Children's Med Ctr 1 Children's Plaza Dayton OH 45409

BERRY, ROBERT HUNT, psychologist; b. Mpls., Apr. 25, 1945; s. Robert Edward Lee and Virginia Elinor (Hunt) B. B.A. cum laude, Tulane U., 1967; M.A., UCLA, 1971; M.S., U. Miami, 1976; postgrad. Fielding Inst., Santa Barbara, 1979—. VISTA vol., Ogden, Utah, 1968-70; tchr. spl. schs. for Aborigines, Alice Springs, Australia, 1972-73; clin. psychology instr. Adrian Coll. (Mich.), 1976-77; alcoholism therapist Beyer Hosp., Ypsilanti, Mich., 1978-79; correctional psychologist So. Mich. Prison, Jackson, 1979—; program cons. U. Mich.; mem. biomed. com. Mich. Tech. Council. Mem. Am. Psychol. Assn., Friends of Mich. Psychoanalytic Soc., Mich. Psychol. Assn., Internat. Transactional Analysis Assn., Mich. Assn. Profl. Psychology, U. Mich. Alumni Assn. Clubs: U. Mich. Pres.', Exchange of Am. Home: 2109 Pauline Ct Ann Arbor MI 48103 Office: 4000 Cooper St Jackson MI 49201

BERRY, ROBERTA MILDRED, civic worker; b. Medinah, Ill., Feb. 27, 1926; d. Judson Stewart and Anna Doretha (Neddermeyer) Lawrence; m. Moses Berry, June 29, 1948; children—Scott, Mark. B.Mus., Cornell Coll., 1948. Choir dir. Presbyterian, Methodist Chs., Cedar Rapids, Iowa, 1949-71; tchr. assoc. Cedar Rapids Community Schs., 1963-73; bd. dirs. Pioneer Village, Cedar Rapids, 1982-83, Linn Community Food Bank, Cedar Rapids, 1983-85; pres. Chs. United, Cedar Rapids, 1984-85; orginator Grade Sch. Picture Lady Program, Cedar Rapids, 1968-69; pres. Seminole Valley Farm, Cedar Rapids, 1980-81; v.p. Ch. Women United, Cedar Rapids, 1984-85. Bd. dirs. YWCA, Cedar Rapids, 1970-72, Cedar Rapids Symphony Guild, 1983-85, Iowa Rails to Trails, Cedar Rapids, 1983-85, Methwick Manor Aux., Cedar Rapids, 1983-85; sec. Council on Aging, Cedar Rapids, 1984-85. Clubs: Beethoven (pres. 1964-65), College (pres. 1965-66), PEO (pres. 1982-83), Demolay Mothers Aux (pres. 1974-75), Postal Workers Aux (pres. 1974-75) (Cedar Rapids). Avocations: oil painting; needlework; tennis; biking; choir. Home: 1118 Maplewood Dr NE Cedar Rapids IA 52402

BERRY, SHARON ELAINE, interior designer; b. Kansas City, Mo., May 27, 1945; d. Ralph Epping Hohmann and Ruth Justine (Sturm) Hohmann Gibson; m. Max Allen Berry, Apr. 8, 1984. Grad. high sch., Kansas City, Mo. Designer Danie Dunn Interiors, Kansas City, Mo., 1972-76, 1980-83; co-owner, operator Clift-Willard Interiors, Leawood, Kans., 1976-80; head decorating dept. Carpets by Johnson and Johnson, Overland Park, Kans., 1983-84; owner, operator Nouveau Interiors, Shawnee Mission, Kans., 1984—; publicity dir. Design Excellence Awards, Kansas City, Mo., 1982—; designer Designers Showhouse, Kansas City, Mo., 1975—; participant Design '81 Congress, Helsinki, Finland, 1981. Mem. Jr. Women's Symphony Alliance, Kansas City, Mo., 1983—. Recipient Gold medal Home Builders Assn. of Kansas City, 1977, Silver medal, 1978, 79, 81. Mem. Am. Soc. Interior Designers (assoc.). Office: Nouveau Interiors 9321 W 74th St Shawnee Mission KS 66204

BERSCHE, JOSEPH EDWIN, construction executive; b. Fairmont, W.Va., Oct. 17, 1931; s. G. Joseph and Jessie Naomi (Darling) B.; student Mich. State Normal Sch., 1949-50, Nyack Coll., 1950-51, U.S. Navy Engring. Sch., 1952; m. Barbara Carol Stegmaier, June 9, 1956; children—Craig, Chris, Kimberly Jo, Curt, Barbi Jo. Pres., Bersche Constrn. Co., Pontiac, Mich., 1956-66; exec. v.p., dir. Hannan Co., Cleve., 1967-77; pres. Inland Constrn., Inc., Chgo., 1977—; dir. Christian Publs. Inc., Harrisburg, Pa.; trustee pension fund Urban Investment and Devel. Co., Chgo. Trustee, Nyack (N.Y.) Coll., Stow Alliance Fellowship, Alliance Theol. Sem., Nyack; bd. mgrs. Christian and Missionary Alliance, Nyack; bd. dirs. Shell Point Village Retirement Home, Ft. Myers, Fla. Served with USN, 1951-55. Mem. Builders Assn. Chgo. (bd. dirs.), Assn. Governing Bds. of Univs. and Colls. Clubs: Hudson Country; Carlton, Execs. (Chgo.). Office: 730 N Franklin St Chicago IL 60610

BERST, JANET ROSE, data processing executive; b. Hammond, Ind., June 25, 1937; d. John Albert and Mary Ruth (Barnes) B.; B.A. in Speech, Taylor U., Upland, Ind., 1959; diploma in programming Internat. Data Processing Inst., Cin., 1967. Lead programmer analyst Midland Mut. Life Ins. Co., Columbus, Ohio, 1969-72, Ohio Dept. Edn., Columbus, 1972-75; sr. programmer analyst Ohio Youth Commn., Columbus, 1975-77; sr. devel. analyst Lincoln Nat. Life Ins., Fort Wayne, Ind., 1977-79; tech. analyst Washington Nat. Ins., Evanston, Ill., 1979—. Active, Evanston Hist. Soc.; bd. dirs. Mental Health Assn. Evanston. Fellow Life Mgmt. Inst.; mem. Assn. Systems Mgmt. (pres. Chgo. chpt.), Assn. Computing Machinery (pres. Central Ohio chpt.), Internat. Platform Assn., AAUW. Methodist. Club: Photography. Author: Christianity and the Real World. Office: 1630 Chicago Ave Evanston IL 60201

BERTELSON, ROBERT CALVIN, chemical company executive, research chemist; b. Milw., Nov. 5, 1931; s. Edward and Ida Clara (Ruskin) B.; m. Mary Lee Johnson, Jan. 21, 1960; children—Thomas Edward, Kenneth Andrew. B.S. in Chemistry, U. Wis.-Madison, 1952; Ph.D., MIT, 1957. Sr. research chemist NCR Corp., Dayton, Ohio, 1957-73; sr. research assoc. NSF, Wright-Patterson, Ohio, 1972-74; pres. ChromaChems. Inc., Dayton, 1974—. Contbr. articles to profl. jours., also book chpts. Patentee in field. Served with U.S. Army, 1957-60. Mem. Am. Chem. Soc., AAAS, Soc. Photog. Scis. Engrs., N.Y. Acad. Scis., InterAm. Photochem. Soc., Sigma Xi. Avocation: music. Office: Chroma Chems Inc PO Box 20273 Dayton OH 45420

BERTHELSEN, JOHN ROBERT, printing company executive; b. Albert Lea, Minn., July 23, 1954; s. Robert Eugene and Erna Catherine (Petersen) B.; m. Debra Denise Peterson, June 29, 1974; children—Angela Marie, Derek John. Student public schs. Albert Lea, Minn. Prodn. worker Arrow Printing Co., Albert Lea, 1972-73; journeyman Munson Printing Co., Red Wing, Minn., 1973-75; prep. foreman O'Connor Printing Co., Sioux Falls, S.D., 1975-76; preparation supr. Modern Press Inc., Sioux Falls, 1976-79; gen. mgr. Suttle Press, Inc., Waunakee, Wis., 1979-82, pres., 1982—. Recipient 1st place Nat. Skill Olympics (printing), Vocat. Indsl. Clubs Am., 1972, Gold award best managed printing co. Nat. Assn. Printers and Lithographers, 1983. Mem. Madison Craftsmen (pres. 1983-85), Internat. Assn. Printing House Craftsmen (gov. 6th dist. 1985—). Club: Madison Ben Franklin. Home: 6334 Clovernook Rd Middleton WI 53562 Office: Suttle Press Inc 806 S Division St PO Box 308 Waunakee WI 53597

BERTING, ROBERT JAMES, advt. agy. exec.; b. Indpls., July 4, 1931; s. Herman Phillip and Vada Melodine (Coleman) B.; student John Herron Art Inst., 1950-52; m. Barbara Jean Freije, Dec. 27, 1975. With Indpls. Times Newspaper, 1950-51, Armour & Co., Indpls., 1951-55, Arthur Murray Dance Studios, Indpls., 1955-58, Hook Drug Co., Indpls., 1958-62, Topics Newspapers, Indpls., 1962-76, Format. Inc., Indpls., 1976-80; pres. Central Ind. Advt., Indpls., 1980—; pres. Berting Seminar Prodns., 1980—; instr. advt. Ind. U., Indpls., 1981—. Mem. Ind. Bus. Communicators, Central Ind. Suburban Newspapers Assn. (exec. dir. 1977), Ind. Soc. Assn. Execs. Club: Advt. of Indpls. Home: 6330 Woburn Dr Indianapolis IN 46250

BERTINI, ROBERT HINES, public relations executive; b. Charlotte, N.C., Sept. 29, 1951; s. Robert Hines and Ann (Smith) B.; m. Olivia Maxine Upright, Aug. 24, 1974; 1 son, Robert Scott. B.A. in English, Applachian State U., 1973. Reporter Times, Thomasville, N.C., 1973-76, Greensboro (N.C.) News, 1976; mgr. pub. relations Miller Brewing Co., Eden, N.C., 1976-80, community liaison mgr., Milw., 1980-81, community relations mgr., 1982—. Mem. publicity com. Milw. Council, Boy Scouts Am. Mem. Pub. Relations Soc. Am. Democrat. Baptist. Office: 3939 W Highland Blvd Milwaukee WI 53201

BERTOG, EUGENE TRACY, educator; b. Chgo., Nov. 29, 1930; s. Frank Carl and Grayce (Tracy) B.; B.S., Loyola U., Chgo., 1952, M.Ed., 1973; m. Elaine Kohl, June 25, 1955; children—Eugene, Elaine, Joseph, Steven, Robert. Dir. edn. and tng. Continental Casualty Co., Chgo., 1955-69; dir. ednl. services CNA Fin. Corp., Chgo., 1969-72; gen. mgr. Lake Shore Club Chgo., 1972-74; prof., chmn. dept. hotel mgmt. Oakton Community Coll., Des Plaines, 1974—. Mem. deans adv. council Loyola U., 1976—, also mem. citizens bd.; pres. PTA, 1971-73. Served as lt. AUS, 1953-55; Korea. Named Alumnus of Yr., Loyola U., 1967; mem. Loyola U. Athletic Hall of Fame; recipient service to youth through athletics awards, Teaching Effectiveness award Oakton Community Coll. Mem. Hotel Sales Mktg. Assn. (dir.), Am. Acad. Polit. and Social Sci., Am. Soc. Tng. and Devel., Ins. Co. Edn. Dirs. Soc., U.S. Olympic Soc., Loyola U. Alumni Assn. (pres. 1969-72), Ill. Tng. Dirs. Assn., U.S. Navy League, Blue Key, Alpha Kappa Psi, Beta Gamma Sigma, Tau Kappa Epsilon. Clubs: North Shore Country; Lake Shore (pres. dir.), Executives (Chgo.); Internat. (Chgo.). Home: 2314 Sussex Ln Northbrook IL 60062 Office: 1600 E Golf Rd Des Plaines IL 60016

BERTRAND, LOUIS ROBERTSON, lawyer; b. Wilmington Del., July 16, 1942; m. Sharon Ann Clark, June 1966; children—Robertson, Elisa, Laura. B.A. in History, SUNY-Buffalo, 1965; J.D., U. Toledo, 1968. Bar: Ohio 1968, Mich. 1969, U.S. Dist. Ct. (no. dist.) Ohio 1970; diplomate Nat. Bd. Trial Advocacy. Investigator, Toledo Police Dept., 1967-68; probation officer Portage County Juvenile Ct., Ravenna, Ohio, 1968-69; asst. pros. atty. Portage County, 1969-72; instr. Dept. Mgmt. Kent State U., Ohio, 1969-70; ptnr. Bertrand & Zavinski, Ravenna, 1971—. Councilman, Hiram (Ohio) 1973—, mem. finance com., chmn. safety com., pres. Village Council, 1976-78. Mem. Assn. Trial Lawyers Am., Ohio Acad. Trial Lawyers, Akron Bar Assn., Portage County Bar Assn. (chmn. grievance com. 1975), Summit-Portage Football Offcials Assn. (assoc.) Clubs: Ohio State Athletic Assn. (lic. official baseball, 1983, football, 1980). Office: Bertrand & Zavinski PO Box 268 409 S Prospect Ravenna OH 44266

BERUBE, PHILLIP, state senator; b. Belcourt, N.D., Apr. 6, 1905; s. Arthur and Victorine (Mongeon) B.; ed. public schs.; m. Alma Casavant, 1929; children—Leonel, Vivian Beruve Cote, Delina Berube Grossal, Loreeta Berube Leanard, Harvey, Julian Berube Lentz, Adrien, Jackie. Farmer, 1927-30; mem. N.D. State Senate, 1952—. Mem. County Sch. Reorgn. Com. N.D., 1947-69. Mem. Farmers Union. Roman Catholic. Club: Commercial. Office: State Capitol Bismarck ND 58505*

BERZINS, ANDREJS, engineering administrator; b. Latvia, Feb. 3, 1924; s. Peter and Lydia (Neiland) B.; m. Velta Jonson, Dec. 24, 1948; children—Michael, Diana. Diploma in Civil Engring., Riga (Latvia) State Tech. Inst., 1943; B.S. in Mech. Engring., Baltic U., Hamburg, W.Ger., 1947. Registered engr. Ohio, Ontario. Design engr. Davy McKee Corp., Cleve., 1957-63, project engr., 1964-67, mgr. engring., 1967-74, v.p. engring., 1974—. Sustaining mem. Rep. Nat. Com. Mem. Assn. Iron and Steel Engrs., AIME. Patentee: charging apparatus with removable bell, charging apparatus for receptacle, method and appartus for cooling reduced metal agglomerates; contbr. articles to profl. jours. Office: 6200 Oak Tree Blvd Cleveland OH 44131

BERZINS, ERNA MARIJA, physician; b. Latvia, Nov. 27, 1914; d. Arturs and Anna (Steckenbergs) Meilands; came to U.S., 1951, naturalized, 1956; M.D., Latvian State U., 1940; m. Verners Berzins, Aug. 24, 1935; children—Valdis, Andis. Mem. pediatric faculty Latvian State U., 1940-44; intern Good Samaritan Hosp., Dayton, Ohio, 1951-52; resident in pediatrics Children's Hosp. of Mich., Detroit, 1953-55; practice medicine specialising in pediatrics, Detroit, 1956-60; with ARC, Cleve., 1961-63; physician pediatric outpatient dept. Cleve. Met. Gen. Hosp., 1963—; asst. prof. Case-Western Res. U., Cleve. Trustee Women's Gen. Hosp., Cleve. Mem. AMA, Ohio Med. Assn., Acad. Medicine, No. Ohio Pediatric Soc., Am. Women's Med. Assn., Am. Med. Polit. Action Com. Lutheran. Address: 5460 Friar Circle Cleveland OH 44126

BESCHLOSS, MORRIS RICHARD, valve manufacturing exec.; b. Berlin, Mar. 7, 1929; s. Otto and Manya (Levine) B.; B.S., U. Ill., 1952; m. Ruth Greenwald, Nov. 13, 1954; children—Michael, Steven. Advt. mgr. Hammond Valve Corp. (Ind.), 1956-58, asst. sales mgr., 1958-61, field sales mgr., 1961-62, v.p. sales, 1962-63, pres., 1963-68, chmn. bd., 1968—, also dir.; pres. Condec Flow Control 1968-84; v.p., dir. Condec Corp.; pres. Plumbing-Heating-Cooling Info. Bur., 1971-72, chmn. bd., 1973-80. Sec.-treas. Flossmoor-Homewood (Ill.) Area Sch. Bd., 1969-73. Served from 2d lt. to capt. AUS, 1952-54. Recipient Distinguished Eagle award Boy Scouts Am., 1974. Mem. Valve Mfrs. Assn. (dir. 1971—, pres. 1971-73), Assn. Industry Mfrs. (charter pres.), World Bus. Council, Tau Delta Phi, Sigma Delta Chi, Alpha Phi Omega. Clubs: Execs., Econ. (Chgo.). Home: Chicago IL 60611 Office: 840 N Michigan Ave Chicago IL 60611

BESS, TIMOTHY ALAN, school psychologist; b. Clarksville, Ark., Mar. 30, 1950; s. George William and Agnes (Allen) B.; B.A. in Psychology, Butler U., Indpls., 1974, M.S. in Counseling, 1977; M.S. Ed., U. Wis.-River Falls, 1983; m. Nancy Helen Jaracz, Mar. 11, 1977; children—Jonathan, Jeffrey. Assoc. instr. communication and cognitive devel. Marion County Assn. Retarded Citizens, Indpls., 1975, employment specialist, 1975-76: coordinator psychol. services and spl. edn. Plainfield (Ind.) Community Sch. Corp., 1977-78; coordinator 3-R program emotionally disturbed/behavioral problems students Ind. Sch. Dist. 834, Stillwater, Minn., 1978-79; sch. psychologist Ind. Sch. Dist. 191, Burnsville, Minn., 1979-80, Ind. Sch. Dist. 833, Cottage Grove, Minn., 1980—; coordinator Alternative Learning Ctr. Ind. Sch. Dist. 833, Cottage Grove. Mem. Nat. Assn. Sch. Psychologists, Assn. Specialists Group Work, Butler U. Alumni Assn., Phi Delta Kappa. Home: 7781 Inskip Trail Cottage Grove MN 55016 Office: Park Sr High Sch 8040 80th St S Cottage Grove MN 55016

BESSER, HOWARD RUSSELL, lawyer; b. Cleve., Sept. 12, 1941; s. Morris Milton and Florence Helen (Sandler) B.; m. Barbara Kaye, Sept. 3, 1972; 1 son, Matthew Emerson Douglas. B.A., Ohio State U., 1963, J.D., 1966. Bar: Ohio 1966, U.S. Dist. Ct. (no. dist.) Ohio 1967, U.S. Ct. Appeals (6th cir.) 1975, U.S. Supreme Ct. 1977. Assoc., Griff, Weiner & Orkin, Cleve., 1966-68; asst. dir. law, counsel to mayor City of Cleve., 1968-71; U.S. dist. counsel EEOC, 1971-76; trial atty. Ohio Bell Telephone Co., 1976—; lectr. law Cleve. State U., 1971-85, adj. prof. law, 1985—. State pres. ACLU, 1973-75, 83—, v.p., 1982-83, 70-73, bd. dirs., 1968-77, 80—; mem. adv. council Musical Arts Assn., 1983—; vice-chmn. New Democratic Coalition Cuyahoga County, 1969-71; trustee No. Ohio, Am. Jewish Congress, 1983—. Recipient Outstanding Civil Libertarian of Yr. award ACLU, 1975. Mem. ABA, Ohio Bar Assn. (chmn. civil rights com. 1980—), Cuyahoga County Bar Assn. (trustee 1983—), Cleve. Bar Assn., Sphinx, Tau Epsilon Rho. Contbr. articles to profl. jours. Home: 3554 Stoer Rd Shaker Heights OH 44122 Office: Ohio Bell Telephone Co 45 Erieview Plaza Room 1448 Cleveland OH 44114

BESSIRE, HOWARD DEAN, foundation executive, consultant; b. Missouri Valley, Iowa, Mar. 1921; s. Howard Dean and Etta Blanche (Pound) B. B.S. in Bus. Adminstrn., U. Neb., 1948; grad. Organization Mgmt. Inst., Economic Devel. Inst., Sec. C. of C., Colby, Kans., 1948-49, exec. dir., Clinton, Iowa, 1949-53, El Paso County Texas Ind. Devel. Corp., 1962-66, Cofco Indsl. Found., Council Bluffs, Iowa, 1953-57; economic developer, chief operating officer Walla Walla County Port Dist., Washington, 1957-59; exec. v.p. Idaho East Oreg. Economic Devel. Council, Boise, 1959-62, Indsl. Devel., Inc., Wichita Falls, Tex., 1966-70; exec. dir., chief operating officer Indsl. Found., Inc., South Bend, Ind., 1973; sec. H & S Cons., Inc., South Bend, 1969—; also dir.; dir. Am. Economic Devel. Council, Chgo.; chmn. Ind. Area Devel. Council, Indpls., 1979; v.p. Pacific Northwest Industrial Devel. Council, 1961. Author: Techniques of Industrial Development, 1964, Practice of Industrial Development, 1970, A Handbook for the 80s Industrial Development, 1981. Served as 1st sgt. U.S. Army, 1940-45, ETO. Fellow Am. Economic Devel. Council (bd. dirs. 1981—); mem. Ind. Area Devel. Council (chmn. 1979), Mid-Am. Econ. Devel. Council. Democrat. Lodges: Masons, Shriners. Avocations: writing; indsl. park and building designer. Home: PO Box #765 South Bend IN 46624

BESTERFIELD, DALE HAMLYN, engineering educator; b. Harvey, Ill., Sept. 19, 1930; s. E. Howard and Maude (Hamlyn) B.; m. Helen Hratko, Oct. 12, 1957; children—Carol, Glen, Mary. B.S. in Indsl. Engring., Washington U., St. Louis, 1953; M.S., Ill. Inst. Tech., 1965; Ph.D., Soc. Ill. U., 1971. Registered profl. engr., Mo., Calif.; cert. mfg. engr. Indsl. engr. Union-Camp Corp., Trenton, N.J., 1955-61; mem. faculty So. Ill. U., Carbondale, 1962—, prof. engring., 1964—, chmn. dept., 1983—; research prof. Nat. Chengchi U., Taipei, Taiwan, 1982-83; seminar leader Am. Mgmt. Assn., N.Y.C., 1982—; instr. Union Carbide Corp., Paducah, Ky., 1983. Author: Quality Control, 1979; Technical Sketching, 1983; chpt. in handbook. Scoutmaster, Boy Scouts Am., Carbondale, 1973-74. Served with AUS, 1953-55. Recipient Amoco Teaching awards So. Ill. U., 1974, 77. Mem. Am. Soc. Quality Control (instr. 1980—), Soc. Mfg. Engrs., Nat. Assn. Indsl. Tech. Avocations: golf; swimming; woodworking. Office: Coll Engring and Tech Southern Ill Univ Carbondale IL 62901

BETHEL, KATHLEEN EVONNE, librarian; b. Washington, Aug. 4, 1953; d. Frederick Errington and Helen Evonne (Roy) B. B.A., Elmhurst Coll., Ill., 1975; M.A.L.S., Rosary Coll., River Forest, Ill., 1977. Receptionist, Newberry Library, Chgo., 1975-77; br. and reference librarian Maywood Pub. Library, Ill., 1977-78; asst. librarian Johnson Pub. Co., Chgo., 1978-81; librarian African-Am. studies Northwestern U., Evanston, Ill., 1982—. Mem. ALA, Nat. Black Caucus Librarians, NAACP. Office: Northwestern Univ Library 1935 Sheridan Rd Evanston IL 60201

BETSCHMAN, RICHARD FRANK, locksmith, hardware executive; b. Norwalk, Ohio, May 25, 1932; s. Cyrillus N. and Martha (Egle) B.; m. Dolores Catherine Seifker, Aug. 25, 1951; children—David Paul, Ronald Gerard, Sharon Marie, Kathy Ann, Diane Marie. Foreman outboard finishing line Lyman Boats Co., Sandusky, Ohio, 1953-57; shipping clk. Rotary Printing Co., Norwalk, Ohio, 1957-63; service mgr. appliance repairs P & R Electric Co., Norwalk, 1963-67; owner, operator Hess Hardware Co., Monroeville, Ohio, 1970—; lectr. security. Pres. Monroeville Hist. Soc., 1974—; sec. Mayor's Area Devel. Com., Monroeville, Ohio, 1975-76; chmn. Town Meeting Monroeville, 1977; organizer, gen. chmn. Community Picnic Day, 1979—; v.p. Monroeville Community Affairs Com., 1983—. Mem. Asso. Locksmiths Am., Pa.-Ohio Locksmiths Assn., Am., Ohio hardware assns., Am. Hardware Probe Panel, Sentry Hardware Dealer Probe, Huron County (Ohio) Am. Heritage Com. Democrat. Roman Catholic. Clubs: Lockmasters Tru-Center, Kiwanis (sec.-treas. Monroeville 1973-77). Home: 142 E Main St Norwalk OH 44857 Office: 2 N Main St Monroeville OH 44847

BETTAN, ANITA ESTHER, public relations specialist, writer; b. Cin., Nov. 30, 1928; d. Israel and Ida Judith (Goldstein) B. B.A., U. Cin., 1950; M.A., Columbia U., 1951. Copywriter, Shillito's, Cin., 1953-55; continuity dir. Sta. WSAI, Cin., 1955-57; copywriter, jr. account exec. William F. Holland Agy., Cin., 1957-61; account coordinator Stockton-West-Burkhart, Inc., Cin., 1962-67; asst. to info. officer U. Cin. Coll-Conservatory of Music, 1967-71; info. services writer U. Cin., 1971—, mem. com. on aging, 1981—. Contbr. articles to mags. Dep. foreman Hamilton County Grand Jury, Cin., 1979, foreman petit jury, 1980; pres. career div. Council Jewish Women, Cin., 1962-64; vol. Jewish Hosp., Cin., 1954-59; mem. Sr. Olympics Com., Cin., 1981—. Mem. Women in Communications. Home: 2101 Grandin Rd Cincinnati OH 45208 Office: U Cin Mail Location No 65 Cincinnati OH 45221

BETTENDORF, JAMES BERNARD, clergyman, church association administrator; b. Jackson, Mich., Oct. 22, 1933; s. Bernard Anthony and Kathryn Marie (Vaughan) B. B.A., Sacred Heart Sem., 1955; postgrad. U. Detroit, 1956, U. Notre Dame, 1957, Cath. U. of Am., 1958; S.T.B., St. John Sem., 1959; M.A., Western Mich. U., 1970; postgrad. St. Mary Coll., 1981—. Assoc. pastor Holy Trinity Ch., Fowler, Mich., 1959-60, St. Phillip Ch., Battle Creek, Mich., 1960-63, Sacred Heart Ch., Flint, 1963-66; dir. Flint Newman Ctr., Flint Cath. Info. Ctr., Mich., 1966—; pastor Good Shepherd Ch., Montrose, Mich., 1983—. Mem. exec. bd. dirs. Genesse-Lapeer-Shiawasee Health Planning Commn., Flint, 1971—, Urban Coalition, Flint, 1973-74; mem. Tall Pine council Boy Scouts of Am. Mem. Lansing Cath. Campus Ministry Assn. (diocesan bd. dirs. 1971—), Mich. Cath Campus Ministry Assn., Nat. Assn. Diocesan Dirs. Campus Ministry (mem. exec. bd.), Cath. Campus Ministry Assn. (recipient Charles Forsyth award 1983). Home: 1802 E Court St Flint MI 48503 Office: Flint Newman Ctr 609 E Fifth Ave Flint MI 48503

BETZ, RONALD PHILIP, pharmacist; b. Chgo., Nov. 26, 1933; s. David Robert and Olga Marie (Martinson) B.; B.S., U. Ill., 1955; m. Rose Marie Marella, May 18, 1963; children—David Christian, Christopher Peter. Asst. dir. of pharmacy U. Ill., Chgo., 1959-62; dir. pharmacy Mt. Sinai Hosp., Chgo., 1962—; pres. Pharmacy Systems, Inc., 1982—; teaching asso. Coll. of Pharmacy, U. Ill., Chgo., 1977—; pres. Pharmacy Service and Systems, 1972-81; dir. Ill. Coop. Health Data Systems, 1976-80. Bd. dirs. Howard-/Paulina Redevel. Corp., 1983—. Served with U.S. Army, 1956-58. Mem. Am. Pharm. Assn., Am. Soc. Hosp. Pharmacists, Ill. Pharm. Assn. (pres. 1975), Ill. Acad. Preceptors in Pharmacy (pres. 1972), No. Ill. Soc. Hosp. Pharmacists (pres. 1966), Kappa Psi. Democrat. Lutheran. Contbr. articles in field to profl. jours. Home: 7505 N Sheridan Rd Chicago IL 60626 Office: 2750 W 15th Pl Chicago IL 60608

BETZOLD, BARBARA ANN, hospital food services administrator, consultant; b. Hillsboro, Ill., Dec. 4, 1954; d. Clifford Lyle and Dorothy Joan (Sorrells) Betzold. Student Western Ill. U., 1973-75; B.S. cum laude in Home Econs., Kans. State U., 1977. Clin. dietitian St. Mary's Hosp., Centralia, Ill., 1977-78, dir. dietetic services, 1978—; dir. dietetic services med. cons. firm, 1982—; mem. food service adv. com. Ill. Hosp. Assn.; freelance cons.; preceptor for correspondence courses. Bd. dirs. ARC, 1979-81; mem. comml. cooking adv. com. Centralia Correctional Ctr., 1980—. Named Outstanding Working Woman of Ill., 1985. Mem. Am. Dietetic Assn., Am. Diabetes Assn., Am. Soc. Hosp. Food Service Adminstrs., So. Ill. Dietetic Assn., Gateway Dietetic Assn., Bus. and Profl. Women's Club (treas. 1983-84, Young Careerist award 1983, individual devel. award 1984, v.p. 1984-85), Dist. Bus. Profl. Womens Club (chmn. individual devel. program 1984-85), Omicron Nu (treas. 1983-87), Kappa Omicron Phi. Republican. Methodist. Developer teaching informational pamphlets for diabetic patients. Office: Saint Mary's Hosp 400 N Pleasant St Centralia IL 62801

BEUC, RUDOLPH, JR., architect, real estate broker; b. St. Louis, Nov. 7, 1931; s. Rudolph M. and Lillian Ann (Rethemeyer) B.; B.Arch., Washington U., St. Louis, 1955; m. Mildred Hild, Jan. 25, 1968; children—Rudolph III, Ralph M. Archtl. draftsman Bank Bldg. & Equipment Corp. Am., St. Louis, 1950, Hammond & Gorlock, architects, St. Louis, 1957-58; designer Schwarz & Van Hoefen, architects, St. Louis, 1958; architect George E. Berg Architects, St. Louis, 1958-60; architect R. Beuc, Architects, Inc., St. Louis, 1960—, pres., 1960—, also dir.; pres., dir. Hilterdevco, Inc., St. Louis, 1964—; dir. Rethemeyer Coffee Co., Inc., St. Louis. Dir. pub. works Peerless Park, 1967—; deacon Webster Groves Presbyn. Ch. Served with AUS, 1955-57. Mem. AIA, Soc. Am. Registered Architects, Mo. Council Architects, Mo. Assn. Bldg. Ofcls. and Inspectors, Bldg. Ofcls. Council Am., Webster Groves C. of C., Am. Legion (past comdr.). Clubs: Mason, Lion (past pres.); Order Eastern Star, DeMolay, High Twelve (past state pres.), Scottish Rite, Washington University, Westborough Country. Home: 138 W Glendale Rd St Louis MO 63119 Office: 142 W Glendale Rd St Louis MO 63119

BEUGEN, JOAN BETH, communications executive; b. Chgo., Mar. 9, 1943; d. Leslie and Janet (Glick) Caplan; B.S. in Speech, Northwestern U., 1965; m. Sheldon Howard Beugen, July 16, 1967. Founder, prin., pres. The Creative Establishment, Chgo., San Francisco, Tokyo and N.Y.C., 1969—; speaker on entrepreneurship for women at seminars and workshops; del. White House Conf. Small Bus., 1979. Trustee Mt. Sinai Hosp. Med. Ctr., Chgo. Network, Nat. Women's Forum; v.p. region Com. of 200; mem. women in bus. com. Overseas Edn. Fund. Recipient numerous awards for films and multi-media presentations; named Woman Entrepreneur of Yr., Women in Bus., 1984. Mem. Nat. Assn. Women Bus. Owners (pres. Chgo. chpt. 1979), Chgo. Film Council, Chgo. Audio-Visual Producers Assn., Ill. Women's Agenda. Club: Commercial (civic com. task force). Contbr. articles on multi-media to profl. jours. Office: 1421 N Wells St Chicago IL 60610

BEUMER, ORIAN FRANKLIN, personnel director; b. Holland, Ind., Nov. 14, 1926; s. Frank Emil and Lydia Clara (Linstrot) B.; student Butler U., 1947-48; B.A. in English, U. Evansville, 1952, M.A. in continuing Studies, 1982; children—Toni Lynn, Steven Laune. Pub. relations aide Internat. Harvester Co., Evansville, Ind., 1952-55; employee communications editor Mead Johnson & Co., Evansville, 1955-58, supr. profl. employment, 1958, mgr. new product scheduling and coordination, 1958-66; franchised distbr. Vanda Cosmetics, Evansville, 1966-67; personnel dir. St. Mary's Med. Center, Evansville, 1967—; tchr. nursing home adminstrn. Lockyear Bus. Coll. Pres. bd. dirs. Youth Emergency Service, Inc., Evansville, 1977-80. Served with USN, 1944-46. Mem. Am. Soc. Personnel Adminstrn. (dist. dir. 1980—, accredited exec. in personnel), Ind. Health Careers Inc. (dir. 1972-79), Ind. Soc. Hosp. Personnel Adminstrn. (pres. 1969-70, editor newsletter 1971-73), Am. Soc. Hosp. Personnel Adminstrn., Am. Hosp. Assn., Ind. Personnel Assn. (dir. 1981-82, pres. 1985), Evansville Personnel Assn. (pres. 1976-77), Vis. Nurse Assn. Southwestern Ind. (dir. 1976-79, pres. 1981-85), Profl. Secs. Internat. (mem. exec. adv. bd. Ind. div., Exec. of Yr. 1982), Ind. State C. of C. (personnel and indsl. relations com. 1981—). Home: 1566 Old Plank Rd Newburgh IN 47630 Office: St Mary's Med Ctr 3700 Washington Ave Evansville IN 47750

BEUTEL, ERNEST WILLIAM, surgeon; b. Chgo., Feb. 14, 1946; s. Ernest and Hazel Augusta (Zachow) B.; B.S. magna cum laude, Loyola U., Chgo., 1967, M.D., 1971, J.D., 1985; m. Anita Paul Harrison, June 11, 1976; children—Ernest Wiley, William Andrew. Intern, St. Joseph Hosp., Chgo., 1971-72, resident in surgery, 1972-76; resident in thoracic surgery Cook County Hosp., 1976-78; commd. lt. comdr. USN, 1978-80; staff thoracic surgeon Naval Regional Med. Center, Great Lakes, 1978-80, cons. thoracic surgeon, 1980—; attending staff thoracic surgery St. Joseph Hosp., Chgo., 1978—, Ravenswood Hosp. Med. Center, Chgo., Resurrection Hosp., Chgo., St. Francis Hosp., Evanston, Ill.; surg. assoc. Northwestern U. Mem. health law adv. bd. Loyola U. Law Sch., Chgo. Diplomate Am. Bd. Surgery, Am. Bd. Thoracic Surgery. Fellow A.C.S., Am. Coll. Cardiology (assoc.), Am. Coll. Chest Physicians; mem. AMA, Am. Soc. Parenteral and Enteral Nutrition, Alpha Omega Alpha, Phi Sigma Tau, Phi Beta Pi. Address: PO Box 31130 Chicago IL 60631-0130

BEVANS, DOUGLAS LEONARD, automotive accessories manufacturing company executive; b. Leicester, Eng., Aug. 29, 1925, came to Can., 1948; s. Leonard Arthur and Edna Alice (Leach) B.; m. Amy Scott, June 28, 1947 (div. 1980); children—Phillip Granville, Gerald Alan; m. 2d, Louisette Marie Paquet, Aug. 28, 1981. C.I.M., U. Toronto, 1965. Sales product mgr. Mastex Ltd., Master Textiles Ltd., Winnipeg, Man., Can., 1949-60; product mgr. CIL, Toronto, Ont., Can., 1960-63; pres. D.L. Bevans, Can. Ltd., 1962; gen. mgr. Kurly Kate Ltd., Toronto, 1963-66; gen. mgr. Dylex Diversified Ltd., Toronto, 1966-69; pres. Powerflow Products Ltd., Toronto, 1969—, Powerflow, Inc., Buffalo, 1978, Adastra Ltd., Toronto, 1983—. Served with RAF, 1944-47. Mem. Can. Indsl. Mgmt. Anglican/Episcopal. Club: Bd. of Trade (Toronto). Patentee in field. Office: 21 Apex Rd Toronto ON M6A 2V6 Canada

BE VIER, WILLIAM A., teacher educator; b. Springfield, Mo., July 31, 1927; s. Charles and Erma G. (Ritter) BeV.; B.A., Drury Coll., 1950; Th.M., Dallas Theol. Sem., 1955, Th.D., 1958; M.A., So. Meth. U., 1960; Ed.D., A.B.D., Wayne State U., 1968; m. Jo Ann King, Aug. 11, 1949; children—Cynthia, Shirley. With Frisco Ry., 1943-45, 46-51, John E. Mitchell Co., Dallas, 1952-60; instr. Dallas Theol. Sem., 1958-59; teaching fellow So. Meth. U., Dallas, 1959-60; prof. Detroit Bible Coll., 1960-74, registrar, 1962-66, dean, 1964-73, exec. v.p., 1967-74, acting pres., 1967-68; prof., dean edn., v.p. for acad. affairs Northwestern Coll., Roseville, Minn., 1974-80, prof., 1980—. Bd. dirs. Religious Analysis Service, Mpls., 1979—. Served with USMC, 1945-46, 50-51; col. Army Res. Mem. Res. Officers Assn., Ind. Fund Chs. of Am., Huguenot Hist. Soc., Bevier-Elting Family Assn., Phi Alpha Theta. Office: Northwestern Coll Roseville MN 55113

BEYER, BALDWIN MARTIN, clergyman, counselor; b. Chgo., Apr. 30, 1926; s. Casimir and Helen (Wozniak) B.; B.A., Mary Immaculate Coll., Garrison, N.Y., 1950; M.A. in Theology, St. Anthony Sem., 1954. Joined Capuchin-Franciscan order Roman Catholic Ch., 1945, ordained priest, 1953; asst. pastor chs., Milw., 1954-58, Appleton, Wis., 1959-61; prof. theology Victory Noll Coll., Huntington, Ind., 1961-65, St. Francis Bros. Sch., Mt. Calvary, Wis., 1967-69; hosp. chaplain, Detroit, 1969-73; alcoholism counselor Sacred Heart Ch., Detroit and Friendship House, Bay City, Mich., 1973-74; dir. Human Aid, Inc., Gladwin, Mich., 1974-85; mem. Mich. Credentialing Bd. Addiction Profls.; cons. Saginaw Diocesan Health Panel. Cert. hosp. chaplain, addictions counselor, social worker, Mich. Mem. Mich. Assn. Alcoholism and Drug Abuse Counselors, Nat. Alcohol and Drug Problems Assn., Nat. Assn. Alcoholism Counselors, Cath. Hosp. Chaplains.

BEYER, EMIL E., JR., state legislator; b. Omaha, May 20, 1929; m. Barbara; children—Linda, Diane, Randall, Vicki. Real estate exec.; mem. Nebr. Legislature, 1980—; mem. state officeholder for safety com. U.S. Dept. Transp. Bd. dirs. Gretna Parent-Tchr. Orgn.; chmn. Gretna Planning Bd.; pres. Gretna Civic Orng. Mem. Nebr. Motor Carriers Assn. (bd. dirs.). Club: Optimists (dir.). Address: Gretna NE *

BEYER, KAREN ANN, social worker; b. Cleve., Jan. 30, 1942; d. William Pryor and Evelyn Ann Haynes; B.A., Ohio State U., 1965; M.S.W., Loyola U., Chgo., 1969; postgrad. Family Inst., Northwestern U., 1979; 1 dau., Jennifer. with Cuyahoga County Div. Child Welfare, Cleve., 1965, Dallas County Child Welfare Unit, Dallas, 1966; with Lutheran Welfare Services Ill., Chgo., 1967-73; pvt. practice psychotherapy, family mediation, Barrington, Ill., 1975—; therapist Family Service Assn. Greater Elgin (Ill.), 1973-77, dir. profl. services, 1977—; fieldwork social work instr. for Loyola U., U. Ill., 1977-80. Bd. dirs. Talkline, 1982—; mem. mental health adv. bd. Elgin Community Coll. Mem. Nat. Assn. Social Workers, Acad. Cert. Social Workers, Am. Assn. Marriage and Family Therapy, Am. Orthopsychiat. Assn. Unitarian. Home: 1809 Dumont Ln Schaumburg IL 60194 Office: 164 Division St Elgin IL 60120

BEYERL, MERRILL CHARLES, university dean, educational administrator; b. Malone, N.Y., Sept. 13, 1921; s. Roy and Ruth (Stewart) B.; m. Eunice Ledger, Nov. 19, 1944 (dec.); children—Cynthia Ann, Todd Douglas, Gregory Scott. B.S., Syracuse U., 1946, M.S., 1948, Ph.D., 1953. Lic. psychologist, Ind. Tchr. elem. sch., Plattsburgh, N.Y., 1941-42; Regimental High Sch., Baldwinsville, N.Y., 1946-48; instr. Syracuse U., N.Y., 1949-51; instr., counselor U. Ill.-Urbana, 1951-53; asst. prof. Ball State U., Muncie, Ind., 1953-57, prof., 1957-62, dean students, v.p. student affairs, 1962—; psychol. testing Pub. Schs., Syracuse; psychol. cons. Marsh Foodliner Chain, Owens, Ill., cons. psychologist Sheltered Workshop, Muncie; cons. State Hosp., Fort Wayne, Ind., 1969-75. Bd. dirs. Muncie Boys Club, 1968, Ind. Retarded Childrens Assn., Muncie, 1971-78; past pres., bd. dirs. Muncie YMCA, 1975; active in Govs. Commn. Handicapped, Indpls., 1965—. Served to capt. USMC, 1942-46. Recipient Nat. Gold Medallion Boys Club Am., Govs. Award Outstanding Profl. in Rehab. State of Ind.; named Hon. Outstanding Hoosier State of Ind., Hon. Ky. Col. State of Ind. Mem. Am. Assn. Counseling & Devel. (exec. bd. 1975, 76), Am. Coll. Personnel Assn. (pres. 1973-74), Nat. Assn. Student Personnel Adminstrn. (exec. bd. 1967-71), Ind. Coll. Personnel Assn. Am. Psychol. Assn. Avocations: travel, golf. Office: Ball State U 2000 University Ave Muncie IN 47304

BEYNEN, GIJSBERTUS KOOLEMANS, bibliographer, educator; b. Surabaya, Indonesia, June 12, 1935; s. G.J.W. and Froukje (de Jong) Koolemans Beijnen; Jur. Cand., Leiden (Netherlands) U., 1957, Lit. Slav. Cand., 1959; Ph.D., Stanford U., 1967; M.L.S., SUNY-Geneseo, 1974; m. Patricia Joan McBride; children—Johanna, Margaret, Axel, Sophia, Andrew, Elisabeth Blake Warner. Asst. prof. Russian, Emporia State U., 1963-66; asst. prof. Fordham U., N.Y.C., 1966-69; asst. prof. U. Rochester (N.Y.), 1969-73; assoc. prof., Slavic bibliographer Ohio State U., Columbus, 1974—; vis. asst. prof. Kent State U., 1983—; chmn. Slavic and East European sect. Assn. Coll. and Research Libraries, 1983-84. Recipient 1300 Yrs. Bulgaria medal, 1982; Internat. Research and Exchanges Bd. fellow Moscow State U., 1970-71; Nat. Endowment Humanities translation grantee 1981-82; Midwest Consortium for Internat. Activities exchange fellow Moscow State U., 1981-82; NDEA Title VI fellow, 1962-63. Mennonite. Club: Toastmasters (pres. 1962-63). Contbr. articles to profl. jours. Home: 686 Neil Ave Columbus OH 43215 Office: 1858 Neil Ave Columbus OH 43210

BEYNON, DIANE ELIZABETH, archaeologist, educator; b. Pitts., Mar. 18, 1952; d. William John and Evelyn (Hayden) B. B.A., Muskingum Coll., 1974; Ph.D., U. Pitts., 1981. Teaching asst. U. Pitts., 1976-79; instr. Pa. State U., 1979; lectr. Muskingum Coll., New Concord, Ohio, 1980; asst. prof. anthropology Ind.-Purdue U., Ft. Wayne, 1981—; cons. and contract archaeology. Dept. Interior grantee, 1982-84; grantee Fox Island Alliance for Archaeol. Excavation, 1982-83. Mem. Soc. Am. Archaeology, Council for Conservation of India Archaeology. Contbr. article in field to Am. Antiquity. Office: Dept Anthropology Ind Univ Fort Wayne IN 46805

BEZ, BERT MARVIN, anesthesiologist, pharmacist, osteopathic physician and surgeon; b. Detroit, Dec. 15, 1935; s. David M. and Yetta (Ostrow) B.; m. Carol Ehrenfeld, June 21, 1962; children—Douglas, Joel. B.S. in Pharmacy, U. Mich., 1957; D.O., Coll. Osteo. Medicine and Surgery, Des Moines, 1961. Diplomate Am. Osteo. Bd. Anesthesiology. Intern, Doctors Hosp., Columbus, Ohio, 1961-62; resident in anesthesiology Detroit Osteo. Hosp., 1963-65; gen. practice medicine, Columbus, 1962-63; practice anesthesiology, Detroit and Battle Creek, Mich., 1965-72; prof. osteo. medicine Mich. State U., East Lansing, 1972-76, assoc. prof. and chmn. div. anesthesiology Coll. Human Medicine, 1980—, also chmn. anesthesia dept. Ingham Med. Center, Lansing, Mich. and chmn. pharmacy and therapeutics, dir. cardio-thoracic tng. for residents in anesthesiology. Recipient Charles H. Stocking award U. Mich., 1957, Merit cert. Mich. State U. Coll. Human Medicine, 1975. Fellow Am. Coll. Osteo. Anesthesiologists; mem. Am. Soc. Anesthesiologists, Internat. Research Soc. Anesthesiologists, Mich. Assn. Osteo. Physicians and Surgeons. Jewish. Club: Masons. Office: 401 W Greenlawn Suite 120 Lansing MI 48910

BEZKOROVAINY, ANATOLY, medical educator, biochemist; b. Riga, Latvia, Feb. 11, 1935; s. Ignatius and Olga (Solovey) B.; m. Marilyn Grib, June 14, 1964; children—Gregory, Alexander. B.S., U. Chgo., 1956; Ph.D., U. Ill., 1960; J.D., Ill. Inst. Tech., 1977. Bar: Ill. 1977. Research assoc. Oak Ridge Nat. Lab., Tenn., 1960-61; chemist U.S. Dept. Agriculture, Ames, Iowa, 1961-62; mem. faculty Rush-Presby. St. Lukes' Med. Center, Chgo., 1962—, asst. prof., 1962-67, assoc. prof., 1967-73, prof. biochemistry, 1973—, assoc. chmn., dir. ednl. programs biochemistry dept., 1980—. Author: Basic Protein Chemistry, 1970; Biochemistry of Nonheme Iron, 1980; (with Rafelson and Hayashi) Basic Biochemistry, 1980. Contbr. articles to profl. jours. Grantee numerous NSF, NIH, Am. Heart Assn., 1973-80. Fellow Nat. Acad. Clin. Biochemistry (bd. dirs. 1984—); mem. Am. Soc. Biol. Chemists, Am. Chem. Soc., Am. Inst. Nutrition. Eastern Orthodox. Home: 6801 Kilpatrick Ave Lincolnwood IL 60646 Office: Rush-Presbyn-St Luke's Med Center Biochemistry Dept 1753 W Congress Chicago IL 60612

BHAKTHAVATHSALAN, AMRUTHA, physician, educator; b. Mysore State, India, Mar. 1, 1933; d. K. and Uma (Devi) Marilingappa; came to U.S., 1966; B.S., Maharani's Coll. for Women, Bangalore, Mysore State, India, 1950; B.Medicine, B. Surgery, Univ. Med. Coll., Mysore, India, 1955. House surgeon, rotating intern Meml. Hosp., Niagara Falls, N.Y., 1966-67; resident ob-gyn and pathology St. Thomas Hosp., Akron, Ohio, 1967; resident ob-gyn Med. Coll. Ohio at Toledo and Asso. Hosps. Program, Toledo Hosp., 1968, Maumee Valley Hosp., 1969, St. Vincent Hosp., 1969, Toledo Hosp., 1970; chief resident ob-gyn Maumee Valley Hosp., 1970-71; instr. dept. ob-gyn Med. Coll. Ohio, Toledo, 1971-73; fellow perinatology Nassau County Med. Center, East Meadow, N.Y., 1973-74; research assoc., 1974-75; asst. prof. dept. ob-gyn SUNY-Stonybrook, 1975-76; physician-in-charge div. obstetrics, dept. ob-gyn Queens Hosp. Center Affiliation L.I. Jewish-Hillside Med. Center, Jamaica, N.Y., 1975-76; perinatologist N.W. Ohio Regional Perinatal Center, Toledo Hosp., 1976-84; dir. maternal-fetal medicine Mt. Sinai Hosp., Chgo., 1984—; clin. asst. prof. dept. ob-gyn Med. Coll. Ohio, Toledo, 1976-77, clin. assoc. prof., 1977-80, clin. prof., 1980—. Diplomate Am. Bd. Ob-Gyn, subsplty. cert. in Maternal-Fetal Medicine. Fellow Am. Coll. Obstetricians and Gynecologists; mem. Am. Med. Women's Assn., Inc., Nat. Perinatal Assn., Ohio Perinatal Assn., Soc. Perinatal Obstetricians. Contbr. articles to profl. jours. Office: Mount Sinai Hosp Dept Ob-Gyn California Ave at 15th St Chicago IL 60608

BIAGINI, ESTHER PIER, interior designer, retailer, graphoanalyst consultant; b. Chgo.; d. Silvio and Ilia (Paganelli) Nannini; student U. Ill., 1951-52; grad. Harrington Inst. Interior Design; m. Giulio J. Biagini, Oct. 5, 1952; children—Marc, Nannette, Lisa. Graphoanalyst; personal cons. in field; pub. relations cons. Bevmar Co., 1976; pres. Design Factory, Inc.; mgr. Fenco Galleries, Imports. Active PTA; pres. Brookfield (Ill.) Library Bd., 1969-70, 72-73, treas., 1970-71, sec., 1967-68, 73-74. Recipient Am. Legion award, 1950. Mem. ALA, Ill. Library Assn., Ill. Dirs. Library Assn., Am. Soc. Interior Designers, Brookfield Woman's Club. Home: 116 Princeton Rd Hinsdale IL 60521

BIALLAS, LEONARD JOHN, religious educator; b. Pontiac, Mich., May 3, 1939; s. Leonard John and Elizabeth (Mansfield) B.; m. Martha Susan Weedman, June 15, 1974. A.B., U. Notre Dame, 1961; M.A., Holy Cross Coll., 1965; S.T.D., Inst. Catholique,-Paris, 1970. Asst. prof. U. Notre Dame, Ind., 1970-73; faculty Quincy Coll. Ill., 1973—, prof. dept. theology, 1982—. Contbr. articles to profl. jours. Editor, Bulletin of Council on Study of Religion, 1977—. Mem. Am. Acad. Religion, Coll. Theology Soc., Cath. Theol. Soc. Am. Roman Catholic. Home: 20 Spring Lake Quincy IL 62301 Office: Quincy Coll Quincy IL 62301

BIANCHI, CHRISTOPHER ANTHONY, lawyer; b. Cape May, N.J., Sept. 19, 1955; s. Anthony James and Marguerite Rose (Grande) B.; m. Suzanne Renne Slover, Apr. 28, 1984. B.S., Widener, U., 1977; J.D., Cleve.-Marshall Law Sch., 1980. Bar: Ohio 1980, U.S. Dist. Ct. (no. dist.) Ohio 1980, U.S. Dist. Ct. (so. dist.) Ohio 1982, U.S. Ct. Claims 1983. Assoc. Russo, Roth & Co. L.P.A., Cleve., 1980-81; lawyer transp., Ohio Atty. Gen.'s Office, Columbus, 1981—. Mem. Ohio Acad. Trial Lawyers, Columbus Bar Assn., ABA, Pi Gamma Mu. Omicron Delta Epsilon. Roman Catholic. Home: 4787 Kilcary Ct Apt C Columbus OH 43220 Office: Ohio Atty Gen's Office 25 S Front St Columbus OH 43215

BIASI, THOMAS LOUIS, hotel manager; b. Chgo., Nov. 21, 1952; s. Louis and Vera Marie (Barucca) B.; m. Terry Lee Meehan, June 25, 1977; children—Peter Thomas, Tony Matthew, Rebecca Marie. Student Ohio State U., 1971-73. Maintenance worker Holiday Inns, Inc., Des Plaines, Ill., 1975-77, asst. chief engr., 1977-79, chief engr., 1979-83, dir. of facilities, 1983, exec. housekeeper, Chgo., 1983-84, gen. mgr., Milw., 1984—; cons. Mount Prospect Joint Venture, Ill., 1983; lectr. Chgo. Assn. Commerce and Industry, 1984. Mgr. Schaumburg Youth Hockey, Ill., 1978-79, Chgo. Downtown Softball League, 1984. Mem. Wis. Innkeepers Assn., Milw. Hotel/Motel Assn. Roman Catholic. Avocations: handcrafted fishing; tackle; camping; contact sports; photography. Home: 5423 N Port Washington Rd Milwaukee WI 53217 Office: Holiday Inn Northeast 5423 N Port Washington Rd Milwaukee WI 53217

BIBBO, MARLUCE, physician, educator; b. Sao Paulo, Brazil, July 14, 1939; d. Domingos and Yolanda (Ranciaro) Bibbo; M.D., U. Sao Paulo, 1963, Sc.D., 1968. Intern, Hosps. das Clinicas, U. Sao Paulo, 1963, resident in ob-gyn, 1964-66; instr. dept. morphology and ob-gyn U. Sao Paulo, 1966-68, asst. prof., 1968-69; asst. prof. sect. cytology dept. ob-gyn U. Chgo., 1969-73, asso. prof., 1973-77, asso. prof. pathology, 1974-77, prof. ob-gyn and pathology, 1978—; asso. dir. Cytology Lab., Approved Sch. Cytotech. and Cytocybernetics, AMA-Am. Soc. Clin. Pathologists, 1970—. Mem. research com. Ill. div. Am. Cancer Soc., 1976—. Fellow Internat. Acad. Cytology (chmn. com. lab. cert. 1977—); mem. Am. Soc. Cytology (exec. com. 1972—, pres. 1982-83). Contbr. numerous articles to profl. jours. Home: 400 E Randolph St Apt 2009 Chicago IL 60601 Office: 5841 S Maryland Ave Chicago IL 60637

BIBBS, CAROLYN ANDERSON, art educator, free lance designer; b. Moline, Ill., Mar. 28, 1949; d. Fredrick Douglas and LaJune (Barlow) Anderson; m. Ronnie Lee Bibbs, Aug. 19, 1972; children—Kyle Whitney, Klyne Michael B.A., Augustana Coll., 1971; M.S. Bank Street Coll. Edn., Parsons Sch. Design, 1985. Cert. art tchr., Ill. Art tchr. East Moline (Ill.) Pub. Schs., 1971—; art tchr. to sr. citizens; calligrapher; graphic designer. Charter mem. Quad Cities (Ill.) chpt. Jack and Jill, Inc. Mem. Ill. Edn. Assn., NEA, Alpha Kappa Alpha. Democrat. Home: 817 24th Ave Rock Island IL 61201 Office: 600 19th St East Moline IL 61244

BIBBY, JAMES JOHN, mental health agency administrator; b. Milw., Oct. 3, 1947; s. James Elias and Marion (Herrmann) B.; m. Kathleen Denise (Jones), Nov. 8, 1980. B.A., Marquette U., 1969; M.S., Purdue U., 1972. Psychology trainee Marion VA Hosp. (Ind.), 1971-73; therapist Child and Adult Mental Health Center, Youngstown, Ohio, 1973-74, emergency mgr., 1974-75; with Four County Comprehensive Mental Health Center Inc., Logansport, Ind., 1975—, adminstr., 1978-79, exec. dir., 1979—. Bd. dirs. United Way of Cass County (Ind.), 1980-84, pres., 1982-83. Mem. Am. Psychol. Assn. Republican. Roman Catholic. Clubs: Logansport Jaycees, Rotary, Elks. Office: 1015 Michigan Ave Logansport IN 46947

BIBLE, RICHARD LEE, business executive; b. Bryan, Ohio, Mar. 15, 1947; s. Earl Leroy and Lillian Marie (Weber) B.; m. Sandra Sue Johnston, Apr. 12, 1969; children—Christopher, Suzette. Student, Lain Tech. Inst., Indpls., 1966, Tri State Coll., Angola, Ind., 1967. Design draftsman The Aro Corp., Bryan, Ohio, 1967-71, tech. mktg. supr., 1971-74, dist. sales mgr., Chgo., 1974-77; nat. sales mgr. Indsl. Pumping & Petroleum Systems Products., Bryan, 1977-83; v.p. mktg. Reelcraft Industries, Inc., Columbia City, Ind., 1984—. Mem. Petroleum Equipment Inst. (bd. dirs.), Motor Equipment Mfrs. Assn. Mem. Ch. of Christ. Club: Orchard Hills Country. Home: Oak Borough of Coventry 2925 Smugglers Cove Fort Wayne IN 46804

BICE, DONALD ALLEN, millwork executive, engineer, consultant; b. Flushing, Ohio, Sept. 30, 1929; s. Jacob Leroy and Myrtle Viola (Howard) B.; m. Clara B. Bigger, June 6, 1950; children—Thomas, Ted, William, Donald, Tamra. Student Coll. Steubenville, 1952, Cleve. Enging. Inst., 1953, Western Mich. U., 1957, Earlham Coll., 1962, Ind. U.-South Bend, 1966-67. Exec. v.p. Benson Mfg. Corp., Milw., 1969-74; pres. Anson & Gilckey, Inc., Merrill, Wis., 1974-79; Clairmar Homes, Inc., Aetna Green, Ind., 1978-81; gen. mgr. Rockwell of Randolph, Inc., Wis., 1981—. Patentee desk docking system, 1957; teaching wall system, 1959; shutter mounting method, 1967; door hinging system, 1964. Avocations: golf; travel. Home: 110 We Go Trail Fox Lake WI 53933 Office: Rockwell of Randolph Inc 334 W Stroud St Randolph WI 53956

BICK, DAVID GREER, health care marketing consultant; b. Toledo, June 29, 1953; s. James D. and Carol Jean (Herrmann) B.; m. Laurie Kay Cuprys, Nov. 7, 1976; children—Jennifer Kelly, Jesse Quinn, Matthew Adam. B.E., U. Toledo, 1975; cert. health cons. Purdue U., 1981. Dist. mgr. Blue Cross Northwest Ohio, Tiffin, 1977-79, regional mgr., Sandusky, 1979-81, dir. sales, Toledo, 1981-82; v.p. mktg. Blue Cross/Blue Shield Central N.Y., Syracuse, 1983; exec. dir. Preview-Health Benefits Mgmt. of Ohio, Toledo, 1984—. Author: Paupers and Profiteers (poetry), 1977. Mem. Found. for Life, Toledo, 1978-85, PTA, 1983-85. Mem. Toledo C. of C. Roman Catholic. Lodge: Rotary. Avocations: photography; golf; basketball. Home: 1658 Kalida Toledo OH 43612 Office: 3737 Sylvnia Ave PO Box 887 Toledo OH 43696

BICKEL, ERMALINDA, real estate broker; b. Casole Bruzio Provincia di Cosenza, Italy, Nov. 8, 1919; d. Saverio and Emilia (Fortino) Fortino; came to U.S., 1927, naturalized, 1927; student pub. schs., Italy, Elkhart, Ind.; Grad. Real Estate Inst., Purdue U.; m. William E. Bickel, Aug. 10, 1946; 1 dau., Patricia Ann Heiser. Office clk. Gen. Telephone, Elkhart, 1939-41; sec. to pres. Ames Co. div. Miles Labs., Inc., Elkhart, 1941-52, tech. sec. pharmacy research dept., 1962-82; freelance legal sec., 1956-61; owner, founder Blue Chip Realty, Inc., Elkhart, 1968-83. Mem. Nat., Ind., Elkhart real estate bds., Delta Theta Tau, Elkhart C. of C. Roman Catholic. Club: Zonta. Office: 26258 Cottage Ave Elkhart IN 46514

BICKEL, FLOYD GILBERT, III, investment counselor; b. St. Louis, Jan. 10, 1944; s. Floyd Gilbert II and Mary Mildred (Welch) B.; B.S. in Bus. Adminstrn., Washington U., St. Louis, 1966; M.S. in Commerce, St. Louis U., 1968; m. Martha Wohler, June 11, 1966; children—Christine Carleton, Susan Marie, Katherine Anne, Jennifer Anne. Andrew Barrett (dec.). With research dept. Yates, Woods & Co., St. Louis, 1966-67; asst. br. mgr. E.F. Hutton & Co., Inc., St. Louis, 1967-70; asst. v.p., resident mgr. Bache & Co., Inc., St. Louis, 1970-72; pres. Donelan-Phelps Investment Advisors, Inc., St. Louis, 1972-80; v.p., dir. consulting services E.F. Hutton & Co., Inc., St. Louis, 1980—; founder Brentwood Bancshares, Inc.; pres., dir. Drew Petroleum, Inc. Biclan, Inc., Gilmar Realty, Inc.; chmn., dir. Data Research Assos., Inc., St. John's Bancshares, Inc., Maverick Tube Co. Mem. City of Des Peres (Mo.) Planning and Zoning Commn., 1975-76; chmn. St. Louis County Bd. Equalization, 1976-79; pub. safety commr. City of Des Peres, 1977-80, mem. audit and fin. com., 1980-84; mem. Gov.'s Crime Commn., 1981-84; bd dirs. Care and Counseling, Inc. Mem. Internat. Soc. Cert. Employee Benefit Specialists (dir.), Internat. Found. Employee Benefit Plan, St. Louis Soc. Fin. Analysts. Republican. Presbyterian. Clubs: Bellerive Country; St. Louis; Commanderie de Bordeaux. Contbr. bus. articles to mags. Home: 12120 Belle Meade Saint Louis MO 63131 Office: 100 S Brentwood Blvd Saint Louis MO 63105

BICKFORD, THOMAS EDWARD, civil engr.; b. Newton, Mass., May 22, 1929; s. Edward Milton and Mabel Etta (Eldridge) B.; B.S. in Civil Enging., Northeastern U., 1957; postgrad. Ohio State U., 1960-72; m. Edna Harriett Thompson, Oct. 22, 1955 (div. 1979); m. Carol Schar Shay, May 24, 1981; children—Douglas Thomas, Linda Kathryn. Civil engr. Columbia Gas System Service Corp., Columbus, Ohio, 1957-60, Scioto Conservancy Dist., Columbus, 1962-64; civil engr. Burgess & Niple, Ltd., Columbus, 1961-62, 64-70, asst. personnel dir., 1966-70, personnel dir., 1971—. Vice-pres. PTA, Columbus, 1969-70, pres., 1971-72; chmn. engrs. group, profl. div. United Way, 1969-70; trustee Forest Park Civic Assn. Registered profl. engr., Ohio, Fla. Mem. Ohio Soc. Profl. Engrs., ASCE, Personnel Soc. Columbus (v.p. 1972, treas. 1977), Am. Soc. Personnel Adminstrn., Nat. Soc. Profl. Engrs. Independent Republican. Home: 6060 Springburn Dr Dublin OH 43017 Office: 5085 Reed Rd Columbus OH 43220

BICKLE, FRANKLIN M., optometrist; b. Newark, Ohio, Dec. 22, 1953; s. Walter K. and Margaret E. (Sepos) B.; D.Optometry, Ohio State U., 1978. Group practice optometry, Newark, 1978—; pres. Pro Care Vision Centers, Inc.; clin. instr. Ohio State U. Coll. Optometry, Columbus, 1978—; instr. cardio-pulmonary resusitation, 1978—. Ohio State U. undergrad. scholar, 1972-74, Wildermuth Meml. scholar, 1976-78. Mem. Am. Optometric Assn., Nat. Eye Research Found., Am. Public Health Assn., Ohio Optometric Assn., Ohio Public Health Assn., Am. Optometric Found., Beta Sigma Kappa, Newark Jaycees. Home: 1737 Stonewall Dr Newark OH 43055 Office: 305 Deo Dr Newark OH 43055

BICKLEY, JOHN HOWARD, JR., lawyer; b. Chgo., May 12, 1929; s. John H. and Letta (McGraw) B.; student Evanston Twp. Community Coll., 1948; J.D., Chgo. Kent Coll. Law, 1951; children—John H., III, Lisa F., Kathryn M. Admitted to Ill. bar, 1952; partner Peterson, Bogucki & Bickley, Attys., Chgo., 1957-67, individual practice, Chgo., 1968—; mem. firm Bickley &

Bickley; spl. asst. atty. gen. Ill., 1968-69; chief environ. control div. Ill. Atty. Gen.'s Office, 1970-71; asst. U.S. atty. No. Dist. Ill., 1955-57; trial atty. Forest Preserve Dist. Cook County; spl. prosecutor Chgo. Police Burglar Scandal, 1961; mem. lecture forum MidWest U.S. Attys. Conf., 1963; apptd. to dist. performance assistance com. U.S. Dist. Ct. for No. Dist. Ill. to determine qualifications of applicants for admission to trial bar of ct. Mem. dist. council SBA, 1971-72; legal cons. Ill. State Bd. Elections. Trustee, Village of Mount Prospect (Ill.), 1961-63, 1st v.p. Regular Republican Orgn., Elk Grove Twp., 1961-62; candidate for state's atty. Cook County, 1964. Served with USMCR, now lt. col. (ret.). Named one of Chgo.'s 10 Outstanding Young Men, Chgo. Jaycees, 1964; One of Outstanding Young Men U.S., 1965; named to alumni honor council Chgo. Kent Coll. Law, 1978. Mem. Internat. Acad. Law and Sci., Ill., Chgo., Fed. (pres. Chgo. chpt. 1972-73, nat. v.p. 1973-74) bar assns., Am. Arbitration Assn. (nat. panel arbitrators), Am., Ill. (pres. 1971-72), trial lawyers assns., Trial Lawyers Club Chgo., Soc. Trial Lawyers, Law Club Chgo., Legal Club Chgo., Globe and Anchor Soc. Ill. (past pres.), Chgo. Kent Coll. Law Alumni Assn. (dir.), Am. Legion. Episcopalian. Clubs: Masons (32 deg., Shriner), Tavern, Plaza (Chgo.). Secured conviction of syndicate crime leader Paul (The Waiter) Ricca, 1957. Home: 6 Ct of Bucks County Lincolnshire IL 60015 Office: 230 N Michigan Ave Chicago IL 60601

BIDDINGER, JOHN WESLEY, financial exec.; b. Indpls., May 5, 1940; s. Noble L. and Eleanor Jane (Lynch) B.; B.S., Ind. U., 1963; m. Margaret Jo Hunt, Sept. 1, 1962; children—Karen Elizabeth, Katherine Jane. With City Securities Corp., Indpls., 1963—, salesman, 1963-67, v.p., 1967-69, exec. v.p., dir., 1969-79, pres., dir., 1979-80; pres. Biddinger Investment Capital Corp., Global Tech., Inc., Access Tech., Inc., Retrieval Systems, Inc., Capital Corp., Ind. Ventures, Inc., Internat. Transaction System Inc., U.S.A. Vault Corp.; chmn. bd. Crime Control Inc.; dir. Asbury Mgmt. & Fin. Corp. Crime Control, Inc., Media Omaha, Inc., U.S.A. Communications Inc., Media South, Inc., So. Hospitality Corp., Starlight Musicals; treas., chmn. exec. com. SunGroup Inc. Bd. dirs. Found. Assos. Hon. Ky. col., col. a.d.c. Tenn.; cert. gen. agt., life ins. agt. Mem. Confrerie des Chevaliers du Tastevin, Internat. Wine and Food Soc., Confrerie de la Chaine des Rotisseurs, Indpls. Bond Club, Nat. (nominating com., affiliate liaison com., bd. govs. 1978—, chmn. publ. com.), Indpls. (inaugural pres.) security traders assns., Indpls. Jaycees, Well House Soc., Second Century Club of Indpls. Mus. Art, Cousteau Soc., Oceanic Soc., Ind. U. Sch. Bus. Alumni Assn., Ind. U. Alumni Assn. (bd. mgrs., chmn. nominating com., mem. dues, ins. and outdoor edn. coms.), Dean's Assos. Ind. U. Bus. Sch., Ind. U. Varsity Club, Ind. U. Hoosier 100, Sigma Chi. Clubs: Pacesetters, Pointe Golf and Tennis, Meridian Hills Country, Manor House, Andre's. Lodge: Masons. Home: 9121 Spring Hollow Dr Indianapolis IN 46260 Office: 9102 N Meridian St Indianapolis IN 46260

BIDDISON, JACK MICHAEL, oil company executive, geologist, engineer; b. Columbus, Ohio, Feb. 27, 1954; s. Jack Carpenter and Betty Yvonne (Mollette) B. B.S. in Geology and Mineralogy, Ohio State U., 1977; M.B.A., Kent State U., 1985. Cert. profl. geol. scientist. Geologist, Inland Drilling Co., Ravenna, Ohio, 1978-81; geol. engr. Gasearch, Inc., Girard, Ohio, 1981; geotech. engr. CER Corp., Las Vegas, Nev., 1981-82; mgr. petroleum engring. and geol. services Energy Devel. Ops., Gen. Electric Co., Kent, Ohio, 1982—. Mem. Am. Inst. Profl. Geologists, Am. Assn. Petroleum Geologists, Soc. Petroleum Engrs., Ohio Geol. Soc. Methodist. Avocations: Basketball; rock collecting; cross country skiing. Home: 3852 Nautilus Trail Aurora OH 44202 Office: Gen Electric Co Energy Devel Operation 2007 State Rte 59 Kent OH 44240-4113

BIDDLE, JAMES HAROLD, lawyer; b. Cin., Aug. 10, 1947; s. Harold D. and Luella E. (Kress) B.; m. Linda Williams, Nov. 22, 1969 (div. 1976; m. Pamela F. Harris, May 26, 1979; 1 child, Megan Elizabeth. B.A., Capital U., 1969; J.D., Northern Ky. State U., 1975. Bar: Ohio 1975, U.S. Dist. Ct. (so. dist.) Ohio 1982, (we. dist.) Mo. 1982. City planner City of Cin., 1969-73, bldg. official, 1973-76; sole practice, Cin., 1976-81; with McNabb & Pursley, Butler, Mo., 1981-82, sole practice, Butler, 1982-85; trust adminstr. United Mo. Bank of Kansas City, 1985—. Pres., St. Matthew Lutheran Ch., Butler, Mo., 1984. Mem. ABA, Mo. Bar Assn., Ohio Bar Assn. Republican. Lodge: Elks (sec. 1984). Office: 10th and Grand PO Box 226 Kansas City MO 64141

BIDEAU, EDWIN H., III, lawyer, state legislator; b. Chanute, Kans., Oct. 1, 1950; s. Edwin H. and Beverly M. (Semon) B.; m. Margaet E. Fritton, June 30, 1973; children—Scott, Sarah, Jenney. A.A., Neosho Community Coll., 1970; B.B.A., Washburn U., 1972, J.D., 1975. Bar: Kans., U.S. Dist. Ct. Kans., U.S. Dist. Ct. Okla. Law clk. Kans. Dept. Ins., Topeka, 1973-75; asst. county atty. Neosho County, Chanute, 1975-76, county atty., 1976-85; sole practice, Chanute, 1975—; mem. Kans. Ho. of Reps., 1985—; law office mgmt. cons. Profl. Software Assocs., Inc., Rep. precinct committeeman, 1984—; mem. Chanute Library Bd.; dirs. Neosho Valley Hist. Soc. Mem. Neosho County Bar Assn. (pres. 1977-79), Kans. County Attys. Assn. (law enforcement com. 1979-81), Kans. Bar Assn., ABA, Southeastern Kans. Bar Assn., Assn. Trial Lawyers Am., Kans. Dist. Attys. Assn. Presbyterian. Lodge: Rotary (Chanute). Avocations: horseback riding; hunting; fishing; computers; sailing. Home: 14 S Rutter St Chanute KS 66720 Office: 123 W Main St Chanute KS 66720

BIDWILL, WILLIAM V., football executive; Mng. gen. partner, now chmn. St. Louis Cardinals Football Team. Office: Saint Louis Cardinals 200 Stadium Plaza Saint Louis MO 63102*

BIEBER, OWEN F., labor union official; b. North Dorr, Mich., Dec. 28, 1929; s. Albert F. and Minnie (Schwartz) B.; m. Shirley M. Van Woerkom, Nov. 25, 1950; children—Kenneth, Linda, Michael, Ronald, Joan. H.H.D., Grand Valley Coll. Internat. rep. Internat. Union, UAW, Grand Rapids, Mich., 1961-72, asst. regional dir. Reg. 1D, Internat. Union, 1972-74, regional dir., 1974-80, v.p. Internat. Union, UAW, Detroit, 1980-83, pres., 1983—. Mem. Kent County Dem. Com. Exec. Bd., Wyoming, Mich., 1966-80; chmn. Kent County Dem. Com., 1964-66, del. Nat. Dem. Convs., 1968, 76. Named Labor Man of Yr. Kent County AFL-CIO, 1965. Mem. NAACP, Grand Rapids Urban League. Roman Catholic. Club: Econ. (Detroit) Office: Internat Union UAW 8000 E Jefferson Detroit MI 48214

BIEBER, PAUL JOHN, lawyer; educator, consultant; b. Davenport, Iowa, June 26, 1954; s. Otto Albert and Corinne Helen (Lense) B.; m. Connie Sue McGinnis, Aug. 8, 1976. B.A., St. Ambrose Coll., 1976; J.D., Drake U., 1979. Bar: Iowa 1980, U.S. dist. Ct. (so. dist.) Iowa 1980. Assoc. Wells & Brubaker, Davenport, 1979-80; ptnr. Christie & Bieber, Davenport, 1980—; instr. in bus. law St. Ambrose Coll., Davenport, 1981—; cons. Morning Hill Reflection Studios, Davenport, 1982—; farmer. Mem. bd. Christian edn. Trinity Lutheran Ch., Davenport, 1984—; v.p., dirs. Davenport Citizens for Responsible Devel., Inc. Mem. Scott County Bar Assn., Iowa Bar Assn. Home: 5022 NW Blvd Davenport IA 52806 Office: Christie & Bieber 1203 Jersey Ridge Rd Davenport IA 52803

BIEBERLE, GORDON FRANKLIN, publishing company executive, marketing consultant; b. Ellinwood, Kans., May 31, 1943; s. Nick Louis and Rose Elizabeth (Schartz) B.; m. Patricia Y. George (div. 1980). B.A., Kans. State U., 1965; postgrad. Sam Houston State U., 1965-66. Editor Nat. 4H News, Chgo., 1969-76; owner Bieberle Assocs., Lawrence, Kans., 1976-77, Des Plaines, Ill., 1977—; v.p. Color Market, Northbrook, Ill., 1984—; pub. Publishing Trade, Northfield, Ill., 1982-84; tchr. Fla. Keys Jr. Coll., Key West, 1968-69; faculty Face to Face Publishing Co., N.Y.C., 1984. Contbr. articles to profl. jours; editor: Profl. Photographer, 1979-84. Served to lt. (j.g.) USNR, 1967-69. Mem. Am. Soc. Bus. Press Editors (bd. dirs. 1982-83), Am. Pub. Works Assn. (dir. publs. 1977-79), Chgo. Soc. Bus. Press Editors (pres. 1981-83), Profl. Photographers Am. Avocations: antique furniture; music. Home: 1495 Oakwood Des Plaines IL 60016 Office: Color Market 3177 MacArthur Blvd Northbrook IL 60064

BIEDERMAN, EARL DONALD, explosive powder mfg. co. exec.; b. Cleve., May 28, 1935; s. Hy and Sally Ann (Simon) B.; B.S., Miami U., 1957; M.S., Purdue U., 1959; m. Marianne Miller, June 13, 1959; children—Scott. Asst. football, basketball, baseball coach Wabash Coll., 1957-58; head football coach, dept. head social studies Toronto (Ohio) Bd. Edn., 1958-60, Mentor (Ohio) Bd. Edn., 1960-63; sales rep. Texaco, Inc., Cleve., 1963-65, dist. sales supr., 1965-70; sales coordinator Ammonium Nitrate sales, West Coast regional mgr., nat. acct. mgr. Seismic and Pipeline Explosives div. Austin Powder Co., Cleve., 1970—; area scout Cin. Bengals, 1967—. Recreation commnr., Solon, Ohio, 1972-74; bd. dirs. Grantwood Municipal Golf Course, Solon, 1972-75. Mem. AIME, Soc. Exploration Geophysicists, Permian Basin Geophys. Soc., Geophys. Soc. Alaska, N.Mex. Mining Assn., Calif. Mining Assn., Colo. Mining Assn., Casper Geophys. Soc., Delta Kappa Epsilon. Home: 408 Mill Pond Rd Aurora OH 44202 Office: 3690 Orange Place Beachwood OH 44122

BIEDRON, THEODORE JOHN, newspaper advertising executive; b. Evergreen Park, Ill., Nov. 30, 1946; s. Theodore John and Ione Margaret B.; B.A. in Polit. Sci., U. Ill., 1968; m. Gloria Anne DeAngelo, Nov. 7, 1970; children—Jessica Ann, Lauren. Recruitment advt. mgr. Chgo. Sun-Times, 1968-74; classified advt. mgr. Pioneer Press, Wilmette, Ill., 1974-76; classified mgr., v.p. Lerner Newspapers, Chgo., 1976-79, assoc. pub., 1980-82, advt. dir., 1982—; dir. Lerner Cable TV. Mem. Assn. Newspaper Classified Advt. Mgrs. (past bd. advisors), Suburban Newspapers of Am. (award for best classified advt. sect. 1975, cert. of excellence 1979), Ill. Press Assn., Nat. Newspaper Assn. Home: 1130 Lake St Wilmette IL 60091 Office: 7519 N Ashland St Chicago IL 60626

BIEHN, LAWRENCE HENRY, educational administrator; b. Mankato, Minn., Sept. 29, 1931; s. Simon Michael and Marguerite Dorothy (Doran) B.; m. Dorothy Ann Frederick, June 20, 1953; children—Douglas, Christopher, Gary, Lori Ann. B.S., Minn. State U., 1955; M.A., U. Minn., 1962. Tchr., prin. Sioux Valley Schs., Lake Park, Iowa, 1955-58; prin. Rapidan (Minn.) Schs., 1958-63, Am. Dependent Schs., Seoul, Korea, 1963-66, Centennial Sr. High Sch., Circle Pines, Minn., 1966—; v.p. Hager Mfg. Co., Mankato, 1979—. Mem. City Council, Circle Pines, 1971-78; mem. adv. com. Minn. Dept. Corrections, 1978-80. Served with U.S. Army, 1950-52. Mem. Nat. Assn. Secondary Sch. Prins., Minn. Assn. Secondary Sch. Prins., Am. Legion (comdr. 1960-63). Roman Catholic. Club: Lions. Home: 77 West Rd Circle Pines MN 55014 Office: North Rd and Lever St Circle Pines MN 55014

BIEN, STANLEY DANIEL, accountant; b. Gary, Ind., Nov. 13, 1954; s. Stanley E. and Lillian Bien; B.S., Ferris State Coll., 1977; M.P.A., Western Mich. U., 1982; m. Jean Ann Lotoszinski, Oct. 13, 1979; children—Nicholas James, Katie Marie. Program accountant fin. mgmt. sect. Dep. Dir.'s Office, Mich. Dept. Public Health, Lansing, 1977-82, chief system and procedures for acctg., 1982—. Recipient Hoosier State Scholarship award, 1973-74. Mem. Nat. Assn. Accts., State Govtl. Accts. Assn. Mich., Mich. State Employees Assn., Assn. Govt. Accts., Fellowship Christian Athletes, Delta Sigma Pi. Clubs: Canoe, Accounting. Home: 1085 Craig St Lansing MI 48906 Office: Mich Dept Public Health Finance and Grants Mgmt-Acctg 3500 N Logan St Lansing MI 48909

BIERMEIER, PETER CHARLES, real estate executive; b. Eau Claire, Wis., Feb. 24, 1952; s. Frank and Monica Augusta (Masek) B.; m. Joan Lee Galloway, Aug. 9, 1975. B.S., U. Wis.-Eau Claire, 1974. Lic. real estate broker, Wis. Asst. city planner City of Eau Claire, 1974-78; dir. community devel. Owen Ayres & Assocs., Eau Claire, 1978-80; pres. Interval Resorts, Inc., Brookfield, Wis., 1981—; dir. U. Wis. Eau Claire U. Alumni Assn., 1981-83; founder, spokesperson Wis. Timesharing Assn., 1982. Mem. Wis. Bd. Realtors, Nat. Bd. Realtors, Nat. Timeshare Council. Roman Catholic. Club: Lake Forest Country. Office: 640 N Brookfield Rd Brookfield WI 53005

BIERY, JOHN CARL, physician; b. Columbus, Ohio, Nov. 10, 1944; s. Richard J. and Evelyn Joy (Bowman) B.; m. Kathleen Ford, June 1, 1968; children—John Carl Jr., Allison Kathleen. B.S., Northeast Mo. State U., 1972; D.O., Kirksville Coll. Osteo. Medicine, 1974. Team physician Bowling Green State U., 1976-77; ptnr. Ottawa Med. Ctr., Ohio, 1975—; emergency room physician Fostoria City Hosp., Ohio, 1982—, St. Rita's Med. Ctr., Lima, Ohio, 1975—. Served with USAF, 1964-68. Fellow Am. Coll. Sports Medicine; mem. Ohio Osteo. Assn. (pres. Acad. Dist. II 1982-85), Am. Osteo. Assn., Am. Coll. Family Practice, VFW. Avocations: swimming; golf; reading. Home: 9086 Cherokee Pl Ottawa OH 45875 Office: 110 Selhorst Dr Box 326 Ottawa OH 45875

BIESER, IRVIN GRUEN, JR., lawyer; b. Dayton, Ohio, June 17, 1941; s. Irvin Gruen and Catharine (French) B.; m. Tracy Hegamaster, Feb. 14, 1976. B.A., Harvard U., 1963, J.D., 1966. Bar: Ohio 1966. Instr. law, interim dean U. Liberia Sch. Law, Monrovia, 1967-69; assoc. Bieser, Greer & Landis, Dayton, 1969—, ptnr., 1974—, dir., sec. French Oil Mill Machinery Co. and Subs., Piqua, Ohio, 1975—. Trustee Dayton Art Inst., 1980—; trustee, treas. Dayton Philharmonic Orch., 1984—; trustee Ohio Preservation Alliance, 1983—; active Little Miami, Inc. (conservation nat. scenic river), Dayton, 1973—; mem. Montgomery County Pub. Defender Commn. Republican. Clubs: Buz Fuz, Miami Valley Hunt and Polo (Dayton). Lodge: Rotary of Dayton. Avocations: adventure travel; collecting African art; squash; skiing. Home: 790 E Schantz Ave Dayton OH 45419 Office: Bieser Greer & Landis 400 Gem Plaza Dayton OH 45402

BIGELIS, RAMUNAS, microbiologist, research scientist; b. Wunsiedel, W.Ger., May 28, 1947; came to U.S., 1949, naturalized, 1958; s. Vincent and Liudvina (Raustis) B.; B.S., U. Ill.-Chgo., 1969; Ph.D., Purdue U., 1974. Research asst. Purdue U., West Lafayette, Ind., 1970-74; postdoctoral fellow Cold Spring Harbor Lab., N.Y., 1975-78; postdoctoral assoc. Cornell U., Ithaca, N.Y., 1975-79; asst. prof. Wake Forest U., Winston-Salem, N.C., 1979-83; research scientist Miles Labs., Inc., Elkhart, Ind., 1983-85, sr. research scientist, 1985—. Contbr. chpts. to books, articles to profl. jours. Ill. State scholar, 1969. Mem. Am. Soc. Microbiology (newsletter ed. Ind. branch 1983—), AAAS, AAUP, Sigma Xi. Office: Miles Labs Inc Biotechnol GRP 1127 Myrtle St Elkhart IN 46515

BIGELOW, M. PENNY, printing equipment company executive, leasing company executive, video company executive, seminar company executive; b. New Eagle, Pa., Apr. 16, 1941; d. Clifford Marion and Frances Virginia (Gillingham) W.; m. James Howard Bigelow, Jan. 29, 1966; 1 child, David. B.S., U. Pitts., 1961; postgrad. edn. Temple U. Sch. Medicine, 1961-62, U. Pa., 1962-64, Ind. U.-Purdue U., Indpls., 1965—. Research chemist anatomy Ind. U., Indpls., 1964-66, preventive dentistry Sch. Medicine, 1966-70; co-owner, sec.-treas. Astro Offset Sales & Service, Inc., Indpls., 1967—. Editor Tropical Topics mag., 1971; in-house newsletter Ampersand, 1979—. Mem. Dealer Communicator (bd. advisors 1980—), Ind. Assn. Credit Mgmt. (edn. com. 1981—), Nat. Graphic Arts Dealers Assn. (founder, bd. dirs., sec. 1982—), Profl. Telemarketing Mgmt. Assn. (bd. dirs. 1983- 85, chmn. 1983-84), Graphic Arts Equipment and Supply Dealers Assn. (video com. 1985—). Republican. Avocations: reading; cooking; backgammon; sailing; swimming. Home: 1424 Sandi Dr Indianapolis IN 46260 Office: Astro Inc 5750 W 79th St Indianapolis IN 46278

BIGELOW, MARTHA MITCHELL, historian; b. Talladega Springs, Ala., Sept. 19, 1921; B.A., Ala. Coll., 1943; M.A., U. Chgo., 1944, Ph.D., 1946; children—Martha Frances, Carolyn. Assoc. prof. Miss. Coll., Clinton, 1946-48; assoc. prof. Memphis State U., 1948-49; asso. prof. U. Miss., 1949-50; assoc. curator manuscripts Mich. Hist. Collections, U. Mich., Ann Arbor, 1954-57; prof. history Miss. Coll., 1957-71, chmn. dept. history and polit. sci., 1964-71; dir. Mich. history div., Mich. Dept. State, sec. Mich. Hist. Commn., state historic preservation officer for Mich., Lansing, 1971—. Julius Rosenwald fellow, 1945-46. Mem. Am. Assn. State and Local History (v.p. 1976-78, pres. 1978-80), So. Hist. Assn., Orgn. Am. Historians, Mich. Hist. Soc., Miss. Hist. Soc., Nat. Assn. State Archives and Records Adminstrs. Contbr. articles to profl. jours. Office: 208 N Capitol 3d Fl Lansing MI 48918*

BIGGAR, EDWARD SAMUEL, lawyer; b. Kansas City, Mo., Nov. 19, 1917; s. Frank Wilson and Katharine (Rea) B.; A.B., U. Mich., 1938, J.D. with distinction, 1940; m. Susan Bagby, July 9, 1955; children—John Edward, Julie Anne, Nancy Rea, William Bagby, Martha Susan. Admitted to Mo. bar, 1940; assoc. firm Stinson Mag, Thomson, McEvers and Fizzell, attys., Kansas City, Mo., 1948-50, partner, 1950—; dir. Western Chem. Co., Kansas City, Cereal Food Processors, Inc., Kansas City, Mission Hills Bank, N.A., Kansas City. Chmn. Citizens Assn. Kansas City, Mo., 1959-60; bd. dirs. Greater Kansas City YMCA, 1965—, pres., 1979-81; chmn. Transp. Planning Commn. Greater Kansas City, 1964-65; mem. Met. Planning Commn., Kansas City Region, 1966-67; pres. Kansas City (Mo.) unit Am. Cancer Soc., 1956-58. Trustee, Sunset Hill Sch., Kansas City, Mo., 1971-77; mem. visitors com. U. Mich. Law Sch., 1977—; pres. Kansas City (Mo.) Bd. Police Commrs., 1981—. Served to 1st lt. USAAF, 1942-45. Mem. Lawyers Assn. Kansas City (pres. 1966-67), Mo. Bar, Am., Kansas City bar assns., Order of Coif, Phi Beta Kappa, Phi Delta Phi, Phi Delta Theta. Republican. Presbyterian. Home: 1221 Stratford Rd Kansas City MO 64113 Office: 2100 Charter Bank Center Kansas City MO 64105

BIGGS, BILLY LEE, school superintendant; b. Ft. Scott, Kans., Jan. 4, 1943; s. Arthur LeRoy and Edythe Bell (Bendure) B.; m. Martha Jane Hutchins, Aug. 19, 1967; children—Tiffany, Kristin. B.S., Pittsburg (Kans.) State U., 1966, M.S., 1967, Ed.S., 1978; Ed.D., Okla. State U., 1981. Cert. sch. adminstr., Kans. Secondary tchr., Carthage, Mo., 1967-68, Joplin, Mo., 1970-80; prin. Moundridge (Kans.) High Sch., 1980-83; supt. schs., Axtell, Bern and Summerfield, Kans., 1983—. Pres. Mid-Kans. League; sec. Jasper County Democratic Party. Served with U.S. Army, 1968-70. Decorated Bronze Star. Mem. Nat. Council for Accreditation Tchr. Edn., Nat. Assn. Secondary Sch. Prins., Assn. Supervision and Curriculum Devel., Phi Delta Kappa, Phi Kappa Phi. Lutheran. Lodge: Lions (Moundridge). Home: Box 13 Axtell KS 66403

BIGGS, JUDITH ANGELA, university adminstrator; b. Kingman, Kans., May 28, 1959; d. Daniel and Angeline Catherine (Martin) B.; B.S. in Edn., Emporia State U., 1981; M.A., Bowling Green State U., 1984. Student sec. Emporia State U., Kans., 1977-81; field rep. Alpha Sigma Alpha Nat. Sorority, Springfield, Mo., 1981-82; alumni affairs coordinator Bowling Green State U., Ohio, 1982-83, Panhellenic grad. advisor, 1983-84, unit dir. Alpha Gamma Delta, 1982-84, Pi Kappa Phi, 1984—, asst. dir. small group housing and Greek life, 1984—; career planning and placement intern Wichita State U., Kans., 1983, Findlay Coll., Ohio, 1983. Tchr. religious edn. St. Thomas More, Roman Catholic Ch., Bowling Green, Ohio, 1984. Mem. Am. Coll. Personnel Assn. (mem. commn. IV 1984—), Assn. Frat. Advisors (liason com. 1984—), Am. Assn. Counseling and Devel. Republican. Avocations: tennis, touch football, reading, conversation. Home and Office: 425 Student Services Bowling Green State U Bowling Green OH 43403-0152

BIGGS, NANCY ANN, computer programmer; b. Springfield, Ill., Feb. 27, 1941; d. Ralph Calvin and Grace Florence (Stephens) Buecker; m. John David Biggs, June 3, 1960; 1 child, Kent Edward. M.A. in Math. Systems, Sangamon State U., 1982. Computer programmer Ill. Dept. Revenue, Springfield, 1982-83, Ill. Community Coll. Bd., Springfield, 1983-84; computer programmer/analyst Horace Mann Ins. Cos., Springfield, 1984—. Mem. Assn. Systems Mgmt. (treas. 1983—), Assn. Computing Machinery. Democrat. Avocations: antiques; traveling; computer graphics; sewing. Home: 3005 Arlington Dr Springfield IL 62704 Office: Horace Mann Ins Cos One Horace Mann Plaza Springfield IL 62715

BIGGS, ROBERT WILDER, JR., mfg. co. exec.; b. Lorain, Ohio, Jan. 21, 1934; s. Robert Wilder and Eleanor (Hughes) B.; B.S. in Bus. Adminstrn., Ind. U., 1958; m. Dolores Bonnadine Ward, July 9, 1955; children—Robert Wilder, Adrienne. In retail industry, 1958-60; asst. purchasing agt. Oglebay Norton Co., Cleve., 1960-64; mgnt. cons. Case & Co., Cleve., 1964-68; with Pickands Mather & Co., Cleve., 1968—, treas., 1974—, v.p., 1981—; mem. adv. bd. Arkwright Boston, 1978—. Trustee, Cleve. Inst. Music, 1979—. Served with U.S. Army, 1954-56. Mem. Fin. Execs. Inst., Nat. Assn. Accts., Am. Iron and Steel Inst., U.S. Power Squadron, Cleve. Treas.'s Club (dir.). Clubs: Cleve. Athletic, Mid-Day, Sandusky Yacht. Office: 1100 Superior Ave Cleveland OH 44114

BIGHAM, DARREL EUGENE, history educator; b. Harrisburg, Pa., Aug. 12, 1942; s. Paul D. and Ethel B.; B.A., Messiah Coll., 1964; postgrad. Harvard Div. Sch., 1964-65; Ph.D., U. Kans., 1970; m. Mary Elizabeth Hitchcock, Sept. 23, 1965; children—Matthew, Elizabeth. Asst. prof. history U. So. Ind., Evansville, 1970-75, assoc. prof., 1975-81, prof., 1981—. Exec. dir. Leadership Evansville, 1976-79; dir. archives div. Conrad Baker Found., 1971-85; chmn. Evansville Bicentennial Council, 1974-77; bd. dirs. Evansville Mus., 1972—, sec., 1977-78, pres., 1979-81; trustee Evansville Vanderburgh County Pub. Library, 1971-80; bd. dirs. Met. Evansville Progress Commn., 1981—, chmn., 1983—; bd. dirs. Evansville Arts and Edn. Council, 1982—, pres., 1984-85; pres. Vol. Action Ctr., 1983-85; bd. dirs. Conrad Baker Found., 1971—, Planned Parenthood S.W. Ind., 1978-79. Rockefeller Brothers Theol. fellow, 1964-65; NDEA fellow, 1965-68. Mem. Soc. Ind. Archivists (dir. 1972-75, pres. 1977-79), Am. Hist. Assn., Orgn. Am. Historians, Ind. Hist. Soc., So. Hist. Assn., Vanderburgh County Hist. Soc. (pres. 1981-84). Mem. United Ch. of Christ. Clubs: Rotary, Petroleum, Oak Meadow Country. Contbr. articles to scholarly jours. Home: 8215 Kuebler Rd Evansville IN 47712 Office: Dept History Univ So Ind Evansville IN 47712

BIGUS, LAWRENCE WEAVER, lawyer; b. Kansas City, Mo., Apr. 2, 1955; s. Kenneth Eli and Elma (Weaver) B. B.B.A. magna cum laude, U. Houston, 1977, J.D., 1980. Bars: Mo. 1980, U.S. Dist. Ct. (we. dist.) Mo. 1980. Ptnr., Bigus & Bigus, Kansas City, Mo., 1980-82, Kaplan, Shanberg, Bigus & Osman, Kansas City, Mo., 1982—; legal counsel Mo. Jaycees (Greater Kansas City chpt.), 1982—. Contbr. articles to profl. jours. Trustee, Menorah Med. Ctr., Kansas City, Mo., 1983—. Named one of Outstanding Young Men Am., 1984; recipient scholarship Trust div. Kansas Bankers Assn., 1980. Mem. Mo. Bar Assn., ABA, Kansas City Bar Assn., Kansas City Area Hosp. Lawyers Assn., Jaycees (keyman Kansas City chpt. 1983, 84, keyman Mo. chpt. 1984), Order of Coif, Phi Kappa Phi, Beta Gamma Sigma. Republican. Jewish. Office: Kaplan Shanberg Bigus & Osman 1101 Walnut St Suite 1402 Kansas City MO 64106

BILBREY, DAVID MASTON, contracting company executive; b. Dayton, Ohio, Sept. 25, 1950; s. Percy Bilbrey and Margie Kathryn (Goss) B.; B.B.A., U. Cin., 1972; student Ohio Coll. Applied Sci., Cin., summer 1971; postgrad. Sinclair Community Coll., Dayton, 1973-74; m. Julia Rosario Delgado, Feb. 12, 1977; 1 dau., Jennifer René. Mgr. indsl. and spl. projects group div. Danis Industries Corp., Dayton, 1973-74, equipment scheduler, 1974, field engr., 1974-75, job engr., 1975, office engr., 1975-76, mgr. indsl. and spl. projects div., 1976—. Lic. real estate agt., Ohio. Mem. Oakwood Community Jaycees (external v.p. 1978-79), Dayton Builders Exchange (pres.). Mem. Disciples of Christ. Office: BG Danis Co 1801 E 1st St Dayton OH 45403

BILBRUCK, EDWARD E(UGENE), industrial auctioneer and appraiser, real estate broker; b. Terre Haute, Ind., Jan. 20, 1922; s. Charles J. and Martha (McClain) B.; m. Jeanne Day, Oct. 20, 1962. Student Central Y Coll.-Chgo., 1962-63. Cert. machinery appraiser. Exec. pres. Samuel L. Winternitz Co., Chgo., 1953-67; pres. Edward Bilbruck, Inc., Des Plaines, Ill., 1967—. Served with USAAF, 1941-45. Mem. Am. Soc. Appraisers (assoc.), Internat. Soc. Appraisers, Machinery Dealers Nat. Assn. (cert.), Nat. Auctioneers Assn. Presbyterian. Club: St. Paul Athletic (Minn.). Home: 482 Fairfax Ct Asheboro NC 27203 Office: Edward Bilbruck Inc 3158 Des Plaines #118 Des Plaines IL 60018

BILD, FRANK, state senator; b. Romania, Sept. 30, 1911; s. Anton and Katerina (Schiebel) B.; came to U.S., 1913, naturalized, 1937; B.S. in Edn., Ind. U., 1934; J.D., St. Louis U., 1942; m. Flora Huss, Sept. 18, 1937; children—Brian Alan, Karen Ann, Norman Anton, Kathleen Ann. Dir. athletics Southside St. Louis YMCA, 1936-42; admitted to Mo. bar, 1946, since practiced in St. Louis. Republican committeeman Concord (Mo.) Twp., 1956-66; mem. Mo. Ho. of Reps. from 47th Dist., 1963-64, 67-72; mem. Mo. Senate from 15th Dist., 1973—, chmn. Republican caucus; mem. Mo. Atomic Energy Commn. Served to capt. AUS, 1942-46. Recipient Meritorious award St. Louis Globe Democrat. Lutheran. Club: Concord Village Lions. Office: 11648 Gravois Rd Saint Louis MO 63126

BILDERBACK, GILBERT DEAN, printing company executive; b. Murphysboro, Ill., Dec. 9, 1935; s. Lester J. and Wanda M. (Berkbigler) B.; m. Carolyn Janice Rench, June 10, 1956; 1 child, Stephen E. B.S. in Bus. So. Ill. U., 1962. Salesman, Orchard Corp., St. Louis, 1957-66, dir. purchasing and traffic ops., 1966—. Mem. City Zoning Commn., Crestwood, Mo., 1984. Named Citizen of Yr. Crestwood/Sunset Hills C. of C., 1984. Pres. Watson Elem. Sch. PTA, 1978-79; v.p. Truman Middle Sch. PTA, 1982-83; chmn. Troop 581 Gravois council Boy Scouts Am., 1982—. Lodges: Rotary (pres. 1984), Masons. Avocations: golf, travel. Home: 9068 Laurel Crest Saint Louis MO 63126 Office: Orchard Corp 1154 Rece Saint Louis MO 63126

BILEYDI, SUMER MEHMET, advt. agy. exec.; b. Antalya, Turkey, Feb. 7, 1936; s. Abdurrahman M. and Neriman (Akman) B.; B.A., Mich. State U., 1961, M.A., 1962; m. Lois Elloine Goode, Dec. 30. 1961; children—Can M., Sera N. Mktg. cons. Export Promotion Center, Ankara, Turkey, 1962; planner Gardner Advt. Agy., St. Louis, 1963-65; planning supr. Batten, Barton,

Durstine & Osborn, N.Y.C., 1965-69; asso. dir. Ketchum, Macleod & Grove, Pitts., 1969-73; sr. v.p., dir. Carmichael Lynch, Inc., Mpls., 1973—. Pres., Turkish Am. Assn., 1974-75. Mem. Am. Mktg. Assn., Advt. Research Found., Advt. Fedn. Minn. Islam. Club: Minn. Turkish Am. Contbr. articles to profl. jours. Home: 16670 Baywood Terr Eden Prairie MN 55344 Office: 100 22d St E Minneapolis MN 55404

BILKEY, WILLIAM WALTER, JR., industrial engineer; b. St. Louis, Sept. 21, 1943; s. William W. and Romona (Foosey) B.; student S.E. Mo. State U., 1962, Jefferson Coll., 1967-75; B.S. in Indsl. Mgmt. and Psychology, Washington U., St. Louis, 1983. With Carter Carburetor div. A.C.F. Industries, St. Louis, 1963—, gen. foreman carburetor assembly, 1976-78, mgr. tooling and indsl. engring., 1978-82, mgr. statis. mfg. analysis, 1982, dir. quality assurance and statis. programs, 1982—. Mem. Am. Inst. Indsl. Engrs., Am. Soc. Quality Control. Club: Moo do Kwan. Office: 9666 Olive Blvd Saint Louis MO 63132

BILLE, DONALD ALLEN, nurse, educator; b. Waupun, Wis., Feb. 10, 1943; s. Arthur and Ada (Wellhouse) B.; grad. St. Luke's Hosp. Sch. Nursing, 1964; B.S.N., U. Wis., Madison, 1966, Ph.D., 1975; M.S.N., Marquette U., 1971. Mem. faculty Coll. Nursing, Marquette U., Milw., 1970-72; coordinator intensive care unit VA Med. Center, Wood, Wis., 1973-74; dir. nursing edn. Mercy Hosp., Chgo., 1975-77; asst. prof. U. Ill. Med. Center, Chgo., 1978-79; asso. prof. nursing DePaul U., Chgo., 1979-84, prof., 1984—, chmn. grad. program, 1980-81. Served with Nurse Corps, U.S. Army, 1966-70. Mem. Ill. League Nursing (chmn. program com., dir.), Nat. League Nursing, Chgo. Council Fgn. Relations (patron), Assn. Supervision and Curriculum Devel., Am. Soc. Health Edn. and Tng., Phi Delta Kappa, Sigma Theta Tau (Zeta Sigma chpt.) Congregationalist. Author: Staff Development: A Systems Approach, 1982. Editor: Practical Approaches to Patient Teaching, 1981. Mem. editorial bd. Quality Rev. Bull., Jour. Nursing Edn., Nursing Adminstrn. Quar.; editorial bd., book rev. editor Today's OR Nurse; contbr. numerous articles to profl. jours. Home: 3749 N Wilton Ave Chicago IL 60613 Office: DePaul U 2323 N Seminary Ave Chicago IL 60614

BILLESBACH, ANN ELIZABETH, historical center curator; b. Grand Island, Nebr., Aug. 14, 1953; d. Mattias Benedict and Elizabeth Jean (Bottorff) B. B.A., U. Nebr.-Lincoln, 1975; M.A., SUNY-Oneonta, 1983. Intern, Nat. Endowment Humanities Inst. Texan Cultures, San Antonio, 1976-77; curator Willa Cather Found., Red Cloud, Nebr., 1978, Willa Cather Hist. Ctr., Red Cloud, 1978—; cons. humanist Nebr. Com. for Humanities, Lincoln, 1978-83; grant reviewer Inst. Mus. Services, Washington, 1983—, Nebr. Arts Council, 1981—; humanist-in-residence, project dir. Nebr. Museums Coalition, 1981-82; bd. dirs. Webster County Hist. Mus., Red Cloud, 1979-82. Pres., Red Cloud Arts Council, 1983; sec., bd. dirs. Prairie-Plains Resource Inst., 1980-83. Recipient Nebr. Regents Scholarship award, 1971; Smithsonian Instn. Nat. Museums Act Fellowship award, 1975. Mem. Am. Assn. State and Local History, Am. Assn. Museums, Internat. Com. on Museums, Nat. Trust for Historic Preservation, Assn. Living Hist. Farms and Agrl. Museums. Address: Willa Cather Hist Ctr PO Box 326 Red Cloud NE 68970

BILLIG, THOMAS CLIFFORD, publishing company executive, marketing consultant; b. Pitts., Aug. 20, 1930; s. Thomas Clifford and Melba Helen (Stucky) B.; student Montgomery Jr. Coll., 1948-49, Am. U., 1950-51; B.S. summa cum laude, Northwestern U., 1956; m. Helen Page Hine, May 14, 1951; children—Thomas Clifford III, James Frederick. Asst. ins. mgr. Montgomery Ward & Co., Chgo., 1951-54; ins. mgr., asst. dir. personnel, asst. to chmn. Butler Bros. (now City Products Corp.), Chgo., 1954-59; market research mgr. R.R. Donnelley & Sons, Chgo., 1959-61; pres., dir. Indsl. Fiber Glass Products Corp., Scottville and Ludington, Mich., 1962-68; mass mktg. mgmt. cons., Mpls., 1968-71; v.p. Mail Mktg. Systems & Services, St. Paul and Bloomington, Minn., 1971-74; pres., dir. Nat. Ins. Advt. Regulation Service Corp., Mpls., 1974—, Fins & Feathers Pub. Co., Mpls., 1977—, Billig & Assos., Mpls., 1979—; dir. Total Life Clinics. Served with USNR, 1948-56. Recipient Samuel Dresner Plotkin award Northwestern U., 1956. Mem. Delta Mu Delta, Beta Gamma Sigma. Home: 3445 Zenith Ave S Minneapolis MN 55416 Office: Fins & Feathers Pub Co 318 W Franklin Ave Minneapolis MN 55404

BILLINGHAM, DAVID RALPH, social service administrator; b. Rockford, Ill., Apr. 10, 1949; s. Ralph B. and Elfrieda K. (Muehleisen) B.; B.S. in Psychology, Rockford Coll., 1971; M.S.W., U. Ill., Chgo., 1975; m. Jean Caughey, June 2, 1973; 1 son, Matthew David. Social worker Ill. Dept. Children and Family Services, 1971-73; lead social worker Mental Health Advocacy Project, Chgo., 1975-76; forensic psychiatry program social worker Ill. State Psychiat. Inst., Chgo., 1977-80; grant specialist Region II, Ill. Dept. Mental Health, 1980-81; dir. residential services Victor C. Neumann Assn., Chgo., 1981—; chmn. human rights com. W.A. Howe Center for Developmentally Disabled. Cert. social worker, Ill. Mem. Acad. Cert. Social Workers, Alt. Living Mgrs. Assn., Am. Orthopsychiat. Assn., Nat. Assn. Social Workers, Am. Assn. Mental Deficiency, Ill. Assn. Retarded Citizens. Office: 1608 N Milwaukee Ave 6th Floor Chicago IL 60647

BILLINGS, CHARLES HARRY, lawyer; b. St. Louis, Sept. 17, 1952; s. Charles Patrick and Mary Eileen (Hixson) B.; m. Kathleen Ann Bruntrager, July 30, 1976; children—Charles, Daniel, Anne. B.A., St. Louis U., 1975; J.D., St. Mary's U., San Antonio, 1978. Bars: Mo. 1978, U.S. Dist. Ct. (ea. and we. dists.) Mo. 1978, U.S. Supreme Ct. 1982. Prosecutor, St. Louis Circuit Atty., 1978-80; assoc. Bruntrager & Billings, St. Louis, 1980-82, ptnr., 1982—. Judge, City of Pine Lawn, Mo., 1979—, City of Des Peres, 1985—. Mem. Am. Trial Lawyers Am., ABA, Mo. Bar Assn., St. Louis Bar Assn., Phi Kappa Psi. Roman Catholic. Club: C.Y.C. St. Gerard Majella. Home: 13025 Winding Trail St Louis MO 63131 Office: Bruntrager Bruntrager & Billings PC 1015 Locust St Suite 1140 St Louis MO 63101

BILLINGS, DOUGLAS GLEN, corporate executive; b. Creston, Iowa, Mar. 9, 1942; s. Glen Dale and Nancy Jane (Wilhelm) B.; m. Annette Louise Sellergren, June 21, 1969; children—Melissa Smith, Abigail Fleming. B.A., Parsons Coll., 1963. Assoc. instr. Parsons Coll., Fairfield, Iowa, 1965-66; retail operator Men's Wear, Red Oak, Iowa, 1967-71; innkeeper Holiday Inn, Red Oak, 1971-80; pres. Red Coach Enterprises Inc., Red Oak, 1980-82, chmn., pres., 1982—; pres. Acorn Devel. Co., Red Oak, 1981—; chmn. Internat. Assn. Holiday Inns Inc. Polit. Action Com., Memphis, 1982-84. Mem. Iowa Devel. Commn., 1976-80; chmn. Housing Agy. of Red Oak, 1981-84; mem. fin. com. Iowa Democratic Com., 1982—, chmn. bus. council, 1983—; dist. chmn. Mid.-Am. council Boy Scouts Am., 1983—. Served with U.S. Army, 1967-72. Recipient Outstanding Achievement award Internat. Assn. Holiday Inns Inc., 1979-82. Mem. Internat. Assn. Holiday Inns Inc. (com., bd. dirs. 1984—), Am. Hotel and Motel Assn., Iowa Hotel-Motel Assn. (past dir.), Iowa Restaurant Assn., Sigma Phi Epsilon. Episcopalian. Club: Embassy (Des Moines). Lodge: Elks. Home: 802 8th St Red Oak IA 51566 Office: Red Coach Enterprises Inc US Hwy 34 Red Oak IA 51566

BILLINGS, WILLIAM HOWARD, See *Who's Who in America,* 43rd edition.

BILLINGSLEY, GARY LEE, medical homecare company executive, respiratory therapist; b. Anderson, Ind., Nov. 14, 1956; s. Grady Lee and Eula George (Hunt) B.; m. Laura Dana Harrell, Nov. 7, 1976 (div. July 1979). Respiratory therapist, Ind. Voc. Tech. Coll., 1976. Staff therapist Condell Meml. Hosp., Libertyville, Ill., 1976-79; critical care therapist St. Vincent's Hosp., Indpls., 1977-82, West View Osteo. Hosp., Indpls., 1982-84; mgr. Stat Med. Homecare, Anderson, 1984—. Mem. Ind. Soc. Respiratory Therapy, Anderson C. of C. Democrat. Avocations: art; music; golf; micro-computing; travel. Home: 1534 Edgewood Dr Anderson IL 46011 Office: Stat Med Homecare of Am Inc 3690 State Rd 9 N Anderson IN 46012

BILLINGSLEY, JOHN SMITH, radiologist; b. Newton, Iowa, Jan. 16, 1929; s. John William and Mary Mable (Smith) B.; B.A., Simpson Coll., 1951; M.D., Western Res. U., 1955; m. Cleo Eloise Jones, Aug. 25, 1952; children—John Elliott, James William, Joseph Crane. Intern, Iowa Meth. Hosp., Des Moines, 1955-56; fellow in radiology Mayo Clinic, Rochester, Minn., 1956-59; practice medicine specializing in radiology, Ft. Wayne, Ind., 1961—; asso. Duemling Clinic; staff Luth. Hosp.; asso. faculty Ind. Sch. Medicine, Ft. Wayne Center Med. Edn. Served to capt. M.C., AUS, 1959-61. Mem. Am. Coll. Radiology, AMA, Ind. Med. Assn., Ind., Iowa hist. socs., Am. Def. Preparedness Assn., Nat. Rifle Assn. Club: Ft. Wayne Country. Home: 4720 Crestwood Dr Fort Wayne IN 46807 Office: 2828 Fairfield Ave Fort Wayne IN 46807

BILLINGSLEY, ROGER DALE, food company executive; b. Oak Park, Ill., Feb. 8, 1952; s. William Glenn and Pauline Evelyn (Kirby) B.; m. Belinda Consuela Perry (div. 1977); children—Christina Lynn, Eric Noel. B.S., So. Ill. U., 1975, M.S., 1977; Ph.D., U. Tenn., 1979. Researcher U. Ill., Urbana, 1979-80; biostatistician research dept. Kellogg Co., Battle Creek, Mich., 1980-82, supr. stats. and sensory evaluation, 1982-83, mgr. evaluation services, 1983, mgr. stats. and food products devel., 1983-84, dir. cereal product devel. and product evaluation, 1984—. Mem. Am. Mgmt. Assn., Am. Statis. Assn. Methodist. Lodge: Masons. Home: 6994 18 1/2 Mile Rd Marshall MI 49068 Office: Kellogg Co 235 Porter St Battle Creek MI 49015

BILLMAN, FRED LEO, mfg. co. exec.; b. Hebron, Nebr., June 19, 1941; s. Elsworth Leo and Ruth Marie (Livergood) B.; student Omaha U., 1958-59; B.S. in Chemistry and Math., Fla. State U., 1963; M.S., Wayne State U., 1965, Ph.D., 1969; m. Mary Renee Hagarty, Aug. 7, 1971; children—Thomas Lloyd, Aaron Donald, Ellen Marie. Research asst. Wayne State U., 1963-69; research chemist basic organic research Johnsons Wax, Racine, Wis., 1969-74, sr. research chemist Johnson Wax Internat., 1974-77, research and devel. dir., Mex., 1977-80, Chile, 1980-81, internat. research and devel. mgr., 1981—. Mem. Coledonia Twp. (Wis.) Planning Bd., 1975-76. Mem. Am. Chem. Soc., Mexican Aerosol Soc. Patentee fabric softening agts. Home: 4840 Three Mile Rd Racine WI 53406 Office: 1525 Howe St Racine WI 53403

BILLOW, MICHAEL ALAN, osteopathic physician; b. Homestead, Pa., Oct. 5, 1955; s. Joseph and Rita Louise (Persichitti) B.; m. Vicki Jane Cooper, June 5, 1976; children—Damien Grant, Megan Renae. B.A., Case Western Res. U., 1977; D.O., Des Moines Coll. Osteo. Medicine and Surgery, 1980. Intern, Brentwood Hosp., Warrensville Heights, Ohio, 1980-81; resident in pediatrics Rush-Presbyn. St. Lukes Med. Ctr., Chgo., 1981-83, chief resident pediatrics, 1983-84, fellow pediatric critical care, 1984; practice medicine specializing in pediatrics, Bloomingdale, Ill., 1984—. Fellow Am. Acad. Pediatrics; mem. AMA, Nat. Assn. Residents and Interns (mem. interns com. for care of children), Ill. Med. Soc., Chgo. Med. Soc. Republican. Roman Catholic. Club: Lincoln Park Trap and Skeet (Chgo.). Home: 2000 N 74th Ave Elmwood Park IL 60635

BILLS, EDWIN LYNN, training specialist; b. Delaware, Ohio, Dec. 20, 1942; s. Harold Lynn and Lucille (Sharp) B.; B.S. in Edn., U. Cin., 1973, M.Ed., 1975; Ohio Vocat. Edn. Adminstrn. intern, Kent State U., 1977-78; m. Shirlee Costello, June 9, 1972; children—Amylynn, Nathan. Computer ops. shift supr. U.S. Shoe Corp., Cin., 1970-73; communications electronics instr. Great Oaks Joint Vocat. Sch. Dist., Cin., 1973-77, trade and indsl. edn. supr., 1977-80; assoc. dir. Scarlet Oaks Career Devel. Center, Cin., 1980-82; mgr. internal tng. Cin. Milacron Electronic Systems, 1982—. Bd. dirs. Ripley County Ind. ARC, 1978-83, Public Service award, 1978; rep. Ripley County Disaster Council; bd. dirs. Catholic Charities, Indpls. Served with USN, 1962-69. Mem. Am. Radio Relay League (Public Service award), Nat. Alumni Assn. Coll. Edn. U. Cin. (v.p., mem. exec. bd.). Roman Catholic. Clubs: Laughery Valley Amateur Radio (past pres.), U. Cin. Vets. (charter, past sec.). Home: Rt 1 Box 195A Sunman IN 47041 Office: Rt 48 and Mason Rd Lebanon OH 45036

BILLS, MARK MCEWEN, dentist, management consultant; b. Flint, Mich., July 6, 1946; s. Mark Whitzel and Sara Elizabeth (McEwen) B.; m. Nancy Lynn Wycoff, Mar. 12, 1972 (div. 1978); m. Martha Elaine Weaver, Dec. 22, 1984. B.S., Ill. State U., 1974, M.S., 1976; D.M.D., So. Ill. U., 1980. Cert. Ill., Fla. Dental component dir. St. Francis Med. Ctr., Community Clinic, Peoria, Ill., 1980-83; chief dental services VA Out-Patient Clinic, Peoria, 1983-84; gen. practice dentistry, Peoria, 1980—; cons., specialist comprehensive hemophiliac treatment team St. Francis Med. Ctr., 1982—; instr. Dental Hygiene Sch., Ill. Central Coll., Peoria, 1981-82. Chmn. auction com. Pub. TV, Peoria, 1983; fundraiser Multiple Sclerosis Assn., 1983. Served to capt. U.S. Army, 1966-70, Vietnam. Mem. Ill. State Dental Soc., Peoria Dental Soc., Am. Dental Assn., Acad. Gen. Dentistry, Fedn. Dentair Internationale, Ill. Acad. Dental Practice Mgmt. Republican. Methodist. Lodge: Kiwanis. Avocations: sailing; scuba diving; offshore powerboat racing; skiing. Home: 1116 W Loucks Ave Peoria IL 61604 Office: Profl Mgmt Cons 1627 Clower Creek Dr T-170 Sarasota FL 33581

BILLY, GERRY DEE, sheriff, law enforcement instructor; b. Zanesville, Ohio, Feb. 6, 1951; s. Paul and Jean (Drake) B.; m. Mary Lynn Bibart, June 19, 1976; children—Angela Mishonne, Paul James. Assoc. Applied Sci. cum laude, Muskingum Area Tech. Coll., Zanesville, 1975; B.A. cum laude, Ohio Dominican Coll., 1980. Detective Muskingum Sheriff Dept., Zanesville, 1974-76; agent-in-charge Tri-County Anti-Crime Program, Newark, Ohio, 1976-78; investigator Porter, Wright Law Office, Columbus, Ohio, 1978-80; sheriff Licking County, Newark, 1981—; instr. criminal justice law enforcement Central Ohio Tech. Coll., Newark, 1978—; con. Varasso & Assocs. Architects/Planners, Newark, 1981—. Asst. dir. Licking County Spl. Olympics, 1980—; chmn. Ohio Police Olympics, Columbus, 1976—; bd. dirs. Licking County chpt. ARC, 1983—; trustee Licking County Hist. Soc., 1982—; apptd. mem. Commn. on Prison Crowding, 1984. Served as mil. police investigator AUS, 1971-73. Named Outstanding Young Man of Am., U.S. Jaycees, 1981, 82, 83, Outstanding Young Man of Licking County, Newark Area Jaycees, 1982; recipient Disting. Service award Newark Area Jaycees, 1980, 81, 82; Appreciation award Ohio Spl. Olympics, 1983, Cert. Accomodation, Am. Legion, 1983, Presidential Award of Honor, Granville Jaycees, 1983, Disting. Service award U.S. Jaycees, 1982; Appreciation award Nat. Child Safety Council, 1981, Outstanding Instr. award Muskingum County Law Enforcement Acad., 1976. Mem. Narcotic Assn. of Regional Coordinating Officers of Ohio (pres. 1984—, Exec. Service award 1982), Buckeye State Sheriff's Assn. (tng. coordinator 1982—), Nat. Sheriff's Assn., Ohio Auto Theft Investigator's Assn., U.S. Dept. Justice Drug Trafficking Commn. (law enforcement coordinating com.), Am. Correctional Assn., Am. Jail Assn. (speaker nat. conf. 1985), VFW. Republican. Lutheran. Lodges: Masons, Honorable Order Ky. Colonels. Avocations: golf; basketball; hunting; painting and design. Home: 14 Richards Rd Newark OH 43055 Office: Licking County Sheriff's Dept 46 S Third St Newark OH 43055

BILSEL, YILMAZ CELIK, physician; b. Istanbul, Turkey, May 17, 1927; s. Huseyin Sabri and Makbule (Ahmet) B.; m. Zeliha Tanriover, Oct. 29, 1960; children—Deniz, Kurt. M.D., U. Istanbul, 1949. Physician, R.R. Co., Adana, Turkey, 1951-53; resident in internal medicine Eskisehir, Turkey, 1953-56; internist, R.R. Hosp., Izmir and Istanbul, Turkey, 1956-58; resident, Homer G. Phillips Hosp., St. Louis, 1958-61; fellow in hematology, Med. Coll. Ga., Augusta, 1961-63; practice medicine, Kirklareli, Turkey, 1963-66; supr. City Hosp., 1966-70; practice medicine specializing in internal medicine, East St. Louis, Ill., 1970—; bd. mem. St. Mary's Hosp., East St. Louis; pres. staff Centreville Twp. Hosp. (Ill.). Served to lt. M.C. Turkish Army, 1949-50. Mem. AMA, Ill. State Med. Soc., Mo. Med. Soc., Clair County Med. Soc., So. Ill. Med. Soc. Co-author: Angiotensin II and Erythropoiesis, 1963. Home: 25 Huntleigh Woods Saint Louis MO 63131 Office: 4601 State St East Saint Louis IL 62205

BILSKY, EARL, textile/apparel company executive; b. Fall River, Mass., Sept. 26, 1928; s. David and Rose (Nulman) B.; B.S., S.E. Mass. U., 1952; M.S. (research fellow), Inst. of Textile Tech., 1954; m. Betty Ann Funk, Dec. 5, 1954; children—Edward Scott, Karen Lee, Matthew Kolman. Engr. specialist Goodyear Aerospace Corp., Akron, Ohio, 1960-62; merchandise mgr. apparel and indsl. Am. Cyanamid Co., N.Y.C. and Wayne, N.J., 1962-71; exec. v.p. Aileen, Inc., N.Y.C. and Abilene, Tex., 1971-76, also dir.; pres. Eagle Knitting Mills, Milw., 1976—. Bd. dirs. United Way, Abilene, 1975-76, YMCA, Abilene, 1973-76, Abilene Art Mus., 1974-75, Milw. Council on Drug Abuse, 1981-83. planning/zoning commr. City of Abilene, 1975-76. Served with USMC, 1946-48. Patentee in field. Office: 507 S 2d St Milwaukee WI 53204

BINGHAM, MARJORIE JEAN WALL, educator; b. St. Paul, Nebr., May 27, 1936; d. George Richard and Fay Maugerite Wall; B.A., Grinnell Coll., 1958; M.A., U. Minn., 1959, Ph.D., 1969; m. Thomas Egan, Feb. 28, 1975. Tchr. public schs., Davenport, Iowa, 1959-62, St. Louis Park, Minn., 1963-77; dir. women in world area studies St. Louis Park and Robbinsdale (Minn.) schs., 1977—. Mem. Minn. Humanities Commn., 1983—. Woodrow Wilson fellow, 1958-59; recipient Minn. Bus. award for excellence in edn. Mem. Women Historians of Midwest (pres. 1980—, mem. exec. bd. 1978—), Minn. Hist. Soc. (mem. edn. bd. 1979—), Minn. Council of Social Studies (mem. exec. bd. 1977—), Am. Hist. Soc. (teaching div.), Phi Beta Kappa. Co-author: Women in the U.S.S.R., 1980; Women in Islam, 1980; Women in Israel, 1980; Women in China, 1980; Women in India, 1980; Women in Africa, 1982; Women in Ancient Greece and Rome, 1983; Women in Medieval and Renaissance Europe, 1984; Women in Latin America, 1985. Mem. editorial bd. The History Tchr. Home: 5732 Lake Rose Dr Minnetonka MN 55343 Office: 6425 W 33d St Saint Louis Park MN 55426

BINNING, WILLIAM CHARLES, political scientist, educator; b. Boston, Mar. 8, 1944; s. Kenneth William and Josephine Agnes (Crotty) B.; B.A. in Politics, St. Anselm's Coll., 1966; Ph.D. in Govt. and Internat. Relations (NDEA fellow), U. Notre Dame, 1970; m. Maureen G. Fannon, Nov. 26, 1966; children—Patrick, Catherine. Asst. prof. polit. sci. Youngstown (Ohio) State U., 1970-77, asso. prof., chmn. polit. sci., 1977-84, prof., 1984—; project dir. NSF, 1978-79, grant evaluator, 1979. Trustee Internat. Inst., Youngstown, 1972—, Children and Family Services Bd., Mahoning County, 1977—; vice chmn. Mahoning County Republican Central Com., 1973-74, chmn., 1980—; chmn. Mahoning County Rep. Exec. Com., 1980—; mem. Mahoning County Bd. Elections, 1980—. Mem. Am. Polit. Sci. Assn., Internat. Studies Assn., Latin Am. Studies Assn., Midwest Polit. Sci. Assn., AAUP. Home: 2893 Algonquin Dr Poland OH 44514 Office: Dept Polit Sci Youngstown State U Youngstown OH 44555

BINOTTI, DAVID ALLEN, orthodontist; b. Chgo., Apr. 8, 1943; s. Evo Joseph and Anne (DiVita) B.; D.D.S., Loyola U. (Chgo.), 1967, M.S. in Oral Biology, 1969, Certificate Specialty Orthodontics, 1969; m. Barbara J. Rizzo, June 24, 1967; children—Eric David, Nicholas Allen. Practice orthodontics, Oak Lawn, Ill., 1969—, Lombard, Ill., 1971—; asso. with Dr. Ernest Panos, Chgo., 1969-74; clin. instr. dept. orthodontics Sch. Dentistry, Loyola U., 1969-72. Mem. ADA, Chgo. Dental Soc., Am. Assn. Orthodontists, Ill. Soc. Orthodontists. Roman Catholic. Office: 5208 W 95th St Oak Lawn IL 60453 also 805 S Main St Suite 2 Lombard IL 60148

BIRD, MELVIN RONALD, pharmacist; b. Hannibal, Mo., Nov. 2, 1945; s. Edward Melvin and Margaret Etta (Bloom) B.; divorced. B.S. in Pharmacy, St. Louis Coll. of Pharmacy, 1968. Pharmacist, St. Marys Pharmacy, Hannibal, 1968—. Mem. Am. Pharm. Assn., Nat. Assn. Retail Druggists, Mo. Pharm. Assn., Northeast Mo. Pharm. Assn. (pres. 1975-84). Roman Catholic. Club: Hannibal Country. Lodges: Lions, Elks. Avocations: hunting; fishing; card playing; antique collecting. Office: St Marys Pharmacy 2900 St Marys Ave Hannibal MO 63401

BIRD, MERLE KENDALL, steel processing company executive; b. Mt. Pleasant, Iowa, July 1, 1927; s. Eugene Clifford and Freida Fern (Kerr) B.; m. Helen Marie Hohn, June 16, 1951; children—Stephen Kent, Cynthia June, David Kurt, Kim Marie, Kevin Lee, Rebbecca Susan. Student, U. Minn., 1945-46; B.S. in Edn., Western Ill. U., 1949; M.S. in Edn., No. Ill. U., 1956. Basketball ofcl. Ill. High Sch. Assn., Colusa and Crystal Lake, Ill., 1949-67, football ofcl., 1952-67; tchr., coach, athletic dir. Sch. Dist. 311, Colusa, 1949-52, Sch. Dist. 47, Crystal Lake, 1952-57; prodn. mgr. TC Industries, Inc., Crystal Lake, 1957-65, personnel mgr., 1965-74, dir. employee and pub. relations, 1974—. Pres., McHenry County Tb Assn., 1962-65, St. Thomas Sch. Bd., 1967-68, DuPage-McHenry Lung Assn., 1968-71; Crystal Lake Park Dist., 1970, 73, Four Colonies Townhouse Assn., 1981-83; cubmaster Blackhawk Area council Boy Scouts Am., 1964-66; sec. McHenry Hosp. Bd., 1974-79; v.p. Am. Lung Assn. Ill., 1980, 83. Served with USN, 1945-46. Mem. McHenry County Mfg. Assn. (pres. 1961), McHenry County Personnel Mgrs., Crystal Lake Jr. C. of C. (pres. 1960-61, awards 1959, 62), Am. Legion. Republican. Roman Catholic. Club: Lions. Editor, Terra Cotta Newsletter, 1966—. Home: 601 Cress Creek Crystal Lake IL 60014 Office: TC Industries Inc PO Box 477 Crystal Lake IL 60014

BIRD, MILFORD GILBERT, mechanical engineer; b. Algona, Iowa, Jan. 21, 1917; s. Henry Francis and Verona May (Gilbert) B.; student Chgo. Tech. Coll., 1938-41, U. Minn., 1949-53; m. Bernice Laura Stoeckel, Sept. 9, 1944; children—Ronald Gilbert, Bonnie Laura. With CCC, Grand Rapids, Minn., 1934; asst. to ednl. adviser Roberts-Hamilton Co., Mpls., 1935-38; draftsman Tri-City Roofing & Sheet Metal Works, Whiting, Ind, 1938-41; office mgr. Honeywell, Inc., Mpls., 1944-45; field research engr. Reese Assos., Mpls., 1945-49; v.p. Bird, Bird & Assos., Mpls., 1949-73; sr. mech. engr., pres. U.S. Postal Service Design & Constrn., St. Paul, 1973—. Served with U.S. Army, 1941-44. Mem. Minn. Assn. Cons. Engrs. (pres. 1966-67), Am. Cons. Engrs. Council (nat. dir. 1970-72), Nat., Minn. socs. profl. engrs., Profl. Engrs. In Govt., Assn. Energy Engrs. Republican. Lutheran. Home: 3200 46th Ave N Robbinsdale MN 55422 Office: 180 E Kellogg Blvd Saint Paul MN 55169

BIRDSALL, WESTON DONALD, utilities company official; b. Cleve., Dec. 28, 1920; s. Albert Barton and Mary Helen (McCreery) B.; m. Anne Marie Wodder, May 29, 1943; children—Susanne, Sonne, Scott, Shan, Steven. B.S. in Edn., Ohio State U., 1942; B.S.M.E., U. Nebr., 1949. Engr., Phillips Petroleum Co., 1949-53; gen. mgr., ptnr. Davidson Gas & Electric Co., 1953-66; v.p. Mgmt. Computer Network, 1966-72; gen. mgr. Osage Mcpl. Utilities (Iowa), 1972—; dir. Home Trust & Savs. Bank. Co-chmn. indsl. devel. bd. Community Chest. Served with AUS, 1944-47; ETO. Recipient Pres.'s award for energy efficiency, 1980; Energy Innovators award Am. Pub. Power Assn., 1981; Community citation Iowa VFW, 1981; award for excellence in energy conservation Gov. of Iowa, 1982; Seven Hats award Am. Pub. Power Assn., 1982, nat. award for energy innovation Dept. Energy, 1984. Mem. Iowa Assn. Mcpl. Utilities (pres. 1979-81), VFW, Am. Legion. Republican. Lutheran. Club: Rotary. Contbr. articles to Pub. Power Mag., various newspapers. Home: Route 2 Osage IA 50461 Office: 720 Chestnut St Box 207 Osage IA 50461

BIRG, LAURA DARNELL, sociologist, educator; b. Milw., May 11, 1939; d. Shapley B. and Margaret (Austin) Darnell; m. Herwart G. Birg, Apr. 9, 1963; children—Carter Frederick, Erika Clarke. B.S., Northwestern U., 1961; M.S. in Sociology with honors, Roosevelt U., Chgo., 1977; Ph.D., U. Ill.-Chgo., 1981. Promotion mgr. Northwestern U. Press, Evanston, Ill., 1960-61; editor Fact-index Compton's Ency., Chgo., 1961-64, 72-73; freelance writer Marquis Who's Who, Inc., Chgo., 1964—, writer, editor, 1968—; asst. prof. St. Xavier Coll., Chgo., 1980-84, assoc. prof., 1984—, chmn. dept. sociology and anthropology, 1982—; cons. editor New Standard Ency., Chgo., 1966—; cons. Ency. Brit., Chgo., 1982-83; lectr. U. Ill.-Chgo., Barat Coll., Roosevelt U., Northeastern Ill. U., others. Author: Support Systems of Female Felons, 1981. Editor: Midwest Feminist Papers V, 1984-85. Contbr. articles to profl. jours. Active PTA, Elmhurst, Ill., 1970-76, pres. local chpt., Elmhurst, 1975-76; active Girl Scouts U.S., Boy Scouts Am., LWV. Grantee NIMH, 1978-80; Small Projects grantee St. Xavier Coll., 1982—. Mem. Am. Sociol. Assn., Ill. Sociol. Assn. (treas. 1983—), Midwest Sociol. Assn. (com. status of women 1983—), Sociologists for Women in Soc. (chair 1983-84), AAUP, Women in Research, So. Sociol. Soc., others. Democrat. Home: 217 Geneva Ave Elmhurst IL 60126 Office: St Xavier Coll Dept Sociology and Anthropology 3700 W 103d St Chicago IL 60655

BIRK, ROBERT EUGENE, physician; b. Buffalo, Jan. 7, 1926; s. Reginald H. and Florence (Diebolt) B.; A.B., Colgate U., 1948; M.D., U. Rochester, 1952; m. Janet L. Davidson, June 24, 1950; children—David Eugene, James Michael, Patricia Jean, Thomas Spencer, Susan Margaret. Intern, resident Henry Ford Hosp., Detroit, 1952-57, chief 2d med. div., 1961-66, asst. to chmn. dept. medicine, 1965-66; practice medicine, specializing in internal medicine, Grosse Pointe, Mich., 1966—; sr. active staff St. John Hosp., 1966—, chief dept. medicine, 1967-70, dir. health edn., dir. grad. med. edn., 1975—, exec. dir. continuing med. edn., 1975—; dir. med. affairs St. Clair Ambulatory Care Corp., 1980—, bd. dirs., 1984—; dir. St. Clair Home Care Services, 1980—, St. Clair Exec. Diagnostic Services, 1980—; v.p. clin. affairs St. Clair Health Corp., 1985—; assoc. medicine Wayne State U., 1969—. Mem. trustee's council U. Rochester, 1973-75, Med. Center alumni council, 1974-75; corp. mem. bd. Boys Clubs Met. Detroit, 1973—; trustee Mich. Cancer Found., 1980—, bd. dirs., 1982-84. Served with Army of U.S., 1943-46. Diplomate Am. Bd. Internal Medicine. Fellow ACP, Detroit Acad. Medicine; mem. AMA, Assn. Hosp. Med. Edn., Acad. Physician Med. Dirs., Alpha Tau Omega. Republican. Episcopalian. Clubs: Grosse Pointe (Mich.); Carleton (Chgo.). Contbr. articles to profl. jours. Home: 10 Stratford Pl Grosse Pointe MI 48230 Office: 22151 Moross Rd Suite G33 Detroit MI 48236

BIRKHAHN, RONALD HUGO, clinical nutrition educator; b. Marshalltown, Iowa, Dec. 4, 1939; s. Hugo Robert and Florence Grace (Lyon) B.; m. Gertrude Oi-Yee Chan, Nov. 22, 1969; children—Ronald Henry, Robert Hugo. B.A., Cornell Coll., Mt. Vernon, Iowa, 1962; Ph.D., Purdue U., 1967. Asst. prof. Hanover Coll., Ind., 1967-73; research assoc. SUNY-Buffalo, 1973-76; asst. prof. Med. Coll. Ohio, Toledo, 1976-81. assoc. prof., 1981—; cons.

Travenol Labs., Deerfield, Ill., 1982—. Contbr. articles to profl. jours. and chpts. to scholarly texts. Inventor of synthetic compounds. Active Anthony Wayne council Boy Scouts Am., 1980—. Mem. Am. Inst. Nutrition, Am. Physiology Soc., Am. Soc. Clin. Nutrition, Am. Chem. Soc., N.Y. Acad. Sci. Office: Med Coll of Ohio CS 10008 Toledo OH 43699

BIRKHOLZ, GABRIELLA SONJA, communication agency executive; b. Chgo., Apr. 11, 1938; d. Ladislav E. and Sonja (Kosner) Becvar; student U. Wis., 1969-71; B.A. in Communications and Bus. Mgmt., Alverno Coll., 1983. Editor, owner Fox Lake (Wis.) Rep., 1962-65, McFarland (Wis.) Community Life and Monona Community Herald, 1966-69; bur. reporter Waukesha (Wis.) Daily Freeman, 1969-71; community relations staff Waukesha County Tech. Inst., Pewaukee, Wis., 1971-73; public relations specialist JI Case Co., Racine, Wis., 1973-75, corp. publs. editor, 1975-80; v.p. and dir. publs. Image Mgmt., Valley View Center, Milw., 1980-82; pres. Communication Concepts, Unltd., Racine, 1982—; guest lectr. Alverno Coll., U. Wis.; adj. faculty U. Wis.-Parkside. Bd. dirs. Big Bros./Big Sisters Racine County; mem. Downtown Racine Devel. Corp., Downtown Racine Assn. Recipient awards Wis. Press Assn., Wis. Press Women, Nat. Fedn. Press Women, Internat. Assn. Bus. Communicators. Mem. Women in Communication, Internat. Assn. Bus. Communicators (accredited mem.; bd. dirs. 1982-85), Wis. Women Entrepreneurs, Nat. Assn. Female Execs., Sigma Delta Chi. Contbr. articles in field to profl. jours. Home: 901 Kingston Ave Racine WI 53402 Office: 312 Main St Racine WI 53403

BIRLA, SUSHIL KUMAR, automotive manufacturing executive; b. Sirsa, Haryana State, India, Oct. 1, 1943; came to U.S., 1969, naturalized, 1978; s. Mahabir Prasad and Lalita Devi (Mohunta) B.; B.S.M.E., Birla Inst. Tech. and Sci., Pilani, India, 1965; M.S.E.E., Wayne State U., 1971; m. Pramila Kela, Dec. 14, 1972; children—Jyoti, Asheesh, Preeti. Mng. partner Madhu Woodcraft Industries, Jaipur, India, 1965-66; supt. prodn. planning and control Hindustan Motors, Uttarpara, India, 1966-69; proposal, controls engr. Cross Co., Fraser, Mich., 1969-73; design engr. Excello Machine Tool Products, Detroit, 1973-76; staff devel. engr. Gen. Motors Mfg. Devel., GM Tech. Center, Warren, Mich., 1976—; mem. Machine Tool Task Force for U.S. Air Force Materials Lab., Dept. Def., 1978-80. Vol. probation aide Macomb County, Mich., 1976-77; vol. probation counselor Sterling Heights, Mich., 1979—; pres. Macomb County (Mich.) chpt. Mothers Against Drunk Drivers, 1983. Recipient Outstanding Contbn. award Dept. Def.; cert. mfg. engr. Mem. Soc. Mfg. Engrs., IEEE (sr.), ASME. Home: 42380 Buckingham Dr Sterling Heights MI 48078 Office: Gen Motors Mfg Devel Gen Motors Tech Center Warren MI 48090

BIRNBAUM, PHILIP HARVEY, business administrator educator; b. San Diego, Jan. 21, 1944; s. Louis and Ruth Laureen (Bay) B.; B.A., U. Calif.-Berkeley, 1965; Ph.D., U. Wash., 1975; m. Marlin Sue Van Every, Dec. 26, 1964; 1 son, Brian Philip. Personnel analyst Los Angeles County Civil Service Commn., 1965-67; teaching assoc. U. Wash., Seattle, 1972-74; asst. prof. bus. adminstrn. Ind. U., Bloomington, 1975-80, assoc. prof., 1980—; resident dir. J.F.K. Inst., Tiburg U., The Netherlands; vis. scholar Polish Acad. Scis. Served with USAF, 1967-71. NSF fellow, 1974-75; N.Y. Acad. Scis. fellow, 1981; sr. Fulbright scholar, U. Hong Kong, 1981-82; recipient DBA Assn. teaching award Ind. U., 1978. Mem. Acad. of Mgmt., AAAS, Am. Inst. for Decision Scis., Am. Sociol. Assn., Soc. for Social Study of Sci., Inst. of Mgmt. Sci., Internat. Assn. for Study of Interdisciplinary Research, Beta Gamma Sigma, Beta Alpha Psi, Sigma Iota Epsilon. Democrat. Methodist. Co-author: Organization Theory: A Structural and Behavioral Analysis; Modern Management Techniques for Engineers and Scientists; contbr. book reviews, articles to profl. publs., sect. to book, invited papers Germany, Poland, Eng., Can., Thailand, Hong Kong. Office: Grad Sch Bus Ind Univ Bloomington IN 47405

BIRNIE, EMALEE, real estate company executive; b. Grand Rapids, Mich., Nov. 7, 1947; d. Samuel Patterson and Eleanor Louise (Slykhouse) Gordon; m. Jan Gilbert Vonk, Sept. 9, 1966 (div. 1980); children—Charles Gordon, David Gerrit; m. John Matthews Birnie, Nov. 15, 1980. Student Grand Rapids Jr. Coll., 1965-67, Grand Valley State U., 1978; grad. Real Estate Inst., Mich. Assn. Realtors, 1978, Real Estate Alumni U. Mich., 1980. Teller, Old Kent Bank, Grand Rapids, 1967-69; sales assoc. R.J. Ide, Grand Rapids, 1974-76, Red Apple Real Estate, Grand Rapids, 1976-79; sales rep. Am. Title Ins. Co., Grand Rapids, 1979; sales mgr. Century 21 Packard, Grand Rapids, 1979-80, pres., broker, 1984—; owner, broker The Property Shop, Grand Rapids, 1980-83; instr. Grand Rapids Jr. Coll., 1977-78, Forest Hills Adult Edn., Grand Rapids, 1979-80; v.p. Broker's Council Century 21, Grand Rapids, 1984—; founder, sec. Alliance of Women Entrepreneurs, Grand Rapids, 1984—; faculty Entrepreneurial Inst., Grand Rapids, 1984. Mem. Nat. Assn. Realtors, Mich. Assn. Realtors, Grand Rapids Real Estate Bd. (chmn. edn. com. 1979-80), Women's Council Realtors (pres. 1980-83), Grand Rapids C. of C. Republican. Avocations: reading; travelling. Office: Century 21 Packard Inc 2135 Wealthy St SE Grand Rapids MI 49506

BIRO, JOHN EDWARD, mgmt. and mktg. analyst; b. Chgo., Sept. 1, 1952; s. Arpad Anthony and Dorothy Jane (Hock) B.; B.S., U. Ill., Chgo., 1974. With United Parcel Service, Northbrook, Ill., 1972-76; dir. Seeker Enterprises, Oak Brook, Ill., 1976—; ops. mgr. Automobile Purchasing Specialists, Chgo., 1977—; pres. Midwest Diversified Services Inc., Oak Brook, 1978—; pres. Affiliated Nat. Systems, Inc., Oak Brook, 1980—; dir. Smart Buyers Shopping Systems Inc., Schaumburg. Mem. Am. Mgmt. Assn. Roman Catholic. Home: 430 N Brainard St LaGrange Park IL 60525 Office: 999 Plaza Dr Schaumburg IL 60195

BIRO, NICHOLAS GEORGE, public relations executive; b. Budapest, Hungary, Nov. 30, 1929; came to U.S., 1936; s. Nicholas M. and Margaret (Mager) B.; m. Joan Brynda, Feb. 20, 1965; children—Michael, Nancy, David. B.S., U. Ill., 1952. Editor Billboard Pub. Co., Chgo., 1957-65; dir. pub. relations Sta. WCFL, Chgo., 1965-66; v.p. Martin Janis & Co., Chgo., 1966-69; dir. pub. relations Wilson Foods Corp., Oklahoma City, 1969-77; group dir. R.J. Reynolds, Inc., Winston-Salem, N.C., 1977-78; v.p. Holiday Inns, Inc., Memphis, 1978-81; sr. v.p. Ruder Finn & Rotman, Chgo., 1981—. Vice chmn. small bus. group United Way, Memphis, 1979; mem. faculty adv. com. Oklahoma City U., 1973-77; bd. dir. Oklahoma City Beautiful, 1975-77; chmn. pub. relations com. Am. Meat Inst., 1974-76. Served to 1st lt. USMCR, 1952-54. Mem. Pub. Relations Soc. Am. (accredited, pres. Oklahoma City chpt. 1975, chmn. 5 state S.W. dist. 1976-77, chmn. Chgo. chpt. counselor acad. 1984, chmn. profl. devel. com. 1985), Nat. Investor Relations Inst. (v.p., dir. Chgo. chpt. 1985). Office: 444 N Michigan Ave Chicago IL 60601

BIRR, DANIEL HOWARD, interior architect; b. Coffeyville, Kans., Nov. 22, 1951; s. Daniel Harry and Olive Jean (Perkins) B.; m. Christina M. Carden. B.Interior Architecture, Kans. State U., 1974. Registered architect. Designer, G Interiors, Rapid City, S.D., 1974-76; space planner/designer Alpha Techne, Rapid City, 1976-80; project designer Comml. Builders of Kans., Wichita, 1980-81, Pizza Hut Inc., Wichita, 1981—. Mem. AIA. Episcopalian. Home: 3607 N Clarence Wichita KS 67204 Office: Pizza Hut Inc 9111 E Douglas Wichita KS

BISCHOF, MILTON J., JR., architect; b. St. Louis, Aug. 17, 1929; s. Milton and Catherine (Kersting) B.; m. Evelyn M. Bright, June 28, 1952; children—Deborah Ann, Lauri Ann, Mark Richard. B.Arch., Washington U., 1952; Energy Auditor, U. Mo., 1978. Registered architect, Mo. Architect, Bernard Bloom, St. Louis, 1954-57; architect, ptnr. Manske-Dieckmann & Ptnrs., St. Louis, 1957-70; architect, v.p. mktg. Hellmuth, Obata & Kassabaum, St. Louis, 1970-79; architect, dir. mktg. The GCE Internat. Inc., Cons. Engrs., St. Louis, 1979-83; exec. v.p. Russell & Axon, Engring-Architects-Planners, Inc., 1983—. dir. Home Fed. Savs. & Loan. Chmn., Met. St. Louis Sewer Dist., 1978—; mem. St. Louis County Council, 1968-76; pres. St. Louis County Grand Jury Assn.; co-chmn. City-County Bi-centennial Commn., 1976; mem. adv. bd. St. Louis Council YWCA; mem. Regional Commerce & Growth Assn. Served with U.S. Army, 1952-54. Recipient various awards C. of C., 1975, 77, Am. Revolution Bi-centennial Adminstrn., 1977, Conv. and Visitors Bur. Greater St. Louis, 1977. Mem. AIA, Mo. Council Architects, St. Louis AIA, Engrs. Club St. Louis, Soc. Mktg. Profl. Services, Soc. Am. Mil. Engrs. Republican. Roman Catholic. Clubs: Media, Mo. Athletic, St. Louis Advt., St. Louis Ambassadors. Contbr. articles to profl. jours. Home: 6 Elmcrest Acres Saint Louis MO 63138 Office: 319 N 4th St Saint Louis MO 63102

BISCIGLIA, ANTHONY FRANK, junior high school administrator; b. Kenosha, Wis., May 28, 1938; s. Joseph Thomas and Marie (Bruno) B.; m. Rita Frances Savaglio, Aug. 22, 1964; children—Anthony J., Susan M., Linda A. B.S. in History, U. Wis.-Madison, 1960; M.S. in Guidance, Marquette U., 1968, doctoral student in Sch. Adminstrn., 1980—. Elem. tchr. Milw. Pub. Schs., Wis., 1962-68, elem. sch. guidance counselor, 1968-69; elem. sch. principal Kenosha Unified Sch. Dist., Wis., 1969-75, jr. high sch., 1975—; bd. mem. Wis. Dept. Pub. Insts. State Superintendents Adv. Com. on the Deaf, 1984—; sch. chmn. Effective Schs. Research Lance Jr. High Sch., Kenosha, 1984—; co-chmn. Modern Tech. Conf. for Educators, U. Wis., 1983. Bd. dirs. Kenosha United Way, 1972-79, pres., 1975-76, campaign chmn., 1974-75; campaign chmn. Archbishop's Funds Appeal, Kenosha, 1970-71; mem. commonwealth parent com. Carthage Coll., 1984; v.p. pub. relations Kenosha Civic Vet.'s Parade com., 1984, v.p., 1985; chmn. Kenosha Plus Task Force, 1985. Recipient Distng. Service award Girl Scouts of U.S., Kenosha, 1974. Mem. Kenosha Schs. Administrn Assn. (pres. 1976), Kenosha Industrial Task Force (bd. mem. 1984—), Kenosha Econ. Devel. Commn., Nat. Soc. Study Edn., U. Wis. Alumni Club (pres. 1977), Rotary West Found. (bd. dirs. 1981-86), Marquette U. Alumni Assn. (rep. for Kenosha, 1982), Phi Delta Kappa, Delta Sigma Phi. Roman Catholic. Lodge: Rotary (pres. 1982, Paul Harris award 1983, bd. mem. 1973—, rep. SE Wis. in New South Wales, Australia 1972). Home: 4470 Harrison Rd Kenosha WI 53142 Office: Bullen Jr High Sch 2804 39th Ave Kenosha WI 53142

BISEL, HARRY FERREE, physician, educator; b. Manor, Pa., June 17, 1918; s. George Culbertson and Mary Stotler (Ferree) B.; B.S., U. Pitts., 1939, M.D., 1942; m. Sara Louise Clark, Oct. 30, 1954; children—Jane, Clark, Harold. Intern, U. Pitts. Med. Center, 1942-43; resident, U. Pa. Grad. Sch. Medicine, 1948-49, Harvard Med. Sch. (Boston City Hosp.), 1949-50; resident physician Meml. Sloan Kettering Cancer Center, 1951-53; cancer coordinator medicine U. Pitts., 1953-63; chmn. div. med. oncology Mayo Clinic, Rochester, Minn., 1963-72, sr. cons. div. med. oncology, 1972—, prof. oncology Mayo Med. Sch., 1967—; cons. Nat. Cancer Inst. Served to capt. MC USNR, 1943-47. Recipient Philip S. Hench Disting. Alumnus award, U. Pitts. Sch. Medicine, 1972. Mem. Am. Soc. Clin. Oncology (past pres.), Soc. Surg. Oncology, Am. Assn. Cancer Edn., Am. Assn. Cancer Research. Presbyterian. Rotarian. Home: 1223 Skyline Dr Rochester MN 55902 Office: Mayo Clinic Rochester MN 55905

BISH, MILAN DAVID, land development company executive, diplomat; b. Harvard, Nebr., July 1, 1929; s. Charles and Mabel Etta (Williams) B.; B.A., Hastings Coll., 1951; m. Allene R. Miller, Mar. 17, 1951; children—Cynthia, Linda, Charles. Pres., Bish Machinery Co., Grand Island, Nebr., 1965-73, Mid-Continent Enterprises, 1974—; pres. Bish Inc., investment cons., Grand Island; pres. Comml. Nat. Bank, Grand Island; state chmn. Nebr. Republican Party, 1971-72; mem. Rep. Nat. Com., 1971-72; mem. Rep. Exec. Com. Nebr., 1972-74; Nebr. chmn. Citizens for Reagan, 1976; chmn. Nebr. del. Rep. Nat. Conv., 1976; mem. steering com. Citizens for the Republic; Nebr. chmn. Reagan for Pres., 1980; Reagan-Bush polit. dir., fall 1980; mem. presdl. transition team, Dec. 1980-Jan. 1981; U.S. ambassador to Barbados, St. Vincent, St. Lucia, Dominica, Antigua and Barbuda; spl. rep. for pres. of U.S. to various Caribbean nations; mem. Nebr. Hwy. Commn., 1979—. Named Ambassador of Nebr. Mem. C. of C. (pres. 1977). Mason (32 deg., Shriner), Elk, Eagle, Rotarian (dist. gov. 1970-71). Clubs: Riverside Golf, Liederkranz, Platt Deustch. Home: 2012 W Louise St Grand Island NE Office: PO Box 2156 Grand Island NE 68802

BISHARA, SAMIR EDWARD, orthodontist, educator; b. Cairo, Oct. 31, 1935; s. Edward Constantin and Georgette Ibrahim (Kelela) B.; B. in Dental Surgery, Alexandria U., Egypt, 1957, diploma in Orthodontics, 1967; M.S., U. Iowa. 1970, certificate in Orthodontics, 1970, D.D.S., 1972; m. Cynthia Jane McLaughlin, July 3, 1975; children—Dina Marie, Dorine Gabrielle, Cherine Noelle. Practice gen. dentistry, Alexandria, Egypt, 1957-68, specializing in orthodontics, Iowa City, Iowa, 1970—; fellow in clin. pedodontics Guggenheim Dental Clinic, N.Y.C., 1959-60; resident in oral surgery Moassat Hosp., Alexandria, Egypt, 1960-61, mem. staff, 1961-68; asst. prof. Coll. Dentistry, U. Iowa, Iowa City, 1970-73, asso. prof., 1973-76, prof., 1976—. Fellow Am. Coll. Dentists, Internat. Coll. Dentists. Mem. ADA, Am. Assn. Orthodontics, Internat. Dental Fedn., AAAS, Internat. Assn. for Dental Research, Am. Cleft Palate Assn., Assn. of Egyptian Am. Scholars, Omicron Kappa Upsilon, Sigma Xi. Contbr. articles on orthodontics to profl. jours. and book chpts. Home: 1014 Penkridge Dr Iowa City IA 52240 Office: Orthodontic Dept College of Dentistry Iowa City IA 52242

BISHOP, ALLEN JOHN, savs. and loan assn. exec.; b. Berwyn, Ill., Feb. 17, 1948; s. John Edward and Mildred Alice (Chovancek) B.; B.S., Eastern Ill. U., 1971, M.B.A., 1972; m. Christine Ann Orbeck, June 8, 1974. With Clyde Savs. and Loan Assn., North Riverside, Ill., 1973—, dir. mktg., 1975-76, asst. v.p., dir. mktg., 1976-80, v.p., dir. mktg., 1980—; instr. Inst. Fin. Edn., Morton Coll., 1973-74. Mem. Savs. Assn. Council (dir.), Savs. Instns. Mktg. Soc. Am. (dir. chpt. 1, v.p. 1981, pres. 1982 Mktg. award 1976), Eastern Ill. U. Alumni Assn. Chgo. Fin. Advertisers, Delta Chi, Delta Mu Delta. Roman Catholic. Home: 9645 W 57th St Countryside IL 60525 Office: 7222 W Cermak Rd North Riverside IL 60546

BISHOP, BUDD HARRIS, museum official; b. Canton, Ga., Nov. 1, 1936; s. James Monroe and Eula (Ponder) B.; A.B., Shorter Coll., Rome, Ga., 1958; M.F.A., U. Ga., 1960; m. Julia Crowder, Nov. 30, 1968. Art dir. Ensworth Sch., Nashville, 1961-63; lectr. art history Vanderbilt U., 1962; dir. creative services Transit Advt. Assn., Inc., N.Y.C., 1964-66; dir. Hunter Mus. Art, Chattanooga, 1966-76; dir. Columbus (Ohio) Mus. Art, 1976—; juror, lectr. and cons. in field. Trustee Columbus Acad., 1976-82; mem. adv. bd. Jr. League Hist. Restoration Project, 1977—; trustee Franklin Art Fund; chmn. Commn. for Public Art Projects, 1980-82. Recipient Gov.'s award Tenn. Arts Commn., 1971; Alumni award Shorter Coll., 1979. Mem. Assn. Art Mus. Dir. Ohio Museums Assn., Midwest Museums Assn., Am. Assn. Museums. Club: Review (Columbus). Lodge: Rotary. Office: 480 E Broad St Columbus OH 43215

BISHOP, GEORGE FRANKLIN, political social psychologist; b. New Haven, July 26, 1942; s. George Elwood and Mary Bridget (Trant) B.; B.S. in Psychology, Mich. State U., 1966, M.A., 1969, Ph.D., 1973; m. Lucille C. Minervini, Aug. 14, 1971; 1 dau., Kristina Marie. Instr., Multidisciplinary Social Sci. Program, Mich. State U., E. Lansing, 1972-73; asst. prof. Dept. Sociology and Anthropology, U. Notre Dame (Ind.), 1973-75; research assoc. behavioral sci. lab. U. Cin., 1975-77, sr. research assoc., 1977—, co-dir. Greater Cin. Survey, U. Cin., 1978-82, dir., 1982—, assoc. prof. polit. sci., 1982—; research cons. Community Mental Health/Mental Retardation bd., Hamilton County, Ohio, 1979-81. Served with U.S. Army, 1961-62. NSF grantee, 1977-84; Nat. Council Sr. Citizens grantee, 1977-78. Mem. Midwest Assn. Pub. Opinion Research (pres. 1977-78), Am. Assn. Pub. Opinion Research, Am. Polit. Sci. Assn., Midwest Polit. Sci. Assn., Soc. Advancement of Social Psychology, World Assn. Pub. Opinion Research (treas. 1983—). Sr. editor: The Presidential Debates: Media, Electoral, and Policy Perspectives, 1978; sr. author various articles profl. jours. Home: 459 Karenlaw Ln Cincinnati OH 45231 Office: ML 132 Univ of Cin Cinnati OH 45221

BISHOP, GILBERT CLARE, surgeon; b. Leonard, Mich., Sept. 30, 1899; s. Frank Leo and Genevieve (Thomas) B.; student Oberlin Coll., 1919-21, U. Mich., 1918-23; M.D., U. Chgo. (Rush), 1926; postgrad. U. Pa., 1944-45; m. Jane Lucile Wise, Sept. 22, 1925; children—Robert, Dean, Barbara, Donald, Malcolm, David. Intern, Henry Ford Hosp., Detroit, 1925-26; student surgery Elizabeth Hosp., Vienna, Austria, 1927-28, Allgemeines Krankenhaus, Vienna, 1930-31; founder, adminstr. Bishop Hosp., Almont, Mich., 1935-59; resident in surgery Guthrie Clinic, Sayre, Pa., 1945-46; surgeon-in-chief Community Hosp., Almont, 1959-70; ret., 1973. Diplomate Am. Bd. Surgery. Fellow A.C.S.; mem. AMA, Mich. Med. Soc., Detroit, Flint acads. surgery. Republican. Congregationalist. Home: 5331 Van Dyke Rd Almont MI 48003

BISHOP, JACK LAWSON, JR., management consultant; b. Rockville Centre, N.Y., Dec. 3, 1939; s. Jack Lawson and Elizabeth Janet (Blee) B.; B.S. in Chem. Engring., U. Colo., 1961; Ph.D., U. Ill., 1972; m. Donna Norine Leavens, June 24, 1962; children—Elizabeth Anona, Jack Lawson, Kathleen Anne, Caroline Donna Van Alstine. Product devel. engr., mgmt. scis. specialist Dow Corning Corp., Midland, Mich., 1961-72; instr. Central Mich. U., Mt. Pleasant, 1969-70; mgr. mgmt. scis. Ky. Fried Chicken, Louisville, 1972-73; mgr. econ. and gen. research May Dept. Stores Inc., St. Louis, 1973-76; mgr. strategic and econ. planning Brunswick Corp., Skokie, Ill., 1976-83; prin. Bishop Assocs., Evanston, Ill., 1983—; adv. Purchasing Mgmt. Assn. Chgo.; producer monthly TV programs. Mem. exec. com., community relations com. Midwest regional office Am. Friends Service Com., 1978-83; exec. bd. dirs., treas. Midwest Friends Housing Corp., 1980-82; mem. policy com. Friends Com. on Nat. Legislation. Mem. Ops. Research Soc. Am., Chgo. Council Fgn. Relations, Inst. Mgmt. Sci., Am. Econ. Assn., Am. Statis. Assn., Nat. Assn. Bus. Economists, Am. Inst. Decision Scis. Author: Insect, Disease and Weed Control, 1972; Practical Emulsions, 1968. Home: 2000 Sherman Ave Suite 202 Evanston IL 60201 Office: 2000 Sherman Ave Suite 100 PO Box 311 Evanston IL 60204

BISHOP, JERRY DANIEL, import-export executive; b. Bay City, Tex., Feb. 13, 1943; s. Edward Jerome and Dorothy Elizabeth (Ford) B.; m. Yolanda Rivera Tugues, Jan. 6, 1980; 1 stepdau., Linda D. Hollyfield. Student U. Nebr.-Omaha, 1962-64, M.S. in Polit. Sci. Pub. Adminstrn., 1972; B.A. in Mil. Sci. Affairs, U. Ky., 1966; postgrad. U. Tex., 1966; Ph.D. in Internat. Trade Devel. (hon.), U. Burma, 1979. Mgr. Beemaster Apiaries, Snelling, Calif., Bellevue, Nebr., 1972-75; queen breeder, bus. ptnr. Beemaster, Inc., Arroyo Grande, Calif. and Bellevue, Nebr., 1975-77, Asbury-Bishop Apiaries, Merced, Calif., 1977-78; mgr., ptnr. Cal-Alaskan Apiaries, Azusa, Calif., 1978-80; pres. Cal-Alaskan Internat., Manna Foods Co., La Verne, Calif., 1980—; ptnr. Golden Harvest, Inc., Omaha, 1982—; chmn., bd. dirs. No. Am. Internat. Trading & Devel. Assocs. Ltd., Bermuda, 1981—; master, instr. Kung-fu Karate Martial Arts U. Ky., also Mil. Tng. Ctrs., 1964-70; skydiving instr. U.S. Parachute Assn., Lexington, Ky., 1964-70; scuba and marine diving instr. Internat. Skindiver's Assn., St. Petersburg, Fla., 1964-70. Served to capt. Intelligence Corps, U.S. Army, 1967-70; Vietnam. Decorated Bronze Star, Bronze Star with V, Combat Air Medal with two clusters, Purple Heart (U.S.); Chung-Mi-Bos-Tin, Meritorious Service medal, Cross of Gallantry with gold, silver and bronze stars; Medal of Honor 1st class, Nat. Police merit medal 2d class, Civic-Action medal with palm, Revolutionary-Devel. medal with palm, Psychol.-Warfare Ops. medal of honor, Staff-Service medal 1st class, Air medal with silver star (Vietnam). Mem. Acad. Polit. Sci., UN Assn., Am. Beekeeping Fedn., So U.S. Trade Assn., Nat. Assn. Export Mgmt. Co's., U. Ky. Alumni Assn., Nebr. Honey Producers Assn., Calif. Honey Producers Assn., Republican. Clubs: Internat. Skindiver's Assn., U.S. Parachute Assn., Biblical Archaeology Soc. (Washington). Inventor-designer, heating equipment for honeybees in agr., 1975; styrafoam shipping container for overseas bee shipments, 1977; developer 1st comml. disease-resistant strain of honey bees, 1975-77, 1st internat. computer trading-exchange, 1984; inventor new computer programming lang. Simplicity, 1984. Office: No Am Internat Trading & Devel Assocs Ltd Bermuda also Houston TX

BISHOP, JOYCE ANN ARMENTROUT, counselor, educator; b. West Mansfield, Ohio, June 16, 1935; d. Frederic J. and Marjorie Vere (Stephens) Armentrout; A.B., Albion Coll., 1956; M.A., Western Mich. U., 1969; children—Belinda Lee, Thomas James. Tchr. phys. edn. Walled Lake (Mich.) Jr. High Sch., 1956-58; tchr. adult edn. pub. sch., Milw., 1959-65, Lakeview Schs., Battle Creek, Mich., 1966—; dir. student activities, Olivet (Mich.) Coll., 1969-71, also asst. prof., counselor; counselor Kellogg Community Coll., Battle Creek, 1971—. Sec. adult bd. Teens Inc., 1965-68; bd. dirs., pres. Battle Creek Day Care Ctrs., 1984-85. Mem. Com. to Rev. Articulation Matters (charter), Mich. Assn. Coll. Registrars and Admissions Officers, AAUW, Am., Mich. personnel and guidance assns., Am. Sch. Counselors Assn., Am. Coll. Personnel Assn., Am. Assn. Collegiate Registrars and Admissions Officers (interassn. liaison with Am. Assn. Community and Jr. Colls.), Mich. Assn. Coll. Registrars and Admissions Officers (com. on coll. articulation, pres. 1979-80), Beta Beta Beta, Alpha Chi Omega. Lutheran. Clubs: Altrusa, Battle Creek Road Runners (v.p.). Home: 721 Eastfield Dr Battle Creek MI 49015 Office: 450 North Ave Battle Creek MI 49016

BISHOP, MARSHALL EDWARD, chemistry educator; b. Amsterdam, N.Y., Aug. 3, 1942; s. Raymond Murle and Muriel Katherine (Johnson) B.; B.A., Oakland U., 1964, M.S., 1967; Ph.D., SUNY, 1975; m. Jacqueline Ann Winter, July 13, 1968; children—Eric Alan, Kathryn Ann. Exptl. spectroscopist Gen. Motors Corp., Pontiac, Mich., 1964-66, 67-69; instr. chemistry Oakland U., Rochester, Mich., 1968; research fellow SUNY, Albany, 1969-75; instr. chemistry, spl. projects cons. to pres. Southwestern Mich. Coll., Dowagiac, 1975—, coordinator chem. tech. program; instr. continuing edn. Oakland U., 1968-69. Mem. adv. com. Southwestern Mich. Coll. Mus.; mem. sci. cons. com. Sci. for Citizens, Western Mich. U. Named Student of Distinction, Oakland U., 1961, 62, 64; NDEA Title IV grad. fellow, 1970-73; cert. profl. chemist Am. Inst. Chemists. Mem. Am. Chem. Soc., Chem. Soc. London, Mich. Coll. Chemistry Tchrs. Assn., Mich. Assn. Computer Users in Learning, Mich. Hist. Soc., Cass County Hist. Soc., Dowagiac Hist. Soc., Am. Canal Soc., Sigma Xi. Republican. Methodist. Club: Grange. Contbr. articles to profl. jours. Home: 54255 Twin Lakes Rd Dowagiac MI 49047 Office: Dept Chemistry Cherry Grove Rd Dowagiac MI 49047

BISHOP, MARY JO, editor, writer; b. Washington, Ohio, Mar. 27, 1956; d. Dean Eugene and Mary Belle (Keener) Burris; m. William Michael Bishop, Sept. 23, 1980. B.S. in Journalism, summa cum laude, Ohio U., 1978. Lifestyle editor Eagle-Gazette, Lancaster, Ohio, 1978; bus. editor Marion Star, Ohio, 1978-81, Sunday editor, asst. city editor, 1981-82; publ. editor Mich. Tech. U., Houghton, 1982—; editor Mag. Mich. Tech Research, 1983—. 1984. Mem. Council Advancement and Support Edn. Dem. Roman Catholic. Avocations: cross-country skiing. Office: Mich Tech Univ Houghton MI

BISHOP, RALPH JOHN, III, anthropologist, bookseller; b. Cleve., July 20, 1944; s. Ralph John and Margaret (Young) B.; B.A., Cornell U., 1966; M.A., Northwestern U., 1971, Ph.D., 1974; m. Leslie Anne Griffin, Sept. 23, 1972; children—John Kenneth, Russell Glen. Instr., Roosevelt U., Chgo., 1972-75, 79—; mgr. trade dept. Kroch's & Brentano's, Chgo., 1975-81; founder, pres., Bookchoice, Evanston, Ill., 1981—; prin. Ralph J. Bishop Ednl. Resources, 1984—; lectr. Northwestern U., 1985—; scholar-in-residence, Vicksburg, Miss., 1985-86. Fellow Soc. Applied Anthropology; mem. Nat. Assn. for Practice of Anthropology (co-founder), Am. Anthropol. Assn., Council on Anthropology and Edn. Episcopalian. Office: 1430 Crain St Evanston IL 60202

BISHOP, ROBERT DEANE, nuclear engineer; b. Emporia, Kans., June 23, 1946; s. Clarence Dwight and Cora Frances (Foley) B.; m. Sheila Roberts, Dec. 18, 1976; B.S., Kans. State U., 1969; M.B.A., U. Chgo., 1977. Engr. in tng. State of Kans., 1969; nuclear engr. Commonwealth Edison Co., Dresden sta., 1971-75, tech. staff supr. LaSalle County sta., 1975-80, asst. supt. sta., 1980-85, services supt., 1985—. Served to 1st lt., inf. U.S. Army, 1970-71. Decorated Bronze Star medal; licensed nuclear reactor operator. Mem. Am. Nuclear Soc. Home: 113 Prairie Dr Minooka IL 60447 Office: LaSalle County Station Box 240 Marseilles IL 61341

BISHOP, ROBERT LEWIS, pianist-vocalist, songwriter, publisher; b. Peoria, Ill., Nov. 8, 1955; s. Thomas James and Mary Ellen Bishop. Grad. Spalding Inst., Peoria, 1973. Founder, pres. LeVec Pub. Co., Peoria, 1976—; mem. cons. faculty Ill. State U., pianist/vocalist, 1975; rec. artist, 1977—; composer numerous songs, 1974—, including If I Can't Hold You in My Arms, 1975; Lady in My Corner, 1976; Stay, 1977; Middle of the Night, 1980; Winner numerous music competitions as pianist and singer, Midwest, N.Y., Calif.; Coll. Performing Arts grantee Harvard U., 1973. Mem. Am. Fedn. Musicians, ASCAP. Republican. Roman Catholic.

BISHOP, WARNER BADER, business executive; b. Lakewood, Ohio, Dec. 13, 1918; s. Warner Brown and Gladys (Bader) B.; A.B., Dartmouth Coll., 1941, M.B.A., Amos Tuck Grad. Sch., 1942; grad. Advanced Mgmt. Program, Harvard U., 1955; m. Katherine Sue White, Dec. 15, 1944; children—Susan, Judith, Katharine, Jennifer; m. Barrie Osborn, Feb. 4, 1967; children—Wilder, Brooks; m. 3d, Susan Bragg Howard, June 3, 1982. With Archer-Daniels-Midland Co., Cleve., 1946-59, successively sales rep., export mgr., sales mgr., divisional gen. mgr., asst. v.p., 1946-56, v.p., 1956-59; pres. Fed. Foundry Supply Co., 1957-59, Wyodak Clay & Chem. Co., 1957-59, Basic, Inc., until 1963; pres. Union Fin. Corp., Cleve., 1963-74; pres. Union Savs. Assn., 1963-74, chmn., 1970—; chmn., pres. Transohio Fin. Corp., Cleve., 1974-84; dir. Port Clinton Nat. Bank, Akron Savs. Assn., Cin. Savs. Assn., United Savs. Assn.; trustee Med. Met. Cleve. Sec. Foundry Ednl. Found., 1956-60; gen. campaign mgr. Cleve. Area Heart Soc., bd. chmn., 1960-61; mem. corp. Fenn Coll.; bd. dirs. Ohio Heart Soc.; chmn. Highland Redevel. Corp., 1963-68; pres. Council High Blood Pressure, 1964-69. Served to lt. USNR, 1942-45; comdg. officer escort vessels. Clubs: Union, India House (N.Y.C.); Meadow (Southampton, N.Y.); Chagrin Valley, Union, Tavern (Cleve.); Bath and Tennis, Everglades (Palm Beach, Fla.). Contbr. articles to trade jours. Address: Two

Bratenahl Pl Suite 140 Bratenahl OH 44108 also 300 S Ocean Blvd Palm Beach FL 33480

BISSEY, WILLIAM KARL, bank exec.; b. Columbus, Ind., Aug. 18, 1940; s. Harry Carl and Mary M. (Fleming) B.; B.S. (Ford fellow), Ind. U., 1962, M.B.A., 1964. Purchasing agt. Arvin Industries, Inc., Columbus, 1964-68; instr. Ohio No. U., Ada, 1968-73; credit analyst Mchts. Nat. Bank, Indpls., 1974-78; asst. v.p., mgr. internat. econ. research Am. Fletcher Nat. Bank, Indpls., 1978—. Served with U.S. Army, 1963-64. Mem. Alpha Kappa Psi, Delta Sigma Phi, Beta Gamma Sigma, Omicron Delta Epsilon. Presbyterian. Home: 8305 Sobax Dr Indianapolis IN 46268 Office: 111 Monument Circle Indianapolis IN 46277

BITELER, CORNELIUS ROYAL, electronic co. exec.; b. Flint, Mich., Oct. 20, 1931; s. Royal Cornelius and Maude Melvia B.; B.S. in Mech. Engring., Purdue U., 1956; grad. Gen. Electric Mfg. Tng. Program, 1959; m. Jean Elaine Moyer, Sept. 27, 1958; children—Mark Christian, Dawn Christina. Mfg. engr., Gen. Electric, 1956-62, Bohn Aluminum, 1962-66; gen. foreman All Steel Equipment, 1966-69; asst. plant mgr. North Electric, Kenton, Ohio, 1969-75; v.p. Gleason Assos., Chgo., 1975-77; ops. analyst GTE Automatic Electric, Northlake, Ill., 1977-78, mgr. mfg. ops. analysis, 1978-80, productivity mgr., 1980—. Active Yokefellows Internat. Home: 141 Joyce Chicago Heights IL 60411 Office: 400 N Wolf Northlake IL 60164

BITHER, PAUL PRESTON, optometrist, educator; b. Houlton, Maine, Oct. 14, 1954; s. Preston Maurice and Christie (Gavel) B.; m. Carol Louise Alexander, Sept. 22, 1984. B.A., Colby Coll., 1976; D.Optometry, New Eng. Coll. Optometry, Boston, 1980. Resident in low vision VA Hosp. Blind Rehab. Ctr., West Haven, Conn., 1980-81; asst. prof. Sch. Optometry, Ind. U., Indpls., 1981—. Mem. Am. Optometric Assn., Ind. Optometric Assn., Am. Assn. Workers for the Blind, Ind. Low Vision Soc. (ednl. chmn.), Central Ind. Optometric Soc. Methodist. Office: Indiana Univ Optometry Clinic 1802 N Illinois St Indianapolis IN 46202

BITKER, MARJORIE MARKS (MRS. BRUNO VOLTAIRE BITKER), writer, editor; b. N.Y.C., Feb. 9, 1901; d. Cecil Alexander and Rachel (Fox) Marks; A.B. magna cum laude (Caroline Duror Meml. fellow), Barnard Coll., 1921; M.A., Columbia U., 1922; m. James C. Jacobson, 1922 (div. 1942); children—Emilie J. Jacobi, Margaret J. Strange, Elizabeth J. Hahn; m. 2d, John C. Mayer, Oct. 24, 1942 (dec. June 1945); m. 3d, Bruno Voltaire Bitker, Oct. 10, 1957 (dec. 1984). Free lance writer, 1922—; editor Farrar Straus, N.Y.C., 1946-47, G.P. Putnam's Sons, N.Y.C., 1947-53, David McKay Co., N.Y.C., 1953-55; now editorial cons., book reviewer, feature writer. Lectr., Hunter Coll., Coll. City N.Y., 1949-53; Women's Chair for Humanistic Studies, Marquette U., 1972-73. Mem. pres.'s council Alverno Coll., 1975-77; bd. visitors U. Wis., 1962-68; alumnae trustee Barnard Coll., 1964-68, Barnard-in-Milw.; co-founder, past pres., hon. bd. dirs. in perpetuity Bookfellows: Friends Wis. Libraries. Recipient Barnard Alumnae Recognition award, 1978. Mem. AAUW, Women's Nat. Book Assn., Bookfellows Milw. (pres. 1971-73, dir.), Phi Beta Kappa. Author: (novels) Gold of Evening, 1975, A Different Flame, 1976; contbr. articles, and book revs. to mags. and newspapers. Address: 2330 E Back Bay Milwaukee WI 53202

BITTING, PHYLLIS DIANE, real estate broker; b. Kosciusko County, Ind., Oct. 11, 1935; d. Earl Vance and Edna Ruth (Powers) Davis; student Ind. U., 1971, 75-77; m. James Duane Bitting, June 26, 1953; 1 son, Andrew Vance. Real estate broker Center Realty, Warsaw, Ind., 1973—; operator real estate appraisal service, 1980—; sec., treas. Kosciusko Bd. Realtors, Warsaw, 1975-76, v.p., 1977-78, pres., dir., 1978—; state sec. by law com. Ind. Assn. Realtors, Indpls., 1977—. Trustee, Walnut Creek United Methodist Ch., Warsaw, 1977—. Mem. Nat. Bd. Realtors, Ind. Realtors Assn. (state dir. 1979-82, state public relations and communications com. 1981—, mem. honor soc.), DAR (regent Anthony Nigo chpt. 1974-75). Home: Route 2 Box 88 Warsaw IN 46580 Office: Route 2 Box 88 Warsaw IN 46580

BITTINGER, BILLY MOODY, educator, consultant; b. Frankfort, Ky., June 7, 1933; d. Lloyd Franklin and Margaret Maria (Carter) Moody; m. Dale Austin Bittinger, June 25, 1951; children—Margaret Dale, Mary Laurance, Bradley Lloyd, Mark Carter. Student Ohio Wesleyan U., 1950-51, Hardin Simmons Coll., 1960-61, Valley Coll., 1966-67; B.A., Wright State U., 1969, M.Ed., 1972. Lic. tchr., Ohio. Tchr., Mad River Twp. Schs., 1969-74, curriculum coordinator K-12, 1974-77, dir. secondary edn., 1978-81, dir. curriculum, 1981—; cons. in field; presentor ednl. conf. Wright State U. Ednl. Leadership Adv. Council. Mem. Southwestern Ohio Assn. for Supervision and Curriculum Devel. (pres. 1982-83), Ohio Assn. for Supervision and Curriculum Devel. (pres. 1984—), Assn. for Supervision and Curriculum Devel. (div. 1983—), Phi Delta Kappa, Kappa Alpha Theta. Republican. Contbr. articles to profl. jours. Office: 801 Harshman Rd Dayton OH 45431

BITTLE, BONNIE JEAN, communications executive; b. Elkhorn, Wis., June 30, 1950; d. Peter John and Betty Jean (Kuhl) Robertson; m. James Michael Bittle, July 3, 1981; m. Irvinn Nathan, Dec. 23, 1973; (div. May 1979); 1 child, Peter David. Student U. Wis.-Whitewater, 1968-73; student DePaul U., 1984—. Cert. industry cons. communications. Broker, Town and Country Properties, Appleton, Wis., 1976-78; market adminstr. Wis. Tel. Co., Appleton, Wis., 1978-79; account exec. Wis. Tel., Milw., 1979-81; account exec. Southwestern Bell Co., Houston, 1981-83; account exec. industry cons. AT & T Communications, Chgo., 1983—. Bd. dirs. Friends of the Library, Appleton, 1978. Methodist. Mem. Nat. Assn. Female Exec. Office: AT & T Communications 1701 East Woodfield Rd Suite 220 Schaumburg IL 60195

BIVINS, BRACK ALLEN, surgeon, researcher; b. Nashville, Nov. 28, 1943; s. Brack Amos and Marjorie Rose (Belcher) B.; m. Brenda Kingston, Feb. 3, 1973; children—Brack David, Berkley Kingston. B.S., Western Ky. U., 1966; M.D., U. Ky., 1970. Diplomate Am. Bd. Surgery. Resident in surgery U. Ky. Med. Ctr., Lexington, 1970-77; asst. prof. surgery U. Ky. Coll. Medicine, Lexington, 1977-80, assoc. prof. surgery, 1980-82; div. head trauma surgery, dir. nutrition support service Henry Ford Hosp., Detroit, 1983—. Contbr. articles to profl. jours. Served to lt. col. USNG, 1970-81. Am. Cancer Soc. Clin. fellow, 1972; F.A. Coller Soc. Travelling fellow, 1976; recipient Am. Soc. Hosp. Pharm. Research award, 1976; Parenteral Drug Assn. Research award, 1976. Fellow A.C.S., mem. Central Surg. Assn., Am. Assn. Surgery Trauma, Am. Soc. Parenteral and Enteral Nutrition, Soc. Surgery Alimentary Tract, Sigma Xi, Alpha Omega Alpha. Avocations: golf; hunting; fishing; Office: Henry Ford Hosp 2799 W Grand Blvd Detroit MI 48202

BIXBY, RICHARD WILLIAM, human resources specialist; b. Waterloo, Iowa, June 1, 1941; married, 2 children. B.A. in Phys. Edn. and Secondary Edn., Wartburg Coll., Waverly, 1963; M.A., U. Wis., Platteville, 1970. Tchr., coach, high sch., Manitowoc, Wis., 1963-65, Lancaster, Wis., 1965-69; asst. prof., coach U. Wis., Platteville, 1969-70; dir. guidance Sheboygan Falls (Wis.) Dist. #1, 1970-79; mgr. employee devel. John Deere Product Engring., Waterloo, 1979-84, human resource devel. program mgr., 1984—. Mem. Am., Wis. personnel and guidance assns., Am. Soc. Tng. and Devel., Am. Football Coaches Assn., Wis. Coaches Assn. Certified sch. counselor. Named Football Coach of Year, 1966, 68, 69, Wis. Outstanding Educator of Year, 1975. Home: 220 Angie Dr Cedar Falls IA 50613 Office: PO Box 3500 Waterloo IA 50704

BJELDANES, MITCHELL NORMAN, consulting engineer; b. Sheboygan, Wis., Apr. 22, 1933; s. Ole Mitchell and Angela P. (Mersch) B.; m. Marion Francis Zuehlsdorf, Aug. 31, 1957; children—Lynn Francis, Steven Mitchell. B.M.E., U. Minn., 1960. Registered profl. engr., Minn., Wis., N.D., Mich., Conn., Kans. Chief nuclear engr. No. States Power Co., Mpls., 1960-74; project mgr. Black and Veatch Cons. Engrs., Kansas City, Mo., 1974—. Served with USN, 1951-55, Korea. Mem. Am. Nuclear Soc., ASME. Republican. Lutheran. Avocations: Golf; hunting. Home: 14907 Rosehill Rd Olathe KS 66062 Office: Black and Veatch Engrs and Architects 1500 Meadowlake Pkwy Kansas City MO 64114

BJORGAARD, ETHEL LOUISE, lawyer; b. Kansas City, Kans., July 18, 1957; d. Ernest Oscar and Wanda Christine (Malcom) B.; 1 dau., Jennifer Christine Bjorgaard-Garlow. B.G.S. in History, Kans. U., 1978; J.D., Washburn U., 1981. Bar: 1981. Sole practice, Bonner Springs, Kans., 1981—. Mem. Wyandotte County Bar Assn., Nat. Fedn. Republican Women, Bus. and Profl. Women (Young Careerist 1982). Baptist. Home: Rural Route 1 Bonner Springs KS 66012 Office: Law Office of Lou Bjorgaard 118A Warner Bonner Springs KS 66012

BJORK, CARL KENNETH, SR., chemical company executive, chemist, patent agent; b. Burlington, Iowa, Mar. 16, 1926; s. Algot Eric and Madeline Esther (Anderson) B.; m. Joyce Catherine Dornacher, Sept. 25, 1947; children—Stephanie, Sherri, Carl, Catherine, Jeffrey, Jeremy, Michelle. B.A., Augustana Coll., 1947; M.A., DePauw U., 1950; Ph.D., U. Ky., 1953. Registered U.S. patent agent. Research chemist Internat. Mineral & Chem. Corp., Mulberry, Fla., 1953-54; researcher, developer, engr. Dow Chem. Co., Midland, Mich., 1954-59, patent agent, 1959-63, group leader patent dept., 1963-70, mgr. bioproducts sect., 1970-78, mgr. internat. patent sect., 1978—. Author (booklet) Record Books, Their Generation, Maintenance, and Safekeeping, 1983. Contbr. articles to profl. jours. Patentee in field. Commr. Parks and Recreation, Midland, 1970-79. Mem. Am. Chem. Soc. (mem. Nat. Com. Patents and Related Matters, 1978—, vice chmn. Div. Chemistry and the Law, 1983-84, chmn., 1984—). Sigma Xi, Alpha Xi Sigma. Lutheran. Avocations: outdoor sports; travelling. Home: 2712 Lambros Dr Midland MI 48640 Office: Patent Dept Dow Chem Co 1776 Bldg Midland MI 48640

BJORK, KENNETH O., ret. educator, editor; b. Enderlin, N.D., July 19, 1909; s. Theodore S. and Martha (Arneson) B.; B.A., St. Olaf Coll., 1930; M.A., U. Wis., 1931, Ph.D., 1935; Ph.D. (hon.), U. Oslo, 1976; m. Thora Lie, Apr. 1, 1960; children—Kenneth T., Arnold L.; children by previous marriage—Herum P., Mark P.; stepchildren—Ellen, Jon T. Asst. prof. history U. Mont., Havre, 1935-37; asst. prof. St. Olaf Coll., Northfield, Minn., 1937-39, asso. prof., 1939-44, prof., 1944-74, prof. emeritus, 1974—, chmn. dept. history, 1960-65; vis. asso. prof. U. Nebr., Lincoln, summers 1938, 40, U. Mich., Ann Arbor, 1940-41, U. Wis., Madison, 1943-44; Rockefeller Found. rep., prof. U. East Africa, 1965-67; editor Norwegian-Am. Hist. Assn., Northfield, 1960-80, editor emeritus, 1980—, pres., 1973-75. Chmn. Gov.'s Com. on Refugee Relief, State of Minn., 1955-58. Decorated knight 1st class Order St. Olav (Norway). Social Sci. Research Council fellow, 1947-48, 51-52; Fulbright scholar, 1959-60. Democrat. Lutheran. Author: Saga in Steel and Concrete, 1947; West of the Great Divide, 1958; editor books; contbr. articles to profl. jours. Address: 500 W Woodley Apt 302 Northfield MN 55057

BJORNCRANTZ, CARL EDUARD, retail company executive; b. Evanston, Ill., Sept. 16, 1944; s. Carl Gustav and Julia Elizabeth (Merriam) B.; m. Leslie Francis Benton, Aug. 31, 1968; 1 child, William Benton. A.B. in Polit. Sci., Colgate U., 1966; M.B.A., U. Va., 1970. With Sears Roebuck & Co., Chgo., 1970—, exec. personnel mgr., 1976-78, group catalog mktg. mgr., 1978-80, nat. mgr. circulation, 1981-82, nat. mgr. advt., circulation, prodn. and distbn., market devel., 1982—; cons. Talent Assistance Program, Chgo., 1970-74; instr. retail mktg. Northeastern Ill. U., Chgo., 1978-79; speaker in field. Bd. dirs. Internat. Visitor's Ctr., Chgo., 1974-80; fin. chmn. Chgo. Father's Day Council, 1976—. Recipient Maroon citation Disting. Alumni award Colgate U., 1981. Mem. Direct Mktg. Assn. (exec. bd. 1982—), Mail Order Assn. Am. Republican. Methodist. Clubs: North Shore Country (Glenview, Ill.); Metropolitan (Chgo.). Lodge: Brotherhood of Knights of Vine. Avocations: tennis; platform tennis; golf; study of wine. Home: 2146 Forestview Rd Evanston IL 60201 Office: Sears Roebuck & Co Sears Tower Chicago IL 60684

BJORNDAL, ARNE MAGNE, endodontist; b. Ulstein, Norway, Aug. 19, 1916; s. Martin I. and Anne B.; B.S., State Coll. Volda, 1939; D.D.S., U. Oslo, 1947; D.D.S., U. Iowa, 1954, M.S., 1956; m. Katharine G. Benson, Jan. 12, 1952; children—Katharine, Kari, Lee. Instr., Coll. Dentistry U. Oslo, 1948-50, 51-53; intern Forsyth Dental Infirmary, Boston, 1950-51; mem. faculty U. Iowa, Iowa City, 1954—, prof., 1964—, founder, head dept. endodontics, 1956-80. Served to maj. Army NG, 1963-70. Decorated King Hakon 7th medal (Norway); diplomate Am. Bd. Endodontics; Fulbright scholar, 1950-51. Fellow Am. Coll. Dentistry; mem. ADA (service fgn. countries award 1979), Iowa Dental Assn. (life), Am. Assn. Endodontics, N.Y. Acad. Sci., Omicron Kappa Upsilon. Republican. Lutheran. Clubs: Optimists, Elks. Author: Anatomy and Morphology of Human Teeth, 1983. Home: 3 Washington Pl Iowa City IA 52240 Office: Coll Dentistry U Iowa Iowa City IA 52242

BJUGAN, LESLIE ARNOLD, social worker; b. Mpls., Mar. 5; s. Leonard Nels and Amanda Jane (Carley) B.; B.S., Moorhead State Coll., 1949; M.A. in Public Adminstrn., U. Minn., 1971, M.S.W., 1980; m. Maxine Lorraine Bolser, Nov. 21, 1944; children—Carley Jo Bjugan Watts, Jody Lynn Everson. Social worker Polk County Welfare Dept., Crookston, Minn., 1949-50; various positions in mental health, child welfare Hennepin County Welfare Dept., Mpls., 1950-77; dir. Crest Homes, Am. Baptist Homes for the Midwest, 1977-78; pre-petition screener Office County Atty., Hennepin County Dept. Community Services, Mpls., 1978-81; social worker VA Med. Ctr., Mpls., 1981—. Mem. Model City Protective Service Adv. Com., 1971-73; adv. U.S. Navy Recruiting Sta., Mpls., 1980; vol. Assn. for Alzheimer's Disease and Related Disorders, 1980. Served with USN, 1942-45. Recipient Outstanding Community Service commendation Am. Acad. Human Services, 1975, citation of honor Hennepin County, 1976. Mem. Nat. Assn. Social Workers, Gerontol. Soc. (charter mem. Minn. chpt.), Nat. Council on Aging. Democrat. Mem. Christian Ch. (Disciples of Christ). Home: 9700 Portland Ave S Bloomington MN 55420 Office: Outpatient Clinic VA Fort Snelling Bldg 17 Saint Paul MN 55111

BLAAUW, RUSSELL WAYNE, legislative liaison; b. Chgo., July 20, 1944; s. John Joseph and Bernice (Rabusch) B.; m. M. Bernadette Lynch, June 20, 1981. B.A. So. Ill. U., 1968, M.S., 1974. Legis. budget analyst Ill. Ho. of Reps., Springfield, 1972-77; legis. fiscal analyst La. Legis. Fiscal Office, Baton Rouge, 1977-78; exec. dir. Commn. on Welfare Law Revision, Springfield, 1978-80; assoc. dir. Washington office, Ill. Legislature, 1980-81; legis liaison Dept. Mental Health Devel. Disabilities, Springfield, 1981—; cons. Ill. Council on Nutrition, Springfield, 1980, Legis. Adv. Commn. on Welfare, Springfield, 1975-77; speaker-panelist Nat. Legal Services Corp., Kansas City, Mo., 1977. Vol. Big Brother/Big Sister of Sangamon County, Springfield, 1979-78, bd. dirs. 1979-80; vol. Family Court East Baton Rouge Parish, 1978-79; co-dir. Elem. Ed. Tutoring Program, Springfield, 1976-77. Avocations: traveling; photography; skiing; canoeing; running. Home: 220 Cranmer Dr Springfield IL 62704 Office: Ill Dept of Mental Health & Developmental Disabilities 401 Spring St Springfield IL 62706

BLACH, PHYLLIS ANN, pharmacist; b. Yuma, Colo., June 12, 1954; d. Sherman Clair and Joan Elaine (McCormick) B. B.S. in Pharmacy, Creighton U., 1977. Regis. pharmacist, Mo. Staff pharmacist St. John's Hosp., Springfield, Mo., 1977-78, Dillon's Pharmacy, Springfield, 1978-80, head pharmacist, 1980—. Mem. Am. Pharm. Assn. Republican. Roman Catholic. Avocations: snow skiing; catamaran sailing; bicycling. Home: 4521 S Graystone Ct Springfield MO 65807

BLACK, ASA CALVIN, JR., anatomist, educator; b. Clarksville, Tenn., Jan. 2, 1943; s. Asa C. and Josephine Elizabeth Black; m. Cynthia Woods, Apr. 3, 1971; B.A., Vanderbilt U., 1965, Ph.D. in Anatomy (NIH predoctoral fellow), 1974. Asso., U. Iowa, Iowa City, 1973-74, NIH postdoctoral fellow Coll. Medicine, 1974-75, asst. prof. dept. anatomy Coll. Medicine, 1975—; instr. anatomy Vanderbilt U., Nashville, 1972-73. Mem. AAAS, Am. Assn. Anatomists, Am. Chem. Soc., Am. Soc. Neurochemistry, Brit. Brain Research Assn., European Brain Behavior Soc., Internat. Soc. Neurochemistry, Sigma Xi. Contbr. chpts. to books, articles to biol. jours. Home: 537 Terrace Rd Iowa City IA 52240 Office: U Iowa Coll Medicine 1-402 Basic Science Bldg Dept Anatomy Iowa City IA 52242

BLACK, BERT, state administrator, lawyer; b. N.Y.C., Mar. 6, 1956; s. Thomas and Evelyn Gretel (Florio) B. B.A. in Biology, SUNY-Buffalo, 1976; J.D., U. Minn., 1979. Bar: Minn. 1979, U.S. Dist. Ct. Minn. 1979. Reporter Adv. Task Force on Minn. Corp. Law, Mpls., 1979-81; dir. corp. div. State of Minn., St. Paul, 1981—; lectr. various continuing legal edn. programs, 1981-84. Chmn. Democratic Farmer Labor 59th Dist., Mpls., 1982-84; chmn. Mpls. Dem. Farmer Labor Party, 1983—; mem. state central com. Minn. Dem. Farm Labor, 1982—. Mem. Citizens League, Ams. for Dem. Action (bd. dirs. local chpt. 1982—). Jewish. Home: 3524 Pillsbury Ave S Minneapolis MN 55408 Office: State of Minn Corp Div 180 State Office Bldg St Paul MN 55155

BLACK, CHARLES EDWARD, physician; b. Schneider, Ind., Mar. 24, 1922; s. Louie Alexander and Erma May Bell (Allison) B.; m. Judith M. Brawner, Aug. 18, 1951; children—Theo W., Timothy E., Beverly S., Patricia E., Daniel A., Jennifer M. B.S., Ind. U.-Bloomington, 1948, M.D., 1951. Diplomate Am. Bd. Ob-Gyn. Intern, Ind. U.-Indpls., 1951-52; resident in Ob-Gyn, U. Ill.-Chgo., 1955-58; pvt. practice medicine, Hammond, Ind., 1953-55, specializing in Ob-Gyn, Gary, Ind., 1958-59, Monroe, Mich., 1963—; mem. staff Ob-Gyn, Toledo Clinic, Ohio, 1959-63; chief dept. Ob-Gyn Mercy Meml. Hosp., Monroe, Mich., 1965—, Flower Hosp., Toledo, 1960-63. Sec., v.p., pres. Monroe Pub. Schs., 1970-78. Served with AUS, 1940-45. Fellow Am. Coll. Ob-Gyn; mem. Monroe County Med. Soc. (past pres.). Methodist. Lodge: Masons. Home: 5412 Timber Ln Monroe MI 48161 Office: 721 N Macomb St Monroe MI 48161

BLACK, DANIEL ALBERT OLEISKY, industrial engineer; b. Mpls., Jan. 17, 1954; s. Albert Samuel and Shirley Jean (Peterson) Oleisky B.; B.Math. with distinction, U. Minn., 1975, M.S. with honors, 1976; m. Vicki Ann Reed, Dec. 18, 1976. Loan collector First Nat. Bank Mpls., 1975-76; quality control engr. Graco Inc., Mpls., 1976-79; quality assurance mgr. Webster Electric Co. div. Sta-Rite Industries, Inc., Racine, Wis., 1979-80, mgr. planning and prodn. control, 1980-81; mfg. supt. Fairbanks Morse Engine div. Colt Industries, Beloit, Wis., 1981-82, prodn. and inventory control mgr., 1982-84; mgr. materials program Rockwell Internat, Automotive, Troy, Mich., 1984—. Advisor, Jr. Achievement, Mpls., 1977-79; mem. ARC Safety Services, Mpls., 1968-75; trustee Minn. Phi Gamma Delta Ednl. Found., 1975-80; bd. dirs. Phi Gamma Delta House Corp., 1975-80. Named Minn. Young Engr. of Yr., 1978; recipient U. Minn. Outstanding Student Leadership award, 1975; Phi Gamma Delta Weum and Devaney awards, 1975; cert. quality engr., cert. reliability engr., cert. prodn. and inventory mgmt. Mem. Am. Soc. Quality Control, Am. Inst. Indsl. Engrs., Am. Prodn. and Inventory Control Soc., Automotive Industry Action Group. Home: 4279 Whisperway Troy MI 48098 Office: 2135 W Maple Rd Troy MI 48084

BLACK, DENISE LOUISE, educator; b. Ft. Sill, Okla., Apr. 16, 1950; d. Nelson Arthur and Virginia Mary (Smith) Taber; A.A., Community Coll. of Allegheny County, Boyce campus, 1970; B.S., Slippery Rock State Coll., 1972; M.A., Eastern Mich. U., 1978; m. Robert Paul Black, Aug. 12, 1972; children—Paula Ann, Jennifer Lea. Adult edn. tchr. ecology and physiology Huron Valley Schs., Milford, Mich., 1973-74; tchr. gen. biology and earth sci. Howell (Mich.) Public Schs., 1974-75; adult edn. tchr. life sci. Holly (Mich.) Area Schs., 1978-80, Hartland (Mich.) Consol. Schs., 1978—; tchr. biology Walled Lake (Mich.) Consol. Schs., 1980-83. Coach, Milford Youth Athletic Assn., 1973-85. Cert. guidance and counselor. Mem. Nat. Assn. Biology Tchrs., Mich. Assn. Biology Tchrs., Beta Beta Beta, Phi Kappa Phi, Phi Theta Kappa. Methodist. Home: 2576 Shady Ln Milford MI 48042

BLACK, JAMES ROBERT, industrial engineer; b. Davenport, Iowa, Feb. 17, 1948; s. Robert James and Anne Louise (Johnson) B.; B.S. in Indsl. Engring. (Fisher Governor scholar 1968-69, Maytag scholar 1969-70), Iowa State U., 1970, M.S., 1971; M.B.A., U. Chgo., 1976; m. Mary Ann O'Malley, June 5, 1971; 1 son, Robert Joseph. Indsl. engr. Inland Steel Co., East Chicago, Ind., 1971-76, sr. indsl. engr., 1976-77; indsl. engring. supr. Clark Equipment Co., Jackson, Mich., 1977-78; indsl. engring. mgr. Harrison Plant, Graphic Systems div. Rockwell Internat., Rockford, Ill., 1978-83; corp. supr. indirect work measurement Kohler Co. (Wis.), 1983—; co-leader, guest lectr. Am. Mgmt. Assn., 1979-80. Cons. Project Business div. Jr. Achievement, 1980; pack com. chmn. Cub Scouts, Boy Scouts Am., 1980-83, Webelos leader, 1982-83, asst. scoutmaster, 1983-84, scoutmaster, 1984-85; asst. soccer coach, 1981-83, coach, 1984. Mem. Am. Inst. Indsl. Engrs. (sr. mem.; treas. 1979-80, pres. 1980-81, past pres. 1981-82, seminar speaker 1984). Contbr. articles to profl. jours. Home: 4500 Prairie View Rd Sheboygan WI 53081 Office: Kohler Co 44 Highland Dr Kohler WI 53044

BLACK, JOHN BUNYAN, civil engineer; b. Kansas City, Mo., Dec. 25, 1927; s. Ernest Bateman and Faye Irene (Bunyan) B.; B.S., U. Kans., 1949; m. Marilyn McConnell, Feb. 2, 1957; children—Katherine Faye, Helen Winslow, Robert Winslow II. Asst. resident engr. Black & Veatch, cons. engrs., Los Alamos, 1949-50; engr. Alvord, Burdick & Howson, engrs., Chgo., 1953-65; project mgr. Greeley & Hansen, engrs., 1966-67, asso., 1968-74; owner John B. Black Cons. Engrs., 1975—. Served with AUS, 1951-52. Registered profl. engr., Calif., Iowa, Ill., Mich., Mo., Man., N.Y., Ind., Wis., Va. Fellow ASCE (com. water laws 1977—; dir. Ill. sect. 1977-78, sec. 1979-80, pres. 1982-83); mem. Am. Water Works Assn. (life), Central States Water Pollution Control Assn., Man. Assn. Profl. Engrs., Sigma Alpha Epsilon. Republican. Episcopalian. Club: Colo. Mountain (Boulder). Contbr. articles to profl. publs. Home: 595 Washington Ave Glencoe IL 60022 Office: 2 N Riverside Plaza Chicago IL 60606

BLACK, J(OHN) ROY, agricultural economics educator, consultant; b. Great Falls, Mont., Aug. 21, 1941; s. John Wing and Kathleen (Bartley) B.; m. Lois J. Karl. B.S., Mont. State U., 1963; Ph.D., U. Minn., 1975. Asst. prof. agrl. econs. Mich. State U., East Lansing, 1970-76, assoc. prof., 1976-80, prof., 1980—; cons. Internat. Harvester, Chgo., 1975, Am. Cyanamid, Princeton, N.J., 1984, Tex. A&M U., College Station, 1984. Contbr. articles to profl. jours. Advisor, Fed. Extension Service, U.S. Dept. Agr., 1975, 77, 78, 80, 85, Gov.'s Conf. on Mich. Agr., Lansing, 1979, Fact Finding Com., Mich. Legislature, Lansing, 1979-80, Fed. Crop Ins. Adv. Com., Washington, 1982. Recipient John A. Hannah award Mich. State U., 1972, Superior Service award U.S. Dept. Agr., 1974, Outstanding Contbr. award Am. Assn. Crop Insurers, 1984. Mem. Am. Agrl. Econs. Assn. (Outstanding Specialist award 1979), Am. Statis. Assn., Am. Assn. Animal Scientists, Sigma Xi, Gamma Sigma Delta. Avocations: golf; tennis; gardening. Home: 3861 New Salem Okemos MI 48864 Office: Mich State U East Lansing MI 48824

BLACK, LOUIS ANTHONY, physician; b. Kenton, Ohio, July 29, 1920; s. Louis Walker and Mary (Lundy) B.; B.A., Ohio State U., 1941, M.D., 1944; student U. Pa. Grad. Sch. Medicine, 1958-59; m. Roberta Mae Johnson, Sept. 29, 1942; children—Linda Ann Black Terwilliger, Thomas J. Intern, Los Angeles County Gen. Hosp., 1944-45; pvt. practice medicine specializing in internal medicine, Kenton, Ohio, 1948-59, specializing in internal medicine and cardiology, Kenton, 1959—; mem. staff Hardin Meml. Hosp., Kenton. Pres., Central Ohio Heart Assn., 1971-72; mem. Kenton Sch. Bd., 1956-60. Served to capt. MC AUS, 1946-47. Diplomate Am. Bd. Internal Medicine. Mem. Ohio State Med. Assn. Office: Philips Med Park 405 N Main St Kenton OH 43326

BLACK, MARY ELLEN STEWART, jewelry store executive, buyer, bookkeeper; b. Ind., Sept. 21, 1903; d. George Thomas and Sarah Victoria (Demaree) Stewart; m. E.J. Black, July 7, 1928; children—George H., Vincent L. Student Central Bus. Coll., 1922. Stenographer, J.C. Hume Fuel Saver Corp., Indpls., 1921-22; receptionist funeral home, Osgood, Ind., 1928-47; stenographer, bookkeeper Prudential Ins. Co., Madison, Ind., 1922-28; mgr. Black's Jewelry Store, Lawrenceville, Ill., 1947—. Recipient Retailer of Yr. award Lawrence County C. of C., 1983-84. Mem. Lawrence County Bus. and Profl. Women's Club (named Woman of Yr. 1983-84), D.A.R. Republican. Methodist. Lodge: Order Eastern Star. Avocation: reading.

BLACK, NEAL FRANCIS, trade association executive, editor, columnist; b. Preston, Iowa, Jan. 14, 1928; s. Edwin Brandon and Gertrude (Mertens) B.; m. Margaret Mary Gerlach, Jan. 22, 1951; children—Rebecca Ann, John Joseph, Angela Mary, Patrick Neal. B.A., State U. Iowa, 1949. Reporter, farm editor Courier, Waterloo, Iowa, 1949-57; mng. editor Nat. Hog Farmer, St. Paul, 1957-72, editor, 1973-79; pres. Livestock Conservation Inst., South St. Paul, 1980—; editor Internat. Pigletter, South St. Paul, 1981—; columnist Hog Farm Mgmt., Mpls., 1985—. Mem. U.S. Sec. Agr.'s Adv. Com. on Fgn. Animal and Poultry Diseases. Served as M/sgt. U.S. Army, 1950-52, Korea. Recipient Meritorious Service award Livestock Conservation Inst., 1979, Service to Pork Industry award Nat. Hog Farmer, 1982, award for Service Am. Assn. Swine Practitioners, 1983, Meat Industry Advancement award Am. Meat Inst., 1984. Republican. Roman Catholic. Home: 2825 Vilas Ln Eagan MN 55121 Office: Livestock Conservation Inst 239 Livestock Exchange Bldg South Saint Paul MN 55075

BLACK, ROBERT STITT, public utility executive; b. Newport News, Va., Oct. 31, 1951; s. William Holmes and Catherine Louise (Stitt) B.; B.A. cum laude in Econs., Kenyon Coll., 1973; M.B.A. in Fin., U. Mich., 1975; m. Christine Carr, Aug. 17, 1974; children—Robert Stitt II, Michael Todd. Regulatory affairs analyst El Paso Natural Gas Co. (Tex.), 1975-76; asst. to pres. Waterville Gas and Oil Co. (Ohio), 1976-77, pres., 1977—; spokesman for gas cos. at legis. and regulatory agy. hearings, 1978—. Mem. Ohio Gas Assn. (trustee 1981—, v.p. 1983-84, pres. 1984-85), Waterville C. of C. (dir. 1977-78, pres. 1983). Republican. Episcopalian. Clubs: Toledo, Waterville Rotary (bd.

dirs. 1981-84, pres. 1985-86), Belmont Country, Masons. Home: 26623 W River Rd Perrysburg OH 43551 Office: PO Box 259 Waterville OH 43566

BLACK, STEVEN BITTERS, plastic surgeon; b. Rochester, Minn., June 4, 1946; s. Albert Seward and Madge Marie (Bitters) B.; B.S., U. Nebr., Lincoln, 1969, M.D., Omaha, 1972; m. Joyce Marie Graupmann, July 14, 1979; children—Jonathan Steven, Kathryn Joyce; 1 dau. by previous marriage, Michelle Marie. Diplomate Am. Bd. Plastic Surgery, Am. Bd. Surgery. Intern, Mayo Clinic, Rochester, Minn., 1972-73; surg. resident Mayo Grad. Sch. Medicine, Rochester, 1973-77, plastic surgery resident, 1977-79; practice medicine specializing in plastic surgery, Omaha, 1979—; instr. U. Nebr. Coll. Medicine; mem. staff Bishop Clarkson Meml., Nebr. Meth., Immanuel, Children's hosps. (all Omaha), U. Nebr. Hosps. and Clinics. Fellow ACS; mem. AMA, Nebr. Med. Assn., Met. Omaha Med. Soc., Am. Soc. Plastic and Reconstructive Surgeons. Contbr. articles to med. jours. Home: 1306 S 218th St Elkhorn NE 68022 Office: Suite 219 Doctors Bldg 44th and Farnam Sts Omaha NE 68131

BLACK, THOMAS ALEXANDER, JR., dentist; b. Pitts., Jan. 10, 1943; s. Thomas Alexander and Griselda (Best) B.; B.S., Purdue U., 1965; D.M.D., Washington U., St. Louis, 1975, M.B.A., 1975; m. Sandra Jean Gredys, May 10, 1969. Prodn. supr. Proctor & Gamble, St. Louis, 1968-69; with Mallinckroft Chem. Works, St. Louis, 1969-71; gen. practice dentistry, Marlborough, Mo., 1976—; clin. instr. dentistry Washington U., St. Louis, 1976-78, asst. prof., 1978-82; staff dentist Bethesda Dilworth Meml. Home. Deacon, mem. choir Webster Groves (Mo.) Presbyn. Ch.; pres. York Village Assn. Served to capt. C.E., AUS, 1965-68. Mem. Am., Mo. dental assns., Greater St. Louis Dental Soc., Am. Philat. Soc., Soc. Am. Mil. Engrs., Xi Psi Phi, Am. Revenue Assn., other philat. socs., Alpha Phi Omega. Club: Rotary (dir.). Home: 70 York Dr Brentwood MO 63144 Office: 8460 Watson Rd Suite 112 Marlborough MO 63119

BLACK, WALTER KERRIGAN, lawyer; b. Birmingham, Ala., Jan. 27, 1915; s. Timuel Dixon and Mattie (McConner) B.; A.B., U. Ill., 1939; LL.B., John Marshall Law Sch., 1952; m. Dorothy E. Wickliffe, July 2, 1950 (dec. Apr. 1983); m. 2d, Buthynah Ammar, June 23, 1983. Admitted to Ill. bar, 1952; partner firm McCoy & Black, Chgo., 1952-59; partner firm McCoy Ming & Leighton, Chgo., 1959-64; partner firm McCoy, Ming & Black, Chgo., 1965-77; prin. firm Mitchell & Black, Chgo., 1977—; village atty. Robbins (Ill.), 1952-69, 81—, East Chicago Heights (Ill.), 1954-69, 77—; hearing examiner Ill. Fair Practices Commn.; arbitrator Am. Arbitration Assn., 1971—. Mem. governing bd. Cook County Legal Assistance Found., Inc. Served with AUS, 1942-46. Mem. Ill., Chgo., Cook County bar assns., Kappa Alpha Psi. Mem. A.M.E. Ch. (atty., trustee). Home: 2231 E 67th St Chicago IL 60649 Office: 343 S Dearborn St Chicago IL 60604

BLACK, WILLIAM A., See *Who's Who in America,* 43rd edition.

BLACK, WILLIAM G., clergyman. Bishop So. Ohio region Episcopal Ch., Cin. Office: 412 Sycamore St Cincinnati OH 45202*

BLACKBURN, CATHERINE ELAINE, lawyer, pharmacist; b. Columbus, Ohio, Nov. 5, 1953; d. Robert Jerome and Patricia Ann (Buchman) B. B.S. in Pharmacy with high honors, U. Ky., 1978; J.D. with honors, Ohio State U., 1982. Bars: Ohio 1982, U.S. Dist. Ct. (so. dist.) Ohio 1983. Chief pharmacist Louisa Community Hosp., Ky., 1978; pharmacist Riverside Meth. Hosp., Columbus, Ohio, 1978-82; law clk. Michael F. Colley Co., L.P.A., Columbus, 1980-82, assoc., 1982—; workshop leader Ohio Drug Studies Inst., Columbus, 1982, 83, 14th Nat. Conf. on Women and the Law, Washington, D.C., 1983; lectr./speaker Iowa Trial Lawyers Assn., Iowa City, 1984. Staff writer, editor Ohio State U. Law Jour., 1980-82. Trustee Women's Outreach for Women, Columbus, 1982-85. Mem. Assn. Trial Lawyers Am. (lectr./speaker 1982—), Ohio Acad. Trial Lawyers, Columbus Bar Assn., Ohio Bar Assn., Am. Soc. Pharmacy Law, Order of Coif, Phi Beta Kappa, Rho Chi Soc. Democrat. Home: 2648 Summit St Columbus OH 43202 Office: Michael F Colley Co LPA 536 S High St Columbus OH 43215

BLACKBURN, JAMES HOMER, physicist; b. Mansfield, Ohio, Nov. 25, 1929; s. Adam Homer and Eleanor Jane (Jones) B.; m. Marla Kay Bose, Mar. 17, 1957; children—Heidi J., Jamie T. B.Sc., Ohio State U., 1955, M.Sc., 1957. Scientist, Los Alamos Sci. Lab., 1957-65; asst. dir. lab. Stanford Research Inst., Menlo Park, Calif., 1965-69; prin. engring. fellow Honeywell, Inc., Hopkins, Minn., 1970—. Contbr. articles to profl. jours. Served with USN, 1948-52. Mem. Am. Phys. Soc., Combustion Inst., AAAS Am. Def. Preparedness Assn. Home: 4003 Hull Rd Minnetonka MN 55343 Office: 600 2d St NE Hopkins MN 55343

BLACKFAN, CYRUS LINTON, specialty chemicals company executive; b. Phila., Sept. 10, 1935; s. Cyrus Linton and Ethel Carrel (Hobensack) B.; m. Barbara Lee Hance, Dec. 17, 1960; children—Barbara May, John Cyrus, David Lyle. B.S., Lafayette Coll., 1957; postgrad. Northwestern U., 1973, MIT, 1982. Sales engr. Union Carbide, N.Y.C., Cleve., 1957-66; product mgr. B.F. Goodrich, Cleve., 1967-72, mgr. new products, 1972-74, mgr. corp. planning, Akron, Ohio, 1974-75, dir. planning, Cleve., 1977-78, v.p. mktg., Akron, 1978-80, v.p., gen. mgr., 1980-82; pres. Chemionics Corp., Tallmadge, Ohio, 1982—. Mem. Akron Regional Development Bd., 1982—. Served to 1st lt. U.S. Army, 1957-59. Mem. Comml. Devel. Assn., Am. Chem. Soc. Republican. Presbyterian. Club: Cascade. Contbr. articles to profl. jours.

BLACKMAN, ANNE DUFF, newspaper editor; b. San Francisco, Oct. 2, 1936; d. Price Hope and Pauline (Lehning) Duff; m. Edward Galbreath Blackman, III, Aug. 31, 1956; children—Paula Blackman Thrasher, Edward Galbreath IV, Cristan, Tallie. Student Lindenwood Coll., St. Charles, Mo., 1954-55, Vanderbilt U., 1955-57, U. Nebr., 1973. Advt. mgr. Goldstein/Chapmans, Omaha, 1967-75; mng. editor Gautier (Miss.) Ind., 1975-79, Citizen Newspapers, St. Louis, 1980—. Mem. adv. com. Pascagoula (Miss.) Schs., 1976-79; mem. festival com. Judevine Ctr. Autistic Children, St. Louis, 1983—; editor stories for St. Louis chpt. Am. Cancer Soc., 1981. Recipient Outstanding Woman award St. Louis-Marketplace Forum, 1983; named 1st Mardi Gras Queen, Gautier Jaycees, 1979; Best Story award Miss. Press Assn., 1979; 1st place Media award Nat. Mental Health Assn., 1981; 2d place award Suburban News Assn., 1980; 1st Media award St. Louis chpt. Am. Cancer Soc., 1982. Mem. Creve Coeur Area C. of C. (dir. 1981—, v.p. 1984—), Chesterfield C. of C. Home: 15344 Thistlebriar Ct Chesterfield MO 63017 Office: Citizen Newspapers 12520 Olive Blvd Creve Coeur MO 63141

BLACKMAN, KENNETH EUGENE, microbiologist; b. Ilion, N.Y., June 30, 1938; s. Harold Scott and Ida Blackman LaFayette; m. Doris Rowen, Apr. 20, 1963; childen—Deborah, Colleen, Teresa. B.S., Georgetown U., 1963; M.S., U. Cin., 1967, 1970. Research assoc. with Dr. Albert Sabin, Children's Hosp. Research Found., Cin., 1963-65; instr. Coll. Medicine, U. Cin., 1967-70; scientist Meloy Labs., Inc. subs. Revlon Corp., Springfield Va., 1970-71, tech. mgr. Life Scis. div., 1971-73, dir. Life Scis. div., 1973-76; v.p. Life Scis. div., 1976-81; v.p. sci. devel. Gibco div. Dexter Corp., Chagrin Falls, Ohio, 1981-83; v.p. comml. devel. Life Technologies, Inc., 1983-84; exec. v.p., chief operating officer BW Biotec, Chgo., 1984—. Served with USAF, 1956-60. Recipient Pres.'s award Am. Soc. Microbiology, 1969; Spl. award Am. Cancer Soc., 1969; U. Cin. scholar, 1965-70; NIH summer fellow, 1961-63. Mem. Am. Soc. Microbiology, Tissue Culture Assn., Licensing Execs. Soc. Roman Catholic. Contbr. articles to profl. jours. Home: 35036 Cannon Rd Chagrin Falls OH 44022 Office: BW Biotec 3570 Avondale Ave Chicago IL 60618

BLACKMAR, CHARLES BLAKEY, judge; b. Kansas City, Mo., Apr. 19, 1922; s. Charles Maxwell and Eleanor (Blakey) B.; A.B. summa cum laude, Princeton U., 1942; J.D., U. Mich., 1948; m. Ellen Day Bonnifield, July 18, 1943 (dec. 1983); children—Charles A., Thomas J., Lucy E. Blackmar Alpaugh, Elizabeth S., George B.; m. Jeanne Stephens Lee, Oct. 5, 1984. Bar: Mo. 1948. Practiced in Kansas City; mem. firm Swanson, Midgley, Jones, Blackmar & Eager, and predecessors, 1948-66; professorial lectr. U. Mo. at Kansas City, 1949-58; prof. law St. Louis U., 1966-82, prof. emeritus, 1982—; apptd. judge Supreme Ct. of Mo., 1982—; spl. asst. atty. gen. Mo., 1969-77; labor arbitrator. Chmn., Fair Pub. Accommodations Commn. Kansas City (Mo.), 1964-66; mem. Commn. Human Relations Kansas City, 1965-66; mem. Jackson County Republican Com., 1952-58, Mo. Rep. Com., 1956-58. Served to 1st lt., inf., AUS, 1943-46. Decorated Silver Star, Purple Heart. Mem. Am. Law Inst., Nat. Acad. Arbitrators, Mo. Bar (spl. lectr. insts.), Disciples Peace Fellowship, Order of Coif, Phi Beta Kappa. Mem. Disciples of Christ Ch. Author (with Volz and others) Missouri Practice, 1953, West's Federal practice Manual, 1957, 71; (with Devitt) Federal Jury Practice and Instructions, 1970, 3d edit., 1977; contbr. numerous articles on probate law to profl. publs. Office: Supreme Ct Bldg Jefferson City MO 65101

BLACKORBY, EDWARD CONVERSE, historian, educator; b. Hansboro, N.D., May 30, 1911; s. Charles Edward and Clara Ellen (Converse) B.; B.S., Mayville State Tchrs. Coll., 1930; Ph.D., U. N.D., 1958; postgrad. Am. U.; m. Jewel Catherine Barenscheer, Nov. 24, 1937; 1 son, Charles Edward. Tchr. public schs., Russell, Niagara, Pembina and New Rockford, N.D., 1930-49; prof. history Dickinson (N.D.) State Tchrs. Coll., 1949-59; prof. history U. Wis., Eau Claire, 1959-81, prof. emeritus, 1981—. Mem. City Council Eau Claire, 1966-68, chmn. Cable TV Adv. Com., 1975-82; mem. Park Bd.; clk. Sch. Dist. Named Tchr. of Yr., U. Wis., Eau Claire, 1968; Edward C. Blackorby award for excellence in history named in his honor, 1982. Mem. Orgn. Am. Historians, Am. Hist. Assn., State Hist. Soc. Wis., N.D. Hist. Soc., Western History Assn., Agrl. History Assn., Nat. Council Social Studies, AAUP, Wis. Council Social Studies, NEA, SAR, Phi Alpha Theta, Phi Delta Kappa, Phi Kappa Phi, Phi Eta Sigma (hon.). Democrat. Congregationalist. Club: Masons. Author: Prairie Rebel: The Public Life of William Lemke; George B. Winship: Progressive Journalist of the Middle Border; contbr. to Ency. Americana, Dictionary of Am. Biography, profl. jours. Home: 1004 Village Sq Altoona WI 54720 Office: Dept History HHH 729 U Wis Eau Claire WI 54701

BLACKWELDER, MURRAY MAX, director of devolopment; b. Newton, Kans., Apr. 3, 1947; s. Max William and Blanche (Murray) B.; m. Diane Frances Wilson, June 27, 1970; children—Brett Wilson, Karsten Max. B.S., Baker U., 1969; M.P.A., U. Mo.-Kansas City, 1975. Line planeer Hallmark Cards, Kansas City, Mo., 1969-74; dir. alumni affairs, Baker U., Baldwin City, Kans., 1974-77; pres., owner Arend-Miller Pharm., Inc., Gardner, Kans., 1977-78; dir. of devel. Baker U., Baldwin City, 1978-81, Rockhurst Coll., Kansas City, 1981—; dir. Ecumenical Christian Ministries, Inc., Lawrence, Kans., 1984—, Greater Kansas City Council Philanthropy, Mo., 1984—; v.p. Nat. Soc. Fund Raising Execs., Kansas City, 1984—. Commr. Olathe, Kans. Planning Commn., 1981—; guardian Kans. Advocacy and Protective Assn., Topeka, 1981—; fundraising chmn. Blue Valley Citizens for Bond Passage, Stanley, Kans., 1983—. Recipient Baker U. Alumni Citation Baker U., 1978. Mem. Am. Council on Planning, Ind. Colls. and Univs. Mo., Mo. Ind. Colls. Found., Council for Advancement and Support of Edn., Kans. Real Estate Bd., Delta Tau Delta (Alumni of the Year, 1976). Republican. Presbyterian. Club: Optimist (Stanley). Home: 11901 W 149th St Olathe KS 66062 Office: Rockhurst Coll 5225 Troost Kansas City MO 64110

BLACKWELL, KENNETH EMERSON, chem. engr.; b. Clendenin, W.Va., Dec. 13, 1930; s. John Ervin and Ava (Strickland) B.; student N.C. State Coll., 1950-51, Tri-State Coll., 1959-60; B.S., Fla. State Christian Coll., 1972; M.S., Tenn. Christian U., 1977, Ph.D., 1978; m. Harriet Pauline Anderson, Feb. 10, 1953; children—Vicky Jo, Yma Yvonne. Chem. processing supr. Am. Viscose Corp., Nitro, W.Va., 1953-59; chem. processing supr. Purex Corp., St. Louis, 1960-67, sr. project engr., 1967-80, sr. field engr., 1980-81, regional project engr., 1981—. Served with USAF, 1948-52. Mem. Inst. for Cert. of Engring. Technicians. Mem. United Ch. Christ. Home: 12040 Larimore Rd Saint Louis MO 63138 Office: Purex Corp 6506 N Broadway Saint Louis MO 63147

BLACKWELL, ROBERT WALLINGFORD, printing company executive; b. Oak Park, Ill., Oct. 28, 1952; s. Clifford Earl and Abigail (Gunderson) B.; m. Laurie Ann Munoz, Dec. 30, 1975; children—Jennifer Ross, Christopher Miles. B.A., Coe Coll., 1974. Research analyst Rocliff Assocs., Delavan, Wis., 1975; customer service rep. Deluxe Check Printers, Milw., 1976, sales rep., 1977-80, asst. plant mgr., 1980-82, methods and procedures mgr., St. Paul, 1982-84, nat. dir. customer service, 1984—; cons. Jr. Achievement, St. Paul, 1984. Bd. dirs. Delavan Lake Improvement Assn., Delavan, 1980-82. Mem. Internat. Customer Service Assn., Soc. Consumer Affairs Profls. in Bus. Republican. Lutheran. Clubs: Delavan Lake Yacht (vice chmn. 1980-82), Delavan Lake Sailing Sch. (sec. 1980-82). Avocations: competitive sailing, golf, tennis, skiing. Home: 1149 Amble Dr Arden Hills MN 55112 Office: Deluxe Check Printers 1080 West County Rd F Shoreview MN 55112

BLACKWOOD, R(OBERT) ROSS, metallurgical co. exec.; b. Windsor, Ont., Can., Sept. 12, 1928; came to U.S., 1929; s. Robert Alexander and Annie (Beecroft) B.; B.S. in Metall. Engring. U. Wis., 1953; m. Beverly Joy Svenson, June 21, 1953; children—Kari Lynn, Scott Andrew. Metall. engr. A.C. Spark Plug Co., Flint, Mich., 1953-54; mgr. T. H. Cochrane Labs., Milw., 1954-60, pres., owner, 1960-74; pres. Tenaxol Inc., Milw., 1965—, chmn. bd., 1967—. Served with U.S. Army, 1946-48; Japan. Recipient Outstanding Engring. award U. Wis., 1977; registered profl. engr., Wis. Mem. Am. Soc. Metals, AIME (chmn. Wis. chpt. 1962-63), Soc. Automotive Engrs., Soc. Mfg. Engrs., Nat. Soc. Profl. Engrs. Republican. Presbyterian. Clubs: Lions, (Wauwatosa, Wis.); Masons, Shriners. Patentee metal quenching medium. Home: 2877 N 122d St Wauwatosa WI 53222 Office: 5801 W National Ave Milwaukee WI 53214

BLADDY, CHARLEN LECRONE, special educator; b. Tiffin, Ohio, Dec. 4, 1943; d. Charles Relna and Luella Adeline (McCracken) LeCrone; m. Jerome Stanley Bladdy, Feb. 17, 1968. B.A., Heidelberg Coll., 1965; M.S. Edn., No. Ill. U., 1974. English, Spanish tchr. Columbian high sch., Tiffin, Ohio, 1965-67; stewardess United Airlines, Chgo., 1967; exec. sec. Frederick Chusid, Chgo., 1968; tchr. hearing impaired Chgo. Bd. Edn., 1968—. Mem. Delta Kappa Gamma (membership chmn. 1982-83). Home: 1233 Colgate Wilmette IL 60091 Office: Jamieson School 5650 N Mozart Chicago IL 60659

BLAIES, JOSEPH WILLIAM, III, township administrator; b. East St. Louis, Ill., Sept. 10, 1932; s. Joseph William Jr. and Magdalen Mary (Hermann) B.; m. Margaret Ann Meyer, July 10, 1954; children—Patricia Jolene, Joseph William. Student Belleville Coll., Ill., So. Ill. Univ., 1970-73. Acct., Esmark, National City, Ill., 1950-71; mgr. wastewater treatment facilities, Caseyville Township, O'Fallon, Ill., 1971—; dir. Investors Savs. and Loan, Fairview Heights, Ill., 1973-83; aide Ill. State Senator James H. Donnewald, Springfield, 1973-80; vice chmn. Fairview Heights Econ. Devel. Commn., 1982—; dir. Caseyville Township, 1960, St. Clair County, Belleville, Ill., 1966; dir. Ill. EPA Mgmt. Bd., 1978. Bd. dirs. United Way, Greater St. Louis, Belleville, 1984, Greater St. Louis chpt. ARC, 1985—. Recipient Service to City award Fairview Heights, 1972. Mem. Water Pollution Control Fedn. Democrat. Roman Catholic. Lodges: Optimist, K.C. Avocations: Camping; fishing; gardening. Home: 105 Palm Dr Fairview Heights IL 62208 Office: Caseyville Township #1 Ecology Dr O'Fallon IL 62269

BLAIN, ALEXANDER, III, surgeon, educator; b. Detroit, Mar. 9, 1918; s. Alexander William and Ruby (Johnson) B.; student Washington and Lee U., 1935-37; B.A., Wayne U., 1940, M.D., 1943; M.S. in Surgery, U. Mich., 1948; m. Josephine Woodbury Bowen, May 3, 1941; children—Helen Bowen, Alexander IV, Bruce Scott Murray, Josephine Johnson; m. 2d, Mary E. Mains, 1968. House officer, Halsted fellow in surgery Johns Hopkins, 1943-46; resident surgeon U. Hosp., Ann Arbor, Mich., 1946-50; instr. surgery U. Mich., 1950-57; chief surgeon 14th Field Hosp., Bad Kreuznach, W. Ger.; clin. asst. prof. surgery Wayne State U., 1962—; also surgeon-in-chief Alexander Blain Hosp., Detroit, 1953-78; cons. surgeon Highland Park Gen. Hosp., St. Joseph's Hosp., Otsego Meml. Hosp., Gaylord, Mich.; med. dir. The Budd Co., 1977-82. Pres., Met. Detroit Family Service Assn., 1962-63, Detroit Museum Soc., 1961-62; staff Harper Hosp., Detroit, Crittenton Hosp., Rochester, Mich., Detroit Deaconess Hosp. Mem. Detroit Zool. Park Commn., 1974-82 pres., 1978-82; surgeon Detroit Urban Indian Health Center, 1982—, Am. Cancer Detection Ctr., Farmington Hills, 1984—. Trustee Alexander Blain Meml. Hosp., 1942-67, Ostego Meml. Hosp. Found., Gaylord, Mich., 1976—; bd. dirs. Detroit Zool. Soc., 1972-75, 82—; pres. W. J. Stapleton Found. Health Edn., 1978-84. Served as lt. M.C., AUS, 1942-44, maj., 1955-57. Recipient Wayne State U. Med. Alumni award, 1968. Diplomate Am. Bd. Surgery. Fellow A.C.S., N.Y. Acad. Scis.; mem. Internat. Cardiovascular Soc., F.A. Coller Surg. Soc., Am. Fedn. for Clin. Research, Cranbrook Inst. Sci., Soc. Vascular Surgery, Am. Thyroid Assn., Société Internationale de Chirurgle, Mich. Med. Soc. (chmn. surg. section 1963), Assn. Clin. Surgery, Pan-Pacific Surg. Assn., Acad. Am. Poets, Am. Poetry Assn., Mich. Poetry Soc., Nu Sigma Nu, Phi Gamma Delta. Clubs: Grosse Pointe, Otsego, Prismatic (pres. 1967), Detroit, Detroit Racquet (pres. 1976-80), Cardio-Vascular Surgeons (pres. 1961-62). Clubs: Acanthus, Waweatonong (pres. 1978), Circumnavigators. Author: (with F. A. Coller) Indications For and Results of Splenectomy, 1950; Prismatic Papers and an Ode, 1968; Prismatic Haiku Poems (Remembered Voices), 1973; (poems) Shu Shu Ga, 2d edit., 1983, Clackshant, 1982; also contbr. numerous articles surg. jours. Editorial bd. Review Surgery, 1959-79. Home: 8 Stratford Pl Grosse Pointe MI 48230

BLAIN, CHARLOTTE MARIE, physician; b. Meadeville, Pa., July 18, 1941; d. Frank Andrew and Valerie Marie (Serafin) B.; student Coll. St. Francis, 1958-60, DePaul U., 1960-61; M.D., U. Ill., 1965; m. John G. Hamby, June 12, 1971 (dec. May 1976); 1 son, Charles J. Hamby. Intern, resident U. Ill. Hosps., Chgo., 1967-70; practice medicine specializing in internal medicine, Elmhurst, Ill., 1969—; instr. medicine U. Ill. Hosp., 1969-70; asst. prof. medicine Loyola U., 1970-71; mem. staff Elmhurst Meml. Hosp., 1970—; clin. asst. prof. Chgo. Med. Sch., 1978—. U. Ill. fellow in infectious diseases, 1968-69. Bd. dirs. Classical Symphony. Diplomate Am. Bd. Family Practice, Am. Bd. Internal Medicine. Fellow A.C.P., Am. Acad. Family Practice; mem. AMA, Am. Med. Women's Assn., Am. Soc. Internal Medicine, Am. Fedn. Clin. Research, Am. Profl. Practice Assn., AAAS, Royal Soc. Medicine, DuPage Med. Soc. Roman Catholic. Club: Univ. (Chgo.). Contbr. articles and chpts. to med. jours. and texts. Home: 320 Cottage Hill Elmhurst IL 60126 Office: 135 Cottage Hill Elmhurst IL 60126

BLAIN, DONALD GRAY, physician; b. Detroit, Feb. 27, 1924; s. Alexander and Ruby (Johnson) B.; ed. Princeton, 1946; M.D., Wayne State U., 1950; m. Grace Carpenter, June, 1954; children—Elizabeth, Ian, Patricia. Intern, Union Meml. Hosp., Balt., 1950-51; gen. surg. resident Ch. Home Hosp., Balt., 1953-55, Henry Ford Hosp., Detroit, 1955-56, Alexander Blain Hosp., Detroit, 1956-58; staff Blain Hosp.; resident urology N.C. Bapt. Hosp. and instr. urology Bowman Gray Sch. Medicine, Winston-Salem, 1962-65; pvt. practice urology, Mount Clemens, Mich., 1965—; pres. Oakland Macomb Profl. Standards Rev. Orgn., 1973-79. Mem. Gov.'s Conf. on Health Manpower, 1973; bd. dirs. Mich. MDPAC. Served to capt. USAF, 1951-53. Diplomate Am. Bd. Urology. Fellow A.C.S.; mem. Macomb County Med. Soc. (past pres.), Am. Assn. Clin. Urologists, Am. Urologic Assn., Societe Internationale d'Urologie, Detroit Surg. Soc. (council), St. Andrews Soc. Republican. Presbyterian. Clubs: Country of Detroit, Metamora Hunt, Sedgefield Hunt. Home: 34136 E Jefferson St Clair Shores MI 48082

BLAINE, WILLIAM MCKINLEY, JR., sales executive; b. Chgo., Apr. 9, 1931; s. William McKinley and Edith Alvina (Charbonnier) B.; A.B. in Sociology/Anthropology, U. Ill., 1954; M.A. in Edn., U. Chgo., 1955; postgrad. U. Wis., 1962-63; M.B.A., Northwestern U., 1980; m. Tokiko Tanabe, Mar. 24, 1956; children—William McKinley III, James. Elem. tchr. Dept. Public Instrn., Territory Hawaii, 1955-56; area mgr. World Book Childcraft Internat., Inc., 1957-58, dist. mgr., 1958-59, div. mgr., 1959-62, div. mgr., Hayward, Calif., 1962-76, asso. sales tng., Chgo., 1976-80, dir. mktg. services/ins. projects, 1980-83; nat. sales dir. Nationwide Legal Services, Inc., 1984-85, v.p. bus. devel., 1985—; guest lectr. Chabot Community Coll., Hayward, 1973. Sec., Oahu Democratic County Com., 1959-60; mem. Sch. Adv. Com., Hayward, 1972; bd. dirs. East Bay Youth Symphony, Hayward, 1973-76; neighborhood commr. Boy Scouts Am., Hayward, 1964-66; pres. Woodland Estates Community Assn., 1973; bd. dirs. Mt. Prospect Public Library, 1979—. Mem. ALA (mem. library trustee div.), C. of C. Democrat. Methodist. Clubs: Des Plaines Yacht, Rotary. Home: 119 N Emerson St Mount Prospect IL 60056 Office: 1000 Northern Blvd Great Neck NY 11021

BLAIR, CHARLES VINCENT, lawyer, educational administrator; b. Long Island City, N.Y., June 16, 1933; s. Clarence Vincent Blair and Vera Marie (Myskowski) Campbell; m. Janis Joann Rigdon, Oct. 7, 1955; children—Scott Lincoln, Todd Vincent, David Douglas, Nancy Alison. B.A., U. Akron, 1955, M.A., 1963, J.D., 1983; postgrad. State U. Iowa, 1966. Bar: Ohio 1983. Dean, Evening Coll., U. Akron, 1967-70, dean adminstrn., 1970-72, asst. to pres., 1972-74; charter vice provost Northeastern Ohio U. Coll. Medicine, Rootstown, 1974-82; assoc. Buckingham, Doolittle & Burroughs, Akron, 1983-84, McDowall & Whalen, Cuyahoga Falls, Ohio, 1984—; cons. in field; mem. rev. panel HEW, Washington, 1979; pres. Med. Edn. Found., Northeastern Ohio U. Coll. Medicine, 1985. Contbr. articles to profl. publs. Chmn. Western Res. Acad. Upward Bound, Hudson, Ohio, 1973—; mem. Tallmadge Bd. Edn., Ohio, 1974—, pres., 1978, 79, 84, 85. Served to 1st lt. USAF, 1956-59, lt. col. Air N.G., USAFR, 1961-80. Recipient Disting. Service award Jr. C. of C., 1966, Alumni Honor award U. Akron, 1980, Disting. Service award Northeastern Ohio U. Coll. Medicine, 1982; Am. Council Edn. fellow, 1972-73. Mem. Ohio Sch. Bds. Assn. (trustee 1982—, pres. northeast region 1985), Res. Officers Assn. U.S., ABA, Akron Bar Assn., Ohio State Bar Assn. Lodge: Rotary. Avocations: stamp collecting; travel. Home: 96 N Village View Rd Tallmadge OH 44278 Office: McDowell & Whalen 135 Portage Trail Cuyahoga Falls OH 44222

BLAIR, D. KEVIN, lawyer; b. Garrett, Ind., Jan. 9, 1949; s. Leon B. Blair and Margaret (Hyde) Blair Muhn; m. Sandra Cordes, Oct. 14, 1967 (div. Apr. 1979); 1 child, Scott Alan. B.S., Ind. U., 1972, J.D., 1978. Bar: Ill. 1978, U.S. Dist. Ct. (no. dist.) Ill. 1978, U.S. Dist. Ct. (no. dist.) Ind. 1980, U.S. Ct. Appeals (7th cir.) 1980. Assoc. Rooks, Pitts and Poust, Chgo., 1978—; arbitrator Am. Arbitration Assn., Chgo., 1983—. Office: Rooks Pitts and Poust 55 W Monroe Suite 1500 Chicago IL 60603

BLAIR, ETCYL HOWELL, chem. co. exec.; b. Wynona, Okla., Oct. 15, 1922; s. Tunice Wilbur and Ruby (Wilson) B.; A.B., Southwestern Coll., Winfield, Kans., 1947, D.Sc. (hon.), 1974; M.S., Kans. State Coll., 1949, Ph.D., 1952; m. Ruth Gross, Sept. 4, 1949; children—David, Ronald, Kevin. Research chemist Dow Chem. Co., Midland, Mich., 1951-56, group leader, 1956-65, div. leader, 1965-66, asst. dir. E.C. Britton Research Lab., 1966-67, dir. lab., 1967-68, mgr. research and devel., agrl. dept., 1968-71, dir. research and devel., ag-organics dept., 1971-73, dir. health and environ. research Dow Chem. U.S.A., 1973-78, v.p., dir. health and environ. scis. Dow Chem. Co., 1978—. Bd. dirs. Chem. Industry Inst. Toxicology; chmn. sci. sub-com. Matrix:Midland, 1978—. Served in USAF, 1943-46. Mem. Am. Chem. Soc. (chmn. Midland sect. 1959; sect. award 1979), Fedn. Am. Scientists, Internat. Acad. Environ. Safety, Research Soc. Am., Am. Inst. Chemists, AAAS, N.Y. Acad. Scis., Soc. Ecotoxicology and Environ. Safety, Soc. Chem. Industry, Sigma Xi. Republican. Methodist. Author: Chlorodioxins—Origin and Fate, 1973. Patentee in field. Home: 4 Crescent Ct Midland MI 48640 Office: 2020 Dow Center Midland MI 48640

BLAIR, JOSEPH SKILES, JR., educator; b. Niles, Ohio, Dec. 16, 1919; s. Joseph Skiles and Elizabeth Leo (Higgins) B.; B.S., Kent State U., 1942; M.A., Columbia U., 1948; Ph.D. (Danforth Found. fellow), Ohio State U., 1962; m. Marjorie Ella Jacot, June 15, 1946; children—Brenda Ruth, Lawrence Paul. Exec. dir. City Coll. N.Y. YM-YWCA and N.Y. U. Med. Students Club, 1948-52; coll. exec. Ohio-W.Va. area YMCA, 1952-59; ednl. services mgr. Nationwide Ins. Co., 1962-68; prof. Franklin U., Columbus, Ohio, 1968-83, prof. emeritus, 1983—; cons. mgmt., 1983—; owner, mgr. Brookside Conf. Center; pres. Vicinia, Inc. Moderator, Univ. Bapt. Ch. Mem. Religious Speech Communication Assn., Assn. Edn. and Communication Tech., Am. Mgmt. Assn. Home: 254 E Torrence Rd Columbus OH 43214

BLAIR, LACHLAN FERGUSON, urban planner, educator; b. Lakewood, Ohio, Sept. 6, 1919; s. Neil Ferguson and Rebecca Henderson (Gunn) B.; student Cleve. Sch. Architecture, Western Res. U., 1936-40; B.City Planning, M.I.T., 1949; m. Mary Anne Novotny, Dec. 12, 1942; children—Douglas MacLachlan, Marilyn Ruth. Archtl. designer various firms, Cleve., 1940-43; sr. planner Providence City Plan Commn., 1949-51; chief state planning div. R.I. Devel. Council, 1952-56; pres. Blair Assos., Planning Cons., Providence, Syracuse, N.Y., Washington, 1957-66; prof. urban and regional planning U. Ill., Urbana, 1966—. Mem. Ill. Hist. Sites Adv. Council, 1969-77, 84-86; chmn. Urbana Plan Commn., 1973-80; mem. Champaign County Regional Planning Commn., 1974—. Served with C.E., U.S. Army, 1943-46. EPA public adminstrn. fellow, 1972-73. Mem. Am. Inst. Cert. Planners (past pres. New Eng., Ill. chpts., gov.), Am. Planning Assn., Partners for Livable Places, Nat. Trust for Hist. Preservation, Preservation Action, Tau Beta Pi. Democrat. Unitarian. Editor: Cape Cod 1980, 1962; College Hill: A Demonstration of Historic Area Renewal, 1959, 67. Author: The Distinctive Architecture of Willemstad, 1961. Home: 506 W Illinois St Urbana IL 61801 Office: 1003 W Nevada Urbana IL 61801

BLAIR, VIRGINIA ANN, public relations executive; b. Kansas City, Mo., Dec. 20, 1925; d. Paul Lowe and Lou Etta (Cooley) Smith; m. James Leon Grant, Sept. 3, 1943 (dec. July 1944); m. 2d, Warden Tannahill Blair, Jr., Nov. 7, 1947; children—Janet, Warden Tannahill, III. B.S. in Speech, Northwestern

U., 1948. Free-lance writer, Chgo., 1959-69; writer, editor Smith, Bucklin & Assocs., Inc., Chgo., 1969-72, account mgr., 1972-79, account supr., 1979-80, dir. pub. relations, 1980-85; pres. GB Pub. Relations, 1985—; judge U.S. Indsl. Film Festival, 1974, 75; instr. Writer's Workshop, Evanston, Ill., 1978; dir. Northwestern U. Library Council, 1978—. Emmy nominee Nat. Acad. TV Arts & Scis., 1963; recipient Service award Northwestern U., 1978, Creative Excellence award U.S. Indsl. Film Festival, 1976, Gold Leaf merit cert. Family Circle mag. and Food Council Am., 1977. Mem. Pub. Relations Soc. Am. (counselors acad.), Women's Advt. Club Chgo. (pres.), Publicity Club Chgo., Nat. Acad. TV Arts & Scis., Zeta Phi Eta (Service award 1978), Alpha Gamma Delta. Author dramas (produced on CBS): Jeanne D'Arc: The Trial, 1961; Cordon of Fear, 1961; Reflection, 1961; If I Should Die, 1963; 3-act children's play: Children of Courage, 1967. Home and Office: 463 Highcrest Dr Wilmette IL 60091

BLAIR, WILLIAM TRAVIS, association executive; b. Canton, Ohio, Dec. 17, 1925; s. George Neely and Helen Irene (Travis) B.; m. Eleanor Reid, Mar. 16, 1954; children—Carol, Tim, Anne, Linda. B.A., Ohio Wesleyan U., 1950; A.M.P., Mich. State U., 1964. Sales rep. indsl. and consumer sales Columbus Coated Fabrics (Ohio), 1950-57; asst. legis. affairs Ohio C. of C., Columbus, 1957-58, assoc. dir. legis. affairs, 1958-61, dir. indsl. devel., 1961-77, dir. social legis., 1963-77, dir. legis. affairs, 1973-77, exec. v.p., 1977-80, pres., 1980—; sec., mem. exec. com. Ohio Med. Indemnity, Inc., 1966-79; dir. 88 Fund Inc. Chmn. bd. dirs. Central YMCA, Columbus, 1974; trustee Ctr. Sci. and Industry, Columbus, 1962—; pres. Gt. Lakes Area Devel. Council, 1971. Served with USCGR, 1943-46. Mem. Council State Chambers of Commerce (chmn. 1980-82), Ohio Soc. Assn. Execs. (dir. 1979-82), C. of C. Execs. of Ohio (dir. 1977). Republican. Presbyterian. Clubs: Columbus Rotary, Columbus Athletic, University (dir. 1980-83), York Temple Country. Lodge: Masons. Editor: Structure and Functions of Ohio State Government, 1958. Office: 35 E Gay St Columbus OH 43215

BLAKE, BRIAN FRANCIS, psychologist; b. Jersey City, Aug. 26, 1942; s. Andrew Aloyisius and Mary Agnes (White) B.; m. Ann Marie Sicola; children—Kristin, Eric, Sean, Kevin. A.B., St. Peter's Coll., 1964; M.S., Purdue U., 1966, Ph.D., 1969. Asst. prof. psychology St. John's U., N.Y.C., 1969-72, assoc. prof., 1972-73; asst. prof. psychology and agrl. econs. Purdue U., West Lafayette, Ind., 1973-75, assoc. prof., 1975-79, prof., 1979-81; prof. psychology Cleve. State U., 1981—; pres. Decision Dynamics, Inc.; cons. market research-pub. opinion surveys. Mem. Am. Psychol. Assn., Am. Mktg. Assn., Eastern Psychol. Assn., Midwestern Psychol. Assn., Sigma Xi. Contbr. articles to profl. jours. Office: Dept Psychology Cleve State U Cleveland OH 44115

BLAKE, CHARLES LEE, pharmacist; b. Akron, Ohio, Aug. 13, 1955; s. Harvey Lee and Garnett Verdeal (May) B.; m. Crystal Lynn Triplett, June 12, 1976; children—Christopher Lee, Charla Lynea. B.S. in Pharmacy, Ohio No. U., 1978. Registered pharmacist, Ohio. Asst. mgr. Gray Drug Stores, Inc., Akron, 1978-79, Parkwood Plaza Pharmacy, Akron, 1979-85; owner Blake Family Pharmacy, Inc., Akron, 1985—. Mem. Am. Pharm. Assn., Ohio State Pharm. Assn., Summit County Pharm. Assn. Republican. Avocations: philately, fishing, bowling. Home: 230 Van Buren Ave Cuyahoga Falls OH 44221-1427 Office: Blake Family Pharmacy Inc 426 W Turkey Foot Lake Rd Akron OH 44319

BLAKE, ELIZABETH STANTON, university dean, French educator; b. N.Y.C., Apr. 28, 1930; d. William Harold and Elizabeth Cady (Stanton) B. A.B., Barnard Coll., 1953; A.M., Middlebury Coll., 1953; Ph.D., Columbia U., 1967. Instr. French, Barnard Coll., N.Y.C., 1956-63; instr. French, Wellesley Coll., Mass., 1963-67, asst. prof. French, 1967-73, dean acad. programs, 1974-79; acad. dean, prof. French, U. Minn.-Morris, 1979—; commr. Minn. Humanities Commn., St. Paul, 1983—; commr. at large North Central Assn. Colleges and Schs., Chgo., 1982—; mem. Minn. State Planning Commn. Am. Council on Educ. Nat. Identification Program for Advancement Women in Higher Educ. Admin., Mpls., 1981-84. Contbr. articles to profl. jours. Danforth Found. faculty assoc., 1970—; Fulbright scholar U.S. and French Govt. U. Paris, 1952-53; teaching asst. French govt. College Moderne de Jeunes Filles, 1953-54; recipient Woman of Achievement award Bus. and Profl. Women's Club, 1983. Mem. Modern Language Assn., Am. Assn. Tchrs. French, Am. Council Tchrs. Fgn. Languages, AAUP, Phi Beta Kappa, Pi Delta Phi. United Church of Christ. Club: Morris Area Bus. and Profl. Women's. Avocations: sports, music, reading, theatre, opera. Home: 704 Imperial Dr Apt 309 Morris MN 56267 Office: U Minn College Ave and 4th St Morris MN 56267

BLAKE, FAYE SIDES, physical education educator; b. Dora, Ala., Dec. 26, 1935; d. Victor Hugo and Clara Lucy (King) Sides; m. Thomas Edison Blake, Feb. 3, 1956; children—Thomas Craig, Victor Bruce, David Alan. B.S., Jacksonville State U., 1957; M.A., George Peabody Coll. for Tchrs., 1962. Tchr. math. Wildwood (Fla.) Pub. Schs., 1957-58; tchr. phys. edn. Bethany (Ill.) Pub. Schs., 1958-60, Matteson (Ill.) Pub. Schs., 1960-68; tchr. Homewood Flossmoor (Ill.) High Sch., 1968—, coach basketball, tennis and golf, 1970-80, athletic equipment mgr., 1983-86; chmn. North Central Evaluation Com., Homewood Flossmoor, 1983-84. Author: Shaping Your Child into an Athlete, 1978; co-author phys. edn. curriculum guide. Mem. NEA (life), Women's South Inter-Conf. Assn. (pres. 1967-68), Ill. Edn. Assn., Homewood Flossmoor Athletic Assn. Democrat. Baptist. Home: 3534 W 218th St Matteson IL 60443 Office: Homewood Flossmoor High Sch 999 Kedzie Ave Flossmoor IL 60422

BLAKE, FRANK BURGAY, medical record librarian; b. N.Y.C., Feb. 10, 1924; s. Francis Gilman and Marguerite (Burgay) B.; B.S., U. Minn., 1947; B.S. in Med. Record Library Sci., St. Louis U., 1948; M.S., N.Y. U., 1951; diploma Air U., 1960; m. Filomena Yolanda Ciaccio, Dec. 15, 1962; children—Anthony Francis, Robert Burgay. Staff U.S. Army Hosp., Ft. Ord, Calif., 1964-65; med. record librarian County of Tulare, Visalia, Calif., 1966-69, Winnebago (Wis.) Mental Health Inst., 1970-81; preceptor U. Minn. ind. study program in mental health adminstrn., 1977; exec. dir. Medica, Inc., Tulare, Calif., 1968-70, 1968-70; cons. Brown County Mental Health Center, Green Bay, Wis., 1971-76; cons. Med. record program evaluation Herzing Insts., Inc., Milw., 1971-73, mem. bd. advisers med. stenographer program, 1971-72; bd. advisers med. record technician program Moraine Park Tech. Inst., Fond du Lac, Wis., 1974—. Mem. Northeastern Assn. Med. Record Librarians (v.p. 1970-71). Author: Medical Terminology Source Book, 1983; An Instruction Manual for the Problem Oriented Medical Record in Correctional Institutions, 1984. Contbr. artices to profl. jours. Home: 1607 Hazel St Oshkosh WI 54901 Office: Bur Correctional Health Services 110 E Main St Madison WI 53703

BLAKE, HAYWARD ROBERT, graphic design consultant; b. West Haven, Conn., Aug. 29, 1925; s. Floyd Brewer and Marie Clara (Kuehl) B.; m. Simone Louise Roussy, July 21, 1948; children—Paul Andre, Christophe Henri, Yvonne Elizabeth. Degree in Visual Design, Ill. Inst. Tech., 1958. Staff designer Container Corp. Am., Chgo., 1952-53, Raymond Loewy Assoc., Chgo., 1953-54, Sears Roebuck & Co., Chgo., 1954-55; design dir. Ekco-Alcoa Containers, Wheeling, Ill., 1955-60; v.p. design Low's Inc., Chgo., 1961-63; pres. Hayward Blake & Co., Evanston, Ill., 1964—; mem. 27 Chgo. Designers, 1961—; lectr. Am. Press Inst., Reston, Va., 1978-81, U. Ill., Chgo., 1981-84; exhbn. judge Chgo. Book Clinic, 1980-81. Designer: (graphic neon) Color-Ed, Whitney Mus., 1974; (sculpture) No Right Turn, Ryder Gallery, 1976; (book) Discoveries from Kurdish Looms, Chgo. Book Clinic, 1984. Bd. dirs. Evanston Art Ctr., 1976, Design/Evanston, 1981, Evanston Library Friends, 1985. Served to sgt. U.S. Army, 1943-46; ETO. Recipient Disting. award Am. Inst. Graphic Arts, N.Y.C., 1976; Merit award N.Y. Type Dirs. Club, 1980; Award of Excellence, Art Mus. Assn., San Francisco, 1984. Fellow Soc. Typographic Arts (pres. 1959-60, dir. 1970-75, ex-officio 1980-85, cert. excellence 1982). Club: Caxton (Chgo.) (council 1981-84). Home: 1017 Ridge Ct Evanston IL 60202-2269

BLAKE, JOSEPH ALFRED, sociology and social psychology educator, researcher, consultant; b. Ware, Mass., Nov. 24, 1938; s. Joseph Maxim and Dorothy Lillian (Decoteau) B.; m. Dorothy Louise Nixon, Feb. 23, 1963; children—Adrienne Dorothy, Joseph Ervin. A.S., Jr. Coll. Broward County, 1965; B.A., Fla. Atlantic U., 1967; M.A., Northwestern U., 1969, Ph.D., 1973. Asst. prof. U. N.Mex., Albuquerque, 1971-73; asst. prof. Va. Poly. Inst. and State U., Blacksburg, 1973-78; vis. asst. prof. Wright State U., Dayton, Ohio, 1979; asst. prof. sociology and social psychology Ind. U.-East, Richmond, 1980-83, assoc. prof., 1984—; dir., project mgr. Ind. Area IX Agy. on Aging Needs Assessment Project; CD cons. on human response to disaster. Mem. Ind. Area IX Agy. on Aging Policy Bd.; mem. Miami Valley (Ohio) Gerontology Council. Served with U.S. Army, 1958-60. Mem. Inter-Univ. Seminar on Armed Forces and Soc., Am. Sociol. Assn., Ind. Acad. Social Scis., Soc. Sci. Exploration. Contbr. articles on collective behavior, war and mil., organizational behavior and sociology of knowledge to profl. jours. Home: 6835 Hubbard Dr Dayton OH 45424 Office: Ind U-East Richmond IN 47374

BLAKE, RUTH RICHARDS, real estate developer; b. Kansas City, Mo., Jan. 11, 1926; d. Alva Kenneth and Anna Jane Richards; m. Russell Storr Blake, Jan. 19, 1946; children—Rhayma Ann, Roger Thomas, Brian Richard. B.A., U. Mo., Columbia, 1945, M.A., Kansas City, 1954. Pres., Blake Devel. Co., Kansas City, Mo., 1968—; part owner, dir. RMI Media Prodns., Inc., Kansas City, Mo., 1967-83; mem. consumer adv. planning group Kansas City Power & Light Co., 1984—. Bd. dirs. Susan B. Anthony Found., 1980-82, Mo. Corp. Sci. and Tech., 1983—, CORO Found., 1983—; chmn. Jackson County Econ. Devel. Commn., 1980-83, mem., 1977-83.; chmn. alumni support group Mo. Council Pub. Higher Edn., 1979-81; chmn. bd. dirs. Kansas City Civic Orch., 1971-75; bd. dirs., founding mem. Dimensions Unltd., 1973-79; mem. adminstrv. bd. Central United Meth. Ch. Recipient Community Service award U. Mo. Kansas City, 1974, Alumni Achievement award 1963. Mem. U. Mo. Alumni Alliance (chmn. 1980-82), Greater Kansas City C. of C. (dir. 1977-80, chmn. govt. relations council 1978-80, chmn. state affairs com. 1977), Nat. Assn. Women Bus. Owners (v.p. Mid-Am. chpt. 1979), U. Mo. Kansas City Alumni Assn. (pres. 1968), Women's C. of C. Greater Kansas City (v.p. 1971), Music Tchrs. Nat. Assn., Sigma Alpha Iota. Methodist.

BLAKE, THOMAS GAYNOR, chemist; b. Nashville, Sept. 24, 1917; s. Robert Edwin and Dorothy (Gaynor) B.; student Princeton U., 1935-38; B.A., Central Meth. Coll., Fayette, Mo., 1940; postgrad. Washington U., St. Louis, 1942-44; m. Jane Elizabeth Spore. May 2, 1942; children—Dorothy Gaynor, Thomas Gaynor. Project engr. Explosives div. Olin Mathieson Chem. Corp., East Alton, Ill., 1941-48, head explosives chem. sect., 1948-54, dir. research and devel. explosives div., 1954-56; asst. dir. research and devel. armament div. Universal Match Corp., Ferguson, Mo., 1956-58; pres., dir. research Hanley Industries Inc., St. Louis, 1958—; lectr., cons. in field. Mem. Am. Def. Preparedness Assn. (life), Am. Soc. Indsl. Security, Mo. Athletic Club, Engrs. Club St. Louis, Mo. State Hist. Soc., St. Louis Westerners. Congregationalist. Patentee in field. Home: 16430 Old Jamestown Rd Florissant MO 63034 Office: 3640 Seminary Rd PO Box 1058 Alton IL 62002

BLAKE, WILLIAM HENRY, former credit executive, civic leader; b. Jasonville, Ind., Feb. 18, 1913; s. Straude and Cora (Pope) B.; m. Helen Elizabeth Platt, Jan. 2, 1937; children—William Henry, Allen Howard. Student Knox Coll., 1932-35; B.S., U. Ill., 1936, MS., 1941, postgrad., 1946; postgrad. NYU, 1950-51, Am. U., 1955-56, 58; grad. Columbia U. Grad. Sch. Consumer Credit, 1956, Northeastern Inst., Yale U., 1957. Tchr. pub. schs., Champaign, Ill., 1936-41; exec. sec. Ill. Soc. C.P.A.s, Chgo., 1941-44; dean men, assoc. prof. bus. adminstrn. Catawba Coll., 1947-51; dir. research Nat. Consumer Fin. Assn., Washington, 1954-59; exec. v.p. Internat. Consumer Credit Assn., St. Louis, 1959-78; ret., 1978; trustee Internat. Consumer Credit Assn. Ins. Trust and Retirement Program. Author: Good Things of Life on Credit, 1960; How To Use Consumer Credit Widely, 1963; Home Study Courses in Credit and Collections, 1968; Human Relations, 1969; Communications, 1970; Administrative Office Management, 1972. Chmn. pub. relations com. Ill. Heart Assn., 1980—; bd. dirs., sec. Salvation Army, Decatur, 1978—; chmn. fin. com., chmn. bd. trustees, session mem. Westminster Presbyn. Ch., Decatur, 1980—; mem. president's adv. cabinet Southeastern U.; advisor Office Edn. Assn.; chmn. bd. trustees Alta Deana div. University City, 1970-73, congl. liaison, 1959—; mem. council U. Ill. Sch. Edn. Alumni, 1979—; bd. dirs. Decatur Consumer Credit Assn., 1978—. Served to lt. USNR, 1944-47; to lt. comdr., 1951-54. Named Mo. Consumer Credit Exec. of Yr., 1977; William Henry Blake Found. Consumer Credit established in his honor by Internat Consumer Credit Assn., 1978. Fellow Soc. Cert. Consumer Credit Execs. (hon.); mem. Credit Grantors Assn. Can. (dir. 1959-72), U.S. C. of C. (banking and currency com. 1968-71, trade assn. com. 1964-67), Am. Soc. Assn. Execs. (dir. 1965-68), Pub. Relations Soc. Am. (dir., treas. Ill. chpt.), Internat. Platform Assn., Washington Trade Assn. Execs., U. Ill. Alumni Assn., Phi Sigma Kappa. Republican. Clubs: Press (St. Louis); Capitol Hill Exchequer (Washington). Lodge: Rotary (Paul Harris fellow; dir. 1980—, pres. 1985-86). Home: 5 Edgewood Ct Decatur IL 62522

BLAKEMORE, WILLIAM ROSS, communications company executive; b. San Antonio, July 27, 1944; s. James Edward and Margaret Elizabeth (Wylie) B.; m. Shirley Ilene Johns, Mar. 20, 1971; children—William Scott, Bethany Brooke. B.B.A. in Personnel Mgmt., North Tex. State U., 1966. Sales rep. Word Inc., Waco, Tex., 1970-71; owner, mgr. Agape Booksellers, Jackson, Mich., 1971-74; dist. sales mgr. Nelson Communications, Nashville, Tenn., 1974—. Treas., Christian Bus. Men's Com., Jackson, Mich., 1977, South Central Youth for Christ, Jackson, 1982—. Served with USN, 1967-68. Republican. Free Methodist. Avocations: sailing; reading. Home: 6110 Browns Lake Rd Jackson MI 49203

BLAKSLEE, GEORGE WARREN, retired geologist; b. Llanerch, Pa., July 12, 1921; s. Leigh Wallace and Grace Belle (Lamb) B., Sr.; m. Kathleen Jeanette Peterson, Sept. 16, 1948; children—Warren Leigh, Sharon Lee Blakslee Curtis. B.A., Pa. State U., 1943; postgrad. U. Pa., 1946, Pa. State U., 1951. Geologist, ARAMCO, Dhahran, Saudi Arabia, 1946-51; subsurface geologist Tidewater Assoc. Oil, Regina, Sask., Can., 1952-57, Ankara, Turkey, 1957-60, Tidewater Oil Co., Madrid, 1960, chief geologist, Karachi, Pakistan, 1960-62, gen. mgr., 1962-63; liaison rep. Getty Oil Co., Tehran, Iran, 1963-65, chief geologist, 1965-67, mgr. dir., 1967-70; mng. dir. Getty Petroleum Co., Algiers, Algeria, 1970-73; chief geologist internat. div., Los Angeles, 1973-77; dir. Bank of Brodhead, Wis. Contbg. Author: Jurassic and Carboniferous of Western Canada, 1958. Trustee Greenwood Cemetery, Brodhead, 1980—; town bd. supr.. Decatur Twp., Green County, Wis., 1980—. Served to 2d lt. USAAF, 1943-46. Fellow Royal Geog. Soc.; mem. Pa. State Alumni Assn., Nat. Holstein-Friesian Assn., Wis. Holstein-Friesian Assn., Am. Assn. Petroleum Geologists, Wis. Farm Bur., Am. Legion (comdr. Gehr post 1984), Phi Kappa Sigma. Republican. Episcopalian. Club: Karachi Yacht (Pakistan) (life); Decatur Lake Country (Brodhead). Lodge: Lions (Pakistan) (charter). Avocations: golf; photography; history; travel; painting. Home: N 3976 Park Rd Brodhead WI 53520

BLAKUT, MITCHELL ANTHONY, manufacturing company executive; b. Chgo., Feb. 15, 1921; s. Anthony and Anna (Ducal) B.; student North Park Coll., 1950; m. May 1, 1943; children—Mary Ann, Charles Mitchell. Process and mfg. engring. Pioneer Tool Co., Chgo., 1958-61; sr. process engr. Pyle Nat. Co., Chgo., 1961-64; quality control supr. Bell & Howell Co., Chgo., from 1964; now with Memorex-Bell & Howell Home Video, Northbrook, Ill. Served with Inf., AUS, 1944-46. Asst. scoutmaster, commr. Chgo. Area council Boy Scouts Am. Mem. Soc. Mfg. Engrs. (v.p., cert. mfg. engr.), Am. Soc. Quality Control, Internat. Biog. Assn. Democrat. Roman Catholic. Registered profl. engr., Calif. Home: 5725 N Marmora St Chicago IL 60646 Office: 3055 MacArthur Blvd Northbrook IL 60062

BLAMEY, RICHARD LYLE, accountant; b. Fond du Lac, Wis., Dec. 13, 1941; s. Lyle Donald and Lucille Hazel (Immel) B.; B.B.A., U. Wis., 1964; m. Ann-Elizabeth McCallum, Aug. 14, 1977; children—Richard Scott, Heather Lynn, Jennifer Ann. Staff acct. Ronald Mattox & Assos., Madison, Wis., 1965-71, audit mgr., Fond du Lac, 1971-74, ptnr., 1974-75; ptnr. Alexander Grant & Co., Fond du Lac, 1975—; v.p., treas. Ledgeview Devel. Corp., Fond du Lac, 1971-77, pres., 1977—; ptnr. Mt. Calvary Assos., 1979—. Mem. Fond du Lac Civic Center Com., 1972—; adviser Jr. Achievement, 1974-75; chmn. accts. div. Dane County United Fund drive, 1970-71; first reader First Ch. of Christ Scientist, Fond du Lac, 1975-78, chmn. bd., 1980-81; bd. dirs., treas. Student Center Found., Madison, 1969-71. Mem. Nat. Assn. Accts. (pres. Sheboyan Lakeshore chpt. 1977-78), Wis. Inst. C.P.A.s, (chmn. practice mgmt. com. and seminar 1972), Fond du Lac Jaycees (v.p. 1974-75), U. Wis. Alumni Assn. (pres. 1977-78). Republican. Clubs: South Hills Country (treas. 1978-81), Wis. Region Classic Car, Antique Auto Club Am., Rotary. Home: Route 4 Ledgeview Springs Fond du Lac WI 54935 Office: 131 S Main St Fond du Lac WI 54935

BLANCHARD, ALAINA GALE, biostatistician; b. Waltham, Mass., Mar. 24, 1955; d. Ralph S. Jr. and Marie T. (Neugebauer) Blanchard. B.S., Northeastern U., 1979; M.P.H., U. Mich., 1982. Clin. lab. technician Mass. Eye and Ear Infirmary, Boston, 1977-79; research asst. Sch. Medicine, Boston U., 1979-80; biostatistician Standard Oil Co Ind., Chgo., 1982—. Contbr. articles to profl. jours. Vice pres. New Eng. Luth. Student Movement, Boston, 1978. USPHS trainee, 1980-82. Mem. Am. Statis. Assn., Am. Pub. Health Assn., Phi Sigma. Lutheran. Club: Am. Youth Hostels (Chgo.). Avocations: Sailing, weight lifting. Office: Amoco Corp Indiana 200 E Randolph Dr PO Box 5910-A Chicago IL 60680

BLANCHARD, JAMES J., governor; b. Detroit, Aug. 8, 1942; m. Paula Parker; 1 son, Jay. B.A., M.B.A., Mich. State U., Lansing; J.D., U. Minn. Bar: Mich. 1968. Legal aid elections bur. Office Sec. State, State of Mich., 1968-69; asst. atty. gen. State of Mich., 1969-74, adminstrv. asst. to atty. gen., 1970-71, asst. dep. atty. gen., 1971-72; mem. 94th-96th Congresses from 18th Mich. Dist.; gov. State of Mich., 1983—; mem. Pres.'s Commn. on Holocaust. Mem. Oakland County exec. club Mich. State U. Mem. Assn. Asst. Attys. Gen., Ferndale Jaycees, State Bar Mich., Am. Bar Assn., LWV, U. Minn. Law Sch. Alumni Club, U. Detroit Titan Club. Democrat. Office: Office of the Governor Exec Office Capitol Bldg Lansing MI 48909

BLANCHARD, THOMAS EARLE, business owner, consultant; b. Schenectady, Mar. 14, 1943; s. Edward W. and Elanor A. (Butler) B.; m. Janet Lee Marsh, Oct. 10, 1946; children—Marcy Lee, Michael Thomas. A.A.S., Paul Smith's Coll., 1964. Regional credit ctr. mgr. W.T. Grant Co., Albany, N.Y., 1964-72, store mgr., 1972-75; distbn. mgr. Central Warehouse Corp., Albany, 1975-80; gen. mgr. Toledo Cold Storage Inc., 1980-81; chmn., pres. Great Lakes Cold Storage Inc., Toledo, 1981—, Blanchard Oil Co., 1984—, Brew Thru Corp., 1983—, cons. Served with Air N.G., 1964-70. Mem. Internat. Assn. Refrigerated Warehouses, Toledo Chamber of Commerce, Maumee Valley Petroleum Dealers Assn., Ohio Petroleum Mktg. Assn., Toledo Area Small Bus. Assn. Home: 2383 Hubbard Rd Monroe MI 48161 Office: 355 Morris St Toledo OH 43602

BLAND, E. A., moving van co. exec. Pres., chief operating officer Atlas Van Lines, Inc., Evansville, Ind. Office: Atlas Van Lines Inc 1212 St George Rd Evansville IN 47711

BLAND, EVERETT RUDOLPH, transportation company executive; b. Pana, Ill., Mar. 26, 1946; s. James Harold and Pauline (Smart) B.; m. Diane Shirley Wilczynski, Jan. 30, 1970; children—Michele H., Kimberly K., Colette M. B.S. in Bus., Eastern Ill. U., 1968. With dept. customer services/claims Inland Steel Co., Chgo., 1968-71; sales mgr. Consolidated Freightways, Highland, Ind., 1971-74; terminal mgr. Tucker Freight Lines, South Bend, Ind., 1974-76; asst. gen. mgr. Ind. Trucking, Inc., Gary, Ind., 1976-78, gen. mgr., 1980-84; operation central mgr. Artim Transp., Merrillville, Ind., 1978-80; dist. mgr. Burnham Trucking Co., East Chgo., Ind., 1984—. Century mem. Chicago Area council Boy Scouts Am., 1983. Recipient Sons of Am. Revolution award, 1968, Support award Lake Area United Way, 1984. Mem. Calumet Transp. Assn., Michiana Transp. Assn., Kanakkee Transp. Assn., South Suburban Traffic Assn., Delta Sigma Phi. Democrat. Roman Catholic. Home: 9427 Olcott St Saint John IN 46373 Office: Burnham Trucking Co PO Box 578 E Chicago IN 46312

BLAND, ROBERT DANIEL, educator; b. Terre Haute, Ind., Aug. 23, 1937; s. William Frank and Pearl Averil (Morgan) B.; B.S., Ball State U., 1960, M.S., 1964; Ph.D., U. Minn., 1971; m. Mary Ellen Anderson, July 28, 1968; children—Cynthia, Stephanie. Coordinator gen. biol. program U. Minn., Mpls., 1970-74; faculty dept. biology Coll. St. Thomas, St. Paul, 1974—. Author: General Biology Laboratory Guide, 1973; Freshwater Biology, 1974; Dissertation Abstracts, 1971; contbr. articles to profl. jours. Home: 1639 Ridgewood Ln Saint Paul MN 55113 Office: Dept Biology Coll of St Thomas Saint Paul MN 55105

BLANEY, DORIS RUTH, nursing educator; b. Gary, Ind., Sept. 5; d. Frank Albert and Ruth Elnora (Carlson) Papke; m. Karter Robert Blaney, Mar. 10, 1956; children—James Michael, Thomas Karter. B.S. Nursing, Ind. U., 1955, Ed.D., 1973; M.A., U. Chgo., 1959. Instr., Meth. Hosp., Gary, Ind., 1955-58, asst. dir. Sch. Nursing, 1958-64; faculty Ind. U. Sch. Nursing-Norhtwest-Campus, Gary, 1966—, prof. Maternal Child Nursing, 1967—, dir., 1967-81, asst. dean. sch., 1981—. Bd. dirs. Am. Lung Assn. of Ind., 1978—, pres. 1985-86; bd. dirs. Ind. Statewide Health Coordinating Council, 1981—, v.p., 1984-85; N-CAP coordinator Ind.'s 1st Congl. Dist., 1981—. Fellow Am. Acad. Nursing; mem. Am. Nurses Assn. (mem. cabinet on nursing edn. Kansas City, Mo. 1976-84, Cert. of Service award 1984), Ind. State Nurses Assn. (commn. on nursing edn. 1977-81, Cert. of Service award 1981), Nat. League for Nursing (accreditation visitor/alt. mem. bd. rev. 1980—), Sigma Theta Tau, Alpha Chi Omega, Kappa Kappa Kappa. Lutheran. Avocation: gourmet cooking. Office: Indiana U Sch Nursing-Northwest Campus 3400 Broadway Gary IN 46408

BLANK, MICHAEL KENNETH, physician; b. Cape Girardeau, Mo., Oct. 16, 1942; s. Walter E. and Dortha M. (Silsby) B.; A.B., Central Meth. U., 1964; M.D., U. Kans., 1968; m. Kathleen P. Goff, Sept. 6, 1969; children—Jennifer, Michael, Missy. Intern, St. Luke's Hosp., St. Louis, 1968-69; resident in gen. surgery St. John Mercy Med. Center, St. Louis, 1969-73; practice medicine specializing in surgery, De Soto, Mo., 1979—; chief staff Jefferson Meml. Hosp., Festus, Mo., 1979—, chief of surgery, 1983-84; asst. prof. Baylor U., Waco, Tex., 1973-74. Vice pres., Dist. 73 Sch. Bd., De Soto, 1974-76, dir., 1976-80; med. adv. nursing program Jefferson Coll., 1976-78; adv. bd. Blue Cross of St. Louis County, 1978-80. Served to maj. M.C., U.S. Army, 1973-75. Diplomate Am. Bd. Surgery. Fellow A.C.S., Internat. Coll. Surgeons, S.W. Surg. Congress; mem. Jefferson County Med. Soc. (pres. 1978-79). Republican. Methodist. Club: Elks. Address: 111 Easton St De Soto MO 63020

BLANK, ROBERT HENRY, political science educator; b. Milw., Mar. 28, 1943; s. Orville Albert and Sylvia (Linnemeier) B.; m. Mallory Scott, July 15, 1967; children—Jeremy, Mai-Ling, Maigin. A.B., Purdue U., 1965; M.A., U. Md., 1969, Ph.D., 1971. Faculty U. Idaho, Moscow, 1971—, prof. polit. sci., 1980—, chmn. polit. sci. dept. 1977-82; sr. Fulbright lectr. U.S. Edn. Found., Taiwan, Republic of China, 1976-77; U. Canterbury, N.Z., 1985; summer fellow Ctr. Advanced Study in Behavioral Sci., Stanford, Calif., 1978; scholar-in-residence Ctr. for Biopolit. Research, DeKalb, Ill., 1979-80. Author: Political Parties: An Introduction, 1980; The Political Implications of Human Genetic Technology, 1981; Redefining Human Life, 1983. Editor: Biological Differences and Social Equality, 1983. Contbr. articles to profl. jours. Served to lt. USN, 1965-67, Vietnam. Fellow State of Md., 1968-71, NEH, Vanderbilt U., 1981, Earhardt Found., 1983. Mem. Am. Polit. Sci. Assn., Western Polit. Sci. Assn. (exec. council 1981-83), Pacific NW Polit. Sci. Assn. (pres. 1984-85), Assn. Politics and Life Scis. (editorial bd. 1982—), Policy Studies Assn. Home: 634 N Hayes Moscow ID 83843 Office: Dept Polit Sci U Idaho Moscow ID 83843

BLANK, ROLF ALLAN, communications company executive; b. Appleton, Minn., Dec. 17, 1937; s. Taalkeus Alfred and Anita Frank (Houltzhouser) B.; m. Rachel Lynn Hampton, Apr. 11, 1937; children—Elizabeth, Mark. B.S., Northwestern U., 1959. With Armstrong Cork Co., Lancaster, Pa., 1963-66, Young & Rubicam, Inc., Chgo., 1966-73; pres. Rolf Blank Communications, Inc., Chgo., 1973—. Chmn. pub. relations Winnetka (Ill.) Community House, 1980-81; mem. council Winnetka Congregational Ch. Served to lt. (j.g.) USNR, 1960-63. Mem. Pub. Relations Soc. Am. (accredited), Soc. Automotive Engrs., Northwestern U. Sch. Speech Alumni (dir.). Republican. Clubs: Indian Hill (Winnetka, Ill.); Arts (Chgo.). Office: Rolf Blank Communications Inc 225 N Michigan Ave Chicago IL 60601

BLANK, WALLACE JAMES, manufacturing executive; b. Neenah, Wis., Apr. 16, 1929; s. Julius August and Caroline Ann (Werner) B.; B.S. in Mech. Engring., U. Wis., 1952; m. Margaret Mary Schultz, June 7, 1958. Registered profl. engr., Wis. Staff engr. Fairbanks Morse & Co., Beloit, Wis., 1952-59; sr. engr. Thiokol Chem. Co., 1960, N. Am. Aviation Atomics, internat. div., 1961; dir. mil. engring. FWD Corp., Clintonville, Wis., 1962-68; tech. dir. Oshkosh Truck Corp. (Wis.), 1968-74, v.p. engring., 1974—. Patentee in field of truck suspensions and transmissions. Mem. Soc. Auto Engrs., Am. Def. Preparedness Assn., Assn. U.S. Army, Air Force Assn. Roman Catholic. Home: 5352 Iahmaytah Rd Oshkosh WI 54901 Office: 2300 Oregon St Oshkosh WI 54903

BLANKENBAKER, RONALD GAIL, physician, educator; b. Rensselaer, Ind., Dec. 1, 1941; s. Lloyd L. and Lovina (Anderson) B.; B.S. in Biology, Purdue U., 1963; M.D., Ind. U., 1968, M.S. in Pharmacology, 1970. Intern, Meth. Hosp. Grad. Med. Ctr., Indpls., 1968-69, resident in family practice, 1969-71; med. dir. Indpls. Home for Aged, 1971-77, Am. Mid-Town Nursing

Ctr., Indpls., 1974-77, Home Assn., Tampa, Fla., 1977-79; asst. prof. family practice Ind. U., Indpls., 1973-77, clin. prof., 1980—; prof. dept. family medicine U. South Fla. Coll. Medicine, Tampa, 1977-79, chmn. dept., 1977-79; health commr. State of Ind. and sec. Ind. Bd. Health, Indpls., 1979—; dir. family practice edn. Meth. Hosp. Grad. Med. Ctr., 1971-77; family practice editor Reference and Index Services, Inc., Indpls., 1976-77, sr. editor, 1977-79; legis. lobbyist Ind. Acad. Family Physicians, 1973-77; med. adv. New Hope Found. of Am., Inc., 1974-79. Bd. dirs. Meals on Wheels, Inc., Peoples Health Ctr., Indpls., Marion County Cancer Soc., Ind. Sports Corp. Served to lt. col. USAF Res., 1971—. Decorated Meritorious Service medal; recipient Service to Mankind award Sertoma Club, 1976, Outstanding Alumnus award Mt. Ayr (Ind.) High Sch., 1976; named Sagamore of the Wabash, Gov. Ind., 1980. Diplomate Am. Bd. Family Practice. Fellow Am. Acad. Family Physicians, Am. Coll. Preventive Medicine, Soc. Prospective Medicine (v.p., pres. 1978-80, dir.); mem. AMA, Ind. State Med. Assn., Marion County Med. Soc., Ind. Acad. Family Physicians (v.p. 1977), Ind. Allied Health Assn. (pres. 1973-74), Ind. Acad. Sci., Soc. Tchrs. Family Medicine, Ind. Arthritis Found. (dir.), Ind. Lung Assn. (dir.), Assn. Am. Med. Colls., Assn. Depts. Family Medicine, Fla. Acad. Family Physicians (dir.). Republican. Office: Ind Bd Health 1330 W Michigan PO Box 1964 Indianapolis IN 46206

BLANKENSHIP, SAMMY DELANO, computer specialist, educator; b. Chattanooga, Mar. 25, 1936; s. William Doyle and Daisy Irene (Alford) B.; B.S., Murray State U., 1960, M.S. 1968; postgrad. (Bus. Research fellow) Ind. U., 1976-77, Miss. State U., 1978; m. Shirley Elaine Morlock, Sept. 10, 1955; children—Susan Elaine, James Kelley. Systems engr. IBM, Evansville, Ind., 1968-69; tchr. Evansville-Vanderburgh Sch. Corp., 1969-70; systems rep. Honeywell Info. Systems, Evansville, 1970; asst. prof. in bus. Ind. State U., Evansville, 1970-81; sr. applications specialist Gen. Electric Co., 1981—; info. systems cons. to bus., govt. and edn. Precinct committeeman Democratic Party, Vanderburgh County, 1978—; mem. Vanderburgh County Election Bd., 1978-79; candidate Ind. Legislature, 1972. Methodist. Club: Masons. Contbr. articles to newspapers and Midwest Bus. Adminstrn. Assn. Home: Rural Route 1 Box 351C Evansville IN 47712 Office: 1 Lexan Ln Mount Vernon IN 47620

BLANKENSHIP, VIRGINIA RADER, psychology educator; b. Washington, Ind., Jan. 2, 1945; d. Owen Richard and Kathleen Virginia (Eads) Rader; m. Timothy Sims, Feb. 8, 1963; 1 son, Mark Alan; m. 2d, Bruce Blankenship, May 25, 1974. B.S., Ind. State U., 1974, Ph.D., U. Mich., 1979. Asst. prof. sch. edn. Ind. U., Bloomington, 1979-81; asst. prof. psychology, coordinator women's studies program Oakland U., Rochester, Mich., 1981—. Recipient Spencer Found. award, 1980. Mem. Am. Psychol. Assn., Am. Ednl. Research Assn., Internat. Soc. for Study Behavioral Devel., Sigma Xi. Democrat. Contbr. articles to profl. jours. Home: 30701 Stellamar St Birmingham MI 48010 Office: Dept Psychology Oakland U Rochester MI 48063

BLANTON, DAVID ANDERSON, III, public relations company executive; b. St. Louis, Dec. 9, 1942; s. David A., Jr. and Bernard (Corrigan) Blanton. A.B., Georgetown U., 1964, M.A., 1968. Vice pres. G.H. Walker, Laird, Inc., 1970-75, A.G. Edwards & Sons, Inc., 1975-80; v.p. and dir. investor relations div. Fleishman-Hillard, Inc., St. Louis, 1980—. Active United Way of Greater St. Louis, Kammergild Chamber Orch., Theatre Project Co. Mem. Fin. Analysts Fedn., Nat. Investor Relations Inst., Internat. Assn. Bus. Communicators, Pub. Relations Soc. Am. Roman Catholic. Clubs: St. Louis Country, Noonday; Jonathan (Los Angeles). Home: 2 Lenox Pl Saint Louis MO 63108 Office: 1 Memorial Dr Saint Louis MO 63102

BLANTON, HELEN IRENE, nurse; b. Maryville, Tenn., Jan. 12, 1946; d. William Justian and Emily Irene (Hendry) B. Diploma, St. Mary's Sch. Nursing, Knoxville, 1967; B.S., U. Md., 1977; M.S., U. So. Calif., 1979; M.A., Webster Coll., 1981; M.A., Webster U., 1984. Staff nurse operating room U. Tenn. Hosp., 1967-68; from staff nurse to supr. hosps. U.S. Army, U.S., Vietnam, W.Ger., 1968-80; asst. chief nursing service Hines (Ill.) VA Hosp., 1981-83, utilization rev. mgr., 1983—; adj. prof. Surgical Tech. Program, Triton Coll. Res. dep. sheriff Lake County, Ill. Served to capt. U.S. Army, 1968-80, to maj. Res. Decorated Bronze Star, Vietnam Cross Gallantry, Vietnam Civic Action medal. Mem. Assn. Operating Room Nurses (cert.), Assn. Advancement Med. Instrumentation, Am. Nurses Assn. (cert.), Nat. Assn. Quality Assurance Profls. (cert.), Ill. Assn. Quality Assurance Profls., Res. Officers Assn. (life). Contbr. articles to profl. jours. Home: PO Box 351 Mundelein IL 60060 Office: 00A3 Hines VA Hosp Hines IL 60141

BLANTON, HENRY PAUL, JR., consumer products company sales executive; b. Natchez, Miss., Mar. 20, 1938; s. Henry Paul and Helen (Kennedy) B.; m. Rhonda Melita Price, July 1, 1972; children—Marla Lauren, Dana Nicole. B.S. in Bus. Adminstrn., Roosevelt U., 1971; M.B.A., Governors State U., 1975. Salesman, key account mgr. Lever Bros. Co., N.Y.C., 1971-76; dist. sales mgr. Cool-Ray Inc., Morris Plains, N.J., 1976-77; nat. accounts mgr. Carborundum Co., Niagara Falls, N.Y., 1978-81; regional sales mgr. Interpace Corp., Seattle, 1981; nat. accounts mgr. Rain Bird Nat. Sales Corp., Glendora, Calif., 1981—. Mgr. bus. and public relations Greater Grand Crossing Organizing Com., 1983. Served with U.S. Army, 1955-58. Mem. Am. Mgmt. Assn. Roman Catholic.

BLASCO, ALFRED JOSEPH, financial firm executive; b. Kansas City, Mo., Oct. 9, 1904; s. Joseph and Mary (Bevacqua) B.; student Kansas City Sch. Accountancy, 1921-25, Am. Inst. Banking, 1926-30; Ph.D. (hon.), Avila Coll., 1969; m. Kathryn Oleno, June 28, 1926; children—Barbara (Mrs. Charles F. Mehrer III), Phyllis (Mrs. Michael R. O'Connor). From office boy to asst. controller Commerce Trust Co., Kansas City, Mo., 1921-35; controller Interstate Securities Co., Kansas City, 1935-45, v.p., 1945-53, pres., 1953-61, chmn. bd., 1961-68; sr. v.p. ISC Fin. Corp., 1968-69, hon. chmn. bd., 1970-77, pres., 1979—; chmn. bd. Red Bridge Bank, 1966-72; chmn. bd. Mark Plaza State Bank, Overland Park, Kans., 1973-77; spl. lectr. consumer credit Columbia, N.Y.C., 1956, U. Kans., Lawrence, 1963-64. Mem. Fair Pub. Accomodations Com., Kansas City, Mo., 1964-68; pres. Catholic Community Library, 1955-56; ward committeeman, Kansas City, Mo., 1972-76. Pres. hon. bd. dirs. Baptist Meml. Hosp., 1970-74; chmn. bd. dirs. St. Anthony's Home, 1965-69; chmn. bd. trustees Avila Coll., 1969—. Decorated papal knight Equestrian Order Holy Sepulchre of Jerusalem, 1957, knight comdr., 1964, knight grand cross, 1966, knight of the collar, 1982, lt. No. Lieutenancy U.S., 1970-77, vice gov. gen., 1977-82; named Bus. Man of Year, State of Mo., 1957; named Man of Yr., City of Hope, 1973; recipient Community Service award Rockne Club of Notre Dame, 1959, Brotherhood award NCCJ, 1979, Wisdom award of honor, 1979. Mem. Soc. St. Vincent de Paul (pres. 1959-67), Am. Indsl. Bankers Assn. (nat. pres. 1956-57), Am. Inst. Banking (pres. Kansas City chpt. 1932-33), Bank Auditors and Controllers Assn., Fin. Execs. Inst. Am. (pres. Kansas City chpt. 1928-29), Nat. Assn. Accountants, Kansas City C. of C. Clubs: Kansas City, Hillcrest Country, Serra (pres. 1959-60). Lodge: Rotary. Contbr. articles to profl. jours. Home: 11705 Central St Kansas City MO 64114 Office: 8080 Ward Pkwy Kansas City MO 64114

BLASDEL, JEFF ERVIN, pharmacist; b. Cin., July 11, 1956; s. John Edgar and Clara Wilma (Fondong) B.; m. Michelle Elaine Wiedeman, June 27, 1981; children—Carey, Jacob. B.S., Purdue U., 1979; postgrad. Ball State U., 1983-84. Registered pharmacist, Ind. Pharmacist, asst. mgr. Hook Drugs, Inc., Brookville, Ind., 1979-81, pharmacist, mgr., Connerville, Ind., 1981—. Treas., bd. dirs. Regenstrief Boys Club, Connersville, 1984—; chmn. bus. div., bd. dirs. Fayette County United Way, Connersville, 1983—; chmn. council on ministries First United Methodist Ch., Connersville, 1984—. Recipient Eli Lilly Achievement award, 1979, Silver Knight award Hook Drugs, Inc., 1983, 84, Gold Key award, 1983, 84, President's award, 1983-84. Mem. Ind. Pharmacists Assn. (employer-employee relations com. 1982—), Purdue U. Alumni Assn. (life mem.), Connersville C. of C. (diplomat 1984—), Rho Chi (award 1978). Republican. Lodge: Kiwanis (v.p. 1984—). Avocations: tennis, golf, photography, basketball, community service. Home: 1201 S Cherokee Ln Connersville IN 47331 Office: Hook Drugs Inc 309 Central Ave Connersville IN 47331

BLASIAR, DAVID ANTHONY, consulting engineer; b. Rawlins, Wyo., Jan. 18, 1941; s. Frank Carl and Lois LaVivian (Burk) B.; m. Virginia Lee Jantz, June 6, 1965; children—David Anthony, Darin Ashley, Daniel Allen. B.S. in Archtl. Engring., Kans. State U., 1965; M.S. in Civil Engring., U. Mo., 1973. Profl. engr. Kans., Mo., Ill., Ind., Ky. Architect Black & Veatch, Kansas City, Mo., 1965-66; project engr., 1969-73, project mgr., 1974-77, regional mgr., St. Louis, 1978-84, engr. in charge, Dallas, 1984—; cons. engr. Indpls. Water Co., 1972-77, Met. Sewer Dist., St. Louis, 1978-83, City of Dallas, 1984—. Designer Eagle Creek water purification system, Ind., 1974, Bissell System sewer collection system, St. Louis, 1981; engr. in charge Long Range Program, Dallas, 1984; author articles, reports. Pres. PTO Parkway Sch. Dist., St. Louis County, Mo., 1981, mem. sch. reorgn. com., 1982-83. Served to capt. U.S. Army, 1966-68, Germany. Recipient Landscape Architect Achievement award, U.S. Corps Engrs., 1981, Mech. Engring. Installation award, Mech. Contractors Assn., Indpls., 1974. Fellow Am. Acad. Environ. Engrs.; mem. Nat. Soc. Profl. Engrs., ASCE (com. chmn. 1975, Outstanding Civil Engr. Achievement award 1982), Water Pollution Control Fedn. (com. chmn. 1977-84), Am. Water Works Assn. Club: Engrs. (St. Louis). Avocation: Black powder rifle and handgun building and shooting. Office: Black & Veatch 1415 Elbridge Payne Rd Chesterfield MO 63017

BLASSINGAME, LURTON WYATT, urban studies educator; b. N.Y.C., Mar. 18, 1935; s. Edmund L. and Catherine (Shaw) B.; m. Carolyn Mockridge, Aug. 25, 1962; children—Wyatt, Curtis. A.B., Harvard U., 1956; Ph.D., NYU, 1968. Asst. prof. U. Wis.-Oshkosh, 1969-72, assoc. prof. urban studies, 1973—, asst. dean, 1972-75, assoc. dean, 1975-79, coordinator urban studies program, 1980—. Contbr. articles to profl. jours. Chmn., Oshkosh Planning Commn., 1978—; bd. dirs. Oshkosh Comml. Devel. Corp., 1982-84; mem. housing adv. com. East Central Wis. Regional Planning Commn., 1980-83; trustee 1st Congregational Ch., Oshkosh, 1984; exec. v.p. Oshkosh Symphony, 1981-82. Served to 1st lt. USN, 1956-59. U. Wis.-Oshkosh grantee, 1982, 83; NYU grantee, 1966-67. Mem. Am. Planning Assn., Nat. Assn. Housing and Rehab. Ofcls., Urban Affairs Assn., Wis. City Mgmt. Assn. (sec. 1982—), Microcomputers in Planning. Club: Harvard (Madison). Home: 1926 E Murdock Ave Oshkosh WI 54901 Office: U Wis-Oshkosh Halsey Science 215 Oshkosh WI 54901

BLASZKIEWICZ, CYNTHIA BERNADETTE, insurance company analyst; b. Detroit, Sept. 23, 1949; d. Albert Joseph and Alma Rose (Miller) Allen; m. Daniel Alexander Blaszkiewicz, June 6, 1976 (div. 1984). Counter clk. Gil's Cleaners, Detroit, 1965-66; coop. student Mich. Blue Cross, Detroit, 1966-67; sec. Blue Cross Blue Shield Mich., Detroit, 1967-77, analyst, 1977—; cosmetologist, 1974—. Mem. Women's Econ. Club of Detroit, Health and People Pac. Avocations: snow skiing; bowling; tennis; racquet ball; swimming; needlecraft. Office: Blue Cross Blue Shield Mich 600 Lafayette E Detroit MI 48226

BLATT, SIDNEY ISRAEL, chemical company executive, container company executive; b. Columbus, Ohio, June 5, 1921; s. Rudolph S. and Clara (Mattlin) B.; m. Selma Mae Kantor, July 11, 1943; children—Meredith Gail, Cynthia Blatt Paine, Laura Jo Blatt Paul. Vice pres. Columbus Barrell Cooperage Co., 1947-50, pres., 1950-55; pres. Columbus Steel Drum Co. div. Franklin Steel Co., 1955—, Surface Research Corp., Columbus, 1959—. Bd. dirs., mem. exec. com. Columbus Jewish Fedn., 1966—, v.p., 1968-74, pres., 1974-76; bd. dirs. Big Bros. Assn., Columbus, 1967-70, Heritage House, Columbus, Jewish Ctr., Columbus; chmn. Jewish Community Relations Com., Columbus, 1969-73; v.p. found. Temple Israel, Columbus, 1970-72, pres. temple, 1977-78; mem. campaign cabinet United Way Franklin County, 1978. Served with inf. AUS, 1943-45. Recipient plaque for outstanding leadership State of Israel Bonds, 1968, Centennial Man of Yr. award ORT, 1980; named Ohio Small Bus. Man of Yr., Columbus C. of C., 1970, Temple Man of Yr., Temple Israel Brotherhood, 1979, co-honoree New Mem. Class, Temple Israel, 1980. Mem. Nat. Barrel and Drum Assn. (dir., treas., exec. com., chmn. bd. dirs. 1981-84), Pres. Assn., Nat. Assn. Indsl. and Office Parks. Clubs: Winding Hollow Country (pres. 1973-75), Renaissance, Firestone Country, Jockey. Address: 330 Stanberry Ave Columbus OH 43209

BLATTNER, JOHN FRANCIS, clinical therapist; b. Chgo., Aug. 16, 1948; s. Oscar J. and Marian C. Blattner; B.A., Quincy Coll., 1970; M.A., Ill. State U., Bloomington, 1975; m. Kathy M. Smialek, June 12, 1976; children—Brian, William, Joseph. Therapist, Leyden Family Service and Mental Health Center, Franklin Park, Ill., 1975-77; therapist alcohol program and edn. center Loretto Hosp., Chgo., 1977-81; coordinator outpatient alcohol center The Roth Group, Northbrook, Ill., 1978-81; pres. Centre City Assocs., 1982—; cons. Catholic Charities, 1979-85. Mem. subarea council Suburban Health Systems Agy., 1980-81; v.p. Ill. Alcoholism Certification Bd., 1981-82. Served with U.S. Army, 1971-73. Mem. Am. Psychol. Assn., Ill. Psychol. Assn., Nat. Assn. Alcoholism Counselors, Assn. Labor-Mgmt. Adminstrs. and Cons. on Alcoholism (bd. dirs. 1980-82), Ill. Alcoholism Counselors Alliance. Home: 102 Rugeley Rd Western Springs IL 60558 Office: 405 N Wabash Ave Suite 1510 Chicago IL 60611

BLAZER, SONDRA KAY GORDON, employee contract specialist, writer; b. Middletown, Ohio, June 2, 1937; d. John Charles and Ora Lillie (Stewart) Gordon; A.A. magna cum laude, U. Cin., 1975; m. Ralph J. Bays, Feb. 17, 1956 (dec. 1969); children—Sherry Kay, Cynthia Rae, Robert Jay. Reporter, ch. editor Middletown Jour., 1955-56; mng. editor Warren County Reporter, Lebanon, Ohio, 1966-72; corr. Franklin (Ohio) Chronicle, 1974-78; free lance journalist, 1973—, family therapist Mary Haven Youth Center, Lebanon, Ohio, 1980-83; spl. places ops. Supr. U.S. Bur. Census, 1980. Mem. Ohio Gov.'s Traffic Safety Com., 1972-76; mem. Warren County Bd. Mental Health and Retardation, 1972-80, chmn., 1974-80; chmn. dist. one planning council Ohio Dept. Mental Health 1977-80; mem. exec. bd. Ohio Community Mental Health Assn., 1979-80; mem. citizens adv. com. Lebanon Correctional Instn., Lebanon, 1971—; sec. Warren County Safety Council, 1972-76; mem. citizens com. Ohio Dept. Rehab. and Corrections 1976-82; bd. dirs. Warren County com. Ohio Easter Seal Soc. for Crippled Children and Adults, 1967—; mem. Warren County Bd. Elections, 1974-80, Warren Profl. Health Adv. Com.; bd. dirs. Warren United Appeal; asst. to organizer Warren County Disaster Services, 1975; former sec. Warren County Disaster Services Orgn.; sec., Warren County Democratic Women's Club, 1963-67, Warren County Dem. Central and Exec. Com., 1965-80; precinct committeeman Dem. party, 1964-80; mem. land use subcom. Ohio-Ky.-Ind. Council Govts., 1975—; sec. Warren County Interagy. Council, editor newsletter; Sunday sch. tchr. Methodist Ch., 1963-72. Winner 1st pl. Beta Sigma Phi internat. short story contest, 1964, Ohio Dept. Hwy. Safety Media contest, 1970. Mem. Ohio Corrections and Ct. Assn., Nat. Council Crime and Delinquency, Internat. Platform Assn., Ohio Assn. Bds. County Visitors (pres. 1981), Phi Kappa Epsilon, Alpha Sigma Lambda. Address: 3730 Beatrice Dr Franklin OH 45005

BLAZOWSKI, PHILLIP, county government official; b. Tomahawk, Wis., Jan. 6, 1943; s. Thaudeus S. and Phyllis E. (Egtvedt) B.; m. Roberta H. Schontag, July 24, 1971. B.S. cum laude, Northland Coll., 1971; M.S., So. Ill. U., 1973; cert. Harvard U., 1983. Planner, Southeastern N.H. Regional Planning Commn., Exeter, 1972; cons. Ill. Dept. Local Affairs, Springfield, 1973; county planner, Rock County, Janesville Wis., 1973-75, dir. planning and devel., 1975—; chmn. Rock County Econ. Devel. Tech. Com., Janesville, 1974—. Editor: Illinois Planning Enabling Legislation, 1973. Chmn. legis. com. Wis. Planning Assn., Madison, 1976-84. Recipient Disting. Service award Wis. Hist. Soc., 1976. Local Asst. Achievement award Nat. Assn. Counties, 1982. Mem. Am. Planning Assn., Internat. City Mgmt. Assn., Am. Inst. Cert. Planners, Wis. Econ. Devel. Assn., Nat. Assn. County Planning Dirs., Wis. Planning Assn. (bd. dirs. 1980—, pres. 1983—), Janesville C. of C., Ducks Unltd. (pres. 1974). Clubs: Janesville Country, Blackhawk Curling (bd. dirs. 1984—). Lodge: Rotary (bd. dirs. 1979-81). Avocations: curling; hunting; fishing; golf. Home: 1118 Grace Ct Janesville WI 53545 Office: Rock County Planning and Devel Agy 51 S Main St Janesville WI 53545

BLECHMAN, GERALD AARON, psychologist; b. Detroit, Jan. 11, 1941; s. Morris and Clara (Taub) B.; children—Mari Suzanne, James Michael, Jonathan Miles; m. 2nd Doris Knoche, Sept. 4, 1983. B.A., Wayne State U., 1963; M.A., Northwestern U., 1965, Ph.D., 1968. Staff psychologist Children's Meml. Hosp., Chgo., 1967-72; dir. outpatient psychology services Northwestern U. Med. Sch., Evanston, Ill., 1971-72; dir. psychol. services Project Head Start, City of Chgo., 1972-76; pvt. practice clin. psychology, Skokie, Ill., 1975—; dir. outpatient dept. Old Orchard Hosp., Skokie, Ill.; cons. Northwestern U. Speech and Lang. Clinic, 1976-81. Mem. Am. Psychol. Assn., Ill. Psychol. Assn. Office: 4711 Golf Rd Skokie IL 60076

BLECKE, ARTHUR EDWARD, principal; b. Oak Park, Ill., Sept. 21, 1926; s. Paul Gerard and Mathilda (Ziebell); m. June Audrey Eckholm, Jan. 22, 1949; children—William, Robert, Carol. B.S. in Phys. Edn., U. Ill., 1950; M.Edn., Loyola U., 1967. Tchr., coach Buckley High Sch., Ill., 1951-52, Paxton High Sch., Ill., 1952-53, Luther High Sch. North, Chgo., 1953-65, also dept. chmn.; asst. coach football and basketball Elmhurst Coll., Ill., 1965-66; dean, prin. Antioch Community High Sch., Ill., 1966—; cons. in field; lectr. Contbr. articles to profl. jours. Mem. sanitary dist. Village of Lindenhurst, Ill., 1968—; planning commn., 1967-77. Served with U.S. Army, 1945. Recipient Hon. Mention "Those Who Excel", Ill. State Bd. Edn., 1980. Mem. Lindenhurst Sanitary Dist. (pres. 1976—), Ill. Prins. Assn. (dir. 1980-81, 83-84), Nat. Assn. Secondary Sch. Prins. Lutheran. Avocations: Golf; bowling; model railroading. Office: Antioch Community High Sch 1133 S Main St Antioch IL 60002

BLEDSOE, WILLIAM THOMAS, financial executive, accountant; b. Memphis, Mar. 26, 1947; s. Walter Lee and Estell (Robinson) B.; m. Eleanor Laverne Walker, Aug. 17, 1974; 1 son, Ellery Theon. B.S. in Acctg., Tenn. State U., 1972; cert. U. Cin., 1971; M.B.A., U. Chgo., 1974. C.P.A. Staff acct. Peat, Warwick, Mitchell & Co., Memphis, 1972; intern No. Trust Bank, Chgo., 1973; instr. acctg., Chgo. State U., 1974; fin. analyst Bendix Corp., Southfield, Mich., 1974-76; fin. mgr. Am. Hosp. Supply, Evanston, Ill., 1976—; vis. prof. Black Exec. Exchange Program, Nat. Urban League, Inc., N.Y.C., 1978—; cons. Youth Motivation Task Force, Nat. Alliance Bus., Washington, 1982. Trustee 2d Baptist Ch., Evanston, 1981—, fin. sec., 1982, fin. adviser, 1983—. Served with U.S. Army, 1965-68; Vietnam. Council Opportunities in Grad. Mgmt. Edn. fellow, 1972-74; recipient cert. of appreciation Nat. Urban League, 1978, Nat. Alliance Bus., 1982, Tenn. State U. Career Devel. Ctr., 1982. Mem. Ill. C.P.A. Soc., Am. Inst. C.P.A.s, Nat. Black M.B.A. Assn. Home: 4014 N Mitchell Ave Arlington Heights IL 60004 Office: American Hospital Supply Corp 1 American Plaza Evanston IL 60201

BLEGSTAD, JEROME PAUL, sales executive; b. Manchester, N.H., Oct. 16, 1944; s. Melford S. and Wanda (Peterson) B.; m. Sandra Hollis, July 28, 1948; children—Kareston M., Dustin J. B.B.A., Wichita State U., 1970. Sales rep. Mattel Toy Corp., Hawthorne, Calif., 1970-71; sales rep. Econs. Lab., St. Paul, 1971-73, dist. sales mgr., 1973—. Chmn., Park & Recreation Dept., City of Blue Springs, Mo., 1983—, mem. park bd., 1981—; pres. Blue Springs Powderpuff Softball, 1981-82, 84—. Served with U.S. Army, 1965-67. Urantia. Avocations: Oil Painting; running; softball. Home and Office: 1017 Canterbury Rd Blue Springs MO 64015

BLEICH, ALLAN LYNN, communications products executive, system and business planning consultant; b. Paxton, Ill., Aug. 9, 1946; m. Rosemary Petersen, June 20, 1968; children—Angela, Laurel, Aaron. B.S. in Math., U. Ill., 1968. Cons. analyst Product Mktg., Dayton, Ohio, 1976-79; product mgr. Fin. Systems, Dayton, 1979-80; mgr. product mgmt. Communication Systems, Dayton, 1980-82; dir. product mgmt. Fin. Systems, Dayton, 1982-84; program dir. communications Gen. Purpose Computers, Dayton, 1984—. Campaign coordinator United Way, Dayton, 1983; advisor Victim Witness Ctr., Dayton, 1978. Avocations: soccer; tennis; racquetball; duplicate bridge. Home: 2036 Meadow Side Ln Centerville OH 45459

BLESCH, CHRISTOPHER JOHN, computer systems engineer; b. Whittier, Calif., Jan. 9, 1958; s. William Robert and Beverly Jean (Schurman) B.; m. Melinda Catherine Lewis, Aug. 25, 1979. B.S. in Mech. Engring., Ohio State U., 1979, M.S. in Mech. Engring., 1981, M.B.A., 1985. Engr. Owens-Corning Fiberglas, Granville, Ohio, 1980-85; computer systems engr. Electronic Data Systems, Dallas, 1985—. Mem. ASME, ASHRAE. Republican. Methodist. Avocations: reading; photography; bicycling.

BLESSING, CLARENCE WILLARD, civil engineer, city administrator, consultant; b. Canton, Mo., Jan. 27, 1925; s. Roswell Henery and Opal Pearl (Wheelock) B.; m. Virginia Rebecca Dotson, July 6, 1947; children—Wilham Ross, Clarence Willard, Martha Rebecca, Virginia LeeEtta, Angela Kay, Susan Lynn, Joseph Paul. B.S. in Civil Engring., U. Mo., 1950, postgrad., 1979-83; postgrad. in edn. N.E. Mo. State U., 1961. Registered profl. engr., Mo. Designer Silas Mason Co., Burlington, Iowa, 1951-52; field office mgr. Cameron Joyce & Co., Keokuk, Iowa, 1952; field engr. Ebasco Service & Bechtel Corp., Joppa, Ill., 1952-54; paving foreman Skranka Constrn. Co., Scott AFB, Ill., 1954-55; sr. constrn. insp. Mo. Hwy. Dept. Hannibal, 1955-76; owner, operator The Pharm, New London, Mo., 1976-77; asst. dir. pub. works City of Hannibal, 1977—. Author: Campin', Cookin', and Stuff, 1982. Served with U.S. Army, 1943-45, 50-51; PTO, Korea. Recipient Arrowhead Honor award Gt. Rivers council Boy Scouts Am., 1981, Silver Beaver award Nat. council, 1982. Mem. Nat. Soc. Profl. Engrs., Mo. Soc. Profl. Engrs., Am. Pub. Works Assn., Mo. Land Surveyors Assn. Mem. Christian Ch. (Disciples of Christ). Club: Hi-Twelve (pres. 1983) (Hannibal). Lodges: Rotary (songleader 1982-83) (Hannibal); Masons (master 1962), Shriners. Home: Rural Route 1 New London MO 63401 Office: City Engr's Office 320 Broadway Hannibal MO 63401

BLEWITT, RICHARD FRANCIS, management consultant; b. Scranton, Pa., Mar. 26, 1947; s. Frank Joseph and Margaret (Kearney) B.; B.S. in Govt. and Politics, U. Md., 1973; M.B.A., U. Chgo., 1981; m. Dec. 7, 1968; children—Mar Lynn and Carrie Ann (twins). Staff writer Scranton Times-Sunday Times, 1966-68; press relations asst. Am. Trucking Assns., Washington, 1970-72; mgr. press relations Mfg. Chemists Assn., Washington, 1972-75; mgr. public relations FMC Corp. Chem. Group, Phila., 1975-78; v.p. corporate affairs Velsicol Chem. Corp., Chgo., 1978-84; prin. Rowan & Blewitt, Inc., mgmt. cons., Washington, 1984—; prin. Blewitt & Cefalo, Inc., advt./pub. relations agy., Scranton, Pa., 1981—. Served with USN, 1968-70. Mem. Profl. News Media Assn. Northeastern Pa. (founder, charter pres.), Public Relations Soc. Am., Chgo. Fgn. Relations Council (com. on fgn. affairs), Pennsylvania Soc. Democrat. Roman Catholic. Club: Chgo. Press. Contbg. editor World Book Ency., 1973—. Home: 9459 Drake Ave Evanston IL 60203 Office: 1899 L St NW Washington DC 20036

BLEZNICK, DONALD WILLIAM, romance languages educator; b. N.Y.C., Dec. 24, 1924; s. Louis and Gertrude (Kleinman) B.; m. Rozlyn Burakoff, June 15, 1952; children—Jordan, Susan. B.A., CCNY, 1946; M.A., Univ. Nacional de México, 1948; Ph.D., Columbia U., 1954. Instr. Ohio State U., 1949-55; prof. romance langs. Pa. State U., University Park, 1955-67; head romance langs. U. Cin., 1967-72, prof., 1967—; vis. prof. Hebrew U., Jerusalem, 1974. Contbr. articles to profl. jours. Bibliographer: Modern Lang. Assn. Internat. Bibliography, 1966-81. Editor: Hispania, 1974-83, El Ensayo Español, 1964, Madrugrada, 1969, (with T. Pattison) Representative Spanish Authors, 1971; Sourcebook for Hispanic Literature and Language, 1974, 2d edit., 1983; Cin. Romance Review, 1982—; Studies on the Quixote and Other Cervantine Works, 1984; others. Served with CIC, U.S. Army, 1946-47. Decorated knights cross Order Civil Merit (Spain); recipient Rieveschl award U. Cin., 1980, others; Downer fellow CCNY, 1947-48; Taft grantee U. Cin., 1972-75, 78, 83; Am. Philos. Soc. grantee, 1964. Mem. Am. Assn. Tchrs. Spanish and Portugese (exec. com. 1975—), MLA, Los Ensayistas (adv. bd. 1976—), Comediantes, AAUP, Midwest MLA, Conf. Editors Learned Journs. (exec. com. 1978-79), Celestinesca, Cervantes Soc. Am., Phi Beta Kappa, Sigma Delta Pi (Order Don Quijote 1970, v.p. Midwest 1975-83, José Martel award 1980), Phi Sigma Iota, Kappa Delta Pi. Home: 7870 Elbrook Ave Cincinnati OH 45237 Office: U Cin Dept Romance Langs and Lits Cincinnati OH 45221

BLIESE, KATHLEEN ANDERSON, physician, nutrition consultant; b. Elk Horn, Iowa, Mar. 23, 1940; d. Arnold and Leona Christine (Gregersen) Anderson; m. Arthur Paul Bliese, Jr., Sept. 2, 1959. Student Lutheran Bible Inst., Mpls., 1958-59; B.A. in Gen. Sci., Dana Coll., Blair, Nebr., 1962; M.D., U. Nebr., 1967; postgrad. Nancy Bounds, Internat., Omaha, 1985. Diplomate Am. Bd. Family Practice. Practice medicine specializing in family practice, Omaha, 1968-69; med. dir. refugee camps, mem. med. team Lutheran World Relief, Nigeria, 1969-70; med. dir., founder Lamb Hosp., Bangladesh, 1970-80; practice medicine Northwest Clinic, Omaha, 1980—; med. dir., assoc. dir. World Wide Ministries, Omaha, 1981—; nutrition cons. Shaklee, Inc., Omaha, 1983—; speaker on religion and nutrition. Author, dir. program on rural health devel. in Bangladesh, 1976-80 (Best Internat. Program award 1983). Speaker radio program Kindle the Flame, 1981—. Adviser to women's ministry bd. Christ Luth. Ch., Omaha, 1981—; bd. dirs. children's tv program Jean's Story Time, 1983—. Named Nebr. Outstanding Young Woman of Yr., 1968; recipient Disting. Alumnus award Dana Coll., 1978, Woman of Achievement award Mrs. Nebr. Pageant, 1984. Fellow Am. Acad. Family Practice; mem. AMA (nat., state and county chpts.), Women's Am. Med. Assn., World Med. Assn. Republican. Lutheran. Avocations: writing music; sewing; knitting; swimming; skiing. Home: 6024 N 110th Plaza Omaha NE 68164 Office: Northwest Clinic 2734 N 61st St Omaha Ne 68104

BLIN, RANDY ALAN, plastic company executive; b. Cedar Rapids, Iowa, July 26, 1959; s. James Lee Blin and Yvonne Marie (Burbach) Blin Leibrand;

m. Deborah Lynn Johnson, Nov. 27, 1982; 1 child, Jonathan James. Student Mont. State U., 1977-79. Purchasing agt. Triangle Plastics, Inc., Winthrop, Iowa, 1977-78, materials mgr., 1978-80, customer service mgr., 1980-82; customer service mgr. Superior Plastics, Inc., Winthrop, 1982-83, gen. mgr., Independence, Iowa, 1984—. Del. Republican County Conv., 1980. Recipient Presdl. award of honor Iowa Jaycees, 1984. Mem. Soc. Plastics Engrs. (assoc.), Independence Jaycees (pres. 1983, 84, chmn. bd. 1984, 85), Ducks Unltd. Methodist. Clubs: Wapsipinicon Country, Exchange (charter sec. 1984, 85). Avocations: Alpine skiing; swimming; travel. Office: Superior Plastics Inc PO Box 350 Independence IA 50644

BLINN, GILBERT EUGENE, national park executive; b. Spokane, Apr. 18, 1938; s. Harold Eugene and Katherine (Gilbert) B.; m. Barbara Jean Freese, June 8, 1963; children—Grant Eugene, Alan David. B.A. in Geography, Wash. State U., 1960. Seasonal ranger Mt. Rainier Nat. Park, Longmire, Wash., 1960, seasonal park ranger, 1961-65; naturalist Joshua Tree Nat. Monument, Twentynine Palms, Calif., 1960-61; dist. ranger Death Valley Nat. Monument, Death Valley, Calif., 1965-69; supt. Katmai Nat. Monument, King Salmon, Alaska, 1969-79, Badlands Nat. Park, Interior, S.D., 1979—. Served with U.S. Army, 1961-62. Lodge: Masons (sr. deacon 1981—), Lions (pres. 1971-79). Club: Toastmaster (pres. 1979—) (Wall, S.D.). Home: Badlands Nat Park Interior SD 57750 Office: Nat Park Service Badlands Nat Park Interior SD 57750

BLINZLER, ALAN PATRICK, lawyer; b. Bartlesville, Okla., June 26, 1954; s. Glenn Frederick and Jane (Kirkpatrick) B.; m. Kelly Lynn Connelley, Dec. 31, 1977; children—Adam Frederick, Erin Lynn. B.A. cum laude in History, Southwestern Coll., 1976; M.B.A., J.D., U. Kans., 1979. Bars: Kans. 1979, U.S. Dist. Ct. Kans. 1979, Mo. 1980, U.S. Dist. Ct. (we. dist.) Mo. 1980, U.S. Ct. Appeals (10th cir.) 1982. Assoc. Blackwell, Sanders, Matheny, Weary & Lombardi, Overland Park, Kans., 1980—. Asst. scoutmaster Heart of Am. council Boy Scouts Am., Boy Scouts Am., 1977-80, scoutmaster, 1980-83; Republican precinct committeeman, Prairie Village, Kans., 1980-84; mem. Rep. Central Com., Johnson County, Kans., 1980-84; treas. Johnson County Fire Dist. No. 2, Prairie Village, 1981-82; chmn. Prairie Village Rep. Party, 1982-84, Johnson County Rep. Policy Com., 1982-84; mem. Kansas City Consensus, Mo., 1983-84, Johnson County Rep. Exec. Com., 1983-84, Internat. Relations Council, Kansas City, Mo., 1983-84; del. to Rep. State Central Com. of Kans., 1983-84, 3d Congl. Dist. Rep. Central. Com., 1983-84; com. mem. Explorer Post, Boy Scouts Am., Olathe, Kans., 1984. Named Eagle Scout Boy Scouts Am., 1969; recipient Best Brief in Nation award ABA Appellate Advocacy Contest, 1978. Mem. ABA (com. on discovery reform 1983-84), Kans. Bar Assn., Mo. Bar Assn., Kansas City Bar Assn., Johnson County Bar Assn. Mem. Disciples of Christ. Lodge: Lions (v.p. 1984). Home: 7701 Chadwick Prairie Village KS 66208 Office: Blackwell Sanders Matheny Weary & Lombardi 9401 Indian Creek Pkwy Overland Park KS 66225

BLIWAS, PHILIP R., insurance executive; b. Milw., June 28, 1920; s. Rubin and Caroline B.; student U. Wis., 1937-40; LL.B., Marquette U., 1947; postgrad. Columbia U., 1942, Ind. U. Law Sch., 1946-47; cert. farm estate planning U. Minn., 1977; cert. Keypact Inst. Advanced Studies, 1979; m. Joyce Shirley Strauss; children—James Charles, Janice M. Sec., Charles Strauss Shoes, Milw., 1947-51; pres., gen. mgr., chief exec. officer Korbe Shoe, Inc., Mpls., 1951-74; field underwriter N.Y. Life Ins. Co., 1975-79; gen. agt., owner Philip Bliwas Agy., Chaska, Minn., 1978—; founder, chief exec. officer Janus: Fin. Mktg. Corp., Von Hertzen Fin. Services, Inc. chief exec. officer Concepts for Profl. Benefits, Inc., Concepts for Profl. Benefits of Calif. Del. to county and state convs. Minn. Democratic Farm Labor Party, 1972, 76, 80; vol. work Carver County Family Services. Served to lt. USN, 1941-46; PTO. Recipient Life Ins. Nat. Sales Achievement ann. award Nat. Assn. Life Underwriters, 1978-82, Nat. Quality award, 1977, 78, 81; named Top Life Ins. Producer of 1981, Nat. Travelers Life Co. Mem. Nat. Assn. Life Underwriters, Million Dollar Round Table (Top of Table 1982). Home: 110922 Von Hertzen Circle Chaska MN 55318

BLIX, SUSANNE, psychiatrist; b. Crawfordsville, Ind., Oct. 29, 1949; d. Fred Mayor and Marjorie Marie (Durst) Blix; m. William Charles McGraw, June 20, 1971; children—Annmarie Blix McGraw, Annalisa Ruth McGraw. B.A., DePauw U., 71; M.D., Ind. U., 1975. Intern internal medicine Ind. U. Med. Sch., Indpls., 1975-76, resident psychiatry, 1977-79, fellow child psychiatry, 1979-81, asst. prof. psychiatry, 1981—, asst. dir. psychiat. services Riley Children's Hosp., 1981-85, dir. psychiat. services, 1985—; cons. Ind. Pastoral Counselling Ctr., Indpls., 1978-79; cons. Cummins Mental Health Ctr., Danville, Ind., 1981-84, Midtown Mental Health Ctr., Indpls., 1984-85. Named Miss DePauw U., Greencastle, Ind., 1969. Mem. Ind. Psychiat. Soc. (membership sec. 1983-84), Am. Psychiat. Assn., Am. Acad. Child Psychiatry, Marian County Med. Soc., Ind. State Med. Assn., Kappa Alpha Theta, Phi Beta Kappa. Mem. Disciples of Christ Ch. Contbr. articles to profl. jours.

BLIZMAN, PAUL J., lawyer, social worker; b. Wyandotte, Mich., June 4, 1940; s. Paul J. and Olga G. (Rudenko) B.; student U. Mich., 1958-62; A.B., Wayne State U., 1966, M.S.W., 1969; J.D., Detroit Coll. Law, 1980; m. Leah Snyder, Sept. 3, 1967; 1 dau., Alexis. Counselor, Reception Center W.J. Maxey Sch., Whitmore Lake, Mich., 1969-71, dir., 1972-74, social work supr., 1971-72; licensing cons. Mich. Dept. Social Services, 1974-78; clin. social worker Health Care Inst., Detroit, 1979-80, Detroit Receiving Hosp., Univ. Health Center, 1980-82; ptnr. Melamed & Blizman, P.C., 1983-84, Melamed Blizman & Dailey, P.C., 1984—; pvt. practice social work, Birmingham, Mich., 1975—; field instr. social work Wayne State U., 1979-82. Mem. ABA, Mich. State Bar, Oakland County Bar Assn., Delta Theta Phi. Home: 28700 Herndonwood Dr Farmington Hills MI 48018 Office: 24901 Northwestern Hwy Suite 314B Southfield MI 48075

BLOCH, RALEIGH EDWARD, paper company executive; b. Oshkosh, Wis., Nov. 19, 1933; s. Nestor Julian and Irene Marie (Burgett) B.; m. Jean Alice Nelson, Jan. 8, 1955; children—Diana Norieka, Julie Orloski. B.S.M.E., Milw. Sch. Engring., 1960. Capital investment coordinator Am. Can Co., Greenwich, Conn., 1969-71, indsl. engring coordinator, 1971-72, plant supt., Scranton, Pa., 1972-75, plant mgr., 1975-80, assoc. dir., Neenah, Wis., 1980-82; dir. research/devel. James River Corp., Neenah, 1982—; tchr. engring. U. Wis., Wausau, 1961-63; cons. editor Aspen Systems Corp., Germantown, Md., 1977-78; seminar speaker U. Wis. Ext., Madison, 1970. Contbr. articles to profl. jours. Served with USAF, 1952-56. Recipient award for Excellence in Mgmt. Pa. Gas and Electric, 1976. Mem. Am. Mgmt. Assn., Soc. of Research Adminstrs., C. of C. Republican. Methodist. Club: Soc. for Preservation and Encouragement of Barber Shop Quartet Singing in Am. Avocations: Singing; boating skiing. Address: James River Corp 1915 Marathon Ave Neenah WI 54956

BLOCHOWSKI, THOMAS KENNETH, manufacturing engineer; b. Toledo, Oct. 27, 1942; s. Edmund Eugene and Helen Alice (Sobieralski) B.; Asso. Mfg. Tech., U. Toledo, 1965; m. Judith Ann Gasiorowski, Aug. 24, 1963; children—Kenneth Robert, Cynthia Ann, Kevin Michael. Sales mgr. Block Indsl. Service, Toledo, 1964-69; chief tool engr. Mather Co., Milan, Mich., 1969-71; mfg. engr. machine shop M-S/Tillotson Co., Toledo, 1971-74; sr. lead process engr. Harley Davidson Motor Co., Milw., 1974-75; mfg. engr. corp. staff Prestolite Co., Toledo, 1975-81; pres. Bisel Mfg. Inc., screw machine plant, Toledo, 1981—; mem. faculty Monroe County (Mich.) Community Coll. Bd. dirs. Goodwill Industries, Toledo, cons. sheltered workshop program. Registered profl. mfg. engr., Calif. Mem. Soc. Mfg. Engrs. (sr. mem., chmn. Toledo chpt. 1971-72), St. Francis De Sales Alumni Assn., Toledo Jr. C. of C. Roman Catholic. Club: Tamaron Country. Home: 6014 Tetherwood Dr Toledo OH 43613 Office: 1121 Hazelwood St Toledo OH 43605

BLOCK, REBECCA, lawyer; b. Bklyn., June 28, 1947; d. Albert S. and Lottie (Cohn) Gorman; m. David N. Block, May 27, 1967; children—Justin, Gareth. B.A., Bklyn. Coll., 1968; M.A. in Psychology, Ea. Ill. U., 1977; J.D. with honors, DePaul, 1981. Bar: Ill. 1981, U.S. Dist. Ct. (no. dist.) Ill. 1981, U.S. Ct. Appeals (7th cir.) 1982, U.S. Dist. Ct. (cen. dist.) Ill. 1983. Assoc., Friedman & Koven, Chgo., 1981-83; sole practice, Charleston, Ill., 1983—; dir. Bank of Charleston. Bd. dirs. Coles County Mental Health Ctr., Mattoon, Ill., 1984, Am. Cancer Soc., Charleston, 1984. Recipient Decalogue award, 1980, Searle award 1980. Mem. Ill. State Bar Assn., Coles-Cumberland Bar Assn. Home: Rural Route #2 Box 241 Charleston IL 61920 Office: 418 6th St PO Box 739 Charleston IL 61920

BLOCK, SANFORD LEE, oral surgeon; b. Chgo., Aug. 30, 1943; s. Harry Leo and Sophie (Dombek) B.; m. Noal S. Blender, May 30, 1966; children—Jared Gavin, Darren Randall, Nicole Suzanne. Student U. Ill., 1964; D.D.S., Loyola U., Chgo., 1969; LL.B., Blackstone Law Sch., 1973. Cert. Am. Bd. Dental Examiners. Asst. prof. oral surgery U. Ill. Coll. Dentistry, Chgo., 1972—, clinic coordinator Temporomandibular Joint and Facial Pain Research Ctr., 1974-84; dir. dentistry/oral surgery Swedish Covenant Hosp., Chgo., 1976—; cons. Office of Med. Examiner Cook County, Chgo., 1980—. Co-author: The Temporomandibular Joint, 1980. Contbr. articles to profl. jours. C.V. Mosby scholar, 1969; Marcus Levy scholar Chgo. Jewish Fedn., 1967-68; Alpha Omega scholar, 1969. Fellow Acad. Implants and Transplants; mem. ADA, Ill. Dental Soc., Chgo. Dental Soc., Am. Assn. Dental Research, Internat. Assn. Study of Pain, Blue Key. Jewish. Avocations: archeology; computers; guitar. Office: Swedish Covenant Hosp 5145 N California Ave Chicago IL 60625

BLOCK, SHAUN CUDAHY, food manufacturing executive; b. Chgo., Aug. 28, 1941; s. Michael and Annie May (Henry) C.; m. Andrew Keith Block, Jan. 4, 1964; children—Andrew Keith, Christopher P., Shauna B. B.A., Northwestern U., 1964. Vice pres. Top Hat, Chgo., 1982—; v.p., dir. Open Lands Project, Chgo., 1975—. Mem. Ill. Commn. on State Banks & Trusts, 1980-84; exec. com. Women's Bd. U. Chgo., 1983-84. Roman Catholic. Avocations: reading; golf; skiing.

BLOCKER, CECIL ARLO, JR., manufacturing executive; b. Columbus, Ohio, Feb. 15, 1931; s. Cecil Arlo and Elizabeth Agusta (Davis) B.; B.Mining Engring., B.Petroleum Engring., Ohio State U., 1956, M.B.A., 1964; M.Bus.Mgmt., Frostburg State Coll., 1978; m. Virginia Travis Wakeman, Sept. 2, 1978; children by previous marriage—Debra, Victoria, Craig, Jacqueline. Refinery lab head, petroleum engr. Standard Oil of N.J., Sumatra, Indonesia, 1958-63; mgr. quality assurance Cummins Engine Co., Columbus, Ind., 1965-68; dir. quality assurance Levinson-Hayes, Pitts., 1968-70; plant mgr. Levinson-Levco, Pitts., 1970-73; dir. quality assurance Pullman Trailmobile, Chgo., 1973-75; dir. quality control Pullman-Standard, Chgo., 1975-76; operations mgr., prodn. control mgr., quality control mgr. Frick Co., Waynesboro, Pa., 1976-78; dir. ops. Frick Forest Products, Waynesboro, Pa., 1978; dir., v.p. quality assurance Campbell-Hausfeld Group of Scott Fetzer, Harrison, Ohio, 1978-82, corp. dir. quality improvement, 1982—; pres. Ultramax Corp., 1982—; cons. high tech. Served with USAF, 1956-58. Registered profl. engr., Ohio. Mem. Am. Soc. Quality Control (Cin. chmn. 1979-81, Pitts. chmn. 1972, mem. Chgo. bd. 1974-75). Republican. Unitarian. Club: Elks. Home and Office: 6245 Twinwillow Ln Cincinnati OH 45247

BLODGETT, JOHN WOOD, former lumber company executive; b. Grand Rapids, Mich., May 24, 1901; s. John Wood and Minnie (Cumnock) B.; A.B., Harvard, 1923; m. Sarah Reed Gallagher, Sept. 28, 1939 (div. Dec. 1963); children—Julia Reed (Mrs. John R. Curtis, Jr.), Katherine Blodgett Winter, Sarah Wood (Mrs. Prescott Nelson Dunbar); m. 2d, Edith Irwin Ferris, June 21, 1967. Dir. U.S. Nat. Bank, 1929-52; chmn. Blodgett Co., Ltd., 1932-37; pres. Mich.-Calif. Lumber Co., Camino, Calif., 1936-65; pres. Consol. Timber Co., Portland, Oreg., 1934-49; chmn. Wright-Blodgett Co., Ltd., Grand Rapids, Mich., 1936-47; pres. Western Mgmt. Co., Grand Rapids, 1937-55; sec., mem. bd. mgrs. Hill-Davis Lumber Co., Arcata, Calif., 1937-58; dir. Arcata Redwood Co., 1947-67, sec., 1959-66; dir. Arcata Nat. Corp., 1967-68, Booth-Kelly Lumber Co., 1941-59. Trustee, Blodgett Meml. Hosp., Grand Rapids, 1941—; mem. overseer com. to visit Harvard Library, 1972—, to visit Harvard dept. athletics, 1973-83; hon. curator Spanish Civil War Collection, Harvard Coll. Library, 1983-84; mem. com. on univ. resources Harvard Coll. Bd. Overseers, 1980-83; adv. com. Harvard Fund Council, 1952-55; mem. overseers com. to visit Harvard Forest, 1949-62. Mem. U.S. Naval Inst., USN League, Am. Ordnance Assn., S.A.R. Mason. Clubs: River, Harvard (N.Y.C.); Bohemian (San Francisco); Chicago, Racquet (Chgo.); Kent Country, University, Peninsular (Grand Rapids); University (Portland, Oreg.). Home: 250 Plymouth Rd SE Grand Rapids MI 49506

BLODGETT, VIRGINIA JUNE BALLARD (MRS. RALPH WESLEY BLODGETT), ednl. adminstr.; b. Detroit; d. William King and Marie (Crossley) Ballard; A.B., Asbury Coll., 1935; M.S., Butler U., 1962; postgrad. U. Louisville, Ind. State U., Ball State U., Ohio State U., San Francisco State U.; Ph.D. (hon.), Colo. State Christian Coll.; m. Ralph Wesley Blodgett, Sept. 25, 1935; children—Vivian Sue Shields, Rebecca June Downing, Judith Elaine (Mrs. David Purvis). Tchr. Dependent Schs., Europe, 1951-54, English various high schs., Ind., Va., Fla., 1942—, chmn. English dept. Woodview Sch., Indpls., 1961—, dean girls, 1964—; instr. evening div. Ind. Central Coll., Indpls., 1964-69, adult counselor, 1965—. Active various community drives. Gen. Electric Co. fellow, 1967. Mem. Am., Ind. (sec. 1969) assns. women deans and counselors, NEA, Ind. State Tchrs. Assn., Warren Twp. Classroom Tchrs., Central Ind., Ind. personnel and guidance assns., Alpha Delta Kappa. Methodist (tchr. ch. schs. 1935—). Office: 901 N Post Rd Indianapolis IN 46219

BLOEMER, HUBERTUS (HUGH) LUDWIG, cartography and remote sensing educator, director; b. Dinklage, Oldenburg, Germany, Nov. 15, 1939; came to U.S., 1960, naturalized, 1976; s. Clemens August and Regina Louise Bloemer. B.A., U. Cin., 1966; M.A., Kent State U., 1968; Ph.D., Union Grad. Sch., 1977. Instr. cartography Ohio U., Athens, 1971-77, asst. prof., 1977-84, assoc. prof., 1984—; cons. Sands Hill Coal Co., Wellston, Ohio, 1981—. Contbr. articles to profl. jours. Recipient Spl. Recognition award U.S. Orienteering Fedn., 1973; named Univ. Prof., Ohio U. Student Body; fellow NASA, Am. Soc. Engring. Edn., 1979-80. Mem. Am. Congress Surveying Mapping, Internat. Soc. Photogrammetry Remote Sensing, Am. Space Found., Ohio Remote Sensing Steering Com. (charter), Sigma Xi-Sci. Research Soc. Roman Catholic. Avocations: art metal work; wood working; landscaping; racquetball; hiking. Home: Route 3 Box 263 Simms Rd Athens OH 45701 Office: Ohio Univ Porter Hall 507B Athens OH 45701

BLOEMER, JOHN WILLIAM, mechanical engineer; b. Indpls., June 5, 1935; s. Frank William and Bonnie Grace (Smith) B.; B.S. in Mech. Engring., Purdue U., 1957; M.S. in Mech. Engring., Ohio State U., 1963; M.S. in Mgmt., Case Western Res. U., 1971; m. Sandra A. Updike, Sept. 1, 1956; children—Sherrie, Jennifer, John, Joseph, Kristen. Research engr. Battelle Meml. Inst., Columbus, Ohio, 1957-65; prin. engr. Eaton Corp., Willoughby Hills, Ohio, 1965—. Served with C.E., U.S. Army, 1960. Registered profl. engr., Ohio, Fla.; cert. master hazardous materials mgr. Mem. ASME, Inst. Noise Control Engrs. Mem. Church of Christ. Home: 8217 Yorkshire Dr Mentor OH 44060 Office: Eaton Corp 32500 Chardon Rd Willoughby Hills OH 44094

BLOMGREN, EMMA JEAN, educator; b. Elkton, S.D., Sept. 7, 1938; d. Clarence Edward and Margaret Lucille (Houselog) B.; B.S., Dakota State U., 1971; postgrad. U. S.D., 1980—. Tchr., Oldham Pub. Schs., S.D., 1958-61; tchr./coach Sioux Falls Pub. Schs. (S.D.), 1961-65, Sacred Heart Sch., Ft. Dodge, Iowa, 1966-69; tchr./coach Ind. Dist. 514, Ellsworth, Minn., 1969—, mem. continuing edn. com., 1974—; negotiator Local Tchrs. Union, Ellsworth, 1982-83; HAMEE dir. Social Studies Consortium, Adrian, Minn., 1976—. U.S. Office Edn. fellow, 1981. Mem. NEA, Minn. Coaches Assn., Nat. Volleyball Coaches Assn., Minn. Edn. Assn., Dist. 8 Coaches. Republican. Roman Catholic. Address: PO Box 172 Ellsworth MN 56129

BLOMGREN, HOLTON EUGENE, association executive; b. Mpls., Mar. 22, 1916; s. Henning Alfred and Jean (Holton) B.; B.A., U. Minn., 1938; M.B.A., Harvard U., 1940; M.A., George Washington U., 1965; grad. Army Command and Gen. Staff Coll., 1956, Army War Coll., 1963; m. Elouise Breckenridge, Nov. 14, 1942; children—Peter Frederick, Donna Lynne (Mrs. Ralph Askren), Philip Michael, Diane Elizabeth. Joined U.S. Army, advanced through grades to col., 1971; faculty Adj. Gen. Sch., 1942-47; gen. staff Hdqrs. Europe, 1948-51; faculty Army Fin. Sch., 1952-55; comdt., 1967-71; gen. staff Army Hdqrs., Washington, 1956-60, 63-65, Vietnam, 1965-66, ret., 1971; chief exec. Ind. Manufactured Housing Assn., Indpls., 1971-80; exec. dir. Nat. Manufactured Housing Fedn., Washington, 1977-79, pres., 1980—; fin. advisor Minister Def. Thailand, 1960-62; zoning cons. County Plan Commns. State Ind.; registered lobbyist U.S. Congress; govtl. affairs rep. manufactured housing industry. Decorated Legion Merit with oak leaf cluster, Air medal, Bronze Star medal. Named Sagamore of Wabash, Legion of Hoosier Heroes. Mem. Ret. Officers Assn., Harvard Alumni Assn., Chi Psi. Club: Harvard (Washington). Editor, pub. nat. distributed newsletter; editorial writer nat. trade mag. for manufactured housing industry. Office: 1015 15th St NW Suite 1240 Washington DC 20005

BLOMMEL, HENRY HOWARD, archivist; b. Connersville, Ind., Jan. 17, 1924; s. William and Hazel Marie (Riggs) B.; m. Emma Catherine Richards, Aug. 14, 1948; children—Linda Joyce Blommel Howard, John Curtis. Grad. high sch., Connersville, Ind. Gen. foreman Avco, Connersville, 1942-56; letter carrier U.S. Postal Service, 1956-84; archivist My Data Collection, Connersville, 1928—. Author: Indiana'a Little Detroit, 1964; What Was the McFarlan, 1967; Cord Connersville, 1969; Errett Lobban Cord Holdings, 1980. Chmn. Hist. Connersville, Inc., 1965, Cord Factory Meet, 1975, Founders Festival, 1980. Served with U.S. Army, 1943-46. Named Man of Yr., Jr. C. of C., Connersville, 1967. Mem. Automotive Old Timers, Am. Legion. Democrat. Methodist. Lodge: Masons. Avocations: state and local history; automobiles. Home: Route 5 Connersville IN 47331

BLOMQUIST, ROGER VINCENT, environment engineering company executive; b. Iron Mountain, Mich., Feb. 11, 1944; s. William Thure and Ellen Dagmar (Johnson) B.; B.S. with honors, Mich. State U., 1966; Ph.D., U. Wis., 1971; Exec. Devel. Program, Cornell U., 1976; m. Patricia Ann Beaty, Sept. 6, 1969; children—Jason, Matthew. Agronomist, Internat. Minerals and Chem. Co., Libertyville, Ill., 1966; research assoc. U. Wis., Madison, 1966-70; postdoctoral research fellow U. Guelph (Ont., Can.), 1971; v.p., treas., dir. Nat. Biocentric Inc., St. Paul, 1971-79; br. mgr. Environ. Research Group, St. Paul, 1979-82; v.p., gen. mgr. Braun Environ. Labs., 1982—; mem. adv. com. Rice Creek Watershed Dist.; mem. Ramsey County Engring. and Environ. Adv. Com. Precinct vice chmn. Democratic Farm Labor Party, 1976-78, del., dist. conv., 1972, 74, 76, del. county conv., 1972; mem. New Brighton City Council, 1978-84, acting mayor, 1978-84; pres. Ramsey County League of Local Govts., 1984; mem. Park Bd., 1977-79. Bush Found. fellow, 1976; Wis. Alumni Research Found. fellow, 1967-70; Louis Ware scholar, 1966; 4-H scholar, 1962-66. Mem. Nat., Minn. assns. environ. profls., Water Pollution Control Fedn., Air Pollution Control Assn., Izaak Walton League, Am. Soc. Agronomy, Sales and Mktg. Execs., New Brighton Jaycees (v.p. 1973), Sigma Xi, Alpha Zeta. Lutheran. Home: 2023 Pleasant View Dr New Brighton MN 55112

BLOMSTEDT, ERIK RAGNAR, library administrator; b. Lulea, Sweden, May 10, 1947; came to U.S., 1956, naturalized, 1965; s. Ragnar Johan and Anna Viktoria (Sundkvist) B.; m. Lily Anna Yakich, May 18, 1974; children—James, Jennifer. B.A., Northeastern Ill. U., 1969; M.S., U. Ill., 1973; M.P.A., Roosevelt U., 1976; student Universidad de las Americas, 1967. Reference librarian Chgo. Pub. Library, 1973-75; dir. Cook County Corrections Library Program, Chgo., 1975-77; dir. Three Rivers Pub. Library Dist., Channahon, Ill., 1977—. Contbr. articles on folk music to profl. jours. Mem. exec. bd. Sunny Ridge Family Ctr., Wheaton, Ill., 1982—, Midwest Baptist Conf., Park Ridge, Ill., 1981—. Served with U.S. Army, 1969-72; Vietnam. Decorated Bronze Star. Ill. State Library scholar, 1972. Mem. Am. Library Assn., Ill. Library Assn. (treas. DLRT 1978-79), Beta Phi Mu, Psi Chi. Home: 1111 C Gael Dr Joliet IL 60410 Office: Three Rivers Pub Library Dist 210 Channon Dr Channahon IL 60410

BLONDIS, ERNEST RICHARD, physician, surgeon; b. Cleve., Mar. 9, 1908; s. Harry Leonard and Sarah Alice (Reznick) B.; m. Mary Claire Steffen, Oct. 14, 1935; children—Stephanie, Sara, Ernest Richard, Robert, Thomas, Margaret, Rose, John. A.B. in Biochemistry magna cum laude, Harvard U., 1929; M.D., Case Western Res. U., 1933. Diplomate Am. Bd. Surgery (lifetime fellow in abdominal surgery). Intern, Cleve. City Hosp., 1933-34, resident in surgery St. Joseph Hosp., Joliet, Ill., 1934-35; practice medicine specializing in family practice and gen. surgery, Lemont, Ill., 1935-43, 46-78, Wewoka, Okla., 1978-79, Lemont, 1983—; chmn. dept. surgery Northlake (Ill.) Hosp., 1979-82; mem. staff Suburban Hosp.; dir., co-founder Lemont Savs. and Loan Assn., 1957—; dir. Thomas Steel Corp., Lemont. Bd. dirs. Northlake Community Hosp., 1979-83. Served to capt. M.C., U.S. Army, 1943-46. Fellow Internat. Coll. Surgeons; mem. AMA (Physicians Recognition award 1982), Am. Acad. Family Physicians (pres. county chpt. 1964-68), Am. Soc. Occupational Medicine, Am. Soc. Contemporary Medicine and Surgery, Royal Soc. Medicine, N.Y. Acad. Scis., Lemont C. of C., Lemont Area Hist. Soc., Am. Legion, Phi Beta Kappa. Republican. Roman Catholic. Club: Harvard (Chgo.). Lodge: KC. Office: 201 Stephen St Lemont IL 60439

BLONIGAN, WILLIAM ANTHONY, lawyer; b. Wichita, Kans., Nov. 7, 1953; s. Fabian Adrian and Mary Joan (Cavanagh) B.; m. Teresa Michele Brown, Aug. 8, 1975; children—William J., Maria T., Michelle J. B.A. in Polit. Sci., U. Minn., 1975; J.D., William Mitchell Coll. Law, 1978. Bar: Minn. 1979, U.S. Dist. Ct. Minn. 1979. Constrn. foreman Arrow Tech. Sales, Golden Valley, Minn., 1972-74; assoc. Korba & Blonigan, P.A. and predecessor Korba Law Office, St. Anthony, Minn., 1979-82, ptnr., 1982—. Author: Blonigan Children's Poems, 1984. Mem. Robbinsdale City Council, Minn., 1981—; commr. Robbinsdale Housing and Redevel. Authority, 1981-83, chmn., 1983—; mem. legis. com. League Minn. Cities, St. Paul, 1981, mem. budget com., 1984; mem. N.W. Suburbs Cable Communications Commn., Crystal, Minn., 1981—; commr. Suburban Rate Authority, Mpls., 1981-83. Recipient C. William Brownfield award New Hope Jaycees, 1980; mem. Robbinsdale Jaycees. Roman Catholic. Home: 4004 Quail Ave N Robbinsdale MN 55422 Office: Korba & Blonigan PA 4001 Stinson Blvd NE Saint Anthony MN 55421

BLOODWORTH, WILLIE ETHEL, realty company executive, accountant, appraiser; b. Marion, Ala., Sept. 18, 1936; d. Willie and Ezelle (Edwards) White; m. William C. Bloodworth, May 29, 1958; children—Titus Jerome, William Darryl. Student Cleveland Community Coll., 1974-77, LaSalle Extension U., Chgo., 1974-78, John Carroll U., 1980-81, Real Estate Appraising Inst., 1980-81. Cert. real estate broker, pub. acct., appraiser. Pres., B&B Bookkeeping Taxes, East Cleveland, Ohio, 1965—, W.E. Bloodworth Realty Co., East Cleveland, 1976—, Midwestern Indsl. Ctr. Inc., East Cleveland, 1980—, Ethel's Enterprise, East Cleveland, 1980—, W.E. Bloodworth Appraising Co., East Cleveland, 1981—; chairwoman Apollo Bedding Inc., Cleve. Pres., Voters Service Club, Cleve., 1977; v.p. Citizens Against Neighborhood Deterioration and Overcrowding, East Cleveland, 1980—; com. mem. East Cleveland Democratic Club, 1983—; bd. dirs. East Cleveland LWV; com. mem. Ann. Jud. Scholarship Fund Inc. Recipient achievement awards U.S. Congress, 1977, Cuyahoga Community Coll., Cleve., 1980, City of Cleve., 1983; cert. of achievement Cleve. Pub. Schs., 1984; cert. Ann. Jud. Scholarship Fund Inc., 1984. Mem. Real Estate Appraisers Inst. (award 1981), Am. Bus. Women's Assn., Cleve. Area Bd. Realtors, Cleve. Area Real Estate Brokers Assn. (sec. 1981), Nat. Assn. Female Execs., East Cleveland C. of C. (a founder, dir. 1984—), Euclid-Lee Bus. Assn. (sec.-treas.). Baptist. Club: Supper (Cleve.). Home: 1106 Mt Vernon Blvd Cleveland OH 44112 Office: B&B Bookkeeping & Tax Service/W E Bloodworth Realty Co 14916 Euclid Ave East Cleveland OH 44112

BLOOM, HERBERT J., oral surgeon, educational director; b. Chgo., Feb. 15, 1912; s. Joseph A. and Sophia B. (Lebin) B.; m. Alice L. Gilbert, Jan. 17, 1982; children by previous marriage—Stephen, Michael, Linda. D.D.S., U. Mich., 1935, M.S., 1937, M.S. in Surgery, 1943, Ph.D., 1940. Diplomate Am. Bd. Oral and Maxillofacial Surgery. Pvt. practice oral and maxillofacial surgery, 1944-72; faculty U. Mich., Ann Arbor, 1944-62; adj. prof. Wayne State U., 1962—; dept. chmn. Mt. Carmel Mercy Hosp., Detroit, 1944-72, Sinai Hosp., 1950-72, dir. Center for Continuing Med. Edn., 1974—, dir. Cleft Palate Center, Head and Neck Team, editor Sinai Hosp. Bull., 1972—; mem. staff Sinai, Mt. Carmel, Providence, Grace/Harper, Samaritan hosps.; cons. in field; regional cons. Am. Bd. Oral Surgery; cons. Council on Dental Edn., ADA, others; assoc. editor Detroit Dental Bull., 1945-48, editor, 1969—; assoc. editor Jour. Oral Surgery, 1983—. Pres., Detroit Bd. Health, 1974-77; cons. Detroit House Correction, 1949-50; v.p. United Health Orgn., 1979—; bd. dirs. Detroit Area Council on World Affairs, 1970-73, Mich. Found. for Infectious Diseases, 1978—; bd. dirs. Project Hope, 1962—, mem. med. bd., 1966—; trustee Mich. Cancer Found., 1969—, pres., 1978, v.p. bd. dirs., 1973—, dir. Oral Cancer Detection Center and Head and Neck Service, 1976—. Recipient Health award, Vietnam, 1961; Medal of Honor, Peru, 1963; Health Contbn. award, Ecuador, 1964; Internat. Service award Am. Soc. Oral Surgeons; Nat. Alpha Omega Achievement award, 1967; Alpha Omega Recognition award, 1965, 69; named Mich. Citizen of Yr., Mich. Dental Assn., 1969; Disting. Achievement award Mich. Cancer Found., 1971; Knights of Charity award Maryglade Coll., 1973; Ben Gurion award A-O-Israel, 1975; Alfred C. Fones Award, Conn. Dental Assn., 1975. Fellow Am. Acad. Oral Pathology, Am. Coll. Dentists, Internat. Coll. Dentists; mem. Mich. Soc. Oral Surgeons (pres. 1970-71), Detroit Acad. Oral Surgery (pres. 1963-64), Am. Soc. Oral Surgeons, Am. Acad. Oral Pathology, ADA, Am. Cleft Palate Assn., Am. Med. Writers Assn., Am. Assn. Dental Editors, Great Lakes Acad. Oral Surgery, Internat. Assn. Oral Surgeons (founder fellow), Chalmers Lyons Acad. Oral Surgery, AAAS, Fedn. Dentaire

Internationale, Mich. Assn. of the Professions, Pan Am. Med. Soc., Am. Coll. Dentists, Am. Coll. Oral and Maxillofacial Surgeons (pres. 1976-79, editor, regent 1979—), Am. Acad. Med. Adminstrs., Sigma Xi, Omicron Kappa Upsilon. Contbr. numerous articles to profl. jours. Office: Sinai Hosp Detroit MI 48235

BLOOM, STEPHEN I., banker; b. Bklyn., July 15, 1945; s. David H. and Estelle (Braunstein) B.; m. Rochelle Malkin, June 11, 1967; children—Alisa, Stacy, Jaime. B.B.A., Ohio State U., 1967; postgrad. in econs. and fin., Cleve. State U., 1972. Pres. U.S. Mortgage Co., Inc., Cleve., 1975—, Capcom, Inc., Cleve., 1977—; gen. ptnr. Hampton Hills Assn., Newark, 1982—, U.S. Ventures, Ltd., Cleve., 1984—, Newport Ptnrs., Hilton Head Island, S.C., 1984—. Chmn. Adopt-a-Sch., Cleve. Jewish Fedn., 1983-84, U.S. Com. Sports for Israel, Phila., 1984—, Housing Our Citizens, Cleve., 1984—; pres. Menorah Fed. Credit Union, 1977-78. Served to 2d lt. U.S. Army, 1967-68. Mem. Mortgage Bankers Assn. Am., Nat. Assn. Review Appraisers and Underwriters, Internat. Inst. Valuers, Nat. Assn. Home Builders, Urban Land Inst., Internat. Council Shopping Ctrs. Clubs: Univ. (pres. 1974-75), Interlodge (pres. 1977-78). Lodge: B'nai B'rith (Label Katz Young Leadership award 1978, Univ. Lodge Man Yr. 1980). Avocations: Marathon running; boating; public speaking. Home: 2890 NW 28th Terr Boca Raton FL 33434 Office: US Mortgage Co Inc 3401 N Federal Hwy Boca Raton FL 33431

BLOOM, STEPHEN JOEL, vending company executive; b. Chgo., Feb. 27, 1936; s. Max Samuel and Carolyn (Gumbiner) B.; B.B.A., U. Mich., 1958; m. Nancy Lee Gillan, Aug. 24, 1957; children—Anne, Bradley, Thomas, Carolyn. Salesman. then gen. mgr. Cigarette Service Co., Countryside, Ill., 1957-65, pres., chief exec. officer, i965—; pres., dir. Intercontinental Cons. Corp., Balt., chmn. bd., 1978—; vice chmn., chief adminstrv. officer Core-Mark Internat.; dir. Ford City Bank & Trust Co. Bd. dirs. Clarendon Hills (Ill.) United Fund, 1975—; mem. Chgo. Crime Commn.; finance chmn. DuPage County Republican Com., 1976. Named Man of Year, Chgo. Tobacco Table, 1972. Mem. Nat. Automatic Mdsg. Assn. (Minuteman award 1974), Nat. Assn. Tobacco Distbrs. (Young Exec. of Year award 1973, dir. 1978, nat. legis. chmn.), Nat. Tobacco Council (bd. dirs.), Young Pres.' Orgn., Ill. Assn. Tobacco Distbrs. Club: Standard. Lodge: Chgo. Rotary. Home: 3 Hamill Ln Clarendon Hills IL 60514 Office: 5401 S Dansher Rd Countryside IL 60525

BLOOM, VICTOR, psychiatrist; b. N.Y.C., Aug. 17, 1931; s. Hyman and Anna (Victor) B.; m. Shirley Dobie, June 30, 1973; children—Dorcas D., Claire B., Gordon D., David B., Elizabeth D. B.S. U. Mich., 1953, M.D., 1957. Diplomate Am. Bd. Psychiatry and Neurology. Intern Sinai Hosp. of Detroit, 1958; psychiat. resident Lafayette Clinic, Detroit, 1959-61, chief adult inpat. service, 1968-72; clin. assoc. prof. Wayne State U., Detroit, 1972—; pvt. practice psychiatry, Detroit, 1961-85, Grosse Pointe Park, Mich., 1973—. Mem. AMA, Am. Psychiat. Assn., Mich. State Med. Soc., Wayne County Med. Soc., Mich. Psychiat. Soc., Friends of Mich. Psychoanalytic Soc. Contbr. articles on psychotherapy, group psychotherapy, bioenergetic analysis, liaison psychiatry, death and dying, prevention of suicide, psychotherapy of schizophrenia to profl. jours. Home and Office: 1007 Three Mile Dr Grosse Pointe Park MI 48230

BLOOMFIELD, COLEMAN, insurance executive; b. Winnipeg, Man., Can., July 2, 1926; s. Samuel and Bessie (Staniloff) B.; came to U.S., 1952, naturalized, 1958; B.Commerce, U. Man., 1948; m. Shirley Rosenbaum, Nov. 4, 1948; children—Catherine, Laura, Leon, Diane, Richard. With Commonwealth Life Ins. Co., Louisville 1948-51; actuary, sr. v.p. Minn. Mut. Life Ins. Co., St. Paul, 1952-70, exec. v.p., 1970-71, pres., chief exec. officer, 1971—, chmn. bd., 1977—; pres., dir. Fin. Life Ins. Co.; dir. Minn. Title Corp., 1st Nat. Bank St. Paul. Bd. dirs. N. Star Research Inst., Minn. Orch. Assn., United Hosps., Inc.; v.p., bd. dirs. St. Paul United Way. Fellow Soc. Actuaries; mem. St. Paul C. of C., Am. Council Life Ins. (dir.). Office: Minn Mut Life Ins Co 400 N Robert St Saint Paul MN 55101*

BLOOMFIELD, DAVID SOLOMON, lawyer, educator; b. Cleve., Dec. 13, 1944; s. Jerome P. and Anne M. (Knoll) B.; m. Sally Ward, June 4, 1969; children—David S., Paul W. B.S., Ohio State U., 1966, J.D., 1969; postgrad. NYU Grad. Sch. Law, 1969-70. Bar: Ohio 1969, U.S. Supreme Ct. 1973, U.S. Tax Ct. 1970, U.S. Dist. Ct. (so. dist.) Ohio 1970, U.S. Dist. Ct. (no. dist.) Ohio 1972, U.S. Ct. Appeals (6th cir.) 1973. Mem. staff Lybrand Ross Bros. & Montgomery, N.Y.C., 1969-70; chief tax sect. Atty. Gen. Ohio, Columbus, 1970-71; assoc., then ptnr. Ward Kaps Bainbridge Maurer Bloomfield & Melvin, and predecessor, Columbus, 1971—; lectr. Capital U., 1972-78, Ohio Paralegal Inst., 1979; adj. prof. Capital U. Coll. Law, Columbus, 1980—. Contbr. articles to profl. jours. Active Columbus United Way, 1979—; bd. dirs. N.W. Mental Health Assn., 1979-82; campaign chmn. Price for Judge, Columbus, 1980. Named Adj. Prof. of Yr., Capital U. Law Sch., 1982-83, 83-84, 84-85; recipient Merit award Ohio Law Inst., 1975. Mem. ABA, Ohio Bar Assn. (coms.), Columbus Bar Assn. (chair coms.). Democrat. Jewish. Clubs: University, Athletic, Ohio State U. President's (Columbus). Avocation: woodworking. Home: 3741 Romnay Rd Columbus OH 43220 Office: Ward Kaps et al 199 S 5th St Columbus OH 43215

BLOOMFIELD, SAUL SOLOMON, academic physician, clinical investigator, clinical pharmacologist; b. Montreal, Can., June 30, 1925; came to U.S., 1965, permanent resident; s. Oscar H. and Tillie S. (Schoilovitch) B.; m. Ellen S Steinberg, Jan. 9, 1949; children—Laurence, Patricia, Matthew. B.S., McGill U., Montreal, 1946, M.S., 1948; M.D., U. Geneva, 1953; M.S., U. Montreal, 1965. Intern Montreal Gen. Hosp., 1953-54; resident in internal medicine Queen Mary Vets. Hosp., Montreal, 1954-55; gen. practice medicine, Montreal, 1955-63; instr. pharmacology U. Montreal, 1963-65; from asst. to assoc. prof. U. Cin., 1965-77, prof. medicine and pharmacology, 1977—; vis. scientist Merrell Internat., Strasbourg, France, 1972-73; acting dir. div. clin. pharmacology U. Cin., 1979-81; vis. prof. Oxford U., 1980. Contbr. articles to profl. jours. Mem. Com. Human Research, Cin., 1969-77; del. U.S. Pharmacopeia Conv., Cin., 1972-80; pres.-elect U. Cin. Coll. Medicine Faculty Forum, 1983-85, pres., 1985-87. NIH research grantee, 1968-72; research fellow Can. Found. Advancement Therapeutics, 1964-65, NIH, 1966-68. Mem. Am. Soc. Clin. Pharmacology and Therapeutics, Am. Soc. Pharmacology and Exptl. Therapeutics, Am. Fedn. Clin. Research, Am. Pain Soc., Cin. Soc. Internal Medicine. Club: Faculty. Home: 57 Carpenter's Ridge Cincinnati OH 45241 Office: U Cincinnati Med Ctr 5502 Med Scis Bldg Cincinnati OH 45267-0578

BLOOMQUIST, ROSS FRANCE, college administrator; b. Willmar, Minn., Apr. 29, 1923; s. Aldrich Albin Carl and Leola (France) B.; m. Lavinia Carolyn Bloom, Oct. 6, 1946; children—Timothy, Marcia, Betsy. B.A., Gustavus Adolphus Coll., 1946. Bus. mgr. Gustavus Adolphus Coll., St. Peter, Minn., 1955-75, v.p., treas., 1975—; chmn. bd. First Nat. Bank, St. Peter, 1974—. Bd. dirs. St. Peter C. of C., 1952—; exec. bd. Twin Valley Council Boy Scouts Am., Mankato, Minn., 1972—. Served to lt. j.g. USN, 1942-46. Recipient Eagle award Boy Scouts Am., 1940, Silver Beaver award, 1972. Republican. Lutheran. Home: 708 Valley View Rd St Peter MN 56028 Office: Gustavus Adolphus Coll St Peter MN 56082

BLOSER, DIETER, radiologist; b. Yugoslavia, Aug. 17, 1944; came to U.S., 1947, naturalized, 1954; s. Peter and Eva Helen B.; A.B., Princeton U., 1966; M.D., Case Western Res. U., 1970; m. Deborah Pierce Forbes, Nov. 25, 1967; children—Peter Forbes, Timothy Philip. Intern dept. medicine U. Hosps. of Cleve., 1970-71, resident in radiology, 1971-72, 74-76, chief resident, 1975-76; practice medicine specializing in radiology, Parma, Ohio, 1976—; mem. staff Parma Community Gen. Hosp., 1976—, chief nuclear medicine, 1977—, chief radiology, 1984—; mem. staff U. Hosps. of Cleve., Cleve. Met. Gen. Hosp. Served to lt. comdr. USN, 1972-74. Diplomate Am. Bd. Radiology. Mem. Am. Coll. Radiology, Radiol. Soc. N. Am., Ohio Radiol. Soc., Cleve. Radiol. Soc., Am. Inst. Ultrasound in Medicine, Cleve. Acad. Medicine, AMA, Ohio Med. Assn., Princeton Alumni Assn. No. Ohio, Phi Beta Kappa, Alpha Omega Alpha. Lutheran. Home: 1251 Oakridge Dr Cleveland Heights OH 44121 Office: 7007 Power Blvd Parma OH 44129 also 18660 Bagley Rd Middleburg Heights OH

BLOSSOM, JOHN SEIBERT, consulting engineer; b. Detroit, Aug. 10, 1917; s. John and Catherine (Seibert) B.; m. Enid Foege, May 13, 1940 (dec. Aug. 1973); 1 child, John Albert; m. Harriet Snowdon, July 28, 1974. Student in mech. engring. Lawrence Inst. Tech., 1942, 46-47. Registered profl. engr., Mich., Ohio, Ind., Ky., Md., N.Y., D.C., Pa., W.Va., S.C. Chief instr. Thermal Inst., Detroit, 1937-39; chief engr., sec. Mech. Heat & Cold, Inc., 1939-44, 46-57; ptnr. Ziel-Blossom & Assoc., Cin., 1957-71; pres. ZBA, Inc. and Ziel-Blossom & Assocs., Inc., 1971-84; v.p., treas. ZBA, Inc., Cin., 1984—. Contbr. articles to profl. jours. Mem. ad hoc com. on solid wastes Nat. Acad. Scis.-Bldg. Research Adv. Bd., Washington, 1967-74; trustee Shadybrook House of Laymen's Movement, Cleve., 1964-71, arbitrator Am. Arbitration Assn., Cin., 1968—. Served with USNR, 1944-46. Fellow ASHRAE (chmn. handbook, pub., research and tech. coms. 1960-84, Wolverine Diamond Key award 1959, tech. council 1985—); mem. Nat. Soc. Profl. Engrs., Mich. Soc. Profl. Engrs. (chmn. bldg. code com. 1953-56). Presbyterian. Avocations: squash racquets; tennis. Home: 7351 S Mingo Ln Madeira OH 45243 Office: ZBA Inc 23 E 7th St Cincinnati OH 45202

BLOUGH, JOHN PHILIP, consulting engineering executive; b. Detroit, July 2, 1934; s. John Philip and Kathleen (Koenig) B.; m. Joanna Emma Petracci, Apr. 7, 1956; children—John Philip, Angela Marie, Mark Edmund, James Peter (dec.). B.S., U. Detroit, 1957. Cert. health care safety profl. With Pharm. sales dept. Wyeth Labs., Macomb County, Mich., 1957-61; systems engr. IBM, Detroit, 1961-64; project mgr. Detroit Pub. Schs., 1964-67; mem. adminstrv. staff Henry Ford Hosp., Detroit, 1967-76; pres. Med. Instrumentation Systems-Hosp. Shared Engring. Services, Inc., Grosse Pointe, Park, Mich., 1976—. Bd. dirs. Eastern Wayne County Heart Unit of Mich. Heart Assn.; pres. St. Clair Shores (Mich.) Baseball Assn., 1981—. Mem. Engring. Soc. Detroit, Assn. for Advancement of Med. Instrumentation, Mich. Hosp. Assn., Am. Hosp. Assn., Grosse Pointe Park Bus. and Profl. Assn. (pres. 1983). Roman Catholic. Home: 23440 Playview Ave Saint Clair Shores MI 48082 Office: 15133 Kercheval Ave Grosse Pointe Park MI 48230

BLUE, ROBERT LEE, educator; b. Columbiaville, Mich., Apr. 23, 1920; s. Arthur Floyd and Elma (Ellis) B.; B.A., Mich. State U., 1941; M.A., U. Mich., 1952; m. Dorothy L. Seward, July 15, 1961. Tchr., Chesaning (Mich.) High Sch., 1941-42, 45-57; prin. Ricker Jr. High Sch., Saginaw, Mich., 1957-59, Buena Vista High Sch., Saginaw, 1960-69; asst. prof. secondary edn. Central Mich. U., Mt. Pleasant, 1969—. Bd. dirs. Hartley Edn. Nature Camp, 1957-69. Served with U.S. Army, 1942-45. Decorated Bronze Star. Mem. NEA (life), Mich. Edn. Assn., Assn. Tchr. Educators, Mich. Assn. Tchr. Educators, Nat. Assn. Secondary Sch. Prins., Mich. Assn. Secondary Sch. Prins., Mich. PTA (hon. life), Am. Legion, Mich. Hist. Soc., Saginaw County Hist. Soc., Lapeer County Hist. Soc., Phi Delta Kappa. Republican. Methodist. Clubs: Optimist, Knife and Fork, Pit and Balcony, Masons. Author: Footsteps Into The Past, A History of Columbiaville, 1979, also articles. Home: 4584 Colonial Dr Saginaw MI 48603 Office: 115 W Genesee Saginaw MI 48602

BLUESTEIN, JUDITH ANN, diversified industry executive, educator, rabbi; b. Cin., Apr. 2, 1948; d. Paul Harold and Joan Ruth (Straus) B.; B.A., U. Pa., 1969; postgrad. Am. Sch. Classical Studies, Athens, Greece, 1968, Vergilian Soc., 1970, 76, 77, 78, Hebrew Union Coll., Jewish Inst. Religion, Jerusalem, 1971, 1979-80, Am. Acad. in Rome, 1975; M.A.H.L., Hebrew Union Coll.-Jewish Inst. Religion, Cin., 1983; M.A. in Religion (Univ. fellow), Case Western Res. U., 1973, M.A. in Latin, 1973. Sec., Paul H. Bluestein & Co., Cin., 1964—; v.p. Panel Machine Co., 1966—, Blujay Corp., 1966—, Ermet Products Corp., 1966—; partner Companhia Engenheiros Industrial Bluestein do Brasil, Cin., 1971—; rabbi, 1984; with Jewish Theol. Sem. Am., 1984—; rabbi Temple Israel, Marion, Ohio, 1980-84, Temple Sholom, Galesburg, Ill., 1985—; tchr. Latin, Cin. Public Schs., 1973-79. Mem. Archeol. Inst. Am., Classical Assn. Middle West and South (v.p. Ohio 1976-79), Am. Classical League, Ohio Classical Conf. (council 1976-79), Vergilian Soc., Soc. Bibl. Lit., Cin. Assn. Tchrs. Classics (pres. 1976-78), Am. Philol. Assn., Central Conf. Am. Rabbis, N.Y. Bd. Rabbis, Assn. Reform Rabbis N.Y.C. Address: 3420 Section Rd Cincinnati OH 45237

BLUESTEIN, PAUL HAROLD, management engineer; b. Cin., June 14, 1923; s. Norman and Eunice D. (Schullman) B.; B.S., Carnegie Inst. Tech., 1946, B. Engring. in Mgmt. Engring., 1946; M.B.A., Xavier U., 1973; m. Joan Ruth Straus, May 17, 1943; children—Alice Sue Bluestein Greenbaum, Judith Ann. Time study engr. Lodge & Shipley Co., 1946-47; adminstrv. engr. Randall Co., 1947-52; partner Paul H. Bluestein & Co., mgmt. cons., 1952—, Seinsheimer-Bluestein Mgmt. Services, 1964-70, Companhia Engenheiros Industrial Bluestein do Brasil, 1970—; gen. mgr. Baker Refrigeration Co., 1953-56; pres., dir. Tabor Mfg. Co. 1953-54, Blujay Corp., 1954—, Blatt & Ludwig Corp., 1954-57, Jason Industries, Inc., 1954-57, Hamilton-York Corp., 1954-57, Earle Hardware Mfg. Co., 1955-57, Hermas Machine Co., Panel Machine Co., Ermet Products Corp. Tyco Labs., Inc., 1968-69, All-Tech Industries, 1969, Del. Tisco Corp., 1970-71; gen. mgr. Hafleigh & Co., 1959-60; sr. v.p., gen. mgr. McCauley Ind. Corp., 1959-60; v.p., gen. mgr. Farmco Machine div. Worden-Allen Co., 1974-75; gen. mgr. Am. Art Works div. Rapid-Am. Corp., 1960-63; sec.-treas., dir. Liberty Baking Co., 1964-65; pres. Duguesne Baking Co., 1964-65, Goddard Bakers, Inc., 1964-65; pub. Merger and Acquisition Digest, 1962—; exec. v.p. Peck, Stow & Wilcox Co., 1976-77; dir. Norameo, Inc., 1964-67. Served from pvt. to tech. sgt. AUS, 1943-46. Registered profl. engr., Ohio. Mem. ASME, Internat. Inst. Indsl. Engrs., Joint Engring. Mgmt. Conf., Am. Soc. Engring. Mgmt., N.Am. Mgmt. Council, World Council Mgmt. (world bd). Lodge: B'nai B'rith. Home: 3420 Section Rd Amberley Village Cincinnati OH 45237 Office: 3420 Section Rd Cincinnati OH 45237

BLUHM, GENE ROBERT, mechanical engineer; b. Quincy, Ill., Aug. 30, 1959; s. Robert Martin and Larine Evelyn (Flesner) B.; m. Nancy Anne Ruppin, Nov. 28, 1981. B.S. in Mech. Engring., Valparaiso U., 1981. Design engr. Cooper Industries/Cooper Petroleum Equipment, Quincy, 1981—. Mem. ASME, Applicon/Scattered Midwest User Group. Lutheran. Office: Cooper Industries/Cooper Petroleum Equipment 1800 Gardner Expressway Quincy IL 62301

BLUM, KENNETH CLARKE, newspaper executive; b. Detroit, June 3, 1946; s. John Robert and Harriette Regina (Miller) B.; m. Nancy Ann Caputo, Aug. 29, 1969; children—Shane Ann, Matthew Joseph. B.S., Baldwin-Wallace Coll., 1968. Editor, The Courier-Crescent, Orrville, Ohio, 1968-76, mgr., 1975—; mgr. The Farmer- Hub, Millersburg, Ohio, 1976—, The Main St. Press, Rittman, Ohio, 1980—, The Marketeer, Wooster, Ohio, 1975—; columnist Pub. Aux., Washington, 1981—. Contbg. author: The Newspaper, 1981. Vice-pres. Orville (Ohio) Hist. Soc., 1974-77. Recipient awards Ohio Newspaper Assn., Nat. Newspaper Assn., Ohio News Photographers Assn., Nat. Assn. Advt. Pubs. Mem. Nat. Newspaper Assn. (state chmn. 1982—), Soc. Profl. Journalists, Buckeye Press Assn. (pres. 1977-79). Republican. Club: Exchange (Orrville, Ohio). Home: 909 N. Crown Hill Rd Orrville OH 44667 Office: The Daily Record 409 N Main St Orrville OH 44667

BLUM, KENNETH DALE, candy and tobacco company executive; b. Columbus, Ohio, July 24, 1956; s. Joseph and Nancy Joyce (Cooper) B. B.B.A., Colo. U., 1979. Mktg. rep. Four-Phase Systems, Inc., Cin., 1979-82; v.p., gen. mgr. Peerless Candy and Tobacco Co., Inc., Columbus, 1982—. Program chmn. Jewish Nat. Fund, Columbus, 1984, Bonds for Israel, Columbus, 1983-85. Lodge: B'Nai B'Rith. Avocations: Skiing, jogging, racquetball. Office: Peerless Candy and Tobacco Co Inc 970 Freeway Dr N Columbus OH 43229

BLUM, STEVEN EDWARD, osteopathic physician, medical educator; b. Detroit, July 18, 1953; s. Maurice Bernard and Joan Rae (Stevens) B.; m. Andrea Gail Rosenberg, Aug. 1, 1982. B.S. in Zoology and Anthropology with distinction, U. Mich., 1975; D.O., Mich. State U., 1978. Intern Botsford Gen. Hosp., Farmington, Mich., 1978-79, mem. staff, 1980—; gen. practice osteo. medicine, Novi, Mich., 1980—; assoc. clin. prof. family medicine Mich. State U. Coll. Osteo. Medicine, 1982—. Mem. Am. Osteo. Assn., Mich. Osteo. Assn., Oakland County Osteo. Assn., Am. Soc. Colposcopy and Cervical Pathology. Jewish. Home: Farmington Hills MI Office: Novi MI

BLUME, HERBERT EDWARD, accountant; b. Tripoli, Iowa, Sept. 20, 1917; s. William C. and Hulda D. (Hagenow) B.; student LaSalle Extension U., 1943-44; m. Elvera E. Kelling, Sept. 25, 1938; children—Carol (Mrs. Merlin H. Franzen), Marjorie (Mrs. Arthur F. Maynard), Marilyn (Mrs. Robert F. Seefeld). Farmer, nr. Tripoli, 1938-40; pvt. tax practice, Tripoli, 1944—; pvt. practice accounting, 1945—; treas. Tripoli Devel. Corp., 1959—; pres. Aids for Handicaps, Inc., 1958—; pub. Farm Record. Sec. Bremer County Zoning Commn., 1963-80; presdl. elector 3d Dist. Iowa, 1980. Accounting practitioner, 1975—. Sec. finance Iowa dist. east Lutheran Ch.-Mo. Synod, 1960-66; chmn. St. John Luth. Ch., Denver, Iowa, 1980. Mem. Nat. Soc. Pub. Accountants (accredited), Accts. Assn. Iowa (pres. 1970-71), Nat. Assn. Tax Practitioners, Iowa Soc. Acctg. Practitioners, Luth. Laymen's League, Farm Bur. Republican. Patentee stairwalking crutches, 1945. Address: Tripoli IA 50676

BLUMENTHAL, D. JEFFREY, management consultant; b. Evanston, Ill., June 12, 1940; s. Harold and Jeanne (Newberry) B.; m. Joan Hartstein, Aug. 21, 1966; children—Andrew Samuel, Marianne. B.Eng. in Physics, Cornell U., 1963; M.S., Stanford U., 1964, Engr., 1969. Sr. engr. Sylvania Elect. Co., Mt. View, Calif., 1965-69; v.p. Planmetrics, Inc., Chgo., 1969-78; pres., mgmt. cons. The Jeffrey Corp., Deerfield, Ill., 1978—; adj. mem. faculty Northwestern U., Evanston, Ill., 1980-84. Chmn. CATV Com., Village Deerfield, Ill., 1980; trustee Village Bd., Deerfield, 1976. Mem. Nat. Assn. Bus. Economists, Am. Statis. Assn. Republican. Jewish. Clubs: Executive's (Chgo.); Abbey Springs Yacht. Home: 1043 Peachtree Lane Deerfield IL 60015 Office: The Jeffrey Corp PO Box 643 Deerfield IL 60015

BLUMENTHAL, DAVID LIONEL, psychoanalyst; b. Chgo., Apr. 22, 1926; s. Sol and Ida (Schniederman) B.; B.S. in Mech. Engring., Purdue U., 1948; M.S.W., U. Chgo., 1949, postgrad., 1950; M.A., Butler U., Indpls., 1959; postgrad. Nat. Psychol. Assn. for Psychoanalysis, N.Y.C., 1955-70; M.A., Christian Theol. Sem., 1982; Sc.D. (hon.), Lincoln Coll., Indpls., 1962; Rel.D., Ind. Christian U., 1984; m. Patricia Louise Wright, Apr. 19, 1968; 1 dau., Jill Ann. Psychiat. caseworker Ind. U. Med. Center, 1950-51; caseworker, supr., adminstrv. asst. Family Service Assn. Indpls., 1951-54; pvt. practice psychotherapy and psychoanalysis, Indpls., 1954—; psychotherapist, dir. Shelby County Mental Health Center, Shelbyville, Ind., 1955-58; mem. faculty Ind. U., Purdue U., Butler U., Lincoln Coll., 1954-74. Served with USNR, 1944-46. Recipient Public Relations award Family Service Assn. Indpls., 1952, 54. Mem. Acad. Cert. Social Workers, Nat. Assn. Social Workers (charter), Am. Acad. Psychotherapists, Am. Group Psychotherapy Assn., Am. Soc. Group Psychotherapy and Psychodrama, Ind. Soc. Clin. Social Workers, NAACP. Jewish. Author articles in field. Address: 8100 Sargent Rd Indianapolis IN 46256

BLUMENTHAL, W. MICHAEL, manufacturing company executive; b. Germany, Jan. 3, 1926; s. Ewald and Rose Valerie (Markt) B.; B.Sc., U. Calif. at Berkeley, 1951; M.A., M.P.A., Princeton, 1953, Ph.D., 1956; m. Margaret Eileen Polley, Sept. 8, 1951. Came to U.S., 1947, naturalized, 1952. Research asso. Princeton, 1954-57; labor arbitrator State of N.J., 1955-57; v.p. dir. Crown Cork Internat. Corp., 1957-61, also dir. overseas affiliated cos.; became dep. asst. sec. state for econ. affairs Dept. State, 1961; apptd. President's dep. spl. rep. for trade negotiations with rank of ambassador, 1963-67; pres. Bendix Internat., 1967-70; dir. Bendix Corp., 1967-77, vice chmn., 1970-71, pres., chief operating officer, 1971-72, chmn., pres., chief exec. officer, 1972-77; sec. of Treasury, Washington, 1977-79; vice chmn., chief exec. officer Burroughs Corp., Detroit, 1980-81, chmn., chief exec. officer, 1981—, also dir.; dir. Equitable Life Assurance Soc. U.S., 1972-77, 79—, Pillsbury Co., 1979—, Chem. N.Y. Corp. and subs. Chem. Bank, 1979—; U.S. rep. commn. internat. commodity trade UN Econ. and Social Council, 1961, 1962; U.S. adviser spl. meeting Inter-Am. Econ. and Social Council, 1961; chmn. U.S. del. UN Coffee Conf., 1962; bd. dirs. Bus. Com. for Arts; trustee Rockefeller Found. Charter trustee Princeton. Mem. Bus. Council, Am. Econ. Assn., Council Fgn. Relations, Atlantic Council U.S. (dir.), Phi Beta Kappa. Clubs: Princeton, Century (N.Y.C.); Econ. of Detroit (dir.). Office: Burroughs Corp Burroughs Plaza Detroit MI 48232

BLUNT, ROY D., state government official. Sec. of State, State of Mo., Jefferson City. Office: Office of the Sec of State PO Box 778 Jefferson City MO 65102*

BLUTZA, STEVEN JAY, marketing executive; b. N.Y.C., Oct. 4, 1945; s. Charles and Anne (Rosenberg) B. B.A., CCNY, 1966; M.A., U. Calif.-Berkeley, 1967, Ph.D., 1978. Instr. polit. sci. U. Ill., Urbana, 1972-75; pres. Consumer Services Orgn., Chgo., 1978-81, Profl. Services Mktg. Corp., Chgo., 1982—. Mem. Am. Prepaid Legal Services Inst., Nat. Resource Ctr. for Consumers of Legal Services, Phi Beta Kappa. Home: 5020 S Lake Shore Dr Apt 3415 Chicago IL 60615 Office: 1 Quincy Ct Suite 1622 Chicago IL 60604

BOAND, CHARLES W., lawyer; b. Bates County, Mo., Aug. 19, 1908; s. Albert and Edith Nadine (Pipes) B.; A.A., Jr. Coll. Kansas City; J.D. summa cum laude, U. Mo.-Kansas City; M.B.A., LL.B. cum laude, U. Chgo.; m. Phoebe Bard, Aug. 2, 1980; children—Bard, Barbara. Bar: Mo. 1931, D.C. 1936, Ill. 1937, U.S. Supreme Ct. 1935, U.S. Ct. Appeals (1st, 2d, 5th, 7th, 9th, 10th, 11th and D.C. Cirs.), trial bar of U.S. Dist. Ct. (no. dist.) Ill. Assoc., Moore & Fitch, St. Louis, 1933; atty. Gen. Counsel's Office, U.S. Treasury Dept., 1933-36; assoc. Wilson & McIlvaine, 1937-42, ptnr., 1945—, sr. ptnr., chmn. exec. com., 1974—. Mem. council Grad. Sch. Bus., U. Chgo., 1961-68, mem. vis. com. to library U. Chgo., 1985—; mem. citizens bd. U. Chgo.; trustee Muskingum Coll., 1965-79. Served as officer USNR, 1942-45; lt. comdr. Res. (ret.). Mem. Nat. conf. lawyers and C.P.A.s, Ill. Bar Assn. (chmn. exec. com. corp. securities law sect. 1954-56), Chgo. Bar Assn. (chmn. com. corp. law 1963-64), Fed. Bar Assn., 7th Circuit Bar Assn., U. Chgo. Alumni Assn. (pres. 1975-80, alumni cabinet 1964-70, 72-80, v.p. 1973-74, 1st Alumni Disting. Service award 1981), U. Chgo. Law Sch. Alumni Assn. (pres. 1968-70, dir. 1950-72), Order of Coif, Beta Gamma Sigma, Sigma Chi, Phi Alpha Delta. Presbyterian (stated clk. 1962-65). Clubs: Chicago, Mid-Am., Metropolitan, Law, Legal (Chgo.); Barrington Hills (Ill.) Country (dir. 1947-55); Los Caballeros Golf (Ariz.). Editor: Case Notes, U. Chgo. Law Rev., 1932-33. Home: 250 W County Line Rd PO Box 567 Barrington Hills IL 60010 Office: 135 S LaSalle St Chicago IL 60603

BOBB, JUDITH KAY, educator; b. Seymour, Ind., Jan. 27, 1941; d. Albert Carl and Grace Ione (Persinger) Judd; m. Louis Earl Bobb, July 23, 1961; children—Douglas Allen, Julia Ann. B.A. in Elem. Edn., Purdue U., 1964, postgrad. in Spl. End. for Gifted Children, 1979-81; M.S., Ind. U., 1970. Cert. elem. tchr., Ind. Second grade tchr. Brownstown (Ind.) Elem. Sch., 1964—; organizer activities for gifted pupils. Mem. NEA, Ind. State Tchrs. Assn., Brownstown Classroom Tchrs. Assn., Assn. for Supervision and Curriculum Devel., Ind. Assn. for Supervision and Curriculum Devel., Delta Kappa Gamma. Lutheran. Club: Tri Kappa, Seymour, Ind. Home: RR 3 Seymour IN 47274

BOBER, MARY LOU, steel company consultant; b. East Chicago, Ind., July 13, 1955; d. Joseph F. and Myrtle (Bessler) B.; A.B., Ind. U., 1977, M.B.A., 1979. Staff cons. Inland Steel Co., East Chicago, Ind., 1979-81, cons., 1981—. Home: 3130 N Lake Shore Dr Apt 907 Chicago IL 60657 Office: Inland Steel Co 30 W Monroe St Chicago IL 60603

BOBINET, LOUIS GEORGE, insurance company manager; b. Chelsea, Iowa, Aug. 11, 1937; s. William Antone and Helen Anna (Seidel) B.; B.A., Simpson Coll., 1960; M.S., Drake U., 1968; m. Claire Whinery, Feb. 23, 1974; children—Kyle, Kayla. Jr. high sci. tchr. Indianola (Iowa) Community Sch., 1960-70; adjustor IMT Ins. Co., Des Moines, 1970-71, personnel mgr., 1971-82; personnel mgr. Farmers Mut. Hail Ins. Co., Des Moines, 1982—. Mem. Adminstrv. Mgmt. Soc. (pres. 1983-84), Sigma Alpha Epsilon (life). Republican. Methodist. Clubs: Kiwanis, Masons, Shriners. Home: 201 N J St Indianola IA 50125 Office: Farmers Mut Hail Ins Co 2323 Grand Ave Des Moines IA 50305

BOBOWICK, MORTON, lawyer; b. Bklyn., Oct. 8, 1942; s. Norman and Shirley B. (Jacobs) B.; m. Susan Beth Liber, Feb. 21, 1965; children—Marla Jill, Michelle Lynn. B.A. magna cum laude, Bklyn. Coll., 1962; J.D. cum laude, Harvard U., 1965. Bar: Ohio 1966, D.C. 1966. Atty., CAB, Washington, 1965-1966; clk. U.S. Ct. Appeals (6th cir.), Dayton, Ohio, 1966-1968; ptnr. Eastman and Smith, Toledo, 1968—; trustee Toledo Estate Planning Council. Mem. ABA, Ohio Bar Assn., Toledo Bar Assn., Phi Beta Kappa. Jewish. Avocations: Tennis; traveling; skiing. Home: 4601 Beaconsfield Ct Toledo OH 43623 Office: Eastman and Smith 800 United Savings Bldg Toledo OH 43604

BOCCIA, EDWARD EUGENE, fine arts educator, artist; b. Newark, June 22, 1921; s. Cono and Frances (Jacobitti) B.; m. Madeleine Jean Wysong, July 14, 1945; 1 child, Alice. Cert. Pratt Inst., 1942; student Art Students League, N.Y.C., 1938, 46; B.S., Columbia U., 1948, M.A., 1952. Dean Columbus Art Sch., Ohio, 1948-51; asst. dean Washington U., St. Louis, 1951-54, assoc. prof. drawing, 1954-66, prof. art, 1966—; guest instr. U. Sask, Regina, 1960, Webster Coll., Webster Groves, Mo., summer 1965, Fontbonne Coll., St. Louis, summer 1970. Painter murals Newman Chapel, Washington, U., St. Louis, 1964, First Nat. Bank, 1966, Brith Sholom Kneseth Israel Temple, St. Louis, 1970. Served with U.S. Army, 1942-45, ETO. Recipient Cavaliers Al Merito, Republic of Italy, 1979; named hon. v.p. St. Louis U., 1979. Mem. St. Louis Poetry Ctr. (hon. mention awards 1983). Roman Catholic. Avocation: swimming. Home: 600 Harper Ave Webster Groves MO 63119

BOCK, LEO LOUIS, electrical engineer; b. Poole, Nebr., Jan. 7, 1927; s. Louis Alex and Mary (Heerman) B.; B.S.E.E., U. Nebr., 1951; m. Verona Velma Hafner, Dec. 18, 1951; children—Diane, Gerald, Karen, Michael, Lawrence. Elec. engr. Sperry Univac, 1951-55, engring. mgr., 1955-61, product planning mgr., 1961-65; sr. engr. IBM Corp., Owego, N.Y., 1965-68; product planning mgr. Mohawk Data Scis., Herkimer, N.Y., 1968-69; coordinator for product planning Sperry Univac, St. Paul, 1969-70, mktg. mgr., 1970-77, navy systems market planning mgr., 1977-79; staff systems engr. Sperry DPG Computer Systems, 1979—. Served with USAF, 1945-46. Mem. IEEE. Republican. Lutheran. Home: 10824 York Ave S Bloomington MN 55431 Office: Sperry Park Saint Paul MN 55165

BOCKELMAN, J(OHN) RICHARD, lawyer; b. Chgo., Aug. 8, 1925; s. Carl August and Mary (Ritchie) B.; student U. Wis., 1943-44, Northwestern U., 1944-45, Harvard U., 1945, U. Hawaii, 1946; B.S. in Bus. Adminstrn., Northwestern U., 1946; M.A. in Econs., U. Chgo., 1949, J.D., 1951. Admitted to Ill. bar, 1951; atty.-adviser Chgo. ops. office U.S. AEC, 1951-52; asso. firm Schradzke, Gould & Ratner, Chgo., 1952-57, Brown, Dashow & Langeluttig, Chgo., 1957-59, firm Antonow & Weissbourd, Chgo., 1959-61; partner firm Burton, Isaacs, Bockelman & Miller, Chgo., 1961-69; individual practice law, Chgo., 1970—; prof. bus. law Ill. Inst. Tech., Chgo., 1950-82; lectr. econs. De Paul U., Chgo., 1952-53; dir., v.p., sec. Secretaries, Inc., Chgo., Beale Travel Service, Inc., Chgo.; dir., sec. Arlington Engring. Co., Chgo.; dir., v.p. Universal Distbrs., Inc., Chgo. Served with USNR, 1943-46. Mem. Am., Ill. Chgo. bar assns., Catholic Lawyers Guild Chgo., Phi Delta Theta. Clubs: Lake Point Tower, Barclay Ltd., Execs., Whitehall, Internat. (Chgo.); Anvil (East Dundee, Ill.). Home: 1212 Lake Shore Dr Chicago IL 60610 Office: 104 S Michigan Ave Chicago IL 60603

BODDIE, DON O'MAR, records company executive, producer, recording artist; b. St. Louis, Nov. 22, 1944; s. George Palmer and Lucille (Boddie) Johnson; m. Martha Lee Brown, Oct. 9, 1970 (div. 1979); children—Don O'Mar, Anthony, Shawn, Shellie. Student Forest Park Community Coll., Jr. Coll. Dist., St. Louis, 1980-82, U. Mo.-St. Louis, 1982-84. Rec. artist, Bamboo Records, St. Louis, 1966-70; chmn. bd. Puzzletown Prodns., St. Louis, 1970-85; producer, writer, artist Hi Records, Memphis, 1976-79; producer, writer Motown Records, Los Angeles, 1976-78; producer, writer, artist Chrome Records, St. Louis, 1979—; cons. Archway Studios, St. Louis, 1970-85; v.p. Scorpio Prodns., Pine Lawn, Mo., 1980-82, producer music, 1980-84; promotions JD Mgmt. and Assocs., St. Louis, 1979-85. Entertainment, Com. to Elect Irene Smith, St. Louis, 1982. Democrat. Roman Catholic. Home: 6112 Hancock Saint Louis MO 63134 Office: Chrome Records 6112 Hancock Saint Louis MO 63134

BODE, SANDRA JEAN, educational administrator; b. Warren, Ohio, Apr. 20, 1941; d. Gilbert Vernon and Clara Helen (Mount) Reed; student Kent (Ohio) State U., 1959-62; B.S. in Edn., Youngstown (Ohio) State U., 1964; postgrad. Purdue U., 1969-70; M.S. in Edn., No. Ill. U., 1977; m. Glen Harold Bode, June 6, 1964. Tchr. elem. sch., Mineral Ridge, Ohio, 1962-66, Kent pub. schs., 1966-68, Duneland Sch. Corp., Chesterton, Ind., 1969-70, Overseas Dependent Schs., Germany, 1971-73; coordinator career edn. Thornton Area Pub. Sch. Corp., 1973-76; dir. DuPage Career Edn. Center, Wheaton, Ill., 1976—; sex equity cons. Ill. Bd. Edn.; mem. teaching staff Nat. Coll. Edn., Evanston, Ill., Governors State U., Park Forest, Ill., No. Ill. U., DeKalb; cons. to Cook and DuPage Counties, SBA, U.S. Office of Career Edn., Washington. Home: 726 S Adams St Hinsdale IL 60521 Office: Dir Office for Computer Literacy No Ill U DeKalb IL 60115

BODENSTEIN, KENNETH ALAN, financial executive; b. N.Y.C., Feb. 25, 1937; s. William and Sylvia (Halperin) B.; m. Susan Sims, Sept. 4, 1960; children—Todd, Leslie, A.B., Columbia U., 1957, B.S. in Chem. Engring., 1958, M.B.A., 1960. Asst. to treas. Air Products and Chems. Co., Allentown, Pa., 1960-64; sr. investment analyst Armour & Co., Chgo., 1964-68; mgr. midwest region Goodbody & Co., Chgo., 1968-70; dir. bus. research CNA Fin. Co., Chgo., 1970-74; sr. v.p. Duff & Phelps Inc., Chgo., 1975—. Mem. Assn. Corp. Growth (bd. dirs. 1982-84), Investment Analyst Soc. Chgo. (bd. dirs. 1984-87). Chartered Fin. Analyst. Clubs: University, Midtown Tennis, Fullerton Tennis (Chgo.). Home: 340 Diversey Pkwy Chicago IL 60657 Office: Duff & Phelps Inc 55 E Monroe St Chicago IL 60603

BODENSTEINER, ROBERT THEODORE, trucking industry executive; b. Decorah, Iowa, May 14, 1933; s. Cyril Mathew and Acquin Marie (Kilcoin) B.; B.S., Iowa State U., 1955; postgrad. Iowa U., 1957; postgrad. N.Y. City Coll., 1958; m. Amalia Frances Valenti, Nov. 28, 1959; children—Theodore Girard, David Neil, Susan Frances. Internal auditor N.Y. Life Ins. Co., N.Y.C., 1957-59; adminstrv. asst. Ft. Dodge (Iowa) By-Products Co., 1960-63; spl sales agent Lincoln Nat. Life Ins. Co., Ft. Dodge, 1963-67; stock and commodity broker Lamson Bros. and Co., Ft. Dodge, 1967-73, pres., gen. mgr. Center Line, Inc., Ft. Dodge, 1973—; chmn. bd. Internat. Mining and Devel., Inc., Ft. Dodge By-Products Co., Webster Rendering Co., Hot Line, Inc., Bowlerama, Inc., Air Lanes, Inc., Center Line, Inc. Pres., Sertoma Club of Ft. Dodge, 1967, gov. West Iowa dist. Sertoma Internat., 1970-72; bd. dirs., treas. Lakota Council Girl Scouts U.S.A., 6 yrs. Served to lt. (j.g.) USN, 1955-57. Recipient various sales awards, Lincoln Nat. Life Ins. Co. and Lamson Bros. & Co. Mem. Ft. Dodge C. of C., Nat. C. of C. Republican. Roman Catholic. Club: Barbershoppers (div. v.p.). Home: 2222 22d Ave N Fort Dodge IA 50501 Office: Box 1275 Fort Dodge IA 50501

BODIE, LLOYD LEWIS, school principal; b. Phila., Mar. 11, 1941; s. Lloyd Lewis and Ruth (Miller) B.; m. Carol June Ousky, Sept. 12, 1965; children—Douglas Allen, Blair Elizabeth, Gregory Reed. B.S., Ind. State U., 1965, M.S., 1969, Ph.D., 1979. Tchr., Otter Creek Jr. High Sch., Terre Haute, Ind., 1969-71; planetarium dir. Vigo County Schs., Terre Haute, 1971-75; asst. prin. Terre Haute South Vigo High Sch., 1975-79; prin. Brownsburg High Sch., Ind., 1979-82, Southport High Sch., Indpls., 1982—. Home: 1001 E Edgewood Ave Indianapolis IN 46227 Office: Southport High Sch 941 E Banta Rd Indianapolis IN 46227

BODMAN, GERALD RICHARD, consulting engineer; b. Catawissa, Pa., May 22, 1944; s. Gerald Frederick and Betty Mae (Stevenson) B.; B.S., Pa. State U., 1966, M.S., 1968; m. Mary Ellen Ahler, July 21, 1973; children—Lee, Melanie, Julian. Self-employed as irrigation system designer, Catawissa, Pa., 1964-67; instr. Pa. State U., University Park, 1966-68; engr./constrn. supr. New Eng. Pole Builders, Inc., Ludlow, Mass., 1968-70: self-employed in home bldg. and remodeling, Ludlow, Mass., 1970-71; extension agrl. engr., asst. prof. Pa. State U., University Park, 1971-78; pvt. practice cons. agrl. and structural engring. Space Preceptors Assocs., State College, Pa., Ludlow, Mass., Lincoln, Nebr., 1970—; specialist on farmstead engring., livestock housing, milking systems and procedures, grain drying, solar energy for livestock housing, extraneous voltage; assoc. prof., extension agrl. engr. U. Nebr., Lincoln, 1978—; vis. prof. dept. home econs. Ind. U., Bloomington, 1972. Mem. bd. deacons State College Presbyn. Ch., 1974-78, chmn., 1978; deacon Eastridge Presbyn. Ch., Lincoln, 1981-83. Recipient Excellence in Extension Programming award for Solar livestock housing U. Nebr., 1983. registered profl. engr., Pa. N.Y., Mass., Ind., Calif., Maine, N.H., Vt., Md., Colo., Iowa, Kans., Tenn., Del., Conn., Ill., Mo., Minn., Nebr., Ohio, N.J., Va., R.I., W.Va., Minn., S.D., Tex., Oreg.; lic. land surveyor, Pa. Mem. Am. Soc. Agrl. Engrs. (mem. exec. com. North Atlantic region 1975-78, 1st vice-chmn. program 1977-78, chmn.-elect Pa. sect. 1977-78, Blue Ribbon awards in Ednl. Aids Competition, 1975, 77, 78, 79, 80, 81, 82, 83, 84 Young Extension Engr. of Yr. 1982, chmn. ad hoc applications publ. com. 1982—, profl. devel. dept. 1983-84, cons. guidelines subcom., milk handling equipment com. 1985-86, meetings com. 1985-86), Profl. Engrs. in Pvt. Practice, Nat., Nebr. socs. profl. engrs., AAAS, N.E. Dairy Practices Council (chmn. practical plumbing for milking centers subcom.), Nebr. Dairymen's Assn. (bd. dirs. 1983—), ASHRAE. Republican. Contbr. 200 articles to profl. jours. and popular publs. Home and Office: 5911 Sunrise Rd Lincoln NE 68510

BOECK, LAVERNE DWAINE, fermentation microbiologist; b. Johnson, Nebr., May 16, 1930; s. Otto Bernhard and Alma Marie (Stutheit) B.; student U. Nebr., 1947-49, Wartburg Coll., 1949-50; B.S. in Biology, Butler U., 1958, M.S. in Microbiology, 1963; m. Fredia Mae Jarrett, Oct. 25, 1953; children—Deborah, Kirk, Bruce, Eric, Gregg, Craig. Clerical engring. analyst Allison div. Gen. Motors Corp., Indpls., 1953-57; asso. microbiologist Eli Lilly & Co., Indpls., 1958-63, microbiologist, 1963-65, asst. sr. microbiologist, 1965-67, asso. sr. microbiologist, 1967-72, sr. microbiologist, 1972—. Served to lt., Anti-aircraft Arty., U.S. Army, 1951-53. Mem. Am. Soc. Microbiology, Soc. Indsl. Microbiology, Am. Chem. Soc., Sigma Xi. Republican. Lutheran. Contbr. articles to profl. jours.; patentee in field. Home: 741 Chapel Hill West Dr Indianapolis IN 46224 Office: Eli Lilly Research Labs Indianapolis IN 46285

BOEDDEKER, TIMOTHY MARK, postal executive; b. St. Louis, Aug. 16, 1948; s. Clyde and Constance Faye (McCollum) B.; m. Margaret Mary Botts, May 15, 1971; children—Abigail Faye, Timothy Mark. Student, William Jennings Bryan Coll., 1967-70; B.A., Webster Coll., 1976, M.A., 1981. Supr. mails U.S. Postal Service, St. Louis, 1977-80, mgmt. trainee, 1980, mgr. Creve Coeur br., 1981-85, mgr. Wheeler Sta., 1985—. Deacon, West County Christian Ch., 1979—; trustee Internat. Soc. Christian Endeavor, 1979—; 2d v.p. Traditional Sch., Pattonville Sch. Dist. PTA, 1983-85, pres., 1985-86. Served with USCG, 1970-74, USCGR, 1974—. Mem. Nat. Assn. Postal Suprs., Am. Assn. Individual Investors, Res. Officers Assn. Republican. Home: 11115 Morrow Dr St Ann MO 63074

BOEHM, ROBERT JOHN, manufacturing company executive; b. Cleve., Sept. 13, 1948; s. Arthur Andrew and Emilie (Fleps) B.; m. Bonny Katrina Bauer, July 10, 1971. B.S.B.A., Xavier U., 1970. Buyer, Boehm Pressed Steel Co., Cleve., 1971-74, prodn. planner, 1974-76, v.p., 1976-84, pres., 1984—. Mem. operating com. Pvt. Industry Council Cuyahoga, Parma, Geauga, Cleve., 1983. Mem. Am. Metal Stamping Assn. (Cleve. dist. chmn. 1982-83, dir. 1982-83, bd. dirs. Charitable Found. 1982-83), Purchasing Mgmt. Assn., Cleve. Engring. Soc., Cleve. Machine Trades Assn. (bd. dirs. 1982—). Clubs: Westwood Country (Rocky River, Ohio); Rockwell Springs Trout (Castalia, Ohio). Office: The Boehm Pressed Steel Co 2219 W 63d St Cleveland OH 44102

BOEHM, THEODORE REED, lawyer; b. Evanston, Ill., Sept. 12, 1938; s. Hans George and Frances (Reed) B.; m. Natalie Joss, June 17, 1961; children—Elisabeth, Jennifer, Sarah, Macy. A.B. summa cum laude, Brown U., 1960; J.D. magna cum laude, Harvard U., 1963. Bar: D.C. 1964, Ind. 1964, U.S. Supreme Ct. 1975. Law clk. to Chief Justice Warren, Justice Reed, Justice Burton, U.S. Supreme Ct., Washington, 1963-64; assoc. Baker & Daniels, Indpls., 1965-70, ptnr., 1970—. Pres., Ind. Sports Corp., 1980—; chmn. organizing com. Nat. Sports Festival, 1982. Mem. ABA, Ind. Bar Assn., 7th Fed. Cir. Ct. Bar Assn. Home: 8639 Emerald Ln Indianapolis IN 46260 Office: 810 Fletcher Trust Bldg Indianapolis IN 46204

BOEHMAN, ROBERT URBAN, rubber company financial executive; b. St. Meinrad, Ind., Aug. 11, 1944; s. Louis Edward and Evelyn Frances (Fischer) B.; m. Sylvia Frances Mehling, May 20, 1966; 1 son, Gregory Allen. B.S. in Acctg., Brescia Coll., Owensboro, Ky., 1967; M.B.A., U. Evansville, 1972. Sr. internal auditor Akzona, Inc., Asheville, N.C., 1973-74; controller Interstar Chems., New Brunswick, N.J., 1974-78, Paoli Chair Co. (Ind.), 1978-80; div. controller N.Am. Products, Jasper, Ind., 1980; controller Jasper Rubber Products, Inc., 1981-82, dir. fin., 1982—. Bd. dirs. Marian Heights Acad., Ferdinand, Ind., 1981—; pres. Holy Family Parent Tchr. group, Nasper; coach Jasper Youth Soccer League, 1981-83, v.p. bd. dirs. 1981—; coach Little League, Jasper, 1983; active fundraising campaign Brescia Coll., 1983. Named to Outstanding Young Men Am., U.S. Jaycees, 1974. Mem. Nat. Assn. Accts. (pres. Brunswick area chpt. 1976, nat. acctg. research com. 1977—). Jaycee Roosters. Republican. Roman Catholic. Club: Patora Lake Sailing (treas., bd. dirs., founder) Jasper. Lodges: KC, Hon. Order Ky. Cols. Home: R3 Box 692H University Dr Jasper IN 47546 Office: Jasper Rubber Products Inc 1010 First Ave Jasper IN 47546

BOEING, CHARLENE ADELLE, veterinarian; b. Chgo., Feb. 20, 1947; d. Paul J. and Penny (Adelle) B.; m. Ronald A. Price, Oct. 20, 1973; 1 dau., Michele. D.V.M., U. Ill., 1972. Assoc. veterinarian Prospect Animal Hosp., Mt. Prospect, Ill., 1972-74; clin. veterinarian U. Ill. Biol. Resource Lab., Chgo., 1974-75; asst. veterinarian Antioch Animal Hosp. (Ill.), 1975-76; dir., owner Grove Animal Hosp., Buffalo Grove, Ill., 1976—. Mem. Chgo. Vet. Med. Assn., Women's Vet. Assn., AVMA, Feline Practitioners Assn., NOW, Sierra Club. Office: Grove Animal Hosp Route 83 and Buffalo Grove Rd Prairie View IL 60069

BOEKE, ROBERT WILLIAM, manufacturing company executive; b. Hubbard, Iowa, July 28, 1925; s. John Henry and Elizabeth A. (Schwartz) B.; B.S., Iowa State Coll., 1948, M.S., 1950; postgrad. Columbia U., 1966, Aspen Inst., 1976; m. Roberta Starbuck, Sept. 6, 1947; children—Lee Anne Boeke Burke, Linda Sue Boeke Day, John Robert. Instr., Iowa State U., Ames, 1947-51; with Deere & Co., various locations, 1951-79, sr. v.p. components design and mfr., Moline, Ill., 1979—, also dir.; dir. Banks of Iowa. Active Boy Scouts Am., Moline, 1972-81; active United Way of Rock Island and Scott Counties; pres. Iowa State U. Found., 1983—. Served with USN, 1943-45. Mem. Am. Soc. Quality Control, Farm and Indsl. Equipment Inst. Presbyterian. Home: 2895 W Court Bettendorf IA 52722 Office: Deere & Company John Deere Rd Moline IL 61265

BOELTER, ROBERT, advertising agency executive; b. Eau Claire, Wis., Nov. 21, 1940; s. Robert H. and La Vyne M. (Sherman) B.; B.S., U. Wis., Madison, 1965; 1 son, Christopher. Art dir. Waldbilling & Besteman, Inc., Madison, 1966-67; creative dir. Stephan & Brady, Inc., Madison, 1967-70; art dir. Hoffman, York, Baker & Johnson, Chgo., 1970-71, Milw., 1971-73; pres. Advt., Boelter & Lincoln, Madison and Milw., 1973—; tchr. Madison Area Tech. Coll., 1966-67, mem. comml. art adv. bd., 1976—. Recipient numerous awards for advt. creative work, including: Madison Advt. Club, 1967-70, 74—, Milw. Advt. Club, 1977, Milw. Art Dirs. Club, 1966-71, Milw. Soc. Communicating Arts, 1972-76, Am. Advt. Fedn., 1975-81, Am. Bus. Press Assn., 1972, CLIO, 1979, N.Y. One Show, 1981, Bank Mktg. Assn., 1979-81, Rockford Advt. Club, 1980. Mem. Am. Mktg. Assn. (chpt. pres. 1981), Madison Advt. Club, Madison Art Center, Downtown Madison Inc. (dir. 1979-84), Greater Madison C. of C., North Central Briarders (founding pres. 1976-77), Briard Club Am. (pres. 1983-84), Nat. Dog Breed Club, Nat. Model Railroaders Assn., Chgo. and Northwestern Hist. Soc., Mid-Continent Ry. Mus., Pro-Com. Home: 4383 Windsor Rd Windsor WI 53598 Office: PO Box 1665 123 E Doty St Madison WI 53701

BOEMI, A. ANDREW, banker; b. N.Y.C., Mar. 3, 1915; s. S. and Marietta (Boemi) B.; B.C.E., Coll. City N.Y., 1936, M.C.E., 1938; m. Flora Dorothy DeMuro, Apr. 26, 1941; children—Andrew A., Marcia Rosamond Buchanan. Engr., Gibb & Hill, Cons. Engrs., N.Y.C., 1937; city planner N.Y. Planning Comm., 1938-41; cons. U.S. Bur. Budget, Exec. Office of President, Washington, 1942; asst. loan officer, planning cons., asst. v.p., v.p. First Fed. Savs. & Loan, Chgo., 1946-57; pres., chief exec. officer Madison Bank & Trust Co., Chgo., 1957-84, chmn. bd., 1974—; pres., chmn. bd. Madison Financial Corp., Chgo., 1974-84, chmn. bd., chief exec. officer, 1985—; chmn. bd. Madison Nat. Bank of Niles (Ill.), 1976—, 1st Nat. Bank of Wheeling (Ill.), 1978—, MFC Mortgage Co., 1983—. Mem. exec. com. Archdiocesan Commn. Human Relations and Ecumenism, 1969-72; mem. Mayor's Commn. Landmarks Preservation Council, 1972-75. Bd. dirs. Met. Housing and Planning Council, 1950—, pres., 1975-76; mem. Elementary Sch. Bd., Park Ridge, Ill., 1953-59, pres., 1956-59; citizens bd. Loyola U., Chgo.; chmn. Joint Action Com. Civic Assns. for location Chgo. campus U. Ill., 1960-61; chmn. Gateway Com., Chgo., 1958-63; bd. dirs. Duncan YMCA, 1964-77. Served to lt. comdr. USNR, 1942-46. Recipient commendation from sec. navy, World War II; decorated Knight Order Holy Sepulchre of Jerusalem. Mem. Am. Bankers Assn., ASCE, Am. Inst. Planners, Navy League U.S., Newcomen Soc. N. Am., Am. Legion, Lambda Alpha, Alpha Beta Gamma. Republican. Roman Catholic. Clubs: Economic, Bankers, University (Chgo.); Park Ridge Country. Home: 1110 N Lake Shore Dr Apt 7-S Chicago IL 60611 Office: 400 W Madison St Chicago IL 60606

BOENDER, EDWARD, banker, investor; b. Oskaloosa, Iowa, Mar. 21, 1933; s. William Martin and Christine (DeVries) B.; m. Helene Marilyn Kelderman, Apr. 25, 1952; children—Patricia, Michael, John, Carol. B.A., Am. Inst. Bus., Des Moines; grad. diploma Savs. & Loan Inst., Chgo. Pres., chmn. Pioneer Fed. Savs. & Loan, Mason City, Iowa, 1961—; pres., Pioneer Service Corp.; dir. Savs. and Loan Computer Trust, Des Moines. Bd. dirs. North Iowa Area Community Coll., Mason City Devel. Assn., North Iowa Auditorium Found.; mem. Mayors Downtown Redevel. Task Force, Mason City. Home: 1011 6th SE Mason City IA 50401 Office: Pioneer Fed Savs 124 North Washington Mason City IA 50401

BOERGER, WILLIAM GEORGE, oral and maxillofacial surgeon; b. St. Cloud, Minn., May 30, 1941; s. Milton Carl and Geneva Marie (Spaniol) B.; student Crosier Sem., Onamia, Minn., 1959-61, St. Cloud State Coll., 1961-63; B.S., U. Minn., 1965, D.D.S., 1967; m. Hiroko Hamada, Nov. 16, 1968 (div. 1978); 1 son, Jeffrey; m. Theresa M. Wagner, Nov. 3, 1978; children—Megan, John. Resident in oral surgery U. Minn., Mpls., 1969-72; practice oral surgery, Wayzata, Minn., 1972—, also Edina and Burnsville, Minn.; mem. staffs Methodist Hosp., St. Louis Park, Minn., Fairview Southdale Hosp., Edina, Fairview Ridges Hosp., Burnsville, Waconia Ridgeview Hosp., also Children's Health Center, Mpls. Served with USNR, 1967-69. Fellow Am. Dental Soc. Anesthesiology, Am. Assn. Oral and Maxillofacial Surgeons; mem. ADA, Minn., Mpls. Dist. dental socs., Mpls., Minn. socs. oral and maxillofacial surgeons, Minnetonka, Bloomington dental study clubs, Southdale Dental Soc., Omicron Kappa Upsilon. Office: 250 N Central Ave #214 Wayzata MN 55391

BOERNER, WOLFGANG-MARTIN, electrical engineer, educator; b. Finschhafen, Papua New Guinea, July 26, 1937; s. Martin Ernst and Ilse Louise (Stoss) B.; came to U.S., 1963; m. Eileen Annette Hassebrock, Dec. 23, 1967; children—Vaughan W., Juergen A., Joanna E. Arbitur, A. von Platen Gymnasium, Ansbach, Bavaria, W. Ger., 1958; Dipl.-Ing., Technische U. Munich, 1963; Ph.D. in Elec. Engring., U. Pa., 1967. Postdoctoral research and teaching fellow U. Man. (Can.), 1968-69, asst. prof. dept. elec. engring., 1969-71, assoc. prof., 1971-76, prof. and research prof., 1976-82; prof., dir. communications lab., dept. elec. engring and computer sci. U. Ill.-Chgo., 1978—; pres. Polarimetrics, Inc., Northbrook, Ill., 1982—; vis. prof. U. Canterbury, Christchurch, N.Z., 1976; vis. lectr. U. Auckland (N.Z.), 1976; del. Gen. Assembly of Union Radio-Sci. Internat., Washington, 1981, Florence, Italy, 1984; Gen. Assembly Internat. Commn. on Optics, Graz, Austria, 1981; dir. NATO Workshop on Inverse Methods in Electromagnetic Imaging, W. Ger., 1982; invited speaker in field. Spl. advisor U.S. Congl. Adv. Bd. Fulbright exchange scholar and Moore Sch. fellow, 1963-66; U. Pa. dissertation fellow, 1966-67; Alexander von Humboldt fellow, 1978; 1980; NATO sr. scientist fellow, 1982; Winnipeg Rh Inst. grantee, 1976; Alexander von Humboldt Found. sr. scientist award, 1985; vis. prof. award Govt. of Netherlands, 1979; vis. scientist award German Aero. and Space Research Establishment, Oberpfaffenhofen, 1980-83; Japan Soc. Promotion Sci. fellow, 1984. Fellow IEEE; mem. Antennas and Propagation Soc. (S64, M67, SM75, F84, guest editor spl. issue trans. 1979-81, assoc. editor 1980), Soc. Engring. Scis., Soc. Exploration Geophysicists, Optical Soc. Am., Remote Sensing Soc., AAAS, Soc. Photo-optical Instrumentation Engrs., Assn. Profl. Engrs. of Province of Man. (cert.), Electromagnetic Soc., Fulbright Alumni Assn., Funnel, Nat. Soc. Profl. Engrs., German Fulbright Soc., Am. Def. Preparedness Assn. Republican. Contbr. numerous articles and reports to profl. pubs.; patentee in field. Home: 1021 Cedar Ln Northbrook IL 60062 Office: Communications Lab Dept Elec Engring and Computer Sci Univ of Ill SEL-4210 Chicago IL 60680

BOESCH, CHARLES HERMAN, JR., lawyer; b. Dayton, Ohio, Dec. 22, 1943; s. Charles Herman and Kathryn (Saum) B. B.A., St. Josephs Coll., 1966; J.D., Akron U., 1969. Bar: Ohio 1972. Salesman, Allied Wines, Dayton, 1969-70; ins. adjustor Ohio Claims Service, Dayton, 1970-72; ptnr. Boesch & Boesch, Dayton, 1972—. Sec. Dayton Bus. Form, Inc., Dayton, 1975-79; chmn. com. YMCA, Dayton, 1981-84. Mem. Dayton Bar Assn. Democrat. Roman Catholic. Avocations: Gardening, house restoration, computing. Home: 139 Jackson St Dayton OH 45402 Office: 1005 Third Nat Bldg Dayton OH 45402

BOESCHENSTEIN, WILLIAM WADE, glass products manufacturing executive; b. Chgo., Sept. 7, 1925; s. Harold and Elizabeth (Wade) B.; B.S., Yale U., 1950; m. Josephine H. Moll, Nov. 28, 1953; children—William W., Michael, Peter, Stephen. With Owens-Corning Fiberglas Corp., 1950—, exec. v.p., 1967-71, pres., 1971—, chief exec. officer, 1972—, chmn., 1981—, also dir.; dir. FMC Corp., Hanna Mining Co., Prudential Ins. Co. Am. Trustee Toledo Mus. Art, Phillips Acad., Andover, Mass. Mem. Bus. Council, Conf. Bd. Clubs: Econ. (N.Y.C.); Econ. (Detroit); Inverness (Toledo); Belmont Country (Perrysburg, Ohio); Augusta (Ga.) Nat. Office: Owens Corning Fiberglas Corp Fiberglas Tower Toledo OH 43659

BOESE, GILBERT KARYLE, zoo director; b. Chgo., June 24, 1937; s. Carl Henry and Winifred (Mack) B.; children—Ann, Peter. B.A., Carthage Coll., 1959; M.S., No. Ill. U., 1960; Ph.D., Johns Hopkins U., 1973. Asst. prof. biology Elmhurst Coll., Ill., 1967-69; curator research and edn. Brookfield Zoo, Ill., 1971-73, assoc. dir. devel. and edn., 1973-77, v.p., 1976-80, dep. dir., 1977-80; dir. Milwaukee County Zoo, 1980—. Bd. dirs. Greater Milw. Conv. and Visitors Bur.; mem. Pres.'s Council Carthage Coll. Recipient Disting. Alumni award Carthage Coll., 1982. Mem. Am. Assn. Zool. Parks and Aquariums (bd. dirs. 1984—). Club: University. Lodge: Rotary (Milw.). Avocations: tennis; cross-country skiing; game fishing; nature photography. Home and Office: Milw County Zoo 10001 W Bluemound Rd Milwaukee WI 53226

BOESE, VIRGINIA ELLEN, curator; b. Troy, Ohio, July 16, 1907; d. William Harry and Virginia Grace (Meeker) Gilbert; student Western Coll. for Women, Oxford, Ohio, 1924-26; B.A., Ohio Wesleyan U., Delaware, 1928; m. Carl Wimmler Boese, Aug. 5, 1929. Tchr. Latin and English, Concord Twp. Sch., Miami County, Ohio, 1928-29; legal sec. to William Harry Gilbert, Troy, 1931-45; dir. Troy Hist. Soc., 1965-76, archivist-librarian, 1966-76, genealogist, 1966—, dir. hist. room, 1966-76, asst. archivist-librarian, 1976—; dir., curator Overfield Log Tavern Mus., 1966-75, asst. curator, 1975—. Pres., violinist Troy Music Club, 1932-33; pres. Troy Altrurian Club, 1933-34, Current Events Club, 1954-55. Co-recipient (with husband) Community Service award Troy Jaycees, 1972. Mem. DAR, Colonial Dames XVII Century, LWV, Daus. of Founders and Patriots Am., Phi Mu, Kappa Delta Pi. Republican. Presbyn. (deacon). Author: Overfield Genealogy Research Notes, 1968, rev., 1970; Revolutionary Soldiers of Miami County, Ohio, 1976, rev., 1979; Meeker Genealogy, 1975; Genealogy of Knoop Family of Miami County, Ohio, 1981; Ball Family of England and America, 1982; Thomas Family of St. Mary's County, Md. Compiler, Index to Beers 1880 History, of Miami County, Ohio, 1973. Home: 106 S Plum St Troy OH 45373 Office: 201 E Water St Troy OH 45373

BOESEL, MILTON CHARLES, JR., lawyer, bus. exec.; b. Toledo, July 12, 1928; s. Milton C. and Florence (Fitzgerald) B.; B.A., Yale U., 1950; LL.B., Harvard U., 1953; m. Lucy Laughlin Mather, Mar. 25, 1961; children—Elizabeth Parks, Charles Mather, Andrew Fitzgerald. Admitted to Ohio bar, 1953, Mich. bar, 1953; counsel firm Ritter, Boesel, Robinson & Marsh, Toledo, 1956—; pres., dir. Michabo, Inc.; dir. First Nat. Bank Toledo. Served to lt., USNR, 1953-56. Episcopalian. Mason. Clubs: Toledo, Toledo Country (Toledo); Leland (Mich.) Country. Home: 2268 Innisbrook Rd Toledo OH 43606 Office: 240 Huron St Toledo OH 43604

BOESNE, ROBERT ALAN, forensic chemist; b. Chgo., Mar. 30, 1934; s. Fred W. and Adeline B. (Kondrad) B.; A.A. in Chemistry, Wright Jr. Coll., 1960; B.S. in Chemistry, Ill. Inst. Tech., 1969, M. Pub. Adminstrn., 1974; m. June C. Franke, Dec. 10, 1955; children—Mark A., Brian A. Patrolman, Chgo. Police Dept., 1956-58, investigator crime lab., 1958-60, firearms examiner, 1960-63, sr. firearms examiner, 1963-65, chemist, crime lab., 1965-71, chief chemist, 1971-74, tech. coordinator, 1974—; pres. B and W Cons. Forensic Chemists, Inc.; part time faculty St. Xavier Coll., 1978-79; lectr. Northwestern U., Ill. Inst. Tech., U. Notre Dame, Loyola U., Chgo. Police Acad.; state instr. in use of breathalyzer; mem. Task Force for Evaluation of Ill. Crime Lab System, 1974-75; mem. Ill. Arson Adv. Com. Fellow Am. Acad. Forensic Scis. (criminalistics sect.); mem. Am. Chem. Soc., Internat. Assn. Arson Investigators (chmn. forensic lab. com. Ill. chpt.), Midwestern Assn. Forensic Scientists (founder, pres. 1976-77), Am. Firearms and Tool Marks Examiners (charter), Chgo. Gas Chromatography Discussion Group, Am. Soc. Pub. Adminstrn. Lodges: Masons, Shriners. Expert witness in firearms identification and forensic chemistry municipal, county, fed. cts.; contbr. articles to profl. jours. Office: Chicago Police Dept 1121 S State St Chicago IL 60605 also 2901 Finley Rd 5 Suite 110 Downers Grove IL 60515*

BOETTGER, MARY ANN, educational administrator; b. Kawkawlin, Mich., Oct. 27, 1936; s. Jacob Joseph and Genevieve Irene (Garstecki) Gorzinski; m. Boyd Rex Boettger, Oct. 17, 1959; children—William, Joseph, Patrica. B.A., Madonna Coll., 1959; M.A., U. Mich., 1965; Ed.S., Mich. State U., 1981. Tchr., Bay City Pub. Schs., Mich., 1959—, elem. prin., 1985—. Mem. human services com. City of Bay City. Hilda Maehling fellow NEA, 1982. Mem. Bay City Assn. Suprs. and Admistrators., LWV, Nat. Assn. Elem. Sch. Prins., Democratic Women Orgn. Home: 505 Harold St Bay City MI 48708 Office: Dolsen Elem

Sch 1201 Fourth St Bay City MI 48708 also Woodside Elem Sch 201 Woodside Ln Bay City MI 48708

BOEWE, JOHN FREDRICK, purchasing director; b. Olney, Ill., Feb. 4, 1933; s. Fred Earnest and Susan (Woltors) B.; m. Louise Brown, June 19, 1955. B.A. in Music, U. Wis.-Madison, 1955; M.A., U. Ill., 1957. Mgr. labor relations Ill. Central Gulf R.R., Chgo., 1960-75, adminstr. corp. service, 1975-80, dir. purchasing dept., 1980—. Served to 1st lt. U.S. Army, 1957-60. Mem. Purchasing Mgmt. Assn. Chgo. Avocations: fishing; golf; skiing. Home: 2447 Clyde Rd Homewood IL 60430 Office: Ill Central Gulf RR 233 N Michigan Ave Chicago IL 60601

BOGACZYK, STANLEY JOHN, stainless steel fabricating company executive; b. Blossburg, Pa., May 18, 1942; s. Stanley H. and Mary M. (Beaderman) B.; m. Claire Marie Crosson, Sept. 19, 1970; children—Mark, Lauren, Michelle. B.S., Rider Coll., 1964. Mgr. employee relations Okonite Co., Ramsey, N.J., 1965-70; mgr. labor relations U.S. Postal Service, N.Y.C., 1970-73; v.p. personnel and indsl. relations ITT Grinnell, Elmira, N.Y., 1973-78; v.p. Mueller Co., Decatur, Ill., 1978-83; pres. Superior Stainless, Inc., Delavan, Wis., 1983—; chmn. bd. Macon Metal Products Co., Blue Mound, Ill., 1981—. Bd. dirs. Decatur Boys' Club, 1983, Janesville Youth Hockey, Wis., 1984. Mem. Am. Mgmt. Assns., Decatur C. of C. (bd. dirs. 1983), Delta Sigma Pi. Roman Catholic. Club: Trout Unlimited. Avocations: fly fishing; woodworking. Office: 611 Sugar Creek Rd Delavan WI 53115

BOGG, RICHARD ALLAN, sociology educator; b. Grosse Pointe, Mich., May 31, 1934; s. Sydney Elmer and Dorothy Marie B.; B.B.A., U. Mich., 1956, Ph.D., 1971; postgrad. U. Exeter (Eng.), 1957-58; M.H.A., Washington U., St. Louis, 1960. Asst. adminstr. Port Huron (Mich.) Hosp., 1960-62; research asso. U. Mich. Sch. Pub. Health, 1965-69; asst. prof. dept. community medicine Faculty Medicine, U. Alta., Edmonton, Can., 1969-72; asst. prof. dept. sociology Ball State U., Muncie, Ind., 1972-77, assoc. prof., 1977—; contbr. papers to profl. confs. Bd. dirs. Planned Parenthood of Delaware County, 1973-75. USPHS trainee, 1962-65; HEW Childrens Bur. research grantee, 1966-68, Mich. Ho. of Reps. spl. research grantee, 1968. Mem. Am. Sociol. Assn., ACLU. Contbr. articles to profl. jours. Home: Rural Route 2 Daleville IN 47334 Office: Dept Sociology Ball State U Muncie IN 47306

BOGGESS, THOMAS PHILLIP, III, reprographics and graphics arts co. exec.; b. Greenville, Ky., Jan. 22, 1921; s. William C. and Gertrude Lucille (Lumpkins) B.; grad. high sch.; m. Ann Marie Mossner, Sept. 1, 1942; children—Thomas Phillip IV, Nancy L. Vice-pres. Alfred Mossner Co., Chgo., 1945-70, pres., chief operating officer, 1970—, also dir.; treas., dir. Blue Printers Supply Corp., Chgo. Chmn. zoning bd. of appeals, Village of River Forest, Ill., 1950—; mem., past bd. dirs. Westchester (Ill.) Bible Ch. Served with USNR, 1942-45. Decorated Purple Heart, Bronze Star (5). Mem. Blue Print Club of Chgo. (pres. 1957-62), Disabled Am. Vets. Club: Oak Park Country. Home: 335 Gale Ave River Forest IL 60305 Office: 137 N Wabash Ave Chicago IL 60602

BOGINA, AUGUST, JR., state senator; b. Girard, Kans., Sept. 13, 1927; s. August and Mary (Blazic) B.; B.S., Engring., Kans. State U., 1950; m. Velma M. Rank, 1949; children—Kathleen A., August III, Michael E., Mark A. Owner, Bogina & Assocs., Lenaxa, Kans., 1962-70; pres. Bogina Cons. Engrs., 1970—; partner Bogina Petroleum Engineers, 1983—; mem. Kans. Ho. of Reps., 1974-80, Kans. Senate, 1980—. Precinct committeeman Kans. Republican party, 1970-74, chmn. city com., 1972-74. Served with U.S. Army, 1946-48. Registered profl. engr., Kans., Mo., Colo., Okla. Mem. Nat., Mo. socs. profl. engrs., Kans. Engring. Soc., Kans. Soc. Land Surveyors, Mo. Registered Land Surveyors. Roman Catholic.

BOGOMOLNY, RICHARD J., retail food chain executive. Chmn., chief exec. officer First Nat. Supermarkets Inc., Maple Heights, Ohio, also dir. Office: First Nat Supermarkets Inc 17000 Rockside Rd Maple Heights OH 44137*

BOGUE, ANDREW WENDELL, federal judge; b. Yankton, S.D., May 23, 1919; s. Andrew S. and Genevieve Bogue; B.S., S.D. State U., 1941; LL.B., U. S.D., 1947; m. Florence Elizabeth Williams, Aug. 5, 1945; children—Andrew Stevenson, Laurie Beth, Scott MacFarlane. Bar: S.D. 1947. States atty. Turner County (S.D.), from 1952; judge 2d Jud. Circuit S.D., 1967-70; judge U.S. Dist. Ct. S.D., Rapid City, 1970—, chief judge, 1980—. Mem. ABA, S.D. Bar Assn. Episcopalian. Address: Fed Bldg Room 318 515 9th St Rapid City SD 57701*

BOGUSKY, RACHEL M., physician, counseling psychologist; b. Throop, Pa., Mar. 10, 1939; d. John Paul and Veronica (Farkas) Bogusky; student pvt. schs.; B.S., So. Conn. State Coll.; M.A., U. Conn.; Ed.S., Columbia U., Ed.D.; M.D., Universidad Autonoma de Ciudad Juarez, Mex. Tchr. East Haven (Conn.) Bd. Edn., 1961-62; dir. program for gifted, coordinator sci., master tchr. Greenwich (Conn.) Bd. Edn., 1962-69, 71-72; counseling therapist Psychol. Consultation Center, Columbia U., N.Y.C., 1970-71, instr. applied human devel., 1970-71; asst. prof. edn. U. Mich., Ann Arbor, 1973-76; behavior therapist, assertive tng. cons. Inst. for Behavior Change, Ann Arbor, 1975-76; ednl. psychologist, ednl. mgr. Med. Corp., Ann Arbor, 1976-77; pvt. cons. and counseling practice, Ann Arbor, 1975—. Recipient certificate recognition for ednl. contbns. Greenwich C. of C., 1969. Mem. Am. Psychol. Assn., Am. Personnel and Guidance Assn., Council for Exceptional Children (pres. chpt. 359, Fairfield County 1968-69), Assn. Advancement Behavior Therapy, Am. Soc. Tng. and Devel., Kappa Delta Pi. Author books, monographs and articles. Home and Office: 1 Haverhill Ct Ann Arbor MI 48105

BOHLEY, PAUL BRANCH, pump products manufacturing company executive; b. Medina, Ohio, Dec. 14, 1923; s. Christian Gotleib and Bessie Louise (Dickerman) B.; student Ohio State U. Coll. Agr., 1941-43, 46-47; m. Dorothy Louise Persons, May 26, 1944; children—Donna Allyn (Mrs. Larry Alan Davis), Keith Persons. Owner-operator Crestview Farms, producers hybrid corn and certified small grain, Medina, 1945-62; gen. sales mgr. O-Y-O Seed Assos., Inc., Marysville, Ohio, 1962-65; sales mgr. agrl. and petroleum equipment divs. Gorman Rupp Co., mfr. pumps and associated products, Mansfield, Ohio, 1965—. Mem. Buckeye Consol. Sch. Bd., 1952-64, pres., 1952-53, 61-62. Served with USAAF, 1942-45; lt. col. Res. (ret.). Decorated D.F.C., Air medal with 5 oak leaf clusters. Mem. Nat. Fertilizer Solutions Assn. (dir. 1972, nat. v.p. 1970-73), Sprinkler Irrigation Assn. (chmn. membership com. 1972, chmn. Waste Water resources com. 1973-74, dir. 1974-75, pres. 1978), Ohio Flying Farmers Assn. (dir. 1947-48, 74-76, sec. 1978), Am. Legion, V.F.W., Medina C. of C., Air Force Assn., Ohio Future Farmers Assn. (hon.), Nat. Security Council, Alpha Zeta. Republican. Methodist (lay minister 1955-60). Lion (sec. 1948-52). Contbr. to profl. publs. in field. Home: 5986 Branch Rd Medina OH 44256 Office: 305 Bowman St Mansfield OH 44902

BOHLIM, RICHARD CHARLES, civil engineer; b. Michigan City, Ind., Sept. 5, 1952; s. George A. and Margaret (Elias) B.; B.S.C.E., Ind. Inst. Tech., 1974. Registered profl. engr., Kans.; lic. pvt. pilot. Service engr. Combustion Engring., Martins Creek, Pa., 1974, Boston, 1974-75, St. Louis, 1975-76, lead service engr. for combustion engring., Lawrence, Kans., 1976-78, resident service engr., Overland Park, Kans., 1978-80, resident supr. tech. services Kansas City Dist., 1980—, dist. mgr. tech. services, Kansas City, 1981—. Mem. ASCE (citation award 1974), Alpha Sigma Phi. Roman Catholic. Club: Moose. Home: 11521 Mastin Overland Park KS 66210 Office: 6362 College Blvd Overland Park KS 66211

BOHLMANN, RALPH ARTHUR, clergyman church official; b. Palisade, Nebr., Feb. 20, 1932; s. Arthur Erwin and Anne Fredericka (Weeke) B.; student St. Johns Coll., Winfield, Kans.; B.A., Concordia Sem., 1953; M.Div., 1956, S.T.M., 1966; Fulbright scholar U. Heidelberg, 1956-57; Ph.D., Yale U., 1968; m. Patricia Anne McCleary, Apr. 19, 1959; children—Paul, Lynn. Ordained to ministry Lutheran Ch., Mo. Synod, 1958; instr. history and religion Concordia Coll., 1957-58; pastor Mt. Olive Luth. Ch., Des Moines, 1958-60; prof. systematic theology Concordia Sem., St. Louis, 1960-71; acting pres., 1974-75, pres., 1975-81; pres. Luth. Ch.-Mo. Synod, 1981—; exec. sec. Commn. Theology and Ch. Relations Luth. Ch. Mo. Synod St. Louis, 1971-74; mem. Faith and Order Commn. Nat. Council Chs., 1973-76. Author: Principles of Biblical Interpretation in the Lutheran Confessions, 1968. Office: 1333 S Kirkwood Rd Saint Louis MO 63122

BOHM, MILFORD MILES, consumer services company executive; b. Sharon, Pa., Oct. 29, 1921; s. Joseph and Irene Golda B.; m. Leona Cytron, June 15, 1952; children—Miriam G., Vicki L., David R., Robert D. Student U. Pa., U. Paris. Chmn., dir. CPI Corp., St. Louis, 1942—; dir. Mark Twain State Bank, St. Louis, 1968—; chmn., chief exec. officer Cencit Inc., St. Louis, 1983—; mem. adv. bd. Early Stages Co., San Francisco, 1985—. Chmn., Jewish Fedn. Council, St. Louis, 1984; dir. St. Louis Metro RCGA,; chmn. City Venture Inner City Devel. Commn., St. Louis; trustee Internat. Bd. Govs. for Technion U., Haifa, Israel, Recipient Prime Minister's award State of Israel; Appreciation award Better Bus. Bur., 1979; CPI Corp. Founders scholar, 1982. Mem. Profl. Photographers Assn. Am., Master Photo Finishers and Dealers Assn., Met. Assn. Philanthropy (St. Louis). Jewish. Clubs: Creve Coeur Racquet, Washington U., B'nai B'rith (St. Louis). Avocations: tennis; swimming; jogging; boating; reading. Office: CPI Corp 1706 Washington Ave Saint Louis MO 63103

BOHNERT, WILLIAM PEACE, JR., agronomist; b. Los Angeles, Apr. 27, 1944; s. William Peace and Eleanor (Kohake) B.; B.S. in Agr., U. Mo., 1966, M.S. in Soils, 1967; cert. profl. agronomist; m. Ann Marie Kramper, Oct. 17, 1980. Area agronomy specialist U. Mo., Plattsburg, 1970-76; tech. service specialist research and devel. Chevron Chem. Co., Omaha, 1976—. Sec., Clinton County Soil and Water Conservation Dist., 1970-76. Served with U.S. Army, 1968-70. Nat. Plant Food Inst. Soil Sci. scholar, 1965. Mem. Am. Soc. Agronomy, Crop Sci. Soc. Am., No-Till Farmer Assn., Gamma Sigma Delta, Alpha Zeta. Democrat. Roman Catholic. Clubs: Dominic (v.p. 1978, treas. 1979), LaSalle. Home: 10550 Clark St Des Moines IA 50322 Office: Chevron Chem Co Rural Route Box 173 Dallas Center IA 50322

BOHON, ELLIS G(RAY), accountant, management and tax consultant; b. LaBelle, Mo., Sept. 1, 1902; s. Frank W. and Lee (Ellis) B.; student Westminster Coll., Fulton, Mo., 1920-21; B.S. cum laude, Knox Coll., Galesburg, Ill., 1924; postgrad. Walton Sch. Commerce, 1927-29, Northwestern U., 1930-33, 1935, 1965-66, YMCA Community Coll., 1963-71, Chgo. Bd. Trade Grain Inst., 1955, 56 (all Chgo.); C.P.A., U. Ill., 1935; m. Joyce L. Finlayson, Apr. 15, 1939; children—Walter Duncan, Ellis Gray, II (dec.). Staff accountant Ernst & Ernst, C.P.A.'s, Chgo., 1927-30; partner R. L. Pearce & Co., C.P.A.s', 1930-36; propr. E. G. Bohon & Co., C.P.A.'s, 1936—; former lectr. Am. Inst. Banking, Walton Sch. Commerce, Ill. Inst. Tech., Chgo., Lake Forest (Ill.) Coll. Former advisor, treas. Lakes chpt. Order DeMolay, bus. men's adv. council Jones Comml. High Sch. (Chgo.). Enrolled as atty. Tax Ct. U.S.A.; C.P.A., Ill., Ky., Iowa, Mo. Member Am. Inst. C.P.A.'s, Am. Accounting Assn., Ill. (past chmn. tech. com.), Ia. socs. C.P.A.'s, Nat. Assn. Accountants, Am. Arbitration Assn., Accounting Research Assn., Am. Inst. Laundering, Ky. Hist. Soc., Midwest Bus. Adminstrn. Assn., Phi Delta Theta. Presbyterian. Clubs: Masons, Monroe, Shriners (treas. club 1978), Order Eastern Star, Union League, Univ. of Evanston, Swedish Glee. Author papers. Home: 523 E North Ave Lake Bluff IL 60044 Office: 53 W Jackson Blvd Room 824 Chicago IL 60604

BOILEAU, OLIVER CLARK, JR., aerospace executive; b. Camden, N.J., Mar. 31, 1927; s. Oliver Clark and Florence Mary (Smith) B.; B.S.E.E., U. Pa., 1951, M.S.E.E., 1953; Sc.M. in Indsl. Mgmt. (Sloan fellow), MIT, 1964; m. Nan Eleze Hallen, Sept. 15, 1951; children—Clark Edward, Adrienne Lee, Nanette Erika, Jay Marshall. Mgr., Boeing Aerospace Co., Seattle, 1953-66, v.p., 1967-72, mgr. Minuteman, 1966-70, pres., 1972-80; pres., dir. Gen. Dynamics Corp., Clayton, Mo., 1980—; dir. Centerre Bank. Mem. vis. com. dept. aeros. MIT; trustee St. Louis U.; bd. overseers Sch. Engring., U. Pa., Lawrence Inst. Tech. Corp.; v.p., mem. exec. bd. St. Louis Area council Boy Scouts Am.; bd. dirs. Jr. Achievement. Served with USN, 1944-46. Fellow AIAA; mem. Navy League, Air Force Assn., Am. Def. Preparedness Assn., Assn. U.S. Army, Nat. Aeros. Assn., Nat. Acad. Engring., Naval War Coll. Found., Eta Kappa Nu, Sigma Tau, Theta Xi. Club: Nat. Space. Office: 7733 Forsyth Blvd Clayton MO 63105

BOILLOT, JAMES BENJAMIN, agricultural administrator; b. Columbia, Mo., July 17, 1935; s. Buell Francis and Dorcas Elizabeth (Downing) B.; m. Phyllis Mae Aufderheide, Aug. 30, 1959; children—Douglas, Kristen, Karen. B.S., U. Mo., 1958, M.S., 1959. Dir. agr. State Mo., Jefferson City, 1973-77, 81-84; dir. agribus. program Mo. C. of C., Jefferson City, 1977-79; pres. Mo. Fin. Adv. and Resource Mgmt. Support, Columbia, 1984—; mem. nat. agrl. research and extension users, adv. bd. U.S. Dept. Agr., 1984—, dir. intergovtl. affairs, 1985—, mem. task force farm income protection ins., 1982-83, fed. grain inspection service adv. com., 1981-82, tech. adv. com. multilateral trade negotiations on oil-seeds, 1975-76, task force nonpoint pollution policy EPA, 1984, adv. com., 1974-76; various positions and offices Nat. Assn. State Depts. Agr., 1976-84; mem. transp. policy commn. State Mo., 1976; pres. Mid Am. Internat. Agri Trade Council, 1976; advisor to com. agr. Nat. Govs. Assn., 1983-84. Mem. Boone County Home Rule Charter Drafting Commn., 1982; chmn. Callaway County Extension Council, 1972; adv. com. dept. agronomy Coll. Agr., U. Mo., Columbia, 1979-82. Recipient Am. Farmer Degree award Future Farmers Am., Merit award Gamma Sigma Delta, Centennial award U. Mo., Man of Yr. award Mo. Agr. Industries Council, Hon. State Farmer award Mo. Assn. Future Farmers Am., Citation, Jefferson City Prodn. Credit Assn., Builder of Men award Mo. Farmhouse Assn.; named Outstanding Mo. Comml. Pork Producer. Republican. Presbyterian. Lodge: Rotary (bd. dirs. 1983-84). Home: Route 6 Box 241 Columbia MO 65202

BOISSY, THOMAS JOSEPH, trucking company executive; b. Forest Park, Ill., Mar. 30, 1930; s. Alphonce Narciss and Alice Rose (LaChaplle) Plan Commn. m. Violet June Johnson, Jan. 25, 1963; children—Ronald, Kathy, Roxanne, Tracy; m. 2d, Betty Carol Ewing, Feb. 5, 1950 (div. Mar. 1958). Student Freight Traffic Inst., 1952-53. Dispatcher, Argo Collier Truck Lines, Chgo., 1952-54; ops. mgr. Hancock Trucking, 1954-58, Arbet Truck Lines, Inc., Chgo., 1958-64; asst. terminal mgr. Holland Motor Freight, Inc., Chgo., 1964-66; terminal mgr. Lincoln Dixie Freight Lines, Inc., Chgo., 1966-77; gen. mgr. D.A. Express, Inc., Calumet Park, Ill., 1977—; dir. Metalstich, Inc., Alsip, Ill., Danny's Express, Inc., Worth, Ill. Pres. Twp. Orgn., 1938-84. Served to cpl. U.S. Army, 1948-52; Korea. Chmn. Country Club Hills Plan Commn., 1971; commr. Country Club Hills Park Dist., 1970-72; youth commr. Bremen Twp., 1977; alternate del. Republican Conv., 1980. Mem. Freight Traffic Alumni, VFW (comdr. 1965). Republican. Home: 15812 S 86th Ave Orland Park IL 60462 Office: 11937 S Page Ave Calumet Park IL 60643

BOJARSKI, RONALD HENRY, priest, educator; b. Cleve., Nov. 15, 1934; s. Henry Edward and Frances Pauline (Ruszkowski) B. Ph.B., Borromeo Coll., 1957; postgrad. St. Mary Sem., 1957-61; M.Elem. Edn. and Adminstrn., St. John Coll., 1972; Ph.D., U. Md., 1974. Ordained priest Roman Catholic Ch., 1961. Counselor, Erieview and St. Edward High Sch., 1970-72; tchr. Cleve. Central Cath. High Sch., 1963-65; asst. supt. edn. Diocese Cleve., 1974-83, regional supt. Cuyahoga West region, 1975-83. Mem. Assn. Am. Sch. Adminstrs., Assn. Supervision and Curriculum Devel., Nat. Cath. Edn. Assn., Univ. Counseling Ednl. Adminstrs. (adv. bd. Pa., Md., Va.). Author: The Christian Code of Ethics for the Catholic Education Profession, 1976; Evaluation of Adminstrators, 1974.

BOKUNIEWICZ, LEN, JR., advertising executive; b. Detroit, Feb. 28, 1947; m. Debra, Nov. 29, 1979; 1 child, Nick. B.A., Mich. State U., 1969. Contbg. editor Auto Club Mich., Dearborn, 1970-80, sr. writer Ross Roy Inc., Detroit, 1981-83, creative supr., 1985—; sr. writer Wunderman, Ricotta & Kline subs. Young & Rubicam, 1984-85. Capt., Westmoreland Block Club, Detroit, 1980-85; chmn. pub. relations, pub. safety com. North Rosedale Park Civic Assn., Detroit, 1977-85. Mem. Direct Mktg. Assn. Detroit (editor newsletter 1981-85), Adcraft Club Detroit. Avocations: antiquing; weight training; jazz; Detroit renaissance. Home: 16710 Westmoreland St Detroit MI 48219 Office: Ross Roy Inc 2751 E Jefferson Detroit MI 48207

BOLAS, GERALD DOUGLAS, art museum administrator; art history educator; b. Los Angeles, Nov. 1, 1949; s. Norman Theodore and Elizabeth Louise (Douglas) B.; m. Deborah Jean Wohletz, Nov. 25, 1978; 1 dau., Ellen Claire. B.A., U. Calif.-Santa Barbara, 1972, M.A., 1975; postgrad. CUNY, 1984—. Teaching asst. U. Calif.-Santa Barbara, 1973-74; Nat. Endowment Humanities mus. intern Yale U. Art Gallery, New Haven, 1975-76, asst. to dir., 1976-77; dir. Washington U. Gallery of Art, St. Louis, 1977—; adj. asst. prof. art history Washington U., 1982—; field reviewer Inst. Mus. Services, Washington, 1980-83; advisor Mo. Arts Council, St. Louis, 1981-82; bd. dirs. Asian Art Soc. of Washington U., 1983—. Author: Illustrated Checklist, 1981; numerous catalog forwards. Organizer numerous exhbns. Mem. Assn. Art Mus. Dirs., Coll. Art Assn., Am. Assn. Museums, Midwest Art History Soc. Home: 5544 Waterman 1W Saint Louis MO 63112 Office: Washington U Gallery Art Steinberg Hall Campus Box 1214 Saint Louis MO 63130

BOLEN, CHARLES WARREN, university dean; b. West Frankfort, Ill., Sept. 27, 1923; s. William B. and Iva (Phillips) B.; B.M.E., Northwestern U., 1948; M.Mus., Eastman Sch. Music, Rochester, N.Y., 1950; Ph.D., Ind. U., 1954; m. Maxine Sheffler, Aug. 1, 1948; children—Ann, Jayne. Chmn. dept. music, prof. music Ripon (Wis.) Coll., 1954-62; dean Sch. Fine Arts, U. Mont., Missoula, 1962-70; dean Coll. Fine Arts, Ill. State U., Normal, 1970—; chmn. Mont. Arts Council, 1965-70; instr. Interlochen Music Camp, summers 1954-62; mem. Bloomington-Normal Symphony Soc., 1970—, pres., 1984-85; past mem. adv. bd. J.F. Kennedy Center Arts. Served with USAAF, 1942-46. Decorated Commendation medal; named Outstanding Tchr. of Year, Ripon Coll., 1962. Mem. Internat. Council Fine Arts Deans (chmn. 1969-70). Office: Ill State U Normal IL 61761

BOLENDER, TODD, See *Who's Who in America,* 43rd edition.

BOLES, CHRIS A., columnist; b. Purdy, Mo., Feb. 4, 1944; d. Alvin J. and Wilma Agnes (Parrigan) Ceselski; m. James Hugh Boles, July 6, 1963; children—Tammy Jo, Rana Dawn, Russell James. Student Wichita Bus. Coll., Crowder Coll. With Farm and Ranch World, Tulsa, 1971-81; stringer Country World, Tulsa, Joplin Globe, 1972-82; columnist Calif. Horse Rev., Fla. Horse Country, Tex. and So. Quarter Horse Jour., Horses Unltd., Valley Horse News, Continental Horseman; contbr. over 500 articles to horse mags.; advt. cons.; press sec. Mo. Parimutuel Horse Racing, 1983—; pub. relations chairperson Quarter Horse Racing Assn. Mo., 1981—; regional dir. Quarter Horse Racing Owners Am., Ft. Worth. Address: PO Box 225 Stark City MO 64866

BOLES, EDGAR HOWARD, II, lawyer; b. Cleve., Mar. 2, 1947; s. Laurence Huey and Blossom (Miller) B.; m. Elizabeth Young, Dec. 27, 1974; children—Gwendolyn H., Edgar H. III, Mary H., Elizabeth A. B.A., Ohio Wesleyan U., 1969; J.D., Case Western Res. U., 1973. Bar: Ohio 1973. Law clk. Ct. of Appeals of Ohio, Cleve., 1973-75; asst. county prosecutor Cuyahoga County, Cleve., 1975-76; mem. firm Calfee, Halter & Griswold, 1976-84; ptnr. Thomas & Boles, Chagrin Falls, 1985—. Mem. bd. govs. Case Western Res. U. Sch. Law, Cleve., 1981—. Mem. ABA, Ohio Bar Assn., Greater Cleve. Bar Assn. Republican. Episcopalian. Club: Hermit. Home: 2221 Delaware Dr Cleveland Heights OH 44106 Office: Thomas & Boles 36 S Franklin St Chagrin Falls OH 44022

BOLGER, T(HOMAS) MICHAEL, lawyer; b. Minocqua, Wis., Dec. 23, 1939; s. Patrick Edward and Mary Frances (McConville) B.; B.A., Marquette U., 1961; M.A., St. Louis U., 1966, Ph.L., 1966; J.D., Northwestern U., 1971; m. Virginia Kay Empey, Aug. 24, 1968; children—John, Jennifer. Admitted to Wis. bar, 1971; mem. firm Quarles & Brady, Milw., 1971—, partner, 1978—; instr. philosophy Marquette U., Milw., 1967-68. Vice chmn. United Performing Arts Fund drive, 1976-77; bd. dirs. Kearney Negro Welfare Found., 1974—, Milw. Repertory Theatre, 1977—, Milw. Ballet Found., Inc., 1981—, Permanent Diaconate Program of Milw. Archdiocese, 1977—; pres. Artreach, Inc., 1979—, Milw. Repertory Theater, 1980—; pres. bd. trustees Highland Community Sch., 1976—; trustee, sec.). U. Wis.-Milw. Found., 1976—; pres. bd. dirs. Hickory Hollow, 1978—. Mem. Am. Bar Assn., Milw. Bar Assn., Wis. Bar Assn., Fed. Bar Assn., Marquette U Alumni Assn. (pres. 1982-84), Alpha Sigma Nu, Phi Sigma Tau. Clubs: Univ., The Town. Contbr. articles in field to profl. jours.; editor Northwestern Jour. of Criminal Law, 1970-71. Home: 137 E White Oak Way Mequon WI 53092 Office: 780 N Water St Milwaukee WI 53202

BOLIN, SHARON ELAINE, college dean; b. Pontiac, Mich., Dec. 16, 1936; d. William R. and Betty C. (Fremed) B. Diploma in Nursing, W. Suburban Sch. Nursing, 1957; B.S., Wheaton Coll., 1959; M.S., DePaul U., 1963; Ed.D., Loyola U. Instr., West Suburban Hosp. Sch. of Nursing, Oak Park, Ill., 1959-67, dir. sch., 1967-84; dean West Suburban Coll. Nursing, Oak Park, 1982—; dir., sec. Evang. Child & Family Agy. Mem. editorial bd. Jour. Christian Nursing, 1984—; contbr. articles to profl. jours. USPHS grantee, 1961-62. Mem. Christian Nurse Educators (sec.-treas. 1983—), Am. Nurses Assn., Ill. Nurses Assn. (several offices), Nat. League Nursing, Ill. League Nursing (v.p. 1984—), Sigma Theta Tau, Baptist. Home: 7558-C Crawford Ave Skokie IL 60076 Office: W Suburban Coll Nursing Erie at Austin Oak Park IL 60302

BOLING, LAWRENCE H., See *Who's Who in America,* 43rd edition.

BOLLENBACHER, HERBERT KENNETH, steel company official; b. Wilkinsburg, Pa., Apr. 16, 1933; s. Curtis W. and Ebba M. (Frendberg) B.; m. Nancy Jane Cercena, June 29, 1957; children—Mary E., Kenneth E. A.B., U. Pitts., 1960, M.Ed., 1963. Cert. safety profl. Staff asst. tng. J & L Steel Co., Pitts., 1963-66; mgr. tng., devel. and accident prevention Textron Corp., Pitts., 1966-72; supr. safety Copperweld Steel Co., Warren, Ohio, 1972-75, mgr. safety, security, 1975-78, mgr. human resources conservation, 1978—; mem. adj. faculty Pa. State U. Served with U.S. Army, 1954-56. Mem. Am. Soc. Safety Engrs. (past pres. Ohio-Pa. chpt., Ohio Safety Profl. of Yr. 1983-84), Ohio Soc. Safety Engrs. (past pres.), Am. Iron and Steel Inst., Mfrs. Assn. Eastern Ohio and Western Pa. (safety chmn. 12 yrs.; Safety Profl. of Yr. award 1984), Trumbull Camp Gideons Internat. (past pres.), Ohio Gideons (area coordinator, membership cabinet). Presbyterian (elder). Lodge: Rotary. Author suprs. monthly discussion guide, article for tech. publ. Avocations: softball; volleyball; reading.

BOLLER, TIMOTHY CHARLES, lawyer; b. Waterloo, Iowa, July 17, 1956; s. Galen Charles and Marione Lucille (Ross) B.; m. Jean Louise Friar, June 19, 1982. B.A. in Polit. Sci. with honors, U. Iowa, 1978, J.D. with distinction, 1981. Bar: Iowa 1981, U.S. Dist. Ct. (no. dist.) Iowa 1981. Assoc. Charles F. Hinton Law Firm, Waterloo, 1981-83; ptnr. Hinton, Boller and Huisinga Law Firm, Waterloo, 1983—; bd. dirs. Iowa State Bar Rev. Sch. Inc., Des Moines, 1982—. Active Alan Vestal Scholarship Fund Drive, Iowa City, 1983; capt. Waterloo Art Assn. Fund Dr., 1984. Mem. Iowa State Bar Assn., Assn. trial Lawyers Iowa, Assn. Trial Lawyers Am., Black Hawk County Bar Assn., Phi Beta Kappa. Roman Catholic. Lodge: Exchange (bd. dirs. local club 1982—). Home: 4109 Heritage Cedar Falls IA 50613 Office: Hinton Boller and Huisinga Law Firm 751 Progress Waterloo IA 50701

BOLLING, ROBERT LEE, detective agency executive; b. Nashville, Apr. 4, 1929; s. Robert Lee and Maude (Turner) B.; m. Patricia Rose McLaughlin, Dec. 17, 1962. B.S. in Bus., Westminster Coll., Fulton, Mo., 1952; Assoc. in Law Enforcement, Meramec Community Coll., Kirkwood, Mo., 1975. Owner, pres. Bolling Ins. Co., Clayton, Mo., 1962-69; acct. rep. Wells-Fargo, Clayton, 1970-72; pres. L&R Security, St. Louis, Mo., 1972-73, Citadel Security, Chesterfield, Mo., 1974—, also dir.; pres. Mo. Assoc. Mut. Ins. Agts., 1968-69. Named Agt. of Yr. Mo. Assoc. Mut. Ins. Agts., 1969. Club: Terre Du Lac Country (Bonne Terre, Mo.). Office: Citadel Security Co Inc 263 Lamp and Lantern Village Chesterfield MO 63017

BOLLMEIER, EMIL WAYNE, manufacturing executive; b. Hurst, Ill., Jan. 16, 1925; s. Emil Philip and Flossie Louise (Swain) B.; B.S. in Chem. Engring., U. Nebr., 1947; postgrad. U. Minn., 1949-51; m. Nancy Lee Mercier, Feb. 9, 1972; children—David Wayne, Ann Louise, Paul Wesley. With 3M Co., St. Paul, 1947—, div. v.p. electro products div., 1965-72, group v.p. elec. products group, 1973-82, mem. 3M mgmt. com.; chief exec. officer, gen. ptnr. C-TEK Ltd. Partnership, 1982—; pres. Dynex Research, Inc., 1982—. Mem. Planning Commn., Mendota Heights, Minn., 1960-65; chmn. Republican Party, Dakota County, Minn., 1965-68. Served with USNR, 1945-46. Fellow IEEE; mem. Nat. Elec. Mfrs. Assn. (bd. govs.), Sigma Xi, Sigma Tau, Theta Xi. Presbyterian. Numerous patents in U.S. and fgn. countries spring reserve elec. wire connectors dispensing packages for insulating resins, resin injection splicing techniques, self-cleaning, high-tension elec. insulators for contaminated areas, magnetic remote control switches. Office: C-TEK Ltd Partnership 3615 29th Ave NE Minneapolis MN 55418

BOLTRES, H. WILLIAM, investment and financial consultant; b. Canton, Ohio, Apr. 7, 1936; s. Henry W. and Sarah A. Boltres; student Malone Coll., Ohio State U.; m. Doris Jean Kaufman, Aug. 9, 1958; children—Martin W., Christine A. With Addressograph-Multigraph Corp., Cleve., 1957-63, H.W. Boltres & Assos., Canton, 1963-65, Ohio Dept. Natural Resources, Columbus, 1965-75; pres. The Boltres Co., Columbus, 1975—; cons. Mem. fin. com.

Licking County Republican party, 1978-80. Served with USMC, 1953-54, U.S. Army, 1954-56. Mem. Nat. Rifle Assn. Methodist. Clubs: Columbus Touchdown, Big Red Touchdown, Ducks Unltd. Home: 123 W Broadway Granville OH 43023 Office: 1919 Lancaster Rd Box 454 Granville OH 43023

BOLWELL, HARRY JAMES, See *Who's Who in America,* 43rd edition.

BOLYARD, CHARLES WESLEY, behavioral scientist; b. Ft. Wayne, Ind., May 28, 1937; s. Charles Wesley and Virginia Maxine Bolyard; B.B.A., Ind. Central U., 1960; M.A., Ball State U., 1962; Ph.D., Purdue U., 1971; m. Martha E. Hudson, Aug. 14, 1960; children—Mark Gregory, Todd Andrew. Sch. counselor MSD Perry Twp., Indpls., 1963-68; univ. adminstr. Purdue U., 1968-70; prof., univ. adminstr. Ind.-Purdue U., Ft. Wayne, 1970-77; behavioral sci. cons. Lincoln Nat. Life Ins., Ft. Wayne, Ind., 1977—. Pres. exec. bd. Allen County Mental Health Assn., 1983-84; mem. adv. bd. Jr. League of Ft. Wayne, 1977—; adminstrv. bd., sec.-treas. Parent Club, Homestead High Sch., 1977-79; mem. area com. Internat. Yr. of Disabled Persons; mem. adv. com. Ind. Vocat. Services; mem. adv. bd. Nat. Spinal Cord Injury Found.; bd. dirs. ARC; mem. Ft. Wayne Area Council on Employment of Handicapped; mem. Ind. State Exec. Fellows Program Adv. Com.; bd. dirs. United Way Allen County, 1983-84; mem. edn. com. McMillen Health Ctr. NDEA fellow, 1964. Mem. Organizational Devel. Network, Am. Soc. Personnel Adminstrn., Am. Psychol. Assn., Personnel Assn. Ft. Wayne. Methodist. Club: Optimists (v.p.). Author: (with Robert S. Barkhaus) Threads: A Tapestry of Self and Career Exploration, 1980; Career Development in the 1980's: Theory and Practice, 1981; contbr. chpt. to book, articles to profl. jours. Home: 11626 Indigo Dr Fort Wayne IN 46804 Office: 1300 S Clinton St Fort Wayne IN 46801

BOLZ, CARL JOHN, brewery executive; b. Milw., Mar. 9, 1934; s. Carl August and Adele Erna (Martens) B.; m. Marilyn Ruth Counihan, June 29, 1957; children—Jennifer Ruth, Laura Ann. B.S., U. Wis., 1959. Staff instr. personnel benefits adminstrn. AC Electronics div. Gen. Motors Corp., Oak Creek, Wis., 1959-66; sales rep. Office Products div. IBM, Milw., 1966-69; br. office sales mgr. Office Products div. Saxon Industries, Milw., 1969-71; mgr. employee communications Miller Brewing Co., Milw., 1971-74; dir. corp. communications Anheuser-Busch Cos., St. Louis, 1975—. Bd. dirs. United Way of Greater St. Louis. Served with U.S. Army, 1956-58. Mem. Internat. Assn. Bus. Communicators (accredited), Pub. Relations Soc. Am., Internat. TV Assn. Republican. Methodist. Clubs: Ballwin Golf (Mo.), Rotary.

BOMAN, STANLEY MARK, public affairs executive; b. Joplin, Mo., July 23, 1951; s. Johnnie Ray and Billie Clorene (Wyrick) B.; m. Cynthia Louise Nelson, Nov. 24, 1973 (div. Feb. 1980); m. Nellrena Dee Boyer, Oct. 30, 1980; children—Tawni Jean, Darren Todd, Christi Dawn, Regenia Louise, Stacy Leigh. B.D., Central Mo. State U., 1973. Lobbyist pub. relations John Britton Assocs., Jefferson City, Mo., 1972-76; dir. info. and organizational relations Mo. NEA, Jefferson City, 1976-79; polit. cons. Boman/Purkey Assocs., Jefferson City, 1979-80; regional dir. Mo. and Kans., Ky., Tenn., Ala., Miss., La., Okla. The Tobacco Inst., Joplin, Mo., 1980—. Mem. Mo. State Democratic Com., 1972—. Mem. Pub. Relations Soc. Am., Mo. Soc. Assn. Execs., Okla. Retail Tobacco Dealers Assn. (ex-officio dir.). Baptist. Office: PO Box 2309 Joplin MO 64803

BOMKAMP, LORAINE MARY, educator; b. Cedar Rapids, Iowa, July 9, 1930; d. Frank William and Kathryn (Seifert) Bomkamp; student Clarke Coll., 1948-49; A.A. with distinction, Mt. Mercy Coll., 1950; B.A., U. Iowa, 1958, M.A. in Bus. Edn. and Office Mgmt., 1965. Sec., Simmons, Perrine, Albright, Ellwood and Neff, attys., Cedar Rapids, 1950-51, Century Engring. Corp., Cedar Rapids, 1951-56; tchr. Wausau (Wis.) Tech. Inst., 1958-63, Cedar Rapids Community Sch. Dist., 1964—, coordinator data processing edn., 1964-65. Co-chmn. Donnelly Nursing Edn. Center, Mt. Mercy Coll., Cedar Rapids, 1975; chmn. Sister Immaculata Meml., 1972. Recipient Distinguished Alumni award Mt. Mercy Coll., 1972; Individual Performance award Data Processing Mgmt. Assn., 1978; Women's Equality Day award Cedar Rapids Civic Groups, 1978. Mem. NEA, Nat. Secs. Assn. (award 1967), Am., Iowa (award 1970) vocat. assns., Bus. and Profl. Women's Club (dir. 1967-70, Woman of Year award 1977), AAUW, Cath. Daus. Am., Iowa State, Cedar Rapids edn. assns., Nat., Iowa (award 1969) bus. edn. assns., Iowa Office Edn. Assn., Internat. Fedn. Catholic Alumnae (regent 1968-69), Mt. Mercy, Clarke Coll., U Iowa alumni assns., Delta Kappa Gamma (pres. 1976-78). Roman Catholic. Contbr. articles on bus. edn. to profl. jours. Home: 1352 Hinkley Ave NW Cedar Rapids IA 52405 Office: Jefferson Sr High Sch 1243 20th St SW Cedar Rapids IA 52404

BONACH, LOUISE AHLFORS, consultant; b. Eveleth, Minn., June 14, 1948; d. George F. and Mary (Gornik) Ahlfors; B.A., U. Minn., Duluth, 1970; m. Joseph V. Bonach, Aug. 27, 1971. Mem. admissions staff Augsburg Coll., Mpls., 1970-71; personnel asst. Fairview Hosp., Mpls., 1971-73, personnel officer, 1973-75, dir. employee relations, 1975-80, dir. human resources, 1980-82; profl. services cons. Brim & Assocs., Mpls., 1982—. Mem. Am. Soc. Tng. and Devel., Am. Soc. Personnel Adminstrs., Am. Soc. Hosp. Public Relations Assn., Minn. Soc. Hosp. Public Relations, Twin Cities Personnel Assn., Am. Hosp. Assn., Mpls. Soc. Fine Arts. Home: 15665 S Woodgate Rd Minnetonka MN 55343 Office: Brim & Assocs 5775 Wayzata Blvd Minneapolis MN 55454

BONAFIGLIA, JOSEPH C., plastics company executive; b. Phila., Dec. 6, 1938; s. Ralph and Theresa (Severino) B.; m. Dolores Jean Niccoletti, Mar. 7, 1973; children—Maria Kristine, Ruppert, Jeffrey, Scott. B.A. in Math., Temple U., 1979. Research lab. mgr. Rohm & Haas Co., Bristol, Pa., 1974-77, salesman, N.Y.C., 1977-78, Mich., 1978-80; mktg. mgr. CertainTeed Corp., Troy, Mich., 1980-81, regional sales mgr., 1981—. Patentee in field. Vol. Project Concern-Walk for Mankind, Troy, 1980-84. Mem. Soc. Plastics Industry (chmn. Houston conf. 1983-84, Expo II 1985—), Soc. for Advancement of Materials and Process Engring. (chmn. 1984, bd. dirs. 1985), Soc. Plastics Engrs., MENSA, Troy C. of C. Roman Catholic. Avocations: sketching; oil and acrylic painting; woodworking; electronics; reading. Home: 1500 Brentwood Dr Troy MI 48098 Office: CertainTeed Corp 1450 Souter Troy MI 48083

BONAHOOM, YVONNE JANE, industrial testing company executive; b. Chgo., Aug. 28, 1940; d. Herbert Joseph and Margaret (Saddy) B.; B.S., Elmhurst Coll., 1980. Sr. sec. Nalco Chem. Co., Oak Brook, Ill., 1965-76, product safety specialist, 1976-77; mgr. quality assurance unit Indsl. Bio-Test Labs., Northbrook, Ill., 1977-78, mgr. validation team, 1978-80, pres., 1980—1980-85. Fellow Chgo. Council Fgn. Relations. Republican. Club: Zonta (fellow mem. N.W. Cook County chpt.). Office: Indsl Bio-Test Labs 1810 Frontage Rd Northbrook IL 60062

BONAVENTURA, LEO MARK, gynecologist, educator; b. East Chicago, Ill., Aug. 1, 1945; s. Angelo Peter and Wanda D. (Kelleher) B.; student Marquette U., 1963-66; M.D., Ind. U., 1970; married; children—Leo Mark, Dena Anne, Angela Lorena, Nicole Palmira, Leah Michelle, Adam Xavier. Intern in surgery, Cook County Hosp., Chgo., 1970-71; resident in ob-gyn., Ind. U. Hosps., 1973-76, fellow in reproductive endocrinology and infertility, 1976-78; asst. prof. ob-gyn., Ind. U., 1976—, asst. head sect. reproductive endocrinology and infertility, 1978-80, head sect., 1980-81. Served with USN attached to USMC, 1971-73. Named Intern of Yr., Cook County Hosp., 1971. Diplomate Am. Bd. Obstetrics and Gynecology, Am. Bd. Reproductive Endocrinology and Infertility. Mem. Central Assn. Ob-Gyn., Am. Coll. Obstetricians and Gynecologists, Am. Fertility Soc., Can. Fertility Soc., Soc. Reproductive Endocrinologists. Roman Catholic. Contbr. articles to profl. jours. Office: 8330 Naab Rd Indianapolis IN 46260

BONBRISCO, DANIEL EUGENE, physician; b. Detroit, Jan. 24, 1946; s. Eugene Charles and Mary (Juliano) B.; m. Diane Cantrell, Dec. 23, 1968; children—Denise Marie, Dana Lynn. B.S., Wayne State U., 1968; D.O., Kirksville Coll. Osteo. Medicine. Diplomate Nat. Bd. Examiners for Osteo. Physicians and Surgeons. Cert. Am. Osteo. Bd. Gen. Practice. Postdoctoral U. Mich. and Harvard Med. Sch.; Intern Flint Osteo. Hosp., Mich., 1974-75; gen. practice osteo. medicine, Fenton, Mich., 1974—; staff physician Hurley Med. Center, Flint Osteo. Hosp., Genesee Meml. Hosp., McLaren Hosp., Flint, 1974—; adj. faculty Coll. Osteo. Medicine Des Moines; asst. clin. prof. dept. family practice Coll. Osteo Medicine, Mich. State U., East Lansing; aviation med. examiner FAA. Co-med. dir. Hospice of Fenton, 1982; med. dir. Stan Marie Nursing Home, Argentine, Mich., 1984. Mem. Am. Osteo. Assn., Mich. Assn. Osteo. Physicians and Surgeons, Internat. Soc. Philos. Enquiry, Med. Amateur Radio Assn. Mensa, Internat. Legion of Intelligence. Republican. Roman Catholic. Lodge: K.C. Avocations: photography; ham radio; tennis; table tennis; world travel. Office: 329 Silver Lake Rd Fenton MI 48430

BOND, ALICE ELIZABETH, counselor for special services; b. Portland, Ind., Mar. 24, 1945; d. Russel Edmund and Margaret E. (Brown) Rouch; m. Byron Duane Bond, Dec. 17, 1966; children—Korinne Elizabeth, Ryan Duane. B.S., Ball State U., 1966; M.Ed., Ind. State U., 1985. Tchr. Three Rivers High Sch., Mich., 1967-71; counselor Vincennes U., Ind., 1978—. Mem. Mid-Am. Assn. Edn. Opportunity Personnel, Am. Assn. Counseling and Devel. Methodist. Avocations: Painting, needlepoint, reading. Home: 2637 Turley Ave Vincennes IN 47591 Office: Spl Services Vincennes U Vincennes IN 47591

BOND, CHARLES MORRIS, insurance company executive; b. St. Louis, Apr. 27, 1941; s. Conley Charles and Viva Bond (Bryant) B.; A.S., Connors State Coll., 1961; B.S., Panhandle State U., 1969; M.S., Pitts. State U., 1973, Ed.S., 1978; m. Paula Joan Case, Jan. 20, 1962; children—Monica, Moreena, Tyrone. Tchr., Argentine High Sch., Kansas City, 1969-73; indsl. tng. coordinator Kansas City Pub. Schs., 1973-75; edn. adminstr. Kansas City Area Vocat.-Tech. Schs., 1975-79; ins. agt. Prudential Ins. Co. Am., Prairie Village, Kans., 1979-80, devel. mgr., 1980—. Served with USAR, 1962-68. Mem. Johnson-Wyandott Life Underwriters Assn., Nat. Assn. Life Underwriters. Democrat. Baptist. Club: Optimist Internat., Masons, Shriners. Home: 6828 Georgia St Kansas City KS 66109 Office: 1900 W 75th St Prairie Village KS 66208

BOND, EPPERSON ELLIS, chemist; b. Nashville, Apr. 5, 1923; s. Epperson Porter and Margaret (Reed) B.; B.A., Fisk U., 1944, postgrad., 1945; postgrad. DePaul U., 1946; m. Marian Ruth Phillips, June 9, 1950; 1 son, Michael Ellis. Research asso. Glidden Co., Chgo., 1946-47, Med. Sch., U. Ill., Chgo., 1947-50, Northwestern U., Chgo., 1950-53; chemist VA Hosp., Hines, Ill., 1953—, now research chemist, chmn. research safety com. Chmn. credit com. Hines Fed. Credit Union, 1963-73, pres., 1973—; chmn. Hines Hosp. EEO com.; chmn. Med. Dist. 17 EEO program council. Bd. dirs., pres. Roseland Heights Community Assn. Fellow Am. Inst. Chemists; mem. Am. Assn. Clin. Chemists (dir.), Am. Chem. Soc., Ill. Kidney Found., Alpha Phi Alpha. Methodist (vice chmn. bd. stewards). Club: Men's (Chgo.). Home: 9835 Forest Ave Chicago IL 60628 Office: PO Box 41 Hines IL 60141

BOND, JUDY GRANEY, insurance company executive; b. Seneca, Kans., July 31, 1948; d. Thomas Patrick and Irene Mildred (Carroll) Graney; m. Michael Ray Bond, June 8, 1974; children—Thomas, Elizabeth. B.A. in Math., Benedictine Coll., 1970. Systems analyst AT&T Long Lines, Kansas City, Mo., 1970-73, Xerox Corp., Rochester, N.Y., 1973-74; systems analyst Blue Cross of Kansas City, Mo., 1974-81, supr. claims systems, 1982-83, mgr. claims systems, 1984—. Mem. Data Processing Mgmt. Assn., Assn. Systems Mgmt., Assn. Women in Computing. Democrat. Roman Catholic. Office: Blue Cross & Blue Shield of Kansas City PO Box 169 Kansas City MO 64141-0169

BOND, MORRIS LINDSAY, banker; b. Columbia, S.C., Sept. 30, 1936; s. Lindsay Johnson and Lossie Mae (Johnson) B.; B.S., Clemson U., 1958; M.B.A., St. Louis U., 1967; postgrad. Southwestern Grad. Sch. Banking, So. Meth. U., 1980; m. Patricia Jeanne Hunter, June 14, 1962; children—Stephanie Jane, Michael Morris. Research technologist Corp. Research and Devel. Center, Pet, Inc., Greenville, Ill., 1959-61, supr. project control, 1961-66, sect. chief, 1966-68, mgr. adminstrv. services, 1968-73; ops. improvement officer Centerre Bank N.A., St. Louis, 1974-76, asst. v.p., 1976-78, v.p. account services div., 1978-81, v.p. info. systems devel., 1981-83, v.p. account services div., 1983—; instr. bus. mgmt. Greenville Coll., 1977—, Am. Assn. Indsl. Mgmt., St. Louis, 1977—. Mem. Am. Inst. Indsl. Engrs., Am. Inst. Banking. Methodist. Clubs: Masons, Shriners. Home: Springwood Estates Route 2 Box 145C Greenville IL 62246 Office: One Centerre Plaza St Louis MO 63101

BOND, ROBERT LANCE, rehabilitation center executive, vocational consultant; b. Franklin, Ind., Feb. 4, 1954; s. Allen Dale and Lois Jean (Chitwood) B.; m. Kathy Lynn Moberly, Sept. 8, 1973; 1 child, Robert Ryan. B.S. in Edn., Auburn U., 1976, M.Ed., 1977; Ed.D., Ball State U. Dir. rehab. services Anthony Wayne Rehab. Ctr., Fort Wayne, Ind., 1977—; vocat. cons., Fort Wayne, 1979—; vocat. expert Social Security Adminstrn., Washington, 1982—. Mem. adv. bd. Purdue U. Mental Health Tech. Program, Fort Wayne, 1980—; exec. bd. Fort Wayne Area Adv. Council for Employment Handicapped, 1984. Named Disting. Hoosier, Gov. Ind., 1972. Mem. Nat. Rehab. Assn., Vocat. Evaluation and Work Adjustment Assn., Ind. Vocat. Evaluation and Work Adjustment Assn. (pres. Indpls. 1983—), Ind. Assn. Rehab. Facilities (chmn. rehab. services div. 1983—), Rho Sigma Epsilon. Avocations: coin collecting; sports. Home: 1105 W Oakdale Fort Wayne IN 46807 Office: Anthony Wayne Rehabilitation Ctr 2826 S Calhoun St Fort Wayne IN 46807

BONDA, ALVA TED, electronics executive; b. Cleve., June 1, 1917; s. Jacob Nathan and Nettie (Wasserman) B.; m. Marie C., Oct. 27, 1940; children—Penny Bonda Solomon, Joel, Thomas. Grad. Glenville High Sch., Cleve. Owner, operator car rental bus., 1945-49; pres. Airport Parking Co. Am., Cleve., 1949-68; pres. Cleve. Indians Baseball Inc., 1974-78; chmn. Avis Rent-A-Car, 1968-72, Penril Corp., 1978—; dir. MCI Communications Corp., Washington, Cleve. Indians, Consolidated Products Inc., Indpls. Active, NCCJ, Am. Cancer Soc.; vice chmn. Greater Cleve. Growth Assn.; mem. Ohio Bd. Regents, Cleve. 500 Found.; bd. dirs. ACLU; trustee Am. Mus. Immigration, Police Athletic League, Cleve. Mt. Sinai Hosp.; co-chmn. United Appeal; civilian aide Sec. Army; pres. Cleve. Bd. Edn., 1982-85. Served with U.S. Army, 1941-45. Recipient John F. Kennedy award, Variety Club Super Citizen award; named to Glenville Hall of Fame. Democrat. Clubs: Oakwood Country (Cleve.); Palm Beach Country (Fla.). Avocations: golf; tennis; boating. Home: 2 Bratenahl Pl Cleveland OH 44108 Office: 1700 Ohio Savings Plaza Cleveland OH 44114

BONDAR, ANDREW ARTHUR, dentist; b. Manchester, N.H., Oct. 23, 1914; s. Arthur George and Anna (Greneshen) B.; student U. N.H., 1932-34; D.M.D., Tufts U., 1938; diploma U.S. Army Med. Field Service Sch., 1969; cert. Command and Gen. Staff Coll., 1972; m. Ellen Ferguson Stewart, July 24, 1953; 1 dau., Billie Arlene. Pvt. practice dentistry, Manchester, 1939-42, 46-49; dentist VA Hosp./Dental Service, 1949-82. Lectr., clinician dist. and local dental socs. in N.H., N.Y., Que., Can. Asst. coach Jr. Am. Legion Baseball Team, Manchester, 1947-49; nat. chmn. Nat. German Prisoner of War Meml. Service, Ft. Custer, Mich., 1973-75. Served to capt. AUS, 1942-46, now col. Res. ret. Recipient cert. of commendation United War Vets. Council Battle Creek, 1979. Fellow Am. Acad. Gen. Dentistry, Midwest Acad. Prosthodontics; mem. ADA, New Eng. Dental Soc., Northeastern Dental Soc., Assn. U.S. Army, Tufts Coll., U. N.H. alumni assns., Assn. Mil. Surgeons U.S., Am. Soc. Geriatric Dentistry (nat. treas. 1975-81), Fedn. Am. Scientists, AAAS, Am. Legion, VFW, DAV, Vets. of Battle of the Bulge, Res. Officers Assn. U.S. (brigade of vols., past pres. chpt.; dental surgeon Mich. dept. 1973-77, 79—), 40 and 8. Club: Elks. Home: 519 Alvena Ave Battle Creek MI 49017

BONE, VIDA MARIE, employment consulting company executive; b. Vero Beach, Fla., Feb. 14, 1926; d. Raymond Lee and Emma Evangeline (DeFoe) Gore; student schs. Vero Beach; m. Charles Northington Bone, Oct. 11, 1944; children—Charles Raymond, Leonard Olin. With Winn Dixie Grocery Co., Miami, Fla., 1948-59; pvt. practice as beautician, 1960-66; supr. Servomation of Chgo., 1966-67; employment counselor Hallmark Personnel, Chgo., 1967-69; pres., owner, operator Employment Consultants Inc., Lansing, Ill., 1970—. Mem. Nat. (certified), Ill. employment assns. Republican. Lutheran. Club: Lansing Sportsman. Home: 3445 176th St Lansing IL 60438 Office: 1965 Bernice Rd Suite A Lansing IL 60438

BONEBURG, ANITA STROETZ, educator; b. Hammond, Ind., Feb. 23, 1920; d. Earl S. and Gertrude M. (Willarson) Stroetz; B.S. in Home Econs., Milw. Downer U. (now Lawrence U.), 1942; M.S. in Edn., Cleve. State U., 1978; postgrad. John Carroll U., 1970-75; Kent State U., 1979; m. Chester J. Boneburg, Aug. 25, 1942; children—Katharine D. Karawas, Thomas J., Peter K. With Gallup-Robinson Opinion Surveys, Cleve. and Princeton, N.J., 1957-59; U.S. census taker U.S. Dept. Commerce, Washington, 1960; with Cleve. Public Schs., 1960-85, substitute tchr., 1960-63, tchr. Blossom Hill Correctional Facility, 1963-68, tchr. home econs. dept. Lincoln-West High Sch., 1968—, newspaper advisor, 1984-85; mem. textbook com. Greater Cleve.; participant Martha H. Jennings Econ. Edn. Interface Program, 1981-82; mem. facilitators team High Schs. for the Future, 1984-85. Mem. Future Homemakers Am. Task Force, 1980-83, Ohio regional com. Juvenile protection chmn. PTA, 1964; active West Shore Rep. Club, 1959-64; mem. World Hunger Com., 1979-80; adv. ARC and Human Relations Clubs, 1970-78, Welcome Club, 1980-81, Swords to Plowshares Com.; mem. Urban League Aux., 1983-84. Recipient Martha Holden Jennings tchr. leadership award, 1972; scholar award, 1966; ARC service award, 1975, 80; Quincy Washington Reading award; Sohio Tchrs. award, 1981-82; Am. Assn. Christians and Jews human relations grantee, 1970. Mem. Am. Vocat. Assn. (public relations com., legis. com. nat. network), Am. Home Econs. Assn., Ohio Vocat. Assn., Greater Cleve. Home Econs. Assn., Cleve. Council on Human Relations, Cleve. Econ. Council, Cleve. Teachers Union (conf. com., del. assembly rep., 1970-75), Lawrence U. Alumni Assn., Cleve. State U. Alumni Assn. Episcopalian. Clubs: Pinehurst Country (Pinehurst, N.C.), Coll. Club West. Active curriculum devel., task forces, research coms. in field; fund raising, Lawrence U., 1973—. Home: 18429 Sloane Lakewood OH 44107

BONÉE, JOHN RAOUL, information technologies company executive; b. New Orleans, Nov. 11, 1923; s. John Raoul and Lucille Evelyn (Schwarzenbach) B.: student Loyola U., New Orleans, 1940-42; M.A., Aquinas Inst., 1946, 50; Ph.D., U. Fribourg (Switzerland), 1953; m. Mavis Long Heyl, Dec. 22, 1967; children—Mavis Heyl McClung, Larrye Heyl Steldt. Joined Dominican Order, Roman Catholic Ch., 1942, ordained priest, 1949, laicized, 1967; prof. modern and contemporary philosophy Aquinas Inst., River Forest, Ill., 1953-61; prof. communications and homiletics St. Rose Priory, Dubuque, Iowa, 1961-67; mgr. Ill. Bell Tel. Co., Chgo., 1967-83, mgr. corp. communications, 1970-83; pub. relations mgr. exec. support Ameritech, 1983—; lectr. DePaul U., 1968-82; adj. assoc. prof. communications Rosary Coll., River Forest, Ill., 1984—; cons. VISCAM, Cameroon, Africa, 1980-82. Mem. Community Relations Commn. Oak Park (Ill.), 1973-74. Mem. Public Relations Soc. Am., Chgo. Pub. Relations Clinic, Chgo. Press Club. Roman Catholic. Home: 801 S Kenilworth Ave Oak Park IL 60304 Office: 30 S Wacker Dr Chicago IL 60606

BONEZZI, WILLIAM DAVID, lawyer; b. Cambridge, Eng., Nov. 25, 1945; s. Robert Michael and Nina Kathleen (Cromack) B.; m. Janine Roberta Burke, Oct. 29, 1977; children—Shannon, Christopher. B.S., Bowling Green State U., 1970; J.D., Cleve. State U., 1973. Bar: Ohio 1973. Lawyer with York, Bonezzi & Thomas, Cleve., 1973-78; div. gen. atty. Liberty Mutual Ins. Co., Cleve., 1978-85; prin. Jacobson Maynard, Tuschman & Kalur, Cleve., 1985—. Served with USMC 1966-68. Mem. ABA, Ohio Acad. Trial Attys., Cleve. Bar Assn., Am. Arbitration Assn., Cleve. Acad. Trial Attys. Republican. Episcopalian. Avocations: golf; racquetball; reading. Home: 25988 Byron Dr North Olmsted OH 44070 Office: Jacobson Maynard Tuschman & Kalur 100 Erieview Plaza 14th Floor Cleveland OH 44114

BONGIORNO, JOHN ANTHONY, sales manager; b. Chgo., Sept. 29, 1951; s. John Anthony and Stephanie Marie (DiTusa) B.; A.S. in Accounting and Bus. Adminstrn., Triton Coll., 1971; student in Mktg., U. Ill., Chgo., 1969-73; m. Sharon Louise Bernath, July 12, 1975. Sales rep. electronic data processing Chgo. office Reynolds & Reynolds Co., Elk Grove Village, 1973-75, sales rep. automotive forms, 1975-81, Eastern div. sales mgr. automotive forms, Dayton, Ohio, 1981-83, N.E. regional sales mgr. bus. forms and systems div., 1983—. Named to 300 Club for sales excellence Reynolds and Reynolds Co., 1975-77, 79-80. Mem. Dayton Sales and Mktg. Club. Roman Catholic. Home: 7540 Pelway Dr Dayton OH 45459 Office: 800 Germantown PO Box 1005 Dayton OH 45401

BONGIORNO, JOSEPH SALVATORE, lawyer; b. Chgo., Nov. 13, 1953; s. Philip S. and Marie (Termini) B.; m. Margaret Rohde, Apr. 23, 1983. B.A., Elmhurst Coll., 1975; J.D., Northern Ill. U., 1979. Bar: Ill. 1979, U.S. Dist. Ct. (no. dist.) Ill. 1981. Asst. states atty. Du Page County States Attys. Office, Wheaton, Ill., 1979-83; assoc. Daniels & Faris, Elmhurst, Ill., 1983-84; legal counsel to minority leader Ill. Ho. Reps., Springfield, 1984—; trustee Addison Fire Protection Dist., Ill., 1984—. Precinct committeeman Du Page County Republican Central Com., Wheaton, 1980—. Roman Catholic. Office: 180 W Park Elmhurst IL 60126

BONHAUS, LAURENCE ALLEN, lawyer, urban planner; b. Cin., May 27, 1949; s. Alphonse Lawrence and Mary Kathryn (Muchmore) B.; B.S. in Architecture cum laude, U. Cin., 1973, J.D., 1976; m. Jacquelyn Lea Arck, Oct. 11, 1981; 1 son, Andrew Laurence. Bar: Ohio 1976, U.S. Supreme Ct. 1982. Draftsman, designer Arend & Arend Architects, Cin., 1969-72; designer Kral, Zepf, Frietag and Assos., Architects & Engrs., Cin., 1972-73; designer, OSHA specialist offices Robert Harter Snyder, Cin., 1973-76; OSHA and bldg. code specialist, Project Designer AEDES Assos., Inc., 1973-76; individual practice archtl. and planning law, Cin., 1976—; v.p., urban planner Citysystems, Inc., Cin., 1976—; arbitrator Am. Arbitration Assn.; sec. P.D.A., Inc. Co-chmn. Ohio Confederation, 1970-72, lobbyist for state and state affiliated univs.; mem. Gradison Campaign com., N.Avondale Neighborhood Assn.; pres., trustee NAPA; v.p. Fairview/Clifton Heights housing devel. corp.; v.p. Asbury property mgmt. non-profit housing corp.; mem. Greater Cin. Beautiful Com., Contemporary Arts Center; first violinist, concertmaster, chmn. bd. dirs. Cin. Civic Orch.; mus. dir., condr. Gilbert and Sullivan Soc., Cin., also bd. dirs.; condr. Cin. Young Peoples Theater; co-chmn., treas., bd. dirs., exec. com. Ohio Solar Resources Adv. Panel; v.p. Cin. Archtl. Found.; sustaining mem. Republican Nat. Com. Mem. AIA (co-chmn. nat. conv. com. 1980, nat. codes and standards com., Henry Adams cert., 1973, chmn. Cin. chpt. speakers bur., by-laws com.), ABA, Cin. Bar Assn. (chmn. OSHA com., mem. constrn. and engring. law com.), Architects Soc. Ohio, Lawyers Club of Cin., Southwest Ohio Alt. Energy Assn. (founding mem., dir., exec. com.), Ohio Solar Energy Assn. (pres. dir.), Nat. Passive Solar Conf. Planning Com., Cin. Energy Network (co-founder), Cin. Engrs. Club (bd. dirs.), SCARAB (v.p., 1970-71), Greater Cin. C. of C. (energy com.), Phi Alpha Delta (alumni justice Cin. chpt., dep. internat. justice, Outstanding Service cert. 1980, 82). Methodist (mem. adminstrv. bd.). Clubs: Cin. CINgles (dirs., dir. devel.), Updowntowners (Oktoberfest planning com.), Cincinnatus, Metro. Works include interior design and execution of mosaic panel Forest Chapel United Meth. Ch., 1969, restoration Fleischman mansion, 1974-76, Conroy mansion, 1977-79; new zoning code and land use plan Union Twp., Clermont County, Ohio, 1977-78; handicapped accessibility study Montgomery County, Ohio, 1979-81; urban renewal study Newark, Ohio, 1977-78; ind. living facility Total Living Concepts, Inc., Cin., 1980-81, solar zoning ordinances, 1982-83. Home: 948 Dana Ave Cincinnati OH 45229

BONI, ROBERT EUGENE, steel products company executive. Pres., chief exec. officer Armco Inc., Middletown, Ohio, also dir. Office: Armco Inc 703 Curtis St Middletown OH 45043*

BONIOR, DAVID EDWARD, congressman; b. Detroit, June 6, 1945; s. Edward John and Irene (Gaverluk) B.; B.A., U. Iowa, 1967; M.A., Chapman Coll., 1972. Mem. Mich. Ho. of Reps., 1973-76; mem. 95th-99th Congresses from 12th Mich. Dist. Home: 37549 Charter Oaks Blvd Mount Clemens MI 48043 Office: 2242 Rayburn House Office Bldg Washington DC 20515

BONNER, PAUL ANTHONY, medical group executive; b. Boston, Aug. 19, 1944; s. John Joseph and Adela Ann (Krupovesas) B.; B.S. in Mktg. Mgmt., Boston Coll., 1966; M.P.H. in Hosp. Adminstrn. (Yale scholar), Yale U., 1968; Sc.D. in Health Services Adminstrn., Harvard U., 1976; m. Patricia Ann Kenney, June 22, 1968; children—Alison M., Andrew D. Adminstrv. resident Beth Israel Hosp., Boston, 1968; health center adminstr. Harvard Community Health Plan, Boston, 1968-71; mem. profl. staff health care group Arthur D. Little, Inc., Cambridge, Mass., 1971-76; asst. supt., chief operating officer Wrentham (Mass.) State Sch., 1976-77; v.p. profl. services Greater Cleve. Hosp. Assn., 1977-82; v.p. bd. trustees Central Med. Emergency Dispatch, Inc., Cleve., 1980-82; v.p., chief operating officer Cancer Data System, Inc., Cleve., 1980-82; dir. health systems planning Cleve. Clinic Found., 1982-83, dir. strategic planning, 1983-84, dir. regional health care systems, 1985—; trustee Pvt. Accent on Quality, Inc., Cleve., 1981-82; USPHS trainees, 1966-67, 73-75. Mem. Am. Hosp. Assn., Am. Public Health Assn., Am. Coll. Hosp. Adminstrs., Group Health Assn. Am. Club: Chagrin Valley Athletic. Home: 119 Southwyck Chagrin Falls OH 44022 Office: Cleve Clinic Found 9500 Euclid Ave Cleveland OH 44106

BONNER, THOMAS NEVILLE, history educator, former university president; b. Rochester, N.Y., May 28, 1923; s. John Neville and Mary (McGowan) B.; A.B., U. Rochester, 1947, M.A., 1948; Ph.D., Northwestern U., 1952; LL.D. (hon.), U. N.H., 1974; children—Phillip Lynn, Diana Joan. Acad. dean William Woods Coll., 1951-54; prof. history, chmn. dept. social sci. U. Omaha, 1955-62; Fulbright lectr. U. Mainz (W. Ger.), 1954-55; prof., head history dept.

U. Cin., 1963-68, v.p. acad. affairs, provost, 1967-71; pres. U. N.H., Durham, 1971-74; pres. Union Coll., chancellor Union U., Schenectady, 1974-78; pres. Wayne State U., Detroit, 1978-82, Disting. prof. history, 1983—; vis. prof. U. Freiburg, 1982-83. Democratic candidate for Congress, 1962; legis. aide to Senator McGovern, 1962-63. Served with Radio Intelligence Corps, AUS, 1942-46; ETO. Guggenheim fellow, 1958-59, 64-65. Mem. Am. Hist. Assn., Orgn. Am. Historians, Phi Beta Kappa, Pi Gamma Mu, Phi Alpha Theta. Author: Medicine in Chicago, 1957; The Kansas Doctor, 1959; (with others) The Contemporary World, 1960; Our Recent Past, 1963; American Doctors and German Universities, 1963. Editor, translator: Journey Through the Rocky Mountains (Jacob Schiel), 1959. Office: Dept History Wayne State U Detroit MI 48202

BONNIWELL, GEORGE BARTON, investment banking executive; b. Battle Creek, Mich., May 21, 1939; s. Calvin Hartley and Margaret Beatrice (Goslin) B.; m. Charlotte Ann Yost, Mar. 21, 1964; children—Jed, Kent, Ann. B.S., Macalester Coll., 1961. Mgr. Investors Diversified Services, Mpls., 1964-69; investment analyst Craig-Hallum, Inc., 1969-71, v.p., 1971-75, pres., chief exec. officer, 1976—, dir., 1981—; dir. Minn. Cooperation Office, Mpls. Mem. Golden Valley, Minn. Human Rights Commn., 1967-70, Minn. DeMolay Found., 1974-77. Recipient Legion of Honor award 1967. Served with U.S. Army, 1961-63. Mem. Fin. Analysts Fedn., Twin Cities Soc. Security Analysts. Lodge: Masons. Home: 18107 Woolman Dr Minnetonka MN 55345 Office: Craig-Hallum Inc 133 South 7th St Minneapolis MN 55402

BONOMO, DAVID MICHAEL, data processing executive; b. Peoria, Ill., June 5, 1948; s. Richard Stephen and Evelyn (Stengle) B. B.A. in Govt., So. Ill. U., 1970; B.S. in Computer Sci., Ill. State U., 1979. Co. exec. part time Bonomo Tool & Die Inc., Delavan, Ill., 1965-70, 1972-77; sr. systems analyst Owens-Corning Fiberglas Corp., Toledo, Ohio, 1980-83; analyst II Fermi Nat. Accelerator Lab., Batavia, Ill. 1983—. Vol. Republican Campaign Com., Carbondale, Ill., 1968, 70. Served with U.S. Army, 1970-72. Mem. Data Processing Mgmt. Assn., Assn. Computing Machinery, Am. Mgmt. Assn. (corp. affiliated). Presbyterian. Club: Four Lakes Ski (treas. 1984-85). Home: 5900 Oakwood Dr Lisle IL 60532 Office: Fermi Nat Accelerator Lab PO Box 500 M S III Batavia IL 60510

BONSETT, GLEN LEO, former educator, organization official; b. Scott County, Ind., July 29, 1924; s. Leo and Glen Anna (Mahan) B.; student Hanover Coll., 1942-43, Berea Coll., 1943-44; B.S., Ind. U., 1948, M.S., 1949, P.E.D., 1957; postgrad. Mich. State U., 1966-67, U. Calif-Santa Barbara, 1978; m. Melba June Mace, Feb. 21, 1980; children by previous marriage—Sandra Marie, Andrea Lee, Candace Lynn. Tchr., coach Ind. U. Lab. Sch., 1948-53; mem. faculty Hanover (Ind.) Coll., 1953-61, prof., 1955-61, coach intercollegiate athletics, 1953-61, student personnel adminstr., dean of men, 1961-75, v.p. for devel., 1975-81; with Goettler Assocs., Columbus, Ohio, 1981-83; spl. asst. to chief exec. officer estate preservations trusts and endowment ARC, 1984—; vis. lectr. Ind. U., 1954-60. Served with USNR, 1943-46; to comdr. Res. Mem. Council Advancement and Support Edn., Ind. Coll. Personnel Assn. (pres. 1971), Nat. Assn. Student Personnel Adminstrn., Ind. Personnel Guidance Assn., Ind. High Sch. Athletic Assn., AAHPER, Ind. Assn. Health, Phys. Edn. and Recreation (chmn. research sect.), Health, Phys. Edn. and Recreation Alumni Assn. Ind. U. (pres.), Ind. U. Alumni Assn. (dir.), Phi Epsilon Kappa, Lambda Chi Alpha, Phi Delta Kappa, Sigma Pi Sigma, Alpha Phi Omega. Republican. Methodist. Clubs: Masons, Elks, Moose, Shriners.

BONSIB, RICHARD EUGENE, marketing services executive; b. Ft. Wayne, Ind., Nov. 8, 1931; s. Louis William and Marietta Anna (Jacobs) B., Sr.; B.S. in Mktg., Ind. U., 1953; postgrad course Am. Mgmt. Assn., 1966; m. Gretchen Allen, Aug. 23, 1958; children—Gregory Allen, Stephen Richard. Owner, pres. The Century Press, Ft. Wayne, 1948-53; with Bonsib Inc., Ft. Wayne and Indpls., 1953—, pres., chmn., 1975-85, chmn., chief exec. officer, 1985—; v.p., dir. L.W. Bonsib Found., Inc., Ft. Wayne, 1961-74; v.p. Prodn. Concepts Ltd., Creative Concepts, 1980-81; treas. HPL, Inc., Ft. Wayne, 1965-66; pres. Leemark Tours, Inc., Chgo., 1968-70. Founding dir. Ft. Wayne Horizons Econ. Devel. Council; past v.p., dir. Allen County-Ft. Wayne YMCA; former v.p., dir. fathers bd. Culver (Ind.) Mil. Acad.; bd. dirs., pres. Allen County-Ft. Wayne Hist. Soc.; v.p., bd. dirs. United Way Allen County; past chmn. steering com. Leadership Prayer Breakfast; past chmn., founding dir. Summit Tech. and Research Transfer, Inc.; bd. dirs. Harold W. McMillen Ctr. for Health Edn. Served with U.S. Army, 1955-57; Korea. Mem. Ft. Wayne Advt. Club (pres. 1963), Pub. Relations Soc. Am., Greater Ft. Wayne C. of C. (dir.), Phi Gamma Delta. Republican. Presbyterian. Home: 5511 Covington Rd Fort Wayne IN 46804 Office: Bonsib Bldg 927 S Harrison St Fort Wayne IN 46802

BONSKY, JACK ALAN, tire mfg. corp. exec., lawyer; b. Canton, Ohio, Mar. 12, 1938; s. Jack H. and Pearl E. Bonsky; B.A., Ohio U., 1960; J.D., Ohio State U., 1964; m. Carol Ann Portmann, Sept. 2, 1960; children—Jack Raymond, Cynthia Lynn. Bar: Ohio 1964. With Metcalf, Thomas & Bonsky, Marietta, Ohio, 1964-69, Addison, Fisher & Bonsky, Marietta, 1969-70; asst. counsel GenCorp., Inc. (formerly Gen. Tire & Rubber Co.), Akron, Ohio, 1970-75, assoc. gen. counsel, 1975—, asst. sec., 1977—. Mem. Marietta Income Tax Bd. of Rev., 1966-67; mem. Traffic Commn., 1966-69, chmn., 1967; mem. Civil Service Commn., 1969; trustee Urban League, 1978-81, pres., 1980-81; trustee Akron Community Service Center, 1978-81, United Way of Summit County, 1981—; bd. dirs. Washington County Soc. for Crippled Children, 1964-70; bd. dirs. S.E. Ohio unit Arthritis Found., 1967-70, chmn., 1968-70; mem. Washington County Health Planning Com., 1968-70; mem. ho. of dels. Ohio Easter Seal Soc., 1968-70. Recipient Akron Community Service Center and Urban League Leadership award, 1981. Mem. Ohio State Bar Assn. Home: 4234 Idlebrook Dr Akron OH 44313 Office: GenCorp Inc 1 General St Akron OH 44329

BONTE, JOHN LEE, chemistry educator; b. Belmond, Iowa, Dec. 7, 1946; s. Merle John and Peggy Joyce (Anderson) B.; m. Martha Kay Anderson, May 30, 1969; children—Benjamin, Krista. B.A., St. Olaf Coll., 1969; Ph.D., Iowa State U., 1976. Instr. chemistry Clinton Community Coll., Iowa, 1976—; asst. prof. Iowa State U., Ames, 1984. Contbr. articles to profl. jours. Served with U.S. Army, 1969-72. Mem. Am. Chem. Soc., Iowa Acad. Sci. Democrat. Lutheran. Avocations: gardening; sailing; reading. Home: 872 14th Ave NW Clinton IA 52732 Office: Clinton Community Coll 1000 Lincoln Blvd Clinton IA 52732

BOODEN, JOHN MORRIS, pharmaceutical company official; b. Kalamazoo, July 25, 1939; s. Marinus and Anna (Brunsting) B.; married; children—Scott Alan, Michael John. B.B.A., Western Mich. U., 1963. Salesman, NCR, Kalamazoo, 1963-65; European fin. analyst Upjohn Internat., Kalamazoo, 1965-72, controller R&D, 1972-80, mgr. corp. budgeting, 1980-83, mgr. corp. fin. planning, 1983-84, dir. corp. fin. planning and analysis, 1985—. Mem. Kalamazoo Hist. Commn., 1980-83; bd. dirs. Kalamazoo Child Guidance Clinic, 1983-85. Served with U.S. Army, 1957-58. Mem. Planning Forum. Republican. Home: 1803 Greenview Ave Portage MI 49002

BOOE, JAMES MARVIN, chemical engineer; b. Austin, Ind., Nov. 12, 1906; s. James Ross and Grace (Hesler) B.; B.S., Butler U., 1928; m. Dortha Maud Weaver, July 30, 1938; children—James Marvin, Ann Marie, John Weaver. Chemist, Indpls. Plating Co., 1929; chief chemist P. R. Mallory & Co., 1929-45, dir. electrochem. research, 1945-51, exec. chem. engr., 1951-53, dir. chem. and metall. research corp. labs., 1953-63; dir. chem. labs. Mallory Capacitor Co., Indpls., 1963-72, cons., 1972—. Advisory bd. Am. Security Council; bd. dirs. Irvington Benton House Assn.; pres., bd. dirs. Irvington Hist. Landmarks Found. Accredited profl. chemist Am. Inst. Chemists. Recipient Army-Navy E civilian award, Naval Ordnance Devel. award. Fellow Am. Inst. Chemists; mem. Am. Chem. Soc., Electrochem. Soc., Irvington Hist. Soc., Am. Def. Preparedness Assn., Indpls. Scientech Soc. (bd. dirs.), Smithsonian Instn. (asso.), Indpls. Mus. Art, Goodwill Industries, Ransburg YMCA, Presbyterian (elder, trustee). Lodge: Kiwanis. Patentee in field (38). Research on electrolytic capacitors, batteries, resistors, semiconductors. Home: 548 N Audubon Rd Indianapolis IN 46219 Office: 3029 E Washington St Indianapolis IN 46201

BOOHER, MICHAEL ROBERT, lawyer; b. Dayton, Ohio, Aug. 5, 1956; s. Robert W. and Jeannine G. (Houck) B.; m. Marcia L. Moore, Aug. 23, 1980. B.A., Miami U., Oxford, Ohio, 1978; J.D., Ohio State U., 1981. Bar: Ohio 1981, Fla. 1982, U.S. Dist. Ct. (so. dist.) Ohio 1981. Assoc. Earl H. Moore Co., L.P.A., Dayton, Ohio, 1981-82, Finkleman & Forshaw, Middletown, Ohio, 1982-83; ptnr. Finkleman, Forshaw, Milbauer & Booher, Middletown, 1983—. Mem. Butler County Bar Assn., Dayton Bar Assn., Middletown Bar Assn. Republican. Club: Dayton Ski. Home 2524 Oak Park Ave Kettering OH 45419 Office: Finkleman Forshaw Milbauer & Booher 405 Savs and Loan Bldg Middletown OH 45042

BOOHER, ROBERT BONKE, dentist; b. Indpls., Sept. 8, 1949; s. Norman R. and Olga M. (Bonke) B.; m. Joyce A. Friend, Aug. 4, 1973. B.S., Purdue U., 1971; D.D.S., Ind. U., 1975. Assoc. dentist Dental Health Assocs., Indpls., 1977-79, co-owner, 1979-80; owner Assocs. in Family Dentistry, Indpls., 1980—. Bd. dirs. Julia Jameson Health Camp for Children, Indpls., 1978—. Served to capt. U.S. Army, 1977—. Mem. ADA, Ind. Dental Assn., Indpls. Dist. Dental Soc. Presbyterian. Lodge: Masons. Avocations: singing; golf; tennis. Home: 5094 Greensview Way Plainfield IN 46168 Office: 62 S Girls School Rd Indianapolis IN 46231

BOOKER, DEBORAH SHANNON, educator; b. Washington, Apr. 6, 1937; d. Angus R. and Barbara (Stratton) Shannon; B.A., U. Mo., 1959; m. Paul Booker, Nov. 26, 1960; children—Margaret, Sarah, Charles. Psychol. technician U. Mo., Columbia, 1959-61; owner, mgr. The Horse Fair, Columbia, 1965—; asst. prof. equestrian sci. William Woods Coll., Fulton, Mo., 1972—; nat. examiner, mem. instrn. council U.S. Pony Clubs, Inc., 1978—. Mem. Am. Horse Shows Assn. (tech. del. for combined tng. and dressage, recorded steward), U.S. Combined Tng. Assn., U.S. Pony Clubs, Inc. Episcopalian. Home: Route 9 Columbia MO 65202 Office: William Woods Coll Fulton MO 65251

BOOKER, JAMES ARTHUR, German language educator; b. Cheyenne, Wyo., June 17, 1938; s. James Arthur and Adeline (Hansen) B.; m. Elaine Marie Glammeier, July, 1, 1960; children—Michael James, Robert Glenn. B.S., U.S. Mil. Acad., 1960; M.A., U. Nebr., 1970, Ph.D., 1975. Instr. English Mayen Gymnasium, W. Germany, 1971-72; prof. German lang. Whitworth Coll., Spokane, Wash,. 1972-73, Wheaton Coll., Ill., 1973-76, Mankato State U., Minn., 1976—. Assoc. editor Schatzkammer jour., 1984. Contbr. articles to profl. jours. Served to capt. U.S. Army, 1960-67. Mem. MLA, Am. Assn. Tchrs. German. Clubs: German-AM., Stammtisch (Mankato). Avocations: fishing, hunting, racquetball, running, music. Home: 318 Floral Ave Mankato MN 56001 Office: Fgn Lang Dept Mankato State U Mankato MN 56001

BOOKSHESTER, DENNIS S., retail company executive. Vice chmn., dir. Carson Pirie Scott & Co., Chgo., chmn., chief exec. officer dept. stores div. Office: Carson Pirie Scott & Co 1 S State St Chicago IL 60603*

BOOKSTEIN, FRED LEON, statistician; b. Detroit, July 27, 1947; m. Edith M. Leavis; children—Victoria, Amelia. B.S., U. Mich., 1966, Ph.D., 1977; M.A., Harvard U., 1971. Asst. to assoc. research scientist U. Mich., Ann Arbor, 1977-84, assoc. prof., 1982-84, research scientist, 1984—; pres. Growth and Form, Inc., Ann Arbor, 1980—. Author: Measurement of Biological Shape & Shape Change, 1978; Morphometrics in Evolutionary Biology, 1985. Contbr. articles to profl. jours. Junior fellow U. Mich., 1974. Office: Center for Human Growth 300 N Ingalls Bldg Ann Arbor MI 48109

BOOKWALTER, RICHARD LEROY, aluminum products manufacturing company executive; b. Mansfield, Ohio, Feb. 6, 1942; s. John Leroy and Leatha Ardella (Lutz) B.; B.S. in Bus. Adminstrn., Franklin U., 1974; m. Beverly Tean Shaarda, Mar. 23, 1961; children—Terri Lynn, Bradley Allen, Derrick Roy. Mgr. mfg. acctg. Faultless Rubber Co., Ashland, Ohio, 1972-76; controller Tubelite Archtl. div. Consol. Aluminum Co. (now Tubelite div. Indal Inc.), Reed City, Mich., 1976-79, plant mgr., 1979-81, v.p. ops. and fin., 1981-84, v.p. ops., 1984—. Treas., United Methodist Ch., Reed City, 1980-83; mem. Reed City Zoning Bd. Appeals, 1981—, W. Central Mich. Pvt. Industry Council, 1981-83 Mem. Reed City C. of C. (v.p.). Author short stories. Home: 423 W Todd Ave Reed City MI 49677 Office: Tubelite div Indal Inc Old US 131 PO Box 118 Reed City MI 49677

BOONE, LESTER VERLIN, agronomist; b. Mount Vernon, Ill., Sept. 5, 1931; s. Charles Lester and Sylvia Mae (Mullinax) B.; B.S., So. Ill. U., 1956; M.S., U. Ill., 1972; m. Norma Jean Anderson, Dec. 22, 1954; children—Andrew V., Dawn E. Area agronomist for So. Ill., U. Ill., 1956-67, research and extension agronomist, Champaign-Urbana campus, 1967—; state coordinator agronomy field research. Mem. Field Consol. Sch. Bd. Edn., Texico, Ill., 1964-67. Served with USAF, 1950-54. Mem. Am. Soc. Agronomy, Soil Sci. Soc. Am., Internat. Soc. Soil Sci., AAAS, Council Agrl. Sci. and Tech., Am. Registry Cert. Profls. in Agronomy, Crops and Soils (cert. profl. agronomist and soil scientist). Republican. Baptist. Author: (with others) Producing Farm Crops, 1975, 2d edit., 1980; contbr. numerous articles to profl. jours. Home: 2514 Stanford Dr Champaign IL 61820 Office: AW-109 Turner Hall 1102 S Goodwin Ave Urbana IL 61801

BOONKHAM, CHOTCHAI, internist; b. Cheingrai, Thailand, May 29, 1943; s. Boonsing and Homhuon (Yantadilok) B.; came to U.S., 1969; M.D., Siriraj Med. Sch. and Hosp., Bangkok, Thailand, 1968; m. Sumalee Ratanagorn, May 1, 1972; children—Martin, Monica. Intern, N.Y. Poly-clinic Hosp., N.Y.C., 1969-70; resident in internal medicine Shadyside Hosp., Pitts., 1970-71, St. Mary's Health Center, St. Louis, 1971-73; practice medicine specializing in internal medicine, Overland, Mo., 1973-76, Bridgeton, Mo., 1976—. Diplomate Am. Bd. Internal Medicine. Mem. ACP, AMA, Mo., St. Louis med. assns., Am., Mo. socs. internal medicine. Buddhist. Home: 15424 Highcroft Dr Chesterfield MO 63017 Office: 3478 Bridgeland Dr Suite 1 Bridgeton MO 63044

BOORMAN, PAUL HAROLD, diversified manufacturing company executive; b. Kenosha, Wis., Aug. 22, 1931; m. Alyce Marie Woods; children—Susan, Patricia, Pamela. B.A., Miami U.-Oxford, Ohio, 1953; M.S., Cornell U., 1958. Mgr. indsl. relations Westinghouse Electric Co., Cheswick, Pa., 1958-70; dir. labor relations ITT Fed. Electric, Paramus, N.J., 1970-72, ITT Rayonier Co., N.Y.C., 1972-74; v.p. human resources Hitchiner Corp., Milford, N.H., 1974-79, Copeland Corp., Sidney, Ohio, 1979—.

BOOS, FREDERICK CARPENTER, hotelier, tourism consultant; b. Mpls., Aug. 2, 1933; s. George W. and Elizabeth (Carpenter) B.; m. Mary Cote, June 10, 1960; children—Julia, Carolyn, Cynthia. B.A., Colgate U., 1955. Sales rep. Foote Lumber, Mpls., 1958-63; sales rep. Grand View Lodge, Brainerd, Minn., 1963-65, asst. mgr., 1965-70, gen. mgr., owner, 1970—; Chmn. Minn. Assn. of Commerce and Industry, St. Paul, 1984—; pres. Minn. Heartland Assn., 1978-80. Served to sgt. U.S. Army, 1956-58, Korea. Named Tourism Man of Yr., Minn. Dept. Tourism. 1984. Mem. Minn. Resort Assn. (pres. 1971-73, Man of Yr. 1982), Upper Midwest Hospitality Assn. (chmn. 1982—), Minn. Hotel Assn. (bd. dirs. 1980—). Avocations: reading; tennis; fishing; skiing. Home: 4618 Edgebrook Pl Edina MN 55424 Office: Grand View Lodge Route 6 Box 22 Brainerd MN 56401

BOOSALIS, ELSIE, real estate management executive; b. Cedar Rapids, Iowa, Dec. 1, 1913; adopted dau. of Peter and Rose (Halleck) B.; student Phoenix Bus. Coll., 1943-44, Northwestern U., 1952-53, U. Minn. Property mgr. Peter Boosalis Bldg. Trust, Mpls., 1953—, trustee, 1960—. Bd. dirs. Greater Lake St. Council; sustaining mem. council Girl Scouts U.S.A.; bus. mem. Powderhorn Devel. Corp.; donor Guthrie Theater; active ARC, YWCA, WAMSO. Mem. Mpls. Soc. Fine Arts, Minn., Hennepin County hist. socs., Mpls. C. of C., Minn. Orch. Assn. (guarantor, chmn.), English Speaking Union, Am. Swedish Inst. Home: 4551 Dupont Ave S Minneapolis MN 55409 Office: 2951 Chicago Ave Minneapolis MN 55407

BOOTH, GEORGE D., business, marketing and merchandising services executive, publisher; b. Highland Park, Mich., Jan. 4, 1927; s. George H. and Gladys L. (Rich) B.; m. Marie Newberry, July 17, 1948; children—Glenn A., Rick L. Student, Graceland Coll., 1947, Drake U., 1948. Owner, operator Booth Dept. Stores, Garden City, Mich., 1948-50, Booth Motor Sales, Monroe, Mich., 1950-56; merchandising exec. Chrysler Corp., Highland Park, 1956-77; pres. Merchandising Bus. Services, Inc., Southfield, Mich., 1978—, Nat. Bus. Opportunities Ctrs., Inc., 1980-84, Nat. Print & Copy Marts, Inc., 1980—, Channel 1 Video Prodns., 1981—; editor, pub. The Mini Shopper, Internat., 1969-77, Idea-Motives, 1977-78, The Am. Merchandising Report, 1983—; mktg. cons., speaker. Served with USAF, 1945-47. Mem. sales Promotion Execs. Assn. (past pres. Detroit chpt., Sales Promotion Exec. of Yr. 1967). Lodge: Kiwanis. Author materials on motivation, careers. Home: 1570 Forest Ln Birmingham MI 48010 Office: Merchandising Bus Services 24611 Greenfield Rd Southfield MI 48075

BOOTHE, JACQUELINE ANN, nursing educational administrator; b. Terre Haute, Ind., May 5, 1931. Student Maryville Coll. of Sacred Heart, 1948-50, Washington U., St. Louis, 1950-51; B.S. in Nursing, diploma, Johns Hopkins U., 1954, M.Ed., 1970. Assoc. dir. nursing edn. Deaconess Hosp. Sch. Nursing, St. Louis, 1954-66; adminstrv. asst. Johns Hopkins Hosp. Sch. Nursing, Balt., 1966-70; dir. nursing edn. Good Samaritan Hosp. Sch. Nursing, Cin., 1970—; regional group on nursing Ohio Commn.'s Study on Nursing Needs and Resources, 1979-82; mem. Ohio Commn. on Nursing, 1984—. Mem. ednl. com. Am. Cancer Soc.; bd. dirs. Cin. Cancer Control Council; mem. adv. com. Council on Aging; mem. adv. com. Cin. Continuing Edn. Com.; mem. women's com. Cin. Symphony Orch., 1970—. Mem. Nat. League for Nursing (program com. 1975-81, accreditation team 1976-78, chmn. nominating com. 1981-83), Ohio League for Nursing (dir. 1975-79), Assembly of Hosp. Schs. of Nursing, Cin. Dirs. Conf. Group of Nursing Leadership, Ohio Council Diploma Nurse Educators (chmn. 1984—), Buckeye State Nurses Orgn. (co-founder), Am. Assn. for Higher Edn., AAAS, Assn. for Supervision and Curriculum Devel., Friends of Cin. Parks. Presbyterian (pres. bd. trustees Cin. Presbytery). Home: 2380 Madison Rd Cincinnati OH 45208 Office: Good Samaritan Hosp Sch Nursing Cincinnati OH 45220

BORANYAK, MARK, brewing company executive; b. Topeka, Kans., Jan. 6, 1950; s. Rudolph and Atha M. (Rounkles) B.; m. Sharon Rae Etzel, Apr. 20, 1974. Student Washburn U., 1968-69; B.S., Kans. State U., 1972. Cert. assn. exec. Mgr. pub. and govtl. affairs Topeka C. of C., 1972-75; exec. dir. Kans. Beer Wholesalers Assn., Topeka, 1975-83; mgr. industry and govt. programs Anheuser Busch Cos., St. Louis, 1983, mgr. state affairs, 1984—; speaker Leadership Manhattan (Kans.), 1982. Officer, Nat. Council on Alcoholism, Topeka, 1983, bd. dirs., 1982-83; mem. Topeka-Shawnee County Litter Control Commn., 1977; mem. Topeka Friends of the Zoo, 1980-83; team capt. United Way of Greater Topeka, 1979; mem. Topeka Assn. for Retarded Citizens, 1980-83; vol. fundraiser Boys Club of Topeka, 1977; mem. Topeka Jaycees, 1972-73; bd. dirs. Jr. Achievement of Northeast Kans., Topeka, 1973-75; mem. Shawnee County Manpower Commn., Topeka, 1974. Mem. Wholesale Beer Assn. Execs. (officer 1981-82), Kans. Soc. Assn. Execs. (chmn. com. 1980, speaker 1982), Am. Soc. Assn. Execs. (cert. 1983), Pub. Relations Soc. Topeka, Kans. Assn. Commerce and Industry (Leadership Kans. 1982), Kans. State U. Alumni Assn. Republican. Roman Catholic. Home: 5808 Mango Dr St Louis MO 63129 Office: Anheuser Busch Cos One Busch Pl St Louis MO 63118

BORANYAK, SHARON ETZEL (MRS. MARK BORANYAK), writer, editor; b. Topeka, Kans., May 2, 1951; d. Raymond Francis and Julia Elizabeth (Porubsky) Etzel; B.S., Kans. State U., 1973; m. Mark Boranyak, Apr. 20, 1974. Assoc. editor Capper's Weekly, Topeka, Kans., 1973-76; pub. info. specialist Stormont-Vail Hosp., Topeka, 1976; informational writer Water Quality Mgmt. sect. Kans. Dept. Health and Environment, Topeka, 1976-77, pub. relations dir. div. environment, 1977-79; editor Kans. Legis. Div. of Post-Audit, 1979-83; tech. writer McDonnell Douglas Corp., St. Louis, 1983—; cons. Topeka Broadcast Council. Mem. Women in Communications (treas. Topeka chpt. 1975-79), Nat. Fedn. Press Women (v.p. Topeka chpt. 1978-79, pres. 1980—), Topeka Home Econs. Assn., People to People. Republican. Roman Catholic. Contbr. articles to profl. jours. Home: 5808 Mango Dr Saint Louis MO 63129

BORATYN, GEORGE MICHAEL, JR., lawyer, banker, Doberman Pinscher breeder and trainer; b. Chgo., Feb. 24, 1947; s. George Michael and Joane Mary (Sterczek) B.; m. Judith F. Gawlik, June 22, 1975. Grad. Loyola U., 1970; J.D., Lewis U., 1979; J.D., No. Ill. U., 1981; postgrad. Northwestern U. Tchr., St. Thecla Elem. Sch., Chgo., 1969; with comml. loan div. Colonial Bank & Trust Co. of Chgo., 1973-78; asst. v.p. comml. loan div. First Nat. Bank & Trust Co. of Barrington (Ill.), 1979-80; v.p., comml. loan officer Mt. Prospect State Bank (Ill.), 1981-83; sr. loan workout specialist F.D.I.C., Knoxville, Tenn., 1984; v.p. comml. loan div. Bank of Ravenswood, Chgo., 1985—; pres. Juris Canis Inc.; cons. to contbg. editor Dog World, Dog Sports, others. Served with U.S. Army, 1969-75. Recipient letters of accomodation. Mem. Midwest Credit Conf., Robert Morris Assos., Am. Kennel Club, Can. Kennel Club, Doberman Pinscher Club Am. and Breeders Assn., Owner-Handlers' Assn., Tau Kappa Epsilon, (past pres.), Tau Epsilon Rho. Roman Catholic. Designer, distbr. Guard Dog Sign; contbr. articles to publs. including Barrington Courier Rev., Crain's Chgo. Bus., Nat. Inquirer, Dog World, Doberman Quar., Doberman Monthly, Belmont-Central Leader, Barrington Leader Publs., Paddock Publs.; author case study for NIMH, HEW.

BORCHERT, JOHN RAMSEY, construction equipment company executive; b. Mpls., Jan. 27, 1919; s. Carl G. and Grace B. (Ramsey) B.; m. Jeane Ledin, Nov. 29, 1947; children—James, Ellen, Ann, Peter. B.B.A., U. Minn., 1940. Prodn. expeditor GarWood Industries, Detroit, 1940-41; br. mgr. Borchert-Ingersoll, Inc., Duluth, Minn., 1946-50, v.p., St. Paul, 1950-51, pres., 1951—; pres. Assoc. Equipment Distbrs., Chgo., 1963; chmn. St. Paul Employer's Assn., 1978-80. Pres., North Oaks Home Owners Assn., Minn., 1961, St. Paul Goodwill Industries, 1960-62, Dakota County Devel. Assn., Eagan, Minn., 1975. Served to lt. (s.g.) USNR, 1942-46, PTO. Republican. Presbyterian. Home: 3 Dogwood Lane North Oaks MN 55110 Office: Borchert-Ingersoll Inc 3275 Dodd Rd Eagan MN 55121

BORCHERT, ROGER NORMAN, geologist; b. Faribault, Minn., Jan. 10, 1947; s. August Fredrick and Wimona Shirley (Kirkman) B.; m. Nancy Ann Kotlarz, Dec. 20, 1969; children—Heather Leigh, Shelley Christine. B.S., Winona State Coll., 1969. Tchr. Sch. Dist. No. 1, Schaumberg, Ill., 1970; tchr., head sci. dept. Sch. Dist. No. 1, Hulett, Wyo., 1970-73; chemist, applications engr. Pesek Engring Co., Golden Valley, Minn., 1973-75; petroleum engr. II, N.D. Geol. Survey, Grand Forks, N.D., 1975-80; geologist Harris, Brown & Klemer, Bismarck, N.D., 1980-83, v.p., 1983—. Mem. Am. Inst. Mining Engrs., Am. Assn. Petroleum Geologists (del. Rocky Mountain sect. 1984, alternate nat. chpt. 1984), Am. Inst. Profl. Geologists, N.D. Geol. Soc. (sec. 1978-79), N.D. Archeol. Assn. Republican. Lutheran. Lodge: Elks. Avocations: hunting; fishing; camping; fossil collecting; trap shooting. Home: 826 N 5th St Bismarck ND 58501 Office: Harris Brown & Klemer Inc PO Box 5006 Bismarck ND 58502

BORCHERT, STEVEN JOHN, chemist; b. Madison, Wis., Jan. 20, 1950; s. Willard W. and Beatrice N. Borchert; B.A., U. Wis., 1972; A.M. (NSF fellow 1972-74, Standard Oil Co. Calif. scholar 1971), Harvard U., 1973, Ph.D., 1977. Research chemist Upjohn Co., Kalamazoo, 1977—. Mem. Am. Chem. Soc., Parenteral Drug Assn. Home: 1706 Whitby Ave Portage MI 49002 Office: Upjohn Co 7000 Portage Rd Kalamazoo MI 49001

BORDEN, ERNEST CARLETON, oncologist, educator; b. Norwalk, Conn., July 12, 1939; m. Louise Dise, June 24, 1967; children—Kristin Louise, Sandra Lanneau. A.B., Harvard U., 1961; M.D., Duke U., 1966. Intern, Duke U., Durham, N.C., 1966-67; resident U. Pa., Phila., 1967-68; postdoctoral fellow Johns Hopkins U. Sch. Medicine, Balt., 1970-73; asst. prof. dept. human oncology and medicine U. Wis. Clin. Cancer Ctr., Madison, 1973-79, assoc. prof., 1979-83, prof., 1983—; chief clin. oncology Meml. Vets. Hosp., Madison, 1977-81; mem. interferon adv. com. Am. Cancer Soc., N.Y.C., 1979—, jr. faculty fellow, 1975-78, prof. clin. oncology, 1984—; mem. biol. response modifiers program, decision network com. Nat. Cancer Inst., Bethesda, Md., 1982—. Contbr. articles to profl. publs. Davison scholar Oxford U., 1966. Mem. Eastern Coop. Oncology Group (chmn. com. 1980-84, award merit 1984), Soc. Biol. Therapy (bd. dirs. 1984—), Wis. Clin. Cancer Ctr. (chmn. edn. com. 1979—). Office: U Wis Clin Cancer Ctr 600 Highland Ave Madison WI 53792

BORDLEY, ROBERT FRANCIS, automotive company researcher; b. Columbus, Ohio, Aug. 15, 1955; s. Robert Guy and Ann Mary Bordley. B.S. in Physics, Mich. State U., 1975, B.A. in Pub. Policy, 1976, M.S. in Systems Sci., 1976; M.S. in Ops. Research, U. Calif.-Berkeley, 1977, M.B.A., 1979, Ph.D. in Ops. Research, 1979. Intern Coop. League, Washington, 1975; assoc. sr. research Gen. Motors Research Labs., Warren, Mich., 1978-80, sr. researcher, 1980-82, staff researcher, 1982—mem. mission analysis group GM trelly design project, 1985—; adj. prof. U. Mich.-Dearborn, 1980. Recipient Wildlife Conservation award Va. Game Commn. Assn., 1973, speaking awards Am. Legion, 1971, 73; Nat. Merit scholar, 1973-76; Mich. State U. alumni disting. scholar, 1973-76; NSF fellow, 1976-79. Mem. Ops. Research Soc. Am., Am. Inst. Indsl. Engrs., Pub. Choice Soc., Inst. Mgmt. Scis., Am. Econ. Assn., Soc. for Promotion Econ. Theory, Soc. Risk Analysis, AAAS, James Madison Coll. Alumni Assn. (dir. 1982-84, pres. 1984—), Cosmos Soc., Phi Beta Kappa, Sigma Xi, Phi Kappa Phi. Contbr. articles to profl. publs. Home: 803 W 4th

St Royal Oak MI 48067 Office: Dept Societal Analysis Gen Motors Research Labs Warren MI 48090

BOREN, ARTHUR RODNEY, JR., commercial banker; b. Dayton, Ohio, June 25, 1946; s. A. Rodney and D. Charlotte (Polk) B.; m. Susan Stansfield; 1 son, Justin S. B.A., Washington and Lee U., 1968; M.I.M., Am. Grad. Sch., Phoenix, 1973. Tchr., Miami Valley Sch., Dayton, 1968-70, adminstr., 1970-71; internat. banker Norwest Bank Mpls., N.A., 1974-78, nat. banker, 1978-81, v.p. nat. dept., 1980, v.p. treasury div., 1981-83, sr. v.p. security sales dept., 1983—. Mem. Am. Inst. Banking. Republican. Episcopalian. Clubs: Miami Valley Hunt and Polo (Dayton); Minneapolis (Mpls.). Office: Norwest Bank Mpls NA 255 2d Ave S Minneapolis MN 55479

BORENSTINE, ALVIN JEROME, search company executive; b. Kansas City, Mo., Dec. 14, 1933; s. Samuel and Ella C. (Berman) B.; m. Roula Alakiotou, Dec. 31, 1976; Ella Marie and Sami (twins). B.S. in Econs., U. Kans., 1956; M.B.A., U. Pa., 1960. Analyst, Johnson & Johnson, New Brunswick, N.J., 1961-62; systems mgr. Levitt & Sons, Levittown, N.J., 1962-66; dir. mgmt. info. services Warren Brothers Co., Cambridge, Mass., 1966-71; mgr. fin. and adminstrv. systems Esmark, Inc., Chgo., 1971-72; pres. Synergistics Assocs. Ltd., Chgo., 1972—. Mem. Assn. for Systems Mgmt. (pres. Boston chpt. 1969, Disting. Service award 1970), Soc. Mgmt. Info. Systems, B'nai B'rith. Systems and Procedures Assn. research fellow, 1959-60; Eddie Jacobson Found. scholar, 1958-60. Clubs: Carlton, Whitehall. Home: 6033 N Sheridan Chicago IL 60660 Office: 320 N Michigan Ave Suite 1002 Chicago IL 60601

BORGER, FREDERICK HOWARD, manufacturing company executive; b. Jamaica, N.Y., Apr. 2, 1946; s. Howard Francis and Irene Albie (Koucky) B.; B.B.A., St. John's U., 1967; M.B.A., N.Y. U., 1970; m. Joan A. Manning, June 24, 1967; children—Kristin, James. Orgn. devel. cons. Western Electric Co., N.Y.C., 1968-72; v.p., cons. Cin. Comml. Cons., Cin., 1972-73; mgr. corp. staffing Borden Inc., Columbus, 1973-78; dir. human resources O.M. Scott & Sons, Marysville, Ohio, 1978—. Vice pres. Homeowners Assn., Norwich, 1974-75; trustee Homeowners Assn., Columbus, Ohio, 1974-76, sec.-treas. Grandview Hts. Youth Athletic Assn., 1983, v.p., then pres., 1983-85. Mem. Am. Soc. Tng. and Devel., Am. Soc. Personnel Adminstrn., Central Ohio Personnel Assn., Midwest OD Network. Republican. Roman Catholic. Home: 1149 Ashland Ave Columbus OH 43212 Office: 14111 Scottslawn Rd Marysville OH 43041

BORGWARDT, ROBERT G., pastor, TV preacher; b. Milw., Aug. 7, 1922; s. Erwin R. and Hilda M. (Meier) B.; m. Ruth Fossum, June 14, 1947 (dec. 1963); children—Kathryn, John, Stephen; m. Joan Renee Gullickson, Sept. 25, 1964; children—Anne, Eric. B.A., St. Olaf Coll., Minn., 1944; M.T., Luther Sem., St. Paul, 1947; D.D. (hon.), Carthage Coll., Wis., 1975. Ordained: Minister, Am. Lutheran Ch. Sr. pastor Trinity Lutheran Ch., Madison, Wis., 1947-53; assoc. pastor Central Lutheran, Mpls., 1953-55; sr. pastor First Lutheran Ch., Sioux Falls, S.D., 1955-63, Bethel Lutheran Ch., Madison, 1963—; pub. relations com. Lutheran Council, U.S.A., 1964-67; pres. Madison Area Council Chs., 1969-70; bd. regents Wartburg Coll., Waverly, Iowa, 1972-77; cert. visit Bethel Bible Series, Japan, Korea, 1975. Author: Men Who Knew Jesus, 1958; Kind and Heavenly Father, 1967; Don't Blow Out The Candle, 1969; I am Hurting...Please Help Me. Mem., Gov.'s Bd. Ethics, Wis., 1980—. Recipient Young Man of Yr. award C. of C., Sioux Falls, 1958; Disting. Alumni award St. Olaf Coll., Minn., 1985; British Fgn. Office Conf. Participant, Wilton Park, Sussex, Eng., 1974, 84. Club: Rotary (bd. dirs. Madison 1964—). Avocations: cycling; golf; tennis; travel. Home: 938 Waban Hill Madison WI 53711 Office: Bethel Lutheran Ch 31 Wisconsin Ave Madison WI 53703

BORITZKI, BASIL JEROME, telephone holding company executive, lawyer; b. Springfield, Mo., Nov. 30, 1924; s. Bruno O. and Madalene A. (Robertson) B.; m. JoAnn McCarty, May 7, 1955. B.S., S.W. Mo. State U., 1948; J.D., Ohio State U., 1951. Bar: Ohio 1951, U.S. Supreme Ct. 1963, N.Y. 1965. Atty. examiner, sec. Ohio Pub. Utilities Commn., Columbus, 1952-63; mgr. div. toll revenues and rate structures Rochester Telephone Corp. (N.Y.), 1963-66; staff dir. rates and toll settlements United Telephone Systems Hdqrs., Westwood, Kans., 1966-72, asst. v.p., 1972, v.p., 1972—; chmn. adv. bd. Inst. Pub. Utilities, Grad. Sch. Bus., Mich. State U.; mem. Telephone Ind. Policy Task Force, 1979-81. Served with AUS, 1943-45. Recipient S.W. Mo. State U.'s Outstanding Alumnus award, 1982. Mem. ABA, Ohio Bar Assn., U.S. Ind. Telephone Assn. (research and analysis task force, citation 1967, 75, 78, 82), Telephone Industry-Exchange Carriers Assn. (ad hoc com.). Office: 2330 Johnson Dr Westwood KS 66205

BORKHOLDER, FREEMON, construction executive, developer; b. Bremen, Ind., Oct. 11, 1932; s. Daniel J. and Emma (Coblentz) B.; student pub. schs.; m. Margaret Hershberger, Apr. 26, 1956; children—Lorene Kaye, Sueetta, Dwayne Alan, Jonathan Jay, Cheryl Elaine. With Coppes Inc., Nappanee, Ind., 1955-62; owner, pres. F.D. Borkholder Co., Nappanee, 1960—; v.p. Borkholder Bldgs., Nunica, Mich., 1967—; sec.-treas. Newmar Industries, Nappanee, 1968—; developer indsl. parks, 1967—. Bd. dirs. No. Youth Programs, Hope Rescue Mission, South Bend, Ind. Mem. Nat. Frame Builders Assn. (pres. 1971-72, dir., pres. Ind. chpt. 1979), Internat. Platform Assn. Mennonite. Home: RD 1 Bremen IN 46506 Office: PO Box 32 Nappanee IN 46550

BORKOWSKI, IGOR, real estate executive; b. Baranov, Poland, Mar. 17, 1928; came to U.S., 1950; s. Peter and Larissa (Korolko) B.; m. Ludmilla Biloprosowa, Aug. 4, 1957; children—Michael, Tamara. B.C.E., U. Ill., 1957. Designer, Monsanto Chem. Corp., Chgo., 1957-65; ptnr., dir. ops. Remex Corp., Mt. Prospect, Ill., 1969—. Served with U.S. Army, 1951-54, ETO. Recipient Humanitarian award City of Hope, 1983. Mem. Multi-Housing Assn. (sec.). Republican. Eastern Orthodox. Avocations: boating; golf; flying. Home: 1650 Balmoral Circle Inverness IL 60067 Office: 500 W Central Rd Mount Prospect IL 60056

BORLAND, BRUCE HENNINGER, transportation equipment management and leasing company executive; b. Butler, Pa., Dec. 28, 1929; s. Bruce Sylvester and Mary Elizabeth (Henninger) B.; m. Beatrice Anne Buckler, Nov. 25, 1952; children—Cheryl Borland McClure, Bruce David. B.S., Northwestern U., 1951. Sales promotion staff Bell & Howell, Chgo., 1952-53; mgr. Hotpoint Co., Chgo., 1956-58; sales rep. GATX Corp., Chgo., 1958-60, dist. mgr., 1960-79, sales mgr., 1979-80; pres., chmn., chief exec. officer Temco Corp., Lake Bluff, Ill., 1981—; dir. Omnicard Internat., Wheeling; mem. Shippers Adv. Bd. Mem. U.S. Congl. Adv. Bd. Served with JAGC, U.S. Army, 1952-54. Mem. Am. Petroleum Inst., Chgo. Traffic Club, Covered Hopper Car Shippers Assn., Fertilizer Inst., Traffic Clubs Internat., Internat. Platform Assn., Am. Mgmt. Assn., Am. Legion. Republican. Clubs: Forge; Evanston Golf; Union League (Chgo.); Post and Paddock. Home: 2801 Orange Brace Rd Riverwoods IL 60015 Office: Temco Corp 100 E Scranton Lake Bluff IL 60044

BORMAN, EDWARD HENRY, assn. exec.; b. Webster Groves, Mo., Sept. 26, 1926; s. Edward Henry and Lillian M. B.; B.S. in Bus. Adminstrn., Washington U., St. Louis, 1950; J.D., St. Louis U., 1965; m. Janet A. Borman, Nov. 19, 1949; children—Anne, Keith, Bethany, Michael. Cashier, Equitable Life Ins. Co., U.S., St. Louis, 1950-57; dir. Medicare, Gen. Am. Life Ins. Co., St. Louis, 1966-70; admitted to Mo. bar, 1965; exec. dir. Mo. Assn. Osteo. Physicians and Surgeons, Jefferson City, 1970—; dir. Mid-Mo. Med. Found., 1978-83; dir. Charles Still Hosp., Mo. Health Data Corp. Chmn., Mo. Health Council, 1971-72; chmn. adv. com. Mo. Center for Health Stats., 1973-75. Served with USNR, 1944-46. Mem. Am. Osteo. Assn. (com. on continuing med. edn.), Assn. Osteo. State Exec. Dirs. (pres.), Mo. Bar Assn., Cole County Bar Assn., Mo. Soc. Assn. Execs., Am. Legion, Phi Alpha Delta, Sigma Nu. Republican. Editor: Jour. of Mo. Osteo. Assn., 1970—. Home: 2413 Cheryl Dr Jefferson City MO 65101 Office: PO Box 748 Jefferson City MO 65102

BORMAN, PAUL, See *Who's Who in America,* 43rd edition.

BORN, CHRISTOPHER PAUL, ophthalmologist; b. Evansville, Ind., Sept. 25, 1951; s. Harold Joseph and Betty Jean (Rasche) B.; m. Vicki Rae Mohr, Aug. 9, 1975; children—Ryan Christopher, Amy Elizabeth. B.S., U. Ill., 1973; M.D., Washington U., St. Louis, 1977. Diplomate Am. Bd. Ophthalmology. Intern, Mayo Clinic, Rochester, Minn., 1977-78; ophthalmology resident U. Minn., Mpls., 1979-81; ophthalmologist Gundersen Clinic, La Crosse, Wis., 1981—. Mem. Am. Acad. Ophthalmology, Tau Beta Pi, Triangle. Roman Catholic. Avocation: scuba diving. Home: 128 S 14th St La Crosse WI 54601 Office: Gundersen Clinic 836 South Ave La Crosse WI 54601

BORNE, HENRY, sociology educator, airline agent; b. N.Y.C., Apr. 19, 1952; s. Stanford and Ruth (Collins) B.; m. Cynthia Steinacker, July 12, 1975; children—Benjamin, Abigail. B.A., Coll. Wooster, 1975; M.A., U. Notre Dame, 1979, Ph.D., 1983. Farm worker Wickhams Fruit Farm, Cutchogue, N.Y., intermittently, 1969-76; customer service agt. United Airlines, South Bend, Ind., 1977—; instr. sociology and anthropology Holy Cross Jr. Coll., Notre Dame, Ind., 1980—. Vol. day care Child Abuse and Neglect Orgn., South Bend, 1978-80; bd. dirs. Children's Ctr., South Bend, 1984. NIMH research asst., 1976-77; United Presbyn. Ch. grantee, 1974-75. Mem. Am. Social. Assn., Nat. Council Family Relations. Unitarian. Avocation: Jogging. Home: 2722 Hartzer St South Bend IN 46628 Office: Holy Cross Jr College Dept Social and Behavioral Scis US 31 Notre Dame IN 46556

BORNHOEFT, JACK HARRY, construction company executive; b. Chgo., July 16, 1923; s. Elmer J. and Lilliam M. (Matthias) B.; B.S., Northwestern U., 1947; m. Sept. 6, 1947; children—Nancy, Susan, Gregg. With Gerhardt F. Meyne Co., Chgo., 1945—, chmn., 1978—. Bd. dirs. Chgo. Bldg. Congress, 1978—. Served with USAAF, 1942-45, USAF, 1950-51. Decorated Air medal. Mem. Western Soc. Engrs. Republican. Presbyterian. Clubs: Tower, Rotary, East Bank; Park Ridge Country. Office: Gerhardt F Meyne Co 345 N Canal St Chicago IL 60606

BORNHOEFT, JOHN WILLIAM, III, microbiologist; b. Lakewood, Ohio, Apr. 24, 1943; s. John William and Billie Louise (Parshall) B.; B.A., Beloit Coll., 1965; M.S., Chgo. Med. Sch., 1972; Ph.D. (fellow), Loyola U., 1980; m. Margaret Teresa, June 13, 1971 (dec. 1981); 1 son, John William IV. Research asst. U. Ill. Med. Ctr., Chgo., 1967-69, Chgo. Med. Sch., 1970-71; clin. instr. Loyola U. Dental Sch., 1974-75; research asst. Loyola U., Chgo., 1976-79, research assoc., 1979-81; applied microbiologist, mgr. Am. Convertors Co., Evanston, Ill., 1981-85; pres. J.W.B. Assocs., cons. to healthcare industry, 1985—; cons. Rapid Med. Services, 1976-77; mem. faculty Mundelein Coll. Chgo., part time 1980; clin. microbiologist Loyola Student Health Services, 1976-81. Mem. Am. Soc. Microbiology, Am. Inst. Biol. Scis., Sigma Xi. Club: Alfa Romeo Owners. Office: 643 Hillside Elmhurst IL 60126

BORNS, ROBERT AARON, real estate developer; b. Gary, Ind., Oct. 24, 1935; s. Irving Jonah and Sylvia (Mackoff) B.; m. Sandra Solotkin Mar. 30, 1958; children—Stephanie, Elizabeth, Emily. B.S., Ind. U., 1957. Account exec. Reynolds & Co., Chgo., 1957-59, Francis I. duPont Co., Indpls., 1960; owner, operator Borns & Co., Indpls., 1960-63; chmn. Borns Mgmt. Corp., Indpls., 1963—; dir. Heritage Venture Group, Inc. Bd. dirs. Indpls. Mus. of Art-Life, Children's Mus. of Indpls., Jewish Welfare Fedn., Indpls. Conv. and Visitors Bur., Corp. Community Council; trustee Marion Coll., Indpls. Symphony Orch.; bd. dirs., mem. exec. com. St. Vincent's Hosp. Found.; mem. adv. bd. Butler U. Bus. Sch.; mem. bd. visitors Jewish Studies Program, Ind. U. Recipient Enterprise award Indpls. Bus. Jour., 1982. Jewish. Clubs: Economic (bd. dirs.), Univ. Office: 200 S Meridian St Indianapolis IN 46225

BORRESEN, C. ROBERT, psychology educator, consultant; b. Chgo., July 12, 1926; s. Kristian and Dagny (Mathiesen) B.; m. Thelma Jasper Meacham, Dec. 28, 1966; 1 stepson, Michael Robert Meacham. B.S., Northwestern U., 1953; M.A., U. Mo., 1958, Ph.D., 1968. Cert. psychologist, Kans. Instr. psychology U. Mo., Columbia, 1962-63; asst. prof. Memphis State U., 1963-65; asst. prof. psychology Wichita State U. (Kans.), 1965-73, assoc. prof., 1974—, chmn. psychology dept., 1978-83; cons. psychology of perception, 1968—; cons. and court expert witness, 1977—; mem. Kans. Bd. Examiners of Psychologists, 1977-80, chmn. bd., 1979-80; mem. adv. com. Kans. Bd. Behavioral Scis., 1980—; regional rep., evaluator continuing edn., mem. supervisory bd. Behavioral Scis. Regulatory Bd., 1984-86. Author: Human Factors Manual, 1974, 76; papers presented at profl. meetings, internat. confs. Treas. mem.'s campaign 4 elections Kans. Ho. of Reps. Served with USN, 1944-46. Mem. Am. Psychol. Assn., Southwestern Psychol. Assn., Midwestern Psychol. Assn., Kans. Psychol. Assn., Wichita Area Psychol. Assn., Internat. Sci. Soc. for Polit. Psychology. Contbr. numerous articles to psychology jours.

BORTOLOTTI, NORMA MAY, investment exec.; b. Omaha, Apr. 8, 1931; d. Isidoro and Michelina (Cominoli) B.; Dickinson Secretarial Sch., Omaha, 1958; B.A., Duchesne Coll., 1954; postgrad. Creighton U., 1957, 58, 77, 78; Typist, W.O.W. Life Ins. Co., Omaha, 1948; with Universal Terrazzo & Tile Co., Omaha, 1949-77, sec., receptionist and acct., 1954-70, v.p., 1964-77; acct., hostess 7301 Corp., night club, Omaha, 1964-69, also dir.; v.p. NND Investment Co., Omaha, 1957—; mgmt. v.p. NND Investment Corp., Omaha, 1957—. Active local ward and precinct work Republican Party, 1975. Recipient Outstanding Service award Republican Party, 1975. Mem. E de M, Catholic Soc. Sacred Heart, Nat. Assn. Female Execs. Home: 9904 Florence Heights Blvd Omaha NE 68112

BORUCKI, WALTER C., distribution company executive; b. Detroit, June 11, 1916; s. Adam J. and Agata (Hardy) B.; student U. Poznan (Poland), 1937-39; m. Helen Jeza, Jan. 6, 1954; children—Judith Ellen, Mary Elizabeth. Prof. chemistry St. Mary's Coll., Orchard Lake, Mich., 1944-46; pres. Vets. Supply & Distbg. Co., Hamtramck, Mich., 1946—. Served with M.C., U.S. Army, 1941. Clubs: Polish Nat. Alliance, Polish Falcons, Alliance Poles, Amvets, Am. Legion. Author: Historia Stanow Zjednoczonych Ameryki Polnocnej, 1955. Home: 26420 Saint Josaphat Dr Warren MI 48091 Office: 3225 Caniff St Hamtramck MI 48212

BORUFF, DONALD VICTOR, mfg. co. exec.; b. Greene County, Ind.; s. Harvey Victor and Perla Clara (Wonder) B.; ed. Ind. Central U.; m. Berniece Hagaman, 1934; children—Donna Carpenter, Roma Carrick. Personnel dir. Mitts & Merrill, Saginaw, Mich., 1951-65, Am. Hoist Co., Bay City, Mich., 1966-68, KC Engring. & Machine Co., Saginaw, 1969-81; lectr. in field. Active YMCA; bd. dirs. Saginaw City Rescue Mission; leader fund drives Saginaw United Way; mem. steering com. Saginaw Intermediate Sch. Dist.; leader vol. programs Bay City Pubs. Schs.; tchr. Bible Sch. Mem. Am. Soc. Personnel Adminstrn. (accredited exec. in personnel, cert. in A.E.P., Superior Merit award 1978), Valley Soc. Personnel Adminstrs. (pres. 1977—), Saginaw Employment Mgrs. Club (officer). Clubs: Indsl. Exec., Masons. Address: 3358 Nottingham Dr Bay City MI 48706

BORUFF, JOHN DAVID, government official; b. Lakewood, Ohio, July 8, 1930; s. Glenn Tourner and Edith (Weybright) B.; A.B. in Biology, Ind. U., 1953, M.S. in Health and Safety Edn., 1965; m. Martha Lois Myers, June 12, 1953; children—Martha Yvonne Boruff Wyatt, Audrey Elaine, David Paul, Kenneth Edward. Sanitarian, Ind. State Bd. Health, 1957-60, tng. officer Div. Food and Drugs, 1960-63, health edn. cons. Div. Health Edn., 1963-65; health-housing coordinator Associated Migrant Opportunity Services, Inc., Indpls., 1965-66; extension health edn. specialist Purdue U., 1966-69; statistician div. pub. health records, coordinator health data unit pub. health stats. Ind. Bd. Health, 1969-83, health planner, statistician office health planning and policy devel., 1983—; former state data mgr. Nat. Public Health Program Reporting System, Assn. State and Territorial Health Ofcls. Served as hosp. corpsman USCGR, 1953-57; sr. asst. health service officer USPHS Res. Mem. USPHS Commd. Officers Assn., No. Nut Growers Assn., Ind. Nut Growers Assn. (editor bull.), Theta Xi. Presbyterian (elder, past stated clk., organist, choir dir.). Club: Masons (32 deg.; mem. Indpls. Valley Scottish Rite Orch. and Athenaeum Turners Orch.). Author: Health Trends in Indiana 1900-1973; Indiana Health Profile 1968-80; contbr. Ind. State Bd. Health Bull. Home: RR 1 Box 128 Roachdale IN 46172 Office: 1330 W Michigan St Indianapolis IN 46206

BORYC, NICHOLAS MICHAEL, transportation company executive; b. Waukegan, Ill., Oct. 30, 1952; s. Louis J. and Cecile D. B.; B. Applied Scis. with honors, Western Ill. U., 1975; m. Mary C. Rushforth, Nov. 12, 1977; 1 child, Sarah Anne Agnes. Sales rep. Roadway Express Inc., Chgo., 1976-78, mgr. terminal, 1979-82; pres., account mgr. Consol. Freightways, McCook, Ill., 1982—. Active Boy Scouts Am. Mem. Better Govt. Assn. Home: 112 Woodstock St Clarendon Hills IL 60514 Office: Consol Freightways McCook IL 60625

BORYCZKA, RAYMOND STANLEY, history educator, writer, researcher; b. Detroit, Aug. 23, 1947; s. John Joseph and Francis Cecilia (Tykocski) B.; m. Margaret Ann Kettles, Dec. 27, 1980; 1 dau. by previous marriage, Jocelyn Marie. B.A., Wayne State U., 1968; M.A., U. Mich., 1974, postgrad., 1976. Cert. secondary edn. tchr., Mich. Tchr. social studies Monroe (Mich.) Pub. Schs., 1971-73; teaching fellow U. Mich., Ann Arbor, 1973-75; asst. prof. history U. Tex.-San Antonio, 1977-79; resident historian-curator Ohio Hist. Soc., Columbus, 1979—; guest lectr. Am. labor history; cons. oral history; oral history interviewer; audio-visual cons. in Am. history. Baseball coach Westerville (Ohio) Little League, 1982, St. Paul Parish Jr. Varsity, Westerville, 1983. John D. Pierce research fellow, 1975-76; Alvin M. Bentley Found. doctoral scholar, 1976-77. Mem. Am. Hist. Assn., Orgn. Am. Historians. Roman Catholic. Author: No Strength Without Union: An Illustrated History of Ohio Workers, 1803-1980, 1982. Office: 1982 Velma Columbus OH 43211

BORYSEWICZ, MARY LOUISE, editor; b. Chgo.; d. Thomas J. and Mabel E. (Zeien) O'Farrell; B.A., Mundelein Coll., 1970; postgrad. in English lit. U. Ill, 1970-71; grad. exec. program U. Chgo., 1982; m. Daniel S. Borysewicz, June 11, 1955; children—Mary Adele, Stephen Francis, Paul Barnabas. Tchr. advanced level English for fgn.-speaking adults Evanston Twp. (Ill.) High Sch., 1969-71; editor sci. publs. AMA, Chgo., 1971-73; exec. mng. editor Am. Jour. Ophthalmology, Chgo., 1973—; guest lectr. U. Chgo. Med. Sch., 1979, Harvard U. Med. Sch., 1978, Northwestern U. Med. Sch., 1979, Am. Acad. Ophthalmology, 1976, 81. Mem. Am. Soc. Bus. Press Editors, Am. Soc. Profl. and Exec. Women, Council Biology Editors, Internat. Fedn. Sci. Editors Assns., Soc. Scholarly Pub. Contbr. articles to sci. publs.; editor: Ophthalmology Principles and Concepts, 4th edit., 1978, 5th edit., 1982. Home: 4415 N California Ave Chicago IL 60625 Office: 435 N Michigan Ave Chicago IL 60611

BOS, CAROLE DIANNE, lawyer; b. Grand Rapids, Mich., May 31, 1949; d. James and Alberdean (Kooiker) Berkenpas; m. James Edwin Bos, Apr. 3, 1969; B.A. with high honors, Grand Valley State Coll., 1977; J.D. cum laude, T.M. Cooley Law Sch., Lansing, Mich., 1981. Bar: Mich. 1981. Asst. mgr. Army & Air Force Base Exchange, Soesterberg, Netherlands, 1969-73; mgmt. asst. Selfridge Air Nat. Guard Base, Mt. Clemens, Mich., 1973-74; legal asst. John Boyles, Grand Rapids, 1974-77; law clk. Cholette, Perkins & Buchanan, Grand Rapids, 1977-82; trial atty. Hecht, Buchanan & Cheney, Grand Rapids, 1982-84; ptnr. Buchanan & Bos, Grand Rapids, 1984—; mem. adv. bd. Grand Valley State Coll., 1981—. Co-author: Video Techniques in Trial and Pretrial, 1983; Video Technology: Its Use and Application in Law, 1984; contbr. articles to profl. jours. Bd. dirs. Jellema Ho., Grand Rapids; trustee Grand Valley State Coll. Found. Breen scholar, 1977. Mem. Grand Rapids Bar Assn. (library com. 1983—), Mich. State Bar Assn. (communications com. 1983—), ABA, Fed. Bar Assn. (regional dir. 1984—), Am. Trial Lawyers Assn. Home: 1502 Hawthorne Hills Dr Ada MI 49301 Office: Buchanan & Bos 6th Floor Frey Bldg Grand Rapids MI 49503

BOSCARINO, JOSEPH ANGELLO, marketing company executive; b. Paterson, N.J., Jan. 24, 1946; s. George and Rose B.; m. Sandra Cornetto, Oct. 20, 1968; children—Karen, Katherine, David. B.A., Fordham U., 1974; M.A., NYU, 1975, Ph.D., 1977. Postdoctoral research fellow health services research Yale U., New Haven, 1977-79; health research dir. Market Opinion Research, Detroit, 1979-81; v.p. research Allied Research Assocs., Chgo., 1981—; cons. VA, NIMH, 1977-81. Served with U.S. Army, 1964-67; Vietnam. Decorated Vietnam Service medal. Schaenman fellow, 1976. Mem. Am. Mktg. Assn., Am. Sociol. Assn., Am. Psychol. Assn., Alpha Sigma Lambda. Editor, Jour. Health Care Mktg. Contbr. articles to med. and sci. jours. Office: Allied Research Assocs 75 E Wacker Dr 18th Floor Chicago IL 60601

BOSCHWITZ, RUDY, U.S. Senator; b. Berlin, Germany, Nov. 7, 1930; came to U.S., 1935; B.S., N.Y. U., 1950, LL.B., 1953; m. Ellen Lowenstein, 1956; children—Gerry, Ken, Dan, Tom. Admitted to N.Y. bar, 1954, Wis. bar, 1959; practiced in N.Y.C., from 1956; founder, operator Plywood Minn., 1963-77; U.S. senator from Minn., 1979—. Del., Minn. Republican Conv., 1968-78; del. Rep. Nat. Conv., 1972, 76. Served with Signal Corps, U.S. Army, 1954-55. Home: Plymouth MN Office: 419 Robert St N Saint Paul MN 55101 also 506 Hart Senate Office Bldg Washington DC 20510*

BOSEKER, BARBARA JEAN, educator; b. Milw., Dec. 2, 1944; d. Edward Herbert and Alice Margaret (Maas) B.; student U. Nigeria, Nsukka, 1966; B.S. (hon.) in Secondary Edn. (Elks Nat. and State Youth scholar), U. Wis., Milw., 1968; M.A. in Anthropology (Ford Found. fellow 1968-69, NDEA fellow 1970-71), U. Wis., Madison, 1971, Ph.D. in Edn. (NDEA fellow), 1978; m. Dale Leslie Sutcliffe, Aug. 8, 1975. Chemistry lab. technician Allen-Bradley Corp., Milw., 1963; coordinator Neighborhood Youth Corps, Madison, 1970; program devel. specialist Tchr. Corps, Madison, 1976-77; asst. prof. edn. Occidental Coll., 1978-80, Moorhead State U., 1980—; cons. Inst. Latin Am. Studies, U. Tex., Austin, 1980. Grant writer Fargo-Moorhead (N.D.) Indian Center, 1980. Cert. English tchr. grades 7 through 12, Wis. Mem. NEA, Am. Assn. Colls. Tchr. Edn., Mortar Bd., Phi Kappa Phi, Pi Lambda Theta, Kappa Delta Pi, Sigma Tau Delta, Sigma Epsilon Sigma. Democrat. Christian Scientist. Contbr. articles to profl. jours. Home: 2709 S 15th St Apt 301 Fargo ND 58103 Office: Moorhead State U Moorhead MN 56560

BOSHART, DONNA LOU, educational administrator; b. Galena, Kans., Nov. 20, 1939; d. Randolph Daniel and Nola Mae (Turrentine) Commons; m. Donald Lee Boshart, Nov. 27, 1964; children—Douglas Lee, Dustin Lane. B.S., Pittsburg (Kans.) State U., 1963, M.S., 1976, Ed.S., 1981; Ed.D., Okla. State U., 1983. Tchr. elem. sch. Jefferson County (Colo.), 1963-68; tchr. art Columbus (Kans.) High Sch., 1968-69; tchr. elem. sch. Riverton, Kans., 1969-74, Joplin, Mo., 1974-78; adminstr., supr. curriculum, dir. fed. programs, clk. of bd. Galena Unified Sch. Dist., Kans., 1978-83; asst. supt. curriculum and personnel Derby (Kans.) Unified Sch. Dist., 1983—. Mem. profl. standards com. Spiva Art Ctr., 1980. Mem. Am. Assn. Sch. Adminstrs., Assn. Supervision and Curriculum Devel., United Sch. Adminstrs. Kans., Kans. Assn. Sch. Adminstrs., Kans. Assn. Curriculum Devel., Cherokee County Sch. Adminstrs. Assn. Republican. Clubs: Art, Soroptimists. Office: 120 E Washington St Derby KS 67037

BOSLAUGH, LESLIE, state judge; b. Hastings, Nebr., Sept. 4, 1917; s. Paul E. and Ann (Herzog) B.; B.B.A., U. Nebr., 1939, LL.B., 1941; m. Elizabeth F. Meyer, Aug. 10, 1943; children—Marguerite Ann, Sarah Elizabeth, Paul Robert. Admitted to Nebr. bar, 1941. Mem. staff Nebr. Statute Revision Commn., 1941-43; pvt. practice law, Hastings, 1946-47; asst. atty. gen. Nebr., 1947-48; mem. firm Stiner & Boslaugh, Hastings, 1949-60; judge Nebr. Supreme Ct., Lincoln, 1961—. Served to lt. AUS, 1943-46. Mem. Am., Nebr. bar assns., Am. Judicature Soc., Inst. Jud. Adminstrn., Appellate Judges Conf., Order of Coif. Office: Supreme Ct Box 4638 Lincoln NE 68509*

BOSLER, MARK STEVEN, lawyer; b. Detroit, May 17, 1953; s. Francis Edward and Joan Marie (Sullivan) B. B.A., Mich. State U., 1975; J.D., U. Detroit, 1981. Bar: Mich. 1982, U.S. Dist. Ct. (ea. dist.) Mich. 1982, Ill. 1983. Ins. auditor Equifax, Inc., Southfield, Mich., 1979-84; sole practice, Southfield, 1982-84; atty. UAW-GM Legal Services, Pontiac, Mich., 1984—; real estate broker, Southfield, 1984—. Vice pres. Farmington Area Jaycees, Mich., 1985-86; cand. dist. judge 47th Dist. Ct. Mich., 1984. Mem. ABA, Am. Trial Lawyers Assn., Comml. Law League, Oakland County Bar Assn., Am. Judicature Soc. Roman Catholic. Office: 140 S Saginaw Suite 700 Pontiac MI 48058

BOSMANN, HAROLD BRUCE, geriatric educator, university dean; b. Chgo., June 17, 1942; s. Harold William and Gladys (Hoagland) B.; m. Maureen O'Pray, Oct. 29, 1966; children—Geoffrey, Katharine. A.B., Knox Coll., 1964; Ph.D., U. Rochester, N.Y., 1966; M.S. (hon.), Cambridge U., 1968. NSF postdoctoral fellow Strangeways Lab., Cambridge U., Eng., 1966-67; NIH postdoctoral fellow Salk Inst. Biol. Studies, San Diego, 1967-68; asst. prof. pharmacology and toxicology U. Rochester Sch. Medicine & Dentistry, N.Y., 1968-74, assoc. prof., 1974-76, assoc. prof. oncology, 1976-78, prof., 1978-80, chmn., prof. dept. pharmacology and toxicology, 1980-82, vis. prof., 1982-83; assoc. dean, dir. PAGER, prof. geriatrics U. Cin. Coll. Medicine, 1982—; cons. and lectr. in field. Contbr. articles to profl. jours. Editor: Invasion and Metastasis 1981-85; Internat. Ency. of Pharmacology and Therapeutics, 1982—. Bd. trustees Retired Sr. Vol. Programs, Cin., 1981—; sec. Tristate Cancer Council, 1984—. Recipient numerous fellowships and awards including: George F. Baker Found. scholar, 1960-63; U.S. Nat. Inst. Gen. Med. Scis. fellow, 1963-66; Sidney Sussex Coll. life fellow, Eng., 1967; U.S. Nat. Inst. Gen. Med. Scis. Research Career Devel. award, 1969-74; Leukemia Soc. Am. scholar award, 1974-79; U.S. Nat. Inst. Aging, Geriatric Medicine Acad. award, 1979-82. Mem. Am. Chem. Soc., Biophys. Soc., Am.

Soc. Pharmacology and Exptl. Therapeutics, Gerontology Soc. Am. (biol. scis. and clin. medicine sub-sects., research com.), Am. Soc. Microbiology (antimicrobial chemotherapy sub-sect.), Am. Soc. Regional Anesthesia. Office: U Cin Coll Medicine 231 Bethesda Ave Cincinnati OH 45267

BOSS, BERTRAM JOAB, medical clinic administrator, consultant; b. Marcus, Ia., Oct. 1, 1917; s. Joab Bertram and Sarah (Gurley) B.; m. Helen Ivah Metcalf, Aug. 13, 1938, (div. 1946); m. Agnes Emogene Gronlund, Apr. 17, 1949; children—Beverly, Susanne, David. B.A. in Acctg., Nat. Bus. Coll., Ia., 1938; cert. indsl. bus. adminstrn, U. Neb., 1948. Acct. and office mgr. Fairmont Foods Co., Sioux City, Ia., 1938-48, controller, Devils Lake, N.D., 1949-55; Imperial Dairy Co., Rock Island, Ill., 1955-60, Fairmont Foods Co., Moorhead, Minn., 1960-63; administr. Neuropsychiat. Clinics, Fargo, N.D., 1963-70; administr. assoc. Dakota Clinic, Fargo, 1971-72; adminstr. Albert Lea Clinic, Minn., 1972—; cons. various med. groups, 1976—. Author: Tall are the Hills, 1972. Fellow Am. Coll. Med. Group Administrs.; mem. Med. Group Mgmt. Assn. (various coms.), Minn. Med. Group Mgmt. Assn. (various coms.), Southeastern Minn. Med. Group Mgmt. Assn., Fargo Chamber Commerce, Moorhead Chamber Commerce, Albert Lea Chamber Commerce, Sons Confederate Vets., Sons Am. Revolution. Republican. Lutheran. Club: Moorhead (pres. 1971-72); Albert Lea (pres. 1985-86. Lodge: Kiwanis. Avocations: woodworking, photography, writing, SW radio. Home: 1201 Richway Dr West Albert Lea MN 56007 Office: Albert Lea Clinic P A 1602 Fountain St Albert Lea MN 56007

BOSSE, JAMES PAUL, auditor, educator; b. St. Louis, Mo., Mar. 8, 1946; s. Paul Otto and Anna Mary (Buecher) B. B.S. in Applied Math., U. Mo.-Rolla, 1970. Cert. info. systems auditor; cert. systems profl.; cert. quality analyst. Sr. electronic data processing auditor Gen. Am. Life Ins. Co., St. Louis, 1977-82; sr. electronic data processing auditor ITT Fin. Corp., St. Louis, 1982-85, audit supr. EDP, 1985—; instr. Meramec Community Coll., St. Louis, 1985. Mem. Electronic Data Processing Auditors Assn. (pres. St. Louis chpt. 1984-85, Outstanding Service award 1984). Avocation: long distance running. Office: ITT Fin Corp 12555 Manchester Rd Des Peres MO 63131

BOSTER, JOLYNN BARRY, lawyer, state legislator; b. Maricopa County, Ariz., Aug. 21, 1951; d. Jack and M. Jackie (Hamilton) Barry. B.S., Ohio State U., 1973, J.D., 1976. Bar: Ohio 1976. U.S. Tax Ct. 1976, U.S. Dist. Ct. (so. dist.) Ohio 1977, U.S. Supreme Ct. 1981. Assoc. Emens, Hurd, Kegler & Ritter, Columbus, Ohio, 1976-78; asst. city solicitor City of Gallipolis, Ohio, 1978-81; ptnr. Eachus & Boster, Gallipolis, 1978-81, Cowles & Boster, Gallipolis, 1981—; mem. Ohio Ho. of Reps., Columbus, 1983—. Mem. adv. council Ohio U. Sch. Nursing, Athens; trustee Big Bros./Big Sisters, Gallipolis. Named Woman of Yr., Gallipolis Bus. and Profl. Women, 1983, Mental Health Adv., Athens Hocking Vinton Mental Health Bd., 1984. Mem. Ohio State Bar Assn., ABA, Gallia County Bar Assn., Ohio Assn. Trial Attys. Democrat. Presbyterian. Avocations: jogging; tennis; snow skiing; bicycling. Office: Cowles & Boster Co LPA 26 Locust St Gallipolis OH 45631

BOSTON, DAVID A., city manager; b. Jan. 17, 1947; s. Anna Lou (Koperski) B. B.B.A., U. Toledo, 1969, M.B.A., 1977. With City of Toledo, 1970—, asst. dir., 1975-77, div. head, 1977-79, asst. city mgr. adminstrn., 1979-81, city mgr., 1981—. Mem. Internat. City Mgmt. Assn., Internat. Personnel Mgmt. Assn., U. Toledo Alumni Assn., Am. Soc. Public Adminstrn., Municipal Fin. Officers Assn. Office: City of Toledo One Government Center Toledo OH 43604

BOSTON, DEANNA KAY, hospital financial administrator; b. Carlinville, Ill., Jan. 29, 1945; d. Floyd Young and Christina Louise (Polo) Wheeler; m. Lynn Eldon Boston, June 2, 1973. Assoc. Sci., Lincoln Land Community Coll., Springfield, Ill., 1983. Lab technician Motorola Semicondr., Scottsdale, Ariz.; bookkeeper Macoupin Service Co., Carlinville; bookkeeper Bellm Farm Supply, Carlinville, 1969-71; bus. office mgr. Carlinville Area Hosp., 1972-79, dir. fin., 1979-84; dir. fin. St. Francis Hosp., 1984—. Bd. dirs. Ill. South Conf. United Ch. of Christ, 1982-84, chmn. fin. St. Paul's United Ch. of Christ, dir. choir, 1968—; active Ecumenical Christmas Sing, Carlinville; bd. dirs. Macoupin County Fair Queen Pageant, 1970—. Recipient Wall St. Jour. award Lincoln Land Community Coll., 1983. Mem. Nat. Matrix/Healthcare Fin. Mgmt. Assn., Healthcare Fin. Mgmt. Assn. So. Ill. Chpt. (advanced mem., pres. 1982, Outstanding Achievement awards 1980, nat. award 1979, 1982), Phi Theta Kappa, Alpha Beta Gamma. Republican. Home: 305 N High St Carlinville IL 62626 Office: St Francis Hosp 1215 E Union Ave Litchfield IL 62056

BOSTROM, HARVEY RADER, clergyman, college president; b. Chgo., Jan. 1, 1919; s. Albert and Ruth (Hawkinson) B.; m. Naomi Butcher, Aug. 24, 1944; children—Stephen, Daniel. B.S. Econs. and Bus. Wheaton Coll., 1940; diploma in missions Nyack Coll., 1943; M.A. Christian Ed., Wheaton Coll., 1944; Ph.D. in Higher Ed. Adminstrn., N.Y. U., 1960. Ordained to ministry Christian and Missionary Alliance, 1947. Missionary, Christian Missionary Alliance, Ecuador, 1945-58; faculty Wheaton Coll., Ill., 1960-65, Trinity Coll., Deerfield, Ill., 1967-72; v.p. adminstrn. Trinity Evang. Div. Sch. & Trinity Coll., Deerfield, 1973-75; v.p. devel. and pub. relations Trinity Coll., Deerfield, 1976-80; pres. Fort Wayne Bible Coll., Ind., 1980—. Lodge: Rotary. Home: 4626 Beaver Ave Fort Wayne IN 46807 Office: Fort Wayne Bible Coll 1025 W Rudisill Blvd Fort Wayne IN 46807

BOSWELL, NATHALIE SPENCE, speech pathologist; b. Cleve., May 9, 1924; d. Harrison Morton and Nathalie Muriel (Clem) Spence; student Skidmore Coll, 1941-42; Mus.B. in Edn., Northwestern U., 1945; M.A., Western Res. U., 1961; m. June 15, 1946; children—Louis Keith, Donna Spence, Deborah Anne. Speech therapist Highland View Hosp., Cleve., 1961-64; speech pathologist Cleve. VA Hosp., 1964—; chmn. Equal Employment Opportunity Counselors, 1969-74, Fed. Women Speakers Bur., 1968—, Fed. Career Info. Program, 1970-72, Fed. Coll. Relations Council, 1970-74, Fed. Exec. Bd., 1972-73; adj. instr. Case Western Res. U., 1982—. Mem. Cleve. Orch. Chorus, 1969-82; vol. Seamen's Service, 1976—; patron Police Athletic League. Recipient Performance award Equal Employment Opportunities, 1973; Quality Increase award, 1980; others; lic. speech pathologist, Ohio. Mem. Am. Speech and Hearing Assn. (cert. clin. competence), Ohio Speech and Hearing Assn., Aphasiology Assn. Ohio, Chi Omega Alumni Assn., Musical Arts Assn., Western Res. Hist. Soc., Cleve. Mus. Natural History, Cleve. Mus. Art, Smithsonian Assos., Nat. Wildlife Fedn., Audubon Soc., Nat. Trust Hist. Preservation, Am. Heritage Soc. Mem. Ch. Reformed Latter-Day Saints. Author: Guidelines for EEO Counselors in their Training Program, 1973; prin. author: Laryngectomy-Orientation for Patients and Families, 1981. Home: 2946 Berkshire Rd Cleveland Heights OH 44118 Office: 10701 East Blvd Cleveland OH 44106

BOSWELL, ROBERT BOWEN, automobile company executive; b. Washington, Feb. 14, 1920; s. Roscoe Conkling and Ida Blanche (Fowler) B.; B.S. in Metall. Engring., U. Mich., 1942; m. Ruth Ione Capron, Aug. 16, 1942; children—Robert Capron, James Russell, John Richard. Research metallurgist Chrysler Corp., Highland Park, Mich., 1946-50, chief metallurgist Tank Engine div., New Orleans, 1951-54, chief engr. Forge and Foundry div., Highland Park, 1955-60, mgr. product engring. various mfg. divs., Detroit, 1961-75, mgr. material cost analysis, Highland Park, 1975-80, mgr. chassis cost analysis, 1980-82, program mgr. Mich. div. Barnes & Reinecke, Inc., Madison Heights, 1982—; evening sch. instr. Wayne State U., 1948-51. Served to lt. Ordnance, USNR, 1942-45. Mem. Am. Soc. Metals (chmn. Detroit chpt. 1961-62), Soc. Automotive Engrs. (governing bd. Detroit sect. 1964-66). Republican. Presbyterian. Club: C.I.T. (Detroit) Contbr. articles trade jours. Patentee in field. Home: 4332 MacQueen Dr Orchard Lake MI 48033 Office: Barnes & Reinecke Inc 30335 Stephenson Hwy Madison Heights MI 48071

BOTSAS, ELEFTHERIOS NICHOLAS, economics educator; b. Achladine, Greece, Apr. 6, 1931; came to U.S., 1956, naturalized, 1971; s. Nicholas Themistokles and Helen J. (Karabetsos) B.; B.S., U. Detroit, 1960; Ph.D. (grad. fellow 1960-64, Mendelson research fellow 1962, 64), Wayne State U., 1965; m. Chrysoula G. Kyriakou, Dec. 26, 1965; children—Helena G., Nicholas George. Asst. prof. Lafayette Coll., Easton, Pa., 1964-66; asst. prof. Oakland U., Rochester, Mich., 1966-70, assoc. prof., 1970-76, chmn. econs. dept., 1972-78, prof. econs. and mgmt., 1976—; mem. Council of Econ. Advisors Oakland County, Mich., 1966-68. Exec. bd. Am. Hellenic Congress, 1974—, chmn. exec. bd., 1979-80; mem. Diocesan Council, Greek Orthodox Ch. N.Am. and S.Am. Served with Greek Army, 1953-55. Recipient Teaching Excellence award Gold Key Soc., 1981. Mem. Am. Econ. Assn., AAAS, Am. Assn. S.E. European Studies, Mich. Acad. Arts, Letters and Scis., AAUP, Modern Greek Studies Assn., Am. Hellenic Ednl. Progressive Assn. Contbr. writings in field to publs. Home: 2539 Yorkshire Ln Bloomfield Hills MI 48013 Office: Sch Econs and Mgmt Oakland Univ Rochester MI 48063

BOUCHARD, DONALD WALTER, tool manufacturing company executive, engineer; b. Central Falls, R.I., Nov. 18, 1942; s. Maurice Roland and Lucille Jeanne (Seddon) B.; m. Charlene Joyce Branch, Feb. 1960 (div. 1970); 1 child, Lauren Jeanne; m. Wendy Kathlene Weise, June 23, 1973; children—Scott Douglas, Tiffany Ann. Assoc. Sci., Roger Williams Coll., 1969, B.S., 1971. Engr., Brown & Sharpe, North Kingstown, R.I., 1960-70, Leesona Corp., Warwick, R.I., 1970-72; product mgr. Engis Corp., Morton Grove, Ill., 1972—. Contbr. articles to profl. jours. Mem. ASME. Avocations: scuba diving, archery, firearms, woodworking. Home: 5712 Greenview Rd Cary IL 60013 Office: Engis Corp 8035 Austin Ave Morton Grove IL 60053

BOUDOULAS, HARISIOS, cardiologist, educator; b. Velvendo, Kozani, Greece, Nov. 3, 1935; came to U.S., 1975; s. Konstantinos and Sophia (Manolas) B.; M.D., U. Salonica, Greece, 1959, doctorate diploma, 1967; m. Olga Paspati, Feb. 27, 1971; children—Sophia, Constantinos. Intern, 401st Gen. Army Hosp., Greece, 1960; resident in cardiology 424th Military Hosp., Salonica, 1961; resident in internal medicine First Med. Clinic, U. Salonica, 1962-64, resident in cardiology, 1964-66, attending physician renal unit, 1966-67, coronary care unit, 1967-69, lectr. in medicine, 1969-70, sr. lectr., head coronary care unit, 1973-75; fellow, instr. div. cardiology Ohio State U., 1970-73, fellow, 1975, asst. prof. medicine, 1975-78, asso. prof., 1978-80; dir. cardiac non-invasive lab., 1978-80; prof. medicine, chief clin. cardiovascular research, div. cardiology Wayne State U., Detroit, 1980-82; chief Cardiovascular Diagnostic and Tng. Center, VA Med. Center, Allen Park, Mich., 1980-82; prof. medicine, dir. research div. cardiology Ohio State U., 1983-85, prof. pharmacy, 1983—; co-dir. Overstreet Teaching and Research Labs., 1983—; disting. research investigator Central Ohio chpt. Am. Heart Assn., 1983—. Fellow Am. Coll. Cardiology, Council Clin. Cardiology, Am. Coll. Clin. Pharmacology, Am. Coll. Angiology, A.C.P.; mem. Med. Assn. Salonica, Greek Soc. Biochemistry, Greek Renal Assn., European Dialysis and Transplant Assn., Am. Heart Assn., Greek Heart Assn., Greek Com. Against Hypertension, Am. Fedn. Clin. Research, Central Soc. Clin. Research. Greek Orthodox. Mem. team which performed first successful kidney transplantation in Greece; contbr. numerous articles to profl. jours. Home: 4185 Mumford Ct Columbus OH 43220 Office: Ohio State U Columbus OH

BOUDREAU, EDWARD DAVID, JR., physician; b. Hartford, Conn., Nov. 21, 1951; s. Edward David Sr. and Margaret (Murphy) B.; m. Susan Kathleen Giblin, Sept. 17, 1978; children—Kristen, Michael. B.S. in Chemistry, Bates Coll., 1973; D.O., Mich. State U., 1977. Diplomate Am. Bd. Emergency Medicine. Intern Doctors Hosp., Columbus, Ohio; staff physician emergency dept. Point Pleasant Hosp., N.J., 1981-82; dir. emergency dept. Doctors Hosp., Columbus, 1982—, chmn. dept. emergency medicine, 1984—. Served to capt. U.S. Army, 1978-81. Dana scholar Bates Coll., 1970. Fellow Am. Coll. Emergency Physicians (Ohio chpt.); mem. Phi Beta Kappa. Roman Catholic. Avocation: sailing catamaran. Home: 5204 Ashford Rd Dublin OH 43017 Office: Emergency Dept Doctors Hosp North 1087 Dennison Ave Columbus OH 43201

BOULANGER, RODNEY EDMUND, pipeline company executive; b. Detroit, Apr. 4, 1940; s. Howard Louis and Mildred (Oblak) B.; m. Nancy Ann Ewigleben, Dec. 29, 1962; children—Brent, Karla, Melissa. B.S., Ferris State U., 1963; M.B.A., U. Detroit, 1967. Econ. analyst Mich. Consolidated Gas Co., Detroit, 1963-70, mgr. econ. and fin. planning, 1970-73; dir. energy econs. Am. Natural Service Co., Detroit, 1973-77, dir. system econs. and diversification, 1977-78, v.p. system econs. and diversification, 1978-80; v.p. fin. adminstrn. ANG Coal Gasification Co., Detroit, 1980-82; treas., chief fin. officer Gt. Plains Gasification Assocs., Detroit, 1982-84; v.p. fin., sec. ANG Coal Gasification Co., Detroit, 1982-84; exec. v.p. ANR Pipeline Co., 1985—. Bd. dirs. Eastwood Clinics, Detroit. Mem. Beta Gamma Sigma. Clubs: Detroit Athletic, Renaissance (Detroit); Duck Lake Country (Albion, Mich.). Home: 592 University Grosse Pointe MI 48230 Office: ANR Pipeline Co 500 Renaissance Ctr Detroit MI 48243

BOULGER, WILLIAM CHARLES, lawyer; b. Columbus, Ohio, Apr. 2, 1924; s. James Ignatius and Rebecca (Laughlin) B.; m. Ruth J. Schachtele, Dec. 29, 1954; children—Brigid Carolyn, Ruth Mary. A.B., Harvard Coll., 1948; LL.B., Law Sch. Cin., 1951. Bar: Ohio, 1951, U.S. Dist. Ct. (so. dist.) Ohio 1952, U.S. Supreme Ct. 1957. Ptnr. with Thomas A. Boulger, Chillicothe, Ohio, 1951-73; sole propr. Law Offices of William C. Boulger, Chillicothe, 1974—. Pres. Ross County Welfare Assn., Chillicothe, 1954-60; mem. Chillicothe. ARC, 1958-84, chmn., 1959-63; mem. Democratic Exec. Com., Chillicothe, 1950s. Served as pfc. U.S. Army, 1943-45, ETO. Mem. Ross County Bar Assn. (pres. 1971), Ohio Bar Assn., ABA. Roman Catholic. Clubs: Sunset, Symposiarchs (pres.). Avocations: tennis, golf. Home: 31 Club Dr Chillicothe OH 45601 Office: Law Offices of William C Boulger 10-14 Foulke Block Chillicothe OH 45601

BOULTINGHOUSE, JANE ELLEN, principal; b. Rockport, Ind., Feb. 15, 1947; d. Oscar Wayne and Anna Ellen (Gentry) B. B.A., U. Evansville, 1969, M.A., 1974. Lic. adminstr. and supr., Ind. Elem. tchr. Ella Williams Sch., Boonville, Ind., 1969-72; 1st grade tchr. Chandler Elem. Sch., Ind., 1973-75; second grade tchr. Loge Sch., Boonville, 1975-80; prin. Oakdale Elem. Sch., Boonville, 1980—. Assn. Childhood Edn. Internat. fellow, 1972-73; named Outstanding Tchr. Warrick County, Boonville Jaycees, 1975, Outstanding Boss of Yr., 1982. Mem. Ind. Assn. Elem. Sch. Prins., Assn. Supervision and Curriculum Devel., Ind. Reading Assn., Warrick County Reading Assn., Warrick County Adminstrs., Warrick County Assn. Retarded Citizens, Boonville Bus. and Profl. Women, Old Rockport Civic Theater Assn., Alpha Delta Kappa, Phi Delta Kappa, Pi Lambda Theta. Methodist. Clubs: Boonville Women's, Rebekah Lodge. Home: 1773 Covey Dr Boonville IN 47601 Office: 802 S 8th St Boonville IN 47601

BOULTON, EDWIN CHARLES, bishop; b. St. Joseph, Mo., Apr. 15, 1928; s. Glen Elwood and Elsa Adina Elizabeth (Person) B.; m. Betty Ann Fisher, July 17, 1949; children—Ann Lisa, Charles Mitchell, James Clay, Melanie Beth. A.B., William Jewell Coll., 1950; M.Div., Duke U., 1953; D.Div., Iowa Wesleyan Coll., 1974, Rust Coll., 1982; D.H.L., Simpson Coll., 1980, Westmar Coll. Ordained to ministry Methodist. Ch., 1953; pastor chs., West End-Vass, N.C., 1953, Republic Community, Iowa, 1954-57, Pocahontas, Iowa, 1957-64, Bettendorf, Iowa, 1964-70; dist. supt., Dubuque, Iowa, 1970-73; adminstrv. asst. to bishop, Des Moines, 1973-80, bishop of Dakotas Area, Mitchell, S.D., 1980—; bd. dirs. World Meth. Council. Named Disting. Alumnus, Duke U. Divinity Sch., 1980. Office: 1721 S University St Fargo ND 58103 also PO Box 460 Mitchell SD 57301

BOUMA, GERALD DALE, educator; b. Orange City, Iowa, Oct. 8, 1944; s. Ralph and Jenny Marjory (Reinsma) B.; student Dordt Coll., 1962-65; A.B., Northwestern Coll., 1967; M.Mus., Ariz. State U., 1969, Ed.D., 1982; m. Donna Mae Duistermars, July 14, 1966; children—Tonya Nicole, Caron Leigh. Ch. choir dir. Calvary Christian Ref. Ch., Orange City, 1962-66, 72-75; music instr. Unity Christian High Sch., Orange City, 1964-68; prof. music Dordt Coll., Sioux Center, Iowa, 1969-85, condr. of bands, 1974-85; prof. music Westmont Coll., Santa Barbara, Calif., 1985—. Mem. fin. bd. Orange City Christian Sch., 1969-72; bd. dirs. Sioux County Concert Series, 1969-72; dir. musicals Sioux County Arts Council, 1976, Orange City Community Prodns., 1968-79. Mem. Music Educators Nat. Conf., Nat. Band Assn., Iowa Bandmasters Assn. Republican. Christian Ref. Ch. Composer: Sonnet for Brass Choir, 1969; March Mae, 1971; Sketch for Euphonium and Band, 1969. Home: 615 Second St SW Orange City IA 51041 Office: Dordt Coll Sioux Center IA 51250

BOUNDY, JOHN EDWARD, hospital administrator; b. Peoria, Ill., Dec. 14, 1937; s. Donald Albert and Marguerite Mary B.; m. Janice Fay Russell, June 26, 1965; children—Timothy, Jeffrey, Darren. A.A., Midstate Coll. Commerce, 1961. Asst. credit mgr. St. Francis Med. Ctr., Peoria, 1960-65, credit mgr., 1965-77, patients accounts mgr., 1977—. Pres. bd. dirs., emergency med. technician Rescue Squad 702, Tremont, Ill. Served with USN, 1955-58. Recipient William G. Follmer award Health Care Mgmt. Assn., 1976; named Boss of Yr., Internat. Credit Women's Club, 1977. Mem. Healthcare Fin. Mgmt. Assn., Internat. Consumer Credit Assn. (cert. exec.), Nat. Registry Emergency Med. Technicians. Roman Catholic. Club: K.C. Author: How To Collect From the Township Form of Government, 1974. Home: Route 1 Tremont IL 61568 Office: 530 NE Glen Oak Ave Peoria IL 61637

BOURBON, ARCHIE THEODORE, association administrator; b. Granite City, Ill., Dec. 11, 1945; s. Archie Theodore and Grace Estelle (Geist) B., Sr.; m. Jane Culver Jones, June 10, 1972; children—Todd Wesley, Travis Culver. B.A., Central Meth. U., 1968; M.B.A., Southwest Mo. State U., 1978; Med. Technologist U.S. Naval Med. Sch., 1970. Dir. tech. services ARC, Springfield, Mo., 1973-80, plasma cons., 1980-82, tech. adviser, 1979-81, lic. reviewer, 1980-82; dir. catering service Western Food Enterprise, Springfield, 1982-84; dir. mktg. Springfield Area C. of C., 1985—; mgmt. cons. Clin. Lab. Services, Springfield, 1980-82. Tech. adviser jour. Blood Bank, Mgmt., 1980. Chmn. bd. trustees United Meth. Ch., Springfield, 1974-78; loaned exec. United Way of Ozarks, Springfield, 1977-80; blood bank coordinator Internat. Soc. Clin. Lab. Technologists, 1976. Served with USN, 1969-72. Gen. Steel Industries scholar, 1963. Mem. Am. Mgmt. Assn., Assn. Mil. Surgeons, Am. Assn. Blood Banks (bd. dirs. 1975-78), U.S. Naval Res. Assn., Res. Officer Assn. Democrat. Lodges: Masons, Kiwanis. Avocations: jogging; bowling; camping; tennis. Home: 2458 E Barataria Springfield MO 65804 Office: Springfield Area C of C PO Box 1687 SSS 320 N Jefferson Springfield MO 65805

BOURG, JOHN PATRICK, computer industry executive; b. Harlingen, Tex., Oct. 26, 1938; s. Adam Lee and Sabrina (Doris) B.; m. Suzanne Tidwell; 1 son, Steven Mark; m. Molly Metz, Nov. 29, 1980; 1 stepson, Andrew Prentis Brown. B.E.E., Rice U., 1961; M.B.A. with honors, U. Chgo., 1968. Engring. mgr. AT&T, Chgo., 1961-66; mgmt. services cons. Price Waterhouse, Chgo., 1966-68; mgmt. cons. McKinsey, Chgo., 1968-72; v.p., gen. mgr. Avery Internat., San Marino, Calif., 1972-80; planning dir. motor div. Gen. Electric, Indpls., 1980-83; pres. Wabash DataTech, Rolling Meadows, Ill., 1983—. Named Outstanding Engr., Tex. Soc. Profl. Engrs., 1960: fellow Weiss Coll., Rice U., 1958-60. Mem. Pres. Assn., Internat. Radio Engrs., Am. Inst. Elec. Engrs. Republican. Home: 20 Country Oaks Dr Barrington Hills IL 60010 Office: Wabash DataTech Inc Two Continental Towers Suite 400 Rolling Meadows IL 60008

BOURN, PATRICIA MCANULTY, educator; b. Shelbina, Mo., Apr. 19, 1929; d. Clarence A. and Fannie E. (Sharp) McAnulty; m. Benjamin Wayne Bourn, Apr. 22, 1951; 1 son, Peter Bradley. B.S., N.E. Mo. State U., 1951, M.A., 1968; postgrad. U. Mo., 1970-78. Sec., Hort. div. U. Mo., Columbia, 1949; sec. Carter Oil Co., Tulsa, 1949-50; tchr. bus. edn. New London (Mo.) High Sch., 1952-55; instr. bus. edn. Hannibal (Mo.) High Sch. and Hannibal Area Vocat.-Tech. Schs., 1955—. Mem. Hannibal Arts Council, 1979—, Mo. Adv. Council Vocat. Edn., 1983—. Recipient Outstanding Bus. Edn. award Mo. Bus. Edn. Assn., 1977. Mem. Am. Vocat. Assn., Mo. Vocat. Assn., Hannibal Edn. Assn., Nat. Bus. Edn. Assn. Christian Ch. Home: 3206 Marsh Ave Hannibal MO 63401 Office: 4550 McMasters Ave Hannibal MO 63401

BOURNE, GODFREY RODERICK, wildlife ecologist; b. Georgetown, Guyana, Mar. 20, 1943; came to U.S., 1966, naturalized, 1981; s. Layton George and Edna Rubina (Thompson) B.; B.A., Ohio Wesleyan U., 1971; M.En., Miami U., 1976; Ph.D., (fellow 1976-79), U. Mich., 1983; m. Carol Elizabeth Mulligan, Dec. 21, 1968. Avian researcher, artist, Guyana, 1962-64; asst. tchr. Christ Ch. Secondary Sch., Guyana, 1964-66; writer-illustrator, U.S., 1971—; cons. LGL Ltd., Edmonton, Alta., Can., 1975; teaching fellow U. Mich., Ann Arbor, 1976-79, lectr., 1977-79, 81, research scientist, lectr., 1983—; cons. Man and the Biosphere Com., Guyana, 1980. Active Boy Scouts of Guyana, 1952-59, patrol leader, 1957-59; mem. Kamoa Art Group, 1961-65, v.p., 1964-65; mem. Christ Ch. Young People's Movement, 1964-66, pres., 1965-66; mem. Ohio Wesleyan U. Internat. Student Assn., 1967-71, Wheaton Club, 1970-73; hon. mem. Langdon Club, 1975-76. Welder Wildlife Found. fellow, 1973-75, Rackham Block fellow, 1979-81, grantee, 1979-80; research grantee Fred and Jane Stevens, 1974, 80; Chapman Meml. Fund grantee, 1973, 74, 80; NSF grantee, 1983—; recipient Marcia Brady Tucker award Am. Ornithol. Union, 1972; Samuel Trask Dana award Sch. Natural Resources, U. Mich., 1982. Mem. AAAS, Interciencia Assn., Am. Ornithologists Union, Wilson Ornithol. Soc., Cornell Lab. of Ornithology, Wildlife Soc., Sigma Xi (research grantee, 1979-80), Phi Kappa Phi. Artist, oil painting Abary Wetland, 1961 (Guyana Nat. Mus.); contbr. research papers on ecology of neotropical birds to publs. Home: 1142 Nielsen Ct Apt 9 Ann Arbor MI 48105 Office: School Natural Resources Univ Michigan Ann Arbor MI 48109

BOUSEMAN, JOHN KEITH, entomologist, naturalist; b. Clinton, Iowa, Aug. 11, 1936; s. Thomas Elmer and Kathryn Teresa (Van Buer) B.; m. Barbara Ann Busby, Aug. 21, 1956; children—Karen, David, Thomas, Lynn, Paul; m. 2d, Tamara Faye Moore, Oct. 15, 1977; 1 child, William. B.S. in Entomology, U. Ill., 1960, M.S. in Entomology, 1962. Registered profl. entomologist, Ill. Expdn. entomologist Am. Mus. Natural History, Uruguayan Expdn., 1963, Bolivian Expdn., 1964, 65; instr. U. Ill., Urbana, 1965-66; asst. entomologist agrl. entomology Ill. Agrl. Expt. Sta., Urbana, 1972—; asst. entomologist Ill. Natural History Survey, Champaign, 1972-84, assoc. entomologist, 1984—; entomological expdns. to Bolivia, Brazil, Paraguay, Zambia, Uruguay, Venezuela, W.I., Mex.; cons. Zambia Ministry Agr. and Water Devel., 1984. Sci. Research Soc. Am. grantee, 1961; NSF grantee, 1982. Mem. Entomol. Soc. Am., Coleopterists Soc., N.Y. Entomol. Soc., Entomol. Soc. Washington, Kans. Entomol. Soc., Sigma Xi. Club: Ill. Field Entomologists (Champaign). Contbr. numerous publ. to profl. jours. Office: Ill Natural History Survey 607 E Peabody Champaign IL 61820

BOUSSETA, MOHAMED, computer center director; b. Casablanca, Morocco, June 25, 1940; s. Ahmed Allal and Fatima (Lourak) B.; m. Beverly J. Sadden, Nov. 28, 1964; 1 child, Stephen. B.A., Morningside Coll., 1964; M.A., U. Mont., 1969. Instr. Nat. Coll., pub. schs., Sioux Falls, S.D., 1965-79; system analyst Eros Data Center, Sioux Falls, 1980-83; dir. computer ctr. Briar Cliff Coll., Sioux City, Iowa, 1983—. Mem. Nat. Council Tchrs. Math., Data Processing Mgmt. Assn., Digital Equipment Corp. Users Soc., Siouxland DPMA (edn. dir. 1980, cert.) Democrat. Moslem. Home: 520 E Lotta St Sioux Falls SD 57105

BOUZA, ANTHONY VILA, See *Who's Who in America,* 43rd edition.

BOUZEK, ROBERT EDWARD, communications executive; b. Prairie du Chien, Wis., Sept. 24, 1933; s. Edward James and Emma Regina (White) B.; B.S.J., U. Wis.-Madison, 1962; m. Mary Elizabeth Scott, Dec. 20, 1960; children—Michaelle, Elizabeth Mary, Lisa Diane, Jane Ann. Editor, Courier-Press, Prairie du Chien, 1957-58; govtl./bus. reporter Waukesha (Wis.) Freeman, 1958-59; reporter, copy editor Wis. State Jour., Madison, 1959-63; copy editor supr. Milw. Jour., 1963-67; pub. relations specialist Am. Mut. Ins. Alliance, Chgo., 1967-68; pub. relations counsel Carl Byoir & Assos. Inc., Chgo., 1968-70; account supr. Harshe-Rotman & Druck Inc., Chgo., 1970-77, v.p., 1977-79; mgr. media relations Ill. Bell Telephone Co., Chgo., 1979-81, mgr. advt., 1981-83; v.p. Bernard E. Ury Assocs., Inc., 1983—. Home: 69 E Quincy St Riverside IL 60546 Office: 307 N Michigan Ave Chicago IL 60601

BOVEE, EUGENE CLEVELAND, protozoologist, educator; b. Sioux City, Iowa, Apr. 1, 1915; S..s. Earl Eugene and Martha Nora (Johnson) B.; B.A., U. No. Iowa, 1939; M.S., U. Iowa, 1948; Ph.D., UCLA, 1950; m. Maezene B. Wamsley, May 18, 1942; m. 2d, Elizabeth A. Moss, May 9, 1968; children—Frances, Gregory, Matthew; stepchildren—Lynne, Lisa. Instr. zoology Iowa U., 1940-41; biology tchr. Greene (Iowa) High Sch., 1941-42; instr. biology U. No. Iowa, 1946-48; instr. zoology UCLA, 1948-50, research zoologist, 1962-68; asst. prof. biology Calif. Poly. U., 1950-52; asso. prof. zoology, dept. chmn. N.D. State U., 1952-53; asst. prof. biology U. Houston, 1953-55; asso. prof. U. Fla., 1955-62; prof. physiology and cell biology U. Kans., Lawrence, 1968—, counseling officer div. biol. sci., 1974-80; cons. Am. Type Culture Collection, 1980-82, W.C. Brown, Pub., 1978-82. Served to 1st lt. U.S. Army, World War II. Research grantee, NIH, 1957-62, NSF, 1970-74, NIH, NSF, and ONR, 1962-68, Kans. Fed. Water Resources Inst. and U. Kans., 1968-81; recipient Disting. Alumni award, U. No. Iowa, 1980. Mem. Soc. Protozoology (pres. 1979-80, v.p. 1970-71, treas. 1972-78, exec. com. 1970-81), Am. Inst. Biol. Sci., Am. Microscopy Soc. (mem.-at-large exec. com. 1959-62), Western Soc. Naturalists, Iowa Acad. Sci., Kans. Acad. Sci. (life mem., pres. 1979-80, exec. com. 1975-81), Sigma Xi. Editor Kans. Sci. Bull., 1974-79; co-author: How to Know the Protozoa, 2d edit., 1979; co-editor: Illustrated Guide to the Protozoa, 1984-85; contbr. chpts. to books, articles to jours. Office: 154 Snow Hall Univ Kansas Lawrence KS 66044

BOVEE, JOAN GUILDENBECHER, home economist, educator; b. Muncie, Ind., May 8, 1946; d. Robert and Kathryn E. (Bullock) Guildenbecher; B.S., Purdue U., 1968; M.S., St. Francis Coll., 1972; postgrad. Ind. U., 1979-80; m. Norman Alan Bovee, Dec. 28, 1967. Jr. fashion merchandizing cons. Montgomery Wards, Fort Wayne, Ind., 1963-67; clothing and textile lab. technician Purdue U., w. Lafayette, Ind., 1966-67; vocat. home econs. tchr. Prairie Heights Community High Sch., LaGrange, Ind., 1968—, also dir. student activities, 1972—; cons. for local 4-H workshops, 1968—; mem. staff Student Leadership Inst., Ind. U., Bloomington, 1983—, advisor workshop coordinator, 1984—; staff mem., tchr. Wood Youth Ctr. for Population Edn. Project. Mem. adv. com. Prairie Heights Outdoor Community Edn. Center, 1979—, Sol D. Wood Ctr., 1984—; mem. planning com. Prairie Heights Ann. Fall Farm Festival, 1972—. Mem. Nat. Assn. Vocat. Home Econs. Tchrs. (state contact person 1980, sec. candidate 1983), Am. Home Econs. Assn. (mem. ho. of dels. 1978-79), Am. Vocat. Assn. (mem. ho. of dels. 1978-80), Ind. Vocat. Assn. (mem. awards com. 1981), Ind. Vocat. Home Econs. Assn. (pres. 1979-80, dist. pres. 1978), Ind. Home Econs. Assn. (mem. public relations com. 1979—, liaison com. with Ind. Vocat. Home Econs. Assn. 1982—, dist. 2 newsletter editor and nominating com. 1983—, state nominating com. 1984—), NEA, Ind. State Tchrs. Assn., Prairie Heights Edn. Assn., Nat. Council of Family Relations, Ind. Council of Family Relations, LaGrange County Mental Health Assn., Kappa Delta Pi, Omicron Nu. Mem. Apostolic Christian Ch. Contbg. author: Indiana State Interpersonal Relations Curriculum Guide, 1977, Indiana State Human Development Curriculum Guide, 1979. Home: Rural Route 1 PO Box 320 Wolcottville IN 46795

BOVEE, PHYLLIS ELLEN, nurse, hospital executive; b. Cozad, Nebr., Feb. 21, 1932; d. Mac H. and E. Blandena (Johnson) B. B.S., Nebr. Wesleyan U., 1958; M.S., U. Nebr., 1978. Staff nurse Meth. Hosp., Omaha, 1951-52; med. surg. instr. Bryan Hosp. Sch. Nursing, Lincoln, Nebr., 1952-61, assoc. dir. nursing edn., 1961-71, dir. nursing edn., 1971-82; v.p. Div. A, Bryan Meml. Hosp., Lincoln, 1982—. Mem. Nat. League Nursing, Fedn. for Accessible Nursing Edn. and Licensure, Nebr. Consortium Hosp. Schs. Nursing, Assn. Nursing Service Dirs., AAUW, DAR. Republican. Methodist. Office: Bryan Meml Hosp 4848 Sumner St Lincoln NE 68506

BOWDEN, DOUGLAS IVES, accountant; b. Marceline, Mo., Nov. 4, 1953; s. Homer Ives, Jr., and Betty Jo (Burgener) B.; B.S. in Bus. Adminstrn., U. Mo., Columbia, 1976. Acct., Dept. Natural Resources, State of Mo., Jefferson City, 1977-78; mgr. acctg. Four Seasons Lakesites, Inc., Lake Ozark, Mo., 1978—. Vol. coll. tutor, tax preparation counselor, disc jockey stas. KLDN-FM, Eldon, Mo., KCOU-FM, Columbia, Mo. Mem. U. Mo. Alumni Assn., Am. Bowling Congress, Phi Eta Sigma. Mem. Christian Church (Disciples of Christ). Home: Route 2 Box 179-22 Osage Beach MO 65065 Office: PO Box 408 Lake Ozark MO 65049

BOWDEN, GEORGE FRANCIS, engineering educator, consultant; b. Chgo., Mar. 3, 1925; s. George J. Bowden and Helen E. (Havlik) Wade; m. Barbara Caryl, Oct. 30, 1948; children—Alane, Gale, Philip, Carl. B.S.C.E., Purdue U., 1948, M.S.C.E., Wayne State U., 1974. Registered profl. engr., Mich., Ill. Field engr. Commonwealth Edison Co., Chgo., 1948-59; v.p., dir. research and devel. Symons Corp., Des Plaines, Ill., 1959-70; chmn. constru. engring. dept. Lawrence Inst. Tech., Southfield, Mich., 1971-83, prof., 1971—; cons., Milford, Mich., 1974—. Patentee in field (25). Contbg. author: Handbook of Heavy Construction, 1969. Pres., Timber Trails Assn., Northbrook, Ill., 1967-68; bd. dirs. West Northfield Sch., Northbrook, 1970-71; arbitrator Am. Arbitration Assn., 1974. Served as aviation cadet USN, 1943-45. Mem. ASCE (adv. 1977-85), Am. Concrete Inst., Engring. Soc. Detroit, Tau Beta Pi, Chi Epsilon, Am. Youth Hostels, Mich. Radio Control Soc. Avocations: radio controlled sail planes; hiking; scuba diving. Home: 2694 Parkway Pl Milford MI 48042 Office: 21000 W Ten Mile Rd Southfield MI 48075

BOWDEN, OTIS HEARNE, II, management consulting firm executive; b. Stuttgart, Ark., Jan. 2, 1928; s. Otis Hearne and Donna (Trice) B.; B.S. in Bus. Adminstrn., Washington U., 1950, M.B.A., 1953; m. Helen Carol Lamar, June 25, 1949. Financial analyst St. Louis Union Trust Co., St. Louis, 1950-53; dist. mgr. TRW, Inc., Cleve., 1953-63; dir. Mass Transit Center, B.F. Goodrich Co., Akron, Ohio, 1963-67; v.p. E.A. Butler Assocs., Inc., Cleve., 1967-71; pres. Bowden & Co., Inc., Cleve., 1972—; guest lectr. Akron U., 1972—. Nat. promotion dir. Laymen's Hour Radio Broadcast, 1959-63; chmn. commerce and industry div. United Fund of Greater Cleve., 1962; pres. Am. Baptist Men of Ohio, 1962-63; trustee Alderson-Broaddus Coll., Philippi, W.Va., 1965-76, Eastern Coll., Phila.; alumni bd. govs. Washington U., St. Louis; bd. dirs. Am. Bapt. Fgn. Mission Soc., 1962-71; regional dir. Project Winsome Internationale; vice chmn. adv. bd. Salvation Army of Greater Cleve., 1979—, also chmn. program com. Served with USMCR, 1951. Mem. Am. Mgmt. Assn., Ohio Cons. Assn. (pres. 1982), Am. Mktg. Assn. Clubs: Rotary (trustee 1975-77, Paul Harris fellow 1978), Union. Office: 5000 Rockside Rd Cleveland OH 44131

BOWDLE, FREDERICK CHARLES, obstetrician, gynecologist; b. Napoleon, Ohio, Mar. 31, 1934; s. Charles P. and Reta Belle (Stuempel) B.; student U. Mich., 1952-55, M.D., 1959; m. Sandra Kay Lowe, June 22, 1963; children—Brian Frederick, Julie Rochelle. Intern, St. Vincent Med. Center, Toledo, 1959-60, resident, 1962-65, now mem. staff, chmn. dept. obstetrics and gynecology, 1971-75, practice medicine specializing in obstetrics and gynecology, Toledo, 1965—; mem. staffs Toledo Hosp., Med. Coll. Ohio; clin. asst. prof. ob-gyn Med. Coll. Ohio, Toledo, 1972-84, clin. assoc. prof., 1984—; mem. profl. edn. com. Lucas County (Ohio) unit Am. Cancer Soc., 1971. Served as capt. M.C. USAF, 1960-62. Diplomate Am. Bd. Obstetrics and Gynecology. Fellow Am. Coll. Obstetrics and Gynecology, A.C.S.; mem. Acad. Medicine of Toledo and Lucas County, Toledo, Mich. socs. obstetrics-gynecology, Central Assn. Obstetrics-Gynecology, AMA, N. Am. Gynecol. Soc., Am. Assn. Gynecologic Laparoscopists, Am. Fertility Soc., U. Mich. Alumni Assn., Ohio State Alumni Assn. Republican. Methodist. Clubs: Royal Order Jesters, Masons, Shriners (potentate 1979). Home: 4629 Beaconsfield Ct Toledo OH 43623 Office: Sunforest Med Bldg 3900 Sunforest Ct Toledo OH 43623

BOWEN, GARY ROGER, architect; b. Page, Nebr., Apr. 24, 1942; s. Roger David and Eugenia (Luben) B.; m. Elizabeth Ann Humphrey, Aug. 4, 1962; children—Ann, Leslie. Student Wayne State Coll., 1950-52; B.Arch., U. Nebr., 1964, M. Arch., 1974. Registered architect, Nebr., Iowa; cert. Nat. Council Archtl. Registration Bds. With Howell, Killick, Partridge, Amis, London, 1963, F.W. Horn Assocs., Quincy, Ill., 1964-66; design architect Leo A. Daly Co., Omaha, 1966-72; ptnr. Hartman Morford Bowen, Omaha, 1972-74, Bahr Vermeer Haecker, Omaha, 1974—; vis. critic Coll. Architecture, U. Nebr.; vis. lectr. Coll. Architecture, Kansas State U.; dir. Landmarks Inc., Omaha. Bd. dirs. Western Heritage Soc., Omaha. Am. Collegiate Schs. of Architecture Fgn. Work Exchange scholar, 1963; recipient Housing Mag. Homes for Better Living Nat. Design award, 1981. Mem. AIA (nat. com. on design), Nebr. Soc. Architects (honor award 1979). Republican. Methodist. Club: Field of Omaha. Project architect Central Park Mall, Omaha. Home: 6007 Lafayette Ct Omaha NE 68132 Office: 1209 Harney St Omaha NE 68102

BOWEN, GEORGE HAMILTON, JR., astrophysicist, educator; b. Tulsa, June 20, 1925; s. George and Dorothy (Huntington) B.; m. Marjorie B. Bowen, June 19, 1948; children—Paul, Margaret, Carol, Dorothy, Kevin. B.S. with honors, Calif. Inst. Tech., 1949, Ph.D., 1953. Research assoc. Oak Ridge Nat. Lab., Tenn., 1952-54; asst. to assoc. prof. Iowa State U., Ames, 1954-65, prof. astrophysics, 1965—. Contbr. articles to profl. jours. Served with USNR, 1944-46. Recipient Iowa State U. Outstanding Tchr. award, 1970; Faculty Service citation, Iowa State U. Alumni Assn. Mem. Am. Astron. Soc., Astron. Soc. Pacific, AAAS, Sigma Xi. Avocations: Photography; gardening. Home: 1919 Burnett Ave Ames IA 50010 Office: Dept Physics Iowa State Univ Ames IA 50011

BOWEN, RICHARD L., See *Who's Who in America,* 43rd edition.

BOWEN, ROBERT KENDALL, farmer; b. Ewa Oahu, Hawaii, Feb. 8, 1948; s. Robert Wesley and Gertrude (Benevides) B.; m. Susan Marie Leutloff, Sept. 14, 1968; children—Kenneth J., Keith A., Kyle E. Student Ill. State U., 1967, A.A. in Agrl. Prodn. and Mgmt., Kankakee Jr. Coll., 1968. Cert. emergency med. service 1st responder, Ill. Farm mgr. DeYoung & Mercier, St. Anne, Ill., 1968-77, Hoekstra Farms, St. Anne, 1978-79; owner, operator Highland Farms, St. Anne, 1980—. Patrol officer Kankakee River Police Dept., 1979—, 4-H club leader. Served to staff sgt. Army N.G., 1968-76. Mem. Profl. Farmers Am. Republican. Lutheran. Lodge: Elks. Avocations: riflery; marksmanship instructor. Home: Rural Route #3 Box 491 St Anne IL 60964

BOWEN, WILLIAM J., management consultant; b. N.Y.C.; B.S., Fordham U., 1956; M.B.A., NYU, 1963. Trainee, Smith, Barney & Co., N.Y.C., 1959-61; asst. v.p. investments 1st Nat. City Bank, N.Y.C., 1961-67; instl. salesman Hayden Stone, Inc., N.Y.C., 1967-69; successively v.p. and Eastern regional sales mgr., 1st v.p. and instl. sales mgr. Shearson, Hammill & Co., Inc., N.Y.C., 1969-73; assoc. Heidrick and Struggles, Inc., Chgo., 1973-77, ptnr., 1977—, v.p., 1977-78, sr. v.p. and mgr., 1978-80, sr. v.p. and central regional mgr., 1980-81, pres. and chief exec. officer, 1981-83, vice-chmn., 1983—. Office: Heidrick & Struggles Inc 125 S Wacker Dr Chicago IL 60606

BOWER, ROBERT HEWITT, surgeon, surgical educator, researcher; b. Omaha, Aug. 20, 1949; s. John Walter and Dorothy May (Sibert) B.; m. Debra Lea Goettsche, July 4, 1980; children—Timothy Conrad, Michael Harvey. B.A., Grinnell Coll., 1971; M.D., U. Nebr., 1975. Diplomate Nat. Bd. Med. Examiners, Am. Bd. Surgery. Intern, U. Nebr., 1975-76, resident in surgery, 1976-80, chief resident, 1979-80; clin. and research fellow U. Cin., 1980-81; asst. prof. surgery, dir. nutritional support service U. Cin., 1981-85, assoc. prof. surgery, 1985—. Fellow ACS; mem. AMA, Assn. Acad. Surgery, Am. Soc. Parenteral and Enteral Nutrition, Ohio Med. Assn., Acad. Medicine Cin., Cin. Surg. Soc. Mem. United Ch. of Christ. Contbr. articles to profl. jours., chpts. to books. Office University Cincinnati Dept Surgery Cincinnati OH 45267

BOWER, SHIRLEY MAE (MRS. JAY R. BOWER), Realtor; b. Marshfield, Mo., Apr. 2, 1935; d. James Oliver and Ruth Irene (Hyde) Day; B.A. in Speech and Dramatics cum laude, Culver-Stockton Coll., 1957; grad. Ill. Inst. Real Estate Brokers, 1972; m. Jay R. Bower, Aug. 5, 1956; 1 dau., Lisa Lynne. Tchr. speech, drama and English Quincy (Ill.) Jr. High Sch., 1951-58; tchr. speech and drama Central High Sch., Camp Point, Ill., 1958-60, 65—; real estate broker, 1976-78; relocation dir. and co-owner Bower Realtors, ERA, Quincy, Camp Point, Ill., 1967—. Co-dir. Quincy Jr. Theater, 1957-58, bd. dirs.; bd. dirs. Family Service Agy., Quincy, 1967-68, Quincy Jr. High Sch. PTA, 1973; alumni bd. dirs. Culver-Stockton Coll., 1967—, pres., 1965-66. Mem. Quincy Bd. Realtors, Nat. Assn. Real Estate Brokers, Nat. Inst. Real Estate Brokers, Quincy Service League. Chi Omega. Presbyterian. Home: 2828 Southfield Dr Quincy IL 62301 Office: 503 Maine St Quincy IL 62301

BOWER, WILLIAM WALTER, scientist; b. Hammond, Ind., Jan. 9, 1945; s. William Walter and Frances Anita (Good) B.; B.S. in Mech. Engring., Purdue U., 1967, M.S., 1969, Ph.D., 1971. Sr. engr. Propulsion Dept., McDonnell Aircraft Co., St. Louis, 1971-74, sr. scientist Flight Scis. Dept., Research Labs., 1974—; grad. instr. mech. engring. Purdue U., 1970-71. NDEA Title IV fellow, 1967-70; recipient Meritorious Tech. Contbn. award St. Louis sect. AIAA, 1977. Asso. fellow AIAA; mem. ASME (fluid mechanics com.). Presbyterian. Club: McDonnell Douglas Corp St Louis Mgmt. Contbr. articles to tech. jours. Home: 4575 Whisper Lake Dr Apt 8 Florissant MO 63033 Office: McDonnell Douglas Corp PO Box 516 Saint Louis MO 63166

BOWERS, EUGENE DYER, JR., insurance company executive; b. Monmouth, Ill., June 14, 1944; s. Eugene Dyer Bowers and Madeline Bernice (Britt) Young; m. Joyce Ann Demarais, June 10, 1967; children—Denise Michelle, Eugene Dyer. B.Acctg., Midstate Coll.-Peoria, 1975. Margins clk. Hayden Stone & Co., Chgo., 1962-64; foundry insp. Caterpillar Tractor Co., Peoria, Ill., 1968-70; field auditor Home Ins. Co., Peoria, 1970-74, field office audit supr., 1974-77, field office audit mgr., Charlotte, N.C., 1977-80, regional audit mgr., Mpls., 1980-84, sr. processing services officer premium audit, 1984—. Contbr. articles to publs. Served with USAF, 1964-68. Named Jaycee of Month, Riverview Germantown Hills Jaycees, 1972, Key Man, 1973. Mem. Nat. Soc. Ins. Premium Auditors (local v.p. 1978-79, com. chmn. 1982—). Republican. Roman Catholic. Home: 375 Blevens Dr Manchester NH 03104 Office: Home Ins Co 3000 Goffs Falls Rd PO Box 5160 Manchester NH 03108

BOWERS, FRANK DANA, botany educator; b. Fayetteville, Ark., Mar. 21, 1936; s. Frank M. and Bess Ann (McDonald) B.; m. Donna Jaye Olsen, Mar. 18, 1967. B.S., Southwest Mo. State U., 1966; M.S., U. Tenn., 1968, Ph.D., 1972. Asst. curator herbarium U. Tenn.-Knoxville, 1968-72; research assoc., 1973-75; asst. prof. botany, U. Wis.-Stevens Point, 1975-80, assoc. prof., 1980—. Contbr. articles to profl. jours. Mem. Am. Bryological and Lichenological Soc. (sec.-treas. 1978-80), Am. Soc. Plant Taxonomists, Internat. Assn. Plant Taxonomists, Soc. Econ. Botany. Baptist. Avocations: fishing, camping, painting. Home: 848 Oak Ridge Ln Stevens Point WI 54481 Office: U Wis Biology Dept Stevens Point WI 54481

BOWERS, MAYNARD CLAIRE, botanist; b. Battle Creek, Mich., Nov. 5, 1930; s. Frederick Claire and Elnora Alice (Hard) B.; A.B., Albion Coll., 1956; M.Ed., U. Va., 1960; Ph.D., U. Colo., 1966; m. Leenamari Kangas, Aug. 16, 1970; children—Maynard Claire, Janet Louise, Piiamari Riikka, Eerik Maynard Johannes. Tchr., Whittier Jr. High Sch., Flint, Mich., 1956-57, Meadowlawn Jr. High Sch., St. Petersburg, Fla., 1957-59; asst. prof. Towson (Md.) State Coll., 1960-62, Catonsville (Md.) Community Coll., 1961-62; prof. botany No. Mich. U., Marquette, 1966—; seasonal naturalist Nat. Park Service, Shenandoah Nat. Park, 1956, Glacier Nat. Park, 1957-66. Served with USAF, 1951-52. U. Colo. scholar, 1965-66; NSF grantee, 1959-60. Mem. Am. Bryological and Lichenological Soc., Internat. Assn. Bryologists, Internat. Assn. Plant Taxonomists, Internat. Orgn. Plant Biosystematists, Mich. Bot. Club, Nordic Bryoloigal Soc., Sigma Xi. Clubs: Am. Legion, Masons. Contbr. articles to profl. jours. Home: 2 Northwoods Ln Marquette MI 49855 Office: Dept Biology No Mich U Marquette MI 49855

BOWERS, NEIL AUSTIN, chemical company executive; b. Detroit, Mar. 16, 1936; s. Earl Austin and Thelma (Goodwin) Bowers Cullen; m. Patricia Kathleen Borland, Sept. 14, 1957; 1 dau., Cathleen Marie. Student Fla. State U., Eastern Mich. U.; A.B.A. in Fin., B.S.M.E., U. Okla.; M.S. in Edn., U. Mich. Area supr. Marathon Oil Co., Detroit, 1958-69; sales engr. Bowers-Siemon Chems., Coal City, Ill., 1969-72, mktg. mgr., 1972-74, v.p. engring., 1974-78, exec. v.p., Livonia, Mich., 1978-83; pres., chief exec. officer ACTS-BSC Inc., Plymouth, Mich., 1983—, also dir.; dir. Acts-BSC Inc., Livonia. Editor: Men of Steel, 1980; author articles for profl. jours.; holder patents abrasive cutting Hydra-clene, 1970, 81. Hon. sheriff Will County, Ill.; sustaining mem. Republican party; charter mem. Rep. Senatorial Task Force. Served with AUS, 1959-63. Mem. Wire Reinforcement Inst. (dir. 1978-82, chmn. continuing edn. com. 1983), Am. Soc. Metals, Wire Assn. Internat. (chmn. edn. com. 1983, long range planning and suppliers adv. com. 1985), Sigma Chi. Roman Catholic. Lodge: KC (3d degree). Office: ACTS-BSC Inc 1176 S Main St Plymouth MI 48170

BOWERSOX, HAROLD JONATHAN, osteopathic physician, surgeon; b. Youngstown, Ohio, May 23, 1941; s. David Frederick and Janis Mary (Hanna) B.; children from previous marriage—Laura Maureen, Stephanie Ann; m. Noelia Ester Rivera, Apr. 23, 1982; 1 child, Noelia Johanna. R.N., NYU, 1963; B.S., Mo. State U., 1965; D.O., Kirksville Coll., 1969. Diplomate Am. Bd. Osteo. Examiners. Intern York Meml. Hosp., Pa., 1969-70; practice medicine specializing osteo., Hanover, Pa., 1970-82; ind. health practioner Northeastern Ohio Gen. Hosp., Madison, 1982—. Mem. Nat. Republican Senatorial Com., Washington, 1984. Recipient Chase award Bellevue Sch. Nursing, 1963; Mosby scholar, 1969; Perrin T. Wilson scholar, 1969. Mem. Madison-Perry Co. of C., Northeastern Ohio Gen. Hosp. Assn., Am. Coll. Clin. Pharmacologists, Am. Osteo. Assn., Am. Coll. Osteo. Gen. Practioners, Lake County Hospice (trustee). Republican. Lutheran. Avocations: martial arts; art; drawing; painting; music. Home: 996 Dock Rd Madison OH 44057 Office: Justin Wise Med Bldg 3750 Center Rd Perry OH 44081

BOWLBY, RICHARD ERIC, computer systems analyst; b. Detroit, Aug. 17, 1939; s. Garner Milton and Florence Marie (Russell) B.; m. Gwendoline Joyce Coldwell, Apr. 29, 1967. B.A., Wayne State U., 1962. With Ford Motor Co., Detroit, 1962-65, 66—, now computer systems analyst; pres. 1300 Lafayette East-Coop., Inc., 1981-82. Mem. Antiquaries, Friends Asian Art, Friends Detroit Pub. Library, Friends Orch. Hall. Club: Founders Soc. (Detroit). Office: Ford Motor Co 300 Renaissance Ctr Suite 3000 Box 43314 Detroit MI 48243

BOWLING, DAVID SAMUEL, geophysicist; b. Bennett, Ky., July 10, 1929; s. Reece Madison and Nancy Elizabeth (Knipp) B.; B.A., Berea Coll., 1956; m. Anna Louise Ogle, Dec. 22, 1955; children—Marla Lucille, Theresa Anne, David Reece, John Anthony. Computer trainee Geophys. Service Inc., Dallas, 1956-56, 2d computer, 1956-57, 1st computer, 1957-59, seismologist, 1959-60, party chief, 1960-62; cons. geophysicist Bowling, Roberson and Ward Seismic Assos., Norman, Okla., 1962-63; area supr. explosives product group Monsanto Co., St. Louis, 1963-68; project engr. G.W. Murphy Industries Inc., Houston, 1968-70, ops. mgr., 1970; ptnr. White Engring. Assos. Inc., Joplin, Mo., 1970—, pres., 1972—; pres., prin. owner White Indsl. Seismology, Inc., 1983—. Served to sgt., U.S. Army, 1948-52. Registered geophysicist, Calif.; certified geologist Maine; certified profl. geol. scientist Am. Inst. Profl. Geologists. Mem. Soc. Exploration Geophysicists, AAAS, ASTM, Soc. Mining Engrs. of AIME, Soc. Am. Mil. Engrs., Seismol. Soc. Am., Am. Assn. Petroleum Geologists (assoc., founding mem. energy minerals div.). Methodist. Clubs: Masons, K.T. Patentee in field. Home: Route 7 Box 145 Joplin MO 64801 Office: PO Box 1256 Joplin MO 64801

BOWLING, WILLIAM GLASGOW, emeritus English language educator; b. St. Louis, May 7, 1902; s. William Walter and Mary Susan (Glasgow) B.; A.B., Washington U., St. Louis, 1924, A.M., 1925; postgrad. Harvard U., 1930-31; m. Violet Whelen, Aug. 3, 1933; 1 son, Townsend Whelen. Instr., asst. prof., assoc. prof. English, Washington U., 1925-70, prof. emeritus, 1970—, asst. to dean, acting dean, dean Univ. Coll., 1928-42; dean Coll. Liberal Arts, 1942-46; dean men, 1942-44; civilian adminstr. Pre-professional Unit of Army Specialized Tng. Program, Washington U., St. Louis, 1943-44, dean admissions, 1946-65, univ. historian, 1965-70, univ. grand marshal, 1960-68. Part-time drama critic St. Louis Times, 1929-30; pioneer at Washington U. in radio in edn., alumni insts. and ednl. motion pictures; exec. sec. Washington U. Assn. Lecture Series, 1940-47. Pres., Maryland PTA, Clayton, Mo., 1946-47. Recipient Washington U. Alumni award, 1960. Mem. Greater St. Louis Council Tchrs. of English (pres. 1936-39; exec. sec., 1939-41), Am. Assn. Collegiate Registrars and Admissions Officers (hon.; book rev. editor quarterly jour., College and University 1955-66), St. Louis Audubon Soc. (pres. 1950-52, mem. bd. dir., 1944—), Phi Delta Theta, Omicron Delta Kappa, Phi Delta Kappa. Republican. Episcopalian. Club: University (St. Louis). Contbr. to jours. Address: 7408 Washington Ave Saint Louis MO 63130

BOWMAN, MARK DOUGLAS, structural engineer; b. Logansport, Ind., Aug. 9, 1952; s. John Robert and Mabel Louise (Nelson) B.; B.S.C.E. (Elks scholar), Purdue U., 1974, M.S.C.E. (Nellie Munson award), 1975; Ph.D. (C.P. Siess award), U. Ill., 1981; m. Barbara Baerwald, Aug. 6, 1977; children—Katherine Elaine, Benjamin Robert. Civil engr. Chgo. Bridge & Iron Co., Oakbrook, Ill., summer 1974; teaching and lab. asst. Purdue U., West Lafayette, Ind., 1974-75; structural design engr. Precast/Schokbeton Inc., Kalamazoo, 1975-77; asst. prof. civil engring. Purdue U., 1981—. Mem. ASCE (chmn. com. fatigue and fracture of steel structures), Am. Concrete Inst. (com. fatigue concrete structures), Nat., Ind. socs. profl. engrs., Am. Soc. Engring. Edn., Nat. Geog. Soc., Sigma Xi, Phi Kappa Phi, Chi Epsilon, Tau Beta Pi, Triangle Frat. (chpt. advisor 1982—). Lutheran. Asst. editor Mich. Civil Engr., 1976-77. Contbr. articles to profl. jours. Home: 16 N 20 St Lafayette IN 47904 Office: Civil Engring Bldg Purdue U West Lafayette IN 47907

BOWMAN, MONROE BENGT, architect; b. Chgo., Aug. 28, 1901; s. Henry William and Ellen Mercedes (Bjork) B.; m. Louise Kohnmann, Nov. 1944; 1 son, Kenneth Monroe; B.Arch., Ill. Inst. Tech., 1924. Registered architect, Ill., Wis., Ind., Ohio, Colo. Asso., Benjamin H. Marshall, Chgo., 1926; exhibited models and photographs of Bowman Bros. comtemporary designs at Mus. Modern Art, N.Y.C., 1931; pvt. practice architecture, Chgo., 1941-44; asso. Monroe Bowman Assos., Chgo., 1945—; cons. Chgo. Dept. City Planning, City of Sparta (Wis.), Alfred Shaw, Architect. Mem. Navy League U.S. Important works include Boeing Aircraft bldgs., Wichita, Kans., Emerson Electric bldgs., St. Louis, Maytag Co., Newton, Iowa, Douglas Aircraft bldgs., Park Ridge, Ill., Shwayder Bros. bldgs., Denver, Clark Equipment Co., Buchannon, Mich., Radio-TV Sta. WHO, Des Moines, Foote, Cone & Belding offices, Chgo., Burridge Devel., Hinsdale, Ill., Yacht Club and recreational facilities, Lake Bemiji, Minn., United Airlines offices downtown Chgo., Automatic Sprinkler Corp., Chgo., King Machine Tool div. Am. Steel Foundries, Cin., Marine Terr. Apts., Chgo., Dorchester Park Apts., Chgo., Manteno (Ill.) State Hosp., No. Ill. Gas Co. bldgs., LaGrange, Joliet, Streator and Morris, 1340 Astor St. Apt. Bldg., Burnham Center, Chgo., NSF, Green Bank, W.Va., Naval Radio Research Sta., Sugar Grove, W.Va., Columbus Boy Choir Sch., Princeton, N.J., office bldg. and hotel, Charleston, W.Va. Home: 730 Ridge Ave Evanston IL 60201

BOWMAN, PASCO MIDDLETON, II, federal judge. U.S. cir. judge U.S. Ct. Appeals Eight Cir., Mo., 1983—. Office: US Ct Appeals 819 US Courthouse 811 Grand Ave Kansas City MO 64106*

BOWMAN, ROBERT ALLOTT, state treasurer; b. Evanston, Ill., Apr. 12, 1955; s. John Benjamin and Constance (Judkins) B. B.A., Harvard Coll., 1977; M.B.A., U. Pa., 1979. Spl. asst. domestic fin. U.S. Treasury Dept., Washington, 1979-81; assoc. mcpl. fin. Goldman, Sachs & Co., N.Y.C., 1981-83; state treas. State of Mich., Lansing, 1983—. Democrat. Methodist. Office: PO Box 15128 Lansing MI 48901

BOWMAN, SUZZANNE KUHN, phys. therapist; b. Durham, N.C., Sept. 13, 1948; d. Harold Hunter and Beatrice Laura (Hart) Kuhn; student U. Miami, 1966-69; cert. in phys. therapy, Ohio State U., 1971; married. Staff phys. therapist Highland View Hosp., Cleve., 1971-73; chief phys. therapy Sunny Acres Hosp., Cleve., 1973-78; asst. chief phys. therapy Highland View Hosp., Cleve., 1976-78; dir. phys. therapy Friendship Village Health Center, Schaumberg, Ill., 1978; phys. medicine mgr. Good Samaritan Hosp., Downers Grove, Ill., 1978—; chmn. bd., dir. phys. therapy Ill. Therapeutic Assocs., Ltd., 1980—; pres. Midwest Therapeutic Assocs., Ltd.; pvt. practice phys. therapy; instr. trainer CPR, 1977—. Recipient Outstanding Service award U. Miami, 1968. Mem. Am. Phys. Therapy Assn. (Ill. quality assurance com. 1979-80, Eastern dist. edn. com. 1979-80), Chicagoland Phys. Therapy Dirs. Forum, Mortar Board. Quaker. Home: 939 Cherry Hills Naperville IL 60540

BOWMAN-DALTON, BURDENE KATHRYN, educator, computer consultant; b. Magnolia, Ohio, July 13, 1937; d. Ernest Mowles and Mary Kathryn (Long) Bowman; B.M.E., Capital U., 1959; M.A. in Edn., Akron U., 1967, postgrad. 1976—; m. Louis W. Dalton, Mar. 13, 1979. Profl. vocalist, various clubs in the East, 1959-60; music tchr. East Liverpool (Ohio) City Schs., 1959-62; music tchr. Revere Local Schs., Akron, Ohio, 1962-75, elem. tchr., 1975-80, elem. team leader/computer cons., 1979-85, tchr. middle sch. math., gift-talented, computer literacy, 1981—; local and regional dir., Olympics of the Mind, also program chmn. for computer problem for world finals. Mem. Citizen Com., Akron, 1975-76; profl. rep. Bath Assn. to Help, 1978-80; audit com. BATH, 1977-79; volunteer chmn. Antique Car Show, Akron, 1972-81. Martha Holden Jennings Found. grantee, 1977-78; Title IV ESEA grantee, 1977-81. Mem. Assn. for Devel. of Computer-Based Instructional Systems, Assn. Supervision and Curriculum Devel., Ohio Assn. for Gifted Children, Phi Beta. Republican. Lutheran. Home: 353 Retreat Dr Akron OH 44313 Office: 3195 Spring Valley Rd Bath OH 44210

BOWSER, EMILIE LOUISE, nurse, educator; b. Newark, Ohio, July 16, 1941; d. James Elbert and Geraldine Mae (Utts) Drumm; m. Gary L. Bowser, June 6, 1964 (div. July 1980); children—Deborah, Diana, David. B.S.N. in Nursing, Ohio State U., 1964; M.S. in Nursing, Wayne State U., 1984. R.N., Ohio. Charge nurse West Paces Ferry Hosp., Atlanta, 1972-73; clin. instr. St. Vincent's Hosp., Toledo, Ohio, 1976; staff nurse Toledo Hosp., parttime 1976—; staff nurse Flower Hosp., Toledo, 1978-79; clin. instr. U. Toledo, 1979; asst. prof. nursing Owens Tech. Coll., Toledo, 1979—, cons. continuing edn., 1981—; advisor Nat. Student Nurses Assn., Toledo, 1981—. Cub scout com. chmn. Wolverine council Boy Scouts Am., 1983—; mem. youth com. Trinity Episcopal Ch. Mem. Ohio Nurses Assn. (publicity com. 1980-82), Bedford Band Boosters, Alpha Delta Pi. Republican. Club: Tamaron Country (Toledo). Home: 1765 Heather Temperance MI 48182 Office: Owens Tech Coll Oregon Rd Toledo OH 43699

BOXWELL, GEORGE FREDERICK, osteopathic physician; b. Detroit, July 20, 1951; s. Norman Lloyd and Rebecca (Manning) B.; m. Grace L. Hoerauf, June 23, 1973; children—Jennifer Ann, Daniel F., Katherine P. B.A., Olivet Coll., 1973; D.O., Kirksville Coll. Osteo. Medicine, 1976. Diplomate Nat. Bd. Examiners. Intern Art Centre Hosp., Detroit, 1976-77; pvt. practice medicine St. Helen Med. Ctr., Mich., 1979—; dir. continuing med. edn. Tolfree Hosp., West Branch, Mich., 1980—, v.p. med. staff, 1983-85, pres., 1985—. Served with USPHS, 1977-79. Mem. Am. Osteo. Assn., Mich. Assn. Osteo. Physicians and Surgeons. Avocations: Landscaping, cross country skiing, golf, camping. Home: 9272 Tippedy St Saint Helen MI 48656 Office: Saint Helen Med Ctr 1360 N St Helen Rd Saint Helen MI 48656

BOYCE, STANLEY EDMAN, educator; b. Glendale, W.Va., Nov. 11, 1947; s. Marion Stanley and Aurelia Eudoris (Wickham) B.; B.A. in Speech, David

Lipscomb Coll., 1970; postgrad. Muskingum Coll., 1975-76, Kent State U., 1975-76, Bowling Green State U., 1980; m. Marlene Ann Maxwell, July 5, 1968; children—Tasha Dawn, Tanya Beth. Jailer, Coshocton County Sheriff's Office, Coshocton, Ohio, 1975; tchr. English Riverview Local Sch. Dist., Warsaw, Ohio, 1976-77; tchr. Licking County Joint Vocat. Sch., Newark, Ohio, 1977-79; tchr. English, Coshocton County Joint Vocat. Sch., 1979—, also advisor student newspaper and yearbook; mem. East Central Uniserv Com. Served with USN, 1971-75. Mem. Ohio Vocat. Assn., Am. Vocat. Assn., NEA, Ohio Edn. Assn., Eastern Ohio Edn. Assn., Internat. Platform Assn., Coshocton County Joint Vocat. Sch. Edn. Assn. Republican. Mem. Ch. of Christ. Clubs: Coshocton County Sportsmen Assn., Masons. Home: 602 Hill St Coshocton OH 43812 Office: 23640 County Rd 202 Coshocton OH 43812

BOYD, ALAN CONDUITT, lawyer; b. Indpls., Aug. 19, 1926; s. Alan Wilson and Dorothy Rodman (Lee) B.; m. Anne Crete Fuller, Aug. 30, 1947; children—Anne Margaret Boyd McKisson and Amy Lucretia Boyd Garrett. B.B.A., U. of Mich., 1947, J.D. cum laude, 1951. Bar: Ind. 1951, Ohio 1958. Assoc., Barnes, Hickam, Pantzer & Boyd, Inpls., 1951-58; atty. Owens-Illinois, Toledo, 1958-77, asst. gen. counsel and asst. sec., 1977-83, assoc. gen. counsel and asst. sec., 1973—. Dir., sec. Lucas County Unit Am. Cancer Soc., Toledo; sec. Greater Toledo Corp. Mem. ABA, Ohio State Bar Assn., Toledo Bar Assn. Republican. Club: Inverness (Toledo) Home: 5348 Northbrook Ct Sylvania OH 43560 Office: Owens-Illinois Inc One Seagate Toledo OH 43666

BOYD, CHRISTOPHER S(TEPHEN), lawyer; b. Saginaw, Mich., Sept. 4, 1951; s. Leo Joseph and Betty Jean (Meyer) B.; m. Virginia Margaret Michelson, Oct. 5, 1979; 2 children. B.S. in Bus. Adminstrn., Central Mich. U., 1974; J.D., Wayne State U., 1978. Bar: Mich. 1978, U.S. Dist. Ct. (ea. dist.) Mich. 1978. Staff investigator Mich. Jud. Tenure Commn., Detroit, 1976-78, staff atty., 1978-79; asst. city atty. City of Saginaw, 1979; assoc. Gorte, Williams & Wellman, P.C., Saginaw, 1979-81; ptnr. Bay/Saginaw Law Ctrs., P.C., Saginaw, 1981-84; pros. atty., Saginaw County, 1985—. Hall of Fame inductee S. S. Peter and Paul High Sch., Saginaw, 1983. Mem. Assn. Trial Lawyers Am., Mich. Trial Lawyers Assn. Democrat. Roman Catholic. Office: Pros Atty Office Govtl Ctr 111 S Michigan Saginaw MI 48602

BOYD, DOROTHY RUTH, musician, educator; b. Atlantic City, Oct. 20, 1907; d. Herbert C. and Alice Frambes (Boice) Doughty; pvt. student of music, 1923-25; student Progressive Series Piano Inst., Jenkintown, Pa., 1924, Muskingum Coll., summers 1926-30; m. Merton Greer Boyd, June 24, 1930; children—Alys J. Boyd Carpenter, Merilyn J. Boyd Drumm, Merton Greer, Mildred K. Boyd Hibbard. Propr. pvt. music studios in N.J. and Ohio, 1924—, Mansfield, Ohio, bgng. 1957, now in Lexington, Ohio; adjudicator, condr. music workshops; pres. Coshocton (Ohio) Music Club, 1944-45; organist, choir dir. Cambridge (Ohio) First Baptist Ch., 1930-37; organist Newcomerstown (Ohio) Methodist Ch., 1938-41, Coshocton Evang. and Reformed Ch., 1942-46, St. Paul Lutheran Ch., Mansfield, 1958-80, South Side Christian Ch., Mansfield, 1983—; choir dir. Bucyrus (Ohio) First Meth. Ch., 1947-57. Active local Camp Fire Girls, Girl Scouts, 4-H Club; mem. bd. Mansfield YWCA, 1960-62, 74-76; mem. women's com. Mansfield Symphony Soc. Mem. Nat. Guild Piano Tchrs., Nat. Organ and Piano Guild, Nat. Guild Auditions (chmn. Mansfield area 1978—), Music Tchrs. Nat. Assn., Ohio Music Tchrs. Assn. (county chmn. 1957-60, vice chmn. N. Central dist. 1976—, chmn. 1961-67), Richland County Music Tchrs. Assn. (sec.-treas. 1980-82 83-84), Nat. Fedn. Music Clubs, Independent Music Tchrs. Forum (state chmn. 1977-80), Am. Coll. Musicians, Mansfield Music Study Club (sec. 1972-77). Republican. Mem. Christian Ch. Club: Order Eastern Star. Address: 30 Darby Dr Lexington OH 44904

BOYD, GLENDA LORENE, home economics educator; b. Evansville, Ind., Feb. 14, 1937; d. James Glendale and Helen Marie (Johnson) Riney; m. Gerald David Boyd, Aug. 30, 1968. B.A., U. Evansville, 1971, M.A., 1975. With Mead Johnson & Co., 1957-68, lab. asst. pharm. product devel. Research Center, 1961-68; educator vocational day care and child devel. classes, vocat. class Central High Sch., Evansville, 1971—. Mem. Am. Home Econs. Assn., Nat. Tchrs. Assn., Ind. Home Econs. Assn. (dist. pub. relations chmn.), Ind. Tchrs. Assn., Evansville Home Econs. Assn., Evansville Tchrs. Assn. Home: 13201 Woodland Ln Evansville IN 47711 Office: 5400 1st Ave Evansville IN 47710

BOYD, GREGORY ALLAN, business systems equipment company manager; b. Detroit, Aug. 21, 1951; s. John L. and Frieda R. Boyd; B.S. in Bus. Adminstrn., Wayne State U., Detroit, 1973; M.B.A. in Fin., U. Detroit, 1978. Asst. credit mgr. Hughes & Hatcher, Inc., Detroit, 1973-76; acct. Cadillac div. Gen. Motors Corp., Detroit, 1976-78; credit supr. Fed.-Mogul Corp., Southfield, Mich., 1978-79, credit mgr., 1979-82; group credit and collection mgr., Burroughs Corp., 1982—; membership recruiter Jr. Achievement Southeastern Mich., 1978. Mem. Am. Mgmt. Assn., Nat. Assn. Credit Mgmt., Nat. Black M.B.A. Assn., Assn. M.B.A. Execs., Omega Psi Phi. Home: 30200 Southfield Rd Apt 208 Southfield MI 48076 Office: Burroughs Corp Burrough Pl Detroit MI

BOYD, JANET SCOTT, nursing school administrator, nursing education and nursing research consultant; b. Haverstraw, N.Y., July 21, 1921; d. Russel Thomas and Nora (Burke) S.; m. Robert David Boyd, Mar. 21, 1953; children—Robert Jr., Bruce Scott, Keith Ian. B.S.N., Case-Western Res., 1948; M.A., U. Chgo., 1952; Ph.D., U. Wis., 1976. Asst. prof. U. Wis., Madison, 1961-65, dept. head nursing, 1965-69; asst. exec. adminstr. Wis. Nurses Assn., Madison, 1972-75; dir. nursing sch. Eastern Mich. U., Ypsilanti, 1976—; bd. dirs. Midwest Alliance Nursing, Indpls., 1982-84; pres. Mich. Colls. Nursing, 1978-82; v.p. Mich. League Nursing, Detroit, 1978-84; chmn. legis. com. Mich. Nurses Assn., East Lansing, 1977-83. Office: Eastern Mich U Dept Nursing Baccalaureat Ypsilanti MI 48197

BOYD, JOHN KENT, advt. exec.; b. Portsmouth, Ohio, Oct. 17, 1910; s. Lambert Thomas and Faery Ann (Ritter) B.; student Tulane U., New Orleans, 1927-29; m. Jeanne Marie Dunlap, Dec. 26, 1935; children—John Kent, Barbara Ann. Mem. staff advt. dept. Am. Rolling Mill Co., Middletown, Ohio, 1929-31; advt. mgr. Pitts. and Midway Coal Mining Co., Kansas City, Mo., 1932-35; v.p. Ferry-Hanly Co., 1935-44; partner Bruce B. Brewer & Co., Kansas City and Mpls., 1944-66; pres., chief exec. officer Bruce B. Brewer Co., Inc., 1967-72, chmn. bd., chief exec. officer, 1972-75; dir. Marco Mfg. Co.; past pres., dir. Quivira, Inc.; pres. Kaybee, Inc. Co-chmn. United Funds publicity com., 1953; dir. United Cerebral Palsy Assn. of Kansas City; active Boy Scouts Am.; bd. govs. Starlight Theatre Assn., YMCA, Quiet Birdmen; bd. dirs. Kansas City Crime Commn. Control adv. com. FAA Kanas City Air Traffic. Named Man of Yr. in Gen. Aviation, 1969; recipient silver medal Am. Advt. Fedn., 1972. Mem. AIM, Nat. Aero. Assn., Am. Legion, Kansas City Sr. Golf Assn., Kansas City Promotion Com., Airplane Owners and Pilots Assn. (nat.). Am. Mktg. Assn. (dir. Kansas City chpt.), Am. Royal Assn. (gov.), C. of C., Snipe Class Internat. Racing Assn., Nat. Pilots Assn. (dir.) Am. Bonanza Soc., Air Force Assn., Silver Wings. Clubs: Kansas City, Advt., Sales Execs., Quivira Country, Mission Hills Country, Aero of Kansas City, OX5 of Am.; Capital Hill (Washington); Quivira Sailing (past commodore); Diamondhead Yacht and Country; Bay-Waveland Yacht. Author: Jerry Dalrymple, 1931. Home: 3400 Yacht Club Circle Bay Saint Louis MS 39520 Office: 849 W 52d Terr Kansas City MO 64112

BOYD, WILLARD LEE, museum executive; b. St. Paul, Mar. 29, 1927; s. Willard Lee and Frances L. (Collins) B.; B.S.L., U. Minn., 1949, LL.B., 1951; LL.M. (William W. Cook fellow 1951-52), U. Mich., 1952, S.J.D., 1962; LL.D., Buena Vista Coll., 1969, Coe Coll., 1969, Marycrest Coll., 1974, U. Fla., 1976; L.H.D., Cornell (Iowa) Coll., 1974, U. Iowa, 1981; Litt.D., Simpson Coll., 1976; m. Susan Kuehn, Aug. 28, 1954; children—Elizabeth Kuehn, Willard Lee III, Thomas Henry. Admitted to Minn. bar, 1951, Iowa bar, 1958; assoc. firm Dorsey, Windhorst, Hannaford, Whitney & Halladay, Mpls., 1952-54; mem. faculty U. Iowa Coll. law, 1954-81, prof., 1961—, assoc. dean Coll. Law, 1964, v.p. acad. affairs, dean faculties at univ., 1964-69, pres., 1969-81, pres. emeritus, 1981—; pres. Field Mus. of Natural History, Chgo., 1981—. U.S. del. to Spl. Commn. on Succession of The Hague Conf. Pvt. Internat. Law, 1970-72; mem. commn. on fed. relations Am. Council Edn., 1971-74, bd. dirs., 1978-81; chmn. Iowa Gov.'s Com. for Assemblies on Future of Iowa, 1972-74; chmn. Iowa 2000 Com., 1975-78; mem. Nat. Council on Arts, 1976-82; mem. Iowa Coordinating Council for Post High Sch. Edn., 1968-81, chmn., 1976-77; mem. U.S. Senate Commn. on Operation of the Senate, 1975-76; mem. Nat. Com. on Careers for Older Ams., 1978—; mem. Arts, Humanities and Older Ams. Steering Com., 1981—. Bd. dirs. Center for Research Libraries, 1965-68, chmn. 1968; bd. commrs. Nat. Commn. on Accrediting, 1970-74, pres., 1974; bd. dirs. Harry S. Truman Library Inst., 1969-81; bd. dirs. Council Post-secondary Accreditation, 1977-81, exec. com., 1978-81; adv. bd. Met. Opera Assn., 1978—; exec. com. div. baccalaureate and higher degree programs Nat. League Nursing, 1979-81. Served with USNR, 1945-46. Recipient Outstanding Achievement award U. Minn., 1972. Mem. Am. Bar Assn. (past chmn. com. social, labor and indsl. legislation 1963-65, chmn. 1965-66, comparative law sect., chmn. ednl. policy com. legal edn. sect. 1975-78, mem. council 1975-82, chmn. 1980-81, mem. clin. legal edn. guidelines project 1977-80, task force on lawyer competency 1978-79), Iowa Bar Assn., Am. Assn. UN, Nat. Assn. State Univs. and Land Grant Colls. (commn. arts and scis. 1969-73, adv. com. Office Advancement Pub. Negro Colls. 1972-79), Assn. Am. Univs. (exec. com. 1977-81, chmn. 1979-80), Order of Coif. Congregationalist. Contbr. articles to profl. jours. Home: 3800 N Lake Shore Dr Apt 3A Chicago IL 60613 Office: Field Mus Natural History Roosevelt Rd at Lake Shore Dr Chicago IL 60605

BOYD, WILLIAM MICHAEL, educational administrator; b. Starkville, Miss., Aug. 23, 1941; s. Billie and Edna Mae (Everette) B.; m. Eliza Ackers, Feb. 12, 1962 (div. May 1967); children—Stacey Diane, Alicia Ann. B.A., Harris Tchrs. Coll., 1964; M.Ed., U. Mo.-St. Louis, 1972. Cert. tchr., prin., Mo. Janitor Hawk Janitor Service, St. Louis, 1959-62; postal clk. U.S. Postal Service, St. Louis, 1962-64; tchr. St. Louis Pub. Schs., 1964-70, adminstr., 1970—. Treas. LaSalle United Methodist Ch., St. Louis, 1977—; usher LaSalle Usher Bd., 1977. Mem. Adminstrs. Assn., Kappa Alpa Psi. Lodge: Prince Hall Masons. Avocations: home decorating, hunting, fishing, camping. Home: 3212a Rutger St Saint Louis MO 63104 Office: Toussaint L'Ouverture Middle Sch 3021 Hickory St Saint Louis MO 63104

BOYER, BRUCE HATTON, writer, corporate executive; b. Evanston, Ill., Oct. 5, 1946; s. Paul Frederick and Betty (Hatton) B.; m. Janice R. Muhr, July 25, 1982; 1 child, Samuel David. B.A. cum laude, Amherst Coll., 1968; M.A., Ph.D., UCLA, 1973. Asst. prof. Amherst Coll., Mass., 1972-74; copywriter J. Walter Thompson, Chgo., 1978-79; freelance writer William Morris Agy., N.Y.C., 1974—; exec. creative dir. Hammacher Schlemmer & Co., Chgo., 1984—. Author: The Solstice Cipher, 1979. Producer Brillianteen youth program McGaw YMCA of Evanston, 1983—; bd. dirs. Ctr. for French Colonial Studies, Prairie du Rocher, Ill., 1983—. Recipient Edward Poole Lay fellow Amherst Coll., 1968-69, Nat. Def. Edn. Act Title IV fellow UCLA, 1969-72. Mem. Mystery Writers of Am., Chgo. Assn. Direct Mktg. Home: 1242 Asbury Ave Evanston IL 60202 Office: Hammacher Schlemmer & Co 212 W Superior St Chicago IL 60626

BOYER, DANIEL BRUCE, dentistry educator; b. Esterville, Iowa, Apr. 21, 1944; s. Bruce D. and Shirley L. (Yager) B.; m. E. Marcia Hazelett, June 13, 1970; 1 child, Daniel F. B.A., U. Iowa, 1966, D.D.S., 1970; Ph.D., Poly. Inst. N.Y., 1975. Asst. prof. U. Iowa, Iowa City, 1974-78, assoc. prof. dentistry, 1978—; cons. Council Dental Edn., Council Dental Therapeutics Am. Dental Assn., 1983—. Contbr. articles to profl. jours. U. Iowa scholar 1967-69. Fellow Acad. Dental Materials; mem. Internat. Assn. Dental Research (pres. Iowa sect. 1985—), Am. Dental Assn., Iowa Dental Assn., Univ. Dist. Dental Soc., Johnson County Dental Soc., Dental Materials Group Am. Assn. Dental Research, Sigma Xi, Psi Omega, Omicron Kappa Upsilon. Democrat. Avocations: micro computer programming; travel; reading; fishing. Home: 1004 Penkridge Dr Iowa City IA 52240 Office: Coll Dentistry U Iowa Iowa City IA 52242

BOYER, DENNIS LEE, lawyer, lobbyist; b. Allentown, Pa., July 13, 1949; s. Erwin A. and Grace Benner (Choyce) B. B.A., Kutztown State Coll., 1975; J.D., W.Va. U., 1978. Bar: W.Va. 1978, Wis. 1981. Legal counsel W.Va. Dept. Labor, Charleston, 1978-79; cons. labor, Weirton, W.Va., 1979-80; legis. dir. Am. Fedn. State, County, and Mcpl. Employees, Madison, Wis., 1980—. Author: Public Employee Bargaining, 1978; Prevailing Wages, 1979. Del. Democratic Nat. Conv., Miami, Fla., 1972; candidate for Pa. State Assembly, 1974. Served to sgt. USAF, 1967-71; Vietnam. Dept. Labor grantee, 1977. Mem. Labor and Farm Party. Home: 410 Rogers Madison WI 53703 Office: AFSCME 5 Odana Ct Madison WI 53719

BOYER, DOROTHY MARGARET, railroad co. exec.; b. Kochville, Mich., Nov. 23, 1910; d. Herbert Adams and Mary Barbara (Gerber) Otto; student U. Mich., 1929-31; B.A., Central State Tchrs. Coll., 1933; m. Harold C. Boyer, Oct. 12, 1940 (dec. May 1965); children—Marjorie J. Boyer Wheaton, Joan B. Boyer Corner, Herbert C. Tchr., Jewett Sch., Kochville, 1933-35, Herig Sch., Saginaw, Mich., 1935-40; chmn. bd. Iowa Terminal R.R. Co., Mason City and Charles City, Iowa, 1965—. Pres. woman's assn. Westminster Presbyn. Ch., Detroit, 1963, elder, 1973-75, sec., 1978, bd. trustees, 1976-78. Club: Lathrup Village (Mich.) Woman's. Home: 18525 Roseland Blvd Lathrup Village MI 48076 Office: PO Box 450 Mason City IA 50401

BOYER, JAMES RAYMOND, manufacturing company executive, engineering, manufacturing consultant; b. St. Louis, Sept. 9, 1949; s. Richard Lynn and Cecilia (Thebeau) B.; m. Christine Marie Kohler, May 8, 1969; children—Jamie Christine, Julie Caryn, Joyce Carol. B.S. in Bus. Adminstrn., U. Mo., 1971. Cert. mfg. engr. Asst. mgr. Kelly Tire, St. Louis, 1970-71; asst. gen. mgr. Mound City Screw, St. Louis, 1972-79; v.p., gen. mgr. Essex Industries, St. Louis, 1979—. Bd. dirs. Jefferson Community Coll., St. Louis, 1984-85; mem. PTA bd. Notre Dame High Sch. Pres. Holy Name Soc., St. Gabriel's St. Louis, 1979. Mem. Soc. Mfg. Engrs. (past treas., sec., chmn.). Office: Essex Screw Products Co 6477 Manchester St St Louis MO 63139

BOYKE, BRUCE CARL, contractor, concrete and masonry; b. Chgo., May 12, 1930; s. Carl and Elsie Marie (La Ffin) B.; student public schs., Zion, Ill.; m. Kathleen J. McManaman, Sept. 16, 1950;children—Laura, Karen, Bruce, Blair, Kerry. Founder, pres. Bruce Concrete Constrn., Inc., Skokie, Ill., 1959—; formed Bruce Boyke Masonry Corp., Skokie, 1963—. Bruce Boyke Imperial Manor, Waukegan, 1964 (pres.); founder Bruce Boyke's Imperial Towers, Waukegan, 1968—. Spl. mem. Boy Scouts America. Republican committeeman Waukegan, 1951-53; pres. Village of Green Oaks, 1977-81. Served with AUS, 1947-51. Mem. Chgo. Assn. Commerce and Industry (indsl. devel. com.), Lake County Contractors Assn., Zion Benton C. of C., Waukegan-North Chicago C. of C. Home: Green Oaks Libertyville IL 60048 Office: 805 Baldwin Waukegan IL 60085

BOYKIN, NANCY MERRITT, school administrator; b. Washington, Mar. 20; d. Matthew and Mary Gertrude (White) Merritt; m. Ulysses Wilhelm Boykin, Apr. 17, 1965; 1 dau. by previous marriage—Taunya Lovell Banks. B.S., D.C. Tchrs. Coll.; M.A., Howard U., M.S.W., 1965; Ph.D., U. Mich., 1976. Employee relations counselor Office Chief of Fin., U.S. Army, Washington; adminstrv. asst. to Civilian Aide to Sec. of Def., Washington; policewoman Met. Police Dept., Washington; social worker Dept. Pub. Welfare, Washington; adminstrv. asst. to dir. Active Community Teams, Inc., Detroit, 1965-66; dir. continuing edn. for girls program Detroit Pub. Schs., 1966—; cons. U.S. Dept. Edn., 1982; presdl. appointee Nat. Adv. Council on Extension and Continuing Edn., 1973-80. Mem. Mich. Bd. Examiners of Social Workers, 1978-83; mem. Mich. Republican Com., 1975-80, 83—; presdl. appointee to nat. adv. bd. Community Coll. of Air Force, 1984—; gov.'s appointee Mich. Youth Adv. Com., 1984-87; sec. 1st Rep. Dist., 1973-77; mem. Nat. Black Republicans., 1972—. Named Educator of Yr., Nat. Black Women's Polit. Leadership Caucus, 1981; recipient Placque in recognition distinguished contbn. post-sec. edn. Pres.'s Nat. Adv. Com., 1973-80; Spirit of Detroit award, 1979; others. Mem. Profl. Women's Network, Nat. Assn. Supervision and Curriculum Devel., Detroit Orgn. of Sch. Adminstrs., Nat. Assn. Black Sch. Educators, Detroit Assn. Univ. Mich. Women, Sch. Edn. Alumni Assn. Wayne State U. (bd. govs.), U. Mich. Alumnae Assn., Mich. Assn. Concerned with Sch. Age Parents, Phi Delta Kappa. Contbr. articles to profl. jours. Home: 17224 Fairfield Ave Detroit MI 48221 Office: 2200 Ewald Circle Detroit MI 48238

BOYLAN, BRIAN RICHARD, author, theatre director, photographer; b. Chgo., Dec. 11, 1936, s. Francis Thomas and Mary Catherine (Kane) B.; student Loyola U., 1954-58; children—Rebecca, Gregory, Ingrid. Editor, Jour. AMA, Med. World News, The Statesman, 1956-64; author, 1965—; works include: The New Heart, 1969; Infidelity, 1971; Benedict Arnold: The Dark Eagle, 1973; A Hack in a Hurry, 1980; Final Trace, 1983; works include 12 books, 3 plays, 2 screenplays; photographer, 1966—; theatre dir., 1970—; works include 31 plays, videotapes and films. Home: 1530 S 6th St Minneapolis MN 55454

BOYLE, KAMMER, management psychologist; b. New Orleans, June 17, 1946; d. Benjamin Franklin and Ethel Clair (Kammer) B.; m. Edward Turner Barfield, July 23, 1966 (div. 1975); children—Darren Barfield, Meloe Barfield. B.S. in Mgmt., magna cum laude, U. West Fla., 1976; Ph.D. in Indsl./Organizational Psychology, U. Tenn., 1982. Lic. psychologist, Ohio, Tenn. Pvt. practice mgmt. psychology, Knoxville, 1978-81; teaching and research asst. U. Tenn., Knoxville, 1977-81; mgmt. trainer CIA, Washington, 1978; cons. PRADCO, Cleve., 1982-83; pres., cons. Mgmt. and Assessment Services, Inc., Cleve., 1983—; author and presenter ann. Conf. Am. Psychol. Assn., 1980, Southwestern Psychol. Conf., 1979. Mem. Jr. League Am., Pensacola, Fla., 1970-75; treas. Bar Aux., Pensacola, 1971. Recipient Capital Gifts Stipend, U. Tenn., 1976-80; Walter Bonham fellow, 1980-81. Mem. Cleve. Psychol. Assn., Orgn. Devel. Inst., Am. Psychol. Assn., Acad. of Mgmt., Soc. of Advancement of Mgmt. (pres. 1974-75), Am. Soc. Tng. and Devel. (chpt. rep. career devel. 1984—). Office: Mgmt & Assessment Services Inc Four Commerce Park Sq Suite 600 Cleveland OH 44122-5403

BOYLE, MICHAEL, mayor; b. Los Angeles, Jan. 19, 1944; s. Harold James and Ethel Loretta (Ryan) B.; m. Anne C. Howell, Apr. 22, 1965; children—Maureen A., Michael E., Patrick G., James T., Margaret Mary. B.A. in Bus., Creighton U., Omaha, 1973, J.D., 1977. Bar: Nebr. Assoc., Erickson, Sederstrom, Omaha, 1983—; mayor City of Omaha, 1981—; chief dep. Douglas County Election Commr. (Nebr.), 1968-72, commr., 1972-81; chmn. Omaha Pub. Sch. Com. to Investigate Election Irregularities; dir. Greater Omaha Corp. Bd. dirs. Met. Area Planning Agy., Omaha; bd. dirs. Combined Health Agencies Drive; bd. dirs. Boys Town Boosters; mem. City of Omaha Elmwood Park Task Force; mem. St. Cecilia's Cathedral Parish Council, Omaha; mem. St. Cecilia's Elem./Cathedral High Bd. Edn., Omaha. Mem. ABA, Nebr. State Bar Assn., Omaha Bar Assn., Nebr. League Municipalities (v.p. 1983, pres.-elect), U.S. Conf. of Mayors (community, housing and econ. devel. com.). Democrat. Roman Catholic. Office: Office of Mayor 1819 Farnam St Suite 300 Omaha NE 68183

BOYLE, PATRICIA J., state justice. Justice Mich. Supreme Ct., Lansing. Office: Supreme Ct Law Bldg PO Box 30052 Lansing MI 48909*

BOYLES, LARRY REX, retail and mail order photographic marketing company executive; b. Whiting, Iowa, Mar. 31, 1936; s. Rex Slater and Dorothy May (Crossley) B.; student Morningside Coll., 1956-60, 62-64; m. Olga Jo Dobler, Aug. 10, 1963; children—Michael Rex, Kimberly Sue Daniels, Spencer Ryan. Area mgr. Marquette Corp., Sioux City, Iowa, 1965-66; dist. mgr. Continental Albums, Inc., Sioux City, 1967-70, area mgr., Mpls., 1970-72, nat. sales mgr., Omaha, 1972-80; nat. sales mgr. Am. Family Products, Omaha, 1973-80; pres., editor Merit Pubs., Inc., Omaha, 1976-80; pres. C. & B. Enterprises, Sioux City, 1968-81; pres., nat. sales mgr. Am-Fam Corp., Omaha, 1980—; cons. Scherling Corp., 1972-80, A & A Photo Service, 1973—, Kemmer Assocs. Inc., 1983—. Mem. Greater Omaha C. of C., Photo Mktg. Assn. Republican. Clubs: Blair County, Masons. Editor, pub. bicentennial edit. Who's Who in Nebraska, 1976-77. Home: Route 2 Pioneer Hills Blair NE 68008 Office: PO Box 14075 W Omaha Station Omaha NE 68114

BOYSAW, HAROLD EDWARD, former public welfare administrator; b. Joliet, Ill., Oct. 28, 1912; s. John and Julia (Fleming) B.; B.A., Ill. Wesleyan U., 1938, L.H.D., 1965; M.A., U. Chgo., 1952; m. Lucille Williams, Aug. 10, 1941. Caseworker, City Chgo. Relief Adminstrn., 1938-41; with Cook County Dept. Pub. Aid, Chgo., 1941-75, supervising caseworker, 1948-52, asst. office supr., 1952-60, office supr., 1960-62, adminstrv. field supr., 1962-69, dep. dir. adminstrv. services, 1969-74, asst. to dir. community services, 1974-75. Mem. Citizens Com. Juvenile Ct. Bd. dirs. Chgo. chpt. Am. Cancer Soc.; former bd. dirs. Big Bros. Met. Chgo., Chgo. Lung Assn.; trustee Ill. Children's Home and Aid Soc.; adv. council Ill. Council Aging, Chgo. Office for Sr. Citizens; bd. dirs. Exec. Service Corps, Chgo. Served with U.S. Army, 1943-45. Mem. Nat. Assn. Social Workers, Acad. Certified Social Workers, Am. Pub. Welfare Assn., Am. Sociol. Assn., Ill. Welfare Assn., Chgo. Urban League, NAACP, Nat. Conf. Social Welfare, Alpha Phi Alpha. Club: City (gov.) (Chgo.). Home: 11360 S Aberdeen St Chicago IL 60643

BOYSEN, THOMAS J., podiatrist; b. Chgo., Feb. 25, 1946; s. Vernon L. and Irene B.; B.S., No. Ill. U., 1968; D. Podiatric Medicine, Ill. Coll. Podiatric Medicine, 1972; m. Stephanie Hutter, Oct. 9, 1970; 1 dau., Wendi. Resident in surgery St. Bernard Hosp., Chgo., 1972-73; practice podiatry Oak Forest, Ill., 1974—, mem. staff St. Anne's Hosp. West, Northlake, Ill., Northwest Surgicare, Arlington Heights, Ill., St. Anne's Hosp., Chgo., Mercy Health Center, Justice, Ill. Diplomate Am. Bd. Podiatric Surgery. Mem. Ill. Podiatry Soc., Am. Podiatry Assn., Am. Public Health Assn., Ill. Podiatry Soc. (past pres. Zone 11, 2d v.p., del. to bd., sec.). Office: 5601 W Victoria Dr Oak Forest IL 60452

BOZZOLA, JOHN JOSEPH, botany educator, researcher; b. Herrin, Ill., Oct. 22, 1946. Ph.D., So. Ill. U., 1977. Instr. Med. Coll. Pa., Phila., 1976-79, asst. prof. microbiology, 1979-83; dir. Electron Microscopy Ctr., So. Ill. U., Carbondale, 1983-85, assoc. prof. botany dept., 1985—. Contbr. research articles on electron microscopy to prof. jours. Recipient Young Investigator award Nat. Inst. Dental Research, Washington, 1978. Mem. Electron Microscopy Soc. Am., Am. Soc. Microbiology, Ill. State Acad. Sci., Sigma Xi, Phi Kappa Phi, Kappa Delta Pi. Avocations: Photography, bicycling, gardening, painting, computers. Office: Ctr Electron Microscopy Neckers 146-B So Ill U Carbondale IL 62901

BRAATEN, KATHLEEN ANN, nurse, educator; b. South Milwaukee, Wis., Sept. 1, 1945; d. Edward S. and Alice F. Weinstock; student Edgewood Coll., Madison, Wis., 1963-64; R.N., St. Marys Sch. Nursing, Madison, 1966; lic. nursing home adminstr., U. Wis., 1976; B.S. (Nursing scholar), Coll. of St. Francis, Joliet, Ill., 1977; M.S., U. Wis., 1983; m. Lyle D. Braaten, Aug. 6, 1966; children—Todd Allen, Jennifer Lynn, Sara Ann. Staff nurse, supr., dir. nurses, asst. adminstr. Mt. Carmel Nursing Home, Greenfield, Wis., 1966-79; instr. nursing Milw. Tech. Coll., 1979-84; dean allied health Waukesha Tech. Inst., Pewaukee, Wis., 1985—; operating room nurse St. Marys Hosp., Manhattan, Kans., 1966; staff nurse Irwin Army Hosp., Ft. Riley, Kans., 1967-68; dir. nursing Woodstock N.W. Health Center, 1971-73. Mem. Nat. League for Nursing, Wis. League for Nursing, Am. Fedn. Tchrs. Roman Catholic. Home: W332 N5543 Linden Circle W Nashotah WI 53058 Office: 800 Main St Pewaukee WI 53072

BRABSON, HOWARD VICTOR, social worker, educator; b. Knoxville, Tenn., Sept. 18, 1925; s. Alfred L. and Fannie Ruby Brabson; B.S. in Social Scis., Coll. of Ozarks, 1956; M.S.W. Catholic U. Am., 1962, D. Social Work (fellow), 1975; m. Rudienne Houston, Sept. 13, 1952. Asst. supt. Cedar Knoll Schs., Laurel, Md., 1958-61; supt. vocat. edn. Boys Indsl. Sch., Lancaster, Ohio, 1962-63; dep. commr. Ohio Youth Commn., Columbus, 1963-65; area supr. Vista, Washington, 1965-67, program mgr., Great Lakes region, Chgo., 1967-69; asso. prof. social work U. Mich., Ann Arbor, 1969—; cons. to various community orgns. and schs., 1969—; mem. planning com. Internat. Conf. Social Welfare, 1978. Mem. mayor's Com. for Community Revitalization, Ann Arbor, 1975-76; bd. dirs. Octagon House, 1976-77, chmn., 1977-78. Served to capt. inf., U.S. Army, 1946-58; PTO. Recipient Man of Yr. award Willow Run Adversary Club, 1978; Faculty Recognition award U. Mich., 1981. Mem. Acad. Cert. Social Workers, Mich. Assn. Black Social Workers (Outstanding Service award 1978), Assn. Voluntary Action Scholars (dir. 1976-78), Nat. Assn. Black Social Workers (nat. pres. 1978—, mem. steering com. 1971—, founder 1968), Huron Valley Assn. Black Social Workers (pres. 1973—), Zeta Chi Beta. Roman Catholic. Contbr. articles to social work jours. Home: 1325 S Maple St Apt 301 Ann Arbor MI 48103 Office: School of Social Work Univ Michigan 1065 Frieze Bldg Ann Arbor MI 48109

BRACCO, ROBERT ARMANDO, lawyer; b. Chgo., Sept. 12, 1953; s. Armando and Antoinette (Smoljan) B. B.A., Ind. U., 1975; M.P.A., Ohio State U., 1977; J.D., Capital U., Columbus, Ohio, 1981. Bar: Ohio 1982, U.S. Dist. Ct. (no. dist.) Ohio 1982. Criminal justice adminstr. Ohio Pub. Defender, Columbus, 1977-79; asst. dir. Indsl. Commn. Ohio, Columbus, 1979-82; sole practice, Columbus, 1982—; cons. on state govt. NE/MW Assocs., Cleve., 1983—. Recipient Meritorious Service award State of Ohio, 1982. Mem. Assn. Trial Lawyers Am., Ohio State Bar Assn., Columbus Bar Assn. Republican. Roman Catholic. Club: Columbus Athletic. Office: 1660 NW Professional Plaza Suite B Columbus OH 43220

BRACIALE, VIVIAN LAM, immunologist; b. N.Y.C., June 5, 1948; d. Wing Ching and Wai Ching (Li) Lam; m. Thomas J. Braciale Jr., Aug. 5, 1972; children—Kara, Michael Stephen, Laura. A.B., Cornell U., 1969; Ph.D., U.

Pa., 1973. Postdoctoral fellow U. Pa., Phila., 1974-75, Washington U. Med. Sch., St. Louis, 1975-76, research instr. immunology, 1978-83, research asst. prof. pathology, 1983—. Contbr. articles in immunology to profl. jours. N.Y. State Regent scholar; NIH Research Service awardee; vis. fellow Australian Nat. U., Canberra, 1976-78. Mem. Am. Assn. Immunologists, Am. Diabetes Assn. Lutheran. Office: Washington Univ Med Sch Dept Pathology 660 S Euclid St Louis MO 63110

BRACKEN, JOSEPH ANDREW, theology educator; b. Chgo., Mar. 22, 1930; s. Andrew Joseph and Agnes Patricia (Ryan) B. Litt.B., Xavier U., Cin., 1953; M.A., Loyola U., Chgo., 1960; Ph.D., U. Freiburg, W.Ger., 1968. Asst. prof. St. Mary of Lake Sem., Chgo., 1968-74; assoc. prof. Marquette U., Milw., 1974-82; prof. theology Xavier U., Cin., 1982—, chmn. dept., 1982—. Author: Freiheit und Kausalität bei Schelling, 1974; What Are They Saying about the Trinity, 1979; The Triune Symbol-Persons, Process and Community, 1985. Contbr. articles to profl. jours. Mem. Am. Acad. Religion, Cath. Theol. Soc. Am., Metaphys. Soc. Am. Roman Catholic. Avocations: tennis; swimming. Home: 3800 Victory Pkwy Cincinnati OH 54207-1096

BRACKETT, EDWARD BOONE, III, orthopedic surgeon; b. Fort Worth, Jan. 5, 1936; s. Edward Boone and Bessie Lee (Hudgins) B.; student Tex. Tech. Coll., 1957; M.D., Baylor U., 1961; m. Jean Elliott, July 11, 1959; children—Bess E., Geoffrey, Elliott Mencken, Edward Boone IV, Anneke Gail. Intern, Cook County Hosp., Chgo., 1961-62; resident Northwestern U., Chgo., 1962-66; practice medicine specializing in orthopedic surgery, Oak Park, Ill., 1966—, Westgate Orthopaedics Ltd., Oak Park, 1969—; mem. staff Loyola U., Oak Park Hosp., Loretto Hosp., Rush Med. Sch.; chmn. dept. orthopedics West Suburban Hosp., pres. med. staff, 1982—; clin. assoc. prof. orthopedics Loyola U.; chmn. bd. Chgo. Loop Mediclinic, 1973-75; cons. orthopedic surgery City Service Oil Co., 1970. Guarantor, Lyric Opera Chgo., 1971-84; guest condr. Chgo. Symphony Orch., 1979, Chgo. Chamber Orch., 1980; mem. humanities adv. council Triton Coll., 1983-84; charter mem. vis. com. Northwestern U. Sch. Music, 1982—. Served as lt. comdr. USNR, 1967-69; Vietnam. Recipient Outstanding Tchr. award Dept. Orthopedic Surgery, West Suburban Hosp., 1978, 79. Diplomate Am. Orthopedic Bd. Surgery, Am. Bd. Neurol. Orthopedic Surgeons. Fellow A.C.S., Am. Acad. Orthopedic Surgeons, Inst. of Medicine of Chgo., Am. Acad. Neurol. and Orthopedic Surgeons, Am. Assn. for Hand Surgery, Internat. Coll. Surgeons; mem. Am. Trauma Soc. (founder), Royal Soc. Medicine, Ill. Orthopedic Soc., Chgo. Orthopedic Soc., AMA, Chgo. Med. Soc. (alt. councilor), Clin. Orthopedic Soc., Internat. Platform Assn., Civil War Round Table, Friends Chgo. Symphony Orch., Chgo. Chamber Orch. Assn. (dir.), Symphonia Musicale (dir.), Sigma Alpha Epsilon, Phi Eta Sigma, Phi Chi, Alpha Epsilon Delta. Cons. orthopedic editor Jour. Indsl. Medicine, 1966-67. Home: 1407 Ashland Ave River Forest IL 60305 Office: 1125 Westgate St Oak Park IL 60301

BRACKHAHN, DONALD GARLAND, university administrator; b. Kansas City, Mo., Nov. 2, 1936; s. James Alexander and Mary Jeannette (Garland) B.; B.A., U. Mo., Kansas City, 1958, M.A. in History, 1965; m. Nancy Lee Dunbar, Feb. 24, 1962; children—Dawn Renee, Diane Michelle. Grad. asst. history dept. U. Kansas City, 1958-60; social sci. tchr. Kansas City (Mo.) Sch. Dist., 1960-66, athletic dir., tennis coach, 1964-66; asst. dir. devel. U. Mo., Kansas City, 1966-70, dir. devel., alumni and constituent relations, 1970-80, dir. alumni and constituent relations, asst. to pres. for alumni relations, 1980-84; exec. dir. alumni relations U. Mo., Rolla, 1985—. Trustee, Kansas City Mus. History and Sci., 1972-80, Johnson County (Kans.) Library, 1972-73; mem. Johnson County Charter Commn., 1974-76; bd. dirs. Shawnee Civic Band, 1971-85; pres. Johnson County Friends of Library, 1976-78; mem. transition com., nominating com., chmn. speakers bur. Heart of Am. United Way; bd. dirs., pres. Johnson County United Community Services, 1980-82; sec., pres. standing com. Episcopal Diocese of Kans., 1980-83; mem. vestry, lay reader, liturgical asst., lay pastor Christ Ch., Overland Park, Kans. Served with USNG, 1959-65. Mem. ALA, Kansas City Council for Social Studies (pres. 1965-66), Greater Kansas City Council on Philanthropy (pres. 1980-81), Council for Advancement and Support of Edn., Assn. of Vol. Bds., U. Mo. Kansas City Internat. Alumni Assn. (pres. 1965), Kansas City C. of C., Omicron Delta Kappa (faculty advisor), Phi Delta Kappa, Phi Mu Alpha Sinfonia, Tau Kappa Epsilon. Republican. Club: Rockhill Tennis. Home: Route 4 Box 319 Rolla MO 65401 Office: U Mo Rolla 108 Harris Hall Rolla MO 65401

BRACKIN, JOHN FRANK, mowing equipment manufacturing company executive; b. Wahpeton, N.D., Apr. 19, 1944; s. George B. and Clarice R. (Rollofson) B.; m. Paulette K. Tisch, Dec. 26, 1970; children—Jill E., Jollyne K., Product mgr. Toro Mfg., Bloomington, Minn., 1973-75, chief engr., 1975-79, mgr. product evaluation, 1979-81, dir. engring., 1981-82; v.p. engring. Simplicity Mfg., Port Washington, Wis., 1983—; dir., v.p. Toro Credit Union, Bloomington, 1979-83; dir., treas. Brackin Auto and Implement Co., 1981-85. Inventor design patent for commercial rotary mower, 1976, design patent mower deck belt adjustor, 1976. Campaign chmn. Toro United Way, Bloomington, Minn., 1974. Mem. Soc. Automotive Engrs., Outdoor Power Equipment Inst. (tech. adv. com.). Republican. Roman Catholic. Office: Simplicity Mfg Co 500 N Spring St Port Washington WI 53074

BRADBURN, THOMAS LYLE, safety engineer; g. Detroit, Jan. 6, 1942; s. James Lyle and Lucile Irene (Cushing) B.; m. Sandra Caroline Stover, July 27, 1963; 1 son, Travis Lyle. B.S. in Indsl. Mgmt., Lawrence Inst. Tech., 1977. Cert. Bd. Cert. Safety Profls. Service coordinator Dennison Copier div. Dennison Mfg. Co., Orlando, Fla., 1966-68; jr. engr. Truck and Coach div. Gen. Motors Corp., Pontiac, Mich., 1968-76, safety rep. truck and bus mfg. div., 1976—. Asst. scoutmaster troop 134 Boy Scouts Am., 1979-82. Served with USAF, 1962-66. Mem. Am. Soc. Safety Engrs. (profl.), Inst. Indsl. Engrs., Soc. Mfg. Engrs., Engring. Soc. Detroit, Mich. Indsl. Hygiene Assn. Baptist.

BRADBURY, DANIEL JOSEPH, library administrator, educational administrator; b. Kansas City, Kans., Dec. 7, 1945; m. Mary F. Callaghan, May 10, 1967; children—Patricia, Tracy, Amanda, Anthony, Sean. Student Rockhurst Coll., 1964-65, Kansas City Metro Jr. Coll., 1965-66; B.A. in English Lang. and Lit., U. Mo.-Kansas City, 1971; M.L.S., Emporia State U., 1972. Assoc. dir. extension services Waco-McLennan County Library, Waco, Tex., 1972-74; library dir. Rolling Hills Consol. Library, St. Joseph, Mo., 1974-77, Janesville Pub. Library, Wis., 1977-83; dir. leisure services City of Janesville, 1982-83; dir. Kansas City Mo. Pub. Library, 1983—; interim, exec. dir., Pub. Library, 1985—; mem. faculty Baylor U., Waco, 1973-74; dir. Janesville Library System, Janesville, 1978-83; participant Gov.'s Conf. on Library and Info. Sci., Wis., 1979; mem. council Kansas City Metro Library Network, 1984—. Bd. dirs. St. John's Sch., Janesville, 1980-83. Mem. Greater Kansas City C. of C., Mid-Town Troost Assn. (bd. 1984—), ALA, Mo. Library Assn. (legis. chmn. 1984-85), Library Adminstrn. and Mgmt. Assn. (sec. chmn. 1983-85), Wis. Library Assn. (pres. 1982). Roman Catholic. Lodges: Rotary, Lions (pres. 1981-82). Home: 3630 Holmes St Kansas City MO 64109 Office: Kansas City Mo Pub Library 311 E 12th St Kansas City MO 64106

BRADBURY, JAMES CLIFFORD, geological researcher, administrator; b. Oregon, Ill., July 7, 1918; s. Guy Ira and Gertrude (Coffey) B.; divorced 1965; children—Sarah, Peter, Jean. A.B., U. Ill., 1941; M.A., Harvard U., 1949, Ph.D., 1958. Geologist, State Geol. Survey, Urbana, Ill., 1949-82, head indsl. minerals sect., 1968-82, prin. geologist, head geol. group, 1982-84, prin. geologist emeritus, 1984—. Contbr. articles on mineral deposits to profl. jours. Bd. editors: Industrial Minerals & Rocks, 4th and 5th editions, 1975, 83. Served as specialist 4 U.S. Army Engrs., 1941-45. Fellow Geol. Soc. Am., AAAS; Mem. Soc. Mining Engrs. (bd. dirs. 1970-73), Am. Inst. Mining, Metall. and Petroleum Engrs. (Hal Williams Hardings award 1984), Soc. Econ. Geologists, Internat. Assn. on Genesis of Ore Deposits, Ill. State Acad. Sci.; Roman Catholic. Lodge: Kiwanis (bd. dirs. 1983—). Avocations: skiing, hiking, fishing. Office: State Geol Survey 615 E Peabody Dr Champaign IL 61820

BRADEN, BERWYN BARTOW, lawyer; b. Pana, Ill., Jan. 10, 1928; s. George Clark and Florence Lucille (Bartow) B.; student Carthage Coll., 1946-48; student U. Wis., 1948-49, J.D., 1959; m. Betty J.; children—Scott, Mark, Mathew, Sue, Ralph, Ladd, Brad. Bar: Wis. 1959, U.S. Supreme Ct. 1965. Ptnr. Genoar & Braden, Lake Geneva, Wis., 1959-63; individual practice law, Lake Geneva, 1963-68, 72-74; ptnr. Braden & English, Lake Geneva, 1968-72, Braden & Olson, Lake Geneva, 1974—; counsel Citizens Nat. Bank, 1959—; city atty. Lake Geneva, 1962-64; tchr. Law Sch., U. Wis., 1977. Bd. dirs. Lake Geneva YMCA. Served with USMCR, 1945-46. Mem. Walworth County (pres. 1962-63), Am., Chgo. bar assns., State Bar Wis. (chmn. conv. and entertainment com. 1979-81), Bar Assn. 7th Fed. Circuit, Wis. Acad. Trial Lawyers (sec. 1975, treas. 1976, dir. 1977-79), Assn. Trial Lawyers, Phi Alpha Delta. Home: 103 Curtis St Lake Geneva WI 53147 Office: 705 Pine Tree Ln Lake Geneva WI 53147 also PO Box 512 Lake Geneva WI 53147

BRADFORD, KIMERLEE JAY, mechanical engineer; b. Putnam, Conn., Mar. 22, 1932; s. H. Jay and Dorothy Gertrude (Martin) B.; B.S., U. N.H., 1965; postgrad. U. Ariz., 1970-73; m. Shigeko Shikuma, June 18, 1955; children—Jon Chandler, Karyl Ann, William Jay, Charles Martin. Enlisted USAF, 1950, advanced through grades to maj., 1965; missile ops. officer, N.Mex., W.Ger., 1957-60; missile maintenance officer, W.Ger., 1960-62; program mgmt. specialist, Los Angeles, 1965-70; ret., 1970; reliability engr. Control Data Corp., St. Paul, 1973-81; mgr. receiving insp. No. Telecom Inc.-EOS, 1981-82, mgr. in-process quality engring., 1982-83, sr. engr. reliability assurance, 1983—. Committeeman, Boy Scouts Am., 1972-73. Recipient Tech. Excellence award Control Data Corp., 1977. Mem. ASME, Am. Soc. Quality Control, Ret. Officers Assn. Home: 310 107th St W Bloomington MN 55420 Office: 245 E 6 St Saint Paul MN 55101

BRADFORD, WILLIAM STEPHEN, orthodontist; b. Boston, July 23, 1912; s. Joseph S. and Anna (Hogarty) B.; B.S., Harvard U., 1934, postgrad. Engring. Sch., 1934-35; D.D.S., Northwestern U., 1944; M.S., U. Kansas City Dental Sch., 1948; m. Barbara Ann Kennedy, May 30, 1942; children—Martha Ann, William Stephen. Researcher, neurologic unit Harvard Med. Sch., 1935-36; researcher New Eng. Lime Co., Canaan, Conn., 1936-38; chem. rep. for New Eng., Ohio Chem. Co., 1938-41; practice dentistry specializing in orthodontics, Highland Park, Ill., 1948—; prof. orthodontics Loyola U., Chgo., 1969—; dir., pres. Midwest Seminar in Dental Medicine. Vice pres. Suburban Arts Center; mem. Zoning Bd. Appeals Highland Park. Mem. Harvard Assn. Chemists, Harvard Grads. Soc., Field Museum Natural History, Am. Assn. Orthodontists, ADA, Highland Park C. of C. (dir., pres.), Ill. Doberman Pinscher Club (pres.), Finishing Touch Dog Tng. Group (pres.). Club: Rotary (dir., pres.). Home: 3001 Ridge Rd Highland Park IL 60035 Office: 1964 Sheridan Rd Highland Park IL 60035

BRADLEY, DANNY, educator; b. Atlanta, Nov. 26, 1945; s. Robert and Gloria (Milner) B.; B.A., Clark Coll., 1967; M.A.T., Northeastern Ill. U., 1976; postgrad. Loop Coll., 1982—. Tchr., Atlanta Bd. Edn., 1973-75; tchr. Chgo. Bd. Edn., 1967-73, 1975—, now mathematics/computer programming tchr. Percy L. Julian High Sch.; cons. Profl. Computer Applications, Inc., summer 1982; geomath instr. City Colls. Chgo., S. Shore Evening High Sch., 1982—; part-time instr. Calumet Evening Sch., 1975-77, Dunbar Evening Sch., 1977-80, others. Mem. Assn. for Supervision and Curriculum Devel., Nat. Council Tchrs. Math., Ill. Council Tchrs. Math., Ill. Assn. for Supervision and Curriculum Devel., Assn. for Ednl. Data Systems, Minn. Ednl. Computer Consortium, Assn. Math. Advanced Placement Tchrs., World Future Soc., Phi Delta Kappa, Omega Psi Phi. Democrat. Baptist. Contbr. articles to profl. jours. Home: 7616 S Shore Dr Apt 307 Chicago IL 60649 Office: 10330 S Elizabeth St Chicago IL 60643

BRADLEY, LARRY E., school administrator; b. East McKeesport, Pa., June 19, 1941; s. Edwin Shaw and Dorthy B. (Montz) B.; m. Connie Mae Heiple, Nov. 12, 1965; 1 child, Lisa M. B.S., Ind. U. Pa., 1963; M.Ed., U. Wyo., 1968; Admin. Cert., Chadron State Coll., 1974; postgrad. U. Nebr., 1978—. Cert. administrator. Geography tchr. Hempfield Pub. Schs., Greensborg, Pa., 1963-68; guidance counselor Scottsbluff Pub. Schs., Nebr., 1968-70, asst. prin., 1970-73; jr. high prin. Columbus City Schs., 1974—; peer reviewer Profl. Practices Com., Lincoln, Nebr., 1976—. Grad. fellow Idea Inst., Columbia, Mo., 1978-80; named for Exemplary Sch. Discipline Nat. Sch. Resource Network, 1981, Phi Delta Kappan, 1981. Mem. Nat. Assn. Secondary Sch. Prins., Nebr. Council Sch. Admins. (chmn. legis. com. 1983-84, cons. evaluation 1983-84, disting. service award 1983), Northeast Secondary Prins. (pres. 1980-81), Columbus C. of C. (chmn. educl. com. 1982); fellow Inst. Devel. Educl. Activities. Lodge: Kiwanis (bd. dirs. 1984—). Office: Columbus Jr High Sch 1661 25th Ave Columbus NE 68601

BRADLEY, LEON CHARLES, music educator; b. Battle Creek, Mich., Sept. 8, 1938; s. Leon Harvey and Sigrid Pearl (Anderson) B.; B.A., Mich. State U., 1961, M.M. Brass Specialist, 1967; postgrad. U. Okla., summer 1974, U. Wis., summer 1975; m. Mary Elizabeth Bradley, Dec. 23, 1968; children—Kyle Newman, Shannon Sigrid, Karl Norman, Charles Nathan. Band dir. Owosso-St. Paul, Mich., 1958-61, Hopkins (Mich.) Public Schs., 1961-62, Cedar Springs (Mich.) Public Schs., 1962-65; grad. asst. music theory-aural harmony Mich. State U., East Lansing, 1965-67; asst. prof. asst. dir. bands Minot (N.D.) State Coll., 1967-69; asso. prof. instrumental music & music edn., dir. bands Sch. of the Ozarks, Point Lookout, Mo., 1969—; clinician low brass instruments Selmer, Inc., 1979—. Active, Springfield Symphony Orch., 1969-72, 81-82, Springfield Regional Opera Orch., 1981—; dir. Abou Ben Adhem Shrine Band, 1978-80. Mem. Coll. Band Dir.'s Nat. Assn. (nat. chmn. Sacred Wind Music commn.), Music Educators Nat. Conf., Nat. Assn. Jazz Educators, Nat. Assn. Wind & Percussion Instrs. (new music reviewer, assn. jour. 1968-71), Mo. Music Edn. Assn., Mo. Bandmasters Assn., Percussive Arts Soc., Music Tchrs. Nat. Assn., Mo. Music Tchrs. Assn., Branson Arts Council, Am. Fedn. Musicians (local 150), Ducks Unltd. (mem. com. 1978-81, chmn., 1981), Phi Mu Alpha (life). Episcopalian. Lodges: Masons, Lions (pres. 1983-84), Scottish Rite. Contbr. articles in field to profl. jours. Home: SR 2 Box 3079 119 South Dr Branson MO 65616 Office: Music Dept Sch of the Ozarks Point Lookout MO 65726

BRADLEY, ROBERT MARK, educational administrator; b. Eldorado, Ill., Apr. 23, 1956; s. Edward A. and Margaret Carolyn (Winterberger) B.; m. Cheryl Diane Moore, Feb. 14, 1975; 1 child, Jeffrey Mark. A.A.S. in Bus. Edn., Southern Ill. U., 1976, B.S. in Elem. Edn., 1980, M.S. in Ednl. Leadership, 1983. Jr. high sch. tchr., coach, Merrian Sch. Dist. #19, Fairfield, Ill., 1980-81; 2d grade tchr., coach Enfield Sch. Dist., Ill., #4, 1981-83; regional supt. of schs., regional gifted coordinator, 4 county area, Ill., 1983-84; high sch. prin. North Wayne (Consol. Unit Dist. #200, Cisne, Ill., 1984—; cons. Area Gifted Service Ctr., Benton, Ill., 1983-84. Mem. Nat. Assn. of Secondary Sch. Prins., Ill. Prins. Assn., So. Ill. Planning Commn. for Gifted Edn. (bd. dirs. 1983-84). Democrat. Baptist. Club: Nat. Wildlife Assn. Lodge: Rotary. Avocations: water skiing; snow skiing; ornathology; hiking; basketball; softball; canoeing. Home: PO Box 474 Cisne IL 62823 Office: Cisne High Sch PO Box 98 Cisne IL 62823

BRADLEY, RONALD HOWARD, neuro-anatomist; b. Detroit, Aug. 21, 1950; s. Clarence Edward and Lorraine Day (Moyers) B.; B.A., Wayne State U., 1973, M.S., 1978; Ph.D., Mich. State U., 1983, D.O., 1984. Chef, Hotel St. Regis. Detroit, 1968-70; chief lab. mgr. Mich. Cancer Found. Electron Microscopy Lab., 1973-76; sr. research asst. anatomy Wayne State U., 1976-80; with neurosci. program Mich. State U., 1980-84, intern, 1984-85; resident U. Mich., 1985—; Mem. Am. Assn. Cell Biologists, Electron Microscopy Soc. Am., N.Y. Acad. Sci., AAAS, Am. Osteo. Assn., Am. Assn. Anatomists, Sigma Xi, Sigma Sigma Phi, Methodist. Mason. Home: 14580 Stofer Ct Chelsea MI 48118 Office: Mich State U 5th Floor Fee Hall East Lansing MI 48824

BRADLEY, WILLIAM ARTHUR, educator; b. Lansing, Mich., Nov. 11, 1921; s. Arthur and Amy F. (Barringer) B.; B.S. in Civil Engring., Mich. State U., 1943; M.S., U. Ill., 1947; Ph.D., U. Mich., 1956; m. Elizabeth G. Ewing, June 29, 1949; children—David, Nancy, Susan. Engr., Douglas Aircraft, El Segundo, Calif., 1943-44; engr. G.M. Foster, Bridge Cons., Lansing, 1945-46; mem. faculty Mich. State U., East Lansing, 1947—, prof. mechanics and civil engring., 1961—; cons. Dow Chem. Corp., 1959-61. Bd. dirs. West Side Neighborhood Assn. Recipient Disting. Faculty award Mich. State U., 1963; Western Electric Fund award, 1966. Mem. ASCE, Am. Concrete Inst., Internat. Assn. Bridge and Structural Engrs., Am. Soc. Engring. Edn., Sigma Xi, Phi Kappa Phi, Tau Beta Pi, Chi Epsilon. Home: 1919 W Kalamazoo St Lansing MI 48915 Office: Coll Engring Mich State U East Lansing MI 48824

BRADNER, JAMES EDWARD, science educator; b. Evanston, Ill., Aug. 16, 1933; s. Eric John and Florence Hester (Thompson) B.; m. Jane Binding, Oct. 18, 1957; children—Michael, Christopher. B.A., Albion Coll. (Mich.), 1955; M.A., Wayne State U., 1965. Cert. tchr., Mich. Tchr. sci. Berkley Schs., Mich., 1960-62, chmn. dept. sci., 1962-65; instr., chmn. dept. Oakland Community Coll., Bloomington Hills, Mich., 1965-66, dir., coordinator, researcher, 1966-70, prof. sci., 1970—; pvt. practice consulting, Royal Oak, Mich., 1970—. Author: Theories of Relativity Geologic Time, 1965-66. Served with U.S. Army, 1957-59. Mem. Mich. Assn. Computer Use in Learning, Phi Mu Alpha Symphonia, Phi Delta Kappa. Avocations: computer programming, sailing, hiking. Home: 1031 Edgewood St Royal Oak MI 48067 Office: Oakland Community Coll Southeast Campus System Science & Health 22322 Rutland St Southfield MI 48075

BRADSHAW, LAWRENCE JAMES, artist, educator; b. St. Paul, Kans., Sept. 21, 1945; s. James Lawrence and Pauline Marie (Nunnink) B.; B.F.A., Pittsburg (Kans.) State U., 1967, M.A., 1971; M.F.A., Ohio U., Athens, 1973. Designer, Union Oil Co., Honolulu, summer 1967; proofreader, typist CBS-TV, Hollywood, Calif., 1967-69; prodn. artist Writers Service, Hollywood, 1969: advt. mgr. J.C. Penney Co., Pittsburg, 1970-71; teaching asst. Pittsburg State U., 1970-71, Ohio U., 1971-73; instr. Akron (Ohio) Art Inst., summer 1973; assoc. prof. art U. Nebr., Omaha, 1973—, dir. univ. galleries, 1974-76; visual arts rep., designer Met. Arts Council, Omaha, 1976; art dir. Akron City Scholarship Program, 1973; juror various art exhbns., 1974—; one-man exhbns. include Hillel House, Athens, Ohio, 1973, U. Nebr., 1974, Pittsburg State U., 1974, 77; group exhbns. include Museo Nazionale dell' Accademia Italia, 1983, Pa. State U., 1983, Stuhr Mus., Grand Island, Nebr., 1983, Esta Robinson Gallery, N.Y.C., 1982, others. Recipient Spl. award Internat. Platform Assn., 1981; Purchase award Eppley Competition, U. Nebr., 1982; named Outstanding Young Alumnus Pitts. State U., 1982; recipient Gold medal for artistic merit Internat. Parliament, Salsamaggiore, Italy, 1983. NDEA fellow, 1967; Nebr. Arts Council grantee 1976. Mem. Nat. Coll. Art Assn., Artists Equity, Nat. Accademia Italia, Mid-Am. Coll. Art Assn., Joslyn Art Mus., World U. Roundtable, Accademia Europa, Visual Artists and Galleries Assn., Visual Individualists United (bd. dirs.). Office: Room 391A Adminstrn Bldg Univ Nebr Omaha NE 68182

BRADT, DONA MARY SONTAG, corporate information center manager; b. Hastings, Minn., Oct. 17, 1930; d. Edwin Gervase and Maude Marie (Hatten) S.; student Mt. St. Marys Coll., 1948, Library Sch. U. Minn., 1968-70; B.A., Met. State U., 1975; Mt. m. Arnold L. Bradt (div.); children—Michael Edwin, Robert Dana, Jeffrey Arnold, Peter Matthew, Andrew Hatten. Legal sec. Langevin & Langlais, 1964-65; librarian Econ Lab., Inc., St. Paul, 1965—, head librarian, 1979-80, mgr. corp. info. center, 1980—. Mem. Am. Soc. Info. Sci., Spl. Libraries Assn., ALA, Minn. Library Assn., AAAS. Republican. Roman Catholic. Home: 7981 115th St S Cottage Grove MN 55016 Office: Econ Lab Inc 840 Sibley Meml Hwy Saint Paul MN 55118

BRADWAY, RAYMOND WILLIAM, JR., surgeon; b. Phila., June 17, 1932; s. Raymond William and Anne (Hannum) B.; student Mansfield State Coll., 1950-52; D.O., Phila. Coll. Osteo. Medicine, 1956; m. Barbara Moffitt, Feb. 25, 1961; children—Beverly Anne, Robert Alan, Karen Denise, Alison Jane. Intern, Detroit Osteo. Hosp., 1956-57, resident in surgery, 1957-61; postgrad. tng. in thoracic surgery, Phila. and Boston, 1961-62; practice medicine specializing in thoracic surgery, Detroit, 1962-63, in gen. and thoracic surgery, Columbus, Ohio, 1963—; sr. attending surgeon, cons. Doctors Hosp., Columbus, 1963—, chmn. div. thor. surgery, 1966—, chmn. dept. gen. surgery, 1979-81; clin. prof. surgery and thoracic surgery Ohio U., 1977—. Trustee, Columbus Acad. Recipient C.L. Ballinger Disting. Osteo. Surgeon award, 1979; diplomate Am. Osteo. Bd. Surgery, Am. Osteo. Bd. Thoracic Surgery. Fellow Am. Coll. Osteo. Surgeons (chmn. continuing surg. edn. com. 1973-80, bd. govs. 1980—, pres. thoracic-cardiovascular sect. 1974), mem. and chmn. numerous coms.); mem. Am. Osteo. Assn. (vice chmn. continuing med. edn. com. 1973-78), Am. Osteo. Bd. Surgery, Ohio Osteo. Assn., Columbus Acad. Osteo. Medicine, Am. Thoracic Soc., Ohio Thoracic Soc., Am. Soc. Contemporary Medicine and Surgery, Am. Soc. Parenteral and Enteral Nutrition, Royal Soc. Medicine. Republican. Presbyterian. Clubs: Scioto Golf and Country, Masons, Shriners. Editorial cons. Jour. Am. Osteopathic Assn., 1966—. Office: 50 Old Village Rd Columbus OH 43228

BRADY, DARLENE ANN, artist, researcher; b. Ft. Hood, Tex., Aug. 4, 1951; d. Egbert Leo, Jr. and Eleanor Rose Marie (Wollenhaupt) B. B.F.A. summa cum laude, Ohio U., 1976; M.L.S. summa cum laude, U. Pitts, 1978, M.F.A. summa cum laude, 1980. Painter stained glass artist, 1976—; ptnr. Archi-Textures, Cin., 1984—; vis. asst. prof. design U. Cin., 1984-85; grad. and teaching asst. U. Pitts., 1977-80; fine arts bibliographer Tulane U., 1981-83; guest curator of stained glass from Mellon Collection, U. Pitts., 1979, intern Frick Library, 1978; instr. Ohio U., winter 1976, curator B.F.A. Grad. Exhibit, 1976, asst. curator fine arts slide library, 1973-77. Group exhbns. include Fest for All '81, Broussard Galleries, Baton Rouge, 1981, Assocs. Exhibit, Stained Glass Assn. Am., 1980-84, Glass on Holiday, Gazebo Gallery, Gatlinburg, Tenn., 1981, Ark.-La.-Tex. Glass Invitational, La. Tech. U. Art Gallery, 1981; commns. include stained glass panel Athens Humane Soc., 1976, Athens Landscape painting for McDonald's Restaurant, 1976, Transitions stained glass windows Tompson residence, Athens, 1977. La. Cypress stained glass panels entrance door Hainesworth residence, Ruston, La., 1979, stained glass triptych Marybell Holstead residence, Ruston, 1981, solar room with 7 stained glass panels wollenhaupt residence, Lima, Ohio, 1984, others. Author: Stained Glass Index, 1906-77, 1979; Stained Glass: A Guide to Information Sources, 1980; Le Corbusier: An Annotated Bibliography, 1985. Contbr. articles to profl. jours. Scholar Phi Kappa Phi, 1977, J.W. Morgan, 1977, Deans fall 1978, Provost, 1978. Mem. Coll. Art Assn., Glass Arts Soc., Stained Glass Assn. Am. (assoc., rep. 1980-81), Beta Phi Mu, Phi Kappa Phi. Home: 1665 Pullen Ave Cincinnati OH 45223

BRADY, GERALD WILLIAM, JR., lawyer; b. Galesburg, Ill., Mar. 27, 1949; s. Gerald William and Mary Teresa (McQuire) B.; m. Susan Irene Olson, Aug. 7, 1976; 1 child, Ryan. B.S., Bradley U., 1972; J.D., St. Louis U., 1981. Bar: Ill. 1981. Supr. sports and community facilities Peoria Park Dist., 1972-78; instr. moot ct. program St. Louis U., 1980-81; asst. state's atty. felony div. Peoria County State's Attys. Office, Peoria, Ill., 1981—. Served with U.S. Army, 1970-76. Mem. ABA, Ill. Bar Assn., Peoria County Bar Assn. Democrat. Roman Catholic. Lodge: Kiwanis. Home: 111 Fairway Dr Peoria IL 61604

BRADY, MARK EDWARD, insurance business executive; b. Minneola, N.Y., Dec. 25, 1931; s. Edward Patrick and Vivian Evelyn (Vizard) B.; B.A., A.A., Passionist Fathers Sem., 1954; postgrad. Yale U., 1956, Hudson Coll., 1957-58, Suffolk U Sch. Law, 1959; m. Anne M. Sughrue, Feb. 11, 1956; children—Pamela, Kent, Joy, Sean. Mgmt. trainee State St. Trust Co., Boston, 1954-55; with Universal C.I.T., Inc., N.Y.C., 1959-65, br. mgr., 1961-63, dist. mgr., 1963-65; dist. mgr. Yegen Assocs., Teaneck, N.J., and Pitts., 1965-67, div. head, 1967-72, v.p., 1972; founder, chmn. Columbus Assocs., Inc. (Ohio), 1972—, Brady Ins. Co. (Ohio), 1972—, Nat. Crown Life Ins. Co., 1974—; dir. Britannia Ins. Co. Ltd. (B.W.I.); chmn. Brady Cons. Assocs. Inc., N.Y. State, Mass., CAI Acceptance Corp., Tara Cons., Tara Fin. Services. Mem. Pres.'s Council, Georgetown U. Served with USAF, 1955-58. Recipient Freedoms Found Bronze George Washington medal, 1958. Mem. Ohio Mobile Home Assn., U.S. Savs. and Loan League, Ohio Savs. and Loan League, Am. Bankers Assn., Ohio Bankers Assn. Republican. Clubs: Columbus Acad., Pillars, Buckeye, Ohio State U. Pres. Home: Top O' The Mornin' Pataskala OH 43062 Office: 1303 S High St Columbus OH 43206

BRADY, MAUREEN ELIZABETH, educator; b. Chgo., Mar. 15, 1945; d. William James and Gertrude (Hunter) B.; B.S. in Edn., Ill. State U., Normal, 1967, M.S. in Ednl. Media, 1971; postgrad. Nat. Coll. Edn. Librarian, Sch. Dist. 47, Crystal Lake, Ill., 1967-69, Sch. Dist. 155, Crystal Lake, 1969-70; learning center tchr. Rugen Elementary Sch., Glenview, Ill., 1971-73; library media specialist Sunny Hill Elem. Sch. Dist. 220, Barrington, Ill., 1974—. Mem. Friends of Minocqua (Wis.) Library; mem. aux. Good Shepherd Hosp., Barrington. Recipient Alumni Achievement award Dept. Communications Ill. State U., 1983. Mem. ALA, Ill. Library Assn., Ill. Assn. Media in Edn., Assn. Ednl. Communications and Tech., (sec. div. sch. media specialists), Ill. Assn. Ednl. Communications and Tech. (div. com.), NEA, Ill., Barrington (dir.) edn. assns., Chgo. Suburban Audiovisual Roundtable (sec.), No. Ill. Media Assn., Ill. Computer Users in Edn. (pres. elect), AAUW (dir. Barrington area br.), Friends of Barrington Area Library, Ill. St. Andrew's Soc., Elgin Scottish Soc. (pres.), Alpha Beta Alpha (life), Kappa Delta Pi (dir.), Phi Delta Kappa. Cert. geography, library sci., ednl. media, Ill. Office: 2500 Helm Rd Carpentersville IL 60110

BRADY, WILLIAM ARTHUR, speech pathologist; b. Titusville, Pa., May 13, 1942; s. Walter Robert and Alma Cecelia B.; B.S. in Speech and Speech Correction, Clarion State Coll., 1966; M.Ed. in Speech Pathology (Office Edn. fellow), Pa. State U., 1967; Ph.D. in Speech Pathology, Kent State U., 1978. Speech therapist Lawrence County (Pa.) Pub. Schs., 1966-68, Titusville (Pa.)

Area Schs., summer 1966, Ellwood City (Pa.) Area Schs., 1968; instr. speech pathology dept. Edinboro State Coll., summer 1968, Clarion State Coll., 1968-69, Ill. State U., 1969-70, Allegheny Coll., 1970-71; teaching fellow in speech pathology Kent State U., 1971-74, adj. asso. prof. speech pathology, 1976-77; dir. speech pathology St. Elizabeth Hosp. Med. Center, Youngstown, Ohio, 1974—. Mem. Am. (certified in clin. comptence in speech pathology), Ohio (chmn. com. clin. and hosp. affairs 1976-77), Mahoning Valley (v.p. 1976-77) speech and hearing assns., Aphasiology Assn. Ohio. Contbr. articles to profl. jours. Home: 4521 Washington Sq Apt 2 Youngstown OH 44515 Office: 1044 Belmont Ave Youngstown OH 44501

BRADY, WILLIAM EDWARD, educator; b. Newark, Dec. 24, 1926; s. William Edward and Alice Fuller (Quinby) B.; m. Sydney Stradley Graham, Apr. 4, 1959; children—Elizabeth, Mary Catherine, William Edward. B.A., Hobart Coll., 1950; M.A., Brown U., 1953, Ph.D., 1958. Instr. English, Hobart & William Smith Colls., 1950-51, Brown U., Providence, 1953-56, U. Chgo., 1957-58, asst. prof., 1958-62; asst. prof. Knox Coll., 1962-65, assoc. prof., 1965-72; prof. English, Knox Coll., Galesburg, 1972—; vis. prof. Colo. Coll., Hobart and William Smith Coll., trustee, 1965-72. Contbr. articles to profl. jours. Author: Death in the Stacks. Served with USN, 1944-46. Brown U. fellow, 1956-57. Mem. Renaissance Soc., MLA, Shakespeare Soc., Bodelian Library Life Friend. Democrat. Episcopalian. Club: Quadrangel. Avocations: Cooking; swimming. Home: 1160 N Cherry St Galesburg IL 61401 Office: Knox Coll Galesburg IL 61401

BRAGAW, RICHARD SHERMAN, public relations counselor, writer; b. Evanston, Ill., Aug. 7, 1940; s. James Berry and Sylvia Elizabeth (Callender) B.; m. Lenore Kathleen Gonzales, May 6, 1972; children—Richard Ernest, Kevin Patrick, Daniel Berry. B.A., Dartmouth Coll., 1962; M.A. in Eng. Lit., U. Minn., 1964; postgrad. Wayne State U., 1968-69. Reporter Detroit Free Press, 1964-67; pub. relations mgr. Chrysler Corp., Detroit, N.Y.C. and Los Angeles, 1967-70; reporter, bur. chief Dayton Daily News, Dayton and Columbus, Ohio, 1971-74; campaign press sec., research dir., U.S. Sen. John H. Glenn, 1974; v.p. Food Mktg. Inst., Chgo., Washington, 1974-78; pub. affairs dir. Cereal Inst. Inc., Schaumburg, Ill., 1978-81; prin. Bragaw Pub. Relations Services, Palatine, Ill., 1981—; teaching asst. U. Minn., 1962-64; dir. Inner City Bus. Improvement Forum, Detroit, 1967-69. Vestry, St. Hilary's Episcopal Ch., 1982-85. Recipient Perkins prize Dartmouth Coll., 1962; awards Ohio AP, Outdoor Writers of Ohio, 1972; shared Pulitzer Prize, Detroit Free Press, 1967. Mem. Pub. Relations Soc. Am., Publicity Club Chgo., Northwest Suburban Assn. Commerce and Industry. Contbr. numerous articles to profl. jours.

BRAGG, THOMAS ARTHUR, physician; b. Cairo, Mo., Nov. 28, 1951; s. Thomas Edward and Mary Sue (Graves) B.; m. Janet Lynn McCale, Mar. 22, 1980. A.A., Moberly Jr. Coll., Mo., 1971; B.S., No. Mo. State U., 1973; D.O., Kirksville Coll. Osteopathic Medicine, 1977. Intern, Charles Still Hosp., Jefferson City, Mo., 1978; family physician Nat. Health Service Corp., USPHS, Seymour, Iowa, 1978-81, Kirksville Coll. Osteo. Medicine, Macon, Mo., 1981-83; dir. emergency services Moberly Regional Med. Ctr., Mo., 1983—; emergency dept. dir. Moberly Regional Med. Ctr. and Trauma Ctr., 1983—; dir. rural satellite clinics Moberly Regional Med. Ctr., 1984, dir. skilled nursing facility, 1984. Served to 2d lt. USPHS, 1978-81. Recipient award USPHS, Seymour, Iowa, 1981, Scholarship, USPHS, Seymour, 1981. Mem. Am. Osteo. Assn., Mo. Osteo. Assn. Democrat. Mem. Christian Ch. Avocations: music; hunting; fishing; camping. Home: RFD 1 Cairo MO 65239 Office: Moberly Regional Med Ctr 1515 Union St Moberly MO 65270

BRAGNO, EDWARD ALBERT, vintner; b. Chgo., Sept. 30, 1910; s. Francesco and Josephine (Mustari) B.; m. Molly Netcher, Aug. 9, 1947. Student parochial schs., Chgo. Assoc. with wine industry, 1933—; pres. Larkmead Vineyards, Inc., St. Helena, Calif., 1943-46, Salmina Lands, Inc., St. Helena, 1943-46; v.p. Bragno & Co., Chgo., from 1938; pres. Bragno & Co., Riverbank, Calif., Edward A. Bragno & Co., Inc., Bragno World Wines Ltd., Chgo. Bd. dirs., trustee Italian Welfare Council; active Arthritis and Rheumatism Found. Mem. Assoc. Vintners of Middle West (past pres.), Acad. Wine at Bordeaux (Grand Council award). Club: Racquet (Palm Springs, Calif.). Home: 1200 Lake Shore Dr Chicago IL also Paw Paw Lake MI Office: 40 E Walton Pl Chicago IL 60611

BRAGUE, NORMAN EVERETT, lawyer; b. Marietta, Ohio, Oct. 16, 1946; s. Clive Levi and Kate (Bircher) B. B.B.A. cum laude, Ohio U., 1968; J.D., Ohio State U., 1971. Bar: Ohio. Assoc. Parker & Parker, Akron, Ohio, 1971-72; pvt. practice, Wadsworth, Ohio, 1972-76; asst. city solicitor City of Wadsworth, 1973-75, city solicitor, 1976-77, dir. law, 1977—; trustee Community Improvement Corp., Wadsworth, 1976—. Active Medina County Republican Central Com., 1974—. Mem. ABA, Ohio State Bar Assn., Medina County Bar Assn., Phi Alpha Delta, Pi Kappa Alpha. Republican. Episcopalian. Clubs: University (Akron), Rotary (Wadsworth), SAR. Lodges: Masons, Elks. Avocation: History. Home: 324 Portage St Wadsworth OH 44281 Office: City of Wadsworth 145 High St Wadsworth OH 44281

BRAHAM, ROSCOE RILEY, JR., meteorology educator; b. Yates City, Ill., Jan. 3, 1921; s. Roscoe Riley and Edith L. (Bowman) B.; m. Mary Ann Moll, Mar. 12, 1943; children—Ruth Ann Braham Ashton, Nancy Kay Braham Billingslea, Richard Riley, Jean Lou Braham Barwig. B.S. in Geology, Ohio U., 1942; S.M., U. Chgo., 1948, Ph.D., 1951. Sr. analyst U.S. Weather Bur. Thunderstorm Project, Fla., Ohio, Ill., 1947-49; staff meteorologist U. Chgo., 1949-50, 51-54; meteorologist N.Mex. Inst. Tech., Socorro, 1950-51; dir. Inst. Atmospheric Physics, U. Ariz., Tucson, 1954-56; assoc. prof. U. Chgo. and U. Ariz., 1954-56; prof. meteorology U. Chgo., 1956—; trustee Univ. Corp. Atmospheric Research, Boulder, Colo., 1965-67, 73-76, 79—, mem. exec. com., 1973-76, 79—; mem. adv. panels, coms. NSF, Dept. Commerce, Nat. Acad. Sci., NRC, 19—. Author: (with H.R. Byers) The Thunderstorm, 1949. Contbr. sci. papers to profl. lit., sects. to encys., books. Served to 1st lt. USAAF, 1942-46. Recipient Losey award Inst. Aero. Sci., 1950, Silver medal Dept. Commerce, 1950. Fellow Am. Meterol. Soc. (assoc. editor 1953-69, Rossby medal 1981, councilor 1969-72, 79-82), Royal Meteorol. Soc.; mem. Am. Geophys. Union, AAAS, Internat. Assn. for Gt. Lakes Research, Phi Beta Kappa, Sigma Xi. Avocations: stamp collecting; gardening; woodworking. Home: 57 Longcommon Rd Riverside IL 60546 Office: Dept Physics Univ Chgo 5734 S Ellis Ave Chicago IL 60637

BRAHE, NEIL BENTON, dentist; b. Appleton, Wis., June 21, 1926; s. Ralph Bertrand and Mary Jesse (O'Brien) B.; student Ripon Coll., 1946-49; D.D.S., Loyola Coll., Chgo., 1953; m. Barbara Hughes, May 28, 1983; children by previous marriage—Alison Ann, David Carlton, Bruce Benton. Mem. faculty Marquette U., Milw., 1961—, asst. prof. dental practice adminstrn., 1961-65; gen. practice dentistry, Appleton, 1953—; founder, pres. Project D, Appleton, 1961—. Mem. Am. Greater Milw. dental assns., Wis. State, Chgo. (asso.) dental socs., Outagamie Dental Soc., A.V. Purinton Acad., Am. Legion, Appleton C. of C. Clubs: Rotary, Northside Bus., Appleton Yacht, Oshkosh Power Boat, Elks, Masons. Author: Dental Assistants' Self Training Program, 1967; Executive Dynamics in Dental Practice, 1969; We Like These Ideas, 1970, Wonderful World of Modern Dentistry, 1971, Great Ideas for Dental Practice, 1972; (with Alison A. Brahe) Dental Letter Book, 1975; Marketing/Public Relations Letters for the Dental Practice, 1983. Office: 335 E Wisconsin St Appleton WI 54911

BRAINERD, GERTRUDE PERKINS, educator; b. Canton, Ill., Feb. 19, 1924; d. Keith Carey and Eva C. (Eggert) Perkins; B.S., Western Ill. U., 1945, M.S., 1955; postgrad. Bradley U., 1950, 62-63, Washington U., 1964, Ind. U., 1965-68; m. Robert W. Brainerd, May 22, 1968. Tchr. Augusta Community High Sch., 1945-47, Canton (Ill.) Jr. and Sr. High Sch., 1948-63, Belleville Twp. High Sch. W., 1963-65; instr. Belleville (Ill.) Area Coll., 1963-66, instr. English, 1970-82, chmn. dept., 1977-79; teaching assoc. Ind. U., 1966-68. Pres. bd. dirs. YWCA, Canton. Mem. AAUW (Ill. div. dir. 1974-77, 2d v.p. pub. info. 1975-77, corr. sec. 1977, project dir. 1979), AAUP (br. v.p. 1974), Pi Lambda Theta. Home: 1411 Princeton Dr O'Fallon IL 62269

BRAKE, OLEN ARTHUR, industrial safety equipment company executive; b. Cozad, Nebr., July 4, 1922; s. Ulysses Grant and Cora M. (Bullock) B.; m. Helen Margaret, Sept. 27, 1943. Student U. Nebr., 1939-41. With Sprague Electric Co., Beatrice, Nebr., 1946-51; salesman Interstate Machinery & Supply, Omaha, 1951-61; founder, ptnr. Ebco Safety Service Co., Omaha, 1961—. Served with Q.M.C., U.S. Army, 1942-45. Mem. Am. Soc. Safety Engrs., Am. Legion. Republican. Presbyterian. Clubs: Masons, Rotary, Order of Eastern Star, Shriners, Lincoln University.

BRAKER, WILLIAM PAUL, aquarium dir.; b. Chgo., Nov. 3, 1926; s. William Paul and Minnie (Wassermann) B.; m. Patricia Reese, Sept. 2, 1950; children—Helen Elizabeth, William Paul, III, Nancy Carol, Gretchen Patricia; B.S., Northwestern U., 1950; M.S., George Washington U., 1953; postgrad. U. Chgo., 1954-58. Aquarist, John G. Shedd Aquarium, Chgo., 1950, asst. curator, 1953-60, asst. dir., 1960-64, dir., 1964—; tissue culture research Nat. Cancer Inst., Bethesda, Md., 1952; cons. various aquariums and marine parks. Auditor, Rich Twp. Govt., 1975-79; trustee Prairie State Coll., 1970-74. Mem. Shedd Aquarium Soc. (trustee, sec.), Am. Assn. Zool. Parks and Aquariums (past pres., past chmn. legis. com., past chmn. ethics com.), Internat. Union of Dirs. Zool. Gardens, Am. Soc. Ichthyologists and Herpatologists, Am. Fisheries Soc., Kennicott Club (past pres.). Author, cons. books, columns and encys. on aquatic subjects. Home: RFD 1 Sunset Rd Matteson IL 60443 Office: 1200 S Lake Shore Dr Chicago IL 60605

BRAM, ISABELLE MARY RICKEY MCDONOUGH (MRS. JOHN BRAM), clubwoman; b. Oskaloosa, Ia., Apr. 4; d. Lindsey Vinton and Heddy (Lundee) Rickey; B.A. in Govt., George Washington U., 1947, postgrad., 1947-49; m. Dayle C. McDonough, Jan. 20, 1949; m. 2d, John G. Bram, Nov. 24, 1980. Dep. tax assessor and collector Aransas Pass Ind. Sch. Dist., 1939-41; sec. to city atty., Aransas Pass, Tex., 1939-41; info. specialist U.S. Dept. State, Washington, 1942-48. Treas. Mo. Fedn. Women's Clubs, Inc., 1964-66, 2d v.p., 1966-68, 1st v.p., 1968-70, pres., 1970-72; bd. dirs. Gen. Fedn. Women's Clubs. Mem. steering com. Citizens Com. for Conservation; mem. exec. com. Missourians for Clean Water. Pres., DeKalb County Women's Democratic Club, 1964. Bd. dirs. DeKalb County Pub. Library, pres., 1966; bd. dirs. Mo. Girls Town Found. Mem. AAUW, Nat. League Am. Pen Women, DeKalb County Hist. Soc., Internat. Platform Assn., Zeta Tau Alpha, Phi Delta Delta, Phi Delta Gamma. Democrat. Episcopalian. Mem. Order Eastern Star. Clubs: Tri Arts, Shakespeare, Wimodausis, Gavel, Ledgers. Editor: Mo. Clubwoman mag. Home: Sloan and Cherry Sts Maysville MO 64469

BRAMA, RICHARD LEROY, construction company executive; b. Mpls., Mar. 23, 1935; s. August and Flora (DeGidio) B.; m. Angela Ann Walrod, July 8, 1977; children—Cheryl Ann, Robert LeRoy, Thomas Anthony, Lisa Michelle, Kathleen Marie, Christy Ann, Flora Angela, Gina Maria, Richard LeRoy II. Student U. Minn., 1952-54. With mgmt. staff, salesman Boutells-Leaders, Mpls., 1951-60; salesman, investor Petruzza Realty, Mpls., 1960-62; owner Brama Constrn., Mpls., 1962—. Bd. dirs. St. John's Prep. Sch., Collegeville, Minn., 1975—. Mem. Italian Am. Club (treas. 1959-69). Republican. Roman Catholic. Avocations: softball; boating; hunting; volleyball; fishing. Office: Brama Constrn Suite 1 800 W County Rd D New Brighton MN 55112

BRAMAN, DONALD WILLIAM, public relations consultant; b. Mpls., June 19, 1917; s. Maurice I. and Ida (Garber) B.; B.A. cum laude, U. Minn., 1937; m. Sally Davidson, June 16, 1946; children—Stuart, Sandra, Richard. With Mpls. Star, 1937-41; dir. public relations Manson-Gold Advt. Agy., Mpls., 1946-47; public relations staff, publs. editor Toni Co., St. Paul, 1947-49; assoc. dir. public relations Olmsted & Foley, Mpls., 1950-58; co-founder, pres. Don Braman & Assos., Inc., Mpls., 1958-77; v.p. Doremus & Co., N.Y.C. 1977-82; pub. relations cons., 1982—; cons. Internat. Exec. Service Corps.; teaching asst., lectr. Sch. Journalism U. Minn.; dir. Minn. Advt. Fedn. Chmn. Mayor's Com. for Employment of Handicapped, 1950's; chmn. Mpls. Symphony Orchestra Guaranty Fund Campaign, 1960's; fin. com. Mpls. LWV, 1970's; dir. Am.-Israel Chamber of Commerce & Industry of Minn., 1980's. Served with USMC, 1941-45. Mem. Public Relations Soc. Am. (dir., pres. Minn. chpt., mem. exec. com. counselors acad., Disting. Service award 1973, accredited), Nat. Investor Relations Inst. (dir., pres. Minn. chpt.), Mpls. Area C. of C. (chmn. coms. various dates), Marine Corps Combat Correspondents Assn., U. Minn. Alumni Assn., Nat. Audubon Soc., Ariz. Archeol. Soc., Sigma Delta Chi, Zeta Beta Tau. Clubs: Minn. Press, Masons, Scottish Rite, Shrine. Contbr. articles in field to profl. publs., travel articles to popular publs. Home and Office: 19 S First St B-402 Minneapolis MN 55401

BRAMHALL, ROBERT RICHARD, consultant; b. Ft. Smith, Ark., Oct. 30, 1927; s. Richard Marion and Ima Lucille (Stovall) B.; A.B., Harvard U., 1951, M.B.A., 1960; m. Mary Margaret Bundy, Aug. 10, 1957; children—Robert Richard, Laura Louise. With Gen. Electric Co., N.Y.C., 1954-66, Philco-Ford subs. Ford Motor Co., Phila., 1966-68, Warwick Electronics subs. Whirlpool Corp., Niles, Ill., 1968-70; exec. chmn. Robert R. Bramhall & Assos., Lake Forest, Ill., 1970—; cons. to Rockwell Internat., Bunker-Ramo Corp., Dan River Inc., TRW, Memorex, J.P. Stevens, G.D. Searle, Molex, Spartan Mills, Simpsons-Sears Ltd. (Toronto, Ont., Can.), Rollins, Inc., GSW, Inc., Lubrizol Corp., State of Ill. Pres. Chgo. Tennis Patrons, Inc., 1974-75. Served with U.S. Army, 1946-48. Republican. Presbyterian. Clubs: Bath and Tennis (Lake Forest); Harvard of Chgo. Home: 855 Buena Rd Lake Forest IL 60045 Office: 222 Wisconsin Bldg Lake Forest IL 60045

BRAMLET, GEORGIA LOU, physical education instructor; b. Eldorado, Ill., May 9, 1928; d. Horace Green and Mamie Grace (Bays) Bramlet. B.S.E., So. Ill. U., 1952. Phys. edn. instr. Olney Jr. High Sch. East Richland Unit (Ill.), 1952-53; instr. Ridgway High Sch. North Gallatin Unit (Ill.), 1953-64; instr. Carmi High Sch. (Ill.), 1964—, girl's sports coordinator, 1973—, coach, 1973-78. Mem. White County Tchr.'s Assn., N. Central Assn. Secondary Schs. (visitation and evaluation com.). Republican. Baptist. Lodge: Eastern Star. Home: RR 3 Eldorado IL 62930

BRAMLETT, DERALD LEE, executive management consultant, seminar speaker; b. Omaha, Jan. 9, 1938; s. William S. and Alma D. (Evans) B.; m. Paula Mae Carlson, June 14, 1958; children—Terri, Carol, David, Karen. B.S.B.A., U. Minn., 1960; M.B.A., U. Nebr., 1968. Sales rep. Jello div. Gen. Foods Corp., Omaha, 1964-66; dir. personnel Bishop Clarkson Meml. Hosp., Omaha, 1966-68; cons. A.T. Kearney & Co., Chgo., 1968-71; exec. v.p. Monarch Printing Co., Chgo., 1971-74; pres., owner Lamson/Griffiths Assocs., Chgo., 1974—; exec. and profl. recruiter and cons. Served to capt., USAF, 1961-64. Mem. Chgo. Exec. Club. Republican. Baptist. Contbr. articles profl. jours. Home: 1 Cedar Glen Rd Rolling Meadows IL 60008 Office: 1 E Northwest Hwy Suite 102 Palatine IL 60067

BRANAGHAN, RICHARD LEROY, SR., health agency executive; b. Providence, Feb. 10, 1923; s. Roy and Agnes (Bush) B.; ed. Kent State U.; m. Catherine R. McMahon, May 4, 1946; children—James R., Paula J. Branaghan Suveges, Patricia H. Branaghan Wise, Virginia M. Branaghan Janc, Richard Leroy, Russell J. On-the-job trainer passenger service United Air Lines, Cleve. Hopkins Airport, 1957-65; exec. dir. Nat. Hemophilia Found., No. Ohio chpt., 1965-69, regional dir., 1969-71, dir. field services, asst. exec. dir., N.Y.C., 1971-73; exec. dir. Nat. Commn. to Combat Huntington's Disease, N.Y.C., 1973-75, v.p. N.E. Ohio chpt., 1981; dir. devel. Child Guidance Center, Cleve., 1975-76; exec. v.p. Nat. Huntingtons Disease Assn., Cleve., 1975-77; dir. devel. Better Health Assn. Am., Lakewood, Ohio, 1983-84, exec. v.p., 1984—; pres. B. & R. & Assos. Inc., hearing aid dealers, sales and rental sick room equipment, Parma Heights, Ohio. Dir. vets. affairs, vol. asst. to mayor Pawtucket (R.I.), 1948-53; spl. asst. to U.S. Senator J. Howard McGrath, R.I. office, 1946-48. Served with U.S. Army, 1943-45; ETO. Recipient Vol. awards United Air Lines, 1966, Nat. Hemophilia Found., 1970. Mem. Nat. Soc. Fund Raisers, Ohio Council Fund Raising Execs., Am. Vets. (past state dept. vice comdr. R.I.). Democrat. Roman Catholic. Club: Roadrunner's (exec. sec. 1969-70) (Cleve.). Home: 1545 Elmwood Ave Lakewood OH 44107 Office: Detroit-Warren Bldg 14805 Detroit Ave Lakewood OH 44107

BRANCAFORTE, CHARLOTTE LANG, language educator; b. Munich, Fed. Republic Germany, July 26, 1934; came to U.S., 1958; d. Christoph and Marieluise (Unglert) Knobl-Lang; m. Benito Brancaforte, Nov. 11, 1961; children—Elio Chsristoph, Daniela Beatrix, Stephanie Andrea. D. in Teaching, Landshut Coll., Germany, 1954; B.A. in Edn., Denver U., 1958; Ph.D. in German and Polit. Sci., U. Ill., 1967. Asst. prof. German, U. Wis., Madison, 1966-73, assoc. prof., 1973-78, prof., 1978—, dir. Max Kade Inst. German-Am. Studies, 1984—. Author: Venus, critical study, 1974; Partial Latin Translation of Lazarius De Tormes, 1983; co-author: Lazarillo De Tormes, 1977. Chmn., Western European Area Studies Program, U. Wis., 1980—. Mem. Modern Lang. Assn., Soc. Renaissance and Baroque Studies, Nat. Assn. Dept. Fgn. Langs. (pres. 1984). Home: 1727 Summit Ave Madison WI 53705 Office: U Wis Dept German 1220 Linden Dr Madison WI 53706

BRANCH, MARJORIE BEATRICE, ednl. adminstr.; b. Chgo., Mar. 31, 1927; d. Foster Raymond and Josephine Beatrice (Statum) B.; B.A. in Christian Edn., Wheaton Coll., 1955; M.A. in Edn., U. Chgo., 1959; student Northwestern U., 1946-48; postgrad. Atlanta U., 1956-57, Chgo. Tchrs. Coll., 1959-61. Instr., Carver Bible Inst., 1955-57; tchr. Chgo. Bd. Edn., 1957-66, adminstr. dept. human relations, 1966-72, adminstr. dept. govt. funded programs, 1972-73, prin. Leif Ericson Elem. Sch., 1973-82; dist. supt. Dist. #20, 1982—. Instr. community organizing and citizenship tng., 1966-71. Adv. council Met. Comprehensive Health Care Orgn., 1970-71; bd. dirs. LWV Citizen Info. Service, 1966-72, Tri-Community Day Care Center. Chgo.. 1973-79. Mem. Assn. Adminstrv. Women (dir. Met. Chgo. chpt.), Chgo. Prins. Assn., Phi Delta Kappa (Educator of Yr., 1979). Mem. Christian Ch. (dir. religious edn. 1969-72, vice-moderator 1982—). Home: 3021 S Michigan Ave Chicago IL 60616 Office: 10538 S Langley Ave Chicago IL 60628

BRANCH, RAYMOND LEE, nursing home administrator; b. Balt., Aug. 3, 1928; s. Augustus Lee Branch and Irene Frances (Colbert) Branch Gilmore; B.S. in Health Care Adminstrn., Wichita State U., 1980; m. Idaline Clark, Dec. 27, 1963; children—Joan L. Branch Roberts, Pamela L. Branch Gilyard, Pamela J. Branch Whitaker, Bonnie F. Branch Marshall. Served as enlisted man U.S. Air Force, 1947-74, advanced through grades to master sgt., 1971; various supervisory positions in personnel and records, U.S., Korea, Eng. and Vietnam, 1951-72; personnel supt., chief customer service center 81st Combat Support Group RAF Bentwaters, Eng., 1972-74; ret., 1974; data intern Health Systems Agy. S.E. Kans., Wichita, 1978-79; asst. adminstr. Stafford Homes, Wichita, Kans., 1980-81; nursing home adminstr. Medicalodg South of Kansas City (Kans.), 1981-82, Spl. Care Devel. Ctr., Haven, Kans., 1982-83, Heartland Care Ctr., Belleville, Kans., 1983-84, Directions Unltd., Winfield, Kans., 1985, Hill Haven of Wichita, 1985—. Decorated Bronze Star medal, Meritorious Service medal, Air Force Commendation medal with oak leaf cluster. Democrat. Baptist. Club: Am. Legion. Home: 615 E Maywood Wichita KS 67216 Office: 932 N Topeka St Wichita KS 67214

BRAND, GLENN CHRISTIAN, lawyer, oil company executive; b. Lamberton, Minn., Apr. 1, 1914; s. John Frank and Mary Louise Brand; m. Evelyn Lenore Hauge, Sept. 7, 1940; children—Marshall, Sherman, Spencer, Shadley. Student Augsburg Coll., 1937; LL.B., Mpls.-Minn. Law Sch., 1942. Bar: Minn. 1942. Pub. Lake St. Jour., Mpls., 1940; tax rep. Standard Oil Co. Ind., 1941-75; owner Brand Travel Trailers, Wayzata, Minn., 1957-70; pres. GLEVCO, Marcell, Minn., 1976—. Planning adv. commn. Itasca County; pres. Deer River Citizen Action Group; active Arrowhead Regional Devel. Commn. Served to lt. j.g. USN, 1943-45. Mem. Internat. Assn. Assessing Officers, S.D. Assn. Assessing Officers, Minn. Assn. Assessing Officers, S.D. and N.D. Petroleum Council, Minn. Petroleum Council (pres. 1956-75). Republican. Club: VFW (Talmoon, Minn.). Patentee coin operated timer, 1977. Home and Office: Star Route Box 65 Marcell MN 56657

BRANDEL, PAUL WILLIAM, lawyer, business executive; b. Chgo., Oct. 7, 1911; s. Carl P. and Christine (Johnson) B.; grad. North Park Acad., Chgo., 1928; grad. North Park Coll. 1930, LL.D., 1972; J.D., Chgo. Kent Coll. Law, 1933; LL.D., Trinity Coll., 1968, Ill. Benedictine Coll., 1973; m. Bernice Peterson Stege, Jan. 3, 1976; 1 dau., Carola Ruth (Mrs. Loren Anderson). Admitted to Ill. bar, 1933, since practiced in Chgo.; ptnr. firm Brandel & Johnson; dir. Barrington State Bank, Countryside Bank; pres. Paul W. Brandel Enterprises, Inc. Chmn. bd. Stone-Brandel Center; bd. dirs. Interlocken Music Acad., Religious Heritage Am.; life trustee Ill. Inst. Tech.; adv. bd. Salvation Army, Goodwill Industries. Decorated commdr. Kungl. Nordstjärneorden (Sweden). Mem. Am., Ill., Chgo. bar assns., Gideons. Mem. Evangelical Covenant Ch. America Clubs: Union League, Mich. Shores, Svithoid, Nordic Law, Chgo. Athletic Assn., Swedish (Chgo.); Lauderdale Yacht; Everglades (Palm Beach, Fla.); Kiwanis. Home: 2515 Mayapple Ct Northbrook IL 60062 Office: 641 Landwehr Rd Northbrook IL 60062

BRANDENBURG, HENRY LEE, mfg. co. exec.; b. Secaucus, N.J., Feb. 5, 1925; s. Henry Herman and Nathalie Estelle (Ackerman) B.; student Fairleigh Dickinson U., 1946-47, U. Colo., 1947-48, Cleve. State U., 1968-72; m. Sherrill Ann Overton, June 23, 1973; children—Sherry Lee, Henry Lance, Kim Bowen, Kit Archer, Kevin Dixon, Heidi Lalani. Project engr. Gibson Refrigerator Co., Greenville, Miss., 1952-61; mgr. def. products Mueller Brass Co., Port Huron, Mich., 1961-63; mgr. Ordnance Devel. Center, TRW, Cleve., 1964-68; dir. Tech. & Bus. Services, Cleve. State U., 1968-73, also lectr.; pres. Prontour Co., Dennison, Ohio, 1973—; dir. Lashle Enterprises, Dover, Ohio, 1972—, First Name, Inc., Ft. Pierce, Fla. Pres., Small World Credit Union, Dennison, 1981—; indsl. dir. Dennison Growth Assn., 1976—; Served with USAAF, 1943-46. Mem. Cleve. Engring. Soc., AIAA, Buckeye State Sheriff's Assn., Full Gospel Businessmen's Fellowship Internat. (v.p.). Republican. Methodist. Club: Kiwanis. Patentee in field. Home: 635 N Water St Uhrichsville OH 44683 Office: PO Box 269 Dennison OH 44621

BRANDES, ANNETTE THERRIEN, educator, consulting psychologist; b. Cokato, Minn., Nov. 6, 1940; d. Frederick George and Geneva Orcella (Therrien) B.; B.S., U. Minn., 1962, M.A., 1967; postgrad. Ariz. State U., 1969; Ph.D., U. Chgo., 1981. Lic. cons. psychologist. Tchr. phys. edn. Meml. High Sch., Eau Claire, Wis., 1962-64; phys. edn. specialist Stillwater (Minn.) Schs., 1964-66; counselor Centennial High Sch., Circle Pines, Minn., 1966-68, St. Louis Park (Minn.) Schs., 1968-69; dir. counseling Rhein-Main Am. Schs., Frankfurt, West Germany, 1969-71; asst. dean students (dean of women) Westminster Coll., Salt Lake City, 1971-72; head counselor, instr. dept. psychology St. Scholastica Coll., Duluth, Minn., 1972-74; research cons. dept. research and evaluation Chgo. Bd. Edn., 1978-79; asst. to v.p. acad. affairs U. Minn., 1981-84; pvt. practice mgmt./ednl. cons., Mpls., 1981—; owner Brandes Step Family Services; cons. psychologist Met. Med. Ctr., Mpls.; cons. edn. and human relations, Duluth. Leader, Girl Scouts U.S.A., Duluth, 1972-74. Laverne Noyes Found. scholar, 1974-75. Recipient Arrowhead Leadership award U. Minn., Duluth, 1961. Mem. Am. Psychol. Assn., Minn. Psychol. Assn., Am. Sociol. Assn., Minn. Psychologists in Pvt. Practice, Minn. Ind. Scholars Forum, Pi Lambda Theta. Author novels under pseudonym. Home: 826 Main St NE Minneapolis MN 55413

BRANDIN, DONALD NELSON, bank holding company executive; b. N.Y.C., Dec. 28, 1921; s. Nils F. and Dorothy May (Mead) B.; A.B., Princeton U., 1944; children—Robert N., Patricia A. Brandin Barnes, Douglas M.; m. Mary Elliott Keyes, Jan. 1, 1982; 1 stepdau., Elisabeth E. White. With Bankers Trust Co., N.Y.C., 1946-56; v.p. Boatmen's Nat. Bank, St. Louis, 1956-67, sr. v.p., 1967-68, chmn. exec. com., 1968-70, pres., chief operating officer, 1971-72, chmn., pres., chief exec. officer, 1973-78, chmn. bd., 1973—, chief exec. officer, 1973-84, also dir.; exec. v.p. Boatmen's Bancshares, Inc., St. Louis, 1969-72, chmn. bd., chief exec. officer, 1973—, also dir.; dir. Boatman's 1st Nat. Bank of Kansas City, Boatmen's Life Ins. Co., Phoenix, Mo. Mortgage & Investment Co., Petrolite Corp., William S. Barnickel & Co., Laclede Gas Co. (all St. Louis). Bd. dirs. Arts and Edn. Council of Greater St. Louis, St. Louis Symphony Soc., Washington U., St. Louis; pres. Civic Progress. Served to capt. U.S. Army, 1943-46. Mem. Assn. Bank Holding Cos., Assn. Res. City Bankers (bd. dirs.), Am., Mo. bankers assns., Bank Adminstrn. Inst., Internat. Fin. Conf. (bd. dirs.), Robert Morris Assocs. Clubs: Old Warson Country, St. Louis, Stadium, Bogey, Deer Creek (St. Louis); Metropolitan (Chgo.); Kansas City; Blind Brook (Purchase, N.Y.); Garden of Gods (Colorado Springs, Colo.). Home: 60 Briarcliff Saint Louis MO 63124 Office: 100 N Broadway PO Box 236 Saint Louis MO 63166

BRANDSTETTER, DAVID ALBERT, telephone product sales cos. exec.; b. St. Louis, Apr. 7, 1937; s. Edward Otto and Jeannette Eleanor (Leitner) B.; B.S.B.A., Washington U., St. Louis, 1958; m. Holly Nylander, Dec. 28, 1975; children—Sheri, Scott, Kevin, Jason, Troy. Sales rep. S.G. Adams Printing & Stationery, St. Louis, 1958-61; regional mgr. Allied Carbon and Ribbon Mfg. Co., N.Y.C., 1961-65; founder, pres. Electronic Communications Ltd., St. Louis, 1965—, Phone World, St. Louis, 1978—. Recipient Dictaphone Achievement awards, 1975-82. Mem. Adminstrv. Mgmt. Soc., St. Louis Jaycees, Sales and Mktg. Execs., Regional Commerce and Growth Assn. Contbr. articles to Progressive Mgmt. mag., 1979, 80, 81. Home: 1652 Foxleigh Ct Saint Louis MO 63131 Office: Electronic Communications Ltd 1325 Hampton Ave Saint Louis MO 63139 also Phone World 12730 Olive Street Rd Saint Louis MO 63141 also Phone World 1327 Hampton Ave Saint Louis MO 63139 also Phone World 4127 Union Saint Louis MO

BRANDSTRADER, FRED LUCAS, clergyman; b. Chgo., Nov. 30, 1938; s. Fred Lucas and Agnes (Golden) B.; B.A. in Sociology, Loyola U., Chgo., 1962;

B.D., St. Mary-Mundelein, 1964; M.A. in Urban Studies, Loyola U., 1972. Ordained priest Roman Catholic Ch., 1968. Assoc. pastor Our Lady of Angels Ch., Chgo., 1970-76; pastor San Miguelito-Panama, Panama City, 1976-77; assoc. pastor Queen of Angels, Chgo., 1976-81; pastor Providence of God, Chgo., 1981—; mem. Chgo. Priest Senate, 1982—. Bd. dirs. Better Boys Found., Chgo., 1970—, Centro de la Causa, Chgo., 1981—, Saffer Found., Chgo., 1982; mem. Hispanic Caucus, Chgo., 1970—. Home: 717 W 18th St Chicago IL 60616 Office: Providence of God Ch 717 W 18th St Chicago IL 60616

BRANDT, GENE STUART, college fundraising administrator; b. Bklyn., Aug. 29, 1950; s. Eugene Charles and Elsie Virginia (Williams) B.; m. DeSha Doiron, Aug. 11, 1979. A.B. in Polit. Sci., Knox Coll., 1972. Asst. dir. admissions Knox Coll., Galesburg, Ill., 1972-75, dir. alumni affairs, 1975-77; dir. univ. devel. U. Nev., Reno, 1977-79; dir. devel. Lake Forest Coll., Ill., 1979-81, v.p. for devel., 1981—. Mem. Council for Advancement and Support of Edn. Named Outstanding Young Man of Am., 1981. Clubs: Bath and Tennis (Lake Bluff) (bd. govs. 1984—); Mid-Day (Chgo.). Avocations: tennis; golf; photography. Office: Lake Forest Coll College and Sheridan Rds Lake Forest IL 60045

BRANDT, ROBERT LEE, JR., educational administrator; b. Greenville, Ohio, Oct. 3, 1942; s. Robert Lee and Glenna Mae (Hill) B.; m. Marilyn Lou Hartman, Aug. 1, 1964; children—Kimberly, Tamara. B.S., Ohio State U., 1964; M.S. Mich. State U., 1966; Ed.D., U. Cin., 1972. Vocat. tchr., Spencerville (Ohio) schs., 1963-68; vocat. supr. Greene Vocat. Sch., Xenia, Ohio, 1968-70, vocat. dir. 1970-74; supt. Vantage Joint Vocat. Sch., Van Wert, Ohio, 1974—; sch. pres., 1974—. Active United Way (past pres.); v.p. St. Thomas Lutheran Ch. Mem. Ohio Assn. Vocat. Sch. Supts. (past pres.), Buckeye (Ohio) Assn. Sch. Adminstrs., Am. Assn. Sch. Adminstrs. Club: Rotary (Van Wert). Home: Route 5 Box 280 Van Wert OH 45891 Office: 818 N Franklin St Van Wert OH 45891

BRANDT, WILLIAM ARTHUR, JR., consulting executive; b. Chgo., Sept. 5, 1949; s. William Arthur and Joan Virginia (Ashworth) B.; B.A. with honors, St. Louis U., 1971; M.A., U. Chgo., 1972, postgrad., 1972—; m. Patrice Bugelas, Jan. 19, 1980; 1 child, Katherine Ashworth. Asst. to pres. Pyro Mining Co., Chgo., 1972-76; commentator on bus. and polit. affairs Sta. WBBM-AM, Chgo., 1977; with Melaniphy & Assocs., Inc., Chgo., 1976-78; pres., cons. Devel. Specialists, Inc., Chgo., 1978—; dir. Lafayette Coal Co., Pyro Mining Co., Black Tam Mining Co., Harper Sq. Housing Corp., C-Way Industries, Inc., Nu-Door, Inc., Smith Tool Co., Central Transfer Corp., Ashworth Interiors, Ltd. Mem. adv. bd. Sociological Abstracts, Inc., San Diego, 1979—. LaVerne Noyes scholar, 1971-74. Mem. Am. Sociol. Assn., Am. Coll. Real Estate Cons., Internat. Sociol. Assn., Nat. Assn. Housing and Redevel. Ofcls., Nat. Assn. Real Estate Counsellors, Brit. Sociol. Assn., Chgo. Council Fgn. Relations, Ill. Sociol. Assn., Midwest Sociol. Soc., Soc. Social Research, UN Assn., Aircraft Owners and Pilots Assn. Democrat. Roman Catholic. Clubs: Petroleum (Evansville, Ind.); Amelia Island (Fla.) Plantation. Contbr. articles to profl. jours. Office: 53 W Jackson Blvd Suite 1122 Chicago IL 60604

BRANDYS, ROBERT, home furnishings store executive, pharmacist; b. Hammond, Ind., Dec. 10, 1938; s. Frank Edward and Ann (Smolen) B.; m. Lynn Diane Poplawski, June 30, 1962; children—Robert F., Todd A. B.S. in Pharmacy, Purdue U., 1960. Registered pharmacist, Ill., Ind. Pharmacist Hotz Drugs, Lansing, Ill., 1960-61, Ford Hopkins Drug Co., Melrose Park, Ill., 1961-71, Johnson Drug Co., Batavia, Ill., 1969-71; owner, operator Potpourri, Calumet City, Ill., 1971—; v.p. L. Brandys, Inc., Naperville, Ill., 1983—. Served to capt. U.S. Army, 1962-65. Decorated Army Commendation medal. Mem. Phi Eta Sigma, Rho Chi. Roman Catholic. Avocations: playing piano, fishing. Office: L Brandys Inc 1163 Ogden Ave Naperville IL 60540

BRANN, EDWARD R(OMMEL), editor; b. Rostock, Mecklenburg, Germany, May 20, 1920; s. Guenther O.R. and Lilli (Appel) B.; came to U.S., 1938, naturalized, 1966; B.A., Berea Coll., 1945; M.A., U. Chgo., 1946; postgrad. U. Wis., 1948-56; m. Helen Louise Sweet, Dec. 9, 1948; children—Johannes Weidler, Paul George. Asst. membership sec. central YMCA, Chgo., 1946-48; asst. editor Credit Union Mag., Madison, Wis., 1955-65; dir. hist. projects, asst. dir. publs. CUNA Internat., Inc., Madison, 1965-70, staff historian, 1958-65; asst. dir. publs. Credit Union Nat. Assn., Inc., Madison, 1970-72, 83-84, asst. dir. communications, 1973-83, sr. editor Credit Union mag., 1973-84, coordinator Innovative Ideas Center, 1980-84; contbg. editor Credit Union Exec. mag., 1982-84; dir. hist. projects World Council of Credit Unions, Inc., 1970-79, dir. European relations, 1972-83. Active ARC, bd. dirs. Dane County chpt., vol. cons., 1984—. Recipient Christo et Ecclesiae award Concordia Coll., Milw., 1968, Distinguished Alumnus award Berea Coll., 1977, Risser award Dane County chpt. ARC, 1983; named Ky. col. Mem. Am. Hist. Assn., NEA, Assn. Higher Edn., Luth. Laymen's League, Wis. Hist. Soc., Delta Phi Alpha, Pi Gamma Mu. Lutheran. Contbr. articles to profl. jours. Home: PO Box 383 Madison WI 53701 Office: PO Box 5905 Madison WI 53705

BRANNEN, STEPHEN ANTHONY, lawyer; b. Shenandoah, Iowa, Sept. 20, 1955; s. Charles Howard and Beatrice Davis (Williams) B.; m. Sheila Joy Scheib, May 28, 1977; 1 child, Gina Lee. B.S.B.A., Creighton U., 1977, J.D., 1979. Bar: Iowa 1979, U.S. Dist. Ct. (no. dist.) Iowa 1979, U.S. Dist. Ct. (so. dist.) Iowa 1983. Assoc. Gustafson Law Firm, Denison, Iowa, 1979—; asst. county atty. Crawford County, Denison, 1979—. Pres. Denison Youth Found., 1984; bd. dirs. Denison Community Chest, 1982—. Mem. Iowa Bar Assn., Crawford County Bar Assn. (sec.-treas. 1981-83), Iowa County Atty. Assn., Denison Jaycees (v.p. and bd. dirs. 1980-81), Denison C. of C. (v.p. 1984). Democrat. Roman Catholic. Lodge: K.C. Home: 1431 City View Dr Denison IA 51442 Office: c/o Gustafson Law Firm 27 S Main Denison IA 51442

BRANNOCK, MICHAEL CARL, geologist; b. Cambridge, Md., Mar. 9, 1949; s. Edgar Wright Sr. and Betty Irene (Rumbley) B.; m. Beverly Hathaway, May 31, 1971; children—Kristina, Kathryn. B.S., Marshall U., 1971. Geologist Ky. and W.Va. Gas Co., Prestonsburg, Ky., 1972-74; engr. Quaker State Oil Refining Corp., Belpre, Ohio, 1974-77, sr. geologist, 1977—, dist. geologist, 1985—. Mem. Am. Assn. Petroleum Geologists (cert. petroleum geologist), Ohio Oil and Gas Assn., Ohio Geol. Soc., Appalachian Geol. Soc. Democrat. Methodist. Avocations: swimming; woodworking. Home: 1901 Niagara St Parkersburg WV 26101 Office: Quaker State Oil Refining Corp 1226 Putnam Howe Dr Belpre OH 45714

BRANNON, VICTOR DEWITT, retired research inst. exec.; b. Des Moines, Aug. 26, 1909; s. Ralph William and Carrie Pearl (Hamblin) B.; A.B., U. Ariz., 1931, A.M., 1932; student U. Wis., 1935-36; Ph.D., U. Mo., 1938; m. Dorothy Ellen Webb, Aug. 20, 1933; children—Vicki Rae, Richard Carlyle. Instr. polit. sci. U. Ariz., summers 1931, 33; tchr. social scis. San Simon High Sch., 1933-34; research asst. N.Y. Bd. Regents Inquiry into the cost and character of pub. edn., 1936-37; researcher and statistician Mo. State Hwy. Dept. and Mo. State Planning Bd., 1938-39; asst. dir. St. Louis Govtl. Research Inst., 1939-46, dir., 1947-83; research cons. St. Louis, St. Louis County Bd. Freeholders, 1954, bd. trustees Met. St. Louis Sewer Dist., 1955, St. Louis Charter Bd. Freeholders, 1956-57; research cons. St. Louis Police Dept., 1947-49, 1957-65; sec. Constl. Revision Study Com., 1962; research cons. Com. on Municipalities and Services in St. Louis County, 1958, St. Louis County Charter Com., 1979. Adv. council U. Mo. Sch. Bus. and Pub. Adminstrn., 1965-66. Mem. Govtl. Research Assn. (trustee 1950, 51, pres. 1961-62), Phi Kappa Phi, Phi Delta Kappa. Author articles on polit. sci. Home: 7 Hillard Rd Glendale MO 63122

BRANOVAN, LEO, emeritus mathematics educator; b. Kishinev, Romania, Apr. 17, 1895; came to U.S., 1914, naturalized, 1926; s. Itzik and Sophia (Swartz) B.; B.S. in Elec. Engring., U. Wis., 1924; M.S. in Applied Math., U. Chgo., 1927; postgrad. (part-time) Columbia U., 1935-38; m. Pearl Lhevine, July 7, 1933; 1 dau., Rosalind Branovan Turner. Engr., Gen. Electric Co., Ft. Wayne, Ind., 1924-26; instr., cons. math. U. Minn., 1927-31; math. cons. J.D. Goode Co., Chgo., 1932-34; full-time cons. mathematician, N.Y.C., 1935-38; instr., cons. Bklyn. Poly. Inst., 1939-44; mem. faculty Marquette U., Milw., 1944—, assoc. prof. math., 1955-70, prof. emeritus, 1970—; math. cons., research in global differential geometry, Milw., 1970—. Mem. Am. Math. Soc., AAUP, Am. Soc. Engring. Edn., AAAS, Wis. Acad. Arts, Letters and Sci., Pi Mu Epsilon. Clubs: Wis. Alumni, Statesman's; Loyalty, Quarter Century (Marquette U.). Author research paper: Umbilics on Hyperellipsoids in Four Dimensions. Office: William Wehr Physics Bldg 428 Marquette U Milwaukee WI 53233

BRANSDORFER, STEPHEN CHRISTIE, lawyer; b. Lansing, Mich., Sept. 18, 1929; s. Henry and Sadie (Kohane) B.; A.B., Mich. State U., 1951; J.D., U. Mich., 1956; LL.M., Georgetown U., 1958; m. Peggy Ruth Deisig, May 24, 1952; children—Mark, David, Amy, Jill. Admitted to Mich. bar, 1956, U.S. Ct. Appeals D.C., 1959, U.S. Supreme Ct. bar, 1959; trial atty. U.S. Dept. Justice, Washington, 1956-58; spl. asst. U.S. atty. for D.C., 1958-59, also atty.-editor U.S. Dept. Justice, Washington; assoc. Miller, Johnson, Snell & Cummiskey, Grand Rapids, Mich., 1959-63, partner, 1963—; vis. instr. Mich. State U., 1973—; lectr. Inst. Continuing Legal Edn., 1973-75; mem. Mich. Supreme Ct. com. on standard jury instructions, 1963-72, com. on rules of evidence, 1975-76; mem. Mich. Civil Service Commn., 1975-78, chmn., 1977-78; Republican candidate for atty. gen. Mich., 1978; trustee, sec. Mich. State Bar Found.; Pres., Grand Rapids Child Guidance Clinic; mem. council legal advisors Rep. Nat. Com., 1981—; mem. Mich. State Bd. Canvassers, 1983—; mem. 6th Circuit Adv. Com., 1983—. Served with AUS, 1951-53. Fellow Am. Bar Found.; mem. Am., Grand Rapids (trustee) bar assns., State Bar Mich. (commr. 1968—, pres. 1974-75), Bar Assn. D.C., Fed. Bar Assn. (pres. W. Mich. chpt. 1983-84), 6th Circuit Jud. Conf. (life), Phi Alpha Delta, Delta Chi. Presbyterian (elder, trustee). Club: Rotary. Home: 7250 Bradfield Rd Ada MI 49301 Office: 800 Calder Plaza Bldg Vandenberg Center Grand Rapids MI 49503

BRANSON, JAMES R., bank official; b. Springfield, Mo., Sept. 18, 1940; s. Ivan Roland and Freida Elizabeth (Baker) B.; student MacMurray Coll., Abilene, Tex., 1961-62; B.A. in Psychology, Drury Coll., 1966; m. Mary Diane Kempker, Nov. 7, 1964; children—Andrew Franklin, Susan Marie. With outing products div. Coleman Co., Wichita, Kans., 1966-67; with ammunition plant Nat. Gypsum Co., Parsons, Kans., 1967-69; dir. personnel Boatmens Nat. Bank, Springfield, Mo., 1969—; personnel cons. 7-11 Corp.; instr. Am. Inst. Banking. Exec. advisor Jr. Achievement, 1979-80; chmn. March of Dimes, 1971-77; adv. bd. Bridgway Program, St. John's Hosp., 1983—; chmn. personnel adv. bd. ARC, 1982—; commr. Ozark council Boy Scouts Am., 1969-71, scoutmaster, 1980-82, adv. Order of Arrow, 1982-84; mem. personnel com. YMCA, 1984—; mem. guidance and counseling bd. Springfield Pub. Schs., 1984—; mem. Mid Continent Bank Video Edn. Bd., 1984—, Springfield Personnel Bd., 1984—. Served with USAF; 1959-63. Mem. Springfield C. of C. (loaned exec. program dir. 1982-83), Am. Soc. Personnel Adminstrs., Nat. Audubon Soc., Sierra Club. Republican. Home: 2218 E Cardinal St Springfield MO 65804 Office: PO Box 1157 Southside Station Springfield MO 65807

BRANSTAD, TERRY E., governor of Iowa; b. Leland, Iowa, Nov. 17, 1946; grad. U. Iowa and Drake U. Law Sch.; married Chris Branstad; 3 children. Sr. ptnr. Branstad & Schwarm, until 1982; mem. Ho. of Reps., 1972-74, 74-76, 76-78; lt. gov. State of Iowa, 1979-82, gov., 1982—. Del. to dist. and state Republican convs., 1968, 70, 72, 74, 76, 78, 80, 84; alt. del. Rep. Nat. Conv., 1976, del., 1980; mem. Truman Scholarship Found. Served with U.S. Army, 1969-71. Recipient Army Commendation medal. Mem. Nat. Govs. Assn. (com. on agr., com. on transp.), Farm Bur., Lake Mills C. of C., Am. Legion, Ducks Unltd., Sons of Norway. Lodge: Lions. Office: Office of Gov State House Des Moines IA 50319

BRANSTOOL, CHARLES EUGENE, state senator, farmer; b. Mt. Vernon, Ohio, Dec. 13, 1936; s. Charles H. and Bonnie (Motter) B.; m. Mary Jo Torrens, Sept. 19, 1958; children—Mary Martha, Marshall, John, David, Chuck. B.S. in Agr., Ohio State U., 1958. Ptnr., Branstool Bros. Gen. Farming, Utica, Ohio, 1962—; mem. Ohio Ho. of Reps., 1974-81; mem. Ohio Senate, 1982—. Mem. North Fork Bd. Edn., Utica, 1968-74, pres., 1974. Served to lt. USN, 1959-62. Named Outstanding Utica Area Jaycee, 1968, One of 10 Best Ohio Legislators, Columbus Monthly, 1984. Mem. Jaycees, Grange, Am. Legion. Presbyterian. Lodge: Masons. Home: 6360 Johnstown-Utica Rd Utica OH 43080 Office: Statehouse Columbus OH 43216

BRANT, RICHARD ROSS, manufacturing company official; Cin., Sept. 29, 1934; s. Albert Herman and Alice (Gard) B.; m. Helen Baukin, Sept. 4, 1954; children—Kristen, Mark, Eric. B.A., DePauw U., 1956; M.B.A., Western Mich. U., 1967. Mgr., Comfast Ill. Tool Works, Des Plaines, Ill., 1977—; dir. Wells Mfg. Co., Wells Corp., Three Rivers, Mich. Active Boy Scouts Am. Served to capt. USAF, 1957-60. Mem. Soc. Cable TV Engrs., U.S. Ind. Telephone Assn., Am. Mgmt. Assn. Republican. Lutheran. Club: Rotary (Elgin, Ill.).

BRASS, WINSTON JOHN, law enforcement official; b. Vizagapatam, India, May 3, 1938; came to U.S., 1959; naturalized, 1966; s. Baden Anthony and Alice (Abraham) B.; m. Pauline Marie Caronm, June 30, 1962; children—Renee, Denise, Andre, Elise, Yvonne, Dianne, Jeanette. A. Applied Sci., Kishwaukee Coll., Malta, Ill., 1978; grad. FBI Nat. Acad., 1976, So. Police inst., U. Louisville, 1972. Patrolman, Rochelle Police Dept., Ill., 1968-70, sgt., 1970-76, lt., 1974, chief of police, 1974—; mem. adv. bd. Kishwaukee Coll. Law Enforcement, 1980—. Area coordinator Blackhawk area Boy Scouts Am., 1982—. Mem. Ill. Assn. Chiefs of Police (pub. works com. 1980-82, legis. com. 1982-84), Internat. Assn. Chiefs Police. Republican. Roman Catholic. Home: 401 S 3d St Rochelle IL 61068 Office: 416 N 6th St Rochelle IL 61068

BRATEK, MICHAEL ANDREW, airline executive; b. Superior, Wis., Jan. 21, 1953; s. Andrew Jacob and Florence Jenette (Sislo) B.; m. Catherine Ann Maxwell, Sept. 12, 1981. A.A., Triton Coll., River Grove, Ill., 1975; B.S., Elmhurst Coll., Ill., 1977. Service supr. Flying Tigers, Chgo., 1977-79, account exec., 1979-80, dist. sales mgr. Mpls., 1980-83, regional sales dir., 1983-84, dir. services central U.S., Mpls., 1984—. Named Outstanding Speaker, Delta Nu Alpha Transp. Club, 1982, Dist. Sales Mgr. of Yr., Flying Tigers, 1982. Mem. Mpls. C. of C. (aviation com.), Apple Valley Jaycees, Toastmasters Internat. (v.p. 1984-85). Republican. Roman Catholic. Clubs: Decatholon, Athletic (Bloomington, Minn.). Avocations: racquetball; squash; golf; fishing. Home: 8725 144th St Ct Apple Valley MN 55124 Office: Flying Tigers 7100 34th Ave S Minneapolis MN 55411

BRATT, ALBERTUS DIRK, biology educator; b. Bozeman, Mont., Apr. 2, 1933; s. Albert H. and Anna (Visser) B.; m. Marilyn Joyce De Graaf, Sept. 7, 1955; children—Debra Lynn, Linda Sue, Pamela Kay, Dirk Alan. A.B., Calvin Coll., 1955; B.S., Mich. State U., 1957; Ph.D., Cornell U., 1964. Grad. asst. Cornell U., Ithaca, N.Y., 1961-64, research assoc., summers 1964, 65, 66; instr. biology Calvin Coll., Grand Rapids, Mich., 1958-61, prof., 1964—. Contbr. articles to profl. jours. Mem. Mich. Entomol. Soc. (pres. 1976-77), Am. Inst. Biol. Scis. Democrat. Mem. Christian Ref. Ch. Avocation: photography. Office: Calvin Coll Dept Biology Grand Rapids MI 49506

BRATTEN, DAVID LEE, beer and wine distributing and import company executive; b. Indpls., Dec. 18, 1943; s. Max Hinds and Dorothy Frances (Bartlett) B.; m. Kim Kay, Dec. 22, 1982; children—Matthew S. Mostrom, Kristine Kay. B.A. in Humanities, Purdue U., 1968. Asst. sales mgr. Nat. Liquor Corp., Indpls., 1971-76; v.p. sale and mktg. United Independents, Indpls., 1976-77; mgr., cons. Cut-Rate Liquors, Jeffersonville, Ind., 1977-79; factory rep. Nutone div. Scovill Co., Cin., 1979-82; sales engr. Champion Tool & Engring., Mishawaka, Ind., 1982-83; owner, v.p. Premium Beer & Wine Imports Co., Carmel, Ind., 1983—. Served with U.S. Army, 1968-70; Vietnam. Republican. Methodist. Lodges: Elks, Eagles. Home: Box 128 2d and Hanna Sts McCordsville IN 46055 Office: Premium Beer & Wine Imports Co 598 Industrial Dr Carmel IN 46032

BRAUDE, MICHAEL, board of trade executive; b. Chgo., Mar. 6, 1936; s. Sheldon and Nan (Resnik) B.; B.S., U. Mo., 1957; M.S. (Samuel Bronfman fellow), Columbia U., 1958; m. Linda Miller, Aug. 20, 1961; children—Peter, Adam. Vice pres. Merc. Bank, Kansas City, Mo., 1965-70, Commerce Bank of Kansas City, 1970—; exec. v.p. Am. Bank, Kansas City, 1979-83; pres. Republic Bank Kansas City, 1983-84; pres., chief exec. officer Kansas City Bd. Trade, 1984—; tchr. evening div. U. Kans., 1967-70, Avila Coll., 1974-77; host radio show Managing Your Money, Nat. Pub. Radio, Kansas City. Vice chmn. dean's adv. com. U. Mo. Sch. Bus., 1977-79; v.p. Kansas City Philharm. Orch., 1977-79; trustee Metro Community Coll. Found., Kansas City, 1978-78. Mem. Bank Mktg. Assn., Mo. Bankers Assn. Jewish. Clubs: Homestead Country (Shawnee Mission, Kans.); Kansas City. Author: Managing Your Money, 1969; author 12 children's books. Home: 5319 Mission Woods Terr Shawnee Mission KS 66205 Office: Bd Trade 4800 Main St Suite 303 Kansas City MO 64112

BRAUN, ROBERT ALEXANDER, psychiatrist; b. Chemnitz, Germany, Dec. 14, 1910; s. Leo and Bertha (Eisenschiml) B.; came to U.S., 1939, naturalized, 1946; M.D., U. Vienna (Austria), 1937; m. Gertrud E. Mittler, Jan. 6, 1946; children—Eleanor, Ronald. Intern, William McKinley Meml. Hosp., Trenton, N.J., 1940-41; resident in psychiatry Rochester (Minn.) State Hosp., 1950-51, staff psychiatrist, 1951-56; resident in psychiatry Lafayette Clinic, Detroit, 1956-58, staff psychiatrist, 1958-60; clin. dir. Clinton Valley Center (formerly Pontiac State Hosp.), Pontiac, Mich., 1960-63, dir. Oakland Div., 1963-80; pvt. practice psychiatry, 1980—; clin. assoc. prof. dept. psychiatry Mich. State U., 1969-80. Diplomate Am. Bd. Psychiatry. Life fellow Am. Psychiat. Assn. Home: 27835 Berrywood Apt 52 Farmington Hills MI 48018 Office: 25882 Orchard Lake Rd Suite 203 Farmington Hills MI 48018

BRAUN, ROBERT CLARE, association executive; b. Indpls., July 18, 1928; s. Ewald Elsworth and Lila (Inman) B.; B.S. in Journalism-Advt., Butler U., 1950; postgrad. Ind. U., 1957, 66. Reporter, Northside Topics Newspaper, Indpls., 1949, advt. mgr., 1950; asst. mgr. Clarence E. Crippen Printing Co., Indpls., 1951; corp. sec. Auto-Imports, Ltd., Indpls., 1952-53; pres. O. R. Brown Paper Co., Indpls., 1953-69; Robert C. Braun Advt. Agy., 1959-70, Zimmer Engraving Inc., Indpls., 1964-69; former chmn. bd. O. R. Brown Paper Co., Zimmer Engraving, Inc.; advt. cons. Rolls-Royce Motor Cars, 1957-59; exec. dir., chief exec. officer Historic Landmarks Found., Ind., 1969-73; exec. v.p., Purchasing Mgmt. Assn. Indpls., 1974—; pres. A.P.S. Industries, Inc., 1979—; nat. v.p. Associated Purchasing Publs., 1981—; gen. mgr. Midwest Indsl. Show, 1974—, Midwest Office Systems and Equipment Show, 1974—, Grand Valley Indsl. Show, 1974—, Evansville Indsl. Show, 1981. Chmn., Citizens' Adv. Com. to Marion County Met. Planning Dept., 1963; pres. museum com. Indpls. Fire Dept., 1966—; mem. adv. com. Historic Preservation Commn. Marion County, 1967-73; Midwestern artifacts cons. to curator of White House, Washington, 1971-73; mem. Mayor's Contract Compliance Adv. Bd., 1977—; mem. Mayor's Subcom. for Indpls. Stadium, 1981—; mem. Met. Mus. Art, Indpls. Mus. Art. Bd. dirs. Historic Landmarks Found. Ind., 1960-69; dir., sec. Ind. Arthritis and Rheumatism Found., 1960-67, pres., 1969, dir., 1970—, dir. Asso. Patient Services, 1976—; pres. Amanda Wasson Meml. Found., 1961-72, Huggler-Ault Meml. Trust, 1961-72. Recipient Meritorious Service award St. Jude's Police League, 1961; citation for meritorious service Am. Legion Police Post 56, 1962; Tafflinger-Holiday Park appreciation award, 1973; Nat. Vol. Service Citation, Arthritis Found., 1979; Margaret Egan Meml. award Ind. Arthritis Found., 1980; Indpls. Profl. Fire Fighters meritorious service award, 1982. Mem. Marion County Hist. Soc. (dir. 1964—, pres. 1965-69, 74-76, 1st v.p. 1979), Am. Guild Organists (mem. Indpls. chpt., charter mem. Franklin Coll. br.), Indpls. Humane Soc., Ind. Museum Soc. (treas., dir. 1967-74), Internat. Fire Buff Assos., Indpls. Second Alarm Fire Buffs (sec.-treas. 1967, pres. 1969), Ind. Hist. Soc., Nat. Hist. Soc., Nat. Trust Historic Preservation, Smithsonian Assn., Soc. Archtl. Historians, Am. Heritage Soc., N.A.P.M. Editors Group (nat. sec. 1979-81, nat. chmn./pres. 1981—), Am. Assn. State and Local History, Decorative Arts Soc. Indpls., Ind. Soc. Assn. Execs., Nat. Assn. Purchasing Mgmt. (W.L. Beckham internat. pub. relations award 1983), Purchasing Mgmt. Assn. Indpls. (dir. 1974—), Victorian Soc. Am. (nat. sec. 1971-74), Lambda Chi Alpha, Alpha Delta Sigma, Sigma Delta Chi, Tau Kappa Alpha. Club: Indpls. Press, Rolls-Royce Owners. Author: The Mr. Eli Lilly that I Knew, 1977. Editor: Historic Landmarks News, 1969-74; Hoosier Purchasor mag., 1974—. Contbr. articles to profl. jours. Home: 1415 W 52d St Indianapolis IN 46208 Office: 527 Glendale Bldg 6100 N Keystone Ave Indianapolis IN 46220

BRAUN, VICKI ANN COSTAN, public relations specialist, public speaker; b. Cleve., Aug. 31, 1949; d. Lewis Costan and Victoria (Borza) C.; m. Raymond Richard Braun, Jan. 8, 1972. B.S., U. Dayton, 1970; postgrad. U. Hawaii, 1972, Wright State U., 1982. Coordinator Sta. KTHI-TV, Grand Forks, N.D., 1973-74; continuity asst. Avco Broadcasting Co./Grinnell Broadcasting Co., Dayton, Ohio, 1974-76, continuity dir., 1976-78; devel. project mgr. Greater Dayton Pub. TV, 1978-79, membership dir., 1980-81; devel./pub. relations coordinator Hearing and Speech Ctr., Dayton, 1981-84; asst. dir. hosp. communications Children's Med. Ctr., Dayton, 1984—; speaker United Way Speaker's Bur. Mem. adv. council Community Services for Deaf; mem. communications adv. council United Way Greater Dayton. Recipient Golden Mike award, 1978; Ohio Edn1. Broadcasting Commn. award, 1981, Golden Quill award for feature writing, 1985. Mem. Nat. Acad. TV Arts and Scis. (dir., officer), Women in Communications, Internat. Assn. Bus. Communicators. Office: 1 Children's Plaza Dayton OH 45404

BRAVOS, THOMAS WILLIAM, data processing executive, accountant; b. Chgo., Feb. 4, 1947; s. William John and Violet (Kachiroubas) B.; m. Mary Louise Soboleski, Sept. 13, 1969; children—Christina, Stephanie, Carolyn, William (dec.), Joanna. B.A., McConmar Coll., 1969; postgrad. Lewis U., 1971, DePaul U., 1972. C.P.A., Ill. Staff acct. Arthur Greenman & Co., C.P.A.s, Chgo., 1968-71; mgr. audit Philip Rosenstrock & Co., C.P.A.s, Chgo., 1971-75; mgr. audit/MAS, Coleman, Epstein, Berlin & Co., C.P.A.s, Chgo., 1975-77; mgr. audit Schwartz, Frumm & Millman, C.P.A.s, Chgo., 1981; v.p., asst. corp. sec., dir. data processing Mercury Metal Products, Inc., Schaumburg, Ill., 1981-84; audit mgr. Schwartz, Frumm & Millman, C.P.A.s, 1984—; fin. and tax cons. Mem. Am. Inst. C.P.A.s, Ill. C.P.A. Soc. Home: 153 Braintree Dr Bloomingdale IL 60108 Office: Schwartz Frumm & Millman CPAs 6 N Michigan Ave Chicago IL 60612

BRAXTON, JOHN LEDGER, judge; b. Phila., Feb. 6, 1945; s. John L. and Sylvia (Trotman) B. B.S., Pa. State U., 1966; J.D., Howard U., 1971. Bar: Pa. 1971, D.C. 1972. Chief municipal ct. unit Dist. Atty.'s Office City of Phila., 1978-81; judge Ct. of Common Pleas, Phila., 1981—. Dir. Pa. Minority Bus. Devel. Authority, Harrisburg, 1976-81, Phila. Citywide Devel. Corp., Phila., 1981—; pres. Homemaker Services of Met. Area, 1985. Served to 1st lt. U.S. Army, 1966-68, Vietnam. Decorated Bronze Star. Mem. Nat. Bar Assn. (jud. council). Episcopalian. Club: Racquet (Phila.). Home: 514E S Randolph St Philadelphia PA 19147 Office: Ct Common Pleas 203 One East Penn Square Philadelphia PA 19107

BRAY, ANDREW MICHAEL, graphics company executive; b. Norway, Mich., July 31, 1938; s. Andrew John and Ethel Mary (Cronick) B.; B.S.M.E., Mich. Tech. U., 1960; postgrad. U. Wis., Milw., 1961-63; registered profl. engr.; children—Susan Mary, Mark Andrew. Engr., AC Electronics Co., 1960-63; engr. research and devel. Paper Converting Machine Co., Green Bay, Wis., 1963-67; chief engr. Magna-Print Co., Green Bay, 1967-68; sales engr. J.M. Grimstad Inc., Green Bay, 1968-74; pres. OEM Devel. Corp., Oconto Falls, Wis., 1974-77; pres. Tech Draulics Ltd., Oconto Falls, 1975-84; ABAH Sports, Ltd.; mgr. research Magna-Graphics Corp.; pres. Abah Sports, Ltd.; instr. mech. engring. U. Wis., Green Bay, 1964-69; coach Howard-Suamico High Sch. Hockey. Town chmn. Town of Suamico (Wis.), 1974-81; sec. Suamico San. Dist., 1972-84; bd. dirs. Brown County Youth Hockey Bd.; pres. Howard-Suamico Youth Hockey Assn.; active Big Bros./Big Sisters of Brown County. Mem. Fluid Power Soc. Roman Catholic. Clubs: K.C., Elks, Optimists. Contbr. articles to profl. publs. Inventor in field. Home: 3244 Maple Grove Ln Suamico WI 54141 Office: Magna-Graphics Corp 229 Van Buren Oconto Falls WI 54154

BRAY, MICHAEL JOSEPH, magnet manufacturing company executive, city fire official; b. Ft. Harrison, Ind., Oct. 12, 1939; s. James and Martha (Mock) B.; m. Sharon Joyce Worley, June 10, 1960; 1 child, Kimberly Ruth. Student indsl. mgmt. Purdue U., 1961-64. Cert. master firefighter in tactics, Ind.; cert. instr. fire service, Ind. Draftsman, machine repair Permanent Magnet Co., Inc., Indpls., 1957-59, staff cost acctg. and quality control, 1959-62, sales and inventory control, 1962-67, sales, inventory and prodn. control, 1967-72, purchasing agt., mgr. traffic, engr. security prodn., 1972—. Vol. fireman City of Lawrence, Ind., 1955—; corp. pres. Lawrence Vol. Fire Dept., Inc., Ind., 1966-67, 69-70, 72-73, 76-79, 83-84, corp. treas., 1981-83, adminstr. asst. chief, 1984—; chief pit fire detail Indpls. Motor Speedway, 1983—; coach Lawrence Little League program, 1969; candidate sch. bd. Met. Sch. Dist., Lawrence Twp., 1970, textbook selection com., 1974-75; candidate Lawrence City Council, 1971. Recipient Cert. of Recognition, ARC, 1963, named Fireman of Month, Kiwanis, 1971. Mem. Assn. Prodn. and Inventory Control (treas. 1968-69), Am. Foundrymen's Assn., Ind. Firefighters' Assn. (chmn. affairs of vols. 1976-79). Republican. Avocations: scuba diving and rescue; fishing; theatre; tennis. Home: 7405 E 50th St Lawrence IN 46226 Office: Permanent Magnet Co Inc PO Box 26226 4437 Bragdon St Indianapolis IN 46226

BRAY, PIERCE, telephone company executive; b. Chgo., Jan. 16, 1924; s. Harold A. and Margaret (Maclennan) B.; B.A., U. Chgo., 1948, M.B.A., 1949; m. Maud Dorothy Minto, May 14, 1955; children—Margaret Dorothy, William Harold, Andrew Pierce. Fin. analyst Ford Motor Co., Dearborn,

Mich., 1949-55; cons. Booz, Allen & Hamilton, Chgo. and Manila, 1955-58; mgr. pricing Cummins Engine Co., Columbus, Ind., 1958-61, controller, 1961-66; v.p. fin. Weatherhead Co., Cleve., 1966-67; v.p. Mid-Continent Telephone Corp. (now ALLTEL Corp.), Hudson, Ohio, 1967-70, treas., 1967-70, v.p. fin., 1970-81, exec. v.p., chief fin. officer, 1981—, dir., 1976—, also chmn. various subs.; dir., trustee Cardinal Group of Funds; instr. fin. and econs. U. Detroit, 1952-54. Trustee Beech Brook, treatment center for disturbed children, Pepper Pike, Ohio, 1972—, treas., 1976-79, pres., 1979-81. Served with AUS, 1943-46; PTO. Mem. Fin. Execs. Inst., U.S. Telephone Assn. (chmn. investor relations com. 1974—), Inst. Public Utilities (exec. com. 1978-83, chmn. 1981-82), Cleve. Treasurers Club, Delta Upsilon. Presbyterian (elder). Clubs: Downtown Athletic (N.Y.C.); Union, Midday (Cleve.); Walloon Lake (Mich.) Yacht (commodore 1982), Walloon Lake Country. Home: 31173 Northwood Dr Pepper Pike OH 44124 Office: 100 Executive Pkwy Hudson OH 44236

BRAY, RICHARD DANIEL, retail book company executive; b. Albany, N.Y., June 19, 1945; s. Harry and Sylvia Jeanette (Weiss) B.; m. Suzannah Greentree, Aug. 17, 1980. A.A., Pasadena City Coll., 1966; B.A., San Francisco State U., 1969. Pres. Guild Books, Inc., Chgo., 1979—. Judge, Carl Sandburg award Friends of Chgo. Pub. Library, 1985; mem. lit. adv. bd. Ill. Arts Council, 1985; mem. multi-arts adv. com. Chgo. City Arts Program, 1985; bd. dirs. Friends of Chgo. Pub. Library. Mem. Am. Booksellers Assn., Nat. Assn. Coll. Stores, Nat. Writers Union, Am. Writers Congress (exec. 1981-82), Midwest Book Travelers. Avocation: magic. Office: Guild Books 2456 N Lincoln Ave Chicago IL 60614

BRAY, SYLVIA CECILE, tax practitioner, bookkeeper, insurance agent; b. Sidney, Ohio, Dec. 10, 1929; d. Joseph Carter and Emma Faye (Barlow) Bedford; m. Robert Bray, Aug. 17, 1946; children—James Ray, Linda Faye Dubois. Cert. proficiency Southwestern Acad., 1967. Owner, pres. Bray's Income Tax Service, Sidney, 1964—; auditor Copeland Corp., Sidney, 1969-73; ins. agt. Rumbaugh & Assocs., Lima, Ohio, 1977—; rep., mem. adv. com. Women Bus. Owners; cons. in tax savs. field. Recipient Millionaires Club award Am. Bankers Life Ins. Co., 1980-81, Women of Yr. award, 1979; one of three women bus. owners present at presdl. signing of exec. order establishing adv. com. on women's bus. ownership. Buckeye Mem. Nat. Assn. Income Tax Practitioners (cert., pres. Ohio chpt.), Nat. Fedn. Ind. Bus. Mem. Ch. of God. Club: Altrusa Internat. (Sidney). Home and office: 1359 S Main Ave Sidney OH 45365

BRAYER, ROGER CHARLES, metallurgist; b. Aubervilliers, Seine, France, July 26, 1923; came to U.S., 1946, naturalized, 1952; s. Jules Ernest and Rachel Eloise (Leloup) B.; B.S., U. Paris, 1944; Certificate d'Etudes Superieures, Sorbonne, 1945; M.S., St. Louis U., 1950; postgrad. Rensselaer Poly. Inst., 1959-63; m. Edith Marie Silies, Dec. 27, 1947; children—Michel Roger, Mark Jean, Patrick Charles, Anne-Marie Suzanne. Spectrographer, analyst, devel. engr. Vickers Electric Div., 1951-58; devel. spectrographer, research chemist, nuclear metallurgist, project engr. Combustion Engring. Nuclear Div., 1958-66; chief metallurgist Vactec, Inc., Maryland Heights, Mo., 1966-69, research and devel. mgr., 1969-73, product mgr., 1973—, safety coordinator, 1976-80, safety dir., 1980—. Mem. disaster team ARC, 1979; scoutmaster Boy Scouts Am., 1979. Served with French Arty., 1945. Chaplain Grady Scholar, 1946. Mem. Am. Chem. Soc., Soc. for Applied Spectroscopy, Am. Soc. for Metals, French Soc. St. Louis (v.p. 1949-50), Sigma Xi. Roman Catholic. Home: 214 Stoneyview Ct Creve Coeur MO 63141 Office: Vactec Inc 10900 Page Blvd Saint Louis MO 63132

BREAM, HARVEY CLEVELAND, JR., seminary president; b. Champaign, Ill., July 23, 1924; s. Harvey C. and Maude (Harbaugh) B.; m. Mary Ann Work, Aug. 7, 1949; children—Deborah, Christine, Harvey C., Scott. A.B., Cin. Bible Sem., 1944, postgrad., 1945-47; D.Div. (hon.) Ky. Christian Coll., 1979. Ordained to ministry, 1944. Pastor, Montgomery Road Ch. of Christ, Cin., 1948-52; evangelist, then dir. The Christian Restoration Assn., Cin., 1952-70; pastor Forest Dale Ch. Christ, Cin., 1957-60; pres. The Cin. Bible Sem., 1970—; mem. com. N.Am. Christian Conv., Cin., 1982—. Editor: Restoration Herald, 1960-70, The Anchor, 1947-48; contbr. articles to Christian Standard and The Lookout. Avocations: Gardening, stamp collecting, hunting. Office: The Cincinnati Bible Sem 2700 Glenway Ave Cincinnati OH 45204

BRECHEISEN, KURT DALE, broadcasting executive, radio announcer; b. Garnett, Kans., Oct. 10, 1956; s. Adell Warren and Jean Elane (Estep) B. B.S. in Radio-TV, Theatre Kans. State U., 1979. Announcer Sta. KSDB, Manhattan, Kans., 1978-79, Sta. KJLS, Hays, Kans., 1980-81, music dir., 1981—. Republican. Methodist. Avocations: computer programming; electronics; reading; snow skiing. Home: 120 Vicki Ln Hays KS 67601 Office: KJLS Radio Rural Route 1 Hays KS 67601

BRECHER, ARTHUR SEYMOUR, biochemistry educator, researcher; b. N.Y.C., Mar. 30, 1928; s. Harry Benjamin and Mollie (Rudich) B.; m. Laura Alma Lyman, June 19, 1966; children—Benjamin, Sharon. B.S., City Coll. N.Y., 1948; Ph.D., UCLA, 1956; postdoctoral. Purdue U., 1956-58. Jr. research scientist N.Y. State Dept. Mental Hygiene, N.Y.C., 1948-52; biochemist FDA, Washington, 1958-60; assoc. research biochemist Bklyn. State Hosp., 1960-63, asst. prof. biochemistry George Washington U. Med. Sch., Washington, 1963-69; assoc. prof. chemistry Bowling Green State U., Ohio, 1969-75, prof., 1975—. Contbr. articles to profl. jours. Pres. Wood County Heart Br., Bowling Green, 1974-75; trustee Wood County Cancer Unit, Bowling Green, 1972-84, Northwest Ohio Heart Assn., Bowling Green, 1980-84. Recipient Research and Devel. award Bowling Green State U., 1974, Special Achievement award, 1975. Fellow AAAS; mem. Am. Soc. Biol. Chemists, Internatl. Soc. Neurochemistry, Am. Chem. Soc., Am. Heart Assn., Sigma Xi. Avocations: cycling, reading, lapidary, hunting. Office: Bowling Green State U Bowling Green OH 43403

BRECHER, FRANKLIN RAYMOND, pathologist; b. Bklyn., Dec. 14, 1933; s. Max and Anne (Wolfe) B.; m. Terez Birk, Sept. 27, 1970; stepchildren—Carolyn Hopkins, Angela Birk. B.A., NYU, 1956; D.O., Kirksville Coll. Osteo. Medicine, 1964. Intern Grandview Hosp., Dayton, Ohio, 1964-65, resident in anatomic and clin. pathology, 1965-69, chmn. pathology dept., 1977—; resident in clin. pathology Mayo Clinic, Rochester, Minn., 1969-70; dir. labs, Southview Hosp., Centerville, Ohio, 1978—, Grandview Hosp., Dayton, Ohio, 1977—; asst. clin. prof. Wright State U. Sch. Medicine, Dayton, 1975—; assoc. clin. prof. Ohio U. Coll. Osteo Medicine, Athens, 1978—. Trustee Community Blood Ctr., Dayton. Served with U.S. Army, 1957-59; with USAR, 1959-65. Fellow Coll. Am. Pathologists, Am. Soc. Clin. Pathologists; mem. Ohio Soc. Pathologists, Dayton Area Pathologists, Am. Assn. Blood Banks, Am. Osteo. Coll. Pathologists. Office: Grandview Hosp 405 Grand Ave Dayton OH 45405 also Southview Hosp 1997 Miamisburg-Centerville Rd Centerville OH 45459

BRECKENRIDGE, ROBERT JERALD, insurance executive; b. Kansas City, Mo., Dec. 7, 1933; s. Robert R. and Ruth W. (Rigg) B.; m. Martha C. McKittrick, July 18, 1965; children—Bruce R., William R. B.S.B.A., U. Mo., 1955. C.P.A., Mo. With Arthur Young & Co., Kansas City, Mo., 1957-67; with Employers Reins. Corp., Overland Park, Kans., 1967-81, comptroller, 1971-81, treas., 1977-81; comptroller, treas. ERC Mgmt. Corp., Overland Park, 1981-83; v.p. Employers Reins. Corp., Overland Park, 1983—; dir. First Fidelity Equity Corp., Bates-Turner, Inc. Served to 1st lt. USAF, 1955-57. Rhodes Clay scholar. Mem. Fin. Execs. Inst., Am. Inst. C.P.A.s, Mo. Soc. C.P.A.s, Nat. Assn. Accts., Alpha Kappa Psi, Beta Gamma Sigma, Phi Eta Sigma. Methodist. Office: 5200 Metcalf Ave PO Box 2991 Overland Park KS 66201

BRECKON, DONALD JOHN, educator; b. Port Huron, Mich., June 11, 1939; s. Robert Joseph and Margaret Elizabeth (Wade) B.; A.A., Port Huron Community Coll., 1959; B.S., Central Mich. U., 1962, M.A., 1963; M.P.H. (USPHS trainee), U. Mich., 1968; Ph.D., Mich. State U., 1977; postgrad. U. Wis., 1965-66, Western Mich. U., 1968; m. Sandra Kay Biehn, Sept. 4, 1959; children—Lori E., LeeAnne M., Lisa C., Lynanne W. Instr. health edn. Central Mich. U., Mt. Pleasant, 1963-68, asst. prof., 1968-72, assoc. prof., 1972-81, prof. health edn., 1978-81, asst. dean health, phys. edn. and recreation, 1981-82, assoc. dean edn., health and human services, 1982—; cons. hosps. and health agencies. Mem. governing council Health Systems Agy., Region 6, Mich., 1976-79; bd. dirs. Am. Cancer Soc., 1977-79, Community Council on Drug Misuse, 1976-78. Recipient Central Mich. U. Teaching Effectiveness award, 1975; Disting. Service award Mich. Alcoholism and Addiction Assn., 1977; Mich. Dept. Edn. scholar, 1971; Yale U. Drug Dependence Inst. scholar, 1973; Midwest Inst. Alcohol Studies, Mich. Dept. Public Health scholar, 1974; Am. Council on Edn. Leadership Devel. program fellow, 1979. Mem. Mich. Public Health Assn. (pres. 1976-77), Am. Public Health Assn., Soc. Public Health Edn. (pres. 1978-79), Internat. Soc. Pub. Health Edn., Coalition of Mich. Health Edn. Orgns., Mich. Alcohol and Addiction Assn., Am. Alliance for Health and Phys. Edn. Contbr. articles to profl. jours.; author: Hospital Health Education: A Guide to Program Development, 1982; Community Health Education: Setting, Roles and Skills, 1985. Home: 1413 Crosslanes St Mount Pleasant MI 48858 Office: Central Mich Univ Mount Pleasant MI 48859

BRECKON, PATRICK WILLARD, real estate executive, investment consultant; b. Whitewater, Wis., Dec. 13, 1944; s. Fred S. and Dorothy M. (Vivian) B.; m. Mary Alice Edge, Apr. 1, 1972; children—Sean, Mark. B.S. in Anthropology, U. Wis., 1976. Lic. realtor, Wis. Salesperson, Parkwood Realty, Madison, Wis., 1977-78, Casey, Carney & White, Madison, 1978-80, First Realty, Madison, 1980-81; owner, pres. Real Estate Clearinghouse, Madison, 1981—. Developed real estate brokerage system for residential sales. Served in USAF, 1965-69. Named Airman of Yr., Edwards AFB, 1967. Mem. Greater Madison Bd. Realtors, Wis. Realtors Assn., Nat. Assn. Realtors.

BREDE, ARDELL FREDERICK, hospital executive; b. Austin, Minn., June 23, 1939; s. Fred and Linda Bertha (Scheel) B.; A.Commerce, Austin Jr. Coll., 1957-59; postgrad. U. Minn., 1970-71, Brigham Young U., 1974; m. Judith Ellen Nelson, Mar. 24, 1961; children—Leslie, Scott, Jennifer. With Rochester (Minn.) Methodist Hosp., 1959—, dir. admissions and bus. services, 1975—. Mem. utilization review com. Mayo Clinic, 1970—; chmn. Olmsted County United Way, 1982, pres. elect, 1984; mem. citizens adv. task force Rochester Attraction Center, 1979—; mem. adv. panel Minn. State Arts Bd., 1983. Mem. Hosp. Fin. Mgmt. Assn., Southeastern Minn. Health Systems Agy. Lutheran. Club: Rochester Quarterbacks. Home: 431 14th Ave SW Rochester MN 55902 Office: Rochester Methodist Hospital 201 W Center St Rochester MN 55901

BREDENKAMP, NORMAN LOUIS, elec. engr.; b. Peoria, Ill., Jan. 2, 1944; s. John Louis and Dagmar (Soyring) B.; student DeVry Tech. Inst., 1962-64. Self-employed radio technician, Browns, Ill., 1958-62, radio and TV technician, Browns, 1964-65; elec. engr. Pacific Press & Shear, Mount Carmel, Ill., 1967-70; computer analyst RCA, Palm Beach Gardens, Fla., 1967-70; self-employed radio and TV technician, Palm Beach Gardens, 1970-72; radio announcer, program dir. WVMC-WSAB, Mt. Carmel, Ill., 1972-73; self-employed trouble shooter, Grayville, Ill., 1973—. Mem. Grayville Days Com.; vol. Fire Dept.; active Civil Defense. Mem. IEEE, Instrument Soc. Am., C. of C., Am. Sunbathing Assn. Clubs: CB Radio; Traveliers (Lake Geneva, Wis.). Home: Route 1 Grayville IL 62844 Office: Alexander Ln Grayville IL 62844

BREECE, ROBERT WILLIAM, JR., lawyer; b. Blackwell, Okla., Feb. 5, 1942; s. Robert William and Helen Elaine (Maddox) B.; B.S.B.A., Northwestern U., 1964; J.D., U. Okla., 1967; LL.M., Washington U., St. Louis, 1970; m. Elaine Marie Keller, Sept. 7, 1968; children—Bryan, Justin, Lauren. Admitted to Okla. bar, 1967, Mo. bar, 1969, U.S. Supreme Ct. bar, 1976; practice law, St. Louis, 1968—. Mem. Mo. Bar Assn., ABA, Am. Soc. Corp. Secs. Inc. Presbyterian. Clubs: Forest Hills Country (pres. 1978), Mo. Athletic, University. Home: 35 Crown Manor Chesterfield MO 63017 Office: 7777 Bonhomme Suite 1500 Saint Louis MO 63105

BREED, EILEEN JUDITH, educator; b. Chgo., Sept. 18, 1945; d. John Joseph and Helen Agatha (Hoy) Kennedy; B.A., Northeastern Ill. U., 1966, M.A., 1976, postgrad., 1980-81; postgrad. Nat. Coll. Edn., 1981, 83; m. Harvey Breed, Feb. 3, 1973; 1 dau., Diana Marie Parks. Tchr., Canty Elem. Sch., Chgo., 1967-76; tchr. St. Raymond's Sch., Mt. Prospect, Ill., 1976-78; pvt. practice diagnosis and remediation learning disabilities, cons. spl. edn., Des Plaines, Ill., 1976-78; prin. Angel Town Pvt. Sch., Des Plaines, 1978-79; tutoring, coop. work tng. coordinator Nipper Sch., spl. edn. facility, Des Plaines, 1979—; tchr. parent-edn. classes; cons. pvt. schs. Mem. Council Exceptional Children, Council on Understanding Learning Disabilities, Nat. Assn. Retarded Citizens, Ill. Assn. Vocat. Edn. Spl. Needs Personnel. Initiated various spl. edn. programs. Home: 1011 W Grant Dr Des Plaines IL 60016 Office: 1101 E Gregory Des Plaines IL 60016

BREED, STERLING LARUE, college educator, counselor; b. Paw Paw, Mich., Oct. 9, 1928; s. LaRue H. and Eda L. (Ayars) B.; m. Betty Hansen, June 17, 1953; 1 child, Thomas Sterling. B.S., Western Mich. U., 1955; M.A., 1958; postgrad. Mich. State U., 1960-65, U. Mich., 1974-81. Trooper, Mich. State Police, Traverse City, 1950-53; tchr. Paw Paw Jr. High Sch., 1955-56; asst. dean of men Western Mich. U., Kalamazoo, 1956-60, counselor, coordinator acad. advising, 1960-73, dir. counseling ctr., 1973-76, counselor, prof., 1976—. Served with U.S. Army, 1946-48; ETO. Recipient Meritorious Service award Mich. State Police, 1952, Disting. Service award Western Mich. U., 1985. Mem. Mich. Coll. Personnel Assn. (Outstanding Service award 1978, pres. 1971-72, bd. dirs. 1979-85), Am. Coll. Personnel Assn. (state membership chmn. 1966-77), Mich. Personnel and Guidance Assn. (bd. dirs. 1984-85), Kalamazoo County Personnel and Guidance Assn. (exec. bd. 1976-77), Am. Assn. Counseling and Devel., Nat. Vocat. Guidance Assn., Mich. Vocat. Guidance Assn., Mich. League Nursing (pres. 1979-81, Outstanding Service award 1981), Nat. League Nursing (region vice-chmn. 1981-83, nat. bd. dirs. 1983—), AAUP, Assn. Humanistic Edn. and Devel., Phi Delta Kappa, Sigma Tau Gamma (pres. 1964-66), Western Mich. U. Alumni Assn. (pres. 1980-82). Republican. Episcopalian. Avocations: tennis; travel; photography. Home: 867 Dobbin Dr Kalamazoo MI 49007 Office: Western Mich U Counseling Ctr Kalamazoo MI 49008

BREEDEN, CHARLES GARY, SR., business executive, consultant; b. Miami, Fla., Mar. 20, 1935; s. Daniel S. and Ida M. (McCormick) B.; m. Jacqueline L. Tidmore, Nov. 5, 1956; children—Charles, Debbie, Brett, Mitch, Frances. Student U. N.C., 1954-55, UCLA, 1957. Exec. v.p. B & E Sales, Detroit, 1977-81; owner, pres. Glenlore Golf Club, Milford Mich., 1978-83; owner, pres. Breeden Enterprises, Milford, 1981-83; exec. v.p., gen. mgr., prin. System Specialist Inc., Arlington, Tex., 1983—; exec. v.p., prin. Kelley & Co., Dallas, 1983—; cons. bus. mgmt., computer sales, and mgmt. techniques. Chmn. Cotacawa council Boy Scouts Am., 1962-65. Recipient Outstanding Sales and Merchandising award Nabisco, 1958; Pres.'s award for outstanding sales mgmt. B & E Sales, 1970; other sales and sales mgmt. awards. Clubs: Adcraft, Shady Hollow Country.

BREEN, JOHN GERALD, manufacturing company executive; b. Cleve., July 21, 1934; s. Hugh Gerald and Margaret Cecelia (Bonner) B.; B.S., John Carroll U., 1956; M.B.A., Case Western Res. U., 1962; m. Mary Jane Brubach, Apr. 12, 1958; children—Kathleen Anne, John Patrick, James Phillip, David Hugh, Anne Margaret. With Clevite Corp., Cleve., 1957-73, gen. mgr. foil div., 1969-73, gen. mgr. engine parts div., 1973-74; group v.p. indsl. group Gould Inc., Rolling Meadows, Ill., 1974-77, exec. v.p., 1977-79; pres. Sherwin-Williams Co., Cleve., 1979-81, chmn., pres., chief exec. officer, 1981—, also dir.; dir. Parker-Hannifin Corp., Cleve., LTV Corp., Cleve., Nat. City Bank, Cleve. Served with U.S. Army, 1956-57. Clubs: Pepper Pike, Union, Cleve. Skating. Office: Sherwin-Williams Co 101 Prospect Ave NW Cleveland OH 44115

BREEN, KATHERINE ANNE, speech and language pathologist; b. Chgo., Oct. 31, 1948; d. Robert Stephen and Gertrude Catherine (Bader) Breen; B.S., Northwestern U., 1970; M.A. (U.S. Rehab. Services trainee), U. Mo., Columbia, 1971. Speech/lang. pathologist Fulton (Mo.) pub. schs., 1971-73; co-dir. Easter Seal Speech Clinic, Jefferson City, Mo., summers 1972, 73; speech/lang. pathologist Shawnee Mission (Kans.) pub. schs., 1973—; staff St. Joseph's Hosp., Kansas City, Mo., 1978-81, Midwest Rehab. Ctr., Kansas City, 1985—; pvt. practice speech therapy; cons. East Central Mo. Mental Health Center; guest lectr. Fontbonne Coll., St. Louis. Clin. certification in speech pathology. Mem. Am., Kans. speech and hearing assns., NEA, Mo. State Tchrs. Assn., Kansas City Alumni Assn. of Northwestern U. (dir. alumni admissions council, Outstanding Leadership award for work on alumni admissions council 1981), Friends of Art Nelson/Atkins Art Gallery and Museum (vol.), Nat. Trust Hist. Preservation, Kansas City Hist. Found., Zeta Phi Eta. Methodist. Home: 6865 W 51st Terr Apt 1C Shawnee Mission KS 66202 Office: 7235 Antioch Shawnee Mission KS 66204

BREES, ANTON DURHAM, electronics company executive; b. Durham, N.C., June 23, 1936; s. Anton and Josephine Y. (Yarnell) B.; m. Sharon S. Phillips, Dec. 18, 1983; children: Jacquelyn Brees McNicholos, Anton D., III, Douglas K., David Kovac, Timothy Kovac. Mus.B., U. Miami, Coral Gables, Fla., 1958; M.S., George Washington U., 1968. Commd. 2d lt., U.S. Air Force, 1958, advanced through grades to col., 1977, ret., 1982; chief electronics, warfare div. Headquarters U.S. Air Force, Pentagon, Washington, 1976-79, dep. for ops., Eglin Air Force Base, 1979-82; dir. F-15 program DSD, Northrop, Rolling Meadows, Ill., 1982-83, dir. mktg., 1983-84, dir. spl. projects, 1984—; guest speaker Italian Air Force War Coll., Milano, Italy, 1974, 75, French Air Force War Coll., Paris, 1975, 76. Author: Formulation of Foreign Policy With Red China, 1967. Contbr. articles to profl. publs. Regional adviser Ramstein, Fed. Republic Germany council Boy Scouts Am., 1974; bd. dirs. Handicapped Olympics, Eglin Air Force Base, 1980. Decorated Legion of Merit. Mem. Assn. Old Crows (nat. bd. dirs. 76—, nat. pres. 1978-80). Soc. Preservation and Encouragement of Barbershop Quartet Singing in Am. Republican. Roman Catholic. Lodge: K.C. Avocations: Barbershop chorus, running, stunt flying. Home: 23049 Bonny Riggs Ct Mundelein IL 60060 Office: Northrop DSD 600 Hicks Rd Rolling Meadows IL 60008

BREEST, FRANCES ANN, educator; b. Milw., Mar. 1, 1949; d. Edward Bernard and Virginia Mary (Jablonowski) Popa; m. Robert Allen Breest, Aug. 6, 1971. B.A., Alverno Coll., Milw., 1971; M.A. in Exceptional Edn., Cardinal Stritch Coll., Milw., 1981, M.A. in Reading, 1983. Elem. sch. tchr. Pub. Schs., Milw., 1972-77, learning disabilities tchr., 1977—. Mem. Internat. Reading Assn., Wis. Council for Learning Disabilities, Milw. Area Reading Council, Wis. State Roads Assn., Council for Exceptional Children, Assn. Children with Learning Disabilities, Women's Aux. of Am. Soc. Concrete Constrn., Milw. Tchrs. Union (blg. rep., reading and exceptional edn. coms.), Delta Epsilon Sigma. Lutheran. Club: Concordia Century (Milw.). Home: 10928 N Lake View Rd 6E Mequon WI 53092 Office: 3618 N 53d St Milwaukee WI 53216

BREGSTEIN, RICHARD FREDRIC, marketing executive; b. N.Y.C., Apr. 25, 1936; s. Samuel Joseph and Muriel (Rubine) B.; B.A., U. Vt., 1957; m. Jane Bell Henning, Dec. 18, 1968; children—Alison Ruth, Jared Joseph. Mgr. community relations Prudential Ins. Co., Newark, 1960-71; mgr. public info. Coll. of Medicine and Dentistry of N.J., Newark, 1971-73; pres. Aspen Group, Inc., Newark, 1973-74; dir. community relations and health info. Martland Med. Center, 1974-76; dir. pub. affairs Ill. Hosp. Assn., Oak Brook, 1976-79; dir. public and profl. relations Joint Commn. on Accreditation of Hosps., Chgo., 1979-82; regional dir. Planco, 1982—; pres. Chippewa Grap, Inc., 1985—; lectr. on mktg., public relations governing bds. and fin. planning. Pres. bd. New Well Narcotic Rehab. Center, 1971-72; bd. dirs. Urban League Essex County, 1973-76; bd. dirs. Interracial Council for Bus. Opportunity of N.J., 1965-68; bd. dirs. Am. Lung Assn. of N.J., 1975-76; mem. City of Newark Narcotic Adv. Council, 1971-76; bd. dirs. Newark dist. ARC, 1973-76. Mem. Am. Mktg. Assn., Chgo. Mktg. Assn., N.Y. Acad. Scis., Acad. Hosp. Public Relations. Home: 606 Chippewa Ln Darien IL 60559 Office: 606 Chippewa Ln Darien IL 60559

BREHM, SHARON STEPHENS, psychology educator; b. Roanoke, Va., Apr. 18, 1945; d. John W. and Jane C. (Phenix) Stephens; m. Jack W. Brehm, Oct. 25, 1968 (div. Dec. 1979). B.A., Duke U., 1967, Ph.D., 1973; M.A., Harvard U., 1968. Lic. psychologist, Kans. Asst. prof. psychology Va. Poly. Inst. and State U., Blacksburg, 1974-75; asst. prof. psychology U. Kans., Lawrence, 1975-78, assoc. prof., 1978-83, prof., 1983—. Author: The Application of Social Psychology to Clinical Practice, 1976; Intimate Relationships, 1985; (with others) Psychological Reactance, 1981. Co-editor: Developmental Social Psychology, 1981. Fulbright scholar, Paris, 1981-82. Mem. Am. Psychol. Assn., Soc. Exptl. Social Psychology, Nat. Council on Families. Democrat. Office: Dept Psychology U Kans Lawrence KS 66045

BREHM, WILLIAM ALLEN, JR., urban planner; b. Neenah, Wis., Jan. 18, 1945; s. William Allen and Katharine (Gilbert) B.; B.A., Lawrence U., 1967; M.U.P. (Richard King Mellon fellow 1967-68), Mich. State U., 1973; m. Patricia Lee Kelley, Dec. 30, 1967; children—Laura Kelley, William Hunt, Katharine Ann. Dir. planning Charter Twp. of Meridian (Mich.), 1969-72; v.p., treas. Planning Cons. Services, Inc., Lansing, Mich., 1972-76; dir. planning Manson, Jackson, Kane, Architects, Inc., Lansing, 1974-76; dir. planning and devel. City of Appleton (Wis.), 1976—, exec. dir. Redevel. Authority, 1979—; dir. Appleton Gallery of Arts, 1984—. Trustee, Charter Twp. of Meridan, 1972-74, supr., 1974-76; dist. chmn. Boy Scouts Am., 1979-81. Lic. profl. community planner, Mich. Mem. Am. Inst. Cert. Planners, Am. Planning Assn., Urban Land Inst., Nat. Trust Historic Preservation, Council Urban Econ. Devel., Assn. Wis. Planners (treas. 1977-79, pres. 1981-82), Wis. Econ. Devel. Assn., Delta Tau Delta. Mem. United Ch. of Christ. Club: Rotary. Home: 716 S Fidelis Dr Appleton WI 54915 Office: 200 N Appleton St Appleton WI 54911

BREIER, HAROLD A., law enforcement official. Police chief, City of Milw. Office: Milwaukee Police Dept Office of the Chief of Police Milwaukee WI 53201*

BREIHAN, CARL WILLIAM, JR., electrical engineer, supply company executive; b. St. Louis, Sept. 9, 1949; s. Carl William, Sr. and Ethel (Venarde) B.; m. Maeme Yee, July 23, 1973; children—Eric, Marc, Tara. B.S. in Elec. Engring., Mich. State U.; M.A. in Thermal and Fluid Dynamics, U. Del. Registered profl. elec. engr. Sales mgr. Ogden Mfg. co., Chgo., 1973-78; ptnr. Tac, Inc., Greenwood, Ind., 1980—; pres., ARC, Inc., Greenwood, 1982—, CEM Electric, Inc., Greenwood, 1978—; chmn. bd. and chief exec. officer CEMCO Enterprises, Greenwood, 1982—. Served to USN, 1968-73. Mem. Soc. of Plastics Engrs., Soc. of Plastic Industry. Republican. Roman Catholic. Club: St. Louis Water Safety (pres. 1963-68). Lodges: Elks, Moose. Avocations: scuba diving; boating; race car building and driving. Home: 1802 Davis Dr Franklin IN 46131 Office: CEM Electric Co Inc 1747 Industrial Dr Greenwood IN 46142

BREIHAN, EDNA MARIA THIES, retired educator; b. Flossmoor, Ill., Jan. 22, 1911; d. Henry Frederick and Anna (Cohrs) Thies; student Valparaiso U., 1928-30; A.B., Coll. of St. Francis, 1953; M.Ed., De Paul U., 1957; certificate advanced study in reading U. Chgo., 1966; m. Armin Henry Breihan, June 26, 1937; children—Joanne, James. Tchr., Lutheran Parochial Schs., Detroit, Chgo., 1930-37; pvt. tchr. remedial reading, Homewood, Ill., Flossmoor, 1945-51; tchr. Culbertson Sch., Joliet, Ill., 1953-57, Central Sch., Lockport, Ill., 1955-58; reading cons. Lockport Twp. High Sch. 1958-66; reading coordinator Lockport Twp. Sch. Dist. 205, 1966-71, chmn. reading dept., 1971-75. Mem. Lockport Woman's Club (hon.), NEA, Nat. Soc. for Study Edn., Internat. Reading Assn. (past pres. Will County council), Ill. Edn. Assn., Internat. Platform Assn., Lockport Bus. and Profl. Women's Assn., Assn. Supervision and Curriculum Devel., Am. Inst. Mgmt. (exec. council), AAUW, Delta Kappa Gamma, Chi Sigma Xi. Lutheran. Home: 1512 Briggs St Box 344 Lockport IL 60441

BREITBORDE, LAWRENCE BART, anthropology educator; b. Worcester, Mass., Feb. 20, 1949; s. Abraham and Sylvia (Berman) B.; m. Sandra Lee Kachagian, June 8, 1971; 1 child, Nicholas. B.A., Clark U., 1971; M.A., U. Rochester, 1973, Ph.D., 1978. Asst. prof. Beloit Coll., Wis., 1977-83, assoc. prof. anthropology, 1983—, chmn. dept., 1982—, assoc. dean coll., 1985—; assoc. in African ethnology, linguistics Logan Mus. of Anthropology, Beloit, 1977—. Contbr. articles to profl. jours. Grantee Nat. Endowment Humanities, 1982-83; fellow NSF, NIMH, Fulbright-Hays, 1974-76. Fellow Am. Anthrop. Assn., Royal Anthropology Inst., Liberian Studies Assn. (v.p., sec. 1984-85). Jewish. Office: Dept Anthropology Beloit Coll Beloit WI 53511

BREITENBERGER, ERNST, scientist, educator; b. Graz, Austria, June 11, 1924; came to U.S., 1958; s. Julius Johann and Anna (Wiesinger) B.; m. Janine Dufaure, 1954 (div. 1974); children—Roland, Caroline, Gisela, Erich. Dr. phil., U. Vienna, 1950; Ph.D., Cambridge U., 1956. Research assoc. Radium Inst., Vienna, 1950-51, Cavendish Lab., Cambridge, Eng., 1951-54; mem. faculty U. Malaya, Singapore, 1954-58, U. S.C., Columbia, 1958-63; prof. physics Ohio U., Athens, 1963—; guest prof. U. Bonn, W. Ger., 1969-70. Contbr. articles to profl. jours. Mem. Am. Phys. Soc., Math. Assn., History Sci. Soc., N.Y. Acad. Sci., Sigma Xi. Office: Ohio U Clippinger Labs Athens OH 45701

BREMS, HANS JULIUS, educator; b. Viborg, Denmark, Oct. 16, 1915; came to U.S., 1951, naturalized, 1958; s. Holger and Andrea (Golditz) B.; Ph.D., U. Copenhagen, 1950; hedersdoktor Swedish Sch. Econs., 1970; m. Ulla C. Simoni, May 20, 1944; children—Lisa, Marianne, Karen Joyce. Asst. prof. U. Copenhagen, 1943-51, U. Calif.-Berkeley, 1951-54; mem. faculty U. Ill.-Champaign, 1954—, prof. econs., 1955—; vis. prof. UCLA, 1953, U. Mich., 1957, U. Calif., Berkeley, 1958, Harvard U., 1960, U. Kiel (W. Ger.), 1961, 72, U. Colo., 1963, Gottingen (W. Ger.) U., 1964, Hamburg (W. Ger.) U., 1967, U. Uppsala (Sweden), 1968, U. Lund (Sweden), 1970, 75, U. Goteborg (Sweden), 1972, U. Copenhagen, 1975, Stockholm, 1980, 82, U. Zurich, 1983. Mem.

Royal Danish Acad. Scis. and Letters, Am. Econ. Assn., Royal Econ. Soc. Author: Product Equilibrium under Monopolistic Competition, 1951; Output, Employment, Capital and Growth, 1959; Quantitative Economic Theory, 1968; Labor, Capital and Growth, 1973; A Wage Earners' Investment Fund - Forms and Economic Effects, 1975; Inflation, Interest and Growth, 1980; Dynamische Makrotheorie - Inflation, Zins und Wachstum, 1980; Fiscal Theory—Government, Inflation and Growth, 1983; Pioneering Economic Theory 1630-1980—A Mathematical Restatement, 1986. Home: 1103 S Douglas Ave Urbana IL 61801 Office: Commerce W 1206 6th St Champaign IL 61820

BRENAN, KATHLEEN MULVANEY, computer and accounting educator; b. Waynesburg, Pa., July 21, 1952; d. Bernard Blair and Mary Margaret (Knoer) M.; m. Michael Ray Brenan, Sept. 9, 1978; children—Erin, Andrew. B.S. in Math., Miami U., Oxford, Ohio, 1974; M.Acctg., Bowling Green State U., 1982. Dress buyer Wren Dept. Store, Springfield, Ohio, 1974-76; internal auditor Huntington Bancshares, Columbus, Ohio, 1977-80; instr. Bowling Green State U., Ohio, 1982-84; system analyst United Telephone Co., Mansfield, Ohio, 1984; asst. prof. Ashland Coll., Ohio, 1984—. Author: Introduction to Computers and BASIC Programming, 1984. Mem. Data Processing Mgmt. Assn. Republican. Lutheran. Home: 1217 Springbrook Dr Mansfield OH 44906

BREND, RUTH MARGARET, linguistics educator, consultant; b. Winnipeg, Man., Can., Jan. 8, 1927; naturalized, 1964; d. Willie and Margaret (Hodgson) Brend. B.A., U. Manitoba, 1946, diploma in social work, 1947; M.A. in Linguistics, U. Mich., 1960, Ph.D. in Linguistics, 1964. B. Theology (hon.), Multnomah Sch. of the Bible, 1972. Social worker Provincial Govt., Winnipeg, 1947-49; linguistic teaching asst. Summer Inst. Linguistics, Norman, Okla., 1955-65; research asst. Prof. K. L. Pike, Ann Arbor, Mich., 1960-75; visiting lectr. Monash U., Melbourne, Australia, 1969-70; Fullbright prof. U. Tromso/-Trondheim, Norway, 1975-76; prof. linguistics Mich. State U., East Lansing, 1964—; cons. in linguistic workshops Summer Inst. Linguistics, Peru, Ecuador, India, Mex., Colombia, 1960—. Author: A Tagmemic Analysis of Mexican Spanish Clauses, 1968. Editor: Advances in Tagmemics, 1974, Kenneth L. Pike, 1972; co-editor (with Kenneth L. Pike): Tagmemics (2 volumes), 1976; managing editor WORD, 1984—. Mem. Linguistic Soc. Am., Linguistics Assn. Can. and U.S., Women's Research Club (pres. 1984-85). Mem. Christian Ref. Ch. Home: 3363 Burbank Dr Ann Arbor MI 48105 Office: Mich State U Dept Linguistics Wells Hall A-618 East Lansing MI 48824-1027

BRENEMAN, DAVID WORTHY, college president; economist; b. Albuquerque, Oct. 24, 1940; s. Clement Daniel and Muriel Ruth Breneman; m. Judith Dodge, June 10, 1962; children—Erica, Carleton. B.A., U. Colo., 1963; Ph.D., U. Calif.-Berkeley, 1970. Asst. prof. econs. Amherst Coll., 1970-72; staff dir. Nat. Acad. Sci., 1972-75; sr. fellow Brookings Instn., 1975-83; pres. Kalamazoo Coll., 1983—; professorial lectr. econs. George Washington U., 1979-82; trustee Woodrow Wilson Nat. Fellowship Found., 1980—, W.E. Upjohn Inst., 1983—; dir. Nat. Ctr. for Higher Edn. Mgmt. Systems, 1980-84. Author: Public Policy and Private Higher Education, 1978; Financing Community Colleges, 1981. Exec. editor Change Mag., 1980-84. Woodrow Wilson fellow 1963, Danforth fellow 1963, NDEA fellow 1967; recipient Buchanan prize U. Calif., 1970. Mem. Am. Econ. Assn., Am. Assn. Higher Edn. (dir. 1982—). Democrat. Club: Kalamazoo Country; Park, Univ. (N.Y.C.). Home: 136 Thompson St Kalamazoo MI 49007 Office: Kalamazoo Coll Kalamazoo MI 49007

BRENGEL, FRED L., automation systems manufacturing company executive. Chmn., pres., chief exec. officer, dir. Johnson Controls, Inc., Milw. Office: Johnson Controls Inc 5757 N Green Bay Ave Milwaukee WI 53201*

BRENIZER, NED WICKLIFFE, management information specialist; b. Ft. Wayne, Ind., Oct. 20, 1930; s. Leo Cletus and Hazel Elizabeth (Wickliffe) B.; student Drake U., 1948-50; m. Adeline P. Sylvia, July 15, 1978; children—(by previous marriage) Scott R., Beth A.; stepchildren—Christine, Michael, James. With Capehart-Farnsworth Materials Mgmt., Ft. Wayne, 1951-57; PERT specialist ITT Fed. Div., Ft. Wayne, 1957-65; with Tokheim Corp., Ft. Wayne, Ind., 1965—, mgr. info. systems, mgr. sales adminstrn., 1978—; lectr., cons. in field. Recipient Assn. Systems Mgmt. Merit award, 1974, Achievement award, 1979, Disting. Service award, 1983; Am. Prodn. and Inventory Control Soc. Best Jour. Article of Year award, 1978; winner essay contest Adminstrv. Mgmt. Assn. and IAM of London, 1985; cert. systems profl. Mem. Assn. Systems Mgmt., Internat. Customer Service Assn. Presbyterian. Contbr. articles to profl. jours. Home: 6312 Dumont Dr Fort Wayne IN 46815 Office: 1602 Wabash Ave Fort Wayne IN 46802

BRENNAN, CORINNE PATRICIA, nurse; b. St. Louis, June 23, 1954; d. Thomas Patrick and Audrey Sybil (Bryce) Sullivan. R.N., Barnes Hosp., 1974. Staff nurse Barnes Hosp., St. Louis, 1974-76; charge nurse orthopedics St. Louis City Hosp., 1977-81, charge nurse CCU, 1983-85; charge nurse, acting dir. nursing Mo. Eastern Corrections Ctr., Pacific, 1981-83, Jewish Hosp., 1985—; CPR instr. Mo. and St. Louis Heart Assns., 1982—. Mem. Am. Assn. Critical Care Nurses, St. Louis Assn. Critical Care Nurses. Republican. Roman Catholic. Home: 11162C Gravois St Saint Louis MO 63126 Office: Jewish Hosp 216 S Kingshighway Saint Louis MO 63178

BRENNAN, EMMET JAMES, III, personnel consultant; b. St. Louis, Oct. 4, 1945; s. Emmet James and Rita Katherine (Perkinson) B.; student St. Louis U., 1963-65, Washington U., St. Louis, 1965-70, U. Mo., St. Louis, 1975; B.A. with honors in Mgmt., Webster U., 1978; m. Elizabeth Jane Webb, Mar. 7, 1970. Personnel specialist Otto Faerber & Assos., St. Louis, 1965-70; indsl. relations personnel mgr. Rexall Drug Co., St. Louis, 1970-71; compensation analyst Dart Industries, Los Angeles, 1971-74; corp. wage and salary adminstr., personnel devel. assoc. Mallinckrodt, Inc., St. Louis, 1974-78; dir. St. Louis office Sullivan, Eisemann & Thomsen, St. Louis, 1978-80; pres. Brennan, Thomsen Assocs., Inc., Chesterfield, Mo., 1980—; asst. dir. Compensation Inst., 1981-82; guest lectr. various univs. and profl. socs. Lector, Incarnate Word Roman Cath. Parish. Served with U.S. Army, 1966-68. Mem. Am. Compensation Assn., Am. Soc. for Personnel Adminstrn., Nat. Com. on Pay Equity, Chesterfield C. of C., St. Louis Regional Com. and Growth Assn., Phi Kappa Theta. Author: Geographic Salary and Cost of Living Differentials, 1980; The Compensation Audit, 1981; The Complete Handbook of Wage and Salary Administration, 1986; contbg. editor, founding mem. bd. editorial advisors Personnel Jour., 1984—; St. Louis mgr. Today's Mgr., 1985—; contbr. articles to profl. jours. Office: Brennan Thomsen Assos Inc 106 Four Seasons Center Chesterfield MO 63017

BRENNAN, JOSEPH MICHAEL, nuclear security coordinator; b. Lowell, Mass., Oct. 31, 1944; s. Joseph Thomas and Eileen (Greeley) B.; m. Paula Rene Paulson, Aug. 28, 1971; children—Michael J., Patrick R. B.S. in Bus. Adminstrn., Providence Coll., 1966. Supervisory spl. agt. FBI, Detroit, Mich., Newark, Washington and San Juan, P.R., 1970-83; sr. nuclear security coordinator Commonwealth Edison Co., Chgo., 1983—. Co-chmn. small gifts com. Marianjoy Rehab. Hosp., Wheaton, Ill., 1983; mem. Chgo. Crime Commn., 1983. Served to capt. USMC, 1966-69; Vietnam. Mem. Soc. Former Spl. Agts. FBI. Roman Catholic. Clubs: Glen Ayre (Wheaton); Old Wayne (West Chicago, Ill.). Office: Commonwealth Edison Co 72 W Adams St Chicago IL 60690

BRENNAN, MARY THERESE, city ofcl.; b. St. Louis, Apr. 12, 1951; d. Francis Charles and Beulah Mary (Tornatore) B.; student parochial schs., St. Louis. Stenographer, Council on Human Relations, City of St. Louis, 1969-71, sec. Mcpl. Bus. Devel. Commn., 1971-73, exec. sec. to dir. Community Devel. Agy., 1973-80, exec. sec., adminstrv. asst. to mayor's exec. asst. Mayor's Office, 1980—. Home: 3410 McCausland Ave Saint Louis MO 63139 Office: Room 200 City Hall Mayor's Office Market and Tucker Sts Saint Louis MO 63103

BRENNAN, NANCY HOUGH, space designer; b. Evanston, Ill., Nov. 15; d. Charles F. and Nancy Pope (Browning) Hough; m. James Gordon Brenna, Apr. 15, 1950 (div. Oct. 1970); children—Margot, David, James, Stephen, Peter; m. Peter Joseph Byrne, Aug. 29, 1978. B.A., Manhattanville Coll., 1948; M.F.A., Catholic U. Am., 1951; diploma in interior design Harrington Sch., Chgo., 1980. Designer, Meredith Beals Interiors, Chgo., 1971-73, Watson & Boaler, Inc., Chgo., 1973-76; designer, pres. Nancy H. Brennan, Inc., Chgo., 1976—; lectr. Art Inst. Chgo., 1962-78. Hon. v.p. St. Joseph's U., Phila, 1982. Mem. Am. Soc. Interior Designers (assoc.). Republican. Roman Catholic. Clubs: Saddle and Cycle, Woman's Athletic (Chgo.). Avocations: art; antiques; seashore. Home: 2430 Lakeview Chicago IL 60614 Office: 501 N Wells St Chicago IL 60610

BRENNAN, RICHARD SNYDER, financial company executive, lawyer; b St. Louis, Mar. 18, 1938; s. Clarence Rosso and Anna (Snyder) B.; m. Margaret McDonald Wilson, July 23, 1963; children—George, Joseph, Sophie. A.B., Princeton U., 1960; J.D., U. Mich., 1963. Bar: Ill. Assoc., Shearman & Sterling, N.Y.C., 1963-64; assoc., ptnr. Mayer, Brown & Platt, Chgo., 1964-82; exec. v.p, gen. counsel, sec. Continental Ill. Corp., Chgo., 1982—. Office: Continental Illinois Corp 231 S LaSalle St Chicago IL 60093

BRENNAN, ROBERT LAWRENCE, psychometrician; b. Hartford, Conn., May 31, 1944; s. Robert and Irene Veronica (Connors) B.; B.A., Salem State Coll., 1967; M.A.T., Harvard U., 1968, Ed.D., 1970; m. Sandra Lee Spychala, Aug. 16, 1969; 1 son, Sean Michael. Research asso., lectr. Grad. Sch. Edn., Harvard U., Cambridge, Mass., 1970-71; asst. prof. edn. SUNY-Stony Brook, 1971-76; sr. research psychologist Am. Coll. Testing Program, Iowa City, 1976-79, dir. measurement research dept., 1979-84, asst. v.p. for measurement research, 1984—; adj. faculty Sch. Edn. U. Iowa, 1979—; cons. Office Child Devel., HEW, 1975-79. Harvard prize fellow, 1967. Mem. Am. Ednl. Research Assn. (Div. D award 1980), Am. Statis. Assn., Am. Psychol. Assn., Am. Ednl. Research Assn., Nat. Council Measurement Edn., Psychometric Soc. Assoc. editor Jour. Ednl. Measurement, 1978-83, Applied Psychological Measurement, 1982—; contbr. articles to profl. jours. Home: 85 N Westminster St Iowa City IA 52240 Office: PO Box 168 Am Coll Testing Program Iowa City IA 52243

BRENNAN, ROBERT WALTER, assn. exec.; b. Chgo., Mar. 12, 1934; s. Walter R. and Grace A. (Mason) B.; B.S., U. Wis., Madison, 1957; m. Mary J. Engler, June 15, 1962; children—Barbara, Susan (twins). Tchr., coach Waukesha (Wis.) High Sch., 1960-63; track coach U. Wis., Madison, 1963-71; exec. asst. to mayor City of Madison, 1971-73; pres. C. of C., Madison, 1973—; dir. Cherokee Park, Inc. Chmn. bd. dirs. Clyde Dupin Reachout Ministries, 1974—; bd. dirs. Bill Glass Evangelistic Assn., 1972—. Named Madison Favorite Son, 1971. Mem. Wis. C. of C. (dir.), Madison Urban League, U. Wis. Alumni Assn., Nat. W Club, Wis. Urban League, C. of C. Execs., Wis. Hist. Soc., Fellowship Christian Athletes, Theta Delta Chi, Phi Epsilon Kappa. Club: Rotary. Midwest corr. Track & Field News, 1963-71; spl. events cons. Letterman Mag., 1971. Home: 5514 Comanche Way Madison WI 53704 Office: PO Box 71 Madison WI 53701

BRENNAN, THOMAS EMMETT, JR., lawyer, judge; b. Detroit, Mar. 20, 1952; s. Thomas Emmett and Pauline Mary (Weinberger) B.; m. Julie Schafer, Apr. 23, 1977; children—Thomas Emmett, Patrick Joseph. B.S., Mich. State U., 1974; J.D., Thomas M. Cooley Law Sch., 1978. Bar: Mich. 1978. Asst. city atty. City of East Lansing, Mich., 1978-79; ptnr. Klug & Brennan, P.C., East Lansing, 1979-81; dist. judge 55th Dist. Ct., Mason, Mich., 1981—; 9th Dist. commr. Ingham County Bd., Mason, 1979-81; bd. dirs. Thomas M. Cooley Law Sch. Lansing, 1980—, adj. prof., 1983—; adj. prof. Mich. State U., 1983—. Mem. Ingham County Bar Assn., ABA, Ingham County Trial Judges Assn., Mich. Dist. Judges Assn., Thomas M. Cooley Law Sch. Alumni Assn. (Disting. Alumnus award 1983). Clubs: Mich. State U. (Lansing), Downtown Coaches (Lansing) (bd. dirs.). Lodge: Rotary (charter Mason). Office: 55th Dist Ct 700 Buhl Ave Mason MI 48854

BRENNECKE, GARY DAVID, sales representative; b. Chanute, Kans., June 8, 1942; s. Paul T. and Frances I. (Letcher) B.; m. Martha B. Cooper, July 25, 1964; children—Janese, Mike. A.A., Neosho County Community Coll., 1962; B.S., Pittsburg State U., Kans., 1964. Sales rep. Upjohn Co., Kalamazoo, 1964—; 1st v.p. Health System Agy., Wichita, 1982—. Pres. Parsons USD 503 Sch. Bd., Kans., 1984—; mem. Human Relations Commn., Parsons, 1983—. Presbyterian. Avocations: golf, hunting. Home: 3100 Johnston Rd Parsons KS 67357

BRENNEMAN, FLEET B., lawyer; b. Canton, Ohio, Feb. 14, 1932; s. Fleetus Ingram and Maxine (Wollam) O'Mara; m. Carol E. Perlowski, Nov. 18, 1954; children—Kathryn, Paula, Lisa, Laura, Peggy. B.A., Ohio No. U., 1954, J.D., 1959. Bar: Ohio 1959. Dep. clk. Juvenile Ct., Cuyahoga County Cleve., 1959-61; sole practice, Orrville, Ohio, 1961-65; ptnr. Brenneman & Waltman, Orrville, 1966—; corporate atty. First Savings and Loan, Orrville, 1964—; gen. counsel Orrville Community Centennial Com. Inc., 1963-64. Trustee, Orrville United Way, 1968-74, 80—, pres., 1968-70, 80-82; trustee, gen. counsel Orrville Area Devel. Found., Inc., 1985—. Served with U.S. Army, 1954-56. Mem. Orrville C. of C. (trustee 1975-79), Wayne County Bar Assn. (pres. 1982), Nat. Rifle Assn., Ohio Rifle and Pistol Assn. Republican. Roman Catholic. Lodge: Rotary (pres. 1971-72). Avocations: hunting, fishing, rifle marksmanship, photography. Office: Brenneman & Waltman 144 N Main St Orrville OH 44667

BRENNEMAN, RICHARD REXFORD, sales manager; b. Pitts., Nov. 27, 1943; s. Rexford William and Katherine Sylvia (Pasacic) B.; m. Elsa Lillie Dougherty, Sept. 4, 1965; children—Susan Denise, Sharon Michelle. Student Frostburg State Coll., Akron U. Product devel. engr. Gen. Tire and Rubber Co., Akron, Ohio, 1965-68; engring. sales cons. Bruning div. AM Corp., Akron, 1968-73; sales engr., Diebold Inc., Canton, Ohio and Buffalo, 1973-76; security analyst, Buffalo, 1976; br. mgr. Océ Industries, Inc., Cleve., 1976—; mem. mgmt. bd. Cleve. Bus. Show, 1978—, chmn. mgmt. bd., 1981—. Named Dir. of Yr., Ohio Jaycees, 1969, 72. Served with Ohio N.G., 1966-72. Mem. Nat. Micrographics Assn. (pres. Ohio chpt., v.p., exec. bd. 1978—), Assn. Info. and Image Mgmt. (exec. bd. Ohio chpt., Nat. Disting. Service citation). Republican. Lutheran. Home: 915 Kenner Dr Medina OH 44256 Office: 6930 Snowville Rd Brecksville OH 44141

BRENNER, ROBERT LAWRENCE, geology educator, researcher; b. N.Y.C., Dec. 13, 1940; s. William and Mildred (Rothstein) B.; m. Vida Louise Allweiss, July 29, 1973. B.S. in Geology, CCNY, 1963; M.S. in Geology, U. Mont., 1964; Ph.D. in Geology, U. Mo., 1973. Assoc. scientist Marathon Oil Co., Littleton, Colo., 1964-69; research scientist Conoco Oil Co., Ponca City, Okla., 1973-77; asst. prof. geology U. Iowa, Iowa City, 1977-82, assoc. prof., 1982—. Author: Petroleum Stratigraphy, 1984. Contbr. articles to profl. jours. Mem. Soc. Econ. Paleontologists and Minerologists, Geol. Soc. Am., Am. Assn. Petroleum Geologists. Office: U Iowa Trowbridge Hall Iowa City IA 52242

BRETHOUR, JOHN RAYMOND, animal scientist; b. Junction City, Kans., Sept. 30, 1934; s. Raymond U. and Ruth (Wolfe) B.; m. Carol June Thomas, Aug. 16, 1964; 1 child, John R., Jr. B.S., Kans. State U., 1955; M.S., Okla. State U., 1956. Technician, U. Tenn.-AEC, Oak Ridge, 1956-57; instr. beef cattle sci. Kans. State U., Hays, 1957-62, asst. prof., 1962-68, assoc. prof., 1968-75, prof., 1975—. Contbr. articles to profl. publs. Mem. Kans. Livestock Assn., Nat. Cattlemans Assn., Am. Soc. Animal Sci., Sigma Xi. Methodist. Lodge: Lions. Home: Hall at Frontier Hays KS 67601 Office: Fort Hays Exptl Sta Hays KS 67601

BRETT, GEORGE HOWARD, See *Who's Who in America*, 43rd edition.

BRETT, RANDALL PHILIP, mgmt. cons.; b. Balt., June 14, 1950; s. Herbert Saul and Muriel (Berns) B.; B.A., U. Ill., 1972; M.Mgmt., Northwestern U., 1977; m. Deborah L. Lieber, May 20, 1973. Personnel mgr. Interstate Service Corp., Chgo., 1972-74; personnel mgr. Motorola, Inc., Schaumburg, Ill., 1974-77, 79; sr. cons. asso. Drake-Beam & Assos., Inc., Des Plaines, Ill., 1977-79; prin. Employee Relations Assos., Chgo., 1979-82; v.p. Drake Beam Moran, Inc., 1982—; mem. adj. faculty Elmhurst Coll. Center for Spl. Programs. Mem. Am. Mgmt. Assn., Soc. Personnel Adminstrs. Greater Chgo., Am. Soc. Profl. Cons., Am. Soc. Personnel Adminstrn., Am. Soc. Tng. and Devel. Democrat. Mem. editorial rev. com. Am. Soc. Personnel Adminstrn. Contbr. articles to profl. jours.

BRETT, RICHARD JOHN, speech pathologist; b. Chgo., Sept. 5, 1921; s. Richard J. and Emily (Salter) B.; B.Ed., No. Ill. State Tchrs. Coll., 1943; M.S., U. Ill., 1947; student U. Amsterdam (Holland), 1949, U. Chgo., 1948-49, 62, 66-67, Northwestern U., 1967. Speech supr. Summer Residential Clinic, U. Ill., Urbana, 1948, 50, 52; speech pathologist Waukegan (Ill.) High Schs., 1946—; chmn. Chgo. Regional Interviewing Com. for Exchange of Tchrs., U.S. Dept. Edn., 1962—; del. to Internat. Fedn. of Free Tchr. Unions, Switzerland. 1953. Founder, Pub. Sch. Caucus, Chgo., 1973, chmn., 1973-76. Served with U.S. Army, 1943-45. Fellow Am. Speech-Lang.-Hearing Assn. (membership com. 1975-77, conv. program com. 1974, 77); mem. Ill. Speech and Hearing Assn. (chmn. legis. com. 1964-65, treas. 1977-78, v.p. bus. affairs 1978-79), Internat. Council Exceptional Children (pres. Chgo. suburban chpt. 1949-50), Am. (co-chmn. internat. relations com. 1952-63), Ill. (chmn. profl. standards com. 1952-57), Lake County (pres. 1949-51, 64-67) fedns. tchrs., UN Assn., Mus. Contemporary Art, ACLU, Common Cause, Art Inst. Chgo., Chgo. Symphony Soc. Club: National Travel. Compiler: World Study and Travel for Teachers, 1952—; editor Five-O-Format, 1951-56, 66-69. Home: 616 4th St Waukegan IL 60085 Office: Waukegan East High School 1011 Washington St Waukegan IL 60085

BREUER, COY LEBURN, civil engr.; b. Phelps County, Mo., Apr. 3, 1924; s. Thomas Franklin and Minnie Mae (Agee) B.; B.S. in Civil Engring., U. Mo., Rolla, 1949; m. Ruby Irene Wycoff, Jan. 19, 1946; children—Rhonda Jean, Randal Coy, Rodney Kent. With Mo. Hwy. and Transp. Dept., and predecessor, 1949—, sr. engr., 1964-69, asst. div. engr., Jefferson City, 1969—. Bd. dirs. Meml. Community Hosp., Jefferson City, Mo., 1979. Served with AUS, 1943-45. Registered profl. engr., Mo. Mem. Acad. Civil Engrs., ASCE, Nat. Soc. Profl. Engrs., Hwy. Engrs. Assn. Mo., Mo. Soc. Profl. Engrs. Office: State Hwy Bldg Jefferson City MO 65102

BREVER, THOMAS EDWARD, lawyer; b. Sauk Centre, Minn.; s. Donald Charles and Darlene Mildred (Rehkamp) B.; m. Bonita Mae Voit, Aug. 30, 1975; children—Eric, Nathan. B.A. summa cum laude, St. John's U., Collegeville, Minn., 1975; J.D. cum laude, U. Minn., 1978. Bar: Minn. 1978, U.S. Dist. Ct. Minn. 1978, U.S. Tax Ct. 1978, U.S. Ct. Appeals (8th cir.) 1978. Sr. trial atty. Office Chief Counsel, IRS, St. Paul, 1978-84; instr. in tax acctg. St. John's U., 1982; spl. asst. U.S. atty. Dept. Justice, Mpls., 1983-84; sr. state and local tax specialist Pillsbury Co., Mpls., 1984-85; atty. Head & Truhn, Mpls., 1985—; vol. atty. So. Minn. Regional Legal Aid, St. Paul, 1980-84. Mem. Fed. Bar Assn. (dir. Minn. chpt.), Minn. Bar Assn., Hennepin Co. Bar Assn., Inst. Property Taxation, Can. Property Tax Agt.'s Assn., Internat. Assn. Assessing Officers. Roman Catholic. Office: Head & Truhn 2110 First Bank Place W Minneapolis MN 55402

BREWER, A. KEITH, physicist, cancer researcher; b. Richland Center, Wis., Oct. 20, 1893; s. Edward and Hattie (Dove) B. B.A., U. Wis., 1915, M.S., 1921, Ph.D., 1924; NRC fellow, Calif. Inst. Tech., 1924-27. Physicist, Fixed Nitrogen Research Lab., Washington, 1927-39; chief, mass spectrometer and isotope lab. Nat. Bur. Standards, Washington, 1932-46, chief sci. sect., naval ops., 1946-68; cons. physicist, Washington, 1968—. Co-founder, Richland Jr. Acad. Scis., 1973. Bd. dirs. A. Keith Brewer Found., Inc. Donor A. Keith Brewer Library, Richland Center. Fellow Am. Phys. Soc.; mem. Am. Chem. Soc., Cancer Control Soc., N.Y., Washington acads. sci., Washington Philos. Soc., Sigma Xi, Phi Kappa Phi. Republican. Clubs: Masons, Shriners. Contbr. articles to profl. jours.; developer high pH therapy for cancer. Address: Sci Room A Keith Brewer Library Richland Center WI 53581

BREWER, EDWARD EUGENE, tire and rubber products company executive. Chmn., dir. Cooper Tire & Rubber Co., Findlay, Ohio. Office: Cooper Tire & Rubber Co Lima & Western Aves Findlay OH 45840*

BREWER, F. ANDREW, state official; b. New London, Conn., Apr. 7, 1943; s. F.V. and Alice (Tierney) B.; m. Maureen C. Mogen, Sept. 14, 1979. B.A. in Polit. Sci., Coll. St. Thomas, 1965; postgrad. U. Minn. Law Sch.-Mpls., 1965-66, Coll. St. Thomas, 1967-68. Info. dir. Minn. Pub. Service Commn., St. Paul, 1973; pub. relations dir. Minn. Bicentennial Commn., St. Paul, 1973-75; exec. asst. to majority leader Minn. Ho. of Reps., St. Paul, 1975; legis. asst. Gov. Wendell Anderson, St. Paul, 1976; legis. dir. Minn. Dept. Natural Resources, St. Paul, 1976—. Dept. dir. United Way of St. Paul Area, 1981-84. Recipient Outstanding Service award, St. Paul United Way, 1982. Democratic Farmer Labor. Roman Catholic. Avocations: Hunting; fishing; amateur athletics; Irish history and culture. Home: 5141 10th Ave S Minneapolis MN 55417 Office: Minn Dept Natural Resources 500 Lafayette Rd Saint Paul MN 55146

BREWER, GEORGE EUGENE FRANCIS, chemical consultant; b. Vienna, Austria, Jan. 23, 1909; s. Ernest and Sophia (Segalla) B.; A.B., State Coll. Vienna, 1928; M.Sc., U. Vienna, 1930, Ph.D. in Chemistry, 1932; m. Frances Joan Werner, June 29, 1933 (dec. Nov. 1965); m. Maxine R. Levin, Mar. 4, 1967. Came to U.S., 1940, naturalized, 1945. Asst. lectr. U. Vienna (Austria), 1933-36; tech. mgr. S. Wolf & Co. Textile Refining Mill, Erlach, Austria, 1936-38; lectr. Inst. de l'Industrie Textile de Brabant, Brussels, 1939; prof. Rosary Coll., River Forest, Ill., 1940-43; biochemist NRC project Elgin (Ill.) State Hosp., 1943-44; prof. chemistry, head dept. Marygrove Coll., Detroit, 1944-67; cons. Ford Motor Co., Detroit, 1957-67, staff scientist Mfg. Devel. Center, Dearborn, Mich., 1968-72; now coating cons.; Matiello Meml. lectr. Fedn. Socs. Paint Tech., 1973; mem. NRC com. ciphers, codes and punched card techniques, Washington, 1957-59; abstractor Chem. Abstracts, 1948-63. Recipient Midgley medal Detroit sect. Am. Chem. Soc., 1969, Doolittle award div. organic coatings and plastics chemistry, 1969; cert. cons. chemist, profl. chemist, mfg. engr. Fellow Am. Inst. Chemists (chmn. Mich. inst. 1969, pres. 1977-81, Chem. Pioneer award 1978), Inst. Metal Finishing Eng., Engring. Soc. Detroit (Engr.'s Week Gold award 1981); mem. Am. Chem. Soc. (councillor 1951-83; chmn. Detroit sect. 1960, sec. div. organic coatings and plastics chemistry 1971, chmn. 1974), Met. Detroit Sci. Club (dir. 1948), N.Y. Acad. Sci., Nat. Sci. Tchrs. Assn., Catholic Austrian Confraternity, Chem. Coaters Assn. (program chmn. 1971-73, dir. 1974-77, pres. 1976), Assn. Analytical Chemists (pres. 1959), Mich. Coll. Chem. Tchrs. Assn. (pres. 1954), Assn. Cons. Chemists and Chem. Engrs. Contbr. articles to profl. jours. Patentee electrophoretic deposition organic coatings. Home and office: 6135 Wing Lake Rd Birmingham MI 48010

BREWER, PAUL HUIE, advertising executive, artist; b. Alexandria, La., Jan. 24, 1934; s. Ralph Wright and Margot (Riviere) B.; B.A., La. Coll., Pineville, 1956; degree in advt. design and Famous Artists Schs., Westport, Conn., 1959; m. Anita Hines, May 16, 1953 (div. 1971); children—Anita Joy (dec.), Laura Riviere; m. Carole Lynn Kuhrt, July 8, 1972; children—Nicole Renee, Brett Kuhrt. Artist, Ralph Brewer's Studio and Engraving Co., Alexandria, 1952-54; art dir. Sta. KALB-TV, Alexandria, 1954-56; designer New Orleans Public Service Co., 1956; artist King Studio, Chgo., 1957; asst. art dir. Continental Casualty Co., Chgo., 1957-58; designer, art dir. Field Enterprises div. Chgo. Sun-Times, then dir. design; art dir. State Farm Ins. Cos., Bloomington, Ill., 1973, dir. art and design, 1973-77; prodn. mgr. and exec. art dir. U.S. Savs. and Loan League, Chgo., 1977—, corp. v.p., 1983—; pres. PBAdvt., Highland Park, Ill., 1982—; one-man shows: La. Coll., 1963, Chgo. Public Library, Chgo. Press Club, 1972; illustrator: Who Am I?, 1973; represented in permanent collections: Union League Club, Chgo., Ill. Bell Telephone Co., Chgo., others; portraits include: Jack Benny, Danny Kaye, Danny Thomas, Pablo Picasso, Mrs. Marshall Field IV, Phil Silvers, David Susskind, Leonard Bernstein, Merv Griffin, Bob Newhart, others; advt. dir. Artists Guild Bull., 1965; chmn. Artists Guild Chgo. Watercolor Show, 1967. Bd. dirs. Artists Guild Chgo. Credit Union, House of Wray Corp. Ill., N. Shore Art League. Recipient awards Am. Newspaper Guild, Artists Guild Chgo., Chgo. III, Famous Artists Sch., Graphic Arts Council Chgo.; Hartford Illustration award, 1968; Chgo. III award, 1970; Nat. award Louisville Rotogravure Assn., 1975; SIMSA nat. award, 1977 (3), 1979 (2); Union League Chgo. award; award of excellence Hopper Paper Co., 1978, 79; Addy awards State of Iowa, 1980 (2); Nat. Merchandising award P.O.P.A.I., 1980; 2 nat. awards Fin. Instns. Mktg. Assn., 1984; Internat. Paper Co. award, 1984. Mem. Artists Guild Chgo., Famous Artists Sch. Alumni Assn., Am. Watercolor Soc. (asso.), Chgo. Soc. Communicating Arts (dir.), Chgo. Soc. Typographic Arts, N. Shore Art League, La. Coll. Alumni Assn. Presbyterian (elder). Designer and illustrator: New in the City; Count a Lonely Cadence. Home: 41 Red Oak Ln Highland Park IL 60035 also 2358 North Shore Route 5 Box 134-A Delavan WI 53115 Office: 111 E Wacker Dr Chicago IL 60601

BREWER, RUTH RUSSELL (MRS. JOHN I. BREWER), civic worker; b. Great Bend, Kan., June 21, 1904; d. Francis Vernon and Jettie (McBride) Russell; B.A., U. Wis., 1921; M.A., Columbia, 1923; m. John I. Brewer, June 2, 1928; 1 son, John V. Instr., Bradley U., Peoria, Ill., 1923-26; service rep. Trift Inc., Oak Park, Ill., 1927. Head surg. dressing unit ARC, Denver, 1943-44; chmn. women's div. Joint Appeal, Chgo., 1957; mem. woman's planning bd. Crusade of Mercy, 1957-69; treas. Kenwood Social Service Club, Chgo., 1953, 1st v.p., 1954, pres., 1955; treas. women's bd. Women's Aux. of Goodwill Industries, 1962-63. Bd. dirs., corr. sec., 1st v.p. woman's aux. Infant Welfare

Soc., Chgo., 1960-63, pres., 1965-66, bd. advisers woman's aux., 1967-69, bd. dirs., 1968-71. Mem. Woman's bd. YWCA-Met. Chgo., 1968—. Mem. Kappa Alpha Theta. Club: Woman's Athletic (Chgo.). Home: 860 Lake Shore Dr Chicago IL 60611

BREWER, THELMA MAE, nurse; b. Ohiopyle, Pa., Jan. 31, 1921; d. Binger Addison and Ada (Burnworth) Show; m. Forest Salyer, Dec. 15, 1952; 1 son, James Allen; m. 2d, Kenneth Wilson Brewer, Jan. 19, 1955; children—Geoffrey Lynn, Mary Elizabeth. Grad. Massillon City Hosp. Sch. Nursing, 1942; postgrad. St. John's Hosp., Springfield, Ill., 1949, Mary Manse Coll., 1970. R.N., Ohio, Mo. Gen. duty nurse Massillon (Ohio) City Hosp., 1942-44, asst. operating room supr., 1950-53; operating room supr. Burge Meth. Hosp., Springfield, Mo., 1944-46; operating room supr. Riverside Hosp., Toledo, Ohio, 1950-53, head nurse, recovery room, 1957-77, dir. central supply dept., 1977—; central supply dept. supr. St. Charles Hosp., Oregon, Ohio, 1953-56. Mem. Massillon Community Hosp. Alumnae Assn.

BREWER, WARREN WESLEY, principal; b. Portage, Wis., Nov. 20, 1936; s. Thomas Wesley and Myrtle Goldie (West) B.; m. Lois Eleanor Jentz, Nov. 3, 1957, (div.); children—Molana May, Loranda Louise, Warren Benjamin; m. Marilyn Jane Messer, Dec. 19, 1970. B.S. in Secondary Edn., U. Wis.-Platteville, 1961; M.A. in Ednl. Adminstrn., Roosevelt U., 1969; specialist cert. in ednl. adminstrn. U.Wis.-Milw., 1976. Tchr. pub. schs., Ill., 1957-67; adminstrv. asst. Woodland Sch., Gages Lake, Ill., 1967-70; curriculum cons CESA 3, Gillette, Wis., 1970-71; asst. prin. Sheboygan Pub. Sch., Wis., 1971-77, prin. jr. high sch., 1977-82, prin. middle sch., 1982—; cons. Wis. Renewal and Improvement of Secondary Edn., U. Wis+Madison, 1980—. Mem. Wis. Secondary Sch. Adminstrs. Assn., Assn. Wis. Sch. Adminstrs. (Service award 1983), Wis. Middle Level Edn. Commn., Nat. Assn. Secondary Sch. Prins., Nat. Com. on Middle Level Edn. (chmn. 1984—), Phi Delta Kappa (pres. 1981-82). Lodge: Lions (pres. 1980-81). Avocations: hunting, fishing, travel, model ship building. Home: 4019 N 30th St Sheboygan WI 53081 Office: Horace Mann Middle Sch 2820 Union Ave Sheboygan WI 53081

BREWSTER, DONALD ELLIOTT, association executive; b. Paterson, N.J., Jan. 29, 1924; s. Benjamin John and Sarah Neille (Elliott) B.; student U. Ill., 1942; B.S., Bradley U., 1950; postgrad. Ind. U., 1968, Washington U., St. Louis, 1971; m. Jerre Owens, Nov. 1958; children—Stephanie, Barbara Jean, Dawn. With Am. Cancer Soc., 1960—, exec. v.p. Mich. Div., Lansing, 1970—; asso. dir. Ketchum, Inc., Pitts., 1956-60. Chmn. fund raising campaign St. Paul Episcopal Ch., 1976, sr. warden vestry, 1978. Served with USN, 1943-46. Mem. Nat. Soc. Fund Raising Execs., Am. Soc. Assn. Execs., Mich. Soc. Assn. Execs., U.S. Power Squadron, U.S. Coast Guard Aux. Republican. Clubs: University, Muskegon Yacht, Lansing Racquet. Home: 843 Longfellow Dr East Lansing MI 48823 Office: Am Cancer Soc 1205 E Saginaw St Lansing MI 48906

BREY, GARY ROBERT, plastics company executive; b. Grand Rapids, Mich., Nov. 13, 1946; s. Herman Fredrick and Doris (Streb) B.; m. Mary Miller, Nov. 4, 1971; 1 son, Gary Robert. B.A., Mich. State U., 1968; postgrad. law Wayne State U., 1969-71. With sales dept. Dun and Bradstreet, Chgo., 1971-75; sales mgr. Univex Internat., Los Angeles, 1975-78; gen. ptnr. Mid Am. Resources, Denver, 1983; v.p. Mid Am. Techs., Denver, 1981; chmn. Mid Am. Plastics Corp., Denver, 1978—. Clubs: Cascade Country (Grand Rapids); Woodland Hills Country (Los Angeles). Home: 2461 Westboro Dr NE Grand Rapids MI 49506 Office: Mid Am Plastics Corp 1805 S Bellair #300 Denver CO 80222

BREZINA, DAVID CHARLES, lawyer, educator; b. Berwyn, Ill., Sept. 11, 1953; s. John Charles and Virginia (Nelson) B.; married, Jan. 4, 1980. J.D. with honors, Chgo.-Kent Law Sch., 1978; student John Marshall Law Sch., 1978-84. Bars: Ill. 1978, U.S. Dist. Ct. (no. dist.) Ill. 1978, Trial Bar (no. dist.) Ill. 1982, U.S. Ct. Appeals (7th cir.) 1978, U.S. Ct. Customs and Patent Appeals 1980, U.S. Ct. Appeals (D.C. cir.) 1982, U.S. Supreme Ct. 1981. Assoc. Brezina & Buckingham, P.C., Chgo., 1978—; instr. Columbia Coll., Chgo., 1983—. Author: Cases and Materials on Intellectual Property Law for AEMMP, 1984. Editor: Antitrust and Misuse Aspects of Intellectual Property Law, 1985. Intellectual property cons. Ill. Inst. Tech./Chgo. Kent Law Rev., 1979-83; guest commentator Columbia Coll. Chronicle, 1984; patentee composite vehicle manufacture, 1985; contbr. articles on trademarks to profl. publs. Mem. staff Dick Clark Senate Campaign, Marion, Iowa, 1972; intern 66th Iowa Gen. Assembly, Des Moines, 1975; incorporator Concerned Citizens of Brookfield, Ill., 1976; election troubleshooter Project LEAP, Chgo., 1977—. Mem. ABA, Ill. State Bar Assn., Chgo. Bar Assn., Lawyers Pilots Bar Assn. Clubs: Chgo. Area Rugby Football Union (discipline chmn. 1980-81), Lincoln Park Rugby Football (asst. coach 1981-82). Office: Brezina & Buckingham PC 135 S LaSalle St Chicago IL 60603

BREZINSKI, THADDEUS WILLIAM, insurance company executive; b. Chgo., Jan. 19, 1937; s. Edward Alexander and Cecelia (Chilicki) B.; m. Barbara Elaine Hagg, Dec. 1, 1962; children—Steven E., Lisa M. Student Ill. Inst. Tech., 1954-57. Sales rep. Zurich Ins., Co., Chgo., 1962-70, sr. sales rep., 1970-72, prodn. mgr., Chgo., 1972-75, branch mgr., Pitts. and Palatine, Ill., 1975-84, regional v.p., 1984—; founder, pres. Suburban Mgrs. Group, Chgo., 1980—; Mem. Ins. Execs. of Chgo., 1984—. Served as SP/4 U.S. Army, 1960-62. Mem. Soc. Chartered Property and Casualty Underwriters. Roman Catholic. Avocations: philatelics, hunting, fishing. Home: 944 W Gilbert Ave Palatine IL 60067 Office: Zurich Ins Co 120 S Riverside Plaza Chicago IL 60606

BREZNAI, THEODORE ANDREW, lawyer; b. Rochester, Pa., Nov. 9, 1948; s. Joseph and Mary (Lazar) B.; m. Julia Mary Tamoney, July 15, 1978; children—Matthew James, Kathleen Ann, Nora Ann. B.A., John Carroll U., 1970; J.D., Cleve. State U., 1975. Bar: Ohio 1975, U.S. Dist. Ct. (no. and ea. dists.) Ohio 1976. Legal counsel Bissell Co., Cleve., 1975-82, title counsel Midland Title Security, 1980-82; counsel Harvest Ins. Cos., 1982-84; v.p., counsel Surety Title Agy., Inc., Cleve., 1984—. Contbr. articles to profl. jours. Trustee, scholar chmn. Waterford Soc., 1980-81. Mem. Ohio State Bar Assn., Cleve. Bar Assn. (asst. chmn. real estate jud. com. 1981), ABA, Cleve Title Assn. (pres. 1981-82), Mortgage Bankers Assn. Avocations: reading; music; sports. Home: 20715 Stratford Ave Rocky River OH 44116 Office: Surety Title Agy Inc 450 Leader Bldg Cleveland OH 44114

BRICCETTI, THOMAS BERNARD, conductor; b. Mt. Kisco, N.Y., Jan. 14, 1936; s. Thomas Bernard and Joan Therese (Filardi) B.; student of Jean Dansereau, 1948-60, Richart Lert, 1963-64; student U. Rochester Eastman Sch. Music, 1953-54, Columbia Grad. Sch. Fine Arts, 1954-55; m. Billie Lee Mommer, July 10, 1978; children—Katherine Anne, David Clark. Pianist, composer, 1955-62; mus. dir. Pinellas County (Fla.) Youth Symphony, 1962-68, St. Petersburg (Fla.) Philharm. Orch., 1963-68, St. Petersburg Civic Opera Co., 1964-68; asso. condr. Indpls. Symphony Orch., 1968-78; mus. dir. Ft. Wayne (Ind.) Philharm. Orch., 1970-78, Univ. Circle Orch., Cleve. Inst. Music, 1972-75, Omaha Symphony Orch., 1975—, Nebr. Sinfonia, from 1977, Festival 1000 Oaks, from 1978; internat. guest condr., from 1972; prin. guest condr. Nat. Orch., Luxembourg, 1977; prin. condr. Stavanger Orch., Norway, 1984—. Recipient Prix de Rome for mus. composition Italian Govt., 1958-59; Ford. Found. fellow, 1961-62; Yaddo grantee, 1963; named Profl. Artist of Yr., Indpls., 1970. Mem. ASCAP, Phi Mu Alpha Sinfonia. Nat. Endowment for Arts commn. to compose Violin Concerto, 1967; other compositions.

BRICE, L. RIDER, architect; b. Toledo, Ohio, Dec. 9, 1943; s. Leonard Rider Brice and Peggy Jean (Neale) Phillips; student Principia Coll., 1961-63; B.F.A., Ohio State U., 1968, B.Arch., 1975; m. Kristine Kay Artopoeus, Sept. 21, 1968; children—Trey, Colin, Tina. Design expeditor Richardson/Smith Inc., Worthington, Ohio, 1965-67, design service salesman, 1967-68; project designer Artolier Lighting & Sound div. Emerson Electric Co., Garfield, N.J., 1968-72; div. sales mgr. Electrolux div. Consol. Foods Corp., Fairfield, N.J., 1971-73, cons. designer, 1971-73; salesman Kenco Security Systems, Columbus, Ohio, 1974-76; archtl. designer Gene Swartz & Assocs., Chillicothe, Ohio, 1976-77, C. Curtiss Inscho & Assocs., Columbus, 1978-83, Noverre Musson Assocs., 1983—; v.p. Delta Tau Delta House Corp., 1973—; cons. residential design, 1976—. Mem. AIA. Christian Scientist. Home: 2164 Fairfax Rd Upper Arlington OH 43221 Office: 965 E Broad St Columbus OH 43215

BRICKELL, RICHARD ALLEN, computer systems consultant; b. Los Angeles, Sept. 4, 1941; s. Herschel Raymond and Lillian Kathern (Arnold B.; m. Jean Kendall, Oct. 31, 1962; children—Shanna, Sean, Dawn, Michael. Sales rep. Central Sch. Supply, Louisville, 1962-73; sales rep. Batesville Casket Co. (Ind.), 1973-80; sales mgr. Simmons Casket Co., Welsley, Mass., 1980-82; owner Forecast Trend Cons., Inc., Valley City, N.D, 1982—. Served with USN, 1959-62. Republican. Baptist. Office: Forecast Trend Cons Inc 801 5th Ave NW Valley City ND 58072

BRICKLEY, JAMES H., state supreme court justice; b. Flint, Mich., Nov. 15, 1928; s. J. Harry and Marie E. (Fischer) B.; 6 children. B.A., U. Detroit, 1951, LL.B., 1954, Ph.D. (hon.), 1977; LL.M., NYU, 1957; hon. degrees: Ph.D., Spring Arbor Coll., 1975, Detroit Coll. Bus., 1975, Ferris State Coll., 1980, Saginaw Valley State Coll., 1980, Schoolcraft Coll., 1981, Detroit Coll. Law. Bar: Mich. 1958. Spl. agent FBI, 1954-58; practice law, Detroit, 1959-62; mem. Detroit City Council, 1962-66, pres. protem, 1965-66; chief asst. prosecutor Wayne County (Mich.), 1967-69; U.S. atty. U.S. Dist. Ct. (ea. dist.) Mich., 1969-70; lt. gov. State of Mich., Lansing, 1971-74, 79-82; pres. Eastern Mich. U., Ypsilanti, 1975-78; justice Mich. Supreme Ct., Lansing, 1982—; lectr., adj. prof. U. Detroit, Wayne State U., U. Mich., Cooley Law Sch., 1958-73. Republican. Roman Catholic. Office: Mich Supreme Ct Law Bldg 2d Floor Lansing MI 48909

BRICKMAN, ROBERT OTTO, landscape company executive; b. Chgo., Jan. 22, 1938; s. Theodore William and Amy Edith (Kitzelman) B.; B.A. in Bus. Adminstrn., Lake Forest Coll., 1960; m. Gail Field Walkemeyer, Aug. 29, 1959; children—Jill, Barbara, Cynthia. Sales rep. UARCO, Inc., Chgo., 1960-61; landscape supr. Theodore Brickman Co., Long Grove, Ill., 1961-63, sales mgr., 1964-67, v.p., sec., 1967—; dir. Mid. Am. Hort. Trade Show, 1983—. Mem. exec. bd. N.W. Council Boy Scouts Am., 1976-77; trustee Immanuel Ch. New Jerusalem, Glenview, 1971—; bd. dirs. Buehler YMCA. Recipient distinguished service award Countryside Center Handicapped. Mem. Asso. Landscape Contractors Am., Ill. Nurserymen's Assn. (treas., v.p.). Republican. Club: Rotary (sec. 1963-65, pres. 1973-74, dist. gov.'s rep. 1974-77 dist. gov. 1981-82, chmn. internat. youth activities com. 1983-84). Home: 1025 Gladish Ln Glenview IL 60025 Office: Long Grove Rd Long Grove IL 60047

BRIDGEFORTH, JACQUI WEAVER, chemist, information scientist; b. Indpls., Feb. 2, 1946; d. Richard O. and Norris (Shane) Tanner; B.S., Marian Coll., 1970; M.S., Ball State U., 1982; children—Patrick Mahaffey, David Bridgeforth, Regina Easley, Darla Smith, Mark Young. With Union Carbide, Indpls., 1965-68; with Eli Lilly & Co., Indpls., 1968—, sr. patent specialist, 1978—. Bd. dirs., hosp. counselor Marion County Victims Advocates Program, 1978—; mem. youth adv. bd. Ctr. for Leadership Devel., 1979—; mem. adv. bd. Walker Career Ctr., 1981—; mem. Warren Twp. (Ind.) Sch. Improvement Council, 1980—; mem. Warren Twp. curriculum study steering com., 1982—. Mem. Am. Statis. Assn., Assn. Info. Mgrs., Am. Soc. Info. Sci., Spl. Library Assn., ALA, Am. Chem. Soc. Roman Catholic. Office: Eli Lilly & Co 307 E McCarty St Indianapolis IN 46285

BRIDGELAND, JAMES RALPH, JR., lawyer; b. Cleve., Feb. 16, 1929; s. James Ralph and Alice Laura (Huth) B.; m. Margaret Louise Bates, March 24, 1950; children—Deborah, Cynthia, Rebekah, Alicia, John. B.A., U. Akron, 1951; M.A., Harvard U., 1955, J.D., 1957. Bar: Ohio 1957. Mem. internat. staff Goodyear Tire & Rubber Co., Akron, Ohio, 1953-56; ptnr. Taft, Stettinius & Hollister, Cin., 1957—; dir. and mem. exec. com. First Nat. Bank Cin.; dir. Consol. Biscuit Co., SHV N.Am., Inc., Robert A. Cline Co., Art Stamping, Inc., Seinau-Fisher Studios, Inc.; sec. Vortec, Inc. Trustee of Cin. Symphony Orchestra (mem. exec. com.), Louise Taft Semple Found. (sec.), Hillside Trust Co., Jobs for Cin. Grads.; past dir. Cin. Legal Aid Soc. past vice chmn. men's com. Great Rivers Girl Scouts U.S. Council. Served to 1st lt. USAF, 1951-53, Korea. Fellow Aspen Inst.; mem. ABA, Ohio Bar Assn., Cin. Bar Assn., Am. Arbitration Assn., Harvard Law Sch. Assn. (past pres. Cin. chpt.), Harvard Alumni Assn. (nat. v.p. 1978-85). Republican. Episcopalian. Clubs: Harvard (pres. 1983-84), Queen City, Commonwealth (treas. 1984-86). Home: 8175 Brill Rd Cincinnati OH 45243

BRIDGENS, JAMES GETTY, forensic pathologist, medical legal consultant; b. Kansas City, Mo., Oct. 29, 1922; s. Haskell Elwyn and Helen (Getty) B.; m. Ruth Hamilton, May 14, 1948 (div. 1966); m. Mary Isabelle Berkey, Sept. 2, 1966. B.S., U. Kans., Lawrence, 1945; M.D., U. Kans.-Kansas City, 1947. Diplomate Am. Bd. Pathology. Intern, Kansas City Gen. Hosp., Mo., 1947-48, resident, 1948-52, assoc. pathologist, 1951-52; pathologist Alaskan Air Command, Anchorage, Alaska, 1953-55, Independence Sanitarium and Hosp., Mo., 1955-61; assoc. pathologist St. Joseph's Hosp., Kansas City, 1961-66; dir. labs. Shawnee Mission Med. Ctr., Kans., 1962-83, med. legal cons., Kansas City, 1983—; presenter in field. Contbr. articles, reports to profl. publs. Founding mem. Nat. Orgn. to Counter Sexual Assault, Kansas City, 1974-78. Served to capt. USAF, 1953-55. Fellow Coll. Am. Pathologists, Am. Soc. Clin. Pathologists, Am. Acad. Forensic Scis.; mem. Kans. Med. Soc. (councilor 1980—), AMA. Democrat. Lodge: Rotary. Avocations: travel, arts, antiques, photography. Home and office: 1025 Huntington Rd Kansas City MO 64113

BRIDGES, NORMAN VALETTE, college administrator; b. Newaygo County, Mich., Apr. 2, 1938; s. Guy Norman and Nellie (Ackley) B.; m. Janice Kay Stephey, Sept. 3, 1959; children—David, Jonathan, Daniel. B.S., Bethel Coll., 1960; A.M., U. Mich., 1964, Ph.D., 1970. Tchr. high sch. English Ind. pub. schs., 1960-62; tchr. jr. high sch. social studies Mich. pub. schs., 1962-63; dean students, prof., v.p. Bethel Coll., Mishawaka, Ind., 1966-76; pres. Friends Bible Coll., Haviland, Kans., 1976-85; v.p. univ. relations Friends U., Wichita, Kans., 1985—. Vice chmn. Kiowa County Meml. Hosp. Bd., Greensburg, Kans., 1979—. Mem. Nat. Assn. Evangelicals, Am. Assn. Bible Colls. Quaker. Home: 1900 Univ Wichita KS 67213

BRIDGEWATER, BERNARD ADOLPHUS, JR., business executive; b. Tulsa, Mar. 13, 1934; s. Bernard Adolphus and Mary Alethea (Burton) B.; A.B., Westminster Coll., Fulton, Mo., 1955; LL.B., U. Okla., 1958; M.B.A., Harvard, 1964; m. Barbara Paton, July 2, 1960; children—Barrie, Elizabeth, Bonnie. Admitted to Okla. bar, 1958, U.S. Supreme Ct. bar, U.S. Ct. of Claims bar; asst. county atty., Tulsa, 1962; assoc. McKinsey & Co., mgmt. cons., Chgo., 1964-68, prin., 1968-72, dir., 1972-73, 75; assoc. dir. nat. security and internat. affairs Office Mgmt. and Budget, Exec. Office Pres., Washington, 1973-74; exec. v.p. Baxter Travenol Labs., Inc., Chgo. and Deerfield, Ill., 1975-79, now dir.; pres., chief exec. officer Brown Group, Inc., Clayton, Mo., 1979—, chmn., 1985—; dir. FMC Corp., Chgo., Celanese Corp., N.Y.C., Baxter Travenol, Chgo., Centerre Bancorp., St. Louis; cons. Office Mgmt. and Budget, 1973, 75—. Trustee Rush-Presbyn.-St. Luke's Med. Center, 1974—, Washington U., St. Louis, 1983—. Served to lt. USNR, 1958-62. Recipient Rayonier Found. award Harvard, 1963; George F. Baker scholar, 1964. Mem. Beta Theta Pi, Omicron Delta Kappa, Phi Alpha Delta. Clubs: Chgo., Econ. (Chgo.); River (N.Y.C.); St. Louis Country, Log Cabin (St. Louis); Indian Hill Country (Winnetka, Ill.). Author: (with others) Better Management of Business Giving, 1965. Home: 35 Overhills Dr Ladue MO 63124 Office: Brown Group Inc 8400 Maryland Ave Clayton MO

BRIDGMAN, CHARLES JAMES, engineering educator; b. Toledo, Ohio, May 6, 1930; s. Charles Donald and Wilhelmina E. (Everett) B.; m. Lucy Stella Hull, May 15, 1954; children—Kathleen M. McFadden, Stephanie A. Danahy, Charles James, Kenneth M., Paula J., Thomas A. B.S., U.S. Naval Acad., 1952; M.S., N.C. State U., 1958, Ph.D., 1963. Asst., asso. prof. nuclear engring. Sch. Engring., Air Force Inst. Tech., Dayton, 1959-74, prof., chmn. nuclear engring. and chmn. Sch. Engring. Ph.D. Council, 1974—. Served to capt. USAF, 1952-63. Recipient Gage Crocker Outstanding Prof. award A.F. Inst. Tech., 1980. Mem. Am. Nuclear Soc., Health Physics Soc., Am. Soc. Engring. Edn., AAUP. Contbr. articles to profl. jours. Office: Dept Physics Sch Engring Air Force Inst Tech Wright Patterson AFB Dayton OH 45433

BRIDSON, SUSAN NIGHTINGALE, librarian; b. Reno, Nev., May 10, 1945; d. Herbert Larned and Hannah Jeanne (Gates) Dorrance; m. James Alan Bridson, June 23, 1973; children—Christopher Kenneth, Rebecca Noelle. B.A. in English, Fla. State U., 1967; M.A, U. Ariz., 1972; M.L.S., Emporia State U., 1983. Instr. U. Ariz., Tucson, 1970-72; tchr. Amphitheater High Sch., Tucson, 1972-74; instr. Washburn U., Topeka, Kans., 1977-80; tchr. Seaman High Sch., 1980-82; librarian Hayden High Sch., 1982—. Founder, Hayden Friends of the Library, 1982—. Mem. ALA, Kans. Library Assn., Kans. Assn. Sch. Librarians, Beta Phi Mu. Democrat. Roman Catholic. Home: 3002 Wisconsin Topeka KS 66605 Office: Hayden High Sch 401 Gage St Topeka KS 66606

BRIDWELL, BERNICE WAYNETTE, nurse; b. Zanesville, Ohio, Feb. 21, 1943; d. Wayne Everett and Marjorie Elsie (Monteith) Fitz; student Wittenberg U., 1960-61; dipl., Springfield City Hosp. Sch. Nursing, 1965; student Ohio State U., 1972; B.S.N., Ohio U., 1979; m. John Robert Bridwell, Jan. 8, 1966; children—Sherry Lu, Robert John. Staff nurse surg. intensive care unit Ohio State U. Hosps., Columbus, 1965; pediatric staff nurse Bethesda Hosp., Zanesville, Ohio, 1966, asst. clin. instr. Sch. Nursing, Zanesville, 1966-67, adult practical nursing instr., 1967-69, instr. pharmacology, 1970-77, jr. instr. high sch. practical nursing, 1972-74, instr. practical nursing Muskingum Area Vocat. Sch. Sec., mgr. Girl's Youth Slowpitch Softball League, Zanesville, 1973; tchr. Sun. sch. St. John Luth. Ch., Zanesville, 1967-68, 74-77, planner area Bible Sch., 1977, pres. St. John Luth. Ch. Women, 1973-75, altar chmn., 1977-79, circle leader, 1969-70. Mem. Muskingum Valley Dist. Nurses Assn., Ohio Nurses Assn., Am. Nurses Assn., Muskingum Area Vocational Sch. Edn. Assn., Ohio Edn. Assn., NEA, Ohio Vocat. Assn., Am. Vocat. Assn., Ohio Orgn. Practical Nurse Educators. Clubs: Vocat. Indsl. Clubs of Am. (asst. advisor Muskingum Area chpt. 1980-81), Nat. Vocat. Clubs of Am., Ohio Vocat. Indsl. Clubs of Am. Home: 5585 Kenny Dr Zanesville OH 43701 Office: 400 Richards Rd Zanesville OH 43701

BRIER, JACK HAROLD, state official; b. Kansas City, Mo., June 25, 1946; s. Marshall W. and M. Pearl (Munden) B.; student U. Kans., 1964-67, 77—; B.B.A., Washburn U., Topeka, 1970. Dep. asst. sec. state for legis. matters State of Kans., Topeka, 1969-70, asst. sec. state, 1970-78, sec. state, 1978—. Nat. v.p. Muscular Dystrophy Assn.; trustee Kans. Jaycees Found.; mem. exec. com. Council State Govts. bd. advisors CloseUp Kans.; adv. bd. Greater Univ. Fund, U. Kans. Named Outstanding Young Topekan, 1979; Outstanding Young Kansan, 1979; communications and leadership award Toastmasters Internat. Mem. Kans. Jaycees, Topeka Jaycees, Council State Govts. (exec. com.), Nat. Assn. Secs. State (exec. com., past pres.), Kans. State Hist. Soc. (bd. dirs., nominating com.), Shawnee County Hist. Soc., Am. Council Young Polit. Leaders Council (planning and coordinating com. council state govts.), Order of Police (assoc.), Sagamore Nat. Honor Fraternity (hon.), Blue Key (hon.), Fraternal Order Police (assoc.), Washburn U. Alumni Assn. (bd. dirs.). Republican. Office: Office of Secretary of State 2d Floor Capitol Bldg Topeka KS 66612

BRIERTON, DAVID LAWRENCE, housing developer; b. Milw., Sept. 25, 1942; s. Bernard Lawrence and Ruth Margaret (Conway) B.; B.B.A., Wis. State U., Whitewater, 1969; M.S. (HUD fellow), U. Wis., 1970; m. Judith Ann Ruch, Aug. 20, 1966; children—Kristin, Kerry, Kevin, Keely, Kolin, Korey. Project mgr. Gene B. Glick Co., Indpls., 1970-72; pres. Dominion Group Inc., Mpls., 1972—; mem. adv. bd. Ann. Nat. Apt. Builders and Developers Conf. and Exposition, Atlanta, 1978. Served with USAF, 1962-65. Mem. Nat. Leased Housing Assn. (dir. 1979—), Minn. Multi-Housing Assn. (dir. 1979—), Wis. Assn. Housing Authorities. Roman Catholic. Clubs: Rolling Green Country, Calhoun Beach. Office: 3140 Harbor Ln Plymouth MN 55441 Home: 3020 Jewel Ln Plymouth MN 55391

BRIGDEN, ROBERT CAMPBELL, investment broker; b. Cleve., May 19, 1942; s. James H. and A. Margaret (Campbell) B.; B.S. in Indsl. Tech., Ohio U., 1967; m. Nancy Romain Schwarzmann, Feb. 24, 1973. Asst. sales engr. Westinghouse Elec. Co., Columbus, Ohio, 1967-68; securities broker J.N. Russell Co., Cleve., 1969-74, Blyth Eastman Dillon, Cleve., 1974-75, Cleve-Corp Securities, Cleve., 1975-79, Affiliated Investors Service, 1979—; developer, partner Manor Apts., Alexander Apts.; advisor Newark Wire Cloth Co., Verona Realty; pres. Video Depot, 1981-83; pres., founder Video H.Q., 1983—; owner Robert C. Brigden Investments, 1980—; prin. Affiliated Investors Service, 1979—. Active Big Bros. Greater Cleve., 1973-83; past mem. adv. bd., past dir. Salvation Army, 1977-79; past bd. dirs., v.p. Cleveland Heights Housing Preservation Center, 1977-79; founder, pres. Playhouse Sq. Bus. Council. Served as paratrooper AUS, 1962-64. Mem. Theosophical Soc., Jr. C. of C. Presbyterian. Clubs: Cleve. Athletic, Jewish Community Center, Cleve. Rotary (bd. dirs. 1981-83), Cleve. Bond. Home: 3455 Edison Rd Cleveland OH 44121 Office: 1278 Euclid Ave Cleveland OH 44115

BRIGGS, DENNIS HERBERT, orthodontist; b. Cedar Rapids, Iowa, Feb. 17, 1942; s. Carroll T. and Virginia (Mohler) B.; m. Carol Ann Starrett, July 3, 1965; children—Sean Colin, Chad Michael. B.A., U. Iowa, 1964, D.D.S., 1969, M.S. in Orthodontics, 1973. Practice dentistry specializing in orthodontics, Neenah, Wis., 1972—; owner Carden Quarter Horses, Neenah, 1979—. Mem. Neenah Planning Commn., 1983—. Served to capt. USAF, 1968-70. Kinnick Athletic scholar U. Iowa, 1960-64. Mem. Wis. Dental Assn., Winnebago County Dental Assn., Neenah-Menasha Dental Assn., Am. Assn. Orthodontists, Wis. Soc. Orthodontists, Am. Quarter Horse Assn., Wis. Quarter Horse Assn., N.E. Wis. Quarter Horse Assn. Club: Optimists. Home: 1330 Woodenshoe Rd Neenah WI 54956 Office: 151 E Forest Ave Neenah WI 54956

BRIGGS, MARJORIE CROWDER, lawyer; b. Shreveport, La., Mar. 26, 1946; d. Rowland Edmund and Marjorie Ernestine (Biles) Crowder; m. Ronald J. Briggs, July 11, 1970; children—Sarah, Andrew. B.A., Carson-Newman Coll., 1968; M.A., Ohio State U., 1969, J.D., 1975. Bar: Ohio 1975. Asst. dean of women Albion Coll., Mich., 1969-70; dir. residence hall Ohio State U., Columbus, 1970-71, acad. counselor, 1971-72; assoc. Porter, Wright, Morris, Arthur, Columbus, 1975-83, ptnr., 1983—; legal aid Community Law Office, Columbus, 1973-74. Trustee, pres. Epilepsy Assn. Central Ohio, Columbus, 1977-84; bd. dirs. Columbus Speech & Hearing, 1977-82; mem. allocation com. United Way Franklin County, 1984-85. Mem. ABA, Ohio Bar Assn., Columbus Bar Assn. (com. chmn. 1979-83, editor 1981-83), Am. Arbitration Assn., Nat. Assn. Women Lawyers, Women Lawyers Franklin County, Columbus Def. Assn. Clubs: Columbus, Metropolitan. Home: 233 Erie Rd Columbus OH 43214 Office: Porter Wright Morris & Arthur 41 S High St Columbus OH 43215

BRIGGS, WILLIAM BENAJAH, aeronautical engineer; b. Okmulgee, Okla., Dec. 13, 1922; s. Eugene Stephen and Mary Bettie (Gentry) B.; B.A. in Physics, Phillips U., 1943, D.Sc. (hon.), 1977; M.S. in Mech. Engring., Ga. Inst. Tech., 1947; m. Lorraine Hood, June 6, 1944; children—Eugene Stephen II, Cynthia Anne, Julia Louise, Spencer Gentry. Aero. scientist Nat. Adv. Commn. Aeros., Cleve., 1948-52; propulsion engr. Chance Vought Aircraft/LTV, Dallas, 1952-64; mgr. advanced planning McDonnell Douglas Co., St. Louis, 1964-80, dir. program devel. fusion energy, 1980—; mem. NASA Planetary Quarantine Adv. Panel. Chmn. bd. Christian Bd. Publ., St. Louis, 1974—; chmn. Disciples Council of Greater St. Louis, 1969-73. Served with USN, 1943-46. Asso. fellow AIAA (dir. region 5 1974-77, v.p. mem. services 1978-79); mem. Am. Nuclear Soc. Mem. Disciples of Christ Ch. Club: Masons. Contbr. articles on aero. engring. and energy to profl. jours. Patentee in field. Home: 1819 Bradburn Dr Saint Louis MO 63131 Office: PO Box 516 McDonnell Douglas Astronautics Co Saint Louis MO 63166

BRIGHAM, WILLIAM FRANK, optometrist; b. Portland, Ind., Jan. 20, 1942; s. William F., Sr. and Roberta (Gray) B.; divorced; children—Kris, Ben, Nate, Cindy. A.B., Ind. U., 1965, O.D., 1967. Sole practice optometry, Ft. Wayne, Ind., 1968—. Named Boss of Yr., Ind. Paraoptmetrics, 1984. Mem. Ind. Optometric Assn. (chmn. vision therapy com. 1972-75), Allen County Headstart (cons.). Home: 902 W Wayne Fort Wayne IN 46804 Office: 902 W Wayne St Fort Wayne IN 46804

BRIGHT, JON BRANSON, environmental engineer; b. Fairfield, Ill., Jan. 9, 1953; s. Edward Merle and Julia (Lubker) B. M.C.E., Tex. A&M U., 1977. Registered profl. engr., Tex. Assoc. environ. engr. Marathon Oil Co., LaFayette, La., 1977-81, environ. engr., Houston, 1981-83, advanced environ. engr., Findlay, Ohio, 1983—. Author (thesis) Evaluation of Coastal Waters from Landsat Satellite Imagery, 1977. Recipient Carnegie Hero Fund medal, 1967. Mem. ASCE, Am. Soc. Safety Engrs., Am. Indsl. Hygiene Assn. Presbyterian. Avocations: collecting early 20th century prints; antique refinishing. Home: 2616 S Main St Findlay OH 45840 Office: Marathon Oil Co 539 S Main St Findlay OH 45840

BRIGHT, MARY KATHERINE, university administrator; b. Waukegan, Ill., Oct. 30, 1925; d. William Lincoln and Edna Belle (Wardlow) Manny; B.A. in English with honors, Calif. State U., Northridge, 1965; M.A. in English, U. So. Calif., 1968, postgrad. in linguistics and higher edn.; m. William Herbert Bright, Dec. 22, 1978; children—Marianne, Kurtina, Kristina. Instr., sr. lectr. English, English as second lang. Calif. State U.-Northridge and U. So. Calif., 1965-68, asst. dean summer session, exec. dir. summer session evening coll., 1969-74; dir. continuing edn. Calif. State U.-Long Beach, 1974-78; assoc. dir. urban extension and non-credit programs Ohio State U., 1978-80; dir. office mgmt. devel. U. Ill. Coll. Bus. Adminstrn., Chgo., 1980—; v.p. Bright's Bytes Unltd., Inc., computer-assisted mgmt. cons. firm.; conf. presenter; pres. Council Non-Traditional Studies, 1972-78; cons. W.Va. Bd. Regents, 1978. Mem. Nat. Univ. Continuing Edn. Assn., Sigma Alpha Alpha. Presbyterian. Office: 2426 UH Box 4348 U Ill Chicago IL 60680

BRIGHT, MYRON H., See *Who's Who in America,* 43rd edition.

BRILL, KENNETH GRAY, JR., geology educator, researcher; b. St. Paul, Nov. 16, 1910; s. Kenneth Gray and Laura (Cooke) B.; m. Priscilla Ritchie, July 28, 1939; children—David, Thomas. B.A., U. Minn., 1935; postgrad. Yale U., 1935-37; M.S., U. Mich., 1938, Ph.D., 1939. Inst., asst. prof. U. Chattanooga, 1939-45; geologist U.S. Geol. Survey, Washington, 1942-44; from asst. prof. to prof. St. Louis U., 1946-79, prof. emeritus, 1979—; contract geologist Gulf Oil Corp., Tulsa, summer 1952, 54, 55, 56, Pan Am. Petroleum Corp., Tulsa, summer 1961, 62, 63, 65; spl. coal cons. Econ. Cooperation Adminstrn., Republic of Korea, 1949; Fulbright lectr. U. Tasmania, Hobart, 1952, hon. research assoc., 1978. Contbr. articles to profl. jours. James Dwight Dana Fellow Yale U., 1935-36. Fellow Geol. Soc. Am. (emeritus; sec., treas. North Central sect. 1980—), AAAS (council mem. 1952-53); mem. Paleontol. Soc. (emeritus), Am. Assn. Petroleum Geologists, Mo. Acad. Sci. (pres. 1968), Sci. Tchrs. Mo. (Sci. Educator award 1974-75), Explorers Club. Episcopalian. Home: 360 S Gore Ave Webster Groves MO 63119

BRILL, RICHARD B(ENJAMIN), public relations co. exec.; b. N.Y.C., Aug. 29, 1944; s. David and Augusta (Harrison) B.; B.S.M.E., Lafayette Coll., 1966; M.B.A., Northwestern U., 1968; m. Marlene Targ, Feb., 1973; 1 dau., Alison Targ. Account exec. Anthony M. Franco & Assocs., Detroit, 1973-75, Burson-Marsteller, Chgo., 1978; account exec. Selz, Seabolt & Assocs., Inc., Chgo., 1975-77, dir. fin. relations, 1979, group supr., 1982, v.p., 1983—. Mem. Public Relations Soc. Am., Chgo. Assn. Commerce and Industry, Chgo. High Tech Assn., Execs. Club Chgo., Northwestern U. Mgmt. Alumni Assn., Condominium Assn. (pres.). Home: 3180 Lake Shore Dr Chicago IL 60657 Office: 221 N LaSalle St Chicago IL 60601

BRINER, DONALD HEILMAN, medical educator, physician; b. Phila., Nov. 9, 1919; s. Robert M. and Catherine R. (Heilman) B.; m. Betty J. Biddle, Oct. 21, 1945; children—Barbara, Thomas, Beth, William. B.S., Lehigh U., 1944; D.O., Phila. Coll. Osteo. Medicine, 1944. Diplomate Am. Osteo. Bd. Internal Medicine; cert. Am. Osteo. Bd. Rheumatology. Intern, Bashline-Rossman Hosp., Grove City, Pa., 1944-45; resident in internal medicine Detroit Osteo. Hosp., 1953-56; gen. practice family medicine, Mercer, Pa., 1945-53; sr. attending physician Grandview Hosp., Dayton, Ohio, 1956-79; fellow in clin. immunology Cin. Gen. Hosp., 1976-77; prof. and chmn. dept. internal medicine Coll. Osteo. Medicine Mich. State U., East Lansing, 1979—; tchr.; adminstr. Named Earl F. Riceman Lectr., Eastern Study Conf. 1970; recipient Disting. Service award Am. Coll. Osteo. Internists, 1974. Fellow Am. Coll. Osteo. Internist; Am. Osteo. Assn., Mich. Osteo. Assn., Am. Rheumatism Assn., Ohio Rheumatism Assn. Republican. Presbyterian. Contbr. articles to profl. jours. Home: 3905 Raleigh St Okemos MI 48864 Office: B-305 West Fee Hall Mich State U East Lansing MI 48824

BRINGE, BERNARD GLENN, airline exec.; b. Northwood, Iowa, Feb. 11, 1934; s. Melvin Theodore and Gladys Joy (Pangburn) B.; B.S., U. Wis., Whitewater, 1961; M.B.A., Roosevelt U., Chgo., 1968; m. Erna Lynne Tripp, May 29, 1965. Tchr. high sch. bus., Slinger and Salem, Wis., 1961-65; with United Airlines, 1966—, mgr. passenger revenue systems, Chgo., 1978—. Served with U.S. Army, 1955-57. Mem. NEA, Nat. Bus. Edn. Assn., Chgo. Mgmt. Club, Pi Omega Pi. Republican. Presbyterian. Home: 1588 Clover Dr Inverness IL 60067 Office: United Airlines EXOKA PO Box 66100 Chicago IL 60666

BRINGHAM, WILLIAM TALBERT, SR., fraternity executive; b. Normal, Ill., Dec. 16, 1924; s. Russell Wilson and Sarah E. (Talbert) B.; Ph.B., Illinois Wesleyan University, 1948; J.D., Vanderbilt University, 1951; grad. trust devel. school Northwestern U. Sch. Commerce, 1953; m. Ruth Irene Jaeger, Jan. 10, 1947; 1 son, William Talbert. Spl. agt. FBI, 1951-52; exec. sec. Sigma Chi Frat., 1954—; exec. dir. Sigma Chi Found., 1956—, also sec.; also sec. bd. grand trustee of Sigma Chi, exec. v.p., sec. exec. com., and sec. grand council Sigma Chi Fraternity (name later changed to Sigma Chi Corp.); bd. dirs., treas. Nat. Interfrat. Found. Bd. dirs., treas. Kendall Coll.; bd. dirs. Soc. Assn. Execs. Found.; del. Sch. Bd. Caucus. Del. Ill. Republican Conv., former Northfield Twp. Rep. committeeman, former trustee Wilmette, Ill. Former chmn. and Police Commn., Wilmette, Ill. Served with USNR, 1942-46. Named flying col. Delta Airlines, ambassador Trans World Airlines, admiral Am. Airlines; recipient Grand Consul's Citation, Order of Constantine award, Significant Sigaward Mem. Am. Personnel and Guidance Assn., Nat. Assn. Student Personnel Adminstrs., Am. Soc. Assn. Execs. (Key award 1973; vice chmn. ann. meeting com.; dir. Found.), Wilmette, Evanston hist. socs., Travelers Protective Assn., Am. Legion, Frat. Execs. Assn. (pres., exec. com.), Evanston C. of C. (past dir.), S.A.R., Chgo. Soc. Assn. Execs. (dir., pres.), Phi Delta Phi. Lodges: Mason (Shriner, 33 deg., K.T., Red Cross of Constantine), Royal Order Scotland. Clubs: Kiwanis, University (pres.) (Evanston); Westmoreland Country (Wilmette, Ill.). Author booklet on alumni chpts. Sigma Chi. Chmn. com. that edited Visitation Manual for College Fraternities. Address: 4020 Bunker Ln Wilmette IL 60091

BRINK, BRUCE CARLETON,, JR., osteopathic physician; b. Kirksville, Mo., Sept. 2, 1949; s. Bruce C. and Lois J. (McClure) B. B.S., U. Evansville, 1972; D.O., Kirksville Coll. Medicine, 1977. Diplomate Am. Osteo. Bd. Gen. Practice. Intern, Grandview Hosp., Dayton, Ohio, 1977-78, resident, 1978-79; gen. practice osteo. medicine, Princeton, Ind., 1979—; mem. staff Gibson Gen. Hosp., Princeton, 1979—, chief obstetrics, 1983—, also v.p. med. staff; mem. Gibson County Bd. Health; chmn. Ind. Osteo. Conv., 1983; del. Am. Med. Peer Rev., 1984. Mem. Ind. Assn. Osteo. Physicians, Am. Cancer Soc., Am. Osteo. Assn., Ind. Assn. Osteo. Physicians and Surgeons (trustee), Am. Coll. Gen. Practitioners, Ind. Peer Rev. Orgn., Porsche Club Am., Porsche Club Western Ky., U.S. Hang Gliding Assn., Exptl. Aircraft Assn. (ultralight div.), Aircraft Owners and Pilots Assn. Republican. Presbyterian. Lodge: Elks. Home: Old Petersburg Rd Princeton IN 47670 Office: 410 N Main St Princeton IN 47670

BRINKLEY, GEORGE ARNOLD, JR., educator; b. Wilmington, N.C., Apr. 20, 1931; s. George Arnold and Ida Bell (West) B.; A.B., Davidson Coll., 1953; M.A., Columbia U., 1955, Ph.D., 1964; m. Ann Mae Kreps, Aug. 9, 1959; 1 dau., Heidi Ann. Instr. polit. sci. Columbia U., N.Y.C., 1957-58; with dept. govt. U. Notre Dame, 1958—, prof., 1970—, dir. Program of Soviet & East European Studies, 1969—, chmn. dept., 1969-77, dir. Inst. Internat. Studies, 1975-78. Ford Found. fellow, 1954-57; Internat. Affairs fellow Council on Fgn. Relations, 1968-69. Mem. Am. Assn. Advancement of Slavic Studies (chmn. membership com. 1978-81); Midwest Slavic Assn. (chmn. exec. com. 1979-81), Phi Beta Kappa. Methodist. Author: The Volunteer Army and Allied Intervention in South Russia, 1917-1921, 1966. Office: Dept Govt U Notre Dame Notre Dame IN 46556

BRINKLEY, WILLIAM JOHN, educator; b. Shawneetown, Ill., Dec. 8, 1925; s. William Henry and Frances (Leath) B.; B.S., U. Ill., 1945. Tchr. high sch., McLeansboro, Ill., 1945—, high sch. coordinator vocations, 1968—; owner Brinkley Interiors and Galleries, antique porcelain, McLeansboro. Mem. adv. bd. Ill. Edn. Council, 1967—; mem. Pres.'s Com. 100, 1968; mem. Hamilton County Bicentennial Com.; chmn. rehab. com. McCoy Meml. Library and Hamilton County Hist. Soc. Bldg.; mem. Friends of Mus., Mitchell Mus., Mt. Vernon, Ill., 1978-84; mem. Hamilton County Republican Com., 1950-68. Recipient Tchr. of Year award U. Ill. Edn. Dept., 1963; Merit award Gov. Ill. 1964; Disting. Service award Future Farmers Am., 1967; George Washington medal honor Freedoms Found. Am., 1966, 69; Outstanding Vocat. Edn. award Ill. State Vocat. Edn. Service, 1981; Presbyn. Service award, 1984. Mem. NEA, Ill. Edn. Assn., Hamilton County (pres. 1970), Gallatin County hist. socs., Nat., Ill. (Tchr. of Tchrs.) assns. vocat. agr. tchrs., Rend Lake Symphony Soc., Arts and Humanities Soc., SAR (bd. govs. Ill., state chmn. constructive citizenship com.), Hereditary Register of U.S., Phi Beta Kappa, Delta Sigma Phi. Presbyn. Mason, Kiwanian, Elk, Lion. Home: 401 Washington St S McLeansboro IL 62859 Office: 200 S Pearl St McLeansboro IL 62859 also 401 S Washington Ave McLeansboro IL 62859

BRINKMAN, JOHN ANTHONY, orientalist, educator; b. Chgo., July 4, 1934; s. A(dam) John and Alice (Davies) B.; A.B., Loyola U. Chgo., 1956, M.A., 1958; Ph.D., U. Chgo., 1962; m. Monique E. Geschier, Mar. 24, 1970; 1 son, Charles E. Research assoc. Oriental Inst., U. Chgo., 1963, asst. prof. Assyriology and Ancient History, 1964-66, assoc. prof., 1966-70, prof., 1970—, chmn. dept., 1969-72, dir. Oriental Inst., 1972-81, Charles H. Swift Disting. Service prof., 1984—; mem. staff of Chgo. Assyrian Dictionary, 1963—; ann. prof. Am. Schs. Oriental Research, Baghdad, 1968-69, chmn. Baghdad Schs. com., 1970—, mem. exec. com., 1971-75, 82—, chmn., 1973-75, trustee, 1975—. Mem. vis. com. dept. near Eastern langs. and civilizations Harvard, 1973-80. Fellow Am. Council Learned Socs., 1963-64, Am. Research Inst. Turkey, 1971; NEH fellow, 1973-74; Guggenheim fellow, 1984-85. Mem. Am. Oriental Soc. (br. v.p. 1970-71, pres. 1971-72), Brit. Inst. Persian Studies, Brit. Inst. Archaeology at Ankara. Roman Catholic. Author: Political History of Post-Kassite Babylonia, 1968; Materials and Studies for Kassite History, Vol. 1, 1976; Prelude to Empire, 1984; mem. editorial bd. Chgo. Assyrian Dictionary, 1977—; editor-in-charge Royal Inscriptions of Mesopotamia Project, Babylonian sect., 1979—. Contbr. articles to profl. jours. Home: 5535 S University Ave Chicago IL 60637 Office: Oriental Inst 1155 E 58th St Chicago IL 60637

BRINKMAN, PAUL DEL(BERT), journalism educator, university dean; b. Olpe, Kans., Feb. 10, 1937; s. Paul Theodore and Delphine Barbara (Brown) B.; m. Evelyn Marie Lange, Aug. 5, 1961; children—Scott Michael, Susan Lynn. B.S., Emporia State Coll., 1958; M.A., Ind. U.-Bloomington, 1963, Ph.D., 1971. Reporter, Emporia (Kans.) Gazette, 1954-59; instr. journalism Leavenworth (Kans.) High Sch., 1959-62; lectr. Ind. U.-Bloomington, 1962-65, 68-70; asst. prof. Kans. State U., 1965-68, prof., dean Sch. Journalism, 1970—, dir. William Allen White Found., 1974—, faculty rep. Bigh Eight Conf., Nat. Collegiate Athletic Assn., 1978—. Contbr. articles to profl. jours., newspapers. Mem. Assn. Edn. in Journalism and Mass Communications (past pres.), Assn. Schs. Journalism and Mass Communications (past pres.), Inland Daily Press Assn., Kappa Tau Alpha, Sigma Delta Chi. Avocations: Golf, softball. Home: 2553 Missouri St Lawrence KS 66044 Office: William Allen White Sch Journalism Univ Kans 200 Stauffer-Flint Hall Lawrence KS 66045

BRINKMEYER, LOREN JAY, data processor, college administrator; b. Udall, Kans., Apr. 21, 1925; s. William Frederick and Verna Christina (Mead) B.; student U. Kans., 1943, 50-51, U. Wis., 1943-44; D. Mus. Dramatics, U. Heidelberg (Germany), 1954; D. Internat. Comml. Law, U. Poitiers (France), 1964; B.S.B. with honors, Emporia State U., 1972, M.S.B. with honors, 1978; Ph.D. in Computer Info. Systems, Loyola U., Paris, 1983; also student numerous data processing and computer sci. courses; m. Helen Josephine Walkemeyer, Mar. 10, 1946; 1 son, Karl Phillip. Served as enlisted man U.S. Army, 1943-45, commd. 2d lt., 1945, advanced through grades to lt. col., 1962; data processing supr., Hawaii, 1945-51, W. Ger., 1951-54, U.S., 1955, 60-61, Alaska, 1956-59, France, 1962-64, ret., 1964; dir. data processing Butler County Community Coll., El Dorado, Kans., 1964—; cons. data processing. Pres. El Dorado Mcpl. Bd., 1971-83; mem. choir United Methodist Ch., El Dorado, 1964—; mem. Kans. U. Alumni Band, 1972—. Decorated Army Commendation medal, Bronze Star with two oak leaf clusters, Purple Heart. Mem. NEA, Kans. Higher Edn. Assn., Am. Vocat. Assn., Kans. Vocat. Assn., Kans. Bus. Occupations Assn., Kans. Bus. Edn. Assn., Kans. Bus. Computerized Student Follow-up (adv. bd.), Data Processing Edn. Kans., Assn. Ednl. Data Systems, Data Processing Mgmt. Assn. (cert.), Assn. Computing Machinery, Soc. Data Educators, Internat. Assn. Computer Programmers, Ret. Enlisted Assn., Ret. Officers Assn., 96th Inf. Div. Assn., Nat. Assn. Uniformed Services, Am. Legion, VFW. Independent Republican. Author: Electrical Accounting Machines, 2d edit., 1964; Automated Inventory and Financial Systems, edit., 1976; Punched Card Business Data Processing, 3d edit., 1974. Office: Data Center Butler County Community Coll Haverhill and Towanda El Dorado KS 67042

BRINKMEYER, WILLIS ROBERT, farm corp. exec.; b. Beatrice, Nebr., Jan. 4, 1931; s. Henry and Amelia Marie (Helmke) B.; graduate Bus. Adminstrn., Lincoln (Nebr.) Sch. Commerce; m. Shirley Louis Mitchell, Jan. 1, 1961; children—Renee, Mae Marie. Pres. Brinkmeyer Farms, Inc., Cortland, Nebr., 1972-80. Mem. 18th Dist. Jud. Nominating Commn., 1973—. Mem. Top Farmers of Am. Republican. Lutheran. Home: Route 1 Cortland NE 68331

BRINSON, DAVID LEE, industrial engineer; b. Brazil, Ind., Apr. 14, 1956; s. Russell Leslie and Vera Patricia (All) B.; m. Cheryl Ann Searcy, Oct. 11, 1980; 1 child, Anthony Schuyler. B.Indsl. Adminstrn., Gen. Motors Inst., 1979; M.B.A., Ind. State U., 1984. Assoc. indsl. engr. Detroit Diesel Allison div. Gen. Motor Corp., Indpls., 1979-82; indsl. engr., 1982—. Trustee, Harmony United Meth. Ch., 1980-82, supt. Sunday Sch., 1980-81. Mem. Inst. Indsl. Engrs. Republican. Lodge: Masons. (master). Avocations: band; golf; biking. Home: PO Box 185 Harmony IN 47853 Office: Detroit Diesel Allison Div GMC PO Box 894 L26 Indianapolis IN 46206

BRINTON, WILLIAM RAYMOND, writer, public relations consultant; b. Lewistown, Pa., Dec. 18, 1932; s. William Addison and Evelyn Irene (Hawk) B.; m. Wendy Byers, Aug. 18, 1973; children—Reed Collins, David Byers. Student Southeastern La. State, 1953-54; student Tulane U., 1954-56. Sports writer Times Picayune, New Orleans, 1956-58; reporter Daily Advertiser, Lafayette, La., 1958-60, Nonpareil Council Bluffs (Iowa), 1960-62; writer, reporter, bur. mgr. UPI, New Orleans, Baton Rouge, Kansas City, Mo., Topeka, 1962-67; writer, producer sta. KMBC-TV Kansas City, 1967-69; freelance writer, Kansas City, Mo., 1969-70; pub. relations cons., writer, prin. Bill Brinton Assoc., Kansas City, Mo., 1970; bd. govs. Am. Royal; lectr. Penn Valley Community Coll. Bd. dirs. Child World Sch. for Gifted Children, Old Westport Improvement Assn. Served with USAF, 1949-53. Recipient Cert. of Recognition Mo. Dental Assn., 1981; Disting. Service award City of Kansas City, 1972; Ky Col. Mem. Pub. Relations Soc. Am. (PRISM award, Kansas City chpt. 1981), Internat. Assn. Bus. Communicators. Democrat. Editor, pub. Editors Forum. Office: 4050 Broadway Suite 219 Kansas City MO 64111

BRISCOE, KEITH G., college president; b. Adams, Wis., Oct. 16, 1933; B.S., U. Wis., La Crosse, 1960; M.Ed., U. N.H., 1968; postgrad. Case Western Res. U., Iowa State U., U. Wis., Okla. State U.; LL.D. (hon.), Coll. Idaho, 1978, Buena Vista Coll., 1979; m. Carmen Irene Schweinler, Aug. 15, 1956; 1 dau., Susan Ann. Asst. dir. Coll. Union, Wis. State U., Stevens Point, 1960-62, U. N.H., 1962-64; dir. Coll. Union, dir. student activities, asst. prof. student life Baldwin Wallace Coll., Berea, Ohio, 1964-70; v.p. Coll. Steubenville (Ohio), 1970-74; pres. Buena Vista Coll., Storm Lake, Iowa, 1974—; higher edn. cons. Cuyahoga Community Coll., Coll. Wooster; v.p., treas. Ednl. Task, Inc., Berea, 1967-69; mem. nat. adv. bd. Coll. Transition Program, Berea, 1967-69; mem. adv. bd. Coll. and Univ. Partnership Program. Bd. dirs. Council Ind. Colls., 1981-83; bd. dirs., pres. Assn. Presbyn. Colls. and Univs.; exec. com., vice chmn. Nexus; adv. to program bd. Presbyn. Ch. U.S.A.; bd. dirs., officer Coll. of Mid-Am.; mem. Am. Council on Edn., mem. coordinating com., 1981—; co-chmn. Sino-Am. Inst. Higher Edn., Republic of China, 1981. Served with AUS, 1956-58. Mem. Assn. Coll. and Univ. Concert Mgrs. (trustee), UN Assn., Iowa Assn. Ind. Colls. and Univs. (pres., exec. com. 1977—), Iowa Assn. Coll. Presidents (pres. exec. com.), Phi Epsilon Kappa, Phi Delta Kappa. Republican. Methodist. Clubs: Masons, Des Moines, Order of the Arch, Rotary. Author: Directory of College Unions, 1963; An Annotated Bibliography of the College Union, 1967; A Study of Alternatives to Financing Private Higher Private Education, 1973; contbr. articles to profl. jours. Address: Office of Pres Buena Vista Coll Storm Lake IA 50588

BRISKIN, MADELEINE, oceanographer, climatologist, micropaleontologist; b. Paris, Sept. 4, 1932; came to U.S., 1951, naturalized, 1956; d. Michel and Mina B.; B.S., CCNY, 1965; M.S., U. Conn., 1967; Ph.D., Brown U., 1973. Asso. prof. geology Old Tech. U. Cin., 1980—. Recipient award Research Support, 1971-72, NSF Support award, 1978, Old Tech. U. Cin. Dean's award, 1978, Research Council award, 1978. Mem. Climap, Am. Geophys. Union, Am. Quaternary Assn., AAAS, Paleontologist Soc., Cin. Engrs. and Scientists Soc., Woods Hole Oceanographic Instn., Lamont-Doherty Geol. Obs., N.Y. Acad. Sci., Sigma Xi. Contbr. articles to profl. jours. Office: Dept Geology U Cin Cincinnati OH 45221

BRISTER, FRANK RAYFIELD, media educator; b. Gloucester, Mass., May 8, 1928; s. Frank John and Gladys Mae (Reid) B.; B.A. in Humanities (Rotary scholar), U. Hartford (Conn.), 1965; M.S. in TV-Radio, Syracuse U., 1966, cert. advanced studies, Instructional Tech., 1969. Coordinator audiovisual services Univ. Coll., Syracuse (N.Y.) U., 1966-69; dir. audiovisual services Ferris State Coll., Big Rapids, Mich., 1969-74, asso. prof. Sch. Edn., coordinator media tech. program, 1974—; cons. media utilization modules to improve classroom instruction; author ednl. mediated programs. Home: 403 Maple St Big Rapids MI 49307

BRISTOL, BENTON KEITH, agriculture educator, consultant; b. Ansley, Nebr., Feb. 21, 1920; s. Clyde Cecil and Ima Ethel (Davis) B.; m. Bettyjo Moore, Sept. 14, 1941; 1 son, Larry Benton. B.S., Colo. State Coll. A&M Arts, 1946; M.S., Okla. A&M Coll., 1950; Ed.D., Pa. State U., 1959. Cert. vocat. agr. tchr., Colo. Tchr. vocat. agr. Rocky Ford (Colo.) High Sch., 1946-49; tchr. vocat. agr. and chemistry Collbran (Colo.) High Sch., 1950-51; instr. agrl. edn. Pa. State U., University Park, 1955-60, asst. prof. agrl. edn., 1960-63; prof. edn. Ohio State U. (Faculty of Edn. in India), 1963-65; assoc. prof. agr. Ill. State U., Normal, 1965-75, prof. agrl. mechanics, 1975—; cons. creativity Creative Problem-Solving Inst. Chmn. cons. com. YWCA Sr. Services, 1978-84. Served to 1st lt. U.S. Army, 1946-49; to capt. USAF, 1951-54. Recipient Hon. State Farmer Degree Ill. Future Farmers Am. Assn., 1966; Kellogg Found. grantee, 1977, 78, 79. Mem. Ill. Assn. Vocat. Agr. Tchrs. (service award 1979, 84), Ill. Vocat. Assn., Am. Vocat. Assn., Am. Soc. Safety Egnrs., Nat. Inst. for Farm Safety, Inc. Republican. Methodist. Co-author 2 books; contbr. numerous articles on agrl. edn. to profl. jours. Office: Dept Agr Ill State U Normal IL 61761

BRITT, RONALD LEROY, mechanical engineer; b. Abilene, Kans., Mar. 1, 1935; s. Elvin Elbert and Lona Helen (Conn) B.; B.S.M.E., Wichita State U., 1963; m. Judith Ann Salter, June 29, 1957; children—Brett Gavin, Mark Damon, Melissa. Product engr. to product planner Hotpoint div. Gen. Electric Co., Chgo., 1963-68; product planner Norge Co., Chgo., 1968; product mgr., asst. dir. engring. Leigh Products Inc., Coopersville, Mich., 1968-74; mgr. research and devel. MiamiCarey div. Jim Walter Corp., Monroe, Ohio, 1974-84; dir. engring. div. SICO, Belvedere Co., Belvidere, Ill., 1984—; industry rep. for electric fans Underwriters Labs. Active, Boy Scouts Am., 1970-73, PTA, 1973—; exec. adviser Jr. Achievement, 1984—. Served with U.S. Army, 1958-60. Recipient Inventor's award Gen. Electric Co., 1967. Mem. ASME, Home Ventilation Inst. (engring. com. 1975-84). Republican. Congregationalist. Clubs: Free Blown Glassblowing, Carnival and Art Glass Collectors. Patentee in field. Home: 2605 Central Ave Middletown OH 45044 Office: 203 Garver Rd Monroe OH 45050

BRITT, RUSSELL WILLIAM, utility executive; b. 1926. B.S. in Elec. Engring., U. Wis., 1946, B.B.A., 1948. With Wis. Electric Power Co., 1948—, asst. controller, 1960-62, controller, 1962-77, treas., 1969-73, v.p. fin. and controller, 1973-75, exec. v.p., controller, 1975-77, exec. v.p., 1977-82, pres. chief operating officer, 1982—. Office: Wis Electric Power Co Inc 231 W Michigan St PO Box 2046 Milwaukee WI 53201

BRITT, RUTH EVANGELINE BURGIN, civic worker; b. Fayette, Mo., Mar. 15, 1907; d. Samuel Herschel and Lora (Miller) Burgin; student Wesleyan Woman's Coll., 1926-27; A.B., Tallahassee Woman's Coll., 1928; m. James T. Britt, Sept. 18, 1930; children—Thomas Burgin, Robert McCammon. Bd. dirs. Spofford Home for Children, 1937-38, Della Lamb Neighborhood House, 1937-38, YMCA, 1938-39; mem. Woman's City Club, Kansas City, Mo., 1931—, chmn. hosp. com., 1931-35; mem. Guild Friends Art at William Rockhill Nelson Gallery, 1961—; mem. fireside com. Kansas City Art Inst., 1948-49; mem. women's div. Kansas City Philharmonic Assn., 1966—, Kansas City Mus. Assn., 1966—; bd. mgrs. George H. Nettleton Home for Aged Women, 1968-73. Chmn. Christian-social relations Women's Soc. Christian Service, 1946-48, pres., 1937-38, chmn. missions, 1961-63; chmn. St. Francis Aux. of St. Francis Home for Boys, Salina and Ellsworth, Kan., 1946-48, supplies com. Community Chest Dr., 1951; vol. visitor for aged Mattie Rhodes Settlement House, 1948; Hosp. Gray Lady, 1948-50. Pres., Young Women's Democratic Club, 1931-33. Mem. UDC, D.A.R. (regent 1942-43). Methodist (mem. adminstrv. bd.). Address: 409 W 58th Terr Kansas City MO 64113

BRITTAIN, WILLIAM LYLE, restaurant franchise executive; b. Woodward, Okla., July 22, 1956; s. Lyle Brittain and Kathryn (Dotson) Nickels; m. Kenna Gale Alley, July 12, 1980 (div. Jan. 1982); 1 child, Chasity Dawn. Student pub. schs. Cook, Pizza Hut, Fort Scott, Kans., 1973-74, mgr., 1974-75, Woodward, 1975-76, floating mgr. Ft. Scott and Nevada, Mo., 1976-79, dist. supr., Ft. Scott, 1979—. Fund raising project leader Muscular Distrophy Assn., Ft. Scott, 1982-84. Mem. Motel-Restaurant Assn. (pres. 1980—), Ft. Scott Jr. C. of C. (pres. 1983-84, plaque 1984), Ft. Scott C. of C., Ft. Scott Nat. Hist. Site (fund raiser 1984). Republican. Avocations: fishing; community orgns. Home: 830 S Judson St Fort Scott KS 66701 Office: Pizza Hut 15 E Huntington Fort Scott KS 66701

BRITTEN, WILLIAM HARRY, editor, publisher; b. Zearing, Iowa, Aug. 25, 1921; s. Harry William and Gertrude Alice (Lehman) B. B.A., Western Union Coll., 1943; student Iowa State Coll., summer 1942; M.A., State U. Iowa, 1948. Reporter, Worcester (Mass.) Telegram, 1948-55; landscaper John F. Keenen, Leicester, Mass., 1956; sales dept. clk. Reed & Prince Mfg. Co., Worcester, 1957-63, inventory control clk., 1964, chief expeditor, 1965; state editor Marshalltown (Ia.) Times-Republican, 1965-66, staff writer, 1966-67; news editor Denison (Ia.) Bull. and Rev., 1967-68; city editor Boone News Republican, 1968; editor, pub., owner The Tri-County News, Zearing, 1968—; editor, pub. Hubbard (Iowa) Rev., 1969-72; Sec., Young Men's Republican Club, Worcester, 1957; corr. sec. Young People's Rep. Club, 1958; mem. Ward 8 Rep. Com., Worcester, 1960-65; Rep. candidate Mass. state legislature, 1960; ward chmn. to elect Edward W. Brooke atty. gen. Mass., 1962, 64; bd. dirs. Story County Cancer Soc., 1976-81. Served with AUS, 1943-45. Mem. Iowa Press Assn., Nat. Newspaper Assn., Am. Fedn. Arts., Am. Legion (post comdr. 1982-83), Westmar Coll., U. Iowa alumni assns. Mem. Ch. of Christ. Home: 416 S Pearl St Zearing IA 50278 Office: Main St Zearing IA 50278

BRITTON, CARMELITA VIOLA, physician; b. Kansas City, Mo., Nov. 26, 1949; d. Daniel Lavelle and Lucinda Marie (Barnes) B.; B.S., Rensselaer Poly. Inst., Troy, N.Y., 1973; M.D., Albany (N.Y.) Med. Coll., 1973. Intern, then resident in pediatrics St. Louis Children's Hosp., 1973-75, fellow in pediatric cardiology, 1975-77; dir. pediatric services St. Luke's Med. Bldg., St. Louis, 1979-84; asst. pediatrician Washington U. Med. Sch., St. Louis, 1979-84; co-dir. dept. pediatrics St. Louis City Hosp., 1978-80, dir. house-staff edn., 1980-84; asst. pediatrician Columbia U., N.Y.C., 1984—; asst. dir. pediatric service St. Lukes-Roosevelt Hosp., N.Y.C., 1984—. Fellow Am. Acad. Pediatrics; mem. Internat. Platform Assn. Author articles in field. Home: 1733 Teaneck Rd Teaneck NJ 07666 Office: Dept Pediatrics Columbia U New York NY 10025

BRITTON, CLARK VEAZIE, designer, educator; b. Balt., Oct. 11, 1930; s. Clark Veazie and Eleanor (Musgrove) B.; m. Regina Johnston, Aug. 27, 1952; 1 child, Dana Clark. B.A., Auburn U., 1952, M.A., 1955; postgrad. Ohio State U., 1961. Instr., Auburn U., Ala., 1955-57; from instr. to prof. design Wichita State U., Kans., 1957—, chmn. graphic design, 1972-85; ptnr. Design Assocs., Wichita, 1957—. Exhbns. include: Nat. Univ. and Coll. Designer Exhbn. (Silver award of Excellence for Best Book Design), 1975; Images USA (1st prize animation 1975), Tulsa Art Dirs. Club Ann. (Bronze award for book design), 1976, Kansas City Art Dirs. Club Ann. (Bronze award, Silver award, 7 Best of Show awards), 1976, 77, (Bronze award), 1980, (Merit award), 1981, Wichita Art Dirs. Club Ann. (2 Silver award), 1976, (Silver award), 1977, (Silver award), 1981, Wichita Advt. Club (Merit award), 1981, Mexico City Internat. Film Festival, 1981. Served to capt. USAF, 1952-54. Home: 8307 Peach Tree Ln Wichita KS 67207 Office: Wichita State U 1845 Fairmount Ave Wichita KS 67208

BRITTON, KENNETH RAY, osteopath; b. Walla Walla, Wash., Aug. 25, 1953; s. William Edward and Betty Lou (Eccles) B.; m. Rita Marie Schell, Mar. 2, 1950; children—Abigail, Benjamin. B.A. in Biology, U. No. Iowa, 1976; D.O., Coll. Osteo. Medicine and Surgery, 1979. Rotating intern Des Moines Gen. Hosp., 1979-80; gen. practice osteo. medicine, Albia, Iowa, 1980-82, 82—; chief staff and chmn. ob-gyn dept. Monroe County Health Care Ctr., Albia, also chmn. nutritional support team and mem. utilization rev. com. Community medicine preceptor for Coll. of Osteo. Medicine and Surgery. Served with USPHS, 1980-82. Mem. Am. Osteo. Assn., Iowa Soc. Osteo. Physicians and Surgeons. Home: 515 E Benton Ave Albia IA 52531 Office: 15 N Main St Albia IA 52531

BRIX, KELLEY ANN, medical educator; b. Tulsa, Feb. 18, 1952; d. Gerald Oliver and Shirley Ann (Hayenga) Brix. B.S. in Biology, Purdue U., 1972; M.S. in Zoology, U. Mich., 1974, M.D., 1978; M.P.H., U. Ill., 1980. Diplomate Am. Bd. Preventive Medicine. Resident in internal medicine Northwestern U. Hosp., Chgo., 1978-79; resident in preventive medicine U. Ill. Hosp. and Cook

County Hosp., Chgo., 1979-81; asst. prof. occupational medicine and instr. internal medicine U. Mich., Ann Arbor, 1981—, cons. dept. family practice, 1982—; cons. United Auto Workers, Detroit, 1981—, Mich. State Dept. Pub. Health, 1982—, Mich. Dept. Natural Resources, 1983— Mich. Toxic Substance Control Commn., 1983—, Mich. Dept. Edn., 1985—; chmn. Mich. Occupational Health Standards Commn., 1984—. Mem. Physicians for Social Responsibility, 1982—. Fellow Am. Coll. Preventive Medicine; mem. Mich. Indsl. Hygiene Soc. (dir. 1982—), Am. Pub. Health Assn. (program com. 1982—), Am. Occupational Medicine Assn., AAAS, Phi Beta Kappa, Delta Omega. Office: U Mich Sch Pub Health M6218 SPH II Bldg Ann Arbor MI 48109

BRIXIUS, FRANK JOSEPH, lawyer; b. St. Cloud, Minn., May 23, 1938; s. Albert J. and Mary Kathryn (Thiesen) B.; B.S. (William scholar), U. Minn., 1961; J.D., William Mitchell Coll. Law, 1966; m. Suzanne DeLong, July 14, 1962; children—Elizabeth Ann, Mary Alanah, Frank Joseph. With First Nat. Bank Mpls., 1962-66; admitted to Minn. bar, 1966; assoc. Hvass, Weisman & King, Mpls., 1966-69, ptnr., 1969—, v.p., chief fin. officer, 1984—. Mem. Greenwood (Minn.) City Council, 1970-71, 71-83, chmn. adv. com., 1970, council rep. to Hennepin County League Municipalities and Met. League Municipalities, 1972-76; mayor, Greenwood, 1973-83; co-chmn. Hennepin County Criminal Justice Council, 1974-75. Dir. Suburban Rate Authority; dir., mem. exec. com. Suburban League Municipalities, 1974-75, also chmn. pub. safety dept. 1974-75, 77-78, 80-82. Trustee Alpha Nu Trust Fund, 1974—. Recipient West Publishing Outstanding Law Student award, 1965. Fellow Internat. Soc. Barristers; mem. Am., Minn., Hennepin County bar assns., Am., Minn. trial lawyers assns., Assn. Met. Municipalities (dir., exec. com. 1974-75), Am. Judicature Soc., Chi Psi. Home: 21720 Fairview Greenwood MN 55331 Office: 715 Cargill Bldg Minneapolis MN 55402

BRO, KENNETH ARTHUR, plastic manufacturing company executive; b. Tsingdao, Shandung, China, Aug. 28, 1921 (parents Am. citizens); s. Albin Carl and Marguerite (Harmon) B.; m. Patricia Welch, May 6, 1944; children—William, Peter, Kenneth M., Patricia, Elizabeth, A. Charles. B.S., Northwestern U., 1949. Purchasing agent Welch Mfg. Co., Chgo., 1950-56; v.p. Welch Sci. Co., Chgo., 1957-64; v.p., co-owner Webb Plastic Co., Northbrook, Ill., 1965—; dir. Sargent-Welch Sci. Co., Skokie, Ill., 1957—. Chmn. bd. trustees Northland Coll., Ashland, Wis., 1957, 70-74; pres. bd. dirs. Chgo. Commons Assn., 1962, 70-74; dist. chmn. bd. dirs. Jr. Achievement, Chgo., 1970, 72-74; pres. Found. for Sci. Relaxation, 1965—. Served to pvt. 1st class U.S. Army, 1944-46, ETO. Decorated Bronze Star, Purple Heart. Mem. Am. Vaccum Soc., Am. Assn. Physics Tchrs. Republican. Congregationalist. Clubs: Indian Hill (Winnetka); University, Chgo. Yacht, Economic, Executive (Chgo.). Avocations: sailing; flying; traveling. Home: 375 Sheridan Rd Winnetka IL 60093 Office: Webb Plastic Inc 2820 Old Willow Rd Northbrook IL 60062

BROACH, ALGNER EUGENE ADOLPHUS, III, podiatrist; b. Cin., June 2, 1933; s. Algner Eugene Adolphus II and Susie Belle Broach (Lindsey) B.; B.S., Central State U., 1958; D.P.M., Ohio Coll. Podiatric Medicine, 1966; m. Lillie Mae Morton, Aug. 15, 1959; children—Connie M., Charisse M., Cheryl A., Cynthia L., Algner E. A.IV. Practice podiatry, Cin., 1967—; mem. staff, dept. med. dir. Walnut Hills-Evanston Med. Center, 1975-78; mem. staff West End Health Center, 1975—; mem. Cin. Health Dept. Task Force; pres. bd. dirs. Walnut Hills-Evanston Med. Center. Mem. Walnut Hills Community Council, 1980-81. Served with M.C., USAF, 1951-53, U.S. Army Res., 1978—. Diplomate Nat. Bd. Podiatry Examiners. Fellow Am. Acad. Podiatric Laser Surgery, Am. Assn. Hosp. Podiatrists; mem. Am. Podiatry Assn., Ohio Podiatry Assn., So. Ohio Acad. Podiatry, Jewish Hosp. Assn., Assn. Mil. Surgeons, Nat. Podiatry Assn., Res. Officers Assn., Greater Cin. Minority Bus. and Profl. Assn., Alpha Phi Alpha, Pi Delta, Phi Alpha Pi. Clubs: Masons. Home: 1139 Cheyenne Dr Cincinnati OH 45216 Office: 2916 Gilbert Ave Ideal Medical Bldg Cincinnati OH 45206

BROADHURST, KENNON EMANUEL, surgeon; b. Wayne County, N.C., Mar. 12, 1935; s. King E. and Ethel (Greenfield) B.; m. Perlita Atienza, Dec. 23, 1965; children—Kennon, Kristina, Karyna. B.S., N.C. Agrl. & Tech. Coll., 1957; M.D., Meharry Med. Coll., 1963. Diplomate Am. Bd. Surgery. Intern, resident in surgery U. Iowa Hosps., Iowa City, 1963-68; resident in cardiovascular, thoracic surgery U.S. Calif. Los Angeles County Med. Ctr., 1968-70; attending staff St. Mary's Hosp., Detroit Lakes, Minn., 1970-71, St. Luke's Hosp., Aberdeen, S.D., 1971—, Dakota Midland Hosp., Aberdeen, 1971-74, 1977—; practice medicine specializing in thoracic and vascular surgery Aberdeen, 1971—. Mem. AMA (Physician's Recognition award, 1970, 74, 78, 82), Am. Coll. Chest Physicians, John Paul North Surg. Soc., S.D. State Med. Assn.; fellow Am. Coll. Surgeons. Served to capt. M.C. USAR, 1959-69. Democrat. Congregationalist. Avocation: flying. Home: 711 Willow Dr Aberdeen SD 57401 Office: Cardiovascular & Thoracic Services Ltd 201 S Lloyd St Aberdeen SD 57401

BROCK, CHARLES MARQUIS, lawyer; b. Watseka, Ill., Oct. 8, 1941; s. Glen Westgate and Muriel Lucile (Bubeck) B.; m. Elizabeth Bonilla, Dec. 17, 1966; children—Henry Christopher, Anna Melissa. A.B. cum laude, Princeton U., 1963; J.D., Georgetown U., 1968; M.B.A., U. Chgo., 1974. Bar: Ill. 1969, U.S. Dist. Ct. (no. dist.) Ill. 1969. Asst. trust counsel Continental Ill. Nat. Bank, Chgo., 1968-74; regional counsel Latin Am., Can. Abbott Labs., North Chgo., Ill., 1974-77, regional counsel, Europe, Africa and Middle East, 1977-81, div. counsel, 1981—. Mem. New Trier Republican Orgn., Kenilworth, Ill., 1982—. Served with Inter-Am. Def. Coll., U.S. Army, 1964-66. Mem. ABA, Ill. State Bar Assn., Chgo. Bar Assn., Phi Beta Kappa. Republican. Clubs: Chgo. Curling, Princeton (Chgo.); Princeton (N.Y.C.). Home: 1473 Asbury Ave Winnetka IL 60093 Office: Abbott Labs Abbott Park North Chicago IL 60064

BROCK, JOHN E., bank holding company executive. Pres. Landmark Bancshares Corp., St. Louis. Office: Landmark Bancshares Corp 10 S Brentwood Blvd Saint Louis MO 63105*

BROCK, RUSSELL L., marketing and management consulting firm executive; b. Milngavie, Scotland, Jan. 19, 1946; came to U.S., 1948, naturalized, 1962; s. George and Emily L. U. (Cranston) B.; married; children—Travis, James, Elizabeth. B.A., Bowling Green State U., 1968, M.A., 1976. Marketing rep. 3M Co., Toledo, Ft. Wayne, Ind., 1971-72; tchr. coordinator Toledo pub. schs., 1972-76; dir. Owens Tech. Coll., Perrysburg, Ohio, 1976-77; exec. dir. Bowling Green State U., Ohio, 1977-82; pres. BG Mgmt. Group, Bowling Green, 1982-84, R. L. Brock & Assocs., Columbus, Ohio, 1984—. Columnist (corporate newsletter) Innovative Management Systems, Targeted Selling Techniques. Dir. ward campaigns 9th dist. 1978 U.S. Congressional Election. Recipient Outstanding Tchr. award Detroit News, 1968. Mem. Columbus Area C. of C. ASTD (chpt. officer 1977-79), Internat. Mgmt. by Objectives Inst. (bd. dirs. 1977-82). Club: Sales Executives (chair) (Columbus). Avocations: running; music; photography. Office: R L Brock & Assocs PO Box 872 Dublin OH 43017

BROCK, THOMAS WALTER, glass company administrator; b. Marion, Ind., Feb. 15, 1931; s. Richard Mark and Beulah Blanch (Gransinger) B.; B.S., Ball State Tchrs. Coll., 1953; M.S., U. Toledo, 1962; children—Teresa Eileen, William Jeffrey. With Owens Illinois Inc., Toledo, 1953—, materials and process engr., 1966-74, contract adminstr., 1974-83, mgr. Kimble research and devel., 1983—. Pres., Mt. Vernon PTA, 1963. Mem. Am. Ceramic Soc., Nat. Contract Mgmt. Assn., Sigma Xi. Republican. Methodist. Patentee in glass-ceramic materials and products. Home: 1439 Creekwood Ln Toledo OH 43614 Office: One Sea Gate Toledo OH 43666

BROCKERT, KENNETH LEE, hosp. lab. adminstr., med. technologist; b. Springfield, Mo., June 15, 1932; s. Thomas Edward and Lula Rachel (Love) B.; clin. lab. technician certificate U.S. Navy, 1952; A.A. in Liberal Arts, Kent State U., 1973; m. Marilyn Lois Noll, Sept. 29, 1956; children—Ann Marie, Mark Alan, Matthew Lee, Nina Jane. Histology technician U.S. Naval Hosp., North Chicago, Ill., 1956; adminstrv. technologist Timken Mercy Hosp. Lab., Canton, Ohio, 1956-72; lab. dir. Alliance (Ohio) City Hosp., 1972—; mem. nat. lab. panel Market Potential Corp. Bd. dirs. Alliance chpt. ARC, 1972-77; mem. St. Michael's Men's Choir, 1977—; lay dir. Canton Cursillo Center, 1978-80; mem. adv. bd., med. lab. technologists program Stark Tech. Coll., 1980—; treas. Irish Oaks Homeowners Assn., 1981—. Served with USN, 1950-56. Mem. Am. Soc. Clin. Pathologists (certified histology technician), Registry Med. Technologists, Am. Heart Assn. (certified in basic cardiac life support), Am. Soc. Med. Technologists, Ohio Soc. Med. Technologists (treas. dist. 1, 1983—), Citizens Hosp. Assn. Alliance. Democrat. Roman Catholic. Clubs: St. Michaels Men's (sec.); Kiwanis (dir. local club 1974-77, pres. 1977-78, div. chmn. spiritual aims 1982-83) (Alliance). Participant in designing lab. for Alliance City Hosp. Home: 5055 Tralee Circle NW Canton OH 44720 Office: 264 E Rice St Alliance OH 44601

BROCKHAUS, ROBERT HEROLD, SR., business educator, consultant; b. St. Louis, Apr. 18, 1940; s. Herold August and Imogene Martha (McKenzie) B.; m. Joyce Patricia Dees, June 13, 1970; children—Cheryl Lynn, Robert Herold. B.S. in Mech. Engring., U. Mo.-Rolla, 1962; M.S.I.A., Purdue U., 1966; Ph.D., Washington U., St. Louis, 1976. Mgr. Ralston-Purina, St. Louis, 1962-69; pres. Progressive Mgmt. Enterprises, Ltd., St. Louis, 1969—; asst. prof. mgmt. sci. St. Louis U., 1972-78, assoc. prof., 1978-84, prof., 1984—; dir. Small Bus. Inst., St. Louis U., 1976—; state adminstr. Mo. Small Bus. Devel. Ctrs., St. Louis, 1982—; Schoen prof. entrepreneurship Baylor U., 1981; McAninch prof. entrepreneurship Kans. State U., 1985—. Co-author: Encyclopedia of Entrepreneurship, 1982; Building A Better You, 1982; Nursing Concepts for Health Promotion, 1979; also contbr. articles to profl. jours. Bd. dirs. City Venture, St. Louis, 1982—. Recipient Disting. Service award Pi Kappa Alpha, 1972; Fulbright fellow, U. Waikato, N.Z., 1985. Fellow Internat. Council for Small Bus. (sr. v.p. 1981-83, internat. pres. 1983-84), Nat. Small Bus. Inst. Dirs. Assn. (nat. v.p. 1980-82, nat. pres. 1982-83), Acad. Mgmt. (nat. program chmn. 1977-78), Fenton Jaycees (treas.). Mem. United Ch. of Christ. Club: Executive (St. Louis) (moderator 1973—). Avocations: swimming; sailing; camping. Home: 10000 Hilltop Dr Saint Louis MO 63128 Office; St Louis U 3674 Lindell Blvd Saint Louis MO 63108

BROD, DONALD FREDERICK, journalism educator, magazine editor, professional association executive; b. St. Charles, Mo., May 10, 1932; s. Theodore Frank and Caroline (Hammer) B.; m. Nancy Lee Schelker, Sept. 28, 1957 (div. 1983); children—Andrew, Stephen. B.A., Southeast Mo. State Coll., 1954; M.A., U. Mo., 1958; Ph.D., U. Minn., 1968. Reporter, editor Montezuma Valley Jour., Cortez, Colo., 1958-60; mem. journalism faculty U. Wis., River Falls, 1960-69, No. Ill. U., DeKalb, 1969—; editor Grassroots Editor, DeKalb, 1981—; exec. sec. Internat. Soc. Weekly Newspaper Editors, DeKalb, 1981—; tchr. journalism classes, Britain, China, Ger., 1982-84. Contbr. numerous articles to profl. jours. Served to cpl. U.S. Army, 1955-57. Recipient 1st place photojournalism award Colo. Press Assn., 1960. Mem. Assn. for Edn. in Journalism and Mass Communication, Soc. Profl. Journalists, Internat. Soc. Weekly Newspaper Editors. Home: 43 White Oak Circle Saint Charles IL 60174 Office: Dept Journalism Northern Ill Univ DeKalb IL 60115

BRODD, JOEL WILLIS, lawyer; b. Hutchinson, Minn., Nov. 7, 1951; s. Willis Burton and Grace Mary (Smith) B.; m. Deborah Roberts Townsend, Sept. 3, 1977; children—Christopher Joel, Peter Townsend. B.A. in Polit. Sci., Moorhead State Coll., 1973; M.S.J.A., Sch. Law, U. Denver, 1976; J.D., William Mitchell Coll. Law, 1982. Bar: Minn. 1982, U.S. Ct. Appeals (8th cir.) 1983, U.S. Dist. Ct. (ea. dist.) Mich. 1984, U.S. Claims Ct. 1984. Ct. planner Wyo. Supreme Ct., Cheyenne, 1977-78; staff assoc. Nat. Ctr. for State Cts., St. Paul, 1978-79; assoc. Robins Zelle Larson & Kaplan, Mpls., 1982—. Mem. Assn. Trial Lawyers Am., Am. Judicature Soc. Democrat. Episcopalian. Office: Robins Zelle Larson & Kaplan 1800 International Centre 900 2d Ave S Minneapolis MN 55402

BRODEUR, LEON RODOLPHE, rubber manufacturing company executive; b. Manchester, N.H., July 12, 1927; s. Frederic A. and Bertha (Baril) B.; m. Helen M. Silvia, Nov. 17, 1955; children—Kenneth, Stephen, Michele. B.S., St. Anselm's Coll., 1951. With Firestone Tire & Rubber Co., 1951—, mgr. foam products, Corry, Pa., 1961-65, mgr. urethane foam prodn., Milan, Tenn., 1965-68, v.p. foam products div., Fall River, Mass., 1968-69, pres. 1969-72, pres. electric wheel co. div., Quincy Ill., 1972-73, v.p. diversified products, Akron, Ohio, 1973-78, v.p. subs. and domestic tire divs., 1978-82, exec. v.p., pres. N.Am. tire group, 1982, pres., 1982-84, vice chmn., 1984—. Pres., Akron Area Jr. Achievement, 1982. Served with AUS, 1945-46. Mem. Am. Def. Preparedness Assn. Roman Catholic. Office: Firestone Tire & Rubber Co 1200 Firestone Pkwy Akron OH 44317*

BRODHUN, ANDREW R., banker; b. 1940. B.A., Mich. State U., 1965. Pres. Mich. Nat. Bank-West Metro, 1974-80; v.p. Mich. Nat. Corp., 1980—; group v.p. Mich. Nat. Bank of Detroit Inc., Troy, 1965-74, pres., 1981—. Served with USN, 1962-64. Office: Mich Nat Bank of Detroit 1000 W Maple PO Box 1059 Troy MI 48099*

BRODY, BRUCE B., ophthalmologist; b. Chgo., Nov. 24, 1942; s. Bernard Benjamin and Florence Lydia (Schriebier) B.; m. Renee Mari Jacover, June 19, 1969 (div. Mar. 1978); Eslieie Norma Schrager, Oct. 2, 1979; children—Joshua Ethan, Alexis Barbara, Louis Andrew, Alison Elizabeth. B.A. Northwestern U., 1964; M.D., Chgo. Med. Sch., 1969. Diplomate Am. Bd. Ophthalmology. Practice of medicine specializing in ophthalmology S. Chgo. Eye Assocs., Ltd., 1978—. Served as surgeon USPHS, 1970-74. Fellow Am. Acad. Ophthalmology; mem. Chgo. Ophthalmological Soc., Chgo. Med. Soc., Ill. State Med. Soc. Home: 1103 Sunset Rd Winnetka IL 60093 Office: 2315 E 93rd Chicago IL 60617

BRODY, MYRON, artist; b. N.Y.C., Apr. 5, 1940; B.F.A., Phila. Coll. Art, 1965; student Nat. Inst. Fine Arts, Mexico City, 1961, Ateneum, Helsinki, 1968-69, U. Va. Sch. Continuing Edn., 1970-71; M.F.A. (scholar), U. Pa., 1968; cert. advanced grad. study in arts adminstrn. Harvard U., 1975; m. Senta Brody; 1 dau., Heather. Substitute tchr. art Phila. Bd. Edn., 1966-67; tchr. Phila. Coll. Art, summer 1968; Total Action against Poverty, Roanoke, Va., 1970-71; mem. faculty U. Va. Sch. Continuing Edn., Charlottesville, 1970-76; tchr., head sculpture program Yeovil (Somerset, Eng.) Tech. Coll., 1973-74; lectr. art dept. Hollins (Va.) Coll., 1975; asst. prof., chmn. art dept. Va. Western Community Coll., Roanoke, 1969-76; prof., chmn. visual art dept. Avila Coll., Kansas City, Mo., 1976-85; chmn. art dept. U. Ark., Fayetteville, 1985—; one-man shows USIA, Helsinki, 1969, Va. Mus. Fine Arts, Richmond, 1975, Roanoke Fine Arts Center, 1976; Bedyk Gallery, Kansas City, Mo., 1982; two-man shows Hollins Coll., 1970, 73, Va. Poly. Inst. and State U., Blacksburg, 1970, 73, Washington and Lee U., 1970, Va. State Coll., Petersburg, 1971, Richard Bland Coll., Petersburg, 1971, Salem Coll., Winston-Salem, N.C., 1971, William and Mary Coll., Williamsburg, 1972; exhibited in numerous group shows, 1968—, including Va. Mus. Fine Arts, Roanoke Fine Arts Center, Philbrook Art Center, Tulsa, Southeastern Center for Contemporary Art, Winston-Salem, Wichita Art Mus., Kansas City Art Inst., Inst. Contemporary Art, Phila.; represented in permanent collections: Prudential Ins. Co. Am., U. Va., Princeton U., State Dept., also others. Founder, mem. steering com., mem. bd. Roanoke Valley Arts Council, 1975-76; founder, mem. steering com. Kansas City Arts Council, 1978—, Arts and Bull Soc., Kansas City, 1979—; vp. bd., chmn. fin. com. Kansas City Artists Coalition, 1979-81; ednl. and mktg. cons. Friends of Jazz, Kansas City, 1978-83; pres. bd., chmn. state com. for cultural arts Mo.-U.S.A./Para Brazil, Partners of the Americas, Inc., U. Mo., Rolla, 1981-83; exec. dir. Arts Exchange Internat., 1983—. Served with U.S. Army, 1961-63. Recipient Dimensional Design award Phila. Coll. Art, 1965, 2d prize for sculpture Piedmont chpt. Va. Mus. Art, Martinsville, 1970, purchase award for sculpture Roanoke Summer Art Festival, 1970, cert. of distinction Va. Mus. Fine Arts, 1973, 75, sculpture prize Festival in Park, Roanoke, 1976, Best in Show award Lynchburg Fine Arts Center, 1976, resolution Kansas City Mcpl. Art Commn., 1979; cert. of disting. service Maseu Nacional de Belas Artes, Rio de Janeiro, Brazil, World Culture prize Art Centro Studie Richerche delle Nazioni Salsomaggiore, Italy; Fulbright-Hays fellow, 1968-69, 73-74. Mem. Coll. Art Assn. Am., Nat. Assn. Art Adminstrs., Fulbright Alumni Assn. Office: U Ark FNAR 116 Fayetteville AR 72701

BRODY, ROBERT, dermatologist; b. Cleve., June 15, 1948; s. Melvin and Nancy Elizabeth Brody; A.B. with distinction, Stanford U., 1970; M.D., U. Mich., 1974. Intern in internal medicine, Cleve. Clinic, 1974-75, resident in dermatology, 1975-78; practice medicine specializing in dermatology, Cleve., 1978—; staff physician Kaiser-Permanente Med. Center, 1978-82, mem. profl. edn. com., 1978-82, chmn., 1980-82, also sec. exec. com., 1980; pvt. practice, 1982—; asst. clin. prof. Case Western Res. U. Med. Sch., 1978-80, 83—, clin. instr., 1980-83, dermatology dept. rep. to gen. faculty, 1980-82; asst. physician Univ. Hosps. Cleve., 1979—. Sec., Cleve. Play House Men's Com., 1979-82; mem. ann. fund com. Stanford U., 1978—, regional co-chmn., 1981-82. Diplomate Am. Bd. Dermatology. Mem. Am. Acad. Dermatology, Cleve. Acad. Medicine. Contbr. articles to med. jours. Club: Cleve. Skating. Home: 13415 Shaker Blvd Cleveland OH 44120 Office: 3461 Warrensville Ctr Rd Shaker Heights OH 44122

BROEKER, DAVID TERRY, dental health program executive; b. Hermann, Mo., Jan. 26, 1948; s. Harvey William and Mabel Kathryn (Langenberg) B.; m. Suzanne Douglas, June 11, 1977 (div. June 1983); 1 child, Bart. B.S., Central Mo. State U., 1970. Dir. transition Auditors Transition Office, Jefferson City, Mo., 1978-79; adminstrv. mgr. Office State Auditor, Jefferson City, 1979-80; outstate coordinator Bond for Gov. Com., Kansas City, Mo., 1980; dir. personnel and adminstrn. Gov. Transition Office, Jefferson City, 1980-81; asst. to gov. Office of Gov., Jefferson City, 1981-85; sr. v.p. Preferred Dental Health Plan Mo. Inc., Jefferson City, 1985—; trustee Mo. State Employees Retirement System, Jefferson City, 1981-85. Named Outstanding Young Men Am. 1971, 74, 83; Outstanding Young Civic Leader Jefferson City Jaycees 1981; Optimist of Year Sunrise Optimist Club, 1984. Mem. Central Mo. State U. Nat. Alumni Assn. (pres. 1981-82), Alpha Phi Sigma, Phi Kappa Phi. Republican. Lodges: Optimists, Masons. Home: Box 313 Linn MO 65051 Office: Preferred Dental Health Plan Mo Inc 600 Monroe St Jefferson City MO 65101

BROFFMAN, MORTON HOWARD, management and media consultant; b. N.Y.C., Aug. 17, 1920; s. Samuel L. and Fannie B. (Mack) B.; B.A. cum laude, CCNY, 1940; M.A., N.Y. U., 1943; M.A. (teaching fellow 1949-50), Harvard U., 1950, M.P.A., 1951, Ph.D., 1953; m. Louise Hargrove, Dec. 24, 1969; children—Trudy, Jane, Michael. Vice pres., dir. mfg. and engring. Rayco Co., 1953-56, sr. v.p., dir. mktg. and retail stores, 1956-61; exec. v.p., gen. mgr. L.A. Darling Co., 1961-63; exec. v.p., chief operating officer United Brands Corp., N.Y.C., 1964-70; pres. Am. Biltrite, Inc., Boston, 1970-74; pres., chief exec. officer Combined Mgmt. Services Corp., N.Y.C., 1975-80, Public Media Inc., Wilmette, Ill., 1980—; pres. Sound Video Unlimited Inc., Niles, Ill., 1985—; dir. Sterndent Corp., Films, Inc., Public Media Corp., Bldg. Materials Distbrs. Co.; mem. faculty Northeastern U., Boston, 1950-51, Rutgers U., 1955-56. Bd. dirs. Save the Children Fedn., 1978—. Served with USN, 1944-46. Mem. Am. Mgmt. Assn., Conf. Bd., Am. Mktg. Assn., Inst. Indsl. Engrs. Clubs: Harvard (Boston and N.Y.C.); Manhattan, Drug and Chem., Internat., Whitehall, Touhy Tennis. Author, cons. editor profl. publs. Home: 1410 Sheridan Rd Wilmette IL 60091 Office: Sound Video Unlimited Inc 7000 N Austin Ave Niles IL 60648

BROGAN, CLAUDIA WHALEY, university official; b. Cherry Point, N.C., July 13, 1955; d. Clark Whaley and Barbara Ann (Hashbarger) B. B.F.A., Ill. Wesleyan U., 1977; M.S.Edn., U. Wis.-Platteville, 1980. Cert. secondary tchr., Ill., Bus. mgr., asst. dir. Girl Scout Council Camp, Jonesboro, Ark., 1977-78; high sch. tchr. Highland Community Schs., Ill., 1977-78; resident dir. U. Wis., Platteville, 1978-80, residence hall dir., Oshkosh, 1980-83, student affairs coordinator, Madison, 1983-85; coordinator residence life Ind. U., Bloomington, 1985—; mediator, cons. Ctr. Conflict Resolution, 1983—. Contbr. articles to profl. jours. Chairperson Leadership Devel. Com., Madison, 1983-85; vol. Local Democratic Com., Oshkosh, 1980, 81, 82, Hosp. Hospice Assn., 1982, 83; church organist Wesley United Methodist Ch., 1982, 83. Ill. PTA grantee, 1973; Nat. Merit scholar, 1973. Mem. Upper Midwest Region Assn. Coll. Univ. Housing Officers (exec. officer), Am. Assn. Counseling and Devel., Wis. Coll. Personnel Assn., Student Personnel Assn. Wis. Methodist. Avocations: piano, poetry writing, correspondence, church choir. Home: Apt 218-C Briscoe Center Bloomington IN 47406 Office: Coordinator Office McNutt Center Ind U Bloomington IN 47406

BROGAN, JAMES AUSTIN, judge; b. Chgo., Oct. 23, 1939; s. Austin John and Mary Belle (Edmiston) B.; m. Sheila Ann Straining, May 8, 1982; children—Aaron, Kara, Kelly. A.B., Notre Dame U., 1961; J.D., Georgetown U., 1964. Bar: Ohio, 1964. First asst. proc. atty. Montgomery County, Ohio, 1969-81; presiding judge Ct. Appeals (2d dist.) Ohio, Dayton, 1981—; adj. instr. Cinclair Community Coll., Dayton, 1969—. Pres. Catholic Social Services, Dayton, 1984—, Man-Man Assocs., Dayton, 1984—. Fellow Am. Coll. Trial Lawyers; mem. Dayton Bar Assn., Ohio State Bar Assn., ABA. Lodge: Optimists (v.p. 1984—). Avocations; golf, tennis. Home: 1104 Deer Run Rd Dayton OH 45459

BROH-KAHN, LAWRENCE EARL, lawyer; b. Cin., Dec. 27, 1903; s. A. Bernard and Marie Leone (Broh) K.; m. Esther Weil Broh-Kahn, June 11, 1932; 1 son, Jere. A.B., U. Cin., 1924, A.M., 1926; J.D., Harvard U., 1936. Bar: Ohio 1936, U.S. Supreme Ct. 1938. Practice, Cleve., 1936—; tchr. John Carroll U., 1975-81, Case Western Res. U., 1955-75. Decorated comdr. de l'Ordre du Bontemps de Medoc et des Graves, comdr. de la Jurade de St. Emilion. Mem. ABA, Ohio State Bar Assn., Bar Assn. Greater Cleve. Jewish. Home and office: 16200 Fernway Rd Shaker Heights OH 44120

BROIHIER, CHARLES EDWARD, manufacturing company official; b. Decorah, Iowa, Nov. 28, 1943; s. Marcellus George and Genevieve Loraine (McManus) B.; m. Eileen Carol May, Oct. 1, 1944; children—Mark, Ann, Matthew. B.S., Dominican Coll. of Racine, 1966; M.S., Mich. State U., 1969; M.B.A., U. Wis.-Milw., 1980. Tchr. biology Racine Unified Sch. Dist. (Wis.), 1969-74; successively time keeper, mfg. foreman, prodn. control supr., user rep. EDP system implementation, buyer J.I. Case Co., Racine, 1974-83, prodn. control supr., 1982—. Sec., Racine County Youth Baseball; lector and basketball coach St. Sebastian Parish. Mem. Am. Prodn. and Inventory Control Soc. (cert.). Republican. Roman Catholic. Home: 2832 92d St Sturtevant WI 53177 Office: J I Case Co 24th and Mead Sts Racine WI 53403

BROMAN, ROBERT FABEL, corporation executive; b. Aitkin, Minn., Oct. 19, 1939; s. Elmer Martin and Marcella M. (Fabel) B.; m. Carol Ann Schaefer, Dec. 29, 1961; children—Elizabeth, Erika, Andrew, Karl. B.A. Carleton Coll. 1961; Ph.D. Northwestern U., 1965. Asst. prof. U. Nebr., Lincoln, 1965-71, assoc. prof. chemistry, 1971-80, freshman chem. coordinator, 1967-72; field sales mgr. Isco, Inc., Lincoln, Nebr., 1979-81, sales mgr., 1982—; adv. Jr. Achievement, Lincoln, 1980-81. Author: (with others) Lab Experiments for Elementary Analytical Chemistry, 1984. Rep. alumni admissions Carleton Coll., 1982—; chmn., fin. drive Unitarian Ch., Lincoln, 1979, 82, bd. dirs., 1978-81. Mem. AAAS, Am. Chem. Soc. (adv. bd. Nebr. sect. 1977-79), Sigma Xi. Democrat. Avocations: computer programming, home repair. Office: Isco Inc 4700 Superior St Lincoln NE 68504

BROMMER, JANE KAY, nurse; b. Hastings, Nebr., Nov. 12, 1940; d. Oliver E. and Irene (Stamer) Wendell; m. Robert Lee Brommer, Sept. 2, 1960; children—Laura Lee, John Lindsey. R.N., Mary Lanning Meml. Hosp. Sch. Nursing, 1971; student Hastings Coll. R.N., Nebr. Staff nurse Home Health Dept. Mary Lanning Hosp., Hastings, 1972-75, coordinator recruitment and student affairs, 1982-83; supr. Medicare Unit, Good Samaritan Village, Hastings, 1975-78, dir. in-home services, 1983—; staff nurse Hastings Med. Clinic, 1978-82; career counselor Mary Lanning Sch. Nursing, 1982-83. Pres., Hastings Jr. Women's Club, 1964-66; bd. dirs. Hastings Community Theatre, 1967. Mem. Am. Nurses Assn., Fedn. for Accessible Nursing Edn. and Licensure. Republican. Methodist. Lodges: Order Eastern Star, Daus. of Nile. Home: Rt 2 PO Box 76 Juniata NE 68955

BRONN, DONALD GEORGE, radiation oncologist, medical researcher; b. Karlsruhe, W.Ger., Oct. 12, 1948; s. Count Jakov Ivanovich and Agnes (Pervak) Broschnovsky; came to U.S., 1950; m. Leslie Joan Boyle, Aug. 21, 1973; children—Jacob Alexander, Natasha Nisa. B.A., Ohio State U., 1972, M.S., 1976, Ph.D. in Cell Physiology, 1979, M.D., 1982. Grad. teaching assoc. zoology Ohio State U., Columbus, 1973-75, grad. research assoc. in surgery, 1975-79, research coordinator Lab for Breast Cancer Research, Ohio State U. Hosps., 1977—, research assoc. ultrasound and nuclear medicine divs., dept. radiology, 1980-82; Samuel J. Roessler Found. Med. Research fellow, 1980-82; Am. Cancer Soc. fellow in clin. oncology, 1985-86; clin. instr. div. of radiation oncology, dept. radiology Ohio State U., 1982—; bd. dirs. Inst. for Energy Funding Ltd., N.Y.C., 1983—. Named to Landacre Soc. Ohio State U. Coll. Med., 1979, Outstanding Research Presentation, 1979; pres., 1981-82; grantee Am. Cancer Soc., Elsa U. Pardee Found., Bremer Found., 1975—; recipient Nat. Student Research Forum 1st prize, 1979; Mead Johnson Excellence of Research award, 1979; Surgery award Ohio State U. Coll. Medicine, 1982, Robert M. Zollinger Research award, 1982; Am. Radium Soc. young oncologist travel grantee, 1985. Fellow Royal Micros. Soc.; mem. AAAS, AMA, Am. Soc. for Cell Biology, N.Y. Acad. Scis., Ohio State Med. Assn., Acad. Medicine Columbus and Franklin County, Am. Coll. Radiology, Radiol. Soc. N. Am., Soc. for Magnetic Resonance Imaging, Am. Soc. Therapeutic Radiology and Oncology, Sigma Xi. Author: The Hormonal Characterization of Breast Cancer By Oxygen Consumption Levels, 1979; contbr. articles on cancer biology and medicine to profl. publs.; inventor Bronn intraoperative treatment unit for Microtron generated long distance electron beam radiation in the operative suite. Office: N 082 Doan Hall University Hosps 410 West 10th Ave Columbus OH 43210

BRONTON, ARNE WIGGO, designer; b. Esbjerg, Denmark, July 31, 1930; came to U.S., 1952, naturalized, 1957; s. Soren Peter and Camilla (Jensen) B.; degree in architecture, Tech. Coll., Esbjerg, 1949; postgrad. U. Chgo., spl. courses; m. Elsa Louise Drenning, Sept. 17, 1960; children—Christian, Allen. Founder, Crown Custom Designs, Inc., Barrington Hills, Ill., 1952—, pres., chief exec. officer, chmn. bd., 1975—; pres. Bank Bldg. Cons.; cons. fin. instns. Past pres., chmn. Danish Nat. Com.; bd. dirs. Royal Danish Guards, Danish Lang. Found., Sovereign Order St. John. Served to 2d lt. Royal Danish Guards, 1950-51. Decorated Knight of Malta, Yugoslav Commemorative War Cross, Knight Order Dannebrog (Denmark), Ordre de la Liberation (France), Badge of Ravna Gora, Royal Order White Eagle III, (Serbia); recipient bronze and gold medal in design, 1949-50. Mem. Pres.'s Assn., Am. Mgmt. Assn., AIA, Am. Soc. Interior Designers, Constrn. Specifications Inst., Exec. Club Chgo., Internat. Assn. Architects. Republican. Lutheran. Clubs: Turnbery Country, Marco Island Country, Marco Island Yacht, Sertoma (life). Lodges: Masons, Shriners. Office: Crown Custom Design Inc 409 W Countyline Rd Barrington Hills IL 60010

BROOKBANK, SHERRY ANN, librarian, researcher; b. Batesville, Ind., Sept. 19, 1952; d. James A. and Betty (Reamer) B. B.Gen. Sci., Ind. U., 1980, M.L.S., 1980. Reference asst. and verifier, reference desk, Ind. U., Bloomington, 1979-81, sr. library asst. interlibrary services, 1981, interlibrary loan librarian, 1981-82, circulation librarian edn. library, 1982—, employment dir., 1982—, res. circulation librarian, 1982—, info. specialist library info. program service, 1979—. Organizer Ind. U. Library Booksale, 1981—. Ford P. Hall scholar, 1978-79; Kappa Kappa Kappa scholar, 1970. Mem. ALA, Kappa Kappa Kappa. Home: 3650 Leonard Springs Rd Apt 47 Bloomington IN 47401

BROOKS, CHARLES DAVID, political and business consultant; b. Highland Park, Ill., May 13, 1957; s. Norman Melvin and Dorothy (Price) B. B.A. in Polit. Sci., DePauw U., 1979; cert. in Internat. Law., Hague Acad. Internat. Law, Netherlands, 1980; M.A. in Internat. Relations, U. Chgo., 1981. Cons., Am. Export Mgmt. Co., Cambridge, Mass., 1982-83; v.p. Creative Impact Group, Glencoe, Ill., 1981-84; cons. Balboa Constrn. Co., Chgo., 1983-84, Marketplace Internat., Highland Park, 1983-85, Brooks Cons. Internat., Inc., Arlington, Va. and Highland Park, 1985—. Contbr. articles to profl. jours., chpt. to book. Chmn. Citizens for Am., Ill., 1984; mem. Republican Nat. Assembly, Chgo., 1984; pub. relations March of Dimes, Chgo., 1984; mem. Scholars for Regan-Bush, 1984. Mem. Delta Chi. Jewish.

BROOKS, CLIFFORD WRIGHT, JR., optometry educator, author; b. Cin., Jan. 23, 1946; s. Clifford Wright and Ruth Louise (Henize) B.; m. Vickie Lynn Murphy, June 4, 1968; children—Deborah, Clifford III. B.A., Ind. U., 1969, O.D., 1971. Practice optometry Salem, Orleans, Ind., 1971-72; guest lectr. Hoheren Fachschule Fur Augenoptik, Cologne, Germany, 1972-74; asst. prof. Ind. U. Sch. Optometry, Bloomington, 1974-80, assoc. prof., 1980—, dir. optometric tech. programs, 1977—. Co-author: System for Ophthalmic Dispensing, 1979. Author: Essentials for Ophthalmic Lens Work, 1983. Contbr. articles to profl. jours. Mem. Am. Optometric Assn., Ind. Optometric Assn., Stonebelt Optometric Soc. Office: Ind Univ Sch Optometry 800 E Atwater Ave Bloomington IN 47405

BROOKS, FRANK MARSHALL, petroleum geologist; b. Wichita, Kans., Oct. 7, 1912; s. Herman O. and Stella M. (Thompson) B.; m. Carolyne Ann, Feb. 26, 1938 (dec. Feb. 1958); children—Stephanie Ann, Rodger Alan; m. Lena Mae Downs, Mar. 27, 1976. B.A., U. Wichita, 1934; postgrad. U. Iowa, 1936-37. Geologist, Gulf Oil Corp., Wichita, 1934-39, Indpls., 1939-43, Bridgeport Oil Co., Wichita, 1943-46; geologist El Dorado Refining Co., Kans., 1946-56, v.p., 1948-56; v.p., geologist Sterling Drilling Co., Hutchinson, Kans., 1956-58; ind. geologist, Wichita, 1958—. Mem. Wichita State U. Alumni Assn. (bd. dirs. 1980—, v.p. 1981-83), Kans. Geol. Soc. (pres. 1950), Soc. Ind. Profl. Earth Scientists (chpt. pres. 1974), Am. Inst. Profl. Geologists (chpt. pres. 1980), Shocker Alumni and Faculty Club (bd. dirs. 1981-84, sec. 1983-84), Wichita Petroleum Club (bd. dirs. and v.p. 1949-51). Republican. Congregationalist. Lodge: Masons (Wichita). Avocations: golfing; travel. Office: 1735 KSB Bldg Wichita KS 67202

BROOKS, GENE EDWARD, See *Who's Who in America,* 43rd edition.

BROOKS, GLADYS SINCLAIR, management consultant; b. Mpls., June 8, 1914; d. John Franklin and Gladys (Phillips) Sinclair; student U. Geneva, Switzerland, 1935; B.A., U. Minn., 1936; LL.D., Hamline U., 1966; m. Wright W. Brooks, Apr. 17, 1941; children—Diane (Mrs. Roger Montgomery), John, Pamela (Mrs. Jean Marc Perraud). Dir. Farmer's and Mechanics Bank, 1973-82; mem. Met. Council, 1975-83; lectr. world affairs, 1939-—; mem. Mpls. City Council, 1967-73; mem. Met. Airports Commn., 1971-74; pres. World Affairs Ctr. U. Minn., 1976—; instr. continuing edn. for women U. Minn.; lectr. on world tours as Am. specialist U.S. Dept. State, 1959-60; pres. Brooks/Ridder & Assocs. Mem. Mpls. Charter Commn., 1948-51; pres. YWCA, 1953-57, mem. nat. bd., del. world meeting, Denmark; pres. Minn. Internat. Ctr., 1953-63; chmn. Minn. Women's Com. for Civil Rights, 1961-64; mem. U.S. Com. for UNICEF, 1959-68; mem. Gov.'s Adv. Com. Children and Youth, 1953-58, Minn. Adv. Com. Employment and Security, 1948-50; Midwest adv. com. Inst. Internat. Edn.; mem. nat. com. White House Conf. Children and Youth, 1960; chmn. Gov.'s Human Rights Commn., 1961-65; dir. Citizens Com. Delinquency and Crime, 1969-81; chmn. Mpls. Adv. Com. on Tourism, 1976-82; vice chmn. Nat. Community Partnerships Seminars, 1977-82; mem. Midwest Selection Panel, White House Fellows, 1981. Del. Rep. Nat. Conv., 1952; state chmn. Citizens for Eisenhower, 1956; founder, pres. Rep. Workshop; co-chmn. Mpls. Bicentennial Commn., 1974-76; pres. Internat. Center for Fgn. Students; dir. Minn. Alumni Assn.; trustee United Theol. Sem., YWCA, Met. State U.; bd. dirs. Hamline U.; mem. pres.'s adv. council St. Catherine's Coll. Recipient Centennial Women of Minn. award Hamline U., 1954; Woman of Distinction award AAUW, Mpls. 1956; Woman of Yr. award YWCA, 1973; Brotherhood award NCCJ, 1975; Service to Freedom award Minn. State Bar Assn., 1976; Community Leadership award YWCA, 1981. Mem. World Affairs Council (pres. 1942-44), Minn. LWV (dir. 1940-45), Mpls. Council Ch. Women (pres. 1946-48), Nat. Council of Chs. (mem. gen. bd., v.p. 1961-69), Minn. Council of Chs. (1st woman pres. 1961-64, Christian service award 1967), Mpls. Council of Chs. (v.p. 1946-48), United Ch. Women (bd. mgrs.), Minn. UN Assn. (dir.), Nat. League Cities (human resources steering com. 1972-73), Am. Acad. Polit. Sci., Mpls. C. of C., Minn. Women's Polit. Caucus, Minn. Women's Econ. Roundtable, AAUW, Women's Symphony Assn., Delta Kappa Gamma (hon.). Presbyn. Clubs: Zonta, Women's, Lafayette (Mpls.). Home: 5056 Garfield Ave S Minneapolis MN 55419

BROOKS, GWENDOLYN, author; b. Topeka, June 7, 1917; d. David Anderson and Keziah Corinne (Wims) B.; m. Henry L. Blakely, Sept. 17, 1939; children—Henry L., Nora. Grad., Wilson Jr. Coll., Chgo., 1936; L.H.D., Columbia Coll., 1964. Instr. poetry Columbia Coll., Chgo., Northeastern Ill. State Coll.; Mem. Ill. Arts Council. Author: poetry A Street in Bronzeville, 1945, Annie Allen, 1949, Maud Martha; novel, 1953, Bronzeville Boys and Girls; for children, 1956, The Bean Eaters; poetry, 1960, Selected Poems, 1963, In the Mecca, 1968, Riot, 1969, Family Pictures, 1970, Aloneness, 1971, To Disembark, 1981; autobiography Report From Part One, 1972, The Tiger Who Wore White Gloves, 1974, Beckonings, 1975, Primer for Blacks, 1980, Young Poets' Primer, 1981. Named One of 10 Women of Year Mademoiselle mag., 1945; recipient award for creative writing Am. Acad. Arts and Letters, 1946; Guggenheim fellow for creative writing, 1946, 47; Pulitzer prize for poetry, 1950; Anisfield-Wolf award, 1969; named Poet Laureate of Ill., 1969. Mem. Soc. Midland Authors. Home: 7428 S Evans Ave Chicago IL 60619

BROOKS, KEN EDWIN, fitness center owner; b. Coldwater, Mich., Nov. 26, 1952; s. Kinyon Edwin and Patricia (Simpson) B.; m. Elaine A. Thompson, July 29, 1972 (div. Dec. 1982); 1 child, Jerri Christine. Student Platte Coll., 1972-73. Asst. instr. Am. Taekwondo Assn., Columbus, Nebr., 1973-74, instr., 1974-80; owner, mgr. ATA Fitness Ctr., Columbus, 1982—; regional judge Am. Taekwondo Assn., Omaha, 1979-83, chief of publs., Little Rock, 1981-83, nat. judge, 1984—. Roman Catholic. Home: 2313 1/2 11th St Columbus NE 68601 Office: ATA Fitness Ctr Pershing Ctr Columbus NE 68601

BROOKS, KENNETH, publishing executive; b. N.Y.C., Nov. 20, 1950; s. Clarence Edward and Barbara (Thomas) B. B.B.A., L.I. U., 1974. Promotion mgr. Charter Pub. Co., N.Y.C., 1976-79; fulfillment mgr. Webb Pub. Co., St. Paul, 1979-82; circulation dir. PJS Publs. Inc., Peoria, Ill., 1982—. Avocations: tennis; sailing; skiing. Office: PJS Publs Inc News Plaza Peoria IL 61606

BROOKS, MICHAEL LYNN, advertising agency executive; b. Lafayette, Ind., Feb. 9, 1943; s. Ray Daniel and Velda Deane (Smith) B.; B.S., Ind. State U., 1965; postgrad. Ind. U., 1966. Spl. assignment writer Indpls. News, 1965-68; advt. dir. Eastern Express, Inc., Terre Haute, Ind., 1968-72; pres., chmn. bd. CRE, Inc., Indpls., 1972—. Bd. dirs. Katherine Hamilton Mental Health Center, Inc., Terre Haute, 1980-84. Ford Found. grantee, 1966. Mem. Nat. Agri-Mktg. Assn., Ind. Fedn. Advt. Agys. (past dir.), Bank Mktg. Assn., Advt. Club Indpls. Clubs: Indpls. Press, Columbia, Skyline. Office: 400 Victoria Centre 22 E Washington Indianapolis IN 46204

BROOKS, ROBERT ALEXANDER, oil company executive; b. Ft. Knox, Ky., Sept. 12, 1944; s. Robert and Meredith (Boller) B.; m. Carol Mateer, Aug. 13, 1966; children—Alison, Joy, Robert, Deborah. B.S., U. Ill., 1966; M.S., La. State U., 1969, Ph.D., 1970. Assoc. La. Water Resources Research Inst., Baton Rouge, 1966-70; scientist Conoco, Ponca City, Okla., 1970-74; team leader uranium exploration U.S. Geol. Survey, Denver, 1974-77; v.p. minerals Energy Res. Group, Wichita, Kans., 1977-82, v.p. oil exploration, 1982—; rep. uranium resource com. UN, Rome, 1976. Contbr. articles to profl. jours. Mem. Am. Assn. Petroleum Geologists, Soc. Econ. Geologists, Denver Regional Exploration Geologists (pres. 1977-80), Kans. Geol. Soc. Republican. Presbyterian. Clubs: Wichita Country, Wichita; Hiwan (Evergreen, Colo.). Avocations: skiing, tennis, swimming, scuba. Home: 646 Edgewater St Wichita KS 67230 Office: Energy Res Group 217 N Water PO Box 1201 Wichita KS 67201

BROOKS, ROGER ALAN, political scientist; b. Ann Arbor, Mich., Aug. 9, 1944; s. Warren Wilfred and Sylvia May (Burrell) B.; B.A., U. Mich., 1966; postgrad. U. Strathclyde, Glasgow, Scotland, 1969-70; Ph.D. (NDEA fellow), Mich. State U., 1973; m. Ronnie Lee Durchlag, May 8, 1966; children—Kirsten, Russell. Instr. polit. sci. U. Fla., Gainesville, 1970-71; asst. prof. polit. sci. Macalester Coll., St. Paul, 1971-78; adj. prof. polit. sci. U. Minn., Mpls., 1978-82, Augsburg Coll., Mpls., 1979-82; prin. program evaluator Minn. Office of Legis. Auditor, St. Paul, 1978-84, dep. legis. auditor, 1984—. Mem. St. Paul Cable Communications Bd., 1979-81, Metro Council Aviation Com., 1984-85. Woodrow Wilson fellow, 1969-70; European Parliamentary fellow, 1977-78; William Warner Bishop prize U. Mich., 1965. Mem. Am. Polit. Sci. Assn., Minn. Polit. Sci. Assn. (mem. exec. com. 1978-80), Am. Soc. for Public Adminstrn., Evaluation Research Soc., Citizens League. Club: Sierra (vice chmn. Northstar chpt. 1979-81). Home: 1671 Pinehurst Ave Saint Paul MN 55116 Office: 122 Veterans Service Bldg Saint Paul MN 55155

BROOKS, ROGER KAY, insurance company executive; b. Clarion, Iowa, Apr. 30, 1937; s. Edgar Sherman and Hazel (Whipple) B.; m. Marcia Rae Ramsey, Nov. 19, 1955; children—Michael, Jeffrey, David. Student Drake U., 1955-57; B.A. magna cum laude, U. Iowa, 1959. With Central Life Assurance Co., Des Moines, 1959—, asst. sec., 1963-64, asst. actuary, 1964-66, asst. to pres., 1966, asst. to pres., assoc. actuary, 1967-68, v.p., 1968-71, exec. v.p., 1971-72, pres. and chief operating officer, 1972-74, pres. and chief exec. officer, 1974—; dir. Norwest Bank, 1974—, Iowa Meth. Med. Ctr., 1981—. Bd. dirs. Des Moines Art Ctr.; gen. chmn. United Way, 1983. Fellow Soc. Actuaries; mem. Am. Acad. Actuaries, Des Moines Actuaries Club (past pres.), Des Moines C. of C. (bd. dirs., appeals rev. steering com., bd. dirs. Des Moines Devel. Corp., Greater Des Moines com.), Phi Beta Kappa. Clubs: Des Moines (bd. dirs.), Wakonda. Lodge: Rotary.

BROOKS, TAMMY LEE, fashion design firm executive; b. Kansas City, Mo., Sept. 24, 1958; d. Harland Ray and Melba Nell (Newton) B.; m. Anthony Hugo Bartolomi, Aug. 13, 1979 (div. July 1981); 1 child, Anthony Hugo. Student pub. schs. Model, Stix Boar, Fuller, Macy's, Woolf Bros., Swansons, Sasson, others, Kansas City, Dallas, N.Y.C., 1973—; designer, owner T.L. Brooks Inc., Branson, Mo., 1980—; dir., owner T.L. Brooks Beauty/Charm Seminars, Springfield, Mo., 1983—. Republican. Avocations: water skiing; gardening; Bible study; travelling; cooking. Office: T L Brooks Inc PO Box 4916 Springfield MO 65808-4916

BROOKS, THOMAS WILLIAM, chemical company executive, chemistry researcher; b. Wyandotte, Mich., Nov. 11, 1933; s. Buford Wallace and Jessie (Hindley) B.; m. Flora Lucretia Smith, June 9, 1956; children—Lucretia Collette, Stephanie Kay, Thomas Webster. B.S., The Citadel, 1956; M.S., U. Fla., 1959, Ph.D., 1961. NSF postdoctoral fellow U. Fla., 1961-62; research fellow Pulp Chems. Assn., 1963-64; mgr. research and devel. Calgon-Havens Systems, Merck & Co., Inc., 1964-73; assoc. dir. chemistry div. North Star Research and Devel. Inst., 1973-74; tech. dir. environ. chems. group Albany Internat. Corp. (N.Y.), 1974-82; dir. research and devel. Franklin Internat., Inc., Columbus, Ohio, 1982—. Mem. ofcl. bd. United Methodist Ch., Gainesville, Fla., 1967-69, Franklin, Mass., 1975-76. Served to capt. Chem. Corps, USAR, 1956-65. Recipient IR100 award Indsl. Research and Devel. Mag., 1977. Mem. Am. Chem. Soc., Entomol. Soc. Am., AAAS, Controlled Release Soc. (founding bd. govs. 1975-76), Comml. Devel. Assn., Adhesion Soc., Assn. Citadel Men, Audubon Soc. Democrat. Methodist. Contbr. articles to profl. publs.; patentee in field. Home: 6639 Stenten St Worthington OH 43085 Office: 2020 Bruck St Columbus OH 43085

BROOMFIELD, TYREE SIMS, police chief, consultant, lecturer; b. Feb. 11, 1938; s. Tyree Sims and Emma (Anderson) B.; m. Geri Jackson, July 2, 1966; 1 child, Tyree Sims, III. B.A., Central State U., 1973; H.H.D. (hon.), Wilberforce U., 1983. Intergroup relations specialist human relations dept., City of Dayton, Ohio, 1969-70; adminstrv. asst. to police chief Dept. of Police, City of Dayton, 1970-72, dir. conflict mgmt., 1970, supt., 1972-76, dep. dir., 1976-83, dir., chief of police, 1983—; cons. U.S. Dept. Justice, Washington, 1969—; bd. dirs. Nat. Orgn. Human Rights Workers, 1969-74; mem. Nat. Minority Council on Criminal Justice, Washington, 1976-80; charter bd. mem. Nat. Orgn. Police/Community Relations Officers. Contbr.: Police and the Behavioral Sciences, 1974; Police Community Relations, 1974; The Inequality of Justice, 1982. 2d v.p. ARC, Dayton, 1976—; chmn. personnel com. Dayton Art Inst., 1979—; bd. dirs. Montgomery County Council on Aging, 1980-83; bd. trustees Dayton Soc. Natural History, 1984—. Named One of Top Ten Outstanding Young Men, Greater Dayton Area Jaycees, 1969, Outstanding Young Man, 1969; Exec. of Yr., Dayton Area Exec. Club, 1983; recipient Brotherhood award Frontier's Internat., 1972. Mem. Am. Arbitration Assn. (panelist 1972-75), Internat. Assn. Chief of Police, Ohio Assn. Chiefs of Police, Nat. Orgn. Black Law Enforcement Execs. (charter). Democrat. Mem. African Methodist Episcopal Ch. Club: Boule. Lodge: Rotary. Home: 4501 Greenleaf Dr Dayton OH 45417 Office: Dept Police City of Dayton 335 W 3d St Dayton OH 45402

BROOMFIELD, WILLIAM S., congressman; b. Royal Oak, Mich., Apr. 28, 1922; s. S. C. and Fern (Taylor) B.; student Mich. State U.; m. Jane Smith Thompson, 1951; children—Susan, Nancy, Barbara. Mem. Mich. Ho. of Reps., 1948, 50, 52, speaker pro tem, 1953; mem. Mich. Senate, 1954-56; mem. 85th-99th congresses from 19th Mich. Dist., ranking Republican on Com. Fgn. Affairs, mem. Small Bus. Com.; U.S. del. NATO Parliamentarians' Conf., Paris, 1960, NATO Conf., Denmark, 1975, U.S.-U.K. Parliamentary Conf., Bermuda, 1962, Can.-U.S. Interparliamentary Conf., 1961-64, 67-69, 72, 74-79, Mex.-U.S. Interparliamentary Group, 1969-74, 22d UN Gen. Assembly; congressional adviser Conf. of Com. on Disarmament, Geneva, 1970, 83. Pres., Nat. Rep. Club of Capitol Hill, 1970-74; mem. Nat. Fgn. Relations Council of Am. Legion, 1974. Presbyterian. Clubs: Masons, Lions, Odd Fellows, Optimists. Home: Birmingham MI Office: Room 2306 Rayburn House Office Bldg Washington DC 20515*

BROSE, MERLE LEVERNE, physician; b. Cedar Falls, Iowa, Aug. 23, 1922; s. Robert Lisle and Amy Belle (Shedd) B.; B.S., U. Wis., 1943; M.D., 1946; m. Phyllis Marie Magill, Jan. 10, 1948; children—Linda (Mrs. Steven Kleinsteiber), Cheryl (Mrs. William Zieman), Pamela (Mrs. Thomas Zembal), Sandra (Mrs. Gerald Jackson), William. Intern, Columbia Hosp., Wilkinsburg, Pa., 1946-47, resident in surgery, 1947-48; gen. practice medicine, Irwin, Pa., 1950-63; med. dir. Nat. Union Ins. Co., Pitts., 1962-63; gen. practice medicine, Menomonee Falls, Wis., 1963-65; physician Health Service, U. Wis., Madison, 1965-—; mem. faculty U. Wis. Med. Sch., 1965-—. Served to capt. USAF, 1948-50. Mem. U.S. Power Squadrons (Madison squadron sec. 1969, treas. 1970, adminstrv. officer 1971, exec. officer, 1972, dist. adminstrv. officer 1972, comdr. 1973, grade Navigator 1970, dist. exec. officer 1974, dist. comdr, 1975). Club: Four Lakes Yacht (commodore 1978) (Madison). Lodges: Masons, Shriners (pres. Shrine Concert Band). Home: 4517 Gregg Rd Madison WI 53705 Office: 1552 University Ave Madison WI 53705

BROSE, PHYLLIS MARIE, nurse; b. Stewartsville, Pa., Sept. 20, 1925; d. George Allan and Roberta Fern (Lintner) Magill; R.N., Columbia Hosp. Sch. Nursing, Wilkinsburg, Pa., 1946; certificate Sch. Anesthesia St. Francis Hosp., Pitts., 1948; m. Merle LaVerne Brose, Jan. 10, 1948; children—Linda Brose Kleinsteiber, Cheryl Brose Zieman, Pamela Brose Zembal, Sandra Brose Jackson, William. Nurse, Columbia Hosp., 1946-47, anesthetist, 1948, staff nurse, 1949-50; nursing supr., coordinator dialysis U. Wis. Hosp., Madison, 1966—. Mem. med. and sci. bd. Kidney Found. Wis., 1970—; mem. adv. council Nat. Center Health Care Tech.; bd. dirs. S. Central chpt. Wis. Kidney Found., 1980-81; mem. Network 13 Coordinating Council End-Stage Renal Disease, Inc. Recipient Exceptional Performance award in nursing U. Wis., 1977. Mem. Am. Assn. Nephrology Nurses and Technicians (pres. Wis. chpt. 1978-79). Club: Four Lakes Yacht. Home: 4517 Gregg Rd Madison WI 53705 Office: 600 Highland Ave Madison WI 53706

BROSNAN, MARGARET ANNE, hospital executive; b. Cleve.; d. Patrick J. and Mary Loretta (Barrett) B.; B.A., Ursuline Coll., 1960; M.S., St. Louis U., 1962; M.B.A., Kent State U., 1968; J.D., U. Akron, 1971. Mem. faculty St. John Coll., Cleve., 1960-62; dir. dietary service St. Vincent Charity Hosp., Cleve., 1960-62; pres. St. Thomas Hosp. Med. Center, Akron, Ohio, from 1962; admitted to Ohio bar, 1973; exec. council Northeastern Ohio U. Coll. Medicine, 1979—; mem. North Akron Bd. Trade, 1981—. Mem. Akron Planning Commn., 1972-77, Akron Historic Preservation Com., 1976-79, Summit County Bd. Visitors, 1980-82; trustee Akron Regional Devel. Bd., 1973—. Fellow Am. Coll. Hosp. Adminstrs.; mem. Am. Hosp. Assn., Ohio Hosp. Assn. (mem. various coms. 1968—), Akron Regional Health Assn. (pres. 1977-78), ABA, Ohio State Bar Assn., Akron Bar Assn., Nat. Health Lawyers Assn., Am. Soc. Hosp. Attys. of Am. Hosp. Assn., Soc. Ohio Hosp. Attys. of Ohio Hosp. Assn., Am. Soc. Law and Medicine. Contbr. articles profl. jours. Home: 444 N Main St Akron OH 44310 Office: St Thomas Med Center 444 N Main St Akron OH 44310

BROSSART, RONALD FRANK, agricultural management specialist; b. Rugby, N.D., Aug. 18, 1951; s. Valentine Frank and Alice Catherine (Walters) B.; B.S., N.D. State U., 1973. Asst. county supr. Farmers Home Adminstrn., U.S. Dept. Agr., Wahpeton, N.D., 1973-74, Lamoure, N.D., 1974-78, Rugby, 1979—. Mem. Orgn. Profl. Employees Dept. Agr. Roman Catholic. Clubs: Rugby Jaycees, Rugby Country, Eagles, KC. Home: 1020 3d Ave SE Rugby ND 58368 Office: 406 3d Ave SW Rugby ND 58368

BROSSEAU, TERRANCE GENE, medical center administrator; b. Drayton, N.D., Apr. 11, 1942; s. Franklin Hubert and Jean Ethel (Brown) B.; m. Alane Marie Oster; children—Bradley, Tracy, Steven. B.B.A., U. N.D., 1964, M.P.A., 1977; grad. Res. Officers Tng. Coll., 1964, U.S. Army Command and Gen. Staff Coll., 1976. Acct. Grand Forks Creamery Co., N.D., 1964-65; controller Medcenter One (formerly Bismarck Hosp.), Bismarck, N.D., 1968-72, asst. adminstr., 1972-79, adminstr., 1979-80, pres., 1980—; dir. Blue Cross of N.D., Dakota Bank and Trust Co., Bismarck; exec. officer U.S. Army 311th Evacuation Hosp., Bismarck, 1976—. City commr. City of Bismarck, 1978—; pres. bd. dirs. United Way, Bismarck, 1984; bd. dirs. Bismarck Devel. Assn., 1982, YMCA, Bismarck, 1984. Fellow Healthcare Fin. Mgmt. Assn. (pres. N.D. chpt. 1972, nat. bd. examiners 1976-79, William G. Follmer award 1973, Robert H. Reeves award 1976, Frederick T. Muncie award 1979), Am. Coll. Hosp. Adminstrs.; mem. N.D. Hosp. Assn. (v.p. 1985). Republican. Roman Catholic. Avocations: hunting; fishing; carpentry; ranching. Home: 3304 Winnipeg Dr Bismarck ND 58501 Office: Medcenter One 300 N Seventh St Bismarck ND 58501

BROST, EILEEN MARIE, guidance counselor; b. Medford, Wis., July 18, 1909; d. Peter and Pauline (Rudolph) Brost; B.A., Loyola U., 1939; M.A., St. Xavier U., 1954; M.Ed., Loyola U., 1970; postgrad. Alverno Coll., Milw. State Tchrs. Coll., DePaul U., Lewis U., Marquette U., Alfred Adler Inst., Chgo., Marylhurst Coll., Oreg. Joined Sch. Sisters of St. Francis, Roman Cath. Ch., 1925; tchr. various locations, Ill., Oreg. and Wis., 1927-68; religious edn. coordinator St. Anne's Parish, Barrington, Ill., 1968-72; guidance counselor, various schs., Chgo. Public Sch. System and Chgo. Archdiocese, 1972—; parish minister, 1982—. Active parish orgns., Pro-Life Orgn. Cert. tchr., Ill., Wis.; Braille cert. Mem. Nat. Ret. Tchrs. Assn., Chgo. Ret. Tchrs. Assn., Am. Guidance and Personnel Assn., Am. Sch. Counselor Assn. Roman Catholic. Home: 1925 Kedvale St Chicago IL 60639 Office: 4131 W Cortland Chicago IL 60639

BROSTROM, ELAINE MADISON, college administrator; b. Poy Sippi, Wis., April 29, 1928; d. Raymond Andrew and Isabel Barbara (Godson) Madison; m. Carl Milton Brostrom, June 8, 1952; children—James Madison, Jennifer Ruth. B.A., Dana Coll., 1951; M.S., Mankato State U., 1972. Dir. pub. affairs Gustavus Adolphus Coll., St. Peter, Minn., 1977—. Lutheran. Office: Gustavus Adolphus Coll St Peter MN 56082

BROTHERS, DELORES MAY, controller; b. Evansville, Ind., June 12, 1926; d. Joseph Gilbert and Loretta Katherine (Heinz) Cook; m. Damian Louis Brothers, July 24; children—Jerry, Ronald, Nancy. A.A., Lockyears Bus. Coll., 1965; B.S., U. Evansville, 1972. Tax acct. Al Umbach C.P.A. Co., Evansville, 1967-69, Klein Acctg. Co., Evansville, 1969-72; with Evana Tool & Engring., Inc., Evansville, 1972—, controller, 1983—; tchr. cost acctg. Ind. State U., Evansville; cons. to small bus. firms. Active Freedom Festival, YWCA fund raising, ARC blood bank drive. Named Jr. Achievement Leader, 1981. Mem. Am. Soc. Women Accts. (mem. yr. award 1983), Am. Inst. Corp. Controllers, Nat. Assn. Accts. Roman Catholic. Clubs: Altrusa Internat. Bus. Profl. Women's (Evansville). Office: 5825 Old Boonville Hwy Evansville IN 47715

BROTJE, ROBERT J., JR., spark plug company executive. Pres., chief operating officer Champion Spark Plug Co., Toledo, Ohio, also dir. Office: Champion Spark Plug Co 900 Upton Ave Toledo OH 43661*

BROUGH, JOHN HERBERT, occupational therapist, ednl. adminstr.; b. Danville, Ill., June 11, 1945; s. John C. and Elsie B. (Trimby) B. B.S. in Occupational Therapy, U. Ill., 1968; postgrad. Nat. Coll. of Edn., Evanston, Ill., 1969. Tchr. health edn. Sch. Dist. 303, Ill., 1968-71; remedial specialist Camp Arrowhead, Wis., summers, 1969-71; vocat. evaluator Vermilion County (Ill.) Rehab. Center, 1971-72; dir. remedial program Camp Algonquin, Ill., summers, 1972-79; dir. Brough Learning Center, Danville, Ill., 1972—, dir. occupational therapy, 1984—; dir. occupational therapy Kankakee (Ill.) Area Spl. Edn. Co-op, 1980-84; cons. to United Cerebral Palsy, Bur. of Indian Affairs, Children's House, Adolph Meyer Center, Progress Sch., 1974-84; mem. adv. com. Area Health Edn. System for Continuing Edn., 1973-79. Bd. dirs. N. Am. Riding for the Handicapped Assn., 1975—. Recipient Vol. Service award VA, 1962, Meritorious Service citation Am. Legion, 1962; James scholar, 1964-68. Mem. Am. Occupational Therapy Assn., Kickapoo Dist. Occupational Therapy Assn. (pres. 1972-76), Ill. Occupational Therapy Assn. (treas. 1976-79), Vermilion Assn. for Learning Disabilities (treas. 1980-84), The U.S. Capitol Hist. Soc. (founding mem.). Contbr. articles on therapy to profl. publs. Office: 1027 S Washington St Kankakee IL 60901 Home: 1027 S Washington St Kankakee IL 60901

BROUK, J. JOHN, bldg. and insulation material mfg. co. exec.; b. St. Louis, Apr. 30, 1917; s. Joseph John and Marie (Hilgert) B.; B.S. in Ceramic Engring., U. Ill., 1938: m. Ruthe Garman, Nov. 1, 1946; children—Joseph John, Joanne Marie. Refractory researcher metallurgy dept. Naval Research Lab., Washington, 1943-46; pres. Precast Slab & Tile Co., St. Louis, 1951-54, Perlite Insulation Co., St. Louis, 1951-54; v.p. Fed. Cement Tile Co., Chgo., 1954-57; pres. Brouk Co., St. Louis, 1957—; pres. Perlite Inst., 1950-52; nat. sales agt. perlite ore Great Lakes Carbon Co., 1952-72, Grefco, Inc., 1966-72. Bd. dirs. Mt. St. Rose Hosp., St. Louis Conservatory and Sch. for Arts, Multiple Sclerosis Soc.; mem. nat. bd. Young Audiences. Mem. Internat. Vermiculite Assn. (pres. 1976-80), Young Presidents Orgn. (pres. St. Louis chpt. 1959, lectr. mgmt. seminars). Contbr. numerous articles on perlite insulation to profl. and trade jours.; patentee perlite brick veneer wall panel; developer combined perlite and vermiculite concrete and corrugated metal roof-deck system. Office: Brouk Co 1367 S Kingshighway Saint Louis MO 63110

BROUMAND, HORMOZ K(HALIL), food company executive, consultant; b. Teheran, Iran, Aug. 29, 1924; came to U.S., 1944, naturalized, 1962; s. Khalil and Farangis (Daneshgar) B.; m. Rachel Tour, Oct. 28, 1956; children—Clifton, Stafford. M.S., U. Mass., 1950; Ph.D., Rutgers U., 1954. Research chemist Continental Can Co., Chgo., 1953-54; postdoctoral fellow Purdue U., Lafayette, Ind., 1955; research chemist Nabisco Co., N.Y., N.J., 1956-59; dir. research Stark Wetzel, Indpls., 1959-61; pres. N.Am. Lab. Co., Inc., Indpls., 1961—. Contbr. articles to profl. jours. Patentee in field. Bd. dir. Ind. Symphony Soc., Indpls., 1976-80, Internat. Ctr., Indpls., 1976—, Catheral Art, Indpls., 1984—. Recipient proclamation City of Indpls., 1983. Fellow Institute Food Technologist (chmn., various positions Ind. sect. 1959—, cert. of recognition 1977), Purdue Food Sci. Club (hon. 1973); mem. Sigma Xi, Phi Tau Sigma. Democrat. Mem. Bahai Ch. Avocations: music; activites internat. understanding. Home: 3853 Nesbitt Rd Indianapolis IN 46220 Office: North Am Lab Co Inc 1717 W 10th St Indianapolis IN 46222

BROWMAN, DAVID L(UDVIG), archeologist; b. Missoula, Mont., Dec. 9, 1941; s. Ludvig G. and Audra (Arnold) B.; m. M. Jane Fox, Apr. 24, 1965; children—Lisa, Tina, Becky. B.A., U. Mont., 1963; M.A., U. Wash., 1966; Ph.D., Harvard U., 1970. Hwy. archeologist Wash. State Hwy. Dept., Olympia, 1964-66; field dir. Yale U., New Haven, 1968-69; tutor Harvard U., 1969-70; mem. faculty Washington U., St. Louis, 1970—, prof. archeology, 1984—; dir. Cons. Survey Archeology, St. Louis, 1976—, Inst. Study of Plants, Food and Man, Kirkwood, Mo., 1979-84; cons. St. Louis Dept. Parks and Recreation, 1978—. Editor/author: Advances in Andean Archeology, 1978; Economic Organization of Prehispanic Peru, 1984. Editor: Cultural Continuity in Mesoamerica, 1979; Early Native Americans, 1980. Charter mem. Confluence St. Louis, 1983; mem. Gov.'s Adv. Council Hist. Preservation, 1982—. NSF fellow, 1967, grantee, 1974-75, 85—. Mem. Soc. Profl. Archeologists (sec.-treas. 1981-83), AAUP (chpt. pres. 1980-82), Mo. Assn. Profl. Archeologists (v.p. 1981-82), Mo. Archeology Soc. (trustee 1977—), Sigma Xi (chpt. sec. 1984—). Roman Catholic. Avocations: hiking; gardening. Office: Campus Box 1114 Washington U Saint Louis MO 63122

BROWN, ALAN CRAWFORD, lawyer; b. Rockford, Ill., May 12, 1956; s. Gerald Crawford and Jane Ella (Herzberger) B.; m. Judy Ellen Bourn, Dec. 28, 1978. B.A. magna cum laude, Miami U., Oxford, Ohio, 1978; J.D. with honors, U. Chgo., 1981. Bar: Ill. 1981, U.S. Dist. Ct. (no. dist.) Ill. 1981. Assoc., Kirkland and Ellis, Chgo., 1981—. Mem. Order of Coif, Phi Beta Kappa. Office: Kirkland & Ellis 200 E Randolph Dr Suite 5600 Chicago IL 60601

BROWN, ARVILL BUELL, civil engineer; b. Wetonka, S.D., Aug. 5, 1923; s. Arvill Clay and Anna (Gunderson) B.; B.S., Tri-State U., Angola, Ind., 1946; certificate small homes council course U. Ill., 1954; m. June Strong, Oct. 13, 1944; children—Duane Arvill, LuReign Anne, Anita June. Asst. project engr. Ind. State Hwy. Dept., 1946-47; project engr. Tri-State Coll., Angola, Ind., 1947-48; field engr. James Stewart Corp., Chgo., 1948-50; chief engr., gen. field supt. and estimator Fisher-Stoune, Inc., Decatur, Ill., 1950-60; chief engr. aluminum bldg. products div. Maco Corp., Huntington, Ind., 1960-64; partner B & K Engring. Company, Huntington, 1963-64, v.p., 1964-65, pres. B & K Engring., Inc., Kendallville, Ind., 1966-77, also dir.; pres. Brown Cons. Engrs., Inc., Kendallville, 1977—; owner Arvill B. Brown, profl. engr., Kendallville, 1971——; constrn. mgr., engr. Great Lakes Bible Coll., Lansing, 1971-76; pres. Noble County (Ind.) Plan Commn., 1967-71; hwy. engr. Noble County, 1965-71, surveyor, 1967-71; mem. Noble County Drainage Bd., 1967-71. Active Boy Scouts, Cub Scouts; trustee, sec., forwarding agt. Christian Edn. Assn. of Orient, Inc., 1965—; mem. exec. com. New Chs. Christ Evangelism, 1965——; dir. Lake James Christian Assembly, Angola, Ind., 1970-75; nat. alumni dir. Tri-State Coll., Angola, Ind., 1971-75; trustee Gt. Lakes Bible Coll., Lansing, 1982—. Served with USNR, 1944-46. Registered profl. engr., Ill., Ind., Ohio, Mich., Ky., Minn., Wis., Ga.; profl. land surveyor, Ind.; certified fallout shelter analyst U.S. Dept. Def.; certificates on energy-comml. and residential bldgs., Wis. Mem. Decatur Contractors Assn. (past sec.-treas.). Mem. Ch. of Christ (elder). Patentee in field. Home: 357 N Main St Kendallville IN 46755 Office: 212 S Main St Kendallville IN 46755

BROWN, BAIRD, ret. ins. co. exec.; b. Chgo., Aug. 8, 1922; s. George Frederic and Irene (Larmon) B.; A.B., Washington and Lee U., 1949; student U. Chgo., 1946-48. Vice pres. Geo. F. Brown & Sons, Inc. Chgo., 1948-52, dir., sec., 1952-70, v.p., 1957-70; exec. v.p., dir. Interstate Nat. Corp., 1970-74; pres. Internat. Visitors Center, 1964-65, Lyric Opera Guild, 1958-59; mem. Ill. Arts Council, 1966-67; mem. Joseph Jefferson Awards Com., 1971-79, 81—. Served with USAAF, 1943-45. Mem. UN Assn. (dir. Chgo. br. 1967-73), Sigma Chi. Club: Arts. Home: 2440 N Lakeview Ave Chicago IL 60614

BROWN, BARBARA LYNN, publishing company executive; b. Cleve., Sept. 16, 1951; d. Lennart Uno and Louise Ulla (Borenius) Gunnerfeldt; m. Bronnie D. Brown, July 16, 1983; 1 child, Elyse; stepchildren—Joseph Paul, Sharon Sue. B. Mus., Mich. State U., 1975; M.Ed., Fla. Atlantic U., 1976, Ed.S., 1980, Ed.D., 1982. Editor's asst. Mich. State U., East Lansing, 1969-70; instr. flute Lansing Conservatory of Music, Mich., 1970-73; instrumental tchr. Music for Am. Inc., 1974; research asst., editor monthly newsletter Ctr. for Econ. Edn., Fla. Atlantic U., 1976-77; founder, pres. Lynnco Publs., Boca Raton, Fla., 1978—. Author: Guidebook to Happiness, Multiple Sclerosis (The Guide to Successful Coping), 1980; The Art of Talking: A Handbook of Marital Communication, 1979. Mem. Nat. Assn. Female Execs., Mensa, Phi Delta Kappa. Democrat. Lutheran. Home and Office: 206 E Chimney Hill Dr DeWitt MI 48820

BROWN, BETTY ANN, university administrator; b. What Cheer, Iowa; d. William F. and Anna (Kelley) Tinsley; B.A., Iowa Wesleyan Coll., 1943; M.A., Ill. State U., 1971, postgrad., 1971—; m. Forrest Edwin —Dick— Brown, Nov. 19, 1943; children—Joanne Kelley, Thomas Edwin, Kenneth Scott (dec.), Richard Scott (dec.). Placement counselor Ill. State U. Placement Service, Normal, 1966-67; employment interviewer Ill. State Employment Service, 1967-68; fin. aid adv. Ill. State U., Normal, 1968—. Bd. dirs. Family Services of McLean County, 1979—; mem. Ill. N.G. Scholarship Bd., 1979—; mem. Ill. State U. Adult Learners Scholarship Com., 1985-86. Mem. Nat. Assn. Student Employment Adminstrs. (historian 1983-84), Midwest Assn. Student Employment Adminstrs. (service award 1980, sec. 1982-84), Ill. Guidance and Personnel Assn. (treas. 1976-77), Am. Coll. Personnel Assn., Nat. Assn. Women Deans, Adminstrs. and Counselors, Nat. Assn. Work and the Coll. Student, Ill. Assn. Fin. Aid Adminstrs., Ill. State Univ. Adminstrs. Club, Kappa Delta Pi (pres. Mu chpt. 1979-81). Presbyterian. Club: Altrusa (chpt. pres. 1979). Home: 1907 Owens Dr Bloomington IL 61701 Office: Hovey 211 Ill State Univ Normal IL 61761

BROWN, BILL, architect, author, liturgical consultant; b. Pitts., June 2, 1950; s. Vincent J. and Rose C. (Schillinger) B.; m. Dawn Ellen Gardner, June 23, 1973; children—Krista Ann, Lori Catherine. B.Arch. with high honors, U. Notre Dame, 1973. Lic. architect, Ind.; cert. Nat. Council Archtl. Registration Bds. Archtl. grad. Leroy Troyer and Assocs., Mishawaka, Ind., 1973-76, architect, 1976—, ptnr., 1979—. Recipient Reynolds Aluminum Prize for Design, 1972; Notre Dame Dept. of Architecture thesis prize, 1973; —Bene— award Modern Liturgy mag., 1982. Mem. AIA (pres. No. Ind. chpt., 1980), Ind. Soc. Architects (pres. 1984). Roman Catholic. Editor, contbg. author: Building and Renovation Kit for Places of Catholic Worship; contbg. author books on places of worship. Office: 202 S 5th St Goshen IN 46526

BROWN, BRUCE CARTER, park developer; b. Lansing, Mich., Aug. 17, 1938; s. Alvin Raymond and Myrtle Fern (Carter) B.; m. Lynne Marie Ahlberg, Aug. 23, 1963; children—Susan Marie, Sarah Lynne. B.S., Mich. State U., 1962, M.Urban Planning, 1965. Dir. city planning City of Kalamazoo, 1969-73, city mgr., 1973-76; comml. realtor, Grand Rapids, Mich., 1977; dir. city planning City of Indpls., 1978-79; exec. dir. White River Park Devel. Commn., Indpls., 1979—; planning cons. to various cities; vis. lectr. various colls. and univs. Mem. exec. com. Ind. Sports Corp.; bd. dirs. Maranatha Bible Conf., 1977—; mem. Ind. Olympic Com., 1980—, Mayor's Clean City Com. Mem. Urban Land Inst., Internat. City Mgrs. Assn. Baptist. Lodge: Rotary. Office: White River Park Development Commission 801 W Washington St Indianapolis IN 46204

BROWN, CHARLES ASA, lawyer; b. Woodsfield, Ohio, Oct. 17, 1912; s. Charles A. and Anna Miriam (Hayes) B.; A.B. Va. Mil. Inst., 1931-35; student U. Mich., 1937; J.D., Western Res. U., 1938 children—Charles A. III, Ridgley. Admitted to Ohio bar, 1938, pvt. practice Portsmouth, 1938——; asst. atty. gen. State of Ohio, 1963; owner Raven Rock Farm and Feurt Farm, Scioto River Farm Tract, Winters Farm. Lectr. Indian lore. Active Boy Scouts Am., 1946——, serving as merit badge counsellor, exec. bds. Scioto Area council, Portsmouth dist. commr., scout master troop 12, 1966-80; developer, adviser Indian dance team Portsmouth dist., 1964-78, v.p. Scioto Area council, 1967-68, nat. rep. Nat. council, 1967-68; advisory council Girl Scouts of Am., 1947-48; advisory chief Indian Tribes, 1961-63; councilman Western Black Elk Keetowah, Cherokee Nation, 1964——; mem. Cedar River Tulsa Muskogee Band. Bd. dirs. Portsmouth Little League Baseball Assn., 1957-58, Scioto County unit Am. Cancer Soc., 1973-80; advisory bd. Practical Nurses Assn., 1960-61; sr. warden Episcopal Ch., lay reader, 1950-76; lay reader Anglican Orthodox Ch., 1976-77, Anglican Ch. N. Am., 1977-81. Served from 1st lt. to capt. U.S. Army, 1941-46; lt. col. Res. (ret.). Decorated Bronze Star with oak leaf cluster, Purple Heart, Am. Defense medal, Victory medal, three battle stars, Occupational medal, European theatre ribbon. Named Ky. Col.; recipient Silver Beaver award Boy Scouts Am., 1968, Vigil Order of Arrow, 1971. Mem. Am. Indian Bar Assn., Ohio Bar Assn., Portsmouth Bar Assn. (trustee 1966-71), Am. Legion, VFW, DAV, Nat. Rifle Assn., Ohio Farm Bur., various Am. Indian orgns. Club: Daniel Boone Muzzle Loading Rifle. Lodges: Odd Fellow, Redman, Mason (32 deg., master of lodge 1965, Shriner, past comdr.; trustee lodge 1966-71, excellent high priest chpt. 1976-77, illustrious master council 1978-79, pres. 5th dist. Royal Arch Masons 1979, arch adjutant 6th arch council 1979-81, dist. dep. grand high priest 1980-83, anointed high priest RAM, recipient silver trowel, Royal Order Scotland, Knight Masons Ireland, Nat. Sojourners, Order of Corks, Tall Cedars Lebanon, York Cross of Honour, K.T. priest), Knight Masons of USA, Order of the Bath, K.P. (grand tribune Ohio 1961, past chancellor comdr.), Ohio Masonic Vets., Philalethes Soc., Elk, Eagle, Fraternal Order of Police, Order Eastern Star (patron 1966, trustee 1967-70), White Shrine of Jerusalem. Designer flood wall, Portsmouth, Ohio, 1936. Office: 721 Washington St Portsmouth OH 45662

BROWN, CHARLES ERIC, biochemistry educator, analytical instrumentation consultant; b. Spangler, Pa., Nov. 23, 1946; s. Charles E. and Dorothy R. (Riddle) B.; m. Kathy Louise Houck, July 24, 1971; 1 son, Eric Nathaniel. B.A. in Chemistry, SUNY-Buffalo, 1968, Ph.D. in Biochemistry, Northwestern U., 1973. Instr., postdoctoral fellow depts. chemistry, biochemistry and molecular biology Northwestern U., Evanston, Ill., 1973-75; research fellow Roche Inst. Molecular Biology, Nutley, N.J., 1975-77; asst. prof. biochemistry Med. Coll. Wis. Milw., 1977-83, assoc. prof., 1983—; cons. Nicolet Instrument Corp., Metriflow, Inc., 1984—. NIH predoctoral fellow, 1968-72; Cottrell Research grantee, 1979-82; Arthritis Found. grantee, 1984. Mem. Soc. Neurosci., Am. Chem. Soc., AAAS, Internat. Soc. Magnetic Resonance, Am. Soc. Pharmacology and Exptl. Therapeutics, Sigma Xi, Phi Lambda Upsilon. Contbr. articles in field to profl. jours. and chpts. to books; developer biomedical equipment and techniques. Office: Med Coll Wis Dept Biochemistry 8701 Watertown Plank Rd Milwaukee WI 53226

BROWN, CLIFFORD F., justice Supreme Court Ohio; b. Bronson Twp., Ohio, Jan. 21, 1916; s. Ignatius A. Brown; m. Katherine; children—Charles, Margaret Brown Kramb, Sheila, Ann Brown Playko; A.B. magna cum laude, U. Notre Dame, 1936, LL.B. cum laude, 1938. Admitted to Ohio bar, 1938, Mich. bar, 1939; practice law, Norwalk, Ohio, 1938-64; judge Huron County Ct., 1958-65, Ohio Ct. Appeals, 1965-80; justice Ohio Supreme Ct., 1980—. Served with U.S. Army, World War II. Mem. Am., Ohio, Lucas County, Toledo bar assns., Toledo Old Newsboys Goodfellow Assn., Internat. Inst. Great Toledo, VFW. Democrat. Clubs: Kiwanis, Eagles, YMCA Athletic, Torch. Address: Supreme Court State Capitol Columbus OH 43215*

BROWN, DANIEL, company executive, art critic, artists' model; b. Cin., Nov. 4, 1946; s. Sidney H. and Genevieve Florence (Elbaum) B.; m. Ellen Neveloff, May 24, 1970; m. 2d, Jane Felson, Sept. 14, 1980; stepchildren—Christopher Minton, Scott Minton. A.B. cum laude, Middlebury Coll., 1968; A.M., U. Mich., 1970; postgrad. Princeton U., 1971-72. Dir. cultural events U. Cin., 1972, spl. asst. to pres., 1973; v.p., corp. sec. Brockton Shoe Trimming Co., Cin., 1974—; art critic Cin. Mag., 1980-83, Cin. Art Acad. Newsletter; art reviewer Dialogue Mag., 1983—; art commentator Sta. WKRC-TV, Cin. Mem. exhbns. com. Contemporary Arts Ctr.; mem. membership com. Cin. Art Mus., Mercantile Library; trustee Contemporary Arts Ctr. 1984—, Vocal Arts Ensemble, 1984, Enjoy the Arts, 1985—. Mem. Shoe and Leather Club, Two-Ten Nat. Found., Internat. Platform Assn. Club: University (Cin.). Home: 3900 Rose Hill Ave Apt 401B Cincinnati OH 45229 Office: Brockton Shoe Trimming Co 212 E 8th St Cincinnati OH 45202

BROWN, DARMAE JUDD, librarian; b. Jefferson City, Mo., Sept. 14, 1952; d. William Robert and Dorothy Judd (Curtis) B. B.A., W.Va. Wesleyan Coll., 1974; M.A., U. Denver, 1975; postgrad. Odessa Coll., 1982-84, U. No. Ia., 1984—. Organist numerous chs. in Md., W.Va., Colo., Tex., 1969-84 St. Barnabas Episcopal Chapel, Odessa, 1981-84; searching assoc. Bibliog. Center for Research, Denver, 1975-76; librarian N.E. Colo. Regional Library, Wray, 1976-81; head tech. services Ector County Library, Odessa, Tex., 1981-84. Mem. ALA, Iowa Library Assn., Library and Info. Tech. Assn., Beta Phi Mu, Sigma Alpha Iota. Head tech. services dept. Waterloo pub. Library, Iowa, since 1984—. Home: 1143 Lantern Sq #12 Waterloo IA 50701-5746

BROWN, DENNIS ALLEN, financial executive; b. Chariton, Iowa, Nov. 21, 1952; s. Melvin O. and Maxine L. (Jeffries) B.; m. Marcia A. Steinfeldt, Feb. 6, 1978; 1 child, Stacey. B.S., Drake U., 1974, postgrad. 1974. Several positions to vice pres. Norwest Bank Des Moines (formerly Iowa-Des Moines Nat. Bank), 1974-83; treas. Fin. Info. Trust and predecessor co. S & L Computer Trust, Des Moines, 1983—. Worker Muscular Dystrophy Assn., Des Moines, Variety Club Iowa, Des Moines, United Way, Des Moines. Mem. Am. Mgmt. Assn., Iowa Cash Mgmt. Assn. Avocations: Golf, photography, personal computing. Office: Fin Info Trust 907 Walnut St Des Moines IA 50309

BROWN, DON LYNN, bank loan officer, farm management consultant; b. Houston, Mo., Sept. 27, 1953; s. Dwaine Sheridan and Thelma May (Parmenter) B.; m. Mary Kathryn Kell, Apr. 4, 1953; children—Krista Dawn, Kelly Anna. B.S. cum laude, U. Mo., 1976, postgrad., 1977-82. Instr., cons. in farm mgmt., Chillicothe, Mo., 1977-82; loan officer Bank of Houston (Mo.), 1982—; farm mgmt. cons.; seminar instr. in estate planning. Past pres. Boone County (Mo.) Fair; livestock supt. Mo. State Fair, 1977-78. Mem. Houston C. of C., Nat. Republican Com., Am. Bankers Assn., Mo. Bankers Assn., Alpha Tau Alpha. Republican. Baptist. Clubs: Rotary; State Young Farmer Advisors (Jefferson City, Mo.). Contbr. articles to agrl. mags. Home: 508 Ozark St Houston MO 65483 Office: PO Box 160 Houston MO 65483

BROWN, DONALD JAMES, lawyer; b. Herman, Minn., Aug. 18, 1954; s. Lawrence Joseph and Violet Irene (Twait) B. B.A., U. Minn., 1977, J.D., 1981. Bar: Ill. 1981, U.S. Dist. Ct. (no. dist.) Ill. 1981, Minn. 1981, U.S. Ct. Appeals (7th cir.) 1981. Instr., U. Minn. Law Ctr., Mpls., 1980-81; assoc. Jacobs, Williams & Montgomery, Ltd., Chgo., 1981-84, Winthrop, Weinstine & Sexton, St. Paul, 1984—. Mem. ABA, Ill. Bar Assn., Minn. Bar Assn., Chgo. Bar Assn. Home: 4016 16th Ave S Minneapolis MN 55407 Office: Winthrop Weinstine & Sexton 1800 Conwed Tower 444 Cedar St Saint Paul MN 55101

BROWN, DONALD PATRICK, investment company executive; b. St. Louis, Nov. 25, 1935; s. Patrick and Margaret (Paschen) B.; m. Mary Ellen Georgevitch, June 17, 1961; children—Donald J., Mary M., John P., Maureen E. B.S. in Commerce, St. Louis U., 1963, M.S., 1969. Statis. analyst Westinghouse Electric Corp., 1955-57; ins. mgr., project mgr. Monsanto Co., 1957-68; dir. planning Dain Kalman & Quail, Inc., 1968-70; v.p. fin. and ops. U. Minn., Mpls., 1970-80; pres. Munsingwear, Inc., 1980-83; pres. The EntreSource Cos., Mpls., 1983-84, FBS Mcht. Banking Group, Mpls., 1984—; dir. First Am. Money Fund, Profl. On-Line Systems, Inc. Bd. dirs., pres. Minn. Opera Co., 1980—; mem. fin. com. Mpls. Soc. Fine Arts, 1981—. Served with Air N.G., 1960-64. Mem. Fin. Execs. Inst. Republican. Roman Catholic. Clubs: Mpls., Town and Country of St. Paul. Home: 2222 S Rosewood Ln Saint Paul MN 55113 Office: 1300 First Bank Pl W Minneapolis MN 55402

BROWN, DONALD RICHARD, software company executive; b. Sioux Falls, S.D., Apr. 23, 1938; s. Donald Meeker and Thelma (Fish) B.; m. Margaret Marie Bearss, Jan. 25, 1958; children—Todd Alan, Laura Marie. B.S.E., U. Mich., 1961, M.S., 1964, postgrad., 1965-67. Research mathematician Conductron Corp., Ann Arbor, Mich., 1961-67, research engr. Ford Motor Co., Dearborn, Mich., 1967-69; tech. mgr. ADP Network Services, Ann Arbor, Mich., 1969-75; sr. cons. ADP, Clifton, N.J., 1975-76; v.p. ADP Network Services, Roseland, N.J., 1976-81; pres. Database Design, Inc., Ann Arbor, Mich., 1981—; dir. Securities Research Ltd., Hamilton, Bermuda, 1982—, James Martin Investments Ltd., Hamilton, 1982—. Co-author: Methods of Radar Cross-Section Analysis, 1968. Mem. Tau Beta Pi. Home: 2981 Devonshire Ann Arbor MI 48104 Office: Database Design Inc 2006 Hogback Rd Ann Arbor MI 48104

BROWN, DONALD ROBERT, psychology educator; b. Albany, N.Y., Mar. 5, 1925; s. J. Edward and Natile (Rosenberg) B.; m. June Gole, Aug. 14, 1945; children—Peter Douglas, Thomas Matthew, Jacob Noah. A.B., Harvard U., 1948; M.A., U. Calif.-Berkeley, 1951, Ph.D., 1951. Mem. faculty Bryn Mawr (Pa.) Coll., from 1951, prof. psychology, from 1963; sr. research cons. Mellon Found., Vassar Coll., 1953-63; part-time vis. prof. Swarthmore (Pa.) Coll., U. Pa., also U. Calif.-Berkeley, 1953-63; prof. psychology, sr. research scientist Ctr. Research Learning and Teaching, U. Mich., Ann Arbor, 1964—; cons. Peace Corps, 1965-71; hon. research fellow Univ. Coll., London, 1970-71. Ctr. for Advanced Study Behavioral Scis. fellow, 1960-61; Fulbright sr. research fellow, 1982; Netherlands basic sci. fellow, 1983. Served with AUS, 1943-46; ETO. Fellow Am. Psychol. Assn.; mem. Soc. Psychol. Study of Social Issues, AAAS, AAUP, Sigma Xi, Psi Chi. Editor: Changing Role and Status of Soviet Women, 1967; contbr. articles, chpts. in books. Home: 2511 Hawthorn Ann Arbor MI 48104

BROWN, D(ONALD) WARREN, snack food manufacturing company executive; b. Marion, Ohio, Nov. 23, 1939; s. W. Hoover and Ava (King) B.; m. Barbara Vennard, Dec. 2, 1962 (div. Jan. 1984); children—Katherine L., Douglas W. B.S., Miami U., Oxford, Ohio, 1961. Asst. sales mgr., Popped-Right, Inc., Marion, 1961-62, sales mgr., 1962-64, v.p., treas., 1964-67, exec. v.p., 1967-69, pres. Wyandot, Inc. (new name for Popped-Right, Inc.), 1969—. Bd. dirs. Harding Area council Boy Scouts Am., Marion, 1969—, Community MedCtr Complex Coordinating Council, 1984-86; chmn. Marion County Home Health Services; pres. YMCA Endowment Bd., 1983—. Recipient Disting. Service award Jaycees, 1972, Silver Beaver award Boy Scouts Am., 1981. Mem. Potatoe Chip Snack Food Assn. (treas. 1985-87), Popcorn Inst. Methodist. Lodges: Symposiarchs, Rotary (pres. Marion club 1984—). Club: Marion Country (pres. 1975). Avocations: golf; tennis; snow skiing. Home: 840 Vernon Heights Blvd Marion OH 43302 Office: Wyandot Inc 135 Wyandot Ave Marion OH 43302

BROWN, DOUGLAS RICHARD, businessman; b. Cleve., Mar. 28, 1951; s. Edward Austin and Mary (Westerman) B.; A.S. in Bus. Adminstrn., Rock Valley Coll., Ill., 1976; m. Susan L. Clark, Sept. 18, 1971; children—Kevin Patrick, Steffany Lynn. Dist. sales mgr. Radio Shack div. Tandy Corp., 1972-77; founder, 1977, gen. mgr. Handi-Fix Stores, Inc., Cleve. and Indpls., 1977-79; founder, pres. Corp. Personnel, Inc. (merged with R.J. Evans & Assoc. Inc.), Cleve., Mng. dir., banking div., 1983—; speaker in field. Served with U.S. Army, 1969-71. Cert. personnel cons. Mem. Am. Mgmt. Assn. Home: 831 Cedar Grove Circle Sagamore Hills OH 44067 Office: RJ Evans & Assocs Inc 26949 Chagrin Blvd Beachwood OH 44112

BROWN, EDITH, community development agency administrator; b. Milw., Nov. 25, 1935; d. Anton J. and Elizabeth K. (Kribitsch) Volk; m. Edward S. Brown. B.S., U. Wis., 1958, M.S. in Social Work, 1964; M.S. in Mgmt., Cardinal Stritch Coll., Milw., 1985. Hosp. admissions worker, 1958-60; welfare worker, 1960-62; with Kiwanis Children's Ctr. and Children's Hosp. Psychiat. Clinic, Milw., 1962-64; social worker Lutheran Social Services, Milw., 1964-67; foster care supr. Milwaukee County Dept. Social Services, 1967-71, social services adminstr. child protection and parent services, comprehensive emergency services and a coordinated community edn. and support services, 1971-79; assoc. dir. Community Devel. Agy., City of Milw., 1979—; tech. advisor for child abuse, neglect, woman abuse, domestic violence; grantswriter, tchr., cons. in field. Mem. Summerfest Adv. Council, Mayor's Beautification Com.; chmn. Summerfest Planting, 1972—; chmn. Milwaukee County Child Abuse and Neglect Task force, 1976-78; chmn. adv. council Milw. Boy's Club, 1981-84; vice chmn. Internat. Yr. for Disabled Persons, 1982; liaison Nat. Yr. for Disabled Persons, City of Milw., 1982-83; asst. chairperson City of Milw. United Way Campaign, 1983; mem. Mayor's Youth Initiatives Task Force, 1984-85; mem. adv. panel M.P.A. degree program U. Wis., 1984—. Office of Vocat. Rehab. scholar, 1962-64; Successful Women in Mgmt. award J. Wis., 1977; award Community Tchrs. Corps, 1977; Changemaker award Wis. Fed. Jr. Women's Clubs, 1978; Outstanding Community Services award Milwaukee County, 1979, Outstanding Services award, 1979, Exemplary Service award, 1982; Woman of Yr. award Mcpl. Women's Assn., 1981. Mem. Acad. Cert. Social Workers, Nat. Assn. Social Workers, Internat. Council on Social Welfare, Internat. Fedn. Social Welfare, Am. Soc. for Pub. Adminstrn. (pres. Milw. chpt., Outstanding Service and Dedication award 1984-85), Research Clearinghouse, Am. Bus. Women's Assn. (Woman of Yr. award 1975), Internat. Graphoanalysis Soc. (pres. Wis. chpt.). Club: Variety of Wis. Tech. contbr. to profl., community, resource documents, 1971—; author print and broadcast programs. Office: Community Devel Agency 200 E Wells St Milwaukee WI 53202

BROWN, EDWARD LEE, postal service official; b. St. Louis, July 5, 1937; s. Rainey A. and Cleola Irene (Shepard) Bernard; B.S. in Bus. Adminstrn., U. Mo., 1973; postgrad. So. Ill. U., 1975-77; M.A. in Computer Data Mgmt., Webster U., 1985; m. Allie Stark Crawford, June 4, 1961; children—Stevon A., Byron E., Robin M. Procurement officer U.S. Postal Service, St. Louis, 1967-69, adminstrv. officer, 1969-77, gen. mgr. mgmt. services, 1977—. Bd. dirs. King-Fanon Community Mental Health Center, St. Louis, 1978—; active Mathews Dickey Boys Club. Served with USAF, 1956-60. Mem. St. Louis Assn. of Black Psychologists (fin. sec. 1976—). Mem. African Meth. Episcopal Ch. Home: 1814 Cambridge Ln Saint Louis MO 63147 Office: 1720 Market St Saint Louis MO 63180

BROWN, EDWARD LINUS, patent agent, civil engineer; b. Erie, Pa., July 30, 1906; s. William George and Anna Josephine (Metz) B.; B.S. in Civil Engring., Case Inst. Tech., 1928; m. Doris Anne Maloy, Apr. 11, 1931; children—Anne Brown Manning, Edward Linus, Constance Brown Guild. With Pa. R.R., 1926-35; various position in sales, product design and devel., constrn. Armco Steel Corp., Middletown, Ohio, also Denver, 1936-71; cons. engr., 1971-75; admitted to practice U.S. Patent Office, 1975; patent agt., Middletown, Ohio, 1975—. Chmn. traffic com. Middletown Area Safety Council, 1952; chmn. advancement com. Boy Scouts Am., 1952-60; pres. Friends of Library, 1979-80. Fellow ASCE; mem. Nat. Soc. Profl. Engrs. (life), Ohio Soc. Profl. Engrs. (life, Outstanding Service award 1951, 75), Engrs. Found. Ohio, Sigma Alpha Epsilon. Roman Catholic. Patentee in field of steel products. Home and Office: 3011 Central Ave Middletown OH 45044

BROWN, EDWARD RANDOLPH, lawyer; b. Cleve., Sept. 17, 1933; s. Percy Whiting and Helen F. Campbell (Hurd) B.; m. Sally Reed, Sept. 9, 1961; children—Rosalind Whiting, Jocelyn Gayden. B.A., Harvard Coll., 1955; LL.B., Case Western Res. U., 1962. Bar: Ohio 1962, U.S. Dist. Ct. Ohio 1963, U.S. Ct. Appeals (6th cir.) 1966, U.S. Supreme Ct. 1972. Assoc., Squire, Sanders & Dempsey, Cleve., 1962-64; staff atty. Legal Aid Defenders Office, Cleve., 1964-67; assoc., ptnr. Arter & Hadden, Cleve., 1967—; pres. Cleve. Legal Aid Soc., 1978-81. Trustee Cleve. Inst. Music, 1984—. Served with U.S. Army, 1955-58. Mem. Am. Law Inst., ABA (bus. bankruptcy com.), Cleve. Bar Assn. (bankruptcy and commercial law sect.). Democrat. Avocations: foreign languages; swimming. Home: 15901 Chadbourne St Shaker Heights OH 44120 Office: 1100 Huntington Bldg Cleveland OH 44115

BROWN, EDWIN LEWIS, JR., lawyer; b. Parker, S.D., Mar. 15, 1903; s. Edwin Lewis and Lucy Elizabeth (Lowenberg) B.; J.D., U. Nebr., 1926; m. Faye Hulbert, May 8, 1926; children—Betty Lou (Mrs. Philip Trainer), Lewis Charles. Admitted to Nebr. bar, 1926, Ill. bar, 1933, U.S. Supreme Ct., 1960; practice in Chgo., 1933——; partner firm Brown, Stine & Cook (now Brown, Cook & Hanson), 1950-81. Mem. wills and bequests com. Shriners Crippled Children's Hosp., Chgo.; bd. dirs. Comml. Law Found. Mem. Am., Ill., Chgo. bar assns., Am. Judicature Soc., Comml. Law League Am. (pres. 1963-64), Phi Alpha Delta. Republican. Presbyterian. Mason (32 deg., K.T., Shriner). Clubs: Union League (Chgo.); Westmoreland Country (Wilmette, Ill.). Home: 2617 Hurd Ave Evanston IL 60201 Office: 135 S La Salle St Chicago IL 60603 also 2114 Central St Evanston IL 60201

BROWN, ELLSWORTH HOWARD, museum administrator; b. Ashland, Wis., Mar. 27, 1943; s. Harold Frederick and Isabel (Ellsworth) B.; B.A., Hillsdale Coll., 1965; M.A., Western Mich. U., 1966; Ph.D., Mich. State U., 1975; m. Dorothy Alice Boyse, June 26, 1965; 1 son, Lincoln Frederick. Asst. prof. Dickinson (N.D.) State Coll., 1970-71; dir. Dacotah Prairie Mus.,

Aberdeen, S.D., 1971-76; asst. prof. history No. State Coll., Aberdeen, 1975-76; adj. prof. Vanderbilt U., 1978-81, U. Tenn., Nashville, 1978-79; dir. Tenn. State Mus., Nashville, 1976-81, Chgo. Hist. Soc., 1981—. Trustee Chgo. Met. History Fair. Mem. Am. Assn. State and Local History (council), Am. Assn. Museums (council), Lincoln Park C. of C. (bd. dirs.). Office: Chgo Hist Soc Clark St and North Ave Chicago IL 60614

BROWN, EMMA JEAN MITCHELL, educator; b. Marshall, Tex., June 1, 1939; d. Johnnie D. and Elvia L. Mitchell Nickerson. B.S., Bishop Coll., 1961; M.S., Boston State Coll., 1967; postgrad. Boston U., 1963, 66, Howard U., 1974, U. Dayton, 1979, 80, 81, Miami U., Oxford, Ohio, 1980, Wright State U. Tchr. English, N.E. Jr. High Sch., Kansas City, Kans., 1961-62; info.-mail clk. Boston U., 1962-63; service rep. New Eng. Tel. & Tel., Boston, 1963-65; tchr. Harvard Elem. Sch., Boston, 1965-66, Carter Avery Elem. Sch., Needham, Mass., 1966-67; instr. Sinclair Community Coll., 1971-73, Wright State U., 1971-75; vis. lectr. U. Ibadan (Nigeria), 1975-76; tng. coordinator Dayton (Ohio) Job Corps., 1979; reading specialist Colonel White High Sch., Dayton, 1979-81, Int. Alt. Sch., 1981-82, Martyrs Cath. Sch., 1983-84, Patterson Co-Op High Sch., 1984—. Third v.p. Dayton Urban League Guild, 1977. Recipient medallion City of Dayton, 1981. Mem. Internat. Reading Assn., Dayton Edn. Assn., Western Ohio Edn. Assn., Ohio Edn. Assn., NEA, Miami Valley African Assn., City Folk, Miami Valley Literacy Assn., Ch. Women United, Zeta Phi Beta. Methodist. Author: Come Sit at My Table: A Mini African Cookbook, 1980; (poetry) Network Africa, 1984 contbr. articles to profl. jours. Home: 473 Marathon Dayton OH 45406

BROWN, FREDERICK DOUGLAS, physiologist, educator; b. Springfield, Ohio, June 3, 1929; s. Charles David and Ruth Noami B.; m. Joyce Louise Burton, June 11, 1955; children—Fred, Sharon, Michael Regina, Stephan, Monica. B.S., U. Dayton, 1956; M.S., Miami U., Ohio, 1958; postgrad. Case Western Res. U., 1963-66; Ed.D., Nova U., 1981. Researcher artificial organs and exptl. heart surgery Cleve. Clinic, 1958-63; predoctoral fellow Case Western Res. U., Cleve., 1963-66; instr. sci. Cleve. Bd. Edn., 1966-69; asst. prof. St. John's Coll., Cleve., 1969-73; instr. Sch. Anesthesia Cleve. Clinic, 1973-74; prof. anatomy and physiology Cuyahoga Community Coll., Warrensville, Ohio, 1973—. Pres., Bd. Catholic Edn., Diocese of Cleve., 1972-73; chmn. CSC Warrensville Heights (Ohio), 1970-72; councilman Warrensville Heights, 1982—. Served to 2d lt. U.S. Army, 1952-54. NIH fellow, 1963-66. Mem. AAUP, N.Y. Acad. Scis., Nat. Assn. Advisors of Sci., Ohio Coll. Biology Tchrs. Assn., Alpha Phi Alpha. Democrat. Contbr. articles to profl. jours.

BROWN, FREDERICK LEE, health care executive; b. Clarksburg, W.Va., Oct. 22, 1940; s. Claude Raymond and Anne Elizabeth (Kiddy) B.; m. Mary Ruth Price, Aug. 22, 1964; children—Gregory Lee, Michael Owen-Price. B.A. in Psychology, Northwestern U., 1962; M.B.A., in Health Care Adminstrn., George Washington U., 1966. Various adminstrv. positions Methodist Hosp. Ind., Inc., Indpls., 1965-71, assoc. adminstr., 1971-72, v.p. ops., 1972-74; exec. v.p., chief operating officer Meml. Hosp. DuPage County, Elmhurst, Ill., 1974-82; pres., chief. exec. officer Christian Hosp. Northeast-Northwest, St. Louis, 1982—; pres. Christian Health Care Systems, Inc., St. Louis, 1983—; pres. CH Allied Services, Inc., St. Louis, 1983—; lectr. Ind. U. Sch. Health Care Adminstrn., 1972-74; chmn. Chgo. Hosp. Risk Pooling Program, 1980-82; dir. Central Eastern Mo. Profl. Review Orgn., St. Louis, 1982—; adj. instr. health care adminstrn. Washington U. Sch. Medicine, St. Louis, 1982—. Bd. dirs. Marion County Community Shelter, Planning Policy Council, 1968-69; bd. dirs. Alpha Home, Indpls., 1969-74; chmn. Allied Health Sub-Com. Ind. div., Am. Cancer Soc., 1972-74; mem. Allocations Com. United Fund Greater Indpls., 1972-74; mem. Task Force Project Understanding, 1973-74; mem. Task Force on Future Sch. System, Elmhurst, Ill., 1982; co-chmn. hosp. div. United Way Greater St. Louis, 1983—. Served with USAR, 1962-69. Named to Outstanding Young Men Am., 1974; recipient Alumnus Yr. award George Washington U. Alumni Assn., 1981. Fellow Am. Coll. Hosp. Adminstrs.; mem. Am. Acad. Med. Adminstrs., Am. Hosp. Assn., George Washington U. Alumni Assn. Health Services Adminstrn. (dir., pres. 1979-80), Am. Pub. Health Assn., Advt. Club Greater St. Louis. Republican. Methodist. Club: Norwood Hills County (St. Louis). Lodge: Rotary. Contbr. articles in field to profl. jours. Home: 150 Rue Grand Lake Saint Louis MO 63367 Office: Christian Hosp Northeast Northwest 11133 Dunn Rd Saint Louis MO 63136

BROWN, GARY MICHAEL, university administrator; b. Watervliet, N.Y., Dec. 21, 1959; s. Ronald J. and Shelia H. (Liquid) B.; m. Laura Ellen Niznik, July 14, 1984. B.A. in Biology and Chemistry, Coll. St. Rose, 1982; M.S. in Higher Edn., So. Ill. U., 1984. Head resident So. Ill. U. Housing, Carbondale, 1982-83, acting program coordinator, 1984, program coordinator, 1984—. Mem. Am. Personnel and Guidance Assn. (asst. chairperson placement 1982), Nat. Assn. Student Personnel administrators, Coll. St. Rose Alumni Assn. (named Outstanding Jr. of Yr. 1981), Phi Delta Kappa Pi. Roman Catholic. Avocations: woodworking, hiking, canoeing, camping. Home: Rural Route 1 Box 80 Makanda IL 62958 Office: University Housing Washington Square Carbondale IL 62901

BROWN, GLADYS SADDLER, educator; b. Memphis, Jan. 27, 1923; s. Henry Rutherford and Edith Estee (Hawkins) Saddler Mahone; m. Joseph L. Brown, Nov. 10, 1950; children—Lorelle Joan, Karen Renee. B.S. in Edn., Central State U., 1947; M.S. in Counseling, Chgo. State U., 1968. Asst. to library film advisor ALA, Chgo., 1947-53; sec. to sec. Musicians Union Local 208, Chgo., 1953-60; tchr. Chgo. Bd. Edn., 1960-68; asst. prof. Chgo. City Coll., 1968—, mem. adv. council Olive-Harvey campus, 1978-82; sr. sponsor Hyde Park High Sch., Chgo., 1964-68, coordinator coop. edn., 1967-68. Mem. Chgo. Bus. Tchrs. Assn., Ill. Edn. Assn., Am. Fedn. Tchrs., Phi Beta Lambda, Alpha Kappa Alpha. Democrat. Episcopalian. Club: Merry Eight Bridge. Office: Olive Harvey College 10001 S Woodlawn Chicago IL 60628

BROWN, GLYNN PRATHER, interior designer; b. Dyersburg, Tenn., Feb. 3, 1940; s. George Wesley and Mamie Charlotte (Prather) B.; student Fullerton Coll.; m. June 1, 1977; 1 son, Sean Hunter Designer, Crossroads Co., Whittier, Calif., 1964-65; owner, designer Diversified Design Co., Orange, Calif., 1965-70, Innerscape Co., Newport Beach, Calif., 1970-76; dir. interior design The Ramos Group Architects, Kansas City, Mo., 1977-79; pres. Glynn Brown, Designer, Inc., Kansas City, Mo., 1978—; owner, developer Design Exchange, Kansas City. Pres. bd. dirs. Woodgate Homes Assn., 1979; mem. Quality Hill Residential Task Force; pres. Hist. Garment Dist. Group. Served with USAF, 1960-64. Recipient Davidson award as Interior Designer of Yr., 1983. Mem. Am. Soc. Interior Designers (dir. 1979, chmn. program com. 1979, v.p.-elect 1980, pres. 1981). Republican.

BROWN, GORDON MARSHALL, research engineer; b. Detroit, Feb. 17, 1934; s. Everett J. and Agnes (Craig) B.; student Greenville Coll., 1952-54; B.M.E., Gen. Motors Inst., 1958; M.S., U. Mich., 1959; m. Sharla A. Smith, Aug. 16, 1958; children—Gordon C., Julie Marie. Tooling project engr. Fisher Body div. Gen. Motors Corp., Pontiac, Mich., 1954-58; grad. asst. nuclear engring. U. Mich., 1960-61; project engr. nuclear scis. Bendix Aerospace Systems, Ann Arbor, Mich., 1961-67; dir. engring., mgr. mfg. GCO, Inc., Ann Arbor, 1967-73; prin. research engr., mem. research staff Ford Motor Co., Dearborn, Mich., 1973—; optical systems cons. Recipient Gen. Motors Grad. fellowships in nuclear engring., 1960-61. Mem. Am. Soc. Non-Destructive Testing (Achievement award 1970), Soc. Photo-Optical Instrumentation, Soc. Automotive Engrs., Optical Soc. Am. Contbr. to Holographic Nondestructive Testing, 1975. Patentee holographic method for testing tires, 1971. Home: 3191 Bluett St Ann Arbor MI 48105 Office: Ford Motor Co Room S-1023 SRL PO Box 2053 Dearborn MI 48121

BROWN, HARRY FRANCIS, educational administrator; b. Chgo., Feb. 4, 1930; s. Harry Francis and Genevieve Inez (Kirchens) B.; m. Marilyn Ann Brown, July 25, 1953; children—James, Kathleen, Thomas, Patricia, Colleen. B.A., DePaul U., 1952, M.Ed., 1959. Reporter, Dun & Bradstreet, Inc., 1954-57; tchr. Wilmot Elem. Sch., Wilmot Jr. High Sch., Deerfield, Ill., 1957-61, prin. Wilmot Elem. Sch., 1960—. Vice pres. Tamarack Civic Assn., 1975-77. Served with AUS, 1952-54. Holder age-group world record in 60-yard dash; Nat. Masters Track and Field Champion in 60-yard dash, 1985. Mem. Assn. Supervision and Curriculum Devel., Ill. Prins. Assn., Nat. Elem. Sch. Prins. Assn. Home: 610 Hillside Ave Wauconda IL 60084 Office: 795 Wilmot Rd Deerfield IL 60015

BROWN, HERBERT CHARLES, chemistry educator; b. London, May 22, 1912; s. Charles and Pearl (Stine) B.; came to U.S., 1914; A.S., Wright Jr. Coll., Chgo., 1935; B.S., U. Chgo., 1936, Ph.D., 1938, D.Sc., 1968; m. Sarah Baylen, Feb. 6, 1937; 1 son, Charles Allan. Asst. in chemistry U. Chgo., 1936-38; Eli Lilly postdoctoral research fellow, 1938-39, instr., 1939-43; asst. prof. chemistry Wayne U., 1943-46, assoc. prof., 1946-47; prof. inorganic chemistry Purdue U., 1947-59, Richard B. Wetherill prof. chemistry, 1959, Richard B. Wetherill research prof., 1960-78, emeritus, 1978—; vis. prof. UCLA, 1951, Ohio State U., 1952, U. Mexico, 1954, U. Calif.-Berkeley, 1957, U. Colo., 1958, U. Heidelberg, 1963, SUNY, Stonybrook, 1966, U. Calif.-Santa Barbara, 1967, Hebrew U., Jerusalem, 1969, U. Wales, Swansea, 1973, U. Cape Town, South Africa, 1974, U. Calif.-San Diego, 1979, U. Fla., 1982, U. Auckland (N.Z.), 1983; Harrison-Howe lectr., 1953; Friend E. Clark lectr., 1953; Freud McCormack lectr., 1954; Centenary lectr. (Eng.), 1955; Thomas W. Talley lectr., 1956; Falk-Plaut lectr., 1957, Julius Stieglitz lectr., 1958, Max Tishler lectr., 1958; Kekule-Couper Centenary lectr., 1958, E.C. Franklin lectr., 1960, Ira Remsen lectr., 1961; Edgar Fahs Smith lectr., 1962; Seydel-Wooley lectr. 1966; Baker lectr., 1969; Chem. Soc. lectr., Australia, 1972; Armes lectr., 1973; Henry Gilman lectr., 1975; Randolph T. Major lectr., 1978; Clifford B. Purves lectr., 1979; chem. cons. to indsl. corps. Served as co-dir. war research projects U. Chgo. for U.S. Army, Nat. Def. Research Com., Manhattan Project, 1940-43. Bd. govs. Hebrew U., 1969—. Recipient Purdue Sigma Xi research award, 1951; Nichols medal, 1959; award Am. Chem. Soc., 1960; S.O.C.M.A. medal, 1960; H.N. McCoy award, 1965; Linus Pauling medal, 1968; Nat. medal of Sci., 1969; Roger Adams medal, 1971; Charles Frederick Chandler medal, 1973; Chem. Pioneer award, 1975; Madison Marshall award, 1975; Sci. Achievement award medal CCNY, 1976; C.K. Ingold medal, 1978; Elliott Cresson medal, 1978; Nobel prize in Chemistry, 1979; Priestley medal, 1981; Perkin medal, 1982; Gold medal Am. Inst. Chemists, 1985. Fellow Royal Chem. Soc. (hon.), Indian Nat. Acad. Sci. (fgn.); mem. Nat. Acad. Scis., Am. Acad. Arts and Scis., Am. Chem. Soc. (chmn. Purdue sect. 1955-56), Chem. Soc. Japan (hon.), Pharm. Soc. Japan (hon.), AAAS, Phi Beta Kappa, Sigma Xi, Alpha Chi Sigma, Phi Lambda Upsilon (hon.). Author: Hydroboration, 1962; Boranes in Organic Chemistry, 1972; Organic Synthesis via Boranes, 1975; The Nonclassical Ion Problem, 1977. Contbr. articles to chem. jours.; awarded patents (with others) on preparation of borohydrides, diborane, hydroboration, synthesis of aliphatic derivatives; research in phys., organic, inorganic chemistry relating chem. behavior to molecular structure; selective reductions, hydroboration; chemistry of organoboranes. Office: Dept Chemistry Purdue Univ West Lafayette IN 47907

BROWN, HORACE LUDWIG, civil engineer, land surveyor; b. Newark, Ohio, Dec. 20, 1906; s. Horace Randolph and Mary Anna (Steubs) B.; m. Ruth Elizabeth Anne, Nov. 28, 1936. Registered profl. engr., Ohio; profl. land surveyor. Rodman Chmn. City of Newark, 1928-41, engr. surveyor, 1945—, design engr., 1950—; surveyor Indsl. Gas Corp., Newark, 1941-45; pvt. practice engring.-surveying, Licking County, Ohio, 1944-75. Composer vocal, piano and symphonic music. Contbr. Devel. Fund, Ohio State U., Columbus; mem. N.Y. Philharmonic Soc., Friends of N.Y. Philharmonic, Met. Opera Guild of N.Y. Mem. Am. Congress Surveying-Mapping (life). Republican. Avocations: microscopy; astronomy; photography; electricity; electronics. Home: 135 N 21st St Newark OH 43055 Office: City of Newark 40 W Main St Newark OH 43055

BROWN, HOWARD EARL, community college president; b. Springfield, Ill., June 22, 1922; s. Lorenza Dee and Zona (Sharp) B.; m. Helen Rebecca Bundy, Apr. 10, 1944; children—Bill Wayne, Becky Louise Flora, Sally Elizabeth Schepper. B.S., Ill. State U.-Normal, 1948; M.S., Colo. State U., 1953; Specialist Edn., Eastern Ill. U., 1971; postgrad. Columbia U., 1967, U. Ill., 1976. High sch. coach, tchr., Blue Mound, Ill., 1948-55, prin., 1957-59, sch. supt., 1959-65; county supt. Macon County Ednl. Service Region, Decatur, Ill., 1965-80, regional supt., 1980-85; pres. Richland Community Coll., 1985—; tchr. Richland Community Coll., 1979-82, pres., 1985—; prof. Millikin U., 1976-78; mem. Ill. State Tchr. Certification Bd., 1970-74; chmn. Ill. Task Force-Study of Declining Enrollment, 1975-76. Pres., Mental Health Assn. Macon County; pres. Decatur Area Arts Council; mem. United Fund Bd.; chmn. Farm Bur. Rural/Urban Com. Youth Program; bd. dirs. Salvation Army, Decatur Macon County United Way; chmn. High Risk Infant Screening Com. Macon County; chmn. Billy Graham Golden Prairie Crusade for Christ, Decatur, 1967. Served with U.S. Army, 1942-45. Decorated Bronze Star medal; recipient Voice of Democracy Service award VFW, 1968-69, 79-80, 81-82, Nat. Schoolman's award Freedoms Found., 1971, Disting. Service award Macon County Council Exceptional Children, 1975. Mem. Am. Assn. Sch. Adminstrs., Ill. Assn. Sch. Adminstrs., Ill. Assn. Regional Supts. Schs. (past pres.), Ill. Assn. County Ofcls., VFW, Am. Legion, Macon County Hist. Soc. Methodist. Lodges Rotary (pres. 1971; pub. speaking award) (Decatur), Masons (32 deg.), Shriners. Home: 1989 W Macon St Decatur IL 62522 Office: 2425 Federal Ct Decatur IL 62526

BROWN, JAMES E., banker; b. St. Louis, 1919. Sr. v.p. Merc. Trust Co., St. Louis, 1954-70; pres., dir. Merc. Bancorp., St. Louis, 1970-84, also dir.; banking cons., 1984—. Pres., bd. dirs. Downtown St. Louis, Inc., 1975-77; bd. dirs. Deaconess Hosp., 1975—; chmn. Better Bus. Bur., 1970-72. Served with AUS, 1941-45. Office: 1130 Hampton Ave Saint Louis MO 63139

BROWN, JAMES FRANCIS, insurance company executive; b. Mpls., May 8, 1920; s. James Colonel and Frances Eva (Heil) B.; m. Peggy Elaine Gildehouse, Dec. 4, 1953 (div., 1977); children—Nancy, Heather. Student Carleton Coll., 1938-39, Culver-Stockton Coll., 1939-41; J.D., Washington and Lee U., 1948. Bar: Mo. 1948, U.S. Supreme Ct. 1971. Atty., investigator HEW, Kansas City, Mo., 1951-75; pres., chief exec. officer, chmn. bd. dirs, Jim Brown, Inc., 1976—, Warranty Service Co., St. Louis, 1976—; chmn. bd. dirs. Pembroke Omega Corp. Served with AUS 1942-45. Mem. Mo. Bar Assn. Baptist.

BROWN, JAMES LEHMON, chem. co. exec.; b. Detroit, Nov. 20, 1929; s. Abram Lehmon and Donnabelle (Chenoweth) B.; A.B., U. Mich., 1951, M.B.A., 1952; m. Judith Marsh Sinclair, June 28, 1952; children—Kirk, Scott, Kim, Carrie, Elizabeth. Propr. constrn. firm, Ann Arbor, Mich., 1955-58; sales mgr. Sinclair Mfg. Co., Toledo, 1958-64, pres., 1964—, also chmn. bd.; chmn. bd. Sinclair Mfg. Assos., WGTE-TV-FM, 1980—; dir. Monroe, Mich., Mather Co., Craft House Corp., Hunt Chem., Inc., St. Paul. Mem. Toledo Citizens Com. for Effective Govt., 1971-72; pres. Toledo Area Govtl. Research Assn., 1974-75; trustee Toledo Area council Boy Scouts Am., 1971—, exec. bd., 1970—, pres., 1975—; trustee U. Toledo Corp., 1975—, Toledo chpt. ARC, 1977-79. Served with AUS, 1952-55. Mem. Phi Eta Sigma, Theta Delta Chi, Sigma Delta Chi. Club: Toledo. Home: 30 Meadow Ln Toledo OH 43623 Office: 5644 Monroe St Sylvania OH 43560

BROWN, JAMES MARTIN, railroad executive; b. Lancaster, N.Y., Apr. 10, 1945; s. David and Christine (Anzie) B.; m. Patricia Ann Willison, Nov. 4, 1967; 1 son, Michael Todd. Student pub. schs., Depew, N.Y. Dispatching foreman Penn Central, Selkirk, N.Y., 1970-75, gen. foreman, New Haven, Conn., 1975-76; gen. foreman Nat. R.R. Passenger Corp., New Haven, 1976, gen. supr. N.E. corridor, 1976-79, supt. locomotives, 1979-80, facility mgr., Chgo., 1980-84; plant mgr. Chrome Locomotive, Silurs, Ill., 1984—. Cubmaster Quinnipiac council Boy Scouts Am., 1978, scoutmaster, 1979; trustee Calvary Baptist Ch., Meriden, Conn., 1979. Served with USN, 1963-66. Recipient Order of Arrow, Boy Scouts Am., 1980. Mem. Locomotive Maintenance Officers Assn. Democrat. Lodge: Masons. Home: 3525 56th Street Ct Moline IL 61265 Office: Chrome Locomotive PO Box 197 Silurs IL 61282

BROWN, JAY EDWARD, insurance company executive; b. Mason City, Iowa, June 17, 1924; s. Artemas and Ruth (Sunberg) B.; m. Norma Gae Vorse, Mar. 10, 1945; children—Terrell Jay, Barbara Ann, Marianne Kay Cary. Student Jr. Coll., Mason City, Iowa, 1942-43, N.W. Mo. Coll., 1943-44; B.S. in Math., U. Nebr., 1947; M.B.A. in Actuarial Sci., Drake U., 1949. Sr. v.p., sec., dir. Nat. Travelers Life Co., Des Moines, 1948—, Nat. Travelers Investment Co., Des Moines, 1981—, Am. Travelers Assurance Co., Des Moines, 1982—; dir. Nat. Assn. Life Cos., Atlanta. Bd. dirs. Polk Des Moines Taxpayer Assn., 1963—. Served with USN, 1942-46. Mem. Des Moines Actuaries Club, Des Moines Fin. Analysts, Des Moines Fin. Exec. Inst. Republican. Presbyterian. Avocations: hunting; fishing. Home: 2100 Woodland St West Des Moines IA 50265 Office: Nat Travelers Life Co 820 Keosauqua Way Des Moines IA 50308

BROWN, JOAN LEE, social worker, nurse clinical specialist; b. Jackson, Mich., Oct. 13, 1945; d. Jack Winton and Alma Florence (Gibbard) Brown; m. Thomas H. Shultz, Dec. 21, 1975; children—Jennifer Lee, Sandra Joan. B.S. in Nursing, Spalding U., Louisville, 1968; M.S. in Nursing, U. N.C., 1972. Nurse intensive-care units various instns.; instr. med. surg. nursing U. N.C., Chapel Hill, 1972-73; evening supr. Addison (Mich.) Community Hosp., 1973-74; clin. specialist in psychiatry Chelsea (Mich.) Community Hosp., 1976-82; mental health specialist St. Joseph's Mercy Hosp., Ann Arbor, Mich., 1982—; psycho-therapist group and individual therapy; lectr. in field. Lic. cert. social worker. Mem. U. N.C. Alumni Assn., Spalding Coll. Alumni Assn., Sigma Theta Tau. Methodist. Home: 3978 Scio Church Rd Ann Arbor MI 48103

BROWN, JOHN L., state legislator, farmer, rancher; b. Rapid City, S.D., July 22, 1952; s. Lawrence M. and Helen D. (Davis) B.; m. Roberta Jean Haskell, Aug. 11, 1979; children—Erin Susanne, Colin Elliot. B.S. in Animal Sci., S.D. State U., 1974. Sec.-treas. Cave Hills Cattle Co., Buffalo, S.D., 1974—; mem. S.D. Legislature, 1978-80, mem. S.D. Senate, 1980—. Chmn. Harding County Republican Party, S.D., 1974-78; alt. del. Rep. Nat. Conv., 1976. Lutheran. Lodge: Lions (pres. Buffalo 1977-78).

BROWN, JOSEPH ANDREW, JR., transportation consultant; b. Bristol, Conn., July 28, 1915; s. Joseph Andrew and Emma Virginia (Robey) B.; student Morse Coll., 1934-35; m. Edythe E. Hill, May 2, 1942 (div.); children—Michael R., Peter D., Stephen J., Kathleen V., Julie Ann, Anthony R. Freight service mgr. Eastern Express Inc., Terre Haute, Ind., 1947-56; v.p. ops., mem. exec. com. Mchts. Motor Freight, Inc., St. Paul, 1957-60; dir. freight claim prevention Spector Freight System, Inc., Chgo., 1960-63; salesman Callner Corp. and Ken-Di Realty Co., Chgo., 1964-70; search cons. Cadillac Assos., Inc., Chgo., 1971-84. Mem. transp. adv. com. Richard J. Daley Coll., Chgo., 1979-84. Served to lt. col. OSS, AUS, 1941-47. Decorated Legion of Merit; recipient cert. of meritorious service Am. Trucking Assn. Mem. Am. Soc. Traffic and Transp. (a founder, emeritus), Nat. Council Physical Distbn. Mgmt. Patentee cargo cart conveyor. Home: 445 W Barry St Apt 524 Chicago IL 60657

BROWN, JOSEPH DAVID, business educator, marketing executive; b. Columbus, Ohio, Dec. 19, 1937; s. William Elvin and Jessie Mae (Wrightsel) B.; m. Marcia Lee Hahn, June 10, 1964; children—Rhonda, Jeffrey, Scott, Douglas. B.S., Ohio State U., 1959, M.S., 1960, Ph.D., 1964. Asst. prof. mktg. U. Ga., 1963-68; assoc. prof. dept. mktg. Ball State U., Muncie, Ind., 1963-70, dir., prof. Bur. Bus. Research, 1970—; pres. Brown & Assocs., Inc., Muncie. Contbr. articles to profl. jours. Elder Presbyterian Ch.; pres. bd. dirs. Jr. Achievement-Ind., Muncie, 1977-78; pres. Ind. Redevel. Commn., Muncie, 1970-78. Recipient research grants: Outstanding Research award Sears and Roebuck Found. U. Ga. Mem. Assn. for Univ. Bus. and Econ. Research, Am. Mktg. Assn., Ind. Econ. Forum, Eastern Ind. Econs. Club. Home: Rural Route 11 PO Box 97 Muncie IN 47302 Office: Bur Bus Research Ball State U Muncie IN 47306

BROWN, KEVIN CLARK, retail jeweler; b. Bay City, Mich., Oct. 10, 1953; s. Julius Junior and Marva Fae (Kephart) B.; m. Jacklyn Sue Prince, Oct. 20, 1979. B.S. cum laude, Central Mich. U., 1975. Youth counselor County Probate Ct., Rogers City, Mich., 1975-78; employment counselor Northeast Mich. Manpower, Onaway, 1978-81; mgr. retail sales J.F. Reusch Co., Cheboygan, Mich., 1982—. Mem. Cheboygan Downtown Bus. Assn., 1985—. Mich. Competitive scholar, 1971. Mem. Gemological Inst. Am. (cert. diamond appraiser), Am. Gem. Soc. (student affiliate). Methodist. Avocations: stained glass, hunting; fishing; gardening. Home: Box 242 Forest St Onaway MI 49765 Office: JF Reusch Jewelers 324 N Main St Cheboygan MI 49721

BROWN, LEE JORGENSEN, retailer; b. Cadillac, Mich., Jan. 17, 1940; s. Thaddeus James and Marian Katherine (Jorgensen) B.; m. Pamela Sue Cochran, Feb. 25, 1967 (div.); 1 dau., Susannah Jane; m. Roberta Ann Preston, Apr. 7, 1984; stepchildren—Jane Marie, Jacqueline Lee. B.A., Augustana Coll., 1962; M.A., Western Mich. U., 1966, M.A., 1967. Head dept. English, Loy Norrix High Sch., Kalamazoo, 1963-72; pres. Brown's Men's Wear, Inc., Cadillac, Mich., 1972—; dir. NBD Evart Bank, Mich., Pantree Restaurants. Lutheran. Home: 408 E Harris St Cadillac MI 49601 Office: 109 N Mitchell St Cadillac MI 49601

BROWN, MABEL ESTLE, retired educator; b. Muscatine County, Iowa, Oct. 6, 1907; d. Chester Millar and Mayme (Bell) Estle; m. Robert G. Brown, Dec. 30, 1931; children—Patricia Jane Brown Hoback, Linnaeus Estle. B.A., U. Iowa, 1929; M.S., Iowa State U., 1953. Cert. secondary tchr., guidance counselor, sch. librarian, Iowa. High sch. tchr., Conesville, Iowa, 1930-32, 42-48, Nichols, Iowa, 1949-50; grad. asst. journalism Iowa State U., Ames, 1950-53; tchr., librarian Lone Tree High Sch., (Iowa), 1953-60, guidance counselor, 1960-70; chmn. Carrie Stanley Scholarship Com., Lone Tree, 1962-70. Author: The Fork of the Rivers: History Is People, 1978. Chmn., Muscatine County Farm Bur. Women, Muscatine, Iowa, 1938-42; judge, clk. Twp. Election Com., Conesville, 1970—. Mem. NEA (life), Iowa Edn. Soc. (life), ALA, Iowa Acad. Sci., Theta Sigma Phi. Republican. Home: Rural Route Conesville IA 52739

BROWN, MALCOLM HAMRICK, musicology educator; b. Carrollton, Ga., Nov. 9, 1929; s. Ralph Sebastian and Gertrude (Hamrick) B.; m. Shirley Anne Wood, July 5, 1952; children—Shirley Dollens, Jeannette Tarleton. B.Mus., Converse Coll., Spartanburg, S.C., 1951; M.Mus., U. Mich., 1956; Ph.D., Fla. State U., 1967. Head div. piano Mt. Union Coll., Alliance, Ohio, 1956-59; lectr. in music Ind. U., Bloomington, 1962-67, assoc. prof., 1967-76, prof., 1976—, chmn. musicology, 1972-79, 85—. Series editor: Russian Music Studies, 1981—; editor: Musorgsky: In Memoriam 1881-1981, 1982; Russian & Soviet Music: Essays for Boris Schwarz, 1984; Slavonic & European Music: Essays for Gerald Abraham, 1984. Contbr. articles to profl. jours. Participant in profl. confs. Ford Found. fellow, 1961-62; Rockefeller Found. grantee, 1969-70; Lilly Endowment fellow, 1981-82; Am. Council Learned Socs. fellow, 1969-70, 82. Mem. Am. Musicological Soc. (council 1981-83), Am. Assn. Advancement Slavic Studies (editorial bd. 1982—). Avocations: tennis, jogging. Home: 6701 E Bender Rd Bloomington IN 47401 Office: Ind U Sch Music Bloomington IN 47405

BROWN, MARVIN, advertising executive; b. Boston, Mar. 17, 1926; s. Frank A. and Frances (Caplan) B.; student Cornell U., 1943-44, U. Mo., 1946-49; B.J., N.Y. U., 1955; m. Constance Ruth Kaminsky, Sept. 5, 1948; children—Valerie Kay, Mark Kenneth, Randall Craig. Reporter, asst. city editor Shreveport (La.) Times, 1949-53; pub. relations mgr. Glenn Mason Advt., Shreveport, 1953-54; advt. and pub. relations dir. Radio-TV Tng. Assn., N.Y.C., 1954-57; creative services mgr. Nationwide Ins. Cos., Columbus, Ohio, 1957-64; pub. Key Mag., Columbus, 1959—; pres. Marbro Advt., Inc., Columbus, 1965—; pub. Columbus Scene Mag., 1981—, Columbus Bride and Groom Mag., 1985—. Pres., Columbus Quincentennial Expn., 1970—; bd. dirs. Columbus Conv. and Visitors Bur., 1981—. Served with U.S. Army, 1944-46. Mem. Columbus Advt. Fedn. (pres. 1972-73), Columbus Area C. of C. (dir. 1972-73). Clubs: Columbus Athletic, Winding Hollow Country. Home: 180 S Harding Rd Columbus OH 43209 Office: 303 E Livingston Ave Columbus OH 43215

BROWN, MARY ANNE, state memorial curator; b. Chillicothe, Ohio, May 29, 1942; d. Floyd Arthur and Ann Rosalie (Weisenberger) B. B.A. in History, Ohio Dominican Coll., 1964; M.A. in Am. History, Ohio U., 1981. Teaching cert. Tchr. Bishop Flaget High Sch., Chillicothe, 1964-74; interpreter Adena State Meml., Chillicothe, summers 1959-76, curator, 1976—. Author site brochure Adena State Meml., articles on Adena. Bd. trustees, sec. bd. St. Margaret's Cemetery Assn., Chillicothe, 1984—; chmn. interim decoration portion ch. renovation project, 1983—; active local sewer issues; bd. trustees Chillicothe-Ross Vis. and Conv. Bur., 1983—; mem. planning com. Bicentennial of Northwest Territory, 1985—. Summer fellow, Winterthur/U. Del., Newark, 1967. Mem. Ross County Hist. Soc., Jefferson County Hist. Soc. (W.Va.), Ross County Geneal. Soc., Berkeley County Hist. Soc. (W.Va.), Chillicothe C. of C. (recreational devel. com. 1980—). Avocation: Research genealogy of Worthington family of Adena and other locations. Home: 636 Cherokee Rd Chillicothe OH 45601 Office: Adena State Memorial Ohio Historical Soc PO Box 831-A Chillicothe OH 45601

BROWN, MICHAEL JAMES, psychologist; b. Phila., Mar. 14, 1947; s. Richard Lynn and Gertrude May (McTamany) B.; B.A., Mich. State U., 1969, M.A., 1971, Ph.D., 1974; m. Susan Brady, Dec. 30, 1967, div. Nov. 21, 1983; children—Jennifer, Emily. Counselor, Lansing (Mich.) Boys Tng. Sch., 1968-71; psychologist Ingham Community Mental Health Center, Lansing, 1971-73; dir. tng. Tri-County Drug Treatment Programs, Lansing, 1973-74; dir. tng. Huron Valley Inst., Ann Arbor, Mich., 1974-81; dir. Spectrum

Psychol. Services, 1979—; adj. prof. Sch. Community Medicine, Mich. State U., 1972-73; lectr. Oakland U., Rochester, Mich., 1973-74; lectr. social work Mich. State U., 1974-75. Cert. psychol. examiner, cert. psychologist, cert. cons. psychologist, lic. psychologist, Mich. Mem. Am. Rehab. Counselors Assn. (mem. research com. 1972-73), Internat. Transactional Analysis Assn. (mem. sch. com. 1974-76, mem. tng. standards com. 1976-79, treas. 1979-81), Am. Psychol. Assn., Phi Beta Kappa, Phi Eta Sigma. Author: Psychodiagnosis in Brief, 1977; co-author (with Stanley Woollams and Kristyn Huige) Transactional Analysis in Brief, 1974; (with Taibi Kahler) NoTAtions: A Guide to Transactional Analysis Literature, 1977; (with Woollams) Transactional Analysis, 1978; TA: The Total Handbook of Transactional Analysis, 1979. Contbr. to Transactional Analysis jour. Office: Spectrum Psychol Services 2046 Washtenaw Ypsilanti MI

BROWN, MICHAEL JOE, educational administrator, musician, real estate agent; b. Galesburg, Ill., Jan. 26, 1941; s. Harold A. and Vivian I. (Spilman) B.; m. Mary Jane Youngblood, Mar. 21, 1964; Marcia Jo, Mark Joseph. B.S., Western Ill. U., 1964; M.A., Bradley U., 1969. Cert. elem. tchr., Ill. Tchr., Yates City Schs., Ill., 1963-64, Lewistown Sch. Dist. 141, Ill., 1964-78; prin. Beardstown Jr. High Sch., Ill., 1978—. Author: Computer Programs-The Data Compiler, 1984; Computer Programs for School Principals, 1984. Mus. dir. Community Chorus, Beardstown, 1980. Mem. Nat. Assn. Elem. Prins., Ill. Prins. Assn. (pub. relations com. 1980-81), Beardstown Prins. Assn. (pres. 1983—), Phi Delta Kappa, Phi Mu Alpha. Lodge: Rotary (pres. Beardstown club 1983). Avocations: Music; golf; computers. Home: Rural Route 1 Box 173 Beardstown IL 62618 Office: Beardstown Jr High Sch 200 E 15th St Beardstown IL 62618

BROWN, MONTAGUE, health care consultant, lawyer; b. Whitmire, S.C., Sept. 14, 1931; s. Barney and Minnie (Vaughn) B.; m. Janet Pearson, Dec. 27, 1957 (div. Feb. 1974); children—Julia, Helene, Laura; m. Barbara P. McCool, Aug. 16, 1974. A.B., U. Chgo., 1959, M.B.A., 1960; Dr.P.H., U. N.C., 1972, J.D., 1981. Bars: D.C. 1981, Kans. 1982. Assoc. prof. health adminstrn./urban affairs, dir. studies in hosp. and health services adminstrn. Northwestern U., Evanston, Ill., 1971-75; prof. dept. health adminstrn. Duke U., Durham, N.C., 1975-80; sole practice, Shawnee Mission, Kans., 1982—; pres. Strategic Mgmt. Services, Inc., Shawnee Mission, 1982—. Author: (with others) Hospital Management Systems: Multi-Unit Organization and Delivery of Health Care, 1976; Management Response: Conceptual Human and Technical Skills of Management, 1977; Multihospital Systems: Strategies for Organization and Management, 1979; Strategy Planning in Health Care Management, 1979. Editor Health Care Mgmt. Rev., 1976. Served to capt. USAFR, 1967. Recipient traineeship USPHS, 1973, 74, Dean Conley award Am. Coll. Hosp. Adminstrs., 1976, Alumni Leadership award U. N.C., 1984; scholar Ford Found., 1960-61; fellow W.K. Kellogg Found., 1961-62, Alfred P. Sloan Found., 1966, spl. research fellow Nat. Ctr. for Health Services Research and Devel., 1975-76. Fellow Am. Pub. Health Assn.; mem. Am. Hosp. Assn., Hosp. Adminstrs. Correspondence Club, Delta Omega (Theta chpt.). Office: Strategic Mgmt Services Inc 6803 W 64th St Shawnee Mission KS 66202

BROWN, NORMAN STEPHEN, artist; b. Chgo., June 21, 1912; s. Norman Charles and Anna (Kirchner) B.; student Art Inst. Chgo., Comml. Art Inst., Chgo., DePaul U.; m. Helen M. Schilf, May 4, 1938 (dec.); children—Mary Ellen, Norman Stephen, Michael, Mark, Edward. Portraits include: Pope Pius XII, Samuel Cardinal Stritch, George Cardinal Meyer, Gov. Dan Walker of Ill., Robert F. Joyce, bishop of Burlington, Vt.; World War II Meml., 103d Gen. Hosp. AUS, Burlington. Served with AUS, 1943-46. Recipient medal U.S. Flag Assn. Mem. Artists Guild Chgo., Palette & Chisel Acad., Chgo. Municipal Art League. Home: PO Box 106 Deerfield IL 60015 Studio: 1012 Dearborn St N Chicago IL 60610

BROWN, ORIL IRENE, psychologist; b. Maumee, Ohio, Sept. 16, 1908; d. Edwin J. and L. Irene (Remelsbecker) Brown; student U. Toledo, 1926-28; B.S. cum laude, Northwestern U., 1930; M.A., George Washington U., 1951, Ph.D., 1965. Asst., Medill Sch. Journalism, Northwestern U., 1930-36; copyreader European edit. N.Y. Herald-Tribune, Paris, France, 1936-37; editorial work, free-lance writing, Chgo., 1930-36, 37-42; asst. editor Fgn. Broadcast Intelligence Service, Washington, 1942-51; research asst. Human Resources Research Office, Washington, 1952-53; pub. sch. psychologist, Portsmouth, Va., 1953-54; staff psychologist N.D. State Hosp., Jamestown, 1955-57; instr. psychiatry Med. Coll. of Va., 1957-60; staff psychologist Danville (Pa.) State Hosp., 1960-64; staff psychologist Mental Hygiene Clinic, Toledo, 1964, acting chief psychologist, 1965-68, psychologist dir. I, 1968-70, psychologist dir. II, 1970-77; pvt. practice psychology, Toledo, 1977—. Mem. LWV (dir. 1966-67), Am., Ohio, Midwestern, Southeastern psychol. assns., AAUW (dir. 1973-75), Ohio Hist. Soc., Maumee Valley Hist. Soc., ACLU, Alliance Française, Sigma Xi. Episcopalian. Contbr. articles to profl. jours. Home: 2270 Townley Rd Toledo OH 43614 Office: 2500 W Central Ave Toledo OH 43606

BROWN, PATRICIA JANE, tire company executive; b. Bluffton, Ohio, June 24, 1948; d. James Cletus Cornely and Mary Jeanne (Farrell) C.; m. Jack Eugene Brown, Jan. 24, 1967; children—Douglas Eugene, Jennifer Lynne. A.A. in Mgmt., Findlay Coll., 1983, B.A. in Mktg., 1985. Sales Analyst Cooper Tire & Rubber Co., Findlay, Ohio, 1968-69, sales analysis supr., 1969-77, Supr. advt. and mktg. services, 1977-78, asst. advt. mgr., 1979—. Mem. United Way (Speakers Bureau, 1979-80, Budget & Admissions Com. 1979-81), Hancock County, Ohio, Liberty-Benton Bd. of Edn. (pres. 1982, 83, 85), Hancock County. Mem. Toledo Advt. Club. Republican. Clubs: Liberty-Benton Athletic Boosters, Liberty-Benton Parent, Tchrs. Org. Home: 300 N Infirmary Rd Findlay OH 45840 Office: Cooper Tire & Rubber Co Lima & Western Ave Findlay OH 45840

BROWN, PATRICIA LYNN, information scientist, laboratory executive; b. Lafayette, La., Oct. 1, 1928; d. William Madison and Maude Juanita (Thomas) Brown; B.S. in Chem. Engring., U. Southwestern La., 1947; M.A. in Chemistry, U. Tex., 1949. Instr. analytical chemistry Smith Coll., Northampton, Mass., 1949-50; chemist R&M Labs., Peabody, Mass., 1950; research asso. indsl. toxicology Albany (N.Y.) Med. Coll., 1950-51; mem. info. services staff Ethyl Corp., Ferndale, Mich., 1951-55; sr. tech. writer, editor, staff engr. Westinghouse Atomic Power Div., Pitts., 1955-57; supr., then mgr. info. services, tech. info. cons. Tex. Instruments, Dallas, 1957-66; sr. info. scientist, sr. researcher Battelle Columbus (Ohio) Labs., 1966-76; mgr. sci. services, assoc. dir., info. counselor Travenol Labs., Morton Grove, Ill., 1976—. Loaned exec. United Way Campaign, 1972, 73. Bd. dirs. Engring. Socs. Library, 1961-63, 66-71. Mem. Soc. Women Engrs. (pres. 1961-63), Am. Chem. Soc., Spl. Libraries Assn., Am. Soc. Info. Sci., Soc. Tech. Communication. Author publs. in field. Home: 1109 Skylark Dr Palatine IL 60067 Office: 6301 Lincoln Ave Morton Grove IL 60053

BROWN, PAUL, football executive; b. Norwalk, Ohio, July 9, 1908; ed. Ohio State U., Miami U. (Ohio). Coach, Severn (Md.) Prep. Sch., 1930-32; coach football and basketball Massillon (Ohio) High Sch., 1932-41; coach Ohio State U., Columbus, 1941-43, Great Lakes Coll., 1944-45; coach profl. football team Cleve. Browns, 1946-62; coach Cin. Bengals, 1968-76, v.p., gen. mgr., 1976—. Office: care Cincinnati Bengals 200 Riverfront Stadium Cincinnati OH 45202*

BROWN, PAUL EARNEST, college official and dean, minister; b. Paragould, Ark., Oct. 19, 1931; s. Henry Silas and Lora Mae (Shettles) B.; m. Cornelia Smith, June 6, 1956; children—Lynn, Mark, Dan, Beth. B.A., Miss. Coll., 1953; B.D. New Orleans Bapt. Theol. Sem., 1956, Th.M., 1972; M.A., U. Miss., 1972, Ph.D., 1974. Pastor Kilmichael Bapt. Ch., Miss., 1956-59, Oakhaven Bapt. Ch., Memphis, 1959-68; admissions rep. Union U., Jackson, Tenn., 1968-70; instr. bible and art, chmn. div. langs. and arts Clarke Coll., Newton, Miss., 1970-76; exec. v.p., acad. dean Hannibal-LaGrange Coll., Mo., 1976—. Pres. Bd. Ministerial Edn., Miss., 1974-76; mem. Hannibal Hist. Commn., 1982—. Lodge: Rotary. Avocations: jogging; reading. Office: Hannibal-LaGrange Coll Hannibal MO 63401

BROWN, PHILIP KIMBLE, business executive; b. Lorain, Ohio, Nov. 27, 1937; s. Harold August and Hildred Opal (Jones) B.; A.B. in Sociology, Coll. of Wooster, Ohio, 1957; postgrad U. Mich., 1962, (U.S. Dept. Agr. scholar) Nat. Rural Devel. Leaders Sch., Cin., 1976; m. Deborah Ann Manning, Sept. 7, 1976; 1 son, Derek Nolan; children by previous marriage—Philip Kimble Dane, Stuart Kipling Zane. Mgmt. trainee United Parcel Service, Cleve., 1957-59; mgr. Montgomery Ward, Cin., 1959-61; case worker Lucas County (Ohio) Child Welfare Bd., Toledo, 1961-63; owner, operator farm, Warsaw, Ohio, 1963—; owner, operator Warsaw (Ohio) Milling Co., 1967-75; manpower adminstr. Kno-Ho-Co, Warsaw, 1969-75, exec. dir., 1975—; pres. Muskingum Coach Co., 1981—; pres. Insulation Supply Co., Mt. Vernon, Ohio, 1983—; dir. Corp. for Ohio Appalachian Devel. Bd. dirs. Area Six Health Planning Systems Agy., Marietta, Ohio, 1977. Recipient Govs. award for community action, 1975. Mem. Nat. Assn. Transp. Disadvantaged, Ohio Assn. Community Action Agys. (trustee 1975—), Nat. Assn. R.R. Passengers, Am. Motorcycle Assn. Home: 53192 TR 170 Fresno OH 43824 Office: Rural Route 3 Warsaw OH 43844

BROWN, PHILIP ROBERT, cable television company manager-technician; b. Arkansas City, Kans., Feb. 24, 1953; s. Earle Berkley and Muriel Doris (Woolger) B.; m. Carol Wain Hesket, Dec. 7, 1973; children—Janelle, Evan, Ethan. Student Cowley County Community Coll., 1971-73. Installer, technician Cowley Cablevision, Winfield, Kans., 1973-78; mgr. technician Sumner Cable TV, Wellington, Kans., 1978—. Bd. dirs. Kansas Cable TV Assn., Junction City, 1982—. Baptist. Avocations: amateur radio, photography. Home: 421 N Poplar Wellington KS 67152 Office: Sumner Cable TV 117 W Harvey Wellington KS 67152

BROWN, PHILLIP HERBERT, history educator; b. Chgo., Sept. 3, 1952; s. Phillip Herbert Brown and Louise Alice (Chilton) Brown Johnson; m. Wanda Faye Pitts, Mar. 27, 1976. B.A., U. Ill.-Chgo., 1977. Mgr. Chgo. Tribune Newspaper, 1977; instr. Roosevelt U., Chgo., 1977-79; case mgr. Methodist Youth Services, Chgo., 1979-82; instr. Columbia Coll., Chgo., 1984—. Patentee appliances. Counselor, dep. registrar Mayor's Polit. Edn. Project, Chgo., 1984-85; active Inventor's Council, Chgo., 1985—. Democrat. Methodist. Avocations: chess; reading; swimming; basketball; nautilus. Home: 6811 S Claremont Chicago IL 60636

BROWN, RALPHAEL LANGSTON, chemical company executive, accountant; b. Winston-Salem, N.C., Sept. 1, 1942; s. Warner Baxter and Annie (Davis) B. m. Elsie Nash, Sept. 5, 1963; children—Ralphael, Reuben Lemar. B.S. acctg., N.C. A&T State U., 1973; M.B.A., Ala. A&M State U., 1977. Prod. line acct. Honeywell, Inc., Mpls., 1973-75; supr. project acct. Monsanto Co., St. Louis, 1975-78, various controller positions, 1978-81, supr. internat. audit, 1981-84, mgr. planning, 1984—. Chmn. fiscal com. United Way, Greater St. Louis, 1981—, cons. Jr. Achievement, 1984. Grantee Am. Inst. C.P.A.s. Mem. Nat. Assn. Accts., Assn. M.B.A. Execs., Inst. Internal Auditors, Am. Mgmt. Assn., Kappa Alpha Mu, Kappa Alpha Psi (treas. 1979-81). Lodges: Masons, Shriners. Avocations: golf; tennis; bowling. Home: 793 Amolac Dr Creve Coeur MO 63141

BROWN, RICHARD EUGENE, accounting educator, consultant; b. Little Falls, N.Y., June 30, 1937; s. Edward Stanislaus Brown and Mary Elizabeth (Metz) Brown Lynch; A.B. (Coll. scholar), Hope Coll., 1959; M.P.A. (Mich. Fellow), U. Mich., 1960; D.P.A. (Littauer Fellow), Harvard U., 1968; m. Beverly Ann Shaffer, Feb. 25, 1961; children—Kelly Christine, Christopher Richard, Kirsten Marie. With TVA, Knoxville, 1961-69, asst. to gen. mgr., 1967-69; dir. audit ops. Legis. Commn. on Expenditure Rev., Albany, N.Y., 1970-75; state auditor Kans. Legislature, Topeka, 1975-83; prof. non-profit acctg. Kent State U., 1983—; spl. cons. Price Waterhouse, 1983—; prof. or adj. prof. fin. and adminstrn. William and Mary Coll., U. Kans., U. Tenn., Kans. State U., SUNY, Albany; cons. GAO, various state legislatures. Scoutmaster, Boy Scouts Am. Mem. Am. Soc. Public Adminstrn. (chmn. mgmt. sci. sect.), Nat. Conf. State Legislatures (exec. com.), Public Adminstrn. Soc. (pres. Topeka), Am. Inst. C.P.A.s (task force on operational auditing). Author: The GAO; Untapped Source of Congl. Power, 1970; editor: The Effectiveness of Legislative Program Review, 1979; co-author: Auditing the Performance of Government; contbr. articles to profl. jours.; editorial bd. Govt. Accts. Jour., 1983—, Public Adminstrn. Rev., 1980-83; co-editor Public Budgeting and Finance. Home: 2373 Glenn Echo Dr Hudson OH 44236 Office: Coll Bus Adminstrn Kent State U Kent OH 44242

BROWN, RICHARD MURRAY, statistician; b. Plymouth, Mich., Mar. 7, 1943; s. Harold Richard and Flossie Lorenz (Rowland) B.; m. Diana Kay Ausbon, Aug. 15, 1969; children—Tammy, Candy, Kimberly, Richard, Jessica. Assoc., Wastenaw Community Coll., 1978; B.S., Eastern Mich. U., 1975. Cert. quality engr., quality technician. Quality technician Ford Motor Co., Ypsilanti, Mich., 1966-76, supr. mfg., 1976-77, exptl. quality technologist, Dearborn, Mich., 1977-83, design engr., 1982-83, statis. specialist, 1983-85; design assurance specialist Chrysler Corp., Highland Park, Mich., 1985—; instr. Wastenaw Community Coll., Ypsilanti, 1980—, advisor, 1981-84. Mem. Am. Soc. Quality Control (chmn. Ann Arbor sect. 1983-84), Am. Statis. Assn. Avocations: Toy trains; old cars. Home: 8705 Westchester Ln Canton MI 48187 Office: Chrysler Corp CIMS 417-39-02 PO Box 1118 Detroit MI 48288

BROWN, RICHARD OSBORNE, physician; b. Detroit, May 20, 1930; s. Richard Wells and Flossie Eva (Osborne) B.; B.A., Wayne State U., 1953; M.D., Howard U., 1959; m. Dolores Debro, Jan. 23, 1954; children—Richard Debro, Kevin Michael; m. 2d, Martha Evelyn McGregor, Oct. 6, 1973; children—Vincent, Tiffany Diane. Intern, Wayne County Gen. Hosp., 1959-60; resident ophthalmology Homer G. Phillips Hosp., St. Louis, 1962-65; staff ophthalmologist CHA-Met. Hosp., Detroit, 1965-67; practice medicine specializing in ophthalmology, Detroit, 1967—; chief med. staff Kirwood Gen. Hosp., 1974-76, now trustee, Cons., Met., SW Detroit, Lakeside, Kirwood, St. Joseph hosps. Mem. Draft Bd., 1971-76. Served with AUS, 1953-55. Mem. Am. Assn. Ophthalmology, Nat. Med. Assn. (2d v.p. 1981-83, 1st v.p. 1983—), AMA, Wayne County, Detroit (treas. 1972-78, pres. 1978-80), Mich. State med. socs., Detroit C. of C., Am. Profl. Practice Assn., Council Med. Staffs Mich. (dir. 1971—). Episcopalian. Home: 22854 Newport Southfield MI 48075 Office: 3800 Woodward St Detroit MI 48201

BROWN, RICHARD RALPH, lawyer, business and marketing educator; b. Tiffin, Ohio, Aug. 22, 1941; s. Ralph Clair and Freda Mae (Bacon) B.; m. Carolyn Sue Curlis, Aug. 22, 1964; children—Timothy Richard, Eric Lee. B.A., Heidelberg Coll., 1962; M.Ed., Bowling Green State U., 1964; J.D., Cleve. Marshall U., 1968; postgrad. Case Western Res. U., 1967, Ohio State U., 1980. Bar: Ohio 1968. Ptnr. Elyria & Findlay, Upper Sandusky, Ohio, 1968—; atty. Ameritrust (Cleve. Trust Co.), Cleve., 1969-72; sr. real estate atty., analyst Firestone, Akron, Ohio, 1972-75; v.p. trust officer Bancohio, Sandusky, 1975-76; assoc. prof. law Ohio No. U., Ada, 1976-79; adj. prof. Bowling Green State U., Ohio, 1979-82; instr. Marion Tech. Coll., Ohio, 1982—; dir. privately held corps., Upper Sandusky. Com. mem. Put-Han-Sen council Boy Scouts Am. Mem. Wyandot County Bar Assn., Ohio Bar Assn. Republican. Methodist. Home: 551 S Sandusky Ave Upper Sandusky OH 43351 Office: PO box 403 114 E Wyandot Ave Upper Sandusky OH 43351

BROWN, ROBERT ORDWAY, food products co. exec.; b. Tyler, Minn., July 31, 1917; s. Peter J. and Ella M. (Hansen) B.; B.Chem. Engring., U. Minn., 1939; m. Margrethe Frederiksen, June 12, 1943; children—Rolf, Linnea (Mrs. Lauren Berg), Karla, Paul, Grete. Sect. head. Pillsbury Mills, Mpls., 1939-56; cons. engr. Robert O. Brown Co., Mpls., 1956—. Mem. Am. Inst. Chem. Engrs., AAAS, Am. Assn. Cereal Chemists, N.Y. Acad. Scis., Inst. Food Technologists, ASHRAE, Am. Chem. Soc., Am. Soc. Cons. Engrs., Nat. Soc. Profl. Engrs., Assn. Energy Engrs. Home: 4500 Morningside Rd Minneapolis MN 55416 Office: 6885 Washington Ave S Suite 200 Edina MN 55435

BROWN, ROBERT S., bank executive executive. Chmn., pres., chief exec. officer, dir. First Savings Assn. of Wis., Milw. Office: First Savings Assn of Wis 700 N Water St Milwaukee WI 53202*

BROWN, ROBERT VENTON, government official; b. Oklahoma City, June 10, 1936; s. David L. and Grace A. B.; B.A. in Bus., U. Md., 1969; M.B.A., U. Utah, 1971; grad. Air Command and Staff Coll., 1972; sr. exec. fellow, Harvard U., 1980; student U. Okla., 1957-63; m. Barbara Lee Garrett, Sept. 1, 1957; children—Lee-Anita, Jennifer Lynne, Yvonne Kathleen, Denise Ladele. With maintenance and materiel mgmt. Air Force Logistics Command, Okla. and Calif., 1959-66; logistics staff U.S. Air Force Europe, Germany, 1966-71; chief tech. support sect. Inventory Mgmt. Div., Tex., 1972-77; chief product performance evaluation div. Air Force Acquisition Logistics div. Air Force Logistics Command, Wright-Patterson AFB, Ohio, 1977-78, dir. acquisition control Air Force dep. for avionics control, 1978-81, asst. to comdr., 1981; mem. Fed. Sr. Exec. Service; instr. logistics Our Lady of the Lake U., San Antonio, 1973-77; part-time faculty local colls. Safety com. PTA; adv. bd. Order of Rainbow for Girls; booster High Sch. Math. and Sci. Club; advisor 4-H Clubs Am. Served with USN, 1954-57. Mem. Soc. Logistics Engrs. (ednl. chmn. Tex. 1975-76), Am. Def. Preparedness Assn., Air Force Assn., Assn. of Grads. Air Force Inst. Tech. (charter). Clubs: VFW, Masons, Scottish Rite, Shrine. Contbr. papers to profl. seminars and symposia. Office: HQ AFALC/CA Wright-Patterson AFB OH 45433

BROWN, (ROBERT) WENDELL, lawyer; b. Mpls., Feb. 26, 1902; s. Robert and Jane Amanda (Anderson) B.; A.B., U. Hawaii, 1924; J.D., U. Mich., 1926; m. Barbara Ann Fisher, Oct. 20, 1934; children—Barbara Ann (Mrs. Neil Maurice Travis), Mary Alice (Mrs. Alfred Lee Fletcher). Admitted to Mich. bar, 1926; Supreme Ct. Mich., U.S. Supreme Ct., 6th U.S. Circuit Ct. of Appeals, U.S. Dist. Ct., Eastern and Western Dists. Mich., U.S. Bd. Immigration Appeals, U.S. Tax Ct.; lawyer firm Routier, Nichols & Fildew, Detroit, 1926, Nichols & Fildew, 1927-28, Frank C. Sibley, 1929, Ferguson & Ferguson, 1929-31; asst. atty. gen. Mich., 1931-32; with legal dept. Union Guardian Trust Co., Detroit, 1933-34; sole practice law, Detroit, 1934-81, Farmington Hills, Mich., 1981—. Legal adviser Wayne County (Mich.) Graft Grand Jury, 1939-40; asst. pros. atty. civil matters Wayne County, 1940; spl. asst. city atty. to investigate Police Dept. Highland Park, Mich., 1951-52; pres. Detroit Bar Assn., 1948-49. Chmn. citizens com. to form Oakland County (Mich.) Community Coll., 1962-63. Pres. Farmington (Mich.) Sch. Bd., 1952-56; chmn. Oakland County Republican County Conv., 1952; trustee Farmington Twp., Oakland County, 1957-61; pres. Oakland County Lincoln Rep. Club, 1958. Treas., bd. dirs. Friends of Detroit Library, 1943-44; bd. dirs. Farmington Friends of Library, Inc., 1952-58, pres., 1956-57. Hon. mem. Farmington Hist. Soc., 1966, St. Anthonys Guild, Franciscan Friars, 1975. Mem. ABA, State Bar Mich. (chmn. or mem. various coms. 1935-72), Oakland County Bar Assn. (life). Presbyn. (elder). Home: 29921 Ardmore St Farmington Hills MI 48018 Office: 32969 Hamilton Ct Farmington Hills MI 48018

BROWN, ROGER TRUMAN, veterinarian; b. Slater, Iowa, Sept. 2, 1938; s. Truman Mark and Ruth Theressa (Olson) B.; D.V.M., Iowa State U., 1963; m. Nancy Lee Dunham, Dec. 29, 1961. Gen. practice veterinary medicine, Bethesda, Md., 1965-70, Omaha, 1970—; owner Bel Air Animal Clinic, Omaha, 1970—; chmn. bd. dirs., veterinary practice cons. Ancom, Inc.; chmn. bd. dirs. Ornamental Fish Industries, Cartel, Inc., Filing Systems Design, Inc. Served with Veterinary Corps, U.S. Army, 1963-65. Mem. Am., Nebr. veterinary med. assns., Am. Animal Hosp. Assn., Nebr. Acad. Veterinary Medicine, Am. Maltese Assn., Nebr. Kennel Club, Internat. Platform Assn., Kappa Sigma. Republican. Lutheran. Co-author monthly syndicated maltese column Popular Dogs mag., 1973-75, also audio-visual client edn. filmstrips. Home: 1417 S 136th St Omaha NE 68144 Office: 12100 West Center Rd Suite 600 Omaha NE 68144

BROWN, RONALD DEAN, electrical engineer, consultant; b. Mt. Pleasant, Iowa, Dec. 10, 1936; s. John Swiers and Frances Irene (Foster) B.; m. Roberta Lynne Rich, June 17, 1961; children—Barry, John, Maria. B.S. in E.E., U. Iowa, Iowa City, 1960. Registered profl. engr., Iowa, 10 other states. Engr. in tng. Stanley Cons., Muscatine, Iowa, 1960-64, engr., 1968-77, chief elec. engr., 1977—, vice pres., 1979—, dir. tech. staff, 1982—; systems engr. Western Ill. Power Coop, Jacksonville, 1964-68; mem. Iowa State Bd. Engring. Examiners, Des Moines, 1974-83; mem. Engring. accreditation Commn. Accreditation Bd. for Engring. and Tech., 1979-82. Named Engr. of the Yr. Quint Cities Joint Engring. Council, 1979. Mem. IEEE (Centennial medal 1984), Am. Soc. Engring. Edn., Iowa Engring. Soc. (chpt. pres. 1984-85), Nat. Soc. Profl. Engrs. Presbyterian. Avocations: amateur radio, travel, spectator sports. Office: Stanley Cons 225 Iowa Ave Muscatine IA 52761

BROWN, ROWINE HAYES, hospital administrator, physician, lawyer; b. Harvey, Ill., Feb. 15, 1913; d. Robert and Nancy Detrich (Steel) Hayes; m. William L. Brown Jr., June 12, 1943 (dec.). B.S., U. Ill.-Chgo., 1938, M.D., 1938, D.Sc. (hon.), 1975; J.D., Chgo. Kent Coll. Law, 1961. diplomate Am. Bd. Pediatrics. Bar: Ill. 1963. Asst. med. supt. Mcpl. Contagious Disease Hosp., Chgo., 1944-50; asst. med. supt., assoc. dir. pediatrics Cook County Hosp., Chgo., 1950-73, med. dir., 1973—. Contbr. articles to profl. jours. Bd. dirs. Womens Share Pub. Service; bd. dirs., sec. Chgo. Foundlings Home, 1972—. Named to Hall of Fame, Ill. Inst. Tech., 1984; named U. Ill. Coll. Medicine Alumnus of Yr., 1977; others. Mem. Womens Bar Assn. Ill. (pres. 1975), Chgo. Kent Coll. Law Alumni Assn. (pres. 1975-76), U. Ill. Alumni Assn. (bd. dirs. 1975—), Chgo. Bar Assn. Republican. Presbyterian. Clubs: Quadrangle, 500 (Chgo.). Avocations: collecting pushers and stamps; needlepoint; music. Home: 1700 E 56th St Chicago IL 60637 Office: Cook County Hosp 1825 W Harrison St Chicago IL 60612

BROWN, SHARON GAIL, data processing executive; b. Chgo., Dec. 25, 1941; d. Otto and Pauline (Lauer) Schumacher; B.G.S., Roosevelt U.; m. Robert B. Ringo, Aug. 2, 1984; 1 dau. by previous marriage, Susan Ann. Info. analyst Internat. Minerals & Chems., Northbrook, Ill., 1966-71, programmer analyst, 1971-74; programmer analyst Procon Internat. Inc. subs. UOP Inc., Des Plaines, Ill., 1974-76, systems analyst, 1976-77, project leader, 1977-78; mgr. adminstrv. services, 1978-82; spl. cons. to pres. IPS Internat., Ltd., 1982-83; spl. cons. to pres. CEI Supply Co. div. Sigma-Chapman, Inc., 1984—; data processing cons. Mem. Buffalo Grove (Ill.) Youth Commn., 1978-82; mem. adv. com. UOP Polit. Action Com., 1979-82; Mem. Rep. Senatorial Com. Inner Circle. Mem. Am. Mgmt. Assn., Chgo. Council on Fgn. Relations, Lake Forest-Lake Bluff Hist. Soc. Home: 1381 N Lake Rd Lake Forest IL 60045

BROWN, SHERROD CAMPBELL, state official; b. Mansfield, Ohio, Nov. 9, 1952; s. Charles G. and Emily (Campbell) B.; m. Larke Ummel, 1979; children—Emily, Elizabeth. B.A., Yale U., 1974; M.A., Ohio State U., 1979, 81. Mem. Ohio Ho. of Reps., 1975-82; sec. of state State of Ohio, 1983—. Mem. Ohio Democratic Central Com., 1976—. Recipient Outstanding Chief Elections Officer award Midwest Voter Registration Edn. Project, 1984. Presbyterian.

BROWN, SORREL (MARTHA), agronomist; b. Frankfurt, Germany, Nov. 5, 1949; parents U.S. citizens; d. Arthur William and Luisa Margarita (Badaracco) B.; student Tex. Christian U., 1967-69, U. Tex., Austin, 1969-70; B.S. in Psychology, Ariz. State U., 1972, M.S. in Soil Sci., 1977. Plant pathologist Ariz. Public Service Utilities Co., Phoenix, 1976, 77; field agronomist Chevron Chem. Co., Des Moines, 1977-80; crop prodn. specialist Iowa State U. Extension, Des Moines, 1980—; speaker in field. Mem. Iowa Sister-State Friendship Com.; v.p. Iowa-Yucatan Ptnrs. of Am. Recipient McVickar Agronomy Achievement award Chevron Chem. Co., 1978; Sarah Tyson Bradley Meml. fellow, 1973-74; Laura M. Bohem Found. scholar, 1974-75. Mem. Am. Soc. Agronomy, Soil Sci. Soc. Am., Nat. Assn. County Agrl. Agts. (Career Guidance award 1981), Alpha Zeta. Home: 2806 Adams Des Moines IA 50310 Office: 109 W Winds 1454 30th St West Des Moines IA 50265

BROWN, SPENCER HUNTER, historian, educator; b. Knoxville, Tenn., June 10, 1928; s. John Orville and Edith Frances (Hunter) B.; B.A. in Teaching Social Studies magna cum laude, U. Ill., 1954, M.A. in History (fellow), 1955; Ph.D. in History (African studies fellow), Northwestern U., 1964; m. Doris Lucille Craig, Aug. 4, 1951; 1 dau., Rebecca Lee. Tchr., then tchr./chmn. social scis. dept. Carl Sandburg High Sch., Orland Park, Ill., 1955-59; mem. faculty Western Ill. U., Macomb, 1962—, prof. history, 1971—, chmn. dept., 1976-84. Served with USNR, 1945-47. Ford Found. fellow, 1961-62. Mem. African Studies Assn., Am. Hist. Assn., AAUP, Phi Beta Kappa. Gen. editor Jour. Developing Areas, 1965-76, bus. mgr., 1976—, assoc. editor, 1984—. Home: Box 47 Tennessee IL 62374 Office: Dept History Western Ill Univ Macomb IL 61455

BROWN, STEVEN DOUGLAS, psychologist; b. Troy, Ohio, Feb. 17, 1947; s. Irvin Russell and Elma Mae (Lamka) B.; m. Linda Heath, 1985. B.A., Muskingum Coll., 1969; M.A., U. Va., 1972; Ph.D., U. Calif., Santa Barbara, 1977. Psychologist, Central State Hosp., Petersburg, Va., 1971-73; mental health cons. San Mateo County (Calif.) Mental Health Services, San Mateo, 1973-74; cons. drug abuse program Fed. Correctional Instn., Lompoc, Calif., 1976-77; fellow dept. psychiatry U. Wis., Madison, 1977-78; dir. counseling psychology clinic, counseling psychology program U. Calif., Santa Barbara, 1978-79; asst. prof. psychology U. Minn., Mpls., 1979-84; assoc. prof. counseling psychology and higher edn. Loyola U. Chgo., 1984—; cons. in field. Cora I. Orr fellow, 1968-69. Mem. Am. Psychol. Assn., Am. Personnel and Guidance Assn., Assn. for Advancement of Behavior Therapy, N.Y. Acad.

Scis., Sigma Xi, Psi Chi, Phi Sigma, Kappa Delta Pi. Home: 1415 Lincoln St Evanston IL 60626 Office: Dept Counseling Psychology and Higher Edn Loyola U 820 N Michigan Ave Chicago IL 60611

BROWN, STEVEN RAY, insurance executive; b. Cedar Rapids, Iowa, June 27, 1946; s. Charles Gabriel and Nina Wilson) B.; m. Cynthia Joyce Corless, Jan. 31, 1969; children—Rebecca Ellen, Jeffrey Tyler. B.B.A., U. Iowa, 1968, postgrad., 1968-69. CPCU. Agt., Charles Brown Inc., Oskaloosa, 1972-77; pres. Brown Ins. Services, Oskaloosa, 1977—. Pres., Oskaloosa Indsl. Devel. Bd., 1983-84; chmn. Oskaloosa Public Housing Authority, 1982-83; chmn. Mahaska County Red Cross, 1977-79; chmn. Oskaloosa Civil Service Commn., 1974-77. Mem. Ind. Ins. Agts. Iowa (dist. bd dirs. 1974-75, young agt. of yr. 1977-78); Ind. Ins. Agts. Mahaska County (pres. 1975, 76, 79, 80, 83—), Profl. Ins. Agts. Iowa., Mahaska Amateur Radio Club (sec. treas. 1984—). Republican. Episcopalian. Lodge: Kiwanis (pres. 1982-83). Avocations: amateur radio; photography; railroad enthusiast. Home: 602 N Park Ave PO Box 1088 Oskaloosa IA 52577 Office: Brown Ins Services Inc 212 1st Ave E PO Box 1088 Oskaloosa IA 52577

BROWN, SUZANNE WILEY, mus. exec.; b. Cheyenne, Wyo., Aug. 28, 1938; d. Robert James and Catharine Helen (Schroeder) Wiley; B.S. with honors, U. Wyo., 1960, M.S., 1964; postgrad. U. Cin. Med. Sch., 1965-66, U. Ill., 1969-72; m. Ralph E. Brown, July 19, 1968; 1 dau., Nina M. Research asst. Harvard Med. Sch., 1962-63; research asst. U. Cin. Med. Sch., 1964-65; sr. lab. asst. U. Chgo., 1966-67; research assoc. U. Colo. Med. Sch., 1968; teaching asst. U. Ill., 1971-73; exec. asst. Chgo. Acad. Scis., 1974-82, asst. dir., 1982—. NDEA fellow, 1960-62. Mem. Mus. Educators of Greater Chgo., Am. Assn. Museums, Internat. Council Museums, Brookfield Zool. Soc. (bd. govs.), Pub. Relations in Service to Muslims, Midwest Mus. Conf., Phi Beta Kappa, Sigma Xi, Phi Kappa Phi. Office: 2001 N Clark St Chicago IL 60614

BROWN, THOMAS FRANCIS, village official; b. Cicero, Ill., Feb. 3, 1923; s. Thomas Francis and Mary Gertrude (McCartin) B.; Ph.B., Loyola U., Chgo., 1947; m. Helen Irene Sauer, June 10, 1944; children—Helen Anne, Thomas Francis, Joachim, Christine, Kathleen, Beth, Timothy, Martin, John. Personnel counselor Western Electric, Chgo., 1947-52; pres. T.F. Brown Co., Chgo., 1952—; trustee Village of LaGrange, Ill., 1966-73, chmn. police and fire com., 1966-73, village pres., 19—; chmn. bd. T.F. Brown Co., 1976. Trustee Plumbers Pension Fund, 1970—; chmn. Selective Service Bd. #111, Ill., 1967-74. Served to lt., USAAF, 1943-46. Decorated D.F.C., Purple Heart, Air Medal with two oak leaf clusters. Recipient distinguished citation, Father of Year award, 1966. Mem. Chgo., Ill., Nat. plumbing contractors assns., W. Central Assn. Chgo., Cook County Community Devel. advisory bd., Cook County Council Govts. (exec. bd.). Roman Catholic. Clubs: Executive of Chgo., K.C., Serra Internat. Author: To Thine Own Self Be True, 1960. Home: 101 N Catherine Ave LaGrange IL 60525 Office: 1345 W Washington Blvd Chicago IL 60607

BROWN, VIRGIL ENNIS, county official, insurance agent; b. Louisville, Aug. 12, 1920; s. George Ennis and Sarah (Neighbors) B.; m. Lurtissia D. Spencer; children—Veretta Brown Garrison, Virgil E., Jr. Student Fenn Coll. (now Cleve. State U.), 1947-49. Supr., Wolf Envelope Co., Cleve., 1942-59; owner, operator Firestone Tire franchise, Cleve., 1959-61; owner, prin. Virgil E. Brown Ins. Agy., Cleve., 1961—; councilman City of Cleve., 1967-72; dir. Bd. Elections, Cuyahoga County, Cleve., 1972-79, county commr., 1979—; mem. adv. bd. St. Lawrence Seaway Devel. Corp., Washington, 1984—; dir. Nat. Assn. Counties, Washington, 1979—, County Commr. Assn. Ohio, 1979—, Northeast Ohio Areawide Coordinating Agy., Cleve., 1979—. Vice chmn., mem. exec. com. Cuyahoga County Republican Orgn., Cleve.; pub. service sector chmn. United Way Campaign, Cleve., 1983, 84; bd. dirs. Rose-Mary Home for Crippled Children, Cleve., 1975—. Recipient Cert. Nat. Recognition HUD, 1983; recognized for Contbns. to County Citizens Assn. Black Social Workers, Cleve., 1983; Outstanding Merit/County Leadership award Cuyahoga Community Coll., 1982; various citations, awards Kiwanis, Rotary, Cleve., 1967—. Mem. Ind. Ins. Agts. Lodge: Mason. Office: Bd of Cuyahoga County Commrs 1219 Ontario St Cleveland OH 44113

BROWN, VIRGINIA, system program manager; b. Knippa, Tex., Nov. 13, 1933; d. Ralph and Hedwig Deely; stepfather James L. Stevenson; m. Larry Foster Keith, Nov. 30, 1957 (div. 1965); children—William Scott, Joyce Marie, Bradford Jay, Keith Brown; m. James Clarence Brown, June 25, 1965 (div. 1979). Clk., Ft. Sam Houston, Tex., 1951-58, Kelly AFB, Tex., 1964-67; clk. Aero. Systems div. Wright-Patterson AFB, Ohio, 1973-74, chief adminstrv. orders, 1974-76, program analyst Avionics Lab. Air Force Wright Aeronaut. Labs., 1976-81, program analyst Directorate Aircraft Modification, 4950th Test Wing, 1981-83; fin. specialist Aero. Systems div. Wright-Patterson AFB, Ohio, 1983-84. Mem. Am. Soc. Mil. Comptrollers, Engring. Mgmt. Soc. (exec. com.), Am. Bus. Women's Assn. Lutheran. Home: 4360 Pinecastle Ct Dayton OH 45424 Office: Wright Patterson AFB OH 45433

BROWN, VIVIAN KEYS, elementary school administrator; b. Wisner, La., Nov. 24, 1946; d. Eugene and Ethel (Neal) Keys; m. Willie Brown, Sept. 4, 1982. B.S., Grambling State U., 1968; M.A., Central Mich. U., 1975; student U. Mich., 1980. Tchr., Franklin Parish Schs., Winnsboro, La., 1968-72; tchr. Buena Vista Pub. Schs., Saginaw, Mich., 1972-77, sch. adminstr., 1977—, dir. spl. programs, student personnel, 1977—. Mem. NAACP, Mich. Assn. State and Fed. Program Specialists, Assn. for Supervision and Curriculum Devel., Mich. Reading Assn., Buena Vista Adminstrs. Assn. (v.p.), Delta Sigma Theta. Home: 4672 S Gregory Pl Saginaw MI 48601 Office: 705 N Towerline Rd Saginaw MI 48601

BROWN, WAYNE ALLAN, maintenance/construction executive; b. Oklahoma City, Okla., May 15, 1945; s. William J. and Mary Jean (Senft) B.; m. Elizabeth Ann Cowling, Aug. 1, 1975; children—Kristi, Michael, Donna. Student Tex. A. and M. U., 1964, Lee Coll., 1965. Gen supr. Min-Co., Inc., Texas City, Tex., 1978-80; constrn. coordinator Good Hope Refinery, La., 1980; mgr. spl. projects TCP, Inc., Good Hope, 1980-82; maintenance mgr. Aldev Maintenance, Inc., Destrehan, La., 1982-83; maintenance analyst, sr. constrn. engr. Fermi 2 Nuclear Power Plant, Bechtel, Monroe, Mich., 1983—. Served with USNR, 1968-74. Mem. Solar Energy Soc., Am. Nuclear Soc. Democrat. Episcopalian. Avocations: woodcarving; photography.

BROWN, WILLIAM BOYD, tax firm executive, educator; b. Sioux Falls, S.D., June 19, 1939; s. Leo and Florence (Mullen) B.; m. Annette McDonald, June 18, 1966; children—Brenda, Bridget, Elizabeth. B.S.B.A., State U. S.D., 1961; J.D., U. Minn., 1966. Bar: Minn. With Deliotte Haskins & Sells, N.Y.C., 1966-69, Mpls., 1969—, now ptnr. in charge taxes Minn. offices; mem. faculty U. Minn. Served to 1st lt. U.S. Army, 1961-63. Mem. Minn. Soc. C.P.A.s (ethics com.), Am. Inst. C.P.A.s, ABA, Minn. Bar Assn., Internat. Fiscal Assn., Minn. Assn. Commerce and Industry, Assn. Gen. Contractors, C.P.A. Tax Roundtable (former chmn.), Mpls. Aquatennial Assn., Citizens League, Hennepin County Bar Assn., Sigma Alpha Epsilon, Delta Theta Phi. Independent Republican. Clubs: Libbs Bay Boat (vice commodore); Mpls. Athletic, Interlachen Country. Address: 625 4th Ave S Suite 1000 Minneapolis MN 55415

BROWN, WILLIAM DARREL, mechanical engineer; b. Portland, Oreg., June 2, 1939; s. Charles Frank Lafollette and Mildred Caroline (Bredenbeck) B.; B.S. in M.E., Oreg. State U., 1961; M.S., U. Wash., 1970; m. Sharon Lee Hawley, July 14, 1961; children—Shannon, Ross, Robby. Project engr., Esco Inc., Portland, Oreg., 1961-62; prin. engr. Silver Eagle Co., Portland, 1963-64; design engr. Omark Industries Inc., Portland, 1965-66; mech. engr. Sandwell Intrnat., Inc., Portland, 1967-68; mech. engr. Pacific Rim Inc., Tacoma, Wash., part time 1968-70; mech. engr. Sargent & Lundy, Chgo., 1970-73; sr. nuclear engr. Fluor Pioneer Inc., Chgo., 1973-78; sr. mech. engr. Laramore Douglass and Popham, Cons. Engrs., Chgo., 1978-79; assoc. M.W. Brown & Assocs., Chgo., 1979-82; propr. Darrel Brown, Profl. Engr., 1983—; cons. Inst. Cultural Affairs. Mem. Village of Oak Park Econ. Devel. Com., 1973; co-founder Beye Neighborhood Council, Oak Park, 1973—; mem. Townmeeting Task Force, 1975-76. Mem. ASME, Am. Nuclear Soc. Democrat. Mem. First Ch. of Religious Science. Home: Box 893 Oak Park IL 60303

BROWN, WILLIAM EVERETT, chemical engineer; b. Auburn, N.Y., Nov. 9, 1927; s. Everett Lawton and Helen May (Rasmussen) B.; B.S., Syracuse U., 1951; m. Natalie Smith, Oct. 3, 1953; children—Matthew, Kevin, Paul, Lorraine, Rebecca. With Dow Chem. Co., Midland, Mich., 1951—, head testing sect., 1956-62, head performance and design, 1962-66, sr. sect. head automotive sect., 1967, new applications devel., 1967-70, tech. mgr. new ventures research and devel., 1970-74, research mgr. Saran and Converted Products research, 1974-80, sr. research mgr., 1980-83, sr. research mgr. plastics dept., 1983—. Chmn. planning com. Bay-Midland OEO, 1970-72; pres. Men of Music, Midland, 1979-80. Served with U.S. Army, 1946-47. Mem. ASTM, Inst. Food Technologists, Research and Devel. Assocs., Sigma Xi. Contbr. articles to profl. jours. Editor: Testing of Polymers, book series, 1965-70. Home: 4950 Grandview Circle Midland MI 48640 Office: Plastics Dept Dow Chemical USA Midland MI 48640

BROWN, WILLIAM MILTON, scientific administrator, educator; b. Wheeling, W.Va., Feb. 14, 1932; s. John David and Marjorie Jennie (Walter) B.; m. Norma Jean Hulett, Aug. 24, 1963; children—Cheryl Lynn, Mark William, Jennifer Christine. B.S. in Elec. Engring., W.Va. U., 1952, M.S., Johns Hopkins U., 1955, Dr. Eng., 1957. Engr., Air Arm div. Westinghouse ElectricCorp., Balt., 1952-54; lectr. Johns Hopkins U., Balt., 1954-57, project supr. radiation lab., 1954-57; mem. tech. staff Inst. Def. Analysis, Pentagon, 1957-58; mem. faculty U. Mich., Ann Arbor, 1958—, prof. elec. engring., 1963—, dir. Willow Run Labs., 1970-72, pres. Environ. Research Inst. Mich., 1973—, adj. prof., 19—; vis. prof. Imperial Coll. U. London, 1968; v.p. Chain Lakes Research Corp., Detroit, 1969-70; cons., 19—. Author: Analysis of Linear Time-Invariant Systes, 1963; Random Processes, Communications, and Radar, 1969; contbr. articles to profl. jours. Fellow IEEE. Avocation: long distance running. Home: 525 Huntington Dr Ann Arbor MI 48104 Office: Environ Research Inst Mich PO Box 8618 Ann Arbor MI 48107

BROWN, WILLIAM TERRENCE, oil company executive; b. Kansas City, Mo., Dec. 6, 1941; s. William Francis and Ninalee (Timmons) B.; B.S., Rockhurst Coll., 1963; J.D., U. Mo., Kansas City, 1969; m. Kathleen Rae Ball, May 28, 1966 (div.); children—Stephen M., Christopher M. Admitted to U.S. Tax Ct. bar, 1972; with Sernes, Chandler, Schupp & Conneally, C.P.A.s, Kansas City, 1962-64; mng. partner Brown & Co., C.P.A.s, Kansas City, Mo., 1964-81; chmn. Sterling Oil and Exploration, Inc., Kansas City, Mo., 1981—; pres. Brown Energy Corp., Kansas City, 1983—; J.R. Stewart Constrn. Co., Inc., Independence, Mo., 1985—. Lay mem. mediation bd. Jackson County Med. Soc., 1975; treas., bd. dirs., mem. exec. com. Legal Aid of Western Mo., 1974-84; bd. dirs. Pre-Trial Diversion Services, Inc., 1975-78, Estate Planning Assn. Kansas City, 1966-68. Mem. Am. Inst. C.P.A.s. Home: 525 E 129th Terr Kansas City MO 64145 Office: 8080 Ward Pkwy Suite 440 Kansas City MO 64114

BROWNE, ALDIS JEROME, JR., real estate broker; b. Chgo., Mar. 21, 1912; s. Aldis J. and Elizabeth (Cunningham) B.; B.A., Yale U., 1935; m. Bertha Erminger, Oct. 22, 1938; children—Aldis J. III, Howell E., John Kenneth. Vice pres., dir. Browne & Storch Inc., and predecessors, Chgo., 1935-81, dir., 1961-81; with Quinlan & Tyson, Evanston, Ill., 1981-84, L.J. Sheridan Co., 1985—. Bd. dirs. English Speaking Union, Civic Fedn., Mil. Order World Wars; chmn. Bldg. Rev. Bd. Lake Forest; vestryman, St. James Episcopalian Ch., 1947-60; trustee, Old People's Home, Chgo.; bd. dirs. Key West Art and Hist. Soc. Served to capt. USNR. Mem. Chgo. (dir.), Ill., N. Side Chgo. real estate bds., Nat. Realtors Assn., Order Founders and Patriots (gov. Ill. chpt.), Soc. Colonial Wars (gov. Ill. chpt.), Order St. Lazarus, Mil. Order World Wars (past comdr. Chgo. br.), Chgo. Art Inst. (governing life), Navy League (past dir.). Republican. Clubs: Chgo., Tavern, Army Navy Washington, Masons. Home: 165 W Onwentsia Rd Lake Forest IL 60045 Office: LJ Sheridan & Co 30 N LaSalle St Chicago IL 60602

BROWNE, JAMES EDWARD, dentist, consultant; b. Abbeville, S.C., Feb. 5, 1939; s. Jack Edward and Magnolia (Green) B.; m. Elaine Parker, Apr. 1, 1967 (div. 1978); 1 child, Jacquelyn; m. Leatrice Parker, June 30, 1979; 1 child, Courtney. B.S., N.C. Agrl. and Tech. State U., 1962; M.B.A., U. Mo.-Jefferson City, 1973; D.D.S., Ohio State U., 1976. Vice pres. Evanston Community Council, Cin., 1978-79; sec. Ohio Valley Dental Soc., Cin., 1978-79, v.p. 1981—; v.p. Buckeye Dental Soc., Columbus, Ohio, 1980-81; cons. Practice Mgrs., Cin., 1984—, Mem. View Place Civic Org., Cin., 1984—; cons. Coalition of Neighborhoods, Cin., 1984—. Served to capt. U.S.A.F., 1963-73. Mem. Am. Orthodontic Soc., Beta Kappa Chi, Kappa Alpha Psi. Presbyterian. Avocations: racquetball; tennis; computer programming. Home: 7834 View Place Cincinnati OH 45224 Office: 1618 Cedar Ave Cincinnati OH 45224

BROWNE, JANE COTTON, family planning consultant; b. St. Paul, Nov. 19, 1912; d. Donald Reed and Grace (Gillette) Cotton; student Wells Coll., 1930-32; m. Harry C. Browne, May 17, 1941 (div. May, 1954); 1 son, Marshall Gillette. Adminstrv. asst. Cargill, Inc., Mpls., 1944-45; office mgr., dir. spl. gifts Am. City Bur., Portland, Oreg., 1947-48; dir. field cons. Planned Parenthood, N.Y. State (Eastern League), 1956-58; exec. dir. Planned Parenthood of Mpls., 1951-56; exec. dir. Planned Parenthood Assn. of Chgo. Area, 1958-69; sr. fellow Adlai Stevenson Inst. Internat. Affairs, 1969; chmn. exec. dirs. council Planned Parenthood-World Population, 1965-68; mem. steering com. N. Cook County Office Econ. Opportunity, 1966-69; gov. bd. Cook County, Office Econ. Opportunity, 1966-69, founder, mem. Family Planning Coordinating Council Met. Chgo., 1967-71; mem. health com., welfare com., Evanston Anti-Poverty Council, 1967-69; mem. Gov.'s State-Wide Advisory Council Ill. Div. Health Planning and Resource Devel., Com. Health Care Facilities, 1968-71; mem. profl. advisory panel Welfare Council Met. Chgo., 1969-71; advisory council Comprehensive Health Planning, Inc., Met. Chgo., 1969-71; family planning cons., research asso. Center for Population Studies, U. Minn., 1970—. U.S. del. Internat. Planned Parenthood Conf., Singapore, 1963 Bangdung, Indonesia, 1969; cons. Near East South Asia div. AID, 1968; project dir. Ark. Family Planning Council, 1970-71, spl. cons., 1971-73; family planning cons. Office Econ. Opportunity, Washington, 1970-73; cons. Nat. Center Family Planning Services, Region VIII, Dept. Health, Edn. and Welfare, 1972-73; program adviser Naomi Gray Assos., 1970—; internat. traveler, lectr. Bd. dirs. Opportunity Workshop, Mpls., 1972—; budget allocations com. United Way of Mpls., 1974-77; bd. dirs., chmn. pub. affairs com. Met. YWCA, Mpls., 1977—. Mem. Mpls. Bd. Realtors (asso.), Am. Pub. Health Assn., Nat. Conf. Social Welfare. Episcopalian. Home: 205 S Barry Ave Apt #310 Wayzata MN 55391

BROWNELL, MELVIN RUSSELL, retail druggist, pharmacist, mayor; b. Grand Meadow, Minn., Sept. 1, 1925; s. Howard Russell and Helen Frances (Doten) B.; m. Ann Linden, Nov. 10, 1952; children—Thomas, James, John, Richard, Mary, Christopher, Paul. B.S. in Pharmacy, U. Minn., 1950. Registered pharmacist. Pharmacist, mgr. Ted Maier Drug, Inc., Winona, Minn., 1950-55; pres., pharmacist Brownell Drug, Inc., St. Charles, Minn., 1955—. Alderman, City of St. Charles, 1965-77, mayor, 1977—; vice chmn. Winona County Planning and Zoning Commn., 1976—; chmn. Dover, Eyota, St. Charles Sanitary Dist., 1968—; mem. Minn. Peace Officers Standards and Tng. Bd., 1982-84, Milti-County Housing-Rehab. Authority, Wabasha, Minn., 1982—. Served with USN, 1944-46. Recipient C. C. Ludwig award Minn. League Cities, 1985. Mem. Nat. Assn. Retail Druggists, Minn. State Pharm. Assn. (chmn. dist. 1 1979), U. Minn. Century Mortar Club, St. Charles C. of C. (pres. 1958), Am. Legion. Republican. Roman Catholic. Club: Lions (pres. St. Charles 1960). Lodge: Moose. Avocation: Photography. Home: 161 W 5th St Saint Charles MN 55972 Office: Brownell Drug Inc 925 Whitewater Ave Saint Charles MN 55972

BROWNING, EARL DEAN, sch. adminstr.; b. Annawan, Ill., Jan. 21, 1926; s. Earl F. and Velma L. Browning; B.S., Western Ill. U., 1951; M.A., U. Ill., 1957; advanced cert. of specialist So. Ill. U., 1968; m. Ardythe A. Machesney, June 23, 1951; 1 dau., Lexa Linn. Indsl. arts tchr. Alton (Ill.) Community Sch. Dist., 1951-57, dir. adult edn., 1957-67, adminstrv. asst. vocat. edn., 1967—. Served with U.S. Army, 1944-46. Decorated Bronze Star; recipient Those Who Excel award Ill. Bd. Edn., 1976; named Outstanding Vocat. Adminstr. of Yr., Ill. Council Local Adminstrs., 1981. Mem. Am. Vocat. Assn., Ill. Vocat. Assn., Ill. Indsl. Arts Assn., Nat. Council Local Adminstrs., NEA. Methodist. Home: 5502 Ladue St Godfrey IL 62035 Office: Alton Community School Dist 1854 E Broadway Alton IL 62002

BROWNING, REED, history educator; b. N.Y.C., Aug. 26, 1938; s. Arthur M. and Martha P. (Reed) B.; m. Susan Lee Lampley, Jan. 8, 1963; 1 child, Stephen. B.A., Dartmouth Coll., 1960; student U. Vienna, Austria, 1962-63; Ph.D., Yale U., 1965. Asst. in instr. Yale U., New Haven, Conn., 1964, instr. to asst. prof. Amherst Coll., Mass., 1965-67, asst. prof. to prof. Kenyon Coll., Gambier, Ohio, 1967—. Author: The Duke of Newcastle, 1975; Political and Constitutional Ideas of the Court Whigs, 1982. Mem. Am. Hist. Assn., Ohio Acad. Hist., North Am. Conf. British Studies, Soc. Am. Baseball Research, Am. Soc. Eighteenth Century Studies. Home: Box 382 Gambier OH 43022 Office: Kenyon Coll Gambier OH 43022

BROWNING, ROBERT DOYLE, construction company executive; b. Daviess County, Ind., Sept. 30, 1917; s. Ray and Pearl (Browning) B.; grad. high sch.; student Internat. Corr. Sch.; m. Betty Overton, Sept. 2, 1942; children—Sondra Chapman, Larry, Gerald. Farmer, Washington, Ind., 1936-41; asst. engr. roads Ind. State Hwy., 1945-50; with Thompson Constrn. Co., Inc., Indpls., 1950—, field engr., 1961, office engr., estimator, 1961-70, exec. v.p., 1970—, also dir. Bd. dirs. Patton Park. Treas. Young Republicans, Daviess County, Ind., 1946-50; trustee Camby (Ind.) Community Ch. Served to master sgt. USAF, 1941-45. Decorated Bronze Star. Mem. V.F.W., Ind. Constructors Inc. (sec.-treas. 1978-79), Am. Legion. Clubs: Masons, K.P. Home: 8641 Camby Rd Camby IN 46116 Office: 3840 Prospect St Indianapolis IN 46203

BROWNING, ROBERT LYNN, educator, clergyman; b. Gallatin, Mo., June 19, 1924; s. Robert W. and Nell J. (Trotter) B.; B.A., Mo. Valley Coll., 1945; M.Div., Union Theol. Sem., 1948; Ph.D., Ohio State U., 1960; postgrad. Columbia U., 1951-53, Oxford (Eng.) U., 1978-79; m. Jean Beatty, Dec. 27, 1947 (dec. 1977); children—Gregory, David, Peter, Lisa; m. 2d. Jackie L. Rogers, Aug. 26, 1979. Ordained to ministry Disciples of Christ Ch., 1949, transferred to United Meth. Ch., 1950; minister edn. Old Stone Ch., Meadville, Pa., 1946-51, Community Ch. at the Circle, Mt. Vernon, N.Y., 1951-53, North Broadway United Meth. Ch., Columbus, Ohio, 1953-59; prof. Christian edn. Meth. Theol. Sch., Delaware, Ohio, 1959-72, William A. Chryst prof. Christian edn., 1972—; pres. Meth. Conf. on Christian edn., 1967-69; exec. dir. Commn. on Role of the Professions in Soc., 1974-76, cons., 1976—. Bd. dirs. Southside Settlement, Columbus, 1968-74, Tray-Lee Center, Columbus, 1955-59, Ohio State U. Wesley Found., 1960-78, vice chmn. 1976-78. Served with USN, 1942-45. Recipient Paul Hinkhouse award Religious Public Relations Council Am., 1971. Mem. Assn. for Profl. Edn. for Ministry (editor proc. 1980—), Religious Edn. Assn., Assn. of Profs. and Researchers in Religious Edn. Author: Communication with Junior Highs, 1968; Guidelines for Youth Ministry, 1970; What on Earth Are You Doing, 1966; (audiotape) (with Charles Foster) Communicating the Faith with Children, 1971; Ways the Bible Comes Alive, 1975; Ways Persons Become Christian, 1976; (with Charles Foster, Everett Tilson) Looking at Leadership with the Eyes of Biblical Faith, 1978; (with Roy Reed) the Sacraments in Religious Education and Liturgy: An Ecumenical Model, 1985; contbg. author: Preventing Adolescent Alienation: An Interprofessional Approach, 1983; editor: Integration: Objective Studies and Practical Theology, Proc. Assn. Profl. Edn. for Ministry, 1981; contbr. articles on religious edn. to profl. jours. Home: 6613 Hawthorne St Worthington OH 43085 Office: 3081 Columbus Pike Delaware OH 43015

BROWNING, STERLING EDWIN, II, chemist; b. Ardmore, Okla., Aug. 27, 1933; s. Sterling Edwin and Viola Mae (Jones) B.; student Okla. A&M U., 1951-56, Tulsa U., 1961-62; B.A., Okla. State U., 1967; m. Merlene Fox, Sept. 29, 1962; children—Melissa Anne, Sterling Edwin III, Jonathan Brian. Lab. helper Pan Am. Oil Corp., Tulsa, 1956-57; partner Browning's Carpet Co., Tulsa, 1957-61; research asst. chemistry Dowell div. Dow Chem. Co., Tulsa, 1961-63; tech. corr. Fisher Sci. Co., St. Louis, 1963-65; lab. technician Okla. State U., Stillwater, 1965-67; analytic chemist Sci. Assocs., St. Louis, 1967-68; chief chemist Sherwood Med. Industries, St. Louis, 1968-74; sr. analytical chemist, spectroscopist Sigma Chem. Co., St. Louis, 1974—; staff Applied Sci. Cons., St. Louis, 1972—. Trustee Greenmar Subdiv., Mo., 1972-73; active Boy Scouts Am., Girl Scouts U.S.A., 1975—. Mem. Am. Chem. Soc. (treas. gen. topics group St. Louis sect. 1981-82), St. Louis Soc. Analysts, Soc. for Applied Spectroscopy, Coblentz Soc., St. Louis Chromatography Discussion Group, Sigma Study Group, Sigma Alpha Epsilon. Republican. Presbyterian.

BROWNSCOMBE, WILLIAM EDWARD, dentist; b. McKeesport, Pa., Apr. 23, 1947; s. Robert James Brownscombe and Nancy Lee (Bell) Kalb; m. Judy Ellen Perkins, June 14, 1969; children—Brett Evan, Tyler James, Darby Lee. B.S., U. Mich., 1969, D.D.S., 1974. Gen. practice dentistry, Grosse Pointe, Mich., 1974-79, St. Clair Shores, Mich., 1979—; hosp. staff Cottage Hosp., Grosse Pointe, 1983—. Editor Jour. Eastern Dental Soc., 1976-79. Officer Cub Scouts Pack 19, Grosse Pointe, 1978—; councilman Grosse Pointe Meml. Ch., 1978-81; mem. Grosse Pointe PTO, PTA, 1980-83. Mem. ADA, Mich. Dental Assn., Detroit Dist. Dental Soc. (Outstanding Merit award 1984), Am. Acad. Oral Medicine, Am. Acad. Sports Dentistry. Republican. Presbyterian. Avocations: windsurfing, water skiing, downhill snow skiing. Home: 364 University Pl Grosse Pointe MI 48230 Office: 24055 Jefferson St Saint Clair Shores MI 48080

BROYHILL, ROY FRANKLIN, indsl. turf and agrl. equipment mfg. exec.; b. Sioux City, Iowa, June 20, 1919; s. George Franklin and Effie (Motes) B.; B.B.A., U. Nebr., 1940; m. Arline W. Stewart, Jan. 30, 1943; children—Lynn Diann (dec.), Craig G., Kent Bryan, Bryce Alan. Trainee mgr. Montgomery Ward Co., 1940; semi-sr. acct. L. H. Keightley, 1941-42; chief accountant Army Exchange Service, Sioux City, 1942-46; pres., chmn. Broyhill Co., 1946—; pres., dir. Star Printing & Pub. Co., South Sioux City, 1949—; pres., chmn. Broyhill Corp., 1953—; v.p. Broyhill Mfg. Co., 1978—; pres., chmn. bd. Broyhill Inc.; dir. 1st Nat. Bank, Sioux City. Mem. U.S.A. Exec. Res.; mem. Nebr. dist. adv. council SBA, 1971—. Mayor of Dakota City, 1951-53; mem. Nebr. Republican Central Com., 1954-56. Past mem. local sch. bd. Trustee U. Nebr., U. Nebr. Found. Served with AUS, 1940-41. Mem. Nitrogen Solutions Assn. (dir. 1956-60), Farm Equipment Mfrs. Assn. (dir., pres. 1971-72), Atokad Racing Assn. (past dir.), N.A.M., U.S., South Sioux City chambers commerce, Nebr. Assn. Commerce and Industry (dir. 1972-73), Alumni Assn. U. Nebr. (dir.), Beta Theta Pi, Alpha Kappa Psi. Presbyn. (elder). Mason (Shriner), Kiwanian. Home: 1610 Broadway Dakota City NE 68731 Office: Broyhill Co N Market Sq Dakota City NE 68731

BROYLES, PATRICK JAMES, government official; b. Columbus, Ohio, July 5, 1950; s. Nick and Elzetta Pearl (Presson) B.; m. Phyllis Caughman, July 5, 1981; 1 dau., Brenda Gail Caughman. B.S., Okla. State U., 1975; M.S., 1978. Cert. profl. soil erosion and sediment control specialist. Grad. asst. Okla. State U., Stillwater, 1975-77; range conservationist Soil Conservationist Service, U.S. Dept. Agr., Pawhuska, Okla., 1977-80, Cheyenne, Okla., 1980-81, dist. conservationist, Columbus, Kans., 1981-85, Cottonwood Falls, Kans., 1985—. Deacon, First Christian Ch., 1978-80. Served with M.I., U.S. Army, 1970-73. Mem. Soc. for Range Mgmt. (life; chmn. producer affairs com. Kans.-Okla. sect. 1980—, sec.-treas. 1978), Nat. Wildlife Fedn. (life), Council for Agrl. Sci. and Tech., Kans. Livestock Assn. (natural resources com.), Okla. Cattlemen's Assn., Nat. Assn. Conservation Dists., Kans. Assn. Conservation Dists., Am. Legion, Nat. Rifle Assn. (life). Republican. Mem. Disciples of Christ Ch. Lodge: Lions (pres. Pawhuska 1979-80). Home: 522 S Indiana Columbus KS 66725 Office: Box F 336 Broadway Cottonwood Falls KS 66845

BROZOVIC, RICHARD, mfg. co. exec.; b. Briar Hill, Pa., Apr. 2, 1932; s. Albert Elmer and Emily Louise (Yelinek) B.; student pub. schs., Jefferson, Pa.; m. Jean E. Heverling, Apr. 18, 1953; 1 son, Robert A. Served from pvt. to 1st sgt. U.S. Army, 1947-71, ret., 1971; pres., gen. mgr. Geyer Bros. Brewing Co., Frankenmuth, Mich., 1975—. Decorated Bronze Star medals (2), Purple Heart. Mem. Am. Legion. Roman Catholic. Clubs: Frankenmuth Conservation, Men's of Blessed Trinity Cath. Ch. Home: 448 Sunburst Dr Frankenmuth MI 48734 Office: 425 S Main St Frankenmuth MI 48734

BRUBAKER, KARL EUGENE, solar manufacturing executive; b. Columbis, Ohio, Nov. 6, 1956; s. Kenton Kaylor and Emma Margaret (Shetler) B.; m. Marcia Plett, June 9, 1984. B.S., Eastern Mennonite U., 1978. Mgr. Earthkeepers, Harrisonburg, Va., 1975-78; asst. gen. mgr. Sunflower Energy Works, Lehigh, Kans., 1978-83, gen. mgr., 1983—. Bd. dirs. Crossroads Fed. Credit Union, Goessel, Kans., 1984—. Mem. Kans. Solar Energy Soc., Kans. Natural Resources Council. Democrat. Mennonite. Avocations: stamp collecting; chess; tennis; hiking. Home: Box 71 Goessel KS 67053 Office: Sunflower Energy Works 101 Main St Lehigh KS 67073

BRUBAKER, VICTORIA LYN, physical education educator; b. La Jolla, Calif., Feb. 1, 1954; d. Gene Duane and Donna Lee (Grant) B. B.S. with honors in Edn., N.W. Mo. State U., 1976. Cert. tchr., Mo., Iowa. Tchr., coach Rock Port High Sch. (Mo.), 1977—; basketball, softball ofcl. Iowa High Sch. Girls' Assn., 1973-82; softball coach Essex High Sch. (Iowa), summer, 1973-77, Shenandoah High Sch. (Iowa), summer, 1976-77; basketball coach Tarkio High Sch., Mo., 1984-85; sports writer Shenandoah Evening Sentinel, 1976-77; mem. adv. com. Mo. State High Sch. Activities Assn., Columbia, 1981—. Named Dist. Coach of Yr., Dist. Press Assn., 1981; Nodaway Empire Coach of Yr.,

Daily Forum, 1981. Mem. Mo. State Tchrs. Assn. (chmn. phys. edn. sect. 1980-81), Community Tchrs. Assn. (bldg. rep. 1981), Tchrs.-Adminstrs.-Sch. Bd. Com., AAHPER, Mo. Basketball Coaches Assn., Fellowship Christian Athletes, Kappa Delta Pi, Delta Psi Kappa. Republican. Baptist.

BRUBECK, ANNE ELIZABETH DENTON, artist; b. Beardstown, Ill., Mar. 5, 1918; d. Harry B. and Helen Jean (Gibbs) Denton; student Christian Coll., 1935-36; B.Design, Newcomb Coll., Tulane U., 1939; postgrad. Art Inst. Chgo., 1939-40; A.A. (hon.), Wabash Valley Coll., 1981; m. William E. Brubeck, Dec. 14, 1940; children—Jean Brubeck Stayman, William E. Instr. painting Wabash Valley Coll., Mt. Carmel, Ill., 1962-67; painter; one-man shows include N.Y.C., 1961, 63-67, Evansville, Ind., 1963-69; retrospective, Wabash Valley Coll., 1980; juried exhbns. include: Evansville Mus., 1963, 64, 65, Swopes Gallery, Terre Haute, Ind., 1964, 68, Nashville, 1967. Trustee, Mt. Carmel Pub. Library, 1954—, chmn., 1975-6; mem. cultural events com. Wabash Valley Coll., 1976-80. Brubeck Art Center named in her and her husband's honor, 1976; named to Mt. Carmel High Sch. Centennial Hall of Fame, 1982. Mem. Ill. Library Assn., Nat. League Am. Penwomen, PEO. Methodist. Club: Reviewers Matinee. Home and office: 729 Cherry St Mount Carmel IL 62863

BRUCE, CAROLYN CORRINGTON, nurse; b. North Vernon, Ind., Apr. 28, 1936; d. Ottis C. and Ruth E. (Davis) Corya; R.N., Methodist Hosp., Indpls., 1956; B.S. in Health Edn., Ind. U., 1975, postgrad., 1976; spl. course in respiratory therapy U. Chgo., 1973; m. Reginald A. Bruce, July 16, 1976; children by previous marriage—Douglas Corrington, Judith Corrington, Carla Corrington. Charge nurse metabolic unit Meth. Hosp., Indpls., 1956-59, head nurse metabolic unit, 1959-63, head nurse ICU, 1968-69, head nurse med. unit, 1969-70, dir. respiratory therapy, 1970-75, asst. dir. nursing, 1975-76; dir. nursing Paris (Ill.) Hosp., 1976-77, Crawford Meml. Hosp., Robinson, Ill., 1978-79; adminstr. Lincolnland Vis. Nurse Assn., 1980—; pres. DECCCA Health Planning Agy., 1982-84; pres., chief exec. officer Jennings Vis. Nurse Assn., Inc., 1983—, Home Health Care Inc.; camp nurse diabetics, office nurse Dr. J.H. Warvel, 1958; indsl. nurse Cummins Engine Co., Columbus, Ind., 1963; head nurse psychiatry, Madison, Ind., 1965-68; former faculty mem. CPR; v.p. Health Planning Bd.; vol. ARC, Am. Cancer Soc. Mem. Am. Nurses Assn. (cert. nursing adminstr.), Ill. Nurses Assn., Coles-Cumberland Med. Soc. Aux. (pres. 1981-82), Meth. Hosp. Nursing Alumnae (pres. 1970-74). Presbyterian. Home: 15 Doral Ct Route 3 Mattoon IL 61938

BRUCE, JAMES FRANKLIN, publishing company executive; b. Indpls., Mar. 25, 1930; s. Albert Lee and Myrtle Elizabeth (Horne) B.; B.S., Ind. U., 1953; m. Mary Bruce. Mgr. consumer affairs dept. Indpls. Better Bus. Bur., Inc., 1958-59; with Ency. Brit., Chgo., 1959—, dir. co. relations, 1979—. Mem. Spl. Task Force Pres.' Council for Phys. Fitness and Sports, 1973—; mem. spl. adv. group U.S. Bicentennial Adminstrn.; mem. spl. adv. council Better Bus. Bur., Washington. Served as capt. USAF, 1953-55. Mem. Wedgewood Soc. Chgo., U.S. C. of C. (mem. bus. consumer council), Chgo. Sales and Mktg. Club, Nat. Premium Advt. Assn. Am., Council Fgn. Relations, Conf. Consumer Orgns., Soc. Consumer Affairs Profls. in Bus. Direct Selling Assn., Ind. U. Alumni Assn., Soc. Consumers and Profls. in Bus. Club: Army-Navy (Washington). Office: Ency Brit 310 S Michigan Ave Chicago IL 60604

BRUCE, TERRY L., congressman; b. Olney, Ill., J.D., U. Ill., 1969; m. Charlotte Roberts; children—Emily Anne, Ellen Catherine. Farm labor staff U.S. Dept. Labor, Washington, mem. staff Congressman George Shipley, Ill. State Senator Philip Benefiel; legis. intern, 1969-70; mem. Ill. Senate, from 1970, asst. majority leader, from 1975; now mem. 99th Congress from Ill. Named Outstanding Legislator of Year, Ill. Edn. Assn., 1972-78, Spl. Recognition award, 1980; winner Right to Know award Ill. Press Assn., 1975, service awards, 1977, 78; award Ill. Community Coll. Trustees Assn., numerous others. Democrat. Address: Olney IL

BRUCKEN, LINDA BOGGS, school administrator; b. Maysville, Ky., Jan. 19, 1949; d. John Bayard and Mae Lucille (Craycraft) Boggs; m. William Louis Brucken, Apr. 4, 1975; children—William Patrick, Scott David. B.S., Bowling Green State U., 1972; M.S. in Edn., U. Dayton, 1980. Cert. tchr. elem. and spl. children; cert. prin. for spl. children, Ohio. Tchr. Warren County Bd. Mental Retardation, Lebanon, Ohio, 1972-74; tchr. Montgomery County Bd. Mental Retardation, Dayton, Ohio, 1974-82; asst. prin. Southview Sch., Montgomery County, Dayton, 1981—. Mem. levy com. Montgomery County Bd. Mental Retardation, 1977, Bellbrook High Sch., 1981. Recipient Citizenship award Waynesville High Sch., 1967. Mem. Assn. Supervision and Curriculum Devel. Republican. Developer programs for handicapped students. Office: 25 Thorpe Dr Dayton OH 45420

BRUCKER, EDMUND, artist, portrait painter, educator; b. Cleve., Nov. 20, 1912; s. Ludwig and Theresa (Strung) B.; diploma in portrait painting Cleve. Inst. Art, 1934, postgrad., 1934-36; m. Marcelline B. Spencer, Jan. 28, 1939; 1 son, Robert. Instr., Cleve. Inst. Art, 1936-38, John Herron Art Sch., Indpls., 1938-67; lectr. painting Herron Sch. Art, Ind. U., Indpls., 1967-68, assoc. prof., 1968-73, prof., 1973-83, prof. emeritus, 1983—; one-man shows: Herron Art Inst., 1947, 63, Hoosier Art Gallery, Indpls., 1953; group shows include: Carnegie Art Inst., Pitts., 1941, Library of Congress, 1945, Met. Mus. Art, N.Y.C., 1952, Ind. State Mus., 1979; represented in permanent collections: Eli Lilly & Co., Indpls., Northwestern U., Ind. U., Purdue U., Cleve. Mus. Art, Dartmouth Coll., Evansville (Ind.) Mus. Arts and Scis., City of Cleve. Warner Collection, Scholl Mfg. Co., Chgo., Phillips Oil Co., Bartlesville, Okla., Weir Cook Internat. Airport, Indpls., Indpls. Motor Speedway Hall of Fame Mus., Taylor U.; numerous others; portrait cover artist Ind. Bus. and Industry Mag., 1960-71. Recipient Milliken award Art Assn. Indpls., 1963; named Sagamore of the Wabash, Gov. of Ind., 1965. Mem. Ind. Artists Club, Hoosier Salon Patrons Assn., Indpls. Museum Art. Club: Riviera. Home: 545 King Dr Indianapolis IN 46260

BRUCKER, MICHAEL ARTHUR, pharmacist; b. Cape Girardeau, Mo., June 15, 1948; s. Otto Celestine and Zita Josephine (Heuring) B.; m. Connie Jean Light, Nov. 14, 1968; children—Michael D., Melissa D. B.S. in Pharmacy, Northeast La. U., 1971. Registered pharmacist, Mo., Ind. Pharmacist, Kneibert Clinic Pharmacy, Poplar Bluff, Mo., 1971-76; sales rep. Eli Lilly & Co., Indpls., 1976—. Asst. leader Southeast Mo. council Boy Scouts Am., 1981—. Recipient Recognition Poplar Bluff Region Diagnostician Assn., 1974. Mem. Mo. Jaycees (Outstanding pres. 1975, Jaycee of Yr. 1975), Southeast Mo. Pharm. Assn., Cape Girardeau Pharm. Assn. (v.p. 1981—), So. Ill. Hosp. Pharmacy Assn. Club: Missouri. Lodge: K.C. Republican. Avocations: water and snow skiing; racquetball; hunting. Home: 2014 Pamela Cape Girardeau MO 63701

BRUCKNER, CLARENCE AUGUST, real estate exec.; b. Chgo., Aug. 7, 1931; s. Clarence R. and Elizabeth K. (McCarl) B.; student U. Ill., 1949-51; m. Leta Fox; children—Linda, Lisbeth, Paul, Curt; stepchildren—Jennifer, Douglas, Stephen, Stuart, Jamie. Vice pres. Donald F. Moore, Inc., 1955-67; pres. C.A. Bruckner & Assos., Inc., Oak Brook, Ill., 1967—, Bruckner, Fitts & Assos., Inc. 1977-80; sec. Woodsmyth Corp., 1977-80; gen. partner Commerce Sq., 1975—. Served with USAF, 1951-52. Mem. Soc. Real Estate Appraisers (past pres. Chgo. chpt.), Am. Inst. Real Estate Appraisers, Am. Soc. Real Estate Counselors, Jr. Real Estate Bd. Chgo. (past pres.). Methodist. Club: Masons (Medinah Temple Shrine). Home: 2408 Shasta Dr Lisle IL 60532 Office: 901 W Liberty Dr Wheaton IL 60187

BRUEGGEMANN, WALTER GEORGE, physician, ophthalmologist; b. Ft. Wayne, Ind., July 21, 1930; s. Walter Carl and Loraine Marie (Goeglein) B.; m. Marguerite Joan Hamman, Oct. 27, 1957; children—Stephen, Gregory, Jane, Thomas. B.S. in Pharmacy, Purdue U., 1952; M.D., Ind. U.-Indpls., 1967. Diplomate Am. Acad. Ophthalmology. Asst. mgr. Dan Purvis Drugs, New Haven, Ind., 1954-60; owner, mgr. Medical Clinic Apothecary, Ft. Wayne, Ind., 1960-63; intern Meth. Hosp., Indpls., 1967-68; resident Ind. U. Hosps., Indpls., 1968-71; pvt. practice medicine specializing in ophthalmology, Columbus, Ind., 1971—; mem. staff Bartholomew County Hosp., Columbus, Wishard Hosp., Indpls., Meth. Hosp., Indpls. Named Intern of Year, Meth. Hosp. Ho. Staff, Indpls., 1968. Mem. AMA, Ind. State Med. Assn., Ind. State Ophthalmol. Assn., Indpls. Ophthalmol. Assn., Bartholomew-Brown County Med. Assn. Republican. Lutheran. Club: Lions (past pres., zone chmn., dep. dist. gov.). Avocations: Fishing, photography, spectator sports. Home: 11953 W Locust Ln Columbus IN 47201 Office: 411 Plaza Dr F Columbus IN 47201

BRUENING, WILLIAM PAUL, controls co. exec.; b. St. Louis, Mar, 8, 1935; s. Francis Joseph and Crystal Verda (Baumgartner) B.; B.E.E., U. Dayton, 1957. Sales engr. Cutler-Hammer Inc., St. Louis, 1957-63, O'Brien Equipment Co., St. Louis, 1963-69; v.p., sec. Central Controls Co., Inc., St. Louis, 1969-76; pres. Process Controls Co., Inc., St. Louis, 1976—; dir. Bannes-Sheughnessy Inc. Bd. dirs. St. Louis Area chpt. March of Dimes Birth Defects Found. Served with U.S. Army, 1957-63. Mem. Instrument Soc. Am. (sr.), Confrerie des Chevaliers du Tastevin, Newcomen Soc. N.Am., Mercedes-Benz Club Am., Commanderie de Bordeaux. Republican. Roman Catholic. Clubs: St. Louis, Mo. Athletic. Home: 6813 Aliceton Ave Saint Louis MO 63123 Office: 20 American Industrial Dr Maryland Heights MO 63043

BRUGLER, RICHARD KENNETH, steel and iron mfg. co. exec.; b. Warren, Ohio, Oct. 28, 1928; s. Herman Kenneth and Mildred Marrietta (Fell) B.; B.S. in Mech. Engring., Case Inst. Tech., 1952, B.S. in Elec. Engring., 1954; m. Jean Elizabeth Brooks, Dec. 22, 1951; children—David Kenneth, Diane Jean, Eric Paul, Kurt Ernst. Draftsman, Perfection Stove Co., Cleve., 1951-52; lab. machinist Thompson Products Co., Cleve., 1952-54; with Heltzel Co., Warren, 1954—, chief engr., 1962-65, v.p. engring., 1965-78, v.p. ops., 1978-80, exec. v.p., 1980-83, pres., 1983—; chmn. Concrete Plant Mfrs. Bur., 1975-78. Served with USNR, 1946-48. Mem. Nat. Readymix Assn. (dir.), Nat., Trumbull County (sec. 1976-78, pres. 1979) socs. profl. engrs., IEEE (sr.), Nat. Scalemens Assn., Antique Wireless Assn., Palatine Soc. Methodist. Club: Masons. Patentee in field. Home: 1359 Beechcrest St Warren OH 44485 Office: 1750 Thomas Rd Warren OH 44484

BRUHNKE, PAUL EDWARD, appliance mfg. co. exec.; b. Chgo., June 11, 1946; s. Edward G. and Viola Ellen (Krueger) B.; B.S. in Mktg., U. Ill., 1969; M.B.A., DePaul U., Chgo., 1970; m. Joan Mary Murphy, Aug. 29, 1970. Sales rep. Dun & Bradstreet, Inc., 1972-73; account exec. GR Co. div. Kelvinator, Inc., Grand Rapids, Mich., 1973-74; nat. accounts mgr. Kelvinator Appliance Co., Grand Rapids, 1974-75, div. sales mgr., 1975—. Served with U.S. Army, 1970-72. Decorated Army Commendation medal. Office: 930 Ft Duquesne Blvd Pittsburgh PA 15222

BRUINS, ELTON JOHN, college dean, religion educator; b. Fairwater, Wis., July 29, 1927; s. Clarence Raymond and Angeline Theodora (Kemink) B.; m. Elaine Ann Redeker, June 24, 1954; children—Mary Elaine Bruins Plasman, David Lewis. B.A., Hope Coll., 1950; B.D., Western Theol. Sem., 1953; S.T.M., Union Theol. Sem., 1957; Ph.D., NYU, 1962. Ordained to ministry Reformed Ch., 1954. Pastor, Reformed Ch., Elmsford, N.Y., 1955-61, Flushing, N.Y., 1961-66; prof. religion Hope Coll., Holland, Mich., 1966—, chmn. religion dept., 1977-84, dean arts and humanities, 1984—; archivist Western Theol. Sem., Holland, 1967-78, Netherlands Mus., Holland, 1968—, also v.p., 1980—. Author: The Americanization of a Congregation, 1970. Contbr. articles to profl. jours. Chmn. Hist./Cultural Commn., Holland, 1978-82. Served with USNR, 1945-46. Named to Evert J. and Hattie E. Blekkink Chair of Religion, Hope Coll., 1980. Mem. Assn. for Advancement Dutch-Am. Studies (pres. 1983), Am. Soc. Ch. History, Presbyn. Hist. Soc., Midwest Archives Conf., State Hist. Soc. Wis. Democrat. Mem. Reformed Ch. Home: 191 W 15th St Holland MI 49423 Office: Hope Coll Holland MI 49423

BRULL, HANS FRANK, social worker; b. Berlin, Germany, May 17, 1921; s. Victor and Ellen (Berendsen) B.; came to U.S., 1933, naturalized, 1943; B.A., CCNY, 1949; M.S.W., U. Pa., 1951; postgrad. U. Chgo., 1962; m. Rose Weiss, May 3, 1953 (div.); children—Ellen Sandra, Steven Victor; m. 2d, Olive Rue, Dec. 20, 1969. Caseworker Childrens Ct. Clinic, Melbourne, Australia, 1951, Jewish Family and Childrens Service, Mpls., 1951-53, Jewish Children's Bur., Chgo., 1953-56; head sch. social work dept. New Trier High Sch.-West, Northfield, 1963-82; clin. asst. prof. Sch. Social Work, Smith Coll., Northampton, Mass., 1975. Pvt. practice as psychiat. social worker, Winnetka. Mem. citizens adv. com. Youth Employment Service, 1965—; pres. Glenview Human Relations Com., 1963-64; mem. bd. Gates House Inc., 1970-73; mem. New Trier Twp. Com. on Youth, 1980—. Served with M.I., AUS, 1943-46. Mem. Nat. Assn. Social Workers (mem. state bd. 1976-77, del. nat. assembly 1977). Contbr. articles to profl. publs. Home: 1416 Edgewood Ln Winnetka IL 60093 Office: 525 Winnetka Ave Winnetka IL 60093

BRUMBAUGH, PHILIP SLOAN, quality control consultant; b. St. Louis, Nov. 14, 1932; s. Richard I. and Grace L. (Lischer) B.; A.B., Washington U., St. Louis, 1954, M.B.A., 1958, Ph.D., 1963; postgrad. Univ. Coll. London, 1963-64; m. Bettina Ann Viviano, Feb. 25, 1978. Ops. analyst Humble Oil & Refining Co., Houston, 1961-62; indsl. engr. Falstaff Brewing Corp., St. Louis, 1963; asst. prof. Sch. Engring., Washington U., St. Louis, 1964-70; asso. prof. U. Mo., St. Louis, 1970-74; pres. Qualtech Systems, Inc., Maryland Heights, Mo., 1974—. Mem. indsl. engring. adv. com. St. Louis Community Colls. Served with U.S. Army, 1954-56. Mem. Am. Statis. Assn., Am. Inst. Indsl. Engrs. (past nat. dir., past pres. St. Louis chpt.), Am. Soc. for Quality Control (cert. quality engr., past chmn. St. Louis sect.). Clubs: Univ., Engrs. (St. Louis). Home: 1359 Mason Rd Saint Louis MO 63131 Office: Qualtech Systems Inc 100 Progress Pkwy Suite 221 Maryland Heights MO 63043

BRUMBAUGH, WILLIAM JAY, coal and hard rock minerals company executive; b. Pittsburg, Kans., Aug. 21, 1930; s. John A. and Leona Geneva (Finley) B.; m. Geraldine Ponchur, June 18, 1953; children—Teri L. Forsythe, Curtis A., W. Kent, John V. B.S. in Edn., Pittsburg State U., 1951; postgrad. Okla. State U., 1974. Mathematician engring. dept. McNally Pittsburg Inc., Kans., 1951-52, chief process engr., 1954-71, asst. to pres., 1971-73, v.p., gen. mgr., 1973-80, corp. mgr. tech. services, 1980-82, corp. v.p. tech. services, 1982—; bd. dirs. McNally Australia Proprietary Ltd., North Ryde, New South Wales, 1982—; chmn. bd. dirs. Kans. div. McNally Pittsburg Inc., 1973-80. Bd. dirs. Pittsburg United Way, 1978-84, v.p., 1983; active Jr. C. of C., Pittsburg, 1955-65, v.p., 1962, pres. 1963. Served to lt. comdr. USNR, 1949-72. Mem. Pittsburg State U. Alumni Assn. (bd. dirs. 1960-62, pres. 1962, trustee, 1976-79), Soc. Mining Engring. of AIME, Rocky Mountain Coal Mining Inst., Nat. Assn. Mfrs., Pittsburg C. of C. Republican. Avocations: tennis; golf; bowling; hunting; waterskiing. Home: 802 Lakeview Dr Pittsburg KS 66762 Office: McNally Pittsburg Inc PO Box 651 100 N Pine St Pittsburg KS 66762

BRUMMETT, ANNA RUTH, biology educator; b. Fort Smith, Ark., Mar. 25, 1924; d. James Harlan and Lila Margaret (Etter) B.; A.A., Fort Smith Jr. Coll., 1946; B.A. with honors, U. Ark., 1948, M.A., 1949; Ph.D., Bryn Mawr Coll., 1953. Instr. biology Bryn Mawr Coll. (Pa.), 1952-53, Carleton Coll., Northfield, Minn., 1953-56, asst. prof. biology, 1956-61; asst. prof. biology Oberlin Coll. (Ohio), 1961-67, assoc. prof. biology and assoc. dean Coll., 1967-68, assoc. prof., 1968-73, prof. biology, 1974—, chmn. dept., 1974-83; chmn. biol. achievement com. Coll. Bd., Ednl. Test Service, 1979-83, mem. Coll. Bd. Sci. adv. com., 1980-83. Mem. AAAS, Am. Soc. Zoologists, AAUW, Am. Soc. Cell Biology, Soc. Developmental Biology, N.Y. Acad. Scis. Democrat. Contbr. articles on biology to profl. jours. Home: 50 Glenhurst Dr Oberlin OH 44074 Office: Biology Dept Kettering Hall Oberlin OH 44074

BRUNDIDGE, NANCY CORINNE, social worker; b. Louisville, Miss., Sept. 27, 1920; d. Elijah and Roberta (May) Thompson; m. Roy Lee Brundidge, Dec. 24, 1937; children—Carlita J. Nickson, Adrienne Nickson. A.A., Ind. U., 1956; B.A., Roosevelt U., 1960, M.A., 1973. Caseworker I and II, Cook County Dept. Pub. Aid., Chgo., 1960-69; social worker Gary Sch. Corp., Ind., 1969-70; job specialist social worker Ind. State Employment, Hammond, 1970-73; social worker, attendance officer Hammond pub. schs., Ind., 1973—; cert. drug edn. cons. Hammond Sch. City, 1976—; guest lectr. Ind. State U., 1980-81. Chmn. adv. bd. Salvation Army program com. Named Ind. State Social Worker of Yr., Midwest Social Workers Council, 1983-84. Mem. AAUW (cultural chmn.). Home: 137 Porter St Gary IN 46406

BRUNE, LINDA RUTH, educator; b. DuQuoin, Ill., Aug. 13, 1947; d. Louis John and Martha Frieda (Zinke) B. B.S. in Edn., So. Ill. U., 1969. Tchr. Community Consol. Dist. 204, Pinckneyville, Ill., 1969—. Tchr. Sunday Sch., Lutheran Ch. Home: Rural Route 3 Box 25 Nashville IL 62263 Office: Community Consol 204 Sch Pinckneyville IL 62274

BRUNER, JERE WAITE, political scientist, educator; b. Akron, Ohio, Mar. 5, 1928; s. Harold Edwards and Evelyn Berenice (Waite) B.; student Harvard U., 1946-48; B.S., Northwestern U., 1962, M.S., 1963; Ph.D. (Woodrow Wilson nat. fellow 1963-64, Univ. dissertation fellow 1965-66, NSF fellow 1966-67), Yale U., 1973; m. Ann Fairchild White, July 3, 1960 (div. 1971); 1 child, Erika Susan; m. Katharina Sabina Kleiner, Aug. 28, 1971; 1 child, Franziska Renata Corinthia. Tchr., Soc. of Bros., Paraguay, 1951-55, translator, 1951-58, engr., 1949-59, editor, 1954-57; acting asst. prof. govt. Oberlin Coll., 1967-73, asst. prof., 1973-76, assoc. prof., 1976—, govt. dept. chair, 1981-85; participant NSF Faculty Workshop, summer 1974. Campaign cons. to state legislator Donald Pease, Ohio (now congressman), 1968-71. Mem. Am. Polit. Sci. Assn., Midwest Polit. Sci. Assn., Internat. Transactional Analysis Assn. Author: (with others) Political Socialization Across the Generations, 1975; editorial bd. Am. Jour. Polit. Sci., 1979-82. Office: Govt Dept Oberlin Coll Oberlin OH 44074

BRUNER, LEE ROY, pharmacist; b. Civil Bend, Mo., Feb. 14, 1936; s. Homer Russell and Minnie (Reck) B.; m. Vivian Mariett Carl, Apr. 6, 1973; children—Michael Lane, Lori Ayn, Penny Eleeza Jessica. B.S., U. Mo.-Kansas City, 1957. Owner, operator Bruner's Pharmacy, Greenfield, Mo., 1959-66, Pill Box Pharmacy, Willard, Mo., 1971—. Home: 400 Watson Dr Willard MO 65781

BRUNER, PHILIP LANE, lawyer; b. Chgo., Sept. 26, 1939; s. Henry Pfeiffer and Marjorie (Williamson) B.; A.B., Princeton U., 1961; J.D., U. Mich., 1964; M.B.A., Syracuse U., 1967; m. Ellen Carole Germann, Mar. 21, 1964; children—Philip Richard, Stephen Reed, Carolyn Anne. Admitted to Wis. bar, 1964, Minn. bar, 1968; mem. firm Hart and Bruner, Mpls., 1983—; adj. prof. William Mitchell Coll. Law, St. Paul, 1970-78, 81; lectr. law seminars univs.; bar assns. and industry. Mem. Bd. Edn., Mahtomedi Ind. Sch. Dist. 832, 1978—. Served to capt. USAF, 1964-67. Recipient Disting. Service award St. Paul Jaycees, 1974; named One of Ten Outstanding Young Minnesotans, Minn. Jaycees, 1975. Fellow Nat. Contract Mgmt. Assn.; mem. Internat. Am., Fed., Minn., Wis., Ramsey, Hennepin bar assns., Internat. Assn. Ins. Counsel, Am. Arbitration Assn. (nat. panel arbitrators). Club: Mpls. Athletic. Contbr. articles to profl. jours. Home: 8432 80th St N Stillwater MN 55082 Office: 1221 Nicollet Mall Minneapolis MN 55403

BRUNER, TIMOTHY LEE, college administrator; b. Hutchinson, Kans., Nov. 18, 1950; s. Norval Eugene and Alberta Helen (Davis) B.; m. Kathy Ann Shappley, Aug. 4, 1972; children—Sharla Kristine, Olivia Joy, Karis Leigh. B.A., Harding U., 1973. Tchr., missionary Namwianga Secondary Sch., Kalomo, Zambia, Africa, 1973-75; dir. info. Harding U., Searcy, Ark., 1975-77; dir. coll. relations York Coll., Nebr., 1977-84, asst. to the pres., 1984—. Deacon, East Hill Ch. of Christ, York, 1982—. Mem. U.S. Basketball Writers Assn., U.S. Coll. Baseball Writers Assn., Coll. Sports Info. Dirs. Assn. Avocations: Basketball; tennis; golf; sportswriting. Home: 1012 Delaware Ave York NE 68467 Office: York Coll 9th and Kiplinger York NE 68467

BRUNER, WILLIAM EVANS, II, ophthalmologist, educator, researcher; b. Cleve., Oct. 10, 1949; s. Clark Evans and Pauline (Schrenk) B.; m. Susan Lee Fraser, June 7, 1975; children—Amanda Lee, Andrew Evans. B.A., Wesleyan U., 1971; M.D., Case Western Res. U., 1975. Diplomate Am. Bd. Ophthalmology. Intern in surgery Univ. Hosps., Cleve., 1975-76; resident in ophthalmology, 1976-79; fellow in cornea and anterior segment surgery Johns Hopkins Hosp., Balt., 1979-81; asst. prof. ophthalmology Case Western Res. U., Cleve., 1981—; chief ophthalmology VA Med. Ctr., Cleve., 1981—. Contbr. chpts. to med. textbooks and articles to profl. jours. Recipient Alfred S. Maschke award Case Western Res. U. Sch. Medicine, 1975. Fellow Am. Acad. Ophthalmology; mem. AMA, Assn. Research in Vision and Ophthalmology, Wilmer Residents Assn., Cleve. Acad. Medicine, Alpha Omega Alpha. Republican. Clubs: Cleve. Skating, The Kirtland. Avocations: snow skiing; tennis; golfing; music; art. Home: 2906 Weybridge Rd Shaker Heights OH 44120 Office: Univ Suburban Health Ctr 1611 S Green Rd Cleveland OH 44121

BRUNETTE, JOHN S., sales executive; b. Chgo., June 10, 1930; s. William B. and Mary Alice (Nolan) B.; m. Patricia Reese, Jan. 23, 1954; children—Steven, Cynthia, Gregory, Michael, William, Robert. Student Northwestern U., 1957. Sales engr. Maxon Corp., Muncie, Ind., 1958-68, br. mgr., Detroit, 1968-75, gen. sales mgr., Muncie, 1975-79, v.p., 1979—, also dir.; dir. Ind. Heating Equipment Assn. Served to 1st lt. USAF, 1950-55, Korea. Roman Catholic. Office: Maxon Corp 201 E 18th St Muncie IN 47302

BRUNK, SAMUEL FREDERICK, med. oncologist; b. Harrisonburg, Va., Dec. 21, 1932; s. Harry Anthony and Lena Gertrude (Burkholder) B.; B.S., Eastern Mennonite Coll., 1955; M.D. (Mosby scholar) U. Va., 1959; M.S. in Pharmacology, U. Iowa, 1967; m. Mary Priscilla Bauman, June 24, 1976; children—Samuel, Jill, Geoffrey, Heather, Kirsten, Paul, Barbara. Straight med. intern U. Va., Charlottesville, 1959-60; resident in chest diseases Blue Ridge Sanatorium, Charlottesville, 1960-61; resident in internal medicine U. Iowa, Iowa City, 1962-64, fellow in clin. pharmacology (oncology), 1964-65, fellow in clin. pharmacology (oncology), 1966-67, assoc. in medicine, 1966, asst. prof. internal medicine, 1966, asso. prof., 1972-76; fellow in medicine (oncology) Johns Hopkins U., Balt., 1965-66; vis. physician bone marrow transplantation unit Fred Hutchinson Cancer Treatment Center, U. Wash., Seattle, 1975; practice medicine specializing in med. oncology, Des Moines, 1976—; attending physician Iowa Luth. Hosp., 1976—, Iowa Meth. Med. Center, 1976—, NW Community Hosp., 1976—, Mercy Hosp. Med. Center, 1976— (all Des Moines); cons. physician Des Moines Gen. Osteo. Hosp., 1976—; prin. investigator Iowa Oncology Research Assn. in assn. with N. Central Cancer Treatment Group and Eastern Coop. Oncology Group, 1978-84. Bd. dirs. Iowa div. Am. Cancer Soc., 1971—, Johnson County chpt., 1968-72. Diplomate Am. Bd. Internal Medicine. Fellow ACP, Am. Coll. Clin. Pharmacology; mem. AMA, Iowa Med. Soc., Polk County Med. Soc., Iowa Thoracic Soc., Am. Thoracic Soc., Iowa Clin. Med. Soc., Am. Fedn. Clin. Research, AAAS, Iowa Heart Assn., Am. Assn. Cancer Edn., Am. Soc. Hematology, Am. Soc. Clin. Pharmacology and Therapeutics, Central Soc. Clin. Research. Raven Soc., Alpha Omega Alpha. Roman Catholic. Contbr. articles to med. jours. Home: 3940 Grand Ave West Des Moines IA 50265 Office: Penn Med Place Suite 308 1301 Pennsylvania Ave Des Moines IA 50316

BRUNKE, SCOTT MOORE, plastic manufacturing company executive; b. Evanston, Ill., June 14, 1947; s. Wallace Charles and Janice Marie (Moore) B.; m. Susan Virginia Lund, Oct. 21, 1967; children—Eric Moore, Aaron Mart, Adam Paul, David Ryan. Student Western Ill. U., 1965-66, Coll. of DuPage, 1966-67, Central YMCA Coll., 1967-68. With research and devel. dept. Am. Can Co., Batavia, Ill., 1967-69; plant engr. Borse Plastic Products, Hinsdale, Ill., 1969-71; plant mgr. A&G Plastic Products, Sturgis, Mich., 1971-75; plant mgr. Leon Plastics div. U.S. Industries, Grand Rapids, Mich., 1975-79; co-owner, exec. v.p. B&G Plastics Inc., Grand Rapids, Mich., 1979—, B&G Industries, 1983—; co-owner B&G Helicopter Co., 1982—, B&G Machinery Co., 1979—, Cachia & Brunke Constrn. Co., Yucca Valley, Calif., 1983—, B&G Export Co., 1981—. Mem. Soc. Plastics Industry, Aircraft Owners and Pilots Assn., Grand Rapids C. of C. Republican. Mem. Ch. of Christ. Patentee in field. Office: B&G Plastics Inc 220 Front St SW Grand Rapids MI 49504

BRUNNER, KAY LORRAINE, human resource specialist; b. Columbus, Ohio, July 17, 1949; d. Clarence Edward and Virginia Belle Yahn; B.S., Bowling Green (Ohio) State U., 1970, M.Ed., 1976; postgrad. U. Toledo, 1977—; m. David W. Brunner, Jr., June 24, 1972. Elem. tchr. public schs., Sylvania, Ohio, 1971-75; adminstrv. masters intern, grad. asst., acad. counselor U. Toledo, 1976-78; asst. employment mgr. Ohio Citizens Trust Co., Toledo, 1978-79, personnel devel. mgr., 1979-81; cons. Career Devel., Inc., 1982-85; human resource planning specialist Blue Cross/Blue Shield Mich., 1985—. Chmn. bloodmobile ARC, 1979—. Mem. Internat. Assn. Personnel Women, Am. Soc. Tng. and Devel., Toledo Personnel Mgmt. Assn., Bowling Green State U. Alumni Assn., Phi Delta Kappa, Gamma Phi Beta, Pi Lambda Theta, Sigma Alpha Iota, Phi Kappa Phi. Methodist.

BRUNO, THOMAS ANTHONY, lawyer; b. Berwyn, Ill., Feb. 8, 1954; s. Alexander Nicholas and Mildred Mary (Biciste) B.; m. Elizabeth Ann Matthias, June 12, 1976. B.A., U. Ill. 1976, J.D., 1979. Bars: Ill. 1980, U.S. Dist. Ct. (cen. dist.) Ill. 1980, U.S. Supreme Ct. 1985. Prin. Thomas A. Bruno and Assocs., Urbana, Ill., 1980—; lectr. U. Ill. Law Sch., Urbana, 1981—. Author (newspaper column) Honest Lawyer, 1983. Bd. dirs. Devel. Services Ctr., Champaign, Ill., 1979-82; vice chmn. bd. Disabled Citizens Found., Champaign, 1982—; mem. Humane Soc. Champaign County, 1984. Ill. Legis. scholar, 1972-76. Mem. ABA, Ill. Bar Assn., Champaign County Bar Assn., Assn. Trial Lawyers Am., Champaign County Assn. Criminal Defense Lawyers (past pres. Champaign chpt. 1982—), Nat. Assn. for Prevention Child Abuse (v.p. Champaign county chpt.), Phi Eta Sigma. Democrat. Roman Catholic. Clubs: U. Ill. Quarterback, U. Ill. Rebounder. Lodge: K.P. Home: 1109 W Park Ave Champaign IL 61821 Office: Thomas A Bruno and Assocs 303 W Green St Urbana IL 61801

BRUNO, THOMAS RALPH, orthopedic surgeon; b. Chgo., Oct. 7, 1939; s. Albert and Ann (Broccolo) B.; m. Sharon Marie Kelly, June 13, 1964; children—Maria, Thomas Jr., Anna, Leah, Michael, Caroline, Matthew. Student Loyola U.-Chgo., 1957-70, M.D., 1964. Diplomate Am. Bd. Orthopedic Surgery. Intern Cook County Hosp., Chgo., 1964-65; resident in orthopedic surgery, Northwestern U., Chgo., 1965-70, fellow hand surgery, 1970-71; staff orthopedic surgeon, hand cons. N.W. Community Hosp., Arlington Heights, Ill., 1972—; cons. hand surgery, orthopedic surgery O'Hare Ind. Clinic, Elk Grove Village, Ill., 1973—; asst. prof. orthopedic surgery Rush Presbyn. St. Luke's Med. Ctr., Chgo., 1973-84. Contbr. articles to profl. jours. Coach, med. cons. Palatine Basketball Assn., (Ill.), 1980-82; v.p. Inverness Soccer Assn. (Ill.), 1982—. Served to maj USAF, 1970-72. U.S. Govt. fellow, 1969-70. Fellow Am. Acad. Orthopedic Surgeons; mem. Ill. Orthopedic Soc., Midwest Orthopedic Soc., ACS (com. trauma 1977—). Roman Catholic. Clubs: Inverness Golf; Right Tennis (Shaumburg, Ill.). Avocations: tennis; aerobic conditioning. Office: Orthopedic Assocs SC 2010 S Arlington Heights Rd Arlington Heights IL 60005

BRUNOW, EDWIN EDWARD, metall. cons.; b. Milw., July 28, 1912; s. John Johann and Anna Henrietta (Radmann) B.; student U. Wis., Milw., 1931-38, Marquette U., 1933-36; m. Grace Gladys Alma De Sham, June 27, 1942; children—Barry W., Nancy G. Brunow Hornsby. Plant metallurgist Sivyer Steel Co., Milw., 1938-59, metall. engr., 1959-63, tech. dir., 1963-69; metall. engr. Ervin Industries, Adrian, Mich., 1969-74, tech. dir., 1974-77; metall. cons., 1977—. Vice-chmn. Potawatomi council Boy Scouts Am.; mem. local sch. bds., 1953-58. Mem. Am. Foundrymen's Soc., Am. Soc. Metals, ASTM, Steel Founders Soc. Am. Research included cast armor plate, early warning system, minuteman silos, nuclear reactors; developed 450 and 250 micron size steel balls for xerography. Home: 1343 Feeman Ct Adrian MI 49221

BRUNS, BILLY LEE, consulting electrical engineer; b. St. Louis, Nov. 21, 1925; s. Henry Lee and Violet Jean (Williams) B.; B.A., Washington U., St. Louis, 1949, postgrad. Sch. Engring., 1959-62; m. Lillian Colleen Mobley, Sept. 6, 1947; children—Holly Rene, Kerry Alan, Barry Lee, Terrence William. Supt., engr., estimator Schneider Electric Co., St. Louis, 1950-54, Ledbetter Electric Co., 1954-57; tchr. indsl. electricity St. Louis Bd. Edn., 1957-71; pres. B.L. Bruns & Assos., cons. engrs., St. Louis, 1963-72; v.p., chief engr. Hosp. Bldg. & Equipment Co., St. Louis, 1972-76; pres., prin. B.L. Bruns & Assos. cons. engrs., St. Louis, 1976—; tchr. elec. engring. U. Mo. St. Louis extension, 1975-76. Mem. Mo. Adv. Council on Vocat. Edn., 1969-76, chmn., 1975-76; leader Explorer post Boy Scouts Am., 1950-57. Served with AUS, 1944-46: PTO, Okinawa. Decorated Purple Heart. Registered profl. engr., Mo., Ill., Wash., Fla., La., Wis., Minn., N.Y., Iowa, Pa., Miss., Ind., Ala. Mem. Nat., Mo. socs. profl. engrs., Profl. Engrs. in Pvt. Practice, Am. Soc. Heating, Refrigeration and Air Conditioning Engrs., Illuminating Engrs. Soc., Am. Mgmt. Assn. Baptist. Club: Masons. Tech. editor The National Electrical Code and Blueprint Reading, Am. Tech. Soc., 1959-65. Home: 1243 Hobson Dr Ferguson MO 63135 Office: 10 Adams Suite 111 Ferguson MO 63135

BRUNSDALE, MITZI LOUISA MALLARIAN, English language educator, book critic; b. Fargo, N.D., May 16, 1939; d. Gregory Starn and Phyllis (Grobe) Mallarian; B.S. with honors (Nat. Merit scholar), N.D. State U., 1959, M.S., 1961; postgrad. Ind. U., 1959-60; Ph.D. (Danforth fellow), U. N.D., 1976; m. John Edward Brunsdale, Dec. 2, 1961; children—Margaret Louisa, Jean Ellen and Maureen Lois (twins). Departmental tchr. N.D. State U., 1958-59, grad. asst., 1960-61, instr. English and French, 1961; grad. asst. Ind. U., 1959-60; book critic Houston Post, 1971—; instr. English, Mayville (N.D.) State Coll., 1975-76, asst. prof., 1976-78, assoc. prof., 1978-83, prof., 1983—. Sec., 20th Dist. N.D. Republican Party, 1963-70; chmn. N.D. Humanities Council, 1980, 81-82; grant rev. panelist Nat. Endowment for Humanities. Mem. MLA, Rocky Mountain MLA, D.H. Lawrence Soc. Am., AAUP, Fgn. Lang. Assn. Red River, Linguistic Circle Man. and N.D., P.E.O., Phi Kappa Phi, Sigma Alpha Iota, Kappa Alpha Theta. Republican. Contbr. articles to profl. jours. and reference encys. Home: Rural Route 1 Mayville ND 58257 Office: Dept English Mayville State Coll Mayville ND 58257

BRUNSTING, ALBERT, physicist, optical engineer; b. Trenton, N.J., Mar. 24, 1945; s. Bernard Robert and Alice Clare (Nixon) B. m. Joyce Elaine Weener, Jan. 27, 1967; children—David, Michael. B.A., Hope Coll., 1967; M.S., U. N.Mex., 1969, Ph.D., 1972. Asst. prof. Auburn U., Ala., 1972-74; prin. physicist Coulter Electronics, Hialeah, Fla., 1974-81; supr. optical engring Miles Labs., Mishawaka, Ind., 1981—; mem. patent rev. bd. Applied Optics, Washington, 1982—. Contbr. articles to profl. jours. Patentee in field. Mem. Optical Soc. Am., Soc. Photo-optical Instrumentation Engrs. Home: 51718 Northfield Dr Elkhart IN 46514

BRUNSWICK, WILFRED LAWRENCE, physician; b. Ft. Recovery, Ohio, Mar. 19, 1929; s. Lawrence Henry and Justina Mary (Braun) B.; m. Joyce Marie Colbeck, June 9, 1955; children—Kim, Lawrence, Robert, Craig, Douglas, Susan, John. B.A., Ohio State U., 1951; M.D., St. Louis U., 1955. Diplomate Am. Bd. Internal Medicine. Intern St. Elizabeth's Hosp., Dayton, Ohio, 1955-56; resident in medicine Henry Ford Hosp., Detroit, 1958-61; practice medicine specializing in internal medicine Link Clinic, Mattoon, Ill., 1961—; asst. clin. prof. medicine U. Ill. Sch. Med., Urbana-Champaign, 1980—. Served to capt. U.S. Army, 1956-58. Fellow Am. Coll. Chest Physicians; mem. Am. Coll. Physicians, Am. Soc. Internal Medicine. Roman Catholic. Lodge: Knights of Columbus. Avocations: Fishing, gardening. Office: Link Clinic 1710 Wabash Mattoon IL 61938

BRUSADIN, RINALDO ANTONIO, pharmacist, educator; b. Columbus, Ohio, July 15, 1937; s. Antonio Pietro and Teresa Lucretia (Aluffo) B.; m. Eileen Patricia Angst, Dec. 23, 1960; children—Mark R., Deanna E., Maria L., Anne M. B.S., Ohio State U., 1959, M.S. in Pharmacy Adminstrn., 1975. Registered pharmacist, Ohio, Fla. Owner, pharmacist The Apothecary, Inc., Columbus, Ohio, 1966—; mng. ptnr. Brusadin, Dicello & Assocs., Columbus, Ohio, 1982—; sr. ptnr. Impact Mgmt. Assocs., Springfield, Va., 1983—; pres. Coop. of Ohio Pharmacies, 1984—; owner, pharmacist RonMor Corp., Columbus, 1972-81; adj. ast. prof. Ohio State U., 1975-80; clin. assoc. prof. Ohio State U. Columbus, 1983—; lectr. McNeil Labs. Ltd., Ontario, 1981—; cons. Ross Labs., Columbus, 1982—. Served to 1st lt. USAF, 1960-63. Recipient Disting. Alumni award Ohio State U., 1982; Merck Sharp & Dohme Co. award, 1981; named Retailer of Yr., Ohio Drug Travelers, Honolulu, 1974. Mem. Am. Pharm. Assn. (trustee 1976-77, 83-85), Acad. Pharm. Practice (pres. 1982), Ohio Pharm. Assn. (pres. 1976-77; Keys award 1977), Am. Assn. Colls. Pharmacy. Republican. Mem. Grace Brethren Ch. Home: 6870 Oakfair Ave Worthington OH 43085 Office: The Apothecary 1230 Morse St Columbus OH

BRUSIUS, BETTY LORRAINE, religious and educational organization administrator; b. Didsbury, Alta., Can., Sept. 2, 1935; s. Alexander and Mathilda (Schuhart) Weitz; m. Ronald William Brusius, June 17, 1953; children—Cathy Merrill, Ronda Carlson, Paula, Krista. Student Concordia Tchrs. Coll., Seward, Nebr., 1968-72. Exec. dir. Nat. Lutheran Parent-Tchr. League, St. Louis, 1979; co-developer Mo. Synod Luth Ch. marriage, family enrichment experiences; nat. trainer leader couples marriage enrichment; leader couple, marriage communications labs., effective tng., stress mgmt. Mem. Council Affilliated Marriage Enrichment Orgns., Assn. Couples Marriage Enrichment; program leader Active Parenting. Cons. Concordia Sex Edn. series; contbr. articles to religious publs.; producer videotape parenting program. Office: 123 W Clinton Pl Room 102 Saint Louis MO 63122

BRUSS, CAROL LOUISE, educator, actress; b. Milw., May 30; d. Walter Julius and Erna Caroline (Pieplow) Bruss. B.A., Carthage Coll., 1951; postgrad. Alverno Coll.-Milw., 1971-72. Life cert. secondary tchr., Wis. Personnel clk. Sears & Roebuck Co., 1951-55; mgr. Security Nat. Ins. Agy., Milw., 1955-60; student, dir., producer Sta. WMUS, Milw. Area Tech. Coll., 1960-65; office mgr. Stat Tab Corp., Milw., 1965-71; career specialist Milw. Pub. Schs., 1971—; theatre career specialist, 1977-84; tchr. English and speech Bay View High Sch., 1984—; actress, dir. Milw. community theatres; soprano soloist Lake Park Ch., Milw. Active South Div. Civic Assn., Milw.; mem. Marquis Library N.Y Soc.; life mem. (hon.) Lutheran Ch. Women. Recipient producer's award for best program Channel 10 Milw. Area Tech. Coll., 1962; Best Artistic award Act One Theatre Co., Milw. Pub. Schs., 1981. Mem. Wis. Theatre Assn., Impresarios-Milw. Performing Arts Ctr., AAUW, South Div. Civic Assn., Phi Lambda Omega, Alpha Mu Gamma, Alpha Psi Omega. Club: Coll. Women's. Home: 2216 S 28th St Milwaukee WI 53215

BRUSSEE, C. ROGER, marketing specialist; b. Cleve., Feb. 4, 1928; s. Casper B. and Sophia (Depta) B.; m. Anne Davidson, June 20, 1953; children—Frederic Carl, David Charles. B.S., Miami U., Oxford, Ohio, 1951. Mktg. dir. Whitin Machine, Worcester, Mass., 1960-65; dir. corp. planning Mead Corp., Dayton, Ohio, 1968-71; internat. mktg. dir. Am. Optical Co., Southbridge, Mass., 1971-79; v.p. bus. planning Itek Corp., Lexington, Mass., 1979-80, v.p. mktg./internat. sales, Ft. Lauderdale, Fla., 1980-81; market planning specialist 3M Co., St. Paul, 1982—; pres. owner Brussee Assocs., Ft. Lauderdale, 1981-82; cons. Mass. Bay Transp. Authority, Boston 1965-67. Author: U.S. Consumer Eyewear, 1979-83. Contbr. articles to mktg. jours. Served with USN, 1947-49. Mem. Am. Mktg. Assn. Republican. Unitarian. Avocations: reading; travel; photography. Home: 111 E Kellogg Blvd Saint Paul MN 55101 Office; 3M Bldg 223-4W 3M Ctr Saint Paul MN 55144

BRYAN, A(LONZO) J(AY), service club official; b. Washington, N.J., Sept. 17, 1917; s. Alonzo J. and Anna Belle (Babcock) B.; student pub. schs.; m. Elizabeth Elfreida Koehler, June 25, 1941 (div. 1961); children—Donna Elizabeth, Alonzo Jay, Nadine; m. 2d, Janet Dorothy Onstad, Mar. 15, 1962 (div. 1977); children—Brenda Joyce, Marlowe Francis, Marilyn Janet. Engaged as retail florist, Washington, N.J., 1941-64; now spl. asst. adminstrv. services Kiwanis Internat., Indpls. Fund drive chmn. ARC, 1952; bd. dirs. Washington YMCA, 1945-55, N.J. Taxpayers Assn., 1947-52; mem. Washington Bd. Edn., 1948-55. Mem. Washington Grange, Sons and Daus. of Liberty, Soc. Am. Florists, Nat. Fedn. Ind. Businessmen, Florists Telegraph Delivery Assn., C. of C. Methodist. Clubs: Masons, Tall Cedars of Lebanon, Jr. Order United Am. Mechanics, Kiwanis (pres. Washington (N.J.) 1952, lt. gov. internat. 1953-54, gov. N.J. dist. 1955, sec. N.J. dist. 1957-64, sec. S.E. area Chgo. 1965-74; editor The Jersey Kiwanian 1958-64); Breakfast (pres. 1981-82) (Chgo.). Home: Crooked Creek Community 4095 Point Bar Rd Apt 2C Indianapolis IN 46268 Office: Kiwanis Internat 3636 Woodview Terr Indianapolis IN 46268

BRYAN, ARTHUR ELDRIDGE, JR., lawyer; b. Webster City, Iowa, July 28, 1924; s. Arthur Eldridge and Grace Lillian (Glassburner) B.; B.A., State U. Iowa, 1949, J.D., 1951; m. Elizabeth Ann Stubbings, Oct. 18, 1958; children—Elizabeth Grace, Arthur Eldridge III, John Milner, Daniel Franklin. With U.P. R.R. Co., Omaha, 1942-54; capital ptnr., mem. exec. com., chmn. tax dept. McDermott, Will & Emery, Chgo., 1954—; dir. Gits Bros. Mfg., Chgo., 1967-68; dir., v.p., sec. Yuma Mesa Devel. Co., Yuma, Ariz., 1967-79; chmn. bd. dirs., chief exec. officer Lake Arrowhead Devel. Co. (Calif.), 1971-80. Lectr. taxation U. Chgo., Marquette U., No. Ill. U. Mem. com. on legis. action New Trier (Ill.) High Sch., 1974-78; active Boy Scouts Am., Glencoe, Ill., 1968-74; mem. adv. bd. United Settlement Appeal, Chgo., 1962. Bd. dirs., treas., pres. chmn. fin. com. Erie Neighborhood House, Chgo., 1958—; trustee N. Central Coll., Naperville, Ill., 1974-79; sec., chmn. bd. trustees, sec. prudential bd. Glencoe Union Ch., 1969-79. Served with inf. AUS, 1942-46; ETO, PTO. Decorated Bronze Star, Combat Inf. badge. Mem. Am. (chmn., spl. adviser sect. taxation com. on comml. banks and financials 1966-74), Ill., Iowa Chgo. bar assns., Ill. C. of C. (chmn. fed. tech. tax com.), Chgo. Assn. Commerce and Industry (fed. appropriations and expenditures com. 1968—), Am. Coll. Tax Counsel. Clubs: Chgo., Mid-Day, Monroe, Executive (Chgo.); Skokie Country (Glencoe, Ill.); Quail Creek Country (Naples, Fla.). Contbr. articles to profl. jours. Home: 565 Washington St Glencoe IL 60022 Office: 111 W Monroe St Chicago IL 60603

BRYAN, HENRY C(LARK), JR., lawyer; b. St. Louis, Dec. 8, 1930; s. Henry Clark and Faith (Young) B.; A.B., Washington U., St. Louis, 1952, LL.B., 1956; m. Sarah Ann McCarthy, July 28, 1956; children—Mark Pendleton, Thomas Clark, Sarah Christy. Admitted to Mo. bar, 1956; law clk. to fed. judge, 1956; asso. firm McDonald & Wright, St. Louis, 1956-60; partner firm McDonald, Bernard, Wright & Timm, St. Louis, 1961-64, McDonald, Wright & Bryan, 1964-81, Wright, Bryan & Walsh, 1981-84; v.p., dir. Harbor Point Boat & Dock Co., St. Charles, Mo., 1966-80, Merrell Ins. Agy., 1966-80; dir. Stanley Hanks Painting Co. Served to 1st lt. AUS, 1952-54. Mem. Am., Mo., St. Louis (past chmn. probate and trust sect., marriage and divorce law com.) bar assns., Kappa Sigma, Phi Delta Phi. Republican. Episcopalian. Elk. Home: 41 Ladue Terr Ladue MO 63124 Office: 11 S Meramec St Saint Louis MO 63105

BRYAN, HENRY EDWARD, JR., land surveyor, transitman; b. Boonville, Mo., Dec. 4, 1947; s. Henry Edward and Jessie Ferris (Simpson) B.; m. Dorris Eilene Stowers, May 3, 1969. Student U. Mo., 1965-68, Rend Lake Jr. Coll., 1968-82. Registered land surveyor, Ill., Ky., Ind. Party chief J & E Surveys, Odin, Ill., 1974-79; party chief, land surveyor Woodfall & Assocs., Mt. Vernon, Ill., 1979-81; transitman Inland Steel Coal Co., Sesser, Ill., 1981—; land surveyor, owner Egyptian Surveying Services Co., Benton, Ill., 1982—. Mem. Am. Congress on Surveying and Mapping (Nat. Soc. Profl. Surveyors div.), Ill. Registered Land Surveyors Assn. (dir. 1982-83, past pres. Little Egyptian chpt.), Mo. Assn. Registered Land Surveyors. Mem. Assemblies of God Ch. Avocations: gardening; old books on surveying and surveying history. Home: 208 Burkett Benton IL 62812 Office: Inland Steel Coal Co Rural Route 5 McLeansboro IL 62859

BRYAN, JOHN H., JR., food company executive; b. West Point, Miss., 1936. B.A. in Econs. and Bus. Adminstrn., Southwestern at Memphis, 1958. With Consol. Foods Corp., Chgo., 1960—, exec. v.p. ops., 1974, pres., 1974—, chief exec. officer, 1975—, chmn. bd., 1976—, also dir.; dir. Standard Oil Co. (Ind.), 1st Chgo. Corp., 1st Nat. Bank Chgo. Bd. dirs. Nat. Merit Scholarship Corp., United Way of Chgo., Catalyst, Nat. Women's Econ. Alliance; bus. adv. Council Chgo. Urban League; trustee com. for econ. devel. Rush-Presbyn.-St Luke's Med. Ctr.; rep. to Bus. Council; mem. nat. corps. com. United Negro Coll. Fund. Mem. Grocery Mfrs. Am. (chmn., dir.). Office: Consolidated Foods Corp Three First Nat Plaza Chicago IL 60602

BRYAN, ORPEN W., public school system administrator; b. Chgo., Mar. 17, 1931; s. Roland and Alberta (Davis) B.; m. Mary L. Washington, Aug. 21, 1967. A.A., Wilson Jr. Coll., 1950; B.Ed., Chgo. Tchrs. Coll., 1952; B.E., Loyola U., Chgo., 1959, M.Ed., 1963; Ed.D., Nova U., 1975. Cert. tchr. and prin., Ill. Elem. tchr., Chgo. Bd. Edn., 1954-61, counselor, asst. prin., 1961-65, prin., 1965-73, dist. supt., 1973-81, dep. supt., 1981-85, asst. supt., 1985—; mem. State of Ill. Edn. Adv. Council, 1976-81. Vice pres., Joint Negro Appeal; bd. dirs. Beatrice Caffrey Youth Services, Inc. Served with U.S. Army, 1952-54. Recipient Outstanding Service award State of Ill. Commn. on Delinquency, 1979. Mem. Am. Assn. Sch. Adminstrs., Assn. Curriculum and Supervision Devel., Nat. Assn. Black Sch. Educators, Urban League, NAACP, Phi Delta Kappa. Methodist. Club: City (Chgo.). Office: 160 W Wendell Chicago IL 60610

BRYANT, BETTY JANE, shopping center exec.; b. Camden, Ind., June 19, 1926; d. Claude Raymond and Louise (Eckert) Wickard; B.S., Purdue U., 1947; m. Harry R. Bryant, Aug. 21, 1949; children—Susan, Patricia. Retail mgmt. and advt. L.S. Ayres, Indpls., 1947-49, Burdine's, Miami, Fla., 1950-51, Joske's, San Antonio, 1968, Dillard's, San Antonio, 1968-70; with Sterling Advt. Agy., N.Y.C., 1949; mktg. dir. Mary Ann Fabrics and Designer's Fabrics By Mail, Evanston, Ill., 1971-75; instr. Ray-Vogue Sch., Chgo., 1976; mktg. dir. Woodfield Shopping Center, Schaumburg, Ill., 1977—. Mem. council Fashion Group of Chgo. Bd. dirs. Northwest Area council Girl Scouts Am., 1982—, Greater Woodfield Conv. and Visitors Bur., 1984-85. Mem. N.W. Suburban Assn. (dir.), Commerce and Industry (v.p. 1981-82), Chgo. Area Shopping Center Mktg. Dirs.'s Assn., Women in Mgmt., Mortar Board, Kappa Kappa Gamma. Home: 2008 Bayberry Ln Hoffman Estates IL 60195 Office: Woodfield Merchants Assn 5 Woodfield Mall Schaumburg IL 60195

BRYANT, DENNIS GENE, professional services manager; b. Kirksville, Mo., May 17, 1957; s. Paul Everett and Ruth Anita (Davis) B.; B.S., Northeast Mo. State U., 1980. Programmer, analyst Grange Mut. Columbus, 1980-82; telecommunication specialist Blue Cross of Central Ohio, Columbus, 1982-83; mgr. Comtech Systems, Inc., Columbus, 1983—. Mentor Central Ohio Rehab. Ctr., Columbus, 1983—. Mem. Assn. Systems Mgmt. Avocations: fishing, painting, reading. Office: Comtech Systems Inc 250 E 5th St Suite 1500 Cincinnati OH 45202

BRYANT, DONALD LOYD, JR., insurance executive; b. Mt. Vernon, Ill., June 30, 1942; s. Donald Loyd and A. Eileen (Galloway) B.; B.A., Denison U., 1964; J.D., Washington U., 1967; M.S.F.S., Am. Coll., 1978; m. Barbara Murphy, July 9, 1981; children—Derek Lawrence, Christina Murphy. Admitted to Mo. bar, 1967; agt. Equitable Life Assurance Soc. U.S., St. Louis, 1968—; pres. Donald L. Bryant & Assos., 1969-74, Bryant Planning Group, Inc., St. Louis, 1974—. Bd. dirs. St. Louis Area council Boy Scouts Am., 1974—; bd. dirs. United Way, St. Louis. Served with U.S. Navy, 1967. Mem. Am. Bar Assn., Mo. Bar Assn., Assn. Advanced Life Underwriting (dir. 1979-82, asso. v.p. 1979-82), St. Louis Estate Planning Council, Million Dollar Round Table, The Forum. Republican. Presbyterian. Clubs: Bellerive Country, St. Louis, Mo. Athletic. Home: 3 Picardy Ln Saint Louis MO 63124 Office: Suite 1770 100 N Broadway Saint Louis MO 63102

BRYANT, DOROTHY TAYLOR, educator; b. Indpls., Mar. 22, 1931; d. George E. and Lalla Marie (Bass) Taylor; m. Alvin Jones, Dec. 6, 1958; 1 dau., Pamela M.; m. 2d, William J. Bryant, June 27, 1974. B.S. in Edn., Ind. U., 1953; M.A., Northeastern Ill. U., 1968; Ed.D., Vanderbilt U., 1982. Tchr. pub. schs., Gary, Ind., 1953; tchr. elem. sch. Chgo. Bd. Edn., 1954-68, 80-83, evaluator ECIA Chpt. 1 programs, 1984—, lang. arts cons., 1968-75, instrn. coordinator Dists. 11, 23, 1976-80. Founding mem. Profl. Women's Aux. Provident Hosp.; bd. dirs. Beatrice Coffery Youth Services. Recipient 20 yr. service award Profl. Women's Aux. Provident Hosp. Mem. Assn. Supervision and Curriculum Devel. (trustee), Chgo. Assn. for Supervision and Curriculum Devel. (founder), AAUW, Neal Marshall Alumni of Ind. U., Phi Delta Kappa, Delta Sigma Theta. Mem. United Ch. of Christ. Home: 2246 W 91st St Chicago IL 60620

BRYANT, JAMES WESLEY, investment executive; b. Kingston, Ont., Can., Nov. 8, 1921; came to U.S., 1953, naturalized, 1961; s. Victor Wesley and Martha (Stewart) B.; m. Joy Gibson, Feb. 25, 1950; children—James David, Mary Ruth, John Victor, Douglas Andrew, Barbara Ann. B.Commerce Queen's U., Can., 1949; Diploma Stonier Grad. Sch. Banking, 1968. Second v.p. Lincoln Nat. Life, Ft. Wayne, Ind., 1953-56; exec. v.p. Old Stone Bank, Providence, R.I., 1965-71; sr. v.p. Salk, Ward and Salk, Chgo., 1971-72, Washington Nat. Ins. Co., Evanston, Ill., 1972—; dir. Wash. Nat. Ins. Co., mem. fin. com.; chmn., dir. Wash. Nat. Devel. Co., Ill. Mortgage Banks Assn.; trustee Wash. Nat. Benefit Plans; chmn. investment sect. Am. Council Life Ins.; chmn. bd. regents Life Officers Investment Seminar Am. Council Life Ins. Rockford Coll. Served with RCAF, 1942-46, Royal Can. Ordinance Corp. (Res.), 1951-53. Republican. Presbyterian. Clubs: Mich. Shores, Chgo. Curling, Indian Hill Curling, Can. Club of Chgo. Home: 1007 Lake Ave Wilmette IL 60091 Office: Washington Nat Ins Co 1630 Chicago Ave Evanston IL 60201

BRYANT, JERRY DOYLE, lawyer; b. Whitley City, Ky., Mar. 12, 1947; s. Fred and Myrtle Roberta (Vanover) B.; B.S., Cumberland Coll., 1969; J.D., Ind. U., 1973; m. Glenna J. Mattingly, Aug. 31, 1968; children—Laura, Jennifer, Jeremy. Mgr., Sears Roebuck & Co., Cin., 1969-70; indsl. relations rep. Westinghouse Co., Bloomington, Ind., 1970-71; admitted to Ohio bar, 1974, Fla. bar, 1984; individual practice law, Wilmington, Ohio, from 1974; now sr. ptnr. firm Bryant, Chappars, Rose & Dobyns, Wilmington; vis. asst. prof. Wilmington Coll., 1975-79; spl. counsel Ohio Atty. Gen., 1975-79. Chmn. Clinton County Bd. Elections, 1976-80; mem. exec. com. Democratic party, Wilmington, 1975-79. Mem. Am. Bar Assn., Am. Trial Lawyers Assn., Ohio Bar Assn., Clinton County Bar Assn. (pres.), Wilmington C. of C. Democrat. Methodist. Lodges: Eagles, Rotary, Masons, Shriners. Home: 317 Indian Ripple Rd Wilmington OH 45177 Office: 121 W Main St PO Box 470 Wilmington OH 45177

BRYANT, PEGGY LYNN, lawyer, judge; b. Marion, Ohio, July 31, 1951; d. Ralph and Mary Grace (Fazio) B.; m. Thomas Leslie Long, Apr. 24, 1982. B.A. magna cum laude, Miami U., Ohio, 1973; J.D. cum laude, Ohio State U., 1976. Bar: Ohio 76, U.S. Dist. Ct. (no. and so. dists.) Ohio 1977, U.S. Ct. Appeals (6th cir.) 1980. Assoc., Alexander Ebinger Fisher McAlister & Lawrence, Columbus, Ohio, 1976-81, ptnr., 1982-85; judge Franklin County Mcpl. Ct., 1985—; lectr. Mem. Ptnrs. in Edn., Ohio State U., 1978—; bd. dirs. Bridge Found. and Bridge Counseling. Recipient Donald B. Becker award Ohio State U. Coll. Law, 1974, Judge Joseph M. Harter award, 1976. Mem. ABA (health care com. of antitrust sect.), Ohio Bar Assn. (health care com. of antitrust sect.), Columbus Bar Assn. (media com., chair interprofl. com.), Phi Beta Kappa, Phi Kappa Phi. Democrat. Roman Catholic. Clubs: Capital, Metropolitan (nominating com.) (Columbus). Avocations: reading; music; theatre; travel. Home: 1271 W 1st Ave Columbus OH 43212 Office: Franklin County Mcpl Ct 375 S High St Columbus OH 43215

BRYANT, TERRY LYNN, counselor; b. Parsons, Kans., Mar. 26, 1952; d. Earl Morris and Neva L. (Sissel) B.; A.A., Labette Com. Jr. Coll., 1972; B.S., Kans. State Coll., 1974, M.S., 1975; Ed.S., Pittsburg (Kans.) State U., 1981; m. Debra Kay Brown, June 14, 1980; 1 son, Kyle David. Counselor, Kans. State Dept. Human Resources, Pittsburg, 1975—, handicapped applicant specialist, 1983—; owner, operator lic. foster child care facility, Arma, Kans.; manpower generalist State of Kans., 1976-77. Mem. Am. Personnel and Guidance Assn., Kans. Assn. Pub. Employees, Assn. Specialists in Group Work, Internat. Assn. Personnel in Employment Security, S.E. Kans. Assn. Personnel in Employment Security, Phi Theta Kappa. Baptist. Home: PO Box 457 Arma KS 66712 Office: 104 S Pine St Pittsburg KS 66762

BRYANT, VIVIAN CHILLIS, educator; b. Detroit, June 25, 1938; d. Ollie and Elizabeth Chillis; B.A., Mich. State U., 1959; M.Ed., Wayne State U., 1965; Ed.S., U. Mich., 1975; m. William Russell Bryant, July 16, 1971; 1 dau., Darmetta Annese. Tchr. Spanish, Inkster (Mich.) High Sch., 1959-62; tchr. English, asst. prin. Carver Jr. High Sch., Los Angeles, 1962-67; guidance counselor, tchr. speech, music Christ the King High Sch., Okinawa, 1967-69; tchr. English, River Rouge (Mich.) High Sch., 1969—, chmn. dept. English, fgn. langs. and art, 1974—. Treas., chmn. Southfield Parent Youth Guidance Commn., 1978—; mem. Southfield Pub. Schs. Task Force, 1975, Southfield Citizens Adv. Bd. on Sex Edn., 1979—; mem. Women's Conf. of Concern; mem. Human Relations Council, 1981. Recipient VFW award, 1976; Mother of Yr. award Ohio U., 1983. Mem. Nat. Assn. Women Deans, Adminstrs. and Counselors, Assn. Supervision and Curriculum Devel., Nat. Council Tchrs. English, Delta Sigma Theta. Mem. African Methodist Episcopal Ch. Clubs: Oak Grove Ensemble (pres.), Ravine's Women's of Southfield. Home: 23100 Staunton Dr Southfield MI 48034 Office: 1411 Coolidge Hwy River Rouge MI 48218

BRYANT, WILLIAM H., association executive; b. Albany, N.Y., June 21, 1933; s. James W. and Olma A. (Bryant) B.; m. Nancy McClurg, Aug. 26, 1972; children—Dana, Alethea, Jeff. B.S.B.A., Akron U., 1960. Trainee Mohawk Tire Co., Akron, Ohio, 1954; dir. research Tri County Planning Assn., Akron, 1957-63, Ohio Dept. Devel., Columbus, 1963-69; with Greater Cleve. Growth Assn., 1969—, pres., 1980—; bd. dirs. Conv. and Visitors Bur., 1980—, Cleve. Area Devel. Corp., 1980—. Served with USAF, 1952-56. Mem. U.S. C. of C. (bd. dirs.), Ohio C. of C. Office: 690 Union Commerce Bldg Cleveland OH 44115*

BRYANT-BOOKER, DELORIS, educator; b. Fort Valley, Ga., Sept. 11, 1938; d. Henry Edward and Marion (Pendleton) Bryant; children—James A. Booker, Karla L. Booker. B.S., Hampton Inst., 1959; cert. edn. Dominican Coll., 1973; M.A., San Francisco State U., 1982. Cert. tchr. elem., spl. edn. Computer programmer Dept. Def., Washington, 1959-64; computer systems analyst Tech. Ops. Research, Inc., 1964-68; tchr. elem. sch. Kentfield Sch. Dist. (Calif.), 1973-78; tchr. Glen Ellyn 89 Sch. Dist. (Ill.), 1979—. Bd. dirs. West Suburban YWCA, Lombard, Ill., 1980—, vice-chair, 1984—; bd. dirs. Dist. 89 Edn. Assn., Glen Ellyn, 1980—, sec., 1980-82. Recipient literacy award West Suburban Reading Council, 1985; Calif. Edn. Assn. scholar, 1972. Mem. Ill. Edn. Assn. (ethnic minority rep. regional council), Council Exceptional Children, Internat. Reading Assn., Alpha Kappa Alpha (most sisterly Lambda Alpha Omega chpt. 1981), Nat. Hampton Alumni Assn. Democrat. Home: 137 Mill Pond Dr Glendale Heights IL 60139

BRYCE, GARY LYNN, educator; b. Detroit, Mar. 28, 1941; s. David and Ingrid (Saastomian) B.; B.S., U. Mich., 1963, M.A., 1975, labor relations certificate, 1975; children—Amy Lynn, David Vincent. Faculty, U. Pitts., 1963-64; tchr. St. Williams Sch., Walled Lake, Mich., 1964-65, Clawson (Mich.) pub. schs., 1965-67; tchr., coach Royal Oak (Mich.) pub. schs., 1967-85; mem. faculty, coach women's basketball and softball Wayne State U., Detroit, 1985—; clinic organizer Mich. Softball Coaches, 1979. U. Pitts. fellow, 1963-64; named Mich. High Sch. Softball Coach of the Yr., 1979; Wayne State U. Softball Coach of Yr., Gt. Lakes Interscholastic Conf., 1982. Mem. Mich. High Sch. Softball Assn. (dir. 1981—), Nat. High Sch. Coaches Assn., Mich. High Sch. Coaches Assn., Mich. Softball Assn., NEA, Mich. Edn. Assn., Internat. Platform Assn., Am. Security Council, Am. Def. Preparedness Assn. Democrat. Unitarian. Address: 101 Matthae Wayne State U Detroit MI 48202

BRYSON, HENRY HOWARD, computer company executive; b. Greenwood, S.C., Aug. 18, 1934; s. Benjamin Broadus and Rosa Lee (Parker) B.; m. Eleanor Ann Holmes, Dec. 25, 1955; children—Henry Howard Jr., Kenneth, Tracy. B.A. in Math., Morehouse Coll., 1956; postgrad., U. Dayton, 1959-60. Mathematician U.S. Air Force, Wright Patterson AFB, Ohio, 1956-67; with Control Data Corp., Mpls., 1967—, now gen. mgr. Pres. Roads Men's Civic Club, St. Paul, 1976-83; bd. dirs. St. Paul Urban League, 1981-84, Turning Point (Halfway House), Mpls., 1981-83. Fellow Am. Mgmt. Assn. Democrat. Baptist. Avocations: Golf, spectator sports, reading. Home: 10249 Berkshire Rd Bloomington MN 55437 Office: Control Data Corp PO Box O Bloomington MN 55440

BRYSON, WILLIAM RONALD, state regulatory program official, engineering geologist; b. Manhattan, Kans., Dec. 29, 1934; s. Harry Ray and Gladys Winifred (Musser) B.; m. Betty Ann Dinkel, Apr. 28, 1962; 1 child, Stewart Clayton. B.S., Kans. State U., 1958, M.S., 1959. Teaching asst. Kans. State U., Manhattan, 1958-59; dist. geologist Kans. Dept. Health and Environ., Topeka, 1959-61, Dodge City, 1961-74, asst. dir. oil field sect., Topeka, 1974-78, dir. Bur. Oil Field and Environ. Geology, Topeka, 1978—, dir. Office Environ. Geology, 1985—; bd. dirs. Kans. Mined Land Bd., Pittsburg, 1980-85; mem. EPA Groundwater Strategy Task Force, 1980-81; dir. Underground Injection Practices Council, Oklahoma City, 1984—; mem. steering com. Interstate Oil Compact Commn., 1978—; dir. conservation div. Kans. Corp. Commn., 1985—. Author tech. papers and bulletins. Dist. commr. Boy Scouts Am., Dodge City, 1972-74, Lawrence, Kans., 1975-76; vice chmn. Dept. Geology Adv. Council, Manhattan, 1982-85. Mem. Assn. Engring. Geologists (sect. chmn. 1972-73, Plaque award 1973, sect. mem. 1965—, nat. legis. affairs chmn. 1984—, chmn. nat. ann. meeting 1983—), Kans. Water Well Assn. (Key Man award 1984). Avocations: philately; bowling; gardening. Home: 709 Lawrence St Lawrence KS 66044 Office: Bur Oil Field and Environ Geology Kans Dept Health and Environment Bldg 740 Forbes Field Topeka KS 66620

BRZEZINSKI, I(GNATIUS) FRANK, dentist; b. Chgo., Nov. 15, 1919; s. Frank Anthony and Mary (Orlowski) B.; D.D.S., Loyola U. (Chgo.), 1944; m. Therese Victoria Istok, Nov. 23, 1950; children—Paul Frank, Daniel Steven, Carol Ann. Practice gen. dentistry, Chgo., 1947—; asso. clin. prof. operative dentistry Sch. Dentistry Loyola U., 1970—. Served to lt. Dental Corps, USNR, 1944-46. Fellow Am. Coll. Dentists, Acad. Gen. Dentistry, Internat. Coll. Dentists; mem. Chgo. Dental Soc. (dir., past pres. N.W. br.), Dental Arts Club Chgo., Am. Prosthodontic Soc., Pierre Fauchard Acad., Odontographic Soc., Omicron Kappa Upsilon. Club: Polish Am. Comml. Home: 5440 N Panama St Chicago IL 60656 Office: 5301 W Fullerton St Chicago IL 60639

BUA, NICHOLAS JOHN, federal judge; b. Chgo., Feb. 9, 1925; s. Frank and Lena (Marino) B.; J.D., DePaul U., 1953; m. Camille F. Scordato, Nov. 20, 1943; 1 dau., Lisa Annette Bua Krinch. Admitted to Ill. bar, 1953; trial atty., Chgo., 1953-63; judge Village Ct., Melrose Park, Ill., 1963-64; asso. judge Circuit Ct. Cook County, Chgo., 1964-71, circuit judge, 1971-76; justice Ill. Appellate Ct.-1st Dist., from 1976; now U.S. dist. judge; northern dist. ILLINOIS vice chmn. exec. com. Jud. Conf. Ill., also mem. supreme ct. rules com., 1970—; lectr. DePaul U.; mem. faculty Def. Tactics Seminar, Ill. Def. Counsel Seminar, 1971. Trustee Goltlieb Meml. Hosp., Schwab Rehab. Hosp. Fellow Nat. Coll. State Trial Judges, U. Nev., 1966. Served with Armed Forces, World War II. Contbr. articles to legal publs. Office: Everett McKinley Dirksen Bldg 219 S Dearborn St Chicago IL 60604

BUBB, HENRY AGNEW, savings and loan association executive; b. Williamsport, Pa., Mar. 26, 1907; m. Elizabeth Black, June 26, 1929; 1 child, Betty Bubb Dicus. D.B.A., Washburn U.-U. Kans., 1928. Chmn. bd. Capitol Fed. Savings and Loan Assn., Topeka, Kansas; dir. Security Benefit Life Ins. Co., Capitol Funds, Inc., Columbian Nat. Title Ins. Co.; mem. U.S. Treas. Adv. Com.; chmn. emeritus MGIC Investment Corp. Trustee Kansas U. Endowment Assn. past nat. pres. Kans. U. Alumni Assn.; past pres. and dir., Downtown Topeka, Inc.; chmn. Higher Edn. Loan Program of Kansas, 1977; pres. emeritus Kansas Masonic Found., Inc. Recipient Distinguished Kansan award Native Sons and Daughters, 1974, Distinguished fellow Internat. Union of Bldg. socs. and Savings and Loan Assns., 1971, Fred Ellsworth medallion U. Kansas, 1977. Mem. Newcomen Soc. in N.A., U.S. League of Savings Assns. (legisl. cons., mem. 1975 internat. devel. com., mem. sr. adv. group of the com. on polit. action), C. of C. (past pres.), S.A.R., 35th Div. Assn., Alpha Kappa Psi, Sigma Chi. Clubs: Topeka Country (past pres.), Garden of the Gods (Colo. Springs), Paradise Valley Country (Ariz.). Lodge: York Rite Bodies, Cabiri, Royal Order of Jesters (past bd. dirs.), Shriners, Masons, Rotary, Scottish Rite (33 deg.; past potentate). Home: 2323 Mayfair Place Topeka KS 66611 Office: Capitol Fed Savings and Loan Assn 700 Kansas Ave Topeka KS 66603

BUBENIK, OLDRICH VENCESLAS, surgeon, oncologist; b. Nove Mesto, Czechoslovakia, Sept. 16, 1943; came to U.S., 1980; s. Oldrich and Bozena (Seidel) B.; m. Jana Marie Vesselova, Aug. 10, 1968; children—Jeanne Beatrice, Jacob Andre. Grad. Purkinje U. (Czechoslovakia), 1967; M.D., Queen's U. (Can), 1972; M.Sc., McGill U. (Can.), 1977; postgrad., E. Fischel State Cancer Hosp., Columbia, Mo., 1980-82. Instr. surgery and oncology Univ. Health Scis., Kansas City, Mo., 1984—; cons. Lakeside Hosp., Kansas City, 1984—. Fellow Royal Coll. Surgeons. Contbr. articles to profl. jours. Avocation: stamp collecting. Office: Univ Health Sciences 2105 Independence Kansas City MO 64124

BUBLITZ, JEROME ERNEST, agricultural cooperative executive; b. Montevideo, Minn., Dec. 19, 1948; s. Elmer Ernest and Norma Charlotte (Olson) B.; B.S., U. Chgo., 1970; student (NSF grantee), U. Iowa, 1966. Rebuyer, Western Auto Supply Co., Kansas City, Mo., 1970-71; asst. inventory control mgr. Western Auto Supply Co., Kansas City, Mo., 1971-72, asst. corp. inventory control mgr., 1972-73, asst. to corp. v.p. inventory control, 1973-75; dist. mgr. MFA Livestock Assn., Inc., Marshall, Mo., 1975-78, asst. gen. mgr., 1978—; instr. Nat. Inst. for Coop. Edn., U. Mo., 1979—. Mem. Kansas City-Jackson County Drug Abuse Task Force, 1974-75; mem. Kansas City Mayor's Corps of Progress, 1972-75; mem. Saline County Republican Com., 1976—. Mem. Saline County Hist. Soc. (v.p. 1976-80), Marshall C. of C. (mem. agribus. com.), Am. Swedish Inst., Am. Soc. Tng. and Devel., Am. Inst. Cooperation, Indsl. Mgmt. Soc., Am. Inst. Indsl. Engrs., Psi Upsilon. Republican. Lutheran. Clubs: The Kansas City Club, Vasa Order, Sons of Norway, Germania, Vesterheim, Rotary, Optimists. Home: 100 Ridgecrest Rd Marshall MO 65340 Office: PO Box 278 West Hwy 20 Marshall MO 65340

BUCHANAN, GERALD SNYDER, physician; b. Albert Lea, Minn., Jan. 28, 1920; s. Frank Merton and Verian Almeda (Snyder) B.; B.S., Union Coll., 1949; M.D., Loma Linda U., 1949; m. Laura Mae Martin, Sept. 9, 1945 (div. Jan. 1975); children—Gerald Duane, Douglas Lee, Randall Stuart; m. 2d, Edith Ellen Wheelock, Sept. 16, 1977. intern Hurley Hosp., Flint, Mich., 1949-50; practice gen. medicine, Fenton, Mich., 1950-51, Deer River, Minn., 1951-54, Ithaca, Mich., 1956-57, Holly, Mich., 1957—; mem. staff Hurley, McLaren, Genesee Meml. hosps. (all Flint). Pres. North Oakland unit Mich. Cancer Found., 1968-70. Served to capt. USMC, 1954-56. Home: 3258 Grange Hall Rd Holly MI 48442 Office: 3741 Grange Hall Rd Holly MI 48442

BUCHANAN, LARRY DEE, advertising agency executive; b. Atlantic, Iowa, Aug. 13, 1937; s. William Howard and Harriet Elizabeth (Simpson) B.; student So. Meth. U., 1958; B.A., N.Tex. State U., 1960; m. Frankie L. Henderson, Mar., 1961 (div.); 1 dau., Lauri Dee; m. 2d Karen P. Daniels, July, 1975 (div.); m. 3d, Joan C. Gidney; 1 stepson, Jason M. Writer graphic services dept. Collins Radio Co., Cedar Rapids, Iowa, 1961-63, writer, public relations dept., 1964; co-founder, sec., treas., dir. writer-producer Three Arts, Inc., Cedar Rapids, 1964-70, sr. v.p., dir., creative dir., 1970—. Mem. Cedar Rapids Symphony Orch. Assn., 1967-74, 81—, pres., 1970-71; search and rescue pilot CAP, 1969-71. Served with USMCR, 1955-61. cert. airline transport pilot. Mem. Advt. Fedn. of Cedar Rapids (pres., 1971), Nat. Agri-Mktg. Assn., Sigma Delta Chi, Phi Mu Alpha Sinfonia. Republican. Office: 425 2d SE 11th Floor Cedar Rapids IA 52401

BUCHE, MARY PATRICIA, hospital official; b. Chgo., Mar. 12, 1922; d. Thomas Frederick and Bertha Adelaide (Rife) Murphy; m. William John Buche, Jan. 3, 1942 (dec.); children—Mark, Monica Buche Dux. Student Earlham Coll., 1939-40. Joined 3d Order of St. Francis, 1965; receptionist, Richmond, Ind., 1944-45; dept. mgr. J.C. Penney Co., Frankfort, Ind., 1962-64; employment counselor Rose Personnel Agy., Lafayette, Ind., 1968-69; patient rep. St. Elizabeth Hosp. Med. Ctr., Lafayette, 1969-74, dir. patient relations, 1974—; cons. Purdue U. Pres. Lafayette in Ind. Deanery, Council of Catholic Women, 1968; mem. parish council St. Boniface Ch., Lafayette, 1971-75, active Ladies Soc., 1965—; coordinator Widow to Widow mental health assn., 1981. Mem. Nat. Soc. Patient Reps., Ind. Soc. Patient Reps. (charter, pres. 1977), Ind. Hosp. Assn., Am. Hosp. Assn., Psi Iota Xi (v.p. 1965-66). Home: 907 N 20th St Apt 4 Lafayette IN 47904 Office: St Elizabeth Hosp Med Ctr 1501 Hartford St Lafayette IN 47903

BUCHER, GLENN RICHARD, collelge dean; b. Mechanicsburg, Pa., May 20, 1940; s. K. Ezra and Esther (Markley) B.; m. Mary K. Gladfelter, June 12, 1963; children—Christina Hope, Timothy Jon. A.B., Elizabethtown (Pa.) Coll., 1962; M.Div., Union Sem., N.Y.C., 1965; Ph.D., Boston U., 1968. Vis. instr. Emerson Coll., Boston, 1967-68; asst. prof. Howard U., 1968-70; vis. scholar Union Sem., N.Y.C., 1975-76; acting dir. Ctr. for Program and Instl. Renewal, Sherman, Tex., 1980-82; Lincoln prof. religion Coll. of Wooster, 1970-85, dean of faculty, 1985—; higher edn. cons. Ind. and Assn. Am. Colls., 1980—. Author, editor: Straight/White/Male, 1976, Confusion and Hope, 1974; contbr. articles to profl. jours. Fellow Soc. Values in Higher Edn., Am. Acad. Religion. Home: 426 Pearl St Wooster OH 44691 Office: Dean of Faculty Coll of Wooster Wooster OH 44691

BUCHER, HENRY HALE, JR., educator; b. Hainan Island, China, Mar. 7, 1936; s. Henry Hale and Louise Catron (Scott) B. (parents Am. citizens); student Davidson Coll., 1954-56; B.A., Am. U. of Beirut, 1958; postgrad. Univ. Coll., Legon, Ghana, 1960-61, Sorbonne U. Paris, 1962-63; M.Div., Princeton Theol. Sem., 1962; M.A. (Ford fellow), U. Wis., Madison, 1971, Ph.D., 1977; m. Emily Orr Clifford, June 22, 1969; 1 son, Clifford Hale. Ordained to ministry United Presbyterian Ch., U.S.A., 1962; intern service and study project in Gabon, under World Student Christian Fedn. of Geneva, 1962-65; mem. staff dept. higher edn. Nat. Council of Chs., N.Y.C., 1965-68; program dir. Ams. for Middle East Understanding, N.Y.C., 1969; curriculum specialist African studies program U. Wis., Madison, 1977-80; cons. in global edn., 1980—; lectr. on So. Africa; mem. Madison Area Com. on So. Africa, 1969—, Madison Friends of Internat. Students, 1975—; Fulbright/Hays doctoral dissertation research abroad fellow, Gabon, Senegal, France, 1973-74. Mem. Am. Hist. Assn., African Studies Assn., Societe des Africanistes, Societe Francaise d'Histoire d'Outre-Mer, Soc. Intercultural Edn., Tng. and Research, Wis. Council Social Studies. Author: The Third World: Middle East, 1973, rev., 1984; contbr. articles on Africa, Middle East to profl. publs. Home: 223 W Oak St Cottage Grove WI 53527 Office: 229 N Main St Cottage Grove WI 53527

BUCHER, OTTO NORMAN, clergyman, educator; b. Milw., June 3, 1933; s. Otto A. and Ida (Smazal) B.; B.A., Capuchin Sem. of St. Felix, Huntington, Ind., 1956; postgrad. Capuchin Sem. of St. Anthony, Marathon, Wis., 1956-60; S.T.L., Catholic U. Am., 1963; S.S.L., Pontifical Bibl. Inst., Rome, 1965. Joined Capuchin Franciscan Order, 1952; ordained priest Roman Catholic Ch., 1959; lector in scripture Capuchin Sem. of St. Anthony, Marathon, 1966-70; asso. prof. Bibl. studies St. Francis Sem., Sch. Pastoral Ministry, Milw., 1970-73; asso. prof. Bibl. studies Sacred Heart Sch. of Theology, Hales Corners, Wis., 1973—, acad. dean, 1979-85, vice rector, 1984—; mem. exec. com. Midwestern Assn. Theology Schs., 1973-74. Mem. Cath. Bibl. Assn. Am., Soc. Bibl. Lit. Democrat. Home: St Fidelis Friary 528 N 31st St Milwaukee WI 53208 Office: Sacred Heart Sch Theology 7335 S Lovers Lane Rd PO Box 429 Hales Corners WI 53130

BUCHHOLZ, RONALD LEWIS, architect; b. Milw., Jan. 14, 1951; s. Raymond LeRoy and Della (Krause) B.; B.S. in Architecture, U. Wis., Milw., 1973; m. Mary Lou Stockhausen, May 20, 1972; children—Lauren Robert, Geoffrey Alan. Archtl. appraiser Am. Appraisal Co., Milw., 1973; plan examiner, bur. bldgs. and structures, div. safety and bldgs. Wis. Dept. Industry, Labor and Human Relations, Madison, 1973-76, staff architect, 1976, architect, adminstrv. code cons., bur. code devel., 1976-80, dep. dir., 1980-83, asst. dir., 1983—; instr. U. Wis., Madison Ext., also state certification courses for bldg. and dwelling insps.; mem. Wis. Bldg. Code Adv. Rev. Bd., 1976—, Fire Prevention Council, 1978—, adv. com. Alternative Energy Tax Credits, 1978, 80; mem. Interagy. Com. on Spills of Hazardous Materials, 1981—; mem. adv. com. Wis. Electric Supply, 1984—. Vol. leader Boy Scouts Am. Served with Army N.G., 1970-76. Registered architect, Wis. Mem. Resdl. Facilities Council (exec. sec. 1976-78), Bldg. Ofcls. and Code Adminstrs. Internat. Inc., Nat. Eagle Scout Assn. Roman Catholic. Author tech. reports. Home: 4925 Knox Ln Madison WI 53711 Office: 201 E Washington Ave Room 103 Madison WI 53702

BUCHSIEB, WALTER CHARLES, orthodontist; b. Columbus, Ohio, Aug. 30, 1929; s. Walter William and Emma Marie (Held) B.; B.A., Ohio State U., 1951, D.D.S., 1955, M.S., 1960; m. Betty Lou Risch, June 19, 1955; children—Walter Charles II, Christine Ann. Pvt. practice dentistry specializing in orthodontics, Dayton, Ohio, 1959—; cons. orthodontist Miami Valley Hosp., Childrens Med. Center, Dayton; asst. prof. dept. orthodontics Ohio State U. Coll. Dentistry, 1984—. Mem. fin. and program com. United Health Found., 1971-73; mem. dean's adv. com. Ohio State U. Coll. Dentistry; bd. dirs. Hearing and Speech Center, 1968-82, 2d v.p., 1976-78, pres., 1978-79; orthodontic advisor Ohio Dept. Health Bur. Crippled Children's Services, 1983-84. Served to capt. AUS, 1955-58. Mem. ADA (alt. del. 1968—, council on internat. relations 1984—), Ohio Dental Assn. (sec. council legislation 1969-78, v.p. 1978-79, pres.-elect 1979-80, pres. 1980-81), Am. Coll. Dentists, Dayton Dental Soc. (pres. 1970-71), Great Lakes Soc. Orthodontists (sec.-treas. 1972-75, pres. 1977-78), Internat. Coll. Dentists, Am. Assn. Orthodontists (chmn. council legislation 1976, speaker of house 1982-85), Pierre Fauchard Acad., Ohio State U. Alumni Assn., Delta Upsilon, Psi Omega. Republican. Lutheran (elder 1965-68, v.p. 1974). Clubs: Masons, Rotary (pres. 1973-74, Paul Harris fellow). Home: 1520 Brittany Hills Dr Dayton OH 45459 Office: 5335 Far Hills Ave Dayton OH 45429

BUCHTEL, FORREST LAWRENCE, college dean, musician, composer; b. St. Edward, Nebr., Dec. 9, 1899; s. Charles Stanton and Frances Marian (Stephens) B.; A.B., Simpson Coll., 1921; M.S. in Edn. (scholar), Northwestern U., 1931; B.Mus.Ed., VanderCook Coll. Music, Chgo., 1932, M.Mus.Ed., 1933; D.F.A., Simpson Coll., 1983; m. Jessie Helene Macdonald, June 6, 1925; children—Bonnie Buchtel Cataldo, Helene Buchtel Adams, Beverly Buchtel Platt, Forrest Lawrence. Tchr., South High Sch., Grand Rapids, Mich., 1921-25, Emporia (Kans.) State U., 1925-30, Lane Tech. High Sch., Chgo., 1930-34, Amundsen High Sch., Chgo., 1935-54; tchr. VanderCook Coll. Music, Chgo., 1931-81, dean of students, 1960; composer, works include: 30 sets of bandbooks, 800 solos and ensembles for sch. bands, 30 marches, 30 overtures. Served with S.A.T.C., 1918. Recipient Alumni award Simpson Coll., 1961, VanderCook Coll., 1965. Mem. Am. Bandmasters Assn., ASCAP, Bandmasters Hall of Fame, Phi Beta Mu, Phi Mu Alpha Sinfonia, Kappa Kappa Psi, Delta Upsilon. Methodist. Club: Univ. (Chgo.). Home: 1116 Cleveland St Evanston IL 60202 Office: 3209 S Michigan Ave Chicago IL 60616

BUCHTEL, MICHAEL ALFRED, civil engineer, realtor associate; b. Barberton, Ohio, Apr. 22, 1925; s. Percy Elberta and Dortha Opal (Lowery) B.; B.S. in Civil Engring., U. Akron, 1971; m. Pauline Margaret Slee, Dec. 30, 1948; children—Preston Carl, Michele Darlene. Utility boilers Babcock & Wilcox Co., Barberton, 1947-54, draftsman, layout man for power boilers, 1954-73, structural engr., stress analyst on power boilers, 1974-82; realtor assoc. Century 21: McElroy Realty Inc., Brunswick, Ohio, 1982—. Active Boy Scouts Am., 1952-56, Jr. Achievement, 1956, Chapel in University Park, Akron, Ohio, 1952-68. Served with U.S. Army, 1949-50. Recipient Jr. Achievement award, 1956. Mem. ASCE (pres. Akron sect., award 1978). Republican. Clubs: Hilltoppers, Masons, Kiwanis, Gideons Internat. (sec. Medina County camp 1968—). Home: 875 Andrews Rd Medina OH 44256 Office: 4171 Center Rd Brunswick OH 44212

BUCK, BERNESTINE BRADFORD, school counselor; b. Altheimer, Ark., July 25, 1924; d. Henry Walker and Dora Lois (Sims) Bradford; B.A., Stowe Tchrs. Coll., 1950; M.Ed., U. Mo., 1973; m. Joseph Wellington Buck, Oct. 1, 1950; children—Stanley W., Linda Carol, Debra Lois. Tchr. pub. schs., St. Louis, 1950-73, sch. counselor, 1973—. Mem. U. Mo. scholarship com., 1974-84. Mem. Am., Mo. personnel and guidance assns., St. Louis Guidance Assn. (pres. 1979-80), Mo. Guidance Assn. (exec. council 1980-81, v.p. elem. sect.). Baptist.

BUCK, EARL CHRIS, clinical laboratory administrator; b. Duluth, Minn., Sept. 6, 1947; s. Earl Chris and Mabel Alice (Frame) B.; m. Teresa Ann Lindholm, Apr. 6, 1968; children—Sharie, Nichole, Earl. B.A., U. Minn.-Duluth, 1973; postgrad. U. No. Iowa. Vice pres., treas. Consol. Regional Labs., Inc., Waterloo, Iowa, 1978—. Served to lt. comdr. USNR, 1970-78. Mem. Clin. Lab. Mgmt. Assn. (pres. Iowa chpt., nat. bd. dirs. 1983-84, treas. 1983-85), Am. Soc. Clin. Pathologists (assoc.), Am. Legion (post bingo treas., chaplain, pres. bldg. com.). Mem. Ch. of Christ. Club: Willow Run Country (Denver, Iowa). Home: Box 609 Denver IA 50622 Office: 618 Allen St Waterloo IA 50702

BUCK, JAMES ROY, engineering educator, researcher, consultant; b. Big Rapids, Mich., Feb. 22, 1930; s. John Robert and Lois Jenieve (Lane) B.; m. Marie Neola Gilbertson, Aug. 26, 1962; children—Carolyn Marie, John Gilbert, James Roy II. Student Ferris State Coll., 1948-49; B.S., Mich. Technol. U., 1952, M.S. in Civil Engring., 1953; Ph.D., U. Mich., 1964. Materials engr. U.S. Naval Civil Engrs. Research Lab., Port Hueneme, Calif., 1952-53; structural engr. Austin Engrs. Ltd., Midland, Mich., 1956-57; field engr. Calumet Flexicore Corp., East Chicago, Ill., 1957-58; instr. Ferris State Coll., Big Rapids, 1958-59; research asst. U. Mich., Ann Arbor, 1959-62, asst prof., Dearborn, Mich., 1962-65; assoc. prof. Purdue U., Lafayette, Ind., 1965-79, prof., 1979-81; prof. indsl. and mgmt. engring., chmn. dept. indsl. and mgmt. engring. U. Iowa, Iowa City, 1981—; cons. in field. Served to lt. (j.g.) Civil Engring Corps, USNR, 1953-56. Recipient Eugene Grant award Am. Soc. Engring. Edn., 1979; Best Tchr. award Sch. Indsl. Engring., Purdue U., 1979. Mem. Inst. Indsl. Engrs., Human Factors Soc., Inst. Mgmt. Sci. Lutheran. Clubs: Rotary, Elks. Author: Economic Risk Decisions in Engineering and Management, 1984. Contbr. chpts. to books, articles to profl. publs. Home: 2353 Cae Dr Iowa City IA 52240 Office: Room 4132 EB U Iowa Systems Div Iowa City IA 52242

BUCK, MAYNARD ARDEEN, JR., printing and publishing executive; b. Warren, Ohio, May 21, 1929; s. Maynard Ardeen and Gertrude Wilhelmina (Reuss) B.; m. Anne Williams, Aug. 27, 1950; 1 child, Maynard Ardeen III. B.Sc., Kent State U., 1953, M.A., 1954. Pres. Freeport Press, Ohio, 1957—, Carrollton Graphics, Inc., Ohio, 1975-83, chmn., 1983—; pub. Harrison News-Herald, Cadiz, Ohio, 1968—, Free Press standard, Carrollton, 1975—. Bd. dirs. Muskingum Watershed Conservancy Dist., Ohio, 1978—; sch. bd. mem. Cadiz Local Schs., 1971-76; trustee Harrison Community Hosp., Ohio, 1969-81. Served to lt. USAF, 1954-56. Mem. Ohio Newspaper Assn. (pres. 1982-83, chmn. bd. 1983—). Presbyterian. Lodge: Masons. Office: Carrollton Graphics Inc 707 Canton Rd Carrollton OH 44615

BUCK, ORLIN EDWARD, health insurance consultant; b. Laporte, Iowa, June 19, 1928; s. Charles Arthur and Nellie Etta (Border) B.; m. Mary Ellen Charest, Aug. 25, 1947 (div. 1970) children—Anthony Edward, Roberta Jane, Schlichting, Rebecca Ann Ripley; m. Daisy Lee Shinn, July 1, 1971; stepchildren—Lester Dale Shinn, Cindy Shinn Reynolds, Sandy Kay Shinn. Student, U. Northern Iowa, 1965-66. Sales mgr. Walnut Dairy, Waterloo, Iowa, 1948-65; owner, operator restaurant, Waterloo, 1962-70; asst. mgr. Mutual of N.Y., Waterloo, 1962-70; cons. to Blue Cross/Blue Shield, Davenport, Iowa, 1970—; cons. to various cities and counties regarding health info. Profl. clown for Crippled Children and Blind Insts.; cons. Democratic Party, locally and nationally; chmn. Cultural Exchange Student Program, City of Davenport. Club: High Twelve (Davenport) Lodges: Masons (past master 1982), Shriners, Lions (past pres.), Order Eastern Star (past patron). Avocations: amateur photography. Home: 3835 Kelling Davenport IA 52806 Office: Blue Cross/Blue Shield Iowa 1910 E Kimberly 3 Corporate East Davenport IA 52808

BUCKENMYER, JAMES ALBERT, college dean, educator; b. Toledo, Nov. 11, 1932; m. Susan Loughlin; 4 children. M.B.A. in Indsl. Mgmt., U. Toledo, 1962; Ph.B. in Commerce, U. Notre Dame, 1954; D.B.A. in Orgn. Behavior, Washington U., St. Louis, 1970; M.A. in Communication Sci., Govs. State U., 1983. Instr. Bowling Green State U., Ohio, 1964-65; assoc. prof. U. Dayton, Ohio, 1965-73; asst. dean grad. programs Govs. State U., Park Forest South, Ill., 1973-75, prof. mgmt., 1973-82, acting dean, 1977-78, acting assoc. dean. acad. affairs, 1977-79, chmn. div. mgmt. and adminstrv. scis., 1980-82; dean, prof. mgmt. S.E. Mo. State U., Cape Girardeau, 1982—; vis. prof. Purdue U., Calumet, 1982; cons. numerous orgns. and colls. Contbr. articles to profl. jours. Mem. Acad. Mgmt., Am. Assn. Higher Edn., Work Edn. Council (project com. 1977), Phi Delta Kappa. Home: Route 1 Box 171 Northland Acres Jackson MO 63755 Office: Southeast Mo State U Cape Girardeau MO 63701

BUCKINGHAM, ALBERT WILLIAM, college administrator, physical education educator; b. Westfield, Iowa, Apr. 1, 1914; s. James W. and Sophie E. (Seamen) B.; B.A., Morningside Coll., 1939; M.A., Stanford U., 1950; postgrad. Notre Dame U., Northwestern U., 1942; m. Marian Marjorie Miller, Oct. 31, 1942; children—Susan Elizabeth, Rosemary, James William. Prin. and coach, Sergeant Bluff, Iowa, 1939-41; athletic dir. and coach, Mapleton, Iowa, 1941-42; basketball coach Morningside Coll., Sioux City, Iowa, 1945-56, dir. phys. edn. and athletics, 1945-69, asst. prof. phys. edn., 1945-55, assoc. prof., 1956—, dir. pub. relations, 1956-68, v.p. estate planning, 1962—. Bd. dirs. U.S. Olympic Com., 1965-77, Iowa United Methodist Found., 1975—; pres. U.S. Collegiate Sports Council, 1973-77; chief of missions World Univ. Games, 1977, 79. Served with USN, 1942-45. Named to Hall of Fame, Greater S.C. Athletic Assn., 1970, North Central Intercollegiate Athletic Conf., Helms Hall of Fame, Nat. Assn. Intercollegiate Athletics, 1969. Fellow Am. Sch. Health Assn.; mem. Nat. Assn. Intercollegiate Athletics (pres. 1965-66), Iowa Dirs. Coll. Public Relations (pres. 1955), Sioux City C. of C. (chmn. recreation com. 1954). Republican. Methodist. Clubs: Lions (pres. local club 1954-55), Sioux City Boat, Shriners, Masons (Sioux City). Contbr. articles to phys. edn. mags. Home: 1504 Morningside Ave Sioux City IA 51106 Office: 1501 Morningside Ave Sioux City IA 51106

BUCKINGHAM, BETTY JO, library media consultant; b. Prairie City, Iowa, Aug. 6, 1927; d. Irvin Amos and E(lsie) Dean (Webb) B. B.A., Iowa State Tchrs. Coll., 1948; M.S. in Library Sci., U. Ill.-Urbana, 1953; Ph.D., U. Minn.-Mpls., 1978. Tchr. English, Earlham Community Sch., Earlham, Iowa, 1948-50; tchr., librarian Harlan (Iowa) Community Sch., 1950-54; librarian Ft. Madison (Iowa) Community High Sch., 1954-60; librarian Kurtz Jr. High Sch., Des Moines, Iowa, 1960-64; cons. Iowa Dept. Pub. Instrn., Des Moines, 1964—; lectr. U. Minn.-Mpls., 1970. Mem. ALA, Am. Assn. Sch. Librarians (past sec., pres., councillor 1984-85), Nat. Edn. Assn., Iowa Ednl. Media Assn. (cons. 1973-83), Iowa Library Assn., Intellectual Freedom Found., Women's Fellowship Prairie City (past pres.), Beta Phi Mu, Kappa Delta Pi. Democrat. Church of the Brethren (mem. steering com. women's caucus 1977-80, editor Cistern periodical 1980—, bd. dirs. No. Plains dist. 1984—). Avocations: Reading, classical music, writing. Home: RR 2 Box 111 Prairie City IA 50228 Office: Iowa Dept Pub Instrn Grimes State Office Bldg Des Moines IA 50319

BUCKINGHAM, WILLIAM BRICE, physician; b. Chgo., July 25, 1924; s. Brice Albert and Mary (Ahern) B.; student John Carroll U., Cleve., 1942-44; M.D., U. Ill., 1947, B.S., 1956; m. Margery L. Cross, Sept. 16, 1950; children—Cathlin, Megan, Gillian, William Brice, Peter, Michael, John, Maura, Mark, David, Dierdre. Intern, Cook County Hosp., Chgo., 1947-49, resident, 1950-52; fellow Northwestern U., 1951-52. Diplomate Am. Bd. Internal Medicine. Practice medicine, specializing in internal medicine, Chgo., 1952—; attending physician Oak Park Hosp., 1952—, Augustana Hosp., Chgo., 1954-66; staff physician Oak Forest Tb. Hosp., 1952-55; asso. attending pulmonary disease sect. Cook County Hosp., 1952-56, attending physician, 1956-64, chief pulmonary sect., 1963-64, attending physician dept. medicine, 1964-66; cons. DeKalb County Tb. Hosp. and Clinic, 1954-60; attending physician St. Elizabeths Hosp., Chgo., 1954-65, St. Josephs Hosp., Chgo., 1964-68; attending physician VA Research Hosp., Chgo., 1960-70, cons. pulmonary diseases, 1970; attending physician Northwestern Meml. Hosp., 1966—, dir. pulmonary lab., 1968-75; clin. asst. Northwestern U. Med. Sch., 1952-56, instr., 1956-59, asso. in medicine, 1959-68, asst. prof., 1968-70, asso. prof., 1970—, chief, sect. gen. medicine, 1975-78; mem. sci. adv. com. Municipal Tb. Sanitarium, 1968-72; cons. in tb. Ill. Dept. Pub. Health, 1973—; tb. control officer Chgo. Bd. Health, 1974-84; vis. prof. medicine Universidad Autonoma de Guadalajara Med. Sch., 1975, 80; cons. med. editor Quality Rev. Bull., Joint Commn. on Accreditation of Hosps., 1975. Fellow A.C.P., Am. Coll. Chest Physicians (pres. Ill. chpt. 1966-67, gen. chmn. First Fall Sci. Assembly, Chgo. 1969), Inst. of Medicine Chgo.; mem. AMA, Am. Soc. Internal Medicine, Ill. Soc. Internal Medicine (exec. council 1965-85, pres. 1973-75), Chgo. Soc. Internal Medicine (pres. 1977-78), Am. Thoracic Soc., Ill., Chgo. med. socs., Chgo. Tb. Inst. (dir.), Am. Assn. Inhaalation Therapists (bd. med. advisers 1969-72), Riverside Golf Club. Contbr. articles to profl. jours. Home: 319 Linden Ave Oak Park IL 60302 Office: 233 E Erle St Chicago IL 60611

BUCKLEY, RALPH EUGENE, minister; b. Parma, Mo., Sept. 8, 1931; s. Homer Clarence and Ruby Jewel (Oliver) B.; m. Faye Laverne Snider, July 24, 1951; 1 child, Paul Talmadge. Th.B., Th.M., Faith Baptist Coll., 1971; postgrad. Midwestern Bapt. Sem., 1971-72; D.Ministry, Crossroad Div. Sem., 1978. Owner, mgr. Standard Oil Co., Bernie, Mo., 1951-54; salesman Kirksey Pontiac Co., Malden, Mo., 1954-57; supr. Internat. Harvestor, St. Louis, 1958-60; owner, operator Buckley Farms, Bernie, 1960-66; minister So. Baptist, Malden, 1966-67, educator, minister, Jonesboro, Ill., 1967—; exec. mem. George Hutching Evang. Assn., St. Louis, 1974-78; trustee Mid-Continent Bapt. Coll., Mayfield, Ky., 1976-78; dir. Faith Christian Schs., Morgantown, Ky., 1974-79; exec. mem. Mo. Bapt., Jefferson City, 1981-82. Author: Sunday School Re-fueling Station, 1975, Commentary Matthews Gospel, 1980. Dir. Area Wide Crusade, Lawson, Mo., 1972; cert. state umpire Mo. Softball Assn., Jefferson City, 1977. Home: 2841 Bethel Blvd Zion IL 60099 Office: 1st Bapt Ch 1727 N 27th St Zion IL 60099

BUCKLEY, ROBERT MICHAEL, clinical psychologist; b. Chgo., Oct. 20, 1927; s. Michael Francis and Lillian Ruth (Johnson) B.; B.S., Ill. Inst. Tech., 1960, M.S., 1963, Ph.D., 1970; m. Alice Kay Hanson, Oct. 17, 1959; children—Michelle, Tamara, Shawn. Chemist, metallurgist, Nalco, Chgo., 1952-56; psychologist, Chgo. Bur. Child Study, 1964-66, Speed Ednl. Coop., Chicago Heights, Ill., 1966-77; clin. psychologist, pres. Buckley-Long Assos. Ltd., Homewood, Ill., 1974-77. Served with USN, 1945-47. Mem. Am., Midwest, Ill. psychol. assns., Biofeedback Socs. Am., Ill. (chmn. instrumentation com). Club: VFW. Contbr. research reports on biofeedback to confs. Home: 4732 W 176th St Country Club Hills IL 60477 Office: 18019 Dixie Hwy Suite 1-D Homewood IL 60430

BUCKMAN, CHARLES EDWARD, JR., information systems executive; b. Kansas City, Mo., Sept. 27, 1943; s. Charles Edward and Geraldine Clara (Herold) B.; student Ill. State U., 1961-64; B.S., Quincy Coll., 1966; postgrad. U. Ill., 1967-68; m. Judith Brosi, Nov. 19, 1966; children—Christina Elaine, Erin Noel, Brian Charles. Juvenile parole agent Ill. Youth Commn., 1966-67, regional supr., Springfield, 1967-68; account salesman Ill. Bell Telephone, Moline, 1967-70, communications cons., 1970-72, data communications specialist, 1972-74, account mgr., 1974-76, mgr. data tech. support, Chgo., 1976-77, product mgr., 1977-80, industry mgr., 1980-82; nat. account mgr. Am. Bell, Inc., 1983; pres. Blythe-Nelson Midwest, Inc., 1983—. Treas. Christian Family Movement, 1975-76; mem. religious edn. bd. Sacred Heart Ch., Moline, 1975-76; mem. curriculum adv. com. Black Hawk Coll., Moline, 1973-76; pres. Hobson Village Assn. Mem. Data Processing Mgmt. Assn., Am. Mgmt. Assn., Nat. Eagle Scouts Assn. Roman Catholic. Lodge: Kiwanis. Home: 1081 Challdon Ct Naperville IL 60540 Office: 1 Naperville Plaza Naperville IL 60540

BUCKMAN, JEFFREY, physician; b. Chgo., Sept. 22, 1942; s. Morris and Ethel (Warter) B.; m. Myrna Elaine Saltzman, May 29, 1968; children—Ari Daniel, Lori Sue, Tami Michelle, Jodi Hollis. B.A., Northwestern U., Evanston, Ill., 1964; M.S., Syracuse U., 1965; M.D., Chgo. Med. Sch., 1969. Diplomate Am. Bd. Internal Medicine. Intern, Cleve. Clinic, 1969, resident in internal medicine, 1969-70, resident in hypertension, nephrology, 1970-73; dir. Research Cardiorehab, Ltd., Niles, Ill., 1977—; attending staff Luth Gen. Hosp., Park Ridge, Ill.; dir., pres. Vascular Diagnostics, Ltd., DesPlaines, Ill., 1982—. Pres., Maine Twp. Jewish Congregation, DesPlaines, 1981-84. Mem. Am. Soc. Internal Medicine, Am. Inst. Ultrasound in Medicine, Am. Soc. Nephrology, AMA, Chgo. Med. Soc., N.Y. Acad. Scis. Avocation: video, hifi. Office: North Suburban Med Cons 1875 Dempster Ave Suite 410 Park Ridge IL 60068

BUCUR, NICHOLAS ANTHONY, III, data processing exec.; b. Managua, Nicaragua, Oct. 11, 1950 (parents Am. citizens); s. Nicholas A. and Jacoba (Galo) B.; student Cuyahoga Community Coll., 1969-71. Propr., Infinity Co., pub., Cleve., 1968—, data processing cons., 1973—; editorialist WZAK Radio, Cleve., 1969-73, dir. pub. affairs, 1975—, moderator, announcer People's Voice program, 1973—; pub. Cleve. Feminist mag., 1973; systems mgr. Systems Info. Services, Cleve., 1976-78; sr. systems analyst Picker Corp., Cleve., 1978—; instr. data processing Cuyahoga Community Coll. Vice pres. Greater Cleve. Young Republican Club, 1971; mem. human relations com. Fedn. for Community Planning, 1973. Cert. computer profl. Mem. Nat. Mgmt. Assn. Mensa. Club: Cleve. City. Home: 10206 Clifton St Cleveland OH 44102 Office: 600 Beta Dr Cleveland OH 44143

BUDD, GITA BLUMENTALS, health care management consultant; b. Mpls., Nov. 2, 1955; d. Janis and Ausma Blumentals; m. J. Mark Budd, Apr. 28, 1979. B.A., Northwestern U., 1976, M. Mgmt., 1978. Adminstr. critical care Lutheran Gen. Hosp., Park Ridge, Ill., 1978-79, therapy services, 1979-80; assoc. Amherst Assocs. Inc., Chgo., 1980-81, sr. assoc., 1981-83, mgr., 1983—; preceptor hosp. and health services mgmt. program, Northwestern U., Evanston, 1982—. Mem. Healthcare Fin. Mgmt. Assn., Soc. Hosp. Planning, Women Health Execs. Network (membership chmn.), Lincoln Park Zool. Soc., Frank Lloyd Wright Home and Studio Found., Alpha Chi Omega. Republican. Lutheran. Home: 2151 Decook Ave Park Ridge IL 60068 Office: Amherst Associates Inc 140 S Dearborn St Chicago IL 60603

BUDDIG, THOMAS ROBERT, meat processing company executive; b. Chgo., Mar. 25, 1952; s. Robert Charles and Mary Jane (Brittain) B.; B.S. in Bus. Adminstrn., U. Denver, 1974; m. Alexis C. Evanoff, Nov. 29, 1975. Mem. gen. sales and merchandising staff Carl Buddig & Co., Chgo., 1974-76, new product devel. dept. 1976-77, advt. mgr., 1977-78, nat. sales dir., 1978—. Mem. Am. Mktg. Assn., Am. Mgmt. Assn., Sales and Mktg. Execs. Assn. Chgo., Order of Omega. Presbyterian. Club: Univ. (Chgo.). Office: 11914 S Peoria St Chicago IL 60643

BUDZAK, KATHRYN SUE (MRS. ARTHUR BUDZAK), physician; b. Racine, Wis., May 6, 1940; d. Raymond Philip and Emma Kathryn (Sorensen) Myer; student Stephens Coll., 1957-58, Luther Coll., 1958-59; B.S. with honors, U. Wis. at Milw., 1962; M.D., U. Wis., 1969; m. Arthur Budzak, Dec. 21, 1961; children—Ann Elizabeth, Lynn Marie. Intern, Madison (Wis.) Gen. Hosp., 1969-70; emergency physician, emergency suite St. Mary's Hosp., Madison, 1971-75; urgent care physician Dean Clinic, Madison, 1975—. Recipient Disting. Alumnae award Stephens Coll., 1979. Mem. Am. Coll. Emergency Physicians, Am. Coll. of Sports Medicine, AMA, Am., Wis. (pres. south central chpt. 1979-81), acads. family physicians, Wis., Dane County med. socs., Am. Med. Women's Assn., Women in Medicine in Wis., Wis. Med. Alumni Assn. (dir. 1979-82, pres. 1983-84), Sigma Sigma Sigma. Presbyterian. Mem. editorial bd., asst. editor Wis. Med. Alumni Quar. Home: 6110 Davenport Dr Madison WI 53711 Office: 1313 Fish Hatchery Rd Madison WI 53715

BUECHE, WENDELL FRANCIS, manufacturing company executive; b. Flushing, Mich., Nov. 7, 1930; s. Paul D. and Catherine (McGraw) B.; B.S. in Mech. Engring., U. Notre Dame, 1952; m. Virginia M. Smith, June 14, 1952; children—Denise, Barbara, Daniel, Brian. With Allis-Chalmers Corp., 1952—, utility group sales mgr., Cleve., 1959-62, dist. mgr., Detroit, 1962-64, sales and mktg. mgr., 1964-69, gen. mgr. crushing and screening equipment div., Appleton, Wis., 1969-73, group exec. and v.p. aggregate and coal processing group, West Allis, Wis., 1973-76, exec. v.p. elec. groups, 1976-77, exec. v.p., chief adminstrv. and fin. officer, 1977-80, exec. v.p., head solids process equipment sector and fluids processing group, chief fin. officer, 1980-81, pres., chief operating officer, 1981—, chief exec. officer, 1984—, also dir.; dir. Fiat-Allis, Siemens-Allis, M&I Marshall & Ilsley Bank. Mem. Greater Milw. Com., 1981—, Chgo. Com., 1981—. Mem. Am. Inst. Elec. and Electronic Engrs., ASME, Am. Inst. Mining Engrs., Nat. Sand and Gravel Assn. (dir.), Nat. Elec. Mfrs. Assn. (gov.). Clubs: Milw. Country; Westmoor Country. Office: Allis Chalmers Corp PO Box 512 Milwaukee WI 53201*

BUEDINGEN, WILLIAM M., paper mill executive; b. Milw., Nov. 10, 1925; s. Wilmer Edward and Clara Alma (Kroening) B.; m. Mary Frances Valiquette, Dec. 18, 1949; children—Kim Keri, Todd. Student engring. Marquette U., 1946-48; B.S. in Phys. Edn., U. Wis.-LaCrosse, 1951. Tchr., coach Tomahawk High Sch., Wis., 1951-55; paper mill supt. Owens-Ill. Inc., Big Island Va., 1955-56, Valdosta, Ga., 1956-65, mill mgr., Big Island, 1965-68, Valdosta, 1968-70, Tomahawk, 1970—; v.p. bd. trustees, mem. exec. com. Paper Sci. Found., Stevens Point, Wis., 1975—. Contbr. articles to trade mags. Vice pres. Tomahawk Area Corp., 1971—; bd. dirs., mem. exec. com. Wis. Valley Improvement Co., Wausau, 1971—; trustee U. Wis. Found. Bd., LaCrosse, 1975—; trustee, mem. exec. com., chmn. scholarship com. Pulp and Paper Sch., U. Wis.-Stevens Point, 1980—; former bd. dirs. Tomahawk Civic Ctr. Assn., Trees for Tomorrow, Eagle River, Wis. Recipient Community Leader award Sta. WDEZ, 1975, 78. Mem. Tomahawk C. of C. (bd. dirs. 1975, Disting. Service award 1976), Wis. Paper Council (vice chmn. 1983-84, chmn. 1984—), Paper Industry Mgmt. Assn., Tech. Assn. Pulp and Paper Industry. Republican. Congregationalist. Lodges: Lions (bd. dirs. 1974-78), Optimist (v.p. 1975-76). Avocations: lapidary; coin collecting; golfing; swimming; water skiing. Office: Owens-Ill Inc N9090 Hwy E Tomahawk WI 54487

BUEHRIG, JAMES OTTO, JR., real estate company executive; b. St. Louis, Mar. 30, 1954; s. James O. and Shirley M. (Peters) B.; m. Nancy A. Striebel, Aug. 16, 1974; children—Matthew, Gregory, Amanda. B.S., Northeast Mo. State U., 1976. C.P.A., Mo. Sr. acct. Peat, Marwick & Mitchell, St. Louis, 1975-79; controller Mason-Cassilly Inc., 1979-81; sr. v.p., chief fin. officer J.L. Mason Group, Inc., St. Louis, 1981—, also dir.; dir. Brentwood Bank, Mo., 1983—. Mem. devel. bd. Cardinal Glennon Children's Hosp., St. Louis, 1984—. Mem. Am. Inst. C.P.A.s, Mo. Soc. C.P.A.s, Nat. Assn. Accts., Am. Mgmt. Assn. Roman Catholic. Office: J L Mason Group Inc 1215 Fern Ridge Pkwy Saint Louis MO 63141

BUENZ, JOHN BUECHLER, architectural planning and design company executive; b. North Platte, Nebr., June 9, 1933; s. Harold Richard and Catherine Louise (Buechler) B.; m. Olga Marie Lindfors, June 19, 1960; children—Theodore, Anne. B.A., Iowa State U., 1957; M.A., Ga. Inst. Tech., 1958. Designer, Eero Saarinen & Assocs., Birmingham, Mich., 1958-59, Harry Weese & Assocs., Chgo., 1960-61, Keck & Keck, Chgo., 1961-63; head archtl. planning and design Solomon, Cordwell, Buenz & Assocs., Inc., Chgo., 1970—, pres., 1984—. Mem. Chgo. Com. on Hi-Rise Bldgs., 1965-84; mem. Lincoln Park Conservation Assn., 1960-84. Fellow AIA; mem. North Michigan Ave. Assn. Clubs: Chicago Yacht, Rotary. Office: 444 W Grant Pl Chicago IL 60614

BUER, HOWARD HENRY, coll. adminstr.; b. Milw., Jan. 14, 1922; s. Henry William and Hertha Martha (Hinz) B.; B.C.E., M.C.E., U. Wis.; m. Raymir Behrens, Feb. 23, 1946; children—Karen Diane, Scott Howard. Instr. civil engring. U. Wis., Madison, 1948-51; analyst Chance Vought Aircraft Co., Dallas, 1951-52; asst. prof. civil engring. U. Del., Newark, 1952-54; instr. engring. mechanics U. Wis., Madison, 1954-55; asst. to chief structural engr. Mead & Hunt, cons. engrs., Madison, 1955-64; sci. programmer U. Wis. Phys. Scis. Lab., Stoughton, 1964-67; dir. adminstrv. data processing The Principia, St. Louis, 1968-80; dir. Computer Center, Lindenwood Coll., St. Charles, Mo., 1980-82; computer specialist Webster U., St. Louis, 1982—; structural engr. mem. City of Madison Bd. Bldg. Examiners and Appeals, 1963-64. Served with C.E., U.S. Army, 1942-46. Registered profl. engr., Wis.; cert. computer programmer, cert. data processor. Mem. Assn. Computer Machinery, Assn. Systems Mgmt., Data Processing Mgmt. Assn., Soc. Preservation and Encouragement of Barber Shop Quartet Singing in Am., Chi Epsilon, Tau Beta Pi. Republican. Christian Scientist. Club: Masons. Home: 3025 Headland Dr Saint Charles MO 63301 Office: Webster U Saint Louis MO 63119

BUERK, HANS GUENTHER, retired wholesale trade company executive; b. Rottweil, Germany, Nov. 23, 1924; s. Christian and Johanna Anna (Martin) B.; M.B.A., U. Tuebingen, 1949; m. Utta Santo-Passo, Aug. 4, 1961; 1 dau., Joan Cristina. Came to U.S., 1961, naturalized, 1967. With Dr. Treude Assn., Stuttgart, West Germany, 1950-54; controller A.G. Messerschmitt, Munich, West Germany, 1955-57; jr. partner Koeck, Baden-Baden, West Germany, 1958-61; cost accountant Harris Trust & Savs. Bank, Chgo., 1962-63; auditor Chemetron Corp., Chgo., 1963-66; with Robert Bosch Corp., Broadview, Ill., 1966-82, v.p. finance, 1971-79; v.p. fin., treas., sec. Robert Bosch N. Am. Inc., co. hdqrs., Broadview, 1980-82, also dir.; now mgmt. cons. Served with German Army, 1942-45. Mem. Am. Mgmt. Assn. (presidents council 1973—). Home: 3300 N Lake Shore Dr Chicago IL 60657

BUERLING, SIEGFRIED FRIEDEL, historic village official; b. Essen, Germany, Jan. 29, 1932; s. Friedrich and Bertha Wilhelmiene (Wackermann) B.; came to U.S., 1959, naturalized, 1968; grad. trade sch.; m. Heidi Elisabeth Heid, Aug. 31, 1957; children—Peter Johannes, Curt Tracy. With Buerling Cabinet Shop, Essen, 1945-56; furniture restorer Canadiana Antiques, Montreal, Que., Can., 1956-59; preparator Western Reserve Hist. Soc., Cleve., 1959-62, supr. ops., 1962-66, mgr. ops., 1966-70, mgr. properties, 1970-74, dir. Hale Farm and Village, Bath, Ohio, 1975—, dir. dept. properties and preservation, 1977—; v.p. ops. Cuyahoga Valley Preservation and Scenic R.R. Assn.; restoration cons. Bd. dirs. Hower House Found., Akron, Ohio, 1974—. Recipient Woodrow Wilson award Woodlawn Conf., Nat. Trust for Historic Preservation, 1971; Outstanding Citizen award Nationality Services Center Greater Cleve., 1975. Mem. Internat. Council Crafts and Interpretation. Home: 2743 Oak Hill Rd Bath OH 44210 Office: 2686 Oak Hill Rd Bath OH 44210

BUESING, OLIVER R., surgeon, retired army officer; b. Grand Rapids, Mich., Jan. 19, 1910; s. William Desmond and Katherine Elizabeth (Schantz) B.; m. Chris O. Schott, Dec. 7, 1948 (dec. 1973); children—Mary A., Russel, Suzy Buesing Blaine; m. Inez P. Love, Aug. 7, 1981. M.D., U. Mich., 1936. Diplomate Am. Bd. Surgery. Intern Butterworth Hosp., Grand Rapids, 1936-37, jr. attending surg. staff, 1938-42; commd. to lt., U.S. Army, 1942, advanced through grades to col., 1962; served as chief surg. service 97th Gen. Hosp., Tilton Gen. Hosp., 2d Gen. Hosp.; basic sci. course Walter Reed Research and Grad. Sch., Washington, 1947; fellow surg. pathology Emory U., Atlanta, 1948, fellow surgery, 1949-51; cons. surgeon 9th Army, 1959-60, 1st Army, 1965-66; chief dept. surgery Munson Army Hosp., 1960-65, Patterson Army Hosp., 1965-67; ret. 1967; asst. chief surg. service VA Ctr., Leavenworth, Kans., 1967-79; asst. clin. prof. surgery U. Kans., Leavenworth, 1967-79, emeritus, 1979—. Decorated Legion of Merit, 1967. Fellow ACS; Southwestern Surg. Congress (sr.); mem. AMA, Ft. Leavenworth Officers Club. Republican. Address: 230 9th Ave Leavenworth KS 66048

BUESSER, ANTHONY CARPENTER, lawyer; b. Detroit, Oct. 15, 1929; s. Frederick Gustavis and Lela (Carpenter) B.; B.A. in English with honors, U. Mich., 1952, M.A., 1953, J.D., 1960; m. Carolyn Sue Pickle, Mar. 13, 1954; children—Kent Anderson, Anthony Carpenter, Andrew Clayton; m. 2d, Bettina Rieveschl, Dec. 14, 1973. Admitted to Mich. bar, 1961; asso firm Chase, Goodenough & Buesser, Detroit, 1961-66; partner firm Buesser, Buesser, Snyder & Blank, Detroit and Bloomfield Hills, 1966-81. Trustee, chmn. bd. Detroit Country Day Sch., Birmingham, Mich., 1970-82, 84—. Served with AUS, 1953-55. Recipient Avery Hopwood award major fiction U. Mich., 1953. Mem. Am., Mich., Detroit (pres. 1976-77), Oakland County bar assns., Am. Judicature Soc., Am. Arbitration Assn. (arbitrator), Alpha Delta Phi, Phi Delta Phi. Clubs: Thomas M. Cooley, Detroit, (Detroit). Home and Office: 32908 Outland Trail Birmingham MI 48010

BUESSER, FREDERICK GUSTAVUS, III, lawyer; b. Detroit, Apr. 30, 1941; s. Frederick Gustavus and Betty A. (Ronal) B.; B.A., U. Mich., 1964, J.D., 1966; m. Julia Forsyth Guest, June 28, 1963; children—Jennifer, Katherine, Frederick. Admitted to Mich. bar, 1966; asso. firm Buesser, Buesser, Snyder & Blank, Detroit, Bloomfield Hills, 1966, partner, 1967—; lectr. and mem. faculty legal seminars. Fellow Am. Bar Found.; mem. Am. Bar Assn., State Bar of Mich., Am. Judicature Soc., Sigma Chi, Phi Delta Phi. Episcopalian. Home: 242 N Glengarry St Birmingham MI 48009 Office: 4190 Telegraph St Bloomfield Hills MI 48013

BUETTEMEYER, KIM EDWARD, health educator, athletic trainer; b. Robinson, Ill., June 7, 1952; s. Charles Edward and Mary Evelyn (Hanna) B. A. Sci., Lincoln Trail Coll., 1973; B.S., Eastern Ill. U., 1976, M.S., 1978. Athletic trainer Chgo. Cubs, 1978—, Newton High Sch. (Ill.), 1979—; health educator Newton High Sch., 1980—. Advisor sports medicine Jasper County, Newton, Ill., 1980—. Mem. Ill. Edn. Assn., Nat. Athletic Tng. Assn. (cert. mem.), NEA, Ill. Athletic Tng. Assn. Home: PO Box 195 Stoy IL 62464 Office: Newton High Sch West End Ave Newton IL 62448

BUGG, ROBERT, state administrator; b. June 3, 1941; s. Walter and Mattie C. (Sturgis) B.; m. Jacquie C., May 31, 1970; children—Glen, Chris, Anton. B.A., Washburn Coll.-Kans., 1974; M.P.A., U. Kans., 1976. Police officer, 1966-68; field rep. Topeka (Kans.) Human Relations, 1968-69; counselor, Topeka, 1969-70; exec. dir. Big Brothers, Big Sisters, Topeka, 1970-82; dir. div. motor vehicles State of Kans., Topeka, 1982—. 2d vice chmn. Shawnee County Democratic Com., 1978—, minority rep., 1978—, chmn. black caucus, 1982—. Mem. Leadership of Kans. Commerce and Industry. Baptist. Home: 3721 Evans St Topeka KS 66609

BUGGY, STEVEN JAMES, paper company advertising executive; b. Milw., July 31, 1957; s. William J. and Jacqueline L. (Boudreau) B.; m. Janet L. Dallas, June 5, 1982; children—Lindsey, Erin. B.A., U. Wis.-Oshkosh, 1980. Account exec. Geer-Murray, Inc., Oshkosh, 1981-83; adv. mgr. Appleton Papers Inc. (Wis.), 1983—; owner Master/Stroke Innovations, Oshkosh, 1984—. Recipient awards Milw. Ad Club, 1983-84. Mem. Advt. Assn. Fox River Valley (several awards 1982-84). Roman Catholic. Avocations: skiing, boating, antiques, tennis, golf, classic autos. Home: 4726 Bay View Ln Oshkosh WI 54901 Office: Appleton Papers Inc 825 E Wisconsin Ave Appleton WI 54911

BUHL, ROBERT CARL, manufacturing executive; b. Detroit, Nov. 27, 1931; s. Carl F. and Louise C. (Horning) B.; m. Jane Ferris Johnston, Dec. 1, 1972; children—Deborah, Carrie Robyn. B.S. in Engring. and Mgmt., U. Mich., 1956. With Bower Roller Bearing div. Fed. Mogul Corp., Detroit, 1955-67; plant mgr. Formsprag Co., Mt. Pleasant, Mich., 1967-70, v.p. ops., 1970-78; dir. mfg. Ind. div. Dana Corp., Warren, Mich., 1978—; cons. in field. Vice-pres. S.E. Park Assn., Grosse Pointe Park Civic Assn.; mem. planning commn. City of Grosse Pointe Park, 1984—; dir. fin. St. James Lutheran Ch., 1981-83. Served with U.S. Army, 1953-55. Mem. Soc. Mfg. Engrs., Engring. Soc. Detroit. Club: Lakeslands Golf & Country (Brighton, Mich.).

BUILTA, HOWARD CLAIRE, real estate development company executive; b. Lawton, Okla., Apr. 29, 1943; s. Howard Phillip and Alice Ann (Stimpert) B.; m. Claudia Lynn Mastalio, Sept. 3, 1966; children—Jeffrey B., Lindsey M. B.S., U. Ill., 1965; M.B.A., No. Ill. U., 1967. Project adminstr. Seay & Thomas, Chgo., 1969-71; v.p. Rauch & Co., Chgo., 1971-77; v.p., gen. mgr. The Whiston Group, Chgo., 1977-79; v.p. corp. devel. Marathon U.S. Realties, Chgo., 1979—. Mem. adv. council Lutheran Social Services, Chgo., 1976-81, Salvation Army Community Counseling Service, Chgo., 1982—; trustee Palatine Twp. Govt., Ill., 1979-81; bd. dirs. Palatine Twp. Republican Orgn., 1979-81. Served to 1st lt. U.S. Army, 1967-69, Vietnam. Decorated Bronze Star, Army Commendation medal. Mem. Inst. Real Estate Mgmt. (cert. property mgr.), Bldg. Owners and Mgrs. Assn. Internat. (real property adminstr., pres. Suburban Chgo., Des Plaines, 1977-79, pres. North Central region 1984), Urban Land Inst., Chgo. Real Estate Bd. (sec. 1985), Ill. Assn. Realtors (bd. dirs. 1985), Lambda Alpha (pres. Ely chpt. 1984), Am. Legion. Club: Attic (Chgo.). Lodge: Masons. Avocations: reading; fishing. Home: 2316 Sunset Rd Palatine IL 60074 Office: Marathon US Realties Three First National Plaza Suite 5700 Chicago IL 60602

BUJAKE, JOHN EDWARD, JR., beverage company executive; b. N.Y.C., May 23, 1933; s. John E. and Mary B.; m. Gail Cruise, Aug. 1, 1964; children—John E., III, Laura, Jacquelyn, William. B.S. in Chemistry, Manhattan Coll., N.Y.C., 1954; M.S., Holy Cross Coll., Worcester, Mass., 1955; Ph.D. in Phys. Chemistry, Columbia U., 1959; M.B.A. in Mgmt., NYU, 1963. Research assoc. Lever Bros., Edgewater, N.J., 1959-68; dir. research and devel. Coke Foods, Houston, 1968-72; dir. research and devel. Quaker Oats Co., Barrington, Ill. 1972-77; v.p. research and devel. The Seven-Up Co., St. Louis, 1977—. Contbr. articles to profl. jours. Mem. Calorie Control Council, Internat. Life Scis. Inst., Indsl. Research Inst., Am. Chem. Soc., Inst. Food Technology. Office: The Seven-Up Co 121 S Meramec St Saint Louis MO 63105

BUJARSKI, JOZEF JULIAN, molecular biologist; b. Poznan, Poland, Mar. 19, 1948; came to U.S., 1981; s. Wiktor and Helena (Domanska) B.; m. Aleksandra A. Dzianott, July, 1971; children—Krzysztof, Marek, Lukasz. M.Sc. in Chemistry, U. Poznan, Poland, 1971, M.S. in Biology, 1978, Ph.D. in Chemistry, 1977. Research asst. U. Poznan, Poland, 1975-76, research assoc., 1976-77; sr. research assoc. Polish Acad. Sci., Poznan, 1978-80; sr. research assoc. U. Wis., Madison, 1981-83, project assoc., 1984—. Contbr. articles to sci. jours. Mem. Polish Chem. Soc., Polish Biochem. Soc., Am. Soc. Virology, Internat. Soc. Plant Molecular Biology. Avocations: Biking, swimming and carpentry. Home: 23A University Houses Madison WI 53705 Office: Biophysics Lab 1525 Linden Dr U Wis Madison WI 53706

BUJKO, LESTER GEORGE, energy company manager; b. Hamburg, Germany, June 10, 1947; came to U.S., 1950, naturalized, 1955; s. William and Helena B.; B.S. in Econs., Ill. Inst. Tech., 1972; postgrad. Ill. Inst. Tech., 1973-74; M.B.A., U. Nebr., 1984; m. Deborah Susan Saikley, Mar. 26, 1977; 1 dau., Lesley Renae. Fleet mgr. Diversey Chem. Co., 1968; acctg. supr. Atlantic Richfield, 1969-72; mgr. fin. reporting control InterNorth Corp., Omaha, 1972-84; with United Petroleum Gas, Omaha, 1984—. Recipient Exec. Recognition award No. Petrochem., 1979. Mem. Nat. Assn. Accts., Omaha Zool. Soc., Joslyn Art Assn. Republican. Episcopalian. Club: Knights of Ak-Sar-Ben. Research on econ. devel. of East and West Germany after World War II, control of contractors in antifreeze ops., mgmt. compliance to Fgn. Corrupt Practices Act of 1977. Office: UPG Inc 1815 Capitol Ave Omaha NE 68102

BULDAK, GERALD E., public relations executive; b. Joliet, Ill., Sept. 26, 1944; s. Casmer and Sue B. A.B., Marquette U., 1966; postgrad. Loyola U., Chgo., 1966-67, Roosevelt U., 1967-68. Writer, reporter Joliet (Ill.) Herald News, 1962-66; public relations asst. Armour & Co., Chgo., 1966-69; mgr. spl. projects CNA Fin. Corp., Chgo., 1969-72; with Continental Ill. Nat. Bank, 1972-84, v.p. corp. affairs/pub. relations, 1980-84; mgr. pub. affairs Detroit Edison, 1984—. Mem. Internat. Pub. Relations Assn., Pub. Relations Soc. Am., Sigma Delta Chi. Clubs: Publicity, Headline. Home: 743 Pemberton Rd Grosse Pointe Park MI 48230

BULL, LAWRENCE MYLES, engineer; b. Aliquippa, Pa., Feb. 20, 1931; s. Thomas Leslie and Gertrude Margaret (Miller) B.; B.S.E.E., Ind. Inst. Tech., 1955; m. Emily Jane Antal, June 7, 1958; children—L. Michael, Louis A., Laura A., James C. Transmission corrosion engr. Manufactures Light & Heat Co., Pitts., 1955-64; corrosion engr. Columbia Gas System-Pitts. Group Co., Pitts., 1964-68; project engr. Columbia Gas Systems Service Corp., Marble Cliff, Ohio, 1968-73; mgr. corrosion and leakage control Columbia Gas Distbn. Cos., Columbus, Ohio, 1973—. Served with U.S. Navy, 1948-52. Mem. ASME, ASTM, Nat. Assn. Corrosion Engrs., Nat., Ohio socs. profl. engrs. Republican. Roman Catholic. Club: Northington Athletic Assn. Home: 829 Pipestone Dr Worthington OH 43085 Office: 200 Civic Center Dr Columbus OH 43215

BULL, ROBERT KEITH, soil scientist; b. Eckert, Colo., Mar. 10, 1927; s. Ernest Atwood and Dorothy (Nelson) B.; B.S. in Agronomy, Colo. State U., 1951, postgrad. in soil sci., 1960; M.S. in Agrl. Econs., N.Mex. State U., 1971; m. Fern Eileen Quiggle, July 21, 1962; children—Karin Elisabeth, Gretchen Louise, Lisa Irene. Soil scientist Soil Conservation Service, U.S., 1951-53; with Morrison Knudsen, Afghanistan, 1953-56, Tams, Iraq, 1956-58; soil scientist Bur. Reclamation, Dept. Interior, 1960-62, Internat. Engring. Co., Bangladesh, 1962-65, Ralph M. Parsons, Saudi Arabia, 1965-67, Internat. Engring. Co., Peru, 1967-69; with Harza Engring. Co., 1971—, Guatemala, Jamaica, Dominican Republic, Haiti, Guyana, Venezuela, Colombia, Honduras, Iran, Thailand, Senegal, Pakistan, Saudi Arabia. Served with U.S. Army, 1945-47. Mem. Am. Soc. Agronomy, Soil Sci. Soc. Am. Home: 1325 E Sanborn Dr Palatine IL 60067 Office: Harza Engring Co 150 S Wacker Dr Chicago IL 60606

BULLARD, MERYL AUDREY, occupational therapist; b. Chgo., Apr. 12, 1933; d. Melville Allan and Helen (Logsdon) Snyder; B.S. cum laude, U. Wis., Madison, 1955, O.T.R., 1956; M.P.A. cum laude, Drake U., 1983; children—Linda, Michael, Steven, Alison. Dir. occupational therapy Burlington (Iowa) Med. Center, 1966-74; cons. occupational therapist, Spencer, Iowa, 1975-76; dir. partial hosp. program NW Iowa Mental Health Center, Spencer, 1976-78; cons. Iowa Health Dept., Des Moines, 1978-79; dir. occupational therapy Broadlawns Med. Center, Des Moines, 1980-81; chief occupational therapy VA Med. Center, Knoxville, Iowa, 1981—, coordinator VA Occupational Therapy Task Force; lectr.; cons. VA. Bd. dirs. Polk County Public Health Nursing, Des Moines, 1980-82. Pres. bd. dirs. Clay County Assn. Retarded Citizens, 1975-79; founder Pre-Sch. for Handicapped, Spencer, Iowa, 1976; bd. dirs. Sunshine Workers, Inc., 1975-79; mem. adv. com. Iowa Found. Med. Care, 1979-83. Mem. Iowa Occupational Therapy Assn. (chmn. com. on practice, 1978-83), Am. Occupational Therapy Assn., Met. Women's Network, Pi Alpha Alpha, Pi Beta Phi. Congregationalist. Contbr. articles to profl. jours. Home: 212 Dickman Des Moines IA 50315 Office: VA Med Ctr Knoxville IA 50138

BULLARD, THOMAS ROBERT, retail book executive; b. Chgo., May 6, 1944; s. Henry M. and Ethel (Munday) B.; B.S., Ill. Inst. Tech., 1966; M.A., Northwestern U., 1968; Ph.D., U. Ill., Chgo., 1973. Teaching asst. history U.

Ill. at Chgo. Circle, 1969-73; head nautical dept. Owen Davies, bookseller, Chgo., 1973-80, owner, Oak Park, Ill., 1980—; instr. history Sch. Art Inst. Chgo., 1975-77; cons. in field. Nat. Merit scholar, 1961-62, Hon. Ill. State scholar, 1962. Mem. U.S. Naval Inst., Internat. Naval Research Orgn., Navy Records Soc. (U.K.), Central Electric Railfans Assn., Electric Railroaders Assn., Nat. Ry. Hist. Soc., Ry. and Locomotive Hist. Soc. (dir. Chgo. chpt.). Mem. United Ch. Christ. Author: Street, Interurban and Rapid Transit Railways of the United States: A Selective Historical Bibliography. Contbg. author: Biographical Dictionary of American Mayors. Home: 228 N Lombard Ave Oak Park IL 60302 Office: Owen Davies Bookseller 200 W Harrison St Oak Park IL 60304

BULLARD, WADE ARTHUR, JR., corp. exec.; b. Wilmington, N.C., Jan. 23, 1931; s. Wade Arthur and Mildred (Anderson) B.; student Columbus U. (Washington), 1949-51; B.B.A., U. Mich., 1957; m. Genie Bassage; children—Linda Kay, Cynthia Ann. Pres. gen. mgr. Patterson's, Sturgis, Mich., 1957—, also dir.; v.p., dir. Clark Plastic Engring. Co., Sturgis, 1967-73; pres. dir. Plastek Co., 1968—, Colonial Motor Inn, Inc., 1964-76, Wade Bullard, Inc. chmn. bd. Aronco Plastics, Inc., 1974-75. (all Sturgis), 1969-77; Mem. Sturgis Bd. Zoning Appeals, 1967-77; Sturgis city commr., 1975-77; dir. Bd. Pub. Works, St. Joseph County, 1976-77; pres. Klinger Lake Assn., Sturgis, 1969-71; pres., dir. Sturgis Improvement Assn., 1966—, Sturgis Econ. Devel. Corp., 1978—. Served with CIC, AUS, 1951-54; Korea. Decorated Bronze Star medal, UN Service medal, Nat. Def. Service medal. Episcopalian. Elk. Club: Klinger Lake Country (Sturgis). Home: Klinger Lake Sturgis MI 49091 Office: 1106 W Chicago St Sturgis MI 49091

BULLMER, KENNETH, psychology educator; b. St. Louis, Sept. 14, 1923; s. George and Mildred Bullmer; B.S. in Bus. Adminstrn., Washington U., St. Louis, 1949; A.M., U. Mich., 1967; Ed.D., Ind. U., 1970; m. Carole Marie Hartnett, Jan. 1, 1975; children—Casey, Victoria, Elizabeth, Christina. Dir. admissions Montecello Coll., Godfrey, Ill., 1960-62, Franklin (Ind.) Coll., 1962-64; admissions officer Flint Coll., U. Mich., 1964-67; participant NDEA Inst., Ind. U., 1967-68, counselor counseling and psychol. services, 1968-69, research assoc. Inst. Sex Research, 1969-70; assoc. prof. psychology Western Mich. U., Kalamazoo, 1970—; pvt. practice psychol. counseling, 1970—; dir. Portage Community Outreach Center, 1978-84. Served with AUS, 1943-46; PTO. Decorated Bronze Star. Mem. Am. Psychol. Assn., Am. Soc. Clin. Hypnosis, Am. Assn. Sex Educators, Counselors and Therapists, Mich. Psychol. Assn., Western Mich. Psychol. Assn. Author: The Art of Empathy, 1975, Empathie, 1978. Home: 6738 Rothbury St Portage MI 49002 Office: 3109 Sangren Hall Western Mich Univ Kalamazoo MI 49008

BULLOCK, JOHN DAVID, ophthalmic surgeon; b. Cin., July 31, 1943; s. Joseph Craven and Emilie Helen (Woide) B.; A.B., Dartmouth Coll., 1965, B.M.S., 1966; M.D., Harvard U., 1968; postgrad. Armed Forces Inst. Pathology, 1970; M.S. in Microbiology and Immunology, Wright State U., 1982; m. Gretchen Hageman, June 25, 1966; children—John David, Katherine Ann, Richard Joseph. Intern, asst. in medicine Washington U., St. Louis, 1968-69; resident in ophthalmology and plastic surgery Yale U., 1971-74; clin. instr. ophthalmology, 1974; Heed fellow U. Calif., San Francisco, 1974-75; Orbital fellow Mayo Clinic, Rochester, Minn., 1975; clin. instr. ophthalmology Stanford (Calif.) U., 1974-75; assoc. prof. microbiology and immunology, chmn. dept. ophthalmology Wright State U. Sch. Medicine, 1984—; lectr. law and medicine U. Dayton Law Sch., 1981—; practice medicine specializing in ophthalmic surgery, Dayton, Ohio; mem. staff Miami Valley Hosp., Children's Med. Center, Kettering Med. Center, St. Elizabeth Hosp., Good Samaritan Hosp., Sycamore Med. Ctr. Trustee, Children's Med. Center, Dayton, 1977-80; bd. dirs. Lions Eye Bank W. Central Ohio, 1982—. Diplomate Am. Bd. Ophthalmology (bd. examiner 1979—). Mem. Am. Assn. Ophthalmology, Am. Acad. Ophthalmology, A.C.S., AMA, Am. Coll. Cryosurgery, Am. Soc. Ophthalmic Plastic and Reconstructive Surgery, Am. Assn. Pediatric Ophthalmology and Strabismus, Assn. for Research Vision and Ophthalmology, Keratorefractive Soc., Am. Soc. Ophthalmic Ultrasound, Am. Intraocular Implant Soc., Orbit Soc., Am. Acad. Facial Plastic and Reconstructive Surgery, Internat. Soc. Orbital Disorders, Internat. Corneal Soc., Castroviejo Soc., Frank Walsh Soc., Soc. Heed Fellows, Ocular Microbiology and Immunology Group, Soc. of Geriatric Opthalmology, Internat. Oculoplastic Soc., Am. Soc. Microbiology, Am. Soc. Laser Medicine and Surgery, Am. Ophthal. Soc. (assoc.), Soc. Eye Surgeons, Theobald Soc. Clubs: Dayton Country, Dayton Racquet. Contbr. articles to profl. jours. Home: 1155 Ridgeway Rd Dayton OH 45419 Office 1520 S Main St Dayton OH 45419

BUMAGIN, VICTORIA EDITH WEROSUB, social services executive; b. Free City of Danzig, June 20, 1923; d. Isaac A. and Zinaida (Towbin) Werosub; came to U.S., 1938, naturalized, 1941; B.A., City U. N.Y., 1945; M.S. Social Work, Columbia U., 1969; postgrad. U. Chgo., 1974—; m. Victor I. Bumagin, Mar. 16, 1946; children—Louisa, Susan, Elizabeth, Deborah, Jennifer. Caseworker to intake supr. to case supr. N.J. Bur. Children's Services, 1962-69; sr. social worker Dept. Social Services, Berkshire, Eng., 1970-73; dir. social services Council for Jewish Elderly, Chgo., 1974—; dir. Ctr. Applied Gerontology; assoc. prof. Loyola U., Chgo.; instr. Summer Inst., U. Chgo., univ. sr. clin. assoc.; mem. Task Force on Age Discrimination; manifesto for Brit. Nat. Conf. on Aging, 1971-73; mem. tech. adv. com. Protective Service to Aged, 1977—; spl. advisor White House Conf. on Aging, 1981. Bd. dirs. ctr. for Applied Gerontology; pres. Children's Mus. Met. Chgo. Fellow Gerontol. Soc. Am.; mem. Soc. for Life Cycle Psychology, Nat., Brit. (sec., v.p.) assns. social workers, Columbia U. Sch. Social Work Alumni Assn. (dir.), Acad. Certified Social Workers, Registry Clin. Social Workers. Author: The Appliance Cookbook, 1971; co-author: Aging Is a Family Affair, 1979; also articles in profl. jours. Home: 1224 North Branch Dr Wilmette IL 60091 Office: 1015 W Howard St Evanston IL 60202

BUMGARDNER, RENA JEWELL, mental health executive, clinical social worker; b. Athens, Tex., Nov. 28, 1940; d. Willie and Eula Ellen (Bass) Jewell; m. Thomas Arthur Bumgardner, Aug. 25, 1962; children—Melody, Susan, Judy. Student Tex. Woman's U., 1959-62; B.S. with honors, U. Minn., 1964, M.S.W., 1966. Instr. sociology, social work U. Wis.-Superior, 1966-67; family therapist Duluth (Minn.) Family Services, 1967-68; clin. social worker Human Resource Center of Douglas County, Superior, 1970-82, exec. dir., 1982—. Chmn. bd. dirs. Children's Corner Day Care, Superior, 1975-77; bd. dirs. Spectra, Inc., Duluth, 1983-85; mem. Superior Community Housing Resource Bd., 1985—. Mem. Nat. Assn. Social Workers, Acad. Cert. Social Workers, Am. Bus. Women's Assn. (charter chpt. woman of yr. 1984), Nat. Assn. Female Execs., Mental Health Assn. (dir. 1982—). Democrat.

BUMP, MILO SHANNON, info. systems cons.; b. Topeka, Kans., Oct. 26, 1922; s. Wilson Raymond and Pearle Julia (Pickering) B.; m. Reba Mae McCaleb, July 19, 1974; 1 son, Shannon Kevin. Parts and material handler Boeing Airplane Co., Wichita, Kans., 1942-47, expediter, 1947-52, sr. supr., exptl. prodn. control, 1952-55, programmer, analyst, 1955-60; systems analyst Martin-Marietta Co., Denver, 1960-62; mgr. engring. systems Gen. Electric Co., Huntsville, Ala., 1962-66, internal cons. systems, Phoenix, 1967-69; sr. cons. Computer Scis. Corp., St. Louis, Chgo. and London, 1969-71; dir. info. systems Du Quoin Packing Co. (Ill.), 1971-80; cons. info. systems, 1980—. Served with USAAF, 1942-45; ETO. Mem. St. Louis Honeywell Users Group (past treas.). Home: 207 S 3d St Elkville IL 62932 Office: PO Box 306 Elkville IL 62932

BUMP, WILBUR NEIL, lawyer; b. Peoria, Ill., July 12, 1929; s. Wilbur Earl and Mae (Nelson) B.; B.S., State U. Iowa, 1951, J.D., 1958; m. Elaine Bonneval, Nov. 24, 1951; children—William Earl, Jeffrey Neil, Steven Bonneval. Admitted to Iowa bar, 1958; solicitor gen. Iowa Atty. Gen. Office, Des Moines, 1961-64; practiced in Des Moines, 1964—; gen. counsel Iowa Luth. Hosp. Served with USAF, 1951-54. Mem. Am., Iowa (bd. govs. 1976-81), Polk County (pres. 1976-77) bar assns. Club: Kiwanis (pres. 1974-75). Presbyterian (elder). Home: Route 2 Winterset IA 50273 Office: 2 Corporate Pl 1501 42d St West Des Moines IA 50265

BUNCE, PETER H., company executive. Student Princeton U., 1951. Founder, The Bunce Corp., St. Louis, 1959—, chmn. bd. Served with USAF. Bd. dirs. V.P., Fair Found., Care and Counseling, St. Louis; pres. Repertory Theatre of St. Louis; chmn. bd. Monmouth Coll., Ill., trustee of bd.; chmn. St. Louis chpt. Young Pres.'s Orgn. Mem. Am. Arbitration Assn. (mem. nat. panel). Address: The Bunce Corp 1266 Andes Blvd Saint Louis MO 63132

BUNCH, THOMAS EDWARD, lawyer; b. Chillicothe, Ohio, Oct. 8, 1949; s. Booker P. and Marjory (Neal) B.; m. Kathie Meyer, Aug. 7, 1971; children—Jonathon, Ryan, Brooke Marie. B.S., U. Dayton, 1971; M.B.A., U. Fla., 1972; J.D., U. Toledo, 1980. Bars: Ohio 1980, U.S. Dist. Ct. (so. dist.) Ohio 1981. Assoc. Bunstine, Mowrey & Moore, Chillicothe, 1980-81; ptnr. Bunstine, Moore, Corzine & Bunch Co., L.P.A., Chillicothe, 1981—. Note and comment editor U. Toledo Law Rev., 1980. Mem. Bishop Flaget Sch. Bd., Chillicothe, 1983—; pres.-elect St. Peters Parish Council, Chillicothe, 1983—. Served to capt. U.S. Army, 1972-76. Mem. Ohio Assn. Civil Trial Attys., Defense Research Inst., Ohio Bar Assn., Ross County Bar Assn. Democrat. Roman Catholic. Club: Flaget Parents (pres. 1981-82). Lodge: K.C. Home: 389 W 4th St Chillicothe OH 45601 Office: Bunstine Moore Corzine & Bunch Co LPA 38 S Paint St Chillicothe OH 45601

BUNDRA, NANCY ANN, automotive company executive; b. Cabin Creek, W.Va., Nov. 1, 1938; d. Lester Thompson and Olive Marie (Duncan) T.; m. Stephen F. Bundra, Oct. 31, 1956; children—Stephen, Michael, Alan. B.S. in Mgmt. and Mktg., Davis and Elkins Coll., 1980. Project engr. Truck Coach, Gen. Motors Corp., Pontiac, Mich., 1973-75, sect. engr., 1975-78, staff engr., 1978-81, chief engr. medium duty trucks, 1981-85, chief engr.-overseas, imports, exports, joint ventures, 1985—. Mem. Soc. Automotive Engrs. Office: 660 S Boulevard E Pontiac MI 48053

BUNDSCHUH, JAMES EDWARD, university administrator, chemistry educator; b. St. Louis, Nov. 13, 1941. B.S., St. Louis U., 1963; Ph.D., Duquesne U., 1967; Faculty chemistry Western Ill. U., Macomb, 1968-75, chmn. chemistry dept., 1975-81; dean sci.-humanities Indiana-Purdue U., Fort Wayne, 1981—; vis. prof. U. Stuttgart, Fed. Republic Germany, 1973-74. Mem. Am. Chem. Soc. (pres. elect NE Ind. sect.), Sigma Xi. Office: Indiana-Purdue Univ Dean Sci-Humanities 2101 Coliseum Blvd E Fort Wayne IN 46805

BUNDY, BLAKELY FETRIDGE, educator, writer; b. Chgo., Aug. 31, 1944; d. William Harrison and Bonnie Jean (Clark) Fetridge; m. Harvey Hollister Bundy, III, Aug. 20, 1966; children—H. Hollister, IV, Clark Harrison, Elizabeth Lowell, Reed Fetridge. B.A. cum laude, Wheaton Coll., Mass., 1966; M.Ed., Nat. Coll. Edn., 1985. Tchr. Norwich Kindergarten, Vt., 1966-67, WillowWood Pre-Sch., Winnetka, Ill., 1983—, bd. dirs., 1972-81, adv. bd., 1981-83; bd. dirs. North Ave. Day Nursery, Chgo., 1970-76. Author (pamphlet) What an Executive Should Know About Industry Sponsored Day Care, 1984. Contbr. articles to Redbook, Glamour, Dartnell Inst. Bus. Research. Mem. United Republican Fund, Chgo., 1968—; active N.E. Ill. council Boy Scouts Am., 1976-80, Illinois Shore council Girl Scouts U.S.A., 1981—. Mem. Chgo. Assn. Edn. Young Children. Episcopalian. Clubs: Indian Hill (Winnetka); Stevensville Yacht (Mich.). Avocations: golf, sailing. Office: Willow Wood Pre-School 1255 Willow Rd Winnetka IL 60093

BUNDY, HOWARD, elementary school principal, language arts supervisor; b. Dix, Ill., Sept. 24, 1913; s. Raleigh Oran and Retha Pearl (Sanders) B.; m. Frances Arlene Petrea, July 18, 1939; children—Michael, Vicky. B.S., So. Ill. U., 1947, M.S., 1964; M.S., U. Ill., 1949. Tchr. elem. rural one-room sch., Ill., 1934-38; prin., tchr. two-room sch., Walnut Hill, Ill., 1938-40, Centralia, Ill., 1940-43; prin. Centralia Elem. Sch., 1944-74, lang. arts supr., 1965-74; instr. McKendree Coll., Lebanon, Ill., 1952-62. Author (with others): History of Education in Centralia, Ill., 1949. Chmn. Marion County Draft Bd., Centralia, 1945; Kaskaskia Reading Council Organizer, 1960; co-chmn. community devel. program, Centralia, 1962; chmn. Marion County Welfare Com., 1983. Mem. Painters Union (sec-treas. 1953, conv. del. 1974, 79, 84), Am. Legion (life mem.; commr. Post 446 1965), Ill. Ret. Tchrs. Assn. (life), Marion County Ret. Tchrs. (pres. 1983—), Phi Delta Kappa. Named Outstanding Educator of So. Ill. U., 1963. Republican. Elder 1st Christian Ch. Lodge: Optimists. Club: Greenview Golf. Home: 6 Mitchell Dr Centralia IL 62801

BUNGE, JOHN ARTHUR, market research co. exec.; b. Elgin, Ill., Mar. 14, 1941; s. Arthur August and Gracia Vinina (Webster) B.; B.S. in Mktg. Mgmt., Northwestern U., 1963; m. Barbara Jean Nall, Aug. 28, 1972; 1 son, Jason Todd. Research analyst Ben Franklin div. City Products Corp., Des Plaines, Ill., 1965-68; mgr. mktg. services Cargill, Wilson & Acree, Richmond, Va., 1968-70; dir. mktg. services Glenn Advt., Dallas, 1970-72; v.p. Message Factors, Inc., Dallas, 1972-74, Atlanta, 1974-75; sr. project dir. Britt and Frerichs, Inc., Chgo., 1975-76, br. mgr. and sr. project dir., Denver, 1976, gen. mgr., Chgo., 1977-78; partner Britt Mktg., Evanston, Ill., 1978-79; pres. Legal Mktg. Research, Inc., Evanston, 1979—; speaker at assn. meetings, seminars. Served with USN, 1963-65. Mem. Am. Mktg. Assn., Mktg. Research Assn., Council Am. Survey Research Orgns., United Comml. Travelers Am. Home and office: 1606 Central St Evanston IL 60201

BUNGE, ROBERT PIERCE, language educator; b. Oak Park, Ill., Sept. 24, 1930; s. George Herbert and Caroline Elizabeth (Pierce) B.; M.A., Roosevelt U., 1973; Ph.D., DePaul U., 1982; m. Muriel Perlman, Mar. 17, 1956; step-children—Harmon Berns, Hilary Berns. Tchr. adult evening sch. Maine Twp., Park Ridge, Ill., 1962-74; with Bunge Movers, Evanston, Ill., 1968-72; lectr. Roosevelt U., Chgo., 1971, 73, 75, 77, DePaul U., Chgo., 1974-79; prof. Lakota (Sioux Indian lang.), U. S.D., Vermillion, 1979—; cons. in Indian culture States of S.D., Iowa and Nebr.; ct. interpreter for Lakota lang. Lectr., women's groups, bus. groups; commencement speaker North Shore Country Day Sch., Winnetka, Ill., 1974; convocation speaker Morningside Coll., 1984. Served with AUS, 1952-54; PTO. Mem. Internat. Platform Assn., Am. Philos. Assn., Theosophical Soc., Siouan and Caddoan Linguistic Soc., Rocky Mountain Lang. Soc. Author: Sioux Language Phrase Book, 1976; An American Urphilosophie, 1983; contbg. author: Sioux Collections, 1982; contbr. articles to profl. jours. Home: 6 Cherrywood Ct Vermillion SD 57069 Office: Dept Modern Langs U SD Vermillion SD 57069

BUNGUM, JOHN LEWIS, economist, educator; b. Kasson, Minn., Dec. 17, 1942; s. Gustav Norman and Elsie Charlotte (Throndson) B.; B.A., Luther Coll., Decorah, Iowa, 1963; M.A. (univ. scholar 1968-69), U. Iowa, 1969; Ph.D. (univ. fellow 1974-76), U. Nebr., 1977; m. Lorna Jean Thiesen, Aug. 13, 1977; children—John Lewis II, Bethany Lorna. From instr. to assoc. prof. econs. U. Wis., Platteville, 1969-79; assoc. prof. econs. Gustavus Adolphus Coll., St. Peter, Minn., 1979—, chmn. dept. econs. and bus., 1984—, chmn. faculty senate, 1983-85; instr. U. Wis. Liberal Arts Center, Copenhagen, 1973. Served with USAR, 1964-67; Vietnam. Govt. of Norway scholar, summer 1963. Mem. Am. Econ. Assn., AAUP, Midwest Econ. Assn., Western Econ. Assn., Atlantic Econ. Assn., Assn. Am. Colls., Minn. Econ. Assn. Lutheran. Contbr. articles to profl. jours. Home: 841 Church St Saint Peter MN 56082 Office: Dept Econs Gustavus Adolphus Coll Saint Peter MN 56082

BUNKER, PAUL RICHARD, orchestra executive; b. Cleve., Feb. 1, 1952; s. Norman Fredrick and Mary Catherine Bunker. B.A. in Communications and Music History, Cleve. State U., 1977. Gen. mgr. radio sta. WCSB-FM, Cleve., 1976-78; dir. pub. relations Norfolk Symphony (Va.), 1978-79; gen. mgr. Evansville Philharmonic Orch. (Ind.), 1979-82; gen. mgr. Youngtown Symphony Orch. (Ohio), 1982—. Trustee Orgn. Ohio Orchs., 1982—; chmn. music panel Ind. Arts Commn., 1982; mem. Ohio Citizens Com. for the Arts. Mem. Youngstown Area C. of C. Lodge: Kiwanis. Office: 260 Federal Plaza West Youngstown OH 44503*

BUNTE, FREDERICK JOSEPH, university president; b. Columbus, Ohio, Dec. 19, 1937; s. Fred Joseph and Margaret Louise (Murday) B.; m. Judith Schueneman, June 27, 1964; children—Susan, Rebecca. B.S., Ohio State U., 1959, M.A., 1964, Ph.D., 1972; A.S.B.A., Franklin U., 1974. Chmn., tchr. social studies Upper Arlington Sr. High Sch., Columbus, Ohio, 1959-65; instr. sociology Franklin U., Columbus, 1965-72, prof., chmn. div. social and behavioral sci., 1972-74, dean Gen. Coll., 1974-78, dean acad. affairs, 1975-78, pres., 1978—. Trustee Columbus Area Leadership Program, Ohio affiliate Nat. Soc. Prevent Blindness, Central Ohio council Boy Scouts Am. Mem. Am. Sociol. Assn., Am. Assn. for Higher Edn., Am. Acad. Polit. and Social Sci., Nat. Council on Family Relations, Newcomen Soc. N. Am. Clubs: Kiwanis (pres. elect), Metropolitan, Torch, Executives, University, Faculty (Ohio State U.). Home: 287 Frontenac Pl Worthington OH 43085 Office: 201 S Grant Ave Columbus OH 43215

BUNTROCK, DEAN L., waste management company executive. Chmn., chief exec. officer, dir. Waste Mgmt., Inc., Oak Brook, Ill. Office: Waste Mgmt Inc 3003 Butterfield Rd Oak Brook IL 60521*

BUNTZ, ROBERT ARTHUR, JR., real estate development, publishing companies executive; b. Kingston, Pa., Jan. 13, 1952; s. Robert Arthur and Helen (Catanwzaro) B. Student Franklin & Marshall Coll., 1970-71, Harvard U., 1972; B.A., Grinnell Coll., 1974. Admissions officer MacAlester Coll., St. Paul, 1974-76; pres. Buntz Devel. Co., St. Paul, 1976-81, River Basin Pub. Co., St. Paul, 1979—; gen. ptnr. Rysdahl, Buntz & Assocs., St. Paul, 1981—; v.p. Bluefin Resorts, Inc., Tofte, Minn., 1983—; cons. Boisclair Corp., Mpls., 1984—. Contbr. articles to newspapers. Mem. Dist. 8 St. Paul Planning Council, 1980-82, Ramsey Hill Assn., St. Paul, 1978—; cons. Cook County Bd. Commns., Grand Marais, Minn., 1984. Mem. Nat. Homebuilders Assn., St. Paul Area Bd. Realtors, Minn. C. of C., Aircraft Owners and Pilots Assn. Avocations: flying; running; cross-country skiing; biking. Office: Rysdahl Buntz & Assocs Suite 209 370 Selby Ave Saint Paul MN 55102

BURCH, HAROLD DEE, educator; b. Vernon County, Mo., Sept. 9, 1928; s. Harry A. and Florence L. (Coonrod) B.; student Fort Scott (Kans.) Jr. Coll., 1947; B.Music Edn., Pittsburg (Kans.) State U., 1950; M.Music Edn., U. Kans., 1964, Ed.D., 1974; m. Dolores Elaine Reilley, Dec. 20, 1958; children—Stephanie Dee, Angela Kay. Music dir. elem. and secondary pub. schs., Kans., 1950-66; instr. dept. fine arts Kellogg Community Coll., Battle Creek, Mich., 1966-68; mem. faculty curriculum and instrn. dept. Mankato (Minn.) State U., 1969—, prof., 1979—, chairperson dept. curriculum and instrn., 1982—, co-dir. Center for Personal Devel. in Teaching, 1978-83; mem. Minn. State Univ. Bd. Task Force Tchr. Edn., 1984—. Bd. dirs. United Christian Campus Ctr., Mankato State U., 1982—; mem. adminstrv. bd. Centenary United Meth. Ch. Faculty research grantee, Mankato U., 1972, 78, 82. Asst. dir., Project HEED (U.S. Office Edn. grant project), 1974-77. Mem. Assn. of Tchr. Educators, Assn. for Supervision and Curriculum Devel., Minn. Council on Quality Edn., Minn. Assn. Tchr. Educators (past pres.), Phi Delta Kappa, Phi Mu Alpha Sinfonia. Contbg. author: (curriculum handbook) Humanizing Environment and Educational Development, 1975; contbr. articles on edn. to profl. publs. Home: 120 Rita Rd Mankato MN 56001 Office: PO Box 52 Mankato State Univ Mankato MN 56001

BURCH, JAMES HENRY, graphic designer; b. Ashtabula, Ohio, Aug. 2, 1938; s. Reed Holtz and Agnes Belle (Shank) B.; student U. Dayton, 1957-59, Miami U., Oxford, Ohio, 1972-78; B.F.A., Dayton Art Inst., 1975; m. Darlene Hazel Samuelson, May 10, 1959; children—Kandy, Lisa, Reed. Advt. artist, designer NCR Corp., Dayton, Ohio, 1961-68; art dir., account rep. Brown & Kroger Pub. Co., Dayton, 1968-70; graphics supr., art dir. Miami U., 1970—; owner, operator James Burch and Assos., Oxford, 1976—. Bd. dirs. Miami U. Fed. Employees Credit Union, 1979—, chmn. fin. and property com., 1979; bd. dirs. Wesley Found. at Miami U., 1976—, treas., 1978-79. Served with USAF, 1956-60. Recipient award of merit for design, silver and bronze award Univ. and Coll. Designers Regional Design Competition, 1977; 1st place award for design of direct mail campaign Dayton Advt. Club, 1968. Mem. Indsl. Graphics Internat. (dir., pres. 1979, award for design excellence, best of show trophy in poster design category), Univ. and Coll. Designers Assn., Graphic Artists Guild. Methodist. Clubs: Art Dirs. (Cin.); Oxford Arts (past pres.). Home: 550 S Main St Oxford OH 45056

BURCHELL, EDWARD V., manufacturing company executive; b. Chgo., Dec. 26, 1939; s. Edward O. and Marjorie F. (Hathaway) B.; B.A., Hamline U., 1961; m. Mary G. Cossack, Dec. 2, 1961; children—Laurie Ann, Edward R., Susan M. Marketing specialist 3M Co., St. Paul, Minn., 1961-63, sales rep., Louisville, 1963-66, sales rep. converter trades-new products, Cin., 1966-68; mktg./sales specialist Conwed Corp., St. Paul, Minn., 1968-75, sales mgr., 1975-79, mktg. mgr., 1979-81; v.p. Internet, Inc., Mpls., 1981—. Basketball and baseball coach Community Youth Program, 1972-77. Named Outstanding Converter-New Product Salesman, 3M Co., 1967, Outstanding Salesman plastics div. Conwed Corp., 1973, Outstanding Mktg. Contbr., Conwed Corp., 1976. Republican. Methodist. Patentee in field. Office: 2730 Nevada Ave N Minneapolis MN 55427

BURCHFIELD, JAMES RALPH, lawyer; b. Vincennes, Ind., Feb. 6, 1924; s. James R. and Doris (Marchal) B.; m. Dorothey Alice Underwood, July 31, 1949; children—Susan Burchfield Holiday, J. Randolph, Stephanie D. B.A., Ohio State U., 1947, J.D., 1949. Bar: Ohio 1949, U.S. Supreme Ct. 1960. Sole practice, Columbus, Ohio, 1949-77; ptnr. Burchfield & Burchfield, Columbus, 1978—; pres. Ohio Bar Liability Ins. Co., 1978—, also dir. Exec. dir. Franklin County Eisenhower Orgn., Ohio, 1952; mem. Mayor's Spl. Com. on Transit, Columbus, 1955-58; trustee Columbus Goodwill, 1970; mem. Ohio Soc. Colonial Wars, 1972. Served with USAF, 1943-45. Recipient Outstanding Young Man award Columbus Jaycees, 1956, Mil. Hon. award, Scabbard & Blade, 1948. Mem. Bexley Am. Legion (post comdr. 1954), Columbus Bar Assn., Am. Arbitrator's Assn., ABA, Ohio State Bar Assn. (chmn. 1970—), Am. Jud. Assn., Eastside Bus. Assn. (pres. 1955); fellow Ohio State Bar Found.; mem. Phi Alpha Theta. Republican. Clubs: Sertoma Internat. (pres. 1967), Sertoma Found. (pres. 1977-79). Lodges: Masons (treas. 1952—), Shriners. Avocations: world travel; hiking; fishing; reading. Home: 42 Park Dr Columbus OH 43209 Office: Burchfield & Burchfield 1313 E Broad St Columbus OH 43205

BURCHINAL, ALBERT WILLIAM, social work dir.; b. Connellsville, Pa., Oct. 6, 1920; s. John Henry and Anna Eliza (Gaster) B.; B.S. in Econs., Thiel Coll., 1952; M.S.W., U. Pitts., 1954, M.P.H., 1961; m. Katharina Berta Lutz, Nov. 10, 1948; children—John Robert, James Albert, Charles Stephen, William Leighton, David Lutz. Dir. family service dept. Luth. Community Services, Springfield, Ohio, 1954-60; med. social work research asso., birth defects clin. study center Children's Hosp., Columbus, Ohio, 1961-63; instr. Ohio State U. Sch. Social Work, Columbus, 1963-64; research dir. United Community Council, Columbus, 1964-68; project dir. div. adminstrn. on aging Ohio Dept. Mental Hygiene and Corrections, Columbus, 1968-69; coordinator mental retardation services Richland County Mental Health and Mental Retardation Bd., Mansfield, Ohio, 1969-70; dir. social services Mt. Vernon (Ohio) Devel. Center, 1970—; mem. central humanization com. Ohio Dept. Mental Health and Mental Retardation, 1973-75, inst. advocate; Mem. tech. advisory com. Franklin County Regional Planning Commn., 1965-69; mem. Mid-Ohio Health Planning Fedn., 1971-81; mem. Columbus Met. Census Tract Com., 1964-69, Knox County Health Planning Council, 1971—, Knox County Mental Health Assn., 1971—, Knox County Assn. for Retarded Citizens, 1971—; life mem. Parents and Friends Vol. Assn. Mt. Vernon Devel. Center, program chmn., 1972-82; mem. program and facilities coms. Columbus Met. Area Community Action Orgn., 1965-66; active Boy Scouts Am.; mem. Clark County com. Gov.'s Commn. on Aging, 1960; mem. Citizens' Advisory Com. Knox County Regional Planning Commn., 1973—, vice chmn., 1976—; mem. Knox County Disaster Support Group, 1982—; trustee Clark County Mental Health Assn., Planned Parenthood Clinic, Springfield. Served with U.S. Army, 1945-47. Mem. Nat. Assn. Social Workers (register of clin. social workers, state com. Ohio chpt., exec. com., charter, chpt. chmn. med. and health services council 1963-65, chpt. treas. 1968-69), Am. Assn. Social Workers, Am. Assn. Med. Social Workers, Acad. Certified Social Workers, Ohio Assn. for Children with Learning Disabilities, Performing Arts for Exceptional Children, Ohio Citizens Council, Ohio State Social Workers Assn., Knox County Community Services Roundtable (1st v.p., treas.), ARC (Knox County chpt.), Am. Legion (life; post comdr. 1979-80, chaplain 1982-83), Am. Assn. Sex Educators, Counselors and Therapists, Luth. Welfare League Cent. Ohio (mem. family service advisory com. 1967-70), Luth. Conf. Social Concern, Nat. Conf. Social Welfare (life), Am. Assn. for Mental Deficiency, Ohio Assn. for Retarded Citizens Parents Vol. Assn. Apple Creek Devel. Center (life), Mt. Vernon Area C. of C., Am. Pub. Health Assn. (nat. and Ohio chpt.), Ohio Welfare Conf., Amvets (life), Alpha Phi Omega (life). Club: Rotary. Lutheran (mem. Ohio dist. social service com. 1965-68). Home: 346 Illinois Ave Westerville OH 43081 Mailing Address: PO Box 622 Mount Vernon OH 43050

BURCHMORE, ROBERT NORRIS, JR., banker; b. Evanston, Ill., s. Robert Norris and Margaret (Wegner) B.; m. Lynn Rogers, Mar. 18, 1960 (div. 1971); m. Lynn Weldon, Apr. 16, 1977; children—John Stewart, Anne Allen. B.A., Lake Forest Coll., 1961; grad. Sch. Banking, 1975; grad. B.M.A. Sch. Banking, 1973. Bus. services rep. Harris Bank, Chgo., 1964-70; asst. v.p. Glenview Bank, Ill., 1970-73; v.p. 1st Nat. Bank Winnetka, Ill., 1973—. Mem. Ill. Bankers Assn., Chgo. Fin. Advertisers Assn., Bank Mktg. Assn., Coast Guard Aux., Navy League, Lake Mich. Yachting Assn. Republican. Methodist. Clubs: Chgo. Corinthian Yacht, Waukegan Yacht, Execs. Avocations: Sailing. Home: 171 Riverside Dr Northfield IL 60093 Office: 1st Nat Bank Winnetka 520 Greenbay Rd Winnetka IL 60093

BURD, JOHN STEPHEN, educational administrator, music educator; b. Lock Haven, Pa., Apr. 6, 1939; s. John Wilson and Lily (Fye) B.; m. Patricia Ayers, June 3, 1961; children—Catherine Elizabeth, Emily Susanne. B.M.E., Greenville Coll., 1961; M.S.M., Butler U., 1964; Ph.D., Ind. State U., 1971. Adj. music instr. Rose Hulman Inst. Tech., Terre Haute, Ind., 1969-71; assoc. prof., Greenville Coll., Ill., 1971-76; prof. educ. Lindenwood Coll., St. Charles, Mo., 1976-80; v.p. acad. affairs Maryville Coll., St. Louis, 1980—; team evaluator Nat. Council Accreditation Tchr. Edn., 1979—; cons. colleges, 1979—. Editor: New Voices of Educatiion, 1969-71. Contbr. articles to profl. jours. Choir dir. Central Presbyterian Ch., St. Louis, 1984—, Maryville Coll., St. Louis, 1984—; v.p. Christian Arts, Inc., N.J., 1965—. Recipient Outstanding Alumnus award Greenville Coll., 1982. Mem. Am. Assn. Tchr. Educ., Am. Assn. Higher Educ., Mo. Assn. Coll. Tchrs. Educ. (pres. 1979-80). Presbyterian. Lodge: Rotary (sergeant at arms 1983-84, treas. 1984—, pres.-elect 1985). Avocations: tennis, painting, travel, singing in a male quartet. Office: Maryville College 13550 Conway Rd St Louis MO 63141

BURDICK, BRUCE FRANCIS, computer retailer; b. Shenadoah, Iowa, Oct. 11, 1939; s. Francis Dale and Elizabeth Dorothy (Petersen) Witt B.; m. Mary Eda Tishendorf, July 30, 1967; children—Bryan Alfred, Bryce Francis, Heather Elizabeth, Branden David. Student U. Colo., 1957-58, U. Denver, 1959-60; LL.B., Blackstone Sch. Law, Chgo., 1964; postgrad. Dupage Hort. Sch., 1967-68. Bar: Calif. 1964. Sales mgr. Forest Olson Real Estate, Santa Ana, Calif., 1964-66; pvt. investigator, Los Angeles, 1966-67; ptnr. Harrison & Co. Greenhouse, Sioux City, Iowa, 1967-77; pres. Burdick's Wormery, Sioux City, 1977-78; pres., chief exec. officer Burdick's Computer Stores, Overland Park, Kans., 1978—; dir. Bio Med. Research, Overland Park, Kans., 1983—; mem. network adv. council Computerland, Hayward, Calif., 1983—; mem. dealer adv. council Apple Computer, Cupertino, Calif., 1980-82, IBM, Boca Raton, Fla., 1980-81, ITT, Phoenix, Ariz., 1983—. Mem. Fellowship of Christian Athletes, Kansas City, Mo., 1983; trustee Westmar Coll., LeMars, Iowa. Served with USMC, 1960-64. Recipient Highest Sales award Computerland Corporate, 1980-81, 82-83, Pres. Cup, 1980; named Bus. Man of Yr. Kansas City, Small Bus. Assn., 1983. Mem. Computerland Corporate (mem. pres. adv. council 1980—), C. of C. Republican. Lutheran. Club: Johnson County Youth Hockey Assn. (commr. 1982-83) (Overland Park, Kans.). Office: Burdick's Computer Stores Inc 9119 Barton St Overland Park KS 66214

BURDICK, EUGENE ALLAN, judge; b. Williston, N.D., Oct. 15, 1912; s. Usher Lloyd and Emma Cecelia (Robertson) B.; m. May Picard, Feb. 14, 1939; children—William Eugene, Elizabeth Jane Cantarine. B.A., U. Minn., 1933, J.D., 1935. Bar: N.D. 1935, U.S. Dist. Ct. N.D., 1943. Sole practice, Willison, 1935-53; state's atty. Williams County, N.D., 1939-45; judge Dist. Ct. Northwest 5th Jud. Dist., N.D., 1953-78; surrogate judge N.D. Supreme Ct., 1981—; commr. Uniform State Laws, N.D., 1959; mem. exec. com. Nat. Conf. State Trial Judges, 1968-71, 75, state del. 1959-74; pres. nat. Conf. Commrs. on Uniform State Laws, 1971-73, chmn. com. on style, 1975—; chmn. Govs. Com. Children and Youth, 1965-71. Editor N.D. Pattern Jury Instrns.-Criminal, 1985. Pres. James Meml. Library, Williston, 1948-65. Recipient Outstanding Trustee award ALA, 1956; N.D. Nat. Leadership award, 1972. Mem. ABA, State Bar Assn. N.D. (pres. 1951-52; Disting. Service award 1983), N.D. Jud. Council, Nat. Council Juvenile and Family Ct. Judges, Am. Judicature Soc. (bd. dirs. 1967-68, 74-78, Herbert Harley award 1985), N.D. Conf. Social Welfare (exec. com.), Juvenile Ct. Judges Adv. Council to N.D., Am. Law Inst., Inst. Jud. Adminstrn., Assn. Trial Lawyers Am., N.D. Farm Bur., N.D. Farmers Union, Am. Contract Bridge League, Boat Owners Assn. of U.S., Order of Coif (hon.), Phi Alpha Delta, Sigma Nu. Club: Toastmaster (hon. mem.). Lodges: Elks (hon. life), Kiwanis (past pres.). Home: 405 E 14th St Williston ND 58801-4499

BURDICK, MARY LUELLA, hospital executive; b. Olean, N.Y., Sept. 22, 1929; d. Leone Leslie and Ida Florence (Tompkins) Sturtevant; student public schs.; m. Kenneth Gerald Burdick, Aug. 31, 1946; children—Ronald Leone, Anna Marie, Gerald Ralph. Bookkeeper, cashier Things Shoe Store, Lockport, N.Y., 1954-55; mgr. trainee Joanlee Dress Shop, Lockport, 1958; supr. Syncro Corp., Hicksville, Ohio, 1960-67; various positions Tribune Printing Co., Hicksville, 1969-77; seamstress, Hicksville, 1976-79; mgr. forms, mgmt. Parkview Meml. Hosp., Fort Wayne, Ind., 1979—. Treas., Hicksville Missionary Ch., 1970-80, 82—, now dir. children's group. Home: 04512 State Route 18 Hicksville OH 43526 Office: Parkview Meml Hosp 2200 Randallia Dr Fort Wayne IN 46805

BURDICK, QUENTIN NORTHROP, U.S. senator; b. Munich, N.D., June 19, 1908; s. Usher Lloyd and Emma (Robertson) B.; B.A., U. Minn., 1931, LL.B., 1932. Admitted to N.D. bar, 1932, practiced in Fargo, 1932-58; mem. 86th Congress, N.D. at large; member U.S. Senate from N.D., 1960—. Democrat. Home: 1110 S 9th St Fargo ND 58102 Office: 511 Hart Senate Office Bldg Washington DC 20510*

BURDON, WILLIAM FONTAINE, advertising executive; b. Ware, Mass., Dec. 21, 1926; s. Paul P. and Dorothy S. (Schaninger) B.; Assoc. B.A., Curry Coll., Boston, 1951; m. Leonora Foronda, Sept. 10, 1954; children—Susan Lee, Linda Marie. With NBC, 1952-54; exec. v.p., creative dir. Marvin Hult & Assos., advt., Peoria, Ill., 1955-61; pres. Burdon Advt., Inc., Peoria, 1962-82; pres. Burdon/Tull/Oakley Ltd., Peoria, 1982—. Mem. adv. bd. YWCA. Landmarks Found. Served with U.S. Army, 1945-47. Author published poetry. Home: 1827 W Sunnyview Dr Peoria IL 61614 Office: 2523 W Reservoir Blvd Peoria IL 61615

BUREMAN, JAMES EDWARD, optometrist; b. Oklahoma City, Okla., Apr. 15, 1954; s. Ralph Edward and Thelma J. (Hamlin) B.; m. Sherry Kathryn Classen, June 9, 1984. B.A. in Bio., Central Methodist Coll., 1976; O.D., Ill. Coll. Optometry, 1980. Optometrist, Springfield, Mo., 1984—. Coach Youth Baseball, West Ger., 1980-83. Served as capt. U.S. Army, 1980-84. Army Optometry scholar, 1976. Mem. Am. Optometric Assn., Mo. Optometric Assn., Armed Forces Optometric Assn. Republican. Roman Catholic. Lodge: Rotary. Avocations: sports; reading. Home: 1032 W Cherokee Springfield MO 65807-2585 Office: 1923 E Kearny Springfield MO 65803

BUREN, STEPHEN RAYMOND, corporate controller; b. Festus, Mo., Dec. 9, 1943; s. Arthur Stanton and Alice Catherine (Rhyneer) B.; m. Lynn Maria Byington, Apr. 4, 1964; children—Stephen, Jr., Jason, Theresa, Angela. B.S. in Acctg., Washington U., St. Louis, 1973; M.B.A., Wichita State U., 1984. Acct. St. Joe Minerals Corp., Herculaneum, Mo., 1965-71, asst. controller, 1971-74; acctg. mgr. The Cessna Aircraft Co., Wichita, Kans., 1974-75, div. controller, 1975-81, dir. finance, 1981-84, corp. controller, 1984—. Mem. Budget Review Com., United Way, Wichita, 1975-76. Mem. Nat. Assn. Accts., Am. Acctg. Assn., The Controllers' Council. Home: 11601 Valley Hi Dr Wichita KS 67209 Office: The Cessna Aircraft Co PO Box 1521 Wichita KS 67201

BURESH-REIST, DIANE KAY, pharmacist; b. Cedar Rapids, Iowa, Mar. 21, 1958; d. Edwin Wesley and Martha Mary (Blazek) B.; m. Jeffrey Clark Reist, Mar. 30, 1985. B.S. in Pharmacy, U. Iowa, 1981. Registered pharmacist, Iowa. Sec. Best Plumbing and Heating, Cedar Rapids, 1976-80; staff pharmacist Mercy Hosp., Cedar Rapids, 1980—; relief pharmacist Claxton Pharmacy, Cedar Rapids, 1984—; pharmacy-nursing liaison Mercy Hosp., Cedar Rapids, 1980—. Linn County Speakers Bur. rep., 1982—. Mem. Iowa Pharmacists Assn. (dist. rep. to Ho. of Dels.), Iowa Soc. of Hosp. Pharmacists. Republican. Presbyterian. Club: Chandon. Avocations: gourmet cooking, skiing, bowling, travel. Home: 1620 Seminole Ave NW #8 Cedar Rapids IA 52405 Office: Mercy Hospital Pharmacy 701 10th St SE Cedar Rapids IA 52403

BURFORD, MARY ANNE, medical technologist; b. Paris, Ark., Aug. 24, 1939; d. Anthony John and Julia Elizabeth (Hoffman) Elsken; B.S. in Biology, Benedictine Coll., 1961; grad. in med. tech. St. Mary's Sch. Med. Tech., 1962; m. Joseph Paul Burford, May 11, 1968 (div. Feb. 1983); children—Sarah Elizabeth, Shawn Anthony, Joseph Paul, Daniel Aaron. Evening supr. St. Vincent's Infirmary, Little Rock, 1962-65; med. technologist Holt-Krock Clinic, Ft. Smith, Ark., 1966-68, Ball Meml. Hosp., Muncie, Ind., 1971-72, Pathologist Assoc., Muncie, 1972-73; chief technologist Ob-Gyn Inc., Muncie, 1975—; instr. microbiology St. Vincent's Infirmary, 1962-65, Sparks Med. Ctr., Ft. Smith, 1966-68. Chmn. liturgical life, St. Mary's Catholic Ch.; treas Met. Football League, 1983-85. Mem. Am. Soc. Clin. Pathologists (affiliate mem., registered med. technologist), Am. Assn. Clin. Chemists, Am. Soc. for Microbiology. Club: Muncie Altrusa (chmn. materials and records com., constn. and by-laws com. 1985-86). Home: 1509 W Buckingham Dr Muncie IN 47302 Office: 2501 W Jackson St Muncie IN 47302

BURG, LAWRENCE EDWARD, stockbroker; b. LaPorte, Ind., Apr. 2, 1913; s. Clifford Ash and Hazel D. (Russell) B.; student bus. coll., spl. courses Northwestern U., 1946-47; m. Mary Ewing Glickauf, Jan. 10, 1942; children—Kenneth, Bruce, Louise, Mary. Salesman, Commonwealth Edison Co., Chgo., 1931-32, dist. rep., 1937-51; salesman Burg Typewriter Service, 1933, Williams & Meyer Co., 1934-35, Standard Oil Co. (Ind.), 1935-36; owner Minit-Fry Potato Co., 1951-54, pres., 1954-61; mgr. research dept., asst. sec. Wm. H. Tegtmeyer Co., 1961-65; registered rep., research cons., mut. funds specialist Woolard & Co., Chgo., 1965-79, Altorfer, Podesta, Woolard & Co., 1979-81, Stifel, Nicolaus & Co., 1981-82, Bacon Whipple & Co., Inc. subs. Stifel, Nicolaus & Co. Inc., Chgo., 1982—; owner Minit Calculator; former partner St. Lawrence Chem. Products Co. Registered rep. Nat. Assn. Security Dealers. Served with AUS, 1941-45. Mem. Am. Security Council (nat. adv. bd.), Am. Contract Bridge League, Internat. Platform Assn., Am. Legion, U.S. Chess Fedn., Aerial Phenomena Research Orgn., Christian Scientist (1st reader 1959-62, asst. com. on publ. for Ill. 1962—). Clubs: Homewood-Flossmoor Chess, Beverly Social. Home: 820 Elder Rd Apt 214 Homewood IL 60430 Office: 135 S LaSalle St Chicago IL 60603

BURGE, JOHN LARRY, executive staffing and personnel consultant; b. Mayfield, Ky., June 18, 1918; s. Edwin and Laura (Staten) B.; B.S., U. Kans., 1941; M.A., Villanova U., 1959; postgrad. in mgmt. Stanford U., 1962, U. Mich., 1977; m. Melva I. Grant, 1938; children—Sharon Burge Womack, Penny Burge Johansen. Dir. personnel, public relations and safety Lucky Lager Brewing Co., San Francisco, 1962-66; corp. personnel mgr., dir. pub. relations and safety MJB Coffe Corp., San Francisco, 1966-69; co-owner Ulrich Personnel Agy., Palo Alto, Calif., 1969-70; personnel mgr., area public relations dir. Bechtel Power Corp., Ann Arbor, Mich., 1970-80; exec. staffing cons. Fluor Corp., Irvine, Calif., 1981—, Procon Corp., Des Plaines, Ill., Soil Testing Services, Chgo., Domino's Pizza Corp. Ann Arbor, Mich., Ditty-Lynch & Assocs., Inc., Royal Oak, Mich., 1982—; prof. naval sci. Villanova U., 1956-59; mem. faculty St. Louis Community Coll., 1981—. Airport commr., Ann Arbor, Mich., 1975-77; mem. President's Com. on Handicapped, 1970—; coordinator Explorer Post, Boy Scouts Am. Served to comdr. USN, 1941-62. Decorated Air medal with six oak leaf clusters. Mem. Am. Soc. Personnel Adminstrn., Ann Arbor Personnel Assn. (pres. 1979-80), Navy League, C. of C. (edn. com.). Republican. Baptist. Clubs: Quiet Birdmen, K, Exchange. Middle weight Golden Gloves champion, 1937. Office: 14722 Greenleaf Valley Dr Chesterfield MO 63017

BURGE, JOHN WESLEY, JR., mgmt. cons.; b. Mobile, Ala., Sept. 11, 1932; s. John W. and Mary Jo (Guest) B.; student Centenary Coll., 1955-57, San Antonio Coll., 1958-63, UCLA, 1965; m. Shirley P. Roberts, Mar. 29, 1958; children—John W., Carol Delene, Eric W., Kurt R., Karen K. With ITT Gilfillan, Los Angeles, 1954-69; pres., gen. mgr. RANTEC, Calabasas, Calif., 1969-70; pres. electronics and space div., group v.p. govt. and def. Emerson Electric Co., St. Louis, 1970-80; pres. John W. Burge & Assos., St. Louis, 1981—; mgmt. cons.; adv. dir. Emerson Electric Co.; dir. Emerson Systems, Internat., Emerson Systems Corp.; lectr. in field. Bd. dirs. Progressive Youth Center, St. Louis, 1975-80. Served with USAF, 1950-54. Decorated Grand Cordon of Order of Al-Istiqlal of the 1st order King Hussein of Jordan, 1978. Mem. U.S. Navy League, Am. Mgmt. Assn., Am. Def. Preparedness Assn. Home: 11711 Chanticleer Ct Pensacola FL 32507 Office: 8100 W Florissant St Saint Louis MO 63136

BURGER, MARY LOUISE, psychologist, educator; b. Chgo., Nov. 3; d. Robert Stanley and Margaret Agnes (Brennan) Hirsh; B.A., Mundelein Coll.; M.Ed., Loyola U.; Ed.D. No. Ill. U., 1972; m. William Bronson Burger, Mar. 16, 1968. Tchr., Chgo. Bd. Edn., 1954-68; mem. faculty DePaul U., 1960-61, Roosevelt U., 1967-70; cons. psychologist Worthington-Hurst & Assos., Headstart Program, Chgo., 1972-74; prof. dept. early childhood edn. Northeastern Ill. U., 1968—, chmn. dept., 1972-80, chmn. faculty assembly Coll. Edn., 1981; chmn. subcom. Chgo. region White House Conf. on Children, 1979-81; ednl. dir., owner Childhood Edn. Nursery and Day Care Center, Evanston, Ill., 1974—; cons. Chgo. Mayor's Office Child Care Services. Chmn. bd. dirs. Univ. Community Care Center. Mem. Assn. Childhood Edn. Internat. (past pres. Ill. and Chgo. brs., chmn. nominating com. 1980-81, internat. v.p., mem. exec. bd.), Nat. Assn. Edn. Young Children, Assn. Higher Edn., NW Assn. Nursery Schs., AAUP, Phi Delta Kappa, Delta Kappa Gamma (past pres. Gamma Alpha chpt.). Club: Zonta Internat. (v.p. Chgo. Loop club 1983-85, pres. elect 1984-86). Editor bull. and pamphlets Assn. Childhood Edn. Internat., 1975-77. Home: Fairfax Village 1 Kittery on Auburn Rolling Meadows IL 60008 Office: Northeastern Ill U 5500 N St Louis Ave Chicago IL 60025 also Childhood Edn Center 2727 Crawford St Evanston IL 60201

BURGER, WILLIAM ROBERT, picture frame company executive; b. La Porte, Ind., Mar. 21, 1942; s. Walter Theodore and Mary Alice (Gregory) B.; m. Marcella Beigel, July 31, 1965; children—Michele, Tonia, Gwen. B.S., Northwestern U., 1964. Foreman, Thanhardt-Burger Corp., La Porte, 1965-68, v.p., 1969—. Dir. La Porte Walther League Chorus; ch. pipe organist. Served with U.S. Army, 1966-72. Lutheran. Office: Thanhardt-Burger Corp 1105 Washington St La Porte In 46350

BURGERT, ALFRED LELAND, banker; b. Lawrence, Kans., Mar. 14, 1924; s. Alfred Leander and Myrtle Alma (Atkinson) B.; student Sterling Coll., 1942, Muskingum Coll., 1943; B.S., U. Kans., 1948, J.D., 1950; diploma Stonier Grad. Sch. Banking of Rutgers U., 1964; m. Betty Jane Koontz, Aug. 21, 1946; children—Maretta Kay, Alfred Lee, Philip Lynn. With 1st State Bank & Trust Co., Pittsburg, Kans., 1950—, exec. v.p., chief exec. officer, 1972-73, pres., chief exec. officer, 1973—, trust officer, dir., 1967—. Trustee Pittsburg YMCA, also past pres.; treas., bd. dirs. Mid-Am. YMCA; treas., adv. trustee Mt. Carmel Hosp. Planning Com.; past mem., past pres. Pittsburg Pub. Library Bd.; past pres. Pittsburg State U. Endowment Assn., 1975-77. Served with AUS, 1943-46. Mem. Kans. Bankers Assn. (governing council, bank mgmt. com., past pres. trust div., past exec. com.), Pittsburg C. of C. (pres. 1971-72), Kans., Crawford County bar assns., Phi Alpha Delta. Republican. Presbyterian (elder). Clubs: Lions (pres. Pittsburg 1965-66), Crestwood Country, Kansas City, U. Kans. Chancellors. Home: 1406 S Catalpa St Pittsburg KS 66762 Office: 417 N Broadway Pittsburg KS 66762

BURGESS, JANET HELEN, interior designer; b. Moline, Ill., Jan. 22, 1933; d. John Joseph and Helen Elizabeth (Johnson) B.; student Augustana Coll., Rock Island, Ill., 1950-51, U. Utah, Logan, 1951-52, Marycrest Coll., 1959-60; m. Richard Everett Guth, Aug. 25, 1951; children—John Joseph, Marshall Claude, Linnea Ann Guth Layman; m. Milan Andrew Vodick, Feb. 16, 1980. One-person shows: El Pao, Bolivar, Venezuela, 1952-62; represented in pvt. collections, U.S., Europe, S.Am.; producer, designer Playcrafters Barn Theatre, Moline, Ill., 1963-65; designer, gen. mgr. Grilk Interiors, Davenport, Iowa, 1963—; dir. Fine Arts Gallery, Davenport, 1978-84; chmn. bd. Product Handling, Inc., Davenport, 1981—; owner mail order bus. Amazon Vinegar & Pickling Works Drygoods, Davenport. Contbr. articles to profl. jours.; design work featured in Gift & Decorative Accessories mag., 1969, 80, Decor mag., 1979. Bd. dirs. Rock Island Art Guild, 1974—, Quad Cities Arts Council, 1980—; bd. dirs. Village of East Davenport (Iowa) Assn., 1973—, pres., 1981; bd. dirs. Neighborhood Housing Services, Davenport, Davenport Area Conv. and Tourism Bur., 1981; mem. adv. bd. interior design dept. Scott Community Coll., 1975—; mem. Mayor's Com. Historic Preservation, Davenport, Iowa, 1976-77, 85—; bd. dirs. retail com. Operation Clean Davenport, 1981; mem. 16th Iowa Civil War Re-enactment Union. Mem. Gift and Decorative Accessories Assn. (nat. merit award 1969), Am. Soc. Interior Designers (asso.), Davenport C. of C., Nat. Trust Historic Preservation, Preservation Group, State Iowa Hist. Soc., Rock Island Arsenal Hist. Soc. Home: 2801 34th Ave Ct Rock Island IL 61201 Office: 2200 E 11th St Davenport IA 52803 also 2218 E 11th St Davenport IA 52803

BURGETTE, JAMES MILTON, dentist; b. Toledo, Aug. 18, 1937; s. James Martin and Louise (Milton) B.; A.B., Lincoln U., 1959; D.D.S., Howard U., 1964; m. Carolyn Harris, Aug. 24, 1963; children—Stephanie, James, Ngina. Practice dentistry, Detroit, 1967—. Sec. Wolverine Polit. Action Com., Detroit, 1971—. Mem. Detroit Pub. Sch. Health Council. Bd. dirs. Comprehensive Neighborhood Health Services; mem. coordinating council Black Christian Nationalist Ch.; mem. exec. bd. Congl. Dist., Democratic Party Orgn.; mem. deacon bd. Shrine of Black Madonna; trustee Comprehensive Health Planning Council Southeastern Mich. Served to lt. Dental Corps, USNR, 1964-67. Mem. Nat. Dental Assn. (mem. ho. of dels., parliamentarian 1977), Wolverine Dental Soc. Mich. (editor news jour. 1971; recipient meritorious service award 1972, pres. 1976), Acad. Gen. Dentistry, Am. Profl. Practice Com., Orgn. Black Scientists (v.p. 1979), Howard Alumni Assn. (sec. 1969-70), Am. Legion (exec. bd. Post 77), Chi Delta Mu, Omega Psi Phi. Club: Masons. Home: 1660 Lincolnshire Dr Detroit MI 48203 Office: 5050 Joy Rd Detroit MI 48204

BURGHER, LOUIS WILLIAM, physician, educator; b. Centerville, Iowa, Oct. 31, 1944; s. Wendell and Dorothy (Probasco) B.; B.S., U. Nebr., 1966, M.D. with honors, 1970, M.Med. Sci., 1972, Ph.D. in Med. Sci., 1978; m. Susan Stephens, May 20, 1979; children—Tanya Jo, Tara Lynn, Lucas William, Rachel Elizabeth. Intern, U. Nebr. Coll. Medicine, 1970-71, resident in internal medicine, 1971-72; practice medicine specializing in pulmonary medicine, Omaha, 1974—; NIH fellow in pulmonary diseases Mayo Grad. Sch. of Medicine, Rochester, Minn., 1972-74, assoc. prof., 1981—, chief sect. pulmonary medicine, 1980-84; clin. research assoc. in pulmonary disease U. Nebr. Coll. of Medicine, 1969-72; med. dir. pulmonary medicine Bishop Clarkson Meml. Hosp., Omaha, 1974—; mem. pulmonary-allergy drugs adv. FDA, 1984—; Tb cons. to Nebr. Dept. Health, 1972—. Med. dir. Nebr. Opportunity for Vols. in ACTION, 1971-72; trustee Nebr. Found., 1982—. Recipient Upjohn award Nebr. coll. Medicine, 1970. Diplomate Am. Bd. Internal Medicine, subsplty. bd. pulmonary medicine. Fellow Am. Coll. Chest Physicians; mem. AMA (council on med. edn. 1973-78, mem. liaison com. on med. edn. 1974-79), Nebr. Med. Assn., Am. Thoracic Soc., Zumbro Valley Med. Soc. (exec. com. 1973-74), Univ. Med. Center House Officers Assn. (pres. 1971-72), Mayo Fellows Assn. (pres. 1973-74), Nat. Acad. Scis. (mem. task force study Inst. Medicine), Nebr. Thoracic Soc. (pres. 1980-81), Alpha Omega Alpha. Contbr. articles on pulmonary disease to profl. jours. Home: 139 N Elmwood Rd Omaha NE 68132 Office: Bishop Clarkson Meml Hosp Dewey Ave and 44th St PO Box 3328 Omaha NE 68103

BURI, JOHN ROBERT, psychology educator, clergyman, Christian counselor; b. Dubuque, Iowa, Feb. 8, 1950; s. Robert Francis and Catherine (Pierick) B.; m. Kathleen Marie Dodds, June 3, 1972; children—Nicholas J., Joseph J., Mark J., Daniel J. B.A. in Psychology, Loras Coll., 1972, M.A., Loyola U., Chgo., 1975, Ph.D. in Cognitive Psychology, 1976. Teaching, research asst. Loyola U., Chgo., 1972-75, instr. 1975-76; asst. prof. Coll. St. Thomas, St. Paul, 1976-82, assoc. prof., dept. chmn., 1982—. Chmn. precinct caucus. Nat. Collegiate Athletic Assn. scholar athlete fellow Loyola U., 1972-73; named Tchr. of Yr., Coll. St. Thomas, 1976-81. Mem. Am. Psychol. Assn., Midwestern Psychol. Assn., Minn. Psychol. Assn., Christian Assn. for Psychol. Studies, Delta Epsilon Sigma. Democrat. Roman Catholic. Home: 1718 Lincoln Ave Saint Paul MN 55105 Office: 2115 Summit Ave Saint Paul MN 55105

BURICK, JOSEPH PETER, physician; b. Youngstown, Ohio, June 28, 1951; s. Joseph and Carole (Vlasic) B.; m. Jacquelyn Elaine Edgar, June 26, 1980; children—Joseph Timothy, Christina Nicole, Nichole Marie. A.B., Youngstown State U., 1969; D.O., Chgo. Coll. Osteo. Medicine, 1973. Resident in family practice St. Thomas Family Practice Center, Akron, 1977-80, dir. alcohol detoxification unit, 1980-82, chmn. family medicine, 1985—; dir. Summit County Drug Bd., 1982—; emergency rm. physician St. Thomas Hosp. Med. Ctr., Akron, Robinson Meml. Hosp., Ravenna, Ohio, part-time 1980—; mem. staff St. Thomas Hosp., Akron Gen. Med. Ctr., Children's Hosp. Med. Ctr., Akron, Akron City Hosp.; clin. instr. Northeastern Ohio Univs. Coll. Medicine, 1982—; clin. preceptor Kent State U. Coll. Nursing, 1982—; cons. alcoholism and drug abuse Edwin Shaw Hosp. Rehab. Ctr., 1982—. Mem. AMA, Am. Acad. Family Physicians, Summit County Med. Soc., Sigma Sigma Phi. Office: 578 N Main St Akron OH 44310

BURINGRUD, TERRY NILS, educator; b. Fargo, N.D., Aug. 6, 1952; s. Nils Martin and Elaine Annabell (Ponto) B.; m. Mary Ellen, June 23, 1973; children—Eric, Nicole. A.S., Wahpeton State Sch. Sci. (N.D.), 1972, B.S., Minot State Coll., 1974. Tchr., coach Esmond Pub. Sch. (N.D.), 1974-76, Maple Valley Pub. Sch., Tower City, N.D., 1976-85; sales rep. Harcourt Brace Jovanovich, 1985—. Bd. dirs. Tower City Park, 1978-80; supr. St. Paul Lutheran Sunday Sch., Tower City, 1982—. Named Dist. 4 Coach of Yr., 1983. Mem. N.D. High Sch. Coaches Assn., Nat. High Sch. Coaches Assn., N.D. Edn. Assn., NEA. Club: Tower City Summer Recreation (pres. 1984). Home: PO Box 93 Tower City ND 58071 Office: Maple Valley Pub Sch Buffalo ND 58011

BURK, H., market research company executive. Chmn., chief exec. officer, dir. A.C. Nielsen Co., Northbrook, Ill. Office: A C Nielsen Co Nielsen Plaza Northbrook IL 60062*

BURK, KEITH EUGENE, management consultant; b. Albion, Mich., May 31, 1941; s. Wilson Eugene and Ruth Elizabeth (Chamberlain) B.; B.S., Western Mich. U., 1969; m. Darlene Carole Nelson, Feb. 2, 1963; children—Linnea Ruth, Eric Eugene. Lab. technician U.S. Plywood (name now Champion Internat.), 1965-67, mgr. tech. engring., 1967-69, tech. service mgr., 1969-70; engring. mgr. Dover Corp., Portage, Mich., 1970-71; engr. A.B. Cassedy & Assos., Ridgefield, Conn., 1971-73, group engr., 1973-74, asst. chief, 1974-76, chief, 1976-80; co-founder KAMACO, Inc., v.p. ops., 1981—. Mem. Kalamazoo Civic Theater, 1973—; cubmaster Boy Scouts Am., 1982—. Served with U.S. Army, 1961-63. Mem. Am. Mgmt. Assn., AIAA, Am. Inst. Indsl. Engrs., Nat. Assn. Profl. Consultants, Am. Security Council. Republican. Christian Scientist. Club: Coterie Dance. Lodge: Rotary. Patentee in field.

BURK, WILLIAM LEE, optometrist; b. Callao, Mo., Apr. 20, 1935; s. William F. and Stella (Baker) B.; m. Barbara Burlew, June 11, 1983; children—Christopher, Jason. B.S., Northeast Mo. State U., 1959; O.D., So. Calif., Coll. Optometry, 1972. Lic. optometrist, N.Mex., Mo., Calif., Ariz.; cert. tchr. and community coll. instr., Ariz., Calif. Instr., Los Angeles Trade-Tech. Coll., 1969-72, Yavapai Coll., Cottonwood, Ariz., 1975-76; sole practice optometry, Ozark, Mo., 1983—. Served with U.S. Army, 1955-56; Ger. Mem. Better Vision Inst., Am. Optometric Assn. Office: Riverview Plaza Ozark MO 65721

BURKE, EMMETT CHARLES, educator; b. Montgomery, Ala., Jan. 30, 1920; s. William J. and Ethel (Scott) B.; A.B., B.S., Roosevelt U., 1945; M.A., Loyola U., 1953; M.Ed., DePaul U., 1954; O.D., Ill. Coll. Optometry, 1947; m. Sarah Scott, Aug. 14, 1949. Sr. caseworker Ill. Pub. Aid Commn., Chgo., 1948-56; asst. prin. Wm. Carter Pub. Sch., Chgo., 1957—; asst. prof. Nat. Coll. of Edn., Chgo., 1969-85; dir. Washington Pk. YMCA, Afro-Am. Family and Community Services. Active Nat. Urban League, NAACP. Served with USAAF, 1942-45. Certified social worker, Ill. Mem. Nat. Assn. of Black Profs. (dir.), Chgo. African-Am. Tchrs. Assn. (dir.), Chgo. Asst. Prins. Assn. (dir.), Chgo. Council for Exceptional Children (dir.), AAUP, NEA, Phi Delta Kappa, Alpha Phi Alpha. Home: 601 E 32nd St Chicago IL 60616 Office: 5740 S Michigan Ave Chicago IL 60637

BURKE, JAMES CHARLES, automobile company assembly repairman, geophysical and geologic consultant; b. Indpls., Mar. 25, 1954; s. Charles August and Mary Jo (Shelby) B.; m. Laura Leigh Davis, Aug. 26, 1978; children—Brandon C., Brenna L., Bryce D., Brin A. B.S., Youngstown State U., 1981; M.S., U. Akron, 1985. Repairman Gen. Motors, Lordstown, Ohio, 1974—; teaching asst. U. Akron, Ohio, 1982-83; instr. geology Youngstown State U., Ohio, 1984-85; cons., Youngstown, 1984—. Student mem. Soc. Exploration Geophysicists, Am. Assn. Petroleum Geologists. Republican. Methodist. Lodge: Masons. Avocations: reading, golf, racquetball, softball. Home: 4205 Pembrook Youngstown OH 44515

BURKE, JAMES DONALD, art historian, museum director; b. Salem, Oreg., Feb. 22, 1939; s. Donald James and Ellin Anne (Adams) B.; B.A., Brown U., 1962; M.A., U. Pa., 1966; Ph.D., Harvard U., 1972; m. Diane E. Davies, May 17, 1980. Vis curator Fitzwilliam Mus., Cambridge, Eng., 1970-71; curator, Allen Art Mus., Oberlin Coll., 1971-72; curator Yale U. Art Gallery, New Haven, 1972-78; asst. dir. art St. Louis Art Mus., 1978-80, dir., 1980—. Author: Charles Meryon: Prints and Drawings, 1974; Jan Both (1618-1652): Paintings, Drawings and Prints, 1976. Fulbright-Hayes fellow U. Amsterdam, Netherlands, 1968-69; Paul Sachs travelling fellow Harvard U., 1970; Nat. Endowment Arts mus. profl. fellow Europe, 1973. Mem. Am. Assn. Museums, Print Council Am. (trustee), Coll. Art Assn. Am. Office: St Louis Art Mus Forest Park Saint Louis MO 63110

BURKE, JOE, professional sports team executive; m. Mary Burke; children—Joe, Mary Ann, Jimmy, John, Alice, Bobby, Vincent. Ticket mgr., bus. mgr., gen. mgr. Louisville Colonels, 1948-66; with Washington Senators (now Tex. Rangers), as asst. gen. mgr., bus. mgr., treas., v.p., 1961-73; v.p. bus. Kansas City Royals, 1973-74, exec. v.p., gen. mgr., 1974-81, pres., 1981—. Office: care Kansas City Royals Box 1969 Kansas City MO 64141*

BURKE, JOHN EDWARD, communications educator; b. Huntington, W.Va., Aug. 10, 1942; s. Charles Joseph and Eloise Marie (Sang) B.; B.A., Marshall U., 1965; M.F.A., Ohio U., 1966, Ph.D., Ohio State U., 1971; children—John Lindsey, Elizabeth Ann. Intern, U.S. Ho. Reps., 1960-61; news writer, editor Sta. WSAZ-TV, Huntington, 1962-65; instr. Kent State U., 1966-69; dir. TV Arts dept. Cleve. Summer Sch. for Arts, 1967-68; asst. to dir. Ohio State U. Telecommunications Center, 1969-71; project dir. Ohio Valley Med. Microwave TV System, Columbus, 1971-73; dir., asso. prof. biomed. communications Ohio State U. Coll. Medicine, asso. prof. communications Coll. Social and Behavioral Scis., 1972-84; assoc. dean acad. affairs, prof. U. Ill. Coll. Associated Health Professions, Chgo., 1984—; cons. univs., bus., industry, including U. Tenn., Nat. Med. Audio-Visual Center, Upjohn Co., N. Central Assn. Colls. and Univs. USPHS grantee, 1972-77. Fellow Am. Soc. Allied Health Professions; mem. Health Scis. Communications Assn., Assn. Biomed. Communications Dirs., Am. Med. Writers Assn., Alpha Psi Omega, Alpha Epislon Rho. Democrat. Roman Catholic. Author: History of Public Broadcasting Act of 1967, 1979; contbr. articles to profl. jours.; editor Jour. Allied Health, 1978—. Home: 1111 N Dearborn St Chicago IL 60610 Office: 808 S Wood St Chicago IL 60612

BURKE, JOHN JOSEPH, JR., real estate developer; b. Milw., Oct. 10, 1941; s. John J. and Marnie (Katholing) B.; m. Kathryn Murphy, Aug. 20, 1966; children—Wendy, John, Molly, Patrick, Rory. B.Sc., Spring Hill Coll., 1963; postgrad. Marquette U., 1963-65. Pres. Burke Assocs., Milw., 1966—; chmn. bd., chief exec. officer Midwest Ctr. Housing Mgmt., 1976—, Nat. Ctr. for Housing Mgmt., Washington, 1980—; ptnr. The Beer Baron's, Milw., 1983—, 18 Ltd. Partnerships, Milw., 1970—. Mem. Planning Commn., Village of Fox Point, Wis., 1980—. Fellow Nat. Ctr. Housing Mgmt. Republican. Roman Catholic. Clubs: Ozaukee Country, Milw. Athletic. Avocations: skiing; golf; sailing. Office: N81 W12920 Leon Rd Menomonee Falls WI 53051

BURKE, JOHN MICHAEL, chem. physicist; b. Takoma Park, Md., Apr. 27, 1946; s. John Richard and Doris Jean (Waltman) B.; A.B., Thomas More Coll., 1966; Ph.D. (NASA trainee, 1967-69, grad. fellow, 1969-71), Case Western Res. U., 1971; m. Mary Jane Elenewski, May 24, 1975; children—Alexander, Mairead. Presdl. intern, Nat. Bur. Standards, Washington, 1972-73; research asso. Princeton (N.J.) U., 1973-77; staff scientist Procter & Gamble, Cin., 1977—. NIH postdoctoral fellow, 1975-76. Mem. Optical Soc. Am., Soc. Mfg. Engrs. Contbr. articles in field to profl. publs. Office: 6300 Center Hill Rd Cincinnati OH 45224

BURKE, JOHNNY WILLIAM, broadcaster; b. Cleve., Apr. 23, 1954; s. William Patrick and Joyce Helen (Smeltz) B.; m. Genevieve Elaine Vandeweel, Aug. 9, 1980; children—Steven, Daniel. Student Kent State U., 1972-75. With various radio stas., Ohio, 1972-80; with Sta. WGAR, Cleve., 1978-80; morning personality Sta. WTRX, Flint, Mich., 1980—, program dir., 1982—; lectr. in field. Active Flint's Downtown Devel. Authority, Center City Assn., 1981-83. Recipient Billy Durant Civic award and Spl. award Easter Seal Soc., 1981. Mem. AFTRA.

BURKE, KENNETH ANDREW, advertising agency executive; b. Cleve., Sept. 9, 1941; s. Frank F. and Margret M. (Tome) B.; B.S. in B.A., Bowling Green State U., 1965; m. Karen Lee Burley, July 1, 1968; children—Allison Leigh, Aric Jason. Account exec. Lang, Fisher, Stashower, Cleve., 1967-69; account supr. Tracy Locke, Dallas, 1969-72, Grey Advt., N.Y.C., 1972-76; v.p. Griswold Eshleman, Cleve., 1976-79; v.p., gen. mgr. Simpson Mktg. Communications Agy., Columbus, Ohio, 1979-81; pres., chmn. bd. Martcom, Inc., Columbus, 1981—; dir. Berkshire Product Inc., Cleve., 1979—. Adv. bd. Am. Cancer Soc., Columbus, 1980—. Recipient Navy Achievement in Advt. award, 1975; Cleve. Advt. Club award, 1968. Mem. Am. Mktg. Assn., Columbus Advt. Fedn., Columbus C. of C., Theta Chi. Roman Catholic. Clubs: Rotary, Cleve. Advt., Brookside Country, Agonis Athletic Found. Author: Children's Stories, 1970. Home: 1753 Bedford Rd Upper Arlington OH 43212 Office: 2000 W Henderson Rd Columbus OH 43220

BURKE, PAUL E., JR., state senator, manufacturing company executive; b. Kansas City, Mo., Jan. 4, 1934; s. Paul E. and Virginia (Moling) B.; children—Anne Elizabeth, Kelly Patricia, A. Catherine, Jennifer Marie. B.S. in Bus. Adminstrn., U. Kans., 1956. Exec. v.p. Webb Belting & Supply Co., Inc., Kansas City, Mo., 1959—; dir., mem. internal audit com. Anchor Savs. Assn., Leawood, Kans.; dir., officer MidAm. Packing and Seals, Inc.; mem. Kans. Ho. of Reps., 1972-74; mem. Kans. State Senate, 1975—, majority floor leader, 1985—; mem. exec. com., chmn. adv. com. on fiscal affairs Nat. Conf. State Legislators. Councilman, City of Prairie Village (Kans.), 1959-63; mem. Kans. Turnpike Authority, 1965-69, chmn., 1969; mem. adv. bd. Sec. of Corrections, 1973-78. Served to capt. USAF, 1956-59; capt. USNR, 1963—. Mem. Kans. Assn. Commerce and Industry (dir. industry div.). Republican. Episcopalian. Lodges: Masons, Shriners. Home: PO Box 6867 Leawood KS 66206 Office: Box 1268 Kansas City MO 64141

BURKE, PAUL STANLEY, JR., ins. co. exec.; b. St. Paul, Aug. 5, 1926; s. Paul Stanley and Loretta Josephine (Bertrang) B.; B.B.A., U. Minn., 1956; m. Irene Marie Wagner, Apr. 22, 1950; children—John, Steven, Nancy, Lawrence, Linda, James, Thomas. Regional mgr. Minn. Mutual Life Ins. Co., Los Angeles, 1950-61; pres. Paul Burke & Assos., Inc., ins. consultants and adminstrs., Mpls., 1961-73, Trust Life Ins. Co. Am., Scottsdale, Ariz., 1968-73, Purchase & Discount Buying Service Corp., 1977-80, Am. Reliance Corp., 1967-85; chmn. bd. Larson & Burke Inc., 1980—. dir. Lindbom & Assos., Inc., St. Paul. Pres., Boys Clubs of Mpls., 1974-76. Served with USAAF, 1944-47. Mem. Pilots Internat. Assn. (pres. 1966-73). Republican. Roman Catholic. Clubs: Mpls. Athletic, N. Am. Hunting (pres. 1978—). Home: 27 Circle W Edina MN 55436

BURKE, ROBERT P., English language educator; b. Kincaid, Ill., Dec. 1, 1930; s. Michael J. and Alice A. (Manuel) B.; m. Roberta L. Brown, Aug. 4, 1929; children—John, Kelly. B.S., N.Mex. Western U., 1955, M.S., 1956; M.A., U. Ill., 1959; Ph.D., So. Ill. U., 1971. Elem. sch. tchr., Tovey, Ill., 1950-52; asst. prof. Ark. State Tchrs. Coll., Conway, 1957-60; instr., chmn. dept. English, Joliet Jr. Coll., Ill., 1960—; text reviewer various pubs. Editor, Will County Ednl. Region, 1979-80. Author: Manual for the Reading/Writing Lab, 1975; also articles. Mem. Joliet High Sch. Bd., 1974-80, v.p., 1978-79; bd. dirs. Will County Counseling Agy., 1974-78; chief coordinator Will County Democratic party, 1974-78; trustee Will County Regional Edn. Bd., 1981—, v.p., 1984-85. Served as 2d lt. U.S. Army, 1952-54, PTO. Mem. Nat. Council Tchrs. of English, Coll. Council on Composition and Communication, Am. Fedn. Tchrs., Assn. Depts. English, Blue Key. Episcopalian. Club: Ingalls Park Athletic (Joliet) (trustee 1979-81). Avocations: reading; photography.

BURKE, STEVEN CHARLES, healthcare administration executive; b. Atlanta, May 23, 1951; s. Charles Hulett and Carole Ruth (Mason) B.; m. Margaret Hudgins, Aug. 9, 1975; 1 child, David. B.A., U. South Sewanee, 1973; M. Health Adminstrn., Duke U., 1975. Planning analyst Greenville Hosp., S.C., 1975-78, asst. dir. facility devel. and constrn., 1978-79, asst. v.p. planning, 1979-83; dir. planning and mktg. Western Res. Health System, Youngstown, Ohio, 1983-84, v.p. planning and mktg., 1984—. Mem. Am. Coll. Hosp. Adminstrs., Am. Soc. Hosp. Planning and Mktg. of Am. Hosp. Assn., Ohio Soc. Hosp. Planning and Mktg., Soc. Strategic Healthcare Mgmt. of Hosp. Assn. Pa. Episcopalian. Avocations: choral singing; racquetball. Home: 4627 Pinegrove Ave Youngstown OH 44515 Office: Western Reserve Health System 345 Oak Hill Ave Youngstown OH 44501

BURKE, THOMAS JOSEPH, civil engineer; b. Grosse Pointe Park, Mich., Sept. 1, 1927; s. Cyril Joseph and Marie Estelle (Sullivan) B.; B.C.E., Villanova U., 1949; m. Elaine Kiefer, Nov. 10, 1951; children—Judy Lee Burke Brooks, Kathleen Marie Harness, Maureen Elaine, Thomas P. Pres., Burke Rental Service, Sterling Heights, Mich., 1949—, Cyril J. Burke, Inc., Sterling Heights, Mich., 1949—. Trustee Villanova U., 1980—. Served to lt. USAF, Korea. Mem. ASCE, Detroit Builders Exchange (v.p. 1976-78, dir. 1975-78), Associated Equipment Distbrs. (dir. 1955-58, 75-78), Associated Underground Contractors (dir. 1965-68), Mich. Ready Mix Concrete Assn. (dir. 1960-65), Villanova U. Alumni Assn. (nat. v.p. 1978-79, nat. pres. 1980), Detroit Engring. Soc. Roman Catholic. Clubs: Grosse Pointe Yacht, Otsego Ski, Ocean Reef, Detroit Athletic, Villanova U. of Detroit (pres. 1955-65). Home: 578 Shelden Rd Grosse Pointe Shores MI 48236 also 688 N Lake Shore Rd Port Sanilac MI Office: 36000 Mound Rd Sterling Heights MI 48077

BURKE, THOMAS RICHARD, community college administrator; b. St. Louis, Oct. 2, 1944; s. Lloyd Richard and Frances Elizabeth (Yelton) B.; m. Sara Lou Jones, July 3, 1969; 1 child, Kimberly Ayre. B.A., U. Miss., 1970, M.A., 1972, Ph.D., 1981. Instr., Mountain Empire Community Coll., Big Stone Gap, Va., 1972-74, asst. prof., 1974-77, assoc. prof. history, 1977-80, acting pres., 1977, dean instrn., 1976-80; v.p. Three Rivers Community Coll., Poplar Bluff, Mo., 1980—. Chmn. City of Poplar Bluff Hist. Commn. Served with USAF, 1965-69. Edn. Professions Devel. Act fellow, 1970-72. Mem. Am. Assn. Community and Jr. Colls., Am. Vocat. Assn., Mo. Assn. Community and Jr. Colls. (chmn.), Mo. Hist. Assn., Mo. Vocat. Assn., Nat. Council Local Adminstrs., Phi Delta Kappa. Methodist. Lodges: Scottish Rite, Masons, Shriners. Home: 2101 Birkhead Rd Poplar Bluff MO 63901 Office: Three Rivers Blvd Poplar Bluff MO 63901

BURKEMPER, JAMES J., real estate executive; b. St. Louis, Sept. 25, 1931; s. Joseph Francis and Agnes Virginia (Seymour) B.; m. Jane Elizabeth Berry, May 28, 1960; children—Ira, Paul, Bruce, Hilary, Caroline. Student U. Chgo., 1955-56; B.A. (HEW scholar), Washington U., 1959. With N.Y., Chgo. & St. Louis R.R., St. Louis, 1950-51; with Ira E. Berry, Inc., real estate, St. Louis, 1959—, exec. v.p., 1970—. Bd. dirs. United Cerebral Palsy Assn., Greater St. Louis, Loretto-Hilton Repertory Theatre, St. Louis. Served with USNR, 1951-55. Mem. Internat. Real Estate Redn., Real Estate Bd. Met. St. Louis. Club: St. Louis, Univ., Algonquin Country (St. Louis). Home: 26 Brentmoor Park Clayton MO 63105 Office: 7711 Bonhomme Saint Louis MO 63105

BURKERT, ROBERT RANDALL, artist, educator; b. Racine, Wis., Aug. 20, 1930; s. Clarence G. and Margaret Ann (Sorenson) B.; m. Nancy Ekholm, Aug. 29,. 1953; children—Claire, Rand. M.S., U. Wis.-Madison, 1955. Cert. tchr. Instr., Bur. Audio-Visual Instrn., Madison, 1953, Denison U., Granville, Ohio, 1956; prof. U. Wis.-Milw., 1956—. One-man shows include: Wustom Mus. Art, Racine, Rubiner Galleries, Detroit, Bradley Galleries, Milw.; group shows include: Mus. Modern Art, N.Y.C., Art Inst. Chgo. & Phila. Mus., Milw. Art Mus., Tate Gallery, London; represented in permanent collections: Tate Gallery, Met. Mus., Phila. Mus. Trustee, Milw. Art Mus., 1978-82. Wis. Arts Bd. grantee, 1976; recipient Gov.'s award Wis. Arts Found., 1983; Friends of Art award, 1972. Avocations: tennis; fishing; mushrooming; photography.

BURKET, GAIL BROOK, author; b. Stronghurst, Ill., Nov. 1, 1905; d. John Cecil and Maud (Simonson) Brook; A.B., U. Ill., 1926; M.A. in English Lit., Northwestern U., 1929; m. Walter Cleveland Burket, June 22, 1929; children—Elaine (Mrs. William L. Harwood), Anne, Margaret (Mrs. James Boyce). Pres. woman's aux. Internat. Coll. Surgeons, 1950-54, now bd. dirs. Mus.; nat. vice chmn. Am. Heritage of DAR, 1971-74; pres. Northwestern U. Guild, 1976-78; sec. Evanston women's bd. Northwestern U. Settlement, 1979-81, pres., 1984—. Recipient Robert Ferguson Meml. award Friends of Lit., 1973. Mem. Nat. League Am. Pen Women (Ill. state pres. 1952-54, nat. v.p. 1958-60), Soc. Midland Authors, Poetry Soc. Am., Women in Communications, AAUW (pres. N. Shore br. 1961-63), Ill. Opera Guild (bd. dirs. 1982—), Daus. Am. Colonists (state v.p. 1973-76), Colonial Dames Am. (chpt. regent 1974-80), Phi Beta Kappa, Delta Zeta. Author: Courage Beloved, 1949; Manners Please, 1949; Blueprint for Peace, 1951; Let's Be Popular, 1951; You Can Write a Poem, 1954; Far Meadows, 1955; This is My Country, 1960; From the Prairies, 1968. Contbr. articles, poems to lit. publs. Address: 1020 Lake Shore Dr Evanston IL 60202

BURKET, GEORGE EDWARD, JR., physician; b. Kingman, Kans., Dec. 10, 1912; s. George Edward and Jessie May (Talbert) B.; student Wichita State U., 1930-33; M.D., U. Kans., 1937; m. Mary Elizabeth Wallace, Nov. 12, 1938; children—George Edward III, Carol Sue, Elizabeth Christine. Intern, Santa Barbara (Calif.) Gen. Hosp., 1937-38, resident, 1938-39; grad. asst. in surgery Mass. Gen. Hosp., Boston, 1956-57; pvt. practice medicine, Kingman, Kans., 1939-73; preceptor in medicine U. Kans. Med. Sch., 1950-73, asso. prof., 1973-78, clin. prof., 1978-84. Mem. Kingman Bd. Edn., 1946-58; mem. Kans. State Bd. Health, 1960-66. Diplomate Am. Bd. Family Practice. Mem. Kans. Med. Soc. (pres. 1966-67), Am. Acad. Family Physicians (pres. 1967-68; John Walsh founders award 1979), Inst. Medicine, AMA, Assn. Am. Med. Colls., Soc. Tchrs. Family Medicine, Alpha Omega Alpha. Republican. Episcopalian. Mason (Shriner). Clubs: Garden of Gods (Colorado Springs, Colo.); Wichita, Wichita Country. Contbr. articles to profl. jours. Home: Spring Lake Route 1 Kingman KS 67068

BURKET, RICHARD EDWARD, food technology company executive; b. Sandusky, Ohio, Apr. 25, 1928; s. Firm C. and Marie (Bock) B.; m. Carolyn Anne McMillen, Feb. 22, 1951 (div.); children—Leslie, Buffie, Lynn Murphy. B.A., Oberlin Coll., 1950. Sales mgr. Rhoades Equipment Co., Fort Wayne, Ind., 1954; various exec. positions central Soya Co., Fort Wayne, 1955-69; v.p., asst. to pres. Archer Daniels Midland Co., Decatur, Ill., 1969-80, v.p., asst. to chmn., 1980—. Mem. Decatur Macon County Devel. Found., 1983—; bd. dirs. St. Mary's Hosp. Bd., 1975—, ARC., 1975—; mem. adv. council Purdue U., Ill. Ednl. Devel. Found.; active Boy's Club of Decatur, 1975—, Decatur Area Arts Council, 1971—, Macon County Rep. Com., Macon County Conservation Bd. Served to lt. U.S. Army, 1950-53. Mem. Soy Protein Council, Inst. Food Technologists, Am. Soybean Assn., Metro Decatur C. of C. Home: Route 1 Box 84A Blue Mound IL 62513 Office: 4666 Faries Pwy Decatur IL 62525

BURKEY, LEE MELVILLE, lawyer; b. Beach, N.D., Mar. 21, 1914; s. L. M. and Mina (Horner) B.; B.A., U. Ill., 1936. M.A., 1938; J.D. with honors, John Marshall Law Sch., 1943; m. Lorraine Burghardt, June 11, 1938; 1 son, Lee Melville. Tchr., Princeton, Ill., 1937-38. Harvey, 1938-43; admitted to Ill. bar, 1944; atty. Office of Solicitor. U.S. Dept. Labor, 1944-51; lectr. bus. law Roosevelt Coll., 1949-52; ptnr. law firm Asher, Pavalon, Gittler & Greenfield and predecessor firms, Chgo., 1951—; dir. La Grange Fed. Savs. and Loan Assn., 1975—. Mem. Northeastern Ill. Planning Commn., 1969-73, pres., 1970-—; mem. Employment Security Adv. Bd., 1970-73; life mem. assoc. bd. Community Meml. Gen. Hosp., La Grange, Ill.; mem. bd. dirs. for homeland ministries United Ch. of Christ, 1983—; bd. dirs. Better Bus. Bur. Met. Chgo., 1975-82, Plymouth Place, Inc., 1973-81. Trustee, Village of LaGrange, 1962-68, mayor, 1968-73, village atty., 1973-—. Served to 2d lt. Ill. Nat. Guard. Recipient Disting. Alumnus award John Marshall Law Sch., 1973. Mem. ABA Ill., Chgo., bar assns., Order of John Marshall, SAR (state pres. 1977), S.R. Congregationalist. Clubs: LaGrange Country, Masons. Author numerous articles on lie detector evidence. Home: 926 S Catherine St LaGrange IL 60525 Office: 2 N La Salle St Chicago IL 60602

BURKHARDT, JUDITH CAROL, employee relations specialist; b. Highland Park, Mich., Aug. 1, 1940; d. Edward Anthony and Angela Margarita (Gebell) B.; 1 dau., Barbara. B.A., Marygrove Coll., 1963; postgrad. Mich. Technol. U., 1968, U. Detroit, 1974; M.Ed., Wayne State U., 1974. Tchr., Holy Redeemer Sch., Detroit, 1964-67, St. Bede Sch., Southfield, Mich., 1967-69, St. Hugo Sch., Bloomfield Hills, Mich., 1969-73; children's supr. Oakland County Childrens Village, Pontiac, Mich., 1974; youth advisor Pontiac (Mich.) Police Dept., 1974-85; in employee relations Blue Cross-Blue Shield of Mich., 1985—. Pres. Bloomfield Youth Guidance, Bloomfield Hills, 1971-73; sec. Cath. Social Services, Royal Oak, Mich., 1969-73; mem. community adv. bd. Woodland Hills Ctr., Troy, Mich.; founding mem. Bloomfield-Birmingham Ctr. for Human Devel., Bloomfield Hills, 1971; mem. Women's Polit. Caucus, Washington, 1983—. Mem. AAUW, Am. Assn. Female Execs. Democrat. Roman Catholic. Office: Blue Cross Blue Shield Mich 600 Lafayette E Detroit MI 48226

BURKHART, DAMA MARTIN, educator; b. Woodsfield, Ohio, Mar. 16, 1926; d. Wilbert Earl and Carrie Mildred (Doan) Martin; B.S. cum laude, Taylor U., Upland, Ind., 1950; M.S., Butler U., Indpls., 1965; Ph.D. (grad. fellow), Purdue U., 1968; m. George F. Burkhart, Apr. 11, 1981; children by previous marriage—Paige Elizabeth Cofield, Malvin Scott Cofield. Mem. pub. relations dept. Taylor U., 1950-51; tchr., curriculum cons. Howard County (Ind.) Council Chs., 1955-65; staff counselor, psychol. services Purdue U., 1965-68, vis. prof. edn., 1969-70, human devel. specialist, dept. child devel. and family life, 1970-74, staff and program devel. specialist Sch. Home Econs. and Coop. Extension Service, 1974—, asst. dir. Coop. Extension Service, also asst. dean Sch. Consumer and Family Scis.; adult edn. supr. Asso. Migrant Opportunities Services, 1967; v.p. Ind. Council Family Relations, 1972-74, pres., 1980—, bd. dirs., 1975-77; mem. Task Force on Career Devel. for Women, 1975-76; condr. workshops, cons. in field. Recipient Ecumenical citation Howard County, 1965. Council Chs. grantee. Mem. Nat. Council Family Relations, Am. Home Econs. Assn. Democrat. Presbyterian. Author articles, bulls. Home: 222 N Main St Woodsfield OH 43793

BURKHART, JACQUELINE LOUISE, business educator; b. St. Louis, Jan. 1, 1939; d. John Henry and Minnie Louise (Brammeier) Spauldin; m. Kenneth Lee Burkhart, June 6, 1970; children—Toby Lee, Kendra Lynn. B.S. in Bus. Edn., U. Mo., 1962; M.A. in Office Edn., Central Mo. State U., 1971. Tchr. Warrenton (Mo.) High Sch., 1962-63; sec. Rocketdyne div. N.Am. Aviation, Canoga Park, Calif., 1963-64; tchr. Brookfield (Mo.) Area-Vocat. Sch., 1964-65, Roosevelt High Sch., St. Louis, 1965-67; exec. sec. Lakeside Hosp., Kansas City, Mo., 1967-69; tchr./coordinator dist. dept. chairperson Consol. Sch. Dist. No. 1, Kansas City, Mo., 1969—. Mem. NEA, Mo. Edn. Assn., Mo. Bus. Edn. Assn., Mo. Vocat. Assn., Am. Vocat. Assn., Nat. Bus. Edn. Assn. Baptist. Home: 7606 E 127th St Grandview MO 64030 Office: 9010 Old Santa Fe Rd Kansas City MO 64138

BURKHOLDER, RICHARD JOSEPH, educator; b. Toledo, July 27, 1949; s. Joseph Fred and Isabelle Marie (Harbauer) B. B.S., Ohio State U., 1971, M.S., 1980. Teaching. cert., Ohio. Tchr. vocat. agrl. Elmwood (Ohio) local schs., 1971-74, Bowling Green (Ohio) City Schs., 1974—. Mem. NEA, Ohio Edn. Assn., Nat. Vocat. Agr. Tchrs. Assn., Ohio Vocat. Assn., Ohio Vocat. Agr. Tchrs. Assn., Bowling Green Edn. Assn., Wood County Farm Bur., Wood County Agrl. Soc. (treas.), Future Farmers Am. Alumni Assn. (life), Gamma Sigma Delta. Lutheran. Home: 7628 Sugar Ridge Rd Pemberville OH 43450 Office: 530 W Poe Rd Bowling Green OH 43402

BURKLEY, JOHN HAYWARD, lawyer; b. Columbus, Ohio, Sept. 15, 1951; s. Walter Raymond and Martha Van Riet (Hayward) B.; m. Nancy Gale Gumerlock, June 26, 1982. B.A., U. Notre Dame, 1973; J.D., U. Mich., 1976. Bar: Ohio 1976, U.S. Dist. Ct. (so. dist.) Ohio 1976. Ptnr., Carlile, Patchen, Murphy & Allison, Columbus, 1976-82; corp. atty. OCLC Online Computer Library Ctr., Inc., Dublin, Ohio, 1982—. Composer of numerous songs, instrumentals and musical compositions for piano and guitar. Founding chmn. planned giving program Central Ohio Cystic Fibrosis Found., 1982; active mem. Big Bros. Assn., 1976—. Recipient Eagle Scout award, Boy Scouts Am., 1969. Mem. Man-To-Man Assn. (past bd. dirs.), Columbus Bar Assn. (chmn. corp. counsel com. 1983-84, founding chmn. computer law inst. 1982-84), Phi Beta Kappa. Avocations: Chess; guitar; reading; music; football.

BURKY, RICHARD CLAYTON, educator; b. Canton, Ohio, Sept. 8, 1948; s. Clayton Lawrence and Sarah Alice (Geisey) B.; m. Patricia Pauline Arcinio, Dec. 20, 1967 (div.); children—Charles Richard, Denise Marie; m. 2d, Linda Rose Chartier, July 31, 1976; children—Heather Marie, Erica Rose. B.A., Kent State U., 1981. Service mgr. George Weikem Volvo Village, Massillon, Ohio, 1974; head sch. bus mechanic Jackson Local Schs., Massillon, 1974-76, auto mechanics instr. vocat. dept., 1976—, instr. adult edn., 1977-83; regional adviser Vocat. Indsl. Clubs Am., 1980-83. Served with USAF, 1966-74. Mem. NEA, Am. Vocat. Assn., Ohio Educators Assn., Ohio Vocat. Assn., Jackson Meml. Educators Assn., Iota Lambda Sigma. Home: 2300 Manchester Ave SW Massillon OH 44646 Office: 7600 Fulton Dr NW Massillon OH 44646

BURLEIGH, BRUCE DANIEL, JR., biochemist, endocrinologist; b. Augusta, Ga., June 23, 1942; s. Bruce Daniel and Billie Ann (Carter) B.; m. Dorothy Jean Roskos, Sept. 4, 1962 (div. 1981); 1 son, Michael Eugene. B.S., Carnegie-Mellon U., 1964; M.S., U. Mich., 1967, Ph.D., 1970. With MRC Lab, Cambridge, Eng., 1970-73; asst. prof. biochemistry M.D. Anderson Hosp., U. Tex. Cancer Ctr., Houston, 1973-79, assoc. biochemist, 1979-81; research scientist Internat. Mineral & Chem. Corp., Terre Haute, Ind., 1981-82, sr. research scientist, 1983—. NIH fellow, 1968-70; Am. Cancer Soc. fellow, 1970-72; Robert A. Welch grantee, 1979-81. Mem. Am. Chem. Soc., Am. Soc. of Biol. Chemists, Endocrine Soc., AAAS, N.Y. Acad. of Sci., Sigma Xi, Tau Beta Pi, Phi Lambda Upsilon. Episcopalian. Contbr. articles to profl. jours. Home: 075 Oak Ave Oak Terr Div Mundelein IL 60060 Office: Internat Minerals & Chem Corp R&D Labs 1810 Frontage Rd Northbrook IL 60062

BURLISON, JOHN FRANKLIN, dentist; b. Christopher, Ill., May 30, 1949; s. Raymond Eugene and Martha Ann (Krajnik) B.; m. Christy Ranell Sadler, June 13, 1971; 1 child, Jared Sadler. B.S., U. Ill.-Chicago Circle, 1972, D.D.S., 1974. Gen. practice dentistry John F. Burlison, D.D.S., Ltd., Benton, Ill., 1974—. Mem. Omicron Kappa Upsilon. Lodges: Lions, Elks. Avocations: boating; skiing; golf; racquetball; hunting; jet-skiing. Home: 405 E Park St Benton IL 62812 Office: John F Burlison DDS LTD Route 2 Benton IL 62812

BURMEISTER, CLARENCE EDWARD, business executive; b. Clarkston, Mich., May 5, 1929; s. Alfred John and Mary Eleanor (Brief) B.; m. Pauline Bernice Sherman, June 16, 1943 (div. Sept. 1962); children—Paula Kay Burmeister Waling, Clarence, Rose Mary Burmeister Cooper; m. Sharon Kathleen Scott, May 5, 1973; children—Stephanie Kathlee, Tiffany Lynne. Student pub. schs., Pontiac, Mich. Owner, Burmeister Lumber Co., Union Lake, Mich., 1948-66; sales mgr. GAC, Southfield, Mich., 1967-75; owner Handprint Farms, Kings Mill, Mich., 1959-66, Van Stuff by Burmeister, Troy and Royal Oak, Mich., 1976—. Chmn. U.S. Congl. adv. bd. dirs. Republican party, Washington, 1982—, nat. congl. com., 1983—. Named Top Salesman Worldwide, GAC, 1971. Mem. Automotive Parts and Accessories Assn. (chmn. com. seminars; 1st advocate award 1978). Roman Catholic. Office: Burmeister Co PO Box 99129 Troy MI 48099

BURMEISTER, RAY WILLIAM, internist; b. New Haven, Mo., Nov. 22, 1929; s. William Henry and Ella Caroline (Kissling) B.; B.S. in Biology and Chemistry, St. Louis U., 1950, M.D., 1954; m. Edna Florene Struck, June 6, 1953; children—William Alan, Robert Christian, Brenda Lynn, Brian Edward. Intern, St. Louis U. Hosp., 1954-55; resident in internal medicine St. Louis U. Hosps., 1955-57; chief resident in internal medicine St. Louis City Hosp., 1957-58; trainee in microbiology St. Louis U., 1960-61; asso. dir. unit II med. service St. Louis City Hosp., 1961-71; dir. div. health care adminstrn. St. Louis U. Sch. Medicine, 1971-77; pres. InterMed Med. Consultants, Inc., St. Louis, 1977—, Qual-T-Med, Inc., 1980—; cons. infectious disease St. Louis U. Hosp., 1971-77; med. dir. Mt. St. Rose Hosp. Geriatric Rehab. Center, 1961-80; pres. RTD Med., Inc., 1966—; mem. clin. faculty Joint Commn. Accreditation of Hosps.; dir. Luth. Med. Center. Served to capt. M.C., AUS, 1958-60; col. M.C., USAR. Fellow ACP; mem. N.Y. Acad. Scis., Am. Soc. Internal Medicine, Mo. Soc. Internal Medicine (past pres.), AAAS, Am. Fedn. Clin. Research, AAUP, AMA, Mo. Med. Assn., St. Louis Met. Med. Soc., St. Louis Internists Club (past pres.). Republican. Lutheran. Contbr. articles on internal medicine, infectious disease and patient care rev. to profl. jours. and textbooks. Home: 10834 Forest Circle Dr Saint Louis MO 63128 Office: 2900 Lemay Ferry Rd Suite 208 Saint Louis MO 63125

BURNETT, HENRY BRUCE, banker; b. Raleigh, Ill., May 25, 1912; s. Rex Corwin and Fayette (Wesley) B.; student U. Ill., 1930-32, U. Wis., 1950-52; m. Virginia Stinson, June 6, 1931; 1 son, Hal Bruce; m. 2d, Joan Stroub, Aug. 23, 1963. Chevrolet dealer, Eldorado, Ill., 1941-58; registered rep. Newhard, Cook & Co., St. Louis, 1960-61; chmn. Norris City State Bank (Ill.), 1962—; pres. C.P. Burnett & Sons, Bankers, Eldorado, Ill., 1969-75, dir., 1950-78; chmn. Egyptian State Bank, Carrier Mills, Ill., 1968-72; chmn. Gallatin County State Bank, Ridgway, Ill., 1975—; dir. So. Ill., Inc. Mayor, Eldorado, 1943-47; former trustee Shrutleff Coll., Alton, Ill.; bd. dirs., v.p. Ferrell Hosp., Eldorado; chmn. Ill. Indsl. Devel. Authority, Marion, 1974-79; chmn. bd. deacons Calvary Baptist Ch., 1957-58, bd. trustees, 1950-60; bd. dirs. So. Ill. U. Found., 1979—. Served with inf. AUS, 1944-46; ETO. Mem. Eldorado C. of C. (pres. 1957-59). Lodges: Rotary (pres. Eldorado 1950-51), Lions (pres. Eldorado 1939-40). Home: 1201 Pine St Eldorado IL 62930 Office: PO Box 450 Norris City IL 62869

BURNETT, JEAN BULLARD (MRS. JAMES R. BURNETT), biochemist; b. Flint, Mich., Feb. 19, 1924; d. Chester M. and Katheryn (Krasser) Bullard; B.S., Mich. State U., 1944, M.S., 1945, Ph.D. (Council fellow), 1952; m. James R. Burnett, June 8, 1947. Research assoc. dept. zoology Mich. State U., East Lansing, 1954-59, dept. biochemistry, 1959-61, acting dir. research biochem. genetics, dept. biochemistry, 1961-62, assoc. prof., asst. chmn. dept. biomechanics, 1973-82, prof. dept. anatomy, 1982-84, prof. dept. zoology, Coll. Natural Sci. and Coll. Osteo. Medicine, 1984—; assoc. biochemist Mass. Gen. Hosp., Boston, 1964-73; prin. research assoc. dermatology Harvard, 1962-73, faculty medicine, 1964-73, also spl. lectr., cons., tutor Med. Sch.; vis. prof. dept. biology U. Ariz., 1979-80. USPHS, NIH grantee, 1965-68; Gen. Research Support grantee Mass. Gen. Hosp., 1968-72; Ford Found. travel grantee, 1973; Am. Cancer Soc. grantee, 1971-73; Internat. Pigment Cell Conf. travel grantee, 1980; recipient Med. Found. award, 1970. Mem. AAAS, Am. Chem. Soc., Am. Inst. Biol. Sci., Genetics Soc. Am., Soc. Investigative Dermatology, N.Y. Acad. Scis., Sigma Xi (Research award 1971), Pi Kappa Delta, Kappa Delta Pi, Pi Mu Epsilon, Sigma Delta Epsilon. Home: PO Box 308 Okemos MI 48864 Office: Dept Zoology Natural Sci Bldg Mich State U East Lansing MI 48824

BURNETT, JOSEPH A., accountant, educator; b. Covington, Ky., Oct. 27, 1943; s. Joseph A. and Mildred L. (Yeager) B.; m. Karen L. England, Mar. 19, 1966; children—Kara, Aimee, Laura. B.B.A., U. Cin., 1966, M.B.A., 1969; M.A. (hon.), Brown U., 1975. C.P.A., Ohio. Dir. research adminstrn. Brown U., Providence, 1969-75; instr. acctg. U. Cin., 1975-77, asst. prof., 1977—, sr. grant and contract specialist, 1975-83; pvt. practice acctg., Cin., 1977—; cons. on small bus., taxes, indirect costs; lectr. for Nat. Assn. Coll. and Univ. Bus. Officers, 1978—. Mem. Nat. Council Univ. Research Adminstrs., Ohio Soc. C.P.A.s, Soc. Research Adminstrs., Pi Kappa Alpha, Omicron Delta Kappa. Club: 3 Rivers Swim (treas. 1980—). Author: (with Kahn) Compound Interest and Present Value, 1978, Problems & Solutions in Accounting, 1980; Fundamentals of Grant and Contract Administration, 1978. Office: U Cin 3007 Clifton Ave Cincinnati OH 45220

BURNETT, PATRICIA HILL, artist, lecturer; b. Bklyn., Sept. 5, 1920; d. William Burr and Mimi (Uline) Hill; student U. Toledo, 1937-38, Goucher Coll., 1939-40; student Master's program Inst. D'Allende, Mexico, 1967, Wayne State U., 1972; student of John Carroll, Detroit, 1941-44, Sarkis Sarkisian, Detroit, 1956-60, Wallace Bassford, Provincetown, Mass., 1968-72, Walter Midener, Detroit, 1960-63; m. Harry Albert Burnett, Oct. 9, 1948; children—William Hill Lange, Harry Burnett III, Terrill Hill, Hillary Hill. Actress, Lone Ranger program Radio Blue Network, 1941-45; tchr. of painting and sculpture U. Mich. Extension, Ann Arbor, 1965—; lectr. N.Y. Speakers Bur., 1971—; propr. Burnett Studios, Detroit, 1962—, mgr., 1962—. Numerous one-woman shows of paintings and sculpture include: Scarab Club, Detroit, 1971, Midland (Mich.) Art Center, Wayne State U., Detroit, The Gallery, Ft. Lauderdale, Fla., Agra Gallery, Washington, Salon des Artes, Paris; numerous group shows including: Palazzo Pruili Gallery, Venice, Italy, 1971, Detroit Inst. of Arts, 1967, Butler Mus., N.Cleve., 1972, Windsor (Ont., Can.) Art Center, 1973, Weisbaden (Germany) Gallery, 1976; represented in permanent collections: Detroit Inst. of Arts, Wayne State U., Detroit, Wooster (Ohio) Coll., Ford Motor Co., Detroit, Bloomfield Art Assn., Bloomfield Hills, Mich., also private collections; numerous portrait paintings including portraits of Indira Ghandi, Benson Ford, Joyce Carol Oates, Mrs. Edsel Ford, Betty Ford, Roman Gribbs, Princess Olga Mrivani, Lord John Mackintosh, Marlo Thomas, Viveca Lindfois, Betty Freidan, Gloria Steinem, Congresswoman Martha Griffiths, Margaret Papandreou, Valentina Tereshkova. Chairwoman of Mich. Women's Commn., 1972—; pres. Detroit House of Correction Commn., 1975—; treas. Republican Dist. 1 of Mich., 1973—; mem. Issues Com., Republican State Central Com., 1975-76; sec. Republican State Ways and Means Com., 1975—; mem. Mich. State Adv. Council Vocat. Edn.; mem. Mich. Arts in Edn. Council, 1978—; mem. New Detroit Arts Com., 1979—; chmn. World Feminist Commn., 1974—. Recipient Silver Salute award Mich. State U., 1976, Most Popular award San Diego Sculpture Show, 1971, First prize award Cape Cod Artists Show, 1968; named Distinguished Woman of Mich., Bus. and Profl. Women's Orgn., 1974, Distinguished Woman Northwood Inst., 1977. Mem. Detroit Inst. Arts (dir. membership com. 1958—), Nat. Assn. of Commns. for Women (sec., dir. 1976-78), Mich. Acad. of the Arts, Detroit Soc. of Women Painters and Sculptors, Women in the Arts, Scarab Club (dir. 1962-63), Ibex Club (pres. 1951), NOW (nat. bd. 1971-75, del. UN conf., Mex., 1975), Women's Econ. Club, N.Y. Portrait Club (nat. com. 1978—), French Am. C. of C. (v.p.), Alpha Phi. Episcopalian. Clubs: Zonta Internat., Detroit (bd. dirs.). Contbr. articles to art jours. Home: 18261 Hamilton Rd Detroit MI 48203 Office: 217 Farnsworth Detroit MI 48202

BURNETT, ROBERT A., publisher; b. Joplin, Mo., June 4, 1927; s. Lee Worth and Gladys (Plummer) B.; A.B., U. Mo., 1948; m. Gloria M. Cowden, Dec. 25, 1948; children—Robert A., Stephen, Gregory, Douglas, David, Penelope. Salesman, Cowden Motor Co., Guthrie Center, Iowa, then Equitable Life Assurance Soc., Joplin, Mo.; now pres., chief exec. officer Meredith Corp.; dir. Whirlpool Corp., Norwest Bank, Des Moines, Dayton Hudson Corp., ITT, Iowa Resources Inc. Bd. dirs. Grinnell Coll. Served with AUS, 1945-46. Mem. N.A.M. (dir.), Phi Delta Theta. Congregationalist. Home: 315 37 St Des Moines IA 50312 Office: 1716 Locust St Des Moines IA 50303

BURNETTE, RAND, history educator; b. Evansville, Ind., Aug. 10, 1936; s. Charles Dent and Mary Frances (Wertz) B.; m. Patricia Lou Bauer, June 14, 1958; children—Patrick, Catherine, Mark. A.B. in History, Wabash Coll., Crawfordsville, In., 1958; M.S. in History, U. Wis.-Madison, 1959; Ph.D. in History, Ind. U., 1967. Instr. Carthage Coll. (Ill.), 1962-63, asst. prof. in history, Carthage and Kenosha, Wis., 1963-64, 64-68; asst. prof. MacMurray Coll., Jacksonville, Ill., 1968-71, assoc. prof., 1971-75, prof., 1975—. Bd. dirs. Jacksonville Pub. Library, 1976-82; pres. Morgan County Hist. Soc., Jacksonville, 1977-81, Friends of Jacksonville Pub. Library, 1982-84; dist. chmn. Abraham Lincoln council Boy Scouts Am., 1981-83. Grantee NEH, 1980, 84. Mem. Am. Hist. Assn., Orgn. Am. Historians, AAUP, Renaissance Soc. Am., Am. Soc. Reformation Research, Am. Soc. 18th Century Studies, Phi Alpha Theta. Democrat. Lutheran. Rotary. (treas. 1978-80). Home: 234 N Webster Jacksonville IL 62650 Office: MacMurray Coll Dept History 425 E College Ave Jacksonville IL 62650

BURNISTON, KAREN SUE, nurse; b. Hammond, Ind., May 20, 1939; d. George Hubbard and Bette Ruth (Ambler) B.; R.N., Parkview Methodist Hosp., Ft. Wayne, Ind., 1961; B.S. in Nursing, Purdue U., 1974; M.S., No. Ill. U., DeKalb, 1976. Staff nurse Parkview Meml. Hosp., 1961-63, 71-73; physician office and operating room nurse, 1963-67; nurse N.W. Ind. Home Health Services, 1974; mem. faculty Michael Reese Hosp. Sch. Nursing, Chgo., 1977-79; asst. dir. nursing Mt. Sinai Hosp. Med. Center, Chgo., 1977-79; asst. adminstr. patient services St. Margaret Hosp., Hammond, 1980-85; asst. adminstr. patient services St. Catherine Hosp., East Chicago, Ind., 1985—. Bd. dirs. South Lake Ctr. Mental Health. Served with Nurse Corps, USAF, 1967-71. Mem. Am. Nurses Assn., Am. Soc. Nursing Service Adminstrs., N.W. Ind. Council Nursing Service Adminstrs., Ind. Nurses Assn., Lake County Mental Health Assn. (bd. dirs.), Ind. Soc. Hosp. Nursing Service Adminstrs., Sigma Theta Tau. Mem. Christian Ch. (Disciples of Christ). Club: Altrusa. Home: 1601 Anna St Schererville IN 46375 Office: 5454 Hohman Ave Hammond IN 46320

BURNS, BRUCE PALMER, psychologist; b. Jamestown, N.Y., Mar. 5, 1922; s. Harold Fletcher and Genevieve Margaret (Erickson) B.; B.A., Coll. Wooster, 1965; M.A., Mich. State U., 1967, Ph.D., 1972. Gen. mgr. Burns Case Goods Corp., Jamestown, 1949-54, 59-64; pres., owner Show Off Inc., Jamestown, 1954-59; asst. program dir. Detroit Substance Abuse Treatment Program, 1972-78; pvt. practice clin. psychology, Detroit, 1976—; dir. Renaissance Psychol. Services, 1978—; vis. lectr. Eastern Mich. U., Ypsilanti, 1971-72; cons. Methadone Clinic, 1975-78. Served to lt. (j.g.) USNR, 1943-46. Cert. health service provider in psychology; lic. psychologist, Mich. Mem. Am., Canadian, Mich. psychol. assns., Am. Rehab. Counselors Assn., Am. Soc. Clin. Hypnosis, Mich. Personnel and Guidance Assn., Soc. Clin. and Exptl. Hypnosis, Mich. Soc. Lic. Psychologists, Mich. Assn. Marriage Counselors, Nat. Registry Health Service Providers in Psychology, SAR, Beta Theta Pi. Club: Renaissance. Office: 100 Renaissance Center Suite 1480 Detroit MI 48243 also 755 W Big Beaver Suite 416 Troy MI 48084

BURNS, C(HARLES) PATRICK, hematologist-oncologist; b. Kansas City, Mo., Oct. 8, 1937; s. Charles Edgar and Ruth (Eastham) B.; B.A., U. Kans., 1959, M.D., 1963; m. Janet Sue Walsh, June 15, 1968: children—Charles Geoffrey, Scott Patrick. Intern, Cleve. Met. Gen. Hosp., 1963-64; asst. resident in internal medicine, Univ. Hosps., Cleve., 1966-68, sr. resident in hematology, 1968-69: instr. medicine Case Western Res. U., 1970-71; asst. chief hematology Cleve. VA Hosp., 1970-71; asst. prof. medicine U. Iowa Hosps., Iowa City, 1971-75, assoc. prof. medicine, 1975-80, prof. medicine, 1980—, also dir. sect. on med. oncology, co-dir. div. hematology-oncology; vis. scientist Imperial Cancer Research Fund Labs., London, 1983; cons. U.S. VA Hosp.; mem. study sect. on exptl. therapeutics NIH. Served to capt. M.C., AUS, 1964-66. Am. Cancer Soc. fellow in hematology-oncology, 1968-69; USPHS fellow in medicine, 1969-70; USPHS career awardee, 1978. Diplomate Am. Bd. Internal Medicine, subsplty. bds. hematology, med. oncology. Fellow A.C.P.; mem. Am. Soc. Hematology, Am. Assn. Cancer Research, Internat. Soc. Hematology, Central Soc. Clin. Research, Am. Soc. Clin. Oncology, Soc. Exptl. Biology and Medicine, AAAS, Am. Fedn. Clin. Research, Royal Soc. Medicine, Lambda Chi Alpha, Phi Beta Pi, Alpha Omega Alpha. Research and publs. on hematologic malignancies, tumor lipid biochemistry, leukemia and oncology. Home: 2046 Rochester Ct Iowa City IA 52240 Office: Dept Medicine University Iowa Hospitals Iowa City IA 52242

BURNS, CHARLES R(OBERT), lawyer; b. St. Louis; s. Robert J. Burns and Shirley Mae (Bouril) Burns Pederson; m. Sharon K. Urban, Aug. 3, 1974 (div. Oct. 1982). Student Lewis and Clark Coll., 1972-73; B.S., Western Ill. U., 1975; J.D., Golden Gate U., 1980. Bar: Ill. 1981, U.S. Dist. Ct. (so. dist.) Ill. 1981. Realtor, Burns Realty, Edwardsville, Ill., 1975-78; law clk. Union Bank, San Francisco, 1979, Kayser Aluminum, Oakland, Calif., 1980; asst. states atty. Madison County States Atty.'s Office, Ill., 1980; sole practice, Edwardsville, 1981—; spl asst atty. gen., 1984—; dir. MADCO Credit Union, Edwardsville. Mem. Madison County Bd., Ill., 1982—; mem. Madison County Democratic Com., 1982—. Mem. Assn. Trial Lawyers Am., Ill. Trial Lawyers Assn., Bar Assn. Met. St. Louis, ABA, Ill. State Bar Assn. Roman Catholic. Home: Rural Route 3 Box 347 Edwardsville IL 62025 Office: 318 Hillsboro Ave Edwardsville IL 62025

BURNS, DONALD CLARE, community college president; b. Hubbardston, Mich., Jan. 4, 1943; s. Michael Louis and Florence Leona (Hogan) B.; B.A., Aquinas Coll., Grand Rapids, Mich., 1965; M.A. in Guidance and Counseling, Mich. State U., 1969, Ph.D. in Adminstrn. and Curriculum, 1982; m. Maureen Ann Empey, Aug. 19, 1967; children—Daniel, Colleen, Donna, Cara. Tchr., coach St. Thomas Sch., Grand Rapids, 1965-68; dir. guidance and admissions Am. Sch. Madrid, 1969-71; counselor, dir. area guidance center Montcalm Community Coll., Sidney, Mich., 1971-74, dean student and community services, 1974-80, v.p. for instrn., 1980-84, pres., 1984—. chmn. Mich. Sch. Counselor Legis. Com., 1973, Career Edn. Planning Dist. 22, 1975-78; vice chmn. Community Action Agy., 1976—; cons. in field. Mem. Am. Assn. for Higher Edn., Am. Personnel and Guidance Assn., Mich. Assn. Community Coll. Instrnl. Adminstrs., Mich. Assn. Community Student Personnel Adminstrs. Roman Catholic. Author articles in field. Office: Montcalm Community Coll Sidney MI 48885

BURNS, JERRY FRANK, educator; b. Clio, Iowa, Aug. 11, 1934; s. John William and Maxine Hazel (Rogers) B.; student N.E. Mo. State U., William Jewell Coll., Grandview Coll.; B.S. in Edn., S.W. Mo. State U., 1959; M.Ed., U. Mo., 1962; postgrad. U. Nebr., Eastern Mont. Coll., U. S.D.; m. Phyllis Idell Petty, Feb. 28, 1954. Tchr., asst. prin. Des Moines Public Schs., 1959-67; sch. psychologist Warren and Marion County Bd. Edn., Indianola, Iowa, 1967-75; coordinator spl. edn. Heartland Edn. Agy., Ankeny, Iowa, 1975-78, asst. dir. spl. edn., 1978—. Former sec.-treas., bd. trustees, bd. deacons Assembly of God Ch. Lic. psychologist, Iowa. Mem. NEA (life), Nat. Assn. Sch. Psychologists (charter), Iowa Sch. Psychologists Assn. (charter), Iowa Psychol. Assn., Council Exceptional Children, Des Moines Radio Amateur Assn. Republican. Club: Greater Des Moines FM. Home: 3842 Brinkwood Rd Des Moines IA 50310 Office: 1932 SW 3d St Ankeny IA 50021

BURNS, MARIAN M., lawyer; b. Burlingame, Kans., Apr. 18, 1931; d. Victor S. Mussatto and Janet Mussatto Hotchkiss; m. Clyde M. Burns; children—Janet, Richard. A.B., Kans. U., 1952, LL.B., 1954. Bar: Kans. Ct. atty. Osage County, Kansas, 1955-61; mcpl. judge Osage City, Kans., 1961—. Pres. U.S. Dist. 421 Sch. Bd., Lyndon, Kans.; past pres. Lincoln Day Club, Independence, Kans.; Republican Party candidate State Senate 17th Dist., 1984. Mem. Kans. Bar Assn., Osage County Bar Assn., Am. Legion Aux. Lodge: Masons. Avocations: barrel racing (mem. Nat. Old Timers Rodeo Assn., Kans. State Horse Show cir. 1965—, finalist 1982, 83, 84). Home: Box 641 Lyndon KS 66451 Office: Burns & Burns Box 641 Lyndon KS 66451

BURNS, MICHAEL KENT, educator, chemical dependency counselor; b. Sarasota, Fla., Jan. 4, 1945; s. Richard Andrew and Lilian Ida (Kent) B.; B.A. (Univ. scholar), Capital U., 1967; M.A., Ohio State U., 1969; ednl. staff personnel adminstrv. specialist cert., Cleve. State U., 1978; cert. sch. counselor Cleve. State U., 1982; m. Brenda Carolyn Bingham, Dec. 24, 1973. Grad. teaching fellow Ohio State U., 1967-69; instr. Wright State U., 1969-70; tchr. Spanish, social studies Euclid (Ohio) High Sch., 1970—, tchr. social studies, 1977—; summer intern Euclid Fisher Body Plant, Gen. Motors Corp., 1978; fellow Taft Inst. Govt., 1978, 79; career guidance inst. intern Cleve. Met. Jobs Council, 1980; tchr. Cleve. State U., 1980-81; group facilitator insight and aftercare chem. dependency programs, peer counseling co-facilitator, 1981; chem. dependency counselor Glenbeigy Adolescent Hosp., Cleve., 1983—. Cert. drug counselor. Mem. Euclid Tchrs. Assn. (v.p. 1974-76, pres. 1977-78), Ohio Edn. Assn., NEA, Assn. Supervision and Curriculum Devel., World Future Soc., Penticulus, Pi Lambda Theta. Democrat. Unitarian. Home: 19345 Riverview Ave Rocky River OH 44116 Office: 711 E 222d St Euclid OH 44123

BURNS, MICHAEL PAUL, auditor; b. Highland Park, Mich., Dec. 2, 1935; s. Gerald Dennis and Stella Marie Stanislaw B.; A.A. cum laude, Chgo. City Coll., 1961; B.S. in Bus. Adminstrn., cum laude, Roosevelt U., 1962; m. Rosemarie Klem, Aug. 25, 1962; children—Dennis Anthony, Michael Paul, Mary Therese. Mem. staff Peat Marwick Mitchell & Co., C.P.A.s, Chgo., 1962-65, Pullman Bank & Trust Co., Chgo., 1965-68, Scot Lad Foods Inc., Chgo., 1968-72; auditor I.C. Industries Inc., Chgo., 1972-80, Michael Reese Hosp. and Med. Center, 1980—. Trustee Village of Thornton (Ill.), 1970-72, treas., 1972-77; regional coordinator Health Care Internal Audit Group, 1983—. Served with AUS, 1954-57. Mem. Am. Inst. C.P.A.s, Ill. State C.P.A.s (health care com. 1981—), Nat. Acctg. Assn., Health Care Fin. Mgmt. Assn. Home: 16730 Clyde Ave South Holland IL 60473 Office: 29th St and Ellis Ave Chicago IL 60616

BURNS, RICHARD DON, orthodontist; b. Leon, Iowa, Nov. 29, 1939; s. Leslie Warren and Ethel (Shafer) B.; D.D.S. summa cum laude, State U. Iowa, 1963; M.S.D. in Dentistry, Ind. U., 1966. Practice orthodontics, Elkhart, Ind., 1967—; founder, pres., treas., dir. OrthoTek, Inc., Elkhart, 1968—, Westwood Realty Elkhart, Inc., 1968—, Lancer Advt. Agy. Inc., Elkhart, 1971—; founding pres. Richard D. Burns Orthodontics, Inc., 1970—, Am. Dentactrs., Inc., P.C. Trustee Richard D. Burns Orthodontics Profit Sharing and Pension Trusts, OrthoTek Profit Sharing and Pension Trust; founder, chmn. trustees Midwest Mus. Am. Art. Served with USPHS, 1963-64, USAF, 1966-67. Mem. Am., Ind. dental assns., Elkhart County Dental Soc. (past pres.), Am. Assn. Orthodontists, Ind. Soc. Orthodontists (past pres., past sec.), Great Lakes Soc. Orthodontists, Am. Soc. Dentistry for Children, Omicron Kappa Upsilon, Psi Omega, Sigma Phi Epsilon. Methodist. Kiwanian. Inventor dental appliance; designer orthodontic pub. relations products. Home: 2413 Greenleaf Blvd Elkhart IN 46514 Office: 1750 Kilbourn St Elkhart IN 46514

BURNS, RICHARD HOWARD, food preparation equipment manufacturing company manager; b. Ridgewood, N.J., Sept. 26, 1930; s. Robert Orr and Opal May (Shirreffs) B.; B.S. in Applied Art (Indsl. Design), Auburn U., 1953; m. Beverly Duncan Ritchie, Sept. 9, 1953; children—Richard Howard, Laura Elizabeth Burns Scarff. Mgr. indsl. design Hobart Corp., Troy, Ohio, 1955-57, project engr., 1957-66, mgr. indsl. design, 1966—; owner, pres. Richard H. Burns's Assos., indsl. design and engring. cons. Mem. Miami County Planning Commn., Troy City Council, 1978—. Served with U.S. Army, 1953-55, capt. Res. ret. Mem. Indsl. Designers Soc. Am., Troy C. of C., Am. Def. Preparedness Assn. Republican. Presbyterian (elder). Lodge: Kiwanis. Patentee in field. Home: 662 Clarendon Rd Troy OH 45373 Office: World Hdqrs Ave Troy OH 45373

BURNS, ROBERT EDWARD, editor, publisher; b. Chgo., May 14, 1919; s. William Joseph and Sara (Foy) B.; student DePaul U., 1937-39; Ph.B., Loyola U., 1941; m. Brenda Coleman, May 15, 1948; children—Maddy F., Martin J. Public relations dir. Cath. Youth Orgn., Chgo., 1943-45, 47-49; exec. dir. No. Ind. Region, NCCJ, South Bend, Ind., 1946; exec. editor U.S. Cath. Mag., gen. mgr. Claretian Pubs., Chgo., 1949-84. Mem. Thomas More Assn. (dir. 1960—). Author: The Examined Life, 1980; Catholics on the Cutting Edge, 1983. Home: Route 2 Box 277J Montello WI 53949

BURNSIDE, JULIAN BERNARD, electrical safety specialist; b. Tampa, Fla., Jan. 8, 1924; s. Edgar G. and Clara L. (Justen) B.; m. Ailene M. McIver, Mar. 8, 1953 (div.); children—Julian, Lorretta Gale, Ronald P.; m. 2d, Lidia Maria Myslinska, Mar. 19, 1976; 1 stepson, Mark Stys. Student in elec. engring., Auburn U., 1943-44. From meter reader to field engr. Tampa Electric Light and Power Co., 1941-57, insp., 1957-58, engr. relay tester, 1958-61; chief electric insp., city elec. engr., City of Tampa, 1961-71; code specialist, coordinator UL/inspection authority relations Underwriters Labs., Inc., Northbrook, Ill., 1971—. Served with U.S. Army, 1943-45. Mem. Internat. Assn. Elec. Insps. (cert. electric safety engr. 1965), Am. Soc. Safety Engrs., DAV, Am. Legion. Republican. Roman Catholic. Home: 8321 N Elmore St Niles IL 60648 Office: Underwriters Labs 333 Pfingsten Rd Northbrook IL 60062

BURNSTEIN, HAROLD ROBERT, lawyer; b. Chgo., May 28, 1919; s. Samuel and Fay (Fine) B.; B.S.C., Northwestern U., 1940; J.D., DePaul U., 1950; m. Harriet Kahn, May 25, 1946; children—Clifford Nolan, Joan Ellen. Pub. accountant Katz, Wagner & Co., Chgo., 1940-41; tax accountant Consol. Vultee Aircraft Corp., San Diego, 1941-45; tax accountant Hughes and Hughes, Chgo., 1946-50, counsel, 1950-79; of counsel firm Schwartz and Freeman; admitted to Ill. bar, 1950, since practiced in Chgo. Past chmn. Highland Park Voters Assn.; mem. Dist. 108 Sch. Bd., Highland Park, 1967-73, pres., 1972-73; mem. Highland Park Library Bd., 1974-80; bd. dirs. North Suburban Library System, 1976-79, Lay Response Council, 1979-81; bd. dirs. Jewish Children's Bur., 1978—, v.p., 1982—. Mem. Am., Chgo. (com. fed. taxation, past chmn.) bar assns., Ill. Soc. C.P.A.'s, Am. Inst. C.P.A.'s, DePaul Bd. Assos., Chgo. Council on Fgn. Relations, Beta Alpha Psi. Jewish. Clubs: Birchwood (past pres.) (Highland Park); Standard, Economic (Chgo.). Contbr. articles on fed. taxation to profl. jours. Home: 510 Ravine Dr Highland Park IL 60035 Office: 401 N Michigan Ave Chicago IL 60611

BURPULIS, EUGENIA G., telephone company executive; b. Salem, N.J., Nov. 21, 1942; s. George S. and Thelma (Pirovolos) B.; student Kent State U., 1961-62, Cuyahoga Community Coll., 1977. With Ohio Bell Tel. Co., Cleve., 1961—, Supr., 1964-71, asst. mgr. multi-media, 1971-75, asst. mgr. course devel., 1975-78, mgr. course devel., 1978—. Mem. Nat. Soc. Performance and Instrn., Am. Bus. Woman's Assn. (editor bull., newsletter editor 1982—, edn. chmn. 1982; Woman of Year), Ohio Bell Pioneers (editor newsletter 1980-81), St. Demetrios Philoptochos Soc., Nat. Chios Soc. (cmv. sec.). Club: Women's City (Cleve.). Greek Orthodox (mem. choir, past pres., treas.). Home: 1273 W 108th St Cleveland OH 44102 Office: 45 Erieview Plaza Cleveland OH 44114

BURR, HENRY EDWIN, molecular biology educator, researcher; b. Chillicothe, Ohio, Feb. 25, 1939; s. Henry E. Gorney and Genevieve Burr. Student Washington and Lee U., 1957-59; B.A., Miami U., Oxford, Ohio, 1962, M.S., 1964; Ph.D., U. Cin., 1973. Scientist NIH-Nat. Cancer Inst. Bethesda, Md., 1965-67; fellow Stanford U., Calif., 1972-74, research assoc., 1974-82; assoc. prof. Wayne State U., Detroit, 1982—; cons. Nat. Genosciences, Detroit, 1982-83. Contbr. articles to profl. jours. Instr. Given Inst. Workshop, Aspen, Colo., 1976. Fellow NIH, 1968-72, Damon Runyon Found., 1973-75. Mem. Soc. Study of Evolution, Internat. Star Class Yacht Racing Assn. (life), Am. Amateur Radio Relay League (life), Sigma Xi, Delta Upsilon. Club: Richmond Yacht (Calif.). Avocations: Yacht racing; amateur radio operator. Office: Wayne State Univ Dept Biol Sci Detroit MI 48202

BURR, JAMES EDWARD, hotel manager; b. Utica, N.Y., July 20, 1941; s. James I. and Virginia Ellen (Davidson) B. B.S., Cornell U., 1963. Asst. budget control dir. Plaza Hotel, N.Y.C., 1963-65; asst. mgr. Danbury Motor Inn (Conn.), 1965-66; cons. to mgr. Harris, Kerr, Forster, Chgo., 1966-75, prin., Miami, Fla., 1975-77; dist. dir. Holiday Inns, Inc., Miami, 1978-79, dir. franchise relations, Toronto, Ont., Can., 1980, dist. dir., Chgo., 1981-83, gen. mgr. Holiday Inn Lake Shore Dr., Chgo., 1983—. Cons. editor tng. manual. Neighborhood campaign ctr. chmn. Percy for Senator, Chgo., 1966; v.p. Chgo. Hospitality Council for City of Hope, 1982-83; hon. mem. Ye Hosts Hon., Ithaca, N.Y., 1962. Mem. Cornell Soc. Hotelmen (dir. 1971-72), Greater Chgo. Hotel and Motel Assn. (bd. dirs. 1985—), Confrerie de la Chaine des Rotisseurs., MENSA. Republican. Presbyterian. Club: Canadian of Chgo. Home and office: 644 N Lake Shore Dr Chicago IL 60611

BURRELL, BARBARA, advertising agency executive; b. Chgo., Mar. 19, 1941; d. Wiley Jones; children—Bonita Aldridge, Alexandra Burrell, Jason Burrell. B.S., No. Ill. U., 1963. Tchr., Chgo. Bd. Edn., 1963-65, 66-67; media estimator Needham, Harper, Steers, Chgo., 1965-66; personnel counselor Continental Bank, Chgo., 1973-74; sr. v.p., sec.-treas. Burrell Advt., Chgo., 1974—; dir. Hyde Park Fed. Savs., Chgo., 1979-82; dir. South Shore Bank, Chgo., 1982—. Mem. aux. bd. Hyde Park Art Ctr., Chgo.; mem. Hyde Park-Kenwood Devel. Corp., Chgo., S.E. Chgo. Commn.; mem. adv. com. DuSable Mus. African Am. History, 1983—. Mem. Inst. Psychoanalysis (edn. fund 1983—), Alpha Gamma Pi, Club: Chgo. Network (program chmn. 1983-84).

BURRELL, DONALD JAMES, photofinishing company executive; b. Gary, Ind., Oct. 31, 1936; s. Frank and Anna (Bonko) B.; m. Alice M. Shema, Oct. 3, 1959; children—John J., James A., Mary A., Robert M., Donna M. Cert. profl. photographer N.Y. Inst. Photography, 1958. Photographer, Spasoff Studio, Gary, 1956-57; indsl. photographer Rockwell Internat., East Chicago, Ind., 1957-59; owner DNJ Color Lab., Gary, 1959-69; gen. mgr. KMS Industries, Ann Arbor, Mich., 1969-73; owner Burrell Colour Inc., Crown Point, Ind., 1973—; owner, cons. mgr. D & S Color Inc., Bradenton, Fla., 1980—; bd. dirs. Citizens Fed., Hammond, Ind. Bd. dirs. St. Anthony Hosp., Crown Point, 1970-78; mem. lay adv. bd. St. Matthias Catholic Ch., Crown Point, 1975-78. Recipient outstanding photography award Profl. Photographers Assn., 1959. Mem. Assn. Profl. Color Labs. (founder, pres. 1970-71), Photo Mktg. Assn. (trustee), Profl. Photographers Am., Crown Point C. of C. (dir. 1967-69). Lodge: Rotary (Crown Point). Office: Burrell Colour Inc 1311 Merrillville Rd Crown Point IN 46307

BURROUGHS, WAYNE ROBERT, packaging company executive; b. Sherbrooke, Que., Can., Nov. 12, 1939; s. Selah Eugene and Olive Elizabeth (Turnbull) B.; m. Alice Elizabeth Philip, May 9, 1964; children—Tracey, Catherine, Michael. B.Comm., Loyola of Montreal, 1972. Cert. Can. Inst. Mgmt. Mgr. indsl. engring. Atlas Asbestos Co., Montreal, Que., 1967-69; plant mgr. Perkins Papers Ltd., Laval, Que., 1969-71; mgr. mfg. Converted Papers div. Domtar Packaging Ltd., Toronto, Ont., Can., 1972-76; v.p., gen. mgr. Diamond Nat. of Can. Ltd., Brantford, Ont., 1976-82, v.p., gen. mgr. moulded products div. Reid Dominion Packaging Ltd. (successor to Diamond Nat. of Can.), Brantford, 1982—. Chmn. Brantford Devel. Bd., 1981-82. Mem. Am. Inst. Indsl. Engrs., Can. Mfrs. Assn., Brantford Regional C. of C. (dir.). Mem. United Ch. of Can. Clubs: Brantford, Brantford Golf and Country, Kiwanis (dir. Brantford). Home: 29 Summerhayes Crescent Brantford ON N3R 5J2 Canada Office: 81 Elgin St Brantford ON N3T 5T6 Canada

BURROWS, FRANK LOWELL, pharmacist, pharmaceutical sales; b. Waterloo, Iowa, May 25, 1932; s. Francis Lowell and Eva R. (Roberts) B.; m. Vesta Jean Donahue, June 3, 1953; children—Kay, John, Joan, Mary Margaret, Jane. B.S. in Pharmacy, Drake U., 1956. Registered pharmacist Iowa. Pharmacist Montross Pharmacy, Winterset, Iowa, 1956-59, Bauder Pharmacy, Des Moines, Iowa, 1959-74; med. rep. Merrell-Dow, Cin., 1974—; speaker on drug abuse, Iowa; lectr. Drake U.; tchr. drug abuse Des Moines Adult Edn. Adv. council Gov. Council Drug Abuse, Iowa, 1974; bd. dirs. Mid Iowa Drug Abuse Council, chmn. edn. com., med. com.; pres. Byron Rich Sch. PTA, 1973, 74. Recipient Pres. award Merrell-Dow Pharms. 1975, Pace Setter award Merrell-Dow Pharms., 1976. HEW Grant 1972.. Mem. Am. Pharm. Assn., Iowa Pharm. Assn. Republican. Presbyterian. Lodge: Masons. Avocations: furniture making; woodworking; fishing. Home and Office: 4305 Ashby Ave Des Moines IA 50310

BURROWS, HAROLD HENRY, financial consultant; b. Mpls., Oct. 18, 1942; s. Harold Henry and Emily (Sirotiak) B.; B.S. in Math. and Physics, Iowa State U., 1964; M.S. in Physics, U. Minn., 1967, M.B.A., 1972; m. Renée Ruth Marko, Dec. 18, 1965; children—Jason, Sonja, Suzanne. Research physicist Honeywell Inc., Mpls., 1967-69; account exec. Merrill Lynch Inc., Mpls., 1969-76; fin. cons. Shearson/Am. Express Inc., Mpls., 1976—, v.p. investments, 1981-83, 1st v.p. investments, 1983—. Lutheran. Home: 5135 Fern Dr Loretto MN 55357 Office: 625 4th Ave S Suite 1125 Minneapolis MN 55415

BURSLEY, GILBERT EVERETTE, former college president, former state senator, former army officer; b. Ann Arbor, Mich., Feb. 28, 1913; s. Philip Everett and Flora (Peters) B.; m. Vivette Mumtaz, Jan. 15, 1949; 1 son, Philip. A.B., U. Mich., 1934; M.B.A., Harvard U., 1936; postgrad. in internat. relations George Washington U., 1953-54. Commd. 1st lt. U.S. Army, 1940, advanced through grades to lt. col., 1954; mil. attache, Istanbul, Turkey,

1946-49; with Joint U.S. Mil. Missions, Athens, 1949-52, UN Truce Supervision Orgn., Palestine, sr. mil. advisor Israel-Jordon and Israel-Egypt Mixed Armistice Commns., 1954; Am. consul, pub. affairs officer in charge USIA program, Belgian Congo, French Equatorial Africa, Ruanda, Urundi, Cameroons, Angola, 1955-57; cons. World Wide Broadcasting Found., 1957; asst. dir. U. Mich. Devel. Council, 1957-64; mem. U.S. Trade and Investment Mission to Cameroons and Ivory Coast, 1968; pres. Cleary Coll., Ypsilanti, Mich., 1978-83, chancellor, 1984, trustee, 1985—, pres. and chancellor emeritus, 1985—. Adviser policy com. Nat. Assessment Edn. Progress, 1976-83, Mich. Higher Edn. Capital Investment, 1980, Fund for Improvement Postsecondary Edn., 1976-79; mem. Interstate Migrant Edn. Task Force, 1976-81; mem. Edn. Commn. of States, 1973-85; chmn. Mich. Edn. Council, 1973-79; mem. Mich. Bicentennial Commn., 1976; mem. Mich. Ho. of Reps., 1960-64; mem. Mich. Senate, 1964-78, asst. pres. pro tem, 1974-78, asst. majority leader, 1970-74, also chmn. 15 legis. coms.; pres. Mich. Internat. Council, 1978-80; chmn. Mich. UN Day, 1970-80; bd. dirs. Mich. Artrain, 1974—, Washtenaw County Hospice, 1980, Ann Arbor Citizens Council, Mich. Council on Arts; chmn. Mich. Vocat. Edn. Task Force, 1980; pres. Gulf Pines Home Owners Assn., Sanibel, 1984-85. Recipient award of merit Mich. Agrl. Conf., 1968; commendation Mich. Senate, 1973, 85; Disting. Service award Assn. Ind. Colls. and Univs. in Mich., 1976, Edn. Commn. of States, 1978; Ednl. Leadership award Mich. Assn. Elem. Prins., 1978. Mem. Mich. Hist. Soc., Mich. Soc. Mayflower Descs. (gov. 1965-71), SAR (past pres. Washtenaw chpt.), Sanibel Com. of The Islands (chmn.), Fgn. Policy Assn., Ann Arbor C. of C. (legis. com. 1982—, Disting Service award 1978), VFW, Am. Legion, Soc. Am. Magicians. Republican. Episcopalian. Clubs: Harvard Bus. Sch., Economic (Detroit); U. Mich. Alumni, Ann Arbor. Lodge: Rotary (Paul Harris fellow). Contbr. articles on edn. and fgn. commerce to profl. publs. Home: 2065 Geddes Ave Ann Arbor MI 48104 also 900 Gumbo Limbo Ln Sanibel FL 33957 Office: 2107 Washtenaw Ave Ypsilanti MI 48197

BURT, FRANK N., JR., vascular surgeon; b. Freeport, Ill., Apr. 30, 1943; s. Frank N. and Betty N. (Becker) B.; B.S., Northwestern U., 1965, M.D., 1967; m. Connie Grange, Feb. 8, 1969; children—Kristin, Mitchell. Intern, Latter-day Saints Hosp., Salt Lake City, 1967-68, resident, 1968-70; resident St. Agnes Hosp., Balt., 1970-72; fellow in peripheral vascular surgery Providence Hosp., Southfield, Mich., 1975; peripheral vascular surgeon, ptnr. Northland Vascular Clinic, Southfield, 1975-80; asso. Woodland Med. Group, 1980-82; med. dir. intensive and spl. care units Providence Hosp., 1976-78, chief sect. vascular surgery, 1979-83; guest physician first surg. clinic U. Vienna, 1967; founder, chmn. bd. dirs. Data-Med Corp., Southfield, 1979—; founder, chmn. Cogensys Corp., 1982; lectr. grad. sch. engring. George Washington U., 1976-79. Troop leader Detroit council Boy Scouts Am., 1975-77. Served with USAF, 1972-74. Recipient Michael E. DeBakey research award in vascular surgery, 1977. Diplomate Am. Bd. Surgery. Mem. AMA, Mich. Med. Soc., Oakland County Mich. Med. Soc., Internat. Coll. Angiology, Am. Med. Soc. of Vienna. Mormon. Developer ICU patient data mgmt. system Providence Hosp.; inventor, developer Data-Med profl. practice mgmt. system; researcher vascular surgery and artificial intelligence in medicine. Home: 2178 Coach Way Bloomfield Hills MI 48013 Office: 31390 Northwestern Hwy Farmington Hills MI 48018

BURTCH, ROBERT CHARLES, JR, surveying mapping educator; b. Toledo, Dec. 6, 1947; s. Robert Charles and Dorothy Ann (Link) B.; m. Carol Christine Cobb, Sept. 21, 1974; children—Justin, Nathan. B.S. in Surveying, Ferris State Coll., 1977; M.S. in Geodetic Sci., Ohio State U., 1983. Asst. prof. Ferris State Coll., Big Rapids, Mich., 1979—. Contbr. articles to profl. jours. Served to sgt. USAF, 1966-70. Mem. Am. Congress on Surveying and Mapping, Am. Soc. Photogrammetry, Am. Geophys. Union, Can. Inst. Surveying, Urban and Regional Info. Systems Assn. Avocations: photography, furniture refinishing. Home: 507 S Michigan Big Rapids MI 49307 Office: Ferris State Coll Surveying and Mapping Program Big Rapids MI 49307

BURTON, CHARLES VICTOR, physician, surgeon; b. N.Y.C., Jan. 2, 1935; s. Norman Howard and Ruth Esther (Putziger) B.; m. Noel Michelle Kleid, Aug. 26, 1961; children—Matthew, Timothy, Andrew; student Johns Hopkins U., 1952-56; M.D., N.Y. Med. Coll., 1960. Intern surgery Yale U. Med. Center, 1961-62; asst. resident neurol. surgery Johns Hopkins Hosp., Balt., 1962-66, chief resident, 1966-67; asso. chief surgery, chief neurosurgery USPHS Hosp., Seattle, 1967-69; vis. research affiliate Primate Center, U. Wash., 1967-69; asst. prof. neurosurgery Temple U. Health Scis. Center, Phila., 1970-73, asso. prof., 1973-74, neurol. research coordinator, 1970-74; dir. dept. neuroaugmentive surgery Sister Kenny Inst., Mpls., 1974-81, med. dir. Low Back Clinic, 1977—; med. dir. Inst. Low Back Care, Mpls., 1980—; co-chmn. Joint Neurosurg. Com. on Devices and Drugs, 1973-77; chmn. Internat. Standards Orgn., 1974-76, FDA adv. panel on neurologic devices, 1974-77; mem. U.S. Biomed. Instrumentation Del. to Soviet Union, 1974. Research fellow Nat. Polio Found., 1956, HEW, 1958; neurosurg. fellow Johns Hopkins Hosp., 1960-61, 62-67, 69-70; Diplomate Am. Bd. Neurol. Surgery, Nat. Bd. Med. Examiners. Fellow ACS; mem. Congress Neurol. Surgeons (chmn. com. materials and devices 1972-79), Am. Assn. Neurol. Surgeons, Minn. Neurosurg. Soc., AAAS, ASTM (chmn. com. materials 1973-78), Internat. Soc. Study of Lumbar Spine, Am. Nat. Standards Inst. (med. device tech. adv. bd. 1973-78), Philadelphia County Med. Soc. (med.-legal com. 1970-74), Minn. Med. Assn. (Gold medal award for best sci. presentation at 1975 Meeting, subcom. on med. testimony 1978—), Hennepin County Med. Soc. (med.-legal com. 1975—), Mpls. Acad. Medicine, Cor et Manus Soc., Alpha Epsilon Delta. Home: 148 W Lake St Excelsior MN 55331 Office: Inst Low Back Care 2737 Chicago Ave Minneapolis MN 55407

BURTON, COURTNEY, mining and shipping co. exec.; b. Cleve., Oct. 29, 1912; s. Courtney and Sarita (Oglebay) B.; student Mich. Coll. Mining and Tech., 1933-34, B.S., 1956; m. Marguerite Rankin, Sept. 7, 1933 (dec. Apr. 1976); children—Sarita Ann Burton Frith, Marguerite Rankin Burton Humphrey; m. Margaret Butler Leitch, Dec. 20, 1978. Dir. E.W. Oglebay Co., Cleve., 1934-57, pres., 1947-57; v.p. Ferro Engring. Co., Cleve., 1950-57; pres. Fortuna Lake Mining Co., Cleve., 1950-57; treas., dir. Columbia Transp. Co., Cleve., 1950-57; v.p. Montreal Mining Co., Cleve., 1950-57; pres. North Shore Land Co., Cleve., 1950-57; v.p., dir. Brule Smokeless Coal Co., Cleve., 1950-57; chmn. bd., chmn. exec. com. Oglebay Norton Co., Cleve., 1957—. Dir. Ohio CD and Rationing, 1941-42; exec. asst. Office Coordinator Inter-Am. Affairs, 1942-44; mem. bd. commrs. Cleve. Met. Park Bd., 1969-74. Mayor, Village of Gates Mills (Ohio), 1948-61; chmn. Ohio Republican Fin. Com., 1954-61, Rep. Nat. Fin. Com., 1961-64; trustee Bethany Coll.; past trustee Nat. Park Found.; hon. trustee Univ. Hosp., Cleve., Oglebay Inst., Wheeling, W.Va.; pres. Am.'s Future Trees Found., Cleve. Zool. Soc. (pres. 1968-76). Served to lt. USNR, 1944-46. Mem. Am. Iron and Steel Inst., Nat. Coal Assn. Episcopalian. Clubs: Chagrin Valley Hunt (master of hounds 1946-54) (Gates Mills); Tavern, Union (Cleve.); Rolling Rock (Ligonier, Pa.); Fort Henry, Wheeling Country, Ye Olde Country (Wheeling); Kirtland (Willoughby, Ohio). Office: 1100 Superior Ave Cleveland OH 44114

BURTON, DANNY L., congressman b. Indpls., June 21, 1938; s. Charles W. and Bonnie Lee (Hardisty) B.; ed. Ind. U., 1958, Cin. Bible Sem., 1959-60; m. Barbara J. Logan, 1959; children—Danielle, Danny L. Owner, Dan Burton Agy., from 1967—; mem. Ind. Ho. of Reps., 1967-69, 77-79, Ind. Senate, 1969-70, 81-82, 98th-99th U.S. Congresses, 6th Dist., Ind. Served with U.S. Army, 1956-57. Republican. Office: 120 Cannon House Office Bldg Washington DC 20515*

BURTON, DARRELL IRVIN, engineering executive; b. Ashtabula, Ohio, Sept. 21, 1926; s. George Irvin and Barbara Elizabeth (Streyle) B.; B.S. in Radio Engring., Chgo. Tech. Coll., 1954; m. Lois Carol Warkentien, Apr. 14, 1951; children—Linda Jean Burton Clinton, Lisa Ann Burton Watts, Lori Elizabeth. Research and devel. engr. Motorola, Inc., Chgo., 1951-60; devel. engr. Hallicrafters, Chgo., 1960-62; chief engr. TRW, Inc., Des Plaines, Ill., 1962-65; devel. engr. Warwick, Niles, Ill., 1965-68; systems mgr. Admiral Corp., Chgo., 1968-76; elec.-electronics lab. mgr. Montgomery Ward & Co., Chgo., 1976-82; staff engr. Wells-Gardner Electronics Corp., Chgo., 1982—; tchr. electronics and math. Pres. Addison Homeowners Assn., 1958-60, v.p., 1960-62; mem. Addison Plan Commn., 1960-63. Served with USNR, 1944. Mem. IEEE, ASTM. Club: York Amateur Radio (pres. 1984-86). Republican. Lutheran. Patentee in field. Home: 112 Lawndale Ave Elmhurst IL 60126

BURTON, DOROTHY HOPE, educator; b. Norwood, Ohio, Apr. 7, 1928; d. Osber Franklin and Ina Belle (Sears) Zachary; student Olivet Nazarene Coll., 1945-49; B.S. in Edn., Ball State U., 1960, M.A. in Edn., 1967; M.A. in Edn., Ohio State U., 1984; m. Roy Dean Burton, Nov. 28, 1947 (div.); children—Jennifer D. Burton Dooley, Sally Jo Hunley. Classroom tchr. Aroma Park (Ill.) Sch., 1954-56, Bradley (Ill.) Schs., 1957, Crawfordsville (Ind.) City Schs., 1957-58, Muncie (Ind.) City Schs., 1960-77; field placement coordinator, asst. prof. edn. Mt. Vernon (Ohio) Nazarene Coll., 1977—; substitute tchr. Kankakee Community. Mem. Assn. Supervision and Curriculum Devel., Ohio Assn. Gifted Children, Ind. Ret. Tchrs. Assn., Am. Assn. Colls. Tchr. Educators, Assn. Tchr. Educators, Nazarene Assn. Colls. Tchr. Edn., Ohio Assn. Tchr. Educators, Kappa Delta Pi. Republican. Nazarene. Home: 9 Claypool Dr Mount Vernon OH 43050 Office: 800 Martinsburg Rd Mount Vernon OH 43050

BURTON, MARY ELIZABETH, beauty company executive; b. Richmond, Va., Dec. 18, 1951; d. Samuel Bayard and Dottie (Brown) Jeter; 1 dau., Jennifer Ann. B.A. in Sociology, Coll. William and Mary, 1973; M.B.A., U. Chgo., 1975. Corp. trainee Jewel Cos., Chgo., 1975-82, mdse. mgr. Osco Drug div., 1980-82; pres. Bee Discount, Hillside, Ill., 1982-83, Victory Beauty Systems (parent of Bee Discount), Hillside, 1983—. Mem. mental health task force United Methodist Ch., Naperville, Ill., 1982. Grantee NSF, 1972, George Hay Brown Found. U. Chgo. Grad. Sch. Bus., 1975. Mem. U. Chgo. Women's Bus. Group, Com. of 200. Republican. Avocations: aerobics, jogging. Home: 6186 Hickory Dr Lisle IL 60532 Office: Victory Beauty Systems 205 Fencl Ln Hillside IL 60162

BURTON, THOMAS ARTHUR, instrument manufacturing company executive; b. Richmond, Va., Dec. 29, 1934; s. Arthur Nunlay and Mary (Hamilton) B.; m. Mary Frances Pierce, June 5, 1956; children—Thomas Arthur, Elizabeth Frances, Michael Pierce. B.S. with honors in Indsl. Engring., U. Fla., 1956. Project engr. Union Carbide Corp., Charleston, W.Va., 1956-60; sales engr. Flo-Tronics, Inc., Mpls., 1960-62, sales mgr., 1962-64, div. mgr., 1964-70; v.p. Waters Instruments, Rochester, Minn., 1970-76, pres., chief exec. officer, 1977—. Dir. United Fin. Inc. Trustee, St. Mary's Hosp., 1976-83, v.p., 1978-83. Mem. Am. Mgmt. Assn., Young Presidents Orgn. Republican. Episcopalian. Clubs: Rochester Golf and Country; Decathlon (Mpls.). Patentee in field. Home: 822 Sierra Ln NE Rochester MN 55904 Office: Waters Instruments Inc PO Box 6117 Rochester MN 55903

BURTON, VERONA DEVINE, botanist; b. Reading, Pa., Nov. 23, 1922; d. John Edward and Verona Anna Marie (Dillman) Devine; m. Daniel Frederick Burton, July 22, 1950; 1 child, John. A.B., Hunter Coll., 1944; M.S., State U. Iowa, 1946, Ph.D., 1948. Faculty, Mankato State U., Minn., 1948—, prof. biology. Contbr. articles to profl. jours. Mem. Adv. Council, Minn. Bd. Investment, St. Paul, 1984—; trustee Minn. Tchrs. Retirement Assn., 1981—; mem. adv. council for Voc. Edn., Mpls., 1984—. Elsie Seringhaus scholar, 1944; Mankato YWCA Leadership award, 1973; Woman of Achievement Bus. and Profl. Women, 1983. Mem. Internat. Soc. for Plant Morphologists, Mankato State U. Faculty Assn., Bus. and Profl. Women, Sigma Xi. Democratic-Farmer-Labor. Episcopalian. Avocations: Gardening; canning. Home: 512 Hickory St Mankato MN 56001 Office: Mankato State Univ Mankato MN 56001

BURTON, WALTER ERVIN, writer; b. McMechen, W.Va., Nov. 18, 1903; s. David William and Mary Lucinda (Yoho) B.; student U. Akron, 1922-23, Johns Hopkins, 1923-24, 27-28. Editorial staffs Evening Times, Times-Press, Herald Pub. Co., Akron, 1922-23, 24-27. Mem. Nat. Assn. Home and Workshop Writers. Club: Portage Camera (Akron). Contbr. numerous articles to mags. including Popular Mechanics, Popular Sci., others. Author: Home-Built Photo Equipment, 1947; The Story of Tire Beads and Tires, 1954, others. Editor: Engineering with Rubber, 1949. Patentee in field. Address: 1032 Florida Ave Akron OH 44314

BURTON, WAYNE NORMAN, bank executive, physician, medical educator; b. Portland, Oreg., Nov. 14, 1947; s. Meyer and Pearl (Feves) B.; m. Cheryl Ann Costel, Sept. 7, 1981; children—Jason Bernard, Lindsay Julia. B.A., U. Calif.-Santa Barbara, 1969; M.D., U. Oreg., 1974. Resident in internal medicine Northwestern U. Med. Ctr., Chgo., 1974-77; staff physician Internat. Harvester Co., Chgo., 1977-82; v.p., med. dir. First Nat. Bank Chgo., 1982—; cons. Northwestern Meml. Hosp., Chgo., 1978—, asst. prof. clin. medicine, 1979—, asst. prof. psychiatry, 1984—. Contbr. articles to profl. jours. Active fitness com. Chgo. Heart Assn. Fellow ACP, Am. Occupational Med. Assn., mem. AMA, Chgo. Soc. Internal Medicine, Am. Med. Soc. Alcoholism. Avocations: stamp collecting; golf; racquetball; swimming. Home: 175 E Delaware Pl Apt 7610 Chicago IL 60611

BUSBY, NANCY CAROLYN, real estate executive; b. Muncie, Ind., Apr. 11, 1949; d. John Eldon and Nina Mae (Perdue) B. Student Purdue U., 1967-69. Adminstrv. asst. FCH Services, Inc., Indpls., 1969-78; v.p. Triangle Assocs., Inc., Indpls., 1978—. Mem. Inst. Real Estate Mgmt., Met. Indpls. Bd. Realtors. Democrat. Mem. Christian Ch. Office: Triangle Assocs Inc 921 E 8th St Suite 111 Indianapolis IN 46240

BUSCH, ARTHUR ALLEN, lawyer, educator; b. Flint, Mich., July 25, 1954; s. William Allen and Anna Elizabeth (York) B.; m. Bernadette Marie-Therese Regnier, Aug. 28, 1982. B.A., Mich. State U., 1976, M.L.I.R., 1977; J.D., T.M. Cooley Law Sch., 1982. Bar: Mich. 1982, U.S. Dist. Ct. (ea. dist.) Mich. 1984. Personnel supr. Nat. Gypsum Co., Gibsonburg, Ohio, 1977-78; instr. C. S. Mott Community Coll., Flint, Mich., 1978—, Mich. State U., East Lansing, 1980-82; sole practice, Flint, 1982—; counsel Flint City Council, 1982-84; mem. transition team for Mayor, Flint, 1983; cons. labor atty. City of Flint, 1984. Mem. com. to elect James A. Sharp Jr., Flint, 1983; treas., campaign mgr. Judge Donnellan, Flint, 1984. Mem. Mich. Bar Assn., Genesee County Bar Assn., Assn. Trial Lawyers Am., ABA, Internat. Inst. Flint. Democrat. Baptist. Office: 317 E Fifth St Flint MI 48502

BUSCH, AUGUST ADOLPHUS, III, brewery executive; b. St. Louis, June 16, 1937; s. August Anheuser and Elizabeth (Overton) B.; student U. Ariz., 1957-59, Siebel Inst. Tech., 1960-61; m. Virginia L. Wiley, Dec. 28, 1974; children—Steven August, Virginia Marie; children by previous marriage—August Adolphus, Susan Marie. With Anheuser-Busch, Inc., St. Louis, 1957—, sales mgr., 1962-64, v.p. mktg. ops., 1964-65, v.p., gen. mgr., 1965-74, pres., 1974—, chief exec. officer, 1975—, also dir.; now also pres., chmn. bd. Anheuser-Busch Cos., Inc.; dir. St. Louis Nat. Baseball Club, Gen. Am. Life Ins. Co., Mfg. R.W. Co., Norfolk So. Ry., Southwestern Bell Telephone Co., Campbell Taggart, Inc. Mem. adv. bd. St. John Mercy Med. Center, Busch Center U. Pa.; trustee Washington U.; mem. pres.'s council St. Louis U.; bd. dirs. United Way Greater St. Louis, St. Louis Symphony Soc., Jr. Achievement Mississippi Valley; dir. emeritus Coll. William and Mary; sponsor Coll. William and Mary, C. of C. U.S.; bd. overseers Wharton Sch., U. Pa.; mem. exec. bd. Boy Scouts Am. Mem. U.S. Brewers Assn. (dir.), Grocery Mfrs. Am. (dir.). Clubs: St. Louis, Racquet (St. Louis), Log Cabin, Stadium, Noonday, St. Louis Country. Office: One Busch Pl Saint Louis MO 63118

BUSCH, MERRILL J., business, public relations and publishing executive; b. Jordan, Minn., July 25, 1936; s. Albert Meinrad and Hildegarde (Bauer) B.; student St. Thomas Coll., St. Paul, 1954-57; B.A. summa cum laude, U. Minn., 1958, postgrad., 1958-59; m. Mary Daphne Meteraud, Oct. 16, 1965; children—Christopher, Jennifer, Amy. Pres. Busch & Partners, 1979—; chmn. Prime Publs., Inc. Bd. dirs. Am. Endeavour, Inc. Served with AUS, 1959-60. Work included in tricentennial time capsule Minn. Bicentennial Commn., 1976. Mem. Phi Beta Kappa. Republican. Roman Catholic. Club: Mpls. Athletic. Home: 2120 Girard Ave S Minneapolis MN 55405 also 87 Shorewood Dr St Michael MN 55376 Office: 1111 W 22d St Minneapolis MN 55405

BUSCH, ROBERT MICHAEL, insurance company executive; b. Rice Lake, Wis., Nov. 3, 1950; s. Leonard Albert and Rosalie Susan (Schutz) B.; B.S., U. Wis., Eau Claire, 1974, B.S. in Environ. and Public Health, 1976; M.S., U. Wis., Stout, 1978; postgrad in public health U. Minn., 1978-80; m. Leah Ellan Masterson, Dec. 13, 1980. With Wausau Ins. Cos., Mpls., 1980, loss control specialist, Oshkosh, Wis., 1981-82, Green Bay, 1982-83, sr. safety cons., 1982—. Mem. Am. Soc. Safety Engrs. (cert. safety profl., chpt. v.p. 1984-85), Am. Indsl. Hygiene Assn., Green Bay (Wis.) C. of C. (chmn. safety and health com.), Phi Kappa Phi. Clubs: Green Bay Golf League. Office: PO Box 19030 Green Bay WI 54307

BUSCH, THEODORE NORMAN, cons. shooting range design; b. Cleve., Dec. 29, 1919; s. Theodore S. and Norma B.; student pub. schs. Cleve.; m. 2d, Sené Rosene, June 30, 1961; 1 dau. by previous marriage, Kathy. Dir. tech. communications DoAll Co., Des Plaines, Ill., 1952-62; v.p. Shooting Equipment, Inc., Chgo., 1962-69; v.p. Caswell Equipment Co., Inc., Mpls., 1969—; v.p. Seneb, Inc. Mpls., 1976—. Served with USAAF, World War II. Mem. Am. Soc. Quality Control, Soc. Mfg. Engrs., Internat. Assn. Law Enforcement Firearm Instrs., Internat. Soc. Law Enforcement and Criminal Justice Instrs., Soc. Am. Mil. Engrs., Internat. Assn. Chiefs of Police. Author: Fundamentals of Dimensional Metrology, 1963; Guidelines for Police Shooting Ranges, 1977; Guidelines for Commercial Shooting Ranges, 1979. Contbr. articles to profl. jours. Patentee in field. Home: 910 Mt Curve Ave Minneapolis MN 55403 Office: 1221 Marshall St NE Minneapolis MN 55413

BUSCHBACH, THOMAS CHARLES, geologist; b. Cicero, Ill., May 12, 1923; s. Thomas Dominick and Vivian (Smiley) B.; B.S., U. Ill., 1950, M.S., 1951, Ph.D., 1959; m. Mildred Merle Fletcher, Nov. 26, 1947; children—Thomas Richard, Susan Kay, Deborah Lynn Buschbach Baker. Geologist, structural geology, stratigraphy, underground storage of natural gas Ill. Geol. Survey, 1951-78; coordinator New Madrid Seismotectonic Study, U.S. Nuclear Regulatory Commn., 1976—; research prof. geology St. Louis U., 1978—. Geologic cons. petroleum, seismic hazards. Served to lt. comdr. USNR, 1942-47. Fellow Geol. Soc. Am.; mem. Am. Assn. Petroleum Geologists (chmn. stratigraphic correlations com. 1970-73), Assn. Engring. Geologists, Am. Geophys. Union. Home: 604 Park Ln Champaign IL 61820 Office: St Louis U PO Box 8099 Laclede Sta Saint Louis MO 63156

BUSH, DAVID MICHAEL, financial consultant; b. Pontiac, Mich., Apr. 9, 1943; s. Lyman Albert and Dorothy Beatrice (Hibbler) B.; m. Linda Dorothy Brobst, July 20, 1968; children—Christine, David, Deborah, Steven. B.S. in Metall. Engring., Mich. Tech. U., 1965; M.B.A., Bradley U., 1975. With quality control U.S. Steel Corp., Gary, Ind., 1965-66; with mfg. and engring. mgmt. Caterpillar Tractor, Peoria, Ill., 1968-82; fin. cons. Merrill Lynch Pierce Fenner & Smith, Peoria, 1982—. Active Cub and Boy Scouts groups W.D. Boyce council Boy Scouts Am., 1979-84. Served with U.S. Army, 1966-68. Mem. Am. Soc. for Metals. Republican. Presbyterian. Club: Kiwanis. Office: 456 Fulton St Suite 400 Peoria IL 61602

BUSH, DOROTHY JEAN BOHN, counselor; b. Dayton, Ohio, Apr. 18, 1932; d. David William and Carrie May (Tilton) Bohn; A.B., Wittenberg U., 1954, B.S. in Edn., 1954, M.Ed., 1958; postgrad. Miami U., Oxford, Ohio, 1954-55, Antioch Coll., 1963, Wright State U., 1970-74; m. Ralph Royal Bush, Jr., May 23, 1954 (dec. Mar. 1984); children—Rebecca Renee (Mrs. Anton Simon Zink, Jr.), Cynthia Colette. Tchr., Fairborn (Ohio) City Schs., 1954-61, Beavercreek Twp. Schs., Xenia, Ohio, 1962-65, Dayton (Ohio) City Schs., 1965-80; guidance counselor Belmont High Sch., Dayton, 1973-80. Clk.-treas. Village of Enon, 1961-62; mem. Bicentennial Com., City of Fairborn. Mem. NEA, Ohio Edn. Assn., Dayton Edn. Assn., DAR, Nat. Soc. Colonial Dames XVII Century, Nat. Soc. Daus. Am. Colonists, Mayflower Desc. in State of Ohio, Soc. Sons and Daus. of the Pilgrims, Nat. Soc. New Eng. Women, Women Desc. of Ancient and Hon. Arty. Co., Nat. Soc. Children of Am. Revolution (sr. state pres. 1978-82, sr. nat. v.p. Great Lakes region 1982-84), Nat. Soc. Dames of Ct. of Honor, Nat. Soc. Flagon and Trencher, Nat. Soc. Desc. of Colonial Clergy, Nat. Soc. Desc. Colonial Govs., Desc. Old Plymouth Colony, Nat. Soc. Daus. of Colonial Wars, Nat. Soc. U.S. Daus. of 1812, Delta Zeta. Home: 318 Ridgewood Dr Fairborn OH 45324

BUSH, GUY LOUIS, biology educator; b. Greenfield, Iowa, July 9, 1929; s. Guy Louis and Fausta Louise (Gibbs) B.; m. Dolores Theresa Alpisa, June 28, 1959; children—Lisa Alexandra, Guy Louis Gibbs, Eliana Elsbeth. B.S. in Entomology, Iowa State U., 1953; M.S. in Entomology, Va. Poly. Inst., 1960; Ph.D. in Biology, Harvard U., 1964. Research entomologist U.S. Dept. Agr., Mexico City, 1955-57; research asst. dept. entomology Va. Poly. Inst., Blacksburg, 1957-60; teaching fellow biology Harvard U., Cambridge, 1960-62, NSF predoctoral fellow, 1963-64; NIH postdoctoral fellow dept. zoology U. Melbourne, Parkville, Australia, 1964-66; asst. prof. zoology U. Tex., Austin, 1966-71, assoc. prof., 1971-76, prof., 1976-81; Hannah disting. prof. evolutionary biology, depts. zoology, entomology and Kellogg Biol. Sta., Mich. State U., East Lansing, 1981—; vis. research scientist Swiss Fed. Research Sta. for Arborculture, Horticulture and Vitaculture, Wadenswil, Switzerland, 1971; vis. prof. U. Sao Paulo, Brazil, 1977, Mus. Vertebrate Zoology, U. Calif.-Berkeley, 1977-78; cons. in field. Bd. dirs. Zero Population Growth, Inc., 1968-70, Austin Natural Sci. Ctr., 1972-75. Served to 1st lt. Med. Service Corps, U.S. Army, 1953-55. Guggenheim fellow, 1977-78; grantee NIH, NSF, 1966—. Fellow AAAS; mem. Soc. Study of Evolution (pres. 1981), Am. Soc. Naturalists (v.p. 1980), Genetics Soc. Am., Entomol. Soc. Am. (chmn. sect.), Cambridge Entomol. Club. Club: Ephraim Yacht (Wis.). Contbr. numerous articles to profl. jours. and chpts. to books.

BUSH, MARION HAROLD, JR., consultant; b. Joliet, Ill., Sept. 10, 1945; s. Marion Harold and Ella Mae (Deaton) B.; B.S. in Bus. Adminstrn., U. Md., 1969; m. Jeanne Carol Cofran; children—Jason Scott, Amy Sue. Apprentice, Liniger Co., Inc., Marion, Ind., 1964, supt., 1978—; v.p. B.&M. Tech. Cons., Marion, 1970-72, pres., 1973—. Public safety dir. City of Marion, 1975-76. Served with Spl. Forces U.S. Army, 1966-69; master sgt. U.S. Army N.G., 1972-82, 1st sgt., 1982-84, command sgt. maj., 1984—. Decorated Bronze Star, Combat Inf. badge, Joint Service Commendation medal; recipient commendation Mayor of Marion, 1976, Gov. Bowen, 1978. Mem. Am. Welding Soc., Ind. Vol. Firemen's Assn. (Midwest award, 1978, 79), Spl. Forces Assn., N.G. Assn., Plumbers and Pipefitters Local 166, Spl. Ops. Assn. Democrat. Mem. Bethel Ch. Lodges: Masons, Ft. Wayne Scottish Rite.

BUSH, MARTIN H., university administrator, museum director. B.A., SUNY-Albany, 1958, M.A., 1959; Ph.D., Syracuse U., 1966. Sr. historian N.Y. State Edn. Dept., Albany, 1961-62, cons., 1962-63; instr. Syracuse U., N.Y., 1963-65, asst. dean, 1965-70; assoc. prof. Wichita State U., Kans., 1970—, asst. v.p., 1970-74, dir. mus., 1974—, v.p. acad. resources, 1974—; art cons. Fourth Fin. Corp., Wichita, 1974—; dir. Mid-Am. Arts Alliance, Wichita, 1973-76; vice-chmn. Kans. Pub. TV, Wichita, 1973-79; mem. Wichita Air Mus. Task Force, 1984-85; vice chmn. Kans. Com. for the Humanities, Wichita, 1971-74, Univ. Press Kans., Wichita, 1972-73; dir. Wichita Festivals, Inc., 1972-74. Author: Ben Shahn: The Passion of Sacco and Vanzetti, 1968; Revolutionary Enigma, 1969; Doris Caesar, 1970; Ernest Trova, 1977; Robert Goodnough, 1981; Philip Reisman: The People Are His Passion, 1985; Roy Carruthers, 1985; Sculptures by Duane Hanson, 1985. Served with U.S. Army, 1953-54, Korea. Recipient George S. Patton medal and Legion of Honor, Govt. of Luxembourg, 1969; Recognition award Wichita State U. Alumni Assn., 1982; award of excellence Met. Arts Council, 1983; Excellence in the Arts award The Wichita Wagonmasters, 1984; named Wichita of Yr., The Wichita Sun, 1976, Outstanding Educator, Kans. Art Edn. Assn., 1979; Syracuse U. fellow, 1961-62, N.Y. State Regents War Service scholar, 1959-63. Mem. Phi Kappa Phi. Avocations: writing; art collection; tennis, skiing; travelling. Office: Wichita State U Box 46 Wichita KS 67208

BUSH, ROBERT EMERSON, university administrator, educator; b. St. Joseph, Mo., May 30, 1935; s. Emerson Ellsworth and Marie Anne (Doring) B.; m. Betty Jean Johnson, June 30, 1960; children—Gregory R., Jeffrey B., Traci A. B.S., N.W. Mo. State U., 1957; M.S. in Edn., U. Mo., 1967, Ed.D., 1973. Adminstrv. intern U. Mo.-Columbia, 1970-72; instr., dir. admissions N.W. Mo. State U., Maryville, 1968-70, dean admissions and student records, 1972-79, asst. to pres., 1977-79, v.p. environ. devel., 1979—; cons. Sta. WRC-TV, Washington, 1967, NASA, 1963-68, Stanford Research Internat. (Calif.), 1982. Vice chmn. Maryville Housing Authority, 1980; mem. dist. com. Boy Scouts Am., Maryville, 1981; v.p. Maryville Airport Bd., 1981—. Served to lt. col. Air N.G., 1956—. Recipient Gov.'s Disting. Service award State of Mo., 1978; Exec. of Year award Nat. Secs. Assn., 1981, Comdr.'s Disting. Service award 139th Tactical Airlift Group, 1983. Mem. Maryville C. of C. (pres. 1980, Leadership award 1980), Am. Council Edn., Assn. Phys. Plant Adminstrn., Res. Officers Assn. (pres. 1976-77), Nat. Assn. Coll. and Univ. Bus. Officers, Phi Delta Kappa. Methodist. Club: Eagle Nest Officers. Author: Aviation, The First Step, 1965, Developmental Process, 1973; Implementation and Mgmt. Jour., 1983. Office: NW Mo State Univ Maryville MO 64468

BUSH, SARGENT, JR., English educator; b. Flemington, N.J., Sept. 22, 1937; s. Sargent and Marion Louise (Roberts) B.; m. Cynthia Bird Greig, June 18, 1960; children—Charles Sargent, James Jonathan. A.B., Princeton U., 1959; M.A., U. Iowa, 1964, Ph.D., 1967. Asst. prof. English, Washington and Lee U., Lexington, Va., 1967-71; asst. prof. English, U. Wis., Madison, 1971-73, assoc. prof., 1973-79, prof., 1979—, chmn. dept. English, 1980-83; vis.

prof. U. Warwick, Coventry, Eng., 1983-84. Served with U.S. Army, 1959-60, 61-62. Fellow Coop. Program in Humanities, 1969-70, Am. Council Learned Socs., 1974, Inst. for Research in Humanities, 1978; grantee NEH, summer, 1969, Am. Philos. Soc., 1979. Mem. MLA, Nathaniel Hawthorne Soc., Assn. Documentary Editing, Cambridge Bibliog. Soc. Presbyterian. Author: (with George H. Williams, Norman Pettit and Winfried Herget) Thomas Hooker: Writings in England and Holland, 1626-1633, 1975; The Writings of Thomas Hooker: Spiritual Adventure in Two Worlds, 1980; (with Carl J. Rasmussen) The Library of Emmanuel Coll., Cambridge 1584-1637, 1986; contbr. articles on lit. to profl. jours. Home: 4146 Manitou Way Madison WI 53711 Office: Helen C White Hall Univ Wis Madison WI 53706

BUSHBACHER, CATHERINE ONOFRIO, educator; b. Chgo., Mar. 8, 1953; d. Louis and Margaret Sophie (Nichkolson) O.; B.S.E.E., DePaul U., 1974, M.A. with distinction, 1979; postgrad. U. Chgo., 1980—. Tchr., Bernard Moos Sch., Chgo. Bd. Edn., 1974-76, Duke Ellington Br. Sch., 1976-78, basic skills resource tchr. Burbank Sch., 1978-79, basic skills tchr., 1979-82, also volleyball coach, girl's basketball coach, tchr. sign lang.; tchr. Sayre Lang. Acad., Chgo., 1982—; instr. Inst. Fin. Edn. Cert. K-9 tchr., supr., adminstr., Ill; cert. K-3 tchr., prin., Chgo. Mem. Assn. for Supervision and Curriculum Devel., Council for Basic Edn., Assn. Tchrs. Educators, Chgo. Prins. Assn., Ella Flagg Young Assn., Aquin Guild, Gregorians (sec.), Phi Delta Kappa, Kappa Delta Phi. Clubs: Cath. Alumni, De Paul Booster. Office: 1850 N Newland Ave Chicago IL 60635

BUSHBAUM, MARIANNE LUCILLE, social worker; b. Portland, Oreg., June 10, 1923; d. Frank Olaf and Alma Bertina (Dahl) Walbom; student U. Minn., 1942-43, 75-76, St. Mary's Jr. Coll., 1976-77; m. Richard Leonard Bushbaum, Aug. 10, 1944; children—Holly, Timmi Li, Kimla, Joan, Jill, Dirk, Laurie. Mgr. Parkview Pain Rehab. Unit, Mpls., 1977-78; chem. dependency counselor Parkview Treatment Center, Mpls., 1977; counselor Parkview Pain Clinic, Mpls., 1978, asst. dir., 1979-80, program dir., 1981—. Eden Prairie (Minn.) chpt. pres. Am. Field Service, 1965-66. Mem. Internat. Platform Assn., Midwest Pain Soc., Assn. Humanistic Psychology, Minn. Assn. Rehab. Providers, AAAS. Republican. Lodge: Rosicrucian. Home: 14230 Chestnut Dr Eden Prairie MN 55344 Office: 3705 Park Center Blvd Minneapolis MN 55416

BUSHING, WILLIAM HENRY, acquisitions and mergers consulting co. exec.; b. Oak Park, Ill., Apr. 12, 1925; s. William G. and Rose (Hilgendorf) B.; student Mont. Sch. Mines, 1943-44; B.S. in Bus. Adminstrn., Northwestern U., 1946; postgrad. Harvard U., 1946; m. Barbara Gallond, Mar. 2, 1946; children—William Walter, Barbara Lee, Judith Ann, Nancy Jean. With A.B. Dick Co., Chgo., 1946-62; nat. sales mgr. Allstate Ins. Co., Northbrook, Ill., 1964-70; pres. W.H. Bushing & Co., Inc., Northbrook, 1970—. Served with U.S. Navy, 1943-46. Office: 1161 Walnut Ln Northbrook IL 60062

BUSHNER, THERESE, educational administrator; b. Allentown, Pa., Feb. 11, 1950. B.S., Duquesne U., 1972; M.A., Bowling Green State U., 1973; postgrad. U. Wis.-Milw. Dir. residence hall Bowling Green State U., Ohio, 1972-73; asst. dir. student activities Marquette U., Milw., 1973-78; trainer mgmt. devel. Blue Cross Blue Shield, Milw., 1978-80; adj. faculty Cardinal Stritch Coll., Milw., 1982—; faculty Waukesha County Tech. Inst., Pewaukee, Wis., 1980-83, dept. chmn., 1983—; evaluator Wis. Dept. Pub. Instrn., Madison, 1984. Mem. Assn. Study of Higher Edn., Am. Assn. Higher Edn., Nat. Orgn. Legal Problems in Edn., Phi Beta Kappa. Office: Waukesha County Tech Inst 800 Main St Pewaukee WI 53072

BUSHO, ELIZABETH MARY, nurse, educator; b. Ellendale, Minn., Feb. 26, 1927; d. Ruben Oscar and Lillian Katherine (Gahagan) Busho. R.N., Kahler Hosps. Sch. of Nursing, 1948. R.N., Minn. Operating room staff nurse, Minn., Calif., Colo., 1948-53; operating room head nurse, Mt. Sinai Hosp., Mpls., 1953-61; asst. supr. operating room St. Barnabas Hosp., Mpls., 1961-71; asst. dir. surg. services St. Mary's Hosp., Rochester, Minn., 1971-80, dir., 1980—; instr. Rochester Community Coll. Mem. editorial bd. Perioperative Nursing Quar. Adv. bd. Rochester Area Vocat. Tech. Inst., Rochester Community Coll. Republican. Methodist. Developer course in operating room nursing. Office: St Mary's Hosp 1216 2d St Rochester MN 55901

BUSKIRK, PHYLLIS RICHARDSON, economist; b. Queens, N.Y., July 19, 1930; d. William Edward and Amy A. Richardson; A.B. cum laude, William Smith Coll., 1951; m. Allen V. Buskirk, Sept. 13, 1950; children—Leslie Ann, William Allen, Carol Amy, Janet Helen. Clk. technician W.T. Grant Co., N.Y.C.; 1948-49; research asst. W.E. Upjohn Inst. for Employment Research, Kalamazoo, 1970-75, research assoc., 1976-83, sr. staff economist, 1983—. Mem. Civil Service Bd. City of Kalamazoo, 1977—, chmn., 1981—; trustee First Presbyterian Ch., Kalamazoo, 1984—, chmn., 1985; trustee Sr. Citizens Fund, Kalamazoo, 1984—. Mem. Am. Statis. Assn., Indsl. Relations Research Assn., Nat. Assn. Bus. Economists. Clubs: P.E.O., Kalamazoo Network. Co-editor Business Conditions in the Kalamazoo Area, Quar. Rev., 1979-84; asst. editor Bus. Outlook, The Quar. Report for W. Mich., 1984—. Office: 300 S Westnedge Ave Kalamazoo MI 49007

BUSS, RICHARD MILTON, economic development executive; b. Detroit, Sept. 26, 1942; s. Rex Herbert and Margaret Elizabeth (Hurson) B.; m. Bettie Jeanne Bollinger, Dec. 16, 1977; children—Justin Adams, Mathew Gordon. Student Mich. Tech. U., 1960; B.A., Western Mich. U., 1967; M.S., U. Mich., 1969; postgrad., Oreg. State U., 1970-71, Mich. State U., 1971-73. Instr. Western Mich. U., Kalamazoo, 1969-70; adminstrv. asst. Wayne County, Detroit, 1972-79; analyst SEM Health Assn., Southfield, Mich., 1979-80; econ. devel. dir. Downriver Community Conference, Southgate, Mich., 1980—. Campaign mgr. Congl. Campaign 16th Dist., Detroit, 1974; v.p. Mich. Emergency Services Health Council, 1978-79; bd. dirs. Mich. Environmental Council, Lansing, 1983—. Served with U.S. Army, 1962-65. Grantee Harder Found., 1984, U.S. Small Bus. Adminstrn., 1982, Nat. Trout and Salmon Found., 1982, Dept. HEW, 1975. Episcopalian. Club: Trout Unlimited (Vienna, Va.) (chmn. Mich. Council 1983—). Avocations: fishing, conservation, volunteer work. Home: 16803 Westmoreland Detroit MI 48219 Office: Downriver Community Conference 15100 North Line Southgate MI 48195

BUSSARD, H. KENNARD, architect; b. Clarinda, Iowa, July 9, 1936; s. Harry Kenneth and Lois (Davidson) B.; m. Judith Evans, June 14, 1958; children—Lisa, Kevin, Brian. B. Arch., Iowa State U., 1960. Registered architect, Iowa, Calif., Minn., Colo.; cert. Nat. Council Archtl. Registration Bds. Project architect Pereira-Jones & Emmons-Blurock-Ellerbroeck, Corona del Mar, Calif., 1963-65; assoc. Wilson-Williams, Corona del Mar, 1965-66; pres. Bussard/Dikis Assocs. Ltd., Des Moines, 1966—; dir. Hawkeye Bank & Trust; lectr. Iowa State U., also past chmn. dept. architecture profl. adv. bd. Past deacon and ruling elder Central Presbyn. Ch. Served as 1st lt., C.E., U.S. Army, 1961-63. Recipient profl. achievement citation in Engring., Iowa State U., 1977. Fellow AIA (chmn. nat. architecture for edn. com., past pres. Iowa chpt., past chmn. Iowa intern devel. program, nat. bd. dirs. 1985-87), Council Ednl. Facility Planners, Des Moines C. of C. (Bur. Econ. Devel., Friday Forum), U. No. Iowa Parents Assn. (bd. dirs. 1983-86), Order of Knoll, Phi Delta Theta. Republican. Club: Cyclone (Iowa State U.). Home: 7687 SW 52d Ave Des Moines IA 50321 Office: 300 Homestead Bldg 303 Locust St Des Moines IA 50309

BUSSEY, RONALD JOSEPH, real estate consultant; b. Lake Leelanau, Mich., Aug. 10, 1933; s. Urban John and Cecelia Agnes (Hahnenberg) B.; m. Linda Coyle, Jan. 7, 1961; children—Brian Keith, Kevin Scott, Scott Christopher, Eric Gregory. B.S. in Gen. Bus., U. Detroit, 1957; M.Retailing, U. Pitts., 1959. Cert. counselor of real estate. Retail market analyst Flannery & Assocs., Pitts., 1959-61; v.p., office mgr. Larry Smith & Co., Inc., Chgo., 1961-74; sr. v.p. Urban Projects, Inc., Los Angeles, 1974-77; pres., owner Metro-Econs., Inc., Northbrook, Ill., 1977-79; v.p. and dir. real estate counseling Arthur Rubloff & Co., Chgo., 1979-82; sr. v.p., dir. Landauer Assocs., Inc., Chgo., 1982-84; owner, pres. Metro-Econs., Inc., Chgo., 1984—; real estate broker. Bd. dirs. Greater State Street Council, 1983. Mem. Am. Soc. Real Estate Counselors, Urban Land Inst., Internat. Council Shopping Centers, Chgo. Real Estate Bd., Nat. Assn. Realtors, Ill. Assn. Realtors, Lambda Alpha. Republican. Roman Catholic. Clubs: Mid-Day, Realty (Chgo.). Home: 845 Greenwood Ave Glencoe IL 60022 Office: 123 W Madison St Suite 1200 Chicago IL 60602

BUSTER, WILLIAM FRANK, business equipment manufacturing company executive; b. Oak Creek, Colo., Nov. 20, 1927; s. Frank Lafayette and Francis (Lamb) B.; m. Evelyn Marie Johnson, Sept. 15, 1951; children—Barbara Anne, Patricia Johanna. B.S.E.E., Milw. Sch. Engring., 1953. With NCR Corp., 1974—, gen. mgr., San Diego, 1974-76, v.p., 1976-77, v.p., Dayton, Ohio, 1977-80, sr. v.p., 1980-83, exec. v.p., 1983—; dir. Computer Peripherals, Inc., Centronics Data Computer Corp. Served with USAF, 1946-49. Office: NCR Corp 1700 S Patterson Blvd Dayton OH 45479

BUTCHER, DOUGLAS BRENT, container company executive; b. Atlantic, Iowa, Aug. 8, 1946; s. Parker Holbrook and Majorie (Welch) B.; m. Sherry Flaugh, Dec. 1, 1979; children—Brandie, Liebchen, Malisa, Douglas Brent. A.A. in Bus., Des Moines Area Community Coll., 1982. Dock worker Great Plains Bag Co., Des Moines, 1968-79, shipping supr., 1979-82, shipping and warehouse supr., 1982-84; materials mgr. Stone Container Corp., Des Moines, 1984—. Served with USN, 1964-65. Democrat. Mem. Des Moines Area Community Coll. Alumni Assn. Club: Drake Mktg. (Des Moines). Avocations: home computer, photography, tropical fish. Home: 545 Gepke Pkwy Des Moines IA 50320 Office: Stone Container Corp Bag Div 2201 Bell Ave Des Moines IA 50315

BUTCHER, GRACE MARY, English language educator, writer; b. Rochester, N.Y., Jan. 18, 1934; d. Lyman Lorenzo and Mary Hindman (Spencer) Lamb; m. Robert Claar Butcher, Dec. 15, 1951 (div. 1967); children—Robert, Daniel. B.A., Hiram Coll., 1966; M.A., Kent State U., 1967. Instr. English, Cleve. State U., 1967-68; Assoc. prof. Kent State U., Geauga Campus, Burton, Ohio, 1968—; lectr. workshops, poetry readings, 1960—. Author: (poems) The Bright Colored Dark, 1966, More Stars Than Room For, 1966, Rumors of Ecstasy, 1971, 81, Before I Go Out on the Road, 1979. Contr. poems to lit. mags. Vis. poet Ohio Arts Council (creative writing award 1979). Grantee Nat. Endowment for Arts, 1969. Avocation: track (nat. champion 1958, 59, 60). Home: PO Box 274 Chardon OH 44024 Office: Geauga Campus Kent State Univ 14111 Claridon-Troy Rd Burton OH 44021

BUTIN, JAMES WALKER, physician; b. Fredonia, Kans., July 13, 1923; s. James A. and Berenice Marie (Walker) B.; A.B., U. Kans., 1944, M.D., 1947; M.S. in Medicine, U. Minn., 1952; m. Betty Belle Launder, June 29, 1949 (dec. Oct. 1981); children—Richard Edward, Philip Walker, Lucy Elizabeth, John Murray; m. Patricia L. Guinan, June 10, 1984. Intern, U. Kans. Med. Center, 1947-48; resident in pathology, 1948; fellow in internal medicine Mayo Found., 1949-52; practice medicine specializing in internal medicine and gastroenterology, Wichita, Kans., 1952—; mem. staff Wichita Clinic, St. Francis Hosp., Wesley Med. Center; asso. prof. Kans. U. Sch. Medicine, Wichita. Summerfield scholar, 1940-44. Diplomate Am. Bd. Internal Medicine (gastroenterology). Mem. A.C.P., AMA, Am. Gastroenterol. Assn., Am. Assn. History Medicine, Kans. Med. Soc., Sedgwick County Med. Soc. (past pres.) Christian Med. Soc., Wichita Med. Edn. Assn. (chmn. 1973-74), Mayo Alumni Assn., Wichita Audubon Soc. (past pres.), Kans. Ornithol. Soc. (past pres.), Phi Beta Kappa, Alpha Omega Alpha, Nu Sigma Nu, Beta Theta Pi. Republican. Episcopalian. Contbr. articles to med. jours. Home: 38 Mission Rd Wichita KS 67206 Office: 3311 E Murdock Ave Wichita KS 67208

BUTLER, BILLY BURCHELL, educator, researcher; b. Corinth, Miss., July 4, 1930; s. Chester Plaught and Nancy Cordellia (Blankenship) B.; m. Crystal Mae Bragg, Jan. 2, 1959; children—Clifton Eugene, Timothy Chad. B.S., Middle Tenn. State U., 1965; M.A., Mary Crest Coll., 1976; Ed.S., Western Ill. U., 1982. Child care supr. Tenn. Orphan Home, Spring Hill, 1963-65; welfare worker Tenn. Dept. Pub. Welfare, Franklin, 1965-68; tchr. Rock Falls (Ill.) Elem. Sch., 1968—; religious educator. Served with AC, U.S. Army, 1946-47. Mem. Rock Falls Elem. Edn. Assn., NEA, Ill. Edn. Assn., Assn. Supervision and Curriculum Devel. Democrat. Mem. Ch. of Christ.

BUTLER, DENNIS ARTHUR, psychologist, clinical mental health counselor; b. Kansas City, Kans., May 19, 1940; s. Ben Arthur and Naomi Mae (Bernard) B., Jr.; B.S., U. Kans., 1966; M.S., Emporia State U., 1969, Ed.S., 1976; Ph.D., Kans. State U., 1980; m. Reve Marie Gnuse, Sept. 2, 1978; 1 dau. by previous marriage, Diana Dawn. Acct., auditor Trans World Airlines, Kansas City, Mo., 1959-63; elem. tchr. Shawnee Mission (Kans.) Sch. Dist., 1966-69, tchr. psychology/anthropology, 1969-75, career devel. cons., 1975—; clin mental health counselor Inst. for Marriage & Family Counseling, 1979-82; pvt. practice counseling, 1982—. Lic. psychologist. Mem. NEA, Greater Kansas City Psychol. Assn., Am. Psychol. Assn., Am. Assn. Counseling and Devel., Am. Mental Health Counselors Assn. Kans. Mental Health Counselors Assn. (pres.). Republican. Episcopalian. Office: 7920 Ward Pkwy Suite 207 Kansas City MO 64114

BUTLER, EDWARD DEAN, lens crafting company executive; b. Phila., Jan. 31, 1945; s. Edward E. and Christella May (Campbell) B.; m. Brenda Benzar, Sept. 13, 1969; 1 child, Kira Benzar. B.S., Bob Jones U., 1965; M.S., Mich. State U., 1969, M.B.A., 1968. Assoc. advt. mgr. Procter & Gamble, Cin., 1969-82; pres. Precision Lens Crafters, Cin., 1982—. Republican. Avocation: antique auto racing. Home: 4325 Drake Rd Cincinnati OH 45243 Office: Precision Lens Crafters 10200 Alliance Rd Cincinnati OH 45242

BUTLER, GERALDINE HEISKELL (GERRI), designer, artist; b. Detroit, Sept. 6, 1930; d. Artist Kavassel and Geraldine Gentle (Heiskell) B.; student Wright Jr. Coll., 1946; B.E., Chgo. U., 1948; B.A. in Edn. (Delta Sigma Theta Scholar), Chgo. Art Inst., 1949, M.A. in Edn., 1950; postgrad. Harvard U., 1962-64. Tchr. pub. elementary schs., Chgo., 1949-52; tchr. art Chgo. pub. high schs., 1953-61; supr. art Chgo. Bd. Edn., 1962-75; graphic art and media coordinator, dept. instrn. Chgo. Bd. Edn., 1976-77; founder, prin. Gehebu-AK, design cons. services, Chgo., 1976—; founder, prin. Butler Studios, creative designer, Chgo., 1977—; one-man shows include: Saxon Gallery, Chgo., Roosevelt Hotel, N.Y.C., Henri IV Restaurant, Cambridge, Mass., Hilton Trinidad, B.W.I., Goldstein Gallery, Chgo.; group shows include: Triangle Gallery, Chgo., McCormick Pl., Chgo., Hyde Park Art Center, Chgo., Ill. State Fair, Peninsula Exhbts., Door County, Wis.; represented in permanent collections: rental gallery Art Inst. Chgo., Huntington Hartford Collection, N.Y.C.; judge numerous exhbts. and competitions; art cons. and designer. Mem. Ill. wing CAP, 1963—. Huntington Hartford fellow, 1956-58. Mem. Internat., Ill., Nat. art edn. assns., Western Arts Assn., Am. Craftsmen Assn., Alumni Chgo. Art Inst., Soc. Typog. Arts, Artists Guild Chgo., Chgo. Soc. Artists, N. Shore Art League, Hyde Park Art Center, Evanston Art Center, USAF Art Corps, Triangle-Lincoln Park Art Center, Am. Youth Hostels, Delta Kappa Gamma, Delta Sigma Theta. Episcopalian. Office: PO Box 11360 Chicago IL 60611

BUTLER, JAMES MARTIN, educator; b. Freeport, Ill., Apr. 20, 1948; s. Martin Harvey and Elizabeth Ann (Hillebrecht) B.; B.S., U. Ill., 1970; M.S., Northeastern Ill. U., 1978; M.A., Chgo. State U., 1982; m. Ruth Ann Dratwa, Dec. 17, 1972; children—Dawn Marie, Christine Ann, Kimberly Ann, James Martin, Jennifer Lynn. Tchr. sci., chmn. dept. Thornton Fractional North High Sch., Calumet City, Ill., 1979—. Vice pres. Holy Name Soc., St. Andrew Ch., 1979-81, pres., 1982-83. Mem. Nat. Assn. Biology Tchrs., Am. Assn. Physics Tchrs., Assn. Supervision and Curriculum Devel., Ill. Assn. Biology Tchrs., Ill. Chess Assn., U.S. Chess Fedn., U. Ill. Alumni Assn. (life), Northeastern Ill. U. Alumni Assn., Chgo. State U. Alumni Assn. Club: KC (4 deg.). Home: 426 155th St Calumet City IL 60409 Office: 755 Pulaski Rd Calumet City IL 60409

BUTLER, KENNETH B., business exec.; b. Richland, Mich., Aug. 27, 1902; s. Ross S. and Jennie (Blain) B.; B.A., U. Wis., 1925; m. Wilma Steinberg, Nov. 5, 1925; 1 son, Roger Lee; m. Doris Sibigtroth, 1969. Reporter, Madison (Wis.) Capital Times, 1923-25; editor Mendota (Ill.) Sun-Bull., 1925-27; pub. Constantine (Mich.) Advertiser Record, 1927-31; mgr. Conco Press, Mendota, 1931-41; pres. Wayside Press, 1941-78; pres. Kenneth B. Butler and Assos., 1938—; founder Butler Typo-Design Research Center, 1951, Time-Was Village Mus., 1967; lectr. Medill Sch. Journalism, Northwestern U., 1950-75; bus. mgr. P.E.O. Record, 1931-78. Gen. chmn. Mendota Centennial Jubilee, 1953, Mendota Autorama, 1955, 57, 59, 61, Constantine (Mich.) Centennial, 1928; mem. Sweet Corn Festival Com., 1962; chmn. Nat. Glidden Tour., 1963. Bd. dirs. LaSalle County unit Am. Cancer Soc. Named Kiwanis Man of Year, 1953; recipient Community Service award C. of C., 1976. Mem. Mendota Athletic Booster Soc., Ill. State, Mendota (dir. 1947-53) chambers of commerce, Am. Bell Assn., Farm Bur., Ill. Mfrs. Assn., Mark Twain Soc., LaSalle County Hist. Soc., Sigma Delta Chi. Republican. Presbyterian (elder). Elk. Clubs: Horatio Alger (co-founder, pres. 1965-67); Antique Automobile Am. (dir. Ill. region, pres. 1960-61, treas. 1967-68, nat. bd. dirs., dir. activities Central region), Steam Car, Classic Car, Pierce Arrow Society, Rolls Royce Owners, Model T Ford, Horseless Carriage, Men's Garden Am. Author: Headline Design, 1949; Effective Illustration, 1952; 101 Layouts, 1954; Double Spreads, 1955; Back of the Book Makeup, 1957; Ken Butler's Layout Scrapbook, 1958; Display Type Faces, 1959; Back of the Book Makeup, 1960; Borders, Boxes and Ornamentation, 1961; How To Stage an Oldtime Auto Event, 1961. Co-author: Magnificent Whistlestop. Editor Sidelights. Contbr. articles to profl. publs. Speaker and lectr. Home: 1325 W Burlington Rd Mendota IL 61342 Office: 700 14th Ave Mendota IL 61342

BUTLER, KERN, constrn. co. exec.; b. Peru, Ind., July 15, 1936; s. M. Auber and Ruth H. Butler, B.S., Ind. U., 1962; m. Anna Mae Greenfield, July 31, 1955; children—Victoria Elizabeth, Roxanne Dawn, Teena Gay. Bookkeeper, M.A. Butler, Spencerville, Ind., 1955-62; gen. mgr. Butler & Butler Constrn. Co., Auburn, Ind., 1962-64, sec., treas., gen. mgr., 1964—; pres. Butler Real Estate, Inc., 1972—; bus. mgr. Vanguard Pub. Co., Auburn, 1968—. Trustee, Eckhart Public Library, 1968—, treas., 1972—; trustee Auburn Presbyterian Ch., 1966-69. Republican. Clubs: Fort Wayne Summit, Gideons. Home: 207 S Dewey St Auburn IN 46706 Office: 207 S West St Auburn IN 46706

BUTLER, LAVONNE RUTH GRASLIE (MRS. WARREN ELMER BUTLER), former mayor, former newspaper publisher; b. Faith, S.D., Aug. 22, 1922; d. Ludwig Martin and Lilly Regina (Ness) Graslie; first grade certificate Spearfish Normal Sch., 1942; m. Warren Elmer Butler, Dec. 29, 1942; children—Richard, James. Tchr., Cherry Creek Dist. 2, Ziebach County, S.C., 1943-45; sec. to supr. schs., Faith, 1966-68; editor, pub. Faith Independent, 1969-79; mayor City of Faith, 1981-85. Pres., PTA, 1953-54. Mem. Republican State Central Com., 1970—. Mem. Nat. Newspaper Assn., S.D. Press Assn., C. of C. (v.p. 1970—), Beta Sigma Phi. Methodist. Mem. Order Eastern Star. Co-editor Faith Country Book, 1960, editor, 1984; editor, project dir. Faith Country Heritage Book, 1985. Home: Faith SD 57626

BUTLER, LINDA CAROL, artist; b. Houston, Dec. 27, 1948; d. James Bernard and Annie Louise (Goodman) B. Student Stephen F. Austin Tchrs. Coll., 1967, Birmingham (Ala.) So. Coll., 1969; B.F.A., Pratt Inst., 1971. Owner, designer Fresh Ideas Needlepoint Co., Houston, 1971-73, Design and Illustration Studios, Houston, 1970-77, Bright Idea Gallery, 1975-76; staff artist Alban Corp., Houston, 1973; artist House of Coleman, Houston, 1975-76; artist Houston Creative Kitchens, 1977, Houston Post 1977, Hallmark Cards Co., Kansas City, Mo., 1977—; lectr., seminar leader artistic creativity. Vol. Easter Seal Soc., Am. Cancer Soc.; vol. clown, art instr. Children's Mercy Hosp., Kansas City; lay minister Unity Sch. Practical Christianity. Recipient 1st prize Easter Seal Design Contest, 1965; Radcliffe Club Award Excellence in Writing, 1967; Scholastic Mag. Gold Key Award, 1966. Mem. Kansas City Artist's Coalition, Friends of Art, Nelson Art Gallery. Club: Toastmasters. Designer, illustrator numerous books.

BUTLER, LOUIS ALLEN, sales, marketing manager grain trade company; b. Independence, Ky., June 6, 1935; s. Allen Woodrow and Catherine (Brown) B.; m. Muriel Ann Shepherd, Jan. 25, 1964; children—Douglas , Scott, David. B.S. in Agrl. Engring., U. Ky., 1962; M.S. in Econs., N.C. State U., 1976. Test engr. Internat. Harvester, Hinsdale, Ill., 1962-65; v.p., mgr. Culligan Soft Water, Zeeland, Mich., 1965-71; plant mgr., chief engr. Maes, Inc., Holland, Mich., 1971-72; sales engr. Aeroglide Corp., Raleigh, N.C., 1972-77; sales and mktg. mgr. Dickey-john Corp., Auburn, Ill., 1977—; pres. Grain Equipment Mfg. Assn., Chgo., 1984—. Contbr. articles to profl. jours. Vestryman St. Perers Episcopal Ch., Bettendorf, Iowa, 1979-81, Christ Episcopal Ch., Springfield, Iowa, 1983—; soccer ofcl. YMCA, Bettendorf, 1978-80, YMCA, Springfield, 1981-83; mem. Springfield Art Assn., 1981—, Vachel Linsey Assn., Springfield, 1981—. Served with U.S. Army, 1959-61. Mem. Internat. Water Conditioning Assn. (bd. dirs. 1968-70), Am. Soc. Agrl. Engring., Am. Assn. Cereal Chemists, Grain Elevator and Processing Soc., Am. Feed Industries Assn. (bd. dirs. 1984—), Farm Implement Equipment Inst. (bd. dirs. 1985—), Cereal Chemistry Mktg. Internat. (bd. dirs. 1985—), Assn. Operating Millers. Avocations: travel, oil and geology work, reading. Home: 1936 Noble Ave Springfield IL 62704 Office: Dickey-john Corp PO Box 10 Auburn IL 62615

BUTLER, LOUIS BENNETT, JR., lawyer; b. Chgo., Feb. 15, 1952; s. Louis Bennett and Gwendolyn (Prescott) B.; m. Irene Marianne Hecht, Aug. 30, 1981; children—Jessica Marianne, Erika Nicole. B.A., Lawrence U., 1973; J.D., U. Wis.-Madison, 1977. Bar: Ill. 1978, Wis. 1979, U.S. Dist. Ct. (no. dist.) Ill. 1978, U.S. Dist. Ct. (ea. dist.) Wis. 1979, U.S. Ct. Appeals (7th cir.) 1979, U.S. Supreme Ct. 1983. Teaching asst. legal writing U. Wis. Law Sch., Madison, 1974-76; patient rights adv. Bur. Mental Health, Madison, 1976; hearing examiner, 1976-77; legal intern Prisoner's Legal Assistance, Chgo., 1977-78; atty. Independence Bank, Chgo., 1978-79; appellate atty. Office State Pub. Defender, Milw., 1979—. Active South Shore Community Orgn., Chgo., 1978; pres. adv. bd. Adaptive Behavior Ctr., Chgo. Reed Mental Health Ctr., 1978. Mem. Wis. Bar Assn., Ill. State Bar Assn., Wis. Black Lawyer's Assn. (treas. 1984-85). Democrat. Roman Catholic. Office: Office State Pub Defender 819 N 6th St Room 821 Milwaukee WI 53203

BUTLER, OWEN BRADFORD, chemical company executive; b. Lynchburg, Va., Nov. 11, 1923; s. James Herbert and Ida Virginia (Garbee) B.; A.B., Dartmouth, 1947; m. Erna Bernice Dalton, Mar. 7, 1945; children—Nancy Butler Brown, James. With Procter & Gamble Co., Cin., 1945—, v.p. sales, 1968-70, v.p., group exec., 1970-73, exec. v.p., 1973-74, vice chmn. bd., 1974-81, chmn. bd. dirs., 1981—; dir. Hosp. Corp. Am., Armco, No. Telecom Ltd. Trustee Good Samaritan Hosp. Served with USNR, 1941-45, 50-51. Mem. Phi Beta Kappa. Republican. Clubs: Metropolitan (Washington); Queen City (Cin.). Home: 4346-S State Route 123 Morrow OH 45152 Office: PO Box 599 Cincinnati OH 45201

BUTLER, PAUL THURMAN, college administrator; b. Springfield, Mo., Nov. 17, 1928; s. Willard Drew and Verna Lois (Thurman) B.; Th.B., Ozark Bible Coll., 1961, M.Bibl. Lit., 1973; m. Gale Jynne Kinnard, Nov. 20, 1948; children—Sherry Lynne, Mark Stephen. Non-commd. officer U.S. Navy, 1946-56, mem. staff Amphibious Forces, Pacific, 1947-51, guided missile unit 41, Point Mugu, Calif., 1951-56; ret., 1956; ordained to ministry Christian Ch., 1958; minister Washington Christian Ch., Lebanon, Mo., 1958-60; dean admissions Ozark Christian Coll., Joplin, Mo., 1960—, prof. Bible and philosophy, 1960—. Mem. Am. Legion, SAR, Mo. Territorial Pioneers. Republican. Author: The Gospel of John, 1961; The Minor Prophets, 1968; Daniel, 1976; Isaiah, 3 vols., 1978; Esther, 1979; The Gospel of Luke, 1981 (trans. into Korean, French, Portuguese, East Indian-Tamil); Revelation, 1982; I Corinthians, 1984. Home: 2502 Utica St Joplin MO 64801 Office: 1111 N Main St Joplin MO 64801

BUTLER, WILFORD ARTHUR, fraternity executive; b. Grand Rapids, Mich., Apr. 17, 1937; s. Wilford A. and Dorothy (French) B.; B.A., Western Mich. U., 1961; M.B.A., Fla. Atlantic U. Dir. pub. relations Preferred Ins. Co., Grand Rapids, 1961-62; asst. to chmn. Delta Upsilon fraternity, N.Y.C., 1962, exec. sec., Indpls., 1963-76, exec. dir., 1976—; advisor Mid-Am. Interfrat. Assn., 1965—. Mem. Am. Coll. Frat. Bicentennial Commn. study, 1975-77; bd. dirs. Greater Indpls. Republican Fin. Com., 1981—. Recipient Salisbury-Scott award Tau Kappa Epsilon, 1975, citation of honor Theta Chi, appreciation citation Delta Chi, 1979; Sagamore of Wabash award State of Ind., 1982. Mem. Assn. Coll. Frats. (pres. 1974), Frat. Execs. Assn. (sec., editor 1974, pres. 1976-77), Commn. on Fraternity Research (treas. 1972-75), Am. Soc. Assn. Execs. (cert.; mem. editors and pubs. sect. adv. bd., chmn. membership dirs. sect. council bd. 1979-82, mem. membership promotion com. 1979-81, Key award 1982), Ind. Soc. Assn. Execs. (chmn. cert. program 1979-81, bd. dirs., mem. exec. com. 1980; Disting. Service award 1980, pres.-elect 1982), Ind. Conv. and Visitors Assn. (bd. dirs. 1981—), Delta Upsilon (editor monthly Newstrends 1971—, quar. 1973—). Clubs: Indpls. Alumni of Delta Upsilon, Columbia (gen. membership chmn. 1979—, dir. 1981—, sec. 1982-84 chmn. Columbian Lit. and Arts Found. Inc., pres. Columbian Hist. Found. Inc.) (Indpls.). Author: Executive Compensation Trends. Editor, Our Record, 1963—, Provision of Leadership corp. officers guide. Office: PO Box 40108 Indianapolis IN 46240

BUTLER, WILLIAM JOHN, biostatistics educator; b. San Francisco, July 16, 1952; s. Francis Xavier and Eileen Evelyn (Ricks) B.; m. Janice Lynn Patton, July 5, 1980. B.A. in Math., U. Calif.-Irvine, 1974; M.S. in Biostats., U. Wash., 1977, Ph.D. in Biostats., 1979. Research asst. U. Wash., Seattle, 1974-79; asst. prof. U. Mich., Ann Arbor, 1979—; advisor Toxic Substance Control Com., Lansing, Mich., 1984-85; ad hoc mem. occupational health study sect. NIH, Bethesda, Md., 1984; lectr. EPA, Washington, 1985. Contbr. articles on biostats. and environ. epidemiology to profl. jours. Vol. Neighborhood Sr. Services, Ann Arbor, 1983, Los Angeles Olympic Organizing Com.,

1984. Trainee NIH, 1975-79. Mem. Biometric Soc., Am. Statis. Assn. (officer local chpt. 1980), Soc. Epidemiol. Research Am. Pub. Health Assn. Clubs: Friends of the Irvine Crew (Calif.); Stanford Crew (Palo Alto, Calif.). Home: 120 Crest St Ann Arbor MI 48103 Office: Dept Biostats Sch Pub Health U Mich 109 S Observatory Way Ann Arbor MI 48109

BUTLER, WILLIAM JOSEPH, JR., ins. broker; b. Chgo., Feb. 24, 1942; s. William Joseph and Emily Jane (Mockenhaupt) B.; B.S., Coll. of the Holy Cross, Worcester, Mass., 1964; M.B.A., St. Louis U., 1969; m. Helen Katherine O'Malley, Aug. 28, 1965 (div. 1976); children—Charlotte Anne, Emily Jane. Mgmt. trainee Clinton E. Frank Inc., Chgo., 1969-70; dist. agt. Prudential Ins. Co., Evanston, Ill., 1970-74, spl. agt., Skokie, Ill., 1974—. Mem. fin. com. St. Mary's Ch., Lake Forest, Ill., 1980-81. Served to capt. USAF, 1964-68. C.L.U. Mem. Chgo. Assn. Life Underwriters. Republican. Roman Catholic. Home: 570 N Sheridan Rd Lake Forest IL 60045 Office: Prudential Insurance Co 5150 Golf Rd Skokie IL 60076

BUTTEL, THEODORE LYLE, science educator; b. Centerville, Iowa, May 26, 1939; s. Peter George and Matida Maxine (Green) B.; B.A., U. Iowa, 1966; M.A., N.E. Mo. State U., 1970; Ph.D., Walden U., 1979; children—Lisa Michele, Patricia Ann, Denise Kathleen. Tchr. sci., math. English Valley's Schs., North English, Iowa, 1960-67; tchr. sci., chmn. dept. sci. Washington Sch., Ottumwa (Iowa) Public Schs., 1967-72, tchr. sci., interdisciplinary team leader Walsh Sch., 1972-75, tchr. sci., chmn. dept. sci., 1975—, tchr. sci. Ottumwa High Sch., 1982-85; mem. Iowa Instructional and Profl. Devel. Com., 1972-74; trainer for Performance Learning Systems, 1975—; human relations cons. and tchr. Area Edn. Agy. #15, 1977-81, vice chmn. staff devel. com., 1977-80; county chmn. and mem. Iowa Bd. Polit. Action for Edn., 1966-81; dir. Washington Ednl. Field Trips for Walsh Students, 1972-81; cons., trainer in field. Mem. Nat. TEACH Cadre (charter), U. Iowa Alumni Assn. (life), N.E. Mo. State U. Alumni Assn. (life), Ottumwa Edn. Assn., Iowa State Edn. Assn. (chmn. bd. State Unit 9 Ednl. Div. 1973-75), NEA (life), Nat. Sci. Tchrs. Assn., Iowa Assn. Supervision and Curriculum Devel., Assn. Supervision and Curriculum Devel., Assn. Tchr. Educators, Phi Delta Kappa. Democrat. Roman Catholic. Home: 122 E Alta Vista Ottumwa IA 52501 Office: 549 E 4th St Ottumwa IA 52501

BUTTERS, ELIZABETH AGNES, epidemiology nurse; b. Rock County, Wis., Apr. 30, 1934; d. Thomas James and Elizabeth Margaret (Doran) B. Grad. Mercy Hosp. Sch. Nursing, 1956. Staff nurse Mercy Hosp. of Janesville (Wis.), 1956-61, head nurse, 1961-64, asst. dir. nursing, 1964-70, epidemiology and employee health nurse, 1971—; participant Hosp. Accreditation Standards Program. Mem. Mercy Hosp. Alumni Assn., Assn. for Practitioners in Infection Control. Democrat. Roman Catholic. Home: 2210 Mineral Point Ave Janesville WI 53545 Office: Mercy Hosp Janesville 1000 Mineral Point Ave 5th Floor Janesville WI 53545

BUTTERY, JANET LOUISE, movie theatre co. exec.; b. Columbus, Ohio, May 19, 1953; d. Thomas William and Pauline Adelaide (Burgess) B.; B.A., U. Kans., 1975, M.B.A., 1978; Troisième Degré, Université de Bordeaux (France), 1975. Real estate devel. Am. Multi Cinema, Kansas City, Mo., 1978—. Home: 7510 Lamar St Apt 66 Prairie Village KS 66208 Office: 106 W 14th St Suite 1700 Kansas City MO 64105

BUTTRAM, JAMES DAVID, religious publishing company executive; b. Springfield, Mo., May 7, 1941; s. Lester Leo and Ethel Bernice (Thiemer) B. B.S., Central Mo. State U., Warrensburg, 1971. Police officer City of Independence, Mo., 1965; controller Gospel Tract Soc. Inc., Independence, 1965—; pres. Bethel Bible Sch., Port au Prince, Haiti, 1976—; supt. Ebenezer Christian Schs., Haiti, 1983—. Author numerous religious tracts. Editor: Gospel Tract Harvester, 1978—. Served with USAFR, 1964-70. Mem. Independence C. of C. Republican. Mem. Assembly of God Ch. Club: Kiwanis (pres. 1982-83). Office: Gospel Tract Soc Inc 1105 S Fuller St Independence MO 64050

BUTTREY, DONALD WAYNE, lawyer; b. Terre Haute, Ind., Feb. 6, 1935; s. William Edgar and Nellie Madaline (Vaughn) B.; B.S., Ind. State U., 1956; J.D., Ind. U., 1961; children—Greg, Alan, Jason. Bar: Ind. 1961. Law clk. to chief judge U.S. Dist. Ct. So. Dist. Ind., 1961-63; mem. firm McHale, Cook & Welch, P.C., Indpls., 1963—; chmn. Central Region, IRS-Bar Liaison Com., 1983-84. Chmn. Marion County Dem. Fin. Com., 1984—. Served with AUS, 1956-58. Mem. Am. (coms. taxation, real property, probate and trust law sect.), Ind. (chmn. taxation sect. 1982-83, mem. probate sect.), Indpls. (chmn. legal econs. com. 1985, mem. long-range planning com. 1985—), 7th Circuit bar assns., Ind. Soc. Chgo., Phi Delta Phi, Theta Chi. Methodist. Clubs: Indpls. Athletic (bd. dirs. 1982—), Univ., Highland Country. Editor Ind. Law Jour., 1960-61. Home: 2215 Rome Dr Indianapolis IN 46208 Office: 1122 Chamber of Commerce Bldg 320 N Meridian St Indianapolis IN 46204

BUTZ, BEVERLY GRAHAM, financial executive; b. Chgo., Nov. 10, 1948; d. William Otto and Catherine (Graham) B.; student Hollins Coll., 1966-68; B.A., U. Mich., 1970; M.B.A. program, U. Chgo., 1975-78. Programmer trainee No. Trust Co., Chgo., 1970-72; analyst/programmer Zurich Ins. Co., Chgo., 1972-74; programmer/analyst First Nat. Bank of Chgo., 1974-76, lead programmer/analyst, 1976-79, project mgr., 1979-82, internat. product devel. officer, 1982—, officer of corp., 1981—, asst. v.p., 1984—. Bd. dirs. Lakeview Mental Health Council; active Jr. League of Chgo., 1970-79; vol. Presbyn. St. Luke's Hosp., Chgo., 1970-72, Planned Parenthood, 1980; vol. Una Puerta Abierta, 1972-74, treas. cookbook com., 1975-76; mem. Jr. Bd. of Youth Guidance, 1977-79. Mem. Nat. Assn. Bank Women, Nat. Assn. Female Execs. Congregationalist. Club: Midtown Tennis. Office: 1 First Nat Plaza Chicago IL 60670

BUZBY, SCOTT HAINES, tire and rubber company executive; b. Phila., Feb. 5, 1929; s. Jesse Milton and Helene B.; m. Anne Elizabeth Ellis, July 14, 1956; children—Cynthia, Scott H. B.A., Middlebury Coll., 1951. With Goodyear Tire & Rubber Co., Akron, Ohio, 1954-56, Goodyear Internat. Corp., 1956-57, Brazil, 1957-62, sales mgr., Colombia, 1962-66, sales dir., Australia, 1966-67, mng. dir., 1967-71, v.p., Akron, 1971-74, asst. to pres., 1974-76, pres. Kelly-Springfield, 1976-78, exec. v.p., pres. tire div., 1978-84; pres., cheif exec. officer Goodyear Can. Inc., Toronto, Ont., 1984—. Served with USCG, 1951-54. Mem. Rubber Assn. Can. Clubs: Portage Country (Akron); Mississauga Golf and Country (Toronto, Ont.). Office: 21 Four Seasons Pl Islington ON M9B 6G2 Canada

BYARS, ANNIE MARIE, educator; b. Decatur, Ala., Nov. 19, 1944; d. Alphonso and Mary Ann (Bevels) B.; B.S., Ala. Agrl. and Mech. U., 1967; M.A., U. Detroit, 1975; postgrad. Wayne State U., 1972-73, Mich. State U., 1982-84. Vol., U.S. Peace Corps, Jamaica, West Indies, 1967-69; tchr. Lewis Bus. Coll., Detroit, 1970; life ins. sales agt. Franklin Life Ins. Co., Detroit, 1978-81; tchr. bus. edn. Detroit Public Schs., 1970—. Mem. Nat. Bus. Edn. Assn., Am. Vocational Assn., North-Central Bus. Edn. Assn.

BYBEE, RODGER WAYNE, education educator; b. San Francisco, 1942; s. Wayne and Genevieve (Mungon) B.; B.A., Colo. State Coll., 1966; M.A., U. No. Colo., 1969; Ph.D., NYU, 1975; m. Patricia Brovsky, May 28, 1966. Sch. tchr. public schs. Greeley, Colo., 1965-66; sci. instr. U. No. Colo., 1966-70; teaching fellow NYU, N.Y.C., 1970-72; instr. in edn. Carleton Coll., Northfield, Minn., 1972-75, asst. prof., 1975-81, assoc. prof. edn., dept. chmn. 1981—; cons. D.C. Heath Spl. Edn. for Elem. Sci., Nat. Assessment of Ednl. Progress, Biol. Scis. Curriculum Study. Bd. dirs. Acid Rain Found., Ctr. Sci. and Tech. Edn. Fellow AAAS (mem.-at-large); mem. Nat. Sci. Tchrs. Assn., Nat. Assn. Biology Tchrs., Nat. Assn. for Research in Sci. Teaching, World Future Soc. Editorial bd. Jour. of Research in Science Teaching, The Am. Biology Tchr.; co-author: Becoming a Better Elementary Science Teacher, 1975, Becoming a Secondary School Science Teacher, 1981, Violence, Values and Justice in the Schools, 1982; Piaget for Educators, 1982; Science and Society, 1984; Teaching About Science and Society, 1984; Redesigning Science and Technology Education, 1984; Human Ecology: A Perspective for Biology Education, 1985; editor, contbr. articles to numerous profl. publs. Home: 212 Maple Northfield MN 55057 Office: Education Dept Carleton College Northfield MN 55057

BYERLY, DEAN LYLE, mechanics instructor; b. Fayette, Iowa, Aug. 4, 1936; s. William Henry and Vesta Lucille (Meyer) B.; m. Phyllis Maye Follmer, Aug. 4, 1962; 1 son, Robert Dean. B.S., Upper Iowa U., 1966; postgrad. U. No. Iowa, 1982, Iowa State U., 1972. Service instr. Allis-Chalmers Mfg. Co., Des Moines, 1966-67; shop mgr. Brubaker Co., Prairie City, Iowa, 1967-68; instr. Northeast Iowa Tech. Inst., Calmar, Iowa, 1968—. Bd. dirs. Ft. Atkinson Library, 1976—; mem. ann. observance com. Friends Ft. Atkinson Hist., 1976—. Served with USAF, 1956-60. Recipient Disting. Service award Iowa Future Farmers Assn., 1982; Disting. Service award Northeast Iowa Dist. Future Farmers Assn., 1975. Mem. Assn. Diesel Specialists, Am. Vocat. Assn., Nat. Vocat. Agr. Tchrs. Assn., Iowa Vocat. Assn., Iowa Vocat. Agr. Tchrs. Assn. Methodist. Home: Route 2 Fort Atkinson IA 52144 Office: Northeast Iowa Tech Inst Calmar IA 52132

BYERLY, ELEANOR LILL, librarian; b. Durango, Colo., Jan. 26, 1940; d. John Louis and Ethel S. (Dillabaugh) Lill Lynch; m. Donald G. Byerly, July 26, 1960; children—Scott, Shannon. B.A., Ohio Dominican Coll., 1979; M.L.S., Kent State U., 1980. Reference librarian Ohio State U., Columbus, 1980-81; adminstrv. asst. Columbus Area Library Info. Council Ohio, 1981-82; reference and bibliographic instrn. librarian Pontifical Coll. Josephinum, Columbus, 1982—; instr. library sci., Ohio Dominican Coll. Trustee Delaware County Dist. Library; pres. Friends of Delaware County Dist. Library; mem. bd. Delaware Children's Home. Mem. Ohio Library Assn., ALA, Franklin County Library Assn., Beta Phi Mu, Delta Epsilon Sigma. Republican. Roman Catholic. Home: 169 Deven Rd Delaware OH 43015 Office: Pontifical College Josephinum 7835 High St Columbus OH 43085

BYERS, HAROLD RALPH, violinist; b. Portland, Oreg., Aug. 16, 1944; s. Irwin Lyle and Elma Vera (Parkhurst) B.; m. Dorothy Furber, Dec. 26, 1970; children—Eric Furber, Mark Parkhurst. B.Mus., Oberlin Coll., 1966; postgrad. Juilliard Sch. Mus., 1966-68. Violinist, Chamber Symphony Phila., 1968, Syracuse (N.Y.) Symphony and Cazenovia String Quartet, 1968-70, Atlanta Symphony and Atlanta Spring Quartet, 1971-72, Columbus Symphony and Columbus String Quartet, 1972-74, Cin. Symphony Orch., 1974—; recital debut, Washington, 1984; mem. faculty Miami U., Oxford, Ohio, 1980—; mem. Baroque Chamber players, 1979—; treas. Cin. Symphony Players Com., 1980-82, mem. artistic adv. com., 1980; pvt. violin tchr. Mem. bd. U Kids Coop., 1981-82. Mem. Am. Fedn. Musicians, Historic Keyboard Soc. Office: 1241 Elm St Cincinnati OH 45210

BYERS, STEPHEN WALTER, dentist; b. Freeport, Ill., June 1, 1946; s. Willard D. and Mary June (Grassau) B.; m. Debby Lynn Wasmund, Mar. 16, 1978; children—Stephanie Diane, Erich Stephen. D.D.S., U. Iowa, 1971. Diplomate Nat. Bd. of Dental Examiners; Iowa State Bd. of Dental Examiners. Gen. practice dentistry Community Health Care Ctr., Davenport, Iowa, 1982-84; gen. practice dentistry, LeClaire, Iowa, 1984—. Bd. dirs. YMCA, Davenport, Iowa, 1982—; chpt. com. Ducks Unlimited, LeClaire, 1983—, area chmn., 1985—. Served to maj. USAF, 1971-82. Mem. ADA, Scott County Dental Soc., Davenport Dist. Dental Soc., LeClaire C. of C. (treas. 1984—). Republican. Methodist. Lodge: Elks. Avocations: duck and pheasant hunting; fishing; canoeing; camping; hiking. Office: 126 S Cody Rd LeClaire IA 52723

BYINGTON, RICHARD PRICE, surgical supply company executive; b. Grand Rapids, Mich., July 24, 1940; s. Stanley J. and Constance Y. (Des Noyer) B.; B.S. in Pharmacy, Ferris State Coll., 1962; m. Margaret Ellen Evert, Aug. 26, 1961; children—James, Michael, Connie. Pub. relations rep. Mich. State Pharm. Assn., Lansing, 1962; pharmacist White & White Pharmacy Inc., Grand Rapids, 1962-63; sales rep. White & White Surg. Supply Inc., Grand Rapids, 1963-67, sales mgr., 1967-70, exec. v.p., 1970-74, pres., 1974—; mem. Nursing Home Adminstrs. Licensure Bd., 1970—. Mem. Health Industries Distbrs. Assn. (bd. dirs., sr. v.p.), Am., Mich., Kent County pharm. assns. Roman Catholic. Clubs: Lions, Peninsular. Home: 3341 Ashton Rd SE Grand Rapids MI 49506 Office: 19 La Grave Ave SE Grand Rapids MI 49503

BYRD, AUDREY MITCHELL, educator; b. Middlesboro, Ky.; d. James Allen and Emma Frances (Hardy) Mitchell; m. Winston Byrd, June 30, 1968; children—Audrey Frances, Winston. B.S., Central State U., M.S. in Edn., 1968; student Putman Modeling Sch., 1960; postgrad. Columbia U., 1965, Purdue U., 1982. Tchr., Carver Sch., Gary, Ind.; resource tchr. Parent Outreach Program, Gary, Ind., 1979-82; instr. lit. for gifted and talented Tolleston Sch., Gary, 1982—, reading specialist, 1982—; real estate salesperson; beauty cons. Miss Black Teenage World Pageant, 1980-81; condr. workshops in field. Founder, Shangri-La Social and Civic Club, 1960. Recipient Successful Woman award Ednl. Aides and Tutors, 1982. Mem. Internat. Reading Assn., Realtor Assn., Assn. Supervision and Curriculum Devel. Roman Catholic. Club: Women on the Move. Writer children's stories and poems; developer formula for Audra Youth Cream, 1970. Home: 2033 Chase St Gary IN 46404 Office: 2700 W 19th Ave Suite M11 Gary IN 44404

BYRD, RICHARD EDWARD, behavioral scientist, clergyman; b. St. Petersburg, Fla., Jan. 23, 1931; s. Eldo and Louise Gould (Parker) Lawton; m. Helen Mandeville Penn, Aug. 30, 1950; children—Jackie Louise, Richard Edward. B.A., U. Fla., 1952; M. Div., Va. Theol. Sem., 1956; Ph.D., NYU, 1970. Ordained to ministry Episcopal Ch., 1956. Various religious positions, Fla., 1956-60; pres. Richard E. Byrd Co., Faribault, Minn., 1966—, Mpls., 1980—; dir. E.W. Cook Sch. Psychotherapy, 1972-77; exec. v.p. Wilson Ctr. Edn. and Psychiatry, Faribault, 1977-80; dir. SHARE Minn., health maintenance orgn. Author: Managing Risk in Changing Times, 1982; A Guide to Personal Risk-Taking, 1974; multi-media series Participative Management, 1982. Chmn. Edina Human Rights Commn., Mpls., 1972; asst. pastor St. Stephen's Episcopal Ch., Mpls., 1979—; pres. Enablers, St. Paul, 1980. Named Orgn. Devel. Cons. of Yr., Am. Soc. Tng. and Devel. 1984. Mem. Assn. Creative Change (pres. 1971-73), Am. Psychol. Assn., NTL Inst. Applied Social Sci., Minn. Psychol. Assn., D.C. Psychol. Assn. Republican. Club: Minneapolis. Lodge: Rotary. Home: 4900 W Sunnyslope Rd Edina MN 55424 Office: 5200 Willson Rd Suite 402 Minneapolis MN 55424

BYRNE, DIANE MARIE, statistical specialist; b. Detroit, Nov. 11, 1952; d. Romeo Fredrick and Patricia Ann (Murphy) Bernard; m. Larry Eugene Byrne, Aug. 20, 1971; children—Jennifer Leigh, Ryan Michael. B.S., U. Mich-Dearborn, 1981. Research assoc. laser technologist Sinia Hosp., Detroit, 1979-80; coordinator math. Nat. Inst. Tech., Livonia, Mich., 1981-83; cons., trainer Schoolcraft Coll., Livonia, 1983—, Argyle Assocs., Inc., New Canaan, Conn., 1983-85; adminstr. Quality Inst. Eaton Corp., 1985—. Mem. Am. Soc. Quality Control (regional counselor automotive div. 1985—), Am. Statis. Assn., Math. Assn. Am., Schoolcraft Coll. Found. Roman Catholic. Home: 10948 Edington St Livonia MI 48150

BYRNE, MICHAEL JOSEPH, business executive; b. Chgo., Apr. 3, 1928; s. Michael Joseph and Edith (Lueken) B.; B.Sc. in Mktg., Loyola U., Chgo., 1952; m. Eileen Kelly, June 27, 1953; children—Michael Joseph, Nancy, James, Thomas, Patrick, Terrence. Sales engr. Emery Industries, Inc., Cin., 1952-59; with Pennsalt Chem. Corp., Phila., 1959-60; with Oakton Cleaners, Inc., Skokie, Ill., 1960-70, pres., 1960-70; pres. Datatax Inc., Skokie, 1970-74, Dataforms & Midwest Mktg. Assn., 1970—, Metro Tax Service Inc., 1975—, Midwest Synthetic Lubrication Products, 1978—. Served with ordnance U.S. Army, 1946-48. Mem. A.I.M., VFW, Alpha Kappa Psi. Club: Toastmasters Internat. Home: 600 Grego Ct PO Box 916 Prospect Heights IL 60070

BYRNS, TIMOTHY CHESTER, educator; b. Cleve., Nov. 13, 1947; s. Chester A. and Evelyn S. (Grodzynski); B.A. and B.S.Ed., Bowling Green (Ohio) State U., 1970; A.A. and A.A.B., Cuyahoga Community Coll., 1978, M.B.A. candidate in Internat. Mgmt., Baldwin-Wallace Coll.; student Touraine First, France, U. Salzburg, Austria, Spanish Cultural Inst., Spain. Cert. tchr., Ohio. Instr. fgn. langs. Parma (Ohio) City Schs., 1975—. Creator, producer career exploration ednl. TV series, 1983. Named Tennis Coach of Yr., New Lake Erie League, 1977. Mem. Parma Edn. Assn., Ohio Edn. Assn., NEA. Roman Catholic. Home: 454 Georgia Ave Elyria OH 44035 Office: Parma Sr High Sch W 54th St Parma OH 44129

BYRON, MARY MORRISSY, court reporter; b. Chgo., June 15, 1952; d. Eugene Vincent Morrissy and Margaret Mary (Lucitt) Leonard; m. Robert Anthony Schmitt, Sept. 25, 1971 (div. Nov. 1974); m. Jeffrey Byron, July 23, 1978; children—Matthew Jason, Daniel Scott. Student MacCormac Jr. Coll., 1973, Chgo. Coll. Commerce, 1974, Daley Jr. Coll., 1972, Southwest Sch. Bus., 1971. Cert. shorthand reporter; registered profl. reporter. Court reporter Central Reporters, Chgo., 1973-74; co-owner Morrissy & McGuire, Chgo., 1974-78; owner Morrissy & Others, Chgo., 1978-83; pres. Morrissy & Others, Ltd., Chgo., 1982—. Sec., Del Mar Woods Improvement Assn., Deerfield, Ill., 1980-82. Mem. Nat. Shorthand Reporters Assn., Ill. Shorthand Reporters Assn. Home: 2620 Wildwood Ln Deerfield IL 60015 Office: Morrissy & Others Ltd 189 W Madison Chicago IL 60602

BYRON, RITA ELLEN COONEY, travel executive, publisher, real estate agent; b. Cleve.; d. Harry James and Marie (Hakey) Cooney; m. Carl James Byron Jr., Nov. 27, 1954 (dec.); children—Carey Lewis, Carl James, Bradford William. Student Cleve. Coll., 1954, Western Res. U., 1955, John Carroll U., 1956; Ph.D. (hon.), Colo. State Christian Coll., 1972. Mgr. European Immigration dept. U.S. Steamship Lines, Cleve., 1956; real estate agt. W.I. White Realtor Inc., Shaker Heights, Ohio, 1965-67, J.P. Malone Realtors Inc., Shaker Heights, 1967-70, Thomas Murray & Assocs., 1971-76, Mary Anderson Realty, Shaker Heights, 1978-79, Barth Brad & Andrews Realtors Inc., Shaker Heights, 1979—; v.p., co-owner Your Connection To Travel, Kent, Ohio, 1980—; v.p., gen. mgr. World Class Travel Agy., 1985—; dir. Travel One div. Quaker Sq., Akron, Travel Trends for Singles, 1985. Mem. U.S. Figure Skating Assn., 1960—, Wightman Cup Women's Com., 1965—; mem. women's com. Cleve. Mus. of Art, 1969—; co-chmn. Cleve. Invitational Figure Skating Competition, 1972—; chmn. Gold Rush Rush, U.S. Ski Team, 1982, Cleve. benefit U.S. Olympic Teams; chmn. Midas Touch, 1983; patron Cleve. 500, 1983; originator Benefits Unltd., Exceptional Single Person's, Connections Unltd., 1983; founder, coordinator Singled Out Club, 1983; co-ptnr., adv. bd. The Service Service, 1984; benefit chmn., patroness various balls and fund-raising events; vol. Foster Parents Inc., 1983; vol. Council on World Affairs, 1983, Bellefaire Home for Spl. Children, 1983, Big Sisters Greater Cleve., 1983, Camp Cheerful, 1983, Chisholm Ctr., 1983, Children's Diabetic Camp Ho Mita Koda, 1984, Young Audiences, 1985; adv. trustee Friends of Fairmount Theatre of the Deaf, 1983; mem. Greater Cleve. Growth Assn., 1983. Mem. Western Res. Hist. Soc., Garden Ctr. Greater Cleve., Friends Cleve. Pub. Library, UN Assn. of U.S., Cleve. Council World Affairs, U.S. Ski Ednl. Fund (chmn. benefits), English Speaking Union (jr. bd.), Travel Age Exchange, Globetrotters Internat. Fedn. Women's Travel Orgns., North Coast Exec. Women's Network, Growth Assn., Council on Small Enterprises. Cleve. Real Estate Bd. Clubs: Cleve. Skating, Broadmoor World Arena Figure Skating, Colony Beach and Racquet, Suburban Ski, Cleve. Advertising, Communicator's, Towne Hall, Women's City, Gilmour Acad. Women's, Mid-Day, Cleve. Wellesley, Arctic Circle. Co-pub., exec. editor The Single Register, other publs.; featured in numerous publs. Home: 3520 Ingleside Rd Shaker Heights OH 44122

BYRUM, JAMES EDGAR, agricultural association executive; b. Jackson, Mich., June 18, 1953; s. Richard Rossman and Frances (Morehouse) B.; m. Dianne Yvonne Byrum, Dec. 28, 1974; children—Barbara A., James R. Student, Lansing Community Coll., 1970-72, Mich. State U., 1972-74. Senate aide Mich. State Senate, Lansing, 1971-72; load adjuster Peoples Bank of Leslie, Mich., 1972-72; sales rep. Monsanto Agrl. Products Co., St. Louis, 1974-77, product supr., 1977-79; exec. sec. Mich. Bean Commn., Lansing, 1979—. Project AIM coordinator Ag's Amazing Acre Coordinator, Mich. State Fair, 1981; mem. Ingham County Democratic exec. com., 1980-81; bd. dirs. Lansing Conv. Bur., 1981—. Named Star State Farmer, Mich. Future Farmers of Am., 1971. Congregationalist. Home: 4933 Bellevue Rd Onondaga MI 49264 Office: 1020 Long Blvd Suite 13 Lansing MI 48910

CABLE, STEPHEN JAMES, investment executive; b. Canton, Ohio, May 7, 1924; s. Davis Arthur and Gail (Watson) C.; B.S. in Chem. Engring., Case-Western Res. U., 1950; advanced mgmt. tng. Emory U., 1966-67; m. Jane Irwin Purdy, June 24, 1948; children—Nancy Jane, Davis James. Plant engr. Sparta Ceramic Co., 1950-54, plant mgr., 1954-56; successively mgr., sec., group v.p. Spartek, Inc. (formerly U.S. Ceramic Tile Co.), Canton, 1956-82, also dir.; chmn. bd., chief exec. officer Polywood Corp., North Canton, 1982—; pres., chief. exec. officer; SPR Fund, Inc.; v.p., dir. Joseph A. Locker Co., Canton. Trustee Canton YMCA. Served to 2d lt. Transp. Corps, AUS, 1943-46. Mem. Sigma Xi, Tau Beta Pi, Alpha Chi Sigma. Clubs: Canton (trustee), Congress Lake (Hartville, Ohio). Contbr. articles trade jours. Patentee in field. Home: 558 N Prospect St Hartville OH 44632 Office: 6903 Promway NW North Canton OH 44720

CABOT, JOSEPH, pedodontist; b. Detroit, Oct. 15, 1921; s. Benjamin and Ethel (Gutkovsky) C.; B.S., Wayne State U., 1942; D.D.S., U. Mich., 1945, M.S., 1947; m. Ruth Weiner, Aug. 19, 1945; children—Bonnie Cabot Kaufman, Gary Michael, Elizabeth Ann Cabot Stenvig, Jon Elliott. Mott fellow U. Mich., 1945-46; pedontic fellow Hurley Hosp., Flint, Mich., 1946-47; individual practice pedontics, Detroit, 1947-55, Lathrup Village, Mich., 1969—. Mem. bd. Delta Dental Plan Mich., 1959—, pres., 1963-66; pres., Detroit Dental Aid, 1952-55. Local bd. chmn. Selective Service, 1959-67, appeal bd. chmn., 1969—, dental adviser to state dir., 1968—; assemblyman United Community Services, 1971-77; pres. Nat. Found. Dentistry for the Handicapped. Served to maj. Dental Corps, AUS, 1955-57. Fellow Internat. Coll. Dentists, Am. Coll. Dentists, Am. Acad. Pedodontics; mem. ADA (ho. of dels. 1965-76, trustee 1977-83, 1st v.p. 1983-84), Mich. Dental Assn. (pres. 1975-76), Mich. Soc. Dentistry for Children (pres. 1953-54), Detroit Dist. Dental Soc. (Merit award 1964, pres. 1966-67), Kenneth A. Easlick Grad. Soc. (pres. 1973-75), Pierre Fauchard Acad., Omicron Kappa Upsilon, Alpha Omega. Lion. Home: 3199 Interlaken Rd Orchard Lake MI 48033 Office: 18239 W 12 Mile Rd Lathrup Village MI 48076

CABRAL, GALILEU, internist; b. Minas, Brazil, Feb. 19, 1941; came to U.S., 1969, naturalized, 1976; s. Joaquim Azevedo and Alice Tasca (Sartori) C.; M.D., Univ. Juiz de Fora, Brazil, 1964; postgrad. cert. U. Mo., Columbia, 1973; m. Kathleen Ann Fries, May 10, 1974; children—Anthony Eugene, William Lee. Intern, Mo. Bapt. Hosp., St. Louis County, 1969, resident, 1970-73, chief med. resident, 1973, mem. active staff, 1974—, asso. chief med. staff, 1980—; pres. St. Francois Med. Center, Florissant, Mo., 1979-80; mem. continuing edn. com. Christian Hosp. N.E., 1978—. Served to lt. Brazilian Navy, 1965-68. Diplomate Am. Bd. Internal Medicine. Mem. AMA (Physician Recognition award 1972—), A.C.P., Mo. State Med. Assn., Met. St. Louis Med. Soc., Midwest Internists (v.p.). Roman Catholic. Home: 15244 Lochcrest Ct Ballwin MO 63011 Office: 14377 Woodlake Dr Suite 109 Chesterfield MO 63017

CABRERA, HUGO ALFREDO, microbiologist, epidemiologist; b. Naguabo, P.R., Sept. 17, 1921; came to U.S., 1940; s. Alfredo and Francisca Cabrera; m. Mildred Van Overen, June 10, 1946; children—Hugo, Francisca, Jean Marie, Mary, Patricia, Noelita, Michael, John, Paul, Margaret, Catherine. A.B., W.Va. U., 1946; M.S., U. Mich., 1950, M.P.H., 1951, Ph.D., 1954. Diplomate Am. Bd. Med. Microbiology. Postgrad. Ohio Dept. Health, Columbus, 1954-55; microbiologist, epidemiologist Mount Carmel Med. Ctr., Columbus, 1955—; cons. microbiology St. Ann's Hosp., Columbus, 1959-71, St. Anthony Hosp., Columbus, 1963-71, Mount Carmel East Hosp., Columbus, 1971—. Contbr. articles to profl. jours. Mem. Am. Soc. Microbiology, Assn. Practitioners in Infection Control., South Central Assn. Clin. Microbiology. Roman Catholic. Avocations: tennis; jogging. Home: 1245 Langston Dr Columbus OH 43220 Office: Mount Carmel Med Ctr 793 W State St Columbus OH 43220

CACIOPPO, JOHN TERRANCE, psychology educator, researcher; b. Marshall, Tex., June 12, 1951; s. Cyrus Joseph and Mary Katherine (Kazimour) C.; m. Barbara Lee Andersen, May 17, 1981. B.S. in Econs., U. Mo.-Columbia, 1973; M.A. in Psychology, Ohio State U., 1975, Ph.D., in Psychology, 1977. Asst. prof. psychology U. Notre Dame (Ind.), 1977-79; asst. prof. psychology U. Iowa, Iowa City, 1979-81, assoc. prof. psychology, 1981-85, prof. psychology, 1985—; assoc. and cons. editor various profl. jours. NSF grantee, 1979—. Mem. Soc. Exptl. Social Psychology, Soc. Psychophysiol. Research, Soc. Advancement Social Psychology, Midwestern Psychol. Assn., Am. Psychol. Assn., AAAS, Sigma Xi. Author, editor 4 books. Contbr. articles to profl. jours.

CADE, VICTOR ROSCOE, osteopathic surgeon; b. Larned, Kans., Apr. 7, 1911; s. Albert Benton and Minnie H. (Goodman) C.; m. Helen G. Shore, 1933; children—Sonya Marie Cade Steiner, Steven Ray Cade. D.O., U. Health Scis., Kansas City, Mo., 1934; diploma Am. Inst. Hypnosis, 1977; Postgrad. in surgery U. Vienna, Diplomate Am. Osteo. Bd. Surgery, Kans. State Bd. Healing Arts. Gen. practice osteo. medicine, Larned, 1934—, also Corpus Christi, Tex.; mem. staff St. Joseph Meml. Hosp., Larned, Corpus Christi Osteo. Hosp.; mem. faculty U. Health Scis. Mem. Coll. Osteo. Surgeons, ACS, Kans. Assn. Osteo. Medicine (hon. life mem.), Am. Osteopathy Assn., Am. Med. Soc. Vienna. Lodge: Masons. Office: Cade Bldg 820 Broadway Larned KS 67550

CADIEUX, EUGENE ROGERS, insurance company executive; b. Detroit, Feb. 14, 1923; s. Harold S. and Nadia (Rogers) C.; student U. Detroit Coll.

Commerce and Finance, 1941-42, Sch. Law, 1952; m. Leontine R. Keane, May 10, 1975. With bond dept. Standard Accident Ins. Co., Detroit, 1951-54; bond mgr. Am. Ins. Co., Detroit, 1954-65, Fireman's Fund, Cin., 1965-66, Md. Casualty Co., Detroit, 1966-75, Zervos Agency, Inc., 1975; cons. to contractors, 1957—. Asst. dir. boys work Internat Assn. Y's Mens Clubs, 1953; committeeman YMCA, Detroit; mem. citizens council Internat. Inst., 1977—; trustee Joint Meml. Day Assn. Served with AUS, World War II. Mem. Surety Assn. Mich. (sec. 1958), Am. Assn. State and Local History, Mich., Detroit (sec. 1970—, trustee), Cin. (com. on library and acquisitions), Grosse Pointe (pres. 1980-82) hist. socs., SAR (pres. Mich. soc. 1961-62, bd. mgrs., nat. Americanism com.), Friends Pub. Library Cin., Friends Pub. Library Grosse Pointe (hist. com.), Delta Sigma Pi, Gamma Eta Gamma. Clubs: Country (Detroit), Algonquin, Grosse Pointe Ski. Home: 208 Ridgemont Rd Grosse Pointe Farms MI 48236 Office: 24724 Farmbrook St Southfield MI 48034

CADIEUX, R. D., chemical company executive. Pres. Amoco Chems. Corp., Chgo., also dir. Office: Amoco Chems Co 200 E Randolph Dr Chicago IL 60601*

CADIGAN, RUFUS JONES, theatre educator, producer; b. Salem, Mass., May 31, 1946; s. George Leslie and Jane Margaret (Jones) C.; m. Helen Elise Huckabee, Aug. 17, 1979; children—Matthew Ryan; 1 stepchild, Kent Bradley Lindstrom. B.A., Lawrence U., 1968; M.A., U. Mass., 1973; Ph.D., U. Kans., 1979. Prof. theatre Ottawa U., Kans., 1976-79; chmn. theatre dept. Rockford Coll., Ill., 1979—, producer Rockford Coll. Summer Theatre, 1979—. Active Rockford Civic Theatre, 1982-83; bd. dirs. New Am. Theatre, Rockford, 1985, Spectrum Sch., Rockford, 1984-85; vestry mem. Emmanuel Episc. Ch., Rockford, 1983-85. Mem. Am. Theatre Assn., Ill. Theatre Assn. Democrat. Avocations: reading; writing; fiction; running; swimming. Home: 6878 Paddock Ln Rockford IL 61111 Office: Rockford Coll 5050 E State St Rockford IL 61101

CADOGAN, EDWARD JOHN PATRICK, mfg. co. mktg. exec.; b. London, Dec. 22, 1939; came to U.S., 1959, naturalized, 1964; B.S. in Mktg., L.I. U., 1971; M.B.A., U. Dayton, 1977; m. Wanda Maxine Evans, Dec. 30, 1975. Sr. field engr. Fairchild Camera & Instrument Corp., Syosset, N.Y., in Vietnam and Okinawa, 1964-69; mgr. Honeywell Mut. Alarm Corp., N.Y.C., 1971-72; sales engr. CAI/div. Recon-Optical, Barrington, Ill., 1972-75; mktg. engr. Cin. Electronics Corp., 1977-78; mktg. mgr. electro-optics Electronic Warfare Centre, Systems Research Labs., Dayton, Ohio, 1978-82; regional mgr. Fairchild Weston Systems, Inc., Dayton, 1982—. Mem. Republican Nat. Com. Served with USAF, 1959-63. Mem. Assn. M.B.A. Execs., Assn. Old Crows, Tech. Mktg. Soc. Am., Am. Def. Preparedness Assn., Air Force Assn., Assn. Unmanned Vehicle Systems, Nat. Contract Mgmt. Assn. Home: 5420 Pentland Circle Huber Heights OH 45424 Office: 4032 Linden Ave Dayton OH 45432

CADWELL, JAMES BURTON, information systems management executive; b. Berwyn, Ill., Oct. 10, 1942; s. Charles Stewart and Louise (Beilby) C.; m. Kathleen Anne Holland, Feb. 22, 1969; children—Kathleen M., Megan M., James P. B.A., St. Mary's Coll., 1968. Mem. mktg. staff GTE Automatic Electric, Northbrook, Ill., 1968-72; ops. analyst Cook Electric Co., Morton Grove, Ill., 1972-76; systems analyst Kitchens of Sara Lee, Deerfield, Ill., 1976-79; project mgr. Walgreen Co., Deerfield, 1979-82; project leader Culligan Water Treatment div. Beatrice Foods, Northbrook, 1982—. Bd. dirs. Youth Services, Glenview, Ill., 1976; mem. fin. com. Sam Young for U.S. Ho. of Reps., Glenview, 1979. Served with U.S. Army, 1963-66. Republican. Roman Catholic. Clubs: Olph Mens; St. Mary's Veterans (Winona, Minn.) (pres. 1967-68). Lodges: Optimists, Kiwanis. Home: 1939 Palmgren St Glenview IL 60025

CADY, DARREL ROBERT, historian, educator; b. Waterloo, Iowa, Apr. 17, 1933; s. Harold Frank and Rosalie Pearl (Shobe) C.; m. LaVonne Marilyn Gross, June 11, 1955; children—Shawn, Sarah. B.A., U. No. Iowa, 1958; M.A., U. Ill., 1962; Ph.D., U. Kans., 1974. Tchr. history Tipton High Sch. (Iowa), 1958-60; tchr. history, head dept. Roseburg High Sch. (Oreg.), 1962-63; tchr. history Clinton High Sch. (Iowa), 1963-65; assoc. prof. history Western Ill. U., 1969—. Served with USNR, 1953-56. Harry S. Truman Library Inst. grantee, 1967; Merchant scholar, 1966-67; NDEA fellow, Kans., 1968-69. Mem. Orgn. Am. Historians, Univ. Profls. of Ill. Office: 445 Morgan Hall Western Ill Univ Macomb IL 61455

CADY, RICHARD HAROLD, rare books and autographs dealer; b. Tulsa, Mar. 25, 1943; s. Francis H. and Mozelle (McClure) C.; m. Denise Abad, July 29, 1964; 1 child, Anthony Bowen. B.A., Northwestern U., 1965. First asst. buyer Marshall Field & Co., Chgo., 1966-72; assoc. Hamill & Barker, Rare Books, Chgo., 1973-75; home accessories personnel officer, buyer decorative accessories, buyer book dept., asst. group merchandise mgr., buyer rare books and autographs prints and maps Marshall Field & Co., Chgo., 1976-80; sole propr. Richard Cady - Rare Books, Chgo., N.Y.C., 1980—. Bd. dirs. Channel 11 (WTTW) Art Auction, 1980, Field Mus., both Chgo. Mem. Bibliog. Soc. Am., Art Inst. Chgo., 1890's Soc. London, Manuscript Soc., Pvt. Libraries Assn. London, Oxford Bibl. Soc. Club: Caxton. Avocations: tennis; archaeology; collecting canes; armadillos. Address: 1927 N Hudson Ave Chicago IL 60614

CAFFARELLI, ROBERT N., lawyer; b. Chicago Heights, Ill., Mar. 20, 1933; s. Joseph and Emma (Bramanti) C.; m. Patricia McNally, Feb. 17, 1962; children—Michael, Mary Beth B.D. magna cum laude in Acctg., U. Notre Dame, 1955; J.D., DePaul U., 1958. Bar: Ill. 1958. Asst. U.S. atty. No. Dist. of Ill., Chgo., 1959-62; assoc. McDermott, Will & Emery, Chgo., 1962-63; assoc. Walsh & Case, Chgo., 1964-68; ptnr Caffarelli & Wiczer, Chgo., 1968-74; sole practice Chgo., 1974—; ptnr Boodell, Sears, Giambalvo & Crowley, Chgo., 1975—; dir., sec. Nagle Pumps, Inc., Chicago Heights, Ill., 1972—; dir. sec. Vulcan Tube & Metals, Chicago Heights, 1965-82; chmn. bd., 1973-74. Mem. editorial bd. DePaul Law Rev., 1956-57-58. Bd. dirs. Infant Jesus of Prague Ch., Flossmoor, Ill., 1974-76; pres., bd. dirs. Montessori Children's Home, Park Forest, Ill., 1969-70. Mem. ABA, Fed. Bar Assn., Ill. State Bar Assn., Chgo. Bar Assn., Justinian Soc. Lawyers. Roman Catholic. Club: Olympia Fields Country (bd. gov. 1977-83, pres. 1981-83) Avocations: Golf; reading; athletics Office: Boodell Sears Giambalvo & Crowley 69 W Washington Chicago IL 60461

CAFFEY, JACQUELYN SWEETNER, educator; b. Meridian, Miss., Oct. 23, 1938; d. Oraton Vanderbuilt and Maggie Augusta (Buckingham) Sweetner; m. Leroy Clementi Caffey, Feb. 26, 1960; 1 son, Derwin Clementi. B.S., Tenn. State U., 1959; M.Ed., Wayne State U., 1966. Tchr., Meridian Pub. Schs., 1959-61; substitute tchr. St. Louis Pub. Schs., 1961-62; tchr. Ypsilanti (Mich.) Pub. Schs., 1962-64; tchr. Detroit Pub. Schs., 1962-72, reading tchr., 1972—, dir. Davison Reading Ctr., R2R Project and Resource Ctrs. Sec., Detroit Meridianites, Inc., 1974-76. Recipient Right To Read Outstanding Service award, 1977-78. Mem. Assn. Supervision and Curriculum Devel., NAACP, Am. Fedn. Tchrs., Mich. Fedn. Tchrs., Detroit Fedn. Tchrs., Internat. Reading Assn., Detroit Met. Reading Council, Phi Delta Kappa. Methodist. Clubs: Bridge Friends, Two Plus Two Couples, Les Cosmopolis Bridge. Author: I Remember Mrs. Sadie, 1980; The Black Hostage, 1981; 20-Sure Fire Ways to Produce Creative Writers, 1980; 30 Super Ideas to Produce Better Readers, 1981; The Lives of Jack and Jackie, 1982; Drops of Gold, 1981; My Roots, 1981; Martin Luther King, Jr., 1982; Buckingham Palace, 1982; The Descendants of Tom and Maude Caffey, 1983. Home: 19441 Snowden St Detroit MI 48235 Office: 2800 Davison St Detroit MI 48212

CAGLE, ALBERT WAYNE, engineering consultant; b. High Point, N.C., May 25, 1924; s. Grady Carson and Mary (Davis) C.; B.S., High Point Coll., 1948; M.S., U. Louisville, 1950; m. Bessie Valeria Kivett, Sept. 16, 1949; children—Albert Wayne, Lynne, Deborah, Mark. Research chemist Cone Mills Research, Greensboro, N.C., 1950; with AT&T Tech. Inc., Lee's Summit, Mo., 1951—, sr. staff engr., 1970—. Served with U.S. Army, 1943-46. Decorated Bronze Star. Fellow Am. Soc. for Metals; mem. Am. Chem. Soc., Soc. Plastics Engrs., Soc. Mfg. Engrs. Methodist. Clubs: Masons, Shriners. Home: 6622 Englewood Raytown MO 64133 Office: AT & T Tech Inc 777 N Blue Parkway Lee's Summit MO 64063

CAGLE, CHARLES HARMON, educator, author; b. Colorado City, Tex., Sept. 28, 1930; s. William Wallace and Bonnie Belle (Cansler) C.; B.A., Southwestern Okla. State U., 1952; M.A., U. Okla., 1954, postgrad., 1957-58; M.F.A., U. Iowa, 1965. Free lance television writer, N.Y.C., 1956-57; prof. journalism/English, Cameron (Okla.) State U., 1959-60; prof. creative writing Pittsburg (Kans.) State U., 1960—; free lance profl. writer fiction, screenplays. Active Crawford County (Kans.) Hist. Soc., Pittsburg Area Arts and Crafts Players. Served with Signal Corps, U.S. Army, 1952-54; Korea. Recipient citation ALA, 1970; Seaton award for fiction, 1981. Mem. AAUP, Nat. Assn. Tchrs. English, Kans. Assn. Tchrs. English, Am. Film Inst., Am. Humanist Assn. Democrat. Author: (play) The Sudden Truth, 1957; author eighty paperback novels, 1967—, including The Beast, 1970. Office: English Dept Pittsburg State U Pittsburg KS 66762

CAHALEN, SHIRLEY LEANORE, educator; b. LaHarpe, Kans., Aug. 20, 1933; d. Hugh E. and Irma Eunonia (Russell) Pearman; m. Keith E. Cahalen, Sept. 2, 1953; 1 child, Keith P. Student Iola Jr. Coll., 1951-52, McPherson Coll., 1952-53, Pratt Community Coll., 1963-64; B.S., Northwestern State U., Alva, Okla., 1966; M.S., Kans. State U., 1981; postgrad. Emporia State U., summer 1982. With Kans. Power & Light Co., McPherson, 1952-53, State Farm Ins. Co., Jacksonville, Fla., 1957-59, Kans. Fish and Game Commn., Pratt, 1960-62; home econs. tchr. Kirby-Smith Jr. High Sch., Jacksonville, Fla., 1966-67, Unified Sch. Dist. 254, Medicine Lodge, Kans., 1968-71, Sch. Dist. 259, Wichita East, Wichita, Kans., 1971-73, Dist. 490 El Dorado, Kans., 1975-82; tchr. Augusta (Kans.) Sr. High Sch., 1982—. Mem. edn. com. First United Meth. Ch., 1981-84. Mem. Walnut Valley Edn. Assn., Kans. Edn. Assn. (state rep.), NEA, Am. Vocat. Assn., Kans. Vocat. Assn., Butler County Spl. Edn. Assn., AAUW (pres. 1979-81), Kappa Delta Pi, Am. Legion Aux. Methodist. Home: 318 School Rd El Dorado KS 67042 Office: Augusta Sr High Sch Augusta KS 67010

CAHILL, CLYDE S., See *Who's Who in America*, 43rd edition.

CAHILL, MARY FRAN, journalist; b. Milw.; d. Morgan Joseph and Claire Catherine (Warnimont) C.; B.A., M.A., Marquette U. Photojournalist Cedarburg (Wis.) News Graphic, 1965-67; photojournalist Milw. Jour., 1967-76, feature writer, 1976-83, food writer, 1983—; mem. unit holders council Jour. Co., 1977-79. Hon. mem. Milw. Fire Dept. Recipient Disting. Service award Milw. Fire Dept., 1972, 74, 75, 77, 78, 79, 80; cert. of appreciation USCGR, 1975, 77. Mem. Nat. Press Photographers Assn., Wis. News Photographers Assn. (sec. 1973-75), Women in Communications, Milw. Press Club, Zool. Soc. Milwaukee County, Zoo Pride, Wis. Emergency Med. Technicians Assn. (Woman of Yr. award 1975), Nat. Assn. Emergency Med. Technicians, Milw. Fire Hist. Soc. (dir. 1982—, treas. 1982-83, sec. 1983—), Sigma Delta Chi, Phi Mu, Phi Alpha Theta, Pi Gamma Mu. Club: Nordic Ski. Office: 333 W State St Milwaukee WI 53201

CAHILL, RICHARD JOHN, advertising executive; b. Mpls., Dec. 30, 1938; s. Edward Leroy and Marjorie Marie (Dolbec) C.; m. Elda Theresa Zachman, May 3, 1969; children—Kimberly Ann, Brian Edward. A.A., U. Minn., 1958, B.A., 1960. Cert. advt. specialist, Minn. Sales corr. Shedd-Brown, Mpls., 1964-68, asst. gen. sales mgr., 1968-79, v.p., gen. mgr. Shedd-Brown, Trend Devel. Corp. Subs., 1979-82, exec. v.p. Shedd-Brown, 1982-84, pres., 1984—. Served to 1st lt. U.S. Army, 1961-63. Recipient Merit award Specialty Advt. Assn., 1981, 1982, Most Beneficial Sales and Mgmt. Aids award Specialty Advt. Assn., 1980, Best Catalog award Specialty Advt. Assn., 1981, First Pl. in Offset Printing award Specialty Advt. Assn., 1982, Sales Talk Championship award Dale Carnegie & Assoc., Inc., 1968. Mem. Mfrs. Agents Nat. Assn. Roman Catholic. Lodge: Lions Home: 7209 Shannon Dr Edina MN 55435 Office: Shedd-Brown 13911 Ridgedale Dr Minnetonka MN 55343

CAIN, CHARLES ALAN, electrical engineering educator, researcher; b. Tampa, Fla., Mar. 3, 1943; s. Charles Franklin and Bernice Virginia (Harvey) C.; m. Yoshiko Hill. B.E.E., U. Fla., 1965; M.S. in Elec. Engring., MIT, 1967; Ph.D., U. Mich., 1972. Registered profl. engr. Tech. staff Bell Telephone Labs., Inc., Naperville, Ill., 1965-68; teaching fellow U. Mich., Ann Arbor, 1968-72; asst. prof. U. Ill., Urbana, 1972-78, assoc. prof., 1978-83, prof., 1983—, chmn. bioengring. faculty, 1983—. Contbr. articles to profl. jours. Recipient Outstanding Grad. Student Elec. and Computer Engring. award U. Mich., 1972; U. Ill. fellow, 1981-82; Hitachi Central Research Lab. vis. research fellow, 1984-85. Sr. mem. IEEE; mem. Bioelectromagnetics Soc. (bd. dirs. 1984—, charter mem.), Radiation Research Soc. Avocations: hiking; mountain climbing. Office: Dept Elec and Computer Engring U Ill 1406 W Green St Urbana IL 61801

CAIN, ROBERT BARR, computer graphics company executive; b. Detroit, July 19, 1941; s. Alexander and Bernadine (Kaiser) C.; m. Mary Elaine Kendall, Apr. 2, 1960; children—Robert A., Gary R., Sandra D. B.A. in Indsl. Mgmt., Lawrence Inst. Tech., 1967. Tech. engr. Xerox Corp., Detroit, 1965-69; pub. relations dir. Bendix Corp., Southfield, Mich., 1970-73; creative dir. Maritz Inc., St. Louis, 1973-75; pres., founder Symtec Inc., Farmington, Mich., 1974—, Mich. Sci. Systems, Inc., Farmington, 1984—; cons. Sandy Corp., Troy, Mich., 1975—. Author: Numerical Control Handbook, 1967. Publ. newsletter: Numerical Control Newsletter, 1967-69. Patentee flash activated laser. Served with USAF, 1959-64. Recipient Product of Yr. award Gov. State Mich., 1983. Mem. Numerical Control Soc. (Outstanding Contribution award 1964), Soc. Mfg. Engrs. (Instr. Yr. award 1970). Republican. Presbyterian. Avocations: art; travel; computer graphics design; computer programming. Home: 33132 Shiawassee Farmington MI 48024 Office: Symtec Inc 15933 W 8 Mile Rd Detroit MI 48235

CAINE, CLIFFORD JAMES, educational administrator, consultant; b. Watertown, S.D., May 28, 1933; s. Louis Vernon and Elizabeth Matilda (Holland) C. B.A., Macalester Coll., 1955; J.D., U. Minn., 1958, Ph.D., 1975; postgrad. Harvard U., 1976. Bar: Minn. 1958. Dir. men's residence halls and student union Macalester Coll., 1959-63, dir. adminstrv. policies study, 1969-70; lectr. U. Minn., 1966-68, also coordinator Neighborhood Seminar program; asst. headmaster St. Paul Acad. and Summit Sch., St. Paul, 1970-85; dir. student services Breck Sch., Mpls., 1985—. Bd. dirs. Hallie Q. Brown Community Center, 1972-73, Family Service of St. Paul, 1973-79; ruling elder United Presbyn. Ch., 1962—; clk. of session House of Hope Presbyn. Ch., 1983-84. Mem. Am. Acad. Polit. and Social Sci., Am. Studies Assn., Nat. Assn. Coll. Admissions Counselors, Minn. Bar Assn., U.S. Profl. Tennis Assn., Minn. Assn. Secondary Sch. and Coll. Admissions Officers (pres. 1978-79). Club: Univ. (St. Paul). Home: 456 Summit Ave Saint Paul MN 55102 Office: 1712 Randolph Ave Saint Paul MN 55105

CAIRNS, DONALD FREDRICK, engineering and management consultant; b. Coulterville, Ill., Sept. 9, 1924; s. Fred Barton and Elsie Loretta (Barbary) C.; B.S., U. Ill., 1950; M.B.A., St. Louis U., 1966, Ph.D., 1972; m. Marion Grace Huey, Sept. 2, 1950; 1 son, Douglas Scott. Asst. engr. Mo. Pacific R.R. Co., St. Louis, 1950-56; project engr., plant engr., asst. to pres., v.p. Granite City Steel Co. (Ill.), 1956-79; pres. Nat. Inter-Tech, Inc., subs. Nat. Intergroup, Inc., St. Louis, 1979—; pres., chmn. bd. Indsl. Waste Control Council; mem. Mo. Bd. Architects, Profl. Engrs. and Land Surveyors, 1983; guest lectr. Washington U. Grad. Sch. Bus. Chmn. Webster Groves (Mo.) City Planning Commn., 1958; mem. St. Louis County Traffic Commn., 1960-61, Webster Groves Bus. Devel. Commn., 1962, St. Louis County Charter Commn., 1979; mem., chmn. St. Louis County Planning Commn., 1968-76; pres., dir. Edgewood Children's Center, 1963-72. Served with AUS, 1943-46. Decorated Bronze Star; recipient recognition for control of air pollution Pres.'s Johnson and Nixon, 1970; registered profl. engr., Mo., Ill. Mem. Nat. Soc. Profl. Engrs., Mo. Soc. Profl. Engrs., Am. Iron and Steel Inst., ASCE, Air Pollution Control Assn., Assn. Iron and Steel Engrs., Southwestern Ill. Indsl. Assn. (chmn. bd.). Club: Algonquin Golf. Home: 17 E Swon Ave Webster Groves MO 63119 Office: 425 N New Ballas Rd Saint Louis MO 63141

CALAPAI, LETTERIO, artist; b. Boston; s. Biagio and Emanuela (Planeta) C.; m. Jean Hilliard, Jan. 5, 1962. Grad. Mass. Sch. Art, Boston Sch. Fine Arts and Crafts, Art Students League N.Y.C. Head graphics Albright Art Sch., Buffalo, 1949-54; assoc. Contempories Graphic Arts Ctr., 1956-57 (name changed to Pratt-Contemporaries 1957); faculty mem. New Sch. Social Research, N.Y.C., 1957-61; founder, dir. Intaglio Workshop, N.Y.C., 1960-65; lectr. art edn. NYU, 1962-65; assoc. prof. Brandeis U., 1964-65; vis. assoc. prof. Kendall Coll., Evanston, Ill., 1965-69; lectr. art and architecture U. Ill., Chicago Circle, 1966; mem. com. Field Mus. Natural History, Chgo., 1973-74; mem. adv. panel Ill. Arts Council, 1971-73. Publications: 25 Wood Engravings by Letterio Calapai, 1948, A Portfolio of Wood Engravings: 30 Aesop's Fables Printed by Letterio Calapai from the Original Blocks of Thomas Bewick, 1973, A Negro Bible; wood engravings, 1946; Mural Historical Development of Military Signal Communication, commd. by, Works Progress Adminstrn., 1939; acquired by U.S. Signal Corps Mus., Fort Gordon, Ga., 1980. One man shows in N.Y.C., Nat. Gallery of Art, Smithsonian Instn., Washington, Paris and London; represented in permanent collections, Met. Mus. Art, Boston Mus. Fine Arts, Chgo. Art Inst., Fogg Mus., Bklyn. Mus., Albright Art Gallery, Library of Congress, N.Y. Pub. Library, Boston Pub. Library, Free Library Phila., Rose Mus., Brandeis U., The Biblioteque Nationale, Paris, Princeton U. Library, The Houghton Library (Harvard), Va. Mus. Fine Arts, Columbia U., Wichita State U., Kans., Washington U. Gallery Art, St. Louis, Ill. State Mus., Nat. Mus. of Bezalel, Nat. Mus. Jerusalem, Israel, Tokyo Mus., Japan, Civic Gallery Modern Art, Palermo, Italy, Gorakhpur U. Mus. Art, India, Kunsthaus, Zurich, Switzerland, Rosenwald Collection. Illustrator: (with wood engravings) One Hundred Years Ago. Recipient prize award America In the War Exhibition, 1943; work chosen for Fifty Best Prints of the Yr., 1944; Albert H. Wiggins purchase prize First Boston Printmakers Exhbn., 1948; John Taylor Arms prize Soc. Am. Graphic Artists, 1954; Library of Congress purchase prize, 1950, 51, 54; William J. Keller prize Western N.Y. Exhbn., 1954; Tiffany Found. grant in graphic arts, 1959; Audubon Artists medal for creative graphics, 1967; purchase prize 27th Ill. Invitational Exhbn. Ill. State Mus., 1974; purchase awards Art Inst. Chgo., 1972-73; Gold medal for graphics Italian-Am. Artists in U.S.A., 1977, 79; hon. mention Ill. Regional Print Show, 1977; Purchase award Northwestern U., 1978, U. Ill., 1978; Excellence award N. Shore Art League, Chgo., 1982; numerous other awards. Mem. Soc. Am. Graphic Artists (hon. mem. council), Print Council Am., Calif. Soc. Etchers, Boston Printmakers, Coll. Art Assn., Internat. Assn. Art, Deer Isle Artists Assn. (pres. 1979—). Home: 1458 Wilmette Ave Wilmette IL 60091 Office: The Workshop Gallery (344 Tudor Ct) PO Box 158 Glencoe IL 60022

CALARCO, DONALD CHARLES, marketing executive; b. Chgo., Jan. 3, 1948; s. Dominic N. and Lucille F. (Balsano) C.; m. Cynthia Lou Zon, Aug. 13, 1965; children—Laura, Kimberly, Regina. Br. mgr. fin. div. Kemper Ins. Co., Chgo., 1968-72; v.p. mktg. Wilshire Mktg., Chgo., 1972-76; dir. sales Travel Incentives, Oak Brook, Ill., 1976-79; v.p. sales Nat. Creative Merchandising, Arlington Heights, Ill., 1979-82; founder, pres. Am. Mktg., Oak Brook, 1982—; founder, dir. Success Planners Inst., Chgo., Gt. Am. Mktg. Assn., Oak Brook. Author: (job search guide) Forever Upward, 1978. Bd. dirs., trustee Goodwill Industries, Chgo., 1983. Mem. Am. Mgmt. Assn. Republican. Roman Catholic. Avocations: golf; skiing; reading; writing. Home: 5640 W Pershing Rd Cicero IL 60650 Office: 1315 W 22d St Oak Brook IL 60521

CALDER, GEORGE ALEXANDER, educator; b. Detroit, Oct. 1, 1937; s. Alexander and Janette (Wolcott) C. B.A., Wayne State U., 1959, M.Ed., 1960. Cert. tchr., Mich. Math. tchr. Emerson Jr. High Sch., Livonia, Mich., 1960-79; tchr. Franklin High Sch., Livonia, 1979—, chmn. math. dept., 1980—. Recipient Outstanding Service award Livonia Edn. Assn., 1965, 1976, 1978; Outstanding Young Educator award Livonia Jaycees, 1969. Mem. NEA, Livonia Edn. Assn., Mich. Edn. Assn., Nat. Council Tchrs. Math., Detroit Council Tchrs. Math., Mich. Council Tchrs. Math., Hist. Soc. Livonia, Mich. Hist. Soc., Detroit Hist. Soc., Detroit Soc. for Geneal. Research, SAR (membership chmn. Detroit 1976-83, Nat. Membership award 1979, 81, 82). Methodist. Author: (with others) Discoveries in Modern Mathematics, Courses 1, 2, 1968, 1972; Daily Thoughts for the Classroom, 1974. Office: Franklin High Sch 31000 Joy Rd Livonia MI 48150

CALDERON, EDUARDO FIEGEHEN, neurologist; b. Santiago, Chile, May 14, 1932; came to U.S., 1974, naturalized, 1980; s. Pedro N. and Teresa F. Calderon; B.Sc., Catholic U. Chile; M.D., U. Chile, 1958; m. Yolanda Urrejola, Nov. 27, 1958; children—Eduardo Tomas, John Paul, M. Alexandra, M. Pauline, Francisco. Intern, Cath. U. Clin. Hosp., Santiago, 1958; gen. practice medicine, Chile, 1958-63; trainee, then instr. in neurology U. Chile, 1963-68, asst. prof. neurology, 1971-74; postdoctoral fellow Stanford U. Med. Sch., 1968-71; practice medicine specializing in neurology, Toledo, 1974—; mem. staff St. Luke's Hosp., Mercy Hosp.; clin. asso. prof. Med. Coll. Ohio, Toledo; bd. dirs. Multiple Sclerosis Soc. N.W. Ohio, Toledo, 1974—. Diplomate Am. Bd. Psychiatry and Neurology, Am. Bd. EEG Qualification. Mem. Am. Acad. Neurology, Am. EEG Soc., Ohio Med. Assn., Lucas County Acad. Medicine. Roman Catholic. Home: 5815 Swan Creek Dr Toledo OH 43614 Office: 3949 Sun Forest Ct Toledo OH 43623

CALDWELL, DIANNE DEE, cosmetic company executive; b. Youngstown, Ohio, Jan. 24, 1946; d. Leo William and June Marie (Gakel) Difford; B.S. in Edn., Kent (Ohio) State U., 1968; m. Thomas R. Caldwell, June 22, 1968; children—Ryan Thomas, Reed Jason. High sch. English tchr., Mogadore, Ohio, 1968-69; librarian Ann Arbor (Mich.) Public Schs., 1969-72; cons. Jafra Cosmetics, Inc.-Gillette, Saline, Mich., 1974-79, cons., mgr., 1977-79, regional dir., 1979-82; v.p. The Creative Circle, Saline, 1982—; divisional sales mgr. Jafra Cosmetics, Inc., Saline, 1982—. Pres. Ann Arbor Police Wives Assn., 1971-75; mem. Republican Nat. Com.; mem. Saline Vocat. Edn. Adv. Com., 1979-80; spl. events chmn. Saline March of Dimes, 1973-75. Named Outstanding Mgr., Jafra Cosmetics, Inc.-Gillette, 1978; recipient Jan Day award, 1978, Saline Edn. Adv. award, 1979, 80. Mem. Nat. Assn. Female Execs., Nat. Ruffled Grouse Soc. Methodist. Office: 213 E Michigan Ave Saline MI 48176

CALDWELL, GILBERT RAYMOND, III, lawyer; b. Newton, Iowa, June 14, 1952; s. Gilbert Raymond and Francis Elizabeth (Ellingsworth) C.; m. Jeanne Sharon Myerscough, Dec. 23, 1974; 1 son, Kyle Myerscough. B.A., U. Tulsa, 1974, J.D., 1977. Bar: Iowa 1978, U.S. Dist Ct. (no. and so. dists.) Iowa 1978. Asst. city prosecutor, legal intern City of Tulsa, 1976-77; asst. county atty. Jasper County, Iowa, 1978; assoc. Caldwell, Caldwell & Caldwell, Newton, 1978-79, ptnr., 1979—. Republican precinct chmn. Fairview Twp, Iowa, 1982-83. Mem. Am. Judicature Soc., ABA, Iowa Bar Assn., Jasper County Bar Assn., Assn. Trial Lawyers Iowa, Assn. Trial Lawyers Am., Newton Jaycees (sec. 1978-79, pres. 1979-80), Newton C. of C., Iowa Jaycees (state legal council 1979-80). Clubs: Monroe Community (Iowa); Jasper County Farm Bur. (Newton). Lodge: Kiwanis. Home: RFD 2 Monroe IA 50170 Office: Caldwell Caldwell & Caldwell 203 Midtown Bldg Newton IA 50208

CALDWELL, JAMES MARSHALL, accountant; b. Chillicothe, Ohio, Aug. 1, 1939; s. Marshall and Emma (Gillette) C.; B.B.A., Ohio U., 1963; m. Pamela Lynne Marsh, June 13, 1963; children—Jennifer Lynne, James Patrick. Dep. auditor Ross County (Ohio), 1960-63, county commr., 1977—; tchr. Jackson (Ohio) City Schs., 1963-64; accountant, Chillicothe, 1961—; pres. James M. Caldwell & Assos. Inc., public accts.; sec. Huston Gifts, Dolls & Flowers Inc. City councilman, City of Chillicothe, 1968-75; pres. Ross County Young Republican Club, 1968-69; bd. dirs. Ross County Community Improvement Corp.; trustee Mid-Ohio Health Planning Fedn., 1975-77, Ohio Valley Health Services Found.; pres. Bd. Ross County Commrs., 1979; mem. Ross County Planning Commn.; exec. bd. Ohio Valley Regional Devel. Commn.; mem. citizens policy adv. com. Scioto River Basin, Ohio EPA. Mem. Nat. Soc. Public Accts., Public Acctg. Soc. of Ohio (pres. So. Ohio chpt. 1974-79), Chillicothe-Ross C. of C. (dir. 1970-73, pres. 1973), Chillicothe Jaycees (Citizen of Year 1973). Methodist (mem. adminstrv. bd. 1971-74, chmn. council ministries 1975-76, trustee 1985—). Lodges: Kiwanis, Elks. Home: 306 Fairway Ave Chillicothe OH 45601 Office: 84 W 2d St PO Box 1640 Chillicothe OH 45601

CALDWELL, JAMES WILLIAM, drugstore chain executive; b. Fallis, Ky., Apr. 24, 1935; s. James Hugh and Estelle Bernice (Drugan) C.; m. Delinda Jane Reeves, Mar. 29, 1959. B.S. in Pharmacy, Purdue U., 1957. Registered pharmacist. Asst. mgr. Hook Drugs, Inc., Indpls., 1958-62, mgr., 1962-69, divisional coordinator, 1969-77, asst. v.p. ops. 1977-83, asst. v.p. health care, 1983-84; v.p. health care, 1985—. Bd. dirs. Indpls. Sr. Citizens Ctr., 1984—, chmn. bldg. com., 1984—; fin. chmn. Southport United Methodist Ch., Ind., 1980-83. Served with U.S. Army, 1959-61. Mem. Ind. Pharmacist Assn. Democrat. Lodge: Masons. Avocations: farming; Tennessee walking horses; miniature animals. Home: 8930 Baker Rd Indianapolis IN 46259 Office: Hook Drugs Inc 2800 Enterprise St Indianapolis IN 46226

CALDWELL, PHILIP, automobile manufacturing company executive; b. Bourneville, Ohio, Jan. 27, 1920; s. Robert Clyde and Wilhelmina (Hemphill) C.; B.A. in Econs., Muskingum Coll., Concord, Ohio, 1940, L.H.D. (hon.), 1974; M.B.A., Harvard U. Grad. Sch. Bus., 1942; D.B.A. (hon.), Upper Iowa U., 1978; LL.D. (hon.), Boston U., 1979, Eastern Mich. U., 1979, Miami U., Oxford, Ohio, 1980, Davidson Coll., 1982, Lawrence Inst. Tech., 1984, Ohio U., 1984, U. Mich., 1984; m. Betsey Chinn Clark, Oct. 27, 1945; children—Lawrence Clark, Lucy Hemphill Caldwell Stair, Desiree Branch Caldwell Armitage. Civilian, Navy Dept., 1946-53, dep. dir. procurement policy div., 1948-53; with Ford Motor Co., Dearborn, Mich., 1953—, v.p., gen. mgr. truck ops., 1968-70, pres., dir. subs. Philco-Ford Corp., 1970-71, v.p. mfg. group N.

Am. automotive ops., 1971-72, exec. v.p. internat. automotive ops., 1973-77, vice chmn. bd., 1977-79, dep. chief exec. officer, 1978-79, pres., 1978-80, chief exec. officer, 1979—, chmn. bd., 1980—, also dir.; chmn. chief exec. officer Ford of Europe, Inc., 1972-73; dir. Ford Latin Am., Ford Mid-East and Africa, Ford Asia-Pacific, Ford Motor Credit Co., Ford of Europe, Ford Can.; mem. internat. adv. com. Chase Manhattan Bank; dir. Digital Equipment Corp., Chase Manhattan Bank N.A., Chase Manhattan Corp., Federated Dept. Stores, Russell Reynolds Assocs. Inc. Mem. Trilateral Commn.; trustee Com. Econ. Devel.; bd. dirs. Harvard U. Assocs. Grad. Sch. Bus. Adminstrn., Detroit Renaissance, Detroit Symphony Orch.; exec. com. Bus.-Higher Edn. Forum; trustee Muskingum Coll.; vice chmn. bd. trustees New Detroit, Inc. Served to lt. USNR, 1942-46. Recipient 1st William A. Jump Meml. award, 1950, Meritorious Civilian Service award Navy Dept., 1953; Internat. Exec. of Yr. award Sch. Mgmt., Brigham Young U., 1983; Bus. Statesman award Harvard Bus. Sch. Club N.Y., 1984; named Outstanding Citizen of Yr., Mich. Assn. Broadcasters, 1984, Automotive Leader of Yr., Automotive Hall of Fame, 1984, Businessman of Yr., Harvard Bus. Sch. Club of Columbus, Ohio, 1984. Mem. Motor Vehicle Mfrs. Assn. (sec.), Bus. Council, Bus. Roundtable, Conf. Bd. Clubs: Detroit, Detroit Athletic, Renaissance (Detroit); Bloomfield Hills (Mich.) Country. Address: Ford Motor Co American Rd Dearborn MI 48121

CALDWELL, WILL M., See *Who's Who in America,* 43rd edition.

CALE, MICHAEL GLENN, grocery company executive; b. Laharpe, Ill., Aug. 19, 1959; s. Joseph G. and Joyce J. (Haley) C.; m. Maxi J. Scott, Nov. 14, 1981. Grad. Macomb High Sch., 1977. Vice pres. merchandising C.F.C. Wholesale Grocery Co., Eldridge, Iowa, 1985—. Home: 6069 34th Ave Moline IL 61265 Office: CFC Wholesale Grocery Co 2951 S 1st St Eldridge IA 52748

CALENDINE, RICHARD ALLEN, pharmacist; b. Zanesville, Ohio, Oct. 1, 1948; s. Billy Arthur and Mildred Nevada (Hayes) C.; m. Sheriel Susan Fogt, July 26, 1975; children—Paula Michelle, Pamela Renee. B.S. in Pharmacy, Ohio No. U., 1972. Intern, M. M. Sear's Pharmacy, McConnelsville, Ohio, 1966-69, Price & Richardson Pharmacy, McConnelsville, 1969-71; intern Shanely Pharmacy, Covington, Ohio, 1971-72, staff pharmacist, 1972-82; staff pharmacist Piqua Med. Ctr., Ohio, 1972-80, sr. staff pharmacist, 1980—. Bd. dirs. Miami County ARC, Piqua, Ohio, 1984—, Miami County Am. Cancer Soc., Troy, Ohio, 1979. Fellow Ohio State Pharm. Assn. (assoc. dir.), Am. Pharm. Assn., Ohio Soc. Hosp. Pharmacists, Am. Soc. Hosp. Pharmacists, Dayton Area Soc. Hosp. Pharmacists. Republican. Methodist. Lodge: Eagles. Avocations: jogging; golf; softball; bowling. Home: 1814 Carol Dr Piqua OH 45356

CALENDINE, RICHARD HARLEY, college administrator; b. Parkersburg, W.Va., Oct. 25, 1939; s. Harley William and Margaret Irene (Armstrong) C.; B.A., W.Va. Wesleyan Coll., 1962; M.A., Ohio State U., 1966; m. Georgeann Allard, Aug. 22, 1964; children—Caren Ferree, Michelle Louise. Terminal clk. Am. Bitumals and Asphalt Co., Marietta, Ohio, 1959-61; asst. dir. student financial aids Ohio State U., Columbus, 1964-67, counseling psychologist Counseling Center, 1967-74; financial aids officer Columbus Tech. Inst., 1974—. Individual practice psychology, Columbus, 1973—. Bd. dirs. Columbus Campaign for Arms Control. Mem. Am., Ohio psychol. assns., Nat., Ohio assns. student financial aid adminstrs., First Families of Ohio, Order Crown of Charlemagne in U.S.A., Ohio Geneal. Soc. (v.p. chpt. 1979), Phi Delta Kappa, Omicron Delta Kappa, Psi Chi, Theta Xi, Alpha Phi Omega (chair sect. 58, 1968-70). Presbyterian (chmn. bd. deacons 1973, elder 1980-83). Lodge: Masons (pres. club). Author: College Majors as a Guide to Career Planning, 1972. Home: 111 Webster Park Columbus OH 43214

CALHOUN, DONALD EUGENE, JR., judge; b. Columbus, Ohio, May 15, 1926; s. Donald Eugene and Esther (Cope) C.; m. Shirley Claggett, Aug. 28, 1948; children—Catherine C., Donald E. III, Elizabeth C. B.A. in Polit. Sci., Ohio State U., 1949, J.D., 1951. Bar: Ohio 1951. Sole practice, Columbus, Ohio, 1951-68; sr. ptnr. Folkerth, Calhoun, Webster, Maurrer & O'Brien, Attys., Columbus, 1968-82, ptnr. Guren Merritt, Feibel, Sogg & Cohen, Attys., Columbus, 1982-84; counsel Lane Alton & Horst, Attys., Columbus, 1984-85; U.S. bankruptcy judge, 1985—; exec. com. Columbus Bar Found., 1984-85; arbitrator Am. Arbitration Assn., Cin., 1953-85. Mem. exec. com. Franklin County Republican Orgn., Columbus, 1963-85; bd. dirs. Columbus Pub. Schs., pres., 1963-72; bd. dirs., exec. com. bd. homeland ministries United Ch. Christ., N.Y.C., 1978-85. Served with USN, 1944-46. Recipient Outstanding Young Man award Columbus Jr. C. of C., 1957. Fellow Ohio State Bar Found., Columbus Bar Found. (chmn. 1974); mem. Columbus Bar Assn. (pres. 1967-68, Community Service award 1972), Ohio State Bar Assn., ABA. Congregationalist. Club: University (pres. 1977). Lodge: Masons. Home: 216 W Beechwold Blvd Columbus OH 43214 Office: US Courthouse 85 Marconi Blvd Columbus OH 43215

CALHOUN, JAMES LAWRENCE, IV, metalworking company executive; b. East Orange, N.J., Jan. 8, 1931; s. James Lawrence and Lewie Blakeslee C.; m. Joanne Louise Tesch, Aug. 8, 1953; children—Natalie Patricia, Julia Gail, Susan Elisabeth, James Lawrence V. B.S. in Mech. Engring., Northwestern U., 1953. Various middle mgmt. positions Continental Foundry & Machine Co., 1953-56; with Blaw-Knox Co., 1956-74, mgr. engring., 1969-70, plant mgr. East Chicago (Ind.) works, 1970-74; with White Consol. Industries, Inc., Cleve., 1974—, v.p. energy and environ. affairs, 1976—, v.p. foundries, 1980—, v.p. productivity and environ. affairs, 1985—. Mem. Council on Energy and Environ. Balance, Cleve. Served with U.S. Army, 1954-55. Mem. Am. Foundrymen's Soc. (dir. Northeast Ohio), Cast Metals Fedn., Iron Casting Soc., Steel Founders Soc. Am., MAPI Hazardous Waste Council (vice chmn.). Episcopalian. Home: 592 Welshire St Bay Village OH 44140 Office: 11770 Berea Rd Cleveland OH 44111

CALHOUN, JOHN CHARLES, civil and structural engineer; b. Omaha, May 9, 1941; s. John Harlan and Opal Mae (Leonard) C.; m. Mary Camille Case, Aug. 5, 1962; children—Michael John, Ann Christine. B.S. in C.E., U. Iowa, 1964; M.S., U. Iowa, 1966. Registered profl. engr., Iowa, Mich., Minn., Nebr. Engr.-in-tng. Powers & Assocs., Iowa City, 1964-66; cons. engr. Powers-Willis & Assocs., Iowa City, 1968-73; county engr. Madison County (Iowa), Winterset, 1973-77; v.p. Terry A. Shuck Structural Engrs., Inc., Des Moines, 1977-82; pres. Calhoun-Britson-Assocs., Inc., West Des Moines, 1982—. Mem. Iowa Hwy. Research Bd., 1974-76; dir. Iowa Good Rds. Assn., 1982—. Active United Way of Greater Des Moines; participant Joint Civilian Orientation Conf. 47, 1982. Served to 1st lt., C.E., U.S. Army, 1966-68. Decorated Bronze Star; Nile Kinnick Meml. scholar U. Iowa, 1959. Mem. ASCE (sect. past pres.), Am. Cons. Engrs. Council, Cons. Engrs. Council Iowa, Nat. Soc. Profl. Engrs., Iowa Engring. Soc. (pres. 1985-86), Am. Ry. Engring. Assn., Am. Pub. Works Assn., Am. Concrete Inst., Am. Inst. Steel Constrn., Def. Orientation Conf. Assn. Republican. Mem. United Ch. of Christ. Lodge: Masons. Office: 929 9th St West Des Moines IA 50265

CALHOUN, LILLIAN SCOTT, public relations co. exec.; b. Savannah, Ga., June 25, 1925; d. Walter Sanford and Laura (McDowell) Scott; B.A., Ohio State U., 1944; m. Harold William Calhoun, Sept. 20, 1950; children—Laura, Harold, Walter, Karen. Columnist, feature editor Chgo. Defender, 1963-65; asso. editor Jet, Ebony, mags., 1961-63; reporter Chgo. Sun-Times, 1965-68; mng. editor Integrated Edn. mag., 1968-71; info. officer, acting info. dir. Dept. Labor, 1971-73; co-editor Chgo. Reporter, 1973-76; pres., founder Calmar Communications, Inc., Chgo., 1978—; columnist Crain's Chgo. Bus., 1978-80, Chgo. Journalism Rev., 1969-74. Vice-chairperson Ill. Commn. on Human Relations, 1973-75; mem. Gov.'s Commn. on Status of Women, 1965-67, Gov.'s Adv. Council on Manpower, 1973-75. Recipient YWCA Leader award, 1984. Mem. Soc. Midland Authors, Chgo. Network, Alpha Gamma Pi. Episcopalian. Clubs: Chgo. Press, Publicity, Arts. Office: 500 N Dearborn St Suite 1302 Chicago IL 60610

CALHOUN, SALLY HANSON, clinical psychologist, educator; b. Wauwatosa, Wis., July 7, 1939; d. Lee Delbert and Olive Elizabeth (Congdon) Hanson; B.A. with distinction in English, U. Mich., 1961, M.A. in English, 1963; M.A. (USPHS fellow), Northwestern U., 1967, Ph.D. in Clin. Psychology, 1970; m. David Redfearn Calhoun, Sept. 5, 1964; children—Douglas David, Julie Katherine. Clin. clk. Hines VA Hosp., 1964; psychologist Ill. State Psychiat. Inst., 1965-69; cons. Nelson Hall Pub. Co., 1972-78, also lectr. Northeastern Ill. U., 1972-77; with Assoc. Psychotherapists of Chgo., 1973-74; pvt. practice clin. psychology, Glenview, Ill., 1978—; asst. prof., core faculty Forest Inst. Profl. Psychology, 1979—. Recipient awards for fiction Scholastic Mag., 1954, 56, Avery Hopwood writing award U. Mich., 1958. Mem. Am. Psychol. Assn., Ill. Psychol. Assn., Nat. Council Health Service Providers Psychology, Nat. Soc. Arts and Letters, Mortar Bd., Pi Beta Phi. Office: 1717 Glenview Rd Suite 200 Glenview IL 60025

CALHOUN, SHERYL LYNNE, nurse; b. Des Moines, Apr. 15, 1956; d. Joe Louis and Patricia Lou (Wyant) C. A.A., Grand View Coll., 1978, B.S.N., 1979. Staff nurse Broadlawns Med. Ctr., Des Moines, 1979-82; unit mgr. Des Moines Gen. Hosp., 1982-83, chief patient care coordinator, 1983—. Mem. Am. Assn. Critical Care Nurses, Iowa Nurses Assn., Assn. Nurses in Osteo. Medicine. Democrat. Home: 1338 E 15th St Des Moines IA 50316

CALICO, PAUL BRENT, lawyer; b. Berea, Ky., Aug. 24, 1954; s. Thurman E. and Norma Jean (Brandenberg) C.; m. Ann Carol Rutherford, June 2, 1979; 1 child, Austin Clay. B.S. magna cum laude, Western Ky. U., 1976; J.D. with distinction, U. Ky., 1980. Bar: Ohio 1980, Ky. 1981, U.S. Dist. Ct. (so. dist.) Ohio 1980, U.S. Dist. Ct. (ea. dist.) Ky. 1981. Assoc. Strauss, Troy & Ruehlmann Co., L.P.A., Cin., 1980—. Contbr. legal/med. articles to profl. jours. Decorated Order of the Coif U. Ky.; mem. ABA, Ohio Bar Assn., Ky. Bar Assn., Cin. Law Library Assn., Cin. Bar Assn. (arbitrator 1982—, participant vol. lawyers for the poor project 1983—, mem. common pleas ct. com. 1985—, mcpl. ct., civil law and procedure com. 1985—, domestic relations com. 1985—), No. Ky. Bar Assn. Presbyterian. Home: 1227 Laurence Rd Wyoming OH 45215 Office: Strauss Troy & Ruehlmann Co LPA 201 E 5th St Suite 2100 Cincinnati OH 45202

CALIENDO, EMIL PHILIP, lawyer, state hearing officer and adviser; b. Chgo., May 22, 1954; s. Rocco Frank and Angeline (Davolio) C. B.A. in Sociology and Polit. Sci., Rosary Coll., 1976; J.D., No. Ill. U., 1979. Bar: Ill. 1980, U.S. Dist. Ct. (no. dist.) Ill. 1980, U.S. Ct. Appeals (7th cir.) 1981. Sole practice, Chgo., 1980—; atty., hearing officer, tech. adviser to Ill. Sec. of State, Chgo., 1981—, mem. bd. rev., Springfield, 1983—; mem. hearing com. Rosary Coll., River Forest, Ill., 1975, 76. Atty. 36th Ward Regular Democratic Orgn., Chgo., 1982. Mem. Chgo. Bar Assn. Roman Catholic. Clubs: Marro-Caliendo Softball (co-capt. 1976—), Randolph Tower (Chgo.); Oak Park Ct. Ho. (Oak Park, Ill.). Office: 180 N LaSalle Chicago IL 60601

CALIGIURI, VINCENT JOSEPH, quality engineer; b. Toledo, Oct. 2, 1951; s. Vincent Angelo and Mary Lou (Hohl) C.; m. Donna Marie Hackworth, May 1, 1982; 1 dau., Deanna Marie. B.B.A., U. Toledo, 1975. Cert. quality engr., Ohio Sr. process technician Imperial Clevite Inc., Milan, Ohio, 1975-81; quality engr. Gen. Tire & Rubber, Wabash, Ind., 1981—; tchr. statis. quality control courses to plant personnel. Mem. Am. Soc. Quality Control. Democrat. Roman Catholic. Home: 473 N Wabash St Wabash IN 46992 Office: 1 General St Wabash IN 46992

CALIMAFDE, GEORGE JOHN, paper company executive; b. N.Y.C., May 28, 1920; s. Michael John and Nellie (Fuglewicz) C.; m. Laurie Ann Wintle, Nov. 19, 1955; 1 child, Deirdre Ann. B.B.A., St. John's U., 1942; LL.B., St. John's U. Law Sch., 1949. Bar: N.Y., 1949. Asst. mgr. tax dept. Diamond Internat. Corp., N.Y.C., 1949-52; mgr. tax dept. U.S. Plywood Corp., N.Y.C., 1953-56; v.p., gen. mgr. Fisherman Press Corp., Oxford, Ohio, 1956-58; asst. to pres. Nationwide Papers, Inc., Chgo., 1958-68; pres. United Mchts. Inc., Atlanta, 1968-76; exec. dir. Paper Industry Mgmt. Assn., Arlington Heights, Ill., 1976—. Served as tech. sgt. USAF, 1942-46. Mem. Am. Soc. Assn. Execs., TAPPI, Can. Pulp and Paper Assn. Republican. Roman Catholic. Avocations: reading; golf; model building; gardening. Home: 35 Walnut Lane Dundee IL 60118 Office: Paper Industry Mgmt Assn 2400 E Oakton St Arlington Heights IL 60005

CALIRI, JOSEPH LOUIS, lawyer, corp. exec.; b. Rochester, N.Y., Mar. 16, 1916; s. Salvatore and Maria Teresa (Bottazzi) C.; A.B., U. Rochester, 1938; LL.B., Cornell, 1941; m. Dorothy Ann McGrath, Aug. 19, 1944; children—Robert Redmond, Barbara Jane. Admitted to N.Y. bar, 1941, Ill. bar, 1974; law dept. Kraft, Inc. (formerly Nat. Dairy Products Corp.), N.Y.C., 1941-51, asst. sec., 1951-52, sec., 1952-71, v.p., 1971—, dir., 1980—; v.p., sec. Dart & Kraft, Inc., 1980-81; ret., 1981. Past pres. Bd. Edn., Union Free Sch. Dist. No. 9, West Islip, L.I. Mem. Am. Judicature Soc., Am. Soc. Corp. Secs., Am., Ill., Chgo. bar assns., Cornell Law Assn., Phi Beta Kappa, Alpha Phi Delta. Clubs: Magoun Landing Yacht (West Islip, N.Y.); Cornell (N.Y.); Mich. Shores, Westmoreland Country (Wilmette, Ill.). Home: 1500 Sheridan Rd Wilmette IL 60091

CALK, RICHARD EDWARD, jewelry executive; b. Cin., Feb. 13, 1938; s. Joseph and Frances Earl (Reese) C.; m. Barbara Anne Towhey, July 1, 1961; children—Richard E., Stephen, Matthew, Margaret Frances, John Towhey. A.A., U. Cin., 1960; B.A., Nat. Coll. Edn., 1982, M.S., 1983. Region mgr. Internat. Playtex, N.Y.C., 1973-74, European sales dir., Slough, Eng., 1974-75; mktg. mgr. Playtex U.K. Ltd., London, 1975-77; gen. mgr. Playtex Scandanavia, Copenhagen, 1977-78; v.p., chief operating officer STP Internat. Inc., Fort Lauderdale, Fla., 1978-80; v.p. mktg. and sales Pakula & Co., Chgo., 1980—. Trustee Commerce Twp., Mich., Walled Lake, 1968, Town of Lincolnshire, Ill., 1985—. Mem. Union Lake Jaycees (Mich.; v.p. 1967-68), Delta Sigma Pi. Republican. Roman Catholic. Clubs: East Bank, Merchants and Mfrs. (Chgo.). Home: 17 Victoria Ln Lincolnshire IL 60015 Office: Pakula & Co 166 Apparel Center Chicago IL 60654

CALKINS, MYRON DONALD, city public works administrator; b. Tacoma, Wash., Oct. 1, 1919; s. Donald James Fernando and Mabel Bryant (Adams) C.; m. Nettie Alice Overman, June 21, 1942 (dec. 1978); children—Susan Jean, Ronald James, Donald Cyrus; m. 2d E. Lenore Jacob, May 5, 1979. B.S. in C.E., Wash. State U., 1942; B.S. in Mgmt. Engring. (hon.), U. Mo.-Rolla, 1975. Registered Profl. Engr., Mo., Wash. Hydraulic engr. U.S. Geol. Survey, Portland, Oreg., 1942-44, 46-47; bridge design engr. Wash. Hwy. Dept., Olympia, 1947-48; project engr. City of Tacoma, Wash., 1948-55, city engr., 1955-64; dir. pub. works City of Kansas City, Mo., 1964—. Contbr. articles to tech. jours. Active Boy Scouts Am., 1955-57, 61-64; mem. Speakers Bur., United Way, Kansas City, 1979-82. Served with USNR, 1944-46. Mem. Am. Pub. Works Assn. (past pres.), Am. Acad. Environ. Engrs. (trustee 1981-84), ASCE (recipient Edmund Friedman Profl. Recognition award 1979), Am. Rd. & Transp. Bldrs. Assn. (div. pres. 1979-80), Nat. Soc. Profl. Engrs. (pres. Mo. chpt. 1979-80), Soc. Am. Mil. Engrs. (pres. Kansas City post 1978-79), Hwy. Engrs. Assn. Mo. (past pres.), Pub. Works Hist. Soc. (past pres.). Club: Engineers (past pres.). Avocations: Travelling; stamp collecting; music. Office: Pub Works Dept 414 E 12th St Kansas City MO 64106

CALLAHAN, CECIL, financial analyst; b. Atlanta, Minn., May 1, 1954; s. Henry F. Sr. and Juanita (Davis) C. B.A. in Econs., Polit. Sci. and History, Macalester Coll., 1976; M.S. in Mgmt., Carnegie-Mellon U., 1978. Fin. analyst State of Minn., St. Paul, 1979-81; bank lender Norwest Bank, Mpls., 1981-83; fin. planning analyst Fed. Reserve, Mpls., 1983—, mgmt. sci. analyst, 1983—. Bd. dirs. Minn. Inst. Black Chem. Abuse, Macalester Coll. Alumni Bd.; del. local Democratic conv. caucus, 1984. Avocations: marathon running, cooking, racquetball. Office: Fed Reserve Bank 250 Marquette Ave Minneapolis MN 55404

CALLAHAN, CHARLES, III, economics educator, consultant; b. Fairmont, W.Va., Feb. 24, 1949; s. Charles, Jr., and Lucille Geneva (Beasley) C.; children—JoAnn, Andrew. A.B., Otterbein Coll., 1971; A.M., U. Ill., 1974, Ph.D., 1979. Programmer, Rockwell Internat., Columbus, Ohio, 1971-72; teaching asst. U. Ill., Urbana, 1973-75; asst. prof. Denison U., Granville, Ohio, 1976-83; assoc. prof. econs. No. State Coll., Aberdeen, S.D., 1983—; cons. Served with USAR, 1982-83. Grantee Order Eastern Star, 1968, U. Ill., 1972; recipient award U.S. Jaycees, 1982. Mem. Am. Econ. Assn., Missouri Valley Econ. Assn., Indsl. Relations Research Assn., Midwest Econ. Assn., Western Econ. Assn., Pi Gamma Mu, Omicron Delta Epsilon, Sigma Iota Epsilon, Sigma Phi Omega. Mem. Assembly of God Ch. Contbr. articles to publs. Home and Office: Northern State College Aberdeen SD 57401

CALLAHAN, FRANCIS JOSEPH, manufacturing company executive; b. Lima, Ohio, July 8, 1923; s. Francis J. and Bertha E. (Falk) C.; m. Mary Elizabeth Krouse, June 30, 1945; children—Francis Joseph III, Cornelia S. Callahan Richards, Timothy J. Student U. Dayton, 1941; B.S., U.S. Naval Acad., 1945; B.S.E.E., MIT, 1948, M.S., Nuclear Engring., 1953. Commd. ensign U.S. Navy, 1945, advanced through grades to capt. USNR, 1976, project officer USS Nautilus, USS Seawolf, 1954-58; pres. Nupro Co., Willoughby, Ohio, 1958—; v.p. Crawford Fitting Co., Solon, Ohio, 1959-81, pres., 1981—; pres. Whitey Co., Cleveland Heights, Ohio, 1960—; dir. Midwest Bank & Trust Co., 1969—, Midwestern Nat. Life Ins. Co., 1970—, Tappan Co., 1977-80, Invacare Co., 1980—, Environ. Growth Control Co., 1970—, Royal Appliance Co., 1984—, Applied Concrete Tech., 1984—. Chmn. bd. trustees Gilmoor Acad., 1973-79, recipient Man of Yr. award, 1973; chmn. bd. dirs. Marymount Hosp., 1983; trustee Cleve. Boys Clubs, 1970—; bd. dirs. Jr. Achievement, 1963—. Mem. Atomic Indsl. Forum, NAM, ASME. Roman Catholic. Clubs: Kirtland Country, Pepper Pike, Union, Hillbrook (Cleve.); Quail Creek Country (Naples, Fla.). Patentee valves, fittings. Home: 3195 Roundwood Rd Hunting Valley OH 44022

CALLAHAN, MICHAEL THOMAS, construction consultant, lawyer; b. Kansas City, Mo., Oct. 7, 1948; s. Harry Leslie and Venita June (Yohn) C.; B.A., U. Kans., 1970; J.D., U. Mo., 1973, LL.M., 1979; postgrad. Temple U., 1976-77; m. Stella Sue Paffenbach, Mar. 21, 1970; children—Molly Leigh, Michael Kroh. Admitted to Kans. bar, 1973, N.J. bar, 1975, Mo. bar, 1977; v.p. T.J. Constrn., Inc., Lenexa, Kans., 1973-74; sr. cons. Wagner-Hohns-Inglis, Inc., Mt. Holly, N.J., 1974-77, v.p., Kansas City, Mo., 1977—; adj. prof. U. Kans.; arbitrator, lectr. in field; mem. Bldg. Industry Adv. Bd. Mem. Am. Bar Assn., N.J. Bar Assn., Mo. Bar Assn., Am. Arbitration Assn., Project Mgrs. Inst., Fed. Bar Assn., Internat. Wine and Food Soc., Congregationalist. Clubs: Kansas City, Indian Hills Country. Lodge: Rotary Internat. Author: Desk Book of Construction Law, 1981; Discovery in Construction Litigation, 1983; Construction Schedules, 1983; contbr. articles to profl. jours. Home: 9011 Delmar St Prairie Village KS 66207 Office: 8700 State Line Rd Suite 310 Leawood KS 66206

CALLIHAN, HARRIET K., medical society executive; b. Chgo., Feb. 8, 1930; d. Harry Louis and Josephine (Olstad) Kohlman; B.A., U. Chgo., 1951, M.B.A., 1953; m. Clair Clifton Callihan, Dec. 17, 1955; 1 dau., Barbara Claire Eloy-Callihan. Personnel dir. Leo Burnett Co., Chgo., 1953-57, John Plain & Co., 1957-62, Follett Pub. Co., 1962-64, Needham, Harper & Steers, N.Y.C., 1966-68, Bell, Boyd, Lloyd, Haddad & Burns, 1964-66; Hume, Clement, Hume & Lee, 1968-70, owner, operator PersD, 1970-75; exec. dir. Inst. Medicine Chgo., 1975—, mng. editor ofcl. med. publ. Proceedings, 1975—. Sec./treas. Interagy. Council on Smoking and Disease. Mem. Chgo. Soc. Assn. Execs., Conf. Med. Soc. Execs. Greater Chgo. (pres.), Am. Med. Writers Assn. (pres.), Women in Health Care, Lincoln Park Zool. Soc., Field Mus. Soc. Natural History, Nat. Soc. Fund Raising Exec. Profl. Conv. Mgrs. Assn., Women in Mgmt., Chgo. Council Fgn. Relations, Chgo. Connection, Met. Chgo. Coalition Aging, Midwest Pharm. Advt. Club. Clubs: Westmoreland Country, Michigan Shores; Publicity of Chgo. Office: Inst of Medicine of Chicago 332 S Michigan Ave Chicago IL 60604

CALLIN, DIANE TOMCHEFF, English educator; b. Melrose Park, Ill., May 15, 1935; d. Demeter Stephen and Frosa (Buteff) Tomcheff; m. Charles Ovington Callin; 1 dau., Erin Leigh. B.A., U. Ill.-Urbana, 1957, Ph.D., 1975; M.A., Northwestern U., 1966. Cert. high sch. and jr. high sch. tchr., Ill. English tchr. Chgo. Pub. Schs., 1957-58, Los Angeles Pub. Schs., 1959-61; tchr., honors dir. Fenton High Sch., Bensenville, Ill., 1961-68; prof. English, William Rainey Harper Coll., Palatine, Ill., 1968—, also dir. honors program. Author: Perceptions and Reflections, 1973; also articles. Patentee doll's house with unique locks. Grantee in field. Mem. Nat. Council Tchrs. of English, Ill. Council Tchrs. of English, Tchrs. Union, AAUW, Frontiers, Signs LWV, Popular Culture Assn., Phi Theta Kappa, Phi Beta Kappa, Phi Kappa Phi, Alpha Lambda Delta. Mortar Bd. Democrat. Home: 10 S Addison St Bensenville IL 60106 Office: Harper College Roselle and Algonquin Rds Palatine IL 60067

CALLIS, KENNETH EDWARD, psychologist; b. Nashville, Mar. 31, 1948; s. Ken J. and Jane (Smith) C.; m. Gail Herndon, March 22, 1970; children—Chad, Andy. B.S., U. Tenn., 1971; M.A., Southeast Mo. State U., 1975. Cert. psychologist, Mo. Tchr.-coach, Washington County (Mo.) schs., 1971-74; tchr.-coach Jackson Public Schs., Mo., 1974-75, guidance counselor, 1975-77; assoc. dir. community services St. Francis Mental Health Ctr., Cape Girardeau, Mo., 1977—; cons. Region 8 Community Mental Health Ctr. Tech. Assistance Program, Lawrence, Kans. Mem. Am. Psychol. Assn. Baptist. Home: Rt 3 Jackson MO 63755 Office: St Francis Mental Health Ctr Cape Girardeau MO 63701

CALLIS, KENNETH RIVERS, clergyman; b. Louisville, Aug. 26, 1925; s. George Washington and Fannie Lou (Hutcherson) G.; student Berea Coll., 1943-44; B.S. in Mech. Engring., U. Mich., 1947, postgrad. (Margaret Kraus Ramsdell fellow), 1947-48; M.Div., Asbury Theol. Sem., 1950; D.D. (hon.), Albion Coll., 1975; m. Annie Ruth Smith, Sept. 1, 1949; children—Kenneth Rivers, Annette, Cheryl Lynn. Ordained to ministry United Methodist Ch., 1949; minister, Mich., 1950—, sr. minister Ypsilanti 1st Meth. Ch., 1965-72, Court St. Meth. Ch., Flint, 1972-77, Utica United Meth. Ch., Sterling Heights, 1977—; trustee Asbury Theol. Sem., 1979—; pres. bd. trustees United Meth. Retirement Homes, Detroit conf., 1979—; dean Mich. Pastors Sch., 1972-75; mem. World Meth. Council, 1971-76; del. Gen. Conf., 1976. Mem. Sterling Heights Housing Commn., 1978—; exec. bd., council advancement chmn. Clinton Valley council Boy Scouts Am., 1978-80, exec. bd. Tall Pine council, 1974-77; mem. Ypsilanti Housing Commn., 1969-72. Served to ensign USN, 1943-46. Mem. Utica Ministerial Assn. Contbr. articles to religious mag. Home: 8506 Clinton River Rd Sterling Heights MI 48078 Office: Utica United Meth Ch 8650 Canal Rd Sterling Heights MI 48078

CALLISON, ANN LONG, health care accounting manager; b. Wilmington, Del., Aug. 3, 1956; m. Michael R. Callison, Dec. 1, 1979. B.A. in Social Sci., Drake U., 1977, postgrad., 1981. C.P.A., Iowa; cert. tchr., Iowa. Substitute tchr. Des Moines Ind. Sch. Dist., 1977-78; gen. ledger coordinator Am. Republic Ins. Co., Des Moines, 1978-80; facility acctg. mgr. Life Care Services, Des Moines, 1980—. Mem. Health Care Fin. Mgmt. Assn., Phi Beta Kappa, Alpha Lambda Delta. Office: Life Care Services 800 2d Ave Des Moines IA 50309

CALLOW, WILLIAM GRANT, justice Wis. Supreme Ct.; b. Waukesha, Wis., Apr. 9, 1921; s. Curtis Grant and Mildred G. C.; Ph.B. in Econs., U. Wis., 1943, J.D., 1948; m. Jean A. Zilavy, Apr. 15, 1950; children—William Grant, Christine S., Katherine H. Admitted to Wis. bar, 1948; asst. city atty. City of Waukesha, 1948-52, city atty., 1952-60; judge Waukesha County (Wis.) Ct., 1961-77; justice Supreme Ct. Wis., 1978—; asst. prof. law U. Minn., 1951-52; mem. faculty Wis. Jud. Coll., 1968-75. Served with USMC, 1943-45, USAF, 1951-52; Korea. Recipient Disting. Service award Waukesha Jr. C. of C., 1955, Good Human Relations award Dale Carnegie, Disting. Service award Lawyers Wives of Wis. Assn., Outstanding Alumnus award U. Wis., 1973. Fellow Am. Bar Found.; mem. Am. Bar Assn., State Bar Wis., Dane County (Wis.) Bar Assn., Nat. Conf. Commrs. on Uniform State Laws (chmn. Wis. Commn.). Episcopalian. Author State Bar of Wis. pamphlet for teenagers, used as curriculum for all 9th grade students: You and The Law, 1974; contbr. articles to Am. Bar Jour., S.D. Law Rev. Office: State Capitol Box 1688 Madison WI 53701*

CALLOWAY, ROBERT QUINCY, school supply company executive; b. Logansport, Ind., Oct. 14, 1927; s. Charles Quincy and Gladys Fern (Maxson) C.; m. Patricia Louise Sims, Nov. 12, 1950; children—Cynthia Louise, Carol Ann, James Quincy. Student Ind. U., 1948. Founder, pres. Imperial Enterprises Corp., Lafayette, Ind., 1961—, Imperial Ednl. Programs Co., Lafayette, 1970—, Imperial Travel Service, Lafayette, 1974—; dir. Marengo State Bank, Milltown Nat. Bank, Rushville Nat. Bank. Served with USN, 1945-46; ETO. Mem. Nat. Sch. Supply and Equipment Assn., Ind. Sch. Distbrs. Assn. Republican. Lodges: Masons, Shriners, Elks. Home: 3616 Cypress St Lafayette IN 47905 Office: 3440 Kossuth St Lafayette IN 47903

CALLOZZO, FRANK PAUL, orthodontist; b. Chgo., Mar. 24, 1923; s. Frank and Frances (Bruno) C.; 1 child, Mary Gina Trail. D.D.S., Loyola U., Chgo., 1953; postgrad. U. Chgo., 1953-54; M.S. in Orthodontia, U. Ill.-Chgo., 1971. Practice dentistry, Chgo., 1954-69; practice dentistry specializing in orthodontics, Oak Forest, Ill., 1969—. Served with USN, 1942-46. Mem. Chgo. Dental Soc., Ill. Dental Soc., Am. Dental Assn., Ill. Orthodontic Soc., Midwest Orthodontic Soc., Am. Assn. Orthodontics, Blue Key, Omicron Kappa Upsilon. Club: Midlothian Country (Ill.). Republican. Roman Catholic. Lodge: Rotary. Avocation: Stained glass. Home: 1321 Heather Hill Crescent Flossmoor IL 60422 Office: Oak Forest Profl Ctr 15510 S Cicero Ave Oak Forest IL 60452

CALOMENI, DALE ANTHONY, lawyer; b. Detroit, Mar. 31, 1952; s. Anthony David and Annette (Bayliff) C.; B.A. cum laude, Seattle U., 1974; J.D., Thomas M. Cooley Sch. Law 1979. Bar: Mich. 1980, U.S. Dist. Ct. (we. dist.) Mich. 1981. Intern commerce div. Mich. Atty. Gen.'s Office, Lansing, 1977, City Atty.'s Office, Jackson, Mich., 1978-79; asst. pros. atty. Kent County Prosecutor's Office, Grand Rapids, Mich., 1979-81; ptnr. Henkel & Calomeni, P.C., Grand Rapids, 1981—. Active Rockford Jaycees, Mich., 1982-83. Mem. Grand Rapids Bar Assn., Mich. Bar Assn., Assn. Trial Lawyers Am. Republican. Office: Henkel & Calomeni PC Fountain Hill Profl Offices 72 Ransom St NE Grand Rapids MI 49503

CALVERT, GARY ROSS, insurance company official; b. Columbus, Ohio, Jan. 15, 1947; s. H. Ross and Betty Carol (Wood) C.; B.S., U.S. Mil. Acad., 1969; m. Judith Carolyn Calvert, Nov. 30, 1979; 1 dau., Jennifer Niccole; children from previous marriage—Christiana Lynn, Geoffrey Ross. Commd. 2d lt. U.S. Army, 1969, advanced through grades to capt., 1971; ret., 1974; mgr. tng. and devel. Procter and Gamble Paper Products, Mehoopany, Pa., 1974-77; dir. tng. and devel. Arthur Treacher's Fish and Chips, Columbus, 1977-79; dir. tng. and devel. J.C. Penney Casualty Ins., Westerville, Ohio, 1980—. Mem. Am. Soc. Tng. and Devel. (editor Central Ohio newsletter 1982-83), Nat. Ins. Cos. Edn. Dirs. Soc., Assn. Grads. U.S. Mil. Acad., Phi Delta Kappa. Methodist. Home: 1860 Knollridge Ct Columbus OH 43229 Office: 800 Brooksedge Blvd Westerville OH 43081

CALVERT, NANCY ANN, public relations executive; b. Michigan City, Ind., Oct. 26, 1939; d. E. Preston and Eloise (Worthington) C. B.A. in Communication Arts, Lindenwood Coll., 1961; postgrad. U. Ariz., summers 1962-64. Dir. pub. relations, tchr. journalism, pub. schs., Michigan City, 1962-65; asst. dir. radio and TV, Batz Hodgson Neuwoehner Advt. and Pub. Relations, St. Louis, 1965-68; dir. pub. relations, pub. sch. dist., St. Charles, 1968-76; staff asst. pub. relations, Electro-Motive div. Gen. Motors Corp., LaGrange, Ill., 1976-79, asst. dir. pub. relations, 1979, dir. pub. relations and advt., 1979—, mem. Gen. Motors Chgo. pub. affairs com., 1979—, mem. steering com. Gen. Motors civic involvement program, 1982—. Trustee Chgo. 4-H Found. Mem. Am. R.R. Found. (chmn. advt. subcom.), Ry. Progress Inst. (pub. relations adv. com.), Assn. Am. R.R.s (pub. relations adv. com.), R.R. Pub. Relations Assn. (v.p. 1982-83, program chmn. 1984, sr. v.p. 1985, pres. 1985-86), Assn. R.R. Advt. Mgrs., Women's Advt. Club Chgo., Pub. Relations Soc. Am., Pub. Relations Clinic, Alpha Epsilon Rho. Episcopalian. Clubs: Chgo. Press; Pottawattomie Country (Michigan City). Office: Gen Motors Electro-Motive Div LaGrange IL 60525

CALVIN, ROBERT JOSEPH, management consultant; b. Chgo., Dec. 28, 1936; s. Joseph K. and Pauline (Harris) C.; m. Jane L. Levy, Apr. 27, 1940; children—Susan D., Amy E. B.A., Conn. Wesleyan U., 1956; M.B.A., Columbia U., 1957. Salesman, acct., prodn. mgr. Cryovac div. W.R. Grace Co., Boston, 1958-60; asst. to pres. Lab. for Electronics, Boston, 1960-62; gen. mgr. Mid Continent Leasing, Chgo., 1963-65; pres. Hayward Marum Inc., Lawrence, Mass., 1970-80, Mgmt. Dimensions Inc., Chgo., 1962—. Guest lectr. Grad. Sch. Bus., U. Chgo., 1968—. Pres. bd. dirs. Jane Addams Ctr., Chgo.; bd. dirs. Hull House Assocs., Author: Profitable Sales Management and Marketing for Growing Businesses, 1983.

CALVIN, STAFFORD RICHARD, retail mail order house executive; b. St. Paul Apr. 6, 1931; s. Carl and Zelda Ida (Engelson) C.; m. Phyllis Lotwin, Sept. 15, 1958 (div 1970); m. Nancy Pistner, Sept. 21, 1974 (div.); children—Lawrence, Carlton, Loran. B.A., U. Minn. 1952. Pres. Sibley Co., St. Paul, 1953-58, Dealers Distbrs., St. Paul, 1958-65; v.p. Internat. Systems Assn., N.Y.C., 1965-70, Carlson Cos., Mpls., 1970-74; chmn. bd. Calhoun's Collectors Soc., Inc., Mpls., 1974—. Vice pres. Jewish Family Services, St. Paul, 1982; bd. dirs. Little Bros. of Elderly, Chgo., 1984. Democrat. Home: PO Box 35733 Edina MN 55435 Office: Calhoun's Collectors Soc Inc 7401 Cahill Rd Minneapolis MN 55435

CAMBPELL, CHARLES DAVID, college administrator; b. Midland, Mich., May 14, 1953; s. Charles David and Ida Margaret (Tovey) C.; m. Susan Goethel, Aug. 20, 1977; 1 child, Morgan. B.A., Alma Coll., 1975; M.A., Central Mich. U., 1981. Asst. dean students Alma Coll., Mich., 1976-77, assoc. dean students, 1977-80; dean students Ctr. for Creative Studies, Coll. Art and Design, Detroit, 1980—. Profl. rep. arts adv. com. U. Liggett Sch., Grosse Pointe Woods, Mich., 1981—. Chmn. Med. Ctr. Citizens Dist. Council, 1984—. Mem. Am. Assn. Counseling and Devel., Am. Coll. Personnel Assn., Mich. Personnel and Guidance Assn., Detroit Inst. Arts Founders Soc. Home: 10085 LaSalle St Huntington Woods MI 48070 Office: Coll Art and Design Ctr Creative Studies 245 E Kirby St Detroit MI 48202

CAMBRE, LEON ANTONIO, forest manager; b. Jackson, Miss., Oct. 31, 1932; s. Leonce Antonio and Veronica Anna (Grohoski) C.; m. Elizabeth Ann Phillips, Sept. 3, 1955; children—John, Mary Ann, Donna Sue, Cheryl Lee, Joseph David. B.S. in Forest Mgmt., Miss. State U., 1958. Dep. forest supr. Daniel Boone Nat. Forest, Winchester, Ky., 1969-71; congl. fellow U.S. Congress, 1971-72; forest supr. Nat. Forests in Miss., Jackson, 1972-75; dir. legis. affairs U.S. Forest Service, Washington D.C., 1975-77, dir. coop. forestry, 1977-79; forest supr. Mark Twain Nat. Forest, Rolla, Mo., 1979—. Served to staff sgt. USAF, 1951-55, Korea. Recipient Miss. Conservationist of Yr. award Nat. Wildlife Fedn., 1974; Outstanding Alumnus award Miss. State U. Sch Forest Resources, 1980; Nat. Energy Efficiency award Dept. Energy, 1982; Superior Service award Dept. Agr., 1983. Mem. Soc. Am. Foresters, Wildlife Soc., Audubon Soc., Nat. Wildlife Fedn., Ruffled Grouse Soc. Roman Catholic. Lodge: Rotary. Avocations: sports, woodworking. Office: Mark Twain Nat Forest 401 Fairgrounds Road Rolla MO 65401

CAMBURN, MARVIN EDWIN, mathematics educator, educational administrator; b. Stockbridge, Mich., Apr. 1, 1938; s. Burtis Harmon and Gertrude Lillian (Stephens) C.; m. Joyce Carol Weeman, June 7, 1959; children—Eric Marvin, Stephen Arthur. B.A., Albion Coll., 1960; M.A., U. Detroit, 1964; Ph.D., Mich. State U., 1971; postdoctoral Harvard U., 1982. Tchr. math. pub. high schs., Mich., N.Y., 1960-66; instr. Wayne State Coll., Nebr., 1966-68; assoc. prof. Mercyhurst Coll., Erie Pa., 1971-78, chmn. dept. math., 1974-75, chmn. sci. div., 1975-77, coordinator instl. devel., 1976-78; dean faculty and instrn. Ill. Benedictine Coll., Lisle, 1978—; sec. Consortium West Suburban Colls., Lisle, 1979-80, 1984—; chmn. Acad. Adv. Panel, 1980-81; mem. exec. bd. Associated Colls. Chgo. Area, River Forest, Ill., 1979-84, treas., 1980-82, chmn., 1982-83. Contbr. articles to profl. jours. Summer Inst. fellow NSF, 1962-63, 1963-64, 1968, teaching fellow Mich. State U., 1969-71; Sch. Natural Sci. Scholarship Mich. State U., 1970-71. Mem. Am. Math. Soc., Math. Assn. Am., Am. Assn. Higher Edn., Am. Council Acad. Deans, Lisle C. of C., Kappa Mu Epsilon. Home: 542 Gamble Dr Lisle IL 60532 Office: Ill Benedictine Coll 5700 Coll Rd Lisle IL 60532

CAMCAM, GLORIA AMAGO, dietitian; b. Manila, Philippines, Jan. 15, 1929; came to U.S., 1968, naturalized, 1974; d. Emilio N. and Dolores A. (Almendrala) Amago; B.S., U. Philippines, 1953; M.S. in Nutrition, U. Ia., 1954; m. Nicolas G. Camcam, Jr., Apr. 21, 1963; children—Nicolas III, Nathan. Staff dietitian, U. Iowa Hosps., Iowa City, 1954-55; research dietitian Philippine Gen. Hosp., Manila, 1955-68; therapeutic dietitian St. Elizabeth Hosp., Chgo., 1968-71, chief therapeutic dietitian, 1971-79, chief nutritional services, 1980—; 1st chmn. Bd. Examiners for Dietitians, Philippines, 1963-65; cons. dietetic internship Philippine Gen. Hosp., 1965-68. U. Iowa fellow, 1953; 25th Anniversary Certificate of Appreciation as Pres., Dietetic Assn. Philippines, 1957-61. Mem. Ill. Dietetic Assn., Am. Dietetic Assn., Chgo. Dietetic Assn., Am. Soc. Hosp. Food Service Adminstrs. (Chgo.-Midwest chpt.), Am. Soc. Parenteral and Enteral Nutrition, Ill. Food Service Execs. Assn. Mem. Philippine-Am. Ecumenical Ch. Home: 3731 W Windsor St Chicago IL 60625

CAMERON, J. DOUGLAS, ophthalmic pathologist, ophthalmologist; b. Erskine, Minn., Jan. 7, 1943; s. John H. and Annette L. (Larson) C.; m. Barbara Ruth Hauser, Sept. 17, 1967; children—Jason, Stuart, David. B.A., St. Olaf Coll., 1965; M.D., Northwestern U., 1969. Diplomate Am. Bd. Ophthalmology. Intern Montefiore Hosp. and Med. Ctr., N.Y.C., 1969-70; in pub. health service Navajo Indian Reservation, Crownpoint Indian Hosp., N.Mex., 1970-72; fellow ophthalmic pathology Scheie Eye Inst. U. Pa., Phila., 1972-74; clin. resident in ophthalmology, 1974-77; Heed fellow Armed Forces Inst. Pathology, Washington, 1978; asst. prof. Dept. Ophthalmology U. Minn., Mpls., 1978—; chief Dept. Ophthalmology Hennepin County Med. Ctr., Mpls., 1978—; dir. Lab. Ophthalmic Pathology U Minn., Mpls., 1978—; mem. faculty ophthalmic pathology, ophthalmologist course AFIP, Washington, 1978—; Am. Acad Ophthalmology Basic and Clinic Sci., 1980-83, chmn., 1983—; clinic dir. Nat. Eye Inst. Visual Acuity Impairment Pilot Study, Mpls., 1980-82. Author book chpts., abstracts. Contbr. numerous articles to profl. jours. Mem. Assn. for Research in Vision and Ophthalmology (recipient travel fellowship award, 1976), U. Pa. Ophthalmology Alumni Assn. (recipient best resident paper award 1975-76, trustee 1979—), Soc. Heed Fellows, AMA, Armed Forces Inst. Pathology Ophthalmic Branch, Am. Assn. Ophthalmic Pathologists, AAAS, Theobald Soc., Hennepin County Med. Soc., Minn. Med. Soc., Minn. Ophthal. Soc., Minn. Acad. Ophthalmology, Minn. Soc. Clin. Pathologists, Mpls. Med. Research Found. Democrat. Avocations: viola; woodworking; photography. Home: 1720 Humboldt Ave So Minneapolis MN 55403 Office: 701 Park Ave So Minneapolis MN 55415

CAMERON, JOHN JAMES, hardware company executive; b. Milw., Mar. 5, 1933; s. Paul and Frances (Schweda) Chmielewski; m. Ruth Sharon Racette, Oct. 8, 1955; children—John James, Robert, Annemarie. B.S., Marquette U., 1957. News editor Cudahy Reminder-Enterprise, Wis., 1957-63; pub. relations mgr. Met. Milw. Assn. Commerce, 1963-69; pub. relations dir. Marqeutte U., Milw., 1969-73; pub. relations mgr. Miller Brewing Co., Milw., 1973-78, Kraft, Inc., Glenview, Ill., 1978-79; dir. corp. communications Ace Hardware Corp., Oak Brook, Ill., 1979—. Past bd. dirs. Urban Day Sch., Cath. Social Services, Milw. Served with U.S. Army, 1953-55. Recipient Nat. award Am. Coll. Pub. Relations Assn., 1973. Mem. Internat. Assn. Bus. Communicators, Pub. Relations Soc. Am., Am. C. of C. (past pres. publs., Execs. award 1964). Home: 23904 N Quentin Rd Lake Zurich IL 60047 Office: Ace Hardware Corp Oak Brook IL 60521

CAMERON, OLIVER GENE, psychiatrist, educator, psychobiology researcher; b. Evanston, Ill., Aug. 28, 1946; s. Gene Oliver and Elizabeth Marie (Burns) C.; m. Susan Linda Friedman, June 22, 1972; children—Leah Victoria, Peter Sean. B.A., U. Notre Dame, 1968; Ph.D., U. Chgo., 1972, M.D., 1974. Diplomate Am. Bd. psychiatry and Neurology. Med. intern U. Mich., Ann Arbor, 1974-75, psychiatry resident, 1975-78, psychiatry fellow, 1978-79, asst. prof. psychiatry, 1979—, dir. anxiety disorders program, dept. psychiatry, 1984—. Contbr. articles to profl. jours. Mem. Am. Psychiatric Assn., Am. Psychosomatic Soc., AAAS, Sigma Xi. Avocations: photography; travel; golf. Home: 1505 Harbrooke Ann Arbor MI 48103 Office: U Mich 1405 E Ann St Ann Arbor MI 48109

CAMERON, ROY EUGENE, scientist; b. Denver, July 16, 1929; s. Guy Francis and Ilda Annora (Horn) C.: B.S., Wash. State U., 1953 and 1954; M.S., U. Ariz., 1958, Ph.D., 1961; D.D. (hon.), Ministry of Christ Ch., Delavan, Wis., 1975; m. Margot Elizabeth Hoagland, May 5, 1956 (div. July 1977); children—Susan Lynn, Catherine Ann; m. 2d, Carolyn Mary Light, Sept. 22, 1978. Research scientist Hughes Aircraft Corp., Tucson, Ariz., 1955-56; sr. scientist Jet Propulsion Lab., Pasadena, Calif., 1961-68, mem. tech. staff, 1969-74; dir. research Darwin Research Inst., Dana Point, Calif., 1974-75; dep. dir. Land Reclamation Lab. Argonne (Ill.) Nat. Lab., 1975-77, dir. energy resources tng. and devel. 1977—; cons. Lunar Receiving Lab. Baylor U., 1966-68, Ecology Center Utah State U., Desert Biome, 1970-72, Tundra Biome, 1973-74, U. Maine, 1973-76. Served with U.S. Army, 1950-52; Korea, Japan. Recipient 3 NASA awards for tech. briefs; Paul Steere Burgess fellow U. Ariz., 1959; NSF grantee, 1970-74; Dept. Interior grantee, 1978-80. Mem. AAAS, Soil Scientists Soc. Am., Ecol. Soc. Am., Phycological Soc. Am., Am. Soc. Agronomy, Antarctican Soc., Polar Soc. Am., Am. Scientist Affiliation, World Future Soc., Internat. Soc. Soil Sci., Ariz. Acad. Sci., Am. Inst. Biol. Sci., Sigma Xi. Mem. Christian Ch. Contbr. numerous articles to sci. books; 7 Antarctic expdns., 1966-74. Home: 3433 Woodridge Dr Woodridge IL 60517 Office: 9700 S Cass Ave Argonne IL 60439

CAMERON, WILLIAM SCOTT, technical engineer, project manager; b. Chgo., May 10, 1948; s. Robert Joseph and Vivienne Agnes (Keir) C.; m. Barbara Elaine Slonneger, June, 1982. B.S. in Civil Engring. Iowa State U., 1970, M.S. in Sani. Engring., 1974. Registered profl. engr., Ohio. Environ. engr. Procter and Gamble Co., Cin., 1970-76, tech. engr., 1976-81, project mgr., 1981—. Served to SP4 U.S. Army, 1970-76. Methodist. Avocation: bicycling. Office: Proctor and Gamble Co 6250 Center Hill Rd Cincinnati OH 45224

CAMFIELD, LIONEL DALE, construction firm executive; b. Dayton, Ohio, May 6, 1954; s. Lester Wayman and Ella (Chafin) C.; m. Katharine Louise Moessinger, June 23, 1973; children—Christopher Scott, Rebecca Lynn, Douglas Allen. Ptnr. C & C Constrn. Co., Fairborn, 1972—. Parade chmn. Fairborn Festival Com., 1982, mem., 1983-84; mem. Parks and Recreation Adv. Bd., Fairborn, 1984, sec., 1983, chmn., 1985. Mem. Fairborn C. of C., Jaycees (Fairborn chpt., chmn. 1982-83, pres. 1981-82, v.p. 1980-81, state dir. 1984, numerous local awards including Jaycee of Yr. 1982, Spark Plug of Yr. 1983, Presdl. award of honor 1980, 81, Outstanding Young Men in Am. 1982, 84), Jaycees (Ohio chpt., dir. dist. 16-B, numerous awards including Dist. Dir. of Yr. 1984, Togetherness award 1984). Avocations: model railroading; bowling; softball. Home: 161 E Diana Ln Fairborn OH 45324 Office: C & C Constrn Co 2049 Triumph Dr Fairborn OH 45324

CAMMA, ALBERT JOHN, neurosurgeon; b. Cleve., Dec. 27, 1940; s. August and Amelia (Catalioti) C.; B.S. cum laude, John Carroll U., 1963; M.D., Western Res. U., 1967; m. Sheryl Virginia Doptis, Aug. 27, 1966; children—August Leon, Albert David. Intern, surg. resident U. Pitts., 1967-69, resident in neurosurgery, 1971-75; practice medicine specializing in neurosurgery, Zanesville, Ohio, 1975—. Trustee Zanesville YMCA, 1976-82. Served with M.C., USN, 1969-71. Diplomate Am. Bd. Neurol. Surgeons, Nat. Bd. Med. Examiners. Mem. AMA, Ohio State Med. Assn., Muskingum County Acad. Medicine, Congress Neurol. Surgeons, Am. Acad. Thermology, Midwest Pain Soc., Soc. Behavioral Medicine, ACS, Am. Assn. Neurol. Surgeons, Ohio State Neurosurg. Soc., Mid-Atlantic Neurosurg. Soc., Am. Pain Soc. Office: 2835 Maple Ave Zanesville OH 43701

CAMMA, PHILIP, accountant; b. Phila., May 22, 1923; s. Anthony and Rose (LaSpada) C.; B.S., U. Pa., 1952; m. Anna Ruth Karg, July 21, 1956 (dec. Aug. 1960); 1 son, Anthony Philip. Accountant, Main and Co., C.P.A.s, Phila., 1952-53; in charge accountant Haskins & Sells, C.P.A.'s, Phila., St. Louis, Cin. and Columbus, Ohio, 1953-60; controller Marvin Warner Co., Cin., 1960-61; controller Leshner Corp., 1961-63; mng. ptnr. Camma & Patrick, C.P.A.s, 1963-66; founder Philip Camma & Co., C.P.A.s, Cin., 1966—. Served with USAAF, 1942-45; ETO. Mem. Am. Legion, Am. Inst. C.P.A.s, Ohio, Ky. socs. C.P.A.s, Am. Acctg. Assn., Nat. Assn. Accts. Republican. Clubs: Cincinnati; University Pa.; Hamilton City. Home: Phelps Townhouse Cincinnati OH 45202 Office: 700 Walnut St Suite 603 Cincinnati OH 45202

CAMMARATA, WALTER THOMAS, publishing company executive; b. St. Louis, July 2, 1940; s. Walter and Anne (Tucciarello) C.; B.S., St. Louis U., 1964, M.B.A., 1968; m. Gail Ann Leiendecker, Feb. 11, 1961; children—Mark, Dana, Christy. Office mgr. McGraw Hill Book Co., Manchester, Mo., 1967, staff asst., 1968, gen. mgr., 1969, regional v.p., 1980—. Bd. dirs. YMCA. Served with U.S. Army, 1962-68. Mem. Associated Industries of Mo., C. of C., Ballwin Athletic Assn. Republican. Club: Rotary. Home: 651 Tanglewilde Dr Manchester MO 63011 Office: 13955 Manchester Rd Manchester MO 63011

CAMMIN, WILLIAM BENJAMIN, clin. psychologist; b. Saginaw, Mich., Jan. 16, 1941; s. Howard John and Beulah Ione Cammin; B.S., Central Mich. U., 1964; M.A., Western Mich. U., 1966; Ph.D., U. S.C., 1969; m. Joanne Marie Seidel, July 23, 1966; children—Darren William, Kiena Marie, Clane Joseph. Chief psychologist outpatient services Carter Meml. Hosp., Ind. Med. Center, Indpls., 1968-70; cons. clin. psychology Quinco Community Mental Health Center, Columbus, Ind., 1969-70; cons. Community Mental Health Planning, Kokomo, Ind., 1970; exec. dir. Bay-Arenac Community Mental Health Services Bd., Bay City, Mich., 1971—; mem. mental health com. E. Central Mich. Health Systems Agy., 1973—; co-chmn. psychiat. tech. com. Emergency Med. Services Eastern Mich., 1975-78. Mem. Am. Psychol. Assn., Mich. Psychol. Assn., Mich. Assn. Community Mental Health Dirs. (exec. com.). Home: 5578 Mackinaw Rd Saginaw MI 48604 Office: 201 Mulholland St Bay City MI 48706

CAMP, ALIDA DIANE, law educator; b. N.Y.C., Feb. 14, 1955; d. Seymour and Pearl (Aisen) C.; m. Roger Morris Arar, June 3, 1984. B.A., SUNY-Binghamton, 1976; J.D., Columbia U., 1980. Bar: N.Y. 1981, U.S. Dist. Ct. (so. and ea. dists.) N.Y. 1981. Student intern U.S. Atty.'s Office, N.Y.C., 1979-80; assoc. Kaye, Scholer, Fierman, Hays & Handler, N.Y.C., 1980-83; asst. prof. bus. law Grad. Sch. Bus. Adminstrn., U. Mich., Ann Arbor, 1983—, sr. faculty adviser Mortarboard, 1983—; vol. atty. Vol. Lawyers for Arts, N.Y.C., 1982-83; alumni adviser Columbia U. Sch. Law, 1985—. Editor Columbia Jour. Law and Soc. Problems, 1979-80. Mem. Am. Mus. Natural History, N.Y.C., 1983—. Harlan Fiske Stone scholar Columbia U. Sch. Law, 1978, 80. Mem. Am. Bus. Law Assn., ABA, Midwest Regional Bus. Law Assn., Tristate Regional Bus. Law Assn., Columbia Law Sch. Alumni Assn. Jewish. Home: 555 E William St Ann Arbor MI 48104 Office: U Mich Grad Sch Bus Adminstrn 904 Monroe St Ann Arbor MI 48109

CAMP, ERICK JAMES, army officer; b. St. Louis, Dec. 31, 1942; s. Francis Jackson' and Bernice Joanna (Siems) C.; m. Ruth Ann Gallagher, Jan. 6, 1968; children—Laura Lynn, Ericka Lynn. Ph.B., Cardinal Glennon Coll., 1964; M.S. in Econs., S.D. State U., 1973. Enlisted U.S. Army, 1965, advanced through grades to maj., 1985; ops. officer 52nd signal bn., Federal Republic Germany, 1968-80; dep. dir. automation U.S. Army Recruiting Command, Ft. Sheridan, Ill., 1980-81, chief systems div., 1981-84, chief computer support, 1984—. Decorated Bronze Star. Mem. Computer Mgmt. Group, Gamma Sigma Delta. Republican, Roman Catholic. Avocations: cross-country skiing; hunting. Home: 3475B McCormick Dr Ft Sheridan IL 60037 Office: USARCAM CS Bldg 65 Fort Sheridan IL 60037

CAMPBELL, BRIAN PHILLIP, manufacturing company executive; b. Oak Park, Ill., Aug. 23, 1940; s. Andrew Frank and Elizabeth (Gabris) C.; B.S.C., DePaul U., 1963; M.B.A., Northwestern U., 1966; M.S. in Fed. Income Taxation, DePaul U., 1973; m. Mary Lucina Lincoln; 1 child, Elizabeth L. With No. Trust Co., Chgo., 1963; asst. v.p. Walston & Co., Inc., Chgo., 1963-65; v.p. Glore Forgan Staats, Inc., Chgo., 1965-70; v.p. duPont Glore Forgan Inc., Chgo., 1970-73; v.p. Masco Corp., Taylor, Mich., 1974-77, group v.p., 1977—; lectr. DePaul U., 1972-73. Bd. dirs. Chgo. Boys Clubs, 1972-73, Boys Clubs Met. Detroit, 1974—; mem. bus. adv. council DePaul U., 1984—. Mem. Inst. Chartered Fin. Analysts, Fin. Execs. Inst., Planning Execs. Inst. Episcopalian. Clubs: Chicago, Univ. (Chgo.); Chgo., Barton Hills Country. Office: 21001 Van Born Rd Taylor MI 48180

CAMPBELL, BRUCE CRICHTON, hospital administrator; b. Balt., July 21, 1947; s. James Allen and Elda Shaffer (Crichton) C.; m. Linda Page Cottrell, June 28, 1969; children—Molly Shaffer, Andrew Crichton. B.A., Lake Forest Coll., 1969; M.H.A., Washington U., St. Louis, 1973; D.P.H., U. Ill., 1979. Adminstrv. asst. Passavant Meml. Hosp., Chgo., 1970-71; adminstrv. resident Albany (N.Y.) Med. Ctr. Hosp., 1972-73; adminstrv. asst. Rush-Presbyn.-St. Luke's Med. Ctr., Chgo., 1973-75, asst. adminstr., 1975-77, asst. v.p., 1977-79, v.p. adminstrv. affairs, 1979-83; chmn. dept. health systems mgmt. Rush U., Chgo., 1977-81, dean Coll. Health Scis., 1981-83; exec. dir. U. Chgo. Hosps. and Clinics, 1983-85; pres. Campbell Assocs., 1985—. Leadership fellow Greater Chgo., 1985; W.K. Kellogg Found. fellow, 1977. Mem. Young Adminstrs. Chgo. (pres. 1977), Assn. Univ. Programs in Health Adminstrn., Ill. Hosp. Assn., Chgo. Hosp. Council. Home: 1806 N Sedgwick St Chicago IL 60614 Office: 1806 N Sedgwick St Chicago IL 60614

CAMPBELL, CALVIN ARTHUR, JR., mining, tunneling and plastics molding equipment manufacturing company executive; b. Detroit, Sept. 1, 1934; s. Calvin Arthur and Alta Christine (Koch) C.; B.A. in Econs., Williams Coll., 1956; B.S. in Chem. Engring., MIT, 1959; J.D., U. Mich., 1961; m. Rosemary Phoenix, June 6, 1959; 1 dau., Georgia Alta. With Exxon Co., N.Y.C., 1961-69; chmn. bd., treas. John B. Adt Co., York, Pa., 1969-70; with Goodman Equipment Corp., Chgo., 1971—, pres., chief exec. officer, 1971—, chmn. bd. Improved Plastics Machinery Corp. subs. Goodman Equipment Corp., 1979—, Goodman Conveyor Co., 1984—. Mem. Chgo. Econ. Devel. Commn., 1980—, Ill. Devel. Bd., 1983—, Ill. Commn. Sci. and Tech., 1983—, Pres.'s Council, Mus. Sci. and Tech., Chgo., 1984—. Mem. Am., N.Y. bar assns., Am. Mining Congress (gov. from 1972, chmn. bd. govs. mfrs. div. 1980-83, dir. 1980—), Ill. Mfrs. Assn. (bd. dirs. 1978-84), Am. Inst. Chem. Engrs., Young Pres.'s Orgn., Chief Execs. Orgn., Newcomen Soc. N.Am., Psi Upsilon, Phi Delta Phi. Clubs: Econ., Chicago, Chgo. Commonwealth, Racquet (Chgo.); Glen View; Skytop (Pa.). Office: 4834 S Halsted St Chicago IL 60609

CAMPBELL, CHARLES GEORGE, banker; b. Andover, Eng., July 16, 1895; s. William T. and Grace (Calder) C.; came to U.S., 1901, naturalized, 1919; grad. Ind. Bus. Coll., 1916; student U. Chgo., 1920-22; hon. degree Wabash Coll., 1980; m. Helen I. Thompson, June 14, 1926; children—Claire E. (Mrs. David Locke, Jr.), Joyce C. (Mrs. Rodney Beals). Sec.-treas. Kamp Motor Co., Mt. Carmel, Ill., 1923-26, pres., 1926-59; v.p. Vigo Motor Co., Terre Haute, Ind., 1944-50; v.p. Security Bank and Trust Co., Mt. Carmel, 1937-59, pres., 1959-64, chmn. bd., 1969—, also dir.; pres. Am. Savs. & Loan Assn., Mt. Carmel, 1939-59, dir., 1937—; dir. Camray, Inc., Mt. Carmel, Mt. Carmel Area Devel. Corp.; dir. Tri-Country Indsl. Com., 1965-67. Mem. Mt. Carmel City Commn., 1963—; mayor City of Mt. Carmel, 1965-67. Served with U.S. Army, 1917-19; AEF in France. Named to Mt. Carmel High Sch. Hall of Fame, 1983. Mem. Mt. Carmel C. of C. (dir. 1959-62, 65-68), Am. Legion (comdr. Wabash post 1937), 40 and 8, Wabash Valley Assn. Presbyterian. Lodges: Masons, Shriners, Elks (lodge trustee 1979-80), Moose, Eagles, Kiwanis (pres. Mt. Carmel 1935, dir. 1936). Home: 323 Cherry St Mount Carmel IL 62863 Office: 400 Main St Mount Carmel IL 62863

CAMPBELL, CHARLES INGALLS, JR., savs. and loan assn. exec.; b. Casper, Wyo., Jan. 9, 1923; s. Charles Ingalls and Ann Marie (Ryan) C.; student U. Mo., 1940-41, U.S. Naval Acad., 1941-43, Marine Corps Schs., 1943, Armed Forces Staff Coll., 1962; m. Kathryn Ryan, Feb. 7, 1953; children—Ann, Charles Ingalls III, Mary Kay, John. Commd. 2d lt. U.S. Marine Corps, 1943, advanced through grades to lt. col., 1970; ret., 1970; asst. sec. dir. personnel and purchasing Safety Fed. Savs. & Loan, Kansas City, Mo., 1971—. Hon. bd. dirs. Rockhurst Coll.; dep. election commr., Kansas City, Mo., 1972-78. Decorated Air medal with three gold stars, Purple Heart, Navy commendation medal. Mem. Mo. Council Retired Officers Assn. (pres. 1975-76), Am. Soc. Personnel Adminstrn. (accredited), Mil. Order World Wars, U. Mo. Alumni Assn., U.S. Naval Acad. Alumni Assn., Mo. Sheriffs Assn., DAV, Sigma Chi. Democrat. Roman Catholic. Clubs: Army-Navy Country (Washington); Brookridge Country, Homestead Country (dir. 1978-81) (Kansas City, Mo.). Home: 421 Westover Rd Kansas City MO 64113 Office: 910 Grand St Kansas City MO 64106

CAMPBELL, D'ANN MAE, history educator; b. Denver, Dec. 30, 1949; d. Bernard Edward and Eleanor Louise (Mahoney) Campbell; B.A., Colo. Coll., 1972; Ph.D. in History, U. N.C., Chapel Hill, 1979; m. Richard Jensen, July 16, 1976. Asst. dir. Family and Community History Center, Newberry Library, Chgo., 1976-78, assoc. dir., 1978-79; adj. prof. history U. Ill., Chgo. Circle, 1977-79; dean for women's affairs Ind. U., asst. prof. history, 1979—. Newberry Library fellow, 1975-76, NEH grantee, 1976-79, 81-84; Dept. Edn. grantee, 1979-81, 83-85. Mem. Am. Studies Assn. (nat. council 1979-81), Orgn. Am. Historians (chair com. status women 1977-79, chmn. nominating bd. 1980-82), Am. Hist. Assn., So. Hist. Assn., Social Sci. Hist. Assn. (chmn. nominating bd.), Nat. Hist. Communal Socs. Assn. (pres.), Quantum Internat. Orgn., Coalition for Women in Humanities and Social Scis., Phi Beta Kappa. Author: Women at War with America, 1984; contbr. articles to profl. jours.; mem. editorial bd. Newberry Papers, Teaching History. Home: 1109 Longwood Dr Bloomington IN 47401 Office: Meml Hall E Ind U Bloomington IN 47405

CAMPBELL, DAVID MCKENDREE, pharmacist, grain farmer; b. Marengo. Ill., June 24, 1956; s. John Gifford and Emily Jane (Dewhirst) C.; m. Linda Ann Walkowicz, June 23, 1984. Student Monmouth Coll., 1974-77; B.S. in Pharmacy, Purdue U., 1981. Registered pharmacist, Ill., Ind. Research asst. Purdue Pharmacy Sch., West Lafayette, Ind., 1979-80; pharmacist St. Mary's Hosp., Decatur, Ill., 1981, Decatur Meml. Hosp., 1982—; farm owner/operator, Maroa, Ill., Mem. Am. Fedn. Aviculture, Farm Bur., Am. Pharm. Assn., Ill. Pharm. Assn., Ill. Sheriffs Assn., Audobon Soc., Phi Lambda Upsilon. Republican. Methodist. Lodge: Lions (2d v.p. 1984). Avocations: aviculture; photography; skiing. Home: Rural Route #1 Maroa IL 61756

CAMPBELL, DAVID MICHAEL, motion picture company sales executive; b. Columbus, Ohio, June 7, 1949; s. Thurl Garfield and Mary Janice (Thompson) C.; B.S., Fla. State U., 1972; m. Catherine A. Jacobs, Jan. 6, 1979. Studio operator Sta. WPTV, West Palm Beach, Fla., 1968-69; mem. prodn. staff sta. WCTV, Tallahassee, Fla., 1970-71; producer, dir. Sta. KPHO-TV, Phoenix, 1973-74; buyer, semiconductor products div. Motorola, Phoenix, 1972-74; regional dir. Tele-Tronics Corp., Scottsdale, Ariz., 1975; exec. producer Sta. WKEF-TV, Dayton, Ohio, 1975-76; dir. sales Columbia Pictures TV, Chgo.,

1976-81; exec. sales dir. Metromedia Producers Corp. Inc., Chgo., 1981-82; exec. dir. sales Midwest div. Viacom Enterprises Inc., Chgo., 1982—. Mem. Nat. Acad. TV Arts and Scis., Am. Film Inst., Broadcast Advt. Club Chgo., Phi Theta Kappa. Home: 815 Arlington Heights Rd Itasca IL 60143 Office: Viacom Enterprises 10 S Riverside Plaza Chicago IL 60606

CAMPBELL, EDWARD L., lawyer; b. Elgin, Ill., Dec. 24, 1950; s. James R. and Marguerite A. (Sterling) C.; m. Karla K. Heyl, June 18, 1977; children—James Edward, Shawn William. A.A., Trenton Jr. Coll., 1974; B.A., NE Mo. State U., 1976; J.D., U. Mo.-Columbia, 1979. Bars: Mo. 1979, U.S. Dist. Co. (we. and ea. dists.) Mo. 1979. Ptnr. Adams & Campbell, Kirksville, Mo., 1979-84, sole practice, Kirksville, 1984—. Bd. dirs. Adair County YMCA, Kirksville, 1984—, Adair County Red Cross, Kirksville, 1984—. Served as specialist 4th class U.S. Army, 1970-72, Vietnam. Named 1982 Citizen of the Yr., City of Kirksville. Mem. Assn. Trial Lawyers Am., ABA, Mo. Bar Assn., Mo. Assn. Trial Lawyers (regional pub. interest chmn. 1984), Adair County Bar Assn. (pres. 1982-84), Jaycees (pres. Kirksville chpt. 1982-83, bd. dirs. Mo. chpt. 1984, Outstanding Young Missourian Mo. chpt. 1983, Jaycee Internat. senator 1983—, Charles Kulp Jr. Meml. award 1983). Roman Catholic. Lodges: Moose, VFW. Home: #8 Center Rd Kirksville MO 63501 Office: 304 S Franklin Suite 100 Kirksville MO 63501

CAMPBELL, F(ENTON) GREGORY, university administrator, historian; b. Columbia, Tenn., Dec. 16, 1939; s. Fenton G. and Ruth (Hayes) C.; A.B., Baylor U., 1960; postgrad. (Fulbright grantee), Philipps U., Marburg/Lahn, W. Ger., 1960-61; M.A. (Woodrow Wilson fellow), Emory U., 1962; postgrad. (Exchange fellow) Charles U., Prague, Czechoslovakia, 1965-66; Ph.D., Yale U., 1967; postgrad. Inst. for Ednl. Mgmt., Harvard U., 1981; m. Barbara D. Kuhn, Aug. 29, 1970; children—Fenton H., Matthew W., Charles H. Research staff historian Yale U., New Haven, 1966-68, spl. asst. to acting pres., 1977-78; asst. prof. history U. Wis., Milw., 1968-69; asst. prof. European history U. Chgo., 1969-76, spl. asst. to pres., 1978—, sec. bd. trustees, 1979—; fellow Woodrow Wilson Internat. Center for Scholars, Smithsonian Instn., Washington, 1976-77; mem. E. European selection com. Internat. Research and Exchanges Bd., 1975-78; rev. panelist NEH, 1983-84. Fulbright grantee, 1973-74; U.S.A.-Czechoslovakia exchange fellow, 1973-74, 85. Mem. Am. Hist. Assn., Am. Assn. for Advancement Slavic Studies, Czechoslovak History Conf. (pres. 1980-82), Conf. Group on Central European History (sec.-treas. 1980-83), Chgo. Council on Fgn. Relations (com. on fgn. affairs 1979—, exec. com. 1984—), Phi Beta Kappa. Clubs: Mid-Day, Quadrangle (Chgo.). Author: Confrontation in Central Europe, 1975. Contbr. articles, revs. to profl. jours. Joint editor Akten zur deutschen auswartigen Politik, 1918-45, 1966—. Home: 5830 Stony Island Ave Chicago IL 60637 Office: Office of Pres U Chgo 5801 S Ellis Ave Chicago IL 60637

CAMPBELL, GREGORY SCOTT, real estate development executive; b. Blue Earth, Minn., May 5, 1948; s. Dallas L. and Ida G. (Leland) C.; m. Elizabeth Barnett, Jan. 1, 1972; children—Elizabeth, Jonathan. B.A., Wheaton Coll., 1970. Regional mgr. Service Master, Inc., Downers Grove, Ill., 1970-72; v.p. J. Emil Anderson & Son, Des Plaines, Ill., 1972-79; sr. v.p. Richard Ellis, Inc., Chgo., 1979-84, Homart Devel. Co., Chgo., 1984—. Mem. Wheaton Youth Outreach, 1980; bd. dirs. Overseas Athletics, Wheaton; chmn. bd. dirs. Honey Rock Camp, Three Lakes, Wis. Mem. Internat. Council Shopping Ctrs., Chgo. Real Estate Bd., Nat. Assn. Realtors, Execs. Club Chgo. Home: 1726 Milton Ln Wheaton IL 60187 Office: Homart Devel Co 55 W Monroe Chicago IL 60603

CAMPBELL, HARRY DUANE, college business officer; b. St. Louis, Dec. 19, 1932; s. Harry I. and Ruth E. (Triplett) C.; m. Anna Lee, Sept. 7, 1957; 1 dau., Maryann. B.S., Central Mo. State U., 1981. Acct. Rolla Fed. Savs. & Loan, Mo., 1959-62; asst. bus. mgr. Southwest Baptist U., Bolivar, Mo., 1962-66; bus. mgr. Crowder Coll., Neosho, Mo., 1966-69, East Central Coll., Union, Mo., 1969—. Elected mem. Bolivar City Council, 1964-66. Served to cpl. U.S. Army, 1953-55, Korea. Mem. Nat. Assn. Ednl. Buyers, Mo. Assn. Pub. Purchasing (bd. dirs. 1976-78), Nat. Assn. Coll. and Univ. Bus. Officers., Central State Regional Assn. Baptist. Lodges: Masons, Lions, Rotary. Home: RR1 Box 345 Union MO 63084 Office: East Central Coll Hwy 50 and Prairie Dell Rd PO Box 529 Union MO 63084

CAMPBELL, HELEN WOERNER (MRS. THOMAS B. CAMPBELL), librarian; b. Indpls., Oct. 17, 1918; d. Clarence Julius and Gertrude Elizabeth (Colley) Woerner; student Ind. U., 1935-38; B.S., Butler U., 1967; m. Thomas B. Campbell, Jan. 17, 1942; 1 dau., Martha (Mrs. L. Kurt Adamson). Asst. order librarian Ind. U., Bloomington, 1937-42; librarian Ind. U. Sch. Dentistry, Indpls., 1942-46, cataloger, part-time, 1960-65, asst. librarian, 1965-66, librarian, 1966-80. Mem. Med. Library Assn., Spl. Libraries Assn. (chpt. pres. 1972-73). Home: 1865 Norfolk St Indianapolis IN 46224

CAMPBELL, JAMES ARTHUR, professional baseball team executive; b. Huron, Ohio, Feb. 5, 1924; s. Arthur A. and Vanessa (Hart) C.; B.S., Ohio State U., 1949; m. Helene G. Mulligan, Jan. 16, 1954 (div. July 1969). Bus. mgr. Thomasville (Ga.) Baseball Club, 1950, Toledo Baseball Club, 1951, Buffalo Baseball Club, 1952; bus. mgr. Detroit Minor League System, 1953, asst. farm dir. Detroit Baseball Club, 1954-56, v.p., farm dir., 1957-61, v.p., gen. mgr. 1962-65, exec. v.p., gen. mgr. Detroit Tigers, 1965-78, pres., gen. mgr., 1978-83, pres., chief exec. officer, 1984—. Served with AC, USNR, 1943-46. Named Maj. League Exec. of Year, 1968. Mem. Ohio State U. Varsity O Assn., Delta Upsilon. Presbyterian. Clubs: Detroit Athletic, Detroit Press. Office: Tiger Stadium 2121 Trumbull St Detroit MI 48216*

CAMPBELL, JO ANN, university official; b. Bethesda, Md., Jan. 1, 1957; d. Ira John and Yvette (Hanlon) C. B.A., U. S.C., 1978, M.Ed., 1980. Hall advisor, residence hall dir. U. S.C., Columbia, 1975-79; resident counselor Coker Coll., Hartsville, S.C., 1979-80; resident dir. Cath. U., Washington, 1980-81; patient clk. U. Mich. Hosp., Ann Arbor, 1981-82; area coordinator U. Ill.-Chgo., 1982—. Blood drive coordinator ARC, Columbia, S.C., 1979; women's advocate Safe House, Ann Arbor, 1982. Recipient Caroline McKissick Belser award U. S.C., 1975; Outstanding Com. Mem. award U. S.C., 1977-78, Outstanding Sr. award, 1977-78. Mem. Assn. Coll. and Univ. Housing Officers (ednl. programs com. 1985-86), Am. Assn. Counseling and Devel., Am. Coll. Personnel Assn., Nat. Assn. Student Personnel Adminstrs., Nat. Assn. Women Deans, Adminstrs. and Counselors, Great Lakes Assn. Coll. and Univ. Housing Officers (program com. fall 1985 conf.), Chgo. Area Small Coll. Housing Adminstrs. Democrat. Avocations: swimming; trivia games; movies. Office: U Ill-Chgo Campus Housing Office 1933 W Polk St Chicago IL 60612

CAMPBELL, JOEL RODERICK, lawyer; b. Cleve., Dec. 10, 1946; s. Ralph L. and Jean M. (Roderick) C.; m. Anne Medick, Aug. 25, 1968 (div. July 1981); children—Kristie A., Scott R.; m. Robin Ann Rentfrow, Jan. 22, 1982. B.A. in Bus. Adminstrn., Ohio State U., 1968; J.D., U. Akron, 1972. Bar: Ohio 1972. Asst. pros. atty. Franklin County, Columbus, Ohio, 1972-73; ptnr. Britt, Campbell & Nagel, Columbus, 1973—. Contbr. articles to profl. jours. Recipient, Merit award Ohio Legal Ctr. Inst., Columbus, 1978. Mem. ABA, Ohio State Bar Assn., Columbus Bar Assn., Franklin County Trial Lawyers, Am. Judicature Soc. Clubs: Sawmill Athletic, Ohio State U. Pres.'s (Columbus). Avocations: Basketball; volleyball; softball; racquetball. Office: 490 City Park Ave Columbus OH 43215

CAMPBELL, M. DONALD, JR., university administrator; b. Mpls., Oct. 8, 1944; s. M. Donald and Elsie Lillian (Denham) C.; m. Louise Matthews, Aug. 14, 1976; children—David, Andrew. B.A., U. Minn., 1966, M.A., 1973; postgrad. Bethel Theol. Sem., 1966-68; Ph.D., U. Wis., 1977. Continuing edn. specialist U. Ill., Urbana, 1977-80, dir. continuing med. edn., 1980-83; dir. extended edn. U. Wis., LaCrosse, 1983—. Pres. bd. dirs. Coulee Region Christian Sch., 1984—. Served with U.S. Army, 1968-71. Mem. Nat. Univ. Continuing Edn. Assn. Office: U Wis Office Extended Edn LaCrosse WI 54601

CAMPBELL, MALCOLM BYRON, educator; b. Flint, Mich., May 25, 1938; s. Malcolm and Marian Marguerite (Smith) C.; m. Lynn Mildred Ufholz, June 29, 1968 (div. 1977); children—Alycia Lynn, Courtney Jessica. A.B., U. Mich., 1960, A.M., 1961, Ph.D., 1966. Tchr., English elem. schs., Bloomfield Hills (Mich.) Dist. Schs., 1965-66; asst. prof. edn. Bowling Green State U. (Ohio), 1966-70, assoc. prof., 1970-75, prof., 1975—; cons. Tiffin Devel. Ctr. (Ohio). Lyndon Baines Johnson Found. grantee, 1974. Mem. Comparative and Internat. Edn. Soc., Ohio Valley Philosophy of Edn. Soc., Am. Ednl. Studies Assn., Am. Ednl. Research Assn., Spl. Interest Group on Internat. Studies. Democrat. Author: Non-Specialist Study in the New Universities and Colleges of Advanced Technology in England, 1966; co-editor: Jour. of Abstracts in Internat. Edn., 1971—, Ednl. Impressions: Readings, 1977. Home: 227 Mercer Rd Apt 20B Bowling Green OH 43402 Office: 556 Ednl Bldg Bowling Green State U Bowling Green OH 43403

CAMPBELL, MALCOLM DAVID, dentist; b. Detroit, Sept. 23, 1926; s. Malcolm Duncan and Mabel Edith (White) C.; B.A., Wayne State U., 1951, teaching cert., 1951; D.D.S., U. Detroit, 1955, postgrad., 1962-63; m. Janet Cauhorn, Nov. 14, 1958; children—Mary Catherine, David, Elizabeth, Douglas. Pvt. practice dentistry, Dearborn, Mich.; mem. staff Harper Hosp., Detroit, 1957—; instr. Sch. Dentistry U. Detroit, 1961-65, U. Mich., 1966-74; adviser Wayne County Welfare Dept. Sponsor Detroit council Boy Scouts Am.; bd. dirs. Dearborn Community Health; deacon First Presbyterian Ch. of Dearborn. Fellow Acad. Gen. Dentistry, Internat. Coll. Dentists, Am. Coll. Dentists, Acad. Dentistry Internat., Royal Soc. Health; mem. Southwestern Dental Club (treas., corr. sec. 1957, pres. 1960), Dental Aid Commn. (pres. 1959-61), Chgo., Detroit Dist. dental socs., Mich. Soc. Psychosomatic Dentistry (v.p. 1962-63, pres. 1964), Am. Acad. Dental Medicine (pres. Mich. sect. 1964-65), Am. Acad. Oral Medicine, Am. Assn. Dental Schs., Orgn. Tchrs. Dental Practice Adminstrn., Am. Acad. Dental Practice Adminstrn., Mich. Dental Assn. (trustee). Office: 23601 Ford Rd Dearborn MI 48128

CAMPBELL, RAYMOND WILLIS, patent lawyer; b. Ashland, Wis., May 5, 1952; s. Willis David and Anne Agnes (Kriskovich) C.; m. Bonnie Lee Newell, June 29, 1974; children—Nicholas, Rebecca, Benjamin, Adam. B.A. magna cum laude, Northland Coll., 1974; J.D. cum laude, Notre Dame U., 1980. Bars: Ind. 1980, U.S. Dist. Ct. (no. dist.) Ind. 1980, U.S. Ct. Customs and Patent Appeals 1982. Patent atty. Hobbs & Campbell, South Bend, Ind., 1980-81, Trane Co., La Crosse, Wis., 1981-84; asst. patent counsel Beloit Corp., Wis., 1984—. Roman Catholic. Office: Beloit Corp 1 St Lawrence Ave Beloit WI 53511

CAMPBELL, RICHARD ALDEN, industrial and energy company executive; b. Bend, Oreg., July 31, 1926; s. Corlis Eugene and Lydia Amney (Peck) C.; m. Edna Mary Seaman, June 12, 1948; children—Stephen Alden, Douglas Niall (dec.), Carolyn Joyce. B.S. in E.E., U. Ill, 1949, M.S., 1950. With TRW, Inc., Redondo Beach, Calif., 1954—, exec. v.p. TRW Inc. Electronics Sector, 1979—, exec. v.p. TRW Inc. Indsl. and Energy Sector, Cleve., 1984—; ptnr. Calif. Investment Assocs.; dir. Tylan Corp., Cetec Corp. Patentee in radio communications. Trustee Nat. Multiple Sclerosis Soc.; mem. U. Ill. Bd. Overseers for Microelectronics Ctr. and U. Ill. Corp. Resources Council. Served with USN, 1944-46. Recipient Alumni Honor award U. Ill. Coll. Engring. Mem. Am. Electronics Assn. (pres. 1969, bd. dirs. 1970), IEEE (sr.), Sigma Xi, Phi Kappa Phi, Tau Beta Pi, Eta Kappa Nu, Sigma Tau, Pi Mu Epsilon, Phi Eta Sigma. Republican. Clubs: Rolling Hills Country, Rancheros Visitadores, Los Caballeros. Lodge: Kiwanis. Office: TRW Inc 30050 Chagrin Blvd Cleveland OH 44124

CAMPBELL, RICHARD GEORGE, manufacturing company official; b. Detroit, Nov. 14, 1932; s. Richard George and Eva Naomi (Johnson) C.; m. Marie Evelyn Campbell; children—Richard George, Jay Lamont, Steven Ray. B.S.M.E., Calif. State U., 1967; M.M.S., West Coast U., 1972; M.B.A., U. Chgo., 1979. Chief engr. Falcon Plastics, Oxnard, Calif., 1966-69, plant mgr., 1969-72; engring. mgr. Johnson & Johnson, N. Brunswick, N.J., 1972-73, mgr. equipment and facilities, 1973-76; plant mgr., Chgo., 1976-81; dir. mfg. Abbott Labs., North Chgo., 1981-85; pres. Venture Plastics, Inc., Santa Ana, Calif., 1985—. Address: Venture Plastics Inc 2420 W 3d St Santa Ana CA 92703

CAMPBELL, ROBERT COULTER, ophthalmologist; b. Millville, N.J., Jan. 24, 1946; s. Howard Eakin and Dorothy Irene Campbell; m. JoAnn Nalevanko, Aug. 22, 1970; children—Scott, Ian. B.A., Franklin and Marshall Coll., 1967; M.D., Temple U., 1971. Intern, Geisinger Med. Ctr., Danville, Pa., 1971-72; resident in ophthalmology Mayo Clinic, Rochester, Minn., 1974-77; corneal fellow Harvard Med. Sch., Boston, 1977-79; practice medicine specializing in ophthalmology, Mpls., 1979—. Diplomate Am. Bd. Ophthalmology. Home: 6537 Navaho Trail Edina MN 55435 Office: 5000 W 39th St Minneapolis MN 55416

CAMPBELL, ROBERT HALLER, educational administrator; b. East Alton, Ill., Nov. 13, 1939; s. Joseph A. and Margaret R. (Haller) C.; m. Edith Marlene Leonard, Apr. 9, 1960; children—Susan Marie, Jeffrey Robert. A.B., McKendree Coll., 1961; M.A., Carnegie Inst. Tech., 1967; postgrad. So. Ill. U., 1972-73. Cert. tchr. supr., adminstr., Ill. Tchr. High Mount Sch., Belleville, Ill., 1961-63, Roxana Pub. Schs. (Ill.), 1964-66; gifted program dir. Community Unit Sch. Dist. No. 2, Marion, Ill., 1967-71, dir. curriculum and instructional services, 1973—, area service ctr. dir. John A. Logan Coll., Carterville, Ill., 1971-73. Active United Way, YMCA, Methodist Ch. commr. Marion Park Dist., v.p., 1982-83. Recipient Disting. Service award Marion Jaycees, 1972. Mem. Assn. Supervision and Curriculum Devel., Ill., Assn. Supervision and Curriculum Devel., Nat. Assn. for Gifted Children; Marion C. of C. (Citizen of Yr. award 1979), Schoolmasters, Phi Delta Kappa. Lodge: Kiwanis (pres. Marion 1978-79). Home: 904 N Market St Marion IL 62959 Office: Community Unit Sch Dist No 2 1410 West Hendrickson St Marion IL 62959

CAMPBELL, ROBERT L., management consultant; b. Haverford, Pa., Jan. 6, 1944; s. Robert L. and I. Lee (Groah) C.; B.S. in Mktg., Loyola U., Chgo., 1964; M.M., Northwestern U., 1978; m. Elizabeth A. Powers, Dec. 20, 1975; 1 dau., Elisabeth Powers. Mgmt. cons. Quirsfeld, Hussey & Manes, Chgo., 1964-70, Peat, Marwick, Mitchell & Co., Chgo., 1970-73, Booz, Allen & Hamilton, Chgo., 1973; founder, owner, mgr. Robert Campbell & Assocs., Chgo., 1973—; lectr. Loyola U., part-time, 1976—, Fin. Inst., part-time, 1972—. Bd. dirs. Youth Guidance Chgo., 1977—; chmn. devel. com. Ill. Republican Com., 1970—. Mem. Assn. Bus. Economists, Am. Econometric Assn., Nat. Small Bus. Assn., Am. Prodn. and Inventory Control Soc., Am. Mktg. Assn., Northwestern U. Alumni Assn. (dir. 1978—). Clubs: Chgo. Yacht, University (Chgo.). Contbr. articles on labor econs. to profl. publs. Home: 470 Deming Pl Chicago IL 60614 Office: 18 S Michigan Ave Chicago IL 60603

CAMPBELL, THOMAS PATRICK, educator; b. Gary, Ind., Sept. 19, 1942; s. John Joseph and Mary (Ledreau) C.; m. Evelyn Carol Waichulis, June 14, 1969; children—Jennifer Lynn, Christopher Scott. B.S. Ed., Ind. U., 1964, M.S.Ed., 1968. Tchr. Gary Pub. Schs., Ind., 1964-72; guidance dir. Lake Station Community Schs., Ind., 1972—; mem. North-Central Evaluation Team, Rochester, Ind., 1983; chmn. North-Central Rev. Team, Lake Station, Ind., 1985-86. City chmn. Hobart Democratic Precinct Orgn., Ind., 1980-84; pres. bd. dirs. N.W. Ind. Cath. Youth Orgn., Gary, 1982-84, pro deo et juventute, 1984; pres. park bd. City of Hobart, 1984; chmn. cancer drive City of Hobart, 1983. Mem. Am. Assn. Counseling and Devel., Ind. Assn. Coll. Counselors and Admissions, Phi Delta Kappa. Democrat. Roman Catholic. Lodges: Lions (treas. 1983-84), KC.

CAMPBELL-PHEBUS, CAROLYN, retail store executive; b. Champaign, Ill., Jan. 28, 1941; d. John Henry Bates and Mable Lillas (Stiebner) Smith; m. John Michael Campbell, July 27, 1960 (div. Jan. 1977); children—David Michael, John Jeffrey; m. Joseph William Phebus, Apr. 19, 1980. Student Parkland Jr. Coll., LaSalle Coll. Designer Interiors, Monticello, Ill., 1975-77; owner Campbell House Interiors, Champaign, 1977-81; owner, pres. Interiors Ltd., Champaign, 1981-83, Interiors II Ltd., Champaign, 1983-85; bus. mgr. Custom Flooring and Acoustics, Inc., Champaign, 1985—. Pres. Jr. League, Champaign, 1976; bd. dirs. Champaign County Exec. Club, 1982-84, exec. intership program Urbana High Sch., Ill., 1983-85. Named Bus. Woman of Yr., YWCA, 1982. Republican. Presbyterian. Avocations: tennis; sailing; reading; weightlifting. Home: #3 Persimmon Circle Urbana IL 61801 Office: Custom Flooring and Acoustics 508 S First Champaign IL 61820

CAMPBELL-THRANE, LUCILLE WISSOLIK, educational research center administrator; b. Pitts., Jan. 3, 1921; d. Albert and Roselda Blacksmith (Frances) Wissolik; m. Roland George Campbell, June 25, 1943; children—Melanie Campbell Dragan, Kaaren (dec.), George Crawford, Heidi Campbell Fay; m. 2d, William John Thrane, May 5, 1975. B.S. in Home Econs., Carnegie Mellon U., 1942; M.Ed., U. Pitts., 1953; Ed.D., Pa. State U., 1967. Dir., coordinator vocat. edn. State of Pa., 1964; program officer Region 3, Office of Edn., HEW, Phila., 1973-75; assoc. dir. resource devel. Nat. Ctr. for Research in Vocat. Edn., Columbus, Ohio, 1975-79, assoc. dir. devel. research, 1979—; founder, dir. Pitts. Skill Ctr.; cons. Middle State Accreditation. Bd. dirs. Allegheny council Girl Scouts Am., 1955-60, scout leader, 1950-62; supr. jr. vols. St. Margaret Hosp., Pitts., 1958-62; trustee Franklin County Mental Health Assn., Columbus, 1981—. Named Homemaking Tchr. of Yr., Seventeen Mag., 1963; recipient Carnegie Mellon U. merit award, 1971; disting. alumna in edn. award U. Pitts., 1971, 72, 74. Mem. Am. Home Econs. Assn., Am. Vocat. Assn., Pa. Vocat. Adminstrs., Omicron Nu, Pi Lambda Theta, Delta Kappa Gamma, Phi Delta Kappa, Omicron Tau Theta. Episcopalian. Clubs: Lakeview Country (Morgantown, W.Va.); Order of Eastern Star. Contbr. articles to profl. jours. Home: 1000 Urlin Ave Summit Chase Suite 1006 Columbus OH 43212 Office: 1960 Kenny Rd Columbus OH 43210

CAMPION, FRANK DAVIS, editorial and public relations executive; b. Columbus, Ohio, Oct. 30, 1921; s. Edward Winslow and Ruth Baird (Johnson) C.; m. Ann Cornell, 1948 (div. 1963); children—Frank Davis, Ann Baird; m. Georgene Haney, 1964; children—Kate, Geoffrey. B.A., Yale U., 1943. Reporter, editor Life mag., 1946-60; copywriter Young & Rubicam, 1960-68; pub. relations exec. N.Y. Stock Exchange, 1968-70; communications dir. AMA, Chgo., 1970-77, spl. asst. pub. relations, 1977-84, div. consumer book program 1985—. Served to lt. U.S. Army, 1943-45. Decorated Bronze Star. Mem. Pub. Relations Soc. Am. Club: Indian Hill. Author: The AMA and U.S. Health Policy Since 1940, 1984. Office: 535 N Dearborn St Chicago IL 60610

CAMPION, RUSSELL RICHMOND, food service equipment manufacturing company executive; b. Milw., Oct. 9, 1930; s. Russell Henry and Anna (Winne) C.; student U. Wis., 1948-49; m. Marguerite Schubert, Sept. 15, 1951; children—Jill Mary, Thomas Richmond, Jon Winne. Sales mgr. F.W. Boelter Co., Milw., 1952-62; sales mgr. Bastian Blessing Co., Chgo., 1962-67, mktg. mgr., Grand Haven, Mich., 1967-76, pres., 1976—, also dir.; dir. Service Action Corp. Mem. Nat. Assn. Food Service Equipment Mfrs. (dir. 1967—, pres. 1974, 83, sec. 1980), West Mich. Mfg. Assn. (dir. 1976—, sec.), Tri-City C. of C. Roman Catholic. Clubs: Century (Muskegon, Mich.); Rotary (Spring Lake, Mich.). Home: 18183 Fruitport Rd Spring Lake MI 49456 Office: 422 N Griffin St Grand Haven MI 49417

CAMPLIN, FORREST RALPH, architect; b. Shirley, Ind., June 28, 1917; s. Russell and Mae C.; ed. pub. schs.; m. Viola Faye Reed, June 15, 1947; children—Gloria Jean, Mary Darlene, Rita Ann. With Russell Camplin, masonry contractor, 1936-42; with Gen. Motors Corp., Anderson, Ind., 1942-51; with Edward D. James, Inc. (now James Assocs. Architects-Engrs., Inc.), Indpls., 1951-82, architect, 1961—. Served with C.E., U.S. Army, 1942-45. Mem. AIA (emeritus), Ind. Hist. Soc., Methodist. Mason. Chief archtl. works include St. Thomas Episcopal Ch., Franklin, Ind., 1968, Central Nat. Bank, Greencastle, 1971, Chapel, Ft. Benjamin Harrison, 1976, Morgan County (Ind.) Courthouse, Martinsville, 1976, 1st United Meth. Ch., Crawfordsville, Ind., 1977, Camp Atterbury N.G. Tng. Facilities, 1980, East Coll. restoration DePauw U., Greencastle, Ind., 1981. Home: PO Box 27 Wilkinson IN 46186

CAMPNEY, MARK EUGENE, city parks superintendent; b. Curlew, Iowa, Sept. 30, 1924; s. James Elmer and Ethel Adella (Corle) C.; m. Lola Lusher, July 3, 1951; children—Owen, Nancy, Bruce, David. B.S. in Agronomy, Iowa State U., 1951. Unit game mgr. State Conservation Commn., Ruthven, Iowa, 1955-60; research asst. U. Calif. Davis, 1963-67; supt. parks City of Spencer, Iowa, 1968—. Dir. Parker Hist. Soc. of Clay County, Spencer, 1978—. Mem. Am. Forestry Assn., Iowa State Arboretum, Iowa State Rose Soc. (v.p. 1981—) Clay County Garden Club (pres. 1980-81), Federated Garden Club Iowa (dist. dir. 1982-83, chmn. Blue Star Highways 1984—). Clubs: Izaak Walton, Toastmasters (Spencer). Lodge: Lions (pres. 1983-84). Methodist. Avocations: gardening; carpentry. Home: 913 W 5th St Spencer IA 51301

CAMULLI, STEPHEN JOHN, electronics corporation official; b. N.Y.C., July 7, 1943; s. Otto and Johanna Maria Elizabeth (Wolters) C.; B.B.A. in Prodn. Mgmt., Hofstra U., 1976; m. Yvette Linda Jacobs, July 26, 1964; children—Elyse Danielle, Eric Ian. Contract adminstr. Electrospace Corp., Glen Cove, N.Y., 1965-66; program adminstr. Hazeltine Corp., Greenlawn, N.Y., 1966-70, mgr. project services, 1970-73, mgr. prodn. planning, 1973-77, mgr. prodn. and inventory control, 1977; asst. nat. parts mgr. Sony Corp. Am., Kansas City, Mo., 1977-82, East Central regional service mgr., Cleve., 1982-84, regional service mgr. Central Region, Niles, Ill., 1984—. Mem. Am. Prodn. and Inventory Control Soc. (employment chmn. 1974-76, dir. membership retention 1976-77, v.p. membership 1977-78), Japanese Bus. Assn. Greater Kansas City (v.p. 1979-80), Internat. Trade Club of Greater Kansas City. Club: K.P. Office: 7540 Caldwell Ave Niles IL 60648

CANARY, KATHRYN HELGESEN, real estate company executive; b. Janesville, Wis., Aug. 23, 1943; d. Lester A. and Phyllis (Morgan) Helgeson; m. Paul Anthony Canary, Apr. 19, 1969. B.S., U. Wis., 1965. Vice pres. Helgesein Realty, Janesville, 1965-76, Advanced Housing Co., Delavan, Wis., 1976—, Dublin Investments Ltd., Delavan, 1976—; mem. adv. council SBA, Madison, Wis., 1966-79; dir., mem. exec. com. Wis. Bus. Devel. Fin. Corp., Madison, 1981-84. Supr., Delavan Town Bd., 1976-79; U.S. Congl. candidate from 1st Dist., Wis., 1979-80; vice chmn. Walworth County Republican Club, 1977-78. Mem. AAUW, Wis. Women in Bus. (bd. dirs., mem. steering com. 1983—), U. Wis. Alumni Assn., Alpha Phi. Avocations: tennis; auto racing. Address: 3535 S Shore Dr Delavan WI 53115

CANDEE, RICHARD ALEXANDER, JR., diversified manufacturing corporation executive; b. Milw., Dec. 13, 1947; s. Richard Alexander and Vi (Egan) C.; m. Mary Linda Brown, May 26, 1979. B.A. magna cum laude, Lawrence U., 1970; M.B.A., Harvard U., 1978; student Mich. State U./Barcelona, Spain, 1968. Sales coordinator, asst. plant mgr. Barton Mfg., Inc., Wis. and P.R., 1970-72; v.p., treas. Cormac, S.A., Panama and Wis., 1972-73; export sales mgr. Latin Am., Gehl Co., West Bend, Wis., 1973-76; mktg. analyst Deere & Co., Moline, Ill., summer 1977; mktg. assoc. Eaton Corp., Cleve., 1978-83, planner, sales mgr., mktg. mgr., Brussels and Aurora, Ohio, 1983—; pres. Vintage Motorpress, Inc., Shaker Heights, Ohio, 1982—; dir. Bill's Sporting Goods Inc., Lomira, Wis., Wolf's Auction Galleries, Cleve. Author, pub.: Aston Martin in America (Davis award 1983), 1982; Facel Vega-The Glory That Was France..., 1975. Exec. producer video tape Austin Healeys-On the Road, 1985. Capt. fund raising Cleve. Orch., 1978—, Cleve. Ballet, 1980-82; trustee Friends of Shaker Square, Cleve., 1980—; jud. candidate rev. com. Citizens League, 1984. Recipient Conn./Pa. driver Aston Martin Owners Club, Lakeville, Conn., 1982, S.C.H. Davis Publs. award, London, 1983. Mem. Phi Delta Theta. Clubs: Harvard Bus. Sch. (v.p. 1980-85), Skating, University (Cleve.). Avocation: vintage automobile racing. Home: 13623 Larchmere Blvd Shaker Heights OH 44120 Office: Indsl Polymer Products Div Eaton Corp 1199 S Chillicothe Ave Aurora OH 44202

CANE, ROY DOUGLAS, anesthesiology educator, researcher; b. Johannesburg, South Africa, Jan. 29, 1945; s. Francis John and Ruby (Nicholas) C. M.B.B.Ch., U. Witwatersrand, South Africa, 1969. Registered specialist anesthetist. Intern, Coronation Hosp., Johannesburg, 1970; registrar in anesthesia Baragwanath Hosp. and U. Witwatersrand Med. Sch., Johannesburg, 1971-73, sr. med. officer, 1974, anesthetist, dir. intensive care, 1975, prin. anesthetitist, dir. intensive care, 1976-77; resident in anesthesia Northwestern U., Chgo., 1974, asst. prof. clin. anesthesia, 1978-81, assoc. prof., asst. dir. respiratory/critical care, 1981—, pres. med. faculty senate, 1983-84; mem. assoc. attending staff Northwestern Meml. Hosp., 1979-84, attending staff, 1984—, asst. med. dir. dept. respiratory therapy, 1978-84, assoc. med. dir. dept. respiratory therapy, 1985—; lectr. Cook County Grad. Sch. Medicine, 1980—. Fellow Faculty Anesthetists of Coll. Medicine South Africa, 1973. Fellow Am. Coll. Chest Physicians; mem. Am. Assn. Respiratory Therapy, Ill. Soc. Respiratory Therapy (med. adviser 1980-83), Nat. Assn. Med. Dirs. of Respiratory Care, Soc. Critical Care Medicine, Am. Soc. Anesthesiologists, South African Critical Care Medicine Soc. (founder), South African Soc. Anesthetists (Atherstone prize 1972), South African Med. and Dental Council, Assn. Univ. Anesthetists, Med. Grads. Assn. Johannesburg, Chgo. Thoracic Soc., Ill. Soc. Anesthesiology, Sigma Xi. Co-author: Case Studies in Critical Care Medicine, Clinical Application of Respiratory Care, 3d edit. Reviewer for Jour. AMA, Critical Care Medicine, Chest and Respiratory Care, Am. Inst. Biol. Scis., 1982—, NIH, 1983—; editorial cons. Yr. Book Med. Pubs.; editor Year Book of Anesthesia, 1981; contbr. articles, abstracts to profl. jours., chpts. in books. Office: 250 E Superior St Suite 676 Chicago IL 60611

CANEPA, JOHN CHARLES, financial executive; b. Newburyport, Mass., Aug. 26, 1930; s. John Jere and Agnes R. (Barbour) C.; A.B., Harvard U., 1953; M.B.A., N.Y.U., 1960; m. Marie Olney, Sept. 13, 1953; children—Claudia, John J., Peter C., Milissa L. With Chase Manhattan Bank, N.Y.C., 1957-63;

sr. v.p. Provident Bank, Cin., 1963-70; pres. Old Kent Fin. Corp., also Old Kent Bank & Trust Co., Grand Rapids, Mich., 1970—. Served with USN, 1953-57. Office: Old Kent Bank & Trust Co 1 Vandenberg Center Grand Rapids MI 49503

CANGANELLI, MICHAEL ANTONIO, lawyer, emergency management program specialist; b. Indpls., Dec. 1, 1951; s. Vincent G. and Beverly Janice (Neal) C.; m. Debra Ellen Krulik, Feb. 9, 1982; children—William, Joseph, Michael, Anastasia, Eli, Robert, Alexandra. B.A., Ind. U.-Bloomington, 1974; J.D., Ill. Inst. Tech./Chgo.-Kent Coll., 1978. Bar: Ill. 1982, U.S. Ct. Appeals (7th cir.) 1982, U.S. Dist. Ct. (no. dist.) ill. 1982. With Fed. Emergency Mgmt. Agy., Chgo., 1981—; sole practice, Chgo., 1982—; assoc. Klimek & Richiardi, Ltd., Chgo., 1984—. Recipient Founders' Day Acad. Achievement award Ind. U., 1974; Outstanding Performance award Fed. Emergency Mgmt. Agy., 1983. Mem. Assn. Trial Lawyers Am., Fed. Bar Assn., Chgo. Bar Assn. Democrat. Roman Catholic. Club: Sierra. Lodge: K.C. Home: 1510 119th St Whiting IN 46394 Office: Klimek & Richiardi Ltd 3 First National Plaza 14th Floor Chicago IL 60602

CANJAR, PATRICIA MCWADE, psychologist, marriage counselor; b. Pitts., Mar. 14, 1932; d. Robert Malachai McWade and Lillian Kathryn (Seidenstricker) Robb; m. Lawrence N. Canjar, Aug. 4, 1951 (dec. Nov. 1972); 1 son, R. Michael; m. James M. McDonald, Sept. 24, 1977. A.A., Carlow Coll., 1951; B.A., U. Detroit, 1973, M.A., 1975. Lic. psychologist, Mich. Psychologist, Robinwood Clinic, Detroit, 1973-77, Psychol. Resources, Birmingham, Mich., 1977-80, Realistic Living Ctr., Warren, Mich., 1983-85, Behavior Ctr., Birmingham, 1980-84. Mem. Nat. YWCA Spl. Commn., Boston, N.Y.C. and Washington, 1967; bd. dirs. YWCA, Pitts., 1961-65, Detroit, 1965-67; asst. coordinator United We Sing, Pitts. Music Festival, 1955-65; pres. Carnegie Mellon Women's Club, Pitts., 1963-65, U. Detroit Faculty Wives' Club, 1968-70. Fellow Am. Psychol. Assn.; mem. Mich. Assn. Profl. Psychologist, Mich. Assn. Alcohol and Drug Abuse Counselors. Democrat. Roman Catholic. Office: Eastwood Community Clinic 888 W Big Beaver Troy MI 48084

CANNADY, EDWARD WYATT, JR., physician; b. East St. Louis, Ill., June 20, 1906; s. Edward Wyatt and Ida Bertha (Rose) C.; A.B., Washington U., St. Louis, 1927, M.D., 1931; m. Helen Freeborn, Oct. 20, 1984; children by previous marriage—Edward Wyatt III, Jane Marie (Mrs. Starr). Intern internal medicine Barnes Hosp., St. Louis, 1931-33, resident physician, 1934-35, asst. physician, 1935-74, emeritus, 1974—; asst. resident Peter Bent Brigham Hosp., Boston, 1933-34; fellow in gastroenterology Washington U. Sch. Medicine, 1935-36, instr. internal medicine 1935-74, emeritus, 1974—; cons. internal medicine Washington U. Clinics, 1942-74; physician St. Mary's Hosp., East St. Louis, 1935-77, pres. staff, 1947-49, chmn. med. dept., 1945-47; physician Christian Welfare Hosp., 1935-77, chmn. med. dept., 1939-53, dir. electrocardiography, 1936-77; dir. electrocardiography Centreville Twp. Hosp., East St. Louis. mem. staff Meml. Hosp., Belleville, Ill., St. Elizabeth Hosp., Belleville. Dir. 1st Nat. Bank, East St. Louis; pres. C.I.F. Dir. health service East St. Louis pub. schs., 1936-37; chmn. med. adv. bd. Selective Service, 1941-45; pres. St. Clair County Council Aging, 1961-62; chmn. St. Clair County Home Care Program, 1961-68, St. Clair County Med. Soc. Com. Aging, 1960-70; del. White House Conf. Aging, 1961, 71, 81; mem. Adv. Council Improvement Econ. and Social Status Older People, 1959-66; bd. dirs., exec. com. Nat. Council Homemaker Services, 1966-73, chmn. profl. adv. com. 1971-73; bd. dirs. St. Louis Met. Hosp. Planning Commn., 1966-70; mem. Ill. Council Aging, 1966-74; mem. Gov.'s Council on Aging, 1974-76; mem. Ill. Regional Heart Disease, Cancer and Stroke Com.; mem. exec. com. Bi-State Regional Com. on Heart Disease, Cancer and Stroke; pres. Ill. Joint Council to Improve Health Care Aged, 1959-61; dir. Ill. Council Continuing Med. Edn., 1972-77, v.p., 1974-75. Trustee McKendree Coll.; adv. bd. Belleville Jr. Coll. Sch. Nursing, 1970-78; bd. dirs. United Fund Greater East St. Louis, 1953-58. Recipient Disting. Service Award Am. Heart Assn., 1957, Disting. Achievement award, 1957; award Ill. Public Health Assn., 1971; Greater Met. St. Louis award in geriatrics, 1976. Diplomate Am. Bd. Internal Medicine. Fellow Am. Coll. Cardiology, Am. Geriatrics Soc., A.C.P. (gov. 1964-70); mem. AMA (ho. dels. 1961-71, mem. aging com.; editorial adv. bd. Chronic Illness News Letter 1962-70, chmn. Ill. delegation 1964-66, mem. council vol. health agys.), Am. (dir. 1956-62, personnel and personnel tng. com. 1956-60), Ill. (pres. 1950-51) heart assns., St. Clair County (pres. 1952, bd. censors 1953-57), Ill. (sec. cardiovascular sect. 1957, chmn. sect., 1958-59; chmn. com. on aging, 1959-69, speaker Ho. Dels. 1964-68, pres. 1969-70) med. socs., Beta Theta Pi, Nu Sigma Nu, Alpha Omega Alpha. Presbyn. Mason. Clubs: St. Clair Country, Mo. Athletic, Media; Palmbrook Country (Sun City, Ariz.). Contbr. articles to med. jours. Home: 7500 Claymont Ct Apt 2 Belleville IL 62223

CANNADY, ROGER LEON, manufacturing company executive; b. St. Louis, June 5, 1946; s. Wilford Leon and Dorothy Alene (Williams) C.; m. Vicki Storme, Sept. 21, 1966; children—Michael Leon, Marcia Lynn. B.S. in E.E., U. Mo., Rolla, 1968. Service supr. Southwestern Bell Telephone, Kansas City, Mo., 1968-69, service supr., Eldon, Mo., 1975-76, service mgr., Hannibal, Mo., 1976-79; regional service mgr. Gen. Dynamics Communications Co., Chgo., 1979-82; nat. service mgr. Thermotron Industries, Holland, Mich., 1983—. Served to capt., USAF, 1969-74. Decorated Nat. Def. Service medal USAF, 1969; USAF Outstanding Unit award, 1972; Armed Forces Expeditionary medal Republic of Korea, 1973; Vietnam Service medal with 2 battle stars. Mem. Inst. Environ. Sci., Nat. Assn. Service Mgrs., Nat. Rifle Assn. Club: Michigan United Conservation. Home: 372 Evergreen Dr Holland MI 49423 Office: Thermotron Industries 291 Kollen Park Dr Holland MI 49423

CANNELLA, VINCENT J., accountant; b. N.Y.C., Jan. 19, 1939; s. Matthew and Dorothy (Davies) C.; m. Anne Nucciarone, Dec. 30, 1961; children—Joanne Marie, Jennifer Anne, James Michael. B.B.A., St. John's U., 1961. With Peat, Marwick, Mitchell & Co., St. Louis, 1956—, ptnr., Chgo., 1970, mng. ptnr., St. Louis, 1984—, also dir. Bd. dirs. and officer Nat. Alzheimers Disease and Related Disorders Assn.; pres. Kidney Found. of Ill., 1973; others. Elected one of Chgo.'s ten outstanding Young Citizens by Jaycees, 1973. Mem. Am. Inst. C.P.A.'s, Nat. Assn. Accts., Ill. Soc. C.P.A.'s, Mo. Soc. C.P.A.'s. Home: 9858 Litzsinger St Saint Louis MO 63124 Office: 1010 Market St Saint Louis MO 63101

CANNELLO, STEVEN JOSEPH, lawyer; b. Sault Ste. Marie, Mich., July 13, 1955; s. Frank and Theresa Beatrice (LaLonde) C. B.S. with honors, Mich. State U., 1977; J.D. cum laude, Wayne State U., 1980. Bars: Mich. 1980; U.S. Dist. Ct. (we. dist.) Mich. 1980. Pntr. Moher, Andary & Cannello, Sault Ste. Marie, 1980—. Dir. Le Sault de Ste. Marie Historic Sites, 1983—; dir., chmn. City of Sault Ste. Marie Recreational Bldg. Authority, 1985—. Mem. Mich. Trial Lawyers Assn., Am. Trial Lawyers Assn., Tau Beta Pi. Democrat. Roman Catholic. Club: Christopher Columbus Mutual Benefits Soc. (fin. sec. 1982—). Home: 719 E Easterday Sault Ste Marie MI 49783 Office: Moher Andary & Cannello 150 Water St Sault Ste Marie MI 49783

CANNEY, DONALD JAMES, mayor of Cedar Rapids; b. Iowa City, Iowa, Oct. 8, 1930; s. John Joseph and Alice Elizabeth (Mickle) C.; m. Gloria O. Canney, Aug. 20, 1955; children—Kevin Patrick, Timothy Francis, Michael S. Student Oceanside-Carlsbad Coll., Oceanside, Calif., Iowa State U.; B.C.E., U. Iowa, 1959. Commr. streets and pub. improvements City of Cedar Rapids (Iowa), 1965-69, mayor, 1969—; chmn. Iowa Hwy. Research Bd. Served with USMC. Recipient Cert. of Appreciation 9th Naval Dist. Mem. Iowa Good Rds. Assn., Am. Pub. Works Assn., Nat. League of Cities, U.S. Conf. Mayors. Roman Catholic. Office: City Hall Cedar Rapids IA 52401*

CANNING, FRED FRANCIS, drug store chain executive; b. Chgo., Apr. 1, 1924; s. Fred and Lillian (Popiolek) C.; Registered Pharmacist, Hynes Sch. Pharmacy, 1950; m. Margaret Luby, Nov. 23, 1944; children—Jeanette, Laura, Debbie, Terry, Patrick, Marggie, Timothy, Kathleen. With Walgreen Co., Deerfield, Ill., 1946—, v.p. Drug Store div., 1975-76, sr. v.p., 1976-78, exec. v.p., 1978, pres., 1978—, also chief operating officer, dir. Served with USCG, 1942-45. Mem. Am. Pharm. Assn., Am. Mktg. Assn. Roman Catholic. Office: Walgreen Co 200 Wilmot Rd Deerfield IL 60015*

CANNING, KATHERINE MARIE BECKMAN, civic leader; b. Des Moines, Aug. 24, 1913; d. Herman Henry and Emily Amelia (Swanson) Beckman; student Grinnell Coll., 1930-31; A.B., Drake U., 1934; postgrad. U. Iowa; m. John Canning, Aug. 22, 1939; children—John Beckman, Emily Jane Canning Blankinship. Pres., Beckman Bros., Inc., Des Moines, 1959—; pres. Homewood (Ill.) PTA, 1954-56; mem. Homewood Elem. Bd. Edn., 1957-68; vol. Am. Field Service, 1960-80; vol. worker South Suburban Hosp.; mem. resource com. Flossmoor Elem. Schs., 1980; sec. petition com. for new Homewood-Flossmoor High Sch., 1955; mem. troop com. Girl Scouts U.S.A., 1959-61; den. mother Cub Scouts Am., 1950-52; 2d v.p. Homewood-Flossmoor High Sch. PTA, 1964-65; elder, former supt. ch. sch. 1st Presbyterian Ch., Homewood; bd. dirs. Homewood-Flossmoor High Sch. Found., 1984-85; bd. dirs. YWCA, Chgo., 1966-68, Flossmoor Community Fund. Mem. AAUW, PEO (planning com. Chgo. internat. conv. 1977, treas. Ill. state conv. 1981), LWV, Mortar Bd., Zeta Phi Eta, Delta Gamma, Theta Sigma Phi. Home: 2245 Flossmoor Rd Flossmoor IL 60422

CANNING, WILLIAM MATTHEW, psychologist, educator; b. Chgo., Sept. 14, 1921; s. William J. and Edith E. (Williams) C.; B.S. in Edn., Northwestern U., 1947, M.A., 1948, Ph.D., 1955; m. Marian H. Connor, Apr. 23, 1955; children—David, Paul, Peter. Instr. psychology St. Louis U., 1949-51; asst. dean, dir. student counseling Northwestern U., Evanston, Ill., 1951-54; tchr., asst. dean Chgo. Tchrs. Coll., 1954-56; dir. Bur. Child Study, Chgo. Bd. Edn., 1956-81; pvt. practice psychology, Barrington, Ill., 1960—; cons. VA, univs., Am. Psychol. Assn., city public sch. systems, Mayor's Commn. on Human Relations, Gov.'s Commn. on Mental Retardation, State Dept. Mental Health, Office State Supt. Public Instrn., State Psychol. Adv. Com. Served to capt. Chem. Corps, U.S. Army, 1943-46. Diplomate Am. Bd. Profl. Psychology. Fellow Am. Psychol. Assn. (mem. exec. bd. div. sch. psychology); mem. Midwestern Psychol. Assn., Phi Delta Kappa. Contbr. articles in field to profl. jours. Home and Office: 1280 Oak Hill Road Lake Barrington Shores Barrington IL 60010

CANNON, ALLEN E., music educator, violinist; b. Crystal Falls, Mich., June 24, 1920; s. Lester H. and Lena (Tobin) C.; m. Marilyn Levy, June 22, 1945; children—David, Michael. B.S. in Music Edn., Mus. B., U. Ill., 1941, M.Mus., 1942; D.Mus. Edn., Chgo. Mus. Coll., 1954. Cert. tchr., Ill. Music tchr., orch. dir. Alvin High Sch., Ill., 1941-42; faculty mem. Bradley U., Peoria, Ill., 1945—, assoc. prof., 1949-56, prof. violin, 1956—, dir. Sch. Music, 1957-84; concertmaster Peoria Symphony Orch., 1946—, soloist subscription concerts, 1948-80. Contbr. articles to profl. jours. Founding bd. dirs. Peoria Civic Ballet, Central Ill. Youth Orch. Served with USAAF, 1942-45. Mem. Nat. Assn. Sch. Music (chmn. region IV 1979-82), Assn. Ill. Music Schs. (pres. 1980-82), Music Industry Educators Assn., Am. String Tchrs. Assn., (regional chmn. 1965-67). Jewish. Avocations: swimming; Bridge. Home: 2721 W Parkridge Dr Peoria IL 61604 Office: Sch Music Bradley Univ Peoria IL 61625

CANNON, BENJAMIN WINTON, lawyer, business executive; b. Muncie, Ind., Sept. 17, 1944; s. Zane William and Gloria Gene (Phillips) C.; B.A., Western Mich. U., 1965; postgrad. Notre Dame Law Sch., 1966-67; J.D., Wayne State U., 1969; M.B.A., Mich. State U., 1979; m. Diane Joan Koenig, June 24, 1967; children—Matthew Zane, Christine Elizabeth, Leslie Joan, Todd Graham. Admitted to Mich. bar, 1970; law clk. labor relations staff Gen. Motors Corp., Detroit, 1966-69; tax atty. Plante & Moran, C.P.A.s, Southfield, Mich., 1969-71; atty. Burroughs Corp., Detroit, 1971-72; assoc. Nine and Maister, Attys., Bloomfield Hills, Mich., 1972-73; atty. Chrysler Fin. Corp., Troy, Mich., 1973-78, sr. atty., 1978-80; corp. counsel CF Industries Inc., Long Grove, Ill., 1980-81; asst. gen. counsel, asst. sec. COMDISCO, Inc., Rosemont, Ill., 1981-82, asst. v.p. and gen. mgr. internat., 1983—, pres. COMDISCO Internat. Sales Corp., 1983—; asst. sec., gen. counsel Microtron, Inc., Barrington, Ill.; instr. law Oakland U., Rochester, Mich., 1980. Mem. State Bar Mich., Ill. State Bar, Chgo. Bar Assn., ABA Gray's Inn Legal Soc., Omicron Delta Kappa, Kappa Delta Pi. Republican. Presbyterian. Home: 21265 N Pheasant Trail Barrington IL 60010 Office: 6400 Shafer Ct Rosemont IL 60018

CANNON, CHARLES EARL, research chemist; b. Sylacauga, Ala., Jan. 30, 1946; s. Eugene and Carrie Lue (Clemons) C.; B.S., Ala. A&M U., 1968; postgrad. Vanderbilt U., 1968-69; Ph.D., U. Wis., Milw., 1974. Chemist, Amoco Chems. Corp., Naperville, Ill., 1974-78, Standard Oil Co. Ind., Amoco Research Center, 1978—; career day speaker high schs.; sci. fair judge. Recipient John Phillip Sousa music award, 1967; Pres.'s trophy for acad. excellence Ala. A&M U., 1968; Knapp Dissertation award, 1974; Ford Found. fellow, 1973-74. Recipient Alumni award Nat. Assn. Equal Opportunity in Higher Edn., 1983. Mem. Am. Chem. Soc. (vice chmn. Chgo. sect. 1980-81, chmn. 1982-83), Am. Inst. Chemists, Nat. Assn. Negro Musicians (bd. dirs. Central region), So. Christian Leadership Conf., NAACP, Nat. Assn. Advancement Black Chemists and Chem. Engrs., Ala. A&M U. Alumni Assn. (pres. 1984—), Beta Kappa Chi, Alpha Kappa Mu. Democrat. Club: R. Nathaniel Dett Club Music and Allied Arts. Home: 3 S 081 Barkley Ave Warrenville IL 60555 Office: Amoco Corp PO Box 400 Naperville IL 60566

CANNON, JOHN LOWER, III, monument company executive; b. Cleve., Oct. 30, 1944; s. John Lower, Jr. and Florence Dennis (Fuller) C.; B.S. in Bus. Adminstrn., Tri State U., Angola, Ind., 1967; M.S. in Bus. Adminstrn., St. Francis Coll., Ft. Wayne, Ind., 1970; postgrad. Ind. U.-Purdue U. Extension, Ft. Wayne, 1970; m. Patsy Joan Grooms, Feb. 1, 1969; children—John Lower IV, Collier Fuller. Sr. cost acct. Gen. Telephone Co., Ft. Wayne, 1968; mgmt. trainee Cooper Indsl. Products Co., Auburn, Ind., 1968-70; sr. adminstrv. engr. ITT, Ft. Wayne, 1971; nat. contract coordinator contract sales, supr. warehouse planning Magnavox Co., Ft. Wayne, 1972-75; pres. Heritage Energy Savers, Inc., Auburn, 1973-82; owner, pres. Tri State Memls., Auburn, 1976—. Treas. Auburn Community Theatre, 1971, v.p., 1978, pres., 1979-80, bd. dirs., 1979-81, 1971-74; mem. Auburn Econ. Commn., 1982—; asst. scout master Anthony Wayne council Boy Scouts Am., 1970-72, treas., 1972-79, coordinator, 1978-80; deacon Auburn Presbyterian Ch., 1971-74, elder, 1978-80, trustee, 1981-83. Mem. Better Bus. Bur., Monument Builders N.Am., Ind. Monument Builders (v.p. 1979-81), Auburn C. of C. Republican. Club: Rotary (v.p. 1981-82, dir. 1982—). Home: 711 N Main St Auburn IN 46706 Office: 300 E 7th St Auburn IN 46706

CANNON, JOSEPH GERALD, chemistry educator; b. Decatur, Ill., Sept. 30, 1926; s. Linn Howard and Lennie Evelyn (Gehm) C.; m. Carolyn Abrahams, July 15, 1960; children—Janet H., Douglas L., Barbara J., Steven A. B.S. with high honors, U. Ill.-Chgo., 1951, M.S., 1953, Ph.D., 1956. Asst. prof. U. Wis.-Madison, 1956-60, assoc. prof., 1960-62; assoc. prof. U. Iowa, Iowa City, 1962-65, prof. chemistry, 1965—; prof., head div. medicinal chemistry and natural products Coll. Pharmacy, U. Iowa, 1972—. Contbr. sci. articles to reference jours. Patentee in field. Served to sgt. armored. U.S. Army, 1944-46. Recipient Merit award U. Wis., 1982, Soine Meml. award in medicinal chemistry, 1982; named Steelman Distg. Lectr. Lenoir-Rhyne Coll., 1983. Fellow Acad. Pharm. Scis., Am. Inst. Chemists; mem. Am. Chem. Soc. (councillor 1979—), Div. Medicinal Chemistry (nat. chmn. 1971-72), N.Y. Acad. Scis. Democrat. Unitarian. Home: 920 Highwood St Iowa City IA 52240 Office: U Iowa Coll Pharmacy Iowa City IA 52242

CANNON, ZANE WILLIAM, educator; b. Kenyon, Minn., Nov. 18, 1922; s. William Joseph and Floreen (Sanders) C.; student Ball State U., 1940-43; B.S., Western Mich. U., 1960, M.A., 1966; m. Gloria Gene Phillips, July 4, 1943; children—Benjamin W., Russel J., Thomas F. Guest lectr. mktg. Western Mich. U., Kalamazoo, 1963-64, asso. prof. mktg., 1965—; art specialist Portage (Mich.) Pub. Schs., 1964-65; promotion dir. Jour. Advt., 1974-75. Vice-chmn. Kalamazoo Zoning Bd. Appeals, 1967-73. Served in U.S. Army, 1943. Recipient commendation USIS, 1958; Aid Advt. Edn. award, 1969; Bernstein Advisor award, 1971; Direct Mail Spokesman award Direct Mail Mktg. Assn., 1972; Teaching Excellence award, Western Mich. U., 1976; Silver medal award Am. Advt. Fedn., 1977. Mem. Am. Acad. Advt., Am. Advt. Fedn. (dir. 1974-75, acad. adv. com. 1975-83), AAUP, Am. Mktg. Assn., Am. Assn. Editorial Cartoonists, Direct Mktg. Assn., Internat. Assn. Printing House Craftsmen, Point-of-Purchase Advt. Inst., Mktg.-Advt. Roundtable, Kalamazoo Advt. Club, Western Mich. U Ad Club. Republican. Presbyterian. Designed, illustrated Living in Kalamazoo, 1958. Home: 3300 Woodstone Rd #217 Kalamazoo MI 49008 Office: Western Michigan U Coll Bus Mktg Dept Kalamazoo MI 49008

CANTON, IRVING DONALD, management consultant; b. N.Y.C., Feb. 10, 1918; s. Louis and Mollie (Wolf) C.; B.Chem. Engring., Coll. City N.Y., 1940; m. Shelly Terman, Sept. 28, 1958; children—Larry, Diana. Engr., U.S. Navy Dept., 1941-45; research group leader Foster D. Snell Inc., N.Y.C., 1945-49; chem. engring. cons. S.Am., 1949-53; asst. dir. Internat. div. Ill. Inst. Tech., Chgo., 1953-61; founding stockholder, v.p. Indsl. Research Mag., Beverly Shores, Ind., 1961-62; dir. comml. devel. and planning Internat. Minerals and Chem. Co., Skokie, Ill., 1962-67; founder, pres. Strategic Decisions Co. mgmt. cons., Chgo., 1968—. Mem. Am. Mktg. Assn. (dir.; v.p. mktg. mgmt. Chgo.), Midwest Planning Assn. (founding; v.p. 1975), Am. Chem. Soc. Contbr. articles to Harvard Bus. Rev., other bus. and profl. jours. Home: 4141 Grove St Skokie IL 60076 Office: 1 Northfield Plaza Northfield IL 60093

CANTONI, LOUIS JOSEPH, psychologist, poet; b. Detroit, May 22, 1919; s. Pietro and Stella (Puricelli) C.; A.B., U. Calif.-Berkeley, 1946; M.S.W., U. Mich., 1949, Ph.D., 1953; m. Lucile Eudora Moses, Aug. 7, 1948; children—Christopher Louis, Sylvia Therese. Personnel mgr. Johns-Manville Corp., Pittsburg, Calif., 1944-46; social caseworker Detroit Dept. Pub. Welfare, 1946-49; counselor Mich. Div. Vocational Rehab., Detroit, 1949-50; conf. leader, tchr. psychology, coordinator family and community relations program Gen. Motors Inst., Flint, Mich., 1951-56; from assoc. prof. to prof., dir. rehab. counseling Wayne State U., Detroit, 1956—. Judge Mich., regional and nat. essay and poetry contests, 1965-77. Served to 2d lt. AUS, 1942-44. Recipient award for leadership and service Mich. Rehab. Assn., 1964; South and West Ann. Poetry award, 1970; award for meritorious service Wayne State U., 1971, 81. Fellow AAAS; mem. AAUP, Council of Rehab. Counselor Educators (sec. 1957-58; chmn. 1965-66), Am. Psychol. Assn., Am. Assn. for Counseling and Devel., Nat., Mich. (pres. 1963-64), Detroit (pres. 1958), rehab. assns., Detroit Inst. Arts, Poetry Soc. Mich. (Outstanding service award 1984), Soc. for Study Midwestern Lit., Acad. Am. Poets, World Poetry Soc., Phi Kappa Phi, Phi Delta Kappa. Democrat. Episcopalian. Author books including: A Follow-up Study of the 1939-43 Flint, Michigan Guidance Demonstration, 1953; Marriage and Community Relations, 1954; (with Mrs. Cantoni) Counseling Your Friends, 1961; Supervised Practice in Rehabilitation Counseling, 1978; Writings of Louis J. Cantoni, 1981; (poetry) With Joy I Called to You, 1969, Gradually the Dreams Change, 1979; editor: Placement of the Handicapped in Competitive Employment, 1957; co-editor: Preparation of Vocational Rehabilitation Counselors through Field Instruction, 1958; editor Mich. Rehab. Assn. Digest, 1961-63, Grad. Comment, 1963-64; poetry editor Cathedral Digest, 1973-75; co-editor: (poetry) Golden Song Anthology, 1985; contbr. articles and poems to jours. Home: 2591 Woodstock Dr Detroit MI 48203 Office: Wayne State Univ Detroit MI 48202

CANTOR, ALAN BERNARD, biostatistician; b. N.Y.C., Feb. 13, 1942; s. Sam and Beatrice (Klansky) C.; m. Lee Twitty, May 24, 1970; children—David, Raya. B.S., U. Fla., 1962; M.S., Appalachian State U., 1964; Ph.D., U. S.C., 1972. Assoc. prof. math. Benedict Coll., Columbia, S.C., 1971-78; asst. prof. biometry Med. Coll. S.C., Charleston, 1978-83; asst. chief Coop. Studies Program Coordinating Ctr., Hines VA Hosp., Ill., 1983—. Contbr. articles to profl. publs. Recipient summer research award AEC, Savannah River Lab., 1974; NIH postdoctoral fellow, Columbia, S.C., 1976-78. Mem. Am. Statis. Assn., Soc. for Clin. Trials. Jewish. Office: CSPCC 151-K Hines VA Hosp Hines IL 60141

CANTOR, BERNARD JACK, patent lawyer; b. N.Y.C., Aug. 18, 1927; s. Alexander J. and Tillie (Henzeloff) C.; B. Mech. Engring., Cornell, 1949; J.D., George Washington U., Washington, 1952; m. Judith L. Levin, Mar. 25, 1951; children—Glenn H., Cliff A., James E., Ellen B., Mark E. Examiner U.S. Patent Office, Washington, 1949-52; admitted to D.C. bar, 1952, U.S. Patent Office bar, 1952, Mich. bar, 1953; practice patent law, Detroit, 1952—; partner firm Cullen, Sloman, Cantor, Grauer, Scott & Rutherford, Detroit, 1952—; lectr. in field. Mem. Council Detroit Area Boy Scouts Am., 1972—; trustee Fresh Air Soc. of Detroit; bd. dirs. Jewish Vocat. Service of Detroit. Served with AUS, 1944-46. Recipient Ellsworth award patent law George Washington U., 1952; Shofar award Boy Scouts Am., 1975, Silver Beaver award, 1975. Mem. Am. Technion Soc. (v.p. Detroit 1970—), Am., Mich., Detroit bar assns., Mich. Patent Law Assn., Am. Arbitration Assn., Cornell Engring. Soc., Pi Tau Sigma, Phi Delta Phi, Beta Sigma Rho. Contbr. articles on patent law to profl. jours. Home: 5685 Forman Dr Birmingham MI 48010 Office: 3200 City Nat Bldg Detroit MI 48226

CANTOR, HARVEY, insurance company executive; b. N.Y.C., Oct. 19, 1928; s. Daniel and Anna (Finkelstein) C.; m. Edna Sylvia, May 28, 1950; children—Jeffrey W., Beth S., Richard B. M.B.A., Met. Coll. Inst., London, 1976, Ph.D., 1976; J.D., Blackstone Sch. Law, 1973. Pres., New Frontier Assn. Inc., St. Louis, 1964-73; managing dir. Growth Mgmt. Investment Corp., S.A., Luxemburg, 1973-74; mgr. br. office Provident Mutual Life Ins. Co., St. Louis, 1975-78; regional agy. dir. Summit Nat. Life Ins. Co., St. Louis, 1978—; cons. New Frontier Assn. Inc., 1964—, also dir., dir. Growth Mgmt. Investment Corp., S.A., 1973-74. Author: How To Acquire The Selling Habit (All Star awards 1968, 71), 1968. Del. Mo. State Democratic Conv., Jefferson City, 1968. Served to sgt. U.S. Army, 1944-48, ETO. Named Life Mem. Pres.'s Club, Beneficial Standard Life Ins. Co., 1967, Regional Agy. Dir. Yr., Summit Nat. Life Ins. Co., Akron, Ohio, 1979, 80, group Ambassador Gen. Am. Mo. Assn. Life Leaders, 1978; named to Nat. Aviation Hall Fame, 1981, 82, 83, 84; recipient Top Man award No. Life Ins. Co., 1968, 71. Mem. Nat. Assn. Life Underwriters, Mo. Life Underwriters Assn., Life Ins. Mktg. and Research Assn. (cert. sch. in agy. mgmt. 1977), Internat. Assn. Registered Fin. Planners (recipient Registered Fin. Planner 1985), Jewish War Vets. Democrat. Club: Creve Coeur Dem. Lodge: Masons. Avocations: photography; numismatics; golf. Home: 639 Fairways Circle Creve Coeur MO 63141 Office: Summit Nat Life Ins Co 9390 Olive Blvd Saint Louis MO 63132

CANTWELL, LOUIS YAGER, lawyer; b. Oak Park, Ill., Nov. 16, 1918; s. Robert Emmett and Anna Harrison (Yager) C.; B.S., Northwestern U., 1940, J.D., 1943; m. Janet Marie Hanssen, Nov. 9, 1956 (div. Sept. 1979); children—Thomas (dec.), Andrea Lee, David Y. Admitted to Ill. bar, 1944; partner firm Cantwell & Cantwell, Chgo., 1946-63. Dir. Faith at Work Inc., N.Y.C., 1965-67, 70—, Ruth Carter Stapleton Ministries, Behold, Inc. Mem. Am. (interstate custody com. 1959-60), Ill. (mem. joint com. with Chgo. bar on codification family law), Chgo. (chmn. matrimonial law com. 1959-60) bar assns., Am. Acad. Matrimonial Lawyers, Phi Delta Phi, Phi Kappa Psi. Contbr. articles to mags. Home: Rancho Santa Fe CA 92067 Office: 1 N LaSalle St Chicago IL 60602

CAPEN, ROBERT BERNARD, architect; b. Kansas City, Mo., Dec. 14, 1924; s. Lester Edwin and Mae Cathern (Draney) C.; m. Mary Margaret Hurt, Mar. 14, 1953; children—Nancy Patrice, Ann Elizabeth, Melissa Ellen, Catherine Renee, John Edwin, Julie Christine. B.Arch., U. Kans., 1951. Registered architect, Kans., Mo. Project architect Burns & McDonnell Archtl. Engring. Co., Kansas City, Mo., 1953—. Served to 1st lt. USAAF, 1942-45; PTO. Recipient hon. mention Morton Arboretum AIA Internat. Archtl. Competition, 1956. Mem. AIA, Constrn. Specifications Inst., Nat. Sculpture Soc. Democrat. Roman Catholic. Home: 2405 Red Bridge Rd Kansas City MO 64131 Office: Burns & McDonnell 4800 E 63rd St Kansas City MO 64130

CAPIN, JAMES EDWARD, petroleum geologist; b. Princeton, Ind., Mar. 12, 1935; s. George Merril and Calista Ann (Morris) C.; m. Rose Ann Nossett, Jan. 13, 1955; children—Carolyn Sue, Linda Kay, James Kevin, Martha Ann. Student, U. Ala.-Tuscaloosa, 1953; B.A., Hardin Simmons U., 1958. Geologist, Devel. Assocs., Inc., Mt. Carmel, Ill., 1958-60, So. Triangle Oil, Mt. Carmel, 1960-68; cons. geologist, Mt. Carmel, 1968-84; pres. Spartan Petroleum Co., Mt. Carmel, 1969—, Viking Oil Co., Mt. Carmel, 1977—, Saturn Drilling Co., Mt. Carmel, 1980—. Mem. Am. Petroleum Inst., Ohio Oil and Gas Assn., Ind. Producer Assn. Am. Republican. Methodist. Lodge: Elks. Office: 111 E 5th St Mount Carmel IL 62863

CAPIN, JOHN RICHARD, engineer, consultant; b. Fort Wayne, Ind., Mar. 21, 1949; m. Peggy Haist, June 3, 1972. B.S. in Engring., Purdue U., 1971; M. Engring., Stevens Inst. Tech., 1973; M.B.A., Bellarmine Coll., 1985. Registered profl. engr., Ind., Ky. Grad. research asst. Stevens Inst. Tech., Hoboken, N.J., 1971-73; sr. engr. Gen. Dynamic Electrical Boat Co., Groton, Ct., 1973-74; naval architect Brown & Root, Houston, 1977-79; project engr. Jeffboat, Inc., Jeffersonville, Ind., 1979—; cons. Jeffersonville, 1980—. Mem. Inland Wetlands Zoning Commn., Groton, 1976. Mem. Soc. Naval Architects & Marine Engrs. (v. chmn. 1984—), AIAA. Republican. Methodist. Club: Propeller (Louisville). Avocations: fly fishing; jogging. Home: 1209 Allison Ln Jeffersonville IN 47130 Office: Am Comml Barge Line PO Box 610 1030 E Market Jeffersonville IN 47130

CAPLIS, MICHAEL EDWARD, biochemist, toxicologist, educator; b. Ypsilanti, Mich., July 25, 1938; s. John Joseph and Marie Kathrine (Hochrein) C.; B.S., Eastern Mich. U., 1962; M.S., Purdue U., 1964, Ph.D., 1970; m. Lucille Marie Truitt, Feb. 11, 1956; children—Kathleen Ann, Michelle Marie, Maureen Marie, Therese Marie, Michael Edward, Matthew Clifford, Philip Patrick. Sci., math. tchr. St. John Prep Sch., 1958-62; analytical biochemist Ind. Chemist Office, 1962-67; grad. research asst. Purdue U., 1967-69; dir. clin.

biochemistry St. Mary Med. Ctr., Gary, Ind., 1969-83; asst. prof. Ind. U. Med. Sch. div. allied scis., 1969—; instr. Ind. Law Enforcement Tng. Bd., 1973-76; assoc. faculty N.W. Center for Med. Edn., Ind. U. Sch. Medicine; dir. N.W. Ind. Criminal Toxicology Lab., Gary, 1969—. Pres., Holy Angels Cathedral Sch. Home and Sch. Assn., 1972-73. Fed. grantee for establishment regional toxicology lab., 1970-74; diplomate Am. Bd. Forensic Toxicology. Fellow Am. Acad. Forensic Scis., Am. Acad. Clin. Toxicology, Nat. Acad. Clin. Biochemistry; mem. N.Y. Acad. Scis., AAAS, Midwest Assn. Forensic Scis., Am. Assn. Clin. Chemists, Am. Acad. Clin. Toxicology, Am. Chem. Soc., Am. Assn. Crime Lab. Dirs., Am. Assn. Ofcl. Analytical Chemists, Sigma Xi. Roman Catholic. K.C. Home: 676 N 50 W Valparaiso IN 46383 Office: 1400 S Lakepark Ave Hobart IN 46342

CAPONE, JAMES JOSEPH, health care executive, marketing director; b. White Plains, N.Y., Jan. 14, 1945; s. Charles Anthony and Minerva (Udice) C.; m. Robin Silverman, Dec. 22, 1968; children—Michael, Melissa. B.A., NYU, 1967; M.S., Fla. State U., 1969, Ph.D., 1971. Dir. ops. Kallestad Labs., Chaska, Minn., 1971-74; dir. research and devel. Inolex Biomed., Glenwood, Ill., 1974-76; dir. quality assurance Hyland/Baxter Travenol, Round Lake, Ill., 1976-80; dir. mktg. Packard Inst. Co., Downers Grove, Ill., 1980—. Editor Med. Devices/Diagnosis, 1984, contbr. articles; patentee, U.S. and abroad. Mem. Am. Soc. Clin. Pathology. Avocations: Photography; micro-processors; relational databases. Home: 1110 Thackeray Dr Palatine IL 60067

CAPONIGRI, WINIFRED FRANCO, science educator; b. Jersey City, Apr. 1, 1924; d. Franklin Aloysius and Catherine (Lione) Franco; m. A. Robert Caponigri, Oct. 6, 1946 (dec. 1983); children—Victoria, Robert John, Lisa. A.B., Western Mich. U., 1967; M.S., Notre Dame U., 1971. Cert. tchr., Ind. Instr. St. Mary's Acad., South Bend, Ind., 1957-68; prof. sci. Holy Cross Jr. Coll., Notre Dame, 1968—; adj. prof. Ind. U., South Bend, 1977—; prof. Lake Mich. Coll., Benton Harbor, Mich., 1974-75; vis. prof. Saddleback Coll., Mission Viejo, Calif., summer 1976. Bd. dirs. Christ Child Soc., South Bend, 1959-60, South Bend Symphony Assn., 1960—, St. Joseph Valley Scholarship Found., South Bend, 1975—. Mem. Ind. Acad. Sci., Nat. Assn. Geology Tchrs., Am. Chem. Soc. (2-yr. coll. div.), South Bend Hoosier Art Assn., Ladies of Notre Dame (pres. 1953-54), Delta Kappa Gamma (grantee 1980, 84). Republican. Roman Catholic. Avocations: music; art appreciation; bridge. Home: 317 E Napoleon Boulevard South Bend IN 46617 Office: Holy Cross Jr Coll Notre Dame IN 46556

CAPONIGRO, JEFFREY RALPH, public relations counselor; b. Kankakee, Ill., Aug. 13, 1957; s. Ralph A. and Barbara Jean (Paul) C.; m. Ellen Colleen Kennedy, Oct. 15, 1982; 1 child, Nicholas J. B.A., Central Mich. U., 1979. Sports reporter Observer and Eccentric newspapers, Rochester, Mich., 1974-75, Mt. Pleasant (Mich.) Times, 1975-77, Midland (Mich.) Daily News, 1977-79; account exec. Desmond & Assocs., Oak Park, Mich., 1979-80; v.p., corp. officer Anthony M. Franco, Inc., Detroit, 1980-84; sr. v.p., corp. officer MG and Casey Communications, Inc., Southfield, 1984—. Mem. Pub. Relations Soc. Am. (bd. dirs. Detroit chpt.), Adcraft Club of Detroit. Club: Detroit Athletic. Contbr.: Best Sports Stories, 1978. Home: 2873 Mayfair Troy MI 48084 Office: MG and Casey Communications Inc 17117 Nine Mile Rd Suite 1545 Southfield 48075

CAPORALE, D. NICK, See *Who's Who in America,* 43rd edition.

CAPPELLETTI, GRACE, publishing company executive; b. Chgo., Mar. 5, 1939; d. Albert Victor and Rose Agnes (Ryan) Potter; children—Jenny, Julie, John, Nick, Melody. Student pub. schs., Chgo. Chem. processing table top coordinator Putman Pubs., Chgo., 1977-78; pres. Putman Pub. Co., Chgo., 1981—; dir. Am. Bus. Press, N.Y.C. Bd. dirs. Builders of Skills, No. Ill. Mem. Nat. Assn. Women Bus. Owners, Press Assn., Inst. Food Technologists, Am. Soc. Bakery Engrs. Republican. Roman Catholic. Club: Algonquin Women's. Home: 3217 N River Algonquin IL 60102 Office: Putman Pub Co 301 N Erie St Chicago IL 60611

CAPPS, NORMAN E., computer education executive; b. Topeka, June 25, 1933; s. Thomas P. and Mae (McCabe) C.; m. Shirley Lytle, Nov. 24, 1956; children—Linda, Leane. B.S.A., U. Kans., 1955; B.A. in Fgn. Trade, Am. Inst. Internatl. Mgmt., 1956. Internatl. sales staff Wilson & Co., Inc., Chgo., London, 1956-65; pres. Electronic Computer Programming Inst., Kansas City, Mo., 1966—; pres. Mo. Assn. Private Career Schs., Kansas City, 1974. Mem. Mo. Job Training Coordinating Council, Jefferson City, 1983—; v.p. Lyric Opera Kansas City, 1984—. Recipient Meritorious Service award Kansas City Police Dept., 1975. Mem. Data Processing Mgmt. Assn. (pres. 1969-70, Performance award), Assn. for Systems Mgmt. (pres. 1977-78, Disting. Service award), Greater Kansas City C. of C. (vice chmn. 1984—), Omicron Delta Kappa. Clubs: Carriage (Kansas City), Kansas City (pres. 711 Club 1984—). Lodge: Rotary (pres. 1979-80). Home: One Dunford Circle Kansas City MO 64112 Office: Electronic Computer Programming Inst 611 W 39th St Kansas City MO 64111

CAPRARO, MICHAEL ANTHONY, chemical engineer; b. Detroit, Nov. 19, 1948; s. Anthony and Lucille (Caporosso) C.; B.S., Wayne State U., 1970, M.S., 1974; m. Myrna Lee Bolton, Aug. 28, 1971; children—Ernest Anthony, Rachel Elaine, Ellen Janelle. With BASF Wyandotte (Mich.) Corp., 1970—, plant technologist, 1979-83, research assoc., 1983-84, research supr., 1984—. Mem. Am. Inst. Chem. Engrs., Tau Beta Pi. Roman Catholic. Home: 13998 Kingswood St Riverview MI 48192 Office: BASF Wyandotte Corp 1609 Biddle St Wyandotte MI 48192

CAPRINI, JOSEPH ANTHONY, surgeon; b. Upper Darby, Pa., Aug. 20, 1939; s. Joseph G. N. and Teresa C. (Cerra) C.; B.S., Villanova U., 1961; M.D., Hahnemann Med. Coll., 1965; M.S. in Surgery, Northwestern U., 1972; m. Stella Mary Evans, June 12, 1965; children—Michelle, Lara, Carol. Intern, Evanston (Ill.) Hosp., 1965-66; resident Northwestern Univ. Med. Center, Evanston, Chgo., 1966-67, 69-73, Owen L. Coon Found. fellow in surg. hematology, 1973-74; practice medicine specializing in surgery, 1974—; instr. surgery Northwestern U., 1972, clin. asst., 1971, asst. prof., 1973-80, assoc. prof., 1980—; mem. staff Evanston Hosp., dir. clin. admissions, 1972-74, assoc. attending, 1974-76, attending, 1976-78, sr. attending surgeon, 1978—, dir. blood flow lab., 1975, dir. surg. research, 1974—, attending surg. ward service, 1973-76, dir. coagulation research lab., 1970—; attending staff VA Research Hosp., Chgo., 1974—; sr. attending surgeon Glenbrook Hosp. Served to capt. USAF, 1967-69. Diplomate Am. Bd. Surgery, Nat. Bd. Med. Examiners. Fellow A.C.S.; mem. AMA (del. council on thrombosis), Ill. State, Chgo. Med. socs., Am. Trauma Soc., Am. Heart Assn. (mem. council on thrombosis), Chgo. Heart Assn., Midwest Blood Club, Central Surg. Assn., Western Surg. Assn., Assn. for Academic Surgery, Am. Fedn. Clin. Research, N.Y. Acad. Scis., Chgo. Inst. Medicine, Chgo. Surg. Soc., MW Surg. Soc., Internat. Soc. Thrombosis Haemostasis, Ill. Surg. Soc. Producer movie: Repair of Giant Epigastric Hernia, 1973; contbr. 100 articles to med. jours. Home: 28 Coventry Rd Northfield IL 60093 Office: 2050 Pfingsten Rd Glenview IL 60025

CAPUTO, WILLIAM PETER, lawyer; b. Chgo., July 1, 1951; s. Otto Salvatore and Elizabeth (Simonetti) C.; m. Barbara Lynn Glaser, Aug. 29, 1980; children—Jennifer Lynn, William Alan, Brian Peter. B.S.Ed., No. Ill. U., 1972, M.S.Ed., 1974; LL.B., DePaul U., 1982. Bar: Ill. 1982, U.S. Dist. Ct. (no. dist.) Ill. 1982. Tchr. Ridgewood High Sch., Norridge, Ill. 1972-82; assoc. Hinshaw Culbertson, Chgo., 1982—. Mem. ABA, Ill. State Bar Assn., Chgo. Bar Assn. Office: Hinshaw Culbertson 69 W Washington Chicago IL 60602

CARANO, JOHN JOSEPH, JR, foundry products sales manager; b. Warren, Ohio, Oct. 19, 1954; s. John Joseph and Theresa Rose (Mattinat) C.; m. Teresa Helen Scott, Oct. 4, 1980. B.S. in Edn., Youngstown State U., 1979. Sales trainee Midland Ross Corp., Sharon, Pa., 1979-80, coordinator mktg. services, 1980-81, sales rep., Chgo., 1981-82, dist. sales mgr., Columbus, Ohio, 1982—. Mem. Hubbard Vol. Fire Dept., Ohio, 1979; active Ohio Hist. Soc., Columbus, 1984—. Mem. Am. Mktg. Assn., Am. Foundrymen's Soc., Am. Acad. Polit. Scis. and Social Sci., Youngstown State U. Alumni Soc. Democrat. Roman Catholic. Clubs: Toastmasters (v.p. 1984—, Best Pub. Speaker award 1984, Pub. Debate speaker award 1984) (Columbus), Columbus Italian. Avocations: race walking; book collecting. Home: 1752 Pinetree South Unit D Columbus OH 43229 Office: Nat Castings Inc 1400 S Laramie Ave Cicero IL 60650

CARBARY, JONATHAN LEIGH, lawyer; b. Elgin, Ill., Nov. 6, 1949; s. Warren Edward and Barbara Jean (Leigh) C.; m. Janice Kay Weingartner, Dec. 29, 1973; children—Nicole, Dana. B.A., Knox Coll., 1972; J.D., Hamline U., 1978. Bar: Ill. 1978, U.S. Dist. Ct. (no. dist.) Ill. 1979. Assoc., Robert A. Chapski, Ltd., Elgin, Ill., 1978-83; ptnr. Roeser, Vucha & Carbary, Elgin, 1984—. Served to 1st lt. U.S. Army, 1972-73. Recipient Am. Jurisprudence award Lawyer Co-op Pub. Co., 1978. Mem. ABA, Ill. State Bar Assn., Kane County Bar Assn. Republican. Home: 33 Lockman Circle Elgin IL 60120 Office: Roeser Vucha & Carbary 920 Davis Rd Suite 100 Elgin IL 60120

CARBIENER, WAYNE ALAN, nuclear engineering executive; b. Bremen, Ind., Feb. 21, 1936; s. Marvin and Zelma Ruth (Kaley) C.; m. Jacqueline Jean Eaton, Sept. 20, 1958; children—Wayne A., Jr., Jody J., Jill A., Michael S. B.S. in Mech. Engring., Purdue U., 1958, M.S. in Nuclear Engring., 1962; Ph.D. in Nuclear Engring., Ohio State U., 1975. Registered profl. engr., Ohio. Project dir. Battelle Columbus Labs., Ohio, 1969-71, sect. mgr., 1971-76, program mgr., 1976-78; dept. mgr. Battelle Project Mgmt. Div., Columbus, 1978-82, mgr. office nuclear integration, 1982-83, mgr. office nuclear waste isolation, 1984—. Contbr. articles to tech. jours. Mem. troop com. Boy Scouts Am., 1974-83. Served to lt. (j.g.) USN, 1958-61. Mem. ASME, Purdue U. Alumni Assn. (pres. Central Ohio chpt.). Lodge: Masons. Avocations: antique cars; collectible restorations. Office: Battelle Project Mgmt Div Office of Nuclear Waste Isolation 505 King Ave Columbus OH 43201

CARBONE, ALFONSO ROBERT, construction executive; b. Cleve., Jan. 17, 1921; s. Rosario P. and Carmela (Mandalfino) C.; student Sch. Architecture, Western Res. U. and Case Inst. Tech., 1940-42; B.Arch., Western Res. U., 1946; m. Anna Mae Simmons, June 16, 1945; children—Carmela, Florence Roberta, Rosario P. II, Anne Marie. Partner, v.p. estimator R.P. Carbone Constrn. Co., Cleve., 1940-77, owner, pres., 1977-82, chmn. bd., 1983—. Alt. builder rep. mem. City of Cleve., Bd. Bldg. Standards and Bldg. Appeals, 1953-64, builder rep. mem., 1964-74, chmn., 1965-74; past chmn. Cleve. Air Pollution Appeals Bd. Mem. Business Men's Club, Central YMCA, Cleve.; mem. Nat. UN Day Com., 1971-80; trustee, past chmn. resources and personnel com. Alta House, pres. bd. trustees, 1981-83, chmn. devel. and govt. relations com., 1983—; bd. dirs. Neighborhood Ctrs. Assn., 1981-84; del. Assembly of United Way Services of Cleve., 1981-84. Served with U.S. Coast and Geodetic Survey, Washington, 1942-45. Recipient Alpha Rho Chi medal, 1946; decorated cavalier Order Star Solidarity (Italy); papal cavaliere Order St. Gregory. Mem. Cleve. Engring. Soc., Assn. Gen. Contractors Am., Builders Exchange Cleve., Holy Name Soc., Ohio Bldg. Insps. Assn., Citizen League Cleve., Greater Cleve. Growth Assn., Order Sons Italy Am. (past grand orator, past pres. lodge, grand trustee officer, state parliamentarian), Epsilon Delta Rho. Roman Catholic (councilman; commd. extraordinary minister for adminstrn. Holy Communion 1974). Home: 3324 Aberdeen Rd Shaker Heights OH 44120 Office: 3185 E 79th St Cleveland OH 44104

CARBONE, PAUL PETER, physician, cancer researcher, educator; b. White Plains, N.Y., May 2, 1931; s. Antonio and Grace (Capileri) C.; m. Mary Iamurri, Aug. 21, 1954; children—David, Kathryn, Karen, Paul J., Kimberly, Mary Beth, Matthew. Student Union Coll., Schenectady, 1949-52; M.D., Albany Med. Coll., 1956. Intern, USPHS Hosps., Balt., 1956-57, resident in internal medicine, 1958-60; resident in med. oncology Nat. Cancer Inst., NIH, Bethesda, Md., 1960-63, sr. investigator, 1960-65, head solid tumor service, 1965-69, chief medicine br., 1968-72, assoc. dir. med. oncology, 1972-74; Am. Cancer Soc. prof. clin. oncology U. Wis.-Madison, 1976-81, prof. medicine and human oncology, 1976—, chmn. dept. human oncology, 1977—; dir. Wis. Clin. Cancer Ctr., Madison, 1978—; Clowes lectr. Roswell Park Meml. Inst., 1979; bd. dirs. Frontier Sci. & Tech. Research, Brookline, Mass., 1977—, Nat. Found. Cancer Research, 1984—; mem. sci. adv. bd. St. Jude Children's Hosp., Memphis, 1981-83; mem. med. adv. bd. Triton Bioscis./Cetus, Alameda, Calif., 1983—. Editor: Estrogen Receptors in Breast Cancer, 1975; co-editor: Perspectives on Prevention and Treatment of Cancer in the Elderly, 1983; assoc. editor: Current Therapy in Hematology/Oncology, 2d edit., 1985. Served to dir. USPHS, 1956-76. Recipient Albert Lasker award Albert Lasker Found., 1972, Richard and Hilda Rosenthal Found. award, 1977. Mem. Eastern Coop. Oncology Group (chmn. 1971—), Am. Soc. Clin. Oncology (pres. 1972-73), Am. Assn. Cancer Research (v.p. 1978-79, pres. 1979-80). Roman Catholic. Office: Wis Clin Cancer Ctr 600 Highland Ave Madison WI 53792

CARDEN, TERRENCE STEPHEN, JR., physician; b. Scranton, Pa., Mar. 12, 1938; s. Terrence S. and Jean (McGuire) C.; B.S., U. Scranton, 1960; M.S. in Journalism, Columbia U., 1961; M.D., Jefferson Med. Coll., 1971; m. Coralie Hall; children—Terrence Stephen III, Andrea. Copy editor Phila. Inquirer, 1961-63; wire editor Scranton (Pa.) Times 1963-66; public relations dir. Mercy Hosp., Scranton, 1966-67; copy editor Phila. Bull., 1967-69; intern Duke U. Med. Center, Durham, N.C., 1971-72, resident, 1972; practice medicine specializing in emergency medicine and family practice, Highland Park, Ill., 1973—, Lake Forest, Ill., 1974—, Ingleside, Ill., 1978-81, Round Lake, Skokie, Ill., 1980—, Atlanta, 1981—; Glenview, Ill., 1983—, Chgo., 1983—; dir. emergency services Highland Park Hosp., since 1974—; med. dir. South Lake County Mobile Intensive Care Program, 1974—; dir. emergency services Lake Forest Hosp., 1974-80; pres. Emergency Physicians Group, Ltd., Prairie View, Ill., 1974—; clin. asso. prof. dept. surgery Chgo. Med. Sch., Downey, Ill., 1977—; mem. adv. bd. Statewide Mobile Intensive Care, Ill. Dept. Health, 1977-78; dir. First Nat. Bank of Lincolnshire, 1978-81. Bd. dirs., chmn. emergency care com. Lake County Heart Assn., 1977—; state conv. publicity aide Pa. Assn. for Retarded Children, 1966. Diplomate Am. Bd. Family Practice, Am. Bd. Emergency Medicine. Mem. Am. Coll. Emergency Physicians, Am. Acad. Family Physicians, Inst. of Medicine Chgo., Ill. Med. Soc., Am. Trauma Soc., Lake County Med. Soc., U. Assn. Emergency Med. Services, Gibbon Surg. Soc., Physicians Nat. Housestaff Assn. (alt. regional rep. 1972-73), U. Scranton Alumni Soc. (nat. sec. 1967), Jefferson Med. Coll. Alumni Assn., Hobart Amory Hare Honor Med. Soc., Alpha Omega Alpha, Alpha Sigma Nu (v.p. Scranton chpt. 1959-60). Clubs: Gordon Setter Am., Gordon Highlanders, Fox River Valley Kennel. Author: (with R.H. Daffner and J.A. Gehweiler) Case Studies in Radiology, 1975; contbr. editorials to New Physician publ., 1971-75; contbg. editor Jour. Am. Med. Assn., 1977-80; copy editor Introduction to History of General Surgery, 1968. Home: 23636 N Elm Rd Mundelein IL 60060 Office: 430 Milwaukee Ave Prairie View IL 60069

CARDINELL, JENNIFER LYNN, computer company executive; b. Corry, Pa., Mar. 16, 1955; d. Robert Borden and Martha Elinor (Elston) Moore; m. William Joseph Cardinell, July 17, 1982 (div. Dec. 1984); 1 dau., Christine Elizabeth. B.A., Guilford Coll. Tech. cons. Control Data Corp., Mpls., 1979—. Mem. Nat. Assn. Female Execs. Republican. Roman Catholic. Avocations: racquetball, volleyball, biking, backpacking, swimming, cooking, reading. Home: 3635 Blackhawk Rd Eagan MN 55122 Office: Control Data Worldtech 7600 France Ave S Edina MN 55435

CARDUCCI, BERNARDO JOSEPH, psychology educator, consultant; b. Detroit, May 20, 1952; s. Edward and Mary (Bosco) C.; 1 dau., Rozana. A.A., Mt. San Antonio Coll., 1972; B.A., Calif. State U.-Fullerton, 1974, M.A., 1976; Ph.D., Kans. State U., 1981. Asst. prof. psychology Ind. U.-S.E., New Albany, 1979—; textbook, jour. reviewer; textbook mktg. cons.; stress workshop dir.; research supr., tchr. Recipient Most Cert. of Merit award Mt. San Antonio Coll. Associated Men Students, 1971; Service award Ingleside Mental Health Ctr., 1976; Outstanding Faculty Contbn. award Ind. U.-S.E., 1981. Mem. Am. Psychol. Assn., Soc. for Personality and Social Psychology, Midwestern Psychol. Assn., Council Undergrad. Psychology Depts., Southeastern Psychol. Assn., Soc. for Psychol. Study Social Issues, Psi Chi (recipient cert. recognition for outstanding research 1974). Author: Instructor's Manual to Accompany Mehr's Abnormal Psychology, 1983; contbr. numerous articles to psychol. jours. Home: 4002 Summer Pl New Albany IN 47150 Office: Dept Psychology Ind U SE New Albany IN 47150

CARDWELL, MICHAEL STEVEN, obstetrician/perinatologist; b. Salem, Ind., Apr. 3, 1954; s. Carlie and Gladys (Shepard) C.; B.S., Purdue U., 1974; M.D., Ind. U., 1978; m. Dannette M. Littell, Oct. 8, 1983; children by previous marriage—Megan, Zachary. Resident in ob-gyn St. Francis Hosp., Peoria, Ill., 1979-82, chief resident, 1981-82; fellow in maternal-fetal medicine Baylor Coll. Medicine, Houston, 1982-84; dir. maternal-fetal medicine Rockford Meml. Hosp., 1984—; dir. Rockford Perinatal Ctr., 1984—. Scoutmaster Boy Scouts Am., Livonia, Ind., 1972-74; leader 4-H, Ind., 1970-75. Mem. Am. Coll. Ob-Gyn, Am. Public Health Assn., AMA, Am. Inst. Ultrasound in Medicine, Ill. State Med. Assn., Soc. Perinatal Obstetricians, Alpha Omega Alpha. Mem. Christian Ch. Home: 2120 Harlem Blvd Rockford IL 61103 Office: 2400 N Rockton Rockford IL 61103

CAREW, JAN RYNVELD, African-American studies educator, writer; b. Guyana, S.Am., Sept. 24, 1925; s. Alan Charles and Kathleen Ethel (Robertson) C.; m. Joan Murray, June 14, 1952 (dec.); m. Joy Gleason, Sept. 28, 1975; children—Lisa Macbeth, David, Shantoba. Student Howard U., 1945-46, Western Res. U., 1946-48, Charles U., Prague, Czechoslovakia, 1949-50; Dip. Advanced Sci. Research Sorbonne (France), 1950-52. Lectr. extramural dept. London U., 1952-54; broadcaster BBC, 1952-65; lectr. third world lit. Princeton U., 1968-72, sr. fellow Council for Humanities; prof. African-Am. studies Northwestern U., 1972—. Recipient Ill. Arts Council award, 1973; cert. of Excellence Am. Inst. Graphic Arts, 1974; Pushcart prize, 1979; Can. Council grantee, 1968; Princeton U. summer grantee, 1970-71; Rutgers U. summer grantee, 1970-72. Mem. Assn. Caribbean Studies (pres.), Caribbean Soc. Culture and Sci., AAUP, Found. Sci. Ednl. Coop. Author: Black Midas, 1958; The Wild Coast, 1958; The Last Barbarian, 1962; Green Winter, 1965; The Third Gift, 1974; Children of the Sun, 1980; Sea Drums in My Blood, 1972; Origins of Racism, 1976; Caribbean Writer and Exile, 1975; Grenada: The Hour Will Strike Again, 1985. Mem. editorial bd. Jour. African Civilization, Obsidian, Caliban, Jour. Assn. Caribbean Studies. Office: African-Am Studies Dept Northwestern U 2003 Sheridan Rd Evanston IL 60201*

CAREY, EDWARD MARSHEL, JR., accounting co. exec.; b. Washington, Pa., June 12, 1942; s. Edward Marshel and Mildred Elizabeth (Bradley) C.; B.S. in Bus. Adminstrn., Greenville (Ill.) Coll., 1964; m. Naomi Ruth Davis, June 1, 1964; children—Martha Ann, Mary Louise. Accountant, Gen. Motors Corp., Anderson, Ind., 1964-68, supr. accounting, 1968-70; staff accountant Carter, Kirlin & Merrill, C.P.A.s, Indpls., 1970-74, partner, 1974—. C.P.A., Ind. Mem. Am. Inst. C.P.A.s (mgmt. of accounting practice com. 1976-80, chmn. com. 1978-80, mgmt. adv. services com. 1980-83, chmn. com. 1982-83, dir. Indpls. chpt. 1977-83, treas. 1978-79, pres. 1979-80), Nat. Assn. Accountants, Am. Mgmt. Assn., Inst. Internal Auditors (dir.), Greenville Coll. Alumni Assn. (dir., treas. Ind. chpt. 1980-82). Republican. Methodist. Club: Indpls. Athletic. Home: 215 Royal Oak Ct Zionsville IN 46077 Office: 9102 N Meridian St Indianapolis IN 46260

CAREY, GERALD EUGENE, veterinarian; b. St. Joseph, Mo., July 12, 1944; s. Earl Victor and Emma Jean (Ensign) C.; B.S., U. Mo.-Columbia, 1966, D.V.M., 1968; m. Donna Louise Graf, June 3, 1967; children—Jeffrey Jay, Mark Christopher, Allison Beth, Amanda Christine. Unit head dog and cat quarantine unit NIH, Bethesda, Md., 1968-70; individual practice small animal medicine, surgery Kansas City, Mo., 1970-73, Blue Springs, Mo., 1973—. Bd. dirs. Jackson County (Mo.) United Way, 1975-78, Chapel Hill Early Childhood Center; active Boy Scouts Am. Served with commd. corps USPHS, 1968-70. Recipient Pizer award, 1967. Mem. Kansas City (pres. 1977), Mo. (alt. dist. del. 1978—, chmn. small animal disease control com. 1978-79), Am. vet. med. assns. Mo. Acad. Veterinarians. Presbyterian (elder, pres. bd. trustees 1978), Club: Kiwanis. Home: Route 2 Box 58 Blue Springs MO 64015 Office: 938 S 7 Hwy Blue Springs MO 64015

CAREY, HENRY G., fin. mgmt. cons.; b. Dunblane, Sask., Can., July 8, 1923; s. George P. and Clara (Amerud) C.; B.S.C., U. Iowa, 1952; m. Marian E. Steninger, Sept. 2, 1950; children—Henry G., James A., Paul R., John R. Mem. audit and systems staff Arthur Andersen & Co., Chgo., 1952-58; dir. systems New Haven R.R., 1958-60; dir. systems, asst. controller telecommunications div. ITT, Chgo., 1960-63; with Chgo. Blue Cross/Blue Shield, Chgo., 1963-81, v.p., controller, 1963-76, asst. treas., 1976-81; prin. Henry G. Carey & Assos., Downers Grove, Ill., 1981—. Pres., Downers Grove Village Forum Bd., 1972-73. Served with USAAF, 1943-46. C.P.A., Ill. Mem. Fin. Execs. Inst., Am. Inst. C.P.A.'s, Ill. Soc. C.P.A.'s. Republican. Home and office: 522 59th St Downers Grove IL 60516

CAREY, JAMES JOSEPH, government official; b. Berlin, Wis., Apr. 9, 1939; s. Robert Emmet Carey and Ruth Margaret (Harrison) Carey Johnson; B.S. in Bus. Adminstrn., Northwestern U., 1960, postgrad. 1969-70; children—Lynn Margaret, Sarah Ann. Pres., Chgo. Offset Printing Co., 1972-74; exec. v.p. Total Graphic Communication, Inc., Addison, Ill., 1974-76; pres. Coordinated Graphics, Inc., Waukegan, Ill., 1976-78; dir. internat. mil. tng. Telemedia, Inc., Chgo., 1978-81; commr. Fed. Maritime Commn., Washington, 1981—, vice chmn., 1983—. Candidate for asst. sec. Navy, 1981, for dep. asst. sec. def., 1981. Served as surface warfare officer USN, 1962-65, capt. Res. Life mem. Bluejackets Assn. (nat. pres. 1980-81, mng. editor The Bullhorn 1977-81), Navy League of U.S. (dir. 1979-80, v.p. 1980-81), Mil. Order of World Wars (bd. dirs.), U.S. Naval Inst., Am. Def. Preparedness Assn., Fleet Res. Assn., Combat Pilots Assn., Assn. Naval Aviation (v.p. 1981—), Naval Order of U.S., Ret. Officers Assn., Naval Res. Assn. (9th dist. exec. v.p. 1980-81), Non-Commd. Officers Assn., Res. Officers Assn., Naval Res. Enlisted Assn. (area advisor); mem. Armed Forces Communication Electronics Assn., N.G. Assn. Ill., Marine Corps League, Res. Enlisted Assn., USAF Assn., Coalition for Peace Through Strength, Nat. Security Council, P.T. Boats Assn., Transport Aircraft Assn., U.S. Naval Sea Cadet Corp. (nat. bd. dirs. 1978-81, regional dir., 1979-81, nat. v.p. 1981—), Am. Legion, VFW, Zeta Psi (nat. bd. dirs. 1967-71). Republican. Roman Catholic. Clubs: Capitol Hill, Capitol Hill Yacht, Nat. Press, Army and Navy, Officers Service (pres. 1983—). Office: Fed Maritime Commn 1100 L St NW Suite 11502 Washington DC 20573

CAREY, JOHN MICHAEL, lawyer; b. Toledo, Mar. 4, 1951; s. John Quinn and Marcella Anastasia (Hiermeier) C.; m. Terese Marie Anderson, Feb. 7, 1970; children—Jeremy, Elizabeth, Patrick. B.A., Williams Coll., 1973; J.D., U. Toledo, 1977. Bar: Ohio 1978, U.S. Dist. Ct. (no. dist.) Ohio 1978, U.S. Dist. Ct. (ea. Dist.) Mich. 1982, U.S. Ct. Appeals (6th cir.) 1984. Assoc. Fuller & Henry, Toledo, 1978-83, ptnr., 1983-84, Watkins, Bates & Handwork, 1985—. Office: Watkins Bates & Handwork 1200 Nat Bank Bldg Toledo OH 43604

CAREY, RICHARD JAMES, health educator, athletic trainer; b. Aberdeen, Wash., Aug. 9, 1949; s. Robert H. and Harriet R. (Lee) C.; m. Linda Kay Bannister, June 21, 1975. A.A., Grays Harbor Community Coll., 1969; B.A., U. Wash., 1971; M.S., Pa. State U., 1980. Cert. athletic trainer. Research trainer U. Wash. Med. Sch., Seattle, 1972-75; tchr., trainer Lyons Twp. High Sch., LaGrange, Ill., 1976—; instr., examiner Northwestern Sports Med. Ctr., Chgo., 1978-79; mem. Gov.'s Task Force on Sports Medicine, 1980. Co-author: Athletic Training, 1975. Developer: Sports Trauma Management Inventory, 1982. Mem. St. Barbara's Ch. Choir, Brookfield, Ill., 1976—. Mem. AAHPERD, Nat. Athletic Trainers Assn., Inc. (High Sch. Trainer of Yr. award 1984), Ill. Athletic Trainers Assn., Inc. (treas. 1982-86). Democrat. Roman Catholic. Avocations: philately; hiking; camping. Home: 1393 W 52d Pl LaGrange IL 60525 Office: Lyons Twp High Sch 100 S Brainard Ave LaGrange IL 60525

CAREY, SUSAN FRANCES JARRETT, nurse; b. Manhattan, Kans., Jan. 27, 1945; d. Robert Maxwell and Frances Elizabeth (Jennings) Jarrett; R.N., St. John's Hosp. Sch. Nursing, Springfield, Ill., 1968; student Lincolnland Community Coll., 1978; M.A. in Human Devel. Counseling, Sangamon State U., 1978-81; m. Charles Timothy Carey, Apr. 23, 1966; children—Patrick Blair, Dennis Michael, Nolan Kelly. Staff nurse, charge nurse St. John's Hosp., Springfield, 1968-79, 80—; head nurse Meml. Med. Center, 1979-80. Mem. Springfield Desegregation Monitoring Commn., 1977—; precinct election judge, 1978—; treas. Pack 352 Cub Scouts, Springfield. Recipient Public Service award U.S. Dist. Ct., Springfield, 1978; lic. R.N., Ill. Mem. Am. Personnel and Guidance Assn., Ill. Geneal. Soc., Ind. Hist. Soc., Ill. Congress Parents and Tchrs. (life), St. John's Hosp. Sch. of Nursing Alumni Assn., Forum for Death Edn. and Counseling, Prairie Preservation Soc. Ogle County. Democrat. Roman Catholic. Home: 839 Percy Ave Springfield IL 62702

CARL, EARL GEORGE, social worker; b. Wooster, Ohio, Sept. 14, 1924; s. Earl George and Effie (Weible) C.; B.S., Ohio U., 1951; M.S., Simmons Coll., 1955; m. Mary J. Sheehan, Dec. 25, 1950; children—Earl George III, Christopher T., Mary Lisa, Richard S. Boys's supr. Youth Service Bd., State Mass., Boston, 1952-54; psychiat. social worker VA Hosp., Coatesville, Pa., 1955-57, Family Service Chester County, West Chester, Pa., 1957-59; exec. dir. Family Service Pottstown, Pa., 1959-63; asst. dir. social service dept. Newberry (Mich.) State Hosp., 1963-66, dir. field offices, Marquette, Mich., 1966-70; dir. outpatient dept. Coldwater (Mich.) State Home and Tng. Sch., 1970-73; dir. continued care unit Kalamazoo State Hosp., 1973—; guest lectr. in social work No. Mich. U., supr. field lab. in social work, 1967-69; supr. field lab. in social work Western Mich. U., 1974—. Bd. dirs. McKercher Rehab. Center, Kalamazoo. Served with USNR, 1943-46. Mem. Nat. Assn. Social Work, Acad. Cert. Social Workers, Cert. Marriage Counselors Mich., Mich. State

Employees Assn. Home: 3815 Oakridge Rd Kalamazoo MI 49008 Office: Kalamazoo Regional Psychiat Hosp Kalamazoo MI 49008

CARLEN, ROSALINE ANN, financial analyst, accountant; b. Detroit, July 5, 1938; d. Joseph Aloyious and Hedwig Theresa (Jakubiak) Kowalewski; B.B.A., U. Detroit, 1963; A.Indsl. Engring., Lawrence Inst. Tech., 1973; m. Bernard Albert Carlen, Dec. 31, 1973. Delivery coordinator internat. div. Vickers div. Sperry Rand Corp., 1962-67; supr. prodn. control and inventory control Bryant Computer Products div. Excello Corp., 1968-71; acctg. clk. to sr. fin. analyst, mem. devel. team performance measurement system Vought Corp., 1971-75; sr. fin. analyst EECSG div. Bendix Corp., 1977-78; supr. fin. and cost analysis F. Joseph Lamb Co., Warren, Mich., 1979-83; mgr. cost acctg. Cadillac Products, Inc., 1983—; sec.-treas. Evergreen Fin. Services, Sterling Heights, Mich., 1984-85. Mem. St. Clair Shores (Mich.) Budget Com., 1979. Lic. real estate broker, Mich. Mem. Am. Mgmt. Assn. Republican. Roman Catholic. Author mil. maintenance manuals. Home: 23221 Doremus Ave Saint Clair Shores MI 48080 Office: 7000 E Fifteen Mile Rd Sterling Heights MI 48077

CARLIN, JOHN WILLIAM, governor Kansas; b. Salina, Kans., Aug. 3, 1940; s. Jack W. and Hazel L. (Johnson) C.; B.S. in Agr., Kans. State U., 1962; children by previous marriage—John David, Lisa Marie. Farmer, dairyman; mem. Kans. Ho. of Reps. from 92d Dist., 1971-73, from 73d Dist., 1973-79, asst. minority leader, 1975, minority leader, 1975-77, speaker, 1977-79; gov. Kans., 1979—. Democrat. Lutheran. Club: Lions. Office: 2d Floor The Statehouse Topeka KS 66612*

CARLIN, MAYNARD ROGER, lawyer; b. Noel, Mo., Aug. 7, 1955; s. Maynard Ralph and Huelene (Alexander) C. B.A., Mo. Southern State Coll., u., 1977; J.D. cum laude, U. Ark., 1980. Bar: Mo. 1980, U.S. Dist. Ct. (we. dist.) Mo. 1981. Law clk., Pineville, Mo., 1977-80, Riverside, Mo., 1980; assoc. Robert W. Evenson, Pineville, 1980-81, ptnr., 1981-83; pros. atty. McDonald County, Pineville, 1982—; city atty. City of Anderson, Mo, 1981-83, Pineville, 1981-83. Staff, Law Rev. U. Ark., 1979. Mem. McDonald County Booster Club. Mem. ABA, Assn. Trial Lawyers Am., Mo. Bar Assn., Newton/McDonald Counties Bar Assn., Anderson Jaycees, Pineville C. of C., Sigma Mu Alumni Assn. Democrat. Mem. Christian Ch. Office: PO Box 776 Pineville MO 64856

CARLISLE, PATRICIA ANN, educational administrator; b. Flint, Mich., Jan. 20, 1943; d. Warren J. and Clara Jane (Burns) Davis; m. John C. Carlisle, Apr. 8, 1967; children—Danielle Erin, Shauna Rosan. B.S., Central Mich. U., 1965; M.A., Mich. State U., 1969; postgrad. U. Mich., 1971. Research asst. Central Mich. U., Mount Pleasant, 1964-65; tchr., counselor Oakland Community Coll., Oakland County, Mich., 1975-82; counselor, adminstr. Purdue U., Hammond, Ind., 1973-82; acting dir. non-credit programs Purdue U. North Central, Westville, Ind., 1982-84, dir. spl. services, 1984—, chmn. women's conf., 1985. Mem. N.W. Ind. Open Housing Ctr., Gary, 1980—; v.p., bd. dirs. Contact Cares, Northwest Ind., Merrillville, 1983—; bd. dirs. Gifted and Talented Consortium, Northwest Ind., 1984—; chmn. Mich. City Adult Edn. Adv. Com. (Ind.), 1983-84. Mem. Am. Assn. Counseling and Devel., Am. Assn. Women in Community and Jr. Colls., Am. Coll. Personnel Assn., Mid-Am. Assn. Ednl. Opportunity Program Personnel, Phi Kappa Phi, Kappa Delta Pi. Democrat. Unitarian Universalist. Avocations: cross country skiing; gardening; reading, country/folk music. Office: Purdue U N Central Westville IN 46391

CARLOCK, PHILIP DEAN, college dean; b. Effingham, Ill., Mar. 11, 1940; m. Janet L. Schack, Apr. 13, 1963; children—Cindy, Cathy. B.S. in Edn., Eastern Ill. U., 1962, M.S. in Ednl. Administrn., 1964; postgrad. Northwestern U., 1964, U. Mo., 1966, So. Ill. U., 1968, Fla. Atlantic U., 1976; M.A. in Mgmt., Webster U., St. Louis, 1979; Ed.S., So. Ill. U., 1972. Tchr., Catlin Jr. High Sch., Ill., 1962-63; audio-visual staff Arlington Heights Pub. Schs., Ill., 1963-65; asst. coordinator dist. instructional resources St. Louis-St. Louis County Jr. Coll. Dist., 1965-68; lectr. So. Ill. U., Edwardsville, 1972, 74, 75; assoc. mem. grad. faculty Eastern Ill. U., Charleston, 1975; asst./assoc. dean instrn. St. Louis Community Coll. at Forest Park, 1968-70, assoc. dean instrn., 1970-75, dean research and devel. 1974-77, dir. ednl. devel., 1977, acting interim pres., 1977-78, asst. to pres., 1978-79, assoc. dean instrn. life sci. div., 1979—; seminar leader; mem. exec. bd. Mo. Dept. Audio-Visual Edn., 1968-71; mem. Ill. Audio-Visual Assn., 1963-75. Mem. Lindbergh Sch. Dist. Bd. Edn., 1980—, v.p., sec.-treas., bd. dirs.; mem. alumni nominating com. Webster U., 1983-84; mem. coms. Webster Hills United Methodist Ch., Webster Groves, Mo., 1965—. Mem. Eastern Ill. U. Alumni Assn. (v.p. 1979) chpt. exec. com. 1976-79), Adminstrs. Assn. St. Louis Community Coll. Dist. (vice-chmn. 1976-77), Community Coll. Assn. Instrn. and Tech., Assn. Ednl. Communications and Tech., Nat. Community Coll. Assn. (sec.-treas. 1970-71), Ednl. Film Libraries Assn., Greater St. Louis Area Media Roundtable, Assn. Edn. Communications Tech., Tau Kappa Epsilon, Alpha Phi Omega. Home: 9739 Cambrook Dr Saint Louis MO 63123 Office: 5600 Oakland Ave Saint Louis MO 63110

CARLSEN, TED, manufacturing company executive; b. Mpls., Feb. 16, 1930; s. Charles Eugene and Carolyn Mae (Mason) C.; m. Catherine Stickney Relf, Feb. 28, 1953; children—David Relf, Mary Ellen, Daniel Christian, Jane Charlotte. B.A., U. Minn., 1952. Sales engr. Satterlee Co., Mpls., 1954-60; pres. Carlsen Standard Parts Co., Fairbault, Minn., 1960-63; pres., chief exec. officer Upper Midwest Industries, Inc., Hopkins, Minn., 1963—; dir. Fidelity Bank & Trust Co., Mpls. Pres. Lichenhearth Condominium Assn., Snowmass Village, Colo., 1980—; mem. Minn. Elephant Club, St. Paul, 1980—; bd. dirs. Hopkins Crime Commn., 1983—; pres. Viking council Boy Scouts Am., 1979; committeeman Many Waters Area council Boy Scouts Am., 1982—; High Adventure Bases, Boy Scouts Am., 1985—. Served with U.S. Army, 1952-54. Recipient 1984 Minn. Small Businessperson of Yr. award SBA, 1984. Mem. Assn. Rotational Molders (founder 1976), Expanded Metal Mfg. Assn. (pres. 1977). Republican. Episcopalian. Club: Decathlon Athletic (Mpls.). Lodge: Rotary (Hopkins) (pres. 1971-72). Avocations: skiing; fishing; swimming. Home: 6512 Indian Hills Rd Edina MN 55435 Office: Upper Midwest Industries Inc 1520 S Fifth St Hopkins MN 55343

CARLSON, ARTHUR EUGENE, accounting educator; b. Whitewater, Wis., May 10, 1923; s. Paul Adolph and Dorothy Adeline (Cooper) C.; m. Lorraine June Bronson, Aug. 19, 1944; 1 child, George Arthur. Ed.B., U. Wis., Whitewater, 1943; M.B.A., Harvard U., 1947; Ph.D., Northwestern U., 1954. Instr., Ohio U., 1947-50; lectr. Northwestern U., 1950-52; from asst. prof. to prof. acctg. Washington U., St. Louis, 1952—; vis. prof. U. Hawaii, 1963-64. Author: College Accounting, 1967, 2d edit., 1972, 3d edit., 1977, 4th edit., 1982; Accounting Essentials, 1973, 2d edit., 1978, 3d edit., 1983. Trustee, Robert Meml. Endowment Fund., University City, Mo., 1972—, Police and Fire Pension Bd., 1979—. Mem. Nat. Assn. Accts. (past pres.), Assn. Systems Mgmt. (past pres., Disting. Service award 1973). Republican. Episcopalian. Lodge: Kiwanis (pres. 1969). Avocation: bowling. Home: 8023 Gannon St St Louis MO 63130

CARLSON, BARTLEY JAMES, computer software company executive; b. Rockford, Ill., Mar. 4, 1944; s. Alvin B. and Doris E. (Nelson) C.; B.S., No. Ill. U., 1969; children—Jill C., Barbara J., Brenda J. Customer engr. IBM Corp., Glendale, Calif., Janesville, Wis., and Evanston, Ill., 1962-64; field engr. Xerox Corp., Phoenix, 1964-65; systems coordinator Sundstrand Corp., Rockford, 1965-66; programming mgr. No. Ill. Corp., DeKalb, 1966-68; mem. faculty, dir. computer services Waubonsee Coll., Sugar Grove, Ill., 1968-78; dir. computer services Coll. of DuPage, Glen Ellyn, Ill., 1978-80; sr. cons. Deloitte, Haskins & Sells, Chgo., 1980-83; pres. Nat. Systems Labs., Inc., 1983-85, cons. Nat. Systems Labs., Inc.; mem. Nat. Commn. on Software; chmn. Nat. Task Force on Edn. and Tng. of Software Profls., 1981-82; chmn. Task Force on Adminstrv. Computing, Ill. Higher Bd. Edn., 1971. Cert. data educator. Mem. Internat. Word Processing Assn. (cons. adv. council 1982-83), Data Processing Mgmt. Assn., Coll. and Univ. System Exchange (dir.), Word Processing Soc.; Ill. Assn. Ednl. Data Systems (dir. 1973-76), Ill. Community Council of Pres.'s, Nat. Ednl. Computer Network, EDUNET Task Force on Electronic Mail, Coll. and Univ. Machine Records Assn. Club: Big Foot Country. Home: 6705 Innsbruck Ct Lisle IL 60532 Office: Computer Network Corp One Energy Ctr Naperville IL 60566

CARLSON, CRAIG EUGENE, lawyer; b. Iowa City, June 24, 1941; s. Carl Edwin and Evelyn Marie (Temple) C.; m. Sherry Ann Reynolds, Jan. 26, 1963; children—Curt, Tonya, Marc. B.S., Iowa State U., 1963; J.D., Drake U., 1966. Bar: Iowa 1966. Mem. Carter & Carlson Attys., Mitchellville, Iowa, 1966-68; trust officer 1st Nat. Bank, Racine, Wis., 1968-70; sr. v.p. State Bank, Fort Dodge, Iowa, 1970-74; mem. Johnson, Erb, Latham, Gibb & Carlson, Fort Dodge, 1974—. Chmn. YMCA Charitable Found., Grace Lutheran Ch. Found.; trustee Blanden Art Gallery Charitable Found. Named Student Most Outstanding in Scholastic Progress, Drake U. Law Sch., 1966. Mem. Webster County Bar Assn., ABA, Iowa State Bar Assn., Iowa Mcpl. Attys. Assn., Iowa Soc. Hosp. Attys., Iowa Trial Lawyers Assn., Wis. State Bar Assn., Am. Acad. Hosp. Attys. Clubs: Country, Racquet. Lodge: Elks (Ft. Dodge). Office: Johnson Erb Latham Gibb & Carlson 600 Boston Centre Fort Dodge IN 50501

CARLSON, DONALD T(IMMS), printing company executive; b. Chgo., June 22, 1932; s. C. Melvin and Margaret (Timms) C.; m. Shirley Ann Wennerstrand, Jan. 30, 1954; children—Donald T., Marcy Ellen, Jennifer Mallory. B.S. in Mktg., U. Ill., 1954. Account exec. Tempo Communications Inc., Chgo., 1961-71, nat. accounts mgr., 1971-73, dir. mktg., Chgo. and Milw., 1973-75, v.p. for East, Trumbull, Conn. and N.Y.C., 1975-79; v.p. field sales div. Alden Press, Chgo., 1979—; pub. Action Time mag., 1963-72, Mktg. News, 1972-74. Served to 1st lt. U.S. Army, 1955-56. Mem. Direct Mktg. Assn., Delta Kappa Epsilon. Republican. Unitarian. Clubs: Westmoreland Country, Stamford Yacht. Office: 2000 Arthur Ave Elk Grove Village IL 60007

CARLSON, JOHN DAVID, engineer; b. Elgin, Ill., Dec. 28, 1951; s. John E. and Ruth J. (Berg) C.; m. Karen Anne Lee, Aug. 28, 1976; children—Erik, Justin. A.A.S., Elgin Community Coll., 1972; B.S., So. Ill. U., 1974; student Trinity Evang. Sem., 1976. Sales/indsl. engr. Omega, Arlington Heights, Ill., 1974-75; cons. devel. engr. Baxter Travenol Labs., Round Lake, Ill., 1977-79; owner Nature's Pantry, Elgin, 1978-81; test technologist Elgin Sweeper Co., 1980-84, test supr., 1984-85, test mgr., 1985—. Patentee method of repair capillary fiber diffusion device. Deacon Trout Park Bapt. Ch., Elgin, 1984-85, Rolling Meadows Bapt Ch., Ill., 1978-79. Mem. Soc. Automotive Engrs. (assoc.; program chair 1984-85, div. chair 1985-86, sect. officer 1985-86), Seekers Christian Fellowship (pres. 1974-75). Avocations: fishing; woodworking; photography. Office: Elgin Sweeper Co 1300 W Bartlett Rd Elgin IL 60120

CARLSON, LOREN MERLE, university administrator, lawyer, educator; b. Mitchell, S.D., Nov. 2, 1923; s. Clarence A. and Edna M. (Rosenquist) C.; B.A., Yankton Coll., 1948; M.A., U. Wis., 1952; J.D., George Washington U., 1961; m. Verona Gladys Hole, Dec. 21, 1950; children—Catherine Ann, Bradley Reed, Nancy Jewel. Asst. dir. Govtl. Research Bur., U. S.D., 1949-51; orgn. and methods examiner U.S. Dept. State, Washington, 1951-52; asst. dir. legis. research State of S.D., 1953-55, dir., 1955-59; research asst. to Francis Case, U.S. Senator from S.D., 1959-60, adminstrv. asst., 1960-63; admitted to S.D. bar, 1961, U.S. Supreme Ct. bar, 1976; budget officer State of S.D., 1963-68; dir. statewide ednl. services U. S.D., Vermillon, 1968-74, dean continuing edn., 1974—, assoc. prof. polit. sci., 1968-79, prof., 1979—, hwy. laws study dir. Law Sch., 1963; on leave as adminstrv. asst. to Congressman Larry Pressler, 1975-76; sec. Missouri Valley Adult Edn., 1978-79. Chmn. Model Rural Devel. Commn., Dist. II, State of S.D., 1972-74; chmn. Region VII Planning Commn. on Criminal Justice, S.D., 1969-74; mem. Vermillion City Council, 1980—. Served with USN, 1945-46. Named Outstanding Young Man, Pierre Jaycees, 1959. Mem. S.D. State Bar, Am. Soc. for Public Adminstrn., Nat. U. Continuing Edn. Assn., S.D. Adult Edn. Assn. (chmn. 1973-74), Vermillion C. of C., Am. Arbitration Assn., Am. Legion, Pi Sigma Alpha, Pi Kappa Delta. Republican. Lutheran. Clubs: Lions, Eagles, Author: (with W.O. Farber and T.C. Geary) Government of South Dakota, 1979; contbr. articles to profl. publs. Home: 229 Catalina St Vermillion SD 57069 Office: State Wide Educational Services U South Dakota Vermillion SD

CARLSON, O. NORMAN, metallurgy educator; b. Mitchell, S.D., Dec. 21, 1920; s. Oscar Sigfried and Ruth Belle (Gammill) C.; m. Virginia Lucille Jyleen, July 30, 1946; children—Gregory, Richard, Karen. B.A., Yankton Coll., 1943; Ph.D., Iowa State U., 1950. Research asst. Iowa State U., Ames, 1943-46, grad. asst., 1946-50, asst. prof., 1950-55, assoc. prof., 1955-60, prof., chmn. dept. metallurgy and div. chief metallurgy Ames Lab., 1962-66, prof. materials sci., engring. and sr. metallurgist Ames Lab., 1966—; vis. scientist Max Planck Inst., Stuttgart, W.Ger., 1974-75, 83; del. Indo-U.S. Workshop on Extractive Metallurgy, Udaipur, India, 1981. Recipient Iowa State U. Faculty citation Alumni Assn., 1971. Mem. Am. Chem. Soc., Am. Inst. for Metall. Engrs., Am. Soc. Metals, AAAS, Sigma Xi, Phi Kappa Phi, Phi Lambda Upsilon. Lutheran. Lodge: Lions (Outstanding Service award 1985). Co-author: Thorium: Preparation and Properties; Extractive Metallurgy of Refractory Metals. Contbr. articles on metallurgy to profl. jours. Office: 122 Met Devel Bldg Iowa State U Ames IA 50011

CARLSON, PATRICIA BROWN, lawyer; b. Pasadena, Calif., Mar. 11, 1953; d. Levy Aloysius and Barbara Ellen (Buckley) Brown; m. Stephen Curtis Carlson, Aug. 21, 1976; 1 child, Elizabeth Buckley. A.B. cum laude, Princeton U., 1975; M.A., U. Minn., 1980; J.D. cum laude, Northwestern U., 1980. Bar: Ill. 1980, U.S. Dist. Ct. (no. dist.) Ill. 1980. Assoc. Reuben & Proctor, Chgo., 1980-84. Mem. steering com. parish council Old St. Mary's Ch., Chgo., 1984; Handbook Com. of Dearborn Park Preschool, Chgo., 1984. Mem. Chgo. Bar Assn., Order of Coif, Phi Beta Kappa. Republican. Roman Catholic. Home: 1132 S Plymouth Ct Chicago IL 60605

CARLSON, RICHARD FRANK, employee benefit consulting company executive; b. Austin, Tex., Nov. 6, 1939; s. Gilbert Frank and Birdie Elaine (Wilt) C.; B.B.A, Tex. Tech U., 1961; M.B.A., U. Dallas, 1974. Bank examiner, Fed. Res. Bank Dallas, 1965-67; mgr. adminstrn. Recognition Equipment Inc., Dallas, 1967-74; v.p. adminstrn. and personnel A.S. Hansen, Inc., Deerfield, Ill., 1974—. Chmn., United Fund, Dallas, 1972-73. Served with USNR, 1962-64. Mem. Am. Soc. Personnel Adminstrn., Adminstrv. Mgmt. Soc., Am. Compensation Assn., Sigma Chi, Sigma Iota Epsilon. Republican. Home: 2242 N Bissell Chicago IL 60614 Office: 1417 Lake Cook Rd Deerfield IL 60015

CARLSON, RICHARD GEORGE, chemical company executive; b. Chgo., Sept. 26, 1930; s. Gustav George and Mildred Elisabeth (Englund) C.; student Purdue U., 1948-49; B.S., Ill. Inst. Tech., 1956; m. S. Diane Russell, Oct. 10, 1948; children—Richard G., Pamela, Kurt D.; m. 2d, Barbara Jenni, Nov. 1979. With Waterway Terminal, Argo, Ill., 1949-56; with Dow Chem. Co., Midland, Mich., 1956—, prodn. mgr. organic chems., 1968-71, bus. mgr. organic chems., 1971-73, dir. process research, 1973—; mem. fossil energy adv. com. U.S. Dept. Energy, 1976—. Pres., Midland Newcomers Club, 1957-58; scoutmaster Paul Bunyon council Boy Scouts Am., 1956-64; adviser Jr. Achievement, 1956-64; program chmn. P.T.A., 1962-63. Mem. adv. group dept. chem. engring. Ill. Inst. Tech., 1974-77. Inst. Gas Tech. scholar, 1954-56. Mem. Am. Inst. Chem. Engrs., Mich. Energy and Resource Research Assn. (trustee 1974-78), Tau Beta Pi. Methodist. Office: Dow Chem Co Midland MI 48640

CARLSON, ROBERT GEORGE, pharmaceutical company executive, veterinarian, consultant; b. Grand Rapids, Mich., Apr. 1, 1922; s. Harry and Hilda (Carlson) Chapman; m. M. June Bryant, Sept. 14, 1942; children—Margaret Anne, Carrie Jean. D.V.M., Mich. State U., 1952; M.S., Purdue U., 1954, Ph.D., 1956. Diplomate Am. Coll. Vet. Pathologists, Am. Coll. Lab. Animal Medicine. Instr., asst. prof. Purdue U., West Lafayette, Ind., 1952-56; research scientist Upjohn Co., Kalamazoo, Mich., 1956-61, sect. head, 1961-74, dir. pharm. research and devel. Japan Upjohn Ltd., Tokyo, 1974-85, research mgr., 1978-80, group mgr., 1980-84, dir., 1984—. Served to capt. USAAF, 1943-45, ETO. Mem. Am. Coll. Vet. Pathology, Am. Coll. Lab. Animal Medicine, Soc. Toxicology, Euorpean Soc. Toxicology. Home: 1720 Embury Rd Kalamazoo MI 49008 Office: Upjohn Co 301 Henrietta St Kalamazoo MI 49001

CARLSON, ROBERT GERALD, thoracic surgeon; b. Mpls., Dec. 22, 1929; s. Henry John and Agnes Emily (Fagerstrom) C.; B.A., U. Minn., 1951, M.D., 1954, M.S., 1969; m. Florence Ilene Fairbairn, Aug. 4, 1951; children—David, James, Diane, Joel. Intern, U. Oreg. Hosps., Portland, 1954-55; gen. practice medicine, Wadena, Minn., 1955-56; resident in gen. surgery Wayne County Gen. Hosp., Eloise, Mich., 1958-62; practice medicine specializing in gen. surgery, Willmar, Minn., 1962-65; resident in cardiovascular surgery U. Minn., Mpls., 1965-68; research fellow, dept. cardiac pathology Charles T. Miller Hosp., St. Paul, 1966; resident in cardiovascular surgery Cornell U., N.Y.C., 1968-69; instr. surgery Cornell U. Med. Center, 1968-69, asst. prof. surgery, 1969-73; practice medicine specializing in cardiovascular and thoracic surgery, Green Bay, Wis., 1974-79; mem. staffs Bellin Meml. Hosp., St. Vincent's Hosp., St. Mary's Hosp., 1974-75, Theda Clark Hosp., Neenah, Wis., 1979—, St. Elizabeth Hosp., Appleton, Wis., 1979—; mem. com. on coronary artery surgery Inter-Soc. Commn. for Heart Disease Resources. Publicity chmn. Friends of Garden City Library, 1961; active Boy Scouts Am.; publicity dir. Anoka County Republican Com., 1963; publicity chmn. Rep. Caucus, Anoka, Minn., 1966-67. Served with USAF, 1956-58. Diplomate Am. Bd. Surgery, Am. Bd. Thoracic Surgery, Nat. Bd. Med. Examiners. Fellow ACS (certificate of appreciation 1971), Am. Coll. Cardiology, Soc. Thoracic Surgeons, Soc. Vascular Surgeons, Am. Coll. Chest Physicians (Regents' award 1971, certificate of merit 1971), Am. Coll. Angiology; mem. Am. Heart Assn., N.Y. Cardiol. Soc., Internat. Cardiovascular Soc., Internat. Surg. Soc., AMA (certificate of merit 1971, Billings silver medal 1972), AAAS, Brown County Med. Soc., Audubon Soc., Phi Beta Kappa, Alpha Omega Alpha. Republican. Lutheran. Clubs: Green Bay Downtown Rotary (v.p. elect 1979), Neenah Rotary (bd. dirs.), Oneida Country. Contbr. articles to profl. jours. Home: 811 Neff Ct Neenah WI 54956 Office: 104 E Wisconsin Neenah WI 54956

CARLSON, ROBERT GUSTAV, metallurgical engineer; b. Bklyn., June 6, 1928; s. Axel O. and Meta (Heise) C.; m. Eleanore Yourdon, June 9, 1951; children—Sheryl, Lawrence, Robert. B.S. in Metall. Engring., N.Y. Poly. Inst., 1951; M.S. in Metall. Engring., Rensselaer Poly. Inst., 1955; Ph.D., U. Cin., 1963. Registered Profl. Engr., Ohio. Engr. aircraft engine dept. Gen. Electric Corp., Cin., 1951—; mayor, Greenhills, Ohio, 1971-72, 79—. Republican. Presbyterian. Avocations: jogging; pilot. Home: 141 Junedale Dr Greenhills OH 45218 Office: Gen Electric Corp Aircraft Engine Dept Cincinnati OH 45215

CARLSON, ROBERT MARSHALL, hosp. ofcl.; b. Jamestown, N.Y., Oct. 6, 1950; s. Marshall Lawrence and Alice (Christine) C.; B.S., Bowling Green (Ohio) State U., 1972; postgrad. in public health U. Utah, 1972; M.Ed. in Health Edn., U. Toledo, 1977; m. Margaret Swigart, June 10, 1972 (div. 1985); children—Todd Marshall, Scott Thomas. Planning analyst, then found. dir. Riverside Hosp., Toledo, 1975-78; hosp. planning coordinator Med. Coll. Ohio, Toledo, 1978-80, asst. hosp. dir. for ambulatory programs, 1980-81; cons. P.M.S. (Planning & Mgmt. Services) Inc., Bloomington, Minn., 1981-82, dir. health tech. mgmt., 1982-83; dir. health tech. mktg., sr. cons. Ellerbe Cons. Group, Bloomington, 1983—. Active local Boy Scouts Am.; affiliate mem. Blue and Gold program U.S. Naval Acad. Served to lt. (j.g.), Med. Service Corps, USNR. 1972—. Mem. Am. Coll. Hosp. Adminstrs., Am. Hosp. Assn., Am. Soc. Hosp. Planners, Assn. Mil. Surgeons of U.S., Profl. Ski Instrs. Am., Res. Officers Assn., Phi Kappa Phi, Kappa Sigma. Lutheran. Office: One Appletree Sq Bloomington MN 55420

CARLSON, RONALD VAN, rancher, farmer, board of education president; b. Oshkosh, Nebr., Mar. 3, 1939; s. Darrel Kenneth and Kathleen (Delatour) C.; m. Annette Kae Johnson, Sept. 22, 1963; children—Ronda, Kelli, Troy. Farmer, rancher, Lewellen; Nebr., 1960—; mem. Lewellen Bd. Edn., 1965—, pres., 1975—. Served with USNR, 1956-60. Republican. Lutheran. Club: Lions. Address: RR 1 Box 17 Lewellen NE 69147

CARLSON, STANLEY DAVID, entomology educator; b. St. Paul, Sept. 4, 1934; s. Lorien Austin and Sarah Victoria (Book) C.; m. Agneta L. Hedenstrom, Oct. 20, 1969 (div. 1976); 1 child, Anders Tage; m. 2d, Che Chi, Jan. 31, 1977; 1 child, Christy May. B.S., U. Minn., 1956; M.S., U. Nebr., 1961; Ph.D., Kans. State U., 1964. Research entomologist USDA, Manhattan, Kans., 1959-64; asst. prof. Va. Poly. Inst. and State U., Blacksburg, 1964-67; NIH spl. fellow Karolinska Inst., Stockholm, 1967-69, Yale U., New Haven, 1969-70; USPHS fellow U. Ill., Urbana, 1970-71; from asst. prof. to prof. entomology, U. Wis., Madison, 1971—, prof. neuroscis. tng. program, 1971—, dir. scanning electron microscope lab., 1972—. Co-author: Scanning Electron Microscope Atlas of the Honeybee, 1985; also book chpts., articles. Recipient grants NSF, NIH, Nat. Eye Inst. Mem. Entomol. Soc. Am., Assn. Research in Vision and Ophthalmology, Sigma Xi, Gamma Sigma Delta. Democrat. Avocations: classical records; softball; reading; golf; piano playing. Home: 1 Foxboro Circle Madison WI 53717 Office: U Wis Dept Entomology Madison WI 53706

CARLTON, FRANK ALFRED, printing and publishing company executive; b. Chgo., Apr. 6, 1949; s. Howard A. and June (Overlock) C.; m. Caroline F. Szathmary, June 13, 1981; children—Edward A., Robert F. B.A. summa cum laude with exceptional distinction in Classics Yale U. 1970; M.B.A., J.D., Harvard U., 1974. Bar: Ill. 1974. Asst. to sr. v.p., fin. No. Trust Co., Chgo., 1974-75; assoc. atty. Sidley and Austin, Chgo., 1975-78; asst. to pres. Rand McNally & Co., Skokie, Ill., 1978—. Mem. Ill. State Bar Assn., Chgo. Council Fgn. Relations, Phi Beta Kappa. Club: Harvard Bus. Sch. (Chgo.). Home: 3000 N Sheridan Rd Chicago IL 60657 Office: Rand McNally & Co 8255 N Central Park Skokie IL 60076

CARMAN, RICHARD LEE, optometrist; b. Fort Wayne, Ind., Dec. 29, 1934; s. Albert Leo and Goldie Sarah (Chapman) C.; m. Phyllis Marie Dilley, May 14, 1976; children—Tim, Steven, Christopher. O.D., Ind. U., Bloomington, 1962. Practice optometry, Warsaw, Ind., 1962—; pres., prin. Carman Enterprises, Inc., franchise of Country Kitchen Restaurants, Fort Wayne, 1979; v.p., sec. Microcomputer Bus. Applications, Inc., Ft. Wayne, 1982—. Mem. Am. Optometric Assn., Ind. Optometric Assn., Omega Epsilon Phi (chpt. pres. 1961). Served with USNG, 1957-63. Presbyterian. Lodges: Lions (pres. 1980, state dir. eye bank 1970-78), Masons. Avocations: pilot; wilderness fisherman; music; basketball; football. Home: 1316 Country Club Dr Warsaw IN 46580

CARMI, SHLOMO, educator, scientist; b. Cernauti, Rumania, July 18, 1937; s. Shmuel and Haia (Marcovici) C.; student Technion, Haifa, Israel, 1958-60; B.S. cum laude, U. Witwatersrand, Johannesburg, South Africa, 1962; M.S., U. Minn., 1966, Ph.D., 1968; m. Rachel Aharoni, Dec. 23, 1963; children—Sharon, Ronen-Itzhak, Lemore. Came to U.S., 1963, naturalized, 1978. Research engr. W. Rand Gold Mining Co., Krugersdorp, South Africa, 1962-63; research asst., research fellow U. Minn., 1963-68; asst. prof. mech. engring. Wayne State U., 1968-70, 72-73, assoc. prof., 1973-78, prof., 1978—, chmn. faculty assembly Coll. Engring., 1979-80, chmn. univ. research com., 1982-84; sr. lectr. Technion, Israel Inst. Tech., 1970-72, sabbatical, I. Taylor chair, 1977-78; research specialist Ford Motor Co., summer 1973, 74, 76, 77, Detroit Edison Co., summer 1983; speaker sci. meetings, Israel, Can. and U.S.; mem. Mich. Trade Mission to Africa, 1985. South African Technion Soc. scholar, 1960-62; recipient prize Transvaal Chamber of Mines, 1961, faculty research award Wayne State U., 1970; research grantee U.S. Dept. Energy, U.S. Army Research Office. Mem. Am. Phys. Soc., ASME (com. heat transfer, fluid mechanics), Sigma Xi, Tau Beta Pi, Pi Tau Sigma. Asso. editor Jour. Fluids Engring.; editor book in field; contbr. articles and reviews to profl. jours. Home: 5270 Hollow Dr Bloomfield Hills MI 48013 Office: Wayne State U Detroit MI 48202

CARMICHAEL, CHARLES WESLEY, plant engr.; b. Marshall, Ind., Jan 18, 1919; s. Charles Wesley and Clella Ann (Grubb) C.; B.S., Purdue U., 1941; m. Eleanor Lee Johnson, July 2, 1948; 1 dau., Ann Bromley Carmichael Biada. Owner, operator retail stores, West Lafayette, Ind., 1946-48, Franklin, Ind., 1950-53; mem. staff time study Chevrolet Co., Indpls., 1953-55; indsl. engr. Mallory Capacitor Co., Indpls., 1955-60, Greencastle, Ind., 1960-70, plant engr., 1970-81; contract cons. Northwood Assocs., 1981—; lectr. in field. Chmn. Greencastle br. ARC, 1962-63; bd. dirs. United Way Greencastle, 1976-79, 84—. Served to capt., F.A., U.S. Army, 1941-46; ETO. Decorated Bronze Star, Purple Heart with oak leaf cluster. Mem. Greencastle C. of C. (dir. 1962-64), Am. Inst. Plant Engrs., Ind. Bd. Realtors (dir. 1983-85), Putnam County Bd. Realtors (pres. 1983-84), Ind. Hist. Soc, Am. Legion. Republican. Methodist. Clubs: John Purdue, Soc. Ind. Pioneers, Windy Hill Country. Lodges: Masons, Shriners, Kiwanis (past pres.). Home: 702 Highwood Ave Greencastle IN 46135 Office: PO Box 171 Greencastle IN 46135

CARMICHAEL, GREGORY RICHARD, chemical engineering educator; b. Marengo, Ill., June 16, 1952; s. Elsworth Varnes and F. Margaret (Wallace) C.; m. Candace Jerene Pederson, June 14, 1975; 1 child, Emmett. B.S. in Chem. Engring., Iowa State U., 1974; M.S., U. Ky., 1975, Ph.D., 1979. Asst. prof. U. Iowa, Iowa City, 1978-82, assoc. prof., 1982-85, prof., 1985—, chmn. dept., 1982—; vis. scientist Nat. Inst. Environ. Studies, Tsukuba, Japan, 1983. Contbr. numerous articles to profl. jours. Grantee, EPA, NASA, Electic Power Research Inst. Mem. Am. Inst. Chem. Engrs., Air Pollution Control Assn., Am. Chem. Soc., Am. Geog. Union, Am. Meteorol. Soc., Am. Soc. Engring. Edn., Sigma Xi, Omega Chi Epsilon Lodge: Rotary. Office: Dept Chem Engring U Iowa 125 A CB Iowa City IA 52242

CARMICHAEL, JEFFERY LYNN, lawyer; b. Cedar Falls, Iowa, Sept. 23, 1953; s. Arthur Hugh and Shirley Mae (Swanson) C. B.A., U. No. Iowa, 1976; M.A. in Communication, Wichita State U., 1978; J.D., U. Kans., 1981. Bar: Kans. 1981, U.S. Dist. Ct. Kans. 1981. Assoc. Morris, Laing, Evans, Brock & Kennedy Chartered, Wichita, Kans., 1981—. Mem. Assn. Trial Lawyers Am., Kans. Trial Lawyers Assn., Kans. Bar Assn., Wichita Bar Assn. (exec. com. 1984), Wichita Young Lawyers Assn. (pres. 1985). Democrat. Methodist. Home: 723 Stackman St Apt 2 Wichita KS 67203 Office: Morris Laing Evans Brock & Kennedy 4th floor 200 W Douglas Wichita KS 67202

CARMICHAEL, MICHAEL FORBES, utility executive; b. Chgo., Jan. 3, 1942; s. Glenn Vincent and Mary Edith (Forbes) C.; m. Pamela Jane Lawrence, Aug. 10, 1968; 2 children. B.S. in Speech, Northwestern U., 1964. Profl. lectr. Northwestern U., 1964; writer, producer, dir. Sta. WGN, Chgo., 1965-67; creative supr. Campbell-Mithun, Inc., Chgo., 1967-73; N.Am. pub. relations staff Ford Motor Co., Detroit, 1973-74; mem. pub. affairs staff Am. Natural Resources Co., Detroit, 1974-81, mgr. exec. info. services, 1981—; computer cons. Cranbrook Schs. Mem. pub. affairs com. Acctg. Aid Soc. Met. Detroit; pres. Dads Club Brookside Sch. Cranbrook, Bloomfield Hills, Mich.; bd. dirs. Fathers Club Kingswood Sch. Cranbrook, Bloomfield Hills. Recipient Clio award, 1971. Mem. Nat. Assn. Computer Graphics, Assn. Computing Machinery. Episcopalian. Office: One Woodward Ave Detroit MI 48226

CARMICHAEL, RAYMOND WILLIAM, public relations executive; b. Bethesda, Md., Dec. 16, 1951; s. Richard L. and Connie C.; m. Wendy Arnold, Aug. 18, 1973. B.A. in Communications, Polit. Sci., Wittenberg U., 1974; M.B.A., Loyola U.-Chgo., 1983. Dir. pub. relations ARC, Cin. chpt. 1974-77, Chgo. chpt., 1977-81; dir. pub. relations Chgo. Bd. of Trade, 1981—. Active 1st Presbyterian Ch., Evanston, Ill. Recipient Golden Trumpet award, Publicity Club of Chgo., 1977-83. Mem. Pub. Relations Soc. Am. (dr. of bd. Chgo. chpt.). Office: Chicago Board of Trade 141 W Jackson Blvd Chicago IL 60604

CARMICHAEL, VIRGIL WESLY, retired geologist mining engineer, coal company executive; b. Pickering, Mo., Apr. 26, 1919; s. Ava Abraham and Rosevelt (Murphy) C.; B.S., U. Idaho, 1951, M.S., 1956; Ph.D. in Geol. Engrng. and Mgmt., Columbia Pacific U., 1980; profl. geol. engr., U. Idaho, 1967; m. Emma Margaret Freeman, Apr. 1, 1939; m. Colleen Fern Wadsworth, Oct. 29, 1951; children—Bonnie Rae, Peggy Ellen, Jacki Ann. Asst. geologist Day Mines, Wallace, Idaho, 1950; mining engr., chief mining engr. De Anza Engrng. Co., Troy, Idaho and Santa Fe, 1950-52; hwy. engrng. asst. N.Mex. Hwy. Dept., Santa Fe, 1952-53; asst. engr. U. Idaho, also minerals analyst Idaho Bur. Mines, Moscow, 1953-56; mining engr. No. Pacific Ry. Co., St. Paul, 1956-67; geologist N. Am. Coal Corp., Cleve., 1967-69, asst. v.p. engrng., 1969-74, v.p., head exploration dept., 1974-84, ret., 1984. Mem. No. Gt. Plains Resource Council, 1964-67; asst. chief distbn. CD Emergency Mgmt. Fuel Resources for N.D., 1968—. Mem. N.D. Water Users Assn., 1970-84; bd. dirs. Bismarck-Mandan Orch. Assn., 1979-83; bd. dirs. Bismarck Art and Galleries Assn., 1982—, 1st v.p., 1984-85. Served with USNR, 1944-46; PTO. Recipient award 'A' for Sci. writing Sigma Gamma Epsilon, 1957. Registered geologist, Idaho, Calif.; land surveyor, N.Mex., Minn., N.D., Idaho; profl. engr., Idaho, N.Mex., Utah, Minn., N.D. Mem. Am. Inst. Profl. Geologists (past pres. local chpt.), Rocky Mountain Coal Mining Inst. (past v.p.), N.D. Geol. Soc. (past pres.), Am. Inst. Mining Engrs. (pres. local chpt. 1979-80), Am. Mining Congress (bd. govs. western div. 1973-85), AAAS, N.Y. Acad. Scis., Internat. Platform Assn., Nat. Def. Exec. Res., N.D. Acad. Sci., Sigma Xi. Republican. Lodges: Kiwanis (club dir. 1978-80, 83-84, v.p. 1980-81, pres.-elect 1981-82, pres. 1982-83, lt. gov. 1984-85), Masons (lodge officer), Elks.

CARMICHAEL, WILLIAM EDWARDS, marketing director; b. Bedford, Ind., Jan. 25, 1929; s. Ralph and Millie (Marsey) C.; m. Mary Frances McSoley, Oct. 15, 1950 (div.); children—William Wesley, James Edward, Cathi; m. 2d, Betty Jo Withers, Dec. 3, 1982. B.S.B.A., Ind. U., 1955. Sales rep. Black-Hebert Lumber Co., Indpls., 1955-59; sales engr. Acme Refrigeration, Inc., Indpls., 1959-62, sales mgr., 1962-68, v.p. mktg., 1968-74, exec. v.p., 1974-77; pres. Wm. E. Carmichael & Assocs., Indpls., 1977-85; dir. mktg. Black Lumber Co., Inc., Bloomington, Ind., 1985—; dir. Black-Carmichael-Klein Lumber Co., Inc., Bedford, Ind., Black Lumber Co., Martinsville, Inc., Black Lumber Co. Inc., Bloomington, Ind. Contbr. chpt. to manual. Vice chmn. Wayne Twp. Screening Caucus, Indspl., 1966. Served to lt. U.S. Army, 1950-54. Recipient DeMolay Cross of Honor Internat. Supreme Council of Order of DeMolay, 1972; named Ky. Col., 1980; named Mem. of Honor Bethel 109 Internat. Order Job's Daughters, 1977. Democrat. Methodist. Lodges: Masons, Shriners. Office: Black Lumber Co Inc PO Box 576 Bloomington IN 47402

CARNAHAN, ANNE SCHIAVONE, trust officer, lawyer; b. Akron, Ohio, July 6, 1955; d. Joseph Anthony and Frances Ann (Mandala) Schiavone; m. Timothy David Carnahan, Sept. 1, 1980. B.A., Ohio State U., 1976; J.D., U. Akron, 1979. Bar: Ohio 1979. Law clk. Anthony Tuccillo Co. L.P.A., Akron, 1978-79, assoc., 1979-80; trust assoc. 5th Third Bank, Cin., 1982-83; trust officer Society Nat. Bank, Cleve., 1983—. Mem. Internat. Law Soc. (sec.-treas. 1978-79), Bar Assn. Greater Cleve., Bracton's Inn, U. Akron, Phi Alpha Delta, Alpha Chi Omega Alumnae Club (corr. sec. 1975-76, career. info. facilitator 1984—). Democrat. Roman Catholic. Club: 1st Friday (Cleve.). Office: Society Nat Bank 127 Public Sq Cleveland OH 44114

CARNAHAN, JOHN ANDERSON, lawyer; b. Cleve., May 8, 1930; s. Samuel Edwin and Penelope (Moulton) C.; B.A., Duke, 1953, LL.B., 1955, J.D., 1955; m. Katherine Halter, June 14, 1958; children—Peter Moulton, Allison Eads, Kristin Alexandra. Admitted to Ohio bar, 1955, pvt. practice law, Columbus, 1955-78; partner firm Knepper, White, Arter & Hadden, 1978—; lectr. Ohio Legal Center Inst., 1969, 73, 74. Chmn. UN Day, Columbus, 1960. Pres. Capital City Young Republicans Club, 1960. Bd. dirs. Columbus Cancer Clinic, pres., 1978-81; bd. dirs. Columbus chpt. ARC; governing bd. Hannah Neil Mission, Inc., 1974-78. Named 1 of 10 Outstanding Young Men of Columbus, 1965. Fellow Am. Bar Found., Ohio State Bar Found. (trustee); mem. Nat. Conf. Bar Pres., ABA (ho. of dels. 1984-86), Ohio (council of dels. 1965-67, exec. com. 1977-81, pres.-elect 1982-83, pres. 1983-84), Columbus (bd. govs. 1970-72, sec.-treas. 1974-75, pres. 1976-77) bar assns., Am. Coll. Probate Counsel, Duke Alumni Admissions Adv. Com. (chmn. 1965-79), Phi Delta Theta, Phi Delta Phi. Presbyn. Clubs: University (Columbus); Worthington (Ohio) Hills. Editor: Duke Law Jour., 1954-55; contbr. to profl. publs. in field. Home: 872 Clubview Blvd N Worthington OH 43085 Office: 180 E Broad St Columbus OH 43215

CARNEAL, THOMAS WILLIAM, historian, educator; b. Plattsmouth, Nebr., Apr. 8, 1934; s. Glen Thomas and Frances Elizabeth (Wetenkamp) C.; B.A., U. Kansas City, 1963; M.A., U. Mo., Kansas City, 1966; postgrad. U. Mo., 1966-70. Mem. faculty Jr. Coll. program Kemper Mil. Sch., Boonville, Mo., 1965-68; asst., then asso. prof. history N.W. Mo. State U., Maryville, 1968—. Pres., Nodaway County Hist. Soc., 1971—; chmn. Nodaway County Bicentennial Com., 1975-77. Served with U.S. Army, 1953-56. Mem. Orgn. Am. Historians, State Hist. Soc. Mo., Econ. History Assn., Delta Chi. Methodist. Author: A Historic Inventory of Nodaway County, 1977; A Historic Inventory of Andrew County, 1978; A Historic Inventory of the Tri-County Area, 1979; A Historic Inventory of Daviess County, Mo., 1979; Saint Joseph Mo.: Landmarks, 1978; A Historic Inventory of DeKalb County, 1979; A Historic Inventory of Holt County, 1980; A Historic Inventory of Worth County, 1980; A Historic Inventory of Harrison County, 1981; A Historic Inventory of Buchanan County, 1981; Historical and Architectural Landmarks of Nodaway County, 1980; contbr. articles to profl. jours. Home: 418 W 2d St Maryville MO 64468 Office: 307 Colden Hall Northwest Missouri State U Maryville MO 64468

CARNER, WILLIAM JOHN, banker; b. Springfield, Mo., Aug. 9, 1948; s. John Wilson and Willie Marie (Moore) C.; A.B., Drury Coll., 1970; M.B.A., U. Mo., 1972; m. Dorothy Jean Edwards, June 12, 1976; children—Kimberly Jean, John Edwards Carner. Mktg. rep. 1st Nat. Bank Memphis, 1972-73; asst. br. mgr. Bank of Am., Los Angeles, 1973-74; dir. mktg. Commerce Bank, Springfield, Mo., 1974-76; affiliate mktg. mgr. 1st Union Bancorp., St. Louis, 1976-78; pres. Carner & Assocs., Springfield, Mo., 1977—; instr. Drury Coll., 1975, 84—; dir. Ozark Pub. Telecommunications, Inc. 1982—, sec., 1984-85, treas., 1985—. Bd. dirs. Am. Cancer Soc., Greene County, Mo., 1974-82, crusade chmn., 1982-83, publicity chmn., 1974-78; bd. dirs. Springfield (Mo.) Muscular Dystrophy Assn., 1975-76, Greater Ozarks council Camp Fire Girls, 1980-81. Mem. Bank Mktg. Assn., Fin. Instns. Mktg. Assn. (chmn. service mem. com.), Assn. M.B.A. Execs. Democrat. Mem. Christian Ch. (Disciples of Christ). Club: Hickory Hills Country. Lodges: Masons, Shriners. Home: 3605 S Parkhill Springfield MO 65807 Office: PO Box 1482 SSS Springfield MO 65805

CARNES, JOHN CARLTON, forensic odontologist, consultant; b. Durant, Miss., Aug. 31, 1921; s. John Carlton and Jessie B. (McMillan) C.; m. Billie Louise Chance, Oct. 22, 1942; children—Janet Cathleen, John Carlton III. Student El Dorado Jr. Coll., 1939-41, Yale U., 1944; D.D.S., U. Mo.-Kansas City, 1947; B.A., Washburn U., 1972. Clin. instr. U. Mo.-Kansas City, 1946-49; pvt. practice dentistry, Topeka, 1947—; cons. Coroners Office, 3d Jud. Dist., Topeka, 1970—; cons. 3d Jud. Cts., Topeka, 1960-78, cons. coroner 3d jud. dist., Topeka, 1970-84, sherrif's dept., Shawnee County, Kans., 1970-80. Contbr. articles to profl. jours. Served to capt. U.S. Army, 1950-55. Recipient scholarship award Omicron Kappa Upsilon, 1947, Xi Xsi Phi, 1947. Mem. ADA, Internal Reference Orgn. in Forensic Medicine, Internat. Acad. Pathology. Republican. Episcopalian. Avocations: agriculture; world travel; woodworking; creative writing. Home: 3021 Hunters Ln Topeka KS 66614 Office: Box 112 Maple Hill KS 66507

CARNEY, ANDREW LEWIS, physician; b. Chgo., Jan. 18, 1932; s. Andrew and Helen Kubasek; m. Evelyn M. Anderson, June 23, 1963; 1 child, Alexander Peter. B.S., Loyola-Chgo., 1954, M.D., 1958. Diplomate Am. Bd. Thoracic Surgery. Practice medicine specializing in thoracic, cardiovascular and neurovascular surgery, LaGrange, Ill., 1970—. Contbr. articles to profl. jours. Editor: Diagnosis and Treatment of Brain Ischemia, 1981. Producer movies Surgery of the Vertebral Artery I (Golden Eagle award 1978), Surgery of the Vertebral Artery II (Golden Eagle award 1980). Fellow ACS, Am. Coll. Surgeons; mem. Internat. Coll. Surgeons (bd. dirs. 1983—), Soc. Neurovascular Surgery (pres. 1983—), Neurovascular Soc. N. Am. (founding mem.), AMA. Avocations: Writing, tennis, swimming. Home: 222 Forest Ave Oak Park IL 60302 Office: Blood Flow Dynamics 1323 Community Meml Dr LaGrange IL 60525

CARNEY, BARBARA JOYCE, executive search consultant; b. Chgo.; d. Maurice David and Celia (Baylen) Sachnoff; B.A. cum laude, UCLA, 1964; M.Ed., Nat. Coll. Edn., 1968; children—Michael, Michelle. Tchr., North Suburban Chgo. pub. schs., 1965-68; mfrs. rep. Shardon Mktg. Inc., Chgo., 1976-78; Midwestern regional sales mgr. Superscope, Inc., Chatsworth, Calif., 1977-80; nat. spl. markets sales mgr. Ronco, Inc., Elk Grove Village, Ill., 1980-81; exec. search cons. Womack & Assocs., Inc., Chgo., 1982-85, B. Carney & Assocs., Chgo., 1985—. Bd. dirs. North Shore Mental Health Assn., 1975-76; chpt. v.p., chmn. LWV, 1968-76. Mem. Women in Mgmt., AAUW, Am. Soc. Profl. and Exec. Women, Nat. Assn. Female Execs. Home: 2020 Lincoln Park W Chicago IL 60614

CARNEY, LARRY BRADY, telecommunications manager, accountant; b. Poplar Bluff, Mo., Mar. 15, 1948; s. Brady Elvis and Wanda Pauline (Francis) C.; m. Barbara Sue Foster, June 6, 1968; children—Lisa Anne, Steven Wayne, Karen Brooke. B.S. in Bus. Adminstrn., S.E. Mo. State U., 1970. C.P.A. Auditor, Ernst & Whinney, St. Louis, 1970-73; internal auditor, acctg. mgr., v.p. controller Maritz Inc., St. Louis, 1973-80; staff mgr. Southwestern Bell Telephone, St. Louis, 1980-82; staff mgr., industry mgr. AT&T Info. Systems, St. Louis, 1982—; acctg. instr. Mo. Baptist Coll., St. Louis, 1981-82. Served with Army N.G., 1970-76. Mem. Am. Inst. C.P.A.s, Mo. Soc. C.P.A.s. Republican. Baptist. Office: 10820 Sunset Plaza Suite 5A-13 Saint Louis MO 63127

CARNEY, THOMAS PATRICK, medical instruments company executive, researcher; b. Dubois, Pa., May 27, 1915; s. James Patrick and Margaret Elizabeth (Senard) C.; m. Mary Elizabeth McGuire, Oct. 3, 1942; children—Thomas, Sheila, James, Janet. B.S. in Chem. Engring., Notre Dame U., 1937, LL.D. (hon.), 1969; M.S., Pa. State U., 1939, Ph.D., 1941. Research chemist Reilly Tar and Chem. Corp., Indpls., 1937-39, 41-43; post doctoral fellow U. Wis., Madison, 1943-44; research chemist Eli Lilly & Co., Indpls., 1944-54, v.p., 1954-64; exec. v.p. G.D. Searle & Co., Skokie, Ill., 1964-74; chmn. exec. com. Nat. Patent Devel. Co., N.Y.C., 1974-75; pres. Metatech Corp., Northbrook, Ill., 1976—, also dir., Bioferm, Inc., Northbrook, 1980—, also dir.; dir. ImmunoGenetics, Vineland, N.J.; cons. to Sec. HEW, Washington. Author: Laboratory Fractional Distillation, 1949; Instant Evolution, 1980; False Profits, 1981. Contbr. articles to profl. publs. Patentee in field. Recipient Disting. Service award Assn. Cons. Chemists and Engrs., 1976; Ernest Stewart award Council Advancement and Support of Edn., 1982. Fellow N.Y. Acad. Sci., AAAS, Chem. Soc. London, Am. Inst. Chemists; mem. Am. Chem. Soc. (div. chmn.), Swiss Chem. Soc., London Soc. Chem. Industry, Sigma Xi, Alpha Chi Sigma, Phi Lambda Upsilon. Clubs: Onwentsia; Mid-Am. (Chgo.). Home: 277 Bluff's Edge Dr Lake Forest IL 60045 Office: Metatech Corp 910 Skokie Blvd Northbrook IL 60062

CAROME, EDWARD FRANCIS, physicist, educator, consultant; b. Cleve., May 22, 1927; s. Michele A. and Margaret E. (Zupchan) C.; m. Jeanne Marie Stumpf, Dec. 29, 1977; stepchildren—Dawn Marie, Jennifer Roberts; children by previous marriage—Kevin, Patrick, Michael, Daniel, Brian, Mary Ann. B.S. in Physics, John Carroll U., 1951, M.S. in Physics, 1951; Ph.D., Case Inst. Tech., 1954. Mem. faculty John Carroll U., Cleve., 1954—, prof. physics, 1963—; liaison scientist Office Naval Research, London, 1968-69; sr. research scientist Stanford U., Calif., 1978-79; underwater acoustics chair Naval Postgrad. Sch., Monterey, Calif., 1983-84; cons. Naval Research Lab., Washington, 1975-78. Author: Fiber Optic Sensor Handbook, 1982. Patentee in field. Served with USN, 1945-47. Fellow Acoustical Soc. Am., Am. Phys. Soc., IEEE (assoc.); mem. European Phys. Soc. Home: 24 Arden Rd Berkeley CA 94704 Office: Physics Dept John Carroll U University Heights Cleveland OH 44118

CARON, PHILIP LOUIS, dentist, educator; b. Fall River, Mass., Aug. 23, 1945; s. Philip Louis and Evelyn Aurore (Larrivvee) C.; m. Dorothy D. Darnell, July 7, 1973. B.S., Stonehille Coll., 1967; D.D.S., Georgetown U., 1971. Private practice dentistry, Cranston, R.I., 1973-75; staff dentist VA, Providence, 1975-76; clin. fellow and resident VA and Harvard U., Boston, 1976-78; staff dentist VA Med. Ctr., Marion, Ill. 1978—; adj. clin. asst. prof. Sch. Dental Medicine, Alton, Ill., 1983—; Sch. Dental Hygiene, Carbondale, Ill., 1978—. Exec. v.p. R.I. Jaycees, East Greenwich, 1977. Served to capt. U.S. Army, 1971-73, comdr. Res. Roman Catholic. Club: Harvard (St. Louis). Home: RR 2 Box 207 Carterville IL 62918 Office: VA Med Ctr East Main St Marion IL 62959

CAROTHERS, CHARLES OLMSTED, orthopedic surgeon; b. Medina, N.Y., Aug. 2, 1923; s. Thomas Abbott and Helen Flavia (Olmsted) C.; m. Winifred Ashforth Booker, Dec. 22, 1943 (div. 1970); children—Thomas Abbott, Stephen Cole, Lisa Booker; m. 2d Lucille Klau, June 20, 1971. B.A., Williams Coll., 1944; M.D., Harvard U., 1946; M.S. in Orthopedic Surgery, U. Tenn., 1954. Diplomate Am. Bd. Orthopedic Surgery. Intern Cin. Gen. Hosp., 1946-47; head bone research project Naval Med. Research Inst., Bethesda, Md., 1949; resident in gen. surgery U. Cin., 1949-51, resident in orthopedic surgery U. Tenn., 1951-54; practice medicine specializing in orthopedic surgery, Cin., 1954—; mem. staff Drake Hosp.; chief orthopedic sect. Bethesda Hosps.; pres. Carothers & Carothers Inc., Cin.; mem. staff Univ. Med. Sch., Univ. Hosp. Cin. Dep. gov. Gen. Soc. Colonial Wars of Ohio, 1979-82; gov., 1975-76; pres., chief exec. officer Cin. Playhouse In The Park, 1974—. Served with USN, 1949. Mem. Am. Acad. Orthopedic Surgery, Clin. Orthopedic Soc., ACS, Am. Assn. Surgery Trauma, Mid-Am. Orthopedic Assn., AMA. Episcopalian. Clubs: Cin. Country, U. of Cin., Losantiville Country, Wequetonsing Assn. Literary. Home: 1 Walsh Pl Cincinnati OH 45208 Office: 409 Broadway Cincinnati OH 45202

CAROTHERS, ROBERT LEE, university president; b. Sewickley, Pa., Sept. 3, 1942; s. Robert Fleming and Mary (Skinner) C.; m. Mary Patricia Ruane, Nov. 2, 1974; children—Robert Kennedy, Shelley Rye. B.S., Edinboro U. Pa., 1965; M.A., Kent State U., 1966, Ph.D., 1969; J.D., U. Akron, 1980. Bar: Pa. 1981, Prof. English, dean, v.p. Edinboro U., 1968-83; pres. Southwest State U., Marshall, Minn., 1983—; cons. U.S. Office Civil Rights, 1978-79; dir. Pioneer Pub. TV, Appleton, Minn., 1984. Author: Freedom and Other Times, 1972; John Calvin's Favorite Son, 1980. Served with AUS, 1960-68. Mem. Am. Assn. State Colls. and Univs., ACLU, Minn. Agrigrowth Council, Nat. Farmer's Union, ABA. Avocations: fishing, hunting. Home: RR 1 37B Marshall MN 56268 Office: Office of Pres Southwest State Univ Marshall MN 56258

CARP, RICHARD LAWRENCE, lawyer; b. St. Louis, Jan. 26, 1926; s. Avery and Ruth (Silverstein) C.; Student, U. Mo., 1944; Cert., Sorbonne U., Paris, 1946; A.B., Washington U., St. Louis, 1947, J.D., 1951; Licensié en Sci. Politique, Inst. Internat. Studies, Geneva, 1949. Bar: Mo., U.S. Dist. Ct. (ea. dist.) 1952. Mem. U.S. Dept. State, Washington, 1951-53; mem. staff Senator Paul H. Douglas, Washington, 1953-54; assoc. Fordyce, Mayne, Hartman, Renard and Stribling, St. Louis, 1954-63; assoc. counsel, acting chief counsel U.S. Senate Sub-com. on Constl. Rights, Washington, 1956; sole practice, St. Louis, 1963-68; mem. St. Louis Regional U.S. Export Expansion Council, 1964-72; vice chmn., mem. Mo. Commn on Human Rights, 1966-78; ptnr. Carp & Morris, St. Louis, 1968—. Vice chmn. bd. Pastoral Counselling Inst. Greater St. Louis, 1964—; chmn. Common Cause of Mo., St. Louis, 1966-78; bd. dirs. Internat. Inst. Met. St. Louis, 1973-75; trustee Acad. Sci. St. Louis, 1984—; bd. dirs. St. Louis chpt. Am. Soc. Technion, 1985—. Served with U.S. Army, 1944-46, ETO. Decorated Combat Inf. badge; recipient Outstanding Service award Image, St. Louis, 1984. Mem. ABA, Mo. Bar Assn., St. Louis County Bar Assn., Bar Assn. Met. St. Louis, Acad. Matrimonial Lawyers, Am. Immigration Lawyers Assn. Jewish. Home: 230 S Brentwood Saint Louis MO Office: Carp & Morris Law 225 S Meramec Suite 1100 Saint Louis MO 63105

CARPENTER, CARMEN OLGA, elementary school counselor; b. Detroit, Dec. 20, 1937; d. Montgomery O'Neal Tarrant and Nellie Louise (Jackson) Tarrant Tribble; B.S., Wayne State U., 1960, M.Ed., 1975; children—Spencer III, Kevin O'Neal, Brent Dorian. Nat. cert. counselor Nat. Bd. for Cert. Counselors. Vocal music tchr. Detroit Bd. Edn., 1960-77; model Hawkins Apparel, Inc., Lynette's Inc., March of Dimes Extravaganza, 1974-79; elem. sch. counselor Keidan Sch., Detroit Bd. Edn., 1977—; career edn. liaison com. person Region 3, Detroit Bd. Edn. Pres. Courtis Sch. PTA, 1973-74; public relations chairperson Detroit Council PTA, 1976, 79, corr. sec., 1977-79. Democratic Precinct del., 1976, 78—; pres. Oakman Blvd. Homeowners Assn.; chmn. MacKenzie Area Prevention Project; pub. relations chmn. Broadstreet Unity Presbyn. Ch. Named Woman of Yr., St. Andrews Presbyterian Ch., 1973; Ms. March of Dimes Model, 1977; recipient Outstanding Mich. Citizen award, 1978; Cert. of Appreciation, Wayne County Bd. Commrs., 1980; Cert. of Achievement, Detroit Bd. Edn., Guidance and Counseling Dept., 1981; Appreciation Trophy, God's Humanitarian Garden, 1981; citations MacKenzie Area Prevention Project, named Counselor of Month, 1982. Mem. Detroit Fedn. Tchrs. (bldg. rep. 1969, 73), Am. Assn. for Counseling and Devel., Mich. Personnel and Guidance Assn., Mich. Elem. Sch. Counselor Assn., Mich. Non-White Counselors Assn., Guidance Assn. Met. Detroit, Wayne State U. Alumni Assn., Women of Wayne, State Dem. Educators Caucus, Detroit Assn. to Promote Amateur Boxing (rec.-corr. sec. 1979-82), NAACP (life), Phi Delta Kappa. Presbyterian. Club: Les Cosmopolites Bridge (former pres.). Compiler exhbn., booklet on black scientists and inventors for Afro-Am. Mus., 1974. Office: care Guidance Dept 644 Detroit Schs Center Bldg Detroit MI 48202

CARPENTER, JOHN D., food company marketing executive; b. Zanesville, Ohio, Jan. 8, 1949; s. Alwyn Dale and Eloise Marie (Clapper) C.; m. Pamela S. Brown, Dec. 15, 1968. B.S., B.A. in Mktg. summa cum laude, Bowling Green State U., 1971; M.S. in Advt. summa cum laude, U. Ill., 1972. Media asst. Needham, Harper Advt., Chgo., 1972-73, asst. media supr., 1973-74, supr., 1974-76; communications mgr. J.M. Smucker Co., Orrville, Ohio, 1976-82, dir. mktg. services, 1982—. Recipient Founders award J.M. Smucker Co., 1982; scholar James Webb Young U. Ill., Pres.'s scholar Bowling Green State U. Mem. Am. Mktg. Assn., Assn. Nat. Advertisers, Phi Kappa Phi, Beta Gamma Sigma, Omicron Delta Kappa. Lutheran. Avocations: Running; sporting events; history; travel. Office: J M Smucker Co Strawberry Ln Orrville OH 44667

CARPENTER, JOHN DENNIS, banker; b. Stephen, Minn., Feb. 17, 1933; s. Oscar Dennis and Ingrid Marie (Nilsen) C.; student U. Wis. Sch. Banking, 1967; m. Peggy Eileen Pudil, Dec. 22, 1957; children—Denise, Scott, Daniel. Asst. cashier Grafton Nat. Bank (N.D.), 1956-62; asst. v.p. Northwestern State Bank, Luverne, Minn., 1962-68; v.p. Northwestern State Bank, Slayton, Minn., 1968-71; pres. First Nat. Bank, Hay Springs, Nebr., 1971-73; pres., chmn. bd. Northwestern Bank, Hallock, Minn., 1973—, Norkitt Bancorp. Inc., Greenbush State Bank (Minn.), Greenbush Bancshares, Inc., First Nat Bank of Hay Springs. Served with U.S. Army, 1953-55; Korea. Mem. Minn. Bankers Assn., C. of C. (pres., sec.-treas.). Republican. Lutheran. Clubs: Lions (sec.-treas.), Elks, Masons. Home: 217 N 5th St Hallock MN 56728 Office: 302 S 2d St Hallock MN 56728

CARPENTER, JOHN LORING, clergyman; b. Providence, Oct. 27, 1948; s. Cheslie N. and Delight (Swanson) C.; m. MaryAnne Gorman, June 6, 1970; children—John, Christine, Rebekah. B.S.B.A., Babson Coll., 1969; M.Div., Colgate-Rochester Div. Sch., 1973. Ordained to ministry Am. Bapt. Chs. in the U.S.A., 1972. Pastor, Hague Bapt. Ch., N.Y., 1972-74, Voluntown Bapt. Ch., Conn., 1974-80, 1st Bapt. Ch., Middletown, N.Y., 1980-81; administr. Camp Koinonia, Geneva, Ohio, 1982-84; trainer N.Am. Ch. Camp, Ohio, 1983-85; sr. pastor 1st Bapt. Ch., Bridgeport, Conn., 1985—; mem. dept. camps and confs. Ohio Bapt. Conv., 1982-84. Mem. adv. bd. Parents Anonymous Lake County, Ohio, 1983-84; basketball coach, 1983—. Mem. Ministers Council Am. Bapt. Ch., Am. Camping Assn., Christian Camping Internat. Home: 43 Redding Pl Bridgeport CT 06604

CARPENTER, JOT D., landscape architect educator; b. San Francisco, Mar. 19, 1938; s. Jot Thomas and Gretchen Marie (Johnston) C.; m. Claire Marie Dunn, Aug. 8, 1962; children—Jot David, Sean Michael, Kevin Patrick. B.L.A., U. Ga., 1960; M.L.A., Harvard U., 1962. Landscape architect T.J. Wirth Assoc., Billings, Mont., 1965-68; asst. prof. dept. horticulture Cornell U., Ithaca, N.Y., 1968-71; assoc. prof., chmn. dept. landscape architecture Ohio State U., Columbus, 1972-76, prof., chmn., 1976—; dir., vice pres., sec. Landscape Arch. Found., Washington, 1977—; mem. Ohio Bd. Landscape Architecture Examiners, Columbus, 1973-76, Council Landscape Archtl. Registration Bds. Uniform Nat. Exam. Com., Syracuse, N.Y., 1975-77. Author: Landscape Construction, 1976. Editor: Handbook of Landscape Architectural Construction, 1976. Bd. dirs. Columbus Conv. and Visitors Bur., 1977—; mem. Planning Commn., Upper Arlington, Ohio, 1978-82, Ohio Land Use Planning Task Force, 1974. Served to 1st lt. USAF, 1962-65. Fellow Am. Soc. Landscape Architects (sec. treas. 1973-74, vice pres. 1976-78, pres. 1978-79, Pres.'s medal, 1982, Ohio chpt. medal 1983); mem. Internat. Fedn. Landscape Architects (del. Grand Council 1981—), Phi Kappa Phi, Sigma Lambda Alpha. Roman Catholic. Avocations: gardening; photography; science fiction. Home: 1801 Elmwood Ave Upper Arlington OH 43212 Office: Dept Landscape Architecture Ohio State Univ 190 W 17th Ave Columbus OH 43210

CARPENTER, MARY HOLMES, fine arts appraiser; b. St. Louis, Sept. 12, 1952; d. Foster Walther Holmes and Nan (Thornton) Holmes Jones. Student U. Colo., 1970-73, U. East Africa, Nairobi, Kenya, summer 1971, U. Athens (Greece), 1973; B.A. in Art History, Washington U., St. Louis, 1980; M.A. in Valuation Scis., Lindenwood Coll., 1982. Dir. restoration activities German Sch. Archaeology Excavations, Samos, Greece, 1973-79; conservator of fine arts McCaughen & Burr, Inc., Gallery, St. Louis, 1979-80; dir. Massucci's Gallery, St. Louis, 1980; free-lance fine arts appraiser, St. Louis, 1980—. Mem. Am. Inst. Archaeology, Am. Soc. Appraisers, Internat. Soc. Appraisers. Club: Jr. League (St. Louis). Contbr. to Zygos mag., Athens, Valuation mag. Home and Office: 4646 Pershing Pl Saint Louis MO 63108

CARPENTER, PHYLLIS MARIE ROSENAU, physician; b. Hastings, Nebr., Aug. 2, 1926; d. Alvin Benjamin and Sophia Helen (Schmidt) Rosenau; B.S., Hastings Coll., 1948; M.D., U. Nebr., 1951; cert. Gestalt Inst. Cleve., 1970; m. Charles Robert Carpenter, Mar. 24, 1956 (dec. Mar. 1972); children—Charles Robert, Carole Rose, Lucinda Joy. Intern, St. Luke's Hosp., Chgo., 1951-52; resident in pediatrics Children's Meml. Hosp., Chgo., 1952-54; asst. med. dir., also clin. supr. EEG lab., Mcpl. Contagious Disease Hosp., Chgo., 1955-60; tchr. parenting; staff Well Baby Clinics, Infant Welfare, 1960-70; pvt. practice specializing in Gestalt therapy, preventive medicine and biofeedback, Chgo. and Clarendon Hills, Ill., 1970—; mem. staff Grant Hosp., Chgo.; lectr., workshops on stress mgmt. and biofeedback; founding fellow, mem. faculty Gestalt Inst. Chgo., 1970—, faculty chmn., 1981-83; mem. faculty Coll. DuPage, 1975-79, No. Ill. U., 1979-80, George Williams Coll., Chgo., 1979—; therapist Martha Washington Alcoholic Rehab. Clinic, Chgo., 1969-75. Organizer Community Presbyn. Ch. Nursery Sch., 1965-66. Mem. AAUW, Am. Assn. Biofeedback Clinicians (cert. clinician), Am. Med. Writers Assn., Nat. Writers Club. Author articles in field. Contbg. editor Current Health mag., 1981—. Home: 35 Norfolk St Clarendon Hills IL 60514 Office:

35 Norfolk St Clarendon Hills IL 60514 also 826 W Armitage Ave Chicago IL 60614

CARPENTER, SUSAN KAREN, lawyer; b. New Orleans, May 6, 1951; d. Donald Jack and Elise Ann (Diehl) C. B.A., Smith Coll., 1973; J.D., Ind. U., 1976. Bar: Ind. 1976. Dep. pub. defender Ind., Indpls., 1976-81, pub. defender of Ind., 1981—; chief pub. defender Wayne County Pub. Defenders Office, Richmond, 1981. Mem. Criminal Code Study Commn., 1981—; trustee Ind. Criminal Justice Inst., 1983—; bd. dirs. Ind. Pub. Defender Council, 1981—. Mem. Nat. Assn. Defense Lawyers, Nat. Legal Aid and Defender Assn., Ind. Bar Assn., Phi Beta Kappa. Office: Pub Defender of Ind 309 W Washington St Suite 501 Indianapolis IN 46204

CARPENTER, WAYNE SIDNEY, educator; b. Hudson, Mich., Nov. 20, 1940; s. John Sidney and Florence Lillian (Commers) C.; m. Cecelia Ann Earles, Aug. 11, 1962; children—Matthew, Caroline. B.S., Mich. State U., 1961; M.Ed., Western Wash. State U., 1967; postgrad. U. Mich., Bowling Green State U., Wayne State U., Adrian Coll. Cert. teacher, Mich. Tchr. Hazel Park Schs., Mich., 1961-63; tchr. Madison Sch., Adrian, Mich., 1963—. Author: The Green Family Genealogy, 1971; The Earles Family Genealogy, 1973. Pres. Fairfield Cemetery Assn., Adrian, 1978—; organist Fairfield Bapt. Ch., Adrian, 1955—. Mem. Mich. Edn. Assn., Madison Edn. Assn. (past pres., v.p., treas.), Nat. Council Tchrs. of Math., Mich. Council Tchrs. of Math., Detroit Soc. Geneal. Research. Republican. Lodges: Grange (sec. 1977-), Masons (sec. 1984—). Avocation: genealogy, music. Home: 1700 Fairfield Rd Adrian MI 49221 Office: Madison Sch 3498 Treat Hwy Adrian MI 49221

CARPENTER, WENDELL WOODFORD, psychologist, educator; b. Chgo., Jan. 18, 1942; s. Wendell W. and Ethel J. (Neely) C.; m. Diana Lyn, Feb. 11, 1968; children—Scott, Carrie. B.A., Ottawa U., 1966; M.A., Kans. State Tchrs. Coll., 1968; Ph.D., Ill. Inst. Tech., 1974. Cert. psychologist, Ill. Counselor, Chgo.-Read Mental Health Ctr., 1968-70; psychologist, dir. adolescent boys in-patient unit, 1972-74; asst. prof., clin. psychologist Chgo. Coll. Osteo. Medicine, 1974—; pvt. practice psychology, Chgo., 1977—; cons. Harvard Sch., 1976-81. Mem. Am. Psychol. Assn., Ill. Psychol. Assn., Am. Soc. Clin. Hypnosis. Methodist. Home: 626 S Kenilworth Ave Oak Park IL 60304 Office: 5200 S Ellis St Chicago IL 60615

CARR, BOB, lawyer, congressman; b. Janesville, Wis., Mar. 27, 1943; s. Milton Raymond and Edna (Blood) C.; B.S., U. Wis., 1965, J.D., 1968. Mem. staff Mich. Senate Minority Leader, 1968-69; asst. atty. gen. Mich., 1970-72, adminstrv. asst., 1969-70; counsel Spl. Joint Com. on Legal Edn., Mich. Legislature, 1972; admitted to Mich. bar, 1969; mem. 94th to 96th, 98th-99th Congresses from 6th Dist. Mich.; congressional advisor U.S. SALT del., Geneva, 1976-80. Mem. Am. Bar Assn., State Bar Mich., State Bar Wis. Democrat. Contbr. numerous articles to mags. Office: 2439 Rayburn House Office Bldg Washington DC 20515*

CARR, GENE EMMETT, school superintendent; b. Madison, S.D., Dec. 6, 1937; s. Emmett A. and Phyllis E. (Heitman) C.; B.S., Dakota State Coll., 1961; M.S., U. Utah, 1964; Edn. Specialist, U. S.D., 1975; m. Carolyn Riley, May 25, 1961; children—Catherine, Robert, Michael, Mark, Patricia, Bradley. Tchr. pub. schs., Garretson, S.D., 1961-63, Dell Rapids, S.D., 1964-70; supt. schs., Oldham, S.D., 1970-76, Hamlin Schs., Hayti, S.D., 1976—. Vice pres. Oldham Fire Dept., 1972-76; mem. agr. com. Sioux Empire Farm Show, 1964-79. Mem. Sch. Adminstrs. S.D., S.D. Sch. Supts. Assn. (dir.), Am. Quarter Horse Assn. Club, Center of Nation Appaloosa Horse Club (pres. 1972-74, 82-83), Pony of Ams. Club. Contbr. articles to equine mags. Home: PO Box 25 Hayti SD 57241 Office: PO Box 298 Hayti SD 57241

CARR, HAROLD NOFLET, airline executive; b. Kansas City, Kans., Mar. 14, 1921; s. Noflet B. and Mildred (Addison) C.; B.S., Tex. A&M U., 1943; postgrad. Am. U., 1944-46; m. Mary Elizabeth Smith, Aug. 5, 1944; children—Steven Addison, Hal Douglas, James Taylor, Scott Noflet. Asst. dir. route devel. Trans World Airlines, Inc., 1943-47; exec. v.p. Wis. Central Airlines, Inc., 1947-52; mem. firm McKinsey & Co., 1952-54; pres. North Central Airlines, Inc., 1954-69; chmn., 1965-79; chmn. Republic Airlines, Inc., 1979-84, chmn. exec. com., 1984—, also dir., 1952—; dir. Dahlberg, Inc., Ross Industries, Inc., Republic Energy Inc., Governor's Sound, Ltd., Cayman Water Co., First Nat. Bank of Bryan (Tex.), Cayman Mile Ltd., OMI, Inc. Professorial lectr. in mgmt. engring. Am. U., 1952-62. Trustee, Tex. A&M Research Found.; mem. devel. council Coll. Bus. Adminstrn., Tex. A&M U.; bd. nominations Nat. Aviation Hall of Fame; mem. adv. com. Tex. Transp. Inst., Tex. A&M U. System. Mem. World Bus. Council, Am. Mgmt. Assn., Nat. Def. Transp. Assn., Am. Econ. Assn., Minn. Execs. Orgn., Nat. Aero Assn., Nat. Trust for Historic Preservation, Tex. A&M Former Students Assn., Pine Beach Peninsula Assn., Beta Gamma Sigma. Clubs: Aero, Nat. Aviation (Washington); Stearman Alumnus (Wichita, Kans.); Mpls.; Century, Aggie (dir.) (College Station, Tex.); Briarcrest Country (Bryan, Tex.); Racquet (Miami, Fla.); Wings (N.Y.C.); Gull Lake Yacht (Brainerd, Minn.). Address: PO Box H Bryan TX 77805

CARR, JAMES CHARLES, physician; b. New Hampton, Iowa, Mar. 28, 1939; s. Hubert B. and Anna Mary (McKone) C.; B.A. in English, Loras Coll., 1957-61; M.D., U. Iowa, 1965; m. Mary Kay Peters, June 17, 1961; children—Barbara, Robert, Jane, Susan, David. Intern, Broadlawns Polk County Hosp., Des Moines, 1965-66; resident in family practice, 1966-67; practice medicine specializing in family medicine Med. Assos., New Hampton, Iowa, 1967—; chief staff St. Joseph's Community Hosp., New Hampton, 1972, 1975, 80; instr. family medicine Mayo Med. Sch., U. Minn., Rochester, 1975—; med. advisor Chickasaw Ambulance Service, 1972—. Bd. dirs. N.E. Iowa Council on Substance Abuse, 1976-81. Served to major Iowa N. G., 1966-72. Recipient Distinguished Service Award Jaycees, 1971; recipient Outstanding Young Mem of Am. Award, 1974; diplomate Am. Bd. Family Practice. Fellow Am. Acad. Family Practice; mem. AMA, Chickasaw County, Iowa Med. Socs., N.E. Iowa Emergency Med. Services Assn. (dir. 1979—, chmn. 1980, 81). Roman Catholic. Home: 414 N Chestnut Ave New Hampton IA 50659 Office: 201 S Linn Ave New Hampton IA 50659

CARR, LEON CLEMENT, pub. relations exec.; b. lMilbank, S.D., Sept. 11, 1924; s. Frank B. and Laura A. (Kohl) C.; B.A. in Journalism, U. Minn., 1951; m. Donnie M. Cronin, May 19, 1956; 1 son, John. Wire editor St. Cloud (Minn.) Daily Times, 1951-52; staff writer Assoc. Press, Sioux Falls, Pierre, S.D., 1952-56; copy editor St. Paul Pioneer Press, 1956-57; copy editor St. Paul Dispatch, 1957-60, asst. news editor, 1960-61; with 3M, St. Paul, 1961—, staff publicist, 1965-71, pub. relations coordinator, 1971-73, supr. media relations, 1973-76, mgr. br. pub. relations, 1976—. Mem. Pub. Relations Soc. Am. (accredited), U. Minn. Sch. Journalism Mass Communication Alumni Assn. (charter, past pres.), Soc. Profl. Journalists (life). Roman Catholic. Club: Minn. Press (charter). Home: 21 E Logan Ave West Saint Paul MN 55118 Office: 3M Center Box 33600 Saint Paul MN 55133

CARR, PAUL ALLAN, educational administrator; b. Badkreuznach, Germany, May 11, 1955 (parents Am. citizens); s. Cletus Anthony and Karolyn Rosemary (Klein) C.; m. Judy Ann Mitchell, July 28, 1979; 1 child, Thomas Joshua. B.A. in English, North Central Coll., 1978; M.S. Ed. in Counseling, No. Ill. U., 1980. Grad. asst. No. Ill. U. Residential Life, DeKalb, 1978-79, adv., 1979-80, bldg. dir., 1980-81; residence hall coordinator Ill. State U. Residential Life, Normal, 1982-84, area coordinator, 1984—. Author: ISU Residence Hall Handbook, 1984. Mem. Am. Assn. Counseling and Devel., Am. Coll. and Personnel Assn., Nat. Vocat. Guidance Assn. Roman Catholic. Avocations: photography, creative writing, weight training, music. Home and Office 18 East Manchester Hall Normal IL 61761

CARR, ROBERT FRANKLIN, III, fiduciary management company executive; b. Lake Forest, Ill., July 29, 1940; s. Robert Franklin, Jr. and Vesta Culbertson (Morse) C.; B.S. in Bus. Adminstrn., Babson Coll., Wellesley, Mass., 1962; m. Maude Goldsmith; children—Rebecca, Mimi, Robert. Treas., Murine Co., Chgo., 1966-69; mgr. optical dept. Abbott Labs., Lake Bluff, Ill., 1969-72; exec. v.p. mktg. and client services Investment Capital Mgmt. Co., Chgo., 1973-80; chmn. bd. Fiduciary Mgmt. Assocs., Chgo., 1980—; dir. Quincy Coal, Charleston, W.Va., Makalika, Inc., Vero Beach, Fla. Chmn. bd. Grant Hosp., Chgo., 1978; vice chmn. bd. Chgo. Zool. Soc., 1977; bd. dirs., trustee Babson Coll.; assoc. bd. dirs. Northwestern U., 1975; v.p., trustee Graceland Cemetery, Chgo., 1976; trustee Old People's Home, Chgo., 1979, Lake Forest Acad., 1982—. Served with USAR, 1963-69. Mem. Assn. Investment Mgmt. Sales Execs., Econ. Club Chgo. Clubs: Mid-Day (Chgo.); Onwentsia, Winter (Lake Forest); La Cheneaux (Mich.), Old Elm (Ft. Sheridan). Home: 487 Walnut Rd Lake Forest IL 60045 Office: 135 S LaSalle St Suite 3310 Chicago IL 60603

CARR, ROGER BENNING, adhesives company executive, chemist; b. Newton, Mass., June 30, 1941; s. Reginald W. and Annette (Gile) C.; m. Ann M. Grantham, July 10, 1962; children—Jeffrey Scott, Julie Ann. B.S. in Chemistry, N.Mex. Inst. Mining Tech., 1963. Analytical chemist Dow Chem. Co., Midland, Mich., 1963-67, lab. mgr., Cleve., 1967-74; lab. mgr. Am. Can Co., Cleve., 1974-75, internat. tech. liaison, Neenah, Wis., 1975-81; corp. dir. mktg. Findley Adhesives Inc., Milw., 1981-84, v.p. research and devel., 1984—. NSF grantee, 1962. Avocations: sailing; travel. Office: Findley Adhesives Inc PO Box 3000 Elm Grove WI 53005

CARR, SALLYANN, researcher; b. Aurora, Ill., Jan. 1, 1953; d. John Thurman and Grace May (LeCuyer) C. B.A., Eastern Ill. U., 1974; M.A., Western Mich. U., 1975, M.S. in Librarianship, 1981. Researcher Library of Internat. Relations, Chgo., 1975-76; fin. analyst No. Trust Co., Chgo., 1976-79; legal researcher Karon, Morrison & Savikas, Chgo., 1979-80; research assoc. Arthur Andersen & Co., Chgo., 1981-85, Fleming Assocs., Miami, Fla., 1985—. Mem. Am. Soc. Info. Sci., Spl. Libraries Assn., ALA, Chgo. Council Fgn. Relations, Am. Jewish Com., Beta Phi Mu, Pi Sigma Alpha, Alpha Kappa Delta.

CARR, WILLIAM HENRY ALEXANDER, public relations executive, author; b. Albany, N.Y., Nov. 25, 1924; s. John Joseph and Ruby (Sokol) C.; m. Margaret McCormick, Dec. 19, 1973. Student U. Chgo., 1944-46. Reporter, City News Bur., Chgo., 1943-44, Chgo. Sun, 1944-45, 47-48, Chgo. Times, 1945-46; news editor ABC, 1946-47; pub. relations client counsel John Price Jones Co., N.Y.C., 1949-52; assoc. dir. pub. relations United Community Def. Services, N.Y.C., 1952-55; reporter, columnist, editor N.Y. Post, N.Y.C., 1955-64; pub. relations cons. INA Corp., Phila., 1967-71, 71-72; dir. pub. info. State of Pa., Harrisburg, 1971; sr. speechwriter N.Y. Life Ins. Co., N.Y.C., 1975-76; v.p. Jack Raymond & Co., N.Y.C., 1977—; books include: JFK: A Complete Biography, 1962, rev. edit. 1963, The Emergence of Red China, 1966, The DuPonts of Delaware (award Friends of Am. Writers), 1964, The Basic Book of the Cat, 1963, rev. edit., 1978. Mem. Md. Gov.'s Task Force on Crime Prevention and Community Involvement, 1968-69; mem. exec. com. Pa. Public Com. for Humanities, 1971-76. Served with USAAF, World War II. Recipient Albert Schweitzer medal for Humanitarianism, Animal Welfare Inst., 1961. Mem. hila. Writers Conf. (dir.), Authors Guild Am., Aircraft Owners and Pilots Assn. Clubs: Overseas Press, N.Y. Press, Publicity (N.Y.C.); Press (San Francisco). Contbr. articles to numerous mags; columnist Dog World Mag., 1958-65. Address: 3455 Leatherbury Ln Indianapolis IN 46222

CARRADUS, CRAIG ALLEN, civil engineer; b. Manchester, Iowa, Nov. 21, 1953; s. Ellison Wilbur and Berdina Maxine (Miller) C.; m. Vicki Louise Drinkwater, Aug. 17, 1974; children—Tiffany, Alicia, Natasha. B.S., Iowa State U., 1976, M.S., 1978. Registered profl. engr., Iowa, Ill. Research asst. Iowa State U., 1976-78; staff engr. Patzig Testing Labs., Des Moines, 1978-82, mng. engr., Davenport, 1982—. Contbr. articles to profl. jours. Mem. ASCE, Nat. Soc. Profl. Engrs., Construction Specifications Inst.; C. of C. (com. comml. and indstl. devel. 1983-84); Phi Kappa Phi (hon.) Lutheran. Lodge: Lions (bd. dirs. 1983-84). Avocations: carpentry; cabinetry; canoeing; golfing. Office: Patzig Testing Lab 940 W 3rd St Davenport IA 52802

CARRAHER, CHARLES JACOB, JR., professional speaker; b. Cin., Sept. 22, 1922; s. Charles Jacob and Marcella Marie (Hager) C.; grad. pub. schs., Norwood, O.; m. Joyce Ann Root, June 13, 1947; children—Cynthia A., Craig J. With Cin. Enquirer, 1937-72, office mgr., circulation mgr., adminstrv. asst. to exec. v.p., 1947-66, dir. employee community relations, 1966-72, corp. sec., 1969-72; exec. v.p., partner Cin. Suburban Newspapers Inc., 1973-77; asst. dir. devel. WCET-TV, 1977-79; v.p. Garrett Computer Inc., 1979-81; participant numerous symposia. Mem. bd., v.p. Cin. Conv. and Visitors Bur., 1966-72; mem. Cin. Manpower Planning Council, 1972. Bd. dirs. Central Psychiatric Clinic, 1970-80, Mental Health Assn., 1970-72, Great Rivers council Girl Scouts U.S.A., 1969-74; v.p. bd. dirs. Neediest Kids of All, 1969-72; bd. dirs. Greater Cin. Urban League, 1971-74, 75-78. Served to lt., USAAF, World War II, ETO. Decorated Air medal with cluster. Mem. Greater Cin. C. of C. (chmn. human resources devel. com. 1972), Beta Gamma Sigma. Republican. Methodist. Home and office: 10848 Lake Thames Dr Cincinnati OH 45242

CARRIER, WILFRED PETER, elec. engr.; b. Faulkton, S.D., July 14, 1923; s. Wilfred P. and Mary (Mundy) C.; E.E., Ill. Inst. Tech., 1952; m. Mary M. Mulcahy, July 17, 1943; children—Patrick, Timothy. Dir. quality Standard Coil Products Co., Chgo., 1951-58; dir. quality, reliability Mallory Capacitor Co., Indpls., 1958-74, dir. engring., 1974—. Served with AUS, 1942-46; CBI. Mem. Electronic Industries Assn., Am. Soc. Quality Control (regional award), IEEE, Am. Def. Preparedness Assn., Nat. Security Indsl. Assn. Roman Catholic. Clubs: Indpls. Athletic, K.C. Home: 9861 Chesterton St N Indianapolis IN 46280 Office: 3029 Washington St E Indianapolis IN 46206

CARRINGTON, DOROTHY H., university administrator; b. Chgo., May 6, 1921; d. William James and Lena (Ulbrich) C. M.S. in Psychology, Northwestern U., 1943; Ed.D. in Counseling, Fla. State U., 1961. Lic. psychologist, Ill. Prof. psychology Blackburn Coll., 1957-59; asst. dean women Ill. State U., Normal, 1961-65, asst. dean students, 1965-73, affirmative action officer, 1973—. Mem. AAUW (pres. Bloomington-Normal 1967-69, nat. bd. internat. fellowships 1974-76, corp. rep. bd. dirs. Ill. 1981—), Am. Psychol. Assn., Am. Personnel and Guidance Assn., Am. Assn. for Affirmative Action. Home: 114 Eastview Dr Normal IL 61761 Office: Ill State U 207 Hovey Hall Normal IL 61761

CARROLL, CARMAL EDWARD, clergyman, educator; b. Grahn, Ky., Oct. 8, 1923; s. Noah Washington and Jessie Laura (Scott) C.; Ph.B., U. Toledo, 1947, M.A., 1950, B.Edn., 1951; M.L.S., UCLA, 1961; Ph.D., U. Calif., Berkeley, 1969; postgrad. in theology Duke U., Episcopal Div. Sch.; m. Greta E. Seastrom, June 11, 1960; 1 adopted child, Mehran Sabouhi. Edn. librarian, U. So. Calif., 1961-62; reference librarian U. Calif. at Berkeley, 1962-65; dir. library So. Oreg. Coll., Ashland, 1965-67; dir. libraries Wichita (Kans.) State U., 1967-70; prof. library sci. U. Mo. at Columbia, 1970—. Named Ky. col. Mem. AAUP, ALA, Assn. Am. Library Schs., Mo. Library Assn., N.Y. Acad. Sci., Assn. Info. and Image Mgmt., Internat. Platform Assn., Phi Delta Kappa, Beta Phi Mu. Democrat. Episcopalian. Club: Rotary. Author: Professionalization of Education for Librarianship, 1970. Home: 2001 Country Club Dr Columbia MO 65201

CARROLL, CLARA JEAN, business educator; b. Henry, Ill., Jan. 10, 1934; d. Eugene Cleaver and Sarah Arlene (Miles) Kirby. B.S. in Edn., Ill. State U., 1955, M.S. in Edn., 1966. Instr. Chillicothe High Sch., Ill., 1955-69; instr. Ill. Central Coll., East Peoria, Ill., 1969-80, chmn. dept. secretarial sci., 1977—. Author: Business Education into the 80's, 1979. Mem. Profl. Secs. Internat., Internat. Bus. Edn. Assn., Nat. Bus. Edn. Assn., Ill. Bus. Edn. Assn., Delta Pi Epsilon (pres. 1974-75), Delta Kappa Gamma (treas. 1968-72). Episcopalian. Avocations: woodworking; hiking; cycling. Office: Ill Central Coll East Peoria IL 61635

CARROLL, GEORGE DEEKS, ins. co. exec.; b. Mpls., Mar. 27, 1916; s. Joseph Douglas and Dorothy Elizabeth (Deeks) C.; B.S. in Commerce, Northwestern U., 1937; m. Marguerite Ray, Nov. 19, 1938; children—George Deeks, Judith Ray Carroll Smith. With Spl. Agts. Sch., Employers Liability Assurance Corp., Boston and Chgo., 1938-42; with Marsh & McLennan Inc., Chgo., 1942—, asst. v.p., 1956-58, v.p., 1958—; past pres., dir. Ridge Investors Trust; owner Nawaii Lodge, Lake Tomahawk, Woodruff, Wis. Founder with White Sox, 1st Chgo. Little League, 1952; past pres., bd. dirs. Laguna Woods Home Owners Assn.; mem. exec. bd. Chgo. council Boy Scouts Am., 1962-76. Served with USN, 1942-46. Republican. Congregationalist. Clubs: Union League (Chgo.); Midlothian Country (dir.). Home: Route 3 Box 58 Woodruff WI 54568 Office: 222 S Riverside Dr Chicago IL 60606

CARROLL, GLADA IROLENE HOUSER, hospital food service director; b. Carson, Iowa, May 24, 1923; d. Jacob Henry and Sarah Viola (Frain) Houser; B.S., Iowa State U., 1944, M.S., 1977; m. Leo Warren Carroll, Apr. 7, 1945 (dec.); children—Philip, Linda, Daniel, Timothy, Beverly, Rita. Dietitian, Stouffer's Food Corp., Cleve., Chgo., N.Y.C., 1944-46; dietitian, asst. dir. food service Mercy Hosp., Des Moines, 1967-78, dir. food service, 1978—. Mem. Am. Dietetic Assn. (registered dietitian), Iowa Dietetic Assn. (treas. 1979-83, pres. 1984-85), Des Moines Dist. Dietetic Assn., Am. Soc. Hosp. Food Service Adminstrs., Omicron Nu. Roman Catholic. Office: Mercy Hosp 6th and University St Des Moines IA 50314

CARROLL, HARDY, librarian, educator; b. Kernersville, N.C., Feb. 24, 1930; s. Hardy Abram and Mary Helen (Bailey) C.; m. Mary Kulp Gotwals, July 25, 1959; children—Stephen, Deborah. B.A., Guilford Coll., 1951; B.D., Hartford Sem., 1954; M.S. in L.S., Drexel U., 1965; Ph.D., Case Western Res. U., 1974. Cataloger U. Pa., Phila., 1957-59, 63-65; asst. catalog librarian Pa. State U., University Park, 1965-66, personnel librarian, 1966-67; asst. prof. Sch. Library and Info. Sci., Western Mich. U., Kalamazoo, 1970-77, assoc. prof., 1977-85, assoc. prof. U. Libraries, 1985—; trustee Mich. Library Consortium, Lansing, 1977-85, mem. exec. council, 1983-85. Editor: Environmental Information Programs for Public Libraries, 1974. Trustee People's Ch., Kalamazoo, 1982-85. Mem. Vine Neighborhood Assn., Kalamazoo Folklife Assn., ALA (subcom. on copyright 1975-77), Assn. for Library and Info. Sci. Edn., Am. Soc. Info. Sci. (Spl. Interest Group for Edn. chpt. rep. 1977-85), AAUP, Spl. Libraries Assn. Unitarian-Universalist. Home: 618 Axtell St Kalamazoo MI 49008 Office: Bus Library Western Mich U Kalamazoo MI 49008

CARROLL, LOUISE DOLORES, nurse, administrator; b. St. Clairsville, Ohio, Feb. 12, 1924; d. John Joseph and Louise Caritas (Ebbert) C.; R.N., Wheeling (W.Va.) Hosp., 1945; B.S. in Nursing Edn., Catholic U. Am., 1950; M.Ed., Central State U., Wilberforce, Ohio, 1959. Staff nurse Wheeling (W.Va.) Hosp., 1945-46, asst. dir., instr., 1950-55; instr. St. Mary's Hosp., Clarksburg, W.Va., 1946-47; dir. sch. nursing Community Hosp., Springfield, Ohio, 1955-69, v.p., 1969—. Mem. health techs. adv. com. Clark Tech. Coll.; bd. dirs. United Way; mem. Clark County Chpt. ARC, Community Hosp. Aux. Mem. Nat. League Nursing (sch. visitor, review bd. for accreditation of hosp. schs., 1957-72), Ohio Council Diploma Nurse Educators, Ohio Commn. Nursing Needs and Resources, Ohio League Nursing (pres. 1980-82), Am. Hosp. Assn. (del-at-large 1972-78, Assembly of Hosp. Schs. of Nursing disting. leadership award 1978, Edna A. Fagan Disting. Service award 1983). Democrat. Roman Catholic. Home: 3157 Sherwood Park Dr Springfield OH 45505 Office: 2615 E High St Springfield OH 45501

CARROLL, NORMAN EDWARD, college dean, educator; b. Chgo., Oct. 17, 1929; s. Ralph Thomas and Edith (Fay) C.; m. Ruth Carlton, July 26, 1960; children—Rebecca, Mark, John. B.S., Loyola U.-Chgo., 1956; M.S.A., Rosary Coll., 1983; M.A., DePaul U., 1965; Ph.D., Ill. Inst. Tech., 1971. Prin. Carroll Assocs., River Forest, Ill., 1956-65; prof. bus. and econs. Rosary Coll., River Forest, 1968-70, dean Grad. Sch. Bus., 1977—, v.p., dean faculty, 1970—. Contbr. articles to profl. pubs. Bd. dirs. Oak Park Human Relations Com., Ill., 1965; mem. selection com. Chgo. Archdiocesan Sch. Bd., 1970; mem. adv. com. River Forest Sch. Bd., 1975. Served to cpl. U.S. Army, 1951-53. Mem. Acad. Mgmt., Am. Econ. Assn., Associated Colls. Chgo. Area (pres. 1973-75, treas. 1982—), Indsl. Relations Research Assn., Ill. Tng. and Devel. Assn. (chmn. membership 1983-84). Lodge: Rotary. Office: Rosary Coll 7900 Division River Forest IL 60305

CARROLL, RICHARD P., oculoplastic surgery educator, consultant; b. Pitts., Mar. 4, 1940; m. Darlene Joan Stubitsch, July 3, 1965; children—Slate, Amber. B.S., John Carroll U., 1962; M.D., Loyola-Stritch U., 1966. Diplomate Am. Bd. Ophthalmology. Intern, Cleve Clinic, 1966-67; resident Duke U. Eye Ctr., 1970-73; fellow U. Tex., Houston, 1974; clin. assoc. prof. dept. ophthalmology U. Minn., Mpls., 1974—; cons. oculoplastic surgery, Mpls., St. Paul, 1974—. Contbr. articles to profl. jours. and books. Served to maj. M.C., U.S. Army, 1967-70, Germany. Heed Found. fellow, 1974. Fellow Am. Soc. Ophthalmic Plastic Reconstruction Surgery (pres. 1984), Am. Acad. Ophthalmology, Am. Coll. Surgeons, AM. Acad. Facial Plastic and Reconstructive Surgery, Am. Soc. Cosmetic Surgeons. Club: Minnekahda (Mpls.). Office: Ophthalmic Plastic and Reconstructive Surgery PA 1690 University Ave St Paul MN 55104

CARROLL, VALEREE SUE, speech pathologist; b. Kansas City, Mo., Aug. 29, 1946; d. Middleton Scott and Patricia Pauline (Anderson) C.; B.S. in Edn., U. Kans., 1968, M.A. in Speech Pathology, 1970. Speech/lang. pathologist Clay County Health Dept., Liberty, Mo., 1970-71, Kansas City (Mo.) Pub. Schs., 1971—; mem. spl. edn. placement team Kansas City Public Sch. Dist. U.S. Office Edn. fellow, 1968-70. Mem. Am., Greater Kansas City speech hearing assns., Council for Exceptional Children. Republican. Home: 2115 W 78th St Prairie Village KS 66208 Office: 1211 McGee St Kansas City MO 64106

CARROTHERS, GARY LINN, lawyer; b. Wheeling, W.Va., Oct. 16, 1943; s. Ralph Cecil Carrothers and Thelma Jeannette (Hales) Foura; m. Gayle Caryn McIntosh, Sept. 2, 1967; children—Kelly, Caryn, Halli, Jack. B.A., Western Res. U., 1965, J.D., 1968. Bar: Ohio 1969. Ptnr. Hyman, Hyman & Carrothers, Elyria, Ohio, 1968-80; sole practice, 1981—. Bd. dirs. Vis. Nurses Assn., Lorain County, Ohio, 1976; pres. Midview Local Sch. Bd., Lorain County, 1979. Mem. Lorain County Bar Assn., Ohio State Bar Assn. Democrat. Methodist. Avocations: reading; soccer. Home: 106 Country Pl Grafton OH 44044

CARRUTHERS, PHILIP CHARLES, lawyer, public official; b. London, Dec. 8, 1953; came to U.S., 1962, naturalized, 1971; s. J. Alex and Marie (Calarco) C. B.A., U. Minn., 1975, J.D., 1979. Bar: Minn. 1979, U.S. Dist. Ct. Minn., 1979, U.S. Ct. Appeals (8th cir.) 1979. Assoc., Nichols & Kruger, and predecessor firm, 1979-81; ptnr. Nichols, Kruger, Starks and Caruthers, Mpls., 1982-84; ptnr. Luther, Ballenthin & Carruthers, Mpls., 1985—; pros. atty. City of Deephaven, Minn., 1979—, City of Woodland, Minn., 1980—. Co-author: The Drinking Driver in Minnesota: Criminal and Civil Issues, 1982. Note and comment editor Minn. Law Rev., 1978-79. Mem. Met. Council of Twin Cities Area, St. Paul, 1983—. Mem. Minn. Trial Lawyers Assn. (bd. govs. 1982—), Minn. State Bar Assn., Hennepin County Bar Assn., Assn. Trial Lawyers Am. Mem. Democratic Farmer-Labor Party. Roman Catholic. Home: 7852 Yates Ave N Brooklyn Park MN 55443 Office: Luther Ballenthin & Carruthers 4624 IDS Ctr Minneapolis MN 55402

CARSON, BONNIE L(OU), chemist; b. Kansas City, Kans., Aug. 11, 1940; d. Harold Lee and Lorene Marie (Draper) Bachert; student U. Kansas City, 1958-61; B.A. in Chemistry summa cum laude, U. N.H., 1963; M.S. in Organic Chemistry, Oreg. State U., 1966; m. David M. Carson, June, 1961 (div. 1973); 1 dau., Catherine (Katie) Leslie. Grad. teaching asst. Oreg. State U., 1963-66; organic chem. lab. instr. U. Waterloo, Ont., Can., 1968-69; asst. abstractor in macromolecular chemistry Chem. Abstracts Service, Columbus, Ohio, 1969-71; freelance Russian translator, 1971-73; asst. chemist Midwest Research Inst., Kansas City, Mo., 1973-75, asso. chemist, 1975-80, sr. chemist, 1980—. Mem. Am. Soc. Info. Scientists, Am. Chem. Soc., Am. Inst. Chemists, AAAS, N.Y. Acad. Sci., Soc. Environ. Geochemistry and Health, Am. Translators Assn. (pres. Mid-Am. chpt. 1984-85), Soc. Tech. Communication. Author and Editor: (with others) Trace Metals in the Environment, 1977-81; contbr. in field. Home: 5501 Holmes St Kansas City MO 64110 Office: 425 Volker Blvd Kansas City MO 64110

CARSON, CLAUDE MATTESON (KIT), investment counselor; b. Farley, Mo., Sept. 26, 1907; s. Robert Walter and Mirtle Virginia Carson; student Advanced Mgmt. Program, Harvard U., 1962; m. Helen Long, May 16, 1931. Pres., Hoerner Boxes, Inc., until 1966; sr. v.p. adminstrn., dir. Hoerner Waldorf Corp. (merger Hoerner Boxes, Inc and Waldorf Paper Products Co.), St. Paul, 1966-73, 76—, also chmn. audit co., mem. exec. com.; chmn. audit com., dir. Puritan-Bennett Corp., Kansas City, Mo. Mem. Bus. Climate Task Force Com., State of Minn., 1971-73; active Boy Scouts Am. Bd. mgrs. Parker B. Francis Found.; bd. govs. Interlachen, 1976-82. Served with AUS. Fellow Am. Inst. Mgmt. (pres.'s council); mem. Fibre Box Assn. (chmn. bd., past pres.), TAPPI, Fourdrinier Kraft Board Inst., Internat. Corrugated Case Assn. (dir.). Clubs: Union League, Mid-Am. (Chgo.); Interlachen, Question, Minneapolis, St. Paul Pool and Yacht, Harvard Alumni, Rotary. Home: 5209 Schaefer Rd Edina MN 55436 Office: Northwestern Financial Center 7900 Xerxes Ave S Suite 1200 Minneapolis MN 55431

CARSON, GINGER ROBERTS, financial consultant; b. Austin, Minn., Nov. 30, 1957; d. Sherbun Lee and Joyce Ellen (Lightly) R.; m. Randy Lynn Hanson, July 21, 1978 (div. July 1984); m. John M. Carson, Apr. 19, 1985. B.S. in Acctg., Mankato State U., 1979, postgrad., 1985—. Internal auditor Bretts Dept. Store, Mankato, Minn., 1977-78; staff acct. Morken & Andring, Mankato, 1978-79; tax acct. Morem Gearty, Austin, 1980-82; dir. bus. affairs Gerard of Minn. and Iowa, Austin, 1979-83, cons., 1983; fin. cons. Merrill

Lynch Pierce Fenner & Smith, Rochester, Minn., 1983—; cons. Kessner Electric, Austin, 1982-83. Mem. Zonta Internat., Nat. Assn. of Security Dealers, Bus. and Prof. Women of Austin and Rochester (Young Career Woman award 1981), Rochester C. of C. Mem. Democratic Farm Labor Party. Baptist. Avocations: skiing; raquetball; reading. Home: 3726 9th Ave SW Rochester MN 55902 Office: Merrill Lynch Pierce Fenner & Smith Suite 300 Broadway and 2nd St SE Rochester MN 55904

CARSON, GORDON BLOOM, research institute executive, professional engineer; b. High Bridge, N.J., Aug. 1, 1911; s. Whitfield R. and Emily M. (Bloom) C.; m. Beth Lacy, June 19, 1937; children—Richard W., Emily E. Carson Duffus, Alice L. Carson Allman, Jeanne H. Carson Gable. B.S., Case Western Res. U., 1931, D.Eng. (hon.), 1957; M.S., Yale U., 1932, M.E., 1938; LL.D. (hon.), Rio Grande Coll., 1971. Registered profl. engr., Ohio, Calif. Instr. to assoc. prof. mech. and indsl. engring. Case Inst. Tech., Cleve., 1932-44; research engr., dir. research Cleve. Automatic Machine Co., 1939-44; asst. to gen. mgr. Selby Shoe Co., Portsmouth, Ohio, 1944, mgr. engring., 1945-49, corp. sec., 1949-53; dir. Pyrrole Products Co., Portsmouth, 1948-53; dean engring. Ohio State U.-Columbus, 1953-58, dir. Engring. Expt. Sta., 1953-58, v.p. univ. bus. and fin., treas., 1959-71, v.p. Research Found., 1958-71; exec. v.p. Albion Coll. (Mich.), 1971-77; asst. to chancellor, dir. fin. Northwood Inst., Midland, Mich., 1977-82; v.p. Mich. Molecular Inst., Midland, 1982—. Bd. dirs., Cardinal Fund, Inc., Columbus 1966; trustee Cardinal Govt. Trust, Columbus, 1980; bd. dirs. Goodwill Industries, Columbus, 1959-67; bd. dirs. Midland Community Affairs Council, 1982-84, v.p. bd., 1983, pres., 1984; trustee White Cross Hosp. Assn., Columbus, 1960-71. Recipient Tech. Man of Yr. award Columbus Tech. Council, 1957-58, Disting. Service award Ohio State Univ., 1977, Albion Coll., 1980. Fellow AAAS, ASME, Inst. Indsl. Engrs.; mem. U.S. Naval Inst., Nat. Soc. Profl. Engrs., Mich. Soc. Profl. Engrs., Columbus Soc. Fin. Analysts (pres. 1964-65), Sigma Xi (nat. treas. 1981—), Tau Beta Pi, Alpha Pi Mu, Phi Eta Sigma, Romophos, Sphinx, Omicron Delta Epsilon. Lodge: Masons. Editor: Production Handbook, 1958, sr. cons. editor, 1972; patentee in field; contbr. numerous engring. articles to profl. publs. Home: 5413 Gardenbrook Dr Midland MI 48640 Office: Mich Molecular Inst 1910 W Saint Andrews Rd Midland MI 48640

CARSON, IRWIN KRENGEL, orthopedic surgeon; b. Phila., Dec. 30, 1944; s. George K. and Claire (Althousen) C.; m. Nancy Gilbert Dec. 27, 1969; children—Jonathan, Julie, Joshua. A.B., Harvard U., 1966; M.D., U. Mich., 1970. Diplomate Am. Bd. Orthopedic Surgery. Intern, Kaiser Found. Hosp., San Francisco, 1970-71; resident Michael Reese Med. Ctr., Chgo., 1971-74; fellow U. Toronto, 1974-75; practice medicine, specializing in orthopedic surgery, Arlington Hts., Ill., 1976—; staff N.W. Community Hosp., Humana Hosp., Hoffman Estates, Ill., Children's Meml. Hosp., Chgo. Mem. Sch. Bd. Caucus, Highland Park, Ill., 1978—, Recreation Adv. Com., Highland Park, 1983—. Mem. Ill. Orthopedic Soc., Chgo. Orthopedic Soc. Clubs: Harvard of Chgo., U. Mich. of Chgo., Pres.'s. Home: 290 Briar Ln Highland Park IL 60035 Office: 1120 N Arlington Heights Rd Arlington Heights IL 60004

CARSON, MARY SILVANO, educator, counselor; b. Mass., Aug. 11, 1925; d. Joseph and Alice V. (Sherwood) Silvano; B.S., Simmons Coll., Boston, 1947; M.A., U. Chgo., 1961; postgrad. Ctr. Urban Studies, 1970, U. Chgo., 1970, 72, U. Minn., 1977; m. Paul E. Carson, Feb. 21, 1947; children—Jan Ellen, Jeffrey Paul, Amy Jayne. Cert. Nat. Commn. Counselor Cert. Bd., Ill. sch. counselor, Ill. employment counselor III, career testing. Mgr. S.W. Youth Opportunity Center, Dept. Labor, Chgo., 1966-67; careers counselor Gordon Tech. High Sch., Chgo., 1971-74; dir. Career and Assessment Center, YMCA Community Coll., Chgo., 1974-81; project coordinator Career Ctr., Loop Coll., Chgo., 1981-82; adv. bd. City-Wide Coll. Career Center. Bd. dirs. Loop YWCA, Chgo. Mem. Women's Share in Public Service (dir.), Am. Ednl. Research Assn., Am. Counseling and Devel. Assn., Nat. Vocat. Guidance Assn., Bus. and Profl. Women's Club, Pi Lambda Theta (pres. chpt. 1975). Home: 155 Harbor Dr Apt 812 Chicago IL 60601

CARSON, SANDRA MARIE, school counselor, music educator; b. Maryville, Mo., Feb. 5, 1948; d. Charles Wesley and Marcia Jean (Martin) Cornell; B.M.E., Kans., U., 1970, M.S.E., 1975; postgrad. U. Kans.; m. David Eugene Carson, July 1, 1973; children—Kyle David, Corey Michael, Robert Cornell. Instrumental music tchr. elem. and secondary schs. Shawnee Mission (Kans.) Pub. Schs., 1970-73; substitute Manpower tchr., counselor Kansas City (Kans.) Schs., 1974; elem. counselor Title 111 Spice Program, Ottawa (Kans.) Pub. Schs., 1975-77; counselor, tutor minority high sch. students; prepared childbirth instr. Lawrence Meml. Hosp., 1981—. Mem. NEA, Kans. Music Edn. Assn., Music Educators Nat. Conf., Phi Delta Kappa. Contbr. Career Edn. Learning Packet, 5th grade, 1975. Home: Route 3 Box 56C Lawrence KS 66044

CARSON, WARREN BRADFORD, state education executive; b. Chgo., May 10, 1929; s. A. Bradford and Winifred (Warren) C.; m. Susan Chakmakjian, Dec. 20, 1952; (div. 1972); children—Warren Bradford, Ronald S., Cynthia S., Christopher F.; m. 2d Joan Dempsey, July 8, 1972. B.A., U. Calif.-Berkeley, 1953; M.A., Calif. State U.-San Francisco, 1961; Ph.D., Stanford U., 1965. Tchr. Martinez Pub. Schs., Calif., 1953-56; vice prin. King City Pub. Schs., Calif., 1956-57; supt. Greenfield Pub. Schs., Calif., 1957-63; dir. fin. Oreg. Dept. Edn., Salem, 1965-67; supt. Wood Dale Pub. Schs., Ill., 1967-71, Addison Pub. Schs., Ill., 1971-75; asst. state supt. Ill. Bd. Edn., Springfield, 1975—. Served with USAF, 1951-52. Mem. Ill. Assn. Sch. Adminstrs., Ill. Assn. Sch. Bus. Ofcls., Word Process Info. Systems Am. Avocations: golf; birdge; camping. Office: Ill Bd Edn 100 N 1st St Springfield IL 62777

CARSTENS, JOHN CHRISTOPHER, physics educator, researcher; b. Chgo., Oct. 8, 1937; s. Edward Earl and Sylvia O. (Christopher) C.; m. Frieda M. Durkin, June 29, 1967; children—Edward William, Marie Christine. B.A., Monmouth Coll., 1959; Ph.D., U. Mo.-Rolla, 1966. Research engr. Arnold Air Force Sta., Tullahoma, Tenn., 1965-66; postdoctoral fellow Argonne Labs., Ill., 1966-67; asst. prof. physics Western Ill. U., Macomb, 1967-68; asst. prof. physics U. Mo., Rolla, 1968-74, 1 assoc. prof., 1974-82, prof., 1982—, acting dir. Grad. Ctr., Cloud Physics Research, 1984—. Mem. Am. Geophys. Union, Am. Meteorol. Soc., Mo. Acad. Sci., Sigma Xi. Episcopalian.

CARSTENS, ROBERT LOWELL, civil engineering educator, consultant, researcher; b. Sisseton, S.D., July 31, 1922; s. Fred Andrew and Ava Esther (Kulow) C.; m. Marian Helen Kirkendall, Apr. 24, 1948; 1 son, Michael Robert. B.S., Iowa State U., 1943, M.S., 1964, Ph.D., 1966. Registered profl. engr., Iowa. Constrn. engr. Kramme & Jensen Constrn. Co., Des Moines, 1946-48, Jensen Constrn. Co., Des Moines, 1948-50; maintenance engr., supr. Arabian-Am. Oil Co., Saudi Arabia, 1954-61; hwy. engr. U.S. AID, La Paz, Bolivia, 1962-63; prof. civil engring. Iowa State U., Ames, 1964—; cons. hwy. safety and accident reconstruction; mem. Gov.'s Task Force To Modernize State Transp. System, 1973-74. Contbr. articles to tech. and profl. jours. Served with U.S. Army, 1943-45, 50-54. Decorated Bronze Star; recipient Dir. Annual award Iowa Dept. Transp., 1981. Mem. ASCE, Nat. Soc. Profl. Engrs., Inst. Transp. Engrs., Transp. Research Bd. Republican. Lodges: Masons, Shriners, Kiwanis. Home: 1503 20th St Ames IA 50010 Office: Iowa State U Ames IA 50011

CARTER, ANNA CURRY (MRS. E. KEMPER CARTER), civic worker; b. Kansas City, Mo.; d. William Adams and Susan Maud (Machette) Curry; B.S., U. Mo., 1918; M.A., Columbia U., 1930; postgrad. Oxford U., (Eng.), 1935; m. E. Kemper Carter, Feb. 22, 1936 (dec. Dec. 1951); 1 son, E. Kemper (dec.). Tchr., research Kansas City Pub. Schs., 1919-21; dir. speech and dramatics Westport Jr. High Sch., Kansas City, 1921-26; dir. speech and drama S.W. High Sch., Kansas City, 1926-36. Bd. govs. Kansas City Mus. History and Sci., 1960-76; parliamentarian women's div. Kansas City Philharmonic Assn., 1954—; mem. exec. bd., mem. at large Community Children's Theatre, 1955—. Trustee Kansas City Art Inst. and Sch. of Design, Conservatory of Music, U. Mo. at Kansas City, Rockhurst Coll., Kansas City, Mo., Kansas City Philharmonic Assn., Kansas City Museum History and Sci.; hon. dir. Ch. St. Mary Aldenmanburg, Winston Churchill Meml., Fulton, Mo. Sponsor Winston Churchill Meml.; donar Lenox Hill-Skawhegan Art Projects, N.Y.C. Recipient numerous citations and awards including Skowhegan Sch. Art, Kansas City Art Inst., Rockhurst Coll., others. Hon. fellow Harry S. Truman Library Inst.; Soc. fellows William Rockhill Nelson Gallery Art, 1966-76. Mem. AAUW (del. nat. convs.), Alliance Francaise (exec. bd., parliamentarian 1974—), English Speaking Union, Pres. and Past Pres. Gen. Assembly, Sci. Pioneers, Am. Inst. Parliamentarians, ANTA, Speech Assn. Am., Alpha Phi. Baptist. Clubs: University, Woman's City, Carriage, Mission Hills Country, River, Kansas City, Rockhill Tennis; Capitol Hill (Washington). Home: Wornall Plaza 310 W 49th St Apt 507 Kansas City MO 64112

CARTER, ARNOLD NICK, cassette learning systems company executive; b. Phila., Mar. 25, 1929; s. Arnold and Margaret (Richter) C.; A.A., Keystone Jr. Coll., 1949; B.S. in Speech and Dramatic Art, Syracuse U., 1951; postgrad. Syracuse U., 1951-52; M.A. in Communications, Am. Univ., 1959; m. Virginia Lucille Polsgrove, Oct. 14, 1955; children—Victoria Lynne, Andrea Joy. Actor Rome (N.Y.) Little Theater, summers, 1951-52; mgr. customer relations Martin Marietta, Orlando, Fla., 1959-70; v.p. communications research Nightingale-Conant Corp., Chgo., 1970—. Served with USNR, 1953-59; Korea. Recipient Continuare Professus Articulatus Excellare award, Nat. Speakers Assn., 1978. Mem. Sales and Mktg. Execs. Chgo. (v.p. 1979-81), Nat. Speakers Assn., Am. Soc. Tng. and Devel., Internat. Platform Assn. Republican. Presbyn. Author: Communicate Effectively, 1978; The Amazing Results-Full World of Cassette Learning, 1980; Sales Boosters, 1981. Home: 1315 Elmwood Ave Deerfield IL 60015 Office: Nightingale-Conant Corp 7300 N Lehigh Ave Chicago IL 60648

CARTER, BARRY LINN, pharmacy educator; b. Cedar Rapids, Iowa, Feb. 19, 1955; s. Angelo John and LaVonne (Waterbury) C.; m. Susan K. Decker, Aug. 13, 1977. B.S. in Pharmacy, U. Iowa, 1978; Pharm.D., Med. Coll. Va., 1980. Fellow in family practice clin. pharmacy Coll. Pharmacy, U. Iowa, Iowa City, 1980-81, clin. asst. prof., 1981-85, asst. prof., 1985—. Co-author: Handbook of Family Practice, 1985. Contbr. articles to med. and pharm. jours. Grantee (investigator) Am. Soc. Hosp. Pharmacists, 1982, NIH, 1983, Squibb Research and Devel., 1983, Bristol Meyers, 1984. Mem. Am. Soc. Hosp. Pharmacists (field editor 1984—), Am. Coll. Clin. Pharmacy, Am. Assn. Colls. of Pharmacy, Iowa Pharmacists Assn. Office: Coll Pharmacy U Iowa Iowa City IA 52242

CARTER, CURTIS LLOYD, art museum director, aesthetics and philosophy educator, author; b. Moulton, Iowa, Oct. 1, 1935; s. Lloyd Joseph and Helen Edna (Wood) C.; m. Jean Elaine Watson, June 12, 1960; 1 child, Curtis Lloyd, Jr. B.A., Taylor U., 1960; M.Div., Boston U., 1963, Ph.D., 1971. Instr. Marquette U., Milw., 1969-71, asst. prof., 1971-84, prof., 1984—, chmn. com. fine arts, 1975-84; dir. Haggerty Mus. Art, Marquette U., 1984—; chmn. Nat. Bicentennial Dance Conf., Cambridge, Mass., 1976; panelist, referee NEH Individual Research Project, Washington, 1983, Media Panel, Washington, 1984; chmn., speaker World Congress Aesthetics, Montreal, Can., 1984, Joyce and Vico Conf., Venice, Italy, 1985; advisor Bay View High Sch., Milw., 1982—. Gen. editor and essayist: (Art Mus. Catalogue) Selected Works, 1984. Contbr. articles and essays to profl. jours. and publs. Founding pres., bd. dirs. ARTREACH Milw., 1975—; v.p., bd. dirs. Charles Allis Art Mus., Milw., 1979—; bd. dirs. Music From Almost Yesterday, Milw., 1978—, Wis. Heritages, Inc., Milw., 1979—, Goals for Greater Milw. 2000, 1982—, Studio Watts Artist's Housing Project, Los Angeles, 1982—, Milw. Ctr. Photography, 1982—. Grantee Wis. Arts Bd., 1979, NEA, 1979, 80, 81, Inst. Mus. Services, 1982, 84, Mellon Found., 1982, Wis. Humanities, 1984, J. Paul Getty Trust, 1985. Mem. Am. Assn. Museums, Am. Philos. Assn., Am. Soc. for Aesthetics (nat. conf. chmn. 1980), Am. Dance Guild (chmn. nat. bicentennial dance conf. 1976, mem. nat. exec. com.), Hegel Soc. Am., Semiotics Soc. Am., Coll. Art Assn., Am. Assn. U. Adminstrs., Nat. Dance Critics Assn., Internat. Metaphysical Soc. (chmn.-speaker World Cong. Philosophy, Montreal, Can. 1983), Milw. Area Mus. Assocs. Avocation: travel. Home: 2609 E Menlo Blvd Milwaukee WI 53211 Office: Haggerty Museum Art Marquette U Milwaukee WI 53233

CARTER, DANIEL PAUL, consultant systems management; b. Des Moines, July 7, 1953; s. Delbert Bruce and Doris Jean (Thompson) C.; m. Victoria Lea Kriegler, Sept. 13, 1980; children—Kimberly, Nicholas. B.S., Iowa State U., 1975. Cons. staff Arthur Andersen & Co., Chgo., 1975-79, cons. mgr., 1979—. Mem. Data Processing Mgmt. Assn., Assn. Systems Mgmt. (v.p. 1982-83). Lodge: Elks. Avocations: fishing; racquetball; chess. Home: 108 Roanoke St Rochester IL 62563 Office: Arthur Andersen & Co 1 N Old State Capitol Plaza Springfield IL 62701

CARTER, DEBORAH LYN, pediatrician, consultant; b. Greenwood, Miss., Nov. 6, 1950; s. Fleetwood (stepfather) and Clariece Stinson. B.S., Tex. Tech U., 1971; M.D., U. Ala., 1976. Diplomate Am. Bd. Pediatrics. Intern in pediatrics Grady Meml. Hosp., Atlanta, 1976-77, resident in pediatrics, 1977-78, chief resident in pediatrics, 1978-79; fellow in pediatric hematology-/oncology Emory U., Atlanta, 1979; pvt. practice medicine specializing in pediatrics, East Point, Ga., 1980-82; fellow in pediatric hematology/oncology Children's Hosp. Med. Ctr., Cin., 1983-84; cons., tchr., clin. researcher in pediatric hematology/oncology, 1983—; mem. clin. faculty dept. pediatrics Emory U., 1980—; cons. pediatrics Atlanta region Social Security Adminstrn., 1982-83. Am. Cancer Soc. clin. fellow, 1983. Mem. Am. Acad. Pediatrics, Am. Cancer Soc. Home: 780 Sherwood Rd NE Atlanta GA 30324 Office: Pediatric Hematology/Oncology Assocs PC 993 Johnson Ferry Rd Suite 122 Bldg D Atlanta GA 30342

CARTER, JACK FRANKLIN, agronomy educator; b. Lodgepole, Nebr., Oct. 1, 1919; s. Thomas Baker and Mary Ellen (Watkins) C.; m. Iris Imogene Smith, Oct. 19, 1941; children—Nancy, Steven, Jeffrey, Joel, Brian. B.S., U. Nebr., 1941; M.S., Wash. State U., 1947; Ph.D., U. Wis., Madison, 1950. From asst. to prof. agronomy N.D. State U., Fargo, 1950—, chmn. agronomy dept., 1960—; cons. in field. Editor: Sunflower Science and Technology, 1978, 2d edit., 1980. Contbr. chpt. to book. Held numerous offices Faith Methodist Ch., Fargo, 1954—. Served to chief radio technician USN, 1942-45, PTO. Recipient numerous grants for agronomic research. Fellow Am. Soc. Agronomy, Crop Sci. Soc. (pres. 1972), Council Agrl. Sci. and Tech. (pres. 1978-79). Republican. Methodist. Avocations: gardening; fishing; hunting; woodworking; reading; small construction. Home: 1345 N 11th St Fargo ND 58102 Office: Agronomy Dept ND State Univ Fargo ND 58105

CARTER, JAMES H., See *Who's Who in America,* 43rd edition.

CARTER, JERRY RALPH, feed ingredient co. exec.; b. Springfield, Mo., Jan. 11, 1930; s. Lloyd Ralph and Atrelle (Ward) C.; B.S., Drury Coll., 1951; m. Blanchelen Campbell, June 15, 1951; children—Cheri Ellen, Thomas Lloyd, Timmithoy James. Salesman, Nat. Biscuit Co., Springfield, 1954-59; mgr. Southwest Rendering Co., Inc., Springfield, 1959—; mgr. Southwest By-Products, Inc., Springfield, 1959-83, pres., 1961-83; organizer, dir. Met. Nat. Bank, Springfield, Mo., 1983—. Served with USAF, 1951-54. Mem. Nat. Renderers Assn. (regional pres. 1971-72), Drury Coll. Alumni (pres. 1975). Episcopalian (vestry 1964-65). Mason (K.T., Shriner, Jester). Home: 2732 E Seminole St Springfield MO 65804 Office: PO Box 2876 CSS Springfield MO 65803

CARTER, JOHN DALE, organizational development executive; b. Tuskegee, Ala., Apr. 9, 1944; s. Arthur L. and Ann (Bargyh) C.; A.B., Ind. U., 1965, M.S., 1967; Ph.D. (NDEA fellow), Case Western Res. U., 1974; m. Jana Glenn, Aug. 1, 1970. Dir. student affairs Dental Sch., Case Western Res. U., Cleve., 1974-75, asst. prof. applied behavioral sci., 1974—, asst. dean orgn. devel. and student affairs, 1975-78; pres. Carter's Enterprises, Inc., Cleve., 1970-79; chmn. organizational and systems devel. program, dir. program devel. Gestalt Inst. Cleve., 1980—; mem. exec. bd. Nat. Tng. Labs. faculty Am. U., 1985—; bd. dirs. Behavioral Sci. Found. Cleve. Mem. Internat. Assn. Applied Social Scientists, Cert. Cons. Internat. Author: Counselling the Helping Relationship, 1975. Home: 2995 Scarborough Rd Cleveland Heights OH 44118 Office: PO Box 1822 Cleveland OH 44106

CARTER, JOHN WILLIAM MICHAEL, orthodontist, pedodontist, educator; b. Kansas City, Kans., Nov. 21, 1945; s. William Jay and I'Aleen Gloria (Kramer) C.; m. Colleen Marie O'Rourke, June 25, 1977; children—John Ryan William, Caitlyn Marie. B.F.A., U. Kans., 1967, B.A., 1972; D.D.S. with distinction, U. Mo.-Kansas City, 1978; M.Sc.D. in Oral Biology, grad. cert. in pedodontics, Boston U., 1980; grad. cert. in orthodontics St. Louis U., 1982. Practice dentistry specializing in pedodontics, St. Louis, 1980-82; practice dentistry specializing in pedodontics and orthodontics, Overland Park, Kans., 1982—; asst. prof. orthodontics U. Mo.-Kansas City, 1982—, dir. predoctoral orthodontics, 1984—, asst. prof. grad. orthodontics, 1982—; bd. dirs. St. Louis Edn. and Research Found., 1985—. Author, illustrator: (manual) Practical Biomechanics, 1984; Mixed Dentition Analysis and Treatment, 1984. Contbr. to book Dental Collectables, 1984. Served to capt. USAR, 1978. Mem. ADA, Am. Acad. Pediodontics, Am. Assn. Orthodontists, St. Louis Orthodontic Edn. and Research Found., Kans. State Dental Assn., Phi Lambda Upsilon, Psi Omega (pres. 1977, chpt. adviser 1983— nat. committeeman 1984—). Avocations: jogging, cooking, outdoors activities. Office: 8005 W 110th St Suite 214 Overland Park KS 66210

CARTER, LEONARD MATTHEW, JR., hosp. personnel ofcl.; b. Madera, Calif., Jan. 26, 1953; s. Leonard Matthew and Ruth Chasteen (Brinker) C.; B.A. in Polit. Sci., Tarkio Coll., 1976; M.P.A., Murray State U., 1978. Health planner Lincoln Trail Area Devel. Dist., Elizabethtown, Ky., 1978; dir. Milltown (Ind.) Med. Center, 1978-79; dir. personnel Franklin Hosp., Benton, Ill., 1979-82; v.p. employee relations Lancaster Fairfield Community Hosp., Lancaster, Ohio, 1982—; instr. mgmt. Rend Lake Coll. Active, Lincoln Trail CPR Found., 1978; adv. bd. Rend Lake Coll., 1980—. Served with USMC, 1971-75. Mem. Am. Soc. Hosp. Personnel Adminstrn., Am. Mgmt. Assn., S.E. Ohio Hosp. Personnel Assn., Ohio Soc. Hosp. Human Resource Adminstrs., Author: Financing Emergency Medical Services and Cost Saving Measures, 1978; Adult Day Care Centers, 1978; Small Hospital Recruitment A Positive Approach. Home: 1410 Hillbrook Dr Lancaster OH 43130 Office: 401 N Ewing St Lancaster OH 43130

CARTER, MICHAEL FRANK, urologist; b. Santa Monica, Calif., Sept. 14, 1939; s. Floyd Arthur and Evelyn Elizabeth (Eager) C.; student U. So. Calif., 1957-62; M.D., Georgetown U., 1966; m. Joan Carol Tedford, Aug. 23, 1959; children—Cristen, Timothy, Richard, Gregory. Intern, resident in surgery Harbor Gen. Hosp., Torrance, Calif., 1966-68; resident in urology Johns Hopkins Hosp., Balt., 1968-72; asst. prof. urology Northwestern U., Chgo., 1976—; staff physician Northwestern Meml. Hosp., 1972—, exec. com., 1979—; chief of urology Lakeside VA Hosp.; staff Children's Meml. Hosp. Troop com. chmn. Boy Scouts Am., 1977-79; mem. Wilmette (Ill.) Sch. Bd. Caucus, 1977-79. Named Outstanding Intern, Harbor Gen. Hosp., 1967; Am. Cancer Soc. fellow, 1970-72. Diplomate Am. Bd. Urology. Fellow A.C.S.; mem. Am. Urol. Soc., AMA, Chgo. Urol. Soc. (exec. com. 1979—), Ill. Med. Assn. Episcopalian. Research on uveal micro circulation in rabbits, androgens in cell cycle of prostate gland, prostatic ultrasound, impotence and penile blood pressure. Home: 720 Ashland Ave Wilmette IL 60091 Office: 251 E Chicago Ave Chicago IL 60611

CARTER, ROBERT CORNELIUS, lawyer; b. Chgo., June 4, 1917; s. John Gordon and Ada Christine (Abrahamson) C.; B.S., U. Ill., Champaign, 1946; LL.B., Gonzaga U., Spokane, Wash., 1949, J.D., 1967; m. Georgia R. Richardson, Mar. 9, 1937 (dec. Nov. 3, 1973); m. 2d, Gertrude A. Hetteen, June 3, 1975; 1 son, John M. Bar: Minn. 1971. Individual practice law, Spokane, 1949-51, Roseau, Minn., 1965-81; sr. ptnr. firm Carter & Carter, Roseau, 1980-81; of counsel firm Carter, Mergens, and Hardwick, Rouseau, 1980-81; now mem. Robert C. Carter & Assocs. Sec., Minn. Citizens Com. on Natural Resources, 1960-65. Served with USAAF, 1941-46. Decorated Air medal with 2 oak leaf clusters, Presdl. Unit citation. Mem. Minn. Bar Assn., Wash. Bar Assn., Am. Trial Lawyers Assn., Minn. Trial Lawyers Assn., Am. Judicature Soc., Audubon Soc., Am. Wildlife Assn., Green Peace Soc., Nature Conservancy, Sierra Club, Am. Legion, VFW, Phi Alpha Delta. Home: Beaver Farms Wannaska MN 56761 also 5 Canterbury Dr Grenelefe Golf Club Haines City FL 33844 Office: Robert C Carter & Assocs 101 Main Ave N Roseau MN 56751

CARTER, ROBERT LEROY, engineering educator; b. Leavenworth, Kans., Aug. 22, 1918; s. Joseph LeRoy and Viola Elizabeth (Hayner) C.; m. Jewell Mamie Long, June 3, 1941; children—Roberta, Benjamin, Judy Carter Meadows, Frederick, Camille Carter Ronchetto. B.S., U. Okla., 1941; Ph.D., Kuke U., 1949. Registered profl. engr., Mo. Testing technician Eastman Kodak Corp., Rochester, N.Y., 1940-42; physicist Tenn. Eastman Corp., Oak Ridge, 1945-46; research scientist-engr. Atomics Internat., Canoga Park, Calif., 1949-63; faculty U. Mo., Columbia, 1962—, now prof. elec. engring., nuclear engring.; chmn. Mo. Low-Level Radiation Waste Task Force, Jefferson City, 1983-84. Contbr. sci. articles to profl. jours. Commr., Gov.'s Task Force on Low Level Waste, 1981-84; mem. ofcl. bd. Mo. United Meth. Ch., Columbia, 1985. Served to 1st lt. AUS, 194-45, PTO. Mem. Am. Phys. Soc., Am. Nuclear Soc., Nat. Soc. Profl. Engrs., Mo. Soc. Profl. Engrs. (pres. Central chpt. 1978-79, trustee Ednl. Found. 1983—). Republican. Avocations: violinist, violist chamber and symphonic music. Home: 1311 Parkridge Dr Columbia MO 65203 Office: Dept Electrical and Computer Engineering Univ Missouri Columbia MO 65211

CARTER, ROY JEAN, agricultural organization specialist; b. Mt. Vernon, Mo., June 15, 1933, Vermanus P. and Bertha Jane (Evatt) C.; m. Peggy Sue Hughes, Mar. 29, 1956; children—Jeffrey, Randy J. B.S., SW Mo. State U., 1955; M.S., U. Mo., 1957; grad. student Colo. State U., 1966. Youth specialist U. Mo. Extension Ctr., Neosho, 1957—, office coordinator, 1984—; mem. adv. com., state curriculum com. State 4-H Office, Columbia, Mo., 1973—. Fund raiser Neosho United Fund, 1974—. Named Hon. Chpt. Farmer, Neosho Future Farmers Am., 1984. Mem. U. Mo. Extension Assn. (recipient Disting. Service award 1969, Meritorious Service award 1975), Nat. Assn. Extension Assn. (recipient Disting. Service award 1970), Mo. Extension 4-H Assn., Neosho C. of C. (flower box com. 1960, agr. com. 1969), Epsilon Sigma Phi. Club: Farm Bur. Avocation: Horticulture. Office: Univ Mo Extension Ctr Courthouse Basement Neosho MO 64850

CARTER, SALLY (SOPHIA), art shows consultant; b. Buffalo, Dec. 28, 1914; d. Frank and Caroline Walski; B.A., D'Youville Coll., 1936; postgrad. in Art, So. Ill. U., Edwardsville, 1969-75; m. Thad Robert Carter, Nov. 10, 1945; children—Susan V. Carter Penney, Robert Lloyd. Promoter, cons., curator local art shows, Alton, Ill., 1974—; active Friends of Art, dept. art and design So. Ill. U., Edwardsville, v.p., bd. dirs., 1981-85; chmn. ann. art competition Greater Miss. River Art Council., 1975-84; judge So. Ill. Artists Exhbn., 1982. Served to capt. USAF, 1942-45. Ill. Arts Council Chmn.'s grantee. Mem. Greater Miss. River Art Council. Republican. Roman Catholic. Home: 3750 Aberdeen Ave Alton IL 62002

CARTER, SHIRLEY M. BRYANT, counselor; b. Chgo., Nov. 5, 1949; d. Robert L. and Minnie Ferguson (Amerson) Bryant; B.S. with honors, Chgo. State U., 1974; M.S., 1978; m. Naggie L. Carter, Jr., Nov. 18, 1967; children—Kathryn, Nycole, Tiyaka. Unit leader commn. div. Prudential Ins. Co., Chgo., 1969-71; psychotherapist Jackson Park Hosp., Chgo., 1978; tchr. Chgo. Bd. Edn., 1975—, counselor, 1978—. Pres., St. Elthelreda Sch. Bd., 1978-79; youth coordinator 1st Corinthians Ch., Chgo., 1979; mem. So. Bapt. Assn., 1979—, dir. Vacation Bible Sch., 1981, 82; dir. Christian Pre-Sch. Recipient cert. of honor Black Masters Hall of Fame, Chgo. Mem. Assn. Black Psychologists, Am. Personnel and Guidance Assn., Kappa Delta Pi. Baptist. Club: Brainerd Women's. Home: 8940 S Justine St Chicago IL 60620 Office: 4214 S St Lawrence Chicago IL 60653

CARTER, THOMAS EDWARD, business forms manufacturing company executive; b. Cedar Rapids, Iowa, June 12, 1952; s. Arthur Berry and Mary Alice (Harbor) C.; m. Jane Marie Gietl, Aug. 26, 1978; 1 child, Elizabeth Morgan. B.A. with honors, U. Iowa, 1974. Med. sales rep. Ives Labs., Inc., N.Y.C., 1976-79; regional sales mgr. Star Forms, Inc., Moline, Ill., 1979-83, div. mgr., 1984—. Club: Davenport Country. Avocations: golf; fishing. Office: Star Forms Inc 4414 River Dr Moline IL 61265

CARTER, THOMAS SMITH, JR., railroad executive; b. Dallas, June 6, 1921; s. Thomas S. and Mattie (Dowell) C.; B.S. in Civil Engring., So. Meth. U., 1944; m. Janet R. Hostetter, July 3, 1946; children—Diane, Susan Jean, Charles T., Carol Ruth. With M.-K.-T. R.R., 1946-54, chief engr., 1954-61, v.p. operations, 1961-66; v.p. KCS Ry. Co., L & A Ry. Co., 1966—; pres., dir. K.C.S. Ry., 1973—, chief exec. officer, 1981—, chmn. bd., 1983—; pres., dir. L & A Ry. Co., 1974—, chmn. bd., chief exec. officer, 1981—; dir. Kansas City So. Industries. Served with C.E., AUS, 1944-46. Registered profl. engr., Mo., Kans., Okla., Tex., La., Ark. Fellow ASCE; mem. Am. Ry. Engrs. Assn., Assn. Am. Railroads (dir. 1978—), Nat. Soc. Profl. Engrs. Office: 114 W 11th St Kansas City MO 64105

CARTER, WILLIAM BUTLER, seed co. exec.; b. St. Louis, Nov. 28, 1927; s. Sidney Ernest and Virginia Leah (Butler) C.; student Brown U., 1945-46; A.B., Washington U., 1948; m. Drucilla Davis Bryant, June 20, 1970; children—Nancy, Carolyn, Margaret, Mary, John, Robert, Jason. Pres., Corneli Seed Co., St. Louis, 1965-68; v.p. mktg. Keystone Seed Co., Hollister, Calif., 1968-69; with Asgrow Seed Co., Kalamazoo, Mich., 1969—, group mgr. market devel. and customer services, 1979-82, sr. product mgr., 1982—. Served with USN, 1945-46. Episcopalian. Home: 96 S Lake Doster Dr Plainwell MI 49080 Office: Asgrow Seed Co 5300 N 28th St Richland MI 49083

CARTER-BLUIETT, DEBRA ANN, physician; b. Indpls., Aug. 28, 1952; d. J. Richard and Edna M. Carter; 1 dau., Allyson D. B.A., Northwestern U., 1974; M.D., Ind. U., 1978. Intern, Meth. Hosp., Indpls., 1978-79, resident, 1979-82; practice medicine, specializing in family medicine; mem. staff Meth. Hosp., Winona Hosp., Wishard Hosp. Mem. Nat. Med. Assn., Am. Chem. Soc., Ind. Med. Assn., Alpha Kappa Alpha. Office: 3450 N Illinois St Indianapolis IN 46205

CARTON, THOMAS WILLIAM, JR., lawyer; b. Coshocton, Ohio, Sept. 25, 1948; s. Thomas William and Wanda O'Dell (Patterson) C.; m. Linda Theresa Sodini, June 20, 1970 (div. 1976); 1 child, Thomas William, III; m. Edith Eileen Colgin, Feb. 26, 1977; children—Matthew Christopher, Steven Patrick. B.A. Bowling Green U., 1970; J.D. summa cum laude, Ohio State U., 1973. Bar: Ohio 1973. Assot. Gingher & Christensen, Columbus, Ohio, 1973-76, Moritz & McClure, Columbus, 1976-79, Jones, Day, Reavis & Pogue, Columbus, 1979-81; asst. gen. counsel, asst. sec. Wendy's Internat., Inc., Dublin, Ohio, 1981—; v.p. Wendy's Capital Corp., Dublin, 1982—; faculty mem. Georgetown U., Washington, 1984, Ohio Corp. Counsel Inst., Columbus, 1984; mem. steering com. Ohio State U., Council Franchising Issues, Columbus, 1985. Trustee, Hemingway Homeowners Assn., Dublin, 1983—; mem. governing bd. Children's Hosp., Columbus, 1984—; gen. counsel, sec. Recreation Unlimited for Handicapped, Columbus, 1984—; chmn. fund drive Cystic Fibrosis Central Ohio chpt., Columbus, 1984—; mem. Ohio Dept Devel. Adv. Council. Mem. Ohio State Bar Assn., Columbus Bar Assn., ABA. Republican. Roman Catholic. Club: Ohio State U. Pres.'s (Columbus). Avocations: All sports, reading, triathlete. Home: 7072 Fitzgerald Dr Dublin OH 43017 Office: Wendy's Internat Inc 4288 W Dublin-Granville Rd Dublin OH 43017

CARTWRIGHT, HENRY ARTHUR, physician, urologist; b. Detroit, June 27, 1946; s. Arthur and Thelma Lee (Black) C.; m. Carol Susanne Major; children—Henry II, Michael. Student, U. Mich., 1963-66, M.D., 1972; B.S., Wayne State U., 1968. Diplomate Am. Bd. Urology. Intern Henry Ford Hosp., Detroit, 1972-73; gen. surgery resident, U. Mich., Ann Arbor, 1973-75; urology resident Henry Ford Hosp., Detroit, 1975-78; urologist Harper-Grace Hosps., Detroit, 1978—, Hutzel Hosp., Detroit, 1978—, Southwest Detroit Hosp., Detroit, 1978—. Founder Inner-City Med. Polit. Action Com., Detroit, 1983; sec. Detroit Med. Soc., 1984. Served to maj. USNGR, 1972-80. Recipient Disting. Service award Detroit Med. Soc., 1982. Fellow ACS; mem. Am. Urol. Assn., Wayne County Med. Soc. (legis. com.), Mich. State Med. Soc. (licensure and discipline com.). Avocations: boating; Great Lakes fishing; racquetball. Office: 3011 W Grand Blvd 1067 Fisher Bldg Detroit MI 48202

CARTWRIGHT, INEZ P. GESELL, concrete co. exec.; b. Fosston, Minn., Feb. 25, 1917; d. Elmer Olof and Esther Marie (Peterson) Solberg; student public schs.; m. William John Gesell, Dec. 31, 1938 (dec. 1975); children—William Lester, Gary John, Mary Ann; m. Myron R. Cartwright, Jan. 30, 1982. With Gesell Concrete Products Inc., Bagley, Minn., 1945—, pres., 1975—. Treas. ladies aux. St. Ann Roman Catholic Ch., Bagley. Home: 110 Lakeview Dr Bagley MN 56621 Office: Gesell Concrete Products Inc Route 2 Bagley MN 56621

CARTWRIGHT, MYRON ROGER, accountant, mayor; b. Shevlin, Minn., Apr. 15, 1919; s. Clayton Samuel and Esther Seamuela (Rydeen) C.; m. Winona June Mattson, Oct. 24, 1942 (dec. July 1979); children—Lynn Priscilla, Karen Colette, Tracy April; m. Inez Patricia Solberg, Jan. 30, 1982. Grad. French's Bus. Coll., Bemidji, Minn., 1937; B.A. in Acctg. magna cum laude, Coll. of St. Thomas, St. Paul, 1942. C.P.A., Minn., 1952. Instr. acctg. Coll. of St. Thomas, 1946-53; pvt. practice pub. acctg., St. Paul, 1946-52, as C.P.A., 1952—. Mayor of Bagley, Minn., 1985—; bd. dirs. Bagley Indsl. Devel. Corp. Served to capt. USMCR, 1942-45; maj. Res. Mem. Am. Inst. C.P.A.s, Minn. Soc. C.P.A.s, Am. Legion, Minn. Golf Assn. (dir. 1965-66), Minn. Pub. Golf Assn. (sec. 1965-66). Republican. Lutheran. Club: Twin Pines Golf (Bagley, Minn.). Home: 110 Lakeview Dr Bagley MN 56621 Office: City Hall Bagley MN 56621

CARTWRIGHT, PETER SWAIN, consulting engineer; b. Mpls., Dec. 2, 1937; s. Arvid Chapman and Katherine Elizabeth (Swain) C.; m. Carol Jean Dennison, Sept. 5, 1959; children—Michael, Thomas, Susan. B.S. in Chem. Engring., U. Minn., Mpls., 1961. Registered profl. engr., Minn. With engring. dept. 3M Co., St. Paul, 1960-66; mktg. mgr. Conwed Corp., St. Paul, 1966-69, Possis Corp., Mpls., 1969-72; nat. sales mgr. Plastics, Inc., St. Paul, 1972-74; dir. sales and mktg. Osmonics, Inc., Mpls., 1974-80; pres. C3 Internat., Mpls., 1980—. Mem. Bd. Edn., Ind. Sch. Dist. 282, 1975—. Mem. Am. Inst. Chem. Engrs., Am. Electroplaters Soc., Water Pollution Control Fedn., Am. Water Resources Assn., Water Quality Assn., Am. Cons. Engrs. Council, Water Supply Improvement Assn., Assn. Cons. Chemists and Chem. Engrs. Club: Kiwanis. Contbr. articles to profl. jours. Home: 3423 Maplewood Dr NE Minneapolis MN 55418 Office: 1933 W County Rd C2 Roseville MN 55113

CARTY, ANNE MARIE, educational administrator, nurse; b. Bklyn., May 23, 1925; d. Leo Joseph and Mary Cecelia (Kunsman) Louprette; m. Edward Joseph Carty, Oct. 16, 1948; children—Edward, Judith, Mary Beth, Leo. B.S.N., Adelphi U., 1947; M.A., Webster U., 1976; M.S.N., St. Louis U., 1984. Nursing instr. Wilson Tech. Ctr., Dix Hills, N.Y., 1969-72; nursing instr. St. Mary's Coll., O'Fallon, Mo., 1973-81, dir. dept. nursing, 1981—. Mem. Am. Nurses Assn. (dist. v.p. 1976-78), Sigma Theta Tau. Republican. Roman Catholic. Avocations: equestrian activities; jogging; needlework. Home: #1 Rheims Ct Lake St Louis MO 66367 Office: Saint Mary Coll Dept Nursing 200 N Main St O'Fallon MO 66366

CARUS, MILTON BLOUKE, chemical company executive, publisher; b. Chgo., June 15, 1927; s. Edward H. and Dorothy (Blouke) C.; m. Marianne Sondermann, Mar.3, 1951; children—Andre, Christine, Inga. B.S. in Elec. Engring., Calif. Inst. Tech., 1949; postgrad. Mexico City Coll., 1949, U. Freiburg, Fed. Republic Germany, 1949-51, Sorbonne, Paris, 1951. Devel. engr. Carus Chem. Co., Inc., LaSalle, Ill., 1951-55, asst. gen. mgr., 1955-61, exec. v.p., 1961-64, pres., 1964—; pres. Carus Corp., LaSalle, 1967—; editor Open Ct, Pub. Co., LaSalle, 1962-67, pub., pres., 1967—. Chmn. Ill. Valley Community Coll., Com., 1965-67; chmn. bd. Internat. Baccalaureate N.Am., 1980; co-trustee Hegeler Inst., 1968; mem. Nat. Council Ednl. Research, 1982-85, vice chmn., 1983-85; mem. IBO Council, Geneva, 1977—; bd. dirs. Internat. Bd. Books for Young People, 1984-85. Served with USNR, 1945-46. Mem. Ill. Valley Indsl. Assn. (pres. 1970—), Chem. Mfrs. Assn. (bd. dirs. 1972-77), Ill. C. of C. (edn. com. 1973, task force on future of edn. in Ill 1984), U.S. C. of C. (edn., employment and tng. com. 1981—), Phila Soc., LaSalle County Hist. Soc. (bd. dirs. 1979). Home: 2222 Chartres St Peru IL 61354 Office: Carus Corp 1500 8th St LaSalle IL 61301

CARUTHERS, BARBARA SUE APGAR, physician, educator; b. Guthrie, Okla., Oct. 4, 1943; d. Wallace Duke and Gloria Jayne (Glover) McMillin; m. Charles George Caruthers, Apr. 1, 1976; 1 dau., Larisa Ann. B.A. in Biology, Loretto Heights Coll., 1965; M.S. in Anatomy, U. Mich., 1968; M.D., Tex. Tech. Med. Sch., 1976. Diplomate Am. Bd. Family Practice, Am. Bd. Med. Examiners. Research asst. Parke Davis, Ann Arbor, Mich., 1965-66; research asst. Aerospace Med. Labs Wright-Patterson AFB, Ohio, 1968-70; instr. anatomy dept. Tex. Tech. U. Med. Sch., Lubbock, 1972-74, resident in family practice, 1976-79, clin. asst. prof., 1980-83; physician The Pavilion, Lubbock, 1981-83; sr. physician U. Mich. Hosp., dir. Gynecology Clinic, U. Mich. Health Service, health sci. instr. dept. family practice U. Mich., 1984—; mem. adv. Lubbock chpt. March of Dimes, 1972-74. mem. staff Meth. Hosp., St. Mary of the Plains Hosp., U. Mich. Hosp. Mem. Soroptimist Internat., 1979-81. Recipient Upjohn Achievement award, 1976, Psychiatry Achievement award, 1976; Soroptimist Internat. grantee, 1978-79. Mem. Am. Acad. Family Practice, Lubbock County Med. Soc., Tex. Med. Assn., Alpha Omega Alpha. Democrat. Mem. Ch. Latter Day Saints. Home: 884 Scio Meadow Ann Arbor MI 48103 Office: U Mich 207 Fletcher Ann Arbor MI 48109

CARVER, GERFORD CHESTER, mechanical engineer; b. Battle Creek, Mich., July 11, 1929; s. Chester Gerford and Gertrude Marguerite (Stock) C.; B.M.E., Mich. Technol. U., 1950; M.S., Chrysler Inst., 1956; m. Eleanor Anne Dunne, June 25, 1955; children—John, James, Marguerite, Elizabeth, William, Sara. Shop liaison engr., detailer Clark Equipment Co., Battle Creek, 1950; test engr. Chrysler Corp., Highland Park, Mich., 1952-55, welding engr., 1955-56; div. project engr. Midland Ross Corp., Cleve., 1956-62; chief engr. R.S.L. Corp., Cleve., 1962; account engr. A.O. Smith Corp., Milw., 1962—. Served in arty. U.S. Army, 1950-52. Registered profl. engr., Ohio. Mem. Soc. Automotive Engrs., Am. Welding Soc., Am. Soc. Metals, Engring. Soc. Milw. Clubs: Snowstar Ski (asst. head instr.) (Milw.). Home: 880 E Birch St Milwaukee WI 53217 Office: 3533 N 27th St Milwaukee WI 53216

CARVER, PATRICIA ANN, nurse; b. Hammond, Ind., Feb. 8, 1943; d. Johnie and Julia Mae (Johnson) Williams; m. John L. Glover, June 9, 1962 (div. 1966); children—Terrence B., Juliette R.; m. 2d, Roy A. Carver, July 8, 1972; 1 dau., Tiffany Arletha. Diploma Practical Nursing, Purdue U., 1968; A.S. in Nursing, Ind. U., Gary, 1980. Laundry worker St. Margaret Hosp., Hammond, Ind., 1963-64, lic. practical nurse, 1968-80, staff nurse operating room, 1980—; asst. dir. surgery Meth. Hosp., Gary, Ind., 1984, dir. surgery, 1985—; laundry worker Chapman Laundry, Hammond, 1966-67; mem. nursing audit com. St. Margaret Hosp., Hammond, 1981-83. Pres. Matrons Soc., Mt. Zion Bapt. Ch., Hammond, 1963-64, v.p. missionary dept., 1966-67. Recipient Suggestion award St. Margaret Hosp., 1974, 75, 79; Nursing Scholarship, Midtown Registered Nurses Club, 1979. Mem. Assn. Operating Room Nurses (pres. Northwestern Ind. chpt.), Midtown Registered Nurses Club (corr. sec. 1983, co-chmn. scholarship 1982-83). Democrat. Baptist. Home: 1007 Bauer St Hammond IN 46320

CARVER, RICHARD E., mayor, lumber company executive; b. Des Moines, Aug. 28, 1937; s. Maurice Swan and Alice Cecilia (Ellison) C.; m. Judith S. Corley, July 18, 1959; children—Kathryn, Stephen, Cynthia, Susan. B.S., Bradley U., 1959. Pres., Carver Lumber Co., 1962—; alderman City of Peoria (Ill.), 1969-73, mayor, 1973—; dir. Provident Fed. Savs. & Loan Assn. Peoria, L. R. Nelson Mfg. Co. Bd. dirs. Methodist Med. Ctr. Ill.; mem. nat. council advisors Bradley U. Coll. Bus. Adminstrn.; past mem. Pres.'s Adv. Commn. on Intergovtl. Relations; chmn. energy adv. com. Ill. Dept. Local Govt. Affairs; del. UN Conf. on Human Settlements, 1976; mem. exec. com. Republican Nat. Com.; del. Rep. Nat. Conv., 1976. Served to lt. USAF, 1959-62. Named Tri-County Citizen of Yr., 1974; Peoria's Most Outstanding Man of Yr., 1974; recipient B'nai B'rith Citizenship award, 1974; Citizen of Yr. award Magnificent Gentlemen, Inc., 1974; Citizenship award Peoria C. of C., 1977; Internat. Communication Achievement award Toastmasters, 1979. Mem. Ill. State C. of C. (dir., exec. com.), Nat. League of Cities (adv. council), U.S. Conf. Mayors (exec. com., legislation action com., past pres.), Ill. Employment and Tng. Council, Nat. Conf. Rep. Mayors (past pres.), Ill. Municipal League (v.p.). Office: 207 City Hall Bldg Peoria IL 61602*

CARY, ARLENE D., hotel company sales executive; b. Chgo., Dec. 19, 1930; d. Seymour S. and Shirley L. (Land) C.; student U. Wis., 1949-52; B.A., U. Miami, 1953; m. Elliot D. Hagle, Dec. 30, 1972 (div.). Public relations account exec. Robert Howe & Co., 1953-55; sales mgr. Martin B. Iger & Co., 1955-57; sales mgr., gen. mgr. Sorrento Hotel, Miami Beach, Fla., 1957-59; gen. mgr. Mayflower Hotel, Manomet, Mass., 1959-60; various positions Aristocrat Inns of Am., 1960-72; v.p. sales, McCormick Center Hotel, Chgo., 1972—. Active Nat. Women's Polit. Caucus, Internat. Orgn. Women Execs., membership promotion chmn., 1979-80, bd. dirs., 1980-81. Recipient disting. salesman award Sales and Mktg. Execs. Internat., 1977. Mem. Profl. Conv. Mgmt. Assn., Nat. Assn. Exposition Mgrs., Hotel Sales Mgmt. Assn., Meeting Planners Internat., Chgo. Soc. Assn. Execs. Jewish. Home: 1130 S Michigan Ave Apt 3203 Chicago IL 60605 Office: Mc Cormick Center Hotel 23d and Lake Shore Dr Chicago IL 60616

CARY, JOHN MILTON, physician; b. Ewing, Mo., July 11, 1932; s. Milton Madison and Alice (Sells) C.; A.B., Central Coll. Mo., 1954; M.D., St. Louis U., 1958; m. Barbara Ann Dorsey, June 4, 1955; children—Kimberly Anne Cary Kelce, John Madison. Diplomate Am. Bd. Internal Medicine. Intern, Barnes Hosp., St. Louis, 1958-59, resident in internal medicine, 1959-60, subsequently mem. staff; resident in internal medicine St. Lukes Hosp., St. Louis, 1961-62, subsequently mem. staff; fellow in hematology Washington U., St. Louis, 1960-61; practice medicine specializing in internal medicine, St. Louis, 1962—; mem. staff St. Johns Mercy Med. Center; clin. instr. Washington U., 1966—. Mem. ACP, N.Y. Acad. Scis., AAAS, St. Louis Soc. Internal Medicine, Mo. Med. Assn., St. Louis Med. Soc., Alpha Omega Alpha. Presbyterian. Home: 1541 Arbuckle Dr Saint Louis MO 63017 Office: 224 S Woods Mill Rd Saint Louis MO 63017

CARYER, JAMES LEROY, vocational educator; b. Defiance, Ohio, Dec. 12, 1926; s. Thomas Leo and Thelma Irene C.; m. Ruth Ann Hoffman, Nov. 24, 1972; children—Keith, Randal, Sally. Theol. cert. Olivet Nazarene Coll., Kankakee, Ill. Ordained to ministry Ch. of Nazarene, 1955. Machinist, Wayne Pump Co., Fort Wayne, Ind., 1944-46, IHC, 1946-48, Florance Stove Co., Kankakee, 1948-50, Bradley Improvement Co., Kankakee, 1950-53; salesman Montgomery Ward Co., Portsmouth, Ohio, 1953-63; instr. machine trades Pub. Schs. Marion (Ohio), 1963—. Instr. Sunday sch. Ch. Nazarene, 1948. Mem. Ohio Vocat. Assn., Am. Vocat. Assn., Ministerial Assn., FFA (hon.).

CASADABAN, MALCOLM JOHN, molecular biologist; b. New Orleans, Aug. 12, 1949; s. John Adrian and Dolores Anna (Poche) C.; m. Joany Chou, June 19, 1977; 1 child, Brooke Lori. S.B., MIT, 1971; Ph.D., Harvard U., 1976; postgrad. Stanford U., 1976-69. Research fellow Stanford U., Palo Alto, Calif., 1976-79; asst. prof. molecular genetics and cell biology U. Chgo., 1980-85, assoc. prof., 1985—. Contbr. articles to profl. jours. Mem. Am. Soc. Microbiology, AAAS. Club: Chgo. Prokaryotic Molecular Biology, Midwest Yeast. Home: 5227 S Kimbark St Chicago IL 60615 Office: U Chgo 920 E 58th St Chicago IL 60637

CASALE, OTTAVIO MARK, dean, English educator; b. Cleve., Jan. 23, 1934; s. Ottavio and Natalina (D'Arienzo) C.; m. Linda Lee Lenaway, Jan. 27, 1962; children—Laura, Elizabeth. B.A., Kent State U., 1955; M.A., U. Mich.-Ann Arbor, 1959, Ph.D., 1965. Prof. English Kent State U., Ohio, 1965—, dean honors coll., 1981—; Editor: The Kent Affair, 1971; editor, translator A Leopardi Reader, 1981. Served with U.S. Army, 1955-57. Woodrow Wilson Woodrow Wilson Found. fellow, 1958-59; NEH translation grantee, 1978; Fulbright lectr., Italy, 1971-72. Mem. MLA, Phi Beta Kappa, Omicron Delta Kappa. Democrat. Avocations: opera, Mozart, sports. Home: 815 Bryce Rd Kent OH 44240 Office: Kent State U Kent OH 44242

CASCINO, MARY DORY, business executive; b. Chgo., Dec. 21, 1949; d. V. Paul and Vada L. (Tuttle) Dory; A.B., Loyola U., Chgo., 1971; M.A., U. Chgo., 1972; m. Anthony E. Cascino, Jr., July 28, 1973; children—Anthony E. III, Christine Ann, Caroline Stephanie. Asso. planner, local service specialist Northeastern Ill. Planning Commn., 1972-76; self-employed park and recreation planner, Highland Park, Ill., 1976-80; owner Mary Anne Products, Glencoe, Ill., 1981—. Candidate for alderman City of Chgo., 1971; sec. Glencoe PTA; mem. women's bd. Union League, Chgo. Mem. Am. Planning Assn. Author: Bicycle Safety Planning Guide. Home and Office: 385 Lincoln Ave Glencoe IL 60022

CASE, KEELA IRENE, mental health counselor; b. Lincoln County, Kans., Apr. 29, 1922; d. Glenn Raymond and Atha Jane (Montgomery) Jones; B.A., Ft. Hays (Kans.) State U., 1970, M.S., 1971; m. Cleo Clarence Case, Feb. 9, 1941; children—Colleen, Colin, C. Wayne. Mental health counselor High Plains Comprehensive Community Mental Health Center br. office, Colby, Kans., 1971-77, dir. br. office, 1977-82; cons. in field. Mem. AAUW, Am. Assn. Counseling and Devel., Kans. Assn. Counseling and Devel. Am. Mental Health Counselors Assn., Kans. Mental Health Counselors Assn. Phi Delta Kappa. Democrat. Episcopalian. Club: Order Eastern Star. Home: 550 S Grant Colby KS 67701 Office: 135 W 6th St Colby KS 67701

CASE, NORMAN H., manufacturers representative company executive; b. Cleve., Jan. 29, 1932; s. Maxwell B. and Helen Mildred (Lambert) C.; m. Sally Ann Birchard, Mar. 31, 1956; children—Cheryl Ann, Dale Alan. Student, Nat. Radio Sch., 1957-1961. Pres., sales engr. Norm Case Assocs., Rocky River, Ohio, 1967—. Republican precinct committeemen, Rocky River, Ohio, 1963-64; mem. Rocky River Rec. Commn.; mem., pres. Rocky River Bd. Edn., 1975—. Served to cpl. USMC, 1952-54. Republican. Methodist. Lodge: Masons. Home: 22266 Rivergate Dr Rocky River OH 44116 Office: 21010 Center Ridge Rd Rocky River OH 44116

CASE, WILLIAM ROBERT, county official; b. Mpls., July 15, 1921; s. Delbert V. and Nellie (Castonguay) C.; m. Dorothy A. Sheets, July 15, 1953; children—William, Christopher, Catherine. Student, Grinnell Coll., 1944; B.A. in Polit. Sci., U. Kans., 1949, M.A. in Pub. Adminstrn. (Carnegie fellow), 1950. Assoc., Adache Assocs., Inc., Cleve., 1952-58; sr. assoc., cons. Lawrence-Leiter & Co., mgmt. cons., Kansas City, Mo., 1958-60; asst. to gen. mgr. Pitman Mfg. Co., Grandview, Mo., 1960-62, dir. personnel and indsl. relations, br. mgr., 1964-66; gen. mgr. Case Engring. Assocs., Inc., cons. engrs., 1966-71; dir. dept. pub. works, coordinator EEO Office, County of Midland (Mich.), 1972-74, coordinator CETA office, 1974-79, county treas., 1979—; past chmn. City Commn. on Community Relations. County chmn. Midland County United Way; lector, eucharistic minister Blessed Sacrament Roman Catholic. Ch.; past chmn. Adult Edn. Adv. Council; precinct del. Midland County Republican Exec. Com., 1980, 82, 84; del. Rep. State Conv., 1984, 85. Served with U.S. Army, 1943-46. Decorated European Theatre medal with two bronze stars, Victory medal, Pacific Theatre medal. Mem. Mich. Assn. County Treas. (sec., trustee), United County Officers Assn. (bd. reps.), Midland County Econ. Devel. Corp. (bd. dirs.), Midland County C. of C., Am. Soc. Pub. Adminstrs., Mcpl. Fin. Officers Assn., Internat. City Mgrs. Assn., Mich. Assn. Govtl. Computer Users. Clubs: Kiwanis (pres. 1984-85), Rep. Breakfast, KC. Home: 4416 Concord St Midland MI 48640 Office: County Courthouse 301 W Main St Midland MI 48640

CASEY, EDWARD PAUL, manufacturing company executive; b. Boston, Feb. 23, 1930; s. Edward J. and Virginia (Paul) C.; A.B., Yale, 1952; M.B.A., Harvard, 1955; m. Patricia Pinkham, June 23, 1950; children—Patricia Casey Shepherd, Lucile Tyler Casey Arnote, Jennifer Paul Casey Schwab, Sheila Pinkham Casey McManus, Virginia Louise. With Davidson Rubber Co., Dover, N.H., 1950—, pres., 1965—, dir., 1950—; pres. McCord Corp., Detroit, 1965-78, also dir.; chmn., pres., chief exec. officer Ex-Cell-O Corp., Troy, Mich., also dir.; dir. Mfrs. Nat. Corp. Detroit. Mem. finance com. Citizens Research Council of Mich.; mem. president's council U. N.H.; trustee Henry Ford Health Care Corp., Detroit; bd. dirs. Detroit Symphony Orch., United Found., Machinery and Allied Products Inst., Detroit Renaissance, Econ. Club of Detroit, Automotive Hall of Fame, Inc.; mem. adv. council Jr. Achievement, Detroit Area council Boy Scouts Am., fin. com. Citizens Research Council Mich. Mem. Engring. Soc. Detroit, Soc. Automotive Engrs., Harvard Bus. Sch. Club Detroit. Clubs: Detroit, Yondotega (Detroit); Grosse Pointe; Country Club of Detroit (Grosse Pointe Farms, Mich.); Bloomfield Hills (Mich.) Country; Eastern Yacht (Marblehead, Mass.); N.Y. Yacht (N.Y.C.); Wig and Pen (London, Eng.); Bath and Tennis (Palm Beach, Fla.). Home: 4 Rathbone Pl Grosse Pointe MI 48230 Office: Ex-Cello-O Corp 2855 Coolidge Troy MI 48084

CASEY, JOHN MICHAEL, construction company executive; b. Detroit, Dec.11, 1930; s. Michael John and Agnes Mary (Brodrick) C.; m. Dolores Jean Mancuso, Apr.7, 1954; children—Barbara, Kathleen, Joanne, Sue, Mary, Tim, Martin. B.S., U. Wis.-Madison, 1950; M.B.A., U. Detroit, 1953; postgrad. Harvard U., 1961, Georgetown U., 1966. Vice pres. Perron Constrn. Co., Detroit, 1954-58; pres. Pyramid Constrn. Co., Detroit, 1958-60; mgr. Chrysler Corp., Troy, Mich., 1960-70; pres. Derry Corp., Southfield, Mich., 1970-75, Wellesley Constrn. Co., West Bloomfield, Mich., 1975-82; v.p., dir. mktg. Pioneer Co., Madison Heights, Mich., 1982—; dir. Robotic Peripherals, Troy, Slaco Tool Co., Redford, Mich., Novi Bank and Trust, Mich., Liberty Mfg. Co., Wall Lake, Mich. Author: Building for Profit, 1974; What It Takes To Do Business in China, 1983. Pres. Big Bros., Detroit, 1966-70; bd. dirs. United Way, Detroit, 1971-76, ARC, Detroit, 1974- 78. Named Man of Yr., Jr. C. of C., Detroit, 1966. Mem. Irish-Am. Cultural Inst. (v.p. 1981—), Am. Def. Preparedness Assn., Soc. Automotive Engrs., Am. Home Builders Assn. (v.p. 1974-76), Nat. Home Builders Assn. Republican. Roman Catholic. Clubs: 100, President (Detroit). Lodges: Elks, K.C. Home: 26040 Ivanhoe St Redford MI 48239

CASEY, JOHN P., educator; b. Pitts., May 26, 1920; s. Patrick F. Casey; B.A., Bethany (W.Va.) Coll., 1949; M.Ed., U. Pitts., 1950; Ed.D. in Secondary Edn., Ind. U., 1963; m. Eileen Casey; children—Charles, Carol. Tchr. Columbus (Ohio) public schs., 1950-59; asst. prof. Ill. State U., Normal, 1959-63; div. chmn. dept. social sci. Northwestern Coll., Orange City, Iowa, 1963-64; asst. prof. So. Ill. U., Carbondale, 1964-69, assoc. prof. dept. spl. edn. and profl. edn. experiences, 1969-73, prof., 1973—, dir. Talent Retrieval and Devel. Edn. Project (TRADE), 1965-78. Served with U.S. Army. Mem. Ill. Assn. Curriculum Devel., Ill. Assn. Tchr. Educators, Phi Delta Kappa. Certified tchr., Ill., Ohio. Research supervision, research and teaching gifted children. Co-author: Roles in Off-Campus Student Teaching, 1967. Contbr. articles to profl. jours. Home: 623 Glenview Dr Carbondale IL 62901 Office: Coll Edn So Ill U Carbondale IL 62901

CASEY, JULIA KELLER, lawyer; b. Rochester, N.Y, Sept. 12, 1946; d. Henry and Jane (Palmer) Keller; m. David William Casey, June 10, 1966 (div. Jan. 1976); 1 child, Henry Keller. B.A., U. Wash., 1968; J.D., U. Toledo, 1973. Bar: Ohio 1974, U.S. Dist. Ct. (no. and so. dists.) Ohio 1974, U.S. Dist. Ct. (we. dist.) N.Y. 1974, Assoc. Kaplan & Lehman, Toledo, 1973-75, Casey & Slaybod, Toledo, 1976—; chmn. Advisors Basic Legal Equality, Toledo, 1978-81, dir., 1981—; chmn. Juvenile Law Com., Toledo, 1983—. Author: Julia, 1978. Contbr. articles to profl. jours. Foster mother Ohio Youth Commn., Toledo, 1973—. Recipient, Am. Jurisprudence Price award, 1969-73. Mem. Toledo Bar Assn., Women Involved Toledo. Home: 2557 Greenway Toledo OH 43607 Office: 420 Spitzer Bldg Toledo OH 43604

CASEY, MARY THERESE, nursing educator, nurse; b. Chappell, Nebr., Mar. 28, 1954; d. Lawrence James and Mary Phyllis (Dymond) C. B.S.N., Fort Hays State U., 1975; M.S. in Nursing, U. Tex.-Austin, 1982. Advanced registered nurse practitioner. Aide, grad. nurse, charge nurse obstetrics and surg. St. Anthony's Hosp., Hays, Kans., 1975-78; charge nurse high risk surgery Bay Area Hosp., Coos Bay, Oreg., 1978-79; charge nurse obstetrics St. Anthony's Hosp., Hays, Kans., 1979-80; nursing instr. Fort Hays State U., Hays, 1980-81, asst. prof. nursing, 1982—; staff labor and delivery St. Francis Hosp., Topeka, Kans., 1984-85, clin. nurse specialist in obstetrics, 1985—; cons. Am. Nursing Resources, Kansas City, Kans., 1983—. St. Anthony's Hosp. scholar, 1975; Wagner fellow Fort Hays State U. Sch. Nursing, 1981-82. Mem. Am. Nurses' Found., Am. Nurses Assn. (council high-risk perinatal nurses 1982—), Nat. League Nursing, Nat. Assn. Pro-Life Nurses, Kans. State Nurses' Assn. (dist. sec., bd. dirs., exec. bd. 1983-86, rep. to children's Coalition 1983-86, rep. to Kans. Council on Children and Youth 1983-86), Kans. League Nursing, Fort Hays State U. Faculty Assn., Fort Hays State U. Faculty Women's Assn., LWV, Nat. Wildlife Fedn., Audubon Soc., Sierra Club, Sigma Theta Tau, Phi Kappa Phi, Alpha Lambda Delta. Roman Catholic. Home: 5104 W 33d St Topeka KS 66614 Office: St Francis Hosp 1700 W 7th St Topeka KS 66612

CASEY, MURRAY JOSEPH, physician, educator; b. Armour, S.D., May 1, 1936; s. Meryl Joseph and Gladice (Murray) C.; student Chanute Jr. Coll., 1954-55, Rockhurst Coll., 1955-56; A.B., U. Kans., 1958; M.D., Georgetown U., 1962; postgrad. Suffolk U. Law Sch., 1963-64, Howard U., 1965; m. Virginia Anne Fletcher; children—Murray Joseph, Theresa Marie, Anne Franklin, Francis X., Peter Colum., Matthew Padraic. Intern, USPHS Hosp.-Univ. Hosp., Balt., 1962-63; staff physician USPHS Hosp., Boston, 1963-64; staff asso. Lab Infectious Diseases, Nat. Inst. Allergy and Infectious Diseases, NIH, Bethesda, Md., 1964-66; virologist, resident physician Columbia-Presbyn. Med. Ctr., also Francis Delafield Hosp., N.Y.C., 1966-69; USPHS sr. clin. trainee, 1969-70; fellow gynecol. oncology, resident dept. surgery Meml. Hosp. Cancer and Allied Diseases, Meml. Sloan-Kettering Cancer Ctr., N.Y.C., 1969-71, Am. Cancer Soc. fellow, 1969-71; ofcl. observer in radiotherapy U. Tex. M.D. Anderson Hosp. and Tumor Inst., Houston, 1971; vis. scientist Radiumhemmet Karolinska Sjukhuset and Inst., Stockholm, 1971; asst. prof. ob-gyn U. Conn. Sch. Medicine, 1971-75, asso. prof., 1975-80, dir. gynecologic oncology, 1971-80, also mem. med. bd.; prof., asso. chmn. dept. ob-gyn U. Wis. Med. Sch., 1980—; chief ob-gyn, dir. gynecologic oncology Mt. Sinai Med. Ctr., Milw., 1980-82, also mem. med. exec. com.; chmn. research adv. com., mem. council Conn. Cancer Epidemiology Unit; bd. dirs., mem. exec. com., chmn. profl. edn. com. Hartford unit. Am. Cancer Soc., dir. Milw. div.; mem. med. services 1980 Winter Olympic Games, Lake Placid, N.Y.; mem. med. supervisory team U.S. Nordic Ski Team. Diplomate Am. Bd. Med. Examiners, Am. Bd. Ob-Gyn. Fellow Am. Coll. Obstetricians and Gynecologists, ACS; mem. AAAS, N.Y. Acad. Scis., Am. Soc. Colposcopy, Am. Fertility Soc., Soc. Gynecologic Oncologists, New Eng. Assn. Gynecologic Oncologists (pres. 1980-81), Am. Geriatric Soc., Internat. Menopause Soc., Soc. Meml. Gynecologic Oncologists (pres. exec. bd.; pres. 1982-83), Lake Placid Sports Medicine Soc. (v.p. 1981-84, pres. 1984—), Cedarburg C. of C. (Ambassadors com., dir. 1983—), St. George Soc. Contbr. articles to profl. jours., chpts. to books. Research in oncogenesis and tumor immunology.

Home: Cedarburg WI 53012 Office: Dept Ob-Gyn U Wis Med Sch Milw Clin Campus PO Box 342 Milwaukee WI 53201

CASEY, PATRICK MICHAEL, computer company executive; b. Cazanovia, Wis., Nov. 21, 1930; s. William Robert and Anastasia Veronica (Walsh) C.; grad. Indsl. Mgmt., U. Minn., 1959, Assoc. in Adminstrv. Mgmt., 1966; M.B.A., Nat. Coll. Arts and Scis., 1978; m. Donna Rae Robushin, Apr. 13, 1933; children—Michele Ann, Timothy William, Patrick Sean, Kevin Matthew, Kathleen Marie, Colin Brian, Maureen Bridget. With Sperry, St. Paul, 1956—, v.p. Sperry Tech. Services Div., 1975—; tchr. adult vocat. classes in data processing; cons. on computer aided instrn. systems to sch. dists. Chm. Sch. Dist. 272, 1964-70; dir. Hennepin County Vocational Tech. Dist. 287, 1971-76; mem. Eden Prairie Planning and Zoning Bd., 1974. Served with USN, 1948-52. Republican. Roman Catholic. Club: Lions. Home: 181 Birnamwood Dr Burnsville MN 55337 Office: PO Box 3525 Saint Paul MN 55165

CASEY, ROBERT DILLON, JR., advertising publications company executive; b. Evanston, Ill., Apr. 27, 1955; s. Robert Dillon and Rosemary Ann (O'Riley) C.; m. Joan Elizabeth McCarthy, Sept. 28, 1984. B.A. in Fin., U. Ill., 1977. Spl. agt. Northwestern Mut. Life Ins. Co., Chgo., 1978-79; dist. sales rep. Gordon Publs., Chgo., 1979-85, regional office mgr., 1980-85; ind. sales rep. Walker Davis Publs.-Midwest, Chgo., 1985—; group leader sales course Dale Carnegie, Chgo., 1985. Mem. Bus. and Profl. Advt. Assn. Republican. Club: Adult Outdoors (sec. 1984). Avocations: skiing; camping; horseback riding; jogging; reading. Home: 507 Opatrny Dr Fox River Grove IL 60021 Office: Walker Davis Publs-Midwest Suite 330 1 Northfield Plaza Northfield IL 60093

CASH, JERRY NEAL, food science and nutrition educator; b. Lonoke, Ark., Dec. 16, 1942; s. Neal H. and Lou E. (Gilliam) C.; m. Stella F. Hall, Aug. 25, 1962; children—Shannon Lynn, Stephanie Kai. B.S., Ark. State Tchrs. Coll., Conway, 1965; M.S., State Coll. Ark., Conway, 1967; Ph.D., U. Ark., 1975. Industry mgmt. trainee, 1965-66; grad. teaching asst. biology State Coll. Ark., 1966-67; research asst. hort. food sci. U. Ark., 1967-75; asst. prof., extension specialist food sci. and human nutrition Mich. State U., East Lansing, 1975-79, assoc. prof., extension specialist, 1979—; chmn. Nat. Conf. Highlights in Food Sci., 1978-80; referee, reviewer jour. articles and books; cons. field services div. Sunkist Growers, Inc. of Calif., Calif. Frozen Vegetable Council, Potato Chip/Snack Food Assn. Mem. Inst. Food Technologists (chmn. Gt. Lakes sect.), Potato Assn. Am., Am. Soc. Hort. Sci., Mich. Hort. Soc., Mich. Assn. Extension Specialists, Sigma Xi, Phi Tau Sigma. Methodist. Contbr. articles and abstracts to profl. jours. Home: 2759 Southwood Dr East Lansing MI 48823 Office: 139 Food Science Bldg Mich State U East Lansing MI 48824

CASH, JOSEPH HARPER, coll. adminstr., historian; b. Mitchell, S.D., Jan. 3, 1927; s. Joseph R. and Claudia B. (Harper) C.; B.A., U. S.D., 1949; M.A., 1959; Ph.D., U. Iowa, 1966; m. Margaret Ann Halla, Dec. 18, 1952; children—Sheridan Lisa, Joseph Mark, Meredith Ann. Tchr. public schs., S.D., 1951-62; instr. Black Hills State Coll., summer 1961; grad. asst. U. Iowa, 1962-65; asso. prof. history Eastern Mont. Coll., 1965-68; research asso. Inst. Indian Studies, U. S.D., summer 1967, 68, dir. inst. div. Indian research, 1970-77, acting dir. inst., 1976-77, asso. prof., 1970-74, Duke research prof. history, 1972—, prof., 1974—, dean Coll. Arts and Scis., 1977—; dir. Am. Indian Research Project, State of S.D., 1969-74, dir. S.D. Oral History Project, 1970-74, dir. Oral History Center (merger both projects), 1974-77; chmn. S.D. Bd. Hist. Preservation, 1970-73; chmn. council dirs., cultural pres. div. State S.D., 1975-76; mem. S.D. Council on Humanities, 1975-77, S.D. Hist. Records Adv. Bd., 1976—, S.D. Bd. Cultural Preservation, 1977—, Kampgrounds of Am.-U. Adv. Bd., 1978—. Served with USMCR, 1945-46. Recipient award of merit Am. Assn. State and Local History, 1975. Mem. Am. Hist. Assn., Oral History Assn., Orgn. Am. Historians, S.D. Hist. Soc. (pres. 1977—), Western History Assn., Phi Beta Kappa, Phi Delta Theta. Republican. Author 6 Indian Tribal Series books, 1971-76; author: (with Herbert T. Hoover) To Be An Indian, 1971; Working the Homestake, 1973; The Practice of Oral History, 1974; gen. editor: American Indian Oral History Collection, 1977; bd. editors Rocky Mountain Rev., 1966-68, Midwest Rev., S.D. History. Office: Coll Arts and Scis U SD Vermillion SD 57069

CASILIO-LONARDO, EMILIA ELIZABETH, medical research technologist; b. Buffalo, May 10, 1954; d. Mario C. and Rose (Stefanacci) Casilio; m. Anthony Joseph Lonardo, May 19, 1984. B.S., SUNY-Geneseo, 1975; student in Med. Tech., Buffalo Gen. Hosp., 1977; M.S., Western State U., 1981. Cert. med. technologist. Med. technologist, Buffalo Gen. Hosp., 1976-79; med. research technologist Cleve. Clinic Found., 1979—. Active St. Gregory Family Ctr., S. Euclid Ohio, 1983-85, St. Gregory Cath. Renewal, S. Euclid, 1984-85; mem. S. Euclid Library Assn., 1984-85. Western State Found. research grantee, 1978. Mem. Am. Soc. Clin. Pathologists, Am. Human Genetics Soc., Am. Soc. Histocompatibility and Immunogenetics, N.E. Ohio Transplantation Soc. Roman Catholic. Club: Severance Athletic. Avocations: Gourmet cooking; flying small planes; gardening. Office: Cleveland Clinic Found 9500 Euclid Ave Cleveland OH 44106

CASKEY, HAROLD LEROY, state senator; b. Bates County, Mo., Jan. 3, 1938; s. James Alfred and Edith Irene (Anderson) C.; A.B., Central Mo. State U., 1960; J.D., U. Mo., Columbia, 1963; m. Kay Head, 1974; children—Kyle James. Pros. atty., Bates County, 1967-72; city atty., Butler, Mo., 1973-76; individual practice law, Butler, Mo.; asst. prof. NE Mo. State U., 1975-76; mem. Mo. Senate, 1977—. Mem. Mo. Bar Assn., Am. Judicature Soc., Fellowship Christian Politicians, Am. Criminal Justice Educators, Order Coif, Acacia, Phi Alpha Delta, Kappa Mu Epsilon, Alpha Phi Sigma. Baptist. Lodge: Rotary. Office: State Capitol Jefferson City MO 65101*

CASKEY, JERRY ALLAN, chemical engineering educator; b. Galion, Ohio, Sept. 8, 1938; s. Charles S. and Josephine (Williams) C.; m. Martha Ray Baetzold, Jan. 21, 1963; children—Charles, Larry, Kevin. B.S. in Chem. Engring., Ohio U., 1961; M.S. in Chem. Engring., Clemson U. (S.C.), 1963, Ph.D. in Chem. Engring., 1965. Registered profl. engr., Ind. Research engr. Dow Chem. Co., Midland, Mich., 1965-67; asst. prof. chem. engring. Va. Inst. Tech., Blacksburg, 1967-72; assoc. prof. Rose-Hulman Inst., Terre Haute, Ind., 1973-76, prof., 1976—; vis. research prof. Israel Inst. Tech., Haifa, 1972. Contbr. chpt. to book. Asst. scoutmaster Wabash Valley council Boy Scouts Am., 1977-79; bd. dirs. Wabash Valley Youth for Christ, Terre Haute, 1982-84. NSF grantee, 1974-76, 1977-80; named Outstanding Tchr. Triangle Fraternity, 1979. Mem. Am. Inst. Chem. Engrs. (sec. local chpt. 1977-81), Am. Soc. Engring. Edn. (chmn. div. program 1985). Avocations: Running, swimming. Home: 7016 Wabash Ave Terre Haute IN 47803 Office: Rose-Hulman Inst 5500 Wabash Ave Terre Haute IN 47803

CASLER, JAMES DON, hospital administrator; b. Sanford, Maine, Oct. 20, 1949; s. Donald Faye and Pauline Meta (Koepke) C.; m. Jacqueline Sue Klein, June 12, 1971; children—Scott Allen, Amy Marie. B.A., Hastings Coll. (Nebr.), 1971. C.P.A., Nebr. Mem. audit staff Arthur Andersen & Co., Omaha, 1971-77, audit mgr., 1977-78; controller, chief fin. officer Good Samaritan Hosp., Kearney, Nebr., 1978-80, acting adminstr., 1980-81, sr. v.p., 1981—. Mem. Am. Inst. C.P.A.s, Nebr. Soc. C.P.A.s, Healthcare Fin. Mgmt. Assn. (pres. Ak-Sar-Ben chpt. 1985-86, sec. 1983-84). Democrat. Lutheran. Clubs: Sertoma, Kearney Country. Lodges: Elks. Avocations: golf; racquetball; chess; reading; photography. Home: 4638 Parklane Dr Kearney NE 68847 Office: Good Samaritan Hosp 31st St and Central Ave Kearney NE 68847

CASSIDY, DWANE ROY, insulation contracting co. exec.; b. Bedford, Ind., Oct. 20, 1915; s. Leo Clayton and Lilly Fay (Robbins) C.; student Roscoe Turner's Sch. Aviation, 1944; m. Mary Catherine Shrout, Aug. 28, 1937; children—Gail (Mrs. Gordon Everling), Cheryl, Duane, Nina (Mrs. Robert McAnulty). With L. C. Cassidy & Son, Inc., Indpls., 1934—, now v.p.; v.p. L.C. Cassidy & Sons, Inc. of Fla., 1963—. Served with USN, 1944-45; PTO. Mem. Gideons Internat. Methodist. (dir.). Club: Optimists (Indpls.). Home: 644 Lawndale St Plainfield IN 46168 Office: 1918 S High School Rd Indianapolis IN 46241

CASSIDY, GERALD JOSEPH, restaurant chain executive; b. Chgo., Aug. 16, 1941; s. Joseph Patrick and Mary Rita (Gleason) C.; B.S. in Indsl. Econs., Purdue U., 1964; M.B.A., Old Dominion U., 1970; m. Jennie Jones; children—Lisa Kathleen, Mary Elizabeth, Darrin Christopher, Angela Rhonda, Gerald Joseph II. Fin. analyst Gen. Foods Corp., Lafayette, 1970-72; owner, pres. 7 McDonald's Restaurants, Inc., Tipton, Ind., 1973—, charter mem. McDonald's Corp. Operators' Adv. Bd., 1973-74; pres. Central Ind. McDonald's Operators Assn., 1975-76, advt. chmn., 1977-80, 83—; treas. Ind. bd. dirs. Ronald McDonald House, 1980-83, pres., 1984—; adv. com. Ronald McDonald Children's Charities Found., 1984—; lectr. Purdue U., 1969. Fin. chmn. Tipton County Republican Party, 1976-80, county chmn., 1980-81; founder Eagle Inst., Ctr. Human Growth and Achievement, 1984—. Served to lt. USN, 1966-70. Recipient McDonald's Ronald award for excellence in mktg., 1979; Sagamore of the Wabash award, Gov. of Ind., 1980 Mem. Tipton C. of C., Ind. Restaurant Assn., Purdue Pres.' Council, Sigma Pi. Republican. Roman Catholic. Clubs: Elks, Jaycees. Home: Box 6 Atlanta IN 46031 Office: Cassidy Restaurants PO Box 378 Tipton IN 46072

CASSIDY, JAMES MARK, construction company executive; b. Evanston, Ill., June 22, 1942; s. James Michael and Mary Ellen (Munroe) C.; B.A., St. Mary's Coll., 1963; m. Bonnie Marie Bercker, Aug. 1, 1964 (d. Dec. 1981); children—Micaela Marie, Elizabeth Ann, Daniel James; m. Patricia Margaret Mary Murphy, Sept. 15, 1984. Estimator, Cassidy Bros., Inc., Rosemont, Ill., 1963-65, project mgr., 1965-67, v.p., 1967-71, exec. v.p., 1971-77, pres., 1978—; trustee Plasterer's Health & Welfare Trust, 1971—. Area fund leader constrn. industry salute to Boy Scouts Am., 1975; mem. pres.'s council St. Mary's Coll.; chmn. labor liaison com. Laborers Internat. Union N.Am. and Assn. Wall and Ceiling Industries, 1982—; chmn. Chicagoland Assn. Wall and Ceiling Contractors' Carpenters Union Negotiating Team, 1983—. Served with U.S. Army, 1963-64, N.G., 1964-69. Mem. Chgo. Plastering Inst., Builder Uppers Club (pres. 1973-74), Chicagoland Assn. Wall and Ceiling Contractors (pres. 1976-79), Great Lakes Council, Internat. Assn. Wall and Ceiling Contractors (chmn. 1977), Constrn. Employers Assn. Chgo. (dir. 1976—, chmn. com. labor-mgmt. relations 1983—), Assn. Wall and Ceiling Industries (dir. 1978-81). Roman Catholic. Clubs: Abbey Springs Country (Fontana, Wis.); Park Ridge (Ill.) Country. Office: Cassidy Bros Inc PO Box 596 Rosemont IL 60018

CASSIN, CHARLES JOSEPH, financial executive; b. Chicago, Nov. 9, 1951; s. Edward Thomas and Charlotte Therse (Stack) C.; m. Deborah Marie Zurek. Jan. 5, 1974; children—Rebecca, Charles, Heather, Brian, Joseph. B.A., Lewis U., 1979. C.P.A., Ill. Staff acct. Combine Ins., Chgo., 1979-81; mgr. acctg. Security Casualty Ins., Chgo., 1981-82; mgr. fin. reporting Transamerica, Chgo., 1982—; pres. Cassin Acctg. Services, Lombard, Ill., 1979—. Treas. Pine Meadow Assn., Bolingbrook, Ill., 1977, Lombard Hist. Soc., 1985—. Mem. Am. Inst. C.P.A.'s, Ill. C.P.A.'s Assn., Salt Creek C.P.A.'s Assn. Office: Transamerica 175 W Jackson Chicago IL 60604

CASSOU, JAMES LEON, airline pilot; b. Santa Barbara, Calif., Apr. 2, 1951; s. Leon Joseph and Dorisedna (Forslund) C.; A.A., Santa Barbara City Coll., 1973; postgrad. Calif. State Coll., 1973-74; m. Norita Ellen Besel, Mar. 13, 1976. Ambulance attendant, dispatcher and orderly Santa Ynez Valley Hosp., Solvang, Calif., 1968-73; chief ground instr., asst. chief pilot Gt. Atlantic and Pacific Aeroplane Co., Van Nuys, Calif., 1973-74; personal pilot, adminstrv. asst. to A. Brent Carruth, Counselor at Law, Encino, Calif., 1974-75; v.p. transp. and shipping, head grower Santa Maria Greenhouses, Inc., Nipomo, Calif., 1975-76; chief ground instr. Bud Walen Aviation, Van Nuys, Calif., 1976; flight instr. ATE of Santa Monica (Calif.), 1976; capt. Air Wis., Inc., Appleton, 1976—; ind. distbr. Shaklee Products; owner Sky Portraits by Jim; also freelance photographer. Mem. Air Line Pilots Assn., Assoc. Photographers Internat. Club: Pace Setters Running. Office: Outagamie County Airport Appleton WI 54911

CASTEN, CAROL ELIZABETH, nursing administrator; b. Gary, Ind., Aug. 1, 1934; d. Robert B. and Dorothy E. (Hoover) Miller; m. Richard Wayne Casten, Apr. 7, 1958; children—Lisa Ann, Nina Sue. B.S. in Nursing, Ind. U., 1960; M.S. in Nursing, Loyola U., Chgo., 1967; Cert. in Adminstrn., Nat. Coll. Edn., 1984. R.N. Staff Nurse Bloomington and Methodist Hosps., Gary, 1955-57; pub. health nurse City of Mount Vernon, N.Y., 1958-59; instr. nursing St. Mary's Sch. Nursing, LaSalle, Ill., 1959-66, Triton Coll., River Grove, Ill., 1967-68, chmn. dept. nursing, 1968—; cons. Ind. State Bd. Nursing, Indpls., 1980-81; advisor Midwest Alliance in Nursing, 1980—. Mem. Nat. League Nursing (chmn.), Am. Nurses Assn., Sigma Theta Tau. Avocations: swimming; painting, gardening. Home: 923 S Western Ave Park Ridge IL 60068 Office: Triton Coll Dept Nursing Assoc Degree 2000 5th Ave River Grove IL 60171

CASTER, RICHARD JOHN, educational administrator; b. Canton, Ohio, May 12, 1946; s. Peter and Mary Angelantoni) C.; married, 2 children. B.A. in Edn., Walsh Coll., Canton, 1968; M.S. in Tech. Edn., U. Akron (Ohio), 1973, Ed.D., 1979; m. Kathleen Annette; children—Matthew Adam, Scott Michael. Tchr. Columbus (Ohio) City schs., 1968-69; tchr. Canton City schs., 1969-73, coordinator, 1973-74, supr. career edn., 1974-79; asst. prin. Canton McKinley Sr. High Sch., 1979-84; prin. Newark Sr. High Sch., Ohio, 1984—. Ohio Assn. Secondary Sch. Adminstrs., Nat. Assn. Secondary Sch. Prins., Newark Adminstrs. Assn. Home: 693 Tall Oaks Ct Newark OH 43055 Office: Newark High Sch Wright St Newark OH 43055

CASTIGLIONE, DENNIS JOSEPH, printing company marketing executive; b. Cleve., Oct. 8, 1954; s. Joseph Martin and Antoinette Marie (Piunno) C.; m. Mary Elizabeth Gardner, Aug. 7, 1976; children—Michael A., Lisa E. B.S., Bowling Green State U., 1976. Account exec. Baron Advt., Inc., Cleve., 1976-78; communications mgr. Diamond Shamrock Corp., Cleve., 1978-83; v.p. sales and mktg. Carpenter Res. Printing Co., Cleve., 1983—; dir. dept. mktg. info. and research Printing Industries of Am., Washington, 1983—, adv. mktg. adv. com., 1983—. Chmn. Cleve. Printing Week, 1982. Mem. Cleve. Advt. Club, Bus. Profl. Advt. Assn., Sales Mktg. Exec. Internat., Graphic Arts Council Cleve. (pres. 1982-83). Avocations: jogging; racquetball; golf; bowling. Home: 5730 Janet Blvd Solon OH 44139 Office: Carpenter Res Printing Co 7100 Euclid Ave Cleveland OH 44103

CASTLE, DIAN KIRSCHLING, staff development specialist, consultant; b. Wis. Rapids, Wis., May 24, 1942; d. Roman Anthony and Edna Sophie (Hostvedt) Kirschling. B.A., Mt. Mary Coll., 1969; M.S., Chgo. State U., 1978. Cert. tchr., Wis. Recreation leader City of Phila., 1969-70; tchr., Wis., Pa., 1970-74; social worker Dept. of Pub. Aid, Joliet, Ill., 1974-78; dir., coordinator Joliet Community Anti-Crime Orgn., 1978-79; counselor Joliet Jr. Coll., 1979; guidance dir. Assumption High Sch., Wis. Rapids, 1979-82; counselor Kansas City Sch. Dist., Mo., 1983-84; inservice specialist Kans. State Dept. of Edn., Topeka, 1984—; cons. Global Industries Co., Wis. Rapids, 1980—. Contbr. articles to profl. jours. Mem. Wis. Council of Social Agencies, 1979-82, pres., 1982; mem. Adv. Council for Career Edn., Wis. Rapids, 1979-82, Shawnee Mission, Kans., 1983-84; mem. Mayor's Council on Edn., Kans. City, Mo., 1983-84. S.E. Wis. Sci. Fair scholar, 1965. Mem. Nat. Staff Devel. Council, Am. Assn. Counseling and Devel. (cert.), AAUW, Nat. Vocat. Guidance Assn., Am. Soc. Tng. and Devel., U.S. Tennis Assn., Sigma Tau Delta, Alpha Kappa Delta, Phi Alpha, Phi Delta Kappa. Roman Catholic. Club: Smithsonian (Washington). Avocations: tennis; skiing; ballet; camping; sports.

CASTLE, PAUL RAY, technical illustrator; b. Moline, Ill., Nov. 10, 1938; s. Ross Ray and Elsie Lavina (Barger) C.; m. Marrietta Walden, Mar. 16, 1962; children—Terrina Marie, Selena Rae. Student Moline Community Coll., 1958, St. Ambrose Coll., 1959, So. Baptist Sem., 1976. Line artist J.L. Case Co., Bettendorf, Iowa, 1959-61, artist parts catalog Deere & Co., Moline, 1965-74, sr. artist, 1974-77; tech. illustrator John Deere Plow and Planter Works, 1977—. Served with USAF, 1961-65. Mem. Astron. League (Best Art in show award 1984, regional vice-chmn. 1985), Astronomy Club (pres. 1980-85, editor newsletter 1980-85), Planetary Soc., Mid West Corvette Club (pres. 1960-61, 67). Baptist. Avocations: astronomy, photography, corvettes, hiking. Home: 2535 45th St Rock Island IL 61201 Office: Popular Astronomy Club Inc John Deere Planetarium Augustana Coll Rock Island IL 61201

CASTLES, WILLIAM ALBERT, physician; b. Dallas, S.D., Feb. 1, 1911; s. Thomas Ralph and Edna B. (Pabst) C.; student Albia Jr. Coll., 1928-30; M.D., State U. Iowa, 1935; m. Mildred Alyce Owen, Apr. 16, 1932; children—Thomas Ralph, William Albert II. Intern St. Mary's Hosp., Kansas City, Mo., 1935-30; resident Mo. Pacific R.R. Hosp., St. Louis, 1936-37; practice family medicine, Rippey, Iowa, 1939-46, Dallas Center, Iowa, 1946—; mem. staff Iowa Luth. Hosp., Iowa Meth. Hosp., Des Moines; staff physician Midwestern area A.R.C., 1937-39. Dir. Recreational Vehicles Inc., Des Moines, 1972-73. Mem. City Council, Dallas Center, 1948-52. Served from lt. to lt. col. M.C., AUS, 1941-46. Mem. Iowa Med. Soc. (ho. dels. 1952-66), Iowa Acad. Family Practice (dir. 1956-60, pres. 1963-64), Dallas Guthrie County Med. Soc. (pres. 1958), Am. Acad. Family Practice (ho. of dels. 1964-76, commn. membership and credentials). Rotarian (pres. 1959-60). Home: 105 Rhinehart Ave Dallas Center IA 50063 Office: 515 Sycamore St Dallas Center IA 50063

CASTOR, STEPHEN EUGENE, trading company exec.; b. New Castle, Ind., Feb. 4, 1946; s. Ercie Stanton and Helen (Quckenbush) C.; B.A., Adrian Coll., 1971; M.A., U. Mich., 1972; M.B.A., Northwestern U., 1974; J.D., Chgo.-Kent Coll. Law, 1977; m. Esther Marie Olson, Aug. 3, 1974; 1 dau., Stephanie Tara. Banking rep. No. Trust Co., Chgo., 1974-77; v.p., mgr. Asia, Middle East, Africa Northwestern Nat. Bank, Mpls., 1977-81; v.p., gen. mgr. McLean-Fogg Co., Mundelein, Ill., 1981-83; v.p., mgr. sales/mktg. Sears-First Chgo. Trading Co., 1983—; lectr. Coll. Bus., U. Minn.; dir. Am. Equipment Service, Singapore. Served with U.S. Army, 1964-67. Decorated Air medal, Bronze Star, Purple Heart. Mem. Alpha Kappa Psi, Delta Theta Phi. Republican. Lutheran. Office: Suite 0039 One First Nat Plaza Chicago IL 60670

CATALANO, GERALD, acct., oil co. exec.; b. Chgo., Jan. 17, 1949; s. Frank and Virginia (Kreiman) C.; B.S. in Bus. Adminstrn., Roosevelt U., 1971; m. Mary L. Billings, July 4, 1970; children—James, Maria, Gina. Jr. acct. Drebin, Lindquist and Gervasio, Chgo., 1971; jr. acct. Leaf, Dahl and Co., Ltd., 1971-77, prin., 1978—, ptnr. 1980—; prin. Gerald Catalano, C.P.A., Chgo., 1982-83; ptnr. Barbakoff, Catalano & Assocs., 1983—; v.p. Tri-City Oil, Inc., Addison, Ill., 1983—; corp. officer Bionic Auto Parts and Sales, Inc. Pres. Young Democrats, Roosevelt U., 1967-71; dir. Elmhurst Jaycees, 1976. C.P.A., Ill. Mem. Am. Inst. C.P.A.s, Ill. C.P.A. Soc. Roman Catholic. Office: 5865 N Lincoln Suite 116 Chicago Il 60659

CATALIOTTI, ANTHONY JOHN, air force officer; b. N.Y.C., May 6, 1942; s. Salvator Charles and Bridget Rose (Giordano) C.; m. Marilyn Martha Stroup, July 29, 1972; children—Bridget, John, Joseph. B.S., Fordham U., 1964; M.A., Central Mich. U., 1976. Cert. profl. contracts mgr., 1976. Commd. 2d lt. U.S. Air Force, 1964, advanced through grades to maj., 1974; buyer, contracting officer Arnold AFB, Tullahoma, Tenn., 1964-68; contracting mgr., Turkey, 1968-70; sr. contracting officer, Washington, 1970-73; staff asst. to v.p. Air Force Systems Command, Silver Spring, Md., 1973-76; mgr. equipment div. Dept. Def., Scott AFB, Ill., 1976-80, asst. to dir. telecommunications acquisition policy Air Force Communications, 1980—. Recipient Def. Meritorious Service medal, AF Meritorious Service medal. Mem. Nat. Contract Mgmt. Assn. Roman Catholic. Lodge: KC (dir. youth activities 1980-84). Home: 908 Belpre Dr O'Fallon IL 62269 Office: Hdqrs AFCC/EPKP Scott AFB IL 62225

CATHCART, SILAS STRAWN, manufacturing company executive; b. Evanston, Ill., May 6, 1926; s. James A. and Margaret (Strawn) C.; A.B., Princeton U., 1948; m. Corlene Hobbs, Feb. 3, 1951; children—Strawn, James, David and Daniel (twins), Corlene. With Ill. Tool Works, Inc., Chgo., 1948—, exec. v.p., then pres., 1962-72, chmn. bd., 1972—, also dir.; dir. Bethlehem Steel Corp., Gen. Electric Co., Am. Hosp. Supply Corp., Jewel Cos., No. Trust Co., Quaker Oats Co., Savs. & Profit Sharing Fund Sears Employees. Bd. dirs. Northwestern Meml. Hosp., Chgo., 1959—. Served with USNR, 1944-46. Mem. Bus. Roundtable. Clubs: Onwentsia, Old Elm (Lake Forest, Ill.); Commercial, Commonwealth, Economic, Chicago (Chgo.); Augusta (Ga.) Nat. Golf. Office: Ill Tool Works Inc 8501 W Higgins Rd Chicago IL 60631

CATLETT, SANDRA JUNE, registered nurse; b. Hoisington, Kans., Aug. 29, 1952; d. Harvey Lewis and Ramona June (Palmer) Dirks; m. Donald Ray Catlett, May 10, 1975; children—Stephanie Dawn, Melanie Renae. R.N., Hutchinson Hosp. Sch. Nursing, 1973. Staff nurse cardiovascular ICU, Meth. Hosp., Houston, 1973-74, Bergan Mercy Hosp., Omaha, 1975; staff nurse relief supervision St. Mary's Hosp., Nebraska City, Nebr., 1975—, chmn. coronary care com., 1977-80. Named Nurse of Yr., St. Mary's Hosp., Nebraska City, 1977. Baptist.

CATON, JEFFREY ALAN, cat litter manufacturing company executive; b. Elkhart, Ind., Apr. 13, 1956; s. Carter Luther and Carolyn May (Peterson) C. B.B.A., U. Cin., 1979; M.B.A., Ind. U., 1981. Sales rep. Drackett, Houston, 1979-80; asst. product mgr. Gen. Mills, Mpls., 1982-83; brand mgr. Lowe's, Inc., South Bend, Ind., 1983—. Advisor, Jr. Achievement, Mpls., 1983. Mem. Am. Mktg. Assn. Avocations: tennis; racquetball; skiing; reading. Home: 1405 Wall St South Bend IN 46615 Office: Lowe's Inc 348 S Columbia St South Bend IN 46601

CATRON, PATRICIA D'ARCY, art center administrator; b. Memphis, Tenn., Oct. 19, 1920; d. John and Kathryn (Blalack) D'A.; m. Robert Frank Catron, June 1, 1946; children—Kathryn Valerie, Anne D'Arcy. Student Memphis Acad. Art, 1938, Wittenberg U., 1943. Office mgr. Family Service Agency, Springfield, Ohio, 1966-70; dir. Springfield Art Ctr., Ohio, 1970—. Compiler mus. catalogues, 1977-82; contbr. editor New Concept Mag., 1977-78. Mem. Ohio Mus. Assn., Am. Assn., Mus., Ohio Mus. Assn., Colonial Dames Am. (pres. 1980-82), DAR (regent 1974-76), Colonial Dames XVII Century (registrar 1978-80, v.p. 1985-87), Springfield Symphony Women's Assn. (pres. 1957-59), Nat. Soc. Magna Carta Dames. Clubs: Jamestown Soc., Order of Crown of Charlemagne. Avocations: Geneal. research; bridge; sewing; reading. Home: 2001 N Fountain Blvd Springfield OH 45504 Office: Springfield Art Ctr 107 Cliff Pk Rd Springfield OH 45501

CATTERTON, MARY CHOPIN, advertising agency executive, consultant; b. Appleton, Wis., May 16, 1951; d. William Lloyd and Marcella Alice (Haberman) Chopin; m. Robert Bruce Catterton, Sept. 20, 1975; 1 son, Ryan Taylor. B.A. in Radio-TV-Film Communications and Geology, U. Wis.-Oshkosh, 1973. Weather and news reporter Sta. WLUK-TV, Green Bay, Wis., 1973; promotion mgr. sta. WFRV-TV, Green Bay, 1974; news anchor Sta. WBAY-TV, Green Bay, 1976; prin. salesperson, creative writer Irish Saxe Sound Prodn., Appleton, Wis., 1978-81; founder, pres. The Ad Works, Inc., Appleton, 1981—, Madison, Wis., 1985—; cons. Appleton and Oshkosh Chambers Commerce. Media dir. activities, Appleton, including Fantasy Ave. Event, 1983, co-chmn. media com. Octoberfest Celebration, 1983; council Trinity Lutheran Ch. Recipient best ad of yr. award N.E. Wis. Advt. Assn., 1974, 75. Mem. Advt. Assn. of Fox Valley (Addy awards 1980, 81, 82; 2 bronze awards for print, 1 for radio 1983), Oshkosh Alumni Assn., Fox Cities C. of C., Appleton Downtown Retail Assn., Oshkosh C. of C. Republican. Commencement speaker U. Wis., Oshkosh, 1973. Office: PO Box 235 1221 N Lawe St Appleton WI 54912

CATTRELL, BETTY JANE, librarian; b. Wichita, Kans., Feb. 27, 1927; d. Vern Hamlin and Orpha Jane (Kerr) Welch; m. Melvin Lee Cattrell, June 26, 1945; children—Kary Lee, Kieth Lane, Kelly Jane, Karla Joyce. Student Kans. Newman Coll. Periodical librarian Boeing Aircraft, Wichita, Kans., 1953-60; librarian Unified Sch. Dist. #187, Haysville, Kans., 1961-77, Haysville Community Library, 1977—. Mem. Internat. Reading Assn. (pres. 1983—), ALA, Mountain Plains Library Assn., Kans. Library Assn., DAR. Democrat. Baptist. Home: 132 Wire St Haysville KS 67060 Office: Haysville Community Library 230 E Grand St Haysville KS 67060

CAUCUTT, AMY MEAD CARR, business administration educator; b. Christiansburg, Va., May 12, 1946; d. Francis Lewis and Miriam Mead (Arnold) Carr; m. Greg Caucutt; children—Mary A., Elizabeth M., George N. Student Wellesley Coll., 1964-65, Mich. State U., 1966, U. Wis.-Madison, 1967, U. Md., 1968-69, Rochester Community Coll., 1980-81; B.A. with honors, U. Wis.-Eau Claire, 1969; M.B.A., Winona State U., 1982. Instr. bus. adminstrn. Winona State U., Minn., 1982-84; asst. prof. Winona State U.-Rochester, Minn., 1984—; dir. Small Bus. Devel. Ctr., SBA, Winona, 1985—; cons. Olmsted Co., Rochester, 1982. Pub. mem. admissions com. Mayo Med. Sch., Rochester, 1979-82, Am. Assn. Med. Colls., Washington, 1982-83; bd. dirs., found. mem. Ability Bldg. Ctr., Inc., Rochester, 1984—; chmn., vice-chmn. Rochester Planning and Zoning Comm., 1983—; mem. Rochester Zoning Bd. Appeals, 1984, Recycling Task Force, Olmsted County, Minn., 1980-81; mem. housing com. Rochester- Olmsted Council of Govts., 1978-79; candidate for Olmsted County auditor, 1982; co-chmn. for state legis. campaign, precinct chmn., affirmative action officer Democratic Farmer Labor Party, Rochester, 1972—; active various coms., vol. Rochester Sch. Dist. 535, 1981—; mem. vestry, lay reader, Bible sch. dir., mem. various coms. St. Luke's Episcopal Ch., Rochester, 1970—. Mem. LWV (pres. 1976—, sec. treas. 1980-82, mem. coms., League of Yr. 1982), Minn. Women's Network, Rochester C. of C., Minn. Edn. Assn. Home: 716 28th St NW Rochester MN 55901 Office: Winona State U-Rochester 2220 3d Ave SE Rochester MN 55904

CAULFIELD, JOAN, educational administrator; b. St. Joseph, Mo., July 17, 1943; d. Joseph A. and Jane (Lisenby) Caulfield; B.S. in Edn. cum laude, U. Mo., 1963, M.A. in Spanish, 1965, Ph.D., 1978; postgrad. (Mexican Govt.

scholar) Nat. U. Mexico, 1963. TV tchr. Spanish, Kansas City (Mo.) pub. schs., 1963-68; tchr. Spanish, French Bingham Jr. High Schs., Kansas City, 1968-78; asst. prin. S.E. High Sch., Kansas City, 1984; prin. Nowlin Jr. High Sch., Independence, Mo., 1984—; part-time instr. U. Mo.-Kansas City; dir. English Inst., Rockhurst Coll., summers, 1972-75. Mem. Sister City Commn., Kansas City, 1980—; ofcl. translator to mayor on trip to Seville, Spain, 1969; cons. Possum Trot (hist. soc.), 1979-80. Named Outstanding Secondary Educator, 1973; Delta Kappa Gamma state scholar, 1977-78. Mem. Romance Lang. Assn., Assn. for Supervision and Curriculum Devel., Nat. Assn. Secondary Sch. Prins., Modern Lang. Assn., Am. Assn. Tchrs. Spanish and Portuguese, Westport Hist. Soc., Friends of Seville, Friends of Art, Friends of the Zoo. Phi Sigma Iota, Phi Delta Kappa, Delta Kappa Gamma, Phi Kappa Phi. Presbyterian. Home: 431 W 70th St Kansas City MO 64113 Office: 2800 S Hardy St Independence MO 64052

CAVALIER, DONALD RICHARD, university administrator; b. Walhalla, N.D., Sept. 28, 1943; s. Amos O. and Francis (McCambridge) C.; B.S., Mayville State Coll., 1965; M.S., Bemidji State U., 1970; m. Mary A. Salisbury, July 23, 1966; children—David Cavalier, Todd. Tchr., coach Warren (Minn.) public schs., 1965-67; tchr., counselor Crookston (Minn.) public schs., 1967-75; edn. dir. N.W. Regional Corrections Center, Crookston, 1975-76; dir. counseling, career planning and placement U. Minn., Crookston, 1976—; group leader, facilitator, The Social Seminar, Adventures in Attitude Tng., 1975-76; humanistic cons. Moorehead State U., 1973-78. Bd. dirs. S.O.S. Club for Teens, 1976-77; chmn. Family Living Center, Crookston, 1972-73; team leader Crookston Community Drug edn. program, 1975-76. PTO scholar, 1961-62. Mem. Am. Sch. Counselor Assn., Am. Assn. Counseling and Devel., Minn. Assn. Counseling and Devel. Northwestern Minn. Guidance Assn., Minn. Vocat. Guidance Assn., NEA, Nat. Assn. Vocat. Edn. Spl. Needs Personnel, Minn. Coll. Personnel Assn., Minn. Govt. Coll. Council Assn. of Minn. Recruiters and Placement Dirs., Jaycees (pres. 1978-79, named Outstanding Pres. 1979). Democrat. Roman Catholic. Clubs: Lions, K.C., Elks Country, Dance, Town and Country, Eagles, Elks, Toastmaster 600 (pres.). Home: 614 N Ash Ct Crookston MN 56716 Office: U of Minn Bede Hall Room 107 Crookston MN 56716

CAVALIERI, ERCOLE LUIGI, chemist, educator; b. Milano, Italy, Feb. 10, 1937; came to U.S., 1968; s. Attilio and Clelia (Gaioni) C.; Maturita Scientifica, Leonardo Da Vinci U., Milano, 1955; D.Sci., U. Milan, 1962. Postgrad. research assoc. Poly. Zurich, Switzerland, 1962-63; research assoc., asst. prof. U. Montreal, Canada, 1965-68; postdoctoral research assoc. Lawrence Radiation Lab. U. Calif.-Berkeley, 1968-71; asst. prof., then assoc. prof. Nebr. Med. Ctr., Omaha, Nebr.-Omaha, 1971-76, prof., 1981—. Contbr. articles to profl. jours. Lctrs. in field. Grantee Nat. Cancer Inst. NIH, 1973—. Mem. Am. Chem. Soc., AAAS, Am. Assn. Cancer Research, Fedn. Am. Scientists, N.Y. Acad. Scis., Nat. Cancer Inst. (adv. com. 1977). Home: 22635 Wilson Ave Waterloo NE 68069 Office: Eppley Cancer Inst U Nebr Med Center 42nd and Dewey Omaha NE 68105

CAVANAGH, MICHAEL F., state supreme court justice; b. Detroit, Oct. 21, 1940; s. Sylvester J. and Mary Irene (Timmins) C.; m. Patricia E. Ferriss, Apr. 30, 1966; children—Jane Elizabeth, Michael F., Megan Kathleen. B.A., U. Detroit, 1962, J.D., 1966. Bar: Mich. City atty., Lansing, Mich., 1967-69; ptnr. Farhat, Story et al, Lansing, 1969-73; judge 54-A Dist. Ct., Lansing, 1973-75, Mich. Ct. Appeals, 1975-82, justice Mich. Supreme Ct., 1983—; supervising justice Sentencing Guidelines Com., Lansing, 1983—. Chmn. bd. dirs. Am. Heart Assn., Mich., 1985; hon. mem. bd. dirs. Inst. Judicial Adminstrn., N.Y.U. Thomas M. Cooley Law Sch., Mem. ABA, Mich. State Bar Assn., Ingham County Bar Assn. Democrat. Roman Catholic. Avocations: jogging; racquetball; fishing. Home: 234 Kensington East Lansing MI 48823 Office: Mich Supreme Ct Law Bldg PO Box 30052 Lansing MI 48909

CAVANAGH, MIMI METTE, manufacturing company executive; b. Copenhagen, July 14, 1911; d. Ernest Emmerick and Emilie Wilhelmina Frederikke (Fehrn) Michelsen; m. John Sidney Day, Oct. 1936 (div. 1948); m. 2d John Robert Vaselenak, July 1948 (dec. 1968); children—Michael, Johanne; m. 2d, Raymond Cavanagh, July 2, 1978. B.A. in Polit. Sci. and Econs., U. Toronto (Ont., Can.), 1948; cert. in social welfare U. Alta. (Can.), 1961; B.Ed., U. Calgary (Alta.), 1962, M.Ed. in Adult Edn., 1969. Social worker welfare dept. City of Lethbridge (Alta.), 1955-57; probation officer children's aid dept. City of Calgary, 1957-61; reader dept. ednl founds. U. Alta., Calgary, part-time 1962-66; tchr. history, geography, law, econs. Calgary Sch. Bd., 1962-66, social studies adult div. night sch., 1963-65; sessional instr. history edn. U. Calgary, summer 1966, prof. history, asst. to dean, 1967-72; chmn. social sci. dept. evening coll. Mount Royal Coll., Calgary, 1966-67; pres., gen. mgr. Joki Canada Ltd., Mississauga, Ont., 1972—; cons. planning and mfg. systems for various firms, govtl. facilities. Contbr. articles to ednl. jours. Served with Royal Can. Navy, 1944-45. Decorated Can. Victory medal. Recipient Commendation plaque for judging Oxford debates U. Calgary, 1972. Mem. Alta. Tchrs. Fedn., Internat. Material Mgmt. Soc. Mem. Fed. Liberal Party. Lutheran. Clubs: Univ. Women's (mem. com. on constn. and women's rights); Scandinavian-Can. Club (Toronto). Office: Joki Canada Ltd 2133 Royal Windsor Dr #16 Mississauga ON L5J 1K5 Canada

CAVANAH, GARY LYNN, boiler control systems company executive, engineer; b. Kansas City, Mo., Feb. 1, 1941; s. Zillman Gail and Betty Brooke (Burchett) C.; m. Patricia Jane Armbrecht, May 1, 1976. B.S.E.E., Finlay Engring. Coll., 1966. Registered profl. engr., Calif., Kans. Elec. engr. Bailey Controls Co., Wickliffe, Ohio, 1966-73; cons. Fisher Controls Co., Marshalltown, Iowa, 1973-78; pres. SEGA, Inc., Stanley, Kans., 1973—. Contbg. author: Handbook on Distributed Controls, 1983. Sustaining mem. Republican Nat. Com., 1980—. Mem. Instrument Soc. Am. Office: Sega Inc 15238 Cherry St Stanley KS 66223

CAVANAUGH, DENNIS MILES, transportation executive; b. Los Angeles, Sept. 19, 1937; s. Edward and Louella C.; m. Marilyn J. Scovil, Sept. 11, 1965; children—Ann Louise, Amy Denise. B.S., U. Minn., 1965. Yard clk. Soo Line R.R. Co., Shoreham Yard, Mpls., 1955-57, 61-65, yard clk., asst. trainmaster, 1965-67, indsl. engr., 1969-72, dir. transp. planning, transp. dept., 1972-73, asst. supt. central div., 1974, gen. supt., 1974-77, asst. to exec. v.p., 1977-78, gen. mgr. transp. and maintenance, 1978, v.p. ops., 1978-81, exec. v.p., 1981-83, pres., chief operating officer, 1983-84, pres., chief exec. officer, 1984—; pres., chief exec. officer Soo Line Corp., 1985—; asst. cashier Central Northwestern Nat. Bank, Mpls., 1967-69; dir. Belt Rwy. Co., Chgo., Consol. Papers, Inc., Wisconsin Rapids, Wis., Minn. Bus. Partnership, Inc., Mpls., Remmele Engring., Mpls., Soo Line Credit Union, Mpls., Soo Line R.R. Co., Mpls., Bd. dirs. St. John's Prep. Sch., Collegeville, Minn., YMCA, Mpls. Served with USN, 1957-61. Mem. Assn. Am. R.R.s, Am. Mgmt. Assn., Western R.R. Assn., Locomotive Maintenance Officers Assn., Maintenance of Way Assn., Nat. Freight Transp. Assn., N.Am. Soc. Corp. Planning, Inc., Pres. Assn., Rwy. Fuel and Operating Officers Assn., Transp. Clubs Internat. Roman Catholic. Clubs: Midland Hills Country; Mpls. Athletic; Mpls.; Citizens League of Mpls. Minn. Alumni; Union League (Chgo.). Avocations: sailing; cross-country skiing; skating; golf. Office: Soo Line RR Co Box 530 800 Soo Line Bldg Minneapolis MN 55440

CAVESTRI, ANNA MARIE, pharmacist; b. Pitts., Jan. 23, 1948; d. Steve and Anna (Karaman) Stupak; m. Richard Charles Cavestri, Sept. 15, 1973; 1 child, Juliet Nicole. B.S. in Pharmacy, U. Pitts., 1971. Registered pharmacist. Pharmacist, Gen. Pharmacy, Pitts., 1971-74, Thrift Drug, Pitts., 1975-76, Medshoppe Pharmacy, Columbus, Ohio, 1976-80, Miesse Pharmacy, Columbus, 1980-84. Avocations: Photography; sewing; racquetball. Home: 2935 Dynasty Dr Columbus OH 43220

CAWLEY, LAWRENCE JOSEPH, company executive; b. Cleve., Apr. 9, 1934; s. William J. and Mary K. (Keane) C.; m. Lillian J. Pollack, Aug. 20, 1960; children—Michael, Patrick. B.S. in Mech. Engring., Fenn Coll., 1957. Project engr. Cleve. Graphite Bronze, 1968-71; mgr. new products Gould, Cleve., 1971-73, dir. product devel., 1973-76, v.p. ops., 1976-78; pres., gen. mgr. Clevire, Cleve., 1978—; dir. Bimetal Bearings Ltd., Madras, India, 1978—. Active Seven Hills Planning Commn., 1972; trustee Euclid Gen. Hosp., Cleve., 1977. Democrat. Roman Catholic. Clubs: Shaker Heights Country; Univ. of Cleve. Office: 17000 St Clair Ave Cleveland OH 44110

CAYLOR, TRUMAN E., physician; b. Pennville, Ind., Jan. 10, 1900; s. Charles E. and Bessie (Ferree) C.; student Ind. U., 1917-1919; B.S., Wis. U., 1921; M.D., Rush Med. Coll., 1924; m. Julia Gettle, June 28, 1923 (dec. June 6, 1960); children—Carolyn (Mrs. Herman Wadlington), Charles H., Constance (Mrs. Joseph Carney). m. 2d, Eva Abbott, May 29, 1961 (dec. 1979); m. 3d, Suzanne Black, 1980. Intern, Evanston (Ill.) Gen. Hosp.; practice medicine specializing in urology, Bluffton, Ind., 1924—; co-founder, mem. staff Caylor Nickel Clinic, Bluffton, mem. staff Caylor Nickel Hosp., Bluffton, 1939-81, exec. com., 1939-75, also dir.; dir. Mut. Security Life Ins. Co., Ft. Wayne, Ind. Mem. adv. com. Ind. Commn. on Aging, 1972-80; mem. adv. com. Grace Coll., Winona Lake, Ind., 1970—. Bd. dirs. Yorkfellow Inst., Richmond, Ind., Caylor Nickel Research Found.; pres., co-founder Caylor Nickel Research Inst., 1961. Served with AUS, 1918. Fellow A.C.S.; mem. Ind. Council Sagamores, Ind. State Med. Soc. (50th Year Certificate of Distinction 1974), Am. Urol. Assn., Delta Upsilon, Phi Rho Sigma. Clubs: Masons, Shriners, Scottish Rite, Rotary (dist. gov. 1965-66), Elks. Home: 920 River Rd PO Box 292 Bluffton IN 46714 Office: 303 S Main St Bluffton IN 46714

CECALA, AGNES FRICANO, educator; b. Chgo., Mar. 8, 1939; d. Fred E. and Lillian P. (Celano) Fricano; B.S. in Edn., No. Ill. U., 1961, postgrad., 1979-84; m. John James Cecala, Aug. 5, 1961; children—John Joseph, Fred Edward. Secretarial instr. Elmwood Park (Ill.) High Sch., 1964-65; career edn./adult edn. secretarial/communications instr. Triton Coll., River Grove, Ill., 1968-80, word processing/communications instr., 1980—, tng. coordinator, 1980—; cons. word processing, communications and secretarial tng. Mem. Nat. Bus. Edn. Assn., Ill. Bus. Edn. Assn., Assn. Info. Systems Profls., Chgo. Bus. Edn. Assn., Am. Bus. Communications Assn., Internat. Soc. Wang Users, Wang Users Assn., Phi Delta Kappa. Author: (Wang tng. texts) Book I Basic, 1980; Wang Advanced Training Text—Book II, 1980; Wang Glossary Training Text III, 1981; Word Processing Skills and Applications Using Wang Systems. Office: Triton Coll 2000 5th Ave River Grove IL 60171

CECH, JOSEPH HAROLD, chemical engineer; b. Flint, Mich., Oct. 8, 1951; s. Joseph, Jr. and Margaret Luella (Taphouse) C. B.S. in Chem. Engring., Mich. Tech. U., 1978. Trainee, Menasha Corp., North Bend, Oreg., 1978-79, project engr. molded products div., Watertown, Wis., 1979-84, plastic devel. engr., 1984—. Served with USN, 1971-75. Mem. Soc. Plastic Engrs., Am. Inst. Chem. Engrs., Nat. Geog. Soc., Watertown Conservation Club: Methodist. Office: 426 Montgomery St Watertown WI 53094

CECI, LOUIS J., state supreme court judge; b. N.Y.C., Sept. 10, 1927; s. Louis and Filomena Ceci; m. Shirley Ceci; children—Joseph, Geraldine, David; children from previous marriage—Kristin, Remy, Louis. Ph.B., Marquette U., 1951, J.D., 1954. Bar: Wis. 1954. Sole practice law, Milw., 1954-58, 63-68; asst. city atty. City of Milw., 1958-63; legislator Wis. Assembly, Madison, Wis., 1965-66; judge Milw. County, 1968-73, judge Circuit Ct., 1973-82; justice Wis. Supreme Ct., 1982—; lectr. Badger Boys State, 1961, 82, 83, 84; lectr. Wis. Jud. Confs., 1970-79. Asst. dist. commnr. Milwaukee County council Boy Scouts Am., 1962. Served with USNR, 1945-46. Mem. Am. Legion (comdr. 1962-63), ABA, State Bar Wis., Dane County Bar Assn. 53711 Office: PO Box 1688 Madison WI 53701

CECIL, JOSEPH ALEXANDER, III, retail executive; b. Totz, Ky., June 1, 1938; s. Joseph Alexander and Wilma (Fine) C. B.S., U. Tenn.; M.A., Ohio U. Mgr. recruiting Eastern Airlines, N.Y.C., 1969-74; dean of men Emory U., Atlanta, 1966-69; buyer Bloomingdale's, N.Y.C., 1974-79; mdse. mgr. Robinson's, Los Angeles, 1976-79; v.p. Marshall Field's, Chgo., 1979-85; pres., founder Mallards, Chgo., 1985—. Pres. men's council Mus. Contempoary Art, Chgo., 1984—; bd. dirs. Chgo. Mental Health Assn., 1985; mem. com. Chgo. Opera Theatre, 1984-85. Served with USAR, 1961-67. Avocations: tennis; running. Home: 1322 N Astor St Chicago IL 60610 Office: Mallards 50 E Washington St Chicago IL 60602

CECIL, ROBERT SALISBURY, electronics company executive; b. Manila, Philippines, May 28, 1935 (parents Am. citizens); s. Robert Edgar and Susan Elizabeth C.; B.S., U.S. Naval Acad., 1956; M.B.A., Harvard U., 1962; m. Louise Nuttall Millholland, Nov. 30, 1963; children—Scott Douglass, James Hilliard. Contract negotiator Teledyne, Inc., Los Angeles, 1962-63; br. mgr. IBM, Cleve., 1971-72, regional mktg. mgr., Washington, 1973-75, corp. dir. govt. programs, Washington, 1975-77; v.p., corp. dir. mktg. Motorola Inc., Schaumburg, Ill., 1977-84; v.p. cellular ops. Lin Broadcasting Corp., N.Y.C., 1984—. Served with USAF, 1956-60. Episcopalian.

CEDERQUIST, ELEANOR NICHOLAS (MRS. STANLEY G. CEDERQUIST), civic worker; b. Toledo, Aug. 24, 1918; d. Ralph Forest and Marguerite (Wright) Nicholas; A.B., Ind. U., 1941; m. Stanley G. Cederquist, May 10, 1942; children—Eric Stanley, Robert Alan. Sec. The Nicholas Co., Inc., 1953-75. Indpls. exec. chmn. Met. Opera Nat. Co., 1966, mem. nat. council, 1966-67; mem. nat. bd. Am. Nat. Opera Co., 1967; mem. Friends of Kennedy Center, 1966—. Salvation Army Aux., 1965—, Indpls. Mus. of Art Alliance, 1961—, St. Margaret's Hosp. Guild, 1960—, Boys Club Aux., 1960—; pres. women's com. Clowes Meml. Hall, 1965-66, 66-67, adv. bd., 1978-79; residential chmn. Marion County (Ind.)-Am. Cancer Soc. Crusade, 1970—; bd. dirs. Women's Com. Ind. Symphony Soc., 1972—, Crossroads council Boy Scouts Am., 1975—, Ind. Endowment for Arts, 1977-78; trustee Indpls. Mus. Art, 1975—, Civic theatre Indpls., 1977-79; gen. chmn. operating fund campaign Indpls. Mus. Art. Home: 8502 Bent Tree Ct Indianapolis IN 46260

CEJKA, SUSAN ANN, executive search company executive; b. St. Louis, Apr. 9, 1950; d. John Anthony and Betty Joy (McDaniel) C.; m. Paul R. Hales, June 3, 1978. B.S. in Bus. Acctg., U. Mo., 1972. C.P.A., Mo. Mgmt. trainee Southwestern Bell, St. Louis, 1972-73; staff acct. Touche Ross Co., 1973-75; sr. acct. Rubin, Brown, Gornstein, 1976; sr. cons. Grant, Cooper & Assocs., 1977; exec. v.p. Medicus Search, 1977-81; pres., owner Lawrence-Leiter & Co., St. Louis, 1981—. Contbg. author: Persuading Physicians, 1984. Contbr. articles to profl. jours. Active Leadership St. Louis, 1981; co-chmn. Experience St. Louis, 1984; commr. Bus. and Indsl. Devel. Commn., 1984—; bd. dirs. St. Louis council Girl Scouts Am., 1985—. Mem. St. Louis Forum, Met. St. Louis, Women's Commerce Assn. (hon.), St. Louis Women C.P.A.s (founder, 1st pres. 1977), Nat. Assn. Physician Recruiters (chmn. nominating com. 1984). Home: 7056 Maryland Ave St Louis MO 63130 Office: Lawrence-Leiter & Co 135 N Meramec St St Louis MO 63105

CELEBREZZE, ANTHONY J., JR., attorney general Ohio; b. Cleve., Sept. 8, 1941; s. Anthony J. and Anne M. C.; B.S., U.S. Naval Acad., 1963; M.S., George Washington U., 1966; J.D., Cleve. State U., 1973; m. Louisa Godwin, June 19, 1965; children—Anthony J. III, Catherine, Charles, David, Maria. Bar: Ohio 1973. Ptnr., Celebrezze and Marco, Cleve., 1975-79; mem. Ohio State Senate, 1975-79; sec. of state State of Ohio, Columbus, 1979-83, atty. gen., 1983—; chmn. Ohio Organized Crime Cons. Com. Pres., Joint Vets. Commn. of Cuyahoga County, Ohio, 1977-79; v.p. Lake Erie Regional Transp. Authority, 1972-74; mem. Gt. Lakes Commn., 1975-78, vice chmn., 1977-78; former bd. dirs. Central br. YWCA, Cleve. Served with USN, 1963-68, capt. Res. Decorated Navy Commendation medal; recipient Jeffersonian Lodge award, 1977, Man of Yr. award Delta Theta Phi; named 1 of 5 Outstanding Legislators by 2 Ohio mags., 1978. Mem. LWV. Democrat. Roman Catholic. Office: 30 E Broad St Columbus OH 43215

CELEBREZZE, FRANK D., justice Ohio Supreme Court; b. Cleve., Nov. 13, 1928; s. Frank D. and Mary Delsander Celebrezze; student Ohio State U., 1948-50; B.S., Baldwin-Wallace Coll., 1952; LL.B., Cleve.-Marshall Coll. Law, 1956; m. Mary Ann Armstrong, Jan. 20, 1949; children—Judith, Frank, Laura, David, Brian, Stephen, Jeffrey, Keith, Matthew. Admitted to Ohio bar, 1957; began legal practice, Cleve., 1957; judge Ohio Ct. Common Pleas Cuyahoga County, 1964-72; justice Ohio Supreme Ct., 1972—, now chief justice; mem. Ohio Senate, to 1958. Trustee Freedom Found. at Valley Forge. Served with parachute inf. U.S. Army, 1946-47. Recipient Jud. Service award Ohio Supreme Ct., 1972; Outstanding Alumnus award Cleve.-Marshall Coll. Law, 1973; Community Service award AFL-CIO, 1973, Disting. Citizen of Parma award, 1976; Unita Civic award of Youngstown, 1976. Mem. Inst. Jud. Adminstrn. of Bar Assn. Greater Cleve., ABA, Cuyahoga County Bar Assn., Cuyahoga County Joint Vets. Adminstrn. (past pres., past trustee), Cleve. YMCA, Catholic War Vets. Democrat. Roman Catholic. Office: Supreme Ct Ohio State Office Tower 30 E Broad St Columbus OH 43215*

CELESTE, RICHARD F., governor of Ohio; b. Cleve., Nov. 11, 1937; s. Frank C.; B.A. in History magna cum laude; Yale U., 1959; Ph.B. in Politics (Rhodes scholar), Oxford (Eng.) U., 1962; m. Dagmar Braun, 1962; children—Eric, Christopher, Gabriella, Noelle, Natalie, Stephen. Staff liaison officer Peace Corps, 1963; spl. asst. to U.S. ambassador to India, 1963-67; mem. Ohio Ho. of Reps., 1970-74, majority whip, 1972-74; lt. gov. Ohio, 1974-79; dir. Peace Corps, Washington, 1979-81; gov. of Ohio, 1983—. Mem. Ohio Democratic Exec. Com. Mem. Am. Soc. Pub. Adminstrn., Italian Sons and Daus. Am. Methodist. Address: Office of Governor State Capitol Columbus OH 43215*

CENA, LAWRENCE, See *Who's Who in America,* 43rd edition.

CENTANNI, MICHAEL ANTHONY, physicist; b. Cleve., July 6, 1951; s. Gustave George and Margaret Elaine (Flora) C. B.Engring. Sci. cum laude, Cleve. State U., 1973; M.S. in Physics, Rensselaer Poly. Inst., 1976, Ph.D. in Physics, 1977; J.D., Cleve. Marshall Coll. Law, 1983. Bar: Ohio 1984. Research physicist B. F. Goodrich, Brecksville, Ohio, 1977-80; sr. research physicist Sherwin Williams, Cleve., 1980-83; sr. research scientist Ferro Corp., Independence, Ohio, 1983—. Recipient Rensselaer Teaching award Physics Dept., Rensselaer Poly. Inst., 1977. Mem. Am. Phys. Soc., Am. Chem. Soc. (chmn. profl. relations Cleve. sect.), Ohio Bar Assn., Cuyahoga County Bar Assn., Cleve. Bar Assn., Tau Beta Pi, Pi Mu Epsilon, Sigma Pi Sigma. Club: Rensselaer (Perry, Ohio). Home: 7335 Beresford Ave Parma OH 44130 Office: 7500 E Pleasant Valley Rd Independence OH 44131

CENTNER, ROSEMARY LOUISE, chemist; b. Newport, Ky., Sept 23, 1926; d. Alexis F. and Mary Anne (Cloud) Centner; B.A., Our Lady of Cin. Coll., 1947; M.S., U. Cin., 1949. Library asst., tech. library Procter & Gamble Co., 1949-52, br. librarian Miami Valley labs., Cin., 1952-56, tech. librarian, 1956-66, mgr. tech. info. service, 1966-72, mgr. div. info. cons., 1972-73, mgr. NDA coordination, 1973-75, mgr. biomed. communications, 1975-81, mgr. tech. communications, 1981—. Trustee, Edgecliff Coll., 1975-82. Mem. Am. Chem. Soc., Am. Med. Writers Assn. Iota Sigma Pi. Roman Catholic. Home: 2678 Byrneside Dr Cincinnati OH 45239 Office: Winton Hill Tech Center Cincinnati OH 45224

CENTOLELLA, PAUL ALBERT, lawyer; b. Elkhart, Ind., July 26, 1951; s. Albert Peter and Genevieve (Nolan) C.; m. Diane Marie Frye; children—Kelly Marie, David Lee Frye. B.A., Oberlin Coll., 1973; J.D., U. Mich., 1977. Bar: Wash. 1978, U.S. Dist. Ct. (we. dist.) Wash. 1978, Calif. 1979, U.S. Dist. Ct. (no. dist.) Calif. 1979, Ohio 1981, U.S. Dist. Ct. (so. dist.) Ohio 1981. Staff atty. Unemployment Representation Clinic, Inc., Seattle, 1977-78; sole practice, Hoopa, Calif., 1978-81; cons. Ohio State Legal Services Assn., Columbus, 1981-82; sr. utility atty. Ohio Office of the Consumers' Counsel, Columbus, 1982—. Mem. Ohio State Bar Assn., Calif. State Bar Assn., Wash. State Bar Assn. Office: Ohio Office of the Consumers' Counsel 137 E State St Columbus OH 43215

CERMAK, GREGORY WAYNE, research psychologist; b. Cleve., Oct. 17, 1944; s. Frederick Robert and Florence Margaret (Sicha); m. Yvonne Kathleen Bestgren, Aug. 8, 1965; children—Renee, Adam Jason. B.A., U. Calif.-Santa Barbara, 1968; PhD., Stanford U., 1972. Research scientist G.M. Research Labs, Warren, Mich. 1972—; visiting asst. prof. Ariz. State U., Tempe, 1979; cons. Am. Nat. Standards Inst., N.Y.C., 1979-84. Contbr. articles to profl. jours. Campaign vol. Democratic Party, Palo Alto, Calif., 1970-72; coach, referee, ofcl. Birmingham-Bloomfield Soccer Club, 1977-84. Mem. AAAS, Psychometric Soc., Acoustical Soc. Am., Air Pollution Control Assn., Classification Soc. Democrat. Avocations: Soccer; skiing; swimming. Home: 615 Oakland Ave Birmingham MI 48008 Office: Societal Analysis Dept G M Research Labs Warren MI 48090

CERMAK, LEANDER MARTIN, airship engineer; b. Rochester, N.Y., Sept. 20, 1929; s. Eleanor May Sherman, Sept. 20, 1953; children—Daniel Lee, Cynthia Ellen. B.S. in Aero. Engring., Tri State U., 1956; Flight test engr. Goodyear Aircraft Co., Akron, Ohio, 1956-60, missile liaison engr. Goodyear Aerospace Corp., 1960-63, Akron, erection engr., 1973-82, engr., airship pilot, 1982—; supr., airship pilot Goodyear Tire and Rubber Co., 1963-73. Served with U.S. Army, 1948-52, Korea. Mem. AIAA (council 1983—), Wingfoot Lighter than Air Soc., Quiet Birdmen, Wingfoot Flyers. Avocations: organ, skiing, flying, roller skating, sailing. Home: 550 North Ave Tallmadge OH 44278 Office: Goodyear Aerospace Corp 1210 Massillon Rd Akton OH 44315

CERNACH, JOHN C., university administrator; b. Kansas City, Dec. 19, 1944; s. Clarence M. and Dorothy M. (Winegardner) C.; m. Elizabeth Ann Fox, Oct. 21, 1967; children—Michael C., Cindy Michele. B.A., St. Louis U., 1967, M.Ed., 1969, Ph.D., 1975. Acting dir. housing St. Louis U., 1967, asst. dir., U. Ctr., 1968-71; dir., student activities & asst. dean Quincy Coll., Ill., 1971-75, dean students, 1975-83; v.p. student services Creighton U., Omaha, 1983—. Bd. dirs. Hist. Soc., Quincy, 1981-83; coach Little League Soccer, Basketball, Quincy, 1978-83; chmn. edn. com. St. Francis Parish Bd., Quincy, 1979-81; active mem. com. council Boy Scouts Am., Quincy, 1979-82. Mem. Nat. Assn. Student Personnel Administrs., Assn. Coll. Unions Internat., Nat. Orientation Dirs. Assn., Phi Delta Kappa. Lodge: Rotary. Avocations: boating; softball; tennis. Home: 14936 Cedar Circle Omaha NE 68144 Office: Creighton U California at 24th St Omaha NE 68178

CERNEY, JAMES VINCENT, former medical sports injury and health services co. exec.; b. Detroit, Jan. 27, 1914; s. James and Anna (Hein) C.; student Hiram Coll., 1935; A.B., Miami U., 1939; Dr. Podiatric Medicine, Ohio Coll. Podiatric Medicine, 1943; Dr. Mechanotherapy, Central States Coll. Physiatrics, 1948, D. Chiropractic, 1953; m. Martha Elizabeth French, Nov. 2, 1940; children—James F., Lee Carol Cerney Spitler, Patricia Kay Cerney McIntire, Jeffrey Lynn, Kimberle Laine. Leader dance band, 1931-32; dancer Jack Lynch Revue, 1932-33; writer Northwest Sch. of Air series, stas. WLW, WHK, WCLE, 1939; publicity, promotion and merchandising mgr. Sta. WING, Dayton, 1940; practice podiatric medicine, Dayton, 1943—; pres. Profl. Research, Dayton, 1944—, Sports Injuries Research, Inc., 1978—. Pres. Dayton Triangle Profl. Football Team, 1958. Dir. pub. info. CD, Dayton, 1957-58. Recipient first prize award Nat. Podiatry Assn., 1952, meritorious award CD, 1954; named Ky. col. Mem. Central States Coll. Physiatrics (pres. 1960-61), Ohio Mechanotherapists (pres. 1960-61), County Podiatry Soc. (pres. 1962), Authors Guild, Am. Coll. Sports Medicine, Acad. Chinese Medicine, C. of C. (various coms. 1958-59), Dayton Purple Mask Theatre (pres. 1958), Dayton Ballet Guild (pres. 1958), Phi Kappa Tau. Club: Masons. Author: Athletic Injuries, 1963; How to Develop a Million Dollar Personality, 1964; Confidence and Power for Successful Living, 1966; Dynamic Laws of Thinking Rich, 1967; Stay Younger-Live Longer, 1968; Talk Your Way to Success with People, 1968; Thirteen Steps to New Personal Power, 1969; Complete Book of Athletic Taping Techniques, 1971; Acupuncture Without Needles, 1974; Modern Magic of Natural Healing with Water Therapy, 1974; A Handbook of Unusual and Unorthodox Healing Methods, 1975; Prevent-System for Football Injuries, 1975; How to Sell Yourself to Others, 1979; (novel) Flame Durrell, 1971; (stage plays) Blues in the Night, 1939, Fury, 1960, History of the Shiloh' Church, 1959. Editor Ohio Podiatry Jour., 1944. Contbr. articles to popular mags. Inventor throw away toothbrush, 1945, whirlpool bath system, 1946. Creator Skip Holiday series for radio, 1957.

CERNEY, MARY ELLEN, clin. psychologist; b. Detroit, Apr. 23, 1929; d. Stephen Simon and Mary Anne (Neigoot) Cerney; B.A. summa cum laude, Coll. St. Francis, Joliet, Ill., 1960; M.A., Cath. U. Am., 1962, Ph.D., 1965; grad. Topeka Inst. Psychoanalysis, 1981. Tchr. music pub. and parochial elementary schs., Northwestern Ohio, 1948-62; student Cath. U. Am., Washington, 1963-65, instr. psychology, 1964-67; instr. ednl. psychology Mary Manse Coll., Toledo, Ohio, 1965-66; directress juniorate, Sisters St. Francis, Tiffin, Ohio, 1965-69; instr. ednl. psychology Coll. St. Francis, Joliet, 1966-67; Madonna Coll., Livonia, Mich., 1967-69; postdoctoral clin. psychology Topeka (Kans.) State Hosp., 1969-70; postdoctoral clin. psychology Menninger Found., Topeka, 1970-72, clin. psychologist, psychotherapist, hosp. therapist, supr. psychotherapy vocat. assessment program, 1972—; cons. vocation program, Toledo Diocese, also permanent deacon program. Diplomate Am. Bd. Profl. Psychology; cert. clin. psychologist, Ohio, Kans. Mem. Am. Psychol. Assn., Ohio Psychol. Assn., Soc. Personality Assessment. Contbr. articles to psychol. jours. Home: 900 Lincoln St Topeka KS 66606 Office: Menninger Foundation Box 829 Topeka KS 66601

CERNY, JOSEPH CHARLES, urologist, educator; b. Oak Park, Ill., Apr. 20, 1930; s. Joseph James and Mary (Turek) C.; m. Patti Bobette Pickens, Nov. 10, 1962; children—Joseph Charles, Rebecca Anne. B.A., Knox Coll., 1952; M.D., Yale U., 1956. Diplomate Am. Bd. Urology. Intern U. Mich. Hosp., Ann Arbor, 1956-57, resident, 1957-62; practice medicine specializing in urology,

Ann Arbor, and Detroit since 1962—; inst. surgery (urology) U. Mich., Ann Arbor, 1962-64, asst. prof., 1964-66, assoc. prof., 1966-71, clin. prof., 1971—; chmn. dept. urology Henry Ford Hosp., Detroit, 1971—; pres. Resistors, Inc., Chgo., 1960—; cons. St. Joseph Hosp., Ann Arbor, 1973—. Contbr. articles to profl. jours., chpts. in books. Bd. dirs., trustee Nat. Kidney Found. Mich., Ann Arbor, 1980—; bd. dirs. Ann Arbor Amateur Hockey Assn., 1980-83; pres. PTO, Ann Arbor Pub. Schs., 1980. Served to lt. USNR, 1956-76. Recipient Disting. Service award Transplantation Soc. Mich., 1982. Fellow ACS (pres.-elect Mich. br. 1984-85, pres. 1985—); mem. Am. Urol. Assn. (Best Sci. Exhibit award 1978, Best Sci. Films award 1980, 82, pres.-elect north central sect. 1984—), Am. Assn. Transplant Surgeons; Endocrine Surgeons, Soc. Univ. Urologists, Am. Assn. Urologic Oncology, Am. Fertility Soc. Republican. Methodist. Clubs: Barton Hills Country; Ann Arbor Raquet (Ann Arbor). Avocations: tennis; fishing; Civil War. Home: 2800 Fairlane Dr Ann Arbor MI 48104 Office: Dept Urology Henry Ford Hosp 2799 W Grand Blvd Detroit MI 48202

CESARE, ANTHONY GIORGI, JR., writer, inventor, puppeteer; b. Chgo., July 31, 1943; s. Anthony Giorgi and Genevieve Stephanie (Lucas) C.; B.A. in English, Parsons Coll., 1965; m. Margaret Ann Hooks, Sept. 27, 1981. Tech. writer T.M. Pubs., Chgo., 1965-67; copywriter Hilltop Advt., Battle Creek, Mich., 1967-68; mktg. and pub. relations coordinator Ad Art and Design, Kalamazoo, 1968-69; owner Cesare & Assos., Boulder, Colo., 1969-71; freelance writer, 1973-77; tech. editor Chemetron Fire Systems, Monee, Ill., 1971—; sr. tech. writer Allis-Chalmers Corp., 1979-80; pres. Snaffle, Inc., Morocco, Ind.; with Cole Marionettes, Lake Village, Ind., 1984—. Mem. Internat. Platform Assn., Am. Advt. Fedn., Writers Guild. Roman Catholic. Author: The Feathers Technique, 1980; Capt. Monsewer Weird, 1985. Editor: Chemetron Fire Systems Halon 1301 Design Manual, 1978; inventor card game Snaffle, 1978. Home: Lake Village IN 46349

CESARI, LAMBERTO, educator; b. Bologna, Italy, Sept. 23, 1910; s. Cesare and Amelia (Giannizzeri) C.; Ph.D. in Math., U. Pisa (Italy), 1933; m. Isotta Hornauer, Apr. 2, 1939. Came to U.S., 1949. Assoc. prof. U. Pisa, 1939-42; asso. prof. U. Bologna, 1942-47, prof. math., 1947-48; staff Inst. Advanced Study, Princeton, N.J., 1948; prof. math. U. Calif.-Berkeley, 1949, U. Wis., 1950; prof. math. Purdue U., 1950-60; prof. math. U. Mich., Ann Arbor, 1960—, R. L. Wilder prof. math., 1976—. Corr. mem. Accademie delle Scienze di Bologna, Modena, Milano, Italian Nat. Acad.; mem. Math. Assn. Am., Am. Math. Soc. Author: Surface Area, 1955; Asymptotic Properties, 1959; Optimization, 1983; also articles on differential equations, calculus of variations, real analysis. Editorial bd. Applicable Math. Jour., 1970—, Jour. Differential Equations, 1973—, Rendiconti Circolo Matematico di Palermo, 1960—. Home: 2021 Washtenaw Ave Ann Arbor MI 48104

CESARIO, ROBERT CHARLES, franchise executive, consultant; b. Chgo., Apr. 6, 1941; s. Valentino A. and Mary Ethel (Kenny) C.; m. Emily Carbone (div.); 1 son, Jeffrey; m. Susan Kay DePoutee. B.S. in Gen. Edn., Northwestern U., 1975; postgrad. in bus. adminstrn. DePaul U., 1975. Mgr. fin. ops. Midas Internat. Corp., Chgo., 1968-73; dir. staff ops. Am. Hosp. Supply Corp., McGaw Park, Ill., 1973-76; v.p. Car X Service Systems Inc., Chgo., 1976-78, v.p. oil services, 1983-84; v.p., sr. ptnr. Growth Strategies, Inc., 1984—, v.p. Chicken Unlimited Enterprises Inc., Chgo., 1978-83. Served with USMC, 1960-62. Office: 20 N Wacker Dr Suite 1530 Chicago IL 60606

CEY, RONALD CHARLES, professional baseball player. Third baseman Chgo. Cubs. Office: Chgo Cubs Wrigley Field Chicago IL 60613*

CHA, JAI CHUL, pathologist; b. Seoul, Korea, June 12, 1945; s. Donghwan and Keumyai (Lee) C.; M.D., Seoul Nat. U., 1968; came to U.S., 1971, naturalized, 1978; m. Kwangsoon Nam, Nov. 2, 1970; children—Albert, Jennifer. Teaching fellow, resident in pathology Case Western Res. U., Cleve., 1973-76; asso. pathologist Graham Hosp. Assn., Canton, Ill., 1976—; clin. instr. Peoria Sch. Medicine, 1980—. Served with Korean Air Force, 1968-71. Diplomate Am. Bd. Pathology. Mem. AMA, Ill. Med. Soc., Fulton County Med. Soc. (pres.), Coll. Am. Pathologists, Am. Soc. Clin. Pathologists. Presbyterian. Club: Rotary. Home: 1030 N 1st Ave Canton IL 61520 Office: 210 W Walnut St Canton IL 61520

CHADBOURNE, JAMES MICHAEL, transportation sales and marketing executive; b. Mobile, Ala., Jan. 9, 1947; s. Harry and Hilda Katherin (Fox) C.; m. Carolyn Ann McKay, June 28, 1969; children—Sherri, Dawn, Scott. B.A., Wittenberg U., 1970; M.B.A., Case Western Reserve U., 1980. With B.F. Goodrich Co., Akron, Ohio, 1970-83; mktg. mgr. leasing group Leaseway Transp. Co., Cleve., 1983, corp. dir. mktg., 1983-85, corp. dir. sales and mktg., 1985—. Mem. ch. council Trinity Luth. Ch., Clinton, Ohio, 1981-83, supt. Sunday Sch., 1982. Served with U.S. Army, 1965-72. Named Ohio Boys State Rep., 1964; recipient Fulton County med. award, 1964, Nat. Sci. Def. Program award NASA, 1965. Mem. Am. Mgmt. Assn., Sales Mktg. Execs. Assn., Nat. Rifle Assn. (Nat. Rifle Team Championship 1963), Ohio Nat. Acad. Sci., Lambda Chi Alpha. Lutheran. Avocations: stamp collecting; piano; skiing; reading; computers. Club: B.F. Goodrich Bowling (Akron, Ohio) (pres. 1980-81, v.p. 1979-80). Home: 3026 Serfass Rd Clinton OH 44216

CHADDOCK, CHARLES RICHARD, pharmaceutical company executive; b. Canton, Ohio, April 9, 1914; s. Richard Greer and Dora M. (Elser) C.: m. Bessie Jane Kilgore, Sept. 1, 1948; children—Georgia Kay Bailey, Carole Rae. B.S. in Pharmacy, Ohio State U., 1936; postgrad. Syracuse U., 1959. Registered pharmacist, Ohio. Pharmacist, Bowman Bros. Drug Co., Canton, 1936-57; pres. Bowman Braun Pharm. Co., Canton, 1957-61; pres. Bowman Pharm. Inc., 1961-84; pres. CRC Unit Formulas Inc., Canton, 1985—. Developer of new pharm. products, over the counter and prescription items. Mem. Tri-County Health Career Assn. (pres. 1973), Sigma Phi Epsilon (Clifford B. Scott hon. award), Phi Rho Alpha. Republican. Mem. Trinity United Ch. of Christ. Lodges: Rotary (edn. com. 1945—), Masons (32d degree). Avocations: swimming, bridge. Home: 2110 Red Coach Dr NW North Canton OH 44720 Office: CRC Unit Formulas Inc 914-18th St NW Canton OH 44703

CHADWICK, DOUGLAS KENNETH, floorcovering company sales executive; b. Alexandria, Minn., Dec. 25, 1949; s. Kenneth Harmon and Gladys Muriel (Sorenson) C.; m. Joan May Kline, July 19, 1969; 1 child, Ryan Douglas. B.A. in Bus. Mgmt., Coll. St. Thomas, 1978. Salesman, Plywood Minn., Marshall, Minn., 1968-71, asst. v.p. corp. devel., Mpls., 1973-79, mgr., Sioux Falls, S.D., 1979-81; sales mgr. Warren Supply, Sioux Falls, 1981-84, gen. sales mgr., 1984—. Served with USAF, 1971-73. Republican. Lutheran. Lodge: Moose. Avocations: fishing; hunting; woodworking; reading. Home: 3008 S Holbrook Sioux Falls SD 57106 Office: Warren Supply Co 300 E 50th St N Sioux Falls SD 57104

CHAI, WINBERG, educator, consultant; b. Shanghai, China, Oct. 16, 1932; came to U.S., 1951, naturalized, 1973; s. Ch'u and Mei-en (Tsao) C.; student Hartwick Coll., 1951-53; B.A., Wittenberg U., 1955; M.A., New Sch. for Social Research, 1958; Ph.D., NYU, 1968; m. Carolyn Everett, Mar. 17, 1966; children—Maria May-lee, Jeffrey Tien-yu. Lectr., New Sch. for Social Research, 1957-61; vis. asst. prof. Drew U., 1961-62; asst. prof. Fairleigh Dickinson U., 1962-65; assoc. prof. U. Redlands, 1965-73; prof., chmn. CCNY, 1973-79; disting. prof. polit. sci., v.p. U. S.D., Vermillion, 1979-81; cons. U.S. Dept. Edn., 1982—; vice chmn. U.S.-Asia Research Inst., N.Y.C., 1982—; chmn. 3d World Conf. Found., Inc., Chgo., 1982—; cons. Software System & Tech., Inc., M.I. Trading Co., Tokyo, others. Mem. S.D. Com. on Humanities, 1980. Ford Found. humanities grantee, 1968, 69; Haynes Found. fellow, 1967, 68; Pacific Cultural Found. grantee, 1978; NSF grantee, 1970; Hubert Eaton Meml. Fund grantee, 1972-73; Field Found. grantee, 1973, 75; Henry Luce Found. grantee, 1978; Saudi Arabia Ednl. grantee, 1982-83. Mem. Am. Assn. Chinese Studies (pres. 1978-80), AAAS, AAUP, Am. Polit. Sci. Assn., N.Y. Acad. Sci., Internat. Studies Assn. Democrat. Roman Catholic. Author: (with Ch'u Chai) The Story of Chinese Philosophy, 1961, The Changing Society of China, 1962, rev. edit., 1969, The New Politics of Communist China, 1972, The Search for a New China, 1975; editor: Essential Works of Chinese Communism, 1969; (with James Hsiung) Asia and U.S. Foreign Policy, 1981, U.S.-Asian Relations: The National Security Paradox, 1983; co-translator: A Treasury of Chinese Literature, 1965. Home: Seven Oaks Ranch RR 1 Box 22 Vermillion SD 57069 Office: PO Box 472 Vermillion SD 57069

CHAIREZ, RUBEN, virologist; b. El Paso, Tex., Apr. 20, 1942; s. Paul and Mary C.; B.A., UCLA, 1965; Ph.D., Oreg. State U., Corvallis, 1970; m. Yolanda Fernandez Andrade, Dec. 23, 1978; children—Paul, Monica. Fellow dept. biol. scis. Purdue U., 1970-72; research fellow dept. virology Baylor Coll. Medicine, Houston, 1972-74; asst. prof. biology George Mason U., Fairfax, Va., 1974-77; sr. scientist, sect. head Abbott Labs., North Chicago, Ill., 1977—. Mem. AAAS, Am. Soc. Microbiology, Sigma Xi, Phi Sigma. Roman Catholic. Contbr. articles to profl. jours. Home: 1045 Linden Ave Deerfield IL 60015 Office: 14th St and Sheridan De North Chicago IL 60064

CHAKRABARTI, DEBOPAM, biochemist, researcher; b. Midnapur, West Bengal, India, July 13, 1952; s. Narendra Mohan and Monola (Chatterjee) C.; m. Ratna Datta, Jan. 22, 1981. B.S., U. Calcutta, India, 1973, M.S., 1975, Ph.D., 1983. Research scientist Organon (India) Ltd., Calcutta, 1981-84; research assoc. U. Nebr., Lincoln, 1984—. Mem. Am. Soc. Biol. Chemists, Nat. Geog. Soc. Avocations: Photography, hiking, listening to music, reading, philately. Office: Univ of Nebraska-Lincoln 604 Hamilton Hall Lincoln NE 68588

CHAKRABORTY, ANUP KUMAR, physician; b. Brahmanbaria, Bangladesh, May 23, 1946; came to U.S., 1975; s. Kusum Kumar and Jyotsna (Mayee) C.; m. Sarbani Chakraborty, Feb. 19, 1976; children—Apurba, Amit. M.B.B.S., Bankura Sammilani Med. Coll. Calcutta U., 1969; M.D., Postgrad Inst., Chandigarh, India, 1973. Diplomate Am. Bd. Internal Medicine (pulmonary disease). Resident in medicine VA Med. Ctr., Bklyn., 1975-77; fellow in pulmonary medicine Nat. Jewish Hosp. and U. Colo., Denver, 1977-79; staff physician VA Med. Ctr., Denver, 1979-80, also faculty U. Colo. Med. Ctr. chief med. service VA Med. Ctr., Tomah, Wis., 1980-81; dir. respiratory care VA Med. Ctr., Lincoln, Nebr., 1981-82; practice medicine specializing in pulmonary disease, Lincoln, 1982—; mem. staff Bryan Meml., Lincoln Gen., St. Elizabeth Community Health Ctr. (all Lincoln). Fellow ACP, Am. Coll. Chest Physicians. Contbr. articles to profl. jours. Home: 6510 Skylark Ln Lincoln NE 68516 Office: 120 Wedgewood Dr Suite A Lincoln NE 68510

CHALGIAN, CHARLES, economics educator; b. Union City, N.J., July 8, 1930; s. John and Araxe C.; A.B., Antioch Coll., 1958; M.A., Harvard U., 1959; m. Sara Lou Hemenger, Apr. 1, 1955; children—Elizabeth, Douglas, Johanna, Juliet. Tchr. Algonac Community Schs., 1959-61; prof. econs. Macomb County Coll., Warren, Mich., 1961—, active panels; pub. Brown City Banner, weekly newspaper, Sanilac County, Mich. Chmn. Macomb Essentials Transp. Service, 1980-82, mem., 1976—; mem. Macomb County Bd. Commrs., 1976-80; bd. dirs. Southeastern Mich. Transp. Authority, 1978-80. Served with USAF, 1949-53. Decorated UN medal with two stars. Fulbright award, 1965. Mem. Am. Econ. Assn., Democrat. Presbyterian. Author: Current Economic Issues, 1967; contbr. articles to publs. Home: 35290 Moravian Rd Sterling Heights MI 48077 Office: Macomb County College South Campus Warren MI 48093

CHALGREN, WILLIAM SCHLUTZ, neuropsychiatrist; b. Mpls., July 17, 1915; s. Richard William and Dorothy (Schlutz) C.; m. Patricia Barnhardt, June 14, 1943 (div. 1960); children—Richard William, Robert Douglas, James Eric; m. Marcia McLaughlin, Feb. 20, 1960. B.A. cum laude, U. Minn., 1939, B. Medicine, 1943, M.D., 1939, Ph.D., 1949. Diplomate Am. Bd. Psychiatry and Neurology. Research assoc. U. Pa., Phila., 1939-40; instr. dept. psychiatry, U. Minn., Mpls., 1947-48, prof. dept. neuropsychiatry, 1948-50, clin. prof. neurology, 1950—; cons. St. Peter State Hosp., Minn., 1950—; Bd. dirs. Mankato Rehab. Ctr., (Minn.), 1950-60. Served to capt., U.S. Army, 1945-47. Fellow Am. Acad. Neurology, Am. Psychiat. Assn.; mem. Sigma Psi. Lodge: Kiwanis. Avocations: fishing; golfing; curling. Home: 2011 Roe Crest North Mankato MN 56001 Office: Chalgren and Lund Ltd 400 Martin Bldg Mankato MN 56001

CHALKLEY, THOMAS HENRY FERGUSON, ophthalmic surgeon, educator; b. N.Y.C., Nov. 3, 1933; s. Lyman and Katherine (Ferguson) C.; B.A., U. Wis., 1955, M.D., 1958; m. Cynthia Carroll, Nov. 21, 1975; children—Ellen Elizabeth, Deborah Katherine. Intern, E. J. Meyer Hosp., Buffalo, 1958-59; resident physician Northwestern U. Med. Sch., 1960-62; practice medicine specializing in ophthalmic surgery, Chgo., 1962—; attending physician Northwestern Meml. Hosp., Chgo., 1962—; courtesy staff Lakeland Hosp., Elkhorn, Wis., 1983—; assoc. prof. clin. ophthalmology Northwestern U. Med. Sch., 1962—; assoc. examiner Am. Bd. Ophthalmology, 1965—. Bd. dirs. Ill. Soc. Prevention Blindness, 1978-79. Served to comdr. USNR, 1966-68. Recipient Disting. Merit award Hadley Sch. for Blind, 1979. Mem. Am. Acad. Ophthalmology Pan Am. Ophthal. Soc., Chgo. Ophthal. Soc. (pres. 1977-78), AAUP, Walworth County Med. Soc., Wis. Med. Soc. Author: Your Eyes, 1973, 2d edit., 1981; also articles; mem. editorial bd. Am. Jour. Ophthalmology, 1965-82, cons. editor, 1982—. Home: 160 E Pearson Chicago IL 60611 Office: 233 E Erie Chicago IL 60611

CHALMERS, E(DWIN) LAURENCE, JR., See *Who's Who in America,* 43rd edition.

CHAMBERLAIN, DONALD SHERWOOD, radiologist; b. Cin., May 21, 1935; s. Sherwood Archibald and Christine Carter (Matthews) C.; B.A., Northwestern U., 1956, M.D., 1960; m. Lillian Joyce Knudsen, June 2, 1956; children—Cheryl Ann, Daniel. Intern, U. Cin. Gen. Hosp., 1960-61, resident in radiology, 1961-64; practice medicine, specializing in radiology, Radiology, Inc., South Bend, Ind., 1966—; med. staff Meml. Hosp., South Bend, 1966—, Elkhart (Ind.) Gen. Hosp., 1966—, Parkview Hosp., Plymouth, Ind., 1966-81, South Bend Clinic, 1966—; dir., sec. Ind. Physicians Ins. Co., 1981-83; dir. X-Ray Equipment Inc., South Bend, Radiology, Inc.; chmn. Am. Physicians Life Ins. Co., Nat. Bank & Trust Co. South Bend. Bd. dirs. No. Ind. Health Systems Agy., 1978-83, exec. com., 1979-83; bd. dirs. Ind. Med. Edn. and Devel. Info. Center, 1978-81, Ind. State Wide Profl. Standards Rev. Council, 1978; bd. dirs. Ind. Area 2 PSRO Inc., 1974-81, chmn., 1974-79; bd. dirs., chmn. No. Ind. Found. for Health, 1981—; bd. dirs. Meml. Med. Found., 1982—. Served to capt. M.C., U.S. Army, 1964-66. Diplomate Am. Bd. Radiology. Fellow Am. Coll. Radiology (councilor Ind. 1983—); mem. Ind. Med. Soc. (trustee 1978-83), St. Joseph County Med. Soc. (pres. 1976-77), AMA, Ind. Roentgen Soc. (pres. 1985-86), Radiol. Soc. N.Am., Am. Roentgen Ray Soc., N. Central Ind. Med. Edn. Found., South Bend Med. Found., Am. Radio Relay League, Lambda Chi Alpha, Phi Rho Sigma, Pi Kappa Epsilon. Methodist. Clubs: Profl. Investors, South Bend Country, Masons, Shriners, Signal Point. Contbr. articles to med. jours. Home: 54712 Merrifield Dr Mishawaka IN 46545 Office: 707 N Michigan St South Bend IN 46601

CHAMBERLAIN, JOSEPH MILES, See *Who's Who in America,* 43rd edition.

CHAMBERLIN, MARGARET ELIZABETH, marketing consultant; b. Denver, Oct. 3, 1952; d. Elmer John and Helen Claire (Kilday) Roth; m. Mark Hill Chamberlin, June 22, 1974. B.A. in Journalism, U. Okla., 1974; postgrad. in bus. adminstrn. Wichita State U., 1979-83. Account coordinator Advt. Concepts, Wichita, 1974-76; pub. relations dir. Wichita Symphony, 1976-77; dir. advt. Quik Print, Inc., 1977-78; account service copywriter Stephan Advt., Wichita, 1978-79; communications specialist KG and E, The Electric Co., Wichita, 1979-81; account exec. Lida Advt. Co., Wichita, 1981-84; asst. v.p., dir. mktg. Union Nat. Bank of Wichita, 1984-85; owner Chamberlin Communications, Wichita, 1985—. Bd. dirs. Child Care Assn. Wichita/Sedgwick County, 1984—, Friends of the Library, 1985—; vol. ARC, 1982—. Recipient writing awards Kans. Press Women, 1978, 79, 81; Addy awards Wichita Advt. Club, 1980, 82, 83. Mem. Women in Communications (pres. Wichita chpt. 1978-79), Pub. Relations Soc. Am. (student liaison 1984-85, bd. dirs. 1985—), Wichita Area C. of C. (chair Greater Downtown Wichita Spl. Activities com. 1985—), Sales and Mktg. Execs., Advt. Club Wichita, Kappa Delta. Republican. Congregationalist. Home: 157 N Edgemoor Dr Wichita KS 67208 Office: PO Box 18462 Wichita KS 67218

CHAMBERS, BILLY JOE, ch. ofcl.; b. Ft. Worth, Tex., Dec. 13, 1932; s. Joseph Yancy and Bertha Clara (McMillen) C.; B.A., Baylor U., 1955; postgrad. Golden Gate Bapt. Theol. Sem., 1955-58; B.D., Southwestern Bapt. Theol. Sem., 1960; m. Ima Louise Tyson, Aug. 22, 1954; children—Joseph Thurman, Marc William, Carol Lynn. Ordained to ministry, Bapt. Ch., 1956; pastor, So. Bapt. Chs., Ohio, 1960-73; denominational worker Mich. State Baptists, 1973-77; pastor Bapt. Ch., Burton, Mich., 1977-71; denominational worker, dir. ch. services Minn.-Wis. Bapt. Offices, Rochester, Minn., 1981—; associational Sunday sch. dir. World Mission Confs., 1961-75. Trustee Golden Gate Bapt. Sem., 1970-73, Midwestern Bapt. Sem., 1978-81. Mem. Alpha Kappa Delta. Republican. Office: 519 16th St SE Rochester MN 55901

CHAMBERS, EARL RICHARD, personnel administrator; b. Wyoming, Ill., Nov. 4, 1916; s. John Thomas and Margaret Jane (Lawless) C.; B.Ed., Ill. State Normal U., 1938; M.A., U. Ill., 1947, postgrad., 1948-53; m. Jane Margaret Petersen, May 8, 1954 (dec. May 1982); 1 son, Robert. Profl. personnel work Ill. Civil Service Commn., 1947-53, chief of exams. adminstrng., employee selection, 1951-53; personnel dir. St. Louis County, Mo., 1953—. Mem. Gov. Mo. Citizens Adv. Council Higher Edn. Act, 1972-73. Served from pvt. to tech. sgt. AUS, 1942-46; Philippines, New Guinea. Mem. Pub. Personnel Assn. (exec. bd. local chapter, 1952-53, regional sec.-treas., 1956-57, regional 1st v.p. 1963-64, regional chmn. 1964-65), Am. Soc. Personnel Adminstrn. (accredited); Am. Soc. Pub. Adminstrn. (exec. bd. local chpt. 1951-52, 59-63, 64-65, 70-71, pres. Met. St. Louis 1963-64), Internat. Personnel Mgmt. Assn. (v.p. St. Louis chpt. 1973-74, pres. 1974-75), Kappa Delta Pi, Pi Gamma Mu. Contbr. articles, abstracts and revs. to profl. jours. Home: 12 Armstrong Dr Glendale MO 63122 Office: 7900 Forsyth Blvd Clayton Mo 63105

CHAMBERS, GLENN DARRELL, wildlife photographer, artist; b. Butler, Mo., June 14, 1936; s. E. Glenn and Fern M. (Woods) C.; m. Marilyn Janell Henry, Aug. 29, 1959 (div. Jan. 1980); children—James D., Russell G., Lindell C.; m. Jeannie Bay Erwin, Feb. 27, 1980; stepchildren—Robert Roemer, Matthew Roemer. B.S., Central Mo. State U., 1958; M.A., U. Mo.-Columbia, 1961. Area mgr. Mo. Dept. Conservation, Jefferson City, 1961-62, research biologist, 1962-69, biologist, photographer, 1969-79; regional dir. Ducks Unltd., Columbia, Mo., 1979-83, wildlife photographer, 1984—; pres. Niska Art, Inc., Columbia, 1984—. Films include: (with Charles and Elizabeth Schwartz) Return of the Wild Turkey (2d place award Outdoor Writers Assn. Am.), 1971, The Show-Me Hunter (2d place award Outdoor Writers Assn. Am.), 1972, Wild Chorus: The Story of the Canada Goose (1st place award Outdoor Writers Assn. Am.), 1974, (Best Motion Picture award Wildlife Soc.), 1974; More Than Trees: Ecology of the Forest (2d place award Forestry Film Festival, 1st place award Outdoor Writers Assn. Am.), 1977. Photographs in Audubon mag., others. Contbr. tech. articles to Jour. Wildlife Mgmt., 1961-77. Winner 1984-85 Mo. Waterfowl Stamp Design Contest. Democrat. Baptist. Home: 501 Onofrio Ct Columbia MO 65203 Office: Ducks Unltd 1 Waterfowl Way at Gilmer Long Grove IL 60047

CHAMBERS, ROBERTA NADINE, organist, educator; b. Arcola, Ill., Oct. 29, 1924; d. Horace Watson and Ethel Irene (Bartholomew) Mulliken; Mus.B., U. Ill., 1947; M.S. in Music, Ill. State U., 1970; postgrad. in piano pedagogy U. Ind., U. Ill., 1980-83, 84, 85; m. Mar. 10, 1949; children—Michael Lee, Linda Sue. Asst. instr. keyboard harmony U. Ill., 1946; instr. music Tenn. Wesleyan Coll., Athens, 1947-49; assoc. prof. music Lincoln (Ill.) Christian Coll., 1953—; pvt. music tchr.; organist for ch. and service vol. activities. Mem. Am. Guild Organists, Assn. Christian Coll. Music Educators, Nat. Piano Tchrs. Guild, Pi Kappa Lambda, Sigma Alpha Iota. Mem. Christian Ch. Home: 505 Oglesby St Lincoln IL 62656 Office: Lincoln Christian Coll Box 178 Lincoln IL 62656

CHAMBERS, VIRGINIA ANNE, music educator; b. Middlesboro, Ky., Jan. 28, 1931; d. Jason C. and Virginia Claire (Dobyns) C. Mus.B., U. Louisville, 1952; Mus.M., Eastman Sch. Music, 1964; Ph.D., U. Mich., 1970. Gen. elem. music tchr. Oak Ridge Pub. Schs., 1952-63, Rochester (N.Y.) Sch. Dist., 1963-64; prof. music SUNY-Geneso, 1964-66, Eastern Mich. U., Ypsilanti, 1966-68, U. Wis.-Madison, 1968-75, U. Toledo, 1975—; v.p. Tometic Assocs., Ltd., Buffalo. Mem. Music Educators Nat. Conf., Ohio Music Educators Assn. Club: University (Toledo). Author: Words and Music: An Introduction to Music Literacy, 1976; Tometics: Reading Rhythm Patterns, 1979; Piano Accompaniments for A Nichols Worth, Vols. 3 and 4, 1982; editor: A Nichols Worth, Vols. 3 and 4. Home: 3216 Kylemore Rd Toledo OH 43606 Office: Center for Performing Arts U Toledo Toledo OH 43601

CHAMBERS, WALTER R., investment banker; b. Lancaster, Ohio, May 2, 1931; s. Walter R. and Martha Blanche (Notestone) C.; m. Sue Hartley, Aug. 8, 1953; children—James R., Mark R. B.S., Ohio State U., 1952. With Ohio Co., Columbus, 1961—, adminstr. pub. fin., fixed income and equity trading depts., 1968—, dir., exec. v.p., 1972—; dir. Ohio Equities Inc., Ins. Ohio Co. Agy.; pres., dir. Midwest Parking Inc. Treas., bd. dirs. Health Services Found.; trustee Coll. of Wooster; treas. Upper Arlington Civic Assn., 1966-67; cabinet mem. Franklin County United Way, 1982-83. Served with U.S. Army, 1956-58. Mem. Pub. Securities Assn. (chmn., dir.), Securities Industry Assn. (dir., exec. com.), Mcpl. Fin. Forum Washington, Mcpl. Fin. Forum N.Y. Republican. Episcopalian. Clubs: Muirfield Village Golf, Scioto Country, University (Columbus). Lodge: Masons. Contbr. articles to profl. jours. Office: 155 E Broad St Columbus OH 43215

CHAMPAGNE, BRENDA (JEAN) LAMB, occupational therapist; b. Northampton, Mass., Aug. 14, 1951; d. Frank Gilbert and Gertrude Maria (MacArthur) Lamb; student Winthrop Coll., 1969-70, Boston U., 1970; B.S. in Occupational Therapy, Quinnipiac Coll., 1974; m. Clement Henri Champagne, Nov. 9, 1974; children—Melissa Yolande, Timothée Daniel. Occupational therapist Alexandra Pavilion, Montreal (Que., Can.) Children's Hosp., 1974-75; therapist Area Coop. Ednl. Services, North Haven, Conn., 1975, Trinity Luth. Hosp., Kansas City, Mo., 1976; part time therapist Bethany Med. Center, Kansas City, Kans., 1976-77, dir. occupational therapy, 1977-81; home health therapist, nursing home cons. Crosslands Rehab. Agy., 1984—; part time asst. prof. dept. occupational therapy, U. Kans., 1977; chmn. Greater Kansas City Occupational Therapy Adminstrv. Council, 1978-79; cons. profl. adv. com. Outreach Rehab. Services, Inc., 1979-80; cons. profl. adv. bd. Crossland Rehab. Agy., Inc., 1980—; council pres. U. Kans. Council on Occupational Therapy Edn., 1980-83, chmn. coms., 1978-81. Mem. Am. Occupational Therapy Assn. (registered occupational therapist, elected commn. on edn. 1980—), Kans. Occupational Therapy Assn. (newsletter editor 1977-79, state long range plan chmn. 1979-81, state v.p. 1979-81). Contbg. author, editor: MidTerm Evaluation of Fieldwork Experience, 1979. Home: 8215 Webster St Kansas City KS 66109 Office: 51 N 12th St Kansas City KS 66102

CHAMPEAU, BRUCE EDWIN, legal administrator; b. Mpls., Mar. 11, 1943; s. John Matthew (stepfather) and Alice Marie Wilhelm; B.L.S., U. Okla., 1974; M.B.A., Columbia Pacific U., 1983. Cost estimator Bartley Sales Co., Inc., Mpls., 1961-63; supr. Midwest Bldg. Services, Inc., Mpls., 1963-68; mgr. gen. services Dorsey & Whitney, Mpls., 1968-79; office adminstr. Borgelt, Powell, Peterson & Frauen, S.C., Milw., 1979—; condr. workshops Mpls.-St. Paul chpt. Adminstrv. Mgmt. Soc., 1977, 78. Bd. deacons Emanuel Lutheran Ch., Mpls., 1964-67. Mem. ABA (assoc.), Assn. Legal Adminstrs. (sec. Wis. chpt. 1983, v.p. 1984), Adminstrv. Mgmt. Soc. (past dir.), Acad. Cert. Adminstrv. Mgrs. (cert. 1977), Office Tech. Mgmt. Assn. Home: 811 E State St Milwaukee WI 53202 Office: Borgelt Powell Peterson & Frauen S C 735 N Water St Suite 1500 Milwaukee WI 53202

CHAMPNEY, DON, construction company executive; b. Detroit, Sept. 8, 1927; s. Donald Ole and Marjorie Elaine (Porter) C.; m. Ann Christine Mainland, June 23, 1951; children—Christine Champney Forte, Sarah Ann Champney Sieber. B.Arch., U. Mich., 1951. Design engr. Detroit Steel Products, 1951-52; regional mgr. Lumber Fabricators, Inc., Cin., 1952-53; designer Arcose Homes, Cin., 1953-55; v.p. engring. Style Rite Homes Corp., Columbus, Ohio, 1955-57; regional mgr. Scholz Homes, Cin., 1957-58; br. mgr. Fred M. Cole Corp., Columbus, 1958-66; v.p. engring. Gardner Co., Columbus, 1966—. Pres. pro tem, chmn. fin. com. village council Village of Minerva Park, 1976—; mem. Joint Twp. Hosp. Dist., 1982—. Served with USN, 1945-46; to ensign USNR. Recipient mem. of the Yr. Construction Specifications Inst. (Columbus chpt.), 1975. Mem. Builders Exchange Central Ohio (pres. 1981), U. Mich. Club of Columbus (pres. 1960), Sigma Alpha Epsilon. Republican. Episcopalian. Club: Brookside Country (Worthington, Ohio); Continental Athletic (Columbus). Home: 5386 Park Lane Ct Columbus OH 43229 Office: 4588 Kenny Rd Columbus OH 43220

CHAN, CHUN-WAH, social worker; b. Chao-Young, Kwangtung, China, July 22, 1945; s. Hak-Tang and So-Fong (Yeung) C.; came to U.S., 1969, naturalized, 1978; B.S.Sc. cum laude (scholar) Chinese U. Hong Kong, 1967; M.A. (scholar) U. Chgo., 1971; m. Heidi Kwok-Shun Cheng, June 15, 1968. Social work supr. Family Planning Assn. of Hong Kong, 1967-69; with Cook County Hosp., Chgo., 1971—, divisional dir. psychiat. social service div., 1973—, coordinator staff devel. and quality assurance dept. social service, 1978—; pvt. practice individual and family therapy, Chgo., 1977—. Leader Hong Kong Boy Scout Assn., 1964-69; divisional officer St. John Ambulance Brigade, Hong Kong, 1968-69; bd. dirs. Chinese Am. Service League, Chgo.,

1977-78, chmn. nominating com., 1978, pres. bd. dirs. 1978—. Cert. social worker, Ill. Mem. Nat. Assn. Social Workers, Acad. Cert. Social Workers, Asian Am. Mental Health Research Center. Home: 4946 Sunnyside Dr Hillside IL 60162 Office: Psychiatric Social Service Cook County Hospital 1825 W Harrison St Chicago IL 60612

CHAN, SHAU-KUEN PATRICIA, diversified company executive; b. Hong Kong, Dec. 23, 1943; came to U.S., 1958, naturalized, 1973; d. King Cheong and Ma Soo (Ching) Wong; m. Ping Yuen Chan, Oct. 9, 1958; children—Clayton, Mark. B.S., U. Windsor, Ont., Can., 1969; M.S., Mass. Coll. Pharmacy, 1972; postgrad. Queens U., Ont., 1972-74. Registered pharmacist, Mass. Intern. Mass. Gen. Hosp., Boston, 1970-72; clin. pharmacist Lynn Hosp., Mass., 1972; clin. and intravenous pharmacist Mt. Auburn Hosp., Mass., 1972-76; pres. Bali Hai Inc., Maplewood, Minn., 1976—, fin. cons., 1978-81. Mem. Am. Pharm. Assn., Phi Beta Kappa. Avocations: equity investments; travel; cooking. Home: 2430 Dianna Ln Saint Paul MN 55117 Office: Bali Hai Inc 2305 White Bear Ave Maplewood MN 55109

CHAN, SHIH HUNG, mechanical engineering educator, consultant; b. Chang Hwa, Taiwan, Nov. 8, 1943; came to U.S., 1964; s. Ping and Fu Zon (Liao) C.; m. Shirley Shih-Lin Wang, June 14, 1969; children—Bryan, Erick. Diploma Taipei Inst. Tech., Taiwan, 1963; M.S., U. N.H., 1966; Ph.D., U. Calif.-Berkeley, 1969. Registered profl. engr., Wis. Asst. to assoc. prof. NYU, N.Y.C., 1969-73; assoc. prof. Poly. Inst. N.Y., N.Y.C., 1973-74; research staff mem. Argonne Nat. Lab., Ill., 1974-75; assoc. prof. U. Wis., Milw., 1975-78, prof. mech. engring., 1978—, chmn. dept., 1979—; cons. Argonne Nat. Lab., Ill., 1975—, Allen-Bradley Co., Milw., 1984, Gen. Electric Co., Schenectady, 1980. Contbr. articles to profl. jours. Bd. dirs. Orgn. Chinese Americans, State of Wis., 1983—; v.p. Civic Club, Milw., 1984—, pres., 1985—. Served to 2d lt. Taiwan M.C., 1963-64. Recipient Outstanding Research award U. Wis.-Milw. Research Found., 1983; Research citation Assembly State of Wis., Madison, 1984; grantee NSF, Dept. Energy, Argonne Nat. Lab., 1969—. Mem. Am. Nuclear Soc. (pres. Wis. 1982-83), Profl. Ergrs. State of Wis., ASME. Avocations: fishing; Tae-Kwon-do. Home: 3416 W Meadowview Ct Mequon WI 53092 Office: U Wis-Milw PO Box 784 Milwaukee WI 53201

CHANCE, JOHN HARDIN, financial executive; b. Columbia, Mo., Nov. 30, 1937; s. F. Gano and Anna Lee (Toalson) C.; m. Carol Sutton Slack, June 15, 1962; children—Anthony, Garrison; m. 2d, Linda Carol Barto, Jan. 30, 1975; stepchildren—Bradley, Shanon. Student U. Mo., 1955-57, 60-62; D.Bus. (hon.), Southwest Baptist U., 1983. Vice pres. A.B. Chance Co., Centralia, Mo., 1962-77; pres. Boone Internat. Corp., Centralia, 1977—; dir. Am. Bank, Centralia. Pres. Little Dixie Republicans, 1974-78; exec. com. U.S. Indsl. Council; Bd. dirs. U. Mo. Devel. Fund, 1978-82; chmn. Chance Found., 1974—; bd. dirs. Hannibal LaGrange Coll., 1976-78; exec. com. Great Rivers council Boy Scouts Am., 1974—. Served with USN, 1957-59. Mem. Centralia Hist. Soc., Mo. C. of C. (vice chmn. 1972—). Baptist. Lodge: Kiwanis (past pres.). Home: Rt 4 Centralia MO 65240 Office: 123 N Rollins St Centralia MO 65240

CHANCE, JOHN KENNEDY, marketing executive and educator; b. Urbana, Ohio, Sept. 6, 1928; s. William Burnley and Elizabeth Gardiner (Kennedy) C.; m. Marjorie Belle Robinson, Dec. 1, 1951. B.A., Bladwin-Wallace Coll., 1951; B.S., Carnegie Inst. Tech., 1954; M.B.A., Ohio State U., 1971. Asst. sales promotion mgr. Upjohn Co., Kalamazoo, 1954-61; sales mgr. Belmont Press, Inc., St. Clairsville, Ohio, 1961-69; pres. Scrollcraft, Inc., Urbana, 1969-71, S.R. Dorescher, Inc., Urbana, 1975—; prof. and dept. head Urbana Coll., 1971-75; adj. prof. mktg. Clark Tech. Coll., Springfield, Ohio. Mem. Urbana City Housing Bd. Served to lt. col. U.S. Army, 1946-48, 51-53. Republican. Presbyterian. Clubs: Annapolis Yacht, Urbana Country. Author: Rubber Plates for the Printer, 1954, Introduction to Non-Parametric Statistics, 1974. Home: 463 Scioto St Urbana OH 43078 Office: S R Droescher Inc 1512 S Route 68 Urbana OH 43078

CHANDEL, MAHENDRA KUMAR, surgeon; b. Dhar, India, Jan. 9, 1944; s. C.K. and Yashodhara (Rathore) C.; came to U.S., 1970, naturalized, 1974; B.S., U. Indore (India), 1961; M.D., M.G.M. Med. Coll., Indore, 1966; m. Carol Ann Lennox, Apr. 29, 1977; children—Leena, Madhur, Michael. Intern, St. Luke's Hosp., Fargo, N.D., 1970-71; resident St. Elizabeth Hosp., Youngstown, Ohio, 1971-72, Highland Park (Mich.) Gen. Hosp., 1972-74; chief of surgery McNamara Community Hosp., Warren, Mich., 1975, Clare (Mich.) Osteo. Hosp., 1977, 79; practice medicine, specializing in gen. surgery, family practice, angiology, proctology, Clare, 1976—. Diplomate Am. Bd. Surgery, Am. Bd. Family Practice, Internat. Bd. Proctology. Fellow Internat. Coll. Surgeons, Am. Soc. Abdominal Surgery, Am. Acad. Family Practitioners, Am. Coll. Emergency Physicians, Am. Coll. Internat. Physicians; asso. fellow Am. Coll. Angiology; mem. AMA, Am. Soc. Contemporary Medicine and Surgery, Wayne County Med. Soc., Mich. Med. Soc., Clare/Isabella County Med. Soc. Office: 11128 Mission PO Box 120 Clare MI 48617

CHANDLER, JAMES THOMAS, police psychologist; b. Pontiac, Mich., June 22, 1934; s. Albert Max and Marian (Thomson) C.; B.A., Wayne U., 1958, M.A., 1962; Ph.D., Holy Cross Coll., 1972; m. Kay Kirby, May 11, 1957; children—Lynn, Mark, Lisa, Eric. Staff clin. psychologist Plymouth State Home and Tng. Sch., Northville, Mich., 1965-66; dir. div. childhood mental illness and health Mich. Soc. Mental Health, Lathrop Village, Mich., 1966-68; psychologist Lincoln Park (Mich.) Public Schs., 1968-69; chief psychologist Kent Oaks Hosp. and Clinic, Grand Rapids, Mich., 1969-71; program coordinator, evaluator Kent County (Mich.) Community Mental Health Services Bd., 1971-72; adolescent care dir. Villa Maria, Grand Rapids, Mich., 1972-75; sch. psychologist, guidance officer Cath. Central High Sch., Grand Rapids, 1976-77; police psychologist Law Enforcement Clarification Center, Western Mich., 1977-79; chief psychologist Ill. Dept. Law Enforcement, Springfield, 1981—; cons. to numerous agys., 1962—. Chmn., Mich. Youth Services Info. System, Statewide Application Adv. Group, 1974-75. Served with USNR, 1956-60; comdr. Res. ret. Fellow Am. Acad. Crisis Interveners; mem. Am. Assn. Counseling and Devel., Internat. Assn. Chiefs of Police, Naval Res. Assn., Res. Officers Assn., Ret. Officers Assn., Am. Bus. Clubs. Contbr. articles to various publs. Office: State Regional Office Bldg 4500 S 6th St Rd Springfield IL 62706

CHANDLER, KEITH IRVING, chief of police, educator; b. Lansing, Mich., Sept. 6, 1944; s. Irving Hamilton Chandler and June Eilene (Strayer) Alleman; m. Marilyn Helen Nuffer, Jan. 7, 1966; children—Dori Lynn, Michael Scott. A.A., Lansing Community Coll., 1972; B.A., Mich. State U., 1973; M.A., Western Ill. U., 1982. Police officer, Lansing Twp., Mich., 1965-66, East Lansing, Mich., 1966-74; instr. U. Ill., Champaign, 1974-75; chief of police City of Bourbonnais, Ill., 1975-79, City of Bettendorf, Iowa, 1979—; mem. faculty Lansing Community Coll., Mich., 1973, Kankakee Community Coll., Ill., 1975-79, Scott Community Coll., Riverdale, Iowa, 1980—. Bd. dirs. Scott County Unit Am. Heart Assn., Iowa, 1983-84. Served with USNR, 1984—. Mem. Internatl. Assn. Chiefs of Police, Iowa Police Exec. Forum (v.p. 1983-84, pres. 1985-86), Quad City Council Police Chiefs (pres. 1981-82), Mich. State U. Alumni Assn., Western Ill. U. Alumni Assn., Alpha Phi Sigma. Lutheran. Lodges: Optimist (pres. Bettendorf 1984—), Rotary. Avocations: reading, racquetball, team sports. Office: Police Dept 1609 State St Bettendorf IA 52722

CHANDRA, GIRISH, steel company executive; b. Ballia, Uttar Pradesh, India, July 1, 1941; came to U.S., 1970; s. Vindhyachal Prasad; B.Sc., Banaras Hindu U., India, 1959; M.B.A., Case Western Res. U., Cleve., 1972; m. Chander Kiran Sood, July 8, 1973; children—Ankur, Pravir, Nupur. Prodn. supr. New Central Jute Mills Co., Calcutta, 1964-68; office supr., 1968-69; purchase officer Jaipur Metals and Electricals, Ltd. (India), 1969-70; inventory control analyst Alcan Aluminum Corp., Warren, Ohio, 1972-77; inventory mgr. Wheatland Tube Co. (Pa.), 1978-80, mgr. materials mgmt., 1981, dir. materials and systems, 1982-84, dir. materials mgmt., 1985—. Mem. Am. Prodn. and Inventory Control Soc. (v.p. communications Youngstown chpt.). Hindu. Home: 9061 Altura Dr Warren OH 44484 Office: 1 Council Ave Wheatland PA 16161

CHANDRA, SATISH MISRA, statistician; b. Bhadaicha, Hardoi, India, Jan. 3, 1945; came to U.S., 1967, s. Shambhu Ratan and Fulwasa Misra (Dwivedi) M.; M.S., U. Chgo., 1969; Ph.D., So. Meth. U., 1971; cert. reliability engr.; cert. quality engr.; m. Sheela Misra, Aug. 2, 1974; children—Savita, Kavita, Ankur. Assoc. prof. stats. Tuskegee Inst., 1972-79, dir. Computer Based Edn. Tech., 1976-77; sr. statistician, statis. mgr. Baxter Travenol Labs., Inc., Round Lake, Ill., 1979—; cons. in field. Themis fellow, 1969-71. Mem. Am. Statis. Assn., Biometric Soc., Am. Soc. Quality Control, Nat. Assn. Mathematicians. Home: 1100 Wadsworth Pl Vernon Hills IL 60061 Office: Route 120 and Wilson Rd Round Lake IL 60073

CHANDRA, SUDHISH, biologist; b. Lucknow, India, Nov. 4, 1941; came to U.S., 1970; s. Krishna Mohan and Phool Kunwar (Saxena) Dayal; m. Shusheel Saxena, May 22, 1966; children—Jaya, Adeesh. B.Sc., Agra U., India, 1957; M.Sc., Lucknow U., India, 1960, Ph.D., 1964. Research assoc. ARC, Bethesda, Md., 1970-72, St. Vincent Hosp., Worcester, Mass., 1973-74; fellow Eli Lilly & Co., Indpls., 1974-75; research scientist ARC, 1975-81; sr. devel. scientist Armour Pharm. Co., Kankakee, Ill., 1981—; mem. sci. rev. group NIH, Bethesda, 1982—. Contbr. articles, abstracts to profl. publs. Avocations: reading, driving. Office: Armour Pharm Co PO Box 511 Kankakee IL 60901

CHANDRASEKHAR, SUBRAHMANYAN, theoretical astrophysicist; b. Lahore, India, Oct. 19, 1910; came to U.S., 1936, naturalized, 1953; m. Lalitha Chandrasekhar, Sept. 1936. M.A., Presidency Coll., Madras, India, 1930; Ph.D., Trinity Coll., Cambridge, 1933, Sc.D., 1942; Sc.D., U. Mysore (India), 1961, Northwestern U., 1962, U. Newcastle Upon Tyne (Eng.), 1965, Ind. Inst. Tech., 1966, U. Mich., 1967, U. Liege (Belgium), 1967, Oxford U. (Eng.), 1972, U. Delhi, 1973, Carleton U., Can., 1978, Harvard U., 1979. Govt. of India scholar in theoretical physics Cambridge U., 1930-34, fellow Trinity Coll., 1933-37; research assoc. Yerkes Obs., Williams Bay and U. Chgo., 1937, asst. prof., 1938-41, assoc. prof., 1942-43, prof., 1944-47, disting. service prof., 1947-52, Morton D. Hull disting. service prof., 1952—. Author: An Introduction to the Study of Stellar Structure, 1939; Principles of Stellar Dynamics, 1942; Radiative Transfer, 1950; Hydrodynamic and Hydromagnetic Stability, 1961; Ellipsoidal Figures of Equilibrium, 1969; The Mathematical Theory of Black Holes, 1983; Eddington: The Most Distinguished Astrophysicist of His Time, 1983; mng. editor Astrophys. Jour., 1952-71; contbr. articles to sci. periodicals. Recipient Bruce medal Aston. Soc. Pacific, 1952, 1953; Rumford medal Am. Acad. Arts and Scis., 1957; Nat. Medal of Sci., 1966; Nobel Prize in Physics, 1983; Dr. Tomalla prize Eidgenossische Technische Hochschule, Zurich, 1984; R.D. Birla award Indian Physics Assn., 1984. Fellow Royal Soc. (London) (Royal medal 1962, Copley medal 1984); mem. Nat. Acad. Scis. (Henry Draper medal 1971), Am. Phys. Soc. (Dannie Heineman prize 1974), Am. Philos. Soc., Cambridge Philos. Soc., Am. Astron. Soc., Royal Astron. Soc. (London) (gold medal 1953). Club: Quadrangle (U. Chgo.). Office: Lab for Astrophysics and Space Research 933 E 56th St Chicago IL 60637

CHANEY, REECE, psychology educator; b. Rowdy, Ky., July 27, 1938; s. Roy and Lola (Hays) C.; B.S., Ohio U., 1962, M.Ed., 1965, Ph.D., 1968; children—Tammy Kaye, Ronald Dean; m. 2d, Mary L. Ross, July 20, 1979; stepchildren—Reid Robert, Erin Leigh. Tchr., Scioto Valley Schs., Piketon, Ohio, 1959-64; NDEA Title IV fellow Ohio U., 1964-68; elementary counselor South Western City Schs., Grove City, Ohio, 1965-66; prof. and dir. tng. in counseling psychology Ind. State U., Terre Haute, 1968—; cons. marriage and family therapy, career edn. and pupil personnel services Ind. Dept. Pub. Instrn. Cert. psychologist, Ind. Mem. Am. Psychol. Assn., Am., Ind. (pres. 1977-78) personnel and guidance assns., Assn. Counselor Edn. and Supervision, Nat. Vocat. Guidance Assn., Assn. Measurement and Evaluation in Guidance, Am. Sch. Counselor Assn., Phi Delta Kappa. Home: 243 Hudson Ave Terre Haute IN 47803 Office: School of Education Indiana State University Terre Haute IN 47809

CHANEY, WILLIAM REYNOLDS, forestry and natural resources educator; b. McAllen, Tex., Dec. 2, 1941; s. Harold Glen and Mary (Reynolds) C.; m. Joann Judith Simon, Aug. 24, 1968; children—Brandon, Carey. B.S., Tex. A&M U., 1964; Ph.D., U. Wis., 1969. Research assoc. U. Wis., Madison, 1969-70; prof. dept. forestry and natural resources Purdue U., West Lafayette, Ind., 1970—; vis. prof. Univ. Coll. Wales, Aberystwyth, 1977. Contbr. articles to profl. jours., chpts. to books. Scoutmaster Sagamore council Boy Scouts Am., 1984—. Mem. Am. Soc. Plant Physiologists, Internat. Soc. Tropical Forestry, Internat. Union Forest Research Orgn. Roman Catholic. Avocations: stamp collecting; model railroading. Home: 1536 Summit Dr West Lafayette IN 47906 Office: Dept Forestry and Natural Resources Purdue Univ West Lafayette IN 47907

CHANG, CHEN-KANG, pathologist; b. Miao-Li, Taiwan, Republic China, Sept. 8, 1945; s. Kai-In and Niemei (Wu) C.; came to U.S., 1972, naturalized, 1979; M.D., Nat. Taiwan U., 1971; m. Julie Huang, July 1, 1973; children—Warren, Peter. Intern, Nat. Taiwan U. Hosp., Taipei, 1970-71; resident in pathology U. Wis. Med. Center, Madison, 1972-76, mem. faculty, 1976—, clin. asst. prof. pathology, 1977—; pathologist St. Mary's Hosp. Med. Center, Madison, Methodist Hosp., Madison, Ft. Atkinson (Wis.) Meml. Hosp., St. Clare's Hosp., Baraboo, Wis., Stoughton (Wis.) Hosp., Richland Hosp., Richland Center, Wis. Served as officer M.C., Chinese Army, 1971-72. Dr. Huang scholar, 1966-69. Mem. Coll. Am. Pathologists, Am. Soc. Clin. Pathologists, Internat. Acad. Pathology, Wis. State Soc. Pathologists. Contbr. articles to med. jours. Home: 21 N Harwood Circle Madison WI 53717 Office: 707 S Mills St Madison WI 53715

CHANG, JAE CHAN, physician, educator; b. Chong An, Korea, Aug. 29, 1941; s. Tae Whan and Kap Hee (Lee) C.; came to U.S., 1965, naturalized, 1976; M.D., Seoul (Korea) Nat. U., 1965; m. Sue Young Chung, Dec. 4, 1965; children—Sung-Jin, Sung-Ju, Sung-Hoon. Intern, Ellis Hosp., Schenectady, 1965-66; resident in medicine Harrisburg (Pa.) Hosp., 1966-69, fellow in nuclear medicine, 1969-70; instr. in medicine U. Rochester, N.Y., 1970-72; chief hematology sect. VA Hosp., Dayton, Ohio, 1972-75; hematopathologist Good Samaritan Hosp., Dayton, 1975—, dir. oncology unit, 1976—, coordinator of med. edn., 1976-77, chief oncology-hematology sect., 1976—; asst. clin. prof. medicine Ohio State U., Columbus, 1972-75; assoc. clin. prof. medicine Wright State U., Dayton, 1975-80, clin. prof., 1980—; staff St. Elizabeth Med. Center, Dayton, Miami Valley Hosp., Dayton; cons. in hematology VA Hosp. Mem. med. adv. com. Greater Dayton Area chpt. Leukemia Soc. Am., 1977—; trustee Montgomery County Soc. for Cancer Control, Dayton, 1976—, Community Blood Ctr., 1982—. Nat. Cancer Inst. fellow in hematology and oncology, 1970-72; diplomate Am. Bd. Internal Medicine, Am. Bd. Pathology. Fellow A.C.P.; mem. Am. Soc. Hematology, Am. Fedn. Clin. Research, Am. Soc. Clin. Oncologists, Am. Assn. Cancer Research, AAAS, Dayton Oncology Club, Dayton Soc. Internal Medicine. Contbr. articles to profl. med. jours., essays to newspaper columns. Home: 1122 Wycliffe Pl Dayton OH 45459 Office: Good Samaritan Hosp and Health Center 2222 Philadelphia Dr Dayton OH 45406 also 2200 Philadelphia Dr Dayton OH 45406

CHANG, JUNG-CHING, research chemist; b. Taipei, Taiwan, Jan. 13, 1939; came to U.S., 1967; s. Tien-Gen and Mien (Huang) C.; B.S., Tamkang Coll., 1963; M.S., U. P.R., 1969; Ph.D., U. Mo., Kansas City, 1975; m. Mei-Chu, Nov. 12, 1965; 1 dau., Edith. Chem. engr. Taiwan Sugar Corp., 1964-67; research asst. U. P.R., Rio Piedras, 1967-69; research asst., teaching asst., research fellow U. Mo., Kansas City, 1971-75; postdoctoral research asso. U. Oreg., Eugene, 1976-77; postdoctoral fellow U. Cin., 1977-79; chemist ICN Pharmaceuticals, Inc., Cin., 1979-81; research chemist Ashland Chem. Co., Dublin, Ohio, 1981—. Served with Nat. Chinese Air Force, 1963-64. Fisher scholar, 1961-63; NSF research fellow, 1967-69; postdoctoral fellow, 1976-77; U. Kansas City trustees' fellow, 1973-75; U.Mo., Kansas City summer research fellow, 1971-75; Office Naval Research postdoctoral fellow, 1977-79. Mem. Am. Chem. Soc., N.Y. Acad. Scis., Sigma Xi. Contbr. research articles to sci. jours. Home: 2555 Sawmill Forest Ave Dublin OH 43017 Office: PO Box 2219 Columbus OH 43216

CHANG, LONG F., engineer, applied mathematician; b. Taipei, Taiwan, Jan. 1, 1931; came to U.S., 1958, naturalized, 1973; s. Sui Lai and Chin Soon (Chen) C.; m. Tommie C. Hung, Sept. 7, 1969; children—Julia, Sonya. A.A., Taipei Inst. Tech., 1954; B.S. in Elec. Engring., Shibaura Inst. Tech., Tokyo, 1958; Ph.D., Syracuse U., 1962. Field engr. Taiwan Elec. Power Co., 1954-55; research engr. Syracuse U., N.Y., 1960-62, research fellow, 1962-64, asst. prof., 1964-67; sr. engr. Owens-Ill. Inc., Toledo, Ohio, 1967-83, sr. fellow, 1983—; asst. to patent atty. Wenping & Co., Tokyo, 1956-58; ptnr. Taiwan Internat. Patent Atty's. Office, 1963-71. Patentee in field. Fgn. fellow Syracuse U., 1958-60. Fellow Sigma Xi; mem. N.Y. Acad. Sci., Am. Math. Soc., Soc. Indsl. and Applied Math., Soc. Plastic Engrs. Avocations: gardening; reading. Home: 4704 Weldwood Ln Sylvania OH 43560 Office: One Sea Gate Toledo OH 43666

CHANG, WON SOON, educator; b. Kyunggi-do, Korea, July 30, 1949; came to U.S., 1975; s. Seok Yeon and Yeon Sook (Choi) C.; m. Kil Ja Lee, May 17, 1975; children—Catherine Eunyoung, Andrew Donghyeon. B.S., Yonsei U., Korea, 1972, M.S., 1974; M.S., Okla. State U., 1977; Ph.D., Ga. Inst. Tech., 1981. Grad. teaching asst. dept. mech. engring. Yonsei U., Seoul, Korea, 1972-74, research asso., 1974-75, instr., 1975; grad. teaching asst. sch. mech. and aerospace engring. Okla. State U., 1975-76; grad. research asst. sch. mech. engring. Ga. Inst. Tech., 1977-79, grad. teaching asst., 1979-80; cons. Energy Tech. Div., Lee-Tech Industries, Inc., DeKalb, Ill., 1981—; asst. prof. No. Ill. U., DeKalb, 1980—. Mem. ASME, Ill. Acad. Sci., Sigma Xi. Roman Catholic. Contbr. articles to profl. jours. Home: 833 Ridge Dr Apt 316 DeKalb IL 60115 Office: No Ill Univ DeKalb IL 60115

CHANNER, STEPHEN DYER STANTON, trade assn. exec.; b. Chgo., Nov. 1, 1933; s. George Stanton and Maxine (Dyer) C.; B.A. in Bus. Adminstrn., Colo. Coll., 1956; grad. U.S. Army Officers Sch., 1957; m. Antoinette Persons, June 29, 1957; children—Stephen Persons, Wyndham Harvey. Dir. sales Am. Seating Co., Grand Rapids, Mich., 1958-77; with Bus. and Instn. Furniture Mfrs. Assn., Grand Rapids, Mich., 1977—, exec. dir., 1978—. Served to 1st lt., U.S. Army, 1956-58. Mem. Am. Soc. Assn. Execs. Mem. Christian Ch. Club: Grand Rapids Racquet. Contbr. articles to various mags. Home: 7440 Leyton Dr Ada MI 49301 Office: 2335 Burton St SE Grand Rapids MI 49506

CHAO, MARSHALL S., chemist; b. Changsha, China, Nov. 20, 1924; s. Hen-ti and Huey-ying C.; m. Patricia Hu, July 20, 1968; 1 dau., Anita. B.S., Nat. Central U., China, 1947; M.S., U. Ill., 1958, Ph.D., 1961. Teaching asst. Nat. Central U., 1947-49; tech. asst. Taiwan Fertilizer Co., 1949-55; research chemist Dow Chem. Co., Midland, Mich., 1961-72, research specialist, 1973-79, research leader, 1980—. Deacon First Baptist Ch., Midland, 1974-76. Fellow Am. Inst. Chemists; mem. Am. Chem. Soc., Electrochem. Soc. (chmn. Midland sect. 1973, councilor 1974-76, 81-82, chmn. 1983—), N.Y. Acad. Scis., Soc. Electroanalytical Chemists, Sigma Xi, Phi Lambda Epsilon. Author: Taiwan Fertilizers, 1951; contbr. articles to profl. jours. Patentee in field. Home: 1206 Evamar Dr Midland MI 48640 Office: Inorganic Lab Central Research Dow Chem Co Midland MI 48640

CHAPIN, PAUL THOMAS, airline captain; b. Cleve., Jan. 15, 1953; s. Thomas Goldsmith and Anzle Francis (Adamson) C. B.S. in Speech Communications and Pub. Relations, U. Minn., 1978. Pub. relations exec. Aspen Highlands Ski Corp., Aspen, Colo., 1976-79; flight instr. Wings, Inc., St. Paul, 1981-83; capt. Crown Air, San Juan, P.R., 1983; first officer Midstate Airlines, Stevens Point, Wis., 1984, capt., 1984-85; first officer Am. Airlines, Dallas, 1985—; check airman Crown Air, San Juan, 1984. Advisor, fund raiser Explorers, Boy Scouts Am., St. Paul, 1982-83. Republican. Roman Catholic. Clubs: Bald Eagle Water (pres. 1980-83, dir. 1982-83) (White Bear Lake, Minn.); Minn. Water Ski Assn. (pres. 1980-82). Avocations: water skiing; skiing, skating; tennis; swimming; biking. Home: 5372 E Bald Eagle Blvd White Bear Lake MN 55110

CHAPLIN, DAVID, sociology educator; b. Yonkers, N.Y., Nov. 30, 1930; s. Duncan Dunbar and Catherine (Davis) C.; m. Joyce Marie Whittier, Dec. 28, 1954; children—Duncan, Scott, Alexandra. B.A., Amherst Coll., 1953; M.A., Princeton U., 1958, Ph.D., 1963. Instr., U. Del., Newark, 1959-60; asst. prof. Bucknell U., Lewisburg, Pa., 1960-64; assoc. prof. U. Wis.-Madison, 1964-72; prof., chmn. dept. sociology Western Mich. U., Kalamazoo, 1972—; cons. Peace Corps, 1964-66, Presbyn. Ch., 1968, Ford Found., 1969; mem. nat. fellowship award panel NSF, 1971-73. Author: Peruvian Indsl. Labor Force, 1967; also articles. Editor, contbg. author: Peruvian Nationalism, 1976; Population Policies and Growth, 1971. Served with U.S. Army, 1954-56. Grantee NSF, 1963, Social Sci. Research Council, 1970, Am. Philos. Soc., 1967, Manpower Adminstrn., 1968, Ford Found., 1976, Pvt. Industry Council, 1984. Mem. Am. Sociol. Assn., Latin Am. Studies Assn. (exec. council 1971-73), Population Assn. Am. Home: 2304 Bronson Blvd Kalamazoo MI 49008 Office: Western Mich U Kalamazoo MI 49008

CHAPMAN, ANNE BROWN, adult education coordinator; b. Cleve., Nov. 16, 1939; d. Charles William and Elsie Blanche (Rambo) Brown; m. Robert Anthony Chapman, Aug. 19, 1961; children—Kathleen Anne, Robert Alan. B.S., Ohio State U., 1961. Cert. tchr., Ohio. Tchr. home econs. Eastlake Jr. High Sch., Willoughby, Ohio, 1968-75; dept. mgr. White Sewing Machine Co., Cleve., 1978-79; custom product rep. interior design Kay Trimmer Inc., Mentor, Ohio, 1979-80; coordinator displaced homemaker program Lake County Joint Vocat. Sch., Painesville, Ohio, 1980—. Pres. Ridge Parent Tchrs. Assn., 1976-77; mem. Western Res. Consortium, 1980—; mem. Human Services Forum Geauga County, 1980—. Ohio Vocat. Edn. Dept. grantee, 1981-83. Mem. Am. Bus. Women's Assn., Am. Vocat. Assn., Ohio Vocat. Assn., Ohio State U. Home Econs. Alumni Assn., Ohio State U. Alumni Assn., Zeta Tau Alpha. Club: Parents (liaison 1982—). Home: 7281 Taft St Mentor OH 44060 Office: 8140 Auburn Rd Painesville OH 44077

CHAPMAN, CARL HALEY, anthropologist, educator; b. Steelville, Mo., May 29, 1915; s. William M. and Estelle Madolin (Haley) C.; A.B., U. Mo., 1939; M.A., U. N.Mex., 1946; Ph.D. (Horace H. Rackham fellow), U. Mich., 1959; m. Eleanor Eliza Finley, Mar. 14, 1942; children—Richard Carl, Stephen Finley. Instr. sociology U. Mo., Columbia, 1946-48, instr. sociology and anthropology, 1948-50, asst. prof. anthropology, 1951-56, asso. prof., 1957-60, prof. anthropology, 1960—, research prof. Am. archaeology, 1975—, dir. Mus. of Anthropology, 1949-50, 51-56, dir. Am. archaeology, 1946-65, dir. archaeol. research activities, 1965-75, 79-80; mem. steering com. Miss. Alluvial Valley Archaeol. Program, 1968-72; chmn. adv. council on archaeology to Mo. State Park Bd., 1959-70; ex-officio mem. Adv. Council on Archaeology and History, 1970-72, Adv. Council on Hist. Preservation, 1977-81. Gov.'s rep. to Lewis and Clark Trail Commn. meetings State of Mo., 1966-68; sec. Mo. Lewis and Clark Trail Commn., 1966-67; Democratic committeeman 3rd Ward, Columbia, 1970-72; bd. dirs. Mo. Heritage Trust, 1977—. Served with USAF, 1942-45. Decorated Air medal; recipient Thomas Jefferson award, 1984, cert. of appreciation New World Conf. on Rescue Archeology, 1984; Nat. Park Service grantee, 1952-63, NSF grantee, 1961-63; Nat Endowment Humanities grantee, 1971-75, 82-85. Fellow Am. Anthrop. Assn., AAAS; mem. Soc. Am. Archaeology (Disting. Service award 1975, chmn. com. on public understanding of archaeology 1967-69), Am. Soc. Conservation Archaeology (Conservation award 1980), Soc. Profl. Archaeologists (pres. 1978-79), Mo. Archaeol. Soc. (sec. 1946-50, 51-55, 58-80, honor award 1981), Soc. Hist. Archaeology, Central States Anthrop. Assn., Am. Ethnol. Soc., AAUP, Phi Beta Kappa, Sigma Xi. Democrat. Unitarian. Author: (with Eleanor Chapman) Indians and Archaeology of Missouri, 1964; The Origin of the Osage Indian Tribe, 1974; Archaeology of Missouri, Vol. I, 1975, Vol. II, 1980; (with David Evans and John Cottler) Investigation and Comparison of Two Fortified Mississippi Tradition Sites in Southeastern Missouri, 1977; contbg. author: The Indomitable Osage in Spanish Illinois, 1974; Cultural Change and Continuity, 1976; contbr. articles on Am. archaeology to scholarly jours. Home: 211 Edgewood Columbia MO 65203 Office: 205 Swallow Hall U Mo Columbia MO 65211

CHAPMAN, EMILY ELIZABETH, systems analyst; b. Paris, Ont., Can., Jan. 19, 1921; d. Robert Alexander George and Emily Adabelle (Turnbull) Cale; Asso. in Home Econs., Macdonald Inst., Guelph, Ont., 1941; B.S., U. Wis., Madison, 1957, postgrad. Grad. Sch. Computer Scis., 1966-67; m. R. Keith Chapman, Aug. 22, 1942; children—Robert Wayne, Linda Jean, Susan Gay. Research programmer analyst U. Wis., Madison, 1966-70; exec. sec. Sponsors of Sci. Inc., Madison, 1970-74; programmer analyst Higher Ednl. Aids Bd., State of Wis., 1975-78; systems analyst Bur. Info. Devel., Dept. Adminstrn., State of Wis., Madison, 1978-80, project leader, 1980-84, Computer Support mgr., 1984—; cons. programmer analyst, 1970-73. Chmn. Cancer Soc.-Heart Fund Health Drives, Verona, Wis., 1956-57; bd. dirs. Central YWCA, Madison, 1965-66. Recipient Exceptional Performance award Dept. Adminstrn., State of Wis., 1981, 83. Mem. Assn. for Systems Mgmt. (treas. Madison chpt. 1979-81), Council for Agrl. Sci. and Tech., Univ. League Madison, Daus. of Demeter. Home: 1119 Waban Hill Madison WI 53711 Office: State of Wis Dept Adminstrn Gen Exec Facility II Madison WI 53702

CHAPMAN, FRANCES ELIZABETH CLAUSEN (MRS. WILLIAM JAMES CHAPMAN), civic worker; b. Atchison, Kans., Feb. 27, 1920; d. Erwin W. and Helen (Hackney) Clausen; B.A., Wellesley Coll., 1941; m. W. MacLean Johnson, Aug. 31, 1940 (dec. Nov. 1965); children—Stuart MacLean, Duncan Scott, Douglas Hamilton; m. 2d, William James Chapman, Dec. 5, 1970. Project dir. Women in Community Service, Inc., St. Louis, 1965-66; pres. Nursery Found., St. Louis, 1956-58, dir., 1953-59, 65-68; adv. com. Mo. State Children's Day Care, 1963—; chmn. day care com. Mo. Council Children and Youth, 1961, chmn. foster care sect., 1961-63; spl. asst. to the pres. Webster Coll., 1966-68. Bd. dirs. New City Sch., 1967-69, Mid-County YMCA,

1967-70, St. Louis Conservatory and Sch. Arts, 1978—; mem. Mo. State Coordinating Bd. Higher Edn., 1982—; mem. steering com. Mo. Council on Children and Youth, 1967-69; trustee Jr. Coll. Dist., St. Louis-St. Louis County, 1968-80, pres. bd. trustees, 1971-73, 76-77; trustee John Burroughs Sch., 1973-79, Wellesley Coll., 1976-82; bd. dirs. Assn. Governing Bds. Univs. and Colls., 1970-80, v.p., 1977-78, chmn. bd., 1978-79, hon. dir., 1982-85; bd. commrs. Nat. Commn. on Accrediting, 1971-72; bd. overseers Center for Research on Women in Higher Edn. and Professions, Wellesley, Mass., 1977-82. Mem. Nat. Soc. Arts and Letters, Wellesley Coll. Alumnae Assn. (sec., dir. 1958-61). Club: Wellesley Coll. (pres. 1965-67). Home: 10 Overbrook Dr Saint Louis MO 63124

CHAPMAN, (GEORGE) BRAINERD (III), lawyer; b. Louisville, Oct. 18, 1911; s. George B. and Kathryn (Schneiderhan) C.; B.A., Amherst Coll., 1933; J.D., Harvard, 1936; m. Martha McCaig, June 11, 1948; 1 son, George Brainerd, IV. Bar: Ill. 1936. Assoc. then ptnr. Lord, Bissell & Brook, and predecessors, 1936-58; pvt. practice, 1959-62; ptnr. Chapman, Pennington, Montgomery, Holmes & Sloan, Chgo., 1962-70, Vedder, Price, Kaufman & Kammholz, Chgo., 1971-83, of counsel, 1984—; former dir. various corps., eleemosynary instns. and founds. Former chmn. bd. Presbyn. Home; past bd. dirs., nat. treas. Mil. Tng. Camps Assn. U.S. Served from capt. to col. JAG'S Dept., AUS, 1942-46. Decorated Bronze Star (U.S.); knight officer of Crown (Italy); recipient medal for eminent service Amherst Coll., 1969, Foster and Mary McGaw award, 1977. Mem. Beta Theta Pi. Presbyn. (elder, trustee). Author: Dream Cruise, 1980. Clubs: Chgo., University, Law, Glen View (Golf, Ill.). Office: 115 S LaSalle St Chicago IL 60603

CHAPMAN, HOPE HORAN, psychologist; b. Chgo., Feb. 13, 1954; d. Theodore George and Idelle (Poll) H.; B.S. (Ill. State scholar), U. Ill., Champaign-Urbana, 1976; M.A. (research and teaching asst.), No. Ill. U., 1979. Recreational therapist Evanston (Ill.) Ridgeview Shelter Care Home, summer 1976; psychologist Glenwood (Iowa) State Hosp. Sch., 1979-83. Active Omaha Symphonic Chorus, 1981-83; mem. Omaha Public Schs. Citizens Adv. Com., 1980-81; mem. edn. com. Anti-Defamation League, 1980—, chmn. com. anti-Semitism and Jewish youth, 1981-84. Mem. Am. Psychol. Assn., Midwest Psychol. Assn., Am. Assn. on Mental Deficiency, Assn. for Mental Health Affiliation with Israel, Phi Kappa Phi, Psi Chi. Jewish. Contbr. papers to profl. confs., articles to jours. Home: 4513 26th St Columbus NE 68601

CHAPMAN, JOSEPH DUDLEY, gynecologist, sexologist, author; b. Moline, Ill., Apr. 29, 1928; s. Joseph Dudley and Lillian Caroline (Pruder) C.; m. Mary Kay Sartini, June, 1949 (div.); children—Mary Jo Tucker, Nancy Jo Robinson; m. 2d, Virginia Helene Milius, June, 1958 (div.). B.S., U. Ill. and Roosevelt Coll., Chgo., 1950; D.O., Coll. Osteo. Medicine and Surgery, 1953; D.Sc., 1963; M.D., Calif. Coll. Medicine, 1962. Cert. Am. Osteo. Bd. Ob-Gyn. Intern, resident in ob-gyn Still Coll. Hosp., Des Moines; practice medicine specializing in ob-gyn, North Madison, Ohio, 1973—; clin. prof. ob-gyn Ohio U., 1979—; mem. faculty, acad. bd. Inst. Advanced Study Human Sexuality, San Francisco, 1979—; TV appearances on Phil Donahue Show, Good Morning Am., The Last Word, and others; med. examiner FAA. Active Boy Scouts Am. Mem. Assn. Sexologists, Am. Coll. Osteo. Ob-Gyn (Purdue Frederick awards, editor), Acad. Psychosomatic Medicine (bd. govs.), Am. Med. Writers Assn. Lutheran. Author: The Feminine Mind and Body, 1966; The Sexual Equation, 1977; editor-in-chief O.P., 1968-77; editorial cons. Penthouse Forum; contbr. chpts. to books, articles to profl. jours. Home: Box 340 North Madison OH 44057

CHAPMAN, LARRY ARTHUR, university administrator; b. Mt. Vernon, Ill., Nov. 8, 1946; s. Howard Arthur and Rosamary (Bell) C.; m. Mary Jane Boyer, Aug. 16, 1969; children—Mark Andre, Kevin Arthur. A.A., Mt. Vernon Community Coll., 1966; B.S., Murray State U., 1968; M.Ed., U. Ariz., 1977, Ph.D., 1983. Dist. field rep. Westinghouse Co., Tucson, 1973-74; credit mgr. BEDCO, Tucson, 1974-75; adminstrv. asst. U. Ariz., Tucson, 1975-76, vets. coordinator, 1976-78; asst. registrar Pima Community Coll., Tucson, 1978-84; dir. student affairs Coll. Bus. and Adminstrn., So. Ill. U., Carbondale, 1984—. Mem. disciplinary com. Elem. Dist. #95, Carbondale. Served with U.S. Army, 1969-71. Recipient Service award Nat. Assn. Vets. Program Adminstrs., 1978. Mem. Am. Assn. Counseling and Devel., Am. Coll. Personnel Assn. Republican. Baptist. Avocations: Racquetball; jogging; bowling; basketball; softball. Home: 1211 W Freeman Carbondale IL 62901 Office: Coll Bus and Adminstrn So Ill U Carbondale IL 62901

CHAPMAN, RICHARD ALAN, accountant; b. Beatrice, Nebr., Aug. 29, 1947; s. Glenn Ray and Aelcidean Martie (King) C.; student Milw. Sch. Engring., 1968-70; B.S. in Acctg., U. Nebr., 1973; m. Norma Loi-Moi Leung, May 4, 1974. Internal auditor Gen. Telephone & Electronics, Des Plaines, Ill., 1973-75; internal auditor Internat. Minerals & Chem., Des Plaines, 1975-78, fin. analyst chem. group, 1978-79, chief acct. indsl. chems. div., 1979-82, acctg. mgr. indsl. chem. div., 1982-84, controller indsl. chem. div., 1984—. Mem. Beta Gamma Sigma. Office: 421 E Hawley Mundelein IL 60060

CHAPMAN, RONALD WILLIAM, county official; b. Wyandotte, Mich., Mar. 27, 1957; s. Richard Marvin and Margrate Louise (Maurer) C.; m. Ruth Eve Karbowski, Oct. 22, 1976; children—Erica Lee Ann, Ronald William. A.A., Sacramento City Coll., 1978; B.A. cum laude, Calif. State U.-Sacramento, 1979; M.P.A., U. So. Calif., 1980; J.D., Wayne State U., 1984. Adminstrv. asst. to dep. mayor Dearborn (Mich.), 1980-81, dep. dir. Dept. Pub. Works, 1981-84; data processing cons., 1982-84; dir. mgmt. audit and strategic planning Wayne County, Mich., 1984—; practice law, 1985—. Trustee, Dearborn Sch. Bd., 1984—. Served with USAF, 1976-80. Mem. Am. Mgmt. Assn., Assn. Computer Users, Am. Soc. Pub. Adminstrs., Acad. Polit. Sci., Am. Pub. Works Assn., Internat. Platform Assn., Inst. Internal Auditors, Jaycees. Lutheran. Clubs: Pioneers, Civitan (v.p.), Goodfellows. Contbr. articles to profl. jours. Home: 329 Berkeley Pl Dearborn MI 48124 Office: City-County Bldg Two Woodward Ave Detroit MI 48226

CHAPMAN, VICTORIA CASTON, educator; b. St. Louis, Mar. 14, 1919; d. Jonathan Lyle and Violetta Charlena (Davis) Caston; m. Willie Edward Chapman, Mar. 8, 1946; children—Sharon, Vicki. A.B., Stowe Tchrs. Coll., 1942; M.S., U. So. Calif., 1944; Ed.D., Internat. Grad. Sch., 1985. Tchr., St. Louis Bd. Edn., 1943-45, Stowe Tchrs. Coll., St. Louis, 1945-49, Sumner High Sch., St. Louis, 1951-73; asst. prin. Roosevelt High Sch., St. Louis, 1973-76, Acad. Math. and Sci., St. Louis, 1976-77, Cleveland High Sch., St. Louis, 1977-81; prin. Continued Edn. Project, St. Louis, 1981—; Spanish translator. Active Girl Scouts U.S.A. Mem. Am. Bus. Women's Assn., Nat. Council Negro Women, Nat. Assn. Secondary Sch. Prins., Assn. Supervision and Curriculum Devel., St. Louis Adminstrs. Assn., Delta Sigma Theta, Phi Delta Kappa. Republican. Baptist. Clubs: Top Ladies of Distinction, Gay-Dekkers Bridge, Jack and Jill Am.

CHAPMAN, WALTER HOWARD, artist, educator; b. Toledo, Dec. 7, 1912; s. Ralph Martin and Lillian Minor (Seagrave) C.; m. Marie Louise Repasz, Aug. 29, 1943 (div. Nov., 1962); children—Anne Marie, Patricia Lee; m. Jean Clarice Sayre, Jan. 29, 1963. Pvt. study Cleve. Sch. Art., 1930-34, John Huntington Poly., Cleve., 1933, Art Students League N.Y.C., 1939. Artist-in-residence Toledo Blade, 1937-38; freelance illustrator, N.Y.C., 1938-39; artist-in-residence Jack Binder Studio, N.Y.C., 1943-44; creative dir., Phillips Assocs., Toledo, 1946-79; tchr. Toledo Mus. Sch. of Design, 1952-60, 1978—, Chapman-Kohn Art Seminars, Toledo and Columbus 1978-85; owner, operator Chapman Art Gallery, Sylvania, Ohio, 1969—. Contbr. watercolor paintings and illustrations to books and magazines; exhibited in group shows: Springfield Art Mus., Mo., Mainstream Internat., Marietta, Ohio, Salmagundi Club, N.Y.C., Grumbacher Corp., N.Y.C. Served to sgt. U.S. Army, 1942-45, ETO. Decorated Bronze Star. Mem. Illustrators Club Toledo (pres. 1964), Allied Artists of Am., Ohio Watercolor Soc. (bd. dirs. 1979), Northwest Ohio Watercolor Soc. (pres. 1968), Toledo Fedn. Art Socs. (pres. 1961) Toledo Artists Club (bd. dirs. 1962-64, 85). Republican. Clubs: Toledo Advt.; Salmagundi (N.Y.C.). Lodge: Rotary (Toledo). Avocations: landscape painting; portrait painting. Home: 6001 Gregory Dr Sylvania OH 43560 Office: Chapman Art Gallery 5151 S Main St Sylvania OH 43560

CHAPMAN, WILLIAM FRANCIS, newspaper editor, consultant; b. Powersville, Mo., Mar. 28, 1925; s. William Bryant and Esther (Coddington) C.; student jr. coll., St. Joseph, Mo., 1942-43, Central Mo. State Coll., 1946, Wayne State U., 1955; m. Lillian Louise Fyler, Aug. 10, 1945 (dec. Sept. 1984); children—Robert Earl, Karen Louise, Sharon Frances; m. Karen Ann Moore, July 13, 1985. News editor Warrensburg (Mo.) Daily Star-Jour., 1946-47; mgr. U.P.I., Jefferson City, Mo., 1949, war corr., Korea, 1950-51, mgr. Seattle, 1952-53; asst. city editor Detroit Free Press, 1954-61; exec. editor Daily Times, Chester, Pa., 1961-63; mng. editor The Times, Hammond, Ind., 1964-75, exec. editor, 1975-85; editorial dir. Howard Publs., Oceanside, Calif., 1971-85; pres. Chapman Report, Merrillville, Ind., 1985—. Founding dir. Mid-Am. Press Inst., So. Ill. U. Carbondale (chmn. 1971); mem. Internat. Press Inst. Served with USMCR, 1943-46; PTO. Mem. Am. Soc. Newspaper Editors, A.P. Mng. Editors. Home: 7818 Marshall Pl Merrillville IN 46410 Office: 7818 Marshall Pl Merrillville IN 46410

CHAPPELL, MARY ELIZABETH, insurance company official; b. Indpls., Sept. 25, 1953; d. Edward J. and Miriam Rita (Commons) Walsh; m. Mark B. Chappell, Feb. 9, 1980; children—Claire, Christopher. Student Ind. U./Purdue U.-Indpls. C.P.C.U. Rate endorsement clk. Am. States Ins. Co., Indpls., 1971-75, personal lines policy service supr., 1975-79, personal lines policy service mgr., 1977-79, underwriting systems mgr., 1979-81, personal lines auto staff mgr., 1981—. Advisor, Jr. Achievement, Indpls., 1978-79. Named Ins. Woman of Yr., Indpls. Assn. Ins. Women, 1983; recipient Region IV Edn. award Nat. Assn. Ins. Women, 1983. Mem. Indpsl. Assn. Ins. Women (dir.), Am. Mgmt. Soc., Am. Bus. Women's Assn., Nat. Assn. Ins. Women. Democrat. Roman Catholic. Home: 5333 N Guilford St Indianapolis IN 46220 Office: Am States Ins Co PO Box 1636 Indianapolis IN 46207

CHAREK, ROBERT STANLEY, business executive, financial consultant; b. Cleve., Aug. 8, 1924; s. Stanley Joseph and Lillian Helen (Prosser) C.; grad. St. Ignatius High Sch., 1942; student Center Coll. Ky., 1943, Western Res. U., 1946; m. Hilda Marie Hoffman, Aug. 9, 1944; children—Barbara C. Charek Reesing, Bonita L. Charek McCormick, Ralph K. Prince, Christopher R. Public accountant, 1946-47; Gold Bros. Co., Cleve., office mgr. 1947-49; with Master Builders div. Martin Marietta, Cleve., 1949-84, acctg. dept. mgr., 1954-58, dir. acctg., 1959-73, internat. controller, 1974-82, internat. acctg. mgr., 1982-84; financial cons., 1984—. Served with USAAF, 1943-45. Mem. Data Processing Mgmt. Assn. (past dir. chpt.). Republican. Roman Catholic. Club: K.C. Home: 21941 Briarwood Dr Fairview Park OH 44126

CHAREWICZ, DAVID MICHAEL, photographer; b. Chgo., Feb. 17, 1932; s. Michael and Stella (Pietrzak) C.; student DePaul U., 1957, Northwestern U., 1952; m. Catherine Uccello, Nov. 8, 1952; children—Michael, Karen, Daniel. Trainee, Merill Chase, Chgo., 1950-51; dark room technician Maurice Seymour, Chgo., 1951-52; photographer Oscar & Assos., Chgo., 1955-63; owner Dave Chare Photography, Park Ridge, Ill., 1963—; pres., owner C&C Duplicating, Inc., 1978—. Pres. Oakton Parent Tchr. Club, 1968-69, del. dist. 64 caucus, 1970, 73; mem. centennial photo com., Park Ridge, Ill., 1973. Served with AUS, 1952-54. Mem. Profl. Photographers Assn., Midstate Indsl. Photographers Assn. (treas. 1981, pres. 1984-85). Home: 739 N Northwest Hwy Park Ridge IL 60068 Office: 1045 N Northwest Hwy Park Ridge IL 60068

CHARLA, KATHLEEN G., advertising sales representative; b. Holyoke, Mass., Feb. 13, 1942; d. Frank A. and Lena (La Ruffa) Gerace; B.A., Trinity Coll., Washington, 1964; M.A., Stanford U., 1966; Ph.D., Ind. U., 1979; m. Leonard F. Charla, Feb. 3, 1968; children—Larisa, Christopher. Instr., Upsala Coll., 1969-70; free-lance translator Ardis Pubs., Ann Arbor, Mich., Bloomington (Ind.) Translation Group, also McGregor & Werner, Arlington, Va., 1969-75; art cons., Birmingham, Mich., 1976-77; owner, mgr. Kathleen G. Charla Assos., Birmingham, 1976—, advt. sales rep. periodicals Home, Glamour, Modern Photography, High Fidelity, Los Angeles, San Diego, San Francisco, Palm Springs Life, Chief Executive. Stanford-Warsaw Grad. Exchange fellow, 1965-66; NDEA fellow, 1966-67. Mem. Adcraft Club Detroit, Detroit Mktg. Com., Mag. Pubs. Assn., Am. Assn. Advancement of Slavic Studies, Am. Assn. Tchrs. of Slavic and East European Langs. Contbr. articles and revs. to publs. Address: 21000 W Fourteen Mile Rd Birmingham MI 48010

CHARLES, ANDREW VALENTINE, psychiatrist; b. Chgo., Nov. 5, 1939; s. George and Carol Claire (Goettel) C.; B.A. cum laude, U. Mich., 1961; M.D., U. Ill., 1965. Rotating intern Ill. Masonic Hosp., Chgo., 1965-66; psychiatry resident Presbyn. St. Luke's Hosp., Chgo., 1966-69; practice medicine specializing in psychiatry, Chgo., 1969—; mem. attending staff Presbyn. St. Lukes, Chgo. Lakeshore hosps.; med. dir. Ridgeway Hosp., Chgo., 1976-84; med. dir., mem. bd. dirs. Hartgrove Hosp., Chgo., 1984—; instr. psychiatry Rush Med. Sch., Chgo., 1970—; psychiatrist Chgo. Bd. Edn., 1970-77; clin. dir. Exec. Assessment Corp., 1976-78; v.p., contbg. editor Desmodus Pub. Corp. Diplomate Am. Bd. Psychiatry and Neurology. Mem. AMA, Am. Group Psychotherapy Assn., Am., Ill. psychiat. assns., Chgo. Med. Soc., Am. Acad. Med. Dirs., Am. Assn. Utilization Rev. Physicians, Phi Rho Sigma. Contbr. articles to prof. jours. Office: 8 S Michigan Ave Suite 3102 Chicago IL 60603

CHARLES, REID SHAVER, city official, consultant, urban planner; b. Wichita, Kans., Sept. 16, 1940; s. Harry Lytton and Margaret Virginia (Shaver) C.; m. Mary Elizabeth Rouland, June 1, 1963; children—Reid Shaver II, Rouland Shannon. B.A., U. Wichita, 1964, postgrad., 1964-65; postgrad. Tulane U., 1968-69; M.A., Wichita State U., 1970. Grad. fellow Wichita State U., 1965; asminstrv. asst. to city mgr. Newton (Kans.), 1965-66; planning assoc., New Orleans, 1966-69; adminstrv. asst. to exec. sec. devel. Town of Brookline (Mass.), 1969-73; chief systems planning City of Kansas City (Mo.), 1973-74, acting. dep. dir. city devel., 1974-75; prin. CHJ Assocs., Kansas City, Mo., 1975-78; adminstrv. dir. City of Lincoln (Nebr.), 1976-79; chief adminstrv. officer City of Shreveport (La.), 1979; mgmt. cons., Shreveport, 1980-83; city mgr. City of Ankeny (Iowa), 1983—; lectr., cons. in field; participant Nat. Urban Policy Roundtable IV, 1977; mem. tech. adv. group Urban Econ. Policy and Mgmt. Group, U.S. Conf. Mayors-Nat. League Cities, 1977—. Author mcpl. budgeting manuals. Served with USAAF, 1961. Mem. Am. Polit. Sci. Assn., Am. Inst. Cert. Planners, Am. Acad. Polit. and Social Scis., Internat. City Mgmt. Assn., Am. Planning Assn., Am. Soc. Pub. Adminstrn., Pi Sigma Alpha. Quaker. Home: 1206 S E Cortina Ankeny IA 50021 Office: 211 S W Walnut St Ankeny IA 50021

CHARLET, LAURENCE DEAN, research entomologist, educator; b. Danville, Ill., Oct. 6, 1946; s. Robert Junior and Jean Alice (Mills) C.; m. Kathryn Elizabeth Clyde, Feb. 2, 1969; children—Annette Marie, Suzanne Elizabeth, David Robert. B.S., San Diego State U., 1969; M.S., U. Calif.-Riverside, 1973, Ph.D., 1975. Cert. community coll. tchr., Calif. Postgrad. research entomologist, U. Calif., Riverside, 1975-78; research entomologist U.S. Dept. Agr., Agrl. Research Service, Oilseeds Research Unit, Fargo, N.D., 1978—; adj. prof. entomology N.D. State U., Fargo, 1983—. Contbr. articles to jours. NSF trainee, 1971-74. Mem. Entomol. Soc. Am., Entomol. Soc. Can., Acarol. Soc. Am., Internat. Orgn. Biol. Control (governing bd. Western Hemisphere Regional Sect. 1984—), Sigma Xi. Lutheran. Home: 902 Southwood Dr Fargo ND 58103 Office: USDA ARS Dept Entomology ND State Univ 257 Hultz Hall Fargo ND 58105

CHARLTON, RICHARD EARLE, accounting educator; b. Balt., July 26, 1932; s. Richard Earle and Clara Jane (Faulkner) C.; m. Eleanor Louise Siegle, Aug. 4, 1962; children—Richard Earle III, Eric Frederick, Cheryl Louise. B.S. in Bus., Johns Hopkins U., 1952; M.B.A., U. Pa., 1954; Ph.D., Mich. State U., 1976. Teaching fellow U. Mich., 1954-61; asst. prof. Ferris State Coll., 1961-64, Eastern Mich. U., 1976-77, Wayne State U., 1977-84; instr. Schoolcraft Coll., 1964-69; assoc. prof. acctg. U. Detroit, 1984—; researcher 3rd Jud. Cir. Ct., Wayne County, Mich., 1979-80. Contbr. articles to profl. jours. Mem. Am. Acctg. Assn., Beta Alpha Psi, Beta Gamma Sigma. Republican. Lutheran. Avocation: musical activities. Home: 2844 Oakdale Dr Ann Arbor MI 48104 Office: Univ Detroit 4001 W McNichols Rd Detroit MI 48221

CHAROENYING, CYNTHIA JO CULLEN, pharmacist; b. Springfield, Ill., Sept. 16, 1952; d. Donald French and Jacqueline (Cook) Cullen; m. Boon R. Charoenying, Jan. 27, 1979; children—Adrienne, Jula. A.A., Springfield Coll., 1972; B.S. in Pharmacy, Drake U., 1975. Registered pharmacist, Iowa, Ill. Pharmacist, No. Ill. U. Health Ctr., DeKalb, 1975-79; pharm. cons. Boon R. Charoenying, McHenry, Ill., 1979—, breast feeding and family planning cons., 1979—. Presch. coordinator Resurrection Catholic Ch., Woodstock, Ill., 1983—; mem. La Leche League, McHenry. Mem. Am. Pharm. Assn., Ill. Pharm. Assn. Democrat. Home: 5204-A Woodmar Circle McHenry IL 60050

CHARPENTIER, DONALD ARMAND, psychologist; b. Bklyn., Mar. 8, 1935; s. Joseph Roche and Grace Viola (Adrience) C.; B.A., Hope Coll., 1956; M.A., Ohio U., 1958; Ed.S., George Peabody Coll., 1964; Ph.D., U. Minn., 1972; m. Janice Lee Getting, May 21, 1961; children—Jennifer Diane, Ian Lee Burke. Asso. dir. Westminster Found. Ohio, 1956-57, acting dir., 1957-58; psychologist, probation officer Cook County Family Court, Chgo., 1961-62; asst. prof. psychology State U. N.Y., Fredonia, 1964-65; asst. prof. U. Wis., River Falls, 1965-72, asso. prof., 1974-80, prof., 1980—. Vis. research fellow, Harvard U., 1973-74. Lic. psychologist, Wis. Mem. Am. Assn. Advancement Social Psychology, Am. Psychol. Assn., Am. Sociol. Assn., Internat. Soc. History of Behavioral and Social Scis., Soc. Psychol. Study Social Issues, Soc. for Advancement Am. Philosophy. Home: Rt 4 River Falls WI 54022 Office: Dept Psychology Univ Wis River Falls WI 54022

CHARTIER, DONALD M., agricultural products company executive; b. Dallas Center, Iowa, 1933. Grad. Iowa State U., 1958. Pres., chief exec. officer Far-Mar Co., Inc., Kansas City, Mo.; dir. U.S. Feed Grains Council, Nat. Soybean Processors Assn., Soy-Cot Sales, Inc., Farmers Export Co., Kansas City Terminal Elevator Co. Office: Far-Mar Co Inc PO Box 1667 Hutchinson KS 67501*

CHARTIER, JANELLEN OLSEN, airline inflight service coordinator; b. Chgo., Sept. 12, 1951; d. Roger Carl and Genevieve Ann (McCormick) Olsen; m. Lionel Pierre-Paul Chartier, Nov. 6, 1982. B.A. in French and Home Econs., U. Ill., 1973, M.A. in Teaching French, 1974; student U. Rouen (France), 1971-72. Cert. tchr., Ill. Flight attendant Delta Airlines, Atlanta, 1974—, French qualified, 1974—, Spanish qualified, 1977-82, German qualified, 1980—, in flight service coordinator, 1980—, European in flight service coordinator, 1983—; French examiner In-Flight Service, 1984—; interpreter Formax, Inc., Mokena, Ill., 1976-82. Bd. dirs. One Plus One Dance Co., Champaign, Ill., 1977-78. Mem. Alliance Maison Francaise de Chgo., Phi Delta Kappa, Alpha Lambda Delta. Roman Catholic. Home: 155 N Harbor Dr Apt 4306 Chicago IL 60601 Office: Delta Air Lines Hartsfield Internat Airport Atlanta GA 30320

CHASE, CHARLES AYER, investment advisor; b. Mpls., Oct. 12, 1931; s. Kenneth A. and Irma M. (Brodin) C.; A.B., Ripon Coll., 1954; postgrad. U. Minn., Boston U., Mexico City Coll.; m. Janet Gray, Sept. 17, 1960; children—Anne, Charles Ayer. Contracting officer Boston Ordance Dist., 1955-57; ptnr. Chase Investment Co., 1962-74; owner, propr. Chase Investment Co., Mpls., 1974—; cons. Served with ordnance, AUS, 1955-57. Registered investment advisor. Mem. Nat. Rifle Assn., Exptl. Aircraft Assn. Republican. Congregationalist. Club: Mpls. Athletic. Office: 1115 2d Ave S Minneapolis MN 55403

CHASE, ERNEST ARTHUR, accountant; b. Galien, Mich., Apr. 10, 1931; s. Samuel M. and Mildred Irene (Morley) C.; student LaSalle Extension U., 1953-57, Lake Michigan Coll., 1974-75; m. Joyce Elaine Winney, July 21, 1951; children—Ernest L., Arthur M., Robert J., William R., James R. Assembly insp. David Products Co., Niles, Mich., 1951; gen. acct. Warren Featherbone Co., Three Oaks, Mich., 1953-55; cost acct. Bendix Products Co., South Bend, Ind., 1955-56; officer mgr. Babbitt Lumber Co., Niles, 1956-57; cost acct. Curtiss Wright Corp., South Bend, 1957-58; mgr. credit office Am. Home and Gray Aretz Co., South Bend, 1958; chief acct. Millburg Growers Exchange (Mich.), 1958-59; sales mgr. S.W. Mich. dist. Nat. Fedn. Ind. Bus., 1959-60; owner Chase Pub. Acctg. Service, Galien, 1958—, Chase Ins. Service Center, Galien, 1960—, Family Everyday Clothing and Shoe Store, Three Oaks, 1963-65; salesman Kiefer Real Estate, Berrien Springs, Mich., 1962-76. Leader, Boy Scouts Am., 1957-72; sec., treas., coach Galien Little League, 1964-76; clk. Village of Galien, 1963-64; mem. adv. com. Galien Twp. Schs., 1963-70, chmn., 1966-70; mem. tax allocation bd. Berrien County, 1971-72, mem. key man com., 1971-72, chmn. finance com., 1971-72, chmn. budget com., 1969-70, county commr., 1969-72, 77-79, 83-84; mem. Berrien County Pension Bd., 1977-79; road commr. Berrien County, 1984—; mem. regional key man com. Mich. Assn. Counties, 1971-72. Mem. Berrien County Republican Exec. Com., 1969-72, 77-79, 83-84; mem. Berrien County Road Commn., 1985—. Served with USNR, 1949-50, 52-53. Mem. Ind. Accts. Mich., Mich. Assn. Mut. Ins. Agts., Nat. Soc. Pub. Accts., Am. Legion. Methodist. Lion. Home: Hwy US 12 E Galien MI 49113 Office: 112 N Main St Galien MI 49113

CHASE, FRANK RALPH, management consultant; b. Mpls., Nov. 10, 1925; s. Frank R. and Virginia (Nickerson) C.; m. Jean Ann Fosdick, Sept. 18, 1948; children—Sally, Frank, Anne, Barbara. B.B.A., U. Minn., 1947. Coordinator prodn. Gould Nat. Battery Corp., St. Paul, 1948-55; v.p. sales Torit Corp., St. Paul, 1955-69, pres., 1969-74; v.p., gen. mgr. Donaldson Indsl. Group, Mpls., 1974-84; ptnr. Chase Assocs., Excelsior, Minn., 1985—; dir. Tescom Corp., Mpls., Econo Therm Energy Corp., Mpls. Patentee in field. Bd. dirs. ARC, Mpls. Served with USNR, 1944-46. Mem. ASHRAE. Republican. Congregationalist. Home and Office: 20000 Lakeview Ave Excelsior MN 55331

CHASE, JAMES ARTHUR, construction and refractory company executive; b. Battle Creek, Mich., Sept. 25, 1943; s. Donald Arthur and Mary Helena (VanderWeele) C.; m. Debra Ann Schwenk, Feb. 27, 1980; children—Stephanie Lynn, Steven James, Eric James. B.S., Mich. State U., 1965. Field sales engr. Harbison-Walker Refractories, Inc., Pitts., 1965-70, nat. products mgr., 1970-72; nat. mktg. mgr. MacFarlane & Hays Co., Farmington Hills, Mich., 1972-75; internat. products mgr. McClelland & Co., Birmingham, Mich., 1975-80; pres. Chase-Nedrow Industries, Inc., Farmington Hills, 1980—; pres. Nedrow Refractories Co., Farmington Hills, 1985—. Pres., Orchard Hills Homeowners Assn., Novi, Mich., 1983-85. Mem. Am. Foundrymen's Soc. (bd. dirs. Detroit chpt. 1981-84, pres. 1982-83). Republican. Methodist. Avocations: golf; tennis; fishing. Home: 41620 Tamara Dr Novi MI 48050 Office: Chase-Nedrow Industries Inc 150 Landrow Dr Wixom MI

CHASE, JOYCE ELAINE, accountant, ins. co. exec.; b. Benton Harbor, Mich., Dec. 4, 1931; d. Richard I. and Evelyn Pauline (Hahn) Winney; student Lake Mich. Coll., 1974-75, Mich. State Ins. Sch., 1974, m. Ernest Arthur Chase, July 21, 1951; children—Ernest L., Arthur M., Robert J., William R., James R. Clk. Gillespie's Drug Store, Benton Harbor, 1945, WoolWorth's Store, Benton Harbor, 1946-47; bookkeeper Reeder's Bookkeeping Service, Benton Harbor, 1949; assembler VM Corp., Benton Harbor, 1950; telephone operator Mich. Bell Co., Benton Harbor, 1951; bookkeeper I & M Electric Co., Buchanan, Mich., 1952, Auto Specialties Co., St. Joseph, Mich., 1953; clk. Galien Drug Store, Galien, Mich., 1955; assembler Electro-Voice Corp., Buchanan, Mich., 1958-62; bookkeeper Chase Bookkeeping & Tax Service, Galien, Mich., 1963-78, sr. tax accountant, 1968—; ins. agt. Chase Ins. Service Center, Galien, Mich., 1974—; emergency med. technician and ambulance driver Galien Vol. Ambulance Service, 1974—. Cub. Scout den mother S.W. Mich. council Cub. Scouts Am., 1963-69; mem. Galien Twp. election bd., 1971-78; mem. Galien Sch. Election Bd., 1971—; pres. Galien Athletic Boosters, 1969; mem. Galien High Sch., PTA, 1966—, adv. com., 1965-68. Mem. Nat. Soc. Pub. Accountants, Mich. Emergency Services Health Council, Am. Legion Aux. Republican. Methodist. Home: US Route 12 East at Garwood Lake Galien MI 49113 Office: 112 N Main St Galien MI 49113

CHASTAIN, CHARLES WILLIAM, III, physician, health care executive; b. Plattsburg, Mo., Oct. 17, 1930; s. Charles William and Faith Agnes (Payne) C.; m. Caroline Parker Saunders, Nov. 27, 1954 (div. 1981); children—Charles William, Jane Martindale, John Langdon, Catherine Payne, Carrie Parker, Edward Saunders; m. Barbara Annette Maier, Sept. 20, 1981. A.B. cum laude, Harvard U., 1952; M.D., Columbia U., 1956. Diplomate Am. Bd. Family Practice. Intern Mary Imogene Bassett Hosp., Cooperstown, N.Y., 1956-57; resident Ft. Carson Army Hosp., 1957-58; mem. staff Med. Arts Clinic, Farmington, Mo., 1959-77; dir. Family Practice Residency, North Kansas City, Mo., 1977-79; pres. Family Healthcare of Southeast Mo., Flat River, 1979—; v.p. St. Louis Blue Shield, 1973-77; chief of staff Madison Meml. Hosp., Fredericktown, Mo., 1963-65, Bonne Terre Hosp., Mo., 1981-84; Co-author: Accessibility to Health Care, 1972; In-Patient Planning, 1975. Assoc. editor Medical Times, 1974-82. Chmn. Democratic central com. St. Francois County, Mo., 1971-77; St. Francois County Tb Soc., Farmington, 1960-65. Served to capt. U.S. Army, 1957-59. Harvard nat. scholar, 1948. Fellow Am. Acad. Family Physicians (del. 1972-77); mem. Mo. Acad. Family Physicians (pres. 1977-79, chmn. bd. 1979-80), Mo. State Med. Assn. (chmn. econs. com. 1975-77), Mineral Area Med. Soc. (pres. 1967-69, 79-81), St. Francois County Hist. Soc. (chmn. 1972-75). Roman Catholic. Club: Harvard (St. Louis). Lodge: Elks. Avocations: fly fishing, travel. Home: Rural Route 3 Box 15 Bonne Terre MO 63628 Office: Family Healthcare Southeast Mo 815 E Main St Flat River MO 63601

CHASTAIN, CLAUD BLANKENHORN, educator; b. Stamford, Tex., Oct. 12, 1945; s. Claud Harrison and Jean Ida (Blankenhorn) C.; B.S., U. Mo., 1967, D.V.M., 1969; M.S., Iowa State U., 1972; m. Joyce Busche, June 25, 1977; children—Andrea Lee, Danielle Renee. Instr. public health Taiwan Nat. U., 1971-72; instr. Coll. Vet. Medicine, Iowa State U., 1972-75; asst. prof. La. State U., 1975-76; asst. prof. vet. clin. scis. Iowa State U., 1976-77, assoc. prof., 1977-81, prof., 1981-82; assoc. prof., instructional leader of medicine block Coll. Vet. Medicine, U. Mo., Columbia, 1982—. Served to capt. USAF, 1969-71. Mem. Am. Vet. Med. Assn., Am. Acad. Vet. Dermatologists, Am. Assn. Vet. Clinicians, Am. Animal Hosp. Assn., Am. Coll. Vet. Internal Medicine, Nat. Woodcarvers Assn., Nat. Wildlife Fedn., Phi Zeta. Methodist. Office: U Mo Columbia MO 65211

CHASTAIN, KERRY HUGH, leasing company executive; consultant; b. Wichita, Kans., Aug. 4, 1949; s. Bert Lowel and Irene (Welch) C.; m. Karen Elizabeth McDonough, Feb. 21, 1981. Student Wichita State U., 1979-80, Hutchinson Jr. Coll., 1969-70. Area mgr. Rollins Co., Kansas City, Kans., 1978-82; mktg. v.p. Seven States Mktg., Lanexa, Kans., 1982-84; exec. v.p. Pact, Inc., Lanexa, Kans., 1984—; pres. K.&L. Mktg., Overland Park, Kans., 1983—, Forms of Distinction, Olathe, Kans., 1983—; dir. All About Wood, Kansas City, 1984—. Author mktg. checklist booklet, 1983. Mem. Kansas City Direct Mktg. Assn., Mid-Am. Cons. Baptist. Lodge: Shriners. Avocations: racquetball; softball. Home: 413 Normandy St Olathe KS 66061 Office: Forms of Distinction Inc 2111 E Santa Fe Suite 222 Olathe KS 66062

CHATMAN, WILLIE MAE, educator; b. St. Louis, Nov. 1, 1945; d. James and Mosella (Reed) Artis; m. Lindbergh Chatman, Jr., Aug. 17, 1966 (div. Nov. 1979). Student Jackson Community Coll., 1964, 67; B.S., Western Mich. U., Kalamazoo, 1970, M.A., 1973; postgrad. Wayne State U., 1981—; cert. mgmt. devel. seminars Detroit Pub. Schs. Mgmt. Acad., 1983. Cert. in secondary, continuing, vocat. and competency based edn., Mich. Jr. stenographer Consumers Power Co., Jackson, Mich., 1964-66; clk.-typist Mich. Employment Securities Commn., Jackson, 1966-68; sec. to dir. info. Western Mich. U., 1968-69; sec. Kalamazoo Nat. Bank, 1969-70; tchr. bus. edn. No. High Sch., Detroit, 1971-79, head dept. bus. and vocat. edn., 1979—; evaluator Metro Detroit Typing/Shorthand Ann. Contest; cons. North Central Steering Coms. Recipient Vocat. Edn. and Career Devel. award Mich. Dept. Edn., 1974, cert. of recognition Detroit Pub. Schs., 1974, 77, 79, cert. of achievement Research and Devel. in Edn., 1977; Western Mich. U. scholar, 1968. Mem. Mich. Bus. Edn. Assn., Orgn. Sch. Adminstrs. and Suprs., Met. Detroit Bus. Edn. Assn., Mich.-Detroit Assn. Black Sch. Educators. Democrat. Club: Bus. Office Edn. Home: 20083 Greydale St Detroit MI 48219 Office: Northern High School 9026 Woodward Ave Detroit MI 48202

CHATTEN, ROGER GERALD, psychologist; b. Quincy, Ill., Feb. 8, 1944; s. Ernest M. and Genevieve D. (Welch) C.; B.A., William Jewell Coll., 1966; M.A., U. Mo., 1968, Ph.D., 1977; m. Carol Ruth Ferril, Apr. 16, 1966; children—Michael, Kimberly. Instr. psychology Donnelly Coll., 1968-69; counseling intern U. Mo., Kansas City, 1971-72, 73-74; clin. dir. Associated Psychologists and Counselors, Kansas City, Mo., 1978—; adj. prof. Park and Webster Coll., 1973—, Columbia Coll., 1979—, Ottawa U., 1979—; clin. psychology intern Western Mo. Mental Health Center, 1977-78. Lic. psychologist, Mo.; listed Nat. Register Health Service Providers in Psychology; cert. Biofeedback Cert. Inst. Am. Mem. Am. Psychol. Assn. (div. counseling psychology), Biofeedback Soc. Am., Biofeedback Soc. Mo., Greater Kansas City Psychol. Assn., Mo. Psychol. Assn., Profl. Counselors Assn. Home: Kansas City MO Office: Suite 115 4706 Broadway Kansas City MO 64112

CHATTERTON, ROBERT TREAT, JR., reproductive endocrinology educator; b. Catskill, N.Y., Aug. 9, 1935; s. Robert Treat and Irene (Spoor) C.; m. Patricia A. Holland, June 4, 1956 (div. 1965); children—Ruth Ellen, William Matthew, James Daniel; m. Astrida J. Vanags, June 25, 1966 (div. 1977); 1 son, Derek Scott; m. Carol Jean Lewis, May 24, 1985. B.S., Cornell U., 1958, Ph.D., 1963; M.S., U. Conn., 1959. Postdoctoral fellow Harvard U. Med. Sch., 1963-65; research assoc. div. oncology Inst. Steroid Research, Montefiore Hosp. and Med. Ctr., N.Y., 1965-70; asst. prof. U. Ill. Coll. Medicine, 1970-72, assoc. prof., 1972-79; prof. Northwestern U. Med. Sch., Chgo., 1979—; mem. U.S. AID/Sci Adv. Com. NIH grantee, 1972—. Mem. AAAS, N.Y. Acad. Scis., Am. Chem. Soc., Endocrine Soc., Soc. Gynecologic Investigation, Soc. Study Reprodn. Presbyterian (deacon). Contbr. numerous articles to sci. jours.; patentee on ovulation detection method; new form of oral contraceptive; method for hormone removal from body fluids. Home: 5018 W Agatite Ave Chicago IL 60630 Office: 333 E Superior St Suite 1121 Chicago IL 60611

CHAUDHRY, DEWAT RAM, psychiatrist; b. Rajasthan, India, Jan. 5, 1942; s. Mallu Ram and Gomti (Siyag) C.; came to U.S., 1970, naturalized, 1978; M.B.B.S., Sardar Patel Med. Coll., Bikaner, India, 1966; m. Lalita Beniwal, May 12, 1967; children—Neena, Suneel. Intern J.L.N. Hosp., Ajmer, India, 1966-67; resident in psychiatry VA and Provincial hosps., St. John, N.B., Can., 1968-70; intern Aultman Hosp., Canton, Ohio, 1970-71; resident in psychiatry Med. Coll. Toledo Hosp., 1971-73; fellow child psychiatry Hawthorn Center, Northville, Mich., 1973-74; child psychiatrist, coordinator children's services Comprehensive Community Mental Health Center Rock Island (Ill.) and Mercer County, 1974-80; practice medicine specializing in psychiatry, Moline, Ill., 1980—. Diplomate Am. Bd. Psychiatry and Neurology. Fellow Am. Acad. Child Psychiatry; mem. AMA, Ill. State Med. Soc., Am. Psychiat. Assn., Ill. Psychiat. Soc. Hindu. Office: 2101 47th St Moline IL 61265

CHAUDRY, MUHAMMAD MUNIR, food chemist, editor, author, consultant, researcher; b. Jullundur, India, Jan. 1, 1944; s. Sher Muhammad and Fatima Chaudry; m. Jabeen Akhtar, Jan. 15, 1977; children—Salman, Saad. B.S., Lyallpur, Pakistan, 1966, M.S., 1968; M.S., Am. U. Beirut, 1973, Ph.D., U. Ill.-Urbana, 1980. Research asst. Agrl. Research Inst., Lyallpur, Pakistan, 1969-71, U. Ill., Urbana, 1974-80; sr. food technologist Heller Seasonings, Inc., Bedford Park, Ill., 1980—; research and devel. cons. Vice pres. Islamic Food and Nutrition Council, Chgo. AID fellow, 1971-73. Mem. Inst. Food Technologists, Am. Oil Chemists Soc., Sigma Xi. Ifunca. Contbr. articles to profl. jours. Office: Heller Seasonings Inc 6363 W 73d St Bedford Park IL 60638

CHAVERS, BLANCHE MARIE, pediatrician, educator, researcher; b. Clarksdale, Miss., Aug. 2, 1949; d. Andrew and Mildred Louise (Cox) C.; m. Gubare Robert Mpambara, May 21, 1982; 1 child, Kaita. B.S. in Zoology, U. Wash., 1971, M.D., 1975. Diplomate Am. Bd. Pediatrics. Intern, U. Wash., Seattle, 1975-76, resident in pediatrics, 1976-78; fellow in pediatric nephrology U. Minn., Mpls., 1978-81, instr., 1981-82, asst. prof. pediatrics, 1983—; attending physician dept. pediatrics, U. Minn. Sch. Medicine, Mpls., 1981—. Contbr. articles to profl. jours. Recipient Clin. Investigator award NIH, 1982. Mem. Am. Acad. Pediatrics, Am. Soc. Nephrology, Am. Soc. Pediatric Nephrology, Internat. Soc. Nephrology. Democrat. Mem. African Methodist Episcopal Zion Ch. Avocations: tennis; reading; collecting African artifacts; art. Home: 5425 Grand Ave S Minneapolis MN 55419 Office: U Minn Box 491 Mayo 515 Delaware St SE Minneapolis MN 55455

CHEANEY, WILLIAM D(ONALD), educational administrator; b. Henderson, Ky., Oct. 1, 1940; s. Harrison L. and Flossie (Cunningham) C.; m., Sept. 4, 1976. B.A., U. Evansville, 1962; M.A., Mich. State U., 1967, Ph.D., 1975. Elem. and jr. high sch. tchr., Grand Rapids Pub. Schs. (Mich.), 1962-66, community sch. dir., 1966-67, elem. prin., 1967-71; asst. dir. elem. edn. Flint Community Schs. (Mich.), 1974-80; asst. supt. City of Saginaw Sch. Dist. (Mich.), 1980—. Contbr. article to profl. jour.; photographer. Bd. dirs. Saginaw Art Mus.; mem. NAACP; chair Saginaw chpt. United Coll. Fund. Mem. Am. Assn. Sch. Adminstrs., Saginaw Area Reading Council, Nat. Assn. Elem. Prins., Middle Cities Assn. Home: 2233 Mershon St Saginaw MI 48602

CHEE, CHENG-KHEE, artist, educator; b. Xienyou, Fujian, China, Jan. 14, 1934; came to U.S., 1962, naturalized, 1980; s. Ya-Jie and Xien-chun (Zheng) C.; m. Sing-Bee Ong, Aug. 28, 1965; children—Yi-Hung, Yi-Min, Wan-Ying, Yen-Ying. B.A., Nanyang U., Singapore, 1960; M.A., U. Minn., 1964. Asst. librarian Nanyang U., 1961-62; teaching asst. U. Minn., Mpls., 1963-64, librarian, Duluth, 1965-68, instr., 1968-80, asst. prof., 1981—; one-man shows include: Zhejiang Acad. Fine Arts, 1984, Tweed Mus. Art, U. Minn., 1982-83, Itasca Community Coll., 1981, Northwestern Bank of Commerce, Duluth, 1979, Twin Cities Federal Atrium Gallery, 1978, Lakewood Community Coll. Art Ctr., 1978, North Star Gallery U. Minn., 1975; exhibited in group shows: Nat. Acad. and Salmagundi Club, N.Y.C., 1975, 78, 79, 81, Foothills Art Ctr., Golden, Colo., 1976, 78, 80, 84, Nat. Arts Club, N.Y.C., 1980, 81, 82, 83, Community Arts Ctr., Old Forge, N.Y., 1982, 83, Springfield Art Mus., Mo., 1975, St. Louis County Heritage and Arts Center, 1977, Mitchell Museum, Ill., 1983, Meridian House Internat., Washington, D.C., 1983, Mpls. Inst. Arts, 1978. Author portfolio Cheng-Khee Chee Watercolors, 1984. Author exhbn. catalog, 1973-82, Retrospective Exhibition, 1982. Contributor to book Watercolor Energies, 1983. Named Best in Show Sumi-e Soc. Am., 1984; recipient Gold Medal of Honor, Allied Artists of Am. exhibit, 1980; Colo. Centennial award Rocky Mountain Nat. Watermedia Exhbn., 1976; Grumbacher Gold medal Midwest Watercolor Soc. exhbn., 1984; Gold award Ga. Watercolor Soc. exhbn., 1985; numerous other awards. Mem. Am. Watercolor Soc., Nat. Watercolor Soc., Rocky Mountain Nat. Watermedia Soc., Midwest Watercolor Soc., Sumi-e Soc. Am. Home: 1508 Vermilion Rd Duluth MN 55812 Office: Univ Minn Duluth MN 55812

CHEEKS, DANSBY GOIN, lawyer; b. Peoria, Ill., May 4, 1943; s. John G. and Gertrude Cheeks; m. Patricia Ann Jones, Aug. 17, 1968; children—Joshua G., Jonathan A. B.A. in Sociology, U. Iowa, 1966; J.D., Kent Coll. Law, 1974. Bar: Ill. 1974. Reporter, Decatur (Ill.) Herald & Rev., 1966; tchr. Decatur Bd. Edn., 1966-67, Chgo. Bd. Edn., 1967-74; assoc. E. Duke McNeil & Assocs., Chgo., 1974-76; sole practice, Oak Park, Ill., 1976—. Mem. Oak Park Plan Commn.; mem. South Austin-Madison Corp. Mem. ABA. Methodist. Home: 1220 N Forest Ave Oak Park IL 60302 Office: 108 Madison St Oak Park IL 60302

CHEEVER, HERBERT E., JR., political science educator; b. Brookings, S.D., Aug. 26, 1938; s. Herbert E. and Margaret (Williams) C.; m. Synda Lou Riedesel, Mar. 30, 1959; children—Jason D., Michael L., Gene K. Student Carleton Coll., 1956-59; B.S., S.D. State U., 1959-60; M.A., U. Iowa, 1963, Ph.D., 1966. Asst. prof. polit. sci. Kans. State Coll., Pittsburg, 1963-65, U. Wis., LaCrosse, 1966-68; faculty S.D. State U., Brookings, 1968—, now prof., head dept. polit. sci. Avocations: camping; hiking. Home: 405 20th Ave Brookings SD 57006 Office: SD State U Polit Sci Dept Brookings SD 57007

CHEFFER, ROBERT GENE, counselor; b. Kankakee, Ill., Aug. 9, 1936; s. Herman Joseph and Cecilia Marie (Dion) C.; B.S., Eastern Ill. U., 1958; M.Ed., Chgo. State U., 1962; m. Patricia Paris, June 25, 1960; children—Christian, Scott. Tchr., Oak Lawn (Ill.) Community High Sch., 1958-70; counselor Maine Twp. High Sch., Park Ridge, Ill., 1970—, Monacep Alt. High Sch. Program, 1976—. Named Outstanding Secondary Educator, 1973. Mem. Am. Personnel and Guidance Assn., Nat. Vocat. Guidance Assn., Am. Sch. Counselors Assn., Ill. Guidance and Personnel Assn. (pres. 1978-79, pres. N.W. Suburban chpt. 1974-75), Ill. Vocat. Guidance Assn. (pres. 1974-75), Ill. Guidance and Personnel Assn., NEA, Ill. Edn. Assn., Ill. Assn. Adult and Continuing Edn. Counselors, Eastern Ill. U. Alumni Assn., Chgo. State U. Alumni Assn., Pupil Personnel Service Consortium. Home: 153 Chandler St Elmhurst IL 60126 Office: 1111 Dee Rd Park Ridge IL 60068

CHEHVAL, MICHAEL JOHN, surgeon; b. Racine, Wis., June 30, 1941; s. Michael K. and Iva Alma (Makovsky) C.; m. Marijane S. Jakaitis, Sept. 2, 1967; children—Kelley, Michael, Benjamin, Vincent. B.S., Northeast Mo. State U., 1963; M.D., St. Louis U., 1967. Diplomate Am. Bd. Urology. Intern St. Louis U. Hosp., 1967-68; resident U. Iowa Hosps., Iowa City, 1970-75; fellow Am. Cancer Soc., 1973-74; assoc. clin. prof. urology St. Louis U. Sch. Medicine, 1985—; chmn. Div. Urology, St. John's Mercy Med. Ctr., St. Louis, 1983—; sec. med. staff Cardinal Glennon Hosp. for Children, St. Louis, 1985—; pres. Central Eastern Mo. Peer Rev. Orgn., St. Louis, 1984—; chmn. med. adv. com. Vis. Nurses St. Louis, 1984—; staff St. John's Hosp., St. Louis U. Hosp., St. Mary's Health Ctr. Contbr. articles to med. publs. Served with USN, 1968-70. Mem. ACS, Am. Urologic Assn., Soc. Pediatric Urology, AMA, Mo. State Med. Assn., Am. Fertility Soc., St. Louis Med. Soc., St. Louis Urol. Soc., St. Louis Surg. Soc. Lutheran. Home: 1260 Glenvista Pl St Louis MO 63122 Office: Michael J Chehval Inc 621 S New Ballas Rd St Louis MO 63141

CHEMA, THOMAS V., government official, lawyer; b. East Liverpool, Ohio, Oct. 31, 1946; s. Stephen T. and Dorothy Grace (McCormack) C.; m. Barbara Burke Orr, Aug. 15, 1970; children—Christine, Stephen. A.B., U. Notre Dame, 1968; J.D., Harvard U., 1971. Bar: Ohio 1971, U.S. Supreme Ct. 1977. Assoc. Arter and Hadden, Cleve., 1971-83; exec. dir. Ohio Lottery Commn., Cleve., 1983-85; chmn. Pub. Utilities Commn. Ohio, Columbus, 1985—. Candidate for Ohio Senate, 1980; campaign mgr., Senator Howard M. Metzenbaum, 1976; co-chmn. task force on violence and crime, Cleve., 1981—. Mem. Nat. Assn. Regulatory Utility Commrs., Nat. Assn. State Lotteries (bd. dirs.), Greater Cleve. Bar Assn., Ohio State Bar Assn., Cleve. Legal Aid Soc. Democrat. Roman Catholic. Club: City (Cleve.). Lodge: Ceska Sin Carlin. Avocations: skiing; softball. Home: 18580 Parkland Dr Shaker Heights OH 44122 Office: Pub Utilities Commn of Ohio 180 E Broad St Columbus OH 43215

CHEN, BEN, immunologist, cell biologist, educator; b. Taiwan, China, Aug. 5, 1946; came to U.S., 1970, naturalized, 1982. B.S., Fujen U., Taiwan, 1969; M.S., SUNY-Buffalo, 1972; Ph.D., Vanderbilt U., 1977. Research assoc. Washington U.-St. Louis, 1977-80, instr., 1980-82, asst. prof., 1982-83; asst. mem. Mich. Cancer Found., Detroit, 1983—; asst. prof. Wayne State U., Detroit, 1983—. Author tech. papers. Recipient Nat. Research Service award NIH, 1979-80, New Investigator Research award, 1983-85. Mem. Am. Soc. Cell Biology, Reticuloendothelial Soc., Internat. Soc. Exptl. Hematology, AAAS. Office: Mich Cancer Found 110 E Warren Ave Detroit MI 48201

CHEN, CHONG-MAW, biochemistry educator; b. Taoyuan, Taiwan; m. Gong-rong Chuang, Jan. 29, 1967; children—Sharon, Alice, Howard. B.S., Nat. Taiwan U., 1959; Ph.D., Kans. U., 1967. Postdoctoral fellow McMaster U., Hamilton, Ont., Can., 1967-69, Roche Inst. Molecular Biology, Nutley, N.J., 1969-71; from asst. prof. to prof. Biomed. Research Inst., U. Wis.-Kenosha, 1971—, dir. plant biochemistry research lab., 1972—. Contbr. articles to sci. jours. Mem. sci. socs. Home: 2701 Village Green E Racine WI 53406 Office: U Wis Kenosha WI 53141

CHEN, HOLLIS CHING, computer engineering educator; b. Chekiang, China, Nov. 17, 1935; came to U.S., 1960; naturalized, 1971; s. Yu-Chao and Shui-Tan C.; m. Donna H. Liu, Sept. 3, 1961; children—Deiree, Hollis. B.S., Nat. Taiwan U., 1957; M.S. Ohio U., 1961; Ph.D., Syracuse U., 1965. Instr., asst. prof. Syracuse U., N.Y., 1961-67; asst., assoc. prof. Ohio U., Athens, 1967-75, prof., 1975—, acting chmn. dept. elec. and computer engring., 1984—. Author: Theory of EM Waves, 1983; (with others) Research Topics in EM Wave Theory, 1981. Contbr. articles to profl. jours. Mem. IEEE (sr.), Internat. Union Radio Sci., Am. Soc. for Engring. Edn., Soc. Indsl. and Applied Math., Math. Assn. Am., AAAS. Home: 1 Ball Dr Athens OH 45701 Office: Dept Electric and Computer Engring Ohio U Athens OH 45701

CHEN, JOHN TSAN-HSIANG, engineering technology educator; b. Fuchou, Fukien, China, Feb. 11, 1937; came to U.S., 1964; s. Tze-Hong and Pao-Kaun (Liu) C.; m. Yu-Eng Huang, Jan. 6, 1957; children—James P.C., Susan J.L. B.Ed., Nat. Taiwan Normal U., 1961; postgrad. U. Ill., 1968; M.S. in Indsl. Edn., U. Wis.-Stout, 1965; M.S. in Mech. Engring., Marquette U., 1970; Ph.D., U. Mo., 1973. Cert. mfg. engr. Instr., Nat. Taiwan Normal U., Taipei, 1961-62, 63-64, Gateway Tech. Inst., Racine, Wis., 1977-78, 65-76; chmn. mech. engring. tech. Nat. Taiwan Inst. Tech., Taipei, 1976-77; assoc. prof. Rochester Inst. Tech., N.Y., 1978-81; chmn. tech. dept. Pittsburg State U., Kans., 1981-84, asst. to pres., coordinator grad. studies, 1984—; Regional VII chmn. Mech. Tech. in Engring. Dept. Heads Com. cons. Westinghouse Corp., 1983, others. Contbr. articles to sci. publs. Chinese Student Assn., Pittsburg, 1981—. Scholar, Chinese Buddhist Assn., 1959; fellow Fukiense Assn., 1960. Mem. ASME, Am. Soc. Engring. Edn., Soc. Mfg. Engrs., Am. Soc. Metals, Phi Delta Kappa. Avocations: fishing; table tennis. Office: Pittsburg State U Pittsburg KS 66762

CHEN, PETER FU MING, surgeon; b. Medan, Indonesia, Dec. 3, 1941; s. Ah Sok and Oei Tan; came to U.S., 1968, naturalized, 1977; M.D., Nat. Def. Med. Center, Taiwan, 1968; m. Shueh-Yen Tien, Apr. 9, 1968; children—Vivian, Calvin. Intern, Barberton (Ohio) Citizens Hosp., 1968; resident in surgery Fairview (Ohio) Gen. Hosp., 1969-73; practice medicine specializing in surgery, Mantua, Ohio; staff Robinson Meml. Hosp., Ravenna, Ohio; clin. asst. prof. surgery Neucom (Ohio) U. Recipient Scholar award Chinese Govt., 1968. Diplomate Am. Bd. Surgery. Fellow A.C.S.; mem. Ohio Med. Assn., Cleve. Surg. Soc., Portage County Med. Soc. Baptist. Home: 4692 Streeter Rd Mantua OH 44255 Office: 10683 Maple St Mantua OH 44255

CHEN, SHOEI-SHENG, mechanical engineer; b. Taiwan, Jan. 26, 1940; s. Yung-cheng and A-shu (Fang) C.; B.S., Nat. Taiwan U., 1963; M.S., Princeton U., 1966, M.A., 1967, Ph.D., 1968; m. Ruth C. Lee, June 28, 1969; children—Lyrice, Lisa, Steve. Research asst. Princeton U., 1965-68; asst. mech. engr. Argonne (Ill.) Nat. Lab., 1968-71, mech. engr., 1971-80, sr. mech. engr., 1980—; cons. to Internat. Atomic Energy Agy. to assist developing countries in research and devel. of nuclear reactor system components, 1977, 79, 80, also U.S. Regulatory Commn. Fellow ASME; mem. Am. Acad. Mechanics, Acoustical Soc. Am., Sigma Xi. Contbr. numerous articles to profl. jours. Home: 6420 Waterford Ct Willowbrook IL 60521 Office: 9700 S Cass Ave Argonne IL 60439

CHEN, SIMON K., product development company executive; b. Peking, China, Oct. 13, 1925; s. Hoshien and Lin Sie (Chao) Tchen; came to U.S., 1948, naturalized, 1955; B.S.M.E., Nat. Chiao-Tung U., Shanghai, 1947; M.S.M.E., U. Mich., 1949; Ph.D. in Mech. engring., U. Wis., 1952; M.B.A., U. Chgo., 1964; m. Rosemary Ho; children—Margaret, Lillian, Vivian, Victor. Div. chief engr. diesel engine div. Internat. Harvester Co., Melrose Park, Ill., 1952-69; v.p., gen mgr. large engine operation, then v.p. engring. and application FM power systems div. Colt Industries, Beloit, Wis., 1969-73; pres. Beloit Power Systems, Am. Laminate Products subs. Tang Industries, Beloit, 1973-79; pres. Power and Energy, Internat., Inc., Beloit, 1979—. Mem. Greater Beloit Com. Recipient Alumni Distinguished Service award U. Wis., 1973, Achievement and Service award Chinese Inst. Engrs., 1976, Arch T. Colwell award, 1966. Fellow Soc. Automotive Engrs.; mem. Family Service Assn., ASME, Soc. Naval Architects and Marine Engrs., Sigma Xi, Beta Gamma Sigma. Club: Janesville (Wis.) Indoor Tennis. Home: 953 Racine Delavan WI 53115 Office: PO Box 1064 Beloit WI 53511

CHEN, WAI SUN WILLIAM, mathematics educator, statistical researcher; b. Chien-Ou, Fu-Chien, Republic of China, Dec. 21, 1943; came to U.S., 1969; s. You-Chao and Shui-Tan C.; m. Heng Chang, Dec. 22, 1977; 1 child, Chung-Ping David. B.S., Nat. Normal U. at Taiwan, Taipei, Republic of China, 1969; M.S., Ohio U.-Athens, 1971; M.S., U. Ga., 1975, Ph.D., 1978. Asst. prof. Paine Coll., Augusta, Ga., 1977-79; asst. prof. Morehead State U., Ky., 1979-82, assoc. prof., 1982-83; vis. assoc. prof. math. No. Ill. U., DeKalb, 1983—. Mem. Am. Statis. Assn., Biometric Soc., Inst. Math. Stats., Sigma Xi. Home: 4402 Black Partridge Lisle IL 60532 Office: No Ill U DeKalb IL 60115

CHEN, WEN FU, otolaryngologist; b. Taiwan, China, Apr. 25, 1942; s. Wainan and Wangchien C.; came to U.S., 1969, naturalized, 1977; M.D., Kaohsiung Med. Coll., Taiwan, 1968; m. Huiying Wu, Sept. 13, 1973; children—David W., Jeffrey W., Justin W. Intern, Augustana Hosp., Chgo., 1969-70; resident in surgery VA Hosp., Dayton, Ohio, 1970-72; resident in otolaryngology Homer Phillip Hosp., St. Louis, 1972-75; asst. chief otolaryngology VA Hosp., Kansas City, Mo., 1975-77; mem. staff Kansas Med. Center, Kansas City, 1975-77; practice medicine specializing in otolaryngology, Chillicothe, Ohio, 1977—. Diplomate Am. Bd. Otolaryngology. Fellow Am. Acad. Ophalmology and Otolaryngology; mem. AMA, Ohio State Med. Assn. Home: 22 Oakwood Dr Chillicothe OH 45601 Office: 3 Medical Center Dr Chillicothe OH 45601

CHEN, YU MIN, biochemist; b. I-shing, Kiangsu, China, Dec. 23, 1922; s. Mu Fan and Yueh Wah (Pan) C.; came to U.S., 1954, naturalized, 1976; B.S., Nat. Chekiang U. China, 1946; M.S., Nat. Taiwan U., 1950; Ph.D., U. So. Calif., 1960; m. Jiachun Nei, July 11, 1964; children—Peter, Plato. Asso. prof. biochemistry Nat. Taiwan U., 1960-63; fellow Inst. Chemistry, Academia Sinica, Taiwan, 1960-63; research scientist Wayne State U., Detroit, 1963-68, Mich. Cancer Found., Detroit, 1968-73; prin. investigator Wayne State U., Detroit, 1973-80; sr. research biochemist Providence Hosp., Southfield, Mich., 1981—. Pres., Chinese Cultural Center, Detroit, 1976. U. So. Calif. scholar, 1954-60; NIH grantee, 1971-74, 75-78. Mem. Am. Assn. Cancer Research, China Chem. Soc., Chinese Assn. Agrl. Chemistry, Sigma Xi. Research in immunochemistry and hormone receptors. Home: 30105 High Valley Rd Farmington Hills MI 48018 Office: Providence Hosp Southfield MI 48075

CHENEY, BRIGHAM VERNON, physical chemist; b. Salt Lake City, June 11, 1936; s. Silas Lavelle and Klara (Young) C.; m. Marsali McAllister, Aug. 20, 1964; children—Jill, Mark Vernon, Heather, Karin, Brigham McAllister, John David. B.A., U. Utah, 1961, Ph.D., 1966. Research asst. U. Utah, 1964-66; research scientist Upjohn Co., Kalamazoo, 1966-71, scientist, 1971-75, sr. research scientist, 1975—. Missionary, Ch. Jesus Ch. Latter-day Saints, Germany, 1956-59; high councilor, Lansing, Mich., 1969-75, Grand Rapids, Mich., 1975-78; bishop, Kalamazoo, 1978-84; leader Boy Scouts Am., 1972—. Served with Army N.G., 1959-67. Mem. AAAS, Am. Chem. Soc., N.Y. Acad. Scis., Internat. Soc. Quantum Biology, Sigma Xi, Phi Eta Sigma, Sigma Pi Sigma. Contbr. articles to profl. jours. Home: 3507 Runnymede Dr Kalamazoo MI 49007 Office: Upjohn C Kalamazoo MI 49001

CHENEY, DAVID RAYMOND, English educator; b. Castle Dale, Utah, Jan. 23, 1922; s. Silas Lavell and Klara (Young) C.; student Snow Coll., 1939-41; B.A., U. Utah, 1948, M.A., 1949; A.M., Harvard U., 1951; Ph.D., U. Iowa, 1955; m. Patricia Anne Snow, Dec. 18, 1948; 1 child, Pamela. Teaching asst. in English, U. Iowa, 1953-55; instr. English, Lewis and Clark Coll., 1956-58; asso. prof. English, S.W. Mo. State Coll., 1958-63, prof., 1963-65; prof. U. Toledo, 1965—, dir. grad. studies in English, 1968-79. Advisor, youth council NAACP, Springfield, Mo., 1963-65. Served with U.S. Army, 1941-46; PTO. U. Utah research fellow, 1948; U. Toledo research fellow, 1968, 76, 79; U. Iowa grantee, 1966, 68; U. Toledo grantee, 1968, 70, 73, 74, 79, 81-84; Nat. Endowment Humanities summer grantee, 1983. Mem. Modern Humanities Research Assn., Shakespeare Assn. Am., MLA, Central Renaissance Soc. Am., AAUP, Phi Beta Kappa, Phi Kappa Phi. Mormon. Author: The Correspondence of Leigh Hunt and Charles Ollier in the Winter of 1853-54, 1976; editor: Musical Evenings or Selections Vocal and Instrumental (Leigh Hunt), 1964; research on Leigh Hunt letters, Shakespeare. Home: 2833 Goddard Rd Toledo OH 43606 Office: 2801 W Bancroft St Toledo OH 43606

CHENG, CHEN CHANG, book salesman; b. Yanshan, Jiangxi, China, Oct. 1, 1926; came to U.S., 1957; s. Yi Wu and Tsu Shou (Hou) C.; m. Jane Kan, Oct. 5, 1958. Student Chung Cheng U., Nanchang, China, 1946-49; B.A., Taiwan U., Taipei, 1954-56; Postgrad. U. Mo., 1957; M.A., DePaul U., 1964. Reporter Chung Hwa Daily News, Tainan, Taiwan, 1950-55; writer China Times, Taipei, Taiwan, 1955-57; editor San Min Daily, Chgo., 1958-65; chmn. bus. dept. Internat. Sch., Bangkok, Thailand, 1965-71; pres., owner Peking Book House, Evanston, Ill., 1971—; acctg. instr. YMCA Coll., Chgo., 1960-61; tchr. social studies Immaculate Heart of Mary High Sch. for Girls, Westchester, Ill., 1964-65; Chinese instr. U. Maryland, Bangkok br., 1969-71. Author: Ten Years Overseas, 1967; A Chinese View of America, 1984; My Hometown and I, 1985. Mem. charter U.S.-China Friendship Assn., Chgo., 1972, Chinese-Am. Assn., Chgo., 1975. Served to capt. Army of China, 1944-46. Mem. Small Businessmen Assn., Evanston C. of C. Avocations: singing; writing; lecturing. Home: 2001 Sherman Ave Evanston IL 60201 Office: Peking Book House 1520 Sherman Ave Evanston IL 60201

CHENG, CHIN-CHUAN, linguistics educator; b. Hsin-chu, Taiwan, China, Dec. 30, 1936; came to U.S., 1963, naturalized, 1973; s. Chin-Teh and Szu-Mei (Shen) C.; m. Mu-chin Liang, Aug. 23, 1964; children—Ellen, Perry. B.A., Nat. Taiwan U., 1959, M.A., 1961; student Cornell U., 1963-64; Ph.D., U. Ill., 1968. Lectr. in Chinese Harvard U., Cambridge, Mass., 1967-69; lectr. linguistics U. Calif.-Berkeley, 1969-70; asst., assoc. prof. linguistics and Chinese, U. Ill.-Urbana, 1970-80, prof. linguistics and Chinese, 1980—, dir. language learning lab., 1984—; vis. assoc. prof. Chinese U. Hawaii, Honolulu, spring 1980; mem. linguistics delegation to People's Republic of China, 1974. Author: A Synchronic Phonology of Mandarin Chinese, 1973, Language and Linguistics in the People's Republic of China, 1975. Author computer software. Assoc. editor Jour. of Chinese Linguistics, 1973—; bus. editor Studies in Language Learning, 1984—. Contbr. numerous articles to profl. jours. Mem. Linguistic Soc. Am., Assn. Asian Studies, Assn. Computational Linguistics. Home: 2511 S Lynn Urbana IL 61801 Office: Language Learning Lab U Ill 707 S Mathews Urbana IL 61801

CHENG, CHU YUAN, educator; b. Kwangtung Province, China, Apr. 8, 1927; came to U.S., 1959, naturalized, 1964; s. Hung Shan and Shu Chen (Yang) C.; B.A. in Econs., Nat. Chengchih U., Nanking, China, 1947; M.A., Georgetown U., Washington, 1962, Ph.D., 1964; m. Alice Hua Liang, Aug. 15, 1964; children—Anita Tung I, Andrew Y.S. Research prof. Seton Hall U., 1960-64; vis. prof. George Washington U., Washington, 1963; sr. research economist U. Mich., Ann Arbor, 1964-69; assoc. prof. Lawrence U., Appleton, Wis., 1970-71; assoc. prof. econs., chmn. Asian studies com. Ball State U., Muncie, Ind., 1971-73, prof. econs., 1974—; cons. NSF, Washington, 1964—. Bd. dirs. Dr. Sun Yat-sen Inst., Chgo., 1978—. Grantee, NSF, 1960-64, Social Sci. Research Council, 1965-67, 74; recipient Outstanding Research award Ball State U., 1976; Outstanding Educator in Econs., Ball State U., 1981-82. Mem. Am. Econ. Assn., Assn. Asian Studies, Assn. Comparative Econ. Studies, Am. Acad. Polit. and Social Sci., Chinese Acad. and Profl. Assn. Mid-Am. (pres. 1983-84), Ind. Acad. Social Sci., Omicron Delta Epsilon. Author: Scientific and Engineering Manpower in Communist China, 1966; The Machine-Building Industry in Communist China, 1971; China's Petroleum Industry: Output Growth and Export Potential, 1976; China's Economic Development: Growth and Structural Change, 1981; mem. adv. com. Chinese Econ. Studies Quar., 1966—. Home: 1211 Greenbriar Rd Muncie IN 47304 Office: Room 123 Coll Bus Ball State U Muncie IN 47306

CHENG, FRANCIS SHYUE-TSO, physician; b. Kun-Ming, Yunan, China, July 7, 1943; came to U.S., 1971, naturalized, 1978; s. Wen Lo and Jane (Young) C.; m. Sylvia Y. Lam, May 10, 1973; 1 child, Michael. M.D., Kaohsiung Med. Coll., Taiwan, 1971. Diplomate Am. Bd. Internal Medicine, Am. Bd. Cardiovascular Diseases. Rotating intern Vets. Gen. Hosp., Taipei, Taiwan, 1970-71; straight med. intern U. Ill. Hosp., Chgo., 1971-72, resident, 1972-74; asst. in medicine U. Ill. Sch. Medicine, Chgo., 1972-74; fellow in cardiology Michael Reese Hosp. and Med. Ctr., 1974-75, Rush Presbyn.-St. Luke's Hosp., Chgo., 1975-76; instr. Rush Med. Sch., Chgo., 1975-76; med. dir. Cardiac Rehab. Unit, Alexian Bros. Med. Ctr., Elk Grove Village, Ill., 1978—, audit com. chmn. dept. internal medicine, 1981—. Fellow Am. Coll. Cardiology; mem. ACP, Am. Heart Assn., AMA, Cinese-Am. Health Profls. Assn. (pres. 1984). Republican. Club: Meadow. Avocation: computing. Office: 1000 Grand Canyon Pkwy Hoffman Estates IL 60194

CHENG, KUANG LU, chemistry educator; b. Yangchow, China, Sept. 14, 1919; s. Fong Wu and Yi Ming (Chiang) C.; came to U.S., 1947, naturalized, 1955; Ph.D., U. Ill., 1951; children—Meiling, Chiling, Hans Christian. Microchemist, Comml. Solvents Corp., Terre Haute, Ind., 1952-53; instr. U. Conn., Storrs, 1953-55; engr., Westinghouse Electric Corp., Pitts. 1955-57; asso. dir. research, metals div. Kelsey Hayes Co., New Hartford, N.Y., 1957-59; mem. tech. staff RCA Labs., Princeton, 1959-66; prof. chemistry U. Mo.-Kansas City, 1966—. Recipient Achievement award RCA, 1963; N.T. Veatch award for disting. research and creative activity U. Mo.-Kansas City, 1979; cert. of recognition, Office Naval Research, 1979, Tex. A&M U., 1981; Faculty Fellowship award U. Kansas City Bd. Trustees, 1985. Fellow AAAS, Chem. Soc. London; mem. Am. Chem. Soc., Electrochem. Soc., Soc. Applied Spectroscopy, Am. Inst. Physics. Home: 34 E 56th Terrace Kansas City MO 64113 Office: Dept Chemistry Univ Mo Kansas City MO 64110

CHENG, LESTER C., mech. engr., biomed. engring. cons.; b. China, Apr. 20, 1944; s. Chin-Sun and Lu Cheng; came to U.S., 1967, naturalized, 1977; B.S. in Mech. Engring., Nat. Taiwan U., 1965; M.S. in Mech. Engring., N.D. State U., 1968; Ph.D. in Theoretical and Applied Mechanics, U. Ill., 1971; postgrad. San Diego Coll. System, 1974-75; m. Mei Yao, June 1969; children—Gloria, Helen. Research asso. U. Ill., Urbana, 1970-71, Intersci. Research Inst., Champaign, Ill., 1971; engr. analyst Sargent & Lundy Engrs., Chgo., 1971-72, sr. engr., 1972-74; sr. engr. Gen. Atomic Co., San Diego, 1974-76; asst. prof. dept. mech. engring. Wichita (Kans.) State U., 1976-79, asso. prof., 1979—; condr. biomed. engring. program NSF, 1977-80; cons. dept. theoretical and applied mechanics U. Ill., 1974-76, Wichita VA Med. Center, 1978—, Kans. Energy and Environ. Lab., Wichita, 1978—. Registered profl. engr., Kans. Mem. Am. Acad. Mechanics (hon.), ASME, Am. Soc. Engring. Edn., Soc. Automotive Engrs. (Ralph Teetor award 1980), Sigma Xi, Phi Kappa Phi. Contbr. articles fluid mechanics, biomed. engring. and thermal energy studies to sci. jours. Office: Dept Mech Engring Wichita State U Wichita KS 67208

CHENG, PAUL HUNG-CHIAO, civil engineer; b. China, Dec. 1, 1930; s. Yen-Teh and Shu-Yin (Tsou) C.; came to U.S., 1958, naturalized, 1973; B.S. in Civil Engring., Nat. Taiwan U., 1951; M.S. in Civil Engring., U. Va., 1961; m. Lucial Jen Chen, Aug. 1, 1964; children—Maria, Elizabeth, Deborah, Samuel. Structural engr. Swift & Co., Chgo., 1963-67; sr. structural designer P & W Engring., Inc., Chgo., 1967; sr. structural engr. A. Epstein & Son, Inc., Chgo., 1967-68; staff engr. Interlake, Inc., Chgo., 1968-71, supervising engr., 1971-73, chief structural engr., 1973-80, product engring. mgr., 1980-82, CAD/CAM devel. mgr., 1982-84; CAD/CAM System mgr. Continental Can Co., 1984—. Registered structural engr., Ill.; registered profl. civil engr., Calif. Mem. ASCE, Am. Concrete Inst., Am. Mgmt. Assn. Home: 1620 Lawrence Crescent Flossmoor IL 60422 Office: Continental Can Co 1700 Harvester Rd West Chicago IL 60185

CHENG, SYLVIA FAN (MRS. JOHNSON CHU), physician; b. Shangtung, China, June 26, 1918 (came to U.S. 1948, naturalized 1957); d. Stanley C. and Flora C. (Chu) Cheng; B.S., U. Shanghai, 1938; M.D., Woman's Christian Med. Coll., Shanghai, 1942; postgrad. N.Y. U., 1948, Columbia, 1955; m. Johnson Chu, June 11, 1949; children—Stephen Cheng, Timothy Cheng. Rotating intern Margaret Williamson Hosp., 1942-43; resident in medicine, surgery, obstetrics and gynecology St. Luke's and St. Elizabeth Hosp., St. John's U. Hosp., 1943-47; practice medicine specializing in chest diseases, Shanghai, 1947-48, psychiatry and gen. practice, Logansport, Ind., 1956—; chief female service, dir. Tb unit Weston (W.Va.) State Hosp., 1955; chief female service, admission and intensive service, unit dir. Logansport (Ind.) State Hosp., 1956—; cons. physician White County Meml. Hosp., Monticello, Ind., Cass County Meml. hosps., Logansport, Ind., Southeastern Med. Center, Walton, Ind. Recipient award ARC, 1959. Fellow Am. Coll. Chest Physicians, Am. Psychiat. Assn.; mem. AMA, Am. Thoracic Soc., Mental Health Assn., Cass County Med. Soc., Am. Acad. Gen. Practice, Ind. State Med. Assn. Baptist (deaconess 1956-69, 73-76). Home: E 36 Lake Shafer Monticello IN 47960 Office: Southeastern Med Center Walton IN 46994

CHENG, SYLVIA LAM, physician; b. Chung King, China, Aug. 15, 1946; d. Lam Horng-Yip and Yung Wai-Ching; M.D., Kaohsiung Med. Coll., Taiwan, 1972; m. Francis Cheng, Oct. 5, 1973; 1 son, Michael. Cert. Am. Bd. Quality Assurance and Utilization Rev. Physicians Resident in pediatrics Mercy Hosp. and Med. Ctr., Chgo., 1972-75; practice medicine specializing in pediatrics, Hoffman Estates, Ill., 1975—. Fellow Am. Coll. Utilization Rev. Physicians; mem. AMA, Chgo. Med. Assn., Am. Med. Women's Assn., Orgn. Chinese Am. (hon.). Club: Meadow. Office: 1000 Grand Canyon Pkwy Hoffman Estates IL 60194

CHENG, TA-PEI, physics educator; b. Shanghai, China, Nov. 26, 1941; came to U.S., 1960, naturalized, 1971; m. Leslie Su, Dec. 29, 1982. A.B., Dartmouth Coll., 1964; Ph.D., Rockefeller U., 1969. Mem. Inst. Advanced Study, Princeton, N.J., 1969-71; research assoc. Rockefeller U., N.Y.C., 1971-73; asst. prof. physics U. Mo., St. Louis, 1973-76, assoc., 1976-78, prof., 1978—; vis. assoc. prof. Princeton U., 1977-78; vis. prof. U. Minn., Mpls., 1979-80; vis. scientist Lawrence Berkeley Lab., Calif., 1982-83. Author: Gauge Theory Elementary Particle Physics, 1984. Fellow Am. Phys. Soc. Home: 520 E Polo Dr Clayton MO 63105 Office: Physics Dept U Mo Saint Louis MO 63121

CHENG, YUK-BUN DEREK, electrical engineer; b. Swatow, Kwangtung, China, Aug. 7, 1950; s. Leung-Wing and Wai-Shan (Ma) C.; m. Susanna Wai-Hing Yuen, Aug. 6, 1983. Student E. Tex. State U., 1970-71; B.S.E.E., W.Va. Inst. Tech., 1974; M.S.E.E., W.Va. U., 1976. Grad. research asst. dept. elec. engring. W.Va. U., Morgantown, 1974-77; antenna research engr. Andrew Corp., Orland Park, Ill., 1977-82, sr. antenna research engr., 1982-84, sect. leader antenna analysis, 1984—. Recipient William E. Jackson award Radio Tech. Commn. for Aeronautics, 1976. Mem. IEEE, IEEE Antennas and Propagation Soc., (chmn. joint chpt. with Microwave Theory and Techniques Socs. 1985—), Sigma Xi, Eta Kappa Nu, Tau Beta Pi, Phi Kappa Phi. Mem. Chinese Christian Union Ch. Contbr. articles to profl. jours.; patentee in field. Home: 13905 Cherokee Trail Lockport IL 60441 Office: 10500 W 153d St Orland Park IL 60462

CHENOWETH, ARLENE JOYCE, construction company executive; b. Cass City, Mich., Apr. 1, 1941; d. Robert Melvin and Geraldine Thelma (Bell) Milner; grad. Olivet Nazarene Coll., Kankakee, Ill., 1963; postgrad. U. Mich., 1963-65; m. Robert R. Chenoweth, Sept. 1, 1962; children—Timothy, Eric, Gregg. Tchr. bus. edn. Swartz Creek (Mich.) Sr. High Sch., 1963-67, Flushing (Mich.) Sr. High Sch., 1969-74; v.p. A & B Enterprises, Fenton, Mich., 1974—; co-owner, office mgr. Chenoweth Constrn. Co., Inc., Fenton, 1974—, Chenoweth & Assocs. Architects, Inc., Fenton, 1978—; mem. alumni bd. Olivet Nazarene Coll. Founder Fenton Businesswomen's Breakfast Fellowship; dir. Eastern Mich. Dist., Women's Ministries, 1983. Mem. Am. Mgmt. Assn., Nat. Assn. Female Execs., Fenton Area Bus. and Profl. Women's Club (charter mem., treas. 1979). Nazarene. Clubs: University (Flint, Mich.); Spring Meadows Country; Gaylord Country. Home: 12050 White Lake Rd Fenton MI 48430 Office: Chenoweth Constrn Co Inc 101 N Ally Dr Fenton MI 48430

CHENOWETH, ROBERT DUANE, machinery company executive; b. Bedford, Ind., Oct. 10, 1923; s. Henry Carl and Elizabeth Jane (Barrett) C.; engring. student Internat. Corr. Schs., 1946-48; grad. Approved Supply Pastor's Sch., Garrett Theol. Sch., 1959; B.A., Miami U., 1962, postgrad., 1962-64; m. Shirley Ellen Woods, Sept. 17, 1949; children—Steven Carl, Mark Duane, Paula Jane. Cons. engr. J.E. Novotny Co., Dayton, Ohio, 1955-63; ordained elder United Methodist Ch., 1960, ordained to ministry, 1958; pastor Brookville and Miamitown (Ohio) Meth. Chs., 1958-67; chief tool engr. OPW div. Dover Corp., Cin., 1963-64; chief mfg. engr., mgr. mfg. Campbell-Hausfeld Co., Harrison, Ohio, 1964-68; plant mgr. Sheffer Corp., Blue Ash, Ohio, 1968—. Cons. prodn. engring. Helipebs, Ltd., County of Gloucester (Eng.), 1972. Sec., Brookville Planning Com., 1960-63; mem. adv. com. Great Oaks Joint Vocat. Sch., Warren County (Ohio) Joint Vocat. Sch.; mem. adv. council Miami U. Sch. Applied Sci.; mem. Industry Council, Greater Cin. C. of C.; sec. bd. trustees Thomas Meml. Med. Center, Brookville. Recipient Service award City of Brookville, 1963. Mem. Soc. Mfg. Engrs. (past chmn. Dayton chpt., cert. mfg. engr.). Optimist. Home: 1759 Maplewood Dr Lebanon OH 45036 Office: 6990 Cornell Rd Blue Ash OH 45242

CHERNICOFF, DAVID PAUL, osteopathic physician, educator; b. N.Y.C., Aug. 3, 1947; s. Harry and Lillian (Dobkin) C.; A.B., U. Rochester, 1969; D.O., Phila. Coll. Osteo. Medicine, 1973. Rotating intern Rocky Mountain Hosp., Denver, 1973-74; resident in internal medicine Community Gen. Osteo. Hosp., Harrisburg, Pa., 1974-76; fell in hematology and med. oncology Cleve. Clinic, 1976-78; asst. prof. medicine sect. hematology-oncology Chgo. Coll. Osteo. Medicine, 1978-82, assoc. prof., 1982—; co-chmn. tumor task force Chgo. Osteo. Med. Center, 1978—, dir. clin. cancer edn., 1978—; chmn. tumor task force Olympia Fields (Ill.) Osteo. Med. Center. Trustee, Ill. Cancer Council; bd. dir. Chgo. unit Am. Cancer Soc. Diplomate Nat. Bd. Osteo. Examiners, Am. Osteo. Bd. Internal Medicine, also in Hematology-Oncology. Mem. Am. Osteo. Assn., Am. Coll. Osteo. Internists, Am. Assn. for Cancer Edn., AMA, Ill. Assn. Osteo. Physicians and Surgeons, Ill. Med. Soc., Chgo. Med. Soc., Eastern Coop. Oncology Group (sr. investigator), Am. Soc. Clin. Oncology. Contbr. articles to med. jours. Office: Chgo Coll Osteo Medicine 5200 S Ellis Ave Chicago IL 60615

CHERNISH, STANLEY MICHAEL, physician; b. N.Y.C., Jan. 27, 1924; s. Michael B. and Veronica (Hodon) C.; B.A., U. N.C., 1945; M.D., Georgetown U., 1949; m. Lelia M. Higgins, June 19, 1949; 1 child, Dwight. Intern Washington Gen. Hosp., 1949-51; resident Marion County Gen. Hosp., Indpls., 1953-55; clin. research div. Eli Lilly & Co., Indpls., 1954—, staff physician, 1955-63, sr. physician, 1963-74, clin. pharmacologist, 1974—; clin. research in internal medicine, specializing in gastroenterology; vis. staff Marion County Gen. Hosp., 1965—, also mem. dietary com.; mem. staff Lilly Research Labs.; clin. assoc. prof. medicine Ind. U. Sch. Medicine, 1976-80, assoc. prof., 1980—. Served with USNR, 1943-45, 50-53; comdr. Res.; Diplomate Nat. Bd. Med. Examiners, Am. Bd. Internal Medicine, also recert. Fellow A.C.P., Am. Coll. Gastroenterology, Am. Coll. Clin. Pharmacology and Therapeutics; mem. AMA (Physicians Recognition award in continuing med. edn.), Ind. (mem. com. conv. arrangements, ad hoc data processing com., subcom. on accreditation), Marion County (mem. commn. on ops. and stock ops.) med. socs., Am. Pancreatic Study Group, Assn. Am. Physicians and Surgeons, Am. Fedn. for Clin. Research, Am. Gastroent. Assn., Am. Soc. for Gastrointestinal Endoscopy, Sigma Xi. Contbr. chpts. to books, articles to profl. jours. Office: Lilly Corporate Ctr Indianapolis IN 46285

CHERRY, PAUL ROSS, lawyer; b. Charlotte, Mich., Feb. 24, 1951; s. Harold Ross and Ruby Madge (Rawley) C.; m. Jeanette Ellen Cox, June 1, 1974; children—Tyler Ross, Megan Myree, Erin Elaine. B.A., Huntington Coll., 1973; J.D., Ohio No. U., 1977. Bar: Ohio 1978, Ind. 1978, U.S. Dist. Ct. (no. and so. dists.) Ind. 1978, U.S. Ct. Appeals (7th cir.) 1979, U.S. Supreme Ct. 1981. Ptnr. Kruse, Kruse & Cherry, Auburn, Ind., 1978—; dep. prosecutor Dekalb County, Ind., 1980-82, pros. atty., 1983—; prof. bus. law Huntington Coll., Ind., 1979-83; judge pro tem, spl. judge Dekalb Circuit and Superior Cts., 1980—. Mem. Auburn Community Band, 1982—, Auburn Messiah Prodn., 1983—, Dekalb County Drug Task Force; chmn. candidates com. Dekalb County Republican Com., 1982; chmn. bd. Hopewell United Brethren Ch., Auburn, 1979-84. Named Sagamore of Wabash, Gov. of Ind., 1981. Mem. Dekalb County Bar Assn., Ind. Bar Assn. (trial lawyers div.), Ind. Pros. Attys. Assn. Home: 1302 Garwood Dr Auburn IN 46706 Office: Kruse Kruse & Cherry 255 E 9th St Auburn IN 46706

CHERTACK, MELVIN M., internist; b. Chgo., June 19, 1923; s. Nathan and Anna (Wadoplan) C.; B.S., U. Ill., 1944, M.D., 1946, M.S., 1948; m. Orabelle Lorraine Melberg, May 26, 1948; children—Pamela, Craig, Rhonda. Intern, U. Ill. Hosp., Chgo., 1946-47, fellow and resident in internal medicine, 1947-50; practice medicine specializing in internal medicine, Skokie, Ill., 1950—; mem. attending staff Luth. Gen. Hosp., Park Ridge, Ill.; mem. courtesy staff Skokie Valley Hosp.; clin. assoc. prof. U. Ill. Abraham Lincoln Coll. Medicine; chmn. Bd. Health Skokie. Served with U.S. Army, 1943-45. Recipient Research award Aaron Fox Found. for Diabetes Screening Program, 1976, recognition award for service to Skokie Health Dept., Ill. Assn. Pub. Health Adminstrn., 1981, cert. of merit Village of Skokie, 1982. Diplomate Am. Bd. Internal Medicine. Fellow ACP; mem. Am. Diabetes Assn. (dir. Chgo. and No. Ill. affiliate, chpt., past pres. Chgo. and No. Ill. affiliate, citation for pub. service 1982, nominee Pfizer Clinician of Yr. 1984), Chgo., Ill. med. socs., AMA, Chgo. Soc. Internal Medicine, Chgo., Am. heart assns. Club: Anvil (Dundee). Contbr. articles to profl. jours. Home: 440 Whittier Ln Northfield IL 60093 Office: 64 Old Orchard Skokie IL 60077

CHERVENAK, JOHN JOSEPH, hospital administrator; b. Chgo., Aug. 23, 1924; s. John and Antonette M. (Jurasek) C.; m. Lillian Florence Havlik, Sept. 8, 1951; children—Sharon, Deborah. B.S. in Bus. and Econs., Ill. Inst. Tech., 1949. Cert. safety profl., internat. health care profl. Loss prevention mgr. Am. Mut. Ins. Cos., Milw., 1949-75; dir. safety, security St. Michael Hosp., Milw., 1975—. Vice-pres. Mt. Mary Coll. Parent Assn., 1975-77. Served in U.S. Army, 1943-45. Decorated Purple Heart. Mem. Am. Soc. Safety Engrs., Internat. Assn. Hosp. Security (chmn. So. eastern Wis. chpt. 1981-82, vice chmn. 1979-81), Internat. Healthcare Profls. Am., Wis. Healthcare Safety Assn., Am. Legion. Democrat. Roman Catholic. Home: 10357 W Park Ridge Ave Wauwatosa WI 53222 Office: 2400 W Villard Ave Milwaukee WI 53209

CHESEBROUGH, STEPHEN, accountant; b. Providence, R.I., Feb. 7, 1941; s. Westcote Herreshoff and Nancy Wall (Read) C.; m. Pamela Ann Halewood, June 27, 1967; 1 child, Jonathan W. B.A., Harvard U., 1965, M.B.A., 1967. C.P.A., R.I. Auditor, acct. Peat Marwick, various U.S. locations, and Europe, 1967-76; mem. control staff Gen. Mills, Mpls., 1976—. Commr. Parks Bd., Plymouth, Minn.; race dir. Winter Triathlon, Plymouth, 1985; chmn. Community Ctr. Citizens Com., Plymouth, 1984. Mem. Am. Inst. C.P.A.s. Avocations: running; cross country skiing. Home: 3615 Evergreen Plymouth MN 55441

CHESELDINE, DIANA STAFFORD, financial executive; b. Flushing, N.Y., Sept. 23, 1936; d. Harvey Chace and Marian (Turrill) Stafford; m. Raymond Minshall Cheseldine, 1966 (div. 1973.) A.B., Vassar Coll., 1957. Research asst. econ. research First Nat. City Bank (now Citicorp), N.Y.C., 1957-63; econ. asst. econ. research Am. Bankers Assn., N.Y.C., 1963-64; research analyst fin. research Irving Trust Co., N.Y.C., 1964-66; sr. research assoc. U.S. League Savs. Instns., Chgo., 1966—; dir. Fed. Stats. Users Conf., Washington, 1976-80. Editor: Savings and Loan Source Book, 1973-81; Savings Institutions Sourcebook, 1982-84. Contbr. articles to profl. jours. Mem. Am. Statis. Assn. (pres. Chgo. chpt. 1983-84). Episcopalian. Avocation: bridge. Office: US League Savs Instns 111 E Wacker Dr Chicago IL 60601

CHESKY, JEFFREY ALAN, gerontology educator, physiology researcher; b. Lynn, Mass., May 11, 1946; s. Harold Lester Chesky and Elizabeth (Joseph) Chesky Balter; m. Annette Sternberg, Aug. 19, 1970; 1 child, Barry. A.B., Cornell U., 1967; Ph.D., U. Miami, 1974. Asst. prof. gerontology Sangamon State U., Springfield, Ill., 1977-83, assoc. prof., 1983—; adj. assoc. prof. So. Ill. U. Sch. Medicine, Springfield, 1978-85. Editor: Theoretical Aspects of Aging, 1974. Contbr. chpt. to Aging in Muscle, 1978, Nonmammalian Models for Aging Research, 1985. Vice pres. Ill. Sr. Olympics, 1979-83. Grantee NIH, Am. Fedn. Aging Research, Ill. affiliate Am. Heart Assn. Mem. Gerontol. Soc. Am., Am. Aging Assn., Am. Physiol. Soc. (assoc.), Sigma Xi. Avocation: piano playing. Home: 700 S Durkin Dr Apt 359 Springfield IL 62704 Office: Dept Gerontology Sangamon State Univ Springfield IL 62708

CHESLIN, WILLIAM DANA, maxillofacial surgeon, dentist; b. Detroit, Jan. 9, 1948; s. Sigmund John and Olgamarie (Gyzinski) C.; m. Lynne Rosenthal, Mar. 13, 1976. B.S., U. Detroit, 1970; D.D.S., 1970; M.D., Northwestern U., 1980. Diplomate Am. Bd. Oral and Maxillofacial Surgery. Intern, Northwestern Meml. Hosp., Chgo., 1975-78; resident Med. Ctr. Vt., Burlington, 1974-75; Sinai Hosp. of Detroit, 1980-81; practice medicine specializing in oral and maxillofacial surgery; chmn. dept. oral and maxillofacial surgery William Beaumont Hosp., Royal Oak, Mich., 1982—. Mem. AMA, ADA, Omicron Kappa Upsilon (Univ. Detroit Dental Sch.). Avocations: Scuba diving, flying. Home: 954 Canterbury Birmingham MI Office: Torgerson & Small PC 50 W Big Beaver Birmingham MI 48008

CHESTER, EMMA LEE, educator; b. Starkville, Miss., Nov. 8, 1942; d. Aron and Teadie (Bishop) Devine; m. Elruth Chester, Aug. 7, 1971. B.A., Miss. State U., 1970; M.S., Ind. U., 1978. Mail handler U.S. Post Office, Los Angeles, 1968; high sch. tchr. Starkville (Miss.) Pub. Schs., 1971-72; tchr. biology Indpls. Pub. Schs., 1974-78, tchr. sci. jr. high sch., 1978—. Pres., Young Women Christian Council. Recipient Instructional award H. E. Wood High Sch., 1978. Mem. Nat. Assn. Biology Tchrs., Nat. Sci. Tchrs. Assn., Nat. Assn. Supervision and Curriculum Devel., Smithsonian Assocs., Ind. State Tchrs. Assn., Hoosier Assn. Sci. Tchrs., Ind. Assn. Supervision and Curriculum Devel., Indpls. Edn. Assn. Democrat. Mem. Holiness Ch. Home: 2353 N College Ave Indianapolis IN 46205

CHESTER, MICHAEL EDWARD, optometrist; b. Chillicothe, Ohio, Dec. 4, 1952; s. Dwight Arnold and Oma Marie (Hoag) C.; m. Vicki Patricia Metzger, Aug. 6, 1977; children—Brandon Michael, Ashley Paige. B.A., Miami U., Oxford, Ohio, 1975; O.D., Ohio State U., 1979. Pvt. practice optometry, Chillicothe, Ohio, 1979—, Greenfield, Ohio, 1983—; cons. area nursing homes, Chillicothe, 1979—, Vets. Med. Ctr., Chillicothe, 1983—, Ohio State Coll. Optometry, Columbus, 1983—. Editor, Reflex, monthly publ. Central Ohio Optometric Assn. Bd. dirs. South Central Ohio Speech and Hearing, Chillicothe, 1984; chmn. Jaycee Golf Course, Chillicothe, 1984. Recipient Presdl. awards Ohio Jaycees, 1984, Presdl. award of honor Ohio Jaycees, 1984. Mem. Am. Optometric Assn. (sect. on contact lenses), Ohio Optometric Assn. (keyman to Ohio House 1984, Young Optometrist of Yr. 1984), Central Ohio Optometric Assn. (sec. 1982-83), Ross County Acad. Optometry (pres. 1984—), Ohio State U. Alumni Assn., Epsilon Psi Epsilon, Beta Sigma Kappa, Alpha Phi Omega. Republican. Methodist. Club: Chillicothe Jaycees (pres. 1983-84). Avocations: flying-pilot; golf; tennis; swimming; sailing. Home: 361 Braewood Ln Chillicothe OH 45601 Office: 950 E Main St Chillicothe OH 45601

CHEUNG, FAN-BILL, mechanical engineer; b. Canton, China, Mar. 6, 1949; s. Kong-Kwan and Yu-Mui (Kong) C.; m. Pattie P. Hsieh, Feb. 4, 1975; children—Lily, Simon, Jennifer. B.S. in Chem. Engring., Nat. Taiwan U., Taipei, 1969; Ph.D. in Mech. Engring., U. Notre Dame, 1974. Grad. research asst. U. Notre Dame, Ind., 1970-74; asst. mech. engr. Argonne Nat. Lab., Ill., 1974-78, mech. engr., 1978-82, group leader, 1982—. Contbg. author: Annual Review of Fluid Mechanics, 1983; Advances in Transport Processes, 1984. Mem. Am. Soc. Mech. Engrs., Am. Phys. Soc. Home: 17 W010 Fern St Hinsdale IL 60521 Office: Argonne Nat Lab 9700 S Cass Ave Argonne IL 60439

CHEUNG, HERMAN SING-CHUNG, medical educator; b. Kowloon, Hong Kong, China, Aug. 27, 1944; came to U.S., 1964; naturalized, 1977; s. Benton Y. and Angela (Liu) C.; m. Marilyn Chan, June 24, 1972; children—Jennifer Lynn, Jamie May Lynn. B.S., Loyola Marymount U., 1968; Ph.D., U. So. Calif., 1974. Postdoctoral fellow NIH, Los Angeles, 1974-77; asst. prof. Med. Coll. Wis., Milw., 1977-81, assoc. prof., 1981—. Contbr. research articles to profl. jours. Recipient Research Career Devel. award NIH, 1983-88. Mem. Arthritis Found., Sigma Xi., Phi Sigma. Avocations: tennis; fishing. Office: Med Coll Wis 8700 Wisconsin Ave Milwaukee WI 53226

CHI, RICHARD SEE-YEE, educator, art consultant; b. Peking, China, Aug. 3, 1918; s. Mi Kang and Pao (Ten) C.; B.S., Nankai U., China, 1937; M.A., Oxford (Eng.) U., 1962, D.Phil., 1964; Ph.D., Cambridge (Eng.) U., 1964. Came to U.S., 1965. Exec. industry China and Hong Kong, 1938-56; inst. Air Ministry, Eng., 1957-60; lectr. Cambridge U., 1960-62, U. London, summer 1961; univ. lectr. Oxford U., 1962-65; curator City Art Gallery, Bristol, Eng., 1965; assoc. prof. Ind. U., Bloomington, 1965-71, prof., 1971—, acting chmn., summer 1972; assoc. adviser Centro Superiore di Logica e Scienze Comparate, Italy, 1972—; vis. assoc. prof. U. Mich., summer 1968; fellow-participant Linguistic Inst., U. Calif., Los Angeles, 1966; contbg. specialist Summer Faculty Seminar on Buddhism, Carleton Coll., Minn., 1968; mem. Workshop on Problems on Meaning and Truth, Oakland U., 1968; adviser for film Buddhism in China, New York, 1972; cons. Inst. Advanced Studies World Religions, 1972—; session chmn. East-West Philosophers' Conf., 1973; panelist Internat. Conf. on Indian Philosophy, U. Toronto, 1974, 5th Internat. Symposium Multiple-valued Logic, Ind. U., 1974, Internat. Seminar on History of Buddhism, U. Wis., 1976, 30th Internat. Congress Human Scis. in Asia, Mexico City, 1976; mem. sub-com. Buddhist philos. materials Nat. Endowment for Humanities, 1974; rep. of State of Ind., Nat. Reconstrn. Conf., China, 1975. Fellow China Acad., 1969. Mem. Cambridge U. Buddhist Soc. (v.p. 1961-62), Royal Asiatic Soc., Aristotelian Soc., Mind Assn., Assn. Brit. Orientalists, Assn. for Symbolic Logic, Linguistic Soc. Am., Soc. for Asian and Comparative Philosophy (bd. mem.-at-large 1975—), Oriental Art Soc. (founding mem.), Kings Coll. Assn. (Eng.), Asian Studies Inst. (mem. adv. com. 1975—), Indpls. Mus. Art. Clubs: Lake Havasu Golf and Country, Univ., Rotary. Author: The Bracket Complex in Chinese Architecture, 1946; A General Theory of Operators, 1967; Buddhist Formal Logic, 1968; A Comparative Study of Propositions in the Western and Indian Logic, 1972; Topics on Being and Logical Reasoning, 1974; A Semantic Study of Propositions, East and West, 1976; The Art of Chinese Calligraphy, 1977; Dignaga and Post Russell Logic, 1983; The Art of War of Sun Tzu, 1983. Editor, Jour. Buddhist Philosophy, 1978—; reviewer Nat. Endowment for Humanities, 1979—. Home: PO Box 2717 Bloomington IN 47402

CHIAPELAS, NICHOLAS P., printing/communications executive; b. St. Louis, July 11, 1936; married; children—Diane, Tom. B.Journalism with honors, U. Mo.-Columbia, 1958. With Keeler/Morris Printing Co., Inc., St. Louis, pres.; chief operating officer Lithocraft Studios, Lewin Bookbinding, Fordyce Promotional Services; dir. Nat. Graphics, Inc., St. Louis. Chmn. Sml. Bus. Council, Regional Commerce & Growth Assn., St. Louis; chmn. State of St. Louis Com.; dir. Graphic Arts Edn. and Research Council, Graphic Arts Council N. Am., Graphic Arts Show Corp.; commr. St. Louis County Port Authority; vice chmn. and mem. exec. com. Nat. Assn. Printers & Lithographers; bd. dirs., exec. com. Regional Commerce & Growth Assn., others. Address: Keeler/Morris Printing Co Inc 5800 Fee Fee Rd Saint Louis MO 63042

CHIAPPE, WAYNE THOMAS, packaging and equipment executive; b. Los Angeles, Sept. 24, 1924; s. Thomas and Thomasina Chiappe; m. Joanne Marie Ball, Aug. 13, 1955; children—Carole Elizabeth, Susan Marie, David Thomas. B.S.M.E., U. So. Calif., 1949; postgrad. U. Calif., Stanford U. With Am. Can Corp., Los Angeles, 1942-43; with The Continental Group, various locations, 1949-80, gen. mgr. ops. engring., Chgo., 1964-65, gen. mgr. research and devel. Metal Div., Chgo., 1966-71, v.p. research and engring., corp. officer Metal Div., Chgo., 1971-76, v.p. tech. and mfg. Teepak subs., Chgo., 1976-79, v.p. tech. diverse ops., Stamford, Conn., 1979-84; pres. Chapco, Inc., equipment design and sales, Hinsdale, Ill.; cons. in packaging field. Pres. Hinsdale Swim Assn., 1973, 74; mem. Portola Valley Waste Disposal Com., 1957-58; Served as sgt. U.S. Army, 1943-45; Burma, China, India. Republican. Roman Catholic. Contbr. articles to bus. mags; patentee; designer and developer magnetic side seamer, oval form horn, auto body blank feeder and stacker, hi-speed hi-solids compound liner, wire solder gun, portable and modular can lines, UV curing, two-piece aluminum and steel beverage cans, welded cans, others. Office: 731 E 7th St Hinsdale IL 60521

CHIARO, A. WILLIAM, management consultant; b. Chgo., July 12, 1928; s. Anthony Joseph and Marie Anne (Bonario) C.; B.S., U. Ill., 1954; m. Lyne LaVerne Franke, Aug. 27, 1961; children—David Huntington, Caroline Elizabeth. Acct., IBM, Chgo., 1954-55; with Black & Skaggs Assocs., Chgo., 1955—, pres., 1978—; dir. P.M. Chgo., Inc. Served with U.S. Army, 1946-47, USAF, 1950-52. Mem. Soc. Advancement Mgmt., Soc. Profl. Bus. Cons., Nat. Soc. Public Accts. Presbyterian. Club: Kenilworth (Ill.). Contbr. articles to med. and profl. jours. Home: 2721 Iroquois Rd Wilmette IL 60091 Office: 845 N Michigan Ave Chicago IL 60611

CHIDESTER, JOHN KENT, librarian; b. Toledo, Dec. 14, 1948; s. Christian Kent and Mary Jane (Schneider) C.; m. Marilyn Jean Muntz, May 29, 1971; children—Brian Kent, Robert Christian, Margaret Jean. B.A., Heidelberg Coll., 1970; M.L.S., Case Western Res. U., 1974. City editor Fostoria Review Times, Ohio, 1972-73; adult services librarian Marion Pub. Library (Ohio), 1974-76; dir. Mount Vernon Pub. Library, Ohio, 1976—; pres. Central Ohio Interlibrary Network, Mansfield, 1980; v.p., pres.-elect North Central Library Coop., Mansfield, 1985—. Mem. Knox County Republican Com., Mt. Vernon, 1984. Served to staff sgt. USAF, 1970-72. Mem. Beta Phi Mu. Mem. United Ch. Christ, Lodge: Kiwanis (pres. 1982-83). Avocations: Computer and information science. Home: 518 N Braddock St Mount Vernon OH 43050 Office: Mount Vernon Pub Library 201 N Mulberry St Mount Vernon OH 43050

CHIEN, HENRY HUNG-YEH, chemical engineer, consultant; b. Shanghai, China, Sept. 28, 1935; came to U.S., 1958, naturalized, 1971; s. Richard and Su-mei (Chou) C.; m. Maria Kuan, Dec., 1961; children—Michael, David. B.S., Taipei Inst. Tech., 1956; Ph.D., U. Minn., 1963. Registered profl. engr., Mo. Sr. engr. Monsanto Co., St. Louis, 1963-66, engring. specialist, 1966-70, prin. engr. specialist, 1970, engring. supt., 1970-75, fellow, 1975-82, sr. fellow, 1982—. Editor: Foundations of Computer Aided Process Design, 1984. Contbr. articles to profl. jours. Mem. Am. Inst. Chem. Engrs. Roman Catholic. Club: Forest Lake (St. Louis). Avocations: tennis, photography. Office: Monsanto Co 800 N Lindbergh Blvd Saint Louis MO 63167

CHIGAS, VICTOR, brokerage firm executive; b. Peekskill, N.Y., Aug. 1, 1927; s. Christopher Ernest and Ethel (Irwin) C.; children—Christopher R., William J., Victor J. B.S.B.A., Denver U., 1956. Gen. mgr. Rolling Green Country Club, Arlington Heights, Ill., 1958-61; gen. mgr. No. Shore Country Club, Glenview, Ill., 1961-67; acct. exec. Walston & Comp., Chgo., 1967-69; option coordinator, account exec. Shearson, Hammill & Co., Chgo., 1969-74; 1st v.p. Drexel Burnham Lambert, Chgo., 1974-83; sr. v.p. Drexel Trust Co. of Midwest, 1983—, bd. dirs., 1983—. Pres. Greater Chgo. Denver Alumni Assn., Chgo., 1971; dir. Parent's Bd. Drake U., Des Moines, 1980-82; mem. Ill. Cemetary Advisory Commn., Chgo., 1980-81. Served to sgt. USAF, 1950-52. Mem. Greater Chgo. Club Mgrs. Assn. (pres. 1965). Republican. Office: Drexel Burnham Lambert 1 South Wacker Dr Chicago IL 60606

CHIGNELL, DEREK ALAN, chemistry educator; b. London, July 4, 1943; came to U.S., 1975; s. Francis George and Elsie Mary (Lee) C.; m. Judith Roberta McLean, Aug. 22, 1970; children—Andrew, Jeremy, Jennifer. B.S., Kings Coll., U. London, 1964, Ph.D., 1968; M.A., Wheaton Coll., 1977. Fulbright scholar UCLA, 1968-71; lectr. U. Dundee, Scotland, 1971-75; now prof. chemistry Wheaton Coll., Ill.; adj. prof. Loyola U. Med. Sch., Maywood, Ill., 1983—. Fellow Am. Sci. Affiliation; mem. Am. Chem. Soc. Avocations: bicycling; gardening; reading. Home: 1 N 176 Woods Ave Wheaton IL 60188 Office: Wheaton Coll Chemistry Dept Seminary Ave Wheaton IL 60187

CHILCOTE, ROBERT RALPH, physician, educator; b. Cleve., Oct. 8, 1941; s. Ralph E. and Margaret A. (Fisher) C.; A.B., Cornell U., 1963; M.D., U. Rochester, 1969; m. Denise Buckley; children—Kelly, Krista, Ryan. Intern in pediatrics Strong Meml. Hosp., U. Rochester (N.Y.), 1969-70, resident in pediatrics, 1970-71, chief resident in pediatrics, 1971-72; fellow in pediatric hematology James Whitcomb Riley Hosp. for Children, Ind. U. Sch. of Medicine, Indpls., 1972-75; practice medicine specializing in pediatric hematology and oncology, Chgo., 1975-84; dir. div. pediatric hematology Michael Reese Hosp. and Med. Center, Chgo., 1975-77; co-dir. div. pediatric hematology-oncology Wyler Children's Hosp., 1977-84; asst. prof. dept. pediatrics Pritzker Sch. of Medicine, U. Chgo., 1975-84; assoc. prof. pediatrics U. So. Calif. Diplomate Am. Bd. Pediatrics. Mem. Am. Acad. Pediatrics (sect. on oncology-hematology 1974—), Am. Cancer Soc., Am. Soc. Clin. Oncology, Am. Soc. Hematology. Contbr. articles on pediatric hematology and oncology to profl. jours.

CHILDERS, JOHN HENRY, talent company executive, personality representative; b. Hoopston, Ill., July 26, 1930; s. Leroy Kendal and Marie Ann (Sova) C.; m. JoAnn Uhlar, July 27, 1956; children—Michael John, Mark Joseph. Sales rep. Universal Match Corp., Chgo., 1956-59; v.p. sales to pres. Sales Merchandising, Inc., Chgo., 1959-63; chmn. bd., chief exec. officer Talent Services, Inc. and Talent Network, Inc., Skokie, Ill., 1963—. Served as pilot USAF, 1950-56. Mem. Assn. Reps. of Profl. Athletes (v.p.); Internat. Wine and Food Soc., Chaine des Rotisseurs, Les Amis du Vin, Wine finders, Classic Car Club Am., Auburn-Cord-Dusenberg Club. Republican. Roman Catholic. Clubs: Knollwood Country; Big Foot Country; Lake Geneva Country, PGA Country. Home: Lake Forest IL 60045 also Apt 4G North-of-Nell Aspen CO 81611 also 219 Club Cottages Palm Beach Gardens FL 33410 also Lake Geneva WI 53147 Office: 5200 W Main St Skokie IL 60077

CHILDRES, MARY ROSE, univ. bus. adminstr.; b. Livingston, Ala., Apr. 13, 1936; d. Simon and Mary Magdalene (Sanders) Childress; A.S. in Secretarial Sci., U. Cin., 1973, B.S. in Adminstrv. Mgmt., 1976; m. Robert Walker Greene. Secretarial positions Hamilton County (Ohio) Welfare Dept., 1954-S9, VA Hosp., Cin., 1959-63, Mut. Benefit Life Ins. Co., Cin., 1965-66, Ky. State U., Frankfort, 1966-68; nutrition program asst. W.Va. U., Charleston, 1969-70; with U. Cin., 1970—, bus. adminstr., office of vice provost for continuing edn. and met. services, from 1978, now sr. bus. adminstr. continuing edn. and met. services. Chmn. Cornelius Van Jordan Scholarship Fund, U. Cin. Mem. Nat. Secs. Assn. (charter mem., co-founder Frankfort chpt.), AAUW, United Black Assn. of Faculty, Adminstrs. and Staff U. Cin. (treas.), Mid-Level Mgrs. Assn. U. Cin., Nat. U. Continuing Edn. Assn. (chmn., treas. 1982 conv.), Adminstrv. Women's Assn. U. Cin., Nat. Assn. Female Execs., Delta Tau Kappa. Mem. Ch. of God. Author: Handbook of Office Procedures, 1973, 75. Home: 838 Crowden Dr Cincinnati OH 45224 Office: 341 French Hall Clifton U Cin Cincinnati OH 45221

CHILDRESS, BARRY LEE, child psychoanalyst; b. Chgo., Apr. 19, 1941; s. Affie Sylvester and Dorothy Mildred (Rein) C.; m. Gene Ziupsnys, June 29, 1963; children—Brett Lee, Brian Lee. B.S. with honors, U. Ill., 1961, M.D., 1965; grad. Inst. for Psychoanalysis, Chgo., 1983. Diplomate Am. Bd. Psychiatry and Nuerology. Intern Ill. Masonic Hosp., Chgo., 1965-66; resident in adult psychiatry Presbyn.-St. Lukes Hosp., Chgo., 1966-69, fellow in child psychiatry, 1971-72; dir. child psychiatry sect. Rush-Presbyn.-St Lukes Hosp., Chgo., 1975-76; mem. faculty child and adolescent psychotherapy program Inst. Psychoanalysis, Chgo., 1980—, core faculty, 1985—; cons. Hephzibah Children's Home Assn., Oak Park, Ill., 1984—. Served to capt. USAF, 1969-71. Mem. Am. Psychoanalytic Soc., Ill. Council Child Psychiatry, Ill. Soc. Adolescent Psychiatry, Chgo. Psychoanalytic Soc. Avocations: camping; hiking; running; computer applicatins to psychoanalytic practice. Home: 1221 N East Ave Oak Park IL 60301 Office: 520 N Michigan Ave Suite 1420 Chicago IL 60611

CHILDS, GAYLE BERNARD, educator; b. Redfield, S.D., Oct. 17, 1907; s. Alva Eugene and Dora Amelia (Larsen) C.; A.B., Nebr. State Tchrs. Coll., Wayne, 1931; M.A., U. Nebr., 1936, Ph.D., 1949; M.Ed., Harvard, 1938; m. Doris Wilma Hoskinson, Dec. 22, 1930; children—Richard Arlen, George William, Patricia Ann (Mrs. Ronald Bauers). Tchr. sci. Wynot (Nebr.) High Sch., 1928-30; tchr. sci. Wayne (Nebr.) High Sch., 1931-38, prin., 1938-41; supt. Wakefield (Nebr.) pub. schs., 1941-44, West Point (Nebr.) pub. schs., 1944-46; curriculum specialist U. Nebr. extension div., Lincoln, 1946-49, instr. secondary edn. Tchrs. Coll., also curriculum specialist extension div., 1949-51, asst. prof., 1951-53, asso. prof., 1953-56, prof., head class and corr. instrn., 1956-63, prof., asso. dir. extension div., 1963-66, prof., dir. extension div., 1966-74. Nebr. del. White House Conf. on Aging, 1981. Sr. Fulbright-Hays scholar Haile Sellassie I U., Addis Ababa, Ethiopia, 1974. Mem. Nebr. Edn. Assn. (dist. III sec. 1941-42), Nat. U. Extension Assn. (mem. adminstrv. com., div. corr. study 1952-68, chmn. 1963-65, Assn. dir. 1963-65, mem. joint com. minimum data and definitions 1965-70, chmn. 1970-73; Walton S. Bittner award 1971; establishment Gayle B. Childs award div. ind. study 1969; Gayle B. Childs award 1973), Internat. Council on Corr. Edn. (chmn. com. on research 1961-69, program com. 9th internat. conf. 1971-72), Assn. Univ. Evening Colls. (program com. 1971-72, membership com. 1971-73), Nebr. Schoolmasters Club, Phi Delta Kappa (dist. rep. 1957-63, dir., 1963-69, mem. commn. on edn. and human rights and responsibilities 1963-74, mem. adv. panel on commns. 1970-72; Disting. Service award 1970), North Central Assn. Colls. and Secondary Schs. (cons. def. com. 1953-55, mem. panel vis. scholars 1971-73), U. Nebr. Emeriti Assn. (pres. 1979-80). Club: Kiwanis (bd. dirs. 1978-81). Contbr. articles to profl. jours. Home: 4530 Van Dorn St Lincoln NE 68506 Office: 901 N 17th St Lincoln NE 68508

CHILDS, WILLIAM JEFFRIES, research physicist; b. Boston, Nov. 9, 1926; s. Paul Dudley and Clemence (Jeffries) C.; m. Jean Roberts Mallory, June 17, 1951; children—Linton Jeffries, Lee Tracy. A.B., Harvard U., 1948; M.S., U. Mich., 1949, Ph.D., 1956. Physicist, Argonne Nat. Lab., Ill., 1956—; vis. prof. U. Bonn., Fed. Republic Ger., 1972-73. Contbr. articles to profl. jours. Fellow Am. Phys. Soc.; mem. Am. Optical Soc. Avocation: Performing baroque chamber music. Home: 539 Fairview Ave Glen Ellyn IL 60137 Office: Argonne Nat Labs 9700 S Cass Ave Argonne IL 60439

CHIOU, JIUNN PERNG, mechanical engineering educator. B.S., Nat. Taiwan U., Taipei, 1954; M.S., Oreg. State U., 1960; Ph.D., U. Wis.-Madison, 1964. Research asst. U. Wis.-Madison, 1960-63, instr., 1963-64; engring. specialist AiResearch Mfg. Co., Los Angeles, 1964-69; prof. mech. engring. U. Detroit, 1969—. Contbr. articles to engring. and math. jours. Mem. Am. Soc. Mech. Engrs. (chmn. 1979—, fundamental com., solar energy div.), Soc. Automotive Engrs (chmn. 1980—, climate control and passenger car activity coms.), Internat. Soc. Solar Energy. Office: Mech Engring Dept U Detroit 4001 W McNichols Rd Detroit MI 48221

CHIPMAN, DEBORAH GONDEK, communications executive; b. Phoenix, Apr. 6, 1953; d. Joseph H. and Dorothy E. (Bradac) G.; B.A. cum laude in Journalism, Duquesne U., 1975; m. John A. Chipman, Oct. 6, 1979. Dir., performer The Young Tamburitzans ensemble, Phoenix, 1968-71; reporter Phoenix Gazette, 1970-71; newswriter, broadcaster Sta. WDUQ, Pitts., 1973-74; ensemble performer Duquesne U. Tamburitzans, nat. folk arts ensemble, Pitts., 1971-75, European tours, 1971-72; communications/planning Chipman Design, Chgo., 1979—; owner Custom Sources, Chgo., 1980—; writer-editor Fairburn Assos., Inc., Phoenix, 1977-79. Recipient Piano Solo Excellence award Nat. Fedn. Musicians, 1971; Quill and Scroll nat. editorial writing award, 1971. Mem. Women in Communications (treas. Phoenix chpt. 1976-77), Internat. Assn. Bus. Communicators Phoenix award of merit 1979, Gold Four award 1981, Gold Quill award), 1982 Art Inst. Chgo., Sigma Delta Chi (sec. Duquesne chpt. 1974), Kappa Tau Alpha, Duquesne U. Tamburitzans Alumni Assn. Editor Horizons, 1976-77. Home: 400 S Home Ave Park Ridge IL 60068 Office: 205 W Touhy Ave Suite 104 Park Ridge IL 60068

CHIPMAN, JAMES THOMAS, university official; b. Wichita, Kans., Mar. 28, 1952; s. Edwin E. and Mary A. (Johnson) C. B.S. in Polit. Sci., Kans. State U., 1974, B.B.A., 1974, M.S. in Counseling and Student Personnel, 1976; postgrad. Ind. U., 1982—. Asst. dean students, dir. student activities McPherson Coll., Kans., 1976-78; residence hall dir. U. Kans., Lawrence, 1979-81; coordinator for residence life Ind. U., Bloomington, 1981—, anti-racism trainer, 1985—. Recipient Disting. Service award McPherson Coll., 1978, Outstanding Advisor award U. Kans. Assn. Univ. Residence Halls, 1981; named one of Outstanding Young Men in Am., 1983. Mem. Am. Coll. Personnel Assn. (state membership chmn. 1984—), Ind. Coll. Personnel Assn. (exec. com. 1982—), Nat. Orientation Dirs. Assn. (editorial bd. 1972-78, nat. cons.'s com. 1976-78), Pi Lambda Theta, Phi Delta Kappa. Democrat. Presbyterian. Office: Dept of Residence Life McNutt Residence Ctr Bloomington IN 47406

CHIPMAN, JOHN SOMERSET, economist, educator; b. Montreal, P.Q., Can., June 28, 1926; s. Warwick Fielding and Mary Somerset (Aikins) C.; student Universidad de Chile, Santiago, 1943-44; B.A., McGill U., Montreal, 1947, M.A., 1948; Ph.D., Johns Hopkins U., 1951; postdoctoral U. Chgo., 1950-51; m. Margaret Ann Ellefson, June 24, 1960; children—Thomas Noel, Timothy Warwick. Asst. prof. econs. Harvard U., Cambridge, Mass., 1951-55; asso. prof. econs. U. Minn., Mpls., 1955-60, prof., 1961-81, regent's prof., 1981—; fellow Center for Advanced Study in Behavioral Scis., Stanford, Calif., 1972-73; vis. prof. econs. various colls. and univs. Guggenheim fellow, 1980-81. Fellow Econometric Soc. (council 1971-78, 81-83), Am. Statis. Assn., Am. Acad. Arts and Scis., World Assn. for Internat. Relations; mem. Am. Econ. Assn., Inst. Math. Stats., Can. Econ. Assn., Royal Econ. Soc. Author: The Theory of Intersectoral Money Flows and Income Formation, 1951; editor (with others) Preferences, Utility, and Demand, 1971; (with Kindleberger) Flexible Exchange Rates and the Balance of Payments, 1980; editor Jour. of Internat. Econs., 1977—; asso. editor Econometrica, 1956-69. Office: Dept Econs 1122 Mgmt and Econs Bldg U Minn 271 19th Ave S Minneapolis MN 55455

CHIPOCO, ADOLFO MALMBORG, physician; c. Callao, Peru, Dec. 1, 1929; came to U.S., 1955; s. Adolfo and Elisa (Malmborg) Chipoco Meza; m. June Shreiner Badorf, June 1, 1957 (div. Mar. 1973); m. Gladys Mirta Delgado, Oct. 5, 1973. M.D., San Marcos U., Lima, Peru, 1954. Diplomate Am. Bd. Family Practice. Intern, Grasslands Hosp., Valhalla, N.Y., 1955; resident St. Joseph's Hosp., Lancaster, Pa., 1956-59, Henry Ford Hosp., Detroit, 1959-60, Leila Hosp., Battle Creek, Mich., 1960-61; practice family medicine, Detroit, 1968—; mem. staff Grace-Harper Hosp., Detroit, 1968—. Author: Oro Y Sombras, 1976; Los Heroes Y Grau, 1977; El Arbol, 1978; Meditaciones Fernandinas, 1979; Castilla, 1980; La Esfera Azul, The Blue Sphere, 1984; editor: El Amauta, 1979-83; Pams, 1983; Friends of the Arts of Iberoamerica, 1983. Med. chmn. Oakland County unit Am. Cancer Soc., 1968-71; v.p. Friends of Arts Ibero-Am., Bloomfield Hills, Mich., 1983. Recipient Cruz Castilla, Inst. Libertador Castilla, 1982; Valor Humanitario, Peruvian-Am. Council Good Will, 1983. Fellow Am. Acad. Family Practice; mem. AMA, Mich. State Med. Soc., Wayne County Med. Soc., Peruvian Am. Med. Soc. (pres. 1984-85). Roman Catholic. Club: Peruvian of Mich. (pres. 1979-83). Home: 3015 Spring West Bloomfield MI 48033 Office: 17000 S Eight Mile Rd Southfield MI 48075

CHIPPS, MICHAEL ROBERT, college official; b. Grand Island, Nebr., Mar. 28, 1950; s. Robert C. and Kathryn A. (Seifert) C.; m. Susan G. Wescott, Dec. 5, 1970; children—Sean, Angela. Student, U. Nebr., 1968-69, postgrad., 1983—; student Sioux Falls Coll., 1969-70; B.S., Kearney State Coll., 1972; M.S., 1980. Intern, U. Nebr. Med. Center, Nebr. Psychiat. Inst., Omaha, 1978; counselor-examiner div. rehab. services Dept. Edn., Hastings, Nebr., 1975-79; instr. social scis. and coordinator career devel. center Central Community Coll., Hastings, 1979-82, adminstrv. asst., 1982-84, chmn. health div., 1984—. Served to comdr. USAR, 1974—. Recipient award Assn. U.S. Army, 1977, Outstanding Leader award Officer Candidate Acad., 1977. Mem. Res. Officers Assn., Assn. U.S. Army, Phi Delta Kappa. Lodges: Masons, Scottish Rite. Office: PO Box 1024 Hastings NE 68901

CHISHOLM, GEORGE NICKOLAUS, dentist; b. Pullman, Wash., Sept, 21, 1936; s. Leslie L. and Lila Rene (Cates) C.; D.D.S., U. Nebr., 1960; 1 son, Andrew M. Practice dentistry, Lincoln, Nebr., 1963-83; clin. instr. Coll. Dentistry, U. Nebr., 1976-83. Mem. S.E. Nebr. Health Planning Agy., 1976-82. Served to capt. Dental Corps, USAF, 1960-63. Mem. ADA (del. 1980), Nebr. Dental Assn. (del. 1974-80, trustee 1980-83), Lincoln Dist. Dental Assn. (pres. 1979-80), Sigma Alpha Epsilon, Xi Psi Phi. Mason (32 deg., Shriner). Asst. editor Nebr. State Dental Jour., 1967-69. Home: 1230 Manchester Dr Lincoln NE 68528

CHISHOLM, TAGUE CLEMENT, pediatric surgeon, educator; b. E. Millinocket, Maine, Nov. 6, 1915; s. George James and Victoria Mary (Tague) C.; A.B. cum laude, Harvard U., 1936, M.D., 1940; m. Verity Burnett, 1940 (div. 1975); children—Christopher Tague, Penelope Ann, Robin Francis; m. 2d, Johanna Lyon Myers, Aug. 9, 1975. Intern, Peter Bent Brigham Hosp., Boston Children's Hosp., Boston, 1940-41, resident in gen. and pediatric surgery, 1941-46; Arthur Tracy Cabot fellow in surgery Harvard Med. Sch., 1946; practice medicine specializing in pediatric surgery, Mpls., 1947—; mem. faculty U. Minn. Sch. Medicine, Mpls., 1947—, clin. prof. surgery, 1965-85; trustee Mpls. Children's Health Center Hosp. Trustee Bishop Whipple Schs., Faribault, Minn.; bd. dirs. Wells Found., Mpls. Recipient Presdl. award Minn. Med. Assn., 1978; diplomate Am. Bd. Surgery. Recipient Merit medal U. Rio Grande Norte, Brazil, 1976; Charles Bowles Rogers award Hennepin County (Minn.) Med. Soc., 1976. Editorial bd. Jour. Pediatric Surgery, 1965-76, Pediatric Digest, 1962-82, Jour. Minn. Med. Assn., 1957—; contbr. articles in pediatric surgery to profl. jours. and books. Home: 16617 Black Oaks Ln Wayzata MN 55391

CHISM, JAMES ARTHUR, data processor; b. Oak Park, Ill., Mar. 6, 1933; s. William Thompson and Arema Eloise (Chadwick) C.; A.B., DePauw U., 1957; M.B.A., Ind. U., 1959; postgrad. exec. program Wharton Sch. Bus., U. Pa., 1984. Mgmt. engr. consumer and indsl. products div. Uniroyal, Inc., Mishawaka, Ind., 1959-61, sr. mgmt. engr., 1961-63; systems analyst Miles Labs., Inc., Elkhart, Ind., 1963-64, sr. systems analyst, 1965-69, project supr., distbn. systems, 1969-71, mgr. systems and programming for corporate finance and adminstrv. depts., 1971-73, mgr. adminstrv. systems and corp. staff services, 1973-75, group mgr. consumer products group systems and programming, 1975-79; dir. adminstrn. and staff services Cutter/Miles, 1979-81, dir. advanced office systems and corp. adminstrn. 1982-84; dir. advanced office systems Internat. MIS and Adminstrn., 1984-85, dir. advanced office systems, tng. and adminstrn., 1985—. Bd. dirs. United Way Elkhart County, 1974-75. Served with AUS, 1954-56. Mem. Assn. Systems Mgmt. (chpt. pres. 1969-70, div. dir. 1972-77, recipient Merit award 1975, Achievement award 1977, cert. systems profl. 1984), Dean's Assocs. of Ind. U. Sch. Bus.-Bloomington, Assn. Internal Mgmt. Cons., DePauw U., Ind. U. alumni assns., Delta Kappa Epsilon, Sigma Iota Epsilon, Beta Gamma Sigma. Republican. Episcopalian. Clubs: Morris Park Country. (South Bend, Ind.); Delta Kappa Epsilon Club (N.Y.C.), Yale of N.Y.C., Vero Beach Country (Fla.); Coast (Melbourne, Fla.); Ind. Soc. of Chgo. Home: 504 Cedar Crest Ln Mishawaka IN 46545 Office: Miles Labs Inc PO Box 40 1127 Myrtle St Elkhart IN 46515

CHISM, NEAL ASA, economist; b. Humboldt, Nebr., Nov. 5, 1924; s. Ralph Asa and Jessie Ann (Graham) C.; student Weber Coll., Ogden, Utah, 1942, Wabash Coll., Crawfordsville, Ind., 1944-46, U. Ill., 1946; B.S., U. Calif., Berkeley, 1947; certificate d'Etude, U. Grenoble (France), 1949; M.A., U. Nebr., 1951, secondary teaching cert., 1963, Ph.D., 1967; cert. Sch. Banking, U. Wis., 1978; m. Joan Johnson, Feb. 27, 1965; 1 son, John Neal Asa. Export-import salesman Getz Bros. & Co., San Francisco, 1947-48; research officer U.S. Govt., Washington, 1951-53, fgn. service res. officer, 1953-59; asst. to v.p. Am. Express Co., N.Y.C., 1959-62; asst. prof. to assoc. prof. econs. Nebr. Wesleyan U., Lincoln, 1965—, also head dept. bus. adminstrn./econs., 1977—. Chmn. ednl. com. Nemeco Credit Union, 1967-75; univ. rep. Lincoln Community Concerts, Lincoln Community Chest, 1972, 73; univ. rep. to liaison com. Mayor's Edn. Com., 1971. Served with USN, 1942-46. Recipient Trustee award Nebr. Wesleyan U., 1972; named Gt. Teaching Prof. 1st Nat. Bank, Lincoln, 1982. Mem. AAUP (pres. Wesleyan chpt. 1965-69), SAR (pres. Lincoln chpt. 1975-76, pres. Nebr. state soc. 1977), Chism Family Assn. (exec. sec. 1962—), Am. Econs. Assn., Midwest Econs. Assn., Nebr. Bus. and Econs. Assn. (sec.-treas. 1978—), Clan Chisholm Soc. in Am., Scottish Am. Soc., Lincoln Lancaster Geneal. Soc., Delta Phi Epsilon, Delta Tau Delta, Tau Kappa Epsilon (faculty adv. Beta Gamma 1969-77, Nat. Advisers award 1974), Omicron Delta Epsilon, Pi Gamma Mu (pres. chpt. 1977, gov. Nebr. province 1978, vice chancellor middle western region 1980, chancellor 1984). Republican. Presbyterian (deacon, elder). Clubs: Filson (Louisville); Masons, Shriners. Home: 5243 Huntington St Lincoln NE 68504 Office: Nebr Wesleyan U 50th St Paul Lincoln NE 68504

CHITALEY, ANI DINKAR, manufacturing, quality and technology management consultant; b. Nagpur, Maharashtra, India, Nov. 7, 1942; came to U.S., 1965; s. Dinkar V. and Shyamala D.; m. Shubha S. Patwardhan, May 21, 1965; children—Raajnish, Kanchan. B.E., Nagpur U., 1963; M.E., Indian Inst. Tech., Bombay, 1965; Ph.D., MIT, 1968; M.B.A., Case Western Res. U., 1984. Research asst. Surface Lab, MIT, 1965-66, Materials Lab., 1966-68; sr. engr. B.F. Goodrich Co., Brecksville, Ohio, 1968-70; mng. dir. Chreden Engring., Nagpur, 1971-76, Unmaten Engring, Nagpur, 1971-76; chief quality control and improvement Godrej & Boyce, Bombay, 1976-77; sr. assoc. Booz, Allen & Hamilton, Cleve., 1978-84; pres. Automation Mgmt. Services, Inc., Cleve., 1984—; mem. Adv. Bd. Tech. Edn., Bombay, 1975-76; lectr. in field. Contbr. articles to profl. jours. India Govt. Sci. Found. grantee, 1964. Mem. Am. Soc. Quality Control, Soc. Mfg. Engrs., APICS, Sigma Xi, Beta Gamma Sigma. Office: Automation Mgmt Services Inc 8141 Broadview Rd Broadview Heights OH 44147

CHITWOOD, JULIUS RICHARD, librarian; b. Magazine, Ark., June 1, 1921; s. Hoyt Mozart and Florence (Umfrid) C.; A.B. cum laude, Quachita Baptist Coll., Arkadelphis, Ark., 1942; M.Mus., Ind. U., 1948; M.A., U. Chgo., 1954; m. Aileen Newsom, Aug. 6, 1944. Music supr. Edinburg (Ind.) pub. schs., 1946-47; music and audio-visual librarian Roosevelt Coll., Chgo., 1948-51; humanities librarian Drake U., 1951-53; spl. cataloger Chgo. Tchrs. Coll., 1953; asst. circulation librarian Indpls. Pub. Library, 1954-57, coordinator adult services, 1957-61; dir. Rockford (Ill.) Pub. Library 1961-79, No. Ill. Library System, Rockford, 1966-76; exec. dir. Ill. Regional Library System, Chgo., 1981—. Chmn. subcom. library system devel. Ill. Library Adv. Com., 1965-79; adv. com. Grad. Sch. Library Sci., U. Ill., 1964-68; program adv. com. Sauk Valley Jr. Coll., 1967; cons. in field, participant workshops. Mem. history com. Ill. Sesquicentennial Commn.; mem. Mayor Rockford Com. for UN, 1962-68. Sect. chmn. Rockford United Fund, 1966-70; exec. bd. Rockford Civic Orch. Assn., 1962-70; pres. Rockford Regional Acad. Center, 1974-76. Served to maj., inf. AUS, 1942-45; ETO. Mem. Am. (chmn. standards adult services com., adult services div. 1961-66, chmn. subcom. revision standards of materials, pub. library div. 1965-66, pres. bldg. and equipment sect. library adminstrn. div. 1966-67, chmn. staff devel. com. personnel adminstrn. sect., library adminstr. div. 1964-68, pres. library adminstrn. div. 1969-70), Ill. (v.p. 1964-65, pres. 1965-66, Librarian of Year award 1974) library assns., Rockford C. of C. (mem. bd. Rockford area 1967-69). Unitarian (pres. 1965-67). Rotarian (exec. bd. Rockford 1965-66). Clubs: Professional Men's, Rockford University. Home: 916 Paris Ave Rockford IL 61107 Office: 115 7th St S 209 Rockford IL 61104

CHIU, VICTOR, mathematics and physics educator, software engineer, software consultant; b. Tianjin, People's Republic of China, Nov. 28, 1936; came to U.S., 1959, naturalized 1964; s. Kuno and Vivian W. (Tsao) C.; m. Loretta C. Shih, Sept. 2, 1963; children—Frederic, Cornelius. B.S., Kent State U., 1960; M.S., Cornell U., 1967, Ph.D., 1970. Primary sch. master Edn. Dept., Hong Kong, 1956-59; instr. The Coll. of Wooster, Ohio, 1966-67; research asst. Cornell U., Ithaca, N.Y., 1967-70; from asst. prof. to prof. math. and physics Ind. Central U., Indpls., 1970-85; sr. devel. engr. Structural Dynamics Research Corp., 1985—; cons. software Structural Dynamics Research Corp., Cin., 1983—, Detroit allison, Indpls., 1981-83. Contbr. articles to profl. jours. Fellow summer research NSF, 1971, 1978, 1979, Dept. Def., 1983. Mem. U.S. China People's Friendship Assn. (charter), Am. Phys. Soc., Am. Assn. Physics Tchrs., IEEE Computer Soc., AAUP (chpt. sec. 1976-85), Sigma Xi. Office: Structural Dynamics Research Corp 2000 Eastman Dr Milford OH 45150

CHLAD, DOROTHY CLARA, safety education consultant; b. Cleve., Sept. 21, 1934; d. Stanley and Clara (Stebel) Krzynowek; m. Frank Ludwig Chlad, Sept. 1, 1956; children—Tammy Lynne, Lynne Marie. Student Georgetown U., 1970-71, U. Akron, 1972-73, others. Asst. to fashion dir. Higbee's, Cleve., 1955-58; sec. Officers' Club, U.S. Army, Ft. Hood, Tex., 1958-60; tchr./dir. Safety Town, Bedford, Ohio, part-time 1964-74; co-owner nursery sch., Warrensville Heights, Ohio, 1973-74; dist. rep. Ohio Dept. Hwy. Safety, Columbus, 1972-74; founder, pres. Nat. Safety Town Ctr., Cleve., 1974—; mem. Hwy. Safety Conf., White House, 1976; mem. Nat. Conf. Safety Edn., Washington, 1978; cons. Sesame Street, 1979, state govts., 1974—; condr. workshops. Author instructional books, 8 child safety books. Mem. Greater Cleve. Growth Assn., 1976—; mem. bd. control Greater Cleve. Safety Council, 1976—; mem. Cleve. YWCA, 1980—. Named Activist of Yr., Nat. Ctr. Voluntary Action, 1977; Career Woman of Achievement, YWCA Cleve., 1979; recipient Pres.'s Vol. Action award Pres. U.S., 1983. Mem. Nat. Assn. Female Execs., Nat. Safety Council, Am. Driver/Traffic Safety Edn., Nat. Community Edn. Assn., Nat. Pedestrian Com., Vets. of Safety, Internat. Assn. Bus. Communicators, Am. Soc. Safety Engrs. Roman Catholic. Lodges: Jaycettes (pres. 1970-71) (Bedford, Ohio). Club: Jr. Women's. Home: 10169 Inlet Pointe E Aurora OH 44202 Office: PO Box 39312 Cleveland OH 44139

CHO, ALBERT I. PAO, mechanical engineer, educator; b. China, May 2, 1932; came to U.S., 1953; s. Edward I. Lai Cho and Mildred Chong Chen; m.

Betty Chan, Aug. 17, 1963; 1 son, Lawrence. B.S. in Mech. Engring., U. Ill., 1958, M.S., 1959. Cert. profl. engr. Ill., Calif., Fla., Minn., Ind., Tex., Mass., Colo. Assoc. ptnr. Skidmore, Owings & Merrill, Chgo., 1959-83; v.p. Perkins & Will, Chgo., 1984—; asst. prof. Ill. Inst. Tech., Chgo., 1980—. Mem. Mech. Engring. Soc., ASHRAE, ASME, Pi Tau Sigma. Contbr. chpts. to books and articles to profl. jours. Office: Perkins and Will 2 N LaSalle St Chicago IL 60602

CHO, CHENG TSUNG, physician, educator; b. Kaohsiung, Taiwan, Dec. 2, 1937; s. R.E. and S.M. (Chou) C.; came to U.S., 1964, naturalized, 1976; M.D., Kaohsiung Med. Coll., 1962; Ph.D., U. Kans., 1970; m. Chiou-shya Chen, Dec. 14, 1968; children—Jennifer, Julie. Intern, Norwegian-Am. Hosp., Chgo., 1964-65; resident U. Kans. Med. Center, 1965-67, fellow, 1967-70, asst. prof. pediatrics, microbiology, 1970-74, assoc. prof., 1974-78, prof., 1978—, acting chmn. dept. pediatrics, 1978-79, chief sect. of pediatric infectious disease, dept. pediatrics, 1972—; vis. prof. Tri-Service Gen. Hosp. and Nat. Def. Med. Sch., Taiwan, 1980. Recipient Outstanding Pediatric Teaching award U. Kans. Med. Center, 1975, 83; diplomate Am. Bd. Pediatrics. Fellow Am. Acad. Pediatrics, Infectious Disease Soc. Am.; mem. AAAS, Am. Soc. Microbiology, Soc. Pediatric Research, Soc. Exptl. Biology and Medicine, Kans. Med. Soc., Am. Pediatric Soc., Midwest Pediatric Research Soc., Am. Soc. Virology, Kaohsiung Med. Coll. Alumni Assn. Am. (pres. 1978). Am. Co-author: Pediatric Infectious Diseases; author articles on virology and infectious diseases. Home: 10215 Howe Ln Leawood KS 66206 Office: Dept Pediatrics U Kans Med Center Kansas City KS 66103

CHOATE, JERRY RONALD, zoology educator; b. Bartlesville, Okla., Mar. 21, 1943; s. C.W. and Alyce Joyce (Cox) Marks; m. Rosemary Fidelis Walker, Apr. 13, 1963; 1 child, Judd Randolph. B.A., Pittsburg State U., 1965; Ph.D., U. Kans., 1969. Asst. prof. zoology U. Conn., Storrs, 1969-71; lectr. Yale U., New Haven, Conn., 1970; asst. prof. Fort Hays State U., Hays, Kans., 1971-76, assoc. prof., 1976-80, prof., 1980—, dir. mus., 1980—. Author: Mammals of the Plains States, 1985. Contbr. articles to profl. jours. Numerous grants from fed. and state agencies and pvt. orgns., 1961—. Mem. Am. Soc. Mammalogists (trustee 1984—), Southwestern Assn. Naturalists, Assn. Systematics Collections. Avocation: fishing. Home: RR1 Victoria KS 67671 Office: Fort Hays State Mus Fort Hays State U Hays KS 67601

CHODOS, DALE DAVID JEROME, physician, pharmaceutical company executive; b. Mpls., June 5, 1928; s. John H. and Elvera Isabella (Lundberg) C.; A.B., Carroll Coll., Helena Mont., 1950; M.D., St. Louis U., 1954; m. Joyce Annette Smith, Sept. 8, 1951; children—John, Julie, David, Jennifer. Intern, U. Utah, Salt Lake City, 1954-55, resident in pediatrics, 1955-57, NIH fellow in endocrinology and metabolism, 1957-58; practice medicine specializing in pediatrics, Idaho Falls, Idaho, 1958-62; staff physician Upjohn Co., Kalamazoo, 1962-64, head clin. pharmacology, 1964-65, research mgr. clin. pharmacology, 1965-68, research mgr. clin. services, 1968-73, group research mgr. med. therapeutics, 1973-81, med. dir. domestic med. affairs, 1981—; chief pediatrics Latter-day Saints Hosp., Sacred Heart Hosp., Idaho Falls, 1962; chmn. med. relations operating com. Nat. Pharm. Council, 1977-80, med. sect. steering com. 1977—, chmn., 1984-85. Bd. dirs. Family Service Center, Kalamazoo, 1965-71. Served with AUS, 1945-46. Recipient W.E. Upjohn award for Excellence, 1969, Physician's Recognition award, AMA, 1969, 73, 76, 79, 82; diplomate Am. Bd. Pediatrics. Fellow Am. Acad. Pediatrics; mem. Am. Soc. Clin. Pharmacology and Therapeutics, Am. Coll. Clin. Toxicology, AMA. Contbr. articles to med. and pharm. jours. Home: 619 Aqua View Dr Kalamazoo MI 49009 Office: 7000 Portage Rd Kalamazoo MI 49001

CHOI, YUNG-IN, physician; b. Seoul, May 18, 1942; came to U.S. 1969, naturalized, 1977; s. Myung Jin Choi and Keum Joo Lee; m. Sohee Khang, Sept. 30, 1968; children—Peter, Paul, Amy. Student Yonsei U., Seoul, 1963, M.D., 1967. Diplomate Am. Bd. Internal Medicine, Am. Bd. Endocrinology and Metabolism. Intern Yonsei U., Severance Hosp., Seoul, 1967-68, Ellis Hosp., Schenectady, 1969-70; resident Henry Ford Hosp., Detroit, 1970-72, fellow in endocrinology, 1972-73; fellow in typertension and hyperlipidemia, Univ. Hosp., Ann Arbor, Mich., 1973; attending physician Meml. Med. Ctr. Western Mich., Ludington, 1974—. Mem. AMA, ACP. Home: 1201 Kenowa Dr Ludington MI 49431 Office: Meml Med Ctr 12 Atkinson Dr Ludington MI 49431

CHOICE, MICHAEL JOHN, securities exec.; b. Chgo., Sept. 12, 1942; s. Herbert John and Josephine (DeVoto) C.; B.A., Beloit Coll., 1965; M.B.A., Roosevelt U., 1969; m. Nancy Lamson, July 10, 1965; 1 dau., Cynthia. Group div. underwriting supr. Continental Casualty Co., Chgo., 1965-70; asst. v.p. Merrill Lynch, Pierce, Fenner & Smith, Inc., Chgo., 1970—. Mem. United Ch. Christ. Home: 136 Linden Ave Elmhurst IL 60126 Office: 33 W Monroe Chicago IL 60603

CHOICH, RUDOLPH, JR., pharmacist, educator; b. Ambridge, Pa., Mar. 14, 1945; s. Rudolph and Mary Magdalene (Zgainer) C.; m. Joann Vulich, Apr. 11, 1970; 1 child, Jennifer Ashley. B.S. in Pharmacy, Duquesne U., 1968; M.S., U. Iowa, 1973; M.B.A., Butler U., 1985. Registered pharmacist. Asst. dir. pharmacy Ind. U. Hosps., Indpls. 1973-76, dir. pharmacy, 1976—; affiliate asst. prof. Purdue U. Sch. Pharmacy, West Lafayette, Ind., 1973—; symposium faculty Pfi Pharmecs Corp., Dallas, 1984. Contbr. articles to profl. jours. Lectr. Drug Abuse Awareness Program, Indpls. Pub. Schs., 1982-83. Served with U.S. Army, 1969-71. Mem. Am. Soc. Hosp. Pharmacists, Am. Pharm. Assn., Ind. Soc. Hosp. Pharmacists (pres. 1979, Past Pres. award 1980, Hosp. Pharmacist of Yr. 1984), Rho Chi. Roman Catholic. Lodge: Lions. Avocations: racquetball, music, gardening. Home: 7558 Lindsay Dr Indianapolis IN 46224

CHOJNACKI, MATTHEW JOHN, educational administrator; b. Youngstown, Ohio, Mar. 11, 1945; s. Max and Eleanor (Reichert) C.; m. Carolyn Sue Sevasko, Aug. 20, 1966; children—Sharon, Matthew John. B.S. in Edn., Ohio U., 1962-67, M.Ed., 1970. Tchr. pub. high schs., Ohio, 1967-73; asst. prin., adminstrv. asst. Hubbard High Sch., Ohio, 1973-75, prin., 1983—; prin. Reed Middle Sch., Hubbard, 1975-83; mem. prins. adv. com. Kent State U., Ohio, 1983—. Mem. Ohio Assn. Secondary Sch. Adminstrns., Phi Delta Kappa. Republican. Roman Catholic. Lodge: Lions (pres. Hubbard 1984—). Avocations: car restoration, family travel. Home: 170 Maple Leaf Dr Hubbard OH 44425 Office: Hubbard High Sch 350 Hall Ave Hubbard OH 44425

CHOO, YEOW MING, lawyer; b. Johore Bahru, Malaysia, Aug. 1, 1953; s. Far Tong and Kim Fong (Wong) C.; LL.B. with honors, U. Malaya, 1977; LL.M., Harvard U., 1979; J.D., Chgo.-Kent Coll., 1980. Admitted to Malaysia bar, 1977, Ill. bar, 1980; lectr. law U. Malaya Law Sch., Kuala Lumpur, Malaysia, 1977-78, Monash U. Law Sch., Melbourne, Australia, 1978; internat. atty. Standard Oil Co. (Ind.), Chgo., 1979-82; partner firm Anderson, Liu and Choo, Chgo., 1982-84; ptnr. Baer Marks and Upham, N.Y.C., 1984—; dir. Harvard Bros. Internat. Corp.; Boston; chmn. tax subcom. Nat. Council for US-China Trade, 1980—. Mem. Am. Mining Congress (alt. mem. com. on law of sea 1980-82), ABA, Ill. Bar Assn., Chgo. Bar Assn., Malayan Bar Council, U.S. Chess Fedn., Harvard Law Sch. Alumni Assn. Club: Harvard. Home: 1181 Capodanno Blvd Staten Island NY 10306 Office: 33 N Dearborn St Chicago IL 60602 also 805 3d Ave New York NY 10022

CHOPRA, DHARAM VIR, statistics educator; b. Jalandhar, Panjab, India, Oct. 15, 1930; s. Achhru and Vidya Wati (Sondhi) C.; m. Miran Devi Suri, Jan. 1969; 1 child, Sandeep K. M.A., Panjab U., 1953; M.S., U. Mich., 1961, M.A., 1963; Ph.D., U. Nebr., 1968. Lectr. math D.A.V. Coll., Jalandhar, 1953-59; lectr. math M. Tech. Inst., Jalandhar, India, 1954-55; instr. math U. Nebr., Lincoln, 1963-66; asst. prof. So. Colo. State U., Pueblo, 1966-67; asst. prof. stats. Wichita State U., 1967-71, assoc. prof., 1971-76, prof., 1976—. Contbr. articles to profl. jours. Mem. Am. Statis. Assn., Inst. Math. Stats., Internat. Assn. Survey Statisticians, Indian Math. Soc., Indian Statis. Assn. Avocations: hiking; travel. Office: Wichita State U Dept Math and Stats Wichita KS 67208

CHOU, CHEN-LIN, geochemist; b. Kiangsu, China, Oct. 8, 1943; came to U.S., 1966; s. Yun-Chang and Yu-Ying (Liu) C.; m. Susan S. Wen, June 14, 1970; children—Cynthia, Peter. B.S., Nat. Taiwan U., 1965; Ph.D., U. Pitts., 1971. Postdoctoral scholar UCLA, 1971-72, asst. research geochemist, 1972-75; sr. research assoc. U. Toronto (Ont., Can.), 1975, asst. research prof., 1976-79; postdoctoral fellow McMaster U., Hamilton, Ont., Can., 1979-80; lectr. Calif. State U., Fullerton, 1973-74; asst. geologist Ill. State Geol. Survey, Champaign, 1980-84, assoc. geologist, 1984—. Andrew Mellon fellow, 1967-68; recipient Nininger award Ariz. State U., 1971. Mem. Internat. Assn. Geochemistry and Cosmochemistry, Geol. Soc. Am., Geochem. Soc., Mineral. Soc. Am., Am. Geophys. Union, Meteoritical Soc. Home: 3007 Valley Brook Dr Champaign IL 61821 Office: Ill State Geol Survey 615 E Peabody Dr Champaign IL 61820

CHOU, DAVID HUNG-EN, food scientist; b. Nantou, Taiwan, Dec. 2, 1940; s. Chien-tsai and Shin (Chen) C.; B.S., Nat. Taiwan U., 1966; M.S., U. Minn., 1970, Ph.D., 1973; m. Shuh-Mei Chen, Sept. 18, 1969; children—Cindy, Henry. Research asst., Nat Taiwan U., 1967-68; research asst. U. Minn., 1968-71, research fellow, 1971-73; project leader Ralston Purina Co., St. Louis, 1973-76, sr. project leader, 1976-78, assoc. scientist, 1978-81, scientist, 1981-82, mgr., 1982—. Served to 2d lt. Nationalist Chinese Army, 1966-67. Mem. Chinese Agrl. Chemistry Assn., Inst. Food Technologist, Am. Assn. Cereal Chemists, Soc. Rheology, Am. Chem. Soc., Assn. Chinese Food Scientists and Technologists in Am. (v.p. 1978-79, pres. 1979-80), Sigma Xi, Gamma Sigma Delta. Club: American Formosan. Home: 1024 Van Dyke Dr St Louis MO 63011 Office: Checkerboard Sq St Louis MO 63188

CHOUKAS, NICHOLAS CHRIS, dental educator; b. Chgo., Sept. 5, 1923; s. Chris and Ethel (George) C.; student Wright Jr. Coll., 1941-43, U. Chgo., 1943-44; D.D.S., Loyola U., Chgo., 1950, M.S. in Oral Anatomy, 1958; m. LaVerne Tumosa, Apr. 19, 1951; children—Janet Lynn, Chris Nicholas, Michael John, Nicholas Chris. Fellow in oral surgery Loyola U., 1953; resident in oral surgery Cook County Hosp., Chgo., 1954, 55; practice specializing in oral and maxillofacial surgery, Elmwood Park, Ill., 1956—; asst. prof. Loyola U. Dental Sch., 1957-64, asso. prof., 1964—, chmn. dept. oral and maxillofacial surgery, 1962-83, asso. prof. oral biology Grad. Sch., 1968-69, prof. dept. oral biology, 1969—, prof. dept. oral and maxillofacial surgery, 1969—; attending oral surgeon Hines (Ill.) VA Hosp., 1958-60; asso. attending surgeon Cook county Hosp., 1959-62; cons. VA Hosp., Hines, Ill., 1960—. Served to lt. (j.g.), USNR, 1951-53. Research grantee NIH, 1961, 62, 63. Diplomate Am. Bd. Oral and Maxillofacial Surgery. Fellow Internat. Assn. Oral Surgeons, Am. Coll. Dentists, Inst. Medicine Chgo., Pan Am. Med. Assn., Internat. Coll. Dentists, Internat. Assn. Maxillofacial Surgeons, Am. Coll. Stomatologic Surgeons; mem. Chgo. Soc. Oral Surgeons, Am. Soc. Oral Surgeons, Odontographic Soc., Logan Brophy Meml. Soc., Sigma Xi, Omicron Kappa Upsilon, Delta Sigma Delta. Contbr. articles to profl. jours. Home: 230 Oakdene Rd Barrington Hills IL 60010 Office: 7310 North Ave Elmwood Park IL 60635 also 800 Main St Antioch IL 60002

CHOWDHURY, ASHOK KUMAR, economics educator, researcher; b. West Bengal, India, Aug. 15, 1951; came to U.S., 1980; s. Haradhan and Jyotsna C.; m. Shipra Sikdar, Aug. 12, 1978; 1 son, Soumen. B.Sc. in Agr. and Animal Husbandry with honors, G.B. Pant U. of Agr. and Tech., Pantnagar, India, 1973; M.Sc., Indian Agrl. Research Inst., New Delhi, 1975; Ph.D., Iowa State U., 1980. Research assoc. Ctr. Agrl. and Rural Devel., Iowa State U., Ames, 1978-80, vis. asst. prof., summer 1981; asst. prof. econs. Mankato (Minn.) State U., 1980-83, assoc. prof., 1983—. G.B. Pant U. Agr. and Tech. scholar, 1972-73; Indian Agrl. Research Inst. jr. fellow, 1973-75. Mem. Am. Econs. Assn., Am. Agrl. Econs. Assn., Midwest Econs. Assn., Sigma Xi, Gamma Sigma Delta. Author books, the most recent being: An Analysis of the Government Operated Reserve Program For U.S. Crop Commodities Under Various Export Situations for 1980-1990, 1985. 1981; An Analysis of the Government-Operated Reserve Program for U.S. Crop Commodities Under Various Export Situations for 1980-1990, 1985. Home: 151 Bermuda Dr Mankato MN 56001 Office: Box 14 Econs Dept Mankato State U Mankato MN 56001

CHOYKE, ARTHUR DAVIS, JR., luminous ceiling company executive; b. N.Y.C., Mar. 13, 1919; s. Arthur Davis and Lillian (Bauer) C.; A.B., Columbia, 1939, B.S., 1940; m. Phyllis May Ford, Aug. 18, 1945; children—Christopher Ford, Tyler Van. With indsl. engring. dept. Procter & Gamble Co., S.I., N.Y., 1940-43; instr. Pratt Inst., Bklyn., 1942-45; chief indsl. engr. M & M, Ltd., Newark, 1943-47; partner Ford Distbg. Co., Chgo., 1947-57; incorporator, pres., treas., dir. Artcrest Products Co., Inc., Chgo., 1951—; dir. Gallery Series, Harper Sq. Press. Clubs: Exec., Chgo. Farmers, Arts (Chgo.). Home: 29 E Division St Chicago IL 60610 Office: 401 W Ontario St Chicago IL 60610

CHOYKE, PHYLLIS MAY FORD (MRS. ARTHUR DAVIS CHOYKE, JR.), ceiling systems co. exec.; b. Buffalo, Oct. 25, 1921; d. Thomas Cecil and Vera (Buchanan) Ford; B.S. summa cum laude (Bonbright scholar), Northwestern U., 1942; m. Arthur Davis Choyke, Jr., Aug. 18, 1945; children—Christopher Ford, Tyler Van. Reporter, City News Bur., Chgo., 1942-43, Met. sect. Chgo. Tribune, 1943-44; feature writer OWI, N.Y.C., 1944-45; sec. corp. Artcrest Products Co., Inc., Chgo., 1958—, v.p., 1964—, founder-dir. Harper Sq. Press div., 1966—. Mem. Soc. Midland Authors, Chgo. Press Vets. Assn., Phi Beta Kappa. Club: Arts (Chgo.); John Evans (Northwestern U.). Author: (under name Phyllis Ford) (with others) (poetry) Apertures to Anywhere, 1979; editor: Gallery Series One, Poets, 1967; Gallery Series Two, Poets—Poems of the Inner World, 1968; Gallery Series Three—Poets: Levitations and Observations, 1970; Gallery Series Four, Poets-I am Talking About Revolution, 1973; Gallery Series Five/Poets—To An Aging Nation (with occult overtones), 1977; (manuscripts and papers in Brown U. Library). Home: 29 E Division St Chicago IL 60610 Office: 401 W Ontario St Chicago IL 60610

CHRAPKOWSKI, ROSEMARIE, chemical dependence therapist, art therapist; b. Chgo., Dec. 8, 1935; d. Andrew H. and Charlotte D. (Poterackie) C. B.F.A., U. Chgo. and Sch. Art Inst. Chgo., 1959, postgrad., 1962-63, 78; student Inst. Psychiatry, Chgo., Inst. Psychoanalysis, Chgo., Central States Inst. Addiction; grad. alcoholism counselor tng. program Grant Hosp., Chgo., 1981. Cert. alcoholism counselor, Ill.; cert sr. addictions counselor, Ill. Artist various studios and agys., from 1963; staff artist Soc. for Visual Edn., Chgo., 1965-66; assoc. dir. sketchwriting dept. Marquis Pub. Co., Chgo., 1967-68; supr. picture acquisitions Ency. Brit., Inc., Chgo., 1969-71; alcoholism counselor U. Ill. Alcohol Program, Chgo., 1978; sr. chem. dependence counselor Northwestern Meml. Hosp. Inst. Psychiatry, Chgo., 1979—; pvt. practice therapy, Chgo., 1981—; art therapist Northwestern Hosp., 1982—; exhibited paintings various galleries, from 1958. Mem. Ill. Alcoholism Counselors Assn., Ill. Art Therapy Assn., Chgo. Assn. Psychoanalytic Psychology (assoc.), Assn. Transpersonal Psychology, C.G. Jung Inst., Alumni Assn. Sch. Art Inst. Chgo. (life).

CHRASTIL, ROGER ARTHUR, housing adminstrator; b. Hastings, Nebr., May 22, 1948; s. Clarence Charles and Doris Marie (Debban) C.; m. Mary Lois Markowicz, Aug. 30, 1969; children—Michael J., Rachel A., Elizabeth R. B.A. with honors, Ind. U., 1970; M.A., U. Wash., 1972. Researcher The Rand Corp., South Bend, Ind., 1974; certification supr. The Housing Allowance Office, South Bend, 1974-82, chief client services, 1982—; com. mem. Northeast Neighborhood Housing Services, South Bend, 1983-84. Author poetry, short stories, one-act play. Bd. dirs. Writers and Other Troubadours, South Bend, 1983-84; coach Chet Waggoner Little League, South Bend, 1984. Recipient Meritorious Service award Housing Allowance Office, South Bend, 1980, 81, Cert. Nan McKay and Assocs., Mpls., 1982. Mem. Nat. Assn. Housing and Redevel. Ofcls., Am. Mgmt. Assn., St. Joseph County Agy. Breakfasts. Democrat. Lutheran. Club: Ind. U.Alumni (Bloomington and St. Joseph County) (life). Avocations: writing; jogging; music; reading. Home: 1527 E Colfax Ave South Bend IN 46617 Office: Housing Allowance Office Inc 425 N Michigan Ave PO Box 1558 South Bend IN 46634

CHRISOPULOS, JOHN, food service specialist; b. Oak Park, Ill., Jan. 5, 1946; s. Harry and Nicolette (Kappos) C.; student DePaul U., 1964-65; cert., Washburne Trade Sch., 1968; m. Pamela Sue Towsley, Sept. 17, 1978; 1 dau., Amanda Lynn. Sous-chef Racquet Club of Chgo., 1968-69; food service dir. Szabo Food Service, Chgo., 1970-71; owner Markon's Restaurant and Delicatessen, Chgo., 1971-74; mgr. food service Northwestern Meml. Hosp., Chgo., 1974; dir. food service Holy Family Hosp., Des Plaines, Ill., 1975-78; pres. Connoisseurs Caterers, Inc., Barrington, Ill., 1978-82; dir. food services Westlake Community Hosp., Melrose Park, Ill., 1979-80; assoc. dir. food and nutrition service U. Chgo. Med. Center, 1980-82; food service specialist John Sexton & Co., Elk Grove Village, Ill., 1982—. Recipient Pres.'s Club award, 1984. Mem. Am. Soc. Hosp. Food Service Adminstrs. (bd. dirs. 1975-76, chmn. 10th annual ednl. conf. 1977, pres.-elect 1977, pres. 1978, mem. nat. nominating com. 1978), Internat. Food Service Execs. Assn., Catering Execs. Club. Am. Greek Orthodox. Home: 1330 Chalfont Dr Schaumburg IL 60194 Office: 1099 Pratt Blvd Elk Grove Village IL 60007

CHRISTEN, ARDEN GALE, dental educator, researcher, consultant; b. Lemmon, S.D., Jan. 25, 1932; s. Harold John Christen and Dorothy Elizabeth (Taylor) Deering; m. Joan Ardell Akre, Sept. 10, 1955; children—Barbara, Penny, Rebecca, Sarah. B.S., U. Minn., 1954, D.D.S., 1956; M.S.D., Ind. U., 1965; M.A., Ball State U., 1973. Lic. dentist S.D., Minn., Ind. Commd. 1st lt. U.S. Air Force, 1956, advanced through grades to col., 1972; base dental surgeon Zaragoza Air Base, Spain, 1970-73; dental surgeon, cons. preventive dentistry RAF Bentwaters, Eng., 1973-75; air force preventive dentistry officer Sch. Aerospace Medicine, Brooks AFB, Tex., 1978-80; prof., chmn. dept. preventive dentistry Ind. U., Indpls., 1981—; sr. med. service cons. Surgeon Gen., U.S. Air Force, U.S. and Eng., 1974-80; spl. cons. to asst. surgeon gen. for dental services, Washington, 1975-80. Co-author: Primary Preventive Dentistry, 1986. Contbr. numerous articles to profl. jours. Bd. dirs. Bexar County chpt. Am. Cancer Soc., San Antonio, 1976-80, Marion County chpt., Indpls., 1980—; mem. Ind. div. Pub. Edn. Standing Com., Indpls., 1980. Decorated Service medal with 2 oak leaf clusters; Legion of Merit. Fellow Am. Coll. Dentists; mem. ADA, Am. Acad. Oral Pathology, Internat. Assn. Dental Research, Am. Acad. History of Dentistry (v.p. 1984-85). Democrat. Lutheran. Avocations: photography; classical music; travel; jogging. Home: 7112 Sylvan Ridge Rd Indianapolis IN 46240 Office: Oral Health Research Inst Ind U Sch Dentistry 415 Lansing St Indianapolis IN 46202-2876

CHRISTENSEN, TIMOTHY LEE, electric cooperative executive; b. Des Moines, July 28, 1944; s. Leo Donald and Mildred (Daggy) C.; 1 child, Kristie Rae. Student, U.S. Dept. Agr. Grad. Sch., 1970-71, Superior Tech. Sch., 1970, U. Wis. Extension-Madison, 1975. Acct., Head of the Lakes Coop., Superior, Wis., 1968-71; office mgr. Eau Claire Elec. Coop., Fall Creek, Wis., 1971-73; asst. mgr. Price Electric Coop., Phillips, Wis., 1973-76; exec. v.p., gen. mgr. Cedar Valley Elec. Coop., St. Ansgar, Iowa, 1976-83; exec. v.p., gen. mgr. Ill. Valley Elec. Coop., Princeton, 1983—; dir. Soyland Power Coop., Decatur, Ill., 1983—. Organizer, Phillips Youth Activities, 1975; bd. dirs. St. Ansgar C. of C., 1977-83. Served with USAF, 1962-65. Mem. Am. Legion, Phillips C. of C. (sec. 1976), Wis. REC Office Mgrs. Assn. (pres. 1971-76). Lodges: Lions, Elks. Office: Ill Valley Electric Coop Inc PO Box 70 Princeton IL 61356

CHRISTENSEN, CHERRYL JUNE, physician; b. Muscatine, Iowa, June 7, 1948; d. Wildon Wayne and Lillian June (Hurlburt) H.; m. Doran Michael Christensen, Feb. 14, 1975; children—Julia Anna, Vasthi. B.S. in Pharmacy, U. Iowa, 1971; D.O., Coll. Osteo. Medicine and Surgery, 1975. Head health evaluation occupational medicine service Navy Environ. Health Ctr., Norfolk, Va., 1979-82; occupational and environ. medicine physician U. Cin., 1982—; pres. Occupational and Environ. Medicine Cons., Cin. Contbr. articles to profl. jours. Mem. AMA, Am. Occupational Med. Assn., Am. Pub. Health Assn., Am. Osteo. Assn. Lutheran. Home: 8249 Shadybrook Dr West Chester OH 45069 Office: Univ Cin Med Ctr ML 705 Cincinnati OH 45267

CHRISTENSEN, DONN DOUGLAS, lawyer; b. St. Paul, June 30, 1929; s. Jonas Jergen and Hildur Minerva (Lundeen) C.; B.S., U. Minn., 1950, LL.B., 1952; m. Renee E. Pinet, Aug. 31, 1970; children—Keith, Catherine, Eric. Admitted to Minn. bar, 1952, U.S. Fed. Ct., 1955, U.S. Supreme Ct. bar, 1981; practiced in St. Paul, 1954-68, 70—; dep. atty. gen. State of Minn., 1968-70; justice of peace, City of Mendota Heights, Minn., 1961-66; instr. bus. law Macalester Coll., St. Paul, 1960-67. Served with AUS, 1952-54. Mem. Am., Minn. (chmn. environmental law sect. 1972-73), Ramsey County bar assns., Execs. Assn. St. Paul (pres. 1966), Mendota Heights C. of C. (sec. 1965), Delta Theta Phi. Clubs: Athletic, Torch (pres. 1982-83) (St. Paul). Home: 676 Schifsky Rd Saint Paul MN 55112 Office: 155 Arden Plaza Office Saint Paul MN 55112 also North Branch MN 55056

CHRISTENSEN, JERRY MELVIN, agricultural engineer; b. Volga, S.D., May 5, 1949; s. Melvin Nicholi and Louise (Werner) C.; B.S., S.D. State U., 1972. Engr., Morton Bldgs., Spencer, Iowa, 1972-73, Morton, Ill., 1973—, livestock housing products mgr., 1981-84, design estimator, 1984—. Mem. vocat. adv. council Morton High Sch. Registered profl. engr., Ill., S.D. Mem. Am. Soc. Agrl. Engrs. Democrat. Lutheran. Home: PO Box 681 Delavan IL 61734 Office: Morton Bldgs Inc 252 W Adams St Morton IL 61550

CHRISTENSEN, MARGUERITE ALICE, librarian; b. Trout Lake, Wis., Aug. 24, 1917; d. Peter Carl and Alice (Cady) Christensen; B.A., U. Wis., 1938, B.L.S., 1939. Librarian, high sch. and Pub. Library, Bloomer, Wis., 1939-41; asst. librarian Wis. State U., Superior, 1941-43, Carroll Coll., Waukesha, Wis., 1943-45; asst. reference librarian U. Wis.-Madison, 1945-66, head gen. reference dept., 1967-82. Mem. ALA, Assn. Coll. and Research Libraries. Home: 4469 Hillcrest Dr Madison WI 53705

CHRISTENSEN, ORLA JUNE, educator, psychologist; b. Clarkfield, Minn., June 5, 1934; d. Clifford Arnold and Clara Theoline (Stokke) C.; B.A. in Health and Phys. Edn., Augsburg Coll., Mpls., 1956; M.S. in Counseling (NDEA fellow), Purdue U., 1966; Ed.D. in Counseling and Personnel Services in Higher Edn. (Delta Kappa Gamma scholar), Mont. State U., 1972. Tchr. health and phys. edn. Appleton (Minn.) Pub. Schs., 1956-58, Alexandria (Minn.) Pub. Schs., 1958-65; counselor Irvington (N.Y.) High Sch., 1966-67, Tacoma (Wash.) Pub. Schs., 1967-73; prof. ednl. psychology and human services U. S.D., Vermillion, 1973—; coordinator, internship program in ednl. psychology and counseling, participant workshops in communications, human relations, cultural awareness, career devel. Mem. Am. Psychol. Assn., Am. Am. Counseling and Devel., S.D. Assn. Counseling and Devel. (pres. elect, pres. 1983-85), Nat. Vocat. Guidance Assn., Assn. Counselor Edn., N.Am. Soc. Adlerian Psychology, Delta Kappa Gamma Internat., Phi Delta Kappa. Contbr. articles in field to profl. jours. Office: Dezell Edn Center U SD Vermillion SD 57069

CHRISTENSEN, ROGER WILLIAM, manufacturing company official; b. St. Paul, Oct. 26, 1936; s. James Einer and Helen Caroline (Giefer) C.; m. Kristine Elizabeth Skaret, Feb. 23, 1974; 1 child, Eric Joseph. B.A., U. Mankato, 1960. Mgr. Minn. Mining & Mfg. Co., St. Paul, 1962-68, corp. customer relations mgr., 1968—. Served with U.S. Army, 1960-66. Mem. Nat. Accounts Mktg. Assn., Am. Mgmt. Assn., Better Bus. Bur., Bus. Econ. Edn. Found., Am. Nat. Standards Inst., Soc. Consumer Affairs Profls. in Bus. (officer 1985—), Delta Sigma Pi. Home: 944 Transit Ave Roseville MN 55113 Office: Minn Mining & Mfg Co Saint Paul MN 55144

CHRISTENSON, CHRIS, photographer; b. Bedford, O., Nov. 13, 1925; s. Chris and Ilah (Fivecoate) C.; grad. high sch.; m. Eunice McAdoo, Sept. 1, 1957; children—Jeffrey, Joan, Susan. Photographer, Bedford Pictorial Studio, 1948-58; pres., Chris Christenson Photographer, Inc., Bedford, 1958—; track photographer, Thistledown, Randall Park, Cranwood, Summit, 1961—; staff photographer Ohio Thoroughbred mag., 1971—. Mem. Profl. Photographers Am. Home: 719 Johnson St Bedford OH 44146 Office: 39 Woodrow St Bedford OH 44146

CHRISTENSON, FABIENNE FADELEY, business executive; b. Washington, June 20, 1951; d. James McNelledge and Catherine Shirley (Sweeney) Fadeley; B.S. cum laude, U. Md., 1976; M.B.A. with honors, Boston U., 1979; m. Gordon A. Christenson, Sept. 16, 1979. With Gen. Electric Aircraft Engine Group, Evendale, Ohio, 1979—, contract adminstr., foreman, prodn. control specialist, contract adminstr., now buyer raw materials, flash welded and seamless rings for aircraft engines; pres. Mfg. Tng. Program, 1980. Home: 3465 Principio Ave Cincinnati OH 45226 Office: Mail Drop A-182C 1 Neumann Way Cincinnati OH 45215

CHRISTIAN, EDWARD KIEREN, radio station executive; b. Detroit, June 26, 1944; s. William Edward and Dorothy Miriam (Kieren) C.; student Mich. State U., 1962-64; B.A., Wayne State U., 1966, also postgrad.; M.A., Central Mich. U., 1980; m. Judith Dallaire, Nov. 21, 1966; children—Eric, Dana. Mgr., John C. Butler Co., Detroit, 1968-69; nat. sales mgr. WCAR Radio, Detroit, WSUN Radio, St. Petersburg Fla., 1969-70; v.p., gen. mgr., ptnr. WCER Radio, Charlotte, Mich., 1970-74; pres. Josephson Internat./Radio div. WNIC, WNIC-FM, Detroit, WNOR, WNOR-FM, Norfolk, Va., WVKO, WSNY-FM, Columbus, Ohio, WMGF-FM, Milw., WZKC-FM, Rochester, N.Y., 1974—; vice chmn. Mut. Broadcasting Affiliates Council, 1977-79; chmn. Arbitron Radio Adv. Council, 1978-79; bd. dirs. All Industry Music Licensing Com. Pres., United Way, Charlotte, 1973-74; del. Republican State Conv., 1974; bd. dirs. Greater Detroit Safety Council; bd. dirs. Alpha Epsilon Rho Nat. Adv. Council, 1980—. Mem. Dearborn C. of C. (dir.). Kiwanian. Home: 549 Lakeland St Grosse Pointe MI 48230 Office: 400 Renaissance Ctr Suite 2150 Detroit MI 48243

CHRISTIAN, RICHARD CARLTON, university dean, advertising executive; b. Dayton, Ohio, Nov. 29, 1924; s. Raymond A. and Louise (Gamber) C.; B.S. in Bus. Adminstrn., Miami U., Oxford, Ohio, 1948; M.B.A., Northwestern U., 1949; student Denison U., The Citadel, Biarritz Am. U.; m. Audrey Bongartz, Sept. 10, 1949; children—Ann Carra, Richard Carlton. Mktg. analyst Nat. Cash Register Co., Dayton, 1948, Rockwell Mfg. Co., Pitts., 1949-50; exec. v.p. Marsteller Inc., Chgo., 1951-60, pres., 1960-75, chmn. bd., 1975-84, chmn. emeritus, 1985—; assoc. dean Medill Sch. Journalism, Northwestern U., Evanston, Ill., 1985—; dir., chmn. Bus Publs. Audit of Circulation, Inc., 1969-75; dir. First Ill. Corp., 1st Ill. Bank; speaker, author mktg., sales mgmt., mktg. research and advt. Trustee Nat. Coll. Edn., Northwestern U., 1970-74; chmn. exec. com. James Webb Young Fund Edn., U. Ill., 1962-75; assoc. Bus. Adv. Council, Miami, U.; bd. dirs. Mus. Broadcast Communications, Bus. Press Ednl. Found. Served with inf. AUS, 1942-46; ETO. Decorated Bronze Star, Purple Heart; recipient Gov.'s award State of Ohio, 1978; 1st Disting. Service award Am. Acad. Advt., 1979, adv. council J.L. Kellogg Grad. Sch. Mgmt., Northwestern U., recipient Alumni medal, 1983. Mem. Am. Mktg. Assn. (dir. 1953-54), Indsl. Mktg. Assn. (founder, chmn. 1951), Bus./Profl. Publs. Advt. Assn. (life mem. Chgo.; pres. Chgo. 1954-55, nat. v.p. 1955-58, G.D. Crain Jr. award 1977), Northwestern U. Bus. Sch. Alumni Assn. (founder, pres.), Am. Mgmt. Assn., Am. Assn. Advt. Agys. (dir., chmn. 1976-77), Nat. Advt. Rev. Council (pres. 1976-77), Northwestern U. Alumni Assn. (nat. pres. 1968-70), Better Bus. Bur. Chgo. (council, dir.), Chgo. Assn. Commerce and Industry, Council Fgn. Relations, Alpha Delta Sigma, Beta Gamma Sigma, Delta Sigma Pi, Phi Gamma Delta. Baptist (trustee). Clubs: Sky (N.Y.C.); Chicago, Mid-America, Executives, Economic (dir., chmn. forums com.) (Chgo.); Kenilworth; Westmoreland Country (Wilmette, Ill.); Pine Valley Golf (Clementon, N.J.). Home: 132 Oxford Rd Kenilworth IL 60043 Office: Medill Sch Journalism Northwestern U 1845 Sheridan Rd Evanston IL 60201

CHRISTIANSEN, ERNEST BERT, chemical engineering educator; b. Richfield, Utah, July 31, 1910; s. Ernest Christian and Sarah (Nielsen) C.; m. Susan Mann, Sept. 6, 1935; children—David E., Gale A., Alan Grant, Philip A., Richard L., Lisa B. B.S. in Chem. Engring., U. Utah, 1937; M.S. in Chem. Engring., U. Mich., 1939, Ph.D. in Chem. Engring., 1945. Registered profl. engr., Utah. Design and project supr. E.I. duPont de Nemours, Del., 1941-46; prof. chem. engring. U. Idaho, Moscow, 1946-47; prof., chmn. chem. engring. dept. U. Utah, Salt Lake City, 1947-75, prof., 1975—; cons. various cos. Contbr. articles to profl. jours. Vice chmn. advancement com. Great Salt Lake Council Boy Scouts Am. Recipient Disting. Research award U. Utah, Salt Lake City, 1977; named Outstanding Engr., Utah Engring. Council, 1966; Utah Acad. Sci., Arts and Letters fellow, 1972. Fellow Am. Inst. Chem. Engrs. (founders award 1978, nat. dir. 1965-68, dir. Great Salt Lakes sect. 1982—). Republican. Mormon.

CHRISTIANSEN, PAUL ALGER, business exec.; b. Detroit, July 3, 1928; s. Alger Cornelius and Gladys Marie (Volz) C.; B.S., Wayne State U., 1948, M.A., 1949; postgrad. U. Minn., 1950-60, Harvard U., 1978-79; m. Irene A. Adams, July 16, 1954; children—Paul Alger II, John Adams. Instr., Va. Poly. Inst. and State U., Blacksburg, 1949-51; accountant Arthur Andersen & Co., Kansas City, Mo., 1952-55; sr. tax accountant Arthur Young & Co., Kansas City, 1956-58; prof. acctg. U. Mo., Kansas City, 1958-80; owner Paul A. Christiansen, C.P.A., Kansas City, 1958—; pres. Metal Engineered Structures, Inc., Kansas City, 1963—, Paul A. Christiansen & Co., Blue Springs, Mo., 1966—, Lake Village Corp., Blue Springs, 1975—, Oak Grove Med Center, Inc. (Mo.), 1979—. Mem. Jackson County Bond Adv. Commn., 1967-73; chmn. 4th Congl. Dist. Republican Com., 1968; mem. Jackson County Rep. Com., 1968-72; pres. Independence Rep. Club, 1968-72. Decorated King Fredrik II Medal (Norway); C.P.A., Mo. Mem. Am. Inst. C.P.A.'s, Mo. Soc. C.P.A.'s, AAUP (chpt. pres. 1964-65), Nat. Assn. Home Builders, Eastern Jackson County Builders and Developers Assn., Beta Alpha Psi. Contbr. articles to profl. jours. Home: 3333 Lake Shore Dr Blue Springs MO 64015 Office: 333 Lake Village Blvd Blue Springs MO 64015

CHRISTIANSEN, RAYMOND STEPHAN, librarian, educator; b. Oak Park, Ill., Feb. 15, 1950; s. Raymond Julius and Anne Mary (Fusek) C.; m. Phyllis Anne Dombkowski, Nov. 25, 1972; 1 child, Mark David. B.A., Elmhurst Coll., 1971; M.S. in Edn., No. Ill. U., 1974. Dept. dir. Elmhurst Coll., Ill., 1971-73; asst. law librarian media services Lewis U., Glen Ellyn, Ill., 1974-77; asst.-prof. edn. Aurora U., Ill., 1977—, media librarian, 1977-82, instructional developer, 1982—; media cons., 1977—. Author video series: Rothblatt on Criminal Advocacy, 1975; book: Index to SCOPE the UN Magazine, 1977. Mem. Assn. Ednl. Communications and Tech., Ednl. Film Library Assn. Home: 785 Gerten Ave Aurora IL 60505 Office: Aurora U Library 347 S Gladstone Aurora IL 60506

CHRISTIANSEN, RICHARD DEAN, journalist, critic; b. Berwyn, Ill., Aug. 1, 1931; s. William Edward and Louise Christine (Dethlefs) C. B.A., Carleton Coll., 1953; postgrad. Harvard U., 1953-54. Successively reporter, critic, editor arts and amusements Chgo. Daily News, 1957-73, critic-at-large, 1974-78; editor Chicagoan mag., 1973; critic-at-large Chgo. Tribune, 1978-83, entertainment editor, 1983—; cons., educator, broadcaster. Served with U.S. Army, 1955-57. Recipient Beck award for editorial excellence Chgo. Tribune, 1982. Mem. Headline Club, Sigma Delta Chi. Republican. Lutheran. Club: Arts of Chgo. (dir.). Office: 435 N Michigan Ave Chicago IL 60611*

CHRISTIANSON, ELIN BALLANTYNE, librarian, civic worker; b. Gary, Ind., Nov. 11, 1936; d. Donald B. and Dorothy May (Dunning) Ballantyne; B.A., U. Chgo., 1958, M.A., 1961, certificate advanced studies, 1974; m. Stanley David Christianson, July 25, 1959; children—Erica, David. Asst. librarian, then librarian J. Walter Thompson Co., Chgo., 1959-68; library cons., 1968-—; part-time lectr. Grad. Library Sch., U. Chgo., 1981—, Sch. Library and Info. Sci., Ind. U., 1982—. Chmn. Hobart Am. Revolution Bicentennial Commn., 1974-76; bd. dirs. Hobart Hist. Soc., 1973—, pres., 1980—; pres. LWV, Hobart, 1977-79. Recipient Laura Bracken award Hobart Jaycees, 1976; cert. achievement Ind. Am. Revolution Bicentennial Commn., 1975; Woman of Yr. award Hobart Bus. and Profl. Women, 1985. Mem. Am. Assn. Info. Sci., ALA, Ind. Library Assn., Spl. Libraries Assn. (chmn. advt. and mktg. div. 1967-68), English Spl. Libraries Assn., Assn. Library and Info. Sci. Edn., AAUW (pres. Hobart br. 1975-77), U. Chgo. Grad. Library Sch. Alumni Assn. (v.p. 1971-74, 76-77, pres. 1977-79). Unitarian. Author: Non-Professional and Paraprofessional Staff in Special Libraries, 1973; Directory of Library Resources in Northwest Indiana, 1976; Old Settlers Cemetery, 1976; New Special Libraries: A Summary of Research, 1980; Daniel Nash Handy and the Special Library Movement, 1980; co-author: Subject Headings in Advertising, Marketing and Communications Media, 1964; Special Libraries: A Guide for Management, 1981. Address: 141 Beverly Blvd Hobart IN 46342

CHRISTIANSON, RONALD PAUL, company sales manager; b. Estherville, Iowa, Apr. 13, 1944; s. Clarence and Mary Martine (Thompson) C.; m. Mary Anne Hoelzen, July 2, 1966; children—Eric Paul, Lisa Marie. B.A., U. No. Iowa, 1966, M.A. in Chemistry, 1970. Cert. tchr., Iowa. Tchr. Cedar Rapids Schs., Iowa, 1966-69, Waunakee Schs., Wis., 1970-73; salesman Benlo Chem., West Allis, Wis., 1973-75; product mgr. West Agro Chem., Shawnee Mission, Kans., 1975-79; market mgr. Klenzade, St. Paul, 1979-81; sales mgr., 1981—. Author: Sales Training Manual, 1978. Coach Youth Basketball, Rosemount, Minn., 1979-84, coach, umpire Youth Baseball, Rosemount, 1979-83. Mem. Nat. Edn. Assn. (life), Nat. Mastitis Council, Internat. Assn. Milk and Food Environ. Sanitarians, St. Paul C. of C. (membership drive, 1981-82), Waunakee Tchrs. Assn. (pres. 1972-73), Waunakee Jaycees (sec. 1972-73). Avocations: Racquet ball; golf; coin collector. Home: 13632 Elkwood Dr Apple Valley MN 55124 Office: 13th floor Osborn Bldg Saint Paul MN 55104

CHRISTIE, ADRIAN JOSEPH, pathologist; b. Cardiff, Wales, Dec. 1, 1940; s. Maxwell and Sonia (Samuel) C.; came to U.S., 1973; M.D., Welsh Nat. Sch. Medicine, 1964; m. Mynetta Ann Michaelson, Dec. 12, 1965; children—Helen, Leona, Gavin. Resident in pathology Mt. Sinai Hosp., N.Y.C., 1967-68; asst. lectr. pathology Middlesex Hosp. Med. Sch., London, 1968-69; sr. registrar Southmead Hosp., Bristol, Eng., 1970-73; pathologist Grace and I.O.D.E. hosps., Windsor, Ont., Can., 1973-75, Detroit-Macomb Hosps. Assn., Detroit, 1976, Cottage Hosp., Grosse Pointe, Mich., 1976—; clin. asst. prof. Wayne State U. Med. Sch., Detroit. Diplomate Am. Bd. Pathology. Fellow Royal Coll. Physicians and Surgeons (Can.), Am. Soc. Clin. Pathologists, Coll. Am. Pathologists, Internat. Acad. Pathology, Royal Coll. Pathologists; mem. AMA, Wayne County Med. Soc., Mich. Soc. Pathologists, N.Y. Acad. Scis. Jewish. Club: H.M.C.S. Hunter (Windsor). Author papers complications silicone joint implants. Home: 1010 W Lincoln St Birmingham MI 48009 Office: 11800 E 12 Mile Rd Warren MI 48093

CHRISTIE, WALTER SCOTT, state official; b. Indpls., 1922; s. Walter Scott and Nina Lilian (Warfel) C.; B.S. in Bus. Adminstrn., Butler U., 1948. With Roy J. Pile & Co., C.P.A.s, Indpls., 1948-56, Howard E. Nyhart Co., Inc., actuarial consultants, Indpls., 1956-62; with Ind. Dept. Ins., Indpls., 1962—, dep. commr., 1966-74, adminstrv. officer, 1974-79, sr. examiner, 1979-81, adminstrv. asst., 1981-82, chief auditor, 1982—. Bd. dirs. Delt House Corp., Butler U. Served with AUS, 1942-45. Named Ky. Col.; C.P.A., Ind.; cert. fin. examiner. Mem. Ind. Assn. C.P.A.s, Soc. Fin. Examiners (state chmn.), Indpls. Acturarial Club, Nat. Assn. Ins. Commrs. (chmn. Zone IV life and health com. 1970-75), Internat. Platform Assn. Episcopalian (assoc. vestryman 1948-60). Club: Optimist (dir.). Home: 620 E 53d St Indianapolis IN 46220 Office: 509 State Office Bldg 100 N Senate Ave Indianapolis IN 46204

CHRISTIN, VIOLET MARGUERITE, retired banker; b. Chgo., Oct. 4, 1903; d. Charles A. and Eva M. (Bosse) Christin; student Northwestern U., 1936-37, Am. Inst. Banking, 1955-75; Ph.D., Colo. State Christian Coll. With Nat. Bank Austin, 1922-76, asst. sec., 1953-57, sec., 1957-65, sec., asst. v.p., 1965-75, also cons., sec. mktg. com., 1977-79. Mem. Am. Inst. Banking, Ill. Bankers Assn. (50 yr. club), Assn. Chgo. Bank Women, Nat. Assn. Bank Women, Ill. Group. Nat. Assn. Bank Women, Chgo. Financial Advertisers (life mem.; Eagle award 1977, dir., treas.; First Lady Life Mem. award 1981). Clubs: Executives, Advertising, Press (Chgo.). Home: 805 N Grove Ave Oak Park IL 60302

CHRISTISON, WILLIAM HENRY, III, lawyer; b. Moline, Ill., Aug. 30, 1936; s. William Henry and Gladys Evelyn (Matherly) C.; B.A., Northwestern U., 1958; LL.B., U. Iowa, 1961; m. Mary Proctor Stone, Sept. 16, 1958; children—William Henry IV, Elizabeth S., Caroline S. Admitted to Ill. bar, 1961, Iowa bar; partner firm Baymiller, Christison & Radley, Peoria, Ill., 1961—; permanent trustee in bankruptcy U.S. Dist. Ct., So. Dist. of Ill., Peoria, 1967—. Vice pres., dir. W.H.C., Inc., Moline, 1958—; dir., mem. exec. com., trust investment com. 1st Nat. Bank, Peoria, 1967—; dir. A. Lucas Steel Co., First Nat. Bank Metamora. Mem. Peoria Sesquicentennial Commn., 1968. Bd. dirs. John C. Proctor Endowment, 1964—, pres. 1972—; bd. dirs. Meth. Med. Center Found., Ill. Masonic Youth Found., 1976-82; trustee Meth. Med. Ctr. of Ill. Mem. Am., Ill. (dist. sec. 1966), Iowa, Peoria (dir. 1968-69) bar assns., Greater Peoria Legal Aid Soc. (dir. 1971-74), Peoria Hist. Soc., Phi Gamma Delta, Phi Delta Phi. Clubs: Masons, Shriners (potentate 1984), Jesters, Rotary (dir. 1972-75, pres. 1979-80), Country (Peoria). Home: 3217 W Prince George Ct Peoria IL 61615 Office: 700 1st Nat Bank Bldg Peoria IL 61602

CHRISTMAN, LUTHER PARMALU, educational administrator; b. Summit Hill, Pa., Feb. 26, 1915; m. Dorothy Mary Black; children—Gary James, Judith Ann Christman Kinney, Lillian Jane. Diploma, Pa. Hosp. Sch., Phila., 1939; B.S. in Nursing, Temple U., Phila., 1948, Ed.M. in Clin. Psychology, 1952; Ph.D. in Sociology and Anthropology, Mich. State U., 1965; D.H.L. (hon.), Thomas Jefferson U., 1980. R.N., Pa., Tenn., Ill., S.D. Prof. sociology Coll. Arts and Sci., Vanderbilt U., Nashville, 1967-72; dir. nursing Vanderbilt U. Hosp., Nashville, 1967-72; prof. sociology Rush U., Chgo., 1976—; dean Coll. Nursing, Rush Presbyterian-Saint Luke's Med. Ctr., Chgo., 1972—, v.p. nursing, 1972—. N.Z. Nurses' Edn. and Research Found. fellow, 1978; recipient Edith Moore Copeland Founders' award for Creativity, Sigma Theta Tau, 1981. Mem. Am. Assn. Colls. Nursing, Am. Nurses Assn. (3d v.p. 1966-68), Inst. Medicine, Acad. Scis., Hear Internat (chmn. bd. dirs. 1978-83), Nat. Com. Study Nursing and Nursing Edn. Unitarian. Office: Rush-Presbyn-Saint Luke's Med Ctr 600 S Paulina #474 H Chicago IL 60612

CHRISTOFFERSEN, ARTHUR LYNN, insurance holding company executive; b. Maquoketa, Iowa, Nov. 20, 1946; s. Frank Sorne and Frances Leona (Fayram) C.; m. Theresa Ann Seng, June 6, 1970; children—Dawn, Eric. A.A. magna cum laude, Eastern Iowa U., 1970; B.B.A., U. Iowa, 1972. C.P.A., Iowa. Tax acct. Touche Ross & Co., Mpls., 1972-75; tax dir. Life Investors, Cedar Rapids, Iowa, 1975-81, v.p., sec., 1981-83, exec. v.p., 1983—; dir. Leaseamerica Corp., Cedar Rapids, Electronic Tech. Corp., Life Investors Ins. Co. Am. Served with AUS, 1966-68; Ger. Mem. Iowa C.P.A. Soc., Am. Soc. C.P.A.s, Iowa C.P.A. Fed. Tax Com., Iowa Life Ins. Assn. (steering com. 1983), Cedar Rapids C. of C. (bd. dirs. 1983—, treas. 1984-85), Nat. Assn. O-T-C Cos. (bd. dirs., sec.). Republican. Roman Catholic. Club: Jaycees. Home: 810 E Main St Marion IA 52302 Office: Life Investors Inc PO Box 1447 Cedar Rapids IA 52499

CHRISTOPHER, NORMAN FRANKLIN, engineer; b. Irvine, Ky., Sept. 23, 1930; s. Thomas Ashcraft and Anna Maude (Turner) C.; m. Jane Anne Dean, June 16, 1952; children—Paula, Phyllis. B.A., Ky. Wesleyan Coll., 1952; M.S., Ohio U., 1969. Shift chemist Liberty Powder Def. Corp., Baraboo, Wis., 1952-54; shift supr. Goodyear Atomic Corp., Piketon, Ohio, 1954-57, sect. head mass spectrometry dept., 1957-79, asst. gen. mgrs.' staff, 1979-81, supr. mass spectrometry dept., 1982-84, supr. nuclear materials engring., 1984—. Mem. Inst. Nuclear Material Mgmt. Home: 406 S Market St Waverly OH 45690 Office: PO Box 628 Piketon OH 45661

CHRISTOPHER, PAMELA JOY, nurse; b. Lake City, Iowa, Feb. 25, 1957; d. Harold Allen and Myra Joy (Roseke) Christopher. B.A. in Nursing, Luther Coll., Decorah, Iowa, 1980. R.N., Iowa. Nurse aide Aase Haugen Homes, Decorah, 1979-80; staff nurse pediatrics U. Iowa Hosps. and Clinics, Iowa City, 1980-81; staff nurse orthopedics Mercy Hosp. Med. Ctr., Des Moines, 1981—. Lutheran. Home: PO Box 94012 Des Moines IA 50394 Office: Mercy Hosp Med Ctr 6th and University Des Moines IA 50314

CHRISTOPHERSON, WESTON, banker; b. Walum, N.D., May 5, 1925; s. Carl and Ermie (Larsen) C.; B.S., U. N.D., 1949, J.D., 1951; m. Myrna Christensen, June 8, 1951; children—Mia Karen, Mari Louisa, Kari Marie. Admitted to N.D. bar, 1951, Ill. bar, 1952; with Jewel Cos., Inc., Chgo., 1951-84, pres., 1970-80, Chief exec. officer, 1979-84, chmn. bd. 1980-84, also dir.; chmn. bd., dir., chief exec. officer No. Trust Co., 1984—, No. Trust Corp., 1984—; dir. Ameritech, Quaker Oats Co., Borg-Warner, GATX Corp. Bd. dirs. McCormick Theol. sem.; trustee U. Chgo.; mem. Chgo. Com., Chgo. United, Met. Chgo. United Way/Crusade of Mercy Mem. Northwestern U. Assocs., Bus. Council, U. Ill. Found. Presbyterian. Clubs: Economic, Chicago, Casino, Onwentsia, Old Elm, Commercial, Commonwealth. Office: No Trust Co 50 S LaSalle St Chicago IL 60675*

CHRISTY, LARRY WAYNE, telecommunications company official; b. Vincennes, Ind., June 11, 1948; s. Grover Lee and Dorothy Viola (Hamilton) C.; m. Marie, Aug. 5, 1966; children—Larry Wayne II, Austin Troy. Student schs., St. Francisville, Ill. Installation technician G.T.E. Automatic Electric, North Lake, Ill., 1967-79; central office supr. Continental Telecommunications Ind., Scottsburg, 1979-81, specialist/studies, Seymour, 1981-82; nat. project mgr. Telesphere Network, Rolling Meadows, Ill., 1983; v.p. Switching Nastran, Allen, Tex., 1983—. Home: 930 Sycamore Ln Bartlett IL 60103 Office: Nastran 538 Northridge Allen TX 75002

CHRON, GUSTAV NICHOLAS, principal; b. Chgo., June 6, 1926; s. Nicholas Constantine and Jennie (Athans) C.; B.A., DePaul U., 1952; M.A., Northwestern U., 1954; B.A. in Aeros., Stanton U., 1965, Ph.D., 1976; M.Ed., Loyola U., Chgo., 1969; J.D. (hon.), Clinton U., 1971; D.Phil., Met. Coll. Inst., London, 1974; m. Helen Hoegerl, Sept. 18, 1948; children—Edward, Karen, Timothy. Mem. staff Chgo. Better Bus. Bur., 1954-58; tchr. Northbrook (Ill.) elem. schs., 1958-60, Northbrook Jr. High Sch., 1960-63, Glenbrook South High Sch., Glenview, Ill., 1963-64; adminstrv. asst. Comsat div. trust dept. Continental Ill. Nat. Bank, Chgo., 1964-65; prin. Westmoor Sch., Northbrook, 1966-—; dir. Northbrook Dist. 28 Summer Sch., 1971, 77; asst. prof. aeros. Grad. Research Inst., East Coast U., 1975-79. Mem. adv. bd. Am. Security Council. Served with USNR, 1943-46, 52, 63-64. Decorated Air medal, Purple Heart, Navy Commendation medal, Legion of Merit, Bronze Star; named to Aviation Hall of Fame. Mem. Nat., Ill. sch. prins. assns., Am. Security Council, Navy League, Navy Inst., Am. Legion, Assn. Naval Aviation, Tailhook Assn., Am. Mil. Inst., Nat. Rifle Assn., Am. Def. Preparedness Assn., Vets. OSS, Assn. Former Intelligence Officers, Nat. Intelligence Study Center, Internat. Naval Research Orgn., Am. Hist. Found., U.S. Naval Acad. Found., Am. Ednl. Research Assn., U.S. Parachute Assn., 82d Airborne Div. Assn., Aerospace Edn. Assn., Nat. Eagle Scout Assn., Air Force Assn., Am. Philatelic Soc., Phi Delta Kappa, Delta Theta Phi, Pi Gamma Mu. Club: Moose. Home: Chicago IL Office: 2500 Cherry Ln Northbrook IL 60062

CHRONIC, JANET ELIZABETH, restaurant chain marketing executive; b. Robinson, Ill., Oct. 12, 1953; d. Floyd W. and Cora E. (Coulter) C.; B.S., So. Ill. U., 1975; postgrad. Ind. U.-Purdue U., Indpls. High sch. bus. tchr., Lawrenceville, Ill., 1976-77; asst. restaurant mgr. Burger Chef Restaurant, Robinson, 1977-78, Zionsville, Ind., 1978-79, restaurant mgr., Carmel, Ind., 1979, mktg. services mgr. Burger Chef Systems, Indpls., 1979-81, mgr. systems mktg., 1981-82; sr. mktg. mgr. Hardee's Food Systems Inc., 1982—. Active Big Sisters Indpls. Mem. Am. Mgmt. Assn., Nat. Restaurant Assn., Sigma Kappa (founder Gamma Kappa chpt. So. Ill. U. 1974). Office: Hardee's Food Systems PO Box 927 College Park Indianapolis IN 46206

CHU, ALBERT, motel exec.; b. China, July 10, 1933; came to U.S., 1976, naturalized, 1976; s. Hsi-Drin and Bau-Tsen C.; B.A., Nat. Taiwan U., 1959; m. Chia-Ling Sun, June 15, 1966; children—Bob, Jaime, Sabrina. Supr., gen. agt. Korean Nat. Airlines, Far Eastern Airlines, Taiwan, 1959-61; sales agt. Civil Air Transport, Taiwan, 1961-66; mgr. Chen Chang Wood Industry, Taiwan, 1966-75; pres. Chen Chang Internat. Corp., Taiwan, also Cleve., 1975-77; owner Sheridan and Gateway Motels, Dayton, Ohio, 1977-81; owner York Motor Lodge, 1979-81; pres. Chu's Dayton Motels, Inc., 1979—. Mem. Dayton C. of C., Hotel Motel Assn. Office: Chu's Dayton Motels Inc 1891 Harshman Rd Dayton OH 45424

CHU, JOHNSON CHIN SHENG, physician; b. Peiping, China, Sept. 26, 1918; s. Harry S. P. and Florence (Young) C.; M.D., St. John's U., 1945; m. Sylvia Cheng, June 11, 1949; children—Stephen, Timothy. Came to U.S., 1948, naturalized, 1957. Intern U. Hosp., Shanghai, 1944-45; resident, research fellow N.Y.U. Hosp., 1948-50; resident, physician in charge State Hosp. and Med. Center, Weston, W.Va., 1951-56; chief services, clin. dir. State Hosp., Logansport, Ind., 1957-84; attending physician Meml. Hosp., Logansport, Ind., 1968—. Fellow Am. Psychiat. Assn., Am. Coll. Chest Physicians; mem. A.M.A., Ind. Med. Assn., Cass County Med. Soc., AAAS. Research, publs. in cardiology and pharmacology. Contbr. articles profl. jours. Home: E 36 Lake Shafer Monticello IN 47960 Office: Southeastern Medical Center Walton IN 46994

CHU, JOSEPH Q., mechanical engineer; b. Phanrang, Ninhthuan, Vietnam, May 27, 1955; came to U.S., 1973, naturalized, 1981; s. Thuc Nang and Cuoi Thi (Pham) C. B.A., William Jennings Bryan Coll., 1977; M.S., U. Tenn., 1979, Ph.D., 1982. Lab. asst. William Jennings Bryan Coll., Dayton, Tenn., 1975-77; sr. project engr. Allison Gas Turbine Gen. Motors Corp., Indpls., 1982—. Contbr. articles to profl. jours. Mem. AIAA, ASME (assoc.), Phi Kappa Phi. Republican. Roman Catholic. Avocations: canoeing; soccer; photography; hiking; sailing. Home: 8175 Pascal Ct Indianapolis IN 46268 Office: Allison Gas Turbine PO Box 420 Indianapolis IN 46206

CHU, SAMUEL SHEUNG-TAK, biochemical engineer; b. Hong Kong, Sept. 12, 1950; came to Can., 1973; s. Kwan-leung Chu and Chiu-yah Yu; m. Lily Li-min Lee, July 4, 1973; children—Grace, Joyce. B.Sc., Nat. Chung-Hsing U., Taiwan, 1973; M.Sc., U. Toronto, 1974, Ph.D. in Bio-organic Chemistry, 1978; M.Chem. Engring., Ill. Inst. Tech., 1983. Research assoc. U. Chgo., 1978-80, research assoc. in medicine/instr., 1980-82; biochem. engr. III, Molecular Genetics, Inc., Minnetonka, Minn., 1983-84, biochem. engr. IV, 1984—. Mem. Phi Lambda Upsilon. Home: 10111 Cedar Lake Rd #102 Minnetonka MN 55343 Office: Molecular Genetics Inc 10320 Bren Rd E Minnetonka MN 55343

CHUA, CHENG LOK, educator; b. Singapore, Jan. 5, 1938; s. Yew Cheng and Kuo Hui (Tan) C.; came to U.S., 1956; B.A., DePauw U., 1960; M.A., U. Conn., 1962, Ph.D., 1968; m. Gretchen Taeko Sasaki, July 26, 1965; children—Iu-Hui Jarrell, Poh-Pheng Jaime. Part-time instr. English, U. Conn., Storrs, 1960-65; asst. prof. English, U. Mich., Ann Arbor, 1965-72; lectr., sr. lectr. English, U. Singapore, 1972-74; lectr. English, Calif. State U. at Fresno, 1974-76; Nat. Endowment Humanities postdoctoral fellow Yale U., 1976-77, vis. fellow comparative lit., 1976-77; assoc. prof. Moorhead (Minn.) State U., 1977-81, prof., chmn. dept. English, 1982—. Australasian Univs. Lang. and Lit. Assn. grantee, 1975; Am. Council Learned Socs. grantee, 1978; Nat. Endowment Humanities summer fellow, 1980; fellow East Asia Inst., Hamline U., 1981. Mem. MLA, Nat. Council Tchrs. English, Multi-Ethnic Lit. of U.S., AAUP, Nat. Assn. Interdisciplinary Ethnic Studies. Home: 1102 S 16th St Moorhead MN 56560

CHUA, FELIPE SIA, cardiac surgeon; b. Manila, Philippines, May 26, 1936; came to U.S., 1963; s. Jose Salas and Maxima (Sia) C.; m. Farida Isip, June 21, 1959; children—Sheillah, Philip, Jr., Portia, Rachel, Emily. A.A., U. Philippines, Quezon City, 1956; M.D., Far Eastern U., Manila, 1961. Intern Ravenswood Hosp. Chgo., 1963; resident VA Hosp., Hines, Ill., 1965-72; Denton Cooley fellow in cardiac surgery Tex. Heart Inst., 1972; practice medicine specializing in cardiac surgery, Merrillville, Ind., 1973—; chief of staff, St. Mary Med. Ctr., Gary-Hobart, Ind., 1981, St. Anthony Med. Ctr., Crown Point, Ind., 1982, Methodist Hosps., Inc., Merrillville, 1986; pres., chmn. bd. dirs. Conprehensive Healthcare Utilization Alternative, Inc., Merillville, 1984—, Physicians Choice of Northwest Ind., Inc., 1985—. Editor: The Philippine Surgeon, 1975—. SPL News editor Philippine Am. Med. Bull., 1983—. Founder, Mended Hearts Club, Crown Point, 1982; mem. Ronald Reagan for Pres., Washington, 1983; bd. trustees Benigno S. Aquino Meml. Found., Boston, 1983; pres. Am. Heart Assn., Ind., 1974-75. Recipient Citation of Merit, Sen. Raul Manglapus, Manila, 1962; named Most Outstanding Filipino in Midwest, Cavite Assn., 1983. Fellow Am. Coll. Chest Surgeons, Internat. Coll. Surgeons, Am. Coll. Angiology, Ind. Thoracic Soc.; mem. Internat. Soc. Heart Transplantation, Assn. Philippine Practicing Physicians in Am. (pres. 1986-87), Philippine Med. Assn. (pres. 1966-67, editor bull. 1965-66, award of distinction 1966), C.B. Puestow Surgical Soc. (pres. 1967-68, Leadership award 1967), Denton Cooley Cardiac Soc. (pres. 1972-73), Soc. Philippine Surgeons in Am. (pres. 1981-82), Nat. Rifle Assn., Fraternal Order Police Assocs. Republican. Roman Catholic. Avocations: fishing; hunting; writing; photography. Home: 1830 Mirmar Rd Munster IN 46321 Office: 8684 Conecticut Merillville IN 46410

CHUANG, RICHARD YO, political scientist, educator; b. Shanghai, China, Mar. 9, 1939; came to U.S., 1962; s. Han K. and Rose C.; LL.B., Nat. Taiwan U., 1961; M.A. (fgn. student scholar), U. Minn., 1964, Ph.D. (fgn. student scholar), 1970; cert. (scholar) Parker Sch. Fgn. and Comparative law, Columbia U., 1973; m. Elsie Yao Chuang, Sept. 4, 1965; children—Erik, Cliff, Fleur. Vis. asso. prof. law Nat. Taiwan U., 1971-72; vis. asso. prof. polit. sci. Nat. Chung Hsin U., Taipei, Taiwan, 1973-74; asst. prof. No. State Coll., Aberdeen, S.D., 1968-71, assoc. prof., 1971-76, prof. polit. sci., 1976—, acting chmn. dept. social sci., 1979-81, chmn. dept. social sci., 1981-83, interim chmn. faculty social and natural scis., 1983-84, dean Faculty Arts and Scis., 1984—; NSF vis. prof. Republic of China, 1973-74; participant, scholar Diplomat Seminars, U.S. Dept. State, 1981; cons. Mem. Am. Polit. Sci. Assn., Am. Soc. Internat. Law. Democrat. Buddhist. Club: Mason. Author: The International Air Transport Association, 1972; editor No. Social Sci. Rev., 1975—; contbr. numerous articles to profl. jours. Home: 216 21st Ave NE Aberdeen SD 57401 Office: No State Coll Aberdeen SD 57401

CHUBICK, LESLEY IRWIN, advertising executive; b. Clinton, Iowa, Nov. 17, 1943; s. Delvin Dow and Anna Belle (Nichols) C.; B.S., Central Mo. State U., 1967; seminar cert. Fiway Modular Brace System, 1983; m. Markey Lou Ewing, July 11, 1980; children by previous marriage—Lesley Irwin, Jeannette Louise; 1 stepchild, Carol Ann. Lay-out artist/copywriter Sears, Roebuck & Co., Kansas City, Mo., 1973-75; advt. artist/copy writer Medco Jewelry Corp., Overland Park, Kans., 1975-78; free-lance work in advt., Merriam, Kan., 1978-79; advt. mgr. Knit-Rite Inc., Kansas City, Mo., 1979—, trade show and seminar dir., 1982—. Bd. dirs. Quail Valley Coop., 1980-82, sec., 1980-82, editor bi-weekly Quail Valley Newsletter, 1980-82. Recipient Award of Excellence, Advt. Artists Guild of Kansas City, Mo., 1970; cert. of completion Avila Coll. Seminar in Coop. Mgmt., 1980, course in fitting camp orthotic supports, 1980. Mem. Plains Assn. Clubs: Ad of Kansas City, Art Dirs., Sportscar. Home: 14620 W 93d St Lenexa KS 66215 Office: PO Box 208 2020 Grand Ave Kansas City MO 64141

CHUDOBIAK, WALTER JAMES, electronics company executive, electronics engineer; b. Gliechen, Alta., Can., Apr. 2, 1942; s. John and Clara (Suchy) C.; m. Mary Annetta Budarick, Oct. 11, 1969; children—Michael, Anne. B.Sc. in Elec. Engring., U. Alta., Edmonton, 1964; M.Eng. in Electronic Engring.,

Carleton U., Ottawa, Ont., Can., 1965, Ph.D. in Electronic Engring., 1969. Research officer Def. Research Bd., Ottawa, 1965-69; group leader, research scientist Communications Research Centre, Dept. Communications, Ottawa, 1969-75; assoc. prof. Carleton U., 1975-81; pres., founder Avtech Electrosystems Ltd., Ottawa, 1975—, also dir. U. Alta. scholar, 1960-64; Carleton U. scholar, 1964-65. Mem. IEEE, Assn. Profl. Engrs. (Ont.). Conservative. Mem. United Ch. of Canada. Contbr. numerous articles to profl. jours.; patentee in field; inventor nanosecond pulse circuits. Home: 22 Denewood Crescent Nepean ON K2E 7G5 Canada Office: 15 Grenfell Crescent Suite 205 Nepean ON K2G 0G3 Canada

CHULICK, ANTHONY WAYNE, dentist; b. Litchfield, Ill., Nov. 7, 1948; s. Walter John and Josephine (Dominetto) C.; m. Michaeline Louise Ricchiardi, July 24, 1971; 1 child, Caroline. B.S. (hon.), U. Ill.-Chicago Circle, 1971, D.D.S. (hon.), 1973; student St. Louis U., 1969. Gen. practice dentistry, Dekalb, Ill., 1975—. Bd. dirs. Dekalb United Way, 1983—. Served to lt. USN, 1969-75. Mem. ADA, Ill. State Dental Soc., Chgo. Dental Soc., Acad. of Gen. Dentistry, Fox Valley Dental Soc., Dekalb County Cancer Soc. (pres. 1983—). Lodge: Kiwanis (pres. 1984—). Orthodox. Avocations: tennis; snow skiing; gardening. Home: 114 Mattek Ave Dekalb IL 60115 Office: 2600 DeKalb Ave Sycamore IL 60178

CHULINDRA, WIM, architect; b. Chacheongsao, Thailand, May 9, 1947; came to U.S., 1969, naturalized, 1980; s. Son and Somrat (Liang) L.; m. Supastra, Aug. 30, 1969; children—Witra K., Warisa L. Grad. Chulalongkorn U., 1969; B.Arch. with honors, U. Kans., M.Arch., 1973. Registered architect, Kans. Draftsman, Cushman & Long, Long Beach, Calif., 1969-71; lectr. architecture and urban design U. Kans., Lawrence, 1977-79; with Kiene & Bradley Design Group, Topeka, Kans., 1972—, assoc., 1980—. Mem. AIA, Kans. Soc. Architects. Democrat. Buddhist. Lodge: Rotary. Home: 1524 Clontarf St Topeka KS 66611 Office: Kiene & Bradley Design Group First Nat Bank Bldg Suite 925 Topeka KS 66603

CHUNG, HYUNG DOO, neuropathologist, educator; b. Kyung-Nam, Korea, Nov. 15, 1940; came to U.S., 1970, naturalized, 1976; s. Jae Yul and Yuh Ah (Park) C.; M.D., Pusan Nat. U., 1965; m. Jeung Hie Choi, Apr. 12, 1968; children—Sung Chung, Steven Chung, Cindy Chung. Intern, Bronx-Lebanon Hosp. & Med. Center, Bronx, N.Y., 1970-71; resident, Montefiore Hosp. & Med. Center, Bronx, 1971-75; staff neuropathologist VA Med. Center, St. Louis, 1975—; cons. neuropathologist Firmin Desloge Hosp., Cardinal Glennon Children's Hosp., St. Louis, 1980—; asst. prof. pathology St. Louis U. Med. Sch., 1979-80, asst. clin. prof. pathology, 1980—, asst. prof. neurology, 1984—. Served with Korean Army, 1965-68. Diplomate Am. Bd. Pathology. Mem. Am. Assn. Neuropathologists, Internat. Soc. Neuropathology. Home: 845 Durrow Dr Saint Louis MO 63141 Office: 915 N Grand Blvd Saint Louis MO 63125

CHUNG, OKKYUNG KIM, research chemist; b. Seoul, Korea, Apr. 11, 1936; came to U.S., 1959, naturalized, 1972; d. Changshik and Yoonam (Hahn) Kim; B.S., Ewha Womens U., Korea, 1959; M.S., Kans. State U., 1965, Ph.D., 1973; m. Do Sup Chung, Nov. 22, 1961; children—Clara K., Josephine K. Grad. teaching asst. Kans. State U., Manhattan, 1961-64, research asst., 1964-66, 68-71, postdoctoral research assoc., 1973-74, adj. assoc. prof., 1975-83, adj. prof., 1983—; research chemist U.S. Grain Mktg. Research Lab., U.S. Dept. Agr., Manhattan, 1974—; lectr. in field. Recipient Gold Medal award Ewha Women's U., 1959; W.E. Long Merit award So. Bakers Assn., 1971. Mem. Am. Assn. Cereal Chemists (sect. chmn. 1977-78), Am. Chem. Soc., Am. Oil Chemists Soc. (outstanding paper presentation award 1983), Korean Scientists and Engrs. Assn. in Am. (chmn. chpt. 1983-85), Council for Agrl. Sci. and Tech., Sigma Xi, Phi Lambda Upsilon, Gamma Sigma Delta. Contbr. articles to profl. jours. and books; assoc. editor Cereal Chemistry, 1978-81. Home: 200 Carlisle Terr Manhattan KS 66502 Office: 1515 College Ave Manhattan KS 66502

CHUNG, YIP-WAH, science and engineering educator; b. Hong Kong, Nov. 8, 1950; came to U.S., 1973, naturalized, 1983. B.S., U. Hong Kong, 1971, M. Phil., 1973; Ph.D., U. Calif.-Berkeley, 1977. Asst. prof. Northwestern U., Evanston, Ill., 1977-82, assoc. prof. material sci. and engring., 1982—. Scholar Lee Pui Hing Meml., 1970, Earl C. Anthony, 1974. Mem. Am. Phys. Soc., Metallurgical Soc. Office: Dept Mat Sci & Engring Northwestern Univ 2145 Sheridan St Evanston IL 60201

CHUNG, YOUNG-IOB, economics educator; b. Bihyun, Pyong Huk, Korea, June 21, 1928; came to U.S., 1950; s. Mun Chul and Yoon Sun (Choi) C.; m. Oke Kim, July 2, 1960; children—Jee-Won, Jinwon. B.B.A., UCLA, 1952; M.A., Columbia U., 1955, Ph.D., 1965. Instr. Moravian Coll., Bethlehem, Pa., 1961-63, asst. prof., 1963-66; assoc. prof. Eastern Mich. U., Ypsilanti, 1966-70, prof. econs., head dept., 1970—; cons. Am. Occupational Therapy Found., 1981—. Editor Jour. Modern Korean Studies, 1984—. Contbr. articles to profl. jours., chpts. to books. Mem. Downtown Devel. Authority, Ypsilanti, Mich., 1978-84. Mem. Am. Econs. Assn., Soc. Asian Studies, Midwest Econ. Soc., Mich. Econ. Soc. Home: 1625 Gregory St Ypsilanti MI 48197 Office: Eastern Mich U Dept Econs Ypsilanti MI 48197

CHUPP, LELAND HORACE, jeweler, real estate investor; b. Edinburg, Ind., Apr. 12, 1916; s. Nathan and Bessie Pearl (Parks) C.; m. Ruth Mary Weakley, Jan. 1, 1939 (dec. 1980); children—Patricia Lee Chupp Carrille, Frances Earlene Chupp Justuce, Leland Albert, Phyllis Chupp Waggomann; m. Martha S. Schadener, Feb. 14, 1981. Apprentice clocks H.H. Bishop, Indpls., 1929-36; apprentice watchmaker Rogers Jewelers, Indpls., 1936-37, Purvis Jewelers, Indpls., 1937-38; watchmaker A.S. Rowe Jewelers, Indpls., 1938-40; watchmaker, asst. mgr. Hays Jewelers, Lafayette, Ind., 1940-46; owner Chupp Jewelers, Lafayette, 1946—. Coordinator retail div. United Fund, Lafayette, 1954; organizer, elder, trustee Bethany Presbyterian Ch., Lafayette, 1954-59; com. chmn. New Eagle Lodge Bldg., Lafayette, 1954-64. Recipient Commendation award Gov. Ind., 1985. Mem. Jewelers Vigilance Com. Republican. Lodges: Shriners, Scottish Rite, Elks, Eagles. Avocations: designing; remodeling store. Office: Chupp I Inc 125 N 4th St PO Box 127 Lafayette IN 47902

CHURCH, ANNAMARIA THERESA, pediatrician; b. Detroit, Feb. 1, 1955; d. Gerhard Alois and Barbara Lenore (Siegert) Blass; m. Richard Joseph Church, May 17, 1975; children—Christopher, Sarah. B.S., U. Detroit, 1975; M.D., Wayne State U., Detroit, 1979. Diplomate Nat. Bd. Med. Examiners, Am. Bd. Pediatrics. Pediatric resident William Beaumont Hosp., Royal Oak, Mich., 1979-82; practice medicine specializing in pediatrics Brighton-Ann Arbor Med Assn., Brighton, Mich., 1982-83; dir. ambulatory pediatrics William Beaumont Hosp., Royal Oak, 1983-84; practice medicine specializing in pediatrics Child Health Assocs., Southfield, Mich., 1984—. Mem. Suspected Child Abuse and Neglect Team, Royal Oak, 1983—; mem. Adv. Com. on Parent Edn., Royal Oak, 1983—; mem. Pediatric Utilization Rev. Com., Royal Oak, 1983—; mem. Oakland County Council Children at Risk, Oakland County, Mich., 1983. Fellow Am. Acad. Pediatrics; mem. Ambulatory Pediatric Assn. Roman Catholic. Office: Child Health Assocs 16800 W Twelve Mile Rd Southfield MI 48072

CHURCH, IRENE ZABOLY, personnel services company executive; b. Cleve., Feb. 18, 1947; d. Bela Paul and Irene Elizabeth (Chandas) Zaboly; student public schs.; children—Irene Elizabeth, Elizabeth Anne, Lauren Alexandria. Personnel cons., Cleve., 1965; sec., Cleve., 1966-68; personnel cons., Cleve., 1968-70; owner, pres. Oxford Personnel, Pepper Pike, Ohio, 1973—; chmn. bd. Oxford Temporaries, Inc., Pepper Pike, 1979—; guest lectr. in field. Fund raiser Better Bus. Bur., 1973; troop leader Lake Erie council Girl Scouts Am., 1980—; mem. Christian action com. Federated Ch., 1981—, also mem. Martha Mary Circle, program dir., 1982—. Mem. Nat. Assn. Personnel Consultants (co-chmn. ethics com. 1977-78), Ohio Assn. Personnel Consultants (trustee 1975-80, 1st v.p., chmn. bus. practices and ethics 1976-78, chmn. resolutions com. 1981—), Greater Cleve. Assn. Personnel Consultants (1st v.p., chmn. bus. practices and ethics 1974-76, pres., recipient Vi Pender award 1976-77, adv., chmn. Vi Pender award 1977-78, chmn. award 1980, chmn. arbitration 1980—, chmn. fund raising 1980—, chmn. nominating com. 1983—, state trustee 1975-80), Internat. Platform Assn., Euclid C. of C. (small bus. com. 1981—), Greater Cleve. Growth Assn., Council Small Enterprises, Am. Bus. Women's Assn. Home: 8 Ridgecrest Dr Chagrin Falls OH 44022 Office: Oxford Personnel Exec Commons 29425 Chagrin Blvd Pepper Pike OH 44122

CHURCH, JAY KAY, psychologist, educator; b. Wichita, Kans., Jan. 18, 1927; s. Kay Iverson and Gertrude (Parrish) C.; B.A., David Lipscomb Coll., 1948; M.A., Ball State U., 1961; Ph.D., Purdue U., 1963; m. Dorothy Agnes Fellerhoff, May 21, 1976; children—Karen Patrice Church Edwards, Caryn Annice Church Casey, Rex Warren, Max Roger. Chemist, Auburn Rubber Corp., 1948-49; salesman Midwestern United Life Ins. Co., 1949-52; owner, operator Tour-Rest Motel, Waterloo, Ind., 1952-66; tchr., guidance dir., public schs., Hamilton, Ind., 1955-61; counselor Washington Twp. (Ind.) Schs., Indpls., 1961-62; asst. prof. psychology Ball State U., 1963-67, assoc. prof., 1967-71, prof., 1971—, chmn. dept. ednl. psychology, 1970-74, dir. advanced grad. programs in ednl. psychology, 1978-81; pvt. practice psychology, 1963—. Mem. Am. Psychol. Assn., Midwest Psychol. Assn., Ind. Psychol. Assn., Nat. Assn. Sch. Psychologists. Home: 8501 N Ravenwood Dr Muncie IN 47302 Office: Ball State U Muncie IN 47306

CHURCHILL, DENNIS WILLIAM, monument mfg. co. exec.; b. Dubuque, Iowa, Aug. 23, 1944; s. Willis Bernard and Rita Marie (Miller) C.; asso. Lansing Bus. U., 1964; student Lansing Community Coll., 1963-64; m. Sally Jill Scheidt, Jan. 16, 1965; children—Catherine Anne, Christina Marie, Jared Andrew. Ptnr. div. Churchill Enterprises, C & B Trucking Co., Lansing, Mich., 1964-67; sales mgr. Yunker Memls., Inc., Lansing, 1967-69, asst. v.p., 1969-80, pres., owner, 1980—. Mem. Monument Builders N. Am. (dir. Mich. div.), Lansing C. of C., Lansing Philatelic Soc. Democrat. Roman Catholic. Clubs: Kiwanis, Rosicrucians. Inventor door lock and key-less locking device for automobiles; designer 1st multi-conflict Vets. Memorial in U.S. Home: 12463 Spruce Ln Forest Green Estates Perry MI 48872 Office: 1116 E Mount Hope Ave Lansing MI 48910

CHURCHILL, JAMES PAUL, See *Who's Who in America,* 43rd edition.

CHURCHILL, RUEL VANCE, mathematician, educator; b. Akron, Ind., Dec. 12, 1899; s. Abner Cain and Meldora (Friend) C.; B.S., U. Chgo., 1922; Ph.D., U. Mich., 1929; m. Ruby Sicks, 1922 (dec. 1969); m. 2d, Alice Baldwin Warren, 1972; children—Betty Churchill McMurray, Eugene S. Instr. to prof. U. Mich., Ann Arbor, 1922-65, prof. emeritus, 1965—; researcher U. Freiburg, Germany, 1936; researcher Calif. Inst. Tech., 1950; vis. lectr. U. Wis., Madison, 1941; mathematician USAF, 1944. Mem. Math. Assn. Am., Am. Math. Soc., Phi Beta Kappa. Author: (with J.W. Brown) Complex Variables and Applications, 4th edit., 1983; Fourier Series, 3d edit., 1978; Operational Mathematics, 3d edit., 1972. Home: 1231 Wisteria Dr Ann Arbor MI 48104 Office: U Mich Dept Math Ann Arbor MI 48109

CHURLIN, LAURENCE, systems programmer; b. Chgo., Feb. 23, 1944; s. Dewey Thomas and Mary (Hanslick) C.; A.A.S., Prairie State Coll., 1978; m. Georgia Stewart, July 5, 1969; children—Christine, Scott. Supr. computer ops. Field Enterprises Ednl. Corp., Chgo., 1967-70; mgr. computer ops. Systems Data Processing Center, Chgo., 1970-76; mgr. computer ops. Mercy Hosp. and Med. Center, Chgo., 1976-79; systems programmer Mercy Center for Health Care Services, 1979-80; v.p. Mercy Center Fed. Credit Union, 1983-84. Publicity chmn. Woodgate PTO, 1976-77; mem. Matteson Police and Fire Commn., 1983—; mem. sch. bd. Ill. Sch. Dist. 159, 1983—. Served with USAF, 1963-67. Mem. Matteson Jaycees (sec., Cert. of Merit 1979, Jaycee of Yr. 1979). Roman Catholic. Home: 155 Central St Matteson IL 60443 Office: 1325 N Highland Aurora IL 60506

CHUTE, ROBERT DONALD, electrical engineering educator; b. Detroit, Nov. 29, 1928; s. George Maynard and Josephine Chute; B.S. in Elec. Engring., U. Mich., 1950; M.S., Wayne State U., 1966; m. Marion Louise Price, June 17, 1950; children—Janet Louise, Lawrence Robert. Control engr. indsl heating div. Gen. Electric Co., Shelbyville, Ind., 1950-57; group leader Chrysler Corp., Warren, Mich., 1957-59; chief product engr. internat. div. Burroughs Corp., Detroit, 1959-73; asso. prof. elec. engring. Lawrence Inst. Tech., Southfield, Mich., 1973—; cons. in indsl. controls, 1969—. Instl. rep. Detroit Met. Area council Boy Scouts Am., 1964-68. Registered profl. engr., Mich., Ind. Mem. IEEE, Am. Soc. Engring. Edn., Nat. Soc. Profl. Engrs., Engring. Soc. Detroit. Presbyterian. Clubs: Just Right, Economic of Detroit. Author: (with George M. Chute) Electronics in Industry, 1971, 5th edit., 1979; patentee in field. Office: 21000 W Ten Mile Rd Southfield MI 48075

CHUTIS, LAURIEANN LUCY, social worker; b. Detroit, Nov. 30, 1942; d. Paul J. and Helen Marie (Shilakes) C.; A.B., U. Mich., 1964, M.S.W., 1966. Community worker Tuskegee (Ala.) Inst., 1966; social worker Catholic Sch. Bd. Head Start, Chgo., 1966; community worker Cath. Charities, Chgo., 1966-70; asst. to dir. Ravenswood Hosp. Community Mental Health Center, Chgo., 1970-72, coordinator consultation and edn. dept., 1972, dir. consultation and edn. dept., 1972—, also cons., trainer therapist; instr. Chgo. Bd. Edn., Northeastern Ill. U., 1974—; guest lectr. various profl. assn. groups, corps., 1975—; pvt. practice individual group and family therapy; 1976—; cons. NIMH, mental health centers, bus. and industry, 1977—. Coordinator Nat. Consultation and Edn. Net working; mem. Salvation Army Community Services Bd., 1978-80; mem. com. Chgo. Health Systems Agy., 1980—; mem. Ill. Alcohol Prevention Task Force, 1980-82. Mem. Nat. Assn. Social Work, Acad. Certified Social Work, World Fedn. Mental Health, Registry Clin. Social Workers, Nat. Council Community Mental Health Centers (council on Prevention 1977-79), Assn. Consultation-Edn. Service Providers (pres. 1978-79). Contbg. author: To Your Good Health. Contbr. articles to profl. jours. Office: 4550 N Winchester Chicago IL 60640

CIATTEO, CARMEN THOMAS, psychiatrist; b. Clifton Heights, Pa., May 25, 1921; s. Ralph and Grace (Manette) C.; A.B. in Chemistry, U. Pa., 1947; M.D., Loyola U., Chgo., 1951; m. Lucille Dolores Ranum, Nov. 1, 1957; children—William, Jane, Thomas. Intern, Mercy Hosp., Chgo.; resident Fitzsimons Army Hosp., Denver, 1952-53, Hines (Ill.) VA Hosp., 1957-59; practice medicine specializing in psychiatry, Joliet, Ill., 1959-72; correctional and forensic psychiatrist, 1966, 77—; psychiatrist VA hosps., 1959; cons. Dept. Vocat. Rehab., 1959-72, Matrimonial Tribunal Diocese Joliet, 1959-76; cons. Fed. Prison System, U.S. Dept. Justice, Chgo., 1975-76, 77-82; tchr. nursing tng. Hines VA Hosp., 1957-59. Served with USAF, 1942-46, 51-56. Diplomate Am. Bd. Psychiatry and Neurology. Mem. Ill. Psychiat. Soc., Am. Psychiat. Assn., Am. Acad. Psychiatry and Law, Am. Correctional Assn. Democrat. Roman Catholic. Home: Route 2 135 Little Creek Lockport IL 60441 Office: Crafts-Farrow State Hosp 7901 Farrow Rd Columbia SC 29203

CICCONE, WILLIAM, data processing executive; b. St. Louis, Apr. 11, 1937; s. Gerardo and Frances (Caputo) C.; student parochial schs., St. Louis; m. Marcia L. Ciccone; children—Anna Maria, Anthony William, Mary Frances, Mark Olan. Data processing mgr. Comml. Union-N. Brit. Group, Kansas City, Mo., Chgo., 1958-61; data processing mgr. Electronic Pub. Co., Inc., Chgo., 1961; data processing cons. Mgmt. Assistance, Inc., Chgo., 1961-62; data processing mgr. Cruttenden Podesta & Miller, Chgo., 1962-63; v.p. Data Systems Tng. Corp., Hammond, Ind., 1963; pres., chmn. Illiana Data Processing Services, Inc., Tinley Park, Ill., 1963—. Trustee Twp. of Orland (Ill.), 1977-83, collector, 1976-77, chmn. youth commn., 1976-81, youth service bur. adv. bd., 1978-81; trustee Village of Orland Park, 1983—; Ill. State rep. legis. aide, 1977-81; bd. dirs. Cath. Grad. Sch. Conf., 1975-78; chmn./pres. Cath. Central Parochial Basketball League, 1966-78; chmn. Sch. Dist. 135 Sch. Bd. Caucus, 1978; sec. Village of Orland Park Planning Commn., 1965-69. Served with USAF, 1955-58. Cert. data processor. Mem. Twp. Ofcls. of Ill. (2d v.p. collector div. 1976-77, dir. 1979-83), Twp. Ofcls. of Cook County (hon. mem., dir. 1979-83, sec. 1981-83). Democrat. Roman Catholic. Home: 14535 Greenland Ave Orland Park IL 60462 Office: 16860 Oak Park Ave Tinley Park IL 60477

CILLIE, JOHN JAMES, car rental agy. ofcl.; b. Martins Ferry, Ohio, Jan. 4, 1940; s. John Peter and Margaret C.; student Cleve. State U.; m. Janice Kudley, Sept. 30, 1961; children—Sheila, John James. With City Loan and Savs., Cleve., 1961-65, Avco Delta Corp., Cleve., 1965-70, Bobbie Brooks Inc., Cleve., 1970-74, Allstate Ins., Cleve., 1974-76; accounts receivable mgr. Rent-a-Car Agy., Bedford, Ohio, 1976—. Ky. Colonel. Office: 466 Northfield Rd Bedford OH 44146

CINADR, BERNARD FRANK, research and development engineer; b. Brecksville, Ohio, June 5, 1933; s. Martin James and Julia Marie (Piskula) C.; m. Priscilla Mae Tulley, Apr. 15, 1961; children—Brian David. B.S. in Chem. Engring., Case Inst. Tech., 1955, Ph.D. in Phys. Chemistry, 1960. Research engr. The B.F. Goodrich Co., Brecksville, Ohio, 1960-81, research and devel. fellow, 1981—. Contbr. articles to profl. jours. Patentee in field. Mem. Am. Inst. Chem. Engrs., Am. Chem. Soc. (rubber div.), Sigma Xi, Tau Beta Pi. Avocations: Fishing; golf; bowling; woodworking. Home: 8312 Whitewood Rd Brecksville OH 44141 Office: B F Goodrich Co Research and Devel Center 9921 Brecksville Rd Brecksville OH 44141

CIPOLLA, LAWRENCE JOHN, human resources development services company executive; b. Hartford, Conn., Nov. 30, 1943; s. Anthony Francis and Rose Marie (Alesi) C.; A.A. with honors, Manchester Community Coll., 1968; B.A. with high honors, U. Conn., 1970; M.A. with honors (Regent's Fund scholar), U. Minn., 1972; m. Judith L. Peterka, June 24, 1972. Spencer Found. research fellow U. Minn., Mpls., 1971-72; cons., sr. instructional analyst 3M Co., St Paul, 1972-74, supr., 1974-76; v.p. learning systems div. Golle & Holmes, 1976-79, pres. Cipolla Cos., Inc., Mpls., 1979—; mem. grad. sch. faculty U. Minn., Coll. St. Thomas, St. Paul; cons. in sales and mgmt. performance systems, productivity systems, negotiation strategies, team bldg., communication skills; lectr., author in field. Served with USAF, 1961-65. Mem. Am. Soc. Tng. and Devel., Am. Soc. Performance Improvement, Sales and Mktg. Execs. Internat., Phi Beta Kappa. Home: 7021 Comanche Ct Edina MN 55435

CIPOLLA, SAM JOSEPH, physics educator; b. Chgo., July 24, 1940; s. Joseph John and Florence (Mistretta) C.; m. Virginia Stover, Nov. 5, 1966; children—Mark, Karen. B.S., Loyola U.-Chgo., 1962; M.S., Purdue U., 1965, Ph.D., 1969. Asst. prof. physics dept. Creighton U., Omaha, 1969-73, assoc. prof., 1973-83, prof., 1983—; vis. assoc. prof. U. Nebr., Lincoln, 1982-83, vis. prof., 1983—; cons. Omaha Pub. Power, 1974—. Contbr. articles to profl. jours. NSF grantee, 1970-72, 82-83. Mem. Am. Phys. Soc., Am. Assn. Physics Tchrs., Nebr. Acad. Sci., Nebr. Physics Tchrs. Assn. Home: 2917 S 116th Ave Omaha NE 68144 Office: Physics Dept Creighton U Omaha NE 68178

CIRASO, PATRICIA LOUISE, elementary school principal; b. Portsmouth, Ohio, Dec. 4, 1944; d. Frank and Helen Louise (Conley) C. B.S. in Elem. Edn., Ohio U., 1969, M.Ed., 1978. Cert. prin., tchr., supt., adminstr., Ohio. Tchr. West Portsmouth (Ohio) Pub. Schs., 1962-77; prin. Jenkins Elem. Sch., West Portsmouth, Ohio, 1978—. Mem. Portsmouth Jury Com., 1962-68; mem. dist. com. Ohio Right to Read program; mem. Scioto County Republican Com. Mem. Ohio Assn. Elem. Sch. Adminstrs., Scioto County Elem. Adminstrs. Assn., Ohio Assn. Elem. Supervisors, Internat. Reading Assn. (officer), Scioto County Shawnee Reading Council, Am. Legion (women's aux.), Delta Kappa Gamma, Phi Delta Kappa. Republican. United Methodist. Club: Methodist Women (Portsmouth). Coordinator fund drive for March of Dimes. Home: Rt 2 Box 127 GF McDermott OH 45652 Office: Jenkins Elem Sch West Portsmouth OH 45662

CIRCLE, SYBIL JEAN, psychiatrist; b. Peoria, Ill., July 2, 1945; d. Sidney Joseph and Sydell C.; B.A., Northwestern U., 1967, M.D., 1971. Intern, Passavant Meml. Hosp., Chgo., 1971-72; resident in psychiatry Northwestern U. Med. Sch., Chgo., 1972-74; practice medicine specializing in psychiatry, Maywood, Ill., 1975-82, Chgo., 1982—; mem. faculty Loyola U. Med. Sch., Chgo., 1975—, asst. prof., 1977-81, clin. asst. prof., 1981-82, lectr., 1982—; dir. undergrad. edn., dept. psychiatry, 1977-82; staff psychiatrist West Side VA Hosp., 1982—; asst. prof. dept. psychiatry U.-Ill. Med. Sch., 1982—; staff Ill. Masonic Med. Ctr. Diplomate Am. Bd. Psychiatry and Neurology. Mem. AMA, Am. Psychiat. Assn., Ill. Psychiat. Soc., Chgo. Med. Soc. Office: 600 N McClurg Ct #506A Chicago IL 60611

CIRINO, JOHN MICHAEL, management information services director; b. Detroit, Dec. 31, 1940; s. Louis and Marie Antoinette (Sancolla) C. B.S., U. Detroit, 1965, postgrad., 1965-66, Wayne State U., 1966-68. Cert. systems profl. Systems analyst, programmer Automobile Club of Mich., Detroit, 1965-68; sr. systems analyst Chrysler Corp., Detroit, 1968-69; mgr. data processing Stroh Brewery Co., Detroit, 1969-74; dir. data processing, 1974-82; dir. mgmt. information services B & E Sales Co., Bloomfield Hills, Mich., 1982—. Mem. Assn. Systems Mgmt. Republican. Roman Catholic. Avocations: model bldg.; art; tennis; skiing; handball. Home: 24900 N Cromwell Franklin MI 48025 Office: B & E Sales Co 200 E Long Lake Bloomfield Hills MI 48013

CISLAK, PETER JOHN, computer company executive; b. Indpls., June 26, 1931; s. Francis Edward and Jeannette Grace (Huling) C.; student Swarthmore Coll., 1952; B.S., Purdue U., 1958, M.S., 1958; m. Margaret Frances Noble, June 6, 1953; children—Gregory Noble, Carol Margaret, David John, Susan Marie. Instr., Purdue U., 1958-62; statistician Reilly Tar & Chem. Corp., Indpls., 1962-64, data processing mgr., 1964-69, prodn. mgr. chem. div., 1969-77, sr. mgr. chems., 1977-81; chmn., chief exec. officer Alpha Comp Inc., 1981—; dir. Reilly Chems., Reilly Chem. S.A., Belgium; lectr. Ind. U.-Purdue U., Indpls., 1970; instr. computer sci. Ind. U., Purdue U., Indpls., De Pauw U., Greencastle, Ind. Asst. dist. commr. Boy Scouts Am., 1963—. Served with AUS, 1953-57. Mem. Am. Mgmt. Assn. (chmn. seminar), Am. Statis. Assn., Assn. Computing Machinery, Ops. Research Soc. Am., Soc. Chem. Industry, Am. Inst. Chem. Engrs. (chmn. Indpls. sect. 1978), Ind. Soc. Mayflower Descs. (dep. gov. 1974-79). K.C. (4 deg.). Home and office: 8065 Morningside Dr Indianapolis IN 46240

CISSELL, JAMES CHARLES, lawyer; b. Cleve., May 29, 1940; s. Robert Francis and Helen (Freeman) C.; children—Denise, Helene-Marie, Suzanne, James. A.B., Xavier U., 1962; postgrad. Ohio State U., 1963-64; J.D., U. Cin., 1966; D.T.L. (hon.), Cin. Tech. Coll., 1979. Bar: Ohio 1966. Asst. atty. gen. State of Ohio, Cin., 1971-74; U.S. atty. Dept. Justice, Cin., 1978-82; adj. instr. Chase Coll. Law, Highland Heights, Ky., 1982—; ptnr. Cissell, Smith, Farrish & Stanceu, Cin., 1985—. Author: Oil and Gas Law in Ohio, 1964; Federal Criminal Trials, 1983. Contbr., editor: Proving Federal Crimes, 1981. First v.p. Cin. Bd. Park Commrs., 1973-74; mem. Cin. Recreation Commn., 1974; councilmen City of Cin., 1974-78, vice mayor, 1976-77. Ford Found. fellow, 1963-64. Democrat. Office: Cissell Smith Farrish & Stanceu 1100 Gwynne Bldg 602 Main St Cincinnati OH 45202

CITRIN, PHILLIP MARSHALL, lawyer; b. Chgo., Nov. 1, 1931; s. Mandel Hirsch and Birdie (Gulman) C.; B.S., Northwestern U., 1953, J.D., 1956; m. Judith Goldfeder, Dec. 23, 1967 (div. 1984); 1 son, Jeffrey Scott Levin. Admitted to Ill. bar, 1957; ptnr. firm Davis, Jones & Baer, Chgo., 1961-80; individual practice law specializing in domestic relations, Chgo., 1980—. Republican candidate judge circuit ct., Cook County, Ill., 1976, 78. Served with USNR, 1956-58. Fellow Am. Acad. Matrimonial Lawyers (founding); mem. Chgo. (bd. mgrs. 1974-76, chmn. entertainment com. 1971, co-author ann. satire program Christmas Spirits, 1963—, matrimonial law com. 1963—, permanent home com. 1983—), Ill. (mem. assembly of dels. 1972-73, family law com. 1964—), Am. (gavel awards com.) bar assns., Internat. Soc. Family Law, Phi Delta Phi. Office: 30 N LaSalle St Chicago IL 60602

CIULEI, LIVIU, theatrical dir. Artistic dir. The Guthrie Theater, Mpls. Office: The Guthrie Theater 725 Vineland Place Minneapolis MN 55403*

CIURA, JEAN MARIE, management consultant; b. Kenosha, Wis., July 28, 1948; d. Joseph P. and Lilia (Sfasciotti) Sfasciotti; m. Vincent M. Ciura, Jr., Jan. 17, 1981; 1 child, Vincent Robert. Student Loyola U., Rome, Italy, 1967-68; B.A., Marquette U., 1970, M.A., 1972; Ph.D., U. Rochester, 1981. Archivist, U. Wis.-Kenosha, 1977-78, assoc. project dir. Nat. Archives, U. Wis.-Kenosha, 1979-80; cons. Record Controls, Inc., Addison, Ill, 1981-84; pvt. mgmt. cons., Arlington Heights, Ill., 1985—. Author: The Rentention Book, 1984; also profl. articles. Contbg. editor, columnist Jour. Info. Mgmt., 1984—. Fulbright-Hay fellow, Naples, Italy, 1975-76; teaching fellow Marquette U., 1970-72, U. Rochester, 1974-75. Mem. Women in Mgmt., Oak Brook Chamber Commerce and Industry, Assn. Records Mgrs. and Adminstrs., Newcomers Assn. Arlington Heights. Avocations: history, languages, writing, travel. Address: 1815 N Stratford Rd Arlington Heights IL 60004

CLANCY, DANIEL FRANCIS, retired journalist; b. Logansport, Ind., May 8, 1918; s. Joseph Francis and Daisy C. (Strecker) C.; student pub. schs.; m. Okodell Glads Salyer, Apr. 12, 1947; children—Cassandra Sue, Holly Eve. Reporter Logansport Press, 1942-46, Springfield (Ohio) Daily News, 1946-47, Springfield Sun, 1947-56; reporter, Columbus (Ohio) Dispatch, 1956-80, ret. 1980. Dir. Nat. Com. Against Limiting the Presidency, 1949-54. Served to lt. col. Ohio Def. Corps. Decorated French Nat. Merit, Gold medal, La Renaissance Francaise, medal Honor and Merit, knight Order of Lion of Ardennes, Cross of Lorraine and Compains of Resistance, Soc. Encouragement

Arts, Scis., Letters Silver medal (France); knight Order of Crown of Stuart (Eng.); Assn. Am. Friendship Bronze medal, Trieste; count Ho. of Deols (Italy); knight Delcassian Order (Ireland); medal Institute of Libertador Ramon Castilla (Peru); medal Internat. Eloy Alfaro Found. (Panama); silver medal spl. membership Japanese Red Cross Soc.; Ohio Faithful Service ribbon; recipient Nat. Headliner award, 1948, 49; 1st place award for editorial columns Nat. Found. for Hwy. Safety, 1970; cert. of appreciation Ohio Vets. World War I, 1971; Appreciation plaque Ohio N.G., 1976; Meritorious service medal SSS; spl. recognition award Ohio VFW, 1981; Ohio Disting. Service medal; named hon. Ky. col., hon. adm. Nebr. Navy, hon. adm. Tex. Navy, hon. N.Mex. col., hon. Miss. col., hon. lt. col. Ala., Ga., lt. gov. Ohio, Ind. Sagamore; commodore Okla., Ohio. Mem. Am. Mil. Inst., Orders and Medals Soc. Am., Ohio Def. Officers Assn., Nat. Flag Found., Am. Internat. Acad., Brazilian Acad. Polit. and Social Sci., Nat. Citizens for State 51; (P.R.), Inst. Heraldry (Spain), Internat. Inst. Study and Devel. Human Relations, Brazilian Acad. Econs. and Adminstrv. Scis., Sons Union Vets. Civil War (past state comdr.), Continental Confedn. Adopted Indians (co-founder, past continental chief), Civil War Press Corps (founder, past comdr.), Assn. U.S. Army, Am. Indian Lore Assn. (hon.), U.S. Horse Cavalry Assn., 7th U.S. Cavalry Assn. (assoc. life), Cass County (Ind.) Hist. Soc., My Country Soc. Clubs: National Headliners; Honolulu Press. Author: Two Term Tradition, 1940; Collected Poems, 1937-47, 1948. Columnist; contbr. articles to mags. Home: 2420 Zollinger Rd Columbus OH 43221

CLAPP, CHARLES LAWRENCE, III, lawyer; b. Grand Rapids, Mich., Apr. 26, 1956; s. Charles Lawrence II and Marcia Germaine (Miller) C.; m. Cindy Ray, Aug. 23, 1980; children—Charles Lawrence IV, Sarah Ray. B.A., Aquinas Coll., 1978; J.D., Thomas M. Cooley Law Sch., 1981. Bar: Mich. 1982, U.S. Dist. Ct. (we. Dist.) Mich. 1982. Sole practice, Grand Rapids, 1982—. Sec. Serra Club, Grand Rapids, 1983-85. Mem. Phi Alpha Theta. Roman Catholic. Office: 1100 Four Mile Rd NW PO Box 2824 Grand Rapids MI 49501

CLARE, STEWART, educator, research biologist; b. nr. Montgomery City, Mo., Jan. 31, 1913; s. William Gilmore and Wardie (Stewart) C.; B.A., U. Kans., 1935; M.S., Iowa State U., 1937; Ph.D., U. Chgo., 1949; m. Lena Glenn Kaster, Aug. 4, 1936. Student asst. entomology, also William Volker scholar U. Kans., 1931-35; Rockefeller Research fellow Iowa State U., 1935-36, teaching fellow, 1936-37; Univ. fellow zoology U. Chgo., 1937-40; dist. survey supr. entomology U.S. Civil Service Commn. Bur. Entomology and Plant Quarantine, 1937-40, tech. cons., 1941-42; instr. meteorology USAAF Weather Sch., 1942-43; research biologist Midwest Research Inst., Kansas City, Mo., 1945-46; spl. study, research Kansas City Art Inst., U. Mo., 1946-49; instr. zoology U. Alta., 1949-50, asst. prof. zoology, lectr.-instr. sci. color, dept. fine arts, 1950-53; research grantee Alberta Research Council, 1951-53; interim asst. prof. Kansas City Coll. Osteopathy 1953; lectr. zoology U. Adelaide, S. Australia, 1954-55; sr. research officer entomology Sudan Govt. Ministry Agr., Khartoum, Sudan and Gezira Research Sta., Wad Medani, Sudan, N.Africa, 1955-56; sr. entomologist Klipfontein Organic Products Corp., Johannesburg, Union S.Africa, 1957; prof., head dept. biology Union Coll., 1958-59, chmn. sci. div., prof., head biology, 1959-61, spl. study grantee, 1960; prof., head dept. biology Mo. Valley Coll., Marshall, 1961-62, research grantee, 1961-62; lectr., instr. biology, meteorology, sci. of color Adirondack Sci. Camp div. edn. N.Y. State U. Coll. summers 1962-66, dir. acad. program 1963-66, research facilities grantee, 1963-66; Buckbee Found. prof. biology Rockford (Ill.) Coll., lectr. biology eve. coll., 1962-63, spl. research grantee, 1962-63; prof., chmn. dept. biochemistry, mem. research div. Kansas City (Mo.) Coll. Osteopathy and Surgery, U. Health Scis., 1963-67, also NIH basic research grantee, 1963-67; prof. biology Coll. of Emporia (Kans.), 1967-74, dir. biol. research, 1972-74, prof. emeritus, 1974—, research study grantee, 1967-74, research biologist, cons., 1974—, spl. research grantee Coll. of Emporia and U. Alaska, 1970, No. Research Survey, Arctic Inst. N. Am., 1970, 72, Coll. of Emporia Central Am. and Mexico, 1973; cons. to Vols. for Internat. Tech. Assistance, 1962—, Adirondack Research and Field Sta., 1962-66, Nat. Referral Center for Science and Technology, 1970—. Mem. adv. bd. Fine Art Registry, Soc. N.Am. Artists, 1971—. Served with USNR, 1943-45. Recipient certificate service Vols. Internat. Tech. Assistance, 1970; creativity recognition award Internat. Personnel Research, 1972; Outstanding Educator award Coll. of Emporia, 1973; Distinguished Achievement and Service awards for edn. and research in biology, Certificate of Merit in Art, Internat. Biog. Centre, 1968, 72, 73, 76 numerous other awards. Fellow Intercontinental Biog. Assn. (life), Am. Biog. Inst., Explorers Club, Anglo-Am. Acad. (hon.); mem. Brit. Assn. Adv. Sci. (life), Am. Entomol. Soc. (life), Nat. Assn. Biology Tchrs., Arctic Inst. N.Am., Am. Polar Soc., N.Y. Acad. Scis. (life), Inter-Soc. Color Council, Sigma Xi, Phi Sigma, Psi Chi, numerous others. Contbr. monographs in capillary movement in porous materials, physiology and biochemistry of anthropoda; research on sci. and designing of color; numerous local, nat. and internat. exhibits; also articles to profl. jours. Home: 405 NW Woodland Rd Indian Hills in Riverside Kansas City MO 64150

CLAREY, JOHN ROBERT, executive search consultant; b. Waterloo, Iowa, June 5, 1942; s. Robert J. and Norma (Knox) C.; m. Kathleen Ann Kingsley, June 5, 1965; children—Sharon Diane, Suzanne Marie. B.S.B.A., Iowa State U., 1965; M.B.A., U. Pa., 1972. Fin. analyst Ford Motor Co., Dearborn, Mich., 1972-74; cons. Price Waterhouse, Chgo., 1974-75, mgr., 1975-76; assoc. Heidrick & Struggles, 1976-81, v.p., ptnr., 1981-82; pres. Jack Clarey Assocs., Inc., Northbrook, Ill., 1982—; dir. Stick & Rudder, Waukegan, Ill. Served to lt. USN, 1965-70; Vietnam. Republican. Roman Catholic. Clubs: Mid-Am. (Chgo.); Sunset Ridge Country (Northbrook). Avocations: flying, microcomputers. Home: 1337 Hillside Rd Northbrook IL 60062 Office: Jack Clarey Assocs Inc 1200 Shermer Rd Northbrook IL 60062

CLARK, C. KENNETH, JR., lawyer; b. Youngstown, Ohio, Mar. 11, 1930; s. C. Kenneth and Katharine (Griswold) C.; A.B., Oberlin Coll., 1951; J.D., Harvard U., 1954. Admitted to Ohio bar, 1954; partner firm Harrington, Huxley & Smith, Youngstown, 1963—; dir. WKBN Broadcasting Corp., Youngstown, others. Pres. Vol. Service Bur. Youngstown, 1965-68; Trustee, Lucy R. Buechtner Corp., Penn-Ohio Ednl. Found., Youngstown Playground Assn., Assoc. Neighborhood Centers Youngstown, pres., 1969. Mem. Am., Ohio State bar assns., U.S. Jud. Conf. for Sixth Circuit, Youngstown Area C. of C. Presbyn. Club: Youngstown. Home: 1637 Tanglewood Dr Youngstown OH 44505 Office: Mahoning Bank Bldg Youngstown OH 44503

CLARK, CHARLES AUGUSTUS, dental educator; b. Belhaven, N.C., June 24, 1928; s. Charles Edward and Delilah (Sutton) C.; m. Hiawatha Cynthia Wilborn, Dec. 29, 1957; children—Shawn Marie, Cheryl Lynn, John Charles. B.S., Hampton Inst., 1949; M.Sc., Ohio State U., 1951; D.D.S., Howard U., 1955; M.S., U. Pitts., 1960; M.P.H., U. Mich.-Ann Arbor, 1968. Diplomate Am. Bd. Dental Pub. Health. Oral surgeon, Cleve., 1961-68; dental dir. Cleve. Health Dept., 1968-73; chief dental health planning Met. Health Planning Corp., Cleve., 1973-77; assoc. prof., chmn. com. dentistry Case Western Res. U. Dental Sch., 1977-83, prof., chmn. dept. community dentistry, 1983—; cons. Sunny Acres Skilled Nursing Home, Cleve., 1981—; trustee Golden Age Ctrs. Cleve., 1980—. Contbr. articles to sci. jours., chpts. to books; author numerous lecture presentations; producer films. Mem. adv. com. Cuyahoga Community Coll. Dental Hygiene, Cleve., 1975—, Fedn. Community Planning, Cleve., 1977—, Helen S. Brown Sr. Citizens Ctr., Geriatric Medicine, Ohio Bd. Regents, Columbus, 1978-80, Ctr. for Aging and Health, Case We. Res. U., 1980—. Served to capt. AUS, 1956-58. Mem. Ohio Dental Assn. (chmn. sub-council on underserved 1982—, del. 1957—), Cleve. Coalition on Health Care, Am. Assn. Pub. Health Dentists, Am. Pub. Health Assn., Am. Dental Assn. Jehovah's Witness. Avocation: Music. Home: 19230 Scottsdale Blvd Shaker Heights OH 44122 Office: Case Western Res Univ Dental Sch 2123 Abington Rd Cleveland OH 44106

CLARK, CHARLES EDWARD, arbitrator; b. Cleve., Feb. 27, 1921; s. Douglas John and Mae (Egermayer) C.; student Berea Coll., 1939-41, King Coll., 1945; LL.B., U. Tex., 1948; m. Nancy Jane Hilt, Mar. 11, 1942; children—Annette S. (Mrs. Paul Gernhardt), Charles Edward, John A., Nancy P., Paul R., Stephen C., David G. Admitted to Tex. bar, 1948, Mass. bar, 1956, U.S. Supreme Ct. bar, 1959; practice law, San Antonio, 1948-55; writer legal articles, editor NACCA Law Jour., Boston, 1955-58; legal asst. to vice chmn., chief voting sect. U.S. Commn. on Civil Rights, Washington, 1958-61; spl. counsel Pres.'s Com. on Equal Employment Opportunity, 1961-65; sr. compliance officer Office Fed. Contract Compliance, 1965-66; regional dir. Equal Employment Opportunity Commn., Kansas City, Mo., 1966-79; arbitrator, 1979—; prof. law, asst. dean St. Mary's U. Sch. Law, 1948-55; lectr. Rockhurst Coll., 1980—. Active Boy Scouts Am. Served with AUS, 1943-44. Mem. Soc. Profls. in Dispute Resolution, State Bar Tex., Am. GI Forum (D.C. vice chmn. 1962-63), Indsl. Relations Research Assn. (exec. bd. Kansas City 1976—, v.p. chpt. 1985), Phi Delta Phi (province pres. 1951-55). Contbr. articles to legal jours. Home and Office: 6418 Washington St Kansas City MO 64113

CLARK, CHRISTINE MAY, editor, author; b. Peoria, Ill., Apr. 25, 1957; d. Darrell Ronald and Alice Venita (Burkitt) French; m. Terry Randolph Clark, Aug. 28, 1982. B.A., Judson Coll., 1978. Stringer, Countryside Press, Barrington, Ill., 1978; news reporter Judson Coll., Elgin, Ill., 1978; assoc. editor David C. Cook Pub., Elgin, Ill., 1978-80; editor Humpty Dumpty and Jack and Jill Mags, Indpls., 1980—; assoc. editor Turtle Mag. and Children's Digest, 1980—; asst. workshop condr. Chgo. Sunday Sch. Conv., 1978; speaker Ind. Guild Christian Writers and Poets, Indpls., 1983. Author: (religious curriculum) Come, Follow Me, 1983, Living in Covenant, 1985. Contbr. articles and stories to children's and adult religious mags. Asst. scout leader Fox Valley Council Girl Scouts U.S., 1972; vol. Elgin Mental Health Ctr., 1975-76; big sister Big Sister-Little Sister Program, Elgin, 1980. Aurora Found. scholar, 1975. Mem. Central Ind. Writer's Assn., Ind. Guild Christian Writers and Poets, Ednl. Press Assn., Judson Coll. Alumni Assn. Reorganized Ch. of Jesus Christ of Latter-day Saints. Avocations: Piano; travel. Home: 8345 E 41st St Indianapolis IN 46226 Office: Children's Better Health Inst 1100 Waterway Blvd Indianapolis IN 46206

CLARK, DAVID BAIRD, police chief; b. Clark County, Ill., Nov. 18, 1941; s. Marion Dean and Wilma Elaine (Baird) C.; m. Myrtle I. Canterbury, July 2, 1960; children—Richard E., Greg Paul. Grad. of theology Baptist Bible Coll., 1962; Assoc. Bus. Tech., Tiffin U., 1975. Missionary to Ethiopia, Bapt. Bible Fellowship, Springfield, Mo., 1964-67; with Police Dept., City of Findlay, Ohio, 1967—, police chief, 1979—; instr. Ohio Peace Officer Tng. and Trades and Industries Commn., Columbus, 1973—. Mem. Hancock County Alcoholism Bd., 1981, 82, Hancock County Traffic Commn., 1979—; past chmn. Findlay Blockwatch Com., 1983-84. Mem. Ohio Assn. Chief's of Police (com. on legis., tng. com.), FBI Assn. Republican. Baptist. Office: Findlay Police Dept Room 207 Mcpl Bldg Findlay OH 45840

CLARK, DONALD CAMERON, diversified company executive; b. Bklyn., Aug. 9, 1931; s. Alexander and Sarah (Cameron) C.; B.B.A., Clarkson Coll., Potsdam, N.Y., 1953; M.B.A., Northwestern U., 1961; m. Jean Ann Williams, Feb. 6, 1954; children—Donald C., Barbara Jean, Thomas Robert. With Household Internat., Prospect Heights, Ill., 1955—, treas., 1972-74, sr. v.p., 1974-76, exec. v.p., chief fin. officer, 1976-77, pres., 1977—, chief exec. officer, 1982—, chmn. bd., 1984—; dir. Square D Co., Warner Lambert. Bd. dirs. Chgo. Council on Fgn. Relations, Lyric Opera of Chgo.; trustee Clarkson Coll., Northwestern U. Served with U.S. Army, 1953-55. Mem. Econ. Club (dir.). Clubs: Westmoreland Country, Mid-America, Economic. Office: 2700 Sanders Rd Prospect Heights IL 60070

CLARK, DORA BELLE, business educator; b. Milan, Mo., May 5, 1930; d. William G. and Zulah J. (Davis) Steele; m. James Paul Clark, Aug. 20, 1950; children—Paula June, Steven Eugene, Tami Lynn. B.S.E. in Bus. Edn., Northeast Mo. State U., 1956, M.A., 1964. Sec. Prodn. Credit Assn., Milan, 1947-48; tchr. Sterling Rural Sch., Milan, 1948-49; Milan Pub. schs., 1950-52; clk. stenographer, Fort Belvoir, Va., 1952-54; bookkeeper Bessie's Cafe, Milan, 1957-60; bus. edn. tchr. Novinger Pub. Schs. (Mo.), 1957-64; patient claims supr. Mid. Central Health Services, Kirksville, Mo., 1970-71; bus. and office edn. instr. Northeast Mo. State U., Kirksville, 1964—. Mem. Mo. State Tchrs. Assn., Mo. Bus. Edn. Assn., Nat. Bus. Edn. Assn., Mo. Vocat. Assn., Am. Vocat. Assn. Methodist. Clubs: PEO Sojourners Federated, Kirksville Federated Garden. Office: Div Business 114 Violette Hall Northeast Missouri State University Kirksville MO 63501

CLARK, ELIZABETH ANN, nurse; b. Alton, Ill., Dec. 10, 1950; d. Angelo Thomas and Josephine Ann (Lombardo) Alben; grad. St. Joseph's Sch. Nursing, Alton, 1971; B.S. in Nursing, McKendree Coll., 1985; m. Gary Daniel Clark, Aug. 20, 1970; children—Nicole Leigh, Jason Andrew. Staff nurse obstetrics-gynecology S.W. Tex. Meth. Hosp., San Antonio, 1971; staff nurse operating room Kansas City (Mo.) Gen. Hosp., 1971-73; staff nurse obstetrics, recovery room, med.-surg. Spelman Meml. Hosp., Smithville, Mo., 1974-76; staff nurse operating room Alton Meml. Hosp., 1976-85, head nurse operating room, 1985—; sec. Anestat, Inc., 1975-76. Treas. Alton Area Swim Team, 1985—. Mem. Assn. Operating Room Nurses, Phi Theta Kappa. Roman Catholic. Home: 2915 Gilbert Ln Alton IL 62002

CLARK, GENITHA LUCILLE, nurse, educator; b. Bigelow, Kans., July 29, 1932; d. Stephon Aloysious and Mary Catherine (Henley) Farrell; married (wid. Dec. 26, 1977); children—Pamela J., Cynthia J., Sandra S. B.S. in Psychology, Washburn U., 1971; M.S., Kans. State U., 1973; M. Nursing, Univ. Kans., 1983. Dir. nursing edn. Topeka State Hosp., 1971-73; coordinator nursing VA, Leavenworth, Kans., 1973-75; team nurse Menninger Found., Topeka, 1975-76; instr. Newman Hosp., Emporia, Kans., 1976-80; dir. nursing Kans. Neurological Inst., Topeka, 1980—; adj. prof. U. Kans., Lawrence, 1983—. Contbr. chpt. to Basic Patient Needs, 1985. Campaign mem. Rep. Judy Runnels, Topeka, 1980-84; mem. Democratic Club, Topeka, 1980—; bd. dirs. YWCA, Topeka, 1982—. Mem. Am. Nurses Assn., Kans. State Nurses Assn. (econ. v.gen. 1978-80), Dist. Nurses Assn. (mem. legislative com. 1978—, bd. dirs. 1982—), Sigma Theta Tau. Roman Catholic. Home: 135 Courtland Topeka KS 66606 Office: Shehar Hosp Al Taif Saudi Arabia

CLARK, GEORGE ALEXANDER, ophthalmologist; b. Indpls., Dec. 14, 1927; s. Cecil Pratt and Isabella Mary (Brodie) C.; m. Shirley Lee Sprague, June 14, 1953; children—George Gregory, James Sprague, Karin Lee. B.S., Ind. U., 1951, M.D., Ind. U.-Indpls., 1954; O.D., Wayne State U., 1960. Diplomate Am. Bd. of Ophthalmology 1962. Cons. in ophthalmology U.S. Pub. Health Service, Detroit, 1959-60; instr. dept. of ophthalmology, Ind. U.-Indpls., 1960-72; pres. Ind. Acad. of Ophthalmology, Indpls., 1972; pres. G & S Leasing Co., Indpls., 1964—, C-R Leasing Co., Indpls., 1979—. Served to pfc USMC, 1946-47; capt. USAF, 1955-57. Fellow Am. Acad. of Ophthalmology, Ind. Acad. of Ophthalmology, Am. Intraocular Implant Soc. Republican. Presbyterian. Club: Meridian Hills Country (Indpls.). Avocations: aviation; spectator sports. Home: 10430 Fall Creek Rd Indianapolis IN 46240 Office: 50 E 91st St #104 Indianapolis IN 46240

CLARK, GEORGE MASON, architecture educator, architect; b. Brookline, Mass., Mar. 24, 1923; s. George Lindenberg and Mary Mason (Johnson) C.; m. Jean Flanigan, May 20, 1944; children—Elizabeth Ann Clark Swank, Mary Mason Clark Siebert. Student DePauw U., 1940-42; B.S. cum laude in Archtl. Engring., U. Ill., 1944, M.S. in Architecture, 1947. Registered architect, Ill., 1947, Ohio, 1952. Asst. prof. Syracuse U., 1948-51; asst. prof. Ohio State U., Columbus, 1951-55, assoc. prof., 1955-59, prof. architecture, research supr. bldg. research lab., 1959-81, prof. emeritus, 1981—; founder, prin. emeritus Designs in Context, Libertyville, Ill., 1982—, George Mason Clark, Architect, AIA, Gurnee, Ill., 1982—; mem. constrn. panel Am. Arbitration Assn., 1984. Trustee Family Fin. Found., Columbus, 1979-82; trustee, Douglas Lake Shore Assn., Douglas, Mich., 1983—, pres., 1986—. Chmn. Bd. Zoning Appeal, Upper Arlington, Ohio, 1958-63. Served with USNR, 1944-46. Recipient appreciation award Ohio State U., 1969; citation of merit, silver medal, dept. architecture Ohio State U., 1982. Mem. AIA, Am. Soc. Interior Designers (assoc.), ASTM. Republican. Episcopalian. Clubs: Ohio State U. Faculty, Univ. (Columbus). Heather Ridge Golf (Gurnee).

CLARK, JAMES ROBERT, JR., osteopathic physician, radiologist; b. Harrisburg, Pa., May 19, 1946; s. James Robert and Mary Jane (Rudy) C.; m. Marcia Allerdice, Aug. 17, 1968; children—Benjamin, Emily, Elizabeth. B.S. in Pharmacy, U. N.C., 1969; D.O., Phila. Coll. Osteo. Medicine, 1977. Cert. in radiology Am. Osteo. Bd. Radiology. Rotating intern Grandview Hosp., Dayton, Ohio, 1977-78, resident in radiology, 1978-81; practice osteo. medicine specializing in radiology, Dayton, 1981—; mem. Dayton Assocs. in Radiology, Inc., Grandview Hosp., Southview Hosp., Dayton; mem. vol. faculty Ohio U. Coll. Osteo. Medicine. Served to capt. USAF, 1970-73. Mem. Am. Osteo. Assn., Ohio Osteo. Assn., Dayton Dist. Acad. Osteopathy, Am. Osteo. Coll. Radiology, Radiological Soc. of N.Am. Republican. Episcopalian. Office: 405 Grand Ave Dayton OH 45405

CLARK, JAMES STEPHEN, advertising agency executive, marketing consultant; b. Milw., May 15, 1948; s. Glenn Francis and Joyce Philys (Krieger) C.; m. Susan Lynne Lauber, Sept. 8, 1948; children—Jason Andrew, Jennifer Abbe, Aaron Adrian. B.A., U. No. Iowa, 1971. Mktg. and mgmt. positions midwestern region Lucky Stores, Inc., 1967-77; account exec. Mohawk Advt., Mason City, Iowa, 1977-78, v.p., 1978-81, chmn. bd., pres., 1981—. Cubmaster Boy Scouts Am. Recipient nat. and internat. advt. and mktg. awards. Mem. Am. Advt. Assn., Nat. Agr. Mktg. Assn. Republican. Methodist. Lodge: Lions. Home: 9 Timberlane Dr Clear Lake IA 50428 Office: 1307 6th St SW Mason City IA 50401

CLARK, JANE COLBY, educator; b. Smith County, Kans., July 22, 1928; d. Noel Barclay and Velma Matilda (Helfinstine) Colby; B.S., Kans. State U., 1951; postgrad. Colo. State U., 1955-56, U. Colo., summers 1957-59; m. William Kline Clark, May 27, 1951; children—Courtney, Hilary. Tchr. rural sch., Smith County, 1946-47; sec., home service worker ARC, Boulder, Colo., 1952-55; tchr. public schs., Manhattan, Kans., 1956-59; temporary instr. in English, Kans. State U., 1968-74, instr., 1974—, asst. dir. writing lab. dept. English, 1974-85, dir. writing lab., 1985—. Mem. Nat. Council Tchrs. English, Nat. Writing Ctrs. Assn., Midwest Writing Ctrs. Assn., Riley County Humane Soc., Mortar Bd. Alumnae (pres. 1965-66), Phi Kappa Phi. Methodist. Contbr. book revs. to newspaper, Manhattan Mercury. Home: 1801 Ranser Rd Manhattan KS 66502 Office: 102 Denison Hall Kans State U Manhattan KS 66506

CLARK, JANIS MARIA WEATHERALL, special education teacher; b. Chgo., June 29, 1954; d. Eugene Davies and Lillian (Amison) Weatherall; m. Robert Alexander Clark, May 25, 1973; children—Robert Jr., Stephanie Maria. B.S. in Edn., Ill. State U., 1977, M.S. in Edn., 1983. Cert. spl. edn. tchr., adminstr. Ill. Spl. edn. tchr. Bloomington (Ill.) Alternative Schs., 1978-80; head spl. edn. tchr. Peoria (Ill.) Assn. Retarded Citizens, 1980; spl. edn. tchr. LeRoy (Ill.) High Sch., 1980-83, Scott Ctr. Sch., Bloomington, 1984-85; pre-vocation work coordinator University High Sch., Ill. State U., Normal, 1985—. Mem. Assn. Supervision and Curriculum Devel. Home: 2415 Rainbow Ave Bloomington IL 61701 Office: University High School Ill State U Normal IL 61761

CLARK, JOHN EARL, banker, consultant; b. Columbus, Ohio, June 19, 1951; s. Earl W. and Juanita (Wolford) C.; m. Donna M. Weimann, June 12, 1971; children—Carol, Andrea. A.A., Columbus Tech., 1971; cert. Am. Inst. Banking, 1977, Ohio Sch. Consumer Credit, Kent State U., 1978, Ohio Sch. Banking, Ohio U., 1984. Br. asst. City Loan Co., Newark, Ohio, 1969-74; asst. mgr. Credithrift of Am., Lancaster, Ohio, 1974-75; asst. v.p. Central Trust Co., Lancaster, 1975—; freelance photographer, Lancaster, 1977-84; bd. dirs. Jr. Achievement, Lancaster, 1983—, cons., 1979-83; pres. J.E. Clark & Assocs., Inc., Lancaster, 1984—; ptnr. Gameboard Gallery, Lancaster, 1984—. Recipient Gold award United Way, Lancaster, 1977, Citation of Service, Am. Diabetes Assn., 1983. Mem. Fairfield County C. of C., Buckeye Lake C. of C. Baptist. Lodge: Lions (pres. 1984-85). Avocations: photography; fishing; antique collecting. Home: 333 W Fair Ave Lancaster OH 43130 Office: Central Trust Co PO Box 188 Millersport OH 43046

CLARK, JOHN PETER, III, engineering company executive; b. Phila., May 6, 1942; s. John Peter Jr. and Victoria Mary (McQuaide) C.; m. Nancy Ann Lapin, June 22, 1968; children—Shannon John, Hannah Marie. B.S. in Chem. Engring., Notre Dame U., 1964; Ph.D., U. Calif., 1968. Registered profl. engr., Va. Research engr. Agrl. Research Service, U.S. Dept. Agr., Berkeley, Calif., Washington, 1968-72; from asst. to assoc. prof. Va. Poly. Inst. and State U., Blacksburg, 1972-78; dir. research and devel. ITT Continental Baking, Rye, N.Y., 1978-81; pres. Epstein Process Engring. Inc., Chgo., 1981—. Editor: Exercises in Process Simulation, 1977. Contbr. articles to profl. jours. Patentee in field. Mem. Am. Inst. Chem. Engrs. (div. chmn. 1982), Inst. Food Technologists (div. chmn. 1984—), Am. Chem. Soc. Roman Catholic. Avocations: reading, running, Indian art. Home: 644 N Linden Ave Oak Park IL 60302 Office: Epstein Process Engring Inc 600 W Fulton St Chicago IL 60606

CLARK, JOHN ROBERT, management psychologist; b. Pitts., Oct. 23, 1943; B.A., U. Notre Dame, 1965; M.B.A., Loyola U., 1974; Ph.D., Ill. Inst. Tech., 1979; m. Mary Diorio, Nov. 24, 1966. Supr. manpower procurement Hyster Co., Portland, Oreg., 1967-70, sales rep., Chgo., 1970-79; v.p. Mark Silber Assos. Ltd., 1979-81; v.p. Witt Assos., Inc., Oak Brook, Ill., 1981—. Mem. Am. Psychol. Assn., Am. Theatre Organ Soc. Roman Catholic. Club: Notre Dame (Chgo.). Home: 125 Saddlebrook Dr Oak Brook IL 60521 Office: 724 Enterprise Dr Oak Brook IL 60521

CLARK, JOSEPH FRANCIS, senior citizens organization executive; b. Allegheny, Pa., July 21, 1900; s. Joseph R. and Mary Elizabeth (Tully) C.; m. Lulu Marie Tinsler, May 23, 1936; 1 child, Nancy Lou. Grad. Ill. Wesleyan U. Cost acct. Overland Motor Co., Chgo., 1915-19; office mgr. Great Western Refining Co., Chgo., 1919-24; with Western Electric Co., Chgo., 1924-27, Bates Valve Bag Co., Chgo., 1927-34; owner Midway Press, Chgo., 1934-73; with Inland Steel Co., Indiana Harbor, Ind., 1942-45; pres. Rantoul Sr. Citizens Club, Ill., 1977—. Columnist, 1975—. Recipient award Urban League Champaign County, 1984. Republican. Methodist. Avocations: ceramics; reading; choral singing. Office: Rantoul Sr Citizens Club 520 Wabash St Rantoul IL 61866

CLARK, LARRY DALTON, civil engineer; b. Sask., Can., May 12, 1942; s. Albert Ray and Christina Emily (Marum) C.; B.S. in Civil Engring., S.D. Sch. Mines, Rapid City, 1971; m. Janice Martina Kettleson, Aug. 16, 1969; children—Tamara Dayrie, Laura Janelle, Jennifer Lynette, Daniel Jerod. Engr. in tng. Iowa Hwy. Commn., Ames, 1971-75; asst. resident engr. Iowa Dept. Transp., New Hampton, 1975-79, acting resident engr., 1977-78; county engr. Black Hawk County, 1979—. Active local United Way campaign, 1976-77. Recipient award Nat. Assn. Counties Bridge Rehab. Registered profl. engr., Iowa; registered land surveyor. Mem. ASCE, Nat., Iowa socs. profl. engrs., Sigma Tau. Lutheran. Home: 338 Longview Dr Waterloo IA Office: Black Hawk County Courthouse Waterloo IA 50703

CLARK, LINDA MARIE, cons.; b. Chgo., June 9, 1940; d. Harold Dean and Edith M. (Nystrom) C.; B.S., U. Mich., 1962; M.B.A., U. Chgo., 1969. Analyst, Biol. Scis. Computation Ctr., Billings Hosp., U. Chgo., 1962-65; dir. math. and statis. services Armour & Co., Chgo., 1965-68; pvt. practice cons., Chgo., 1968-69; pres. LMC Cons. Co., Flossmoor, Ill., 1969—; dir. Internat. Computer Edn. Corp., Ill., 1971-75. Bd. govs. Internat. House, U. Chgo., 1976—; sec.-treas. U. Chgo. Alumnae Council Exec. Com., 1976-77; del. White House Conf. Small Bus., 1980; mem. Pvt. Industry Council Suburban Cook County, 1980-81. Mem. Am. Statis. Assn. (pres. Chgo. chpt. 1972-73, dir. 1971-74), Optical Soc. Am. (mem. nat. com. computers 1976-77), AAAS, Ill. Del. Small Bus., Ind. Bus. Assn. Ill. (dir., v.p. state issues 1982-84), Chgo. Assn. Commerce and Industry (dir. 1974-79), U. Chgo. Women's Bus. Group, Alpha Chi Omega. Club: P.E.O. (pres. chpt. HH 1981-83). Contbr. articles to profl. jours. Pub. Met. Chgo. Maj. Employer's Directory, 1977. Home: 1127 Dartmouth Rd Flossmoor IL 60422

CLARK, MARTIN BELL, robotics company executive, consultant; b. Duluth, Minn., Mar. 18, 1955; s. Thomas Ferguson and Barbara Jean (Barclay) C.; m. Leigh Ann Schlich, Sept. 24, 1977; children—Andrew Charles, Megan Leigh, Casey Thomas. B.S. in Bus. Administrn., Miami U.-Oxford, Ohio, 1977. Pres., owner Profl. Flagpole Painting, Dayton, Ohio, 1975-76; mgr., coach Trailsend Club, Kettering, Ohio, 1973-77; sr. sales engr. Kettering Material Handling, Dayton, 1977-81; v.p. mktg. Fabspec, Dayton, 1982—; cons. Sperotech, Spring Valley, Ohio, 1982-84; dir., sec. Fabrication Specialties, Dayton, 1982—. Recipient Salesman of Yr. award Kettering Material Handling, 1979. Mem. Robotics Internat. of Soc. Mech. Engr. Republican. Roman Catholic. Club: Quail Run Leisure Ctr. (v.p., bd. dirs. 1982—). Avocations: swimming; skiing; tennis. Home: 1248 Timber Hawk Trail Spring Valley OH 45370

CLARK, MARY ROMAYNE SCHROEDER, communication consultant, civic worker; b. Fergus Falls, Minn.; d. Christian Frederick and Dorothy Genevieve (Miller) Schroeder; B.A., Coll. St. Teresa, 1944; diploma fine arts Conservatory St. Cecelia, 1944; M.A., Marquette U., 1978; postgrad. U. Salzburg (Austria); m. Donald Arthur Clark, Aug. 24, 1946 (dec. Jan. 1975); children—Donald Arthur, Anne Elizabeth, Christopher John. Instr., Ottumwa (Iowa) Heights Coll., 1944-46; instr. U. N.D., Grand Forks, 1946-48, Marquette U., Milw., 1948-52, Milw. Area Tech. Coll., 1962-66, Mt. Mary Coll., Milw., 1976-81; dir. tng. and devel. First Bank, Milw., 1981-84; instr., seminar leader Div. Continuing Edn., Marquette U., 1984—, U. Wis. Ext., 1984—; communications cons. 1978-80, coordinator community relations, 1980—. Mem. com. on edn. U.S. Cath. Conf., Washington, 1971-75; state vol.

adviser Nat. Found., 1971—; mem. adv. bd. Sickle Cell Disease Center, Deaconess Hosp., Milw., 1970-73; mem. nat. alumnae bd. Coll. St. Teresa, Winona, Minn., 1970—; mem. bd. edn. Archdiocese Milw., 1965-71, pres., 1967-71; bd. dirs. Woman to Woman Inc.; adv. bd. Mgmt. Inst., U.Wis.-Milw., 1983—. Named Wis. Woman of Year, Wis. Cath. War Vets., 1963, Alumna of Year, Coll. St. Teresa, 1969, Outstanding Vol. Nat. Found., 1974, Vol. Activist Germaine Monteil, 1974; Presdl. award Nat. Cath. Edn. Assn., 1981; Excellence in Tng. award Am. Soc. Tng. and Devel., 1983, 84. Mem. Archdiocesan Confraternity Christian Mothers (pres. 1961-63), Archdiocesan League Cath. Home and Sch. Assns. (pres. 1963-65), Archdiocesan Council Cath. Women (dist. pres. 1965-67), Nat. Forum Cath. Parents Orgns. (v.p. 1979), Internat. Fedn. Cath. Alumnae, Am. Soc. Tng. and Devel. AAUW, Marquette U. Women's Club (pres. 1959). Home: 317 N Story Pkwy Milwaukee WI 53208

CLARK, MAXINE, retail executive; b. Miami, Fla., Mar. 6, 1949; d. Kenneth and Anne (Lerch) Kasselman; m. Robert Fox, Sept. 1984. B.A. in Journalism, U. Ga., 1971. Exec. trainee Hecht Co., Washington, 1971, hosiery buyer, 1971-72, misses sportswear buyer, 1972-76; mgr. mdse. planning and research May Dept. Stores Co., St. Louis, 1976-78, dir. mdse. devel., 1978-80, v.p. mktg. and sales promotion Venture Stores div., 1980-81, sr. v.p. mktg. and sales promotion Venture Stores div., 1981-83, exec. v.p. mktg. and softlines, 1983-85; exec. v.p. apparel Famous-Barr, St. Louis, 1985—. Sec., Lafayette Sq. Restoration Com., 1978-79. Mem. Nat. Assn. Female Execs., St. Louis Women's Commerce Assn., Advt. Club Greater St. Louis, St. Louis Forum. Home: 6319 Alexander Dr Clayton MO 63105 Office: 615 Northwest Plaza Saint Ann MO 63074

CLARK, MONTAGUE GRAHAM, JR., former college president; b. Charlotte, N.C., Feb. 25, 1909; s. Montague G. and Alice C. (Graham) C.; student Ga. Inst. Tech. Sch. Engring.; LL.D., Drury Coll., 1957; Ed.D., S.W. Baptist Coll., 1972; Litt.D., Sch. of the Ozarks, 1975; D.D., Missouri Valley Coll., 1977; m. Elizabeth Hoyt, May 2, 1933; children—Elizabeth (Mrs. Joe Embser), Alice (Mrs. Harold Davis), Margaret (Mrs. William Miller), Julia (Mrs. Cecil Hampton). Vice pres. Hoyt & Co., Atlanta, 1934-46; v.p. Sch. of Ozarks, Point Lookout, Mo., 1946-52, pres., 1952-81, sec. bd. trustees, 1957-71, now chmn.; ordained to ministry Presbyn. Ch., 1950; dir. Bank of Taney County; dir., mem. exec. com., sec. corp. Blue Cross; spl. cons. NCCJ. Past mem. Commn. on Colls. and Univs., North Central Assn. Colls. and Secondary Schs.; former moderator Lafayette Presbytery and Synod of Mo., Presbyn. Ch. of U.S. Past mem. nat. adv. council on health professions edn. NIH; mem. Nat. council Boy Scouts Am., also mem. adv. bd. Ozarks Empire Area council; mem. Wilson's Creek Battlefield Nat. Commn., 1961—; hon. mem. Mo. Am. Revolution Bicentennial Commn.; former v.p. Am. Heart Assn., also dir.; mem. exec. com., chmn. fund raising adv. and policy com., Gt. Plains regional chmn.; chmn. planned giving and legacies Mo. div. Am. Cancer Soc.; chmn. Mo. Heart Fund, mem. adv. council Council on Am. Affairs; chmn. bd. Mo. Heart Assn.; trustee Patriotic Edn., Inc.; mem. South Central/Lakes County Med. Services System; v.p. Thomas Hart Benton Homestead Meml. Commn.; bd. dirs. St. Louis Scottish Towers Residence Found.; treas., mem. exec. com. Atlanta Christian Council; mem. Park and Recreation Commn. Fulton County; chmn. burns prevention com. Shrine of N. Am.; hon. edn. chmn. for So. Mo. div. Am. Cancer Soc.; mem. Mo. Commn. on Pub. Schs.; mem. area council Boy Scouts Am.; past pres. Atlanta Youth Council. Served to maj. Internal Security, World War II. Named Ark. traveler, 1962; recipient Silver Beaver award Boy Scouts Am.; Gold Heart award Am. Heart Assn.; George Washington certificate Freedoms Found., 1974, 78; In God We Trust award Family Found.; Disting. Service award Am. Legion, Mo.; numerous other awards; named to Ozark Hall of Fame. Mem. SAR (past pres. gen. nat. soc., hon. v.p. Mo. Soc.; Nat. Soc. Good Citizenship medal, Patriot medal, Minute Man award, Va. Soc. medal), Navy League U.S., Mo. C. of C., Branson C. of C. (econ. devel. com.), Mo. Pilots Assn. (1st chmn. bd.), Civil Air Patrol (dir., adv. bd.), White River Valley Hist. Soc. (past pres.), Soc. Colonial Wars, Acad. Mo. Squires, Order Founders and Patriots Am., Air Force Assn., Assn. U.S. Army, Mo. Assn. State Troopers Emergency Relief Soc. (pres.), Atlanta Sunday Sch. Supts. Assn. (pres., treas.), Internat. Assn. Chiefs of Police. Clubs: Mason (33 deg., Shriner, K.T., Red Cross of Constantine, York Rite, past imperial chaplain Imperial Council, Nobles of Mystic Shrine of N. Am.; grand chaplain Grand Lodge Mo.; honoree various ceremonies), Rotary (past local pres., dist. gov. 1966-67), De Molay. Address: The Sch of the Ozarks Point Lookout MO 65726

CLARK, PAUL EDWARD, publisher; b. Metropolis, Ill., Mar. 7, 1941; s. Paul E. and Lillie Jean (Melcher) C.; B.A., So. Ill. U., 1963, M.A., 1965; M.Div., Northwestern U., 1970; D.Mus., Inst. Musical Research (London), 1973; Ph.D., U. Ill., 1978. Staff accompanist The Story (TV series) and White Sisters (Word Records), 1959-62; staff accompanist voice faculty So. Ill. U., Carbondale, 1961-65; ordained to ministry, Meth. Ch., 1966; pastor Stockland (Ill.) United Meth. Ch., 1966-70; minister of music First United Meth. Ch., Watseka, Ill., 1972-76; dir. choral activities Unit 3, Donovan (Ill.) schs., 1970-79; studio musician Chgo., Nashville, Los Angeles, 1966—; pres. Clark Music Pub. and Prodn., Watseka, 1973—; adminstrv. asst., bus. mgr. Community Unit 3 Schs., 1980—; cons. for workshops, univs. Named Piano Tchr. of the Year, So. Ill. U., 1970; Gospel Music Instrumentalist award, 1971; Ill. Chess Coach award, 1973, 74; U. Calif. at Los Angeles fellow, 1971. Mem. Am. Choral Dirs. Assn. (dist. chmn. 1977-80), Am. Fedn. Musicians, Music Educators Nat. Conf., Ill. Music Educators Assn., U.S. Chess Fedn., So. Ill. U. Alumni Assn., NEA, Broadcast Music Inc., Phi Mu Alpha, Mu Alpha Theta. Republican. Methodist. Contbr. articles in field to profl. jours. music reviewer, critic, columnist The Illiana Spirit (newspaper), 1976—; composer; The Voice That Calls His Name, 1961; Jesus Dear Jesus, 1971; Spring Was But A Child, 1977; Country Living, 1976; Losing is the Hurting Side of Love, 1977; Use Me Lord, 1978; Come On In, 1978; All I Ask of You, 1979. Home: 115 W Locust St Watseka IL 60970 Office: PO Box 299 Watseka IL 60970

CLARK, PAUL THOMAS, hospital administrator; b. Ironton, Ohio, Oct. 13, 1943; s. Charles Nelson and Lucille May (Dudley) C.; B.A. in Journalism, Ohio State U., 1969, postgrad., 1971-73; m. Janice M. Merrill, Oct. 16, 1965; children—Colin, Sean. Editor, Ohio Petroleum Marketers Assn., Columbus, 1969; dir. public relations Otterbein Coll., Westerville, Ohio, 1970-72, Riverside Meth. Hosp., Columbus, 1972-77, Bronson Meth. Hosp., Kalamazoo, Mich., 1977-84; sr. v.p. Deaconess Hosp., Cin., 1984—. Spl. events chmn. Kalamazoo United Way, 1978; pub. affairs Kalamazoo County C. of C., 1977—. Served with AUS, 1961-64. Recipient McEachern award Am. Hosp. Assn., 1974, awards Ohio Hosp. Assn., 1974, 75, 76, awards Columbus Advt. Fedn., 1975, 76. Mem. Public Relations Soc. Am. (Silver Anvil award 1981), Am. Coll. Hosp. Adminstrs. Club: Kalamazoo Rotary. Home: 8718 Apalachee Dr Cincinnati OH 45242 Office: 311 Straight St Cincinnati OH 45219

CLARK, PEGGY DIANE, student personnel administrator; b. Lawton, Okla., Oct. 4, 1954; d. Wallace O. and Anita C. (Pedigo) C. B.A., Purdue U., 1977, M.S., 1985. Cert. tchr., Ind. English, speech tchr. Seeger Meml. High Sch., West Labanon, Ind., 1977-79, Carroll High Sch., Flora, Ind., 1979-80; coll. student personnel specialist Purdue Christian Campus House, West Lafayette, Ind., 1980—. Mem. Univ. Ministers Orgn., Nat. Assn. Christian Student Founds., Am. Assn. Counseling and Devel., Am. Coll. Personnel Assn. Mem. Christian Ch. Avocations: Interior design; needlework; reading. Home: 1003 Hartford St Lafayette IN 47904 Office: Purdue Christian Campus House 1000 State St West Lafayette IN 47906

CLARK, PETER BRUCE, newspaper executive; b. Detroit, Oct. 23, 1928; s. Rex Scripps and Marian (Peters) C.; B.A., Pomona Coll., 1952, LL.D. (hon.), 1972; M.P.A., Syracuse U., 1953; Ph.D., U. Chgo., 1959; H.H.D. (hon.), Mich. State U., 1973; LL.D. (hon.), U. Mich., 1977; m. Lianne Schroeder, Dec. 21, 1952; children—Ellen Clark Brown, James. Research assoc., then instr. polit. sci. U. Chgo., 1957-59; asst. prof. polit. sci. Yale U., 1959-61; with Evening News Assn., Detroit, 1960—, sec., v.p., 1961-63, pres., 1963—; pres. Detroit News, 1963-81; pub., 1963-82, chmn. bd., 1969—, also dir.; dir. Detroit br. Fed. Res. Bank Chgo., 1969-71, chmn., 1971-72, dir. Fed. Res. Bank Chgo., 1973-74, chmn., 1975-77. Bd. dirs. United Found. Met. Detroit, Harper-Grace Hosps. Detroit. Served with AUS, 1953-55. Mem. Am. Newspaper Pubs. Assn. (dir. 1966-74), Am. Polit. Sci. Assn., Am. Soc. Newspaper Editors, Adcraft Club Detroit, Econ. Club Detroit, Pi Sigma Alpha. Clubs: Detroit Country, Detroit, Detroit Athletic. Office: 615 Lafayette Blvd Detroit MI 48231

CLARK, RAY LAWRENCE, JR., public relations counsel; b. Sioux City, Iowa, May 30, 1924; s. Ray L., Sr. and Delia Catherine (Enright) C.; m. Dorothy Ross, Aug. 21, 1948; children—Mark Ross, Deborah Clark Sutor, Jennifer L. B.S., Medill Sch. Journalism Northwestern U., 1949, postgrad., 1950-51. With editorial copy desk Chgo. Tribune, 1948-52; pub. info. dir. Chgo. Chpt. ARC, 1952-56; exec. v.p. Ronald Goodman Pub. Relations, Chgo., 1956-64; pres. Clark Cons. Ltd., Oak Park, Ill., 1964—. Bd. dirs., pub. info. chmn. Am. Cancer Soc., Evanston, Ill., 1984. Served to s/sgt. USAF Weather Service, 1942-46. Mem. Pub. Relations Soc. Am. (recipient Silver Anvil 1963, 1964). Republican. Mem. Congregational Ch. Avocations: painting, music, opera. Home: City Walk 66 E 9th St Saint Paul MN 55101 Office: Clark Cons Ltd Box 76067 Saint Paul MN 55175

CLARK, RICHARD GEORGE, association executive; b. Peekskill, N.Y., Sept. 12, 1943; s. George C. and Dorothy (Starr) C.; m. Deborah Lynn Carr, Jan. 13, 1976; children—Jason, Jeffrey, Lindsay. B.S. in Edn., SUNY-Potsdam. Pres., chief exec. officer C. of C., Manchester, Conn., 1972-74, Plantation, Fla., 1974-76; exec. dir., chief exec. officer Indsl. Bd., Ft. Lauderdale, Fla., 1976-78; pres., chief operating officer, C. of C., Rockford, Ill., 1978-82; chief exec. officer Greater Fort Wayne C. of C., Ind.; faculty mem. Inst. of Orgnl. Mgmt., U.S. C. of C., 1972—. Mem. Am. C. of C. Execs., Ind. Commerce Exec. Assn. (div.), Summit Tech. and Research Transfer Ctr. (pres.), Fort Wayne Area Crimestoppers (vice chmn.). Methodist. Lodges: Lions, Kiwanis, Rotary. Avocations: jazz pianist. Address: Greater Fort Wayne C of C 826 Ewing St Fort Wayne IN 46802

CLARK, RICHARD NORVAL, manufacturing company executive; b. Gulfport, Miss., July 15, 1943; s. Norval F. and Mary Jane (Wells) C.; m. Sue Ann Malcolm, Nov. 8, 1980; 1 dau., Hope. B.S. in Indsl. Mgmt., Mich. State U., 1968. Cert. mfg. engr. With Large Jet Engine Group Gen. Electric Co., Cin., 1965-67; quality control engr. Chevrolet div. Gen. Motors Corp., Detroit, 1968-70; mfg. engr. Tecla Co., Inc., Walled Lake, Mich., 1971-74, v.p. 1974—, also dir. Mem. Usher's Guild, St. James Episcopal Ch.; active Republican party. Served to lt., USAFR, 1968-74. Mem. Soc. Mfg. Engrs. (bull. editor 1980-81, chpt. chmn.), Soc. Plastic Engrs., Inventor's Council Mich. (bd. dirs.), Mich. State Alumni Assn., Lakes Area C. of C., Sigma Delta Chi. Episcopalian. Clubs: MSU Presidents, Cin. Airman's. Patentee animal nail trimmer. Home: 25360 Lynford Dr Farmington Hills MI 48018 Office: Tecla Co Inc PO Box 438 2455 E W Maple Rd Walled Lake MI 48088

CLARK, ROBERT EUGENE, educator; b. Cheyenne, Wyo., Aug. 19, 1931; s. Glen E. and Anna W. (Shaw) C.; B.A., Wheaton Coll., 1961; M.S., U. Nebr., Omaha, 1965; Ed.D., U. Denver, 1968; m. Marian A. Anderson, June 13, 1954; children—Kathleen, Kevin, Kristine, Karen, Ken, Kraig. Dir. Christian edn. Bethel Bible Ch., Hammond, Ind., 1954-58; tchr. Faith Bapt. Bible Coll., Ankeny, Iowa, 1958-59, chmn. Christian edn. dept., 1961-69; prof. Christian edn. faculty Moody Bible Inst., Chgo., 1969—. Recipient Faculty Citation award Moody Bible Inst., 1983. Baptist. Author: (with others) Understanding People, 2d edit., 1981; editor Childhood Education in the Church, 1975; Teaching Preschoolers, 1983; contbr. to publs. in field. Home: 1044 Garner Ave Wheaton IL 60187 Office: Moody Bible Inst 820 N LaSalle St Chicago IL 60610

CLARK, ROBERT LOY, human services adminstr.; b. Kansas City, Mo., July 2, 1937; s. Robert William and Donna Lavonna (Loy) C.; A.B., No. Colo. U., 1959; postgrad. Syracuse U., 1959; M.S. in Psychology, Ft. Hays (Kans.) State U., 1963; postgrad. U. Nebr., 1963; m. Connie Lou Davis, Sept. 3, 1960; children—Vicki Marie, Robert Scott, Angie Linn. Vocational rehab. counselor Hays (Kans.) Div. Rehab. Services, 1960-62, Lincoln (Nebr.) Div. Rehab. Services, 1964-65, Glenwood (Iowa) Hosp.-Sch. for Mentally Retarded, 1965-66; exec. dir. Greater Omaha Assn. Retarded Citizens, 1966-71; dir. Douglas County (Nebr.) Dept. Mental Health Resources, Omaha, 1971-74; asst. dir. human services Eastern Neb. Human Services Agy., Omaha, 1974-75; adminstr. human services Lincoln-Lancaster County (Nebr.), 1975—; co-founder Nebr. Coalition for Community Human Services, 1982, pres., 1982, 1st v.p., 1983; community services cons. U. Nebr. Coll. Medicine, 1971-74, instr. med. psychology, dept. psychiatry, 1975-79; adv. mem. governing bd. Eastern Nebr. Community Office of Retardation, 1970-74; mem. Nebr. Gov.'s Citizens' Study Com. Mental Retardation, 1967-69; mem. Lincoln-Lancaster County Emergency Med. Services Council, 1975-78; bd. dirs. Mental Health Assn. Nebr., 1972—, treas., 1974-76, 84—; bd. dirs. Lincoln Action Program, 1976-80, Combined Health Agencies Drive of Nebr., 1985—. Mem. Rehab. Assn. Nebr. (past dir., treas. 1964-72). Democrat. Home: 1681 Woodsview Lincoln NE 68502 Office: 555 S 10th St Lincoln NE 68508

CLARK, RUSSELL GENTRY, See *Who's Who in America*, 43rd edition.

CLARK, RUSSELL LEWIS, landscape architect; b. Sheridan, Mich., Nov. 28, 1950; s. Erwin Dale and Jo Lena (Ross) C.; m. Karen Sue Yeasley, Mar. 17, 1972; children—R. Jason, Jeremy H., Karyann L. Student Ferris State Coll., 1969-71; B. Landscape Architecture with honors, Mich. State U., 1974. Registered landscape architect, Mich. Landscape architect Grabeck, Bell & Kline, Traverse City, Mich., 1974-75; planner Lellanau County Planning Commn., Leland, Mich., 1975-78; sr. planner Metcalf & Eddy Internat., Al-Khobar, Saudi Arabia, 1983; prin., owner R. Clark Assocs., Inc., Traverse City, 1979-84; v.p. spl. projects Traverse Devel. Co., Acme, Mich., 1984—. Bd. dirs. Traverse City Osteopathic Hosp., 1983-85. Mem. Am. Soc. Landscape Architects, Mich. Soc. Planning Ofcls., Mich. Bd. Landscape Architects (past chmn.), Traverse City C. of C. Home: 2706 Hartman Rd Traverse City MI 49684 Office: Gd Traverse Condominium Developers Inc PO Box 366 Acme MI 49610

CLARK, SAMUEL KELLY, engineering educator, researcher; b. Ypsilanti, Mich., Nov. 3, 1924; s. Floyd A. and Esther L. (Kelly) C.; m. Mary Jean Battelle, Jan. 4, 1952; children—Elizabeth, Samuel, Andrew, Frederic, David. B.S. in Aero. Engring., U. Mich., 1946, Ph.D., 1951. Registered profl. engr., Ohio. Engr., Douglas Aircraft, Santa Monica, Calif., 1946-47, Borg-Warner Corp., Detroit, 1948-51, Ford Motor Co., Detroit, 1951-52; asst. prof. Case Inst. Tech., Cleve., 1952-55; from asst. prof. to prof. U. Mich., Ann Arbor, 1955—; cons. in field. Author: Dynamics of Continous Elements, 1967; editor: Mechanics of Pneumatic Tires, 1977. Served with USN, 1943-46. Fellow Soc. Automotive Engrs.; mem. ASME, Soc. Exptl. Mechanics. Episcopalian. Avocations: travel; squash; sailing. Home: 885 Oakdale Rd Ann Arbor MI 48105 Office: U Mich 315 Automotive Lab Dept Mech Engring Ann Arbor MI 48109

CLARK, SAMUEL SMITH, physician, educator; b. Phila., Sept. 2, 1932; s. Horace E. and Jane (Mullin) C.; B.S., McGill U., 1954, M.D. C.M., 1958; m. Heather Jean Ogilvy, June 22, 1957; children—Ross Angus, Erin, Brian Mullin. Intern, Bethesda (Md.) Naval Hosp., 1958-59; resident Royal Victoria Hosp., Montreal, Que., Can., 1962-67; practice medicine, specializing in urology, Wheaton, Ill., 1976—; attending urologist Central DuPage Hosp., Winfield, Ill., 1976—; dir. urol. services, dir. neurogenic bladder service, both at Marianjoy Rehab. Hosp., Wheaton, 1983—; asst. prof. urology Abraham Lincoln Sch. of Medicine, U. Ill., Chgo., 1968-71, assoc. prof., 1971-73, prof., 1973-80, head div. urology, 1971-77; clin. prof. Loyola U., Chgo., 1980—; med. dir. Crescent Counties Found. for Med. Care, 1979-83. Bd. dirs. Marianjoy Rehab. Hosp., 1979-84. Served to lt. M.C., USN, 1958-62. Diplomate Am. Bd. Urology, Fellow ACS; mem. Am. Urol. Assn. (exec. com. North Central sect. 1974-77), Ill. Urol. Assn. (pres. 1979-80), DuPage Med. Soc., AMA, Chgo. Urol. Soc. (sec. treas. 1974-79, pres. 1979-80). Episcopalian. Clubs: Glen Oak Country. Contbr. articles to profl. jours. Home: 592 Turner St Glen Ellyn IL 60137 Office: 399 Schmale Rd Wheaton IL 60187

CLARK, STANLEY ANDREW, college administrator; b. Oneonta, N.Y., Nov. 18, 1948; s. Douglas Alan and Ruth (Campbell) C.; m. Susan L. Carlton, June 3, 1969; children—Rachel, Russell. Teaching fellow U. Fla., Gainesville, 1970-72; asst. prof. U. Sask., Saskatoon, Can., 1972-74; asst. prof. Gordon Coll., Wenham, Mass., 1974-78, assoc. prof., 1978-81, chmn. dept. sociology, 1974-81; dean acad. affairs Tabor Coll., Hillsboro, 1981—; growth contracting cons. Gordon Coll., 1979-81; leader workshops. Contbr. articles to profl. jours. Pres., bd. dirs. Northridge Homes, Inc., Beverly, Mass., 1977-78; v.p. North Shore Welfare Adv. Bd., Mass. Region IV, 1977-78; tchr. Adult Sunday Sch. Hillsboro Mennonite Brethren Ch., 1982—. Mem. Phi Kappa Phi. Avocations: ham radio operator; bowling. Office: Tabor Coll 400 S Jefferson Hillsboro KS 67063

CLARK, STEPHEN RUSSELL, lawyer; b. St. Louis, Apr. 12, 1949; s. William Albert and Eileen (Seibert) C.; B.A., St. Louis U., 1971, J.D., 1974; m. Joyce Rose Netemeg, July 19, 1984; 1 child Clayton William; 1 child by previous marriage, Kyle William. Admitted to Ill. bar, 1974; atty. firm McRoberts, Sheppard, McRoberts & Wimmer, P.C., East St. Louis, Ill., 1974-77; partner firm Montalvo & Clark, Belleville; Ill., 1977-83, Clark & Sturgeon, 1984—. Treas., bd. dirs. Children, family and Youth Advocacy Council, Belleville, 1978-81; chmn. Young Republican Orgn. Ill., 1977-79; vice chmn. Young Rep. Nat. Fedn., 1979-81, chmn., 1983—, spl. counsel to chmn., 1981-83; pres. St. Clair County Young Rep. Club, 1976-80. Recipient resolution award State of Ill., 1977, Man of Year award Young Rep. Orgn. Ill., 1978. Mem. Am. Bar Assn., Am. Trial Lawyers Assn., Conf. Personal Fin. Law, Ill. Bar Assn., Ill. Trail Lawyers Assn., St. Clair County Bar Assn. Roman Catholic. Home: 134 Kensington Heights Rd Belleville IL 62223 Office: 9425 W Main St Belleville IL 62223

CLARK, THOMAS RALPH, insurance company executive; b. Des Moines, Dec. 3, 1940; s. Thomas McKinstry and Vivian Irene (Lewis) C.; B.A., Drake U., 1980; m. Suzanne David, Aug. 25, 1975; children—Thomas Lewis, Karen Sue, Michelle Patterson, Todd Patterson. With Bankers Life & Assoc. Ins. Services, Inc., 1966-81; pres. Mass. Mut. Life and Mass. Fin. Group, Inc., 1981—. C.L.U. Mem. Internat. Assn. Fin. Planners, Iowa Assn. Life Underwriters (pres. 1975-76, nat. committeeman 1976-85), Des Moines Assn. Life Underwriters (pres. 1980-81), Am. Soc. C.L.U.'s, Polk County Estate Planners, Million Dollar Round Table (life), Des Moines C. of C. Republican. Mem. Christian Ch. (Disciples of Christ) (pres. 1979-81). Club: Des Moines. Home: 3007 Mary Lynn Dr Urbandale IA 50322 Office: 400 UCB Bldg Des Moines IA 50309

CLARK, THOMAS ROLFE, clinical psychologist; b. Detroit, Oct. 30, 1947; s. Edward Rolfe and Ruth Ann (Spurr) C.; m. Mary Franzen, July 15, 1972. A.B. magna cum laude, Greenville Coll., 1963; Ph.D. (Robards Doctoral fellow), U. Windsor (Can.), 1972. Diplomate Am. Bd. Psychology. Intern Wayne County Psychiat. Hosp., Detroit, mem. staff, 1972-77; chief psychologist Heritage Hosp., 1978-81; dir. mental health, program dir. Marian Manor Med. Center, exec. and clin. dir. Alpha Psychol. Services, Livonia, Mich.; pvt. pvt. practice clin., forensic and med. psychology and psychotherapy, Detroit, 1972—; dir. Alpha Psychol. Services, 1982—; faculty Henry Ford Community Coll., Dearborn, Mich., 1972-76; dir. clin. services Met. Guidance Center, Livonia, Mich., 1978—; mental health cons. People's Community Hosp. Authority, various police depts. Organist 1st United Meth. Ch., Dearborn, 1965-83; concert organist, 1975—; bd. dirs. Meth. Children's Home Soc., Livonia, Mich., 1974-84. Fellow Am. Orthopsychiat. Assn., Am. Coll. Psychology, Masters and Johnson Inst., Christian Assn. Psychol. Studies; mem. Am., Southeastern, Southwestern, Western, Mich. psychol. assns., Internat. Therapy Behavior Assn., Am. Assn. Sex Edn. Counselors, Acad. of Psychologists in Marital, Sex, and Family Therapy, Mich. Soc. Lic. Psychologists, Mich. Alcoholism and Addiction Assn., Am. Guild Organists, Internat. Council Psychologists, Mich. Profl. Police Assn., Internat. Law Enforcement Stress Assn. Contbr. articles to profl. jours.; rec. artist. Recipient awards in music, psychology. Office: Suite 150 29555 W Six Mile Rd Livonia MI 48152

CLARK, W. H., JR., chemical company executive. Chmn., pres., chief exec. officer, dir. Nalco Chem. Co., Oak Brook, Ill. Office: Nalco Chem Co 2901 Butterfield Rd Oak Brook IL 60521*

CLARK, WILLIAM FRANCIS, JR., training manager; b. Elizabeth, N.J., Nov. 22, 1943; s. William Francis and Rose Elizabeth (Fisher) C.; m. Patricia Ann Hodgins, June 1, 1971 (div.); m. Gail Peay, Nov. 1, 1976. B.A., Elon Coll., 1970; postgrad. Winthrop Coll., 1972. Sci. tchr., coach Fort Mill (S.C.) High Sch., 1970-72; area mgr. Internat. Harvester, Charlotte, N.C., 1972-74, sales tng. instr., 1974-75, instr., developer, 1975-76, program coordinator, 1976-78; mgr. tng. edn. A.O. Smith Harvestore Products, Inc., Arlington Heights, Ill., 1978—; mgr. sales and product tng. NAP Consumer Electronics Corp.; guest speaker Nat. Agri-Mktg. Assn., Shawnee Mission, Kans., 1983. Mem. Am. Soc. Tng. and Devel., Am. Mgmt. Assn., Mantread Agy., Alpha Pi Delta. Presbyterian. Home: 236 Baltusrol Dr Knoxville TN 37922 Office: AO Smith Harvestore Products Inc 550 W Algonquin Rd Arlington Heights IL 60005

CLARK, WILLIAM GEORGE, chief justice state supreme court; b. Chgo., July 16, 1924; s. John S. and Ita (Kennedy) C.; student Loyola U., Chgo., 1942-43, 44; J.D., DePaul U., 1946; J.D. (hon.), John Marshall Law Sch., Chgo., 1962; m. Rosalie Locatis, Nov. 28, 1946; children—Merrilee, William George, Donald, John Steven, Robert. Admitted to Ill. bar, 1947; mem. firm Crane, Kearney, Korzen, Phelan & Clark, and predecessor, Chgo., 1947-56; atty. for Pub. Adminstr. Ill., 1949-53; mem. Ill. Ho. of Reps. from Austin Dist. of Chgo., 1952-54, 56-60, mem. Senate, 1954-56, majority leader, 1959; atty. gen. Ill., 1960-69; partner firm Arvey, Hodes & Mantynband, Chgo.; justice Supreme Ct. Ill., after 1976, now chief justice. Served with AUS, 1942-44. Mem. Ill., Chgo., bar assns., Celtic Legal Soc., Irish Fellowship Club (pres. 1961-62), Catholic Lawyers Guild Chgo., Delta Theta Phi. Office: Ill Supreme Ct Richard J Daley Center Chicago IL 60602

CLARK, WILLIAM MERLE, baseball scout; b. Clinton, Mo., Aug. 18, 1932; s. Merle William and Beulah (Wilson) C.; student George Barr Umpire Sch., 1950, Central Mo. State U., 1950-51; B.J., U. Mo., 1958; postgrad. Somers Umpire Sch., 1962; m. Dolores Pearl Denny, Aug. 11, 1955; children—Patrick Sean, Michael Seumas, Kelly Kathleen, Kerry Maureen, Casey Connor. Umpire, Central Mexican League, Neb. State League, 1956; sportswriter, Lexington (Ky.) Leader, 1958, Columbia (Mo.) Missourian, 1958-60, Columbia (Mo.) Tribune, 1963—; recreation dir. City of Columbia, Mo., 1962-68. Umpire, Pioneer League, 1962; partner J.C. Stables, Columbia, Mo., 1965—; scouting supr. Pitts. Pirates, 1968, Seattle, 1969, Milw., 1970, Cin., 1971—. Served with AUS, 1951-54. Mem. Amateur Athletic Union (life), Mo. Sportswriter's Assn. (pres. 1958), Mo. Archeol. Soc., Mo. Hist. Soc., Columbia Audubon Soc. Unitarian-Universalist. Address: 3906 Grace Ellen Dr Columbia MO 65202

CLARKE, CHARLES FENTON, lawyer; b. Hillsboro, Ohio, July 25, 1916; s. Charles F. and Margaret (Patton) C.; A.B. summa cum laude, Washington and Lee Coll., 1938; LL.B., U. Mich., 1940; LL.D., Cleve. State U., 1971; m. Virginia Schoppenhorst, Apr. 3, 1945; children—Elizabeth, Margaret, Jane, Charles Fenton IV. Admitted to Mich. bar, 1940, Ohio bar, 1946; pvt. practice law, Detroit, 1942; asso. Squire, Sanders & Dempsey, Cleve., 1946-57, partner, 1957—. Dir. W.M. Brode Co. Trustee Legal Aid Soc., 1959-67; pres. Nat. Assn. R.R. Trial Counsel, 1966-68; pres. Alumni bd. dirs. Washington and Lee U., 1970-72; pres. bd. dirs. Free Med. Clinic Greater Cleve., Inc.; life mem. Sixth Circuit Jud. Conf.; chmn. legis. com. Cleve. Welfare Fedn., 1961-68; trustee Cleve. Citizens League, 1956-62; dir. Citizens adv. bd. Cuyahoga County Juvenile Ct., 1970-73; dir. George Jr. Republic, Greenville, Pa., 1970-73; vice chmn. Cleve. Crime Commn., 1974-75; trustee Fedn. Community Planning, 1984—; mem. exec. com. Cuyahoga County Rep. Orgn., 1950—; councilman, Bay Village, Ohio, 1948-53; pres., trustee Cleve. Hearing and Speech Center, 1957-63; trustee Laurel Sch.; bd. dirs. Bowman Tech. Sch. Served to 1st lt. C.I.C., AUS, World War II. Fellow Am. Coll. Trial Lawyers; mem. Cleve. Civil War Round Table (pres. 1968), Cleve. Zool. Soc. (dir. 1970), Phi Beta Kappa. Republican. Presbyn. (sec. bd. trustees 1965-74, elder). Clubs: Skating, Union (Cleve.); Tavern. Home: 2262 Tudor Dr Cleveland Heights OH 44106 Office: Huntington Bldg Cleveland OH 44115

CLARKE, CHARLES PATRICK, electronics co. exec.; b. Chgo., Oct. 3, 1929; s. James Patrick and Elizabeth (McLaughlin) C.; student U. Ill., 1948-50; B.S., DePaul U., 1953. Auditor, Baumann Finney Co., C.P.A.'s, Chgo., 1953-55; with Cuneo Press, Inc., Chgo., 1955-66, successively asst. gen. accounting supr., asst. chief corp. accountant, gen. auditor, 1955-61, systems, procedures and audit mgr., 1961-64, asst. to treas., 1964-66; comptroller Internat. Couriers Corp. (formerly Bankers Utilities Corp.), Chgo., 1966-69, treas., 1969-72, financial v.p., 1972-75; pres. C.P. Charles & Assos., 1975-76; treas., corp. controller DC Electronics, Inc., Aurora, Ill., 1976—. C.P.A., Ill. Mem. Am. Inst. C.P.A.'s, Ill. Soc. C.P.A.'s, Nat. Assn. Accountants, Financial Execs. Inst. Democrat. Roman Catholic. Home: 36 Parliament Dr W Palos Heights IL 60463 Office: 544 N Highland Aurora IL 60506

CLARKE, OSCAR WITHERS, physician; b. Petersburg, Va., Jan. 29, 1919; s. Oscar Withers and Mary (Reese) C.; B.S., Randolph Macon Coll., 1941; M.D., Med. Coll. Va., 1944; m. Susan Frances King, June 18, 1949; children—Susan Frances, Mary Elizabeth, Jennifer Ann. Intern Boston City Hosp., 1944-45; resident internal medicine Med. Coll. Va., 1945-46, 48-49, fellow in cardiology, 1949-50; practice medicine specializing in internal medicine, cardiology Gallipolis (Ohio) Holzer Med. Center, 1950—. Dir. Ohio

Valley Devel. Co., Gallipolis, Community Improvement Corp. Vice pres. Tri-State regional council Boy Scouts Am., 1957. Pres. Gallipolis City Bd. Health, 1955—, Gallia County Heart Council, 1955—. Trustee, Med. Meml. Found.; Holzer Hosp. Found.; pres. Ohio State Med. Bd.; chmn. Ohio Med. Edn. and Research Found. Served as capt. M.C., AUS, 1946-48; ETO. Recipient John Stewart Bryant pathology award Med. Coll. Va., 1943. Fellow ACP, Royal Soc. Medicine; mem. Gallia County Med. Soc. (pres. 1953), AMA, Am., Central Ohio (recipient medal of merit 1960, trustee) heart assns.; Ohio Med. assn. (pres. 1973-74), Am., Ohio (trustee) socs. internal medicine, Tri-State Community Concert Assn. (pres. 1957-59), Alpha Omega Alpha, Sigma Zeta, Chi Beta Phi. Presbyterian. Club: Rotary (pres. 1953-54). Contbr. articles to profl. jours. Home: Spruce Knoll Gallipolis OH 45631 Office: Box 344 Holzer Med Clinic Gallipolis OH 45631

CLARKSON, HARVEY NORMAN, osteopathic physician, consultant internal medicine; b. Kirksville, Mo., Jan. 19, 1943; s. Burl William and Marvel Melissa (Prather) C.; m. Deborah Lou Craggs, Nov. 27, 1969; children—Veronica Dawn, Wesley Allen, Vanessa D. B.S. in Zoology, N.E. Mo. State U., B.S. and Edn. D.O., Kirksville Coll. Osteo. Medicine, 1970. Intern Ft. Worth Osteo. Hosp., 1970-71; resident in internal medicine Kirksville Osteo. Hosp., from 1971; staff physician, instr. internal medicine Kirksville Coll. Osteo. Medicine. Recipient writing award Am. Coll. Osteo. Internal Medicine. Mem. Am. Osteo. Assn., Mo. Osteo. Assn. Physicians and Surgeons, N.E. Mo. Assn. Osteo. Physicians and Surgeons, Am. Coll. Osteo. Internists, Am. College Emergency Physicians, Am. Heart Assn., Am. Lung Assn. Baptist. Lodges: Rotary, Masons. Contbr. articles to profl. jours. Home: 2304 Northeast St Kirksville MO 63501 Office: Kirksville College Osteopathic Medicine 902 E LaHarpe Kirksville MO 63501

CLARY, ROSALIE BRANDON STANTON, timber farm executive, civic worker; b. Evanston, Ill., Aug. 3, 1928; d. Frederick Charles Hite-Smith and Rose Cecile (Liebich) Stanton; B.S., Northwestern U., 1950, M.A., 1954; m. Virgil Vincent Clary, Oct. 17, 1959; children—Rosalie Marian, Frederick Stanton, Virgil Vincent, Kathleen Elizabeth. Tchr., Chgo. Public Schs., 1951-55, adjustment tchr., 1956-61; faculty Loyola U., Chgo., 1963; v.p. Stanton Enterprises, Inc., Adams County, Miss., 1971—; author Family History Record, genealogy record book, Kenilworth, Ill., 1977—; also lectr. Leader, Girl Scouts, Winnetka, Ill., 1969-71, 78—, Cub Scouts, 1972-77; badge counselor Boy Scouts Am., 1978—; election judge Republican party, 1977—. Mem. Nat. Soc. DAR (Ill. rec. sec. 1979-81, nat. vice chmn. program com. 1980—), Am. Forestry Assn., Forest Farmers Assn., North Suburban Geneal. Soc. (governing bd. 1979—), Winnetka Hist. Soc. (governing bd. 1978—), Internat. Platform Assn., Delta Gamma. Roman Catholic. Home: 509 Elder Ln Winnetka IL 60093 Office: PO Box 401 Kenilworth IL 60043

CLASSEN, LUKE L., savings and loan executive; b. Newton, Kans., Oct. 4, 1956; s. Samuel H. and Lula F. (Nickel) C.; m. Ellen Faye Eckman, June 25, 1977; children—Ryan Mathew, Anthony Dale. B.S.B.A., John Brown U., Ark., 1978. Field rep. Railroad Savs. and Loan Assn., Newton, Kans., 1978-82, savs. mgr., 1982-83, v.p., dir. mktg., 1984—. Bd. dirs. Inst. Fin. Edn., 1983—; funds solicitor United Way, 1984. Mem. Inst. Fin. Edn., Soc. Real Estate Appraisers, Fin. Instns. Mktg. Assn., Newton C. of C. (ambassador 1984—). Republican. Mennonite. Club: Newton Country. Lodge: Jaycees. Avocations: racquetball; tennis; golf. Home: 204 Sherman Dr Newton KS 67114 Office: 129 E Broadway Newton KS 67114

CLAUDER, LINDA MARTIN, radio station manager, music educator; b. Mt. Sterling, Wis., Mar. 25, 1941; d. Clyde O. and Juanita Norma (Vogel) Martin; m. John Charles Clauder, Jan. 29, 1966 (div.). B.A. in Applied Music, U. Wis.-Madison, 1963, M.A. in Applied Music, 1964. Voice tchr. Milton (Wis.) Coll., 1969-70; music programmer, producer Sta. WHA, Madison, 1966-70, music dir., 1970-76, program dir., 1976-79; mgr. projects and prodn. 1979-81, prodn. ctr. dir., 1981—; instr. voice, diction U. Wis. Ext., 1978—; lectr. U. Wis. Sch. Music; dir. features prodn. unit KUSC-FM, 1984. Mem. music panel Wis. Arts Bd., 1973-77, chairperson, 1975-77; mem. grand opening com., Madison Civic Ctr., 1980; Friendship Force, 1977-78; chairperson U. Wis. Opera Bd., 1982-85; bd. dirs. Madison Civic Repertory Theater, 1975-79, Madison Civic Opera, 1978-79. Recipient Disting. Service award Assn. Music Personnel in Pub. Radio, 1982; prodn. award Am. Women in Radio and TV, 1984. Mem. Assn. Music Personnel in Pub. Radio (pres. 1976-78, newsletter editor 1976-79, bd. dirs. 1976-82), Internat. Platform Assn. Phi Beta. Lutheran. Profl. singer appearing in opera, musical comedy on stage, radio and TV. Home: 2849-3 Century Harbor Middleton WI 53562 Office: 821 University Ave Madison WI 53706

CLAUER, CALVIN ROBERT, consulting engineer; b. South Bend, Ind., Sept. 8, 1910; s. Calvin Kingsley and Etta (Fiddick) C.; B.S. in Civil Engring., Purdue U., 1932; postgrad. Columbia U., 1944-45; m. Rosemary Y. Stultz, June 23, 1934; 1 son, Calvin Robert. Project engr. Ind. State Hwy. Commn., 1932-35; engr. Erie R.R. Co., 1935-36; dist. chief engr. Truscon Steel Co., Indpls., 1936-42; chief engr. United Steel Fabricators, Inc., 1945-55, div. sales mgr., 1955-57; pres. Clauer Assos., Engrs. for Industry, Wooster, Ohio, 1957-60, chief product engr. Mfg. group Republic Steel Corp., Youngstown, Ohio, 1960-75; prin. Clauer Assos., Youngstown, 1975-79; prin. Midgley-Clauer & Assos., Youngstown, 1979—. Chmn. civil engring. tech. indsl. adv. com. Youngstown State U., 1971-76. Served to col. USAR, 1932-60. Fellow ASCE; mem. Internat. Assn. for Bridge and Structural Engring., ASTM, Am. Iron and Steel Inst., Am. Concrete Inst., Internat. Materials Mgmt. Soc., Soc. Profl. Journalists-Sigma Delta Chi. Republican. Christian Scientist. Club: Northcliffe. Lodges: Rotary, Masons, Shriners. Holder patent on sheet metal box beam. Home: 3624 Chestnut Ct Cibolo TX 78108 Office: 860 Boardman Canfield Rd Youngstown OH 44512

CLAUSIUS, GERHARD PAUL, optometrist; b. Chgo., Dec. 18, 1907; s. Robert Adolph and Margaret (Reutlinger) C.; Dr. Optometry, Ill. Coll. Optometry, 1932; m. Ella Marie Carlson, July 22, 1933; children—Gerhard Paul (dec.), Donald Robert, Doris Constance Clausius Mosser. Practice optometry, Belvidere, Ill., 1932-80; lectr., writer on Lincoln and Civil War, 1948—. Mem. Belvidere Bd. Edn., 1939-42; bd. dirs. Lincoln Fellowship of Wis. mem. Ill. Sesqui-Centennial Commn. Paul Harris fellow. Mem. Am., Ill. (dir. 1948) optometric assns., No. Ill. Optometric Soc. (v.p. 1958-59), Ill. (v.p.), Boone County (life), Chgo. hist. socs., Chgo. Civil War Round Table (hon. life mem., past pres.), Wis. Lincoln Fellowship (speaker 1979), Phi Theta Upsilon. Lutheran. Rotarian (past pres. Belvidere). Club: Buena Vista (past dir., v.p.) (Fontana, Wis.). Home: 929 Garfield Ave Belvidere IL 61008

CLAUSSEN, VERNE EVERETT, JR., optometrist; b. Wilson, Kans., Aug. 10, 1944; s. Verne E. and Dorothy Louise (Soukup) C.; student (Santa Fe scholar, Union Pacific scholar), 1962-65; B.S., U. Houston Coll. Optometry, 1966, certificate in optometry, 1968; certificate (Gesell fellow) in pediatrics, 1969; D.Optometry, U. Houston, 1970; m. Patricia Mary Williams, Aug. 26, 1966; children—Verne Everett III, Mary Chris. Practice optometry U. Houston Coll. Optometry, mem. clin. staff, 1970; optometrist Wamego and St. Mary's, Kans., 1970—. Lectr. optometry Eastern Seaboard Conf., Washington, U. Houston, 1969; vision cons. Briarwood Sch. for learning problems, Houston, 1967-69. Councilman, Alma City (Kans.), 1971-73. Bd. dirs. Optometric Extension Program Found. Recipient Contest award Kans. Optometric Jour., 1971. Mem. Am., Kans. optometric assns., Heart of Am. Contact Soc., Alma Wamego (dir.), St. Mary's (pres.) chambers commerce, Farm House Assn. (v.p 1976-77), Phi Theta Upsilon, Farm House Frat. (dir.) Republican. Methodist. Club: Dutch Mill Swingers Square Dance. Home: Route 2 Alma KS 66401 Office: 5th and Elm Wamego KS 66547

CLAWSON, ROBERT WAYNE, political science educator; b. Glendale, Calif., Dec. 21, 1939; s. Charles Vernor and Ada Fern (Hower) C.; student Tex. A&M U., 1957-58; A.B., UCLA, 1961. M.A. (Charles Fletcher Scott fellow 1961-64), 1964, Ph.D., 1969; Exchange Scholar U.S. Def. Lang. Inst., 1963-64, State U. Moscow, USSR, 1966; m. Judith Louise Lisy, June 25, 1961; children—Deborah Marie, Gregory Scott. Research asst. Russian and East European Studies Center, UCLA, 1961-65; asst. prof., assoc. prof. polit. sci. Kent (Ohio) State U., 1966-83, prof., 1983—, assoc. dir. Lemnitzer Ctr. NATO Studies, dir. dir. Ctr. Internat. and Comparative Programs; v.p. research, internat. trade INTERAG INC., 1973-75. author Contemporary Soviet Defense Policy. Contbr. editor Houghton Mifflin. Acad. year research fellow Kent State U., spring 1971. Mem. Am. Assn. for Advancement Slavic Studies, Am. Polit. Sci. Assn., AAUP (pres. Kent State chpt. 1975). Democrat. Presbyterian. Club: Sigma Nu. Editor scholarly books;

contbr. articles to profl. publs. Home: 7336 Westview St Kent OH 44240 Office: Center for International Programs Kent State U Kent OH 44242

CLAXTON, ROBERT S(IMON), educator, pharmacist; b. Ottumwa, Iowa, Jan. 28, 1940; s. Robert H. and Kathryn Bunnie (Phillips) C.; m. Maryanna Burke, June 11, 1966; children—Robert Joseph, Cynthia Ann. B.S. in Pharmacy, U. Iowa, 1964, M.A.T., 1966. Registered pharmacist, cert. Minn. Tchr. sci. jr. high sch., Cedar Rapids, Iowa, 1966-69; tchr. chemistry Sch. Dist. 181, Brainerd, Minn., 1969—, advisor Knowledge Bowl Group, 1980-84. Lectr. on drugs Drug Awareness Com., Brainerd, 1980-84. Named Brainerd Tchr. of Yr., Brainerd Edn. Assn., 1983, Honor Roll Tchr., Sta. WTCN-TV, Mpls., 1984, State Tchr. of Excellence, Minn. Edn. Assn., 1984, State Honor Roll Tchr., 1984. Mem. Am. Fedn. Tchrs., Minn. Sci. Tchrs. Assn., Nat. Sci. Tchrs. Assn. Congregationalist. Avocations: swimming, photography, music. Home: 2001 Graydon Ave Brainerd MN 56401 Office: Ind Sch Dist 181 Quince St Brainerd MN 56401

CLAY, HENRY ALLEN, lawyer, systems analyst, consultant; b. Tarentum, Pa., Sept. 10, 1930; s. Henry Clevenger and Mary Eleanor (Shingledecker) C.; m. Christine Ann Brooks, Jan. 3, 1953; children—Stephen Henry, Carol Ann, Andrew Robert. Student Carnegie-Mellon U., 1948-49; B.A., U. Pa., 1952, J.D., 1957. Bar: Washington 1959, Pa. 1961; C.L.U. Trainee, Employee Relations Devel. Program, Gen. Electric Co., Lynn, Mass. and Phila., 1957-59; asst. counsel Provident Mut. Life Ins. Co. Phila., 1959-65, dir. adminstrv. systems, 1965-68; dir. law student div. ABA, Chgo., 1968-69; dir. office mgmt. systems Penn Mut. Life Ins. Co., Phila., 1969-73, dir. variable annuities, pres. Penn Mut. Equity Services, 1973-76; bus. mgr., bd. dirs. Lower Merion Sch. Dist., Ardmore, Pa., 1976-78; ptnr. in charge adminstrn. firm Dykema, Gossett, Spencer, Goodnow & Trigg, Detroit, 1978—; lectr. in work measurement Am. Mgmt. Assn.; circuit exec. qualifier U.S. Circuit Cts. Appeals, 1972-73. Mem. Marple Newtown Sch. Bd., Newtown Square, Pa., 1971-77, pres., 1973-77; judge elections Marple Twp., Broomall, Pa.; pres. Grosse Pointe (Mich.) Newcomers Club, 1982-83; pres. Citizens Against Recall Effort, Grosse Pointe Farms, Mich., 1983-84. Served to maj. JAGC, USAR, 1952-68; Korea. Decorated Army Commendation medal. Fellow Life Mgmt. Inst.; mem. ABA, Phila. Bar Assn., Assn. Internal Mgmt. Cons., Am. Arbitration Assn., Assn. Life Ins. Counsel. Republican. Episcopalian. Clubs: Masons, Shriners (Phila.) Players (Detroit). Office: Dykema Gossett Spencer Goodnow & Trigg 35th floor 400 Renaissance Ctr Detroit MI 48243

CLAY, LOREN PAUL, electronics company executive; b. Wauseon, Ohio, Oct. 4, 1955; s. Richard Louis and Marilyn Bernice (Falor) C.; Asso. in Engring. and Electronics, Valparaiso Tech. Inst. of Electronics, 1976. Electronics technician Swiss Controls, Michigan City, Ind., 1976-77, field engr., Northlake, Ill., 1977-78, quality control technician, Michigan City, 1978, quality control engr., 1978-80, sales engr., 1980-81, mgr. engring. services, 1981; instr. tech. and computer service engring. No. Ind. Pub. Service Co., 1982—. Democrat. Club: Am. Taekwondoe Assn. Home: 2358 Marshall Dr Valparaiso IN 46383

CLAY, WILLIAM LACY, congressman; b. St. Louis, Apr. 30, 1931; s. Irving C. and Luella (Hyatt) C.; m. Carol A. Johnson, Oct. 10, 1953; children—Vicki, Lacy, Michelle. B.S. in Polit. Sci, St. Louis U., 1953. Real estate broker, from 1964, mgr. life ins. co., 1959-61, alderman 26th Ward, St. Louis, 1959-64, bus. rep. state, county and municipal employees union, 1961-64; com. coordinator Steamfitters local 562, 1966-67; mem. 91st-99th congresses from 1st Mo. Dist. Dist. Served with AUS, 1953-55. Mem. NAACP (past exec. bd. mem. St. Louis), CORE, St. Louis Jr. C. of C. Democrat. Office: 2470 Rayburn House Office Bldg Washington DC 20515

CLAYBAUGH, GLENN ALAN, sales executive; b. Lincoln, Nebr., Dec. 10, 1927; s. Joseph H. and Helen (Krause) C.; m. Mary Lou Graham, Aug. 29, 1950; children—Lloyd, Cynthia. B.Sc., U. Nebr., 1949; M.Sc., Mich. State U. 1950; Ph.D., Iowa State U., 1953. Sect. leader Mead Johnson, Evansville, Ind., 1953-63, mktg. dir., 1963-72, dir., 1972-82, group dir., 1982—. Contbr. articles to profl. jours. Patentee in field. Fellow Am. Pub. Health Assn., Royal Soc. Health; mem. Nat. Perinatal Assn., Am. Dairy Sci. Assn., Am. Soc. Microbiology, Nat. Assn. Pediatric Nurse Assocs. and Practitioner (life), Great Plains Orgn. (life), Calif. Perinatal Assn. (life). Republican. Methodist. Lodge: Kiwanis (gov. 1975-76, internat. chmn. 1977-80). Avocations: woodworking; golf; travel. Home: 1612 Russell Ave Evansville IN 47712 Office: Mead Johnson 2404 Pennsylvania Ave Evansville IN 47721

CLAYTON, BRUCE DAVID, educator; b. Grand Island, Nebr., Mar. 9, 1947; s. John David and Eloise Regnier (Camp) C.; student Hastings Coll., 1965-67, B.S., U. Nebr., 1970; D.Pharmacy, U. Mich., 1973; m. Francine Evelyn Purdy, June 19, 1971; children—Sarah Elizabeth, Beth Anne. Asst. prof. clin. pharmacy Creighton U., Omaha, 1974-77; assoc. prof. Coll. Pharmacy, U. Nebr. Med. Center, Omaha, 1978—, vice chmn. dept. pharmacy practice, 1978-84, interim chmn. 1984—; unit coordinator perinatal pharmacy services Univ. Hosps., Omaha, 1978-80; Ciba-Geigy vis. prof., Australia and N.Z., 1979; S.E. Wright traveling fellow Pharm. Soc. Australia, 1983; lectr. in field. Recipient Bristol award for professionalism, 1970; named Nebr. Hosp. Pharmacist of Yr., 1978. Mem. Nebr. Soc. Hosp. Pharmacists (pres. 1978-79, dir. 1979-80), Am. Soc. Hosp. Pharmacists (council on organizational affairs 1979-82, com. on nominations 1980-85, chmn. 1985, ho. of dels. 1980-85), Am. Pharm. Assn., Nebr. Pharm. Assn., Am. Assn. Colls. of Pharmacy, Rho Chi. Author: (with S.A. Ryan) Handbook of Practical Pharmacology, 1977, 2d edit., 1980; (with J.E. Squire) Basic Pharmacology for Nurses, 7th edit., 1981; Handbook of Pharmacology in Nursing, 1984; Basic Pharmacology for Nurses, 1985. Contbr. articles to profl. jours. Home: 5717 Tucker St Omaha NE 68152 Office: 42d and Dewey St Omaha NE 68105

CLAYTON, MILTON LOUIS, educational adminstrator; b. Louisville, Oct. 17, 1948; s. James Samuel and Lucille Marie Moore; m. Deborah Marlene Clayton, Aug. 15, 1970; children—Milton Louis, Janna Marie. B.S., Oakland City Coll., 1971; M.S., Ind. U.-New Albany, 1974; Ed.S., Ind. U.-Bloomington, 1979. Adminstrv. counselor Ind. Vocat. Rehab. Services, Gary, 1971-72; counselor Alternate High Sch., Jeffersonville, Ind., 1972-76; prin. Corden Porter Career Ctr., Jeffersonville, 1976—; dir. adult and vocat. edn. Greater Clark County Schs., 1982—. Den leader Cub Scouts Am.; active Operation Push, Indpls., Jeffersonville Little League. Recipient award Highland Sch. Corp., 1972; award of Achievement JUMP Com., Jeffersonville Citizens for Progress, 1981. Mem. NAACP (Able Adminstr. Clark County 1979). Democrat. Methodist. Home: 4 Cypress St Jeffersonville IN 47130 Office: 601 E Court Ave Jeffersonville IN 47130

CLAY-TURLEY, PAMELA ANN, telephone co. exec.; b. Ames, Iowa, Apr. 22, 1944; d. Roger Leon and Barbara Ruth (Hunt) Clay; B.A., Grinnell Coll., 1966; m. Jack Turley, Sept. 13, 1980; 1 dau., Krista. With Gen. Telephone Co. Ill., Bloomington, 1966—, dir. tng., 1980-82, state mgr. tng., 1982—. Bd. dirs., chmn. personnel McLean County YWCA, 1980—. Mem. Soc. for Tng. and Devel., Bus. and Profl. Women's Club. Home: 1305 Schroeder Normal IL 61761 Office: Gen Telephone Co Ill 404 Brock Dr Bloomington IL 61701

CLEARY, PATRICK JAMES, newspaper editor; b. Momence, Ill., Jan. 20, 1929; s. James Augustine and Nellie DeWitt (Liston) C.; student U. Chgo., 1946-48; m. Alice Marie Duval, Oct. 1, 1955; children—Mary Elizabeth, James Augustine, Michael John. Reporter, wire editor, city editor Kankakee (Ill.) Daily Jour., 1945-52; reporter Gary (Ind.) Post-Tribune, 1952-53; staff asst. Ill. Senate, 1953-57; dir. pub. relations Plumbing Contractors Assn. Chgo. Cook County (Ill.), 1957-59; city clk. City of Kankakee, 1955-57, clk., county and probate cts. County of Kankakee, 1959-63; editor Farmers Weekly Rev., Joliet, Ill., 1963—; editor Compass Newspapers Inc., Kankakee, 1977, Herscher (Ill.) Rev., 1963-69; editor Crete (Ill.) Record, Steger (Ill.) News, 1963-64; chmn. bd. rev. Ill. Dept. Labor, 1969-73. Office: 100 Manhattan Rd Joliet IL 60433

CLEARY, ROBERT EMMET, gynecologist, infertility specialist; b. Evanston, Ill., July 17, 1937; s. John J. and Brigid (O'Grady) C.; M.D., U. Ill., 1962; m. June 10, 1961; children—William Joseph, Theresa Marie, John Thomas. Intern, St. Francis Hosp., Evanston, 1962-63, resident, 1963-66; practice medicine specializing in gynecology and infertility, Indpls., 1970—; head Sect. of Reproductive Endocrinology and Infertility, Chgo. Lying-In Hosp., U. Chgo., 1968-70; head Sect. of Reproductive Endocrinology and Infertility, Ind. U. Med. Center, Indpls. 1970-80; prof. ob-gyn Ind. U., Indpls., 1976-80, clin. prof. ob-gyn, 1980—. Recipient Meml. award Pacific Coast Obstetrical and Gynecol. Soc., 1968; diplomate Am. Bd. Ob-Gyn, Am. Bd. Reproductive

Endocrinology and Infertility. Fellow Am. Coll. Ob-Gyn, Am. Fertility Soc.; mem. Endocrine Soc., Central Assn. Obstetricians and Gynecologists (award, 1974, 79), Soc. Gynecol. Investigation, Pacific Coast Fertility Soc., Soc. Reproductive Endocrinologists, Soc. Reproductive Surgeons, N.Y. Acad. Scis., Sigma Xi. Roman Catholic. Contbr. articles in field to med. jours. Home: 7036 Dubonnet Ct Indianapolis IN 46278 Office: 8091 Township Line Rd Indianapolis IN 46260

CLEARY, RUSSELL GEORGE, brewing company executive; b. Chippewa Falls, Wis., May 22, 1933; s. George and Ruth (Halseth) C.; m. Gail J. Kumm, Jan. 8, 1955; children—Kristine Hope, Sandra Gay. LL.D., U. Wis.-Madison, 1957. Bar: Wis. 1957. Sole practice law, LaCrosse, Wis., 1957-58; dir. sales Hoeschler Realty, LaCrosse, 1958-60; atty., asst. to pres. G. Heileman Brewing Co., LaCrosse, 1960-71, pres., chmn. bd., chief exec. officer, 1971—; dir. Protection Mut. Ins. Co., Park Ridge, Ill., Econs. Lab., Inc., St. Paul, Norwest Bank Mpls., A.O. Smith Co., Milw., Soo Line, Mpls. Past bd. dirs., v.p. LaCrosse Festivals; past bd. dirs. LaCrosse Interstate Fair Assn.; past chmn. LaCrosse Redevel. Authority; past pres. United Fund LaCrosse Area; bd. dirs. Wis. Gov.'s Strategic Devel. Commn., 1984. Named Man of Year, LaCrosse Area C. of C.; named Exec. of Year, Corp. Report mag., 1980. Mem. Wis. Assn. Mfrs. and Commerce (dir. 1983). Presbyterian. Lodge: Masons, Shriners. Office: G Heileman Brewing Co Inc 100 Harborview Plaza LaCrosse WI 54601

CLEGHORN, GEORGE EDWARD, apartment management executive; b. Terre Haute, Ind., Sept. 15, 1950; s. Edward Melle and Dorothy Pearl (Jones) C.; m. Laura Maureen Boyke, Dec. 18, 1971; children—Kathleen Mary, Corey Bruce. A.A.S. in Electronics Engring., SAMS Tech. Inst., 1970; A.A.S. in Mid Mgmt., Coll. Lake County, 1981, A.A.S. in Indsl. Supervision, 1983; Supr. Imperial Towers, Waukegan, Ill., 1976-84, gen. mgr., 1984—. Served with USN, 1970-76. Mem. Waukegan/Lake County C. of C. (investing mem. 1985), Phi Theta Kappa. Republican. Home: 560 Forest View Dr Lindenhurst IL 60046 Office: Gen Mgr Imperial Towers 805 Baldwin Ave Waukegan IL 60085

CLELAND, MARY VALERIE, librarian; b. Budapest, Hungary, Aug. 15, 1942; came to U.S., 1947; d. John William and Edith (Myer) Kapla; m. William Robert Cleland, Aug. 24, 1963; children—Joel Antony, Gregory James. Student Ohio State U., 1961-63; B.A., U. Wash., 1970, M.L.S., 1973. Slide library asst. Seattle Art Museum, 1970-72; adult services librarian Cuyahoga County Pub. Library, Mayfield, Ohio, 1976-82, head adult services So. Euclid Branch, 1982-84; head tech. services Geauga County Pub. Library, Chardon, Ohio, 1984—; pres. Library Staff Assn., Cleve., 1983-84. Mem. ALA, Art Librarians Soc. No. Am. (editor, newsletter 1980-82), Art Librarians Soc. Ohio. Democrat. Roman Catholic. Mailing Address: 11180 Wilson Mills Rd Chardon OH 44024

CLEM, GARY SMITH, lawyer; b. Yellville, Ark., June 18, 1940; s. Leslie G. and Mary Frances (Smith) C. Jr.; m. Judith Ann Koenigsberg, Mar. 25, 1967; children—Deborah Lynn, Lauren Beth. Grad. Washington U., St. Louis, 1962; J.D., U. Mo., 1966. Bar: Mo. 1966, Ill. 1970. Assoc. firm Davis & Morgan, Peoria, Ill., 1969-72, Kavanagh, Scully, Sudow, White & Frederick, Peoria, 1972-76; pres. Clem & Triggs, P.C., Peoria, 1976-85; ptnr. Davis & Morgan, Peoria, 1985—. Vice pres., bd. dirs. Sr. Citizens Found., Inc., 1971-75; bd. dirs. Ill. Valley Pub. Telecommunications, Inc., 1976-78, Community Workshop and Tng. Ctr., 1983—. Served with U.S. Army, 1967-69. Mem. ABA, Mo. Bar Assn., Ill. Bar Assn., Peoria County Bar Assn. (dir. 1982—), Nat. Council Sch. Attys. Republican. Jewish. Clubs: Creve Coeur, Willow Knolls Country. Office: 300 NE Perry Ave Peoria IL 61603

CLEM, NANCY GAYLE, educator; b. Princeton, Ind., Feb. 27, 1941; d. Gaylord Elliott Kirk and Elsie Isabel (Dunning) K.; m. Larry Jay Clem, Aug. 10, 1963; children—Jay Michael, Jana Michelle. B.S. in Vocat. Home Econs., Purdue U., 1963; M.S. in Vocat. Home Econs., Ind. State U., 1966. Vocat. home econs. tchr. Petersburg (Ind.) High Sch., 1963-74; vocat. home econs. tchr., dept. head Pike Central High Sch., Petersburg, 1974—; dist. coordinator Ind. Home Econs. and Future Homemakers Am.; cons. Harcourt, Brace, Jananovich, Inc. Mem. Am. Home Econs. Assn., Ind. Home Econs. Assn. (Home Econs. Tchr. Yr. 1976), Am. Vocat. Assn., Ind. Vocat. Assn., Nat. Assn. Vocat. Home Econs., NEA, Ind. Vocat. Home Econs. Assn. (v.p., pres.-elect), Ind. Tchrs. Assn., Ind. Assn. Future Homemakers Am. Republican. Presbyterian. Lodge: Daus. Nile. Home: Rural Route 2 Princeton IN 47670 Office: Pike Central High Sch Rural Route 3 Petersburg IN 47567

CLEMENS, BRYAN TILLMAN, clergyman; b. Beckum County, Okla., Jan. 22, 1934; s. Ben Tillman and Lou Ella (Thornton) C.; B.S. Wayland Bapt. Coll., Plainview, Tex., 1959; M.S. (NDEA fellow 1962-63), Purdue U., 1963, Ph.D., 1969; m. Odessa Louise Wilson, Dec. 14, 1952; children—Daniel Clay, Kathy Kay, Sharon Sue, Ben Tillman. Public sch. tchr., Tex., 1959-62; asst. dean Purdue U., 1964-67; dean of students Wayland Bapt. Coll., 1967-69; asst. dean of men, then dean of men Purdue U., 1969-74; counselor Southeastern Sch. Corp., 1974-78; ordained to ministry Am. Bapt. Ch., 1964; pastor Blue Ball Ch., Walton, Ind., 1971-78, Metea Bapt. Ch. Lucerne, Ind., 1979—. Club: Grass Creek Lions. Author articles in field. Address: Rural Route 1 Box 54E Lucerne IN 46950

CLEMENS, PAT (TOM), manufacturing company executive; b. Hibbing, Minn., July 26, 1944; s. Jack LeRoy and Mildred (Coss) C.; m. Marianne Paznar, Oct. 1, 1966; children—Patrick Michael, Heather Kristen. B.S. in Econs. and Mgmt., St. Cloud State U., 1968. Sales adminstr. Transistor Electronics Co., Eden Prarie, Minn., 1969; head instnl. sales Chiquita Brands, Edina, Minn., 1970; dist. sales mgr. Menley & James Labs., Phila., 1971-75; owner, pres. T. P. Clemens Labs., Eagan, Minn., 1975—; instr. community edn. Rosemount, Minn., 1982 lectr. econs. to corps., high schs. and colls. in U.S., Scotland, Ireland, and Jamaica. Author, editor: How Prejudice and Narcissism Control Economics of the United States and the World, 1979. Little League coach, 1970-82; high sch. weight lifting coach, 1982—; vol. worker with comatose children. Mem. Internat. Platform Assn. Home and office: 1276 Vildmark Dr Eagan MN 55123

CLEMENT, PAUL PLATTS, JR., educational development company executive; b. Geneva, Ill., Aug. 30, 1935; s. Paul P. and Vera Elizabeth (Dahlquist) C.; A.B., Coe Coll., 1957; m. Susan Alice Aikins, June 7, 1958; children—Paul Platts, Kathleen Elizabeth. Sales tech. rep. Burroughs Corp., Chgo., 1960-63; mgr. EDP, Harding-Williams Corp., Chgo., 1963-65; edn. coordinator Standard Oil Co., Chgo., 1965-69; mgr. product planning Edutronics Systems Internat., Chgo., 1969-71; dir. interactive products devel. Advanced Systems Inc., Chgo., 1971—; cons. Served to capt. USAF, 1958-60. Mem. ACM, Nat. Soc. Performance and Instrn. Home: 4942 Linscott Ave Downers Grove IL 60515 Office: 2340 S Arlington Heights Rd Arlington Heights IL 60005

CLEMENTE, JAVIER LARRANAGA, physician; b. Lima, Peru, Oct. 5, 1940; came to U.S., 1968; s. Hilario and Sabina Clemente; student Nat. Mayor U. San Marcos, Lima, 1959-60; M.D., San Marcos U., Lima, 1967; m. Barbara Pelegrin, May 30, 1970; children—Michael, Daniel, Deanna, Jonathan, Mark. Resident, Cayetano Heredia U., Lima, 1967-68; intern Carney Hosp., Boston, 1968-69, resident, 1969-71; fellow in nephrology U. Chgo. Hosp. and Clinics, 1971-72; sr. resident in nephrology VA Hosp., Hines, Ill., 1972-73, staff physician renal sect., 1973-77, physician-in-charge assisted dialysis, 1974-76, physician-in-charge assisted and ltd. care dialysis, 1976-77; practice medicine specializing in internal medicine and nephrology, Cleve., 1977—; chief nephrology sect. St. John's Hosp., Cleve., 1981—, Fairview Gen. Hosp., Cleve., 1982—; clin. instr. medicine Loyola U., Maywood, Ill., 1973-77, asst. prof., 1977. Diplomate Am. Bd. Internal Medicine, Am. Bd. Nephrology. Mem. AMA (Physician recognition award 1976-79), Cleve. Acad. Medicine, Ohio Med. Assn. Contbr. articles and abstracts to med. jours. Office: 18099 Lorain Ave Suite 316 Cleveland OH 44111

CLEMENTS, STEVEN DON, optometrist; b. Spokane, Wash., Aug. 6, 1953; s. Don Stone and Beverly Jean (Hibbert) C.; m. Janis Gene Madsen, Mar. 18, 1976; children—Scott, Tyler, Susan. B.S. in Visual Sci., Pacific U., 1980, O.D., 1982. Diplomate Am. Bd. Optometrist. With U.S. Army, 1979—, staff optometrist MEDDAC, Ft. Leonard Wood, 1982—; adj. assoc. prof. optometry St. Louis Coll. of Optometry, Ft. Leonard Wood, Mo., 1982—. Recipient J. Harold Bailey award Am. Optometric Found., 1982. Mem. Armed Forces Optometric Soc., Am. Optometric Assn. Morrison. Avocations: Computer programming; shooting; reloading. Home: 1 Williams Fort Leonard Wood MO 65473 Office: US Army MEDDAC Fort Leonard Wood MO 65473

CLEMINS, CHARLES FRANK, financial executive; b. Bluford, Ill., July 28, 1926; s. Artie Oscar and Beulah Ann (Bruce) C.; m. Patricia Stanley, Mar. 31, 1951 (dec. 1981); children—Ellen, Charles, Susan. B.S. in Acctg., U. Ill., 1949. Auditor Touche Ross & Co., St. Louis, 1949-54; mgr. gen. acctng. Packaging Corp. Am., Quincy, Ill., 1954-61; office mgr. Clark, Heldman & Wood, C.P.A.s, Springfield, Ohio, 1961-63; accounts mgr. DeSoto Inc., Des Plaines, Ill., 1963-73, corp. controller, 1974-77, treas., 1977—. Served with U.S. Army, 1944-46, ETO. Mem. Am. Inst. C.P.A.s, Ill. Soc. C.P.A.s, Fin. Execs. Inst. (bd. dirs. 1979-84). Republican. Mem. Ch. of Christ. Club: Meadow (Rolling Meadows). Lodge: Masons. Home: 23 N Tower Rd Oak Brook IL 60521 Office: DeSoto Inc 1700 S Mt Prospect Des Plaines IL 60018

CLEVELAND, DONALD LESLIE, insurance broker reinsurance intermediary and consultant; b. Omaha, Nebr., July 16, 1938; s. Albert Leslie and Lucille Arlene (Fancher) C.; B.S. in Polit. Sci. and Journalism, Creighton U., 1961; M.A. in Polit. Sci., U. Nebr., 1968; m. Christa Anita Wahl, Oct. 9, 1965; children—Christopher Leslie, Stephan Donald. Adminstrv. asst. Clarkson Hosp., Omaha, 1965-67; adminstrv. asst. Assn. Minn. Counties, St. Paul, 1967-68; asst. dir. house research dept. Minn. Ho. of Reps., St. Paul, 1968-71; exec. dir. Iowa State Assn. Counties, Des Moines, 1971-80; chmn. Cleveland Research and Devel. Corp., 1975-84; v.p. domestic ops. GIF Ins. Co. Ltd., 1980-84; chief exec. officer Multi-County Services Agy., Joint County Unemployment Compensation Fund, County Liability Indemnification Fund, Local Govt. Research Found., 1975-80; pres. Cleveland Group, West Des Moines, Iowa, 1980—. Pres., St. Paul Beautiful Coordinating Com., 1970-71; county rep. Mid Continent Fed. Regional Council, Kansas City, 1977-80. Served to capt. U.S. Army, 1961-66. Mem. Am. Soc. Assn. Execs., Am. Soc. Public Adminstrn., Acad. Polit. Sci., Council Fgn. Relations, Internat. Personnel Mgmt. Assn., Nat. Assn. Counties, Nat. Assn. County Assn. Execs. (sec.-treas. 1978—, 2d v.p. 1979-80, 1st v.p. and pres. 1980), Captive Ins. Cos. Assn. (bd. dirs. 1984). Democrat. Roman Catholic. Editor The County, 1971-80. Office: Cleveland Group 1200 35th St Suite 101 West Des Moines IA 50265

CLEVELAND, HELEN BARTH, teaching consultant, civic worker; b. Alliance, Ohio, Aug. 28, 1904; d. Luther Martin and Ella Mae (Forest) Barth; A.B., Mt. Union Coll., 1927; postgrad. Kent State U., 1929-32, Akron U., 1946-48, N.Y. U., 1950-53; M.A., Syracuse U., 1955, Ph.D., 1958; postgrad. London Acad. Arts, 1970, U. San Juan, 1972, Acad. Arts Honolulu, 1973; m. Harold J. Cleveland, Oct. 26, 1946; children—Carol, Ronald, Marilyn, George, Donald. Tchr., cons. Alliance Public Schs., 1927-74; instr. crafts Syracuse U., 1953-60; instr. art, Sierra Leone, 1963-64; pres., dir. Chautauqua (N.Y.) Art Gallery, 1963-76, pres. emeritus, bd. dirs., 1977—; bd. dirs., cons. adminstr. Mabel Hartzel Mus., Alliance, 1974—; bd. dirs. Lighthouse Gallery, Tequesta, Fla., 1970-72, Canton (Ohio) Culture Center, 1970—; trustee Alliance Art Center; mem. Keating (Mich.) Antique Village. Recipient Bronze plaque Community Alliance Bi-Centennial Com., 1976, Community Service award Am. Legion Aux., 1975. Mem. Am. Assn. Ret. Persons (pres. 1980-82), Am. Fedn. Art, Ohio Fedn. Art; life mem. NEA, Ohio Edn. Assn. Republican. Methodist. Clubs: Mt. Union College Women, Alliance Woman, Chautaqua Woman, Univ. Women, Order Eastern Star, K.T. Ladies, Shrine Ladies, DeMolay-Rainbow (Mom of Year 1959). Author: Arts and Crafts, 1955; Art in Poetry, 1959; Creativity in Elementary Schools, 1963. Home: 1192 Parkside Dr Alliance OH 44601

CLEVELAND, JERRY LESTER, hospital official; b. Ft. Dodge, Iowa, Nov. 1, 1949; s. Lester Jessie and Maxine Evelyn (Burch) C.; A.A., Area XI Community Coll., Ankeny, Iowa, 1977; m. Adella Lynn Lara, Dec. 19, 1970; children—Michael, Timothy, Frank. Asst. chief, then chief supply, processing and distbn. VA Hosp., Des Moines, 1973-77; dir. central service St. Luke's Methodist Hosp., Cedar Rapids, 1977—, chmn. safety com., 1979, chmn. products improvement com., 1980-84, chmn. assocs. activities com., 1980, treas., 1981-85. Served with USN, 1969-73. Mem. Am. Soc. Hosp. Central Service Personnel (membership com. 1980-81, dir. region II 1982-83, pres-elect 1984, pres. 1985), Central Service Assn. Iowa (chmn. membership 1978, pres. 1979-81, membership dir. 1985), Am. Legion. Roman Catholic. Club: Los Amigos (v.p. 1978-79 pres. 1980-81) (Cedar Rapids). Office: 1026 A Ave NE Cedar Rapids IA 52402

CLEVEN, DONALD LE ROY, construction company executive; b. Kendall, Wis., Mar. 11, 1931; s. Morris Edward and Anne Marie (Preuss) C.; Master of Accounts, Madison (Wis.) Bus. Coll., 1950; postgrad. Madison Area Tech. Coll., 1968-73, U. Wis., Madison, 1973-77; m. Maxine Eileen Schuchmann, May 18, 1958; children—Gina, Paul, Ruth. Acct. trainee, distbr. sales acct. Borden Co., Madison, Wis., 1950-57, internal auditor, Chgo., 1958; acct. Vogel Bros. Bldg. Co., Madison, 1958-69, treas., 1969-83; controller Munz Corp., Madison, 1983-84; portfolio/property mgr. real estate and mortgages div. State of Wis. Investment Bd., 1984—. Bd. dirs. Leigh Roberts Transitional House, Madison, 1983—. C.P.A. Mem. Nat. Assn. Accts., Am. Inst. C.P.A.'s, Wis. Inst. C.P.A.'s. Lutheran. Home: 1706 Wendy Ln Madison WI 53716 Office: 340 W Washington Ave Madison WI 53703

CLEVENGER, HORACE MARSHALL, operations research analyst; b. Manhattan, Kans., Dec. 21, 1913; s. Charles Henry and Edna (Warren) C.; B.S.A., Purdue U., 1938; M.S., Ohio State U., 1952; postgrad. Harris Tchrs. Coll., St. Louis, 1956-57, So. Ill. U., Alton, 1961, Washington U., 1962-71; m. Roberta Walter, June 8, 1941; children—John Walter, Robert Marshall, Donna Jean. Clk., Bur. Census, Washington, 1940-41; agrl. statistician Bur. Agr. Econs., Trenton, N.J., 1941-42; analytical statistician Bur. Agrl. Econs., Columbus, 1942-52, Doane Agrl. Service, St. Louis, 1953-54; acting asst. traffic mgr. Stix, Baer & Fuller, St. Louis, 1954-56; tchr. St. Louis Bd. Edn., St. Louis, 1956-57; analytical statistician U.S. Army Transp. Materiel Command, St. Louis, 1957-60, operations research analyst, 1960-64; math. statistician U.S. Army Aviation Systems Command, 1964-69; ops. research analyst U.S. Army Troop Support and Aviation Materiel Readiness Command, 1969-79; ret., 1979. Mem. Ops. Research Soc. Am., Am. Soc. Quality Control, Am. Statis. Assn., Am. Econ. Assn. Contbr. articles to profl. jours. Home: 21 Almeda Pl Ferguson MO 63135

CLEVENGER, ROBERT VINCENT, lawyer; b. Hancock, Mich., July 23, 1921; s. Arthur W. and Yolande (Elwood) C.; student Earlham Coll., Richmond, Ind., 1939-41; A.B., U. Ill., 1942, J.D., 1947; m. Dorothy Jean Marsh, Sept. 18, 1943; children—Arthur Eugene, Darley Yolande, Mary Marsha. Bar: Ill. 1947. Practice law, Pekin; asst. state's atty., Tazewell County (Ill.), 1951-52, spl. asst. state's atty., 1956-57; public guardian, conservator of Tazewell County, 1961-69; sec. Pekin Devel. Corp., 1970-74, 83-84, Future Horizons, Inc., Pekin, 1972-80; sec. Celestial Investors, Pekin, 1966—; atty. Village of Mackinaw, Ill., 1967-83, Village of Armington, Ill., 1968-83. Vice chmn. Tomahawk Dist., Creve Coeur council Boy Scouts Am., 1967-68, dean of merit badge counselors, 1969-84, explorer adviser Explorer Post 1776, 1976-77; chmn. Tazewell Citizens Com. on Human Relations, 1967; chmn. Tri-County Anti-Crime Project, 1977-79; pres. Pekin Edison Sch., PTA, 1954-55, 62-63, Pekin council, 1955-56; pres. Greater Peoria area chpt. World Federalists, U.S., 1967-69, 81—, sec., 1969-81; pres. Pekin Safeguard Against Crime Com., 1976-78, sec., 1979-84; v.p. Greater Peoria Area Crime Stoppers, Inc., 1981-82, dir., 1981—, fund appeal chmn., 1985—; mem. Town Bd. of Pekin Twp., 1949-53; pres. Champaign County (Ill.) Young Democrats, 1946-47; Tazewell County chmn. Ill. Com. for Constl. Revision, 1950; Pekin Twp. chmn. Dem. Com., 1950-52; Dem. precinct committeeman, 1972-74; mem. Tazewell County Dem. Central Com., 1972-74; mem. organizing com. Pekin Hope, Inc., 1982-84. Served as master sgt. AUS, 1942-46, 50-53. Recipient Citation for Outstanding Contbn. to Human Relations, Tazewell Citizens Com. on Human Relations, 1968; Order of Arrow, Boy Scouts Am., 1960, Silver Beaver award, 1967. Mem. Am., Ill., Tazewell County (pres. 1955-56, chmn. legal aid com. 1971-72, chmn. ethics com. 1979-83) bar assns., Fedn. Local Bar Assns. (pres. 3d dist. 1963), World Federalists (v.p. Midwest 1969), Pekin C. of C. (chmn. edn. com. 1955-56, chmn. local affairs com. 1959-60, chmn. legis. reform com. 1979-80), Tri-County Urban League, Internat. League for Human Rights, World Peace Through Center (com. on regional orgns. and devel. internat. law 1970, spl. com. on rev. of UN 1970), Alpha Kappa Lambda, Phi Alpha Delta. Methodist (chmn. Christian social concerns commn. 1967-70). Clubs: Kiwanis (pres. 1956, sec. 1963-64, lt. gov. Ill.-Eastern Iowa dist. 1965, mem. internat. relations com. Ill.-Eastern Iowa dist. 1967, chmn. support chs. in spiritual aims Ill.-Eastern Iowa dist. 1966, treas., past lt. gov. div. 20 I-I dist. 1970—, chmn. citizenship services com. Pekin club 1976-77, 79-80, 84-86), Pekin Boat (judge advocate 1957-83). Home: 1011 Monroe St Pekin IL 61554

CLEVEY, JUDITH MARIE, health association administrator, consultant, educator; b. Grand Rapids, Mich., July 24, 1952; d. Sidney Benson and Catherine Elizabeth (Bethune) Younkman; m. Mark H. Clevey, Apr. 27, 1974 (div.). B.A., Western Mich. U., 1974, M.P.A., 1976. Research analyst City of Kalamazoo, 1975-76; grant coordinator Muskegon County (Mich.), 1976-78; project rev. dir. West Mich. Health System Agy., Grand Rapids, 1978-80, Mich. Mid-South Health System Agy., Lansing, 1978-80; dir. Health Planning Cons. Service, Mich. Hosp. Assn. Service Corp., Lansing, 1980—; mem. faculty Western Mich. U., 1980—; cons. on grants for non-profit groups. Chmn., Mich. Reproductive Freedom Council, 1980-81. Recipient D.C. Shilling award Western Mich. U., 1974; named Outstanding Young Woman of Am., 1982. Mem. Am. Soc. Hosp. Planning, Am. Pub. Health Assn., Am. Soc. Pub. Adminstrn., Bus. and Profl. Women's Assn., AAUW (chmn. legis. com. 1979—). Democrat. Roman Catholic. Contbr. article to profl. jour. Office: Mich Hosp Assn Service Corp 6215 West St Joseph Hwy Lansing MI 48917

CLEWLOW, GERALD LEONARD, plastics manufacturing company executive; b. Evansville, Ind., Aug. 18, 1944; s. Thomas Leonard Clewlow and Maxine Marie (Nevitt) Clewlow Loehr; m. Linda Faye Mullen, Dec. 24, 1966; children—Gregory Lee, Dana Mitchelle. Student Ind. State U., 1970-73; B.S., U. Evansville, 1984; postgrad. U.S. Command and Gen. Staff Coll., 1983—. Gen. foreman Crescent Plastics Co., Evansville, 1966-76; material control mgr. Gen. Tire and Rubber Co., Evansville, 1977-78, prodn. mgr., Fort Smith, Ark., 1978-80; prodn. engr. Gen. Corp., Evansville, 1980-82, prodn. mgr., 1982—. Mem. Soc. Mfg. Engrs., Soc. Plastics Engrs., Am. Prodn. and Inventory Control Soc., Evansville Officers Club, Evansville Foremens Club. Republican. Lodge: Masons. Home: 7611 Knottingham Dr Newburgh IN 47630 Office: DiversiTech Gen Plastic Extrusions Div Gen Corp Evansville IN 47710

CLIFFORD, THOMAS JOHN, university president; b. Langdon, N.D., Mar. 16, 1921; s. Thomas Joseph and Elizabeth (Howitz) C.; B.C.S., U. N.D., 1942, J.D., 1948; M.B.S., Stanford, 1957. Stanford exec. fellow, 1958; m. Florence Marie Schmidt, Jan. 25, 1943; children—Thomas John, Stephen Michael. Instr. accounting U. N.D., 1946-47, assoc. prof., 1948-49, prof., 1949—, counselor men, 1947-49, head accounting dept., 1948-49, dean sch. commerce, 1950-71, pres. univ., 1971—. C.P.A., 1949—; dir. First Bank of N.D., Grand Forks, Ottertail Power Co., Fergus Falls, Western States Life Ins. Co., Fargo. Bd. dirs. Greater N.D. Assn., Fargo, Bush Found., St. Paul, Minn.; chmn. bd. Bush Found., 1981—. Served from 2d lt. to maj. USMC, 1942-45. Decorated Purple Heart, Bronze Star medal, Silver Star. Mem. N.D. C.P.A. Soc. (pres. 1953-54), AIM, Am. Inst. Accts., ABA, Beta Gamma Sigma, Beta Alpha Psi, Phi Eta Sigma, Kappa Sigma, Blue Key, Order Coif. K.C. Office: Univ North Dakota Grand Forks ND 58201

CLIFFORD, VIRGINIA ANN, lawyer; b. Bayside, N.Y., May 17, 1954; d. Edward James and Margaret B. (Egan) C.; m. Scott B. Schaffer, Aug. 2, 1980 (div. 1981); m. Robert David Levinson, Apr. 3, 1982. A.B., Vassar Coll., 1977; J.D., Case Western Res. U., 1980. Bar: Ohio 1980, U.S. Dist. Ct. (no. dist.) Ohio 1980. Assoc., J.S. Cook & Assocs., Chesterland, Ohio, 1980-81, Mahle, Mosher & Richer, Painesville, Ohio, 1981-82; mem. Mosher, Richer & Clifford, Painesville, 1982—. Bd. dirs. Neighboring: Supportive Service for Mental Health, Painesville, 1982—. Mem. Bus. and Profl. Women (v.p. 1982—), Lake County Women Bus. Owners, ABA, Assn. Trial Lawyers Am., Ohio State Bar Assn., Lake County Bar Assn. Democrat. Unitarian. Home: 4935 Oakland Dr Lyndhurst OH 44124 Office: 270 E Main St Suite 250 Painesville OH 44077

CLINE, (ALBERT) LESLIE, retail bookseller; b. Mountain Home, Ark., Oct. 25, 1931; s. Albert Leslie and Viva M. (Ray) C.; m. Barbara J. Brunker, June 3, 1951; 1 child: Robbie Gaye. Student Garden City Jr. Coll., Kans., 1949-51. Office mgr. No. Nat. Gas, Holcomb, Kans., 1951-74; pres. Books Etc., Inc., Garden City, Kans., 1974—. Avocations: duplicate bridge, golf. Home: Box 1773 Garden City KS 67846 Office: Books Etc Inc 109 Grant St Garden City KS 67846

CLINE, CHARLES WILLIAM, poet, educator; b. Waleska, Ga., Mar. 1, 1937; s. Paul Ardell and Mary Montarie (Pittman) C.; A.A., Reinhardt Coll., 1957; student Conservatory of Music, U. Cin., 1957-58; B.A., George Peabody Coll. for Tchrs., 1960; M.A., Vanderbilt U., 1963; D.Litt. (hon.), World U., 1981; m. Sandra Lee Williamson, June 11, 1966; 1 son, Jeffrey Charles. Asst. prof. English, Shorter Coll., Rome, Ga., 1963-64; instr. English, W. Ga. Coll., Carrollton, 1964-68; manuscript procurement editor Fideler Co., Grand Rapids, Mich., 1968; asso. prof. English, Kellogg Community Coll., Battle Creek, Mich., 1969-75, prof. English and resident poet, 1975—; condr. poetry readings and workshops; chmn. creative writing sect. Midwest Conf. on English, 1977. Recipient poetry awards from Weave Anthology, 1974, Modus Operandi, 1975, Internat. Belles-Lettres Soc., 1975, Poetry Soc. of Mich., 1975, N.Am. Mentor, 1976, 77; resolutions for recognition Mich. Ho. of Reps., Mich. Senate; diploma di merito Università delle Arti. Founding fellow Internat. Acad. of Poets (award 1983); fellow Internat. Biog. Assn. (life), Internat. Soc. Lit. (life); mem. Tagore Inst. Creative Writing Internat. (life), Assoc. Writing Programs, Nat. Council of Tchrs. of English, Midwest Conf. on English, NEA, Mich. Edn. Assn., Mich. Assn. of Higher Edn., World Poetry Soc. Intercontinental, Centro Studi e Scambi Internazionali (Poet Laureate award, Diploma di Benemerenza, Diploma d'Onore, Diploma de Palme d'Oro Academiche), Accademia Leonardo da Vinci, Poetry Soc. Am., World Univ. Roundtable, Poets and Writers, Acad. Am. Poets. Presbyterian. Author: Crossing the Ohio, 1976; Questions for the Snow, 1979; Ultima Thule, 1984. Editor: Forty Salutes to Mich. Poets, 1975. Contbr. poems to jours. and anthologies. Home: 9866 S Westnedge Ave Kalamazoo MI 49002 Office: Kellogg Community Coll 450 North Ave Battle Creek MI 49016

CLINE, DOROTHY MAY STAMMERJOHN (MRS. EDWARD WILBURN CLINE), educator; b. Boonville, Mo., Oct. 19, 1915; d. Benjamin Franklin and Lottie (Walther) Stammerjohn; grad. nurse U. Mo., 1937; B.S. in Edn., 1939, postgrad., 1966-67; M.S., Ark. State U., 1964; m. Edward Wilburn Cline, Aug. 16, 1938 (dec. May 1962); children—Margaret Ann (Mrs. Rodger Orville Bell), Susan Elizabeth (Mrs. Gary Lee Burns), Dorothy Jean. Dir. Christian Coll. Infirmary, Columbia, Mo., 1936-37; asst. chief nursing service VA Hosp., Poplar Bluff, Mo., 1950-58; tchr.-in-charge Tng. Center No. 4, Poplar Bluff, 1959-66, State Sch. No. 53, Boonville, 1967—; instr. U. Mo., Columbia, 1973-74; cons. for workshops for new tchrs., curriculum revision Mo. Dept. Edn. Mem. Butler County Council Retarded Children, 1959-66; v.p. Boonslick Assn. Retarded Children, 1969-72; sec.-treas. Mo. chpt. Am. Assn. on Mental Deficiency, 1973-75. Mem. NEA, Mo. Tchrs. Assn., Am. Assn. on Mental Deficiency, Council for Exceptional Children, AAUW (v.p. Boonville br. 1968-70, 75-77), Mo. Writers Guild, Creative Writer's Group (pres. 1974—), Columbia Creative Writers Group, Eastern Center Poetry Soc., Laura Speed Elliott High Sch. Alumni Assn., Bus. and Profl. Women's Club, Smithsonian Assn., U. Mo. Alumni Assn., Ark. State U. Alumni Assn., Internat. Platform Assn., Mo. Hist. Soc., Boonslick Hist. Soc., Friends Historic Boonville, Delta Kappa Gamma. Mem. Christian Ch. Home: 603 E High St Boonville MO 65233

CLINE, JAYSON HOWARD, coin dealer; b. Richlands, Va., Sept. 21, 1934; s. George Henry and Rachael Elizabeth (Ray) J.; student public schs., Richlands; m. Vicki Ann Coleman Hyer, Jan. 30, 1981; children by previous marriage—Carlotta Bernard, Quinton Bennett, Carmellia Loyd; stepchildren—Brian Hyer, Keith Hyer. Apprentice, Sunshine Biscuit Co., Dayton, Ohio, 1954-55; with Nat. Cash Register Co., Dayton, 1955-65; owner, operator Cline's Rare Coins, Dayton, 1955—; lectr. numismatics Wilberforce Coll. Cedarville Coll. Mem. Am. Numismatic Assn. (life), Blue Ridge Numismatic Assn. (life), Penn-Ohio Gt. Eastern Numismatic Assn. (life), So. Calif. Numismatists, Tex. State Numismatists, Mich. State Numismatists, Central States Numismatists, Fla. United Numismatists. Republican. Mem. Brethren Ch. Club: Green County Coin, Penn-Ohio Coin, Inc. (v.p.). Author: Standing Liberty Quarters, 1976; contbr. articles to profl. publs. Office: 4421 Salem Ave Dayton OH 45416

CLINE, LANCE DOUGLAS, lawyer; b. Columbus, Ind., Oct. 8, 1951; s. Leon Dale and Jo Ann Alice (Fauser) C.; m. Mary Margaret Nagle, Oct. 8, 1977; children—Rachel Ann, Natalie Brooke. B.A., Ind. U., 1973, J.D., 1980. Bar: Ind. 1980, U.S. Dist. Ct. (so. dist.) Ind. 1980. Ptnr. Townsend Yosha Cline & Price, Indpls., 1980—. Contbr. articles to profl. jours. Mem. Ind. Trial Lawyers Assn. (dir. 1984), Am. Trial Lawyers Assn., ABA, Ind. State Bar Assn., Indpls. Bar Assn., Phi Beta Kappa. Home: 8800 Moore Rd Indianapolis IN 46278 Office: Townsend Yosha Cline & Price 2220 N Meridian St Indianapolis IN 46208

CLINE, RICHARD GORDON, retail distribution company executive; b. Chgo., Feb. 17, 1935; s. William R. and Katherine A. (Bothwell) C.; B.S., U. Ill., 1957; m. Carole J. Costello, Dec. 28, 1957; children—Patricia, Linda, Richard, Jeffrey. With Jewel Cos., Inc., 1963—, pres. Osco Drug, Inc. subs., 1970-79, sr. exec. v.p., 1979, vice chmn., Chgo., from 1979, pres., chief operating officer, 1980-84, chmn., pres., and chief exec. officer, 1984-85, also dir., 1980-85; dir. NICOR, Inc., No. Ill. Gas Co., Pepsi-Cola Gen. Bottlers, Inc. Trustee Rush-Presbyterian-St. Luke's Med. Center; gov. and former chmn. bd. Central DuPage Hosp.; mem. U. Ill. Found. Clubs: Econ., Chgo., Comml., Commonwealth, Chgo. Golf. Office: NICOR Inc PO Box 200 1700 W Ferry Rd Naperville IL 60566

CLINE, WALTER QUAINE, geologist, oil producer, real estate developer and appraiser; b. Mount Vernon, Ill., May 19, 1926; s. Orval Kellous and Vandora (Wheeler) C.; m. Frances Shaw (dec. 1974); children—Cynthia, John, Robert. B.A., Evansville Coll., 1952; postgrad. U. Ga., 1972, U. Colo., 1972, U. Ind., 1974. Scout-geologist Stanford Oil Co., Evansville, Ind., 1952-53; area geologist Cities Service Oil, Midland, Tex., 1953-58, exploration geologist, supr. oil drilling and exploration, Evansville, Ind., 1958—; pres. Kellous Corp., Evansville, 1980—. Contbr. articles to profl. publs. Served as cpl. U.S. Army, 1944-46, Res., 1946-60. Mem. Am. Inst. Profl. Geologists, Am. Assn. Petroleum Geologists, Ill. Geol. Soc., Ind.-Ky. Geol. Soc., Ind. Bd. Realtors, VFW, Am. Legion. Lodge: Eagles. Avocations: swimming, camping, reading. nature study. Office: Kellous Corp Box 363 Evansville IN 47703

CLINE, WILBUR JAMES, educational administrator; b. Centerville, Iowa, May 28, 1918; s. Thomas C. and Nadie (Maring) C.; B.S., Iowa Wesleyan Coll., 1940; M.S. in Edn., Drake U., 1954; Specialists Degree, U. Colo., 1959; m. Olive Lucille Jones, Oct. 25, 1942; 1 dau., Marjorie Anne Cline Holland. Tchr. Centerville (Iowa) Pub. Schs., 1939-41, Ottumwa (Iowa) Pub. Schs., 1941-42, Mason City (Iowa) Pub. Schs., 1942-43; tng. officer VA, Des Moines, 1946-53; guidance counselor Davenport High Sch., Iowa, 1954-60; dir. guidance services Davenport (Iowa) pub. schs., 1960-63; dir. data processing services Scott County (Iowa) schs., 1963-66; dir. Area 9 Schs. Info. Center, Bettendorf, Iowa, 1966-70; v.p. Kempton-Cline Data Systems, Davenport, Iowa, 1970-74; asst. to dir. Bi-State Met. Computer Commn., 1974-75; guidance counselor Pleasant Valley Community Schs., Pleasant Valley, Iowa, 1975-80; vocat. cons. to Social Security Adminstrn., 1963-64. Mem. citizens adv. com. Scott County Mental Health Center, 1977, 1978-79; elder Newcomb Presbyn. Ch., Davenport, 1957-60. Served with USAAF, 1942-46; CBI, with USAF, 1950-52; lt. col. Res. ret. Mem. Iowa Edn. Assn. (life), Ret. Officers Assn., Res. Officers Assn., Am. Assn. Ret. Persons, Beta Beta Beta. Clubs: Masons (32 deg.), Moose, Shriners. Home: 1555 W Garfield St Davenport IA 52804

CLINGAN, MELVIN HALL, lumber exec., publisher; b. Atchison, Kans., July 12, 1929; s. Frank E. and Hazel Ellen (Hall) C.; B.S. in Bus. (Summerfield scholar), U. Kans., 1951; m. Athelia Roberta Sweet, Apr. 7, 1956; children—Sandra, Scott, Kimberly, Marcia. Pres., Holiday Homes, Inc. and Clingan Land Co., Shawnee Mission, Kans., 1956—; former pub. Johnson County Herald, Gardner News, De Soto News, Spring Hill New Era; dir. R.L. Sweet Lumber Co. and subs., Kansas City, Kans., 1959—, exec. v.p., 1973-80, pres., 1981—. Vice pres. Westwood View Sch. Bd., 1965-68; Republican congl. dist. chmn., mem. state exec. com., 1966-72; bd. dirs. Johnson County Community Coll. Found., 1973-82. Served with USAF, 1951-55. Mem. Home Builders Assn. Greater Kansas City (past pres.), Home Builders Assn. Kans. (past pres.), Nat. Assn. Home Builders (nat. life dir.), Mission C. of C. (pres. 1971), Sigma Nu (grand officer 1961-68, ednl. found. 1980—, trustee 1982—), Omicron Delta Kappa, Beta Gamma Sigma, Republican. Mem. Disciples of Christ Ch. Club: Mission Hills Country. Home: 5345 Mission Woods Rd Shawnee Mission KS 66205 Office: 4500 Roe Blvd Kansas City KS 66103

CLINGER, DANIEL WAYNE, architect; b. Bucyrus, Ohio, Oct. 6, 1945; s. Henry A. and Dortha J. (Pool) C.; m. Marsha Lynn Tanner, Aug. 28, 1966; children—Andrea, Philip; m. 2d Charlotte Ann Smith, Mar. 2, 1975; children—Sheri, James, Tracy, Melynda. Student in drafting Stautzenberger Coll., 1964-65. Registered architect, Ohio. Draftsman, Finkbiner, Pettis and Strout, cons. engrs., Toledo, 1966, Warren G. Gallahan, architect, Marion, Ohio, 1966-67; supr., AWA Indsl. Design Ctr., Marion, 1967-68; draftsman, then architect Rooney, Musser and Assocs., Findlay, Ohio, 1968-83; ops. mgr. Archtl. Forum, 1981—, Advisor Archtl. Explorer Post 384 Boy Scouts Am.; mem. com. Friends of Old Mill Stream; pres. Anchor Park Com., adviser 4-H Club. Mem. AIA (cert. 1982, newsletter editor Toledo chpt.), Architects Soc. Ohio, Findlay Jaycees (pres. 1978-79, awards). Office: Archtl Forum 500 S Main St Findlay OH 45840

CLINGERMAN, THOMAS BURDETTE, avionics manufacturing company executive; b. Beech Grove, Ind., Feb. 26, 1948; s. Cleo Burdette and Ruth Veronica (Beach) C.; m. Karen Marie Slanika, May 22, 1976. B.A., Va. Mil. Inst., 1970; M.P.A., Boise State U., 1980; postgrad. in mgmt. USAF Air Command and Staff Coll., 1975-79. Commd. 2d lt. U.S. Air Force, advanced through grades to maj. 1984; assigned Del Rio, Tex., 1970-74, Nellis AFB, Las Vegas, 1974-76, Mt. Home, Idaho, 1977-80; ret., 1980; indsl. engr. Rockwell Internat. Collins div., Cedar Rapids, Iowa, 1980, mgr. process engring., 1980-82, mgr. flight control, 1983, program mgr. Peoples Republic of China, 1984, program mgr. railroad system, 1984—. Advisor, CAP, 1982—. Mem. Robotics Internat. (sr.), Exptl. Aircraft Assn., Iowa Sled Dog Drivers (pres. 1982—). Republican. Roman Catholic. Avocations: flying; scuba diving; sailing; skiing; sled dog racing. Home: RR 1 Box 269C Solon IA 52333 Office: Rockwell Internat Collins Div 400 Collins Rd 108-157 Cedar Rapids IA 52498

CLINTON, FRANK LEE, mayor; b. Chgo., July 29, 1937; s. Francis Ring and Eva (Strohl) C.; B.S., U. Ill., 1960. Credit analyst Marshall Field & Co., Chgo., 1961-62; with trust dept. Edgar County Nat. Bank, Paris, Ill., 1962-64; purchasing mgr., accountant Bastian-Blessing Co., Chgo., 1965-71; production mgr. McCann Engring. & Mfg. Co., Glendale, Calif., 1971-74; exec. v.p. Paris (Ill.) C. of C., 1975-80; pres. Charleston (Ill.) Area C. of C., 1980-81; mayor City of Paris, 1983—. Bd. dirs. Edgar County Fair Assn., 1966-78, v.p., 1970-73; bd. dirs. Covered Bridge council Girl Scouts U.S., 1977—; pres. Young Republican Orgn., Edgar County, 1964. Served to sgt. Army N.G., 1960-66. Execs. Presbyterian. Clubs: U.S. Auto, Masons, Rotary (dir. 1976-80) Sports announcer for Paris Broadcasting Corp., 1953—. Home: 1002 S Main St Paris IL 61944

CLINTON, WILLIAM CHRISTOPHER, physicist; b. Dubuque, Iowa, Aug. 19, 1937; s. William Milford and Mary Avo (Thorpe) C.; B.A., William Jewell Coll., 1966; student Ill. Inst. Tech., 1967, M.I.T., 1968; m. Lisa DeWandel, July 8, 1978. Med. lab. technician U.S. Air Force, Aeromed. Research Lab., Holloman AFB, N.Mex., 1961-65; physicist U.S. Bur. Mines, Rolla (Mo.) Metallurgy Research Center, 1966—. Chmn., Rolla Combined Fed. Campaign, 1976-78, 83—; bd. dirs. Rolla Civic Theatre, 1976-78, Alamogordo (N.Mex.) Players Workshop, 1963-65, Bus. Opportunities for Mo. Blind, 1982—; bd. govs. Eye Research Found. Mo., 1979—. Mem. Microbeam Analysis Soc., Internat. Metallographic Soc., AAAS, Sigma Xi. Club: Rolla Lions (treas. 1971-77, sec. 1977-83, dist. gov. 1979-80). Contbr. articles to tech. jours. Home: PO Box 1125 Rolla MO 65401 Office: Bur Mines PO Box 280 Rolla MO 65401

CLODFELTER, DONALD GLEN, electric utility company executive; b. Lafayette, Ind., Sept. 5, 1933; s. Glen and Emily (Schilling) C.; m. Anne Elizabeth Eyler, June 26, 1965; children—William Glen, Jon Eyler. B.S.M.E., Purdue U., 1955; M.B.A., Ind. U., 1958. Adminstr., mgr. Cummins Engine Co., Columbus, Ind., 1958-69; gen. mgr. Jackson County REMC, Brownstown, Ind., 1969—. Served to lt. (j.g.) USNR, 1955-57. Home: Rural Route 2 Box 14 Brownstown IN 47220 Office: Jackson County REMC PO Box K Brownstown IN 47220

CLOIDT, SUSAN G., roller skating association executive; b. St. Louis, Mar. 9, 1948; d. Ralph B. and Shirley A. (Deal) Shugert; m. Ronald G. Theis, Oct. 4, 1970 (div.); 1 son, Colin C.; m. 2d, Jeffrey M. Cloidt, Dec. 17, 1981. B.A., Nebr. Wesleyan U., 1970; postgrad. U. Nebr., 1975—. Tchr., Centralia (Kans.) High Sch., 1970-71; mental health educator Omaha area, 1973-75; tech. writer computer network U. Nebr., Lincoln, 1975-77; dir. mental health educators State of Nebr., 1977-78; dir. communications Roller Skating Rink Operators Assn., 1978—. Chmn. Nebr. Task Force on Women, Alcohol and Drugs, 1977-79. Mem. Am. Soc. Assn. Execs., Common Cause. Democrat. Contbr. articles to profl. jours. Office: Roller Skating Rink Operators Assn 7700 A St Lincoln NE 68510

CLOKE, THOMAS HENRY, mech. engr.; b. Chgo., Oct. 17, 1921; s. Thomas Henry and Lillian Clara (Krez) C.; B.S., U. Ill., 1943; m. Frances Irene Fox, Dec. 19, 1942; children—Deborah (Mrs. Wayne R. Kalbow), Thomas Myron. With Shaw, Naess & Murphy and Naess & Murphy, architects, Chgo., 1946-62, chief mech. engr., 1954-62; chief engr. Jensen & Halstead, architects, Chgo., 1962-64; prin. Neiler, Rich & Bladen, Inc., cons. engrs., Chgo., 1964-68, Gritschke & Cloke, Inc., cons. engrs., Chgo., 1968-79, Loebl Schlossman & Hackl, architects, Chgo., 1979—. Cons. engr. U.S. Air Force in Japan, 1963. Mem. Glen Ellyn (Ill.) Park Bd., 1957-60, pres., 1961; mem. Recreation Commn., Village of Glen Ellyn, 1965-74, chmn., 1974-75, mem. Bldg. Bd. of Appeal, 1973-77. Served to capt. AUS, 1943-46. Decorated Bronze Star medal. Registered profl. engr., Ill. Fellow ASHRAE (mem. research promotion com. 1969-75, research and tech. com. 1976-77, chmn. 1977-78, tech. council 1980-83, Disting. Service award); mem. Air Pollution Control Assn., Nat. Fire Protection Assn., Am. Mgmt. Assn., Soc. Am. Mil. Engrs., Am. Gas Assn., U.S. Power Squadron, U.S. Naval Inst., U. Ill. Alumni Assn., Theta Chi. Home: 950 Roslyn Rd Glen Ellyn IL 60137 Office: 845 N Michigan Ave Chicago IL 60611

CLONINGER, CLAUDE ROBERT, psychiatric researcher, educator, genetic epidemiologist; b. Beaumont, Tex., Apr. 4, 1944; s. Morris Sheppard and Marie Concetta (Mazzagatti) C.; m. Sharon Lee Rogan, July 11, 1969; children—Bryan Joseph, Kevin Michael. B.A. U. Tex., 1966; M.D., Washington U., St. Louis, 1980, (hon.) U. Umea, Sweden, 1983. Diplomate Am. Bd. Psychiatry and Neurology. Instr. psychiatry Washington U., St. Louis, 1973-74, asst. prof. 1974-84, assoc. prof., 1978-81, prof., 1981—; prof. genetics, 1978—; vis. prof. U. Hawaii, Honolulu, 1978-79, U. Umea, Sweden, 1980; chmn. NIMH psychopathology Review Com., Washington, 1980-84; cons. WHO, Geneva, 1981—, Am. Psychiatric Assn., Washington, 1978—. Editor: Jour. Behavior Genetics, 1980—, Am. Jour. Human Genetics, 1980-83. Contbr. articles to profl. jours. Recipient Research Scientist award NIMH, 1975, 80, 85. Fellow Am. Psychiat. Assn., Am. Psychopathol. Assn. (treas. 1984—); mem. Am. Soc. Human Genetics (editorial bd. 1980-83), Behavior Genetics Assn. (editorial bd. 1980—), Research Soc. Alcoholism. Avocations: gardening; reading; travel. Home: 4 Lynnbrook Frontenac MO 63131 Office: Washington U 4940 Audubon St Saint Louis MO 63110

CLONINGER, FRANKLIN DALE, plant breeder, research director; b. Hartshorn, Mo., Sept. 25, 1938; s. George Franklin and Patsy Jane (Derryberry) C.; B.S., U. Mo., Columbia, 1960, M.S., 1968, Ph.D., 1973; m. Marion Ruth Haas, May 19, 1962; children—Carla Sue, Mary Jane. Materials insp. Mo. Hwy. Dept., Kirkwood, 1964-65; research asst. P.A.G. Seeds Co., Carrollton, Mo., 1965-66; grad. asst. in agronomy U. Mo., Columbia, 1966-68, research specialist, 1968-74; plant breeder Golden Harvest, J.C. Robinson Seed Co., Waterloo, Nebr., 1974-84, dir. research and devel., 1985—. Elder Faith Christian Ch., Omaha, 1983—. Served with AUS, 1960-63. Mem. Am. Soc. Agronomy, Crop Sci. Soc. Am., Genetics Assn. Am., Can. Seed Growers Assn. Plant Breeder, Sigma Xi, Gamma Sigma Delta. Mem. Disciples of Christ Ch. Home: 602 Westridge St Elkhorn NE 68022 Office: JC Robinson Seed Co Waterloo NE 68069

CLOONAN, JAMES BRIAN, investment executive; b. Chgo., Jan. 28, 1931; s. Bernard V. and Lauretta D. (Maloney) C.; student Northwestern U., 1949-52, B.A., 1957, Ph.D., 1972; M.B.A., U. Chgo., 1964; m. Edythe Adrianne Ratner, Mar. 26, 1970; children—Michele, Christine, Mia; stepchildren—Carrie Madorin, Harry Madorin. Prof., Sch. Bus., Loyola U., Chgo., 1966-71; pres. Quantitative Decision Systems, Inc., Chgo., 1972-73; chmn. bd. Heinold Securities, Inc., Chgo., 1974-77; prof. Grad. Sch. Bus., DePaul U., Chgo., 1978-82; pres., founder Am. Assn. Individual Investors, 1979—; chmn. Investment Info. Services, 1981—; cons. Computer Based Decision Systems, Chgo.; pres., founder Am. Assn. Individual Investors, 1979—. Served with U.S. Army, 1951-54. Mem. Ops. Research Soc., Inst. for Mgmt. Sci., Am. Fin. Assn., Am. Mktg. Assn., An. Inst. for Decision Scis., Assn. for Consumer Research. Author: Estimates of the Impact of Sign and Billboard Removal Under the Highway Beautification Act of 1965, 1966; Stock Options - The Application of Decision Theory to Basic and Advanced Strategies, 1973; An Introduction to Decision-Making for the Individual Investor, 1980; Expanding Your Investment Horizons, 1983. Home: 950 N Michigan Ave Chicago IL 60611 Office: 612 N Michigan Ave Chicago IL 60611

CLOUD, JACK LESLIE, realtor, publisher; b. Fremont, Ohio, Mar. 15, 1925; s. Wesley James and Mildred Elizabeth (Miller) C.; grad. Walsh Coll. Acctg., 1948; m. Janet Sorg, Apr. 1, 1944; children—Jack Leslie, Charles Robert. With Nat. Lithograph Co., Detroit, 1946-57; with Shelby Lithograph Co., Detroit, 1957-62; with Calvert Lithograph Co., Detroit, 1962-70; with Litho-Graphics, Detroit, 1970-75; with Odyssey Internat. Gallery, Livonia, Mich., 1975-79, pres., chmn. bd. dirs., 1975-80; with Candle-lite Inc., Birmingham, Mich., 1977-79, pres., chmn. bd. dirs., 1977-80; chmn. bd. dirs. Litho-Graphics, Inc. Realtor, Birmingham, Mich., 1980—. Served with AUS, 1943-46. Mem. Rockport Art Assn., Internat. Platform Assn., Am. Printing History Assn., U. Mich. Artist Guild. Espicopalian (sr. warden 1977-78, trustee endowment trust 1979—). Clubs: Elks (chmn. bd. trustees 1966-67), Detroit Athletic. Home: 4253 Brandywyne Dr Troy MI 48098 Office: 248 S Woodward Birmingham MI 48011

CLOUD, STEPHEN REED, bearing and transmission company executive, state legislator; b. Kansas City, Kans., Mar. 11, 1949; s. Forrest L. and Bonnie L. (Simpson) C.; m. Barbara Anne Verron, Aug. 26, 1972; children—Matthew Brian, Kevin Michael, Jeffrey David. B.S., U. Kans., 1971. Vol., VISTA, 1971-72; with Indsl. Bearing and Transmission Co., Inc., Merriam, Kans., 1972—, corp. v.p., 1977—; mem. Kans. Ho. of Reps., 1980—. Bd. dirs. Turner House, Inc., 1972—; chmn. Johnson County Planning Commn., 1978-81. Named Lambda Chi Alpha of Yr., 1971; recipient Johnson County Service award Johnson County Bd. Commrs., 1980. Mem. Delta Sigma Pi. Republican. Episcopalian. Home: 20885 W 47th St Shawnee Mission KS 66218 Office: 9400 W 55th St Merriam KS 66203

CLOUSE, JOHN DANIEL, lawyer; b. Evansville, Ind., Sept. 4, 1925; s. Frank Paul and Anna Lucille (Frank) C.; A.B., U. Evansville, 1950; J.D., Ind. U., 1952; m. Georgia L. Ross, Dec. 7, 1978; 1 son, George Chauncey. Admitted to Ind. bar, 1952; assoc. firm James D. Lopp, Evansville, 1952-56; pvt. practice law, Evansville, 1956—; guest editorialist Viewpoint, Evansville Courier, 1978—, Focus, Radio Sta. WGBF, 1978-84; 2d asst. city atty. Evansville, 1954-55. Pres., Civil Service Commn. of Evansville Police Dept., 1961-62; pres. Ind. War Memls. Com., 1963-69; mem. jud. nominating com. Vanderburgh County, Ind., 1976-80. Served with U.S. Army, 1943-46. Decorated Bronze Star medal. Fellow Ind. Bar Found.; mem. Evansville Bar Assn. (v.p. 1972), Ind. Bar Assn., Selden Soc., Pi Gamma Mu. Republican. Club: Travelers Century. Home: 819 S Hebron Ave Evansville IN 47715 Office: 1010 Hulman Bldg Evansville IN 47708

CLUTE, RICHARD BOYD, environmental engineer, manufacturing engineer; b. Mpls., June 19, 1950; s. Howard Boyd and Roene Alberta (Brown) C.; m. Diane Marie Mruz, May 20, 1978; 1 child, Nicholas. B.S in Engring. Tech., St. Cloud State U., 1978. Drafting technician III Franklin Mfg. Co., St. Cloud, Minn., 1979-80, mfg. engr., 1980-84, environ. engring. supr., 1984—. Served with U.S. Army, 1970-72. Affiliate mem. Soc. Mfg. Engrs. Methodist. Club: Midwest 4 Wheel Dr. (St. Paul). Avocations: animal husbandry; off-road racing. Home: Route 7 St Cloud MN 56301 Office: Franklin Mfg Co 701 33rd Ave N St Cloud MN 56301

CLYDE, PAYSON JAMES, civil engineer; b. Columbus, Ohio, Sept. 6, 1930; s. Paul Hibbert and Mildred Rebecca (Smith) C.; B.S. in Civil Engring., Pa. State U., 1952; m. Marilyn Jean Ashley, Nov. 19, 1965; 1 dau. by previous marriage, Alberta Ann Sanders. Sales engr. Armco Drainage & Metal Products, Inc., Detroit, Tucson, 1957-63; exec. sec., dir. engring. Wis. Concrete Pipe Assn., Madison, 1963-66; project engr., customer service engr., safety engr., mgr. marine and indsl. spare parts sales aircraft engine group Gen. Electric Co., Cin., 1966—, now spl. programs coordinator; expert witness; vocat. sch. counselor. Served with USN, 1952-55. Registered profl. engr., Wis., Ind., Calif. Fellow ASCE; mem. Naval Res. Assn., Res. Officers Assn., Navy League. Republican. Roman Catholic. Club: Elks. Author: OSHA and the Safety Engineer, 1977; OSHA and Its Impact, 1978. Home: 11269 Marlette Dr Cincinnati OH 45249 Office: Gen Electric Co Mail Drop N-155 Cincinnati OH 45215

COASH, RONALD JAMES, electrical engineer; b. Clifton, Kans., May 15, 1939; s. Russell Francis and Hazel Marie (Scouten) C.; B.S., Kans. State U., 1972, A.M.; m. Linda Ann Dieker, June 26, 1965; children—Russell E., Jennifer M., Christopher J. Engring. technician environ. research Kans. State U., 1968-70; chief engr. Raincat Engring. Co., Greeley, Colo., 1974, Reinke Mfg. Co., Deshler, Nebr., 1974-82; with Notifrer Corp., Lincoln, Nebr., 1982—; applications, service and mfg. engr. IC/MIDWEC, 1978. Served with USAR, 1961-63. Mem. Am. Soc. Agrl. Engrs., Internat. Brotherhood Elec. Workers, Am. Legion. Roman Catholic. Club: K.C. Author handbook, articles in field. Patentee control circuit. Home: 4311 Antelope Creek Rd Lincoln NE 68506 Office: 6050 N 56th St Lincoln NE 68507

COATES, GLENN RICHARD, lawyer; b. Thorp, Wis., June 8, 1923; s. Richard and Alma (Borck) C.; student Milw. State Tchrs. Coll., 1940-42, N.M. A. and M.A., 1943-44; LL.B., U. Wis., 1948, D.Juridicial Scis., 1951; m. Dolores Milburn, June 24, 1944; children—Richard Ward, Cristie Joan. Admitted to Wis. bar, 1949; atty. Mil. Sea Transp. Service, Dept. Navy, 1951-52; pvt. law practice, Racine, Wis., 1952—; dir. Pioneer Savings & Loan Assn., Racine Federated, Inc. Lectr., U. Wis. Law Sch., 1955-56. Chmn. bd. St. Luke's Meml. Hosp., 1973-76; pres. Racine Area United Way, 1979-81. Served with AUS, 1943-46. Mem. State Bar Wis. (bd. govs. 1969-74, chmn. bd. 1973-74), Wis. Jud. Council (chmn. 1969-72), Am. Bar Assn., Am. Law Inst., Order of Coif. Methodist (chmn. finance com. 1961-67). Mason. Club: Racine Country. Contbr. to profl. publs. in field. Author: Chattel Secured Farm Credit, 1953. Home: 2830 Michigan Blvd Racine WI 53402 Office: 840 Lake Ave Racine WI 53403

COATES, ROGER SPENCER, psychologist; b. Ann Arbor, Mich., June 26, 1955; s. Randall Fitzgerald and Pauline Rosanna (Rogers) C.; B.A., Western Mich. U., 1976, M.A., 1978, Ed.S., 1982. Psychologist, Van Buren Intermediate Sch. Dist., Lawrence, Mich., 1978—; resource person Schoocraft Schs., Western Mich. U., 1976-78. Mem. Nat. Assn. Sch. Psychologists, Mich. Assn. Sch. Psychologists, Assn. Behavior Analysis. Office: 701 S Paw Paw St Lawrence MI 49064

COATS, DANIEL R., congressman; b. Jackson, Mich., May 16, 1943; B.A., Wheaton (Ill.) Coll., 1965; J.D., Ind. U., 1971; m. Marcia Anne Crawford, 1965; children—Laura, Lisa, Andrew. Admitted to Ind. bar, 1972; congressional dist. rep., 1976-80; mem. 97th-99th Congresses from 4th Ind. Dist.; Republican leader House Select Com. Children, Youth and Families; mem. House Energy and Commerce com. Pres. Big Bros./Big Sisters Ft. Wayne, 1978-80; bd. dirs. Anthony Wayne Rehab. Ctr. Served with USAR, 1966-68. Mem. Allen County Bar Assn. Club: Quest. Address: 1417 Longworth House Office Bldg Washington DC 20515

COBB, CAROLYN ANN, communications consultant; b. St. Louis, Feb. 21, 1950; d. Vincent Atlee and Margaret Elizabeth (Ottinger) Knopp; B.A., Harris Tchrs. Coll., 1973; M.A., Webster Coll., 1975; m. Richard Joseph Cobb, Aug. 7, 1976; 1 child, Richard Joseph. Tchr., St. Louis Public Schs. 1973-74; programmer Gen. Am. Life, 1974-75, Mercantile Trust Co., N.A. 1975-78; programmer/analyst Mo. Pacific R.R. 1979-81; data base adminstr. staff specialist Southwestern Bell, St. Louis 1981-84; cons., 1984—. Fin. chmn., mem. various coms. United Ch. of Christ, Oakville, Mo., also softball and volleyball coach, mem. choir and adult fellowship; youth group leader Grace United Ch. of Christ; adviser Drop-In Ctr.; data processing adviser Explorer Post, Boy Scouts Am. Mem. Assn. Systems Mgmt., Data Processing Mgmt. Assn., Assn. Women in Computing (charter), Kappa Delta Pi. Republican. Editor: Fundamentals of Data Communications and Networking. Home and Office: 6520 Galewood Ct Saint Louis MO 63129

COBBIN MURPHY, EARLEAN, lawyer; b. Chgo., July 15, 1943; d. Eddie and Lucinda (Watts) Slaughter; A.A. with honors, Thornton Jr. Coll., 1969; B.S.Ed. cum laude (Legal Opportunities scholar, 1970), Chgo. State U., 1970; J.D., DePaul U., 1976; children—Kenneth, Alonzo, Charlean Renee, Twanda Lekecia. Sec., Samuel Miller & Co., Chgo., 1963-66, Sears Roebuck & Co., Chgo., 1966-68; tchr. Chgo. Vocat. High Sch., Chgo. Bd. Edn., 1971-75; admitted to Ill. bar, 1976; sole practice, Harvey, Ill., 1976—; enforcement atty. securities div. Ill. Sec. of State, 1983-84; part time instr. Chgo. State U.; part time atty. Ill. Sec. of State. Mem. ABA, Nat. Bar Assn., Ill. Bar Assn., Cook County Bar Assn., Chgo. Bar Assn., Women's Bar Assn. Unitarian. Office: 15402 S Center Suite 3 Harvey IL 60429

COBERLY, CAMDEN ARTHUR, engineering educator; b. Elizabeth, W.Va., Dec. 21, 1922; s. James G. Blaine and Edith Luella (Simpson) C.; m. Lenore McComas, June 14, 1946; children—Catherine, Elizabeth, Charles, Robert. B.S., W.V.U., 1944; M.S., Carnegie Inst. Tech., 1947; Ph.D., U. Wis., 1949. Engr., Mallinckrodt Chem. Co., St. Louis, 1949-55, chief engr., 1955-64; prof. U. Wis.-Madison, 1964-68, assoc. dir. engring. exptl. sta., 1964-68, chmn. chem. engring. dept., 1968-71, assoc. dean coll. engring., 1971—, exec. dir. engring. exptl. sta., 1971—. Served to lt. (j.g.) USNR, 1944-46. Fellow Am. Inst. Chem. Engrs.; mem. Am. Soc. Engring. Educ., Am. Chem. Soc., AAAS, Am. Assn. Univ. Profs., Nat. Assn. Corrison Engrs. Avocations: recreational reading on archeology, geography and hist., fishing, camping, golf, outside activities. Home: 4114 N Sunset Ct Madison WI 53705 Office: Engring Exptl Sta Coll Engring 1500 Johnson Dr Madison WI 53706

COBLE, PAUL ISHLER, advertising agency executive; b. Indpls., Mar. 17, 1926; s. Earl and Agnes Elizabeth (Roberts) C.; A.B., Wittenberg U., 1950; postgrad. Case-Western Res. U., 1950-53; m. Marjorie M. Trentanelli, Jan. 27, 1951; children—Jeff, Sarah Anne, Doug. Reporter, Springfield (Ohio) Daily News, 1944; reporter, feature writer Rockford (Ill.) Register-Republic, 1947-48; account exec. Fuller & Smith & Ross, Inc., Cleve., 1949-57; dir. sales promotion McCann Erickson, 1957-63; dir. sales devel. Marschalk Co., 1963-65, v.p., 1965-70, sr. v.p., 1970-73; pres. Coble Group, 1973—; chmn. bd., sec.-treas. Hahn & Coble. Inc., advt., mktg. and pub. relations, 1977—; pub. Islander mag., Hilton Head Island, S.C., 1973-83; asst. prof. advt. W.Va. U., 1982-83. Chief instr. Cleve. Advt. Club Sch., 1961-73. Active fund raising drives for various charitable and youth orgns. Served with AUS, 1944-46. Mem. Sales and Marketing Internat., Assn. Indsl. Advertisers, Cleve. Advt. Club, Newcomen Soc. Clubs: River Oaks Racquet; Sea Pines (Hilton Head Island, S.C.); Cleve. Rotary. Contbr. articles to profl. pubs. Home: 22683 Meadowhill Ln Rocky River OH 44116 Office: Hanna Bldg Cleveland OH 44115

COBLER, LOIS BEULAH, educator; b. Garrett, Ind., June 1, 1899; d. Thomas C. and Ida M. (Van Zile) C.; grad. Tri State U., 1923; B.S., Ind. U., 1937; postgrad. Manchester Coll., Clark U., Western Mich. U., Ball State U., Ind. U., 1938-58. Tchr. public schs., Garrett-DeKalb County, Ind., 1918-56, Garrett Jr. High Sch., 1927-28; librarian J.E. Ober Elem. Sch., Garrett, 1956-66; now librarian, organist Garrett Ch. of Christ. Bd. dirs., monthly radio commentator Garrett Hosp. Aux.; chmn. nat. projects Northeastern Ind. Garden Clubs, 1970—, parliamentarian, 1972—; co-chmn. steering com. DeKalb County Internat. Christian Leadership Prayer Breakfast, 1972, sec., chmn. public relations county prayer breakfast, 1973, chmn. county breakfast, 1974; bd. dirs. Garrett Community Hosp. Aid Found., 1974—; chmn. nominations com. Ind. Mother of Year, 1974. Named Bus. and Profl. Hoosier Lady of Year, 1965; Alumni Disting. Service award Tri State Coll. and Alumni Assn., 1969; Sr. Citizen Queen, DeKalp County (Ind.), 1976-77; Citizen of Yr., Garrett C. of C., 1979. Mem. Nat., Ind. ret. tchrs. assns., DeKalb County Ret. Tchrs., Garrett Hosp. Assn., Ind. Sch. Librarians Assn., Ind. State Tchrs. Assn. (life), Garrett Hist. Soc., Bus. and Profl. Women's Club (hon.; pres. 1932-34, 65-66), Delta Kappa Gamma, Tri Kappa (pres. 1974-76). Club: Garrett Roadside Garden (sec.). Author: History of Garrett Church of Christ, 1967; contbr. biographies of Nancy Hanks Lincoln and Gene Stratton Porter to Mothers of Achievement in American History, 1776-1976, 1976. Co-editor: So Grows A City—Greater Garrett Centennial 1875-1975. Contbr. articles to profl. jours. Columnist Garrett Clipper, 1981-82. Home: 301 W King St Garrett IN 46738

COCHRAN, DONALD EARL, lawyer; b. Chgo., Sept. 17, 1939; s. John Roy and Ruth (Miller) C.; m. Nancy Helburn Stein, Dec. 29, 1984. B.S. in C.E., Ind. Inst. Tech., 1961; M.S., Mich. State U., 1963; J.D., DePaul U., Chgo., 1972; Engring., surveying cons., 1964—; dir. engring. and legal depts. Suburban Homes Corp., Valparaiso, Ind.; dir. South Haven Waterworks; engr. Drainage Bd. Adams County (Ind.), 1966-68; asst. prof. Ind. Inst. Tech., 1962-68; asst. prof. constrn. tech. Calumet campus Purdue U., Hammond, Ind., 1968-73; owner Cochran Enterprises Co., Gary; pvt. practice law, Gary and Westville, Ind., 1972—; pres., dir. M.V.M.H.P., Inc., Valparaiso. Registered profl. engr., Ind., Ohio; profl. land surveyor, Ind. Mem. ASCE, Nat. Soc. Profl. Engrs., Am. Congress on Surveying and Mapping, Ind. Soc. Profl. Land Surveyors (chmn. com. on edn. and registration exams 1966-70, v.p. 1968, pres. 1970 Ill., Ind. bar assns. Home: 576 Fargo Rd Jackson Farm Westville IN 46391 Office: 375 W US #6 South Haven Valparaiso IN 46383

COCHRAN, DWIGHT EDWIN, II, veterinarian; b. East Chicago, Ind., May 18, 1948; s. Dwight Edwin and Laura Eileen (Meyer) C.; student Baylor U., 1966-68; D.V.M., Purdue U., 1973; m. Glenda Kay Boyd, May 19, 1973. Gen. practice veterinary medicine, herd health cons., Boswell, Ind., 1973—; cons. Ind. Dairy Goat Assn. Recipient Leadership award 4-H Clubs, 1978. Mem. Ind. Acad. Veterinary Medicine, Acad. Vet. Cons., Am. Assn. Swine Practitioners, Am. Assn. Sheep, Goat Practitioners, Am. Assn. Bovine Practitioners, Am., Ind., West Central Ind. veterinary med. assns., Am. Registry Cert. Animal Scientists, Am. Soc. Agrl. Cons. Presbyterian. Club: Rotary Internat. (dir. Boswell chpt.). Author: Common Diseases of Dairy Goats, A Guide to Their Prevention, Treatment, and Control For the Herdsman, 1977. Home: 402 E North St Boswell IN 47921 Office: 104 E Main St Boswell IN 47921

COCHRAN, MALCOLM LOWELL, psychologist; b. Crawfordsville, Iowa, Oct. 17, 1941; s. Vaun Wesley and Pearl Ida (Robertson) C.; B.A., Iowa Wesleyan Coll., 1963; M.S., Municipal U. of Omaha, 1965; m. Barbara Sue Stotts, Apr. 17, 1966; children—Teresa Marie, Gary Lowell, Debra Sue, Patricia Diane. Intern sch. psychometrist, Child Study Service Municipal U. of Omaha, 1963-64; research psychometrist, sch. psychologist Glenwood State Hosp.-Sch., Glenwood, Iowa, 1964-68, cons. psychologist, diagnostic and evaluation clinic, 1968-74, dir. employee testing program, 1968-72, dir. psychol. testing center, 1974—, lectr.,-in-service training, child devel., 1968-72. Cubmaster Boy Scouts Am., Glenwood, 1976-77. Served with Army N.G., 1961. Recipient Explorer Scouts Silver Award Boy Scouts Am., 1958; certified sch. psychologist, Iowa; licensed psychologist, Iowa. Fellow Am. Assn. Mental Deficiency. Republican. Methodist. Contbr. articles to profl. jours. Home: 225 W Florence Ave Glenwood IA 51534 Office: 711 S Vine St Glenwood IA 51534

COCHRAN, MORRIS WAYNE, assn. exec.; b. Columbus, Ind., Aug. 30, 1941; s. Carl M. and Elfreda M. (Stillinger) C.; B.F.A., U. Cin., 1963; M.S. (Univ. Scholar), U. Ill., 1964; postgrad. Mich. State U., 1968, Syracuse U., 1969, John Marshall Law Sch., 1970-72, Washington U., 1970-72; m. Mary-Ellen Skeen, July 29, 1963; children—Justine Della, Morris Wayne. News dir. WLTH Radio, Gary, Ind., 1964-65; exec. sec., mgr. Better Bus. Bur. N.W. Ind., Gary, 1965—, pres. ednl. found., 1975—; founder, dir. N.W. Ind. Credit Counseling, 1974—. Bd. dirs. Gary Urban Coalition, 1969-70; chmn. town formation Ross Park, Ind., 1973—; bd. dirs. Gary Jr. Achievement, 1978-81; mem. Conf. of Social Concern, 1981; mem. consumer adv. panel No. Ind. Pub. Service Co., 1982—. Recipient U.P.I. News award, 1965; State Broadcaster of Month award, 1967. Mem. Gary Jaycees (dir. 1965-66), Gary Exchange (dir. 1972-74). Office: 4231 Cleveland St Gary IN 46408

COCHRAN, RICHARD MORRISON, biologist; b. West Plains, Mo., July 24, 1941; s. Russell Van and Dulcie Anona (Morrison) C.; student U. Mo., 1959-61; B.S.E., Ark. State U., 1963, M.S.E., 1965; postgrad. Okla. State U., summers 1968-70; m. Connie Lee Garner, Oct. 12, 1963; children—Richard Garner, Gretchen Hallie. Lookout, U.S. Forest Service, Boise (Idaho) Nat. Forest, 1960, 62; tchr. biology Sandia High Sch., Albuquerque, 1963-64; grad. asst. Ark. State U., 1964-65; tchr. Trumann (Ark.) High Sch., 1965-66; instr. biology S.W. Mo. State U., West Plains, 1966-81, asst. prof. life scis., 1981—; owner, operator Rick's Music Shop, West Plains, 1974—; lectr. wild turkey behavior; profl. musician. Pres., Downtown Mcht.'s Assn., West Plains, 1978-79. Recipient Curators award U. Mo., 1959. Mem. Nat. Wild Turkey Fedn. Club: Rotary. Research in wild turkey behavior; contbr. articles to local publs. Home: PO Box 11A D Cr Route West Plains MO 65775 Office: SW Mo State U West Main St West Plains MO 65775

COCHRAN, SHIRLEY ANN, assistant attorney general; b. Akron, Ohio, Apr. 18, 1953; d. Harry Blaine and Ruth Shirley (Keifer) Cool; m. Mitchell Stephen Cochran, Dec. 4, 1982. B.A., U. Akron, 1974, postgrad., 1974-75, J.D., 1979. Bar: Ohio 1979, U.S. Dist. Ct. (so. dist.) Ohio 1980, U.S. Dist. Ct. (no. dist.) Ohio 1981. Rep. Avon Products, Akron, 1972-73; clk. bookstores U. Akron, 1973-74; teaching asst. U. Akron, 1974-75; student dir. Appellate Rev. Office, Akron, 1976-78, legal intern, 1978-79; asst. atty. gen. State of Ohio, Columbus, 1979—. Mem. Ohio State Bar Assn. (chairperson young lawyers sect. 1984—), ABA, Columbus Bar Assn. (com. chairperson 1982-83), Assn. Trial Lawyers Am., Independence Village Civic Assn., Delta Theta Phi (bailiff local chpt. 1983—). Democrat. Club: Aux. United Fellowship (Barberton, Ohio). Home: 2897 Liberty Bell Ln Reynoldsburg OH 43068

COCHRAN, SUSAN CAROL, health promotion consultant; b. Bryan, Texas; d. Floyd Green and Mildred (Holloway) Cochran. B.S., Sam Houston State U., 1976; M.S., Tex. A & M U., 1978. Program dir. Am. Lung Assn., Houston, 1978-80; coordinator Maryland State Health dept., Prince Frederick, Md., 1980-82; account exec. DiversiHealth, Omaha, 1982—; mem. adv. bd. respiratory therapy U. Houston, 1979, Houston Community Coll., 1979. Contbr. articles to profl. jours. Advocacy, Ch. High Blood Pressure Program, Balt., 1981. Mem. Am. Heart Assn. (mem. program com. 1981-82), Community Health Edn. Council (pres. 1979-80), Soc. Pub. Health Edn., Am. Rural Health Assn., Am. Mktg. Assn., Eta Sigma Gamma. Democrat. Methodist. Club: Omaha Ski, (pres. 1984-86). Avocations: reading, sewing, skiing, travel. Office: DiversiHealth 920 S 107 Ave Suite 200 Omaha NE 68114

COCHRANE, LADD LOREN, educator; b. Hastings, Nebr., Feb. 19, 1932; s. Alex Joy and Irma Henrietta (Harris) C.; m. Delores Ann DeJarnett, Aug. 14, 1955; children—Carrie Eileen Cochrane Ciecior, Patrick Gaylen. Registered physical therapist Mayo Clin. Sch. Physical Therapy, 1957; B.A., Hastings Coll., 1958; M.A., Western Mich. U., 1963; Ph.D., Ariz. State U., 1972. Chief physical therapist, pub. schs., Kalamazoo, Mich., 1958-63; sci. tchr. East Jr. High Sch., Casper, Wyo., 1963-66, sr. vice prin., 1966-70; coordinator edn. field experiences U. Northern Colo., 1972-77, dir. external degrees, conferances and insts., 1977-80, coordinator edn. field experiences, 1980-82; chmn. edn. dept. Hastings Coll., Nebr., 1982—, tchr. cert. officer, 1982—; staff assoc. Colo. Assn. Sch. Execs., Aurora, 1978-79; cons. in field. Contbr. articles to profl. jours. Served to cpl. USAF, 1950-54. Mem. Nat. Edn. Assn., Schoolmasters Nebr., Assn. Supervision and Curriculum Devel., Assn. Tchr. Educators, Nebr. Council Tchr. Edn. (statutory com. 1982—), Nebr. Post-Secondary Edn. (ad hoc com. 1982—), Nebr. Assn. Colls. of Tchr. Edn. (chief instl. rep. 1982—), Am. Assn. Colls. of Tchr. Edn. (chief instl. rep. 1982—), Phi Delta Kappa. Republican. Presbyterian. Avocations: furniture refinishing; antique collecting; music; athletics. Home: 310 North Shore Dr Hastings NE 68901 Office: Hastings Coll 7th and Turner Hastings NE 68901

COCKRELL, RONALD SPENCER, scientist, educator; b. Kansas City, Mo., June 26, 1938; s. Robert Spencer and Jean (Hammond) C.; B.S., U. Mo., 1960, B.Med.Sci., 1964; Ph.D., U. Pa., 1968; m. Florence Barbara Hanline, June 17, 1960; children—Richard, Synthia. Asst. prof. biochemistry St. Louis U. Sch. Medicine, 1969-74, assoc. prof., 1974—. Nat. Cancer Inst. grantee, 1970—. Mem. Am. Soc. Biol. Chemists. Home: 9409 Talbot St Louis MO 63123 Office: 1402 S Grand St Louis MO 63104

CODDINGTON, THOMAS TUCKER, automotive co. exec.; b. Columbus, Ohio, Jan. 1, 1938; s. Gilbert Harold and Louise (Hazen) C.; B.M.E., Ohio State U., 1961; M.Automotive Engring., Chrysler Inst., Highland Park, Mich., 1964; m. Cecelia Ann McLaughlin, Aug. 31, 1968; children—Maureen Louise, Kevin Ward. With Chrysler Corp., Detroit, 1961—, engring. coordinator, spl. vehicle devel., 1969-74, supr. fuel metering systems, engring. office, 1974-78, product planner, truck produce planning, 1978-80; partner, v.p. engring. Specialize Vehicles, Inc., Troy, Mich., 1980—. Served in USAF, 1961-62. Mem. Soc. Automotive Engrs., Ohio State U. Alumni Assn., SAR. Club: Economic (Detroit). Patentee fuel filter, rollover valve, emergency fuel line closure. Home: 6179 Herbmoor St Troy MI 48098 Office: 2468 Industrial Row Troy MI 48084

CODY, DOUGLAS THANE ROMNEY, physician, educator; b. Saint John, N.B., Can., June 23, 1932; came to U.S., 1958, naturalized, 1973; s. Douglas F. and Eleanor M. (Romney) C.; m. Joanne Dae Gerow; children—Douglas Thane Romney, II, Romney Joanne. M.D., Dalhousie U., Halifax, N.S., Can., 1957; Ph.D., U. Minn., 1966. Diplomate Am. Bd. Otolaryngology. Intern, St. John Gen. Hosp., 1956-57; resident Mayo Grad. Sch. Medicine, Rochester, Minn., 1958-63, cons. otolaryngology Mayo Clinic, Rochester, Minn., 1963—, chmn. dept., 1966-82, bd. govs., 1977-84; asst. prof. otolaryngology Mayo Grad. Sch. Medicine, Mayo Med. Sch., 1966-70, assoc. prof., 1970-73, prof., 1974—; chief exec. officer Mayo Group Practices Fla., 1984—; bd. trustees Mayo Found., Rochester, 1977-85. Author: Your Child's Ears, Nose and Throat: A Parents Medical Guide, 1974: Diseases of the Ears, Nose and Throat-A Guide to Diagnosis and Management, 1981. Contbr. articles to profl. publs., chpts. to books. Recipient Edward John Noble award for Fgn. Travel, Mayo Found., 1961; named Shall lectr. Mass. Eye and Ear Infirmary, 1975. Mem. Alumni Assn. Mayo Found. Med. Edn. and Research, Am. Acad. Otolaryngology (head and neck surgery sect., bd. dirs. 1979, A.C.S. (bd. govs. 1980—, adv. council otorhinolaryngology 1982—), Ill. Soc. Ophthalmology and Otolaryngology (hon. mem.), Am. Acad. Ophthalmology and Otolaryngology (award merit 1972), Am. Rhinologic Soc. (hon. mem.), Am. Neurotology Soc., Am. Otological Soc. (bd. trustees research fund 1980—, asst. sec.-treas. 1981-82, sec.-treas. 1982—), Assn. Acad. Depts. Otolaryngology (adminstrv. com. 1981-82), Barany Soc., Centurian Club Deafness Research Found., Otosclerosis Study Group, PanAm. Assn. Otorhinolaryngology and Broncho esophagology, Soc. Univ. Otolaryngologists, Sigma Xi. Home: 1001 Skyline Dr SW Rochester MN 55902 Office: Mayo Clin and Mayo Found 200 1st St SW Rochester MN 55905

CODY, SANDRA DIANE, design analyst, educator; b. Omaha, Dec. 1, 1951; d. Vernon Dwaine and Elizabeth Ann (Watson) Andrews; children—Jason, Brandon. B.S., U. Nebr.-Omaha, 1974; A.A., Inst. Computer Sci., 1981. Cert. tchr., Nebr. Tchr. secondary Omaha Pub. Schs., 1974-78; programming instr. Inst. Computer Sci., Omaha, 1982-83; programmer analyst MUD, Corp., 1981-83; design analyst Majer Corp., 1983—. Mem. Assn. Systems Mgmt. Avocations: camping; racquetball; volleyball. Office: Majers Corp 10202 F St Omaha NE 68127

COE, CURTIS JAMES, coal geologist, hydrogeologist; b. Elyria, Ohio, Nov. 9, 1951; s. Criag J. and Lucy (Marsico) C.; m. Susan Ann Levesque, Mar. 21, 1975; children—Melissa Ann, Michael Jason. B.S., Ohio State U., 1975; M.S., Fla. State U., 1978; student U. Ky. Inst. for Mining and Minerals Research, 1983. Cert. profl. geol. scientist. Chief geologist GLM Mapping Inc., Lisbon, Ohio, 1979-81; project geologist Michael Baker Jr., Beaver, Pa., 1981-82; sr. hydrogeologist Fred C. Hart Assocs., N.Y.C., 1982-83, Ground Water Assocs., Westerville, Ohio, 1983-84; cons. in geology, Westerville, 1984—. Contbr. articles to profl. jours. Mem. Am. Inst. Profl. Geologists, Nat. Water Well Assn., Am. Assn. Petroleum Geologists, Ohio Geol. Soc., No. Ohio Geol. Soc. Republican. Roman Catholic. Home and Office: 6408 Goldfinch Dr Westerville OH 43081

COE, JOHN WILLIAM, management consultant; b. Highland Park, Mich., Oct. 2, 1924; s. C. Leroy and Grace Lamont C.; B.S. in Indsl.-Mech. Engring., U. Mich., 1949; m. Sally Childs, Oct. 24, 1953; children—John Childs, Daniel William. Acct., Charles L. Coe and Assos., 1949; buyer J.L. Hudson Co., Detroit, 1950-58, div. mdse. mgr., 1959-81, v.p., gen. mgr. stores, 1981-83; v.p. retail mktg. Champion Home Builders; dir. Champion Home Builders, I.T.C.O. Inc. Dist. chmn. United Found., 1971-72; bd. dirs. Planned Parenthood League, Inc. Served to lt. (j.g.) USNR, 1943-46. Mem. Am. Mgmt. Assn., Northland-Eastland Mchts. Assn. (dir., past pres.), Phi Alumni Assn. Psi Upsilon (dir.). Republican. Anglican. Clubs: Country of Detroit; Pere Marquette Rod and Gun; Rotary (past pres.)(Harper Woods, Mich.). Home: 382 Chalfonte Grosse Pointe MI 48236 Office: Coe & Assocs Grosse Pointe Farms MI 48236

COE, ROBERT WILLIAM, state ofcl.; b. Johnston City, Ill., Feb. 19, 1927; s. Myron John and Lola Oneida (Cothern) C.; B.S., No. Ill. U., 1965, M.S., 1966; m. Dorothy L. Thorson, June 8, 1947; children—Sandra Coe Freedman, Ronald, Cheryl Coe Gray, Dena. Sanitarian, Ill. Dept. Public Health, Carbondale, 1950-54, Rock Island, 1954-64, Aurora, 1964-71, Springfield, 1971-72, exec. adminstr., Chgo., 1972—; prof. mgmt. No. Ill. U. at DeKalb, 1966-67. Asst. scoutmaster Cub Scouts Am., 1957-59; asst. scoutmaster Boy Scouts Am., 1959-61, scoutmaster, 1961-64, dist. commr., 1964-66. Served with AUS, 1945-47. Mem. Ill. Pub. Health Assn., Assn. Ill. Milk, Food and Environmental Sanitarians (sec., treas. 1968-80), AAUP. Author: A Study to Determine the Effect of Appropriations Upon Program Administration, 1966. Editor: Office Management (Clarence Sims), 1965. Home: 206 Boulder Hill Pass Montgomery IL 60538 Office: Ill Dept Public Health 2121 W Taylor St Chicago IL 60612

COELSCH, GERARD CHRISTOPHER, retail executive; b. Plymouth, Mass., Sept. 3, 1943; s. Eugene Gerard and Dolores Eileen (Longhi) C.; m. Joanne Kathryn Epstein, Mar. 21, 1970. B.A. in History and Math., Calif. State U.-Northridge, 1969; postgrad. Pepperdine U., 1979. Store dir. Food Giant Markets, Los Angeles, 1961-70; mktg. mgr. fast foods Southland Corp., Dallas, 1970-80; dir. gen. Visa Group, Monterrey, Mex., 1980-82; v.p. mktg. Lawson Co. div. Con Foods, Cuyahoga Falls, Ohio, 1982—; cons. Cadena Comml., Monterrey, 1980-82; dir. Internat. Soap Box Derby, Akron, Ohio, 1982—. Cons. Jr. Achievement Project Bus., Ohio, 1982—, div. chmn., 1983. Republican. Roman Catholic. Home: 7407 McShu Ln Hudson OH 44236 Office: Lawson Co 210 Broadway E Cuyahoga Falls OH 44222

COFFEE, CHARLENE DAUGHERTY, accountant; b. Athens, Tenn., Feb. 3, 1943; d. Charles McGee and Alma (Millsaps) Daugherty; B.S., U. Tenn., Knoxville, 1964; m. Joe Donald Coffee, Apr. 9, 1966. Buyer trainee Castner-Knott Co., Nashville, 1964-66; asst. buyer, buyer Harvey's, Nashville, 1966-67; mdse. control clk., supr. Sears Roebuck, Nashville, 1967-73, acctg. mgmt. trainee, 1973-74, mem. point of sale implementation team So. ter., 1974-77, controller acctg. and processing center, Atlanta, 1977-80, staff asst., field report consolidation, Chgo., 1980-81, staff asst. acctg. policy and procedure, 1981-83, sr. staff asst. acctg. services, 1983—. Vice-pres. council Ch. of the Living Christ-Lutheran; dist. bd. dirs. Family Care Services Met. Chgo. Mem. DAR (rec. sec. Sarah's Grove chpt.), AAUW, Delta Zeta. Home: 521 Jervey Ln Bartlett IL 60103 Office: Sears Tower BSC 22-12 Chicago IL 60684

COFFEE, JAMES FREDERICK, lawyer; b. Decatur, Ind., Mar. 6, 1918; s. Claude M. and Frances N. (Butler) C.; B.C.E., Purdue U., 1939; J.D., Ind. U., 1947; m. Jeanmarie Hackman, Dec. 29, 1945 (dec. 1978); children—James, Carolyn, Susan, Sheila, Kevin, Richard, Elizabeth, Thomas, Claudia; m. 2d, Marjorie Hansen Masterson, Oct. 4, 1980. Bar: Wis. 1947, Ill. 1952. Patent atty. Allis Chalmers Mfg. Co., Milw., 1947-51; mem. firm Anderson, Luedeka, Fitch, Even & Tabin, and predecessors, Chgo., 1951-64, partner, 1956-64; individual practice law, Chgo., 1964-71; partner law firm Coffee & Sweeney, Chgo., 1971-76; partner, gen. counsel design firm Marvin Glass & Assocs., Chgo., 1973-83. Served to capt. AUS, 1941-46. Mem. Am., Ill., Chgo. (chmn. com. patents, trademark and unfair trade practices 1967) bar assns., Am. Patent Law Assn., Patent Law Assn. Chgo. (chmn. com. copyrights 1969), Am. Judicature Soc. Home: 320 Earls Ct Deerfield IL 60015

COFFEY, AGNES B(ROWN), librarian; b. Pulaski, Tenn., Aug. 12, 1940; d. James Lewis and Edline (Gilbert) Brown; m. Fred Coffey, Jr., July 7, 1960 (div. 1978); 1 child, Cassandra. B.S. in Edn., Chgo. State U., 1974, M.S. in Edn., 1976; M.S., No. Ill. U., 1983. Mail clk. U.S. Post Office, Chgo., 1965-68; tchr. aide James McCosh Elem. Sch., Chgo., 1969-74; substitute tchr. Chgo. Bd. Edn., 1975; tchr.-librarian A.O. Sexton Elem. Sch., Chgo., 1975-77, Reilly Elem. Sch., Chgo., 1977; librarian Chgo. State U., 1978—. Author Bibliography, 1976. Pres. McCosh Schs. PTA, 1969-71. Mem. ALA, Ill. Library Assn., No. Ill. Media Assn., Phi Delta Kappa, Kappa Delta Pi. Democrat. Office: Chicago State Univ 95th St and S King Dr Chicago IL 60628

COFFEY, GEORGE MICHAEL, anesthesiologist; b. Louisville, Oct. 14, 1944; s. George Alma and Irene Katherine (Zollinger) C.; m. Brenda Mary Wilondek, Jan. 3, 1964; children—Mary Katherine, Angela Elizabeth, George Andrew, Geoffrey Wilondek. B.A., Ind. U., 1973, M.D., 1976. Diplomate Am. Bd. Anesthesiology. Intern, Ind. U. Med. Center, 1976-77, resident, 1977-79; practice medicine specializing in anesthesiology, Indpls., 1979—; mem. staff Methodist Hosp., vice chmn. dept. anesthesiology, 1982—, assoc. dir. operating room services, 1982—; mem. teaching staff Meth. Grad. Med. Center, Indpls. Served with USAF, 1966-70. Mem. Marion County (Ind.) Soc. Anesthesiologists, Am. Soc. Anesthesiologists, Ind. Soc. Anesthesiologists, AMA, Internat. Anesthesia Research Soc. Club: Skyline (Indpls.). Office: Meth Hosp Indianapolis IN

COFFEY, JOHN LOUIS, See *Who's Who in America*, 43rd edition.

COFFEY, MAX E., state senator; b. Vermilion County, Ill., 1939; ed. public schs.; 2 children. Farmer, 1957-61; asst. mgr. feed and fertilizer bus., 1961-64; owner, operator Coffey's Flower Shop, 1965-75, also Coffey Apts.; former mem. Ill. Ho. of Reps.; mem. Ill. Senate, 1976—. Mem. Coles County Bd., 1971-74; supr. Charlestown Twp. (Ill.), 1971-74. Mem. C. of C. Lodges: Elks, Moose, Kiwanis. Office: PO Box 625 1504 20th St Charleston IL 61920 also State Capitol Springfield IL 62706*

COFFEY, RICHARD ALAN, business educator; b. New Orleans, Mar. 11, 1950; s. Richard Elwin and Jean (McArthur) C.; m. Paula Kay Bilancio, Mar. 12, 1977; 1 son, Richard Arthur. B.A., DePauw U., 1972; M.B.A., Ind. U., 1974, M.E., 1984. Lic. tchr., Ind. Credit analyst Ind. Nat. Bank, Indpls., 1974-75; sales coordinator Coachmen Industries, Inc., Middlebury, Ind., 1975-76; officer, br. mgr. First Nat. Bank of Elkhart (Ind.), 1976-78; v.p., sec. Liberator Wagons, Inc., Miami, Fla., 1978-81; lectr. St. Mary's Coll. Sch. Bus., Notre Dame, Ind., 1982—; summer youth employment coordinator Comprehensive Employment Tng. Act, 1982—. Lodges: Kiwanis, Moose, Elks. Home: 1526 Sunnymede St South Bend IN 46615 Office: PO Box 76 Madeleva Hall St Marys Coll Notre Dame IN 46556

COFFIN, BERTRAM DWIGHT, power plant engineer, consultant; b. Peabody, Mass., May 7, 1932; s. Bertram Dwight and Margaret (Reid) C.; m. Shirley May Qualman, Oct. 1, 1955; children—Susan Elizabeth, Brian David, Sarah Louise. B.S. in Mech. Engring, Tufts U., 1954. Registered profl. engr., Calif. Vice pres. mktg. Bailey Australia, Sydney, 1968-71; regional sales mgr. Bailey Meter Co., Chgo., 1971-73, nat. sales mgr., 1973-74, program mgr., Wickliffe, Ohio, 1974-76; tech. dir. H.K. Ferguson Co., Cleve., 1976—. Contbr. articles to profl. jours. Patentee in field. Named Boss of Yr., Am. Bus. Women's Assn., 1974. Mem. ASME. Avocation: miniature aircraft. Home: 7100 Brightwood Dr Painesville OH 44077 Office: HK Ferguson Co 1 Erieview Plaza Cleveland OH 44114

COFFMAN, KENNETH MORROW, mechanical contractor; b. Ann Arbor, Mich., Aug 3, 1921; s. Harold Coe and Aletha (Morrow) C.; B.S., Lawrence U., 1943; m. Barbara Ann Porth, Dec. 30, 1943 (dec. 1983); children—Gregory, Deborah Coffman Greene, Jenifer Coffman Dillon. Exec. v.p. Stanley Carter Co. Ohio, Toledo, 1957-59; v.p. sales Wenzel & Henoch Co., Milw., 1959-64; exec. v.p. Milw. W & H Inc., 1964-70; exec. v.p. Downey Inc., Milw., 1970-76, pres., 1977-82, pres., chief officer, 1982—. Bd. dirs. YMCA, Milw., 1965-85, Tri County, 1973-78; chmn. bd. mgrs. Camp Minikani, 1965-82. Served with USMC 1943-46. Named Layman of year, Tri County YMCA, 1973, Disting Service award, 1979. Mem. Nat. Cert. Pipe Welders Bur. Wis. (dir. 1973-85), Mech. Contractors Assn. South East Wis. (dir. 1970-80, pres. 1974-75), Mech. Contractors Devel. Fund. (dir. 1972-85, pres. 1972-73), Wis. Constrn. Employers Council (dir. 1973-85), Mech. Contractors Assn. of Wis. (dir. 1977-85, pres. 1983-84), Nat. Fire Protection Assn., Nat. Assn. Plumbing, Heating, Cooling Contractors, Mech. Contractors Assn. Am. (dir. 1982-85), Nat. Mech. Equipment Service and Maintenance Bur. (dir. 1982-85), Sheet Metal and Air Conditioning Contractors Nat. Assn. Congregationalist. Home: 925 E Wells St Milwaukee WI 53202 Office: Box 1155 Milwaukee WI 53201

COFFMAN, PHILLIP HUDSON, educator; b. Lincoln, Nebr., Nov. 27, 1936; s. Rowland Francis and Elberta (Hudson) C.; B. Music Edn., U. Nebr., 1958; M. Music, U. Idaho, 1962; Ph.D., U. Toledo, 1971; m. Carolyn J. Nimmo, July 23, 1983; children—Phillip C., Catherine L. Tchr. pub. schs., Rushville, Neb., 1958-59; instr. Doane Coll., Crete, Nebr., 1959-60; teaching asst. U. Idaho, Moscow, 1960-62, instr., 1962-65; assoc. prof., chmn. dept. music Jamestown (N.D.) Coll., 1965-68; adminstrv. intern U. Toledo, 1968-71; assoc. prof., head dept. music U. Minn., Duluth, 1971-76, prof., dean Sch. Fine Arts, 1976—. Mem. Lincoln Symphony, 1954-60, Toledo Symphony, 1969-71; guest artist Ednl. TV, 1964; instr. Internat. Music Camp, 1967-68. Pres. Civic Music Assn., 1967, Minn. Coll. and Univ. Council for Music, 1976; music adjudicator, interviewer Bush Leadership Fellows Program, 1977—; chmn. bd. Duluth Festival of Arts, 1979-81; mem. Gov.'s Commn. on Econ. Vitality in the Arts, 1984—. F.E. Olds scholar, 1963, Bush Found. fellow, 1973. Mem. Internat. Council Fine Arts Deans, Duluth C. of C., Theta Xi, Phi Mu Alpha, Pi Kappa Lambda, Kappa Kappa Psi. Home: 4601 Woodland Ave Duluth MN 55803

COGAN, THOMAS PATRICK, clinical psychologist; b. Chgo., Mar. 9, 1948; s. Robert K. and Agnes V. (Vargo) C.; B.A., Lewis U., 1970; Ph.D., Ill. Inst. Tech., 1977; m. Bette Herbert, Sept. 3, 1971. Staff psychologist Mercy Hosp. and Med. Center, Chgo., 1977-82; pvt. practice clin. psychology, Chgo., 1977—. Recipient Aquinas award Lewis U., 1970. Mem. Am. Psychol. Assn. Condr. research on risk taking in psychotherapy, friendship in psychotherapy. Home: 3282 W Wrightwood Ave Chicago IL 60647 Office: 30 N Michigan Ave Chicago IL 60602

COHEN, ALLAN RICHARD, lawyer; b. Chgo., Feb. 25, 1923; s. Louis and Ruth (Cohen) C.; B.A., U. Wis., 1947, J.D., 1949; postgrad. Northwestern U., 1953-54; m. Audrey Doris Levy, Oct. 14, 1960; children—Joseph, David, Gale. Admitted to Ill. bar, 1950, since practiced in Chgo. Served with AUS, 1943-45. Decorated Presdl. citation with oak leaf cluster. Mem. Fed., Ill. (vice chmn. sect. comml. bankruptcy and banking laws 1977-78), Chgo. (vice chmn. com. bankruptcy 1972-73, chmn. 1973-74; panelist seminar on bankruptcy, 1968, 72, 74, 82, 83) bar assns., Zeta Beta Tau, Tau Epsilon Rho. Club: Elms Swim and Tennis (Highland Park, Ill.). Home: 1986 Dale St Highland Park IL 60035 Office: 55 W Monroe St Chicago IL 60603

COHEN, ANTHONY JAN, financial management company executive; b. Winnipeg, Man., Canada, May 29, 1958; s. Albert Diamond and Irena (Kankova) C. B.S.B.A. in Mktg., Creighton U., 1980. Investment analyst Richardson Greenshields Can. Ltd., Winnipeg, Man., 1980-82; U.S. equity analyst Gendis Inc., Winnipeg, 1982—. Bd. dirs. Man. Paraplegic Assn., Winnipeg, 1984—; barker Variety Clubs, Internat., Winnipeg, 1983—; loaned rep. United Way Winnipeg, 1981—. Fellow Fin. Analysts Fedn. Jewish. Club: Glendale Golf and Country (Winnipeg). Avocations: reading; golf; jogging; ice hockey. Office: Gendis Inc 1370 Sony Pl Winnipeg MB R3C 3C3 Canada

COHEN, ASHLEY VAUGHAN, computer executive, consultant; b. Norwich, Norfolk, Eng., Dec. 9, 1954; came to U.S., 1977; s. Maurice and Joan Mary (Pitt) C.; m. Victoria Cohen, Dec. 23, 1984. Test engr. Computing Techniques, Billingshurst, Eng., 1972-75, Transdata Ltd., Havant, Hants, Eng., 1975-77; customer engr. Sweda Internat., Detroit, 1977-78; systems engr. Unitote/Regitel, Detroit, 1978; area supr. Datatrol, Inc., Detroit, 1978-79; supr. Detroit Free Press, 1979—; pres. computer cons. and service Ashley Services, Fairhaven, Mich., 1983—. Mem. IBEW. Office: Detroit Free Press 321 W Lafayette St Detroit MI 48231

COHEN, BURTON DAVID, franchising executive, lawyer; b. Chgo., Feb. 12, 1940; s. Allan and Gussy (Katz) C.; B.S. in Bus. and Econs., Ill. Inst. Tech., 1960; J.D., Northwestern U., 1963; m. Linda Rochelle Kaine, Jan. 19, 1969; children—David, Jordana. Admitted to Ill. bar, 1963; staff atty. McDonald's Corp., Oak Brook, Ill., 1964-69, asst. sec., 1969-70, asst. gen. counsel, 1970-76, asst. v.p., 1976-78, dir. legal dept., 1978-80, v.p. licensing, asst. gen. counsel, asst. sec., 1980--; lectr. Practising Law Inst. Served with AUS, 1963-64. Mem. Am. Bar Assn., Ill. Bar Assn., Chgo. Bar Assn., Internat. Franchise Assn. (lectr.), Assn. Nat. Advertisers, Chgo. Council Fgn. Relations, Tau Epsilon Phi, Phi Delta Phi. Club: Executives (Chgo.). Author: Franchising: Second Generation Problems, 1969. Office: McDonalds Plaza Oak Brook IL 60521

COHEN, EDWIN ROBERT, financial executive; b. St. Louis, Apr. 13, 1939; s. Harry W. and Sally (Robinson) C.; m. Sheilah Renee Aron, Aug. 20, 1961; children—David Brian, Scott Alan, Craig Aron. B.S., Washington U., St. Louis, 1966; C.L.U., 1973. Chartered fin. cons. Pres. Edwin R. Cohen & Assocs., St. Louis, 1966—; gen. agt. Central Life Assurance Co., Des Moines, 1969—; registered rep. Nat. Assn. Securities Dealers. Arbitrator, Better Bus. Bur. St. Louis, 1976—; chmn. local SSS, 1982—. Mem. Million Dollar Round Table, 1972-74; recipient certs. of appreciation Better Bus. Bur. St. Louis, 1979-85. Mem. Am. Soc. C.L.U.s, Nat. Assn. Life Underwriters (Nat. Quality award 1984, Nat. Sales Achievement award 1983), Gen. Agts. and Mgrs. Assn., St. Louis Life Underwriters Assn. (dir. 1978-81), Am. Legion. Jewish. Lodge: Jaycees (v.p. 1963-64) (St. Louis). Home: 10256 Lylewood Dr Ladue MO 63124 Office: 7710 Carondelet Ave Clayton MO 63105

COHEN, GLORIA, business consultant, dentist; b. Leeds, Eng., Jan. 2, 1930; d. Abraham and Sophia (Lipman) Stewart; m. Lawrence Cohen, Dec. 27, 1951; children—Alan Steven, Martin Ian, David Charles. D.D.S., U. Birmingham, Eng., 1952; postgrad. Grad. Sch. Mgmt., Northwestern U., 1975. Gen. practice dentistry, London, 1952-67; mgr. data and info. G.D. Searle Co., Skokie, Ill., 1968-70, dir. info. services, 1970-76, dir. corp. bus. R&D, 1976-77; bus. R&D cons., Wilmette, Ill., 1977—; cons. to govt. and industry, non-profit orgns. Recipient Bronze medal U. Birmingham, 1950, essay prize, 1951; named Outstanding New Citizen of Yr., Citizenship Council Met. Chgo., 1975. Mem. Internat. Assn. Dental Research, ADA, Fedn. Dentaire Internationale. Office: 200 Kilpatrick Ave Wilmette IL 60091

COHEN, JEROME, electronic business equipment company executive; b. Kansas City, Mo., Oct. 9, 1913; s. Rueben and Helen (Silverstein) C.; grad. Kansas City (Mo.) Jr. Coll., 1931; student Huffs Bus. Coll., 1932, Central Bus. Coll., 1933; m. Jeannette Baier, Nov. 25, 1934; children—Rosalyn Jean, Elaine Marie. Asst. mgr. Burts Shoe Store, Kansas City, Mo., 1932-34; sec. to State Senator of Mo., 1934-35; chief clk. Mo. Old Age Assistance Div., 1935-37, Jackson County (Mo.) Welfare Office, Kansas City, 1937-38; founder Tempo Co., Kansas City, Mo., 1938, pres., 1938—, chief exec. officer, 1938—; pres., chief exec. officer Electronic Bus. Equipment, Inc., Kansas City, Mo., 1957—, Jefferson City, Mo., 1960—, Saint Joseph, Mo., 1961—; commr. Kansas City (Mo.) Park Bd., 1955-72. Vice pres. Am. Humanics Found., Kansas City, Mo., 1956-80; chmn. Kansas City (Mo.) Jewish Chautauqua Drive, 1962-64; mem. Nat. Com. for Support of Public Schs., 1967-78; mem. exec. com. Kansas City Safety Council, 1958-81; chmn. Mayor's Christmas Tree Assn., Kansas City, 1955-84; mem. adv. bd. Met. Jr. Coll., 1972-78; Kansas City chmn. Richards Gebaur AFB Community Council, 1960-61; mem. Kansas City Bus. and Indsl. Commn., 1955-62; pres. Temple B'nai Jehudah, 1980-81; mem. exec. bd. Sr. Citizens Corp. of Kansas City, 1954-65, Kansas City Recreation Commn., 1955-70, Citizens Assn., 1940-70, Child's World, 1969-81, Camp Fire Girls, 1956-66, Starlight Theatre, 1950—, v.p., 1978-80; chmn. Kansas City Soap Box Derby, 1947-64; bd. dirs. U. Kans. Sch. of Religion, 1971-76, Scottish Rite Found. of Mo., 1969—; hon. trustee Heart of Am. council Boy Scouts Am., 1960—. B'nai Jehudah Brotherhood Hall of Fame Honoree, 1976; named Kansas City (Mo.) Mktg. Exec. of Year, 1981. Hon. fellow Harry S. Truman Library Inst.; mem. Mo. C. of C., Kansas City (Mo.) C. of C., Kansas City (Kans.) C. of C., Native Sons of Kansas City (Mo.), Conservation Fedn. of Mo., Mo. U. Assos., Bus. Dist. League (pres. 1963-65), Jackson County Execs. (exec. council), Jackson County Hist. Soc., Audubon Soc., Am. Assn. of Zoos and Aquariums, Bus. Products Council Assn. (pres. 1970-72), Mid-Town Assn. (v.p. 1964-65), Friends of the Zoo (pres. 1973-74), Navy League, Kansas City (Mo.) Lyric Theatre Guild, Japan Am. Soc., Jewish Chautauqua Soc., Hebrew Acad. of Kansas City, Hyman Brand Hebrew Acad., Piscator's Soc. (pres. 1970-71), Sci. Pioneers, Friends of Art, NCCJ, Air Force Assn., U.S. China Friendship Assn., Am. Royal Assn. (bd. govs. 1955-81). Clubs: Masons (33 degrees), Shriners, Kansas City Athletic, Meadowbrook Country, Elmers Fishing (pres. 1968-69). Home: 6616 Ward Parkway Kansas City MO 64113 Office: 1500 Grand Ave Kansas City MO 64108

COHEN, LAWRENCE, physician, dentist, educator; b. Leeds, Eng., Nov. 23, 1926; came to U.S., 1967, naturalized, 1975; s. Joseph and Millie (Burnstein) C.; m. Gloria Stewart, Dec. 27, 1951; children—Alan Steven, Martin Ian, David Charles. D.D.S., Leeds U., 1949; M.D., Guys' Hosp., London, 1956; Ph.D., U. London, 1966. Clin. instr. U. Birmingham, Eng., 1949-50; oral surgery resident Middlesex Hosp., London, 1956-59; sr. resident Stoke Mandeville Hosp., Eng., 1959-60; sr. lectr. oral medicine Eastman Dental Sch., London, 1962-67; head dept. oral diagnosis U. Ill., Chgo., 1967-76; chmn. dept. dentistry Ill. Masonic Med. Ctr., Chgo., 1976—; chmn. oral cavity panel FDA, Washington, 1974-80; cons. FTC, Washington, 1984—; mem. legis. and govtl. affairs, 5 hosp. homebound program, 1981-84. Author: A Synopsis of Medicine in Dentistry, 1977. Editor: Oral Diagnosis and Treatment Planning, 1973. Contbr. articles to profl. jours. Served to Squadron Leader, RAF, 1950-52. Fellow Royal Soc. Medicine; mem. Am. Acad. Oral Medicine (pres. 1984-85, Samuel Charles Miller award 1980), AMD, ADA. Avocations: music; gardening; travel. Office: Ill Masonic Med Ctr 927 Wellington Chicago IL 60657

COHEN, LORELEI FREDA, school psychologist; b. Detroit, Nov. 20, 1937; d. Fred M. and Anna (Margolis) Schuman; m. Norton J. Cohen, June 16, 1957; children—Debrah, Sander. B.A., Wayne State U., 1960, Ed.S., 1978, now Ph.D. candidate; M.A., U. Tex., 1965. Tchr., Killeen, Tex., 1960-63, Detroit Pub. Schs., 1964, Temple Israel, Detroit, 1968-82; psychologist Detroit Pub. Schs.-Citywide Psychol. Services, 1980—; instr. child psychopathology Wayne State U., 1980. Mem. exec. bd. Detroit Assn. Retarded Citizens, 1981-84; docent Detroit Inst. Arts, 1972-78. Jesse Jones scholar U. Tex., 1962; Wayne State U. grad. fellow, 1974-76, 84—. Mem. Am. Psychol. Assn., Phi Beta Kappa.

COHEN, MILLARD STUART, diversified manufacturing company executive; b. Chgo., Jan. 17, 1939; s. Lawrence Irmas and Myra Paula (Littmann) C.; B.S. in Elec. Engring., Purdue U., 1960; m. Judith E. Michel, Aug. 2, 1970; children—Amy Rose, Michele Lauren. Design engr. GTE Automatic Electric Labs., Northlake, Ill., 1960-66; chief elec. engr. Nixdorff Krein Industries, St. St. Louis, 1966-68, dir. data processing, 1968-72, treas., 1970—, v.p., 1980-85, pres., 1985—, exec. v.p. Nixdorff Chain, 1972-76, pres. Grape Expectations, 1976—, also dir. Dist. commr. Boy Scouts Am., 1968-72; judge Mo. State Fair; mem. Mo. State Wine Adv. Bd., 1980—, vice-chmn., 1983; mem. St. Louis County Restaurant Commn., 1979—, Augusta (Mo.) Wine Bd., 1981—. Recipient award of merit French Wine Commn., 1972. Mem. ACM, IEEE, Mensa, Les Amis du Vin, Chaine des Rotisseurs, Commanderie de Bordeaux. Jewish (trustee temple). Club: St. Louis. Home: 11233 Ladue Rd Creve Coeur MO 63141 Office: PO Box 27479 Saint Louis MO 63141

COHEN, MYRON AARON, musician; b. Denver, Mar. 28, 1918; s. Goodman and Rose (Cohen) C.; student De Paul U. Sch. Music, 1936-38, Am. Conservatory of Music, Chgo., 1939-42, Juilliard Sch. Music, 1947; B.A., U. Omaha, 1947; Mus.M., U. Nebr., Lincoln, 1960; violin student Richard Czerwonky, Scott Willits, Louis Persinger, others. Concertmaster following orchs.: Omaha Symphony Orch., 1947-77, Omaha Opera Co. Orch., 1959-79, Lincoln (Nebr.) Symphony Orch., 1951-60; organized String Quartet, 1978; asst. condr. Omaha Youth Orch., 1958-66; part-time faculty U. Omaha, 1951-52, U. Nebr., Lincoln, 1958-59, Coll. St. Mary, 1980—; soloist radio, TV; pvt. violin tchr., Omaha, 1946-82. Served with AUS, 1943-45. Winner commencement contest for violinists Am. Conservatory Music, 1940. Mem. Omaha Musicians Assn. (past mem. exec. bd.), Nebr. Music Tchrs. Assn. (past pres.), Am. String Tchrs. Assn., Pi Kappa Lambda. Democrat. Jewish. Author: The Beginning Violinist's Left Hand Technique, 1956; Finger Relationships through Patterns and Keys for Violin, 1964; also revs. and articles. Home: 3925 S 24th St Omaha NE 68107

COHEN, PAUL G(ERSON), management consultant; b. N.Y.C., July 23, 1938; s. Henry A. and Esther (Reiner) C.; B.A., Union Coll., Schenectady, 1960; children—David Mark, Deborah Esther. With Northwestern Bell Tel. Co., Omaha, 1966-74, revenue supr. long distance and WATS, 1971-74; asst. v.p., sec. S. Riekes & Sons, Inc., Omaha, 1974-75, gen. ops. mgr., 1975-76; v.p. ops., Riekes Crisa Corp., Omaha, 1976-81; pres. Mid-Am. Bus. Enterprises, Inc., Omaha, 1981—. Treas., youth sports program Omaha Suburban Athletic Assn., 1976-77; bd. dirs. Cystic Fibrosis Assn. Nebr., 1977-79; bd. dirs. Jewish Fedn. Omaha, 1973-76, v.p., 1977-81, pres., 1982-84; trustee Nat. Jewish Hosp./Nat. Asthma Center, Denver; bd. dirs. Council Jewish Fedns. Served with USAF, 1960-66; col. Nebr. Air N.G., 1967—, now dep. chief staff Hdqrs. Nebr. Air N.G. Mem. Air Force Assn., Nebr. N.G. Assn. (dir. 1973-76, pres. 1979). Clubs: B'nai B'rith (past pres.; regional pres. 1974-75, dist. bd. govs., 1976-78), Rotary. Home: 12406 Burt Plaza #12 Omaha NE 68154

COHEN, PENNIE MYERS, counseling psychologist, consultant; b. Phila., Aug. 16, 1939; d. William Lee and Roberta B. (Appel) Myers; B.A. magna cum laude, Wichita State U., 1973, M.A., 1975; Ed.D., Internat. Grad. Sch., 1983; children—Susan Lee, Robert Lewis. Counselor, Wichita (Kans.) State U., 1975-78, coordinator consulting, 1978—. Chmn., Wichita Sedgewick County Women's Task Force on Alcohol Abuse, 1979; mem. Wichita Sedgewick County Task Force on Drug Abuse, 1976-79; bd. dirs. Residential Homes for Boys, Mid-Kans. Jewish Welfare Fedn., Family Consultation Service. Mem. Am. Psychol. Assn., Am. Assn. Marriage and Family Therapists, Kans. Psychol. Assn., Kans. Alcoholism Counselors Assn. Office: Box 91 Wichita State Univ Wichita KS 67208

COHEN, PHILIP E., social worker; m. Elaine Cohen; 1 child, Miriam Esther. Social work assoc. VA Med. Ctr., Chillicothe, Ohio, 1971—. Mem. ad hoc com. Internat. Year Disabled Persons; pres. Beth Jacob Congregation Brotherhood. Recipient Hands and Hearts award VA, 1984. Lodge: B'nai B'rith. Office: VA Med Ctr Chillicothe OH 45601

COHEN, PHILIP EDWARD, social worker; b. Chgo., May 26, 1948; s. Morris and Miriam Ann (Wolfson) C.; student Parsons Coll., 1966-67; B.S., Murray State U., 1970; m. Elaine E. Biegacz, Oct. 8, 1972; 1 dau., Miriam Esther. Clk., Bur. of Census, U.S. Dept. Commerce, Jeffersonville, Ind., 1970-71; social work asso. VA Med. Center, Chillicothe, Ohio, 1971—; mem. supervisory com. Chivaho Fed. Credit Union, 1976-80, chmn., 1978, sec. credit com., 1983-85. VA Med. Center rep. Internat. Yr. of Child, 1979; mem. ad hoc com. Internat. Yr. of Disabled Persons, VA Med. Center; trustee Beth Jacob Congregation, 1981—; pres. Beth Jacob Brotherhood, 1984-86. Recipient Superior Performance award VA Med. Center, 1978, 83, VA Adminstrs.'s Hands and Heart award, 1984. Mem. Nat. Assn. Social Workers, VA Employees Assn. (pres. 1977-79, dir. 1979-80), Central Ohio Diabetes Assn., Murray State U. Alumni Assn. (life), Fraternal Order Police Assos., Ky. Col. Democrat. Jewish. Club: B'nai B'rith (Pres.'s award 1973, Community Service award 1975, historian 1973-74, community service v.p. 1975-76, v.p. membership 1978-79), Beth Jacob Young Couples. Home: 5114 Teddy Dr Columbus OH 43227 Office: VA Medical Center 17273 State Route 104 Chillicothe OH 45601

COHEN, PHILIP THEODORE, asphalt paving construction company executive; b. Cin., Apr. 20, 1920; s. Mose and Mollie (Neuerman) C.; m. Helene Schwartz, Juen 26, 1948; children—Hildred Cohen Clayton, O.J., Amy Cohen Diamond. M.E., U. Cin., 1942. Pres., Beacon Constrn. Co., Cin., 1946—. Campaign chmn. Jewish Welfare Fund, Cin., 1968; pres. Rockdale Temple, Cin., 1965-67, Jewish Fedn. Cin., 1982-85, United Jewish Cemetery, Cin., Camp Livingston, Cin.; v.p. Jewish Vocat. Service, Cin.; mem. exec. com. Jewish Hosp., Cin.; trustee Glen Manor Home for Aged, Cin. Served to maj. USAF, 1942-46, ETO. Republican. Jewish. Club: Losantiville Country (pres.) (Cin.). Home: 3940 Red Bud Ave Cincinnati OH 45229 Office: Beacon Constrn Co 13 Walnut St Reading OH 45215

COHEN, ROGER LEE, real estate executive; b. St. Joseph, Mo., Oct. 4, 1935; s. Joseph A. and Esther L. (Wienstock) C.; B.S. in Bus. Adminstrn., U. Mo., 1957; children—Robin, Cynthia, Bradley; m. Joni Beechen, May 8, 1983; children—Mark, Julie, Katie. Exec. trainee Sears, Roebuck & Co., Chgo., 1957; partner Karbank & Co., realtors, Kansas City, 1959-68; pres. Roger L. Cohen & Co., realtors, Kansas City, Mo., 1969—; chmn. bd. Cohen & Co., 1981—; dir. Barclay Evergreen Advt., Empire State Bank, Kansas City, Mo., Mark Twain Bank, Mchts. Bank, Tg Cinnamons Ltd.; bd. dirs. Kansas City (Mo.) Real Estate Bd. Chmn. Jackson County (Mo.) Indsl. Commn., 1969; chmn. March of Dimes, Jackson County, 1965-66; mem. bd. govs. Menorah Med. Center, Jewish Fedn., Kansas City, Mo.; v.p. bd. trustees Temple B'nai Jehudah; bd. dirs. Performing Arts Found., NCCJ; bd. assos. Trinity Luth. Hosp. Served with F.A., AUS, 1957-59. Mem. Soc. Indsl. Realtors (pres. Western Mo.-Kans. chpt. 1974-76, nat. dist. v.p. 1976—), Young Pres. Orgn. (chpt. chmn.). Clubs: Carriage, Oakwood Country, Homestead Country, Kansas City. Home: 3700 W 64th Mission Hills KS 66208 Office: City Center Sq 1100 Main St Suite 850 Kansas City MO 64105

COHEN, SANFORD NED, pediatrics educator, university dean; b. N.Y.C., June 12, 1935; s. George M. and Fannie Leah (Epstein) C.; m. Elizabeth Luskind, June 22, 1958 (div. Aug., 1984); 1 child, Andrew B.; m. Elizabeth Leona Prevot, Aug. 19, 1984. A.B., The Johns Hopkins U., 1956, M.D., 1960. Diplomate Am. Bd. Pediatrics. Intern in pediatrics Johns Hopkins Hosp., 1960-61, resident, 1961-63; instr. to assoc. prof. NYU Sch. Medicine, N.Y.C., 1965-74; chmn., prof. pediatrics Wayne State U. Sch. Med., Detroit, 1974-81, assoc. dean, prof. pediatrics, dir. Developmentally Disabled Inst., 1981—; dir. Child Research Ctr., Detroit, 1975-81; pediatrician-in-chief Children's Hosp. Mich., Detroit, 1974-81; adj. faculty U. Mich. Sch. Pub. Health, Ann Arbor, 1980—. Editor: Progress in Drug Therapy in Children, 1981. Contbr. articles to profl. jours. Mem. bd. health, Leonia, N.J., 1972-74; 1982—, mem. com. oral exams., 1983—, ofcl. examiner, 1984—). Avocations: reading, fishing, sailing. Home: 31775 Ridgeside Dr #21 Farmington Hills MI 48018 Office: Wayne State Univ Sch Med 1261 Scott Hall 540 E Canfield St Detroit MI 48201

COHEN, STEPHEN, lawyer; b. Mansfield, Ohio, Mar. 15, 1932; s. Aaron C. and Leona (Bernstein) C.; m. Marcia Ann Josselson, Sept. 2, 1956; children—Gregory, Lisa, Teresa, Michelle. B.A., Marshall U., 1958; J.D., U. Cin., 1959. Bar: Ohio 1960, U.S. Ct. Appeals (6th cir.) 1960, U.S. Dist. Ct. (so. dist.) Ohio 1961, U.S. Supreme Ct. 1968. Assoc. trust officer First Nat. Bank, Cin., 1959-60; sole practice, Cin., 1960-63, 66-73; asst. city prosecutor City of Cin., 1963-66; village solicitor Amberley Village, Ohio, 1978—; mng. ptnr. Wood & Lamping, Cin., 1973—; arbitrator Common Pleas Ct., Cin., 1976—. Author: Appeals from Municipal and County Courts in Criminal Cases, 1967. Vice pres. Jewish Family Service of Cin., 1984-86. Served with U.S. Army, 1952-54. Fellow ABA (del. 1984-86), Ohio Bar Assn. (del. 1984-86); mem. Cin. Bar Assn. (pres. 1983-84), Am. Arbitration Assn. (arbitrator 1977—), Pi Sigma Alpha. Republican. Jewish. Office: Wood & Lamping 900 Tri-State Bldg Cincinnati OH 45202

COHEN, STEVEN RICHARD, government official; b. Haverhill, Mass., Dec. 14, 1940; s. Kaufman and Celia (Richer) C.; B.A. cum laude, U. Mass., 1962, postgrad., 1962-63; m. Carole Simons, Mar. 21, 1970; children—Scott Michael, Lisa Michelle. With U.S. Office Personnel Mgmt. (formerly U.S. Civil Service Commn.), 1962—, investigator, varied personnel mgmt. and staffing positions, Boston region, 1962-65, adminstrv. officer, bur. recruiting and examining, Washington, 1965-70, mgr. Norfolk (Va.) Area Office, 1970-73, asst. to dep. exec. dir., Washington, 1973-75, dep. regional dir. Great Lakes Region, Chgo., 1975-81, regional dir., 1981—. Mem. Chgo. Fed. Exec. Bd., 1981—, chmn., 1983-84; chmn. Chgo. Combined Fund Campaign, 1983; fed. coordinator Ill. Savs. Bonds Campaign, 1984—. Mem. Internat. Personnel Mgmt. Assn., Am. Soc. Public Adminstrs., Chgo. Fed. Exec. Bd., Chgo. Fed. Personnel Council, Tau Epsilon Phi. Home: 1542 Orth Ct Wheaton IL 60187 Office: 230 S Dearborn St Chgo IL 60604

COHILL, DONALD FRANK, surgeon; b. Darby, Pa., Dec. 1, 1934; s. Raymond Harris and Agnes Mae (Smith) C.; A.B. in Chemistry, Haverford (Pa.) Coll., 1956; M.D., U. Pa., 1960; m. Lorna Westcott, Feb. 15, 1957; children—Karen Lea, Linda Lea, Julie Lea, Andrew Scott. Intern, U. Pa.-Presbyn. Hosp., Phila., 1960-61; surg. resident Abington (Pa.) Meml. Hosp., 1966-70, assoc. surgeon, 1969-70; practice medicine specializing in gen. surgery, Racine, Wis., 1970—; surgeon St. Mary's, St. Luke's hosps.; dir. med. edn. St. Mary's Hosp.; exec. com. Kurten Med. Group; adv. bd. Life Line, Racine. Bd. dirs. S.Am. Mission, Lake Worth, Fla. Served with M.C., USAF, 1962-64. Decorated Commendation medal; named Flight Surgeon of Yr., SAC, USAF, 1963-64. Fellow A.C.S., Milw. Acad. Surgery; mem. AMA, Wis., Racine County med. socs., Racine Acad. Medicine, Wis. Surg. Soc. Mem. Evang. Ch. Home: 1902 Crestwood Dr Caledonia WI 53108 Office: 2405 Northwestern Ave Racine WI 53404

COHN, ALVIN W., diversified food company executive; b. 1921. With CFS Continental Inc., Chgo., v.p., 1948-58, pres., 1958-68, chmn. bd., 1968-81, pres., chief operating officer, dir., 1981—. Office: CFS Continental Inc 100 S Wacker Dr Chicago IL 60606*

COHN, AVERN LEVIN, See *Who's Who in America,* 43rd edition.

COHN, BERT MARTIN, fire protection and security engineer, consultant; b. Stralsund, Germany, May 3, 1930; came to U.S., 1941, naturalized 1951; s. Fritz A. and Ilse (Joseph) C.; m. Holly Renald, Feb. 8, 1964; children—Helise, Judith. B.S. in Engring., Ill. Inst. Tech., 1952. Registered profl. engr. Ill., N.Y., N.J., Va.; cert. fallout shelter analyst Fed. Emergency Mgmt. Agy. Engr., Mo. Inspection Bur., St. Louis, 1950-53; chief fire protection br. U.S. Army No. Command, 8th Army, 1955-57; sr. v.p., treas., dir. Gage-Babcock & Assocs. Inc., Elmhurst, Ill., 1963-85, pres., 1985—; v.p., treas., dir. Gage-Babcock Internat. Ltd., Elmhurst, 1982—; mem. rev. panel on Nat. Bur. Standards Fire Research Ctr., NRC; lectr., expert witness, research investigator fire and safety issues. Mem. Bd. Fire and Police Commrs., Elmhurst, 1970-80, 84—, chmn., 1977-80. Served with U.S. Army, 1953-54. Fellow Soc. Fire Protection Engrs.; mem. Am. Soc. Safety Engrs., Am. Soc. Indsl. Security (cert. protection profl.), ASTM (chmn. combustibility standards), Nat. Fire Protection Assn. Home: 346 Prospect Ave Elmhurst IL 60126 Office: Gage-Babcock Internat 135 Addison Ave Elmhurst IL 60126

COHN, MARK BARRY, lawyer; b. Cleve., Dec. 28, 1947; s. David J. and Dorothy (Camin) C.; m. Marlene Sherman, Dec. 27, 1969; children—Mindy D., Laurie A., Jill R. B.S., Ohio State U., 1969, J.D., 1973. Bar: Ohio 1974, Fla. 1976. Assoc. Jones, Day, Reavis & Pogue, Cleve., 1973-76, Trenam, Simmons, Kemkar et al, Tampa, Fla., 1976-79, Kadish & Krantz, Cleve., 1979-82; sole practice, Cleve., 1982—. Author: Smith's Review of Civil Procedure, 1985. Mem. ABA, Cleve. Bar Assn., Ohio Bar Assn., Fla. Bar Assn., Nat. Trial Lawyers Assn., Order of Coif. Democrat. Jewish. Home: 1825 Aldersgate Dr Lyndhurst OH 44124 Office: 843 Terminal Tower Cleveland OH 44113

COHN, ROBERT H., diversified food company executive; b. 1926. With CFS Continental Inc., Chgo., pres., 1968-81, chmn. bd., chief exec. officer, dir., 1981—. Office: CFS Continental Inc 100 S Wacker Dr Chicago IL 60606*

COIN, SHEILA REGAN, management consultant; b. Columbus, Ohio, Feb. 17, 1942; d. James D. Regan and Jean M. (Hodgson) Cook; B.S., U. Iowa, 1964; m. Tasso Harry Coin, Sept. 17, 1967 (div.); children—Tasso Harry, Alison Regan. Staff nurse VA Hosp., Boston, 1964-66; field rep. health services program devel. ARC, Chgo., 1966-67, adminstr. blood program, 1967; asst. div. dir. Am. Hosp. Assn., also sec. Am. Soc. for Hosp. Dirs. of Nursing Service, Chgo., 1967-69; propr., mgmt. cons. Sheila Regan Coin & Assos., Chgo., 1975-77; partner, mgmt. devel. cons. Coin, Newell & Assos., Chgo., 1977—; instr. dept. continuing edn. Loyola U. Chgo., 1975-77, Rock Valley Coll. Mgmt. Inst., Rockford, Ill., 1978-83, Ill. Central Coll. Inst. for Personal and Profl. Devel., Peoria, Ill., 1979—, Continuing Edn. Ctr. for Health Profls., Triton Coll., River Grove, Ill., 1982—. Vol., Art Inst. Chgo., 1968-69; mem. Chgo. Beautiful Com., 1968-73; mem. jr. bd. Girl Scouts Assn., 1975-76; chmn. Mayor Daley's Chgo. Beautiful Awards Project, 1972; mem. jr. governing bd. Chgo. Symphony Orch., 1971—, pres., 1977-78, governing mem. Orchestral Assn. of Chgo. Symphony Orch.; bd. dirs. ARC, Mid-Am. chpt., 1979-81, Chgo. dist., 1981—, chmn. fin. devel. com., 1981-82; bd. dirs. Com. for Thalassomia, 1981-83; mem. Chgo. women's bd. Nat. Com. for Prevention Child Abuse, 1981-82. Mem. Am. Mgmt. Assn., Am. Soc. for Tng. and Devel., Ill. Tng. and Devel. Assn., Chi Omega. Home: 1037 W North Shore Ave Chicago IL 60626 Office: 919 N Michigan Ave Chicago IL 60611

COLAS, ANTONIO ESPADA, biochemist, educator; b. Muel, Zaragoza, Spain, June 22, 1928; came to U.S., 1962, naturalized, 1968; s. Pedro Lagunas and Antonia Romeo (Espada) C.; m. Maria Inmaculada Martin, Feb. 24, 1955; children—Antonio, Juan, Maria, Santiago. Lic. Med. & Surg., U. Zaragoza, Spain, 1951; Dr. Med. & Surg., U. Madrid, Spain, 1953; Ph.D. in Biochemistry, U. Edinburgh, Scotland, 1955. Asst. prof. U. Zaragoza, 1951-55; acting chmn. U. Salamanca, Spain, 1955-57; prof. U. Valle, Cali, Colombia, 1957-62, U. Oreg., Portland, 1962-68; prof. ob.-gyn. and physiol. chemistry U. Wis., Madison, 1968—; extraordinary prof. U. Zaragoza, 1978—. Contbr. articles on sex steroid hormone biochemistry to profl. jours. Recipient Extraordinary Prize, U. Zaragoza, 1951. Mem. Biochem. Soc., Am. Chem. Soc., Endocrine Soc., Am. Soc. Biol. Chemists, Soc. Gynecologic Investigation. Office: Univ Wis 185 Med Sci Bldg 1300 University Ave Madison WI

COLAW, EMERSON S., clergyman. Bishop N. Central jurisdiction United Methodist Ch., Mpls. Office: 122 W Franklin Ave Rm 400 Minneapolis MN 55404*

COLBER, RUSSELL HOWARD, writer, advertising executive; b. Milw., June 21, 1938; s. Ralph Howard and Margaret Marie (Hoppens) C.; B.A. (WLOL Broadcasting scholar), U. Minn., 1965; M.S. (Nat. Acad. of TV Arts and Scis. fellow), Newhouse Sch. Pub. Communications, Syracuse U., 1966; m. Bonita Elizabeth Cheesebrough, Sept. 1, 1963; children—Newell, Geoffrey, Charles, Nelson. Asst. to v.p. corp. communications Dayton Hudson Corp., Mpls., 1966-70; v.p., Advertisers Diversified Services, Mpls., 1970-73; chmn. communications div. The Mpls. Inst. of Arts, 1973-75; pres., Russ Colber & Assos., Mpls., 1975-78; dir. pub. relations Sielaff/Johnson Advt., 1978-79; dir. advt. Salkin & Linoff, 1979-80, EO Inc., 1981-82, PSG Medtronic Inc., Mpls., 1982—; convenor Twin Cities Journalism Conf., Nat. Model Cities Conf.; panelist Minn. Advt. Fedn. Trade Press Day, 1983. Recipient Fisher-Stevens Nat. Mail Works Achievement award, 1983. Mem. Pub. Relations Soc. Am. (health sect., accredited in pub. relations), Am. Med. Writers Assn., Advt. Fedn., Bus. and Profl. Advt. Assn. (Oliver award 1984). Home: The Churchill 111 Marquette Ave Apt 2604 Minneapolis MN 55401 Office: 6951 Central Ave NE Minneapolis MN 55432

COLBURN, DAVID WAYNE, vocational educator; b. Detroit, Aug. 26, 1950; s. Harry Wayne and Leona Irene (Hunter) C.; m. Rosemary Marie Mayer, Jan. 10, 1951. A.S., Macomb County Community Coll., 1970; B.S., Wayne State U., 1972, M.Ed., 1976, Specialist cert. in Edn., 1980, Ed.D., 1982. Detailer, Cross Co., Fraser, Mich., 1973, Proficient Products, Inc., Warren, Mich., 1978-80; drafting tchr. Detroit Bd. Edn., 1972—, tchr. adult edn., 1973—; mem. task force vocat. edn. service Mich. Dept. Edn., 1981-82, mem. task force tchr. facilitator for Vocat. Tech. Edn. Service, 1983. Mem. Am. Vocat. Assn., Mich. Occupational Edn. Assn., Mich. Curriculum Leaders, Mich. Trade and Tech. Edn., Mich. Indsl. Edn. Soc. (regional adminstrv. officer 1984—; Region Tchr. of Yr. 1983-84). Roman Catholic. Lodge: KC. Home: 32814 Beacon Ln Fraser MI 48026

COLBY, DAVID PAUL, optometrist; b. Fargo, N.D., Mar. 7, 1956; s. Everett Dana and Delores (Dulsky) C. B.S., Pacific U., 1979, O.D., 1980. Gen. practice optometry, Kenmare, N.D., 1983—; speaker in field. Served to capt. USAF, 1980-83. Mem. Am. Optometric Assn., Armed Forces Optometric Soc., Aircraft Owners and Pilots Assn., N.D. Optometric Assn., Nat. Rifleman Assn. Lutheran. Club: Ducks Unlimited (Minot, N.D.). Lodges: Lions (sec. 1984), Elks, (Kenmare). Avocations: hunting; hockey; flying. Home: R R PO Box 857 Kenmare ND 58746 Office: Optometry Clinic Kenmare 28 2d St NW Kenmare ND 58746

COLE, DONALD WHEELER, management psychologist; b. Cleve., Dec. 30, 1929; s. Lawrence Chester and Mabel Louise (Wheeler) C.; A.B., U. R.I., 1950; M.S., Boston U., 1952; 3d year cert. Smith Coll., 1955; D.S.W., Washington U., St. Louis, 1964; m. Norma Gale Skoog, July 11, 1953; 5 children. Mgr. mgmt. devel. TRW, Inc., Cleve., 1963-71; mgmt. psychologist, cons., pres. Don Cole & Assocs., Cleve., 1968—; dir. personnel and orgn. devel. Bobbie Brooks, Cleve., 1974-76; mem. sci. and tech. council Am. Industries Corp., Cleve., 1969-71; mem. faculty Cleve. State U., 1966-73; dir. Orgn. Devel. Inst., 1968—; pres. Internat. Registry Orgn. Devel. Profls., Cleve., 1968—, pub., 1974—. Lic. psychologist, Ohio. Fellow Am. Orthopsychiat. Assn. (life); mem. Société Internationale pour le Développement des Organisations (N.Am. dir. 1977—), Am. Psychol. Assn., Cleve. Psychol. Assn., Orgn. Devel. Network (trustee 1978-81). Author: Professional Suicide, 1981; Improving Profits Through Organization Development, 1982; Conflict Resolution Technology, 1983; pub. Orgn. Devel. Jour., 1983—; editor Orgns. and Change, 1974—; assoc. editor Leadership and Orgn. Devel. Jour., 1979—. Home: 11234 Walnut Ridge Rd Chesterland OH 44026 Office: 6501 Wilson Mills Rd Suite K Cleveland OH 44143

COLE, EDYTH LUTICIA, state government official; b. Chgo., Dec. 3, 1942; d. Alfred Jackson and Helen Louise (Dixon) Cole; B.S., Wilberforce U., 1967; M.Ed., U. Ill., 1969; 2 adopted children, Cary Calvin, Cessley Louise. Asst. dean of students LeMoyne-Owen Coll., Memphis, 1969-70; field rep. Ill. Fair Employment Commn., Chgo., 1970-72; affirmative action officer Sangamon State U., Springfield, Ill., 1972-75; personnel/affirmative action dir. Ill. Bd. Edn., Springfield, 1975—. Rehab. fellow, 1967-69. Mem. Am. Personnel and Guidance Assn., Ill. Affirmative Action Officers Assn. (v.p. 1979), Nat. Assn. Affirmative Action Officers (dir.), Delta Sigma Theta (2d v.p. 1976-78, fin. sec.). Methodist. Home: 856 Independence Ridge Springfield IL 62702 Office: 100 N 1st St Springfield IL 62777

COLE, EUGENE ROGER, clergyman, author; b. Cleve., Nov. 14, 1930; s. Bernard James and Mary Louise (Rogers) C.; B.A., St. Edwards Sem., 1954; student John Carroll U., 1957; M.Div., Sulpician Sem. N.W., 1958; A.B., Central Wash. U., Ellensburg, 1960; M.A., Seattle U., 1970; Litt.D. (hon.), 1983. Ordained priest Roman Catholic Ch., 1958; Newman moderator and cons. Central Wash. U., Ellensburg, 1958-59; bus. mgr. Experiment Press, Seattle, 1959-60; chaplain St. Elizabeth Hosp., Yakima, Wash., 1959-61; chmn. English dept. Yakima Central Cath. High Sch., 1959-66, Marquette High Sch., Yakima, 1966-68; poetry critic Nat. Writers Club, Denver, 1969-72; poet in service Poets & Writers Inc., N.Y.C., 1974—; instr. contract bridge, Ind., 1975-79; freelance writer, editor, researcher, 1958—; researcher Harvard, 1970; religious counselor. Recipient Poetry Broadcast award, 1968; Musical Expertise award, 1970; Lorraine Harr Haiku award, 1974; Ann. Mentor Poetry award, 1974; Pro Mundi Beneficio award, 1975; Readers Union award, 1976. Mem. Authors Guild, Poetry Soc. Am. (judge 1970), Western World Haiku Soc., Acad. Am. Poets, World-Wide Acad. Scholars, Internat. Poetry Soc., Soc. for Scholarly Pub., Internat. Platform Assn., Eighteen Nineties Soc. (London), Friends of the Lilly Library, Expt. Group, Soc. for Study of Midwestern Lit., Nat. Fedn. State Poetry Socs., Poetry Soc. (London), Sir Thomas Beechom Soc., Chgo. Symphony Orch. Assn., Cleve. Mus. Art, Ohioana Library Assn., Century Club of Cleve. State Univ., Poets' League Greater Cleve., Am. Contract Bridge League, Kappa Delta Pi. Composer: Werther: Tone Poem for Piano, 1948; Chronicle for Tape, 1960. Author: Which End, the Empyrean?, 1959; April Is the Cruelest Month, 1970; Falling UP: Haiku & Senryu, 1979; Act & Potency (poems), 1980; Ding an sich: anapoems, 1985; Uneasy Camber: Early Poems & Diversions, 1985; lyrics for male prodn. Finian's Rainbow, 1958; 3 hymns on Bach melodies, 1958; editor: Grand Slam: 13 Great Short Stories about Bridge, 1975; In the Beginning, 1978; Saki's Cup: The Wit and Wisdom of H.H. Munro, 1987, Grand Slam Doubled: A Second Collection of 13 Great Bridge Stories, 1987; assoc. editor: The Harvester, 1955; guest editor Experiment: An Internat. Rev., 1961; editorial staff This Is My Best, 1970; contbr. Your Literary I.Q. Saturday Rev., 1970-72; author religious monograph, also contbr. articles, poetry and drama to numerous lit. jours. and anthologies. Home and Office: PO Box 91277 Cleveland OH 44101

COLE, FRANCINE CIMINO, osteopathic physician; b. Cleve., Oct. 17, 1949; d. William and Rose (Leotta) Cimino; m. Raymond Edward Cole, Dec. 19, 1970; children—Christopher, Kimberly. B.S., U. Dayton, 1971; student Chgo. Coll. Osteo Medicine 1971-73; D.O., Mich. State U. Coll. Osteo. Medicine, 1974. Diplomate Am. Bd. Examiners Osteo Physicians and Surgeons. Practice Osteo. medicine specializing in family practice, River Rouge, Mich., 1975; asst. clin. prof. Mich. State U., East Lansing, River Rouge, Mich.; co-med. dir. Downriver Hospice, Inc., Trenton, Mich.; co-dir., instr. Mich. Health and Wellness Inst., River Rouge; sch. bd. physician River Rouge Pub. Schs. Founding bd. dirs. Downriver Hospice, Inc., Trenton, Mich., 1983; mem. Christian Service Commn. St. Cyprian Catholic Ch., Riverview, Mich., 1983. Am. Osteo. Assn. Auxillary scholar Chgo. Coll. Osteo. Medicine, 1970. Mem. Am. Osteo. Assn., Mich. Assn. Osteo. Physicians and Surgeons, Wayne County Osteo. Assn., Riverside Osteo. Hosp. (profl. staff). Avocation: eastern and western philosophies and theologies. Home: 26045 Waterbury Way Grosse Ile MI 48138 Office: Family Practice 11346 W Jefferson River Rouge MI 48218

COLE, FRANK CRUNDEN, mfg. co. exec.; b. St. Paul, May 14, 1922; s. Wallace H. and Mary (Crunden) C.; B.A., Williams Coll., 1943; m. Ardath Starkloff, May 23, 1959; children—Maria C., Catherine L., Wendy F., Mary C., Caroline B. Vice pres. Crunden Martin Mfg. Co., St. Louis, 1954-64, pres., 1964—, chmn. bd., 1971—; mng. partner Riverfront Realty Co. Bd. dirs. Jefferson Expansion Meml., 1965—. Served to lt. (j.g.), USNR, 1943-46. Clubs: St. Louis Country, Noonday, Deer Creek, Stadium. Office: Crunden Martin Mfg Co PO Box 508 Saint Louis MO 63166

COLE, GARRY LEE, physician; b. Ottumwa, Iowa, Feb. 21, 1936; s. Sally Sheehy; children—Jeff, Cathy. B.S., Iowa State U., 1960; D.O., Coll. Osteopathic Medicine and Surgery, Des Moines, 1973. Diplomate Am. Bd. Family Practice. Family practice medicine Med. Assocs., New Hampton, Iowa, 1973—. Served with U.S. Army, 1955-57. Mem. AMA, Am. Acad. Family Practice, Iowa Med. Soc., Chickasaw County Med. Soc. Office: Med Assocs 201 S Linn Ave New Hampton IA 50659

COLE, HUGO JOHN, osteopathic physician and surgeon; b. Rose Hill, Vir., Sept. 9, 1934; s. Henry Lee and Blanche Henrietta (Trent) C.; m. Phyllis Joy Brown, June 5, 1955 (div. 1967); children—Mary Ann, Amelia Joy, Timothy Scot, Velvet Ellen; m. Sharon Ann Gimbel, Nov. 25, 1972; children—Shannon Beth, Suzanne Marie, Trent Lewis, Sarah JeAnn. D.O., Kirksville Coll. Osteo. Medicine, 1963; Cert. Am. Acad. Osteo. Specialists (surgeon). Rotating internship Carson City Hosp., Mich., 1963-64; resident Carson City Hosp., Mich.; pathology intern Harper Hosp., Detroit, 1971; physician, surgeon Hosp. Clinic Group, Elgin, N.D., 1972—; asst. prof. family medicine Coll. of the Pacific, Pomona, Calif., 1984—; assoc. prof. gen. surgery U. Osteo. Medicine and Health, Des Moines, 1983. Mem. N.D. Assn. Osteo. Physicians & Surgeons (v.p.), Am. Acad. Osteo. Specialists, Am. Acad. Osteo. Surgeons. Republican. Lutheran. Avocations: raising thoroughbred horses, traveling. Home: 4 C Farms Elgin ND 58533 Office: Hospital Clinic Group 300 N Main St Elgin ND 58533

COLE, JAMES SILAS, JR., lawyer; b. Cheyenne, Wyo., Sept. 8, 1953; s. James Silas and Joyce Jeanne (Pawson) C.; m. Ann Marie Shoemaker, May 24, 1975; children—Jean Louise, Timothy James, Mary Elizabeth, Stephen Vincent. B.A. summa cum laude, St. Louis U., 1975; J.D. cum laude, Harvard U., 1978. Bar: Mo. 1979, U.S. Dist. Ct. (ea. dist.) Mo. 1979, U.S. Bankruptcy Ct. (we. dist.) Mo. 1983. Law clk. Mo. Supreme Ct., Jefferson City, 1978-79; assoc. Mulford & Cole and predecessor Michael W. Mulford, Kirksville, Mo., 1979-80, ptnr., 1980—. Co-founder, officer Birthright of Kirksville, 1980—; mem. parish council Mary Immaculate Ch., Kirksville, 1980-83. Mem. Assn. Trial Lawyers Am., Mo. Assn. Trial Attys., Phi Beta Kappa, Alpha Sigma Nu. Democrat. Roman Catholic. Lodge: K.C. (officer local lodge). Office: Mulford & Cole PC 113 E Washington St Kirksville MO 63501

COLE, KATHLEEN ANN, social worker, advt. agy. exec.; b. Cin., Nov. 22, 1946; d. James Scott and Kathryn Gertrude (Borisch) Cole; B.A., Miami U., 1968; M.S.W., U. Mich., 1972; M.M., Northwestern U., 1978; m. Brian Brandt, Mar. 21, 1970. Social worker Hamilton County Welfare Dept., Cin., 1969-70, Lucas County Children Services Bd., Toledo, 1970-74, East Maine Sch. Dist., Niles, Ill., 1974-77; account exec. Leo Burnett Advt. Agy., Chgo., 1978—; field instr. Loyola U., Chgo., 1976-77. Mem. Acad. Cert. Social Workers, Nat. Assn. Social Workers, Miami U. Alumni Assn. (dir. 1976—), Northwestern U. Profl. Women's Assn. Home: 414 Kelling Ln Glencoe IL 60022 Office: Leo Burnett Advt Agy Prudential Plaza Chicago IL 60601

COLE, KENNETH DUANE, architect; b. Ft. Wayne, Ind., Jan. 23, 1932; s. Wolford J. and Helen Francis (McDowell) C.; student Ft. Wayne Art Inst., 1950-51; B.S. in Arch., U. Cin., 1957; m. Carolyn Lou Meyer, Apr. 25, 1953; children—David Brent, Denelle Hope, Diana Faith, Dawn Love. Draftsman-/intern Humbrecht Asso., Ft. Wayne, Ind., 1952-57; designer/draftsman Humbrecht Asso., Ft. Wayne, 1957-58; partner/architect Cole-Matott, Architects/Planners, Ft. Wayne, 1959—; mem. adv. bd. Gen. Services Adminstrn., Region 5, 1976, 78. Bd. dirs. Ft. Wayne Art Inst., 1969-74, Arch, Inc., Ft. Wayne, 1975-77, Downtown Ft. Wayne Assn., 1977-82, Hist. Soc. Ft. Wayne and Allen County, 1982—, Izaak Walton League Am., Ft. Wayne, 1970-76. Recipient Citation, Ind. Soc. of Architects for remodeling of Bonsib Bldg., 1978. Mem. Ft. Wayne C. of C., AIA (bd. dirs. No. Ind. 1971-74, pres. 1974), Ind. Soc. Architects (bd. dirs. 1973-76, sec. 1976), Ft. Wayne Soc. Architects (pres. 1970-71), Am. Arbitration Assn. (panel of arbitrators 1980—). Lutheran. Archtl. works include: Weisser Park Jr. High Sch., 1963, Brandt Hall, 1965, Bonsib Bldg., 1967, Lindley Elem. Sch., 1969, Young Elem. Sch., 1972, Study Elem. Sch., 1975, Old City Hall Renovation, 1978, Peoples Trust Bank Adminstrv. Services Center, 1979. Home: 1321 Maple Ave Fort Wayne IN 46807 Office: 123 1/2 W Wayne St Fort Wayne IN 46802

COLE, LARRY GENE, nursing home administrator; b. Neosho, Mo., Nov. 1, 1949; s. Gerald W. and Verna Lou (Randal) C.; Asso. in Edn., Crowder Coll., 1969; postgrad. U. Mo., Columbia, 1976-77; m. Katherine Lee Turner, Aug. 28, 1969; 1 son, Jason William. Residential dir. Big Bros. Inc. Children's Home, Joplin, Mo., 1969-76; adminstr. Fair Acres Nursing Home, Carthage, Mo., 1976-79; adminstr. Elmhurst Nursing Home, Webb City, Mo., 1979—; adminstrv. dir. Jasper County Assn. for Social Service, Inc., 1979—. Mem. Carthage Council of Social Agys. 1976—; bd. dirs. Sunshine Children's Home, Carthage, Ozark Mental Health Center, Joplin, Community Focus, Inc., Joplin, Big Bros., Joplin; mem. adv. bd. Jasper County Civil Def. Lic. nursing home adminstr., lic. funeral dir. Mo. Mem. Mo. League Nursing Home Adminstrs. Home and Office: Route 1 Box 100C Webb City MO 64870

COLE, LOIS HOVINGA, physical education educator; b. Chgo., Sept. 14, 1947; d. Jacob and Jennie (Beukema) Hovinga; m. Dick Taylor Cole, Jan. 23,

1981. B.A., Calvin Coll., 1969; M.S., St. Francis Coll., 1973; Ph.D., Walden U., 1983. Tchr., West Middle Sch., Grand Rapids, Mich., 1969-70, Concord Jr. High Sch., Elkhart, Ind., 1970-74; asst. prof. Trinity Christian Coll., Palos Heights, Ill., 1974—, chmn. dept., 1982—; nat. sports chmn., volleyball tournament dir. Nat. Christian Coll. Athletic Assn., Chattanooga, 1983—. Co-author: An Individualized Approach to Beginning Tennis, 1975. Named Dist. IV Volleyball Coach of Yr., Nat. Christian Coll. Athletic Assn., 1983; recipient Jo-Dunn award for Archery, Calvin Coll., 1968; Teaching Merit award Trinity Christian Coll., 1977. Mem. Nat. Assn. Phys. Edn. in Higher Edn. Mem. Christian Reformed Ch. Home: 1753 W 100th Pl Chicago IL 60643 Office: Trinity Christian Coll 6601 W College Dr Palos Heights IL 60463

COLE, LOUISE ANNE, office manager; b. Battle Creek, Mich., Apr. 29, 1939; d. Earl Burdette and Bernice Lillian (McLeod) Burch; m. Morris E. Cole, Sept. 12, 1958; children—Brian Douglas, Barry Dwight. Student, Gt. Lakes Bible Coll., 1957-59, Grand Rapids Jr. Coll., 1982-85. Sec., reporter Dun & Bradstreet, Inc., Toledo, Ohio, 1971-75; sec. med. records Toledo Hosp., 1975-77; collections mgr. Selby Gen. Hosp., Marietta, Ohio, 1977-78; credit collection mgr. Osteo. Hosp., Grand Rapids, Mich., 1978-81; office mgr. Neurol. Assocs., Grand Rapids, 1981—. Mem. Rockford Bus. and Profl. Women's Assn. (pres. 1981-82), Western Mich. Bus. and Profl. Women Assn. (dist. dir. 1983—), Mich. Bus. and Profl. Women Assn. (chmn. 1985—, rec. sec. 1985-86), Am. Mgmt. Assn., Mich. Hosp. Fin. Mgmt. Assn. Republican. Mem. Christian Ch. Avocations: church organist; choral director. Home: 9270 Myers Lake Rd Rockfod MI 49341 Office: Neurol Assocs 2855 Michigan St NE Grand Rapids MI 49506

COLE, PATRICIA ANN SHANNON, educational administrator; b. Trenton, Mich., Sept. 5, 1948; d. James Norman and Virginia Ruth (Davis) Shannon; B.S., U. Mich., 1970, Ph.D., 1981; M.A., Eastern Mich. U., 1974. Jr. high sch. bus. edn. tchr. Wyandotte (Mich.) Schs., 1970-72, adult edn. tchr. bus. edn., 1970-72, bus. edn. tchr. Roosevelt High Sch., 1972-78, dir. vocat./career edn., 1978-85; dir. state and fed. programs Wyandotte Pub. Schs., 1985—; instr. secretarial sci. Detroit Coll. Bus., Dearborn, Mich., 1974-82. Cert. profl. sec., 1975; recipient certificates of appreciation for service in field; named outstanding bus. edn. student U. Mich., 1970. Mem. Mich. Council Vocat. Adminstrs. (rep. to Vocat. Edn. Study Task Force, 1980-81), Am. Vocat. Assn., Mich. Occupational Edn. Assn., Vocat. Edn. Planning Com. (chmn. Wayne County, Mich. chpt.), S.E. Regional Vocat. Educators (sec./treas.), Mich. Assn. Career Edn., Mich. Bus. Edn. Assn., Nat. Bus. Edn. Assn., Nat. Secs. Assn., AAUW, Delta Pi Epsilon, Pi Omega Pi. Club: Bus. and Profl. Women. Guest speaker profl. confs.; contbr. articles to profl. publs. in field. Home: 3301 Biddle St Apt 2D Wyandotte MI 48192 Office: 1275 15th St Wyandotte MI 48192

COLE, PAUL LEON, equipment company executive, marketing engineer, consultant; b. Lansing, Mich., June 25, 1946; s. Leslie Arthur and Alice Margaret (LeBoeuf) C.; m. Candace Ann Denhof, June 15, 1968; children. B.S.E., U. Mich., 1970; M.B.A., U. Mont., 1975. Registered profl. engr., Mich. Engr., Brunswick Corp., Muskegon, Mich., 1967-70; product planner, crane and hoist ops. Dresser Industries Inc., Muskegon, 1976-78, mgr. product planning, 1978-82; product mgr. Shaw Walker Co., 1983—; cons. Cole & Assocs. Served to capt. USAF, 1970-76. Mem. Nat. Soc. Profl. Engrs., Mich. Soc. Profl. Engrs., Soc. Mfg. Engrs. (sr.). Home: 4283 Carolyn Dr Muskegon MI 49444

COLE, RICHARD THOMAS, state official; b. Detroit, Apr. 20, 1948; s. Clifford Stanley and Lois Elizabeth (Arthurs) C.; m. Deborah E. Peterson, July 24, 1982; children—Angela, Chapin, Rachel. B.A., Western Mich. U., 1969; M.A., Mich. State U., 1972, Ph.D., 1980. Cons., Mich. State Senate, Lansing, 1970-73, majority exec. sec., 1975-76; dir. of sch. law Mich. Dept. Edn., Lansing, 1974; lobbyist Pub. Affairs Assocs., Lansing, 1977-78; cons. Inst. Ednl. Leadership, Washington, 1977-78; chmn. Publicom Pub. Relations, Lansing, 1979-83; dep. dir. Mich. Dept. Commerce, Lansing, 1983; press sec. Gov. James Blanchard of Mich., 1983—; adj. prof. Mich. State U., 1985; lectr. in field. Served with USAFR, 1970-76. Mem. Mich. Assn. Sch. Adminstrs., Mich. Press Assn., Contbr. articles to profl. publs.

COLE, THOMAS TAFT, lawyer; b. Columbus, Ohio, Mar. 13, 1948; s. Thomas Taft and Elizabeth (Carroll) C.; m. Shirley Marshall, Sept. 15, 1971; children—Sarah, Eric, Matthew. B.A., Ohio State U., 1976; J.D. No. Ky. U., 1983. Bars: Ohio 1983, U.S. Dist. Ct. (so. dist.) Ohio 1983. Probation officer Adult Parole Authority, Columbus, 1976-81, Warren County Ct., Lebanon, Ohio, 1981-83; law clk. Herdman, Revelson & Herdman, Lebanon, 1981-83; assoc. Herdman, Cole & Herdman, Lebanon, 1983-85; ptnr. Logsdon & Cole, Lebanon, 1985—. Mem. ABA, Ohio State Bar Assn., Warren County Bar Assn., Cin. Bar Assn., Assn. Trial Lawyers Am. Office: Logsdon & Cole 203 E Main St Lebanon OH 45036

COLEMAN, BERNARD SINCLAIR, pharmaceutical company official, researcher; b. Liverpool, Eng., June 18, 1937; came to U.S., 1978; s. David and Esther (Morris) C.; m. Margot Jenkins, Sept. 25, 1965; children—Paul, David, Jonathan. M.B., Ch.B., Leeds U., 1961. Diplomate in ob-gyn Royal Coll. Obstetricians and Gynecologists; diplomate in pharm. medicine Royal Colls. Physicians U.K. Practice family medicine, Tenby, Wales, 1967-74; mem. advisor Boehringer Ingelheim, Ltd., Bracknell, Eng., 1974-78; dir. clin. research Duphar Labs., Inc., Worthington, Ohio, 1978-82; sr. dir. clin. research Kali-Duphar Labs., Inc., Worthington, 1983—; adj. assoc. prof. pharmacology Ohio State U., Columbus, 1979—. Author sci. articles. Fellow Royal Soc. Medicine; mem. Am. Soc. Clin. Pharmacology and Therapeutics, Am. Coll. Neuropsychopharmacology, N.Y. Acad. Scis., Can. Coll. Neuropsychopharmacology, Brit. Med. Assn. Lodge: Rotary (bd. dirs. 1983-85) (Dublin-Worthington). Avocations: travel; camping; music; cooking; crafts. Home: 1635 Tennyson Ct Worthington OH 43085 Office: 200 Old Wilson Bridge Rd Worthington OH 43085

COLEMAN, BRASCO HERCULES, business educator; b. Harperville, Miss., Mar. 23, 1921; s. Joe and Queen Eva C. B.S., Alcorn State U., 1949; M.A., Roosevelt U., 1972; D.Ed., George Peabody Coll., Vanderbilt U., 1981. Cert. secondary tchr., adminstr., Ind., Miss., Ill., Calif. Adminstr., tchr. Mound Bayou High Sch., Miss., 1949-52, Blue Island Schs., Ill., 1959-72; tchr. Los Angeles Pub. Schs., 1954-56; prof. bus. edn. Chgo. State U., 1972—; bookkeeper St. Claire Paint Co., Los Angeles, 1954-56. Pres., founder Miss. Union Club U.S.A., Chgo., 1972—; bookkeeper Nat. Baptist Assn., Hot Springs, Ark., 1950-53. Served with U.S. Army, 1943-46, ETO. Mem. Ill. Edn. Assn., Nat. Bus. Edn. Assn., Am. Fedn. Tchrs., AAUP, North Central Team Evaluation of Ill. Schs., Phi Delta Kappa. Avocations: public speaking; sales demonstrations techniques; research.

COLEMAN, BRUCE FREDERICK, economist, municipal bond trader; b. Pontiac, Mich., Aug. 13, 1944; s. Frederick George and Edith Maud (Eley) C.; B.S., U. Mich., 1967; m. Diane Marie Base, May 18, 1968; children—Christine, Carrie, Christopher, Craig, Amanda. With Mfrs. Nat. Bank of Detroit, 1975-76; asst. v.p. Ann Arbor Bank and Trust (Mich.), 1976-78; exec. v.p. Mich. Mcpl. Bond Corp., Ann Arbor, 1978-80; gen. partner Roney & Co., Detroit, 1980—. Mem. Fin. Analysts Soc. Detroit, Bond Club Detroit, Nat. Security Traders Assn., Basis Club Detroit. Office: 1 Griswold Detroit MI 48226

COLEMAN, CLARENCE WILLIAM, banker; b. Wichita, Kans., Mar. 24, 1909; s. William Coffin and Fanny Lucinda (Sheldon) C.; degree U. Kans., 1928-32; LL.D. (hon.), Ottawa U., 1973; D.H.L. (hon.), Friends U., Wichita, Kans.; m. Emry Regester Inghram, Oct. 2, 1935; children—Rochelle, Pamela, Kathryn Sheldon. Dir., The Coleman Co., Inc., Wichita, 1932—, v.p. mfg., 1944-51, asst. gen. mgr., 1951-54, vice chmn. bd., 1971—; pres. Union Nat. Bank of Wichita, 1957-72, vice chmn. bd., 1972—; chmn. bd. Cherry Creek Inn, Denver, 1961-69. Bd. dirs. Found. for Study of Cycles, Pitts., 1966—; bd. dirs. Inst. Logopedics, Wichita, 1940-74, chmn. bd., 1947-48; bd. dirs. Wichita Symphony Soc., Inc., 1965—; trustee Wichita Symphony Soc. Found., 1966—; bd. dirs. United Fund Wichita and Sedgwick County, 1957-70; trustee Friends U., 1956-65; bd. dirs. Wichita Crime Commn., 1953—, pres., 1958-59; trustee Peddie Sch., Hightstown, N.J., 1955-76, chmn., 1972-76, chmn. emeritus, 1981—. Mem. NAM, Wichita C. of C. (dir. 1947-60, pres. 1956), Phi Kappa Psi. Club: Rotary. Home: 530 Broadmoor Ct Wichita KS 67206 Office: 1005 Union Center Wichita KS 67202

COLEMAN, E. THOMAS, congressman; b. Kansas City, Mo., May 29, 1943; s. Earl T. and Marie (Carlson) C.; A.B. in Econ., William Jewell Coll., 1965; M.P.A., N.Y. U., 1969; J.D., Washington U., 1969; m. Marilyn Anderson, June 8, 1968; children—Julie Anne, Emily Catherine, Megan Marie. Admitted to Mo. bar, 1969; practiced in Gladstone, 1973-76; asst. atty. gen. Mo., 1969-73; mem. Mo. Ho. of Reps., 1973-77; mem. 95th-99th Congresses for 6th Mo. Dist. Office: US House of Representatives Washington DC 20515

COLEMAN, GEORGE HUNT, chemist; b. San Gabriel, Calif., Oct. 15, 1928; s. Thomas and Grace Muriel (Love) C.; A.B., U. Calif., Berkeley, 1950; Ph.D., UCLA, 1958; m. Lois Mae Tarleton, Feb. 14, 1953; children—David Howe, Thomas George, Margaret Rose. Microanalyst, U. Calif., Berkeley, 1950-51; nuclear chemist Calif. Research and Devel. Corp., 1951-53; sr. nuclear chemist Lawrence Livermore Lab., 1957-69; asso. prof. chemistry Nebr. Wesleyan U., Lincoln, 1969-78, prof., 1979—, acting head dept., 1976-78, head dept. chemistry, 1978-80. Mem. Am. Chem. Soc., AAAS, Am. Platform Assn. Democrat. Presbyterian. Home: 5920 Margo Dr Lincoln NE 68510 Office: Nebr Wesleyan U 50th and St Paul St Lincoln NE 68504

COLEMAN, GERALD CHRISTOPHER, advertising agency executive; b. Boston, Sept. 27, 1939; s. Gerald Christopher and Anna Rose (Dubanevich) C.; m. Kathleen Louise Dolan, June 3, 1967; children—Lisa, Emily, Craig, Mary. A.B., Boston Coll., 1964; M.B.A., Dartmouth Coll., 1966. Asst. nat. retail sales mgr. photog. products Sears Roebuck & Co., Chgo., 1966-68, asst. nat. buyer calculators, 1968-69, staff asst. to v.p., 1969-70, nat. buyer, product mgr. bedding products, 1970-72, nat. retail sales mgr. toy products, 1972-73, nat. retail mktg. mgr. furniture products, 1973-74; v.p. Wilson, Haight & Welch, Inc., Boston, 1974-77; sr. v.p. N.W. Ayer, Inc., Chgo., 1977-83, sr. v.p., N.Y.C., 1983—, also dir. N.W. Ayer Midwest, Chgo., 1982-83; dir. Allied Fin. Instns. Inc., Boston. Rep. at large Kenilworth (Ill.) Citizens Adv. Com., 1982. Mem. Am. Mktg. Assn. (officer chpt. dir. 1983-84). Roman Catholic. Club: Economic of Chgo.; Dartmouth of N.Y.

COLEMAN, JILL ANN, lawyer; b. Pontiac, Mich., Aug. 31, 1955; d. Irving Isaac and Lorraine Mildred (Gettleson) Merkovitz; m. Randall Scott Coleman, May 24, 1980. B.A., U. Mich., 1977, J.D., 1980. Bar: Mich. 1980, U.S. Dist. Ct. (no. dist.) Ill. 1980, U.S. Ct. Appeals (5th and 11th cirs.) 1981, U.S. Dist. Ct. (ea. dist.) Wis. 1983. Assoc. Levy and Erens, Chgo., 1980-84; ptnr. Erens, Hallock & Miller, Chgo., 1985—. Editorial bd. Mich. Law Rev., 1981-83. Mem. Chgo. Bar Assn., AAUW (past sec./treas. and now v.p. Post Grads Group), Order of Coif. Club: Mich. Law Sch. of Chgo. (ad hoc planning com. 1983—). Office: Erens Hallock & Miller 208 S LaSalle St Suite 1100 Chicago IL 60604

COLEMAN, JOHN EDWARD, lawyer; b. Dayton, Ohio, May 28, 1907; s. George Leidigh and Verrell (Chaffin) C.; m. Jean MacMicken, May 16, 1931; children—George L., Chase Coleman Davies. B.A. with honors, Cornell U., 1929, J.D., 1922. Bar: Ohio 1932. Sole practice, Dayton, 1932—. Bd. dirs. Ohio Chapter Nature Conservatory, 1959—, pres., 1960; bd. dirs., treas. Dayton Mus. Natural History, 1959—. Mem. ABA, Dayton Bar Assn., Res. Officers Assn. U.S. (pres. 1951-52). Clubs: Army and Navy (D.C.); Dayton Racquet, Engrs. of Dayton. Lodge: Masons (master 1955, trustee 1962-83). Office: 634 Third Nat Bldg 32 N Main St Dayton OH 45402

COLEMAN, JOYCE JONES, tax examiner, consultant, nurse, civic worker; b. Selma, Ala., Apr. 3, 1941; d. John Wesley and Vera (Thomas) Jones; m. Milton C. Coleman, Jr., Aug. 6, 1966; children—Geoffrey S., Allyson A. Student Villa Madonna Coll., 1958-59, Mercy Sch. Nursing, 1959-61, U. Cin., 1961-63; grad. practical nurse No. Ky. State Vocat. Sch., 1965. Lic. practical nurse. Staff nurse St. Mary's Hosp., Cin., 1961-65; surg. nurse Good Samaritan Hosp., Cin., 1965; med. office nurse, Cin., 1966-67; tax examiner adjustment br., spl. processing refund inquiry group IRS, Cin.; cons. NIH, Washington. Pres., chmn. bd. dirs., coordinator, co-founder Sickle Cell Awareness Group of Greater Cin., 1972—; mem. adv. bd. Comprehensive Sickle Cell Ctr. Cin.; 3d v.p. Nat. Assn. Sickle Cell Disease Inc., 1985; pres. PTA; treas. chpt. 73 Nat. Treasury Employees Union; past sec. hosp. bond issue com. Ohio chpt. Nat. Health Agys.; mem. parish council, bd. dirs. St. Agnes Fed. Credit Union, chmn. supervisory com.; v.p. St. Agnes Bd. Edn., 1977-79; mem. admissions com. for minority students Kent State U. Med. Sch.; co-founder Bond Hill Child Devel. Ctr., 1973; cons. M.E.T. Cons. and Assocs., Indpls., 1974, Ebon Research Assos., 1976; mem. policy and rev. bd. lay pastoral ministry program Mt. St. Mary's Sem., 1976-82; neighborhood writer Paddock Hills Press, 1980-83. Named Fed. Employee of Yr., 1981, Omega Psi Phi Citizen of Yr., 1981, Citizen of Day, Sta. WLW and WCPO; recipient Bicentennial award for community involvement, 1976, Outstanding Achievement in Community Affairs award, 1976, McDonald award, 1978, Excellence in Leadership award Sickle Cell Awareness Group Greater Cin., 1983. Mem. Nat. Treasury Employees Union, Nat. Assn. Sickle Cell Disease, Nat. Assn. Fund Raising Execs. Roman Catholic. Clubs: Parents, Homemakers, Paddock Hills Assembly. Home: 1323 Westminster Dr Cincinnati OH 45229

COLEMAN, LEE ROY, police chief; b. Lebanon, Mo., Nov. 23, 1921; s. Charles Orville and Lillie Dale (Marsh) C.; m. Jeanne Carol Steenblock, May, 1949 (dec. 1957); m. Florence Elsie Millay, June 12, 1959; children—Janet, Susan, Linda, Coleen, Roxane. Graduate, Police Acad., Kansas City. Lumberjack, Lumber Co., Oak Creek, Colo., 1940; moulder Goodyear Tire Co., Los Angeles, 1941; report clk. Kansas City Mo. Police Dept., 1949-50, police officer, 1950-79; police chief Raymore Mo. Police Dept., 1979—. Served with USN, 1942-48. Mem. Mo. Peace Officers Assn. (pres. 1983-84), Kansas City Mo. Police Benefit Assn. (sec. 1966-75, pres. 1975-78), Met. Chiefs. and Sheriffs Assn. (treas. 1980-83), Kansas City Mo. Police Mem. VFW Post 9762 (comdr. 1954, Post Hall of Fame 1955), Raymore C. of C. (bd. dirs. 1981—). Club: Optimist (Raymore) (sec. 1982-83, v.p. 1984). Avocations: cartooning; writing; swimming. Home: 522 London Way Belton MO 64012 Office: Raymore Police Dept 210 Washington Box 160 Raymore MO 64083

COLEMAN, LESTER EARL, chemical company executive; b. Akron, Ohio, Nov. 6, 1930; s. Lester Earl and Ethel Angeline (Miller) C.; B.S., U. Akron, 1952; M.S., U. Ill., 1953, Ph.D., 1955; m. Jean Goudie Moir, Aug. 31, 1951; children—Robert Scott, Kenneth John. With Goodyear Tire & Rubber, Akron, 1951-52; with Lubrizol Corp., Cleve., 1955—, asst. div. head research and devel., 1968-72, v.p. internat. ops., asst. to pres., 1972-74, exec. v.p., 1974-76, pres., 1976-82 chief exec. officer, 1978—, chmn., 1982—, also dir.; dir. Norfolk So. Corp., Roanoke, Va., S.C. Johnson & Son, Inc., Racine, Wis., Harris Corp., Melbourne, Fla. Mem. nat. exec. bd. Boy Scouts Am.; trustee Cleve. Mus. Natural History, Case Western Res. U.; bd. overseers Dartmouth Med. Sch. Served to capt. USAF, 1955-57. Mem. Am. Chem. Soc. (local chmn. 1973), Am. Petroleum Inst., Greater Cleve. Growth Assn., Sigma Xi, Alpha Chi Sigma, Phi Lambda Upsilon, Phi Delta Theta. Methodist. Contbr. articles to profl. jours. Patentee organic and polymer chemistry. Office: 29400 Lakeland Blvd Wickliffe OH 44092

COLEMAN, PAMELA, investment advisor; b. Wichita, Kans., July 17, 1938; d. Clarence William and Emry Regester (Inghram) Coleman; student U. Okla., 1956-57, U. Mo., 1962-65, Wichita State U., 1972-73; children—Cristy Jeanne Coleman, Cathryn Coleman. Teller, Union Nat. Bank, Wichita, 1959, 1st Nat. Bank, Charleston, S.C., 1959-61, 1st Nat. Bank of New London (Conn.), 1961-62; acct., bookkeeper Greenbaum & Assos., Sydney, Australia, 1966-68; pres., chief exec. officer Sweet Peach Prodns. Pty., Ltd., Sydney, 1968-72; fin. mgr. Clarence Coleman Investments, Wichita, 1972-75, registered investment adv., office mgr., 1976—. Formerly active Project Bus. of Jr. Achievement; bd. dirs. Goodwill Industries of Wichita, 1978-80, sec., 1978-79, treas., 1979-80; 1st v.p. Angel Fire Guild, Santa Fe Opera, 1983-84, treas., 1984-85; pres. Guilds of the Santa Fe Opera, 1984-85; 1st v.p. N.Mex. Opera Guilds, Inc., 1985-86. Mem. Midwest Geneal. Soc., DAR, Soc. Mayflower Descs., Daus. Am. Colonists, Nat. Soc. Colonial Dames of Am. (Kans.). Clubs: Wichita, Wichita Country. Home: PO Box 41 Eagle Nest NM 87718 Office: 1005 Union Center Wichita KS 67202

COLEMAN, PATRICK LOUIS, biochemist, researcher; b. Honolulu, Jan. 16, 1946; s. Merlyn Louis and Mary Catherine (Feeney) C.; m. Donna Lynn Miller, Aug. 24, 1968; children—Patrick Louis, Neil Miller, Ryan James. B.A., St. Mary's Coll., 1967; Ph.D., Purdue U., 1972. Postdoctoral fellow NIH, Bethesda, Md., 1972-74; research scientist Brookhaven Nat. Lab., Upton, N.Y., 1974-77, vis. scientist, 1977-80; research biochemist E.I. Dupont Co., Wilmington, Del., 1977-79; asst. research scientist U. Mich. Med. Sch., Ann Arbor, Mich., 1979-84; sr. biochemist 3M, St. Paul, 1984—; cons. E.I. Dupont, Co., Wilmington, 1980-84. Contbr. articles to profl. jours. Patentee in field. Instr. gifted program Willow Run Sch. Dist., Mich., 1981-83, sec. sch. bd., 1982-83; instr. gifted prog. St. Thomas Sch., Mpls., 1984-85. NIH fellow, 1972-74; Mich. Heart Assn. grantee, 1984; Gen. Henry Arnold scholar U.S. Air Force, 1965-67, AEC scholar, 1965-66. Mem. Am. Soc. Biol. Chemists (assoc.), Internat. Soc. Thrombosis Hemostasis, Am. Chem. Soc., Am. Heart Assn. (council on thrombosis), AAAS. Mem. Democratic Farm Labor Party. Roman Catholic. Avocations: genealogy, local history. Office: 3M Ctr Biosci Lab 270-3S-06 St Paul MN 55144

COLEMAN, RAYMOND JAMES, international trade institute administrator, educator; b. Bethel, Kans., Jan. 8, 1923; s. Leonard George and Jo Hannah (Poulsen) C.; m. Katherine Elizabeth Dietrich, Apr. 8, 1945; children—Katherine Anne Coleman Morehead, Jayne Elaine Coleman Lewis, Christopher Lynn. B.B.A., U. Kans., 1948; M.B.A., Central Mo. State U., 1963; Ph.D. in Bus. Adminstrn., U. Ark., 1967. Mem. mktg. staff Gen. Mills Feed Div., Kansas City, Mo., 1949-56; supr. Investors Diversified Service, Mpls., 1956-63; prof. mktg. Kans. State U., Manhattan, 1963—, dir. Internatl. Trade Inst., 1980—; exec. v.p. Internat. Trade Council of Mid-America, Inc., Manhattan, 1980—. Author: M.I.S.: Management Dimensions, 1973. Vice pres. Kans/-Paraguayan Ptnrs., 1984—. Served to lt. (j.g.), USN, 1943-46, PTO. Decorated Air medals (5). Fellow Fin. Analysts Fedn.; mem. Acad. Internat. Bus., Beta Gamma Sigma, Delta Mu Delta. Republican. Presbyterian. Lodge: Masons. Office: Internat Trade Council Mid-Am Inc 1627 Anderson Ave Manhattan KS 66502

COLEMAN, RICHARD WALTER, educator; b. San Francisco, Sept 10, 1922; s. John Crisp and Reta (Walter) C.; B.A., U. Calif., Berkeley, 1945, Ph.D., 1951; m. Mildred Bradley, Aug. 10, 1949 (dec.); 1 dau., Persis C. Research asst. div. entomology and parasitology U. Calif., Berkeley, 1946-47, 49-50; ind. research, 1951-61; prof. biology, chmn. dept. Curry Coll., Milton, Mass., 1961-63; chmn. div. scis. and math. Monticello Coll., Godfrey, Ill., 1963-64; vis. prof. biology Wilberforce U., Ohio; 1964-65; prof. sci. Upper Iowa U., Fayette, 1965—; collaborator natural history div. Nat. Park Service, 1952; spl. cons. Arctic Health Research Center, USPHS, Alaska, 1954-62; apptd. explorer Commr. N.W. Ty., Yellowknife N.W. Ty., Can., 1966. Mem. Iowa Acad. Sci., Geol. Soc. Iowa (affiliate), AAAS, AAUP, Am. Inst. Biol. Scis., Nat. Sci. Tchrs. Assn., Ecol. Soc. Am., Am. Soc. Limnology and Oceanography, Am. Bryological and Lichenological Soc., Arctic Inst. N.Am., N.Am. Benthological Soc., Am. Malacological Union, Assn. Midwestern Coll. Biology Tchrs., Société de Biologie de Montréal, Nat. Assn. Biology Tchrs., Sigma Xi. Methodist. Contbr. articles to profl. reports. Home: PO Box 156 Fayette IA 52142

COLEMAN, ROBERT CHESTER, JR., manufacturing company official; b. Oak Park, Ill., Oct. 14, 1945; s. Robert C. and Loretta F. (Collins) C.; m. Candace Conway, June 26, 1970; children—Robert C., David C. B.S., Syracuse U., 1967. Sales, Am. Can Corp., various locations, 1971-79, market mgr., Greenwich, Conn., 1979-82, regional sales mgr., Chgo., 1983—. Served to lt. USN, 1967-70; Vietnam. Mem. Can Mfrs. Inst. (vice-chmn. aerosol 1980-84), Chem. Splty. Mfrs. Assn., Aerosol Indsl. Devel. Soc. Republican. Club: Lake Point Tower (Chgo.). Home: 166 Stonegate Ct Glen Ellyn IL 60137 Office: Am Can Co 915 Harger Rd Oak Brook IL 60521

COLEMAN, ROBERT EDWARD, orthodontist; b. Detroit, Jan. 16, 1915; s. Edward M. and Kathryn J. (Bolton) C.; B.S., U. Detroit, 1936, D.D.S., 1937; M.S., U. Mich., 1939; m. Marion Purdy, Nov. 30, 1940; children—Carolyn Coleman Sieffert, Edward Michael, Mary Coleman Scarfone, Janet Coleman Palombit. Practice orthodontics, Detroit, 1937—; head dept. orthodontics Dental Sch., U. Detroit, 1951-63. Served as capt. Dental Corps, AUS, 1943-46. Diplomate Am. Bd. Orthodontics. Fellow Am. Coll. Dentistry (pres. Mich. chpt. 1974); mem. Am. Dental Assn., Mich., Detroit Dist. dental socs., Am. Assn. Orthodontists, Great Lakes Soc. Orthodontists (pres. 1964), Edward H. Angle Soc. Orthodontists (pres. Midwest chpt. 1962), A.A.A.S., Charles H. Tweed Found. Orthodontic Research, U. Detroit Alumni Assn. (past dir.), U. Detroit Dental Alumni Assn. (past pres., sec. 1939-49), U. Mich. Orthodontic Alumni Soc. (pres. 1966), Omicron Kappa Upsilon (past pres.), Delta Sigma Delta (past grand master). Lion (past dir.). Clubs: Detroit Dental Clinic (past dir.), Downtown Dental (past pres.), Detroit Athletic, Country of Detroit. Contbr. articles to profl. jours. Home: 69 Webber Pl Grosse Pointe Shores MI 48236 Office: 20166 Mack Ave Grosse Pointe MI 48236

COLEMAN, THOMAS JAMES, physician, educator; b. Wichita, Kans., June 3, 1918; s. Thomas James and Marguerite (Crummey) C.; student Kans. State U., 1940-41, U. Va, 1946-47; M.D., U. Rochester, 1951; m. Amy Desmond Jones, Aug. 27, 1949; children—Thomas James, Pamela Jane, Patricia Lynn, Richard Cahill, Martha Sue, Robert Bruce. Intern, U. Kans. Med. Center, 1951-52, resident, 1952-55; practice medicine specializing in internal medicine; mem. staffs St. Francis Hosp., Wesley Med. Center, St. Joseph Hosp. and Rehab. Center; clin. asst. prof. medicine Wichita State U. br. U. Kans. Sch. Medicine, 1977—; NIH fellow in endocrinology U. Kans., 1954-55. Served to capt. USAAF, 1942-46. Decorated D.F.C., Air medal with oak leaf cluster. Diplomate Am. Bd. Internal Medicine, Nat. Bd. Med. Examiners. Mem. A.C.P., Am. Coll. Cardiology, AMA, Am. Heart Assn., Kans. Heart Assn. (pres. 1974-75). Republican. Club: Wichita State University. Home: 155 N Crestway Wichita KS 67208 Office: 959 N Emporia St Wichita KS 67214

COLL, DENNIS RAYMOND, real estate investment company executive; b. Pitts., Aug. 18, 1943; s. Edward G. and Alice V. (Ebeling) C.; B.S., U.S. Mil. Acad., 1965; M.B.A., U. Chgo., 1973; m. Judith L. Buchanan, June 4, 1966; children—Brian, Shannon, Gavin, Brandon. Sales positions IBM, Chgo., 1969-72, account mgr., 1972-73; pres. Arlington Fin. Services, Arlington Heights, Ill., 1974-75; pres. Murdoch & Coll, St. Louis and Chgo., 1975—; gen. ptnr. Neuberger & Berman, N.Y.C., 1983—. Mem. Assn. Grads. admission com., trustee U.S. Mil. Acad., 1970-84; v.p. South Loop Planning Bd. Served to capt. U.S. Army, 1965-69. Decorated Bronze Star Valor. Registered real estate broker, prin., registered securities dealer, prin., registered ins. broker. Mem. West Point Soc. Chgo. (pres. 1978-81), other orgns. Republican. Roman Catholic. Office: 343 S Dearborn Suite 1700 Chicago IL 60604

COLLEN, SHELDON ORRIN, lawyer; b. Chgo., Feb. 7, 1922; s. Jacob Allen and Ann (Andalman) C.; B.A. cum laude, Carleton Coll., 1944; J.D., U. Chgo., 1948; m. Ann Blager, Apr. 8, 1946; 1 son, John O. Admitted to Ill. bar, 1949, Minn. bar, 1976, U.S. SUpreme Ct., 1965; practiced in Chgo., 1949—; assoc. Adcock, Fink & Day, 1948-51; mem. Simon & Collen, 1952-57, Friedman & Koven, 1958—; specialist fed. antitrust litigation; sec. Jupiter Industries, Inc., Chgo., 1961—. Mem. bd. edn. U. Chgo. Law Rev., 1948-49. Bd. dirs. Lower Northcenter, Chgo. Youth Centers, Union League Found. for Boys, Contemporary Arts Workshop, Edward P. Martin Soc., Center for Study of Multiple Births; sec., bd. dirs. 3750 Lake Shore Dr., Inc.; pres. Union League Civic and Arts Found. Served with AUS, 1943-46. Fellow Norwegian Am. Mus., Decorah, Iowa. Mem. Am., Chgo. (antitrust law and securities law coms., chmn. antitrust 1976-77), Ill. (council corp. and securities law sect.) bar assns., Bar Assn. 7th Circuit, Am. Judicature Soc., Art Inst. Chgo., Mus. Contemporary Art, Chgo. Council Fgn. Relations. Clubs: Union League (Chgo); Lafayette (Minnetonka Beach, Minn.). Mem. adv. bd. Antitrust Bull. and Jour. Reprints for Antitrust Law and Econs. Home: 3750 Lake Shore Dr Chicago IL 60613 also Meadville Rd Excelsior MN Office: 208 S LaSalle St Chicago IL 60604

COLLER, GARY HAYES, osteopathic physician; b. Detroit, June 5, 1952; s. Eldon Hayes and Shirley Elaine (Makima) C.; m. Mary Elaine Irrer, Oct. 15, 1977; children—Christopher, Michael, Kimberly. B.S. with honors, Mich. State U., 1974, D.O., 1978. Diplomate Nat. Bd. Examiners for Osteopathic Medicine. Gen. practice osteopathic medicine, Montague, Mich., 1979—; mem. staff Muskegon (Mich.) Gen. Hosp.; trainee in preventative medicine Farmington (Mich.) Med. Center. Mem. Nat. Republican Com., 1975-83. Mem. Am. Osteo. Assn., W. Mich. Osteo. Assn., Mich. Osteo. Assn., Am. Acad. Med. Preventics, Internat. Acad. Preventive Medicine, Northwest Acad. Preventive Medicine, N.Y. Acad. Scis., Christian Med. Soc., Nat. Health Service Corp., U.S. C. of C. Contbr. articles on osteopathy to profl. jours. Home: 1424 Waukazoo Holland MI 49423 Office: 9883 US 31 N Montague MI 49437 also 720 E 8th St Holland MI 49423

COLLER, RANDY L., airport administrator; b. Jackson, Mich., Jan. 8, 1951; s. William Robert and Burnadine I. (Murfin) C.; 1 child, Jay Donovan. Student, Jackson Community Coll., 1970—. Cert. airport exec., Mich. Light equipment operator Jackson County Airport, Mich., 1968, utility mgr., 1969, airport serviceman, 1970-73, asst. airport mgr., 1973-76, airport mgr., 1976—. Bd. dirs. Jackson County; mem. Jackson Area Comprehensive Transp. Com., 1976—, Hot Air Jubilee Com.; bd. dirs. Jackson Leadership Acad., 1984. Named Adv. Yr., Explorer Program, Boy Scouts Am., 1979. Mem. Mich. Assn. Airport Execs. (pres. 1979-80, program mgr. runway crack sealing program; named Airport Mgr. Yr., 1978), Airport Operators Council Internat., Am. Assn. Airport Executives. Lodge: Moose. Avocations: big band and contemporary music. Home: 711 Oakhill St Jackson MI 49201 Office: Jackson County Airport-Reynolds Field 3606 Wildwood Ave Jackson MI 49202

COLLETT, JOAN, librarian; b. St. Louis; d. Robert and Mary (Hoolan) C.; m. John Edgar Dustin, Nov. 19, 1983. B.A. magna cum laude, Maryville Coll., 1947; M.A., Washington U., St. Louis, 1950; M.S. in L.S., U. Ill., Urbana, 1954. Regional cons. W.Va. Library Commn., Spencer, W.Va., 1954-56; instr. Rosary Coll., River Forest, Ill., 1956-57; head extension dept. Gary (Ind.) Public Library, 1957-64; librarian Grailville Library, 1965; regional librarian USIA, Latin Am., Africa, 1966-78; exec. dir. librarian St. Louis Public Library, 1978—. Mem. ALA. Office: 1301 Olive St Saint Louis MO 63103

COLLETT, JOHN E., physician; b. Ottumwa, Iowa, Nov. 6, 1949; s. Ralph E. and Lou C.; m. Terry Brown, June 1, 1979; children—Jason, Brandon. B.S.E., N.E. Mo. State U.-Kirksville, 1972, B.S., 1974; D.O., Kirksville Coll. Osteo. Medicine, 1978. Intern, Muskegon Gen. Hosp., 1978-79; practice otsteo. medicine, Whitehall, Mich., 1979—, Muskegon, 1980—; mem. staff Muskegon Gen. Hosp., chmn. dept. gen. practice, 1982-84; mem. exec. com., 1981-84; physician, corp. bus. mgr. Northside Family Medstop, P.C., North Muskegon, 1982—. Mem. Am. Osteo. Assn., Western Mich. Osteo. Assn., Whitehall C. of C. Republican. Home: 1314 Moulton Ave North Muskegon MI 49445 Office: 123 W Colby St Whitehall MI 49461

COLLEY, LYNN ALLAN, insurance agent; b. Sanford, Maine, Oct. 31, 1945; s. Leonard V. and Phyllis A. (Treadwell) C.; student S.E. Mo. U., 1963-67; m. Saundra L. Cumpton Brunke, Dec. 14, 1974; 1 dau., Brooke Anne. Owner, Sikeston (Mo.) Coin & Stamp Co., 1965-68; agt. Met. Life Ins. Co., Sikeston, 1968—; owner C & C Stationery Supply, Sikeston, 1968—, Statewide Pest Control, Sikeston, 1979-81. Chmn., Scott County Rep. Com., 1968-74, vice chmn., 1966-68; treas. bd. dirs. Sikeston Activity Center, 1975-81; mem. Channey-Harris Meml. Com., Sikeston, 1978-80; chmn. adv. bd. Chaney-Harris Cultural Ctr., 1980—. Recipient Am. Legion History award, 1962; Dr. Tom L. Chidester award Sikeston Little Theatre, 1965; Nat. Assn. Life Underwriters Nat. Quality award, 1974, 78, 79, 80, 81, 82, 83, 84, Nat. Health Quality award, 1976, Nat. Sales Achievement award, 1976. Mem. Sikeston Assn. Life Underwriters (sec.-treas. 1975—), Mo. Assn. Life Underwriters, Nat. Assn. Life Underwriters, Sikeston Little Theatre (pres. 1967—), Mo. Arts Council (adv. com. 1981—), Sikeston Arts and Edn. Council (treas. 1975—), St. Louis Symphony in Sikeston Com. (treas. 1976—). Jehovah's Witness. Home: 916 Alexander St Sikeston MO 63801 Office: PO Box 74 Sikeston MO 63801

COLLICOTT, PAUL EDWARD, physician; b. Lexington, Nebr., Apr. 21, 1941; s. Kenneth Paul and Ailene Frances (Alberti) C.; m. Karen Joyce Juker, Aug. 17, 1962; children—Wendy J., Michelle A., Nancy L., Jill S. B.S., U. Nebr., 1963, M.D., U. Nebr.-Omaha, 1966. Diplomate Am. Bd. Surgery. Intern Lincoln Gen. Hosp., Nebr., 1966-67; resident U. Wash., Seattle, 1969-73; mem. staff Lincoln Gen. Hosp., Nebr., 1973—, chief trauma service, 1981-83, chief surgery, 1984—; mem. staff Bryan Meml. Hosp., Lincoln, 1973—, Seward Meml. Hosp., Seward, Nebr., 1981—; clin. instr. Surgery U. Nebr.-Omaha, 1981—; cons. VA, Lincoln, U. Nebr. Student Health Ctr., Lincoln Regional Ctr. Contbr. articles to profl. jours. Served to capt. USAF, 1967-69. Recipient Trauma Achievement award ACS, 1982. Mem. AMA, Nebr. Med. Assn., Nat. Bd. Med. Examiners, Nebr. Bd. Examiners in Medicine and Surgery, Lancaster County Med. Soc. (pres. 1985—), Soc. Clin. Vascular Surgery, ACS, Internat. Cardiovascular Soc., Fed. State Med. Bds., Midwestern Vascular Surgical Soc., Central Surg. Assn., Western Surg. Assn., Am. Assn. for Surgery of Trauma, Theta Nu, Kappa Sigma. Home: Route 1 PO Box 71A Walton NE 68461 Office: 4740 A St Lincoln NE 68510

COLLIE, JOHN, JR., insurance agent; b. Gary, Ind., Apr. 23, 1934; s. John and Christina Dempster (Wardrop) C.; student Purdue U., 1953; A.B. in Econs., Ind. U., 1957; m. Jessie Fearn Shaw, Aug. 1, 1964; children—Cynthia Elizabeth, Douglas Allan Hamilton, Jennifer Fearn. Operator, Collie Optical Lab., Gary, 1957-62; owner, operator Collie Ins. Agy., Merrillville, Ind., 1962—; pres. Collie Realty and Investment; lectr. High Frontier. Lt. col. U.S. Army Res., 1957—; instr. Command and Gen. Staff Coll., 1973-77. Mem. Profl. Ins. Agts. Assn. Ind. (dir.), Internat. Platform Assn., Mil. Order World Wars, Res. Officers Assn. (sec., v.p. Ind. chpt., pres. N.W. Ind.), Izaak Walton League, Lake-Porter Leadership Council, Phi Kappa Psi. Republican. Presbyterian. Clubs: Masons (32 deg.), Shriners, Elks. Home: 717 W 66th Pl Merrillville IN 46410 Office: 5600 Broadway PO Box 8049 Merrillville IN 46410

COLLIER, B. BRUCE, jewel co. exec.; b. Mumford, Tex., Apr. 3, 1928; s. Hosea Oscar and Percy Virginia (Moore) C.; B.S., Baylor U., 1948; postgrad., Ohio State U., 1948-49, Purdue U., 1949-50; m. Mary Carollene Gardner, Sept. 9, 1949; children—Suzanne, Rachel, Bryan, Holly. Partner, Gardner-Collier Jewelry Co., Kirksville, Mo., 1950-66; pres. Gardner-Collier Inc., Kirksville, 1966—; pres., chmn. bd. Kirksville Savs. & Loan Assn., 1970—. Pres., Adair County Credit Bur., 1960; fund raising chmn. group to bring industries to Kirksville, 1960-72. Named outstanding young man Kirksville Jaycees, 1957. Mem. Kirksville C. of C. (pres. 1957), Retail Jewelers Am., Mo. Jewelers Assn. Republican. Baptist. Clubs: Kirksville Country, Masons, Shriners. Home: 1302 E Patterson St Kirksville MO 63501 Office: 111 W Washington St Kirksville MO 63501

COLLIER, NATHAN MORRIS, musician, music educator; b. Clinton, Okla., July 23, 1924; s. Lotan Morris and Annie Carletta (Willsey) C.; m. Frances Aleta Snell, June 24, 1955; children—Susan Aleta Kowalski, Ray Morris. Mus.B., U. Okla., 1949; Mus.M., Eastman Sch. Music, U. Rochester, 1951. String music cons. Lincoln (Nebr.) Pub. Schs., 1951-68; asst. concertmaster Lincoln Symphony Orch., 1953—; assoc. concertmaster Omaha (Nebr.) Symphony, 1977-78, first violin, 1956-79; first violinist Lincoln String Quartet, 1951—; concertmaster Lincoln Symphony, Lincoln Little Symphony, 1977-78; asst. prof. violin and theory Nebr. Weslyan U., Lincoln, 1968-84; now string tchr. St. John Luth. Sch., Seward, Nebr., vis. instr. music Concordia Tchrs. Coll., Seward; asst. concertmaster Nebr. Chamber Orch., 1973—, acting concertmaster on occasion; asst. prof. music Kans. State U., Manhattan, 1980-81, condr. symphony orch., 1980-81; pvt. tchr. and ensemble coach, Lincoln, 1951—; cons., lectr. in field. Tchr. co-organizer Brownville (Nebr.) Summer Music Festival, 1977-77. Served with USN, 1943-46. U.S. Govt. grantee 1966-67. Mem. Am. String Tchrs. Assn., Music Tchrs. Nat. Assn., Music Educators Nat. Conf., Violin Soc. Am., Lincoln Music Tchrs. Assn., Nat. Sch. Orch. Assn., NEA, Nebr. State Edn. Assn., Lincoln Musicians Assn., Omaha Musicians Assn., Internat. Soc. of Bassists. Democrat. Methodist. Composer various musical pieces. Home: 4544 Mohawk Lincoln NE 68510

COLLIER, ROBERT GEORGE, educator; b. Stockton, Calif., Aug. 23, 1944; s. Laurence Donald and Dorothy Louise (Braghetta) C.; A.A., San Joaquin Delta Coll., 1965; B.A. in Psychology, U. Calif., Riverside, 1967; M.A. in Elem. Edn., Calif. State U., Los Angeles, 1973; Ph.D. in Edn., Claremont Grad. Sch., 1978; m. Sandra LaVaughn Haller, July 22, 1972; children—Steven Edward, Brian James. Asst. football coach U. Calif., Riverside, 1967-68, instr. univ. extension, 1979; elem. tchr. Riverside Unified Sch. Dist., 1968-74, 75-79; research asst. Claremont Grad. Sch., 1974-75; tchr. Lovett's Presch., Riverside, summer 1979; assoc. prof. early childhood edn. Western Ill. U., 1979—; mem. rev. com. Erikson Inst., Chgo.; mem. McDonough County Council Child Devel.; mem. governing bd. Wee Care Center, Macomb, Ill. Served with USAR, 1968-74. Recipient Peter L. Spencer award Phi Delta Kappa at Claremont Grad. Sch., 1978; Western Ill. U. Faculty Devel. Office mini grantee, 1980; Western Ill. U. Research Council grantee, 1981; cert. elem. tchr., Calif. Mem. Assn. Childhood Edn. Internat., Assn. Supervision and Curriculum Devel., Assn. Anthropol. Study Play, Council Exceptional Children, Nat. Assn. Edn. Young Children, Phi Delta Kappa (v.p.-elect. Western Ill. U. chpt. 1981-82). Home: 30 Briarwood Pl Macomb IL 61455 Office: Elem Edn Dept Western Ill U Macomb IL 61455

COLLIER, STEVEN PAUL, lawyer; b. Deshler, Ohio, Oct. 4, 1955; s. John Paul and Mary Virginia (Tawney) C.; m. Annette Kay Panning, June 23, 1979. B.A. in Econs. and Polit. Sci. cum laude, Wittenberg U., 1977; J.D., U. Cin., 1981. Bar: Ohio 1981, U.S. Dist. Ct. (no. dist.) Ohio 1982, U.S. Ct. Appeals (6th cir.) 1984. Intern U.S. Senate Budget Com., Washington, 1976; program analyst Ohio Legis. Budget Office, Columbus, 1977-78; law clk. U.S. Atty.'s Office, Dept. Justice, Cin., 1979-80; assoc. Connelly, Soutar & Jackson, Toledo, 1981—. Mem. Toledo Bar Assn., ABA, Assn. Trial Lawyers Am. Republican. Lutheran. Office: Connelly Soutar & Jackson 2100 Ohio Citizens Bank Bldg Toledo OH 43604

COLLIER, WILLIAM JEWELL, physician; b. Albany, Mo., Apr. 25, 1925; s. Ora and Mabel (Adkisson) C.; B.S., Tulane U., 1947; M.D., Bowman Gray Sch. Medicine, Wake Forest U., 1949; m. Mary Evelyn Fisher, Mar. 29, 1952; children—William Jewell II, Sherry Lynn, Terri Lee, Linda Lorraine. Intern, U.S. Naval Hosp., Great Lakes, Ill., 1949-50; resident internal medicine VA Hosp., Wadsworth, Kans., 1950-51, resident gen. surgery, 1951-52, 54-57; asst. chief surgery VA Hosp., Wichita, Kans., 1957-58; pvt. practice gen. and thoracic surgery, McPherson, Kans., 1958—. Dir. Home State Bank & Trust. Former mem. aviation adv. bd. McPherson City-County Airport. Served from lt. (j.g.) to lt. M.C., USNR, 1952-54. Diplomate Am. Bd. Surgery. Fellow Southwestern Surg. Congress, ACS, Internat. Coll. Surgeons; mem. C. of C. Mem. Christian Ch. Rotarian. Home: 302 S Walnut St McPherson KS 67460 Office: 400 W 4th St McPherson KS 67460

COLLINGS, RICHARD JAMES, political science educator; b. Owensboro, Kent., Nov. 11, 1946; s. Milton H. and Jean Helen (Ladmore) C.; m. Marilyn Jane Linville, Nov. 24, 1967; children—Kelly Jean, Michael James, Kirsten Jane. A.B. in Internatl. Studies, U. Louisville, 1968; M.A. in Latin Am. Studies, Tulane U., 1972, Ph.D. in Polit. Sci., 1977. Instr. Southeast Mo. State U., Cape Girardeau, 1977, chmn. dept., 1979—. Chmn. bd. Southeast Mo. Wesley Found., Cape Girardeau, 1980—. Served with U.S. Army, 1969-71. NSF trainee Tulane U., 1973. Mem. Mo. Polit. Sci. Assn. (sec.-treas. 1980—), Am. Polit. Sci. Assn., Latin Am. Studies Assn., Southeastern Council Latin Am. Studies, So. Polit. Sci. Assn. Phi Kappa Phi, Pi Sigma Alpha, Woodcock Soc. Home: 1052 Patricia St Cape Girardeau MO 63701 Office: Polit Sci Dept Southeast Mo State Univ Cape Girardeau MO 63701

COLLINS, BEATRICE (SMITH), health care facility administrator; b. Jackson, Miss., Aug. 8, 1925; d. Charles and Susie Belle (Barlow) Smith; m. John Otis Collins, June 17, 1945; 1 son, Alfred Tyrone. B.A., Roosevelt U., 1964; student in nursing home adminstrn. Purdue U.-Calumet, 1973. Substitute tchr. Sch. City of Gary (Ind.), 1961-63; supr. children and family services Lake County Dept. Pub. Welfare, Gary, 1968-73; exec. adminstr. East Chicago Rehab. Ctr. (Ind.), 1978-84, Mother Beulah Health Care Facility Ind., 1984—. Dean Christian Edn., Ind. 1st jurisdiction Ch. of God in Christ, 1973—, adminstrv. asst. to state supr., 1979—, sec. women's dept. Ind., 1963—, dist. missionary, 1978—. Alpha Kappa Alpha scholar, 1957. Mem. Ind. Health Care Assn., Ind. Nursing Home Adminstrs. Assn., Am. Pub. Welfare Assn. Home: 2241 Jennings St Gary IN 46404 Office: 2350 Taft St Gary IN 46404

COLLINS, BRIAN CLAY, interior designer; b. Ann Arbor, Mich., Mar. 24, 1950; s. Max Carven and Jeannette Edith (Clay) C. B.A., Mich. State U., 1972. Interior designer J.L. Hudson Co., Detroit, 1972—. Mem. Am. Soc. Interior Designers (sec. Mich. chpt. 1979-80, pres. 1981-82, nat. bd. dirs. 1984-85). Club: Designers Lighting Forum (bd. dirs. 1984). Home: 494 Saint Clair Grosse Pointe MI 48230 Office: JL Hudson Co Interior Design Studio 21500 Northwestern Hwy Southfield MI 48075

COLLINS, CARDISS, congresswoman; b. St. Louis, Sept. 24, 1931; ed. Northwestern U.; m. George W. Collins (dec.); 1 son, Kevin. Stenographer, Ill. Dept. Labor; sec. Ill. Dept. Revenue, then accountant, revenue auditor; mem. 93d-99th Congresses from 7th Ill. Dist., mem. Govt. Ops. com., Energy and Commerce com.; chmn. Manpower and Housing com., former majority whip-at-large; past chmn. Congressional Black Caucus; former chmn. Mems. of Congress for Peace through Law. Bd. dirs. Greater Lawndale Conservation Commn., Chgo. Mem. NAACP, Nat. Council Negro Women, Chgo. Urban League, Alpha Kappa Alpha. Baptist. Democrat. Office: 2264 Rayburn House Office Bldg Washington DC 20515*

COLLINS, CARY JAMES, lawyer, consultant; b. Gary, Ind., Oct. 23, 1947; s. Richard John and Elizabeth (Cogswell) C.; m. Theresa Susan O'Drobniak, June 25, 1977. B.S. in Bus. Adminstrn., Ind. U., 1970; J.D., John Marshall Law Sch. Bars: Ill. 1979, U.S. Dist. Ct. (no. dist.) Ill. 1979, Regional credit mgr. Florsheim Shoe Co., Chgo., 1972-75; supr. student loans U. Ill., Chgo., 1975-79; ptnr. Hill, Van Santen, Steadman & Simpson, Chgo., 1979-84; equity ptnr. Kane, Worrell & Collins, Chgo., 1984—; chmn. subcom. intellectual property Internat. Bus. Council Midwest, Chgo., 1984—. Editor: Chicago Lawyer's Court Handbook, 1984. Chmn. Young Republicans of Gary, 1968; mem. Police and Fire Commn., Hoffman Estates, Ill., 1984—. Mem. Am. Trial Lawyers Assn., Defense Research Inst., ABA (vice chmn. product liability, torts and ins. sect. 1983-84), Chgo. Bar Assn. (dir. young lawyers sect. 1983—), Chgo. Vol. Legal Services, Phi Delta Phi. Roman Catholic. Office: Kane Worrell & Collins 20 S Wacker Dr Suite 3850 Chicago IL 60606

COLLINS, DAN WHITLEY, dentist; b. Ishpeming, Mich., July 21, 1947; s. George Theodore and Helen Maria (Jensen) C.; m. Fae Emilie Holman, Mar. 5, 1968; children—Kaet Holman, Anne Helen, Jill Lillian, Ben, Daniel, Seth. B.S., No. Mich. U., Marquette, 1969; D.D.S., U. Mich., 1976. Tchr., Flint Community Schs. (Mich.), 1969-70; Mott Found. trainee Mott program, Flint, 1969-70; community sch. dir. White Pine Pub. Sch., Mich., 1970-71, White Pine-Ewen-Trout Creek Schs., 1971-72; gen. practice dentistry, Negaunee, Mich., 1976—. Mem. Marquette County United Way Bd., 1977-81; mem. Negaunee Male Chorus, 1980-82; mem. steering com. Negaunee Citizens for a New High Sch., 1984. Grantee No. Mich. U., U. Mich., 1965-69, 72-76. Mem. Am. Dental Assn., Mich. Dental Assn., Am. Assn. Dentistry for Children, Mich. Assn. Dentistry for Handicapped, Omicron Kappa Upsilon. Lutheran. Avocations: Hunting, fishing, Nordic skiing, bldg. constrn., gardening. Office: 100 Croix Negaunee MI 49866

COLLINS, DANIEL VARNUM, educator; b. Barnesville, Ohio, Aug. 18, 1934; s. Robert Lansing and Madge Madeline (McElfresh) C.; m. Lee Joanne Marcus, Jan. 26, 1956; children—Rebecca Lee, Russell Grant, Benjamin Varnum Clifford. B.A., Coll. Wooster, 1956; M.Div., Pitts. Theol. Sem., 1959; M.A., Mich. State U., 1969, Ph.D., 1976. Instr. O.T., Pitts. Sem., 1959-61; religious educator, Bridgeville, Pa., 1960-61, Sturgis, Mich., 1961-65, Spruce, Mich., 1965-68; instr. to asst. prof. Mich. State U., 1970-72; prof. philosophy of edn. Richmond/Coll. Staten Island, CUNY, 1972-79; asst. prof. philosophy edn. Central Coll., Pella, Iowa, 1979-83; vis. prof. edn. and psychology Dickinson State Coll. (N.D.), 1983-84; vis. team mem. Nat. Council Accreditation Tchr. Edn., 1982, 84. Del., Marion County Democratic Conv., 1980-82, 5th Congl. Dist. Dem. Conv., 1982. Mich. State U. Grad. Council fellow, 1970. Mem. Am. Ednl. Studies Assn. (com. on ednl. studies in liberal arts colls. 1981-83, Iowa rep. to com. on acad. standards and accreditation 1982-83), Am. Assn. Childhood (bd. dirs. 1981—, editorial bd. Childhood 1982—), Assn. for Character, Assn. Supervision and Curriculum Devel., Council on Religion Studies in Iowa Schs., History Edn. Soc., Nat. Council Religion and Pub. Edn., John Dewey Soc., Soc. Profs. Edn., Unicorn Soc., Ltd., N.Y. State Founds. Edn. Assn. (bd. dirs. 1976-79, pres. 1978-79, editorial bd. Foundational Studies 1980-82), Iowa Assn. Coll. Tchrs. Edn., Phi Delta Kappa, Phi Kappa Phi. Democrat. Presbyterian. Home: 1412 W 1st St Pella IA 50219

COLLINS, DAVID RAYMOND, educator, author, lecturer; b. Marshalltown, Iowa, Feb. 29, 1940; s. Raymond Amby and Mary Elizabeth (Brecht) C.; B.S., Western Ill. U., 1962, M.S., 1966. Instr. English, Woodrow Wilson Jr. High Sch., 1962-83, Moline (Ill.) Sr. High Sch., 1983—; founder, dir. Miss. Valley Writers Conf., 1973—, Children's Lit. Festival, 1979—; Sec., Quad Cities Arts Council, 1971-75; pres. Friends of Moline Pub. Library, 1965-66. Recipient writing award Writer's Digest, 1967, writer of the year award Writers' Studio, 1971, award Bobbs-Merrill Pub. Co., 1971, writer of the year award Quad-Cities Writers Club, 1972, writing awards Judson Coll., 1971. Mem. Nat., Ill., Moline (dir. 1964-67) edn. assns., Ill. PTA (life; Outstanding Ill. Educator award 1975), Ill. Hist. Soc., Black Hawk Div. Tchrs. English (pres. 1967-68), Writers Studio (pres. 1967-71), Children's Reading Roundtable, Authors Guild, Soc. Children's Book Writers, Juvenile Forum, Quad-Cities Writers Club (pres. 1973-75, 77-78), Am. Amateur Press Assn., Western Ill. U. Alumni (dir. 1968-74, Outstanding Achievement award 1973), Kappa Delta Pi, Sigma Tau Delta, Alpha Delta, Delta Sigma Phi. Democrat. Roman Catholic. Author: Kim Soo and His Tortoise, 1970; Great American Nurses, 1971; Walt Disney's Surprise Christmas Present, 1972; Linda Richards, America's First Trained Nurse, 1973; Harry S. Truman, People's President, 1975; Football Running Backs, 1975; I, Abraham Lincoln, 1976; Illinois Women: Born to Serve, 1976; Joshua Poole Hated School, 1977; Charles Lindbergh, Hero Pilot, 1978; A Spirit of Giving, 1978; If I Could, I Would, 1979; Joshua Poole and Sunrise, 1979; The Wonderful Story of Jesus, 1980; A Special Guest, 1980; The Only Thing Wrong with Birthdays, 1980; George Washington Carver, 1981; George Meany, Mr. Labor, 1981; Dorothy Day, Catholic Worker, 1982; Thomas Merton, Monk with a Mission, 1982; Super Champ! The Story of Babe Didrick son Zaharias, 1982; Notable Illinois Women, 1982; Francis Scott Key, 1982; Joshua Poole and the Special Flowers, 1982; The Golden Circle, 1983, Florence Nightingale, 1984, John Chapman, 1984, Jane Addams, 1985, Clara Barton, 1985. Home: 3403 45th St Moline IL 61265 Office: 3600 23d Ave Moline IL 61265

COLLINS, DON CARY, lawyer; b. Christopher, Ill., Sept. 10, 1951; s. Everett Hugh, Jr. and Evelyn Loriene (Wootton) C.; student Western Ky. U., 1969-70; B.A., Ill. State U., Normal, 1972; J.D., So. Ill. U., 1976. Bar: Ill. 1976, Mo. 1977, U.S. Supreme Ct. bar, U.S. Ct. Appeals (7th cir.), U.S. Dist. Ct. (so. dist.) Ill. Public relations/media chmn. S.W. Ill. Regional Spl. Olympics, 1979. Mem. Am., Ill., Mo., St. Clair County, East St. Louis, Met. St. Louis bar assns., Am. Trial Lawyers Assn., Ill. Trial Lawyers Assn., Am. Judicature Soc., So. Ill. U. Sch. Law Alumni Assn. (bd. dirs. 1984—). Home: 920 E B St Belleville IL 62221 Office: 126 W Main St Belleville IL 62220

COLLINS, DOROTHY LANHAM, interior designer; b. Chgo., Sept. 26, 1926; d. Cecil Ray and Elizabeth (Billow) Lanham; children—Judith Collins Hunerberg, Tom, John, Patricia Collins Gruggen, Susan. Founder, pres. Dorothy Collins Interiors, Inc., Edina, Minn., 1950—; owner Dorothy Collins Retail Design Studio, Edina, 1968—. Fellow Nat. Home Fashion League (v.p., pres.); mem. Fashion Group. Republican. Club: Calhoun Beach. Home: 6432 Red Fox Ct Edina MN 55436 Office: Dorothy Collins Interiors Inc 7010 France Ave S Edina MN 55435

COLLINS, JOYCE PLOEG, home health agency administrator, consultant; b. Grand Rapids, Mich., July 3, 1930. R.N., Blodgett Hosp., 1951; postgrad. Calvin Coll., 1952, Grand Rapids Rapids Jr. Coll. Adminstr. Med. Personnel Pool, Grand Rapids, 1972-84, v.p., 1985—; ptnr. Alpha Investments, Grand Rapids, 1983—; v.p. Comprehensive Home Services, Grand Rapids, 1985—; bd. dirs. Western Mich. Health Systems, Grand Rapids, 1977—, health expo steering com., 1982-84. Mem. Grand Rapids Dist. Nurses (pres. 1978-82, Service award 1982), Mich. Nurses Assn. (bd. dirs. 1981—), Am. Nurses Assn. Republican. Avocation: reading. Office: Med Personnel Pool Loraine Bldg Suite 200 124 E Fulton Grand Rapids MI 49503

COLLINS, MARY ALICE, psychiatric social worker; b. Everett, Wash., Apr. 20, 1937; d. Harry Edward and Mary (Yates) Caton; B.A. in Sociology, Seattle Pacific Coll., 1959; M.S.W., U. Mich., 1966; Ph.D., Mich. State U., 1974; m. Gerald C. Brocker, Mar. 24, 1980. Dir. teenage, adult and counseling depts. YWCA, Flint, Mich., 1959-64, 66-68; social worker Catholic Social Services, Flint, 1969-71, Ingham Med. Mental Health Center, Lansing, Mich., 1971-73; clin. social worker Genesee Psychiat. Center, Flint, 1974-82, Psychol. Evaluation and Treatment Ctr., East Lansing, Mich., 1982-84; pvt. practice, East Lansing, 1984—; instr. social work Lansing Community Coll. and Mich. State U., 1974; vis. prof. Hurley Med. Center, 1979-84; cons. Ingham County Dept. Social Services, 1971-73. Advisor human relations Youth League, Flint Council Chs., 1964-65; sec. Genesee County Young Democrats, 1960-61, pres. Round Lake Improvement Assn., 1984—. Mem. Nat. Assn. Social Workers, Acad. Cert. Social Workers, Registry Clin. Social Workers, Registry Health Care Workers, Phi Kappa Phi, Alpha Kappa Sigma. Contbr. articles to profl. jours. Home: 5945 Round Lake Rd Laingsburg MI 48848 Office 1451 E Lansing Dr Suite 213 B East Lansing MI 48823

COLLINS, MATTHEW JAMES, illustrator, art director; b. Columbus, Ohio, Dec. 21, 1956; s. James William and Lillian Ruth (Overmyer) C. B.F.A., Washington U., 1979. Illustrator, D'Arcy, MacManus & Masius, St. Louis, 1979-81, art dir., 1981—; illustrator Metro Mag., St. Louis, 1979-81, St. Louis Mirror, 1981-82. Recipient Best of Show, St. Louis Flair awards, 1982, Addy award for best 30-second TV comml., 1984; Conway fellow, 1975. Home: 6252 Southwood Apt A1 St Louis MO 63105 Office: D'arcy MacManus & Masius 1 Memorial Dr St Louis MO 63102

COLLINS, MOIRA ANN, graphics and communications company executive, calligrapher; b. Washington, Dec. 16, 1942; d. Peter William and Louise (Carroll) Collins; m. Andrew Joseph Griffin, Aug. 21, 1965; children—Andrew Fitzgerald, Timothy. B.A., U. Toronto (Ont., Can.), 1964; M.A. in Teaching, Northwestern U., 1965; M.Ed. in Urban Studies, Northeastern U., Chgo., 1968. Tchr., Chgo. Bd. Edn., 1965-68; apprentice to profl. calligraphers, scribes and illuminators, U.S. and Eng., 1971-75; freelance calligrapher, 1974-78; mem. publicity and promotional staff Swallow Press, Chgo., 1978-79; owner Letters, Chgo., 1979—. HEW fellow Northeastern U., 1967-68. Author, contbr.; Celebration: Anais Nin, 1975; contbr. to Goodfellow Rev. of Crafts, 1979. Calligrapher: Erotica, 1976, Chgo. Rev., 1978. Chmn. fund-raising Van Gorder Walden Sch., Chgo., 1979-80. Mem. Chgo. Calligraphy Collective (co-founder, chmn. 1976-77, pres. 1978-79, hon. mem.), Soc. Scribes N.Y., Soc. Calligraphers, Soc. Scribes and Illuminators (Eng.), Friends Calligraphy Calif. Democrat. Roman Catholic. Home: 834 W Chalmers Pl Chicago IL 60614 Office: 429 W Ohio St Chicago IL 60610

COLLINS, WILLIAM JAMES, manufacturing company executive; b. Grand Rapids, Mich., Dec. 1, 1915; s. Frank C. and Aileen (Cary) C.; B.S., U. Mich., 1939; m. Margery Aileen McDevitt, Nov. 23, 1942; children—Margaret Totin, William Jeffrey, C. Casey. With Batesco, Inc., Gary, Ind., 1964—, pres., sales mgr., 1981—; pres., sales mgr. Melt Specialties Co., Gary, 1976-81. Served with AC, U.S. Army, 1942-45, USAF, 51-52. Mem. AIME, Am. Foundrymen's Soc., U. Mich. Alumni Assn., Am. Legion, 8th AF Hist. Soc., 486th Bomb Group Assn. Club: Lions. Patentee in field. Home: 7005 Madison St Merrillville IN 46411 Office: PO Box 10562 Gary IN 46410

COLLINSON, JOHN THEODORE, railroad company executive; b. Pitts., 1926. B.S., Cornell U., 1946. Engr., Dravo Corp., 1946; with Balt. and Ohio R.R. Co., 1946—, asst. gen. mgr. staff, 1966-71, gen. mgr., chief engr., 1971-73, v.p. ops. and maintenance, 1973-76, exec. v.p., 1976-78, pres., 1978—; pres., chief exec. officer, dir. Chesapeake & Ohio Ry., Cleve.; pres., dir. Western Md. Ry. Co.; dir. Nat. Mine Service Co., Nat. City Bank of Cleve., Monumental Corp., Richmond, Fredericksburg & Potomac R.R. Co., Chgo. South Shore and South Bend R.R. Served with USN, 1944-46. Office: Chesapeake and Ohio Ry Co Inc Terminal Tower PO Box 6419 Cleveland OH 44101*

COLLINWOOD, DEAN WALTER, sociology educator; b. Altadena, Calif., Oct. 30, 1949; s. George R. and Sarah (Palmer) C.; m. Linda Gae Robison, Apr. 21, 1973; children—Jana Gae, Benjamin Stuart, Stacy Lynn, Jodi Ann. B.A., Brigham Young U., 1973; M.Sc., U. London, 1974; Ph.D., U. Chgo., 1979. Lectr. sociology Coll. of Bahamas and U. of the West Indies, Nassau, 1977-79; asst. prof., chmn. dept. sociology MacMurray Coll., Jacksonville, Ill., 1980—. NEH fellow Ctr. African and Afro-Am. Studies, Atlanta U., 1984; Fulbright lectr., Japan, 1986-87. Author: Modern Bahamian Society, 1985. Contbr. articles to profl. jours. Mem. Am. Acad. Polit. and Social Sci., Ill. Sociol. Assn., Midwest Assn. Latin Americanists, Caribbean Studies Assn. Democrat. Mormon. Club: The Club. Avocations: Tennis; piano; organ. Home: 340 E Beecher Ave Jacksonville IL 62650 Office: MacMurray Coll Dept Sociology Jacksonville IL 62650

COLLMEYER, WAYNE MELVIN, educational administrator; b. Centralia, Ill., Apr. 17, 1948; s. Melvin W. and Irene A. (Kraus) C.; m. Linda Lou Auld, Nov. 10, 1967; children—Andrea, Matthew, Andrew. B.S., So. Ill. U., 1970, M.S., 1972. Cert. secondary tchr., Ill. Math. tchr. Lincoln Jr. High Sch., Carbondale, Ill., 1970-74; asst. prin. Chester High Sch., Ill., 1974-76; prin. Red Bud High Sch., Ill, 1976—; mem. com. for prins. acad. So. Ill. U., Carbondale, 1984; mem. feasibility study com. Ill. State Bd. Edn., Springfield, 1983-84. Mem. Ill. Prins. Assn., Nat. Assn. Secondary Sch. Prins. (mem. smaller high sch. com. 1983—), Phi Delta Kappa. Lutheran. Home: 1004 Fieldcrest Dr Red Bud IL 62278 Office: Red Bud High Sch 815 Locust St Red Bud IL 62278

COLMENERO, CHARLES, business consultant; b. N.Y.C., Dec. 30, 1931; s. Aurelio and Consuelo María (Fernández) C.; B.S., N.Y.U., 1957; student U. Miami, 1957-58, Fairleigh Dickinson U., 1962-63; m. Sabra Ann Pryor, Feb.

20, 1954; children—Laura, Elena, Charles, Elisa, Mercedes, Anita, Aurelio. Indsl. engr. Pan-American, Miami, Fla., 1957-58; mgr. systems and procedures Radiation, Inc., Palm Bay, Fla., 1958-62; gen. analyst Continental Can Co., N.Y.C., 1962-64; mgr. logistics and ops. Xerox Corp. (Latin-Am.), Rochester, N.Y., 1964-68; dir. ops. Xerox De Mexico, S.A., Mexico City, 1968-71; exec. v.p., chief exec. officer Koehn Mfg. Inc., Watertown, S.D., 1971-77; chmn. bd., pres. Mattson's Inc., Grafton, N.D., 1977-82, Repsel Assos. Inc., Watertown, 1982—; dir. Daktronics, Inc., Brookings, S.D., Baltic Overseas, Watertown, Family Farmers & Ranchers, Watertown. Chmn. Dist. Export Council S.D. Served with USAF, 1951-55. Mem. S.D. Mfrs. Assn. (charter dir., chmn. articles and by-laws com., chmn. membership com.), Watertown Mgmt. Council, Farm Equipment Mfrs. Assn., Nat. Assn. Mfrs., Am. Legion, Alpha Kappa Psi. Republican. Presbyterian. Club: Elks. Author: Technology-Its Impact on Enterprise, 1959. Home: 406 2d Ave SE Watertown SD 57201 Office: PO Box 274 Watertown SD 57201

COLOMBERO, DONALD FRANK, health care products company executive; b. Rochester, N.Y., July 5, 1953; s. Frank S. and Rosemarie D. (Ferrara) C.; m. Patricia I. Thornton, July 5, 1975; children—Corrie B., Brandon A. B.A. in Advt., Western Ky. U., 1975. Expeditor, Harris Corp., Rochester, N.Y., 1975-76, sales adminstr., 1976-77, sales promotion mgr., 1977-79; conv. mgr. Zimmer Inc. div. Bristol Myers, Warsaw, Ind., 1979-81, mktg. services mgr., 1981-83, dir. meeting services, 1983—. Recipient exhibit awards Bus. Mktg. Mag., 1st pl., 1980, 2d pl., 1981, 82. Mem. Nat. Trade Show Exhibitors Assn., Health Care Exhibitors Assn., Alpha Kappa Psi (Indpls.). Roman Catholic. Devised lit. transp. modules for cross country shipments. Office: Zimmer Inc 5522 Dividend Dr Indianapolis IN 46241

COLONESE, JOSEPH SAL, architect, engineer; b. Cleve., Dec. 22, 1921; s. Vincent and Irene (Ross) C.; B.S., Kent State U., 1950; m. Jean Melick, Sept. 16, 1950; children—Mark Gary, Jo-Ean. Engr., architect, Union Carbide & Carbon, Cleve., 1950-51; engr., architect N.Y. Central R.R., Cleve., 1951-53; architect, engr. Chrolet Gen. Motors Corp., Cleve., 1953-65, sr. project engr., architect-engr. Gen. Motors World Hdqrs., Detroit, 1965-80; architect-engr. Arabian Am. Oil Co., Ras Tanura, Saudi Arabia, 1980-82; exec, engr. Fine Line Design and Engring., 1983—; past pres. Exec-U-World; engring. cons., 1974—. Active in Unreached Youth, 1955-75; chief engr. Soap Box Derby, 1955-65. Served with USN, 1942-45, U.S. Army, 1945-58. Recipient Best Design awards Mfrs. Assn., 1955-64. Mem. Detroit Engring. Soc. Author 3 books in field, including Plant Engineering Manual. Home: 4894 Haddington Dr Bloomfield Hills MI 48013

COLONNA, RONALD ALBIN, mental health administrator; b. Beaver Falls, Pa., June 25, 1950; s. Albin Renald and Rose Pauline (Morelli) C.; m. Catherine Amelia Rendine, May 13, 1978; children—Andrew, Julia, Stephanie. B.S., Geneva Coll., 1972; M.S., St. Francis Coll., 1975. Instr. psychology Jefferson Tech. Coll., Steubenville, Ohio, 1976-79; psychotherapist/program coordinator Community Residential Family Treatment Home, Steubenville, Ohio, 1978-79; adult mental health services specialist Eastway Mental Health Ctr., Dayton, Ohio, 1979-81; dir. alcoholism services div. Greene County Health Dept., Xenia, Ohio, 1981; instr. psychology Sinclair Community Coll., Dayton, 1980-81; adult team dir. mental health services Murtis H. Taylor Multi-Services Ctr., Cleve., 1981—; instr. psychology humanities div. Cuyahoga Community Coll., Warrensville Twp. campus and Cleve. campus, 1982—. Mem. Am. Psychol. Assn., Ohio Mental Health Counselors Assn. Lodge: KC. Home: 3982 Princeton Blvd South Euclid OH 44121 Office: 13422 Kinsman Rd Cleveland OH 44120

COLSON, PATRICIA MARY (BECK), insurance administrator; b. Chgo., Mar. 22, 1938; d. Charles Joseph Beck and Katherine Harwood (Norton) Beck Ennis; m. Allan Hilding Hanson, 1962 (div. 1974); children—Terrance Allan, Tracy Michele, Eric Stephen; m. Donald Lee Colson, June 27, 1975. Student Marquette U., 1956-58; R.N., St. Francis Hosp. Sch. Nursing, 1974. Tchr., Holy Cross Sch., Deerfield, Ill., 1960-62; charge nurse Martha Washington Hosp., Chgo., 1974-76; asst. dir. nursing Riverwoods Ctr., Mundelein, Ill., 1976-78; asst. dir., mgr. Concerned Care, Inc., Evanston, Ill., 1979-81; dir. nursing Am. Home Health Service, Arlington Heights, Ill., 1982-83; program innovator, developer Home Care Evaluation, Inc. Subs. Republic Service Bur., Naperville, Ill., 1983-84; disability claim rev. cons. Jewel Food Stores, Franklin Park, Ill., 1984—; cons. New Eng. Mut. Life Ins. Co., Rolling Meadows, Ill., 1983. Fellow Nat. League for Nursing. Roman Catholic. Home: 129 S Harvard Ave Arlington Heights IL 60005 Office: Jewel Food Stores 3030 Cullerton Dr Franklin Park IL 60131

COLTER, ELIZABETH ANN, nurse; b. Norristown, Pa., Jan. 26, 1931; d. Lewis J. and Nancy (Hardy) Coffey; diploma Sacred Heart Hosp., Allentown, Pa., 1951; A.A.S., Meramec Community Coll., St. Louis, 1976; B.S. in Mgmt. Maryville Coll.; M.A. in Mgmt., Central Mich. U., 1983; m. Norman C. Colter, July 4, 1952 (div. Sept. 1979); children—Gregory, Marianne. Nurse, Mercy Hosp., Jackson, Mich., 1954-56, Madigan Meml. Hosp., Houlton, Maine, 1956-59; staff nurse to asst. head nurse operating room Mercy Hosp., Jackson, 1959-69; staff nurse St. Lawrence Hosp., Lansing, Mich., 1969-70; nurse Barnes Hosp., St. Louis, 1970-80, head nurse operating room, 1971-74, asst. dir. operating room, 1974-80; dir. operating rooms U. Mich., Ann Arbor, 1980—. Mem. Assn. Operating Room Nurses (pres. St. Louis 1973-74), Am. Coll. Hosp. Adminstrs. (nominee), Sigma Theta Tau, Phi Theta Kappa. Democrat. Lutheran. Home: 2124 Pauline Blvd Apt 307 Ann Arbor MI 48103 Office: U Mich Hospital 1405 E Ann St Ann Arbor MI 48109

COLTON, FRANK BENJAMIN, chemist; b. Bialystok, Poland, Mar. 3, 1923; s. Rubin and Fanny (Rosenblat) C.; brought to U.S., 1934, naturalized, 1934; B.S., Northwestern U., 1945, M.A., 1946; Ph.D., U. Chgo., 1949; m. Adele Heller, Mar. 24, 1950; children—Francine, Sharon, Laura, Sandra. Research fellow Mayo Clinic, Rochester, Minn., 1949-51; with G.D. Searle & Co., Chgo., 1951—, asst. dir. chem. research, 1961-70, research adviser, 1970—. Recipient Discovery medal for first oral contraceptive Nat. Assn. Mfrs., 1965; Profl. Achievement award U. Chgo., 1978; Achievement award Indsl. Research Inst., 1978. Mem. Am. Chem. Soc., Chgo. Chemists Club. Contbr. profl. jours. Pioneer in organic and steroid chemistries. Patentee first oral contraceptive. Home: 3901 Lyons St Evanston IL 60203 Office: G D Searle Co Searle Pkwy Skokie IL 60203

COLWELL, WILLIAM CLYDE, company executive; b. Chgo., Mar. 22, 1948; s. Daryl L. and Elizabeth A. (Mahoney) C.; m. Susan Yohanan, June 12, 1971; children—Daryl, Aaron. B.S., Bradley U., 1970; postgrad. Pa. State U., 1971-72. Inside sales rep. Bear Brand Hosiery Co., Chgo., 1970-71; gen. mgr. Becker Studies, Chgo., 1972-74; owner Scenery Works, Evanston, Ill., 1974-76; account exec. Omnicon, Ltd., Elk Grove, Ill., 1976-82, v.p. exhibit and design constrn., 1982—. Avocations: golf, travel, reading, theatre, sports. Home: 1320 Gordon Terr Deerfield IL 60015 Office: Omnicon Ltd 900 Lunt St Elk Grove IL 60007

COLYER, CHARLES CONSTANT, II, petroleum company executive; Altoona, Pa., Nov. 14, 1921; s. Charles Constant and Helen Rose (Bingman) C.; m. Virginia May Conrad, Sept. 16, 1941 (dec. Apr. 1973; children—Robert, Charles III, Charlene, Diann; m. Virginia Josephine Schild, Nov. 16, 1974. Cert. toolmaker Westinghouse Electric apprenticeship program, Pitts., 1946. B.S. in Mechanical Engring., Carnegie Inst. Tech., 1947. Project mgr. AMOCO Oil, Whiting, Ind., research dir., Naperville, Ill., mgr. product mgmt. AMOCO Chems., Chgo., 1976-80, research devel. supr., Naperville, Ill., 1980-81; mgr. mktg. devel. Lubrizol, Wickliffe, Ohio, 1982—. Patentee automotive lubricants. Chmn. Lake County Ind. Rep. Party, 1968-72; organizer Little League, Griffith, Ind., 1950; bd. mem. town of Griffith, Ind., 1956-60. Served to 1st lt. navigator, U.S. Army Air Force, 1943-45. Fellow Soc. Automotive Engrs. (dir. 1977-79, pres. 1983, Meritorious Service award 1970); mem. Federation Internationale des Societies d'Ingenieuies des Techniques L'Automobile (council mem. 1984—); ASTM (dir. 1972-74, Disting. Service award 1970). Republican. Lutheran. Lodge: Lions (Ind.) (deputy gov. 1958). Avocations: tennis; bridge; travel. Home: 5901 Mallard Ct Mentor OH 44060 Office: Lubrizol 29400 Lakeland Blvd Wickliffe OH 44092

COLYER, ROBERT ALLAN, medical educator; b. Altoona, Pa., Mar. 27, 1945; s. Charles and Virginia (Conrad) C.; m. Lynne A. Colyer, Aug. 26, 1967; children—Brent, Aaron. B.A., Ind. U., 1966; M.D., Johns Hopkins U., 1970. Lic. physician, Ind.; diplomate Am. Bd. Orthopedic surgery. Intern, Vanderbilt U., 1971; research assoc. biochemistry lab. Nat. Cancer Inst., NIH, 1971-73; asst. prof. orthopedic surgery Ind. U., Indpls., 1976-81, assoc. prof. orthopedic surgery, 1981—, dir. spinal cord unit, 1976-81, cons. growth anomalies clinic, 1976—. Served with USPHS, 1971-73. Berg Sloat Traveling fellow, 1977-78; grantee James Whitcomb Riley Meml. Assn., 1978, Orthopaedic Research and Edn. Found., 1978-80. Mem. Ind. Med. Assn., Marion County Med. Assn., Southeastern Cancer Study Group, Ind. Orthopedic Soc., Am. Acad. Orthopedic Surgeons, Ind. Acad. Sci., Orthopedic Research Soc., Am. Spinal Injuries Assn., AMA, Internat. Coll. Surgeons, Pan Pacific Surg. Assn., Phi Beta Kappa. Contbr. articles to profl. jours. Home: 7317 Normandy Way Indianapolis IN 46278 Office: 545 Barnhill Dr Emerson Hall 239 Indianapolis IN 46223

COMBS, DON EDGAR, banker; b. Reinersville, Ohio, Nov. 2, 1929; s. Everett Alva Combs and Bessie (Gorrell) Young; m. Marilyn Elizabeth Price, Nov. 22, 1962; children—Susan Michelle, Michael Don, James Paul, John Price. Asst. cashier 1st Nat. Bank, McConnelsville, Ohio, 1953-61; chief exec. officer Citizens Bank Co., Beverly, Ohio, 1961-72, pres., 1972-82, Malta Nat. Bank, Ohio, 1983—. Corp. mem. Marietta Meml. Hosp., Ohio, 1969—; pres. Friend of Library, Beverly, 1967—. Served to sgt. U.S. Army, 1951-53, Korea. Recipient Boss of Yr. award, Beverly-Waterford Jaycees, 1966. Mem. M&M Jaycees (pres. 1959), Ohio Bankers Assn., Ohio Community Bankers (treas. 1975-81). Republican. Presbyterian. Lodges: Lions, Rotary, Masons. Home: 530 Mitchell Ave Rt 1 Box 9 Beverly OH 45715

COMER, FREDERICK RAY, education association executive; b. Lapeer, Mich., Aug. 3, 1942; s. Arthur Raymond and Lorraine Helen (Kesler) C.; m. Sally Lou Ost, Dec. 18, 1965; children—Allison Lee, Justin Arthur. B.S., Central Mich. U., 1964; M.A., Western Mich. U., 1968. Tchr. Wayland Union Schs., Mich., 1967-70; UniServ dir. Mich. Edn. Assn., Holland, 1970-73, asst. exec. dir., Traverse City, 1973-78, assoc. exec. dir., East Lansing, 1978-81; exec. dir. Iowa State Edn. Assn., Des Moines, 1981—; evaluator Nat. Council Accrediation Tchr. Edn., Washington, 1982; cons. on instrn. Nat. Edn. Assn., Washington, 1983—. Contbr. to booklets. Com. mem. Legis. Com. Collective Bargaining, 1984, Govs. Com. Local Govt., 1983, Planning com. Iowa Edn. Forum, 1983. Mem. Nat. Council State Edn. Assns., Central Mich. U. Alumni Assn., NOW. Democrat. Mem. United Ch. Crist. Avocations: Travel; reading; college athletics. Home: 600 60th Pl Des Moines IA 50312 Office: Iowa State Edn Assn 4025 Tonawanda Dr Des Moines IA 50312

COMIENSKI, JAMES SIGMON, educator; b. Cleve., Nov. 6, 1948; s. Sigmon James and Martha Helen (Chernus) C.; m. Barbara Ann Lutz, July 1, 1978. B.A. in Geology, Case Western Res. U., 1970; postgrad. Ohio State U., Cleve. State U., U. Akron, 1974—. Traffic checker schedule dept. Regional Transit Authority, Cleve., 1966-68, 69-70, 72; sci. tchr., planetarium dir. Lakewood (Ohio) Schs., 1973—; cons. earth sci. curriculum North Ridgeville, 1977; lectr. bird migration; asst. instr. Ohio Sea Grant Edn., summer, 1981. Ruling elder Lakewood Presbyterian Ch., 1981—. Served with U.S. Army, 1970-72. Mem. Nat. Sci. Tchrs. Assn., Great Lakes Planetarium Assn. (edn. com.), Cleve. Astron. Assn. (exec. council), Assn. Astronomy Educators, Internat. Soc. Planetarium Educators, Cleve. Mus. Natural History, Cleve. Regional Council Sci. Tchrs., Cleve. Regional Assn. Planetarians, Lakwood Tchrs. Assn., Ohio Educators Assn., Nat. Earth Sci. Tchrs. Assn., Aerospace Educators Assn., Western Res. Hist. Soc., Nat. Geog. Soc., Planetary Soc., Ctr. Environ. Edn., NEA. Democrat. Co-writer sci. project activities. Home: 18625 Hilliard Rd Apt 206 Rocky River OH 44116 Office: Lakewood Schs 14100 Franklin Blvd Planetarium Lakewood OH 44107

COMITO, FRANK JOSEPH, lawyer; b. Des Moines, Sept. 8, 1954; s. William J. and Joanne E. (Porto) C.; m. Margaret Katherine Beiter, Aug. 23, 1975. B.S., Iowa State U., 1976; J.D., Georgetown U., 1979. Bar: Iowa 1979, U.S. Dist. Ct. (no. and so. dists) Iowa 1980, U.S. Tax Ct. 1984. Clk. to presiding justice Md. Ct. of Appeals, Annapolis, 1978-80; sole practice Carroll, Iowa, 1980—; asst. county atty. Carroll County, 1981-83, magistrate, 1983—. Pres. Carroll Arts Council, 1982. Mem. Iowa State Bar Assn., ABA. Democrat. Roman Catholic. Office: 322 E 6th St Carroll IA 51401

COMMISSO, ITALIA ANN, cable industry executive; b. Marina di Gioiosa Ionica, Italy, Aug. 30, 1953; came to U.S., 1962; d. Giuseppe and Maria Rosa (Femia) C. A.A.S., Elizabeth Seton Coll., 1973; B.S., Fordham U., 1975. Service mgr. Gimble Bros., N.Y.C., 1975-77; dist. supr. Time, Inc., N.Y.C., 1977-80; asst. gen. mgr. Lake Isle Caterers, Eastchester, N.Y., 1980-81; customer Service mgr. Times Mirror Cable, Hartford, Conn., 1981-82; customer service dir. Cablenet, Inc., Mount Prospect, Ill., 1983—. Mem. Women in Cable. Democrat. Roman Catholic.

COMMITO, RICHARD WILLIAM, podiatrist; b. Chgo., May 2, 1951; s. Mario Fiore and Aileen Margaret (Stang) C. B.S., U. Ill.-Chgo., 1972; D.P.M., Ill. Coll. Podiatric Medicine, 1976. Diplomate Nat. Bd. Podiatry Examiners, Am. Bd. Ambulatory Foot Surgery; cert. Internat. Inst. Reflexology, Am. Bd. Podiatric Surgery. Podiatrist, Chgo., 1976—; dir. Podiatry Services Community Hosp., Evanston, Ill., 1978-80; cons. staff poidatry Ridgeway Hosp., Chgo., 1981—; owner Foot Doc Products. Bd. dirs. Little Village unit Chgo. Boys' Clubs, 1981—, mem. One hundred Club, 1982, mem. 400 Club, Marshall Sq. unit, 1981-82; mem. Art Inst. Chgo., 1980-85, Lincoln Park Zool. Soc., Chgo., 1980-85. Fellow Acad. Ambulatory Foot Surgery; mem. Soaring Soc. Am., Ill. Podiatry Edn. Group, Am. Podiatric Med. Assn., Ill. Podiatry Soc., Am. Med. Soc. of Vienna (life), Nat. Assn. Professions. Roman Catholic.

COMPAAN, ALVIN DELL, physics educator, researcher; b. Hull, N.D., June 11, 1943; s. William and Dena (DeJong) C.; m. Mary Han, June 28, 1969; children—Timothy, Kristina, Deanne, David. A.B. in Physics and Math., Calvin Coll., Grand Rapids, Mich., 1965; M.S., U. Chgo., 1966, Ph.D., 1971. Assoc. research scientist NYU, 1971-73; asst. prof. physics Kans. State U., Manhattan, 1973-77, assoc. prof., 1977-81, prof., 1981—. Contbr. articles to profl. jours. Fellow NDEA, 1968, NSF, 1969-71, A..von Humboldt Stiftung found., 1982-83; grantee NSF, 1975-84, Office Naval Research, 1975-84. Mem. Am. Phys. Soc., AAAS, Materials Research Soc., Sigma Xi. Democrat. Presbyterian. Avocations: tennis, cross country skiing. Office: Kans St U Dept Physics Manhattan KS 66506

COMPAGNONE, NICK PETER, educational administrator; b. Bklyn., Sept. 3, 1952; s. Edward Peter and Cathrine Ann (LoMonaco) C.; m. Cindy Ann Hoffman, Aug. 21, 1973; children—Craig Joseph, Chris Edward. B.A., St. Mary of the Plains Coll., 1974; M.S., Wichita State U., 1978. Acting prin. Sacred Heart, Larned, Kans., 1974-75; asst. prin., coach Blessed Sacrament Sch., Wichita, Kans., 1975-78; sch. adminstr. St. Joseph Sch., Oakley, Kans., 1978-82, St. Mary's Sch., Salina, Kans., 1982—; chmn. Colby Commn. Edn., Bd. Edn., Salina Diocese, 1978-82. Mem. United Sch. Adminstrs., Nat. Assn. Elem. Sch. Prins., Assn. Supervision and Curriculum Devel. Democrat. Roman Catholic. Lodge: K.C. Home: 2503 Robin Rd Salina KS 67401 Office: 304 E Cloud St Salina KS 67401

CONANT, A. ROBERT, marketing consultant; b. Washington, N.J., July 23, 1927; s. William A. and Jane (Stickle) C.; m. Joan Evans, June 10, 1950; children—Charlotte, William, Roger, Jane. B.S. in Chemistry, U. Va., 1953. Field salesman Dow Chem. Co., Midland, Mich., 1953-58, product sales mgr., 1958-64, mktg. mgr., 1964-66, mktg. research mgr., 1966-68, mgr. mktg. research and tng., 1972-83; sales mgr. Dow Quimica de Argentina, Buenos Aires, 1968-72; cons. chem. mktg., Midland, 1983—. Contbr. articles to profl. publs. Active Jr. Achievement, Midland. Served with USN, 1945-49. Mem. Am. Chem. Soc., Am. Inst. Chem. Engrs., Chem. Mktg. Research Assn. Republican. Presbyterian. Clubs: Sud Este Yacht (Buenos Aires); Bay City Yacht. Avocations: skiing; sailing; photography; reading. Home and Office: 4909 Washington Midland MI 48640

CONATON, MICHAEL JOSEPH, company executive; b. Detroit, Aug. 3, 1933; s. John Martin and Margaret Alice (Cleary) C.; m. Margaret Ann Cannon, Sept. 3, 1955; children—Catherine, Macaira, Michael, Margaret, Elizabeth. B.S., Xavier U., 1955. C.P.A., Ohio. C.P.A., Stanley A. Hittner, Cin., 1956-58; controller The Moloney Co., Albia, Iowa, 1958-61; councilman City of Albia, 1959-61; dir. The Midland Co., Cin., 1961—, treas., 1961-73, v.p. fin., 1973-80, exec. v.p., 1980—; dir. Burke Mktg. Services, Inc., Cin., 1970—, The Southern Ohio Bank, Cin., 1981—, United Midwest Bancshares, Inc., Cin., 1981—. Served to lt. USMC, 1955-56. Mem. Cin. Soc. Fin. Analysts, Fin. Exec. Inst. Roman Catholic. Home; 1016 Paxton Ave Cincinnati OH 45208 Office: The Midland Co 111 E 4th St Cincinnati OH 45202

CONAWAY, JAMES DONALD, painter, educator; b. Granite City, Ill., Oct. 9, 1932; s. Larkin W. and Clara Mae (Bond) C.; m. Tomie Ikuta, Sept. 2, 1961; children—Kobi, Tai. B.F.A., So. Ill. U., 1960; M.A., U. Iowa, 1965, M.F.A., 1966. Asst. prof. U. Wis.-Stevens Point, 1966-67; instr. Anoka Ramsey Coll., Coon Rapids, Minn., 1967-75; assoc. prof. Hamline U., St. Paul, 1975—. One-man shows: U. Minn.-Mpls., 1968, Davenport Mcpl. Art Gallery, Iowa, 1978, Reed Whipple Art Ctr., Las Vegas, Nev., 1984, numerous others; group shows include: Walker Art Ctr., Mpls., Smithsonian Instn., Washington, Butler Inst. Am. Art, Youngstown, Ohio, Palace of Fine Arts, Santiago, Chile, Joslyn Art Mus., Omaha, Art Inst. Chgo., Sangre de Christo Art Ctr., Pueblo, Colo., Mus. Contemporary Western Art, Houston. Mem. Minn. State Fine Arts Bd., 1982-83; bd. dirs. North Metro Ctr. for Arts 1982—. Served with USN, 1952-56. Mem. Mid-Am. Art Assn. (treas. 1977).

CONBOY, JANET ELIZABETH, developmental disabilities services administrator; b. Birmingham, Ala., Apr. 8, 1947; d. Faris Lyndle and Thelma Maude (Bolin) C.; B.A., Birmingham-So. Coll., 1968; M.A., U. Mo.-Columbia, 1971, M.Ed., 1972. Tchr. secondary English, Decatur (Ala.) City Schs., 1968-70; sch. counselor Rock Port (Mo.) Schs., 1972-77; successively mental health counselor, br. office mgr. Albany Regional Center Devel. Disabilities, Mo. Dept. Mental Health, Maryville, 1977-79, asst. center dir. for treatment, 1979-81, regional center dir., 1981-83; dir. mentally retarded-developmental disabilities community services State of Mo., 1983—. Mem. Am. Assn. Mental Deficiency, Assn. Mental Health Adminstrs., Mo. Planning Council. Episcopalian. Home: 12-B Clarkson Rd Columbia MO 65201 Office: 2002 Missouri Blvd Jefferson City MO 65101

CONCANNON, ANN WORTH, art center administrator; b. Menominee, Mich., Aug. 17, 1946; d. Jean and Margaret (St. Peter) Worth; m. James Concannon, Feb. 27, 1972; children—Aurora Borealis, Jean Worth. B.A., U. Mich., 1968. Dir. Bonifas Art Ctr., Escabana, Mich., 1976-78, fund raiser, 1980-81; dir. Art Center, Battle Creek, Mich., 1981—; adv. Mich. Council for the Arts, Detroit, 1978—. Columnist for City Scene newspaper, 1984. County organizer John Anderson Presidential campaign, 1980. Mem. Mich. Museums Assn. (sec. 1982-84), Concerned Citizens for Arts (bd. dirs. 1984). Office: Art Ctr Battle Creek 265 E Emmett St Battle Creek MI 49017

CONDRA, ALLEN LEE, lawyer; b. Middlesboro, Ky., Apr. 11, 1950; s. Allen and Dorothy Dell (Douglas) C. B.A., Western Ky. U., 1972; J.D., No. Ky. U., 1978. Bar: Ky. 1979, U.S. Dist. Ct. (we. dist.) Ky. 1980. Staff atty. West Ky. Legal Services, Madisonville, 1979-81; dist. atty. Dept. Transp., Commonwealth of Ky., Paducah, 1981—. Mem. Ky. Bar Assn., McCracken County Bar Assn., Phi Alpha Delta. Democrat. Methodist. Lodge: Elks, Masons, K.T. Home: Route 4 Box 322 Hwy 62 Paducah KY 42001 Office: Dept Transp PO Box 3010 Paducah KY 42002-3010

CONDRY, ROBERT STEWART, hospital administrator; b. Charleston, W.Va., Aug. 16, 1941; s. John Charles and Mary Louise (Jester) C.; m. Mary Purcell Heinzer, May 21, 1966; children—Mary-Lynch, John Stewart. B.A., U. Charleston, 1963; M.B.A., George Washington U., 1970. Asst. hosp. dir. Med. Coll. Va., Richmond, 1970-73, assoc. adminstr., 1973-75; assoc. hosp. dir. F.G. McGaw Hosp., Loyola U., Maywood, Ill., 1975-84, hosp. dir., 1984—; preceptor Tulane U., 1984, St. Louis U., 1984, U. Chgo., 1984, George Washington U., 1985. Served with U.S. Army, 1964-66. Fellow Am. Coll. Hosp. Adminstrs.; mem. Am. Acad. Med. Adminstrs., Am. Hosp. Assn., Catholic Hosp. Assn., Am. Mgmt. Assn., Inter-Hosp. Planning Assn. Western Suburbs (pres. 1983—). Republican. Roman Catholic. Avocations: golfing; tennis; camping. Home: 23W280 St James Ct Glen Ellyn IL 60137 Office: Foster G McGaw Hospital Loyola U 2160 S 1st Ave Maywood IL 60153

CONFORTI, CAMILLE, advertising agency executive; b. Chgo., Jan. 21, 1944; d. John and Connie C.; B.Mus., North Central Coll., Naperville, Ill., 1966; cert. advt. specialist U. Houston; 1 son, Laddie Fromelius. Exec. sec. Bell Labs., Naperville, 1966-67; pvt. piano instr., 1966-74; co-owner mason contracting co., 1969-79; account exec. CK & Assos., mktg. and advt., Naperville, 1979-82; account exec. Ad-Vantage, 1982-84; pres., owner Tandem Advt., Inc., Naperville, 1984—. First v.p. Naperville-North Central Coll. Community Concert Assn., 1979-80, pres., 1983-84; mem. President's Club, North Central Coll. Recipient Young Alumnus Merit award North Central Coll., 1984. Mem. North Central Coll. Alumni Assn. (dir., v.p.), Sigma Alpha Iota (chpt. pres. 1965-66, pres. alumnae chpt. 1977-80; Sword of Honor 1977). Home: 25W431 Johnson Dr Naperville IL 60540 Office: Tandem Advt Inc 25W431 Johnson Dr Naperville IL 60540

CONGER, WILLIAM FRAME, educator, artist; b. Dixon, Ill., May 29, 1937; s. Robert Allen and Florence Catherine (Kelly) C.; m. Kathleen Marie Onderak, May 24, 1964; children—Sarah Elizabeth, Clarisa Lynn. Student Sch. Art Inst. of Chgo., 1956-57; B.F.A., U. N.Mex., 1960; M.F.A., U. Chgo., 1966. Asst. prof. Rock Valley Coll., Rockford, Ill., 1966-71; asst. prof. to prof. art DePaul U., Chgo., 1971-85, chmn. dept., 1971-77, 80-84; adj. prof. So. Ill. U., Carbondale, Apr. 1984; prof. Northwestern U., Evanston, Ill., 1984—, chmn. dept. art, 1985—; vis. artist Sch. Art Inst. Chgo., Apr. 1984; dir. Oxbow Sch. Art, Saugatuck, Mich., 1983—; lectr. in field. One man shows include: Kenyon Gallery, Chgo., 1974-75, Kyannert Ctr. for Arts, Champaign, Ill., 1976, Zaks Gallery, Chgo., 1978, 80, 83, Boyd Gallery, Chgo., 1985; exhibited in numerous mus. group shows; represented in permanent collections Art Inst. of Chgo., Ill. State Mus., State of Ill. Bldg. Recipient Friedman prize U. Chgo., 1965, 66, Bartels award Art Inst. of Chgo., 1971. Cluseman award, 1973; DePaul U. research grantee, 1982. Mem. Coll. Art Assn. Am. Roman Catholic. Club: Arts (Chgo.). Avocations: genealogy; colonial American history. Office: Dept Art Northwestern U 216 Kresge Hall Evanston IL 60201 also care Roy Boyd Gallery 215 W Superior Chicago IL 60610

CONGER HALE, MARTHA (MARTI), retail executive; b. Tillamook, Oreg., Feb. 10, 1950; d. William Madison and Patricia Dale (Boston) Conger; divorced; 1 child, Alan Michael. B.A., Western Wash. U., 1972, M.Edn. Tech., 1977. Tchr. Burlington-Edison Sch. Dist., Burlington, Wash., 1973-80, La Conner Sch. Dist., Wash., 1977-80; salesperson, asst. mgr. That Extra Touch, Inc., Mount Vernon, Wash., 1978-80; owner Yours, Mine and Ours, Mount Vernon, 1980-83; mgr. tng. F.W. Woolworth Co., Milw., 1983-85, dir. tng., 1985—. Active Totem council Girl Scouts U.S., 1957-73. Avocations: self-study reading; needlework. Office: F W Woolworth Co 7800 Browndeer Rd Milwaukee WI 53223

CONKLIN, RICHARD CARL, scouting executive; b. Derby, Conn., May 23, 1945; s. Henry Gilder and Mary Hays (Griffin) C.; m. Deborah Morey, Nov. 29, 1969; children—Amy, Elizabeth, Jill. B.S., Springfield Coll., 1967; M.A., Ohio U., 1971; postgrad., Harvard U., 1981. Service worker Internat. Community YMCA, Athens, Greece, 1967-68; 4-H agt. Ohio Coop. Extension Service, Youngstown, 1971-74; dist. dir. Hemlock Council Girl Scouts U.S., Williamsport, Pa., 1974-77, exec. dir. Shining Trail Council, Burlington, Iowa, 1978—. John R. Mott fellow Nat. Council YMCA Ohio U., 1968; recipient Search for Excellence 4-H award Nat. Assn. County Agrl. Agts., Balt., 1973; named Outstanding Young Man in Am. Youngstown Jaycees, 1975. Republican. Presbyterian. Lodge: Rotary (pres.). Home: 150 Clay St Burlington IA 52601 Office: Shining Trail Council Girl Scouts US Inc 2001 S Main PO Box 814 Burlington IA 52601

CONKLIN, ROBERT EUGENE, electronics engineer; b. Loveland, Ohio, Apr. 21, 1925; s. Charles and Alberta (Reynolds) C.; m. Virginia E. McCann, June 14, 1952; children—Carl Lynn, Jill Elaine Conklin Bradford. B.S. in Edn., Wilmington Coll., 1949, B.S. in Sci., 1949. Electronic scientist Electronic Technol. Lab., Wright-Patterson AFB, Ohio, 1951-55; electronic engr. AF Avionics Lab., Wright-Patterson AFB, 1956-60 supervisory elec. engr., 1960-72, cons. electronic engr., 1972-78, supervisory electronic engr., 1978-82, electronic engr. (VHSIC), 1982-83; cons. engr. REC Electronics, Fairborn, Ohio, 1983—; mem. Inst. Nav., 1968-72. Mgr. Babe Ruth Boys' Baseball, 1969-74; mgr. and pres. Little League, Fairborn, 1965-68. Served with USAAC, 1943-46. Mem. IEEE. Republican. Quaker. Lodge: Lions (Fairborn) Home: 114 Wayne Dr Fairborn OH 45324 Office: 47 N Broad St Fairborn OH 45324

CONKLIN, WILLIAM EARL, JR., hospital administrator; b. Charleston, W.Va., Sept. 12, 1937; s. William Earl and Myrtle Lee (Hanson) C.; m. Leila Darlene Ash, Dec. 15, 1957; children—William Earl, Amy Denise. B.S.B.A., W.Va. U., 1960; M.Pub. Adminstrn., Ind. State U., 1981. Adminstrv. extern, acting personnel dir. Meml. Hosp., Charleston, 1960-61; personnel dir., adminstrv. asst. Luth. Hosp., Cleve., 1961-68; dir. personnel Presbyn. Hosp.,

Charlotte, N.C., 1968-70, Deaconess Hosp., Evansville, Ind., 1970—; cons. in field. Com. chmn., asst. scoutmaster Buffalo Trace council Boy Scouts Am., Evansville, 1973-78; bd. dirs. Lutheran Found., 1974-77. Mem. Evansville C. of C. (legis. com. 1980—), Am. Soc. Hosp. Personnel Adminstrn. (lit. award 1978; charter; dir. 1983-85, pres.-elect 1985-86), Ind. Soc. Hosp. Personnel Adminstrn. (pres. 1978-79), Evansville Personnel Assn. (pres. 1978-79), Am. Soc. Personnel Adminstrn., Ind. Personnel Assn., Profl. Secs. Internat. (dir.). Republican. Co-author: A Basic Guide to Health Care Personnel Policies & Procedures, 1983; contbr. articles to profl. jours. Home: 4155 Pine Dr Newburgh IN 47630 Office: 600 Mary St Deaconess Hosp Evansville IN 47747

CONLEY, BETTY JEAN, insurance executive; b. Omaha, Dec. 23, 1929; d. William Glen and Dorothy Ruth (Moore) Mason; m. Wendell O. Conley, Dec. 13, 1946. Student pub. schs., Omaha. C.P.C.U.; cert. profl. ins. woman. Underwriter, Royal Ins. Cos., Omaha, 1964-67, sr. underwriter, 1967-78, underwriting supr., 1978-84, br. supt., 1984—. Mem. Mayor's Task Force on Status of Women, Omaha, 1975-76. Named Woman of Yr., Omaha Women's Polit. Caucas, 1975. Mem. Soc. Chartered Property and Casualty Underwriters, Nat. Assn. Ins. Women (pres. 1975-76), Ins. Women of Omaha (pres. 1959-60), Omaha Soc. C.P.C.U.s, (pres. 1979-80). Republican. Methodist. Home: 1105 Eldorado Dr Omaha NE 68154 Office: Royal Ins Cos Suite 300 7000 W Center Rd Omaha NE 68106

CONLEY, EDWARD JOHN, preventative medicine and sports physician; b. Owosso, Mich., Sept. 5, 1955; s. Edward Phillip and Rita Marie (Fitzgerald) C. B.S., U. Mich., 1977; D.O., Mich. State U. Coll. Osteo. Medicine, 1981. Intern, Flint Osteo. Hosp., Mich.; emergency physician, Clare, Mich., 1982; gen. practice osteo. medicine Flushing Med. Ctr., Mich., 1983—; sports medicine specialist Greater Flint Sports Med. Ctr., Mich., 1983—, med. dir., 1984—; team physician Mott Community Coll., Flint, 1984—, Carman Sr. High Sch., Flint, 1983—; physician Mich. Spl. Olympics, Flint, 1983—. Collaborator breast cancer research, 1980. Mem. Am. Osteo. Assn., Sports Medicine Assn., Genesee County Med. Assn., Assn. Gen. Practitioners, Sigma Sigma Phi. Club: Century (Flint). Avocations: golf; tennis; sailing; gardening; hot air ballooning. Office: Flushing Med Ctr PC 1434 Flushing Rd Flushing MI 48433

CONLEY, MICHAEL KENNETH, obstetrician-gynecologist; b. Coldwater, Mich., July 2, 1950; s. Kenneth D. and Mary F. (Spence) C.; m. Martha E. Guzlay, Oct. 22, 1977; children—Molly M., Patrick M., Alan F. A.B., U. Mich., 1972, M.D., 1976. Diplomate Am. Bd. Ob-Gyn. Intern, Ind. U. Med. Ctr., Indpls., 1976-77, resident, 1976-80; chief sect., dept. ob-gyn Marquette Gen. Hosp., Mich., 1983-84, mem. staff, 1980—; clin. assoc. prof. Mich. State U., East Lansing, 1980—. Advisor, Upper Peninsula chpt. March of Dimes, Marquette, 1982—. Fellow Am. Coll. Ob-gyn, Am. Fertility Soc.; mem. AMA. Office: Ob-gyn Assoc Marquette 1414 W Fair Ave #255 Marquette MI 49855

CONLEY, NORMAN EDDY, engineer; b. Eureka, Kans., Dec. 18, 1943; s. Otis George and Martha Elizabeth (Dixon) C.; m. Carolyn D. Patton, Nov. 19, 1967; 1 child, Sean Peter. B.S. in Aero. Engring., Wichita State U., 1966. Registered profl. engr., Kans. Sr. engr. Boeing Wichita, Kans., 1966-82; engring. specialist Gates Learjet, Wichita, 1976-82; supr. aero. tech. Boeing Mil. Airplane Co., Wichita, 1982—. Co-inventor aircraft wing with improved leading edge. Com. mem. Wichita Republican party, 1981—. Fellow AIAA (assoc.; sect. chmn. 1981-82, nat. membership com. 1975-80, mem. gen. aviation tech. com. 1980-85); mem. Soc. Automotive Engrs. (membership chmn. 1978), Sports Car Club Am. (regional exec. Wichita 1973), Osborne Portable Enthusiasts Kans. (sec. Wichita chpt. 1984). Mem. United Ch. of Christ. Avocations: sports car rallys; personal computers; flying. Home: 2916 W 21st St Wichita KS 67203 Office: Boeing Mil Airplane Co 3801 S Oliver PO Box 7730 Wichita KS 67277

CONLON, JOHN CHARLES, biostatistician; b. Canton, Ohio, Nov. 15, 1945; s. Francis Patrick and Mary Josephine (Gulling) C.; m. Mary Elizabeth Ambelang, Nov. 11, 1978; children—Joseph Patrick, John Christopher. A.B. in Philosophy, John Carroll U., 1967; M.S. in Stats., Fla. State U., 1975, Ph.D. in Stats., 1977. Asst. prof. Akron U., Ohio, 1977-79; math. statistician Dept. Army, Aberdeen, Md., 1979-81; biostatistician Nat. Cancer Inst.-Frederick Cancer Research Facility, Md., 1981-83; sr. research scientist Bristol-Myers, Evansville, Ind., 1983—. Author: Test and Evaluation of System Reliability, Availability and Maintainability, 1982. Served with U.S. Army 1968-71, Vietnam. Mem. Am. Statis. Assn., Biometric Soc. Clubs: Susquehanna Singers (Aberdeen, Md.); Mejo Tennis League (Evansville, Ind.) (pres. 1984-85). Avocations: tennis; golf; classical music. Home: 1200 S Stockwell Rd Evansville IN 47715 Office: Bristol-Myers-Pharm Research and Devel 2404 W Pennsylvania St Evansville IN 47721

CONNELLY, JOHN DOOLEY, social service organization executive; b. Chgo., Sept. 8, 1946; s. John Joseph and Mary (Dooley) C. B.S., Xavier U., 1968; M.A., Northeastern Ill. U., 1973; Ph.D., Cornell U., 1976. Spl. edn. tchr. Spl. Edn. Dist., Lake County, Gurnee, Ill., 1969-73; asst. prof. spl. edn. Eastern Ky. U., Richmond, Ky., 1973-76; div. dir., acting exec. dir. Coty of Chgo. Health System, 1977-80; exec. dir. Jobs for Youth Chgo., 1980—; mgr. Emergency Loan Fund, Chgo., 1983—. Editor jour. Health and Medicine, 1984. Chmn. Pegasus Players Theatre, Chgo., 1982—; bd. dirs. Health and Medicine Policy Research Group, Chgo., 1983-84; Clarence Darrow Community Ctr., Chgo., 1983-84. Roman Catholic. Office: Jobs for Youth Chicago 67 E Madison St Chicago IL 60603

CONNELLY, SHANNON, lawyer; b. Milw., Feb. 15, 1948; d. Lawrence and Harriet (Madsen) Parker; m. Stephen Dwight Connelly, July 9, 1968; children—Karen, Robert, Marianne. B.A., Northwestern U., 1970; J.D., Georgetown U., 1975. Bar: D.C. 1976, Ill., 1980. Assoc. Wheedon, Harris & Montgomery, Washington, 1976-80; mem. firm Sanderson & Majewski, Chgo., 1980-84; corp. counsel Beatrice Foods, Inc., Chgo., 1984—; lectr. Loyola U., Chgo., 1983-84. Active Girl Scouts U.S., 1981—. Mem. ABA, Ill. Bar Assn., Chgo. Bar Assn., Nat. Assn. Women Lawyers, Phi Beta Kappa. Democrat. Roman Catholic. Office: 200 E Ohio St Chicago IL 60611

CONNELLY, WILLIAM JOSEPH, public relations executive; b. Pottsville, Pa., Sept. 29, 1931; s. Joseph Thomas and Marie Cecelia (Ryan) C.; m. Margaret Ann Scanlan Carl, Oct. 6, 1951; children—Margaret Marie, William Joseph, Colleen; m. 2d, Ellen Marie Bufe, May 20, 1972; 1 son, Sean Ryan. A.B., King's Coll., Wilkes-Barre, Pa., 1966; postgrad. U. Scranton, 1965-66, St. Louis U., 1968-71. Profl. broadcaster and journalist, 1949-66; corp. communications specialist Mgmt. Cons., Kingston, Pa., 1958-63; dir. pub. relations St. Louis U. Med. Ctr., 1967-71; dir. pub. affairs Chgo. State U., 1971-74; dir. pub. relations Schwab Rehab. Hosp., Chgo., 1974-76; dir. mktg. pub. relations Bankers Life and Casualty Co., Chgo., 1976-80; dir. mktg. communications and pub. relations Underwriters Labs. Inc., Northbrook, Ill., 1980-83; sr. cons. JN Co., 1983—; prin. Bufe, Connelly & Ryan, Mktg. & Pub. Relations, 1985—; adj. prof. journalism Chgo. State U., 1973-74. Active Boy Scouts Am., 1951-62, Suburban Cook County-Du Page County Health (Planning) Systems Agy., 1984—. Served with USAF, 1950-51. Mem. Pub. Relations Soc. Am. Democrat. Roman Catholic. Home: 830 Panorama Dr Palatine IL 60067 Office: 311 W Superior St Suite 214 Chicago IL 60610 also 830 Panorama Dr Palatine IL 60067

CONNERS, JOHN D., See *Who's Who in America,* 43rd edition.

CONNERTH, WENDIE FAY, nurse; b. Chgo., Feb. 5, 1951; d. Willard Frederich and Alice Marie (Esnorff) Helsdon; A.A., Coll. of DuPage, 1973; Student North Central Coll., 1973-74; B.S., No. Ill. U., 1975, M.S., 1979, postgrad., 1980—; m. Robert William Connerth, Aug. 23, 1975; children—Mary Anna (dec.), Robert William (dec.), Clifton Morgan (dec.), Christian Daniel. Staff nurse Loyola Hosp., Maywood, Ill., 1973-77; staff nurse ICU, Westlake Hosp., Melrose Park, Ill., 1978-79; research technician U. Ill., Chgo. Ill. Sch. Nursing, 1979-80; clin. coordinator gynecology Mt. Sinai Hosp., Chgo., 1979-80; staff nurse Ill. Hosp. Assn. Med. Registry, 1979-81, Kimberly Nurses, 1982—, Suburban Hosp. and Sanitarium of Cook County, 1982-83; guest soloist Coll. DuPage. Commentator, Be Healthy, It's Good for You, Sta. WGCI, 1980. Ill. State Scholarship Commn. grantee, 1969-73. Mem. Am. Nurses Assn., Ill. Nurses Assn. Republican. Christ Ch. Home: 771 S Chatham Elmhurst IL 60126

CONNETT, JOHN EDGAR, biostatistician; b. Faucett, Mo., Oct. 12, 1941; s. Edgar Leonard and Edna Lee (Lewis) C.; m. Jane Yvonne Anderson, May 24, 1966; 1 child, Laurel. A.B., U. Mo., 1963, A.M., 1964; Ph.D., U. Md., 1969. Asst. prof. No. Ill. U., DeKalb, 1969-75; postdoctoral trainee U. Minn., Mpls., 1975-77, asst. prof., 1977—; cons. stats. Nat. Soc. to Prevent Blindness, N.Y.C., 1983—, FMC, Phila., 1984—; site visitor NIH, Bethesda, Md., 1982-84. Contbr. articles to profl. jours. O.M. Stewart fellow U. Mo., 1963, NSF sr. fellow U. Md., College Park, 1968. Mem. Am. Statis. Soc., Pi Mu Epsilon, Phi Theta Kappa. Democrat. Office: Div Biometry U Minn 1226 Mayo Bldg Minneapolis MN 55414

CONNOLLY, MATTHEW BERNARD, JR., conservationist; b. Norwood, Mass., July 28, 1941; s. Matthew B. and Carolyn Dorothy (Masciarelli) C.; m. Stephanie Ruth Leach, June 27, 1969; children—Allison, Caroline. Student St. Francis Xavier U., Antigonish, N.S., Can., 1959-61; Assoc. degree Stockbridge Sch. Agr., Amherst, Mass., 1964; B.S., U. Mass., 1968. State ornithologist Mass. Div. Fish and Game, Boston, 1968-71; dir. Mass. Div. Conservation, Boston, 1971-73, Mass. Div. Coastal Zone Mgmt., Boston, 1973-76, Mass. Div. Fisheries and Wildlife, Boston, 1976-79; dir. devel. Ducks Unltd., Inc., Long Grove, Ill., 1979-81, group mgr., 1981—; gov.'s alt. New Eng. River Basins Commn., 1973-77; chmn. New Eng. Coastal Zone Mgmt. Task Force, 1974-76; mem. Nat. Outer Continental Shelf adv. com. U.S. Dept. Interior, 1974-76; pres. NE Assn. Fisheries and Wildlife Agys., 1978. Pub., editorialist Mass. Wildlife Mag., 1976-79; chmn. editorial bd., Ducks Unltd. Mag., 1981—. Mem. Internat. Assn. Fisheries and Wildlife Agys. (communications com., water resources com.). Avocations: hunting, fishing, birding, reading. Home: Barrington IL Office: Ducks Unlimited Inc 1 Waterfowl Way Long Grove IL 60047

CONNOR, DONALD PIERCE, railroad executive; b. Cortland, N.Y., Apr. 10, 1935; s. Frank Donald and Caroline Louise (Pierce) C.; m. Jacqueline Roberta Suslovic, Oct. 4, 1958; children—Keith Donald, Kevin Kennedy. B.S. in Indsl. Mgmt., Syracuse U., 1957; M.B.A., Duquesne U., 1965. Indsl. engr. H.J. Heinz Co., Pitts., 1957-63; fin. analyst Westinghouse, Pitts., 1963-64; cost engr. Exxon, Floral Park, N.J., 1964-66; various positions Chessie System R.R.s, Cleve., 1966—, also v.p. Served with Air N.G., 1957-63. Mem. Nat. Council for Phys. Distbn. Mgmt., Nat. Freight Transp. Assn. Episcopalian. Clubs: Chagrin Valley Country (Chagrin Falls, Ohio), Center (Balt.). Avocation: Golf. Home: 23775 Duffield Rd Shaker Heights OH 44122 Office: Chessie System Railroads 3300 Terminal Tower Cleveland OH 44101

CONNOR, JAMES RICHARD, university administrator; b. Indpls., Oct. 31, 1928; s. Frank Elliott and Edna (Felt) C.; m. Zoe Ezopov, July 7, 1954; children—Janet K., Paul A. B.A., U. Iowa 1951; M.S., U. Wis.-Madison, 1954, Ph.D., 1961. Asst. prof. history Washington and Lee U., 1956-57, Va. Mil. Inst., 1958-61; asst. dir. Salzburg Seminar in Am. Studies, 1961-62; mem. joint staff Wis. Coordinating Com. Higher Edn., 1962-63; dir. Inst. Analysis, asst. prof. history U. Va., 1963-66; assoc. prof. history, assoc. provost No. Ill. U., 1966-69; provost, acad. v.p., prof. history Western Ill. U., 1969-74; chancellor U. Wis.-Whitewater, 1974—; assoc. dir. VA Higher Edn. Study Com., 1964-65; staff dir. study of governance of acad. med. ctrs. Josiah Macy Jr. Found., 1968-70; mem. Commn. on Higher Edn., North Central Assn., 1970-75, 79-84, cons.-examiner, 1972—. Served with AUS, 1946-47, 51-53. Woodrow Wilson fellow, 1953-54; So. fellow, 1957-58. Mem. AAUP, Am. Hist. Assn., Orgn. Am. Historians, Phi Beta Kappa, Phi Eta Sigma, Phi Kappa Phi, Phi Delta Kappa, Beta Gamma Sigma, Phi Alpha Theta, Delta Sigma Pi. Home: Route 2 Linden Dr Whitewater WI 53190 Office: 800 W Main St Library Adminstrn 2124 Whitewater WI 53190

CONNOR, MAUREEN FROELKE, nurse, hospital administrator; b. Rush City, Minn., Feb. 4, 1942; d. Leonard Robert and Mary Louise (Delmore) Froelke; m. James Allen Connor; children—Mark Allen, Christopher Wade. Diploma Northwestern Hosp. Sch. Nursing, 1963; B.A., Metro U., 1983. Cert. nursing adminstr. Am. Nurses Assn. Nursing supr. Dakota Hosp., Fargo, N.D., 1966-69; dir. nurses St. Mary's Hosp. and Home, Winsted, Minn., 1970-72; asst. adminstr. Houston N.W. Med. Ctr., 1972-80; assoc. adminstr. St. Croix Valley Meml. Hosp., St. Croix Falls, Wis., 1980—; mem. adv. bd. Polk County chpt. Am. Cancer Soc. Mem. Am. Soc. Hosp. Nursing Services Adminstrs., Wis. Nurses Assn., Wis. Soc. Hosp. Nursing Service Adminstrs. Roman Catholic. Home: 1308 3rd St Hudson WI 54016 Office: St Croix Valley Memorial Hospital Saint Croix Falls WI 54024

CONNOR, WILLIAM STEPHEN, food industry executive; b. Chgo., Oct. 11, 1945; s. William Stephen Jr. and Mary Jane (Sheridan) C.; m. Margaret Cordula Carney, Nov. 25, 1973. B.S., So. Ill. U., 1972. Dist. sales mgr. Pepperidge Farm Inc., Chgo., 1979-83; sales mgr. Evans Food Products, Chgo., 1983—. Served with USMC, 1966-69. Mem. Potato Chip Snack Food Assn. Roman Catholic. Avocations: golf; racquetball. Home: 14450 Country Club Ln Orland Park IL 60462 Office: Evans Food Products 700 W 41st St Chicago IL 60609

CONNORS, DORSEY (MRS. JOHN E. FORBES), TV and radio commentator, newspaper columnist; b. Chgo.; d. William J. and Sara (MacLean) Connors; B.A. cum laude, U. Ill.; m. John E. Forbes; 1 dau., Stephanie. Appeared on Personality Profiles, WGN-TV, Chgo., 1948, Dorsey Connors Show, WMAQ-TV, Chgo., 1949-58, 61-63, Armchair Travels, WMAQ-TV, 1952-55, Home Show, NBC, 1954-57, Haute Couture Fashion Openings, NBC, Paris, France, 1954, 58, Dorsey Connors program, WGN, 1958-61, Tempo Nine, WGN-TV, 1961, Society in Chgo., WMAQ-TV, 1964; floor reporter WGN-TV, Republican Conv., Chgo., 1960, Democratic Conv., Los Angeles, 1960; writer column Hi! I'm Dorsey Connors, Chgo. Sun Times, 1965—. Founder Ill. Epilepsy League; mem. woman's bd. Children's Home and Aid Soc.; mem. women's bd. USO. Mem. AFTRA, Screen Actor's Guild, Nat. Acad. TV Arts and Scis., Soc. Midland Authors, Chgo. Hist. Soc., Chi Omega. Author: Gadgets Galore, 1953; Save Time, Save Money, Save Yourself, 1972. Address: care Chgo Sun Times 401 N Wabash Chicago IL 60611

CONNORS, VICTOR JOSEPH, optometrist; b. Hillsboro, Wis., June 9, 1947; s. Joseph Anthony and Ruby Ruth (Hamburg) C.; m. Rebecca Renee Talg, Aug. 29, 1970; children—Sara Ellen, Colleen Erin, Colin Victor. Student, Wis. State U.-La Crosse, 1965-67; B.S. in Optometry, Ill. Coll. Optometry, 1971, O.D., 1971. Sole practice optometry, Middleton, Wis., 1971—; dir. Bank of Middleton. Mem., chmn. City of Middleton Police Commn., 1977—; pres., bd. dirs. Middleton Area Devel. Corp., 1976—; mem. adv. com. Madison Vocat. Tech. Coll., 1980. Mem. Wis. Optometric Assn. (past bd. dirs., v.p.), Am. Optometric Assn., Madison Area Optometric Soc. (pres. 1971—), Middleton C. of C. (past bd. dirs., pres.). Lutheran. Clubs: Optimist (past pres.), Ducks Unltd. (chmn. 1983—). Home: 6630 Maywood Ave Middleton WI 53562 Office: 6602 University Ave Middleton WI 53562

CONRAD, JEROME ARTHUR, surgeon; b. Grand Rapids, Mich., Dec. 18, 1938; s. Conrad J. and Adele (Graff) C.; B.S., Aquinas Coll., 1960; M.D., Georgetown U., 1964; m. Rita A. Laberteaux, July 28, 1962; children—Amy T., Christopher J., Caroline A. Intern, San Francisco Gen. Hosp., 1964-65; orthopedic resident Henry Ford Hosp., Detroit, 1965-69; fellow in orthopedics Harvard U., 1969; practice medicine specializing in orthopedic surgery Mecosta County Gen. Hosp. (formerly Community Hosp.), Big Rapids, Mich., 1971—; mem. staff Reed City, Kelsey Meml. hosps., Lakeview, Mich. Served to lt. comdr. USNR, 1969-71. Diplomate Am. Bd. Orthopedic Surgery. Fellow Am. Acad. Orthopedic Surgery, A.C.S.; mem. AMA, Am. Trauma Soc., Internat. Arthroscopy Assn., Arthroscopy Assn. N.Am., Mid.-Am. Orthopedic Assn., Mich. Orthopedic Soc. (pres. 1984), Mich. State, Tri-County med. socs. Clubs: Lions, Elks. Home: 302 Division St Big Rapids MI 49307 Office: 413 Mecosta St Big Rapids MI 49307

CONRAD, LORETTA JANE, educational administrator; b. Wooster, Ohio, Aug. 9, 1934; d. Donald William and Celia Irene (Smith) C.; B.Mus.Edn. cum laude, Coll. of Wooster, 1956; M.Mus.Edn., U. Colo., 1969; postgrad. cert. supervision/adminstrn. (Univ. scholar), John Carroll U., 1978. Tchr., Avon Lake (Ohio) public schs., 1956-61; Dept. Def., Europe and Far East, 1961-64, Bay Village (Ohio) Bd. Edn., 1964-73, Elyria (Ohio) public schs., 1973-78; asst. prin. Bay Village Bd. Edn., Bay High Sch., 1978-84, Bay Middle Sch., 1984—; music clinician, adjudicator; pvt. tchr. piano; accompanist, dir. Ch. Choir, Luth. Ch., 1966-80. Area rep. for recruitment, mem. music com. Coll. of Wooster. Presser scholar, 1955-56; Annie Webb Blanton scholar, Delta Kappa Gamma, 1968. Mem. Ohio Assn. Secondary Sch. Prins., Nat. Assn. Secondary Sch. Prins., Assn. Secondary Curriculum Devel., Ohio Middle Schs. Assn., Phi Delta Kappa, Delta Kappa Gamma, Alpha Delta (state music rep.). Democrat. Lutheran. Club: Quota (pres. 1985-86). Home: 1650 Cedarwood St Westlake OH 44145 Office: 27725 Wolf Rd Bay Village OH 44140

CONRAN, PATRICIA CANNON, school superintendent; b. Chgo.; d. Julia A. (Irwin) Cannon; m. Patrick Joseph Conran, Oct. 12, 1957; children—Karen, Kevin, Michael, Michele. B.A., Mundelein Coll., 1957; M.A., McCormick Theol. Sem., 1970; Ph.D., Northwestern U., 1974. Research statistician Wade Advt. Chgo., 1957-60; tchr. St. Francis Borgia Sch., Chgo., 1960-61; asst. curriculum coordinator, tchr. St. Mary Ctr. for Learning, Chgo., 1968-70; instr. Mundelein (Ill.) Coll., summer 1970; asst. prin., dir. curriculum, tchr. Acad. Sacred Heart, Chgo., 1970-73; research asst. Sch. Edn., Northwestern U., 1973-74, asst. prof., summer 1976; prin. Indian Trail Sch., Highland Park (Ill.) Dist. 107, 1974-78; asst. supt. for curriculum and instrn. Community Consolidated Sch. Dist. 146, 1978-81; supt. schs. Benjamin Sch. Dist. 25, West Chicago, Ill., 1981—; cons. in field. Lector, commentator Saints Faith, Hope and Charity Ch., Winnetka, Ill., 1974; chmn., mem. Curriculum Study Com., New Trier East High Sch., 1974—; mem. bd. edn. St. Raymond de Penafort Ch., Mt. Prospect, Ill., 1973-74. Mem. Assn. for Supervision and Curriculum Devel. (pres. 1983-84), Am. Ednl. Research Assn., Am. Assn. Sch. Adminstrs. (mem. talent bank), Ill. Assn. Sch. Bus. Ofcls., Nat. Soc. for Study of Edn., Phi Delta Kappa. Contbr. articles to profl. jours.

CONRY, THOMAS FRANCIS, mechanical engineering educator, consultant; b. West Hempstead, N.Y., Mar. 7, 1942; s. Thomas and Bridget Anne (Walsh) C.; m. Sharon Ann Silverwood, June 10, 1967; children—Christine Elizabeth, Carolyn Danielle, Anne Marie. B.S., Pa. State U., 1963; M.S., U. Wis.-Madison, 1967, Ph.D., 1970. Registered profl. engr., Wis., Ill. Engr., Gen. Motors Corp., Milw., 1963-66; sr. research engr., Indpls., 1969-71; asst. prof. gen. engring. U. Ill., Urbana, 1971-75; assoc. prof. gen. and mech. engring., 1975-81, prof. gen. and mech. engring., 1981—; sr. visitor U. Cambridge (Eng.), 1978; cons. Zurn Industries; staff cons. Sargent & Lundy, Engrs.; cons. indsl. firm on machine dynamics, optimization and tribology. Contbr. articles to profl. jours.; tech. editor Jour. Vibration, Acoustics, Stress and Reliability in Design. Mem. Bd. Edn. St. Matthews Parish Roman Catholic Ch., Champaign, 1981-84. NSF trainee, 1968-69; NASA/ASEE summer faculty fellow, 1974-75. Mem. ASME (chmn. design engring. div. 1979-80), Sigma Xi, Lambda Chi Alpha. Home: 3301 Lakeshore Dr Champaign IL 61821 Office: 104 S Mathews Ave Urbana IL 61801

CONSIDINE, FRANK WILLIAM, container corporation executive; b. Chgo., Aug. 15, 1921; s. Frank Joseph and Minnie (Regan) C.; Ph.B., Loyola U., Chgo., 1943; m. Nancy Scott, Apr. 3, 1948. Ptnr., F. J. Hogan Agy., Chgo., 1945-47; asst. to pres. Graham Glass Co., Chgo., 1947-51; owner F.W. Considine Co., Chgo., 1951-55; v.p. Metro Glass div. Kraftco, Chgo., 1955-60; v.p., dir. Nat. Can Corp., Chgo., 1961-67, exec. v.p., 1967-69, pres., 1969—, chief exec. officer, 1973—, chmn., 1984—, also mem. fin. com., chmn. exec. com., mem. corp. devel. com.; dir. Allis Chalmers Corp., 1st Chgo. Corp., 1st Nat. Bank Chgo., Maytag Co., Internat. Minerals & Chem. Corp., Tribune Co., Ency. Brit. Mem. governing bd. Ill. Council Econ. Edn.; past chmn. U.S. sect Egypt-U.S. Bus. Council; trustee Loyola U., Chgo.; exec. com., trustee Mus. Sci. and Industry of Chgo.; bd. dirs. Can Mfrs. Inst., Evanston Hosp., Lyric Opera of Chgo., Jr. Achievement Chgo., Econ. Devel. Com. Chgo., Field Mus. Natural History; bd. dirs. Com. Ill. Indsl. Devel. Authority. Served to lt. USNR, 1943-46. Mem. U.S. Brewers Assn. (asso. dir.), Econ. Club Chgo., Am. Inst. Food Distbrn. (bd. trustees, chmn.), Chgo. Assn. Commerce and Industry (past pres.). Clubs: Chgo., Econ., Comml., Mid Am. (Chgo.); Glen View. Office: Nat Can Co 8101 Higgins Rd Chicago IL 60631*

CONSIDINE, RALPH DONALD, sales and marketing executive, consultant; b. Chgo., Mar. 30, 1934; s. Ralph James and Gertrude M. (Weller) C.; m. Carol May Jefferies, Sept. 17, 1960; children—Cheryl Ann, Ralph James, Donald Albert. B.S., Coll. Holy Cross, 1956. Dist. sales mgr. Procter & Gamble, Cin., 1958-62, Chgo., 1963-73; regional mgr. Celanese Corp., Chgo., 1973-76; regional mgr. Fuller-O'Brien Corp., Chgo., 1976-79; v.p. sales and mktg. Airguide Instrument Co., Chgo., 1979-81; dir. sales and mktg. Sellstrom Mfg. Co., Palatine, Ill., 1981—; cons. Cons. Capacities Group, Cold Spring Harbor, N.Y., 1982—. Vice-pres. Northbrook Hockey League, 1977—; bd. dirs. Amateur Hockey Assn. Ill., Chgo., 1979—, state tournament chmn., 1984-85. Served to lt. (j.g.) USN, 1956-58. Mem. Sales and Mktg. Execs. Chgo. (mem. com. disting. sales awards 1982—). Republican. Roman Catholic. Lodge: Elks.

CONSIDINE, WILLIAM HOWARD, health care adminstrator; b. Akron, Ohio, July 7, 1947; s. G. Howard and Gene Marie (Nelson) C.; m. Rebecca Diane Krenrick, Oct. 14, 1972; children—Michael, Cathryn, Matthew. B.A., Akron U., 1969; M.S., Ohio State U., 1971. Program cons. USPHS, Bethesda, Md., 1971-73; with patient care mgmt. N.C. Meml. Hosp., Chapel Hill, 1973-75, with gen. services, 1975-76, dir. ambulatory care, 1977-79; pres. Children's Hospital, Akron, Ohio, 1979—; cons. search com. Children's Hosp., Nat. Med. Ctr., Washington, 1982, Robert Wood Johnson Found. on Ambulatory Care Dental Program, 1978-79. Chmn. Akron Health Coordinating Council, 1978-79, EEO com. NIH, 1972-73. Served to lt. USPHS, 1971-73. Recipient Appreciation award Ohio State U. Alumni in Health Services Adminstrn., 1975, Outstanding Hoban Alumni award, 1984; research asst. grantee Kellogg Found., 1971. Mem. Am. Coll. of Hosp. Adminstrs., Am. Hosp. Assn., Assn. of Am. Med. Colls., Nat. Assn. of Children's Hosps. and Related Insts., Children's Hosp. Executive Council, Assn. of Univ. Programs in Health Adminstrn., Ohio Hosp. Assn., Ohio State U. Alumni Assn., North Hosp. Assn., Chapel Hill C. of C. Roman Catholic. Clubs: Casad, University, Portage Country (Akron). Office: Children's Hosp Med Ctr of Akron 281 Locust St Akron OH 44308

CONSTANCE, LISA ANN, accountant; b. Chgo., Apr. 30, 1959; d. Philip and Dorothy (Zmuda) C. B.S. in Acctg. cum laude, U. S.C., 1981. C.P.A., Ill. Accounts payable clk. L.E. Myers, Chgo., 1980; peer adviser U. S.C., Columbia, 1979-81; internal auditor Sara Lee Corp., Chgo., 1981-85; internal auditor Union Carbide Corp., Chgo., 1985—. U. S.C. scholar, 1980. Mem. Ill. C.P.A. Soc., EDP Auditors Assn., Beta Gamma Sigma, Beta Alpha Psi. Democrat. Roman Catholic. Avocation: travel. Home: 462 Ridgewood Glen Ellyn IL 60137 Office: Union Carbide 120 S Riverside Plaza Chicago IL 60606

CONTE, LOU JAMES, artistic director, choreographer; b. DuQuoin, Ill., Apr. 17, 1942; s. John and Floy Mae (Saunders) C. Student Ellis DuBoulay Sch. Ballet, Chgo., 1961-68, So. Ill. U., 1960-62, Am. Ballet Theatre Sch., N.Y.C., 1964-66. Choreographer musicals Mame, 1972, Boss, 1973; choreographer Milw. Melody Top, 1966; dir. Lou Conte Dance Studio, Chgo., 1974—; artistic dir. Hubbard St. Dance Co., Chgo., 1977—; lectr. Mem. Actors Equity Assn., AFTRA. Office: 218 S Wabash Ave Chicago IL 60604*

CONTEE, RICHARD S., orchestra executive. Vice pres., managing dir. Saint Paul Chamber Orchestra. Office: St Paul Chamber Orchestra Ordway Music Theatre Landmark Ctr 75 W Fifth St Saint Paul MN 55102*

CONTIE, LEROY JOHN, JR., judge; b. Canton, Ohio, Apr. 2, 1920; s. Leroy J. and Mary J. (DeSantis) C.; m. Janice N. Zollars, Nov. 28, 1953; children—Ann Benson, Leroy J. B.A., U. Mich., 1941, J.D., 1984. Bar: Ohio 1948. Ptnr., Contie & Contie, Canton, 1948-69; judge Stark County Common Pleas Ct., Canton, 1969-71; judge U.S. Dist. Ct. Ohio, Akron, 1971-82; U.S. Ct. Appeals (6th cir.), Cin., 1982—; law dir. City of Canton, 1951-60. Adv. bd. Walsh Coll., Canton, Akron U. Law Sch. Served with U.S. Army, 1942-46. Mem. Am. Judicature Soc., ABA, Fed. Bar Assn., Ohio Bar Assn., Akron Bar Assn., Stark County Bar Assn., Am. Legion. Republican. Roman Catholic. Lodges: K.C., Elks (Canton). Home: 3120 Westmoreland NW Canton OH 44718 Office: US Ct Appeals 2 S Main St Akron OH 44308

CONYERS, JOHN, JR., Congressman; b. Detroit, May 16, 1929; s. John and Lucille (Simpson) C.; B.A., Wayne State U., 1957, LL.B., 1958. Admitted to Mich. bar, 1959; legis. asst., State of Mich., 1958-61; practice law, Detroit, 1962-64; referee Mich. Workmen's Compensation Dept., Detroit, 1962-64; mem. 89th-99th congresses from 1st Mich. Dist., chmn. criminal justice subcom. of judiciary com. Trustee, Martin Luther King, Jr. Center for Nonviolent Social Change. Mem. NAACP (dir. Detroit chpt.), ACLU (Mich. adv. bd.). Served to 2d lt., C.E., U.S. Army, 1951. Baptist. Office: 2313 Rayburn House Office Bldg Washington DC 20515

COOGAN, ALAN HALL, geology educator, lawyer; b. Bklyn., Dec. 19, 1929; s. Francis Allen and Dorothy (Baker) C.; m. Sylvia Carolyn Smith, Aug. 30,

1960; children—Daniel S., Peter M., Stephen A. B.A., U. Calif.-Berkeley, 1956, M.A., 1957; Ph.D., U. Ill., 1962; J.D., U. Akron, 1977. Bar: Ohio 1977. Geologist, Esso Prodn. Research Co., Houston, 1962-67; sole practice, Ravenna, Ohio, 1967—; prof. geology Kent State U., Ohio, 1967—; cons. in geology, Kent, 1970—; v.p. Gilbert Oil Co. Co-author numerous books on geology, paleontology, sedimentology, and law. Contbr. articles to profl. jours. Mem. Bd. Law and Grad. Rev., Ohio, 1980—. Served with U.S. Army, 1952-54. Mem. Am. Assn. Petroleum Geologists, Soc. Econ. Paleontologists and Mineralogists, Am. Inst. Profl. Geologists, Ohio Bar Assn., Paleontol. Soc. Democrat. Presbyterian. Home: 1993 Brokview Dr Kent OH 44240 Office: Dept Geology Kent State Univ Kent OH 44242

COOGAN, JAMES HENRY, lawyer; b. Cin., Aug. 23, 1937; s. Joseph W. and Vera C. (Wiechman) C.; m. Kathy L. Siebert, Dec. 11, 1971; 1 child, Carrie E. B.A. in Econs., U. Cin., 1959, J.D., 1961. Bar: Ohio 1961, U.S. Dist. Ct. (so. dist.) Ohio 1963. Sole practice, Cin., 1961—; lectr. law U. Cin., 1971-80. Contbr. articles to legal jours. Pres. Mt. Airy Civic Club, Cin., 1975-76; trustee Council on Alcoholism, Cin., 1971-81; mem. Hamilton County Big Bros., Cin., 1962-64. Mem. Ohio State Bar Assn., Cin. Bar Assn. (lawyers assistance com., co-chmn. ethics com. 1982, chmn. 1985—). Republican. Roman Catholic. Avocation: power boating. Home: 4844 Raeburn Ln Cincinnati OH 45223 Office: 2112 Central Trust Tower One W Fourth St Cincinnati OH 45202

COOK, ALEXANDER BURNS, educator, museum curator; b. Grand Rapids, Mich., Apr. 16, 1924; s. Gorell Alexander and Harriette Florence (Hinze) C.; B.A., Ohio Wesleyan U., 1949; M.S., Case Western Res. U., 1967. Editorial cartoonist, artist Cleve. Plain Dealer, 1949-55; account exec. Edward Howard & Co., Cleve., 1955-61; spl. art tchr. Cleve. Pub. Schs., 1964—; curator exhibits Gt. Lakes Mus., Vermilion, Ohio, 1970-78, curator, 1978—, chmn. mus. operating com., 1977—. Trustee, Berkshire Condominium Owners Assn., 1981-83, pres., 1982-83. Served with AUS, 1943-45. Recipient award of honor Ohio Wesleyan U., 1955; Distinguished Achievement award Gt. Lakes Hist. Soc., 1973; 1st pl. award for editorial cartoons Union Tchr. Press Assn., 1980, 81, 82. Mem. Gt. Lakes Hist. Soc. (exec. v.p. 1959-64, v.p. 1964—, trustee, mem. exec. com. 1959—), Ohioana Library Assn., Akron Art Mus., Cleve. Mus. Art, Am. Soc. Marine Artists, Delta Tau Delta, Pi Delta Epsilon, Pi Sigma Alpha. Republican. Episcopalian. Contbr. editorial cartoons to Reid Cartoon Collection, U. Kans. Jour. Hist. Center, The Critique, 1975—; editorial adviser, numerous articles to Inland Seas, 1957—, The Chadburn, 1976—; cover illustrations for Ohioana Quar., 1979—; book cover illustrations Dodd, Mead & Co., 1984. Paintings represented in pvt. collections, 1960—; executed mural depicting Gt. Lakes shipping Gt. Lakes Mus., 1969. Home: 11820 Edgewater Dr Lakewood OH 44107

COOK, BEVERLY BLAIR, political science educator; b. Chgo., Dec. 10, 1926; d. Ross J. and Nita L. (Hanson) Ulman; m. Cornelius P. Cotter, July 31, 1966; children—C. Randall, Linda G., David S., Gary A. B.A., Wellesley Coll., 1948; M.A., U. Wis.-Madison, 1949; Ph.D., Claremont Grad. Sch., 1962. Instr. Iowa State U., Ames, 1949-50; asst. prof. polit. sci. Calif. State U.-Fullerton, 1962-66; assoc. prof. U. Wis.-Milw., 1967-74, prof., 1974—; vis. prof. UCLA, 1984; bd. advisers NOW Legal Aid and Def. Fund Project on Jud. Edn. Bd. overseers NSF Supreme Ct. Project; bd. dirs. Bicentennial Constrn. Project '87. Pendleton scholar, 1944-48, Wellesley scholar, 1948; Ford Found. fellow, 1960-62, 72-73; Fromkin grantee, 1973; Florence E. Eagleton grantee, 1976-77; grantee Am. Philos. Soc., 1967, 71, Social Sci. Research Council, 1969-70. Mem. Am. Polit. Sci. Assn., Internat. Polit. Sci. Assn., Midwest Polit. Sci. Assn. (v.p.), Western Polit. Sci. Assn., Law and Soc. Assn., U.S. Supreme Ct. Hist. Soc., NOW, Am. Judicature Soc., Pi Sigma Alpha (bd. dirs.). Author: The Judicial Process in California, 1967; contbr. chpts., articles to profl. publs. Home: 3965 N Harcourt Pl Milwaukee WI 53211 Office: Dept Polit Sci U Wis Milwaukee WI 53201

COOK, D. S., holding company executive. Pres., dir. Buckeye Fin. Corp., Columbus, Ohio. Office: Buckeye Fin Corp 36 E Gay St Columbus OH 43215*

COOK, DON WHITNEY, SR., telephone company executive; b. Memphis, Nov. 9, 1945; s. Willie and Lillian Louise (Whitney) C.; m. Wilma Robinson, Dec. 29, 1968; children—Kimberly, Don. B.E., Lincoln U., 1967; M.E., U. Mo., 1968. Cert. elem. and secondary tchr. and prin., Mo. Tchr. St. Joseph Pub. Schs., Mo., 1970-73; adminstr. Mo. Western State Coll., St. Joseph, 1973-76; communications cons. Southwestern Bell Telephone Co., Kansas City, Mo., 1976, service supr., 1977, adminstrv. mgr., 1977-80, staff mgr. gen. headquarters, St. Louis, 1980—. Patentee (game) Flip Your Lid, 1983. Mem. adv. council Gateway 70001, St. Louis, 1981—, aux. bd. Mt. Zion Baptist Ch., St. Louis, 1983—; bd. dirs. Carver House, Inc., St. Louis, 1984—, United Way, St. Joseph, 1973-76, Boys' Club, Kansas City, 1976-80. Served as 1st lt. U.S. Army, 1968-70, Vietnam. Decorated Bronze Star. Recipient Chgo. Tribune award. Mem. Lincoln U. Alumni Assn., Nat. Alliance of Businessmen, Phi Mu Alpha, Alpha Phi Alpha. Home: 677 Dougherty Terr Dr Manchester MO 63011 Office: Southwestern Bell Telephone Co One Bell Ctr Suite 8X1 St Louis MO 63101

COOK, JOHN RONALD, consulting civil engineer; b. Evanston, Ill., Sept. 21, 1957; s. Ronald Edward and Shirley Ann (Pregl) C.; m. Linda Marie Olsiewicz, Oct. 11, 1981. B.S. in Civil Engring., U. Ill., 1980; M.B.A., Roosevelt U., 1984. Registered profl. engr., Ill., Calif. Civil engr., Doyen & Assocs., Inc., Chgo., 1980-81, project engr., 1981-83, mgr. computer ops., 1982-83, project mgr., 1983-84; sr. mgmt. engr. Surety Support Services, Inc., Oak Brook, Ill., 1984—; pres. Diversified Mgmt. Cons., Naperville, 1979—. United Airlines scholar, 1975. Mem. U. Ill. Alumni Assn., Am. Concrete Inst., Ill. Soc. Profl. Engrs., Nat. Soc. Profl. Engrs., ASCE, Beta Gamma Sigma. Republican. Lutheran. Office: Surety Support Services Inc 1211 W 22d St Suite 426 Oak Brook IL 60521

COOK, JULIAN ABELE, JR., judge; b. Washington, June 22, 1930; s. Julian Abele and Ruth Elizabeth (McNeill) C.; B.A., Pa. State U., 1952; J.D., Georgetown U., 1957; m. Carol Annette Dibble, Dec. 22, 1957; children—Julian Abele, Peter Dibble, Susan Annette. Law clk. to Judge Arthur E. Moore, 1957-58; mem. firm Bledsoe, Ford and Bledsoe, 1958-60; mem. firm Taylor, Patrick, Bailor and Lee, 1960-61; mem. firm Cook and Hooe, 1961-65; mem. firm Hempstead, Houston, McGrath and Cook, 1965-68; individual practice law, 1968-75; partner firm Cook, Wittenberg, Curry and Magid, 1975; partner firm Cook and Curry, 1976-78; judge U.S. Dist. Ct. Eastern Dist. Mich., Detroit, 1978—; adj. prof. law U. Detroit Sch. Law, 1971-74; gen. counsel WTVS, Public Broadcasting TV, 1973-78; mem. Mich. State Bd. Ethics, 1977-78; labor arbitrator Am. Arbitration Assn. and Mich. Employment Relations Commn., 1975-78; mem. Mich. Law and Media Commn., from 1978. Mem. exec. bd. dirs. Child and Family Services Mich., also pres.; bd. dirs. Todd-Phillips Children's Home, Inc., Camp Oakland, Inc., Franklin-Wright Settlement, Inc., Pontiac Opportunities Industrialization Center; mem. Oak Park (Mich.) Compensation Commn.; bd. advisors East Mich. Environ. Action Council; bd. dirs. Oakland Youth Symphony; chmn. Mich. Civil Rights Commn., 1968-71; bd. dirs., treas. Oakland Livingston Econ. Devel. Corp.; bd. dirs. Mich. ACLU, Mich. United Way; chmn. citizens com. Project Twenty Com., Oakland U.; pres., dir. Pontiac Area Urban League. Served with U.S. Army, 1952-54. Recipient Disting. Citizen of Year award NACCP, 1970; Merit citation Pontiac Urban League, 1971; resolution Mich. Ho. of Reps., 1971; Service award Todd Phillips Children's Home, 1978; Pathfinders award Oakland U., 1977. Mem. ABA, Mich. Bar Assn. (chmn. constl. law com. 1969, vice chmn. civil liberties com. 1970), Nat. Bar Assn., Oakland Bar Assn. (chmn. continuing legal edn. com. 1968-69, vice chmn. dist. ct. com. 1977), Wolverine Bar Assn., Fed. Bar Assn., Indsl. Relations Research Assn. Office: 277 United State Courthouse Detroit MI 48226*

COOK, NOEL ROBERT, manufacturing company executive; b. Houston, Mar. 19, 1937; s. Horace Berwick and Leda Estelle (Houghton) C.; student Iowa State U., 1955-57; B.S. in Indsl. Engring., U. Mich., 1960; children—Laurel Jane, David Robert. Engr. in tng. Eaton Mfg., Saginaw, Mich., 1960-61; mgr. mfg. and contracting J. N. Fauver Co., Madison Heights, Mich., 1961-65; pres. Newton Mfg., Royal Oak, Mich., 1965—; soc. Indsl. Piping Contractors, Birmingham, Mich., 1969-75; pres. RNR Metal Fabricators, Inc., Royal Oak, Mich., 1974-78; chmn. bd. Kim Internat. Sales Co., 1978—; pres. Newton Sales Co., Royal Oak, 1978—, Power Package Windsor Ltd., Windsor, Ont., Can., 1981—. Served with U.S. Army, 1960-61. Registered profl. engr., Mich. Mem. Fluid Power Soc., Nat. Fluid Power Assn., Birmingham Jr. C. of C. (past bd. dirs.). Patentee in field. Home: 4481 W Cherry Hill Dr Orchard Lake MI 48033 Office: 4249 Delemere Blvd Royal Oak MI 48073

COOK, ROBERT E., diversified manufacturing executive. Pres., chief exec. officer, chief. operating officer, dir. Roper Corp., Kankakee, Ill. Office: Roper Corp 1905 W Court St Kankakee IL 60901*

COOK, ROBERT WILLIAM, financial executive; b. Sulligent, Ala., Mar. 11, 1943; s. Murray Ray and Millie Grace (Allman) C.; m. Lenore Y. Pinckney, Aug. 28, 1965; children—Miranda J., Adrienne S.; m. Deborah L. Holmes, Mar. 11, 1982; 1 dau., Nina L. B.A. in Econs. cum laude, Rutgers U., 1970, M.B.A. in Acctg., 1971. Cost acctg. clk. Permacel div. Johnson & Johnson, New Brunswick, N.J., 1968-69; staff acct. Arthur Young & Co., C.P.A.s, N.Y.C., 1971-73; fiscal mgr. Opportunities Industrialization Ctrs., Phila., 1973; mgr. adminstrn. Zion Investment Assocs., Phila., 1973-76; sr. acct., then asst. controller Unified Industries, Inc., Springfield, Va., 1976-79, controller, 1979-82; controller PolyTech, Inc., Cleve., 1982—; cons. in field. Served with USAF, 1964-68. Rutgers U. Bd. Govs. scholar. Mem. Nat. Assn. Accts. Home: 17408 Glenshire Ave Cleveland OH 44135 Office: 1744 Payne Ave Cleveland OH 44114

COOK, STANTON R., newspaper pub.; b. Chgo., July 3, 1925; s. Rufus Merrill and Thelma Marie (Bogerson) C.; B.S. in Mech. Engring., Northwestern U., 1949; m. Barbara Wilson. Dist. sales rep. Shell Oil Co., 1949-51; prodn. engr. Chgo. Tribune, 1951-60, asst. prodn. mgr., 1960-65, prodn. mgr., 1965-67, prodn. dir., 1967-70, dir. ops., 1970, v.p. Chgo. Tribune Co., 1967-70, exec. v.p., gen. mgr., 1970-73, pres., 1973—, pub., 1973—, chief exec. officer, from 1974, chmn., 1974—; v.p., dir. Tribune Co., Chgo., 1973-74, pres., chief officer, 1974—; dir. Newspaper Advt. Bur., Inc., AP. Trustee U. Chgo., Mus. Sci. and Industry, Chgo., Orchestral Assn. (Chgo. Symphony), Field Mus. Nat. History, Chgo., Am. Newspaper Pubs. Assn. Found., Robert R. McCormick Trusts and Founds.; mem. bus. adv. council Chgo. Urban League; mem. Chgo. World's Fair-1992 Authority; past. bd. dirs. Chgo. Found. Pub. Edn. Mem. Am. Newspaper Pubs. Assn. (dir., 2d v.p.). Clubs: Econ. (life, past pres.), Comml. (past pres.). Office: 435 N Michigan Ave Chicago IL 60611

COOKE, ALLAN ROY, gastroenterologist, educator; b. Lismore, N.S.W., Australia, Apr. 30, 1936; came to U.S., 1964; s. Lindsay and Elsie Ellen (Vidler) C.; m. Judith McGuire Cooke, Nov. 21, 1983; children—Ian Russell, Colin Roy. B.Medicine, Sydney U., 1958, B.Surgery, 1958, M.D., 1970. Resident, Prince Alfred Hosp., Sydney, Australia, 1959-64; assoc. prof. to prof. U. Iowa, Iowa City, 1970-76; prof. medicine U. Kans., Kansas City, 1976—. Contbr. articles to profl. jours. Served with Australian Army, 1952-58. Fellow ACP, Australian Coll. Physicians; mem. Soc. Clin. Investigation, Central Soc. Clin. Research, Am. Fedn. Clin. Research (pres. 1976-77). Ch. of England. Avocations: Tennis; jogging; collecting prints. Home: 6436 High Dr Mission Hills KS 66208 Office: Univ Kans Med Center Rainbow Blvd Kansas City KS 66103

COOKE, DAVID WILLIAM, medical group practice executive; b. Detroit, May 31, 1935; s. Edward Goddard and Helen (Vredeveld) C.; m. Mary Kathryn Cooke; children—David W., Judith A., Thomas J. B.S., Franklin U., 1974; M.B.A., U. Dayton, 1975. With sales mgmt. dept. Ciba Pharm. Co., Pitts., Detroit and Columbus, Ohio, 1961-68; adj. prof. Franklin U., 1976—; pres. University Med. Mgmt., Inc., Columbus, Ohio, 1981—; exec. dir. Dept. Medicine Found. Inc., Ohio State U., Columbus, 1981—. Mem. Med. Group Mgmt. Assn., Ohio Med. Group Mgmt. Assn., Central Ohio Med. Group Mgmt. Assn., Am. Mgmt. Assn. Presbyterian. Home: 158 Corbin's Mill Dr Dublin OH 43017 Office: 456 Clinic Dr Columbus OH 43210

COOKE, EVELYN KATHLEEN CHATMAN, educator; b. Jackson, Tenn.; d. Charles Elijah and Josie (Bond) Chatman; B.A. cum laude, Lane Coll., 1955; M.Ed., Xavier U.; m. James T. Cooke, Apr. 21, 1954 (div. Aug. 1970); 1 dau., Madelyn LaRene. Tchr. public schs., Chattanooga, 1957-67, Cin., 1967—; cons. career edn. Public Schs., Cin. Pres., Harriet Tubman's Black Women's Democratic Club; mem. upper grade sch study council. Recipient Spirit of Detroit award, 1981, Outstanding Educator award Phi Delta Kappa. Mem. Fellowship United Meth. Musicians, NAACP, Council for Co-op Action, Am., Ohio Fedn. Tchrs. Cin. Fedn. Tchrs., Cin. Council Educators, Nat. Council Negro Women, Top Ladies of Distinction (outstanding service award 1981, nat. 2d v.p. chmn. info. com., pres. Cin. chpt.), Sigma Gamma Rho (nat. constn. and by-laws com., anti-basileus Epsilon Lambda Sigma chpt.), Gamma Theta, Sigma Rho Sigma. Methodist (dir. music ch.). Home: 6748 Elwynne Dr Cincinnati OH 45236

COOKE, JOHN WILLARD, osteopathic physician; b. Chgo., Nov. 28, 1952; s. Weldon and Frances (Willard) C.; m. Kimberly Ann Radnothy, Oct. 27, 1979. B.S. cum laude, Wheaton Coll., 1974; D.O., Mich. State U., 1978. Diplomate Am. Bd. Internal Medicine. Rotating intern Botsford Hosp., Farmington Hills, Mich., 1978-79; resident in internal medicine Wayne State U., Detroit, 1979-82; staff Redford Hosp. (Mich.), 1983—. Mem. Am. Osteo. Assn., Mich. Osteo. Assn. Home: 11084 Flamingo St Livonia MI 48150

COOKSON, ELOISE GRIES, lawyer; b. Toledo, May 3, 1950; d. Walter John and Marie (Beck) Gries; m. Kenneth R. Cookson, Apr. 28, 1979; 1 child, John Richard. B.A., U. Toledo, 1972, J.D., 1976. Bar: Ohio 1976. Asst. pros. atty. Lucas County, Toledo, 1976-79, Cuyahoga County, Cleve., 1979-81; sr. atty.-officer Bank One, Columbus, Ohio, 1982—. Mem. Ohio Bar Assn., Columbus Bar Assn. Office: Bank One 100 E Broad St Columbus OH 43271-0152

COOKSON, KENNETH RAY, lawyer; b. Bluffton, Ohio, Nov. 8, 1951; s. Richard Ray and Betty Jean (Neuenschwander) C.; m. Eloise Gries, Apr. 28, 1979; 1 child, John Richard. B.A., Kalamazoo Coll., 1974; J.D., U. Toledo, 1977. Bar: Ohio 1977. Assoc. Gold, Rotatori & Schwartz, Cleve., 1979-81, Guren, Merritt, Feibel, Sogg & Cohen, Columbus, Ohio, 1981-84, White, Rankin, Henry, Morse & Mann Co., L.P.A., Columbus, 1984—. Mem. ABA, Ohio Bar Assn., Columbus Bar Assn. Club: Athletic (Columbus). Home: 395 Seranade St Reynoldsburg OH 43068 Office: White Rankin Henry Morse & Mann Co LPA 175 S 3rd St Suite 900 Columbus OH 43215

COOMBS, SHARON MAE, productivity and quality consultant; b. Omaha, Apr. 23, 1950; d. John Norman and Mae Theresa (Ziegweid) Gau; m. Walter Freeman Coombs, Aug. 11, 1973 (div. 1985); 1 child, Julia Anne. B.A. in Sociology, Creighton U., 1972. Tchr. Omaha Pub. Schs., 1972-74, Cherry Creek Sch. Dist., Denver, 1975-76; productivity cons. Control Data Corp., Bloomington, Minn., 1978—. Co-chair People for Environ. Action, Grand Island, Nebr., 1973; v.p. Mpls. Clear Air-Clean Water Unltd., 1980-82; exec. com. North Star chpt. Sierra Club, Mpls., 1984—, chair com. polit. edn., 1984—. Democrat. Unitarian. Avocations: reading, playing piano, photography. Office: MPl Control Data Corp 7801 Computer Ave Bloomington MN 55435

COON, CAROL ANN, lawyer; b. Chgo., June 30, 1945; d. George W. and June (Palmer) C.; m. Paul G. Guistolise. B.A., St. Mary of the Woods Coll., 1968; M.S., George Williams Coll., 1971; J.D., No. Ill. U., 1982. Bar: Ill. 1982, U.S. Dist. Ct. (no. dist.) Ill. 1983. Pvt. practice clin. therapy, Wheaton, Ill., 1971-84; dir. tng. Guidance Ctr. of Meml. Health Services, Lombard, Ill., 1973-84; sole practice law, Wheaton, 1983—; cons. family therapy. Mem. Ill. Bar Assn. Home: 1582 Coloma Ct Wheaton IL 60187 Office: 470 E Roosevelt Rd Lombard IL 60187

COON, MINOR JESSER, biochemistry educator; b. Englewood, Colo., July 29, 1921; s. Minor Dillon and Mary (Jesser) C.; m. Mary Louise Newburn, June 27, 1948; children—Lawrence R., Susan L. B.A., U. Colo., 1943; Ph.D., U. Ill., 1946; D.S. (hon.), Northwestern U., 1983. Postdoctoral fellow U. Ill., Urbana, 1946-47; asst. prof. U. Pa., Phila., 1949-53, assoc. prof., 1953-55; research fellow NYU, 1952-53; prof. biochemistry U. Mich., Ann Arbor, 1955—, chmn. dept. biochemistry, 1970—, Victor Vaughan disting. prof., 1983—; cons. Oak Ridge Inst. Nuclear Studies, 1956-58; mem. adv. council Life Ins. Med. Research Fund, N.Y.C., 1960-65; mem. study sect. NIH, Bethesda, Md., 1963-66; chmn. Interest Group on Oxygenases and Redox Enzymes, Internat. Union Biochemistry, 1981—. Recipient Disting. Faculty Achievement award U. Mich., 1975, Disting. Faculty Lectureship award, 1982. Fellow N.Y. Acad. Scis.; mem. Am. Acad. Arts and Scis., Am. Chem. Soc. (Paul Lewis award in Enzyme Chemistry 1959), Am. Soc. Biol. Chemists (William C. Rose award in Biochemistry 1978), Am. Soc. Pharmacology and Exptl. Therapeutics (B.B. Brodie award in drug metabolism 1980), Biophys. Soc., Nat. Acad. Scis., AAAS, Assn. Med. Sch. Depts. Biochemistry (pres. 1974-75). Avocation: art collecting. Office: U Mich Dept Biol Chemistry Ann Arbor MI 48109

COONEY, DOUGLAS LLOYD, communications executive; b. Portland, Maine, July 15, 1945; s. Cornelius J.M. and Vernita E. (Gilbert) C. B.A., U. Maine, 1967; postgrad. U. Denver, 1967-68. Copywriter, editor, dir. creative services, asst. to dir. advt. and pub. relations Liberty Mut. Ins. Co., Boston, 1970-77; sales promotion mgr., advt. account supr., mgr. editorial services CNA Ins., Chgo., 1977-82; communications dir. United Way/Crusade of Mercy, Chgo., 1982—; dir. Chgo. Access Corp.; pres., treas. Arcom Credit Union. Served with USN, 1968-69. Mem. Pub. Relations Soc. Am. Club: Chgo. Press. Home: 1130 N Dearborn St Apt 503 Chicago IL 60610 Office: United Way/Crusade of Mercy 125 S Clark St Room 1739 Chicago IL 60603

COONEY, GEORGE AUGUSTIN, lawyer; b. Detroit, July 12, 1909; s. Augustin W. and Mary (McBride) C.; A.B., U. Detroit, 1932, J.D., 1935; m. Julia Grace Starrs, Oct. 26, 1940; children—George Augustin, Michael Edward, Timothy John. Admitted to Mich. bar, 1935; since practiced in Detroit. Lectr., U. Mich. Inst. Continuing Legal Edn. Recipient Tower award U. Detroit, 1972. Fellow Am. Coll. Probate Counsel; mem. Am., Mich., Fed., Detroit bar assns., Am. Judicature Soc., Cath. Lawyers Soc. Detroit (dir.), Inc. Soc. Irish-Am. Lawyers, Selden Soc., Mich. Assn. Professions, State Bar Mich. (dir. probate and trust law sect., assoc. editor sect. publ. Probate and Trust Law Jour.). Served as warrant officer USAAF, 1943-46. K.C. Clubs: Detroit Golf, Nat. Lawyers (Washington); Stoney Point (Ont.) Sportsmen. Home: 8831 St Clair Rd Stoney Point ON M0R 1M0 Canada Office: Suite 2329 One Kennedy Sq Detroit MI 48226

COONS, CHARLES WILLIAM, auditor, accountant; b. Springfield, Ill., Oct. 31, 1942; s. George R. and Eunice Irene (Robinson) C.; m. Dorothy Ann Mahe, Nov. 22, 1969; 1 dau., Tracy Lyn. B.A., Sangamon State U., 1978. Acctg. supr. State of Ill. Sec. of State, Springfield, 1969-73, City of Springfield, 1973-74; fin. acctg. mgr. State of Ill. State Lottery, Springfield, 1974-78; acct. State of Ill. Dept. Law Enforcement, Springfield, 1978-79; asst. dir. Ill. Community Coll. Bd., Springfield, 1979-81; internal audit mgr. State of Ill. Dept. Registration and Edn., Springfield, 1981—. Author: Community College Accounting Manual, 1981. Pres., Protestant Ch. League, Fast Pitch, Springfield, 1979-82. Served with U.S. Army, 1964-66. Recipient Eagle Scout award Boy Scouts Am., 1957. Mem. Inst. Internal Auditors, State Internal Mgrs. Group, Am. Legion. Baptist. Lodge: Masons. Home: 9 Red Oak Ln Springfield IL 62703 Office: State Ill Dept Registration and Edn 320 W Washington St Springfield IL 62786

COONS, ELDO JESS, JR., recreational vehicle manufacturing company executive; b. Corsicana, Tex., July 5, 1924; s. Eldo Jess and Ruby (Allison) C.; student engring. U. Calif., 1949-50; m. Beverly K. Robbins, Feb. 6, 1985 children by previous marriage—Roberta Ann, Valerie, Cheryl. Owner C & C Constrn. Co., Pomona, Calif., 1946-48; sgt. traffic div. Pomona Police Dept., 1948-54; nat. field dir. Nat. Hot Rod Assn., Los Angeles, 1954-57; pres. Coons Custom Mfg., Inc., Oswego, Kans., 1957-68; chmn. bd. Borg-Warner Corp., 1968-71; pres. Coons Mfg., Inc., Oswego, 1971—. Mem. Kans. Gov.'s Adv. Com. for State Architects Assn. Served with C.E., AUS, 1943-46. Named to Exec. and Profl. Hall Fame, Recreational Vehicle/Mobile Homes Hall of Fame; recipient Paul Abel award Recreation Vehicle Industry Assn., 1978. Mem. Oswego C. of C. (dir.), Nat. Juvenile Officers Assn., Municipal Motor Officers Assn., Am. Legion, AIM (fellow pres.'s council), Young Pres.'s Orgn. Mason (K.T., Shriner), Rotarian (pres. Oswego 1962-63). Originator 1st city sponsored police supervised dragstrip. Home: PO Box 32 Columbis KS 66725 Office: 2300 W 4th St Oswego KS 67356

COONS, PHILIP MEREDITH, psychiatrist, researcher; b. Indpls., July 7, 1945; s. Harold Meredith and Margaret Louise (Richman) C; m. Elizabeth Sue Bowman, Sept. 5, 1981. A.B., Wabash Coll., 1967; M.D., Ind. U., 1971. Diplomate Am. Bd. Psychiatry & Neurology. Rotating intern Methodist Hosp., Indpls., 1971-72; psychiatry resident Ind. U. Hosp., Indpls., 1972-75; staff psychiatrist Carter Hosp., Indpls., 1975—; asst. prof. psychiatry Ind. U. Sch. of Medicine, Indpls., 1975—; psychiatric cons. Vet. Hosp., Indpls., 1977-78, Wishard Hosp., Indpls., 1979—, Goodwill, Indpls., 1980-83; sec. of med. staff Larue D. Carter Meml. Hosp.; dir. dissociative disorders clinic Ind. U. Sch. of Medicine Psychiatry Dept. Contbr. articles to profl. jours. Deacon, Tabernacle Presbyterian Ch., Indpls., 1981-84, chmn. blood drive, 1981-84; mem. Butler-Tarkington Neighborhood Assn., Indpls., Greater Wabash Coll. Found., Crawfordsville, Ind., 1981—. Worker, United Way Campaign Carter Hosp., 1981—. Worker, United Way Campaign Carter Hosp., 1981—. Fellow Am. Psychiatric Assn., Ind. Psychiatric Soc. (pres. 1984—), Am. Assn. of Social Psychiatry; mem. AMA (recipient Physicians Recognition award 1983), Ind. State Med. Assn., Am. Acad. of Clinical Psychiatrists, Ind. Psychiatric Soc. (membership sec. 1981-83, pres. 1983-84), Am. Acad. of Psychosomatic Medicine, Internat. Soc. for the Study of Multiple Personality (sec. 1984—), Soc. for Clinical and Experimental Hypnosis, Marion County Med. Assn. Republican. Avocations: Photography; genealogy; travel; reading; camping. Home: 5045 N Graceland Ave Indianapolis IN 46208 Office: Larue D Carter Meml Hosp 1315 West Tenth St Indianapolis IN 46202

COOPER, CECIL CELESTER, professional baseball player. First baseman Milw. Brewers. Office: Milw Brewers Milw County Stadium Milwaukee WI 53214*

COOPER, CHARLES ALLEN, financial executive; b. Hartington, Nebr., Dec. 5, 1951; s. Robert Ray and Marie Gertrude (Lorensen) C.; m. Sandra Jean Italia, Oct. 4, 1980; children—Charles Jr., Josie Marie. B.B.A., Wayne State Coll., 1976. Acct. exec. First Data Res., Omaha, 1976-78; stock broker Smith Barney, Omaha, 1978-82; bus. trust developer First Nat. Bank, Omaha, 1982—, chmn. wellness com. 1983—. Leader youth activities YMCA, Omaha, 1979—; Named Top First Yr Broker Smith Barney, 1979. Republican. Roman Catholic. Avocation: Marathon runner. Home: 5007 N 60th Ave Omaha NE 68104 Office: First Nat Bank One First Nat Ctr Omaha NE 68102

COOPER, C(HARLES) E(DWARD), artist, photographer, educator; b. Chgo., Nov. 5, 1922; s. Sam and Rose (Achtman) C.; student Corcoran Gallery Art, 1944-45, Inst. Design, 1946-47, Roosevelt Coll.. 1948-52, Sch. Art Inst. Chgo., 1948-51; B.Art Edn., Loyola U. Chgo, 1964; I.D., Ill. Inst. Tech. 1966. With Jan Smith Gallery, 1950-51, House of Arts, 1952-56, Robert North Gallery, 1958-60, Kerrigan Hendrick Gallery, 1961 (all Chgo.); exhibited one-man shows Club St. Elmo, Morris B. Sachs North Side, 1949, Northwestern U. Hillel Found., Evanston, Ill., 1960, 64, Fisher Hall Gallery, Chgo., Alpha Gallery, 1977, 82; exhibited in group shows Momentum shows, 1948, 49, 51, 52, 54, Am. Jewish Art Club, 1951—, Ill. Inst. Tech., 1963, Navy Pier No-Jury Show, Chgo., 1957, Art Inst. Chgo. Vicinity shows, 1947, 52, 53, 58, 63, Art Inst. Chgo. Rental Gallery, 1960—, Chgo. Soc. Artist Gallery, 1967-69, 70—, Alpha Gallery, 1977, 78, Metanatural Dream Gallery, 1981; represented in permanent collection Spertus Mus. of Judaica, Chgo.; high sch. art tchr. Chgo. Pub. Sch. System, 1952-85; lectr. art pvt. orgns.; art cons. Bd. Jewish Edn., Chgo.; cons. pvt. collectors. Mem. planning com. for arts Am. Jewish Com.; exec. bd. Lane Tech. PTA, to 1985. Served with USMC, 1942-45; PTO. Recipient Raymond Schiff Realtors award, 1961; Morris DeWoskin award 1965; Bekker-Stein award, 1980; Leon Garland award Spertus Mus., 1981. Mem. Chgo. Soc. Artists (dir., pres.), Artists Guild Chgo., Chgo. New Art Assn. (dir.), Am. Jewish Arts Club (Maurice Spertus award 1964, Nathan A. Schwartz award 1970, exhbn. chmn. 1965, 69, rec. sec. 1963, v.p. 1972, 73, co-chmn.), Chgo. Artists Coalition (dir., chmn. fair practices com., internal dir. 1981—, dir., parliamentarian, chmn. 1984—), Artists Equity. Studio: 1142 W Morse Ave Chicago IL 60626

COOPER, CHRISTOPHER PATRICK, hotel manager; b. Whakatane, New Zealand, Mar. 17, 1951, came to U.S. 1976, naturalized 1984; s. George Norman and Maysie (Chitty) C.; m. Mary Jane Kruisenga, Sept. 11, 1982; children—Dustin Christopher, Bryce Daniel. B.S.B.A., Sacred Heart Coll., 1968. Food and banquet dir. Jumers Castle Lodges, Bettendorf, Iowa, 1977-78, food and beverage dir. 1978-79; asst. gen. mgr. Jumers Castle Lodges, Champaign, Ill., 1979-80; gen. mgr. Ramada Inn, Grand Rapids, Mich., 1981—. Mem. Assn. Bus. Clubs Am., Greater Grand Rapids Lodging Assn., Wyo. C. of C. Republican. Roman Catholic. Avocations: racquetball; jogging. Home: 2500 Meyer SW Wyoming MI 49509 Office: 255 28th St SW Grand Rapids MI 49505

COOPER, DONALD EDWARD, advertising agency executive; b. Ann Arbor, Mich., May 28, 1945; s. William D. and Elaine (McWain) C.; m. Virginia Ann Tarnosky, Oct. 8, 1966. B.S., Wayne State U., 1967, M.B.A., 1972. Advt. mgr. Security Bank & Trust, Southgate, Mich., 1970-73; asst. v.p. Met. Savs.,

Farmington, Mich., 1973-76; v.p., dir. Arbor Advt., Ann Arbor, 1976-79; chief operating officer Avis Flowers Worldwide, 1979-80; br. mgr., account supr. Tracy-Loke/BBDO, Inc., Southfield, 1980—. Served with U.S. Army, 1968-69. Mem. Am. Mktg. Assn., Wayne State U. Alumni Assn. Republican. Clubs: Adcraft (Detroit); Bay Harbor (Bay City, Mich.).

COOPER, DOUGLAS KENNETH, lawyer; b. Ithaca, N.Y., June 6, 1947; s. Murray I. and Meta F. Cooper; m. Pamela A. Regan, Aug. 22, 1970; children—James, Sarah. B.A., N.C. State U., 1970; J.D., U. N.C., 1974. Bar: Ohio 1974. Assoc., Shapiro, Persky, Stone & Marken Co., L.P.A., Cleve., 1974-76; of counsel Leaseway Transp. Corp., Cleve., 1976-78, assoc. corp. counsel, 1978-82, corp. counsel, 1982—. Contbr. articles to law reviews. Mem. Cleve. Citizens League, 1974—. Mem. Bar Assn. Greater Cleve., Ohio State Bar Assn., ABA. Home: 3322 Ardmore Rd Shaker Heights OH 44120 Office: Leaseway Transp Corp 3700 Park East Dr Cleveland OH 44122

COOPER, GERALD FRANCIS, JR, lawyer; b. Cleve., Dec. 16, 1954; s. Gerald Francis Sr. and Betty Lou (Costello) C.; m. Karen Ann Staehler, Sept. 27, 1980; 1 child, Kathryn Ann. A.B., Miami U., Oxford, Ohio, 1977; J.D., DePaul U., 1980. Bars: Ohio 1980, U.S. Dist. Ct. (no. dist.) Ohio 1980, Fla. 1981, Ill. 1984, U.S. Ct. Appeals (6th cir.) 1984. Ptnr. Cooper, Spector and Weil Co. L.P.A., Cleve., 1980—; vol. atty. Legal Aid Cleve., 1980—. Mem. Assn. Trial Lawyers Am., Am. Judicature Soc., ABA, Ohio Bar Assn., Fla. Bar Assn., Ill. Bar Assn., Chgo. Bar Assn. Democrat. Roman Catholic. Office: Cooper Spector & Weil Co LPA 531 Leader Bldg Cleveland OH 44114

COOPER, JAMES A., locomotive engineer; b. Decatur, Ill., Apr. 13, 1948; s. Thomas William and Mary Emily (Williams) C.; m. Linda Jane Diesing, June 6, 1970; children—Robert Thomas, Barbara Jane. B. M.Ed., Millikin U., 1970. Musician, Decatur Mcpl. Band, Ill., 1966-69; sports wire filer Lindsay-Schwab Newspapers, Decatur Herald & Rev., Ill., 1966-70; emergency med. specialist Decatur Ambulance Service, 1970-72; communications specialist City of Decatur, Ill., 1972; locomotive engr. Norfolk So. Rwy., Decatur, 1972—; state legis. rep. Bd. Locomotive Engrs., Decatur, 1983—. Supr. ofcls. Decatur Youth Hockey Assn., 1982, 84; mem. St. Louis Zoo Parents and St. Louis Zoo Friends, 1978—, Nat. Mus. Transp., St. Louis, 1975—; v.p. Central Ill. Hockey League, 1980-81. Served with U.S. Army, 1971-77. Mem. Amateur Hockey Assn. U.S. (referee 1979—). Ill. Farm Bur., Phi Mu Alpha Sinfonia (membership chmn. 1969, life). Republican. Methodist. Club: Decatur Shrine. Lodge: Masons. Avocations: hockey referee; church choir. Home: 1749 Burning Tree Dr Decatur IL 62521

COOPER, LINDA DAWN, lawyer; b. Cleve., April 30, 1953; d. Robert Boyd and Catherine S. (Powell) C. B.S. in Psychology with honors, Eastern Ky. U., 1975; J.D., Cleve.-Marshall Law Sch., 1977. Bar: Ohio 1978, U.S. Dist. Ct. (no. dist.) Ohio 1980. Law clk. Vanik, Monroe, Zucco and Klein, Cleve., 1976-78; legal intern Cleve.-Marshall Legal Clinic, 1977; assoc. Vanik, Monroe, Zucco, Klein & Scanlon, Cleve. and Chesterland, Ohio, 1978-79; sr. staff atty. Lake County Pub. Defender, Painesville, Ohio, 1979-80; ptnr. Heffernan & Cooper, Painesville, Cleve., 1980-83; sole practice Painesville, 1983—; lectr. criminal justice seminar, Painesville, 1981. Speaker, adv., counselor Cleve. Rape Crisis Center, 1976; appointee Congressman Eckart's Com. on Health, Environment and Energy, Mentor, Ohio, 1983; chmn. juvenile justice com. LWV, Painesville, 1983; councilwoman Willoughby City Council, Ohio, 1984. Mem. Assn. Trial Lawyers Am., ABA, Ohio Bar Assn., Lake County Bar Assn. Democrat. Episcopalian. Home: 5534 D Wrens Ln Willoughby OH 44094 Office: 174 Main St Painesville OH 44077

COOPER, RICHARD ALAN, lawyer; b. Hattisburg, Miss., July 19, 1953; s. H. Douglas and Elaine (Reece) C.; m. Margaret Jeanne Luth, May 9, 1980. B.A., B.S., U. Ark.-Little Rock, 1976; J.D., Washington U., St. Louis, 1979. Bar: Mo. 1979, Ill. 1980. Law clk. U.S. Dist. Ct., St. Louis, 1979-80; assoc. William R. Gartenberg, St. Louis, 1980-81, Danis, Reid, Murphy, Garvin, Tobben, Schreiber & Mohan, St. Louis, 1983—; liaison to Washington U. Sch. Law, Mo. Assn. Trial Attys., St. Louis, 1983—. Bus. mgr. Urban Law Jour., 1978-79; editor Bankruptcy Law Reporter, 1983-84, co-mgr., editor, 1984—. Recipient Milton F. Napier trial award Lawyers Assn. of St. Louis, 1979. Mem. ABA, Mo. Bar Assn., Am. Assn. Trial Attys., Nat. Orgn. Social Security Claimants Reps., Ill. State Bar Assn. Home: 700 E Jackson Saint Louis MO 63119 Office: Danis Reid Murphy Garvin Tobben Schrieber & Mohan 8850 Ladue Rd Saint Louis MO 63124

COOPER, STANLEY LIVINGSTON, insurance company executive; b. St. Louis, Aug. 19, 1945; s. Glynn and Ruby Marie (Stratman) C.; m. Frances Katherine Huber, Aug. 20, 1966; children—Sarah Marie, Katherine Elizabeth. B.A. in Math., U. Mo.-St. Louis, 1968; M.S. in Computer Sci. and Ops. Research, U. Mo.-Rolla, 1974. Cert. data processor; cert. systems profl. Engr. McDonnell Aircraft, St. Louis, 1968-71; sales rep. United Computing Systems, Kansas City, Mo., 1971-72; systems cons. Bank Bldg. & Equipment Corp., St. Louis, 1972-76; banking specialist Am. Bankers Assn., Washington, 1976-78; mgmt. cons. Ernst & Whinney, Balt., 1978-80; v.p., officer NAVCO Corp., St. Louis, 1980—. Mem. Nat. Assn. Ind. Insurers (nat. EDP com. 1981—), Data Processing Mgmt. Assn. (bd. dirs.), Assn. Systems Mgmt. (bd. dirs.). Home: 15521 Chequer Dr Chesterfield MO 63017 Office: NAVCO Corp 10534 Natural Bridge Rd Saint Louis MO 63134

COOPER, THOMAS JOSEPH, pathologist; b. Lebanon, Ky., Mar. 30, 1924; s. Samuel Phillip and Elizabeth (Hill) C.; m. Barbara Zoe Brann, June 1, 1978 (div.); children—Thomas Joseph, Barbara Anne, John Phillip, Mary F. M.D., U. Louisville, 1946. Diplomate Am. Bd. Pathology. Intern U. Iowa, Iowa City, 1947-48, resident, 1948-52, instr., 1952-53; dir. clin. labs. U.S. Air Force Hosps., Orlando, Fla. and Lackland AFB, Tex., 1953-55; assoc. pathologist Clin. Labs., St. Louis, 1955-63; owner, dir. Cooper Med. Lab., St. Louis, 1964-75; dir. labs. St. Anthony's Med. Ctr., St. Louis, 1965—; dir. MOMEDICO, St. Louis; chmn. Mo. Patient Care Found. Bd. dirs., chmn. med. adv. com. St. Louis chpt. ARC. Served with U.S. Army, 1944-46, to capt. M.C., USAF, 1953-55. Fellow Coll. Am. Pathologists, Am. Soc. Clin. Pathologists; mem. St. Louis Met. Med. Soc. (councilor 1976-81, pres. 1982), AMA, St. Louis Pathology Soc., Mo. State Pathology Soc., Mo. State Med. Assn. (del., councilor). Club: Republican 500. Roman Catholic. Home: 13050 Woodley Ln Saint Louis MO 63128 Office: 10010 Kennerly Rd Saint Louis MO 63128

COOPERRIDER, TOM SMITH, botany educator; b. Newark, Ohio, Apr. 15, 1927; s. Oscar Harold and Ruth Evelyn (Smith) C.; B.A., Denison U., 1950; M.S., U. Iowa, 1955, Ph.D. (NSF fellow), 1958; m. Miwako Kunimura, June 13, 1953; children—Julie Ann, John Andrew. With Kent (Ohio) State U., 1958—, instr. biol. scis., 1958-61, asst. prof., 1961-65, assoc. prof., 1965-69, prof., 1969—, dir. exptl. programs, 1972-73, curator herbarium, 1968—, dir. Bot. Gardens and Arboretum, 1972—, mem. editorial bd. Univ. Press, 1976-79; on leave as asst. prof. dept. botany U. Hawaii, 1962-63; NSF researcher Mountain Lake Biol. Sta., U. Va., summer 1958; faculty mem. Iowa Lakeside Lab., U. Iowa, summer 1965; cons. endangered and threatened species U.S. Fish and Wildlife Service, Dept. Interior, 1976—; cons. Davey Tree Expert Co., 1979-85, Ohio Natural Areas Council, 1983. Served with AUS, 1945-46. YMCA-YWCA Students in Govt., Washington, 1950; NSF predoctoral fellow, 1957-58; NSF research grantee, 1965-72. Fellow AAAS, Explorers Club, Ohio Acad. Scis. (v.p. 1967); mem. Am. Soc. Plant Taxonomists, Internat. Assn. Plant Taxonomists, Bot. Soc. Am., Nature Conservancy, Wilderness Soc., Blue Key, Sigma Xi. Author: Ferns and Other Pteridophytes of Iowa, 1959; Vascular Plants of Clinton, Jackson and Jones Counties, Iowa, 1962; editor: Endangered and Threatened Plants of Ohio, 1983. Home: 548 Bowman Dr Kent OH 44240

COOPERSMITH, JEFFREY ALAN, distribution corporation executive; b. N.Y.C., Mar. 23, 1946; s. Jack J. and Anita S. (Selikoff) C.; m. Ann Pearl Sayetta, Jan. 19, 1969; children—Jarred, Aubrey. B.Mgmt. Engring., Rensselaer Poly. Inst., 1967; M.B.A., Ohio State U., 1979. Security arbitrater Arnhold and S. Bleichroeder, Inc., N.Y.C., 1967-70; with Pfizer, Inc., N.Y.C., 1967-70, asst. controller Minerals, Pigments and Metals div., 1970-72; with Distbn. Ctrs., Inc. subs. Distek, Inc., Westerville, Ohio, 1972—, v.p., controller, 1975-77, v.p., treas., 1977-78, v.p. fin., 1978-80, exec. v.p. Distek, Inc., 1980-83, pres., chief operating officer, 1983—, also pres. Distbn. Ctrs. Inc.; dir. Matryx Corp., Columbus, Ohio. Mem. Nat. Council Phys. Distbn. Mgmt., Warehousing Edn. and Research Council, Fin. Execs. Inst. (past dir.). Office: 229 Huber Village Blvd Westerville OH 43081

COOVER, DANIEL ALAN, civil engineer; b. Chambersburg, Pa., Jan. 9, 1954; s. William Daniel and Helen Louise C.; m. Sonya Kay Fowler, Sept. 5, 1981; 1 dau., Aleischa Louise. B.S. in Civil Engring., Bucknell U., 1975; M.S., Carnegie Mellon U., 1977. Registered profl. engr., Ohio. Structural engr. Korda, Nemeth, Kadakia & Jezerinac, Ltd., Columbus, Ohio, 1976-79; structural engr. United McGill Corp., 1979-82, asst. project mgr., 1982-83, mgr. mech. engring., 1983—. Mem. ASCE. Republican. Presbyterian. Office: United McGill Corp 2400 Fairwood Ave Columbus OH 43216

COPE, ESTHER SIDNEY, history educator; b. West Chester, Pa., Sept. 10, 1942; d. Robert Wellington and Jane Davis (Stanton) C. B.A., Wilson Coll., 1964; M.A., U. Wis.-Madison, 1965; Ph.D., Bryn Mawr Coll., 1969. Instr. history Ursinus Coll., Collegeville, Pa., 1968-70, asst. prof. history, 1970-75; asst. prof. history U. Nebr., Lincoln, 1975-76, assoc. prof., 1976-81, prof., 1981—, chmn. dept. history, 1982—; bd. dirs. Yale Ctr. Parliamentary History, New Haven, 1981—. Author: Life of a Public Man, 1981. Editor: Procs. of Short Parliament 1640, 1977. Fellow Royal Hist. Soc.; mem. Am. Hist. Assn., Conf. Brit. Studies (rec. sec. 1975-81), Internat. Commn. on Hist. Rep. and Parliamentary Instns., Berkshire Conf. Women Historians, Phi Beta Kappa. Mem. Soc. of Friends. Office: U Nebr Dept History Lincoln NE 68588

COPELAND, JOHN ALLEN, food packing company executive; b. Converse, La., Aug. 9, 1923; s. Robert S. and Lou (Leysath) C.; m. Lois A. Hansen, Sept. 24, 1945; children—John A., Wade K., Victor G. B.S. in Bus. Adminstrn., La. State U., 1948. With beef dept. Swift & Co., Sioux City, Iowa, 1948-53, with operating and corp. mgmt. in various locations, 1953-66, v.p., Chgo., 1966-73, pres. Fresh Meats div., Chgo., 1973-80; pres., chief exec. officer Swift Ind. Packing Co., Chgo., 1980, Swift Ind. Corp., Chgo., 1981-83, chmn., chief exec. officer, 1983—; dir. Lukens Steel Corp.; chmn. bd. Nat. Live Stock and Meat Bd., 1972-74, Am. Meat Inst., 1981-83; industry rep. USDA Task Force, 1979. Served to capt. U.S. Army, 1943-45. Republican. Lutheran. Office: Swift Ind Corp 115 W Jackson Blvd Chicago IL 60604

COPELAND, WILLIAM MACK, hospital executive, lawyer; b. Harriman, Tenn., Jan. 21, 1937; s. John Hyder and Margaret Elizabeth (Gardner) C.; B.A., So. Colo. State U., 1965; M.S., U. Colo., 1969; J.D., No. Ky. State U., 1977; m. Barbara Ann Leurck, 1980; children—Elizabeth, William, Brian, George, Carolyn. Commd. 2d lt. U.S. Air Force, 1954, advanced through grades to capt., 1968, ret., 1975; asso. adminstr. St. George Hosp., Cin., 1976-77, adminstr., 1977-78; pres. St. Francis-St. George Hosp., Inc., St. Francis-St. George Health Services, Inc. and subs. corps., St. Francis-St. George Hosp., Found., and Mgmt. Co., Mgmt. Dynamics, Inc. Cin., 1978—; lectr. Patients Right Inst.; admitted to Ohio bar, 1978, Fed. Dist. Ct. bar, 1978; chmn. Greater Cin. Hosp. Council, 1984-85; charter pres. Dayton Area Adminstrs. Group; adj. faculty Xavier U. and InterAm. U. Vice chmn. dept. health affairs Cath. Conf. Ohio, 1981-84, chmn. inst. plan com., 1980-84, legis. com. and task force on govt. Decorated Meritorious Service medal, Air Force Commendation medal with oak leaf cluster; recipient Monsignor Griffin award Ohio Hosp. Assn., 1979. Fellow Am. Coll. Hosp. Adminstrs.; mem. Nat. Health Lawyers Assn., Am. Soc. Hosp. Attys., Cath. Health Assn. U.S. (govt. legis. com. 1980-82, health planning com.), Am. Hosp. Assn., Ohio Hosp. Assn. (chmn. elect S.W. dist. council), Am. Soc. Law and Medicine, Am. Bar Assn., Ohio Bar Assn., Cin. Bar Assn., Cin. C. of C. Lodge: Kiwanis. Contbr. articles to profl. jours. Home: 5411 Timberhollow Ln Cincinnati OH 45247 Office: 3131 Queen City Ave Cincinnati OH 45238

COPLEN, MARY JANE, educational administrator, psychologist; b. Wichita, Kans., Apr. 15, 1940; d. Edward James and Anna Mae (Oatman) Webber; children—Molly Ann, Christian Edward. B.S. in Edn., Pitts. State U., 1962; M.Ed., Wichita State U., 1978, postgrad., 1978. Cert. tchr., Kans.; cert. Nat. Bd. Cert. Counselors. Tchr. Buhler Rural High Sch., Kans., 1962-64, USD #308, Huthcinson, Kans., 1967-77 counselor Huthcinson Community Coll., 1978, dir. spl. services, 1978—; bd. dirs. Mo.-Kans.-Nebr. State Midam. Ednl. Opportunity Personnel Program, 1978-82; cons. U.S. Dept. Edn., Washington, 1979; pres. South Central Kans. K.P.G.A., 1980. Leader Wheatbelt council Girl Scouts U.S.A., 1966-68, Kanza council Boy Scouts Am., 1968-69; bd. dirs. Reno County Mental Health Assn., Hutchinson, 1977-81, Hutchinson Recreation Commn./Handicapped, 1980—. Mem. Am. Assn. Counselor Devel., Am. Coll. Personnel, Am. Assn. Women in Community and Jr. Colls. (regional/-state rep., Disting. Service award 1984), Kans. Assn. Counseling and Devel. (s. central Kans. sect.), Kans. Assn. Counseling Devel., Kans. Coll. Personnel Assn., Delta Psi Kappa. Republican. Reorganized Ch. of Jesus Christ of Latter-day Saints. Club: Womens Recreation Assn. (pres. 1960-61). Avocations: Gardening, golf, swimming, bicycling, spectator sports. Home: 122 Carlton Rd Hutchinson KS 67502 Office: Huthcinson Community Coll 1300 N Plum Hutchinson KS 67502

COPLEY, PATRICK O'NEIL, college president; b. Seneca, Mo., Feb. 4, 1933; s. Charles Milton and Lorraine Lida (McCoy) C.; m. Elizabeth Ann Wheeler, Nov. 8, 1953; children—Chazell, Charlene, Patrice. B.A., Grand Canyon Coll., 1958; M.A., Ariz. State U., 1959, Ed.D., 1966. Dir. edn. and music Parkview Bapt. Ch., Phoenix, 1955-59; tchr. Central High Sch., Phoenix, 1959-65; asst. dean Sch. Edn., U. Mo.-St. Louis, 1965-67; dean Sch. Edn., Southwest Mo. State U., Springfield, 1967-82; pres. Mo. Bapt. Coll., St. Louis, 1982—. Contbr. articles to profl. jours. Bd. dirs. Springfield United Cerebral Palsy, 1979-82. Served with USAF, 1951-55. Mem. Assn. Tchr. Educators (pres. Mo. unit 1969-70), Assn. Tchr. Edn. (pres. 1977-79), Tchr. Edn. Council State Colls. and Univs. (pres. 1980-81), Am. Assn. Colls. Tchr. Edn. (bd. dirs. 1980-83). Democrat. Baptist. Lodge: Rotary. Avocations: swimming, piano, reading, youth work. Home: 14 Ridge Creek Dr Saint Louis MO 63141 Office: Mo Bapt Coll 12542 Conway Rd Saint Louis MO 63141

CORABI, JOSEPH MICHAEL, lawyer; b. Washington, Pa., Aug. 19, 1952; s. Samuel Anthony and Kathryn D. (Santo) C.; m. Kathleen McMenamin, Aug. 3, 1979; children—Craig, Ryan. B.A., U. Steubenville, 1974; J.D., Ohio No. U., 1977. Bar: Ohio. Law clk. to judge Ct. Common Pleas, Steubenville, Ohio, summer 1975; ptnr. Corabi & Corabi, Steubenville, 1977—; bus. law instr. U. Steubenville, 1978-81; solicitor Cross Creek Twp., Wintersville, Ohio, 1979—, Village of Bloomingdale, Ohio, 1980—, Village of New Alexandria, Ohio, 1984—. Chmn. Law Day, Steubenville, 1983. Mem. ABA, Ohio State Bar Assn., Jefferson County Bar Assn. (sec. 1981, exec. com. 1982-83), Ohio Acad. Trial Lawyers, Assn. Trial Lawyers Am. Democrat. Roman Catholic. Avocations: softball, basketball. Home: 157 Stardust Dr Steubenville OH 43952 Office: Corabi & Corabi 424 Market St Steubenville OH 43952

CORBETS, DAVID ANTHONY, accountant; b. Washington, May 16, 1951; s. Eugene Paul and Mildred (Vranesevich) C.; m. Deborah Ann Gillespy, Aug. 5, 1972. B.A., Mt. Union Coll., 1973. C.P.A., Ohio. With Hausser & Heintel C.P.A.s, Cleve., 1973-79; with Swearingen & Swearingen C.P.A.s, Cleve., 1979-81; pvt. practice acctg., Solon, Ohio, 1981—. Trustee Solo Home Days, Inc. Mem. Am. Inst. C.P.A.s, Ohio Soc. C.P.A.s. Methodist. Lodge: Kiwanis (past pres. Solon). Home: 6737 Forest Glen St Solon OH 44139 Office: David Corbets 34200 Solon Rd Solon OH 44139

CORBETT, BARBARA LOUISE, advertising agency executive; b. Sioux City, Iowa, May 6, 1947; d. Bayliss and Shirley Louise (Wiese) Corbett; m. Henry F. Terbrueggen, Jr., Nov. 22, 1976. B.A. in Polit. Sci., Antioch Coll., 1969. Cert. bus. communicator. Copywriter, J.L. Hudson Co., Detroit, 1969-72, Patten Co., Southfield, Mich., 1972-73; copywriter/producer Campbell Ewald, Detroit, 1973-75; free lance writer, 1975-76; pres. Corbett Advt., Inc., Rochester, Mich., 1977—; tchr. Barbizon Sch., Southfield, 1979; prof. advt. Oakland Community Coll., 1980-82; judge Detroit News Scholastic Writing Awards competition, Detroit, 1979-80; lectr. in field. Recipient award for Ad of the Year, J.L. Hudson Co., 1971; Merit award Seklemian, 1971; Gold Award Creative Advt. Club of Detroit, 1974; others. Mem. Greater Rochester C. of C. (dir.), Indsl. Marketers of Detroit (pres.), Mich. Advt. Agy. Council (pres.), Midstates Agy. Network (past pres.), Adcraft. Republican. Unitarian. Home: 6175 Sheldon Rd Rochester MI 48064 Office: Corbett Advt Inc 800 W University Dr Suite F Rochester MI 48063

CORBETT, GERARD FRANCIS, electronics company executive; b. Phila., Apr. 6, 1950; s. Eugene Charles and Dolores Marie (Hoffmann) C.; m. Marcia Jean Serafin, July 9, 1983. A.A., Community Coll. of Phila., 1974; B.A. in Pub. Relations, San Jose State U., 1977. Sci. programmer Sverdrup Inc., NASA Ames Research Ctr., Moffett Field, Calif., 1970-77; sr. writer Four-Phase Systems, Inc., Cupertino, Calif., 1977-78; with Nat. Semicondr. Corp., Santa Clara, Calif., 1978-79; sr. account exec. Creamer Dickson Basford, Providence, 1979-81; mgr. tech. and exec. communications Internat. Harvester Co., Chgo., 1981-82; mgr. corp. tech. communications Gould Inc., Rolling Meadows, Ill., 1982-83, dir. corporate pub. relations, 1983—; pub. relations and communications cons. on high tech. Recipient Vice Presdl. award of honor Calif. Jaycees, 1977. Mem. Pub. Relations Soc. Am. (accredited; Pres.'s citation 1981), AIAA, Nat. Assn. Sci. Writers, AAAS, Kappa Tau Alpha. Republican. Roman Catholic. Clubs: Capital Hill, Commonwealth of Calif. Home: 4610 Tall Oaks Ln Rolling Meadows IL 60008 Office: Gould Inc 10 Gould Center Rolling Meadows IL 60008

CORBETT, JULES JOHN, microbiology educator; b. Natrona, Pa., Apr. 12, 1919; s. Anthony and Theodosia (Kuczynski) C.; m. Gabrielle Ann Wengel, June 24, 1950; children—Brian Lee, Alan Jeffrey, Christine Marie. A.A., North Park Coll., 1941; cert. med. tech. Franklin Sch. Sci. and Arts, 1946; S.B., U. Chgo., 1950; M.S., Ill. Inst. Tech., 1957. Med. technologist St. Bernard Hosp., Chgo., 1947-49; microbiologist Englewood Hosp., Chgo., 1949-52; dir. labs. Beverley Arts Bldg., Chgo., 1954; microbiologist Borden Co., Hammond, Ind., 1955-64; instr. Roosevelt U., Chgo., 1956-59, asst. prof., 1959-64, assoc. prof., 1964-72, prof., 1972—, chmn. biology dept., 1974-79; cons. Metro Labs., Chgo. Served with U.S. Army, 1937-39; with USNR, 1941-45. Grantee HEW, 1969-72, Ill. Bd. Higher Edn., 1971-72. Mem. Am. Soc. Microbiology, Ill. Soc. for Microbiology, AAAS, N.Y. Acad. Scis., Ill. State Acad. Sci., Am. Legion (4th dist. comdr. 1975, dep. vice comdr. 1980), La Societe des 40 Hommes et 8 Chevaux Cheminot, VFW, Sigma Xi. Republican. Roman Catholic. Clubs: Immaculate Conception Men's, Clown Unit, Voiture 220 (Chgo.). Home: 8318 S Komensky Ave Chicago IL 60652 Office: 430 S Michigan Ave Roosevelt U Chicago IL 60605

CORBO, DAVID LOUIS, state official educator; b. Mpls., Sept. 4, 1942; s. Louis John Corbo and Vivian Mae (Faircloth) Geretshclaeger; m. Janet Jean Hummel, Aug. 27, 1965; children—Todd Anthony, Scott Louis, Dena Marie. A.A., U. Minn., 1962; B.A., St. Cloud State U., 1965. Social worker State of Minn., Stillwater, 1966-69, personnel officer, 1970-73, personnel mgr., 1973—; instr. Wis. Vocat. Tech. Inst., New Richmond, 1980—; mem. adv. bd., 1981—. Hockey, baseball and football coach, Somerset and Stillwater, 1970—; asst. leader Indianhead council Boy Scouts Am., Stillwater, 1973-76; adminstr., treas. Our Saviors Lutheran Ch, Stillwater, 1975-84; chmn. Somerset Sch. Bd., 1981—. Mem. St. Croix Valley Employers Assn. Avocations: fishing, skiing, hiking, woodwork, bird carving. Home: Rural Route 1 Box 328 Saint Joseph WI 54082 Office: State of Minn MFC-Stillwater Box 55 Stillwater MN 55082

CORBOY, PHILIP HARNETT, lawyer; b. Chgo., Aug. 12, 1924; s. Harold Francis and Marie (Harnett) C.; student St. Ambrose Coll., 1942-43, U. Notre Dame, 1945; J.D., Loyola U., 1949; m. Doris Marie Conway, Nov. 26, 1949; children—Philip Harnett, Joan Marie, John Richard, Thomas Michael. Admitted to Ill. bar, 1949; asst. corp. counsel City Chgo., 1949-50; individual practice, 1950—; lectr. schs. and profl. assns. Trustee Roscoe Pound Found. Served with AUS, 1943-45. Fellow Am. Coll. Trial Lawyers; mem. Am. (chmn. litigation sect. 1979-80), Ill., Chgo. (pres. 1972-73) bar assns., Law Sci. Acad., Am. Judicature Soc., Am., Ill. (pres. 1963-64) trial lawyers assns., Nat. Inst. Trial Advocacy (chmn.-elect 1983-84), Internat. Acad. Trial Lawyers, Internat. Soc. Barristers, Inner Circle Advs. Clubs: Evanston Golf, Covenant, Chgo. Athletic Assn. Contbr. articles to profl. jours. Home: 180 E Pearson St Chicago IL 60611 Office: Suite 630 33 N Dearborn St Chicago IL 60602

CORCORAN, PATRICK ARNOLD, company executive; b. Mpls., Mar. 15, 1937; s. Alvin Byron and Evelyn Victoria (Jensen) C.; B.A., St. Olaf Coll., 1959; m. Carol Ruth Willard, Jan. 9, 1963; children—Pamela Sue, Patrick Sean. Sales corr. 3M Co., St. Paul, 1961, salesman, Wis., 1961-64, account exec., 1964-66; v.p. Color Arts Inc., Racine, Wis., from 1966, now pres., chief exec. officer; organizer, dir. Village Bank of Elm Grove (Wis.), 1979—. Chmn. Recreation Com., Village of Elm Grove, 1974-82; life mem. Republican Party. Mem. Screen Printing Assn. Internat. (dir., sec., v.p., Certificates of Merit 1973-78, Magnus award 1983 chmn. bd. dirs. 1983-84), Am. Soc. Agrl. Engrs., Alumni Assn. St. Olaf Coll. (bd. mem. 1974-78). Republican. Lutheran. Home: 1005 Verdant Dr Elm Grove WI 53122 Office: 1840 Oakdale Ave Racine WI 53406

CORDELL, GEOFFREY ALLAN, natural product chemist, university adminstrator; b. London, Sept. 1, 1946; s. George Royston and Lily (Snelgrove) C.; m. Debby Ann Braun, Oct. 2, 1981. B.Sc. with first class honors, Manchester U., Eng., 1964-67, M.Sc., 1968, Ph.D., 1970. Postdoctoral fellow MIT, Cambridge, 1970-72; research assoc. U. Ill. Coll. Pharmacy, Chgo., 1972-74, asst. prof., 1974-76, assoc. prof., 1976-80, prof., assoc. dean, 1980—, prof., assoc. dean Grad. Coll., 1984—; pres. Nat. Products, Inc., Glenview, Ill., 1983—; mem. bio-organic and natural products study sect. NIH, Bethesda, Md., 1979-84; temporary adviser WHO, Geneva, 1978, 81, 84, 85. Author: Introduction to Alkaloids: A Biogenetic Approach, 1983. Contbr. articles to profl. jours., chpts. to books. Patentee in field. Grantee Nat. Cancer Inst., Bethesda, Md., 1975—, WHO, 1978—; recipient Travel awards Alexander von Humboldt Found., 1981-82, Internat. Union Against Cancer, 1977, NSF, 1984. Fellow Royal Chem. Soc.; mem. Am. Soc. Pharmacognosy (pres. 1985-86), Am. Chem. Soc., Am. Assn. Coll. Pharmacy, AAAS. Avocations: tennis, soccer, table tennis, gardening. Office: U Ill-Chgo 833 S Wood St Chicago IL 60612

CORDEMAN, DOUGLAS GEORGE, aerospace manufacturing company executive; b. Ft. Sill, Okla., Sept. 3, 1931; s. W. Preston and Virginia (Sandt) C.; m. Joan Jaeckel, Nov. 30, 1974; children—Susan, David, Lisa, John, Jean, Daniel. A.B., Dartmouth Coll., 1952; J.D., Harvard U., 1955; D.S. (hon.), Fla. Inst. Tech., 1976. Contract adminstr. Gen. Dynamics Corp., Rochester, N.Y., 1958-60; mgr. contracts Dresser Industries, Houston, 1960-62; asst. mgr. adminstrn. McDonnell Aircraft Co., St. Louis, 1962-64; mgr. contracts Electronics and Space div. Emerson Electric Co., St. Louis, 1964-69, dir. adminstrn., 1969-71, v.p. adminstrn., 1971-78, sr. v.p., 1978—. Contbr. articles to profl. publs. Mem. vestry St. Timothy's Episcopal Ch., St. Louis, 1975-78, 81-83; mem. alumni council Dartmouth Coll., Hanover, N.H., 1979-81. Fellow Nat. Contract Mgmt. Assn. (nat. pres. 1975-77, Blanche Witte Meml. award 1970, hon. life mem.); mem. Am. Def. Preparedness Assn. (bd. dirs. St. Louis chpt. 1973—, pres. 1981-82), Nat. Security Indsl. Assn. (trustee 1980—, exec. com. 1985—), Navy League (life mem.) Assn. U.S. Army, Air Force Assn. Republican. Club: Norwood Hills Country (St. Louis). Avocations: family, running, skiing, swimming. Office: Emerson Electric Co 8100 W Florisant Ave Saint Louis MO 63136

CORDES, BROCK VALENTINE, publisher; b. Milw., Sept. 1, 1942; s. Henry Carl and Mary Elizabeth (Munk) C.; m. Georgia Felice Church, Feb. 19, 1966; children—Erika Hillary, Trevor Eaton. B.A., U. Alaska, 1965; M.B.A., U. Oreg., 1968. Engring. technician, surveyor Alaska Dept. Hwys., Fairbanks, 1963-67; lectr. U. Man., Winnipeg, 1968-72; life underwriter Monarch Life Assurance Co., Winnipeg, 1972-74, br. mgr., Winnipeg, 1974-78; pres., chief exec. officer Seabrook Industries Ltd., Winnipeg, 1978—; pres., pub. Reliance Press Ltd., 1978—; pres. Web Graphics West Ltd., 1978—, Edan Restaurants Ltd., 1978—. Served with USN, 1960-61, USMCR, 1962-65. Mem. Can. Community Newspaper Assn., Printing Industries Am. Progressive Conservative. Presbyterian. Home: 62 Paradise Dr Winnipeg MB Canada R3R 1L1 Office: 386 Broadway Suite 602 Winnipeg MB R3C 3R6 Canada

COREA, RICHARD THOMAS, optometrist; b. Youngstown, Ohio, Feb. 5, 1947; s. D. Richard and Mary Sarah (Salerno) C.; m. Linda Zimmer, June 14, 1969; children—Anthony, Sarah Kathryn, Nicholas R. B.A. in Psychology, St. Joseph's Coll., 1969; D. Optometry, Ohio State U., 1973. Diplomate Am. Bd. Optomerty. Pvt. practice, Milw., 1973-75, Frankfort, Ind., 1975—. Pres., Clinton County Humane Soc., Frankfort, 1976-78; v.p. Frankfort Airport Authority, 1981—. Recipient Outstanding Young Man of Am. award U.S. Jaycees, 1980, 81. Mem. Tecumseh Optometric Soc. (pres. 1975-77), Ind. Optometric Assn., Am. Optometic Assn. Democrat. Roman Catholic. Lodges: Kiwanis (pres. 1981-82), Elks. Avocations: Tennis; reading Home: 959 Harvard Terrace Frankfort IN 46041 Office: 1303 S Jackson Frankfort IN 46041

COREY, JOHN BURHYTE WILMOT, city official; b. Ft. Sill, Okla., June 8, 1912; s. John Burhyte Wilmot and Katharine Jane (Jones) C.; m. Verna Isaacson; children—Susan B. Corey Newell, Judith A. Corey Johnson, Marcia L. Corey Porter. B.S. in Civil Engring., U. Wash., 1935; M.S. in Civil Engring., Tex. A&M U., 1948; grad. U.S. Army Command and Gen. Staff Coll., 1946, U.S. Army War Coll., 1956. Commd. 2d lt. U.S. Army, 1934, advanced through grades to col., 1952, ret., 1962; dep. commr. Dept. Pub. Works, Chgo., 1965-68; adminstrv. asst. to mayor, Chgo., 1968-70, chief water engr. Chgo. Dept. Water and Sewers, 1970-76, dep. commr., 1976-79; commr. Chgo. Dept. Water, 1979—; asst. prof. U.S. Mil. Acad., 1948-52. Bd. dirs. ARC, USO, Am.

Cancer Soc., Chgo. Heart Assn. Named Civil Engr. of Yr., ASCE, 1980. Mem. Tau Beta Pi, Delta Upsilon. Avocation: Golf. Home: 6733 N Edgebrook Terr Chicago IL 60646 Office: Dept Water 121 N LaSalle St Room 403 Chicago IL 60602

CORL, SAMUEL SHIREY, III, car corporation executive; b. Grand Rapids, Mich., Aug. 25, 1937; s. Samuel Shirey, Jr. and Jane (Brooks) C.; m. Nancy Jane Lorris; children—Elisabeth Jane, Samuel Shirey IV. B.B.A., U. Mich., 1960, M.B.A., 1961, Ph.D., 1969. Cert. secondary tchr., Mich. Loan officer Hartger & Willard, Inc., Grand Rapids, 1961-63; classroom tchr. Grand Rapids Pub. Schs., 1964-66; vis. prof. Kalamazoo Coll., 1967-68; prof. Mich. State U., East Lansing, 1969-81; lectr. U. Mich., 1966-67, 68-69; mgr. field tng. Chrysler Corp., Detroit, 1982—; cons. in field. Co-author; Marketing Professional Services, 1974; Land Development, 1973. Contbr. articles to profl. jours. Mich. State U. faculty tchr.-scholar, 1972; recipient Bronze award N.Y. Film and TV Festival, 1984. Mem. Am. Soc. Tng. and Devel. Democrat. Unitarian. Avocations: furniture craftsman, musician, golf, cooking. Home: 1270 Whittier Dr East Landing MI 48823 Office: Chrysler Corp PO Box 857 Detroit MI 48288

CORLISS, JEAN A., public relations executive; b. Warren, Ohio, Sept. 13, 1952; d. Paul J. and Theresa M. (Loney) C.; m. Donald J. Galbreath, May 22, 1982. B.S. in Bus. Adminstrn., Youngstown State U., 1976. Dir. pub. relations Mahoning chpt. ARC, Youngstown, Ohio, 1979-80; writer Youngstown Hosp. Assn., 1980-81, mgr. community relations, 1981-82, dir. community relations, 1982-83; dir. pub. relations Youngstown Osteopathic Hosp., 1984—; pub. relations cons., 1983—. N.E. Ohio dist. ARC. Named Prominent Pub. Relations Specialist, Whitney McMillan, 1983; recipient various awards Youngstown Advt./Pub. Relations Club. Mem. Pub. Relations Soc. Am. (dir.), Am. Soc. Hosp. Pub. Relations (cert.), Ohio Soc. Hosp. Pub. Relations Assn., East Ohio Hosp. Assn., N.E. Ohio Hosp. Pub. Relations Assn. Home: 1021 Hartzell Ave Niles OH 44446 Office: Youngstown Osteopathic Hosp 1319 Florencedale Ave Youngstown OH 44505

CORN, J(OSEPH) EDWARD, JR., opera company administrator; b. St. Louis, Oct. 20, 1932; s. Joseph Edward and Melba (Goldberg) C. A.B., Yale U., 1954. Mgr., San Francisco Opera, 1972-75; dir. planning and pub. affairs Met. Opera, N.Y.C., 1975-77; mgr. Opera Co. of Phila., 1977-80; dir. opera-mus. theater program Nat. Endowment for the Arts, Washington, 1980-81; gen. dir. Wolf Trap Found., Vienna, Va., 1981-82; exec. producer Minn. Opera Co., St. Paul, 1982—; trustee Nat. Inst. for Music Theater, Washington; mem. adv. council Ctr. for Arts Criticism, St. Paul; mem. Ind. Com. on Arts Policy, N.Y.C. Bd. dirs. Nat. Com. on U.S.-China Relations, Music-Theatre Group, Lenox Arts Ctr., First All-Children's Theater; sec. bd. dirs. Midwest China Ctr. Home: 442 Summit Ave Saint Paul MN 55102 Office: Minn Opera Co 400 Sibley St Saint Paul MN 55101

CORNELIUS, WILLIAM EDWARD, utilities company executive; b. Salt Lake City, Sept. 6, 1931; s. Edward Vernon and Gladys (Bray) C.; B.S., U. Mo., 1953; M.L.A., Washington U., St. Louis; m. Mary Virginia Bunker, June 13, 1953; children—Mary Jean, Linda Anne. Mgr., Price Waterhouse & Co., St. Louis, 1955-62; asst. comptroller Union Electric Co., St. Louis, 1962-64, dir. corporate planning, 1964-67, exec. v.p., 1968-80, pres., 1980—, chief exec. officer, 1984—, also dir.; dir. Electric Energy Inc., Gen. Am. Life Ins. Co., Centerre Bancorp. Bd. dirs. William Woods Coll., Washington U., St. Louis Children's Hosp. Served to 1st lt. AUS, 1953-55. C.P.A., Mo. Mem. Beta Theta Pi. Clubs: Bellerive Country, Noonday, St. Louis, Log Cabin. Office: PO Box 149 Saint Louis MO 63166

CORNELL, JOSEPH ANDREW, research pharmacist; b. Chgo., Dec. 11, 1949; s. Downie J. and Dorothy (Schwieder) C.; m. Judith Ann Clinton, Sept. 16, 1972; children—David J., Brian C. Student Calif. State U.-Rohnert Park, 1968-70; Pharm.D., U. Calif.-San Francisco, 1974. Registered pharmacist, Minn. Pharmacist, St. Mary's Hosp., Rochester, Minn., 1974-75; asst. prof. U. Minn., Mpls., 1975-80; asst. editor Am. Soc. Hosp. Pharmacists, Washington, 1980-82; remote site ops. mgr. U. Minn., Mpls., 1982-84; pres. PharmaSoft, Inc., Mpls., 1983-84; dir. research and devel. Cardinal Health Systems, Mpls., 1984—. Author: Computers in Hospital Pharmacy, 1984. Contbr. articles to profl. jours. Roman Catholic. Home: 7933 Monroe St NE Spring Lake Park MN 55432 Office: Cardinal Health Systems 7562 Marketplace Dr Eden Prairie MN 55344

CORNELL, NANCY VIRGINIA, preschool teacher; b. Steubenville, Ohio, July 4, 1948; d. John Alvin and Wilda Pearl (McMasters) Martin; m. Jack Lee Cornell, Feb. 9, 1967; children—Jack, Jr., Lorie Ann, Charles J., Franklin. Student early childhood courses, Ohio U., Rio Grande (Ohio) Coll., West Liberty (W.Va.) State Coll., W.Va. U. Tchr.'s aide Gallia Meigs CAA Head Start, 1974-75, head tchr., 1975-79; head tchr. No. Panhandle (W.Va.) Head Start, 1979-84, home base supr., 1984—. Mem. W.Va. Assn. for Young Children, Assn. for Supervision and Curriculum Devel. Republican. Protestant. Home: RD 1 Box 317 Steubenville Rd Toronto OH 43964 Office: 401 Commerce St Wellsburg WV

CORNELL, RICHARD GARTH, biostatistics educator; b. Cleve., Nov. 18, 1930; s. Russell Gervas and Grace Emeline (Garlick) C.; m. Valma Yvonne Edwards, June 3, 1961; children—Sharon Yvonne, Russell Glenn, Carol Elizabeth. B.A., U. Rochester, 1948; M.S., Va. Poly. Inst., 1954, Ph.D., 1956. Statistician Communicable Disease Ctr., Atlanta, 1956-60; assoc. prof. stats. Fla. State U., Tallahassee, 1960-68, prof., 1968-71; prof. biostats. U. Mich., Ann Arbor, 1971—, chmn. dept., 1971-84; cons. Upjohn Co., Kalamazoo, Mich., 1983-84. Editor: Statistical Methods for Cancer Studies, 1984. Contbr. articles to statis. and med. jours. Deacon Packard Rd. Baptist Ch., Ann Arbor, 1971—. Served with USPHS, 1956-58. Fellow Am. Statis. Assn.; mem. Biometric Soc. (pres. eastern N.Am. region 1975), Am. Sci. Affiliation. Baptist. Avocation: gardening. Home: 6149 Waterworks Rd Saline MI 48176 Office: Dept Biostats U Mich Ann Arbor MI 48109

CORNELL, WILLIAM DANIEL, mechanical engineer; b. Valley Falls, Kans., Apr. 17, 1919; s. Noah P. and Mabel (Hennessy) C.; B.S. in Mech. Engring., U. Ill., 1942; m. Barbara L. Ferguson, Aug. 30, 1942; children—Alice Margaret, Randolph William. Research engr. Linde Air Products Co., Buffalo, 1942-48, cons. to Manhattan Dist. project, 1944-46; project engr. devel. of automatic bowling machine Am. Machine and Foundry, Buffalo, 1948-55; cons. to Gen. Electric Co., Hanford, Wash., 1949-50; project engr. Brunswick Corp., Muskegon, Mich., 1955-59, mgr. advanced engring., 1959-72; mgr. advanced concepts and tech. Sherwood Med. Industries div. Am. Home Products Corp., St. Louis, 1972—; mem. faculty Coll. Engring., U. Buffalo, 1946-47. Recipient Navy E award, 1945, Manhattan Project Recognition award, 1945, Award of Merit, Maritime Commn., 1945; registered profl. engr., N.Y. Republican. Presbyterian. Holder 48 patents, including automatic golf and bowling game apparatus, med. instruments and developer new method of measuring hemoglobin. Home: 907 Camargo Dr Ballwin MO 63011 Office: 11802 Westline Ind Dr Saint Louis MO 63146

CORNELSEN, PAUL FREDERICK, food and engineering company executive; b. Wellington, Kans., Dec. 23, 1923; s. John S. and Theresa Albertime (Von Klatt) C.; m. Floy Lila Brown, Dec. 11, 1943; 1 son, John Floyd. B.S. in M.E., U. Denver, 1949. With Boeing Airplane Co., 1940-41; with Ralston Purina Co., St. Louis, 1946-81, pres. internat. div., 1963-66, exec. v.p., 1966-78, adminstrn. and fin., vice chmn. bd., chief operating officer, 1978-81, dir., 1966-81; pres. mgmt. firm, 1981—; pres., chief exec. officer Moehlenpah Industries Inc., St. Louis, 1982—; dir. Petrolite Corp., St. Louis, DeKalb Ag Research Inc., DeKalb, Sunmark Cos., St. Louis, Carlin Foods, Inc., Chgo. Founding mem. Latin Am. Agribus. Investment Corp., 1970, Industry Coop. Program UN; mem. Presdl. Com. World Food and Nutrition, Acad. Sci., 1979. Served to 1st lt. AUS, 1942-45, 50-52; Korea. Decorated Silver Star. Republican. Lutheran. Clubs: Saint Louis, University, St. Louis, Algonquin Golf (St. Louis). Co-author 14 volume study World Food and Nutrition Policy, 1980; contbr. articles on bus. to profl. jours. Home: 506 Fox Ridge Rd Saint Louis MO 63131 Office: PO Box 7359 Saint Louis MO 63177

CORNIEA, ROBERT EDWARD, motor parts company executive; b. St. Paul, Sept. 19, 1907; s. Edward Henry and Anna Marie (Munson) C.; ed. public schs., St. Paul; m. Dorothea Ada Townsend, June 18, 1932; children—Robert Edmond, Nancy Rose Ann, Raymond Leo, Donald George, James John. Clk., St. Paul Book and Stationery, 1924-25, Montgomery Ward & Co., 1925-27, Nat. Bushing and Parts Co., 1927-34; owner, operator Motor Parts Service Co., Inc., South St. Paul, 1943-79, pres., 1979—; pres. Motor Parts of Shakopee, Inc. (Minn.), 1956—; owner, pres. Motor Parts of Farmington (Minn.), 1964—; owner, pres. Motor Parts of Hastings (Minn.), 1978—. Mem. Motor and Equipment Wholesalers Assn., C. of C. (past v.p.), Coast Guard Aux. Roman Catholic. Clubs: Kiwanis (past pres.), Moose (gov. South Saint Paul 1941, Minn. pres. 1943, dist. dep. supreme gov. 1946, 47, Pilgrim Degree of Merit 1951); Southview Country, St. Paul Yacht, Pool and Yacht. Home: 1025 W 60th St Invergrove Heights MN 55075 Office: Motor Parts Service Co Inc 1111 S Concord St South Saint Paul MN 55075

CORNYN, JOHN EUGENE, accounting company executive; b. San Francisco, Apr. 30, 1906; s. John Eugene and Sara Agnes (Larkin) C.; B.S., St. Mary's Coll., 1934; M.B.A., U. Chgo., 1936; m. Virginia R. Shannahan, Sept. 10, 1938 (dec. May 1964); children—Virginia R., Kathleen R. Cornyn Arnold, John Eugene, Madeleine A. Cornyn Shanley, Carolyn G. Cornyn Clemons; m. 2d, Marian C. Fairfield, Aug. 21, 1965. Partner, John E. Cornyn & Co., C.P.A.s, Winnetka, Ill., 1951-73; pres. John E. Cornyn & Co. Ltd., 1973—. Exec. sec. North Shore Property Owners Assn., 1953—. C.P.A., Ill. Mem. Am. Inst. C.P.A.s, Ill. Soc. C.P.A.s, Am. Acctg. Assn., Am. Tax Assn., Fellowship Cath. Scholars. Catholic (Byzantine Rite). Home: 126 Bertling Ln Winnetka IL 60093

CORRALES, PATRICK, See *Who's Who in America,* 43rd edition.

CORRELL, BRUCE, accounting firm executive; b. Highland, Mich., Aug. 9, 1943; s. George William and Dorothy Emma (Bunting) C.; m. Janis Elaine Furlonge, Feb. 8, 1964 (div. Apr. 1972). B.S., Wayne State U., 1967. C.P.A., Mich. Ptnr. Plante & Moran, Southfield, Mich., 1963-76; mng. ptnr. Correll, Krywko, Harrell & Davis, Southfield, 1976—. Mem. Am. Inst. C.P.A.s, Mich. Assn. C.P.A.s (Gold medal 1967). Club: Detroit Athletic. Office: Correll Krywko Harrell & Davis 26261 Evergreen Suite 200 Southfield MI 48076

CORSER, GEORGE ALBERT, engineering educator, consultant; b. Hibbing, Minn., June 13, 1934; s. Albert and Mary Ann (Argir) C.; m. Maureen Kay Slagg, Apr. 8, 1962; children—George Patrick, John Kevin, Carin Glendyne. B.S. in Civil Engring., U. Colo., 1958; M.S. in Civil Engring., Wash. State U., 1963. Registered profl. engr., Mich. Asst. prof. Wash. State U., Pullman, 1958-64; assoc. prof. Gen. Motors Inst., Flint, Mich., 1964-81; chmn. mech. engring. Saginaw Valley State Coll., Mich., 1981—. Mem. Mayor's Task Force for Efficiency in City Govt., 1971; mem. Community Edn. Day com., 1980; citizen observer, Interfaith Action Council, 1970-71. Recipient Faculty Innovative Teaching award, Gen. Motors Inst., 1975. Mem. ASCE, AAUP, Am. Soc. Engring. Edn. (chmn. edn. research and methods div. 1973-75, dir. N. Central sect. Effective Tching. Insts., 1972), Mich. Soc. Profl. Engrs. (chmn. profl. engrs. in edn. 1974-76, Engr. of Yr. Flint chpt. 1984), Nat. Soc. Profl. Engrs., Sigma Xi, Phi Delta Kappa. Democrat. Unitarian. Lodge: DeMolay. Author: (with others) Mechanical Engineering Laboratory II, 1974. Office: Pioneer Hall Saginaw Valley State Coll 2250 Pierce Rd University Center MI 48710

CORSO, PATRICK ANTHONY, resort and restaurant executive; b. Logansport, Ind., May 20, 1950; s. Salvatore Antony and Marilyn Louise (Raub) C.; m. Judith Diane Garber, June 1, 1974; children—Claire, Anthony, Michael. B.S. in Speech, Ball State U., Muncie, Ind., 1973. Mgmt. trainee Hilton Shanty Creek, Bellaire, Mich., 1973-74, night mgr., 1975; mgr. Squire's Inn Restaurant, Oak Forest, Ill., 1974-75; gen. mgr., ptnr. Dill's Olde Towne Saloon, Traverse City, Mich., 1975—; dir., gen. mgr. Schuss Mountain Resort, Mancelona, Mich., 1979—; bd. trustees West Mich. Tours and Assn., Grand Rapids, 1984; dir. Schuss Mt., Inc., Mancelona, 1981—. Bd. trustees Traverse City Civic Players, 1979; Pres. No. Mich. Visitors Conv. Bur., Petoskey, 1980; bd. dirs. Mancelona Indsl. Fund, 1980-81; gov. appointee Pvt. Industry Council-Region 10 JTPA, Travense City, 1983. Recipient Outstanding Service award Traverse City Hotel and Motel Assn., 1979. Mem. Am. Hotel and Motel Assn., Mich. Lodging Assn., Nat. Ski Area Assn., W. Mich. Tourist Assn., Traverse City C. of C. (bd. dirs. 1979-81, Spl. Service award 1981). Club: Twin Bay Exchange (Traverse City) (bd. dirs. 1978-79). Avocations: Skiing, boating, fishing, golf, basketball. Office: Schuss Mountain Inc Schuss Mountain Rd Mancelona MI 49659

CORSON, THOMAS HAROLD, recreational vehicle manufacturing company executive; b. Elkhart, Ind., Oct. 15, 1927; s. Carl W. and Charlotte (Keyser) C.; student Purdue U., 1945-46, Rensselaer Poly. Inst., 1946-47, So. Meth. U., 1948-49; m. Dorthy Claire Scheide, July 11, 1948; children—Benjamin Thomas, Claire Elaine. Chmn. bd., chief exec. officer Coachmen Industries, Inc., Elkhart, Ind., 1965—; dir. Canton Drop Forge (Ohio), Midwest Commerce Bank, Elkhart, First State Bank; chmn. bd., sec. Greenfield Corp. Middlebury. Trustee Interlochen Arts Acad. and Nat. Music Camp, Ball State U., Muncie, Ind. Served with USNR, 1945-47. Mem. Ind. Mfrs. Assn. (dir.). Methodist. Mason (Shriner). Clubs: Capital Hill (Washington); Imperial (Naples, Fla.); Elcona Country (past dir.). Home: PO Box 504 Middlebury IN 46540 Office: Coachmen Dr PO Box 30 Middlebury IN 46540

CORTE, JAMES CHARLES, electrical construction company executive; b. Blue Island, Ill., July 17, 1948; s. S. Charles and Amelia (Costalunga) C.; B.A., St. Mary's Coll., Winona, Minn., 1970; m. Darcy L. DeYoung, Oct. 3, 1971; children—Mark Charles, Jaime Leigh. With Super Electric Constrn. Co., Chgo., 1971—, asst. controller, 1975-79, controller, 1979—. Mem. Ill. High Sch. Assn., South Suburban Ofcls. Assn. Roman Catholic. Home: 17010 S Cicero Ave Tinley Park IL 60477 Office: 4300 W Chicago Ave Chicago IL 60651

CORTESE, THOMAS ANTHONY, surgeon; b. Mesoraca, Italy, Feb. 20, 1908 (parents Am. citizens); s. Joseph and Mary (Schipani) C.; A.B., Ind. U., 1930, B.S., 1931, M.D., 1933. Intern, resident in surgery Columbus Hosp., Chgo., 1933-34; intern St. Francis Hosp., Indpls., 1932-33; practice medicine specializing in surgery, Indpls., 1934—; mem. staff St. Francis, Community, Univ. Heights hosps.; mem. Pres. Johnson's Commn. on Cardiovascular Disease, 1966-67. Mem. Pres. Johnson's Council on Youth Opportunity, 1966-67. Served with M.C., U.S. Army, World War II. Recipient Cavaliere di Merito, Republic of Italy, also commendatore. Diplomate Am. Bd. Surgery, Am. Bd. Abdominal Surgery, Internat. Coll. Surgeons. Fellow Internat. Fertility Assn.; mem. Indpls., Marion County med. socs., Am. Soc. Contemporary Medicine and Surgery, Am. Soc. Study of Sterility, Am. Fedn. Scientists, N.Y. Acad. Scis., Am. Assn. Clinics, AAAS, World Med. Assn. (founder), Ind. State Med. Assn., AMA, Fedn. of Italian Am. Socs. Ind. (pres., founder), Am. Legion, St. Francis Pathol. Soc., Am. Atomic Scientists. Club: Indpls. Athletic. Author: Hiatus Hernia, 1947; contbr. articles to profl. jours. Home: 3525 Payne Dr Indianapolis IN 46227 Office: 3901 SE St Indianapolis IN 46227

CORY, D. EARLE, jewelry company executive, designer, importer; b. Clarksburg, W.Va., June 11, 1931; s. Bennette Nathaniel and Mary Elizabeth (King) C. B.S. magna cum laude in Mktg. and Mgmt., U. Charleston, 1963, B.A. in Econs., 1963; M.B.A., Ohio U., 1965. Vice-pres. sales Cory Auto Parts Co., Montgomery, W.Va., 1958-61; mktg. mgr. Ford Overseas Dist. Ops., Wixom, Mich., 1965-67; sr. cons. Trans World Airlines, N.Y.C. and Chgo., 1968-70; dir. mktg. Anderson Co., Gary, Ind., 1970-72; pres. Cory Internat., Chgo., 1971—; bd. dirs. Jewelers Am. Chgo. Show, 1979—. Served with USAF, 1951-57. Recipient Wall St. Jour. Achievement award, 1963. Mem. So. Jewelry Travelers Assn., Jewelry Mfrs. Guild, Pi Gamma Mu (v.p. 1961-63). Republican. Methodist. Avocations: foreign travel; skiing; basketball. Office: Cory Internat 175 E Delaware Pl Chicago IL 60611

CORYELL, ORLANDO T., data processing executive; b. Richmond, Ind., June 11, 1931; s. Orlando F. and Lillian (Wesson) C.; m. Caroline Francis Smith, Sept. 19, 1964; children—Jane Ellen, Catherine Rebecca. Ph.B., Northwestern U., 1964; M.B.A., U. Chgo., 1967. Cert. data processing, system profl. Mgr. data processing Chgo. Rawhide, 1968-70; project mgr. Land & Assoc., Chgo., 1970-73; sr. cons. William Kordsiemon Assoc., Chgo., 1973-74; pres. The Colour Shop, Inc., La Grange, Ill., 1974-78, chmn. bd., 1978—; v.p. Comp-U-Mart, La Grange, 1982—; v.p. C.B.I. Assoc., La Grange, 1977-82. Candidate village pres., La Grange, 1973; treas. La Grange Caucus, 1976-78; dir., treas. bd. dirs. Chamber Ballet Ensemble, Evanston, Ill., 1984—. Mem. Assn. Systems Mgmt. (pres. Chgo. chpt. 1971-72, achievement award 1971), Chgo. Lyric Opera. Republican. Lutheran. Avocations: duplicate bridge; boating; travel. Home: 115 S Spring La Grange IL 60525

CORYELL, WILLIAM HENRY, psychiatry educator; b. Detroit, Dec. 29, 1948; s. William Leonard and Margaret Elizabeth (Nalder) C.; m. Kathryn Rose Goldring, May 1977; children—Matthew William, Julia Elizabeth. B.S., U. Ga., 1970; M.D., Med. Coll. Ga., 1973. Diplomate Am. Bd. Psychiatry and Neurology. Resident in psychiatry Washington U., St. Louis, 1977; instr. U. Iowa, Iowa City, 1977-78, asst. prof., 1978-82, assoc. prof., 1982—; mem. merit rev. bd. VA, Washington, 1984—. Contbr. numerous articles to profl. jours. NIH grantee, 1982; NIMH grantee, 1984. Mem. Psychiat. Research Soc., Am. Psychopath. Assn., Soc. Biol. Psychiatrists, Am. Acad. Clin. Psychiatrists, Am. Psychiat. Assn. Republican. Avocation: music. Home: Rural Route 2 Box 80 Iowa City IA 52240 Office: U Iowa 500 Newton Rd Iowa City IA 52242

CORZIN, HAROLD ALLEN, lawyer, educator; b. N.Y.C., Oct. 29, 1946; s. Michael and Sally (Levine) C.; m. Lee Ann Vogel, Sept. 10, 1978. B.A., U. Akron, 1968; J.D., U. Toledo, 1975. Bar: Ohio 1975. Assoc. Nadler, Sokolsky, Bahas, Balantzow & Holub, Akron, Ohio, 1976-78; ptnr. Meador, Corzin & Lowrey and predecessor firm Meador & Corzin, Fairlawn, Ohio, 1978—; instr. Kent State U., Ohio, 1984—; U.S. bankruptcy trustee U.S. Bankruptcy Ct., No. Dist. Ohio, 1976—; asst. atty. gen. State of Ohio, 1980—. Bd. dirs. United Cerebral Palsy, Akron, 1979. Served with USN, 1968-72. Recipient Am. Jurisprudence award, 1974. Mem. Akron Bar Assn., Ohio State Bar Assn. Democrat. Jewish. Avocation: flying. Home: 2514 Smith Rd Akron OH 44313 Office: Meador Corzin & Lowrey 2770 W Market St Fairlawn Akron OH 44313

COSCO, JOHN ANTHONY, hospital administrator; b. Cin., July 13, 1947; s. Adolph John and Pasqualina Marie (Saluppo) C.; m. Anne Patricia Ward, Aug. 5, 1978; children—Jon Francis, Stephen Ward, Justin Thomas. B.S., Xavier U., Cin., 1969, M.Ed., 1972, M.B.A., 1975; postgrad. U. Cin., 1972, Columbia-Pacific U. Notary public. Asst. dir. edn. and staff devel. Jewish Hosp., Cin., 1972-77; exec. dir. Region IX Peer Rev. Systems, Inc., Portsmouth, Ohio, 1977-78; exec. dir. Region II Med. Rev. Corp., Dayton, Ohio, 1978-81; asst. adminstr. Mercy Hosp., Tiffin, Ohio, 1981—; adj. faculty mem. in bus. mgmt. Xavier U., Sinclair Community Coll., Tiffin U.; v.p. Hos-Con & Assocs. Bd. dirs. Tiffin Area Physicians Placement Fund, Info. Ctr. Served to lt. AUS, 1969-71. Decorated Bronze Star. Mem. Am. Coll. Hosp. Adminstrs., Am. Hosp. Assn., Tiffin C. of C., Ohio Hosp. Assn., 1st Cav. Div. Assn. Lodges: Elks, K.C. (4 degree). Home: 289 Ella St Tiffin OH 44883 Office: 485 W Market St Tiffin OH 44883

COSGRIFF, ROBERT P., fund raising consultant; b. Iowa City, Feb. 16, 1926; s. Harold F. and Elizabeth (Phelan) C.; student Washington U., St. Louis, 1946-48; B.S.C., U. Iowa, 1950; postgrad. St. Louis U., 1950-51; children—Kevin, Ann, Jean. Mem. Beaver Assos., Chgo., 1954-60; founder, pres. Cosgriff Co., Omaha, 1960—. Served with USMC, 1944-46. Mem. Nat. Soc. Fund Raising Execs., Am. Public Relations Assn., Iowa C. of C. Execs. Assn., Omaha C. of C., Am. Fund Raising Council (dir.), Am. Legion. Clubs: Omaha, Happy Hollow Country, Lake Shore Country. Office: 1480 1st Nat Center Omaha NE 68102

COSGROVE, JOHN JAMES, institutional research and planning director; b. St. Louis, Oct. 18, 1955; s. James P. and Marie (Reuter) C.; m. Maggie Schwarz, Aug. 20, 1982. B.S. in Adminstrn. of Justice, U. Mo.-St. Louis, 1978, M.A. in Sociology, 1980. Edn. specialist U. Mo., St. Louis, 1979-80, instr., 1979—; research analyst Bi-State Devel. Agy., St. Louis, 1980-82; mgmt. info. analyst St. Louis Community Coll., 1982—. NIMH predoctoral fellow, Washington, 1978; League of Innovation to Community Colls. fellow, 1984. Mem. Assn. Instl. Research, Soc. Coll. and Univ. Planning, Am. Statis. Assn. Roman Catholic. Avocation: sports. Office: St Louis Community Coll 5801 Wilson St Saint Louis MO 63109

COSGROVE, MICHAEL JOE, retail store executive; b. Richland Center, Wis., June 3, 1957; s. Virgil Leo and Connie Lee (Kellogg) C.; m. Robin Lynn Carter, Mar. 20, 1976; children—Chad Michael, Angela Marie, Emmy Lynn. Diploma Western Tech. Inst. Pres., operator Triangle Kwik Stop, Richland, Wis., 1978—. Chmn. fund raising Steve Gunderson for Congress campaign, Richland, 1984. Mem. Econ. Devel. Assn. Richland County (bd. dirs. 1983-84), Southwest Wis. Pvt. Industry Council (bd. dirs. 1984), C. of C. (pres. 1982-85, bd. dirs. 1982). Republican. Mem. Evangelical Free Ch. Club: Tri-County Flying. Lodge: Rotary (bd. dirs. 1983-84). Avocations: sports, camping, flying, family. Home: Rural Route 5 Box 557 Richland Center WI 53581 Office: Triangle Kwik Stop 845 Sextonville Rd Richland Center WI 52581

COSTA, CATHERINE ANNE, former publishing executive, editor; b. Evanston, Ill., May 16, 1946; d. John Robert and Cythera Elsdon (Guthridge) Moyer; m. Robert Charles Van Slobig, May 14, 1966 (div. Sept. 1971); 1 child, Michael; m. Robert Francis, Mar. 4, 1974 (div. July 1985); children—Elizabeth, Michael, Cathleen, Robert C. Student, Lindenwood Coll., 1964-65. Adminstrv. asst. Wis. Dept. Natural Resources, Woodruff, 1980-82, fish mgmt. field staff, 1980-83; owner, guide Bobcat Guide Service, Eagle River, Wis., 1978-83; pub. relations dir. N. Am. Musky U., Eagle River, 1983-85; owner Rainbow Secretarial Service, Eagle River, 1984-85; editor, co-owner The Outdoor Forum, Eagle River, 1984-85; historian Muskies, Inc. Internat., St. Paul, 1982-84, sec., 1983-84. Author, editor: Internat. Symposium on Muskellunge (service award 1984), 1984. Editor The Muskie Line, 1980-85. Sec. Woodruff Area Mchts. Assn., 1977, 78. Mem. Wis. Outdoor Communicators Assn. (treas. 1983), Muskies, Inc. (sec. Headwaters chpt. 1980, 81, treas. 1985, 1st pl. women's div. 1979, 80, 81, 82, service and excellance award 1983), Lady Anglers Sportsfishing Soc. (co-founder 1982, pres. 1983). Baptist. Avocations: muskie fishing, horseback riding, needlepoint. Home and Office: 215 E Wall St Eagle River WI 54521

COSTANZO, DONALD JAMES, advertising and sales promotion manager; b. Bradford, Pa., Apr. 7, 1934; s. Chrisenzo Ernesto and Vincie Ann (Piscitelli) C.; m. Shirley Ann Dressler, Oct. 10, 1959; children—Kristen, Elizabeth, Jennifer, Donald II. B.A., Pa. State U., 1959. Artist, Zippo, Bradford, Pa., 1959-63; advt. mgr. Sypco, State College, Pa., 1963-64; v.p. advt. and pub. relations Federated Home and Mortgage, State College, 1964-66; dir. mail mgr. and asst. advt. mgr. Zippo, Bradford, 1966-72; advt. and sales promotion mgr. Vernon Co., Newton, Iowa, 1972—; sales promotion cons. Pres. Model Cities, Bradford, Pa., 1971; mem. mktg. com. Des Moines Civic Ctr., 1981-84; bd. dirs. Newton YMCA, 1976-80. Served with U.S. Army, 1952-54. Recipient Golden Circle Advt. award, 1981; Exceptional Service award Vernon Co., 1979. Mem. Splty. Advt. Assn. Internat. (Golden Pyramid award 1978, edn. com. tng. facilitator), Direct Mail Assn. Am. (Creative award 1970, 71), Newton C. of C. (dir. 1983—). Republican. Roman Catholic. Club: Newton Country (bd. dirs. 1976-79, pres. 1979). Creator new product catalogs, sales promotion and incentive programs.

COSTELLO, JERRY F., county government official. Dep. sheriff; county bd. chmn. St. Clair County, Ill., dir. ct. services and probation 20th Jud. Cir. Campaign chmn. Heart Assn., Belleville, 1983; vice chmn. Ill. div. United Way, 1984, chmn., 1985; bd. dirs. Ill. Ctr. for Autism; active St. Clair County Big Bros./Big Sisters, Belleville Women's Crisis Ctr., Children's Ctr. for Behavioral Devel.; helped establish St. Clair County chpt. Vets. Outreach Info. Ctr.; mem. East St. Louis Econ. Opportunity Commn., Ill.; vice chmn. Southwestern Ill. Bus. Devel. Fin. Corp., 1985—; bd. dirs. So. Ill. Leadership Council; pres. Urban Counties Council of Ill. Recipient cert. of Appreciation, Bus. and Profl. Women's Assn., 1985; honored Citizens League for Adequate Social Services; 1985 AAHMES Court #84, Daus. ISIS Ann. Humanitarian award, Gene Hughes award Ill. Ct. Services and Probation Assn. Address: 629 Garden Blvd Belleville IL 62221 Office: 10 Public Sq Belleville IL 62220

COSTELLO, RICHARD JAMES, industrial hygienist, engineer; b. Newton, Mass., Apr. 19, 1945; s. Richard E. and Phyllis Ruth (Burton) C. B.S. in Civil Engring., U. Ariz., 1968; M.S. in Environ. Health Engring., U. Tex., 1973. Registered profl. engr., Tex.; diplomate Am. Acad. Environ. Engrs.; cert. Am. Bd. Indsl. Hygiene. Sr. research indsl. hygienist, Robert A. Taft Labs., Nat. Inst. for Occupational Safety and Health, Cin., 1977—; lectr. Ctr. for Profl. Advancement; also speaker indsl. confs. Served to capt. USAF, 1968-76. Decorated 3 Commendation medals. Mem. Am. Indsl. Hygiene Assn., Am. Soc. Safety Engrs., Am. Conf. of Govtl. Indsl. Hygienists, Air Pollution Control Assn., Am. Chem. Soc. Roman Catholic. Contbr. numerous articles to profl. jours. contbg. author: Hazardous Waste Disposal, 1982, Protecting Personnel at Hazardous Waste Sites, 1984.

COTEFF, CHRIS, latex products co. executive, chemist; b. Lorain, Ohio, Feb. 7, 1951; s. Boris and Victoria (Piros) C.; m. Judith Evelyn Drugan, Nov. 15,

1980; 1 son, Aaron Piros. B.A., Hiram Coll., 1975; M.S., Akron U., 1981. Chemist Eaton Corp., Mantua, Ohio, 1976-80; quality control man, chemist Brunswick Corp., Willard, Ohio, 1980-82; quality control dir., sr. chemist Nat. Latex Products Co., Ashland, Ohio, 1982—. Mem. Union Concerned Scientists, Richland Astronomy Soc. (dir., editor), Am. Chem. Soc., Am. Soc. Quality Control, Astron. League, AAAS. Republican. Greek Orthodox. Office: 246 E 4th St Ashland OH 44805

COTMAN, ROBERT JOHN, food service company executive; b. Cleve., Oct. 31, 1945; s. John Earnest and Esther Marie (Fleischer) C.; m. Janet Christie Muhleman, Mar. 12, 1982; 1 son, John Phillip Muhleman. Student U. Mich., 1963-67; B.S., Ohio State U., 1973, M.F.A., 1978. Research assoc. Ctr. for Vocat. Edn., Columbus, Ohio, 1973-75; founder, pres. Group 243 Design, Inc., Ann Arbor, Mich., 1974-81; sr. v.p. Domino's Pizza, Inc., Ann Arbor, 1981—, also dir.; dir. Visual Communications Processes, Inc., Cubecraft Furniture Makers, Inc. Served with U.S. Army, 1968-70. Decorated Commendation medal. Mem. Am. Inst. Graphic Artists, Ann Arbor C. of C., Sigma Nu. Office: Domino's Pizza Inc 1968 Green Rd Ann Arbor MI 48105

COTRUVO, MARIO, public relations specialist; b. N.Y.C., Oct. 28, 1926; s. Vincenzo and Clara (Cardassi) C.; m. Phyllis Marie Stein, June 21, 1952; children—Richard, Catherine, Paul, Anne Marie; m. Margaret Anne Groth, Dec. 28, 1979. B.A., St. Mary's Coll., Moraga, Calif., 1952. News editor Oakland (Calif.) Tribune, 1955-68; legis. asst. Congressman Jerome Waldie, 1968; editorial writer Sta. KPIX-TV, San Francisco, 1968-69; asst. to gen. mgr. San Francisco Recreation and Parks Dept., 1970-73; with Bechtel Group of Cos., San Francisco, 1973—, now pub. relations mgr. subs. Bechtel Power Corp., Ann Arbor, lectr. Mem. exec. com. Mich. Educators Energy Forum, 1979; mem. adv. com. Mich. Com. for Jobs and Energy, 1980; mem. publicity com. Mich. Tech. Council, 1980; communications adv. Washtenaw County United Way, Ann Arbor, 1983. Recipient Excellence award AP, 1968-69, 78; Phillips award L.I. U., 1982; Appreciation award Eastern Mich. U., 1983. Mem. Pub. Relations Soc. Am., Am. Nuclear Soc. Democrat. Author TV scripts. Home: 1006 Greenhills St Ann Arbor MI 48105 Office: PO Box 1000 Ann Arbor MI 48106

COTTELEER, MICHAEL ALEXANDER, lawyer; b. Chgo., Feb. 4, 1944; s. Alexander Charles and Helen Lucille (Schmitt) C.; B.A., No. Ill. U., 1968; J.D. (Alumni scholar), Loyola U., Chgo., 1971; children—Jennifer, Amy, Kevin. Bar: Ill. 1971. Atty. Chgo. Title & Trust Co., 1971-72; atty. firm Herrick, McNeill, McElroy & Peregrine, Chgo., 1972-74, Daniels, Hancock & Faris, Elmhurst, Ill., 1974-75; asst. dean, assoc. prof. law No. Ill. U. Coll. Law, Glen Ellyn, 1975-78; sole practice law, Wheaton, Ill., 1978-81, 82—; partner Borenstein, Cotteleer, Greenberg & Young, Chgo. and Wheaton, 1981-82. Bd. dirs. No. Ill. U. Found., 1979—, mem. pres.'s legis. action com., 1978—; bd. dirs. Festival Theater, Oak Park, Ill., 1981-82. Served with U.S. Army, 1962-65. Recipient award for service Ill. Bd. Regents, 1979. Mem. Am. Bar Assn., Ill. State Bar Assn. (vice chmn. sect. council on corps. and securities law 1981-82), Chgo. Bar Assn., DuPage County Bar Assn., No. Ill. U. Alumni Assn. (v.p., bd. dirs. 1977-82, pres. 1985—), Sigma Alpha Epsilon. Roman Catholic. Office: 209 N Washington St Wheaton IL 60187

COTTER, BARBARA JOANN, accountant; b. DeKalb, Mo., May 1, 1934; d. Ivyal Paul and Eva Evelyn (Hale) C.; m. Ralph Edward Peasley, Feb. 11, 1952 (div. 1968); children—Rhonda Eileen, Arthur Paul. Student Johnson County Community Coll., 1969-70; B.A., Rockhurst Coll., 1972. Asst. controller Rickel Inc., Kansas City, Mo., 1972-81; acct., mdse. dir. Seaboard Allied Milling, Shawnee Mission, Kans., 1981-82; data processing mgr. Physicians Assoc., Overland Park, Kans., 1982-83; owner, operator B.J. Cotter Services, Shawnee, Kans., 1983; trust acct. Merrigan & Assocs., Kansas City, 1983—. Pres. Bonner Springs Jaycee Jaynes, Kans., 1965-66; music dir. children's choir First Christian Ch., 1960. Mem. Am. Bus. Women's Assn., Nat. Assn. Accts. Republican. Mem. Christian Ch. Clubs: Barcelona Townhomes Assn. (treas. 1976). Lodges: Order Eastern Star, DeMolay Mothers. Avocations: golf; bowling; bridge; reading; acting. Home: 6621 Bluejacket Shawnee KS 66203 Office: Merrigan and Assocs 8900 Ward Pkwy Kansas City MO 64114

COTTER, DANIEL ALBERT, hardware wholesale distribution company executive; b. Duluth, Minn., Dec. 26, 1934; s. John M. and Alice (Germain) C.; children—Cynthia Germain, Megan Julia, Michaela Hamlin. B.A. in Bus. Adminstrn., Marquette U., 1957; M.B.A., Northwestern U., 1960. With Cotter & Co., Chgo., 1949—, v.p., 1966-78, nat. sales mgr., 1976-78, pres., 1978—, chief operating officer, from 1978, now also chief exec. officer. Chmn. Lathrop Chgo. Boys' Club, 1970—. Recipient Silver Keystone award Boys Club, 1976, medallion Boys' Clubs Am., 1977, John F. Atkinson Humanitarian award, 1980. Clubs: Univ., Saddle and Cycle, Racquet (Chgo.). Office: Cotter & Coe 2740-52 N Clybourne Ave Chicago IL 60614*

COTTER, JOHN M., hardware company executive; b. 1904; married. With Dayton's Bluff Hardware Co., 1916-23; salesman Raymer Hardware Co., 1923-38; gen. ptnr. Kohlhoop Hardware, 1928-31; gen. mdse. mgr. Kelly-How-Thompson Co., 1933-42; v.p., gen. mgr. Oakes & Co., 1942-48; chmn. bd., dir. Cotter & Co., Chgo., 1948—, also former chief exec. officer. Office: Cotter & Co 2740-52 N Clybourn Ave Chicago IL 60614*

COTTINGHAM, CARL DEAN, community college administrator; b. McLeansboro, Ill., Dec. 13, 1940; s. James Arthur and Ruby Mae (Hamilton) C.; m. Ella Nanette Grant, June 15, 1962; children—Catherine, Jeffrey, Dana Lynn, Jeremy, Betsy Ruth. B.S. in Edn., So. Ill. U., 1962, M.S. in Edn., 1965. Librarian McLeansboro Twp. High Sch., 1962-65; dir. instructional resources Carbondale Community High Sch., Ill., 1965-68; assoc. dean learning resources John A. Logan Coll., Carterville, Ill., 1968-81, dean for learning resources and continuing edn., 1985—; pres. So. Ill. Learning Resources Coop., 1982-83. Mem. Bd. Edn. Carterville Unit 5 Schs., 1972-75; scoutmaster Troop 77 Egyptian council Boy Scouts Am., 1982—. Mem. Sch. Master's Club, So. Ill. Media Roundtable (treas. 1975-77), Ill. Audiovisual Assn. (bd. dirs. 1965-69), Jaycees, Geneal. Soc. So. Ill. (bd. dirs. 1978—). Baptist. Avocations: camping; hiking; history research. Home: Route 3 Box 166 Carterville IL 62918 Office: John A Logan College Carterville IL 62918

COTTRELL, (WILLIAM) PAUL, lawyer; b. Salem, N.J., Nov. 5, 1951; s. Arvil Earl and Gudbjorg (Gudmundsdottir) C.; m. Carolyn Anne Pokoyski, May 25, 1974; children—Jonathan Paul, Elizabeth Constance. B.A. magna cum laude, U. Del., 1975; J.D., U. Chgo., 1978. Bar: Ill. 1978, U.S. Dist. Ct. (no. dist.) Ill. 1978, U.S. Ct. Appeals (7th cir.) 1980, U.S. Tax Ct. 1982, Pa. 1985. Assoc. Karon, Morrison & Savikas, Ltd., Chgo., 1978-81, Fohrman, Lurie, Sklar & Simon, Ltd., Chgo., 1981-84; assoc. dir. Constrn. Law Inst., Chgo., 1982-85. Contbr. chpt. to Illinois Election Law, 1983. Contbr. articles to profl. jours. Treas. Citizens Coalition, 1973-75; bd. dirs. Saxony Ct. Condominium Assn., Chgo., 1981-82. Named Outstanding Young Man of Am., Jaycees, 1983. Mem. Chgo. Bar Assn. (mem. exec. com. Young Lawyers sect. 1981-85, co-chmn. Fed. Trial Bar task force), ABA (vice chairperson com. on liaison Young Laywers Div., 1982—, mem. exec. com., health care law com., 1982—, del. ABA conv. 1983, editor-in-chief law practice notes Barrister), Phi Kappa Phi, Omicron Delta Kappa, Pi Sigma Alpha. Democrat. Unitarian. Mem. Del. Alumni Assn. (Chgo. area coordinator, 1978—). Home: 1203 Talley Rd Wilmington DE 19809 Offic: Howard M Berg & Assocs PA One Customs House Sq PO Box 33 Wilmington DE 19899

COUGHLIN, TIMOTHY JOHN, hospital administrator; b. Erie, Pa., Nov. 28, 1950; s. Harold John and Doris Alma (Carney) C.; m. Eleanor Marie Kapsiak, Jan. 23, 1970; children—Colleen Marie, Erin Kathleen. B.S. in Mech. Engring., Gannon U., 1973, B.S. in Indsl. Mgmt., 1975, M.B.A., 1979. Registered profl. engr., Pa., Ohio. Mgr. indsl. engring. Bucyrus Erie Co. (Pa.), 1972-77; dir. Brown Meml. Hosp., Conneaut, Ohio, 1977-79; asst. adminstr. Ashtabula Gen. Hosp. (Ohio), 1979-82; v.p. East Liverpool City Hosp. (Ohio), 1982—. Mem. Sch. Bd. Erie, Pa., 1970-74; bd. dirs. Am. Cancer Soc., East Liverpool, 1983, Ashtabula County Day Care Ctr., 1982. Mem. Am. Inst. Indsl. Engrs. (sr. mem., chpt. pres. 1981-82), Am. Coll. Hosp. Adminstrs. (treas. 1980-83, outstanding service award 1983). Republican. Roman Catholic. Recipient Community Service award C. of C. Bowling Green, 1976, 77, 78; award citation 112th Gen. Assembly Ohio, 1978; Service Above Self award Rotary Club, 1976; named Bus. Assoc. of Yr., Am. Bus. Women's Assn., 1980. Mem. Fraternal Order of Police (v.p. 1965-66), Am. Criminal Justice Assn., Internat. Assn. Chiefs of Police, Ohio Assn. Chiefs of Police (exec. com. 1982—), Nat. FBI Acad. Assocs., Ohio Crime Prevention Assn. Lutheran. Club: Falcon (Bowling Home: PO Box 5147 East Liverpool OH 43920

COULSON, CHARLES ERNEST, lawyer; b. Belleville, Ill., Oct. 29, 1944; s. Charles Henry and Genevieve (Bell) C.; B.A., Kent State U., 1970; J.D. U. Akron, 1974. Bar: Ohio 1974, U.S. Dist. Ct. (no. dist.) Ohio 1976. Asst. prosecutor Lake County Prosecutor's Office, Painesville, Ohio, 1975-77, chief asst. prosecutor, 1977-79; ptnr. Coulson and Perez, Mentor, Ohio, 1979-82, Davies, Rosplock, Coulson, Perez, Deeb, and Harrell, Willoughby, Ohio, 1982—; law dir. City of Kirtland, Ohio, 1980—; parttime instr. bus. and real estate law Lakeland Community Coll., Mentor, 1979—. Served to 1st lt. U.S. Army, 1968-70, Vietnam. Mem. Assn. Trial Lawyers Am., Ohio Acad. Trial Lawyers, Ohio State Bar Assn., Lake County Bar Assn. Office: Davies Rosplock Coulson Perez Deeb and Harrell 4230 State Route 306 Willoughby OH 44094

COULSON, JOHN C(ARL), real estate executive, investor; b. Sullivan, Ind., July 10, 1939; s. M. Allan and Mary Ellen (Thompson) C.; m. Sue Ellen Frew, Nov. 4, 1961; children—Dan T., Jeff A., John A. B.S. in Indsl. Econs., Purdue U., 1961; grad. Realtors Inst., 1979. Cert. residential specialist, Territorial mgr. Hess & Clark div. Vick Chems., Ashland, Ohio, 1961-66; dist. mgr. Allis Chalmers Mfg. Co., Columbus, Ohio, 1966-68, dist. mgr., Lansing, Mich., 1969-70; store mgr. Plantation Supply, Ft. Wayne, Ind., 1968-69; lot mgr. Thomas Mobile Homes, Kokomo and Lafayette, Ind., 1970-71; real estate broker Coldwell Banker/Sycamore-Mason, West Lafayette, Ind., 1971—; pres. New Vintage Homes, West Lafayette, 1977—; owner Vintage Investments, West Lafayette, 1979—; sec. SAE House Corp., West Lafayette, 1979—. Chmn. West Lafayette Parks and Recreation Adv., West Lafayette, 1977. Served with U.S. Army, 1961-62. Mem. Lafayette Bd. Realtors (pres. 1980-81, bd. dirs. 1975-84, Realtor of Yr. 1985) Ind. Assn. Realtors (bd. dirs. 1981-83), Greater Lafayette C. of C. (com. chmn.), Jaycees (v.p. 1971-73, keyman 1972, dir. 1971-73). Republican. Presbyterian. Lodges: Kiwanis dirs. 1974-77), Elks. Home: 619 Wilshire Ave West Lafayette IN 47906 Office: Coldwell Banker/Sycamore-Mason 1089 Sagamore Pkwy W West Lafayette IN 47906

COULSON, JOHN SELDEN, market research executive; b. Chgo., Aug. 14, 1915; s. Leonard Ward and Mabel Genevive (Selden) C.; m. Jane Eleanor Rinder, Nov. 28, 1943; children—Jane, Nancy Coulson Hobor, Ann Coulson Hubbard, Sara Coulson Ellis. B.A., U. Chgo., 1936; M.B.A., Harvard U., 1938. Mgr. div. research Montgomery Ward, Chgo., 1938-48; sr. assoc. Joseph White & Assocs., Chgo., 1948-50; research supr., mgr. research dept., v.p.-in-charge research Leo Burnett Co., Chgo., 1950-77; ptnr. Communications Workshop, Inc., Chgo., 1977—; lectr. U. Chgo., 1955, 78-79, Northwestern U.-Chgo., 1960-71, U. Ill.-Urbana, 1977, Columbia Coll., Chgo., 1974-76. Contbr. chpts. to books. Bd. mgrs. Lawson YMCA, Chgo., 1970—; bd. govs. Chgo. Heart Assn., 1978—; citizens bd. WBEZ, Chgo. Pub. Radio, 1980—. Mem. Am. Statis. Assn. (pres. Chgo. chpt. 1954-55), Am. Mktg. Assn. (pres. Chgo. chpt. 1963-64), Assn. Pub. Opinion Research (exec. council 1969-72). Republican. Clubs: Univ. of Chgo., Plaza. Home: 175 E Delaware Pl Apt 9009 Chicago IL 60611 Office: Communications Workshop Inc 168 N Michigan Ave Chicago IL 60601

COULTER, THOMAS H(ENRY), former association executive, management consultant; b. Winnipeg, Man., Can., Apr. 21, 1911; s. David and Sarah Anne (Allen) C.; B.S., Carnegie Inst. Tech., 1933; M.A., U. Chgo., 1935; m. Mary Alice Leach, Nov. 24, 1937; children—Sara, Anne, Jane, Thomas II. Investment analyst Shaw & Co., Chgo., 1935-36; sales engr. Universal Zonolite Insulation Co., Chgo., 1936-39, sales promotion mgr., 1939-40, gen. sales mgr., 1940-41, v.p., 1941-45; mgr. devel. div. Booz, Allen & Hamilton, Chgo., 1945-48, partner, 1948-50; pres. Am. Bildrok Co., 1950-54; chief exec. officer Chgo. Assn. Commerce and Industry, 1954-81; exec. v.p. Lester B. Knight & Assos., Chgo., 1981-84; pub. Commerce mag.; lectr. mktg., exec. program U. Chgo.; dir. Chgo.-Tokyo Bank. Mem. State Dept.'s Top Mgmt. Seminar Team, Israel, 1956, Japan, 1958; mem. Dist. Export Council. Mem. Mayor's Commn. Rehab. Persons; mem. Chgo.-Cook County Criminal Justice Commn., Cook County Real Estate Tax Study Commn., Ill. Gov.'s Council on Health and Fitness, Chgo. Dept. Human Services Bd. dirs. Chgo. Crime Commn.; bd. dirs. Chgo. chpt. ARC, 1953-59, USO of Chgo.; mem. citizens bd., council Sch. Bus. Assn.; bd. govs. Internat. House, U. Chgo.; mem. citizens com. U. Ill.; exec. council Chgo. Civil Def. Corps; exec. com. Ill. Council Econ. Edn.; hon. trustee Skokie Valley Community Hosp., pres., 1955-57, 66-70; bd. dirs. Better Bus. Bur. Met. Chgo., Hosp. Planning Council Met. Chgo., Chgo. Council Fgn. Relations; mem. Northwestern U. Assos.; trustee Village of Golf (Ill.), 1951-55; mem. nat. adv. bd. Am. Security Council Edn. Found.; mem. adv. bd. Chgo. Area council Boy Scouts Am.; mem. Cook County Home Rule Commn.; mem. Rehab. Inst. Chgo. Assos.; mem. adv. com. U. Chgo. Met. Inst.; mem. nat. adv. council Nat. Legal Center for Pub. Interest; mem. Cook County Econ. Devel. Adv. Com., Ill. Devel. Bd. Decorated comdr.'s cross Order of Merit (Germany); knight Order of Merit (Italy); knight Order of Lion (Finland); knight 1st class Royal Order of Vasa, comdr. Royal Order Vasa (Sweden); chevalier Nat. Order of Merit (France); 3d class Order of Sacred Treasure (Japan); recipient Silver Ann. All-American award Sports Illustrated, 1957; Outstanding Civilian Service medal U.S. Army, 1961; Gold Badge of Honor for Merits (Austria), 1962, (Province of Vienna), 1971; citation pub. service U. Chgo.; Alumni merit award for outstanding profl. achievement Carnegie Inst. Tech.; Indsl. Statesman award U.S.-Japan Trade Council, 1976; Citizen Fellowship award Inst. Medicine, 1976. Mem. Nat. Sales Execs., Newcomen Soc. N.Am., U.S. C. of C. (banking, monetary and fiscal affairs com.), Nat. Planning Assn., U.S. Olympians (dir. Midwest chpt.), Geog. Soc. Soc. Chgo. (dir.), Internat. Bus. Council, Midwest-Japan Assn., Japan-Am. Soc. Chgo. (dir.), French-Am. C. of C. in U.S. (dir. Midwest chpt.), Am. Austrian Soc. of Midwest, Finnish Am. C. of C. of Midwest, Ill. Assn. C. of C. Execs., Am. Mgmt. Assn., Royal Hort. Soc., Chgo. Hist. Soc., Chgo. Architecture Found, Field Mus. Natural History, Art Inst. Chgo., Mus. Sci. and Industry, Chgo. Council on Fgn. Relations (Chgo. com.), Mid-Am. Swedish Trade Assn., Lambda Alpha. Clubs: Mid-Am., Comml., Execs. (pres. 1950-51), Sales and Mktg. Execs. (pres. 1953-54, award 1979), Internat. Trade, Canadian Univ., Economic, Univ. (Chgo.); Glenview (Golf, Ill.).

COULTON, MARTHA JEAN GLASSCOE (MRS. MARTIN J. COULTON), librarian; b. Dayton, Ohio, Dec. 11, 1927; d. Lafayette Pierre and Gertrude Blanche (Miller) Glasscoe; student Dayton Art Inst., 1946-47; m. Martin J. Coulton, Sept. 6, 1947; children—Perry Jean, Martin John. Dir., Milton (Ohio) Union Public Library, 1968—. Active, West Milton (Ohio) Cable TV Com. Named Outstanding Woman Jaycees, 1978-1979. Mem. ALA, Ohio Library Assn., Miami Valley Library Orgn. (sec. 1981, v.p. 1982, pres. 1983), Internat. Platform Assn., DAR. Home: 1910 N Mowry Rd Pleasant Hill OH 45359 Office: 560 S Main St West Milton OH 45383

COUNSELL, LEE ALBERT, dentist, educator, hispanist; b. Neillsville, Wis., July 5, 1923; s. Clarion and Henrietta (Clemens) C. D.D.S., Northwestern U., 1948; B.A., U. Wis.-Madison, 1949; diploma grad. pedodontics Forsyth Dental Center, Boston, 1949; M.P.H., U. Mich., 1967; M.A. Spanish, So. Ill. U., 1984. Commd. lt. Dental Corps, U.S. Navy, 1950, discharged, 1952, rejoined, 1955, advanced through grades to comdr., 1961, ret., 1972; intern staff Naval Hosp., Gt. Lakes, Ill., 1950; asst. dir. dept. pedodontics Marquette U., 1952-54; practice pedodontics, Washington, 1954-55; house staff Naval Hosp., Boston, 1959-62; dir. dental dept. Naval Constrn. Bn. Center, Davisville, R.I., 1964-66; head preventive dentistry program Naval Base, Gt. Lakes, Ill., 1968-70; asst. chief clin. investigations div. Naval Dental Research Inst., 1971, chief, 1972; asst. dir. Bur. Dental Health, Div. Health, State of Fla., 1972-73; fellow U. Dundee (Scotland), 1973; research assoc. Am. Dental Assn., Chgo., 1973-74; assoc. prof. So. Ill. U., Carbondale, 1974-77, adj. prof., 1979—; cons. dental health edn., 1977—. Decorated Navy Commendation medal. Fellow Am. Assn. Endodontists; mem. ADA, Am. Assn. Tchrs. Spanish and Portuguese, Am. Guild Organists, Xi Psi Phi (life), Phi Kappa Phi. Episcopalian. Contbr. numerous articles to profl. publs. Home and Office: 204 Pine Ln Carbondale IL 62901

COUNSELL, RAYMOND ERNEST, pharmacology and medicinal chemistry educator, consultant; b. Vancouver, B.C., Can., Aug. 20, 1930; came to U.S., 1954; s. Ernest and Florence Rose (Church) C.; m. Elizabeth Ann Short, Sept. 28, 1957; children—Steven R., Ronald L., Catherine A. B.S. in Pharmacy, U. B.C., 1953; Ph.D. in Medicinal Chemistry, U. Minn., 1957. Lectr. U. B.C., Vancouver, 1953-54; teaching asst. U. Minn., Mpls., 1954-55; sr. research chemist G.D. Searle & Co., Skokie, Ill., 1957-64; assoc. prof. U. Mich., Ann Arbor, 1964-69, prof. pharmacology and medicinal chemistry, 1969—; cons. G. D. Searle & Co., Skokie, Ill., 1973-82, NIH, Bethesda, Md., 1968—, Los Alamos Nat. Labs., N.Mex., 1979-83. Patentee in field. Recipient Research Assoc. award Am. Cancer Soc., 1964, T.O. Soine Meml. award U. Minn., 1981; E. Roosevelt Internat. fellow Internat. Union Against Cancer, 1972. Fellow Acad. Pharm. Scis. (chmn., sect. medicinal chemistry 1971-72), AAAS; mem. Am. Chem. Soc. (chmn. div. medicinal chemistry 1971-72), Soc. Nuclear Medicine (vice-chmn. program 1981-82), Am. Soc. Pharmacology and Exptl. Therapeutics. Home: 2257 Delaware Dr Ann Arbor MI 48103 Office: Dept Pharmacology 6322 Med Sci Bldg I U Mich Med Sch Ann Arbor MI 48109

COUPER, DAVID CORTLAND, police chief; b. Little Falls, Minn., Apr. 5, 1938; s. John V. and Elsa D. Couper; B.A., U. Minn., 1968, M.A. (NIMH fellow), 1970; m. Sabine Lobitz; children—Peter, Catherine, Sarah, Michael, Matthew, Jennifer. Officer, Edina (Minn.) Police Dept., 1960-62; officer, detective Mpls. Police Dept., 1962-69; dir. Burnsville (Minn.) Public Safety Dept., 1969-72; chief police City of Madison (Wis.), 1972—; instr. sociology-criminology U. Minn., 1970-71, U. Wis., 1974-77. Bd. dirs. Group Health Coop., Madison, 1979-81. Served with USMC, 1957-60. U. Minn. grantee to study European police, 1971. Mem. Police Exec. Research Forum, Internat. Assn. Chiefs of Police. Club: Rotary. Author: How to Rate Your Local Police, 1983. Contbr. numerous articles to profl. publs. Office: 211 S Carroll St Madison WI 53710*

COURECH, ARLETTA BERNICE, advertising salesperson; b. Isle, Mich., Nov. 11, 1924; d. John Bernard and Eda Marie (Ziesmer) Carlson; m. Arnold John Courech (div.); children—Raymond, Greggory, Wendy, Renee. Student Cambridge Bus. Coll., 1965, Macomb County Community Coll., 1966-67, U. Mich.-Dearborn, 1976. Real estate sales staff Durbin Co., Birmingham, Mich., 1973-75; payroll supr. ITT, Oak Park, Mich., 1975-76; new home sales rep. Harry Carlson Assocs., Troy, Mich., 1975-77; furniture sales rep. Montgomery Ward Co., Pontiac, Mich., 1977-83; advertising dir. Women's Clubs Pub. Co., Inc., Chgo., 1983—. Home: 114 Waterly Ave Pontiac MI 48053 Office: Women's Clubs Pub Co Inc 323 S Jackson St Chicago IL 60606

COUREY, FRED SAMUEL, management consultant, former mayor; b. Lennox, S.D.; s. Samuel Thomas and Mabel (Salem) G.; student Lennox pub. schs. With Courey's Food Mart, Inc., Lennox, 1934-83, co-owner, 1946-83; city auditor, Lennox, 1948-50, mayor, 1960-80; with Fred Courey & Assocs., gen. cons., 1983—; past mem. Urbanized Devel. Commn., S.Eastern Criminal Justice Commn., S.Eastern Health Planning Council (all of S.E. Council Govts. S.D.); past mem. S.D. State Local Govt. Study Commn.; past mem. S.D. adv. council SBA, 1969-82, ACE mgmt. assistance counselor, 1969-84. Gen. chmn. Lennox Diamond Jubilee, 1954; past mem. parish council St. Magdalen Roman Cath. Ch., Lennox; project coordinator, program dir. Lennox Area Med. Center, 1975—; past mem. bd. dirs. Lennox Area Devel. Corp. Served with AUS, 1941-45; PTO. Decorated Army Commendation medal. Mem. Am. Water Works Assn., S.D. Water and Wastewater Conf. (past dir.), Am. Fedn. Police, Am. Legion. Small Towns Inst., Smithsonian Instn., Nat. Rifle Assn., Nat. Wildlife Fedn., Early Am. Soc., Lennox L.E.E. Com., Inc. (bd. dirs. 1983—), VFW. Republican. Club: Lennox Comml. (past pres.), Nat. Travel, S.D. Auto. Address: Box 56 Lennox SD 57039

COURTEAU, ELMER JOSEPH, JR., newspaperman, writer; b. Mpls., May 7, 1921; s. Elmer Joseph and Laura (Rivard-Dufresne) C.; B.A., Coll. of St. Thomas, 1947; postgrad. U. Md., 1948, U. Paris (Sorbonne), 1949, U. Wis., 1952; U. Minn., 1961-63; m. Constance Ann Dobmeyer, June 26, 1948; children—Michele, Gregory, Marc, Jeffrey, Jennifer, Gretchen, Kristin. With Duluth News-Tribune and Herald, 1947-48, Hibbing (Minn.) Daily Tribune, 1950-61, St. Paul Pioneer-Press & Dispatch, 1961-66, Mpls. Tribune, 1966—, Cath. Digest, 1969—. Past pres., current bd. dirs., worthy fellow N.W. Ter. French and Can. Heritage Inst. Mem. Am. Hist. Assn., Am. Acad. Polit. Sci., Am. Name Soc., Cath. Hist. Soc. Phila., Minn. Geneal. Soc. (past pres., dir., worthy fellow), La Société Historique de Que. Democrat. Roman Catholic. Co-author: French Canadians of the North-Central States. Author: The King's Daughters; The Carignan Regiment. Home: 1148 W 60th St Inver Grove Heights MN 55075 Office: 425 Portland Ave Minneapolis MN 55415

COURTNEY, JAMES EDMOND, mining company executive, lawyer; b. Meadville, Pa., Dec. 28, 1931; s. Alexis James and Marian (Winans) C.; m. Eileen Alman, Nov. 2, 1970; children—Alison, David, Jotham. A.B., Dartmouth Coll., 1953, M.B.A., Amos Tuck Sch. Bus. Adminstrn., 1954; LL.B. magna cum laude, Harvard U., 1959. Bar: Ohio 1960. Assoc. Jones Day Reavis & Pogue, Cleve., 1959-63, prnt., 1963-74; v.p. internat. M.A. Hanna Co., Cleve., 1974-78, sr. v.p. corp. devel., 1978-79, exec. v.p., 1979—, also dir.; chmn. St. John d'el Rey Mining Co., P.L.C., Cleve., 1978—; dir. Midland SouthWest, Tex. Trustee Council of Ams., N.Y.C., 1977—. Served to lt. USN, 1954-56. Mem. Am. Iron Ore Assn., Am. Iron and Steel Inst., Am. Mining Congress, Internat. Econ. Policy Assn. (bd. dirs. 1977—). Clubs: Union, Clevelander. Home: 23120 Roberts Run Bay Village OH 44140 Office: MA Hanna Co 100 Erieview Plaza Cleveland OH 44114

COURTNEY, KATHIE SUE, athletic trainer/consultant; b. Aberdeen, S.D., Aug. 4, 1952; d. Robert Charles and Margaret Malvena (Day) Demery; m. Robert James Courtney, Jr., Mar. 22, 1975; children—Amanda Kathleen, Patrick Michael. B.S., S.D. State U., 1974; M.S., Ind. State U., 1975. Grad. asst. trainer Ind. State U., Terre Haute, 1974-75; tchr., coach, trainer West Vigo High Sch., West Terre Haute, Ind., 1975-76; athletic trainer/instr. Dakota State Coll., Madison, S.D., 1976—; athletic trainer cons. Madison High Sch., 1981—, S.D. State U., 1976—, Parent Tchr. Orgn. Mem. Am. Legion Aux., Am. Heart Assn., S.D. Athletic Trainers Assn. (pres. 1985—), Nat. Athletic Trainers Assn. (program dir. dist. 5), S.D. Emergency Med. Tech. Assn., Nat. Emergency Med. Tech. Assn., AAUW. Democrat. Roman Catholic. Clubs: Dakota State Coll. Women's (pres. 1978-79). Home: 209 NW 7th St Madison SD 57042 Office: Room 8 Fieldhouse Dakota State Coll Madison SD 57042

COURTNEY, NICOLE, broadcasting music director; b. Fort Knox, Ky., June 8, 1954; d. David E. and Ruth M. (Delmar) Bruening. Student Miami Dade Community Coll., Fla. State U. Research asst. Sta. 96X-WMJX, Miami, Fla., 1976-77; announcer Sta. WIFE-AM, Indpls., 1977-78, Sta. KFMK-FM, Houston, 1978-82; music dir. Sta. US99-WUSN, Chgo., 1982—. Author: (radio drama) Dark Lords of Sith, 1983. Mem. Acad. Country Music. Democrat. Lutheran. Avocation: filmmaking. Office: US99 First Media of Illinois 875 N Michigan Ave Chicago IL 60611

COURTRIGHT, JEANNE WASHCO, career planning and placement professional; b. Binghamton, N.Y., Aug. 27, skiing; d. Virgil Nicholas and Teresa Margaret (Pucek) Washco; m. John Mark Courtright, July 10, 1976. A.B., Princeton U., 1979; M.A., Ball State U., 1985. Adminstrv. asst. internat./intercultural programs Am. Field Service, N.Y.C., 1979-81; prodn. mgr. Roger Williams Tech. & Econ. Services, Princeton, N.J., 1981; asst. to dir. Career Devel. Ctr., Marion Coll., Ind., 1981-82, counselor, Counseling and Career Devel. Ctr., 1982-84; asst. dir. career planning and placement North Central Coll., Naperville, Ill., 1984—. Mem. Am. Assn. Counseling and Devel., Am. Coll. Personnel Assn., Assn. for Christians in Student Devel., Nat. Assn. for Women Deans, Adminstrs. and Counselors. Avocations: reading; skiing; traveling; camping; canoeing. Office: North Central Coll 30 N Brainard St Naperville IL 60566

COUSINEAU, TOM, professional football player. Linebacker, Cleve. Browns, NFL. Office: Cleveland Browns Cleveland Stadium Cleveland OH 44114*

COUSINS, ALBERT NEWTON, sociology educator; b. Cleve., May 7, 1919; s. Harry and Anna (Roth) C.; m. Rose Demetra Manitsas, May 18, 1944; children—Julia, Daniel. A.B., Ohio State U., 1942; M.A., Harvard U., 1949, Ph.D., 1951. Asst. prof. sociology Fla. State U.-Tallahassee, 1949-51; asst. prof. to prof. sociology Fenn Coll., Cleve., 1951-65; prof. sociology Cleve. State U., 1965—; co-dir. NDEA tng. project, 1966-69; dir. Anti-Poverty Inst., Cleve., 1967. Pres. bd. trustees United Area Citizens Agy., Cleve., 1978-82. Mem. Am. Sociol. Assn., N. Central Sociol. Assn., Phi Beta Kappa. Author: Urban Life, 1979; editor; Urban Man and Society, 1970. Contbr. articles to profl. jours. Home: 2595 Charney Rd University Heights OH 44118 Office: Cleve State Univ Cleveland OH 44115

COUSTON, EVANGELINE LYNN, international consulting firm executive; b. Harvey, Ill., Mar. 2, 1949; d. George Peter and Athena Lula (Drivas) Melonas (Miller); m. Thomas Stephan Couston, Oct. 24, 1970 (div. June 1981);

children—George Peter, Stephan Thomas, Elaine Anastasia. B.S. in Communications, Northwestern U., 1969. Asst. editor World Book div. Field Enterprises Ednl. Corp., Chgo., 1969-70; claims and rates agt. traffic dept. Solo Cup Corp., Chgo., 1970-71; sr. cons., asst. to mgmt. Bus. Men's Clearing House subs. Gen. Employment Enterprises Corp., Chgo., 1973-81; pres., chief exec. officer, owner, founder ELC Internat. Corp., Chgo., 1982—, Fas-Claim Corp., Chgo., 1983—. Active Spl. Olympics, Spl. Children's Charities; mem. Chgo. Council Fgn. Relations, Art Inst. Chgo., Lincoln Park Conservation Assn., Lincoln Park Zool. Soc. Mem. Iron and Steel Soc. of AIME, Internat. Bus. Council Mid-Am., Pres.'s Assn. of Am. Mgmt. Assn., Women in Internat. Trade, Hellenic Profl. Soc. Greek Orthodox. Club: Executives (youth com., speakers' table com.) (Chgo.). Home: 505 N Lake Shore Dr Chicago IL 60611 Office: ELC Internat Corp One Magnificent Mile 980 N Michigan Ave Chicago IL 60611

COVEY, FRANK MICHAEL, JR., lawyer; b. Chgo., Oct. 24, 1932; s. Frank M. and Marie B. (Lorenz) C.; B.S. with honors, Loyola U., 1954, J.D. cum laude, 1957; S.J.D., U. Wis., 1960; m. Patricia Ann McGill, Oct. 7, 1961; children—Geralyn, Frank M. III, Regis Patrick. Bar: Ill. 1957, U.S. Supreme Ct. 1965. Practice law, Chgo., 1959—; law clk. Ill. Appellate Ct., 1959; asso. Belnap, Spencer, Hardy & Freeman, 1959-60; asso. McDermott, Will & Emery, 1960-65, partner, 1965—; instr. Northwestern U. Sch. Law, 1958-59, Loyola U. Coll., 1958-69, 79-80. Research asso. Wis. Gov.'s Com. on Revision of Law of Eminent Domain, 1958; asso. gen. counsel Union League Civic and Arts Found., 1967-69, mng. dir., 1975—, v.p., 1969-72, 73-75, pres., 1972-73; co-dir. Grant Park study team Nat. Commn. on Causes and Prevention of Violence, 1968; mem. revenue adv. com. Chgo. City Council, 1983-84; mem. Spl. Commn. on the Adminstrn. of Justice in Cook County, 1984—; mem. Chgo. Mus. Natural History, also mem. com. cts. and justice, com. legis. reform; mem. bd. athletics Loyola U., 1970-72, estate planning com., 1969—, mem. com. future law sch., 1975-76, citizen's bd., 1978—, trustee, 1980—. Recipient award Conf. Personal Finance Law, 1955; Founder's Day award Loyola U., 1976, medal of excellence, 1979. Fellow Ill. Bar Found.; mem. ABA, Ill. (Lincoln award 1963), Chgo., 7th Fed. Circuit bar assns., Am. Judicature Soc., Cath. Lawyers Guild, Chgo. Council Lawyers, Internat. Assn. Ins. Counsel, Legal Club Chgo., Law Club Chgo., Def. Research Inst., Better Govt. Assn., Art Inst. Chgo., Terra Mus. Am. Art, D'Arcy Gallery Medieval Art, Chgo. Bldg. Congress (dir. 1978-82, sec. 1982-85), Loyola U. Alumni Assn. (pres. 1965-66, bd. govs. 1966-70), North Shore Bd. Realtors (asso.), Law Alumni Assn. (award 1957, v.p. 1968-69, pres. 1969-70, chmn. fund campaign 1967-68, bd. govs. 1972-73), Thomas More Club (chmn. 1973-75), Ill. Hist. Soc., Air Force Assn., Blue Key, Phi Alpha Delta, Alpha Sigma Nu, Pi Gamma Mu, Delta Sigma Rho. Roman Catholic (parish council 1973-75). Club: Union League (dir. 1977-80, chmn. house com. 1977-80) (Chgo.). Author: Roadside Protection Through Access Control, 1960; also articles, speeches. Contbg. author: Federal Civil Practice in Illinois, 1974, 78, 81, 83, 85; Business Litigation I: Competition and Its Limits, 1978; A Lawyer's Guide to Class Actions, 1979, 85. Home: 1104 W Lonnquist Blvd Mount Prospect IL 60056 Office: 111 W Monroe St Chicago IL 60603

COVINGTON, WILLIAM GARDNER, JR., broadcasting executive; b. Monroe, La., Feb. 5, 1954; s. William G. and Edith Louise (Harris) C. Cert. TV Studio Delta-Ouachita Vocat.-Tech. Sch., 1973; 1st class FCC license Elkins Inst., 1975; B.A., Northeast La. U., 1976, M.A., 1984; postgrad., U. Mo., 1985. Gen. mgr. Sta. KNLU, Monroe, La., 1974-76, Sta. KFAL-KKCA, Fulton, Mo., 1984—; news reporter Sta. KNOE-TV, Monroe, 1976-83; account mgr. Sta. KNAN, Monroe, 1983; gen. sales mgr. Sta. WCCL, Jackson, Miss., 1983-84. Author: (booklet) Thoughts, 1976, Frustrated or Fulfilled, 1983. Republican. Mem. Assembly of God Ch. Club: Toastmasters Internat. Lodge: Kiwanis. Avocations: spectator sports; investing; travel. Home: PO Box 395 Fulton MO 65251

COVONE, JAMES MICHAEL, automotive parts distributor company executive; b. Chgo., May 19, 1948; s. Michael Anthony and Della Libra (Prosio) C.; m. Judy Ann West, Aug. 16, 1969; children—Ann-Marie, Christopher. Student So. Ill. U., 1966-69. Dist. mgr. Chemetron Corp., San Leandro, Calif., 1969-72, Hooker Industries, Ontario, Calif., 1972; v.p. Motor Sport Research Co., Butler, Wis., 1972-77, also dir.; gen. mgr. Bellwether Automotive Co., Aurora, Ill., 1977—. Co-leader Cub Scouts Am., Geneva, Ill., 1984—. Mem. Splty. Equipment Market Assn. (motorcycle cons. 1975), Performance Warehouse Assn. Republican. Roman Catholic. Avocation: automobile racing. Home: 19 N Andover Ln Geneva IL 60134 Office: Bellwether Automotive Inc 1631 Landmark Rd Aurora IL 60506

COWAN, DALE HARVEY, internist, lawyer; b. Cleve., Jan. 25, 1938; s. Milton Jerome and Clara (Umans) C.; m. Deborah Wolowitz, Jan. 28, 1967; children—Rachel, Morris Benjamin, William Ezra. A.B., Harvard U., 1959, M.D., 1963; J.D., Case Western Res. U. Diplomate Am. Bd. Internal Medicine. Bar: Ohio 1981. Intern Cleve. Met. Gen. Hosp., 1963-64, resident, 1964-65, 67-70; practice medicine specializing in internal medicine, hematology and oncology; dir. hematology and oncology Marymount Hosp., Cleve., 1982—; asst. prof. medicine Case Western Res. U., Cleve., 1970-75, assoc. prof., 1975-84, clin. prof. environ. health scis.) 1985—, assoc. Health Systems Mgmt. Ctr., 1982—; of counsel firm Burke, Haber & Berick, 1984—; spl. cons. President's Commn. on Bioethics, Washington, 1981—; mem. nat. adv. council Nat. Heart Lung and Blood Inst., Bethesda, Md., 1982—. Author: Preferred Provider Organizations, 1984. Contbr. articles to profl. jours. Bd. dirs. Bur. Jewish Edn., 1977—, Northeast Ohio affiliate Am. Heart Assn., 1982—. Served to lt. comdr. USPHS, 1965-67. Fellow ACP, Am. Coll. Legal Medicine; mem. Am. Soc. Hematology, Am. Soc. Clin. Oncology, Am. Assn. for Cancer Research, AMA, Am. Acad. Hosp. Attys., Am. Soc. Law and Medicine, ABA. Home: 19600 Shaker Blvd Shaker Heights OH 44122 Office: Marymount Hosp 12300 McCracken Rd Garfield Heights OH 44125

COWAN, JERRY LOUIS, lawyer; b. Des Moines, May 18, 1927; s. William L. and Avis I. (Spencer) C.; m. Lee Steel, June 11, 1955; children—Grant S., Breck M. B.A., Denison U., 1951; L.L.B., U. Va., 1956. Bar: Ohio 1956. Assoc. Frost & Jacobs, Cin., 1956-63, ptnr., 1963—; gen. counsel Greater Cin. C. of C., 1972-84. Contbr. articles to profl. jours. Served with U.S. Army, 1945-46. Mem. ABA, Cin. Bar Assn. (chmn. tax com. 1962-64). Republican. Clubs: Cin. Country, University (Cin.). Avocations: golf, history. Home: 11 Hill and Hollow Ln Cincinnati OH 45208 Office: 201 E 5th St Cincinnati OH 45202

COWGER, GARY L., auto company executive; b. Kansas City, Kans.; m. Kay Cowger; children—Mindy, Chris. B.S. in Indsl. Engring., Gen. Motors Inst.; M.S. in Mgmt., MIT (Sloan Found. fellow). With General Motors Co., 1965—, plant supt. car assembly, Oldsmobile div., Lansing, Mich., 1979, prodn. mgr., St. Louis, 1980, mgr. Wentzville, Mo. plant, 1982—. Vice chmn. bd. mgrs. St. Charles YMCA; bd. dirs. Mo. C. of C.; co-chmn. fin. com. Mo. Gov.'s Com. on Sci. Tech.; mem. exec. com. St. Louis Regional Commerce and Growth Assn.; mem. Gov.'s Hawthorn Found.; bd. dirs. Career Productivity Inst. of Lindenwood Coll., Mo. Incu Tech. Found.; adv. bd. dirs. St. Charles County Council of Chambers; pub. mem. Blue Cross Corp. Assembly; bd. trustees Lindenwood Coll.; pres.'s council St. Louis U. Address: Buick Oldsmobile Cadillac Group PO Box 444 Wentzville MO 63385

COWLES, DOUGLAS MOODEY, lawyer; b. Painesville, Ohio, May 27, 1947; s. Charles Moodey and Marilyn (Greenwood) C.; m. Ruth O'Keefe, Jan. 27, 1979; 1 child, Michael. B.A., Miami U., Oxford, Ohio, 1971; J.D., U. Calif. Hastings Coll. Law, San Francisco, 1975. Bar: Calif. 1975, Ohio 1976, U.S. Supreme Ct. 1980. Referee Franklin County Probate Ct., Columbus, Ohio, 1976-80; adj. prof. Rio Grande Coll., Ohio, 1983-84; ptnr. Cowles & Boster, Gallipolis, Ohio, 1980—; city solicitor City of Gallipolis, 1983—; spl. counsel Ohio atty. gen., Gallipolis, 1983—; author, lectr. on wills. Treas. Boster for State Rep. Com., Gallipolis, 1982—; mem. adv. bd. Gallipolis Devel. Ctr., 1983—. Served with U.S. Army, 1968-70, Vietnam. Mem. Assn. Trial Lawyers Am., Calif. Bar Assn., Ohio State Bar Assn., Ohio Trial Lawyers Assn., ABA. Avocations: flying, tennis, running. Office: Cowles & Boster 26 Locust St Gallipolis OH 45631

COWLES, ERNEST LEE, state official, educator, consultant, researcher; b. Lead, S.D., Aug. 9, 1949; s. Leon Andrew and Freeda (Kaubisch) C.; m. Ellison Bell Fuller, Sept. 4, 1970. B.A., U. So. Fla., 1971; M.S., Rollins Coll., 1976; Ph.D., Fla. State U., 1981. Probation and parole officer I & II Fla. Probation Parole Commn., Central, Fla., 1971-76; psychologist Fla. Dept. Offender Rehab., Clearmont, 1976; asst. prof. Northeast Mo. State U., Kirksville, 1978-1984, assoc. prof., 1984-85; dir. div. classification and treatment Mo. Dept. Corrections and Human Services, Jefferson City, 1985—; cons. Kirksville Police Dept., 1984, 10th Jud. Cir. Juvenile Div., Hannibal, Mo., 1983—; also various other positions. Author: Survey of Detention in Missouri, 1979. Contbr. articles to profl. jours. Active Boy Scouts Am.; mem. Gov.'s Task Force on Rape. Law Enforcement Asst. Adminstrn. fellow, 1976-78. Mem. Am. Soc. Criminology, Acad. Criminal Justice Scis., Am. Correctional Assn., Nat. Council on Crime Deliquency, Mensa. Home: 2013 Wooded Ln Jefferson City MO 65101 Office: Mo Dept Corrections and Human Services PO Box 236 Jefferson City MO 65102

COWLES, JOHN, JR., communications executive; b. Des Moines, Iowa, May 27, 1929; s. John and Elizabeth Morley (Bates) C.; m. Jane Sage Fuller, Aug. 23, 1952; children—Tessa Flores, John, Jane Sage, Charles Fuller. A.B., Harvard U., 1951; Litt.D. (hon.), Simpson Coll., 1965. With Cowles Media Co. (and predecessor), 1953-83, editor Mpls. Star and Tribune, 1961-69, chmn., 1973-79, pres., 1968-73, 79-83, pub. Mpls. Star and Tribune, 1982-83, dir., 1956-84; dir. Des Moines Register and Tribune Co., 1960-84; mem. Pulitzer Prize Bd., 1970-83; pres. Industry Square Devel. Co., Mpls., 1978-81, vice-chmn., 1981-82, chmn., 1982-84. Bd. dirs. Guthrie Theater Found., Mpls., 1960-71, pres., 1960-63, chmn., 1964-65; chmn. Mpls. Stadium Site Task Force, 1977-82. Served with AUS, 1951-53. Mem. Greater Mpls. C. of C. (dir. 1978-81), Council Fgn. Relations. Clubs: Minneapolis, Century Assn., A.D., Signet Assn. Office: 430 1st Ave N Minneapolis MN 55401

COWLEY, DENNIS EUGENE, optometrist; b. Logansport, Ind., Nov. 10, 1954; s. Alfred Richard and Kathleen Mae (Chantell) C.; m. Ginger Lynn Kelley, May 31, 1975; children—Andrea, Austin, Allison. Student Anderson Coll., 1973-75; B.S. in Optometry, Ind. U., 1977, O.D., 1979. Assoc. in pvt. practice, Logansport, 1979-80; pvt. practice optometry, Winamac, Ind., 1980—. Treas. Pulaski Meml. Hosp. Found., Winamac, 1984-85; bd. mem. Gifted/Talented Program, Winamac High Sch., 1984-85; elder Bethel Bible Ch., Winamac, 1982-85. Second Nikon scholar, Nikon Instruments, 1976. Recipient Roy E. Denny Meml. award Ind. Acad. Optometry, 1979, mem. Am. Optometric Assn., Ind. Optometric Assn. (practice placement com. 1983-84), Wabash Valley Optometric Assn. (sec.-treas. 1983—), Winamac C. of C. Republican. Club: Kiwanis (bd. dirs. Winamac 1983—). Avocations: Music; tennis; basketball; softball; reading. Home: R R 3 Box 349A Winamac IN 46996 Office: 117 S Monticello St Winamac IN 46996

COX, ARLIE E., state education administrator; b. Crockett, Ky., Sept. 20, 1928; s. Henry R. and Nola (Conley) C.; m. Ruth Evelyn Dunn, Dec. 22, 1949; children—Barry Wayne, Gary, Douglas. B.A., Morehead State U., 1950, M.A., 1959; student Miami U., Oxford, Ohio, 1960-63. Tchr., Morgan County Bd. Edn., West Liberty, Ky., 1950-51, Montgomery County Bd. Edn., Mt. Sterling, Ky., 1956-58; New Lebanon Bd. Edn., Ohio, 1958-65; coordinator Title 1, Chpt. 1, Ohio Dept. Edn., Columbus, 1965—. Served with USAF, 1951-55. Mem. Nat. Assn. State Coordinators Chpt. 1, Ohio Assn. State and Fed. Edn. Programs. Democrat. Lodge: Masons. Avocation: Gardening. Home: 5860 Hall Rd Galloway OH 43119 Office: Ohio Dept Edn 933 High St Worthington OH 43085

COX, BRADLEY BURTON, physicist; b. Danville, Ky., Oct. 29, 1941; s. Henry Clay and Lucy Kelly (Walker) C.; m. Marguerite Marie Van Flandern, June 11, 1983; 1 child by previous marriage, Charlotte Kelly; Ph.D., Duke U., 1967. Research assoc. Johns Hopkins U., Balt., 1967-69, asst. prof., 1969-73; group leader Fermi Nat. Accelerator Lab., Batavia, Ill., 1973-75, head Proton Lab., 1976-77, project leader High Intensity Lab., 1977-81, head research services dept., 1981-83, dep. chmn. physics dept., 1983—, sci. spokeman for various expts., 1971—, mem. exec. com., coordinating council expts., 1983—. Contbr. articles to profl. jours. Served as capt. U.S. Army, 1967-69. Research Corp. grantee, 1972—; NSF grantee, 1981-83; Woodrow Wilson Found. fellow, 1963, J.B. Duke fellow Duke U., 1963-67. Mem. Am. Phys. Soc., Fermilab User Soc., Tevatron Assn. of Fixed Target Expt. Spokesmen, Stanford Linear Accelerator Users Group, Phi Beta Kappa. Democrat. Presbyterian. Avocations: tennis, basketball, running. Office: Fermi Nat Accelerator Lab PO Box 500 Batavia IL 60190

COX, CHARLES AARON, consulting engineer; b. Milw., June 5, 1943; s. Earle Floyd and Margaret Louise (Randel) C.; m. Marilyn Lucile Baumgartner, Apr. 21, 1980; children—Katherine Tara, Chad Aaron. B.S. in Indsl. Mgmt., Purdue U., 1966; A.S. in Computer Sci., Lansing Community Coll., 1970; postgrad. in agrl. econs. Mich. State U., 1973. Cons., Dept. State, Washington, Bombay, India, 1966-68; reliability engr. Diamond Red Truck Co., Lansing, Mich., 1968-70; mgr. systems, computers White Motors, Lansing, 1970-73; pres. Indamer Co., East Lansing, Mich., 1973—. Mem. Soc. for Internat. Devel. Office: Indamer Co PO Box 23111 Lansing MI 48909

COX, DAVID FRANK, chiropractor, radio executive; b. Kenosha, Wis., Mar. 3, 1946; s. Charles Russell and Ellen E. (Fortimo) C.; m. Sandra Louise Ingram, Aug. 7, 1971; children—Aimee, Angela, Amanda. A.A., Kemper Mil. Sch., 1966; B.S. in Human Biology, D. Chiropractic, Nat. Coll. Chiropractic, 1973. Diplomate Nat. Bd. Chiropractic Examiners, Am. Bd. Chiropractic Cons.; lic. chiropractor Ill., Ind. Pvt. practice chiropractic physician, Winchester, Ind., 1974-76, Lansing, Ill., 1976—; sec., treas. DBC Broadcasting, 1982, also dir.; owner, operator sta. WDND FM, Wilmington, Ill., 1982—; ins. cons.; team physician Thornton Fractional South and St. Francis de Sales High Sch. Trustee, Village of Lansing, chmn. pub. works, 1981-83, chmn. fin. com., 1983—. Recipient Rebel Helmet award, Dedicated Service to Athletes award Thornton Fractional South Booster Club, award Thornton Fractional South Hockey Club; hon. emergency med. technician Ill. Dept. Pub. Health. Mem. Nat. Assn. Disability Evaluating Physicians (charter), Am. Chiropractic Assn., Ill. Chiropractic Soc., (bd. dirs. 1982-84), Chgo. Chiropractic Soc. (treas. 1977-80, pres. 1982-84), Am. Coll. Sports Medicine, Lansing C. of C. (dir.), Am. Coll. Chiropractic Cons., Jaycees (Jaycee of Yr. 1978-79, Presdl. award of honor, 1981, past pres., state dir.). Office: 18037 Torrence Ave Lansing IL 60438

COX, DENNIS DEAN, statistics educator; b. Denver, Apr. 7, 1950; s. Dan Olvir and Ina Ruth (Clements) C.; m. Donna Jean Case, Sept. 15, 1971; 1 child, Elizabeth. B.A., U. Colo., 1972; M.S., U. Denver, 1976; Ph.D., U. Wash., 1980. Asst. prof. stats. U. Wis.-Madison, 1980—. Contbr. articles to profl. publs. NSF grantee, 1982, 84. Mem. Inst. Math. Stats., Am. Statis. Assn., Royal Statis. Soc., Soc. Indsl. and Applied Math., Am. Math. Soc. Home: 26-D University Houses Madison WI 53705 Office: U Wis Dept Stats Madison WI 53706

COX, FREDERICK MORELAND, social worker, university dean; b. Los Angeles, Dec. 8, 1928; s. Frederick Alfred Edward and Ethel (Moreland) C.; m. Gay Campbell, June, 1951; children—Lawrence, Elizabeth, Sherman. B.A., UCLA, 1950, M.S.W., 1954; D.S.W., U. Calif.-Berkeley, 1968. Caseworker child welfare Los Angeles Bur. Pub. Assistance, 1952-53; mental health counselor Los Angeles Superior Ct., 1953; caseworker Family Service Bur., Oakland, Calif., 1954-57; program dir. Easter Seal Soc., Oakland, 1957-60; from asst. prof. to prof. social work U. Mich., Ann Arbor, 1964-76; prof., dir. Sch. Social Work, Mich. State U., East Lansing, 1976-80; prof., dean Sch. Social Welfare, U. Wis.-Milw., 1980—; instr. Contra Costa Coll., San Pablo, Calif., 1956-57. Sr. co-editor: Community-Action Planning Development, A Casebook, 1974; Tactics and Techniques of Community Practice, 1977, 2d edit., 1984; Strategies of Community Organization, 3d edit., 1979. Chmn. Ann Arbor Housing Commn., 1970-71; pres. non-profit housing devel. corp., 1970-75. NIMH spl. research fellow, 1960-63. Mem. Council on Social Work Edn., Nat. Assn. Social Workers (v.p. Wis. chpt. 1983—), Acad. Cert. Social Workers, Am. Sociol. Assn., Am. Assn. Schs. Social Work (sec.-treas. 1984—), Wis. Council on Human Concerns (pres. 1983—). Office: 1099 Enderis Hall Milwaukee WI 53201

COX, JAMES CALVIN, truck center executive, association administrator, consultant; b. East Prairie, Mo., July 15, 1942; s. J.C. and Louise (Smith) C.; m. Linda R. Davies, May 29, 1966; children—Jami Lyn, Staci Lee. B.P.E., Purdue U., 1966; M.A., Central Mich. U., 1972; Ph.D., U. Mich., 1975. Program dir. Lafayette Neighborhood Ctrs., Ind., 1965-67; extension agt. for youth Purdue U., Lafayette, 1967-71; planner, researcher C.S. Mott Found., Flint, Mich., 1972-73; dir. Nat. Community Edn. Ctr., Gallaudet Coll., Washington, 1973-76; farmer, New Richmond, Ind., 1976-84; dir. title XX project Nat. Assn. Deaf, Indpls., 1983—, coordinator community analysts, 1985—; gen. mgr. Lafayette Truck Ctr., Ind., 1985—; adj. prof. Ball State U., Muncie, 1976-82. Contbr. articles to profl. publs., chpts. to books. Chmn. Community Edn. Council, Ind. Dept. Pub. Instrn., Indpls., 1976-78; dir. deaf ministry First Assembly of God Ch., Lafayette, 1980—; pres. bd. trustees Town of New Richmond, Ind., 1980; pres. North Montgomery Community Sch. Corp., Linden, Ind., 1984—. C.S. Mott Found. fellow, 1971-73. Mem. Nat. Sch. Bd. Assn. (cons. leadership devel. 1976—), Ind. Sch. Bd. Assn., Nat. Assn. Deaf, Ind. Assn. Deaf. Home: Route 1 New Richmond IN 47967 Office: Lafayette Truck Ctr 2700 State Rd 25 N Lafayette IN 47906

COX, JAMES STEPHEN, police chief; b. Kansas City, Mo., July 22, 1948; s. McKay Arrelious and Emma (Andulsky) C.; m. Helen Murphy Brown, Aug. 8, 1972; 1 child, Heather McKay; 1 stepchild, Debra Ann Entriken. B.A., U. Mo.-Kansas City, 1973; M. Adminstrn. of Justice, Wichita State U., 1977. Cert. law enforcement officer, Kans.; lic pilot. Police officer Leawood Police Dept., Kans., 1970, 72-74, sgt., 1974-78, capt., 1978-81, chief of police, 1981—; instr. County Police Acad., Overland Park, Kans., 1978-80. Mem. Drug and Alcoholism Council of Johnson County, Shawnee Mission, Kans., 1981—, pres., 1983, 84. Served with U.S. Army, 1970-72, ETO. Named Best Police Chief in Suburbs, Squire Publs., 1982, 83. Mem. Internat. Assn. Chiefs of Police, Kans. Assn. Chiefs of Police, Met. Police Chiefs and Sheriffs Assn. (v.p. 1984), Johnson County Police Chiefs Assn. (pres. 1984). Episcopalian. Club: Kansas City Cloudbusters Hot Air Balloon (pres. 1984, 85) (Shawnee Mission). Avocations: sport ballooning, camping, travel, photography. Office: City of Leawood 9617 Lee Blvd Leawood KS 66206

COX, JOSEPH LAWRENCE, lawyer; b. Trenton, Mo., Dec. 7, 1932; s. Forrest Curtis and Lillian Judson (Ritzenthaler) C.; m. Lois Marie Hubble, May 20, 1956; children—Margaret Marie Cox Frazier, Martha Mae Cox Neal. B.A., U. Mo.-Kansas City, 1961, J.D., 1965. Bar: Kans. 1965, U.S. Supreme Ct. 1970. Ptnr. Cox, Anderson & Covell, Mission, Kans., 1965-70; sole practice, Tonganoxie, Kans., 1968—; city atty. of Tonganoxie, 1967-73, Kinwood, Kans., 1972-78; mcpl. judge, Mission, 1969-80, Tonganoxie, 1983—. Served with USAF, 1952-54. Mem. Kans. Bar Assn., Kans. Mcpl. Judges Assn. (bd. dirs. 1975-79, pres. 1977-78). Democrat. Lodges: Masons, Shriners, Sertoma (pres. 1973-76). Avocations: photography; boating; travel. Home: 910 SE 43d St Topeka KS 66609 Office: 624 E 4th Tonganoxie KS 66086

COX, LESTER LEE, broadcasting executive; b. Springfield, Mo., Nov. 6, 1922; s. Lester Edmund and Mildred Belle (Lee) C.; m. Claudine Viola Barrett, Jan. 19, 1946; 1 son, Lester Barrett. A.B. in Econs., Westminster Coll., 1944, LL.D., 1974; postgrad. U.S. Mil. Acad., 1944-46; M.B.A., Drury Coll., 1965. Pres., Springfield TV Inc. (KYTV), 1958-79, K.C. Air Conditioning, North Kansas City, 1968—; pre. Mid Continent Telecasting Inc. (KOAM-TV), Pittsburg, Kans., Pittsburg Broadcasting Co. (KOAM); pres. Ozark Motor & Supply Co., Springfield, Modern Tractor and Supply Co.; chmn. bd. dirs. Ozark Air Lines, St. Louis; dir. CommerceBank, Springfield, Fed. Home Loan Bank, Des Moines, 1967-71. Mem. Mo. Bd. Health, 1968-73, past chmn.; mem. Commn. on Higher Edn. for Mo., 1977—; pres. Oxark Empire council Boy Scouts Am., 1960; chmn. bd. Lester E. Cox Med. Center bd. dirs. Westminster Coll., 1949-79, Drury Coll., 1965-79, Midwest Research Inst., Kansas City. Served with AUS, 1943-46, to capt., 1951-53. Recipient Silver Beaver award Boy Scouts Am., 1961; named Hon. col. Gov. Mo., 1960-64, 68-72. Mem. Central States Shrine Assn. (pres. 1970). Club: Hickory Hills Country. Lodges: Masons, Shriners.*

COX, MYRON KEITH, educator; b. Akron, May 6, 1926; s. Carney F. and Nina Castilla (Kenny) C.; B.S., Va. Poly. Inst., 1949; B.S., Pa. State Coll., 1952; M.S., M.I.T., 1957; D.Sc., London Coll., Eng., 1964; m. Emma A. Edwards, July 2, 1950; children—Carney K., Myron D., Eric L., Brett W. Commd. staff sgt. U.S. Air Force, 1950, advanced through grades maj., 1964; radar meteorology staff Hanscom AFB, Mass., 1964-66; electronic countermeasures Wright Patterson AFB, Ohio, 1966-69; ret., 1969; faculty Wright State U., Dayton, Ohio, 1969—, prof. mgmt. sci., quantitative bus. analysis, 1981—. Bd. govs. Fairborn (Ohio) YMCA, 1972-73. Served with USN, 1944-46. Registered profl. engr., Mass. Fellow Acad. Mktg. Sci.; mem. Inst. Mgmt. Sci., Am. Statis. Assn., Assn. Inst. Decision Sci., So. Mktg. Assn., Phi Kappa Phi, Tau Beta Pi, Sigma Xi, Eta Kappa Nu, Beta Gamma Sigma, Alpha Iota Delta. Club: Lions, Masons, Shriners. Patentee surface friction tester; contbr. mktg., mgmt., forecast modeling and simulation. Home: 2527 Grange Hall Rd Beavercreek OH 45431 Office: Wright State Univ Dayton OH 45435

COX, NORMA JEANNE, advertising executive; b. Mpls., June 10, 1942; d. Norman L. and Jeanne E. (Barthelemy) Justice; m. Howard S. Cox, Nov. 20, 1970; 1 son, Steven Gile. B.A., U. Minn., 1966, postgrad., 1972-73, postgrad., Mpls. Community Coll., 1983. Co-owner, v.p. Howard Cox & Assocs., Edina, Minn., 1969—. Advt. internship supr. U. Minn., 1979-80; bd. dirs. Minn. Advt. Review Council, 1979-81. Mem. Minn. Gov.'s Task Force/State Planning Agy., 1979; dir. Suburban Alateen chpt., 1976-78; bd. dirs. S.W. Mpls. Neighborhood Council, 1966-71. Named Outstanding Young Woman Am., 1979. Mem. Am. Women in Radio and TV (chpt. pres. 1979-80; nat. com. 1980, nat. dir. 1980-83, nat. pres. 1985-86), Advt. Fedn. Minn. (dir. 1975-79, 82-84, pres. 1984-85), Nat. Fedn. Bus. and Profl. Women (Local Businesswoman of Yr. 1982). Roman Catholic. Home: 6829 Valley View Rd Edina MN 55435 Office: 6950 France Ave S Edina MN 55435

COX, OTIS E., state official; b. Anderson, Ind., June 18, 1941; s. Loer G. and Doris M. (Ritenour) C.; m. Patricia E. Eckstein, Dec. 28, 1968; children—Anjanette Lee, Christopher Edward. B.Indsl Engring., Gen. Motors Inst., Flint, Mich. Engr., Gen. Motors, Anderson, 1964-70; dep. clk., Madison County, Anderson, 1970, county auditor, 1977-82; utilities mgr. City of Anderson, 1971-76; auditor State of Ind., Indpls., 1982—. Author: Processing Materials, 1964. Bd. dirs. Ctr. for Mental Health, Madison County, 1980-81. Mem. Nat. Assn. State Auditors, Nat. Assn. Auditors, Controllers, Treasurers. Democrat. Lodges: Elks, Lions. Avocations: Fishing, travel, collecting political Americana. Office: State of Indiana Statehouse Room 240 Indianapolis IN 46204

COX, RODY P(OWELL), medical educator, internist; b. New Brighton, Pa., June 24, 1926; s. Raymond James and Hazel (Powell) C.; m. Jane Beverly Birks, Sept. 5, 1953; children—Shelley Lea, Rody Powell, Sue Ellen. Student Franklin and Marshall Coll., 1946-48; M.D., U. Pa., 1952. Diplomate Am. Bd. Internal Medicine. Intern U. Mich., 1952-53, resident in medicine, 1953-54; resident in medicine U. Pa., Phila., 1953-57, asst. prof. medicine, 1957-60; research assoc. U. Glasgow, Scotland, 1960-61; prof. medicine NYU, N.Y.C., 1961-79, prof. pharmacology, 1972-79, chief div. human genetics, 1972-79; prof., vice chmn. dept. medicine Case-Western Res. U., Cleve., 1979—; chief med. service VA Med. Ctr., Cleve., 1979—; mem. metabolism study sect. NIH, 1970-74, chmn. genetics study sect., 1978-79, chmn. mammalian genetics study sect., 1979-81; mem. panel on clin. scis. NRC, 1976—. Editor: Cell Communication, 1974; co-editor: Epithelial Cell Culture, 1981. Contbr. numerous articles to profl. publs. Served to sgt. U.S. Army, 1944-46, NATOUSA. Fellow ACP; mem. Am. Soc. Clin. Investigation (emeritus), Assn. Am. Physicians, Central Soc. Clin. Research, John Morgan Soc. of U. Pa., Harvey Soc., Am. Soc. Am. Soc. Human Genetics, Interurban Clin. Club, Alpha Omega Alpha (councillor NYU chpt. 1970-76). Home: 22275 Calverton Rd Shaker Heights OH 44122 Office: VA Med Ctr Dept Medicine 10701 East Blvd Cleveland OH 44106

COYNE, M. JEANNE, See *Who's Who in America,* 43rd edition.

COYNE, TERRANCE CHARLES, pharmaceutical research and development executive; b. Racine, Wis., Mar. 22, 1946; s. Edward Charles and Joyce Lilah (DuBois) C.; m. Gayle Maurine Ryder, June 19, 1971; children—Angelique, Genaviece, Alexander. B.S., U. Wis., 1968, M.D., 1972. Intern, U.S. Pub. Health Service Hosp., New Orleans, 1972-73; practice family medicine Grantsburg Clinic, Wis., 1973-74; assoc. dir. clin. research Abbott Labs., North Chgo., Ill., 1974-76, dir. clin. research, 1976-78; dir. med. affairs Riker Labs., 3M, St. Paul. 1978-82, tech. dir., 1982—. Bd. dirs. Mississippi Valley Chamber Orch., St. Paul, 1984-85; mem. Citizens League, Mpls., 1985; bd. dirs. 3M Polit. Action Com., 1984—. Recipient Physicians Recognition award, AMA, 1984. Fellow Am. Soc. Clin. Pharmacology and Therapeutics; mem. Am. Heart Assn., Drug. Info. Assn., Wis. Med. Alumni Assn., Pharm. Mfrs. Assn. (research and devel. sect. steering com. 1984-85). Republican. Methodist. Avocations: Piano; music; gardening; water sports; tennis. Home: 1355 Medora Rd Mendota Heights MN 55118 Office: Riker Labs Inc 3M 3M Center Saint Paul MN 55144

COZAD, JAMES WILLIAM, oil company executive; b. Huntington, Ind., Feb. 10, 1927; s. Emmett and Helen (Motz) C.; m. Virginia E. Alley, Nov. 25, 1948; children—J. Michael, Catherine Louise, William Scott, Jeffrey A., Amy

Jo. B.A., Ind. U., 1950, B.B.A., 1950. C.P.A., Ind., Ill. With Peat, Marwick, Mitchell & Co., Detroit, 1950-57; treas., then v.p. Hygrade Food Products Corp., Detroit, from 1957; treas. Philip Morris, Inc., N.Y.C., 1967-69; fin. v.p. Amoco Oil Co., Chgo., 1969-71, v.p. fin. ops., Standard Oil Co. (Ind.) Chgo., 1971-76, v.p. fin., chief fin. officer, 1976-78, exec. v.p., chief fin. officer, 1978-83, vice-chmn., 1983—; dir. GATX Corp., No. Trust Corp., No. Trust Co. (all Chgo.). Chmn. adv. bd. Inroads/Chicago Inc.; chmn. comml. and profl. div. Crusade of Mercy Campaign, Chgo., 1984; bd. dirs. Nat. Merit Scholarship Corp., Northwestern Meml. Hosp., U. Chgo.-Chgo. Med. Sch., Ind. U. Found.; mem. dean's adv. council Ind. U. Sch. Bus. Served with USNR, 1944-46. Mem. Conf. Bd., Am. Petroleum Inst. (dir., chmn. gen. com. fin. and accounting div.), Chgo. Council Fgn. Relations. Clubs: Glen View, Mid-America, Commercial, Chicago, Economic, Executives Club of Chgo. Office: Standard Oil Co (Ind) 200 E Randolph Dr Chicago IL 60601

CRABB, BARBARA BRANDRIFF, judge; b. Green Bay, Wis., Mar. 17, 1939; d. Charles Edward and Mary (Forrest) Brandriff; A.B., U. Wis., 1960, J.D., 1962; m. Theodore E. Crabb, Jr., Aug. 29, 1959; children—Julia Forrest, Philip Elliott. Bar: Wis. 1963. Assoc., Roberts, Boardman, Suhr and Curry, Madison, 1962-64; research asst. Law Sch., U. Wis., Madison, 1968-70; research asst. ABA project on criminal justice standards, Madison, 1970-71; U.S. magistrate, Madison, 1971-79; judge U.S. Dist. Ct., Madison, 1979—, chief judge, 1980—. Membership chmn., v.p. LWV Milw., 1966-68; mem. Gov.'s Task Force on Prison Reform, 1971-73; mem. Jr. League Milw., 1967-68. Mem. ABA, Dane County Bar Assn., State Bar Wis., Nat. Council Fed. Magistrates, Wis. Law Alumni Assn. Office: Box 1724 Madison WI 53701

CRABB, WINSTON DOUGLAS, physician; b. Waukegan, Ill., May 15, 1943; s. Wilfred Dayton and Leona Irene (Keckler) C.; m. Millicent B., Sept. 23, 1965; chidlren—Wesley David, Laura Elizabeth, William Charles. B.S. in Medicine, Northwestern U., 1965, M.D., 1967. Diplomate Am. Bd. Ob-Gyn. Rotating intern Evanston Med. Sch. Hosp., Ill., 1967-68; resident in ob-gyn Kans. U. Med. Ctr., Kansas City, 1970-73; attending physician ob-gyn, Lincoln Clinic, Nebr., 1973—; attending physician Bryan Hosp., Lincoln, 1973—, chmn. ob-gyn Dept., 1978-80; mem. courtesy staff Lincoln Gen. Hosp., St. Elizabeth's Hosp., 1973—. Mem. med. adv. bd. Planned Parenthood of Lincoln, 1975—. Served with USNR, 1968-70. Fellow Am. Coll. Ob-Gyn; mem. Lancaster County Med. Soc., Nebr. Med. Soc. Democrat. Presbyterian. Avocations: Duplicate bridge; stamp collecting.

CRABTREE, JOE, financial executive; b. Tompkinsville, Ky., Mar. 1, 1922; s. Chester and Cecil (Seay) C.; B.S., U. Ill., 1943; m. Carolyn West, May 13, 1972; children—Joel John, Pamela Jean, Wendy Anne. Asst. treas. Pyle Nat. Co., Chgo., 1943-47; cons. Cutler Hammer Inc., Milw., 1947-50; dir. applications Univac div. Sperry Rand Corp., Blue Bell, Pa., 1950-63; controller AIL, Deer Park, N.Y., 1963-69; v.p. Mohawk Data Scis. Corp., Herkimer, N.Y., 1969-71; v.p. finance, treas. Midland Coops., Inc., Mpls., 1971—; dir. Seaway Pipeline Inc.; pres. Claims Recovery, Inc.; v.p., treas. Petroleum Resources Co., Trade Credit Corp., Midland Credit Corp., MCI-E, Inc. Pres., Autumncrest Condominium Assn., 1981. Mem. Am. Inst. Accts., Fin. Execs. Inst., Am. Accts. Acctg. Assn. Govt. Accts., Nat. Assn. Accts., Nat. Soc. Accts., for Coops., Ill., N.Y. socs. C.P.A.s, North Central Credit Assn., Delta Sigma Pi, Phi Eta Sigma, Beta Gamma Sigma. Episcopalian. Clubs: Mpls. Athletic, Lions. Home: 15140 Woodruff Rd Wayzata MN 55391 Office: 2021 Hennepin Ave E Minneapolis MN 55413

CRABTREE, ROBERT EUGENE, clergyman, seminary administrator; b. Springfield, July 13, 1934; s. Webster James and Flossie Opal (Mercer) C.; m. Shirley Ann Strickler, May 28, 1955; children—Julia Kay, Ronald Robert. B.A., Olivet Nazarene Coll., 1956; B.D., Nazarene Theol. Sem., 1959; M.A., U. Mo., 1966, Ph.D., 1975. Ordained elder Ch. of Nazarene, 1963. Librarian, Nazarene Theol. Sem., Kansas City, Mo., 1959-77, dir. field edn., 1960-69, dir. fin. affairs, 1971-78, asst. to pres., 1978-80, registrar, dir. admissions, 1980—; minister visitation Overland Park Ch. of Nazarene, Kans., 1972-74, 76-82; pastor Nettleton Community Ch., Mo., 1965-68. Editor bibliography for clergy Sem. Tower. Contbr. articles to profl. jours. Bd. dirs., sec. East Meyer Community Assn., Kansas City, 1981-82. Lilly Found. scholar, 1970-71. Mem. Assn. Sem. Field Edn. Dirs. (historian 1960-69), Mo. Assn. Student Fin. Aid Personnel, Am. Assn. Collegiate Registrars and Admissions Officers. Republican. Avocations: golf, mountain climbing, skiing, trout fishing. Home: 5100 W 102nd St Overland Park KS 66207 Office: 1700 E Meyer Blvd Kansas City MO 64131

CRABTREE, SUSAN FELLOWS, university official; b. Steubenville, Ohio, Nov. 26, 1956; d. Ray Curtis Fellows and Martha Eleanor (Negus) Fellows Sandagata; m. Scott Leigh Crabtree, July 3, 1982. B.A. in Speech Communication and Journalism, Muskingum Coll., 1979. Community relations dir. Muskingum Area Community Mental Health Bd., Zanesville, Ohio, 1979-81; pub. info. dir. Tri-State U., Angola, Ind., 1981—, chmn. centennial bd., 1981-84. Vice pres. Steuben County 101 Lakes Festival, Angola, 1983-84. Mem. Internat. Assn. Bus. Communicators (v.p. programs 1983-84, chmn. edn. 1982-83, excellence ann. reports award 1984, merit award 1984), Angola Bus. and Profl. Women. (com. chmn. 1983-85). Republican. Presbyterian. Avocations: reading, golf, travel, aerobics. Home: Room 223 Stewart Hall Angola IN 46703 Office: Tri-State U S Darling St Angola IN 46703

CRAFT, IRMA THEOLA, vocational trade and technical school administrator, educator; b. Winston Sales, N.C., Sept. 20, 1920; d. Earsie and Ida (Alexander) Threadgill; m. Sept. 26, 1946; children—Milton, Violet Wanda. B.A., Howard U., 1946; M.E., Wayne State U., 1962. Tchr. coordinator Northwestern High Sch., Detroit, Mich., 1957-67; dir. Career Devel. Ctr., Detroit, 1967—; mem. State Adv. Council for Vocat. Edn., Lansing, Mich., 1970-72. Author: Way Up and Out for Ghetto Poor, 1970. Editor (cookbook): Community Recipes, 1979. Exec. v.p. Peoples Community Civic League, Detroit, 1965—; speaker Citizens Research Council, St. Paul, 1968, Lions and Exchange Clubs, Traverse City, Mich., 1968; luncheon coordinator Republican Nat. Com., Detroit, 1979. Grantee Ford Found., 1969; recipient bronze medal Nat. Assn. Mfrs., 1967, state award plaque Mich. State Congress, 1969. Mem. Nat. Assn. Bus. & Profl. Women (Sojourner Truth award, 1971), Howard U. Alumni Assn. (named Howardite of Yr. 1970), Delta Phi Epsilon. Democrat. Methodist. Club: Elliottorian (Detroit). Avocations: travel; dancing; swimming; reading; health foods. Home: 2472 S Annabelle Detroit MI 48217 Office: Career Devel Ctr Peoples Community Civic League 5961-14th St Detroit MI 48208

CRAIB, DONALD FORSYTH, JR., See *Who's Who in America,* 43rd edition.

CRAIG, HARALD FRANKLIN, lawyer; b. Lima, Ohio, Oct. 27, 1930; s. Harald F. and Bessie M. (Rose) C.; m. Kaarina M. Kettunen, Aug. 4, 1979; children—Harald F., Anne M. B.A., Bowling Green State U., 1952; J.D., Ohio State U., 1955. Bar: Ohio 1955, U.S. Dist. Ct. (no. dist.) Ohio 1957, U.S. Ct. Appeals (6th cir.) 1958. Sr. ptnr. Brown, Baker, Schlageter & Craig, Toledo, 1957—; dir., officer Electra Mfg. Corp., Holland, Ohio, Regent Electric, Inc., Toledo, Bernard Engraving Co., Toledo. Served to 1st lt. USMC, 1955-57. Mem. ABA, Toledo Bar Assn., Ohio Bar Assn., Am. Judicature Soc., Assn. Trial Lawyers Am. Republican. Home: 3773 Hillandale E Toledo OH 43606 Office: Brown Baker Schlageter & Craig 711 Adams St Toledo OH 43624

CRAIG, JAMES LYNN, diversified food company executive, physician; b. Columbia, Tenn., Aug. 7, 1933; s. Clifford Paul and Ann Mable (Harris) C.; m. Suzanne Anderson, July 20, 1957 (div. 1979); children—James Lynn, Margaret Ann; m. Roberta Annette Ullberg, May 17, 1980. Student, Middle Tenn. State U., 1951-53; M.D., U. Tenn.-Memphis, 1956; M.P.H., U. Pitts., 1963. Diplomate Am. Bd. preventive Medicine, Am. Bd. Family Practice. Intern U. Tenn. Hosp., Knoxville, 1957; resident U. Pitts., 1962-64; physician TVA, Chattanooga, 1961-66, chief health officer, 1966-69, med. dir., 1969-74; v.p., dir. health and safety Gen. Mills Co., Mpls., 1974—; bd. dirs. Emergency Physician Assocs., Mpls., 1984—. Contbr. articles to med. jours. Bd. dirs. Mpls. chpt. Am. Cancer Soc., 1976-80, Am. Heart Assn., 1978—, War Meml. Blood Bank, 1975—, Minn. Bible Coll., 1977-83. Served to capt. USAF, 1958-60. Fellow Am. Acad. Occupational Medicine (dir. 1974-77, treas. 1982, sec. 1983, v.p. 1984), Am. Occupational Med. Assn. (past dir.), AMA. Christian. Club: Kiwanis. Avocations: Photography; cars. Home: 10008 South Shore Dr Minneapolis MN 55441 Office: Gen Mills 9200 Wayzata Blvd Minneapolis MN 55426

CRAIG, JUDITH, clergywoman. Bishop West Mich. and Detroit confs. United Methodist Ch. Office: 155 W Congress Suite 200 Detroit MI 48226*

CRAIG, MAYBLE ESTHER, nursing director, educator; b. P.R., July 18, 1942; d. Enrique and Gloria Esther (Salaman) Charles; children—Brian Anthony, Kimberly Ann. Diploma, Bellevue Sch. of Nursing, 1963; B.S. in Nursing, U. Mich., 1976, M.S., 1983. Head nurse Los Angeles County-U. So. Calif. Hosp., Los Angeles, 1967-71, asst. dir. nursing, 1971-74; instr. Washtenaw Community Coll., Ann Arbor, Mich., 1977; Wayne County Community Coll., Detroit, 1977; dir. med. nursing U. Mich. Hosps., Ann Arbor, 1978—, lectr. Sch. of Nursing, 1982—. Mem. nursing adv. com. Washtenaw Community Coll.; mem. exec. com. Lake Region Conf. 7th Day Adventists. Johnson and Johnson-Wharton fellow, 1983; recipient Excellence in Nursing award Los Angeles County-U. So. Calif. Med. Ctr., 1974. Mem. Greater Detroit Area Soc. for Nursing Services Adminstrs., Sigma Theta Tau. Democrat. Home: 2271 Placid Way Ann Arbor MI 48105 Office: U Mich Hosps 1409 E Ann St Room A6037 Box 54 Ann Arbor MI 48109

CRAIG, ROBERT CHARLES, psychology educator; b. Sault Sainte Marie, Mich., Mar. 9, 1921; s. Frank Lyle and Sylva Octilla (Crowell) C.; B.S., Mich. State U., 1943, M.A., 1948; Ph.D., Tchrs. Coll. Columbia U., 1952; m. Rosalie Esther Deboer, Sept. 2, 1950; children—Bruce R., Stephen F. (dec.), Jeffrey A., Barbara Anne. Research asso. Tchrs. Coll. Columbia U., 1950-52; asst. prof. State U. Wash., Pullman, 1952-55; research scientist Am. Inst. Research, Pitts., 1955-58; asso. prof. ednl. psychology Marquette U., 1958-62, prof., 1962-66; prof. and chmn. dept. counseling and ednl. psychology Mich. State U., East Lansing, 1967-81, prof., 1981—, dir. Office of Research Consultation, 1966-67, dir. U.S. Office Edn. Grad. Research Tng. program, 1966-72; external evaluator Nat. Council Accreditation of Tchr. Edn., 1970-75; cons. Am. Inst. Research, 1958—. Served with USNR, 1943-46. Fellow Am. Psychol. Assn., AAAS; mem. Am. Ednl. Research Assn., Nat. Council Measurement in Edn., Sigma Xi, Phi Kappa Phi, Phi Delta Kappa. Author: Transfer Value of Guided Learning, 1953; (with A.M. Dupuis) American Education, Origins and Issues, 1963; Psychology of Learning in the Classroom, 1966; (with H. Clarizio, W. Mehrens) Contemporary Issues in Educational Psychology, 1969, 4th edit., 1981, Contemporary Educational Psychology, 1975; (with V.H. Noll, D.P. Scannell) Introduction to Educational Measurement, 1979. Home: 185 Maplewood St East Lansing MI 48823 Office: 461 Erickson Hall Michigan State U East Lansing MI 48824

CRAIN, LARRY WAYNE, telecommunications company executive; b. Poplar Bluff, Mo., June 2, 1949; s. Harry C. and Lola E.C.; B.S. magna cum laude, SE Mo. State U., 1975; M.B.A., U. Mo., 1976. New product planner Hallmark Cards, Kansas City, Mo., 1977-78, bus. planning project mgr., 1978-80; mgr. planning United Telecommunications, Inc., Kansas City, Mo., 1980-83; dir. corp. planning, mktg. and regulatory affairs Republic Telcom, Bloomington, Minn., 1983-84, v.p. corporate planning and mktg., 1984—; bd. dirs. Prime Health, health maintenance orgn., 1980-83; instr. mktg. Served with USN, 1968-72. Gregory fellow. Mem. Am. Mktg. Assn., Altel Industry Assn. (bd. dirs. 1984—), Planning Execs. Inst., Am. Numismatic Assn., Mensa. Club: Kansas City Ski. Author fiction. Home: 7320 Gallagher Dr Apt 321 MN 55435 Office: Republic Telcom 8300 Norman Center Dr Bloomington MN 55437

CRALL, DAVID BROUGHTON, lawyer, accountant, business executive; b. Columbus, Ohio, Dec. 15, 1941; s. Frank and Gertrude (Broughton) C.; m. Leslie Meridith. B.S., Ohio State U., 1965; M.B.A., U. Cin., 1969; J.D., No. Ky. U., 1979. Bar: Ohio 1979, U.S. Dist. Ct. (so. dist.) Ohio 1980, U.S. Tax Ct. 1981. Budget analyst Super X Drugs, Cin., 1969-71; fin. dir. Community Action Commn., Cin., 1971-73; tax mgr. Ohio River Co., Cin., 1973-80; ptnr. Crall & Crall, Cin., 1980—; officer, dir. Parrot Pub. Corp., Cin.; officer-treas. Tri Lab Corp., Cin., 1981—. Co-author: Money Magic, 1980; Songs of Peacock Hills, 1982. Served to lst lt., arty., U.S. Army, 1966-67, Vietnam. Mem. Cin. Bar Assn. (taxation sect.), Nat. Muzzle Loaders Rifle Assn., Nat. Old Time Fiddlers Assn. Republican. Methodist.

CRAMBLETT, HENRY GAYLORD, medical educator, physician, university administrator; b. Scio, Ohio, Feb. 8, 1929; s. Carl Smith and Olive (Fulton) C.; m. Donna Reese, June 16, 1960; children—Deborah Kaye, Betsy Diane. B.S. magna cum laude, Mt. Union Coll., 1950, D.Sc. (hon.), 1974; M.D., U. Cin., 1953. Diplomate Am. Bd. Pediatrics, Nat. Bd. Med. Examiners (exec. bd. 1981—), Am. Bd. Microbiology. Intern in medicine Boston City Hosp. on Harvard Med. Service, 1953-54; resident in pediatrics Children's Hosp., Cin., 1954-55; clin. assoc. pediatric sect., lab. clin. investigation Nat. Inst. Allergy and Infectious Diseases, NIH, 1955-57; chief resident, instr. dept. pediatrics, State U. Iowa, 1957-58, asst. prof., 1958-60; assoc. prof. pediatrics, assoc. in pathology and microbiology, dir. virology lab. Bowman Gray Sch. Medicine, Winston-Salem, N.C., 1960-63, prof., 1963-64; prof. pediatrics Ohio State U., Columbus, 1964—, prof. med. microbiology and immunology, 1966—, chmn. dept. med. microbiology, 1966-73, Pomerene prof. medicine, 1982—, dean Coll. Medicine, 1973-80, acting v.p. for med. affairs, 1974-80, dir. univ. hosps., 1979-80, v.p. for health scis., 1980-82, assoc. to v.p. for health services, 1984—; cons. seminar services div. Ctr. Disease Control, 1966—; mem. Ohio Med. Bd., 1970—, pres., 1979; mem. FLEX Exam. Com., 1972—, mem. FLEX Bd., Fedn. State Med. Bds., 1983—; trustee Children's Hosp. Research Found., 1973—, Children's Hosp., 1973-84, Children's Hosp., Inc., 1982-84; dir. med. and postgrad. edn. Office Acad. and Research Affairs, King Faisal Specialist Hosp. and Research Centre, Riyadh, Saudi Arabia, 1983-84. Editor: Perspectives in Pediatric Virology (Ross Research Conf. Report), 1959. Contbr. numerous chpts., articles to profl. publs. Served with USPHS, 1955-57. Recipient Research Career Devel. award NIH, 1961-63. Mem. Am. Acad. Pediatrics. Home: 2480 Sheringham Rd Columbus OH 43220 Office: Ohio State U Coll Medicine 370 W 9th Ave Columbus OH 43210

CRAMER, WILLIAM ANTHONY, biological science educator; b. N.Y.C., June 11, 1938; s. Robert A. and Sylvia (Blumstein) C.; m. Hanni Aebersold, Sept. 12, 1964; children—Rebecca, Jean-Marc, Gabrielle, Nicholas. B.S., MIT, 1959; M.S., U. Chgo., 1960, Ph.D., 1965. Asst. prof. Purdue U., West Lafayette, Ind., 1968-73, assoc. prof., 1973-78, prof. biol. sci. 1978—, assoc. head dept. biol. sci., 1984—; cons. NSF Grants Panels, Washington, 1977-82, U.S. Dept. Agr. Grants Panel, 1983-84. Editor, Biochem. Biophys. Acta, Archives Biochemistry and Biophysics. Contbr. articles to profl. jours. European Molecular Biology Orgn. fellow, Amsterdam, Netherlands, 1975; NIH Career Devel. grantee, 1970-75; NSF fellow, 1965-67. Mem. Am. Soc. Biol. Chemists, Biophys. Soc. Office: Dept Biol Scis Purdue U West Lafayette IN 47907

CRAMPTON, ROBERT WILLIAM, surveyor; b. Lansing, Mich., July 13, 1942; s. William Robert and Marveline Malvin (Martel) C.; m. Patricia Louise Staffen, July 14, 1979; children—Robert L., David A., Tricia M. Jamie L. Lic. land surveyor. Dir. field ops. Stephens Engring., East Lansing, Mich., 1962-79; dir. surveying div. U.P. Engrs. & Architects, Houghton, Mich., 1979-82; prin. Crampton Surveying, Hubbell, Mich., 1982—. Mem. Mich. Soc. Registered Land Surveyors, Hubbell C. of C. Avocations: skiing, pool, motorcycles. Home and office: 1406 Duncan PO Box 206 Hubbell MI 49934

CRANDALL, JOHN DONALD, state official, retired army officer; b. Chgo., Oct. 5, 1935; s. Edward William and Edith (Smith) C.; m. Linda Ann Pinet, Sept. 1, 1962; children—Jon, Melinda, Kristin. B.S., U.S. Mil. Acad., 1958; M.P.A., Drake U., 1981. Commd. 2d lt., U.S. Army, 1958, advanced through grades to lt. col.; numerous command and staff positions, U.S., Greece, Alaska, Viet Nam, ret., 1979; dir. Iowa Office of Disaster Services, Des Moines, 1979—, lectr., instr., 1979—; cons. Hartman & Assocs., Des Moines, 1983—. Mem. Des Moines Ctr. Sci. and Industry, 1977—; mem. Republican Presdl. Task Force, 1984—. Decorated Bronze Star medal. Mem. Des Moines C. of C., Des Moines YMCA, Nat. Emergency Mgmt. Assn. (treas. 1984—), Ret. Officers Assn. (3d v.p. 1984—), Internat. Platform Assn. Republican. Episcopalian. Avocations: Fishing, jogging, volleyball. Home: 670 44th St Des Moines IA 50312 Office: Iowa Office of Disaster Services Hoover State Office Bldg Des Moines IA 50319

CRANDALL, JOHN LYNN, ins. co. exec.; b. Chgo., Apr. 17, 1927; s. Paul Bertram and Olga (Bliech) C.; B.S. in Fire Protection Engring., Ill. Inst. Tech., 1951; m. Irene Anze Ruenne, Dec. 26, 1973; children by previous marriage—Deborah Crandall Schmude, Jeffrey, Lynne; stepchildren—George Ruenne, Helgi Ruenne Becker. Highly protected risk inspector FIA, Chgo., 1951-53, asst. engring. supr., 1953-56, engring. supr., 1956-59, underwriting supr., special agt., 1959-65; HPR engr., underwriter Kemper Group, Chgo., 1965-67, HPR sales specialist, 1967-71; asst. to dir. underwriting Protection Mutual Ins. Co., Park Ridge, Ill., 1971-73, v.p. underwriting, 1973-78, v.p., dir. underwriting, 1978—. Served with USN, 1945-46. Cert. in Gen. Ins., Ins. Inst. Am., 1969; C.P.C.U., 1972. Mem. Soc. Fire Protection Engrs. (charter), Soc. C.P.C.U.s (chpt. pres. 1980-81). Republican. Lutheran. Home: 24 Lambert Dr Schaumburg IL 60193 Office: 300 S Northwest Hwy Park Ridge IL 60068

CRANDELL, DWIGHT SAMUEL, museum director; b. Parke County, Ind., Nov. 30, 1943; s. Terence Wesley and Alice Ruth (Cox) C.; m. Rachel Louise Wentworth, June 14, 1965; children—Jeremy, Abby, Joanna, Joshua. B.A. in History and Edn., Principia Coll., Elsah, Ill., 1965; M.A. in History Mus. Studies, SUNY-Oneonta, 1972. Asst. in research and adminstrn. Mt. Vernon Ladies Assn. of the Union (Va.), 1965-66; ednl. docent, coordinator temp. exhibits Children's Mus., Indpls., 1972-73, curator exhibits research and planning, 1973-76, dir. collections, 1977-81; dir. devel. St. Louis Mus. Sci. and Natural History, St. Louis Sci. Ctr., 1981-82, asst. dir., 1982, exec. dir., 1982—. Mem. Friends of the St. Louis Carousel, 1981—. Served to capt. USAF, 1966-71; Vietnam. Decorated Air medal with 11 clusters; Nat. Mus. Act grantee, 1974. Mem. Am. Assn. Mus., Assn. Sci. Mus. Dirs., Midwest Mus. Conf., Am. Assn. State and Local History, St. Louis Area Mus. Collaborative, Assn. Sci.-Tech. Ctrs. (bd. dirs.). Republican. Christian Scientist. Lodge: Rotary. Office: 5050 Oakland Ave St Louis MO 63110

CRANE, ALISON ROGERS, jeweler, goldsmith, enamelist; b. Louisville, Ky., Nov. 7, 1940; d. Vincent Muir and Frances (Cheatham) R.; m. Thomas Michael Crane, Sept. 22, 1962; children—Kevin Muir, Brook Jennifer. Student Northwestern U., 1956-59, Pine Manor, 1956; grad. Gemological Inst. Am., 1985. Apprentice goldsmith, salesstaff Michael Banner Inc., Glencoe, Ill., 1972-73; owner, operator Jewels By Alison, Glenview, Ill., 1973—. Recipient Golden Horseshoe award Equestrian Assn., 1961, citation Mayor Daley of Chgo., 1959. Mem. Ill. Jewelers Assn. (vigilante com. 1975—). Republican. Avocations: scuba diving; tennis; horseback riding. Home and Office: 1410 Pleasant Ln Glenview IL 60025

CRANE, CURTIS LE ROY, real estate corporation executive, resort owner, accountant, commercial pilot; b. Clam Falls, Wis., July 24, 1939; s. Oliver Irvin and Hazel Belle (Burch) C.; m. Gloria Jean James, June 21, 1959 (div. 1970); children—Craig Lee, Carla Marie, Brian Scott; m. 2d Treva Rae Buzzard, Aug. 20, 1971. Student LaSalle U.; degree in Tax Acctg., Wis. Tech. Inst.; student in Real Estate Brokerage and Investments, Sauk Valley Coll.; student Air Sch. Lic. real estate broker, Wis.; lic. comml. pilot. Profl. baseball player, Twin City All Stars, 1957-59; dir. shop foreman, 1958-64; charter pilot O'Rarke Flying Service, 1964-68; owner cocktail lounge, 1968-71; resort owner Sunny Bay Resort, Chetek, Wis., 1971—; owner broker Mair-Warner-Crane Realty, Chetek; prin. tax service, 1972—. Bd. dirs. Chetek Mcpl. Airport; PTO chmn., 1974; organizer Rehab. for Industry; Chmn. Chetek Indsl. Devel. Found. Served with U.S. Army. Mem. Barron-Washburn Bd. Realtors (dir. and state dir. Wis.), Nat. Bd. Realtors, Nat. Assn. Appraisers, Chetek Area Progress Assn., Chetek Resort Owners Assn., Chetek C. of C. (pres. 1981-82). Republican. Clubs: Lions, Elks, Masons, Shriners. Address: 137 Pine Grove Ave Chetek WI 54728

CRANE, EDWARD J., airline executive; b. 1928; grad. St. Louis U. Sch. Commerce and Fin., 1951; m. Margaret Struif; children—Steven, Edward J., Mary Ann, John. Accounting dept. comptroller Ozark Air Lines, Inc., St. Louis, 1951-60, v.p., comptroller, 1960-65, v.p., treas., 1965-68, exec. v.p., treas., 1968-71, pres., chief exec. officer, 1971—; dir. Bank of St. Louis, Valley Industries, Gen. Bancshares Corp. Trustee, mem. pres.'s council St. Louis U.; bd. dirs. United Way, 1977-81, Regional Commerce and Growth Assn. St. Louis; trustee Incarnate Word Hosp.; bd. dirs. St. Louis council Boy Scouts Am. Served with USMC, World War II. Mem. Assn. Local Transport Airlines (past chmn., bd. dirs.), Air Transport Assn. (bd. dirs.), Air Conf. (bd. dirs.). Office: Ozark Airlines PO Box 10007 Lambert Field St Louis MO 63145

CRANE, FRANK JAMES, JR., salt company executive; b. Akron, Ohio, Dec. 22, 1938; s. Frank James and Violet Helena (Claussen) C.; m. Theresia Gertrud Köhler, Jan. 16, 1970; children—Corinne P., Nicole C., Michele A. B.A., Lake Forest Coll., 1965. Sales exec. Morton Salt Co., Chgo., 1965—; dir. Western Advertisers Golf Assn., Chgo., 1982—. Bd. dirs. Foxfire Homeowners Assn., Crystal Lake, Ill., 1980-82; mem. steering com. U.S. Senate Republican Bus. Adv. Bd., Washington, 1981-82. Served with U.S. Army, 1959-62. Republican. Roman Catholic. Club: Crystal Lake (Ill.) Country (dir. 1982—).

CRANE, JIMMY CLEVE, pharmacist; b. Shelbyville, Ind., Jan. 23, 1943; s. Walter C. and Lillian Pauline (Spradlin) C.; m. Alicia Virginia Marsano, Mar. 9, 1968; children—Liana, Marella. Student Ind. State U., 1961-63; B.S. in Pharmacy, Purdue U., 1966. Registered pharmacist, Ind. Research pharmacist Dow Pharms., Indpls., 1967-70, quality assurance coordinator, supr. clin. and stability lab., 1970-78, sr. clin research assoc., 1978-81; mgr. profl. relations Merrell Dow Pharms., Inc., Indpls., 1981-85, mgr. med. communications, Cin., 1985—. Coach basketball First Baptist Athletics, Indpls., 1983-84; pres. Deerfield Homeowners Assn., Carmel, Ind., 1983; catechist St. Elizabeth Seton, Carmel, Ind., 1984-85; asst. coach softball Carmel Dad's Club, 1984. Served with USAR, 1967. Mem. Assocs. Clin. Pharmacology (bd. dirs. 1983-85, chmn. continuing edn. com. 1981-85), Am. Pharm. Assn., Ind. Pharm. Assn., Am. Med. Writers Assn., Drug Info. Assn. Roman Catholic. Office: Merrell Dow Pharm Inc 2110 E Galbraith Rd Cincinnati OH 45215

CRANE, PHILIP MILLER, congressman; b. Chgo., Nov. 3, 1930; s. George Washington and Cora (Miller) C.; student DePauw U., 1948-50; B.A., Hillsdale Coll., 1952; postgrad. U. Mich., 1952-54, U. Vienna (Austria), 1953, 56; M.A., Ind. U., 1961, Ph.D., 1963; LL.D. (hon.), Grove City (Pa.) Coll.; Dr. en Ciencias Politicas (hon.), Francisco Marroquin U., 1979; m. Arlene Catherine Johnson, Feb. 14, 1959; children—Catherine Anne, Susanna Marie, Jennifer Elizabeth, Rebekah Caroline, George Washington V, Rachel Ellen, Sarah Emma, Carrie Esther. Advt. mgr. Hopkins Syndicate, Inc., Chgo., 1956-58; teaching asst. Ind. U., Bloomington, 1959-62; asst. prof. history Bradley U., Peoria, Ill., 1963-67; dir. schs. Westminster Acad., Northbrook, Ill., 1967-68; mem. 91st-98th congresses from 12th Ill. Dist., mem. ways and means com. Pub. relations dir. Vigo County (Ind.) Republican Orgn., 1962; dir. research Ill. Goldwater Orgn., 1964; chmn. Ill. Citizens for Reagan Com., 1975; mem. nat. adv. bd. Young Ams. for Freedom, 1965—. Bd. dirs. Intercollegiate Studies Inst.; chmn. Am. Conservative Union, 1977-79; trustee Hillsdale Coll.; bd. dirs. Ashbrook Ctr. for Pub. Affairs, Ashland Coll. (Ohio), chmn. Republican Study Com., 1983-84. Served with AUS, 1954-56. Recipient Disting. Alumnus award Hillsdale Coll., 1968, Independence award, 1974; William McGovern award Chgo. Soc., 1969; Freedoms Found. award, 1973. Mem. Univ. Profs. for Acad. Order, Phila. Soc., ASCAP, Phi Alpha Theta, Pi Gamma Mu. Methodist. Author: Democrat's Dilemma, 1964; The Sum of Good Government, 1976; Surrender in Panama, 1977; contbr.: Crisis in Confidence, 1974; Continuity in Crisis: The University at Bay, 1974; Case Against the Reckless Congress, 1976; Can You Afford This House, 1978; View from the Capitol Dome (Looking Right), 1980. Office: Longworth House Office Bldg Washington DC 20515

CRANE, ROBERT LEE, educational administrator, music educator; b. Mt. Pleasant, Mich., Mar. 22, 1937; s. Lloyd William and Maxine Edna (Duncan) C.; m. Janet-Ann Elizabeth Allen, July 4, 1940; 1 child, Donald Allen. B.M.E., Central Mich. U., 1959, M.A., 1960, Ed.S., 1973; Ph.D., Mich. State U., 1978. Cert. secondary tchr., ednl. adminstr. Asst. supt. Boy's Farm Sch., Durand, Ill., 1963-65; music tchr. Central Jr. High Sch., Saginaw, Mich., 1965-69; asst. prin. Webber Jr. High Sch., Saginaw, 1969-72, prin., 1972-79; dep. dir. Averill Career Ctr., Saginaw, 1979-80; prin. South Intermediate Sch., Saginaw, 1980—; instr. Central Mich. U., Mt. Pleasant, 1985—; instr. trumpet sect. Eddy Concert Band, Saginaw, 1966—. Contbr. articles on edn. to profl. jours. Mem. Mich. Assn. Secondary Sch. Prins. (publicity chmn. 1982—), Nat. Assn. Secondary Sch. Prins., Saginaw Assn. Secondary Sch. Prins. (pres. 1976-76, 83-84), Mich. Assn. Middle Sch. Educators, Phil Delta Kappa (pres. 1983-84). Episcopalian. Club: Pioneer (Saginaw). Lodge: Lions (bd. dirs. 1978—, lion tamer 1982-83, tail-twister 1984—, Three in '83 award). Avocations: music, skiing, antique collecting, journal writing, golf. Home: 19 Iota Pl Saginaw MI 48603 Office: South Intermediate Sch 224 Elm St Saginaw MI 48602

CRANE, WALLEN LOGAN, JR., investment executive; b. Toledo, Ohio, Mar. 22, 1944; s. Wallen L. and Cecelia C. (Szyperski) C.; m. Suzanne Christie, Sept. 15, 1969; children—Adam, Sarah. B.B.A., U. Toledo, 1969. Stockbroker, PaineWebber, Toledo, 1972-76, v.p., 1977—; ptnr. Golden, Garrett & Crane,

Toledo, 1976-77. Pres. Point Place Bus. Assn., Toledo, 1980; chmn. Diocesan Devel. Fund Dr., Toledo, 1984. Served to cpl. USMC, 1963-69. Fellow Fin. Analysts Soc. (sec. 1985). Clubs: Toledo, Bond (v.p. 1985—). Avocations: water skiing; squash; running. Home: 2315 Shoreland Toledo OH 43611 Office: PaineWebber 711 Madison Ave Toledo OH 43624

CRANSHAW, DOUGLAS PATTON, health insurance company executive; b. Worcester, Mass., Feb. 11, 1947; s. John Angel and Edith Ferry (Patton) C.; m. Anne Elizabeth Flood, July 30, 1971; children—Joy Elizabeth, John Douglas. B.B.A., U. Mass., 1970; M.B.A., Northeastern U., 1972. With Blue Cross and Blue Shield, Portland, Maine, 1973-77, market research analyst, Concord, N.H., 1977-78, asst. v.p. mktg., Des Moines, 1978-81, v.p. mktg. services, 1981-82, v.p. external services, 1982-85; exec. dir. Health Plans, Inc., Worcester, Mass., 1985—. Treas. Des Moines Bus. Exchange, 1979-84; mem. adv. bus. com. Iowa Found. for Med. Care, 1984-85. Mem. Am. Mktg. Assn. (pres. Des Moines chpt. 1979-80), Central Iowa Sailing Assn. (rear commodore 1984-85). Congregationalist.

CRAVENS, JAMES HEWITT, pediatrician, educator; b. St. Louis, July 11, 1919; s. Harvey Mudd and Marie Elise (Zingre) C.; m. Ann Schnake, Feb. 12, 1944; children—Patricia Ann Cravens Wichser, Carol Lynn Cravens Johnson, James Charles. B.S., U. Ill., 1941; M.D., Washington U., St. Louis, 1943. Diplomate Am. Bd. Pediatrics. Intern U. Chgo. Clinics, 1944; resident in pediatrics St. Louis Children's Hosp., 1947-48; pediatrician Physicians and Surgeons Clinics, Quincy, Ill., 1948—, chmn. bd., 1957-62; instr. pediatrics Washington U., 1948; clin. assoc. in pediatrics So. Ill. U. Sch. Medicine, 1977—. Served to capt. AUS, 1944-46. Fellow Am. Acad. Pediatrics (mem. com. on hosp. care, sec. Ill. chpt. 1980-83, pres.-elect 1983—), mem. AMA, Ill. Med. Soc., Adams County Med. Soc. (pres. 1965), Downstate Ill. Pediatric Soc. (pres. 1973-75), Soc. for Acad. Achievement, Phi Eta Sigma, Phi Lambda Upsilon, Omega Beta Pi, Delta Chi, Phi Rho Sigma. Republican. Presbyterian. Club: Quincy Country. Lodge: Rotary (pres. Quincy 1953-54). Home: 62 Lincoln Hill NE Quincy IL 62301 Office: 1101 Maine St Quincy IL 62301

CRAWFORD, DOUGLAS NATHAN, community college administrator; b. Ann Arbor, Mich., Oct. 7, 1942; s. Ferris Nathan and Eileen Bessie (Icheldinger) C.; m. Lois Ann Hart, June 19, 1970; children—Nathan Robert, Andrea Marie, Kimberly Diane. B.A., Central Mich. U., 1964; M.Pub.Adminstrn., U. Mich., 1969; Ph.D., Mich. State U., 1979. Tchr. govt. and history Petoskey High Schl., Mich., 1968-70; instr. polit. sci. Jackson Community Coll., Mich., 1970-72; assoc. prof. polit. sci. Lansing Community Coll., Mich., 1971-78; chmn. div. gen. and pub. service studies Edison State Community Coll., Piqua, Ohio, 1979-85, dean acad. services, 1985—, mem. chancellor's adv. commn. on two-yr. acad. programs, 1985—, mem. bd. regents task force on social studies, 1981-82; mem. North Central Assn. visitation team, Greenville, Ohio, 1983. Pres. Human Services Council, Miami County (Ohio), 1984—; instl. rep. and convener Domestic Policy Assn., Piqua, 1984—; capt. membership campaign Miami County YMCA, 1984—; del. Mich. Rep. Conv., 1974. Served as 1st lt. U.S. Army, 1965-67, Vietnam. Mem. Am. Soc. Pub. Adminstrn. (chpt. sec. 1974-76), Community Coll. Humanities Assn., Am. Tech. Edn. Assn., Phi Delta Kappa. Episcopalian. Lodge: Rotary (bull. editor 1983—). Avocations: camping; boating; racquetball; collecting old textbooks. Home: 1052 Fairfield Rd Troy OH 45373 Office: Edison State Community Coll 1973 Edison Dr Piqua OH 45356

CRAWFORD, GEORGE LEROY, JR., civil engr.; b. Davenport, Iowa, Mar. 6, 1928; s. George LeRoy and Florence (Gadient) C.; student U. Wyo., 1945-46; B.S., U. Ill., 1950; m. Patricia Ann Schumann, Aug. 15, 1948; children—George LeRoy III, Catherine Ruth, Nancy Jo; m. 2d, Patareka Elfner Korbly, Apr. 6, 1974. Field traffic engr. Ill. Div. Hwys., East St. Louis Dist., 1950-62, dist. traffic engr., 1962-63, sr. field engr. Bur. Traffic, Springfield, 1963-64; prin. G.L. Crawford & Assos., 1964-66; pres. Crawford, Bunte, Roden, Inc., Springfield, 1966-72; v.p. Alan M. Voorhees & Assos., Inc., St. Louis, 1972-73; pres. George L. Crawford & Assocs., Inc., Maryland Heights, Mo., 1973—. Served with C.E., AUS, 1945-47. Presbyn. (elder). Mason (Shriner). Home: 11620 Heatherdale Dr Creve Coeur MO 63146 Office: 12161 Lackland Rd Saint Louis MO 63146

CRAWFORD, JEAN ANDRE, counselor; b. Chgo., Apr. 12, 1941; d. William Moses and Geneva Mae (Lacy) Jones; student Shimer Coll., 1959-60; B.A., Carthage Coll., 1966; M.Ed., Loyola U., Chgo., 1971; postgrad. Nat. Coll. Edn., Evanston, Ill., 1971-77, Northwestern U., 1976-83; m. John N. Crawford, Jr., June 28, 1969. Med. technologist, Chgo., 1960-62; primary and spl. edn. tchr. Chgo. Pub. Schs., 1966-71, counselor maladjusted children and their families, 1971—; counselor juvenile first-offenders, 1968—. Vol., Sta. WTTW-TV; vol. counselor deaf children and their families. Cert. elem. edn., spl. edn. and pupil personnel services, Ill. Mem. Ill. Assn. Counseling and Devel., Am., Ill. sch. counselors assns., Council Exceptional Children, Am. Assn. Counseling Devel., Coordinating Council Handicapped Children, Shimer Coll. Alumni Assn. (sec. 1982-84), Phi Delta Kappa. Home: 601 E 32d St Chicago IL 60616 Office: 2131 W Monroe St Chicago IL 60612

CRAWFORD, JOHN GEORGE, III, pediatric dentist, orthodontist; b. Evergreen Pk., Ill., Oct. 29, 1945; s. John G. and Helen A. (Skoog) C.; m. Susan Marie Machamer, Aug. 27, 1963; 1 child, Andrea Jean. B.S., U. Ill. Med. Ctr.-Chgo., 1968, D.D.S., 1970, M.S., 1974. Cert. pedodontics, Ill., Orthodontics, Ill. Asst. prof. pedodontics, orthodontics U. Ill. Coll. of Dentistry, Chgo., 1974-79, dir. div. of growth and devel., 1975-79; practice dentistry specializing in pediatric dentistry and orthodontics, Oak Park, Ill., 1979—; pedodontic cons. State of Ill. Dept. of Registration and Edn., Springfield, 1982—. Fellow Am. Acad. Pediatric Dentistry; mem. Ill. Soc. Pediatric Dentists (pres. 1985—), Chgo. Dental Soc. (pres. west side br. 1983-84), Am. Assn. Orthodontists. Home: 155 N Taylor Ave Oak Park IL 60302 Office: 505 N Ridgeland Ave Oak Park IL 60302

CRAWFORD, KENNETH JULIAN, rare book dealer; b. Sentinel Butte, N.D., Jan. 18, 1904; s. Lewis Ferandus and Cora Belle (Hazlitt) C.; m. Ellen Rachel Davis, June 18, 1931; children—Olivia. B.S., U. N.D., 1927. Rare book dealer Ken Crawford Books, North St. Paul, Minn., 1927—; rare book appraiser. Republican. Presbyterian. Avocation: traveling. Address: 2735 E 18th St North Saint Paul MN 55109

CRAWFORD, MARGARET WARD, administrative social worker, consultant social work and children's issues; b. Pontiac, Mich., Apr. 18, 1937; d. Julius McKinley and Eveylena (Mathes) Ward; m. Samuel Crawford, Sr., Feb. 25, 1961; children—Cheryl, Samuel, Gary, Sara, Adrienne. B.S., Wayne State U., 1974. Cert. instr. Christian edn., Mich. Family caseworker Mich. Social Services, 1961-73; adminstrv. asst. Schrock Homes, Washtenaw County, Mich., 1981-82, adminstrv. coordinator, 1982—; cons. student rights and sch. bds., state and fed. legis. ednl. system issues; panelist, lectr. adv. pub. schs. and youth issues. Mem. Sumpter Twp. Rehab. Com., Mich., 1980; trustee Lincoln Schs. Bd. Edn., Ypsilanti, Mich., 1974—, v.p., 1979-81, pres., 1981—; bd. dirs. Corner Health Ctr., Ypsilanti, 1980-81; mem. Ypsilanti Mental Health Edn. Task Force, 1974; trustee; youth mission dir. Mt. Hermon Missionary Baptist Ch., 1984—. Recipient cert. appreciation Mich. Assn. for Gifted and Talented Students, Washtenaw County Chpt., 1980, Corner Health Ctr., 1980, cert. Resolution award Sumpter Twp., 1981, cert. appreciation Detroit chpt. Childrens Def. Fund, 1984. Mem. Mich. Assn. Sch. Bds. (Keys to Boardsmanship award 1984-85), Nat. Sch. Bds. Assn., Mich. Sch. Bds. Assn. (legis. com. 1981-84, resolution com.), Washtenaw County Sch. Officers, Sumpter Young Womens Assn. (hon.). Avocation: reading. Home: 49372 Arkona St Belleville MI 48111

CRAWFORD, MARTHA JEANNE, architectural interior designer; b. Rockford, Ill., June 25, 1925; d. Woodruff Lynden and LaVerna (Means) C. Student Vassar Coll., 1943-45, Rockford Coll., 1945, Parsons Sch. Design, 1945-48, Columbia U. Sch. Architecture, 1951-53. Asst. interior designer Eleanor LeMaire Assocs., N.Y.C., 1948-49; head color dept. Amos Parrish & Co., N.Y.C., 1950-52; contract interior designer Beeston and Patterson, N.Y.C., 1952-53, Welton Becket & Assocs., N.Y.C., 1952-53; cons. interior designer, N.Y.C., 1953-58; owner Martha Crawford and Assocs., comml. design co., N.Y.C., 1958-66; archtl. interior designer, Waukesha, Wis., 1975—; color coordinator Parkwood Laminates, Wakefield, Mass., 1953-58, Timbertone Corp., N.Y.C., 1958-61; cons. color coordinator R.C.A. Rubber Co., Akron, Ohio, 1954-59; brochure cons. Rockcote Paints, Rockford, 1960-61. Contbr. to profl. publs. Vol. Inst. for Crippled and Disabled, N.Y.C., 1950-53; sec. Child Care Found., Fort Lauderdale, Fla., 1968-69; vol. Christmas seals campaign Tb Assn., Fort Lauderdale, 1969-70. Recipient award for outstanding interior of yr. S.M. Hexter Co., Cleve., 1959; 2d place award Dow Chem. Co., N.Y.C., 1960. Mem. Constrn. Specifications Inst. (bd. dirs. 1975, President's plaque 1975), AIA, Archtl. League N.Y. (co-chmn. current work 1959-60). Club: Altrusa (pres. 1969-70) (Fort Lauderdale). Avocations: paint jazz pastels; listening to jazz; book discussion groups. Home and office: W305 S4522 Brookhill Rd Waukesha WI 53188

CRAWFORD, RAYMOND CLARKE, dentist; b. Adena, Ohio, Apr. 4, 1912; s. Homer Campbell and Virgie Emma (Townsend) C.; student Duke, 1932-33; D.D.S., Ohio State U., 1937; m. Hazel Rittenhouse, Dec. 28, 1939 (dec. June 1968); children—Judith Lynn (Mrs. Gerald E. Ingle), Lee Campbell, m. Lou Wilson Stewart, Sept. 19, 1970. Pvt. practice dentistry, Adena, 1937—. Mem. sch. bd., Adena, 1939-43. Served with USAAF, 1943-46. Fellow Internat. Coll. Dentists; mem. Pierre Fauchard Acad., Am., Ohio dental assns., Eastern Ohio Dental Soc., Psi Omega. Mason. Home: 600 Dewey Ave Cadiz OH 43907 Office: 111 Main St Adena OH 43901

CRAWFORD, RAYMOND MAXWELL, JR., nuclear engineer; b. Charleston, S.C., July 28, 1933; s. Raymond Maxwell and Mary Elizabeth (Bates) C.; B.S., Wayne State U., 1958, M.S., 1960; Ph.D., U. Calif. at Los Angeles, 1969; m. J. Denise LeDuc, Mar. 10, 1951; children—Denis, Michael, Deborah, Peter, Elizabeth. Instr., Wayne State U., 1960-63; asst. prof. Calif. State U., Northridge, 1963-66; tech. staff Atomics Internat., 1969-71; nuclear engr. Argonne Nat. Lab. (Ill.), 1971-74; asso. and asst. head nuclear safeguards and licensing div. Sargent & Lundy, Chgo., 1974-80; v.p. Science Applications, Inc., Oak Brook, Ill., 1980-83; engring. dir. NUTECH Engrs., Chgo., 1983—; tech. cons. Atomic Power Devel. Assocs., 1962-63; summer fellow NASA Lewis Research Center, 1965-66. Scoutmaster and counsellor Boy Scouts Am., 1963-66; active YMCA, 1966-69; active Recs. for Blind, 1964-65. Recipient numerous awards. Mem. Western Soc. Engrs., Am. Nuclear Soc., Am. Inst. Chem. Engrs., Am. Chem. Soc., Nat. Soc. Profl. Engrs., Am. Sci. Affiliation, N.Y. Acad. Scis., AAAS, Sigma Xi, Tau Beta Pi, Phi Lambda Upsilon. Contbr. articles to tech. jours. Home: 1005 E Kennebec Ln Naperville IL 60540 Office: 225 N Michigan Ave Chicago IL 60601

CRAWFORD, RICHARD DWIGHT, biology educator, wildlife biology researcher; b. Kirksville, Mo., Nov. 16, 1947; s. John Barton and Ethel May (Kirkpatrick) C.; m. Glinda Carol Bloskovich, Dec. 30, 1966; 1 child, Melanie Contessa. B.S. in Edn., Northeast Mo. State U., 1968, M.S., 1969; Ph.D., Iowa State U., 1975. Instr. Iowa State U., Ames, 1973-75; asst. prof. U. N.D., Grand Forks, 1975-80, assoc. prof., 1980-81, assoc. prof., biology chmn., 1981-82, assoc. prof., 1982—; cons. U.S. Fish and Wildlife Service, Jamestown, N.D., 1977, Three Tribes Indian Reservation, New Town, N.D., 1982. Author: (with others) Wildlife in Southwest North Dakota, 1978. Editor: Wildlife Values of Sand and Gravel Pits, 1982. Contbr. articles to profl. jours. Served with U.S. Army, 1969-71. Recipient B.C. Gamble Award U. N.D. Alumni Found., 1983. Mem. Wildlife Soc. (cert. wildlife biologist; assoc. editor 1981-83, pres. N.D. chpt. 1981-82), Am. Ornithologists' Union (elective, life), Wilson Ornithol. Soc. (life). Avocations: wood carving, gardening, fishing. Home: 436 Campbell Dr Grand Forks ND 58201 Office: U ND Dept Biology Grand Forks ND 58202

CRAWFORD, RONALD LYLE, microbiology educator, consultant; b. Santa Anna, Tex., Sept. 28, 1947; s. Lester Crawford and Doris Delores (Smith) Crawford Norman; m. Onie Ann Thompson, Dec. 30, 1967; 1 child, Lisa Brooks. B.A. in Biology cum laude, Oklahoma City U., 1970; M.S. in Bacteriology, U. Wis.-Madison, 1972, Ph.D. in Bacteriology, 1973. Research assoc. U. Minn. St. Paul, 1973-74; research scientist N.Y. State Dept. Health, Albany, 1974-75; asst. prof. microbiology U. Minn.-Twin Cities, 1975-79, assoc. prof., 1979-83, prof., 1983—; research dir. Chem Waste Control, Wayzata, Minn., 1984-85; cons. to industry, 1975—; adviser on environ. pollution to U.S. Senator David Durenberger, Mpls., 1983. Author: Lignin Biodegradation and Transformation, 1981; also book chpts., numerous articles. Editor: (with R.S. Hanson) Microbial Growth on C1 Compounds, 1984; Applied and Environ. Microbiology, 1982—. Weyerhauser fellow U. Wis.-Madison, 1970-73. Mem. Am. Soc. Microbiology, Blue Key, Sigma Xi, Beta Beta Beta. Democrat. Avocations: playing guitar and banjo, long distance running. Office: U Minn Gray Freshwater Biol Inst PO Box 100 Navarre MN 55392

CRAWFORD, SUSAN YOUNG, library administrator, educator; d. James Y. and S.C. Young; m. James Weldon Crawford, July 4, 1956; 1 child, Robert James. B.A., U. B.C., 1948; B.L.S., U. Toronto, 1951; M.A., U. Chgo., 1956, Ph.D., 1971. Dir. archives library dept. AMA, Chgo., 1960-74; assoc. prof. Columbia U., N.Y.C., 1972-75; dir. div. library and archival services AMA, 1974-81; prof. dir. Med. Library, Washington U., St. Louis, 1981—. Author numerous books and jour. articles. Mem. steering com. Universal Guide for Contributors to Sci. Jours., 1978-79. Bd. regents Nat. Library Medicine, Bethesda, Md., 1971-75. Fellow AAAS (mem. Newcomb prize com. 1977); mem. Med. Library Assn. (editor-in-chief 1983—, Janet Doe lectr. 1983, chmn. panel cons. editors 1983—), Am. Soc. Info. Sci. (assoc. editor 1979-81, mem. editorial bd. 1984—), ALA, Soc. for Social Studies of Sci., AAUP, Spl. Libraries Assn., Assn. Acad. Health Scis. Library Dirs., Sigma Xi, Pi Lambda Theta. Home: 2418 Lincoln St Evanston IL 60201 Office: Washington U Sch Medicine PO Box 8132 660 S Euclid Ave Saint Louis MO 63110

CRAWFORD, TAD EVERING, taxidermist, pharmacist, inventor; b. Massillon, Ohio, Mar. 21, 1947; s. Walter Bry and Aura Rozina (Finger) C.; m. Cathy Jean Covert, Apr. 24, 1982; 1 child, Lisa. B.S. in Pharmacy, Ohio No. U., 1970. Registered pharmacist, Ohio. Pharmacist, independent drug stores, Canton, Ohio, 1970-83; owner, developer Tappan Tree Farms, Bowerston, Ohio, 1973—; taxidermist, East Sparta, Ohio, 1955—, owner, operator Tad's Taxidermy, 1978—. Patentee camo leaves. Advisor, Explorers Post, Buckeye council Boy Scouts Am., 1977-79. Recipient 3d place award World Taxidermy Competition (profl. div.) Williams/Hall Prodns., 1983, honorable mention (master artist div.), 1984. Mem. Ohio State Pharmacy Assn., Ohio Taxidermist Trade Register (1st place award, 3 3d place awards, honorable mention 1984), Nat. Taxidermy Assn. (1st, 2d, 3d place awards 1984). Lutheran. Avocations: bowhunting, travel, carpentry, art, sculpture. Home and Office: 6645 Cleveland S East Sparta OH 44626

CRAWFORD, WESLEY GEORGE, building construction educator, surveyor; b. Cumberland, Md., Mar. 19, 1952; s. Paul Franklin and Merry Elizabeth (Growden) C.; m. Bonnie Lou Zimmerman, Aug. 9, 1974. A.S. in Surveying Tech., Pa. State U., 1972; B.S. in Land Surveying, Purdue U., 1975, M.S. in Surveying, 1980. Profl. surveyor, Pa. Field engr. Green Constrn. Co., Bloomington, Md., 1972-74; draftsman, surveyor Office of City Engr., Lafayette, Ind., 1975-76; instr. drafting Ind. Vocat. Tech. Coll., Lafayette, 1976-78; grad. instr. Purdue U., West Lafayette, Ind., 1978-80, asst. prof., 1980-84, assoc. prof. dept. bldg. constrn., 1984—; faculty dir. Purdue Student Pub. Found., West Lafayette, 1984—. Recipient Best Tchr. award Bldg. Constrn. Students, Purdue U., 1981, D.D. Moss Excellence in Teaching award Students in the Bldg. Constrn. Program, Purdue U., 1982. Mem. Am. Congress on Surveying and Mapping, Nat. Soc. Profl. Surveyors, Am. Inst. Constructors, Ind. Soc. Profl. Land Surveyors, Sigma Lambda Chi (nat. pres. 1985—). Avocations: visiting national parks, canoeing, woodworking. Home: 2719 S River Rd West Lafayette IN 47906 Office: Dept Bldg Constrn Knoy Hall Tech Purdue U West Lafayette IN 47907

CRAWFORD, WILLIAM L., optometrist; b. Fairborn, Ohio, Sept. 27, 1947; s. William and Beth A. (Hammill) C.; m. Laurie Jane Lewis, June 20, 1970; children—Christopher D., Jane D. B.S., Miami U., Oxford, Ohio, 1969; M.A., Ind. U., 1971, O.D., 1980; postgrad., Wichita State U., 1973-74. Teaching asst. math Ind. U., Bloomington, 1969-72; assoc. instr. optics, 1976-80; staff optometrist Prime Health, Kansas City, Mo., 1980—, chmn. med. audit practice standards com. 1984—. Contbr. articles to profl. jours. and books. Coach basketball, soccer and softball, Overland Park, Kans., 1983—; tchr., usher, committeeman, Hillcrest Covenant Ch., Prarie Village, Kans, 1981—. Served to capt. USAF, 1972-76. Mem. Kans. City Optometric Soc. (trustee 1982-84), Mo. Optometric Assn. (pub. health com. 1982-83), Am. Optometric Assn. (multidisciplinary practice sect. 1980—, Optometric Recognition award 1983-84), Kansas City IBM Users Group, Am. Pub. Health Assn., Optometric Extension Program. Republican. Club: Overland Park Racquet. Avocations: personal computers, sports, reading. Home: 9616 Glenwood Dr Overland Park KS 66212 Office: Prime Health 373 W 101st Terr Kansas City MO 64114

CRAYTON, BILLY GENE, physician; b. Holden, Mo., May 15, 1931; s. John Reuben and Carrie Zona (Head) C.; student Central Mo. State Coll., 1948-49; B.S., Stetson U., 1958; postgrad. U. Kansas City, summer 1955; M.D., U. Mo., 1962. Intern, Mound Park Hosp., St. Petersburg, Fla., 1962-63; practice gen. medicine Latham Hosp., California, Mo., 1963-64, Kelling Clinic and Hosp., Waverly, 1964—, vice chief of staff, 1980—; preceptor in community health and med. practice U. Mo. Sch. Medicine, Waverly, 1968—; sec., dir. Kelling Hosp., Inc., 1969-80; pres. Kelling Clinic, 1971—; med. dir. Waverly Ambulance Co., 1985—; pres. Riverview Heights, 1972—. Adviser, Mo. chpt. Am. Assn. Med. Assts., 1973-79. Adviser, Explorer Post Boy Scouts Am., 1968-70. Served with AUS, 1952-54. Fellow Am. Acad. Family Physicians. Baptist. Home: PO Box 41 Waverly MO 64096 Office: Kelling Clinic Inc Waverly MO 64096

CREAHAN, DAVID JOSEPH, lawyer; b. Cleve., July 4, 1916; s. John Thomas and Eva (Grothaus) C.; m. Ruth Janice Winterman, Jan. 15, 1944; children—David, Thomas, Mary, Kathleen, Julie, Kevin, Ann, John. B.B.A., U. Cin., 1939; J.D., No. Ky. U., 1975. Bar: Ohio 1975, U.S. Dist. Ct. 1975, U.S. Supreme Ct. 1984; C.P.A., Ohio. Pres. Techne Corp., Plainview, Tex., 1963-69, Cherokee Nitrogen Co., Pryor, Okla., 1969-75; v.p., treas., assoc. gen. counsel N.Ren Corp., Cin., 1975-78; gen. mgr. Sudan-Ren Chem. and Fertilizer Ltd., Khartoum, 1978-81; assoc. Simon and Namanworth, Cin., 1981—. Served to capt. USN, 1941-45, 52-53. Mem. ABA, Ohio State Bar Assn., Cin. Bar Assn. Democrat. Roman Catholic. Avocations: Politics, civil rights, history. Home: 6600 Corbly Rd Cincinnati OH 45230 Office: Simon and Namanworth 602 Main St Cincinnati OH 45202

CREEKMUR, MIDA REE, educational adminstrator; b. Princeton, Ky., Oct. 17, 1941; d. James Randolph and Margaret Helen (Pruett) Hutchinson; m. George H. Creekmur, Jan. 2, 1959; children—Rebecca Lynn Farmer, James Sidney. B.A., U. Evansville, 1969, M.A., 1972. Tchr. Evansville-Vanderburgh Sch. Corp., Ind., 1970-80, prin. Glenwood Middle Sch., 1980—. Mem. Internat. Reading Assn., Nat. Middle Schs. Assn., Assn. Ednl. Adminstrs., Ind. Reading Assn., S.W. Ind. Council Tchrs. Math., Evansville Reading Assn. (pres.), Vanderburgh Elem. Prins. Assn., Phi Delta Kappa, Alpha Delta Kappa Pi Lambda Theta, Phi Kappa Phi. Home: 4045 Bergdolt Rd Evansville IN 47711 Office: Glenwood Middle Sch Evansville-Vanderburgh Sch Corp 901 Sweetser Evansville IN 47713

CREER-GOSS, BETTIE ANNETTA, learning disability educator, editor; b. Collinsville, Miss., Feb. 22, 1950; d. Luke and Johnny Mae Creer; m. James Milton Goss, Aug. 11, 1973; children—James Milton I, Chandra Nicole. B.S., Central Mich. U., 1974, M.A., 1978, Ed.S., in Ednl. Adminstrn., 1982. Cert. tchr. spl. edn., reading specialist, Mich. Juvenile delinquent guidance counselor 1974-77; reading cons., Saginaw, Mich., 1977-78, learning disability tchr., cons. 1978—. Mem. Mich. Reading Assn. (editor newsletter), Nat. Council Ednl. Children, Exec. Edn., Internat. Reading Assn. (del.), Nat. Assn. Female Execs., Phi Delta Kappa. Democrat. Clubs: Tri-City Links, Jr. League. Home: 4365 Jo Dr Saginaw MI 48601 Office: 3465 N Center Rd Saginaw MI 48603

CREGER, MICHELLE BISENIUS, lawyer; b. Emmetsburg, Iowa, Mar. 26, 1955; d. Bernard E. and Mary Ann (Hamilton) Bisenius; m. Richard J. Creger, Sept. 10, 1977. B.A., Creighton U., 1977; J.D., Case Western Res. U., 1981. Bar: Ohio 1981, U.S. Dist. Ct. (no. dist.) Ohio 1981. Assoc. McDonald, Hopkins & Hardy Co. L.P.A., Cleve., 1981—. Steering com. mem. Ctr. for Profl. Ethics, Cleve., 1982—. Mem. Ohio Bar Assn., Cuyahoga County Bar Assn. (chairperson lawyer client relations com.), Greater Cleve. Bar Assn., Cleve. Acad. Trial Attys. Home: 2592 Saybrook Rd University Heights OH 44118 Office: McDonald Hopkins & Hardy Co LPA 1100 E Ohio Bldg Cleveland OH 44114

CREHORE, CHARLES AARON, lawyer; b. Lorain, Ohio, Sept. 15, 1946; s. Charles Case and Catherine Elizabeth (Kurtz) C.; B.A., Wittenberg U., 1968; postgrad. (Delta Sigma Phi Found. scholar), U. Mich., 1968-69, Cleve. State U., 1972-73; J.D., U. Akron, 1976; m. Kathy Louise Stoecklin, June 28, 1969; 1 son, Charles Case II. Bar: Ohio 1976, U.S. Patent Office 1975. Assoc. chemist B.F. Goodrich Co., Akron, 1969-70, chemist, 1970-72, patent atty. trainee, 1972-74, sr. patent atty. trainee, 1974-75, patent asso., 1975-76, patent atty., 1976-79; atty. regulatory affairs The Lubrizol Corp., Wickliffe, Ohio, 1979-81, corp. counsel environment, health and safety, 1981-85, sr. corp. counsel, 1985—. Kennedy Found. grantee, 1968-69. Mem. Am. Bar Assn., Am. Patent Law Assn., Cleve. Internat. Law Assn., Def. Research Inst., Cleve. Patent Law Assn., Licensing Execs. Soc., Phi Alpha Delta. Mem. Gen. Ch. New Jerusalem. Home: PO Box 371 Chagrin Falls OH 44022 Office: 29400 Lakeland Blvd Wickliffe OH 44092

CREIGHTON, MARSHALL JAY, sartographer, geographer; b. Seattle, June 17, 1953; s. Eldridge and Janet Jean (Harris) C.; m. Valerie Kaye Parker, Mar. 23, 1974 (div. Feb. 1984) children—Jessica, Christopher; m. Laraine Kay Gleason, Nov. 10, 1984. B.A. in Geography, Western Wash. State Coll., 1975. Cartographer, U.S. Dept. Interior, Rolla, Mo., 1976-83, supervisory cartographer, 1983—. Author: War, Peace and International Politics, 1977. Mem. Am. Congress on Surveying and Mapping (sect. sec. 1981-82). Republican. Methodist. Avocation: motorcycle touring. Home: 1806 Meadow Ct Rolla MO 65401 Office: Mid-Continent Mapping Ctr 1400 Independence Rd Rolla MO 65401

CREPEAU, DEWEY LEE, lawyer, educator; b. Richmond Heights, Mo., June 3, 1956; s. Dewey Lee and Floy Evelyn (Lacefield) Crapo m. Susan Jane Stonner, July 15, 1978; children—Elizabeth, Courtney. A.B., U. Mo., 1977, J.D., 1980. Bar: Mo. 1980, U.S. Dist. Ct. (we. dist.) Mo. 1980, U.S. Ct. Appeals (8th cir.) 1984. Assoc. William Johnson, P.C., Versailles, Mo. 1980-81; asst. prosecutor Morgan County, Mo., 1980-81; legal aid atty. Mid-Mo. Legal Services Corp., Columbia, 1982; sole practice, Columbia, 1982—; adj. prof. criminal justice Columbia Coll., 1983—. Active Christian Fellowship of Columbia. Mem. Mo. Bar Assn., Boone County Bar Assn., Mo. Assn. Trial Attys., Mo. Assn. Criminal Def. Lawyers, Order Barristers. Home: 201 Cornerstone Ct Columbia MO 65203 Office: 224 N 8th St Columbia MO 65201

CREPPY, MICHAEL JOHN, lawyer; b. Washington, Jan. 6, 1954; s. Mary Lee Coffee; m. Hazel Thom, Apr. 14, 1984. B.A., Fisk U., 1975; J.D., Howard U., 1978; LL.M., Georgetown U., 1979. Bar: D.C. 1980, U.S. Ct. Appeals (D.C. cir.) 1980, U.S. Ct. Appeals (4th, 5th and 9th cirs.) 1982. Law clk. D.C. Superior Ct., Washington, 1979-81; trial atty. U.S. Dept. Justice Immigration and Naturalization Service, 1981-83; trial atty. U.S. Dept. Justice civil div. Office Immigration Litigation, Washington, 1983-84, chief legal officer Immigration and Naturalization Service, Los Angeles 1985—. Recipient Outstanding Performance award U.S. Dept. Justice, Washington, 1981-83. Mem. Alpha Mu Gamma, Phi Alpha Delta. Office: US Dept Justice Immigration and Naturalization Service 300 Los Angeles St Los Angeles CA 90012

CRESSEY, BRYAN CHARLES, lawyer; b. Seattle, Sept. 28, 1949; s. Charles Ovington and Alice Lorraine (Serry) C.; m. Christina Irene Petersen, Aug. 19, 1972; children—Monique Joy, Charlotte Lorraine. B.A., U. Wash., 1972; M.B.A., Harvard U., 1976, J.D., 1976. Bar: Ill. 1977, Wash. 1976. Sr. investment mgr. First Chgo. Investment Corp., Chgo., 1976-80; ptnr. Golder, Thoma, and Cressey, Chgo., 1980—; chmn., dir. MedPlus, Inc., Dallas; dir. Nu-Med, Inc., Encino, Calif., Advanced Robotics Corp., Columbus, Ohio, Interspec, Inc., Conshohocken, Pa., New Hope Pain Ctrs., Inc., Pasadena, Calif., Crystal Diagnostic Systems, Inc. Bd. dirs., v.p. planning Infant Welfare Soc., Chgo., 1984—. Home: Rural Route 2 Bateman Circle Barrington Hills IL 60010 Office: Golder Thoma & Cressey 120 S La Salle St Chicago IL 60603

CRETSOS, JAMES MIMIS, pharmaceutical company science information executive chemist; b. Athens, Greece, Oct. 23, 1929; s. Basil D. and Chrissa B. (Thomaidou) Kretsos; came to U.S., 1946, naturalized, 1955; B.S. in Chemistry, Am. U., 1960, postgrad., 1960-62; m. Barbara Ann Deitz, Mar. 10, 1952; children—Maurice William, Christopher James. Research chemist Melpar, Inc., Falls Church, Va., 1961-63, info. scientist, 1963-64, head tech. info. center, 1964-65, mgr. info. services lab., 1965-67, dir. instructional materials center, Tng. Corp. of Am., Falls Church, 1966-67; dir. info. systems lab. Litton Industries, Bethesda, Md., 1967-69; head sci. info. systems dept. Merrell Dow Pharms., Cin., 1969—; dir. Infoflow, Inc.; cons OEO, Ohio, Ky.-Ind. Regional Library and Info. Council; lectr. U. Cin., 1973-74, U. Ky., 1976-77, 82. Mem. Creative Edn. Found., Buffalo, 1967—. Served with M.C., AUS, 1954-56. Mem. Am. Chem. Soc., Am. Mgmt. Assn., Am. Soc. Info. Sci. (chmn. So. Ohio chpt. 1973-74, chmn. SIG/BC 1973-74, chmn. profl. enhancement com. 1974-75, chmn. 5th mid-year meeting 1976, Watson Davis award 1976, chmn.

membership com. 1977, exec. com. 1979, nominations com. 1980, pres. 1979, chmn. SIG/NMR 1981, chmn. SIG/MED 1985—), Am. Fedn. Info. Processing Socs. (dir. 1981—, mem. exec. com. 1982—), Assn. Computing Machinery, IEEE Computer Soc., Data Processing Mgmt. Assn., IEEE, Associated Info. Mgrs., Drug Info. Assn., Med., Spl. (pres. Cin. chpt. 1974-75, consultation officer 1976-77) libraries assns., Assn. Computational Linguistics, Pharm. Mfrs. Assn., Assn. Info. Image Mgmt., MEDINFO (dir. 1984—). Club: Indoor Tennis. Editor, Health Aspects of Pesticides Abstract Bull., 1967-69; mem. adv. bd. Chem. Abstracts Service, 1981-83, user council, 1983-84. Home: 10701 Adventure Ln Cincinnati OH 45242 Office: 2110 E Galbraith Rd Cincinnati OH 45215

CREVI, ALLAN RAYMOND, investment counselor; b. N.Y.C., Nov. 2, 1942; s. I. Peter and Ellen (Frey) C.; m. Anne Mulhern, Mar. 10. 1968; 1 child: Alexander. B.S. in Elec. Engring., Cornell U., 1965; M.B.A., U. Pa. Wharton Sch., 1969. Chartered investment counselor. Ptnr. Stein Roe & Farnham, Chgo., 1969—. Served to lt. USN, 1965-67. Mem. Investment Analysts Soc. of Chgo. Republican. Club: Union League (Chgo.). Office: Stein Roe & Farnham 1 S Wacker Dr Chicago IL 60606

CREWS, JOHN ERIC, rehabilitation administrator; b. Marion, Ind., Aug. 4, 1946; s. Odis Earl and Beatrice True (Wright) C.; m. Nancy J. Murphy, Aug. 9, 1975; 1 dau., Katherine. B.A. in English, Franklin Coll., 1969; M.A. in English, Ind. U., 1971; M.A. in Blind Rehab. with honors, Western Mich. U., 1977, postgrad in pub. administrn., 1983—. Mem. English faculty Ball State U., Muncie, Ind., 1971-73, S.W. Mo. State U., Springfield, 1973-76, Western Mich. U., Kalamazoo, 1976-77; rehab. tchr. Mich. Commn. for the Blind, Saginaw, 1977-80, program mgr. Sr. Blind Program, Saginaw, Southeastern Mich. Ctr. for Ind. Living, Detroit, 1980—; v.p. bd. Midland County Council on Aging, 1982—; bd. dirs. Saginaw Valley Spl. Needs Vision Clinic, 1981—; mem. adv. bd. rehab. continuing edn. program So. Ill. U., Carbondale, 1985—. Mem. editorial bd. Jour. Visual Impairment and Blindness, 1984—. Contbr. to book and profl. publs. Mem. Mayor's Commn. on Internat. Yr. of Disabled, Saginaw, 1981, Saginaw County Handicapped Adv. Com., 1982-83. Recipient Disting. Service award Midland County Council on Aging, 1984. Ctr. Ind. Living grantee U.S. Dept. Edn., 1980, 82. Mem. Nat. Council Aging, Assn. Retarded Citizens (pres. Midland 1981—; Ann. Appreciation award 1981). Methodist. Lodge: Lions. Home: 103 W Campbell Ct Midland MI 48640 Office: Mich Commn for the Blind 411-G E Genesee Saginaw MI 48607

CRIBBET, JOHN EDWARD, legal educator; b. Findlay, Ill., Feb. 21, 1918; s. Howard Herbert and Ruth Augusta (Wright) C.; m. Betty Jane Smith, Dec. 24, 1941; children—Pamela Lee Cribbet Steward, Carol Ann Cribbet Bell. B.A., Ill. Wesleyan U., 1940, LL.D. (hon.), 1972; J.D., U. Ill., 1947. Bar: Ill. 1947. Assoc., Costigan, Wollrab & Yoder, Bloomington, Ill.; from asst. prof. to prof. law U. Ill., Urbana, 1947-67, dean Coll. of Law, 1967-79, chancellor, 1979-84, Corman prof. law, 1984—; dir. Bloomington Fed. Savs. & Loan, State Farm Ins. Mem. Champaign Planning Commn., 1960-66. Served to maj. U.S. Army, 1941-45. Decorated Bronze Star; Croix de Guerre (France). Mem. ABA, Ill. Bar Assn., Am. Judicature Soc., Assn. Am. Law Schs. (pres. 1979). Republican. Methodist. Club: Rotary (Urbana). Author: Cases and Materials on Judicial Remedies, 1954; Principles of the Law of Property, 2d edit., 1976; Cases and Materials on Property, 5th edit., 1984. Office: Coll Law 504 E Pennsylvania Ave Champaign IL 61820

CRIDER, ERNEST FORD, anesthesiologist; b. Liggett, Ky., May 8, 1921; s. John Solomon and Lissie (Fee) C.; m. Gladys B. Yeary, May 6, 1944; 1 child, Bruce Allan. B.S., Eastern Ky. State U., 1944; M.D., U. Louisville, 1946. Diplomate Am. Bd. Anesthesiology. Attending anesthesiologist Toledo Hosp., 1953—. Served to capt. M.C., U.S. Army, 1951-53. Mem. AMA, Am. Soc. Anesthesiologists, Internat. Anesthesia Research Soc., Ohio Med. Assn. Republican. Methodist. Club: Torch (Toledo). Avocations: electronics, woodworking. Home: 2664 Drummond Rd Toledo OH 43606 Office: Katchka-Friedman-Crioer Med Corp 3939 Monroe St Toledo OH

CRIDER, ROBERT AGUSTINE, international financier; b. Washington, Jan. 3, 1935; s. Rana Albert and Terasa Helen (Dampf) C.; student law enforcement U. Md., 1959-63; m. Debbie Ann Lee, Nov. 1960. Police officer Met. Police Dept., Washington, 1957-67; substitute tchr., bldg. trades instr. Maries R-1 Sch., Vienna, Mo., 1968-70; vets. constrn. tng. officer VA Dept. Edn., Mo., 1968-70; constrn. mgr. Tectonics Ltd., Vienna, 1970-79; owner, dir. R-A Crider & Assocs., St. Louis, 1979—; dir. TI-CO Investment Corp., Langcaster Corp. Served with USAF, 1952-56. Mem. Assn. Ret. Policemen, Internat. Conf. Police, Internat. Assn. Chiefs of Police, Nat. Police Assn., World Future Soc., Internat. Platform Assn., Nat. Assn. Fin. Cons., Internat. Soc. Financiers, Am. Legion, St. Louis Honor Guard. Roman Catholic. Clubs: Lions, K.C. (4th deg.). Home: PO Box 109 Vienna MO 65582 Office: R-A Crider & Assocs PO Box 3459 2644 Roseland Terr Saint Louis MO 63143

CRILLEY, CHRISTINE LEE, lawyer; b. Cedar Rapids, Iowa, Apr. 18, 1957; d. Charles Robert and Marleen Fern (Hansen) Boots; m. Michael Emmett Crilley, Dec. 27, 1979. B.A. in Speech/Edn., U. No. Iowa, 1979; J.D., U. Iowa, 1983. Bar: Iowa 1983, U.S. Dist. Ct. (no. dist.) Iowa 1983. Tchr. high sch. Marion Ind. Schs., Iowa, 1979-80; assoc. Norris & Assocs., Cedar Rapids, Iowa, 1983-84, Crilley & Stokke Law Offices, 1984—. Mem. Trial Lawyers Am., ABA (young lawyer's sect.), Iowa Bar Assn., Trial Lawyers Iowa, Linn County Bar Assn., Women Attys. Linn, Tomahawk, Purple Arrow, Delta Sigma Rho. Club: Voyagers. Home: 249 12th St Cedar Rapids IA 52405 Office: Crilley & Stokke Law Offices 432 Higley Bldg Cedar Rapids IA 52401

CRISAFI, FRANK RALPH, real estate developer, consultant; b. Cleve., Sept. 24, 1933; s. Anthony and Margaret (Fritzsche) C.; m. Betty J. Gural, June 14, 1954; children—Frank A., Anthony W., David A., Karen A. B.B.A. in Acctg., Case Western Res. U., 1956; J.D., Marshall Law Sch., 1971. Bar: Ohio, Fla. Real estate counselor King & Smith Realty, Cleve., 1956-59; pres. Zepkin & Crisafi Realty, Cleve., 1958-78; owner Crisafi Enterprise, Cleve., 1978—. Mem. Cleve. Area Bd. Realtors (treas. 1977, pres.-elect 1981, pres. 1982). Republican. Roman Catholic. Avocation: music. Home: 31220 Roxbury Pk Dr Bay Village OH 44140 Office: Crisafi Enterprises 1540 Leader Bldg Cleveland OH 44114

CRISMAN, PAMELA KAY, public relations official, college official; b. Galesburg, Ill., Aug. 26, 1952; d. Mildrehn Carl and Norma Jean (Goodrich) Black; d. Gerald R. Crisman, Apr. 9, 1977; 1 child, Brian Matthew. B.S. in Pub. Relations, So. Ill. U., 1974; postgrad. Sangamon State U., 1980. Pub. relations asst. Hansen Photography, Decatur, Ill., 1976; sales mgr., promotion dir. G.E. Cablevision, Decatur, 1976-78; info. and plan coordinator Decatur Mental Health Ctr., 1978-83, asst. adminstr., 1983; pub. relations dir. Lake Land Coll., Mattoon, Ill., 1983—; cons. Ill. Dept. Mental Health and Devel. Disabilities-Beneficiary Awareness Project, Springfield, Ill., 1982, Decatur Mental Health Ctr., 1984; chmn. Mental Health Pub. Awareness Com., Decatur, 1978-80. Author, dir. tv pub. service announcements, 1982. Mem. Pub. Relations Soc. Am. (central Ill. chpt.), Ill. Coll. Relations Council, Nat. Nat. Council for Community Relations. Avocations: photography, writing. Office: Lake Land Coll S Route 45 Mattoon IL 61938

CRISPELL, LAWRENCE STEARNS, physician; b. Brideport, Conn., Feb. 19, 1919; s. Charles W. and Dorothy (Stearns) C. B.S., Yale U., 1941, M.D., 1950. Diplomate Am. Bd. Otolaryngology. Intern Bellevue Hosp., N.Y.C., 1943-44; resident Yale U. Hosp., 1944-45, 48-49; practice medicine specializing in otolaryngology, Hanover, N.H., 1949-53, Joplin, Mo., 1953—; mem. staffs Freeman Hosp., Joplin, Mo., Baxter Springs Meml. Hosp., Kans., Grove Meml. Hosp., Okla. Served to major, U.S. Army, 1945-48. Republican. Episcopalinn. Home: 1512 Pelican Point Dr Sarasota FL 33581 Office: 3302 McIntosh Dr Joplin MO 64801

CRISWELL, DENISE ELAINE, athletic trainer, physical education educator; b. Marion, Ohio, Aug. 29, 1956; d. Jerald Wayne and Betty Jean (Williams) C. B.S. in Phys. Edn./Health, Miami U., Oxford, Ohio, 1978; M.S. in Phys. Edn./Edml. Adminstrn., Ft. Hays State U., Hays, Kans., 1979. Cert. First Aid/CPR, Water Safety Instr., ARC. Asst. athletic trainer Valparaiso U. (Ind.), 1979—, instr. phys. edn., 1979—, athletic trainer Sports Camps, 1980—; athletic trainer-cons. Porter County Schs. (Ind.), 1979—; cons. Nautilus Fitness Club, Merrillville, Ind., 1980-81. Mem. Nat. Athletic Trainers Assn., Inc., Ind. Athletic Trainers Assn., Kappa Psi Omega. Democrat. Lutheran. Office: Valparaiso Univ Hilltop Gymnasium Valparaiso IN 46383

CRITTENDEN, LEE JOHN, finance company executive; b. Kalamazoo, Mich., June 20, 1945; s. Jack L. and Evelyn B. (Wohlfert) C.; m. Mary Ann Frescura, Jan. 31, 1970 (div. Aug. 26, 1982); 1 child, Alexandra N. B.S., No. Ill. U., 1968; cert. modern bus. Alexander Hamilton Inst., N.Y.C., 1973. Publs. editor Uniroyal Inc., Joliet Army Ammunition Plant (Ill.), 1968-70; staff editor Employee Communications, Uniroyal, Inc., N.Y.C., 1970-71, assoc. editor employee publs., Middlebury, Conn., 1971-73, pub. relations mgr., tire and automotive products, Allen Park, Mich., 1973-76; v.p. APC Cons., Inc., Joliet, Ill., 1976-81; pres., gen. mgr. Bee Newspapers, Inc., Joliet, Ill., 1978-80; v.p. corp. communications Assocs. Comml. Corp., Chgo., 1981—. Mem. citizens adv. council Selective Investigation and Prosecution Unit, Will County, Ill., 1979-83; bd. dirs. Profl. Truck Driver Inst. Am., Inc., chmn., fin. com. Mem. Am. Trucking Assn. (communications adv. council), Trucking Industry Alliance (coordinating com., chmn., communications com.), Am. Truckers Benevolent Assn. (bd. dirs.), Truck Renting and Leasing Assn. (supplier adv. council), Pub. Relations Soc. Am. Clubs: Publicity (Chgo.), Chgo. Press Club. Office: Assocs Ctr 150 N Michigan Ave Suite 3500 Chicago IL 60601

CRITZ, NANCY WIER, hospital administrator; b. Cin., Feb. 13, 1954; d. Robert Charles and Judy (Phillips) Wier; 1 dau., Kelly Suzanne. A.S. in Social Work, U. Cin., 1974, B.S. in Social Work, 1976. Children's protective social worker Hamilton County (Ohio) Welfare Dept., 1977-79; dir. social services Our Lady of Mercy Hosp., Cin., 1982—; cons. social work students U. Cin. Mem. Am. Hosp. Assn., Soc. Social Work Dirs., Ohio Hosp. Assn. Hosp. Social Work Dirs., Sigma Delta Tau (alumni pres.). Methodist. Home: 471 McIntosh Dr Cincinnati OH 45230 Office: Our Lady of Mercy Hosp Rowan Hills Dr Cincinnati OH 45227

CRIVARO, PETE FRANK, See *Who's Who in America*, 43rd edition.

CROAT, THOMAS BERNARD, botanical curator; b. St. Marys, Iowa, May 23, 1938; s. Oliver Theodore and Irene Mary (Wilgenbush) C.; m. Patricia Swope, Sept. 16, 1965; children—Anne Irene, Thomas Kevin. B.A., Simpson Coll., 1962; M.A., U. Kans., 1966, Ph.D., 1967. Tchr. sci. pub. schs., Virgin Islands and Iowa, 1962-64; research botanist Mo. Botanical Garden, St. Louis, 1967—, P.A. Schulze curator of botany, 1977—; vis. fellow Smithsonian Tropical Research Inst., Ancon, Canal Zone, 1968-71; adv. com. NSF Resources in Systematic Botany, 1972-74; faculty assoc. biology Washington U., St. Louis, 1970-84; adj. faculty U. Mo., St. Louis, 1974-84; adj. assoc. prof. St. Louis U., 1982-84. Author: Flora of Barro Colorado Island, 1978. Contbr. articles to profl. jours. Served as pfc U.S. Army, 1956-58, Fed. Republic Germany. Recipient Research award Soc. Sigma Xi, 1975. Grantee NSF, 1972-83, Nat. Geog. Soc., 1973, 84, Nat. Endowment Arts, 1975, 79. Mem. Am. Soc. Plant Taxonomists, Assn. Tropical Biology, Internat. Soc. Plant Taxonomists, Internat. Aroid Soc. (hon. bd. 1978-84), Botanical Soc. Am. Republican. Roman Catholic. Club: Republican (St. Louis) (pres. 1982-84). Avocations: Welding; electronics; auto repair; construction. Home: 4043 Parker Saint Louis MO 63116 Office: Mo Botanical Garden Box 299 Saint Louis MO 63166

CROCKER, THOMAS NORMAN, business educator; b. Hardin, Tex., Sept. 1, 1937; s. Marvin C. and Hester V. (Smotherman) C.; m. Theresa Onalee James, Apr. 30, 1966; children—Sarah K., Carla C. B.S., Tex. A&M U., 1958; M.B.A., Auburn U., 1972. Commd. 2d lt. U.S. Air Force, 1958, advanced through grades to lt. col., 1975; served in Thailand and Panama, ret., 1976; asst. prof. bus. Iowa Wesleyan Coll., Mt. Pleasant, 1979-83, chair div. bus., 1983—; ind. cons., 1981-84; sec.-treas. Midwest Central R.R., Mt. Pleasant, 1980-81. Contbr. articles to bus. jours. Mem. central com. Henry County Republican party, 1982-83. Decorated D.F.C., others. Mem. Am. Econ. Assn., Air Force Assn. Republican. Methodist. Avocation: photography. Office: Iowa Wesleyan Coll Mount Pleasant IA 52651

CROCKETT, GEORGE WILLIAM, JR., congressman; b. Jacksonville, Fla., Aug. 10, 1909; A.B., Morehouse Coll., Atlanta, 1931; J.D., U. Mich., 1934; LL.D. (hon.), Morehouse Coll., 1972, Shaw Coll., Detroit, 1973; m. Harriette Clark, 1980; children by previous marriage—Elizabeth Ann Hicks, George W., Ethelene C. Jones. Admitted to Fla. bar, 1934, W.Va. bar, 1935, Mich., 1944; sr. atty. Dept. Labor, 1939-43; hearings officer Fed. Fair Employment Practices Commn., Washington, 1943; founder, dir. fair employment practices dept. Internat. United Auto Workers, adminstrv. asst., sec.-treas., asso. gen. counsel, 1944-46; sr. mem. firm Goodman, Crockett, Eden & Robb, Detroit, 1946-66; elected judge Recorder's Ct., Detroit, 1966, 72, presiding judge, 1974; vis. judge Mich. Ct. Appeals, 1979; acting corp. counsel City of Detroit, 1980; founder, 1st chmn. Jud. Council, Nat. Bar Assn.; mem. 97th Congresses from Mich. 13th dist. Trustee Morehouse Coll. Mem. Nat. Lawyers Guild, Nat. Bar Assn., NAACP, Kappa Alpha Psi. Baptist. Democrat. Office: US House of Reps Washington DC 20515

CROCKETT, JAMES EDWIN, physician, educator; b. Kansas City, Kans., Oct. 20, 1924; s. John Edward and Orva Rose (Ramsey) C.; m. Martha Crockett, June 8, 1949; children—Kevin, Brian, Cara. B.A., Park Coll., 1945; M.D., U. Kans., 1949. Diplomate Am. Bd. Internal Medicine and Cardiovascular Diseases. Intern U.S. Naval Hosp., Long Beach, Calif., 1949-50; resident U. Kans. Med. Ctr., Kansas City 1950-56; asst. prof. medicine U. Kans. Sch. Medicine, Kansas City, 1956-58, assoc. prof., 1958-63, dir. cardiology, 1960-63; clin. prof. medicine U. Mo.-Kansas City Sch. Medicine, 1972—; mem. adv. bd. Chinese Inst. Cardiology, Beijing, 1984—. Author: Your Heart, 1983. Contbr. articles to profl. jours. Bd. dirs. St. Lukes Hosp. Research Found., 1973-75. Served to lt. USN, 1949-57. Fellow ACP, Am. Coll. Cardiology (bd. trustees 1965-67, 71-73, Cummings Internat. Teaching award, 1967). Republican. Episcopalian. Clubs: River, Carriage. Avocations: music; reading; tennis. Home: 1233 W 63 Terr Kansas City MO 64113 Office: Office of Pres Cardiovascular Cons 4320 Wornall Kansas City MO 64111

CROCKETT, RUBIE EILEENE, educational administrator; b. Bakerton, Ky.; d. Sanford Russell and Christine Sprouls; m. Waldo Ralph Crockett, Sept. 1, 1967; children—Christy, Alesa, Elaine, Eric. B.S., Ind. Central U., 1967, M.A., 1969; Ed.S., Butler U., Indpls., 1973; Ph.D., Ind. U., 1977. Lic. elem. supt., adminstr., supr., Ind. Tchr. pub. schs., Coe Ridge, Ky., 1961-62; data processor, Key punch operator U.S. Govt., 1963-67; elem. tchr. Indpls. pub. schs., 1967-70, asst. prin. Robert P. Browing Sch., 1970-73; vice prin. jr. high sch., 1973-77; lectr. lectr. social sci. dept. Ind. Central U., 1977-79; lectr. dept. edn. Ind. U., 1978-79; prin. James Whitcomb Riley Elem. Sch., 1979—. Ky. Library Assn. scholar, 1952; Kroger scholar, 1952; Anna R. Reid scholar, 1969; NSF grantee, 1972. Mem. Assn. Supervision and Curriculum Devel., Ind. Assn. Elem. Prins., Indpls. Assn. Elem. Prins., Ind. Hospice Assn., Ind. Reading Assn., NAACP, Nat. Council Negro Women, Forest Manor Multi-Service Assn., Butler-Tarkinton Neighborhood Assn., Soc. Intensified Edn., Phi Delta Kappa, Pi Lambda Theta, Delta Sigma Theta. Baptist. Club: Fortnightly Literary. Home: 5320 Daniel Dr Indianapolis IN 46226 Office: 150 W 40th St Indianapolis IN 46208

CROFTS, INEZ ALTMAN, composer, contralto; b. Portsmouth, Ohio; d. John Louis and Hazel Opal (Walters) Altman; B.Mus., Chgo. Conservatory, 1958, Mus.M., 1960; m. Philip Hague Crofts; 1 son, Philip Hague. Tchr. piano, Portsmouth; organist, choir dir. Temple Bapt. Ch., Portsmouth; TV program Twilight Time, Sta. WNHC, New Haven, 1951-53; dir. Woman's Dept. Club Chorus, Terre Haute, Ind., 1953-55; toured with N.Y.C. Opera Co. in role of Bertha in Barber of Seville, 1957; contralto soloist North Shore Bapt. Ch., 1959-81; composer opera Mission in Burma, premiered Judson Coll., Elgin, Ill., 1970; faculty mem. music dept. Judson Coll., 1968-74, Chgo. Conservatory Coll., 1967-74; dir. choral activities Sigma Alpha Iota (Sword of Honor 1959, Rose award 1971); composer music centennial pageant, Riverside, Ill., 1975. Active Heart Assn. solicitations; bd. dirs. North Shore Bapt. Ch., 1985—. Mem. Internat. Soc. Contemporary Music (dir. Chgo. chpt. 1961—), Lake View Mus. Soc. (pres. 1977-78, dir.), Chgo. Artists Assn. (pres. 1960-62), Musicians Club of Women (pres. 1982-84, program chmn.), Am. Opera Soc., 19th Century Woman's Club. Home: 277 Gatesby Rd Riverside IL 60546

CROGHAN, HAROLD HEENAN, lawyer, mfg. co. exec.; b. Sioux City, Iowa, May 20, 1924; s. Edmond Harold and Marie (Heenan) C.; A.B., Lawrence U., Appleton, Wis., 1947; J.D., Cornell U., 1953; m. Mary Gertrude Murphy, Feb. 4, 1948; children—Catherine, John, Loretta, Margaret. Admitted to N.Y. bar, 1953, Mo. bar, 1953, Ohio bar, 1967; asso. firms in Kansas City, 1953-56; corp. counsel Kansas City Gas Service Co., 1956-66; house counsel, then asst. sec.-corp. counsel Philips Industries Inc., Dayton, Ohio, 1966-68, v.p., sec., corp. counsel, treas., 1968-78, exec. v.p. adminstrn., gen. counsel, 1978—, also dir.; dir. Dexter Axle Co., Winbro, Inc., Malta Mfg. Co. Served with USMCR, 1942-46, 50-52. Decorated Navy Cross, Silver Star, Bronze Star, Purple Heart. Mem. Mo. Bar Assn., Ohio Bar Assn., Dayton Bar Assn., Pvt. Carriage Conf. (dir.), Phi Beta Kappa, Phi Delta Theta, Phi Delta Phi. Roman Catholic. Clubs: Dayton City, Dayton Racquet, Chancery, Vanguard, Rockhill, Hollinger Tennis (Dayton). Home: 609 Garden Rd Dayton OH 45419 Office: 4801 Springfield St Dayton OH 45401

CROIS, JOHN HENRY, village government official; b. Chgo., Jan. 13, 1946; s. Henry F. and Dorothy M. (Priebe) C.; B.A., Elmhurst (Ill.) Coll., 1969; M.A., U. Notre Dame, 1972. Asst. village mgr. Village of Oak Lawn (Ill.), 1975—; coordinator Oak Lawn Swine Flu Immunization Program, 1976. Mem. Internat. City Mgmt. Assn., Am. Soc. Public Adminstrn., Am. Econ. Assn., Ill. City Mgmt. Assn., Ill. Assn. Mcpl. Mgmt. Assts., Metro-Mgrs. Assn. Roman Catholic. Clubs: St. Germaine's Men's, Cath. Alumni. Home: 10233 S Karlov Ave Oak Lawn IL 60453 Office: 5252 W Dumke Dr Oak Lawn IL 60453

CROLL, ROBERT FREDERICK, educator, economist; b. Evanston, Ill., Feb. 3, 1934; s. Frederick Warville and Florence (Campbell) C.; B.S. in Bus. Adminstrn., Northwestern U., 1954; M.B.A. (Burton A. French scholar) with high distinction, U. Mich., 1956; D.B.A., Ind. U., 1969; D.Litt., John F. Kennedy Coll., 1970; m. Sandra Elizebeth Bell, June 15, 1968; 1 son, Robert Frederick. Instr. Ind. U. Sch. Bus., Bloomington, 1956, researcher in bus. econs., 1960-62; mng. dir. Motor Vehicle Industry Research Assocs., Evanston, 1962-63; personal asst. to speaker Ill. Ho. of Reps., 1963-65; asst. prof. bus. adminstrn. Kans. State U., 1965-66; asst. prof. Inst. Indsl. Relations, Loyola U. Chgo., 1966-70; assoc. prof. Sch. Bus. Adminstrn., Central Mich. U., 1970-76, prof., 1976—. Mem. platform committee Ind. Republican Com., 1958; Ind. del. Young Rep. Nat. Conv., 1959; nat. chmn. Youth for Goldwater Orgn., 1960-61; chmn. coll. clubs Young Rep. Orgn. Ill., 1960-62; asst. chief page Rep. Nat. Conv., 1964; mem. Mt. Pleasant City Charter Commn., 1973-76. Trustee estate of F.W. Croll, Chgo., 1959—. Recipient Grand prize Gov. of Ind., 1958. Accredited personnel diplomate Am. Soc. Personnel Adminstrn. Accreditation Inst. Mem. Soc. Automotive Engrs., Am. Inst. Mgmt., Soc. Advancement Mgmt., Am. Econ. Assn., Mt. Pleasant C. of C., Young Ams. for Freedom (founder 1960, vice chmn. 1962-63), Phila. Soc. (founder 1964), Beta Gamma Sigma, Delta Sigma Pi Key, Phi Delta Kappa, Phi Kappa Phi, Pi Sigma Alpha, Delta Mu Delta, Sigma Pi, Alpha Kappa Psi, Sigma Iota Epsilon, Phi Chi Theta. Episcopalian. Clubs: Little Harbor (Harbor Springs, Mich.); Mount Pleasant Country. Author: Fall of an Automotive Empire: A Business History of the Packard Motor Car Company, 1945-1958, others. Contbr. articles to profl. jours. Address: 1224 Glenwood Dr Mount Pleasant MI 48858

CROMLEY, JON LOWELL, lawyer; b. Riverton, Ill., May 23, 1934; s. John Donald and Naomi M. (Mathews) C.; B.S., U. Ill., 1958; J.D., John Marshall Law Sch., 1966. Real estate title examiner Chgo. Title & Trust Co., 1966-70; admitted to Ill. bar, 1966; practiced in Genoa, Ill., 1970—; mem. firm O'Grady & Cromley, Genoa, 1970—; dir. Genoa State Bank, Kingston Mut. County Fire Ins. Co. Bd. dirs. Genoa Day Care Center, Inc. Mem. Am. Judicature Soc., Am., Ill., Chgo., DeKalb County bar assns. Home: 130 Homewood Dr Genoa IL 60135 Office: 213 W Main St Genoa IL 60135

CROMWELL, NORMAN HENRY, chemistry educator, consultant, researcher; b. Terre Haute, Ind., Nov. 22, 1913; s. Henry and Ethyl Lee (Harkelroad) C.; m. Grace Newell, Jan. 29, 1955; children—Christopher Newell, Richard Earl. B.S. with honors, Rose-Hulman Inst., 1935; Ph.D., U. Minn., 1939. From instr. to prof. chemistry U. Nebr., Lincoln, 1939-60, Regents prof. 1960-83 Regents prof. emeritus, 1983—, chmn. dept. 1964-70, v.p., dean grad. studies and research, 1970-73; dir. Eppley Inst. Cancer Research Med. Ctr., Omaha, 1979-83; cons. various U.S. firms, 1943-69. Co-editor: New Trends in Heterocyclic Chemistry, 1979. Contbr. research articles to profl. jours. Trustee Nebr. Art Assn., 1958-80, v.p., 1971. Recipient Outstanding Alumnus Achievement award U. Minn., 1975, Outstanding Research and Creativity award U. Nebr., 1978; Guggenheim fellow Univ. Coll., London, 1950, 1953; Fulbright Advanced Research scholar U. London, 1950-51. Mem. Am. Chem. Soc. (40th Midwest award 1984), Internat. Soc. Heterocyclic Chemistry, Chem. Soc. London. Club: Round Table (Lincoln). Home: 2417 S 70th St Lincoln NE 68506 Office: Hamilton Hall U Nebr Lincoln NE 68588

CRONENWORTH, CHARLES DOUGLAS, salt company executive; b. Mohawk, Mich., 1921; B.S.M.E., Mich. Tech. U., 1944; married; 4 children. Design engr. Chrysler Corp., 1946-47; with Diamond Crystal Salt Co., Inc., St. Clair, Mich., 1947—, plant mgr., 1957-68, gen. mgr. prodn., 1968-73, v.p. prodn., 1973-75, v.p. mfg. and engring., 1975, now pres., chief exec. officer, dir.; dir. Comml. & Savs. Bank of St. Clair County, Maritek Corp., Worldwide Protein Bahamas Ltd. Served to 1st lt. U.S. Army and USMC, World War II. Mem. NAM (dir.), Nat. Soc. Profl. Engrs. Home: 129 E Meldram Saint Clair MI 48079 Office: Diamond Crystal Salt Co Inc 916 S Riverside Ave Saint Clair MI 48079

CRONICAN, RICHARD ALAN, computer company manager; b. Yonkers, N.Y., Sept. 5, 1943; s. John G. Sr., and Josephine M. (Ness) C.; student U. Ariz., 1966-74; m. Dana S. Yarian, July 3, 1965; children—Kimberly and Kelly (twins), Timothy Alan. Patrolman, police dept. City of Tucson, 1966-69, detective, 1969-70, programmer, analyst dept. fin., 1970-73, sys/prog supr., 1973-74, dir. dept. computer services, 1974-81; exec. dir., regional mgr., gen. mgr. Systems & Computer Technology Corp., Malvern, Pa., 1981—; guest lectr. U. Ariz., 1970—, Pima Coll., 1970—, Western Mich. U.; cons. City of Lincoln, Lancaster County, Nebr., Oakland County, Mich., Union County, N.J., Fresno County, Calif., City of Phoenix, S. Tucson, Shelby County, Tenn., Maricopa County, Ariz., City and County of San Francisco, City of Mpls., Minn. Community Coll. System, Peoria County. Ordained deacon, Roman Catholic Ch., 1976; bd. dirs. Armory Park Found., 1977—, AMIGOS Bibliog. Council, Dallas, 1979-80; chmn. Diocese of Tucson Pastoral Council, 1977-81, also adult religious instr.; mem. advisory council Pima Coll., Tucson, 1975-81. Served with USAF, 1961-65. Mem. Am. Mgmt. Assn., Adminstrv. Mgmt. Soc., Internat. Assn. Chiefs of Police, Lincoln C. of C., Urban and Regional Info. Systems Assn. (chmn. DP mgmt. spl. interest group), Data Processing Mgmt. Assn. Clubs: Rotary, Kiwanis. Home: 654 Thorncraft Dr West Chester PA 19380 Office: 4 Country View Rd Malvern PA 19355

CRONIGER, JAMES DEWEY, electrical engineer; b. Cleve., Apr. 20, 1930; s. Wilbur and Elloree A. (Dewey) C.; m. Patricia A. O'Donnell, Sept. 3, 1960; children—Mary Eileen, Colleen, James. B.Sc., Case Inst. Tech., 1952. Registered profl. engr., Ohio. Control engr. Clark Controller, Cleve., 1952-60; systems engr. Reliance Electric, Cleve., 1961-68, supr. fed. marine dept., 1968-74, product mgr., 1974-80, project mgr., 1980—. Precinct committeeman Republican Party, Euclid, Ohio, 1960-65. Served with U.S. Army, 1953-55. Mem. IEEE, Assn. of Iron and Steel Engrs. Republican. Roman Catholic. Club: Euclid Hockey Assn. (pres. 1979-80). Avocations: photography; skeet; ice skating; baseball; watercolor painting. Home: 75 E 217 St Euclid OH 44123 Office: Reliance Electric 24703 Euclid Ave Euclid OH 44117

CRONIN, JAMES WATSON, educator, physicist; b. Chgo., Sept. 29, 1931; s. James Farley and Dorothy (Watson) C.; A.B., So. Meth. U., 1951; Ph.D., U. Chgo., m. Annette Martin, Sept. 11, 1954; children—Cathryn, Emily, Daniel Watson. asso. Brookhaven Nat. Lab., 1955-58; mem. faculty Princeton U., 1958-71, prof. physics, 1965-71; prof. physics U. Chgo., 1971—; Loeb lectr. physics Harvard U., 1967. Recipient Research Corp. Am. award, 1967; John Price Wetherill medal Franklin Inst., 1976; E.O. Lawrence award ERDA, 1977; Nobel Prize in Physics, 1980; Sloan fellow, 1964-66; Guggenheim fellow, 1970-71, 82-83. Mem. Am. Acad. Arts and Scis., Nat. Acad. Sci. Participant early devel. spark chambers; co-discover CP-violation, 1964. Office: Dept Physics Univ Chicago Chicago IL 60637

CRONIN, RICHARD FRANK, banker; b. Topeka, Nov. 29, 1923; s. Frank J. and Florence M. Miller C.; m. Patricia E. Ellison, June 4, 1949 (dec.); children—Barbara Lovel, Marlynn Young, Michael. B.A., Loyola U., Chgo., 1952. With Northern Trust Bank, Chgo., 1952—; assoc. mgr., 1973, asst. mgr., 1973-81, mgr., 1981—; mgr., sec.-treas. No. Trust Safe Deposit Co., Chgo., 1981—, also dir. Served with USAAF, 1942-46. Mem. Am. Safe Deposit Assn. (exec. bd.), Ill. Safe Deposit Assn. (pres. exec. bd., recipient Presdl. award 1981). Office: Nor Trust Bank 50 S LaSalle St Chicago IL 60675

CROOKS, NORMAN MELVIN, tribal chairman; b. Morton, Minn., May 28, 1917; s. Amos and Ellen (Felix) C.; m. Edith Ross, Jan. 7, 1940; children—Norman W., Stanley R., Danny J., Michael A., George M., Alfred R. Ed. pub. schs. Field supt. Northstar Constrn. Co., Mpls.; laborer Asbestos, Inc., Mich.; line constrn. worker Union 120, Mpls.; chmn. Shakopee Mdewakanton Sioux Community, 1969—; sec.-treas. Minn. Intertribal Bd.; dir. Minn. Sioux Tribe. Served with USN, 1942-45. Recipient Honorable Mention award Intertribal Bd. Task Force on Indian Bingo; award Muscular Dystrophy Assn., 1983. Mem. Nat. Assn. Tribal Chairmen, Nat. Congress Am. Indians. Democrat. Episcopalian. Office: 2330 Sioux Trail NW Prior Lake MN 55372*

CROPSEY, HARMON GEORGE, state senator; b. Marcellus, Mich., Aug. 16, 1917; s. Elvaro and Marie Margaret (Coble) C.; m. Ruth Marian Lindsay, July 29, 1943; children—Robert, David, Chris, Alan, Carolyn, George, Lindsay Jo. B.S. in Agr., Iowa State U., 1938. Instr. animal sci. Mich. State U., East Lansing, 1939; 4-H Club agt. Iowa Extension Service, Vinton, 1939, 40; farm mgr. Iowa Canning Co., Vinton, 1941-42; farmer, Decatur, Mich., 1946-80; mem. Mich. Ho. of Reps., 1981-82, mem. Mich. Senate, 1983—; mem. Am. Legis. Exchange Council, Washington, 1982-85. Mem. Lewis-Cass Intermediate Sch. Dist. Bd., Cass County, Mich., 1959-64, Geneva Sch. Penn No. 1 Dist. Bd., Cass County, 1961-64. Served to lt. (j.g.) A.C., USN, 1942-45; ETO. Decorated D.F.C., Air medal. Mem. Am. Security Council (bd. policy 1975-85). Republican. Baptist. Office: Mich State Senate State Capitol Lansing MI 48909

CROSBY, FRED MCCLELLAN, retail home and office furnishings executive; b. Cleve., May 17, 1928; s. Fred Douglas and Marion Grace (Naylor) C.; grad. high sch.; m. Phendalyne D. Tazewell, Dec. 23, 1958; children—Fred, James, Llionicia. Vice pres. Seaway Flooring & Paving Co., Cleve., 1959-63; pres. Crosby Furniture Co., Inc., Cleve., 1963-; dir. First Intercity Banc Corp. Dir. adv. council Ohio Bd. Workmen's Compensation, 1974-82; chmn. Minority Econ. Devel. Corp., 1972-83; bd. dirs. Council Smaller Enterprise, 1973-80, Goodwill Industries, 1973-80, Woodruff Hosp., 1975-82, Cleve. Devel. Found., Greater Cleve. Growth Assn.; chmn. bd. dirs. Glenville YMCA, 1973-76; bd. dirs., treas. Urban League Cleve., 1971-78; mem. adv. council Small Bus. Assn.; bd. dirs. Forest City Hosp. Found., Cleve. State U. Found.; trustee Cleve. Playhouse, Eliza Bryant Ctr.; mem. Ohio State Boxing Commn., 1984—. Served with AUS, 1950-52. Recipient award bus. excellence Dept. Commerce, 1972; Presdl. award YMCA, 1974; Gov. Ohio award community action, 1973; named Family of Yr., Cleve. Urban League, 1971. Mem. Growth Assn. Cleve. (dir.), NAACP (v.p. Cleve. 1969-78), Ohio Council Retail Mchts. (dir.), Ohio Home Furnishing and Appliance Assn. (pres.). Exec. Order Ohio Commodore. Clubs: Mid-Day, Cleve. Play House, Harvard Bus. Sch., Rotary, Clevelander (Cleve.). Home: 2530 Richmond Rd Beachwood OH 44122 Office: 12435 St Clair Ave Cleveland OH 44108

CROSBY, PETER GERARD, marketing executive; b. Seattle, May 12, 1949; s. Richard Norton and Monica Ann (Hoffman) C.; m. Darlene Marie Hartmann, Apr. 1, 1981. A.B. in Econs., Stanford U., 1971; M.B.A., U. Wash., 1975. Dist. sales rep. Western Constrn. Products div. U.S. Gypsum Co., Chgo., 1971-73, sr. div. analyst Wood Fiber Products div., 1975-77, area mktg. mgr. Metal Products div., 1977-80, mgr. mktg. Gossen div., 1980—. Office: 2030 W Bender Rd Milwaukee WI 53209

CROSBY, ROBERT EUGENE, manufacturing company executive, pre-school corporation executive; m. Merrill, Wis., Feb. 19, 1935; s. Lynn L. and Edna J. (Olson) C.; m. Sandra J. Brugger, June 8, 1963 (div. 1983); children—Curt R., Darcy J. B.B.A., U. Wis., 1964, postgrad., Oshkosh, 1971-72. Prodn. planner Kimberly Clark, Neenah, Wis., 1964-67; operations analyst Consoli. Papers, Wisconsin Rapids, Wis., 1967-68, profn. and inventory control mgr., 1968-75, prodn. mgr., 1975-79; mfg. mgr. Consoweld Corp., Wisconsin Rapids, Wis., 1979—; owner Sunshine Pre Sch., Inc., 1979—. Served with USAF, 1953-57. Mem. Paper Industry Mgmt. Assn. (chmn. MIS com. 1970-75), Nat. Equipment Mfrs. Assn., Composite Cand & Tube Inst. Clubs: Bulls Eye Country, Tri-City Curling, Packs & Paddles Canoe (Wisconsin Rapids). Home: 1431 29th Ave S Apt H Wisconsin Rapids WI 54494 Office: 700 Durabeauty Ln Wisconsin Rapids WI 54494

CROSS, JANET LAVERN, nurse; b. East St. Louis, Ill., Aug. 8, 1944; d. Henry Edward and Gustava Lucille (Titus) Pritchett; m. Robert Lee Cross, Dec. 10, 1967 (div. Dec. 1976); 1 dau., Ja'Net Annette. B.N., So. Ill. U., 1972. Staff nurse Vets. John Cochran Hosp., St. Louis, 1972-73, St. Mary's Hosp., East St. Louis, 1974; staff nurse-pub. health East Side Health, East St. Louis, 1974-76; staff nurse Incarnate Word Hosp., St. Louis, 1976—. Mem. parent group, project follow-through Dunbar Sch., East St. Louis, 1981-83. Mem. Ill. Nurses Assn., Am. Nurses Assn., Am. Nurses Found. Baptist.

CROSS, NANNA AILENE, dietitian; b. Ogallala, Nebr., June 29, 1943; d. Wilsie Logan and Ruth Lillian (Rasmussen) C.; m. Prayoj Promkasetrin, June 22, 1969 (div. Mar. 1973). B.S. in Vocat. Home Econs., Kearney State Coll., 1965; M.S. in Food Sci. and Nutrition, Colo. State U., 1969. Tchr. Ainsworth Pub. Schs., Nebr., 1965-67; clin. and research dietitian U. Mo. Med. Ctr., Columbia, 1970-78; asst. prof. nutrition and med. dietetics U. Ill.-Chgo. Health Scis. Ctr., 1978-84; adminstrv. clin. dietitian St. Luke's Hosp., Kansas City, Mo., 1984—. Contbr. articles to profl. jours. Mem. Am. Dietetic Assn. (registered), Kansas City Dietetic Assn., Nutrition Today Soc., Am. Assn. Diabetes Educators, Sigma Xi. Unitarian. Home: 300 W 46th Terr 2W Kansas City MO 64112 Office: St Luke's Hosp 44th St at Wernall Rd Kansas City MO 64111

CROSS, RAYMOND JOSEPH, JR., energy management executive; b. Ithaca, N.Y., July 3, 1935; s. Raymond Joseph and Janet (Cleveland) C.; B.S.M.E., Ga. Inst. Tech., Atlanta, 1958; postgrad. U. Tampa, 1961; M.S. in Indsl. Mgmt., Purdue U., Hammond, Ind., 1972; m. Marguerite Adele Ciani, Nov. 17, 1956; children—Raymond Joseph, John Alexander, Donald James. With Linde div. Union Carbide Corp., Chgo., 1958—, product mgr., N.Y.C., 1972-74, ops. mgr., Chgo., 1974-76, region mgr. Central U.S., Cleve., 1976-77, Midwest regional mgr., Chgo., 1977-82; dir. Energy Mgmt., Danbury, Conn., 1982—; v.p. UCAR Interam., Danbury, 1983—; dir. East Chicago Machine Tool Corp. Mem. tax adv. council Lake County, Ind., 1969-70; mem. adv. council businessmen Congressman Adam Benjamin, 1978-82; bd. dirs. ARC, 1972; pres. Griffith United Fund, 1967-68; treas. Lake County Young Republicans, 1965-66. Served to capt. U.S. Army, 1958-59. Mem. ASME, Ga. Inst. Tech. Alumni Assn., Purdue U. Alumni Assn. Lake County, Purdue U. Lafayette Alumni Assn. Presbyterian. Author: Guided Missile Propellants, 1959.

CROSSLAND, WILLIAM EDWARD, safety engineer; b. Detroit, July 13, 1932; s. Ernest Edward and Clara Gertrude (Davis) C.; B.S. in Safety Engring., U. Ala., 1960; postgrad. U. So. Calif.; m. Helen Charlene Thompson, July 23, 1976. Founder, chmn. bd. Internat. Safety Cons., Inc., 1969-81; dir. safety Handy Andy Corp., San Antonio, 1972-73; safety engr. Royal Globe Ins. Co., 1973-74; dir. safety U.S. Air Force, Oklahoma City, 1974-77; safety and health mgr. Dept. of Labor, Kansas City, Mo., 1977-84; safety mgr. U.S. Air Force, Hickam AFB, Hawaii, 1984—; tchr. safety engring. Okla. State U.; cons. AF Community Coll.; mem. energy com. Fed. Exec. Bd., 1979-84. Vol. Kansas City chpt. ARC. Served with USAF, 1951-72. Decorated AF Commendation Medal with 3 oak leaf clusters, AF Meritorious Service Medal with 2 oak leaf clusters; named Top Civilian Safety Dir. in AF, 1974; registered profl. engr., Calif.; cert. safety profl., Ill.; lic. pvt. pilot; cert. police officer, Tex.; 3d degree black belt jud. instr. Mem. Assn. Fed. Safety and Health Profls. (past pres.), Am. Soc. Safety Engrs., Vets. Safety Internat. (pres. 1985), Nat. Safety Mgmt. Soc., System Safety Soc., Am. Legion, Baptist. Contbr. articles to profl. jours.; composer: Never, 1958; Is It the Same, 1978. Trumpeter, guitarist.

CROTTY, JOHN WILLIAM, optometrist; b. Henryetta, Okla., Nov. 27, 1951; s. Patrick Herald and Jeanine Emily (Burt) C.; m. Debra Jo Cronin, Aug. 3, 1974; children—Ryan, Robin, Richard. B.S., Pacific U., 1974, O.D., 1976. Pvt. practice optometry Drs. Crotty & Crotty P.C., Auburn, Nebr., 1976—. Mem. Dist. 29 Bd. Edn., Auburn, 1978—. Named Outstanding Jaycee, Auburn Jaycees, 1980. Mem. Am. Optometric Assn., Nebr. Optometric Assn. Republican. Roman Catholic. Lodge: K.C. (fin. sec. 1977—). Avocations: golf, racquetball, basketball, tennis. Home: 711 13th St Auburn NE 68305 Office: Drs Crotty and Crotty PC 909 13th St Auburn NE 68305

CROUCH, ROBERT ALLEN, JR., labor relations official; b. St. Joseph, Mo., Aug. 9, 1955; s. Robert Allen and Arvella Bernadine (Hughes) C. B.S. in Psychology and Communications, Southwest Mo. State U., 1978. Contract tchr. Fed. Med. Ctr. for Prisoners, Springfield, Mo., 1976-78; juvenile program specialist Mo. Council on Criminal Justice, Jefferson City, 1979-81; asst. to dir. State of Mo. Dept. Labor and Indsl. Relations, Jefferson City, 1981—; also gospel minister. Chmn. Black History Week Commn., Southwest Mo. State U., 1973-77; active Human Rights Commn., Springfield, 1973-78. Recipient Outstanding Service award Fed. Med. Ctr. for Prisoners, 1977. Mem. Jaycees Internat., Optimists Internat., NAACP, Mo. Black Leadership Assn., Internat. Assn. Personnel in Employment Security, Employment Security Club, Chi Alpha (pres. 1977), Alpha Phi Alpha. Democrat. Home: 2309 Southridge St Apt E Jefferson City MO 65101 Office: 421 E Dunklin St Jefferson City MO 65101

CROVELLA, MICHAEL LAURENCE, college administrator; b. Flint, Mich., June 7, 1928; s. Raymond Valero and Ernestine (Ellegranza) C.; m. Carole June Dreuth, May 24, 1958; children—Tina, Michele, Michael. B.A., Mich. State U., 1957. Fin. analyst Chrysler Corp., Highland Park, Mich., 1957-60; office mgr. Delta Coll., Univ. Ctr., Mich., 1960-64, bus. mgr., 1964-82, v.p. bus. affairs, 1982—, sec. to bd. trustees, 1965—. Served cpl. U.S. Army, 1950-52. Mem. Mich. Community Coll. Bus. Officers Assn. Republican. Roman Catholic. Avocations: Tennis; racquetball; skiing; softball; trailbiking. Home: 3475 Crestmont St Saginaw MI 48603 Office: Bus Affairs Office Delta Coll Delta Rd University Center MI 48710

CROW, ERNEST WHITAKER, cardiology educator; b. Wichita, Kans., Jan. 6, 1920; s. Ernest and Lena S. Crow; m. Bertha M. Sullivan, Sept. 19, 1943; children—Barbara, John, Marilyn, Richard. A.B., Friends U., 1942; M.D., U. Kans., 1944. Diplomate Am. Bd. Internal Medicine, Am. Bd. Cardiovascular Disease. Intern Wesley Med. Ctr., Wichita, Kans., 1944-45, resident in internal medicine, Wichita, 1945-46, 48-49, mem. staff, 1949—; sr. attending staff Grad. Sch. Medicine, U. Pa., Phila., 1951-52; fellow in cardiology U. Kans., Kansas City, 1959-60, asst. clin. prof. medicine, 1963-72, clin. prof., 1972-73; prof., dept. chmn. U. Kans., Wichita, 1973-74, clin. prof., 1974—; mem. staff VA Ctr. Contbr. articles to profl. jours. Served to capt. M.C., U.S Army, 1946-48. Fellow ACP, Am. Coll. Cardiology; mem. Am. Soc. Internal Medicine, Am. Heart Assn., Sedgwick County Med. Soc. Congregationalist. Lodge: Rotary. Avocations: golf, travel, reading. Home: 402 Longford St Wichita KS 67206 Office: Internal Medicine Assocs PA 3243 E Murdock Suite 500 Wichita KS 67208

CROW, RICHARD RONALD, management consultant; b. Point Marion, Pa., Aug. 19, 1915; s. Benjamin K. and Alice (Richards) C.; B.S., California (Pa.) Coll., 1936; M.A., Ohio State U., 1936; m. Mary Grace Jessup, Aug. 16, 1951; children—Megan Leslie, Philip Edward. Tng. dir. Curtiss-Wright Corp., Columbus, Ohio, 1941-45; corporate tng. dir. U.S. Rubber Co., N.Y.C., 1945-53; mgmt. devel. dir., asst. mgr. indsl. relations, regional mgr. indsl. relations Continental Oil Co., Houston and Ft. Worth, 1953-59; v.p. personnel Stouffer Foods Corp., Cleve., 1959-68; corporate v.p.-human resources Sherwin-Williams Co., Cleve., 1968-78; pres. R.R. Crow Co., Inc., Lakewood, Ohio, 1978—. Mem. council on devel., edn. and tng. Nat. Conf. Bd. Accredited personnel exec. Recipient Laureate citation award Epsilon Pi Tau, 1946. Mem. Am. Mgmt. Assn. (manpower planning and devel. commn.). Home: 3858 W Surrey Ct Rocky River OH 44116 Office: 14701 Detroit Ave Suite 511 Lakewood OH 44107

CROW, SAM ALFRED, federal judge; b. Topeka, May 5, 1926; s. Samuel Wheadon and Phyllis K. (Brown) C.; m. Ruth M. Rush, Jan. 30, 1948; children—Sam A., Dan W. B.A., U. Kans., 1949; J.D., Washburn U., 1952. Bar: Kans. 1952, U.S. Dist. Ct. Kans. 1952, U.S. Mil. Ct. Appeals 1953, U.S. Supreme Ct. 1962, U.S. Ct. Appeals (10th cir.) 1963. Law clk. Rooney, Dickinson & Prager, 1952-53; ptnr. Rooeny, Dikcinson, Prager & Crow, Topeka, 1953-63, Dickinson, Crow, Skoog & Honeyman, Topeka, 1963-70; sr. ptnr. Crow & Skoog, Topeka, 1971-75; U.S. magistrate, part-time 1973-75, full time, 1975-81; judge U.S. Dist. Ct. Kans., Wichita, 1981—; lectr. Washburn U. Sch. Law, assns., convs. Bd. rev. Boy Scouts Am., 1960-70, cubmaster, 1957-60; mem. vestry Grace Episcopal Ch., Topeka, 1960-65; chmn. Kans. March of Dimes, 1959, bd. dirs., 1960-65; bd. dirs. Topeka Council Chs., 1960-70; mem. Mulvane Art Soc., 1965—, Kans. Hist. Soc., 1960—; pres., v.p. PTA. Fellow Acad. Internat. Law and Sci.; mem. ABA (del. Nat. Conf. Spl. Ct. Judges 1978, 79), Kans. Bar Assn. (trustee 1970-76, chmn. mil. law sect. 1965, 67, 72, 74, 75), Assn. Trial Lawyers Am., Kans. Trial Lawyers Assn. (sec. 1959-60, pres. 1960-61), Nat. Assn. U.S. Magistrates (com. discovery abuse), Topeka Assn. (chmn. jud. reform com., chmn. bench and bar com., chmn. criminal law com.), Wichita Bar Assn., Topeka Lawyers Club (sec. 1964-65, pres. 1965-66), Res. Officers Assn., Am. Legion, Delta Theta Phi, Sigma Alpha Epsilon. Served to col. JAGC, USAR, 1973—. Club: Shawnee Country. Lodges: Elks, Kiwanis. Office: 401 N Market St Suite 322 Wichita KS 67202

CROWDER, BARBARA LYNN, lawyer; b. Mattoon, Ill., Feb. 3, 1956; d. Robert Dale and Martha Elizabeth (Harrison) C.; m. Lawrence Owen Taliana, Apr. 17, 1982; children—Paul Joseph, Robert Lawrence. B.A., U. Ill., 1978, J.D., 1981. Bar: Ill. 1981. Assoc., Louis E. Olivero, Peru, Ill., 1981-82; asst. state's atty. Madison County (Ill.), Edwardsville, 1982-84; ptnr. Robbins & Crowder, Edwardsville, 1985—. Named Best Oral Advocate, Moot Ct. Bd., 1979; recipient Parliamentary Debate award U. Ill., 1978. named Outstanding Sr., Phi Alpha Delta, 1981. Mem. Ill. Bar Assn., ABA, Phi Alpha Delta, Women Lawyers Met. East (v.p. 1985), LWV, Edwardsville Bus. and Profl. Women. Democrat. Club: Women of Moose, Order Eastern Star. Home: 982 Surrey Dr Edwardsville IL 62025 Office: PO Box 451 Edwardsville IL 62025

CROWL, SAMUEL RENNINGER, university administrator; English educator; b. Toledo, Oct. 9, 1940; s. Lester Samuel and Margaret Elizabeth (Renninger) C.; m. Susan Richardson, Dec. 29, 1963; children—Miranda Paine, Samuel Emerson. A.B., Hamilton Coll., 1962; M.A., Ind. U., 1969, Ph.D., 1970. Resident lectr. Ind. U., Indpls., 1967-69; asst. prof. English, Ohio U., Athens, 1970-75, assoc. prof., 1975-80, prof., 1980—, dean of Univ. Coll., 1981—; cons. NEH, Washington, 1980—; observer Royal Shakespeare Co. Co-author: Ohio University's Educational Plan, 1977-78. Assoc. editor jour. Ohio Rev., 1974—. Contbr. articles to profl. and Shakespearian jours. Recipient O'Bleness award for pub. broadcasting Ctr. Telecommunications, Ohio U., 1976. Fellow Royal Soc. Arts (London), Nat. Humanities Faculty, Ohio Shakespeare Assn. (founding mem.), Ohio U. Alumni Assn. (hon.), Phi Kappa Phi. Club: University (Chgo.). Avocations: theater, opera, ballet, Detroit Tigers. Office: Ohio U Univ Coll 140 Chubb Hall Athens OH 45701

CROWLEY, ANNE STAHL, advertising agency executive; b. Independence, Mo., Aug. 21, 1921; d. William Thomas and Nellie (Carey) Couser; m. David Warren Stahl, Aug. 30, 1941 (div. 1971); children—John Mitchell, Charlotte Anne Stahl Ameter, Margaret Alisa Greer, Barbara Lynn Stahl Fitzgibbons; m. Joseph A. Crowley, Jan. 5, 1974; children—Patrick, Kathy, Katie. Copywriter, prodn. mgr. Robert L. Wilson Co., Tulsa, 1938-41; copywriter, girl Friday, Ritchie Safford Advt., 1941; clk. Airco, Houston, 1942-43; pres. Stahl Assocs., Inc., Maumee, Ohio, 1959—. Office: 219 W Wayne St Maumee OH 43537

CROWLEY, CORNELIUS JOSEPH, emeritus linguistics educator, publishing company executive; b. N.Y.C., Mar. 21, 1911; s. Florence Francis and Helen (Sheehan) C.; m. Frances Felicia Geyer, Sept. 28, 1948; children—Veronica, Robert. B.A., CUNY, 1938; M.A., NYU, 1941, Ph.D., 1951. Cert. secondary tchr., N.Y. Tchr. English, Spanish and Latin, Kohut Sch., Harrison, N.Y., 1942-43; sr. translator Naval Censorship, N.Y.C., 1943-45; instr. Bergen Coll., Teaneck, N.J., 1946-48; asst. prof. U. Wyo., Laramie, 1948-50; asst. prof. to prof. linguistics St. Louis U., 1950-75, prof. emeritus, 1975—; pres. and editor in-chief Heartland Books, Cape Girardeau, Mo., 1972—. Author: Legend of the Wanderings of the Spear of Longinus, 1972. Translator: A Choice of Propertius, 1976, rev. 1981. Contbr. articles to profl. jours. Recipient Cert. of Merit, U.S. Govt., 1945. Mem. Linguistic Soc. of Am., Renaissance Soc. of Am., Am. Oriental Soc., Medieval Acad. of Am., Internat. Linguistic Assn., Phi Sigma (moderator 1952-60) Romance Language Soc. Democrat. Roman Catholic. Avocations: toy trains; studying unusual languages; attempting to decipher Minoan Linear A. Home: 515 North Sprigg Cape Girardeau MO 63701

CROWLEY, JOSEPH MICHAEL, electrical engineer, educator; b. Phila., Sept. 9, 1940; s. Joseph Edward and Mary Veronica (McCall) C.; B.S., M.I.T., 1962, M.S., 1963, Ph.D., 1965; m. Barbara Ann Sauerwald, June 22, 1963; children—Joseph W., Kevin, James, Michael, Daniel. Vis. scientist Max Planck Inst., Goettingen, W. Ger., 1965-66; asst. prof. elec. engring., U. Ill., Urbana, 1966-69, assoc. prof., 1969-78, prof., dir. Applied Electrostats. Research Lab., 1978—; pres. JMC Inc., 1981—; cons. to several corps. Pres., Champaign-Urbana Bd. Cath. Edn., 1978-80. Gen. Motors scholar, 1958-62; AEC fellow, 1962-65; NATO fellow, 1965-66. Mem. IEEE (sr.), Electrostats. Soc. Am., Am. Phys. Soc., Soc. Inf. Display, Mensa. Roman Catholic. Contbr. articles to profl. jours.; patentee ink jet printers. Office Dept Elec Engring U Ill Urbana IL 61801*

CROWLEY, THOMAS EDWARD, security specialist, consultant; b. Cleve., Feb. 18, 1941; s. Thomas F. and Rita C. (Roach) C.; m. Maureen Ann Ginley, Apr. 11, 1964; children—Beth and Judy (twins), Dawn. Degree in Criminology, U. Calif.-Berkeley, 1962; postgrad. Northwestern U., 1964-65, Cleve. State U., 1970, 71, 72; M.B.A., Ohio State U., 1974. Investigator, Protective Services, 1960-65; security mgr. Dairyman's Milk Corp., 1965-67; asst. dir. Cook United, Inc., Maple Heights, Ohio, 1968-71; security dir. Fairview Gen. Hosp., Cleve., 1971; corp. dir. security and safety Chempack Industries, Inc., Chgo., 1971-74; asst. dir. security and safety Ohio Lottery Commn., Cleve., from 1974, dir., to 1978; dir. security Shaker Sq. Security Program, Cleve., 1978—; security cons. Friends of Shaker Sq., Cleve. Catholic Dioceses. Mem. speakers bur. Cuyahoga (Ohio) Criminal Justice Council; asst. ice hockey coach St. Edward High Sch., Lakewood, Ohio, 1974, 75, 76; coach varsity ice hockey Valley Forge (Ohio) High Sch., 1977, 78, 79. Named One of Ohio's Finest Citizens, Ohio Ho. of Reps.; recipient tribute U.S. Congress. Mem. Internat. Assn. Chiefs of Police, Am. Soc. Indsl. Security, Nat. Assn. Chiefs of Police, ABA, Internat. Assn. Arson Investigators, Internat. Assn. Computer Security, Ohio Crime Prevention Assn., Nat. Assn. Sch. Security Dirs., Inst. for Criminal Justice Ethics, Can. Police Combat Assn., Cleve. Restoration Soc., Nat. Coll. Hock Coaches Assn., Philatelic Soc., Soc. Philatelic Ams. Home: 27450 Cottonwood Trail North Olmsted OH 44070 Office: Shaker Sq Security Program 13221 Shaker Sq Cleveland OH 44120

CROWN, LESTER, business executive; b. Chgo., June 7, 1925; s. Henry and Rebecca (Kranz) C.; m. Renee Schine, Dec. 28, 1950; children—Arie Steven, James Schine, Patricia Ann, Daniel Morris, Susan Martha, Sara Beth, Janet Schine. B.S. in Chem. Engring., Northwestern U., 1947; M.B.A., Harvard U., 1949. Instr. math. Northwestern U., Evanston, Ill., 1946-47; v.p., dir., chem. engr. Marblehead Lime Co., Chgo., 1950-56, pres., 1956-66; v.p., dir. Material Service Corp. div. Gen. Dynamics Corp., Chgo., 1953-66, pres., 1970-83, chmn. bd., 1983—; exec. v.p. Gen. Dynamics Corp., St. Louis, 1970—, dir., 1974—, exec. com., 1983—; pres. Henry Crown & Co., Chgo., 1970—; dir. Trans World Corp., Trans World Airlines, N.Y.C., Chgo. Pacific Corp., Chgo. Profl. SportsCorp.; ptnr. N.Y. Yankees Partnership, 1973—. Trustee Northwestern U., Michael Reese Hosp. and Med. Ctr.; bd. dirs. Lyric Opera Chgo., Children's Meml. Hosp., Chgo.; mem. bd. overseers Jewish Theol. Sem., N.Y.C. Recipient Silver plaque NCCJ, Chgo., 1966; Human Rights medallion Am. Jewish Com., Chgo., 1979; award Jewish Theol. Sem., 1980; Julius Rosenwald Meml. award Jewish Fedn. Met. Chgo., 1983. Clubs: Lake Shore Country (Glencoe, Ill.); Northmoor Country (Highland Park, Ill.); Standard, Econ., Carlton, Chgo., Comml., Mid Am. (Chgo.); Marco Polo (N.Y.C.). Office: Material Service Corp 300 W Washington St Chicago IL 60606

CROWNER, DAVID WELLS, dentist; b. Toledo, Oct. 28, 1935; s. Harold Penniman and Jeanette Helen (Bremer) C.; student Purdue U., 1953-55, U. Toledo, 1955-56; D.D.S., Ohio State U., 1960; m. Barbara Ann Prickman, Dec. 27, 1958; children—Susan Lynne, John David. Pvt. practice dentistry, Toledo, 1962-72, Sylvania, Ohio, 1972—. Pres., Renworc, Inc., Sylvania, 1969—. Finance chmn. Sylvania Sch. Bd. Levy, 1973; pres. St. Paul's Lutheran Ch., Toledo; pres. Sylvania Downtown Bus. Assn.; gen. chmn. Holiday Parade, Sylvania, 1983 Served with Dental Corps, USNR, 1960-62, comdr. Res. Decorated Navy Commendation medal. Mem. Am., Ohio, Toledo (program chmn. 1971-72, clinic day chmn. 1968-69, chmn. continuing edn. 1976-77) dental assns., Beta Beta Beta, Alpha Epsilon Delta, Phi Gamma Delta (bd. dirs.). Club: International Torch (membership chmn. 1975—, dir. 1981—, pres.) (Toledo). Home: 6739 Fifth Ave Sylvania OH 43560

CROWNINSHIELD, ROY DOUGLAS, research scientist, medical device executive; b. Worcester, Mass., Sept. 25, 1948; m. Linda Cunnick; children—Amy, Sara. B.S. in Mech. Engring., U. Vt., 1971, M.S. in Mech. Engring., 1973, Ph.D. in Mech. Engring., 1975. Assoc. research scientist U. Iowa, Iowa City, 1975-80, research scientist 1980-81, assoc. prof., 1981-83; dir. research Zimmer, Inc., Warsaw, Ind., 1983—. Author book chpts. Contbr. numerous articles to profl. jours. Served to capt. USAR, 1971-81. Recipient NIH Research Career Devel. award, 1979-84. Mem. Orthopaedic Research Soc., ASME, The Hip Soc. (Otto E. Aufranc award 1981), Am. Acad. Orthopaedic Surgeons (Kappa Delta Young Investigator's award 1982), Sigma Xi. Avocation: tennis. Home: Rt 9 Box 124 Warsaw IN 46580 Office: PO Box 708 Warsaw IN 46580

CROWSON, WALTER COLLON, dentist; b. Detroit, Oct. 12, 1932; s. Walter Stanley and Leone (Collon) C.; B.A., Mich. State U., 1957; D.D.S., U. Mich., 1958; m. Bonnie Lou Kremer, Nov. 30, 1974; 1 dau. by previous marriage—Jony Collon. Practice dentistry, Ferndale, Mich., 1958—. Dental dir. Detroit Orthopaedic Clinic, 1959—; chmn. Dental Adv. Bd. to Ferndale, 1968-74; chmn. Oakland County Dental Vocational Adv. Com.; cons. Dept. Edn. State of Mich.; cons. dental hygiene program Oakland Community Coll., 1975-76; cons. Hartland Center for Handicapped, 1978—; dental surgery staff Detroit Children's Hosp., 1979—; cons. Spl. project U. Mich., 1981. Pres. Graefield Condominium Assn., Birmingham, Mich., 1972-78; bd. dirs. Tri-County Dental Health Council, 1975—, Spirit of Detroit Assn., 1983—. Recipient Citizen of Year award Clawson Troy Elks Club, 1974. Sigma Gamma Found. grantee, 1972. Mem. Am., Mich. dental assns., Mich. Assn. Professions, Oakland County Dental Soc. (chmn. aux. personnel 1974-76), Acad. of Dentistry for Handicapped, Birmingham Power Squadron, Lambda Chi Alpha, Delta Sigma Delta. Elk. Clubs: Detroit Boat (rear commodore 1982, vice commodore 1984, commodore 1985, bd. dirs. 1982—), Huron Pointe Yacht (Mt. Clemens, Mich.), Detroit River Yachting Assn. Home: 1970 Graefield St Birmingham MI 48008 Office: 26789 Woodward St Huntington Woods MI 48070

CROYDON, MICHAEL BENET, sculptor, design educator; b. Woodford, England, July 2, 1931; came to U.S., 1968; s. Frank Edgar and Amelia (Orchard) C.; m. Blanche Pemberton, Jan. 5, 1956 (div. 1971); children—Lucia Jane and Abigail Elizabeth; m. Beverly Gay Hunter, Feb. 25, 1973. A.R.C.A., Royal Coll. of Art, London, 1956. Lectr., Exeter Coll. of Art, Exeter, Devonshire, England, 1958-62; chmn. dept. of design U. of East Africa, Nairobi, Kenya, 1962-68; prof. art Lake Forest Coll., Ill., 1968—. Author: monograph Ivan Albright, 1978, catalogue Graven Image, 1978. Recipient Inland Steel and Ryerson Steel award, 1981. Mem. Arts Club of Chgo., Internat. Sculpture Ctr., AAUP, Coll. Art Assn. Home: 409 East Illinois Rd Lake Forest IL 60045 Office: Lake Forest Coll Sheridan Rd Lake Forest IL 60045

CRUTCHFIELD, JOYCE ELAINE, nursing educator; b. Hereford, Tex., Jan. 28, 1934; d. Clifford Nolan and Almeda Norine (Witherspoon) Penman; married; children—Shelly Elaine, David Alan. B.S.N., U. No. Colo., 1974; M.S., Colo. U., 1976. R.N., Tex., Colo., Nebr. From staff nurse to head nurse Weld County Gen. Hosp., Greeley, Colo., 1969-76, assoc. dir. nursing, 1976-79; asst. prof., baccalaureate nursing chair U. Nebr. Med. Ctr., Lincoln, 1979-84, asst. prof. grad. nursing faculty U. Nebr. Med. Ctr., Omaha, 1984—. Served to lt. Nurse Corps, USN, 1957-60. Mem. Nebr. Nurses Assn. (1st v.p. 1982-86), AAUW, Sigma Theta Tau. Home: 4825 Goldenrod Ln Lincoln NE 68512 Office: U Nebr Med Ctr 42d and Dewey Ave Omaha NE 68105

CRUTHIRD, ROBERT LEE, sociology educator; b. LeFlore County, Miss., Dec. 10, 1944; s. Harvie and Mary Florence (Black) C.; m. Julie Mae Boyd, Dec. 17, 1965; 1 son, Robert Lee. M.A., U. Ill.-Chgo., 1976. Correctional counselor Ill. Dept. Corrections, Joliet, 1977-78; instr. in sociology Kennedy-King Coll., Chgo., 1978-80, 81-84, asst. prof., 1984—, dir. instl. research, 1980-81; cons. Ednl. Mgmt. Assocs., 1981-82. Served with U.S. Army, 1965-67. Crime and delinquency research tng. fellow U. Ill.-Chgo., 1976-77; NEH fellow, summer 1983. Mem. Am. Sociol. Assn., Assn. Instl. Research, Assn. Study of Afro-Am. Life and History, Phi Theta Kappa (named to Ill. Hall of Honor 1984). Democrat. Baptist. Home: 10250 S Elizabeth Chicago IL 60643 Office: 6800 S Wentworth Suite 326E Chicago IL 60621

CRUTSINGER, ROBERT KEANE, wholesale consumer products executive; b. St. Louis, 1930. Grad. Quincy Coll., 1955. With NCR Corp., 1960-70; with Wetterau Inc., Hazelwood, Mo., 1970—, dir., 1973—; exec. v.p., 1973-79, pres. food services group, 1979, pres., chief operating officer, 1979—, dir., 1973—; dir. Centerre Bank of Florissant, Mo. Served with AUS, 1952-54. Mem. Nat. Am. Wholesale Grocers Assn. (dir.). Office: Wetterau Inc 8920 Pershall Rd Hazelwood MO 63042

CRUZ, ERASMO (EDDIE), broadcasting executive; b. Brownsville, Tex., July 10, 1940; s. Roberto and Melchora (Vélez) C.; divorced; children—Erasmo, Jr., Donnie, Ricardo, María Elena. Diploma in broadcast engring. Elkins Inst., 1973. Lic. broadcaster, Ohio. Owner, operator Ed and Phils Sohio, Fort Seneca, Ohio, 1960-65, LaHacienda Restarant, Fremont, Ohio, 1965-82; staff engr. Sta. WFOB, Fostoria, Ohio, 1973-76; staff engr., producer Sta. WGTE-TV, Toledo, 1973-76; counselor, researcher Sandusky County Health Dept., Fremont, 1976-79; pres., gen. mgr. Sta. WLCO-FM, Clyde, Ohio, 1975—; mem. gov.'s task force on Hispanics, Columbus, Ohio, 1985, gov.'s council travel and tourism, 1984. Recipient Businessman award Mecha-Toledo U., 1985. Mem. Ohio Assn. Broadcasters, Nat. Radio Broadcasters Assn. Avocation: Music. Office: WLCO-FM 1859 W McPherson Clyde OH 43410

CSIZMADIA, GAIL ROSA, retail executive, market consultant; b. Bklyn., Sept. 21, 1957; d. Bela Kenneth and Ellinor Margrete (Finvag) C. Student Ohio State U., 1975. Store mgr. Beehive, Inc., N. Olmsted, Ohio, 1974-79, v.p. ops., 1979—; cons. Collectors' Info. Bureau, Winnetka, Ill., 1982—, Greenbook Soc., East Setauket, N.Y., 1983—; v.p. Great No. Mall Mchts. Assn., North Olmsted, 1984—, mem. exec. com., 1983—. Named for highest sales per sq. foot Great Northern Mall, 1983-85. Mem. North Olmsted C. of C., Royal Doulton, Goebel Coll. Club, Precious Moments, Sebastian Miniatures. Republican. Lutheran. Home: 27427 Westown Blvd Westlake OH 44145 Office: Beehive Gift Shop Inc 5108 Great No Mall North Olmsted OH 44070

CUBBERLY, FRED DONALD, JR., product identification company official; b. Dayton, Ohio, Aug. 10, 1948; s. Fred D. and Lucile R. (Fitzgerald) C.; m. Deborah K. Redrick, Mar. 4, 1972; children—Dana N., Diane M. A.A., Sinclair Community Coll., 1970, Assoc. Sci. in Bus. Adminstrn., 1972, Assoc. Applied Sci. in Mgmt., 1974, Assoc. Applied Sci. in Procurement and Materials Mgmt., 1980; B.S. in Mgmt., Wright State U., 1978. Prodn. scheduler Dayton-Walther Corp., Dayton, Ohio, 1967-69, prodn. control supr., 1969-72, prodn. control specialist, 1978-79, corp. sr. buyer, 1979-81; purchasing mgr. Monarch Marking Co., Dayton, 1981-84, bus. unit mgr., 1984—; adj. assoc. prof. mgmt. Wright State U.; lectr. Sinclair Community Coll. Chmn., Miamisburg (Ohio) Community Devel. Adv. Council, 1979-82; mem. Miamisburg Library Renovation Com., 1982; coach Little League baseball, Miamisburg; chmn. Monarch Marking Co. United Way campaign, 1983, 84. Named Outstanding Mgmt. Grad., Wright State U., 1978. Fellow Am. Prodn. and Inventory Control Soc. (cert.); mem. Purchasing Mgmt. Assn. Dayton, Nat. Assn. Purchasing Mgmt. (cert.), Miami Valley Mgmt. Assn., Phi Theta Kappa, Beta Gamma Sigma. Democrat. Mem. Ch. of Christ. Home: 704 Evans Ave Miamisburg OH 45342 Office: SR 725 and Byers Rd Miamisburg OH 45342 also PO Box 608 Dayton OH 45401

CUDAHY, RICHARD DICKSON, federal appeals judge; b. Milw., Feb. 2, 1926; s. Michael Francis and Alice (Dickson) C.; m. Ann Featherston, July 14, 1956 (dec. Nov. 1974); children—Richard Dickson, Norma Kathleen, Theresa Ellen, Daniel Michael, Michaela Alice; m. Janet Schleeper Stuart, July 17, 1976; children—Marguerite Lois, Patrick George. Student Canterbury Sch., New Milford, Conn., 1943; B.S., U.S. Mil. Acad., 1948; J.D., Yale U., 1955; LL.D., Ripon Coll., 1981. Bar: Conn. 1955, D.C. 1957, Ill. 1957, Wis. 1961. Law clk. to chief judge U.S. Ct. Appeals, 2d Circuit, N.Y.C., 1955-56; asst. to legal advisor Dept. State, Washington, 1956-57; assoc., ptnr. Isham, Lincoln & Beale, Chgo., 1957-61, 1976-79; pres. Patrick Cudahy Inc., Cudahy, Wis., 1961-71; ptnr. Godfrey & Kahn, Milw., 1972; commr., chmn. Wis. Pub. Service Commn., Madison, 1972-75; judge U.S. Ct. Appeals, 7th Circuit, Chgo., 1979—; lectr. Marquette U. Sch. Law, Milw., 1961-66, 1973-74; vis. prof. law U. Wis., Madison, 1966-67; professorial lectr. George Washington U. Law Ctr., 1978-79. Mem. Milw. Harbor Commn., 1964-66; pres. Milw. Urban League, 1965-66; trustee Environ Def. Fund, Washington, 1976-79; mem. vis. com. U. Chgo. Sch. Law, 1984—, Am. Law Inst., Phila., 1984—. Served to 1st lt. USAF, 1948-50. Mem. ABA (spl. com. on energy law 1978-84), Wis. Bar Assn., Milw. Bar Assn., Chgo. Bar Assn., Ill. Bar, Conn. Bar., D.C. Bar. Democrat. Roman Catholic. Office: US Court Appeals 7th Circuit 219 S Dearborn St Chicago IL 60604

CUDDY, PAUL GERARD, pharmacist, educator; b. Boston, Apr. 30, 1954; s. John Donald and Catherine Patricia (Glancy) C.; m. Elizabeth Ann Purcell, Aug. 13, 1977 (div. 1980). B.S. in Pharmacy, Mass. Coll. Pharmacy, 1978; D.Pharmacy, U. Mo., 1980. Registered pharmacist, Mass., Mo. Am. Soc. Hosp. Pharmacists resident New Eng. Med. Ctr., Boston, 1978-79; clin. pharmacy resident Truman Med. Ctr., Kansas City, Mo., 1980-81; asst. prof. clin. pharmacy U. Mo.-Kansas City, 1981—; mem. med. adv. com. Hospice Care Mid Am., Kansas City, 1983—. Contbr. articles to med. jours. Recipient AVIE award U. Mo.-Kansas City, 1982, Hesca award, 1983; Weldon Spring grantee, 1983. Mem. Mo. Soc. Hosp. Pharmacists, Greater Kansas City Soc. Hosp. Pharmacists, Am. Soc. Hosp. Pharmacists, Am. Assn. Colls. Pharmacy, Am. Coll. Clin. Pharmacy. Democrat. Roman Catholic. Avocations: Computer applications, music, aerobic excercise. Office: Med Sch Bldg U Mo 2411 Holmes St Kansas City MO 64108

CULL, DAVID GAIL, structural engineer; b. Louisville, July 15, 1947; s. Franklin David and Margaret Lucille (Moreland) C.; m. Linda Jane Turner, Mar. 23, 1968; children—Daniel, Elizabeth, Kathleen. B.C.E., U. Louisville, 1971, M.Engring., 1975. Registered profl. engr., numerous states. Engr., then asst. chief engr. Caldwell Tanks, Inc., Louisville, 1971-76; structural engr. Universal Tank & Iron Works, Inc., Indpls., 1976-80, chief structural engr., 1980-83; v.p. engring. Tank Industry Cons., Inc., Speedway, Ind., 1984—; guest lectr. Brownsburg Community Sch. Corp. Cons. Jr. Achievement Project Bus., 1977-78; mem. bd. zoning appeals Town of Brownsburg (Ind.), 1983-84, v.p., 1985. Mem. Am. Water Works Assn., (3 revision task forces, D100 steel tanks standard com.), Steel Plate Fabricators Assn., Am. Arbitration Assn. (constrn. arbitrator), Steel Structures Painting Council. Republican. Mem. Christian Ch. Home: 6 Woodstock Dr Brownsburg IN 46112 Office: 4912 W 16th St Speedway IN 46224

CULLUM, HAROLD DONALD, principal; b. Portsmouth Ohio, Nov. 20, 1941; s. Harold Ernest and Leona Laurean (Childers) C.; m. Jo Annette Whitley, Apr. 16, 1981; children—Stephanie, Andrea, Donald. B.B.A., Ohio U., 1964; M.A., Eastern Ky. U., 1968; postgrad. Marshall U., 1972, Ohio U., 1979. Tchr. bus. Glenwood High Sch., New Boston, Ohio, 1964-70, asst. prin., tchr., 1970-75; dir. E.S.E.A. Title I New Boston Sch. Dist., 1968-69; instr. econs. and bus. law Shawnee State Tech. Coll., Portsmouth, 1973-75; park dir. Village New Boston, 1973-75; prin. New Boston Jr. and Sr. High Sch., 1975-80; clk., custodian student activities New Boston Sch. Dist., 1978-79; supt. pro tem New Boston Local Sch. Dest., 1978-80; prin. Circleville Jr. High Sch., Ohio, 1980—; registered football ofcl., 1963—. Pres. pro tem New Boston Bd. Health, 1970-71; sec. Citizens Adv. Com. Urban Renewal, New Boston, 1969-70, pres. 1971-80; bd. dirs. Scito County Tubercolosis and Respitory Disease Assn., 1970-80; exec. bd. dirs. Shawnee Mental Health Center, 1979-80; co-chmn. Heart Fund, Circleville, 1984; chmn. Yuletide Seal, 1979. Named Young Man of the Year Jaycees, 1969, 70; mem. NEA (life), Nat. Bus. Edn. Assn., Ohio Bus. Edn. Assn., Dept. Sch. Adminstrs. (sec. 1982-83), Ohio Edn. Assn. (life), Ohio Assn. Secondary Sch Adminstrs., New Boston Edn. Assn. (pres. 1967, bd. dirs. 1968, 69, treas. 6 terms), Phi Delta Kappa. Democrat. Methodist. Lodges: Kiwanis (pres. 1969-70, sec. 1973-75, bd. dirs. 1982, 83, bd. dirs. housing corp.), Aladdin Temple Shrine, Western Sun, Masons. Avocations: Fishing; stamp and coin collecting. Home: 976 Circle Dr Circleville OH 43113 Office: Circleville Jr High Sch 520 S Court St Circleville Ohio 43113

CULPEPPER, RICHARD GROOM, engineer; b. Norfolk, Va., Mar. 5, 1940; s. August Hume and Olive Gertrude (Birmingham) C.; m. Martha Louise Edwards, Nov. 5, 1966; children—Carolyn Ann, Richard Brian. B.S. in Aerospace Engring., Va. Poly. Inst., 1962. Asst. project engr. U.S. Army Aviation Material Lab., Newport News, Va., 1962-66; flight test engr. NASA-Langley Research Ctr., Hampton, Va., 1966-70, sr. flight test engr., 1970-78, tech. mgr., 1978-80; NASA rep. Wright Patterson AFB, 1981—. Contbr. papers to profl. publs. Com. mem. Pack 56, Tecumseh council Boy Scouts Am., 1981, chmn., 1982-83. Recipient Spl. Achievement award NASA, 1974, 76, 80. Fellow AIAA (assoc.). Avocations: Stamp collecting, gardening, HO trains, model airplanes. Home: 169 Cambria Dr Beavercreek OH 45440 Office: NASA Wright Patterson AFB OH 45433

CULVER, ROBERT ELROY, osteopathic physician; b. Toledo, Oct. 1, 1926; s. Elroy and Helen Mary C.; m. Sallie Jane Corder, June 10, 1972; children—Diana, Galen, Ronald, Richard, Patricia, Robert. B.S., U. Toledo, 1951; D.O., Chgo. Coll. Osteo. Medicine, 1959. Intern, Sandusky (Ohio) Meml. Hosp., 1960; practice medicine specializing in family practice and sports medicine, Oregon, Ohio, 1960—; mem. staff Parkview Hosp., Riverside Hosp., Toledo Hosp.; physician Oreg. Sch. System; Oregon police surgeon; chief dep. coroner, 1978-80; chmn. wrestling div. physicians Nat. AAU; U.S. med. rep. Federation Internationale Lute Amateur; physician U.S. World Wrestling Team; med. dir. World Cup of Wrestling; pres. Northwestern Ohio AAU; 3d v.p. Ohio AAU. Mem. Air Force Mus., Toledo Mus. Art; dir. Toledo Zoo; mem. Smithsonian Instn. Served with C.E., U.S. Army, 1944-46; col. Ohio Def. Service. Recipient commendation Ohio Ho. of Reps, 1983, honor award Oregon Sch. System, 1983; apptd. Ky. Col., 1983; named Outstanding Team Physician, State of Ohio, 1984. Mem. Am. Osteo. Assn., Ohio Osteo. Assn., 1st Dist. Acad. Osteo. Medicine (state trustee, past pres.), Am. Coll. Gen. Practioners in Osteo. Medicine and Surgery, Ohio Osteo. Assn. Physicians and Surgeons, Chgo. Coll. Osteo. Med. Alumni Assn., Nat. Rifle Assn. (life), U. Toledo Alumni Assn. (life mem.), Air Force Assn., Aircraft Owners and Pilots Assn., Nat. Hist. Soc., Ohio Hist. Soc., Am. Legion. Methodist. Club: Atlas. Lodges: Masons, Elks, Shriners. Office: 5517 Corduroy Rd Oregon OH 43616

CUMMENS, JOHN ALBERT, law firm administration director, consultant; b. Corvallis, Oreg., Feb. 15, 1943; s. John Edward and Elsie Marie (Roach) C.; m. Linda Ellyn Talaba, Aug. 29, 1964; 1 child, Michael Sean. B.A., Ill. Weslyan U., 1964; M.A., So. Ill. U., 1968, Ph.D., 1972, M.S., 1981. Disposition officer City of Carbondale, Ill., 1972-74; asst. dir. Ill. Office Manpower, Springfield, Ill., 1974-78; mem. research faculty Ohio State U., Columbus, 1978-79; adminstr. Boodell, Sears & Assocs., Chgo., 1979-82, Schwartz & Freeman, Chgo., 1982-85; dir. adminstrn. Ross & Hardies, Chgo., 1985—; lectr. Inst. Continuing Legal Edn., Ann Arbor, Mich., 1982—. Leopold Schepp Found. scholar, 1969-70; fellow George Washington U., 1975-76, Ohio State U., 1978-79. Mem. ABA (assoc.), Am. Vocat. Assn., Law Office Mgrs. Assn. Chgo. (pres. 1983), Assn. Legal Adminstrs. Episcopalian. Home: 1316 Oxford Rd Deerfield IL 60601 Office: Ross & Hardies 150 N Michigan Ave Chicago IL 60601

CUMMIN, ALFRED S(AMUEL), food company executive, educator; b. London, Sept. 5, 1924; s. Jack and Lottie (Hainesdorff) C.; m. Sylvia E. Smolok, Mar. 24, 1945; 1 dau., Cynthia Katherine. B.S., Poly. Inst. Bklyn., 1943, Ph.D. in Chemistry, 1946; M.B.A., U. Buffalo, 1959. Research chemist S.A.M. Labs., Manhattan Project, Columbia U., 1943-44; plant supr. Metal & Plastic Processing Co., Bklyn., 1946-51; research chemist Gen. Chem. div. Allied Chem. & Dye Corp., N.Y.C., 1951-53; sr. chemist Congoleum Nairn, Kearny, N.J., 1953-54; supr. Dielectrics-advance devel. Gen. Electric Co., Hudson Falls, N.Y., 1954-56; mgr. indsl. products research dept. Spencer Kellogg & Sons, Inc. (Textron), Buffalo, 1956-59; mgr. plastics div. Trancoa Chem. Corp., Reading, Mass., 1959-62; assoc. dir. product devel. service labs. Chem. div. Merck & Co., Inc., Rahway, N.J., 1962-69; dir. product devel. Borden Chem. div. Borden, Inc., N.Y.C., 1969-72, tech. dir., 1972-73, tech. dir. Borden, Inc., 1973-78, v.p. product safety and quality, 1978-81, v.p. sci. and tech., 1981—; mem. exec. com. Food Safety Council, 1976-81, trustee, chmn. membership com., 1976-80; dir. Formaldehyde Inst., 1977—, exec. com., 1981—, mem. med. com., 1977—, steering com., 1977—, adminstrv. v.p., 1982—; instr. Poly. Inst. Bklyn., 1946-47; asst. prof. Adelphi Coll., 1952-54; prof. math. sci. U.S. Mcht. Marine Acad., 1954; seminar leader Am. Mgmt. Assn.; prof. mgmt. NYU, 1968—. Recipient cert. award Fedn. Socs. Paint Tech., 1965. Mem. Am. Chem. Soc., Fedn. Coatings Tech., Inst. Food Tech., ASTM, Synthetic Organic Chems. Mfg. Assn. (dir., gov. 1981—, bd. gov. 1982-84), Paint Research Inst., Oxygenated Fuels Assn. (bd. dirs. 1982—), Inst. Food Technologists, Nat. Paint Coatings Assn. (spray paint com.), Delta Sigma Pi, Gamma Sigma Epsilon, Beta Gamma Sigma, Phi Lambda Upsilon. Contbr. articles to profl. jours; patentee in field. Office: 960 Kings Mill Pkwy Columbus OH 43229

CUMMINGS, LARRY LEE, management educator; b. Indpls., Oct. 28, 1937; s. Garland R. and Lillian P. (Smith) C.; A.B. summa cum laude, Wabash Coll., 1959; postgrad. (Woodrow Wilson fellow) U. Calif., Berkeley, 1959-60; M.B.A., Ind. U., 1961, D. Bus. Adminstrn. (Ford Found. fellow, Richard D. Irwin Dissertation fellow), 1964; children—Lee Anne, Glenn Nelson. Asst. prof. Sch. of Bus., Ind. U., Bloomington, 1964-67, asso. prof., 1967; asso. vis. prof. Columbia, N.Y.C., 1967-68; asso. prof. organizational behavior U. Wis., Madison, 1968-70, prof. Grad. Sch. Bus. and Indsl. Relations Inst., 1970-81, Slichter research prof., 1979-81, Romnes fellow, asso. dean Grad. Sch., 1975-81, lectr. dept. of psychology, 1971-81; J.L. Kellogg disting. research prof. Kellogg Grad. Sch. Mgmt., Northwestern U., Evanston, Ill., 1981—; vis. prof. U. B.C., Can., 1971-72; cons. Eli Lilly and Co., Eli Lilly Internat. in London, Bundy Corp., Samsonite Corp., Touché, Ross, Bailey & Smart, Inc., World U., San Juan, P.R.; research proposal reviewer, Can. Council, 1971-74. Bd. dirs. Center for the Study of Organizational Performance, Madison. Recipient McKinsey Found. Mgmt. Research award, 1970. Ford Found. Sr. Research fellow, 1969-70; Richardson Found. Research grantee, 1969. Fellow Acad. of Mgmt. (mem. publs. planning com. 1973-74, v.p. 1978-79, pres. 1981), Am. Psychol. Assn. (mem. sci. affairs com. div. 14 1973-76), Am. Inst. Decision Scis.; mem. Midwestern Psychol. Assn., Am. Sociol. Assn., Am. Soc. Personnel Adminstrn. (com. chmn. research com. 1969-70), Soc. Personnel Adminstrn., Indsl. Relations Research Assn., Sigma Xi, Phi Beta Kappa, Beta Gamma Sigma, Sigma Iota Epsilon, Tau Kappa Alpha, Delta Phi Alpha. Author: (with W.E. Scott) Readings in Organizational Behavior and Human Performance, 1969, 2d edit., 1973; (with F.A. Shull and A.L. Delbecq) Organizational Decision Making, 1970; (with D.P. Schwab) Performance in Organizations, 1973; (with R.B. Durham) Introduction to Organizational Behavior, 1980; (with D.L. Harnett) Bargaining Behavior: An International Study, 1980; (with B.M. Staw) Research in Organizational Behavior, Vol. II, 1980, Vol. III, 1981, Vol. IV, 1982; cons. editor Richard D. Irwin Series in Mgmt. and Behavioral Sci., 1972—; editor Acad. Mgmt. Jour., 1975-78; asso. editor Decision Scis., 1972—; mem. editorial bd. Organization and Adminstrv. Scis., 1973-78. Contbr. numerous research articles on organizational psychology and personnel mgmt. to profl. jours. Office: Kellogg Grad Sch Mgmt Northwestern U Evanston IL 60201

CUMMINGS, NEIL DAGE, optometrist; b. Carrington, N.D., Feb. 28, 1931; s. Clarence Roy and Lucille (Barber) C.; m. Stephanie Kay Lill, Feb. 10, 1968; children—Scott, Ann. B.S., Jamestown Coll., 1953; O.D., Pacific U., 1960. Cert. optometrist, N.D., Minn. Gen. practice optometry, Valley City, N.D., 1960—; pres. N.D. State Bd. Optometry, 1979-83. Served with U.S. Army, 1953-55. Mem. Am. Optometric Assn., N.D. Optometric Assn. (pres. 1972-73, Optometrist of Yr. 1975), Jaycees (Disting. Service award 1966). Republican. Methodist. Lodges: Elks, Eagles, Kiwanis (pres. 1972.). Avocations: hunting, fishing. Home: Rural Route 2 Box 180 Valley City ND 58072 Office: 202 Central Ave S Valley City ND 58072

CUMMINGS, TERRY (ROBERT TERRELL CUMMINGS), professional basketball player. Forward, Milw. Bucks. Office: Milw Bucks 901 N 4th St Milwaukee WI 53203*

CUMMINGS, WALTER J., See *Who's Who in America,* 43rd edition.

CUMMINS, JOAN TALLEY, paperboard company executive; b. Dayton, Ohio, Feb. 21, 1950; d. John Luthern and Brydell Ann (Henschen) T.; m. Michael David Cummins, Sept. 6, 1980. B.A. U. Cin., 1972, M.A. in Indsl. Relations, 1977. Personnel adminstr. Mead Containers Co., Cin., 1977-80, employee relations rep., 1980-82, mgr., human resources Mead Paperboard Products Co., Dayton, 1983—. Mem. Cin. Indsl. Relations Research Assn., Dayton Women's Network, Omicron Delta Epsilon. Office: Mead Paperboard Products Co Courthouse Plaza NE Dayton OH 45463

CUMMINS, WILLIAM ALLEN, industrial engineer; b. Lakeview, Ohio, May 5, 1931; s. Robert E. and Ruth R. (Burden) C.; m. Phyllis J. Holycross, June 27, 1954; children—Kathryn L., Alanna J., Alan M. Student Ohio No. U., 1953-55; diploma in mech. engring. Internat. Correspondence Sch., 1960; postgrad. Ohio State U., 1969-70. Registered profl. engr., Ohio, Ind., Ky., Miss., Fla., Tex. Indsl. engr. Rockwell Corp., Kenton, Ohio, 1951-57, Philips & Davies Corp., Kenton, 1957-60, Swift-Ohio Corp., Kenton, 1960-61; environ. engr. Alden E. Stilson & Assocs., Columbus, Ohio, 1961-72, Franklin Cons., Inc., Columbus, 1972-78, Malcolm Pirnie, Inc., Columbus, 1978—. Contbr. articles to profl. publs. Judge, 35th Internat. Sci. and Engring. Fair, Columbus, 1984. Mem. Am. Acad. Environ. Engrs. (diplomate), Nat. Soc. Profl. Engrs., Am. Water Works Assn., Water Pollution Control Fedn., Order of Engr. (bd. govs. 1971—). Methodist. Club: Engrs. of Columbus (pres. 1984-85). Home: 1047 Afton Rd Columbus OH 43221 Office: Malcolm Pirnie Inc 6161 Busch Blvd Columbus OH 43229

CUNDIFF, LARRY VERL, animal genetics and breeding researcher; b. Abilene, Kans., Dec. 9, 1939; s. John Verl and Bernice Cleda (Berger) C.; m. Laura Ruth Bathurst, Sept. 10, 1960; children—Rodney Verl, Amber Larae, Crystal Michelle. B.S. in Agr., Kans. State U., 1961; M.S. in Animal Sci., Okla. State U., 1963, Ph.D. in Animal Breeding, 1965. Grad. asst. Okla. State U., Stillwater, 1961-65; asst. prof. U. Ky., Lexington, 1965-67; research geneticist USDA, U.Nebr., Lincoln, 1967-73; research geneticist U.S. Meat Animal Research Ctr., USDA, Clay Center, Nebr., 1973-76, research leader, genetics and breeding, 1976—; dir. Beef Improvement Fedn., Blacksburg, Va., 1973—; lectr. in field. Mem. editorial bd. Jour. Animal Sci., Champaign, Ill., 1975-78. Contbr. articles to profl. jours. Pres. Clay Center Community Club, 1983; chmn. bd. trustees United Ch. Christ, Clay Center, 1983-84, lay leader, 1979-81; chmn troop com. Overland Trails Council Boy Scouts Am., 1976-81. Recipient Service award Beef Improvement Fedn., 1975. Mem. Am. Soc. Animal Sci. (program chmn. genetics com. 1972, 1981, editorial bd. jour 1975-78, J. R. Prentice award in animal breeding and genetics 1983), Am. Genteic Assn., Council Agrl. Sci. and Tech., Clay Center Minutemen, Sigma Xi, Alpha Zeta, Gamma Sigma Delta. Avocations: singing; golfing; skiing; fishing. Home: 308 N Alexander Clay Center NE 68933 Office: US Meat Animal Research Ctr PO Box 166 Clay Center NE 68933

CUNNINGHAM, DALE ELLEN, publishing company executive; b. Lewiston, Maine, Oct. 1, 1952; d. Richard F. and Audrey L. (Braunsdorff) C. B.A., Hood Coll., 1973; publication specialist program George Washington U., 1977. Flagwoman, Md.'s First, Frederick County, 1973-74; adminstrv. asst. Constrn. Mgmt. Inc., Rockville, Md., 1975-76; assoc. editor jours. Aspen Systems Corp., Rockville, 1976-79; mktg. asst. N.Y.C. office Springer-Verlag N.Y., 1980-81, sales rep. western ter., 1981-82; dir. instl. mktg. Year Book Med. Pubs., Chgo., 1982-85; dir. mktg. Marquis Who's Who, Inc., Chgo., 1985—. Office: 200 E Ohio St Chicago IL 60611

CUNNINGHAM, DALE LAKEENE, manufacturing company executive; b. Bucklin, Mo., Oct. 3, 1926; s. Aubrey E. and Elva Lucile (White) C.; m. Willa Lou Wilcoxon, June 15, 1952; children—William Dale, David Scott, Gregory Wayne, Susan Eileen. B.S. in Elec. Engring., U. Mo., 1951; M.B.A. Mich. State U., 1970. Chief engr., mgr. long range planning Bendix, Mishawaka, Ind.; plant mgr. Polygon, Walkerton, Ind., 1974-76; ops. mgr. Harco, Mishawaka, 1976-78; gen. mgr. Fargo Assembly of Ind., Mishawaka, 1978—. Mem. IEEE. Lodge: Elks. Avocations: camping; golfing; canoeing; fishing; biking. Home: 16269 Shamrock Dr Mishawaka IN 46544 Office: Fargo Assembly of Ind 800 S Cleveland St Mishawaka IN 46544

CUNNINGHAM, DAN DOUGLAS, pharmacist; b. New Albany, Ind., Dec. 23, 1946; s. Ralph Maurice and Georgene Evelyn (Ingram) C.; m. Sarah Sue Geimer, Aug. 30, 1975; children—Adam Douglas, Audra Victoria, Ross Anthony. B.S. in Pharmacy, Purdue U., 1970. Lic. pharmacist, Ind., S.C. Staff pharmacist St. Joseph Hosp., Ft. Wayne, Ind., 1971-73; pharmacist Anthony Med. Ctr., Ft. Wayne, 1973-75; pharmacist/mgr. Keltsch Pharamacy, Auburn, Ind., 1975-83; owner/pharmacist Cunningham Family Pharmacy, Auburn, 1983—. Bd. dirs. Am. Cancer Soc. DeKalb unit, Auburn, 1980-84. Mem. Ind. Pharamacists Assn., Allen County Pharmacists Assn. (bd. dirs. 1976-80, 81—, pres. 1980-81), Nat. Assn. Retail Druggists. Republican. Methodist. Lodges: Auburn Rotary (treas. 1980-84), Moose. Avocations: swimming; sailing; photography. Home: 403 Duryea Dr Auburn IN 46706 Office: Cunningham Family Pharmacy 131 W 7th St Auburn IN 46706

CUNNINGHAM, EDWARD PRESTON, JR., food manufacturing company personnel executive; b. Hammond, Ind., Sept. 24, 1945; s. Edward Preston and Louise Catherine (Kohler) C.; B.B.A., U. Wis., Madison, 1968, M.B.A., 1969; children—Scott, Jennifer. Personnel supr. Quaker Oats Co., Rockford, Ill., 1972-75, employee relations mgr., 1975-79, employee and community relations mgr., Lawrence, Kans., 1979—. Met. bd. dirs. Nat. Alliance Bus., 1976-78; bd. dirs. U. Kans. Concert Series, 1980—, Lawrence chpt. ARC, 1983—, Douglas County Vis. Nurses, 1983—; chmn. commerce and industry unit Lawrence Multiple Sclerosis, 1981—. Served to capt. U.S. Army, 1969-72; Vietnam. Decorated Bronze Star; named Outstanding Young Man Am., U.S. Jaycees, 1981. Mem. Ill. Employment Service, Midwest Indsl. Mgmt. Assn. (instr. 1978-79), Am. Soc. for Tng. and Devel., Lawrence C. of C. (chmn. edn. com. 1980), Lawrence Personnel Club. Republican. Congregationalist. Club: Cosmopolitan. Home: 2111 Crossgate Circle Lawrence KS 66044 Office: 727 Iowa St Lawrence KS 66044

CUNNINGHAM, FAY LAVERE, chemical engineer, production director; b. Lansing, Mich., July 26, 1922; s. Ernest Wilbur and Mary Catharine (Remington) C.; m. Geraldine Marie Smokovitz, June 12, 1948; children—Bruce W., Deborah L. Student U. Md., 1943-44; B.S., Mich. State U., 1948. Mech. engr. div. indsl. cooperation, MIT, Cambridge, 1944-46; devel. engr. Upjohn Co., Kalamazoo, 1948-57, research mgr. Separation/Engring. Devel., 1958-72, research mgr. Chem. Engring. Devel., 1972-83, dir. Specialty Chem. Prodn., 1984-85. Patentee purification of sitosterol; author tech. papers. Pres. Kalamazoo Mgmt. Assocs., 1964, Oakwood Jr. High Sch. PTA, 1967; chmn. Troop 5 com. Fruit Belt council Boy Scouts Am., 1967-68. Served with U.S. Army, 1943-46. Recipient The Upjohn award, 1963. Mem. Am. Chem. Soc., Am. Inst. Chem. Engrs., AAAS. Avocations: Skiing; tennis; back packing; woodworking; reading. Home: 4323 Sunset Dr Kalamazoo MI 49008 Office: Upjohn Co 7000 Portage Rd Kalamazoo MI 49001

CUNNINGHAM, NINA, researcher, educator; b. Chgo., Dec. 24, 1947; d. Sidney and Betty (Rosmarin) Strickler; m. H. Stuart Cunningham, Apr. 17, 1975; 1 child, Gwyneth. Ph.D. in Philosophy, DePaul U., 1973; M.A. in Library Sci., Rosary Coll., 1980. Teaching asst. DePaul U., 1970; pres., owner Quidlibet Research, Inc., Oak Park, Ill., 1977—; adminstr. U.S. Dist. Cts., Chgo., 1973-83, cons., 1983; cons. Rosenthal and Schanfield, Chgo., 1983, DePaul U., Chgo., 1984. Editor: Ethics & Advocacy newsletter. Founder, bd. dirs. Ctr. for Legal Ethics, Edn. and Research, Chgo., 1984. Fellow DePaul U., 1970, Inst. for Humane Studies, 1976; Marsden Found. grantee, 1972. Mem. Am. Legal Studies Assn., Am. Soc. Study of Law and Legal Philosophy, Royal Inst. Philosophy, Soc. Study of History of Philosophy. Jewish. Avocations: creative writing; bookselling; genealogy. Home and Office: Quidlibet Research Inc 643 N Elmwood Ave Oak Park IL 60302

CUNNINGHAM, RICHARD THOMAS, lawyer; b. Akron, Ohio, Mar. 19, 1930; s. Ernest L. and Hazel A. (Coates) C.; m. Mary Lou Mackin, June 13, 1953; children—Susan, Elizabeth, Amy, David, Diane, Christine. Student Western Res. U., 1948, Columbia U., 1950; L.L.B., U. Ill., 1953. Bar: Ohio 1953, Ill. 1953. Legal officer USN, Norfolk, 1953-56; asst. atty. gen. State of Ohio, Columbus, 1956-57; mng. ptnr. Amer Cunningham Brennan Co., L.P.A., Akron, 1957—; del. Fed. 6th Jud. Conf., 1983—. Trustee Kent State U., chmn. 1984-86; mem. Family Services of Cuyahoga Falls, Ohio, 1964-70, pres. 1968, Bd. Edn., Cuyahoga Falls, 1972-76. Fellow Am. Coll. Trial Lawyers; mem. Akron Bar Assn. (pres. 1976-77), Ohio State Bar Assn. (del. 1977-79), ABA, Assn. Trial Lawyers Am., Ohio Trial Lawyers Assn. Republican. Office: Amer Cunningham Brennan Co L P A 1100 First National Tower Akron OH 44308

CUNNINGHAM, SHIRLEY JEAN, insurance company official; b. Eldorado, Ark., Nov. 15, 1943; d. Charles Travis and Gracie Lee (Traylor) Marrable; B.A., DePaul U., 1981; m. Wilbur C. Cunningham, Nov. 23, 1974; children—Tracy Jeannee and Leslie Jeannette (twins). Supr. word processing Blue Cross Assn., Chgo., 1971-73, mgr. word processing, 1974-77; mgr. word processing and telecommunications Blue Cross & Blue Shield Assns., Chgo., 1978-80, sr. mgr. office services, 1981—; mem. citizen adv. com. Thornton Community Coll., 1979—. Mem. adv. bd. United Career Action Now, recipient Cert. of Recognition, 1981, 83; mem. Vice Pres.'s Task Force on Youth Motivation. Recipient cert. of recognition Citizens Adv. Com., 1980. Mem. Internat. Info./Word Processing Assn., Am. Mgmt. Assn., Word Processing Mgmt. Assn., In-Plant Printing Mgmt. Assn., Assn. Info. Systems Profls., Chgo. Assn. Commerce and Industry (merit employment com.; cert. of merit 1968). Club:

Pershing Park Tennis. Home: 2901 Martin Luther King Dr 1802 Chicago IL 60616 Office: 676 N St Clair Chicago IL 60616

CUNNINGHAM, STANLEY VERNON, mathematics educator; b. Karlsruhe, W.Ger., Aug. 29, 1953; s. Stanley Vernon and Anna Josephine (Hoffmann) C.; m. Susan J. Wisdom, Mar. 22, 1985; stepchildren—David Loren, Benjamin Robert, Erica Rachell. B.S., Kearney State Coll., 1977, M.S., 1979. Cert. tchr. in math., physics, Nebr. Grad. asst. Kearney State Coll. (Nebr.), 1977-78; mem. programming staff AT&T, Kansas City, Mo., 1979; instr. math. Three Rivers Community Coll., Poplar Bluff, Mo., 1980—. Mem. Am. Math. Assn Two Year Colls., Nat. Council Tchrs. Math., Mo. Assn. Community and Jr. Colls., Three Rivers Amateur Radio Assn., Kappa Mu Epsilon, Sigma Pi Sigma. Democrat. Lutheran. Home: 1102 White Oak Dr Poplar Bluff MO 63901 Office: Dept Math Three Rivers Community Coll Poplar Bluff MO 63901

CUNNINGHAM-BALLARD, LINDA ANNETTE, public relations official; b. Toledo, Ohio, Sept. 29, 1955; d. David and Alberta (Turk) C.; m. E. David Ballard II, June 20, 1981; 1 dau., Jennifer Michele. Student Bowling Green State U., 1973-75; B.A. in Journalism, U. Toledo, 1977. Editor Community News, Toledo, Ohio, 1976-77; news media rep. Owens-Ill. Inc., Toledo, 1977-84; freelance writer, 1984—. Nominating, pub. relations com. YWCA, 1981—; mem. Northwest Ohio chpt. ARC, 1978—; mem. pub. relations com. Toledo Festival, 1981; exec. adviser Jr. Achievement of Northeast Ohio, 1978-81. Mem. Democratic Profl. and Bus. Women, Pub. Relations Soc. Am., Soc. Profl. Journalists, Women in Communication. Democrat. Baptist. Club: Press (Toledo). Home: 4923 Hawaiian Terr Cincinnati OH 45223

CUPPAGE, FRANCIS EDWARD, physician, educator; b. Cleve., Aug. 17, 1932; s. Frank E. and Eunice Agnes (Bartels) C.; m. Virginia Lee Bartch, Aug. 18, 1956; children—Lisa Kay, Peter John, Sharon Elizabeth. B.S., Case Western Res. U., 1954; M.D., Ohio State U., 1959, M.S. in Pathology, 1959. Diplomate Am. Bd. Pathology. Intern U. Hosps. of Cleve., 1959-60, resident in pathology, 1960-64, instr. pathology, 1964-65; asst. prof. pathology Ohio State U. Sch. Medicine, Columbus, 1965-67; asst. prof. pathology U. Kans. Med. Ctr., Kansas City, 1967—, acting chmn. pathology, 1984—. Contbr. articles to profl. jours. Lay leader Luth. Ch. orgns., 1967—; bd. dirs. Trinity Manor & Bethany Coll., 1982—. NIH grantee, 1967-75; U. Kans. Alumni Teaching award, 1972; Fogarty Internat. fellow, 1979. Mem. Am. Assn. Pathologists, Am. Soc. Nephrology, Internat. Assn. Pathologists, AAUP, Group for Research in Pathology Edn. Avocations: Woodcarving; hiking; camping; photography; reading. Home: 4740 Black Swan Dr Shawnee Mission KS 66216 Office: Dept Pathology Univ Kans Med Center 39th and Rainbow Rd Kansas City KS 66103

CURCIO, BARBARA A., physical education educator; b. Sharon, Pa., Mar. 14, 1945; d. Frank Orlando and Irene (Alongi) Curcio. B.S. cum laude, Slippery Rock State Coll., 1967, M.Ed., 1968; D.Edn., Ball State U., 1980. Tchr. Moniteau High Sch., West Sunbury, Pa., 1967-68; tchr., coach Pa. State U.-Behrend, Erie, Pa., 1968-70; assoc. prof., coach Ball State U., Muncie, Ind., 1970—; women's volleyball head coach, 1972-83. bd. dirs. Credit Union, 1983; volleyball master clinician Northeastern Jr. Coll., Sterling, Colo., 1979, various high sch. camps, Wyoming, Mich., Ind., 1973-78; fencing cons. Nat. Thespian Meeting, Muncie, 1982. Mem. Ind. Assn. Intercollegiate Athletics for Women (treas. 1981-83, coach state championship volleyball team, 1973, 77), Am. AHPERD, Collegiate Volleyball Coaches Assn., Delta Zeta, Delta Psi Kappa, Kappa Delta Pi. Roman Catholic. Editor chpt. in Phys. Edn. Handbook, 1980; contbr. articles to profl. jour. Office: Ball State U 200F Ball Gym Muncie IN 47306

CURIEL, GONAZLO PAUL, lawyer; b. East Chgo., Ind., Sept. 7, 1953; s. Salvador and Francisca (Rodriguez) C. B.A., Ind. U., 1976, J.D., 1979. Bar: Ill. 1979, Ind. 1980, U.S. Dist. Ct. (no. dist.) Ind., U.S. Dist. Ct. (so. dist.) Ind. Law clk. Judge James Richards, Hammond, 1977; legal intern Student Legal Services, Bloomington, Ind., 1977-78, U.S. Attys. Office, Chgo., 1978; law clk. Judge S. Hugh Dillin, Indpls., 1979; assoc. James & James, Dyer, Ind., 1979—. Hearing examiner East Chgo. Human Rights Commn., Ind., 1983-84. Mem. Nat. Hispanic Bar Assn., Hispanic Bar Assn., East Chgo. Bar Assn. Home: 3507 Grand Blvd East Chicago IN 46312 Office: James & James 200 Monticello St Dyer IN 46311

CURL, DANIEL ARTHUR, pharmacist; b. Dec. 2, 1953; s. Earl Stanley and Patricia Anne (Schindler) C.; m. Mariann Woodruff, Sept. 17, 1982. B.S. in Pharmacy, Ohio No. U., 1977. Staff pharmacist Hatton & Enright Pharmacy, Urbana, Ohio, 1973-78; chief pharmacist, mgr. St. Paris Pharmacy, Ohio, 1978; staff pharmacist Howards Pharmacy, Huber Heights, Ohio, 1979-80, Community Hosp., Springfield, Ohio, 1980-84, Western Pharmacy, Springfield, 1984; chief pharmacist, mgr. Wendt-Bristol Pharmacy, Springfield, 1984-85; staff pharmacist Ohio Masonic Home, Springfield, 1985—; cons. pharmacist Hatton & Enright Pharmacy, Urbana, 1974—. Mem. Urbana Downtown Bus. Assn., 1984, U Urbana Boosters Club, 1984. Mem. Clark County Pharm. Assn. Republican. Methodist. Clubs: Optimist, Shrine. Lodge: Demolay (order of chevalier). Avocations: collecting auto racing memoribilia, off-road driving. Home: 145 Taft Ave Urbana OH 43078 Office: Ohio Masonic Home Springfield OH 45506

CURLER, HOWARD J., See *Who's Who in America,* 43rd edition.

CURLESS, CHARLES DENNIS, lawyer; b. Lamar, Mo., Aug. 30, 1951; s. Charles Emmett and Janet Marie (Streeper) C.; m. Nancy Ann Nichols, Aug. 26, 1972; children—Amy Michelle, Julie Ann, Ann Elizabeth. B.S. in Fin., B.S. in Mgmt., S.W. Mo. State U., 1973; J.D., Oklahoma City U., 1980. Bar: Mo. 1981, U.S. Dist. Ct. (we. dist.) Mo. 1981. Assoc. Woolsey, Fisher, Whiteaker, McDonald & Ansley, Springfield, Mo., 1981-83; ptnr. Nichols & Curless, Lamar, 1983—. Coach Recreation T-Ball and Basketball Program, Lamar; chmn. fin. com. Barton County Republican Com., Mo., 1984. Named Ky. col. Gov. Ky., 1984. Mem. Assn. Trial Lawyers Am., ABA, Mo. Bar, Barton County Bar Assn. (treas. 1983—), Lamar C. of C. (bd. dirs. 1984—), Phi Alpha Delta (justice dist. VI 1984—, cert. appreciation 1981). Methodist. Club: Metro (Lamar). Lodges: Masons, Shriners. Office: Nichols & Curless 120 W 10th St Lamar MO 64759

CURLESS, LARRY DEAN, tax consultant, farm manager; b. Wabash County, Ind., Dec. 29, 1931; s. Wilbur Tyner and Millie Catherine (Garber) C.; m. Marilyn E. Eltzroth, July 27, 1952; children—Charles Randall, Cynthia Ann. B.S. in Agr., Purdue U., 1953. Ptnr. Curless Farms, Inc., Wabash, Ind., 1955-75, owner, pres., 1975—; owner Curless Bookkeeping and Tax Service, 1956—; pres. Pro Ag Co. Inc., Peru, Ind.; dir. Ind. Farm Bur. Coop.; past pres. Wabash County Farm Bur. Coop; stockholder rep. Farmers Forage Research; mem. Region 5 Soil Erosion Com. Bd. dirs. Honeywell Found. 1978—, Wabash County Fair Assn., 1960-66; pres. Noble Twp. Farm Bur., 1958-60, Wabash County Extension Com., 1960-62, Southwood Parent Tchrs. Orgn. and Music Assn., 1965-70; mem. com. on Future Direction of Met. Sch. Dist., 1981. Served with U.S. Army, 1953-55. Mem. Purdue U. Agr. Alumni Assn., Pork Producers Assn. (research com.), Purdue All Am. Band Alumni, Ind. Cattleman's Assn., Ind. Farm Mgmt. Assn (pres.), Farm Bur. Assn. Republican. Presbyterian (elder, tchr.). Home and Office: Rural Route 5 Wabash IN 46992

CURNUTTE, BASIL, JR., physics educator, researcher; b. Portsmouth, Ohio, Mar. 1, 1923; s. Basil and Lula Alfair (Cooper) C.; m. Mary Leete Lukemire, June 10, 1945; children—William Basil, Gregory Mark. B.S., U.S. Naval Acad., 1945; Ph.D., Ohio State U., 1953. Research assoc. Ohio State U., Columbus, 1953; asst. prof. physics Kans. State U., Manhattan, 1954-55, assoc. prof., 1955-64, prof., 1964—, assoc. head physics dept., 1984—; vis. scientist Am. Inst. Physics, 1965-71, U. Ariz., Tucson, 1968. Contbr. chpt. to book. NSF fellow, 1952-53. Served to lt. USN, 1945-49. Fellow Am. Phys. Soc., Optical Soc. Am.; mem. Am. Assn. Physics Tchrs., Sigma Pi Sigma. Episcopalian. Office: Kans State U Dept Physics Cardwell Hall Manhattan KS 66506

CURNUTTE, JOHN TOLLIVER, III, pediatric hematologist/oncologist, researcher; b. Dixon, Ill., Sept. 9, 1951; s. John Tolliver and Elizabeth Ann (Mueller) C.; m. Karen Diane Northrop, June 21, 1975; children—Jacqueline, John IV, Margaret. A.B. magna cum laude in Biochemistry, Harvard U., 1973; M.D., Harvard Med. Sch., 1979; Ph.D. in Biol. Chemistry, Harvard U., 1980. Diplomate Nat. Bd. Med. Examiners. Pediatric resident Mass. Gen. Hosp. and Harvard Med. Sch., Boston, 1979-81; fellow pediatric hematology/oncology Dana Farber Cancer Inst. and Harvard Med. Sch., Boston, 1981-83; asst. prof. pediatrics U. Mich. Med. Sch., Ann Arbor, 1983—. Contbr. articles to profl. jours. NIH Neutrophil Research grantee, 1983-86; Soc. Pediatric Research Starter Research grantee, 1984-85. Mem. Am. Soc. Cell Biology, AMA, Am. Fedn. Clin. Research, Boylston Med. Soc. (co.-chmn. 1976-78). Roman Catholic. Club: Aesculapian (Boston). Avocations: football; mountain climbing. Home: 3315 Oak Dr Ypsilanti MI 48197 Office: U Mich Hosps Pediatric Hematology/Oncology Room F6515 Box 66 Ann Arbor MI 48109

CUROE, BERNADINE MARY, counselor; b. Cascade Iowa, Nov. 20, 1930; d. Harold Richard and Naomi Cecelia (Dahlem) V. B.A., Clarke Coll., 1959; M.A., Loras Coll., 1969. Tchr. schs. in Iowa, 1950-70; counselor Wahlert High Sch., Dubuque, Iowa, 1970-79, Loras Coll., Dubuque, 1979—; counselor Archdiocesan Deacons, Waterloo, Iowa, 1978—; dir. Sisters of Visitation, Dubuque, 1981—. Mem. Am. Assn. Counseling and Devel., Am. Coll. Personnes. Assn. Religious Value Issues (dir. 1979-82), Nat. Orientation dirs., Iowa Student Personnel Assn. Democrat. Roman Catholic. Avocations: Canoeing; swimming; hiking. Home: 900 Alta Vista Dubuque IA 52001 Office: 1450 Alta Vista Loras Dubuque IA 52001

CURRAN, JAMES FRANCIS, dentist; b. Cleve., Mar. 26, 1932; s. Paul Stanley and Genevieve Agnes (Morgan) C.; m. Phyllis Eisele, Dec. 27, 1955; children—Deborah Ann, Sean Francis, Therese Marie, Patricia Holly. B.S., John Carroll U., 1950; D.D.S., Marquette U., 1959. Gen. practice dentistry, Cleveland Heights, Ohio, 1961-80; gen. dental cons. Gen. Electric Co., Ohio, 1965-80; gen. dentist Euclid Clinic Found. (Ohio), 1980—. Served with U.S. Army, 1959-61. Mem. ADA, Ohio Dental Assn. Office: 18599 Lakeshore Blvd Euclid OH 44119

CURRAN, THOMAS FREDERICK, psychotherapist; b. LaCrosse, Wis., Feb. 6, 1948; s. Lawrence Griggs and Eleanor (Gibson) C.; B.S., U. Wis., 1970; M.S.W., Mich. State U., 1972, Ph.D., 1974. Cons., Ingham Med. Center-Community Mental Health Center, Lansing, Mich., 1973-74; asst. prof. Fla. State U., Tallahassee, 1974-77; psychotherapist Genesee Psychiat. Center, Flint, Mich., 1977-81; pres. Northbank Counseling Services, Flint, 1981—; cons. Nat. Council on Alcoholism, 1978—, St. Joseph Hosp., Hurley Hosp., 1984—. Mich. State U. Dean's Office fellow, 1972, 73. Mem. Nat. Assn. Social Workers, Am. Psychol. Assn., Council on Social Work Edn. Editorial adv. bd. Jour. of Humanics, 1977—; contbr. articles to profl. jours. Office: Suite 300 Northbank Center 400 N Saginaw Flint MI 48502 Home: 5510 Maple Park Dr Flint MI 48507

CURRIE, CHARLES LEONARD, college president; b. Phila., July 9, 1930; s. Charles Leonard and Elizabeth Katherine (Harper) C. A.B., Boston Coll., 1955; M.S., 1956; Ph.L., Weston Coll., 1956; Ph.D., Cath. U. Am., 1961; S.T.B., Woodstock Coll., 1962, S.T.L., 1964; D.Sc. (hon.), Bethany Coll., 1974; LL.D., W.Va. Wesleyan U., 1982; Litt. D., U. Cin., 1984; D. Sc., St. Thomas Inst., 1984. Joined S.J., Roman Cath. Ch., 1950. Postdoctoral researcher Nat. Bur. Standards, 1962, Can. Nat. Research Council, 1963-65; Cambridge U., Eng., 1965-66; asst. prof. chemistry Georgetown U., 1966-72; pres. Wheeling Coll., W.Va., 1972-82, Xavier U., Cin., 1982—; bd. dirs. Am. Council on Edn., Holy Cross Coll. Chmn. W.Va. Bd. Miner Tng., Edn. and Cert., 1974-82; bd. dirs. Oglebay Inst., Wheeling, 1972-82, United Way Upper Ohio Valley, 1973-80, W.Va. Humanities Found., 1978-82, Council Ind. Colls., 1981-82, Cin. Area Community Chest, Cin. Area ARC Grantee Dept. Def. 1968-71, Am. Chem. Soc. Petroleum Research Fund, 1963-65, NSF, 1969-72. Mem. Am. Chem. Soc., Chem. Soc. London, Washington Acad. Sci., N.Y. Acad. Sci., AAUP, W.Va. C. of C. (bd. dirs. 1976-82), Wheeling Area C. of C. (bd. dirs. 1974-80), Greater Cin. Area C. of C., Common Cause, Assn. Jesuit Colls. and Univs. (bd. dirs.), W.Va. Assn. Pvt. Colls. (bd. dirs.), Ohio Coll. Assn. (pres. elect 1984), Assn. Ind. Colls. and Univs. Ohio (sec.), Sigma Xi. Club: Queen City (Cin). Lodge: Rotary. Contbr. articles to chem. jours., 1959-73. Address: Xavier Univ 3800 Victory Pkwy Cincinnati OH 45207

CURRIVAN, JOHN DANIEL, lawyer; b. Paris, Jan. 15, 1947. B.S., Cornell U., 1968; M.S., U. Calif.-Berkeley, 1969, U. West Fla., 1971; J.D. summa cum laude, Cornell Law Sch., 1978. Bar: Ohio 1978. Mng. ptnr. Southwest Devel. Co., Kingsville, Tex., 1971-76; Prosecutor, Naval Legal Office, Norfolk, Va., 1978-79, chief prosecutor, 1979-81; sr. atty. USS Nimitz, 1981-83; trial judge Naval Base, Norfolk, 1983-84; assoc. Jones, Day, Reavis & Pogue, Cleve., 1984—. Recipient Younger Fed. Lawyer award Fed. Bar Assn., 1981. Mem. ABA, Ohio State Bar Assn., Order of Coif. Home: 2842 Sedgewick Rd Shaker Heights OH 44120 Office: Jones Day Reavis & Pogue 1700 Huntington Bldg Cleveland OH 44120

CURRY, ALAN C., insurance company executive; b. Columbus, Ohio, Oct. 15, 1933; s. Harold E. and Martha D. (Dew) C; divorced; children—Diane, Thomas, Steven, Timothy, Jeffrey, Barry. Student U. Ill., 1951-52; B.S. with honors in Edn., Ill. State U., 1957. With State Farm Mut. Ins. Co., Bloomington, 1952—, v.p., actuary, 1970—. Mem indsl. bd. advisers Rose-Hulman Inst. Tech., 1978—. Fellow Casualty Actuarial Soc. (bd. dirs. 1970-74); mem. Am. Acad. Actuaries (bd. dirs. 1977-80), Midwestern Actrarial Forum (pres. 1967-73), Am. Risk and Ins. Assn., Am. Statis. Assn. Home: 7 Canterbruy Ct Bloomington IL 61701 Office: State Farm Automobile Ins Co 1 State Farm Plaza Bloomington IL 61701

CURRY, JOHN PATRICK, insurance company executive, management consultant; b. Logan, W.Va., May 3, 1934; s. Albert Bruce and Mary Naomi (Shugert) C.; m. Patricia Jean Blessington, Oct. 26, 1956; children—Joseph Patrick, Mary Patricia. Kathleen Anne, Carmen Frances, John Gregory. Student St. Charles Coll., Catonsville, Md., 1949-52; B.A., U. Notre Dame, 1956; M.S. in Ops. Research, Western Mich. U., 1976. Lic. profl. cons., Mich. Agt., Conn. Mut. Life Ins. Co., 1959-65; gen. agt. Occidental Life Ins. Co., Los Angeles, 1965-66; pres. Investment Assocs. Inc., 1966-69; gen. agt. Fed. Life Ins. Co., Peoples Home Life Ins. Co. and Home Assurance Cos., 1969-71; actuarial cons. Am.-Brit. Ins. & Annuity Co., Ltd. (Bermuda), Battle Creek, Mich., 1979—; mgmt. cons., 1971—; owner, mgr. Nat. Search Cons., exec. search firm, Kalamazoo and Chgo.; owner, operator Curry Supply Co., Portage, Mich., 1978-83; dir. Anglo-Am. Ins. Co., Ltd. (Bermuda). Served with U.S. Army, 1957-59. U. Notre Dame scholar, 1952-55; Pat O'Brien scholar, 1956. Republican. Roman Catholic. Clubs: Elks, Sertoma (charter dir. 1961-64) (Kalamazoo). Home: 7226 Rockford St Kalamazoo MI 49002

CURRY, JOHN WESLEY, educator; b. Canton, Ill., Nov. 13, 1948; s. Wesley LeRoy and Clara Mae (Hysler) C.; m. Francene Elizabeth Anderson, July 12, 1970; children—Jennifer, Robert, Rachel. B.S., Ill. State U., 1970; M.A., Sangamon State U., 1980. Tchr. math., coach Athens High Sch. (Ill.), 1970-77, tchr. math./athletic dir., 1978—; asst. mgr. Illini Sporting Goods, Springfield, Ill., 1977-78; evening instr. Lincoln Land Community Coll. Bd. dirs. Athens United Meth. Ch., 1978-83, chmn. bd., 1978-81, lay leader, 1972-78, 81-83, chmn. bd. trustees, 1982-83. Mem. Nat. Council Tchrs. Math., Assn. Supervision and Curriculum Devel., NEA (life), Ill. Council Tchrs. Math., Ill. Edn. Assn. Methodist. Home: Rural Route 2 Box 293 Athens IL 62613 Office: Rural Route 1 Box 11 Athens IL 62613

CURTIN, PATRICK DANIEL, educational administrator; b. Arpin, Wis., Jan. 5, 1927; s. Daniel Foster and Gertrude Anna (Grosbeier) C.; m. Mary Joan Dwyer, Aug. 2, 1958; children—Sheila Marie, Kevin Patrick, Molly Ann, Sean Vincent. B.S., Lawrence U., 1951; M.S., Winona State U., 1964. Tchr. English, Lincoln High Sch., Park Falls, Wis., 1951-52, tchr. English and social studies, Alma Center, Wis., 1952-54; tchr., coach D.C. Everest High Sch., Schofield, Wis., 1954-69; middle sch. prin. Lake Mills Middle Sch., Wis., 1969—. Mem. Nat. Assn. Secondary Sch. Prins., Assn. Wis. Sch. Adminstrs., Phi Delta Kappa. Roman Catholic. Lodges: KC (treas. 1982-84), Lions (zone chmn. 1979, 81, dep. dist. gov. 1980). Avocations: Furniture refinishing; skiing. Home: 534 W Lake Park Pl Lake Mills WI 53551 Office: Lake Mills Middle Sch 318 College St Lake Mills WI 53551

CURTIS, CLARA SUE, college counselor, b. Stillwater, Okla., May 22, 1946; d. Wade Haskel and Hazel Irene (Harris) Mercer; m. Gary Richard Curtis, June 6, 1976. B.S., Union Coll., 1969; M.Edn., Middle Tenn. State U., 1975. Cert. Counselor, Ohio. Dean of women Highland Acad., Portland, Tenn., 1969-73, Mt. Vernon Acad., Ohio, 1973-80; career counselor Mt. Vernon Nazarene, Coll., 1980-83, dir. career services, 1983—. Chairperson Mt. Vernon SDA Elem. Sch. Bd., 1982—; bd. dirs. Mt. Vernon Acad., 1984—, Mt. Vernon Hill SDA Ch. Bd., 1982—. Mem. Am. Assn. Counseling and Devel., Am. Coll. Personnel Assn., Coll. Placement Council, Assn. Sch., Coll. and Univ. Staffing, Internat. Mgmt. Council (editor newsletter Mt. Vernon chpt. 1984, Outstanding mem. award 1982-83). Avocations: running, reading, camping. Home: 1749 Vernon View Dr Mount Vernon OH 43050 Office: Mt Vernon Nazarene Coll 800 Martinsburg Rd Mount Vernon OH 43050

CURTIS, DONALD RAY, advertising agency executive, publisher; b. Indpls., Apr. 29, 1951; s. Wendell Ray Curtis and Marilyn Ann (Bleistein) Curtis Layne; m. Christine Ann Carter, June 9, 1984. Student Ind. U., 1969-77. Pres. Graphically Speaking, Inc., Indpls., 1978—, Dining Guide Publications, Inc., Indpls., 1980-84; v.p., dir. creative services Shepard Poorman Communications Corp., Indpls., 1981—. Assoc. publisher, editor Indpls. Dining Guide, annually, 1980—. Assoc. publisher annual calendar Indpls. Entertainment, 1984, 85. Recipient William E. Garrett award, Cavanaugh award Ind. U. Mem. Profl. Telemarketing Mgrs. Assn. (pres. 1984-85), Indpls. Assn. Bus. communicators, Art Dirs. Club Indpls. Mem. United Ch. Christ. Club: Ad (Indpls.). Avocations: volleyball; writing; real estate; cooking. Home: 6645 Hythe Rd Indianapolis IN 46220 Office: Shepard Poorman Communications Corp 7301 N Woodland Dr Indianapolis IN 46278

CURTIS, GARY LYNN, medical educator; b. Bellevile, Ill., Jan. 21, 1944; s. Keith L. and Monica A. (Mauser) C.; m. Donna A. Jamison; children—Andrew, Allison, Ashley. B.A., Nebr. Wesleyan U., 1966; Ph.D., Coll. Medicine, U. Nebr., 1971. Instr. biochemistry, U. Nebr. Med. Ctr., Omaha, 1973-76, asst. prof., 1976-80, assoc. prof., dir. infertility lab., research assoc. prof. ob-gyn., 1980—; lectr., presenter papers at nat. meetings. Contbr. numerous articles to sci. publs., chpts. to books. Grantee NIH, Am. Cancer Inst., VA, others. Mem. Soc. Exptl. Biology and Medicine, AAAS. Home: 1102 S 92d St Omaha NE 68124 Office: U Nebr Med Ctr 42d at Dewey Ave Omaha NE 68105

CURTIS, LORENZO JAN, educator; b. St. Johns, Mich., Nov. 4, 1935; s. Lorenzo F. and Grace Rowena (Cornwell) C.; m. Maj R.L. Rosander, Nov. 23, 1971. B.S., U. Toledo, 1958; M.S., U. Mich., 1961, Ph.D., 1963. Registered profl. engr., Ohio. Vis. scientist Argonne Nat. Lab., Argonne, Ill., 1976—; prof. U. Toledo, Ohio, dept. physics, 1963—; docent Lund U., Sweden, 1976-79. Contbr. numerous articles to profl. jours. Recipient Sigma Xi award for Outstanding Research U. Toledo, 1980. Mem. Am. Phys. Soc., Optical Soc. Am., Am. Assn. Physics Tchrs., European Phys. Soc., Svenska Fysiker Samfundet. Avocations: Music; sports. Home: 721 Bronx Dr Toledo OH 43609 Office: Dept Physics and Astronomy Univ Toledo 2801 W Bancroft Toledo OH 43606

CURTIS, NED SHELDON, superintendent of schools; b. Rogers City, Mich., May 20, 1953; s. Ned Sheldon and Donna Mae (McConkey) C.; m. Verna Mae Cobb, Nov. 15, 1974; children—Mackenzie K., Kyle Sheldon. B.S. in Edn., Central Mich. U., 1976, M.A. in Adminstrn., 1978, Ed.S. in Superintendency, 1981; Ph.D. candidate, Mich. State U., 1981-84. Tchr. elem. grades Portage Twp. Schs., Houghton, Mich., 1976-78; prin., Title I dir. Pine River Area Schs., LeRoy, Mich., 1978-79; prin., state fed. programs dir., Vassar, Mich., 1979-81; supt. schs. Fulton Schs., Middleton, Mich., 1981—; workshop facilitator, 1981—; guest lectr. Central Mich. U., 1981—; guest speaker Mich. Tech. U., 1977-78. Mem. Sch. Alliance Polit. Action Com., 1980—; pub. relations dir. Republican Party, Congl. campaign, 1978; organizer Candidates Address Edn., 1982. Named Outstanding New Prin. Region 7, Mich. Elem. and Middle Sch. Prins. Assn., 1978; NSF scholar, 1978. Mem. Mich. Assn. Sch. Adminstrsn., Mich. Assn. Sch. Bds., Am. Assn. Sch. Adminstrs., Nat. Sch. Bd. Assn., Mich. Sch. Bus. Ofcls., Assn. Supervision and Curriculum Devel. Republican. Methodist. Lodge: Lions. Author: Historical Aspects of the Village of Roscommon, 1975. Home: 4764 Lakeside Dr Perrinton MI 48871 Office: 8060 Ely Hwy Middleton MI 48856

CURTIS-LOPEZ, DONNA, social worker, cleaning products distributing company executive; b. Evanston, Ill., Sept. 4, 1944; d. Don Frederic and Bernardina (Lopez) C.; m. Norman Neal Davis, III, Nov. 22, 1970 (div. May 1980); 1 child, Samantha Alma. A.A., Joliet Jr. Coll., 1965; postgrad. Western Mich. U., 1972-74. Sec., various cos., Chgo., 1967-69; sec. Kalamazoo Child Guidance, Mich., 1969-70; social worker Mich. Dept. Social Services, Kalamazoo, 1970-77, supr. social work, Battle Creek and Albion, Mich., 1977—; owner Lopez & Assocs., Kalamazoo, Mich., 1983—. Bd. dirs. East Side Community Ctr., Kalamazoo, 1972. Mem. Mich. Council Social Service Workers. Democrat. Roman Catholic. Lodge: Lioness (Battle Creek) (2d v.p. 1985—). Avocations: reading; swimming; cycling; movies; ceramics. Home: 920 Albert Kalamazoo MI 49001 Office: Calhoun County Dept Social Services 101 N Albion St Albion MI 49224

CURTISS, CHARLES WALLACE, jeweler; b. Urichsville, Ohio, Mar. 29, 1924; s. LeRoy Osborn and Irma L. (Guthrie) C.; m. Evelyn Mae Keller, May 19, 1946. Student, Kent State U., 1942-43, NYU, 1950—. Pres. Curtiss Jewelers, Newcomerstown, Ohio, 1946—. Mem. area council Boy Scouts Am., 1950-57. Served with USN, 1943-46, ATO, PTO. Mem. Am. Nat. Retail Jewelers, Ohio Retail Jewelers, Ind. Retail Jewelers, Retail Mchts., Ohio Watchmakers Assn. (bd. dirs. 1982—), Am. Watchmakers Assn., Newcomerstown C. of C. Republican. Methodist. Lodges: Masons, Elks, Rotary. Avocations: golf; hunting; fishing; gardening. Office: Curtiss Jewelers 120 Main St Newcomerstown OH 43832

CURTISS, R. G., JR., osteopathic physician and surgeon; b. Barryton, Mich., Nov. 4, 1925; s. R. G. and Hester May (McCaman) C.; m. Irma Jane Howison, June 25, 1949; children—Jane, Rexford, Jill. A.B., Alma Coll., 1949; D.O., Coll. Osteo. Medicine and Surgery, Chgo., 1957. Intern, McLaughlin Osteo. Hosp., Lansing, Mich., 1957-58; gen. practice osteo. medicine, Lansing, 1958—; chmn. exec. com. Lansing Gen. Hosp., 1961, chief of staff, 1963-64, dir. dept. Biomechanics, 1982—; clin. assoc. prof. Coll. Osteo. Medicine, Mich. State U., 1969—; cons. in field. Served with USN, 1944-46. Mem. Am. Osteo. Assn., Acad. Applied Osteopathy, Ingham County Assn. Osteo. Physicians and Surgeons (pres. 1961-62), Mich. Assn. Osteo. Gen. Practitioners (pres. 1976-77), Am. Assn. Ret. Persons, Nat. Rifle Assn., Am. Radio Relay League. Republican. Methodist. Developed program on avoiding back problems for hosp. employees. Home and Office: 2500 E Mount Hope Ave Lansing MI 48910

CURTY, JUDITH A., banker; b. Tuscumbia, Mo., Feb. 10, 1957; d. John Benjamin and Dorothy Ann (Holdt) C. A.A., York Coll., 1977; B.A. in Polit. Sci., U. Mo.-Kansas City, 1979. Cert. real estate agt., fin. planner, Mo. Trust adminstr. Commerce Bank, Kansas City, Mo., 1981-82, trust officer, 1982-84; trust officer Mid Am. Bank & Trust Co., Shawnee Mission, Kans., 1984—. Mem. Nat. Assn. Banking Women (com.), Nat. Assn. Female Execs., Kansas City C. of C. (internat. visitors com.), Chi Omega. Mem. Ch. of Christ. Home: 13204 Kemper Ct Independence MO 64050 Office: 4700 W 50th Terr PO Box 2947 Shawnee Mission KS 66201

CUSCINO, THOMAS, JR., mechanical engineer, adminstrator; b. Pitts., May 31, 1950; s. Thomas and Celestina (Roberto) C.; m. Cathline Elaine Edinger, Jan. 28, 1978; 1 child, Curt. B.S.M.E., Pa. State U., 1972, M.S.M.E., 1976. Registered profl. engr., Mo. Draftsman, U.S. Steel Corp., Pitts., 1969; small particle analyst Ctr. for Air Environment Studies, Pa. State U., State College, 1973-75, instr., 1975, research asst., 1975-76, dir. visible emissions evaluation sch., 1976; asst. environ. engr. Midwest Research Inst., Kansas City, Mo., 1976-79, assoc. environ. engr., 1979-82, sr. environ. research engr., 1982-84; project engr. Wilcox Elec., Inc. subs. Northrop Corp., Kansas City, Mo., 1985—. Contbr. tech. papers and reports to profl. publs. Mem. Air Pollution Control Assn. (vice chmn. midwest sect. 1979, chmn. 1980, dir. 1981). Avocations: automotive maintenance, lawn maintenance, electronics. Office: Wilcox Elec Inc subs Northrop Corp 2001 NE 46th St Kansas City MO 64116

CUSHMAN, ORIS MILDRED, nurse, hospital education administrator; b. Springfield, Mass., Nov. 22, 1931; d. Wesley Austin and Alice Mildred (Vaile) Stockwell; m. Laurence Arnold Cushman, Apr. 16, 1955; children—Lynn Ann Cushman Crandall, Laurence Arnold III. Diploma in nursing Hartford Hosp. Sch. Nursing (Conn.), 1953; B.S., Western Mich. U., 1978, M.A., 1980. Staff nurse Wesson Maternal Hosp., Springfield, 1953-54, acting supr., 1954-55; staff nurse Hartford Hosp., 1955-56, head nurse, 1956, staff nurse, 1957-59; staff nurse, charge nurse Reed City Hosp. (Mich.), 1961-67; supr. Meml. Hosp., St. Joseph, Mich., 1967-75, clin. supr. maternal/child health, 1975-77, dir. maternal/child health 1977-80; dir. edn. Pawating Hosp., Niles, Mich., 1980—. Sec. Women's aux. Reed City Hosp., 1964-65, v.p., 1965-66, pres., 1966-67; mem. adv. bd. on family life edn. St. Joseph Sch. Bd. (Mich.), 1979-80. Mem. Nurses Assn. Am. Coll. Obstetricians and Gynecologists, Perinatal Assn.

Mich., S.W. Mich. Perinatal Assn. (founding; v.p. 1979-80, pres. 1980), S.W. Mich. Healthcare Edn. Council (sec. 1983-85), Tri-County Continuing Edn. Council Southwestern Mich. (founding, chairperson 1983-84), Mich. Soc. Healthcare Edn. and Tng. (sec. 1985), Am. Soc. Healthcare Edn. and Tng., Mich. Health Council. Republican. Office: Pawating Hosp 31 N Saint Joseph Ave Niles MI 49120

CUSHMAN, STEPHEN, music educator, consultant; b. Boston, Aug. 16, 1938; s. David and Harriette (Smith) C.; m. Wasthi M. Brannstrom, May 27, 1966; children—Mark, Erik. A.B. cum laude, Harvard U., 1960; Mus.M., New Eng. Conservatory, 1962; Ph.D. in Musicology, Boston U., 1973. Mem. faculty Sch. Music, Boston U., 1974-75; mem. faculty Wheaton (Ill.) Coll. Conservatory, 1975—, prof. music, 1975—, chmn. dept. music history, 1976—; organ recitalist; cons. organ installation; guest lectr. Boston U. Grad. Sch. travel grantee, 1972. Mem. Am. Guild Organists, Am. Musicol. Soc. Republican. Mem. Evang. Convenant Ch. Office: Wheaton College Conservatory Wheaton IL 60187

CUSKEY, STEPHEN MICHAEL, microbiologist, researcher; b. Lancaster, Pa., Dec. 20, 1953; s. Robert Anthony and Joanne Lois (Ressler) C. B.S., Bucknell U., 1975; Ph.D., Rutgers U., 1982. Research assoc. Med. Coll. Va., Richmond, 1982-84; research fellow U. Mich., Ann Arbor, 1984—. Contbr. articles to profl. jours.; contbr. chpt. to Liquid Fuel Developments, 1983. Mem. Am. Soc. Microbiology. Office: Dept Microbiology and Immunology U Mich Ann Arbor MI 48109

CUTCHALL, GREGORY SCOTT, restaurant franchise executive; b. Tucson, May 26, 1952; s. Raymond Collins and Kathrine (Dawson) C.; m. Susan J. Linn, Sept. 7, 1974; children—Cory Collins, Cydney Rae. B.A. in Mktg., U. Nebr., 1974. Location mgr. Ky. Fried Chicken div. Chix-Inc., Omaha, 1971-74, catering mgr., 1974-78, dir. mktg., 1978-81, v.p., 1981—; speaker Nat. Restaurant Assn. Bd. dirs. Nebr. March of Dimes. Mem. Mid Am. Direct Mktg., Omaha Fedn. Advt., Am. Mktg. Assn., Sigma Phi Epsilon Alumni Assn. (pres. 1980-82). Home: 609 Riverside Dr Waterloo NE 68069 Office: 4315 Frances St Omaha NE 68105

CUTHBERTSON, MRS. GEORGE RAYMOND, club woman; b. Liberty, Mo., Apr. 2, 1911; d. Edgar and Mary Jane (Anderson) Archer; student William Jewell Coll., 1929-31; m. George Raymond Cuthbertson, Sept. 3, 1931. Dist. capt. Mothers' March of Dimes, 1959-60; mem. Bergen County Panhellenic Council 1957-60; mem. woman's com. William Jewell Coll. Mem. Mo. Hist. Soc., Clay County Hist. Soc., DAR, Huguenot Soc. S.C., Clay County Mus. Assn., Alpha Delta Pi. Baptist. Clubs: PEO, Liberty Hills Country, Fortnightly. Home: 1921 Clay Dr Liberty MO 64068

CUTHBERTSON, RICHARD WILEY, advertising executive; b. Warren, Pa., Oct. 21, 1935; s. James Campbell and Virginia (Keyes) Cohill; m. Margaret Ann Sampson, Aug. 25, 1962; children—Craig, Jane, James. B.S., Rider Coll., 1961. C.P.A. Mgr., Arthur Andersen & Co., N.Y.C. and Tokyo, 1961-75; controller Foote, Cone & Belding, Chgo., 1975-80; exec. v.p. FCB Internat., Inc., Chgo., 1981—. Served with USMC, 1952-57. Mem. Am. Soc. C.P.A.s, Fin. Execs. Inst. Republican. Roman Catholic. Club: Adventurers (Chgo.). Home: 2101 Grove St Glenview IL 60025 Office: FCB International Inc 401 N Michigan Ave Chicago IL 60611

CUTHBERTSON, ROBERT ALAN, hospital administrator; b. Pittsburg, Kans., June 17, 1947; s. Robert Allen and Sarah Marie (Grasso) C.; m. Teri Ann Tamson, Dec. 28, 1969; children—Matthew, Staci. B.S. in Edn., Pittsburg State U., 1969; M.S., Kans. State U., 1981. Secondary tchr., Haysville, Kans., 1969-70, Yates Ctr., Kans., 1977-78, long term specialist Southeast Kans. Area Agy., Chanute, 1978-81; hosp. adminstr. Hodgeman County Health Ctr., Jetmore, Kans. 1981—. Contbr. articles to profl. jours. Councilman Jetmore City Council, 1983—; chmn. Jetmore Bus. Boosters, 1981—; pres. Jetmore Devel. Corp., 1981—. Served to sgt. U.S. Army, 1970-77. Mem. Am. Coll. Health Care Adminstrs., Am. Coll. Hosp. Adminstrs. (nominee), Health Care Fin. Mgmt. Assn., Kans. Young Health Care Execs. Kans. Hosp. Assn. Republican. Presbyterian. Lodge: Lions (pres. 1984-85). Avocations: photography; camping; sports. Home: 521 Benton PO Box 475 Jetmore KS 67854 Office: Hodgeman County Health Ctr 809 Bramley PO Box 367 Jetmore KS 67854

CUTLER, JOHN FREDERICK, engineering executive; b. Pitts., Aug. 23, 1937; s. John Frederick and Mildred Dorothy (Underwood) C.; m. Diana Sue Larkin, June 7, 1959; children—Michael Alan, Mark Stephen, Michelle Lynne. B.S. in Mech. Engring., Purdue U., 1959. Registered profl. engr., Ind. Design engr. Uniroyal, Indpls., 1959-62; prodn. engr. Richardson Co., Indpls., 1962-63; various engring. positions Schwitzer, Indpls., 1963-79, v.p. engring. and research, 1979—. Patentee in field. Bd. dirs. Internat. Ctr. Indpls., 1978-79, chmn. layout com., 1979. Mem. Soc. Automotive Engrs. Republican. Presbyterian. Clubs: Hoosier Convertible (sec. 1984), Model A (Indpls.). Avocation: Restoring antique automobiles. Home: 8309 Castlebrook Dr Indianapolis IN 46256 Office: Schwitzer 1125 Brookside Ave Indianapolis IN 46206

CUTLER, NORMAN BARRY, funeral service executive; b. Chgo., Mar. 5, 1942; s. Jerome and Hannah (Feinberg) C.; B.S.B.A., Northwestern U., 1964, M.B.A., 1965; m. Gail Weinstein, June 30, 1965; children—Brett, Rebecca. Mgmt. trainee First Nat. Bank of Chgo., 1965-66; with Weinstein Bros., Inc., Wilmette, Ill., 1966—, v.p., 1972—; v.p. Levitt-Weinstein, Inc., North Miami Beach, Fla., 1979—; gen. ptnr. Wilmette Computer Assocs., Dixie Ptnrs., N.M.B. Assocs.; faculty Worsham Coll., Skokie, Ill., 1981-82. Bd. dirs. North Suburban Jewish Community Center, 1975—, also past pres.; gen. co-chmn. Channel 11 Public TV Auction, 1974-75; bd. govs., v.p. Congregation Am Shalom, Glencoe, Ill., now pres. Mem. Jewish Funeral Dirs. Am. (pres. bd. govs.). Lodge: B'nai B'rith (v.p.). Office: 111 Skokie Blvd Wilmette IL 60091

CUTLER, RICHARD LOYD, psychologist, strategy analyst; b. Nottawa, Mich., Sept. 6, 1926; s. William Loyd and Mary Louise (Beerstecher) C.; m. Polly Burmeister, June 19, 1948; children—Patrice Cutler Mariakle, Scott. B.S. summa cum laude, Western Mich. U., 1949; M.A. in Psychology, U. Mich., 1951, Ph.D., 1954. Lic. cons. psychologist, Mich. Asst. prof. psychology U. Calif.-Berkeley, 1953-55; from assoc. prof. to prof. psychology U. Mich., Ann Arbor, 1955-64, v.p., 1964-70, spl. asst. to pres. urban affairs and urban programs, 1969-71; cons. psychologist, strategy analyst, Ann Arbor, 1971—; lectr. in field. Served with USN, 1943-45. Fellow Am. Psychol. Assn.; mem. Mich. Psychol. Assn. (pres. 1964), Mich. Soc. Cons. Psychologists, Mich. Assn. Professions, Phi Beta Kappa, Sigma Xi. Club: Barton Hills Country (pres. 1980). Author: The Liberal Middle Class, 1973; contbr. articles to profl. publs. Office: 1945 Pauline Blvd Ann Arbor MI 48103

CUTNAW (CUGNEAU), MARY-FRANCES, speech educator, writer; b. Dickinson, N.D., June 15, 1931; d. Delbert A. and Edith (Calhoun Pritchard) Cutnaw; B.S., U. Wis.-Mdison, 1953, M.S., 1957, doctoral candidate, 1959-60, 67-68. Tchr., Community Service Displaced Persons Vocat. Sch., Stevens Point, Wis., 1951-52, Pulaski High Sch., Milw., 1953-55; teaching asst. dept. speech U. Wis.-Madison, 1956-57, spl. asst. Sch. Edn., summer 1957; instr. speech and English, U. Wis.-Stout, Menomonie, 1957-58, dean of women, 1958-59, asst. prof. speech, 1959-64, assoc. prof., 1964-74, prof. emeritus, 1974—; hon. scholar, teaching asst. dept. speech U. Wis.-Madison, 1959-60, hon. scholar dept. speech, 1967-68. Organizer, past adviser Young Democratic Orgn., U. Wis.-Stout. Mem. Internat. Platform Assn., Progressive Round Table, U. Wis. Alumni Assn., Assn. U. Wis. Faculties, Wis. Acad. Scis., Arts and Letters, Wis. Women's Network, Am. Quarter Horse Assn., Nat. Soc. Prevention Cruelty to Animals, Nat. Anti-Vivisection Soc., Nat. Ret. Tchrs. Assn., Am. Personnel and Guidance Assn., Smithsonian Asso., Linus Pauling Inst., Center for Study Democratic Instns., ACLU, Common Cause, NOW, Walker Art Center, Phi Beta, Sigma Tau Delta, Pi Lambda Theta, Gamma Phi Beta. Roman Catholic. Clubs: University (St. Paul); Blaisdell Place (dir.), Calhoun Beach. Contbr. articles to profl. jours. Research in speech proficiency and teaching success, curricular speech for spl. occupational groups, speech as guidance tool. Founder, Edith and Kent P. Cutnaw Scholarship, U. Wis.-Stevens Point. Home: Red Cedar Farm Box 282 Menomonie WI 54751 also Cedars on the St Croix Box 176 Lakeland MN 55043

CUTTER, GEORGE STANLEY, investment banker; b. Detroit, Oct. 22, 1945; s. George Osgood and Ann (Barton) C.; m. Catherine Hacker, July 3, 1971; 1 son, S. Barton. B.A., Bowdoin Coll., 1967; M.B.A., Columbia U., 1975. Mgmt. trainee State St. Bank & Trust Co., Boston, 1970-72; asst. v.p. Citibank N.Am., N.Y.C., 1975-79; v.p. Citicorp Internat. Ltd., Hong Kong, 1979-83; v.p. Citicorp Security Markets Inc., Chgo., 1983—. Served to 1st lt. U.S. Army, 1967-70; PTO. Clubs: American of Hong Kong; East Bank (Chgo.). Office: Citicorp Securities Markets Inc 200 S Wacker Dr Chicago IL 60606

CUYJET, MICHAEL JOHN, university administrator; b. Chgo., Dec. 1, 1947; s. John F. and Edwina (Harris) C.; m. Carol Harris Lawson, July 24, 1977; children—Allison Elizabeth, Leslie Carol. B.S., Bradley U., 1969; M.S., No. Ill. U., 1973, Ed.D., 1983. Asst. dir. programming and activities No. Ill. U., DeKalb, 1972-79, adminstrv. assoc. to v.p. for student affairs, 1979-81, dir. programming and activities, 1981—. Contbr. articles to mag. and chpts. to books. Mem. City of DeKalb Mass Transit Adv. Bd., 1980—; bd. dirs. DeKalb County Am. Cancer Soc., 1979-83. Mem. Am. Coll. Personnel Assn. (mem. exec. council, chmm. com. multicultural affairs 1985—), Nat. Assn. Campus Activities (bd. dirs. 1979-82, vice chmn. 1981-82). Democrat. Roman Cathoic. Lodge: K.C. Avocations: photography, traveling. Office: Programming and Activities No Ill Univ DeKalb IL 60115

CYPERT, SAMUEL ALDEN, acctg. co. exec.; b. Granite, Okla., Aug. 5, 1943; s. Alden E. and Ruth N. (Haynes) C.; B.S. magna cum laude, Southwestern Okla. State U., 1970; m. Merrilee Anderson, May 31, 1975; children—Amelia Lee, Elizabeth Anne; children by previous marriage—Beverly, Clif, Benetta. Editor, pub. Weatherford (Okla.) Advertiser, 1968-70; dir. corp. communications Richardson Co., Des Plaines, Ill., 1970-75; dir. communications Profl. Photographers Am., Des Plaines, 1975-79; dir. planning and devel. Peat, Marwick, Mitchell & Co., 1979—; mem. adv. com. on mgmt. and mktg. Ill. State Bd. Edn., 1974-78; editorial cons. Pulse mag., 1978-81, Mason's Line, 1978-81; public relations cons. Ill. State Vet. Med. Assn., 1979-81; instr. fin. writing seminars. Pres., Echo Lake Community Corp., 1981-84; Ill. Crusade coordinator Am. Cancer Soc., 1981. Served with USN, 1962-66. Mem. Midwest Writers Assn., Chgo. Press Club. Author: Writing Effective Business Letters, Memos, Proposals and Reports, 1983. Contbr. articles to consumer mags. and profl. jours. Home: 514 Logan Ave Geneva IL 60134 Office: 303 E Wacker Dr Chicago IL 60601

CYRUS, HOWARD OLIVER, SR., commercial and industrial real estate broker and developer; b. Hammond, Ind., Jan. 22, 1938; s. Claude C. and Catherine C.; m. Mary Beth Rudolph, Aug. 30, 1957 (dec. 1966); children—Howard, Christopher; m. 2d, Ruth E. Bonczkowski Klein, Jan. 1, 1972; 1 son, Samuel; stepchildren—Thomas, Merry Beth, Gregory, T. Robert Klein. Student, Purdue U., 1957-69; Gen. Mgr. Burger Supermarkets, Hammond, 1969-72; with L.R. Meyers Realtors, Munster, Ind., 1972—; owner, mgr. Cyrus & Assocs., Munster 1973; pres. Cyrus-Weiss Mgmt., Inc.; ptnr. Cyrus-Weiss Auction Co.; owner, mgr. Vermillion Co., Cyrus Properties; dir. Produce packaging Corp. of Ind. Mem. adv. council YMCA, Hammond. Served with USNR, 1954-62. Mem. Calumet Bd. Realtors (past dir.), Nat. Assn. Realtors, N.W. Ind. Home Builders Assn. (past bd. dirs.). Presbyterian. Clubs: Ind. Soc. of Chgo., Optimist (past pres., Hammond), Woodmar Country. Lodges: Mason, Shriners, Jesters. Author mail order shopping pamphlet; mfr. bubble bath with spl. formula. Home: 8830 Parkway Dr Highland IN 46322 Office: Cyrus & Assocs 533 Ridge Rd Munster IN 46321

CZAPLICKI, ROMAN, chiropractic physician; b. Grudziadz, Poland, Aug. 12, 1931; s. Antoni Konstanty and Dominika (Lojewski) C.; came to U.S., 1945; D.Chiropractic, Nat. Coll. Chiropractic, 1960; Diploma in Acupuncture Medicine, Nat. Chinese Taiee Acupuncture Coll., 1971; asso. degree Chinese medicine, Hon Hing Inst. Chinese Medicine, Hong Kong, 1971; diploma in osteopathy New South Wales Osteo. Coll., Sydney, Australia, 1977; cert. chiropractic acupuncturist, Nat. Coll. Chiropractic, Chgo., 1977. Cert. clin. hynotherapist, UCLA, 1980; cert. in electro-acupuncture, Voll method, W. Ger., 1980; postgrad. numerous courses. m. Marrieta Surowka, Mar. 17, 1969; 1 dau., Tatiana Dominika. Pvt. practice chiropractic, Chgo., 1960-68, Sydney, Australia, 1968-71, Warren, Mich., 1972-78, Villa Park, Ill., 1979-84, Oak Brook Terrace, Ill., 1984—; mem. staff Patient and Research Ctr., Lombard, Ill.; instr. Chinese medicine Am. Coll. Chiropractic Internists, Detroit, 1972—; mem. Center for Integral Medicine, UCLA. Served with AUS, 1950-52. Fellow Am. Coll. Chiropractic Internists; mem. Am. Chiropractic Assn., Mich. Chiropractic Assn., (dir. dist. 1, bd. appeals peer review, chmn. com. acupuncture research), Ill. Chiropractic Assn., Orthomolecular Med. Soc., Nat. Assn. Disability Evaluating Physicians (charter), Ill. Chiropractic Soc., Internat. Sports Medicine Inst. Author: Acupuncture—5000 Years of Healing Art, 1975. Office: 1 S 132 Summit Ave Oak Brook Terrace IL 60181

CZARNECKI, CARY JOHN, librarian; b. Chgo., Nov. 21, 1946; s. John Anthony and Irene Therese (Slezak) C.; m. Donna Mae Czarnecki, Aug. 5, 1972. A.B. in English, John Carroll U., 1968; M.A., DePaul U., 1974; M.A.L.S., Rosary Coll., 1983. Tchr. English, Loyola Acad., Wilmette, Ill., 1969-78; account exec. Burroughs Corp., Chgo., 1978-79; employee benefits cons. Martin E. Segal Co., Chgo., 1980-81; adult services librarian Oak Park Pub. Library, Ill., 1982-83; reference librarian Oak Lawn Pub. Library, Ill., 1983—. Book reviewer Internat. Jour. Revs. in Library and Info. Sci. John Carroll U. Pres.'s scholar, 1964. Mem. ALA, Ill. Library Assn. Roman Catholic. Club: John Carroll U. Glee (pres. 1967-68). Home: 400 53d St Western Springs IL 60558 Office: Oak Lawn Pub Library 9427 S Raymond Ave Oak Lawn IL 60453

CZARNIECKI, MYRON JAMES, III, art museum director; b. San Francisco, May 28, 1948; s. Myron James, Jr. and Laura Maxine (Atwood) C.; m. Anne Frances Dixon, Nov. 20, 1976; children—Mark James, Laura Anne, Katherine Elizabeth. Student, Xaverius Coll., Antwerp, Belgium, 1966-67; B.A., Wabash Coll., 1971, Sch. Art Inst. Chgo., 1971-72. Instr. photography Wabash Coll., 1970-71; photographer Art Inst. Chgo., 1971-72, audio/visual supr., 1972-74; dir. edn. and state services The Ringling Museums, 1974-76; dir. Miss. Mus. Art, Jackson, 1976-83, Minn. Mus. Art, St. Paul, 1983—; curator-in-residence USIA, Sofia, Bulgaria, 1982; cons. Nat. Endowment for Arts and Humanities; lectr. Art Inst. Chgo.; founding dir. Miss. Inst. Arts and Letters, 1978-83. Author or editor numerous exhbn. catalogs. Raymond Fund grantee, 1972-73; dir. more than 25 grants from Nat. Endowment Arts, Inst. Mus. Services. Mem. Internat. Council Mus., Am. Assn. Mus., Miss. Mus. Assn. (v.p.), Nat. Trust Hist. Preservation, Midwest Mus. Conf. Office: Minn Mus Art Landmark Ctr 5th at Market St Saint Paul MN 55102

DAAB-KRZYKOWSKI, ANDRE, pharmaceutical/nutritional company engineering administrator; b. Warsaw, Poland, May 16, 1949; came to U.S., 1973, naturalized, 1981; s. Aleksy Czeslaw and Zofia (Dyszkiewicz) Krzykowski; m. Brenda Jane Burke, Sept. 6, 1979. M.S. in Chem. Engring., Tech. U. Warsaw, 1973; M.B.A., Memphis State U., 1979. Research chemist Schering-Plough, Memphis, 1974-77; process control mgr. Ralston Purina Co., Memphis, 1977-80; process engring. mgr. Mead Johnson & Co., subs. Bristol-Myers Co., Evansville, Ind., 1980—. Served to 2d lt. Polish Army Res. Mem. Am. Mgmt. Assn., Am. Chem. Soc. Republican. Lutheran. Club: Toastmasters (adminstrv. v.p. local chpt. 1985). Avocations: sailing; scuba diving; karate. Office: Mead Johnson & Co 2404 Pennsylvania Ave Evansville IN 47721

DAANE, G. WARREN, lawyer; b. Grand Rapids, Mich., Apr. 15, 1911; s. Gilbert Leonard and Mamie (Blocksma) D.; m. Mavis Berry, May 15, 1941; children—Gilbert Warren, Robert B., Charles E. A.B., Princeton U., 1932; J.D., U. Mich., 1935. Bar: Mich. 1935, Ohio 1936, U.S. Dist. Ct. (no. dist.) Ohio 1937, U.S. Ct. Appeals (6th cir.) 1950, U.S. Supreme Ct. 1953. Assoc. Baker & Hostetler, Cleve., 1935-50, ptnr., 1951-81, of counsel, 1982—. Served from 2d lt. to lt. col. USAAF, 1942-46. Mem. ABA, Ohio Bar Assn., Bar Assn. Greater Cleve., Order of Coif, Phi Beta Kappa. Club: Mayfield Country.

DABICH, DANICA, biochemist, educator; b. Detroit, Aug. 6, 1930; d. Milan and Mildred D. B.S. in Chemistry, U. Mich., 1952; M.S., Ohio State U., 1955; Ph.D., U. Ill., 1960. Analytical chemist Phillips Petroleum Co., Bartlesville, Okla., 1952-53; research asst. E.B. Ford Research Inst., Detroit, 1955-56; postdoctoral fellow U. Freiburg, Fed. Republic Germany, 1960-61; research assoc. Wayne State U., Detroit, 1961-63, instr., 1963-65, asst. prof., 1966-70, assoc. prof. biochemistry, 1970—. Contbr. numerous articles to profl. publs. Mem. Am. Chem. Soc., Am. Soc. Biol. Chemists, AAAS, Soc. Exptl. Biology and Medicine. Serbian Orthodox. Avocations: sports; gardening; music. Office: Dept Biochemistry Sch Medicine Wayne State U 540 E Canfield St Detroit MI 48201

DABICH, LYUBICA, hematologist, educator; b. Detroit, May 15, 1929; d. Milan and Mildred (Spoljar) D. B.S. in Chemistry, U. Mich., 1954; M.D., C.M., McGill Montreal U., Quebec, Can., 1960. Diplomate Am. Bd. Internal Medicine. Intern, resident U. Mich., Ann Arbor, 1960-64, Elsa U. Pardee fellow in hematology, 1964-65, research assoc. in internal medicine, 1965-66, instr. internal medicine, 1966-68, asst. prof., 1968-73, assoc. prof., 1973—. Producer tapes for TV, 1980. Contbr. articles to profl. jours., chpts. to books. Am. Cancer Soc. fellow, 1965-66. Fellow ACP; mem. Am. Soc. Clin. Oncology, Am. Soc. Hematology, Am. Fedn. Clin. Research. Avocations: skiing, sailing, gardening. Office: 202A Simpson Meml Inst 102 Observatory Ann Arbor MI 48109

DA COSTA, MARGARET ANNE, packaging executive; b. Elmhurst, Ill., Sept. 13, 1941; d. Malvern J. and Margaret E. (Barrett) Hiler; m. Flavio O. da Costa, Oct. 31, 1964 (div.); children—Kathryn (dec.), Flavio J.; m. 2d, Walter A. Gamble, Jr., Dec. 27, 1982. B.A., Miami U., Oxford, Ohio, 1962. Flight attendant Pan Am., N.Y.C., 1962-65; clk. typist City of East Lansing (Mich.), 1974-75; ct. coordinator East Lansing Police Dept., 1975-77; adminstrv. asst. Mich. Co., Lansing, 1977-78; sec.-treas. ASI Packaging Co., Pontiac, Mich., 1978-82, pres.-treas., Grand Blanc, Mich., 1982—; ptnr. Holly-75, 1982—. Mem. Clarkston Zoning Bd. Appeals, 1985. Mem. Clarkston Community Hist. Soc. (treas., bd. dirs. 1980-82), Delta Zeta. Republican. Office: ASI Packaging Co 9311 Holly Rd Grand Blanc MI 48439

DACUS, MINNIE RUTH, human relations specialist; b. Kansas City, Kans., Nov. 11, 1950; d. Alvin Charles and Luetta (Looney) Charles; m. Wesley Gene Dacus, July 25, 1971; children—Quinci Minnique, Wesley Rashad. B.S., Nebr. Wesleyan U., 1973; M.S., U. Nebr., 1977. Tchr. Omaha Pub. Schs., 1973-78, 80-82, human relations specialist, 1982—; reading specialist Berkeley (Calif.) Unified Sch. Dist., 1979-80. Mem. Nebr. Edn. Assn., Omaha Edn. Assn., NEA. Democrat. Christian. Home: 5926 N 108th Ct Omaha NE 68164 Office: 3902 Davenport St Omaha NE 68103

DADO, RALPH NATALE, JR., physician, ophthalmologist; b. Chgo., Mar. 29, 1949; s. Ralph N. Sr. and Violet M. (Mlejnek) D.; m. Christina K. Nolan, July 25, 1981; 1 child, Ralph N., III. B.S., Loyola U., 1970, M.D., 1974. Diplomate Am. Bd. of Ophthalmology. Intern U. Chgo. Billings Hosp., 1974-77, practice medicine specializing in ophthalmology, 1981— cons. physician Rush Presbyterian St. Lukes Hosp., Chgo., 1977—; attending physician Christ's Hosp., Oak Lawn, Ill., 1977-84, U. of Chgo., 1980—, Palos Hosp. Palos Heights, Ill., 1982—; asst. designer research Intraocular Len, 1975; asst. researcher Ophthalmic Ulthasongraphy, 1976. Mem. AMA, Chgo. Med. Soc., Ill. State Med. Soc., Internat. Soc. of Ophthalmology Ultrosongraphy. Club: Vintage Triumph Register (N.J.), Studebaker Drivers (Tex.). Avocations: Organist; photography; antique automobiles. Home and Office: 9621 SW Hwy Oak Lawn IL 60453

DADY, J. MICHAEL, lawyer; b. Sisseton, S.D., Mar. 9, 1949. B.S., St. John's U., 1971; J.D., U. Minn., 1975. Bars: Minn. 1975, U.S. Dist. Ct. Minn. 1975, U.S. Ct. Appeals (8th cir.) 1976, S.D. 1983. Ptnr. Lindquist & Vennum, Mpls., 1979—. Mem. St. John's U. Alumni Assn. (pres. 1984-85). Office: Lindquist & Vennum 4200 IDS Ctr Minneapolis MN 55402

DAGHESTANI, EDDIE (ADNAN), A.Z., economics educator; b. Kuneitra, Syria, May 20, 1933; naturalized U.S. citizen, 1973; s. Abdulhadi Z. and Haddia (Abu-Baker) D.; m. Maysoun Al-Kateb, Dec. 10, 1967; children—Lena, Linda, Diana, Danny. J.D., Damascus U., 1957; M.S., Colo. State U., 1965, Ph.D., 1971. Research asst. econs. Colo. State U., Fort Collins, 1964-65, 66-69; research assoc. N.C. State U., Raleigh, 1965-66; asst. prof. Angelo State U., San Angelo, Tex., 1969-73; assoc. prof. Fort Hays State U., Hays, Kans., 1973-79; assoc. prof. econs. and fin. U.N.D., Minot, 1979—. Bd. dirs. Minot AFB Fed. Credit Union, 1982—, Small Bus. Adminstrn., 1979—, Communiversity Program in Minot, 1982—. Mem. Am. Inst. Decision Scis., Southwestern Soc. Economists, Midwest Econ. Assn., So. Econ. Assn., Am. Bus. Law Assn. Moslem. Clubs: Kiwanis, Elks. Contbr. articles to profl. jours.

DAGMAN, SHERYL ANN, superintendent schools; b. Fargo, N.D., Sept. 15, 1947; d. C. Maynard and Evelyn Gertrude (Holmgren) Hitchcock; m. Virgil Dean Dagman, Sept. 30, 1972; children—Tara Deann, Travis Vernon. B.S., N.D. State U., 1969. Tchr. home econs. Finley Jr. and Sr. High Sch., N.D., 1969-71; tchr. consumer edn. Bemidji High Sch., Minn., 1971-72; supt. schs. Ransom County Schs., Lisbon, N.D., 1973—; exec. officer Ransom County Spl. Edn. Bd., Lisbon, 1972-75, Ransom County Sch. Reorgn. Com., Lisbon, 1973—; sch. fin. coordinator county supt. com. N.D. Dept. Pub. Instrn., 1981-84; mem. statutory revision com. N.D. County Supts. Council, 1982. Sunday sch. tchr., 1979, 85. Named Lisbon Young Career Woman Lisbon Bus. & Prof. Women, 1975; mem. N.D. County Supts. Assn. (state forms com. 1981-84), N.D. Council Sch. Adminstrs., N.D. Farm Bur. (Young Farmer award 1974), N.D. Farmers Union, Ransom County Sch. Bds. Assn. (sec.-treas. 1973—) (Appreciation award 1976-84). Lutheran. Clubs: Lunch n'Learn Homemakers (Lisbon, N.D.) (pres. 1983-85). Avocations: Sewing; crewel embroidery; working with my children; farming and cattle opns. Home: Route 2 Box 138 Enderlin ND 58027 Office: Ransom County Supt Schs Box 112 Courthouse Lisbon ND 58054-0112

DAGUE, LINDA JO CLARK, lawyer; b. Muncie, Ind., Apr. 12, 1947; d. Gene Phillip and Dorothy Catherine (Griffin) Clark; A.B., Ind. U., 1968, J.D., 1982; m. Jerry Halsey Dague, June 15, 1968 (div. May 1979); children—Mary Louise, Robert Clark. Reporter, Tri City Jour., Delaware County, Ind., 1968; teaching asst. Ind. U. Sch. Journalism, 1968-69; editor RCA, Bloomington, Ind., 1969-70, Tri City Jour., 1970-71; asst. editor Pi Lambda Theta, Bloomington, 1974-75, nat. editor, 1975-80; research asst. Ind. U., 1981-82; atty. Warner, Peckinpaugh, Wallace & McLaren, Muncie, 1982—. Vice pres. Friends of Library, Martinsville, 1975-76; bd. dirs. Tulip Trace council Girl Scouts U.S., 1981-82, Ret. Srs. Vol. Program, 1983—, Wepehani Girl Scouts council, 1984—; bd. dirs. Delaware County Council for Arts, 1984—, sec., 1985—. Mem. ABA, Ind. State Bar Assn., Muncie Bar Assn., Women in Communications (pres. chpt. 1978-79), Soc. Profl. Journalists, Ednl. Press Assn. Am. (regional rep. 1979-80), Am. Soc. Assn. Execs. (communicators sect.), Ind. U. Sch. Journalism Alumni Assn. (dir., treas., class agt. 1975-77, pres. 1982-83), Pi Lambda Theta, Zeta Tau Alpha. Republican. Club: Altrusa. Editor Ednl. Horizons, 1975-80; assoc. Ind. U. Law Jour., 1981-82. Home: 301 Pasture Ln Muncie IN 47304 Office: 400 E Jackson St Muncie IN 47305

DAHL, GERALD LUVERN, consultant; b. Osage, Iowa, Nov. 10, 1938; s. Lloyd F. and Leola J. (Painter) D.; B.A., Wheaton Coll., 1960; M.S.W., U. Nebr., 1962; m. Judith Lee Brown, June 24, 1960; children—Peter, Stephen, Leah. Juvenile probation officer Hennepin County Ct. Services, 1962-65; cons. Citizens Council on Delinquency and Crime, Mpls., 1965-67; dir. patient services Mt. Sinai Hosp., Mpls., 1967-69; clin. social worker Mpls. Clinic of Psychiatry, 1969-82, G.L. Dahl & Assocs., Inc., Mpls., 1983—; asso. prof. social work Bethel Coll., St. Paul, 1964-83; spl. instr. sociology Golden Valley Luth. Coll., 1974-83. Founder, Family Counseling Service, Minn. Baptist Conf.; bd. dirs. Edgewater Baptist Ch., 1972-75, chmn., 1974-75. Mem. Nat. Assn. Social Workers, AAUP, Pi Gamma Mu. Author: Why Christian Marriages Are Breaking Up, 1979; Everybody Needs Somebody Sometime, 1980. Office: 4825 Hwy 55 Suite 140 Golden Valley MN 55422

DAHL, HARRY WALDEMAR, lawyer; b. Des Moines, Aug. 7, 1927; s. Harry Waldemar and Helen Gerda (Anderson) D.; B.A., U. Iowa, 1950; J.D., Drake U., 1955; m. Bonnie Sorensen, June 14, 1952; children—Harry Waldemar, Lisabeth (dec.), Christina. Admitted to Iowa bar, 1955, Fla. bar, 1970, Nebr., 1983; practiced in Des Moines, 1955-59, 70—, Miami, Fla., 1972—; mem. firm Steward & Crouch, Des Moines, 1955-59; Iowa dep. indsl. commr., Des Moines, 1959-62, commr. 1962-71; pres. law firm Harry W. Dohl, P.C., Des Moines, 1970—; mem. firm Underwood, Gillis and Karcher, Miami, 1972-78; adj. prof. law Drake U., 1969—. Exec. dir. Internat. Assn. Indsl. Accident Bds. and Commns., 1972-77; dean Coll. Workmen's Compensation, 1972-76, bd. dirs., 1978—; pres. Workers' Compensation Studies, Inc., 1974—, Workers' Compensation Services, Inc., 1977—, Hewitt, Coleman & Assos. Iowa, Inc., 1975-79; founder, mem. Iowa Workers' Compensation Adv. Com., 1963—. Served with USNR, 1945-46. Recipient Adminstrs. award Internat. Assn. Indsl. Accident Bds. and Commns., 1967. Mem. Assn. Trial Lawyers Am. (chmn. workers compensation sect. 1974-75), ABA (chmn. workers compensation com. 1976-78), Iowa Bar Assn., Minn. Bar Assn., Nebr. Bar Assn., Fla. Bar, Iowa Assn. Workers' Compensation Lawyers (co-founder, pres. 1978—), Internat. Bar Assn., Am. Soc. Law and Medicine (council 1975—), Am. Swedish Inst., Swedish Pioneer Hist. Soc., East High Alumni Assn. (pres. 1975-76), Order of Coif. Lutheran. Mason (Shriner). Clubs: Des

Moines Golf and Country, Sertoma (chmn. bd. 1974-75), Des Moines Pioneer; Marine Meml. (San Francisco). Author: Iowa Law on Workmen's Compensation, 1975; contbr. articles to legal jours. Editor ABC Newsletter, 1964-77. Home: 3005 Sylvania Dr Des Moines IA 50365 Office: 974 73d St Des Moines IA 50312

DAHL, NANCY SUE (FIFE), nursing administrator; b. Charleston, W.Va., Oct. 4, 1947; d. Ernest Dara and Dorothy Ann (Lipscomb) Fife; R.N., Grace Hosp., 1970; grad. Mercy Coll., 1970; m. Earl D. Dahl, Aug. 30, 1972; children—Dale Shannon, Rachael Elizabeth. Staff nurse Grace Hosp., Detroit, 1970; intensive care nurse Peralta Hosp., Oakland, Calif., 1970-72; head nurse Mineo Detoxification Center, Cass Lake, Minn., 1972-75; home care coordinator, home health aide instr. Inter County Nursing Agy., Bagley, Minn., 1975-77; nurse evaluator Minn. Dept. Health, Bemidji, 1977-79; dir. nursing services, interim adminstr. Beltrami Nursing Home, Bemidji, 1979-80; dir. nursing service Ah Gwah Ching (Minn.) State Nursing Home, 1980—; now pres. Dahl & Assocs. nursing instr. vocat. nursing programs; mem. policy task force for long term care com. Found. for Health Care Evaluation. Chmn. North Central Planned Parenthood Bd., 1974-76. Mem. Minn. Gerontol. Soc., Bus. and Profl. Women. Republican. Presbyterian. Home: PO Box 104 Ah Gwah Ching MN 56430 Office: Ah Gwah Ching Nursing Home Ah Gwah Ching MN 56430

DAHLE, JOHANNES UPTON, university director; b. Ada, Minn., Nov. 28, 1933; s. Upton Emmanuel and Marte (Golee) D.; m. Arlene Isabel Powell, Dec. 27, 1956; children—Randall Douglas, Lisa Johanna. B.S., U. Minn., 1956, M.A., 1966. Choral dir. U. Minn., Mpls., 1960-62, 63-66; dir. choirs Macalester Coll., St. Paul, 1962-63; dir. student activities and univ. programs U. Wis.-Eau Claire, 1966-71, dir. univ. ctrs., 1971-84, dir. devel., 1984—. Pres., dir. Eau Claire Conv. Tourism Bur., 1979-84; v.p., dir. Eau Claire Regional Arts Council, 1982-84; bd. dirs. United Way of Eau Claire. Served to capt. USAF, 1956-60. Mem. Internat. Assn. Coll. Unions, Council for Advancement and Support Edn., Phi Kappa Phi (sec. 1982-84), Omicron Delta Kappa (sec. 1981-84), Phi Mu Alpha Sinfonia. Mem. United Ch. of Christ. Lodge: Kiwanis (pres. Eau Claire chpt. 1975-76). Home: 1725 Coolidge Ct Eau Claire WI 54701 Office: U Wis Eau Claire 214 Schofield Hall Eau Claire WI 54701

DAHLEN, ELIZABETH MARGARET, speech and language pathologist; b. Moline, Ill., July 23, 1953; d. William Eric and Dorothy Ellen (Reed) D. B.A. cum laude, Augustana Coll., Rock Island, Ill., 1975; M.S., Eastern Ill. U., 1976. Cert. spl. edn. tchr., Ill., Iowa. Speech and lang. pathologist Wyanet Pub. Schs. (Ill.), 1976—, Wyanet, Tiskilwa, Ladd and Dalzell dist. coop., 1976-81, Wyanet, Tiskilwa, Western and Manlius dist. coop., 1981—. Cons. in field; speech therapy inservice resource person Bureau-Marshall-Putnam Counties Spl. Edn. Coop.; staff Summer Speech and Hearing Clinic, Augustana Coll., 1975, 78, 79, 81. Active Bureau County Chorus, 1977—, bd. dirs., 1982—; active Perry Meml. Hosp. Aux., 1980—. Mem. Ill. Speech-Lang.-Hearing Assn. (sec. 1983—), Am. Speech-Lang.-Hearing Assn. (cert.), Delta Kappa Gamma. Republican. Lutheran. Home: 20 E Peru St Apt 3 Princeton IL 61356 Office: Wyanet Grade Sch Wyanet IL 61379

DAHLGREN, EUGENE H., insurance company executive; b. Seattle, June 25, 1947; s. Eugene and Norma (Baumgart) D.; m. Elaine Sharpe, Dec. 27, 1969; children—Adrienne Jane, Morgann Lynn, Westley Miles. B.A., Black Hills State Coll., 1971; student Ins. Inst. Am., Malvern, Pa., 1977-83. Chartered Property Casualty Underwriter. Adjuster, Crawford & Co., Wichita, Kans., 1971; adjuster-in-charge, Gillette, Wyo., 1972-75; claims mgr. S.D. Farm Bur. Mut. Ins. Co., Huron, S.D., 1975-81; regional supr. Nat. Farmers Union Ins. Co., Huron, S.D., 1981—. Mayor, Virgil, S.D., 1976-78; mem. S.D. Congressman's Mil. Acad. Selection Com., 1981, 82; mem. Beadle County Law Enforcement Commn., 1976-78. Republican. Methodist. Club: Internat. Order Blue Goose. Home: Route 3 Box 165 Huron SD 57350

DAHLGREN, ROBERT BERNARD, wildlife research biologist, biology educator; b. Walnut Grove, Minn., Jan. 27, 1929; s. Albert Leonard and Anna Carolina (Lund) D.; m. Carmen Lee, June 11, 1951; children—Dan L., Dee A., David R., Debra M., Dena M., Darcey L. Student Gustavus Adolphus Coll., 1946-48; B.S., S. D. State U., 1950; M.S., Utah State U., 1955; Ph.D., S.D. State U., 1972. Wildlife research biologist S.D. Dept. Game, Fish, and Parks, Huron, S.D., 1952-61; leader small game and furbearer project, 1961-65, asst. chief game mgmt. for research, 1965-67; asst. leader, assoc. prof. S.D. Coop. Wildlife Research Unit, Brookings, 1967-73; leader, prof. Iowa Coop. Wildlife Research Unit, Ames, 1973—. Contbr. articles to profl. jours. Recipient Disting. Alumnus award S.D. State U., 1981. Mem. Wild Life Soc. (pres. Central Mountain sect. 1966, pres. S.D. chpt. 1973, rep. to council 1977-83), Sigma Xi, Phi Kappa Phi, Xi Sigma Pi, Gamma Sigma Delta. Mormon. Avocation: hunting. Office: Iowa Coop Wild Life Research Unit Iowa State U 9 Science II Ames IA 50011

DAHLKE, JANE BRUSH, child psychiatrist; b. Omaha, Feb. 17, 1945; d. John Hobart Brush and Louise (Mackey) B.; m. Helmuth W. Dahlke, Dec. 18, 1971; children—Ann, Rachel. B.A., Wheaton Coll., Norton, Mass., 1967; M.D., U. Nebr., 1972. Intern, U. Nebr., Omaha, 1972-73, resident in psychiatry, 1973-75, fellow in child psychiatry, 1974-76; staff child psychiatrist Nebr. Psychiat. Inst., 1976-78, part-time, 1978-82; pvt. practice medicine specializing in psychiatry, Omaha, 1978—; asst. prof. psychiatry U. Nebr. Coll. Medicine; cons. psychiatrist Episcopal Diocese Nebr.; cons. child psychiatrist Eppley Chem. Dependency Adolescent Services, Meth. Midtown. Mem. AMA, Am. Psychiat. Assn., Nebr. Psychiat. Soc., Am. Acad. Child Psychiatry (com. pvt. practice). Clubs: North Hills Hunt, Odd Couples Dance. Office: 6801 N 72d St Suite 15 Omaha NE 68122

DAHLKE-SEAMAN, DORIS JUNE, insurance agent; b. Sturgis, Mich., June 7, 1944; d. Frederick Alburn and Myrtle Marie (Smith) Nash; m. James C. Dahlke, Dec. 26, 1960 (div. 1969); children—Dana Will, Karl Frederick; m. Kenneth I. Seaman, Dec. 22, 1984. Social work cert., Lansing Community Coll., 1976, A.A. magna cum laude, 1979; B.A., Mich. State U., 1980; postgrad. DePaul U., 1981-82. Program aide Commn. on Alcohol and Drug Edn., Owosso, Mich., 1971-72; program specialist Shiawassee Commn. Mental Health, Owosso, 1972-73; citizen advocate coordinator Assn. Retarded Citizens, Corunna, Mich., 1974-78; activity therapist Shiawassee Commn. Mental Health, Owosso, 1979-80; program coordinator St. Clair Commn. Mental Health, Port Huron, Mich., 1981-82; rep. Am. Nat. Ins. Co., Lansing, Mich., 1983—; bus. ptnr./gen. agt. Eastern Upper Peninsula Ins. Agy., Detour Village, Mich., 1985—; camp dir. Assn. Retarded Citizens, Corunna, 1978-79; crisis ctr. dir. Common Grounds Crisis Ctr., St. Johns, Mich., 1973-75. Editor: Programs for Aging Retarded Manual, 1982. Active Boy Scouts Am., Lansing, 1979—; Sunday sch. supr. United Ch. Ovid, Mich., 1982—; Koskinen Found. grantee, 1978. Mem. Alpha Phi Omega, Phi Theta Kappa. Methodist. Club: O-E Band Boosters (v.p. 1979-80) (Ovid-Elsie, Mich.). Home: Drummond Island MI 49726 Office: Eastern Upper Peninsula Ins Agy PO Box 243 12 Huron St Detour Village MI 49725

DAHLQUIST, HORTON ALBERT, fire chief; b. Omaha, Mar. 12, 1928; s. Horton and Mercedes D.; m. Catherine Dahlquist, June 15, 1957; children—Robert, Catherine, Mercedes, Patricia, William. B.S., U. Nebr.-Omaha, 1964. Firefighter, Omaha Fire Div., 1955-66, capt. 1966-73, bn. chief, 1973-76, asst. chief, 1976-82, fire chief, 1982—; chmn. fire protection tech. dept. U. Nebr.-Omaha. Served with USNR, 1945-47. Mem. Missouri Valley Fire Chiefs Assn., Tri Mut. Aid Assn., Nebr. Emergency Med. Services Council, Internat. Assn. Fire Chiefs. Democrat. Roman Catholic. Club: Omaha Business Men's. Office: 1516 Jackson St Omaha NE 68102

DAHMS, LESTER LOYD, consultant; b. Gladbrook, Iowa, Mar. 9, 1920; s. Henry August and Alvena Polena (Bern) D.; m. Ardis Alvina Mueller, Oct. 12, 1947; children—Beverly J. Dahms Thompson, Kathleen Ann Dahms Carpenter. Student Marshalltown Community Coll., 1964-65. Clk. and rural mail carrier U.S. Postal Service, Marshalltown, Iowa, 1947-75; exec. dir. Am. Inst. Parliamentarians, Inc., Des Moines, 1972-83; pres. Dahms and Bierbaum Assocs., Inc., Norwalk, Iowa, also Dryden, N.Y., 1983—; cons., profl. parliamentarian to various orgns.; tchr. parliamentary procedure; lectr. in field. Served with USMC, 1941-45. Mem. Am. Inst. Parliamentarians (dir. 1964—, pres. 1970-72). Lutheran. Author parliamentary law charts. Home: 1137 Pinehurst Circle Norwalk IA 50211

DAHN, CARL JAMES, aero. engr.; b. Chgo., June 22, 1936; s. Carl E. and Genevieve (Bardon) D.; B.S. in Aero. Engring., U. Minn., 1959; m. Rose E. Kucenski, May 25, 1974. Rocket propulsion devel. engr. Aerojet Gen. Corp., Azusa, Calif., 1959-61, propulsion and explosives devel. engr., 1962-63; chief engr. Omega Ordanace Co., Azusa, 1961-62; propulsion and explosives specialist Honeywell, Inc., Mpls., 1963-68; system safety research engr. IIT Research Inst. Systems Hazard Analysis, Chgo., 1968-74; hazards engring. specialist Polytechnic, Inc., Chgo., 1974-77; pres. Safety Cons. Engrs., Inc., Rosemont, Ill., 1977—; instr. explosives, guns and ballistics; cons. in same field. Asst. scout master Mpls. St. Paul council Boy Scouts Am., 1962; area dir. Parents Without Partners, 1973; ward chmn. Republican party, 1964; ward chmn. Democratic party, 1973. Mem. Am. Soc. Safety Engrs., ASTM (com. sec.), System Safety Soc., Soc. Explosives Engrs., Nat. Soc. Profl. Engrs. Democrat. Methodist and Roman Catholic. Club: N.W. Divorced Catholic Group. Researcher, patentee in explosives field. Home: 6118 W Melrose St Chicago IL 60634 Office: 5240 Pearl St Rosemont IL 60018

DAILEY, BURKE L., state government official; b. Chgo., July 9, 1929; s. Leo Edmund and Helen May (Gray) D.; m. Mary Clare Hughes, Apr. 14, 1951; children—Lisa Anne, Timothy Burke. B.A., Saint Ambrose, Coll., Davenport, Iowa, 1951. Dep. dir. worker's compensation Mich. Dept. Labor, Lansing, 1967-68, dir. worker's compenstaion, 1968-71, chief adminstrv. officer, 1971—; pres. Detroit Claim Mgrs. Assn., 1962. Chmn. Mich. Worker's Compensation Rewrite Com., Lansing, 1969, Mich. Handicapped Employment Com., Lansing, 1970. Recipient Cert. Merit, Mich. State U., 1969; award of Merit, Mich. Epilepsy Found., 1972. Mem. Assn. State Execs. (pres. 1984—), Adminstrv. Officers Assn. (pres. 1974). Roman Catholic. Club: Lansing Racquet. Avocations: golf, tennis, pool, art. Home: 3792 Sandlewood Okemos MI 48864 Office: Mich Dept Labor 7150 Harris Dr Secondary Complex Lansing MI 48909

DAILEY, FRANK WALTER, lawyer; b. Buffalo, Nov. 7, 1919; s. Charles A. and Christine E. (Ticknor) D.; m. Sara Marie Williamson, Jan. 20, 1943 (dec. Sept. 1964); children—Susan Orr, Sharon Cole; m. Margaret Hoover, June 13, 1969; children—Sue Davis, Theresa Laswell, Mary Margaret Wisner. A.B., Duke U., 1941, J.D., 1948. Bar: N.C. 1948, U.S. Dist. Ct. (ea. dist.) N.C. 1950, Tenn. 1959, U.S. Dist. Ct. (ea. dist.) Tenn. 1959, Ind. 1961, U.S. Dist. Ct. (so. dist.) Ind. 1961. Claim rep. Am. Mut. Ins. Co., Raleigh, N.C., 1948-55, br. claim mgr., Chattanooga, 1955-59, regional claim mgr., Indpls., 1959-61; claim supr. Am. States Ins. Co., Indpls., 1961-66; claim mgr. Wabash Fire & Casualty, Indpls., 1966-68; claims atty. Ind. Lumberman's Mut. Ins. Co., Indpls., 1968-85. Contbr. articles to magic jours. Served to lt. USNR, 1942-46; PTO. Mem. N.C. Bar Assn., Ind. Bar Assn., Soc. Am. Magicians (local sec. 1975-80, nat. pres. 1983-84), Internat. Brotherhood Magicians (local pres. 1973). Democrat. Methodist. Home: 7101 Buick Dr Indianapolis IN 46224

DAILEY, ROBERT FRANCIS, educator, systems engineer; b. Cleve., May 26, 1951; s. Robert Francis and Patricia Jean (Kennedy) D.; B.S. with high honors, U. Notre Dame, 1974; M.S. in Indsl. and Systems Engring., Ohio State U., 1979, Ph.D., 1985. Tchr., head math. dept. Hoban High Sch., Akron, Ohio, 1974-77; asst. to dean Coll. Engring. Ohio State U., Columbus, 1977-79; mem. tech. staff Bell Telephone Labs., Naperville, Ill., 1979-81; counselor Ill. Benedictine Coll., Lisle, Ill., 1979-81; grad. teaching assoc. dept. indsl. and systems engring. Ohio State U., 1981-84; asst. prof. math. scis. Loyola U., Chgo., 1985—. Recipient Grad. Assoc. Teaching award Ohio State U., 1983. Mem. Ops. Research Soc. Am., Sigma Xi, Phi Kappa Phi, Alpha Pi Mu. Roman Catholic. Home: Brothers of Holy Cross PO Box 460 Notre Dame IN 46556 Office: Dept Math Scis Loyola U Chicago IL 60626

DAILY, EUGENE JOSEPH, civil engineer; b. Rolla, Mo., Aug. 18, 1913; s. John J. and Anne (Hanefin) D.; m. Jewell Norris, May 1, 1937; children—Carolyn Dailey O'Conner, Kathleen Dailey Wachoiak, John. B.S. in Civil Engring., U. Mo.-Rolla, 1936, Profl. Civil Engr. (hon.), 1971; M.S., U. Ill., 1951. Registered profl. engr., Ill., Mo., Tenn., Ky., Ind. Prof. U. Ill., Champaign, 1947-56; prin. Clark, Daily & Dietz Engrs., Urbana, Ill., 1956-63; pres. Daily & Assocs. Engrs. Inc., Champaign, 1963-81, chmn. bd., 1981—; trustee Champaign-Urbana Mass Transit Dist., 1983—. Contbr. articles to profl. jours. Fellow ASCE (sec., pres. 1973-74); mem. Cons. Engrs. Council Ill. (pres. 1977-78), Soc. Am. Mil. Engrs. (pres. 1984-85), Nat. Soc. Profl. Engrs., Am. Ry. Engrs. Assn. Roman Catholic. Avocation: golf. Home: 1114 Lincolnshire Champaign IL 61821 Office: 816 Dennison Dr Champaign IL 61820

DAILY, EVELYNNE CHARLIER, artist, educator; b. Indpls., Jan. 8, 1903; d. John A. and Anna Barbara (Geizendanner) Bernloehr; m. George Jo Mess, Apr. 28, 1925 (dec. June 1962); m. Edward R. Daily, May 16, 1969. Diploma Herron Sch. Art, 1924, Chgo. Art Inst., 1938, Ecole Des Beaux Arts (France), 1929; Ph.D. (hon.), Colo. State Christian Coll., 1973. Art supr., tchr. Ladywood Sch., Indpls., 1942-43; art tchr. Art League, Indpls., 1956-70; owner, dir. Summer Art Sch., Nashville, Ind., 1962-80, Central Art Studio, Indpls., 1962—. Artist (sketchbook) Historic Buildings in Nashville, Ind., 1972, (oil painting) In My Studio (1st prize Herron Mus. 1958), Lobster with seaweed (merit award 1983), (etchings) Mother and Babes (Hugh Baker Meml. award 1950). Founder Ind. Soc. of Printmakers, 1934; mem. Ind. Fedn. Art Clubs (hon. life) (pres. 1967-69), Ind. Artists Club (hon.), Watercolor Soc. Ind. (3rd v.p.), Nat. Soc. Arts and Letters (recording sec. 1979-80). Avocation: print collecting. Home: 6237 N Central Ave Indianapolis IN 46220

DAILY, FAY KENOYER, botany educator; b. Indpls., Feb. 17, 1911; d. Fredrick and Camellia Thea (Neal) Kenoyer; A.B., Butler U., 1935, M.S., 1952; m. William Allen Daily, June 24, 1937. Lab. technician Eli Lilly & Co., Indpls., 1935-37, Abbott Labs., North Chicago, Ill., 1939, William S. Merrell & Co., Ohio, 1940-41; lubrication chemist Indpls. Propellor div. Curtiss-Wright Corp., 1945; lectr. botany Butler U., Indpls., 1947-49, instr. immunology and microbiology, 1957-58, lectr. microbiology, 1962-63, mem. herbarium staff, 1949—. Ind. Acad. Sci. research grantee, 1961-62. Mem. Am. Inst. Biol. Sci., Bot. Soc. Am., Phycol. Soc. Am., Internat. Phycol. Soc., Ind. Acad. Sci., Torrey Bot. Club, Sigma Xi, Phi Kappa Phi, Sigma Delta Epsilon. Republican. Methodist. Co-author book on sci. history. Contbr. articles on fossil and extant charophytes (algae) to profl. jours. Home: 5884 Compton St Indianapolis IN 46220

DAITCH, PEGGY, advertising agency executive; b. Detroit, Aug. 20, 1946; d. Stanley B. and Miriam L. Friedman; m. Marvin C. Daitch; children—Joshua, Karen. Degree, Universite de Grenoble (France), 1966; B.A., U. Mich., 1967. Producer Sta.-WTAK, Detroit, 1968-70; pub. relations mgr. Sta.-WTVS-TV, Pub. Broadcasting System, Detroit, 1970-72; broadcast producer/writer Loren/Snyder Advt., Detroit, 1976-78; broadcast producer/writer D'Arcy MacManus & Masius, Bloomfield Hills, Mich., 1978-79, account exec., 1979-84, account supr., 1984—. Bd. dirs. Founders Jr. Council, Detroit Inst. Arts, 1976—, sec., 1978, v.p., 1980. Mem. Adcrat Club Detroit, Women's Advt. Club Detroit, The Fashion Group, Nat. Assn. TV Arts and Scis., Detroit Zool. Soc., Detroit Artists Market, Archives Am. Art. Jewish. Home: 8621 Hendrie Huntington Woods MI 48070 Office: 1725 N Woodward Bloomfield Hills MI 48303

DAKE, ANN BARBRA, insurance and risk manager; b. Edgewood, Iowa, June 18, 1952; d. Raymond George and Gretchen Winona (Taylor) Hochhaus, Robert Neil Dake, Sept. 2, 1972; children—Jennifer Ann, Kimberly Michelle. Clerical records dept. Iowa Nat. Mutual Ins. Co., Cedar Rapids, Iowa, 1970-72; customer service rep. Trissel, Graham & Toole, Inc., Davenport, Iowa, 1972-74; rep. comml. lines Friedman Ins. Inc., Dubuque, Iowa, 1974-78; agent The Dave Harper Agy. Inc., Manchester, Iowa, 1978-84, mgr., owner br. office, Strawberry Point, Iowa, 1980-84; ins. and risk mgr. Seedorff Masonry, Strawberry Point, Iowa, 1985—; cons. in field. Mem. Ind. Ins. Agents Iowa (instr. comml. lines rating 1979—), Ins. Women of Dubuque, Ins. Inst. Am. (cert. gen. ins. 1981), Nat. Assn. Ins. Women (cert. profl. ins. woman 1981), Ind. Ins. Agents Am., Strawberry Point C. of C. (sec./treas. 1982—). Republican. Methodist. Office: Seedorff Masonry Inc 408 W Mission St Strawberry Point IA 52076

DALBEC, PAUL EUCLIDE, physics educator; b. New Bedford, Mass., June 26, 1935; s. Euclide and Alice Marie (Sicard) D.; m. Rosa Dolores Schwaiger, Dec. 28, 1963; 1 child, John P. B.S., Boston Coll., 1957; M.S., Notre Dame U., 1959; Ph.D., Georgetown U., 1966. Physicist, Melpar, Inc., Falls Church, Va., 1959-60; head thin films dept. Gen. Instrument Corp., Newark, 1960-61; asst. prof. Am. U., Washington, 1966-68; faculty Youngstown State U., Ohio, 1968—, prof. physics, 1978—. Contbr. articles to profl. jours. Chmn., troop com. Boy Scouts Am., Youngstown, 1983—. Faculty grantee Youngstown State U., Namur, Belgium, 1978-79; fellow NASA, 1964-66, Georgetown U., 1961-64, Notre Dame U., 1957-59. Mem. ASTM, Am. Vacuum Soc., Am. Phys. Soc., Am. Assn. Physics Tchrs., Ohio Edn. Assn. (exec. com. Youngstown State U. chpt. 1980—). Democrat. Roman Catholic. Clubs: Alliance Franco-Am. du Midwest (bd. dirs.), Le Cercle Francais (Youngstown). Home: 1984 Innwood Dr Youngstown OH 44515 Office: Dept Physics Youngstown U 410 Wick Ave Youngstown OH 44555

DALE, MARVIN, contract negotiator; b. Birmingham, Ala., Mar. 30, 1933; s. Finley and Annie (Boykins) D.; m. Ada Gaines (div. June, 1964); children—Marva, Wanda, Derrick; m. Lucile Jenkins, Nov. 18, 1967; children—Stanley, Marviette. A.A., U. Md., 1974, B.A., 1975; M.S., Troy State U., 1977. Enlisted man U.S. Air Force, 1951-81; adminstrv. officer USAF, Ramstein AFB, Fed. Republic Germany, 1971-73, exec. officer, 1973-78; sr. enlisted advisor fgn. tech. div., Wright-Patterson AFB, Ohio, 1978-81, contract negotiator aero. systems div., 1983—; chief of devel. Dayvest Ohio Bur. Employment, Dayton, 1981-82; procurement agt. Def. Logistics Agy., Columbus, Ohio, 1982-83. Pres. Protestant parish council Chapel Mgmt. Program, Wright-Patterson AFB, 1984—. Decorated Bronze Star, Air Force Commendation medal. Fellow Air Force Assn., Noncommd. Officers Assn., Am. Legion; mem. Nat. Contract Mgmt. Assn., Air Force Sgts. Assn. (trustee 1984). Democrat. Baptist. Avocations: chess, swimming, gardening. Home: 7057 Pine View Dr Huber Heights OH 45424 Office: Hq ASD/RWKRC Wright Patterson AFB OH 45433

DALE, MARYELLEN, marketing executive; b. Bedford, Ohio, Nov. 1, 1947; d. Jessie and Luvenia (Kirkland-Rogers) Rogers; student public schs., Bedford, Ohio; children—Celina Louise, Celia Kimberly, Michelle Lynn, Michael Lawrence. Asst. supr. order dept. Williams & Co., Cleve., 1966-68; sales and engring. sec. Interior Steel Equipment Co., Cleve., 1969-71; owner co., Cleve., 1972-74; mgr. advt. adminstrn. CleCon, Inc., Cleve., 1974-81; pres. Target Direct Mktg., Inc., Cleve., 1981—; mktg./advt. cons.; proposal writer for fed. funding for community devel. project. Promotion cons. Social Services Dept., County Welfare Foster Child Div., Cleve., 1981-82; adv. com. Am. Heart Assn., 1981-82. Recipient awards, Cleve. Bus. and Econs. Devel., 1970, Cleve. Advt. Sch., 1976, Splty. Merchandising Corp., 1977. Mem. Internat. Traders, Am. Mgmt. Assn., Black Profl. Assn., Career Guild, Nat. Assn. Female Execs., Am. Soc. Notaries. Baptist. Clubs: Cleve. Advt., Cleve. Communicators. Contbr. articles to profl. jours. Home: 9407 Easton Ave Cleveland OH 44104 Office: 11420 Woodland Ave Cleveland OH 44104

DALEY, DUANE KENNETH, plastics company executive; b. Canton, Ill., Nov. 1, 1942; s. Charles Kenneth and Ila Marie (Brashear) D.; m. Patricia Ann Spencer, Apr. 6, 1963; children—Karl Spencer (dec.), Deanna Kay. Student Galesburg Bus. Coll. (Ill.), 1960-61. Sec. to gen. mgr. Chgo., Burlington & Quincy R.R., Chgo., 1961-65; salesman Accurate Threaded Fasteners, Chgo., 1965-68; v.p. Verco Mfg. Inc., Webster City Iowa, 1968-71; sales mgr. Riverside Plastics Co., Bonaparte, Iowa, 1971-82, gen. mgr., 1982-84; exec. v.p. Mt. Pleasant Plastics, Inc., Iowa, 1984—. Baptist. Home: Rural Route 2 Bonaparte IA 52620 Office: Mt Pleasant Plastics Inc Box 23-A Mount Pleasant IA 52641

DALEY, JAMES KENT, consultant; b. Chgo., Jan. 25, 1952; s. James LeRoy and Sydney Dorcus (Carlton) D.; B.S. in Math., Ill. State U., 1974; M.S. in Biostats., U. Pitts., 1976; M. in Finance, Northwestern U., 1984. Research asst. Nat. Safety Council, Chgo., 1976-78; research analyst Central States Health, Welfare and Pension Fund, Chgo., 1978-84; pension systems cons. Hewitt Assocs., Lincolnshire, Ill., 1984—. USPHS scholar, 1974-76. Mem. Am. Statis. Assn., Ill. State Alumni Assn., U. Pitts. Alumni Assn., Northwestern U. Alumni Assn., Beta Gamma Sigma, Alpha Kappa Lambda. Republican. Evangelical. Lodge: Lions. Avocations: Bicycling; skiing; tennis; golf. Office: Hewitt Assocs 100 Half Day Rd Lincolnshire IL 60015

DALEY, SUSANNA, insurance underwriter; b. Heilbronn, Ger., Nov. 20, 1947; came to U.S., 1951; d. Stanley Walter and Sophia Maria (Trebik) Weglarz; m. Patrick J. Daley, Jr., July 26, 1969; children—Michelle, Christopher. B.A. in Slavic Studies, Alliance Coll., Cambridge Springs, Pa., 1969. Cert. in auto underwriting, in model-netics. Exec. sec., receptionist Vector Corp., Pitts., 1970; bindery asst., translator Linda Hall Library, Kansas City, Mo., 1972-73; comml. lines coder Royal Globe Ins., Kansas City, Mo., 1973-76; comml. casualty rater Md. Casualty Co., Kansas City, Mo., 1976-79; comml. casualty underwriter Continental Ins. Co., Overland Park, Kans., 1979-81; comml. mult-line underwriter Mid-Am. Preferred Ins. Co., Kansas City, Mo., 1981—. Commr., Ethnic Enrichment commn., Kansas City, Mo., 1983. Mem. Kansas City Underwriters Assn. Democrat. Roman Catholic. Club: Inter-Greek Council (Cambridge Springs, Pa.), Polish Nat. Alliance (pres. 1984-85). Home: 3616 S Hocker Ave Independence MO 64055 Office: Mid-America Preferred Ins Co 2800 Rockcreek Pkwy North Kansas City MO 64117

DALEY, THOMAS JAMES, engineering project manager; b. Milw., May 2, 1947; s. Jerome Francis and Shirley Marie (Hoefling) D.; children—Thomas, Sean, Kate. B.S.M.E., U.S. Naval Acad., 1969; M.S.M.E., U.S. Naval Postgrad. Sch., Monterey, Calif., 1970; M.B.A., U. Chgo., 1981. Registered profl. engr., Calif., Ill., N.Y., Ohio, Ala. Project engr. Sargent & Lundy, Chgo., 1976-80; project mgr. Procon, Inc., Des Plaines, Ill., 1980-82, Sargent & Lundy, Chgo., 1982—. Served to lt. comdr. USN, 1969-76. Mem. ASME, Am. Nuclear Soc. Republican. Roman Catholic. Office: Sargent & Lundy 55 E Monroe St Chicago IL 60603

DALIA, VERA, clinical psychologist; b. Brno, Czechoslovakia, Nov. 19, 1935; d. Aharon and Helen (Grun) Wollner; came to U.S., 1963, naturalized, 1970; m. Zol F. Muskovitch, Dec. 23, 1958 (dec. 1969); children—David, Debby. Student Hebrew U., Jerusalem, 1956-58; B.A., U. Toronto, 1961; M.A., U. Evansville, 1971; Ph.D., U. Mich., 1974. Clin. community psychologist Sudbury (Ont., Can.) Algoma Sanatorium, 1974-76; clin. coordinator Bangor (Maine) Mental Health Inst., 1976-78; dir. behavioral sci. family practice residency St. Joseph Hosp., Flint, Mich., 1978-79; clin. and cons. psychologist Flint, Birmingham, Southfield, Mich., 1979-84; clin. faculty U. Maine, 1978. Horace B. Rackham grantee, 1973-74. Mem. Am. Psychol. Assn., Mich. Psychol. Assn., Mich. Soc. Cons. Psychology, Soc. Tchrs. Family Medicine. Office: 1621 E Court St Flint MI 48503

DALLAS, CONSTANTINE GEORGES, architect, engineer; b. Kerassovo, Greece, July 16, 1918; s. Georges Constantine and Eleni (Dermaris) D.; came to U.S., 1957, naturalized, 1961; m. M. Joan Hassmer, May 6, 1961. B.A. in Math., Physics, Chemistry, Geography and Cosmography, Coll. Gymnasium Carpenissiou State Coll., Greece, 1938; assoc. mem. Brit. Inst. Engring. and Tech., 1949. Assoc. Holabird and Root architects and engrs., Chgo., 1957-62; founder, chancellor Internat. Technol. Inst., Chgo., 1962-66, also dean Sch. Architecture; pvt. practice architecture, engring., Chgo., 1966—. Campaign dir. Hellenic Am. Regular Democratic Orgn. Ill.; vol. Radio Free Europe, Palestine, during World War II. Served with Greek Royal Army, 1939-43. Decorated 3 Iron Crosses of Heroism. Mem. AIA, Hellenic Ednl. and Progressive Assn., Evrytanian Greek Assn. Greek Orthodox. Lodge: Masons. Home: 5722 N Christiana Ave Apt 1 Chicago IL 60659 Office: 4401 N Sheridan Rd Chicago IL 60640

DALLAS, DANIEL GEORGE, social worker; b. Chgo., June 8, 1932; s. George C. and Azimena P. (Marines) D.; B.A., Anderson (Ind.) Coll., 1955; B.D., No. Bapt. Theol. Sem., 1958; M.S.W., Mich. State U., 1963; M.Div., No. Bapt. Theol. Sem., 1972, D.Min., 1981; m. G. Aleta Leppien, May 26, 1956; children—Paul, Rhonda. Mem. faculty Mich. Dept. Corrections, Mich. State U., 1963-66; med. social adminstr. Med. Services div. Mich. Dept. Social Services, 1966-68; cons. Outreach Center of DuPage County, 1976—, also dir. social service Meml. Hosp. of DuPage County, Elmhurst, Ill., 1968—; therapist, lectr. Traffic Sch., Elmhurst Coll.; pvt. practice; indsl. cons. Mem. Elmhurst Sr. Citizen Commn., 1976—. Recipient Outstanding Service award Mental Health Assn. Ill., 1978. Mem. Nat. Assn. Social Workers, Soc. Hosp. Social Work Dirs., Am. Hosp. Assn., Nat. Registry of Health Care Providers, Mental Health Assn. Chgo. Club: Rotary. Contbr. articles to profl. jours. Office: 242 N York St Room 203 Elmhurst IL 60126

DALLMEYER, A(LVIN) RUDOLPH, JR., management consultant; b. St. Louis, Nov. 15, 1919; s. Alvin Rudolph and Sarah Lucille (Ford) D.; B.S. in B.A., Washington U., St. Louis, 1941; M.B.A. with distinction, Harvard U., 1947; children—Richard L., R. Ford, J. Scott, P. Suzanne, Exec. asst.

Automatic Electric Co., Chgo., 1947-52; cons., assoc. Booz, Allen & Hamilton, Chgo., 1952-59; v.p. Spencer Stuart & Assos., Chgo., 1959-63; v.p., pres. Donald R. Booz & Assocs., Chgo., 1963-77; pres. Dallmeyer & Co., Inc., Chgo., 1977—; dir. Maritz, Inc., Federated Foods, Inc., Fidelitone Inc., Microseal, Inc., Consol. Chem. Inc. Served to maj. U.S. Army, 1941-45. Cert. mgmt. cons. Mem. Inst. Mgmt. Cons. (chpt. dir.), Am. Mktg. Assn., Chgo. Assn. Commerce and Industry, Internat. Bus. Council MidAm., Chgo. Council on Fgn. Relations, French-Am. C. of C., German Am. C. of C., Phi Delta Theta. Republican. Presbyterian. Clubs: University, Metropolitan, Harvard Bus. Sch. Chgo. (dir.). Home: 861 Bryant Ave Winnetka IL 60093 Office: 20 N Wacker Dr Chicago IL 60606

DALTON, HARRY, baseball executive; b. Springfield, Mass., Aug. 23, 1928; grad. Amherst Coll., 1950. With Balt. Orioles, 1953-71, v.p. and player personnel dir., 1965-71; exec. v.p., gen. mgr. Calif. Angels, 1971-77; exec. v.p., gen. mgr. Milw. Brewers, 1977—. Served to 1st lt., USAF. Decorated Bronze Star. Office: Milw Brewers Milw County Stadium Milwaukee WI 53214*

DALTON, LEROY CALVIN, educator; b. Blue River, Wis., June 13, 1926; s. Edgar LeRoy and Lona Francis (Dyer) D.; B.S., U. Wis., 1950, M.S. in Edn., 1954; M.S. in Math., Marquette U., 1964; postgrad. U. Chgo., 1958; m. Evelyn Mae DeJean, Sept. 2, 1950; children—Steven LeRoy, Nanci Jean. Tchr. math. and sci. Spring Green (Wis.) High Sch., 1950-52, McHenry Community High Sch. (Ill.), 1952-53; tchr. math. Wauwatosa (Wis.) High Sch., 1953-61; tchr. math., Wauwatosa West High Sch., 1961—, chmn. dept., 1961-84; math. area chmn. Wauwatosa Secondary Schs., 1962-65, 71-84; math. area chmn. Wauwatosa Sch. Dist., 1984—. Mem. Wauwatosa Youth Commn., 1971-73; chmn. council on ministries Wauwatosa Ave. Meth. Ch., 1974-76. Recipient Presdl. award for excellence in math. teaching, 1984; named Math. Tchr. of Year, Wis. Soc. Profl. Engrs., 1975; Dist. Tchr. of Yr., 1977; Disting. Math. Educator of Yr., Wis. Math. Council, 1984; NSF summer fellow Marquette U., 1959-63. Mem. Nat. Council Tchrs. Math. (life, dir. 1977-80, mem. math. curriculum for 1980's com. 1977-80, steering com. priorities in sch. math. project 1977-80, mem. bd. liaison to Math. Tchr. editorial panel 1978-80, mem. election com. 1985—), NEA (honor award 1970), Math. Assn. Am. (com. on high sch. contests 1965-71), Wis. Math. Council (pres. 1962), Wis., Wauwatosa edn. assns., Milw. Area Math. Council, Phi Delta Kappa, Mu Alpha Theta (nat. pres. 1962-65). Author: Algebra I, 1967, Algebra 2 and Trigonometry, 1968; Geometry, 1971; Using Algebra, 3d edit., 1981; Using Advanced Algebra, 3d edit., 1981; Using Geometry, 1978; Algebra in the Real World, 1983; editor Topics for Mathematics Clubs, 1973, 2d edit., 1983; editor Clubs sect. Math. Tchr., 1980-82. Home: 938 N 115th St Wauwatosa WI 53226 Office: 11400 W Center St Wauwatosa WI 53222

DALTON, ROBERTA CHRISTY, educator; b. Viola, Ill., Apr. 12, 1913; d. Benjamin Lowe and Lucy Ellen (Gladman) Christy; m. Hensley Havila Dalton, May 31, 1947; 1 child, Deborah Ann. B.A. in Edn., Western Ill. State U., 1935; student Brown's Bus. Coll., 1938. Tchr. Brooklyn Schs., Ill., 1935-36; clk. typist Dist. W.P.A. Office, Peoria, Ill., 1938-41; comml. tchr. Seaton High Sch., Ill., 1941-42; sec., clerk CB&Q RR, Galesburg, Ill., 1945-52; teletypesetter operator Galesburg Register-Mail, 1952-57; tchr. math., 1957-76. Mem. Galesburg Bd. Edn., 1977—, pres. 1981-82, 83-84, 84-85; bd. dirs. City Planning Commn., Galesburg, 1977-87. Recipient Outstanding Citizen award Phi Delta Kappa, 1985. Mem. Ill. Ret. Tchrs. Assn., Galesburg Retired Tchrs. Assn., Nat. Sch. Bd. Assn., Ill. Assn. Sch. Bds. Republican. Congregationalist. Club: Knox Coll. 50 Yr. Lodges: Elkettes, Am. Legion Aux. Avocations: swimming; painting. Home: 1590 W Main St Galesburg IL 61401 Office: Dist 205 Bd Edn 285 S Farnham St Galesburg IL 61401

DALUZ, JOHN THOMAS, metallurgist, company executive, consultant; b. Fall River, Mass., July 30, 1947; s. John Charles and Mary Delores (Carvalho) DaL.; m. Pamela Lee Noblet, Nov. 25, 1968 (div. July 1984); children—Melissa Beth, John Christopher. A.A., Bristol Community Coll., 1968; B.S., Southeastern Mass. U., 1970; M.B.A., Harvard U., 1973. Adminstrv. mgr. Teledyne Rodney Metals, Phila., 1969-78; gen. mgr. Creusot-Loire Steel Corp., Cleve., 1978-81; v.p. Thermo Systems Inc., Denver, 1981-84; pres., chief exec. officer Enforcement Tech. Inc., Aurora, Colo., 1984—. Policeman Denver Res. Police Force, 1984—. Mem. Nat. Assn. Accts. Republican. Roman Catholic. Avocations: photography; autoracing; running; tennis; police patrol work. Home: 2064 Monaco Pkwy Apt 306B Denver CO 80210 Office: Enforcement Tech Inc 10957-P E Bethany Dr Aurora CO 80014

DALY, CHARLES JOSEPH, See *Who's Who in America,* 43rd edition.

DALY, JOHN FRANCIS, industrial manufacturing company executive; b. N.Y.C., Dec. 13, 1922; s. John F. and Caroline (Pohl) D.; B.S., Rensselaer Poly. Inst., 1943; m. Casilda Boyd, July 18, 1953; children—Jo-Ann, Avis, Carol, Peter, Alexia. Vice pres. Internat. Steel Co., Evansville, Ind., 1956-59; exec. v.p. Universal Wire Spring Co., Bedford, Ohio, 1959-60; v.p. Hoover Ball & Bearing Co. (name Hoover Universal Inc. 1978), Ann Arbor, Mich., 1960-66, exec. v.p., 1966-68, pres., 1968—, chmn., chief exec. officer, 1972—, also dir.; vice chmn. bd., dir. Johnson Controls, Inc., Milw.; dir. Comerica Inc., Comerica Bank Detroit, Comerica Ann Arbor, Amerisure Cos., Mich. Mut. Ins. Co., Detroit, Cross & Trecker Corp., Bloomfield Hills, Handleman Co., Troy, Plasti-Line, Knoxville. Trustee Indsl. Tech. Inst., Ann Arbor, Citizens Research Council of Mich., Siena Heights Coll., Adrian. Served to capt. USAAF, 1943-46. Mem. Theta Xi. Home: 905 Berkshire Rd Ann Arbor MI 48104 Office: PO Box 1003 Ann Arbor MI 48106

DALY, MICHAEL MOSBY, osteopathic physician, b. Grand Forks, N.D., July 9, 1943; s. Jerome Joseph and Alda (Mosby) D.; m. Peggy Nell Millikan, Aug. 17, 1963 (div. May, 1973); children—Michael, Kimberly; m. Marian Jeanne Duncan, June 3, 1973; children—Kathleen, MacKenzie; B.S., St. Louis U., 1965; M.S. in Edn., Eastern Ill. U., 1967; D.O. Kirksville Coll. Osteo. Medicine, 1971. Practice medicine specializing in osteo. medicine, Moberly Med. Clinic, Mo., 1972-77, Northwest Clinic, Moberly, 1977—. Bd. dirs. Am. Heart Assn. County Affiliate, 1984, Randolph County Resource Council, 1982. Named by election Pres. Med. Staff Moberly Reg. Med. Ctr., 1982. Mem. Soc. Critical Care Medicine, Am. Coll. Gen. Practioners. Republican. Roman Catholic. Avocations: aviation; computers; home gardening. Home: 1606 Parkwood Moberly MO 65270 Office: Northwest Clinic 1020 Hwy 24W Moberly MO 65270

DALY, SUZETTE MARIE, nurse; b. Bay City, Mich., Oct. 15, 1957; d. Kenneth George and Donna Lorraine (Rushlow) Villermain; m. Dennis Edward Daly, May 31, 1980; 1 son, Keith Edward. B.S.N., Nazareth Coll., 1979. R.N., Mich. Nurse's aide Shoreham Nursing Home, St. Joseph, Mich., 1975-78; secretarial helper office of v.p. Nazareth Coll. (Mich.), 1975-79; patient care technician Borgess Hosp., Kalamazoo, 1978; nurse Bay Med. Ctr., Bay City, Mich., 1977-80; pub. health nurse Dist. Health Dept. 3, Charlevoix, Mich., 1980—. Mem. Mich. Pub. Health Assn. (sec.-treas. 1982—), Charlevoix County Hospice, Nazareth Coll. Alumni Assn. Roman Catholic. Office: Dist Health Dept 3 203 Antrim St Charlevoix MI 49720

DAMACHI, NICHOLAS AGIOBI, industrial engineer, educator; b. Obudu, Nigeria, Mar. 16, 1953; came to U.S., 1972; s. Justin Jabekong and Justina Lami (Ogar) D. B.S.I.E., Ohio State U., 1976, M.S., 1978; Ph.D., U. Cin., 1981. Tchr., Obudu, Nigeria, 1972; systems engr., Div. of Water, City of Columbus, Ohio, 1977-79; indsl. engring. cons. Dosimeter Corp., of Am., Cin., 1980; grad. research lectr. U. Cin., 1979-81, adj. asst. prof. 1981-82, asst. prof. indsl. engring., mng. dir., 1982—. Mem. bd. trustees, Cin. Freestore; Lamic (Nigeria) Ltd. Mem. Inst. of Indsl. Engrs., Am. Soc. for Quality Engrs., Am. Water Works Assn., Human Factors Soc. (chartered), Alpha Pi Mu. Roman Catholic. Contbr. articles to profl. jours. Home: 2075 Clifton Ave Apt 25 Cincinnati OH 45219 Office: Dept Indsl Engring U Cincinnati Cincinnati OH 45221

DAMASKUS, CHARLES WILLIAM, biochemist; b. Blue Island, Ill., Oct. 28, 1924; s. Frederich and Johanna Damaskus; children—Linda, Craig, Diane. B.A., Valparaiso U., 1949. Research chemist Baxter Labs., Morton Grove, Ill., 1949-51; sr. scientist Armour Pharm. Co., Chgo., 1951-63; clin. research scientist Am. Hosp. Supply Co., Mt. Prospect, Ill., 1963-66; pres. Alper Labs., Inc., LaGrange, Ill., 1966—. Contbr. articles to sci. jours. Patentee in field. Elder St. John's Lutheran Ch., LaGrange, 1950-58, chmn. elders, 1959-61, pres. congregation, 1962-64. Served with USCG, 1942-44, as aviator USNR, 1944-47. Mem. Am. Chem. Soc., AAAS. Home: 132 S Kensington Ave LaGrange IL 60325 also 4745 S Atlantic Ponce Inlet FL 32018 Office: PO Box 232 LaGrange IL 60525

DAMES, JEAN, training centers executive, educator, consultant; b. Chgo., Nov. 3, 1940; d. Nicholas Peter and Patricia (Pavlakos) D.; m. Douglas Ryuchi Susu-Mago, May 17, 1980. Student Pierce Coll., Athens, Greece, 1957-58; B.A., U. Chgo., 1961; M.A. in Counseling Psychology, U. Calif.-Berkeley, 1965, postgrad. in ednl. psychology, 1971-74. Tchr. 2d grade Thornton (Ill.) Elem. Sch., 1961-62; credentials counselor U. Calif.-Berkeley, 1963-64, research analyst Ctr. for Research and Devel. in Higher Edn., 1965-67, lectr. Sch. Social Welfare, 1967, tchr. nursery sch. Child Study Ctr., 1971-72, evaluator tchr. tng., 1973-74; instr. psychology San Francisco State Coll., 1965-67; research analyst Calif. Dept. Corrections, Oakland, 1967-71; instr. Sch. Edn., Northwestern U., Evanston, Ill., 1974-75; evaluator multilingual unit dept. research and evaluation Chgo. Bd. Edn., 1975-76; cons. N.W. Ednl. Coop., Arlington Heights, Ill., 1976-82; owner, dir. EPIcenter, computer learning ctr., Evanston, Ill., 1981—; cons. to Chgo.-area sch. dists.; condr. tchr.-tng. workshops on computer use in schs.; lectr. in field. Mem. Phi Delta Kappa. Greek Orthodox. Author LOGO workbook for elem. students. Office: EPI Center 1612 Central St Evanston IL 60201

DAMICO, ANNETTE MARIE, hospital medical records administrator; b. Chillicothe, Ohio, Jan. 14, 1957; d. Ernest Joseph and Mary Catherine (Fink) D. B.S. in Allied Health Professions, Ohio State U., 1979. Dir. med. records Med. Ctr. Hosp., Chillicothe, Ohio, 1979—; med. record cons. Heartland Nursing Home, Chillicothe, 1982. Mem. Am. Med. Record Assn. (registered record adminstr.), Ohio Med. Record Assn. (chmn. job bank 1982). Roman Catholic. Clubs: Chillicothe Bus. and Profl. Women's (v.p. 1983-84), K.C. Ladies Aux., YMCA. Office: 272 Hospital Rd Chillicothe OH 45601

DAMMANN, ROBERT DONALD, medical school official; b. Chgo., Mar. 13, 1928; s. Henry William and Adela (Kaufmann) D.; student U. So. Calif., 1947-48; Mus.B., Northwestern U., 1949, B.Mus. Edn., 1950, M.B.A., 1959, M.Mgmt. in Hosp. and Health Services Mgmt., 1978; m. Joanne Gubbins, Sept. 5, 1953 (dec. Aug. 1983); children—Kathleen Ellen, Donald Alan; m. Janet Rapp, Nov. 4, 1984. Asst. mgr. imports Great Lakes Overseas, Inc., Chgo., 1953-60; researcher marketing Revere Elec. Mfg. Co., Chgo., 1960-64, advt. mgr., 1964-65, mgr. marketing services, 1965-68; mgr. marketing services MSL Steel Co., 1968-69; marketing mgr. Innovex div. Hammond Corp., 1969-70; adminstrv. mgr. dept. anesthesia Northwestern U. Med. Sch., Chgo., 1970-73, dir. adminstrv. services, 1973-78, dir. adminstrv. and fin. services, 1978—, asst. dean for adminstrn., lectr. div. continuing edn., 1978-80. Bd. dirs., sec.-treas. Northwestern Found. for Research and Edn., 1980. Served with AUS, 1951-53. Mem. Assn. Am. Med. Colls. (exec. com. bus. affairs group Midwest-Gt. Plains region 1974-75, chmn. bus. affairs group Midwest-Gt. Plains region 1976-77, mem. nat. steering com. 1976—), Phi Mu Alpha. Lutheran. Home: 1137 Elm Ridge Dr Glencoe IL 60022

DAMPEER, JOHN LYELL, attorney; b. Cleve., June 3, 1916; s. James W. and Felicia (Gressitt) D.; m. Lucie Augustin Kennerdell, June 30, 1950; children—Lyell B., David K., G. Geoffrey. S.B., Harvard U., 1938, LL.B., 1942; student, New Coll., Oxford, England, U., 1938-39. Bar: Ohio 1946. Practice law, Cleve., 1946—; assoc. Thompson, Hine and Flory, 1946-55, ptnr., 1955—; sec., dir. Van Dorn Co., Cleve., 1956—; dir. Monarch Machine Tool Co., Sidney, Ohio, 1977—, J.M. Smucker Co., Orville, Ohio, 1961—. Trustee Family Service Assn., Cleve., 1951-70. Henry fellow, 1938-39. Mem. ABA, Ohio Bar Assn. (chmn. corp. law com. 1959-62), Greater Cleve. Bar Assn. (exec. com. 1958-61), Phi Beta Kappa. Republican. Baptist. Clubs: Union, Kirtland Country (Cleve.). Home: 246 Marlboro Rd Cleveland Heights OH 44118 Office: 1100 Nat City Bank Bldg Cleveland OH 44114

DAMROW, RICHARD G., advertising executive; s. Donald C. and V. June (Miller) D.; m. Kimberly Anne Millhollin, Oct. 13, 1982; children—Andrew, Anthony, Adam. B.A. cum laude, Hastings Coll., 1970; postgrad. Creighton U., 1970-72. Cert. bus. communicator. Pub. relations assoc. Western Electric Co., Omaha, 1970-71; mgr. employee and pub. relations Gate City Steel Corp., Omaha, 1971-72; advt. mgr. Ag-tronic, Inc., Hastings, Nebr., 1972-74; v.p. Fletcher/Mayo Assocs., St. Joseph, Mo., 1974-80; pres. Mark, Morris & Co., Mpls., 1980-82; sr. v.p., mng. dir. Carmichael Lynch Advt., Mpls., 1982—. Mem. Midwest Direct Mktg. Assn., Bus. and Profl. Advt. Assn., Nat. Agrimktg. Assn., Direct Mktg. Assn. Republican. Presbyterian. Club: Greenway Athletic. Home: 2420 Winter Circle Wayzata MN 55391 Office: 100 E 22d St Minneapolis MN 55404

DANCA, JOHN ARTHUR, psychotherapist, educator; b. Chgo., Apr. 19, 1950; s. John Joseph and Josephine Rose (Bartolotta) D.; 1 son, Matthew John. B.A., DePaul U., 1972; M.A., Governors State U., 1975; C.A.S., No. Ill. U., 1978, Ed.D., 1982. Mem. counseling faculty Fenwick High Sch., Oak Park, Ill., 1973-75; instr. psychology, counselor Triton Coll., River Grove, Ill., 1975-78; assoc. dir. Ball Found., Glen Ellyn, Ill., 1978-79; assoc. prof. student devel. Oakton Coll., Des Plaines, Ill., 1979—; cons., lectr. in field. Bd. dirs. Chgo. Bd. of Mental Health, Northwest, 1974-75; mem. Oakton Coll. Crusade of Mercy Appeal, 1982. Mem. NEA, Ill. Edn. Assn., Am. Psychol. Assn., Midwest Psychol. Assn., N.Am. Assn. Adlerian Psychology, Ill. Guidance and Personnel Assn., Ill. Coll. Personnel Assn., Ill. Assn. Tests and Measurements, Phi Delta Kappa. Contbr. articles to profl. jours. Home: 1588 Timber Trail Wheaton IL 60187 Office: 1600 East Golf Rd Des Plaines IL 60016

DANCHIMAH, STEPHEN UKACHUKWU, podiatrist; b. Aba, Imo State, Nigeria, Dec. 31, 1944; came to U.S., 1965; s. Daniel U. and Juliana D.; m. Elnora Robinson, July 25, 1970; 1 dau., Onyekachi. B.S., Dana Coll., Blair, Nebr., 1968; D.Podiatric Medicine, Ill. Coll. Podiatric Medicine, Chgo., 1973; cert. Inst. Pa. Hosp., 1978, Calif. Coll. Podiatric Medicine, 1979, Ohio Coll. Podiatric Medicine, 1982. Pres., dir. South Side Foot Clinics & Surg. Centers, Chgo., 1973—; co-chmn. div. surgery Provident Hosp.; mem. staffs Franklin Blvd. Community Hosp., St. Bernard's Hosp. Active in Roland Burris campaign for comptroller Ill., 1979, 82. Recipient Appreciation cert. Chgo. Community Health Council, 1981. Mem. Chgo. Assn. Commerce and Industry, Cook County Podiatry Assn., Ill. Coll. Podiatric Medicine, Operation PUSH. Anglican. Club: Masons. Home: 651 W Sheridan Rd Apt 6C Chicago IL 60613

DANDREA, CARMINE, English educator, poet, antique dealer; b. Elmira, N.Y., July 30, 1929; s. Carmine S. and Mary E. (DiPetto) D.; m. Nancy R. McMann, Jan. 1, 1976; children—Michael, Karen, Anne, Jane. B.A. in English summa cum laude, Hobart Coll., 1956; postgrad. in Am. Civilization, Brown U., 1956-57; M.S. in Edn., Elmira Coll., 1961; M.F.A. in Creative Writing, Cornell U., 1969. English tchr. Elmira (N.Y.) Free Acad., 1959-65; spl. lectr. in English and social sci. Elmira Coll., 1961-65, asst. prof. English, 1965-72, mem. faculty evening and summer sessions, 1965-75; lectr. in English and audio-visual lab. coordinator Corning (N.Y.) Community Coll., 1972-73; mem. faculty Independent Study Program, SUNY, 1972-73; mem. faculty Lake Michigan Coll., Benton Harbor, Mich., 1973—, instr. English, 1973-75, English staff coordinator, 1973-75, assoc. prof. English, 1975, prof. English, 1976—, chmn. dept. humanities, 1980—. Served with USMC, 1948-52. Decorated Purple Heart. Spl. univ. scholar, Brown U., 1956-57; N.Y. State Regents War Vet. Scholar, 1959-62; HEW/Fulbright faculty grantee, India, 1970; nat. winner N.Y. Poetry Ctr. Discovery 69 Program, 1969; Mayves Zantell Lyric award N.Y. Poetry Forum, 1972; Nat. Fedn. of State Poetry Socs. awards, Bicentennial Patriotism award, 1976; Tradition Poetry award, 1976; Ariz. State Poetry Soc. award, 1972; Rose Magnoni Marinoni Meml. award, 1972; Tenn. Poetry Contest award, 1974; Ill. State Poetry Soc. award, 1976, 77, Walter Lovel Meml. award, 1976; N.Y. State Poetry Forum award, 1976; Shel McDonald Dramatic Poetry award, 1977; Macomb Fantasy Factory ann. awards, 1976, 77, 81. Mem. N.J. Poetry Soc., Phi Beta Kappa, Pi Gamma Mu, Phi Theta Kappa (hon.). Author: (poetry) Heart's Crow, 1972; contbr. poetry to various anthologies. Home: 153 Windsor Rd Benton Harbor MI 49022 Office: 2755 E Napier Ave Benton Harbor MI 49022

DANELLO, PAUL FRANCIS, lawyer; b. Cleve., Aug. 15, 1949; s. Frank Louis and Lillian Therese (Krizek) D. A.B., Princeton U., 1971; B.A., Oxford U., 1973, M.A., 1977; J.D., Columbia U., 1975. Bar: Ohio 1975, D.C. 1984, N.Y. 1984, Pa. 1984. Assoc. Thompson, Hine & Flory, Cleve., 1975-80, Calfee, Halter & Griswold, Cleve., 1980-83; ptnr. Memel, Jacobs, Pierno, Gersh & Ellsworth, D.C., 1983—; Trustee, sec. exec. com. Cleve. 500 Found., 1982—; vice chmn., trustee, mem. exec. com. Planning Commn. Sisters of Charity St. Augustine Health and Human Services, Inc., Richfield, OH 1982—. Contbr. articles to profl. jours. Mem. ABA (com. forum Health Law), Nat. Health Lawyers Assn., Am. Acad. Hosp. Attys. Republican. Roman Catholic. Clubs: Oxford and Cambridge (London), Gridiron (Oxford, Eng.), Bullingdon (Oxford), Narcissus (Oxford). Home: 1080 Wisconsin Ave NW Suite 2011 Washington DC 20007 Office: 1800 M St NW Suite 1000 N Washington DC 20036

DANEY, WILLIAM CHESTER, physician; b. Pueblo, Colo., Nov. 18, 1934; s. William Lawrence and Isabel (Stevenson) D.; m. Barbara Julia Packan, July 27, 1956; children—Colette Marie, Tamra Kay, William C. Jr., Randall Todd. B.A. magna cum laude in Zoology, U. Colo.-Boulder, 1956; M.D., U. Colo.-Denver, 1960. Diplomate Am. Bd. Emergency Medicine Am. Bd. Family Practice. Intern St. Anthony Hosp., Denver, 1960-61; resident in internal medicine St. Mary-Corwin Hosp., Pueblo, 1961; pvt. practice, Pueblo, Colo., 1962-76; Staff St. Mary-Corwin Hosp., Pueblo, 1972-82, dir. emergency dept., 1976-82; chmn. dept. emergency medicine St. Mary's Hosp., Grand Rapids, Mich., 1982—, dir. Emergency Care Ctr., 1983—; pres. Grand River Emergency Med. Group, Grand Rapids, 1982—; del. to Colo. State Med. Soc., Pueblo, 1968; asst. prof. medicine Mich. State U., Lansing, 1983—; examiner Am. Bd. Emergency Medicine, Lansing, 1981—. Mem. Pueblo Arts Council, Colo., 1969-71; Pueblo Civic Symphony, Colo., 1968-72; patron Grand Rapids Opera, Mich., 1984—. Recipient Physicians Recognition award AMA, 1984; Spl. Recognition award Scenic Trails Council Boy Scouts Am., Mich., 1984. Fellow Am. Coll. Emergency Physicians (Spl. Service award Colo. chpt. 1981); mem. Kent County Med. Soc., Kent County Emergency Med. Services Council. Club: Cascade Country (Grand Rapids). Avocations: Fly fishing; photography; astronomy; camping; travel. Home: 1631 Mont Rue SE Grand Rapids MI 49506 Office: Dir Emergency Care Ctr 200 Jefferson SE Grand Rapids MI 49503

DANFORD, ARDATH ANNE, library administrator; b. Lima, Ohio, Feb. 11, 1930; d. Howard Gorby and Grace Rose (Klug) D.; B.A., Fla. State U., 1951, M.A., 1952. Head tech. services Lima Public Library, 1956-60; librarian Way Public Library, Perrysburg, Ohio, 1960-70; asst. dir. Toledo-Lucas County Public Library, 1971-77; dir., 1977—; bd. dirs. OHIONET, Ohio Library Found. Mem. adv. bd. St. Charles Hosp. Recipient Toledo Headliner award Women in Communication, 1978, Boss of Yr. award PerRoMa chpt. Am. Bus. Women's Assn., 1978. Mem. ALA, Ohio Library Assn., League Women Voters. Maumee Valley Hist. Soc. Methodist. Clubs: Toledo, Zonta (pres. club 1975-76) (Toledo). Author: The Perrysburg Story, 1966. Home: 2025 Sandringham St Toledo OH 43615 Office: 325 Michigan St Toledo OH 43624

DANFORTH, JOHN CLAGGETT, U.S. Senator; b. St. Louis, Sept. 5, 1936; s. Donald and Dorothy D.; B.A., Princeton U., 1958; B.D., Yale U., 1963, LL.B., 1963, M.A. (hon.); L.H.D. (hon.), Lindenwood Coll.; D.D. (hon.), Lewis and Clark Coll., Portland, Oreg.; LL.D. (hon.), Drury Coll., Maryville Coll., Rockhurst Coll., Westminster Coll., Culver-Stockton Coll., St Louis U.; D.Hum., William Jewell Coll.; Litt.D., Ind. Central U.; S.T.D., S.W. Bapt. Coll.; m. Sally Dobson; children—Eleanor, Mary, D.D., Jody, Thomas. Bar: N.Y., Mo. Assoc., Davis, Polk, Wardwell, Sunderland & Kiendl, N.Y.C., 1963-66, Bryan, Cave, McPheeters & McRoberts, St. Louis, 1966-68; atty. gen. Mo., 1968-76; mem. U.S. Senate, 1976—, chmn. Com. Commerce, Sci. and Transp., mem. Fin. Com., Budget Com.; chmn. Mo. Law Enforcement Assistance Council, 1973-74; ordained to ministry Episcopal Ch.; asst., asso. pastor various chs. in N.Y. and Mo.; hon. canon Christ Ch. Cathedral, St. Louis; hon. assoc. rector St. Alban's, Washington. Mem. Yale Corp., 1973-79. Recipient Disting. Missourian award, Brotherhood award NCCJ; Truman Disting. Lectr. award Avila Coll. Mem. Mo. Acad. Squires, Nat. Jesuit Honor Soc., Alpha Sigma Mu. Office: 497 Russell Senate Office Bldg Washington DC 20510

DANFORTH, WILLIAM HENRY, physician, educator, university chancellor; b. St. Louis, Apr. 10, 1926; s. Donald and Dorothy (Claggett) D.; A.B., Princeton, 1947; M.D., Harvard, 1951; m. Elizabeth Anne Gray, Sept. 1, 1950; children—Cynthia Danforth Noto, David, Ann, Elizabeth. Intern Barnes Hosp., St. Louis, 1951-52, asst. resident in medicine, 1954-57, resident, 1956-57, mem. staff, 1958—; asst. resident in pediatrics St. Louis Children's Hosp., 1955-56; fellow in cardiology Washington U., St. Louis, 1957-58, instr. medicine, 1957-60, NIH postdoctoral fellow in biochemistry, 1961-63, asst. prof., 1960-65, asso. prof., 1965-67, prof., 1967—, vice chancellor for med. affairs, 1965-71, chancellor, 1971—; pres. Washington U. Med. Sch. and Asso. Hosps., 1965-71; chmn. Washington U. Med. Center Redevel. Corp., 1973—; program coordinator Bi-State Regional Med. Program, 1967-69; dir., Ralston Purina Co., McDonnell Douglas Corp.; mem. nat. adv. heart and lung council NIH, 1970-74; pres. Ind. Colls. and Univs. Mo., 1979-81; mem. adv. com. Mo. Coordinating Bd. for Higher Edn., 1976—; mem. adv. bd. St. Louis Area council Boy Scouts Am. Chmn. bd. Danforth Found., 1966—; trustee Am. Youth Found., 1963—, Princeton U., 1970-74; pres. St. Louis Christmas Carols Assn., 1958-74, chmn., bd. govs., 1975—. Served with USN, 1952-54. Recipient Newton D. Baker award, 1967; Ann. Brotherhood award NCCJ, 1973; Man of Yr. award St. Louis Globe-Democrat, 1978; Exec. of Yr. award Sales and Mktg. Execs. Met. St. Louis, 1980; Human Relations award St. Louis chpt. Am. Jewish Com., 1980. Fellow AAAS, Am. Acad. Arts and Scis.; mem. Am. Soc. Clin. Investigation, Central Soc. for Clin. Research, St. Louis Med. Soc., Nat. Acad. Scis. Inst. Medicine. (council 1977-79). Office: Washington U Saint Louis MO 63130*

DANGEL, MATTHEW EDWIN, ophthalmologist; b. Wadsworth, Ohio, July 28, 1953; s. William Edwin and Eleanor Ruth (Fiscus) D.; m. Ruth Irene Bope, Nov. 25, 1978. B.A., Wittenberg U., 1975, M.D., Ohio State U., 1977. Diplomate Am. Bd. Ophthalmology. Intern Riverside Meth. Hosp., Columbus, 1977-78; resident Ohio State U., Columbus, 1978-81; fellow Johns Hopkins U. Hosp., Balt., 1981-82; asst. prof. ophthalmology Ohio State U., Columbus, 1982—. Contbr. articles to profl. jours. Office: 456 Clinic Dr #5132 Columbus OH 43210

D'ANGELO, DIANE MARIE, physician; b. Rochester, N.Y., Mar. 11, 1949; d. George Joseph and Mary Ann (Talotta) D'Angelo; m. Daniel Joseph Reddy, May 5, 1984. B.A., Duke U., 1971; B.S.N., U. N.C., 1975; M.D., Wayne State U., 1979. Diplomate Am. Bd. Internal Medicine. Surg. technician Hamot Hosp., Erie, Pa., 1970; nurse Hosp. Med. Coll. Pa., Phila., 1975-76; intern in internal medicine St. Joseph Mercy Hosp., Ann Arbor, Mich., 1979-80, resident, 1980-82; fellow in gastroenterology Henry Ford Hosp., Detroit, 1982-84, physician PM Clinic, 1983-84, chief fellow gastroenterology, 1983-84, sr, staff physician, div. gastroenterology, 1984—. Mem. AMA, Am. Gastroenterology Assn., Am. Soc. Gastrointestinal Endoscopy, Detroit Gastroenterol. Soc., ACP. Roman Catholic. Office: Henry Ford Hosp 2799 W Grand Blvd Detroit MI 48202

DANIEL, ANASSERIL E., child psychiatrist; b. Trivandrum, India, Oct. 18, 1944; came to U.S., 1974; s. A.D. Easo and M. Kunjamma; m. Molly Cheriyan, June 11, 1970; children—Sheeba, Mariam. M.D., Med. Coll. Trivandrum, 1966; D.P.M., All India Inst. Mental Health, 1973; M.R.C. Psych., Royal Coll. Psychiatrists, U.K., 1976. Diplomate Am. Bd. Psychiatry and Neurology. Intern, Med. Coll., Trivandrum, 1967-68; resident Mo. Inst. Psychiatry, St. Louis, 1974-76; child psychiatrist Mid-Mo. Mental Health, Columbia, 1977-81, clin. dir., 1981-83, chief of staff, 1983-85, supt., 1985—; assoc. prof. child psychiatry U. Mo. Sch. Medicine, Columbia, 1984—. Contbr. articles to profl. jours. Nat. Inst. Corrections grantee, 1984-85. Mem. Am. Psychiat. Assn. (br. sec. 1983-84, br. pres. 1984-85), Am. Acad. Psychiatry and Law, Am. Correctional Assn., Sigma Xi. Office: Mid Mo Mental Health Ctr 3 Hospital Dr Columbia MO 65201

DANIEL, BEVERLY A., psychotherapist; b. Oct. 26; d. Theodore and Faye F. (Keller) McCord; m. William R. Daniel, June 22, 1953; children—William, Jr., Stephen, Theresa. B.S., Mercy Coll., Detroit, 1975. R.N., Calif., Mich., Ohio; cert. social worker, Mich. Supr. surgery Children's Hosp., Detroit, 1958-61; supr. ob-gyn Kirwood Hosp., Detroit, 1966-71; dir. student health Mercy Coll., Detroit, 1974—; pres. Health and Career Counseling, Detroit, 1981—; psychotherapist MetroHolistic Health, Southfield, Mich., 1984—, con., 1984—; pres. Healing Support, Detroit, 1984—; cons. Wellness and Health, Detroit, 1978—. C.P.R. Trainer Southeastern Mich. Red Cross, Detroit, 1981—; coordinator voter registration League of Black Students, Mercy Coll., 1980-84; vol. Detroit Urban League, 1982-84; hon. recruiter U.S. Air Force and U.S. Navy, Detroit, 1982-84. Recipient Spl. Tribute, State Mich., 1980; Cert. Appreciation Coll. Prep. Summer Class, 1981, 82, 83, Guidance Dept., Cooley High Sch., 1983, Breitheupt Vocat. Ctr., 1984. Mem. Nurses Assn. Am. Coll. Obstetricians and Gynecologists, Ctr. Chinese Medicine, Acad. Holistic Medicine, Metro Detroit Holistic Health Assn., Venereal

Disease Action Coalition (chmn. pub. policy com. 1983—). Office: Mercy Coll Detroit 8200 W Outer Dr Detroit MI 48219

DANIEL, DAVID LOGAN, retired state welfare agency administrator; b. Columbia, Tenn., Jan. 2, 1906; s. David and Mahalah (Lloyd) D.; B.A., Fisk U., 1928; M.A., U. Chgo., 1954, postgrad., 1955-56; m. Mary Beatrice Evins, Aug. 4, 1935. Caseworker, casework supr., dist. office asst. adminstr. Chgo. Relief Adminstrn., Cook County Bur. Welfare and Dept. Pub. Aid, 1933-48; asst. div. dir., pub. assistance div. Cook County Dept. Pub. Aid, Chgo., 1948-66, dir., services programs, 1966-67, dep. dept. dir., 1967-69, dir., 1969-74; asst. dir. Ill. Dept. Pub. Aid, 1974-83. Mem. bd. mgrs. Youth Guidance, 1948—; bd. dirs. Chgo. Commons Assn., Big Bros./Big Sisters of Met. Chgo., 1970-83, Joint Negro Appeal; mem. citizens' adv. com. Ill. Dept. Pub. Aid; mem. info. and referral com. United Way of Chgo.; chmn. state employees campaign United Way/Crusade of Mercy, 1976-83; bd. dirs. Met. Chgo. Coalition on Aging, 1979—; mem. Exec. Service Corps, 1983; mem. citizens adv. com. Ill. Dept. Pub. Aid. Served with AUS, 1943-46; capt. Res. ret. Recipient Service award Vets. Assistance Commn. Cook County, 1973, Chgo. Area Manpower Planning Council, 1974; Past Pres.'s award City Club Chgo., 1974; Holy Angels award Holy Angels Catholic Ch., 1976; Stamps Service award Joint Negro Appeal, 1976; Golden Alumnus Meritorious award Fisk U., 1982; honors award United Way/Crusade of Mercy, 1984, others. Mem. Nat. Assn. County Welfare Dirs. (pres. 1973-74), Nat. Assn. Social Workers, Acad. Certified Social Workers, Chgo. Urban League, Am. Pub. Welfare Assn., NAACP (life), Ill. Welfare Assn. (pres.), Amvets (comdr. Chgo. post #1), Alpha Phi Alpha (life; past chpt. pres.). Methodist. Clubs: City of Chgo. (dir., past pres.), Chgo. Umbrian Glee (pres. 1946—). Home: 5839 S Michigan Ave Chicago IL 60637 Office: 624 S Michigan Ave Chicago IL 60605

DANIEL, LAWRENCE K(IRBY), trucking company executive, horse breeder; b. Mt. Vernon, Mo., Sept. 5, 1940; s. Raymond E. and Maydelle (Kirby) D.; m. Marilyn Ruth Harless, July 20, 1974. Student S.W. Mo. State Coll., 1958-60. Driver Daniel Truck & Equipment Co., Springfield, Mo., 1960-70, salesman, 1970-73; pres. Daniel Co. of Springfield, 1973—; assoc. Hawthorne Found., Jefferson City, Mo., 1983. Contbr. photos and articles to Morgan Horse Mag., 1983. Company named one of 500 Fastest Growing Privately Held Cos., Inc. Mag., 1982; Ky. col., 1983. Mem. Am. Morgan Horse Assn. (life), Ozark's Morgan Horse Club (pres. 1982-83), Mo. Bus. and Truck Assn., Springfield C. of C. (econ. devel. think tank 1983, bd. dirs. 1985—), Mo. C. of C. Republican. Baptist. Office: The Daniel Co of Springfield 3725 W Division St Springfield MO 65803

DANIEL, ROLF W., psychologist; b. Rochester, N.Y., July 18, 1953; s. Gunther F. and Dorothy (Green) D.; m. Nancy Shippers, Aug. 2, 1975. B.A., St. John Fisher Coll., 1975; M.S., St. Francis Coll., 1977; Ed.D., Ball State U., 1982. Behavioral clinician Ft. Wayne (Ind.) State Hosp., 1977-79, mental health adminstr., 1979; dir. psychology Northeast Ind. Spl. Edn. Coop., Corunna, 1982-83; instr. St. Joseph's Hosp. Sch. Nursing, Ft. Wayne, 1983— instr. St. Francis Coll., Ft. Wayne, 1981—; pvt. practice in psychology, Ft. Wayne, 1984—. Mem. learning disabilities task force Ind. Council Adminstrs. in Spl. Edn. Mem. Am. Psychol. Assn., Nat. Assn. Sch. Psychologists, Ind. Psychol. Assn. Democrat. Roman Catholic. Office: 6079 Stoney Creek Dr Fort Wayne IN 46825

DANIEL, THOMAS MALLON, medical educator, researcher; b. Mpls., Oct. 27, 1928; s. Lewis Morgan and Hannah Neil (Mallon) D.; m. Janet Ewing Smith, June 27, 1953; children—Virginia, Stephen, Laura, Bruce. B.S., Yale U., 1951; M.D., Harvard U., 1955. Diplomate Am. Bd. Internal Medicine, Am. Bd. Pulmonary Disease. Intern, resident in medicine Univ. Hosps., Cleve., 1955-59; fellow in microbiology Case Western Res. U., Cleve., 1961-63, instr., asst. prof., 1963-69, assoc. prof., 1969-77, prof. medicine, 1977—, cons. Tb control Internat. Child Care program, Port-au-Prince, Haiti, 1974—. Contbr. numerous articles to sci. jours. and chpts. to scholarly texts on Tb immunology. Bd. dirs., past pres. Am. Lung Assn. of No. Ohio, Cleve., 1974—. Served to capt. U.S. Army, 1959-61. Markle scholar, 1967; Fogarty fellow, Bolivia, 1980; grantee NIH, NSF. Fellow Infectious Diseases Soc. of Am., Am. Coll. Chest Physicians; mem. Am. Thoracic Soc., Central Soc. Clin. Research, Am. Soc. Microbiology, Mem. United Ch. Christ. Office: Dept Medicine Univ Hosps Cleveland OH 44106

DANIEL, WILLIAM LOUIS, geneticist, educator; b. Wyandotte, Mich., Sept. 20, 1942; s. Lafayette Stephen and Dorothy (Reidy) D.; m. Mary Louise Stace, June 20, 1964; children—Mark, Jennifer, Kathryn. B.S., Mich. State U., 1964, Ph.D., 1967. Diplomate Am. Bd. Med. Genetics. Asst. prof. Ill. State U., Normal, 1967-71, assoc. prof., 1971-72; asst. prof. U. Ill., Urbana-Champaign, 1972-76, assoc. prof. genetics, 1976—; dir. Genetic Counseling Service, Regional Health Research Ctr., Urbana, 1975—. Author: Medical Genetics for Health Professionals, 1979; (With others) Genetics and Human Variation, 1982. Contbr. articles to profl. jours. Recipient Eagle Scout award Boy Scouts Am., 1955, numerous teaching awards U. Ill.; named Outstanding Community Leader, 1972. Mem. Genetics Soc. Am., Am. Genetics Assn., Am. Soc. Human Genetics, N.Y. Acad. Scis., Ill. Acad. Scis., AAAS, Phi Kappa Phi. Roman Catholic. Avocations: athletics, photography. Office: Dept Genetics Devel U Ill 505 S Goodwin Ave 515 Morrill Hall Urbana IL 61801

DANIELL, SANDRAL, physical scientist, educator; b. St. Louis, July 29, 1940; d. Willie Davis and Catherine (Robnett) Allen; m. Maurice Digby Daniell, Jan. 29, 1982. B.S., Lincoln U., 1962; M.A., Webster U., 1975; M.S., Washington U., St. Louis, 1980. Cartographer, Def. Mapping Agy., St. Louis, 1962-74, geodesist, 1974-82, phys. scientist, 1982—; affiliate prof. Civil engring. (geometric geodesy) Washington U., St. Louis, 1982—. Mem. Am. Soc. Photogrammetry (exec. bd. 1978-80), Am. Geophys. Union, Beta Kappa Chi. Methodist. Avocations: playing flute; music; poetry. Home: 85 Depot Dr Edwardsville IL 62025

DANIELS, ARTHUR PRESTON, data processing executive; b. Bklyn., Mar. 7, 1946; s. Arthur Preston and Jeannette (Farina) D.; m. Geraldine Ann Mascari, May 2, 1964; children—Joseph Gerard, Christopher Preston. Transp. technician Tri-State Commn., N.Y.C., 1963-67; systems specialist Ins. Data Processing Ctr., N.Y.C., 1967-69; systems planner Borden Inc., N.Y.C., 1969-71, systems project mgr., Columbus, Ohio, 1971-75, mgr. systems support, 1975-80, mgr. info. ctr., 1980-85, mgr. decision support, 1985—; project mgr., speaker Guide 41, Denver, 1976; cons. Borden Can., Toronto, Ont., 1983-84. Coach Pickerington Athletic Assn., Ohio, 1972, Reynoldsburg Little League, Ohio, 1974; vol., booster Bishop Hartley High Sch., Columbus, Ohio, 1984. Mem. Data Processing Mgmt. Assn., Am. Mgmt. Assn., Columbus Info. Ctr. Assn. Roman Catholic. Lodge: K.C. Avocations: sports; Am. history; music. Office: Borden Inc 180 E Broad St Columbus OH 43215

DANIELS, CHARLES EDWARD, pharmacist, educator; b. Rialto, Calif., Aug. 30, 1952; s. Edward Barton and Alma Marie (Muckerheide) D.; m. Linda Marie Battaglia, Apr. 15, 1973; children—Jason, Eric. B.S., U. Ariz., 1975; M.S., U. Minn., 1978, Ph.D., 1981. Registered pharmacist, Calif., Ariz., Minn. Pharmacist, NIH Clin. Ctr., Bethesda, Md., 1976-77, Hennipen Poison Ctr., Mpls., 1977-78; asst. prof. pharmacy U. Minn., Mpls., 1981—, asst. dir. pharmacy, 1980—. Mem editorial bd. Am. Jour. Hosp. Pharmacy, 1983—. Editor: Institutional Management, 1985. Contbr. articles to profl. publs. Block coordinator Neighborhood Energy Workshops, Mpls., 1983; parent leader YMCA Y-Guides Program, Mpls., 1983; mem. adv. council Nathan Hale Pub. Sch., Mpls., 1984-86. Fellow Am. Found. Pharm. Edn., 1977-79; grantee U. Minn., 1979, Nat. Ctr. Health Services, 1979; recipient Research award Minn. Soc. Hosp. Pharmacists, 1984. Mem. Am. Soc. Hosp. Pharmacy (del. ho. reps., 1982-84), Am. Pharm. Assn., Acad. Mgmt., Rho Chi, Phi Kappa Phi, Kappa Psi. Avocations: running, biking, skiing. Office: U Minn Hosps Box 611 420 Delaware St SE Minneapolis MN 55455

DANIELS, DAVID WILDER, music educator; b. Penn Yan, N.Y., Dec. 20, 1933; s. Carroll Cronk and Ursula (Wilder) D.; m. Jimmie Sue Evans, Aug. 11, 1956; children—Michael, Abigail, Andrew. A.B., Oberlin Coll., 1955; M.A., Boston U., 1956; M.F.A., U. Iowa, 1963, Ph.D., 1963. Instr. music Culver-Stockton Coll., Canton, Mo., 1956-58; music librarian Berkshire Atheneaum, Pittsfield, Mass., 1958-61; asst. prof. U. Redlands, Calif., 1963-64, Knox Coll., Galesburg, Ill., 1964-69; asst. prof. Oakland U., Rochester, Mich., 1969-71, assoc. prof., 1971—, chmn. dept., 1982—; music dir. Warren Symphony, Mich., 1974—, Pontiac-Oakland Symphony, Pontiac, Mich., 1977—. Author: Orchestral Music, 1972, rev. edit., 1982; editor: Avanti newsletter, 1982—. Mem. Am. Symphony Orchestra League, AAUP, Coll. Music Soc., Conductors Guild. Home: 1215 Gettysburg Rochester MI 48064 Office: Oakland U Dept Music Rochester MI 48063

DANIELS, DELOIS DIANE, physician; b. Magnolia, Miss., Feb. 14, 1951; d. Phillip and Willie Pearl (Bates) D.; m. Charles Edward Rutledge, Feb. 18, 1978; children—Cavan Edward, Carla Lynn, Christopher Phillip. B.S., Tougaloo Coll., 1972; M.D., Tufts U., 1976. Intern Wayne State U. Affiliated Hosps., Detroit, 1976-77, resident in internal medicine, 1977-79; attending physician Harper-Grace Hosp., Detroit, 1979—; rev. physician State of Mich., Southfield, 1983. Mem. Wayne County Med. Soc., Mich. State Med. Soc. Democrat. Baptist. Office: 1200 6th St Detroit MI 48201

DANIELS, EDNA MYRTLE, osteopathic physician; b. Stoughton, Sask., Can., Nov. 26, 1935; d. Adam Bruce and Laura Joan (Fletcher) Slimmon; m. Kenneth Gordon Daniels, June 2, 1956 (dec.); children—David Kent, Steven Bruce. R.N., Independence San. and Hosp., Mo., 1957; B.S., U. Mo.-Kansas City, 1977; D.O., U. Health Scis. Coll. Osteo. Medicine, 1981. Nurse, Weiss Meml. Hosp., Chgo., 1957-58, Bapt. Meml. Hosp., Kansas City, Mo., 1959-61; temporary nurse, Kansas City, Mo., 1961-70; intern Doctors Hosp., Columbus, Ohio, 1981-82. Mem. Am. Osteo. Assn., Am. Coll. Gen. Practitioners in Osteo. Medicine and Surgery, Bus. and Profl. Women's Assn., Iota Tau Sigma. Mem. Reorganized Ch. of Jesus Christ of Latter-day Saints.

DANIELS, EDWARD WILLIAM, biomedical scientist, researcher; b. Tracy, Minn., Jan. 19, 1917; s. Azro Ashley and Nellie (Bundy) D.; m. Harriet Catherine Zimmerman, Dec. 23, 1943; children—Edward, Paul, Thomas, Lynell. B.A., Cornell Coll., Mount Vernon, Iowa, 1941; M.S., U. Ill., 1947, Ph.D., 1950. Tchr. high sch. sci., 1941-43; instr., asst. prof. dept. physiology U. Chgo., 1950-54. assoc. biologist Argonne Nat. Lab., Ill., 1954-74, biologist, 1974-81; adj. prof. U. Ill. Coll. Medicine, Chgo., 1984—. Served with USN, 1943-46. Fellow U. Ill., 1949. Fellow AAAS; mem. Soc. Protozoologists, Midwest Soc. Electron Microscopy, Am. Inst. Biol. Sci., Radiation Research Soc. Avocation: swimming. Office: U Ill at Chicago Coll Medicine Dept Anatomy PO Box 6998 Chicago IL 60680

DANIELS, JOEL, II, associate dean of students; b. Mt. Vernon, Ohio, May 29, 1956; s. Edwin Richard and Lillian Lucille (Maloney) D.; m. Sally Ann Eakin, July 18, 1981. B.S., Ohio U., 1978; M.Ed., Ohio State U.-Columbus, 1982. Asst. buyer Cooper Energy, Mt. Vernon, Ohio, 1979-80; hall dir. Ohio State U., 1980-82; assoc. dean students Findlay Coll., 1982—. Mem. Ohio Coll. Personnel Assn. (chmn. campus liaison comm. 1981-83). Republican. Baptist. Avocations: Camping, canoeing, woodworking. Home: 148 Madison Ave Findlay OH 45840 Office: Findlay Coll 1000 N Main St Findlay OH 45840

DANIELS, LACY, microbiology educator; b. Mineral Wells, Tex., Mar. 2, 1950; s. Clay Clarence and Daisy Leota (Lacy) D.; m. Frances Marie Ufkes, May 23, 1984. B.A., U. Tex., 1972; M.S., U. Wis., 1974, Ph.D., 1978. Postdoctoral fellow U. Nijmegen, Netherlands, 1978; NIH fellow U. Wis., Madison, 1979-80, MIT, Cambridge, 1980-81; asst. prof. microbiology U. Iowa, Iowa City, 1981—. Vis. scientist, World Bank project IX, U. Indonesia, Jakarta, 1985—. Contbr. articles to profl. jours. Mem. Am. Soc. Microbiology, Am. Chem. Soc., Am. Inst. Chem. Engrs., Phi Beta Kappa. Avocations: travel; camping. Office: U Iowa Dept Microbiology Iowa City IA 52242

DANIELS, ROBERT WILLIAM, dentist; b. Geneseo, Ill., Mar. 23, 1934; s. William and Blanche I. (Sturm) D.; m. Norma Jean Stenzel, June 19, 1955; children—Robert Scott, Thomas Alan. Student Augustana Coll., 1956; D.D.S., Northwestern U., 1960. Lic. dentist, Ill. Staff, Hammond Hosp., Geneseo, and Geneseo Hosp., 1960—. Bd. dirs. County Cancer Bd., Henry County, 1983-84, Little League Baseball, 1970-74; pres. Community Council, 1962, Band Boosters, 1980-81. Mem. Am. Fedn. Musicians, Rock Island Dental Soc. (dist. dir. 1975-76), ADA, Chgo. Dental Soc., Geneseo Jaycees. Lutheran. Lodge: Kiwanis. Avocations: music; fishing; hunting; dogs. Home: 824 S Spring St Geneseo IL 61254 Office: 216 S Center St Geneseo IL 61254

DANIELSON, GLEN NORMAN, manufacturing company executive; b. Vermillion, S.D., Nov. 23, 1923; s. John Gotfrid and Beda (Norman) D.; m. Catherine Ann O'Connor, Feb. 16, 1949; children—Jean, Dan, Annette, Bruce, Carol, Sharon, Kay, Terese. B.S., U. S.D., 1953. Elec. engr. Magnavox, Ft. Wayne, Ind., 1953-55, Goodyear Aircraft, Akron, Ohio, 1955-56; cons. engr. various cos., 1956-65; pres. Alkota Mfg. Inc., Alcester, S.D., 1965-83, A-M-C, Inc., Beresford, S.D., 1983—. Com. mem. Dept. Commerce Export Council, Omaha. Named S.D. Small Businessman Small Bus. Dept., 1981; recipient —E— Award Export Dept. Commerce, 1971. Mem. S.D. Mfg. Assn. (bd. dirs.), Cleaning Equipment Mfrs. Assn. (bd. dirs.). Lodges: Lions (pres. 1971), Eagles, Elks. Avocations: restoring antique cars; golfing; fishing; hunting; gardening. Home: Box 89 Rural Route 2 Vermillion SD 57069 Office: A-M-C Inc 1407 W Main St Beresford SD

DANIELSON, PHILIP MICHAEL, vacuum technology engineering executive; b. Sept. 11, 1936; s. Carl Emil Theodore and Estelle Eleanor (Berkeland) D.; m. Doris Karen Andresen, June 10, 1961. B.S. in Chemistry, Wesleyan U., Ill., 1960. Registered profl. engr., Wis. Nuclear research scientist Argonne Nat. Lab., 1960-72; vacuum cons. Danielson Assoc., Milw., 1972-75, pres., 1975—. Mem. Am. Vacuum Soc. (sect. chmn. 1970, chpt. treas. 1975). Home: 5620 Main St Downers Grove IL 60516 Office: Danielson Assoc Inc 1989 A University Ln Lisle IL 60532

DANILOV, VICTOR JOSEPH, museum administrator; b. Farrell, Pa., Dec. 30, 1924; s. Joseph M. and Ella (Tominovich) D.; B.A., Pa. State U., 1945; M.S., Northwestern U., 1946; Ed.D., U. Colo., 1964; m. Toni Dewey, Sept. 6, 1980; children—Thomas J., Duane P., Denise S. Reporter, night city editor Pitts. Sun-Telegraph, 1946-47; reporter, rewriteman Chgo. Daily News, 1947-50; instr. in journalism U. Colo., 1950-51, dir. univ. relations, 1957-60; asst. prof. journalism U. Kans., 1951-53; mgr. public relations Ill. Inst. Tech. and Armour Research Found., 1953-57; pres. Profile Co., 1960-62; exec. editor, pub., exec. v.p. Indsl. Research Inc., Beverly Shores, Ind., 1962-71; v.p., dir. Mus. Sci. and Industry, Chgo., 1971-77, pres., dir., 1978—. Chmn., Chgo. Council Fine Arts, 1976-84. Mem. AAAS, Am. Assn. Mus.'s (exec. com. 1975-78), Assn. Sci.-Tech. Centers (dir. 1973-84, pres. 1975-76), Internat. Council Mus.'s (vice chmn. internat. com. for mus.'s sci. 1976-82, 84—, pres. 1982-83), History of Sci. Soc., Soc. Indsl. Archeology, Sci. Mus. Exhibit Collaborative (pres. 1984—), Mus. Film Network (pres. 1984—), Soc. History of Tech. Clubs: Univ., Tavern, Casino (Chgo.). Author: Public Affairs Reporting, 1955; Starting a Science Center, 1977; editor: Applying Emerging Technologies, 1970; Nuclear Power in the South, 1970; The Future of Science and Technology, 1975; Museum Accounting Guidelines, 1976; Traveling Exhibitions, 1978; Towards the Year 2000, 1981; Science and Technology Centers, 1982. Office: Mus Sci and Industry 57th St and Lake Shore Dr Chicago IL 60637

DANNEMILLER, ANN ELIZABETH, nurse, paramedic; b. Akron, Ohio, Jan. 29, 1951; d. John Denver and Arline Louise (Howell) Hamilton; m. James Howard Dannemiller, June 19, 1971; children—John Howard, Christine Louise. Assoc. degree in Nursing, Shawnee State Community Coll., 1979, Paramedic, 1981. R.N., paramedic. Fire policy typist Farm Family Ins. Co., Delmar, N.Y., 1971-72; staff nurse ICU, Scioto Meml. Hosp., Portsmouth, Ohio, 1979-81, staff nurse emergency dept., 1982, staff nurse ICU, 1982—; dir. nursing Golden Years Convalescent Center, Portsmouth, 1981-82; paramedic Porter Twp. Rescue Assn., Wheelersburg, Ohio, 1971—; instr. basic Emergency Med. Tech., Scioto County Vocat.-Tech., Portsmouth, 1981—; CPR instr-trainer Am. Heart Assn., 1977—, instr. advanced cardiac life support, 1983—; coordinator Paramedic Continuing Edn., Portsmouth, 1983—. Mem. Ohio Assn. Emergency Med. Services (rec. sec. 1981-83, former bd. mem.). Home: 1743 Lawson St Route 4 Wheelersburg OH 45694 Office: Scioto Meml Hosp 1805 27th St Portsmouth OH 45662

DANNER, JOHN EMIL, lawyer; b. Dubuque, Iowa, June 12, 1950; s. Emil Frank and Mary Catherine (Crimmins) D.; m. Randi Suzanne Biorn, May 21, 1977; children—Stacey Michelle, Tricia Suzanne. B.A., Loras Coll., 1972; J.D., U. Iowa, 1979. Bar: Iowa 1979, Wis. 1979, U.S. Dist. Ct. (we. dist.) Wis. 1979. Assoc Lund, Harrold, Cook & Danner, Minocqua, Wis., 1979-84; ptnr., shareholder Harrold, Scrobell & Danner, S.C., Minocqua, 1984—. Adv. bd. dirs. Nicolet Coll., Lakeland Campus, Minocqua, 1982—; pres. Northwoods Wildlife Hosp., Minocqua, 1983-85. Recipient 1st place award Interstate Oratory Assn., 1972. Mem. State Bar Wis., Iowa State Bar Assn., Oneida-Vilas-Forest County Bar Assn. Roman Catholic. Lodge: Lions (sec. 1983-85). Office: Harrold Scrobell & Danner SC PO Box 1148 Minocqua WI 54548

DANNHAUSEN, PATRICIA, interior designer; b. Nogales, Ariz., Nov. 7, 1953; d. Pablo L. and Concepcion (Padilla) Conss; m. Richard Alan Dannhausen, June 22, 1974; 1 child, Clinton Alan. Student Ariz. State U., 1971-72, Ohio No. U., 1973-74, Wittenberg U., 1975, Ohio State U., 1976, Lima Tech. Coll., 1983-84. Interior designer trainee Shillito's, Cin., 1975-76; interior designer Johnson's Gift & Interiors, Lima, Ohio, 1976-78, J.C. Penney Design Studio, Lima, 1978-79, McCormick Furniture, Wapakoneta, Ohio, 1979-81, Lazarus Interior Design Studio, Lima, 1981—, Suzanne's Interiors, Ft. Wayne, Ind., 1984—; comml. designer Lima Arts Council, 1984—. Mem. Am. Soc. Interior Design (assoc.), Sigma Beta. Roman Catholic. Avocations: oil painting; art; drafting; traveling; sports. Home: 3380 Spencerville Rd Lima OH 45805 Office: Lazarus Interior Design Studio 2600 Elida Rd Lima Mall Lima OH 45807

DANNOV, FRED, lawyer; b. Chgo., Apr. 30, 1930; s. Edward Louis and Rae Dannov; m. Nita Craft, Dec. 25, 1952; children—David, Dana. B.A., Westminster U., 1953; J.D., U. Mo., 1959; M.A., 1961. Bar: Mo. 1959. Asst. pros. atty. Boone County, Mo., 1959-61; instr. Columbia Coll., Mo., 1975-78; judge Mcpl. Ct., Columbia, 1975-79; sole practice, Columbia, 1960—. Served to lt. U.S. Army, 1953-55. Mem. Boone County Bar Assn. (pres. 1979-80). Office: 1103 E Broadway Columbia MO 65201

DANOFF, I. MICHAEL, museum director; b. Chgo., Oct. 22, 1940; s. Maurice and Matilda (Price) D.; B.A. in English, U. Mich., 1962; M.A., N.C. U., 1964; Ph.D., Syracuse U., 1970; m. Frances Evelyn Colker, May 31, 1964; children—Sharon, Brian. Asst. prof. Dickinson (Pa.) Coll., 1970-73; assoc. dir., chief curator Milw. Art Mus., 1974-80; dir. Akron (Ohio) Art Mus., 1980-84, Mus. Contemporary Art, Chgo., 1984—; acquisition dir. HHK Found., Milw., 1977-82; adj. prof. U. Akron, 1980-84. Mem. Assn. Art Mus. Dirs., Am. Assn. Mus., Intermus. Conservation Assn. Coll. Art Assn. Club: Arts of Chgo. Author: From Foreign Shores, 1976; Nancy Eckholm Burkert, 1977; Emergence and Progression, 1979; Image in American Painting and Sculpture, 1950-1980, 1981; Cindy Sherman, 1984, Robert Longo, 1984; Robert Mongold, 1984. Office: Museum of Contemporary Art 237 E Ontario St Chicago IL 60611 Office: 237E Ontario Chicago IL 60611

DANSBY, EUNICE LILLITH, music educator, consultant; b. Springfield, Mass., Jan. 11, 1927; d. Benjamin and Theo Maud (Amsbury) Heideman; m. Ellsworth Harry Dansby, Jr., Sept. 24, 1949; children—Deborah Dale, Ellsworth Harry. B.Applied Music magna cum laude, Millikin U., 1948; M.Mus. Edn., 1953; postgrad. U. Ill., Roosevelt U., U. Wis. Mem. faculty Millikin U., Decatur, Ill., 1945-49, Maroa (Ill.) High Sch., 1947-48, Cerro Gordo (Ill.) Pub. Schs., 1948-49, Chgo. Pub. Schs., 1952-53, Mattoon (Ill.) Pub. Schs., 1953-55, Decatur Pub. Schs., 1957-59, Bethany (Ill.) Pub. Schs., 1959-69, Wheaton-Warrenville (Ill.) Pub. Schs., 1969-83, ret., 1983; guest condr. orchs. and choruses; judge music contests, Ill., Ind., Wis. Mem. Decatur Mcpl. Bond. Recipient Tchr.'s Writing Contest prizes Reader's Digest and NEA, 1970, 71, 72. Mem. NEA (life), Ill. Edn. Assn., Music Educators Nat. Conf., Ill. Music Educators Assn. (rec. sec. 1978-80, Disting. Service award 1985), Am. String Tchrs. Assn., Ill. String Tchrs. Assn. (editor Scroll 1976-82), In-and-About Chgo. Music Educators Assn., Ill. Project for Sch. Reform, Citizens Utility Bd., NOW, LWV (v.p. Decatur chpt.), Phi Kappa Phi, Sigma Alpha Iota (chpt. pres.). Presbyterian. Contbr. articles to Music Educators Jour., Ill. Music Educators Jour., Scroll, Sch. Musician mag.; editor Southeastern Sounds; composer, arranger woodwind ensembles. Home and Office: 1044 W Tuttle St Decatur IL 62522

DANTO, HAROLD NEWTON, environmental engineer; b. Cleve., Jan. 1, 1927; s. Joseph Bernard and Anna (Stotsky) D.; m. Muriel Elaine Sobol, Sept. 6, 1967; children—Charlotte Elizabeth, Allan Howard. B.S. in Chem. Engring., Case Western Res. U., 1950. Prin., H.N. Danto Cons., Cleve., 1954-70; air pollution engr. Ohio EPA, Cleve., 1970-76; sr. environ. engr. Sherwin Williams Co., Cleve., 1976-78; v.p. Danto Environ. Corp., Cleve., 1978-84, pres., 1985—. lectr. in field. Bd. dirs. Eagle Scout Assn., Cleve., 1973-84; active Boy Scouts Am. Served with U.S. Army, 1944-46. Mem. Am. Pollution Control Assn., Water Pollution Control Fedn. Advocations: swimming; hiking; computer programming. Address: 4022 Stonehaven Rd Cleveland OH 44121

DANZIG, MORRIS JUDAH, organic chemist, research and development company executive; b. Staten Island, N.Y., July 31, 1925; s. Abraham and Sara (Green) D.; m. Faye Schwartz, Mar. 22, 1955; children—Jonathan, David. B.S., U. Miami, Fla., 1949, M.S., 1951; Ph.D., Tulane U., 1953; postdoctoral U. Minn., 1954. Sec., leader research and devel. Am. Viscose, Marcus Hook, Pa., 1962-64; new product analyst Gen. Tire & Rubber Co., Akron, Ohio, 1964-65, mgr. advanced devel., 1965-68; dir. organic and polymer research Corn Products, Argo, Ill., 1968-74, exec. dir. research and devel., 1974-75, v.p. research and devel., 1975—; dir. Corn Products, Englewood Cliffs, N.J., Harris Bank-Argo, Summit, Ill., Enzyme Bio-Systems Ltd., Englewood Cliffs. Contbr. articles to profl. jours. Patentee addition products, macromers, preparation of salts. Mem. Am. Chem. Soc., Research Dirs. Assn. Chgo. Inc. (pres., sec., treas. 1976—), Indsl. Research Inst., Am. Mgmt. Assn. Avocation: Photography. Office: Corn Products-Moffett Tech Center 65th & Archer Rd Argo IL 60501

DANZIGER, GERTRUDE, metal fabricating company executive; b. Chgo., Oct. 24, 1919; d. Isidor and Clara (Fuchs) Seelig; student Northwestern U., 1937-40, U. Wis., 1945; m. Sigmund H. Danziger (dec.); children—Robert S., James C. Sec., Homak Mfg. Co., Chgo. 1955-78, pres., 1979—, also dir. Patentee mech. and design process. Office: 4433 S Springfield St Chicago IL 60632

DAOUST, JOSEPH PATRICK, educator, lawyer; b. Mpls., Aug. 24, 1939; s. Joseph Henry and Bernadette Nan (Gannon) D. A.B., St. Louis U., 1963, Ph.L., 1964, M.A., 1964; M.Div., Woodstock Coll., 1969; M.A., U. Pa., 1966, Ph.D. candidate, 1968; J.D., U. Mich., 1982. Bar: Mich. 1982, U.S. dist. ct. (ea. dist.) Mich. 1982. Social devel. worker Indian Social Inst., Pune, India, and Kandy, Sri Lanka, 1972-73; prof. econs. U. Detroit, 1973—, assoc. prof. law and econs., 1982—, v.p. adminstrn. and student affairs, 1975-77, dean humanities and philosophy, 1977-80. Author articles. Dir. social ministry Detroit Province Jesuits, 1980—, chmn. nat. bd. Jesuit Social Ministry, Washington, 1982—; vol. atty. Wayne County Neighborhood Service, Detroit, 1981-83. NSF fellow, 1964-67. Mem. Am. Econ. Assn., Order of Coif. Roman Catholic. Home: 8809 Schoolcraft Detroit MI 48238 Office: Univ Detroit Law Sch 651 E Jefferson Detroit MI 48226

D'APPOLONIA, BERT LUIGI, cereal chemistry educator; b. Sudbury, Ont., Can., Nov. 6, 1939; came to U.S., 1963, naturalized, 1983. B.S., Laurentian U., 1962; M.S., N.D. State U., 1966; Ph.D., 1968. Research asst. N.D. State U., Fargo, 1963-68, asst. prof. dept. cereal chemistry and tech., 1968-73, assoc. prof., 1973-78, prof., 1978—. Contbr. articles to profl. jours. Mem. Am. Assn. Cereal Chemists (pres. 1984—), Am. Soc. Bakery Engrs., Inst. Food Technologists, Sigma Xi. Roman Catholic. Office: ND State U Dept Cereal Sci and Food Tech Fargo ND 58105

DARBY, HARRY, former U.S. senator, industrialist, farmer, stockman; b. Kansas City, Kans., Jan. 23, 1895; s. Harry and Florence Isabelle (Smith) D.; B.S. in Mech. Engring., U. Ill., 1917, M.E., 1929; LL.D. (hon.), Kans. State U., Manhattan, St. Benedict's Coll., Atchison, Kans., Westminster Coll., Fulton, Mo., Washburn U., Topeka; D.Comml. Sci., Baker U., Baldwin City, Kans.; m. Edith Marie Cubbison, Dec. 17, 1917 (dec.); children—Harriet (Mrs. Thomas H. Gibson, Jr.), Joan (Mrs. Roy A. Edwards), Edith Marie (Mrs. Ray Evans), Marjorie (Mrs. Eugene D. Alford). With Mo. Boiler Works Co., Kansas City, Mo., 1911-19; with Darby Corp., Kansas City, Kans., 1920—, chmn. bd., owner, 1945—; founder, chmn. bd. Leavenworth Steel, Inc., Darby Ry. Cars, Inc.; dir. numerous corps.; U.S. senator from Kans., 1949-50. Mem. Republican Nat. Com. for Kans., 1940-64, chmn. Kans. del., 1948, 56, 60, chmn. credentials com., 1944, ticket com., 1956, 60, transp. com., 1960, rural vote com. for Kans., 1940-64, mem. exec. com. of 15; chmn. Kans. Hwy. Commn., 1933-37; mem. at large nat. council, mem. regional exec. com. Boy Scouts Am. Trustee Nat. Cowboy Hall Fame; exec. com. Agrl. Hall Fame; chmn. Eisenhower Presdl. Library Commn.; chmn. emeritus Am. Royal Livestock and Horse Show; chmn. bd. Eisenhower Found., Abilene, Kans. Served from 2d lt. to capt., F.A., U.S. Army, 1917-19; AEF. Recipient awards for civic activities. Fellow ASME; mem. Navy League U.S., Kansas City Crime

Commn., Profl. Engrs., U. Ill. Found., Am. Soc. C.E., Nat., Kans. socs. profl. engrs., Am. Hereford Assn., Am. Nat. Livestock Assn., Kans. Livestock Assn. (exec. com.), Am. Soc. Agrl. Engrs., V.F.W., Am. Legion, 40 and 8, Military Order World Wars. Episcopalian. Mason (32 deg., Shriner, Jester). Clubs: Kansas City, Automobile of Missouri, Saddle and Sirloin, Rotary, River, Terrace, Man of The Month (Kansas City, Kans.); Chicago; Chevy Chase, Capitol Hill (Washington); Cherry Hills (Denver), Burning Tree (Bethesda, Md.). Home: 1220 Hoel Pkwy Kansas City KS 66102 Office: The Darby Corp 1st St and Walker Ave Kansas City KS 66110

D'ARCO, JOHN A., lawyer, state senator; b. Chgo., Oct. 19, 1944; s. John and Antoniette (Briatta) D'A.; m. Michele Mary Mattucci, June 21, 1969 (div. Nov. 1980); children—John Michael III, Mia Antoniette, Robert Joseph. B.A., Loyola U., 1966; J.D., DePaul U., 1975. Service rep. Ill. Dept. Corrections, Chgo., 1967-69; law clk. Cook County Law Div., Chgo., 1971-73, 75-76; research aide Congresswoman Cardiss Collins, Chgo., 1973; mem. Kugler, De Leo, D'Arco, Ltd., Chgo., 1975—; mem. Ill. Ho. of Reps., 1973-76; mem. Ill. Senate, Springfield and Chgo., 1976—, majority whip, 1985—, mem. elections com., exec. com., ins., pensions and licensed activities com., judiciary I and II coms.; mem. Legis. Study Group on Child and Family Policy, Springfield, 1983—; mem. Gov.'s Task Force on Ill. Horse Racing, Chgo., 1984—; mem. Joint Com. Pub. Utility Regulation, Springfield, 1984—. mem. Gen. Assembly Retirement System Trustees Commn., Springfield, 1985—. Author: The Product of My Thought, 1983. Mem. Near West Side community Com., Chgo., 1965—, Joint Civic Com. of Italian-Ams., Chgo., 1970—, 12th Dist. Police Dept. Athletic Com., Chgo., 1975—; bd. dirs. Near West Side Health Planning Orgn., Chgo., 1975—. Recipient Disting. Service award Ill. Occupational Therapy Assn., 1980; Service to Hungry and Needy award Greater Chgo. Food Depository, 1981; Renaissance award Italo-Am. Nat. Union Paterno Lodge 100, 1981; Citation for Support of Vets., Am. Legion, 1982, 83; Disting. Service award Lions Internat., 1983; Legis. of Yr. award Ill. Assn. Homes for Aging, 1984; named Outstanding Sponsor, El Centro Childrens League, 1982, 83. Mem. Ill. Bar Assn., Nat. Conf. Ins. Legislators (membership com.), Nat. Conf. State Legislatures (pensions com.). Democrat. Roman Catholic. Office: Kugler De Leo & D'Arco Ltd 1 N LaSalle St Suite 2225 Chicago IL 60602

D'ARCY, JOHN M., bishop, Roman Catholic Church. Student St. John's Sem.; Dr. Spiritual Theology, Angelicum-Rome, 1968. Ordained priest, 1957, Aux. Bishop, 1975. Parish priest various locations, 1957-74; vicar spiritual devel. Archdiocese of Boston; spiritual dir. St. John's Sem.; bishop Diocese of Fort Wayne-South Bend, Fort Wayne, 1985—, chmn. Diocesan bd. dirs.; chmn. Cath. Charities bd. dirs., Our Sun. Visitor bd. dirs. Address: Diocese of Fort Wayne-South Bend 1103 S Calhoun St PO Box 390 Fort Wayne IN 46801

DAREHSHORI, NADER FARHANG, sales executive; b. Shiraz, Iran, Dec. 15, 1936; came to U.S., 1961, naturalized, 1972; s. Zaki F. and Rokhsar (Farsimadan) D.; B.A. in B.A., U. Wis., 1966, postgrad., 1966; m. Anne C. Wagnild, Dec. 14, 1968. Supt. village schs., Shiraz, 1959-61; salesman Houghton Mifflin Co., Geneva, Ill., 1966-75, field sales mgr., 1975-77, sales mgr. of Midwest, 1977-84, v.p., gen. mgr. Coll. div. Midwest, 1984—, mem. coll. div. mgmt. com., 1968—. Democrat. Club: Kiwanis. Address: 1900 S Batavia Ave Geneva IL 60134

DARLEY, WILLIAM JOSEPH, fire apparatus and municipal supplies manufacturing company executive, mechanical engineer; b. Chgo., July 17, 1928; s. William Stuart and Mary Josephine (Bartik) D.; children—Stephen, Peter, Thomas, Paul, Krina, James, Anne. M.E., Purdue U., 1950. Engr., W. S. Darley & Co., Chippewa Falls, Wis., 1950-51, Chgo., 1951-55, sales mgr., Melrose Park, Ill., 1955-70, v.p., 1970-79, pres., 1979—; tech. com. Nat. Fire Protection Assn., Quincy, Mass., 1980—. Pres., River Forest Service Club, River Forest, Ill., 1978-80; bd. mem. Soc. Samaritans, Chgo., 1980-84; bd. mem. World Without Wars, Chgo., 1980-84. Recipient Outstanding Service award Cuerpo de Bomberos, Valparaiso, Chile, 1973. Mem. Fire Apparatus Mfrs. Assn. (v.p. 1983—), Internat. Assn. Fire Instrs., Soc. Automotive Engrs., Truck Body and Equipment Assn., Chgo. C. of C. and Industry, Central Am. Fireman's Assn. (hon.). Roman Catholic. Office: WS Darley & Co 2000 Anson Dr Melrose Park IL 60160

DARLING, MIKELL CRAIG, museum director; b. Chgo., July 14, 1941; s. Paul J. and Myrtle H. (Hitchcock) D.; m. Sharon J. Sandling, Apr. 15, 1972. B.A., De Paul U., Chgo. Dir. Evanston Hist. Soc., Ill., 1969—; dir. Mitchel Indian Mus, Evanston, 1975—, Combined Great Lakes Naval Assn., Chgo., 1973-80. Assoc. mem. Evanston Preservation Commn., 1982—, Evanston Place Name Com., 1980—. Served with U.S. Army, 1961-64. NEH fellow, 1973. Mem. Am. Assn. State and Local History.

DARLING, ROBERT HOWARD, lawyer; b. Detroit, Oct. 29, 1947; s. George Beatson and Jeanne May (Mainville) D.; m. Cathy Lee Trygstad, Apr. 30, 1970; children—Bradley Howard, Brian Lee, Kara Kristine. B.S. in Mech. Engring., U. Mich., 1969, M.S. in Mech. Engring., 1971; J.D., Wayne State U., 1975. Bar: Mich. 1975, U.S. Dist. Ct. (ea. dist.) Mich. 1975, U.S. Ct. Appeals (6th cir.) 1975. Engr., Bendix Corp., Ann Arbor, Mich., 1970, Ford Motor Co., Dearborn, Mich., 1972-73; ptnr. Philo, Atkinson, Darling, Steinberg, Harper and Edwards, Detroit, 1975-81; sr. ptnr. Sommers, Schwartz, Silver & Schwartz, Southfield, Mich., 1981—. Author: Michigan Products Liability, 1982; Michigan Premises Liability, 1984. Mem. ABA, Assn. Trial Lawyers Am., Mich. Trial Lawyers Assn. (exec. bd. 1981—, publs. chmn. 1981—), Met. Detroit Trial Lawyers Assn. (mem. exec. bd. 1981—), Oakland County Trial Lawyers Assn., State Bar Mich., Detroit Bar Assn., Plymouth Hist. Soc., Pi Tau Sigma. Episcopalian. Avocations: numismatics; history; golf. Home: 11335 Bellwood St Plymouth MI 48170 Office: Sommers Schwartz Silver Schwartz 1800 Travelers Tower Southfield MI 48076

DARLING, SHARON SANDLING, curator, author; b. Mitchell, S.D., Feb. 28, 1943; d. Joseph Davis Sandling and Barbara M. (Fixmer) Sandling; m. Mikell C. Darling, Apr. 15, 1972. B.A., N.C. State U., 1965; M.A.T., Duke U., 1967. Curator decorative and industrial arts Chgo. Hist. Soc., Ill., 1972—. Author: Chicago Metalsmiths, 1977, Chicago Ceramics and Glass, 1980, Decorative & Architectural Arts in Chicago, 1982, Chicago Furniture, 1984. Mem. Am. Soc. Interior Designers, Am. Ceramics Art Soc. Decorative Arts Soc. Club: Cliff Dwellers. Home: 225 1/2 Greenwood St Evanston IL 60201 Office: Chgo Hist Soc Clark St & North Ave Chicago IL 60614

DARNALL, THOMAS STEELE, JR., financial executive; b. Birmingham, Ala., Aug. 9, 1936; s. Thomas Steele and Janice (Dollins) D.; m. Carol Jane Baker, Sept. 30, 1967. B.A. in Econs., U. of South, 1957. Chartered fin. analyst. Ptnr. W. E. Hutton & Co., N.Y.C., 1963-70; pres. Standard & Poors Counseling Corp., N.Y.C., 1971-73; sr. v.p. Centerre Trust Co., St. Louis, 1973—. Trustee U. of South, Sewanee, Tenn., 1976-84, bd. regents, 1983—. Served with U.S. Army, 1957-58. Republican. Episcopalian. Clubs: Old Warson Country (St. Louis); University (N.Y.C.). Home: 201 Graybridge Saint Louis MO 63124 Office: Centerre Trust Co 510 Locust Saint Louis MO 63101

DARNAUER, TIMOTHY GEORGE, travel consultant; b. Lincoln, Nebr., Sept. 25, 1940; s. Emil George and Esther Pauline (Gies) D.; m. Jeannine Faye Heckman, June 27, 1965; children—Sean, Dana. A.A. in Edn. Sci., Luther Jr. Coll., Wahoo, 1962; B.S.E., Midland Luth. Coll., 1966; M.S. in Phys. Sci., Emporia State U., 1971. Cert. travel counselor. Tchr. Oakland Pub. Schs. (Nebr.), 1965-66; tchr. Topeka Pub. Schs. (Kans.), 1966-71; tchr. Omaha Pub. Schs., 1971-79; travel cons. Travel & Transport, Inc., Omaha, 1974-79, dir. adminstrn. tng., 1979—; dir. Travel Careers Inst., Omaha, 1979—. Mem. curriculum devel. com. Omaha Pub. Schs., 1972-74; pres. Am. Lutheran Ch. of Omaha, 1980-81. Recipient Prominenet Tng. & Devel. Profl. award H. Whitney McMillan & Co., St. Cloud, Minn., 1983. Mem. Inst. Cert. Travel Agents Am. Soc. Tng. & Devel., Nebr. Council Pvt. Vocat. Schs., NEA (chpt. negotiations chmn. 1969-71), Nebr. State Edn. Assn. Republican. Lutheran. Co-author: Earth Science Project, 1974; Training Techniques, 1980. Home: 5528 N 57th Ave Omaha NE 68104 Office: Travel & Transport Inc 9777 M St Omaha NE 68127

DARNELL, LARRY NORMAN, plant manager; b. Aurora, Ill., Dec. 27, 1940; s. Norman F. and Arlene G. (Gee) D.; m. Francis Kaye Hill, July 3, 1959; children—Darren A., Dawn M. Student Aurora Coll., 1959-61. Draftsman, Aurora Pump Co., Ill., 1959-64; applications engr., 1964-70; regional sales mgr. Thrush Products, Inc., Peru, Ind., 1970-72, engring. mgr., 1972-80, mktg. mgr., 1976-80; plant mgr. Amtrol, Inc., Peru, 1980—. Exec. dir. St. John's Lutheran Ch., Peru, 1974-78. Mem. Am. Soc. San. Engrs., Phi Delta Kappa. Avocations: golf; hunting; fishing. Home: 529 Longview Dr Peru IN 46970 Office: Amtrol 8th at Jefferso St Peru IN 46970

DARNELL, PATRICIA ANN, nurse; b. Liberal, Kans., Aug. 22, 1954; d. Bobby Joe and Elberta Lea (Edwards) D. B.S. in Nursing, Ft. Hays State U., Kans., 1981. R.N., Kans., Okla. Nursing asst., S.W. Med. Ctr., Liberal, Kans., 1972-76, Good Samaritan Ctr., Dodge City, Kans., 1977; practical nurse Southwest Med. Ctr., 1977-78, operating room staff nurse, 1982-83; practical nurse St. Anthony Hosp., Hays, Kans., 1979, 81; operating room staff nurse Bapt. Med. Ctr. Okla., Oklahoma City, 1983—. Mem. Assn. Operating Room Nurses. Presbyterian. Home: 3136 Northwest Expressway #127 Oklahoma City OK 73112 Office: Bapt Med Ctr Dept Surgery 3300 Northwest Expressway Oklahoma City OK 73112

DARR, ALAN PHIPPS, curator; b. Kankakee, Ill., Sept. 30, 1948; s. Milton Freeman and Margaret (Phipps) D.; m. Mollie Haydon Fletcher, June 28, 1980. B.A., Northwestern U., 1970; M.A., Inst. Fine Arts, NYU, 1975, Ph.D. in Art History, 1980; Cert., Mus. Tng., Met. Mus. Art, 1976, Mus. Mgmt. Inst., U. Calif., 1980. Grad. intern Met. Mus. Art, N.Y.C., 1976; instr. NYU, 1976; asst. curator Detroit Inst. Arts, 1978-80, assoc. curator, 1980-81, curator in charge European sculpture and decorative arts, 1981—; adj. prof. Wayne State U., Detroit, 1982—. Contbr. articles to profl. jours. Nat. Endowment Arts Mus. Profls. Fellow, 1983; John J. McCloy fellow, 1980-81; Ford Found. fellow, 1975-78; Met. Mus. Art fellow, 1975. Office: Detroit Inst Arts 5200 Woodward Ave Detroit MI 48202

DARRAH, CHARLES PATRICK, investment company executive; b. Cleve., Mar. 10, 1947; s. Charles Mort and Pauline An (Petras) D.; m. Cheryl Anne Darrah, Aug. 30, 1969; children—Charles, Stephanie Cathleen, Allison Ann. B.B.A., Cleve. State U., 1971. Area supr. Travelers Express, Elmnurst, Ill., 1971-77; v.p. Merrill Lynch Co., Cleve., 1977—. Recipient Execs. award Merrill Lynch Co., 1981, Pres.'s award, 1982, 83. Fellow Nat. Assn. Securities Dealers. Roman Catholic. Club: Cleve. Athletic. Lodges: Kiwanis (pres. Willowick 1981, bd. dirs. 1983—), K.C. (fin. sec. 1979-80). Home: 2838 Montgomery Rd Shaker Heights OH 44122 Office: Merrill Lynch Co 225 Superior NW Cleveland OH 44113

DARROW, CLARENCE ALLISON, state legislator; b. Dubuque, Iowa, Mar. 22, 1940; s. Clarence Allison and Joan Kathryn (Reinhart) D.; B.S., Loras Coll., Dubuque, 1962; M.S.W., U. Ill., Champaign, 1966; J.D., Chgo.-Kent Coll. Law, 1971; m. Lili Ruja, Nov. 30, 1963; children—Elizabeth, John, Antoinette, Clarence, Jennifer. Bar: Ill. 1971. Asst. state's atty. Rock Island County (Ill.), 1971-74; mem. Ill. Ho. of Reps., Springfield, 1974-83; mem. Ill. Senate, 1983—. Named freshman legislator of yr. Ill. Edn. Assn., 1976; recipient Legis. Achievement award, 1983; Am. Legion award, 1983. Mem. Am., Ill., Rock Island County bar assns., Hampton Hist. Soc. Democrat. Club: Cornbelt Running. Lodge: Elks, Rotary. Office: County Office Bldg 2d Floor Rock Island IL 61201

DARROW, DEAN J., mechanical engineer, mineral leasing agent; b. Baraboo, Wis., Feb. 2, 1921; s. Harold A. and Lillian Agusta (Rodewald) D.; div., 1 child, Tobin Scott. Student St. Ambrose Coll., 1942; B.S.M.E., U. Wis.-Madison, 1947; postgrad. UCLA, 1954-58. Registered profl. engr., Calif. Sr. test engr. Gen. Dynamics, San Diego, 1954-60; research specialist Lockheed, Inc., Sunnyvale, Calif., 1960-62; Apollo project engr. Rockwell, Inc., Downey, Calif., 1963-68; cons. Land Use Planning, Spearfish, S.D., 1968-73; securities rep. First Investors Corp., N.Y.C., 1968-73; dir. Bellefish, Inc., Rapid City, S.D., 1973-78; lease agt. Teledyne, Inc., Houston, 1978-82. Designer oilless cylinder air compressor, water cooled gas turbine. Contbr. articles to profl. jours. Democratic campaign leader S.D., 1967; survey leader State of S.D., 1977. Mem. ASME (life), AIAA. Unitarian-Universalist. Lodge: Elks. Avocations: golf, fishing, hunting, wildlife conservation. Home: PO Box 443 Newell SD 57760

DAS, RATHIN C., molecular and cellular biologist, research scientist; b. Jorhat, India, Jan. 1, 1948; came to U.S., 1978, naturalized, 1984; s. Ramesh C. and Kadambini Das; m. Sushila Kanodia, Nov. 24, 1979; 1 child, Rishiraj K. B.S., Gauhati U., India, 1967, M.S., 1969, Ph.D., 1975. Lectr. U. Gauhati Coll. System, Shillong, India, 1969-75; research assoc. India Inst. Sci., Bangalore, 1975-78, U. Iowa, Iowa City, 1978-81, MIT, Cambridge, 1981-84; research scientist, Miles Labs., Elkhart, Ind., 1984—. Mem. Am. Soc. Microbiology (co-organizer conf. on molecular aspects of protein secretion and membrane assembly 1985), AAAS, Soc. for Complex Carbohydrates, Soc. Indsl. Microbiology, Nat. Geog. Soc. Avocations: philately; chess. Home: 2321 Kenilworth Dr Elkhart IN 46514 Office: Miles Labs Inc PO Box 932 Elkhart IN 46515

DASCHLE, THOMAS ANDREW, congressman; b. Aberdeen, S.D., Dec. 9, 1947; B.A., S.D. State U., 1969; children—Kelley, Nathan, Lindsay. Fin. investment rep.; chief legis. aide, field coordinator Sen. James Abourzek, 1973-77; mem. 96th-97th Congresses from 1st S.D. Dist., 98th Congress at large. Served to 1st lt. USAF, 1969-72. Democrat. Office: Room 2455 Rayburn House Office Bldg Washington DC 20515

DASH, SITA KANTHA, nutrition and health scientist; b. Tunpur, Orissa, India, Nov. 15, 1942; came to U.S., 1969, naturalized, 1977; s. Nila K. and Duti (Sarangi) D.; m. Kalpana M. Mohapatra, June 18, 1967; children—Rajesh, Dave S. D.V.M., Orissa Vet. Coll., Bhubaneswar, India, 1964; M.S., S.D. State U., 1970, Ph.D., 1973. Cert. animal scientist. Vet. surgeon Kakatpur Vet. Clinic, India, 1964-68; asst. project officer Orissa Vet. Service, Bhubaneswar, India, 1968-69; research asst. S.D. State U., Brookings, 1969-73; dir. regulatory services S.D. Dept. Agr., Pierre, 1973-81; pres. UAS Labs. and United Agri-Services, Inc., Mpls., 1981—. Mem. AVMA, Am. Dairy Sci. Assn., Am. Soc. Animal Sci., Assn. Am. Feed Control Ofcls., S.D. Acad. Sci., Minn. Veterinary Med. Assn., S.D. Veterinary Med. Assn., Council Agrl. Sci. and Tech., North Central Assn. Dairy, Food, Feed and Drug Control Ofcls., Am. Feed Mfrs. Assn., Nat. Feed Ingredient Assn., N. Cen. Food Mfrs. Assn., Sigma Xi. Democrat. Hindu. Club: Lions. Contbr. articles to profl. jours. Developed acidophilus tablets and capsules for human use; Keto-Nutri-Aid, Calf Lacto Bolus, others. Home: 10201 Wentworth Ave S Bloomington MN 55420 Office: 7864 12th Ave S Bloomington MN 55420

DAUB, HAL, congressman; b. Fayetteville, N.C., Apr. 23, 1941; s. Harold John and Eleanor M. (Hickman) D.; B.S. in Bus. Adminstrn., Washington U., St. Louis, 1963; J.D., U. Nebr., 1966; m. Cindy S. Shin, Apr. 7, 1968; children—Natalie Ann, John Clifford, Tammy Rene. Admitted to Nebr. bar, 1966; staff intern to U.S. Senator Roman Hruska from Nebr., 1966; asso. firm Fitzgerald, Brown, Leahy & McGill, Omaha, 1968-71; v.p., gen. counsel Standard Chem. Mfg. Co., Omaha, 1971-80; mem. 97th-99th Congresses from 2d Dist. Nebr. Jr. pres. Nebr. Founders Day, 1971; treas. Douglas County Republican Com., 1971-74, chmn., 1974-77; mem. Nebr. Rep. Central Com., 1974—; mem. exec. com., bd. dirs. Combined Health Agys. Drive, 1976; pres.-elect Douglas-Sarpy unit Nebr. Heart Assn., 1977. Served to capt. U.S. Army, 1963-68. Decorated Commendation medal (2); named One of 10 Most Outstanding Young Omahan's, Omaha Jaycees, 1976; recipient service award SAC, 1976; Outstanding Vol. of Yr. award Douglas-Sarpy unit Nebr. Heart Assn., 1976. Mem. Omaha Bar Assn., Nat. Assn. Credit Mgmt. (1st v.p. 1977), Delta Theta Phi. Presbyterian. Clubs: Optimists, Masons. Office: 1019 Longworth House Office Bldg Washington DC 20515*

DAUBENSPECK, BARBARA DIANE SALMI, psychiatric social worker; b. Lakewood, Ohio, Feb. 11, 1952; d. William and Dorothy Mae Salmi; m. Fred Campbell Daubenspeck, June 24, 1972; children—Adam, Lindsay, Brianne. A.B. cum laude, Ohio U., 1973; M.S.W., U. Ill.-Chgo., 1975. Sch. social worker South Met. Assn., Dolton, Ill., 1975-76; psychiat. social worker Family Service & Mental Health Ctr. of South Cook County, Chicago Heights, Ill., 1976-77, part-time 1977—; part-time pvt. practice psychiat. social work, Frankfort, Ill., 1981—. Vol. Y-Cares program YWCA, 1978-81. Mem. Nat. Assn. Social Workers, Acad. Cert. Social Workers (cert.). Democrat. Lutheran. Developed coll. vol. visitation program to prison inmates, Chillicothe, Ohio, 1973. Home: 307 Meota St Park Forest IL 60466 Office: 1240 Ashland Ave Chicago Heights IL 60411

DAUDLIN, PAUL THOMAS, management consultant; b. Detroit, Jan. 20, 1947; s. Paul Leo and Genevieve M. (Peacock) D.; m. Mary Jane Langlois, Mar. 13, 1982; children—Katherine, Molly. B.A., U. Mich., 1976. Asst. to dir. personnel Mich. Mut. Ins. Co., Detroit, 1970-75; asst. dir. human resources St. John Hosp., Detroit, 1975-79; dir. tng. and devel., asst. dir. human resources Campbell-Ewald Co., Warren, Mich., 1979-83; mgr. human resources cons. Arthur Young & Co., Detroit, 1983—; adj. faculty Oakland Community Coll., Royal Oak, Mich., 1982-83. Mem. Am. Soc. Personnel Adminstrn., Am. Soc. Tng. and Devel., Detroit Personnel Mgmt. Assn. Republican. Roman Catholic. Club: University (Detroit). Lodges: KC (East Detroit); Optimists. Avocations: photography; woodworking; tennis; genealogical research; music. Office: Arthur Young & Co 100 Renaissance Ctr Detroit MI 48243

DAUGHADAY, WILLIAM HAMILTON, physician; b. Chgo., Feb. 12, 1918; s. C. Colton and Marion (Sharpe) D.; m. Hazel Judkins, Jan. 22, 1945; children—Elizabeth Colton Axelrod, John Freer. A.B., Harvard U., 1940, M.D., 1943. Diplomate Am. Bd. Internal Medicine. Intern, Boston City Hosp., 1944; asst. resident Barnes City Hosp., St. Louis, 1946-47, cons. clin. chemistry, mem. staff, 1950-69; mem. faculty Washington U. Sch. Medicine, St. Louis, 1949—, NIH fellow biol. chemistry, 1949-50, instr., then asst. prof. medicine, 1950-56, assoc. prof., 1956-63, prof., 1963—, dir. metabolism div., 1951-85, dir. Diabetes and Endocrinology Research Ctr., 1975-77, dir. Diabetes Research and Tng. Ctr., 1977—; mem. endocrine study sect. NIH, 1967-71; mem. adv. bd. Nat. Pituitary Agy., 1964-70; mem. endocrinology and metabolism adv. com. FDA, 1976-81, chmn., 1980-81. Editor: Jour. Lab. and Clin. Medicine, 1960-66, Jour. Clin. Endocrinology and Metabolism, 1973-77; assoc. editor: Jour. Clin. Investigation, 1977-83. Contbr. articles to profl. jours. Served as capt. M.C., AUS, 1944-46. Mem. Am. Diabetes Assn., Central Soc. Clin. Research, Am. Soc. Clin. Investigation, Endocrine Soc. (pres. 1971-72, Fred Conrad Koch medal 1975), Assn. Am. Physicians. Home: 1414 W Adams St Kirkwood MO 63122 Office: Box 8127 Metabolism Div Washington U Sch Medicine 660 S Euclid Ave Saint Louis MO 63110

DAUGHERTY, BENNA KAYE, optometrist; b. Harrisburg, Ill., May 9, 1958; d. Benjamin Franklin Jr. and C. Lodema (Ferrell) Sisk; m. Timothy S. Daugherty, June 9, 1979. A.S., Southeastern Ill. Coll., Harrisburg, 1977; B.S., Ill. Coll. Optometry and Eastern Ill. U., 1982; D.Optometry, Ill Coll. Optometry, Chgo., 1982. Optometrist, Harrisburg, 1982—. Dir. choir Dorrisville Baptist Ch., Harrisburg, 1982—. Mem. So. Ill. Optometric Assn., Ill. Optometric Assn., Am. Optometric Assn. Home: Route 1 Box 342 Harrisburg IL 62946

DAUGHERTY, CONNIE RUTH, early childhood educator; b. Litchfield, Minn., Aug. 23, 1939; d. Edmund Robert and Ruth Helen (Bengtson) Swanson; m. John Charles Daugherty, Jan. 10, 1960; children—Mary Beth, Stephanie Ann, John Michael. Student North Park Coll., Chgo., 1957-59; B.S. in Primary Edn., U. Minn., 1964; postgrad. Mankato State U. Cert. tchr., Minn. Head tchr. St. Peter (Minn.) Play Group, 1967-68; tchr. Peter Pan Nursery Sch., Mankato, Minn., 1968-70; owner, dir., head tchr. Jack and Jill Nursery Sch., St. Peter, 1970—; v.p. Jacon Inc.; cons., mem. Gustavus Adolphus Coll. Early Childhood Program Cert. Com.; cons. Minn. State Dept. Edn., 1978. Sec., bd. dirs. Community Hosp. Aux., 1965-75; v.p. bd. dirs. St. Peter Play Group, 1965-66; mem. Right to Read com., 1974-76; active Girl Scouts U.S.; mem. council 1st Lutheran Ch., St. Peter, 1977-81, v.p., 1980, chmn. youth com., 1978, mem. mut. ministry com., 1981-83, mem. call. com. for sr. pastor, 1976-77; del. Minn. Synod Luth. Ch. Am., 1978, 79; bd. dirs. St. Peter Dollars for Scholars, 1979-81, v.p., 1980-81; bd. dirs. Gustavus Library Assocs., 1980—, vol. chmn., 1980-83. Mem. Nat. Assn. Edn. of Young Child, Minn. Assn. Edn. of Young Child, Minn. Valley Assn. Edn. of Young Child (treas. 1974-75), 1006 Soc. St. Peter C. of C. Republican. Club: Shoreland Country. Contbr. articles to profl. jours. Home: 722 Sioux Ln Saint Peter MN 56082 Office: 1114 Traverse Rd Saint Peter MN 56082

DAUGHERTY, SUSAN LORRAINE, sales consultant; b. Chgo., Sept. 25, 1955; d. Forest Allan and Betty Grace (Dillman) D. Student Bradley U., 1972-76; B.A., Avila Coll., 1980, B.S., 1981. Hemodialysis technician St. Francis Hosp., Peoria, Ill., 1975-77; saleswoman Environ. Internat., Kansas City, Mo., 1977-78; cons. APC Cons., West Palm Beach, Fla., 1978-79; saleswoman Honeywell Corp., Kansas City, Mo., 1979-81, Computerland, St. Charles, Ill., 1980-84; pvt. practice sales cons., West Chicago, Ill., 1984—. Vol. in edn. Kansas City Sch. Dist., Mo., 1978. Mem. Nat. Assn. Female Execs. Democrat. Avocations: photography; collecting music; collecting artwork. Home: PO Box 336 West Chicago IL 60185

DAUST, JAMES EARL, state police officer; b. L'Anse, Mich., Nov. 9, 1934; s. Earl John and Mildred Elizabeth (Sands) D.; m. Karen Marie Kotila, Sept. 14, 1957; children—Mary F., Timothy G., Michael J., Kathleen A. B.S. summa cum laude, No. Mich. U., 1975; postgrad. Central Mich. U., 1980-85. Soils technician State Hwy. Dept., Lansing, Mich., 1954-63; state trooper Mich. State Police, Lansing, 1963—, capt., 1982—. Served with USNG, 1954-63. Recipient Meritorious Citation Mich. State Police, 1968; named Trooper of Yr., Mich. State Police, 1969. Mem. Central Law Enforcement Assn., State Police Command Officers Assn., State Diversion Council, Mich. Assn. Chiefs Police. Lodges: K.C., Kiwanis (pres. 1978-80). Avocations: Carpentry, hunting. Home: 2649 Melville St East Lansing MI 48823 Office: Mich State Police 300 N Clippert St Lansing MI 48912

DAVENPORT, DONALD LYLE, engring. and real estate co. exec.; b. Eau Claire, Wis., Oct. 9, 1930; s. Douglas Benjamin and Leona Margaret (Fairbanks) D.; B.A. in Social Studies, Coll. St. Thomas, St. Paul, 1955; children—Ann, Martin, John, Donna, Jennifer. Adminstrv. asst. to regional mgr. Butler Mfg. Co., Mpls., 1955-58; corp. sec., gen. mgr. Spencer Corp., Eau Claire, 1958-60; sales mgr. Russell Structures Co., Madison, Wis., 1960; former pres. Bldg. Systems, Inc., Middleton, Wis., from 1960; pres. D Davenport Ltd., engring./real estate firm; bldg. cons. Bldg. Systems Gen. Corp., Madison. Former chmn. bd., pres. Jr. Achievement. Served with USAF, 1950-54. Registered profl. engr., Wis.; lic. real estate broker, Wis. Mem. Metal Bldg. Dealer Assn. (pres. 1971), Profl. Engrs. in Constrn., Wis. Soc. Profl. Engrs. (former pres. practice sect.), Johns Manville Dealer Council (chmn.), ARMCO Steel Corp. Dealer Council. Republican. Roman Catholic. Club: Exchange. Home: 6646 W Chestnut Circle Windsor WI 53598 Office: 6313 Odana Rd Madison WI 53719

DAVENPORT, J. WAYNE, public relations specialist; b. Brookfield, Mo., Aug. 17, 1948; s. Robert E. and Anna L. (Witter) D.; m. Julie Kay Banning, May 31, 1969; children—Robert Wayne, John Austin, Thomas James. B.J., U. Mo.-Columbia, 1970, M.A., 1972; M.B.A. candidate Pittsburg State U., Kans., 1980—. Dir. publs. N.E. Mo. State U., Kirksville, 1972-74; dir. pub. relations Cornell Coll., Mt. Vernon, Iowa, 1974-76; dir. devel. and community relations Mercy Hosps., Cedar Rapids, Iowa, 1976-79; univ. dir. pub. affairs and info. Pittsburg State U., 1979—; cons., 1976—. Active United Way, 1979—, First Christian Ch., Pittsburg, 1979—, Boy Scouts Am., 1980-84. Mem. Council for Advancement and Support of Edn. Republican. Lodge: Rotary (Pittsburg). Avocations: running; camping; woodworking; information systems. Home: 1406 Bitner Terr Pittsburg KS 66762 Office: Pittsburg State U 1701 S Broadway Pittsburg KS 66762

DAVID, CLAYTON CUNNINGHAM, corporation executive, community college administrator; b. Topeka, July 19, 1919; s. James Cunningham and Gladys Faye (Zinn) D. B.S. in Agr., Kans. State U., 1941; student Mo. So. Coll., 1970; postgrad. W.Va. U., 1979, 81, 82. Fieldman, Pet Milk Co., Fremont, Ohio, 1945-46, head fieldman, Bryan, Ohio, 1946-48, area fieldman, Greeneville, Tenn., 1948-61, dist. field supt., Salt Lake City, 1961-65, dist. field supt., Nosho, Mo., 1965-71; owner, pres. The Youcan Co., Neosho, Mo., Columbus, Ohio, and St. Clairsville, Ohio, 1971—; assoc. prof. W.Va. No. Community Coll., Wheeling, 1976—, dir. community edn. and coll. exploration, 1979-81; condr. mgmt. and personal devel. seminars bus. and industry. Pres. Greenville United Way, 1959, Greeneville Exchange Club, 1960; mem. Utah state com. Am. Dairy Assn., 1963-65; mem. dairy adv. com. U. Mo., 1969-70; ruling elder Presbyterian Ch. Served to lt. col. USAAF, 1941-45. Decorated Purple Heart. Mem. Am. Soc. Tng. and Devel., 303d Bomb Group assn., 8th Air Force Hist. Soc., Res. Officers Assn. U.S., Air Forces Escape and Evasion Soc., Am. Legion. Republican. Clubs: Belmont Hills Country, Ft. Henry Res. Officers. Editor, pub. My Life, 1975. Home: 215 Dennis Ln Saint Clairsville OH 43950 Office: 1704 Market St Wheeling WV 26003

DAVID, HERBERT ARON, statistics educator; b. Berlin, Germany, Dec. 19, 1925; came to U.S., 1957; s. Max and Betty (Goldmann) D.; m. Vera Reiss, May 13, 1950; 1 child, Alexander John. B.Sc., Sydney U., Australia, 1947; Ph.D., Univ. Coll., London, 1953. Research officer CSIRO, Sydney, 1953-55;

sr. lectr. dept. stats. U. Melbourne, Australia, 1955-57; prof. dept. stats. Va. Poly. Inst., 1957-64; prof. dept. biostats. U. N.C., Chapel Hill, 1964-72; dir., head statis. Lab. and dept. stats. Iowa State U., Ames, 1972-84, prof. stats., 1972—. Author: Order Statistics, 1970, 81; Editor: Contributions to Survey Sampling, 1978; (with H.T. David) Statistics: An Appraisal, 1984. Recipient J. Shelton Horsley award for Meritorious Research, Va. Acad. Scis., 1963, Samuel Wilks award U.S. Army Research Office, 1983; named Disting. Prof. Scis. and Humanities, Iowa State U., 1980. Fellow Am. Statis. Assn., Inst. Math. Stats., mem. Biometric Soc. (pres. 1982-83, editor jour. 1967-72), Internat. Statis. Inst. Jewish. Home: 460 Westwood Dr Ames IA 50010 Office: Iowa State U Dept Statistics Ames IA 50011

DAVID, RICHARD GEORGE, accountant; b. Detroit, July 29, 1956; s. George Asa and Marie (Kirdahy) D.; m. Denise Ann Anton, Aug. 14, 1983. B.B.A., U. Mich., 1978. C.P.A., Mich. Sr. mgr. Peat, Marwick, Mitchell & Co., Detroit, 1978—; pres. Ascot Assocs., Inc. Editor: Preparing for the National Model United Nations, 1980-81. Pres., Nat. Collegiate Conf., N.Y.C., 1979-82; bd. dirs. UN Assn. U.S.A. Recipient Medal of Merit, U.S. Congress, 1974. Mem. Internat. Assn. Hospitality Accts., Am. Inst. C.P.A.s, Nat. Assn. Accts. (bd. dirs. 1979-80), Retail Fin. Execs. Detroit (bd. dirs.), Mich. Assn. C.P.A.s (com. chmn. 1984-85). Home: 13557 Ascot Dr Sterling Heights MI 48077 Office: Peat Marwick Mitchell & Co 200 Renaissance Ctr Suite 3400 Detroit MI 48243

DAVIDSON, ALAN JOHN, banker, lawyer; b. Pitts., June 17, 1938; s. Alan Ralston and Marie Louise (Zang) D.; m. Louise Carolyn Hjelm, Aug. 25, 1962; children—Louise Karen, Amy Marie, Alan Hjelm. B.A., Pa. State U., 1960; J.D., Harvard U., 1963. Bar: Mass. 1964, Pa. 1965, Ohio 1981. With Mellon Bank, N.A., Pitts., 1964-80; exec. v.p. BancOhio Nat. Bank, Columbus, 1981—. Trustee Columbus Symphony Orch., 1982—; Grant Hosp., 1985—; mem. exec. com. Pilot Dogs, Inc., Columbus, 1982—. Mem. ABA, Ohio Bar Assn. Republican. Presbyterian. Clubs: Athletic, Scioto Country (Columbus); Country of Muirfield Village (Dublin, Ohio). Office: BancOhio Nat Bank 155 E Broad St Columbus OH 43251

DAVIDSON, DALWYN ROBERT, electric utility executive, consultant; b. Lorain County, Ohio, Aug. 10, 1918; s. John Francis and Erma Adele (Hayes) D.; m. Georganna Katherine Sharp, Sept. 12, 1942; children—Karen Joy Davidson Leech, Dale Wynn, Glenn Kirk. Student Kent Sate U., 1936-38; B.S.E.E., Case Western Res. U., 1941. Regis. profl. engr., Ohio. Sr. engr. Cleve. Electric Illuminating Co., 1952-57, gen. supr., 1957-67, mgr., 1967-74, v.p., 1974-82, sr. v.p., 1982-83, cons., 1983—. Active Citizens League, Cleve. Served to capt. USAF, 1943-46. Fellow IEEE; mem. Cleve. Engring. Soc., Nat. Soc. Profl. Engrs., Ohio Soc. Profl. Engrs., Cleve. Soc. Profl. Engrs. Republican. Methodist. Home: 29550 Jackson Rd Chagrin Falls OH 44022 Office: Cleve Electric Illuminating Co 55 Public Sq Cleveland OH 44101

DAVIDSON, DAVID EDGAR, lawyer; b. Louisville, Aug. 24, 1954; s. William R and Bernice Cline (Ashton) D.; m. Sally Anne Marguet, Dec. 27, 1975; 1 child, Katherine Esther. B.A., U. Louisville, 1976; J.D., U. Cin., 1980. Bar: Ky. 1980, Ohio 1981, U.S. Dist. Ct. (ea. dist.) Ky. 1981, U.S. Ct. Appeals (6th cir.) 1981. Assoc. Cobb and Oldfield, Covington, Ky., 1980—. Adv. bd. mem. Cancer Family Care, Covington, Ky., 1981-84; referral atty. ACLU, Louisville, Cin., 1980—; reader Library for Blind, Cin., 1982—, Radio Reading Service, Cin., 1982—; mem. vestry Trinity Episcopal Ch., Covington, 1983—, sr. warden, 1985—; govt. relation com. No. Ky. Community Chest, Newport, 1983-84. Mem. Ky. Bar Assn., Ohio Bar Assn., No. Ky. Bar Assn., Kenton County Pub. Defender, Inc. (atty.), Cin. Bar Assn. Democrat. Episcopalian. Home: 142 Pleasant Ridge Ave Fort Mitchell KY 41017 Office: Cobb and Oldfield 213 E 4th St PO Box 1078 Covington KY 41012

DAVIDSON, DAVID ROBERT, organist, conductor; b. Middletown, Ohio, Sept. 25, 1948; s. William R. and Florence L. D.; m. Judith Anne, Aug. 1, 1970; children—Christopher Allan, Jena Michelle. Mus.B., U. Cin., 1970, Mus.M., 1985. Band dir. West Clermont (Ohio) Pub. Schs., 1970-75; band dir., supr. music Lebanon (Ohio) City Schs., 1975-79; ch. musician Mt. Carmel Presbyn. Ch., Kennedy Heights Presbyn. Ch. and Lebanon United Meth. Ch., 1975-79; minister of music Northminster Presbyn. Ch., Cin., 1979—; also handbell, choral and ch. music Clinician. Mem. Am. Guild English Handbell Ringers (pres. 1981-83), Music Educators Nat. Conf., Presbyn. Assn. Musicians, Choristers Guild, Am. Guild Organists. Office: Northminster Presbyterian Church 703 Compton Rd Cincinnati OH 45231

DAVIDSON, DONALD MINER, JR., geology educator; b. Mpls., Oct. 21, 1939; s. Donald Miner and Bernadine (Dunn) D.; m. Mary Frances Johnson, Oct. 22, 19566; children—Robert Gaylord, Mark Edward. B.A., Carleton Coll., 1961; M.S., Columbia U., 1963; Ph.D., 1965. Prof. U. Minn., Duluth, 1965-78; prof., chmn dept. geol. scis. U. Tex., El Paso, 1978-81; sr. research specialist Exxon Product Research Houston, 1981-84; prof., chmn. dept. geology Northern Ill. U., DeKalb, 1984—. Contbr. articles to prof. jours. Fellow Geol. Soc. Am., Geol. Assn. Can., Mem. Soc. Economic Geology. Office: Dept Geology Northern Ill U 312 Davis Hall DeKalb IL 60115

DAVIDSON, GLEN WILLIAM, medical humanities educator, researcher, author; b. Wendell, Idaho, July 26, 1936; s. W. Dean and Grace (Barnum) D.; m. Shirlee Proctor, Nov. 26, 1971; children—Heather, Kristin. B.A., U. Pacific, 1958; M.Div., Drew U., 1961; Ph.D., Claremont Grad. Sch., 1964. Asst. prof., chaplain Colgate U., Hamilton, N.Y., 1964-67; asst. prof. history of religions U. Chgo., 1968-70; fellow U. Iowa Coll. Medicine, Iowa City, 1970-72; assoc. prof. culture and medicine So. Ill. U., Springfield, 1972—, prof., chmn. dept. med. humanities Sch. Medicine, 1974—; chmn. bd. Park Ridge Ctr. Research, Health/Medicine and the Faith Traditions, Park Ridge, Ill., 1980—. Author: Understanding Mourning, 1984; (also editor) Hospice: Development and Administration, 1985. Editor Caduceus: A Mus. Quar. for the Health Scis., 1985—; So. Ill. U. Med. Humanities Series. Author 10 patient counseling films, 1985. Assoc. editor: Death Studies, 1976—. Dir. Pearson Mus., Springfield, 1972—. Recipient Disting. Alumnus award Claremont Grad. Sch., 1982; named Louis Forman Disting. Lectr., St. Lukes's Hosp., Kansas City, Mo., 1984; grantee Luth. Gen. Hosp., Park Ridge, 1983—. Mem. Dirs. of Human Values Programs (convenor 1980-83), Am. Assn. Marriage and Family Therapists (cert. 1974), Am. Acad. Religion, Internat. Workgroup on Death, Dying and Bereavement, Soc. for Values in Higher Edn. Methodist. Avocations: gardening, philately, music. Home: 13 Pinehurst Dr Springfield IL 62704 Office: So Ill U Sch Medicine PO Box 3926 Springfield IL 62708

DAVIDSON, GORDON ALAN, real estate manager; b. Storm Lake, Iowa, Dec. 2, 1946; s. Everett Claire and Eleanor Lucille (Kaufmann) D.; m. Debra Herby Daman, Dec. 1, 1973; 1 child, Pilar Meggan. B.A., U. No. Iowa, 1974; postgrad. Inst. Real Estate Mgmt., 1980. Accredited resident mgr. Asst. mgr. Kinney Shoes, Omaha, Des Moines, 1974-75; resident mgr. Iowa Realty, Des Moines, 1975-80; property mgr. Elkhorn Property Service, Waterloo, Iowa, 1980—; bus. mgr., pres. Mr. D's Goldsmithy, Dubuque, Iowa, 1984—. Decorated Vietnam Cross of Galantry, Nat. Def. medal, Navy Expeditionary medal. Ruling elder Westminster Presbyterian Ch., Waterloo, 1985. Home: 1521 E Mitchell Ave Waterloo IA 50702 Office: Elkhorn Property Services Corp 1521 E Mitchell Ave Waterloo IA 50702

DAVIDSON, IVAN HUGH, theater educator; b. Cedar Mills, Tex., May 29, 1938; s. Horace Hugh and Iva Myrtle (Bates) Davidson; m. Barbara Janet Kraemer, Jan. 27, 1968; children—Tanya, Keirvan. B.A., Hardin-Simmons U., 1960; M.A., Ind. U., 1965; Ph.D., U. Iowa, 1972. Instr. Midland Coll., Fremont, Nebr., 1962-66; assoc. instr. U. Iowa, Iowa City, 1966-69; assoc. prof., chmn. dept. theater, Knox Coll., Galesburg, Ill., 1969—; actor, dir. numerous plays and musicals, 1961—; dir. summer stock, Mich., Ind., Nebr., Fla., 1961-67; artistic and mng. dir. Trotwood Circle Theatre, Dayton, Ohio, summer 1974; regional adjudicator Am. Coll. Theatre Festival, 1978—; judge Ill. High Sch. Drama Finals, 1976, 78, 80, 82. Bd. dirs. Prairie Players Community Theatre, Galesburg, 1973-77, Galesburg Community Chorus, 1984—. Summer Seminar fellow NEH, U. Iowa, 1978, Cornell U., 1981. Mem. Ill. Theatre Assn. (bd. dirs. 1977-80), Am. Theatre Assn. Democrat. Episcopalian. Avocations: tennis, swimming, music. Office: Knox Coll Box 21 Galesburg IL 61401

DAVIDSON, JAMES DOUGLAS, manufacturer's sales representative; b. Syracuse, N.Y., Aug. 8, 1952; s. James Albert and Elizabeth Ann (Meechan) D.; m. Pamela Jean Mitchell, Aug. 31, 1974; children—Emily Ann, Alison Jean. B.S., Clarkson Coll. Sales rep. Midwest Tech. Sales, Merriam, Kans., 1985—. Mem. Assn. of Old Crows. Republican. Lutheran. Avocations: golf; gardening. Office: Midwest Tech Sales Inc 8015 W 63d St Suite 1 Merriam KS 66202

DAVIDSON, JOHN A., state senator, chiropractor; b. Westpoint, Miss., Aug. 31, 1924; s. Homer F. and Anna (Grosboll) D.; D.C., Nat. Coll. Chiropractic, 1951; m. Shirley Beard, 1953; children—Ann, Jane, John. Chiropractor, Springfield, Ill.; trustee, Found. Chiropractic Edn. and Research, 1967—. Mem. and asst. supr. for Capital Twp., Sangamon County (Ill.) Bd. Suprs., 1959-72, chmn., 1970-72; mem. Ill. State Senate, 1973—. Served in AC, USN, 1943-46; PTO. Decorated Air medal, others. Fellow Internat. Coll. Chiropractic; mem. Ill. Chiropractic Soc. (Chiropractor of Yr. 1962), Am. Chiropractic Assn. (Chiropractor of Yr. 1973), Am. Legion. Methodist. Lodges: Masons, Elks. Office: 718 Myers Bldg Springfield IL 62701

DAVIDSON, JOHN HUNTER, agriculturist; b. Wilmette, Ill., May 16, 1914; s. Joseph and Ruth Louise (Moody) D.; m. Elizabeth Marie Boynton, June 16, 1943; children—Joanne Davidson Hildebrand, Kathryn Davidson Bouwens, Patricia. B.S. in Horticulture, Mich. State U., 1937, M.S. in Plant Biochemistry, 1940. Field researcher agrl. chems. Dow Chem. Co., Midland, Mich., 1936-42, with research and devel. dept. agrl. products, 1946-72, tech. adviser research and devel. agrl. products, 1972-80, tech. adviser govt. relations, 1980-84, cons., 1984—. Active Republican Party, Mich. Served to lt. USNR, 1945. Mem. Am. Chem. Soc., Am. Soc. Hort. Sci., Weed Sci. Soc., Am. Pathol. Soc., N.Y. Acad. Sci., Phi Kappa Phi, Alpha Zeta. Presbyterian. Club: Exchange of Midland. Contbr. articles on plant pathology and weed control to profl. jours. Home: 4319 Andre Midland MI 48640 Office: Dow Chem Co PO Box 1706 Midland MI 48640

DAVIDSON, JOHN KENNETH, SR., family sociologist, sex researcher, family planning consultant, educator; b. Augusta, Ga., Oct. 25, 1939; s. Larcie Charles and Betty (Corley) D.; student Augusta Coll., 1956-58; B.S. Ed., U. Ga., 1961, M.A., 1963; Ph.D., U. Fla., 1974; m. Josephine Frazier, Apr. 11, 1964; children—John Kenneth Jr., Stephen Wood. Asst. prof. dept. psychology and sociology Armstrong State Coll., Savannah, 1963-67; asst. prof. dept. sociology Augusta Coll., Augusta, Ga., 1967-74; acting chmn., asst. prof. dept. sociology Ind. U., South Bend, 1974-76; asso. prof. sociology U. Wis.-Eau Claire, 1976-78, prof., 1978—, chmn. dept. sociology, 1976-80; research cons. dept. obstetrics and gynecology Med. Coll. Ga., Augusta, 1969-74, pediatrics, 1972-73, also asso. dir. health care project, 1971-73, research instr., summer 1971, research asso., summer 1972-73, research cons. dept. community dentistry, 1974-79. Program coordinator Community Devel. in Process Phase II and III, Title I Higher Edn. Act of 1965, 1970; mem. sociology and anthropology com. Univ. System Ga., 1970-74, chmn. curriculum sub-com., 1970-72; dir. Sex Edn. The Pub. Schs. and You project Ind. Com. on The Humanities, 1975; mem., chmn. com. on standards and criteria for cert. Nat. Council Family Relations, 1980-84, chmn. com. on implementation of cert.; bd. dirs., past pres. Wis. Council on Family Relations; chmn. Eau Claire adv. com. Planned Parenthood Clinics Wis.; past bd. dirs. Planned Parenthood North Central Ind., also past chmn. pub. affairs com., 1975-76; former mem. bd. dirs., former 1st v.p. Wis. Family Planning Coordinating Council; bd. dirs., past mem. exec. com., past chmn. com. on research in social scis., past mem. internat. com. Assn. for Vol. Sterilization, Inc.; past mem. resources allocation com. Planned Parenthood of Wis., Inc.; past mem. Eau Claire County Adv. Health forum; past mem. Eau Claire County Task Force on Family Planning; past mem. Western Wis. Task Force on Family Planning. Mem. Am. Sociol. Assn., Wis. Sociol. Assn., Mid-South Sociol. Assn., So. Midwest sociol. socs., Am. Home Econs. Assn., Wis. Home Econs. Assn., Soc. Sci. Study of Sex, Soc. Study of Social Problems, Augusta Coll. Alumni Soc., U. Fla., U. Ga. alumni socs., Groves Conf., Pres.'s Club U. Wis.-Eau Claire, Kappa Delta Pi, Phi Kappa Phi, Phi Theta Kappa, Alpha Kappa Delta (pres. Beta chpt. 1971-72, nat. exec. com. 1972-84, editor nat. newsletter 1979-84). Episcopalian. Assoc. editor Jour. Marriage and the Family, 1975-85, Jour. Deviant Behavior, 1979—, Sociol. Spectrum, 1984—; contbr. articles to profl. jours. Home: 1305 Nixon Ave Eau Claire WI 54701 Office: Dept Sociology Univ Wis Eau Claire WI 54701

DAVIDSON, JUDITH ANNE, physical education educator; b. N.Y.C., Nov. 7, 1944; d. James Harold and Miriam Ruth (Karansky) D. B.S., U. N.H., 1966; cert. Chelsea Coll., Eastbourne, Eng., 1967; M.Ed., Boston U., 1974; Ph.D., U. Mass., 1983. Tchr. high sch. N. Rockland Bd. Edn., Haverstraw, N.Y., 1967-68, Newton (Mass.) Bd. Edn., 1968-76; teaching assoc., head field hockey coach U. Mass., Amherst, 1976-78; asst. prof., head field hockey coach U. Iowa, Iowa City, 1978—; owner, mgr. Atalanta Sports Ltd., Iowa City, 1979—. Contbr. articles to profl. jours. Mem. AAU Jr. Olympics Com., Iowa City, 1985, U.S. Olympic Com. Named Coach of Yr., Field Hockey, Big 10 Conf., Chgo., 1983, Coach of Yr. Big 10 Conf., 1984; nat. runner-up NCAA Final Four Field Hockey, 1984. Mem. N.Am. Soc. Sport History, U.S. Field Hockey Assn. (adminstrv. v.p. 1981-83, pres. 1985—, nat. runner-up in indoor hockey 1985), AAHPER, N.Am. Soc. Sport History, Popular Culture Assn. Jewish. Democrat. Home: 1106 Yewell St Iowa City IA 52240 Office: Carver Hawkeye Arena University of Iowa Iowa City IA 52242

DAVIDSON, LUTHER KENNETH, fire chief; b. Moberly, Mo., June 27, 1924; s. Bert Lee and Leela Fern (Acree) D.; m. Norma Lee Farris, Nov. 8, 1947; 1 dau., Linda Sue. Student Moberly, Mo. pub. schs. Machine operator Brown Shoe Co., Moberly, Mo., 1940-42; machine operator, 1946-55; fireman Moberly Fire Dept., 1955-82, fire chief, 1982—. Served with USN, 1942-46. Mem. Internat. Assn. Fire Chiefs, Mo. Assn. Fire Chiefs, VFW. Avocations: Hunting, fishing, boating, skiing. Home: 624 Grand Ave Moberly MO 65270 Office: Moberly Fire Dept 316 N Clark St Moberly MO 65270

DAVIDSON, RICHARD LAURENCE, geneticist, educator; b. Cleve., Feb. 22, 1941; s. Morris and Bess (Segal) D.; m. Jalane Emilie Christensen, Sept. 10, 1967. B.A., Western Res. U., 1963; Ph.D., 1967. Asst. prof. Harvard Med. Sch., Boston, 1970-73, assoc. prof., 1973-81; prof. genetics U. Ill.-Chgo., 1980—, dir. Ctr. Genetics, 1980—. Editor: Somatic Cell Hybridization, 1974; Somatic Cell Genetics, 1984; editor-in-chief Jour. Somatic Cell Genetics, 1975—. Nat. Acad. Scis. fellow, 1967. Mem. AAAS, Am. Soc. Cell Biology, Am. Soc. Microbiology, Tissue Culture Assn., Phi Beta Kappa, NSF (human cell biology adv. panel), NIH (genetic study sect.). Office: U Ill Coll Medicine Ctr Genetics 808 S Wood St Chicago IL 60612

DAVIDSON, TOM ALLEN, process engineer; b. Indpls., Feb. 10, 1951. B.S.I.E., Purdue U., 1973, M.S.I.E., 1977. Process engr. Diamond Chain Co., Indpls., 1973—. Mem. Soc. Mfg. Engrs. Club: Valle Vista Country (Greenwood, Ind.). Home: 55 N 4th Ave Beech Grove IN 46107 Office: 402 Kentucky Ave PO Box 7045 Indianapolis IN 46207

DAVIDSON, WILLIAM M., professional sports team executive, business executive Mng. ptnr. Detroit Pistons, N.B.A., Pontiac, Mich., pres., chief exec. officer Guardian Industries Corp., Northville, Mich. Office: Guardian Industries 43043 W Nine Mile Rd Northville MI 48167*

DAVIES, DAVID GREER, lawyer; b. Evanston, Ill., Apr. 25, 1933; s. Lewis Allen and Frances Clinton (Greer) D.; m. Adelaide Towne Stephenson, June 15, 1955; children—Amy Greer Murway, Martha, David, Ann. B.S.E., U. Mich., 1955, J.D., 1961. Ptnr., Arter & Hadden, Cleve., 1961-79, Ray, Robinson, Hanninen & Carle, Cleve., 1974—. Contbr. articles to profl. jours. Bd. trustees, pres. Bay Interfaith Housing, Bay Village, Ohio, 1968—; trustee St. John and West Shore Hosp., Westlake, Ohio, 1979—, chmn., 1982-84. Served to lt. USNR, 1955-59. Mem. ABA, Ohio State Bar Assn., Maritime Law Assn., Bar Assn. Greater Cleve. (trustee 1976-68), Soc. Naval Architects and Marine Engrs. Democrat. Episcopalian. Club: Edgewater Yacht (Cleve.). Home: 31263 Lake Rd Bay Village OH 44140 Office: 1050 Huntington Bldg 925 Euclid Ave Cleveland OH 44115

DAVIES, GEORGE JAMES, physical therapist, educator; b. La Crosse, Wis., June 9, 1947; m. Carol J. Riley, June 7, 1969; children—Scott, Steven. B.A. in Health and Phys. Edn., Trenton (N.J.) State Coll., 1969, M.Ed. with high honors, 1972; postgrad. Rutgers U., 1973, Columbia U., 1973-75, Fairleigh-Dickinson U., 1974, U. Wis., 1977, U. Wis.-La Crosse, 1978. Cert. phys. therapist Columbia U., 1975; lic. phys. therapist Wis.; cert. athletic trainer Nat. Athletic Trainers Assn.; cert. exercise technician Am. Coll. Sports Medicine; cert. emergency med. technician Nat. Registry of Emergency Med. Technicians, Wis.; cert. cardiopulmonary resuscitation instr., trainer Am. Heart Assn.; cert. cardiopulmonary resuscitation instr., standard first aid and personal safety instr., advanced first aid and emergency care instr., ARC. Student athletic trainer Trenton (N.J.) State Coll., 1967-79, grad. asst. in health and phys. edn., 1971-72; instr. health and phys. edn. Bergen Community Coll., Paramus, N.J., 1972-74, athletic training cons., 1974-75; mem. faculty, asst. prof. phys. therapy U. Wis.-La Crosse, 1975-80, assoc. prof., 1980—, dept. chmn., 1978-79, clin. supr., 1979—, vis. asst. prof. grad. program Inst. Grad. Health Scis., 1980—; nat. faculty mem. U.S. Sports Acad., Mobile, Ala., 1977—; mem. staff La Crosse (Wis.) Exercise Program, 1976—; assoc. dir., bus. mgr. sole practice Orthopaedic and Sports Phys. Therapy, La Crosse, 1979—; cons. in field. Served with USMC, 1969-70. Recipient Cramer Products Athletic Tng. award, 1981; grantee numerous profl. orgns. and govt. agys. Mem. Am. Phys. Therapy Assn. (sports phys. therapy sect.: editor jour., chmn. publs. com.), Am. Coll. Sports Medicine, Nat. Athletic Trainers Assn., Great Lakes Athletic Trainers Assn., Wis. Athletic Trainers Assn., Nat. Registry Emergency Med. Technicians, Wis. Registry Emergency Med. Technicians, Nat. Jogger's Assn., Phi Epsilon Kappa (nat. merit scholar, key award 1972), Sigma Xi. Am. Baptist. Author: (with J. Tesch, et al) Laboratory and Field Tests for Cross Country Skiers, 1980; co-editor: Textbook of Physical Therapy: Orthopaedics and Sports, 1984; contbr. chpts. to books, articles to profl. jours.; editor Sports Medicine column Cardio-Gram, La Crosse, 1976—; co-editor Jour. Orthopaedic and Sports Phys. Therapy, 1979—. Home: 1707 Jennifer Ct Onalaska WI 54650 Office: U Wis 2036 Cowley Hall La Crosse WI 54601

DAVIES, GRAHAM OVERBY, oral surgeon; b. Chgo., Aug. 9, 1923; s. Clarence Hoover and Lillian (Overby) D.; student Lawrence Coll., 1941-42, U. Chgo., 1948-50; D.D.S., Loyola U., Chgo., 1946; M.S.D., Northwestern U., 1954; m. Suan M. Hartman, Oct. 7, 1957; children—Laura Ann, Julie, Jennifer. Pvt. practice oral surgery, Chgo., 1948—; asso. prof. oral surgery Chgo. Coll. Osteo. Medicine, 1974-77, prof., 1977—; pres. Dagar Products, Inc., 1975; dir. Hydrodyne Corp.; guest lectr. U. Ill., U. Sydney (Australia); spl. cons. Ill. Cancer Detection Program. Bd. dirs. Miss Ind. Scholarship Pageant Corp., 1972-74; trustee Town of Michiana Shores (Ind.), 1960-62; trustee Town of Long Beach (Ind.), 1967-81, pres. bd., 1973, 76; adv. com. Ind. Coastal Zone Mgmt. Program; pres. Long Beach Mcpl. Water Bd., 1981—; commr. pub. works Town of Long Beach, 1981—; mem. No. Ind. Planning Commn., 1983. Served with AUS, 1942-45; capt. USAF, 1946-48. Mem. ADA, Ill., Chgo., Kenwood-Hyde Park (pres. 1958) dental assns., N.W. Ind. Dental Soc., Ill. (charter), Chgo. socs. oral surgeons, Odontographic Soc., Chgo. Inst. Medicine (gov.), Delta Tau Delta, Delta Sigma Delta. Club: Long Beach Country (dir. holding corp. 1972). Author: The Comparative Effects of Various Local Anesthetics on Pulse Wave and Rate, 1954; co-author Phosphate in Lake Michigan, 1974. Home: 2751 Floral Trail Long Beach Michigan City IN 46360 Office: 5200 S Ellis Ave Chicago IL 60615

DAVIES, JOHN ARTHUR, trade association executive; b. Cleve., Feb. 29, 1920; s. William R. and Florence C. (Koch) D.; m. Lina Ruth Keeter, Oct. 27, 1951; children—Janet Carol, Nancy Susan. B.A., Conn. Wesleyan U., 1943. Cert. profl. mgr. Materials devel. mgr. Champion Papers, Inc., Hamilton, Ohio, 1963-66; exec. v.p. Internat. Assn. Printing House Craftsmen, Cin., 1966—. Patentee (2). Served to capt., U.S. Army, 1942-45, 50-52; NATOUSA, ETO. Lodges: Elks, Kenwood Lions (past pres.) (Cin.). Avocations: golf; antique clock repair. Home: 5462 Schiering Dr Fairfield OH 45014 Office: Internat Assn Printing House Craftsmen 7599 Kenwood Rd Cincinnati OH 45226

DAVIES, JOHN WYKOFF, employee benefits consultant; b. Gary, Ind., July 28, 1929; s. John W. and Edith Norma (Presar) D.; m. Nancy Anderson, June 20, 1952 (div. 1974); m. Christine Marie Linley, Oct. 9, 1974; children—Judy, Dottie, Mandy, Christopher. A.B., Depauw U., 1951. C.L.U. Group ins. rep. Aetna Life Ins. Co., Toledo, 1954-56, asst. gen. agt., 1956-59; mgr. group and pension dept. Picton-Cavanaugh, Inc., Toledo, 1959-65; sales agt. Aetna Life Ins, Toledo, 1965-69; co-owner v.p. Findley, Davies and Co., Toledo, 1969—. Pres. Sylvania Bd. Edn., Ohio, 1984-85; 3d v.p. Toledo Soc. for Handicapped, 1984—; bd. dirs. Toledo Humane Soc., 1975—. Served with U.S. Army, 1952-54. Lodge: Rotary. Home: 4116 Corey Rd Toledo OH 43623 Office: Findley Davies and Co 510 United Savings Bldg Toledo OH 43604

DAVIES, ROGER, geoscience educator; b. London, Aug. 29, 1948; came to U.S., 1972, naturalized, 1985; s. Trevor Rhys and Gracie Rhys (Beaton) D.; m. Corinne Marie Scofield, Oct. 29, 1977; 1 child, Colin. B.Sc. with honors, Victoria U., Wellington, N.Z., 1970; Ph.D., U. Wis., 1976. Meteorologist, New Zealand Meteorol. Service, Wellington, 1971-77; scientist U. Wis., Madison, 1977-80; asst. prof. geosci. Purdue U., West Lafayette, Ind., 1980—; mem. Earth Radiation Budget Expt. Sci. Team, 1980—, First Internat. Satellite Cloud Climatology Project, Regional Exptl. Sci. Team, 1984—. Contbr. articles and book revs. to profl. publs. Research grantee NASA. Mem. Am. Meteorol. Soc., Am. Geophys. Union, Optical Soc. Am. Avocation: sailing. Office: Purdue Univ Dept Geoscis West Lafayette IN 47907

DAVIS, A. ARTHUR, lawyer; b. Sioux City, Iowa, Oct. 12, 1928; s. Edward R. and Isabel (Baron) D.; m. Joan Below, Aug. 6, 1955 (div. 1970); children—Pamela Benham, Mark Baron; m. Jessie L. Kuhl, Oct. 28, 1984. B.B.S. with honors, Northwestern U., 1950, J.D., 1952. Bar: Iowa 1952, U.S. Ct. Appeals (8th cir.) 1959, D.C. 1968, U.S. Ct. Appeals (2d cir.) 1975. Assoc. Brody, Parker, Roberts, Thoma & Harris, Des Moines, 1955-59; ptnr. Davis, Hockenberg, Wine, Brown & Koehn and predecessor, Des Moines, 1959—; dir. various publicly-held corps.; lectr. on nat., regional banking issues; mem. vis. com. Northwestern U. Law Sch., 1981—; mem. U.S. 8th Cir. Judge Nominating Commn., 1978-80. Bd. dirs. Des Moines Ind. Community Sch. Dist., 1963-69, pres. 1966-67; mem. Des Moines Commn. Human Rights, 1960-63; mem. Pres.'s Holocaust Meml. Council, 1980—; mem. Democratic Nat. Com.'s Adv. Council on Making Govt. Work Better, 1982—; mem. Lt. Gov.'s Iowa Tomorrow Com., 1983—; mem. Central Iowa Labor-Mgmt. Com., 1984—. Served to 1st lt. AUS, 1953-55. Recipient nat. award People to People Program, 1961; Brotherhood award Des Moines chpt. NCCJ, 1981. Mem. ABA, Iowa State Bar Assn., Polk County Bar Assn., Northwestern U. Law Sch. Alumni Assn. (pres. 1977-78), Greater Des Moines C. of C. (bd. dirs. 1973-75, 80—, pres. 1979), Soc. for Iowa's Future, Order of Coif. Jewish. Clubs: Des Moines, Wakonda (Des Moines). Home: 2880 Grand Apt 304 Des Moines IA 50312 Office: 2300 Financial Ctr Des Moines IA 50309

DAVIS, ALVIN BERT, nuclear engineer, government executive; b. Johnstown, Pa., Oct. 8, 1930; s. Harry George and Grace Beatrice (Adams) D.; m. Donna Jean Brangham, Dec. 20, 1953; children—Marjorie Lynn, Jeffery Bert. B.S. Chem. E., Carnegie Inst. Tech., 1952. Certified nuclear engr. Chief project engr. NASA, Sandusky, Ohio, 1963-67, asst. chief reactor div., 1967-72, chief reactor div., 1972-73; chief pressurized water reactor section USNRC, King of Prussia, Pa., 1973-78, chief, fuel and materials safety, Glen Ellyn, Ill., 1978-80, deputy adminstr., 1980—. Avocations: gardening, bridge. Office: US Nuclear Regulatory Commn 799 Roosevelt Rd Glen Ellyn IL 60137

DAVIS, ALVIN GEORGE, international trade consultant; b. Chgo., May 10, 1918; s. Isadore and Mary (Wasserman) D.; m. Rose Lorber, Dec. 14, 1940 (dec. 1980); children—Fred Barry, Glenn Martin; m. 2d, June Elizabeth, May 24, 1982. With Sears Roebuck & Co., 1936-40; gen. partner, sales mgr. Ritz Mfg. Co., 1940-41; buyer hobby dept. The Fair, 1941-43; mgr. hobby div. Central Camera Co., wholesalers, 1944; pres., gen. mgr. Nat. Model Distbrs., Inc., 1945-63; pres. Hobbycraft Exports, 1946-62; pub., editor Cyclopedia Pub., Inc., 1949-62; dir. internat. operations Aurora Plastics Corp., 1951-62, v.p. internat. div., 1962-70; v.p. Aurora Plastics Can., Ltd., 1963-70; mng. dir. Aurora Plastics Nederland N.V., 1964-70, Aurora Plastics Co. U.K. Ltd., Croydon, Eng.; expert cons. U.S. and Fgn. Comml. Service, Hong Kong; EDP internat. trade and distbn. cons.; internat. trade cons. until 1984; sr. internat. trade specialist U.S. Comml. Service, U.S. Dept. Commerce, 1971-84; lectr. Stuart Sch. of Bus. Adminstrn., Ill. Inst. Tech.; dir. Rowe Industries (HK) Ltd., Rowe Industries (Taiwan) (Singapore), Rowe Industries Ltd. Mem., chmn. People to People Com.; scoutmaster, past mem. fin. com. Chgo. council Boy Scouts Am.; info. officer, dep. comdr. CAP. Recipient Berkeley award, 1957, Hobbies award of merit Hobby Industry Assn., 1960, Meritorious award of honor, 1975. Fellow Inst. Dirs. (London), Hobby Industry Am. (hon. life); mem. Nat. Rifle Assn. (life), Soaring Soc. Am., Airplane Owners and Pilots Assn., Acad. Model Aeros. (contest dir. 1936-70), Nat. Model R.R. Assn. (life), Model Industry Assn. (dir. 1952-60, sec. 1954-57, pres. 1957-59), Hobby Industry Assn. (hon. life; pres. 1957-59), Chgo. Aeronuts (hon.). Lodges: Masons (32 deg.), Shriners. Contbr. articles on internat. merchandising to trade mags. Pub., Cyclopedia of Hobbies, 1946-62; editor Dartnell-Internat. Trade Handbook; contbg. editor Brittanica Jr., 1949. Office: 3601 W Devon 300N Chicago IL 60659

DAVIS, BARBARA SNELL, educator; b. Painesville, Ohio, Feb. 21, 1929; d. Roy Addison and Maybelle Irene (Denning) Snell; div.; children—Beth Ann, James L., Polly Denning. B.S., Kent State U., 1951; M.A., Lake Erie Coll., 1981; postgrad. Cleve. State U., 1982-83. Cert. reading specialist, elem. prin., Ohio. Dir. publicity Lake Erie Coll., Painesville, 1954-59; tchr. Mentor (Ohio) Exempted Village Sch. Dist., 1972—. Trustee Old Mentor Found. Mem. Delta Kappa Gamma (pres. 1982-84), Theta Sigma Phi (charter). Methodist. Contbr. articles to profl. jours. Home: 7293 Beechwood Dr Mentor OH 44060 Office: Headlands Sch 5028 Forest Rd Mentor OH 44060

DAVIS, BOB J., transportation educator; b. Grand Saline, Tex., June 27, 1927; s. Frank H. and Minnie Kathryn (Crocker) D.; B.B.A., U. Houston, 1957, M.B.A., 1961, J.D., 1966; m. Alice Joyce Reagan, Oct. 22, 1948; 1 dau., Paula Lynn. Admitted to Tex. bar, 1966; traffic rep. Texaco, Inc., Houston, 1951-61; traffic mgr. Republic Steel Corp., Cleve., 1961-67; mem. faculty Western Ill. U., Macomb, 1967—, prof. transp., 1970-82, dir. exec. devel., 1970-82; mem. Macomb Planning Commn., 1971-75, Macomb Mcpl. Airport Authority, 1980-84. Served with USNR, 1944-47. Recipient Sam Harper award Purchasing Agts. Assn. Houston, 1957; named Traffic Man of Yr., Transp. Club Houston, 1966; Regional Educator of Yr., Delta Nu Alpha, 1980, 81, Regional Man of Yr., 1982, Mapleton award, 1982; Coll. Bus. Tchr. of Yr., Western Ill. U., 1981. Mem. Assn. ICC Practitioners (Clyde B. Aitchison award 1966), Am. Soc. Traffic and Transp., Internat. Material Mgmt. Soc., Ill. Pub. Airports Assn. (bd. dirs. 1982-84), Phi Kappa Phi (disting. mem. 1982). Methodist. Club: Masons. Author books, bibliographies, reports, articles in field. Home: 1111 E Grant St Macomb IL 61455 Office: 900 W Adams St Macomb IL 61455

DAVIS, BRENDA, employment and training executive; b. St. Louis, Jan. 30, 1941; d. William and Lillie (Lee) Johnson; m. Lucious Hogan, Jr., Apr. 20, 1961 (div. 1965); 1 son, Lucious III; m. 2d Harry Davis, Jr., Mar. 9, 1969; 1 son, Jarrett. Student Harris Tchrs. and Jr. Coll., 1959-61, Webster Coll., 1980-82. Interviewer admitting City Health Div., St. Louis, 1964-67; interviewer housing St. Louis Housing, 1967-70; community program aide City Civil Rights, St. Louis, 1970-71; pub. health rep. City Health Div., St. Louis, 1971-74; ops. mgr. St. Louis Agy. on Tng. and Employment, 1974—; adv. mem. U.S. Conf. Mayors, St. Louis, 1981-82. Sec., Walnut Park Housing Revitalization, 1983; adv. mem. St. Matthew Sch. Bd., St. Louis, 1982—; recruitment chmn. service action com. United Way, 1982. Recipient Appreciation awards Juvenile Recreation Program, City St. Louis Recreational Dept., 1974, Project 70001 Inc., 1979, 80, 81. Democrat. Roman Catholic. Home: 5766 Waterman St Saint Louis MO 63112

DAVIS, BRIANT LEROY, research scientist, educator; b. Brigham City, Utah, Nov. 18, 1936; s. Nephi Kunz and Cordelia Amber (Hanson) D.; m. Dixie Lee Powell, Sept. 5, 1957; children—Julia, Laurence Jeffrey, Jennifer, Briant LeRoy. B.S. in Geology, Brigham Young U., 1958, M.S. in Geology, 1959; Ph.D. in Geology, UCLA, 1964. Research geophysicist and assoc. prof. geophysics S.D. Sch. Mines and Tech., Rapid City, 1970-78, research prof. geophysics, sr. scientist dept. meteorology, Inst. Atmospheric Sci., 1978—, head cloud physics group, 1971-84, acting head dept. meteorology, 1982-83. Author: Nucleation Process in Cloud Physics, 1978; contbr. articles to jours. Pres. Black Hills Chamber Music Soc., Rapid City, 1968-78. Mem. Air Pollution Control Assn., Am. Geophys. Union, Am. Meteorol. Soc., Assn. Aerosol Research, Sigma Xi. Republican. Mormon. Club: Black Hills Racquet. Avocations: music; tennis; camping. Home: 4022 Helen Ct Rapid City SD 57702 Office: SD Sch Mines and Tech 500 E St Joe St Rapid City SD 57701

DAVIS, CELIA FAYE, investment broker; b. Frenchburg, Ky., July 22, 1955; d. Emery C. and Emogene D.; A.A., Ky. Mountain Bible Inst., 1976; B.A., Olivet Nazarene Coll., 1980. Prodn. coordinator Liberty Nat. Pub., Chgo., 1977-78; ops. mgr. The Milw. Co., Chgo., 1980-82; adminstrv. asst. Paine Webber, Jackson & Curtis, Inc., Chgo., 1982-84; office mgr., investment broker TransMarket Group, Chgo., 1984—. Mem. Republican Presdl. Task Force; sustaining mem. Rep. Nat. Com. Mem. Stockbrokers Assn., Council Career Planning, Am. Entrepreneurs Assn., Soc. Bus. and Profl. Women, Nat. Assn. Female Execs., U.S. Consumer Assn., Concerned Women Am., Nat. Right to Life, Moral Majority, Conservative Caucus, Nat. Conservative Found., Nat. Taxpayers Union, Citizens for a Debt-Free Am., Smithsonian Instn., Internat. Platform Assn., Nat. Congl. Club. Mem. Ch. Nazarene (organist 1981—, exec. v.p. Nazarene Youth Internat. 1981-82, adv. mem. worship com. 1981, mem. music com. 1980—). Home: 1529 Vine Ave Round Lake Beach IL 60073

DAVIS, CHARLES SIMON, engineering consulting firm executive; b. Dallas, June 6, 1939; s. Simon and Essie J. (Johnson) D.; m. Loretta C. F. Johnson, June 9, 1958; 1 child, Adrienne J. B.S.C.E., Prairie View A&M Coll., 1961; M.S.C.E., U. Wash., 1967; Ph.D., U. Mo.-Rolla, 1972. Registered profl. engr., Mich. Aircraft engr. Lockheed-Ga. Co., Marietta, 1961-62, N.Am. Aviation Co., Los Angeles, 1964; stress engr. Boeing Co., Seattle, 1964-68, Hlyoh/McDonnell, St. Louis, 1968-70; research engr. Ford Motor Co., Dearborn, Mich., 1972-78; pres. Charles S. Davis & Assocs. Inc., Detroit, 1978—. Mem. adv. bd. Detroit Black United Fund, 1983-84. Served to 1st lt. U.S. Army, 1962-64. Mem. ASCE, Mich. Soc. Profl. Engrs., Cons. Engring. Council (bd. dirs.), Engring. Soc. Detroit, Detroit C. of C., Soc. Engrs. and Applied Scientists, Alpha Phi Alpha, Chi Epsilon, Phi Kappa Phi. Democrat. Baptist. Office: Charles S Davis & Assocs Inc 220 Bagley Suite 700 Detroit MI 48226

DAVIS, CHRISTINE NOELLE, lawn maintenance and equipment sales company executive; b. Nancy, France, Dec. 24, 1955; came to U.S., 1957, naturalized, 1974; d. Frederick and Marguerite (Marchal) Stelmach; m. Robert O. Davis, Mar. 24, 1978 (div. 1982); 1 child, Brian Andrew. B.S., Park Coll., 1977. Membership coordinator Kansas City C. of C., Kans., 1977-78; research dept. mgr. J.E. Stowers & Co., Kansas City, Mo., 1978-79; office services mgr. Watson, Ess, Marshall & Enggas, 1979-81; office services mgr., purchasing buyer Alfa-Laval, Inc., 1981-85; purchasing buyer, office services mgr. Ball Enterprises, Parkville, Mo., 1985—. Republican. Roman Catholic. Avocations: interior decorating; tennis; landscaping. Home: 7705 NW 79th Place Kansas City MO 64152 Office: Ball Enterprises Route 27 Parkville MO 64152

DAVIS, C(LAUD) NEAL, college official b. Moko, Ark., Nov. 3, 1936; s. Claud Delbert and Freda Margaret (Gilliam) D.; m. Frances Patricia Duncan, June 16, 1977; children—Cathy Sue, Claud Michael, Cary Mark, Carol Kim, Connie Beth, Cory Mitchel. B.A., William Jewell Coll., 1958; M.A., N.E. Mo. State U., 1963; Ph.D., U. Mo.-Kansas City, 1970. Cert. fund raising exec. Asst. then mgr. Western Auto Supply Co., Mpls., Kansas City, 1958-59; owner, mgmr. Davis Family Shoe Store, Edina, Mo., 1960-64; dean of men William Jewell Coll., Liberty, Mo., 1961-67; dean students Elmhurst Coll., Ill., 1967-73; pres., prof. Judson Coll., Portland and The Dalles, Oreg., 1973-82; v.p., dean devel. and pub. relations Hannibal-LaGrange Coll., Mo., 1982-83; dir. devel. S.E. Mo. State U., Cape Girardeau, 1985—; dir. Holt Internat. Childrens Services, Eugene, Oreg., lectr. in field. Author (with others) Better People, 1981. Contbr. articles to profl. jours. Vice chmn. Council Related Agys., Hannibal, 1984-85. Lay speaker various chs., Mo., Oreg., 1958—. Rotary Paul Harris fellow Oreg., Wash., 1981. Mem. Nat. Soc. Fund Raising Execs., Am. Assn. Higher Edn. (life). Baptist Pub. Relations Assn., Am. Assn. for Counseling and Devel., Am. Coll. Personnel Assn., Cape Girardeau C. of C.; Phi Delta Kappa. Democrat. Lodge: Rotary (past dist. gov., various offices). Avocations: public speaking, photography, writing, international adoption, church related service. Home: Route 2 Box E 534 Cape Girardeau MO 63701 Office: SE Mo State U Cape Girardeau MO 63701

DAVIS, DON WAYNE, educational administrator, basketball coach; b. Anna, Ill., Nov. 15, 1951; s. John Calvin and Shirley Ann (West) D.; m. Donna Sue Sronce, Oct. 20, 1979; children—Lisa Nicole, Robert Wayne. B.S., So. Ill. U., 1974, M.S., 1985. Cert. secondary vocat. edn. tchr. Ill. Ironworker, Internat. Assn. Ironworkers, Paducah, Ky., 1974-78; instr. Shawnee Coll., 1978-79; dir. edn. projects Region 12 Career Guidance Ctr., Anna, 1979—; constituency council mem. Adult Edn. Service Ctr., Edwardsville, Ill., 1981—; cons. Regional Vocat. System, Tamms, Ill., 1982-83; task force mem. Ill. Assn. for Cons. and Devel., 1984—. Co-author: Illinois Career Guidance Handbook, 1981; A Model for a Career Guidance Delivery System, 1979; A Curriculum Guide for Economic Literacy. Adv. council mem. Southeastern Ill. Coll. Youth Ctr., Harrisburg, 1984. Mem. Ill. Vocat. Assn., Ill. Assn. for Cons. and Devel., Ill. Career Devel. Services Assn. Republican. Lutheran. Avocations: golfing, gardening, home restoration. Home: 402 North Main Anna IL 62906 Office: Regional Supt of Schs 1000 N Main Barnes Hall Anna IL 62906

DAVIS, DONALD ROBERT, accounting educator; b. St. Louis, Apr. 8, 1935; s. Howard Allen and Maude (Crow) D.; m. Mary Susannah Fleenor, July 21, 1962; children—Brian Robert, Valerie Ann. B.E.E., Washington U., St. Louis, 1957, M.B.A., 1960. Corp. sec. Cox-Ware Corp., Kirkwood, Mo., 1960; v.p. Mid-States Bus. Capital Corp., St. Louis, 1960-65; pres. Davco Auto Parts, Inc., Farmington, Mo., 1965-67; faculty St. Louis Community Coll., 1967—, prof. acctg., 1981—; writer software Dryden Press, Chgo., 1984—. Creater acctg. software programs. Served to 1st lt. AUS, 1958-59. Washington U. honor scholar, 1954-57; Boatman's Bank fellow, 1958, Weinheimer fellow, 1959. Mem. NEA, Nat. Assn. Accts., Mo. Bus. Edn. Assn., Mo. Assn. Acctg. Educators, Mo. Assn. Community and Jr. Colls., Tau Beta Pi, Sigma Alpha Epsilon. Office: Dept Acctg St Louis Community Coll at Meramec 11333 Big Bend Blvd Kirkwood MO 63122

DAVIS, EARON SCOTT, editor, publisher, environmental health law consultant; b. Chgo., Sept 7, 1950; s. Milton and Grayce Davis; m. Gilla Prizant, May 29, 1977; children—Jeremy Adam, Jonathan Michael. B.A., U. Ill., 1972; J.D., Washington U., St. Louis, 1975; M.P.H., UCLA, 1978. Bar: Ill., Mo., D.C. Asst. to chmn. Ill. Pollution Control Bd., Chgo., 1975-77; environ. cons. Fred C. Hart Assos., Washington, 1979-80; atty. coordinator Migrant Legal Action Program, Washington, 1980-81; environ. cons., Evanston, Ill., 1981—; editor, pub. Ecol. Illness Law Report, Evanston, 1982—. Exec. dir. Human Ecology Action League, Evanston, Ill., 1983-84; mem. nat. adv. bd. Environ. Task Force, Washington, 1984—. Author: Toxic Chemicals: Law and Science, 1982. Contbr. articles to various publs. Mem. adv. com. D.C. Lung Assn., Washington, 1981; Clean Air Coalition, Phila., 1983. Recipient Presdl. award Am. Acad. Environ. Medicine, 1983. Mem. Environ. Law Inst. (assoc.), Air Pollution Control Assn., Nat. Assn. Environ. Profls., Assn. Trial Lawyers Am., Mo. Bar Am. Pub. Health Assn., ABA. Office: Ecological Illness Law Report PO Box 1796 Evanston IL 60204

DAVIS, EDDIE, psychotherapist, social work educator, consultant; b. Bessemer, Ala., Nov. 7, 1937; s. Dan and Ceola (Williams) D.; A.B., Roosevelt U., 1969; A.M., Sch. Social Service Adminstrn. U. Chgo., 1971; postgrad., U. Utah. With Morgan State U., Balt., 1971-72, Fed. City Coll.-HEW Upward Mobility Coll., Washington, 1972-73; lectr. undergrad. and grad. social work programs Jane Addams Coll. Social Work, U. Ill., Chgo., 1975-81, also acting dir. minority affairs; acad. adviser Chgo. State U., Univ. Without Walls; primary therapist Project Reality, Salt Lake City, 1981-82; assoc. instr. social policy U. Utah, 1982; coordinator adult and family services Englewood Mental Health Ctr., 1984—; Comprehensive Health Orgn., Mental Health Ctr., 1984—; family cons. Served with Army N.G., 1961-67. Mem. Nat. Assn. Social Workers, Acad. Certified Social Workers, Nat. Assn. Black Social Workers, Council on Social Work Edn. Club: Evergreen Bath and Tennis. Home: 3120 W Arthington St Chicago IL 60612 Office: Englewood Comprehensive Health Orgn 938 W 69th St Chicago IL 60621

DAVIS, EDDIE GEORGE, electric company administrator; b. St. Louis, 1947; married; 3 children. Student Lincoln U., St. Louis Community Coll.; B.A. in Finance, St. Louis U., 1975. With Union Electric Co., St. Louis, 1971—, sr. adminstr. community affairs, 1976—. Active Boy Scouts Am.; mem. bd. dirs. Spirit of St. Louis Drum & Bugle Corps.; treas., bd. dirs. Neighborhood Mktg. Services Inc.; chmn., treas. St. Louis Pub. Sch. Vol. Adv. Council; treas., bd. dirs. Neighborhood Assn.; mem. Matthews-Dickey Boys Club Blue Ribbon Com.; mem. adv. council Gateway 70001; mem. budget com. Newstead Baptist Ch.; advisor Southside Jr. Achievement Ctr.; mem. bd. advisors Nat. Energy Edn. Day/Mo. Energy Edn. Com.; mem. Energy & Man's Environment Planning and Implementing Com., St. Louis; mem. Energy & Man's Environment Industry, Pres.'s Adv. Council. Mem. Edison Electric Inst. (ednl. services com.), N. Central Region Electric Utility Educators Com. (chmn.), Pub. Relations Soc. Am. (St. Louis chpt.), Nat. Sci. Tchrs. Assn. Baptist. Home: 4867A Penrose St Saint Louis MO 63115 Office: 1901 Gratiot St PO Box 149 Saint Louis MO 63166

DAVIS, EDWARD REYNOLDS, public relations counselor; b. Pitts., Nov. 26, 1947. Reporter, Valley Dailey News, Los Angeles, 1972-78; city editor Los Angeles Sentinel, 1979-81; pub. relations counselor Fleishman-Hillard, Inc., St. Louis, 1981—. Vol. football coach Mathews-Dickey Boys' Club, United Way, St. Louis; pub. relations cons. Inroads, Inc. Recipient Merit award Nat. Newspaper Pubs. Assn., 1979; Disting. Alumni award Calif. State U.-Northridge, 1980. Mem. Pub. Relations Soc. Am., Urban League, NAACP, 100 Black Men of St. Louis, Omega Psi Phi, Upsilon Omega. Mem. African Methodist Episcopal Ch. Office: Fleishman-Hillard Inc One Memorial Dr Saint Louis MO 63102

DAVIS, ELWYN HERBERT, mathematics educator, consultant; b. Leon, Iowa, Jan. 10, 1942; s. Gerald Victor and Mabel Louisa (Gamet) D.; m. Karen Faye Pratt, Sept. 1, 1963; children—Victor Pratt, Karis Kay. A.A., Graceland Coll., Lamoni, Iowa, 1962; B.S. in Edn., U. Mo.-Columbia, 1964, M.A., 1966, Ph.D., 1969. Assoc. prof. math. Pittsburg State U., Kans., 1969-72, asst. prof., 1972-78, prof., 1978—; cons. Phillips Petroleum, Bartlesville, Okla., 1983—. Author: Introductory Modern Algebra, 1973. Developer software puzzles. Pastor Reorganized Ch. Jesus Christ Latter Day Saints, Pittsburg, 1979-83. Mem. Math. Assn. Am., Nat. Council Tchrs. Math., Soc. Petroleum Engrs. Lodge: Kiwanis (pres. 1973-74, 84-85). Avocations: running, computing. Home: 605 Oakcrest Pittsburg KS 66762 Office: Pittsburg State U Dept Math Pittsburg KS 66762

DAVIS, ERROLL BROWN, JR., utility executive; b. Pitts., Aug. 5, 1944; s. Erroll Brown and Eleanor Margaret (Boykin) D.; m. Elaine E. Casey, July 13, 1968; children—Christopher, Whitney. E.E., Carnegie-Mellon U., Pitts., 1965; M.B.A. in Fin., U. Chgo.,1967. Mem. corp. fin. staff Ford Motor Co., Detroit, 1969-73; mem. corp. fin. staff Xerox Corp., Rochester, N.Y., 1973-78; v.p. fin., Wis. Power & Light Co., Madison, 1978-82, v.p. fin. and pub. affairs, 1982-84, exec. v.p., 1984—; mem. econs. adv. com. Edison Electric Inst., Washington, 1983—; dir. Madison Capital Corp., Pub. Utility Inst., Madison. Mem. Police and Fire Commn., Madison, 1982—; mem. energy steering com. Congressional Black Caucus, Washington, 1982—; Served to lt. U.S. Army, 1967-69. Mem. Am. Assn. Blacks in Energy, Madison C. of C. (bd. dirs. 1981—). Club: Madison. Lodge: Rotary. Avocations: tennis. Office: Wis Power & Light Co 222 W Washington Ave Madison WI 53703

DAVIS, EVELYN MARGUERITE B., artist, organist, pianist; b. Springfield, Mo.; d. Philip Edward and Della Jane (Morris) Bailey; student pub. schs., Springfield; student art Drury Coll.; piano student of Charles Cordeal; m. James Harvey Davis, Sept. 22, 1946. Sec., Shea and Morris Monument Co., before 1946; past mem. sextet, soloist Sta. KGBX; past pianist, Sunday sch. tchr., mem. choir East Avenue Bapt. Ch.; tchr. Bible, organist, pianist, vocal soloist and dir. youth choir Bible Bapt. Ch., Maplewood, Mo., 1956-69, also executed 12 by 6 foot mural of Jordan River; pvt. instr. piano and organ, voice, Croma Harp, Affton, Mo., 1960-71, St. Charles, Mo., 1971—; Bible instr. 3d Bapt. Ch., St. Louis, 1948-54; pianist, soloist, tchr. Bible, Temple Bapt. Ch., Kirkwood, Mo., 1969-71; asst. organist-pianist, vocal soloist, tchr. Bible, Bible Ch., Arnold, Mo., 1969; faculty St. Charles Bible Bapt. Christian Sch., 1976-77; ch. organist, pianist, soloist, Bible tchr., dir. youth orch., music arranger Bible Bapt. Ch., St. Charles, 1971-78; organist, vocal soloist, floral arranger, Bible tchr. Faith Missionary Bapt. Ch., St. Charles, 1978-82; organist Bellview Bapt. Ch., Springfield, Mo., 1984—; tchr. piano, organ, voice, organist, Springfield, Mo., 1983-84; interior decorator and floral arranger. Fellow Internat. Biog. Assn. (life), Am. Biog. Inst. Research Assn. (life). Mem. Nat. Guild Organists, Nat. Guild Piano Tchr. Auditions, Internat. Platform Assn. Composer: I Will Sing Hallelujah, (cantata) I Am Alpha and Omega, Prelude to Prayer, My Shepherd, O Sing unto The Lord A New Song, O Come Let Us Sing unto The Lord, The King of Glory; The Lord Is My Light and My Salvation; O Worship the Lord in the Beauty of Holiness; also numerous hymn arrangements for organ and piano. Home: RFD 2 Box 405 Rogersville MO 65742

DAVIS, FORSTER ADAMS, college administrator; b. Palo Alto, Calif., Apr. 22, 1938; s. Paul Herbert and Helen (Brack) D.; B.A., Mo. Valley Coll., 1968; M.A., U. Oreg., 1970; m. Ina Claire DeGraff, Aug. 27, 1966; children—Heather Lynn, Robert Adams, Evan Paul. Dist. exec. Boy Scouts Am., Fargo, N.D., 1970-76; assoc. dir. career planning and placement Moorhead (Minn.) State U., 1976-79; dir. career services St. Olaf Coll., Northfield, Minn., 1979—; chair Minn. Pvt. Coll. Job Fair, 1986. Bd. dirs. Community Blood Bank, 1975-79. Served with U.S. Army, 1961-64. Mem. Minn. Tchr. Placement Assn. (pres. 1980-83), Twin City Personnel Assn., Meeting Planners Internat., Internat. Assn. Bus. Communicators, Coll. Placement Council, Minn. Govs. Coll. Council, Assn. Minn. Recruiters and Placement Dirs. (pres. 1983-85), Midwest Coll. Placement Assn. Office: St Olaf Coll Northfield MN 55057

DAVIS, F(RANCIS) GORDON, public relations executive; b. Bloomfield, Ind., May 21, 1908; s. Francis Gordon and Grace (Bryan) D.; student Wayne State U., 1925-27, postgrad., 1929-30; B.A., U. Mich., 1929, postgrad., 1930, 42; postgrad. Cleve. Inst. Art, 1936-37, Western Res. U., 1938-39; m. Margaret Aletha Smith, July 13, 1931; children—Margaret Jayne Davis Johnson, Marilyn Davis Johnson. Reporter, aviation editor, editorial writer Buffalo Times, 1930-33; feature, editorial, sci. writer Cleve. Press, 1934-42; pub. relations dir. Mich. Blue Cross-Blue Shield, Detroit, 1942-46; exec. dir. Mich. Health Council, Detroit, 1943-46; owner F. Gordon Davis & Assocs., Roscommon, Mich., 1946—. Mem. Pub. Relations Soc. Am., Am. Hosp. Assn. (life; chmn. pub. relations adv. com. 1965, mem. 1968-71, chmn. Conf. Affiliated Soc. Pres. 1969), Ohio Hosp. Assn. (hon.), Am. Soc. Hosp. Pub. Relations (pres. 1968-69), Mich. (pres. 1975-76), Southeastern Mich. (pres. 1973-74) hosp. pub. relations assns. Club: Higgins Lake Boat (dir. 1962-65). Contbr. articles to profl. jours. Home and Office: Route 3 Box 249 Roscommon MI 48653

DAVIS, F(RANCIS) KEITH, civil engineer; b. Bloomington, Wis., Oct. 23, 1928; s. Martin Morris and Anna (Weber) D.; B.S. in Civil Engring., S.D. State U., 1950; m. Roberta Dean Anderson, May 25, 1957; 1 son, Mark Francis. With firm Howard, Needles, Tammen & Bergendoff, Kansas City, Mo., 1950—, asst. chief structural designer, 1960-65, project mgr., sect. chief, 1965-76, dep. chief structural engr., 1976-79, chief engr., 1979—. Bd. advisers N.W. Kans. Area Vocat. Tech. Sch., 1977-80, chmn., 1979-80. Served with AUS, 1951-53. Registered prof. engr., Mo., Iowa. Fellow ASCE; mem. Nat., Mo. socs. profl. engrs., Am. Ry. Engring. Assn. (tech. com. 1981—). Club: Homestead Country. Home: 5024 Howe Dr Shawnee Mission KS 66205 Office: 9200 Ward Pkwy PO Box 299 Kansas City MO 64141

DAVIS, GEORGE BENJAMIN, business educator; b. Cleve., Jan. 29, 1919; s. Benjamin Franklin and Julia Rebecca (Guilfoyle) D.; m. Margaret Owen Easton, Sept. 10, 1946 (dec. Feb. 1954); 1 son, Benjamin; m. Nancy Bayliss Easton, Sept. 10, 1954; children—William, David, Rachel. B.B.A., Cleve. State U., 1941, M.B.A., 1981. C.P.A., Ohio. Controller Ford Motor Co., Cleve., 1947-59; dir. budgets Lubrizol, Wickliffe, Ohio, 1960-62; v.p., treas. Donn, Inc., Westlake, Ohio, 1962-82; dir. Exec. M.B.A. program Cleve. State U., 1981-82, vis. instr., 1983—; dir. Donn, Inc., Westlake, Ohio. Pres. So. Hills YMCA, Brecksville, Ohio, 1974. Served to 1st lt. USAF, 1942-46, ETO. Decorated DFC. Mem. Fin. Execs. Inst., Cleve. State U. Alumni Assn. (pres.-elect 1984). Lodges: Kiwanis (treas. 1978-82), Masons, Shriners.

DAVIS, GLENN GALLERY, library/museum facility consultant; b. Mexico City, Aug. 29, 1955; s. Glenn Tappenden and Marion Isabel (Gallery) D. B.A., Lake Forest Coll., Ill., 1979; M.A., U. Chgo., 1981; postgrad. Harvard U., 1982, Northwestern U., 1984. Planning asst. Newberry Library, Chgo., 1979-81, planning librarian, 1981-82, dir. planning, 1982—; planning cons. Harvard U./Radcliffe U., Cambridge, Mass., 1983—. Patentee in field. Fellow English Speaking Union; mem. ALA, Am. Mgmt. Club, Chgo. Library Club, Republican. Roman Catholic. Club: Caxton. Home: 3710 N Sheffield #305 Chicago IL 60613

DAVIS, GORDON, apparel manufacturing executive; b. N.Y.C., Feb. 23, 1940; s. Arthur and Miriam (Kastel) D.; A.A. with high honors, Fashion Inst. Tech., 1959; B.S. cum laude in Econs., Albright Coll., 1969; m. Olive Dawn Dunkleberger, June 25; children—Gale, Jed, Cliff. Engr. trainee Terre Hill Mfg. Co. (merged with Superior Lingerie Co., N.Y., 1968), Blue Ball, Pa., 1959-63, plant mgr., 1963-65, asst. gen. mgr., 1965-68, gen. mgr., N.Y.C., 1968-79, v.p. mfg., 1979; sr. v.p. Uniforms To You and Co., Chgo., 1979—. Bd. dirs. Pa. Assn. Children with Learning Disabilities, 1976, Jewish Community Center (Reading), 1972; trustee Temple Oheb Shalom (sec. 1973); instr. aircraft flight theory and nav. CAP Berks County, 1965. Recipient Fashion Inst. Tech. mgmt. award. Lic. real estate salesman, Pa. Mem. Am. Inst. Indsl. Engrs., Aircraft Owners and Pilots Assn., Lingerie Mfrs. Assn. (negotiating com.) Democrat. Jewish. Home: 341 Chatelaine Ct Willowbrook IL 60514 Office: 5600 W 73d St Chicago IL 60638

DAVIS, HARRY ALLEN, artist, art educator; b. Hillsboro, Ind., May 21, 1914; s. Harry A. and Eva (Smith) D.; m. Lois Irene Peterson, Dec. 21, 1947; children—Joanna Ingrid Davis Marks, Mark Frederick. B.F.A., Herron Sch. Art, 1938; F.A.A.R., Am. Acad. in Rome, 1941. Artist-in-residence Beloit Coll., Wis., 1941-42; instr. Herron Sch. of Art, Ind. U.-Purdue U.-Indpls., 1946-67, assoc. prof., 1967-70, prof., 1970-83, prof. emeritus, 1983; instr. Indpls. Art League, Ind., 1983—. Exhibited one-man shows at Ind. Sesquicentennial, 1971, Segment of Hist. Ohio Valley, U.S. Bicentennial, 1976, The Italian Influence, traveling show, 1983. Served to tech. sgt. t-4 U.S. Army, 1942-46. Recipient award of distinction, Mainstreams Internat., 1968, 1970-74; Excellence and Purchase Mo. Sesquicentennial award Watercolor U.S.A., 1971; Best of show award Realism '74, 1974; recipient numerous awards nat. and regional exhibits. Fellow Am. Acad. Rome (Prix de Rome award, 1938), Ind. Acad.; mem. Ind. Artists Club, Inc., Brown County Art Guild, Inc., Hoosier Salon. Republican. Mem. Disciples of Christ. Club: The Portfolio (pres. 1971). Avocations: music, woodworking, travel. Home: 6315 Washington Blvd Indianapolis IN 46220

DAVIS, HARRY LENDALL, marketing educator, university dean; b. Balt., Sept. 18, 1937; s. Lendall Evans and Lydia Marie (Peterson) D.; m. Suzanne Marie Ohlsen, June 22, 1963; children—Jeffrey, Jennifer, Brian, Maria. A.B., Dartmouth Coll., 1959, M.B.A., Amos Tuck Sch. Bus. Adminstrn., 1960; M.A. in Sociology, Northwestern U., 1969, Ph.D. in Mktg., 1970. Asst. prof. mktg. U. Chgo. Grad. Sch. Bus., 1963-71, prof., 1973—, dep. dean, 1983—; prof. behavior sci. European Inst. Advanced Studies Mgmt., Brussels, 1971-73; dir. Aparacor, Evanston, Ill., Golden Rule Ins., Indpls. Editor: Behavioral and Management Science in Marketing, 1978. Mem. Am. Mktg. Assn., Am. Assn. Pub. Opinion Research, Am. Sociol. Assn., Assn. Consumer Research, Inst. Mgmt. Sci., Nat. Council Family Relations. Office: U Chgo Grad Sch Bus 1101 E 58th St Chicago IL 60637

DAVIS, HARRY LEONARD, investment company executive; b. Hammond, Ind., Dec. 15, 1941; s. Harry L. Davis and Helen (Chizmadia) Davis Christian; m. Lissa Knudsen, Dec. 22, 1976; 1 son, Anthony Michael; m. Loretta Nelson, June 15, 1961 (div. 1967); children—Gregory A., Minette. Student pub. schs., Downey, Calif. Account exec. Internat. Precious Metals Corp., Fort Lauderdale, Fla., 1975-77; prin., exec. v.p. First Nat. Monetary Group, Southfield, Mich., 1977—, and subs. First Nat. Securities Corp., First Nat. Trading Corp., First Nat. Prodns., Inc., First Nat. Real Estate Corp., Internat. Registry Systems, Fin. Instns. Div., First Ctr. Office Plaza (all Southfield), First Nat. Home Theatres, Inc., Livonia, Mich., Franklin (Mich.) Savs. Bank. Office: 1st Ctr Office Plaza 26913 Northwestern Hwy 6th Floor Southfield MI 48075

DAVIS, HERBERT HAYWOOD, JR., investment banker; b. Omaha, Mar. 23, 1924; s. Herbert H. and Olga (Metz) D.; m. Nell Evans, Feb. 17,. 1945; children—Herbert H., Deborah Davis Horacek. B.C.E., Cornell U., 1948. Chmn. bd. dirs. Kirkpatrick, Pettis, Smith, Polian, Inc., Omaha, 1948—, Lozier Corp., Omaha, Weigh Tronix, Inc., Fairmont, Minn., Miracle Hill Golf and Tennis Ctr.; dir. Chief Automotive System, Inc., Grand Island, Nebr., Midwest Stock Exchange, Chgo. Bd. dirs. Gov.'s Com. Econ. Devel., Lincoln, Nebr., Nebr. Diplomats. Clubs: Omaha Country, Omaha Press; La Quinta Hotel Golf (Calif.), Shadow Mountain Country (Palm Desert, Calif.), Firethorn Golf (Lincoln, Nebr.). Home: 939 S 106 Pl Omaha NE 68114 Office: Kirkpatrick Pettis Smith Polian Inc PO Box 148 Boys Town NE 68010

DAVIS, JAMES ALLEN, chemist; b. Glasgow, Ky., Oct. 17, 1940; s. James C. and Bernice (Allen) D. B.Sc., Western Ky. U., 1962; M.Sc., U. Akron, 1967. Research asst. Goodyear Aerospace Co., Akron, Ohio, 1964-67; microbiologist Century Pharm. Labs., Metairie, La., 1967-68; adminstrv. microbiologist Baxter Labs., Kingstree, S.C., 1968-69; sr. research scientist Firestone Tire & Rubber Co., Akron, 1969—. Patentee rubber to metal adhesion, tire compound devel. Mem. Akron Rubber Group, Am. Chem. Soc., Phi Sigma. Methodist. Avocations: coin collecting; basketball; jogging, fishing; camping. Home: 10688 Mogadore Rd Uniontown OH 44685 Office: Firestone Tire & Rubber Co S Main and Wilbeth Rd Akron OH 44317

DAVIS, JAMES ALLEN, entertainment consultant, musician; b. Fremont, Nebr., June 1, 1955; s. Jack Gilbert and Janice Elizabeth (Myers) D.; m. Debra Ann Reding, Nov. 24, 1979. Student, U. Nebr., N.D. State U. Band leader NOAH, Omaha, 1973-76; composer, pianist Johnny Holm Band, Mpls., 1979-83; agt., owner Davis Entertainment, Omaha, 1976-79, McCarthy, Davis, Fargo, N.D., 1983-85; entertainment cons. Don Romeo Agy., Omaha, 1985—. Rec. artist The Red Ryder Band, 1979, The Johnny Holm Band, 1981, When Love Made a Fool, 1982. Named to dean' list U. Nebr.; recipient Hubert Humphrey medal Hubert Humphrey Meml. Found., Mpls., 1983. Mem. Nat. Assn. Coll. Artists (assoc.), Am. Fedn. Musicians, Rho Epsilon. Avocations: Furniture building; boating; biking. Home and Office: 8504 Cass St Omaha NE 68114

DAVIS, JAMES CASEY, lawyer, arbitrator; b. Bloomington, Ind., Feb. 23, 1937; s. Frank Vivian and Cornelia Haven (Casey) D.; m. Delores Mae Evans, 1961 (div. 1975); 1 dau., Sarah Haven; m. 2d Frances Joyce Budreck, Aug. 21, 1977; 1 dau., Felicia Louisa Budreck. B.A., U. Iowa, 1959, J.D., 1962. Bar: Iowa 1962, U.S. Supreme Ct. 1976. Ptnr. law firm France, Nady & Davis, Tipton, Iowa, 1963-65; exec. sec., gen. counsel Iowa Jr. C. of C., Newton, Iowa, 1965-66; assoc. firm Swanson & Davis, Newton, Iowa, 1966-69, ptnr., 1969-70; Justice of Peace, Newton, Iowa, 1967-70; asst. atty. gen. Iowa Dept. Justice, Des Moines, 1970-79; pvt. practice law, Des Moines, 1979-84; ptnr. Woodward, Davis & Rossi, 1984—; assoc. Environmental Law Inst., 1980—; mediator Iowa Pub. Employment Relations Bd., 1980—, arbitrator, 1983—. Bd. dirs. Iowa chpt. Arthritis Found., 1971—, mem. exec. com., 1976-81, mem. govtl. affairs com., 1976—, chmn. 1977-83, mem. adv. com. 1981-84, , mem. nat. bd. 1976-77; Nat. Vol. Service citation 1984; mem. Iowa State Central Com. Young Republicans, 1970-75; mem. Polk County Rep. Central Com., 1984—; bd. dirs. Newton Community Theatre, 1970-73; leader Explorer Scouts Am., 1963-65. Mem. ABA (chmn. interface com. computer div. econs. sect. 1984—), Fed. Bar Assn. (pres. Iowa chpt. 1982-83, nat. v.p. 1983—, chmn. computer com. 1984—), Iowa Bar Assn. (computer subcom. 1985—), Polk County Bar Assn., Assn. Trial Lawyers Am., Assn. Trial Lawyers Iowa, Iowa Assn. Arbitrators (treas. 1983—), SAR, Sons and Daus. of Pilgrims, Descs. Colonial Clergy, Order of Crown in Am., Trout Unltd. (pres. Iowa chpt. 1974—), Delta Theta Phi. Home: 931 32d St West Des Moines IA 50265 Office: Skywalk Suite 203 700 Walnut St Des Moines IA 50309

DAVIS, JAMES J., osteopathic physician, educator; b. Niagara Falls, N.Y., Apr. 13, 1923; s. Frank and Antonina (Anteczka) Rogozinski; m. Betty A. Dombrowski, Aug. 10, 1946; children—Kingman P., Bruce J., Bradley J., Douglas P. Student Niagara U., 1941-43, U. Rochester, 1943-44, Cornell U., 1944; B.S., Canisius Coll., 1948; postgrad. U. Buffalo, 1948-50; D.O., Phila. Coll. Osteo. Medicine, 1965. Hosp. rep. Parke, Davis Co., 1951-61; gen. practice osteo. medicine, Grand Rapids, Mich., 1965-75; prof. dept. family medicine Coll. Osteo. Medicine, Mich. State U., East Lansing, 1975—; dir. three ambulatory clinics; developer, coordinator courses. Served to lt. (j.g.) USN, 1943-46. Recipient Rose Bowl prize Parke, Davis Co., 1956, 58; Deans award Phila. Coll. Osteo. Medicine, 1965. Fellow Am. Osteo. Assn., Am. Coll. Gen. Practitioners; mem. Mich. Assn. Osteo. Physicians and Surgeons, Ingham County Assn. Osteo. Physicians and Surgeons, Am. Coll. Gen. Practitioners. Roman Catholic. Club: University (East Lansing, Mich.). Contbr. articles to profl. jours. Home: 4726 Arapaho Trail Okemos MI 48864 Office: Mich State U Coll Osteopathic Medicine Family Medicine Fee Hall East Lansing MI 48824

DAVIS, JAMES KEITH, beef cattle breeder; b. Logan, Ohio, Sept. 29, 1939; s. Delbert Pearl and Frieda Belle (Moore) D.; m. Jan Elaine Henderson, Dec. 28, 1963; children—Kimberly Lynne, Keith Eric, Kristen Leigh. B.S. in Agr., Ohio State U., 1961, Ph.D. in Animal Nutrition and Physiology, Ohio State U., 1970; M.S. in Animal Breeding, U. Ga., 1963. 4-H county extension agt. Ohio Coop. Extension Service, Wilmington, 1965-66; asst. prof., coordinator animal sci. Wilmington Coll. (Ohio), 1966-69; dir. research and mktg. Schearbrook Land & Livestock Inc., Clayton, Ohio, 1969-76, v.p., 1976-83, pres., 1983-84, gen. ptnr., 1984—; pres., chief exec. officer Ankina Breeders, Inc., Clayton, 1975—; pres. Buckeye Beef Improvement Fedn., Columbus, 1978-82, Agridex, Inc., Clayton, 1981-84; v.p., sec. Deramo Properties, Inc., Clayton, 1981—; v.p. Anglais Breeding Herds, Ltd., 1976-83, pres., 1983-84; mem. exec. com., chmn. program com. Buckeye Beef Congress, 1976-78; mem. animal sci. adv. com. Agrl. Tech. Inst., Ohio State U., 1977—. Developer Ankina breed of cattle; research and publs. in field of beef cattle sci. Advisor 4-H Club, Montgomery County, Ohio; mem. Montgomery County Extension Adv. Com., Dayton; mem. prin.'s adv. com. Brookville High Sch.; lay leader Concord United Meth. Ch., 1980-82, chmn. council on ministries, 1983, chmn. pastor-parish relations com., 1984-85. Mem. Am. Soc. Animal Sci., Am. Angus Assn., Am. Chianina Assn. (rec. sec., mem. nat. bd.), Green Key, Sigma Xi, Alpha Gamma Sigma, Gamma Sigma Delta. Avocations: woodworking; gardening. Home: 5229 Diamond Mill Rd Brookville OH 45309 Office: Schearbrook Land & Livestock Co 5803 Oakes Rd Clayton OH 45315

DAVIS, JEFFREY COLLEEN, businessman; b. Morris, Ill., Dec. 2, 1952; s. Clarence Colleen and Eva Mae (Yahnke) D.; m. Karen Anne Hemberger, July 5, 1975; 1 son, Jonathan Allen. B.A. in Bus. Adminstrn., Greenville Coll. (Ill.), 1975. Asst. mgr. S.S. Kresge Corp., Troy, Mich., 1975-76; inside sales rep. David C. Cook Pub. Co., Elgin, Ill., 1976-77; sr. cons. Accu Exec. Search, Inc., Oak Brook, Ill., 1977-79; personnel rep. Travenol Labs., Inc., Deerfield, Ill., 1979-81, asst. to v.p. personnel, 1981-82, sr. compensation analyst, 1982-84; owner Davis Custom Decorators, 1984—. Bd. dirs. Butterfield Manor Homeowners Assn., 1984-85. Republican. Home and Office: 423D Ramblewood Dr Glen Ellyn IL 60137

DAVIS, KEITH MONROE, geologist, consultant; b. Decatur, Ill., June 9, 1949; s. Tedd Monroe and Barbara (Wacaser) D.; m. Connie Sue Yates, June 14, 1975; children—Danielle, Brandon. A.S., Lakeland Coll., 1973; B.S., Eastern Ill. U., 1981. Geologist, Woodward-Clyde Cons., Mattoon, Ill., 1982-83; prin. Davis Cons., Mattoon, 1983—. Mem. Am. Assn. Petroleum Geologists. Home and office: Davis Consulting 1524 Stinson Ave Mattoon IL 61938

DAVIS, KENNETH LEE, travel industry executive; b. St. Charles, Mo., July 5, 1957; s. Wilford L. and Janet M. (Engelby) D. Grad. in Liberal Arts, Florissant Valley Community Coll., 1976. With Eastern Airlines, 1976-80, mktg. rep., 1980; cons. Maritz-St. Louis Travel Firm, 1980-83; ops. mgr., travel inst. dir. West Travel Ltd., St. Louis, 1983—. Active sponsor Big Bros.-Big Sisters; vol. Life Crisis Hotline. Republican. Lutheran. Home: 3314 Russell Blvd Apt 12 Saint Louis MO 63104 Office: 14330 S Outer Rd Chesterfield MO 63017

DAVIS, LAURENCE LAIRD, coal company executive; b. Cin., June 6, 1915; s. Thomas Jefferson and Jane (Brown) D.; grad. St. Mark's Sch., 1934; A.B., Harvard, 1938; postgrad. London (Eng.) Sch. Econs., 1939; m. Charlotte Rowe Nichols, Oct. 12, 1940 (dec. Sept. 1973); children—Sally Laird (Mrs. Arthur D. Pratt), Laurence Laird, Thomas Jefferson IV; m. 2d, Onlee Partin, Nov. 7, 1973; 1 dau., Nancy Matilda Kathleen; stepchildren—Rickey Lee Foland, Stella Logan Turner, Samuel J. Logan, Gregory C. Logan. With First Nat. Bank Cin., 1939-42, 46-70, v.p., 1949-64, vice chmn. bd., 1964-70, also dir.; vice consul, econ. analyst State Dept., 1943-45; financial cons., 1970—; pres., dir. Roberta Coal Co.; pres., dir. Millers Creek Mineral Devel. Co., Burning Springs Land Co. Chmn., English Speaking Union 1965-72; pres. Symphony Orch., 1965-68. Bd. dirs. Christ Hosp. Mem. Greater Cin. C. of C. (pres. 1965-68). Clubs: Commonwealth, Camargo, Queen City (Cin.). Home: Cincinnati OH 45243 Office: 7710 Shawnee Run Rd PO Box 43096 Nat Bank Center Cincinnati OH 45202 also Treasure Cay Abaco Bahamas

DAVIS, LAWRENCE, educator; b. Blossburg, Pa., Aug. 17, 1932; s. Harold Irving and Carrie Mae (Rude) D.; B.S., Black Hills State Coll., 1957; M.A., U. S.D., 1958; m. Shirley Leone Blodgett, May 24, 1957; children—Shirleen Deanna (dec.), Darrell Eugene. Speech clinician Sioux City (Iowa) Pub. Schs., 1958-68; asst. prof. speech and hearing sci. Briar Cliff Coll., Sioux City, 1968-74; instr. gen. edn. Western Iowa Tech. Community Coll., Sioux City, 1974—. Past pres. Sioux City Noon Lions, 1971, zone chmn., 1977, dep. dist. gov., 1978, dist. gov., 1979-80, mem. Dist. 9 Council Govs. Lions of Iowa Dist. 9; v.p. Northwest Iowa Lions Gavel Club, 1982-83, pres., 1983-84; mem. Sioux City Human Rights Commn., 1979-82. Served with USAF, 1950-54. Mem. Am., Iowa vocat. assns., Council for Exceptional Children (past pres. N.W. Iowa chpt.), Sioux City Schoolmasters Club (past pres.), AF Assn., Am. Legion, Phi Delta Kappa (treas. 1978-79, 2d v.p. 1983-84, pres. 1984-85). Methodist (sec. fin. com. 1979, chmn. fin. 1980, trustee 1981-84, adminstrv. bd. 1985—). Home: 3416 Pierce St Sioux City IA 51102 Office: Box 265 Sioux City IA 51106

DAVIS, LAWRENCE CLARK, biochemist, educator; b. London, Aug. 16, 1945; came to U.S., 1946; s. George Hawkins and Olive Edwina (Clark) D.; m. Linda Ann Wiles, July 22, 1967; children—Colin, Jennie Lynn, Steven. B.S. Haverford Coll., 1966; Ph.D., Yeshiva U., 1970. Postdoctoral student U. Wis., Madison, 1970-71, 73-75, Norwich State Hosp. (Conn.), 1971-73; asst. prof. Kans. State U., Manhattan, 1975-80, assoc. prof., 1980-84, prof. dept. biochemistry, 1984—; panelist U.S. Dept. Agr. competitive grants, 1981. Author articles. Grantee NIH, 1976—, NSF, 1976-80, U.S. Dept. Agr., 1983—. Mem. Am. Soc. Biol. Chemists, Am. Soc. Microbiologists, Am. Soc. Plant Physiologists. Democrat. Lutheran. Avocations: Rose breeding; woodworking. Home: 3419 Womack Way Manhattan KS 66502 Office: Dept Biochemistry Kans State Univ Willard Hall Manhattan KS 66506

DAVIS, LESTER WILLIAM, JR., travel executive; b. Indpls., Dec. 12, 1924; s. Lester W. and Geraldine (Gregory) D.; B.S., Eastern Ill. U., 1947; m. Virginia M. Smith, Feb. 2, 1943; children—Shirley Ann Davis Casey, Debra Diann Davis Babbitt. Radio, TV announcer-news dir. WLBH, Mattoon, Ill., WPRS, Paris, Ill., WFRL, Freeport, Ill., WREX-TV, Rockford, Ill., 1947-57; del. leader dir. coordinator People to People Travel Program, Winnebago, Ill., Maupintour, Lawrence, Kans., 1957—; trustee People to People, 1975—. Served with Paratroop Corps, U.S. Army, 1942-45. Mem. VFW. Republican. Presbyterian. Clubs: Lions, Elks, Moose, Masons, Shriners, Am. Legion, Footlighters. Home and office: PO Box 32 306 N Elida St Winnebago IL 61088 also 124 S Island Golden Beach FL 33160

D'AVIS, LUIS M., physician, surgeon, immediate care consultant; b. Cochabamba, Bolivia, June 10, 1944; came to U.S., 1971, naturalized, 1976; s. Luis and Adela (Medeiros) d'A.; m. Amalia Lourdes Reyes, May 16, 1969; children—Monique Marie, John-Andrew, Edward-Joseph. B.S., San Agustin Indsl. Coll., 1961; M.D., San Simon U. Med. Sch., Bolivia, 1969. Postgrad. tng., Evanston, Ill., 1971-80; med. staff Bethany Meth., Ravenswood, Forkosh, Masonic hosps., Chgo.; owner, med. dir. Med. Ctr., Chgo. Pres. Bolivian Friendship Club, 1981-83; hon. mem. Internat. Red Cross. Mem. AMA, Ill. Med. Soc., Chgo. Med. Soc., Am. Acad. Family Practice, Ill. Acad. Family Practice (pres. Lincoln Park br.), Interam. Coll. Physicians and Surgeons, Bolivian Med. Soc. (dir. 1982-83). Republican. Roman Catholic. Home: 8241 N Kildare Ave Skokie IL 60076 Office: 4315 N Lincoln Ave Chicago IL 60618

DAVIS, MAYNARD PARKER, educator; b. Bethlehem, Pa., Apr. 15, 1930; s. William Henry and Gertrude Marion (Brunner) D.; m. Elsie Mai Carpenter, Dec. 31, 1952; children—Jeanette, Deborah. B.S. in Secondary Edn., Austin Peay State U., 1957; M.B.A. in Mktg., Bradley U., 1960; postgrad. U. Tenn., 1961, U. Ill., 1972-75. Tchr., Sch. Dist. 150, Peoria, Ill., 1957—; sales promotion mgr. Modern Home TV & Appliances, Inc., 1963-72; pres., treas., chief exec. officer A.R.M.S. of Ill., Inc., Peoria, 1967—; sec. La Cantina Italiana, Inc., 1975-77; dir. Peoria County Sch. Employees Credit Union, 1985—. Served with USMC, 1948-49, 50-52. Mem. Nat. Rifle Assn. (life), Nat. Assn. Federally Lic. Firearms Dealers, NEA (life), Ill. Edn. Assn., Peoria Edn. Assn. (dir., exec. com. 1968-75, negotiator 1970-75), Am. Legion, Midwest Gun Collectors Assn., Kappa Delta Pi. Republican. Club: River Valley Sportsman's (East Peoria). Office: 624 W Lake St Peoria IL 61614

DAVIS, MICHELE STAR, program assistant; b. Auburn, Ind., Dec. 31, 1946; d. Robert Emmett and April Dawn (Bowser) Davis; B.A. summa cum laude, St. Francis Coll., 1970; M.A., Purdue U., 1972, Ph.D., 1979; m. Richard D. Watman, Sept. 13, 1981. Teaching asst. Purdue U., West Lafayette, Ind., 1970-72, grad. instr., 1973-77; lectr. Ohio State U., Columbus, 1979-80, instr., 1980-83, program assistant, 1983—; faculty adviser La Hermandad Latina, club for Hispanic students, founder, dir. Teatro Unidad, dir. Ohio State U. summer Spanish Lang. Camp, 1982; leader seminars, workshops Office Hispanic Student Programs, 1979—. Leader cultural presentations to elem., jr. high and high sch. students through Internat. Council of Mid Ohio. Recipient Hermandad Latina and MECHA award, Ohio State U., 1981. Mem. Am. Assn. Tchrs. of Spanish and Portuguese, Ohio Theatre Affiliation, Ohio Community Theatre Assn., Am. Council of Tchrs. of Fgn. Lang., MLA. Author: A Dramatist and His Characters, 1983; Un Don Juan del Siglo XX; El Conquistador Conquistado, 1981; Del Realismo a la Vanguardia en Tres Dramaturgos Hispanoamericanos, 1981; Dreams and Reflections: The Cycle of Human Existence. Two Plays by Dantes and Giovaninetti; contbr. articles to profl. jours. Home: 23201 Rapp-Dean Rd Raymond OH 43067 Office: Room 347 Ohio Union 1739 N High St Columbus OH 43210

DAVIS, NEIL RAYMOND, chiropractic physician; b. Carbondale, Ill., May 11, 1951; s. Raymond C. and Alice V. (Turner) D.; m. Tresa Ann Gillman, June 22, 1973. Student John A. Logan Coll., 1969-71; B.S., Nat. Coll. Chiropractic, D. Chiropractic, 1975. Diplomate Nat. Bd. Chiropractic Examiners. Gen. practice chiropractic medicine, Marion, Ill., 1976—. Recipient Vol. Service award Vets. Hosp., 1983. Bd. dirs. Christian Concerts, Inc., 1981-83. Mem. Ch. of God. Lodge: Lions (mem. council on health 1977-79) (Marion, Ill.). Home: 192 Christopher Ln Marion IL 62959 Office: 300 N Market St Suite 3 Marion IL 62959

DAVIS, NICKOLETTE LEOWN, automotive aftermarket company executive; b. Havana, Kans., Mar. 29, 1948; d. Earl and Sarah Alice (Harris) Thompson; m. John Robert Davis, Apr. 19, 1965 (div. May 1984); children—Joni Rene, Derrick N. Student Independence Community Jr. Coll., 1974-76. Catalog mgr. Montgomery Wards, Independence, Kans., 1971-73; prodn. worker Automotive Controls Corp., Independence, 1974-79, purchasing clk., 1979-80, buyer, 1980—. Club: Independence Promenade (pres. 1979-81); Avocations: squaredancing; fishing; walking; gardening. Home: 617 S 6th St Independence KS 67301 Office: Automotive Controls Corp 1300 W Oak St Independence KS 67301

DAVIS, NORMAN BRUCE, accountant, tax and financial consultant; b. Waukegan, Ill., Aug. 6, 1948; s. Bairs Davis and Lenormal (Harden Davis Barnes; m. Brenda Carol Merriweather, Apr. 12, 1969 (dec. Jan. 9, 1977). B.A., Carthage Coll., 1982. Dir., treas. United Christian Community Services, Chgo., 1973; cost analyst Teletype Corp., Skokie, Ill., 1974; ops. asst. Tuskegee Inst. Outpatient Clinic, Ala., 1974-75; owner, mgr. Norman B. Davis, Inglewood, Calif. and North Chicago, Ill., 1976-81; gen. acct. Fansteel-V/R Wesson, Inc., Waukegan, Ill., 1981-82; credit analyst Zion State Bank and Trust Co., Zion, Ill., 1983-85. Served with U.S. Army, 1969-76. Recipient Abbott Lab. Scholarship award, 1975; Highest PCPT award Tuskegee Inst. R.O.T.C., 1975. Mem. Nat. Assn. Accts., Nat. Soc. Pub. Accts., World Future Soc., Am. Fedn. Small Bus. Men (bd. dirs. 1984—), Profl. Fin. Assn. (fin. broker 1985—). Baptist. Avocations: computing; tennis; racquetball; reading; travel. Home: PO Box 31 North Chicago IL 60064 Office: 2725 Glen Flora A Suite 513 Waukegan IL 60085

DAVIS, O. C., diversified energy holding company executive. Chmn., pres., dir. Midcon Corp., Chgo. Office: Midcon Corp 701 E 22nd St Box 1207 Lombard IL 60148*

DAVIS, PHILIP CARL, lawyer; b. Mansfield, Ohio, Mar. 22, 1949; s. Harry O. and Bernice (Tracy) D. B.A., U. Toledo, 1971; J.D., Ohio No. U., 1976. Bar: Ohio 1977. Assoc. DeMuth & John, Toledo, 1977-80, ptnr., 1981—; solicitor Village of Whitehouse, Ohio, 1978—. Mem. Wood County Democratic Exec. Com., Ohio, 1977—. Mem. ABA, Toledo Bar Assn., Ohio Bar Assn. Democrat. Lutheran. Club: Ducks Unltd. Lodge: Masons. Avocations: fly fishing, waterfowl hunting, skiing. Home: 305 Martindale Rd Bowling Green OH 43402 Office: DeMuth & John 626 Madison Ave Suite 700 Toledo OH 43604

DAVIS, PHYLLIS MARIE, counselling educator; b. Topeka, Aug. 27, 1923; d. Harold Morgan and Ethel Irene (Hinchsliff) Porter; m. Orville Milo Davis, Oct. 19, 1957. A.A., North Park Coll., 1943; B.S., Northwestern U., 1945, M.A., 1951. Mathematician, Northwestern U., Evanston, Ill., 1945; asst. application engr. Westinghouse Electric Corp., Chgo., 1945-58; dean girls Bremen High Sch., Midlothian, Ill., 1958-66; counselor Thornton Community Coll., South Holland, Ill., 1966—, dir. guidance, 1967. Mem. Am. Assn. Counselling and Devel., Ill. Assn. Counseling and Devel., Ill. Women Dean Adminstrs. and Counselors, Nat. Women Deans, Adminstrs. and Counselors, Suburban Women Deans and Counselors Assn. (pres. 1963), South Suburban Counselors Assn., AAUW, Phi Delta Kappa, Delta Kappa Gamma. Lodge: Order Eastern Star. Office: Thornton Community Coll 15800 S State St South Holland IL 60473

DAVIS, RALPH, research chemist; b. Huntington, Ind., Aug. 14, 1917; s. Floyd Anderson and Rozella (Burton) D.; m. Muriel Evelyn Wait, Aug. 11, 1940 (dec. 1975); children—Robert S., Norman W. B.A., Huntington Coll., 1939; M.A., Ind. U., 1942. Tchr. Leo High Sch., Ind., 1939-41; research asst. in chemistry Ind. U., Bloomington, 1941-42; analytical chemist Dow Chem. Co., Midland, Mich., 1942-49, chem. researcher, 1949-82, ret. 1982. Patentee in field of fluorine and halogen chemistry. Contbr. articles to sci. jours. Active Boy Scouts Am., 1950-63. Mem. Am. Chem. Soc., AAAS, Sigma Xi. Republican. Methodist. Avocations: gardening; photography. Address: 1160 Poseyville Rd R7 Midland MI 48640

DAVIS, RICHARD ARNOLD, paleontologist; b. Cedar Rapids, Iowa, Apr. 19, 1942; s. Earl Leroy and Leila Hazel (Musgrave) D.; m. Mary Louise Farris; 1 dau., Matilda Mary Elspeth. B.A., Cornell Coll., Mt. Vernon, Iowa, 1963; M.S., U. Iowa, 1965, Ph.D., 1968. Research assoc. U. Coll. Swansea, Wales, 1968-69; asst. prof., curator geology U. Cin., 1969-75, adj. assoc. prof. biol. scis., 1984—; paleontologist, dir. sci. edn. Cin. Mus. Natural History, 1975-78, paleontologist, curator collections, 1978—. Cons. editor Rocks and Mineral's Mag., 1979—; author, editor: Cincinnati Fossils. An Elementary Guide to the Ordovician Rocks and Fossils of the Cincinnati, Ohio, Region, 1981; contbr. articles to profl. jours. Trustee, Cedar Bog Assn., Springfield, Ohio, 1982—. NSF fellow, 1965-67, 68-69. Mem. Am. Assn. Mus., Brit. Micropalaeontol. Soc., Geol. Soc. Am., Ohio Acad. Sci., Ohio Biol. Survey, (adv. bd.), Ohio Mus. Assn., Palaeontol. Assn., Paleontol Research Instn., Paleontol. Soc., Soc. Econ. Paleontologists and Mineralogists, Soc. Vertebrate Paleontology, Systematics Assn. Office: Cin Mus Natural History 1720 Gilbert Ave Cincinnati OH 45202

DAVIS, RICHARD JAMES, typewriter co. exec.; b. Miller, S.D., Nov. 2, 1938; s. Everett Edward and Mildred Louise (Pugsley) D.; A.A., Worthington Jr. Coll., 1958; B.S. in Bus. Adminstrn., U. S.D., 1960; m. Maxine Busch, Feb. 20, 1960; children—Greg, Vicki, Jon, Gary, Jay, Sara, Jerry, Timothy. Asst. stores mgr. S.S. Kresge, Rapid City, S.D., 1960-62, Lincoln, Nebr., 1962-63; founder, Dick Davis Typewriter Co., Mankato, Minn., 1963—, owner, mgr., 1981—. Mem. adv. com. on office equip. repair Fairbault Area Vocat. Sch., 1979-81; bd. dirs. S. Central Minn. Camp Fire, Inc., 1978—, pres., 1979, 80. Recipient Corneia Honors, Jr. C. of C., 1975. Mem. Nat. Office Equip. Dealers Assn., Nat. Fedn. Ind. Bus., Minn. Office Machine Dealers Assn., Mankato Area C. of C., Nat. Office Machine Dealers Assn. Republican. Roman Catholic. Clubs: Sertoma, Bonanza Investment, Hilltop Kiwanis, K.C. Home: PO Box 3071 Mankato MN 56001 Office: 525 S Front St Mankato MN 56001

DAVIS, RICHARD MCVAY, English educator, consultant; b. Moose Lake, Minn., June 21, 1924; s. Hollie McVay and Annamarie (Schweitzer) D.; m. Florence Lita Gianotti, May 30, 1956; children—Scott, Christopher, Holly, Maria. B.A., Ohio State U., 1947, M.A., 1948; cert. Sorbonne U., Paris, 1951; Ed.D., U. Mich., 1962. Instr. Gen. Motors Inst., Flint, Mich., 1948-51; systems analyst Ford Motor Co., Kansas City, Mo., 1951-53, Gen. Motors Corp., Detroit, 1953-55; adminstrv. analyst Champion Spark Plug Co., Toledo, Ohio, 1955-57; prof. English dept. humanities Sch. Engring., Air Force Inst. Tech., Wright-Patterson AFB, Ohio, 1962-79; prof. English, head dept. communications and research methods Sch. of Systems and Logistics, 1979—; referee Tech. Communications, 1980—. Author: Thesis Projects in Science and Engineering, 1980. Contbr. articles to profl. jours. Patentee in field. Served with USAAF, 1943-45. Named Outstanding Tchr., Sch. Engring. Student Body, Air Force Inst. Tech., 1966, 70, 71, 75. Fellow Soc. Tech. Communications (assoc., outstanding publ. 1965, 67, 69, 76); mem. Assn. Tchrs. Tech. Writing, Nat. Council Tchrs. English. Avocations: tennis; bowling; shipbuilding. Home: 4417 Glenheath Dr Kettering OH 45440 Office: Dept Communication and Research Methods Sch Systems and Logistics Air Force Inst Tech Wright Patterson AFB OH 45433

DAVIS, RICHARD PAUL, investment adviser; b. Dayton, Ohio, July 29 1949; s. Harry Carl and Eleanor Josephine (Chmielewski) D.; m. Susan Pleiman, May 20, 1972; 1 child, Richard Bradley. B.S., U. Dayton, 1972; M.S., Wright State U., 1978, M.B.A., 1978. Facility econ. planner Gen. Telephone Co., Marion, Ohio, 1972-73; mgr. cash planning Mead Corp., Dayton, 1973-75, mgr. invetments, 1975-77; v.p. Mead Reinsurance, Dayton, 1979-84; v.p. Mead Money Mgmt., Dayton, 1977-79, pres., 1979-84; pres. Flagship Fin. Inc., Dayton, 1984—, Flagship Resources Inc., 1984—, Flagship Capital Inc., 1984—; dir. Flagship Fin. Inc., Flagship Capital, Flagship Resources Inc. Mem. Charter Fin. Analyst, Investment Co. Inst., No Load Mut. Fund Assn. Avocations: jogging; racquetball; water skiing; reading. Office: Flagship Financial Courthouse Plaza NE Dayton OH 45463

DAVIS, ROBERT LOUIS, lawyer; b. Wichita, Kans., June 16, 1927; s. Carl H. and Maria (Francisco) D.; A.B., U. Kans., 1950, J.D., 1952; m. Marian Frances Larson, June 26, 1955; children—Martha F., Alison L., Carl B., Janet E. Admitted to Kans. bar, 1952, Utah bar, 1953; atty. Gulf Oil Corp., 1952-53; partner firm Davis & Davis, Wichita, 1954-61, Davis, Bruce & Davis, 1962-70, Davis, Bruce, Davis & Cather, 1971-72, Davis, Bruce, Davis & Winkler, Wichita, 1975-77, Bruce, Davis & Gilhousen, Wichita, 1977-85, Bruce & Davis, 1985—; mcpl. judge City of Goddard (Kans.), 1979—; lectr. bus. law Friends U., Wichita, 1967; leader. Kans. Lawyers China Mission, 1981. Pres. Goodwill Industries Greater Wichita, 1965-66, 71-73; mem. Wichita Bd. Edn., 1963-71, also pres., 1969-70; bd. dirs. Wichita Guidance Center, 1964-70, Friends Com. on Nat. Legis., Washington, 1970-82, Community Planning Council Wichita, 1972-76; trustee Friends U., 1959-77, chmn. bd., 1965-74; trustee Mid-Am. Yearly Meeting of Friends, 1973-80. Served with USNR, 1945-46. Mem. Wichita, Kans., Utah, Am. bar assns., Phi Beta Kappa, Omicron Delta Kappa. Clubs: Keystone High-Twelve (pres. 1981), Petroleum, University (pres. 1984-85), Knife and Fork (Wichita). Lodges: Masons (33 deg., KYCH), Lions, Shriners. Mem. Soc. of Friends. Editor The Logos jour. Alpha Kappa Lambda, 1950-60. Office: 2121 W Maple Wichita KS 67213

DAVIS, ROBERT PHELPS, surgeon; b. Evanston, Ill., Nov. 9, 1942; s. Carl Braden and Marianne Williams (Hoover) D.; B.A., U. of the South, 1964; M.D., Northwestern U., 1969; Intern, Chgo. Wesley Meml. Hosp., 1969-70; resident in surgery Northwestern U., Chgo., 1970-75; staff surgeon VA Lakeside Hosp., Chgo., 1975—; sr. attending surgeon Columbus Cuneo Med. Center, Chgo., 1975—; asst. med. dir. research and edn., dir. med. edn. Columbus Hosp.; asst. prof. clin. surgery Northwestern U. Med. Sch., 1975—. Diplomate Am. Bd. Surgery. Fellow A.C.S.; mem. Soc. Acad. Surgery, Assn. Vets. Surgeons, Soc. Surgery of Alimentary Tract, Western Surg. Assn., AMA. Republican. Presbyterian. Clubs: Racquet of Chgo., Saddle and Cycle. Home: 1442 N Dearborn St Chicago IL 60610 Office: 467 W Deming Pl Suite 919 Chicago IL 60614

DAVIS, ROBERT W., congressman; b. Marquette, Mich., July 31, 1932; student No. Mich. U., 1950, 52, Hillsdale Coll., 1951-52; B.S., Coll. Mortuary Sci., Wayne State U., 1954; m. Martha Cole, 1976; children—Robert W., Jr., Lisa, George, Alexandra. Funeral dir. Davis Funeral Home, St. Ignace, Mich., 1954-66; mem. St. Ignace City Council, 1964-66; mem. Mich. Ho. of Reps., 1966-70; mem. Mich. Senate, 1970-78, majority whip, 1970-74 minority leader, 1974-78; mem. 96-98th Congresses from 11th Dist. Mich.; mem. N.E.-Midwest Econ. Advancement Coalition, Congressional Tourism Caucus, Republican Study Club, Conf. Gt. Lakes Congressmen, Environ. Study Conf., Coalition for Peace Through Strength, Congressional Shipyard Coalition, Congressional Steel Caucus. Bd. dirs. Mich. Cystic Fibrosis Assn.; adv. bd. Young Ams. for Freedom. Mem. Mich. Funeral Dirs. Assn., Nat. Rifle Assn. Republican. Clubs: Lions, Eagles, Elks, Masons, Ducks Unlimited. Office: 1124 Longworth House Office Bldg Washington DC 20515

DAVIS, RODNEY OWEN, history educator; b. Newton, Kansas, July 14, 1932; s. Harry W. and M. Antoinette (Dey) D.; m. Norma G. Glass, Aug. 7, 1954; children—Anne Catherine, Margaret Emily, Jane Elizabeth. B.S., U. of Kansas, 1954, M.A., 1959; Ph.D., U. of Iowa, 1966. Instr. history Knox Coll., Galesburg, Ill., 1963-66, asst. prof. history, 1966-71, assoc. prof. history, 1971-77, prof. history, 1977—. Co-editor: Illinois: Its History and Legacy, 1984. Served to 1st lt., USAF, 1954-57. Grantee NEH, 1970, 73, 75. Mem. Orgn. of Am. Historians, Agrl. History Soc., Western History Assn., Social Sci. History Assn., Ill. State Historical Soc. (v.p. 1983—). Democrat. Methodist. Home: 984 North Cherry St Galesburg IL 61401

DAVIS, ROGER EARLDEN, media coordinator; b. Wichita, Kans., Nov. 19, 1952; s. Earlden E. and Lucy (Graves) D.; m. Becki Strait, Dec. 29, 1973. B.A. in Edn., Wichita State U., 1974; M.S. in Communications, U. Pa.-Clarion, 1979. Audiovisual edn. technician Wichita State U., Kans., 1974-78; grad. asst. U. Pa.-Clarion, 1978-79; media coordinator Kent State U.-Stark, Canton, Ohio, 1980—, tchr., 1985—; sec. Community TV Consortium, 1984—. Producer: Videotape series, Media Production Techniques, 1981. Director: TV series Micros, Minis & Mainframes, 1983, TV special, Christian Dior, 1985, Multi Image show, Jackson Twp., 1985. Stark County Found. grantee, 1984. Mem. Ohio Ednl. Library/Media Assn., Canton Preservation Soc. Avocations: camping; hiking; biking; photography. Home: 5190-1 Everhard Rd NW Canton OH 44718 Office: Kent State Univ-Stark Media Ctr 6000 Frank Rd NW Canton OH 44720

DAVIS, ROGER ROY, pharmacist; b. Milw., Oct. 11, 1946; s. Joseph John and Marian Florence (Heglund) D.; m. Judith Ann Penasa, Jan. 14, 1967; children—Joseph R., Jennifer J. B.S., N.D. State U., 1975, M.S., 1977. Registered pharmacist, N.D., Ohio. Staff pharmacist VA, Columbia, Mo., 1977-79, supr. in-patient pharmacy, Cin., 1979-82, asst. chief pharmacy service, VA, Dayton, Ohio, 1982-84, VA, Cleve., 1984—, lectr. alcohol rehab. and psychiatry service, Cin., 1979-82. Author: Hepatic Encephalopathy: A Review, 1977. Recipient 1st place award N.D. Wildlife Fedn. pictorial competition, 1976, Kodak Internat. Newspaper Snapshot award The Fargo Forum, 1976; named Man of Yr., Beta Sigma Phi, 1981. Mem. Am. Soc. Hosp. Pharmacists, N.D. State Pharm. Assn., Cleve. Soc. Hosp. Pharmacists, Cin. Soc. Hosp. Pharmacists, Kappa Psi (v.p. 1974). Roman Catholic. Avocations: travel, stained glass, photography, painting. Home: 966 Acorn Circle Medina OH 44256 Office: VA Med Ctr 10701 East Blvd Cleveland OH 44106

DAVIS, SAMUEL EARL, composer, publisher; b. Taylor, Tex., July 12, 1944; s. Oven Steen and Cecelia Augusta (Smith) D.; m. Kathleen Marie McFarlane, Mar. 6, 1967; 1 dau., Stephanie; m. 2d, Belinda Smith, Sept. 7, 1977; 1 dau., Quina. Student Huston-Tillotson Coll., Austin, Tex., 1963-65, U. Minn., 1971-75. Composer, musician gospel music, 1975—; co-owner, mgr. Cada Record Co. div. Cada Music Inc., Mpls., 1978—; owner, mgr. Sam Davis Gospel Ensemble, 1977—; dir. Negro spiritual workshops including: Alliance Chorale of Canada, 1982, Gospel Music Workshop Am., 1977-82; pres., dir. choir Zion Baptist Ch., Mpls., 1972—. Served with USAF, 1965-69. Mem. Am. Fedn. Musicians. Baptist. Co-author (with Dr. R. Buckner) A 300 Year Anthology of Black Religious Music, 1976.

DAVIS, STANLEY STANTON, real estate developer; b. Janesville, Wis., Sept. 9, 1925; s. Ferrell Thornton and Hazel Gladys (Stevens) D.; m. Eloise Jeanette Larson, Nov. 6, 1949; children—William Allen, Jeffrey Stanton. Student U. Pitts., 1944, U. Wis., 1946-47, Madison Coll., 1948-49. Auditor, Kroger Co., Madison, Wis., 1949-54; realtor Badger and Lucey Realty, Madison, 1954-58; pres., owner Empire Realty Co., Madison, 1958-65, Stanton-Fritz Corp., Madison, 1964-74, Highlander Bldg. Devel. Co., Madison, 1975—; owner, mgr. Interior Design and Supply Studio, Madison, 1969—. Served with USAF, 1944-45. Mem. Greater Madison Bd. Realtors, Nat. Assn. Realtors, Wis. Exchange Club, Fla. Real Estate Exchangors. Republican. Lutheran. Lodge: Rotary. Avocations: aviation; hunting; camera; bowling; golf. Home: 3365 Crystal Ct W Palm Harbor FL 33563 also 3018 Irvington Way Madison WI 53713 Office: Highlander Bldg Devel Co 4343 W Beltline Hwy Madison WI 53711

DAVIS, STEPHEN ROBERT, educational administrator; b. Chester, Pa., Mar. 19, 1923. B.S. in Mech. Engring., Drexel U., 1950; M.S. in Mech. Engring., U. Del., 1955; Ph.D. in Mech. Engring., 1963. Engr. Westinghouse Corp., Phila., 1950-51, Ford Motor Co., Dearborn, Mich., 1963-65; dir. tech. planning research and engring div. Cummins Engine Co., Columbus, Ind., 1965-67; assoc. dean grad. studies and research Coll. Engring., Wayne State U., Detroit, 1968-73; dean Sch. Engring., Lawrence Inst. Tech., Southfield, Mich., 1973-83; provost, dean faculty GMI Engring. and Mgmt. Inst., Flint, Mich., 1984—; mem. faculty U. Del., 1951-54, U. Ill., 1954-63; cons. DuPont Co., others. Recipient Gold award Outstanding Scientist and Engrs. in Mich., 1979. Mem. Soc. Automotive Engrs., Am. Soc. Engring. Edn., Engring. Soc. Detroit, ASME, Soc. Mfg. Engrs., Tau Beta Pi, Sigma Xi, Pi Tau Sigma. Office: GMI Engring and Mgmt Inst 1700 W 3d Ave Flint MI 48502

DAVIS, SUSAN ELIZABETH, optometrist; b. Newton, Iowa, Nov. 18, 1952; d. Harold Elmo and Dorothy Minerva (Van Gilst) D.; m. Trygve Gerald Oydgard, Nov. 19, 1977. Student, Simpson Coll., 1971-73; B.S. and O.D., Ind. U., 1977. Assoc. Optometric Assn. of Warren Co., Indianola, Iowa, 1977-78; practice medicine specializing in optometry, Marengo, Iowa, 1978—. Mem. bd. Marengo Devel. Corp., Iowa, 1979-84; sec., treas. Marengo 125th Celebration Com., 1984. Mem. Am. Optometric Assn. (charter mem. contact lens sect. 1983-84), Iowa Optometric Assn., Marengo C. of C. (sec. 1978-84). Democrat. Unitarian. Avocations: Sailing; gardening; crafts; woodburning. Office: Susan E Davis OD 224 E Main St Marengo IA 52301

DAVIS, THOMAS WILLIAM, college dean, electrical engineering educator; b. Belvidere, Ill., Mar. 14, 1946; s. Thomas William and Charlotte Ann (Schildgen) D.; m. Lyndel Etta Schuettpelz, Apr. 3, 1971; 1 child, Bryan William. B.S.E.E., Milw. Sch. Engring., 1968; M.S.E.E., U. Wis.-Milw., 1971. Registered profl. engr., Wis. Prof. elec. engring. Milw. Sch. Engring., 1968—, head computer engring. tech., 1975-77, chmn. dept. elec. engring., 1977-84, dean research, 1981-84, dean acads., 1984—; lectr. U. Wis.-Milw., 1973-76. Author: Problems in Measurements, 1968; (textbooks) Computer Aided Analysis, 1973; Introduction to Interactive Programs, 1978; Experimentation with Microprocessor Applications, 1981. Warning and communications officer Ozaukee County Emergency Govt., Wis., 1981-82; sgt. reserves Grafton Police Dept., Wis., 1976—. Mem. IEEE (sr., student activity dir. 1972-73), Robotics Internat., Soc. Mfg. Engrs. (sr.), Assn. Computing Machinery, Am. Soc. Engring. Edn., Milw. Sch. Engring. Alumni Assn. (achievement award 1968), Phi Kappa Phi, Tau Alpha Pi, Eta Kappa Nu. Avocations, pvt. pilot; basic-advanced ground instr. flying. Home: 635 11th Ave Grafton WI 53024 Office: Milw Sch Engring 1025 N Milwaukee St Milwaukee WI 53201

DAVIS, ULILLAH ELMORE, pharmacist; b. Ashland, Miss., Mar. 15, 1932; d. Hayse and Graftee (McKenzie) Elmore; m. Edward Davis, Jr., Dec. 5, 1959; children—Karen Lynn, Keith Edward. B.S. in Pharmacy, Xavier U., New Orleans, 1955. Registered pharmacist, La., Ohio. Instr. chemistry, biology, dean of women, Miss. Indsl. Coll., Holly Spring, 1956-57; asst. mgr. Shauter Drug Co., Cleve., 1958-59; staff pharmacist Highland View Hosp., Warrensville, Ohio, 1960-70, asst. dir. pharmacy, 1971-78; sr. staff pharmacist Cleve. Met. Gen. Hosp., 1979; dir. pharmacy Kenneth W. Clement Ctr., Cleve., 1980—. Trustee Lee Seville Ch., 1985. Recipient Super Achievement award Highland View Hosp, 1975. Mem. Cleve. Soc. Hosp. Pharmacists, Ohio Soc. Hosp. Pharmacists, Am. Soc. Hosp. Pharmacists, Nat. Pharm. Assn., Cleve. Pharm. Assn. (sec. 1984—), Xavier Alumni Assn., Cleve. Tots and Teens (v.p. 1973-75, Super Performance award 1979), East End Settle Coop. (pres. 1975-78), NAACP, Nat. Council Negro Women, Phillis Wheatley Aux., Alpha Kappa Alpha Achievement award 1982). Democrat. Baptist. Avocations: gourmet cooking; jogging. Home: 20150 S Woodland Rd Shaker Heights OH 44122 Office: Kenneth W Clement Ctr 2500 E 79th St Cleveland OH 44104

DAVIS, WAYNE KAY, medical educator, researcher; b. Findlay, Ohio, Mar. 23, 1946; s. Albert Wayne and Freida Evelyn (Winkle) D.; m. Patricia Ann Krimmer, May 26, 1967; 1 child, J. Brandon. B.A., Central Bible Coll., 1967; M.A., U. Mich., 1969, Ph.D., 1971. Research scientist Ctr. Research Learning and Teaching, Ann Arbor, Mich., 1971-73; asst. prof. U. Mich. Med. Sch., Ann Arbor, 1973-77, assoc. dir. edn. resources and research, 1976-78, assoc. prof., 1977-82, dir. edn. resources and research, 1978—, prof., asst. dean, 1982—; adv. mem. ad hoc study sect. Nat. Heart, Lung and Blood Inst., NIH, Bethesda, Md., mem. site visit team Nat. Inst. Arthritis, Metabolic and Digestive Diseases, NIH, Bethesda, 1978—; cons. Multipurpose Arthritis Ctr., NIH, Bethesda, 1981-83; vis. scholar U. Calif. Med. Sch., San Diego, 1984-85. Author: A Guide to MTS and Remote Terminal Operation, 1972. Contbr. chpts. and articles to med. jours. Bd. dirs. Washtenaw County unit Mich. Heart Assn., 1977-79. Recipient Best Article 1982 award Assn. Diabetes Educators. Mem. Am. Ednl. Research Assn. (program chmn. div. 1, v.p. 1985—), Assn. Am. Med. Colls., Am. Diabetes Assn., Phi Delta Kappa. Clubs: Travis Pointe Country (Ann Arbor), Bay Point Yacht (Marblehead, Ohio). Avocations: sailing, sculling, watercolor painting, bicycling, tennis. Office: U Mich Med Sch G1111 Towsley Ctr Ann Arbor MI 48109

DAVIS, WILLIAM M., pharmacist; b. Erie, Pa., Apr. 13, 1953; s. Benjamin and Goldie (Colman) D. B.S. in Pharmacy, U. Pitts., 1977. Asst. mgr. Cunningham Drug, Parma, Ohio, 1977-79; pharmacy mgr. Barney's Food and Drug, Wickliffe Ohio, 1979-83, Bernie Shulman's, Mayfield Heights, Ohio, 1983-84, St. Luke's Med. Bldg. Pharmacy, Cleve., 1984—. Mem. Phi Eta Sigma.

DAVIS, WILMA JEAN, nursing home adminstr.; b. Goodland, Mo., Apr. 24, 1931; d. Sherman L. and Bessie Keith; cert. housing mgmt., Community Sch. Practical Nursing, Columbia U., 1977, cert. activity dir., 1977, med. records cert., 1978; m. Billy Davis, Mar. 15, 1968; children—Jackie, David, Joey, Kelly. Adminstr., Colonial Nursing Home, Bismarck, Mo., 1958—, Lone Pine Congregate Center, Ironton, Mo., 1977—, Belleview (Mo.) Nursing Home, 1956—. Mem. Am. Health Care Assn., Mo. Assn. Lic. Practical Nurses, Mo. Health Care Assn., Activity Dirs. Assn. Mo. Methodist. Club: Order Eastern Star. Address: Box 24 Star Route Belleview MO 63623

DAVIS, YVETTE CARMON, lawyer; b. Chgo., Oct. 25, 1950; s. Owen Count and Johnnie Beatrice (Lillard) Carmon; m. Hannibal Anthony Davis, Jr., July 7, 1970 (div. July 1977); children—Richard Anthony, Chandra Omara. B.A. in Collective Bargaining and Labor Relations, U. Without Walls, Dayton, Ohio, 1978; J.D., U. Cin., 1982; B.A. in Bus. Adminstrn., Capital U., Columbus, 1983. Bar: Ky., 1983. Staff rep. Ohio Civil Service Employee Assn., Columbus, 1977-79; law clk. U. Cin. Personnel Services, 1980-82; law clk. Baldwin-United Corp., Cin., 1982-83, staff counsel, 1983—; coordinator writing competition Midwest Region Black Am. Law Student Assn., Cin., 1982. Mem. editorial bd. Human Rights Quar., 1982. Bd. dirs. Ohio Black Womens Leadership Caucus, Cin., 1977-79; v.p. Springfield Black Womens Leadership Caucus (Ohio), 1978-79; bd. dirs. ACLU of Springfield/Green County, 1977-79. Urban Morgan Inst. for Internat. Human Rights fellow, 1981-82. Mem. Ky. Bar Assn., Cin. Bar Assn., Black Lawyers Assn. Cin. Democrat. African Methodist Episcopal. Clubs: Internat. Law Soc., Xeta Phi Beta (Cin.). Office: Baldwin-United Corp 1801 Gilbert Ave Cincinnati OH 45202

DAVISON, ELLEN MARGARET, museum curator, educator; b. Scotland County, Mo., Sept. 16, 1929; d. Myron Barnes and Ethel Margaret (Davis) Kirkpatrick; m. Norman Delbert Korbitz, Dec. 23, 1949 (div. 1960); 1 son, Norman Delbert; m. 2d, Walter Sears Davison, May 26, 1962; 1 dau., Jane Ellen. Student Iowa Weselyan Coll., Mt. Pleasant, 1948-49; B.S. in Edn., U.S.D., 1951; postgrad. U. Mo., 1961, N.E. Mo. State U., 1970-71. Cert. tchr. Mo., Iowa, Ala., Fla., Ohio. Tchr., Garfield High Sch., Garrettsville, Ohio, 1951-52; mem. staff coop. extension service USDA, Fla. State U., Tallahassee, 1952; tchr. Jackson (Ala.) Jr. High, 1953; tchr. Ledbetter Country Day Sch., Dallas, 1959-60; mem. staff coop. extension service USDA, U. Mo., Columbia, 1960-62, extension home economist, 1965-66; sales agt. United Farm Agy., Kirksville, Mo., 1964-65; tchr. Ophelia Parrish Jr. High, Kirksville, 1967; substitute tchr. Kirksville Sch. Dist., 1980-83; curator Adair Co. Hist. Mus. and Library, Kirksville, 1981-83. Mem. United Methodist Women. Mem. Am. Econs. Assn., Mo. Home Econs. Assn. (sec.-treas. NE dist.), Extension Home Economists, NEA, PTA, Kirksville (Mo.) Tchrs. Assn., Alpha Theta Kappa Phi, Alpha Phi Sigma. Methodist.

DAVISON, KENNETH LEWIS, research physiologist; b. Hopkins, Mo., Dec. 27, 1935; s. Harlan R. and Hilda E. (Mendenhall) D.; m. Joyce Y. Schmitt, Sept. 8, 1957; children—Jeanette, Kenneth Jr., Kathryn. B.S., U. Mo., 1957; M.S., Iowa State U., 1959, Ph.D., 1961. Research specialist Cornell U., 1961-65; research physiologist U.S. Dept. of Agr., Fargo, N.D., 1965—. Mem. AAAS, Am. Dairy Sci. Assn., Am. Inst. Nutrition, Am. Soc. Animal Sci. Methodist. Home: 2860 N 2d St Fargo ND 58102 Office: Metabolism & Radiation Research Lab 1605 W College St Fargo ND 58105

DAVISSON, MELVIN THOMAS, consulting engineer; b. Grafton, W.Va., Dec. 23, 1931; s. David Earl and Leona Caroline (Haas) D.; m. Marlene Elaine Krumeich, May 14, 1955; children—James Preston, Diana Marie, Teresa Lynn, Kathleen Elaine. B. Civil Engring., U. Akron, 1954; M.S., U. Ill., 1955, Ph.D., 1960. Registered profl. engr. Ohio, Ill. Structural engr. Clark, Dietz Assn., Urbana, Ill., 1955-56; research asst., instr., Univ. Ill., Urbana, 1956-59, asst. prof., 1960-63, assoc. prof. civil engring., 1963-71, prof. civil engring., 1971-81; cons. engr. M.T. Davisson, Consulting Engring., Champaign, 1958—; chmn. to various tech. coms. Contbr. articles to profl. jours. Recipient Alfred A. Raymond award Raymond Internat. Builders, 1958. Mem. Am. Concrete Inst., ASCE (recipient Collingwood prize 1964), ASTM, Am. Railway Engring. Assn., Nat. Soc. of Profl. Engrs., Internat. Soc. Soil Mechanics and Found. Engring., Deep Found. Inst., Sigma Xi. Home: 14 Lake Park Rd Champaign IL 61821 Office: MT Davisson 4 College Park Court Savoy IL 61874

DAVITO, CHARLENE L., nursing adminstr.; b. Westfield, Ill., Sept. 3, 1947; d. Charles W. and Lola M. Goldsmith; grad. St. Joseph Hosp. Sch. Nursing, 1977; postgrad. Lewis U., 1981—; m. Frank L. Davito, July 8, 1967; 1 son, Frank L. Staff nurse Riverside Hosp., Kankakee, Ill., 1977, Morris (Ill.) Hosp., 1977-78; staff nurse Will County Health Dept., Joliet, Ill., 1978-79; dir. nursing Bradley (Ill.) Nursing Centre, 1979; dir. nursing Americana Nursing Center, Joliet, 1980; dir. nursing Briarcliff Manor, Bourbonnais, Ill., 1980-81. Mem. Am. Nurses Assn., Assn. Rehab. Nurses, Ill. Nurses Assn. Roman Catholic. Home: Box 117 Coal City IL 60416

DAVITZ, DONALD JUNIOR, air force officer; b. Columbus, Ohio, Jan. 21, 1955; s. Donald Herbert and Dorothy Louise (Spencer) D.; m. Cheryl Ann Gothard, Mar. 3, 1984. B.S. in Edn., Ohio State U., 1978; M.A. in Bus. Mgmt., Central Mich. U., 1984. Profl. football player Columbus Winds Football Club, 1976-78; track coach Columbus Pub. Schs., 1976-79, wrestling coach, 1977-79, secondary sch. tchr., football coach, 1978-79; commd. 2d lt. U.S. Air Force, 1980, advanced through grades to capt., 1985; combat pilot, Wurtsmith AFB, Mich., 1980—; soccer coach Oscoda Youth Soccer League, Wurtsmith AFB, 1984. Mem. Air Force Assn. (chpt. pub. affairs officer 1980), U.S. Fencing Assn., Ohio State U. Alumni Assn., Sigma Nu. Republican. Mem. Disciples of Christ. Avocations: athletics; travel; self-improvement. Home: 8025A S Alaska St Wurtsmith AFB MI 48753 Office: 524 Bomb Squadron Wurtsmith AFB MI 48753

DAWES, KENNETH JAMES, professor of social work; b. Grand Forks, N.D., May 16, 1936; s. Harvey C. and Helen M. (Jacobson) D.; M. Marjorie D. (Buchfink) June 9, 1962; children—Christopher, John, Mary. Ph.B. in Social Work, U. N.D., 1958; M.S. in Social Work, Columbia U., 1961; Ph.D. in Sociology, U. Minn.-Mpls., 1969. Child welfare worker N.D. Dept. Human Services, Forman, N.D., 1958-60, child welfare supr., Williston, N.D., 1961-64; clin. dir. N.D. State Indsl. Sch., Mandan, 1964-69; dir. N.D. Law Enforcement Council, Bismark, 1969-74; prof., dept. chmn. social work U. N.D., Grand Forks, 1974—; cons. N.D. Dept. Human Services, 1976—. Author: The Human Condition-Social Indicators for North Dakota, 1983. Contbr. articles to profl. jours. Chmn. N.D. Bd. Social Work Examiners, 1983-84; mem. Legislative Com., N.D., 1975; pres. N.D. Conf. Social Welfare, 1977; mem. N.D. Hist. Soc., 1973—. Recipient Social Worker of the Yr. award N.D. Chapter Nat. Assn. Social Workers, 1984; fellow award U. N.D., 1980; Recipient numerous grants Dept. Health and Human Services, 1984. Mem. Nat. Assn. Social Workers (chmn. N.D. chpt. 1977), Midwest Sociol. Assn., Council on Social Work Edn., Am. Assn. State Social Work Bds. Lutheran. Avocation: historical research. Home: 2516 8th Ave N Grand Forks ND 58201 Office: U N D Main Campus Dept Social Work Grand Forks ND 58202

DAWSON, GLENN V., state senator; ed. S.E. Jr. Coll., St. Joseph's Coll., Calumet Coll., Chgo., Marine Naval Sch. Former mem. Ill. Ho. of Reps.; now mem. Ill. Senate. Past Calumet Dist. council Boy Scouts Am.; active Cook County Democratic Orgn. Recipient Man of Yr. award Kiwanis, 1975, Thornton Twp. Young Democrats, 1977; Exceptional Service award K.C., 1980. Mem. Avalon Trails Improvement Assn., East Side C. of C., Hegewisch C. of C. (past pres.), U.S. Coast Guard Master Marine Pilots, Marine Lic. Pilots Assn. Lodges: Lions, KC, Kiwanis. Address: 13343 Baltimore Ave Chicago IL 60634

DAWSON, PETER JOHN, pathologist, educator; b. Wolverhampton, Eng., Feb. 17, 1928; came to U.S., 1960; s. Sydney and Bertha (Richards) D.; m. Elizabeth Ann Coombs, Mar. 1, 1982; m. Nancy Sexton Taylor, Apr. 10, 1953 (div. 1969). B.A., Cambridge U., 1949, M.A., 1953, M.B.,B.Ch., 1952, M.D., 1960. Diplomate Am. Bd. Pathology. Intern, Royal Berkshire Hosp., Reading, Eng., 1952-53, Victoria Hosp. for Children, London, 1953; resident St. George's Hosp., London, 1953-54, Royal Postgrad. Med. Sch., 1954-55, 58-59; vis. asst. prof. U. Calif., San Francisco, 1960-62; lectr. U. Newcastle, Eng., 1962-64; assoc. prof. U. Oreg., Portland, 1964-67, prof. pathology, 1967-76; prof. pathology, dir. lab. surg. pathology U. Chgo., 1977—. Contbr. articles to profl. jours. Fellow Royal Coll. Pathologists; mem. Chgo. Pathology Soc (v.p. 1984—), Internat. Acad. Pathology, Am. Assn. Cancer Research, Am. Assn. Pathologists. Episcopalian. Clubs: Burnham Park Yacht, Quadrangle. Avocation: sailing. Office: Lab Surg Pathology Univ Chicago 5841 Maryland Ave Chicago IL 60638

DAWSON-SAUNDERS, ELIZABETH KNIGHT, statistics educator, consultant; b. Washington, Jan. 20, 1941; d. William Howard and Virginia Faye (Shelton) Knight Corenflos; m. Lawrence E. Dawson, Aug. 18, 1962 (div. 1977); children—Gregory, Curtis; m. Jeffrey J. Saunders, Sept. 20, 1979. B.A., Sangamon State U., 1972, M.A., 1973; Ph.D., U. Ill., 1977. Instr. So. Ill. U. Sch. Medicine, Springfield, 1975-77, asst. prof., 1977-81; adj. prof. Sangamon State U., Springfield, 1977—; assoc. prof. stats. So. Ill. U. Sch. Medicine, Springfield, 1981—; cons. Harvard U. and Geol. Survey, Pakistan, 1982—, NIH, Washington, 1984. Assoc. editor Am. Statistician, 1981—. Mem. preventive medicine and pub. health test com. Nat. Bd. Med. Examiners, Phila., 1984-86. Health occupations grantee Ill. Bd. Edn., Springfield, 1979-81. Mem. Am. Statis. Assn. (publs. officer subsect. on teaching stats. in the health scis. 1977-84, chmn. elect 1985, chmn. 1986), Soc. Med. Decision Making, Sigma Xi (vice-chmn. Sangamon group 1979-81). Avocations: reading; gardening; canoeing. Home: 12 Carriage Hills Springfield IL 62707 Office: So Ill U Sch Medicine PO Box 3926 Springfield IL 62708

DAY, CHARLES C., publishing company executive, minister; b. Croton, Ohio, May 26, 1923; s. Earl Jackson and Una (Canaday) D.; m. Lucille Fisher, Sept. 1, 1944; children—David, Grace. B.A., Marion Coll., 1944, B.Religion, 1945. Ordained to ministry Wesleyan Ch., 1946; minister, Sunbury, Ohio, 1953-58, Norwood, Ohio, 1958-61; missionary Columbia and P.R., 1946-53, 61-64. Home: 1414 Glendale Dr Marion IN 46953 Office: Wesleyan Publishing House PO Box 2000 Marion IN 46952

DAY, DONALD LEE, auditor; b. Southgate, Ky., Sept. 19, 1941; s. Lee and Leona Irene (Brauntz) D.; m. Constance Louise Pace, Apr. 26, 1979; 1 son, Michael Christopher; m. Mary Barbara Lay, Nov. 2, 1963 (div. Aug. 1978); children—Jennifer Lynn, Donald Lee, Barbara Lee. BS., U. Cin., 1963, M.B.A., 1965. Staff auditor Touche Ross & Co., Cin., 1963-65; sr. auditor Gen. Electric Co., Cin., 1965-70; audit mgr. Copeland Corp., Sidney, Ohio, 1970-73; corp. audit mgr. Philips Industries, Dayton, Ohio, 1973—. Mem. Am. Inst. C.P.A.s, Inst. Internal Auditors. Republican. Lutheran. Home: 5250 Angelita Ave Huber Heights OH 45424 Office: Philips Industries Inc 4801 Springfield St Dayton OH 45401

DAY, EMERSON, physician internal medicine; b. Hanover, N.H., May 2, 1913; s. Edmund Ezra and Emily Sophia (Emerson) D.; m. Ruth Fairfield, Aug. 7, 1937; children—Edmund P., Robert F., Nancy, Bonnie, Sheryl. A.B., Dartmouth Coll., 1934; M.D., Harvard U., 1938. Diplomate Am. Bd. Internal Medicine. Prof. preventive medicine chief div. preventive medicine Sloan-Kettering Inst. Cornell U. Med. Coll., N.Y.C., 1954-63; dir. Strang Clinic Meml. Hosp. and Preventive Medicine Inst., N.Y.C., 1950-69; v.p. and med. dir. Medequip Corp., Park Ridge, Ill., 1969-76; sr. med. cons. Medequip Inc., Rockville, Md., 1976-84; prof. medicine Northwestern U. Med. Sch., Chgo., 1976-81, emeritus, 1981—; assoc. dir. Cancer Ctr. Northwestern U., Chgo., 1976-81; med. cons. services, Northbrook, Ill., 1981—; med. dir. Physicians for Med. Cost Containment Inc., Rosemont, Ill., 1984—. Contbr. Articles to profl. jours. Mem. various coms. Am. Cancer Soc. Ill. Div., Chgo., 1969—; pres. N.Y.C. Div. Am. Cancer Soc. 1963-64. Served as flight surgeon U.S. Air Transport Command, 1942-45. Fellow ACP, Am. Geriatrics Soc.; hon. mem. Am. Soc. Cytology (pres. 1958), Am. Assn. Med. Systems and Informatics (founder), Internat. Health Evaluation Assn. (dir.). Congregationalist. Clubs: Century Assoc. (N.Y.C.), Union League. Home and Office: 320 Pebblebrook Dr Northbrook IL 60062

DAY, HARRY GILBERT, nutritional biochemist, consultant; b. Lovilia, Iowa, Oct. 8, 1906; s. John Freeman and Minta Emma (Spencer) D.; m. W. Marie Miller, July 10, 1933 (dec. 1968); children—Margaret Day Pruden, Barbara Day Baumann, Robert M.; m. Gertrude Elizabeth Parr, Aug. 14, 1969. A.B., Cornell Coll., 1930; Sc.D., Johns Hopkins U., 1933; Sc.D. (hon.), Cornell Coll., 1967. Postdoctoral fellow Nat. Research Council, Johns Hopkins U., Balt., 1933-34; mem. gen. edn. bd., Rockefeller Found., Yale U., New Haven, 1934-36; assoc. biochemistry Johns Hopkins U., 1936-40; from asst. prof. to prof. chemistry Ind. U., Bloomington, 1940-50, prof. chemistry, 1950-76, retired, 1976, chmn. dept. chemistry, 1951-62, assoc. dean research and advanced studies, 1967-72; mem. select com. GRAS Substances, Fedn. Am. Soc. Exptl. Biology, Bethesda, Md., 1973-82. Co-developer fluoridized dentifrice. Contbr. numerous articles to profl. jours. Active Bloomington City Council, 1963-71. AMA grantee, 1940-41; and others. Fellow AAAS, Ind. Acad. Sci. (pres. 1962-63), Am. Inst. Nutrition (pres. 1971-72); mem. Am. Chem. Soc. (exam. com. 1959-85), Am. Soc. Biol. Chemists. Republican. Methodist. Lodge: Kiwanis (pres. 1957-58). Home: 1154 Linden Dr Bloomington IN 47401 Office: Ind U Dept Chemistry Bloomington IN 47405

DAY, HOLLIDAY T., curator, art critic; b. Nashville, Dec. 25, 1936; d. Harry and Margaret (Howes) Trentman; m. Benjamin Downing Day, June 14, 1958; children—Elizabeth, Susan. A.B., Wellesley Coll., 1957; M.A., U. Chgo., 1979. Art critic, assoc. editor New Art Examiner, Chgo., 1976-79; writer Art in Am., N.Y.C., 1978-79; curator Am. art Joslyn Art Mus., Omaha, 1980—; mem. panels for selection of pub. sculpture City of Chgo., Nat. Endowment for Arts, U. Nebr., Omaha Met. Arts Council, Art in the Parks, Chgo., Hinsdale Sch. Dist., 1979—. Author: The Shape of Space: The Sculpture of George Sugarman, 1982; I-80 Series, 1983. Editor: The Joslyn Art Museum: Painting and Sculptures from the Collection, 1985. Mem. steering com. for art Art in the Parks, Chgo., 1978-80; mem. art steering com. Argonne Nat. Labs., Ill., 1983-84; chmn. com. for art Hinsdale Sch. Dist., Hinsdale, 1976. Wellesley scholar Wellesley Coll., 1956; Critics fellow Nat. Endowment Arts, Washington, 1979. Mem. Coll. Art Assn., Mid-West Art Historians Assn., Mid West Coll. Art Assn. Club: Arts (Chgo.). Home: 18 S Park St Hinsdale IL 60521 Office: Joslyn Art Mus 2200 Dodge St Omaha NE 68102

DAY, JAMES MICHAEL, hospital administrator, game designer; b. Toledo, Jan. 26, 1951; s. Cecil W. and Edith (Gaspari) D.; m. Merry Livingston, May 24, 1980; 1 dau., Andrea. B.B.A., U. Toledo, 1973. Inventory analyst, cost acct. Questor Co., Toledo, 1971-75; asst. purchasing agt. Riverside Hosp., Toledo, 1975-76, purchasing agt., 1976-78, dir. purchasing, 1978-81, dir. materiel mgmt., 1981-84, dir. materiel and info. services, 1984—; designer computer software materiel mgmt. system. Mem. Northwest Ohio Hosp. Council (chmn. purchasing dir. com.), Am. Hosp. Assn., Ohio Hosp. Assn., Am. Soc. Hosp. Purchasing and Material Mgmt. (sr.). Republican. Roman Catholic. Clubs: Chgo. Wargamers Assn., Metro Detroit Gamers. Home: 2904 Middlesex Dr Toledo OH 43606 Office: Riverside Hosp 1600 Superior St Toledo OH 43604

DAY, JOHN EDWARD, realtor; b. Saginaw, Mich., Mar. 8, 1908; s. Thomas and Margaret Ann (Cavanaugh) D.; B.A., Central Mich. U., 1931; m. Marian McDonagh, Aug. 25, 1934; children—Thomas Bruce, Patricia Ann, John Edward, Marilyn Jane Day Zaetta. Instr. social sci. Arthur Hill High Sch., Saginaw, 1932-59; partner John Day Realty, Saginaw, 1955—; pres. John Day Co., Saginaw, 1966-73; farmer, Saginaw, 1936—. Mem. Am. Soc. Appraisers, Nat., Saginaw (dir. 1960-66) bds. realtors, Saginaw Agrl. Soc. (pres., dir.), Mich. Real Estate Assn., Carriage Assn. Am. Roman Catholic. Clubs: Fordney, Germania (Saginaw). Home: 1810 Short Rd Saginaw MI 48603 Office: Cabaret Trail Saginaw MI 48603

DAY, LAURENCE CLARK, financial executive; b. St. Louis, Feb. 26, 1934; s. Laurence Sturgis and Alice (Clark) Peddle; m. Barbara Ann Bixby, Nov. 19, 1959, (div. May, 1970); children—Stephen Logan, Ethan Sturgis. A.B., Princeton U., 1955; student Washington U. Law Sch., 1959-60. Account exec. media dept. Gardner Advt. Co., St. Louis, 1957-59; stockbroker G. H. Walker & Co., St. Louis, 1960-72; v.p., dir. investment and securities research Newhard, Cook & Co., St. Louis, 1972—; Bd. dirs. Edgewood Children's Ctr., St. Louis, 1983-84-85. Served with U.S. Navy, 1955-57. Mem. Fin. Analyst Fedn. St. Louis Soc. (bd. dirs. 1980-82). Clubs: Princeton (N.Y.C.), Racquet (St. Louis). Home: #1 Watch Hill Rd Ladue MO 63124 Office: Newhard, Cook & Co Inc 300 N Broadway St Louis MO 63102

DAY, ROBERT JENNINGS, building products and refractories company executive; b. Sharon, Pa., Feb. 19, 1925; s. Burwell Fitch and Marie Clara (Guth) D.; m. Marcia Jean Udine, Sept. 23, 1950; children—Margot Jane, Douglas Bruce, Darcy Gail. B.A., Pa. State U., 1947. Sales trainee salesman U.S. Gypsum Co., Harrisburg and Reading, Pa., 1950-54, dist. sales mgr., Balt. and Harrisburg, 1954-58, corp. mktg. mgr., Chgo., 1958-66, corp. dir. product mgmt., Chgo., 1966-69, div. gen. mgr., Los Angeles, 1969-74, corp. v.p. mktg., 1974-77, sr. v.p., 1977-79, exec. v.p., dir., 1979-81, pres., chief operating officer, dir., Chgo., 1981-85; chmn., chief exec. officer USG Corp., Chgo., 1985—; dir. CBI Industries, Oak Brook, Ill., AP Green Refractories, Mexico, Mo., GATX Corp., Chgo., BPB Industries PLC, London, Canadian Gypsum Co. Ltd., Toronto, Ont.; dir., dep. chmn. Fed. Res. Bank Chgo. Mem. adv. bd. Northwestern U. Grad. Sch. Mgmt., also univ. bd. assocs.; trustee George Williams Coll. Clubs: Union League, Mid-Am., Commercial, Metropolitan, Chicago (Chgo.); Hinsdale (Ill.) Golf. Office: USG Corp 101 S Wacker Dr Chicago IL 60606

DAY, ROLAND BERNARD, state supreme ct. justice; b. Oshkosh, Wis., June 11, 1919; s. Peter Oliver and Joanna King (Wescott) D.; B.A., U. Wis., 1942, J.D., 1947; m. Mary Jane Purcell, Dec. 18, 1948; 1 dau., Sarah Jane. Admitted to Wis. bar, 1947; trainee Office Wis. Atty. Gen., 1947; asso. mem. firm Maloney & Wheeler, Madison, 1947-49; 1st asst. dist. atty. Dane County, 1949-52; partner Day, Goodman, Madison, 1953-57; legal counsel, staff Sen. William Proxmire, Washington, 1957-58; partner Wheeler, Van Sickle, Day & Anderson, Madison, 1959-74; justice Wis. Supreme Ct., 1974—. Mem. Madison Housing Authority, 1960-64, chmn., 1961-63. Regent U. Wis. System, 1972-74. Served with AUS, 1943-46. Mem. Am. Bar Assn., State Bar Wis., Am. Trial Lawyers Assn., Am. Judicature Soc., Ygdrasil Lit. Soc. (pres. 1968). Mem. United Ch. of Christ. Clubs: Madison, Madison Literary. Office: Supreme Ct Chambers 214 E State Capitol Madison WI 53702

DAYANI, ELIZABETH LOUISE CROW, nurse, executive, educator; b. Birmingham, Ala., Apr. 28, 1950; d. Jon Killough and Flora Louise (Worthington) Crow; m. John H. Dayani, June 13, 1970; 1 son, John H. B.S.N., Vanderbilt U., 1971, M.S.N. cum laude, 1972. Instr., Vanderbilt U. Sch. Nursing, Nashville, 1972-74; dir., practitioner Moore County Primary Care Center, Lynchberg, Tenn., 1974-75; family nurse practitioner Metro Health Dept., Nashville, 1975-76; asst. prof. Wayne State U. Sch. Nursing, Detroit, 1976-77; asst. prof. U. Kans. Sch. Nursing, Kansas City, 1977-81, assoc. prof., 1981-82; co-owner, exec. dir. Am. Nursing Resources, Kansas City, Mo., 1982—. Recipient Service award Moore County Health Council, 1975. Mem. Am. Nurses Assn., Am. Pub. Health Assn., Nat. Assn. Home Care, Nat. League Nursing, Nat. Assn. Women Bus. Owners, Sigma Theta Tau. Republican. Presbyterian. Clubs: Central Exchange. Author: (with Betty R. Riccardi) The Nurse Entrepreneur, 1982; contbg. editor: The Nurse Practitioner, 1979-83, mem. editorial bd., 1983—; mem. editorial bd. Nursing Economics, 1983, assoc. editor, 1985—; mem. editorial bd. The Kansas Nurse, 1983—.

DCAMP, CHARLES BARTON, educator, musician; b. Fairfield, Iowa, Feb. 16, 1932; s. Glenn Franklin and Nina Clarice (Larson) DC.; student Bradley U., 1950-51; B.S., U. Ill., 1956, M.S., 1957; Ph.D., U. Iowa, 1980; m. Ruth Joyce MacDonald, June 27, 1953; children—James Charles, Douglas Kevin, David Michael, Richard Manley, Paul Frederick, Jon Barton. Tchr., Watervliet (Mich.) Pub. Sch., 1958-61; tchr. music United Twp. High Sch., East Moline, Ill., 1961-63; band dir. Pleasant Valley (Iowa) Schs., 1963-74; prof. music St. Ambrose Coll., Davenport, Iowa, 1974—, also dir. bands, chmn. div. fine arts and chmn. dept. music; guest dir., adjudicator festivals, music contests Iowa, Ill., Minn.; producer Quad-City Music Guild, 1973-77, music dir., 1967-81; chmn. Iowa All-State Band, 1971-74; tchr. woodwinds Bemidji State Coll. Band Camp, 1969—. Mem. Riverdale Vol. Fire Co., 1966-75, pres., 1971-73. Served with AUS, 1952-55. Mem. Iowa (past pres.), Nat. Cath. bandmasters assns., Coll. Band Dirs. Nat. Assn., Music Educators Nat. Conf., Iowa Music Educators (pres.), Am. Fedn. Musicians, Am. Sch. Band Dirs. Assn., Nat. Band Assn., N.E.A. (life), Phi Mu Alpha Sinfonia, Phi Delta Kappa, Tau Kappa Epsilon. Republican. Methodist. Editor, Iowa Music Educator mag., 1979—; contbr. articles to profl. jours. Home: 301 Circle Dr Riverdale Bettendorf IA 52722 Office: St Ambrose Coll Davenport IA 52804

DEAK, CHARLES KAROL, chemist; b. Budapest, Hungary, Sept. 26, 1928; s. Karoly and Ida (Benes) D.; came to U.S., 1955, naturalized, 1961; B.S., Eotvos Coll., Budapest, 1948; student Sorbonne, Paris, 1949; postgrad. Wayne State U., 1957-61; m. Jenny Bocinski, Apr. 9, 1958; children—James, Christine. With Frankel Co., Inc., Detroit, 1957-73, quality control mgr., 1968-71, mgr. tech. services, 1971-73; pres. Analyatical Assocs., Inc., Detroit, 1973—, pres., 1979—. Cert. profl. chemist. Fellow Am. Inst. Chemists; mem. Am. Chem. Soc., ASTM, Am. Soc. Metals, Assn. Analytical Chemists, Photog. Soc. Am. Roman Catholic. Patentee in chem. firefighting agts. and dense metal separation. Club: Internat. Brotherhood Magicians. Home: 29844 Wagner St Warren MI 48093 Office: 19380 Mount Elliott St Detroit MI 48234

DEAL, MARY HOLMAN, urban planner, writer, historian; b. Evanston, Ill., Feb. 5, 1944; d. George Varnum and Emily L. (Sedlacek) D.; A.B., U. Chgo., 1965, M.A., 1966. Adminstrv. asst. Am. Soc. Planning Ofcls., Chgo., 1966-67; asst. planner Genesee County Met. Planning Commn., Flint, Mich., 1967-70; individual practice as planner and designer, Akron, Ohio, 1970-73; housing planner N.E. Ohio Areawide Coordinating Agy., Cleve., 1973-74; regional planner Miami Valley Regional Planning Commn., Dayton, Ohio, 1974-79; project mgr. nat. competition identifying and promoting urban planning activities and designs for women in urban environments HUD, 1980-81; project mgr. Women and Urban Planning: A Bibliography, HUD and Council Planning Librarians, 1980-81. Mem. Am. Planning Assn. (nat. task force mag.; contbr. to Ency. of Cleveland History. planning for women 1979, dir. planning and women div. 1979-81), NOW (treas. Ohio 1975-77), Ohio Women, Inc. (bd. dirs. 1977-78. treas. 1978-79). Contbr. articles to profl. jours. and nat. mags.; contbr. to Ency. of Cleveland History. Home: 610 A Dodge Ct Dayton OH 45431

DEAL, WILLIAM THOMAS, school psychologist; b. Canton, Ohio, Dec. 18, 1949; s. Richard Lee and Rheta Lucille (Gerber) D.; m. Paula Nespeca, Aug. 5, 1972. B.S., Bowling Green State U., 1972; M.A., John Carroll U., 1977; postgrad. Kent State U., 1979—. Sci. tchr. Westlake Schs., 1972-76, head bldg. sci. dept., 1974-76; intern sch. psychologist Garfield Heights Schs., 1976-77, sch. psychologist, 1977—; pvt. practice psychology, Parma Heights, Ohio, 1982-84. Alternate mem. adv. council Cuyahoga County Spl. Edn. Service Ctr., 1977—. Recipient Cert. of Recognition, Garfield Heights Bd. Edn., 1980; Outstanding Achievement award Cleve. Assn. for Children with Learning Disabilities, Inc., 1980. Mem. Nat. Assn. Sch. Psychologists, Am. Orthopsychiat. Assn., AAAS, United Teaching Profession, Ohio Sch. Psychology Assn., Cleve. Assn. Sch. Psychologists. Republican. Mem. Reformed Ch. Home: 5290 Kings Hwy Fairview Park OH 44126 Office: 5640 Briarcliff Dr Garfield Heights OH 44125

DEALY, MILTON DAVID, III, railroad executive; b. Sikeston, Mo., Feb. 10, 1954; s. Milton David and Lucy (Aufdenburg) D.; m. Karen S. Graham, May 28, 1977; children—Dianna, James David. B.A., Central Meth. U., 1976. Asst. roadmaster Mo. Pacific R.R., North Little Rock, Ark., 1976-77, asst. trainmaster, New Orleans, 1977-78, market analyst, St. Louis, 1978-79, trainmaster, Little Rock, 1979-81, div. supt., Chgo., 1981-82; gen. supt. transp. Union Pacific R.R., Omaha, 1984—. Mem. Am. Assn. Railroad Supts. Republican. Methodist. Home: 13018 Lafayette Omaha NE 78154 Office: Union Pacific RR 1416 Dodge Omaha NE 68102

DEAN, ALBERTA LAVAUN, nurse; b. Lafayette, Ind., Apr. 12, 1925; d. Edward Louis and Leona May (Delong) Anderson; m. Guy Dean, Oct. 16, 1948; children—Gregory A., Rebecca A., Eulonda S., Melissa K., Marcia L., Valerie A. R.N., Hurley Med. Ctr., 1948. Staff nurse Hurley Med. Ctr., Flint, Mich., 1948-53, McLaren Gen. Hosp., 1953-54, Lafayette (Ind.) Home Hosp., 1954—. Mem. Southside Wesleyan Ch. Mem. Nurses Assn. of Am. Coll. Obstetricians and Gynecologists. Republican. Home: 276 Dayton Rd Dayton IN 47941 Office: Lafayette Home Hospital 2400 South St Lafeyette IN 47941

DEAN, ERIC, philosophy and religion educator; b. London, Oct. 30, 1924; came to U.S., 1947, naturalized 1971; s. Francis Ernest and Mabel Johanna (Ritchie) D.; m. Betty Jane Garret, July 30, 1948; children—Daphne, Eric Jr., Jonathan. Student North Park Coll., Chgo., 1947-58; A.B., U. Chgo., 1950, B.D., 1953, Ph.D., 1959; D.D. (hon.) Hanover Coll., 1978, Christian Theol. Sem., 1979. Ordained to ministry Presbyterian Ch., 1955. Instr. philosophy, asst. prof. No. Central Coll., Naperville, Ill., 1956-57; prof. philosophy, religion Wabash Coll., Crawfordsville, Ind., 1957—; overseer St. Meinrad Archabbey, Ind., 1968—. Author: The Good News about Sin, 1982. Contbr. articles to profl. jours. Served with RAF, 1942-47. Mem. Am. Theol. Soc. (pres. 1968-69), Ind. Acad. Religion (pres. 1966-67), Am. Soc. Ch. History, N. Am. Acad. Ecumenists. Democrat. Presbyterian. Avocations: monasteries, bicycle touring, backpacking. Office: Wabash Coll Crawfordsville IN 47933

DEAN, J. THOMAS, lawyer; b. Cleve., Feb. 22, 1933; s. John Ladd and Margaret Caroline (Blakely) D.; m. Patricia Jean Whitmore, Aug. 6, 1960; children—Thomas W., Carol M., Joan G. B.A., Ohio Weslyan U., 1956; J.D., Western Res. U., 1959. Bar: Ohio 1959. Asst. pros. atty. Lake County, Ohio, 1960; assoc. Blakely, Rand, Painesville, Ohio, 1961-67; ptnr. Blakely & Dean, 1967-76, Blakely, Dean, Wilson & Klingenberg, Painesville, 1976—; law dir. North Perry Village, Ohio, 1970—. Mem. Painesville Bd. Zoning Appeals, 1971-76; mem. Planning Commn., 1967-79, chmn., 1970-77; pres. Painesville Sr. Citizens, 1982-84; mem. Lake County Bd. Elections, 1964-84; chmn. Lake County Republican. Com., 1970-74, 82-84; mem. Ohio Rep. Central Com., 1980—; clk. Painesville Twp. Park, 1962—. Mem. Lake County Bar Assn. (pres. 1979-80), Ohio State Bar Assn., ABA, Republican. Methodist. Lodge: Kiwanis (pres. 1980-81). Avocation: swimming. Home: 35 Forest Dr Painesville OH 44077 Office: Blakely Dean Wilson & Klingenberg PO Box 526 Painesville OH 44077

DEAN, JEFFREY MARTIN, historic preservationist; b. Madison, Wis., Mar. 3, 1940; s. Frank K. and Gladys (Paust) D.; m. Jill Louise Weber, July 5, 1966. B.A., Lawrence Coll., 1962; postgrad. Yale U., 1962-66. Reporter, Waterbury (Conn.) Republican, 1966, Wis. State Jour., Madison, 1967; dir. urban design sect. City Planning Dept., Madison, 1967-72; state hist. preservation officer and dir. hist. preservation State Hist. Soc. of Wis., Madison, 1972—; founder, pres. Wooden Canoe Heritage Assn., Ltd. Bd. dirs. Hist. Madison, Inc. Mem. Wis. Soc. Archtl. Historians (founder 1973), Wis. Soc. Architects, Nat. Trust Hist. Preservation, Assn. Preservation Tech., Nat. Conf. State Hist. Preservation Officers (bd. dirs. 1981—), Vintage BMW Motorcycle Owners of Am., Inc. (founder, dir. 1972—). Author: Architectural Photography, 1981; contbr. articles to profl. jours. Office: State Hist Soc 816 State St Madison WI 53706

DEAN, WILLIAM DENARD, religion educator, author; b. South Bend, Ind., July 12, 1937; s. William Stover and Eleanor (Hatcher) D.; m. Patricia Ann Fletcher; children—Jennifer, Colin. B.A., Carleton Coll., 1959; M.A., U. Chgo., 1964, Ph.D., 1967. Asst. prof. philosophy, religion Northland Coll., Ashland, Wis., 1966-68; asst. prof. religion Gustavus Adolphus Coll., St. Peter, Minn., 1968-73, assoc. prof. religion, 1973-80, prof. religion, 1980—, chmn. dept. religion, 1979-83; research fellow Inst. for Advanced Study of Religion, U. Chgo., Ill., 1984-85; Author: Coming To: A Theology of Beauty, 1972; Love Before the Fall, 1976; also articles. Del. Wis. Democratic Nat. Conv. committed to McCarthy, Chgo., 1968. Vis. scholar Lutheran Sch. Theology at Chgo, 1984-85. Mem. Am. Jour. of Theology and Philosophy (editorial Bd. 1983—), Am. Acad. Religion. Methodist. Home: 2718 Stone Circle Minnetonka MN 55343 Office: Gustavus Adolphus Coll Saint Peter MN 56082

DEANE, PAUL DUANE, JR., information specialist; b. Jacksonville, Fla., Dec. 18, 1952; s. Paul Duane and Sue (Foster) D.; m. Carolyn Davis, Oct. 24, 1970; children—Paul Davis, Carrie Elspeth. M.L.S., U. S.C., 1979. Drug counselor Milestone Therapeutic Ctr., Greenville, S.C., 1972-74; suicide counselor Greenville Hosp., 1975-76; religion reference librarian Memphis Pub. Library, 1979-80; dir. Orangeburg Pub. Library (S.C.), 1980-83; mgr. reference dept. Allen County Pub. Library, Fort Wayne, Ind., 1983—; Co-editor selected bibliography Books for Pub. Libraries, 1984. Mem. Leadership Orangeburg, 1982. Mem ALA, S.C. Library Assn., S.C. Pub. Library Assn. (sec. 1983), Am. Pub. Library Assn. Methodist. Office: Allen County Pub Library 900 Webster St Fort Wayne IN 46802

DEANGELIS, ALDO A., state senator; b. Chicago Heights, Ill., Mar. 25, 1931; grad. Knox Coll., Galesburg, Ill., 1954; postgrad. U. Chgo., Govs. State U.; m. Meredith Roberts; 4 children. Founder, pres. Dial Tube, 1961-65; co-founder, past pres. Vulcan Tube and Metals Co., 1969-78; mem. Ill. State Senate, 1978—, now asst. minority leader; dir. 1st Suburban Bank Olympia fields. Bd. dirs. United Way of Chicago Heights, S. Suburban Surgi-Care Center; former dir. Respond Now; former chmn. Citizens Support Com. Sch. Dist. 161. Served with U.S. Army, 1954-56. Mem. C. of C., Mfrs. Assn. Chgo. (dir.). Republican. Office: State Capitol Springfield IL 62706

DEANY, CHARLES FRANCIS, school superintendent; b. Kankakee, Ill., Jan. 29, 1934; m. Karla K. Deany, July 21, 1979; children—Kathleen, Tim, Tricia, Ryan. B.S., No. Ill. State Tchrs. Coll., 1959; M.Ed., U. Ill., 1963, C.A.S., 1965. Cert. supr., Ill. Tchr. coach pub. schs., Kankakee, Ill., 1959-63; prin. pub. schs., Bradley, Ill., 1963-68, Joliet, Ill., 1968-71, Palmyra, Ill., 1971-76; supt. schs., Tonica, Ill., 1976-79, Fremont Sch., Mundelein, Ill., 1979—; condr. workshops. Served with AUS, 1954-56. Mem. Nat. Assn. Sch. Adminstrs., Ill. Assn. Sch. Adminstrs. (hon. mention). Roman Catholic. Home: 327 Hojem Grayslake IL 60030 Office: 28855 Fremont Center Mundelein IL 60660

DEARBORN, DORR GELLATLY, medical scientist, pediatric pulmonologist, educator; b. Ontario, Oreg., Nov. 14, 1939; s. Oris Daniel Dearborn and Margaret Emma (Gellatly) Dearborn Osborn; m. Betty Smallmon, June 10, 1963 (div. July 1974); children—John G., Ulyssa M., D. Perkins, Natalie A., Nathan W.; m. Joyce Protiva, Sept. 24, 1976. B.A., Willamette U., 1961; Ph.D., U. Minn., 1969, M.D., 1970. Pediatric intern U. Minn. Hosps., Mpls., 1970-71; staff assoc. NIH, Bethesda, Md., 1971-74; asst. prof. pediatrics and biochemistry Case Western Res. U., Cleve., 1974-81, assoc. prof., 1981—, assoc. chief pediatric pulmonary div. dept. pediatrics, 1985—; research dir. Cystic Fibrosis Research Inst., Cleve., 1979—. Author: (with others) Cystic Fibrosis: Future Prospectives, 1976; Pulmonary Disease and Disorders, 1980; Methods of Enzymology, Vol. 91, 1983; Cystic Fibrosis, 1984. Trustee Rainbow chpt. Cystic Fibrosis Found. Cleve., 1976—, v.p., 1979—. Served as sr. surgeon USPHS, 1971-74. Recipient young investigator award Nat. Heart, Lung and Blood Inst., N.I.H., 1975. Mem. Biophys. Soc., Cystic Fibrosis Found. (mem. CF Club, pres. 1983-84), Am. Chem. Soc., Am. Soc. Biol. Chemists, Soc. Complex Carbohydrates, Sigma Xi, Phi Lambda Upsilon, Alpha Omega Alpha. Republican. Methodist. Avocations: sailing, fishing. Office: Dept Pediatrics Case Western Reserve Univ 2101 Adelbert Rd Cleveland OH 44106

DEARING, JOEL K., broadcasting executive, audio production company executive; b. East Chicago, Ind., Feb. 15, 1956; s. William Thomas and France Loraine (Cowles) D. A.A., Cleve. State U., 1976; B.S. in Communications, U. Tenn., 1978. Radio announcer Multimedia Inc., Knoxville, Tenn., 1976-78, Sta. WGNI-WAAV, Wilmington, N.C., 1978-80; dir. music research Michiana Telecasting, South Bend, Ind., 1980—; owner, pres. Creative Audio, Mishawaka, Ind., 1981—. Sound technician, actor South Bend Civic Theatre, 1981—, bd. dirs., 85—. Recipient Sound Tech award South Bend Civic Theatre, 1983-84. Republican. Methodist. Clubs: Mercedes Benz (Three Rivers); Club of N.Am. (Branch). Avocations: stock market investing; camping; boating. Home: PO Box 5205 532-M Jefferson Estate Ln Mishawaka IN 46545-5205 Office: Michiana Telecasting 54516 Business 31 N South Bend IN 46634

DEARLOVE, JOHN LONGSTREET, advertising and marketing executive; b. St. Louis, Nov. 1, 1951; s. William E. and Marrion (Hiedbrieder) D.; m. Lori McManoman, Aug. 31, 1974 (div. 1983); children—Jennifer A., Jessica Longstreet. Student Oakton Community Coll., 1972-73; B.F.A., Chgo. Acad. Fine Arts, 1974. Exec. v.p. Clay Dearlove and Affiliates, Chgo., 1979-82; pres. Okura Dearlove and Affiliates, Chgo., 1979-84, Innermark Inc., Chgo., 1981—; BDP Inc., Chgo., 1981—, J. L. Dearlove and Affiliates, Chgo., 1983—. Maj. contbr., developer Jour. of Burn Care and Rehab. Home: 203 E Burr Oak Arlington Heights IL 60004 Office: 307 N Michigan Ave Suite 2012 Chicago IL 60601

DE BARONE, ELISSA N., communications consultant, educator; b. Miami, Fla., June 19, 1949; d. Aldo and Elena (Testa) De B.; A.A., Miami-Dade Jr. Coll., 1970; B.A., U. W.Fla., 1972; M.A., U. Ga., 1974; Ph.D., Ohio State U., 1981; m. Steven J. Ring, June 9, 1973; 1 son, Marc Victor Ring. Acad. advisor, 1974-77, asst. coordinator developmental edn., Wright State U., Dayton, Ohio, 1975-76, prof. dept. communication, 1977—, dir. forensics, 1978-79, dir. cable TV, 1980-81; pres. De Barone Communications, Dayton; advisor The Daily Guardian; cons. Sta. WDTN-TV. Mem. Speech Communication Assn., AAUW, Am. Personnel and Guidance Assn., ACLU, Phi Beta Kappa, Phi Kappa Phi. Democrat. Roman Catholic. Contbr. articles to profl. jours. Office: 5575 Shady Oak St Dayton OH 45424

DEBEAR, RICHARD STEPHEN, library planning consultant; b. N.Y.C., Jan. 18, 1933; s. Arthur A. and Sarah (Morrison) deB.; m. Estelle Carmel Grandon, Apr. 27, 1951; children—Richard, Jr., Diana deBear Fortson, Patricia deBear Talkington, Robert, Christopher, Nancy. B.S., Queens Coll. CUNY, 1953. Sales rep. Sperry Rand Corp., Blue Bell, Pa., 1954-76; pres. Library Design Assocs., Plymouth, Mich., 1976—, Am. Library Ctr., Plymouth, 1981—; bldg. cons. to numerous libraries, 1965—. Mem. ALA, Mich. Library Assn. Office: Library Design Assocs Inc 859 S Main St Plymouth MI 48170

DEBLASE, ANTHONY FRANK, publishing company executive, biology educator, consultant; b. South Bend, Ind., Apr. 3, 1942; s. Stephan and Ida (Macri) D.; m. Alyce Mae Myers, Aug. 19, 1969 (dec. Mar. 1976). A.B., Earlham Coll., 1964; Ph.D. in Zoology, Okla. State U., 1971. Asst. dir. museums Earlham Coll., dir. Conner Prairie Mus. (now Conner Prairie Pioneer Settlement), Noblesville, Ind., 1964-66; chief of security and visitor services Field Mus. of Natural History, Chgo., 1970-78; assoc. prof. biology Roosevelt U., Chgo., 1969-78; pres., pub. Desmodus Publs., Inc., Chgo., 1978—. Named expdn. co-mammalogist W.S. & J.K. Street Expdn. to Iran, Field Mus. Natural History, 1968. Mem. Am. Soc. of Mammalogists (life), Am. Assn. of Mus. Club: CHC (Chgo.). Author (with Robert E. Martin) A Manual of Mammalogy (2d edit.), 1981; author tech. publs., short stories; contbr. articles to profl. jours. Office: Desmodus Publs Inc PO Box 6592 Chicago IL 60680

DE BLASIS, JAMES MICHAEL, opera association administrator; b. N.Y.C., Apr. 12, 1931; s. James and Sarah (De Felice) deB.; B.F.A., Carnegie Mellon U., 1959, M.F.A., 1960; m. Ruth Hofreuter, Aug. 25, 1957; 1 dau., Blythe. Mem. drama faculty Carnegie Mellon U., 1960-62; head dept. drama Onondaga Community Coll., Syracuse, N.Y., 1963-72; head Opera Workshop, Syracuse, 1969-70; advisor opera Corbett Found., Cin., 1971-76; gen. dir. Cin. Opera Assn., 1973—; artistic adv. Pitts. Opera, 1979-83; free lance internat. stage dir. of operas. Served with U.S. Army, 1951-53. Mem. Actors Equity, Am. Guild Mus. Artists, Beta Theta Pi. Republican. Episcopalian. Clubs: Carnegie Mellon Drama Alumni. Office: 1241 Elm St Cincinnati OH 45210

DEBOER, KENNETH FRANK, anatomy educator; b. Verdi, Minn., Nov. 6, 1938; s. Frank and Gertrude (Rysdam) DeB.; m. Catherine Ann Caron, Aug. 22, 1959; children—Gregory, Ann, Thomas, Margaret, David. B.A., U. Minn., 1961; M.A., Mankato State U., 1968; Ph.D., Iowa State U., 1970. Predoctoral fellow Iowa State U., Ames, 1968-70; assoc. prof. biology Western State Coll., Gunnison, Colo., 1970-78, prof. anatomy Palmer Coll. Chiropractic, Davenport, Iowa, 1978—. Editorian bd. Jour. Manipulative and Physiol. Therapeutics, 1982—; contbr. articles to profl. jours. Vice pres. Homeowners Assn., Eldridge, Iowa, 1984. Served to comdr. USN 1961-67, Res. Research grantee Found. Chiopractic Edn. and Research, 1981-83. Mem. Biofeedback Soc. Am., Democrat. Avocations: running, skiing. Home: 122 Crestview Dr Eldridge IA 52748 Office: Palmer Coll Chiropractic 1000 Brady St Davenport IA 52803

DEBOLD, VICKI SUE, insurance broker; b. Macomb, Ill., Sept. 14, 1947; d. Robert Melvin and Laura Mae (Magnuson) Pollock; student public schs.; m. Neil C. Goforth, July 18, 1969 (dec. Mar. 1971); m. 2d, David Loran DeBold, Nov. 18, 1978. Various retail sales and secretarial positions, 1964-70; broker-owner Goforth Ins. Agy., Bushnell, Ill., from 1971; sales exec. WJEQ-FM Radio, McDonough Broadcasting, Inc., 1983; profl. singer with group Life, 1972-74. Judge Miss Quincy Pageant, 1974. Named Young Career Woman of Yr., Bus. and Profl. Women Macomb (Ill.), 1972; Miss Macomb of 1966-67. Lic. ins. broker. Hon. mem. Ill. Assn. Nat. Campers and Hikers Assn. (Wild Life Refuge award 1975); mem. Nat. Fedn. Small Businesses, Nat. Assn. Female Execs., Ind. Ins. Agts. Ill., Profl. Ins. Agts. Ill., Bushnell Ind. Ins. Agts. Assn., Macomb Ind. Ins. Agts. Assn. Republican. Presbyterian. Home: 1227 W Adams St Macomb IL 61455

DEBROSSE, THEODORE ANTHONY, state official, petroleum geologist; b. Piqua, Ohio, June 25, 1930; s. Benjamin P. and Agnes M. (Guillozet) DeB.; m. Betty Lou Johnson, Oct. 12, 1957; children—Richard A., Myron E., Jeffrey L., Nanette M. B.S. in Geology, St. Joseph's Coll., Rensselaer, Ind., 1955. Staff geologist Ohio Geol. Survey, Columbus, 1955-65; tech. asst., div. oil and gas Ohio Dept. Natural Resources, Columbus, 1965-69, asst. chief div., 1969—. Named Energy Conservationist of Yr., Nat. Wildlife Fedn., 1975. Charter mem. Ohio Geol. Soc. (pres. 1964-65), Am. Inst. Profl. Geologists (cert. profl. geologist, pres. Ohio sect. 1971); mem. Am. Assn. Petroleum Geologist (dist. rep. 1962-64), Clintonville Conservation Club (pres. 1972-73). Republican. Roman Catholic. Lodge: Eagles. Avocations: Hunting; fishing; camping; woodworking. Home: 118 Chatham Rd Columbus OH 43214 Office: Dept of Natural Resources Div of Oil and Gas Fountain Sq Bldg A Columbus OH 43224

DE BRULER, ROGER O., justice Indiana Supreme Court; b. 1934; A.B., LL.B., Ind. U. Admitted to bar, 1960; now justice Supreme Ct. of Ind., has also served as chief justice. Office: Supreme Court of Indiana 321 State House Indianapolis IN 46204*

DEBYLE, WOODROW C., rental property executive, electrical engineer; b. Grand Rapids, Mich., Dec. 13, 1918; s. William and Flossie (Stuck) DeB.; m. Esther R. VandenBroeck, July 31, 1945 (div. May 1972); children—Woodrow E., Yolanda S.; m. Norma E. Smallen, Nov. 1, 1975. B.S.E.E., U. Mich., 1943. Registered profl. engr., Ohio. Radio engr. Naval Research Lab., Washington, 1943-45; product engr. Automatic Music Instrument, Grand Rapids, Mich., 1946-47; broadcast engr. Radio WLAV, Grand Rapids, 1947; sr. engr. Western Electric, Columbus, Ohio, 1947-82; pres. T & D Investment Property, Inc., Columbus, Ohio, 1965—; head instr. Hawthorne Evening Sch., Chgo., 1953-59, CRES Evening Sch., Columbus, Ohio, 1961; instr. YMCA Evening Sch., Columbus, 1965-73. Treas. Pine Hills Civic Assn., Columbus, 1975-76; founding mem. Central Ohio Hot Jazz Soc., Columbus, 1981—. Served with USN, 1944-45. Mem. IEEE (life). Democrat. Club: Hawthorne Sc. (Chgo.) (pres. 1953-54), CRES Amateur Radio and Electronics (pres. 1961-62). Lodge: Eagle. Avocations: amateur radio; tape recording; electronic equipment; philatelist. Home: 2684 Sonata Dr Columbus OH 43209

DE CAMP, JOHN WILLIAM, state senator; b. Neligh, Nebr., July 6, 1941; s. Hewitt and Blanche DeC.; B.A., U. Nebr., J.D. m. Ma Thi Nga, Oct. 16, 1978; children—Jennifer, Shanda, Tara. Mem. Nebr. Legislature, Lincoln, 1971—; owner apt. complexes in Nebr. Served to capt. U.S. Army, 1968-70. Mem. Nebr. Bar Assn. Republican. Office: State Capitol Lincoln NE 68509

DECASTRO, MICHAEL ANGELO, design engineer; b. Frontenac, Kans., May 3, 1909; s. Fortunato and Maria Boudino DeCastro; m. Elizabeth Lisa Giacobetti, May 9, 1931; children—Phyllis Marie Hrirar DeCastro Sloan, Joyce A. DeCastro Volmut, Betty Jo Arnold DeCastro Shoddy, Anna DeCastro Potter. Architect, design engr. McNally Group, Pittsburg, Kans., 1934-80; investor, M.A. DeCastro, Frontenac, 1980—; dir. Cnetennial Life Ins. Co., 1962-80. Designer plans and specifications for Frontenac High Sch. gym, football stadium and field, Sacred Heart grade sch., Eagles Bldg. Councilman City of Frontenac, Kans., 1947-67. Lodges: Lions, K.C., Eagles. Home: 101 N Labette Frontenac KS 66762

DECHANT, THOMAS PATRICK, educational administrator; b. Berea, Ohio, Apr. 8, 1955; s. Donald W. and Elizabeth (Mills) DeC. B.S. in Bus. Edn., Miami U.-Oxford, Ohio, 1977; postgrad. Cleve. State U., 1981-84. Cert. tchr., Ohio. Bus. tchr. Bucyrus City Schs., Ohio, 1977-78, Polaris Vocat. Ctr., Middleburg Heights, Ohio, 1978-82; staff pub. relations ICM Sch. of Bus., Cleve., 1982-83, ednl. supr., 1983—; chmn. Polaris Adv. Com., 1983—. Mem. Assn. Info. Systems Profls., Assn. Systems Mgrs., Cleve. Area Bus. Tchrs., Ohio Bus. Tchrs. Assn. (state conf. com. 1984), Data Processing Mgmt. Assn. (membership com. 1984—), Ohio Office Edn. Assn. (Outstanding Advisor region 12 1981), Miami U.-Oxford Alumni Club (v.p. 1980-82, pres. 1984—). Roman Catholic. Office: ICM Sch of Bus One Playhouse Sq Bldg Cleveland OH 44115

DECI, EUGENE CLARK, educator; b. Clifton Springs, N.Y., May 9, 1942; s. Frederick Theodore and Florence Helen (Ashman) D.; m. Mary Francis DePauw, May 26, 1967; children—Todd John, Benjamin Theodore. B.A., Hamilton Coll., 1964; Ph.D. SUNY-Binghamton, 1972. Asst. prof. physics

Bklyn. Coll., CUNY, 1972-78; assoc. prof. Alma Coll., Mich., 1978—; vis. assoc. prof. Nat. Superconducting Cyclotron Lab., East Lansing, Mich., 1984—. Contbr. articles to prof. publs. Mem. Am. Phys. Soc., Sigma Xi. Republican. Presbyterian. Home: 1021 Falkirk Ct Alma MI 48801 Office: Alma Coll Alma MI 48801

DECIO, ARTHUR JULIUS, manufacturing company executive; b. Elkhart, Ind., Oct. 19, 1930; s. Julius A. and Lena (Alesia) D.; m. Patricia George, Jan. 6, 1951; children—Terrence, Jamee, Linda, Jay, Leigh Allison. Student DePaul U., 1949-50; D.B.A. (hon.), Salem Col., (W.Va.); LL.D., U. Notre Dame, Ind. State U.-Terre Haute. Pres., Skline Corp., Elkhart, 1956-59, pres., chmn. bd., chief exec. officer, 1959—; dir. Schwarz Paper Co., Morton Grove, Ill., Am. Fletcher Nat. Bank & Trust Co., Indpls., Midwest Commerce Banking Co., Elkhart, Ind., Rodman & Renshaw Capital Group, Inc., Chgo. Trustee, U. Notre Dame, Aux Chandelles Village Found., Elkhart; mem. Commn. on Presdl. Scholars; pres. Elkhart Gen. Hosp. Found.; bd. dirs. Goshen (Ind.) Coll., Nat. Italian Am. Found., Washington; chmn. adv. council United Way, Elkhart, past bd. dirs., campaign chmn., 1966; bd. dirs. Cath. Diocese Fort Wayne-South Bend, Ind.; life mem. adv. bd. Salvation Army, Elkhart; life mem. bd. trustees Marmion Mil. Acad., Aurora, Ill.; past bd. dirs. Elkhart Urban League, Jr. Achievement, Elkhart Gen. Hosp., N. Central Ind. Med. Edn. Found., South Bend, Nat. Jr. Achievement; past trustee Stanley Clark Sch., South Bend, LaLumiere Sch., Laporte, Ind.; mem. Council on Devel. Choices for the 80s, Urban Land Inst.; mem. Presdl. Task Force on Law Income Housing, 1970; bd. govs. Assoc. Colls. of Ind. Recipient U. Portland (Oreg.) medal, Golden Plate award Acad. Achievement, Dallas, Community Service award Elkhart County br. NAACP, 1980, Marmion Centurion award Marmion Mil. Acad., Achievement award Jr. Achievement, others. Mem. Manufactures Housing (nat. dir.), Mobile Home Mfrs. Assn. (bd. dirs., past pres., past chmn. Washington affairs com.), Assn. Colls. Ind. (bd. govs.), Ind. Acad. Roman Catholic. Lodge: Elks. Office: 2520 By Pass Rd Elkhart IN 46514*

DECKER, BETH FRANCIS, nursing adminstr.; b. Croswell, Mich., Sept. 14, 1923; d. Frank William and Delta Ferne (Francis) Gray; diploma St. Joseph Hosp. Sch. Nursing, 1946; m. K. Ward Decker, Sept. 3, 1949; 1 son, Rex A. Staff nurse Good Samaritan Hosp., Cin., 1946, St. Joseph's Hosp., Mt. Clements, Mich., 1946-47; office nurse, Deckerville, Mich., 1947-50; staff nurse Deckerville Hosp., 1950-70; office nurse, Bad Axe, Mich., 1971-73; inservice dir. Huron Meml. Hosp., Bad Axe, 1973-77, dir. nursing service, 1977—, legis. chmn. hosp. aux.; instr. emergency med. technicians, 1973—; cons. Huron and Sanilac Family Planning Program; instr. expectant parent classes. Bd. dirs. East Central Mich. Emergency Med. Services, 1976-79; pres., 1976—; bd. dirs. Health Systems Agy., 1977-82, v.p., 1977-78; community mem. Extended Care Facility Deckerville Area; mem. adv. com. Med. Explorers Post, Boy Scouts Am.; bd. dirs. Blue Water Hospice; mem. council East Central Mich. Health Systems Agy. Served with Cadet Nurses Corps, 1943-46. Mem. Am., Mich., Sanilac Dist. (pres. 1972-73), ARC nurses assns., Natural Childbirth Assn., Mich. Ambulance Assn., Mich. Hosp. Pub. Relations Assn., Emergency Dept. Nurses Assn., East Central Mich. Dist. Nursing Adminstrs. (1st v.p. 1981—), Mich. Soc. Nursing Adminstrs., Nat., Mich. socs. emergency med. technicians, Hosp. Aux. Huron Meml. Hosp., Hosp. Aux. Deckerville Community Hosp., Mich. Heart Assn., Thumb Area Nursing Dirs., East Central Mich. Quality Assurance Profls. Soc., Am. Legion Aux. (pres., sec. local unit 1955-65), Bus. and Profl. Women's Club. Republican. Methodist. Club: Lioness. Home: 2672 Black River St Deckerville MI 48427 Office: 1100 S Van Dyke Bad Axe MI 48413

DECKER, C(ARL) LAWRENCE, medical services company executive, physician; b. Dayton, Ky., May 27, 1940; s. Carl Louis and Virginia (Cline) D.; m. JoAnn Koff, Dec. 16, 1967 (div. 1972); m. Carol Scribner, Sept. 14, 1984. B.S. U. Cin., 1962, M.D., 1966, postgrad., 1967-69; postgrad. Boston U., 1966-67; M.B.A., Xavier U., 1980. Intern Boston City Hosp., 1966-67; resident Boston U. Hosp., 1967-68, U. Cin. Hosp., 1969-70; practice medicine specializing in nephrology, Cin., 1970-72; dir. emergency medicine Bethesda Hosp., Cin., 1970-82; pres. Ambulatory Med. Care, Inc., Milford, Ohio, 1982—, Doctors' Urgent Care Offices Med. Group Ohio, Doctors' Urgent Care Office P.C. of Pa. Contbr. articles to profl. jours. Fellow Am. Coll. Emergency Physicians; mem. Ohio Med. Assn. Avocations: music; racquetball; art. Home: 780 Carpenter Rd Loveland OH 45140 Office: Ambulatory Med Care Inc 935 St Route 28 Milford OH 45150

DECKER, JEAN CAMPBELL, financial executive; b. Chgo., Mar. 10, 1915; d. Dm and Bertha (Campbell) D.; B.A. in Bus. Adminstrn., U. Chgo., 1937. With Calco Mfg. Co., Addison, Ill., 1950—, treas., 1969-81, plan adminstr., dir. pension plan, 1976-82, cons., 1981—; auditor/acct. Gustafson Enterprises, Inc., Addison, Ill., 1954-71, 1971—, dir., 1971-78, 82—; treas. Environ, Inc., Haines City, Fla., 1971-72. Notary public. Mem. U. Chgo. Alumni Assn., Phi Delta Upsilon. Republican. Home: 885 Smith St Glen Ellyn IL 60137

DECKER, PETER W., Bible college official, former chemical company executive; b. Grand Rapids, Mich., Mar. 20, 1919; s. Charles B. and Ruth E. (Thorndill) D.; B.S., Wheaton Coll., 1941; postgrad. Northwestern U., 1942-43, U. Mich., 1958-60; D.Sc. (hon.), London Inst. Applied Research, 1973, LL.D., 1975; m. Margaret I. Stainthorpe, June 10, 1944; children—Peter, Marilyn, Christine, Charles. Advt. dept. Hotels Windermere, Chgo., 1942, Princess Pat Cosmetics, Chgo., 1943; market research investigator A.C. Nielson Co., Chgo., 1944-48; pres. Peter Decker Constrn. Co., Detroit, 1948-60; sales mgr. Century Chem. Products Co., Detroit, 1961-62, v.p., 1962-63, pres., 1963-75; sr. partner G & D Advt. Assos., 1967-78; v.p., treas., exec. dir. Christian Edn. Advancement, Inc., 1975-77, exec. dir., 1978—; registrar, instr. N.T. Greek and Theology Birmingham (Mich.) Bible Inst., 1973—; instr. Midwestern Baptist Coll., 1984—, dir. student fin. aid, 1984—, trustee, 1985—. Neighborhood commr. Boy Scouts Am., 1961-66, merit badge counselor; emeritus, 1979—; mem. Bd. Rev., Beverly Hills, Mich., 1957-63; chmn. bd. review Southfield Twp., Mich., 1964-67; bd. dirs., past pres. Beverly Hills Civic Assn.; bd. dirs. Mich. Epilepsy Center and Assn., 1957-71, exec. com., 1962-67. Mem. Detroit Soc. Model Engrs. (pres. 1958, 62, dir. 1955-71), Chem. Splty. Mfg. Assn., AAAS, Nat. Geog. Soc., Internat. Platform Assn., ASTM, Smithsonian Instn. Assos., Archaeol. Inst. Am., Bibl. Archaeol. Soc., Bible-Sci. Assn., Creation Research Soc., Mich. Student Fin. Aid Assn., Midwest Assn. Student Fin. Aid Adminstrs. Republican (sustaining mem. Oakland County, Mich.). Baptist (trustee, instr. Bible Inst.). Author: Getting To Know New Testament Greek. Home: 33210 Rosevear Dr Beverly Hills Birmingham MI 48009 Office: 280 E Lincoln Birmingham MI 48009

DECKER, RICHARD HENRY, pharmaceutical company executive; b. Grand Rapids, Mich., Aug. 12, 1934; s. Dennis H. and Helen (Lucille) D.; m. Mary Elizabeth Burris, Aug. 5, 1960; children—Stephen, Richard, Stephanie. A.B., Hope Coll., 1956; M.S., U. Ill., 1958; Ph.D., Okla. State U., 1960. NIH postdoctorial fellow U. Wis., 1960-62; research assoc., instr. Mayo Clinic, Rochester, Minn., 1962-71; research scientist Abbott Labs, North Chgo., 1971-81, dir. research and devel., 1981—. Contbr. chpts. on AIDS research to books. Church elder, Reformed Ch., Rochester, 1962-70; symposium faculty Internat. Hepatitus Symposium, 1984; chmn. USSR Hepatitis Symposium, Moscow, 1984. Served to pfc. USNR, 1952-60. Fellow NIH, 1960-62, grantee, 1965, 68; recipient Chemistry award, Hope Coll., 1956. Mem. Fed. Socs. Expl. Biology, Nat. Com. Lab Standards (hepatitis subcom. 1983—); fellow Abbott Labs (Outstanding Research award 1981). Presbyterian. Avocations: Jogging; traveling; photography; music. Home: 924 Castlewood Ln Deerfield IL 60015 Office: Dept Virology & Immunology Abbott Labs 14th and Sheridan Rds North Chicago IL 60064

DECKER, SCOTT HENDERSON, criminal justice educator; b. Evanston, Ill., July 17, 1950; s. Ralph Howard and Bettie Jean (Henderson) D.; m. Jo Ann Smith, June 15, 1974; children—Sara Ann, Laura Henderson. B.A., DePauw U., 1972; M.A., Fla. State U., 1974, Ph.D., 1976. Asst. prof. adminstrn. justice Ind. U., Ft. Wayne, 1976-77; asst. prof. U. Mo., St. Louis, 1977-81, research fellow, 1980—, assoc. prof., 1981—, chmn. dept., 1983—. Author: Criminalization, Victimization and Structural Characteristics of 26 American Cities, 1980; Juvenile Justice Policy, 1983. Contbr. articles to profl. jours. Editor Am. Jour. Police, 1984—. Cons. Crusade Against Crime, St. Louis, 1983-84. Fellow Nat. Inst. Justice, 1983, 84. Home: 7324 Cornell University City MO 63130 Office: U Mo Dept Adminstrn Justice 8001 Natural Bridge Saint Louis MO 63121

DECKER-SPANGENBERG, BARBARA JEAN, artist, forms analyst, gallery administrator; b. Ft. Snelling, Minn., Sept. 27, 1941; d. Lawrence Joseph and Margaret Christene (Menger) Decker; m. Robert J. Spangenberg, Aug. 31, 1968; children—Linda, Gary. B.A. in Sociology, Coll. St. Catherine, St. Paul, 1963; B.F.A. in Sculpture, U. Minn., 1978, postgrad. in library sci., 1978-82. Caseworker mil. services ARC, St. Paul, 1963-65; adoption caseworker Catholic Welfare Services, Mpls., 1965-67; home finder Wilder-Children Services, St. Paul, 1967-68; assoc. forms analyst St. Paul Cos., 1979-85, analyst, 1985—; trainer spl. projects-graphics, 1981-83; founding mem., gallery coordinator WAVE Art Gallery, St. Paul, 1983-84; exhibited in one-woman show: St. Paul YWCA, 1981; group shows: U. Minn., 1975, 77, 78, Coll. St. Thomas, 1978, St. Paul YWCA, 1980; represented in permanent collections: St. Paul Cos., Winter & Assocs., Mpls.; gallery cons., juror YWCA, St. Paul, 1975, 83; cons. graphics Coll. St. Catherine, 1981. Community organizer Highland Neighbors, St. Paul, 1972-78, cons., 1978-82; cons. Highland Area Resident Bus. Ptnrs., St. Paul, 1982-83. Mem. Minn. Artists Exhbn. Program, Art Librarians, Mpls. Inst. Arts, Walker Art Ctr., Women's Art Registry Movement (assoc.; WAVE coordinator 1983). Home: 2130 Pinehurst Ave Saint Paul MN 55116

DECKMAN, JOSEPH THOMAS, construction supply company executive; b. Balt., Sept. 15, 1943; s. Joseph Harward and Florine (Green) D.; m. Cathy Gale Curtiss, July 15, 1968 (div. June 1975) children—Michael, Jason; m. Marcia Kay Coulter, Nov. 15, 1980; children—Trenton, Kate. B.S. in Civil Engring., Lehigh U., 1966, B.S. in Bus. Adminstrn., 1967. Pres., R. Robinson Inc., Washington, 1967-77; sales mgr. Silver Hill Concrete Co., Washington, 1977-80; mgr. product devel. Master Builders, Martin Marietta Corp., Cleve., 1980-83, mgr. strategic planning, 1983, v.p. internat. ops., 1984—. Mem. ASCE, Am. Concrete Inst. (com. 309, 226). Methodist. Home: 3536 Fenley Cleveland Heights OH 44121 Office: Master Builders Div Martin Marietta Corp 23700 Chagrin Blvd Cleveland OH 44122

DE COSTER, MILES MCCALL, artist, publisher; b. California, Mo., Mar. 13, 1950; s. Richard Joseph and Jane Delores (Herst) DeC. B.F.A., Washington U., 1972; M.F.A., Sch. Art Inst. Chgo., 1979. Editor, printer Sch. Art Inst. Publs. Office, Chgo., 1977-79; editor Argot mag., Chgo., 1979—; artist-in-residence Chgo. Council Fine Arts, 1979-80; asst. dir. Word City, 1980-82; pres. Art Equity Inc., 1980—; vis. faculty U. Ill., Chgo. Circle, 1980-81, Art Inst. Chgo., 1981; co-founder Permanent Press, Chgo., 1978—; dir. Bookspace, 1981-83; art dir. In These Times, 1983—. Bd. dirs. N.A.M.E. Gallery, 1982-83, WhiteWalls, 1983—. Author: Scotoma, 1978; Photoaccuracy, 1978; Coloraccuracy, 1979; The Cereal Wars, 1979; Sleight of Hand, 1980; Iconomics: Money, 1984. Home: 3847 N Lincoln Ave Chicago IL 60613

DECRANE, VINCENT FRANCIS, construction co. executive; b. Cleve., Aug. 27, 1927; s. Alfred Charles and Verona Ida (Marquard) DeC.; m. Flora Elizabeth Friday; children—Barbara Bumbacco, Peter, Donna Panzica, Michael, Melinda, Melissa, Joan, Mary Jean. B.S. in Archtl. Engring., U. Notre Dame, 1950. Field engr., Gt. Lakes Dredge & Dock Co., Cleve., 1950; engr., estimator Dunlop & Johnston, Inc., Cleve., 1952-59, sec.-treas., 1959-75, exec. v.p., sec., 1975—; gen. ptnr. Sawmill Creek Lodge Co., Cleve., 1971—. Chmn. com. United Way Cleve., 1971—; chmn. bd., pres. Brentwood Hosp., 1981-85; pres. Catholic Charities Corp., 1980-82; trustee Community Dialysis Ctr., Inc., Gilmour Acad.; mem. Lyndhurst (Ohio) Planning Commn.; trusteeship com. Greater Cleve. Hosp. Assn. Served with AUS, 1946-47, 50-52. Mem. Builders Exchange (pres. 1981—), Cleve. Engring. Soc., Constrn. Employers Assn., Am. Inst. Constructors, Constrn. Industry Affairs Com., Greater Cleve. Growth Assn., Warrensville Heights C. of C. (hon. dir.). Roman Catholic. Club: Mayfield Country. Office: 17900 Miles Ave Warrensville Heights OH 44128

DE DECKERE, DORIS C., public relations executive; b. Grosse Pointe, Mich., Aug. 21; d. George Joseph and Lillian Anna (Pipper) Clutterbuck; ed. Wayne State U.; student U. Mich. Extension, Detroit Inst. Musical Arts; m. Robert O. DeDeckere, Sept. 9, 1950; children—Robert, David, James, Adrienne. Exec. sec. Recorder's Court, Detroit, from 1968; vice chmn. Mayor's Narcotics Com., Detroit; chmn. Pub. Health Commn.. Detroit, 1970-73; asso. dir. Mayor's Com. Human Resources Devel., 1973-74; dir. pub. relations Metro Detroit March of Dimes, 1974-77, 78-81 Detroit Inst. Tech., 1977-78, Island of Boblo, 1981-84; pres. Jade/Assocs., Inc., 1984—; coordinator ethnic classroom project at Wayne State U.; pub. relations cons. to community theatre groups, colls. and businesses; free lance writer, 1965—. Chmn. Housing Poor Peoples March for Eastside of Detroit, 1967; chmn. Christian Services St. Matthews Ch., 1969-72; pres. bd. trustees Detroit Community Music Sch., 1979-81; trustee Project Headline. Recipient Spirit of Detroit medal, 1973, Gov.'s Minute Man award, 1981; certs. of appreciation Mem. Women in Communication, Women in Advt. Pub. Relations Soc. Am., Univ. Cultural Center Assn., Detroit Press Club, Econ. Club of Detroit, Friends of Detroit Library, Women's Economic Club, Friends of Natural History Mus. Roman Catholic. Club: Breakfast of Detroit. Contbr. poetry to various mags. and articles to community publs. Home: 4842 Audubon Detroit MI 48224 Office: 151 W Jefferson Detroit MI 48226

DEDEURWAERDER, JOSE J., automobile manufacturing company executive; b. Halle, Belgium, Dec. 31, 1932; s. Louis and Philippine (Paternot) D.; m. Nelly Clemens, May 14, 1955; 1 child, Joelle. B.S. in Engring., Ecole Technique Superieure de Schaerbeck, 1952. Mng. dir. Renault Belgium, 1958-67; ind. dir. Renault Argentina, 1967-73; chief exec. officer Renault Mex., 1973-76; dir. Dovai (France) assembly plant Renault, 1976-81; exec. v.p. Am. Motors Corp., Southfield, Mich., 1981, pres., dir., 1982—. Served with Belgian Navy, 1952-54. Office: Am Motors Corp 27777 Franklin Rd Southfield MI 48034

DEEB, GARY JAMES, television commentator, columnist; b. Buffalo, Oct. 23, 1945; s. Michael J. and Elvira R. (Popa) D.; m. Susan E. Prill, May 26, 1984. Student SUNY-Buffalo, 1963-64. Newsman, announcer various TV and radio stas., Buffalo, 1962-69; TV columnist Buffalo News, 1969-73, Chgo. Tribune, 1973-80, Chgo. Sun-Times, 1980-83; syndicated columnist News Am. Syndicate, Irvine, Calif., 1980—; media commentator Sta. WLS-TV, Chgo., 1983—. Contbr. articles to Variety, More, Saturday Review and Playboy Mags. Served with USAR, 1966-72. Recipient Annual Pub. Service award Citizens Com. on the Media, Chgo., 1980, Race Relations in Media award Northeastern Ill. U., Chgo., 1981; nine time Pulitzer Prize nominee for commentary and criticism. Democrat. Roman Catholic. Office: WLS-TV 190 N State St Chicago IL 60601

DE EDWARDS, SHARON YVETTE, physician; b. Panama Canal Zone, Sept. 16, 1953; came to U.S., 1978; d. Eddie and Ismay Leotha (Clarke) Willock; m. Fernando Anthony Edwards, II, June 25, 1977; children—Fernando Anthony III, Dorian Alexander. M.D., U. Panama, 1977. Intern Santo Tomas Hosp., Panama City, 1977-78; ob-gyn resident Hurley Med. Ctr., Flint, Mich., 1979-83; practice medicine specializing in ob-gyn Health Central, Lansing, Mich., 1982—. Fellow Am. Fertility Soc. (assoc.), Am. Coll. Ob-Gyn (jr.); mem. AMA. Episcopalian. Office: Health Central 2316 S Cedar Lansing MI 48919

DEEGAN, JOHN, JR., university administrator, researcher; b. Elizabeth, N.J., Nov. 18, 1944; s. John and Margaret (Pignataro) D.; m. Anita Hope Rochelle, Dec. 19, 1964; children—Michael J., Matthew B. Student, Monmouth Coll., West Long Branch (N.J.), 1962-64; B.S., Evangel Coll., Springfield, Mo., 1967; M.A., U. Mich., 1969, Ph.D., 1972. Asst. prof. Rice U., Houston, 1972-75; asst. prof. U. Rochester, N.Y., 1975-80, assoc. prof., 1980; spl. asst. to dep. adminstr. EPA, Washington, 1980, dir. Love Canal Project, 1980-82; assoc. dean Sch. Pub. Health, U. Ill.-Chgo., 1982-83, acting dean, 1983—; cons. EPA, 1983—; trustee Ill. Cancer Council, 1983—. Contbr. articles to sci. jours. Pres., Williamsburg Village Homeowners Assn., Evanston, Ill., 1985. Recipient EPA Bronze medal award, 1982; U. Rochester fellow in Preventive Medicine, 1979. Mem. Am. Pub. Health Assn., Ill. Pub. Health Assn., Assn. Schs. Pub. Health, Am. Assn. Cancer Edn., AAAS, Delta Omega. Democrat. Presbyterian. Avocations: fishing, sailing. Office: Univ Ill Sch Pub Health Box 6998 Chicago IL 60680

DEER, WILLIAM HENRY, lawyer; b. Indpls., Dec. 20, 1930; s. Leon and Mary Jane (Ostheimer) D.; m. Helen Glende, Aug. 4, 1978. B.A., DePauw U., 1953; LL.B., Harvard U., 1956. Bar: Ind. 1956, Ill. 1958. Assoc., Ross, Hardies, O'Keefe & Babcock, Chgo., 1959-76; sole practice, Dolton, Ill., 1977—. Vice pres., bd. dirs. Dr. K.F. Luke Found., South Holland, 1981—; cons. Episcopal-Chinese Activities, Chgo. Diocese, Nat. Trust Hist. Preservation, 1979-83; mem. Lyric Opera Chgo., 1966-83. Served with AUS, 1956-58. DePauw U. Rector scholar, 1952. Mem. Ill. Bar Assn., Chgo. Bar Assn., South Suburban Bar Assn., Phi Beta Kappa. Office: 1350 E Sibley Blvd Suite 206 Dolton IL 60419

DEFABIIS, SUSANNE MARIE, nurse; b. N.Y.C., Mar. 22, 1943; d. Emidio DeFabiis and Maria Verdiglione. B.S. in Nursing, D'Youville Coll., 1967; M.S. in Psychiat. Nursing, St. Xavier Coll., 1974. Registered profl. nurse, Ind., Ill., N.J., N.Y. Asst. dir. nursing service Nazareth Nursing Home, Buffalo, 1967-69; staff nurse Ill. State Psychiat. Inst., Chgo., 1971; psychiat. supr. Jackson Park Hosp., Chgo., 1971-72; asst. head nurse Little Co. of Mary Hosp., Evergreen Park, Ill., part-time 1972-73; instr. psychiat. nursing DePaul U., Chgo., 1973-75; clin. specialist psychiatry Christ Hosp., Oak Lawn, Ill., 1975-79; clin. coordinator mental health Mercy Hosp. and Med. Ctr., Chgo., 1977-78; cons. psychiat. mental health Bethany-Garfield Park Community Hosp., Chgo., part-time, 1978-79; dir. psychiat. nursing Our Lady of Mercy Hosp., Dyer, Ind., 1979-80; practitioner, tchr. psychiat. nursing Rush-Presbyterian-St. Luke's Med. Ctr., Chgo., 1980-81, practitioner, tchr. med. nursing, 1981-82, coordinator nursing systems mgmt., 1982; med./psychiat. liaison nurse, clin. specialist Loyola U. Med. Ctr., Maywood, Ill., 1982—; instr. nursing Rush U., Chgo., 1980—; lectr. in field to profl. assns. Recipient continuing edn. recognition units Ill. Nursing Assn., 1977-79. Mem. Am. Nurses Assn. (cert. clin. specialist in adult psychiat. nursing), Sigma Theta Tau. Club: Riviera Country (Orland Park, Ill.).

DEFFAA, CLYDE CLIFFORD, garment manufacturing company executive; b. Bend, Oreg., Aug. 9, 1946; s. Edward Louis and Doris Ethel (Hale) E.; m. Susan Marschel, Apr. 12, 1980; children—Kristen Kimberely, Haley Marschel. B.S., St. Louis U., 1969. Security asst. U.S. Dept. State, Washington, 1974-76; chief exec. officer Marine Garment Co., Highland, Ill., 1981—; pres., dir. Demarche Industries Inc., St. Louis. Mem. Williamsburg Found. (Va.), 1983-84, St. Louis Council on World Affairs. Served to maj. USMC, 1978-81. Mem. Am. Mgmt. Assn., Pres.'s Assn. Republican. Presbyterian. Home: 9243 Castle Ragh Ct Saint Louis MO 63132 Office: Marine Garment Co 1317 Pestalozzi St Highland IL 62249 also 710 N Tucker St Suite 309 Saint Louis MO 63101

DEFOSSET, DONALD, wholesale paper sales company executive; b. Cin., Nov. 12, 1921; s. Joseph Gustav and Alice (Sandman) DeF.; student U. Cin., 1945-46; m. Marilyn Herzog, Aug. 24, 1946; children—Donald, Daniel. Salesman Phillips Glass Co., Cin., 1945-46; dist. mgr. Ft. Howard Paper Co., St. Louis, 1947-67; exec. v.p. Royal Papers, Inc., St. Louis, from 1967, now pres. Active P.T.A., Boy Scouts Am. Served with AUS, 1941-45. Presbyn. (deacon). Home: 10228 Thornwood Dr Ladue MO 63124 Office: 1218 S Vandeventer St Saint Louis MO 63110

DE GEEST, RANDY SCOTT, lawyer, magistrate; b. Oskaloosa, Iowa, July 17, 1953; s. Glen L. and Myra Jean (Brubaker) De G.; m. Mindy Joanne Morse, Feb. 22, 1977; 1 child, David Scott. B.A., Drake U., 1974, J.D., 1978. Bar: Iowa 1978, U.S. Dist. Ct. (so. dist.) Iowa. Assoc. Spayde & Rielly, Oskaloosa, 1978-79; ptnr. Morse & De Geest, Oskaloosa, 1979—; jud. magistrate State of Iowa, Oskaloosa, 1979—. Bd. dirs. Mahaska County chpt. ARC, Iowa, 1983—. Democrat. Episcopalian. Office: Morse & De Geest PO Box 316 Oskaloosa IA 52577

DEGERSTROM, JAMES MARVIN, health service orgn. exec.; b. Owosso, Mich., Aug. 9, 1933; s. John Marcellus and Emma Judith (Folkadahl) D.; B.S. in M.E., Mich. State U., 1955; M.B.A., DePaul U., 1966; m. Ann Blandford, July 3, 1964. Adminstrv. asst. Sunbeam Corp., Chgo., 1955-61; mfg. supt. Internat. Register Co., Inc., Chgo., 1961-65; sr. engr. Kitchens of Sara Lee, Inc., Deerfield, Ill., 1965-71; pres. Edmanson Bock Caterers, Chgo., 1972; mgr. bldg. ops. Jewel Cos., Inc., Barrington, Ill., 1972-81; dir. plant ops. Copley Meml. Hosp., Aurora, Ill., 1981—; bd. dirs., treas. Credit Union, Kitchens of Sara Lee, 1966-70. Served with USAF, 1957-65. Recipient cert. of recognition, Am. Inst. Plant Engrs. Nat. Conf., 1977. Mem. Am. Inst. Indsl. Engrs., Am. Inst. Plant Engrs. (sec. 1977-79). Club: Toastmasters (dist. officer 1982—). Toastmasters (pres. 1981, area gov. 1982, lt. gov. 1983-84, dist. gov. 1984-85). Home: 8650 N Elmore St Niles IL 60648 Office: Lincoln and Western Aves Aurora IL 60507

DEGRAVELLES, WILLIAM DECATUR, JR., physician; b. Jennings, La., Feb. 20, 1928; s. William Decatur and Ara May (Zenor) deG.; B.S., S.W. La. Inst., 1949; M.D., Tulane U., 1952. Intern Charity Hosp. La., New Orleans, 1952-53; splty. tng. in phys. medicine, rehab. N.Y. U., Bellevue Med. Center, N.Y.C., 1953-56; practice medicine, specializing in phys. medicine and rehab.; dir. rehab. service Duke Med. Center, Durham, N.C., 1956-58; chief phys. medicine and rehab. Iowa Meth. Hosp., Des Moines, 1958—; chief phys. medicine and rehab. Younker Meml. Rehab. Center, Des Moines, 1958—, med. dir., 1958—. Med. cons. Easter Seal's Camp Sunnyside, Des Moines; chmn. med. adv. com. Polk County (Iowa) Nat. Found., 1958-65; mem. Gov.'s Com. on Employment Handicapped, 1964. Bd. dirs. Goodwill Industries, Inc., Des Moines, Iowa Easter Seal Soc. Named Physician of Yr., Gov.'s Com. on Employment of Handicapped, 1968, President's Com. on Employment of Handicapped, 1978; recipient Cotton award Iowa chpt. Arthritis and Rheumatism Assn., 1965; award Iowa Parks and Recreation Assn., 1974; Public Citizen of Yr. award Nat. Assn. Social Workers, 1977, Iowa Public Citizen of Yr. award, 1977; Disting. Service award Iowa Gov.'s Com. on Employment of Handicapped, 1976; citation Nat. Therapeutic Recreation Soc., 1977; Gallantry award Nat. Easter Seal Soc. and Iowa Easter Seal Soc., 1978; diplomate Am. Bd. Phys. Medicine and Rehab. Mem. A.M.A., Iowa, Polk County med. socs., Muscular Dystrophy Assn. Am. (med. adviser Polk County chpt.), Nat. Multiple Sclerosis Soc. (chmn. med. adv. com. central Iowa chpt., 1958-66), Iowa Rehab. Assn. (bd. dirs., past pres.), Internat. Assn. Rehab. Facilities (dir. 1973-76). Home: 6024 Ronwood Dr Des Moines IA 50312 Office: 1200 Pleasant St Des Moines IA 50308

DEGRAW, WILLIAM ALLEN, biology educator; b. Washington, Apr. 26, 1939; s. Carl B. and Myrtle (Ludwig) deG.; m. Margaret A. Billard, Apr. 1, 1961; children—Elizabeth, Rebecca, Deborah. B.S., Allegheny Coll., 1961; M.S., Colo. State U., 1965; Ph.D., Wash. State U., 1972. Jr. biologist Strasenburgh Labs., Rochester, N.Y., 1961-62; asst. prof. biology U. Nebr., Omaha, 1969-73, assoc. prof., 1973-80, prof., 1980—. Chmn. speakers bur. Physicians for Social Responsibility, Omaha, 1981-85. Mem. Am. Ornithologists Union, Cooper Ornithol. Soc., Inland Bird Banding Assn. Methodist. Office: U Nebr 60th and Dodge Sts Omaha NE 68182

DEHAAN, CHRISTEL, vacation exchange company executive; b. Nordlingen, W.Ger., Oct. 20, 1942; came to U.S., 1962; d. Adolf and Anna M. B. (Engel) Stark; m. Jon H. DeHaan, July 16, 1973; children—Keith, Tim, Kirsten. Student Ind. Central U., 1972, 73, 82. Co-founder Resort Condominiums Internat., Indpls., 1974, exec. v.p., 1974—; pres. Vacation Horizons Internat. (merged with Resort Condominiums Internat. 1984), Indpls., 1981-84. Bd. dirs. Nat. Adoption Exchange. Recipient Bronze medal Internat. Film Festival/Indsl. Film, 1982; Jon and Christel DeHaan Day named and recipient commendation Mayor Indpls., 1983. Mem. Am. Land Devel. Assn. (dir.), Nat. Timeshare Council (vice chairperson governing bd. 1982-83, award 1983), Am. Soc. Travel Agts., C. of C. Indpls., Better Bus. Bur. Indpls., Indpls. Zoo, Children's Museum, Indpls. Mus. Art. Clubs: Meridian Hills Country, Skyline. Pub. Endless Vacation mag., 1975-83. Office: 9333 N Meridian St Indianapolis IN 46280

DEHAAN, JON HOLDEN, vacation exchange executive; b. Ann Arbor, Mich., July 7, 1940; s. William and Kathleen Helen (Holden) DeH.; m. Christel Stark, July 16, 1973; children—Keith, Tim, Kirsten. B.A. with honors, Claremont Men's Coll., 1963; M.B.A. with distinction Ind. U., 1966; postgrad. U. Pa. Wharton Sch. Fin., 1966-69. Cons. Econ. Research Assocs., Los Angeles, 1969-70; dir. camping div. Brynmawr Parks Corp. affiliate Ramada Inns, 1970-71; dir. fin. community devel. div. Intertherm Corp., 1972-73; chmn. bd. Resort Condominiums Internat., Indpls., 1974—; founding dir. Nat. TimeSharing Found.; founding dir., v.p. pub. relations Internat. Found. for TimeSharing; speaker in field. Honored with mayoral proclamations City of Miami (Fla.), 1982, City of Indpls., 1983, 84. Mem. Am. Soc. Travel Agts., Am. Land Devel. Assn. (dir., co-chmn. Camp Coast-to-Coast program), Nat. TimeSharing Council (dir. 1976—), Am. Hotel/Motel Assn., Indpls. C. of C., Fla. C. of C. Republican. Episcopalian. Office: 9333 N Meridian Indianapolis IN 46260

DEHAVEN, DANIEL HOWARD, elementary principal; b. Gary, Ind., Jan. 22, 1951; s. Samuel Howard and Audrey May (Harbit) D.; m. Nikki Sue

Blystone, Oct. 28, 1976; children—Jeremy, Jordan, Ashlie, Daniel. B.S. in Edn., Calumet Coll., 1974; M. Elementary Edn., Ind. U., 1977, Specialist in Edn., 1981. Tchr. 6th grade Polk Elementary, Lake Station, Ind., 1974-77, prin., 1977—; varsity basketball coach Edison High Sch., Lake Station, 1976-77; jr. varsity coach, 1975-76, 77-80. Mem. Nat. Assn. Elementary Sch. Prins. Presbyterian. Avocations: camping; basketball; softball; woodworking. Office: Carl J Polk Elementary Sch 2460 Vermillion St Lake Station IN 46405

DEHAVEN, ERNEST THOMAS, association executive; b. Hiram Twp., Ohio, Aug. 7, 1928; s. Ernest Roy and Bertha Catherine (Thomas) DeH.; m. Barbara Ann Hoskin, Aug. 21, 1955; children—Matthew, Stephen, Catherine. A.B., Hiram Coll., 1949; M.H.A., Va. Commonwealth U., 1957. Lic. nursing home adminstr., Iowa. Adminstr. Albert Schweitzer Meml. Hosp., St. Mark, Haiti, 1958-59, Jackman Meml. Hosp., Bilaspur, India, 1959-64; asst. adminstr. Lake County Meml. Hosp., Painesville, Ohio, 1965-67; adminstr. Carroll County Meml. Hosp., Carrollton, Ky., 1967-77; exec. dir. Wesley Manor, Frankfort, Ind., 1977-82; adminstr. Ramsey Meml. Home, Des Moines, 1982—; regional ops. dir. Nat. Benevolent Assn., 1985—. Served with AUS, 1953-54. Mem. Am. Coll. Health Care Adminstrs., Am. Coll. Hosp. Adminstrs., Am. Mgmt. Assn., Des Moines Choral Soc. Mem. Christian Ch. (Disciples of Christ). Avocation: Choral singing. Home: 7008 Townsend St Des Moines IA 50322 Office: Ramsey Meml Home 1611 27th St Des Moines IA 50310

DEHOUSKE, CHRISTINE ANN, computer consulting executive; b. Erie, Pa., Sept. 14, 1948; d. Joseph C. and Stacy (Czerwinski) Dworakowski; m. William J. Dehouske, Sept. 30, 1972. B.A. in Math., Mercyhurst Coll., 1970; postgrad. Pa. State U., 1972. Programmer, analyst Hammermill Paper Co., Erie, 1970-72; sr. systems analyst Cuyahoga County, Ohio, 1973-77; mgr. systems and programming Computer Scis. Corp., Cleve., 1977-80; supr. cons. Ernst and Whinney, Cleve., 1980-82, mgr. cons., 1982-85, prin., 1985—. Co-chmn. Task Force on Violent Crime, Cleve., 1982—; active Greater Cleve. Growth Assn., 1981—, Citizen's League, Cleve., 1982—. Recipient Career Woman of Achievement award Cleve. YWCA, 1984. Mem. EDP Auditors' Assn., Computer Security Inst., Parma Polish-Am. League (sec. 1978-80). Roman Catholic. Office: Ernst and Whinney 1300 Huntington Bldg Cleveland OH 44115

DEIGHAN, THOMAS EDWARD, accountant, real estate developer; b. Cleve., Jan. 1, 1959; s. William Patrick and Geraldine (Loftus) D.; m. Lee Ann Onder, Sept. 1, 1984. B.B.A., John Carroll U., 1981; M.B.A., Cleve. State U., 1984. Pres., Deighan, Westerkamp & Deighan, Cleve., 1983—. Pres., Catholic Big Bros. and Big Sisters, 1981—. Mem. Iota Beta Gamma (pres. 1979-81). Roman Catholic. Club: Irish (Cleve.). Home: 2345 Grandview Rd Cleveland Heights OH 44106

DEINES, VERNON PHILLIP, planning educator, consultant; b. Bazine, Kans., July 28, 1929; s. David Emil Deines and Vera Mae (Coates) Hodge; m. Doris Marie Dishman, Jan. 1, 1955; children—Debra Anne, Sharon Lee, Carol May, Erich Vernon. A.A., St. John's Coll., 1949; B.S. in Archtl. Engring., Kans. State Coll., 1952; M.R.P. in Planning, Kans. State U., 1962; Ph.D. in Adminstrn., U. Pitts., 1977. Registered profl. engr., Kans. Design engr. Mcdonnel Airplane Co., St. Louis, 1952; research engr. Aberdeen Proving Ground, Dept. Def., Md., 1954-57; planning cons., Manhattan, Kans., 1957—; dir. Ctr. Regional and Community Planning, prof., head dept. regional and community planning Kans. State U., Manhattan, 1966—; cons. to various univs., pvt. orgns., and local, state and fed. govtl. agys. Contbr. articles to profl. jours. Bd. dirs. Kans. Planning and Devel. Assn., 1968-70; mem. adv. com. on community service Kans. Edn. Commn., 1970-74; mem. com. on continuing edn. Kans. Bd. Regents, 1974-75; mem. task force on non-point source pollution Kans. Dept. Environment, 1981-85. Served with U.S. Army, 1952-54. Fellow R.K. Mellon Found., 1964-65, NSF sci. faculty, 1965-66. Mem. Am. Planning Assn. (div. chmn. 1980-84), Assn. Collegiate Schs. Planning (pres. 1971-73), Am. Inst. Planners (chpt pres. 1973-75), Am. Inst. Cert. Planners (chpt. officer 1977-84), Phi Kappa Phi. Lutheran. Avocations: sports; reading; travel. Office: Kans State U Seaton Hall 302 Manhattan KS 66506

DEINZER, GEORGE WILLIAM, charitable organization administrator; b. Tiffin, Ohio, Nov. 1, 1934; s. Harvey Charles and Edna Louise (Harpley) D.; A.B., Heidelberg Coll., 1956; postgrad. Washington U., 1956-57. Asst. to dir. phys. plant Heidelberg Coll., 1957-58, admissions counselor, 1958-60, dir. admissions, 1960-71, dir. fin. aids, asso. dir. admissions, 1971-80; exec. dir. Tiffin-Seneca United Way, 1980—. Voting rep. Coll. Entrance Examination Bd., 1963-80; fin. aid cons. Nat. Collegiate Athletic Assn.; cons. Ohio Scholarship Funds, 1960-61. Pres., chmn. allocations com., bd. dirs. United Way; pres. lay bd. Mercy Hosp.; treas., bd. dirs. N.W. Ohio Health Planning Assn., co-chmn. steering com., 1984; mem. legis. com. Ohio Citizens Council, 1981—, human services task force, 1984—; pres. Seneca County Mus.; treas. Tiffin Theatre, Inc.; mem. Seneca Indsl. and Econ. Devel. Corp. Bd., 1983—; chmn. Tiffin Area Devel. and Pub. Relations Dirs., 1984—. Mem. Nat., Ohio (regional coordinator, treas., state trainer, chmn. needs analysis com.) assns. student fin. aid adminstrs., Ohio Athletic Conf. Fin. Dirs. (past chmn.), Internat. Platform Assn., Am. Personnel and Guidance Assn., Am. Coll. Personnel Assn., Council Ohio United Way Execs., Farm Bur., Ohio Hist. Soc., N. Central Ohio Council on Alcoholism, U.S. Naval Inst., Buckeye Sheriffs Assn., Beta Beta Beta. Republican. Lodges: Rotary (dir., pres. 1982-83), Elks. Contbr. articles to profl. jours. Home: 197 Jefferson St Tiffin OH 44883

DEISTER, CHRISTINE ROSEMARY, airline executive; b. Lowestoft, Eng., Apr. 16, 1949; came to U.S., 1973; d. Douglas Stephen and Vera (Mears) Smith; m. Terrence Leonard Deister, Aug. 28, 1976; 1 dau., Nicole Stephanie. Student Felixstowe High Sch., Eng.; gen. cert. edn. U. London; cert. pianoforte Royal Schs. Music. Supr. revenue acctg. Trans World Airlines, London, 1967-73, supr. air freight systems and acctg., Kansas City, Mo., 1973-79, mgr. credit ops., Kansas City, 1979-81, mgr. disbursements, Kansas City, 1981—; treas., corp. officer Duncourt & Assocs., Kansas City, Mo. Bus. coordinator Heart of Am. United Way, 1981. Recipient Charles C. Tillinghast award; named Employee of Yr., Controller's Dept. TWA, 1978. Mem. Internat. Concerns Com. for Children. Home: RR 27 Box 277D Parkville MO 64152 Office: TWA 11500 NW Ambassador Dr Kansas City MO 64153

DEITERING, JOHN EDWARD, corporate executive; b. Ottoville, Ohio, Aug. 10, 1939; s. Leo Joseph and Rosa Violet Deitering; m. Nioma Martha Kortokrax, Aug. 24, 1940; children—Deborah, Sandra, Jeffrey, Annette, John Edward Jr. B.A. in Acctg., Ind. U., 1966. Acctg. supr. Assocs. Investment Co., South Bend, Ind., 1961-66; mgr. data processing Meml. Hosp., Lima, Ohio, 1966-68; systems engr., regional mgr. NCR Corp., Dayton, Ohio, 1968-82, requirements analyst, Europe, 1982-83; pres. Electroaids Inc., Sidney, Ohio, 1983—; instr. Edison State Coll., 1976-78. Mem. Republican Elections Com., 1979. Served with USN, 1959-61. Mem. Data Processing Profl. Users Assn., Am. Legion, VFW. Republican. Roman Catholic. Lodge: K.C. Office: 315 N Ohio Ave Sidney OH 45365

DEITZ, ROBERT DAVID, protective coatings manufacturing company executive; b. Cleve., Dec. 26, 1926; s. Joseph H. and Irene (Mates) D.; m. Sallie Eisen, Jan. 26, 1950; children—Jo-Anne Deitz Daniels, Diana Deitz Russel. B.B.A., Case Western Res. U., 1948. Export mgr. Consol. Paint and Varnish Corp., Cleve., 1948-57; v.p. Consol. Protective Coatings Corp. and subs. Consol. Inter-Continental Corp., Consol. Protective Coatings Ltd., Cleve., Montreal, Que., Can., 1957, pres., 1958—; dir. Hastings Pavement corp., L.I., N.Y. Chmn. budget com. United Way Services, Cleve., 1972-75; trustee Mt. Sinai Med. Ctr., Cleve., 1971-78; pres. Jewish Vocat. Service, 1970-73; vice chmn. Dist. Export Council, Dept. Commerce, 1975-83; pres. Menorah Park Jewish Home for Aged, Beachwood, Ohio, 1976-78. Served with USMC, 1945-46. Recipient Kane award Jewish Community Fedn., 1965; Man of Yr. award Orgn. Rehab. Tng., 1981. Office: Consolidated Protective Coatings Corp 202 Ohio Savs Plaza Cleveland OH 44114

DEJARNETTE, GLENDA, speech and language pathologist, educator; b. Cleve., May 7, 1957; d. Joseph and Fannie B. (Parker) DeJarnette. B.A. in Speech Communications with honors, Allegheny Coll., 1978; M.A. in Speech-Lang. Pathology, Cleve. State U., 1980; Ph.D., Bowling Green (Ohio) State U., 1984. Lic. speech and hearing pathologist, Ohio. Supr. aspiring speech-lang. pathologists, instr. speech-lang. pathology Bowling Green State U., 1980-84; asst. prof. East Tenn. State U., Johnson City, 1984—. Cleve. scholar, 1974-78; Kiwanis scholar, 1975-78, recipient Outstanding Mem. award Assn. Black Collegians of Allegheny Coll., 1978; Outstanding Speech-Lang. Pathologist award Cleve. State U., 1980. Mem. Am. Speech-Lang. and Hearing Assn., Ohio Speech-Lang. and Hearing Assn., Nat. Black Am. Speech-Lang. and Hearing Assn. Contbr. articles to profl. jours. Office: Communicative Disorders East Tenn State U PO Box 21 790A Johnson City TN 37614

DEKKER, EUGENE EARL, biochemist, educator, researcher; b. Highland, Ind., July 23, 1927; s. Peter and Anne (Hendrikse) D.; m. Harriet E. Holwerda, July 5, 1958; children—Gwen E., Paul D., Tom R. A.B., Calvin Coll., 1949; M.S., U. Ill., Urbana, 1951, Ph.D., 1954. Asst. prof. biochemistry U. Louisville, 1954-56; asst. prof. biochemistry U. Mich., Ann Arbor, 1956-65, assoc. prof., 1965-70, prof., 1970—, assoc. chmn., 1975—. Served with USN, 1945-46. Recipient Amoco Outstanding Teaching award, 1978; Life Ins. Med. Research fellow, 1956-58; Lederle med. faculty award, 1958-61; NIH spl. research fellow, 1965-66, 73-74, 81-82. Mem. Am. Chem. Soc., Am. Soc. Biol. Chemists, Am. Soc. Plant Physiologists, Sigma Xi. Avocations: tennis, fishing, sailing, gardening. Home: 2612 Manchester Rd Ann Arbor MI 48104 Office: Dept Biol Chemistry Box 034 U Mich Med Sch Ann Arbor MI 48109

DEKOSTER, LUCAS J(AMES), lawyer; b. Hull, Iowa, June 18, 1918; s. John and Sarah Katherine (Poppen) DeK.; m. Dorothea LaVonne Hymans, Dec. 30, 1942; children—Sarah K, Jacqueline A., John G., Claire E., Mary D. B.S. in Mech. Engring. Iowa State U., 1939; J.D. cum laude, Cleve.-Marshall Law Sch., 1949. Bar: Iowa, 1952. Aerospace research scientist NASA, Hampton, Va., 1940-44, Cleve., 1944-49; patent atty., agt. J.D. Douglass Co., Cleve., 1949-51; sole practice, Hull, 1952-79; ptnr. DeKoster & DeKoster, Hull, 1979—; mem. Iowa Senate, 1964-82; pres. Mut. Fire and Auto Ins. Co., Cedar Rapids, Iowa, 1979—; mem. Iowa Bd. Pub. Instrn., Des Moines, 1982—, chmn., 1984—. Mem. ABA, Iowa Bar Assn. (chmn. com. 1983—). Republican. Mem. Reformed Ch. in Am. Lodge: Kiwanis (lt. gov. 1984). Avocations: reading, travelling. Office: Dept Pub Instrn Grimes Office Bldg Des Moines IA 50319 also 1106 Main St Hull IA 51239

DELAHANTY, EDWARD LAWRENCE, management consultant; b. South Bend, Ind., Feb. 17, 1942; s. Edward Lawrence and Rosemary Margaret (DeVreese) D.; B.S. in Math., U. Notre Dame, 1963; m. Rebecca A. Paczesny, June 22, 1963; children—David Edward, Debra Ann. Asst. actuary Aetna Life & Casualty Co., Hartford, Conn., 1963-70; mng. partner Hewitt Assocs., Mpls., 1971—, mem. exec. com., 1981—; v.p., sec.-treas., dir. CMI Stores Inc., 1983-85; dir. Brandt Barringmann Inc., 1981-84. Enrolled actuary. Fellow Soc. Actuaries mem. Am. Acad. Actuaries, Am. Soc. Personnel Adminstrs., Twin Cities Actuarial Club, Twin Cities Personnel Assn., Midwest Pension Conf. Clubs: Wayzata Country (dir. 1978-84), Mpls. Athletic, Mpls. Home: 511 N Ferndale Rd Wayzata MN 55391 Office: 1115 1st National Bank Bldg Minneapolis MN 55402

DELAINE, SONIA YVETTE, day care center administrator, educator; b. Cin., Dec. 8, 1957; d. Ben William and Grace Anne (Dangerfield) D.; 1 child, Danielle Renee. B.S. in Edn., U. Cin., 1981. Cert. tchr., Ohio. Maj. med. claims processor Blue Cross and Blue Shield, Cin., 1979-81; dir. Porter Day Care Ctr., Cin., 1981—; instr. Head Start, Cin. Bd. Edn., 1984—. Leader Great Rivers council Girl Scouts U.S.A., 1983—; active Met. C.M.E. Ch., Cin. Mem. Phi Delta Kappa. Democrat. Home: 3935 Zinsle Ave #2 Cincinnati OH 45213

DELANEY, JOHN MARTIN, JR., lawyer; b. Alton, Ill., Aug. 14, 1956; s. John Martin and Joan Margaret (Galloway) D. B.A., St. Louis U., 1978, J.D., 1981. Bar: Ill. 1981, U.S. Dist. Ct. (so. dist.) Ill. 1985. Law clk. Madison County Cts., Edwardsville, Ill., 1978-79, Dunham Boman & Leskera, East St. Louis, Ill., 1980-81; asst. states atty. Madison County States Atty.'s Office, Edwardsville, 1981-84; assoc. Allen, Mendenhall & Assocs., Alton, Ill., 1985—. Bd. dirs. Central Baptist Bd., Collinsville, Ill., 1982-83, Blue Knights Law Enforcement, Edwardsville, 1983—. Named to Outstanding Young Men Am., U.S. Jaycees, 1983. Mem. Assn. Trial Lawyers Am., ABA, Ill. State Bar Assn., Madison County Bar Assn., Alton-Wood River Bar Assn. Roman Catholic. Office: Allen Mendenhall & Associates 2010 State St Alton IL 62002

DELANEY, MARY MURRAY (LANE, MARY D.), author, travel agency executive; b. New Richmond, Wis., Jan. 1, 1913; d. Christopher James Murray and Rachel (Newell) Turner Murray; m. Thomas James Delaney, Jr., June 1, 1932; children—Thomas James III, Joni Mary Delaney O'Connell. Grad. Twin City Bus. Coll., 1931; student Macalester Coll., St. Paul, 1955-56, 1958. Sec. Montgomery Ward & Co., St. Paul, 1930-32; auditor E. I. duPont de Nemours, Rosemount, Minn., 1942; v.p., tour escort Delaney J Joyce & O'Dell Travel, 1963—; author: Of Irish Ways, 19; contbr. short stories mags., U.S., England, Australia, Norway, Sweden, Denmark, Italy. Contbr. articles to profl. jours. Mem. Nat. League Am. Pen Women. Home: 1606 Highland Pkwy St Paul MN 55116 Office: 249 S Snelling Ave Saint Paul MN 55105

DELANEY, PHILIP ALFRED, banker; b. Chgo., Nov. 18, 1928; s. Walter J. and Kathryn M. (McWilliams) D.; m. Patricia O'Brien, June 21, 1952; children—Sharon Ann, Philip Jr., Nancy, Mary Beth. B.S. magna cum laude, U. Notre Dame, 1950; M.B.A, U. Chgo., 1956; postgrad. Grad. Sch. Banking U. Wis., 1960. Trainee securities, broker, dealer A.G. Becker & Co., Chgo., 1950, 51-52; with Harris Trust and Savs. Bank, Chgo., 1952—, successively asst. cashier, asst. v.p., v.p. comml. banking dept., sr. v.p. banking dept., 1971, group exec. fin. group, 1972, group exec. Midwest Group, exec. in charge Internat. Banking Group, exec. v.p., chief credit officer, 1980, exec. v.p. Harris Bankcorp, Inc., dir. Harris Bank and Harris Bankcorp, 1980-84, pres. 1984—; dir. DeSoto, Inc., Des Plaines, Ill. Bd. dirs. Catholic Charities of Chgo., Chgo. Conv. and Tourism Bur.; mem. Chgo. Urban League Bus. Adv. Council; bd. dirs. Ill. Council on Econ. Edn.; chief crusader United Way, Crusade of Mercy; mem. citizens bd. Loyola U. of Chgo., Chgo. Com. Served to 2d lt. USMC, 1951. Mem. Am. Bankers Assn., Am. Inst. Banking, Am. Mgmt. Assn., Assn. Res. City Bankers, Bankers Club of Chgo., Chgo. Assn. Commerce and Industry, Chgo. Counci on Fgn. Relations, Robert Morris Assocs., U. Chgo. Alumni Assn. Roman Catholic. Clubs: Chgo. Athletic Assn., Comml. Club of Chgo., Commonwealth Club of Chgo., Economics, Mid-America, Notre Dame (Chgo.); North Shore Country.

DELANO, WILLIAM RICHARD, switch systems manufacturing company engineer; b. Chgo., Feb. 1, 1951; s. William Stevens and Louise Catherine (Uccello) D. B.E.E., Ill. Inst. Tech., 1973. Sr. automatic test engr. Northrop Def. Systems Div., Rolling Meadows, Ill., 1974-79; sr. project leader Genrad Co., Schaumburg, Ill., 1979-81; systems engr. Tex. Instruments Corp., Arlington Heights, Ill., 1981-82; tech. support mgr. Sun Electric Co., Chgo., 1982-83; sr. automatic test engr. Oak Switch Systems, Inc., Crystal Lake, Ill., 1983—; software designer Delano Cons. Inc., Hoffman Estates, Ill., 1983-84. Designer Tri-Ped robot, 1978, water fall and fountain, 1980. Mem. Republican Task Force, Washington, 1983-84. Roman Catholic. Avocations: music; gardening; movies; sports; robotics. Home: 3730 Whispering Trails Hoffman Estates IL 60195 Office: Oak Switch Systems Inc 100 S Main St Crystal Lake IL 60014

DELATTRE, DWIGHT DAVID, architect; b. Ebensburg, Pa., Apr. 1, 1943; s. Clement George and Mary Marie (Rambeau) DeL.; m. Sheila Mary O'Donnell, Sept. 18, 1965; children—Steven Dwight, Brian David. B.S.A.E., Chgo. Tech. Coll., 1965. Cert. architect, Ill. Draftsman, Jensen & Halstead, Chgo., 1965-66, Kennedy Co., Deerfield, Ill., 1966-69, DelBianco, Schwartz & Donatoni, Chgo., 1969-72; with Kennedy Co., Kennedy Bros., Northbrook, Ill., 1972-75, mgr. drafting dept., 1975-78; owner, architect New Horizons Inc., Arlington Heights, Ill., 1978—. Coach, Little League, Elk Grove Village, Ill., 1975-78; leader Northwest Suburban council Boy Scouts Am., 1975-78. Recipient Archtl. award Des Plaines C. of C., 1982, Mem. AIA, AIA (Chgo. chpt.), Nat. Assn. Home Builders, Home Builders Assn. Greater Chgo. (Bronze Key Design award 1984, 2 Silver Key Design awards 1984). Roman Catholic. Avocations: sailing; scuba diving; skiing; woodworking. Office: New Horizons Inc 3223 N Frontage Rd Suite 2315 Arlington Heights IL 60004

DELAY, WILLIAM RAYMOND, communications executive; b. Texarkana, Tex., June 16, 1929; s. Raymond Wallace and Flora Thomas (Greenwood) DeL.; m. Mary Elinor Dolson, Oct. 2, 1954; children—Martha, Nancy. B.S. in Journalism, U. Kans., William Allen White Sch. Journalism, 1951; postgrad. Mead Johnson Inst., 1958-59, Counter Intelligence Corps. Sch., 1951. Reporter Kansas City Kansan, 1951; reporter, copy editor Kansas City Times, 1953-56; pub. relations mgr. Mead Johnson & Co., 1956-60; dir. pub. relations Am. Acad. Family Physicians, 1960-71, dir. communications div., 1971—, founder Am. Acad. Family Physicians Reporter, 1974; advt. promotion mgr. Am. Family Physician mag., 1962-69; instr. pub. relations U. Mo.-Kansas City, 1979; lectr. pub. relations NYU, U. Kans. U. Nev. Chmn. pub. info. com. and exec. com. Am. Cancer Soc., West Met. Area Mo. div. Served with U.S. Army, 1951-53. Recipient U.S. C. of C. Disting. Achievement award, 1962; Gold medal N.Y. Film Festival, 1967. Mem. Pub. Relations Soc. Am. (Silver Anvil award 1980; Prism award Kansas City chpt. 1980, 85; Profl. of Year award 1982, President's award 1985), Soc. Profl. Journalists, Kansas City Press Club, Nat. Assn. Sci. Writers, Am. Assn. Med. Soc. Execs., Soc. Tchrs. Family Medicine, Acad. Health Services Mktg., Sigma Delta Chi. Roman Catholic. Contbr. to book: Kansas City Out Loud. Office: 1740 W 92d St Kansas City MO 64114

DEL BENE, JANET ELAINE, chemistry educator; b. Youngstown, Ohio, June 3, 1939; d. Anthony Joseph and Elizabeth Josephine (Pastier) Del B. B.S., Youngstown State U., 1963, B.A., 1965; Ph.D., U. Cin., 1968. Postdoctoral fellow U. Wis.-Madison, 1968-69, Mellon Inst., Pitts., 1969-70; asst. prof. Youngstown State U., Ohio, 1970-73, assoc. prof., 1973-76, prof. chemistry, 1976—; research prof. molecular pathology and biology Northeastern Ohio Univs. Coll. Medicine, Rootstown, 1977—; mem. grad. faculty Kent State U., Ohio, 1978—; cons. basic med. scis. Northeastern Ohio Univs. Coll. Medicine, 1976. Mem. Girard Bd. Health, Ohio, 1982—. Recipient Agnes Fay Morgan Research award Iota Sigma Pi, 1972; research grantee NIH, 1974-77, 80-83, 85—, Camille and Henry Dreyfus tchr.-scholar grantee, 1974-79. Fellow AAAS; mem. Am. Chem. Soc. (Irving Langmuir award canvassing com. 1978-83, mem. exec. bd. div. computers in chemistry 1974-76, PRF Type G starter grantee 1971-74), AAAS, N.Y. Acad. Scis., Iota Sigma Pi (award coms.), Phi Kappa Phi. Roman Catholic. Avocations: walking; listening to music. Home: 871 N Ward Ave Girard OH 44420 Office: Dept Chemistry Youngstown State U Youngstown OH 44555

DEL CASTILLO, JULIO CESAR, neurosurgeon; b. Havana, Cuba, Jan. 21, 1930; s. Julio Cesar and Violeta (Diaz de Villegas) Del C.; came to U.S., 1961, naturalized, 1968; B.S., Columbus Sch., Havana, 1948; M.D., U. Havana, 1955; m. Rosario Freire, Sept. 18, 1955; children—Julio Cesar, Juan Claudio, Rosemarie. Intern, Michael Reese Hosp., Chgo., 1955-56; resident Cook County Hosp., Chgo., 1957, Lahey Clinic, Boston, 1957-58, U. Pa. Grad. Hosp., 1958-60; research asst. dept. gen. surgery Jackson Meml. Hosp., Miami, Fla., 1962-64; practice medicine, specializing in neurosurgery, Havana, 1960-61, Quincy, Ill., 1965—; mem. staff Blessing Hosp., Quincy, pres. staff, 1972-74; mem. staff St. Mary's Hosp., Quincy; owner Top Hat Hobbies, Inc., Quincy. Bd. dirs. Western Ill. Found. for Med. Care, 1970—; trustee Blessing Hosp., 1972-74. Mem. Am. Acad. Model Aeros., Congress Neurol. Surgeons, AMA, A.C.S., Adams County Med. Soc. (sec., treas. 1966-75, pres.), Ill. Med. Soc., Exptl. Aircraft Assn. Rotarian (dir. 1970-72, pres. 1976-77). Home: 14 Curved Creek Quincy IL 62301 Office: 1235 Brodway Quincy IL 62301

DELCOMYN, FRED, physiology educator; b. Copenhagen, June 4, 1939; came to U.S., 1947, naturalized, 1960; s. Niels Theodor and Erna A. Delcomyn; m. Nancy Ann Nigg, Dec. 14, 1969; children—Julia C. M., Michael T.W., Erik A.W. B.S., Wayne State U., 1962; M.S., Northwestern U., 1964; Ph.D., U. Oreg., 1969. Research assoc. dept. zoology U. Glasgow (Scotland), 1969-71, lectr. inst. physiology, 1971-72; asst. prof. dept. entomology U. Ill.-Urbana, 1972-77, assoc. prof., 1977—. Contbr. articles to profl. jours., chpts. to books. Fellow U. Ill., 1973; grantee NIH, 1975—. Fellow AAAS; mem. Soc. Exptl. Biology, Soc. Neurosci. Office: U Ill Dept Entomology 505 S Goodwin Urbana IL 61801

DELEE, DENNIS, optometrist; b. Chgo., Dec. 25, 1947; s. Jerry and Jean S. (Garfunkel) DeL.; m. Debra Sue Epstein, Dec. 24, 1970 (div. 1974); m. Karen Lynn Reeves, Apr. 4, 1976; children—Dani, Lindsay. Practice medicine specializing in optometry with Dr. A.H. Udesky, Hoffman Estates, Ill., 1973-75, pvt. practice Chgo., 1975-76, Mundelein, Ill., 1976-81, Tuckerman Optical, Chgo., 1981—, nat. dir. optometric services, Columbus, Ohio, 1984—. Jewish. Avocation: Computing. Home: 3700 N Pine Grove Chicago IL 60613 Office: The Optical Shop/Tuckerman Optical J101 Woodfield Mall Schaumburg IL 60195

DE LEONARDIS, NICHOLAS JOHN, banker; b. Chgo., Nov. 13, 1929; s. John and Marie (Janik) De L.; m. Mary Ellen Kloss, Aug. 17, 1957; children—Deborah Marie, Valerie Ann, Nicolette Mary, Regina Ellen, John Paul. B.S., De Paul U., 1951, M.A., 1968. Salesman, Asher J. Goldfine & Co., Chgo., 1953-55; mem. trust dept. staff First Nat Bank Chgo., 1955-63, with mcpl. sales dept., 1963-65, v.p. money mkt. ctr., 1965-80, v.p., chmn. money mgmt. com., 1980-85; sr. v.p., treas. La Salle Nat. Bank, subs. Algemene Bank Nederland, N.V., 1985—; lectr. De Paul U., Chgo., 1968-78, grad. sch. banking U. Wis.-Madison, 1980—. Contbr. articles to profl. publs. Bd. trustees, past chmn. Found. Hearing and Speech Rehab., Chgo., 1968; pres. Dixon Assn. Retarded Citizens, Ill., 1984. Mem. Investment Analysts Soc. Chgo., Delta Mu Delta. Club: Union League Chgo. Office: La Salle Nat Bank 135 S LaSalle Chicago IL 60603

DE LERNO, MANUEL JOSEPH, elec. engr.; b. New Orleans, Jan. 8, 1922; s. Joseph Salvador and Elizabeth Mabry (Jordan) De L.; B.E. in Elec. Engring., Tulane U., 1941; M.E.E., Rensselaer Poly. Inst., 1943; m. Margery Ellen Eaton, Nov. 30, 1946 (div. Oct. 1978); children—Diane, Douglas. Devel. engr. indsl. control dept. Gen. Electric Co., Schenectady, 1941-44; design engr. Lexington Electric Products Co., Newark, 1946-47; asst. prof. elec. engring. Newark Coll. Engring., 1948-49; test engr. Maschinenfabrik Oerlikon, Zurich, Switzerland, 1947-48; application engr. Henry J. Kaufman Co., Chgo., 1949-55; pres. Del Equipment Co., Chgo., 1955-60; v.p. Del-Ray Co., Chgo., 1960-67; pres. S-P-D Services Inc., Forest Park, Ill., 1967-81, S-P-D Industries, Inc., Berwyn, Ill., 1981—; mem. standards making coms. Nat. Fire Protection Assn. Internat. Served as lt. (j.g.) USNR, 1944-45, to lt. comdr., 1950-52. Registered profl. engr., Ill. Mem. IEEE (sr.), Ill. Soc. Profl. Engrs., Soc. Fire Protection Engrs., Am. Water Works Assn. Home: 67 Warwick Rd Winnetka IL 60093 Office: 3105 S Ridgeland Ave Berwyn IL 60402 also PO Box 96 Kenilworth IL 60043

DELFIN, JOSE BLANCO, physician, surgeon; b. Zambales, Philippines, Jan. 29, 1944; came to U.S., 1970; s. Felix and Vivencia (Blanco) D.; m. Amelia Barba, May 15, 1971; children—Joseph Alexis, Aimee Jo, Annalizza Joy. A.A., U. of East, 1963; M.D., Far Eastern U., 1968. Diplomate Am. Bd. Abdominal Surgery. Assoc. med. dir. Franklin Park Indsl. Clinic, 1982-84; surg. cons. Riis Park Urgent Care and Family Health Ctr., Chgo., 1983—. Mem. Far Eastern U. Dr. Nicanor Reyes Med. Alumni Found., Chgo., 1973-74, bd. govs., 1974-79, chmn. membership com., 1979-81, v.p., 1981-83, pres., 1983-85. Recipient plaque of Appreciation Philippine Week Com., Filipino-Am. Council Chgo., 1983. Mem. AMA, Ill. Med. Soc., Chgo. Med. Soc., Assn. Philippine Practicing Physicians Am., Philippine Med. Assn. Chgo., Ill. Philippine Med. Soc. (bd. govs. 1978-84), Far Eastern U. Med. Alumni Assn. Ill. and Midwest (pres. 1983-85). Republican. Roman Catholic. Club: Philippines Lions (Chgo.). Office: Wells Med Clinic 1532 N Wells Chicago IL 60610

DELGADO, DWIGHD D(UBIED), electric products manufacturing company executive; b. Mayaguez, P.R., June 5, 1950; s. Ramón T. Delgado-Murphy and Rosalina (Ortíz) Delgado; m. Annette Shiflett, Mar. 21, 1975 (div. Dec. 1983). B. Indsl. and Systems Engring., Ga. Inst. Tech., 1977. Specialist in materials and prodn. control Gen. Electric Co., Cleve., 1977-79, prodn. engr. incandescent lamps., 1979-81, mgr. shop ops. Halogen unit, 1981-83, mgr. shop ops. splty. unit, 1983; mgr. spl. projects Gen. Electric Ceramics, Inc., Pepper Pike, Ohio, 1983—; indsl. engring. cons. Am. Inst. Indsl. Engrs., Cleve., 1977—. Recipient managerial award Gen. Electric Co., 1979. Mem. Am. Inst. Indsl. Engrs. (sr. mem., v.p. student and extenal affairs 1983-84, bd. dirs. 1980-83, chmn. chpt. devel., pres.-elect 1984-85, award of Excellence 1980), Theta Chi. Roman Catholic. Home: 14235 Lorain Ave Apt 6 Cleveland OH 44111 Office: Gen Electric Ceramics Inc 30100 Chagrin Blvd Pepper Pike OH 44124

DELGADO, JOSEPH RAMON, business executive; b. Chgo., Mar. 4, 1932; s. Joseph Ramon and Florence (Nelson) D. B.A. in English, U. Ill., 1958. With Campbell-Mithun Advt., Chgo., 1960-68, purchasing agt., dir. office services, 1964-68; purchasing agt., asst. to pres., asst. to treas. Maxant Button & Supply Co., Chgo., 1968-70; asst. purchasing agt., administrv. asst. Soiltest, Inc., Evanston, Ill., 1970-82; v.p., asst. to pres. S.W. Chgo. Corp., 1982—. Mem. Lyric Opera Subscription Com., 1957; observer Joint Civic Com. on Elections, 1965; election judge primary and gen. elections, 1968, 70. Served with AUS, 1952-54. Mem. Purchasing Agts. Assn. Chgo. (co-chmn. publicity and pub. relations com. 1963-64), U. Ill. Alumni, Illiniweks, Chgo. Symphony Soc. (charter). Lutheran. Republican. Clubs: Whitehall, Barclay, Ltd., International

(Chgo.). Dance choreographer for various groups and individuals. Home: 900 Lake Shore Chicago IL 60611 Office: 900 Lake Shore Dr Chicago IL 60611 also 3605 NE 32d Ave Fort Lauderdale FL 33308

DELKS, BARRY LEE, university administrator; b. Crawfordsville, Ind., Dec. 5, 1959; s. Larry Ray and Virginia Kay (Stafford) D.; m. Kim Elaine Au, June 2, 1984. B.S. in Agrl. Econs., Purdue U., 1982, M.S. in Counseling, 1984. Asst. agronomist Agr. Cons., Crawfordsville, Ind., 1980; intern U.S. Dept. Agr., Soil Conservation Service, Danville, Ind., 1981; corn researcher Asgrow Seed Co., Oxford, Ind., 1982; interviewer Gannett Grant, West Lafayette, Ind., 1984; acad. advisor Purdue U., West Lafayette, 1983—, researcher aerial infrared photography agronomy dept., 1980, developer tactile maps, dean students, 1984—, student rep. Placement Ctr., 1985. Chmn. edn. com. Purdue Christian Campus House, 1984-85, chmn. orientation, 1983, 84; vol. worker Cookson Hills Orphanage, Siloam Springs, Ark., 1981, 82. Mem. Am. Assn. Counseling and Devel., Am. Coll. Personnel Assn., Nat. Agrl. Mktg. Assn. Republican. Mem. Christian Ch. Club: Grad. Student Orgn. Home: 5427 Tralee Pl Raleigh NC 27609 Office: Sch Agr Purdue U 121 Agr Adminstrn Bldg West Lafayette IN 47907

DELLA-FERA, MARY ANNE, neurobiologist, veterinarian; b. Wilmington, Del., Mar. 29, 1954; d. Vincent William and Mary (Rickel) D. B.A., U. Del., 1975; V.M.D., U. Pa., 1979, Ph.D., 1980. NIH postdoctoral fellow U. Pa., Phila., 1980-81, research assoc., 1981-82, research asst. prof., 1982; research specialist Monsanto Co., St. Louis, 1982-84, research group leader, 1984—; adj. research asst. prof. Washington, U., St. Louis, 1982—; cons. Monsanto Co., 1981-82. Contbr. articles to profl. jours. Vet. medicine sci. trainee NIH, 1974-80; fellow Alfred P. Slaon Found., 1981-83. Mem. Soc. for Neurosci. (recipient Lindsley prize 1981), AAAS, Am Physiol. Soc., Am. Vet. Medicine Assn., Mo. Vet. Medicine Assn. Home: 17858 Orrville Rd Chesterfield MO 63017 Office: Monsanto Co Route 2 Box 423 Gray Summit MO 63039

DELLANDE, WILLIAM DREW, optometrist; b. Dyersburg, Tenn., Jan. 20, 1926; s. Armand Joseph and Georgianna (Collins) D.; m. Alice Hassebrock, Oct. 1, 1947; children—Brian William, Elaine Alison. O.D. Ill. Coll. Optometry, 1949; M.A. U. Mo., 1966. Diplomate Am. Acad. Optometry. Pvt. practice St. Louis, 1950-54, Columbia, Mo., 1955—; instr. reading improvement progam U. Mo., Columbia, 1963-68; mem. adv. com. Sch. Optometry U. Mo.-St. Louis, 1982-84. Contbr. articles profl. jours. Fellow Am. Acad. Optometry; mem. Am. Optometric Assn. (mem. contact lens com. 1972-73, assoc. editor Contact Lens sect. 1983-84), St. Louis Optometric Soc. (pres. 1952), Heart of Am. Contact Lens Soc. (pres. 1970-71, man of the year 1975), Mo. Chapt. Am. Acad. Optometry (pres. 1983-84). Club: Webster Groves Toastmaster (Toastmaster of Yr. 1953). Home: 811 Cornell Columbia MO 65203 Office: 205 Executive Bldg 601 E Broadway Columbia MO 65203

DELONG, DEBORAH, lawyer; b. Louisville, Sept. 5, 1950; d. Henry F. and Lois Jean (Stepp) DeL.; children—Samuel Prentice, Amelie DeLong. B.A., Vanderbilt U., 1972; J.D., U. Cin., 1975. Bar: Ohio. Assoc., Paxton & Seasongood, Cin., 1975-83, ptnr., 1983—. Contbr. articles to profl. jours. Officer Jr. League Cin., 1979—; bd. dirs. Displaced Homemakers, Cin., 1983—; bd. dirs., officer Children's Psychat. Ctr., Cin., 1979—. Mem. ABA, Cin. Bar Assn., Ohio Bar Assn. Republican. Episcopalian. Office: Paxton & Seasongood 1700 Central Trust Tower 1 W 4th St Cincinnati OH 45202

DELONG, MICHAEL BEN, clergyman, college president; b. Bellefonte, Pa., Sept. 24, 1956; s. Bernard Lincoln and Priscilla (Hobson) DeL.; m. Terry Arlene Stone, Dec. 3, 1978; children—Benjamin, Jonathan, Matthew. Student Centerville Bible Coll., 1975-78; B.A., Temple Baptist Coll., 1981, M.A., 1985. Ordained to ministry Baptist Ch. 1979. Minister of music First Bapt. Ch. Centerville, 1978—; instr., registrar Centerville Bible Coll., 1978—, pres., 1985—; asst. pastor First Bapt. Ch. Centerville, 1983—. Editor The Light, 1981-83. Republican. Avocations: tennis, flying, racquetball. Home: 148 Washington Mill Rd Bellbrook OH 45305 Office: First Baptist Ch Centerville 38 N Main St Centerville OH 45459

DELONG, RICHARD AMES, township official, university administrator; b. Ann Arbor, Mich., Nov. 7, 1926; s. David Albert and Sara M. (Bump) DeL.; m. Maurese Patricia McCarthy, Apr. 10, 1946; children—Patrice, Kathleen, Richard Jr., Susan. B.B.A., U. Mich., 1950, M.B.A., 1966. Chief indsl. engr. Hoover-Universal, Ann Arbor, 1955-58; cons. Albert Ramod, Chgo., 1958-61, Coopers & Lybrand, Detroit, 1961-64; systems mgr. U. Mich., Ann Arbor, 1964-70, maintenance mgr., 1970—; supr. Scio Twp., Washtenaw County, Mich., 1984—, planning commr., 1978-84; exec. com. Huron River Watershed, Ann Arbor, 1980-84; cons. Eric Baum, Chgo., 1974-80. Author: Procedures for Medical Records, 1964. Contbr. articles to profl. jours. Served to sgt. USAF, 1943-47, PTO, Korea. Mem. Am. Inst. Indsl. Engrs., Assn. Phys. Plant Adminstrs. Am. Legion. Republican. Baptist. Club: Toastmasters, Lodge: Rotary. Avocation: marathon running. Home: 2555 Scio Rd Dexter MI 48130 Office: Scio Twp 827 N Zeeb Rd Ann Arbor MI 48103

DELOOF, DONALD JULIUS, JR., manufacturing company executive; b. Lansing, Mich., Mar. 6, 1954; s. Donald Julius and Frances Elaine (Appleton) DeL.; m. Mary Ann Furler, Apr. 12, 1975. Student bus. adminstrn. Sexton Coll., Lansing, 1969-72. Propr., D.J.'s News Ctr., Lansing, 1972-74; account exec. Diane Von Furstenburg, N.Y.C., 1976-79; account exec. James Galanos Perfumes, N.Y.C., 1979-81; pres. Sun Circle Internat., Inc., Haslett, Mich., 1981—. Mem. Red Cedar Cert. Devel. Assn., Internat. Entrepreneurs Assn., Jaycees. Republican. Clubs: Walnut Hills Country (East Lansing, Mich.); Elks (Lansing). Patentee shade tray. Office: 5451 Maple Ridge Rd Haslett MI 48840

DELORBE, WILLIAM J(OSEPH), molecular biologist; b. Waterloo, Iowa, Feb. 21, 1949; s. John Philip and Mary Vivian (Powers) DeL.; m. Terry Vytlacil, July 9, 1977; children—William P., Johnathan E., Jacqueline C. B.S., Loras Coll., 1971; Ph.D., U. Iowa, 1977. Postdoctoral fellow U. Calif. Med. Ctr., San Francisco, 1978-81; sr. scientist Molecular Genetics, Inc., Minnetonka, Minn., 1981-82, dir. adminstrn., 1983-84, sci. group dir., 1984—. Contbr. sci. papers to profl. jours. Fellowships NIH, 1980, Calif. Div. Am. Cancer Soc., 1978, Leukemia Soc. Am., 1978, Am. Cancer Soc., 1978. Mem. AAAS, Am. Soc. Microbiology, N.Y. Acad. Scis. Office: Molecular Genetics Inc 10320 Bren Rd E Minnetonka MN 55343

DELUCA, MICHAEL J., power company executive; b. Montevideo, Minn., July 21, 1959; s. Peter Jack and Ruth Anne (Mahowald) DeL.; m. May 7, 1983; 1 child, Adam. B.A. in Communication, N.D. State U., 1981; M.A. in Tng. and Devel., St. Cloud State U., 1982. Tng. and devel. coordinator United Power Assn., Elk River, Minn., 1982—. Contbr. articles to profl. jours. Treas. St. John's Lutheran Ch., Zimmerman, Minn., 1984—. Mem. Am. Soc. Tng. and Devel. (nat. spl. industry group dir. 1984). Office: United Power Assn Elk River MN 55330

DELUCA, VINCENT THOMAS, television broadcasting executive; b. N.Y.C., Oct. 2, 1926; s. Pasquale and Anna (Causerano) D.; m. Ann Harnaga, May 30, 1954; 4 children. B.B.A. in Mktg., Manhattan Coll., 1951. Mgr. media time buying div. E.W.R.R. Agy., N.Y.C., 1956-60; account exec. Katz Radio, N.Y.C., 1960-61; television account exec. Crosely Broadcasting/AVCO, N.Y.C., 1961-67; v.p., midwest sales mgr. AVCO Television Sales, 1968-71 pres., gen. mgr. Sta. WJRT-TV, Knight Ridder Broadcasting, Flint, Mich., 1982—. Served with USN, 1944-46. Home: 5397 Pepper Mill Rd Grand Blanc MI 48439 Office: 2302 Lapeer Rd Flint MI 48533

DE LUCE, JUDITH, classicist, educator; b. Boston, June 9, 1946; d. Hollinshead and Martha Thacher (Hudson) de L. A.B., Colby Coll., Waterville, Maine, 1968; student Dartmouth Coll., 1967-68; M.A., U. Wis., 1971, Ph.D., 1974. Research editor Grolier Info. Service, N.Y.C., 1968-69; asst. prof. classics Miami U., Oxford, Ohio, 1974-81, assoc. prof., 1981—, coordinator women's studies, 1979—, acting chmn. dept., 1983-84, chmn. dept., 1984—. Mem. Oxford Choral Ensemble; trustee United Campus Ministry, 1980-83. Recipient John B. Foster prize Colby Coll., 1967; Hugh E. Pillinger prize U. Wis., 1972; named Outstanding Univ. Woman, Miami U., 1981; Knapp fellow, 1969-70; Ford fellow, 1971, 72; U. Wis. fellow, 1973-74; Bixler scholar, 1967-78; Miami U. grantee. Mem. Am. Philol. Assn., Archaeol. Inst. Am., Ohio Classical Conf., Vergilian Soc., Classical Assn. Middle West and South, Nat. Women's Studies Assn., Am. Legal Studies Assn., Cin. Assn. Tchrs. Classics, Phi Beta Kappa, Omicron Delta Kappa. Editor: (with Hugh T. Wilder) Language in Primates, 1983; contbr. articles, transls. to classical lit. Home: 4869 Somerville Rd Oxford OH 45056 Office: Classics Dept Miami U Oxford OH 45056

DE LUCIA, JOSEPH JAMES, psychology educator; consultant; b. Jersey City, Apr. 30, 1921; s. Vincent and Catherine (Hughes) De L.; m. Kathleen O'Neil (div.); 1 dau., Kathy Ann De Lucia Hug; m. Elizabeth Loebs Maisack, May 5, 1961. B.S., St. Peter's Coll., 1943; M.S., U. Ill., 1949, Ph.D., 1951. Instr. psychology U. Ill.-Urbana, 1950-52; asst. prof. psychology Marquette U., Milw., 1952-56; pvt. practice psychology, Milw., 1956-63; dir. Area Mental Health Ctr., Garden City, Kans., 1963-66; exec. dir. Douglas County Guidance Ctr., Superior, Wis., 1966-67; prof. psychology U. Wis.-Superior, 1967—, chmn. dept. psychology, 1967-74; tchr., cons. in field. Chmn. adv. bd. Sta. WDSE-TV (pub. TV), Duluth, Minn., 1982—; pres. bd. dirs. Djorkje Kostic Inst. Audiolinguistic Studies, Inc., Superior, 1980—. Served with USMC, 1942-45. Mem. Am. Psychol. Assn. Republican. Roman Catholic. Home: 823 4th Ave E Superior WI 54880 Office: U Wis Superior WI 54880

DELUHERY, PATRICK JOHN, state senator; b. Birmingham, Ala., Jan. 31, 1942; s. Frank B. and Lucille (Donovan) D.; B.A. with honors, U. Notre Dame, 1964; B.Sc. (Econ.) with honors, London Sch. Econs., 1967; m. Margaret Morris, 1973; children—Allison, Norah, Rose. Legis. asst. U.S. Senator Harold Hughes, Washington, 1969-74; legis. asst. U.S. Senator John Culver, Washington, 1975; asst. prof. econs. and bus. adminstrn. St. Ambrose Coll., Davenport, Iowa, 1975—; mem. Iowa State Senate, 1979—. Democrat. Roman Catholic. Home: 129 E Rusholme St Davenport IA 52803 Office: Iowa Senate Statehouse Des Moines IA 50319

DEL VALLE, HELEN CYNTHIA, artist; b. Chgo., Sept. 22, 1933; d. Andrew Jack and Mary Texanna (Cohen) DelValle; student Pa. Acad. Fine Arts, 1952; B.J., Northwestern U., 1960. Tchr. art, math., history, Fla., 1952-54; artist, designer, Chgo., 1954-59; free-lance artist, 1959—; group exhbns. include: Mcpl. Art League of Chgo., U. State Mus., Mid Am. Art Assn., Am. Soc. of Artists, Northshore Art Guild; one woman shows include: Balzekas Mus., Chgo., 1973, Chgo. Public Library, 1972, 73, 75, Combined Ins. Co. Am., Chgo., 1970, 71, 72, 74, 75, Am. Soc. Artists, Chgo., 1971, 1977, also others. Recipient Portraiture award, 1961, 68; internat. award for landscape painting, Switzerland, 1975; 38 merits of honor from U.S. and Europe; award Hollywood Music Co., 1984; Idaho award oriental gardening watercolor, 1984. Mem. Am. Soc. Artists (membership chmn. 1970—, also dir., v.p.), Nat. League Am. Pen Women (Dingle award Chgo. chpt. 1971, traditional in oil award 1971, landscape in watercolor award 1973, 1st award in painting 1979, 3d place award Chgo. br. 1980, 81, award for watercolor state art show), Mcpl. Art League Chgo. (hon. mention 1973), Nat. Soc. Artists, Internat. Poetry Soc., Ill. Poetry Soc., Poets and Patrons. Author poems; poems pub. in 14 edits. New Voices in Am. Poetry. Address: PO Box 958 Chicago IL 60690

DEMAREE, JACK LEE, bank executive; b. Indpls., Aug. 14, 1948; s. Jack H. and Virginia M. (Buis) D.; m. Patricia A. Harrold, June 15, 1967; children—Jeannine, Jay. Student Ball State U., 1967-71; grad. Am. Inst. Banking, 1975; grad. U. Wis. Grad. Sch. Banking, 1981; grad. Jr. Bank Officers Seminar, 1970. With Mchts. Nat. Bank, Muncie, Ind., 1967—, asst. cashier, 1972-75, asst. v.p., 1975-81, v.p., 1981—, mgr. consumer services, 1978-80, mgr. mktg. and bus. devel. dept., 1980—; chmn. underwriting com. WIPB Telesale. Bd. dirs. Delaware County Tb Assn. (Ind.), 1980—, pres., 1982—; chmn. Ball State U. Pres.'s Club, Muncie; chmn. United Way Div. VIII, Muncie; bd. dirs. Muncie-Delaware County ARC, Muncie Children's Mus. Named one of 10 Outstanding Young Hoosiers, Ind. Jaycees, 1981; recipient Benny award Ball State U., 1984. Mem. Ind. Bank Mktg. Assn., YMCA, Muncie-Delaware County C. of C. (chmn. welcome to the community com.), Muncie Jaycees (Disting. Service award 1981), Consumer Bankers Assn. Am. Methodist. Clubs: Cardinal Varsity, Catalina, Muncie Advt. Lodges: Kiwanis, Elks. Home: 3412 Riverside Ave Muncie IN 47304 Office: Merchants Nat Bank PO Box 792 Muncie IN 47305

DEMARINIS, SHARON, restaurateur; b. Milw., Aug. 23, 1936; d. Alice (Wagner) Boeck; m. Vito A. Demarinis, June 10, 1958; children—Anthony, Christopher, Susan. Graduate Gibraltar High Sch. Sec. Allen-Bradley Co., Milw., 1955-57, bookkeeper, 1957-79; co-owner, operator Tony's Fiesta, Fish Creek, Wis., 1964-77, Olde Stage Station, Egg Harbor, Wis., 1980—. Pres. Fish Creek Woman's Club, 1976-80, Fish Creek Community Ch., 1976-80, Gibraltar Area Schs., 1976—. Avocations: sewing, singing. Home: 4113 Main St Fish Creek WI 54212

DEMASCIO, ROBERT EDWARD, See *Who's Who in America*, 43rd edition.

DEMEESTER, TOM RYAN, thoracic surgeon, medical educator; b. Grand Rapids, Mar. 7, 1938; s. Ryan J. and Ruth (Van't Hof) DeM.; m. Carol Walburg, Aug. 29, 1958; children—Steven Ryan, Sara Lyn, Scott Ryan, Susan Lyn. A.B., Calvin Coll., 1959, M.D., U. Mich., 1963. Diplomate Am. Bd. Surgery, Am. Bd. Thoracic Surgery. Intern, Johns Hopkins Hosp., Balt., 1963-64, resident, 1968-71; asst. prof. thoracic surgery U. Chgo. Pritzker Sch. Medicine, 1974-76, assoc. prof., 1976-78, prof., 1978-83, chief thoracic surgery, 1974-83; prof. thoracic and cardiovascular surgery, chmn. dept. surgery Creighton U. Sch. Medicine, Omaha, 1983—; chief of surgery St. Joseph Hosp., 1983—. Served to lt. col. U.S. Army, 1971-74. Fellow ACS, Am. Coll. Chest Physicians; mem. Assn. Acad. Surgery, AMA, Am. Heart Assn., Johns Hopkins Med. Surg. Soc., Lukes Soc., Chgo. Surg. Soc., Soc. Univ. Surgeons, Soc. Surg. Chmn., Assn. Surg. Edn., Soc. Thoracic Surgeons, Am. Assn. Thoracic Surgery, Am. Assn. Cancer Research, Soc. Surgery Alimentary Tract, Internat. Assn. Study Lung Cancer, Pan-Pacific Surg. Assn., Central Surg. Assn., Western Surg. Soc., Am. Thoracic Soc., Met. Omaha Med. Soc., Nebr. Thoracic Soc., Southwestern Surg. Congress, Nebr. Med. Assn., Collegium Internationale Chirurgiae Digestivae, Internat. Cardiovascular Soc., Am. Soc. Clin. Oncology, Omaha Mid-West Clin. Soc. Soc. Clin. Surgery, Surg. Biology Club II, Internat. Bronchoesophagological Soc., Societe Internationale de Chirurgie, Am. Surg. Assn., Inst. Medicine Chgo., Soc. Surg. Oncology. Research in lung cancer. Home: 11127 Woolworth Plaza Omaha NE 68144 Office: Dept Surgery Creighton U 601 N 30th St Omaha NE 68131

DEMERATH, JEFFREY TITUS, lawyer; b. Durham, N.C., July 18, 1948; s. Nicholas Jay and Helen (Titus) D.; m. Barbara Singer, Sept. 2, 1972; children—Michael Essex, Thomas England. B.A., Dartmouth Coll., 1970; J.D., Boston U., 1973. Bar: Mass. 1973, D.C. 1974, Mo. 1980, U.S. Dist. Ct. (ea. dist.) Mo. 1981, U.S. Dist. Ct. (D.C. dist.) 1974. Legal asst. to U.S. Senator Stuart Symington of Mo., Washington, 1973-74; asst. U.S. atty. for D.C., Dept. Justice, 1974-80; mem. firm Thompson & Mitchell, St. Louis, 1980-84, Greensfelder, Hemker, Wiese, Gale and Chappelow, St. Louis, 1984—; vice chmn. Young Lawyers Sect., Washington, 1979-80; co-chmn. Criminal Practice Inst., Washington, 1978-79; mem. Com. on Improving Trial Advocacy, Washington, 1978-79; co-chmn. Nat. Moot Ct. Com., Washington, 1977. Campaign worker Harriett Woods for U.S. Senate, St. Louis, 1982. Urban Affairs fellow Dartmouth Coll., 1969. Mem. Bar Assn. Met. St. Louis. Democrat. Unitarian. Clubs: Mo. Athletic, Frontenac Racquet, Dartmouth of St. Louis (pres. 1985). Home: 7 Dartford Ave Clayton MO 63105 Office: Greensfelder Hemker Gale and Chappelow 10 S Broadway St Louis MO 63102

DEMERS, JACQUES, hockey league coach; b. Montreal, Que., Can., Aug. 25, 1944; s. John Demers and Marie Bergeron; m. Linda Stone, June 24, 1973; children—Brandy, Stefanie, Jason. Student Cote St. Luc High Sch., Montreal. Data processor IBM, Montreal, 1977; coach Quebec Nordiques, Quebec, Can., 1978-83, St. Louis Blues, NHL, 1983—. Recipient Spirit of St. Louis Bus. Community award, 1984. Home: 5700 Oakland Ave Saint Louis MO 63110 Office: St Louis Blues Saint Louis MO

DE MEYER, MICHAEL CHARLES, marketing executive; b. Kalamazoo, Dec. 28, 1949; s. Elliott James and Mary (McAleer) D. B.B.A., Western Mich. U., 1972. Asst. to mgr. charge acct. 1st Nat. Bank, Kalamazoo, 1973-75; assoc. exec. fin. resource devel. United Way of Kent County, Grand Rapids, Mich., 1976-84; sr. mktg. rep. Alloy Tek, Inc., Grandville, Mich., 1984—; cons. in non-profit field. Mem. World Affairs Council, Grand Rapids, 1984—; mem. Kent County Council for Prevention and Treatment of Child Abuse and Neglect, 1984—; vol. fund raiser Channel 35 Pub. TV, Allendale, Mich., 1984—; bd. dirs. Catholic Social Services, 1984—. Clubs: Press of Grand Rapids, Univ. Grand Rapids. Avocations: art appreciation, sports, musical appreciation, interior design, photography. Office: AlloyTek Inc 2900 Wilson Ave SW Grandville MI 49418

DEMLOW, CHARLES EDWARD, police detective; b. Inpls., Dec. 22, 1942; s. Edwin Merritt and Nellie Ester (DeLong) D.; m. Jean Ellen McKinstray, Jan. 22, 1962 (div. Jan. 1970); children—Kevin E., Kenneth J.; m. Jacqueline Kaye Foertsch, Aug. 23, 1972; 1 child, Robert M. Student in criminal justice Ind. U. S.E., New Albany, 1971-74. Trooper, Ind. State Police, Charlestown, 1964-70, detective, Indpls., 1970-74, trooper, 1974-83, detective, Sellersburg, 1982—. Recipient Prosecutors award for Excellence Washington County Inc. Pros. Atty., 1982. Republican. Methodist. Lodge: Masons. Avocations: reading; sports; farming; photography. Home: Rural Route 1 Box 197 Scottsburg IN 47170 Office: Ind State Police 8014 Hwy 311 Sellersburg IN 47172

DEMPSEY, JOHN NICHOLAS, packaging company executive; b. St. Paul, June 16, 1923; s. Mark V. and Mabel M. (Stehly) D.; m. Marian V. Lind, June 5, 1948; children—Barbara Dempsey McCarrier, Mary Dempsey Santiago, Patricia Lee. B.S., St. Thomas Coll., 1948; Ph.D., U. Iowa, 1951. Teaching asst. AEC fellow U. Iowa, Iowa City, 1948-51; research chemist Ethyl Corp., Detroit, 1951-52; research physicist Honeywell, Inc., Mpls., 1952-56, research sect. head, 1956-60, asst. dir. research, 1960-61, dir. research, 1961-65, v.p. research, 1965-67, v.p. sci. and engring., 1967-72; v.p. tech. services Bemis Co., Inc., Mpls., 1972-75, v.p. sci. and tech., 1975—, also dir.; trustee Midwest Research Inst., Kansas City, Mo. Served to lt. (j.g.) USN, 1943-46, PTO. Mem. North Star Research Found. (pres., bd. dirs.). Indsl. Research Inst. (rep.), Dirs. Indsl. Research, Am. Mgmt. Assn. (trustee), Am. Chem. Soc., Inst. Environ. Scis., Sigma Xi, Phi Lambda Upsilon, Gamma Alpha. Clubs: Mpls., Interlachen. Avocations: hunting, skeet shooting. Home: 4926 Westgate Rd Minnetonka MN 55345 Office: Bemis Co Inc 800 Northstar Ctr Minneapolis MN 55402

DEMPSEY, JOHN REXFORD, insurance broker; b. Corry, Pa., Dec. 25, 1935; s. Rexford and Lilah (Hinman) D.; B.S., Cornell U., 1957; C.L.U., 1962; m. Barbara Bentley, Aug. 13, 1960; children—Kimberly, Michael, John. Engaged in ins. bus., 1957—; pres. Jack Dempsey Assos., Inc., Ann Arbor, 1968—; speaker in field. Chmn. devel. council Hospice of Washtenaw. Mem. Am. C.L.U.'s, Million Dollar Round Table (dir.; div. v.p.), Ten Million Dollar Forum, Life Ins. Counselors Mich., Estate Planning and Life Underwriters Assn. Washtenaw County (past pres.), Ann Arbor C. of C. (past pres.). Republican. Presbyterian. Club: Barton Hills Country (past pres.). Home: 2171 S 7th St Ann Arbor MI 48103 Office: 1925 Pauline Plaza Ann Arbor MI 48106

DEN ADEL, RAYMOND LEE, classics educator; b. Pella, Iowa, Apr. 23, 1932; s. John J. and Nellie (DeGeus) D. B.A., Central Coll., 1954; M.A., U. Iowa, 1959; Ph.D., U. Ill., 1971. Latin tchr. Pella High Sch., Iowa, 1954-55; Latin and English tchr. Proviso High Sch., Hillside, Ill., 1958-62; teaching asst. U. Iowa, Iowa City, 1962-63; fellow and asst. in classics U. Ill., Urbana, 1963-67; faculty Rockford Coll., Ill., 1967—, prof., 1975—. Served with CIC, U.S. Army, 1955-57. Fulbright grantee, 1960. Bd. dirs. Rockford Community Concert Assn., 1979-85. Mem. Am. Classical League, AAUP, Am. Philological Assn., Ill. Classical Conf., Classical Assn. Middle West, Classical Assn. South., Rockford Archaeol. Soc. Mem. Reformed Ch. in Am. Avocations: photography; travel; reading; music. Home: 2408 Eastmoreland Ave Rockford IL 61108 Office: Rockford Coll 5050 E State St Rockford IL 61108

DENGER, ELSIE SUE, nursing administrator; b. Iowa Falls, Iowa, July 12, 1936; d. Ray Lester and Elsie Mae (Brighton) Denger. R.N., Broadlawns Polk County Sch. Nursing, 1956; B.S. in Nursing, U. Iowa, 1966, M.A., 1968. Dir. nursing services Emma L. Bixby Hosp., Adrian, Mich., 1969-76; asst. hosp. adminstr., dir. nursing services Milton S. Hershey Med. Ctr., Hershey, Pa., 1976-79; asst. exec. dir. nursing services U. Louisville Hosp., 1979-83; v.p. St. Francis Regional Med. Ctr., Wichita, Kans., 1983—. Mem. Nat. League for Nursing, Am. Nurses Assn., Am. Orgn. Nurse Execs. Home: 9016 Funston Ct Wichita KS 67207

DENKO, CHARLES WASIL, physician, researcher; b. Cleve., Aug. 12, 1916; s. Wasil Stepan and Evodikya (Yakochuk) D.; m. J. Joanne Decker, June 17, 1950; children—Christopher, Nicholas, Timothey. B.S. Geneva Coll., 1938; M.S., Pa. State U., 1939, Ph.D., 1943; M.D., Johns Hopkins U., 1951. Resident in medicine U. Chgo., 1952-55; research assoc. U. Chgo., 1955-56; asst. prof. U. Mich., Ann Arbor, 1956-59, Ohio State U., Columbus, 1959-67; dir. research Fairview Gen. Hosp., Cleve., 1968—; from asst. clin. prof. to assoc. clin. prof. Case Western Res. U., Cleve., 1970—; cons. clin. pharmacology, 1955—; pres. Alcusal N. Am., 1984—. Contbr. chpts. to books, articles to profl. jours. Trustee, Sts. Peter and Paul Russian Orthodox Ch., Lakewood, Ohio, 1970-82; councilor Boy Scouts Am., Rocky River, Ohio, 1975-82; bd. govs. YMCA, Westlake, Ohio, 1975-80; trustee Arthritis Found., Cleve., 1972-75, Lupus Found. Am., Cleve., 1984—. Served to capt. U.S. Army, 1945-47. Recipient Disting. Service award Geneva Coll., 1968, Interurban Arthritis Soc., 1982; Sr. Investigator award Arthritis Found. Ohio State U., 1960-65. Mem. Am. Chem. Soc., Am. Rheumatism Assn., Cleve. Rheumatism Soc. (pres. 1973); hon. mem. Australian Rheumatism Assn. Club: Federated Russian Orthodox (v.p. 1980-81). Lodge: Lions. Avocations: Travel; photography. Home: 21160 Avalon Dr Rocky River OH 44116 Office: Fairview Gen Hosp Research Dept 18101 Lorain Ave Cleveland OH 44111

DENNING, GREGORY JOHN, real estate investment executive; b. Coos Bay, Oreg., Jan. 2, 1946; s. Jack and Evelyn T. (Tretter) D.; m. Cheryl L. Topham (div.). B.A. in Psychology and Sociology, Northeastern Ill. U., Chgo., 1973. With Sta. KWRO, Inc., Coquille, Oreg., 1962-64; sales rep. Mead Papers, Chgo., 1965-67; asst. sales/mktg. mgr. Arvey Corp., Chgo., 1968-72; regional sales mgr. Emerson Electric Co., Chgo. and Seattle, 1973-75; nat. sales mgr. Manoir Internat., Chgo., 1976-78; regional mgr. Becton-Dickinson Co., 1978-80; investment counselor Baird and Warner, Chgo., 1981-82; ptnr., v.p., Equest Real Estate and Fin. Corp., Chgo., 1982-84; v.p. Oak Brook Capital Corp., Ill., 1985—. Recipient numerous top sales producer awards. Mem. Chgo. Symphony Soc. Clubs: Gold Coast Ski, Chgo. (v.p. 1976-79). Home: 3505 N Janssen Chicago IL 60657 Office: 101 Jorie Blvd Suite 124 Oak Brook IL 60521

DENNISON, CORLEY FRANCIS, III, broadcasting executive, educator; b. Sutton, W. Va., Dec. 6, 1953; s. Corley F. and Marge (White) D.; m. Betty Hawker, July 15, 1978; 1 child, Corley, IV. B.A. in Mass Communications, James Madison U., 1976; M.A. in English and Speech, Northwest Mo. State U., 1984; cert. studio recording techniques U. Colo., 1981. Announcer, producer Sta. WMRA-JMU, Harrisonburg, Va., 1974-76; program dir. Sta. WKYY, Amherst, Va., 1976-78; news dir. Sta. WLLL-AM WGOL-FM, Lynchburg, Va., 1978-80; ops. mgr. Sta. KXCV-KDLX Northwest Mo. State U., Maryville, 1980-85; dir. broadcast services Northwest Mo. State U., Maryville, 1985—, mem. learning resources com., 1984—. Co-producer: (radio series) Reflections, 1981-83. Engr., producer: (folk music album) Touch the Past, 1984. Producer: (radio music-narrative) Kansas City JAZZ, 1984. Author: (hist. research) Battle of Lynchburg, 1984. Emcee, organizer Sport-a-Thon, Muscular Dystrophy Assn., Lynchburg, 1979; local host Jerry Lewis Labor Day Tele-Thon, Lynchburg, 1979, 80; concert organizer Nodaway Arts Council, Maryville, 1983-84. Mem. Mo. Broadcast Assn. (1st place Promotional Campaign award 1982, 84), Mo. Pub. Radio Assn., Nat. Assn. Broadcasters, U.S. Jaycees (Outstanding Young Man Am. 1984), Sigma Delta Chi. Home: 815 N Main St Maryville MO 64468 Office: KXCV-KDLX Northwest Mo State U Maryville MO 64468

DENNISTON, GEORGE RORABACK, JR., manufacturing company executive; b. Chgo., Aug. 16, 1942; s. George Roraback and Betty (Bower) D.; m. Ann Rae Bscherer, May 15, 1965; children—Susan Ann, George Roraback III. A.A., Kemper Mil. Sch., 1962; B.A., Westminster Coll., 1964. Mgmt. trainee F.W. Woolworth, Co., Chgo., 1964-66, mgr. store, 1967-72; gen. mgr. Connomac Corp., Lyons, Ill., 1972-74; comptroller Tunnel Electric Constrn. Co., McCook, Ill., 1974-79; corp. comptroller Fennell Corp., Harvey, Ill., 1979—; dir. Internat. Equipment Leasing Co., Riverdale, Ill. Trustee Twp. of Riverside, 1984; bd. dirs. Riverside Twp. Mental Health Bd., 1984. Mem. South Suburban Assn. Commerce and Industry (treas. 1984—), Olmsted Soc. (treas. 1972-73). Avocations: sports, tennis, water skiing, snow skiing. Home: 379 Blythe Rd Riverside IL 60546 Office: Fennell Corp 379 E Sibley Blvd Harvey IL 60426

DENOYER, ARSENE J., former community relations executive; b. Limestone Twp., Kankakee County, Ill., Dec. 21, 1904; s. Arsene and Julia (Clark) D.; student parochial schs. of Kankakee and Bourbonnais, Ill. Field dir. Am. Nat. Red Cross, 1943-48; sales United Educators, Inc., 1932-42, community relations, 1948-63, asst. treas., community relations director, 1963—; asst. treas. Book House for Children, 1963—. Life bd. dirs. NCCJ; past pres. Chgo. Civitan Club; chmn. Lake County chpt. ARC, Lake County Adv. Bd. for Spl. Edn.; mem. Ill. Gov.'s Adv. Bd. for Devel. Disabilities, Commn. for Interstate Edn. Served as 1st sgt. USAAF, 1942-43. Mem. Am. C. of C. Execs., Chairs of Pvt. Enterprise, D.A.V. (life), Ill. Assn. C. of C. Execs., Chgo. Assn. Commerce and Industry (govtl. affairs com., mass transp. com.), Kankakee County Hist. Soc. (life), North La. Hist. Soc. (life), Waukegan-Lake County C. of C. Club: Swedish Glee (Waukegan). Home: 805 Baldwin Ave Waukegan IL 60085

DENSMORE-WULFF, LINDA KIMMONS, educational administrator; b. Clovis, N.Mex., Dec. 10, 1946; d. Lee Hugh and Alta Lou (McDaniel) Kimmons; m. Jerry Paul Densmore, Aug. 21, 1965; 1 son, Stefan Christian; m. 2d., Stephen Wayne Wulff, May 23, 1981; 1 dau., Whitney Abigail Kimmons. B.S., Olivet Nazarene Coll.-Kankakee, Ill., 1968; M.Ed., U. Cin., 1978, Ph.D., 1985. Cert. tchr., supr., elem. prin., personnel dir., ednl. researcher, Ohio. Tchr., Jessamine County, Ky., 1968-69; tchr. Mt. Orab Elem. Sch., Western Brown County, Ohio, 1971-74; tchr. Greenhills-Forest Park Sch. Dist., Cin., 1974-80, instructional specialist, 1980-81, project dir. ednl. adminstrn., 1981-85, curriculum dir., 1985—; hostess PBS-TV series Dragons, Wagons and Wax, 1977—. Mem. adminstrv. bd. United Meth. Ch.; rep. Children's Internat. Summer Village, Stockholm, 1978. Mem. Assn. Supervision and Curriculum Devel., Nat. Coalition Sex Equity in Edn., Am. Ednl. Research Assn., Phi Delta Kappa. Home: 1090 Hickory Ridge Ln Cincinnati OH 45140 Office: 1501 Kingsbury Dr Cincinnati OH 45240

DENTON, RAY DOUGLAS, insurance company executive; b. Lake City, Ark., May 16, 1937; s. Ray Dudney and Edna Lorraine (Roe) D.; B.A., U. Mich., 1964, postgrad., 1969-70; J.D., Wayne State U., 1969, postgrad., 1964-65; m. Cheryl Emma Borchardt, Mar. 9, 1964; children—Ray D., Derek St. Clair, Carter Lee. Claims rep. Hartford Ins. Co., Crum & Forster, Detroit, and Am. Claims, Chgo., 1962-73; partner Chgo. Metro Claims, Oak Park, Ill., 1974-75; founder, pres. Ray D. Denton & Assocs., Inc., Hinsdale, Ill., 1975—. Mem. Pi Kappa Alpha, Phi Alpha Delta. Home: 4532 Howard Western Springs IL 60558 Office: 930 N York 1 Hinsdale IL 60521

DEORE, JAMES HART, association executive; b. Connellsville, Pa., Feb. 9, 1944; s. James F. and Rita H. (Hart) DeO.; B.A. in Psychology, St. Vincent Coll., Latrobe, Pa., 1965; postgrad. in Clin. Psychology, W.Va. U., 1966; M.S. in Rehab. Services Adminstrn., DePaul U., 1969; m. June Williams, May 24, 1969; children—Jeanine, James, Jeffrey. Workshop supr. Jewish Vocat. Service, Chgo., 1966-68; program dir. Countryside Center for the Handicapped, Barrington, Ill., 1968-73; chief exec. officer Ray Graham Assn. for the Handicapped, Elmhurst, Ill., 1985—; exec. dir. Found. for the Handicapped, Elmhurst, 1975—; chief exec. officer Housing for the Handicapped, Inst. Human Devel., Bus. Resources, Inc., Elmhurst, 1985—; mem. Gov.'s Com. for the Handicapped; mem. Pres.'s Com. on Handicapped, 1974—; grad. faculty DePaul U., Chgo., leader workshops in field. Mem. Roselle (Ill.) Bd. Edn., 1980—, pres., 1982—; mem. Commn. Status of Disabled Persons, 1984. Recipient P.J. Trevethan award Ray Graham Assn./DePaul U. Dept. Rehab. Adminstrn., 1980. Mem. Nat. Rehab. Assn. (adminstrv. and supervision div.), Ill. Rehab. Assn., Ill. Assn. Rehab. Facilities (treas. bd. dirs., 1977), Ill. Assn. Retarded Citizens (exec. dir.'s com.). Roman Catholic. Contbr. writings in field to profl. publs. Home: 155 E Granville Roselle IL 60172 Office: 420 W Madison Elmhurst IL 60126

DEPPISCH, LUDWIG MICHAEL, pathologist; b. N.Y.C., May 18, 1938; s. Ludwig Adam and Rose (Moyka) D.; m. Rosemarie Granelli, Sept. 24, 1965; children—Carl, Barbara Ann. A.B. Fordham U., 1960; M.D. Johns Hopkins, 1964. Diplomate Am. Bd. Pathology. Intern, Henry Ford Hosp., Detroit, 1964-65; resident in pathology Mt. Sinai Hosp., N.Y.C., 1967-69, assoc. pathologist, 1971-75, asst. prof., 1971-75; assoc. pathologist William Beaumont Hosp., El Paso, Tex., 1969-71; assoc. pathologist Youngstown Hosp., Ohio, 1975-80, vice chmn. pathology dept., 1980-83, chmn. dept. pathology and lab. medicine, 1983—; assoc. prof. pathology Northeast Ohio U. Coll. Medicine, Rootstown, Ohio, 1977-82, prof., 1982—. Author: (with others) Malignant Alteration in Benign Cystic Teratoma, 1983. Contbr. articles to profl. jours. Bd. dirs. Ballet Western R Reserve, Youngstown, 1979-82; charter class Leadership Youngstown, 1984. Served to maj. U.S. Army, 1969-71. Coll. Am. Pathologists fellow; mem. Am. Soc. Clin. Pathologists, Internat. Soc. Gynecol. Pathologists, Group for Research Pathology Ed., Gastrointestinal Pathology Club. Roman Catholic. Club: Sierra (exec. com. chpt. 1976-80) Avocation: ornithology. Home: 685 Blueberry Hill Dr Canfield OH 44406 Office: Youngstown Hosp Association Youngstown OH 44501

DEPUKAT, THADDEUS STANLEY, optometrist; b. Chgo., Feb. 3, 1936; s. Stanley Frank and Genevieve Josephine (Skorupinski) D.; m. Melanie Ann Gadomski, Sept. 7, 1963; children—Brian Ted, Todd Steven. Student Loyola U., 1954-56; B.S., Ill. Coll. Optometry, 1960, O.D., 1960. Clin. instr. Ill. Coll. Optometry, Chgo., 1960-61, assoc. prof., 1961-66; optometrist, Downers Grove, Ill., 1966—; trustee Ill. Coll. Optometry, 1982—. Contbr. articles to profl. jours. Active mem. United Fund Bd., Downers Grove, 1966-69, Suburban Cook County-Dupage County Health Systems Agy., 1976-77; del. White House Conf. on Children, Washington, 1970. Recipient Tribute of Appreciation Ill. Coll. Optometry Alumni Assn., 1982. Fellow Am. Acad. Optometry, AAAS, Coll. Optometrists in Vision Devel.; mem. Ill. Optometric Assn. (Disting. Service award, 1982; pre. 1978-80, v.p. pub. health 1974-76), Ill. Coll. Optometry Alumni Assn., Am. Optometric Assn., West Suburban Optometric Assn. (pres. 1974), Optometric Extension Program. Lodge: Lions (v.p. 1982-85, pres. 1985—). Avocations: camping; computers; reading. Office: 1043 Curtiss Downers Grove IL 60515

DEPUYDT, CHERYL ANN, physical education educator; b. Marquette, Mich., Dec. 16, 1950; d. John Bernard and Yvonne Marie (Ekstedt) Dorais; m. John Daniel DePuydt, Nov. 10, 1973; children—Jenny, Paul, Matt. B.S. in Edn., No. Mich. U., 1972, M.S. in Ednl. Adminstrn., 1978. Instr. phys. edn. Mich. Tech. U., Houghton, 1972-78, basketball coach, 1974-78, volleyball coach, 1974-80, cheerleading coach, 1972-81, asst. prof., 1978—, skating sch. dir., 1972—; figure skating cons. Portage Lake Figure Skating Club, 1972—. Recipient Service award Marquette Figure Skating Club, 1980; named Disting. Tchr., Mich. Tech. U., 1982. Mem. Houghton-Hancock Bus. and Profl. Women (named Young Careerist 1977, 78, pres. 1983-84), Ice Skating Inst. Am. (instr. 1983) U.S. Figure Skating Assn. (profl. 1969—). Roman Catholic. Home: 904 Portage St Houghton MI 49931 Office: SDC Mich Tech U Houghton MI 49931

DERAMUS, BETTY JEAN, editorial writer, columnist; b. Tuscaloosa, Ala., Mar. 29, 1941; s. Jim Louis and Lucille (Richardson) DeR. B.A., Wayne State U., 1963, M.A., 1977. Reporter, copy editor Mich. Chronicle, Detroit, 1963-67; writer Detroit Bd. Edn., 1967-71; reporter Detroit Free Press, 1972-75, editorial writer, columnist, 1978—; instr. English, Wayne State U., 1976-78; contbr. Essence mag., N.Y.C., 1982—; author: The Constant Search, 1969; contbr. anthologies Sturdy Black Bridges, 1979, The Third Coast, 1982. Recipient 1st prize commentary Edn. Writers Assn., 1981; Ernie Pyle award spl. citation Scripps-Howard Found., 1981; Best Editorial Series award Overseas Press Club Am., 1982; Gen. Excellence award ASCAP, 1983. Mem. Nat. Conf. Editorial Writers, Nat. Assn. Black Journalists (2d v.p. 1982). Home: PO Box 1825 Detroit MI 48231 Office: Detroit Free Press 321 W Lafayette St Detroit MI 48231

DERAMUS, WILLIAM NEAL, III, railroad exec.; b. Pittsburg, Kan., Dec. 10, 1915; s. William Neal and Lucile Ione (Nicholas) D.; A.B., U. of Mich., 1936; LL.B., Harvard, 1939; m. Patricia Howell Watson, Jan. 22, 1943; children—William Neal IV, Patricia Nicholas Fogel, Jean Deramus Wagner, Jill Watson Dean. Transp. apprentice Wabash R.R. Co., St. Louis, 1939-41, asst. trainmaster, 1941-43; asst. to gen. mgr. K.C.S. Ry. Co., Kansas City, Mo., 1946-48, asst. to pres. C.G.W. Ry. Co., Chgo., 1948, pres., dir., 1949-57, chmn. exec. com., 1954-57; pres., dir. M.-K.-T.R.R., 1957-61; chmn. bd. MAPCO, Inc., Tulsa, 1960-73, chmn. exec. com., 1966-81, dir.; pres. Kansas City So. Lines (Mo.), 1961-73, chmn. bd., 1966-80; pres. Kansas City So. Industries, Inc. (Mo.), 1962-71, chmn. bd., 1966—; dir. Bus. Men's Assurance Co. Am., Kansas City Royals (all Kansas City, Mo.). Served to maj. Transp. Corps, Mil. Ry. Service AUS, 1943-46; overseas, India, 1943-45. Mem. Beta Theta Pi. Clubs: Chicago; Kansas City, River, Mission Hills Country, Mercury, Rotary (Kansas City). Office: 114 W 11th St Kansas City MO 64105

DERHAM, ROBERT EMMETT, financial executive, financial and tax consultant; b. Evanston, Ill., Dec. 10, 1944; s. Francis Emmett and Helen (Dreelan) D. B.B.A. in Acctg., Loyola U., Chgo., 1971. C.P.A., Ill. Auditor Arthur Young & Co., Chgo., 1971-74; field controller McDonald's Corp., Oak Brook, Ill., 1975-81; chief fin. officer Mediatech, Inc., Chgo., 1981—; dir. Midcoast Producers Services, Inc., Chgo., 1981-84, Travel Tech. Group, Chgo., 1984—. Served with USMC, 1962-66. Mem. Am. Inst. C.P.A.s, Ill. Soc. C.P.A.s, Beta Alpha Psi, Beta Gamma Sigma, Phi Theta Kappa. Avocations: travel; skiing. Home: 1954 N Fremont St Chicago IL 60614 Office: Mediatech Inc 110 Hubbard St Chicago IL 60610

DERICK, DOROTHY BOSK, banker; b. Boston, Apr. 29, 1943; d. Clifford Lambie and Dorothy Edith (Bosk) Derick. A.B., Mt. Holyoke Coll., 1965; cert. Northeastern U. and Boston Security Analysis Soc., 1971; grad. Nat. Grad. Trust Sch., Northwestern U., 1976; S.M. in Mgmt. (Sloan fellow), MIT, 1981. With Shawmut Bank of Boston, N.A., 1965-82, mgmt. trainee, 1968-70, asst. trust officer, 1970-74, trust officer, 1974-79, sr. trust officer, 1979-82; v.p. The No. Trust Co., Chgo., 1982—; clk., dir. Fabtron Corp., Waltham, Mass., 1973—. Treas., bd. dirs. UNICEF Com. Greater Boston, 1974-80, bd. dirs. Greater Chgo. Area Com., 1982—; mem. vestry Trinity Ch., Newton Centre, Mass., 1975-78, 79-82, mem. fin. com., 1976-78, 79-82, chmn. com., 1980-82, trustee endowment funds, 1979-82; trustee Mt. Holyoke Coll., 1978-83, mem. fin., 1978-83, chmn. Task Force on Giving, 1983—, mem. proxy com., 1978—, mem. resources and priorities and five coll. cooperation coms., 1980—, mem. conf. and devel. coms., 1978-81; bd. dirs. Met. Chgo. Coalition on Aging, 1983—; mem. Evanston Commn. Aging, 1983—. Mem. Nat. Assn. Bank Women (dir. 1978-79; trustee Ednl. Found. 1977-78, vice chmn., trustee 1978-79), Mt. Holyoke Coll. Alumnae Assn. (mem. fin. com. 1976-78, dir. 1978-79), Internat. Soc. Pre-retirement Planners, Nat. Council on Aging. Clubs: Mt. Holyoke (treas. 1975-77), MIT Faculty (Boston); MIT (Chgo.). Author: The Corporate Fiduciary and Securities Subject to Resale Restrictions under the Federal Securities Laws. Home: 830-A Forest Ave Evanston IL 60202 Office: The Northern Trust Co 50 S LaSalle St Chicago IL 60675

DEROUSIE, CHARLES STUART, lawyer; b. Adrian, Mich., May 24, 1947; s. Stuart J. and Helia I. (Juntunen) DeR.; m. Patricia Jean Fetzer; children—Jennifer, Jason. B.A. magna cum laude, Oakland U., 1969; J.D. magna cum laude, U. Mich., 1973. Bar: Ohio, 1973, U.S. Dist. Ct. (so. dist.) Ohio 1974. Ptnr. Vorys, Sater, Seymour and Pease, Columbus, Ohio, 1973—. Trustee Ballet Met., Inc., Columbus, 1978—, v.p., 1984—; trustee Gladden Community House, Columbus, 1975-81, pres., 1979-81. Mem. ABA, Columbus Bar Assn., Ohio Bar Assn., Order of Coif. Office: Vorys Sater Seymour and Pease PO Box 1008 52 E Gay St Columbus OH 43216

DERR, RICHARD LUTHER, educator; b. Hughesville, Pa., Dec. 27, 1930; s. Luther and Nora (Hanlon) D.; m. Evelyn Frances Musielak, Apr. 11, 1953; children—Stephanie, Christopher. B.S. in Educ., SUNY-Brockport, 1951; M.Ed., U. Ill.-Urbana-Champaign, 1955, Ed.D., 1959. Elem. sch. tchr. Niagara Falls Pub. Schs., N.Y., 1951, St. Louis Pub. Schs., 1957-59; asst. prof. Washington U., St. Louis, 1957-59; asst. prof. to prof. dept. edn. Case Western Res. U., Cleve., 1959—, asst. dean, Baxter Sch. Info. and Library Sci., Cleve., 1983-84. Author: Taxonomy of Social Purposes of Public Schools, 1973 (outstanding book in 1973 Am. Sch. Bd. Jour.). Contbr. articles to profl. jours. Served to cpl. U.S. Army, 1951-53. Mem. Am. Educl. Research Assn., Philosophy Educ. Soc., Am. Soc. Info. Sci. Roman Catholic. Avocations: golf, gardening, classical music. Office: Case Western Reserve Univ 2040 Adelbert Rd Cleveland OH 44106

DERRYBERRY, BOBBY RAY, speech communications educator; b. Wardville, Okla., July 19, 1937; s. Byron and Trudy (Elmore) D.; m. Anita Joyce Nettles, Dec. 24, 1958; children—Elisa, Marian. B.A., East Central Okla. State U., 1960, M.Teaching, 1962; M.A., U. Ark., 1966, Ph.D., U. Mo., 1973. Instr., Southwest Bapt. U., Bolivar, Mo., 1961-69, asst. prof., 1970-78, assoc. prof. speech communication, chmn. dept., 1981—; grad. instr. U. Mo.-Columbia, 1969-70; prof., chmn. speech dept. Ouachita Bapt. U., Arkadelphia, Ark., 1978-81, dir. debate-forensics, 1970-78, 81—; Mo. province gov. Pi Kappa Delta, 1976-78, 82-84, teams ranked superior, 1969, 73, 75, 77, 83, ranked 1st, 1985, assoc. editor Forensic, 1978-80. Contbr. chpts. to textbook. Mem. Mo. Speech Assn. (editor Newsletter 1984-85), Speech Communication Assn. Democrat. Baptist. Lodge: Masons. Avocations: Writing; walking; tennis; church activities. Home: 1725 W Northwood St Bolivar MO 65613 Office: Dept Speech Communications Southwest Baptist Univ Bolivar MO 65613

DERTIEN, JAMES LEROY, librarian; b. Kearney, Nebr., Dec. 14, 1942; s. John Ludwig and Muriel May (Cooley) D.; m. Elaine Paulette Mohror, Dec. 26, 1965; children—David Dalton, Channing Lee. A.B., U. S.D., 1965; M.L.S., U. Pitts., 1966. Head librarian Sioux Falls Coll. (S.D.), 1967-69; acting dir. libraries U. S.D.-Vermillion, 1969-70; chief librarian City of Bismarck (N.D.), 1970-75; city librarian City of Bellevue (Nebr.), 1975-81, Sioux Falls Pub. Library, 1981—. Served with U.S. Army, 1966-67. Mem. ALA, Mountain Plains Library Assn. (editor newsletter 1983—), Beta Phi Mu. Democrat. Unitarian. Lodge: Rotary. Home: 1602 Carter Pl Sioux Falls SD 57105 Office: 201 N Main Ave Sioux Falls SD 57102

DESALVO, LOUIS JOSEPH, business education educator, consultant; b. Chgo., Mar. 3, 1944; s. Anthony and Josephine DeSalvo; B.S. in Bus., DePaul U., 1966, M.Ed. in Adminstrn., 1972. Chmn., instr. bus. edn. dept. Providence-St. Mel's High Sch., Chgo., 1966-69; adminstrv. asst. dir. DePaul U., Chgo., 1968-70; instr. bus. edn. Lyons Twp. High Sch., Ill., 1969-75, curriculum workshop coordinator, 1970—, career edn. coordinator, 1975—; tng. specialist Chgo. Skill Ctr., 1970-76; instr. Triton Community Coll., 1973—, Moraine Valley Community Coll., 1982—; auditor Continental Ill. Bank, Chgo., 1967-69, also Cumberland Investment, La Grange, Ill.; cons. in field; lectr. various colls. and univs.; adviser ednl. and bus. agys.; resource person to dir. of consumer affairs, Washington. Author: Consumer Finance, 1977; Graduation, Then What; (with other) several learning packets and microcomputer programs. Contbr. articles to profl. jours. Mem. NEA, Nat. Coop. Work Experiences Edn. Assn. (v.p.), Nat. Bus. Edn. Assn., Ill. Vocat. Assn., Ill. Office Edn. Assn., Ill. Fedn. Consumers, Ill. Edn. Assn., Ill. Consumer Edn. Assn., Cath. Bus. Edn. Assn., Ill. Coop. Vocal. Edn. Coordinators Assn. (pres.), Am. Council on Consumer Interests, Chgo. Area Bus. Educators Assn., Ill. Bus. Edn. Assn., DePaul U. Alumni Assn. in Edn., Kappa Delta Pi. Home: 1550 N Lake Shore Dr Apt 18D Chicago IL 60610 Office: Lyons Township High Sch 100 S Brainard LaGrange IL 60525

DESCHAMPS, ROBERT LOUIS, industrial designer, educator, artist; b. Springfield, Mass., May 19, 1925; s. Louis Henry and Emma Josephine (Rice) D.; m. Nita Clara Grant, Mar. 21, 1944; children—Robin Lynn, Sharon Lee, Denise Marie, Robert Grant. Student Sch. of Art Inst. Chgo., 1948-51. Account designer Palma Knapp Assocs., River Forest, Ill., 1951-60; pres. Deschamps Mills Assocs., Lombard, Ill., 1960-80, Contours Cons. Design Group, Bartlett, Ill., 1980—; asst. prof. indsl. design Sch. of Art Inst. of Chgo., 1954-69. Designer indsl. tractor (exhibit selection 2d ann. Chgo. Area Indsl. Design Show 1956), woodworking machine (annual design award Product Design Mag 1960). Treas. Benjamin Elem. Sch., West Chicago, Ill., 1965; chmn. bldg. com. Episcopal Ch. of the Resurrection, West Chicago, 1968. Served with U.S. Army, 1943-46, U.S. and ETO. Mem. Indsl. Designers Soc. Am. Republican. Club: Rotary. Avocations: Drawing; painting; model airplanes; tennis; golf. Home: 372 B2 Newport Ln Bartlett IL 60103 Office: Contours Cons Design Group Inc 864 Stearns Rd Bartlett IL 60103

DESMOND, KATHLEEN KADON, art educator, artist; b. Marshfield, Wis., Sept. 2, 1950; d. John Charles and Ann (Preller) Kadon; m. William Dean Desmond, Aug. 8, 1970 (dec.). B.A. in Art Edn., Photography, U. Wis.-Madison, 1973; M.A. in Art Edn., Ariz. State U., 1976, Ed.D. in Art Edn., 1981. One woman art exhbns. include: Scottsdale Community Coll., 1980, U. Wis., 1978; various group and juried exhbns., France, Ariz., Colo., Ohio., Ky., Ill.; art instr. Scottsdale (Ariz.) Community Coll., 1974-81; instr. photography dept. art U. Wis., summer 1978; teaching assoc. art edn. Ariz. State U., Tempe, 1978-81; asst. prof. art edn. Ohio State U.-Newark, 1981—; researcher in teaching models, art and photography and photography; photography for exhbns. Recipient Ariz. State U. grad. service award in art edn., 1981. Mem. Nat. Art Edn. Assn., Ohio Art Edn. Assn., Ariz. Art Edn. Assn., Soc. Photog. Edn., Columbus Art League, Coll. Art. Assn., Assn. Supervision and Curriculum Am. Ednl. Research Assn., Phi Delta Kappa. Contbr. articles profl. jours. Home: 5254 Karl Rd Columbus OH 43229 Office: Ohio State U Newark OH 43055

DESOMOGYI, AILEEN ADA, retired librarian; b. London, Nov. 26, 1911; d. Harry Alfred and Ada Amelia (Ponten) Taylor; immigrated to Can., 1966; B.A., Royal Holloway Coll., U. London, 1936, M.A., 1938; M.L.S., U. Western Ont., 1971; m. Leslie Kuti, Nov. 22, 1958; m. 2d, Joseph DeSomogyi, July 8, 1966. Librarian in spl. and public libraries, Eng., 1943-66; sr. instr. Nat. Coal Bd., 1957; charge regional collection S.W. Ont., Lawson Library, U. Western Ont., 1967-71; cataloger Coop. Book Centre Can., 1971; mem. staff E. York (Ont.) Public Library, 1971-74; librarian Ont. Ministry Govt. Services Mgmt. and Info. Services Library, 1975-78, Sperry-Univac Computer Systems, Toronto (Ont.) Central Library, 1980-81. Mem. ALA, Internat. Platform Assn., English Speaking Union, Can. Orgn. for Devel. Through Edn., Royal Can. Geog. Soc., Arctic Soc. (charter), Consumers Assn. Can., Can. Wildlife Fedn., Ont. Humane Soc., Internat. Fund Animal Welfare, Endangered Animal Sanctuary, U. Western Ont. Alumni Assn., Royal Holloway Coll. Assn. Roman Catholic. Contbr. articles to profl. jours. Home: 9 Bonnie Brae Blvd Toronto ON M4J 4N3 Canada

DESPRES, LEO ARTHUR, anthropologist; b. Lebanon, N.H., Mar. 29, 1932; s. Leo Arthur and Madeline (Bedford) D.; B.A., U. Notre Dame, 1954, M.A., 1956; Ph.D., Ohio State U., 1960; m. Loretta LaBarre, Aug. 22, 1953; children—Christine, Michelle, Denise, Mary Louise, Renee. Asst. prof. Ohio Wesleyan U., Delaware, 1961-63; from asso. prof. to prof. anthropology Case Western Res. U., Cleve., 1963-74, also chmn. dept.; prof., chmn. dept. sociology and anthropology U. Notre Dame (Ind.), 1974-80, prof. anthropology, 1980—. Social Sci. Research Council fellow, Guyana, 1960-61; Fulbright fellow, 1970-71; NSF research fellow, Brazil, 1984. Fellow AAAS; mem. Am. Anthrop. Assn., Central State Anthrop. Soc., Am. Ethnological Soc., Soc. Applied Anthropology. Roman Catholic. Author: Cultural Pluralism and Nationalist Politics in British Guiana, 1967; editor and contributor: Ethnicity and Resource Competition in Plural Societies. Office: Dept Sociology and Anthropology Univ of Notre Dame Notre Dame IN 46556

DETWILER, DONALD S., history educator; b. 1933; married; 1 child. B.A. in History, George Washington U., 1954; Dr.phil. cum laude, Göttingen U., Germany, 1961. From instr. to asst. prof. Montgomery Coll., Md., 1962-65; asst. prof. W.Va. U., Morgantown, 1965-67; asst. prof. history So. Ill. U., Carbondale, 1967, now prof. Author: Hitler, Franco und Gibralter, 1962; Germany: A Short History, 1976; Translator, editor: Hitler; The Man and the Military Leader, 1972. Contbr. articles to encys. profl. jours. Editor: World War II German Military Studies (24 vols.), 1979; supplement to Official War Diary of the OKW, 1979; War in Asia and the Pacific (15 vols.), 1980. Am. Philos. Soc. grantee, 1969, 74; Am. Council Learned Socs. and German Acad. Exchange Service grantee, 1978. Mem. Am. Com. on History of Second World War (sec., newsletter editor), Com. on History in Classroom (co-chmn.), Assn. Bibliography History (past pres), Am. Hist. Assn., Conf. Group on Central European History, Inter-Univ. Seminar on Armed Forces and Soc., Soc. for Spanish and Portuguese Hist. Studies, U.S. Commn. on Mil. History, Assn. German Studies, Phi Beta Kappa. Episcopalian. Home: 201 Travelstead Ln Carbondale IL 62901 Office: So Ill U Dept History Carbondale IL 62901

DETWILER, RONALD LEE, optometrist; b. Salem, Ohio, Jan. 17, 1948; s. Donald Lee and Virginia May (Prouty) D.; m. Marilou Douglass, Nov. 26, 1977; children—Kristin, Jeffrey, Daniel. B.S., Kent State U., 1970; B. in Visual Sci., Ill. Coll. Optometry, 1975, O.D., 1975. Gen. practice optometry, East Liverpool, Ohio, 1975—; pres. Vision League of Ohio, Columbus, 1978. Bd. dirs. Columbiana County Mental Health Assn., Lisbon, Ohio, 1982—; exec. bd. dirs. Columbiana County council, Boy Scouts Am. 1984—; county chmn. Columbiana County Cystic Fibrosis Assn., East Liverpool, 1979, 80, 85; bd. dirs. Northeast Ohio Regional Council on Alcoholism, Warren, 1980-82. Mem. Northeast Ohio Optometric Assn. (pres. 1979-80, Zone Activity award 1980), Ohio Optometric Found., Better Vision Inst., Ohio Optometric Assn. (chmn. pub. info. 1979, trustee 1980-84, sec.-treas. 1984, pres. 1985—), Salem Jaycees (pres. 1977-78, Outstanding Local Pres. award 1978, Disting. Service award 1978), Council on Sport Vision. Republican. Methodist. Lodges: Kiwanis (East Liverpool) (trustee 1979-80); Elks. Avocation: breeding Arabian horses. Home: 3437 W Garfield Rd Columbiana OH 44408 Office: 122 W 5th St East Liverpool OH 43920

DEUEL, DAVID JOHN, tool manufacturing company executive; b. Bay City, Mich., Sept. 24, 1945; s. Raymond David and Marie June (Gibas) D.; m. Debra Kay Hugo, May 27, 1972; children—Ashley Lynn, Erik Michael. Sales clk. Walgreen Drugs, Bay City, Mich., 1963-64; insp. Chevrolet Mfg., Bay City, Mich., 1964-67; with Wieland Furniture, Bay City, Mich., 1969-70; tool maker Gil Ray Tools, Bay City, Mich., 1970-80, owner, pres., 1981—. Contbr. articles to tech. jours. Mem. edn. com. Bay City Right to Life, 1981; lay pastor Calvary Fellowship Christian Ch., 1976-82, treas., 1972-81. Served with USNR, 1967-68. Mem. Soc. Mfg. Engrs., Associated Locksmiths Am. (assoc.), Bay Area C. of C. Republican. Lodge: Elks. Home: 204 Sharpe St Essexville MI 48732 Office: Gil Ray Tools Inc 1306 McGraw St PO Box 801 Bay City MI 48707

DEUEL, RUTHMARY SPEAR, neurologist, neuroscientist; b. N.Y.C., Mar. 24, 1935; d. W. Spear and Dorothy Harwood (Smedley) Knebel; m. Thomas F. Deuel, Aug. 27, 1960; children—Julia S., Katherine S., Thomas A. B.A., Mt. Holyoke Coll., 1956; postgrad. in German lang. U. Freiburg, 1957; M.D., Columbia U. Coll. Physicians and Surgeons, 1961. Diplomate Am. Bd. Psychiatry and Neurology. Intern, resident U. Chgo. Hosp., 1961-64; neurology resident Peter Bent Brigham-Children's Hosp., Boston, 1964-66; postdoctoral fellow NIMH, Bethesda, Md., 1966-69; neurol. resident Johns Hopkins Hosp., Balt., 1969-70; postdoctoral fellow Washington U., 1970-71; asst. prof. neurology U. Chgo., 1971-76, dir. neurophysiology lab., 1971-76; asst. prof. neurol. pediatrics, Washington U., St. Louis, 1977-80, assoc. prof. pediatrics and neurology, 1980—; primary investigator distant brain metabolic effects of damage in nervous system, 1979—. Profl. advisor Assn. for Children with Learning Disorders, State of Mo., 1980—. NIH research grantee, 1985. Fellow Am. Acad. Neurology; mem. Child Neurol. Soc., Soc. for Neurosci. Episcopalian. Office: Dept Neurology Washington U 710 S Euclid Ave Saint Louis MO 63110

DEUTSCH, ALLEEN DIMITROFF, educational administrator; b. Cleve., Dec. 5, 1946; d. Joseph A. and Mildred A. (Dimitroff) D. B.A., Bowling Green State U., 1969; M.S., Miami U., Oxford Ohio, 1972, Ph.D., 1978. Asst. dean Coll. Arts and Scis., Miami U., Oxford, 1973-79; asst. to provost Bradley U., Peoria, Ill., 1979-83, dir. div. continuing edn. and profl. devel., 1983—, adj. prof. Coll. Edn. Pres. Planned Parenthood Greater Peoria, 1983-85, bd. dirs., 1981—; mem. com. United Way, 1980—; bd. dirs. Peoria YWCA, 1981-84. Mem. Am. Assn. Higher Edn. (women's caucus), Am. Assn. Adult and Continuing Edn., Am. Soc. Tng. and Devel., Nat. Assn. Women Deans, Adminstrs. and Counselors, Nat. Univ. continuing Edn. Assn. (region IV chmn. women's div.), Nat. Women's Studies Assn., Phi Delta Kappa, Phi Kappa Phi, Alpha Lambda Delta. Home: 1008 W College St Peoria IL 61606 Office: Bradley U 118 Bradley Hall Peoria IL 61625

DEUTSCH, FLORENCE ELAYNE GOODILL, nursing administrator; b. San Diego, Aug. 1, 1923; d. George Ehrlich and Beatrice Marie (Urick) Goodill; m. Edward Thomas Deutsch, June 27, 1953 (dec.); 1 son, George Edward. Student, San Diego State Coll., 1942-43; B.S.N., Villa Maria Coll., 1948; diploma in nursing Evanston Hosp., Northwestern U., 1947; M.Ed., Edinboro U., 1961. Staff nurse St. Vincent Hosp., Erie, Pa., 1947; clin. instr.-supr. Hamot Med. Ctr., Erie, 1948-58, dir. edn., 1958-62, dir. Sch. Nursing, 1962-66, 69-73; exec. dir. Florence Crittenton Home, Erie, 1966-69; asst. adminstr., dir. nursing Capitol Hill Hosp., Washington, 1974-79; assoc. adminstr. profl. services Millcreek Community Hosp., 1980-82; v.p. nursing East Liverpool City Hosp. (Ohio), 1982—; lectr., cons. on nursing and nursing law. Bd. dirs., sec. Columbiana County Cancer Soc. Served with USNR, 1948-53. Named Most Outstanding Nurse Erie County, 1969. Mem. Nat. League Nursing, Am. Orgn. Nurse Execs., Am. Soc. Law and Medicine, East Liverpool C. of C., Sigma Theta Tau, Delta Kappa Gamma. Republican. Presbyterian. Editor: Penn League News, 1968-70; contbr. articles to profl. jours. Address: 13623 Ingles Ave East Liverpool OH 43920

DE VAULT, DENNIS ROBERT, heavy equipment designer; b. Abilene, Tex., July 11, 1941; s. Robert Martin and Muriel Dorothy (Sutherland) DeV.; m. Mary Ann Douglas, Aug. 30, 1963 (div. July 1979); children—Kimberly Jo, Brian Douglas; m. Robyn Renee Suchy, Aug. 25, 1982. B.S. in Agr., U. Ariz., 1968. Factory worker Southwestern Paint Co., Tucson, summers 1956-62; assembler Hughes Aircraft Co., Tucson, 1963; dispatcher El Paso Natural Gas

Co., Tucson, 1963-66; research asst. U. Ariz., Tucson, 1966-68; design engr. Internat. Harvester Co., Memphis, 1968-73; design engr. Melroe Co. div. Clark Equipment Co., Bismarck, N.D., 1973-75, engring. services supr., 1975-83, designer, 1983—. Advisor, Jr. Achievement, Memphis, 1970. Served with USN, 1959-62. Mem. Nat. Mgmt. Assn. (charter, bd. dirs.), Bismarck Mandan Hist. and Geneal. Soc. (pres. 1975, 84, bd. dirs.), Soc. Mayflower Descs. Republican. Methodist. Lodge: Elks. Avocations: genealogy; computers; sports; horseback riding. Home: 1420 E Divide Bismarck ND 58501 Office: Melroe Co Clark Equipment Co 403 Airport Rd Bismarck ND 58501

DEVAULT, ROBERT LARRY, sales specialist in chemicals purification; b. Fairmont, W.Va., Aug. 7, 1936; s. Robert Hugh and Aurieta May (Dalton) D.; m. Julia Sue Hudson, Feb. 1., 1957; children—Adonica Lynne Devault Cross, Robert Larry, Julianna May Devault Jayko, Charlotte Lea. B.S. in Chemistry, Fairmont State Coll., 1958; M.S. in Biochemistry, Purdue U., 1961. Research chemist Bristol Labs., Syracuse, N.Y., 1961-69, Abbott Labs., North Chgo. 1969-81; sales rep. Whatman Inc., Clifton, N.J., 1981-84, AMF, Meriden, Conn., 1984—. Patentee in field of antitumor agts. and antibiotics; contbr. articles to jours. Republican. Presbyterian. Avocations: Drama; choral groups; golf; tennis. Home: 841 E Rockland Rd Libertyville IL 60048

DEVELLANO, JIM, professional sports team executive; b. Jan. 18, 1943. Scout, St. Louis Blues Hockey Team, 1967-72; scout N.Y. Islanders Hockey Team, 1972-74, head scout, 1974-80, asst. gen. mgr., 1981-82; gen. mgr. Detroit Red Wings, NHL, 1982—. Named Exec. of Yr. with Indpls. Checkers of Minor Leagues, Hockey News, 1979-80. Office: Detroit Red Wings Joe Louis Arena 600 Civic Center Dr Detroit MI 48226*

DEVENOW, CHESTER, automobile parts manufacturing executive; b. Detroit, 1919. B.A., NYU, 1941; postgrad. Harvard U. Law Sch. Owner, Devenow News Agy., 1946-48; v.p. Donovan Wire & Iron Co., 1947-60; pres., dir. Globe-Wenicke Industries Inc. (1966 merged with Sheller Mfg. Corp.), 1954-66; pres., chief exec. officer Sheller-Globe Corp., Toledo, 1966-72, chmn. bd., pres., chief exec. officer, 1972-77, chmn. bd., chief exec. officer, dir., 1977—; dir. Blue Cross of Northwestern Ohio, Toledo Trustcorp, Toledo Edison Co., Toledo Trust Co. Chmn. Ohio State U. Served with AUS, 1942-45. Office: Sheller-Globe Corp 1505 Jefferson Ave PO Box 962 Toledo OH 43697

DEVICK, STEVEN DELVERN, optometrist; b. Keokuk, Iowa, Feb. 4, 1952; s. Royce D. and Gayle Elaine (Skyles) D.; m. Susan Diane Roush, Dec. 23, 1978; children—Samantha, Ashley, Lindsay. B.S., Western Ill. U., 1972; D.O., Ill. Coll. Optometry, 1976. Lic. optometrist, Ill. Staff optometrist Western Med. Assn., Chgo., 1976-80, Union Eye Care Ctr., Chgo., 1976-78; staff chmn. contact lenses Chgo. Eye, Ear, Nose and Throat Hosp., Chgo., 1976-79; owner, optometrist Good Samaritan Hosp., Downers Grove, Ill, 1976—. Mem. Am. Optometric Assn., Ill. Optometric Assn. (polit. keyman 1982—), West Suburban Optometric Assn. (v.p. civic and legal affairs 1982-84), Downers Grove C. of C. Republican. Lutheran. Lodge: Lions (Oak Brook). Avocations: golf; scuba. Home: 1106 Midwest Club Pkwy Oak Brook IL 60521 Office: Good Samaritan Hosp 3825 Higland #3B Downers Grove IL 60515

DEVIENCE, ALEXANDER, JR., lawyer; b. Chgo., Nov. 18, 1938; s. Alexander and Charlotte D.; B.A., U. Md., 1964; J.D., Loyola U., Chgo., 1967. Admitted to Ill. bar, 1968; assoc. John H. McCollom, Chgo., 1967-70; sole practice law, Chgo., 1970-81; ptnr. Devience and O'Meara, 1981—; prof. bus. law and bus. adminstrn. DePaul U., Chgo., 1971—. Sec., Regional Recidivist Alcoholism Programs. Served with USN, 1956-64. Mem. ABA Ill. Bar Assn., Chgo. Bar Assn., Am. Bus. Law Profs. Assn. Lutheran. Home: 630 Sylviawood St Park Ridge IL 60068

DE VINE, JOHN BERNARD, lawyer; b. Ann Arbor, Mich., Feb. 5, 1920; s. Frank Bernard and Elizabeth Catherine (Doherty) DeV.; A.B., U. Mich., 1941; J.D., Harvard U., 1948; m. Margaret Louise Burke, Apr. 23, 1949; children—Margaret Louise DeVine Mumby, Ann Elizabeth DeVine Hawkins, Kathleen Kennedy, Susan Joan, John Kennedy. Admitted to Mich. bar, 1948; partner firm DeVine, DeVine & Serr, Ann Arbor, 1948—; asst. pros. atty. County of Washtenaw, Mich., 1948-52; dir. Nat. Bank & Trust Co. of Ann Arbor, Nat. Ann Arbor Corp.; mem. Detroit adv. bd. Mich. Consol. Gas Co. Founder NCCJ, Ann Arbor; chmn. Catholic Social Services, Washtenaw County, 1960-64; bd. dirs. Ann Arbor Devel. Council, Nat. Inst. for Burn Medicine. Served to lt. U.S. Navy, 1942-46. Mem. Am. Bar Assn., Mich. Bar Assn. (dir.), Washtenaw County Bar Assn., Am. Soc. Hosp. Attys. (pres.), Mich. Soc. Hosp. Attys. (past pres.), Mich. Hosp. Assn. Roman Catholic. Club: Barton Hills Country. Home: 2121 Wallingford Rd Ann Arbor MI 48104 Office: 300 National Bank & Trust Bldg Ann Arbor MI 48104

DE VINE, LAWRENCE, theater critic; b. N.Y.C., Sept. 21, 1935; s. John Justin and Hazel (Tippit) DeV.; student Georgetown U., 1953-54; B.S. in Journalism, Medill Sch. Journalism, Northwestern U., 1957; postgrad. (Nat. Endowment for Humanities profl. journalism fellow) U. Mich., 1975-76; m. Jane Christian, 1959 (div. Apr. 1968); children—John Justin, II, Ellen Morse; m. 2d Lucy Memory Williamson, July 26, 1968. Theater critic Miami (Fla.) Herald, 1962-67, Los Angeles Herald-Examiner, 1967-68, Detroit Free Press, 1968—; Critic fellow Eugene O'Neill Theater Center, Waterford, Conn., 1971, asso. dir. Nat. Critics Inst., 1973—; critic-in-residence Am. Coll. Theater Festival, 1978-80, mem. nat. playwrighting jury, 1979; mem. Pulitzer Prize jury for drama, 1981—; lectr. in theater criticism U. Detroit, 1974. Served with CIC, U.S. Army, 1958-62. Mem. Am. Theatre Critics Assn. (chmn. exec. com.), Internat. Assn. Theatre Critics (bd. dirs. 1981—), Beta Theta Pi. Roman Catholic. Contbr. articles to Yale Drama Rev., N.Y. Mag., Los Angeles Times, and Knight-Ridder news wire syndication. Office: Detroit Free Press Detroit MI 48231

DEVINE, MICHAEL BUXTON, lawyer; b. Des Moines, Oct. 25, 1953; s. Cleatie Hiram, Jr., and Katherine Ann (Buxton) D. Student St. Peter's Coll., Oxford U., Eng., 1975; B.A. cum laude, St. Olaf Coll., 1976; M.P.A., Drake U., 1980, J.D., 1980. Bar: Iowa 1980, U.S. Dist. Ct. (no. and so. dists.) Iowa 1980, U.S. Ct. Appeals (8th cir.) 1980. Assoc. Bump & Haesemeyer, P.C., Des Moines, 1980—. Active Common Cause, ACLU, Democratic Nat. Com. Scholar St. Olaf Coll., 1972-76; nat. alt. U.S. Presdl. Mgmt. Intern Program, 1980. Mem. Internat. Law Inst., ABA, Fed. Bar Assn. (chmn. state of Iowa SBA export assistance program 1983—, treas. Iowa chpt. 1984—), Iowa Bar Assn., Internat. Bar Assn., Polk County Bar Assn., Phi Alpha Theta, Pi Alpha Alpha, Phi Alpha Delta. Presbyterian. Home: 3508 49th St Des Moines IA 50310 Office: Bump & Haesemeyer PC 2 Corporate Pl Suite 200 1501 42nd St West Des Moines IA 50265

DEVINE, RICHARD ARTHUR, architect, construction company executive; b. Green Bay, Wis., Sept. 7, 1937; s. Arthur Joseph and Florence Irene (Olson) D.; m. Cynthia von Storch, Aug. 22, 1959; children—Craig Richard, Charlotte Adrienne, Derek Joseph. B.A., Lawrence Coll., 1959; B.Arch., U. Ill., 1963, M.S., 1964. Registered architect, Ill., Calif.; registered profl. engr., Calif. Structural engr. A. C. Martin & Assocs., Los Angeles, 1964-67, constrn. adminstr., 1968-76; project mgr. Conrad Engrs., Van Nuys, Calif., 1967-68; gen. mgr. Contempo Vans, Warren, Ohio, 1976-79; constrn. mgr. L. L. Farber, Inc., Pompano Beach, Fla., 1979-80; owner Devine Constrn. Co., Geneva, Ill., 1980-85; architect, constrn. mgr. Perman Constrn./Goodman Devel., Chgo., 1985—. Dist. chmn. Boy Scouts Am., St. Charles, Ill., 1984-85, vice chmn., 1983, dist. commr., 1982; various dist. and unit positions, St. Charles, Canfield, Ohio and Los Angeles, 1968-82; v.p. Geneva Music Boosters, 1984-85, pres., 1985-86. Inland Steel-Ryerson Found. fellow, 1963-64; recipient award of Merit, Ruberoid Matico Urban Design Competition, 1963; Fidelity award for Outstanding Community Service, Fidelity Fed. Savs. and Loan Assn., 1973; Dist. Award of Merit, Mid-Valley Dist., Gt. Western council Boy Scouts Am., 1974, Wood badge, 1974, Order of Arrow-Ordeal, 1970, Order of Arrow-Brotherhood, 1972, Scouters Tng. award, 1971, Scouters Key, 1976; Top Ten award, Albert C. Martin and Assocs., 1974, 75. Mem. Structural Engrs. Assn. Soc. Calif., Gargoyle (nat. scholastic hon. soc.), Scarab (nat. archtl. profl. hon. soc.), Phi Kappa Tau. Republican. Lutheran. Home: 2244 Pepper Valley Dr Geneva IL 60134 Office: Perman Constrn Co 414 N Orleans IL 60610

DEVINE, VAUGHAN P. (BING), professional baseball team executive; b. Mar. 1, 1917; m. Mary Anderson; children—Joanne Devine Schaumburg, Janice, Jane Devine Pilkington. Grad. Washington U., St. Louis. Mem. staff stats. dept. St. Louis Cardinals Nat. League baseball team, until 1939, asst. pub. relations dept., 1939-41, mgr. bus. Cardinals farm system teams, Johnson City, Tenn., 1941-42, Fresno, Calif., 1942, Decatur, Ill., 1942, mgr. farm system team, Columbus, Ga., 1946-49, gen. mgr. farm system team, Rochester, 1949-55, exec. asst. to gen. mgr. parent orgn., St. Louis, 1955-57, gen. mgr., 1957-64, 67-78; exec. v.p., 1973-78; v.p. adminstrn. St. Louis Cardinals, NFL, 1979-81, pres., chief operating officer, 1982—; pres., gen. mgr. N.Y. Mets, 1965-67; v.p. baseball Montreal Expos, 1981. Served with USNR, 1943-46; PTO. Recipient Major League Exec. of Yr. award, 1963, 64. Office: St Louis Cardinals 200 Stadium Plaza Saint Louis MO 63102*

DEVINEY, MARVIN LEE, JR., chemical company executive, research scientist; b. Kingsville, Tex., Dec. 5, 1929; s. Marvin Lee and Esther Lee (Gambrell) D.; B.S. in Chemistry and Math., S.W. Tex. State U., San Marcos, 1949; M.A. in Phys. Chemistry, U. Tex. at Austin, 1952, Ph.D. in Phys. Chemistry, 1956; cert. profl. chemist; m. Marie Carole Massey, June 7, 1975; children—Marvin Lee III, John H., Ann-Marie K. Devel. chemist Celanese Chem. Co., Bishop, Tex., 1956-58; research chemist Shell Chem. Co., Deer Park, Tex., 1958-66; sr. scientist, head group phys. and radio-chemistry Ashland Chem. Co., Houston, 1966-68, mgr. sect. phys. and analytical chemistry, 1968-71, mgr. sect. phys. chemistry div. research and devel., Columbus, Ohio, 1971-78, research assoc., supr. applied surface chemistry, electron microscopy sect., govt. contracts, 1978—; adj. prof. U. Tex., San Antonio, 1973-75. Mem. sci. adv. bd. Am. Petroleum Inst. Research Project 60, 1968-74. Mem. ednl. adv. com. Columbus Tech. Inst., 1974-84, Central Ohio Tech. Coll., 1975-82. Served to lt. col., USAR. Humble Oil Research fellow, 1954. Fellow Am. Inst. Chemists (pres. Ohio Inst. 1978-82, nat. com. mem. 1985—); mem. N.Y., Ohio, Tex. acads. scis., Am. Def. Preparedness Assn., Am. Carbon Soc., Electron Microscopy Soc. Am., Materials Research Soc., Am. Chem. Soc. (chmn. chpt. exec. bd. 1969, Best Paper award rubber div. 1967, 70. Honorable Mention awards 1968, 69, 73; symposia co-chmn., editor 1975, 85), Engr.'s Council Houston (sr. councilor 1970-71), Sigma Xi, Phi Lambda Upsilon, Alpha Chi, Sigma Pi Sigma. Contbr. numerous articles to profl. jours.; patentee in field. Home: 6810 Hayhurst Worthington OH 43085 Office: Box 2219 Columbus OH 43216

DEVISE, PIERRE ROMAIN, educator, city planner; b. Brussels, Belgium, July 27, 1924; s. Victor Pierre and Madeleine (Cupers) deV.; B.A., U. Chgo., 1945, M.A., 1958, Ph.D., 1985; m. Margaret Ahern, Nov. 16, 1978; children—Peter Charles, Daniel Romain. Came to U.S., 1935, naturalized, 1958. Chancellor, Belgian Consul, Chgo., 1945-47, comml. attache, 1947-56, Belgian Consulate Gen., Chgo.; planning dir. Hyde Park-Kenwood Conf., 1956-57; research planner Northeastern Ill. Planning Commn., 1958-60; sr. planner Chgo. City Planning Dept., 1961-63; asst. dir. Hosp. Planning Council for Met. Chgo., 1964-70; asst. dir. Ill. Regional Med. Program, 1971-73; prof. urban scis. U. Ill., 1972-81; prof. polit. sci. Roosevelt U., 1981—; lectr., De Paul U., 1962-72; vis. lectr. U. Mich., 1966, U. Hawaii, 1968, U. Ill., 1969, 70, U. Ia., 1971, U. Chgo., 1972; prin. investigator Chgo. Regional Hosp. Study, 1966-81; exec. dir. Chgo. Commn. to Study Conv. Week Disorders, 1968-70; cons. Chgo. Commn. on Human Relations, 1966, Chgo. Model Cities Program, 1968, Cook County Council of Govts., 1968, Comprehensive Health Planning, Inc., 1971, Census Bur., 1973, U.S. Senate Health Subcom., 1974, HEW, 1975, House Ways and Means Com., 1975, Senate Banking Com., 1976. Bd. dirs. Old Town Boys Club. Mem. Am. Statist. Assn., Chgo. Assn. Commerce and Industry, Am. Pub. Health Assn., Planned Parenthood Assn. Chgo., Assn. Am. Geographers. Club: City (Chgo.). Author monographs including Suburban Factbook, 1960; Social Geography of Metropolitan Chicago, 1960; Chicago's People, Jobs and Homes, 1963; Chicago's Widening Color Gap, 1967; Chicago's Apartheid Hospital System 1968; Chicago: 1971, Ready for Another Fire, 1971; Misused and Misplaced Hospitals and Doctors, 1973; Chicago's Future, 1976; Chicago: Transformations of an Urban System, 1976; Chicago in the Year 2000, 1978. Office: Roosevelt U 430 S Michigan Chicago IL 60605

DEVOLPI, ALEXANDER, physicist; b. N.Y.C., Feb. 28, 1931; s. Paul Bonaventura and Bertha (Gaber) DeV.; m. Helen Genopolis (div.); children—Paul, Dean, Gregory, Marina; m. Judith Carol Klaye, Jan. 14, 1978. B.A. in Journalism, Washington and Lee U., 1953; M.S. in Nuclear Engring. Physics, Va. Poly. Inst., 1958, Ph.D. in Physics, 1967. Mgr. nuclear diagnostics sect. reactor analysis and safety div. Argonne Nat. Lab., Ill., tech. cons., Author: Proliferation, Plutonium and Policy, 1979; (with others) Born Secret, 1981. Patentee in field. Sec. Alliance to End Repression, Chgo., 1969-80. Served to lt. comdr. USN, 1953-56. Mem. Am. Phys. Soc., Am. Nuclear Soc., AAAS. Office: Bldg 208 Argonne Nat Lab Argonne IL 60439

DEVORE, KIMBERLY K., health care executive; b. Louisville., June 19, 1947; d. Wendell O. and Shirley F. DeV.; student (Florence Allen Scholar), Xavier U., 1972-76; A.A., Coll. Mt. St. Joseph, 1979. Patient registration supr. St. Francis Hosp., Cin., 1974-76; cons., bus. mgr. Family Health Care Found., Cin., 1976-77; exec. dir. Hospice of Cin., Inc., 1977-80; pres. Micro Med, 1979—; v.p. Sycamore Profl. Assn., 1979—; ptnr. Enchanted House, 1979—, sec., 1979-80, treas., 1980-83; bd. dirs. Hospice of the Miami Valley, Inc., 1981—, chmn. personnel, by laws com. Mem. service and rehab. com. Hamilton County unit Am. Cancer Soc., 1977-78. Mem. Nat. (treas., sec.; chmn. longterm planning com.), Ohio (co-founder, pres., state chmn.) hospice orgns., Better Housing League, Nat., Ohio, fedns. bus. and profl. women's clubs, Cin. Bus. and Profl. Women's Club (pres. 1973-75). Club: Cin. Woman's.

DEVOS, RICHARD MARVIN, chemical company executive; b. Grand Rapids, Mich., Mar. 4, 1926; s. Simon C. and Ethel R. (Dekker) DeV.; student Calvin Coll., 1946; LL.D. (hon.), Oral Roberts U., Grove City (Pa.) Coll., 1976, Northwood Inst., Midland, Mich., 1977, Dickinson Sch. Law, Carlisle, Pa., 1980, Pepperdine U., 1980, Lubbock Christian Coll., 1981, Hope Coll., Holland, Mich., 1982; m. Helen J. Van Wesep, Feb. 7, 1953. Partner, Wolverine Air Service, 1945-48; co-founder, pres. Ja-Ri Corp., 1949, Amway Corp., 1959—; pres. Amway Pty. Ltd. Australia, 1970—, Amway Hotel Corp., Amway Global, Inc., Ada, Mich., Amway Internat., Inc., Amway (U.K.) Ltd., Amway (Hong Kong) Ltd.; gen. mgr. Amway GmbH (W.Ger.); pres. Amway (Nederland) Ltd., Nutrilite Products Inc., Buena Park, Calif.; co-chmn. dir. Old Kent Bank & Trust, Grand Rapids, Amway (Malaysia) Sdn. Bhd., Amway (Japan) Ltd.; dir., sec. Amway Distbrs. Assn. U.S., Amway Distbrs. Assn. Can.; co-chmn. MBS, Inc., Amway Communications Corp.; pres. Mut. Sports, Inc.; chmn. bd. Reference Map Internat.; chmn. Gospel Films, Muskegon, Mich.; dir., Midwestern regional chmn. BIPAC. Author: Believe! Bd. dirs. past pres. Grand Rapids Jr. Achievement, 1966-67; past bd. control Grand Valley State Colls.; past bd. dirs. United Way Kent County; bd. dirs. Robert Schuller Ministries, Internat. Yr. of Disabled Person, Nat. Legal Center for Public Interest; founder Nat. Orgn. on Disability, 1982; trustee Butterworth Hosp., Grand Rapids; past chmn. New Grand Rapids Com.; mem. corp. Northwood Inst. bd. advisers Butterworth Hosp.; nat. fin. chmn. America II Challenge. Served with USAAF, 1944-46. Recipient Alexander Hamilton award for econ. edn. Freedoms Found.; Disting. Salesman of Year award Grand Rapids Sales and Mktg. Execs.; Bus. Leader of Yr. award Religious Heritage Am.; Industry Week Excellence in Mgmt. award; Thomas Jefferson Freedom of Speech award Kiwanis Internat.; Mich. Week Vol. Leadership award; Mktg. Man of Yr. award West Mich. chpt. Am. Mktg. Assn.; Am. Enterprise Exec. award Nat. Mgmt. Assn.; George Washington Honor medal Freedoms Found.; Free Enterprise award Americanism Ednl. League, Disting. Alumni award Calvin Coll., 1982, Patron award Mich. Found. for Arts, 1982, Outstanding Bus. Leader award Northwood Inst., 1982; named Nat. Sales Exec. of Yr., Sales and Mktg. Execs. of Washington, 1984. Mem. NAM (dir.), Direct Selling Assn. (past chmn., dir., Champion of Free Enterprise and Knights of Royal Way awards, Hall of Fame award), Newcomen Soc., Round Table, Omicron Delta Kappa (hon.). Mem. Christian Reformed Ch. (elder, chmn. fin. com.; past pres. missionary soc.; mem. bd. missions). Clubs: Economic (dir.), Rotary (Disting. Service award) (Grand Rapids); Pillars (bd. dirs.). Featured in film Believe! Home: Grand Rapids MI Office: 7575 E Fulton Rd Ada MI 49355

DEVRIES, GERRIT HENRY, optometrist; b. Chgo., Sept. 16, 1952; s. Gerrit and Leona (Ebbens) DeV.; m. Dianne Sue Kiekover, Aug. 10, 1974; children—Jennifer Sue, Ryan Gerrit. O.D., Ill. Coll. Optometry, Chgo., 1977. Assoc. Dr. Henry R. DeBoer, Lansing, Ill., 1977-79; ptnr. Drs. Sayre & DeVries, DeMotte, Ind., 1979-83; pres. Dr. Gerrit H. DeVries, Optometrist, DeMotte, Ind., 1984—. Pres., DeMotte Park Bd., 1980-81; mem. DeMotte Bd. Zoning Appeals, 1983—; pres. DeMotte Christian Sch. PTA, 1984-85, mem. sch. bd., 1984—, sec. sch. bd., 1985-86. Mem. Am. Optometric Assn., Ind. Optometric Assn., Northwest Ind. Optometric Soc. (pres.-elect 1985), Beta Sigma Kappa. Republican. Christian Reformed. Avocations: Camping, carpentry. Home: 617 Cedar St NW DeMotte IN 46310 Office: 329 N Halleck St PO Box 154 DeMotte IN 46310

DEW, RANDALL KEITH, ruminant nutritionist; b. Aledo, Ill., Nov. 27, 1954; s. Keith Erskine and Dorothy Virgene (Anderson) D.; m. Nancy Creviston, Sept. 3, 1977. B.S. in Animal Sci., Western Ill. U., 1976; M.S. in Animal Sci., Mont. State U., 1981; postgrad. in ruminant nutrition U. Ky., 1985. Nutrition counselor Moorman Mfg. Co., Quincy, Ill., 1976-79; research asst. Mont. State U., 1979-81; beef projects mgr. Internat. Multifoods, Inc., Mpls., 1981. Mem. Am. Soc. Animal Sci. (cert.), Dairy Sci. Assn., Sigma Xi, Alpha Gamma Sigma. Republican. Office: 800 SW Lincoln St LeMars IA 51031

DEWALD, RONALD L., physician, educator; b. Aurora, Ill., Oct. 4, 1934; s. Lee H. and Elsie (Kellen) DeW.; B.S., U. Ill., 1955, M.D., 1959; m. Mary Lee Johnstone, July 21, 1956; children—Ann Elise, Lee Fraser, Christopher James, Ronald Lee. Intern, Presbyn. St. Lukes Hosp., Chgo., 1959-60; resident U. Ill. Hosp., Chgo., 1960-62, 64-65; asst. prof. orthopaedic surgery, 1965-67, asso. prof., 1967-71; prof., chmn. dept., Stritch Sch. Medicine Loyola at Chgo., 1972-73; prof. Rush Med. Coll., Chgo., 1973—. Cons. surgeon Ill. Div. Services for Crippled Children, 1967—, Ill. Childrens Hosp. Sch., Chgo., 1968-84, Holy Family Hosp., Des Plaines, 1972-78, Hines (Ill.) VA Hosp., 1972—; asso. surgeon Shriners Hosp. for Crippled Children, Chgo., 1972—. Served to capt. M.C., AUS, 1962-64. Diplomate Am. Bd. Orthopaedic Surgery (bd. examiners 1973—). Fellow A.C.S.; mem. A.M.A. (Hektoen Silver medal 1971), Chgo., Ill. med. socs., Chgo., Clin. orthopaedic socs., Scoliosis Research Soc. (founding, dir.), Am. Acad. Orthopadic Surgeons (regional admissions chmn. 1975—), Ill. Orthopaedic Assn., Am. Orthopaedic Assn. Contbr. articles to profl. jours. Office: 1725 Harrison St W Chicago IL 60612

DEWANE, JOHN RICHARD, manufacturing company executive; b. Cooperstown, Wis., Mar. 4, 1934; s. Clarence John and Arvilla Anne (Gannon) D.; B.S.M.E., U. Wis., 1957; M.B.A., U. Minn., 1973; m. Judith Anne Arnold, Mar. 17, 1974; 1 dau., Kelly Susanne. Dir. mktg. planning Honeywell, Inc., Washington, 1974-76, dir. mktg., Mpls., 1976-78, v.p. service engring., 1979-81, v.p. bus. devel., 1981-82, v.p., gen. mgr., 1982—. Vice chmn. Community Long-Range Improvement Com., Maple Grove, Minn., 1980-81, chmn. Econ. Devel. Commn., 1982—; mem. Polit. Action com., Honeywell, 1979-83; mem. U. Wis. Alumni Adv. Council; mem. tech. adv. com. on transp. equipment U.S. Dept. Commerce. Served with USN, 1957-60. Navy scholar, 1952-57. Lic. pvt. pilot. Mem. Assn. Unmanned Vehicles, U.S. Navy League, Air Force Assn., Assn. U.S. Army, Am. Def. Preparedness Assn., Aircraft Owners and Pilots Assn., Gen. Aviation Mfrs. Assn. (dir. 1983—, chmn. forecasting com.). Mpls. C. of C. (aviation com. 1980—). Office: 5775 Wayzata Blvd Minneapolis MN 55440

DEWAR, A. S., judge. Chief justice Ct. Queen's Bench, Manitoba, Can. Office: Ct of Queen's Bench Law Courts Bldg Winnipeg Manitoba R3C 0V8 Canada*

DEWAR, ROBERT EARL, retail company executive. Chmn. exec. and fin. coms. K Mart Corp., Troy, Mich. Office: K Mart Corp 3100 W Big Beaver Rd Troy MI 48084*

DEWEY, JOHN D., college athletics executive; b. Joliet, Ill., May 18, 1929; s. Domer E. and Amber J. (Gilbert) D.; m. Ann D. Lindstrom, June 10, 1967. B.S. in Bus. Adminstr., Northwestern U., 1951. Staff auditor Purdue U., West Layfatte, Ind., 1953-57; asst. commr. Big Ten Conf., Schaumburg, Ill., 1957—; sec.-treas. Collegiate Commrs. Assn., Schaumburg, 1974—. Served to capt. USAF, 1951-53. Mem. Nat. Assn. Collegiate Dirs. of Athletics. Presbyterian. Lodge: Elks. Avocation: fishing. Home: 54 Brookdale Ln Palatine IL 60067 Office: Big Ten Conf 1111 Plaza Dr Schaumburg IL 60195

DEWEY, PATRICK RONALD, librarian; b. Pontiac, Mich., Mar. 4, 1949; s. Wilbur Joseph and Hazel (Stuart) D. A.A., Oakland Community Coll., 1971; B.S. in Psychology, Oakland U., 1971; postgrad. Wayne State U., 1973. Paraprofl. II, Oakland Community Coll., Bloomfield Hills, Mich., 1971-74; editorial librarian Playboy Enterprises, Inc., Chgo., 1974-75; reference librarian Eckhart Park Library, Chgo., 1975-76, Toman Library, Chgo., 1976-78; head librarian North Austin Library, Chgo., 1978-81, North-Pulaski Library, Chgo., 1981—; lectr. in field. Author: Public Access Microcomputers: A Handbook for Librarians, 1984; columnist Wilson Library Bull., Library Software Rev.; contbr. articles to profl. jours. Recipient Career Service award, Chgo. Pub. Library, 1983; Chgo. Pub. Library grantee, 1981. Mem. Pub. Library Assn. (mem. com. task force on microcomputers 1982—). Office: Maywood Pub Library 121 S 5th Ave Maywood IL 60153

DE WINDT, EDWARD MANDELL, See *Who's Who in America,* 43rd edition.

DEWINE, MICHAEL, congressman; b. Springfield, Ohio, Jan. 5, 1947; s. Richard and Jean DeWine; m. Frances Struewing; children—Patrick, Jill, Rebecca, John, Brian, Alice. B.S., Miami U., Oxford, Ohio, 1969; J.D., Ohio Northern U. Coll. Law, 1972. Asst. pros. atty. Greene County, Ohio, 1973-75, pros. atty., 1977-81; mem. Ohio State Senatorial Dist. 10, 1981-83; mem. 98th-99th Congresses from 7th Dist. Ohio, mem. Judiciary Com. and Crime, Civil and Constitution Rights, Courts, Civil Liberties and Adminstrn. Justice subcoms., select com. on Aging, 1983—; mem. Greene County Republican Com.; mem. DeWine, Schenck & Rose, Xenia, Ohio, 1973-82, DeWine, Rose, Haller & Sidell, Xenia, 1982—. Mem. Green County Bar Assn., Nat. Dist. Atty. Assn., Ohio Prosecuting Atty. Assn., Fraternal Order Police Assn. Office: 1519 Longworth House Office Bldg Washington DC 20515*

DEWING, ROLLAND LLOYD, educational administrator; b. Portal, N.D., Apr. 11, 1934; s. Lloyd Jacob and Mary (Dalebout) D.; m. Deloris Marie Filleau, June 16, 1956; children—Bridget, Rolland Dean, Amy, James. B.A., Central Wash. State Coll., 1956, M.Ed., 1963; Ph.D., Ball State U., 1967. Cert. tchr., Wash. jr. high tchr. social studies Port Angles Pub. Sch., (Wash.), 1956, 58-64; grad. teaching fellow Ball State U., Muncie, Ind., 1964-66; asst. prof. history, then assoc. prof. Morehead State U., Ky., 1966-69; chmn. social sci. div. Chadron State Coll., Nebr., 1969—; cons. Nebr. Ednl. TV., Lincoln, 1984—. Author: Wounded Knee: The Meaning and Significance of the Second Incident, 1984. Co-author, editor: Centennial History of Chadron, 1985. Contbr. articles to prof. publs. Served with U.S. Army, 1957-58. Doctoral fellow Ball State U., 1964-66. Mem. Western Social Sci. Assn., Nebr. State Hist. Soc., Dawes county Hist. Soc., Phi Delta Kappa. Democrat. Lodge: Rotary. Avocations: Tennis, bridge, fishing, gardening, reading. Home: 899 E 6th Chadron NE 69337 Office: Chadron State Coll Box 13 CSC 10th and Main Chadron NE 69337

DE WITT, JESSE R., See *Who's Who in America,* 43rd edition.

DEXTRAS, MARY LOU, religious organization coordinator; b. Youngstown, Ohio, Sept. 20, 1922; d. Guido and Catherine (Spagnola) Bernard; m. Albert Raymond Dextras, Feb. 9, 1946; children—Suzanne, Paul A., Cathie, Mary Alice, Dee Anne. Student Youngstown Bus. Sch., Wichita State U., 1984—. Exec. sec. U.S. Air Force, Kadena, Okinawa, 1957-62; youth dir. McConnell AFB, Wichita, Kans., 1963-64; real estate agt. Egan Realtors, Derby, Kans., 1965-80; coordinator Congregation Sisters of St. Joseph Coordinated Services, Wichita, 1980—. Served to sgt. USMCWR, 1942-45. Mem. Derby Arts Council, Kans. Named Mother of Yr., Bergstrom AFB, Austin, 1956; recipient Koza Shi Fujenkai award Women's Fedn., Okinawa, 1960; People-to-People award Pres. Eisenhower, 1961. Mem. Derby Bd. Edn., pres., 1978-79, 84-85. Democrat. Roman Catholic. Lodges: Soroptimists, K.C. Aux. (Derby, Kans.). Avocations: Tap dancing; piano. Office: Congregation of Sisters of St Joseph Coordinated Services 3720 E Bayley Wichita KS 67218

DEYSACH, LAWRENCE GEORGE, pharmaceutical company executive; b. Milw., July 9, 1936; s. Leonard Joseph and Geraldine (Perrigo) D.; m. Mary Jo Bunce, Sept. 10, 1966; children—Seth Lawrence, Sarah Miriam, Rebecca Ayn. B.S. summa cum laude, Marquette U., 1957; A.M., Harvard U., 1963; postgrad. U. Chgo., 1967. Lectr. U. Chgo., 1967-69; med. statistician G.D. Searle & Co., Skokie, Ill., 1969-76, sr. biostatistician, 1976-84, supr. med. statistics, 1984—. Mem. Am. Statis. Assn., Biometrics Soc., Sigma Xi. Avocation: profl. singer-bass. Home: 944 Wesley St Evanston IL 60202 Office: G D Searle & Co 4901 Searle Pkwy Skokie IL

DIAL, ELEANORE MAXWELL, foreign language educator; b. Norwich, Conn., Feb. 21, 1929; d. Joseph Walter and Irene (Beetham) Maxwell; B.A., U. Bridgeport (Conn.), 1951; M.A. in Spanish, Mexico City Coll., 1955; Ph.D.,

U. Mo., 1968; m. John E. Dial, Aug. 27, 1959. Mem. faculty U. Wisc.-Milw., 1968-75, Ind. State U., Terre Haute, 1975-78, Bowling Green (Ohio) State U., 1978-79; asst. prof. dept. fgn. langs. and lits. Iowa State U., Ames, 1979—; reader Latin Am. Theatre Rev., 1973—; cons. pub. co.; participant workshops; del. 1st World Congress Women Journalists and Writers, Mex., 1975, also mem. edn. commn. NDEA grantee, 1967; Center Latin Am. grantee, 1972; Nat. Endowment Humanities summer seminar UCLA, 1982, U. Calif.-Santa Barbara, 1984. Mem. Am. Assn. Tchrs. Spanish and Portuguese, Midwest MLA, MLA, N. Central Council Latin Americanists, Midwest Assn. Latin Am. Studies, Caribbean Studies Assn., Phi Sigma Iota, Sigma Delta Pi. Contbr. articles and revs. to scholarly jours. Home: 3219 Ross Rd Ames IA 50010 Office: Iowa State U Ames IA 50010

DIAMANT, MICHAEL HARLAN, lawyer; b. Cleve., July 30, 1946; s. Eugene and Rita June (Hausman) D.; m. Amy Sarah Bresnick, Nov. 23, 1969; children—Aaron Jeremy, Ethan Ari. B.S. in Engring. with high honors, Case Inst. Tech. Case Western Reserve, 1968; J.D. com laude, Harvard Univ., 1971. Bar: Ohio 1971, U.S. Dist. Ct. No. Dist. Ohio 1973, U.S. Ct. of Appeals 6th Cir. 1977, U.S. Ct. Appeals Fed Cir. 1982, U.S. Supreme Ct. 1977. Prin., Kahn, Kleinman, Yanowitz & Arnson Co., L.P.A., Cleve., 1971—; Pres., Solomon Schecter Day Sch. of Cleve., 1984—; v.p. Cleve. Hillel Found., 1981-84. Mem. Bar Assn. Greater Cleve. (chmn. Computer Law Inst. 1983—, chmn. judicial selection com. 1985), Cuyahoga County Bar Assn., ABA. Democrat. Jewish. Office: Kahn Kleinman Yanowitz & Arnson Co LPA 1300 Bond Ct Bldg Cleveland OH 44114

DIAMOND, DARROUGH BLAIN, marketing executive; b. Kankakee, Ill., July 27, 1941; s. Noel A. and Sarah Lois (Wertz) Johnson; m. Linda Mann, Aug. 1, 1964; children—Laura Lynn, Julia True. B.S. in Communications, U. Ill., 1963; postgrad. Northwestern U., 1963-64; M.S. in Advt., U. Ill., 1967. Account exec. Leo Burnett Co., Chgo., 1967-73; nat. advt. mgr. McDonald's Corp., Oak Brook, Ill., 1974-76; dir. food service mktg. Walgreen Co., Deerfield, Ill., 1976-77; pres., chief exec. officer Arby's Franchise Assn., Pitts., 1977-80; sr. v.p. mktg. Wendy's Internat., Dublin, Ohio, 1980-81; pres. Darrough Diamond Enterprises, Inc., Columbus, 1981—; dir. Concept Care, Inc., Pitts., Chem. Clearinghouse Corp.; chmn. bd. Diamond Energy Corp., 1983—; cons. in field. Mem. James Webb Young Fund, Chgo./Urbana, 1967-74; mem. Ohio State U. Devel. Com., 1981-82. Served to 1st lt. U.S. Army, 1964-66. Named Marketer of Yr., Adweek Mag., 1981; decorated Army Commendation medal; U. Ill. scholar, 1959-63. Mem. Am. Mgmt. Assn., Alpha Delta Sigma, Kappa Tau Alpha, Sigma Nu. Republican. Club: Muirfield Country. Home: 4240 Woodhall Rd Upper Arlington OH 43220 Office: Diamond Energy Corp PO Box 906 Mount Vernon OH 43050

DIAMOND, EUGENE CHRISTOPHER, hospital lawyer and administrator; b. Oceanside, Calif., Oct. 19, 1952; s. Eugene Francis and Rosemary (Wright) D.; m. Mary Theresa O'Donnell, Jan. 20, 1984. B.A., U. Notre Dame, 1974; M.H.A., St. Louis U., 1978, J.D., 1979. Bar: Ill. 1979. Staff atty. AUL Legal Def. Fund, Chgo., 1979-80; adminstrv. asst. Holy Cross Hosp., Chgo., 1980-81, asst. adminstr., 1981-82, v.p., 1982-83, counsel to adminstr., 1980—, exec. v.p., 1983—; cons. Birthright of Chgo., 1979—; mem. exec. bd. Hosp. Risk Mgmt. Soc. of Met. Chgo., 1982—, pres., 1984—. Mem. benefit com. Birthright of Chgo., 1981—. Mem. ABA, Am. Acad. Hosp. Attys., Nat. Health Lawyer's Assn., Ill. State Bar Assn., Chgo. Bar Assn. Roman Catholic. Office: Holy Cross Hosp 2701 W 68 St Chicago IL 60629

DIAMOND, ROBERT JEROME, real estate broker; b. St. Louis, Sept. 18, 1929; s. Benjamin and Mollie (Grossman) D.; m. Doris Jean Ginsberg, Aug. 22, 1965; children—Melissa Faith, Benjamin Michael. B.B.A., Wash. State U., 1951. Sec./treas. Brown-Diamond Inc., St. Louis, 1962-64; ptnr. Del Crest Plaza Bldg. Co., St. Louis, 1964-80; v.p. Wallace McNeill Co. real estate brokerage, St. Louis, 1980—. Bd. dirs., treas. Del Crest Apts., Univ. City, Mo., 1983—. Clubs: Clayton (Mo.); Media (St. Louis). Home: 7756 Davis Dr Clayton MO 63105 Office: Wallace McNeill Co 120 S Central Ave Clayton MO 63105

DIAMOND, SUSAN Z., management consultant; b. Okla., Aug. 20, 1949; d. Louis Edward and Henrietta (Wood) D.; A.B. (Nat. Merit scholar, GRTS scholar), U. Chgo., 1970; M.B.A., DePaul U., 1979; m. Allan T. Devitt, July 27, 1974. Dir. study guide prodn. Am. Sch. Co., Chgo., 1972-75; publs. supr. Allied Van Lines, Broadview, Ill., 1975-78, sr. account services rep., 1978-79; pres. Diamond Assocs. Ltd., Melrose Park, Ill., 1978—; condr. seminars Am. Mgmt. Assn. Mem. Nat. Assn. Accts., Adminstrv. Mgmt. Soc., Assn. Records Mgrs. and Adminstrs., Internat. Records Mgmt. Council, Records Mgmt. Soc. Gt. Britain, Bus. Forms Mgmt. Assn., Assn. Info. and Image Mgmt., Delta Mu Delta. Author: How to Talk More Effectively, 1972; Preparing Administrative Manuals, 1981; How to Manage Administrative Operations, 1981; How to be an Effective Secretary in the Modern Office, 1982; Records Management: A Practical Guide, 1983; co-author: Finance Without Fear, 1983; editor Mobility Trends, 1975-78. Office: 2851 N Pearl Ave Melrose Park IL 60160

DIAMOND, THOMAS EDWARD, air force officer; b. St. Paul, Aug. 1, 1942; s. Robert Edward and Olivia Theresa (Caron) D.; m. Rise' Pegram, Dec. 27, 1965; children—Thomas M., Robin M., Gregory T. B.S., Mont. State U., 1965; M.A., U. Denver, 1969; grad. Squadron Officer Sch., Air U., 1970, Armed Forces Staff Coll., 1977, Commd. 2d lt. U.S. Air Force, 1965, advanced through grades to col., 1970—; dep. dir. combat photography 7th Air Force, Tan Son Nhut Air Base, Vietnam, 1971-72, chief audiovisual div. Air Force, Pentagon, Washington, 1972-76, chief protocol, Hdqrs. Tactical Air Command, Langley AFB, Va., 1977-79, chief audiovisual div. Hqtrs. Mil. Airlift Command, Scott AFB, Ill., 1979-81, dir. pub. affairs, 1983—; comdr. 1369th Audiovisual Squadron, Vandenberg AFB, Calif., 1981-83; dir. pub. affairs hdqrs. Mil. Airlift Command, Scott AFB, Ill., 1983—; cons. Amish Mil. Adv. and Asst. Group, Tehran, Iran, 1966; Air Force rep. Dept. Def. Joint Service Planning Group, Washington, 1976; bd. dirs. Spirit of St. Louis chpt. USO, 1983—. Writer/producer: Tomorrow is Now, 1969; producer news film: Rescue of Downed American Pilots, 1971. Pres., Our Lady of Stars Parish Council, Vandenberg AFB, 1982. Decorated Bronze Star, Air Medal; recipient Air Power award Mont. State U., 1963. Mem. Air Force Assn. Roman Catholic. Club: Advertising. Home: 1469 Starlifter Circle Scott AFB IL 62225 Office: HQ MAC/PA Bldg 1600 Scott AFB IL 62225

DIAS, MARIA HELENA, university administrator; b. Mombasa, Kenya, East Africa, Dec. 6, 1952; came to U.S., 1962; d. R. Felix and Silvia (Menezes) D. B.A., Frostburg State Coll., 1974; M.Ed., U. Va., 1976. Asst. dean of women Ripon Coll., Wis., 1976-78; fin. counselor Biospherics, Inc., Bethesda, Md., 1978-79; asst. mgr. Purdue U., West Lafayette, Ind., 1979—. Contbr. articles to profl. jours. Mem. Poor and Needy Com., West Lafayette, 1982, Lafayette Urban Ministry, Ind., 1982-83. Mem. Nat. Assn. Women Deans, Adminstrs. and Counselors, Nat. Assn. Student Personnel Adminstrs., So. Assn. Coll. Student Personnel Adminstrs. Roman Catholic. Avocations: music; outdoor sports. Home: 3120 Courthouse Dr West Lafayette IN 47906 Office: Purdue U West Lafayette IN 47906

DIAZ, LOUIS ALBERT, mechanical engineering educator; b. St. Croix, V.I., Oct. 31, 1950; s. Louis Albert and Agneta Magdalen (Hansen) D.; B.S. in M.E., Mich. Tech. U., 1972, M.S. in M.E., 1978; Purdue U., 1983; m. Paulette Thompson, Dec. 28, 1974. Mech. engr. Jacksonville (Fla.) Naval Air Sta., 1973-76; heat transfer instr. Purdue U., 1979-83; asst. prof. mech. engring. Mich. Technol. U., Houghton, Mich., 1983-85; asst. prof. mech. engring. U. Tex.-El Paso, 1985—. Mem. ASME, AIAA, Am. Inst. Chem. Engrs., Sigma Xi, Tau Beta Pi. Republican. Roman Catholic. Club: Purdue Camera.

DIB, ALBERT JAMES, lawyer; b. Detroit, Oct. 14, 1955; s. James Benjamin and Salma (Nacoud) D. B.A., U. Mich., 1977; J.D., Wayne State U., 1980; cert. U. Exeter, Eng., 1980. Bars: Mich. 1981, U.S. Dist. Ct. (ea. dist.) Mich. 1981, U.S. Ct. Appeals (6th cir.) 1982. Law clk. Lopatin, Miller, Freedman, Bluestone, Erich, Rosen & Bartnick, Detroit, 1978-80, assoc., 1981—; moot ct. judge Detroit Coll. Law, 1984. Vestryman Christ Episcopal Ch., Detroit, 1974-77; charter mem. Republican Presdl. Task Force, 1985—. Recipient Cert. Achievement Mich. High Sch. Mock Trial Tournament, 1984. Mem. Assn. Trial Lawyers Am. (cert. trial advocacy 1984), ABA, Mich. Trials Lawyers Assn., Detroit Bar Assn., Oakland Bar Assn., Macomb Bar Assn. (speaker 1984). Office: Lopatin Miller Freedman Bluestone Erich Rosen & Bartnick 511 E Larned Detroit MI 48226

DIBBEN, MARTYN JAMES, museum curator, botanist, mycologist; b. Gosport, Hampshire, Eng., Jan. 26, 1943; s. Fred Horace and Elsie (Keech) D.; m. Alison Jane Clark, Aug. 24, 1968; children—Nicole Jane, Allan James. B.Sc. with honors, U. London, 1964, M.A. in Edn., 1966; Ph.D. in Botany, Duke U., 1974. Biology master Barkingside High Sch., Essex, Eng., 1964-68; instr. botany Duke U., Durham, N.C., 1972-74; research fellow in lichenology Harvard U., Cambridge, Mass., 1974-75; head sect. for botany Milw. Pub. Mus., 1975—; mem. Sci. Areas Preservation Council, Wis., 1975-82; adj. prof. cryptogamic botany U. Wis., Milw., 1976—. Dep. dir. UNESCO Commn., Orgn. for Flora Neotropica, 1980—. NSF fellow, 1968-73; Harvard/Farlow fellow, 1974-75; grantee RT. Found., 1966-70, FOM Found., 1975, 76, 78, 80, 83, WSDH film, 1976-78, JMP Found., 1978-80, IMS, 1981-82, NSF/PFA, 1983. Mem. Wis. Mycological Soc. (pres. 1982-84), Internat. Assn. for Lichenology (editor Newsletter 1981—), Am. Bryological and Lichenological Soc., Am. Soc. Plant Taxonomy, Assn. for Tropical Biology, Brit. Bryological Soc., Brit. Lichenological Soc., Internat. Assn. Bryology, Internat. Assn. Plant Taxonomy, Internat. Soc. for Tropical Ecology, Mycological Soc. Am., Orgn. for Tropical Studies, Wis. Acad. Scis., Arts and Letters, Wis. Bot. Club (pres. 1980-82), Sigma Xi. Episcopalian. Author numerous articles. Contbr. articles to profl. jours. Office: 800 W Wells St Milwaukee WI 53233

DIBENEDETTO, STEPHEN LOUIS, university financial executive; b. Chgo., July 31, 1951; s. Stephen and Rochina (Curcio) DiB.; m. Karen Patricia Lauders, Oct. 7, 1978; children—Nicole Susan, Lauren Elizabeth. B.A., Western Ill. U., 1973. Collection supr. Cole-Parmer Inst. Co., Chgo., 1974-76; regional credit mgr. Sony Corp. Am., Niles, Ill., 1976-78; sales rep. Gen. Binding Corp., Lombard, Ill., 1978-80; nat. credit mgr. Globe Amerada Glass Co., Elk Grove Village, Ill., 1980-83; asst. dir. student loans Northwestern U., Evanston, Ill., 1983—. Mem. Chgo. Midwest Credit Mgmt. Assn. Roman Catholic. Office: Northwestern U 1801 Hinman Evanston IL 60201

DICK, DENNIS RAY, accountant; b. Muncie, Ind., June 19, 1956; s. Marvin Rischel Dick and Carole Jean (Bauer) Wade. B.B.A., Western Ill. U., 1978; M.B.A., DePaul U., 1981. Mgmt. trainee Continental Bank, Chgo., 1978-79, budget analyst, 1979-80; acctg. supr. Continental Ill. Leasing, Chgo., 1980-82, acctg. mgr., 1982-84; acctg. mgr. Sanwa Bus. Credit Corp., 1984—. Avocation: Golf. Home: 4751 St Joseph Creek Rd Apt 108 Lisle IL 60532 Office: Sanwa Bus Credit Corp 1 South Wacker Dr Chicago IL 60606

DICK, RUTH ANN HORN, business education and office administration educator; b. Logansport, Ind., Sept. 23, 1949; d. Anthony Murray and Doris (Compton) Horn; m. Andrew David Dick, Sept. 14, 1955; 1 son, Anthony George. B.S., Butler U., 1971, M.S., 1973. Life teaching lic. Tchr., Lawrence (Ind.) Central High Sch., 1971-76; asst. prof. bus. edn. and office adminstrn., Coll. of Edn., Butler U., Indpls., 1976—, also coordinator Instructural Services Ctr.; cons. office automation. Active Bethlehem Lutheran Ch., Bulldog Club, Butler U., also Pres.' Club. Nominated for John Robert Gregg award, 1982. Mem. Assn. Info. Systems Profls., Nat. Bus. Edn. Assn., Ind. Bus. Edn. Assn., Adminstrv. Mgmt. Soc., Profl. Secs. Internat., Indpls. Bus. Edn. Council, Ind. Bus. Educators Club, Nat. Assn. Bus. Tchr. Educators, Phi Delta Kappa, Kappa Delta Pi. Republican. Club: Riviera Swim. Home: 4738 Boulevard Pl Indianapolis IN 46208 Office: 4600 Sunset Ave Indianapolis IN 46208

DICKASON, ROBERT HART, osteopathic physician, surgeon; b. Louisville, Aug. 4, 1948; s. Jack Hart and Carol Matilda (Drake) D.; m. Frieda Ann Koubal, July 17, 1971; 1 son, Karl Hart. B.S. in Biology, Baldwin-Wallace Coll., 1970; med. research asst. Case Western Res. U., 1971; D.O., Chgo. Coll. Osteo. Medicine, 1975. Intern, Detroit Osteo. Hosp., 1975-76; resident in gen. surgery Riverside Osteo. Hosp., Trenton, Mich., 1976-80; fellow in colon and rectal surgery William Beaumont Hosp., Royal Oak, Mich., 1980-81; practice osteo. medicine specializing in gen. surgery, colon and rectal surgery, Trenton, Mich., 1981—; mem. teaching staff Riverside Osteo. Hosp., instr. emergency med. technician, 1977—; asst. clin. prof. surgery Mich. State U.; physician examiner colon and rectal cancer screening program Gen. Motors Corp., 1981—; free-lance photographer, 1969-76; lectr. in field; vol. CPR instr., 1977—; vol. physician Downriver Community Health Service Referral Network, 1982-83; med. examiner Am. Cancer Soc., 1982—; vol. med. advisor, pub. speaker United Ostomy Assn., Nat. Found. for Ileitis and Colitis; instr. emergency med. technician Grosse Ile Fire Dept., 1979; unit chmn. Nat. Cancer Prevention Study II, Am. Cancer Soc., 1982. Mem. St. Thomas Lutheran Ch. Council, 1983. Mem. Am. Osteo. Assn., Mich. Assn. Osteo. Physicians and Surgeons, Am. Acad. Osteopathy, Am. Coll. Osteo. Surgeons, Mich. Soc. of Colon and Rectal Surgeons, Wayne County Osteo. Assn., Jaycees (Grosse Ile pres. 1981-82, numerous awards), Sigma Sigma Phi (pres. 1974), Atlas Club, Alpha Phi Omega. Co-author manual for physicians on hyperalimentation and nutritional support; contbr. articles to local newspapers. Home: 9672 Waterway St Grosse Ile MI 48138 Office: 2171 W Jefferson Suite 203 Trenton MI 48183

DICKENS, ROBERT LEE, design executive; b. Chgo., Apr. 5, 1931; s. Robert Sidney and Ruth (Millard) D.; m. Lu Guerzon, Oct. 4, 1957; children—Lynn, Lance. Student U. Colo., 1949-50; cert. Am. Acad. Art, 1953. Apprentice designer Robert Sidney Dickens & Assoc., Chgo., 1948; designer Robert Sidney Dickens Inc., 1953, v.p., 1963; pres. Dickens Design Group Inc., 1965—, also dir.; founder, pres. Design Dirs. Inc., 1952; founder, v.p. Pax Fax Inc., 1963. Bd. dirs. Rendgart Wildlife Acres, Mt. Vernon, Ill.; cubmaster, scout master Boy Scouts Am., 1941-45, 54-55, 66-70. Served with USNR, 1947-51, U.S. Army, 1953-55. Recipient First Award in retail graphics Master Dairy Assn., 1983; First award in oils div. Wind River Valley Nat. Art Exhibit, 1980; Grumbacher Award, 1982; Cleo award (3); others. Mem. Package Designers Council (chmn. Midwest chpt. 1975, treas. 1983), Packaging Inst. U.S., Indsl. Designers Soc. Am., 27 Chgo. Artists, Guild Chgo., Wind River Valley Artists Guild. Club: Oak Park (Ill.). Patentee bottle design One-A-Day vitamins Miles Lab., 1981; other designs for Toblex-Suchard, Beatrice Foods, Gen. Mills, Safeway Stores, Coca-Cola, Armour-Dial Co., Anheuser-Busch, Inc. Home: 714 Linden Ave Oak Park IL 60302 Office: 13 W Grand Ave Chgo IL 60610

DICKERSON, ALLEN BRUCE, interior designer, consultant; b. St. Joseph, Mich., June 8, 1938; s. Harold Clyde and Lucille Anne (Thornton) D.; m. Arlene Virginia Bator, Mar. 26, 1965; children—Scott Denek, Maribeth Anne. B.S. in Indsl. Engring., U. Mich., 1961, M.B.A., 1962; cert. N.Y. Sch. Interior Design, 1967. Sr. indsl. engr. Bohn Aluminum & Brass Co., Detroit, 1962-65, engring. ctr. adminstr., 1965-68, prodn. mgr., 1968-70, asst. plant mgr., 1970-72; plant mgr. DuWel Products Co., Bangor, Mich., 1972-74, corp. chief indsl. engr., 1974-75; contract and residential interior designer Klingman's, Grand Rapids, Mich., 1975—; tchr. South Haven Community Edn. Program, 1977, Western Mich. U., 1975, Am. Soc. Interior Designers, 1980-81. Author: Rental Condominiums-Interior Design for Fun and Profit, 1978. Trustee First United Meth. Ch., South Haven, Mich.; bd. dirs. Van Buren County (Mich.) ARC, 1965-68. Mem. Am. Inst. Indsl. Engrs., Am. Soc. Interior Designers, Nat. Council Interior Design Qualification, South Haven C. of C. (com. chmn.), Internat. Lightning Class Assn. Republican. Methodist. Clubs: South Haven Yacht; Shrine (Grand Rapids); Rotary. Home: Route 5 999 North Shore Dr South Haven MI 49090 Office: PO Box 888 Eastbrook Mall 28th St Grand Rapids MI 49508

DICKERSON, MARY ANN, judge; b. Tuscumbia, Mo., May 27, 1952; d. Garland Vincent and Alta Lucille (Cotten) Platter; m. James R. Dickerson, June 5, 1976; children—Joshua Williams, Laura Renae. B.A., U. Mo., 1974, J.D., 1977. Bars: Mo., U.S. Dist. Ct. (we. dist.) Mo. Assoc. firm Donnelly, Baldwin, Wilhite, Lebanon, Mo., 1978-81; assoc. circuit-probate judge Camden County Assoc. Circuit Ct., Camdenton, Mo., 1981—. Named Most Likely to Succeed, Local Dist. Bus. and Profl. Women, 1979. Mem. Mo. Bar Assn., Camden County Bar Assn., 26th Jud. Circuit Bar Assn. (non-voting), Assn. Probate and Assoc. Circuit Judges (bd. dirs. 1983—), Camden County Hist. Soc. (bd. dirs. 1980-83). Republican. Baptist. Home: PO Box 126 Camdenton MO 65020 Office: Assoc Circuit Ct PO Box 39 Camdenton MO 65020

DICKEY, JULIA EDWARDS, management and promotional consultant; b. Sioux Falls, S.D., Mar. 6, 1940; d. John Keith and Henrietta Barbara (Zerell) Edwards; student DePauw U., 1958-59; A.B., Ind. U., 1962, M.L.S., 1967, postgrad., 1967—; m. Joseph E. Dickey, June 18, 1959; children—Joseph E., John Edwards. Asst. acquisitions librarian Ind. U. Regional Campus Libraries, 1965-67; head tech. services Bartholomew County Library, Columbus, Ind., 1967-74; dir. reference services Southeastern Ind. Area Library Service Authority, Columbus, 1974-78, exec. dir., 1978-80; pres. Jedco Enterprises, 1981—; legis. strategy chmn. Ind. Library Coop. Devel., 1975; dir. Ind. Library Trustees Assn. Governance Project, 1982. Mem. Columbus exec. bd. Mayor's Task Force on Status of Women, 1973—; del. Ind. Sch. Nominating Assembly, 1973-75, 75-77; sec. bd. dirs. Human Services Inc. (Bartholomew, Brown and Jackson Counties community action program), 1975, pres., 1976, 77, 78; mem. adv. council Ind./Nat. Network Study, 1977-78; bd. dirs. Columbus Women's Center; precinct coordinator Vols. For Bayh, 1974; sheriff Columbus 1st precinct, 1975, clk., 1976-77, insp., 1978, judge, 1980-83; treas. Hayes for State Rep. Com., 1978, 82, 84. Named Outstanding Young Woman Am., 1973. Mem. ALA, Ind. Library Assn. (dist. chmn. 1972-73, chmn. library edn. div. 1980-81, ad hoc com. on legis. effectiveness, 1982), Library Assts. and Technicians Round Table (chmn. 1968-69), Tech. Services Round Table (chmn. 1971-72, sec. library planning com. 1969-72), AAUW (pres. 1973-75), Bartholomew County Library Staff Assn. (pres. 1975-76), Exptl. Aircraft Assn. (charter pres. chpt. 729 1981, pres. Ind. council 1984—, major achievement award Oshkosh), 1983), Ind. EAA Council (pres. 1982-84), Antique Airplane Assn., First Tuesday, Psi Iota Xi. Club: Zonta. Home and office: 511 Terrace Lake Rd Columbus IN 47201

DICKHONER, WILLIAM HAROLD, See *Who's Who in America,* 43rd edition.

DICKIE, JOHN PETER, chemist, corporation executive; b. Waseca, Minn., Apr. 4, 1934; s. John Lewis and Martha (Mortensen) D.; m. Peggy Ann Buhrman, Sept. 6, 1966 (div. 1967); children—Joan E., Anne C.; m. Barbara Lee Brueckman, June 8, 1968 (div. 1978); children—Allison, Kimberly. B.A. cum laude, U. Minn., 1956; M.S., U. Wis.-Madison, 1958, Ph.D., 1960. Postdoctoral fellow U. Wis., Madison, 1960-61; fellow Mellon Inst., 1961-68; group mgr. exploratory research Koppers Co., Monroeville, Pa., 1968-74; dir. basic research Carnation Co., Los Angeles, 1974-78; pres. John Dickie Assocs., St. Paul, 1978-84; v.p., chief operating officer, dir., sec. ATR Electronics Co., St. Paul., 1984—. Contbr. articles to profl. jours. Patentee in field. Advisor, Koppers sci. Explorer Scout Post, Monroeville, Pa. Mem. Am. Chem. Soc. (bd. dirs. 1967-68), Pitts. Chemists Club (pres. (1967), Minn. Alumni Assn. (pres. 1970-71). Presbyterian. Avocation: music. Home: 1261 Ingerson Rd Arden Hills MN 55112 Office: ATR Electronics 280 E Lafayette Frontage Rd Saint Paul MN 55107

DICKINSON, DAVID FREEMAN, lawyer; b. Jackson, Mich., Jan. 23, 1939; s. Dale Freeman and Zelma Mae (Moore) D.; m. Margaret Lee Hicks, Sept. 12, 1964 (div. 1976); children—Jennifer Lynn, Douglas Freeman; m. 2d, Helen Dimanin, Nov. 1, 1980. B.A., Mich. State U., 1962; J.D., Wayne State U., 1967. Bar: Mich. 1967. Trial atty. Giltner & Dickinson, Detroit, 1967-73, Charfoos & Charfoos, Detroit, 1973-79, Lopatin Miller, Detroit, 1979—. Mem. Detroit Bar Assn., Oakland Bar Assn., Mich. Trial Lawyers, ABA, Assn. Trial Lawyers Am. Democrat. Episcopalian. Office: Lopatin Miller et al 547 E Jefferson St Detroit MI 48226

DICKINSON, DAVID WALTER, educator, research executive; b. Troy, N.Y., Mar. 29, 1946; s. Edward Irwin and Charlotte Crescentia (Raschke) D.; m. Christine Ann Donnelly, Nov. 18, 1972; children—Kara Ann, Rebecca Jane, Johanna Lee. B.S. in Materials Engring., Rensselaer Poly. Inst., 1967, Ph.D., 1972. Engring. specialist Olin Corp. Research, New Haven, 1972-74; sr. welding research engr. Republic Steel Research, Independence, Ohio, 1974, group leader welding, 1974-79, supr. cold rolled, 1979-83, sect. chief flat rolled, 1983-84; prof. Ohio State U., Columbus, 1984—; dir. research Edison Welding Inst., 1985—. Author: Welding in the Automotive Industry, 1981. Patentee in field. Mem. adv. bd. Lakeland Community Coll., Mentor, Ohio, 1979-82, Cuyahoga Vocat. Sch., Brecksville, Ohio, 1975-83; mem. acad. bd. Highland Sch. Dist., Hinckley, 1983-84; swim team coach YMCA, Wallingford, Conn., 1972-74; youth advisor Lutheran Ch., Hinckley, 1978-83; synod del. Lutheran Ch. Am., Ohio, 1983; del. Ch. council Lutheran Ch., Hinckley, 1979-84. Recipient Excellence in Oral Presentation award Soc. Automotive Engrs., 1981, Lasting Significance award, 1982; Painter Meml. fellow ASTM, 1970. Mem. Am. Welding Soc. (chmn. Cleve. sect. 1979-80, dir. 1982—; Dist. Meritorious award 1981, McKay-Helm award, 1982), Welding Research Council, Internat. Inst. Welding, Am. Soc. for Metals, Welding Acad. Am. Welding Soc. (chmn. 1980—), Joining Div. Council Am. Soc. Metals, Alpha Sigma Mu (pres. 1970-71). Home: 195 Stonefence Ln Dublin OH 43017 Office: Edison Welding Inst 1100 Kinnear Rd Columbus OH 43212

DICKINSON, GEORGE W., hospital administrator; b. Tulsa, Sept. 10, 1930; s. George and Ruth (Chase) D.; children—Steven D., Michael D., Jeffrey J. B.S. in B.A., Phillips U., 1961; M.H.A., Washington U., 1965. X-ray technologist Hillcrest Med. Ctr., Tulsa, 1954-55; bus. mgr. Enid Clinic, Okla., 1955-63; asst. adminstr. Hillcrest Med. Ctr., 1965-68, assoc. adminstr., 1968-70; adminstr. Trinity Luth. Hosp., Kansas City, Mo., 1970-83, chief exec. officer, 1983—; pres. bd. dirs. Consortium of Health Profs., Kansas City, 1983—; bd. dirs. Midwest Health Congress, 1982—, Trinity Luth. Manor, 1979—, Mo. Hosp. Asns., 1981-84. Served with U.S. Army, 1952-54. USPHS traineeship, 1963. Mem. Am. Coll. Hosp. Adminstrs., Am. Hosp. Assn., Alumni Assn. Washington U., Am. Registry of Radiologic Technologists, Kansas City C. of C. Republican. Avocations: Fishing, boating, photography. Home: 10206 Edelweiss Cir Merriam KS 66203 Office: Trinity Luth Hosp 3030 Baltimore Kansas City MO 64108

DICKINSON, JOHN RICHARD, optometrist; b. Danville, Ill., May 10, 1947; s. Robert Dean and Virginia Ruth (Stanton) D.; m. Pamela Jean Smith, June 12, 1971; children—Corey Samuel and Colin Charles. B.S., Ind. U., 1970, D. of Optometry, 1972. Practice assoc. M.D. Bair & Assoc., Findlay, Ohio, 1972-73; resident Martin Luther King Clinic, Cin., 1973-75 practice medicine specializing in optometry, Dayton, Ohio, 1972-84. Contbr. column to Belmont Times, 1985—. Mem. Am. Optometric Assn., Ohio Optometric Assn., Optometric Extension Program (clinic assoc.). Republican. Methodist. Clubs: Toastmasters Internat. (Dayton) (adminstrv. v.p. 1984, pres. 1985), Sertoma Internat. (Dayton) (corresponding sec. 1972, sec. 1973), Indian Guides (Xenia) (chief 1983-84). Avocations: Golf; bowling; traveling to historically significant destinations. Home: 2493 Coldsprings Dr Beaver Creek OH 45385 Office: Dr John R Dickinson Optometrist 1109 Watervliet Ave Dayton OH 45420

DICKINSON, LANCE DE FORREST, management consultant, educator; b. Johnson City, N.Y., Oct. 31, 1945; s. Clarence B. and Jacqueline A. (Quinn) Sweeney; m. Dorothy L. Burruss, Oct. 5, 1968; children—Nathan K., Lauren W., Sarah A. B.S., U. R.I., 1972; M.A., Central Mich. U., 1981. Personnel mgmt. specialist Naval Underwriter System Ctr., Newport, R.I., 1972-74, Def. Property Disposal Service, Battle Creek, Mich., 1974-76, Def. Contracts Region, Chgo., 1976-78; sr. level personnel mgmt. specialist Def. Logistics Agency, Columbus, Ohio, 1978-82; mng. dir. Lance Dickinson & Co., Columbus, 1982—; adj. prof. Franklin U., Columbus. Bd. dirs. Columbus Opera, 1984—; mem. vestry St. Albans Episcopal Ch., Bexley, Ohio, 1984—. Served with U.S. Army, 1966-69, Vietnam. Decorated Bronze Star, Purple Heart, Air medal. Mem. Am. Soc. Personnel Adminstrn. (accredited), Nat. Speakers Assn., Am. Soc. Tng. Devel., Am. Mgmt. Assn. Republican. Clubs: University (Columbus); Binghamton. Avocations: pilot; polo; building airplanes. Office: Lance Dickinson & Co 150 E Mound St Suite 105 Columbus OH 43215

DICKISON, GEORGE JOHNSTONE, dermatologist; b. Saulte Ste. Marie, Mich., June 15, 1921; s. George Johnstone and Elizabeth Margaret (Sawyers) D.; m. Mary Jeanette Chamberlain; children—Anne, Deborah, George, David, John. A.B., Albion Coll., 1943; M.D., U. Mich., 1946. Intern City Hosp. Cleve., 1947-48; resident in dermatology Univ. Hosp., Ann Arbor, Mich., 1953-57; practice medicine specializing in dermatology, Peoria, Ill., 1957—; asst. prof. dermatology U. Ill. Med. Sch. of Peoria, 1974—. Served to capt. USAF, 1951-53. Fellow Am. Acad. Dermatology; mem. Chgo. Dermatology Soc., Ill. State Dermatology Soc., AMA, Ill. State Med. Soc., Peoria County Med. Soc. Republican. Episcopalian. Club: Ill. Valley Yacht (Peoria). Lodge: Rotary. Avocations: Sailing, antique boats and cars. Home: 4831 Grandview Dr Peoria Heights IL 61614 Office: 416 St Mark Ct Peoria IL 61603

DICKMEYER, KERRY DAVID, land surveyor; b. Ft. Wayne, Ind., June 29, 1948; s. David Paul and Alice Joan (Minser) D.; m. Linda Lou Vonder Haar, Aug. 31, 1968; children—Douglas David, Stacy Theresa. Assoc. Applied Sci. Civil Engring., Purdue U., 1970, B.S., 1972. Registered profl. land surveyor, Ind. Instrument man, draftsman Coil Engrs., Inc., Ft. Wayne, 1970-72, survey crew chief, office mgr., 1972-76, chief surveyor (name changed to Coil & Dickmeyer, Inc.), 1976—; mem. assoc. faculty Purdue U., 1980—. Pres. Hillsboro Community Assn., Ft. Wayne, 1983, 84. Mem. Ind. Soc. Profl. Land

Surveyors (v.p. Northeast chpt. 1983, pres., 1984), Am. Congress Surveying and Mapping, Nat. Soc. Profl. Surveyors, Ft. Wayne Ballet, Friends of Allen County Library. Republican. Roman Catholic. Club: Omni (Ft. Wayne). Avocations: philately; computer programming; racquetball; sports. Home: 6734 Hillsboro Ln Fort Wayne IN 46815 Office: Coil & Dickmeyer Inc 6044 East State Fort Wayne IN 46815

DICKSON, CHARLES WILLIAM, JR., speech and theater arts educator; b. Des Moines, Aug. 9, 1926; s. Charles William and Delta (Snow) D.; children—Emily Ann, Robert Charles, Thomas Frederick. B.F.A., Drake U., 1949; M.A., Western Res. U., 1951. Chmn. speech dept. Wartburg Coll., Waverly, Iowa, 1952-56; producer, dir. KDPS TV/FM, Des Moines, 1956-60; chmn. speech and theater arts dept. Grand View Coll., Des Moines, 1960—; instr. Am. Inst. Banking, Des Moines, 1960-70, Uavs. & Loan League, Des Moines, 1960-70. Author: (with others) Core Knowledge for Successful Speech, 1969; Give a Good Speech, 1979. Precinct committeeman Republican party, Des Moines; bd. dirs. Civic Music, Des Moines; pres. Drama Workshop, Des Moines; treas. Iowa Community Theatre Assn., Des Moines. Served to 1st lt. U.S. Army, 1944-46, 51-52, PTO, Korea. Decorated Bronze Star medal. Mem. Iowa Community Theatre Assn. Republican. Methodist. Lodge: Masons. Home: 3515 Kingman Blvd Des Moines IA 50311 Office: Grand View Coll Dept Speech and Theatre Arts 1200 Grand View Ave Des Moines IA 50316

DICKSON, GENE KENNETH, educational administrator; b. Dec. 12, 1943; s. Floyd Kenneth and Marjorie (Bateman) D.; m. Linda Ann Moeller, Aug. 26, 1967; children—Lisa, Lori, Lynette. B.A., Huron Coll., 1965; M.S., Northern State Coll., 1967. Placement counselor Rehabilitation, Redfield, S.D., 1966-67, cons. on retardation, Pierre, S.D., 1967-74; edn. cons. Exceptional Children, Pierre, 1974-76, program adminstr., 1976-77; program dir. Instructional Services, Pierre, 1977-82, Dept. Edn., Pierre, 1982—. Grad. fellow State S.D., 1965. Mem. Adult, Continuing, and Community Edn. Assn. S.D. (exec. bd.), Assn. State Dirs. Adult Edn., S.D. Rehabilitation Assn. (pres. 1973). Republican. Methodist. Club: Jaycees. Avocations: Reading; hunting; fishing; boating; camping. Home: 309 N Tyler Pierre SD 57501 Office: Dept Edn Cultural Affairs 700 N Illinois Pierre SD 57501

DIDHAM, JAMES RICHARD, educational administrator, management consultant; b. Canton, Ohio, Nov. 6, 1943; s. Robert Hewlitt and Elizabeth (Truscott) D.; m. Cheryl Kay Hoffman, Aug. 12, 1967 (div. 1977); 1 child, Laural Lyn; m. Edieann B. Freeman, Sept. 3, 1978; 1 child, Robert James. B.A., Baldwin-Wallace Coll., Berea, Ohio, 1965; M.A., Kent State U., 1972; postgrad. U. Mich., 1975. High sch. tchr. Strongsville Bd. Edn., Ohio, 1965-67; asst. prof. Spanish lit., counselor Baldwin-Wallace Coll., 1967-70; dir. admissions Mount-Union Coll., Alliance, Ohio, 1970-73; asst. to pres. Findlay Coll. (Ohio), 1975-81; mgmt. cons. Moody-Woodley Mgmt., Inc., Findlay, 1981-84; dir. corporate devel. Bowling Green State U., Ohio, 1984—; mgmt. cons. to numerous colls. and univs., 1975—. Author: La Augustia de la Ciudad en las Obras de Florencio Sanchez, 1972; (with others) Changing Practices in Higher Education, 1976. Vice pres. Findlay Area Arts Council, 1984—, Findlay Swim Bd., 1984—. Carnegie Council Research fellow, 1975. Mem. Am. Assn. Higher Edn., Planning Execs. Internat., Assn. Study Higher Edn., C. of C. Presbyterian. Avocations: Racquetball, snow skiing, gardening, photography, classical music. Home: 430 First St Findlay OH 45840 Office: Bowling Green State U Mileti Alumni Ctr Bowling Green OH 43403

DIDIER, NICHOLAS LEO, real estate developer, consultant; b. White River, S.D., Aug. 24, 1928; s. Nicholas John and Nellie M. (Spear) D.; m. Evelyn E. Beach, Sept. 10, 1949; children—James, Thomas, Barbara. B.B.A., Nat. Coll., Rapid City, S.D., 1948. Dist. mgr. Black Hills Power and Light, Sturgis, S.D., 1952-60, dist. mgr., Hot Springs, S.D., 1960-65, mktg. dir., Rapid City, S.D., 1965-73; owner, gen. mgr. Tip Top Motor Hotel, Rapid City, 1973-83; pres. Interwest Devel. Co., Rapid City, 1983—, Didier and Assoc., Rapid City, 1983—; pres., dir. So. Hills Mining Co., Rapid City, 1981—. Chmn. Fall River County Republican Orgn., Hot Springs, 1962-65. Recipient Disting. Service award Sturgis Jr. C. of C., 1958. Mem. Rapid City C. of C. (bd. dirs., treas. 1979-83). Roman Catholic. Club: Arrowhead. Lodge: Elks. Avocations: golf, swimming. Home: 4618 Ridgewood Dr Rapid City SD 57702 Office: Interwest Devel Co 621 6th St Rapid City SD 57701

DIDIO, LIBERATO JOHN ALPHONSE, college dean, anatomy educator; b. Sao Paulo, Brazil, May 7, 1920, came to U.S., 1960, naturalized 1969; s. Pascoal and Lydia (Cacace) D.; m. Lydia Silva, Mar. 12, 1960; children—Vera, Rubens, Lydia, Arthur. B.S., Dante Alighieri Coll., Sao Paulo, 1936; M.D., Faculty of Medicine, U. Sao Paulo, 1945; Diplomate Nat. War Coll., Rio de Janeiro, 1957. From instr. to assoc. prof. anatomy Faculty Medicine, U. Sao Paulo, Brazil, 1942-1954; prof., chmn. anatomy Faculty Medicine, U. Minas Gerais Belo Horizonte, Brazil, 1954-62, Northwestern U., Chgo., 1963-67; prof., chmn. anatomy Med. Coll. Ohio, Toledo, 1967—, dean grad. sch., 1972—; cons. WHO, Geneva, Switzerland, 1972-77, Pan Am. Health Organization, Washington, 1969—. Editor: (with M.C. Anderson) Sphincters of the Digestive System, 1968; Synopsis of Anatomy, 1970; Hepatology, 1980; Nephrology, 1985. Home: 3563 Edgevale Rd Toledo OH 43606 Office: Med Coll Ohio 3000 Arlington Ave Toledo OH 43699

DIDLAKE, WINFRED LOUIS, JR., automotive executive; b. Detroit, Apr. 19, 1948; s. Winfred Louis and Veta F. (Jordan) D.; m. Carmelita Mable Strong, July 17, 1971; children—Jennifer, Winfred. B.S. in Mgmt., Detroit Inst. Tech., 1974; A.A. in Indsl. Tech., Highland Park Jr. Coll., Mich., 1971. Registered profl. engr., Mich. Tool and die maker supr. Chrysler Corp., Detroit, 1967-77, indsl. engring. supr., 1977-81, gen. supt., 1984—; supt. Gen. Dynamics Corp., Lima, Ohio, 1981-82, prodn. mgr., 1982-84; tax cons. H&R Block, Detroit, 1974-80. Bd. dirs. Fair Housing City of Lima, 1983. Mem. Am. Inst. Indsl. Engrs. Roman Catholic. Club: Management (Lima) (treas. 1982-83). Lodge: Rotary (Lima). Avocations: golfing; bowling; softball. Home: 18740 Goldwin Southfield MI 48075 Office: Chrysler Corp 12200 Jefferson St Detroit MI 48215

DIEDERICHS, JANET WOOD, public relations executive; b. Libertyville, Ill.; d. J. Howard and Ruth (Hendrickson) Wood; B.A., Wellesley Coll., 1950; m. John Kuensting Diederichs, 1953. Sales agt. Pan Am. Airways, Chgo., 1951-52; regional mgr. pub. relations Braniff Internat., Chgo., 1953-69; pres. Janet Diederichs & Assocs., Inc., pub. relations cons., Chgo., 1970—; mem. exec. com. World Trade Conf., 1983, 84. Com. mem. Nat. Trust for Historic Preservation, 1975-79, Marshall Scholars (Brit. Govt.), 1975-79; trustee Northwestern Meml. Hosp., 1985—; bd. dirs., mem. exec. com. Chgo. Conv. and Tourism Bur. 1978-85; bd. dirs. Internat. House, U. Chgo., 1978-84, Com. of 200, 1982-84; com. mem. Art Inst. Chgo., 1980-82; mem. exec. com. Vatican Art Council Chgo., 1981-83; pres. Jr. League Chgo., 1968-69. Mem. Nat. Acad. TV Arts and Scis., Soc. Am. Travel Writers, Chgo. Assn. Commerce and Industry (bd. dirs. 1982—, exec. com. 1985—), Pub. Relations Soc. Am., Publicity Club Chgo., Chgo. Network, Chgo. Press Club. Clubs: Economic, Mid-Am. (dir. 1977-79), Woman's Athletic (Chgo.). Home: 229 E Lake Shore Dr Chicago IL 60611 Office: 333 N Michigan Ave Chicago IL 60601

DIEDRICK, MARCELLA ALICE, educator, reading specialist; b. Vesper, Wis., Dec. 22, 1929; d. William A. and Catherine I. (Wirtz) Brockman; m. Robert W. Diedrick, Dec. 4, 1976. B.S., Edgecliff Coll., Cin., 1968; M.A. in Reading, Cardinal Stritch Coll., Milw., 1975; postgrad. St. Thomas Coll., St. Paul, 1976, U. Wis.-Superior, U. Wis.-Stevens Point, 1977-81. Cert. tchr., prin., reading specialist, Wis. Tchr. St. John the Evangelist Elem. Sch., Deer Park, Ohio, 1959-68, Rhinelander (Wis.) Catholic Central, 1968-74, St. Robert Bellarmine, Merrill, Wis., 1974-75, St. Johns, Edgar, Wis., 1975-76; prin., tchr. St. Peter the Fisherman, Eagle River, Wis., 1976-79; reading specialist, Elcho (Wis.) Pub. Schs., 1979—. Mem. Internat. Reading Assn., Wis. State Reading Assn., Headwater Reading Council (pres. 1970-71, 82-83), Delta Kappa Gamma. Roman Catholic.

DIEHL, ANTONI MILLS, physician, pediatric cardiologist, educator; b. Mpls., Nov. 5, 1924; s. Harold Sheely and Julia (Mills) D.; m. Sybil Reid Bothwell, Sept. 7, 1948; children—Paul, Pamela, Brenda, James. Student, Vanderbilt U., 1942-43; B.S., U. Minn., 1945, M.B., 1947, M.D., 1948. Diplomate Am. Bd. Pediatrics, Am. Bd. Pediatric Cardiology. Rotating intern U. Mich. Hosp., Ann Arbor, 1947-48; pediatric resident U. Minn. Hosp., Mpls., 1948-50, pediatric cardiology fellow, 1950-51; instr. pediatric U. Kans. Sch. Medicine, Kansas City, 1953-55, asst. prof., 1955-58, assoc. prof., 1958-67, prof., 1967-78; clin. prof. pediatrics U. Mo. at Kansas City, 1973—; practice medicine specializing in pediatric cardiology, Kansas City, Mo., cons. pediatric cardiology St. Luke's Hosp. Kansas City, Mo., 1978—; assoc. cardiologist Children's Mercy Hosp., Kansas City, Mo., 1979—; pediatrician, pediatric cardiologist Menorah Med. Ctr., Kansas City, Mo., Providence-St. Margaret Health Ctr., Kansas City, Kans., Shawnee Mission Med. Ctr., Kans., Research Hosp., Kansas City, Mo., St. Joseph Hosp., Kansas City, Mo., Bethany Hosp., Kansas City, Kans., Suburban Med. Ctr., Overland Park, Kans.; cons. pediatric cardiology Munson Army Hosp., Ft. Leavenworth, Kans., Freeman Hosp., Joplin, Mo.; con. in rheumatic fever Kans. Dept. Health and Environment, 1976—; vis. prof. pediatrics and pediatric cardiology U. Guatemala, Hosp. Gen. San Juan de Dios, Guatemala, 1977; dir. sect. pediatric cardiology U. Kans. Med. Ctr. Contbr. articles and abstracts to profl. jours., chpts. to books. Mem. com. on rheumatic fever Am. Heart Assn., 1962-70, mem. heart health in young and pub. edn. task force, greater Kansas City div., 1978—; active Am. Heart Assn., Kansas Affiliate, Inc., 1965—; pres. Kaw Valley Heart Assn., 1965-66, chmn. bd. 1966-67, chmn. program com. 1968-69. Named Cloud L. Cray Prof. Pediatric Cardiology, U. Kansas Med. Ctr., 1967-72. Fellow Am. Acad. Pediatrics (chmn. sect. on cardiology 1965), Am. Coll. Cardiology, Am. Coll. Chest Physicians, Am. Pediatric Soc.; mem. Kansas City Southwest Pediatric Soc., Wyandotte County Med. Soc., Kans. Med. Soc., AMA, Mo. Med. Soc., Midwest Soc. Pediatric Research. Republican. Presbyterian. Avocations: sailing, water skiing, fishing and outdoor activities. Home: 13106 W 75th Terr Lenexa KS 66216 Office: 332 Med Plaza 4320 Wornall Rd Kansas City MO 63111

DIEHL, JAY CORMAN, electrical engineer; b. Detroit, June 26, 1952; s. Corman James and Lucille (DiBacco) D.; m. Barbara Anne Barnes, Sept. 20, 1980. B.E.E., Gen. Motors Inst., 1975; M.B.A., Eastern Mich. U., 1983. Registered profl. engr., Mich. Sr. engr. HydraMatic div. Gen. Motors Corp., Ypsilanti, Mich., 1970-84; mgr. plant and process engring. MAC Valve, Inc., Wixom, Mich., 1984—. Republican. Roman Catholic. Avocation: competitive water skiing. Home: 1272 Clarita St Ypsilanti MI 48197 Office: MAC Valve 30569 Beck Rd Wixom MI 48096

DIEL, VERNON M., dentist; b. Alamotta, Kans., Jan. 8, 1932; s. Jacob and Pauline (Schegel) D.; m. Lois F. Brosemer, Aug. 31, 1957; children—Thomas McKay, Scott Evan. B.A., U. Kans., 1958; D.D.S., Kansas City U., 1962. Diplomate Am. Bd. Denistry. Oral surgery tng. Gen. Hosp., Kansas City, Mo., gen. practice denistry, Lawrence, Kans., 1962-84. Pres. Cosmopolitan Internat., Lawrence, 1973; precinct committeeman Republican Central Com., Lawrence, 1968-70. Served with U.S. Army, 1954-56. Recipient Disting. Service award Cosmopolitan Internat., 1974. Mem. ADA, Kans. State Dental Assn., Douglas County Dental Assn. (pres. 1964-65). Club: Lawrence Country. Lodge: Elks. Avocations: antique and classic atuos; model airplanes. Office: Vernon M Diel DDS 2711 W 6th St Lawrence KS 66044

DIELEMAN, WILLIAM WILBUR, state legislator; b. Oskaloosa, Iowa, Jan. 19, 1931; s. Garret Jan and Jozena (DeGeus) D.; B.A., Calvin Coll., Grand Rapids, Mich., 1959; M.A., State U. Iowa, Iowa City, 1966; m. Emily June Langstraat, Aug. 30, 1951; children—Wendell E., Cynthia E. Dieleman DeYoung, Kristen E. Tchr. social studies Pella (Iowa) Christian High Sch., 1959-74; agt. Guarantee Mut. Life Ins. Co. Nebr., 1974—; mem. Pella City Council, 1970-75; mem. Iowa Ho. of Reps. from 70th Dist., 1974-81, state senator from 35th Dist., 1982—; owner, pub. Diamond Trail News, Sully, Iowa. Del. local and state Democratic Convs., 1963—; mem. Iowa Capitol Planning Commn., 1979-82, 84—. Served with U.S. Army, 1953-55. Asian Affairs Inst. grantee, 1972. Mem. Central Iowa Regional Assn. Local Govt. (vice chmn. 1974), Am. Legion, Iowa Assn. Life Underwriters, Nat. Assn. Life Underwriters, Nat. Conf. State Legislators, Council State Govts., Farm Bur. Democrat. Mem. Christian Reformed Ch. (elder 1978-80, 84—). Office: PO Box 220 1201 High Ave W Oskaloosa IA 52577

DIERCKS, EILEEN KAY, educational media coordinator; b. Lima, Ohio, Oct. 31, 1944; d. Robert Wehner and Florence (Huckemeyer) McCarty; m. Dwight Richard Diercks, Dec. 27, 1969; children—Roger, David, Laura. B.S.Ed., Bluffton Coll., 1962-66; M.S., U. Ill., 1968. Tchr. elem. grades Kettering City Schs. (Ohio), 1966-67; children's librarian St. Charles County, St. Charles, Mo., 1968-69; librarian Rantoul High Sch. (Ill.), 1970-71; elem. tchr. Elmhurst Sch. Dist. (Ill.), 1971-72; media coordinator Plainfield Sch. Dist. (Ill.), 1980—. Founder, treas. FISH orgn., Plainfield, 1975-78; pres. Ch. Women United, 1974; treas. Plainfield Congl. Ch., 1983—; bd. dirs. Cub Scouts, 1983—. Mo. State Library scholar, 1967. Mem. Ill. Library Assn., ALA, NEA, Ill. Edn. Assn., Plainfield Assn. Tchrs., Pi Delta, Beta Phi Mu. Club: LeWood Homemakers (pres. 1973-74). Home: 13440 S Rivercrest Dr Plainfield IL 60544 Office: Plainfield Sch Dist #202 612 Commercial St Plainfield IL 60544

DIERENFIELD, RICHARD BRUCE, education educator; b. Aberdeen, S.D., Oct. 15, 1922; s. Herbert E. and Elizabeth (Brown) D.; m. Yvonne Fahldren, Aug. 19, 1950; children—Bruce, David. B.A., Macalester Coll., St. Paul, 1948, M.Ed., 1951; Ed.D., U. Colo., 1958. Instr. edn. Macalester Coll., St. Paul, 1952-55, asst. prof., 1955-58, assoc. prof., 1958-68, prof., 1968—, dir. evening coll., 1960-66, dir. M.Ed. program, 1962-72, chmn. dept. edn., 1968—. Author: Learning to Teach, 1981; Religion in American Public Schools, 1963; others. Contbr. articles to profl. jours. Served to sgt. USAF, 1942-45, PTO. Mem. AAUP, Assn. Tchr. Edn., Nat. Council Social Studies, Phi Delta Kappa, Kappa Delta Pi. Republican. Presbyterian. Avocations: International travel, woodworking, model ship construction. Home: 1566 Red Cedar Rd Eagan MN 55121 Office: Macalester Coll 1600 Grand Ave Saint Paul MN 55105

DIERMEIER, JEFFREY JAMES, investment manager; b. Appleton, Wis., Oct. 1, 1952; s. Clair Hubert and Mary Helen (Quella) D.; m. Peggy Lynn Kolosso, Jan. 5, 1973 (div. Jan. 1978); m. Julie Margaret Evans, Jan. 16, 1982. B.B.A. with distinction, U.Wis.-Madison, 1974, M.B.A., 1975. Chartered fin. analyst. Staff stratagist and methods First Nat. Bank Chgo., 1975-79, div. head, v.p., 1979-84; mng. dir. First Chgo. Investment Advisors, 1984—. T. Doig fellow U. Wis.-Madison, 1974; W. Kies scholar U.Wis., 1973. Mem. Candidate Curriculum Com., Inst. Chartered Fin. Analysts, Fin. Analysts Fedn., Chgo. Analysts Soc., Investment Tech. Symposium Chgo., Chgo. Options/Futures Soc. Roman Catholic. Club: Young Execs. (Chgo.) (pres. 1982-83). Home: 2650 N Lakeview #902 Chicago IL 60614 Office: First Chicago Investment Advisors 3 First Nat Plaza Suite 0146 Chicago IL 60670

DIESEL, J. P., agricultural machinery manufacturing company executive. Chmn., dir. J.I. Case Co., Racine, Wis. Office: JI Case Co 700 State St Racine WI 53404*

DIESEN, CHARLES ORLEY, archaeologist; b. Farmington, Minn., June 4, 1944; s. Albert Eugene and Viola Estelle (Christie) D.; m. Katherine M. Merrill, Oct. 4, 1975; 1 child, Claire M. B.A., Hamline U., 1974. Asst. archaeologist Minn. Hist. Soc., St. Paul, 1965-67, project archaeologist, 1967-81, collections archaeologist, 1981—; artifact conservator Minn. Hist. Soc., St. Paul, 1977—. Mem. Internat. Inst. Conservation (assoc.), Soc. Hist. Archaeology, Assn. Field Archaeology. Home: 5036 Oliver Ave S Minneapolis MN 55419 Office: Minn Hist Soc Fort Snelling History Ctr Saint Paul MN 55111

DIETRICH, DAVID ROBERT, psychologist, researcher; b. Bonne Terre, Mo., Feb. 13, 1950; s. Francis Robert and Marian Ruth (Becker) D.; m. Nancy Dolin, May 8, 1982. A.B. magna cum laude, Washington U., 1972, Ph.D. in Psychology, 1979; postgrad. New Sch. Social Research, 1972-73. Mem. faculty Jefferson Coll., Hillsboro, Mo., 1974; teaching fellow in psychology Washington U., St. Louis, 1974-77, mem. faculty, 1976-77; intern, Chgo.-Read Hosp., 1977-78; postdoctoral fellow in clin. psychology Wayne State U. Med. Sch., Detroit, 1978-80, mem. faculty dept. psychiatry, 1980—; dir. clin. psychology Triad Mental Health Services, Birmingham, Mich., 1981-83; dir. guest lecture series Detroit Psychiat. Inst., 1983—. Mem. Mich. Psychoanalytic Assn. (assoc.), Council for Advancement Psychoanalytic Edn., Am. Psychol. Assn., Psychologists Interested in Study Psychoanalysis, AAUP. Author: Psychopathology and Death Fear: a Quasi Experimental Investigation of the Relationships between Psychopathology and Death Fear, 1979; contbr. articles to profl. jours. Home: 482 Park St Birmingham MI 48011 Office: Detroit Psychiat Inst 1151 Taylor Detroit MI

DIETRICH, GEORGE CHARLES, chemical company executive; b. Detroit, Feb. 5, 1927; s. George Sylvester and Catherine Elizabeth (Cable) D.; B.S., U. Detroit; m. Dorothy Ann Flanigan, Aug. 21, 1954; children—Linda Marie, Elizabeth Ann, George Charles. Field sales mgr. Allied Chem. Co., Chgo., 1960-64; dir. sales Aerosol Research Co., North Riverside, Ill., 1964—; pres. Aeropres Corp., Chgo., 1964-65, Diversified Chems. & Propellants Co., Westmont, Ill., 1965—, also dir.; chmn. bd. ChemSpec Ins. Ltd.; dir. Am. Nat. Bank, De Kalb, Ill., Diversified CPC Internat., Anaheim, Calif. Served with USNR, 1945-46. Mem. Chem. Splty. Mfrs. Assn. (gov., chmn. bd.), Chgo. Drug and Chem. Assn., Chgo. Perfumery Soap and Extract Assn., Nat. Paint and Coatings Assn., Econs. Club Chgo., Execs. Club Chgo. Roman Catholic. Clubs: Butler Nat. Golf, Boca Raton Hotel and Club, Butterfield Country. Home: 1 Charleston Rd Hinsdale IL 60521 Office: 350 E Ogden Ave PO Box 447 Westmont IL 60559

DIETRICH, LOUIS WILLIAM, JR., lawyer, tax consultant; b. Chgo., Jan. 12, 1910; s. Louis William and Ruth Elizabeth (Howard) D.; m. Barbara Rich, Oct. 12, 1939 (div. 1945); children—William C., Annice; m. 2d Edith Ropiequet, Oct. 6, 1945 (div. Feb. 1981); children—Louis William III, Linda, Richard W. B.A., U. Minn., 1932, J.D., 1935. Bar: Minn. 1935, U.S. Tax Ct. 1957. Sole practice, Mpls., 1935-41; budgetary mgr. Montgomery Ward, Chgo., 1941-46; tax cons. Alexander Grant Co., Chgo., 1946-51, Peat, Marwick, Mitchell, Chgo., 1951-56; self-employed tax cons., Glen Ellyn, Ill., 1956—. Pres. dist. 2 Chgo. Regional Rose Soc., 1966; scoutmaster Boy Scouts Am., Glen Ellyn, 1949-60; cubmaster Cub Scouts, Glen Ellyn, 1947-48. Recipient Silver Beaver award DuPage Area council Boy Scouts Am., 1957. Republican. Methodist. Lodges: Masons, Shriners, Rotary. Office: PO Box 591 516 Main St Glen Ellyn IL 60138

DIETRICH, SUZANNE CLAIRE, instructional designer; b. Granite City, Ill., Apr. 9, 1937; d. Charles Daniel and Evelyn Blanche (Waters) D.; B.S. in Speech, Northwestern U., 1958; M.S. in Pub. Communication, Boston U., 1967; postgrad. So. Ill. U., 1973—. Intern, prodn. staff Sta. WGBH-TV, Boston, 1958-59, asst. dir., 1962-64, asst. dir. program Invitation to Art, 1958; cons. producer dir. dept. instructional TV radio Ill. Office Supt. Pub. Instruction, Springfield, 1969-70; dir. program prodn. and distbn., 1970-72; instr. faculty call staff, speech dept. Sch. Fine Arts So. Ill. U., Edwardsville, 1972—, grad. asst. for doctoral program office of dean Sch. Edn., 1975-78; research asst. Ill. public telecommunications study for Ill. Public Broadcasting Council, 1979-80; cons. and research in communications, 1980—; exec. producer, dir. TV programs Con-Con Countdown, 1970, The Flag Speaks, 1971. Roman Catholic. Home: 1011 Minnesota Ave Edwardsville IL 62025

DIETSCHE, DELMAR ALLEN, business executive; b. Bloomer, Wis., Feb. 11, 1931; s. Harold Charles and Minnie (Boese) D.; m. Irene Alma Tiller, June 8, 1952; children—Catherine, David, James. B.S. in Chemistry, U. Wis.-River Falls, 1952; B.S. in Physics, U. Wash., Seattle, 1953. Project engr. elec. div. Gen. Mills, Mpls., 1956-63; tech. service engr. visual products div. 3M Co., St. Paul, 1963-70, product devel. mgr., 1970-76, lab. mgr. nat. advt. div., 1977-82, sign materials project, 1982—. Team leader overhead projector invention, 1977 (Golden Step award), flexible sign face prodn. system, 1977 (Trade Secret award); patentee in field. Active mem. Parks and Recreation Com., Shoreview, Minn., 1969-70. Served to capt. USAF, 1953-56. Mem. Jaycees. Republican. Lutheran. Club: Hudson Golf (Wis.). Avocations: golf; Canadian fishing. Home: 3976 MacKubin St Saint Paul MN 55126 Office: 3M Sign Materials Lab Bldg 553-D-04 Saint Paul MN 55144

DILCHER, DAVID LEONARD, botanist, educator; b. Cedar Falls, Iowa, July 10, 1936; s. Leonard G. and Hannah E. (Short) D.; m. Katherine Rose Swanson, Sept. 10, 1961; children—Peter Corbin, Ann Katherine. B.S., U. Minn., 1958, M.S. in Botany, Geology and Zoology, 1960; postgrad. U. Ill., 1960-62; Ph.D., Yale U., 1964. NSF postdoctoral fellow Senckenberg Mus., Frankfurt am Main, Fed. Republica Germany, 1964-65; instr. dept. biology Yale U., New Haven, 1965-66; asst. prof. botany Ind. U., Bloomington, 1966-70, assoc. prof., 1970-76, prof., 1977—, bot. field explorations in various localities of North Am., Central Am., Eng., Fed. Republic Germany, Portugal, Afghanistan, Mexico, 1960—. Author: (with D. Redmon, M. Tansey and D. Whitehead) Plant Biology Laboratory Manual, 1973, 2d edit., 1975; (with T. Taylor) Biostratrgraphy of Fossil Plants: Successional and Paleoecological Analysis, 1980. Mem. editorial bd. Am. Jour. Botany, 1973-79. Contbr. articles to profl. jours. Mem. Utility Service Bd., City of Bloomington, 1975-77; ruling elder First Presbyterian Ch., Bloomington, 1975-77; bd. dirs. United Campus Ministries, 1971-72. Recipient Bloomington Audubon award, 1977; Guggenheim fellow, 1972; NSF grantee, 1966-84. Mem. Bot. Soc. Am. (chmn. paleobot. sect. 1974-75, sect. treas. paleobot. sect. 1974-77, sec. 1985—), Paleontol. Assn., Internat. Orgn. of Paleobotanists (North Am. rep. 1975-80), Internat. Assn. Angiosperm Paleobotany (pres. 1977-80), Assn. for Tropical Biology, Am. Assn. Stratigraphic Palynologists, Soc. Vertebrate Paleontology, AAAS, Internat. Soc. Plant Taxonomy, Am. Inst. Biol. Scis., Sigma Xi. Office: Dept Biology Ind U Bloomington IN 47405

DILL, CHARLES ANTHONY, manufacturing company executive; b. Cleve., Nov. 29, 1939; s. Melville Reese and Gladys (Frode) D.; m. Louise T. Hall, Aug. 24, 1963 (dec. Sept. 1983); children—Charles Anthony, Dudley Barnes. B.S.M.E., Yale U., 1961; M.B.A., Harvard U., 1963. With Emerson Electric Co., St. Louis, 1963-77, 80—, Centralia, Mo., 1977-80, corp. group v.p., 1980-82, sr. v.p., 1982—; dir. U. Mo. Coll. Engring., Stout Industries, Inc. Mem. Dist. Export Council, Dept. Commerce, St. Louis, 1983—. Recipient Honor award for disting. service to engring., U. Mo., 1981. Republican. Club: St. Louis Country. Home: 807 S Warson Rd St Louis MO 63124 Office: Emerson Electric Co 8000 W Florissant St St Louis MO 63136

DILL, EVERETT CHARLES, lawyer; b. Deshler, Ohio, May 8, 1929; s. Charles and Anna Maria Katharina (Schilling) D.; m. Karol Ann Kirkpatrick, Feb. 18, 1967; children—Anne Marie, Alyson Ruth, Alyssa Ellen. B.Sc. in Bus. Adminstrn., Ohio State U., 1949, J.D., 1952; M.B.A., U. Toledo, 1962. Bar: Ohio 1952, Mich. 1980. With Marathon Oil Co., Findlay, Ohio, 1954-66; tax adviser Esso Inter-Am., Inc., Coral Gables, Fla., 1966-67; tax atty., mgr. Gerber Products Co., Fremont, Mich., 1968-77; tax counsel Upjohn Co., Kalamazoo, Mich., 1977—. Served with U.S. Army, 1952-54. Mem. Ohio State Bar Assn., Mich. Bar Assn., ABA, Tax Execs. Inst. (nat. bd. dirs. 1975-77). Republican. Methodist. Home: 2917 Coachlite Ave Kalamazoo MI 49002 Office: Upjohn Co 700 Portage Rd Kalamazoo MI 49001

DILLARD, JERRY WAYNE, corporate safety engineer; b. Chattanooga, Oct. 17, 1944; s. John and Sarah Wilma (Witt) D.; m. Susan Michelle Andree, Aug. 31, 1974; children—John M., Stephen C., Jeffrey W. B.A. in Chemistry, U. Chattanooga, 1966; postgrad. in metall. engring. U. Tenn. Space Inst., 1966-67; M.A. in Personnel Mgmt., Central Mich. U., 1982. Cert. safety profl., Ill. Operating engr. City of Chattanooga, 1962-66; research asst. U. Tenn. Space Inst., Tullahoma, 1966-67; safety engr. ARO, Inc., Arnold Air Force Sta., Tenn., 1967-72; sr. safety engr. Ford Motor Co. Nashville (Tenn.) Glass Plant, 1972-75, employee program rep. Dearborn (Mich.) Glass Plant, 1975-76; div. safety engr. Ford Motor Co., Dearborn, 1976-78, corp. safety engr. N.Am. Automotive Ops., 1978—; guest lectr. safety engring. studies Mercy and Madonna Colls.; chmn. suprs. sect. Safety Council Southeast Mich., 1980—. Aide de Camp gov.'s staff Gov. Winfield Dunn, State of Tenn., 1974, Gov. Lamar Alexander, 1979. Mem. Am. Soc. Safety Engrs. (mgmt. div.). Methodist. Lodges: Masons, Shriners. Home: 21248 Summerside Ln Northville MI 48167 Office: Ford Motor Co 900 Parklane Towers W 1 Parklane Blvd Dearborn MI 48126

DILL-DEVOR, REBECCA MARIE, laboratory technician, pharmacist; b. La Porte, Ind., July 24, 1956; d. Glen J. and Jean B. (Kozik) Dill; m. Eric Jeffrey Devor, June 26, 1981; 1 child, Courtney Michelle. B.S. in Pharmacy, U. N.Mex., 1981. Registered pharmacist, N.Mex., Kans., Mo. Pharmacy intern St. Joseph Hosp., Albuquerque, 1976-81; pharmacist Super-X Drugs, Lawrence, Kans., 1981-82, St. Louis, 1982-84; tissue culture technician Washington U. Med. Sch., St. Louis, 1984—. Recipient McGaw Labs. award U. N.Mex., 1981. Mem. Am. Pharm. Assn., Acad. Pharmacy Practice, Kappa Epsilon. Republican. Roman Catholic. Avocations: ceramics, piano, crafts. Home: 7408 Wayne Ave Saint Louis MO 63130 Office: Washington U Med Sch 660 S Euclid Box 8108 Saint Louis MO 63110

DILLER, EROLD RAY, cardiovascular pharmacologist; b. May 4, 1922; s. Waldo and Mary Ann (Zimmerman) D.; m. Geneva W. Wuensch, Mar. 18, 1944; children—Cynthia Ann, David Mark. B.A., Bowling Green U., 1949; M.S., Ind. U., 1951. Biochemist Lilly Research Labs., Indpls., 1955-62, sr. biochemist, 1962-66, research scientist, 1966-71, research assoc., 1971—; mem. adv. bd. Devel. Conf. on Lipids, San Francisco, 1980-85, chmn., 1985—. Contbr. articles to profl. jours. Mem. Council on Arteriosclerosis Am. Heart Assn., N.Y. Acad. Sci., Sigma Xi, Phi Lambda Upsilon, Sigma Nu. Mem.

Christian Ch. Avocation: photography. Office: Lilly Research Labs Lilly Corp Ctr Indianapolis IN 46285

DILLIN, SAMUEL HUGH, See *Who's Who in America*, 43rd edition.

DILLING, KIRKPATRICK WALLWICK, lawyer; b. Evanston, Ill., Apr. 11, 1920; s. Albert W. and Elizabeth (Kirkpatrick) D.; engring. student Cornell U., 1939-40; B.S. in Law, Northwestern U., 1942; student DePaul U., 1946-47, L'Ecole Vaubier, Montreux, Switzerland; Degré Normal, Sorbonne, Paris; m. Betty Ellen Bronson, June 18, 1942 (div. July 1944); m. Elizabeth Ely Tilden, Dec. 11, 1948; children—Diana Jean, Eloise Tilden, Victoria Walgreen, Albert Kirkpatrick. Bar: Ill. 1947. Def. work Am. Steel Foundries, East Chicago, Ind., 1942-43; mem. firm Dilling and Dilling, 1948—; gen. counsel Am. Massage and Therapy Assn.; dir. P.E.P. Industries, Ltd., Ry. Devel. Corp.; v.p. Dillman Labs., Ltd.; spl. counsel Herbalife Australasia, Pty., Ltd. Dir., gen. counsel Nat. Health Fedn.; gen. counsel Cancer Control Soc.; bd. dirs. Nat. Safety Council. Served from pvt. to 1st lt. AUS, 1943-46. Mem. Am., Ill., Chgo. bar assns., Am. Trial Lawyers Assn., Cornell Soc. Engrs., Pharm. Advt. Club, Am. Legion, Air Force Assn., Navy League, Delta Upsilon. Republican. Episcopalian. Clubs: Lake Michigan Yachting Assn.; Cornell U. Club of Chicago; Tower. Contbr. articles to pub. health publs. Home: 1120 Lee Rd Northbrook IL 60062 Office: 150 N Wacker Dr Chicago IL 60606

DILLINGOFSKI, MARY SUE, publishing company executive; b. Madison, Wis., Dec. 27, 1944; d. Albert F. and Camille M. (Blott) D. B.A., Lawrence U., 1967; M.S., U. Wis., 1970, Ph.D., 1980. Tchr. English, Madison Pub. Schs. (Wis.), 1967-70; tchr. reading Niles Pub. Schs. (Ill.), 1971-72, Kamehameha Schs., Honolulu, 1972-77; lectr. U. Wis., Madison, 1977-80; cons. Scott, Foresman & Co., Glenview, Ill., 1980-81, mktg. mgr., 1981—; cons. diagnostician Univ. Hosp. Learning Disability Clinic, Madison, Wis., 1977-80; ednl. cons. Kalihi Palama Adult Edn. Ctr., Honolulu, 1973-75; Author: Nonprint Media and Reading, 1979; Sociolinguistics and Reading (W.S. Gray Research award 1980), 1978; also articles in profl. jours. Active Apollo Chorus, Chgo., 1983—, Friends of Sta. WHA, Madison, 1978-80, Mem. Art Deco Soc. Chgo., Internat. Reading Assn. (com. chmn. 1979-81), Wis. Reading Assn. (membership com. 1978-80), North Shore Reading Assn. Club: City (Chgo.). Office: Scott Foresman & Co 1900 E Lake Ave Glenview IL 60025

DILLON, GARY G., See *Who's Who in America*, 43rd edition.

DILLON, J. PAT, telecommunications marketing engineer; b. Long Beach, Calif., Sept. 10, 1945; s. Joseph C. and Mary (Friend) D.; m. Kathleen Doffing, Sept. 14, 1974; children—Shondra L., Jeffrey J. Student U. Colo., 1963-67. Chemist, Longmont Foundry (Colo.), 1965-67; metallurgist Dow Chem. Co., Rocky Flats, Colo., 1967-68; chemist Great Western Sugar Co., Longmont, Colo., 1968-70; engr. Mountain Bell Co., Boulder, Colo., 1970-72; cons. engr. Henkels & McCoy, Blue Bell, Pa., 1972-80; staff engr. Northwestern Bell Co., Mpls., 1980—; owner, mgr. Papillon Enterprises, Apple Valley, Minn., 1982—; co-owner Butterfly Boutique, Apple Valley, 1981—. Author: (pamphlet) How to Save Money Building Your Own House. Mem. Minn. Ind. Businessmen, Innovators Council (award 1982). Roman Catholic. Home: 13943 Everest Ave Apple Valley MN 55124 Office: Northwestern Bell 200 S 5th St Minneapolis MN 55402

DILLON, PHILLIP MICHAEL, construction company executive; b. Ypsilanti, Mich., July 15, 1944; s. Robert Timothy and Maxine Helen (Elliott) D.; student Mich. State U., 1962-66; m. Phyllis Louise Brooks, Jan. 21, 1978; children—Richard, Debora, Michael, Robert, Karen. Store mgr. Morse Shoe, Inc., Detroit, 1964-68, asst. dir. store planning and constrn., Canton, Mass., 1968-72; dir. store planning and constrn. Stride Rite Corp., Boston, 1972-74; sr. v.p. Capitol Cos., Inc., Arlington Heights, Ill., 1974-81; chmn. bd., chief exec. officer Standard Cos., Inc., Palatine, Ill., 1982-83; co-owner, v.p. Eagle Constrn. Corp., 1983—. Mem. Inst. Store Planners. Roman Catholic. Club: Green Acres Sportsman. Office: 304 E Rand Rd Arlington Heights IL 60004

DILLON, RAY E., JR., supermarket chain executive. Chmn., dir. Dillon Cos. Inc., Hutchinson, Kans. Office: Dillon Cos Inc 700 E 30th Ave Hutchinson KS 67501*

DILLON, RICHARD NEIL, mechanical engineer; b. Alliance, Ohio, May 7, 1954; s. James Richard and Marjorie May (Watson) D.; m. Diane Elise Tate, June 21, 1975; children—Katie Ann, Joshua Richard. Student U. Mo. Rolla, 1972-74; B.S.M.E., U. Akron, 1977; E.M.T., Aultman Hosp., 1984. Registered profl. engr., Ohio. Design engr. Alliance Electric, Ohio, 1977-81, chief engr., 1981-85; chief engr. Davis Engring., Alliance, 1985—; treas. Alliance Electric, 1972-84, Davis Engring., 1984-85; mgr. Speco Investment Services, 1977-85. Co-worker Cystic Fibrosis Found., Alliance, 1981-85; com. mem. First Immanuel United Ch. Christ, 1977—. Mem. ASME, Nat. Soc. Profl. Engrs., Ohio Soc. Profl. Engrs. Mem. Christian Ch. Lodge: Order of DeMolay. Home: 15350 Salem Church St Homeworth OH 44634 Office: Davis Engring Inc 22623 Lake Park Blvd Alliance OH 44601

DILMORE, TERRY ALAN, manufacturing company executive, industrial engineer; b. Elmira, N.Y., Oct. 13, 1937; s. Marcus V. and Elsie (Gore) D.; m. Sharon M. Kinzlow, Sept. 8, 1979; children—Kevin, Stacy, Aaron, Audra. B.S., Canisius Coll., 1961; M.B.A., Syracuse U., 1969. Supr. indsl. engring. Ingersoll-Rand, Painted Post, N.Y., 1963-69; mgr., mfg. engr. Combustion Engring., Abilene, Kans., 1969-73, Joy Mfg. Co., Colorado Springs, Colo., 1973-79; ops. mgr. Nat. Mine Service, Ashland, Ky., 1979-83; mgr. mfg. Marmon Transmotive Co., Knoxville, Tenn., 1983—; instr. night sch. Elmira Coll., N.Y., 1963-65. Worker Republican Nat. Com., Ohio, Tenn., 1980-84; officer Vol. Fire Dept., N.Y., Colo., Tenn., 1960-80. Served with U.S. Army, 1961-63. Named to Sports Hall of Fame, County Commn., Elmira, 1980. Mem. Am. Prodn. and Inventory Control Soc. Avocations: hunting, camping.

DILWORTH, JAMES LEE, ski resort executive, consultant, engineer; b. Charlevoix, Mich.; s. Forest Wesley and Kathryn Lee (Kennedy) D.; m. Mary Dell Saunders, Oct. 18, 1952; children—Wesley James, David Saunders, Susan Marguerite. B.C.E., U. Mich., 1951. Registered profl. engr., Mich., Mont., Ind., Colo., N.Mex., Wis., Nev., Utah. Engr. Charlevoix County Rd. Commn., Boyne City, Mich., 1952-57; forest engr. U.S. Forest Service, Cadillac, Mich., 1957-60; constrn. supt. Kendall Constrn., Cadillac, 1960-61; cons. engr. Norton & Kobbins, Cadillac, 1961-63; area mgr. Boyne Highlands, Harbor Springs, Mich., 1963-77; gen. mgr. Nubs Nob Ski Area, Harbor Springs, 1977—; prin. James L. Dilworth Ltd., Ski Area Cons., Harbor Springs, 1977—. Patentee snow machine equipment, 1976, 81, 83, 84. Mem. Ski Area Safety Bd., Mich., 1981—, vice chmn. 1984—; bd. dirs. Midwest Ski Area Assn., 1984—; mem. Emmet County Planning Commn., 1981-84; bd. dirs. Little Traverse Conservancy, Mich., 1984—. Mem. Mich. Soc. Profl. Engrs., Mich. Assn. Professions. Presbyterian. Home: 901 Sunset Ct Petoskey MI 49770 Office: Nubs Nob Ski Area 4021 Nubs Nob Rd Harbor Springs MI 49740

DIMASCIO, PAUL STEPHEN, experimental mechanics engineer, consultant; b. Bryn Mawr, Pa., Nov. 17, 1958; s. Paul Sylvino and Lillian Ann (Sweeney) DiM.; B.S. in Engring. Sci. and Mechanics with honors, Pa. State U., 1980. Cons. DiMascio Tech. Services, State College, Pa., 1980-84; research aide Pa. State U., State Coll., 1980-84; sr. stress engr. Teledyne Continental Motors, Muskegon, Mich., 1985—; owner DiMascio Tech. Services, State College, 1980—. Contbr. articles to profl. jours. Mem. Soc. Exptl. Mechanics, Tau Beta Pi. Clubs: Exptl. Aircraft Assn., Rider Motorcycle Tring. Office: Teledyne Continental Motors Gen Products Div 76 Getty St Muskegon MI 49442

DIMON, MICHAEL PRATT, metals company executive; b. Atlantic City, Sept. 8, 1949; s. Bruce Pratt and Ruth (Burns) D. B.A., Dickinson Coll., 1971; postgrad. Pace U., 1971-73; M.B.A., Harvard U., 1976. C.P.A., N.Y. Staff acct. Price Waterhouse & Co., N.Y.C., 1971-73; sr. acct. Price Waterhouse & Co., N.Y.C., 1973-74, 76-78; sr. bus. analyst Cabot Corp., Boston, 1978-81; project mgr. High Tech. Materials div. Cabot Corp., Kokomo, Ind., 1981-82, mktg. mgr., 1982-83, mgr. bus. planning and communications Cabot Wrought Products div., 1983-84, mgr. bus. devel. Cabot Stellite div., 1984—; dir. Shanghai-Cabot Hardfacing Co., Ltd. Mem. Am. Mktg. Assn., Am. Soc. Metals, Am. Inst. C.P.A.s, Assn. Bus. Marketers. Methodist. Clubs: Harvard (N.Y.C.); Kokomo (Ind.) Country. Home: 2210 Executive Dr Kokomo IN 46902 Office: 1020 W Park Ave Kokomo IN 46901

DINES, LENNA VICTORIA, surgeon, educator; b. Lansing, Mich., Jan. 8, 1942; d. George Kosta and Nevanka (Valcanoff) D. B.S., Mich. State U., 1965; D.O., Kirksville Coll. Osteo. Medicine, 1970. Intern, Sun Coast Hosp., Largo, Fla., 1970-71; emergency room physician Met. Hosp., Pinnellas Park, Fla., 1971-72; resident in gen. surgery Mount Clemens Gen. Hosp., Mich., 1973-76, mem. staff, 1977—; gen. surgeon, Mount Clemens, 1977—; clin. prof. surgery Mich. State U., East Lansing, 1980—, Des Moines Coll. Osteo. Medicine, 1979-82. Contbr. articles to med. jours. Bd. dirs. Ositiak council Girl Scouts U.S.A., 1983—; res. dep. Macomb County Sheriff's Dept., Mount Clemens, 1984—. Mem. Am. Coll. Osteo. Medicine, Am. Osteo. Assn., Mich. Osteo. Assn., Fla. Osteo. Assn., Mount Clemens C. of C. Republican. Greek Orthodox. Office: 22100 Lester Mount Clemens MI 48043

DINGEE, SARAH ELIZABETH, accountant; b. Rock Hill, S.C., Jan. 8, 1925; d. William Parnell and Charlotte Emilie (Laurey) Branigan; m. William A. Dingee, Oct. 18, 1945; children—William A. Jr., Barbara M., Charles E. Student Winthrop Coll., 1941-42, Ind. Vocat. Tech. Coll., 1980-81. Student acct. So. Bell Telephone Co., 1942-43; clk., acct. White Printing Co., 1943-44; sec., acct. Dingee Co., Hobart, Ind., 1953—; sec., counselor, dir. The Answer, Inc., Hobart, 1980—. Mem. Citizens Action Coalition, United Way Vol. Action Bur. Mem. DAR, VFW Aux, Daus. Confederacy, Daus. Isabella, St. Anns Archconfraternity. Roman Catholic. Office: PO Box 157 Hobart IN 46342

DINGELL, JOHN DAVID, congressman; b. Colorado Springs, Colo. July 8, 1926; s. John D. and Grace (Bigler) D.; B.S. in Chemistry, Georgetown U., 1949. J.D., 1952. Admitted to D.C. bar, 1952, Mich. bar, 1953; asst. pros. atty., Wayne County (Mich.), 1953-55: mem. 84th to 88th Congresses from 15th Dist. Mich., 89-99th Congresses from 16th Dist. Mich., chmn. energy and commerce com., mem. Office Tech. Assessment. Served as 2d lt. inf. AUS. 1945-46. Mem. Delta Theta Phi. Office: 2221 Rayburn House Office Bldg Washington DC 20515*

DINGLE, KEVIN STUART, manufacturing company executive; b. Detroit, May 29, 1952; s. Stuart Frank and Rae Helen (Hansen) G.; m. Joan Nancy Parrott, May 19, 1973 (div. 1979); m. Barbara Annette Chavey, Apr. 18, 1981; children—Meghan Elisabeth, Patrick Kevin. B.S., U. Detroit, 1974, M.B.A., 1981. Exec. asst. J.W. Crusoe Investments, Birmingham, Mich., 1974-77; acctg. mgr. Handleman Co., Clawson, Mich., 1977-79, ops. planning analyst, 1979-82; gen. mgr. Premier Malt Products, Grosse Pointe, Mich., 1982-83; controller, chief fin. officer Foamade Industries, Auburn Hills, Mich., 1983—. Mem. Assn. MBA Execs., Assn. Computer Users, Assn. Planning Execs., Automotive Industry Action Group, Mich. C. of C. Congregationalist. Home: 17386 Avilla Lathrup Village MI 48076 Office: Foamade Industries Inc 2550 Auburn Ct Auburn Hills MI 48057

DINI, ROBERT U., lawyer; b. Evanston, Ill., June 6, 1938; s. Umberto J. and Ida D.; children—Jennifer, Laura, John. A.B., U. Notre Dame, 1960; J.D., U. Chgo., 1963. Bar: Ill. 1963, U.S. Dist. Ct. (no. dist.) Ill. 1963, U.S. Ct. Appeals (7th cir.) 1976. Law clerk Ill. Appellate Ct., Chgo., 1963-64; assoc. Petit, Olin, Fazio & Safeblade, Chgo., 1965-68; corp. atty. Maremont Corp., Chgo., 1968-71; sole practice, Winnetka, Ill., 1971—. Mem. Winnetka Caucus Com., Ill., 1977-78; mem. pres.' council Barat Coll., 1979-80. Mem. Chgo. Bar Assn., Ill. State Bar Assn., Amnesty Internat., U.S.A., Winnetka C. of C. (pres. 1977-78, dir. 1975—). Office: Law Office of Robert Dini 1056 Gage St Winnetka IL 60093

DINKEL, SHARON JO, college dean; b. Toledo, Ohio, July 12, 1936; m. James Edward Dinkel, 1 child, Brent Philip. B.E., U. Toledo, 1965, M.Ed., 1969, Ph.D., 1973. Cert. elem., secondary tchr., Ohio. Asst. prof. Ohio Dominican Coll., Columbus, 1970-73, St. Cloud U., Minn., 1973-74; assoc. prof. Ohio State U., Columbus, 1974-79; dean instl. planning Lourdes Coll., Sylvania, Ohio, 1980—; cons. U. Hawaii, 1979, others. Bd. dirs. Trinity-St. Paul Inner City Program, Toledo, 1968; cons. Ohio Civil Rights Commn., 1972; active Democratic campaigns. U. Toledo fellow, 1967-69; recipient Citation, U. Toledo, 1979, Journalistic Excellence award Columbia Press Assn., N.Y.C., 1954. Mem. Am. Council Edn., Ohio Conf. Coll. and Univ. Planning, Soc. Coll. and Univ. Planning (com. 1984-85), Phi Theta Kappa, Phi Kappa Phi (Citation 1973), U. Toledo Alumni Assn., U.S. Coast Guard Aux. Lutheran. Avocations: fossil and mineral collecting; poetry; horseback riding. Office: Lourdes College 6832 Convent Blvd Sylvania OH 43560

DINNDORF, DONALD JAMES, editor, writer-photographer; b. Anchorage, Nov. 26, 1954; s. Donald Alex and Margaret Jean (Studanski) D.; m. Viola Laura Schlangen, June 5, 1976; children—Catherine Lee, James Donald. Student Saint Cloud U., 1973-1975. Outdoor columnist Stearns-Morrison Enterprise, Albany, Minn., Paynesville Press., Minn., Cold Spring Record, Minn., 1975-83, Saint Cloud Daily Times, Minn., 1977-82; editor Minn. Out-of-Doors, Saint Paul, 1982—. Contbr. articles to mags. Mem. Outdoor Writers Assn. Am., Minn. Waterfowl Assn., Minn. Conservation Fedn. (exec. com. 1984-85). Roman Catholic. Avocations: hunting; fishing; nature study. Office: Minnesota Conservation Federation 1036 - B Cleveland Ave South St Paul MN 55116

DINOS, NICHOLAS, engineering educator, administrator; b. Tamaqua, Pa., Jan. 15, 1934; s. Christophoros and Calliope (Haralambos) D.; m. Lillian Gravell, June 18, 1955; children—Gwen Elizabeth, Christopher Nicholas, Janet Kay. B.S., Pa. State U., 1955; M.S., Lehigh U., 1966, Ph.D., 1967. Engr. E. I. duPont Co., Terre Haute, Ind., 1955-57, research engr., Augusta, Ga., 1957-64; assoc. prof. Ohio U., Athens, 1967-72, prof., 1972—, chmn., 1976—; vis. prof. Chubu U., Nagoya, Japan, 1976. Contbr. articles to profl. jours. Elder Presbyterian Ch., Athens, 1967—. NASA fellow Lehigh U., Stanford U., 1966, 72, 74, U.S. Steel fellow Lehigh U., 1965; Danforth Found. assoc. Ohio U., 1978—. Mem. Am. Inst. Chem. Engrs., Am. Chem. Soc., AAUP, AAAS, Am. Soc. Engring. Edn., Sigma Xi, Phi Kappa Phi. Democrat. Avocations: reading, music, outdoors, travel. Home: 29 Briarwood St Athens OH 45701 Office: Ohio Univ Main Campus Dept Chem Engring Athens OH 45701

DINSDALE, HOWARD ARTHUR, ophthalmologist; b. Palmer, Nebr., May 8, 1930; s. George and Rena Dinsdale; m. Barbara Gilmore, June 19, 1954; children—Nancy, Robert. A.B., U. Nebr., 1951, M.D., U. Nebr.-Omaha, 1954. Diplomate Am. Bd. Ophthalmology. Intern, Charles T. Miller Hosp., St. Paul; resident Charles T. Miller Hosp.-U. Minn., instr. U. Minn. Coll. Medicine, Mpls., 1961-67; instr., then assoc. prof. ophthalmology U. Nebr. Coll. Medicine, Omaha, 1968—; practice medicine specializing in ophthalmology, St. Paul, 1960-67, Lilncoln, Nebr., 1967—; instr. Lincoln Med. Edn. Found., 1980—. Elder Presbyterian Ch.-Westminster, Lincoln, 1984—; chmn. Health Council United Fund, St. Paul, 1965; precinct chmn. Lancaster County Republican Party, Lincoln, 1978; pres. Community Blood Bank, Lincoln, 1984. Recipient Radio Sta. WCCO Good Neighbor award, 1967. Mem. AMA, Nebr. Med. Assn., Lancaster County Med. Assn. (pres. 1983), Nebr. Acad. Ophthalmology (pres. 1982), Am. Acad. Ophthalmology. Club: Univ. (Lincoln). Avocations: music; reading; running; bridge. Home: 1621 Devoe Dr Lincoln NE 68506

DINTER, RUTH MARGARET, insurance agent; b. Leon, N.Y., July 22, 1921; d. Glenn Mason and Irene Mattie (Miller) Forrester; m. John Alexander Dinter, July 14, 1940; children—Dennis Allen, Dorothy Ann Dinter Huerter, Dianne A. Student Drake U., 76, 1974-77. Asst. mgr. Ladies and Children's Clothing Store, Cedar Rapids, Iowa, 1957-60; gen. cashier, office mgr. Motor Hotel, Cedar Rapids, 1960-68; claims sec. Bouslog-Verhille Ins. Inc., Marion, Iowa, 1968-74, agt., 1974—; tchr. ins. Kirkwood Community Coll., Cedar Rapids, 1976-78, chmn. Office Edn. Adv. Bd., 1981-83. Bd. dirs. Community Coll., 1971-81; coordinator activities Muscular Dystrophy, Cedar Rapids, 1973-83; den mother, leader Boy Scouts Am. and Girls' Scouts U.S.A., Cattaraugus, N.Y. and Marion, 1949-52, 57-60; leader 4-H, Cattaraugus, 1949-54. Mem. Ins. Women of Cedar Rapids (bd. dirs. 1974-83, pres. 1979-81), Am. Bus. Women's Assn. (officer 1973-77, Woman of Yr. 1976-77, pres. 1976-77). Democrat. Lodges: Soroptimist (bd. dirs. 1982-83), Order of Eastern Star. Home: 3096 14th Ave PO Box 282 Marion IA 52302 Office: Bouslog-Verhille Ins Inc 360 7th Ave PO Box 385 Marion IA 52302

DI PRIMA, STEPHANIE MARIE, educational administrator; b. Chgo., Aug. 29, 1952; d. Joseph and Ann Marie (Albate) DiP. B.A., Rosary Coll., 1973; M.Ed., Loyola U., Chgo., 1978. Tchr., St. Vincent Ferrer Sch., River Forest, Ill., 1974-78; prin. Our Lady of Hope Sch., Rosemont, Ill., 1978-81, Sacred Heart Sch., Winnetka, Ill., 1981-84, St. Monica Sch., Chgo., 1984—. Mem. Nat. Cath. Educators Assn., Nat. Assn. Elem. Sch. Prins., Assn. Supervision and Curriculum Devel., Women in Mgmt., Prins. Coalition for Arts, Prins. Support Group, Adminstrs. Growth Group, Archdiocesan Prins. Assn. Office: 5115 N Montclare Ave Chicago IL 60656

DIRLAM, GORDON AUBREY, real estate facility planner; b. Mpls., Aug. 28, 1950; s. Aubrey William and Hazelle Marie (Menz) D.; m. Mary Kathryn Johnson, Apr. 20, 1974; children—Alexandra, Adam. B.S., U. Minn., 1973. Mus. photographer Minn. Hist. Soc., St. Paul, 1973-74; with real estate leasing, Northwestern Bell, Mpls., 1974-75, real estate bldg. constrn., 1978-81, real estate facility planning, St. Paul, 1981—. Vol. Ind. Republicans, Redwood Falls, Minn., 1964-72. Mem. Internat. Facility Mgmt. Assn. (profl.), Delta Phi Delta. Avocations: golf; carpentry; reading on investing; swimming. Office: Northwestern Bell 70 W 4th St Room 1-C Saint Paul MN 55102

DI ROCCO, PENNY SUE, corporate executive; b. Mpls., Nov. 6, 1947; d. John Byron and Marion Lydia (Campbell) Watschke; student schs. Bloomington, Minn.; m. Thomas Rudd, Sept. 10, 1966 (div.); children—Jesse, Zak; m. 2d, Tom Di Rocco, Aug. 7, 1983. Cancellation clk., underwriter Gen. Motors Ins. Co., Mpls. 1965-71; payroll clk., accounts payable and receivable, salesperson, pres. personnel div., shipping, fin. officer, computer program design Drag Specialties, Inc., Hopkins, Minn., 1980-83; pres. Property Devel. Spltys., Inc., 1983—; ptnr. Di Rocco Devel. Corp. Mem. Am. Mgmt. Assn., Better Bus. Bur. Republican. Office: 5740 Wayzata Blvd Minneapolis MN 55416

DISABATO, JOHN MICHAEL, marketing education coordinator; b. Cleve., June 21, 1950; s. John Devito and Teresa Marie (Vittantonio) DiS. B.S. in Bus. Adminstrn. and Edn., Bowling Green State U., 1973, M. Ed., 1975. Cert. secondary bus., mktg. edn. tchr. Advt. mgr. Montgomery Ward, Toledo, 1972-73; distributive edn. coordinator pub. schs., Dayton, Ohio, 1973-74, Athens, Ohio, 1976-81; sales cons. Marino Bros. Furniture, Willoughby, Ohio, 1981-82; distributive edn. coordinator city schs., Elyria, Ohio, 1982-83, Lakewood, Ohio, 1983—; mktg. instr. Hocking Tech. Coll., Nelsonville, Ohio. Bloodmobile chmn. Athens County chpt. ARC, 1980-81; participant Ohio Retail Mchts. Anti-Shoplifting campaign, 1976-81, 85. Mem. Distributive Edn. Clubs Am. (dist. chmn.), Am. Vocat. Assn., Ohio Vocat. Assn., NEA, Delta Pi Epsilon, Pi Kappa Alpha. Roman Catholic. Club: Cleveland Darter. Lodges: Moose, K.C. Contbr. articles to profl. jours. Office: Lakewood High Sch 14100 Franklin Blvd Lakewood OH 44107

DISBROW, RICHARD EDWIN, utilities executive; b. Newark, Sept. 20, 1930; s. Milton A. and Madeline Catherine (Segal) D.; m. Patricia Fair Warner, June 27, 1953 (div. Sept. 1972); children—John Scott, Lisa Karen; m. 2d, Teresa Marie Moser, May 12, 1973. B.S. Lehigh U., 1952, M.S. in Elec. Engring., Newark Coll. Engring., 1959, M.S. in Indsl. Mgmt. (Sloan fellow), MIT, 1965. With Am. Electric Power Service Corp., N.Y.C., 1954-80, Columbus, Ohio, 1980—; transmission and distbn. mgr., 1967-70, controller, 1970-71, v.p., controller, 1971-74, exec. v.p., 1974-75, vice chmn. bd., 1975-79, pres., chief adminstrv. officer, 1979-84, pres., chief operating officer, 1985—, also dir.; pres., dir. Am. Electric Power Co.; instr. Newark Coll. Engring., 1959-64. Indsl. commr., Piscataway, N.J., 1960-64; mem. N.J. Engrs. Com. for Student Guidance, 1960-64; vis. com., dept. mech. engring. and mechanics Lehigh U.; trustee Franklin U. Served to lt. USAF, 1952-54. Mem. Edison Electric Inst. (bd. dirs.), Psi Upsilon, Eta Kappa Nu. Clubs: Columbus Athletic Worthington Hills Country. Office: Am Electric Power Service Corp 1 Riverside Plaza Columbus OH 43215

DISHER, PAUL JAMES, insurance company executive; b. Chgo., Apr. 17, 1929; s. Arthur Christopher and Margaret Mary (hester) D.; B.A. in Econs., St. Ambrose Coll., 1951; m. Elizabeth Ann Prellberg, Apr. 16, 1955. Sales trainee Hibbard, Spencer, Bartlett Co., Evanston, Ill., 1951-52; 2d v.p. group ins. adminstrn. Washington Nat. Ins. Co., Evanston, 1954-75, 2d v.p., dir. bus. systems, 1975-77, 2d v.p., head home office services dept., 1977-84, v.p. home office services, 1984—, chmn. mgmt. adv. council, 1963-66; charter capt.; owner P&R Sports Inc., Tyree Lures. Vol. fireman, Park Ridge, Ill., 1958-68. Served with U.S. Navy, 1952-54. Mem. Life Office Mgmt. Assn., Health Ins. Assn. Am., Coll. Life Underwriters, Assn. Gt. Lakes Outdoor Writers, Assn. for Systems Mgmt., Ill. Charter Capts. Assn. Conservative Republican. Roman Catholic. Club: Runaway Bay Yacht. Lodge: Moose. Home: 834 Dee Rd Park Ridge IL 60068 Office: Washington Nat Ins Co 1630 Chicago Ave Evanston IL 60201

DISHOP, RICHARD THOMAS, automotive dealer; b. Wauseon, Ohio, Aug. 24, 1942; s. Albert Henry and Amelia A. D.; student U. Automotive Mgmt., New Orleans, 1980; m. Janice Elain Longstreet, July 5, 1973; children—Teresa, Anthony, Jodi. Barber, 1961-64; gen. mgr. Turnpike Travelers, Bowling Green, Ohio, 1967-71; owner, operator Dishop Ford-Nisson, Bowling Green, 1972—; owner, operator RTD & Assos., collection agy., 1972-75; mem. Mid Am. Bank Adv. Bd., 1971-80, pres., 1972. Named to Outstanding Young Men Am., U.S. Jaycees, 1973; recipient Quality Dealer award Datsun, 1975, 80, 82, 83. Mem. Am. Imported Automobile Dealers Assn., Nat. Auto Dealers Assn., Bowling Green Auto Dealers (sec.-treas. 1978-85), Ohio Auto Dealers Assn. Republican. Lutheran. Clubs: Falcon, Elks, Bowling Green State U. Pres.'s. Home: 14251 Gorrill Rd Bowling Green OH 43402 Office: Dishop Ford-Nisson Route 25 Bowling Green OH 43402

DISILVESTRO, ROBERT ARNOLD, nutritional biochemist, educator; b. Bklyn., July 17, 1953; s. Arnold Robert and Margaret Ann (Devereux) DiS.; m. Janet Kay Spangler, Aug. 30, 1975; 1 child, David Joel. B.S. in Biochemistry, Purdue U., 1975; Ph.D., Tex. A&M U., 1982. Analytical chemist State of Ind., West Lafayette, 1975-78; teaching asst. Tex. A&M U., College Station, 1978-79, research asst., 1979-82; research assoc. U. Fla., Gainesville, 1982-84; asst. prof. Purdue U., West Lafayette, 1984—. Contbr. articles to profl. jours., also chpt. to book. Fundraiser Heart Assn., Farmingdale, N.Y., 1969; Sons of Italy scholar, 1971; NIH fellow, 1981. Mem. Phi Lamda Upsilon. Club: Purdue Volleyball. Avocations: running, church activities. Home: 842 Kent Ave West Lafayette IN 49706 Office: Purdue U Dept Foods and Nutrition West Lafayette IN 49707

DISPENSA, PAUL CHARLES, lawyer; b. Hinsdale, Ill., July 9, 1952; s. Paul Charles and Mary Ann (Ponzo) D.; m. Tripp Olive Hellmuth, Apr. 2, 1976; children—Leslie Katherine, Bradley Paul. B.S.B.A., Denver U., 1974; J.D., Lewis Coll. Law, 1978. Bar: Ill. 1982, U.S. Dist. Ct. (no. dist.) Ill. 1982. Adviser Project Verdict, vets. dept. Coll. Dupage, Glen Ellyn, Ill., 1978-79; adjuster Am. Family Ins. Co., Schaumburg, Ill., 1980-82, in-house counsel, 1982—. Mem. ABA, Ill. State Bar Assn., Dupage County Bar Assn., Am. Judicature Soc. Roman Catholic. Office: Am Family Ins Co 1501 Woodfield Dr Suite 200 W Schaumburg IL 60555

DI SPIGNO, GUY JOSEPH, psychologist, consultant; b. Bklyn., Mar. 6, 1948; s. Joseph Vincent and Jeanne Nina (Renna) DiS.; B.S., Carroll Coll., 1969; M.A. (fellow), No. Ill. U., 1972; M.Ed., Loyola U., 1974; Ph.D., Northwestern U., 1977; m. Gisela Riba, May 23, 1979; children—Michael Paul, Abie Francis. Instr., No. Ill. U., DeKalb, 1969-70; chmn. humanities dept. Quincy (Ill.) Boys' High Sch., 1970-71; dir. religious edn. St. Mary's Ch., DeKalb, 1971-72; dir. edn. Immaculate Conception Parish, Higland Park, Ill., 1972-77; dir. human resources Am. Valuation Cons., Des Plaines, Ill., 1977-79; psychologist Hay Assos., Chgo., 1979-80; v.p. psychol. services Exec. Assets Corp., Chgo., 1980-82; dir. mgmt. devel. and personnel services Borg-Warner Corp., Chgo., 1982-84; cons. psychologist Medina & Thompson, Chgo., 1984—. Mem. Highland Park Human Relations Commn., 1975-77, Home Owners and Businessmen's Assn., Highland Park, 1976-77; mem. legis. com. Vernon Hills (Ill.) Sch. Bd.; soccer coach, Am. Youth Soccer Orgn., Glenview, Ill. Clifford B. Scott scholar, 1967. Mem. Community Religious Edn. Dirs. (nat. vice chmn. 1971-73), Am. Psychol. Assn., Ill. Psychol. Assn., Nat. Registry Health Service Providers in Psychology, Am. Personnel and Guidance Assn., Carroll Coll. Alumni Assn., Phi Alpha Theta, Sigma Phi Epsilon. Contbr. articles to profl. jours. Home: 3710 Maple Leaf Dr Glenview IL 60025 Office: 100 S Wacker Dr Suite 1710 Chicago IL 60606

DISSELKOEN, RANDALL CLARE, jewelrey and coin shop executive; b. Zeeland, Mich., Apr. 28, 1950; s. Clarence Leroy and Lorene (Morren) D.; m. Terri Jean Kammeraad, Dec. 15, 1972; children—Robyn, Kaitlyn, Randall. A.B., Davenport Bus. Coll., 1972; student Calvin Coll., 1968-70. Mgr. Cordon Bleu, Grand Rapids, Mich., 1970-73; owner, mgr. Randy Disselkoen LTD, Grand Rapids, 1973—; cons. career day Calvin Coll., Grand Rapids, 1984;

pres. Praise Inc., Grand Rapids, 1984—; speaker for small bus. seminar C. of C., Grand Rapids, 1985. Chmn. prodical com. Billy Graham Film and Josh McDowell com., 1984-85; M.C. Easter Seals auction, Grand Rapids, 1984; auctioneer Rep. Party Annual Fundraiser, Grand Rapids, 1985; M.C. St. Jude annual show, Grand Rapids, 1984. Winner Nat. Recruiting contest Cordon Bleu, 1972; named Nat. Coll. Sales Leader Cordon Bleu, 1972. Mem. Retail Jewelers Assn., Am. Numismatic Assn., Florida United Numismatic Assn., Mich. State Numismatic Assn. (life), Grand Rapids Coin Club (life), Rep. Congl. Leadership Com., Grand Rapids Econ. Club. Mem. Reformed Ch. Clubs: Blythefield Country, Lotus (Grand Rapids), Great Lakes Investment (pres. 1985—). Office: Randy Disselkoen L&D 3090 28th SE Grand Rapids MI 49508

DISTELHORST, GARIS FRED, trade association executive; b. Columbus, Ohio, Jan. 21, 1942; s. Harold Theodore and Ruth (Haywood) D.; m. Helen Cecilia Gillen, Oct. 28, 1972; children—Garen, Kristen. B.S., Ohio State, 1965. Cert. assn. exec. vice pres. Smith, Bucklin & Assocs., Washington, 1969-80; pres., chief exec. officer NACSCORP, Inc., Oberlin, Ohio, 1980—; exec. dir., chief exec. officer Nat. Assn. College Stores, Oberlin, 1980—; mem. nat. adv. bd. Library of Congress, Washington, 1983—; mem. exec. council Internat. Booksellers Fedn., Vienna, Austria, 1981-85. Author Challenge and the Choice booklet, 1977. Bd. dirs. Choral Arts Soc., Washington, 1975-76; mem. Citizens Cable T.V. Commn., Oberlin, 1982-83; chmn. Sesquicentennial Com., Oberlin, 1983; assn. exec. adv. com. Reagan/Bush campaign, Washington, 1984. Recipient U.S. Navy Achievement medal, 1969. Mem. Inst. Assn. Mgmt. Cos. (treas. 1979-80, award of merit 1979), Am. Soc. Assn. Execs. (bd. dirs. ASAE Found. 1978-80 bd. dirs. 1981—, vice chmn. 1985, Key award, 1984), Greater Cleve. Soc. Assn. Execs., Trade Show Bur. Republican. Presbyterian. Lodges: Rotary (dir. 1983-85), Kiwanis. Avocations: reading, downhill skiing, tennis. Office: Nat Assn of College Stores 528 E Lorain St Oberlin OH 44074

DISTIN, MARK ROBERT, surgical equipment sales executive; b. Kalamazoo, Mich., Sept. 11, 1952; s. Robert Edward and Mary Elizabeth (Olmsted) D.; m. Regina Marie Hipple, July 26, 1975; children—Derek Matthew, Kimberly Ann, Craig Robert. B.S., Lakeland Coll., 1975. Tchr. Hillsboro High Sch., Wis., 1975-77, Richmond High Sch., Ill., 1978-80; sales rep. Codman & Shurtleff, Inc., Randolph, Mass., 1977-78, Waymar Med. Co., Mequon, Wis., 1980-81; sales rep. Stryker Corp., Kalamazoo, 1981-82, sales mgr., 1982—. Mem. Am. Mgmt. Assn. Republican. Mem. United Ch. Christ. Avocations: running; fishing; hunting; camping; skiing. Home: 507 Black Earth Rd Wales WI 53183

DITKA, MICHAEL KELLER, See *Who's Who in America,* 43rd edition.

DITMEYER, STEVEN ROLAND, railroad executive; b. St. Louis, Nov. 4, 1941; s. Roland John and Mabel Elizabeth (Hermeling) D.; m. Martha Stark Draper, May 26, 1979; children—Anne, David. B.S., MIT, 1963; cert. in transp. Yale U., 1965, M.A., 1965. Ops. research analyst Fed. R.R. Adminstrn., Washington, 1968-74, assoc. adminstr. policy, 1977-79, assoc. adminstr. research and devel., 1980-81; transp. economist The World Bank, Washington, 1974-77; acting gen. mgr. The Alaska R.R., Anchorage, 1979-80; dir. research and devel. Burlington No. R.R., St. Paul, 1981—. Co-author pub. reports on R.R. industry. Served to capt. USAR, 1966-68. Recipient Spl. Commendation, Fed. R.R. Adminstrn., 1980. Fellow The Permanent Way Inst.; mem. Am. R.R. Engring. Assn., Tau Beta Pi. Episcopalian. Club: Metropolitan (Washington). Office: Burlington Northern RR 9401 Indian Creek Pkwy Overland Park KS 66201

DITTMER, JOSEPH JOHN, psychologist; b. Butler, Pa., Apr. 21, 1947; s. Joseph Robert and Mary (Raith) D. B.A., Slippery Rock U., 1969; M.A., John Carroll U., 1972, Alfred Adler Inst., 1982; Ph.D., Kent State U., 1982. Psychologist Western Res. Psychiat. Ctr., Cleve., 1969—, Western Res. Human Services, Akron, Ohio, 1982—, Mental Health Bd. Summit County, Ohio, 1985—; adj. faculty Case Western Res. U., Cleve., 1981—. Mem. Am. Psychol. Assn., North Am. Soc. Adlerian Psychology, Assn. Mental Health Adminstrs. Avocation: skiing. Home: 55 Kennedy Blvd Northfield OH 44067 Office: Western Res Psychiat Ctr Box 305 Northfield OH 44067

DITTON, DELORES ELAINE, insurance agent; b. Bedford, Ind., Apr. 6, 1934; d. Haase John and Beulah Glen (Guthrie) Benzel; m. Louis George Ditton, Nov. 8, 1958; children—Cynthia, Ryan. R.N., Lutheran Hosp., Ft. Wayne, 1957; B.S. in Health Arts, Coll. of St. Francis, Joliet, 1980; grad. Bill Miller Sch. Real Estate, 1981, Midwest Ins. Sch., 1983, Ft. Wayne Ground Sch., 1978. Lic. nurse, real estate, ins., Ind.; lic. pvt. pilot. Nurse, surg., coronary, critical care areas, Ft. Wayne, Ind., 1957-83; head nurse geriatric facility, Ft. Wayne, 1983; agt. specializing in cancer/intensive care plans Am. Family Life Assurance Co., 1983—; sales rep. New Era Mfg. Co. energy efficient homes. Sci. Fair judge Aerospace Edn. Council, 1983, 84, 85. Mem. Ninety Nines (co-founder Three Rivers chpt., sec. 1983—, membership chmn.), Aircraft Owners and Pilots Assn., Cherokee Pilots Assn., Fort Wayne Aviation Assn. Active Ft. Wayne area flotilla Coast Guard Aux. Home: 5417 Inland Trail Fort Wayne IN 46825

DITTRICH, MICHAEL THOMAS, soft drink company executive; b. Sheboygan, Wis., Sept. 24, 1951; s. Burt Gene and Theresa Adele (Mulloy) D.; m. Joyce B. Baskin, Apr. 7, 1972; children; Joshua, Samantha. B.B.A., U. Wis.-Madison, 1973, M.B.A., 1974. Research asst. U. Wis. Grad. Sch. Bus., Madison, 1973-74; analyst Residential Planning Corp., Chgo., 1974-76; pres. Vittle Stores, Inc., Oconomowoc, Wis., 1976-82; bus. devel. mgr. Pepsi Cola Bottling Group, Milw., 1982-85, regional sales magr., North Brunswick, N.J., 1985—. dir. Detes, Inc., Oconomowoc, 1972—. Campaign mgr. John Alberts Assembly Com., Wis., 1981; treas. Com. to Elect Steve Foti, Wis., 1982. Recipient Meritorious Mktg. award Am. Mktg. Assn., 1973. Mem. Grocery Mfrs. Reps., Phi Kappa Phi. Republican. Avocations: basketball; racquetball; cross country skiing; bicycling. Home: 629 Washington St Oconomowoc WI 53066

DIUGUID, LEWIS WALTER, editor, reporter, photographer; b. St. Louis, July 17, 1955; s. Lincoln Isaiah and Nancy Ruth (Greenlee) D.; m. Valerie Gale Words, Oct. 25, 1977; 1 dau., Adrianne. B.J., U. Mo., 1977. Reporter, photographer Campus Digest, Columbia, Mo., 1974-75, St. Louis Sentinel, 1976; reporter, photographer, copy and automotive editor Kansas City Times, Mo., 1977—; asst. minority recruiting coordinator Kansas City Times and Star, 1985—. Inst. for Journalism Edn. fellow U. Ariz.-Tucson, 1984. Mem. Nat. Assn. Black Journalists, Kansas City Assn. Black Journalists. Roman Catholic. Avocations: jogging; weight lifting; bike riding; woodworking. Home: 3944 Charlotte St Kansas City MO 64110 Office: Kansas City Times 1729 Grand Ave Kansas City MO 64108

DIVELY, CHARLOTTE LYETH, development and fundraising executive, consultant; b. Bethesda, Md., Dec. 20, 1943; d. John Mortimer Richardson Lyeth and Patricia (Dobson) Webb; m. Michael Augustus Dively, June 17, 1978 (div. 1981). B.A., Principia Coll., 1965; cert. N.Y. Sch. Interior Design, 1966. Asst. to treas. fin. com. to re-elect Pres., Washington, 1972-73; congl. laison Adv. Council on Hist. Preservation, Washington, 1973-74; exec. asst. Capital Fund Campaign, N.Y. Bot. Gardens, 1976-78; regional chmn. Americans for an Effective Presidency, N.Y.C., 1980; pres. Mich. Assn. Community Arts Agys., Lansing, Mich., 1981-82; dir. area devel. U. Mich., Ann Arbor, 1983—; cons. Capital Campaign Albion Coll., Mich., 1978-82; cons. Pathfinder Sch., Traverse City, Mich., 1978-79; dir. Longyear Realty Corp., Marquette, Mich., 1975—; dir., treas. Resource Exploration, Inc., Marquette, 1980—. Past pres. Human Relations Commn., Albion; former dir. Impressions V Mus., Lansing, Neighborhood Playhouse Repertory Theatre, N.Y.C., Richard Morse Mime Theatre, N.Y.C., Women's Nat. Republican Club, N.Y.C.; various positions numerous Jr. Leagues; mem. Marquette Hist. Soc., Albion Hist. Soc., Nat. Trust Hist. Preservation, Washington; bd. dirs., v.p. Hist. Soc. Mich., 1984—; bd. dirs. Artrain, Inc., Detroit, 1984—. Mem. Christian Sci. Ch. Avocations: sailing; skiing. Office: Campaign for Mich U Mich 6000 Fleming Bldg Ann Arbor MI 48109

DIVENERE, ANTHONY JOSEPH, lawyer; b. Bari, Italy, June 20, 1941; came to U.S., 1949; s. Joseph and Don (Montini) DiV.; m. Sylvia Kathleen Scarnati, June 19, 1965; children—Anthony, Diana, John. A.B., John Carroll U., 1964; J.D., Ohio State U., 1967. Bar: Ohio 1967. Atty. in charge Cleve. Legal Aid Soc., 1967-70; prin., v.p. Burke Haber & Berick Co., L.P.A., Cleve., 1971—. Recipient Claude E. Clark award Cleve. Legal Aid Soc., 1968; Community Service award North Olmsted Jaycees, 1972. Mem. Cleve. Assn. Civil Trial Attys. (pres. 1979-80), Def. Research Inst., ABA, Ohio Bar Assn., Cleve. Bar Assn. (Appreciation award 1979-80). Club: Vermilion Yacht (Ohio). Avocations: sailing; marathon running; squash; opera. Home: 310 Rye Gate Bay Village OH 44140 Office: Burke Haber & Berick 300 National City Bank Bldg Cleveland OH 44114

DI VENERE, CATHERINE LENA, administrative manager, planner; b. Chgo., Oct. 6, 1941; d. Joseph and Josephine (Zucchero) Di Venere. Participant Am. Mgmt. Assn., Dible Mgmt. and Applied Mgmt. Inst. programs, 1981, 82. Sales asst. to asst. sales mgr. Blair TV, Chgo., 1961-69, sales asst. to v.p. Midwest Sales Mgr., 1969-74, adminstrv. asst. to pres. market div., 1974-76, adminstrv. mgr. Chgo. office, 1976-80; v.p., mgr. office adminstrn. John Blair and Co., Chgo., 1980—. Pres. Park Ridge Ct. Condominium Assn. Mem. Joint Civic Com. Italian-Ams., Am. Women in Radio and TV, Nat. Assn. Female Execs., Apostolate of Women. Office: John Blair & Co 645 N Michigan Ave Suite 700 Chicago IL 60611

DIVER, JAMES THOMAS, principal; b. Middletown, Ohio, Sept. 9, 1937; s. Wallace Marshall and Minnie Ellen (Akers) D.; m. Barbara Carole Schmidt, July 5, 1958; children—Scott, Robert, James, Elizabeth. B.S. in Edn., Miami U., Oxford, Ohio, 1961; M.S. in Secondary Edn., U. Akron, 1968. Tchr. Parma City Schs., Ohio, 1961-70, adminstrv. asst., 1970-72, asst. prin., 1972-75, jr. high sch. prin., 1975-82, high sch. prin., 1982—. Pres. Ridgewood YMCA, Parma, 1982; county chmn. Am. Cancer Soc., Cleve., 1983. Grad. sch. grantee Miami U., 1961. Named Man of the Year Ridgewood YMCA, 1982. Fellow IDEA Acad. of Fellows: mem. NEA, Ohio Edn. Assn., Nat. Assn. Secondary Sch. Adminstrs., Ohio Assn. Secondary Sch. Adminstrs., Parma Amateur Athletic Fedn. Lodge: Elks. Avocations: golf, trap shooting, travel. Home: 7209 Antoinette Dr Parma OH 44129 Office: Parma City Sch Dist 6726 Ridge Rd Parma OH 44129

DIVINA, HENRY DUKE, accountant, state agency consultant; b. Sorsogon, Philippines, July 30, 1940; s. Gregorio E. and Roberta D. (Detablan) D.; came to U.S., 1968, naturalized, 1975; A.C.S., Philippine Coll. Commerce, 1959; B.S.B.A., U. East, Manila, 1962; M.B.A., Southeastern U., 1979, Ph.D., 1981; postgrad. Ind. U., 1983; m. Caridad P. Barroga, Sept. 6, 1969; 1 dau., Caryn Gemma. Cost estimator Sherwin Williams Co., Dayton, Ohio, 1968-70; accountant firm Joseph F. Glotzbach, C.P.A., Hammond, Ind., 1970-71; auditor Ind. Blue Cross, Indpls., 1971-75; accountant Ind. Dept. Pub. Welfare, 1976-77; asst. controller Ind. Rehab. Services Bd., Indpls., 1977-80; ltd. practice pub. accounting, Indpls., 1973—. Vol. cons. Indpls. Bus. Devel. Found., 1974. C.P.A., Philippines, Tex. Mem. Am. Accounting Assn., Am. Inst. C.P.A.s, Philippine-Am. Accounting Assn. (founder, pres. 1974), Barangay Club of Ind. Inc. (auditor 1974, pres. 1976). Home: 3263 Acacia Dr Indianapolis IN 46224 Office: PO Box 44517 Indianapolis IN 46244

DIX, RALPH EUGENE, office supply company executive; b. Leavenworth, Kans., July 16, 1926; s. Grover Webster and Mary Alice Dix; student public schs., Leavenworth; m. Mary Margaret DeCoursey, Dec. 2, 1944; children—Ralph Eugene, Carey Ann. Grocery store clk., 1947-48; owner Ralph's Grocery, 1948-60; in material control Gen. Motors Corp., 1949-59; salesman Sears Roebuck & Co., Leavenworth, 1959-68; owner Dix & Son Office Supply, Leavenworth, 1968—; sr. partner Platte Office Supply, Parkville, Mo., 1978—; partner Discount Carpet Warehouse, Leavenworth, 1978—; consul for Guatemala, 1981—. Mem. Leavenworth Urban Renewal Bd., 1969—; bd. dirs. Leavenworth Downtown Assn., 1974-75; Guatemalan consul Midwest region. Served with U.S. Army, 1944-46. Mem. Leavenworth C. of C. (dir. 1970-72), V.F.W., Am. Legion. Republican. Lodge: Eagles. Home: 2608 S 14th St Leavenworth KS 66048 Office: 413-415 Delaware St Leavenworth KS 66048

DIXON, ALAN JOHN, U.S. senator; b. Belleville, Ill., July 7, 1927; s. William G. and Elsa (Tebbenhoff) D.; B.S., U. Ill., 1949; LL.B., Wash. U., 1949; m. Joan Louise Fox, Jan. 17, 1954; children—Stephanie Jo Yearian, Jeffrey Alan, Elizabeth Jane. Admitted to Illinois bar, 1950, since practiced in Belleville; police magistrate, Belleville, 1949; asst. atty. St. Clair County, 1950; mem. Ill. Ho. Reps., 1951-63; mem. Ill. Senate, 1963-71, minority whip senate; chmn. Jud. Adv. Council; treas. State of Ill., 1971-77, sec. of state, 1977-81; mem. U.S. Senate from Ill., 1981—. Mem. C. of C., Am. Legion. Clubs: Nat. Democratic, St. Clair Country, Columbia Country. Office: United States Senate Washington DC 20510

DIXON, FRED WAYNE, lawyer, pharmacist, consultant; b. Norwood, Va., Aug. 16, 1933; s. John Madison and Ruth Anna (Ewers) D.; m. Marija Angela Cerovic, June 9, 1973. Pharm. D., U. Calif.-San Francisco; J.D., Wayne State U., 1980. Bar: Mich. 1980, U.S. Dist. Ct. (ea. dist.) Mich. 1980. Researcher, assoc. Shrauger & Dunn, Detroit, 1981-82; sole practice, Birmingham, Mich., 1982—; pvt. cons., Detroit, 1982—; panel mem. Microcomputer Research Group, Princeton, N.J., 1984—; cons. Expert Resources, Inc., Peoria Heights, Ill., 1984—; research pharmacist Parke Davis Co., Detroit, 1969-70; staff pharmacist Holy Cross Hosp., Detroit, 1971-74; chief pharmacist Kern Hosp., Warren, Mich., 1974-77; community pharmacist Borman's Inc., Detroit, 1978—. Served with U.S. Army, 1954-56. Regent's scholar U. Calif.-San Francisco, 1966. Mem. ABA, Am. Pharm. Assn. Lodge: Masons. Home: 130 Waddington St Birmingham MI 48009 Office: 400 W Maple St Suite 300 Birmingham MI 48011

DIXON, GEORGE HALL, banker; b. Rochester, N.Y., Oct. 7, 1920; s. George Hall and Frances (Wheeler) D.; B.S., U. Pa., 1942; M.B.A., Harvard U., 1947; LL.D. (hon.), Carroll Coll., Helena, Mont.; m. Marjorie Freeman, Apr. 3, 1948; children—George E., Andrew T., Candis H. Pres. First Nat. Bank Mpls., 1968-76, chmn., 1972-76, also dir.; dep. sec. treasury Dept. of Treasury, Washington, 1976-77; pres. First Bank System, Inc., Mpls., 1977-81, pres., chief exec. officer, 1981-83, chmn., chief exec. officer, 1983—, also dir.; dir. First Nat. Bank St. Paul, First Trust Co. St. Paul, First Nat. Bank Mpls., Donaldson Co., Inc., Bloomington, Minn., Northwestern Nat. Life Ins. Co., Mpls., Soo Line R.R. Co., Mpls., Internat. Multifoods Corp., Mpls., Minn. Orchestral Assn., Mpls.; pres. Minn. Bus. Partnership, Inc., Mpls.; dir., past pres. United Way Mpls.; chmn., trustee Carleton Coll., Northfield, Minn., Sci. Mus. Minn. Served to capt. U.S. Army. Mem. Assn. Res. City Bankers, Assn. Bank Holding Cos., Atlantic Inst. (gov. Paris), Am. Gas Assn. (mem. banking adv. council). Republican. Presbyterian. Clubs: Links (N.Y.); Mpls., Minn. Office: PO Box 522 Minneapolis MN 55480

DIXON, JAMES JASON, physician; b. Kansas City, Mo., July 6, 1920; s. Otto Jason and Olive (Robertson) D.; A.B., U. Kans., 1943, M.D., 1947; m. Kathryn May Hanna, May 2, 1948; children—David Jason, William Nelson, Robert Grant, Mary Christine. Intern, Toledo Hosp., 1947-48, resident, 1948-50; resident Henry Ford Hosp., Detroit, 1950-52; pathologist, dir. labs. Ashtabula (Ohio) Gen. Hosp., 1952-84, Lake County Meml. Hosp., Painesville, Ohio, 1952-58; pathologist Brown Meml. Hosp., Conneaut, Ohio, 1961-70; cons. pathologist Geneva (Ohio) Meml. Hosp., 1961-68; mem. regional adv. com. Cleve. Red Cross Blood Program; dep. sheriff Ashtabula County. Past v.p. Ashtabula Fine Arts Center; active ARC. Diplomate Am. Bd. Pathology. Mem. Ohio, Ashtabula County (sec., treas. 1956, pres. 1960) med. socs., Am. Soc. Clin. Pathologists, Coll. Am. Pathologists, Ohio, Cleve. socs. pathologists, Am. Cancer Soc. (med. dir. Ashtabula County), Am. Assn. Blood Banks, AAAS, Ashtabula Power Squadron (comdr. 1966), Nat. Rifle Assn. (life), Nat. Assn. Federally Licensed Firearms Dealers, Ohio Gun Collectors Assn., Smith and Wesson Collectors Assn., Ohio Rifle and Pistol Assn. (life), Tau Kappa Epsilon, Nu Sigma Nu. Republican. Episcopalian (sr. warden 1960-63). Elk, Rotarian. Clubs: Ashtabula Country, Ashtabula Yacht; Redbrook Boat, Ashtabula Rod and Gun. Home: 1724 Highland Ln Ashtabula OH 44004

DIXON, MARK JOHN, petroleum geologist; b. Waco, Tex., Dec. 25, 1954; s. Robert Berkeley and Louise (Markhus) D. B.A. in Geology, U. Toledo, 1977. Lic. pilot. Pres. Toledo Helicopter Service, Inc., Sylvania, Ohio, 1978-80, Dixon Exploration Inc., Toledo, 1982—; chief operating officer Royal Petroleum Properties, Inc., Cleve., 1980-82. Co-author: Trenton, 1984. Mem. Am. Assn. Petroleum Geologists (jr. mem.), Am. Inst. Profl. Geologists (assoc.), Soc. Exploration Geophysicists (assoc.). Avocations: comml. rotorcraft, instrument fixed wing flying. Home: 5736 Little Rd Sylvania OH 43560 Office: Dixon Exploration Inc 4024 Lewis Ave Toledo OH 43612

DIXON, ROBERT KENNETH, company executive; b. DeKalb, Ill., Nov. 7, 1937; s. Robert Kenneth and Esther Ella (Boekenhauer) D.; m. Carla Jayne Haagensen, Feb. 7, 1959; children—Jeffrey, Dave, Bryan. B.A., Valparaiso U., 1959. Sales rep. Wyeth Lab., Evanston, Ill., 1959-62; sales rep. 3M Co., Chgo., 1962-66, various positions, 1966-82; pres. R. K. Dixon Co., Davenport, Iowa, 1983—. Mem. Adminstrv. Mgmt. Soc., Nat. Office Machine Dealers Assn., Bus. Products Council Assn., Davenport C. of C., Davenport Better Bus. Bur. Republican. Lutheran. Club: Crow Valley Country. Avocations: Travelling, jogging. Office: 5111 Tremont St Suite C Davenport IA 52807

DIXON, RONNIE EDWARD, lawyer; b. Clarksdale, Miss., Feb. 17, 1955; s. Walter Sylvester and Nellie Ruth (Edwards) D.; m. Nov. 22, 1980. B.A., Washington U., St. Louis, 1977; J.D., St. Louis U., 1980. Bar: Ohio 1980, U.S. Dist. Ct. (so. dist.) Ohio 1981. Staff atty. Legal Aid Soc. Cin., 1980-85, sr. atty., 1985—. Big brother Big Bros. Assn. Cin., 1983—; bd. dirs. Eden Alcoholic Treatment Ctr., Cin., 1983—; trustee African Meth. Episcopal Ch., 1984—. Mem. Cin. Bar Assn., Black Lawyers Assn. Cin. (v.p. 1984). Office: Legal Aid Soc Cin 901 Elm St Cincinnati OH 45202

DIXSON-M'RICERD, RICHARD AUSTIN-KAEL, organization development consultant, health educator; b. June 29, 1952. M.S., No. Ill. U., 1981; M.P.H., George Williams Coll., Downers Grove, Ill., 1984, M.B.A., 1985. Mem. faculty No. Ill. U., DeKalb, 1981; program cons. Ill. Inst. Tech./Mellon Found., Chgo., 1982-84; program and process facilitator U. Ill.-Chgo., 1984—; dir. Inst. for Men's Studies, Evanston, Ill., 1981—. Mem. Residential Consumer Advocacy, Evanston, 1982—; leader task force Community Action Com., Chgo., 1983; speaker Planned Parenthood, Mpls., 1984. Recipient Am. Legion of Honor award; Cong. Merit award Ill. Legislature. Mem. Am. Pub. Health Assn., Am. Soc. Tng. and Devel., Am. Counseling and Devel. Assn. Club: Great Lakes Men's Network (Madison, Wis.). Avocations: skiing, hiking, parasailing, woodworking.

DOBBS, DONALD EDWIN ALBERT, public relations executive; b. Ft. Wayne, Ind., Oct. 8, 1931; s. Edmund F. and Agnes (Stempnick) D.; B.S., Marquette U., 1953; m. Beatrice A. Spieker, July 27, 1957; children—Margaret L. Howard, Christopher E.J., Laura C. Pribe. Reporter, Cath. Chronicle, Toledo, 1953; indsl. editor, pub. relations Nat. Supply Co., Toledo 1955-59; employee communications exec. Prestolite Co., an Eltra Co., Toledo, 1959-61, public relations dir., 1961-80, dir. communications, 1980-83; mgr. external affairs Allied Electronic Components Co., an Allied Corp. Co.; pres. Dobbs & Assocs., 1984—. Past chmn. Maumee Valley Hosp. Sch. Nursing Com.; pres. Internat. Inst., Toledo, 1970-73; past chmn. Child Nutrition Center, Toledo; past mem. Ohio Adv. Council Vocat. Edn.; vice chmn. Mayor's Citizen Devel. Forum; chmn., past pres. Mercy Hosp.; bd. dirs. Frederick Douglass Community Assn.; past pres. bd. dirs. Crosby Gardens; pres. Ohio Friends of Library; past chmn. Salvation Army; past pres. Toledo Council of World Affairs, Toledo Hearing and Speech Center, Friends of Toledo/Lucas County Library; past pres. bd. dirs. Internat. Park. Served with AUS, 1953-55. Mem. Marquette U. Alumni Assn. N.W. Ohio (past pres., area dir.), Soc. Profl. Journalists, Public Relations Soc. Am. (past pres. N.W. Ohio), Automotive Public Relations Council (past pres.), Cath. Interracial Council (past pres.). Democrat (past nat. com. Wis. Young Dems.). Roman Catholic. Kiwanian (past pres. Toledo, Mid-City Athletic League, Kiwanis Youth Found.; lt. gov. 1974-75). Clubs: Toledo Press, Toledo Mud Hens Diamond (charter). Home: 2433 Meadowwood Dr Toledo OH 43606 Office: PO Box 2964 Toledo OH 43606

DOBIE, EDWARD RAYMOND, advertising agency executive, office equipment company executive, business engineering firm executive; b. Lakewood, Ohio, Dec. 8, 1918; s. George Norman and Yerda (Lonn) D.; m. Gertrude A. Getz, Nov. 25, 1938 (dec.); children—Patricia L., Edward R.; m. 2d, Beth Ann Winters, May 25, 1979. Chief engr. ARO Equipment Corp., Bryan, Ohio, 1940-47; owner, operator Supervision Toledo, 1947—; ptnr. Associated Office Supply, Monroe, Mich., 1948—; pres. Dobie Co. of Mich., Monroe, 1949—; sec.-treas. Eazy-Way Corp., Cleve., 1955—, also dir.; v.p. Sales Builders Corp., Detroit, 1956—, also dir.; dir. Erie Shores Corp., Monroe. Patentee in field. Vice chmn. ARC, Monroe, 1973-74, chpt. chmn., 1975-76; trustee St. Paul's Methodist Ch., Monroe, 1976-77; del. Monroe Republican County Conv., 1975-76, Mich. State Repub. Conv., 1976-77. Served with U.S. Army, 1944-45, ETO. Mem. Monroe C. of C., Nat. Office Dealers Assn., Internat. Traders, VFW. Lodge: Masons. Avocations: philatelist; numismatist. Home: 3617 Lake Shore Dr Monroe MI 48161 Office: The Dobie Co 421 S Monroe St Monroe MI 48161

DOBISH, ALEX PHILIP, journalist; b. Claremont, N.H., Sept. 6, 1924; s. Philip Sevasteyev and Mary (Barczak) D.; m. Tina B. Arnold, Nov. 26, 1975; children by a previous marriage—Deborah Ann, Mary Elizabeth, Patrina Sarah. B.J., U. Mo., 1948. Messenger, reporter Boston Globe, 1941-42; reporter Green Bay (Wis.) Press Gazette, 1948-51; with Milw. Jour., 1952—, gen. assignment reporter, police cts. reporter, feature writer, spl. assignment, investigative staff writer; lectr. Marquette U., U. Wis.-Milw. Served with AUS, 1942-46. Recipient Sigma Delta Chi Disting. Journalism award, 1980; Richard S. Davis award, 1970; other awards. Mem. Milw. Press Club, Am. Philatelic Soc., Nat. Audubon Soc., Smithsonian Assoc., Sigma Delta Chi. Russian Greek Orthodox. Office: Milw Journal Square Milwaukee WI 53201

DOBY, PAUL BOYCE, state official, veterinarian; b. Okolona, Ark., Mar. 31, 1923; s. Paul Barringer and Ethel (Boyce) D.; m. Wilma Gene Lewis, Mar. 12, 1950. B.S., Kans. State U., 1949, D.V.M., 1949. Asst. prof. U. Ark., Fayetteville; 1949-51; resident vet. J. Garrett Tolan Farms, Pleasant Plains, Ill., 1951-61; vet. U.S. Dept. Agr., Springfield, Ill., 1961-62; asst. supt. div. meat, poultry and livestock inspection Ill. Dept. Agr., Springfield, 1962-63, supt., 1963—; chmn. subcom. swine brucellosis U.S. Animal Health Assn., Richmond, Va., 1982—. Recipient Outstanding Service award Ill. Pork Producers Assn., 1971, Honor award Nat. Assn. State Depts. Agr., 1975, Superior Service award U.S. Dept. Agr., 1976, Outstanding Contribution award Ill. Dept. Agr., 1978. Mem. Livestock conservation Inst. (chmn. bd. dirs. 1981-83, meritorious service award 1976), Ill. Vet. Med. Assn. (pres. 1967-68). Lodge: Rotary (pres. 1970-71). Home: 19 Blackberry Run Springfield IL 62704 Office: Ill Dept Agr Div Meat Poultry and Livestock Inspection Agr Bldg State Fairgrounds Springfield IL 62706

DOCKHORN, ROBERT JOHN, physician; b. Goodland, Kans., Oct. 9, 1934; s. Charles George and Dorotha Mae (Horton) D.; B.A., U. Kans., 1956, M.D., 1960; m. Beverly Ann Wilke, June 15, 1957; children—David, Douglas, Deborah. Intern, Naval Hosp., San Diego, 1960-61, resident in pediatrics, Oakland, Calif., 1963-65; resident in pediatric allergy and immunology U. Kans., 1967-69; resident in pediatric allergy and immunology Children's Mercy Hosp., Kansas City, Mo., 1967-69, chief allergy-immunology div., 1969—; practice medicine specializing in allergy and immunology, Prairie Village, Kans., 1969—; clin. prof. pediatrics and medicine U. Mo. Sch. Medicine, Kansas City. Diplomate Am. Bd. Pediatrics, Am. Bd. Allergy and Immunology. Fellow Am. Acad. Pediatrics, Am. Coll. Allergists (pres. 1981—), Am. Acad. Allergy; mem. AMA, Kans., Johnson County med. socs., Kans. (pres. 1976-77), Mo. (sec. 1975-76) allergy socs., Joint Council of Allergy and Immunology (pres. 1979). Contbr. articles to med. jours. Home: 8510 Delmar Ln Prairie Village KS 66208 Office: 5300 W 94th Terr Prairie Village KS 66207

DOCKING, THOMAS ROBERT, lawyer, state official; b. Lawrence, Kans., Aug. 10, 1954; s. Robert Blackwell and Meredith (Gear) D.; m. Jill Sadowsky, June 18, 1977; children—Brian Thomas, Margery Meredith. B.S., U. Kans.-Lawrence, 1976; M.B.A., 1980, J.D., 1980. Bar: Kans. 1980. Assoc. Regan and McGannon, Wichita, Kans., 1980-82, ptnr., 1982—; lt. gov. State of Kans., Topeka, 1983—; chmn. Kans. Tax Rev. Commn.; Mem. Kans. Dept. Econ. Devel. Adv. Commn. Mem. U. Kans. Alumni Assn. (treas. 1982-83), Kans. Bar Assn., ABA, Pi Sigma Alpha, Beta Gamma Sigma, Beta Theta Pi. Democrat. Presbyterian. Home: 8525 Limerick Ln Wichita KS 67206 Office: Suite 1400 KSB Bldg 125 N Market St Wichita KS 67202

DOCKTER, ARLA MAE, educator; b. Minot, N.D., Sept. 18, 1953; d. Andrew and Christine (Bosch) D.; m. Jeffrey John Dockter, July 12, 1974 (div. 1978); 1 son, Matthew Gottlieb. B.S., Minot State Coll., 1976. Elem. tchr. South Prairie Sch., Minot, N.D., 1976—. Pres. South Prairie PTO, 1982—. Mem. NEA, N.D. Edn. Assn. (regional dir.), N.D. Reading Assn., South Prairie Edn. Assn. Roman Catholic. Home: 422 N Main St Minot ND 58701

DODDS, DAVID WILLIAM, educational administrator; b. Lakewood, Ohio, June 15, 1945; s. David William and Jean Curtis D.; m. Barbara Andelman, Aug. 17, 1968; children—Amy Lynn, Emily Margaret, Elizabeth Joy. B.A., Millikin U., 1967; M.S., Ind. U., 1968; Cert. Adv. Studies, No. Ill. U., 1972. Tchr. Wheeling High Sch., Ill., 1968-72; asst. prin. McHenry West High Sch.,

Ill., 1972-76; prin. McHenry East High Sch., 1976—; pres. McHenry County Curriculum Council, 1984-85. Mem. Citizens for Community Action, McHenry, Ill., 1983-84. Humanities fellow NEH, Boston U., 1984, I.D.E.A. fellow Kettering Found., Columbia, Mo., 1975. Mem. Nat. Assn. Secondary Sch. Prins., Assn. Supervision and Curriculum Devel., Ill. Prins. Assn., Ill. Assn. Supervision and Curriculum Devel., McHenry County Curriculum Council, Fox Valley County Prins. (sec. 1983-84), Phi Delta Kappa. Lodge: Kiwanis (treas. 1984-85). Avocations: Singer; musician. Home: 3702 W Main St McHenry IL 60050

DODDS, DOROTHYMAE, educator; b. Mankato, Minn., Nov. 4, 1927; d. William McKinley and Frances Mathilda (Leslie) Grimes; B.S., Moorhead (Minn.) State U., 1948, M.S., 1979; m. Robert Warren Dodds, Aug. 21, 1948; children—Laura Leslie, Michael Robert. Elem. instr. Mpls. Public Schs., 1948-53; sec.-treas. Dodds Drug, Inc., Red Lake Falls, Minn., 1954-85; instr. sales, mktg. and mgmt., program head Thief River Falls (Minn.) Area Vocat. Tech. Inst., 1979-84, dir. adult edn., 1984-85; asst. dir. Dakota County Area Vocat. Tech. Inst., Rosemount, Minn., 1985—. Com. chmn. Grand Forks (N.D.) council Girl Scouts U.S.A., 1963-70, neighborhood chmn., 1960, v.p., 1970-75, Thanks badge, 1972; com. chmn. Civic and Commerce Assn. of Red Lake Falls, 1971-74; mem. Region I Minn. Arts Adv. com., 1976-80; bd. trustees Citizens for the Arts, St. Paul, 1978—. Recipient awards for painting. Mem. Am. Vocat. Assn., Distributive Edn. Clubs Am. (cert. of appreciation Minn., nat. plaque of appreciation). Republican. Presbyterian. Home: 14601 Portland Ave S Burnsville MN 55337 Office: 1300 145th St E Rosemount MN 55068

DODGE, DAVID LEE, computer company executive; b. Mpls., Oct. 11, 1947; s. Frank Naylor and Thelma Mae (Stephenson) D.; m. Peggy Lee Virginia Rounds, Mar. 9, 1974; children—Carrie MacKenzie, Jesse Oliver. B.B.A., U. Minn., 1970. Sales mgr. AAE, Inc., Cambridge, Mass., 1970-71, Dayton's Mpls., 1971-73, C.J. Bates & Son, Chester, Conn., 1974-78; salesman Dataserv Equipment Inc., Hopkins, Minn., 1978-79, sales mgr., 1979-82, pres., 1982—, also dir. Mem. Am. Mgmt. Assn., Computer Dealers and Lessors Assn., The Presidents Assn. Club: Edina Country. Avocations: skiing; tennis; golf. Office: Dataserv Equipment Inc 509 2nd Ave S Hopkins MN 55343

DODGE, STEPHEN CHARLES, historian, educator; b. Bronx, N.Y., Dec. 27, 1940; s. Stephen Dearborn and Grace Helen (Havranek) D.; m. Marjorie Ann Ruch, Sept. 7, 1963; children—Jonathan, Jeffrey. B.A., U. Dubuque, 1963; M.A., U. Minn., 1964, Ph.D., 1968. Asst. prof. history Millikin U., Decatur, Ill., 1968-76, assoc. prof., 1976-84, prof., 1984—; dir. Carleton Point Bicentennial Project, Abaco, Bahamas, 1983. Co-pres. New Sch., 1973-74. Mem. Caribbean Studies Assn., Wyannie Malone Hist. Mus. Clubs: Decatur Yacht, Hope Town Sailing. Author: Abaco: The History of an Out Island and Its Cays, 1983; (with V. Malone) Hope Town: A Walking Tour and Brief History, 1985. Office: Millikin Univ Decatur IL 62522

DODHOWER, ROD, professional football coach. Head coach Indpls. Colts, 1985—. Office: Indpls Colts PO Box 20000 Indianapolis IN 46220*

DODSON, ANN THOMPSON, librarian; b. Zanesville, Ohio July 2, 1930; d. Charles H. and Mary L. (Aler) Thompson; m. James Theron Dodson, June 22, 1958 (div. Sept. 1976); 1 child, James Thompson. B.A. in English and Spanish cum laude, Muskingum Coll., 1952; postgrad. Ohio State U., 1953-55, Wright State U., 1971-72; M.L.S., North Tex. State U., 1976. Info. specialist Battelle Meml. Inst., Columbus, Ohio, 1957-65; research analyst U. Dayton Research Inst., Ohio, 1965-67, asst. to dir., 1967-68, cons. to info. systems sect., 1969-70, asst. info. scientist, 1970-72; librarian, tech. editor Inst. Aerobics Research, Dallas, 1974-76; mgr. OCLC Library, Inc., Dublin Ohio, 1977—. Contbr. articles to profl. jours. Mem. Am. Soc. Info. Sci., Spl. Libraries Assn., Beta Phi Mu. Republican. Methodist. Office: PO Box 7777 Dublin OH 43017

DODSON, OSCAR HENRY, emeritus museum director, numismatic consultant; b. Houston, Jan. 3, 1905; s. Dennis Seth and Maggie (Sisk) D.; B.S., U.S. Naval Acad., 1927, postgrad., 1936; M.A., U. Ill., 1953; m. Pauline Wellbrock, Dec. 17, 1932; 1 son, John Dennis. Commd. ensign USN, 1927, advanced through grades to rear adm., 1957, ret. 1957; asst. prof. history U. Ill., 1957-59; dir. Money Museum, Nat. Bank of Detroit, 1959-65, World Heritage Mus., U. Ill., Urbana, 1966-73; acting dir. Champaign County Hist. Mus., 1980; mem. Ann. Assay Commn., 1948. Decorated Silver Star. Fellow Am. Numis. Soc., Royal Numis. Soc. London, Explorers Club; mem. Am. Mil. Inst., Am. Archaeol. Inst., Am. Numis. Assn. (pres. 1957-61; Farren Zerbe award 1968), Internat. Banknote Soc. London (hon.), U.S. Naval Acad. Alumni Assn. (life), U.S. Naval Acad. Found., U. Ill. Found. (pres.' council), U. Ill. Alumni Assn. (life mem., Loyalty award 1966), Internat. Platform Assn. Clubs: Torch, Rotary (pres. Champaign, Ill. 1972-73); Army-Navy (Washington); New York Yacht (N.Y.C.); Champaign Country; Circumnavigators. Author: Money Tells the Story, 1962. Contbg. editor Coinage mag., Bridge mag. Contbr. articles to profl., numismatic jours. Office: 486 Lincoln Hall 702 S Wright St Urbana IL 61801

DOE, EILEEN MARIE, educator; b. St. Louis, Mar. 9, 1953; d. John Andrew and Kathleen Appalona (Layton) Hoffman; m. Larry Junior Doe, Aug. 14, 1976. B.S., U. Mo., 1976, postgrad., 1982—. Tchr. mentally handicapped children Northview Sch., Spl. Sch. Dist. St. Louis County, 1976-84; tchr. Highland Sch., 1984—. Mem. Community Tchrs. Assn., Delta Zeta. Roman Catholic. Home: 2 Locust Dr Florissant MO 63031

DOEHRMAN, STEVEN RALPH, research clinical psychologist; b. Ft. Wayne, Ind., July 12, 1942; s. Ralph C. and Virginia Rita (Drury) D.; children—Eric, David. A.B., U. Mich., 1965, Ph.D., 1971. Lic. psychologist, Mich. Supervising clin. psychologist U. Mich., Ann Arbor, 1974-80, lectr. dept. psychology, 1974-81; project dir. Inst. Social Research, Ann Arbor, 1977-81; clin. psychologist, research dir. Orchard Hills Psychiat. Ctr., Farmington Hills, Mich., 1980-85; pvt. practice clin. psychology, Ann Arbor, 1974-83; lectr. civic and bus. groups. NIMH postdoctoral fellow, 1973-75. Mem. Am. Psychol. Assn., Soc. Psychotherapy Research, Assn. Advancement Psychology, Mich. Heart Assn. Clubs: Ann Arbor Ski, Parents without Ptnrs. Contbr. articles to profl. jours.

D'OENCH, RALPH FREDRICK, real estate consultant; b. St. Louis, Oct. 22, 1901; s. Harry Fredrick and Clara (Schmitz) D'O.; m. Mabel Estelle Nichols, Dec. 30, 1926; children—Gloria Nichols D'Oench James, Jean Linda D'Oench Field. B.A., Washington U., St. Louis, 1922. Cert. property mgr., real estate broker, Mo. Property mgr. R.E. Mgmt. Co., St. Louis, 1927-34; pres. Ralph D'Oench Co., St. Louis, 1934-77, cons., 1978—; instr., lectr. real estate U. Ill.-Belleville, 1958-59; instr. Washington U., 1955-67. Assoc. Miss. River Pkwy. Planning Commn., 1954-69; bd. dirs., trustee Washington U., St. Louis, 1955-57. Mem. Real Estate Bd. Met. St. Louis (recipient plaque; emeritus), Inst. Real Estate Mgmt. (plaque; emeritus). Republican. Club: University (St. Louis). Avocations: color slide shows; historical themes; travelogs. Home: 1 Normton Dr Saint Louis MO 63124

DOERING, GEORGE, agricultural products company executive. Pres., chief operating officer ConAgra, Inc. (ConAgra Agri-Products Cos.), Omaha, Neb. Office: ConAgra Inc One Central Park Plaza Omaha NE 68102*

DOERMANN, PAUL EDMUND, surgeon; b. Kodaikanal, India, Aug. 3, 1926 (parents Am. citizens); s. Carl M. and Cora (Knupke) D.; student Ohio State U., 1944; B.S., Capital U., 1947; M.D., U. Mich., 1951; m. W. Ernestine McPherson, May 3, 1953; children—William McPherson, Marcia, Paula Michelle, Diana, Charles. Intern, Louisville Gen. Hosp., 1951-52, resident in surgery, 1952-53; resident in surgery Milw. County Hosp., 1955-58; med. missionary Luth. Mission Hosp., Madang, New Guinea, 1958-59; surgeon Linvill Clinic, Columbia City, Ind., 1960-61; practice medicine specializing in surgery, Huntington, Ind.; pres. med. staff, chief surg. service Huntington Meml. Hosp.; pres. Huntington Surg. Corp. Served from 1st lt. to capt., AUS, 1953-55. Luth. Acad. scholar. Diplomate Am. Bd. Surgery. Fellow ACS; mem. Huntington County, Christian med. socs., Am. Assn. Physicians and Surgeons, Pvt. Doctors Am., Huntington C. of C. Lutheran. Rotarian. Home: 5503 West 500 North Huntington IN 46750 Office: 1751 N Jefferson Huntington IN 46750

DOERSAM, PAUL HOWARD, school administrator; b. Saginaw, Mich., Feb. 2, 1940; s. Harry Charles and Mary Ann D.; m. Nancy K. Bruening, Aug. 18, 1962 (div. 1983); children—Diane, Mark. B.A., U. Mich., 1962; M.A., Eastern Mich. U., 1966; postgrad., Mich. State U., 1969-75. Cert. elem., secondary tchr., Mich. Tchr. Clintondale Elem. Sch., Mt. Clemens, Mich., 1962-63; tchr., Coach South Lake High Sch., St. Clair Shores, Mich., 1963-68; prin. Clintondale Middle Sch., Mt. Clements, 1968-74, Lakeview Jr. High Sch., Battle Creek, Mich., 1974—. Football scholar U. Mich., 1958-62. Mem. Mich. Assn. Middle Sch. Educators (life, bd. dirs. 1969-75), Mich. Assn. Secondary Sch. Prins., Nat. Assn. Secondary Sch. Prins. Avocations: officiating football and basketball games. Office: Lakeview Jr High Sch 20 S Woodrow Ave Battle Creek MI 49015

DOGGETT, JOHN NELSON, JR., clergyman; b. Phila., Apr. 3, 1918; s. John Nelson and Winola (Ballard) D.; B.A., Lincoln U., 1942; M.Div., Union Theol. Sem., N.Y.C., 1945; M.Ed., St. Louis U., 1969, Ph.D., 1971; m. Juanita Toley, Aug. 2, 1973; children by previous marriage—Lorraine, John, William, Kenneth Riddick. Ordained to ministry United Methodist Ch., 1943; civilian chaplain South Gate Community Ch., San Francisco, 1945-47; organizing pastor Downs Meml. Meth. Ch., Oakland, Calif., 1947-49; pastor Scott Meml. Meth. Ch., Pasadena, Calif., 1950-53, Hamilton Meml. Meth. Ch., Los Angeles, 1953-64, Union Meml. United Meth. Ch., St. Louis, 1964-76; dist. supt. United Meth. Ch., St. Louis, 1976-82; sr. pastor Grace United Meth. Ch., St. Louis, 1982-85; ; staff Pastoral Counseling Inst., St. Louis, 1968—; instr. foundations of edn. Harris Tchrs. Coll., St. Louis, 1971-75; assoc. prof. practical theology Met. Coll., St. Louis, 1976-77; commr. Nat. Council Chs. of Christ, 1981. Pres. bd. dirs. St. Louis Christian Med. Ctr., Central Med. Ctr. Hosps., St. Louis, 1973—; pres. St. Louis NAACP, 1973-81; bd. dirs. United Way St. Louis, 1974-81; mem. Commn. on Alternatives to Prison, 1981, Citizens Com. Mo. Dept. Corrections, 1974-80, Mayor's Task Force on Hunger, 1981; adv. com. St. Louis U. Sch. Social Work; adviser John N. Doggett Scholarship Found.; mem. Interfaith Clergy Council, World Meth. Council; pres. Council St. Louis U.; mem. mayor's ambassadors Regional Commerce and Growth Assn., 1980—. Named Minister of Year, St. Louis Argus Newspaper, 1971; recipient Outstanding Alumni award St. Louis U., 1981. Mem. Am. Assn. Pastoral Counselors, Mo. Council Chs., Met. Ministerial Alliance, UN Assn. (clergy-pub. edn. com.), Chi Alpha Lit. Forum, Phi Delta Kappa, Alpha Phi Alpha (nat. chaplain, D. Bowles/R. Anderson Service award), Democrat. Mason, Shriner. Home: 4466 W Pine Blvd #2C Saint Louis MO 63108 Office: 4411 N Newstead Ave Saint Louis MO 63115

DOGGETT, JOSEPH JAMES, physician, hematologist, oncologist; b. Mexico, Mo., Jan. 17, 1942; s. Joseph D. and Jewell M. (Brown) D.; m. Sharon Lynn Daffron, Oct. 19; children—Melinda Brooke, Natasha Rae. B.A., Central Methodist Coll., 1964; D.O., Kirksville Coll. Osteo. Medicine, 1976. Intern, Still Hosp., Jefferson City, Mo., 1976-77, resident, 1977-79, dir. oncology, 1981—; practice medicine specializing in hematology and med. oncology; assoc. clin. prof. medicine U. Mo. Cancer and Leukemia Group B, N.Y.C., 1981—. Served with U.S. Army, 1965-75. Recipient cert. merit, ednl. award Am. Cancer Soc., 1982. Mem. Am. Osteo. Assn., Am. Coll. Osteo. Internists, Am. Soc. Clin. Oncologist. Home: Route 1 Lake Champetra Hartsburg MO 65039 Office: Still Hosp 1111 S Madison St Jefferson City MO 65101

DOHENY, DONALD ALOYSIUS, lawyer, business exec.; b. Milw., Apr. 20, 1924; s. John Anthony and Adelaide (Koller) D.; student U. Notre Dame, 1942-43; B.Mech. Engring., Marquette U., 1947; J.D., Harvard, 1949; postgrad. indsl. engring. and bus. adminstrn. Washington U., 1950-56; m. Catherine Elizabeth Lee, Oct. 25, 1952; children—Donald Aloysius, Celeste Hazel Doheny Kennedy, John Vincent, Ellen Adelaide, Edward Lawrence II, William Francis, Madonna Lee. Asst. to civil engr. Shipbuilding div. Froemming Bros., Inc., Milw., 1942-43; draftsman, designer The Heil Co., Milw., 1944-46; admitted to Wis. bar, 1949, Mo. bar, 1949, U.S. Supreme Ct., 1970; mem. firm Igoe, Carroll & Keefe, St. Louis, 1949-51; asst. to v.p. and gen. mgr., chief prodn. engr., gen. adminstr., dir. adminstrn. Granco Steel Products subsidiary Granite City Steel, Granite City, Ill., 1951-57; asst. to pres. Vestal Labs., Inc., St. Louis, 1957-63; exec. v.p., dir. Moehlenpah Engring., Inc., Hydro-Air Engring., Inc., 1963-67; pres. dir. Foamtex Industries, Inc., St. Louis, 1967-75; exec. v.p., dir. Seasonal Industries, Inc., N.Y.C., 1973-75; mem. law firm Donald A. Doheny, St. Louis, 1967-81; mem. firm Doheny & Doheny, Attys., 1981—; mem. firm Doheny & Assos., Mgmt. Counsel, St. Louis, 1967—; pres., dir. Mktg. & Sales Counsel, Inc., St. Louis, 1975—; pres., dir. Mid-USA Sales Co., St. Louis, 1976—; lectr. bus. orgn. and adminstrn. Washington U., 1950-74; lectr. Grad. Sch. Bus., St. Louis U., 1980—. Served as pvt. AUS, 1943-44; 1st lt. Res., 1948-52. Registered profl. engr., Mo. Mem. Am. Judicature Soc., Am. Marketing Assn. (nat. membership chmn. 1959), ABA, Mo. Bar Assn., Wis. Bar Assn., Fed. Bar Assn., Bar Assn. St. Louis (gen. chmn. pub. relations 1955-56, vice chmn., sec.-treas. jr. sect. 1950, 51), Marquette Engring. Assn. (pres. 1946-47), Engring. Knights, Am. Legion, Tau Beta Pi, Pi Tau Sigma. Clubs: K.C., Notre Dame (pres. 1955, 56), Marquette (pres. 1961) (St. Louis); Stadium, Engineers, Mo. Athletic. Office: 2284 Weldon Pkwy Saint Louis County MO 63146 also 319 N 4th St Suite 1006 Saint Louis MO 63102

DOHERTY, JOSEPH J(AMES), fiberglas company executive; b. Stamford, Conn., Sept. 18, 1933; s. James P. and Catherine F. (McGurn) D.; m. Paula Sue Craver, July 8, 1961; children—James P., Susan E., Michael C. (dec.). B.S., Auburn U., 1958. With Owens-Corning Fiberglas, 1961—, salesman, New Orleans, 1961-65, br. mgr., Boston, 1965-68, product mgr. for tire cord. corp. hdqrs. Toledo, 1968-71, mgr. corp. mktg. communications services, 1971-73, corp. dir. mktg. communications, 1973-78, v.p. mktg. communications, 1978—. Served with Intelligence, U.S. Army, 1951-54. Mem. Assn. Nat. Advts., Nat. Advt. Rev. Bd. Republican. Roman Catholic. Club: Carranor Hunt and Polo (Perrysburg, Ohio). Office: Fiberglas Tower Toledo OH 43659

DOHMEN, FREDERICK HOEGER, retired wholesale drug co. exec.; b. Milw., May 12, 1917; s. Fred William and Viola (Gutsch) D.; B.A. in Commerce, U. Wis., 1939; m. Gladys Elizabeth Dite, Dec. 23, 1939 (dec. 1963); children—William Francis, Robert Charles; m. 2d, Mary Alexander Holgate, June 27, 1964. With F. Dohmen Co., Milw., successively warehouse employee, sec., v.p., 1944-52, pres., 1952-82, dir., 1947—, chmn. bd., 1952-82. Bd. dirs. St. Luke's Hosp. Ednl. Found., Milw., 1965-83, pres., 1969-72, chmn. bd., 1972-73; bd. dirs. U. Wis.-Milw. Found., 1976-79, bd. visitors, 1978—; asso. chmn. Nat. Bible Week, Laymen's Nat. Bible Com., N.Y.C., 1968-82, council of adv., 1983—. Mem. Nat. Wholesale Druggists Assn. (chmn. mfr. relations com. 1962, resolutions com. 1963, mem. of bd. control 1963-66), Nat. Assn. Wholesalers (trustee 1966-75), Druggists Service Council (dir. 1967-71), Wis. Pharm. Assn., Miss. Valley Drug Club, Beta Gamma Sigma, Phi Eta Sigma, Delta Kappa Epsilon. Presbyn. Clubs: University, Town (Milw.). Home: 3903 W Mequon Rd 112 N Mequon WI 53092

DOHNAL, WILLIAM EDWARD, retired steel company executive, consultant; b. Cleve., May 25, 1912; s. Frank and Anna (Florian) D.; grad. Cleve. Coll. Western Res. U., 1940; m. Alta Louella Bingham, June 1, 1933; children—David, Dennis. Auditor, Lybrand, Ross Bros. and Montgomery, 1942-45; acting auditor Cleveland-Cliffs Iron Co., Cleve., 1946-47, auditor, 1947-53, asst. treas., 1953-58, comptroller, 1958-63, v.p., comptroller, 1963-64, v.p. internat., 1964-73, sr. v.p., from 1973, now ret.; internat. bus. cons. C.P.A., Ohio. Mem. Am. Soc. C.P.A.s, Ohio Soc. C.P.A.s, Cleve. Council World Affairs. Clubs: Clevelander; Weld (Perth, Australia). Home: 2181 Ambleside Dr Cleveland OH 44106 also PO Box 516 Safety Harbor FL 33572 also 1710 Lake Cypress Dr Safety Harbor FL 33572

DOISY, EDWARD ADELBERT, biochemist; b. Hume, Ill., Nov. 13, 1893; s. Edward Perez and Ada (Alley) D.; A.B., U. Ill., 1914, M.S., 1916; Ph.D., Harvard U., 1920; D.Sc., Washington U., 1940, Yale U., 1940, U. Chgo., 1941, Central Coll. 1942, U. Ill., 1960, Gustavus Adolphus Coll., 1963; LL.D., St. Louis U., 1955; Docteur honoris causa, U. Paris, 1945; m. Alice Ackert, July 20, 1918 (dec. 1964); children—Edward Adelbert, Robert Ackert, Philip Perez, Richard Joseph; m. 2d, Margaret McCormick, Apr. 19, 1965. Asst. in biochemistry Harvard Med. Sch., 1915-17; instr., asso. and asso. prof. biochemistry Washington U. Sch. Medicine, St. Louis, 1919-23; prof. biochemistry, dir. dept. St. Louis U. Sch. Medicine, 1923-65, Distinguished Service prof. biochemistry, emeritus, also dir. emeritus Edward A. Doisy dept. biochemistry, 1965—, adminstrv. bd.; dir. dept. biochemistry, biochemist St. Mary's Hosp., St. Louis, 1924—. Served to 2d lt. U.S. Army, 1917-19. Several named lectures at various univs. and soc. meetings. Recipient Gold medal St. Louis Med. Soc., 1935; Philip A. Conne medal Chemists Club N.Y., 1935; St. Louis award, 1939; Willard Gibbs medal, 1941; Am. Pharm. Mfg. Assn. award, 1942; Squibb award, 1944; Barren Found. medal, 1972; shared Nobel Prize in Physiology and Medicine with Dr. Henrik Dam, 1943. Mem. League of Nations com. for standardization sex hormones, London, 1932, 35. Mem. Am. Soc. Biol. Chemists (council 1926-27, 34-37, 40-45, pres. 1943-45), Am. Chem. Soc., Nat. Acad. Scis., Am. Philos. Soc., Pontifical Acad. Scis., Am. Acad. Arts and Scis., Phi Beta Kappa, Sigma Xi, Phi Kappa Phi, Alpha Omega Alpha. Author: Sex and Internal Secretions (with Edgar Allen and Charles H. Danforth), 1939. Contbr. articles on blood buffers, sex hormones, vitamin K. and antibiotic compounds to profl. jours. Home: 4B Colonial Village Ct Webster Groves MO 63119 Office: 1402 S Grand Blvd Saint Louis MO 63104

DOLAN, DONALD EDWARD, chiropractor; b. Breckenridge, Mo., Oct. 11, 1914; s. Edward Dixon and Bonnie Mable (De Vaul) D.; m. Romola Blanche Wantland, July 6, 1936; children—Winnona Marguerite, Karon Pomalee, Sherry Darlene. D. Chiropractic Medicine, Cleve. pvt. trucker, 1936-38; Coll., 1946. Self-employed as cement, constrn. worker, decorator, paper hanger and painter, and fender and body shop worker, Chillicothe, Mo., 1933-34; pvt. trucker, 1936-38; operator Corn Products Co. Refinery, North Kans. City, Mo., 1938-50; gen. practice chiropractic medicine, Kansas City, Mo., 1947-49, Leavenworth, Kans., 1949—. Candidate for Coroner, City of Leavenworth, Kans., 1954. Mem. Kans. Chiropractic Assn. Republican. Mem. Christian Ch. Lodges: Masons (Proficiency Examiner, Dist. 2, Grand Chpt. Kans., 1981-82; Service award 1983), Order Eastern Star.

DOLAN, RICHARD EDWIN, banker, lawyer; b. McKeesport, Pa., Feb. 16, 1933; s. Phillip Francis and Kathryn Elizabeth (Martin) D.; m. Alice Catherine Wernert, July 15, 1967; children—Patrick John, Kelly Kay. B.A., Duquesne U., 1955; LL.D., Villanova U., 1958. Bar: Pa 1960, Ohio 1980. Trust officer Pitts. Nat. Bank, 1961-67; v.p. trust dept. Equibank, Pitts., 1967-78; v.p. in charge trusts Belmont County Nat. Bank, St. Clairsville, Ohio, 1978—; instr. Pa. Bankers Trust Sch., Bucknell U., Pitts., 1975-79; bd. dirs. Estate Planning Council, Wheeling, W.Va., 1982—. Bd. dirs. McKeesport Area Sch. Bd., 1967-69; adv. bd. Presbyn. Retirement Home, St. Clairsville, 1981—; trustee St. Clairsville Pub. Library, 1982—; fin. bd. Diocese of Steubenville, Ohio, 1983—. Counsellorship grantee Villanova Law Sch., 1955-58. Mem. Ohio State Bar, Belmont County Bar Assn., Allegheny County Bar Assn. Roman Catholic. Lodges: Rotary (treas. 1969—), K.C. (4 deg.), (treas. 1970—). Avocation: antique cars. Home: Country Club Estates St Clairsville OH 43950 Office: Belmont County Nat Bank PO Box 277 St Clairsville OH 43950

DOLAN, THOMAS IRONSIDE, manufacturing company executive; b. Hastings, Mich., Mar. 31, 1927; s. Clifford and Katherine (Ironside) D.; m. Barbara Sisson, June 11, 1948; children—Sarah, Nancy. B.S., U. Mich., 1949. Pres., Kelvinator, Inc., Grand Rapids, Mich., 1969-75; sr. v.p. White Cons. Industries, Cleve., 1975-80; sr. v.p. A.O. Smith Corp., Milw., 1980-82, pres., 1982-84, pres., chief exec. officer, 1984, chmn. chief exec. officer, 1984—; dir. First Wis. Nat. Bank, Milw.; mem. Bus. Council, Washington, 1984—. Bd. dirs. Met. Milw. Assn. Commerce, 1982—, Greater Milw. Com., 1982—; mem. campaign cabinet United Way of Greater Milw, 1985. Republican. Clubs: Milw., Univ., Country. Lodges: Rotary (Milw.). Office: AO Smith 11270 W Park Pl Milwaukee WI 53224

DOLE, ROBERT J., U.S. senator; b. Russell, Kans., July 22, 1923; s. Doran R. and Bina Dole; student U. Kans., U. Ariz.; A.B., Washburn Municipal U., Topeka, LL.B.; m. Mary Elizabeth Hanford, Dec. 6, 1975; 1 child by previous marriage, Robin. Admitted to Kans. bar; mem. Kans. Ho. of Reps., 1951; pvt. practice law, Russell, 1953-61; Russell County atty., 1953-61; mem. 87th Congress 6th Dist. of Kans., mem. 88th-90th Congresses, 1st Dist. Kans.; now mem. U.S. Senate from Kans., Senate majority leader, 1985—, majority leader 99th Congress, mem. agr. com., judiciary com., rules com., fin. com.; mem. Nat. Commn. on Social Security Reform; co-chmn. Helsinki commn.; mem. Pres.'s Commn. on Drunk Driving; mem. Senate caucus on the family; mem. senate human rights caucus; hon. co-chmn. congressional coalition for Soviet Jews. Chmn., Rep. Nat. Com., 1971-73; Rep. candidate for v.p., 1976; founder Dole Found. for Handicapped. Served with 10th Mountain Div., 75th Inf. Div., AUS, World War II. Decorated Bronze Star with cluster. Mem. Am. Legion, V.F.W., 4-H Fair Assn., Kappa Sigma. Methodist. Mason (Shriner), Elk, Kiwanian. Home: Russell KS 67665 Office: 141 Hart Senate Office Bldg Washington DC 20510*

DOLEZAL, DALE FRANCIS, truck manufacturing company executive; b. Ronan, Mont., Apr. 9, 1936; s. Henry Lewis and Regina Marie Dolezal; B.S. in Indsl. Engring., Mont. State U., 1961; student Program for Mgmt. Devel., Bus. Sch., Harvard U., 1974; m. Patricia Louise Johnson, Aug. 27, 1960; children—Craig, Kelly, Kathleen, Kari. Indsl. and methods engr. Westinghouse Electric Corp., Sunnyvale, Calif., 1961-63; chief indsl. engr. Clarke Equipment Corp., Spokane, Wash., 1963-65; mgr. materials Freightliner Corp., Portland, Oreg., 1965-67; with Internat. Harvester Co., 1967—, dir. purchasing and inventory mgmt., Chgo., 1977-80, dir. materials and ops. planning, 1980-81; gen. mgr. parts and retail Indsl. Trucks div. Eaton Corp., Phila., 1981—; dir. Real Am. Corp.; mem. bd. bus. and indsl. advisers U. Wis., Madison; bd. dirs. Ops. Tng. Inst. Mem. parents adv. bd. Naperville (Ill.) Central High Sch., 1977—; mem. adv. bd. Sch. Dist. 203, Naperville, 1978—. Served with USMC, 1954-57. Registered profl. engr., Oreg. Mem. Am. Inst. Indsl. Engrs., Am. Prodn. and Inventory Control. Soc. Republican. Roman Catholic. Clubs: Rotary, K.C., Harvard (Chgo.). Contbr. articles to trade jours.

DOLLIMORE, DAVID, chemistry educator; b. London, Apr. 3, 1928; s. Frederick and Lucy Maud (Hall) D.; m. Joyce Gwendoline Wethersley, 1954; children—Janet Ann, Philip James, Andrew Christopher. B.Sc., U. London, 1949, Ph.D., 1952; D.Sc., 1976. Postdoctoral research Exeter U., 1952-54; asst. lectr. Queens Coll., Dundee, St. Andrews U., 1954-56; sr. lectr. Royal Coll. Advanced Tech., Salford U., 1956-60, prin. lectr., 1960-64, sr. lectr., 1964-72, reader, 1972-82; prof. chemistry U. Toledo, 1982—, chmn. dept., 1982-84. Author: (with C.J. Keattch) An Introduction to Thermogravimetry, 1975. Contbr. numerous sci. articles to profl. jours. Editor: procs. symposia on thermal analysis, 1976, 81; procs. 14th internat. conf. on vacuum microbalance techniques, 1978. Recipient Silver medal Il Cemento jour., 1980. Fellow Royal Soc. Chemistry; mem. Am. Chem. Soc., Chem. Soc., Am. Inst. Chemistry, Am. Ceramic Soc., Internat. Confedn. Thermal Analysis, N.Am. Thermal Analysis Soc. (Mettler award 1979), Ohio Acad. Sci., Soc. Chem. Industry, Brit. Ceramic Soc., Brit. Thermal Methods Group, Carbon and Graphite Group, Inst. Physics, Fine Particles Soc. Council (chmn. com. on phys.-chem. properties powders 1978-83), Cement and Concrete Assn. (materials research com. 1978-82), Brit. Standards Instn., Sigma Xi. Avocations: walking; indsl. geology. Home: 4709 Crestridge S Toledo OH 43623 Office: Chemistry Dept Univ Toledo Toledo OH 43606

DOLTON, MARY LOUISE (LU), telephone company manager, consultant; b. Grand Island, Nebr., June 4, 1951; d. Fred Peter and Maryanne (Wardyn) Malulka. Student, Northeast Tech. Community Coll., 1974-76, Metro Tech. Community Coll., 1984. Dist. trainer bus. office Northwest Bell, Grand Island, Nebr., 1974-75, asst. mgr. bus. office, Norfolk, Nebr., 1975-76, mgr. operator services, 1976-78, mgr. profl. mgmt. devel., Omaha, 1978-83, dir. product sales, 1983-84, corp. adminstrv. mgr., 1984—; cons. Operation Bridge, Omaha, 1984—. Loaned exec. United Way Midlands, Omaha, 1979; chmn. Nebr. Ednl. TV Auction, Omaha, 1983, team leader, 1984, 85; participant Leadership Omaha, 1984-85. Named Young Career Woman Bus. and Profl. Women, 1977, Outstanding Young Woman of Yr., Bus. and Profl. Women, 1978. Mem. Bus. for better Omaha Nebr. State EEO (chmn. 1984-85), Affirmative Action Council. Mem. Porsche (Omaha) (treas. 1982-83), Omaha Ski (treas. 1979-81). Avocations: snow skiing, auto racing, nautilus, boating. Home: 316 S 51 St Omaha NE 68132 Office: NW Bell Telephone Co 1314 Douglas on the Mall Omaha NE 68102

DOMBROWSKI, J. LOUIS, public affairs executive; b. Chgo., June 16, 1931; s. Nathan and Anna (Peachin) D.; m. Jo Ann Yount, Oct. 15, 1960 (div.); children—Douglas, Kathy, Nancy, Veronica; m. Paris Lynne Cox Hayduk, Dec. 11, 1982; 1 child, Veronica. B.A., U. Md., 1954; M.B.A., U. Chgo., 1962. Bus. news reporter Chgo. Tribune, 1956-61; cons. Comptroller of Currency, Washington, 1961-62; asst. fin. editor Chgo. Tribune, 1962-66, Washington corr., 1966-72, mem. editorial bd., 1972-75; dir. external affairs Regional Transp. Authority Northeastern Ill., 1975-79; v.p. pub. relations Nat. Assn. Realtors, 1979—. Bd. dirs. Mental Health Assn. Greater Chgo.; assoc. bd. dirs. Mt. Sinai Hosp. Chgo. Recipient Edward Scott Beck award for nat. reporting Chgo. Tribune, 1971. Mem. Public Relations Soc. Am., Am. Soc. Assn. Execs., Publicity Club Chgo., Nat. Assn. Real Estate Editors, Soc. Am. Bus. and Econ.

Writers, Chgo. Press Club. Club: Pickwick Golf (Glenview, Ill.). Office: 777 14th St NW Washington DC 20005

DOMMEL, PAUL ROBERT, political science educator; b. Lancaster, Pa., Aug. 28, 1933; s. James Charles and Erma Irene (Kurtz) D.; m. Frances Mildred Fernandes; children—Paul Alex, David James, Robyn Anne. B.S. in Fgn. Service, Georgetown U., 1959; M.A., George Washington U., 1968; Ph.D., U. Mass., 1970. Adminstrv. asst. U.S. Ho. of Reps., Washington, 1963-65; info. officer U.S. Econ. Devel. Adminstr., Washington, 1965-68; asst. prof. Holy Cross Coll., Worcester, Mass., 1969-76, assoc. prof., 1976-82; sr. fellow Brookings Instn., Washington, 1977-82; prof., chmn. dept. polit. sci. Cleve. State U., 1982—; cons., 1979—. Author: Politics of Revenue Sharing, 1974; Decentralizing Urban Policy, 1982. Contbr. chpts. to books, numerous articles to profl. jours. Served with USAF, 1951-55. Travel grantee German Acad. Exchange Service, 1983, U.S.-Spanish Joint Com. for Edn. and Cultural Cooperation, 1985. Mem. Am. Polit. Sci. Assn., Policy Studies Orgn. Democrat. Office: Dept Political Sci Cleve State Univ 2344 Euclid Ave Cleveland OH 44115

DOMMERMUTH, WILLIAM P., marketing educator, consultant; b. Chgo., June 29, 1925; s. Peter R. and Gertrude (Schnell) D., B.A., U. Ia., 1948; Ph.D., Northwestern U., 1964; m. H. Joan Hasty, June 6, 1959; children—Karin Jo, Margaret, Jean. Advt. copywriter Sears, Roebuck & Co., Chgo., 1949-51, sales promotion mgr., 1951-58; asst., then asso. prof. mktg. U. Tex. at Austin, 1961-67; asso. prof. U. Iowa, Iowa City, 1967-68; prof. So. Ill. U., Carbondale, 1968—; cons. bus. firms. Mem. Am. Mktg. Assn., Am. Inst. Decision Scis., Phi Beta Kappa, Beta Gamma Sigma, Theta Xi, Delta Sigma Pi. Author: (with Kernan and Sommers) Promotion: An Introductory Analysis, 1970; (with Andersen) Distribution Systems, 1972; (with Marcus and others) Modern Marketing, 1975, 2d edit., 1980; Promotion: Analysis Strategy and Creativity, 1984. Contbr. articles to profl. jours. Home: Six Rolling Acres Murphysboro IL 62966 Office: Dept Marketing So Ill Univ Carbondale IL 62901

DOMPKE, NORBERT FRANK, photography studio executive; b. Chgo., Oct. 16, 1920; s. Frank and Mary (Manley) D.; grad. Wright Jr. Coll., 1939-40; student Northwestern U., 1946-49; m. Marjorie Gies, Dec. 12, 1964; children—Scott, Pamela. Cost comptroller, budget dir. Scott Radio Corp., 1947; pres. TV Forecast, Inc., 1948-52, editor Chgo. edit. TV Guide, 1953, mgr. Wis. edit., 1954; pres. Root Photographers, Inc., Chgo., 1955—. Served with USAAC, 1943-47. C.P.A., Ill. Mem. United Photographers Orgn. (pres. 1970-71), Profl. Photographers Am., Profl. Sch. Photographers Am. (v.p. 1966-67, sec.-treas. 1967-69, pres. 1969-70, dir. 1971-78), Ill. Small Bus. Men's Assn. (dir. 1970-73), Chgo. Assn. Commerce and Industry (edn. com. 1966—), NEA, Nat. Sch. Press Assn., Ill. High Sch. Press Assn., Nat. Collegiate Sch. Press Assn., Ill. C. of C. Co-founder T.V. Guide, 1947. Clubs: Carlton, Barclay, Whitehall, International; Tonquish Creek Yacht. Home: 990 N Lake Shore Dr Chicago IL 60611 Office: 1131 W Sheridan Rd Chicago IL 60660

DOMPKE, RICHARD KENNETH, management consultant; b. Chgo., May 13, 1929; s. Bernard Stephen and Margaret Dorothy (Granner) D.; student in Architecture, Ill. Inst. Tech., 1947-49, Wright Jr. Coll., 1949-52; B.S. in Indsl. Engring., Northwestern U., 1955; m. Gayle Mary Kenney, Jan. 18, 1956. Indsl. engr. Reynolds Metals Co., Phoenix, 1956-59, plant indsl. engr., McCook, Ill., 1959-67; partner/dir. Deloitte Haskins & Sells, Chgo., 1967-85, ret. Republican committeeman, 1960-61; mem. Lake Forest (Ill.) Bldg. Rev. Bd., 1981-85. Cert. mgmt. cons.; cert. compensation profl.; registered profl. indsl. engr. Mem. Am. Inst. Indsl. Engrs. (dir. Chgo. chpt. 1962-65), Inst. of Mgmt. Consultants, Am. Production and Inventory Control Soc., Am. Compensation Assn., Tau Beta Pi. Clubs: University Club of Chgo., Northwestern Alumni Club of Chgo., Alpha Delta Phi. Contbr. articles to profl. publs. Home: Lake Forest IL

DONAHOE, BERNARD FRANCIS, history educator, author; b. Madison, Wis., Mar. 16, 1932; s. John Stephen and Mary (Sullivan) D. A.B., U. Notre Dame, 1955, M.A., 1959, Ph.D., 1965. Tchr. Archbishop Hoban High Sch., Akron, Ohio, 1956-57, Cathedral High Sch., Indpls., 1957-61; Master of Novices St. Joseph Novitiate, Rolling Prairie, Ind., 1963-68; asst. prof. Holy Cross Jr. Coll., Notre Dame, Ind., 1967—, St. Mary's Coll., Notre Dame, 1968—; assoc. prof., dept. chmn. Holy Cross Jr. Coll., St. Mary's Coll., Notre Dame, 1974—. Author: Private Plans and Public Dangers: The Story of F.D.R.'s 3rd Nomination, 1965. Chmn., bd. advs. Holy Cross Jr. Coll., 1984. Mem. Am. Hist. Assn., Organ. Am. Historians, Assn. Ind. Historians. Roman Catholic. Avocations: Tennis; golf. Home: Holy Cross Brothers Ctr Notre Dame IN 46556 Office: St Mary's Coll Notre Dame IN 46556

DONAHOE, JOHN PHILIP, veterinarian, educator; b. Hagerstown, Md., Dec. 1, 1944; s. Philip William and Margaret Louise (Gallaher) D.; m. Joyce MacIntyre Rudisill, Aug. 15, 1970; children—Paul Philip, Sharon. B.S., U. Ga., 1967, D.V.M., 1970, M.S., 1973, Ph.D., 1977. Research assoc. U. Ga., Athens, 1970-76; assit. prof. Ohio State U., Columbus, 1976-81, assoc. prof., 1981—. Contbr. articles to profl. jours. Mem. Am. Vet. Med. Assn., N.Y. Acad. Sci., Ohio Vet. Med. Assn., Am. Assn. Avian, Pathologists, Omega Tau Sigma (pres. 1982—). Democrat. Roman Catholic. Home: 85 Montrose Way Columbus OH 43214 Office: Ohio State U Vet Medicine 1900 Coffey Rd Columbus OH 43210

DONAHUE, CHARLES BERTRAND, II, lawyer; b. Hampton, Iowa, Apr. 17, 1937; s. Charles Bertrand and Alta Margaret (Sykes) D.; m. Brenda K. Kumpf, July 18, 1961 (div. 1980); children—Kaylie Elizabeth, Megan Elizabeth. A.B., Harvard Coll., 1959; J.D. cum laude, Cleve.-Marshall Coll. Cleve. State U., 1967. Bar: Ohio 1967, Fla. 1973. Subcontract mgr. Westinghouse Corp., Pitts., 1962-63; contract mgr. TRW, Inc., Cleve., 1963-67; ptnr. Calfee, Halter & Griswold, 1967-79; mng. ptnr. Donahue & Scanlon, Cleve., 1979—; adj. faculty Cleve.-Marshall Coll., 1973-79; dir. DeSantis Coatings Inc., Life Systems, Inc., Lortec Power Systems, Inc., Vitec, Inc. Served to capt. USAF, 1959-62. Delta Theta Phi scholar, 1967; recipient Spl. Merit award, Cleve. State U., 1973, Spl. Merit award, Ohio Legal Ctr. Ins., 1972, 74. Mem. Ohio State Bar Assn., Fla. State Bar Assn., Greater Cleve. Bar Assn., Estate Planning Council, Cleve.-Marshall Law Alumni (pres., trustee 1972). Republican. Episcopalian. Clubs: Harvard (Boston and Cleve.). Avocations: traveling; cooking; reading. Home: 827 Brick Mill Run Rd Westlake OH 44145 Office: Donahue & Scanlon One Erieview Plaza Cleveland OH 44114

DONAHUGH, ROBERT HAYDEN, library administrator; b. St. Paul, May 20, 1930; s. Robert Emmett and Elmyra Elanore (Hayden) D.; B.A., Coll. St. Thomas, 1952; M.A., U. Minn., 1953. Instr. English, speech Robert Coll., Istanbul, Turkey, 1956-57; head tech. services Canton (Ohio) Public Library, 1957-62; asst. dir. Public Library of Youngstown and Mahoning County (Ohio), 1962-79, dir., 1979—. Served with Mil. Police Corps, U.S. Army, 1954-56. Mem. ALA, Ohio Library Assn. (editor assn. bull. 1968-72, pres. 1975), Midwest Fedn. Library Assns. (pres. 1979-83), Internat. Platform Assn. Clubs: Elks, Rotary. Author: Evaluation of Reference Resources in 8 Public Libraries in 4 Ohio Counties, 1970; contbr. book revs. to Library Jour., 1958—; host Books Etc. program Sta. WYSU-FM, public radio, 1975—. Home: 509 Ferndale Youngstown OH 44511 Office: 305 Wick Youngstown OH 44503

DONALD, WILLIAM CLYDE, II, clergyman; b. Battle Creek, Mich., Nov. 28, 1918; s. William Clyde and Louella (Shattuck) D.; A.B., Albion Col, 1940; B.D., Garrett Bibl. Inst., 1943; D.D., Northwestern U., 1947; m. Carolyn Marie Fosberg, July 28, 1943; 1 dau., Pamela Marie (Mrs. John Gislason). Chaplain Deaconess Hosp., Milw., 1948-56; pastor Bethel Evangelical and Reformed Ch., Milw., 1949-57, Bethel Evangelical and Reformed Ch., Detroit, 1957-70, Peoples Ch. Chgo., 1970-73, 1st Congl. Ch., Benton Harbor, Mich., 1973-77; interim pastor specialist Plymouth Congl. Ch., Mpls., 1977-79; part-time faculty Wayne State U., 1950-70; chmn. bd. Third Securities Corp., Rockford, Ill., 1965-77. Mem. Am. Protestant Hosp. Assn. (fellow coll. chaplains), Nat. Assn. Congl. Christian Chs. (commn. on ministry 1978-82), Tau Kappa Epsilon. Mem. B'nai B'rith (hon.). Home: 1116 Lakeside Dr Mackinaw City MI 49701

DONALDSON, LESLIE WELLINGTON (LES), JR., research institute executive; b. Washington, Dec. 29, 1953; s. Leslie W. and Conchita (Newman) D.; m. Karen E. Mitchell, June 19, 1976; 1 dau., Adrienne S. Donaldson. B.S. in Chem. Engring., N.J. Inst. Tech., 1974; postgrad. in bus. Seton Hall U., U. Louisville, Loyola U. Chgo. Research engring. asst. E. I. duPont, Inc., Newark, N.J., 1973; process engr. Airco, Inc., Murray Hill, N.J., 1974-77; project engr. Celanese Corp., Louisville, 1977-83; project mgr. indsl. research and devel. Gas Research Inst., Chgo., 1983—. Mem. Rep. Senatorial Com., 1984. Mem. Am. Inst. Chem. Engrs. Republican. Avocations: Racquetball; softball. Office: Gas Research Inst 8600 W Bryn Mawr Ave Chicago IL 60631

DONALSON, JAMES RYAN, real estate broker; b. Kansas City, Mo., Jan. 7, 1945; s. Joseph Elmer and Betty Lee (Cousins) D.; B.S. (Mo. Real Estate Assn. scholar), U. Mo., 1967; m. Sandra Lynn Yockey, Dec. 26, 1964; children—Kimberly Kay, Debra Lynn, Jennifer Lee. Loan officer City Wide Mortgage Co., Kansas City, 1967; interviewer personnel Panhandle Eastern Pipe Line Co., Kansas City, 1968; partner Donalson Realtors, Kansas City, 1969—; pres. Classic Homes, Kansas City, 1973—, Donalson Devel. Co., 1980—, Diversified Investments (formerly Donalson & Assos. Realtors), 1980—; bd. dirs. Multiple Listing Service Greater Kansas City, 1971-75, treas., 1972-73. Bd. dirs. Platte County unit Am. Cancer Soc., 1973-75. Mem. Nat. Assn. Real Estate Bds., Mo. Assn. Realtors (dir. 1974-75), Real Estate Bd. Kansas City (dir. 1978-80), Platte County Bus. and Profl. Men's Assn., U. Mo. Alumni Assn., Homebuilders Assn. Greater Kansas City. Baptist. Lion (dir. 1974-76). Office: 7526 NW Prairie View Rd Kansas City MO 64151

DONATI, ROBERT MARIO, physician, educator; b. Richmond Heights, Mo., Feb. 28, 1934; s. Leo S. and Rose Marie D.; B.S. in Biology, St. Louis U., 1955, M.D., 1959. Intern St. Louis City Hosp., 1959-60; asst. resident John Cochran Hosp., St. Louis, 1960-62; fellow nuclear medicine St. Louis U., 1962-63; practice medicine specializing in nuclear medicine, St. Louis, 1963—; mem. staff John Cochran Hosp., 1963-83, St. Louis U. Hosp., 1963—, mem. faculty Sch. Medicine, 1963—, asst. prof. internal medicine, 1965-68, assoc. prof., 1968-74, prof., 1974—, prof. radiology, 1979—, dir. div. nuclear medicine, 1968—, sr. assoc. dean, 1983—; exec. assoc. v.p. St. Louis U. Med. Ctr., 1985—; adj. prof. internal medicine Washington U., St. Louis, 1979-83; chief nuclear medicine services St. Louis VA Med. Center, 1968-79, chief staff, 1979-83; mem. interagy. radiation task force HEW, 1978-79. Co-chmn. St. Louis Italian Am. Bicentennial Commn., 1976; mem. St. Louis Citizens Edn. Task Force, 1976-78; mem. desegregation monitoring and adv. com. U.S. Dist. Ct., 1981-82; councilor Federated Council Nuclear Medicine Orgns., 1982-84; del. Am. Bd. Med. Spltys., 1982—; nat. adv. com. Multi-hosp. Systems, 1982-84. Served to capt. AUS, 1966-68. Recipient Army Commendation medal, 1968; Exceptional service award VA, 1983. Diplomate Am. Bd. Nuclear Medicine (dir. 1980—, chmn. 1985-86). Mem. AMA (nuclear medicine residency rev. com. 1978-80, rep. sect. on med. schs.), St. Louis Med. Soc., Am. Fedn. Clin. Research (councilor 1967-70), Central Soc. Clin. Research, Am. Coll. Radiology, AAUP, N.Y. Acad. Scis., Soc. Exptl. Biology and Medicine, Soc. Nuclear Medicine (acad. council 1970—, trustee 1977-80, publs. com. 1978-81, 83—, vice chmn. edn. 1978), Am. Coll. Nuclear Physicians, Am., Internat. socs. hematology, Soc. Med. Consultants to Armed Forces, Sigma Xi. Roman Catholic. Club: Cosmos (Washington); Racquet (St. Louis). Editor: (with W.T. Newton) Radioassay in Clinical Medicine, 1974. Contbr. articles to profl. jours. Research in clin. investigative nuclear medicine and assessment, diffusion, and adoption of technology. Home: 5335 Botanical Ave Saint Louis MO 63110 Office: St Louis U Sch Medicine 1402 S Grand Blvd Saint Louis MO 63104

DONEAUD, ANDRE ALEXANDRU, meteorologist, educator, researcher; b. Bucharest, Romania, June 3, 1929; came to U.S., 1978; s. Ernest Alexandre and Marcella Elena (Macovei) D.; m. Alexandrina Sirbu, 1954 (div.); m. 2d, Doina Armida Stan, Aug. 17, 1958. Diploma in Atmospheric Physics, U. Bucharest, 1952, Ph.D., 1971. Research scientist Meteorol. Inst., Bucharest, 1952-78, sci. dir., 1962-72; assoc. prof. U. Bucharest., 1972-78; research sci. tchr., then assoc. prof. S.D. Sch. Mines and Tech., Rapid City, 1978; cons. World Meteorol. Orgn. Served to lt. Romania Air Force, 1952, Recipient Sci. Merit/award Romania Acad. Sci., 1969. Mem. Am. Meteorol. Soc., Am. Geophys. Union, Sigma Xi. Roman Catholic. Club: 39 (Rapid City). Co-author: Numerical and Graphical Methods, 1962; Synoptic, Dynamic and Aeronautic Meteorology, 1966; Prevention and Control of Frost in Vegetable and Fruit Growing, 1968; The Microclimate in Greenhouses, 1977; others; contbr. numerous articles profl. publs. Home: 507 E Chicago St Rapid City SD 57701 Office: 500 St Joseph St Rapid City SD 57701

DONER, RICHARD, manufacturing company executive; b. Detroit, Feb. 5, 1933; m. Vera Tsiguloff; 3 children. B.S. in Aero. Engring., Ind. Inst. Tech., 1958. With Chrysler Corp., Detroit, 1958-70; with Formscraft & Systems, Fort Wayne, 1970-71; purchasing agt. Palmer-Eckrich, Fort Wayne, 1971-72; dir. purchasing Tokheim Corp., Fort Wayne, 1972, mgr. materials, 1974, mgr. ops., 1976, v.p. mfg., 1977, exec. v.p., 1979, dir., 1980—, pres., 1980, pres., chief exec. officer, 1981, chmn. bd. and pres., 1982—; dir. Fort Wayne Nat. Bank, Mutual Security Life Ins. Co., START, Inc. Bd. dirs. Jr. Achievement Northeast Ind., Fort Wayne Area Youth for Christ. Mem. Ind. Mfrs. Assn. (dir.), Ind. C. of C. (dir.). Episcopalian. Address: Tokheim Corp 1600 Wabash Ave Fort Wayne IN 46802

DONEWALD, MARIAN, speech and hearing clinician, educator; b. St. Louis, July 1911; d. Harry William and Daisy Elizabeth (Eissler) Donewald; student U. Colo., 1937-38; A.B., U. Evansville, 1948; M.S., Purdue U., 1950. Tchr. Wheeler Sch., Evansville, Ind., 1935-48; speech and hearing clinician Evansville-Vanderburgh Sch. Corp., 1948—; lectr. speech Purdue U., Lafayette, Ind., 1952-64, dir. summer workshops, 1952-64; lectr. speech Community Coll., U. Evansville, 1955-76, ret., 1976; cons., pvt. therapist, 1976—. Mem. Christian edn. com. 1st Presbyterian Ch., Evansville, 1965-68, altar com., 1969—; Democratic precinct committeeman, mem. adv. bd. Evansville Knight Twp., 1975-79; trustee Campground Cemetery, Evansville, 1966—, sec. bd., 1970—; historian Old Court House, 1976—. Mem. Am. (state del. 1966-68), Central States, Ind. speech and hearing assns., Internat. Council for Exceptional Children, NEA, Ind. State, Evansville tchrs. assns., Speech Communication Assn., Cleft Palate Assn., Internat. Platform Assn., Assn. Tchr. Educators, Embroiderers Guild Am. (chpt. sec. 1982-83), AAUW, Evansville Rose Soc. (sec. 1969—), Kappa Kappa Iota (Ind. pres. 1977-79, 82-83). Clubs: Flower Growers Garden (pres. 1985-86), Rotary. Author: See and Say Book, 1961. Home: 2900 Bellemeade Ave Evansville IN 47714

DONNELLEY, BARBARA COLEMAN, civic worker; b. Chgo., May 20, 1941; d. Walter Cobb Coleman and Barbara (Stanley) Behr; m. Christopher Bayne Clark, July 3, 1965 (div. 1973); children—Barbara Stanley Coleman, Christopher Bayne; m. Thomas E. Donnelley II, Aug. 18, 1979. B.A., Wheaton Coll., Norton, Mass., 1963. With sales staff Max Futorian, Chgo., 1978-79, Lee Rosenberg, Highland Park, Ill., 1977-78, Bartley Collection, Lake Forest, Ill., 1976-77; pres. Gaylord Lockport Co., Chgo. Vice-pres. Open Lands Project, Chgo., 1983-85, Wetlands Research, Inc., Chgo., 1984-85; chmn. Smith Symposium adv. com. Edward L. Ryerson Conservation Area, Deerfield, Ill., 1984—; hist. preservation adviser Lockport Area Devel. Commn., Ill., 1984—. Recipient Friend award Nat. Assn. County Park and Recreation Ofcls., 1985. Republican. Episcopalian. Clubs: Onwentsia (Lake Forest); Casino (Chgo.). Avocations: travel; photography; fishing; skiing; golf; squash.

DONNELLEY, GAYLORD, retired printing company executive; b. Chgo., May 19, 1910; s. Thomas E. and Laura L. (Gaylord) D.; A.B., Yale U., 1931; postgrad. Cambridge U., 1931-32; LL.D. (hon.), Wabash Coll., 1965, Yale U., 1974, U. Chgo., 1976, U. S.C., Spartanburg, 1979; m. Dorothy Williams Ranney, May 4, 1935; children—Elliott R., Strachan, Laura Donnelley. With R.R. Donnelley & Sons Co., Chgo., 1932—, comptroller, office mgr., 1940-42, sec., 1945-47, exec. v.p., 1947-52, pres., 1952-64, chmn. bd., 1964-75, chmn. exec. com., 1975-83, hon. chmn. bd., 1983—; past dir. Borg-Warner Corp., Dun & Bradstreet Corp., Reuben H. Donnelley Corp., First Nat. Bank of Chgo., First Chgo. Corp., Lakeside Bank; dir. Lantana Boatyard, Inc. Vice chmn. exec. com. Chgo. Community Trust, 1978-79; mem. bus. adv. council Chgo. Urban League, 1969—; adv. bd. Ill. Dept. Conservation, 1978-84; mem. Ill. Bd. Higher Edn., 1979-85; adv. council Jr. Achievement, 1955—; mem. policy com. South Side Planning Bd., Chgo., 1966—; adv. bd. YMCA Met. Chgo., 1963—; pres. Community Fund Chgo., 1969-71, bd. dirs., 1964-73; mem. Ill. Nature Preserves Commn., 1968-74; trustee Savs. & Profit Sharing Fund of Sears Employees, 1976-81, Lincoln Acad. of Ill., 1978-79; trustee Newberry Library, 1953-72, life trustee, 1972—, first v.p. of bd., 1970; mem. governing com. Orchestral Assn., 1971; bd. advisors Council for Fin. Aid to Edn., 1971—; trustee Sarah Lawrence Coll., 1965-73, hon. trustee, 1973—; mem. Com. for Corp. Support of Pvt. Univs., 1977-80; chmn. Am. Friends of Cambridge U., 1977-83, dir., 1969—; bd. dirs. Nat. Wildlife Found., 1981-82; trustee U. Chgo., 1947-80, life trustee, 1980—, chmn. bd. trustees, 1970-76; mem. devel. bd. Yale U., 1964-71; mem. council Children's Meml. Hosp., 1977—; hon. bd. advisers Mercy Hosp., 1971—, lay bd. trustees, 1965-71; chmn. bd. Beverly Farm Found., 1962-64; elder First Presbyn. Ch., Libertyville; hon. governing mem. Art Inst. Chgo., 1980—; dir. Protestant Found. of Greater Chgo., 1970-79; trustee United Presbyn. Found., 1963-75, 1st v.p., 1972-73; trustee N. Am. Wildlife Found., 1980—, Ducks Unltd. Found., Nat. Humanities Ctr., 1984—, Conservation Found., 1982—, 1978—, Nat. Recreation Found., 1969—; mem. nat. com. Ams. for Coast, 1980—; mem. nat. adv. bd. Center for Book in Library of Congress, 1980—. Recipient Yale medal, 1972; The Lambs Good Shepherd award, 1978; Citations to Disting. Citizens award Protestant Found. Greater Chgo., 1977; Oak Leaf award The Nature Conservancy, 1976; Conservation Merit award Ill. Dept. Conservation, 1981; Lewis Meml. award Printing Industries Am., 1976; Philanthropist award Nat. Soc. Fundraising Execs., 1980; Charles H. Wacker award United Charities, 1980; numerous others; hon. Fellow Corpus Christi Coll., Cambridge U., 1979. Fellow Royal Soc. for Encouragement Arts, Mfg. and Commerce; mem. Smithsonian Assos. (nat. dir. 1977-83), Ducks Unltd. (pres. 1975-77, trustee 1962-80, trustee emeritus 1980—; chmn. exec. com. 1978-80, vice chmn. bd. 1977-78), Ducks Unltd. (Can.) (trustee 1968-80, hon. dir. 1980—), Ducks Unltd. de Mexico (trustee 1976-79), Nat. Recreation and Parks Assn. (life trustee, Spl. Recognition award 1975). Clubs: Carolina Plantation Soc. (Charleston, S.C.); Coleman Lake (Goodman, Wis.); Old Elm (Highland Park, Ill.); Onwentsia (Lake Forest, Ill.); Shoreacres Golf (Lake Bluff, Ill.); Links, Grolier (N.Y.C.); Casino, Caxton, Chgo., Chgo. Commonwealth, Comml., Econ., Execs., Quadrangle, Racquet, Univ., Wayfarers (Chgo.). Author: To Be A Good Printer, 1977. Office: 2223 Martin Luther King Dr Chicago IL 60616

DONNELLY, ROBERT TRUE, state supreme court justice; b. Lebanon, Mo., Aug. 31, 1924; s. Thomas and Sybil (True) D.; student U. Tulsa, 1942-43, Ohio State U., 1943; J.D., U. Mo., Columbia, 1949; m. Wanda Sue Oates, Nov. 16, 1946; children—Thomas Page, Brian True. Admitted to Mo. bar, 1949; practiced law, Greenfield, Springfield and Lebanon, Mo., 1949-65; justice Supreme Ct. Mo., 1965—, chief justice, 1973-75, 81-83; city atty. City of Lebanon, 1954-55; asst. atty. gen. State of Mo., 1957-61; mem. bar com. 26th Jud. Circuit, 1956-65. Mem. Lebanon Bd. Edn., 1959-65. Served with inf. U.S. Army, World War II; ETO. Decorated Purple Heart. Mem. Mo. Bar (bd. govs. 1956-63), Order of Coif, Order of Barristers. Presbyterian. Office: Supreme Ct Bldg Jefferson City MO 65101

DONNELLY, THOMAS EDWARD, JR, pharmacology educator; b. Chelsea, Mass., Sept. 16, 1943; s. Thomas Edward and Catherine Sutherland (Ross) D.; m. Thorkatla Thorkelsdottir, Jan. 31, 1975; children—Karina, Erling. B.S., Mass. Coll. Pharmacy, 1966; M.A., Harvard U., 1968; Ph.D., Yale U., 1972. Registered pharmacist. Post-doctoral fellow U. Copenhagen, 1972-73; biochemist Leo Pharm. Products Co., Ballerup, Denmark, 1973-74; research assoc. Emory U., Atlanta, 1974; asst. prof. U. Nebr. Med. Ctr., Omaha, 1974-78, assoc. prof. pharmacology, 1978—. Contbr. articles to profl. jours. Coach soccer YMCA, Omaha, 1984-85. Grantee NIH, 1966-72, 76-81, 84—, Am. Heart Assn., Dept. Health Nebr., 1983-85. Mem. AAAS, N.Y. Acad. Scis., Am. Soc. Pharmacology and Exptl. Therapeutics. Democrat. Home: 10713 Valley St Omaha NE 68124 Office: U Nebr Med Ctr 42d St and Dewey Ave Omaha NE 68105

DONNELLY, THOMAS HENRY, chemistry educator, consultant; b. Endicott, N.Y., Apr. 20, 1928; s. Paul John and Dorcas Alida (Gardiner) Donnelly (Donley); m. Jean Marilyn Saunders, May 14, 1955; children—Mary Kathleen, Susan Jean, James Paul, Sarah Elizabeth. B.S. in Chemistry, Rensselaer Polytech Inst., 1950; Ph.D., Cornell U., 1955. Mgr. phys. chem., research and devel. ctr. Swift & Co., Chgo./Oakbrook, Ill., 1965-72, mgr. gelatin and stabilizers, 1967-72, gen. mgr., sci. services, Oakbrook, 1972-78, mgr. applied chemistry, 1978-79; vis. prof. chemistry Loyola U., Chgo., 1979-84, lectr. chemistry, 1984—; mem. food enzymology del. to China People to People, Spokane, Wash., 1985. Contbr. articles, referee Jour. Phys. Chem., 1959—. Patentee in field. Lector, commentator, cantor St. John of the Cross Parish, Western Springs, Ill., 1961—; pres. Home-owners Assn., Western Springs. Served to lt. USNR, 1950-70. Recipient Merit award Chgo. Assn. Tech. Socs., 1984. Mem. AAAS, Inst. Food Technologists, Am. Chem. Soc. (past chmn. and other offices Chgo. sect., mem. div. agrl. and food chemistry, food biochemistry subdiv.). Democrat. Roman Catholic. Office: Loyola U of Chicago Dept Chemistry 6525 N Sheridan Chicago IL 60626

DONNEM, SARAH LUND, civic worker; b. St. Louis, Apr. 10, 1936; d. Joel Y. and Erle Hall (Harsh) Lund; B.A., Vassar Coll., 1958; m. Roland W. Donnem, Feb. 18, 1961; children—Elizabeth Prince, Sarah Madison. Tech. aide Bell Labs., Whippany, N.J., 1959-60; chmn. placement vol. opportunities N.Y. Jr. League, 1972-73, asst. treas. 1974-75, chmn. urban problems relating to mental health, 1967-69, mem. project research com., 1967-71, chmn., 1973-74, mem. bd. mgrs. 1973-74; chmn. community research D.C. Jr. League, 1970-71, mem. bd. mgrs., 1970-71; mem. Stratford Hall (N.Y.) Com., 1970—; bd. dirs. East Side Settlement House, Bronx, N.Y., 1972—, v.p., 1975-76, chmn. Nat. Horse Show Benefit, 1976; bd. dirs. Stanley M. Isaacs Neighborhood Center, N.Y.C., 1973-76, v.p., 1975-76; bd. dirs. Presbyn. Home for Aged Women, N.Y.C., 1974-76, v.p., 1976; mem. exec. bd. N.Y. Aux. of Blue Ridge Sch., 1971-75, sec., 1965-67, pres., 1973-75; budget and benevolence com. Brick Presbyn. Ch., N.Y.C., 1973-76, mem. social service com., 1973-74, chmn. fgn. students com., 1963-64. Bd. dirs. Search and Care, N.Y.C., 1973-76, Project LEARN, Cleve., 1978-82; mem. Fedn. Community Planning, Cleve., Council on Older Persons, 1978-82, mem. Future Planning Task Force, 1980-81, Commn. on Social Concerns, 1982-84; trustee Golden Age Centers Greater Cleve., 1979—, women's council, 1978—, 1st v.p., 1980-81, pres., 1981-85, chmn. Western Res. Antiques Show, 1979, 80; mem. women's com. Cleve. Inst. Arts, 1983—; mem. women's com. Cleve. Orch., 1979—; bd. dirs. Cleve. Ballet, 1980—, exec. com., 1981, chmn. legis. advocacy com., 1981-83, fin. com., 1982—; co-chmn. Yale Ball, 1983; bd. advisers Ret. Sr. Vol. Program, 1982, trustee, 1983—; trustee Fairmount Presbyn. Ch., 1985—; mem. long range planning com. United Way, Cleve., 1985—. Named Vol. of Year, N.Y. Jr. League, 1975. Mem. Nat. Inst. Social Scis. (mem. memberships com. 1972—, trustee 1984—). Nat. Soc. of Colonial Dames, Western Res. Hist. Soc. (mem. women's advisory council 1977; corr. sec. 1978). Republican. Clubs: Colony (N.Y.C.); Chevy Chase (Washington); Intown, Vassar (sec. 1980-82, v.p. 1983, pres. 1984-86), Jr. League Cleve., Kirtland (Cleve.). Address: 2945 Fontenay Rd Shaker Heights OH 44120

DONNER, BARBARA WOOD, editor, writer; b. Canton, Ohio, Aug. 12, 1936; d. William Barker and Marguerite (Siplon) Wood; children—Theodore, Jennifer. B.A., Heidelberg Coll., 1957; postgrad., Hunter Coll., 1960-61, Bowling Green State U., 1957-58. Asst. editor Sci. Research Assocs., Chgo., 1966-67; assoc. editor Encyclopedia Britannica Ednl. Corp., Chgo., assoc. dir. audio visual planning and devel.; sr. editor Harper & Row, Evanston, Ill., 1974-76, Benefic Press, Chgo., 1977-79; mng. editor VGM Career Horizons, Lincolnwood, Ill., 1980—. Author: (with C.G. Clark) (entire Chgo. Tribune Mag.) Africa, 1973. Contbr. articles and short stories to profl. publs. Mem. Chgo. Women in Pub. Democrat. Presbyterian. Avocations: sculpture; ceramic pottery. Home: 7017 N Greenview Chicago IL 60626

DONNERSTEIN, EDWARD IRVING, communications and psychology educator, researcher, author; b. N.Y.C., May 4, 1945; s. Ben and Elenore D.; m. Marcia Verbick, Aug. 19, 1968; m. 2d, Deborah Levine, June 3, 1981. B.A., U. Fla., 1967; Ph.D., Fla. State U., 1972. Asst. prof. psychology So. Ill. U., Carbondale, 1972-74; assoc. prof. Iowa State U., Ames, 1974-78; prof. communications U. Wis.-Madison, 1978—; cons. state govt.; expert, trial testimony. NIMH Research fellow, 1978-80; Army Research Inst. grantee, 1975, 76; NSF grantee, 1983. Mem. Am. Psychol. Assn., Internat. Communication Assn., Internat. Soc. Research on Aggression, Soc. Exptl. Social Psychology, Speech Communication Assn. Author 4 books, 12 book chpts.; contbr. numerous articles to sci. jours.; presenter over 100 papers at profl. meetings. Home: 5018 Sunrise Ridge Middleton WI 53562 Office: Dept Communication Arts U Wis Madison WI 53706

DONNEWALD, JAMES HENRY, lawyer, state official; b. Carlyle, Ill., Jan. 25, 1925; s. Henry and Cecelia (Luepke) D.; m. Ruth E. Holtgrave, June 24, 1953; children—Eric J., Craig J., Jill Y. Student St. Louis U., 1942-44; LL.B., Lincoln Coll. Law, 1949. Bar: Ill. 1951. Mem. Ill. Ho. of Reps., 1960-64; mem. Ill. Senate, 1964-66, 70-76, 78, asst. majority leader 77th-81st Gen. Assemblies, asst. minority leader 78th Gen. Assembly; treas. State of Ill., Springfield, 1982—; gen. practice law, Breese, Ill., 1951—. Served with U.S. Army, 1950-51. Mem. Ill. Bar Assn., Am. Legion. Democrat. Roman Catholic. Lodge: K.C. Office: 550 N 2d St Box 57 Breese IL 62230 Office: Office of the Treasurer 219 State House Springfield IL 62706

DONOHUE, CARROLL JOHN, lawyer; b. St. Louis, June 24, 1917; s. Thomas M. and Florence (Klefisch) D.; A.B., Washington U., St. Louis, 1939, LL.B. magna cum laude, 1939; m. Juanita Maire, Jan. 4, 1943 (div. 1973); children—Patricia Carol Donohue Stevens, Crhistine Ann Donohue Smith, Deborah Lee Donohue Wilucki; m. 2d, Barbara Lounsbury, Dec. 29, 1978. Admitted to Mo. bar, 1939; asso. law firm Hay and Flanagan, St. Louis, 1939-42, firm Salkey and Cornfeld, St. Louis, 1946-49; partner firm Husch, Eppenberger, Donohue, Elson and Cornfeld, St. Louis, 1949—. Mayor, Olivette, Mo., 1953-56. Campaign chmn. ARC, St. Louis County, Mo., 1950; mem. adv. com. Child Welfare, St. Louis, 1952-55, exec. com. Slum Clearance, 1949, bond issue com., 1955, St. Louis County Bond Issue screening and supervisory coms., 1955-61, county citizen's com. for better law enforcement, 1953-56; chmn. com. on immigration policy, 1954-56. Chmn. County Bd. Election Commrs., St. Louis County, Mo., 1960-65; vice-chmn. bd. Regional Commerce and Growth Assn., 1981. Served from apprentice seaman to lt. USNR, 1942-45. Decorated Bronze Star, Navy and M.C. medal. Mem. Mo. Bar (mem. bd. govs., 1948-50, 52, 54, 56; chmn. ann. meeting), St. Louis Bar Assn., (pres. 1954-55, v.p. 1948-49, treas. 1951-54), Order of Coif, Omicron Delta Kappa, Sigma Phi Epsilon, Delta Theta Phi. Club: Missouri Athletic. Office: 100 N Broadway Saint Louis MO 63102

DONOHUE, WILLIAM FRANCIS, health care administrator; b. Rome, N.Y., June 3, 1935; s. William Francis, Jr., and Selina (Bowen) D.; cert. inhalation therapy Yale Med. Center, 1962; B.A., Antioch Coll., 1973; cert. health care adminstrn. Trinity U., 1978. Chief inhalation therapist Lancaster (Pa.) Gen. Hosp., 1962-63, Western Pa. Hosp., Pitts., 1963-65; tech. dir. respiratory care Edgwater Hosp., Chgo., 1965-69; dean allied health scis. Central YMCA Community Coll., Chgo., 1969-75; asst. adminstr. Louise Burg Hosp., Chgo., 1975-77; dir. material mgmt. and quality assurance Provident Hosp.. Chgo., 1977-82; dir. profl. services Provident Med. Ctr., Chgo., 1982-84; assoc. exec. dir. Provident Med. Ctr., Chgo., 1984; pres., chief exec. officer Health Resources Mgmt. Assocs., Inc., Chgo., 1985—; health scis. adv. com. dept. human relations City of Chgo., 1969-76; health occupations adv. com. Chgo. City Colls., 1974-82; trustee Chgo. Hosp. Risk Pooling Program of Chgo. Hosp. Council, 1984—. Recipient 2d prize for sci. exhibits Pa. Med. Soc., 1965. Mem. Am. Coll. Hosp. Adminstrs., Am. Hosp. Assn., Chgo. Hosp. Council, Risk Mgmt. Assn., Am. Public Health Assn., Royal Soc. Health. Asso. editor Inhalation Therapy, 1964-69; contbr. numerous articles profl. jours. Home: 1030 N State St Chicago IL 60610 Office: 1050 N State St Suite 50K Chicago IL 60610

DONOVAN, FRANK WILLIAM, lawyer; b. Washington, Sept. 12, 1904; s. Frank Dennis and Catherine (Connor) D.; A.B., Notre Dame U., 1926; LL.B., Harvard U., 1929; m. Helen Turner, June 25, 1938 (dec. May 1947); children—Frank William, Julia Donovan O'Meara, Russell Hodges; m. 2d, Elizabeth Chetwoode Hodges, June 19, 1947 (dec. Nov. 1967); m. 3d, Ana Maria Fuentes-Munizaga, Dec. 8, 1969. Bar: Mich. 1930. Partner firm Yerkes, Goddard & McClintock, Detroit, 1932-38; individual practice, Detroit, 1938-41; partner firm Fulton & Donovan, Detroit, 1941-50, firm McClintock, Fulton, Donovan & Waterman, 1950-73, McClintock, Donovan, Carson & Roach, 1973-80, Donovan, Hammond, Carson, Ziegelman, Roach & Sotiroff, 1980-81, Donovan Hammond Ziegelman Roach & Sotiroff, 1981—; dir. D.T. Chase Co., Hartford, Zenith Labs, Inc., Northvale, N.J., Ryerson & Haynes, Inc., Jackson, Context Industries, Inc., Miami, Fla. Chmn. Italian Flood Relief Com., Detroit, 1966; chmn. bd. Detroit Grand Opera Assn., Detroit Symphony Orch., Etruscan Found., David T. Chase Found.; mem. senate Stratford Shakespearean Festival Found. (Can.); mem. Met. Opera Assn. N.Y.; trustee Shakespearean Drama Festival Found., Inc., N.Y.C.; bd. dirs. Fundación Angel Ramos, Inc., San Juan, P.R.; bd. govs. Am. Mental Health Found. Recipient Award Merit, Am. C. of C. for Italy, 1967, Citation Appreciation, Greater Mich. Found., 1963; Frank W. Donovan Dayproclaimed in recognition of cultural contributions, City Detroit, 1963. Clubs: Detroit, Country of Detroit, Renaissance (Detroit); Grosse Pointe (Mich.); La Coquille (Palm Beach, Fla.). Home: 8 Donovan Pl Grosse Pointe MI 48230 Office: 400 Renaissance Center Suite 1100 Detroit MI 48243

DONOVAN, JAMES DEBO, international marketing executive; b. Battle Creek, Mich., Feb. 28, 1955; s. John Vincent and Patricia (Hasselhorn) D.; m. Jane Denise Marchand, Sept. 22, 1979. Student Boston Coll., 1973-75; B.A., U. Calif.-Santa Cruz, 1977; M.B.A., Golden Gate U., 1979. Welder, Firme Kochs, Bremen, Ger., 1975; mktg. analyst/translator Creusot-Loire, Nantes, France, 1977; div. mgr. J. D. Marshall, Skokie, Ill., 1979-81; v.p. Intercon Research Assn., Evanston, Ill., 1981—, dir., 1982—. Mem. Licensing Execs. Soc., Assn. M.B.A. Execs. Office: 1219 Howard St Evanston IL 60202

DONOVAN, JAMES ROBERT, business equipment company marketing executive; b. Wichita, Kans., Apr. 11, 1932; s. Karl Genevay and Louise (Silcott) D.; A.B., Harvard U., 1954, M.B.A., 1956; m. Ottilie Schreiber, July 2, 1955; children—Amy Louise, Robert Silcott; m. Margaret Jones Esty, Oct. 31, 1982. Mgr. sales adminstrn., market research Hickok, Inc., Rochester, N.Y., 1956-59, regional sales mgr., 1959-62, asst. nat. sales mgr., 1963-65; group program mgr. Xerox Corp., Stamford, Conn., 1965-68, mktg. mgr. spl. products, 1968-70, mgr. copier products, 1970-72, dir. corp. pricing and competitive activity, 1972-78, dir. corp. mktg. strategy and planning, 1978-83; sr. v.p. corp. mktg. McDonnell Douglas Automation Co., St. Louis, 1983-84; v.p. mktg., planning Info. Systems Group, McDonnell Douglas Corp., St. Louis, 1984—. Vice pres. Family Service, Rochester, 1971-72; dir. Family and Children's Services, Stamford, 1972-79; dir. Rochester Sales Execs. Club, 1966-71; mem. mktg. adv. bd. Columbia U. Bus. Sch., 1978—; v.p. United Way of New Canaan. Mem. Harvard Alumni Assn. (dir. 1978-83), Harvard Bus. Sch. Alumni Assn. (exec. council). Clubs: Harvard (pres. Rochester 1971-72, pres. Fairfield County 1976-78), Harvard Bus. Sch. (pres. Rochester 1972, chmn. Westchester/Fairfield 1973-74); Old Warson Country (St. Louis); Woodway Country (Darien, Conn.). Home: 9834 Old Warson Rd Saint Louis MO 63124 Office: McDonnell Douglas Corp Saint Louis MO 63166

DONOVAN, MARGARET HENDERLITE, pianist, educator; b. Baird, Tex., May 6, 1925; d. Peter Baxter and Jessie (Newton) Henderlite; A.A., Tarleton State U., 1943; B.Mus. cum laude (T scholar), Am. Conservatory of Music, 1945, M.Mus. cum laude, 1953, postgrad., 1953; m. Russell J. Donovan, Sept. 4, 1949; children—Russell John, Peter Henderlite, Rachel Lynn, Margaret Newton, Tammy Jayne. Duo pianist with Charles W. Froh, Tex. State U., Stephenville, 1939-43; pianist, accompanist New Trier High Sch., Winnetka, Ill., 1945-47, Am. Conservatory of Music, Chgo., 1943-53, mem. faculty, 1954—; mem. piano faculty Park Forest Conservatory of Music, Park Forest, Ill., 1958—; pvt. piano instr., 1954—; organist, pianist United Ch. of Christ, Sauk Village, Ill.; adjudicator Nat. Guild of Piano Playing Auditions, 1960—, Soc. of Am. Musicians, 1962, Ill. Fedn. Music Clubs and Auditions, Chgo., 1962—. Recipient Hattstaedt Gold medal Piano award, 1945. Mem. Lakeview Mus. Soc., Cordon Club, Nat. Soc. Lit. and Arts, Am. Coll. Musicians, Soc. Am. Music, Music Tchrs. Nat. Assn., Internat. Platform Assn., Sigma Alpha Iota. Presbyn. Home: 1872 Reichert Ave Sauk Village IL 60411

DONOVAN, MARK PHILIP, association executive, university lecturer; b. Dayton, Ohio, Jan. 17, 1950; s. Charles Thomas and Phyllis Jean (Fryer) D.; m. Elvira Borgstadt, Sept. 10, 1983; 1 child, Vanessa Bodrie. B.A., Centre Coll., 1972; M.A., U. Ga., 1978; postgrad. U. Chgo., 1978—. Exec. dir. Univ. Village Assn., Chgo., 1981—; cons. Landmarks Preservation Council Ill., Chgo., 1980; lectr. U. Ill.-Chgo., 1981—. Co-author: Urban Housing Resources, 1979. Bd. dirs. Friends of Downtown, Chgo., 1981, Chgo. Assn. Neighborhood Devel. Orgns., 1985. Mem. Assn. Am. Geographers. Home: 706 S Ada St Chicago IL 60607 Office: Univ Village Assn 925 S Loomis St Chicago IL 60607

DONOVAN, PAUL J(ERALD), insurance company executive, investment advisor; b. Corning, Iowa, Nov. 18, 1953; s. Daryl E. and Donna Jean (Woolley) P.; m. Deborah Ann Lewis, Aug. 16, 1974; children—Laura Marie, Michael James. B.B.A., U. Iowa, 1976; M.B.A., U. No. Iowa, 1982. C.P.A., Iowa. Asst. v.p. Century Life Ins. Co. Am., Waverly, Iowa, 1976—. Bd. dirs. United Way, Waverly, 1985-88; mem. ch. council Redeemer Lutheran Ch., Waverly, 1984—. Fellow Inst. Chartered Fin. Analysts; mem. Fin. Analyst Fedn., Iowa Soc. C.P.A.s. Republican. Avocations: golf; reading; gardening. Home: 1308 Hillcrest Dr Waverly IA 50677 Office: Century Life of Am Heritage Way Waverly IA 50677

DOODY, MICHAEL FRANCIS, association executive; b. Oak Park, Ill., Oct. 26, 1946; s. F. A. and Jeanne (Squibbs) D.; m. Mary Jane Appleton, June 8, 1968; children—Megan, Bethany, Ryan. B.A. magna cum laude, Providence Coll., 1968; M.P.H., U. R.I., 1971. Assoc. dir. Hosp. Assn. R.I., Providence, 1968-72; dir. delivery health systems Am. Hosp. Assn., Chgo., 1972-74; pres. Am. Osteo. Hosp. Assn., Arlington Heights, Ill., 1974-83, Am. Coll. Osteo. Hosp. Adminstrs., Arlington Heights, 1974-83, Osteopathic Hosps. Mgmt. Co., Arlington Heights, 1980-83, Healthcare Fin. Mgmt. Assn., Oak Brook, Ill., 1983—. Hon. fellow Am. Coll. Osteopathic Hosp. Adminstrs.; mem. Am. Coll. Hosp. Adminstrs., Am. Soc. Assn. Execs., Healthcare Fin. Mgmt. Assn. Avocations: reading; swimming. Office: Healthcare Fin Mgmt Assn 1900 Spring Rd Suite 500 Oak Brook IL 60521

DOOLEY, EDNA MELLICK, hospital pharmacy director; b. Albia, Iowa, Feb. 25, 1927; d. George and Anna (Zezok) Mellick; m. John W. Dooley, Aug. 13, 1949 (div.); children—Patrick, Michael, Terrance, Ellen, Jane, James. B.S. in Pharmacy, U. Iowa, 1949. Registered pharmacist. Pharmacist Mercy Hosp., Iowa City, 1949-51, Gilmour Danielson Co., Lincoln, Nebr., 1964-66; dir. pharmacy Oakdale Sanatorium, Iowa, 1961-66; asst. dir. Mercy Hosp., Iowa City, 1966-74, Illini Hosp., Silvis, Ill., 1974-79; dir. Mason Dist. Hosp., Havana, Ill., 1979—; dir. Home Health Services, Havana, 1978—. Recipient Pharmacist of Yr., Hosp. Pharmacy Inst., 1981. Mem. Am. Soc. Hosp. Pharmacists, Ill. Council Hosp. Pharmacists, Am. Soc. Enteral and Parental Nutrition, Bus. Profl. Women Assn., Sugar Creek Soc. Ill. Council Hosp. Pharmacists (past pres.), Miss. Valley Ill. Council Hosp. Pharmacists (past pres.), Pilot Club. Democrat. Roman Catholic. Avocations: jogging; needle arts; gardening. Home: Route 1 Havana IL 62644 Office: HPI Pharmacy #526 Mason Dist Hosp 520 E Franklin St Havana IL 62644

DOOLEY, J. GORDON, food scientist; b. Nevada, Mo., Nov. 15, 1935; s. Howard Eugene and Wilma June (Vanderford) D.; B.S. with honors in Biology, Drury Coll., Springfield, Mo., 1958; postgrad. (NSF grantee) U. Mo., Rolla, 1961, (NSF grantee) Kirksville (Mo.) State Coll., 1959; M.S. in Biology (NSF grantee), Brown U., 1966; postgrad. bus. mgmt. Alexander Hamilton Inst., 1973-75, No. Ill. U., 1964. Tchr. sci. Morton West High Sch., Berwyn, Ill., 1963-64; dairy technologist Borden Co., Elgin, Ill., 1964-65; project leader Cheese Products Lab., Kraft Corp., Glenview, Ill., 1965-73; sr. food scientist Wallerstein Co. div. Travenol Labs., Inc., Morton Grove, Ill., 1973-77; mgr. food sci. GB Fermentation Industries, Inc., Des Plaines, Ill., 1977-79, mgr. product devel., 1979-82; group leader Food Ingredients div. Stauffer Chem. Co., Clawson, Mich., 1982-84; sr. research scientist Schreiber Foods, Inc., Green Bay, Wis., 1984—; sci. lectr. seminars, Mexico, 1975; assoc. mem. Ad Hoc Enzyme Tech. Com., 1978—; dairy research adv. bd. Utah State U. Recipient Spoke award Nevada (Mo.) Jr. C. of C., 1960. Mem. Am. Dairy Sci. Assn., Inst. Food Technologists, Am. Chem. Soc., Cousteau Soc., Am. Inst. Biol. Scis., Nat. Sci. Tchrs. Assn., Whey Products Inst., Beta Beta Beta, Phi Eta Sigma. Republican. Presbyterian. Clubs: Toastmasters Internat. (pres. Baxter Labs. club 1976-77); Brown U. (Chgo.). Patentee in food and enzyme tech. field; contbr. sci. articles to profl. jours. Home: 261 W Briar Ln Green Bay WI 54301 Office: 1621 Main St Green Bay WI 54302

DORENDA, STEPHEN, JR., lime and stone company executive, former marine officer; b. Mahony City, Pa., Nov. 29, 1936; s. Stephen and Agnes C. (Gdovic) D.; m. Mary Anthia Lamb, Mar. 12, 1960; 1 dau., Carolynn Renee. B.S., U. Pitts., 1958; grad. Naval Intelligence Sch., 1961; postgrad. U.S. Naval Air Acad., U. N.C.-Wilmington. Commd. 2d lt. U.S. Marine Corps, 1958, advanced through grades to maj., 1969; fighter pilot, from 1960; assigned to Mercury Program, 1962; served in Vietnam, 1969, ret., 1978; pres. Rock Mechanics, Inc., Winston-Salem, N.C., 1978-80; ops. mgr. Nat. Lime & Stone Co., Findlay, Ohio, 1980—. Named Outstanding Citizen of N.C., U.S. Pub. Relations Office, 1974, Outstanding Citizen of South, 1975; recipient Sikorsky Winged S award Sikorsky Aircraft Corp., 1960. Republican. Roman Catholic. Home: 430 Hancock St Findlay OH 45840 Office: Nat Lime and Stone Co PO Box 120 Findlay OH 45840

DORGAN, BYRON L., congressman; b. Dickinson, N.D., May 14, 1942; B.S., U. N.D., 1964; M.B.A., U. Denver, 1966; children—Scott M., Shelly L. Tax commr. State of N.D., 1969-80; at-large mem. 97th-99th Congresses from N.D., mem. ways and means com., agr. com., small bus. com., veterans com., 1980-82, select com. on hunger. Chmn. Multistate Tax Commn., 1972-74, Gov. N.D. Commn. Air Transp.; mem. nat. adv. bd. Tax Action Campaign; mem. Gov. N.D. Energy Council, Gov. N.D. Econ. Devel. Task Force, N.D. Bd. Equalization; exec. com. Nat. Assn. Tax Adminstrs., 1972-75; mem. exec. com. N.D. Democratic Party. Address: 238 Cannon House Office Bldg Washington DC 20515

DORMAN, DAVID KENT, physician; b. Milw., Dec. 1, 1942; s. Clifford Warren and Lassie (Beese) D.; m. Donna Lynn Graff, Nov. 16, 1974; 1 dau., Natalie Lynn. B.S., Marquette U., 1964; M.D., Med. Coll. Wis., 1968. Diplomate Am. Bd. Plastic Surgery. Intern Kern County Gen. Hosp., Bakersfield, Calif., 1968-69; resident in gen. surgery Med. Coll. Wis., Hosp., Milw., 1969-75; resident in plastic surgery U. Tex., Galveston, 1975-78; practice medicine specializing in plastic and reconstructive surgery, Milw., 1978—; mem. staffs Elm Brook Meml. Hosp., Brookfield, Community Meml. Hosp., Menomonee Falls. Served to maj. M.C., U.S. Army, 1970-72. Fellow ACS; mem. AMA, Am. Soc. Plastic and Reconstructive Surgery, Am. Assn. Hand Surgery. Advocations: HO model railroading; weather forecasting; stamp collecting. Home: 3200 Jerri Ct Milwaukee WI 53005 Office: 2323 N Mayfair Rd Suite 503 Milwaukee WI 53226

DORN, RAYMOND EDWARD, publications designer; b. St. Charles, Ill., Aug. 17, 1921; s. August and Ann Sophia (Lukesh) D.; m. Vera Ernestine Hogan, Nov. 20, 1948; children—Michael David, Tamara Jane. Worked in all phases of pub., 1946-76; pres. Dorn Workshops (design studio), Lombard, Ill., 1976—; instr. publ. design Printing Industries Inst. Ill. Served with 13th Airborne, U.S. Army, 1942-45. Decorated Am. Campaign, Good Conduct, Victory medals. Mem. Am. Soc. Bus. Press Editors. Lutheran. Author: How to Design and Improve Magazine Layouts, 1974, 3d edit., 1983; 20/20-Problems and Solutions, 1980; Tabloid Design for the Organizational Press, 1983; designer Universal Layout Sheet for mags. and tabloids, 1983; How to be your own Artist, 1985; contbr. articles on publ. design to profl. jours. Home and Office: 1013 S Ahrens Ave Lombard IL 60148

DORNBLASER, DAVID LEE, options trader; b. La Habra, Calif., May 2, 1957; s. Fred David and Catherine Polly (Vibbert) D.; m. Lynn Carol Rosstedt, June 7, 1980. B.S. in Econs., U. Ill., 1979; postgrad. Chgo.-Kent Coll. Law, 1983—. Campaign cons., 1979-80; mem., market-maker Chgo. Bd. Options Exchange, 1980-83; mgr., ptnr. DGS Options & Co., Chgo., 1983—; mem. facilities com. Chgo. Bd. Options Exchange. Former polit. cons.; sec., chmn. Du Page County Young Republicans. Presbyterian. Home: 513 Forest Ave Glen Ellyn IL 60137 Office: 141 W Jackson Blvd Suite 2900 Chicago IL 60604

DORNER, IRENE MARIE-THERESE, medical technologist; b. Los Angeles, Jan. 6, 1934; d. Otto Urban and Erna Johanna (Schüle) Wilhelm; m. Robert W. Dorner, June 27, 1954 (div. 1977); children—Samuel Robert, Jessica Anne. B.A. in Bacteriology, UCLA, 1957. Cert., lic. med. technologist, Calif. Med. technologist Riverside Community Hosp. (Calif.), 1957-58; sr. med. technologist hematology San Bernardino Community Hosp. (Calif.), 1958-62; supr. blood bank Jewish Hosp., St. Louis, 1962-64; supr. blood bank Barnes Hosp., St. Louis, 1965-79, instr. Sch. Anesthesiology, 1970-79; instr. blood bank specialist program Washington U. Med. Ctr., St. Louis, 1968-79; clin. instr. dept. allied health service St. Louis U., 1968, dept. pathology, 1980—; mgr. lab. services Hosp. Div. City of St. Louis, 1980—; lectr. profl. assns., workshops, seminars. Contbr. articles to publs. in field. Cub master St. Louis council Boy Scouts Am., St. Louis, 1978-79; mem. Soc. for Preservation of Health, St. Louis, 1983—. Recipient L. Jean Stubbins award S. Central Assn. Blood Banks, 1975. Mem. Am. Assn. Clin. Pathologists, Am. Assn. Blood Banks (insp. 1975-80), Heart of Am. Assn. Blood Banks (pres. 1969-70, v.p. 1982-83), Clin. Lab. Mgmt. Assn., ARC (med. adv. bd. 1973-79, tech. adv. bd. 1974-79). Republican. Roman Catholic. Home: 42 Aberdeen Pl Clayton MO 63105 Office: Snodgras Lab 1606 Grattan Saint Louis MO 63104

DOROSCHAK, JOHN Z., dentist; b. Solochiw, Ukraine, Feb. 11, 1928; s. William and Anna (Stroczan) D.; came to U.S., 1950, naturalized, 1954; student U. Minn., 1955-57, B.S., 1959, D.D.S., 1961; m. Nadia Zahorodny, June 30, 1962; children—Andrew, Michael, Natalie, Maria. Pvt. practice dentistry, Mpls., 1961—. Cons., St. Joseph's Home for Aged, Mpls., 1974-77, Holy Family Residence, St. Paul, 1977-84. Mem. steering com. St. Anthony West Neighborhood, Mpls., 1971-72; chmn. Mpls. dentists com. Little Sisters of the Poor Devel. Program, 1975; Webelos leader troop 50, Boy Scouts Am., 1975-76; pres. N.E. Regional Sch. Assn. Parents and Tchrs., 1978-79; bd. dirs. East Side Neighborhood Service, 1972; treas. Plast Inc., Ukrainian youth orgn., Mpls., 1979-83; mem. Sr. Citizen Centers Health Adv. Com., Mpls., 1979-83. Served with AUS, 1953-55. Mem. Am. Dental Assn., Minn. Dental Assn. (com. on dental care access 1980-83), Minn. Soc. Preventive Dentistry (dir. 1977-83, treas. 1979-83), Am. Soc. Dentistry for Children, Mpls. Dist. Dental Soc. (nursing home com. 1974—, chmn. 1979-82, 84—, emergency care com. 1983-84), Ukrainian Med. Assn. (sec.-treas. Minn. chpt. 1971-75), Ukrainian Profl. Club, Psi Omega. Mem. Ukrainian Catholic Ch. (campaign chmn. 1966-80, mem. ch. com. 1965—). Club: University Minnesota Alumni (charter mem.). Home: 919 Main St NE Minneapolis MN 55413 Office: Broadway and University Profl Bldg 230 NE Broadway Minneapolis MN 55413

DORR, ROBERT WILLIAM, osteopathic physician; b. Detroit, May 30, 1952; s. William Curtis and Laurel Jean (Thompson) D.; m. Deborah Jean Boyce, May 30, 1980. B.A., Albion Coll., 1974; D.O., Mich. State U., 1977. Cert. aviation med. examiner. Intern, Southeastern Med. Ctr., North Miami Beach, Fla., 1978; gen. practice osteo. medicine Jackson (Mich.) Northwest Clinic, P.C., 1978—; med. dir. Medistation Jackson P.C., 1982—; chmn. credentials com. Jackson Osteo. Hosp. Bd. dirs. Jackson YMCA; bd. advs. Jackson County chpt. MADD (Mothers Against Drunk Driving). Mem. Southcentral Osteo. Assn., Mich. Osteo. Assn. Physicians and Surgeons, Am. Osteo. Assn., Flying Physicians Assn., Am. Coll. Sports Medicine, Civil Aviation Med. Assn., So. Med. Assn., Am. Coll. Gen. Practitioners in Osteo. Medicine and Surgery, Osteo. Gen. Practitioners Mich. Home: 1786 Lochmoor Blvd Jackson MI 49201 Office: 2200 Springport Rd Jackson MI 49202

DORRELL, LARRY DEAN, educational administrator; b. Chairton County, Mo., Oct. 25, 1943; s. Mrash Edward and Myrtle Marie (Stilwell) D.; m. Janet V. Briggs, Aug. 28, 1948; children—Christopher John, Shawn Michael, Jennifer Elizabeth. B.S. in Edn., Northeast Mo. State U., Kirksville, 1969, M.A. in Reformation History, 1971; Ph.D. in Curriculum and Instrn., U. Mo., Columbia, 1980. Cert. tchr., Mo. Agt. State Farm Ins., Brookfield, Mo., 1971-73; chmn. social studies dept. S. Harrison R-II, Batheny, Mo., 1973-75; media dir. Centralia Pub. Sch., Mo., 1975-79, Columbia Pub. Sch., Mo., 1979-82; ednl. adminstr. Mexico Pub Sch., Mo., 1982—. Contbr. articles to profl. jours. Mem. Democratic Com.-Linn County, Brookfield, 1972-74, Democratic Com.-Boone County, Columbia, 1976-80; chmn. Dem. Com.-Centralia, 1976-80. Served to sgt. U.S. Army, 1961-64. Named Outstanding Tchr. Future Tchrs. Am., 1975, Outstanding Ednl. Leader Columbia Pub. Sch., 1981; Outstanding Ednl. Adminstr. Mexico Pub. Schs., 1983. Mem. Mo. State Tchrs. Assn. (chmn. resolutions 1980—), Northeast Dist. Tchrs. Assn. (pres. 1984), Nat. Assn. Secondary Prins. (chmn. scholarship 1984—). Democrat. Baptist. Lodges: Kiwanis (sec./treas. 1973-75), Rotary. Home: 1788 Quail Hill Mexico MO 65265 Office: Mexico Pub Schs 639 N Wade Mexico MO 65265

DORSTE, THOMAS CHARLES, architect; b. Anderson, Ind., Feb. 12, 1923; s. Louis Thomas and Mary Samantha (Haughton) D.; student Ball State U., 1939; B.Arch., MIT, 1947; m. Eleanor Claire Edwardson, Apr. 8, 1944; children—Robert Edwardson, Sarah Haughton, Craig Thomas; m. 2d, Sandra Lucas Smith, 1979. Designer, draftsman Anderson & Beckwith, Boston, 1947-50; chief draftsman Burns & Burns Indpls., 1950-53; ptnr. Dorste & Pantazi, Indpls., 1953-59; owner Thomas C. Dorste, Indpls., 1959-61; v.p., sec. James Assocs., Indpls., 1961—; v.p. James & Berger, architects, engrs., economists, Indpls., 1967— (dir. both firms); dir. James Assocs., Vincennes, Lafayette and Fort Wayne, Ind. Mem. econ. devel. com. City Indpls., 1972-75, adv. com. Indpls. Dept. Devel., 1960-65, policy com. City Market, 1974. Mem. ednl. council Mass. Inst. Tech., 1965—, Nat. Trust for Historic Preservation, 1974—, Indpls. Mus. Soc., 1971—, Indpls. Symphony Soc., 1971-78. Pres., bd. dirs. Indpls. Leadership Com., 1970-73. Served with C.E., AUS, 1942-46. Mem. AIA, Ind. Soc. Architects, MIT Club Ind., Amateur Fencers League Am. Club: Indpls. Fencing. Architect: Ind. U. Univ. Schs., 1963; Greenwood Shopping Center, 1966; Indpls. Regional Postal Facility, 1971; Indpls. Conv. Center, 1972; Ind. U. Retirement Community, 1981; Recruit Tng. Ctr. and Tech. Inst. Naval Studies, others. others. Home: 765 W Hawthorne Zionsville IN 46077 Office: 2828 E 45th St Indianapolis IN 46205

DOSICK, STEVEN MARTIN, peripheral vascular surgeon; b. Chgo., Sept. 17, 1942; s. Max and Ida (Karlin) D.; m. Sandra Lee Reich, July 8, 1969; children—Melissa, Janine, Cynthia. B.S. in Psychology, U. Ill., 1965, M.D., Chgo., 1969. Diplomate Am. Bd. Surgery. Intern, Presbyterian St. Luke's Hosp., Chgo., 1969-70, resident in surgery, 1970-71; resident gen. surgery Med. Coll. Ohio, Toledo, 1971-74, fellow in vascular surgery, 1974-75; dir. Peripheral Vascular Lab. Toledo Hosp., 1976—, Conrad Jobst Meml. Vascular Lab., Toledo Hosp., 1978—, section head vascular surgery, 1982—, asst. prof. surgery Med. Coll. Ohio, 1976—; pres. Toledo Vascular Inst., 1978—. Inventor (vascular tunneler) Dosick Tunneler, 1980. Pres., founder Toledo Bicycle Touring Soc., 1981, 1982, 1983; co-dir. annual symposium Photography for Physicians, Toledo, 1977—. Jewish. Avocations: bicycling; photography; computer. Office: Toledo Vascular Inst 5700 Southwyck Blvd Toledo OH 43614

DOSS, DANIEL LEE, tool company executive, electrical engineer; b. Albert Lea, Minn., Jan. 14, 1949; s. Alfred Wilhelm and Lillie Ida (Rux) D.; m. Theola Ann Lienke, Aug. 29, 1970; children—Stephanie Ann, Heather Lea. B.E.E., U. Minn., 1971; M.B.A., Mankato State U., 1984. Asst. chief engr. Kato Engring., Mankato, Minn., 1971-73; project engr. Owatonna Tool Co., Minn., 1973-75, elec. design engring. supr., 1975-80, application engring. supr., 1980-84, nat. acctg. mgr., 1984-85, mgr. Detroit Tech. Ctr., 1985—. Patentee in field. Mem. Soc. Automotive Engrs., Truck Maintenance Council, IEEE. Republican. Lutheran. Avocations: trapshooting; woodworking. Office: Owatonna Tool Co 23743 Research Dr Farmington Hills MI 48024

DOSS, HOWARD JAY, agricultural safety educator, consultant; b. Lansing, Mich., June 8, 1926. M.S., Mich. State U., 1969. Agrl. safety specialist dept. agr. Mich. State U., East Lansing, 1969—, mem. faculty dept. agrl. engring., 1969—; agrl. safety cons. Mem. Am. Soc. Safety Engrs., Am. Soc. Agrl. Engrs., Nat. Inst. Farm Safety. Club: Clear Creek Ranch Hunt. Author: Agricultural Machinery Safety, 1974. Office: Agrl Engring Dept Mich State U East Lansing MI 48824

DOSTAL, ELIZABETH THERESA, pharmacist; b. Fort Benton, Mont., May 2, 1958; d. Elmer F. and Mary Patricia (Carr) D.; B.S. in Pharmacy, U. Minn., 1981. Registered pharmacist, Minn. Pharmacist, Nile Riverview, Mpls., 1981-83; pharmacist in charge North Ridge Pharmacy, New Hope, Minn., 1983—. English tutor Minn. Literacy Council, Inc., St. Paul, 1982-83; eucharistic minister Newman Ctr., Mpls., 1982—, reader, breadbaker, 1981—. Mem. Am. Pharm. Assn., Minn. Pharm. Assn. Democrat. Roman Catholic. Avocations: camping, reading, baking, piano playing, dancing. Home: 3526 Girard Ave S Minneapolis MN 55408 Office: North Ridge Pharmacy 5430 Boone Ave N New Hope MN 55428

DOTSON, JOHN ARTHUR, principal; b. Des Moines, Feb. 14, 1957; s. Donald L. and Patty J. (Reeves) D.; m. Nancy J. Griggs, Aug. 19, 1978; children—Kristal Kathaleen, John Ryan. B.S. in Music Edn., Drake U., 1979, M.S. in Edn., 1983. Instr. music dir. Atlantic Community Schs., 1979-83; prin. Preston Community Schs., Iowa, 1983—. Mem. Ednl. Adminstrs. Iowa, Nat. Assn. Secondary Sch. Prins. Republican. Methodist. Lodge: Lions. Avocations: Fishing; hunting; music. Office: Preston Community Schs 321 W School St Preston IA 52069

DOTY, JAMES KENNETH, leasing company executive; b. Rochelle, Ill., Aug. 16, 1950; s. John Kenneth and Ruth Marie (Nord) D.; m. Joël Ann Henning, June 1, 1975. B.S. in Chem. Engring., Rutgers U., 1972; M.B.A., U. Mich., 1974. Mgr. prodn. Dupont Co., Deepwater, N.J., 1974-77, bus. analyst, Wilmington, Del., 1977-80; mgr. mktg. Union Tank Car Co., Chgo., 1980-82, dir. planning, 1982—; lectr. N.J. Colls. Engring., 1971. Active various coms. First United Meth. Ch., Evanston, Ill., 1980—. Mem. Railway Progress Inst. (com. equipment leasing), Am. Railway Car Inst. (com. market forcasting), Am. Inst. Chem. Engrs., Tau Beta Pi. Club: Rutgers (v.p. 1984). Avocations: golf, tennis, travel. Office: Union Tank Car Co 111 W Jackson Blvd Chicago IL 60604

DOTY, KATHLYN ELAINE, university administrator; b. Oak Park, Ill., Jan. 12, 1948; d. Paul Stephen and Helen May (Henderson) Mackey; M.B.A., U. Chgo., 1979; m. Richard Lee Doty, Nov. 27, 1973. Programmer trainee Time-Life, Inc., Chgo., 1967-68; jr. systems analyst Aldens Inc., Chgo.,

1968-69, sr. systems analyst, 1969-71, project mgr., 1971-76; self-employed data processing cons., Chgo., 1976-78; dir. systems devel. Loyola U. Chgo., 1978—, bd. dirs., chmn. membership and edn. com. Loyola U. Employees' Fed. Credit Union, 1979—. Bd. dirs. Coll. and Univ. Systems Exchange, 1984—. Mem. Coll. and Univ. Systems Exchange, Assn. for Systems Mgmt., Assn. Women in Computing (pres. Chgo. chpt. 1983—), Assn. Computer Users. Home: PO Box 919 Oak Park IL 60303 Office: 2160 S 1st Ave Maywood IL 60153

DOTZENROD, JAMES ALLEN, farmer, state legislator; b. Breckinridge, Minn., Dec. 14, 1946; s. Ralph Clarence and Erma Martha (Feistner) D.; m. Emmy Lou Opskar; children—Allen James, Rudy William. A.S., N.D. State Sch. Sci., 1966; B.S.E.E., N.D. State U., 1968; student Squadron Officers Sch., 1971. Owner, operator farm, Wyndmere, N.D., 1972—; mem. N.D. Senate, 1978—, chmn. minority caucus, 1981, 83. Chmn., Wyndmere Airport Authority, 1976—; past pres. Wyndmere Community Club, 1979; mem. council Wyndmere Lutheran Ch. Served to capt. USAF, 1968-72, with Air N.G., 1973. Mem. Am. Legion. Democrat.

DOUGHERTY, CHARLES JOSEPH, retired utility executive; b. Clayton, Mo., Apr. 29, 1919; s. Harry J. and Loretto (Grace) D.; m. Suzanne L. Hamilton, May 1, 1943; children—Charles H., Mary Suzanne Dougherty Helfrich, Amy Louise Dougherty Turissini. B.S.C., St. Louis U., 1941, LL.B., 1950. Bar: Mo. 1950. With Union Electric Co., St. Louis, 1941-84, gen. counsel, 1964, exec. v.p., 1964-66, pres., 1966-80, dir., 1966—, chief exec. officer, 1968-84, chmn. bd., 1980-84; former dir. Boatmen's Nat. Bank St. Louis, Boatman's Bancshares, Inc. Trustee Mo. Pub. Expenditure Survey, 1966-85, Govtl. Research Inst., 1967-78; bd. dirs. Jr. Achievement Mississippi Valley, Inc., 1968-84; mem. exec. bd. St. Louis Area council Boy Scouts Am., 1966-83; mem. pres.'s council St. Louis U.; exec. com. United Fund Greater St. Louis, 1967-77; bd. dirs. Mcpl. Theatre Assn., St. Louis, 1968—; bd. dirs. Civic Ctr. Redevel. Corp., 1970-81, chmn., 1975-81; vice chmn. parents council, bd. dirs. St. Mary's Coll., 1969-70, chmn., 1970-72. Served with USMCR, 1942-46. Recipient St. Louis U. Alumni Merit award, 1966. Mem. ABA, Mo. Bar, Bar Assn. St. Louis, C. of C. of Met. St. Louis (dir. 1962-71, pres. 1970), Civic Progress, Nat. Assn. Electric Cos. (bd. dirs. 1968-71), Edison Electric Inst. (bd. dirs. 1968-71, 72-75, 80-84, vice chmn. 1982-83, chmn. 1983-84), Assn. Edison Illuminating Cos. (exec. com. 1968-82, v.p. 1980, pres. 1981), Mo. Valley Elec. Assn. (exec. com. 1966-71), Southwest Electric Conf. (exec. com. 1969-71, 74-77), Mo. C. of C. (bd. dirs. 1968-72), Atomic Indsl. Forum (bd. dirs. 1981-84), Electric Power Research Inst. (bd. dirs. 1982-84), Alpha Sigma Nu. Clubs: Old Warson Country (St. Louis); Bogey. Office: PO Box 149 1901 Gratiot St Saint Louis MO 63166

DOUGHERTY, CHARLOTTE ANNE, financial planner, insurance and securities representative; b. Canton, Ohio, Nov. 9, 1947; d. Myron Martin and Wilma Rose Brown; m. John Edwin Dougherty, Jr., Feb. 14, 1976; 1 son, John Edwin. B.A., Miami U., Oxford, Ohio, 1969; postgrad. Kent State U. (Ohio), 1971-73. Social worker Summit County Welfare, Akron, Ohio, 1971-73; research coordinator Tufts U., Medford, Mass., 1973-74; corp. recruiter Lincoln Nat. Sales Corp., Ft. Wayne, Ind., 1976-79; agt. Lincoln Nat. Life, Cin., 1980—; registered rep. Lincoln Nat. Pension, Cin., 1981—; v.p. Assocs. Benefit Corp., Cin., 1982—; account exec. Integrated Resources Equity Corp., Englewood, Colo., 1983—. Contbr. articles to profl. jours. Mem. Inst. Cert. Fin. Planners, Internat. Assn. Assn. Fin. Planning, Nat. Assn. Life Underwriters, Cin. Assn. Life Underwriters. Republican. Roman Catholic. Office: Oxford Fin Group 8040 Hosbrook Rd Suite 400 Cincinnati OH 45236

DOUGHERTY, LEO ROBERT, medical technologist, educational administrator; b. St. Louis, Apr. 2, 1951; s. Leo Ferdinand and Marie Frances (Sotiropoulos) D.; m. Teresa Marie Wulfers, Jan. 19, 1974; children—Megan Marie, Nicholas Leo. B.S., Southeast Mo. State U., 1973. Registered med. technologist. Head resident Southeast Mo. State U., Cape Girardeau, 1976-78, instr., 1981-83, adj. prof., 1983—; lab. technician St. John's Med. Ctr., Joplin, Mo., 1978-79, edn. coordinator, 1983—; med. technologist St. Francis Hosp., Cape Girardeau, 1979-83; adj. prof. Pittsburgh State U., Kans., 1983—, Drury Coll., Springfield, Mo., 1983—, Mo. So. State Coll., Joplin, 1983—. Assoc. advisor Mo-Kan area Boy Scouts Am., 1984; pres. parents' assn. Carver Nursery Sch., Joplin, 1984; bd. dirs. Carver Meml. Nursery Sch. Joplin, 1984. Mem. Am. Soc. Clin. Pathologists (a-soc.), Am. Soc. Med. Technologists, Prof. Assn. Diving Instrs. Roman Catholic. Avocations: teaching scuba diving; wood working. Office: St Johns Med Ctr Sch Med Tech 2727 McClelland Blvd Joplin MO 64801

DOUGHERTY, ROBERT WATSON, physiologist, researcher; b. Newcovserton, Ohio, Feb. 5, 1904; s. Robert Watson and Amie D. Dougherty; m. Ardythe Wilson, 1938 (dec. 1943); m. Ruth McKinley, Jan. 1, 1948; children—Michael Robert, Susan Eileen. B.S., Iowa State U., 1927; D.V.M., Ohio State U., 1936; M.S., Oreg. State U., 1941. From instr. to asst. prof. Oreg. State U., 1937-42; assoc. prof. Washington State U., 1946-48; prof. vet. physiology Cornell U., Ithaca, N.Y., 1948-61, Iowa State U., Ames, 1963-74; chief physiopathology lab. Nat. Animal Disease Ctr., Ames, 1961-74; helped organize labs. in tropical and high country of Andes for Coll. Vet. Medicine, San Marcos Univ., Lima, Peru, 1966; chmn. organizing com. Second Internat. Symposium Ruminant Physiology and Nutrition, Iowa State Univ., Ames, 1964; vis. prof. N.C. State U., 1974-75, Tuskegee Inst., Ala., 1977-78, U. Wis.-Madison, 1978; pres. Conf. Research Workers in Animal Diseases, 1973; presenter papers at sci. meetings throughout the world; lectr. in field. Author: Experimental Surgery in Farm Animals, 1981. Contbr. chpts. in sci. books. Served to lt. col. with U.S. Army, 1942-46, PTO. Recipient Borden award Am. Vet. Med. Assn. for Borden Co., 1963, Disting. Alumnus award Ohio State U., 1968. Disting. Physiologist award Am. Assn. Vet. Physiologists and Pharmacologists, 1973; Fulbright scholar, New Zealand, 1956-57. Fellow Am. Coll. Pharmacology and Therapeutics (Disting. Fellow award 1978); mem. World Assn. Vet. Physiologists, Pharmacologists, and Biochemists (charter mem., v.p. 1974), N.Y. Acad. Sci., Am. Acad. Vet. Nutritionists, Am. Soc. Vet. Physiologists and Pharmacologists, Am. Physiol. Soc., Soc. Exptl. Biology and Medicine, Am. Vet. Med. Assn., Sigma Xi, Alpha Gamma Rho, Phi Kappa Phi, Alpha Zeta, Phi Zeta. Republican. Presbyterian. Avocations: tennis; skiing; mountain climbing; gardening; woodworking. Home: Route 2 Ames IA 50010

DOUGHERTY, RONALD WILLIAM, lawyer; b. Canton, Ohio, Dec. 6, 1932; s. Russell Dewey and Agnes Elizabeth (Arnold) D.; m. Carole Dee Stover, Aug. 28, 1954; children—Kerry Jane, Russell Delbert. A.B., Dartmouth Coll., 1954; J.D., U. Va., 1960. Ptnr., Krugliak, Wilkins, Griffiths and Dougherty, Canton, 1960—; asst. solicitor City of Canton, 1966-68; lectr. legal seminars. Sec. bd. trustees Christ Presbyterian Ch., Canton, 1972-74; mem. exec. com. Republican Party, Stark County, Ohio; mem. allocations council United Way of Stark County, Stark County Bluecoats. Served to capt. USAFR, 1954-57. Recipient awards Ohio and Canton Jaycees, Service award Buckeye Council-Boy Scouts Am., 1974. Mem. Stark County Bar Assn. (pres. 1983-84, chmn. pub. defender com. 1976-84), Ohio State Bar Assn. (council of dels. 1978-84, exec. com. 1985—), ABA. Clubs: Shady Hollow County (pres. 1978) (Massilon, Ohio); Canton; Dartmouth Northeast Ohio (pres. 1978—). Home: 340 Lakecrest NW Canton OH 44709 Office: Krugliak Wilkins Griffiths & Dougherty 526 Citizens Savs Bank Canton OH 44702

DOUGHTY, CLYDE CARL, biological chemistry and preventive medicine educator; b. Hutchinson, Kans., July 21, 1924; s. George Carl and Bertha E. (Davis) D.; m. Geraldine Ann Quin, Dec. 23, 1951; children—Wendy Sue, Kent C., Kathleen Erin, Paul Kevin. B.A., U. Kans., 1948, M.S., 1950; Ph.D., Ill. Inst. Tech., 1956; postdoctoral student U. Ill.-Chgo., 1959. Research biochemist Charles F. Kettering Found., Yellow Springs, Ohio, 1956-58; asst. prof. U. Ill., Med. Ctr., Chgo., 1959-69, assoc. prof., 1970-76, prof. 1977—. Contbr. articles on enzyme research to profl. jours. Bd. dirs., conservation worker Prairie Club, Chgo., 1978—. Grantee Nat. Eye Inst., Juvenile Diabetes Found. Mem. Am. Assn. Biol. Chemists, AAAS. Presbyterian. Avocations: bicycling, swimming, nature studies, conservation. Office: U Ill Med Ctr 1853 W Polk St Chicago IL 60612

DOUGHTY, WESLEY MERLE, farmer; b. Streator, Ill., July 1, 1928; s. William Wesley and Zelma Lee (Lentz) D.; m. Mildred Louise Peery, June 12, 1955; children—Douglas Peery, Patricia Lynn. Student pub. schs., Ill. Farmer, Jamesport, Mo., 1953—. Chmn., Citizens for Soil, Water and State Parks, Mo., 1984—. Served with U.S. Army, 1951-53. Recipient Outstanding Farm Mgmt. award Kansas City C. of C., 1982; Resource Steward award Mo. Dept. Natural Resources, 1982. Mem. Mo. Assn. Soil and Water Conservation Dists. (pres. 1982-83). Democrat. Methodist. Lodge: Masons, Shriner. Address: Route 2 Jamesport MO 64648

DOUGLAS, GARY RAY, environmental engineer; b. Davenport, Iowa, Jan. 30, 1946; s. Raymond Eugene and Julia Lydia (Gridley) D.; m. Patricia Vee Denzler, Mar. 18, 1967; children—Valerie, Nathan, Adam, Shannon. B.C.E., U. Ill., 1969, M.S., 1971. Registered profl. engr. Wis., N.C., Iowa. Project engr. Rexnord Inc., Milw., 1970-73; design engr. Morgen Design, Milw., 1973-74; environ. tech. analyst Schlitz Brewing Co., Milw., 1974-77, process ops. engr. Winston Salem, N.C., 1977-79; supr. environ. ops. Deere and Co., Waterloo, Iowa, 1979—. Contbr. articles to profl. jours. USPHS fellow U. Ill., 1970. Mem. Water Pollution Control Fedn. (com. 1979-84), Am. Water Works Assn., Iowa Air Pollution Control Assn. Jehovah's Witness. Avocation: racquetball. Home: 444 Hughes Dr Waterloo IA 50701 Office: Deere & Co 400 Westfield Ave Waterloo IA 50701

DOUGLAS, GEORGE HALSEY, English educator; b. East Orange, N.J., Jan. 9, 1934; s. Halsey M. and Harriet Elizabeth (Goldbach) D.; A.B. with honors in Philosophy, Lafayette Coll., 1956; M.A., Columbia U., 1966; Ph.D., U. Ill., 1968; m. Rosalind Braun, June 19, 1961; 1 son, Philip. Tech. editor Bell Telephone Labs., Whippany, N.J., 1958-59; editor Agrl. Expt. Sta., U. Ill., Urbana, 1961-66, instr. Dept. English, 1966-68, asst. prof. English, 1968-77, assoc. prof. English, 1977—. Mem. Am. Studies Assn., MLA, Am. Bus. Communication Assn. Author: H.L. Mencken Critic of American Life, 1978; The Teaching of Business Communication, 1978; Rail City: Chicago and Its Railroads, 1981; Edmund Wilson's America, 1983; When the Lights Began to Show: Women of the Twenties; editor Jour. Bus. Communication, 1968—; contbr. articles to profl. jours. Home: 1514 Grandview Dr Champaign IL 61820 Office: Dept English English Bldg U Ill Urbana IL 61801

DOUGLAS, THOMAS MICHAEL, lawyer; b. Grayling, Mich., Sept. 10, 1951; s. Thomas Edgar III and Geneva Eileen (Avery) D.; m. Karen Jean Eberly, May 24, 1974; children—Brian Michael, Kristen Michelle. B.S., U. Detroit, 1974, M.A., 1976, J.D. magna cum laude, 1979. Bar: Mich. 1980, U.S. Dist. Ct. (we. dist.) Mich. 1980, U.S. Dist. Ct. (ea. dist.) Mich. 1984. Claims rep. Travelers Ins. Co., Southfield, Mich., 1977-80; assoc. firm Gofrank and Kelman, Southfield, Mich., 1985—. Recipient Am. Jurisprudence awards Lawyers Co-op. Pub. Co., 1976, 79; Farmer's Ins. Co. Scholar, 1977-78, pres.'s scholar U. Detroit, 1978-79. Mem. Mich. Def. Trial Counsel, Assn. Trial Lawyers Am., Grand Traverse Antrim Leelanau Bar Assn., Justice Frank Murphy Honor Soc., Alpha Sigma Nu. Republican. Roman Catholic. Home: 9840 Ingram St Livonia MI 48150 Office: Gofrank and Kelman 26555 Evergreen St Southfield MI 48076

DOUGLAS, W. GLENN, company executive; b. McHenry, Ky., Dec. 22, 1934; s. William Charles and Pearl Mae (Schroader) D.; m. Juanita Lazette Brown, Apr. 25, 1953 (div. 1960); children—Rhonda Kay; m. Marita Karel Short, Mar. 25, 1961, Karen Rene, Terry Glenn. Student Kent State U., 1969. Indsl. engr. Swan Rubber Co., Bucyrus, Ohio, 1954-69 with Pantasote Inc., Seymour, Ind., 1969—, personnel mgr., 1972—; pres. South Central Personnel Assn., 1974-75. Mem. draft bd. Selective Service System, Washington, 1983—; mem. Ind. State Fair Bd., Indpls., 1981—; mem. Jackson County Extension Adv. Council, Brownstown, Ind., 1984—. Recipient Cert. of Appreciation and Tng. Selective Service System, 1982. Democrat. Presbyterian. Lodge: Lions (dir. Seymour Ind. 1983-87, pres. 1980-81, zone chmn. 1981-82, chmn. dist. membership 1982-83, dep. dist. gov. 1984-85, gov. 1985-86). Avocations: camping. Home: 230 Marshall Dr Seymour IN 47274 Office: Pantasote Inc 624 B Ave E Seymour IN 47274

DOUGLASS, CAROL ANN, nurse; b. Cin., Sept. 6, 1947; d. Ernest William and Edna Laverne (Rickels) Hillman; m. Daryl E. Douglass, Feb. 21, 1985; children—Cherie Nadine Russell, George Dennis Russell, Elizabeth Ann Russell, Emily Katherine Williams, Jonathan David Williams. A.A.S. cum laude, Raymond Walters Coll., Cin., 1982. R.N., Ohio, Ky. Nurse asst. Mercy S. Hosp., Fairfield, Ohio, 1981, R.N., 1982-83; nurse ICU, Bethesda N. Hosp., Montgomery, Ohio, 1983-84; nurse spl. care Brown County Gen. Hosp., Georgetown, Ohio, 1984-85; nurse Adams County Hosp., West Union, Ohio, 1985—; substitute instr. Booth Meml. Hosp. Sch. Practical Nursing, Florence, Ky., 1984—. Blood pressure screener Golden Years Sr. Citizens, West Chester, Ohio, 1982. Mem. Am. Assn. Critical Care Nurses, Nat. Assn. Female Execs., Phi Theta Kappa. Home: 811 Eagle Creek Rd West Union OH 45693

DOUGLASS, REBECCA SUSAN, educational administrator, research consultant; b. Springfield, Ill., July 30, 1946; d. Stanley and Mary Geneva (Richards) Posnak; m. Roger Anthony Douglass, Dec. 30, 1968; children—Deirdre, Roger. B.A., Sangamon State U., 1974, M.A., 1975. Editor publs. Ill. State Bd. Edn., 1971-74, head curriculum devel. dept. vocat. edn., 1974-76; dir. East Central Curriculum Mgmt. Ctr., Springfield, Ill., 1976-83; dir. Ill. Vocat. Curriculum Ctr., Springfield, 1980-83; exec. dir. East Central Network Curriculum Coordination, 1983—; exec. dir. Ill. Voc. Studies Ctr., 1985—; tchr. edn. adminstrn. Sangamon State U., 1983-85; chmn. Nat. Network Curriculum Coordination in Vocat. and Tech. Edn., 1980-82. Mem. Nat. Research Coordinating Unit Assn. (past mem. exec. bd.), Am. Vocat. Assn., Assn. Supervision and Curriculum Devel., Am. Vocat. Research Assn. Editor Ill. Career Edn. Jour., 1972-76, Career Edn. Quar., 1976-78, Center Critiques, 1976-78.

DOUGLASS, STEPHEN A., educational services director; b. Couch, Mo., Mar. 3, 1929; m. Bette D. Russell, May 13, 1950; children—Connie Jean, Meribeth. B.S., U. Mo., 1950, M.Ed., 1959, ED.D., 1971. Dir., West Plains Vocat. Tech. Sch., Mo., 1954-68; continuing edn. coordinator U. Mo.-Rolla, 1968-71, assoc. dean, 1971-79, dir. tchrs. edn. program. 1979-80, dir. edнl. services, 1980—. Author: (with others) And Thats The Way It Was, 1981. Ednl. advisor 8th Dist. Congressman, Washington, 1980. Served to HM3 USN, 1953-54. Recipient Mo. Outstanding Adult Edn. award MO. Adult Edn. Assn., 1978, Honorary Am. Farmer award Nat. Future Farmers; Assn., 1966. Mem. Nat. Assn. Parliamentarians, Am. Assn. Adult Continuing Edn., Epsilon Sigma Phi (treas. 1979), Phi Delta Kappa. Republican. Methodist. Club: Blue Key (hon. mem.). Lodges: Rotary (pres. 1964), Masons (32 degree). Avocations: collecting marbles and antique farm equipment.

DOURLET, ERNEST FRANCES, manufacturing company executive; b. Lancaster, Ohio, 1924. Grad. W.Va. U., 1949, U. Pa., 1951. Pres. Cadillac Plastic & Chem. Co., 1957-71; exec. v.p. Dayco Corp., Dayton, Ohio, 1972-73, pres., dir., 1973—, also chief operating officer; dir. Price Bros. Co., Winters Nat. Bank and Trust Co. Served with U.S. Army. Office: Dayco Corp 333 W 1st St Dayton OH 45402*

DOUTHIT, EVAN A., lawyer; b. Oklahoma City, Dec. 29, 1953; s. Arthur James and Margrette Elizabeth (Forbes) D.; m. Melinda Rae McDonald, Nov. 14, 1981. B.A., U. Okla., 1976; J.D., Oklahoma City U., 1979. Bar: Okla. 1979, U.S. dist. ct. (so. dist.) Ga. 1981, Ga. 1982, Mo. 1983, U.S. dist. ct. (we. dist.) Mo. 1983. Assoc. Baker & Sterchi, Kansas City, Mo., 1983—. Contbr. articles to legal publ. Served to capt. JAGC U.S. Army, 1979-83. Mem. Assn. Trial Lawyers Am., Okla. Bar Assn., Ga. Bar Assn., Mo. Bar Assn., Kansas City Bar Assn. Republican. Methodist. Home: 9619 Manor Rd Leawood KS 66206 Office: Baker & Sterchi PO Box 13584 Kansas City MO 64199

DOUTT, GERALDINE MOFFATT, educational administrator; b. Warren, Mich., Apr. 16, 1927; s. Stanford and Wilhelmine (Ewaldt) Moffatt; married, 2 children. B.S. in Occupational Therapy, Eastern Mich. U., Ypsilanti, 1952, M.A. in Edn., 1959; E.D.S. in Spl. Edn., Wayne State U., Detroit, 1968; m. Robert G. Doutt; children—Eric Robert, Gerald George. Tchr., Van Dyke Pub. Schs., Warren, 1963-65, tchr. educable mentally impaired, 1965-67, tchr. cons. for emotionally impaired, 1967-69, dir. spl. edn., 1969—. Chmn. Macomb County Interagy. Council, 1968-69. Mem. Mich. Assn. Dirs. Spl. Edn., Nat. Council Exceptional Children, Delta Kappa Gamma. Home: 22919 Playview St St Clair Shores MI 48082 also: Treasure Island Higgins Lake PO Box 412 Higgins Lake MI 48627 Office: 22100 Federal St Warren MI 48089

DOWD, ANN MARIE, med. technologist; b. Detroit, Oct. 17, 1924; d. Frank Raymond and Frances Mae (Ayling) Sullivan; B.S., Wayne State U., 1947; m. Thomas Stephen Dowd, Apr. 23, 1949; children—Cynthia Dowd Restuccia, Kevin Thomas Dowd. Med. technologist Woman's Hosp. (now Hutzel Hosp.), Detroit, 1946-52, St. James Clin. Lab., Detroit, 1960-62; supr. histo-pathology lab. Hutzel Hosp., Detroit, 1962-72, Mt. Carmel Mercy Hosp., 1972—. Mem. Am. Soc. Clin. Pathologists, Am. Soc. Med. Technology, Mich. Soc. Med. Technology, Nat. Soc. Histotechnology, Mich. Soc. Histotechnologists, Wayne State U. Alumni Assn., Smithsonian Assos., Detroit Inst. Arts Founders Soc. Home: 29231 Oak Point Dr Farmington Hill MI 48018 Office: 6071 W Outer Dr Detroit MI 48235

DOWD, DAVID D., judge. U.S. Dist. Judge Sixth Cir., No. Ohio, 1982—. Office: US Dist Ct US Courthouse Akron OH 44308*

DOWD, JAMES PATRICK, bookseller; b. Chgo., Apr. 26, 1937; s. James Patrick and Mary Margaret (Healy) D.; m. Frances Marie Allevato, Aug. 4, 1962; children—Mary Frances, Daniel James, Matthew Joseph. Student Wright Jr. Coll., 1956-58, Harper Coll., 1984. With Spraying Systems Co., Wheaton, Ill., 1958-78, owner operator Dowd's Book Shoppe, St. Charles, Ill., 1978-80; tech. specialist Fermi Nat. Accelerator Lab., Batavia, Ill., 1980—, time & material coordinator, 1982—, SSC task force, 1984—. Editor: Life of Black Hawk, 1974. Author: Built Like A Bear, 1979; Custer Lives, 1983. Contbr.: Images of the Mystic Truth, 1981. Served with U.S. Army, 1961-63. Mem. Midwest Bookhunters. Roman Catholic. Avocations: collector of scarce and rare western Americana. Home: 38W 281 Toms Trail Dr Saint Charles IL 60174 Office: Fermi Nat Accelerator Lab PO Box 500 MS 316 Batavia IL 60510

DOWELL, GERALD, city official; b. St. Charles, Va., Nov. 25, 1941; s. Emmet and Arminda (Baker) D.; m. Beverly A. Rader, Apr. 12, 1963; children—Michelle, Jeff. A.A., North Central Tech. Coll., 1974; B.S., Heidelberg Coll., 1981; M.B.A., Ashland Coll., 1983. Patrolman, Crestline Police Dept., Ohio, 1968-73, sgt., 1973-77, chief, 1977—; mem. commn. Crawford County Traffic Safety Council, Bucyrus, Ohio, 1979. Bd. dirs. North Central Tech. Coll., Mansfield, Ohio, 1978; Crawford County Schs., Bucyrus; mem. Broken Arrow dist. Boy Scouts Am. Exploring Council., 1982. Recipient, Policeman of the Year award, Kiwanas, 1970 citation for Pedestrian Program Improvement AAA club; Outstanding and dedicated service award Nat. Child Safety Council, 1985; mem. Ohio Assn. Chiefs Police (charter); Internat. Assn. Chiefs Police (charter). Avocations: Karate; reading; weightlifting; coaching softball. Home: 895 Cloverdale Ave Crestline OH 44827 Office: 115 W Bucyrus Crestline OH 44827

DOWELL, JESSE MURRAY, JR., banker; b. Chgo., July 25, 1926; s. Jesse Murray and Lydia (Lacey) D.; B.S., with highest honors, U. Ill., 1949, M.S. in Agrl. Econs., 1969; m. Dorothy Carr, May 6, 1951; children—Ellen, Murray. Farmer, Mahomet, Ill., 1949-51; profl. farm mgr. Dowell Agrl. Service, Champaign, 1952-71; mgr. farm dept. Bank of Ill., Champaign, 1971-79; 2d v.p. in charge land acquisition East half U.S., Continental Bank, Chgo., 1979-81, U.S., 1981—; instr. part-time farm mgmt. U. Ill., 1970-71; bd. dirs. U. Ill. Coll. of Agr. Alumni, Urbana. Bd. dirs. Maynard Lake Sub-div., Champaign. Served with USN, 1944-46. Mem. Ill. Soc. Farm Mgrs. and Rural Appraisers (chmn. legis. com. 1973, pres. 1968), Am. Soc. Farm Mgrs. and Rural Appraisers (mem. legis. com. 1976—, vice chmn. 1979, chmn. 1980, 1st v.p. 1981, pres. 1983), U.S.C. of C. (food and agr. com. 1979—), Jr. C. of C. (pres. Champaign 1958), Am. Legion. Methodist. Clubs: Lincolnshire Fields Country, Masons. Editor: Jour. Am. Soc. Farm Mgrs. & Rural Appraisers, 1965, 66; creator idea Fed. Grains Ins. Corp., 1973. Home: 700 Mountain Rd Lake Bluff IL 60044 Office: Continental Bank 30 N LaSalle St Chicago IL 60693

DOWLEY, JOEL EDWARD, manufacturing executive, lawyer; b. Jackson, Mich., Apr. 27, 1952; s. William J. and Beth E. (Morell) D.; m. Janelle Smith, Nov. 12, 1983; 1 child, Kara Marie. B.A., Spring Arbor Coll., 1974; J.D., U. Notre Dame, 1977. Bar: Mich. 1977. Atty. Fraser, Trebilcock, Davis and Foster, P.C., Lansing, Mich., 1977-83; exec. v.p., gen. counsel Dowley Mfg. Inc., Spring Arbor, Mich., 1983—. Pub. mem. Mich. Bd. Psychology, 1978-82, vice chmn., 1980, chmn., 1981-82; pub. mem. ethics com. Am. Assn. Marriage and Family Therapy, 1980; mem. Ingham County Republican Exec. Com., Mich., 1978-84, 3d Dist. Rep. Exec. Com., 1983-85; Rep. candidate for Ingham County commr., 1978, 82; trustee Highfield's, Inc., youth opportunity camp, Onondaga, Mich., 1983—, sec., 1984-85, pres.-elect 1985-86; trustee Boarshead Theater, Lansing, 1983—. Mem. ABA, Mich. Bar Assn., Ingham County Bar Assn., Jackson County Bar Assn., Spring Arbor Coll. Alumni Assn. (trustee 1979-82, pres. 1981-82, Young Leader award 1983). Methodist. Home: 2115 Cooper Ave Lansing MI 48910 Office: Dowley Mfg Inc 7750 King Rd Spring Arbor MI 49283

DOWNEY, DOUGLAS WORTH, editor, publishing executive; b. Oakland, Calif., Nov. 28, 1929; s. John Joseph and Margaret Cudworth (Perley) D.; m. Anne Storrs Reynolds, July 14, 1956; children—Storrs Whitworth, Donald Reynolds. A.B. cum laude, Kenyon Coll., 1951; M.S., U. Wis., 1952. Asst. editor Assoc. Equipment Distbrs., Chgo., 1954-55; assoc. editor Standard Ednl. Corp., Chgo., 1955-57, asst. editorial dir., 1957-60, mng. editor, 1960-63, editor-in-chief, 1963—, v.p., 1964—. Mem. Northbrook Library Bd. (Ill.), 1963-71, 75-79, treas., 1964-67, pres., 1967-71; pres. Glenbrook High Sch. Caucus, 1973. Served with AUS, 1952-54; Korea. Decorated Bronze Star. Republican. Episcopalian. Author: Things to Make and Do, 1974. Home: 2236 Maple Ave Northbrook IL 60062 Office: 200 W Monroe St Chicago IL 60606

DOWNEY, FLORENCE FAYE, educational consultant; b. Marksville, La., Dec. 27, 1942; d. Russell and Louise (Jones) Barton; m. Paulrice McKinley Downey, Oct. 30, 1972 (div. 1979). B.A. in Edn., Prairie View A&M, 1964; M.A. in Edn., Chgo. State U., 1977, M.S. in Edn., 1980. Cert. elem. tchr., Tex., Ill. Tchr. Pine Island Sch. Dist., Anahuac, Tex., 1964-65, Chester Sch. Dist., Tyler, Tex., 1965-66, Joliet Pub. Schs., Ill., 1966-76, Nat. Coll. Edn., Evanston, Ill., 1980-82; ednl. cons. Joliet Pub. Sch., 1976—, curriculum developer, 1976—, computer trainer, 1976—; adj. instr. Lewis U., Joliet, 1984. Author: Curriculum Handbook, 1979; Operating the Apple Computer, 1982. Pres. Union Sch. Bd., Joliet, 1979. Mem. Bus. and Profl. Women, Phi Delta Kappa (sec. 1981-82), Alpha Kappa Alpha (Most Acad. Soror, 1979, Basileus 1983-85, Grammateus 1982-83), Alpha Delta Kappa. Roman Catholic. Avocations: song writing; piano playing; reading, music appreciation, backgammon, swimming. Home: 1111 Karner Dr Joliet IL 60433 Office: Joliet Pub Sch Dist 86 420 N Raynor Ave Joliet IL 60435

DOWNING, FRANKLIN J., county official; b. Dearborn, Mo., Sept. 24, 1924; s. Franklin Jesse and Jessie Fay (Frakes) D.; children—Ronald P., Melody Lynne. Student Platte Bus. Coll., St. Joseph Jr. Coll. Field rep. U.S. Dept. Agr., Maryville and Chilicothe, Mo., 1966-71; owner, mgr. Dearborn Oil Co., Dearborn and Smithville, Mo., 1971-77; with Platte County Mapping Dept., Platte City, Mo., 1979—, planning and zoning dir., 1980—. Mayor, City of Dearborn (Mo.), 1980—. Democrat. Baptist. Club: Platte-Buchanan Sportsmen. Lodge: Masons. Home: 412 E 3d St Dearborn MO 64439 Office: Platte County Planning Dept 324 Main St Platte City MO 64079

DOWNING, GEORGE JACKSON, finance company executive; b. Waukegan, Ill., Dec. 3, 1940; s. Hicks Albertson and Jeanette Lillian (Omick) D.; m. Paulette Renee Rimas, Aug. 4, 1962; children—Allison, Michele, Maura. B.A. in Sociology, Blackburn Coll., 1962; M.B.A. in Mktg., U. Chgo., 1964. Real estate analyst Shell Oil Co., Chgo., 1963-65; with Household Fin. Corp., 1965—, research analyst, Chgo., 1965-70, v.p. dir. research, Chgo., 1970-77, group v.p. mktg., Prospect Heights, Ill., 1977-80, sr. v.p. office of pres., 1980-83, exec. v.p. internat. ops., 1983—, exec. v.p. U.S. ops., 1984. Chmn. bd. trustees Blackburn Coll., 1982—. Recipient Alumni Achievement award Blackburn Coll., 1981. Republican. Clubs: Thorngate Country, Lincolnshire Swim. Office: Household Fin Corp 2700 Sanders Rd Prospect Heights IL 60070

DOWNS, ROBERT BINGHAM, librarian; b. Lenoir, N.C., May 25, 1903; s. John McLeod and Clara Catherine (Hartley) D.; m. Elizabeth Crooks, Aug. 17, 1929 (dec. Sept. 1982); children—Clara Downs Keller, Roberta Downs Andre; m. Jane Bliss Wilson, Sept. 16, 1983. A.B., U. N.C., 1926, LL.D., 1949; B.S., Columbia U., 1927, M.S., 1929; Litt.D., Colby Coll., 1944, U. Ill., 1973; D.L.S., U. Toledo, 1953; L.H.D., Ohio State U., 1963, So. Ill. U., 1970. Librarian, Colby Coll., Waterville, Maine, 1929-31, U. N.C.-Chapel Hill, 1932-38; dir. library NYU, 1938-43; dir. library U. Ill.-Urbana, 1943-58, dean library adminstrn., 1958-71; cons. Nat. U. Mex., 1952, Nat. Diet Library, Japan, 1948, Ankara U. (Turkey), 1955, Kabul U. (Afghanistan), 1963. Author: Books That Changed the World, 1956, 78; Books That Changed America, 1970; Books That Changed the South, 1976; Famous American Books, 1971; Molders of the Modern Mind, 1961; Famous Books Ancient and Medieval, 1964; Resources of Canadian Academic and Research Libraries, 1967; Resources of Southern Libraries, 1938; Resources of New York City Libraries, 1942; American

Library Resources, 1951-81; In Search of New Horizons, 1978; Australian and New Zealand Library Resources, 1979; British and Irish Library Resources, 1981; Landmarks in Science, 1982; Memorable Americans, 1983; (with Ralph E. McCoy) The First Freedom Today, 1984; (with John Flanagan and Harold Scott) More Memorable Americans, 1984; Perspectives on the Past, 1984. Guggenheim fellow, 1971. Mem. Assn. Coll. and Research Libraries (pres. 1941-42), ALA (pres. 1952-53; Clarence Day award 1963, Lippincott award 1968, Melvil Dewey medal 1974), Ill. Library Assn. (pres. 1955-56). Clubs: Caxton (Chgo.); Dial (Urbana). Lodge: Urbana Rotary (pres. 1962-63). Home: 708 W Pennsylvania Ave Urbana IL 61801

DOYEL, CHARLES LYNN, nursing home administrator; b. Albany, Ga., Mar. 12, 1948; s. Melvin Charles and Oka R. (Fry) D.; m. A. Lea Smith, Oct. 15, 1971; children—Dawn Lea, Ryan Charles. B.S., S.W. Mo. State U., 1975. Machine operator Kraft Inc., Springfield, Mo., 1979-81; asst. adminstr. Chastain's of Highland (Ill.), 1981, adminstr., 1981-82; asst. adminstr. Clayton House Health Care, Manchester, Mo., 1982-83; adminstr. Charlevoix Nursing Ctr., St. Charles, Mo., 1983—. Named Res. Officer of Yr., USAR Med. Service Corps, 1983. Home: 13484 Forestlac Creve Coeur MO 63141 Office: Clayton House 1251 E Clayton Rd Manchester MO 63011

DOYLE, ALMA LUCILLE, construction contracts administration and claims executive; b. Okfuskee County, Okla., Jan. 11, 1929; d. Robert Richard and Chloe Earle (Williams) Klutts; m. Andy Hugh Doyle, Oct. 1945; children—Doris June Doyle Fiorini, James Lee, Robert Jeffrey. Student Pueblo Jr. Coll., 1958-59, So. Colo. State Coll., Pueblo, 1971-72. Sec. to supt. Sch. Dist. #70, Pueblo, 1959-63; sec. to pres. Savs. & Loan Assn., Pueblo, 1971-72; engring. clk., sec. Stearns Roger Inc., Pueblo, 1972-76; sec. CF&I Steel Corp., Pueblo, 1976-79; contract adminstr. Stearns Roger Inc., Beulah, N.D., 1979-83; gen. mgr. Egan & Sons, Co., Mandan, N.D., 1983-85. Pres., bd. dirs. Columbine Girl Scouts, Pueblo, 1956-71; v.p., bd. dirs. United Way, Pueblo, 1972-76; bd. dirs. YWCA, Pueblo, 1978-79. Republican. Clubs: Hazen Ski. Avocations: Skiing, golf, photography.

DOYLE, CONSTANCE TALCOTT JOHNSTON, physician; b. Mansfield, Ohio, July 8, 1945; d. Frederick Lyman IV and Nancy Jean Bushnell (Johnston) Talcott; m. Alan Jerome Demsky, June 13, 1976; children—Ian Frederick Demsky, Zachary Adam Demsky. B.S., Ohio U., 1967; M.D., Ohio State U., 1971. Intern, Riverside Hosp., Columbus, Ohio, 1971-72; resident in internal medicine Hurley Hosp. and U. Mich., Flint, 1972-74, emergency physician Oakwood Hosp., Dearborn, Mich., 1974-76, Jackson County (Mich.) Emergency Services; survival flight physician U. Mich. helicopter rescue service, 1983—; disaster cons., co-chmn. emergency med. services disaster com. Region II EMS, 1978-79; course dir. advanced cardiac life support and chmn. advanced life support com. W.A. Foote Meml. Hosp., Jackson, 1979—, others; clin. instr. emergency services, dept. surgery U. Mich., 1981—; instr. Jackson County Emergency Med. Technician refresher courses, Jackson Community Coll. Bd. dirs. Jackson County Heart Assn., 1979-83. Mem. Am. Med. Women's Assn., Am. Coll. Emergency Physicians (Mich. disaster com., dir. Mich. 1979—, chmn. Mich. disaster com. 1979—; nat. ad hoc disaster com. 1983—; cons. Fed. Emergency Mgmt. Agy. disaster mgmt. course 1982—, treas. 1984-85, pres.-elect 1985), ACP, Mich. Assn. Emergency Med. Technicians (dir. 1979-80), Mich. State, Jackson County med. socs., Sierra Club. Jewish. Contbg. author: Clinical Approach to Poisoning and Toxicology, 1983; contbr. articles to profl. publs. Home: 1665 Lansdowne Rd Ann Arbor MI 48105 Office: WA Foote Hospital East Emergency Dept Jackson MI 49201

DOYLE, DONALD VINCENT, state senator; b. Sioux City, Iowa, Jan. 13, 1925; s. William E. and Nelsine E. (Sparby) D.; B.S., Morningside Coll., Sioux City, 1951; J.D., U. S.D., 1953; m. Janet E. Holtz, Aug. 9, 1963; 1 dau., Dawn Renee. Admitted to S.D., Iowa bars, 1953; pvt. practice, Sioux City, 1953—; mem. Iowa Ho. of Reps. from Woodbury County, 1956-80, Iowa Senate, 1981—. Served with USAAF, 1943-46. Recipient award Woodbury County Peace Officers, 1974, Restoration Club Sioux City, 1964, Outstanding Elected Ofcl. award Iowa Corrections Assn., 1979. Mem. Iowa, Woodbury County bar assns., CBI Vets. Assn. (past nat. judge adv.), Am. Legion, VFW, DAV, 40 and 8. Democrat. Office: PO Box 941 Sioux City IA 51101

DOYLE, GERTRUDE ILEENE, hospital administrator; b. Monon, Ind., Feb. 14, 1933; d. Samuel Elmer and Goldia Mae (Raines) Johns; m. Leo Francis Doyle, Apr. 16, 1955; children—Leo Edward, Phillip Wayne. R.N., Methodist Hosp., 1954; B.S.N., Ind. U., 1970, M.S., 1975. R.N., Ind. Office nurse, Indpls., 1954-55; asst. head nurse urology Meth. Hosp., Indpls., 1955-56; occupational health nurse Western Electric Co., Indpls., 1959-68; clin. instr. cardiovascular nursing Meth. Hosp., 1970-75, patient instr. and coordinator cardiovascular rehab. program, 1975-82, program developer, ednl. coordinator noninvasive testing and edn. dept., 1982—; cons. program devel., cardiac rehab. Vol., mem. exec. com., bd. dirs. Marion County chpt. and Ind. affiliate Am. Heart Assn., also instr. basic and advanced cardiac life support. Mem. U. Alumni Assn., Meth. Hosp. Council Cardiovascular Nursing Assn., Am. Heart Assn. (recipient Vol. Instr. CPR 5-Yr. award, 1981). Democrat. Roman Catholic. Clubs: St. Michael's Ladies Aux. (Greenfield); Our Lady of Fatima Ladies Guild (Indpls.). Author: (with Jack Hall) Manual of Cardiovascular Rehabilitation, 1975. Home: Rural Route 10 Box 309 Greenfield IN 46140 Office: Methodist Hosp 1604 N Capitol Ave Indianapolis IN 46202

DOYLE, JAMES RICHARD, dentist; b. Parker, Ariz., Nov. 3, 1948; s. John Anthony and Mary Ellen (Horton) D.; m. Jean Marie Christensen, June 8, 1974; children—Jack Erwin, Kathleen Anne. B.S., Metro. State U., 1974; D.D.S., U. Nebr., 1980. Lic. dentist, Nebr. Grad. asst. U. Nebr., Omaha, 1975-76; gen. practice dentistry, Norfolk, Nebr., 1980—; Madison County Dental cons. Nebr. Dental Assn., Madison, 1981—; continuing edn. dir. No. Dist., 1983—, access to care council, Lincoln, 1980-83. Vice pres. bd. dirs. Norfolk Pub. Library 1984, Link Halfway House Bd., Norfolk, 1983; chmn. Promote Norfolk Council 1982; bd. dirs. Norfolk Family YMCA, 1984, Norfolk United Fund, 1982-85. Served to E-4 USCG, 1967-71. Named Outstanding Young Man Am. Nat. Jaycees, 1984. Mem. ADA, Nebr. Dental Assn., Am. Soc. Dentistry-Children, Acad. Gen. Dentistry, Norfolk C. of C. (bd. dirs. 1984-85). Republican. Roman Catholic. Lodge: Kiwanis. Avocations: fishing, triathalons, exercise, reading. Home: 702 N 19th Box 1261 Norfolk NE 68701 Office: 109 N 29th Norfolk NE 68701

DOYLE, JAMES WARREN, air transportation executive; b. Oak Park, Ill., Jan. 10, 1943; s. James and Phyllis (Moore) D.; m. Christiane Almuth Jung, Sept. 14, 1965; children—Kirsten, Ian. B.Mus., So. Ill. U., 1964; postgrad. Hamburg U., 1965; M.Mus., Ind. U., 1969. Tchr. pub. schs., Westport, Conn., 1967-68; tchr. Huntington Beach Union High Sch. Dist., Calif., 1968-71; asst. to dean Sch. Music, Ind. U., Bloomington, 1973-77; pres. Indianaero, Inc., Bloomington, 1977—. Pres., Bloomington Town Theater, 1985; musician Bloomington Symphony Orch., 1975—. Ind. U. fellow, 1966. Mem. Aircraft Owners and Pilots Assn., Greater Bloomington C. of C., Phi Mu Alpha. Address: Indianaero Inc 2700 S Kirby Rd Bloomington IN 47401

DOYLE, WILLIAM JAY, II, business consultant; b. Cin., Nov. 7, 1928; s. William Jay and Blanche (Gross) D.; B.S., Miami U., Oxford, Ohio, 1949; postgrad. U. Cin., 1950-51, Xavier U., 1953-54, Case Western Res. U., 1959-60; m. Joan Lucas, July 23, 1949; children—David L., William Jay, III, Daniel L. Sales rep. Diebold, Inc., Cin., 1949-52, asst. br. mgr., 1953-57, asst. regional mgr., Cin., 1957-62, regional mgr., Cin., 1962-74; founder, chief exec. officer Central Bus. Systems & Security Concepts Co. div. Central Bus. Equipment Co., Inc., Cin., 1974—, dir. parent co. and divs.; dir. Perry Broadcasting Co., Beautiful Island Broadcasting Co., Sports Broadcasting Packagers Co.; mem. area controller's council Spacesaver Corp., 1985-86; speaker on bus systems, security concepts. Mem. Armstrong Chapel, Methodist ch., Indian Hill, Ohio. Mem. Bus. Systems and Security Mktg. Assn. (nat. dir. 1977-79, nat. pres. 1981-83), Nat. Assn. Accts. Republican. Clubs: Kenwood Country, Masons, Shriners. Contbr. articles to co. and trade publs.; developer new concepts in tng., cash and securities handling, other areas of bus. Home: 6250 S Clippinger Dr Cincinnati OH 45243 Office: 10839 Indeco Dr Cincinnati OH 45241

DRAEMEL, MICHAEL CHARLES, electric wholesale company executive; b. Fremont, Nebr., Sept. 5, 1946; s. Myron Charles and Donna Joan (Dunbar) D.; m. Pamela Kay Stunkel, Feb. 11, 1978; children—Darren Reese, Grif Lee. B.A., Midland Lutheran Coll., Fremont, 1968; M.A., Pepperdine U., Malibu, Calif., 1969. Tchr. high sch., Santa Ana, Calif., 1968-69; profl. golfer, 1971-74; div. mgr. Kriz-Davis Elec. Wholesale Co., Fremont, 1974—. Served with U.S. Army, 1969-71. Republican. Episcopalian. Home: 21318 Brentwood Rd Elkhorn NE 68022 Office: 810 S Schneider Fremont NE 68025

DRAGE, FLORENCE, social worker; b. Cleve., Sept. 10, 1923; d. Oliver and Rose Kraus; B.S. magna cum laude, Cleve. State U., 1976; M.S.S.A., Case Western Reserve U., 1979. Coordinator social services Sr. Citizens Council Lake County, Eastlake, Ohio, 1975-76; psychotherapist Lake County Mental Health Center, Mentor, Ohio, 1978; dir. aging program Catholic Service Bur. Lake County, Painesville, Ohio, 1979—; cons. sr. citizens area council community orgn., Lake County Area, 1978—. Mem. Nat. Assn. Social Workers, Acad. Cert. Social Workers, Am. Orthopsychiat. Assn., Case Western Res. U. Alumnae Assn., Cleve. State U. Alumnae Assn. Home: 2090 Country Club Dr Wickliffe OH 44092 Office: 455 Ameritrust Bldg 8 N State St Painesville OH 44077

DRAGNA, NICK CHARLES, chemical engineer; b. Beaumont, Tex., Oct. 2, 1938; s. Charles and Katherine (Danna) D.; m. Linda Ann Moss, June 13, 1965; children—Nick Charles, Paul Joseph. B.S. in Chem. Engring., Lamar U., Beaumont, 1963, M.B.A., 1968. Process engr. Olin Chem. Co., Beaumont, 1963-69; engring. mgr. C.J. Patterson Co., Kansas City, Mo., 1969-74; plant mgr. Adams Lab., Coal City, Ill., 1974-76; group leader Union Camp Corp., Savannah, Ga., 1976-80, tech. mgr., Dover, Ohio, 1980—. Served with USAFR, 1961-67. Mem. Am. Oil Chemist Soc. Republican. Roman Catholic. Lodges: Rotary (pres. 1985), Elks. Home: 161 Calico Dr Dover OH 44622 Office: Union Camp Corp Chem Div PO Box 220 Dover OH 44622

DRAGOSH, A. JAMES, chiropractor; b. Milw., Aug. 30, 1951; s. Anthony James and Pearl B. (Tobin) D.; m. Marilyn Rae Breitbach, Oct. 6, 1973; children—Ann, Chris. A.A., U. Wis.-Stevens Point, 1972; D.C., Palmer Coll. Chiropractic, Iowa, 1976; postgrad. Nat. Coll. Chiropractic. Diplomate Nat. Bd. Chiropractic. Practice chiropractic, Kaukauna, Wis., 1976—; head tennis coach Kaukauna High Sch., 1984—. Vice-pres. bd. adminstrn. Methodist Ch., Kaukauna, 1983, 84; bd. dirs. Thousand Island Environ. Ctr., Kaukauna, 1984—. Mem. Am. Chiropractic Assn., Wis. Chiropractic Assn., Northeast Dist. Chiropractic Assn. (pres. 1980). Lodge: Kiwanis (Kaukauna) (pres. 1982-83). Home: 510 Sanitorium Rd Kaukauna WI 54130 Office: 500 Lawe St Kaukauna WI 54130

DRAKE, CARL BIGELOW, JR., financial services company executive; b. St. Paul, July 15, 1919; s. Carl Bigelow and Louise Delano (Hadley) D.; B.A., Yale U., 1941; m. Charlotte Hannaford Day, Mar. 12, 1977; children by previous marriage—Carl Bigelow, Eleanor Drake McLear, Trevor R. Various field and underwriting positions St. Paul Fire & Marine Ins. Co., 1941-63, asst. to pres., 1963-66, v.p., asst. to pres., 1966-68, exec. v.p., 1968-69, pres., 1969-73; pres., chief exec. officer of parent co. The St. Paul Cos., Inc., 1973-78, chmn. bd., chief exec. officer, 1977-84, vice chmn., 1984—; dir. Honeywell, Inc., BMC Industries, Inc. Chmn., St. Paul United Way, 1974, now pres.; trustee Macalester Coll. Served to lt. comdr. USNR, 1942-45. Republican. Presbyterian. Clubs: Minnesota, Minneapolis, Somerset Country; Yale (N.Y.C.). Home: 1695 Delaware Ave Saint Paul MN 55118 Office: 385 Washington St Saint Paul MN 55102

DRAKE, GEORGE ALBERT, coll. pres., historian; b. Springfield, Mo., Feb. 25, 1934; s. George Bryant and Alberta (Stimpson) D.; A.B., Grinnell (Iowa) Coll., 1956; Fulbright scholar, U. Paris, 1956-57; A.B. (Rhodes scholar), Oxford U., 1959, M.A., 1963; B.D., U. Chgo., 1962, M.A., 1963, Ph.D. (Rockefeller fellow), 1965; LL.D., Colorado Coll., 1980; m. Susan Martha Ratcliff, June 20, 1960; children—Christopher George, Cynthia May, Melanie Susan. Instr. history Grinnell (Iowa) Coll., 1960-61, pres., 1979—; asst. prof., asso. prof., prof. history Colo. Coll., Colorado Springs, from 1964, acting dean of Coll., 1967-68, dean, 1969-73. Trustee Grinnell Coll., 1970-79, Penrose Hosp., 1976-79, Grinnell Gen. Hosp., from 1980. Nat. Endowment for Humanities fellow, 1974. Mem. Am. Hist. Assn., Am. Ch. History Soc.

DRAKE, GREGORY BYRLE, pharmacist; b. Cambridge, Ohio, Apr. 25, 1945; s. Earl Bond and Juanita Mae (Marks) D.; m. Nancy Lee Cooper, July 11, 1965; children—Brian Timothy, Carly Nicole. B.S., Ohio State U., 1968. Registered pharmacist, Ohio. Stocker, intern Terrace Pharmacy, Columbus, Ohio, 1964-68, pharmacist, 1968-80, co-owner, 1980—; co-owner Drake & Drake, Columbus, 1976—. Mem. Am. Pharm. Assn., Ohio State Pharm. Assn., Central Ohio Acad. Pharmacy, Real Estate Investors Assn., Robert Allen Nothing Down Group. Republican. Avocations: basketball; tennis. Home: 1400 Winchester So Rd Canal Winchester OH 43110 Office: Terrace Pharmacy 1546 Lockbourne Rd Columbus OH 43207

DRAKE, RICHARD FRANCIS, state senator; b. Muscatine, Iowa, Sept. 28, 1927; s. Frank and Fladys (Young) D.; student Iowa State U.; B.S., U.S. Naval Acad., 1950; m. Shirley Jean Henke; children—Cheryll Dee, Ricky Lee. Commd. ensign U.S. Navy, advanced through grades to lt. comdr., 1954; capt. minesweeper U.S.S. Crow; farmer, mgr., 1954—; mem. Iowa Senate, 1968—. Chmn., Young Republican Orgn. Iowa, 1954-56; adminstrv. asst. Muscatine County Rep. Com., 1956-57, chmn., 1958-66; 1st dist. chmn. Rep. party, 1966—; chmn. Nat. Task Force Rail Line Abandonment and Curtailment; chmn. states and rail problems Midwestern Council State Govts., 1978-79. Mem. Farm Bur. Lutheran. Clubs: Masons, Elks, Order Eastern Star. Office: State Senate Des Moines IA 50319*

DRAKE, RICHARD LEE, anatomy and cell biology educator, research scientist; b. Columbus, Ohio, Feb. 25, 1950; s. M. Richard and Nina Louise (Drake) D.; m. Cheryl Susan Brown, Dec. 23, 1972; children—Miles Richard, Jennifer Lyn. B.S., Mt. Union Coll., 1972; Ph.D., Ind. U., 1975. Postdoctoral fellow MIT, Cambridge, Mass., 1975-77; asst. prof. anatomy Med. Coll. Wis., Milw., 1977-81; asst. prof. anatomy and cell biology U. Cin. Coll. Medicine, 1981-85, assoc. prof. anatomy and cell biology, 1985—, dir. body donation program, 1982—, co-dir. freshman med. gross anatomy course, 1982-84, dir. freshman med. and grad. gross anatomy course, 1984—, course dissection coordinator, continuing edn. course for orthopaedic surgeons, 1983—. Mem. Mt. Union Coll. Alumni Council, Alliance, Ohio, 1980-81. Mem. AAAS, Am. Soc. Cell Biology, Am. Assn. Anatomists, Am. Diabetes Assn., Sigma Xi. Methodist. Contbr. articles, abstracts to profl. pubs.; research in field of insulin regulation of cellular metabolism. Office: Dept Anatomy and Cell Biology U Cin Coll Medicine 231 Bethesda Ave ML 521 Cincinnati OH 45267

DRAKE, THOMAS FRANCIS, ophthalmologist; b. Columbus, Ga., Aug. 28, 1942; s. Truman Guthred and Ruth Frances (Haggenjos) D.; m. Laurie Ann Humphrey, Apr. 27, 1968; children—Matthew Truman, Mary Ruth, Mark Howard. A.B. magna cum laude, Harvard U., 1964; M.D., Western Reserve U., 1968. Diplomate Am. Bd. of Ophthalmology. Intern Hennepin County Gen. Hosp., Mpls., 1968-69; resident in ophthalmology Wills Eye Hosp., Phila., 1969-72; practice medicine specializing in ophthalmology, Mankato, Minn., 1974—; sec. exec. com. Immanuel-St. Joseph's Hosp. of Mankato, Minn., 1976-77; sec., treas. Blue Earth County Med. Soc., Mankato, 1975-76. Soccer coach Mankato Area Recreation System, 1983, 84. Served to lt. commdr., USN, 1972-74. Fellow Minn. Acad. of Ophthalmology; mem. Am. Med. Assn., Minn. Med. Assn. Republican. Presbyterian. Avocations: Running; walking; pocket billiards; soccer; coins. Home: 23 Sumner Hill Rd Mankato MN 56001 Office: Security Office Bldg 510 Long St Suite 109 Mankato MN 56001

DRAKE, THOMAS LEE, safety engineer; b. Bay City, Tex., Sept. 22, 1945; s. Thomas Edwin and Jean Patricia (McLaren) D.; m. Rose Marie Russo, July 14, 1968; children—Patricia Jean, Christopher Lee. B.S., Southwest Tex. State U., 1971; M.S. U. Houston-Clear Lake City, 1979. Excorporeal perfusion supr. U. Tex. Med. Br., Galveston, 1971-75; safety supr. Amoco Chemicals Corp., Texas City, Tex., 1975-80; sr. safety engr. Standard Oil Co. (Ind.), Chgo., 1981—; coordinator product safety, 1983-85, sr. staff safety engr., 1985—; Group leader Crusade of Mercy, 1982. Served with U.S. Army, 1966-69. Mem. Am. Soc. Safety Engrs, Am. Soc. Extracorporeal Circulation Technologists (chmn.). Roman Catholic. Contbr. articles to prof. jours. Inventor cooling device for use in open heart surgery. Home: 2931 Alexander Circle Flossmoor IL 60422 Office: 200 E Randolph Dr MC 4906 Chicago IL 60601

DRAPER, WALTER DILLAWAY, librarian; b. Chgo., Sept. 9, 1928; s. Walter Dillaway and Jessie Durant (Johnston) D. B.A., Amherst Coll., 1950; M.Ed., Nat. Coll. Edn., 1954; M.A.L.S., U. Wis., 1965. Cert. tchr., Ill., Ind., Fla. Tchr. Burbank Sch., Oak Lawn, Ill., 1954-56; tchr. Dade County, Miami, Fla., 1956-57; tchr. Sch. City, Hammond, Ind., 1957-60; tchr. Bd. Edn., Chgo., 1966; asst. librarian Rio Grande Coll. (Oh.), 1967-68; reference librarian Pub. Library, Gary, Ind., 1969—. Choir mem. Chopin Chorus, Merrillville, Ind., 1973—, Millenium Chrous, Munster, Ind., 1976—. Winner Sawyer prize Amherst Coll. (Mass.), 1948. Mem. ALA, Ind. Library Assn. Office: Wildermuth Library 501 S Lake St Gary IN 46403

DRAYTON, V. MICHAEL, lawyer; b. Evansville, Ind., Sept. 13, 1953; s. Vernon M. and Julia M. (Slatton) D.; m. Janet L. Collings, Oct. 10, 1981; 1 child, Christopher Michael. B.A., Valparaiso U., 1976, J.D., 1980. Bars: Ind. 1980, Ill. 1980, U.S. Dist. Ct. (so. and no. dists.) Ind. 1980. Assoc. Sallwasser & McCain, La Porte, Ind., 1980—; adj. prof. law Ind. U., South Bend, 1985—. Mem. Am. Trial Lawyers Assn., ABA, Ind. Trial Lawyers Assn., Ind. Bar Assn., Ill. Bar Assn., LaPorte County Assn., La Porte City Bar Assn. Lodge: Lions. Office: Sallwasser and McCain 820 Jefferson Ave La Porte IN 46350

DREESEN, GLENN, photographer; b. Harvey, Ill., Aug. 22, 1936; s. Walter Charles and Glenora (Algoe) D.; m. Geraldine Wilcox, May 14, 1954 (div. 1963); children—Linda, Diane, Daniel; m. Karen Marie Flamini, Mar. 30, 1973. Student photography Profl. Photographers Am., Des Plaines, 1980-83. Owner, photographer Dreesen Photography, Harvey, Ill., 1959-73, Homewood, Ill., 1973—. Served with USN, 1953-57. Named Senator Jr. Chamber Internat., 1972. Mem. South Suburban Assn. Commerce and Industry (pres. 1984), Profl. Photographers Am. (nat. cert. chmn. 1985, numerous awards for photography 1980—), Assoc. Profl. Photographers Ill. (sec. 1984), No. Ill. Profl. Photographers Assn. (past pres.), Am. Soc. Photographers. Roman Catholic. Home: 18656 Dixie Hwy Homewood IL 60430 Office: Dreesen Photography 18 Dixie Hwy Homewood IL

DREESEN, SANDRA JEAN, social worker; b. Indpls., Jan. 3, 1941; d. Harold O'Dell and Aletha Margaret (Fischer) Vance; m. Robert Gerald Dreesen, July 19, 1963; children—Thomas Russell, Robin Lynn, Christy Rene. B.S.W., Ind. U., 1979, M.S.W., 1980. Cert., Acad. Cert. Social Workers. Intern, VA Med. Ctr., Indpls., 1979-80; dir. social service Tipton (Ind.) County Meml. Hosp., 1979-85; supr. M.S.W. cons. Div. Services for Crippled Children, 1985—. Bd. dirs., chmn. Tipton Council on Aging, 1984-85; mem. Tri-County bd. March of Dimes. VA grantee, 1979. Mem. Nat. Assn. Social Workers, Sigma Pi Alpha. Home: 5847 Bywood Dr Tipton IN 46220 Office: 141 S Meridian St Indianapolis IN

DREGER, PETER FRITZ, architect; b. Milw., Mar. 22, 1942; s. Herbert J. and Marjorie T.(Thiel) D.; m. Colleen Ann Nelson, Sept. 16, 1967; children—Kurt, Kelly. Lic. architect, Mich., Wis., Minn., Tex. Draftsman, Helmut Ajango & Assocs., Fort Atkinson, Wis., 1965-67, Waterman, Fuge, Krauss & Assocs., Fort Atkinson, 1967-69; architect Krueger, Shutter & Assocs., Madison, Wis., 1969-71, Bloomquist, Nelson & Assocs., Iron Mountain, Mich., 1971-73; prin. Dreger & Assocs., P.C., Ironwood, Mich., 1973—; instr. Gogebic Community Coll. Century mem. Lake Superior council Boy Scouts Am., 1980—; bd. dirs., pres. Gogebic Adult Retarded Citizens Assn., 1977—. Mem. Nat. Fedn. Ind. Bus., AIA, Mich. Soc. Architects (v.p. Upper Peninsula chpt.), Bldg. Ofcls. and Code Adminstrs. Internat., Nat. Council Archtl. Registrations Bds. Clubs: Gogebic County, Kiwanis, Elks (Ironwood). Home: 623 E Cloverland Dr Ironwood MI 49938

DRENNAN, PHYLLIS, nursing school dean; m. Robert H. Drennan. Diploma in Nursing, Jennie Edmundson Meml. Hosp., Council Bluffs, Iowa, 1948; Cert. in Instnl. Supervision and Teaching, U. Colo., 1953, M.S., 1961; B.S. in Nursing, U. Denver, 1961; Ph.D. in Ednl. Adminstrn., U. Iowa, 1974. Staff nurse, relief supr. VA Hosp., Denver, 1949-52; head nurse Colo. Gen. Hosp., U. Colo. Med. Ctr., Denver, 1953-56; supr. Swedish Hosp., Englewood, Colo., 1956-59; asst. adminstr. nursing, dir. in-service Galesburg State Research Hosp., Ill., 1961-62; curriculum dir., mem. faculty Cottage Hosp. Sch. Nursing, Galesburg, 1962-65; project dir. St. Joseph Hosp. Sch. Nursing, Denver, 1965-66, dir. nursing service, 1965-69; nursing coordinator Kirkwood Community Coll., Cedar Rapids, Iowa, 1969-72; asst. prof. Coll. Nursing, U. Iowa, Iowa City, 1971-72; dean, prof. Sch. Nursing, U. No. Colo., Greeley, 1974-81; dean, prof. U. Mo., Columbia Sch. Nursing, Columbia, 1981—; cons. and lectr. in field. Contbr. chpts. to books, articles to profl. jours. Mem. numerous civic and govtl. coms. in health and edn. U. Iowa fellow in program for mgmt. of ednl. change Coll. Edn., 1973-74. Mem. Nat. League Nursing (various coms.), Am. Nurses Assn. (various coms.), Midwest Alliance Nursing (nominating com. 1983-84), Midwest Nursing Research Soc., Council Grad. Edn. for Adminstrn. in Nursing, Am. Assn. History of Nursing, Am. Assn. Higher Edn., Am. Ednl. Research Assn. (spl. interest group ednl. research and devel. evaluators), Mo. State Nurses Assn., Mo. Pub. Health Assn., U. Colo. Alumni Assn., U. Denver Alumni Assn., U. Iowa Alumni Assn., U. Mo. Alumni Assn., Sigma Phi Omega, Sigma Theta Tau, Pi Lambda Theta. Address: S 215 Nursing Sch Bldg U Mo Columbia MO 65211

DRESCHER, JON WILLIAM, water pollution control professional, educator; b. Toledo, Sept. 15, 1950. A.S. in Civil Engring, U. Toledo, 1972, B.S. in Environ. Sci., 1974. Supt. water pollution control div. City of Bowling Green, Ohio, 1971—; instr. envirm. proctection U. Toledo, 1982—; chmn. Northwest Ohio Water Pollution Control Conf., 1984-85. Mem. Am. Water Works Assn., Bowling Green C. of C., Water Pollution Control Fedn. Office: Bowling Green Mcpl Utilities Box 388 Bowling Green OH 43402

DRESHFIELD, ARTHUR CHARLES, JR., research and development director; b. Kalamazoo, Nov. 9, 1929; s. Arthur C. and Nanette (Rosenberg) D.; m. Ardeth Miller, Apr. 7, 1957; children—Kenneth, Richard, Gerald. B.S. in Chemical Engring., U. Ill., 1951; M.S., Lawrence U., 1953, Ph.D., 1956. Engr. Scott Paper Co., Chester, Pa., 1955-57; research dir. Fibrebond Corp., Antioch, Calif., 1957-68, dir. product devel., San Francisco, 1968-72; mgr. devel., mgr. research and engring. Potlatch Corp., San Francisco. 1972-80, dir. research and devel., Colquet Minn., 1980—. Mem. Tech. Assn. Pulp and Paper Industry (sect. chmn. 1964). Avocations: Tennis; sailing. Office: Potlatch Research and Devel PO Box 510 Cloquet MN 55720

DRESMAL, JAMES EUGENE, insurance executive; b. Pitts., May 16, 1939; s. Eugene James and Grace Elizabeth (McClurg) Muirhead; m. Sept. 11, 1965 (div. Sept., 1984); m. Jacquelyn Elizabeth Carroll, Sept. 12, 1984. children—Todd Harris, Jennifer Jean. B.S. in Finance, U. Ill., 1962. Vice pres. dept. head Washington Nat. Ins. Co., Evanston, Ill., 1964—; chmn., dir. Washington Nat. Devel. Co., Evanston, 1975—; dir. Bus. Software Corp., Boulder, Colo., Evanston Bus. Investment Corp. Served with U.S. Army, 1962-64, Korea. Fellow Life Office Mgmt Assoc.; mem. Fin. Analyst Fedn., Investment Analysts Soc. Chgo. Republican. Presbyterian. Avocations: bowling; golf; fishing. Office: Washington Nat Ins Co 1630 Chicago Ave Evanston IL 60201

DRESSEL, IRENE EMMA RINGWALD, alcoholism and family therapist; b. Enderlin, N.D., Oct. 26, 1926; d. Albert William and Emma Anna Magdelena (Trapp) Ringwald; m. Clarence Irvin Dressel, Jr., Mar. 13, 1946 (div. Nov. 1972); 1 son, Keith Alan. Student pub. schs., Casselton, N.D. Cert. Master addiction counselor, N.D.; cert. chem. dependency counselor, Minn. Alcoholism counseling trainee Heartview Found., Mandan, N.D., 1974-75, family therapy intern, 1975-76, family counselor, 1976-77, supr. family mems. program, 1978; designer, supr. family program The Meadows, Wickenburg, Ariz., 1978-79; treatment programs cons., dir. consultation dept. Johnson Inst., Mpls., 1979-81; assoc. dir. chem. dependency unit Presbyn. Hosp., Oklahoma City, 1981-83; supr. adolescent counseling staff United Recovery Ctr., Grand Forks, N.D., 1983-85; dir. Irene Dressel Counseling, 1985—. cons. S.W. Inst. Alcohol Studies, Norman, Okla., Kans. Alcoholism Counselors Assn., Okla. Assn. Alcoholism and Drug Abuse; lectr. U. N.D., Grand Forks, N.D. Sch. Alcohol Studies. Mem. N.D. Alcoholism Counselors Assn., Nat. Alcoholism and Drug Addiction Counselors Assn., Am. Assn. Counseling and Devel., Nat. Mental Health Counselors Assn. Democrat. Lutheran.

DREW, WALTER HARLOW, paper company executive; b. Chgo., Feb. 23, 1935; s. Ben Harlow and Marion (Heineman) D.; m. Gracia McKenzie, June 27, 1959; children—Jeffrey McKenzie Drew, Martha Ward Drew. B.S., U. Wis.-Madison, 1957. Sales rep. Kimberly-Clark Corp., Cleve., 1960-64, nat. sales mgr., Chgo., 1964-74, div. n.p., gen. mgr., Kimberly, Wis., 1974-76, sr. v.p., Neenah, Wis., 1976—; dir. Twin City Savs., Neenah. Bd. dirs. Camp Manito-wish YMCA, Boulder Junction, Wis., 1983. Served as lt. (j.g.) USNR, 1957-59. Republican. Episcopalian. Club: North Shore Golf (pres. 1983-85). Lodge: Elks. Avocations: sailing, skiing, tennis, golf. Office: Kimberly-Clark Corp PO Box 2001 Neenah WI 54956

DREWS, ROBERT CARREL, physician; b. St. Louis, Sept. 9, 1930; s. Leslie C. and Sarah (Carrel) D.; m. Lorene Ruth Loewenguth, June 2, 1951; children—Pamela, Belinda, Carl, Jeanmarie. A.B., Washington U., St. Louis, 1952, M.D., 1955. Diplomate Am. Bd. Ophthalmology. Intern, St. Luke's Hosp., St. Louis, 1955-56; resident ophthalmology Washington U., St. Louis, 1956-58, chief resident, 1958-59, practice medicine specializing in ophthalmology, St. Louis, 1961—; lectr. ophthalmology Washington U. Sch. Medicine, 1956-66, asst. prof. clin. ophthalmology, 1966-74, assoc. prof., 1974-79, prof., 1979—; asst. ophthalmologist to med. staff Barnes Hosp. Group, St. Louis, 1961—; mem. attending staff Bethesda Gen. Hosp., St. Louis, 1958—; mem. courtesy staff St. Luke's Hosp., St. Louis, 1961-68, mem. staff, 1971—; mem. courtesy staff St. Mary's Hosp., St. Louis, 1961—; cons. Faith Hosp., St. Louis, 1961—; cons. Frisco Employees Hosp., St. Louis, 1961-68; attending ophthalmologist St. Louis Childrens Hosp., 1961—; attending staff ophthalmology St. Louis County Hosp., 1972—; supervising ophthalmologist div. welfare, State Mo., 1963-81; bd. dirs. St. Louis Soc. Blind, 1961—, sec., 1966-67, v.p., 1967-68, pres., 1968-70, 84—; cons. Spl. Sch. Dist. St. Louis County, Mo., 1967-80; cons. Nat. Eye Inst. Program Staff, Cataract Panel, The Nat. Plan for Vision Research, 1983—; mem. Am. Bd. Ophthalmology, 1985—. Mem. editorial bds. Ophtalmology Jour., 1984—, Pakistan Jour. Ophthalmology, 1984—. Mem. St. Louis Soc. Blind, St. Louis Med. Soc., Mo. State Med. Assn., AMA, St. Louis Ophthalmol. Soc., Assn. Research in Ophthalmology, Assn. Mil. Surgeons, So. Med. Assn., Mo. Ophthalmol. Soc., Contact Lens Assn. Ophthalmologists, Pan-Am. Assn. Ophthalmology, Soc. Mil. Ophthalmologists, Am. Intra-Ocular Implant Soc., Internat. Intraocular Implant Club, Am. Ophthalmol. Soc., Internat. Ophthalmic Microsurgery Study Group, others. Republican. Lutheran. Club: Washington Univ. Faculty. Avocation: Photography. Office: 211 N Meramec Ave Clayton MO 63105

DREZDZON, WILLIAM LAWRENCE, mathematics educator; b. Milw., Feb. 19, 1934; s. Edward Kenneth and Mildred Mary (Schneider) D.; B.S. in Math., St. Mary's U., 1957; M.S. in Math. (Esso Oil Co. fellow), Ill. Inst. Tech., 1964; m. Frances Anita Sikes; children—Gregory Francis, Andrea Louise. Tchr. math., chemistry St. Michael's High Sch., Chgo., 1957-59, Lane Tech. High Sch., Chgo., 1959-66; software design engr. A.C. Electronics div. Gen. Motors, Oak Creek, Wis., 1966-67; prof. math., chmn. dept. Kennedy-King Coll., Chgo., 1967-71; prof. math. and learning lab. coordinator Oakton Community Coll., Des Plaines, Ill., 1971—; vis. prof. U. New Orleans, 1982-84; cons. nat. calculus survey, 1975. NSF grantee, 1961-65; Chgo. Bd. Edn. grantee, summer 1964; NSF coop. program, 1971, 72; Chautauqua Course grantee, 1975—. Mem. Math. Assn. Am. (chmn. jr. coll. com. Ill. sect., 1971-74), No. Ill. Math. Assn. Community Colls. (founding pres., 1971, 72), Am. Math. Assn. Two-Yr. Colls. (chmn., 1975, pres. 1979), Nat., Ill. councils tchrs. math., Ill. Assn. Community Colls. (pres. 1979), Met. Mathematics Club of Gtr. Chgo., Adler Planetarium Soc., Ill. Assn. Personalized Learning Programs, Analytic Psychology Club of Chgo., Delta Epsilon Sigma. Regional editor Math. Assns. of Two-Year Colleges Jour., 1970—; author: Curriculum Guide of Transfer Courses for the Ill. Community College Board, 1974; Math. Research and Teaching Techniques, 1973, 76; contbr. articles to jours. Home: 1600 Ashland Ave Des Plaines IL 60016 Office: Oakton Community College 1600 E Golf Rd Des Moines IL 60016

DRIESBACH, WALTER CLARK, JR., sculptor, art educator; b. Cin., July 3, 1929; s. Walter Clark and Katherine Elizabeth (Howard) D.; m. Nancy Grannen, July 16, 1960 (div. Dec. 1980); children—Stephen, Madeline, Elizabeth. m. Susan Sanders, Sept. 3, 1982. Diploma Sch. Dayton Art Inst., 1952; student Art Acad. Cin., 1955-56. Tchr. sculpture Memphis Acad. Arts, 1956-58, Art. Acad. Cin., 1956, 58, 60, 70—, U. Dayton, 1966-72, Thomas More Coll., 1970-71, 1978—, U. Cin., 1980-81. Spl. exhibits include Huntington Gallery, Columbus, 1972, 76, Nationwide Gallery, Columbus, 1980, 81, 83; exhibited in group shows at Akron and Canton Art Inst., Ohio, 1960, Cin. Art Mus., 1972, 81; Contemporary Art Ctr., Cin., 1982, Cincinnati Zoo, 1983; represented in numerous pub. and pvt. collections. Contbr. articles to profl. jours. Served to sgt. U.S. Army, 1952-54. Mem. Cin. MacDowell Soc. Republican. Club: Cin. Carvers Guild. Home: 2541 Erie Ave Cincinnati OH 45208 Office: Art Acad of Cin Eden Park Cincinnati OH 45202

DRILL, LOIS H., retail jeweler; b. Cin., Oct. 10, 1934; d. Harry H. and Idah (Gelshof) Herrman; m. Edwin L. Drill, June 3, 1956; children—Ann Drill Bernstein; Robert Mark. Student U. Cin. Co-owner, mgr. The Two of Us Fine Jewelry Boutique, Cin. Mem. Alpha Zeta Omega Ladies Aux., Dental Aid Fund for Handicapped Children, Jewish Hosp. Ladies Aux., Adath Israel Sisterhood, Hadassah, Am. Women's Orgn., Ruth Lodge. Mem. Retail Jewelers Am. Republican.

DRIML, RICHARD LEE, music educator; b. Alliance, Nebr., May 11, 1935; s. Louis and Beulah (Sims) D.; m. Shirley Ann Case, Dec. 30, 1957; children—Richard Scott, Eva Lynn, Michele Louise, Darriel Louis. B.Music Edn., Kearney State Coll., 1962; M.S. in Edn., 1971. Instr. music Hildreth Pub. Schs., Nebr., 1963-67, Adams Central High Sch., Hastings, Nebr., 1967-69, Wood River Rural High Sch., Nebr., 1969-79; prof. music McCook Community Coll., Nebr., 1979—; contest judge, instrumental clinician various Nebr. conf. schs. Dir. Nebr. State Future Farmers Am. Band, 1974-79. Mem. NEA, Nat. Assn. Jazz Educators, Nebr. State Edn. Assn., Nebr. State Music Educators Assn., Mid-Plains Edn. Assn. (pres. 1982-83). Republican. Baptist. Lodge: Elks, Lions. Avocations: Auto restoration; golf; fishing. Home: 1312 W 1st St McCook NE 69001 Office: McCook Community Coll 1203 E 3d St McCook NE 69001

DRING, PETER BAILEY, naturalist, nature center administrator; b. Oak Park, Ill., Feb. 20, 1935; s. Nathaniel Hutchison and Mary Elizabeth (Bailey) D.; m. Carolyn Elizabeth Nieman, Sept. 7, 1957; children—Timothy, Cynthia, Andrew, Mark. B.S., DePaul U., 1957. Naturalist I, Cook County Forest Preserve Dist., 1957-60, naturalist II, aquatic biologist, 1960-70, naturalist III, dir. Red Schoolhouse Nature Ctr., 1970—; lectr. bird photography, 1978-81; bird bander U.S. Fish & Wildlife Service, 1960—. Mem. Ill. Audubon Soc. (past pres.), Inland Bird Banding Assn., William I. Lyon Bird Banding Council (past pres.). Roman Catholic. Clubs: Morton Arboretun Nature Study and Camera (past pres.), Chgo. Ornithol. Soc. (past pres.). Avocations: Photography; canoeing; swimming; birding. Office: Cook County Forest Preserve Dist 536 N Harlem Ave River Forest IL 60305

DRINKARD, DEBORAH ANN, educator; b. Tampa, Fla., Mar. 14, 1950; d. Albert Arlington and Lillian Elizabeth (Harper) D.; m. Barry Kent Yocom, Aug. 12, 1978; 1 dau., Samantha Elizabeth Drinkard Yocom. B.A. in English-Edn., U. South Fla., 1972; M.S. in Ednl. Guidance and Counseling, Memphis State U., 1974; M.S. in Indsl. Edn., Bemidji State U., 1982. Tchr., Tyronza (Ark.) High Sch., 1972-74, West Jr. High Sch., West Memphis, Ark., 1974-75; counselor Park Rapids (Minn.) High Sch., 1975-77; counselor Marshall (Minn.) High Sch., 1977-78; supr. spl. needs Bemidji (Minn.) Area Vocat. Tech. Inst., 1978—; cons. spl. needs programs, lectr. Mem. adv. bd. Community Mental Health Project, 1979; vice chmn. Congl. Awards Program Adv. Bd.; mem. steering com. Bemidji Area Women's Network, 1982. Mem. Am. Vocat. Assn., Minn. Vocat. Assn., Nat. Assn. Vocat. Spl. Needs Personnel, Minn. Vocat. Assn. Spl. Needs Personnel (exec. bd.), Minn. Edn. Assn., NEA, Phi Kappa Phi. Methodist. Home: Route 3 Box 804 Bemidji MN 56601 Office: Bemidji Area Vocat Tech Inst Roosevelt and Grant Sts Bemidji MN 56601

DRINKWINE, EDWARD ALLEN, insurance company official; b. Superior, Wis., Aug. 5, 1946; s. Clifford Milton and Ella Marie (Custer) Drinkwine; m. Mary Rose Koss, Jan. 25, 1969; children—Jennifer, Angela, Monica Joy. B.S. in Liberal Arts, Wis. State U., 1969. Field rep. Heritage Mut. Ins. Co., Milw. and Kenosha, Wis., 1969-72; resident field rep. Am. Family Ins. Co., Kenosha and Des Plaines, Ill., 1972-75, claim specialist, Indpls., 1975-76, dist. claim mgr., Schuaumburg, Ill., 1976-79, br. claim mgr., Rolling Meadows, Ill., 1979-81, regional claim mgr., Schaumburg, 1981—. Mem. Casualty Adjusters Assn. (past pres., dir.), Chgo. Claim Mgrs. Council (chmn. med. com.), Chgo. Bd. Underwriters, Ins. Inst. Chgo. (instr. 1978-80). Republican. Roman Catholic. Lodge: KC (recorder 1979-81) (Crystal Lake, Ill.). Office: Am Family Ins 1501 Woodfield Rd Suite 200W Schaumburg IL 60195

DRISCOLL, DANIEL DELANO, photographer, inventor, manufacturer; b. Williamsburg, Iowa, Mar. 19, 1946; s. Vincent Edmund and Hilda Gertrude (Schmidt) D.; student U. Iowa, 1964-66; B.A., Loras Coll., 1969; student Winona Sch. Profl. Photography, summers 1969-71: m. Constance Elizabeth Kelleher, Feb. 28, 1970 (div. 1983); children—Duree Danielle, Darren Daniel. With Hilda's Photography, Williamsburg, Iowa, 1969-72; owner Driscoll Gallery, Williamsburg, 1973—, Kent Studio, Iowa City, 1975-76; founder, owner, pres. Four Horsemen Ltd., 1985—; exhibited Epcot Ctr., 1984. Named Iowa Photographer of Yr., 1975, 76, 77; Iowa Fellow of Photography, 1975; Iowa Master of Photography of Yr., 1979; named Heart of Am. Photographer, 1976, 77; recipient Frank W. Medlar Meml. trophy for best portrait, 1975, 76, 77; Internat. Tetrahedron award Eastman Kodak Co., 1984. Mem. Minn. (sweepstakes winner 1973, 74), Nebr. (photographer of year 1974), Pa. (top out of state photographer 1974), Va., Am. (Master of Photography degree 1977) profl. photographers assns. Contbr. articles to profl. jours. Inventor in bioelectronics field. Home: 302 W State St Williamsburg IA 52361 Office: 302 W State St Williamsburg IA 52361

DRISCOLL, JAMES GEORGE, newspaper editor; b. Milw., Oct. 28, 1933; s. George James and Martha (Mattson) D.; m. Esther A. Foti, Oct. 5, 1957; children—Diane Carol, Amy Elizabeth. B.S., U. Wis.-Madison, 1955; M.A., U. Iowa, 1962; postgrad. (Ford Found. fellow) Columbia U., 1966-67. News reporter Gary Post-Tribune, 1957-60, Milw. Jour., 1960, Louisville Courier-Jour., 1962-66, Nat. Observer, Washington, 1967-74; editor Boca Raton News (Fla.), 1976-81; editor Post-Tribune, Gary, Ind., 1981—. Mem. Am. Soc. Newspaper Editors. Author Survival Tactics, 1973; Elections, 1968. Office: 1065 Broadway Gary IN 46402

DRISKELL, CLAUDE EVANS, dentist; b. Chgo., Jan. 13, 1926; s. James Ernest and Helen Elizabeth (Perry) D., Sr.; B.S., Roosevelt U., 1950; B.S. in Dentistry, U. Ill., 1952, D.D.S., 1954; m. Naomi Roberts, Sept. 30, 1953; 1 dau., Yvette Michele; stepchildren—Isaiah, Ruth, Reginald, Elaine. Practice dentistry, Chgo., 1954—. Adj. prof. Chgo. State U., 1971—; dean's aide, adviser black students Coll. Dentistry U. Ill., 1972—; dental cons., supervising dentist, dental hygienists supportive health services Bd. Edn., Chgo., 1974. Vice pres. bd. dirs. Jackson Park Highlands Assn., 1971-73. Served with AUS, 1944-46; ETO. Fellow Internat. Biog. Assn., Royal Soc. Health (Gt. Britain), Acad. Gen. Dentistry; mem. Lincoln Dental Soc. (editor), Chgo. Dental Soc., ADA, Nat. Dental Assn., (editor pres.'s newsletter; dir. pub. relations, publicity; recipient pres.'s spl. achievement award 1969) dental assns., Am. Assn. Dental Editors, Acad. Gen. Dentistry, Soc. Med. Writers, Soc. Advancement Anesthesia in Dentistry, Omega Psi Phi. Author: The Influence of the Halogen Elements upon the Hydrocarbon, and their Effect on General Anesthesia, 1962; History of Chicago's Black Dental Professionals, 1850-1983. Asst. editor Nat. Dental Assn. Quar. Jour., 1977—. Contbr. articles to profl. jours. Home: 6727 S Bennett Ave Chicago IL 60649 Office: 11139 S Halsted St Chicago IL 60628

DRISKELL, JANET SUE, educator; b. Joliet, Ill., June 11, 1958; d. Elmer and Maria Mercedes (Mignucci) D. A.A., Thornton Community Coll., 1977; A.S., 1978; B.S., Olivet Nazarene Coll., 1979, postgrad., 1981-82. Tchr. elem. sch., Portage (Ind.) Christian Schs., 1979—, pre-sch. dir., 1982—, dir. summer day camp, 1979, 80. Recipient Tchr. of Yr. award Tinley Park Ch. of the Nazarene, 1976, 77, Portage 1st Ch. of the Nazarene, 1983; named Most Dedicated Tchr., Portage Christian Schs., 1982-83. Mem. Ind. Reading Assn., Assn. Christian Schs. Internat., Kappa Delta Pi, Phi Theta Kappa. Republican. Mem. Ch. of Nazarene. Home: 5650 Willowdale Ln Apt 154 Portage IN 46368 Office: 3134 Swanson Rd Box 460 Portage IN 46368

DROGUE, KERRIE LYNETTE, retail store executive; b. Indpls., Aug. 11, 1948; d. Donald Francis and Marjorie Joyce (Riley) Drogue; m. Gary Lynn Anderson, Dec. 17, 1981. Student U. Minn., 1966-70. Bookkeeper, Jonathan Devel., Chaska, Minn., 1970-71; owner, ptnr. Black Swan Country Store, Mpls., 1971—. Mem. Minn. Antique Dealers Assn. (sec. 1973-74), Nat. Assn. Women Bus. Owners. Office: Black Swan Country Store 3020 W 50th St Minneapolis MN 55410

DROPPS, EDWIN ARTHUR, JR., development company executive, builder, real estate broker; b. Sauk Rapids, Minn., Oct. 19, 1936; s. Edwin Arthur and Ella Elizabeth (Carlson) D.; m. Valerie J. Theis, Dec. 18, 1954; children—Edwin, Michael, Dianne, Chris. Painter, Bartlett & Dropps, Minn., 1957-63; v.p., builder White Oak Builders, Minn., 1963-68; pres., builder, broker Pine Tree Builders, Minn., 1968-79; pres., developer Cypress Devel. Co., Minn., 1979—; wage and benefit negotiator Mpls. Home Builders, 1974, 76; treas., sec. Core Properties Inc., Mpls., 1985; ptnr. Carlson Dropps & Assoc., Mpls., 1980—, Roseland Devel., Mpls., 1973—. Bd. dirs. Camp New Hope, Megregor, Minn., 1985. Mem. Mpls. Builders Assn. Award of Excellence 1970, Reggie award 1974, Anoka Bd. Realtors, Mpls. Model "A" Club. Lutheran. Lodges: Lions (pres. Mounds View chpt. 1968-69, sec. Ham Lake chpt. 1980-83). Avocations: old autos; sports. Office: Cypress Devel Co Inc 8535 Central Ave Blaine MN 55434

DROTNING, PHILLIP THOMAS, retired oil company official, business and government consultant; b. Deerfield, Wis., July 4, 1920; s. Edward Clarence and Martha (Skaar) D.; student U. Wis., 1937-41; m. Loretta Jayne Taylor, Nov. 3, 1964; children—Meredith Anne, Maria Kristina, Misya Kerri. Reporter, Wis. State Jour., Madison, 1943-44; editorial page writer Milw. Jour., 1944-45; freelance author, 1945-47; exec. sec. to gov. Wis., 1948-55; v.p. Northwest Airlines, Inc., 1956-61; spl. asst. to adminstr. NASA, Washington, 1961-65; exec. communications cons. Standard Oil Co. (Ind.), 1965-66; mgr. communications Am. Oil Co., Chgo., 1967-68; dir. urban affairs Amoco Corp., Chgo., 1968-72, dir. pub. affairs ops., 1973, dir. corp. social policy, 1973-85; ret., 1985; vis. fellow Am. Enterprise Inst. for Pub. Policy Research, Washington, 1985—; cons. to bus. and govt., 1985—. Bd. dirs., first v.p. Child Care Assn. Ill., 1973-76, pres., 1976-78; bd. dirs. T.R.U.S.T., Inc., 1976—, pres., 1979-81. Served with USMCR, 1941-43. Mem. Pub. Relations Soc. Am., Nat. Assn. Mfrs. (chmn. urban affairs com. 1969-71), Nat. Minority Purchasing Council (dir. 1972-84, pres. 1972-77). Clubs: National Press, International, Federal City (Washington); Plaza (Chgo.). Author: A Guide to Negro History in America, 1968; Black Heroes in our Nation's History, 1969; A Job with a Future in the Petroleum Industry, 1969; Up from the Ghetto, 1970; New Hope for Problem Drinkers, 1977; Taking Stock: A Woman's Guide to Corporate Success, 1977; Putting the Fun in Fundraising, 1979; How To Get Your Creditors off Your Back without Losing Your Shirt, 1979; You Can Buy a Home Now, 1982; editorial advisory bd. The Chicago Reporter, 1971-85. Contbr. numerous articles to pubs. Home: 400 N Washington Rd Lake Forest IL 60045 Office: 360 E Randolph Dr Chicago IL 60601

DRUCKER, RICHARD HARRIS, lawyer, restaurant owner; b. Cleve., Sept. 22, 1957; s. Marvin and Sandra Lee (Harris) D. B.A., Ohio State U., 1978; J.D., Cleve. State U., 1981. Bar: Ohio 1981, U.S. Dist. Ct. (no. dist.) Ohio 1981, U.S. Ct. Appeals (6th cir.) 1981. Mem. Drucker, Drucker and Drucker, Cleve., 1981—. Recipient Trustee award Legal Aid., Cleve., 1982. Mem. ABA, Ohio Bar Assn., Greater Cleve. Bar Assn., Cuyahoga County Bar Assn. Jewish. Home: 2628 Mayfield Rd Cleveland Heights OH 44106 Office: Drucker Drucker and Drucker Suite 1414 75 Public Sq Cleveland OH 44113

DRUEN, WILLIAM SIDNEY, lawyer; b. Farmville, Va., May 5, 1942; s. William Gills and Minnie (Kessler) D.; m. Janet Elizabeth Ward, Dec. 21, 1969; children—Courtney Paige, William Sidney II. B.A., Hampden Sydney Coll., 1964; LL.B., U. Va., 1968. Bar: Ohio 1970. Spl. counsel Govs. Office State of Va., Richmond, 1968-70; with legal dept. Nationwide Ins. Co., Columbus, Ohio, 1970-82, v.p., assoc. gen. counsel, 1982—; ptnr. Wagner, Schmidt, McCutchan, Hank & Birkhimer, 1970-76, McCutchan, Schmidt, Birkhimer & Druen, 1976—. Pres. bd. trustees German Village Found., 1983—. Mem. Am. Land Title Assn., Ohio Bar Assn., Va. Bar Assn., Ohio Land Title Assn., Columbus Bar Assn. Republican. Home: 85 E Deshler Ave Columbus OH 43206 Office: Nationwide Ins Co Office of Gen Counsel One Nationwide Plaza Columbus OH 43216

DRUMMOND, CHARLES HENRY, III, ceramic engineer, educator; b. Greensboro, N.C., Aug. 24, 1944; s. Charles Henry and Evelyn Annette (Meeker) B.S. in Ceramic Engring., Ohio State U., 1969, B.Engring. Physics, M.S., 1969, M.S., Harvard U., 1970, Ph.D., 1974. Asst. prof. ceramic engring. Ohio State U., Columbus, 1974-80, assoc. prof., 1980—; dir. Annual Conf. of Glass Problems, Columbus, 1974—. Editor: (proceedings) Ann. Glass Problems Conf. Contbr. articles to profl. jours. Mem. Am. Ceramic Soc., Keramos, Nat. Inst. Ceramic Engrs., Ceramic Edn. Council, Tau Beta Pi. Office: Dept Ceramic Engring 2041 College Rd Columbus OH 43210

DRUSHAL, JEFF DOUGLAS, lawyer; b. Wooster, Ohio, June 14, 1953; s. J. Garber and Dorothy Loree (Whitted) D.; m. Bonnie Lee Casper, Sept. 1, 1973; children—J. Benjamin, J. Adam. B.A., Northwestern U., 1974; J.D. summa cum laude, Ohio State U., 1977. Bar: Ohio 1977, U.S. Dist. Ct. (no. dist.) Ohio 1977, U.S. Tax Ct. 1980, U.S. Ct. Appeals (6th cir.) 1979, U.S. Supreme Ct. 1981. Law clk. U.S. Ct. Appeals (6th Cir.), Cleve., 1977-79; mem. firm Critchfield, Critchfield, Critchfield & Johnston, Wooster, Ohio, 1979—. Contbr. articles to profl. jours. Elder, Westminster Presbyn. Ch., 1984—. Mem. ABA, Ohio Bar Assn., Order of the Coif. Republican. Lodge: Rotary (dir. 1983—). Avocations: Writing; reading; golf; racquetball. Home: 1137 Forest Dr Wooster OH 44691 Office: Critchfield Critchfield Critchfield & Johnston 225 N Market St PO Box 488 Wooster OH 44691

DRUTCHAS, GREGORY G., lawyer; b. Detroit, June 2, 1949; s. Gilbert Henry and Elaine Marie (Rutkowski) D.; m. Cheryl Aline June 9, 1973; children—Gillian Aline, Gregory Ryan. A.B., U. Mich., 1970; J.D., Duke U., 1973. Bar: Mich. 1973, U.S. Dist. Ct. (ea. dist.) Mich. 1974, U.S. Ct. Appeals (6th cir.) 1978, U.S. Supreme Ct. 1984. Assoc. Kitch & Suhrheinrich, P.C. (now Kitch, Saurbier, Drutchas, Wagner & Kenney, P.C.), Detroit, 1973-78, prin., 1978—; lectr., seminar presenter on med. profl. liability. Served to capt., USAFR, 1972-82. Mem. State Bar Mich., Detroit Bar Assn., Oakland County Bar Assn., Mich. Defense Trial Counsel, Mich. Soc. Hosp. Attys., Am. Acad. Hosp. Attys. Republican. Unitarian. Club: Detroit Golf. Author: (with others) Michigan Court of Appeals Practice: A Primer, 1981; contbr. articles to profl. publs. Home: 1386 Lakeside St Birmingham MI 48009 Office: One Woodward Ave Detroit MI 48226

DRUYAN, MARY ELLEN, biochemist, educator; b. Washington, July 14, 1938; d. Theodore and Anne Beverly (Sherr) Spector; m. Robert Druyan, Nov. 25, 1961 (div. 1979); children—Lara Catherine, Kira Elizabeth; m. Duane Merlin Mills, Apr. 25, 1981. B.A., Wellesley Coll., 1960; M.S., Tufts U., 1962; Ph.D., U. Chgo., 1972. Postdoctoral Argonne Nat. Lab., Ill., 1972-74; research chemist Hines VA Hosp., Ill., 1974-76; asst. prof. biochemistry Loyola U., Maywood, Ill., 1976-82, assoc. prof., 1982—. Contbr. research articles to profl. jours. and chpt. to book. Mem. AAU, Theater of Western Springs, NIH (study sect.), Am. Chem. Soc., AAAS, Am. Crystallographic Assn., Am. Assn. Dental Schs. (biochem. sect., nutrition sect.), Am. Assn. Dental Research, Sigma Xi. Avocations: Theater; antiquing; tennis. Home: 641 W 58th St Hinsdale IL 60521 Office: Loyola Univ Med Ctr 2160 S 1st Ave Maywood IL 60153

DRYDEN, JAMES FREDERICH, financial services company executive; b. Chgo., Aug. 2, 1943; s. Fredrick John and Vicki V. (Cichowski) D.; m. Diane C. Dryden, Nov. 22, 1965; 1 dau., Jill Therese. B.B.A., U. Chgo., 1966. Cons., Daniel D. Howard & Assocs., Chgo., 1966-69; dist. mgr. Ideal Toy Corp., N.Y.C., 1969-76; dist. mgr. Creative Playthings, div. of CBS, N.Y.C., 1976-79; regional sales mgr. Airway Luggage, Ellwood City, Pa., 1979-81; v.p. Comp-U-Check, Inc., Southfield, Mich., 1981—. Office: Comp-U-Check Inc 16250 Northland Dr Southfield RI 48075

DUANE, WILLIAM CHARLES, JR., physician, researcher; b. Mankato, Minn., Mar. 16, 1944; s. William Charles and Susan Mary (Fowler) D.; m. Harriet Campe, Oct. 13, 1980; children—Benjamin, Anna. B.A., Carleton Coll., 1966; M.D., U. Minn., 1970. Diplomate Am. Bd. Internal Medicine. Intern U. Minn. Hosps., Mpls., 1970, resident, 1971-72, 74-75; clinical assoc. NIH, Phoenix, 1972-74; research assoc. VA Hosp., Mpls., 1975-77, mem. staff, 1977—; asst. prof. U. Minn., Mpls., 1975-80, assoc. prof. medicine, 1980—. Contbr. articles to profl. jours. Served to surgeon USPHS, 1972-74. Grantee VA, 1975—, NIH, 1978—, 82-85. Mem. N.Y. Acad. Sci., Am. Gastroenterological Assn., Am. Fed. Clin. Research, Am. Soc. Clin. Investigation. Avocations: Woodworking; golf. Office: VA Medical Ctr 111D 54th St & 48th Ave S Minneapolis MN 55417

DUBAY, SANDRA LOUISE, author; b. Battle Creek, Mich., Oct. 6, 1954; d. Harry Andrew and Reatha Lenore (Bingham) DuB. A.A., Wastenaw Community Coll., Ann Arbor, Mich., 1974; B.A. in Psychology, U. Mich., 1976. Freelance writer, 1978—; owner Just Books, 1984—. Author: Mistress of the Sun King, 1980; Flame of Fidelity, 1981; The Claverleigh Curse, 1982; Fidelity's Flight, 1983; Whispers of Passion, 1984; In Passion's Shadow, 1984; Crimson Conquest, 1984; Where Passion Dwells, 1985; By Love Beguiled, 1985. Methodist. Home: 801 Bradfield St Bay City MI 48706

DUBE, EILEEN MARIE, educator; b. Akron, Ohio, May 23, 1937; d. Patrick Leo and Hazel May (Dishon) McAleese; m. Darrell Eugene Dube, Sept. 17, 1960; 1 son, Brent Alexander. B.A. in English, U. Akron, 1959. Tchr., Buchtel High Sch., Akron Pub. Schs., 1959-60, Central-Hower High Sch., 1965-73, sr. advanced placement English tchrs. East High Sch., 1973—; advisor yearbook, literary mag., Quill and Scroll. Jennings Found. scholar, 1982-83. Mem. Nat. Council Tchrs. English, Greater Akron Tchrs. English, Akron Edn. Assn., Ohio Council Tchrs. English and Language Arts, Phi Mu. Republican. Roman Catholic. Lodge: Ancient Order of Hibernians in Am. (Akron). Club: Akron U. Buchtelles. Office: East High Sch 80 Brittain Rd Akron OH 44305

DUBERT, MARY JULIA, social worker; b. Dubuque, Iowa, July 14, 1949; d. Leo J. and Margaret M. (Garvey) Dubert. B.A., U. Iowa, 1975, M.S.W., 1976. Juvenile parole social worker Dubuque County Dept. Social Services, 1976-77; families and children social worker Tama County Dept. Social Services, Toledo, Iowa, 1977; family therapist Dist. IV Dept. Social Services, Bettendorf, Iowa, 1977-78; adult services supr. Scott County Dept. Social Services, Davenport, Iowa, 1978-82, supr. social work treatment and diversion, 1982—; practicum instr. Sch. Social Work, U. Iowa, Iowa City; mem. Adult Protective Services Com., Elderly Services Task Force; mem. evaluation com. Vis. Nurses Assn., Homemaker Services of Scott County. Sec., chmn. loan com. Inner City Devel. Corp.; mem. allocations panel United Way. Democrat. Roman Catholic. Home: 509 Elm Burlington IA 52601 Office: 428 Western Ave Davenport IA 52801

DUBETS, JEFFREY JOSEPH, computer materials management/service company specialist; b. Morristown, N.J., Mar. 30, 1953; s. Joseph Paul and Anny Maria (Rademacher) DuB. B.S. in Speech Pathology and Audiology, Bradley U., Peoria, Ill., 1974, B.B.A., 1975, M.A. in Learning Disabilities, 1977. Cert. speech pathologist. Learning edn. disabilities specialist Macon-Piatt County Spl. Edn. Coop, Decatur, Ill., 1977-80; learning disabilities specialist Aero Spl. Edn. Coop., Burbank, Ill., 1980-83, Glenview Pub. Schs., Ill., 1983-84; computer edn. specialist, mgr. edn. Enterprise Systems, Inc., Bannockburn, Ill., 1984—; instr. Chgo. State U., 1983-84; computer cons., speaker in field. Contbr. articles to profl. publs. Mem. Chgo.-Andersonville Council, Chgo., 1983—. Mem. Nat. Council for Exceptional Children, Ill. Council for Exceptional Children, Am. Mgmt. Assn., Phi Kappa Phi, Sigma Alpha Eta., Roman Catholic. Avocations: education research with computers; skiing; racquetball. Home: 1428 W Farragut Ave #2 Chicago IL 60640 Office: Enterprise Systems Inc 2333 Waukegan Rd Suite E100 Bannockburn IL 60015

DUBIN, ARTHUR DETMERS, architect; b. Chgo., Mar. 14, 1923; s. Henry and Anne (Green) D.; m. Lois Amtman, Mar. 10, 1951 (dec. Sept. 1980); children—Peter Arthur, Polly Louise Dubin Pollak; m. 2d, Phyllis Vollen Burman, Nov. 27, 1981; stepchildren—Garry Arthur, Jill Meredyth, David Yale, Eric Vollen. Student Lake Forest Coll., 1943-44; B.Arch., U. Mich., 1949. Architect, ptnr. Dubin & Dubin, architects and engrs., Chgo., 1950-65, Dubin, Dubin & Black, architects and engrs., 1965-66, Dubin, Dubin, Black & Moutoussamy, 1966-78, Dubin, Dubin & Moutoussamy, 1978—; v.p. DDBM, Inc., constrn. mgmt. cons., 1975—; v.p., dir. 7337 South Shore Drive Corp., 1958-80; ptnr. 7345 South Shore Drive Corp., 1960-80; mem. adv. com. Amtrak, 1972—; gen. ptnr. 340 Wellington Assocs., 1962-73; mem. Ill. Commn. on High Speed Rail Transit, 1966-68; mem. Met. Housing and Planning Council Chgo.; mem. Nat. Council Archtl. Registration Bds., 1971—; speaker at confs., U.S. and France; hon. research assoc. Smithsonian Instn., 1975. Prin. works include govtl. bldgs., rail transit stas. and transp. facilities, mil. installations, hotels, banks, indsl. plants, schs. and colls., hosps., housing and urban renewal planning; author: Some Classic Trains, 1964; More Classic Trains, 1974; author-editor for N.Am.: The Great Trains, 1973; contbr. articles to mags. Chmn. Civic Beautification Com., Highland Park, Ill., 1965-74; life mem. Art Inst. Chgo.; trustee NORTRAM (transp. dist.), Des Plaines, Ill., 1980—. Served with inf. U.S. Army, 1943-46. Decorated Bronze Star with cluster, Purple Heart. Mem. AIA, Am. Pub. Transit Assn., Ry. and Locomotive Hist. Soc. (dir. 1960—), Train Collectors Assn. Clubs: Cliff Dwellers (dir. 1972-75), Builders (pres. 1970-71, dir. 1970—), Arts, Mchts. and Mfrs. (Chgo.). Office: 221 N La Salle St Chicago IL 60601*

DUBOIS, MARK BENJAMIN, utility official; b. Peoria, Ill., Sept. 27, 1955; s. Benjamin John and Marjorie Abigail (Black) DuB.; m. Jeri Rene Simmons, May 24, 1975; 1 son, Benjamin Robert. B.S. with high distinction, U. Ariz., 1977; M.A., U. Kans., 1981. Research asst. State Biol. Survey Kans., Lawrence, 1978-81; systems programmer Central Ill. Light Co., Peoria, 1982-84, operating software supr., 1984-85, gen. supr. data processing ops. sect., 1985—. Bd. dirs. Spl. People Encounter Christ, Peoria, 1982-83; treas. Religious Edn. Activities for Community Handicapped, Peoria, 1978-81. Mem. AAAS, Internat. Union for Study Social Insects, Central States Entomol. Soc., Kans. Acad. Sci., Soc. Systematic Zoology, Sigma Xi. Contbr. articles on entomology and personal computer software to profl. jours. Home: 208 Oakwood Circle Washington IL 61571 Office: Central Illinois Light Co 300 Liberty St Peoria IL 61602

DUBROFF, WILLIAM, steel company executive; b. Johannesburgh, South Africa, Oct. 1, 1937; s. Alexander E. and Diana (Leibow) DuB.; m. Barbara Lee Paley, June 11, 1960; 1 child, Richard Andrew. B.A. in Chemistry, Columbia U., 1961, M.S. in Metallurgy, 1963, Ph.D. in Metallurgy, 1967. Project dir. NASA, Columbia U., N.Y.C., 1965-67; research engr. Inland Steel Co., East Chicago, Ind., 1967-72, supervising research engr., 1972-76, asst. dir. research, 1976-80, assoc. dir. research, 1980-83, dir. research, 1983-85; prin. scientist EG&G Idaho, Inc., Idaho Falls, 1985—; lectr. tech. soc. coms. Patentee in field. Editor Transaction Iron and Steel Soc., 1984—. Advisor Explorer post 299, Calumet council Boy Scouts Am., asst. scoutmaster troop 551. Served with USN, 1956-58. Am. Soc. Metals scholar, N.Y.C., 1962-63, Campbell fellow Columbia U., 1963-64. Mem. Am. Soc. Metals, AIME, Sigma Xi. Home: 9313 Walnut Dr Munster IN 46321 Office: E G & G Idaho Inc 9313 Walnut Dr Munster IN 46321

DUCHE, GREGORY LEE, pharmacist, educator; b. Warren, Ohio, Dec. 3, 1947; s. George Paul and Rose Mary (Cooper) D.; m. Nancy Jo Van Schoyck, June 8, 1980; children—Kathryn Weber, Amy Lynn, Melissa Anne. B.S. in Microbiology, Ohio State U., 1971, B.S. in Pharmacy, 1974, M.S. in Pharmacy/Hosp. Adminstrn., 1982. Registered pharmacist, Ohio. Pharmacist/mgr. Neil Pharmacy, Columbus, Ohio, 1974-78; pharmacist Riverside Meth. Hosp., Columbus, 1978-80, supr., 1980—; cons. Family Med, Inc., Columbus, 1984—; asst. clin. prof. Ohio State U., Columbus, 1982—. Founding mem. Substance Abuse: Voice for Youth, 1984. Gray Drug scholar, 1973; research grantee. Mem. Am. Soc. Hosp. Pharmacists, Ohio Soc. Hosp. Pharmacists, Phi Delta Chi, Rho Chi. Republican. Methodist. Lodge: Lions (sec. 1984—) (Columbus). Avocations: home remodeling/repair; reading; golf; gardening. Home: 3623 Lieb St Columbus OH 43214 Office: 3535 Olentangy River Rd Columbus OH

DUDA, RICHARD MICHAEL, osteopathic physician; b. Toledo, Aug. 6, 1942; s. Michael Eugene and Margaret Julia (Veselka) D.; m. Deborah Ann Kosakowski, Jan. 14, 1972; children—Richard Michael, Bridget Ann. Student U. Toledo, 1960-63; D.O., Chgo. Coll. Osteo. Medicine, 1967. Intern Doctors Hosp., Columbus, Ohio, 1967-68, Mercy Hosp., Toledo, 1970-71; resident Med. Coll. Ohio, 1971-74; practice specializing in emergency medicine, Toledo, 1974—; dir. emergency services Mercy Hosp., Toledo, 1981—; pres. Mercy Emergency Services, Inc., Toledo, 1981—, Phillips Med. Ctr., Inc., 1984—, Demms Co., 1984—; mem. Monroe Med. Control Bd., Emergency/Med. Service Council, 1985—. Mem. Lucus County (Ohio) Drug Abuse Adv. Bd.; bd. dirs. Med. Direction Lucus County, 1984—; mem. U.S. Senatorial Bus. Adv. Bd.; co-founder, mem. Republican Presdl. Task Force. Served as capt. M.C., U.S. Army, 1967-70. Mem. Am. Coll. Emergency Physicians, AMA, Toledo Acad. Medicine, Soc. Law and Medicine, Ohio State Med. Assn. Roman Catholic. Club: Exchange. Office: 2200 Jefferson Ave Toledo OH 43624

DUDARYK, SHARON DIANN, educator; b. Detroit, Aug. 29, 1945; d. Marion and Nettie (Shishka) Slimak; student Detroit Conservatory of Music, 1965; M.Ed. in Counseling, Wayne State U., 1971; postgrad. Oakland Community Coll.; m. Peter Dudaryk, Sept. 1, 1965 (div., 1975); children—Jeffrey Michael Dudaryk, Linda Helen Dudaryk, Patricia Marie Kelly. Vol. remedial tchr. Royal Oak Twp., 1966; elem. tchr., Detroit, 1967—, kindergarten tchr. Van Zile Elem. Sch., 1978—, adult edn. tchr. Osborn High Sch., 1977; counselor Stellwagen Elem. Sch., 1984. Active family workshops, PTA, Founders Soc. Detroit Inst. of Art, LWV, 1978-79; v.p. Bovenschen Sch. PTO, 1983-84; leader Oakland County 4-H. Served as career counselor USNR, 1979—. Mem. Detroit Fedn. Tchrs., Met. Detroit Reading Council, Warren Assn. Gifted and Talented, Detroit Guidance Assn., LWV, Nat. Pilots Assn., Mich. Assn. Computer Users in Learning, AAUW, Mich. Farm Bur., Nat. Fedn. Republican Women, Wayne State U. Alumni Assn., Navy League. Eastern Orthodox. Club: Federated Russian Orthodox. Condr. research in nutrition. Home: 2725 Saratoga Troy MI 48084 Office: 2915 E Outer Dr Detroit MI 48234

DUDEK, ALFRED, pharmacist; b. Youngstown, Ohio, Apr. 6, 1922; s. Frank and Francis (Sitarchik) D. B.S. in Pharmacy, Ohio No. U., 1952. Registered pharmacist. Pharmacist, Syms Drug, Youngstown, 1952—. Served with U.S. Army, 1942-45, Asia, Pacific. Mem. Ohio State Pharm. Assn., Eastern Ohio Pharm. Assn. Roman Catholic. Avocations: Home movies; video; golf. Home: 940 Larkridge Youngstown OH 44512

DUDEK, CHARLES JOSEPH, marketing executive; b. Chgo., Oct. 31, 1955; s. George and Adeline Lorraine (Stodolny) D.; m. Margaret Mary Murphy, Apr. 1, 1978. B.S., DePaul U., 1977, M.B.A., 1982. Sales rep. DuKane Corp., St. Charles, Ill., 1980-81; market research analyst Am. Roller Co., Bannockburn, Ill., 1981-84, mktg. service mgr., 1984—. Served to 1st lt. U.S. Army, 1977-80. Decorated Army Commendation medal. Mem. Am. Mktg. Assn., Midwest Planning Assn. Republican. Roman Catholic. Avocations: Sailing; photography; golf. Home: 849 Appletree Ln Deerfield IL 60015 Office: Am Roller Co 2223 Lakeside Dr Bannockburn IL 60015

DUDLEY, DURAND STOWELL, librarian; b. Cleve., Feb. 28, 1926; s. George Stowell and Corinne Elizabeth (Durand) D.; B.A., Oberlin Coll., 1948; M.L.S., Case Western Res. U., 1950; m. Dorothy Woolworth, July 3, 1954; children—Jane Elizabeth, Deborah Anne. Librarian, Marietta (O.) Coll. Library, 1953-55, Akron (O.) Pub. Library, 1955-60; librarian Marathon Oil Co., Findlay, O., 1960-74, sr. law librarian, 1974—. Mem. Spl. Libraries Assn., Am. Assn. Law Libraries. Presbyterian (deacon). Home: 865 Maple Ave Findlay OH 45840 Office: Marathon Oil Co 539 S Main St Findlay OH 45840

DUDLEY, ROBERT STANLEY, rubber manufacturing company executive; b. Shanghai, China, Oct. 18, 1925; s. Richard and Mona (Edwards) D.; m. Mary Stewart, Dec. 26, 1953; children—Jane, Moira, Jim, Shelagh. M.Sc. in Chem. Engring., U. B.C., 1951. With Can. Synthetic Rubber Ltd. (now Polysar Ltd.), Sarnia, Ont., Can., 1951—, mgr. bus. devel., 1964-68, gen. mgr. latex, 1968-69, v.p. European ops., 1969-71, group v.p. rubber and latex, 1971-79, exec. v.p. ops., 1979-81, pres., chief operating officer, 1981-83, pres., chief exec. officer, 1983—. Mem. Can. Chem. Producers Assn. (dir.), Chem. Mfrs. Assn. (U.S.), Soc. Chem. Industry, Chem. Inst. Can., Can. Soc. Chem. Engring. (award in indsl. practice 1981), Profl. Engrs. Province Ont. Office: Polysar Ltd 201 Front St N Sarnia ON N7T 7V1 Canada*

DUDUKOVIC, MILORAD P., chemical engineering educator, consultant; b. Beograd, Yugoslavia, Mar. 25, 1944; came to U.S., 1968; s. Predrag R. and Melita Maria (Stancl) D.; m. Judith Ann Reiff, Dec. 27, 1969; children—Aleksandra Anne, Nicole Maria. B.S. in Engring., U. Beograd, 1967; M.S., Ill. Inst. Tech., 1970, Ph.D., 1972. Research ingr. Process Design Inst., Beograd, 1967-68; instr. Ill. Inst. Tech., Chgo., 1970-72; asst. prof. Ohio U., Athens, 1972-74; assoc. prof. Washington U., St. Louis, 1974-80, prof., dir., 1980—; cons. in field. Contbr. articles to profl. jours. Fulbright scholar Inst. for Higher Edn., 1968. Mem. Am. Inst. Chem. Engrs., Am. Chem. Soc., Am. Assn. Engring. Edn., AAAS, Sigma Xi. Serbian Christian Orthodox. Club: Century (St. Louis). Avocations: hiking, swimming, travel. Office: Washington U Campus Box 1198 Saint Louis MO 63130

DUERRE, JOHN ARDEN, microbial physiologist, biochemist; b. Webster, S.D., Aug. 21, 1930; s. Dewey H. and Stella M. (Barber) D.; B.S., S.D. State U., 1952, M.S. (Lederle fellow), 1956; Ph.D., U. Minn., 1960; m. Benna Bee Harris, June 16, 1957; children—Gail, Dawn, Arden. Research asso., AEC fellow Argonne (Ill.) Nat. Lab., 1960-61; research bacteriologist NIH Rocky Mountain Lab., Hamilton, Mont., 1961-63; asst. prof. microbiology U. N.D. Med. Sch., 1963-65, asso. prof., 1965-71, prof. microbiology, 1971—; vis. scientist neuropsychiat. research unit Research Council Lab., Carshalton, Surrey, Eng., 1969-70; vis. prof. Walter Reed Army Inst. Research, Washington, 1984-85. Chmn. Grand Forks County (N.D.) Wildlife Fedn., 1965-67, 77-78, Grand Forks chpt. Ducks Unltd., 1970, 77-78; dist. dir. N.D. Wildlife Fedn., 1976-77. Served with U.S. Army, 1953-55. Recipient Career Devel. award NIH, 1965-75; NIH grantee, 1966, 71-83; NSF grantee, 1963-71. Mem. N.Y., N.D. acads. scis., Am. Soc. Microbiologists, Fedn. Am. Soc. Exptl. Biology, Henrici Soc., Sigma Xi (Outstanding Research award 1977). Democrat. Clubs: Grand Forks Curling, Grand Forks Gun, Elks. Contbr. numerous articles to profl. pubs. Home: 918 N 26th St Grand Forks ND 58201 Office: U ND Med Sch Grand Forks ND 58202

DUFF, WILLARD MOYLE, medical educator, dean; b. Canon City, Colo., July 20, 1939; s. Willard Moyle and Alberta Duff (Culbertson) D.; m. Peggy Scudder, June 6, 1963; children—Robert Scott, Richard Sean. B.S., Midland Coll., 1961; M.S., U. Nebr.-Lincoln, 1963, Ph.D., 1967. Assoc. prof. med. edn. U. Hartford, Conn., 1967-75; dir. edn. Hartford Hosp., 1972-78; assoc. dean Med. Coll. Wis., Milw., 1978—, assoc. prof., 1978—, vice-chmn. dept. family practice, 1985—. Author: Family Practice Source Book for Continuing Education, 1984. Editor: Core Curriculum for Family Practice, 1982. Pack leader Potawameni 128 council, Boy Scouts Am., 1982; pres. Waukesha PTA, 1983; pres. Football Booster Club, Waukesha, 1984. NIH fellow, 1965-66; NIH grantee, 1967-71. Mem. Assn. Hosp. Med. Educators, Soc. Deans Med. Coll. Continuing Edn. (exec. com. 1978—), Accredidation Council Continuing Med. Edn. (review com. 1979—). Republican. Avocation: History. Home: N24W22412 Meadowood Ln Waukesha WI 53186 Office: Dept Family Medicine 1314 N 74th st Milwaukee WI 53226

DUFFNEY, RICHARD EDWARD, architect; b. Detroit Lakes, Minn., Aug. 5, 1937; s. George Anthony and Tillie Bergette (Soreng) D.; m. Joyce Elaine Paulson, July 3, 1959; children—Richard A., Nancy, Paul, Sally. Diploma, N.D. State Sch. Sci., Wahpeton, 1960. Assoc. Winston Larson and Assocs., Detroit Lakes, 1960, Kurke Assocs., Fargo, N.D., 1961-64, Kegel Assocs., Detroit Lakes, 1964-83; prin. Duffney Architecture, Detroit Lakes, 1983—. Mem. drafting dept. adv. com. Detroit Lakes Vocat. Tech. Inst., 1968-75, chmn., 1972-75; bd. dirs. Becker County Day Activity Ctr., Detroit Lakes, 1969-73, pres., 1972-73; mem. ch. council Grace Lutheran Ch., Detroit, 1967-69, 75-77, 80—, pres., 1969, 77, 82; precinct chmn. Becker County Ind. Republicans, 1980—, county vice chmn., 1983—. Mem. AIA, Constrn. Specifications Inst., Minn. Bldg. Ofcls., Nat. Council Archtl. Registration Bds., Detroit Lakes Regional C. of C., Detroit Lakes Jaycees (bd. dirs. 1966-73, pres. 1971-72), Minn. Jaycees (v.p. region 17 1972-73, nat. dir. N.W. region 1973-74, chmn. N.W. Water Carnival 1975, internat. senator 1974), Becker County Hist. Soc., Plains Art Mus., Walker Art Ctr. Club: Toastmasters (v.p. local club 1975). Registered architect, Minn., S.D. Lodges: Gideons Internat. (local v.p. 1975, state zone leader 1976-78, local sec. 1978-81, local pres. 1981—); Sons of Norway Internat (bd. dirs. 1979-82, v.p. 1979-82).

DUFFY, EDWARD W., See *Who's Who in America*, 43rd edition.

DUFFY, NORMAN VINCENT, chemistry educator; b. Washington, Nov. 1, 1938; s. Norman Vincent and Glenn Mae (Drury) D.; m. Marianne Youdell, Oct. 13, 1962; children—Norman Vincent III, Mary Virginia, Joseph Leslie, Anne-Marie, Maureen Glenn. B.S., Georgetown U., 1961, Ph.D., 1966. From asst. prof. to assoc. prof. chemistry Kent State U., Ohio, 1966-1980; from asst. dean arts and scis. to assoc. dean, 1973-1976, prof. chemistry dept. 1980—, chmn. dept., 1981—. Contbr. articles to profl. jours. Contbr. articles to encys. Producer ednl. films in field. Mem. Am. Chem. Soc., The Chem. Soc., Sigma Xi. Roman Catholic. Home: 1317 Denise Dr Kent OH 44240 Office: Kent State U Chemistry Dept Kent OH 44242

DUFFY, RICHARD EDWARD ANTHONY, public relations agency executive; b. Boston, Dec. 2, 1928; s. Leo L. and Margaret (Carey) D.; m. Elizabeth Sara Gifford, Aug. 4, 1951; children—Gifford R., Elizabeth J. A.A., Boston U., 1950; student Sorbonne, 1954, U. Md. Overseas Extension, Frankfurt, W.Ger., 1952. News writer pub. info. div. U.S. Army, Europe, 1951-53; columnist, reporter Am. Daily, Frankfurt, 1953-54; editor, columnist, reporter European edit. N.Y. Herald-Tribune, Paris, France, 1954-55; reporter New Bedford (Mass.) Standard-Times, 1955-56, Boston Post, 1956; account exec., staff writer Carl Byoir & Assocs., N.Y.C., 1957-66, account exec., 1969-78, v.p., 1972-76, sr. v.p., 1976-78, exec. v.p. Mid-Am. region, Chgo., 1981—; dir. alumni affairs Boston U., 1966-69; v.p. pub. relations Burlington No. Inc., St. Paul, 1978-81. Served with AUS 1946-48, 50-51. Recipient Silver Anvil awards, 1958, 65, 66, 71. Mem. Pub. Relations Soc. Am., Counselors Soc. Roman Catholic. Clubs: Chgo. Press; Thorngate (Deerfield, Ill.). Home: 48 Fox Trail Lincolnshire IL 60015 Office: 401 N Michigan Ave Suite 770 Chicago IL 60611

DUFFY, WILLIAM EDWARD, JR., educator; b. Fostoria, Ohio, Aug. 30, 1931; s. William Edward and Margaret Louise (Drew) D.; B.S., Wayne State U., 1958, M.Ed., 1960; Ph.D., Northwestern U., 1967; m. Sally King Wolfe, Nov. 21, 1958 (div. 1978). Tchr., Detroit pub. schs., 1957-61; instr. social studies Northwestern U., Evanston, Ill., 1961-65; asst. prof. edn. U. Iowa, Iowa City, 1965-70, asso. prof., 1970—, coordinator Soc. Found. Edn. program, 1978—, chmn. div. founds., postsecondary edn., 1981—; lectr. in field. Served with USAF, 1951-54. Fellow Philosophy of Edn. Soc.; mem. AAAS, Am. Ednl. Research Assn., History of Edn. Soc., Am. Ednl. Studies Assn. Editorial bd. Ednl. Philosophy Theory, 1969-71; contbr. book revs. and articles to profl. pubs. Home: 376 Samoa Pl Iowa City IA 52240 Office: N 438 LC U Iowa Iowa City IA 52242

DUGAN, CHARLES FRANCIS, II, lawyer; b. Ann Arbor, Mich., Aug. 8, 1939; s. Charles F. and Mary (Minton) D.; m. Janice C. Prior, June 11, 1961; children—Heather, Stephanie, Suzanne, Kathleen. B.A., Miami U., Oxford, Ohio, 1960; J.D., U. Mich., 1963. Bar: Ohio 1963. Assoc., Vorys, Sater, Seymour & Pease, Columbus, Ohio, 1963-69, ptnr., 1970—; dir., sec. Buckeye Fin. Corp., Buckeye Fed. Savs. & Loan Assn.; lectr. in field. Contbr. articles to profl. jours. Trustee, sec. Nat. Ch. Residences of Worthington, 1972—; pres. Seal of Ohio council Girl Scouts Am., 1976-79. Mem. Columbus Bar Assn. (securities law com.), Ohio State Bar Assn., ABA (fed. regulation of securities com.). Presbyterian. Home: 847 Bluffview Dr Worthington OH 43085 Office: Vorys Sater Seymour & Pease 52 E Gay St Columbus OH 43215

DUGAN, RICHARD PIERCE, academic administrator, Christian education educator; b. Montclair, N.J., July 22, 1939; s. David H. Jr. and Marjorie (Stone) D.; m. Carol Y. Young, Aug. 19, 1965; children—Richard Jr., Thomas, Patricia. B.A., Wheaton Coll., 1961; B.D., Conservative Bapt. Theol. Sem., 1966; M.A., NYU, 1969, Ph.D., 1977. Prof. Christian edn. Northeastern Bible Coll., Essex Fells, N.J., 1969-82; v.p. for acad. affairs Ft. Wayne Bible Coll., Ind., 1982—. Contbr. articles to profl. jours. Mem. Nat. Assn. Evangelicals, Religious Edn. Assn. Office: Fort Wayne Bible Coll 1025 W Rudisill Blvd Fort Wayne IN 46807

DUGGINS, FRANK HALL, JR., educational administrator, farmer; b. Marshall, Mo., Dec. 7, 1928; s. Frank Hall and Camille (Wilson) D.; m. Margaret Robbins, Sept. 4, 1964; children—Kathleen Camille. B.S. in Mil. Art and Engring., U.S. Mil. Acad., 1950; B.S. in Aero Engring., Miss. State U., 1962. Commd officer U.S. Army, 1950, advanced through grades to col., 1970; ret., 1978; mayor, Marshall, Mo., 1980-83; pres. Kemper Mil. Sch. and Coll., Boonville, Mo., 1983-84, trustee, 1975—, mem. alumni bd., 1984—. Pres. Saline County Red Cross, Marshall, Mo.; pres. Saline County Hist. Soc., Marshall; pres. Missouri Valley Regional Planning Commn. Decorated Legion of Merit (3), Bronze Star (2), Combat Inf. badge (2), Purple Heart. Methodist. Lodge: Rotary (bd. dirs. 1979—). Home: 534 E Arrow St Marshall MO 65341

DUICK, GREGORY FRANCIS, cardiologist; b. Evanston, Ill., Feb. 6, 1946; s. Emory Lawrence and Rosily Margaret Duick; A.B. in Chemistry, Knox Coll., Galesburg, Ill., 1968; M.D., Loyola U., Chgo., 1972; m. Peggy Ann Cyrier, Sept. 25, 1971; children—Michael, Carrie. Intern, Los Angeles County-U. So. Calif. Med. Ctr. 1972-73, resident in internal medicine, 1973-75, fellow in cardiology, 1975-77; fellow in nuclear medicine Vanderbilt U., Nashville, 1980; practice medicine specializing in cardiology, Wichita, Kans., 1977—; dir. Cardiac Catheterization and Non-Invasive Heart Labs., also co-dir. nuclear cardiology dept. St. Francis Hosp., Wichita; med. dir. Midwest Cardionics Inc., Wichita, North Central Echo Labs., St. Paul; cardiovascular dir. Kans. Emergency Med. Services; assoc. clin. prof. medicine Wichita div. U. Kans.; mem. Wichita Cardiology Assocs.; dir. Bank of Mid-Am. Diplomate Am. Bd. Internal Medicine, Sub-bd. Cardiovascular Medicine. Fellow Am. Coll. Cardiology; mem. ACP, Am. Heart Assn., Kans. Heart Assn., Kans. Med. Soc., Sedgwick County Heart Assn., Knox Coll. Alumni Assn., Loyola-Stritch Alumni Assn. Roman Catholic. Home: 112 Ridgecrest Wichita KS 67218 Office: 1035 N Emporia St Suite 130 Wichita KS 67203

DUKE, KELLY FAUST, JR., optometrist, cytotechnologist; b. Memphis, Dec. 4, 1946; s. Kelly Faust, Sr. and Lillyan (Young) D.; m. Shirley Ann Harris, June 12, 1967; children—Kelly Faust, III and Jennifer Blake. B.S., U. of Arkansas, 1964-69, Clinical Pathology Cert., 1970; O.D., southern Coll. of Optemetry, 1977. Diplomate Nat. Bd. Optometry. Practice of optometry, Bentonville, Ark., 1977—; owner Northwest Ark. Cytology Lab., Bentonville, 1978. Roman Catholic. Avocations: jazz piano, music research, tennis, basketball, running.

DUKE, PEGGY O'NEAL, educator; b. Old Hickory, Tenn., May 23, 1929; d. Cleveland and Louise (Page) Bennett; m. Carlton Menard Duke, Mar. 3, 1955; children—Barbara, Dwayne. B.S., Tenn. State U., 1950; M.A., Northwestern U., 1959; M.S., Chgo. State U., 1966; Ed.D., Vanderbilt U., 1981. Cert. in guidance and counseling, Ill. Tchr. Hampton High Sch., Dickson, Tenn., 1950-52; instr. Nat. Coll. Bus., Nashville, 1952-55; bus. edn. tchr. Chgo. pub. schs., 1955-63; counselor, dept. head Parker High Sch., Chgo., 1963-67, parent coordinator, 1967-69, vice-prin., 1969-72, tchr., coordinator Robeson High Sch. (formerly Parker High Sch., 1972—; evaluator North Central Accreditation Assn. Active LWV, women's bd. Chgo. Urban League, League of Black Women. Mem. Ill. State Vocat. Assn., Am. Personnel and Guidance Assn., Am. Assn. Supervision and Curriculum Devel., AAUW, Phi Delta Kappa, Alpha Kappa Alpha. Club: Saint Philip Neri Women's (Chicago). Contbr. articles to profl. jours.

DUKE, TIMOTHY EARL, manufacturing company executive; b. Marion, Ind., Dec. 5, 1946; s. Earl Eugene and Martha Elizabeth (Gaddis) D.; m. Paula Lane Pedersen, Sept. 29, 1969 (div. 1975); 1 child, Jennifer Lane. B.S. in Indsl. Mgmt., Purdue U., 1972. Salesman Dow Chem. Co., Atlanta, 1972-75; sales engr. Wilson-Fiberfil Internat., Rochester, N.Y., 1976-78, mktg. specialist, 1979-80, Evansville, Ind., 1981, mktg. mgr., 1981-84, mgr. licensing and original equipment mfrs., 1984-85, mgr. Central Region sales, 1985—. Recipient Best Speaker award Dale Carnegie Inst., 1982. Sr. mem. Soc. Plastic Engrs. (program com. 1974-75, appreciation award 1981). Republican. Club: Oak Meadow. Avocations: skiing; tennis; chess. Home: 2335 Bayard Park Dr Evansville IN 47714 Office: Wilson-Fiberfil Internat 2267 W Mill Rd Evansville IN 47712

DUKES, JACK RICHARD, history educator; b. Indpls., Jan. 21, 1941; s. Richard Eugene and Kathleen (Cox) D.; B.A., Beloit Coll., 1963; M.A., No. Ill. U., 1965; Ph.D., U. Ill., 1970; m. Joanne Petty, June 15, 1963; children—Gregory Scott, Richard Aaron. Asst. prof. Macalester Coll., St. Paul, 1969-70; assoc. prof. Carroll Coll., Waukesha, Wis., 1970-75, assoc. prof., 1975-83, prof. 1983—, chmn. dept. history, 1972—, dir. Russian Area Studies program, 1972-75; vis. asso. prof. U. Calif., Santa Barbara, 1980-81; Scholar-Diplomat Program participant U.S. Dept. State. Nat. Endowment for Humanities fellow, 1974; U. Ill. assoc. in Russian history, 1977; fellow in residence, U. Calif., Santa Barbara, 1977-78. Mem. Am. Hist. Assn., Am. Assn. for Advancement Slavic Studies, Conf. Group Study Central European History, Soc. History Am. Fgn. Relations. Contbr. articles to profl. jours. Home: 114 W Laflin St Waukesha WI 53186 Office: Dept History Carroll Coll Waukesha WI 53186

DULAJ, NANCE LILLIAN IRENE KOPER, city official; b. Chgo., Nov. 5; d. John Florian and Anastasia Nancy (Borowa) Koper; m. John Dulaj, Feb. 23, 1952 (div. 1972); children—George John, Glenard Ray, Gloria Janine (dec.). A.A., Bogan Coll., Chgo., 1962; B.A., St. Xavier Coll., Chgo., 1970, 82, postgrad. in bus. adminstrn., 1984; postgrad. in bus. law Northwestern U., Chgo. Tchrs. Coll.; diploma John Robert Powers Sch., Chgo., 1984. Cert. tchr. Ill. Tchr. numerous schs. in Ill.; exec. sec., supr., buyer, salesmen trainer Edward Don & Co., 5 yrs.; adminstrv. asst., sec. to fin. v.p. and corp. counsel Lynon Container Internat., 1970-73; sec. to exec. v.p. and patent counsel Velsicol Chem. Corp., Chgo., 1973-77; evening reservations mgr. Drake Hotel, Chgo., 1973-75, Ritz-Carlton Hotel, Chgo., 1976-79, Raphael Hotel, 1980, Park-Hyatt Hotel, 1981; adminstrv. asst. to sr. ptnr., tax dept. mgr. Thomas Havey & Co., C.P.A.s, Chgo., 1977-80; paralegal, sec. to main ptnr. Maher & Newman Ltd., Chgo., 1980; adminstrv. asst. to asst. commr. of mental health Bur. of Labs., Chgo., 1980-82, adminstrv. asst. to commr. of health, 1982—; free-lance writer. Weekly contbr. Southwest News Herald, The Territory Times; contbr. numerous articles to profl. publs. Capt., ARC Blood Drive, 1983; mem. spl. project bd. St. Xavier Coll., Chgo., 1984; mem. Chgo. Plan Commn.; mem. Chgo. Mayor's Lang. Bank; mem. spl. project bd. St. Xavier Coll., 1984; participant numerous civic and cultural activities. Mem. Chgo. Hist. Soc., Chgo. Council Fgn. Relations, 20th Century R.R. Club, Am-European Student Union, Nature Conservancy, Polish Arts Club, Polish Nat. Alliance, Coalition Polish-Am. Women, Queen's Guild, Troubadours Drama Group, Nat. Assn. Female Execs., Nat. Assn. Legal Secs., Women in Communications, Ill, Assn. Legal Secs., Chgo. Assn. Legal Secs. (asst. treas. 1983, chmn. Law Week 1984, 85), Contact Chgo. Teleministries, Galena C. of C., St. Xavier Coll. Alumni Assn., Epsilon Eta Phi, Phi Chi Theta. Roman Catholic. Club: Kiwi. Home: 7235 S Avers Ave Chicago IL 60629 Office: Suite LL-169 Daley Civic Ctr 50 W Washington St Chicago IL 60602

DULEY, ALVIN JOSEPH, educator; b. St. Joe, Fond du Lac County, Wis., Jan. 12, 1916; s. Marie (Mary) (Steffes) D. Diploma U. Wis.-Oshkosh, 1940; B.S., Brigham Young U., 1951; M.A., Ariz. State U., 1960; B.S., Marian Coll., 1981. Cert. in adminstrn., secondary schs. and counseling, Utah.; sch. psychology, English, social studies, Hawaii; counseling, social studies, N.Y., social scis., counseling, psychology, Calif. Jr. Colls. Tchr., U.S. Indian Service, 1946-60; reading specialist McNary Sch. Dist., Ariz., 1960-64; tchr. and dormitory counselor high schs., Lahainaluna, Maui, Hawaii, and psychol. services, Hilo and Kailua-Kona, Hawaii, 1964-80. Active Cub Scouts, Boy Scouts Am., Utah, Ariz., Mont., Miss., Wis., Hi-Y, Hawaii. Recipient awards from Boy Scouts Am., Hi-Y, Dept. Interior. Mem. Am. Assn. Ret. Persons, Hawaii Psychol. Assn., Can. Psychol. Assn., Nat. Assn. Gifted Children (life mem.), Assn. Supervision and Curriculum Devel., Am. Rabbit Breeders Assn., Pyramid Soc. (Arabian Horses), Hawaii Edn. Assn. Roman Catholic. Author: Adult Education Reading Series (bilingual). Home: 953 Meadow Creek Ln Fond du Lac WI 54935

DULL, PAUL PHELLIS, retired judge; b. Celina, Ohio, May 30, 1907; s. Edgar M. and May (Phellis) D.; A.B., Ohio Wesleyan U., 1929; A.M., Columbia, 1931; J.D., Ohio State U., 1937; m. Dorothy E. Anderson, Dec. 23, 1933 (dec.); children—Peter Phellis, Jill; m. 2d, Alberta B. Buerkle, Apr. 7, 1966. Instr. polit. sci. U. Ky., 1931-32; publicity and student promotion Kan. Wesleyan U., 1933; pvt. law practice, Celina, 1937-44, 46-47; judge Common Pleas Ct., Mercer County, Ohio, 1947-74, ret., 1974; adj. assoc. prof. bus. Western Ohio br. campus Wright State U., 1975-79. Bd. dirs. Mercer County chpt. A.R.C., Soc. Crippled Children. Served with USAAF, 1944-45. Mem. Am., Ohio, Mercer County bar assns., Am. Legion, Am. Judicature Soc., Acad. Polit. Sci., Am. Acad. Polit. and Social Sci., Ohio Hist. Soc., Sigma Alpha Epsilon, Phi Delta Phi, Omicron Delta Kappa, Pi Sigma Alpha, Kappa Delta Pi, Pi Delta Epsilon. Mason, Moose, Eagle, Woodman of the World. Author (books of verse): Sprouts From A Small Potato, 1940; Salt To Taste, 1948; Letting Out the Seams, 1954; Unmarked Intersections, 1966; Back Track, 1976; also jud. opinions and legal articles. Home: 659 N Walnut St Celina OH 45822 Office: Court House Celina OH 45822

DULLE, CATHERINE ANN, rehabilitation agency director, consultant; b. St. Louis, Sept. 27, 1950; d. Oliver Anthony and Mary Constance (Sandweg) Dulle. B.A., Fontbonne Coll., 1973; M.A., St. Louis U., 1978. Lic. speech pathologist, Mo. Speech pathologist St. Louis City Sch. System, 1974-77; grad. fellow speech pathology VA Hosp., St. Louis, 1977-78; speech and lang. pathologist Spl. Sch. Dist. of St. Louis County, 1978-79; coordinator speech pathology services Christian Health Care Systems, Inc., St. Louis, 1979-80; pres., owner Assoc. Rehab. Services, Inc., St. Peters, Mo., 1980—, also dir.; pres., dir. Consol. Health Care; guest lectr. St. Louis U., Fontbonne Coll., So. Ill. U. Mem. adv. bd. Staff Builders Home Care, St. Louis, 1982—, Irene Walter Johnson Home Health Agy., St. Louis, 1983—; mem. St. Charles Assn. Retarded Citizens, 1981—; Mem. Am. Speech/Lang./Hearing Assn., Mo. Speech/Lang./Hearing Assn., Speech and Hearing Assn. of Greater St. Louis, Midwestern Adult Communicative Disorders Group, Nat. Assn. Rehab. Agys., Mo. Health Care Assn., Calif. Speech Pathologists and Audiologists in

Pvt. Practice, St. Peters C. of C., Kappa Gamma Pi, Delta Epsilon Sigma. Roman Catholic.

DULLINGER, DEBRA SHIRLEY, state social services executive, pharmacy educator; b. Little Falls, Minn., Apr. 15, 1954; d. Stanley Daniel and Lucille (Pierskalla) Kolodjeski; m. Robert W. Dullinger, Aug. 20, 1977; 1 child, Chase. B.S., U. Minn., 1977, Pharm.D., 1979. Registered pharmacist, Minn. Instr., U. Minn. Coll. Pharmacy, Mpls., 1979-80, asst. prof., clin. pharmacist, 1980-84, clin. asst. prof., 1985—; asst. dir. pharmacy Hennepin County Med. Ctr., Mpls., 1979-80; clin. pharmacist Mpls. VA Med. Ctr., 1980-85; drug utilization rev. coordinator Dept. Human Services, St. Paul, 1985—. Recipient Bristol Award Bristol Pharm. Co., 1977. Mem. Am. Pharm. Assn., Am. Soc. Hosp. Pharmacists, Minn. Asthma and Allergy Found. Am. (mem. exec. bd., sec. 1981-83), Central Minn. Soc. Hosp. Pharmacists. Office: Dept Human Services 444 Lafayette Rd Saint Paul MN 55101

DULSKI, KATHIE ALLISON, newspaper publishing company manager; b. Chgo., Apr. 5, 1943; s. Howard C. and Dorothy A. (Rowan) Uhlir; m. William J. Gillarde, Oct. 9, 1961 (div. Oct. 1966); children—Kathy Ann, Carol Ann; m. 2d, Jerome Raymond Dulski, Sept. 2, 1967 (div. Jan. 1976); 1 son, David Raymond. Student Harper Coll., 1975-79, Systems Sci. Inst., Chgo., 1980. Keypunch operator Medline Industries, Northbrook, Ill., 1975-77; ops. supr. Meyercord Industries, Carol Stream, Ill., 1977-78; ops. mgr. Extel Corp., Northbrook, 1978-83, Chgo. Sun Times, 1983—. Vol., Spl. Olympics, mem. Spl. Leisure Services. Mem. Art Inst. Chgo., Nat. Geog. Soc. Lutheran. Home: 2149 Heather Ln Palatine IL 60074 Office: Chicago Sun Times 401 Wabash Ave Chicago IL 60611

DUMKE, MELVIN PHILIP, dentist; b. Sleepy Eye, Minn., Jan. 23, 1920; s. Herman Gustav and Else Ida (Battig) D.; D.D.S., U. Minn., 1943; m. Phyllis Lorraine Steuck, June 25, 1950; children—Pamela, Bruce, Shari. Practice dentistry, Sleepy Eye, 1946-50, Morgan, Minn., 1950-66, Mankato, Minn., 1966—. Lectr. dental assts. Mankato State Coll., 1967-69. Mem. Town Council, Morgan, 1960-65. Bd. control Martin Luther Acad., New Ulm, Minn., 1965-79; bd. dirs. The Lutheran Home, Belle Plaine, Minn., 1981—. Served to capt., Dental Corps, AUS, 1943-46. Fellow Royal Soc. Health, Internat. Coll. Dentists, Am. Coll. Dentists; mem. ADA (ho. of dels. 1977—), Minn. Dental Assn. (chmn. peer rev. com. 1973-79, mem. ho. of dels. 1978—, pres. 1983-84), So. Dist. Dental Soc. (exec. council), South Central Dental Study Club (pres. 1970), Fedn. Dentaire Internationale, Pierre Fouchard Acad., Mankato C. of C., U. Minn. Alumni Assn., V.F.W. (recipient Distinguished Service award 1966, comdr. 1965), Am. Legion, Psi Omega. Lutheran (pres. congregation 1970). Lion (pres. 1965, 74, zone chmn. 1975). Clubs: Mankato Golf, U. Minn. Sch. Dentistry Century. Home: 364 Carol Ct Mankato MN 56001 Office: 430 S Broad St Mankato MN 56001

DUMONTELLE, PAUL BERTRAND, geologist; b. Kankakee, Ill., June 22, 1933; s. Lester Vernon and Helen (McKinstry) DuM.; m. Dollie Louise Bridgewater, June 5, 1955; children—John, Jeffrey, Jo, James, Jay. B.S., DePauw U., 1955; M.S., Lehigh U., 1957. Lic. geologist, Calif. Geologist, Lehigh Portland Cement Co., Allentown, Pa., 1956, 57, Homestake Mining Co., Lead, S.D., 1957-63; asst. geologist, then assoc. geologist Ill. State Geol. Survey, Champaign, 1963-70, coordinator environ. geology, geologist, 1975, head engring. geology sect., 1979—; dir. Ill. Mine Subsidence Research Program, 1985—; sec. Ill. Mapping Adv. Com., Springfield, 1979—; mem. Prime 750 Policy Com., Champaign, 1983—. Contbr. brochures, handbooks and articles to profl. jours. Commr. Boneyard Creek, Urbana, Ill., 1984. Fellow Geol. Soc. Am.; mem. Am. Inst. Profl. Geologists (cert.), Assn. Engring. Geologists (nat. awards com. 1974-76), Internat. Assn. Engring. Geologists, AIME, Am. Congress on Surveying and Mapping, Sigma Xi. Methodist. Lodges: Masons, Kiwanis (bd. dirs. 1983-84). Home: 2020 Burlison Dr Urbana IL 61801 Office: Ill State Geol Survey 615 E Peabody St Champaign IL 61820

DUMONT-ROSENBERG, VIRGINIA, public relations counselor, publisher; b. Dearborn, Mich., June 28, 1927; d. Francis J. and Ethel (Smith) Rebholz; m. Albert G. Rosenberg, Mar. 1, 1951 (div.); children—Jonathan, Barbara, Timothy. B.A. in Journalism, Wayne State U., 1948. Accredited pub. relations counselor. With newspapers, including Rochester (Mich.) Clarion, 1948-49, East Sider, Detroit, 1949-53; active pub. relations non-profit and ednl. instns., Ill., La., Ohio, 1954-76; founder Virginia Dumont Assocs., Dayton, Ohio, 1977-81; pub. Something Extra mag. insert, Dayton, 1980; co-owner Baker Dumont McCormack & Pilgrim Inc., Dayton, 1981—. Mem. Women in Communications (past pres., award for profl. excellence 1980), Pub. Relations Soc. Am. (past sec., dir. Dayton chpt.), Counselors Acad. of Pub. Relations Soc. Am., Internat. Assn. Bus. Communicators, Dayton Advt. Club, AAUW (dir. state div.), Sierra Club, Nature Conservancy, Assn. Humanistic Psychology, Amnesty Internat., Council on World Affairs, Dayton Area C. of C., Dayton Opera Assn., Dayton Art Inst., ACLU (dir.). Unitarian. Contbr. articles to newspapers and periodicals. Office: Drawer D Mid City Station Dayton OH 45402

DUMOVICH, LORETTA, company executive, real estate broker; b. Kansas City, Kans., Sept. 29, 1930; d. Michael Nicholas and Frances Barbara (Horvat) D. Lic. real estate broker, Kans., Mo. Vice-pres., corp. sec., dir. Riss Internat. Corp., Kansas City, Mo., 1950—; dir.-corp. sec. Republic Industries, Inc., Kansas City, 1969—; dir. Grandview Bank and Trust Co., Grandview, Mo., also mem. trust com., exec. com.; pres., dir. Columbia Properties, Inc., Kansas City, 1969—; dir., corp. sec. Dominion Banqueshares Ltd., Kansas City, 1980—; dir., corp. sec. Profl. Driving Acad., World Leasing, Inc. Mem. Kansas City Bd. Realtors, Mo. Bd. Realtors, Terminal Properties, Inc., Bldg. Owners and Mgrs. Assn., Am. Royal Bd. Govs. Home: 2510 Grand Ave Apt 2704 Kansas City MO 64108 Office: 215 W Pershing Rd Kansas City MO 64108

DUNBAR, MICHAEL AUSTIN, art administrator; b. Santa Paula, Calif., Sept. 21, 1947; s. Joe Austin and Michele (Deitrich) D.; m. Linda Marie Haacke, Aug. 30, 1969; children—Jennifer, Katherine, Melissa. A.A., Lincoln Land Community Coll., 1971; B.A., Ill. State U., 1973, M.S., 1980; M.A., Sangamon State U., 1976. Dir. State Fair Profl. Art Show, Springfield, Ill., 1974-75; exec. dir. Galesburg Arts Council, Ill., 1975-76; coordinator art in Architecture Capital Devel. Bd., Springfield, 1977—; cons. in field. Prin. works include Ill. Collection for State of Ill. Ctr., 18 Ill. Sculptors Traveling Exhibition, Springfield and Vicinity Show, Ill. for Art Dedication Exhibition. Project dir. Seminar on Downtown Restoration, Springfield, 1974; mem. downtown preservation com. SCADA, 1974; mem. Galesburg Bicentennial Commn., 1976. Ill. Arts Council grantee, 1982, 83; Nat. Endowment for Arts fellow, 1974. Mem. Chgo. Sculpture Internat., Chgo. Sculpture Soc. (bd. dirs.), Springfield Contemporary Art Soc. (bd. dirs., sec. 1980-82). Republican. Avocation: Collector. Home: 400 S Walnut St Springfield IL 62704 Office: Capital Devel Bd 401 S Spring St Springfield IL 62706

DUNCAN, CLARENCE AVERY, JR., savings and loan association executive; b. LaGrange, Ga., Jan. 28, 1917; s. Clarence Avery and Maude (Borders) D.; student San Angelo (Tex.) Jr. Coll., 1935-37, U. Tex., 1937-39; m. Lucy Carolyn Watson, Nov. 14, 1981; children—John Davis, David Ray, Lea Ann, Lucy Carroll, Dempsey Sneed, Melanie Ann. With Farm & Home Savs. Assn., Nevada; Mo., 1945—, v.p. Nevada, 1950-56, pres., dir., from 1956, chmn. bd., 1968—, also chief exec. officer; dir. Citizens State Bank, Equity Investors, Inc., Austin, Stewart Info. Sers., Houston. Mem. U.S. Savs. and Loan League (pres. 1966). Episcopalian. Rotarian. Home: 102 Country Club Dr Nevada MO 64772 Office: care Farm & Home Savings Assn 221 W Cherry St PO Box 1893 Nevada MO 64772

DUNCAN, DAVID FRANK, community health specialist, educator; b. Kansas City, Mo., June 26, 1947; s. Chester Frank and Maxine (Irwin) D.; B.A., U. Mo., Kansas City, 1970; postgrad. Sam Houston State U., 1971; Dr.P.H., U. Tex., 1976; 1 foster son, Kevin Rheinboldt. Research asst. U. Kans. Bur. Child Research, 1967-68; supr. Johnson County Juvenile Hall, Olathe, Kans., 1968-70; asst. to warden Draper Correctional Center, Elmore, Ala., summer 1970; supr. Harris County Juvenile Hall, Houston, 1970-71; project dir. Who Cares, Inc. Drug Abuse Treatment Center, Houston, 1971-73; exec. dir. Reality Island Halfway House, Houston, 1974-75; research asso. Tex. Gov.'s Office, Austin, summer 1975; research asso. Inst. Clin. Toxicology, clin. toxicologist Ben Taub Gen. Hosp., Houston, 1975-76; asst. prof. health sci. SUNY, Brockport, 1976-78, asso. prof., 1978, acting chmn. dept. health sci., summer 1978; prof. health edn., coordinator community health program So. Ill. U., Carbondale, 1978—; chmn. So. Ill. Health Edn. Task Force, 1979—; bd. dirs. Ill. Pub. Health Continuing Edn. Council; cons. to numerous health, edn. instns. Mem. Am. Public Health Assn. (past chmn. sect. mental health, mem. action bd.), Ill. Public Health Assn. (exec. council), Am. Coll. Epidemiology, Soc. Epidemiologic Research, AAAS, Ill. Acad. Sci., N.Y. Acad. Sci. Democrat. Methodist. Author: Drugs and the Whole Person, 1982; contbr. articles to profl. jours.; editorial bd. Health Values, 1980—, Jour. Drug Edn., 1981—, Internat. Jour. Mental Health, 1982-83. Home: 35 Pleasant Valley Rural Route 5 Carbondale IL 62901 Office: Dept Health Edn So Ill U Carbondale IL 62901

DUNCAN, DONALD PENDLETON, university administrator; b. Joliet, Ill., Feb. 24, 1916; s. Kenneth Whitney and Nettie Vivian (Pendleton) D.; m. Mercein Benzie, July 6, 1956; children—Kenneth Houlton, Nancy Susan, Debra Mercein. B.S.F., U. Mich., 1937, M.S., 1939; Ph.D., U. Minn., 1951. Shelterbelt forester U.S. Forest Service, Meade, Kans., 1939-40, jr. forester, 1940-41; instr. Kans. State U., Manhattan, 1941-42; instr. Army U., Florence, Italy, 1945; extension forester, state forester Kans. State U., Manhattan, 1946-47; from instr. to prof., asst. dir. Sch. Forestry, U. Minn., St. Paul, 1947-65; dir. Sch. Forestry, Fisheries and Wildlife, U. Mo., Columbia, 1965-85; cons. U. Tenn., Knoxville, 1984. Contbr. chpts. to books, articles to profl. jours. Mem. exec. com. Boy Scouts Am., Columbia, Mo., 1968-84, dist. chmn., 1968-70; elder Presbyn. Ch., Columbia, 1971-85. Served to tech. sgt. U.S. Army, 1942-45, PTO-ETO. Recipient Outstanding Service award Assn. State Coll. and Univ. Forest Res. Orgns., 1975. Fellow AAAS, Soc. Am. Foresters (chmn. edn. policies com. 1974-75); mem. The Wilderness Soc., Mo. Acad. Sci., Sigma Xi, Xi Sigma Pi, Gamma Sigma Delta (sec.). Avocations: woodworking, music, reading, golf. Home: 221 W Brandon Rd Columbia MO 65203 Office: U Mo Sch Forestry Fisheries & Wildlife Columbia MO 65211

DUNCAN, FRANK MARTIN, educational administrator; b. Blue Earth, Minn., June 30, 1943; s. Frank Martin Duncan and Helen Marie (Houghaling) Peterson; m. Carolynn Lee Swensrud, Aug. 21, 1966; children—Derek Andrew, Darcy Lee. B.A., Mankato State U., 1967, M.A.T., 1969, Ed.S., 1975. Cert. supt., prin., tchr., Minn. Tchr., Prescott Pub. Schs., Ariz., 1970-71; tchr. Fairmont Pub. Schs., Minn., 1971-74; prin. Sherburn Pub. Schs., Minn., 1975-77; supt. Amboy-Good Thunder Schs., Amboy, Minn., 1977-80, Howard Lake-Waverly Schs., Howard Lake, Minn., 1980-85. Bd. dirs. Howard Lake Cable Commn., 1983-85; mem. Community Corrections Task Force, Mankato, Minn., 1979-80. Served with U.S. Navy, 1961-67. Bush Found. fellow, 1984-85. Mem. Minn. Assn. Sch. Adminstrs., Am. Assn. Sch. Adminstrs., Mgmt. Concerned for Pub. Edn., Minn. Assn. Sch. Bus. Ofcls. Lutheran. Avocations: archeology, writing. Office: Howard Lake-Waverly Ind Sch Dist PO Box 708 Howard Lake MN 55349

DUNCAN, JOHN PATRICK CAVANAUGH, lawyer; b. Kalamazoo, Jan. 25, 1949; s. James H. and Colleen Patricia (Cloney) D.; 1 dau., Sarah Ellen. B.A. cum laude (NSF fellow summer 1970), Yale U., 1971; J.D., U. Chgo., 1974. Bar: Ill. 1974, U.S. Dist. Ct. for no. dist. Ill. 1974, U.S. Ct. Appeals for 7th circuit 1975, U.S. Supreme Ct. 1979. Assoc. firm Holleb & Coff, Ltd., Chgo., 1974-79, mem., 1979—; gen. counsel Chgo. Office Leasing Brokers Assn., 1983—; dir. Lombard Bancorp., Inc., 1975—. Contbr. articles to profl. jours. Bd. dirs., treas., chmn. planning com. Lincoln Park Conservation Assn., Chgo., 1979-82. Mem. Chgo. Bar Assn. (chmn., fin. insts. coms. 1985—), ABA (bus. and banking sect.), Ill. Bankers Assn., Ill. State Bar Assn. (council comml., banking and bankruptcy sect. 1983—). Club: Yale (Chgo.). Home: 1825 N Mohawk St Chicago IL 60614 Office: Holleb & Coff Ltd One IBM Plaza Suite 4040 Chicago IL 60611

DUNCAN, ROBERT GENE, lawyer; b. Helena, Mo., Nov. 22, 1932; s. Chester Frank and Maxine I. (Henry) D.; m. Anita Fay Woerz, Dec. 11, 1960 (div. 1981); 1 son, Stephen; m. Mary Carol Bradford, Nov. 10, 1983; stepchildren—Marc, Michelle and Misti Montgomery. A.A., Jr. Coll. Kansas City, 1951; B.S. in Edn., Central Mo. State U., 1953; J.D., U. Mo.-Kansas City, 1950. Bar: Mo. 1959, U.S. Supreme Ct. Assoc. Quinn, Peebles & Hickman, Kansas City, Mo., 1960-62, Simon and Pierce, Kansas City, Mo., 1962-65; ptnr. Pierce, Duncan, Bietling & Shute, Kansas, City, Mo., 1965-72, Duncan & Russell, Gladstone, Mo., 1972-81; of counsel Coulson & Chick, Kansas City, Mo., 1981—; city atty. City of Gladstone, 1961-74, mcpl. judge, 1974-81; v.p. Northland Ct. Referal Service, Kansas City, Mo., 1970-83. Editor: Missouri Criminal Law, 1984 (2 vols.). Chmn. Clay County Sheltered Facilities Bd., Gladstone, 1970—. Served to sgt. U.S. Army, 1953-55. Fellow Am. Bd. Criminal Lawyers; mem. Criminal Def. Lawyers (pres. 1983-84), Nat. Assn. Criminal Def. Lawyers, Clay County Bar Assn. (pres. 1978), Order Bench and Robe. Democrat. Lodge: Elks. Avocations: reading; travel. Home: 4248 NE Davidson Rd Kansas City MO 64116 Office: Coulson & Chick 2601 Kendallwood St Gladstone MO 64119

DUNCAN, ROBERT MORTON, See *Who's Who in America,* 43rd edition.

DUNCAN, ROY KEITH, educational administrator; b. Columbus Junction, Iowa,. Aug. 28, 1928; s. William Tedford and Margaret (Ferguson) D.; m. Nancy Dons, Aug. 19, 1954; children—Jeffrey, Linda. A.A., Washington Jr. Coll., 1949; B.A., U. No. Iowa, 1954, M.A., 1956. Tchr. jr. high math. Columbus Community Sch., Columbus Junction, 1949-51, Keokuk Community Sch., Iowa, 1954-56; prin. jr. high sch. Osage Community Sch., Iowa, 1956—; state com. mem. North Central Assn. of Iowa, 1983-84. Chmn. Osage Community Chest, 1975. Served as cpl. AUS, 1951-53. Mem. Ednl. Adminstrs. Iowa, Nat. Assn. Secondary Prins. Republican. Mem. United Ch. Christ. Club: Osage Country (pres. 1984—). Lodge: Kiwanis (pres. 1973-74). Avocations: golf, gardening. Office: Osage Jr High Sch 7th & Sawyer Dr Osage IA 50461

DUNCAN, THEODORE NORMAN, fluid power company executive; b. N.Y.C., Dec. 18, 1921; s. William F. and Sarah L. (Moore) D.; m. Perdema Mauree Miller, June 15, 1946; children—Claudia Mauree Burckard, Sara Diane Klepper, Jennifer Lynn Salter. B.S.M.E., Stevens Inst. Tech., 1943; postgrad. U. Tulsa, 1950-51, Drury Coll., 1956-57. Registered profl. engr., Okla. Gen. mgr. aerospace div. Sperry Vickers, Troy, Mich., 1965-66, v.p., 1966-68, v.p., gen. mgr. Mobile div., 1968-73, v.p. internat., 1973-80; pres. Vickers, Inc., Troy, 1980—; chmn. Vickers S.Y.S. Can.; dir. overseas subs. Bd. dirs. Milw. Sch. Engring., 1984-85, Master Data Ctr., Inc., Southfield, Mich., 1984-85. Served to lt. USN, 1942-47, PTO. Mem. Am. Soc. Metals, ASME, Soc. Mfg. Engrs., Constrn. Industry Mfg. Assn. (tech. bd. 1984—), Nat. Fluid Power Assn. (bd. dirs. 1983-86, chmn. adv. panel for hydraulic competitiveness and compatability 1983—), Internat. Ops. Council Machinery and Allied Products Inst. (bd. dirs. 1984-85), Internat. Rd. Fedn. (bd. dirs. 1984-85), Am. Nat. Standards Inst. (exec. council 1983-86), Mich. C. of C. (bd. dirs. 1983-85), Greater Detroit C. of C. Club: Bloomfield Open Hunt (Mich.). Avocations: golf; horseback riding; sailing. Office: Vickers Inc 1401 Crooks Rd Troy MI 48084

DUNETZ, ANNELIESE ANTONIE, photographer; b. Dortmund-Hörde, Westfalen, Ger., Feb. 13, 1929; d. August and Erna Anna (Wiemer) Brensing; came to U.S., 1955, naturalized, 1958; student photography Rochester (N.Y.) Inst. Tech., 1967-69; children—Ronald, Roger, Rodney. Owner, photographer Photog. Art by Ann, C.P.P., Kenton, Ohio, 1955—. Cert. profl. photographer; cert. master photographer. Mem. Profl. Photographers Assn. Am. (accorded nat. cert. 1980), Profl. Photographers Assn. Ohio (medal of honor 1978). Democrat. Home and Office: 214 N Detroit St Kenton OH 43326

DUNHAM, MICHAEL DONALD, computer systems company executive, computer scientist, engineer; b. Chgo., July 25, 1945; s. Neil McDonald and Effie (Michael) D.; m. Susan Helminiak, Sept. 7, 1968; children—Patrick, Jonathan, Gregory. B.S. in E.E., U. Denver, 1968; M. Mgmt. Sci., U. Ill., Chgo., 1966, U. N.C., 1970, Stevens Inst. Tech., Hoboken, N.J., 1972. Field engr., Becthel Corp., South Haven, Mich., 1967; planning engr. Western Electric div. Bell Labs., Whippany, N.J., 1968-72; scientist Sci. Applications, Huntsville, Ala., 1972-73; product mgr. A.O. Smith, Milw., 1973-78; pres. Effective Mgmt. Systems, Inc., Milw., 1978—, dir., Naperville, Ill.; dir. Effective Security Systems, Inc., Menomonee Falls, Wis. Pres. Hartford Ave. Sch. PTA, Milw., 1976; del. Com. of 100, Milw. Pub. Sch. System, 1977, Wis. Conf. Small Bus., Madison, 1981. Fellow Am. Prodn. and Inventory Control Soc. (cert.), IEEE, IEEE Computer Soc. Congregationalist. Club: Gyro (Milw.) (dir. 1983—). Office: Effective Mgmt Systems Inc 1200 Park Pl Milwaukee WI 53224

DUNLAP, LARRY ELDON, business executive; b. Tiffin, Ohio, June 5, 1939; s. Carl Dellno and Hellen Christina (Creeger) D.; m. Mary Margaret Ratchen, July 3, 1979; children—Chad Carl, Carly Christina; m. Andrea Jean Stevenson, Apr. 6, 1968 (div. Oct. 1973). Student Bowling Green State U., 1957-58, Ohio State U., 1959-60, 1965-66. Design engr. Fostoria Industries, Inc., Ohio, 1966-67, application engr., 1967-68, contract sales mgr., 1968-70, nat. sales mgr., 1970-75, div. mgr., 1975-85, v.p., 1985—; pres., chmn. Dunlap Bros., Inc., Tiffin, 1983—. Mem. Kiwanis Internat., Fostoria, 1984. Served with USMC, 1962-64. Republican. Home: 408 Burnham Dr Fostoria OH 44830 Office: Fostoria Industries Inc 1200 N Main St Fostoria OH 44830

DUNLOP, MARK GEORGE, sales executive, retailer; b. Osage, Iowa, Oct. 17, 1952; s. David Allan and Ann Marie (Krepelka) D.; B.A. in Bus. Adminstrn., U. Iowa, 1975; M.A. in Indsl. Relations, 1977. Dir. franchising Lindsay div. Mec-O-Matic Co., St. Paul, 1977-80; dist. mgr. Mec-O-Matic div., 1980-82, regional sales mgr., 1982-83, field sales mgr., 1983—; dir. Aquachlor, Inc., Salt Lake City; pres. Excalibur for Men, St. Paul, 1981—. Active United Way Campaign. Mem. Delta Upsilon. Republican. Methodist. Avocations: scuba diving; tennis; backgammon. Home: 415 Springhill Rd White Bear Lake MN 55110

DUNN, FLOYD EMRYL, neurologist/psychiatrist, consultant; b. Wilkes-Barre, Pa., Apr. 25, 1910; s. Adrian Anson and Frances Amanda (Culver) D.; m. Wilda Kathryn Lauer, Aug. 14, 1943; children—Kathryn Alice (dec.), Deborah Lee. Student, Temple U., 1929-32; D.O., Phila. Coll. Osteo. Medicine, 1936. Diplomate Am. Osteo. Bd. Neurology and Psychiatry. Resident in neurology, psychiatry Still-Hildreth Hosp., 1941-45, staff psychiatrist, 1945-49; chmn. div. neurology, psychiatry Kirksville Coll. Osteo. Medicine, 1945-48, Kansas City Coll. Osteo. Medicine, U. Health Scis., Mo., 1949-68; mem. staff VA Hosp., Knoxville, Iowa, 1968-76, chief psychiatry service, 1970-76; clin. prof. neurology, psychiatry Coll. Osteo. Medicine, Des Moines, 1970-74; mem. Nat. Bd. Examiners for Osteo. Physicans and Surgeons, 1965-74, Excellence award, 1974, cons. neurology, psychiatry, Chgo., 1974—. Author: (monograph) History of the American College of Neuropsychiatrists, 1984. Contbr. articles to profl. jours. Mem. Iowa Adv. Council on Mental Health Ctrs., Des Moines, 1972-78, Central Regional Adv. Council for Comprehensive Psychiat. Services, Columbia, Mo., 1978—. Fellow Am. Coll. Neuropsychiatrists (life, sec.-treas. 1948-52, pres. 1954-55, 63-64, Disting. Service award 1967, Disting. Fellow award 1984), Am. Assn. on Mental Deficiency; mem. Am. Osteo. Assn. (life, editorial cons. publs. 1958—, del. 1960-69, pres.'s adv. council 1973), Mo. Assn. Osteo. Physicians and Surgeons (hon. life, del. 1958-69, v.p. 1969-70), Phi Sigma Gamma (pres. grand council 1952-53, council sec.-treas. 1953-59, editor Speculum 1959-65, Meritorious Service award 1965), Alpha Phi Omega. Republican. Methodist. Lodges: Lions (pres. Gravois Mills, Mo. chpt. 1984-85), Masons, Elks. Avocations: photography; travel; journalism. Home: Route 3 Box 504-A Gravois Mills MO 65037

DUNN, FRANCIS GILL, state justice; b. Scenic, S.D., Nov. 12, 1913; s. Thomas Bernard and Mary (Gill) D.; student Dakota State Coll., 1931-34; LL.B., U. S.D., 1937; LL.M., George Washington U., 1948; m. Eldred Elizabeth Wagner, 1942; children—David, Rebecca, Thomas, Carol Dunn Norbeck. Individual practice law, Madison, S.D., 1937-41, Sioux Falls, S.D., 1954-56; sec. to U.S. Senator W. J. Bulow, 1941-42; trial atty. U.S. Dept. Justice, Washington, 1946-50; asst. U.S. atty. for S.D., 1950-54; municipal judge, Sioux Falls, 1956-59, circuit judge, 1959-73; justice S.D. Supreme Ct., Pierre, 1973-84, chief justice, 1974-79. Served to lt. USN, 1942-46. Mem. Am., S.D. bar assns., VFW, Delta Theta Phi. Roman Catholic. Club: Elks. Office: 101 S Main St Suite 620 Sioux Falls SD

DUNN, HORTON, JR., organic chemist; b. Coleman, Tex., Sept. 3, 1929; s. Horton and Lora Dean (Bryant) D.; B.A. summa cum laude, Hardin-Simmons U., 1951; M.S., Ph.D., Case Western Res. U. Research chemist Lubrizol Corp., Cleve., 1953-70, dir. tech. info. center, 1970-79, supr. research div., 1980—; chmn. bd., bus. mgr. Isotopics, Cleve., 1964-67, editor, 1961-63. Mem. Am. Chem. Soc. (chpt. treas. 1968-70), Am. Soc. for Info. Sci. (chpt. pres. 1973-74), A.A.A.S., Beta Phi Mu, Alpha Chi. Contbr. articles to profl. jours. Patentee in field. Home: 530 Sycamore Dr Cleveland OH 44132 Office: 29400 Lakeland Blvd Wickliffe OH 44092

DUNN, MARION, osteopathic psychiatrist; b. LaGrange, Ga., Jan. 3, 1948; d. Doris and Willie Mae (Davis) Gamble; m. David Milton Dunn, June 18, 1978; 1 dau., Lisa. B.S. in Nursing, Wayne State U., 1972; D.O., Mich. State U. Coll. Osteo. Medicine, 1977. Instr. nursing Wayne County Community Coll., 1972-74; mem. Wayne County Mental Health Task Force, 1980; intern Mich. Osteo. Med. Ctr., Detroit, 1978-79; resident in psychiatry Lafayette Clinic, Detroit, 1979-82; pvt. practice psychiatry, Southfield, Mich., 1982—; dir. mental health program Detroit Osteo. Hosp., 1982—; producer host, talk therapy program WLQV-AM, 1983. Mem. Am. Osteo. Assn., Wayne County Osteo. Assn., Mich. Assn. Osteo. Physicians and Surgeons, Nat. Council Jewish Women Detroit, Orgn. Working Mothers Am. (founder, pres.). Methodist. Developer Family Digest TV series, 1982. Office: 12523 3d Ave Highland Park MI 48203

DUNN, ROBERT HARVY, mechanical contractor, quarter horse breeder; b. Robinson, Ill., Apr. 2, 1942; s. Winfred Myron and Mary Maxine (Mullins) D.; m. Mary Jane Kerr, Nov. 1, 1963; children—Robert Scott, Amelia Jo. Student, Ea. Ill. U., 1960-61, A.S., So. Ill. U., 1966. Lic. plumber, Ill. Ops. mgr. Blaise, Inc., Centralia, Ill., 1966-71, Ideal Plumbing Co., Champaign, Ill., 1971-72; pres. Able Mech. Contractors, Homer, Ill., 1972—. Mem. Ill. Plumbing Contractors Assn., Ill. Quarter Horse Assn., Am. Quarter Horse Assn. Democrat. Club: Lions. Home: Route 1 Box 276 Homer IL 61849 Office: 500 W 4th St Homer IL 61849

DUNN, SAMUEL WATSON, marketing and advertising educator, consultant; b. Vanderbilt, Pa., Aug. 24, 1918; s. Arthur Collins and Mary Everett (Baer) D.; m. Elizabeth Carson Schick, Dec. 30, 1949; children—Mary Elizabeth Dunn Zak, Eloise Schick Dunn Stuhr. A.B., Harvard U., 1943, M.B.A., 1946; Ph.D., U. Ill., 1951. Instr. U. Western Ont., 1946-47; asst. prof. U. Pitts., 1947-49; asst. prof. to prof. U. Wis.-Madison, 1951-66; prof., head dept. advt. U. Ill., Urbana, 1966-77; dean Coll. Bus. and Pub. Adminstrn., U. Mo.-Columbia, 1977-80, prof. mktg., advt., 1980—; Dai-Ichi-Kikaku disting. prof. mktg. Keio U., Japan, 1982; Gannett vis. prof. U. Fla., 1982; Newhouse prof. Syracuse U., 1984; cons. Milw. Jour., Madison Newspapers, Young & Rubicam Co., Norman, Craig & Kummel Co., Leo Burnett Co., S.W. Bell Co. Served with Transp. Corps, U.S. Army, 1943-46. Fulbright grantee, 1959-60; Marsteller Found. grantee, 1972, 74; Office Naval Research grantee, 1964-66. Mem. Am. Acad. Advt. (pres. 1970-72), Am. Mktg. Assn. (pres. Madison, Wis., and Central Ill. chpts.). Republican. Presbyterian. Club: Rotary. Author: Advertising Copy and Communication, 1956; Advertising: Its Role in Modern Marketing, 1961, 6th edit., 1986; International Handbook of Advertising, 1964; International Advertising and Marketing, 1979; How Fifteen Transnational Corporations Manage Public Affairs, 1979; Public Relations: A Contemporary Approach, 1986; contbr. numerous articles to acad., trade publ. Home: 117 W Burnam Rd Columbia MO 65201 Office: 135 Middlebush Hall U Mo Columbia MO 65211

DUNN, WINIFRED WIESE, occupational therapist; b. St. Louis, Mar. 26, 1950; d. Ignatius Joseph and Mary Louise (Marxer) Wiese; B.S. in Occupational Therapy, U. Mo., 1972, M.S. in Spl. Edn., 1973; Ph.D. in Neuroscis., U. Kans.; m. Robert G. Dunn, Aug. 17, 1973; children—James Daniel, Jessica Morgan. Staff, Liberty (Mo.) Pub. Schs., 1973-80; instr. psychology of exceptional child William Jewell Coll., 1974-80; instr. exceptional child in classroom, characteristics of learning disabled, whole child, psychoednl. assessment Webster U., 1979—; coordinator of pediatric services St. Luke's Hosp., Kansas City, Mo., 1980-84; instr. neuroanatomy and neurophysiology Rockhurst Coll.; instr. diagnostic process for children and applied neuroscis. U. Mo.-Kansas City, 1982—, dir. exemplary services Inst. for Human Devel., 1984—; cons. Mem. Am. Occupational Therapy Assn., Assn. Children with Learning Disabilities, Council Exceptional Children, Kans. Occupational Therapy Assn., Mo. Assn. Children with Learning Disabilities, Pi Lambda Theta. Roman Catholic. Home: 904 NE 60th Terr Kansas City MO 64118 Office: Inst for Human Devel U Mo at Kansas City 2220 Holmes St Kansas City MO 64108

DUNNE, CHRISTOPHER DAVID, stockbroker; b. Pietermaritzburg, Natal, Republic South Africa, May 13, 1955; came to U.S., June 1978; s. Walter Edward and Patricia Helen (Rowan) D.; m. Shelly Cottrill, Oct. 7, 1983. B.Com. Econ. and Bus. Adminstrn., U. Natal, 1975, L.L.B., 1977. Bar: Republic So. Africa 1977; registered broker Am. Stock Exchange, Nat. Assn. Securities Dealers, N.Y. Stock Exchange. Stockbroker Merrill Lynch, Mpls., 1979-85. Am. Field Service scholar, Minn., 1973. Mem. Lawyers Commn.

Internat. Human Rights. Roman Catholic. Clubs: Commodore, Squash (St. Paul). Avocations: Antique collector; marathons. Special Achievement: First So. African given polit. asylum U.S. for refusal to do military service for apartheid govt. Home: 165 Western Ave #507 Saint Paul MN 55102 Office: 2700 IDS Tower Minneapolis MN 55402

DUNNETTE, MARVIN DALE, psychologist; b. Austin, Minn., Sept. 30, 1926; s. Rodney Arthur and Mildred Geneva (Notestine) D.; B.Ch.E., U. Minn., 1948, M.A., 1951, Ph.D., 1954; m. Leaetta Marie Hough, Feb. 2, 1980; children by previous marriage—Nancy Dawn, Peggy Jo, Sheryl Jean. Research fellow dept. metallurgy U. Minn., 1948-49, research fellow, asst. prof. psychology, 1951-55; adviser employee relations research Minn. Mining and Mfg. Co., St. Paul, 1955-59; vis. asso. prof. U. Calif., Berkeley, 1962; chmn. bd. Decision Systems, Inc., Mpls., 1963-65; pres. Personnel Decisions, Inc., Mpls., 1966-75, chmn. bd., 1975-83, vice chmn., head research group, 1982—; pres. Personnel Decisions Research Inst., Mpls., 1975-83, chmn. bd., dir. research, 1983—; prof. psychology U. Minn., Mpls., 1961—; mem. research and devel. adv. group Army Research Inst. Social and Behavioral Scis., 1972-76, chmn. sci. adv. panel, ad hoc com. on personnel research and tng., 1975; mem. personnel research adv. group Bur. Naval Research, 1970-75. Served with USMC, 1944-46. Ford Found. fellow, 1964-65; recipient James A. Hamilton Outstanding Book award Am. Coll. Hosp. Adminstrs., 1972. Mem. Am. Psychol. Assn. (pres. div. 14, 1966-67, bd. sci. affairs 1975-77, James McKeen Cattell award 1965), AAAS. Author: (with W.K. Kirchner) Psychology Applied to Industry, 1965; Personnel Selection and Placement, 1966; (with J.P. Campbell and E.E. Lawler, K.E. Weick) Managerial Behavior, Performance and Effectiveness, 1970; editor: Work and Non Work in the Year 2001, 1973; Handbook of Industrial and Organizational Psychology, 1976; cons. editor Jour. Applied Psychology, 1950-75; contbr. articles to profl. jours. Home: 370 Summit Ave St Paul MN 55102 Office: 2415 Foshay Tower Minneapolis MN 55402

DUNSOMB, J. RICHARD, university band administrator. Student Millikin U. Dir. bands, dir. jazz program Purdue U., West Lafayette, Ind.; bd. dirs. Midwest Nat. band and Orch. clinic, Great Lakes Arts Alliance, Montreaux/-Detroit Jazz Festival. Reviewer jazz Band Mag.; author; guest conductor in field. Recipient Outstanding Jazz Educator award Nat. Band Assn. Mem. Nat. Assn. Jazz Educators (pres.-elect, internat. chmn., Ind. pres., central states coordinator, nat. recording sec., nat. chmn. for summer jazz studies). Office: Purdue U Banks Hall of Music Room 136 West Lafayette IN 47907

DUPES, PHILIP LOWELL, consulting firm executive; b. Hobart, Ind., Aug. 13, 1937; s. Lowell Edgar and Mary Louise (Cherrington) D.; m. Mary Lou Barrie, June 27, 1970. B.S. in Mech. Engring., Purdue U., 1960; M.B.A., U. Mo.-Kansas City, 1983. Registered engr. in tng., Calif. Project engr. Spreckels Sugar div. Am. Sugar Refining Co., San Francisco, 1960-76; sr. project engr. Russell Stover Candy Co., Kansas City, Mo., 1976-81; pres. Philip Lowell Assocs., Inc., Leawood, Kans., 1984—; computer systems, programming services cons. Author: (with others) Beet Sugar Technology, 1971, 3d edit., 1982. Mem. Am. Statis. Assn., Fin. Mgmt. Assn., Beta Gamma Sigma. Office: Philip Lowell Assocs Inc 12742 Overbrook Rd Leawood KS 66209

DUPUIS, FRANCOISE-ARMANDE, minister, languages and culture educator; b. Paris, Mar. 31, 1924; came to U.S., 1948, naturalized, 1962; d. Armand Alexandre and Genevieve Augustine (Blanchet) D.; m. Edward M. Smith, Feb. 19, 1949 (dec. 1971); 1 child, Michele Dupuis Smith Weyant. B.Philosophy-Lettres, Sorbonne, U. Paris, 1944, P.C.B., Faculte des Sciences de Paris, 1946, postgrad. Faculte de Medecine de Paris, 1947; postgrad. in edn. U. No. Iowa, 1962, Upper Iowa U., 1963; cert. in ministry Seabury Western Theol. Sem., 1983. Chmn. dept. langs. and culture Upper Iowa U., Fayette, 1965—, assoc. prof. langs. and culture, 1968—, chmn. humanities div., 1976-80, acting chmn. dept. religion, 1983—. Layreader, chalice bearer Episcopal Ch., Oelwein, Iowa, 1978—; mem. Fayette Betterment Com., 1982. Mem. AAUP, AAUW, Friends of France-Amerique.

DURAND, RALPH SCOTT, fraternal organization executive; b. St. Paul, Jan. 17, 1933; s. Benjamin Joseph and Grace Mabel (Scott) D.; m. Dolores Helen Langer, Aug. 19, 1957; children—Charles, Susan, Robert, Leslie, Kimberly. B.A. in Acctg., Coll. St. Thomas, St. Paul. Chief acct. North Central Life, St. Paul, 1959-63; ins. cons. Geo. V. Stennes & Assocs., Mpls., 1963-69; chief fin. officer Inter State Assurance, Des Moines, 1969-73; exec. officer Sons of Norway, Mpls., 1973—; dir. Sons of Norway Found., Mpls., 1973—; dir. exec. com. Norwegian-Am. C. of C., Mpls., 1973—, Vinland Nat. Ctr., Loretto, Minn., 1977—, Ski For Light, Inc., Mpls., 1975—. Bd. dirs. Dist. 279 Sch. Dist., Plymouth, Minn., 1973-82. Republican. Roman Catholic. Club: Torske Klubben (Mpls.). Lodge: Oslo. Office: Sons of Norway 1455 W Lake St Minneapolis MN 55408

DURBIN, RICHARD JOSEPH, Congressman; b. East St. Louis, Ill., Nov. 21, 1944; s. William and Ann D.; m. Loretta Schaefer, June 24, 1967; children—Christine, Paul, Jennifer. B.S. in Econs., Georgetown U., 1966, J.D., 1969. Bar: Ill. 1969. Chief legal counsel Lt. Gov. Paul Simon of Ill., 1969; mem. staff minority leader Ill. Senate, 1972-77, parliamentarian, 1969-77; practice law from 1969; mem. 98th-99th Congresses from 20th Dist. Ill.; assoc. prof. med. humanities So. Ill. U., from 1978. Campaign worker Sen. Paul Douglas of Ill., 1966; staff Office Ill. Dept. Bus. and Econ. Devel., Washington; candidate for Ill. Lt. Gov., 1978; staff alt. Pres's State Planning Council, 1980; advisor Am. Council Young Polit. Leaders, 1981; mem. YMCA Ann. Membership Roundup, YMCA Bldg. Drive, Pony World Series; bd. dirs. Cath. Charities, United Way of Springfield, Old Capitol Art Fair, Springfield Youth Soccer; mem. Sch. Dist. 1986 Referendum Com., Springfield NAACP. Democrat. Roman Catholic. Office: 417 Cannon House Office Bldg Washington DC 20515

DURBNEY, CLYDROW JOHN, clergyman; b. St. Louis, Sept. 27, 1916; s. Earl Elmer and Conetta Mae D.; A.B., Gordon Coll. Theology and Missions, 1950; B.D., Eden Theol. Sem., 1953; S.T.M., Concordia Theol. Sem., 1954, postgrad. 1954-59; postgrad Eden Sem., 1973-75; D.D., Am. Bible Inst., 1980; Cultural doctorate in Sacred Philosophy, World U., 1982; m. Mattie Lee Neal, Oct. 27, 1968. Ordained to ministry Nat. Bapt. Ch., 1952. Clk., U.S. Post Office, St. Louis, 1941-54; instr. Western Bapt. Bible Coll., St. Louis, 1954-67; asst. pastor Central Bapt. Ch., St. Louis, 1954, pastor, 1983; ghetto evangelist Ch. on Wheels, 1952-84; pastor, founder Saints Fellowship Ch., 1984—. Served with AUS, 1942-46; ETO. Decorated Bronze Star. Recipient Disting. World Service award Central Bapt. Ch. Prayer Aux., 1974. Mem. Internat. Platform Assn., Inst. Research Assn., Gordon Alumni Assn., Anglo Am. Acad., Nat. Geog. Soc., Smithsonian Instn. Republican. Author: With Him in Glory, 1955; Adventures in Soul Winning, 1966; contbr. to New Voices in Am. Poetry, 1972—. Home: 8244 Addington Dr Berkeley MO 63134

DURBROW, BARBARA HELEN, mgmt. cons.; b. Washington Court House, Ohio, Mar. 29, 1936; d. Roy Lee and Esta Pearl (Sword) Mustain; attended U. Cinn., Central Mich. U., U. Ala.; m. Brian Durbrow; children—Robert E., William D. Sr. cons. B.R. Durbrow & Assocs., Cin., 1969-72; v.p., sec., treas., dir. Barbrisons Mgmt. Systems, Inc., Cin., 1972—; v.p. Mgmt. Research and Devel., Inc. (merged with Barbrisons Mgmt.), Cin., 1975-80; v.p., dir. IE, Inc., 1980—; v.p. Durbrow Assocs. Properties, 1984—; co-developer ACCUTRAC Evaluation Systems. Mem. Republican Presdl. Task Force, U.S. Senatorial Club, U.S. Congl. Adv. Bd. Mem. Nat. Mgmt. Assn., Acad. Mgmt. Co-author: Modern Research on Accident Proneness; contbr. articles to profl. jours.; research on employee selection, honesty, substance abuse and accident predisposition. Office: 10451 Grand Oaks Suite 200 Cincinnati OH 45242 also 3040 Madison Rd Suite 203 Cincinnati OH 45209

DURENBERGER, DAVID FERDINAND, U.S. senator; b. St. Cloud, Minn., Aug. 19, 1934; s. George G. and Isabelle M. (Cebulla) D.; B.A. cum laude in Polit. Sci., St. Johns U., 1955; J.D., U. Minn., 1959; m. Gilda Beth Baran, Sept. 4, 1971; children by previous marriage—Charles, David, Michael, Daniel. Admitted to Minn. bar, 1959; mem. firm LeVander Gillen Miller & Durenberger, South St. Paul, 1959-66; exec. sec. to Gov. Harold LeVander, 1967-71; counsel for legal and community affairs, corp. sec. H.B. Fuller Co., St. Paul, 1971-78; U.S. senator from Minn., 1979—, mem. fin. com., govtl. affairs com., select com. on intelligence, select com. on ethics, com. on environment and pub. works, chmn. intergovtl. relations subcom., health subcom., toxic substances subcom.; mem. presdl. adv. com. on federalism, adv. commn. on intergovtl. relations, from 1981. Co-chmn. NAIA Football Bowl Playoff, 1963; div. chmn. United Fund of South St. Paul, 1965; chmn. citizens sect. Minn. Recreation and Park Assn., 1971-72; mem. South St. Paul Parks and Recreation Commn., 1971-72; chmn. Metro Council Open Space Adv. Bd., 1972-74; commr. Murphy-Hanrehan Park Bd., 1973-75; chmn. Save Open Space Now, 1974, Close-Up Found. Minn., 1975-76, Social Investment Task Force, Project Responsibility, 1974-76, Spl. Ser. div. St. Paul Area United Way, 1973-76; chmn. bd. commrs. Hennepin County Park Res. Dist.; vice chmn. Met. Parks and Open Space Bd.; exec. vice chmn. Gov.'s Commn. on Arts; exec. dir. Minn. Constl. Study Commn., Supreme Ct. Adv. Com. on Jud. Responsibility; pres. Burroughs Sch. PTA, Mpls.; chmn. Dakota County Young Republican League, 1963-64; dir. legal council Minn. Young Rep. League, 1964-65; co-chmn. State Young Rep. League Conv., 1965; del. State Rep. Conv., 1966, 68, 70, 72; 1st vice chmn. 13th Ward Mpls. Rep. Party, 1973-74; bd. dirs. Met. Parks Found., Public Service Options, Inc., St. Louis Park AAU Swim Club, Minn. Landmarks, 1971-73, Public Affairs Leadership and Mgmt. Tng., Inc., 1973-75, U. Minn. YMCA, 1973-75, Community Planning Orgn., Inc., St. Paul, 1973-76, Project Environ. Found., 1974-75, Urban Lab., Inc., 1975, Nat. Recreation and Park Assn., Within the System, Inc., from 1976; trustee Children's Health Center and Hosp., Inc., Mpls.; mem. exec. com. Nat. Center for Vol. Action, Minn. Charities Rev. Council. Served as 2d lt. U.S. Army, 1955-56, as capt. Res., 1957-63. Named Outstanding Young Man in South St. Paul, 1964, One of Ten Outstanding Young Men in Minn., 1965. Mem. Am. Bar Assn., Minn. Bar Assn., Corp. Council Assn., St. Johns U. Alumni Assn. (pres. Twin Cities chpt. 1963-65, nat. pres. 1971-73), Mpls., C. of C., St. Paul Area C. of C., Gamma Eta Gamma (chancellor 1958-59, v.p. Alumni Assn. 1965-75). Roman Catholic. Club: KC. Office: 375 Russell Senate Office Bldg Washington DC 20510

DURHAM, LEON, professional baseball player. First baseman Chgo. Cubs. Office: Chgo Cubs Wrigley Field Chicago IL 60613*

DURN, RAYMOND JOSEPH, lawyer; b. Cleve., Nov. 28, 1926; s. Joseph Frank and Mary (Spenko) D.; m. Emmy Reboly, June 5, 1954; children—David, Sarah, Tamara. B.A., Harvard Coll., 1950; LL.B., Harvard U., 1953. Bar: Ohio 1953, U.S. Dist. Ct. (no. dist.) Ohio 1954, U.S. Ct. Appeals (6th cir.) 1974. Assoc. Jones, Day, Reavis & Pogue, Cleve., 1953-60, ptnr., 1960—. Trustee Cleve. Neighborhood Health Services, Inc., 1969—; twp. trustee Chester Twp., Chesterland, Ohio, 1972-75; mem. Bd. Zoning Appeals, Chester Twp., 1969-72, mem. Zoning Commn., 1984—. Served with USAAF, 1944-46; PTO. Mem. Ohio State Bar Assn., Cleve. Bar Assn. Democrat. Unitarian. Club: City (Cleve.). Home: 13088 W Geauga Trail Chesterland OH 44026 Office: Jones Day Reavis & Pogue 1700 Huntington Bldg Cleveland OH 44115

DURNIL, GORDON KAY, lawyer, political party official; b. Indpls., Feb. 20, 1936; s. J. Ray and E. Merle Durnil; m. Lynda L. Powell, Mar. 1, 1963; children—Guy S., Cynthia L. B.S., Ind. U., 1960, J.D., 1965. Bar: Ind. 1965. Sales rep. Franklin Life Ins. Co., 1956, Moore Bus. Forms, Inc., 1960; sole practice, Indpls., 1965—; active Republican Party, 1960—, publicity com. Marion County com. (Ind.), 1966-67, campaign coordinating com., mem. campaign coordinating com. Ind. State Com., 1968-80, mem. congressional coordinating com., 1973-74, campaign dir., 1978, state chmn., 1981—, campaign mgr. for numerous candidates; v.p. Ind. Ornamental Iron Works, Inc., 1960-65; dep. prosecutor Marion County (Ind.), 1965-66; legal counsel Ind. Fedn. Young Republicans, 1965-68; spl. asst. Office of Bus. Service U.S. Dept. Commerce, 1971. Pres. Emmerich Manual High Sch. Alumni Assn., 1968; justice of peace Washington Twp. (Ind.), 1967-70; bd. dirs. Our House, Inc. (Ind. Ronald McDonald House); chmn. Marion County Election Bd., 1978-81. Served with U.S. Army; Korea. Mem. Ind. Bar Assn., Am. Assn. Polit. Cons. Presbyterian. Editor: The Marion County Republican Reporter, 1966-71. Office: One N Capitol St 1260 Indianapolis IN 46204

DURNIN, JOHN PHILIP, printing company executive; b. Milw., Jan. 30, 1932; s. Joseph Patrick and Beatrice Eulalie (Hardesty) D.; m. Rita Christine Ries, Aug. 20, 1955; children—Michael, Matthew, Timothy, Monica, Marla. B.S., Marquette U., 1956. Mgr. edn. products group, Milw., 1968-72, mgr. cylinder group, 1972-74; pres. Koch Label Co., Evansville, Ind., 1974—. Served to sgt. U.S. Army, 1953-55. Mem. Master Brewers' Assn. Republican. Roman Catholic. Avocations: Golf, barbershop singing. Office: Koch Label Co 1405 W Missouri Evansville IN 47710

DUROSS, WILLIAM JAMES, JR., mortician; b. Detroit, Nov. 6, 1935; s. William James and Mary Augusta (Rotarius) D.; m. Nancy Marie Gipperich, Sept. 28, 1968; children—William James III, Amy Marie. Student, U. Detroit, 1953-54; cert. mortuary sci. Wayne State U.-Detroit, 1956. Lic. mortician, Mich. Resident tng. Weitenberner Funeral Home, Detroit, 1952-56 owner, pres., treas., dir., 1983—; with William R. Hamilton Co., Detroit, 1957, DeSantis Funeral Home, Detroit, 1957-65, owner, pres., treas., dir. Wm. J. Duross Funeral Home, Warren, Mich., 1966—. Mem. Nat. Funeral Dirs. Assn., Mich. Funeral Dirs. Assn., Warren Symphony Assn., Kolping Soc. Roman Catholic. Clubs: Elks, Kiwanis, Optimist, Lions.

DURPETTI, ANTHONY ALDO, broadcasting executive; b. Chgo., Feb. 1, 1944; s. Aldo Domenick and Mary Lucille (Bucci) D.; m. Marion Kathleen Michelotti, Feb. 1, 1969; 1 dau., Michelle Nicole. Student Northwestern U., 1963-65. Media buyer D'Arcy Advt., Chgo., 1967-69; with McGavren Guild Radio, 1969—, account exec., 1969-71, sales mgr., 1971-73, mgr. Chgo. region, 1973-75, exec. v.p. central div., 1975—, also mem. exec. com., chmn. tng. div. Served with AUS, 1965-67. Mem. Sta. Reps. Assn., Broadcast Advt. Club Chgo. Democrat. Roman Catholic. Clubs: Burnham Park Yacht, Chgo. Health. Office: 111 E Wacker Dr Chicago IL 60601

DURRETT, ANDREW MANNING, consulting designer, inventor; b. Clarksville, Tenn., Jan. 7, 1924; s. Andrew Manning and Betty Ann (Empson) D.; m. Jean E. Lanning, May 14, 1949; children—Cheryl A. Durrett Yurs, Griffith Lynn, Susan Elizabeth Durrett Pantle, Robert Tracy, Vicki Jean Durrett Robinson. Student U. Tenn., 1946-48; B.F.A., Art Inst. Chgo., 1951. Mech. engr. Werthan Bag Corp., Nashville, 1951-52; designer C.F. Block, Chgo., 1952-53, Advt. Metal Display, Chgo., 1953-55; artist, poster designer Gen. Outdoor Advt. Co., Chgo., 1956-58; with sales, tng. films and scripts. Ross Wetzel Studios, Chgo., 1958-60; sales mgr. indsl. design Palma-Knapp Design, River Forest, Ill., 1961-65; founder, pres. Manning Durrett Design Assocs., R&D med. equipment, Spring Grove, Ill., 1965—. Author: (with Don Gilbert) Industrial Insectology, 1980; producer films on insect control; patentee in field; exhibited med. and indsl. products Mus. Sci. and Industry, Chgo., 1970. Bd. dirs., sec. Brookfield Citizens Mgmt. Assn. (Ill.), 1953-54; committeeman Oaks Assn., Libertyville, Ill., 1970-76, chmn. service com.; co-author flood plane ordinance, Libertyville, 1975. Served with USN, 1943-46. Recipient Excellence in Design awards Indsl. Design Rev., 1969, 69. Mem. Sch. Art Inst. Chgo. Alumni Assn., Chgo. Assn. Commerce and Industry, Internat. Platform Assn., Phi Kappa Phi. Republican. Methodist. Clubs: Oak Bus. Men's (Ill.); Cambridge Country (Libertyville). Office: Manning Durrett Design Assocs 38625 Forest Ave Spring Grove IL 60081

DUST, ROBERT CARL, utilities official, city official; b. Saginaw, Mich., Jan. 4, 1933; s. Carl Theodore and Olga P. (Dixon) D.; m. Marilyn Ann Heath, June 4, 1954; children—Tobin Howard, Timothy Carl. B.S. in Civil Engring., Mich. State U., 1955. Registered profl. engr., Mich. Methods engr. Saginaw Steering Gear, Mich., 1956; civil engr. City of Saginaw, 1957-62, dir. utilities, 1963—, acting city mgr., 1978—; commr. Saginaw Midland Water System, 1963—. Served to 1st lt. USAR, 1955-63. Mem. Inst. Mcpl. Engrs., Am. Pub. Works Assn., Am. Water Works Assn., Water Pollution Control Fedn., Mich. Soc. Planning Ofcls. Presbyterian. Avocations: sailing, fishing, golf. Home: 32 Victory Ct Saginaw MI 48602 Office: Utilities Dept 1701 S Jefferson Saginaw MI 48601

DUSTER, DONALD LEON, utility company executive; b. Chgo., Feb. 10, 1932; s. Benjamin and Alfreda (Barnett) D.; m. Maxine Porter, Dec. 22, 1962; children—Michelle, David, Daniel. B.S., U. Ill., 1953; M.B.A., DePaul U., 1977. Store mgr. Spiegel, Inc., Chgo., 1955-62; adminstrv. asst. Commonwealth Edison, Chgo., 1962-77, 1979—. Dir. Ill. Dept. Bus. and Econ. Devel., Springfield, Ill., 1977-79; bd. dirs. Chgo. Commons Assn., Taylor Inst., Chgo., Latino Inst., Chgo.; mem. Citizens Commn. on the Juvenile Ct., Chgo., 1984; mem. U.S.-South Africa Leader Exchange Program, Washington, 1972—. Mem. Investment Analyst Soc. Chgo. Club: Econ. (Chgo.). Home: 9046 S Blackstone Ave Chicago IL 60619 Office: Commonwealth Edison 72 W Adams St Chicago IL 60690

DU TEMPLE, OCTAVE JOSEPH, scientific society executive, chemical engineer; b. Hubbell, Mich., Dec. 10, 1920; s. Octave Joseph and Marguerite (Gadoury) DuT.; m. Orpha Jane Servies, June 9, 1943 (div. May 1945); m. Susan Margaret Keach, June 9, 1951; children—Lesley Ann, Octave Joseph. B.S., Mich. Tech. U., 1948, M.S., 1949; M.B.A., Northwestern U., 1955. Chem. engr. Argonne Nat. Lab, Ill., 1949-58; exec. dir. Am. Nuclear Soc., La Grange Park, Ill., 1958—; dir. Am. Assn. Engring. Socs., 1980—; mem. internat. adv. com. AAAS, Washington, 1980—; dir. Council Engring. and Sci. Soc. Execs., 1974-78. Editor: Prehistoric Copper Mining in Lake Superior Area, 1963; editor Nuclear News, 1959—; co-author sci. reports on reprocessing irradiated fuels. Sec. Burr Ridge Planning Com., Ill., 1972-74, Burr Ridge Zoning Bd. Appeals, 1972. Served with USAAC, 1945-46. Recipient Octave Du Temple award Am. Nuclear Soc., 1983, Disting. Service award, 1978; Outstanding Mgmt. award Am. Soc. Assn. Execs., 1972. Mem. Am. Nuclear Soc. (exec. dir. 1958—), Am. Inst. Chem. Engrs., Am. Chem. Soc., Am. Soc. Engring. Edn. Republican. Episcopalian.

DUVAL, DANIEL WEBSTER, See *Who's Who in America,* 43rd edition.

DUVALL, BETTY, educational administrator; b. Everton, Mo., Nov. 29, 1939; s. John Wesley and Tinnie Pauline (Poteet) Funk; m. Richard Duvall, Dec. 27, 1963. B.S. in Edn., S.W. Mo. State U., 1960; M.A. in Librarianship, U. Denver, 1966; M.A. in Humanities, NYU, 1976; Ph.D. in Higher Edn., St. Louis U., 1983. Asst. prof. L.S., St. Louis Community Coll.-Florissant Valley, St. Louis, 1963-66, assoc. dean instrn., 1966-75, dir. Circle Project, 1972-75, acting pres., 1978, dean instrn., 1975—; cons./examiner North Central Assn., Chgo., 1969—. Author: Show-Me Libraries, 1984. Mem. awards com. YMCA, St. Louis, 1981; co-chmn. United Way Greater St. Louis, 1981; bd. dirs., program chmn. St. Louis Metro forum, 1984. Wall St. Jour. fellow 1961; Council Library Resources fellow, 1971; St. Louis Leadership Program fellow, 1978. Mem. Ferguson-Berkeley C. of C., Mo. Vocat. Assn., North Central Assn. Acad. Deans (pres. 1982-83), Mo. Assn. Community and Jr. Colls. Home: 10 N Kingshighway Saint Louis MO 63108 Office: St Louis Community Coll-Florissant Valley 3400 Pershall Rd Saint Louis MO 63135

DUVALL, RUSSEL WILEY, electronics corporation executive; b. Indpls., Sept. 8, 1940; s. Russel Franklin and Margaret Helen (Hedges) D.; m. Gay Lynn Halbert, Oct. 25, 1969. A.B., Wabash Coll., 1962; M.B.A. with distinction, Keller Grad. Sch. Mgmt., 1979. Merchandise handling mgr. Lane Bryant, Inc., Indpls., 1969-71; founder, pres. PerfaClime, Inc., Indpls., 1971-72; v.p., dist. mgr. A.W.D., Inc., Indpls., 1972-74; asst. to pres. Crooks Terminal Warehouses, Inc., Chgo., 1975-76; plant and logistics mgr. Flavor Tree Foods, Inc., Chgo., 1976-77; plant mgr. Lawry's Foods, Inc., Chgo., 1977-79; v.p. prodn. and distbn. Monogram Models, Inc., Chgo., 1979-82; pres., chief exec. officer Reach Electronics, Inc., Lexington, Nebr., 1982-85, also dir.; pres., chief exec. officer Veetronix, Inc., Lexington, 1982-85, also dir.; pres., chief exec. officer CRV Corp., Lexington, 1984—, also dir.; gen. mgr. DRV Sino-Am. Communications Co., Ltd., Beijing, China, 1985—, also dir. Charter mem. Keller Grad. Sch. Alumni Adv. Council, Chgo., 1982. Served to lt. comdr. USN, USNR, 1962-79. Recipient Small Bus. of Yr. Nebr. award Small Bus. Adminstrn., 1984, Boss of Yr. award Jaycees, 1983, —E— award for exporting U.S. Dept. Commerce, 1983. Avocations: reading; flying; writing and playing music; writing poetry; participating in sports. Office: CRV Corp PO Box 308 Lexington NE 68850

DVORAK, DANIEL FRANCIS, information systems executive; b. Joliet, Ill., Dec. 8, 1954; s. Donald David and Joan Marie (McNamee) D.; m. Maureen Therese Dryz, July 12, 1975. B.S. in Mgmt., Elmhurst Coll., 1977; M.B.A. in Info. Systems Mgmt., DePaul U., 1981. Systems analyst Am. Hosp. Supply, Evanson, Ill., 1977-80; mgr. systems and programming Schwinn Bicycle Co., Chgo., 1980-83; dir. bus. systems Newell Cos., Inc., Freeport, Ill., 1983—. Coordinator United Fund, Freeport, 1984. Ill. State Scholarship Commn. scholar, 1972. Mem. Data Processing Mgmt. Assn., Am. Production and Inventory Control Soc. (cert. 1982). Republican. Roman Catholic. Avocations: Golf; racquetball; automobile racing. Office: Newell Cos 29 E Stephenson St Freeport IL 61032

DVORAK, DAVID GRANT, ophthalmologist; b. Cedar Rapids, Iowa, Dec. 28, 1938; s. Otto Joseph and Grace Emma (Munger) D.; m. Carol Diane Braun, Aug. 26, 1961; children—David Scott, Cathy Lynn; B.S., Valparaiso U., 1960; M.D., U. Mich., 1964. Diplomate Am. Bd. Ophthalmology. Bronson Meth. Hosp., Kalamazoo, Mich., 1964-65; resident in ophthalmology Ind. U.-Indpls., 1967-70; practice medicine specializing in ophthalmology, Kalamazoo, Mich., 1970—; asst. clin. prof. surgery Mich. State U., East Lansing, 1973—. Served to capt. U.S. Army, 1965-67, Vietnam. Fellow Am. Acad. Ophthalmology; mem. AMA, Kalamazoo Acad. Medicine, Mich. Ophthal. Soc. Republican. Lutheran. Avocations: tennis, bicycling, photography. Office: Kalamazoo Ophthalmology PC 255 Bronson Med Ctr Kalamazoo MI 49007

DVORIN, HAROLD LEWIS, financial executive; b. Chgo., Dec. 17, 1939; s. Joseph L. and Thelma (Davies) D.; m. Sarah Jane King, July 10, 1982. B.S. in Mgmt., U. Ill.-Urbana, 1961, M.Acctg.Sci., 1967. Staff acct. Alexander Grant & Co., Chgo., 1964-65; profit analyst Inland Steel Co., Chgo., 1965-68; mgr. cost. acctg. Gen. Felt Industries, Chgo., 1968-71, Internat. Products, Palatine, Ill., 1972-73; asst. controller switch div. Oak Industries, Crystal Lake, Ill., 1973-81; controller-treas. Redington, Inc., Bellwood, Ill., 1982—; instr. William R. Harper Coll., Palatine, 1974-77, Triton Coll., River Grove, Ill., 1973. Vol., Chgo. Symphony Orch. Marathon, 1980-83; mem. Jazz Inst. Chgo., Chgo. Symphony Soc. Served in U.S. Army, 1961-64. Home: 801 W Bryn Mawr Ave Roselle IL 60172 Office: 3000 St Charles Rd Bellwood IL 60104

DWORKIN, JAMES BARNET, industrial relations educator, labor arbitrator; b. Cin., July 8, 1948; s. Harry and Beatrice Leah (Steinberg) D.; m. Nancy Elizabeth Hunter, July 20, 1973; children—Sarah, David. B.A. in Econs. with high honors, U. Cin., 1970, M.A. in Indsl. Relations, 1971; Ph.D. in Indsl. Relations, U. Minn., 1976. Mem. faculty Purdue U., West Lafayette, Ind., 1976—, assoc. prof. indsl. relations, 1983—, dir. M.S. in Indsl. Relations program, 19; vis. assoc. prof. U. Minn.-Mpls., 1981-83; arbitrator Am. Arbitration Assn., Nat. Mediation Bd., Pub. Employment Relations Bd., Ind. Edn. Employment Relations Bd. Recipient Outstanding Tchr. award Purdue U. Sch. Mgmt., 1979. Mem. Indsl. Relations Research Assn., Am. Arbitration Assn., Am. Econs. Assn., Soc. Profls. in Dispute Resolution. Democrat. Jewish. Author: Owners Versus Players: Baseball and Collective Bargaining, 1981; contbr. numerous articles to profl. publs. Home: 3103 Decatur St West Lafayette IN 47906 Office: Purdue Univ 489 Krannert Grad Sch West Lafayette IN 47907

DWORKIN, SIDNEY, business executive; b. Detroit, 1921; B.A., Wayne State U., 1942; married. Partner, Dworkin, Boone & Gross, C.P.A.'s, 1950-66; indsl. acct., 1966; Revco D S Inc., Twinsburg, Ohio, 1966-85, chief exec. officer, dir., 1966—, chmn., 1983—; chmn. bd. Fabri-Centers Am., Inc., from 1983; dir. Neutrogena Corp., Eclipse Industries, Inc., No. Instruments Co., Nat. City Bank Corp., Fabric Centers Corp. Mem. Nat. Assn. Chain Drug Stores (dir.). Served in U.S. Army, 1943-45. Office: Revco D S Inc 1925 Enterprise Pkwy Twinsburg OH 44087

DWYER, JOHN COMER, laboratory executive; b. Evergreen Park, Ill., Sept. 5, 1947; s. Frank Joseph and Joan Mary (Edwarde) D.; m. Carlene Gail Pye, Oct. 18, 1975. B.S. in Chemistry U. Ill., 1970. Chemist Travenol Labs, Inc., Morton Grove, Ill., 1970-74, supr., 1974-77, mgr. 1977-82, assoc. dir., 1982—. Mem. Am. Chemical Soc. (cert.), Am. Mgmt. Assn., Parenteral Drug Assn. Avocations: Philately; reading; learning; photography; skiing. Home: 250 Old Oak Dr Buffalo Grove IL 60090 Office: Baxter Travenol Labs 6301 Lincoln Ave Morton Grove IL 60053

DWYER, MARIE RITA ROZELLE (MRS. JOHN D. DWYER), educator; b. N.Y.C., Sept. 4, 1915; d. Charles W. and Agnes (Coyle) Rozelle; student L'Assomption, Paris, 1932-33; B.A., Notre Dame Coll., 1936; M.A., Fordham U., 1938, also postgrad; postgrad. St. Louis U.; student Sorbonne, Paris, summers 1933-37, 52; m. John D. Dwyer, Sept. 8, 1942; children—John Duncan, Joseph Charles, James Gerard, Jerome Valentine. Tchr. French, Sch. of Edn., Fordham U., N.Y.C., 1938-42, Notre Dame Coll., N.Y.C., 1939-40, Coll. of St. Rose, Albany, N.Y., 1949-53, Washington U., St. Louis, 1959-60; faculty French dept. Webster Coll., 1966-74; dir. community services Internat. Students Program, St. Louis U., 1974-83, with internat. programs, 1984—; mem. faculty Meramec Community Coll., St. Louis, 1968-70. Active community fund drives, including Greater St. Louis Fund for Arts and Edn.; bd. dirs. St. Louis Christmas Carols Assn., 1962-64, Parish Council, 1966-67; adult adviser cultural program for young adults Archdiocesan Council Cath. Youth,

1961-67; mem. Archdiocesan Council Laity Charities; chmn. internat. friendship program Archdiocesan Council of Laity of St. Louis, 1984. Mem. Am. Assn. Tchrs. French (pres. St. Louis chpt. 1955-56), Mo. Acad. Sci. (life mem., editorial staff transactions 1969-72, chmn. linguistics sect. 1970-76, past mem. exec. bd.), Alliance Française (past sec. St. Louis), Société Française (past sec.), KC Aux. (past pres.), AAAS (rep. Mo. Acad. Sci. at conv. in Mexico City 1973), Notre Dame Coll. Alumnae Assn. (past pres.), Internat. Fedn. Cath. Alumnae (past pres. Albany), Jesuit Mothers Guild (pres. 1963-65), Cath. Women's League (pres. 1964-66), Archdiocean Council Cath. Women (mem. coms. family life teen-age code, corr. sec. 1963-64, pres. 1964-66 South Central dist., adv. council 1968—), Nat. French Honor Soc., AAUP, MLA, Mo. MLA (pres. 1961-63), Central States Conf. on Teaching Fgn. Langs., Société International de la Linguistique, Linguistic Soc. Am., Fgn. Lang. Assn. Mo. (v.p. 1973, sec. 4-Coll. Consortium (Webster, Fontbonne, Maryville and Lindenwood) 1972-73), Centro Studie Scambi Internazionali (mem. internat. com.), Smithsonian Instn. Nat. Assos., Internat. Platform Assn., Pi Delta Phi, Alpha Sigma Nu. Club: St. Louis University Faculty Women's (pres. 1956-58, dir. 1959—, v.p. 1983-84). Extensive travel for ednl. and linguistic research. Home: 526 Oakwood Ave Webster Groves MO 63119 Office: Internat Programs St Louis U 220 N Grand Blvd Saint Louis MO 63103

DWYER, RUSSELL LEE, chief of police; b. Warren County, Ohio, Jan. 31, 1938; s. Lawrence Corwin and Lillian (Knox) D.; m. Oma Ann Robertson, Mar. 11, 1961 (div. Apr. 1981); children—Robert, Anthony; m. Patricia Ann Roberson, Apr. 22, 1983; stepchildren—Dennis, Dana. Student Miami U., Oxford, Ohio, 1961-1969. Patrolman Middletown Div. of Police, Ohio, 1960-63, detective, 1963-64, sgt., 1964-70, lt., 1970-71, service div. comdr., 1971-75, chief of police, 1975—; pres., bd. dirs. Drug Counseling Services, Butler County, Ohio, 1984—. Contbr. articles to police mags. Bd. dirs. Pokey Griffith council Boy Scouts Am., Middletown; past pres. Middletown High Sch. Athletic Boosters. Recipient Robert Hamilton Bishop medal Miami U., Oxford, Ohio, 1982; Outstanding Contbn. to Edn. award Middletown Tchrs. Assn. Mem. Internat. Assn. Chiefs Police (treas. 1984—), Internat. Narcotics Enforcement Officers Assn., Ohio Assn. Chiefs Police (past pres.) Republican. Roman Catholic. Lodge: Rotary. Avocations: scuba diving; raising horses; music; reading. Home: 7272 Dickey Rd Middletown OH 45042 Office: Middletown Div Police 1 City Centre Plaza Middletown OH 45042

DYBALA, RAY ANTHONY, tax lawyer; b. Chgo., Nov. 6, 1948; s. Roman Anthony and Mary Ann (Bowman) D.; m. Antoinette Marilyn Yucus, Oct. 29, 1972; children—Matthew, Eric, Michelle. B.S., B.A., Roosevelt U., 1971; M.B.A., DePaul U., 1976, J.D., 1980. Bars: Ill. 1980, U.S. Dist. Ct. (no. dist.) Ill. 1980; C.P.A., Ill. Sr. tax analyst Amsted Industries Inc., Chgo., 1970-73; asst. tax mgr. Morton Thiokol, Inc., Chgo., 1973-75; tax dir. Oakbrook Consolidated, Ill., 1975-78; tax counsel Motorola, Inc., Schaumburg, Ill., 1978—. Mem. Tax Execs. Inst., ABA, Ill. Bar Assn., Chgo. Bar Assn., Am. Inst. C.P.A.s, Ill. C.P.A. Soc. Republican. Roman Catholic. Club: Chgo. Tax. Home: 2113 Aberdeen Ct Wheaton IL 60187 Office: Motorola Inc 1303 E Algonquin Rd Schaumburg IL 60196

DYBEL, MICHAEL WAYNE, biochemist, biotechnology company executive, consultant; b. Hammond, Ind., July 19, 1946. B.A., Wabash Coll., 1968; M.S., Northwestern U., 1969; postgrad. U. Notre Dame, 1969-71; M.B.A., U. Chgo., 1978. Biochemist, Internat. Minerals and Chem., Mundelein, Ill., 1971-72; biochemist I, Abbott Labs., North Chicago, Ill., 1972-78; assoc. Technonic Cons., Chgo., 1978-81; v.p. Centaur Genetics Corp., Chgo., 1981; pres. Strategic Techs. Internat., Libertyville, Ill., 1982—; pres. Coal Biotech Corp., Libertyville, 1984—. Lubrizol scholar Wabash Coll., 1968. Mem. Am. Chem. Soc., AAAS. Office: Strategic Techs Internat Inc 800 S Milwaukee Rd Libertyville IL 60048

DYDEK, PAUL ANTHONY, accountant; b. East Chicago, Ind., July 14, 1956; s. Joseph and Sally (Bogucki) D.; m. Stephanie Marie Gavrilos, May 14, 1983. B.S. in Acctg. magna cum laude, Calumet Coll., Whiting, Ind., 1978; M.B.A. in Fin., DePaul U., Chgo., 1982. C.P.A., Ill. Acctg. trainee Republic Steel Corp., Chgo., 1978-80, cost acct., 1981-82, supr. budgets, 1982-84, fin. analyst, 1984-85, supr. gen. acctg., 1985—; v.p. LTV Steel Suprs. Club. Mem. Zeta Beta Tau, Delta Mu Delta. Roman Catholic. Lodge: K.C. Home: 1630 Roberts Ave Whiting IN 46394

DYE, CARL MELVYN, educational association executive; b. Cedar Rapids, Iowa, Oct. 7, 1940; s. Floyd Carmen and Inger Marie (Johansen) D.; B.A., Parsons Coll., 1962; M.S.Ed., No. Ill. U., 1967. Dir. admissions counselors Parsons Coll., Fairfield, Iowa, 1962-68; acad. dean Bryant and Stratton Coll., Milw., 1968-69; pres. Coll. of the South, Pascagoula, Miss., 1969-70; acad. dean Massey Jr. Coll., Atlanta, 1970-71; pres. Am. Schs. Assn., Chgo., 1971—; dir., founder Vocat. Transfer Services, 1982. Served with U.S. Army, 1963-64. Mem. Phi Kappa Phi. Home: 2252 N Fremont St Chicago IL 60614

DYE, DAVID ALAN, lawyer, educator; b. Lexington, Mo., Sept. 11, 1950; s. Donald Alfred and Dorothy Sue D.; m. Julia Yolanda Zapata, June 21, 1979. B.A., U. Mo., 1972, J.D., 1976. Sole practice, Kansas City, Mo., 1976—; prof., coordinator Lawyers' Asst. Program, Mo. Western State Coll., St. Joseph, 1977—. Co-founder, pres. Mid-Coast Radio Project, Inc., 1978-79, bd. dirs., 1978-80, chmn. adv. council, 1980—; legal cons. Greater Kansas City Epilepsy League, pres., 1982-84, mem. exec. com., 1984—, bd. dirs. 1978—; mem. ho. of dels. Epilepsy Found. Am., 1982-83. State of Mo. grantee, 1980, 82. Mem. ABA, Mo. Bar Assn., Mo. Bar Assn. (legal asst. com., subcom. to form legal asst. guideline), Kansas City Met. Bar Assn. (legal asst. com.), Am. Assn. for Paralegal Edn. (organizer, mem. membership com., bd. dirs. 1983-86, chmn. fundraising com. 1984), Nat. Assn. of Legal Assts. (assoc.). Editor: (with John Calvert) Systems for Legal Assistant: A Resource Manual of Selected Articles and Materials., 1980; author articles on paralegal edn. and profession; organizer, condr. seminars, workshops on legal assts. programs. Home: PO Box 6158 Kansas City MO 64110 Office: Mo Western State Coll St Joseph MO 64501

DYE, PATRICIA LYNNE (MCDONALD), lawyer; b. Sinton, Tex., Oct. 30, 1951; d. Carlos Wass and Louise (Burk) McDonald; 1 child, Clovis Lawrence. B.A. in German, Columbia Union Coll., Takoma Park, Md., 1974; J.D., Capital U., 1980. Bar: Ohio 1980, U.S. Dist. Ct. (so. dist.) Ohio 1982. Transfer-in clk. Group Hospitalization, Inc., Washington, 1975-76; work-study asst. Capital U. Law Sch., Columbus, Ohio, 1976-77; legal aide Ohio Dept. Commerce, Columbus, 1977-79, legal intern, 1979-80, atty., 1981—. Republican. Adventist. Home: 5250 Cyprus Dr Delaware OH 43015

DYE, PEGGIE LOU, elementary educator; b. Kennett, Mo., Oct. 20, 1934; d. Henry Curtis Green and Hazel Delia (Sallee) Green Fullerton; m. James David Dye, Jan. 30, 1954; children—Debra Rene Dye McKone, Susan Kay Dye Storms. B.A., Mich. State U., 1974, M.A. in Classroom Teaching, 1977; postgrad. Mich. Montessori Tng. Ctr., 1977-78. Tchr.-aide follow-through program Flint (Mich.) Community Schs., 1968-73, tchr. grades K-2, 1974-77 Montessori tchr. grades K-2 1977—. Mem. state adv. council Women's Missionary Union of So. Baptists in Mich.; Women's Missionary Union dir. Genesee Baptist Assn. Mem. Nat. Assn. Ret. People (assoc.), United Tchrs. Flint (mem. task force for excellence in edn.), NEA, Nat. Audubon Soc., Mich. Edn. Assn., Internat. Inst. Republican. Home: 4420 Old Colony Dr Flint MI 48507

DYE, RICHARD WAYNE, ins. co. exec.; b. Birmingham, Ala., Jan. 31, 1937; s. Arlie and Flora (Donaldson) D.; Asso. in Bus., Flint Jr. Coll., 1958; B.S., Eastern Mich. U., 1961; M.A., Central Mich. U., 1964, ednl. specialist, 1968; m. Sylvia Kathleen McKinsey, June 30, 1962; children—Lora Ann, Amy Elizabeth. Bus. tchr., coach Millington (Mich.) Public Schs., 1962-63; bus. tchr., coach, counselor Blanchard (Mich.) Public Schs., 1963-64, prin., 1964-66; bus. mgr. Essexville (Mich.) Public Schs., 1966-67; supt. Rapid River (Mich.) Public Schs., 1967-69; agent State Farm Ins. Co., Escanaba, Mich., 1969-71, owner, mgr., agt. 1971—. Chmn. ch. council Calvary Luth. Ch., 1969-81; chmn. Delta County Zoning Bd. Appeals, 1976-80; mem. Delta Planning Commn., 1980—; mem. Ensign Fire Dept., 1978-81, fire chief, 1978. Served with N.G., 1959-65. Mem. Central Upper Penninsula Life Underwriters Assn., Nat. Rifle Assn., Nat. Def. Preparedness Assn. Club: Masons. Home: Rural Route 3 Rapid River MI 49878 Office: State Farm Ins Co 1005 Ludington St Escanaba MI 49829

DYER, ROBERT LEE, psychologist; b. Terre Haute, Ind., Sept. 16, 1947; s. Ora and Mary Ethel (Mullen) D.; m. Jane Ellen Martin, Feb. 20, 1971; children—Jason Martin, Joshua Reed, Brody Lee. B.S., Ind. State U., 1969, M.S., 1970, Ph.D., 1978. Correctional diagnostic specialist Johnston Youth Community Ctr., Terre Haute, 1972-73; staff psychologist Hamilton Ctr., Terre Haute, 1973-81; dep. dir. So. Hills Mental Health Ctr., Jasper, Ind., 1981-84; exec. dir. Quinco Cons. Ctr., Columbus, Ind., 1984—. Served with U.S. Army, 1970-72. Mem. Am. Psychol. Assn., Ind. Psychol. Assn., Ind. Council Community Mental Health Ctrs., Am. Mgmt. Assn. Contbr. articles to profl. jours. Office: 2075 Lincoln Park Dr Columbus IN 47201

DYER, SUSAN REBECCA, educator; b. Monongahela, Pa., Aug. 4, 1943; d. Pershing General and Chrystal Rebecca (Edge) Parrish; m. Andrew Gregory Dyer, Aug. 26, 1967 (div. 1974); 1 dau., Pamela Kristin. B.S. in Edn., Central State U., 1966; M.A. in Ednl. Adminstrn., U. Mich., 1975. Social Studies tchr. Beaubian Jr. High Sch., 1966-76; social studies tchr. Mumford High Sch., Detroit, 1976-80, test coordinator, 1980—, facilitator Ford Found. High Sch. Improvement Project, 1982—; Afro-Am. history cons. Detroit Bd. Edn., Archdiocese of Detroit, Mich. State U.; participant competency-based testing hearing U.S. Dept. Edn., Washington, 1981. Mem. Detroit Fedn. Tchrs., Delta Sigma Theta. Baptist. Contbr. articles to profl. jours. Home: 19373 Robson St Detroit MI 48235 Office: 17525 Wyoming St Detroit MI 48221

DYER, WILLIAM ALLAN, JR., newspaper executive; b. Providence, Oct. 23, 1902; s. William Allan and Clara (Spink) D.; grad. Lawrenceville Sch., 1920; B.Ph., Brown U., 1924; LL.D., Ind. U., 1977; D.H.L. (hon.), Butler U., 1983; m. Marian Elizabeth Blumer, Aug. 9, 1934; children—Allan H., William E. Reporter, Syracuse (N.Y.) Jour., 1923; various advt. positions Syracuse (N.Y.) Post-Standard, 1925-41; v.p., gen. mgr. Star Pub. Co., Indpls., 1944-49; v.p. Indpls. Newspapers, Inc., 1949-75, gen. mgr., 1949-74, pres., 1975—; pres. Muncie Newspapers, Inc., 1975—; dir. Central Newspapers, Inc., Indpls., 1949—, exec. v.p. 1964-73; N.Y.C. dir. Met. Sunday Newspapers, 1951-75, pres., 1969-75; dir. Am. Newspaper Pub. Assn. bur. advt., 1963-69, Research Inst., 1955-62, pres., 1963-64; pres. Central Newspapers Found. Indpls. Mem. exec. com. United Fund Indpls., 1954-70, pres. 1970; v.p. Comm. Service Council, Indpls. 1967-68; v.p., bd. dirs. Ind. State Symphony Soc.; pres. Goodwill Industries Found. of Central Ind., 1980—. Trustee, Brown U., 1952-59; pres. Indpls. Community Hosp. Found., 1976-83. Served to lt. comdr., USNR, 1941-44. Recipient Advt. Club Torch of Truth award, 1975; Am. Advt. Fedn. silver medal, 1971. Mem. Better Bus. Bur. Indpls. (dir. 1950-65, pres. 1958, 65), Nat. Better Bus. Bur. (dir. 1950-70), Council Better Bus. Burs. (dir. 1970, 79—), Indpls. C. of C. (dir. 1967—, v.p. 1970-71), Am. Newspaper Publishers Assn. (labor relations com. 1953-63), Indpls. Advt. Club (dir. 1952-54, pres. 1952-53), Indpls. Comm. Hosp. Assn. (dir. 1952-54, 66-69, v.p. 1954). Club: Brown U. Ind. (Brown Bear award, 1968, sec. 1946-52, pres. 1952-54). Home: 401 Buckingham Dr Indianapolis IN 46208 Office: 307 N Pennsylvania St Indianapolis IN 46204

DYER, WILLIAM EARL, JR., newspaper editor; b. Kearney, Nebr., May 15, 1927; s. William Earl and Hazel Maud (Hosfelt) D.; m. Elizabeth M. Meisinger, June 26, 1967; children—Lee Michael, Scott William. B.A., U. Nebr., 1949. Reporter, Nebraska City Daily News Press., 1943-44; reporter, copy editor The Lincoln Star (Nebr.), 1948-50, city editor, 1951-60, exec. editor, 1960—; pres. Nebr. AP Editors, 1964. Pres., Lincoln Unitarian Ch., 1962-63; state chmn. Nebr. We Shake Hands Indian Project, 1958-60; mem. Nebr. Adv. Com. on Indian Law Enforcement, 1960-62; mem. State Adv. Com. to Welfare Dept., 1970-73, 80-84. Served with AUS, 1945-46. Named Hon. Mem., Omaha Indian Tribe. Mem. AP Mng. Editors Assn., Phi Beta Kappa, Sigma Delta Chi. Democrat. Club: Open Forum. Home: 1115 Fall Creek Rd Lincoln NE 68510 Office: 926 P St Lincoln NE 68501

DYKEN, MARK LEWIS, neurologist, medical educator; b. Laramie, Wyo., Aug. 26, 1928; s. Mark L. and Thelma Violet (Achenbach) D.; m. Beverly All, June 8, 1951; children—Betsy Lynn, Mark Eric, Julie Suzanne, Amy Luise, Andrew Christopher, Gregory Allen. B.S., Ind. U., 1951, M.D., 1954. Diplomate Am. Bd. Psychiatry and Neurology. Intern, Gen. Hosp., Indpls., 1955; resident in neurology Ind. U. Hosp., Indpls., 1955-58; clin. dir., dir. research New Castle State Hosp., Ind., 1958-61; asst. prof. Ind. U. Sch. Medicine, Indpls., 1958-61, assoc. prof., 1964-69, prof. neurology, 1969—, chmn. dept., 1971—. Fellow Am. Acad. Neurology; mem. Am. Heart Assn. (chmn. Stroke Council 1984—), Neurology (pres.-elect 1984—), AMA, Ind. Med. Soc., Marion County Med. Soc., Am. Neurol. Assn. Home: 7406 W 92d St Zionsville IN 46077 Office: Dept Neurology Ind U Sch Medicine 545 Barnhill Dr Indianapolis IN 46223

DYKMAN, KERRY RAND, hospital adminstrator; b. Grand Rapids, Mich., Apr. 3, 1942; s. Gerald Elco and Frances Louis (Averill) D.; m. Virginia Kathryn Schawb, Aug. 17, 1968; children—Courtney Elisabeth, Tiffany Nicole. Assoc., Grand Rapids Jr. Coll., 1962; B.S., Western Mich. U., 1964; M.B.A., 1969. Personnel dir. Saratoga Hosp., Detroit, 1975, asst. adminstr., 1975-77, assoc. adminstr., 1977-79, adminstr., 1979-81, exec. dir., 1981—; pres. Saratoga Health Care Corp., 1983—. Council pres. Zion United Ch. Christ, Fraser, Mich.; mem. Greater Detroit Area Health Council Planning Com.; mem. Comprehensive Health Planning Council of Southeastern Mich., Detroit. Mem. Am. Coll. Hosp. Adminstrs., Mich. Hosp. Assn. Southeastern Mich. (planning com.), Alpha Phi Omega. Office: Saratoga Community Hosp 15000 Gratiot Ave Detroit MI 48205

DYKSTERHUIS, JERRY EDSKO, vocational rehabilitation corporation executive, consultant; b. Parsons, Kans., June 21, 1941; s. Edsko Jerry and Margaret Adeline (Cox) D.; m. Myrna Sylvara, July 3, 1965 (div. Nov. 1971); 1 son, Edsko Jerry II; m. Donna Ann Reed, Feb. 16, 1974; children—Christopher Raymond, Dana Lynn, Amy Beth, Douglas David. B.S., Colo. State U., 1965; M.A., U. Nebr., 1970, Ph.D., 1981. Rehab. counselor Glenwood State Hosp. (Iowa), 1962-65; clin. psychometrist Letterman Hosp., San Francisco, 1966-68; dir. pulmonary rehab. U. Nebr. Med. Ctr., Omaha, 1969-72, dir. family services, 1973-75, dir. rehab., 1976-79; pres., dir. rehab. Career Design, Inc., Omaha, Lincoln, Phoenix, 1980—; cons. rehab.; expert witness. Author: (with Irving Kass) Chronic Obstructive Lung Disease, 1973; contbr. chpt., numerous articles to profl. jours., 1970—. Mem. Iowa Gov.'s Task Force on Mental Retardation, 1965; chmn. Nebr. Gov.'s Conf. on Human Resource Devel., 1971; bd. dirs. Nebr. Easter Seal Soc., 1972—, pres., 1980-81, treas, 1984-85; mem. Omaha Mayor's Com. on Employment of Handicapped, 1977-78. Served with U.S. Army, 1966-68. Named to admiralty in hon. navy Gov. Nebr., 1972; recipient Keuthe award Nebr. Easter Seal Soc., 1978, 81, Meritorious Service to State award Gov. Nebr., 1979; U.S. Dept. Edn. Rehab. Services Adminstr. Project with Industry grantee, 1983-86; Nat. Electronics Industries Found. grantee, 1985—, Mem. Nat. Rehab. Counseling Assn. (bd. dirs. 1971-74), Rehab. Assn. Nebr. (bd. dirs. 1977—, pres. 1979, McArtor award 1979), Rehab. Counseling Assn. Nebr. (pres. 1973), Nebr. Assn. Rehab. Profls. in Pvt. Sector (charter; treas. 1982-84). Methodist. Lodges: Kiwanis, Lions. Home: 9852 Louis Dr Omaha NE 68114 Office: Career Design Inc 7359 Pacific St Omaha NE 68114

DYKSTRA, RICHARD KEITH, pharmacist; b. Sioux Center, Iowa, July 27, 1953; s. Dick and Grace (Lems) D.; m. Nancy Gayle Sandbulte, Aug. 14, 1976; children—Tressa Gayle, Anne Gayle. B.S., U. Iowa, 1976. Mgr. Star Drug, Spencer, Iowa, 1977-80; owner, mgr. Hull Pharmacy, Iowa, 1980—; cons. pharmacist Pleasant Acres Nursing Home, Hull, 1980—; relief pharmacist Orange City Hosp., Iowa, 1981—. Pres. Businessman's Assn., Hull, 1984—; vol. EMT Squad, Hull, 1984—. Mem. Hull Jaycees, Iowa Pharmacists Assn., Am. Pharmacists Assn. Democrat. Club: Otter Valley Country (George, Iowa). Avocations: jogging, golf, softball, skiing. Home: 803 2d St Hull IA 51239

DYMACEK, ROSALIE MARIE, educator; b. Laurel, Nebr., June 4, 1940; d. Robert R. and Mildred H. (Anderson) Stone; m. Myles W. Dymacek, Jr., Dec. 22, 1962; children—Myla, Dawn, Dana. B.S., U. Nebr., 1966, M.S., 1975. Tchr. Spanish, English pub. schs., Lincoln, Nebr., 1966-67, 68-70, 75-76, tchr. presch. handicapped program, 1980—; coordinator day care in-service tng. program Southeast Community Coll., Lincoln, 1977-80. Bd. dirs., mem. child care com. YWCA, 1980-83. Mem. Nat. Assn. for Edn. of Young Children, Council for Exceptional Children.

DY-RAGOS, RAMON REYES, physician, surgeon; b. Naga City, Philippines, July 27, 1941; s. Julian and Marciana C. (Reyes) Dy-R.; m. Lydia U. Sy; children—R. Leonard, Julian B., Phillip L., Mark J. M.D., U. St. Tomas, Philippines, 1965. Diplomate Am. Bd. Surgery, Am. Bd. Neurol. and Orthopaedic Surgery. Intern Middlesex Meml. Hosp., Middletown, Ct., 1966-67; resident in gen. surgery St. Joseph Hosp., Houston, 1967-68; resident in neurosurgery U. Va. Med. Ctr., Charlottesville, 1968-73; practice medicine specializing in neurosurgery Kansas City, Mo., 1973—; mem. staff Spelman Meml. Hosp., Trinity Luth. Hosp. Physician vol. Boy Scouts Am., 1982—. Recipient cert. recognition Pan Ednl. Inst., 1976. Mem. AMA (Physician Recognition award 1970-83), Congress Neurol. Surgery, Mo. State Med. Assn. (conv. del. 1982), Clay-Platte County Med. Soc., Kansas City Neurol. Soc., Soc. Philippine Neurol. Surgeons in Am., Mo. Internat. Physicians, Am. Profl. Practice Assn., Filipino Assn. Greater Kansas City (pres. 1976, chmn. ways and means com. 1981, cert. appreciation 1976), Gladstone C. of C. Lodge: K.C. Office: 5700 N Broadway Kansas City MO 64118

DYRDA, ROBERT JOSEPH, electrical engineer; b. Chgo., Apr. 20, 1954; s. Joseph Edward and Eleanor Therese (Leganski) D. B.S., No. Ill. U., 1976; B.S., Elmhurst Coll., 1981; M.B.A., Loyola U., 1984. Elec. engr. Rockwell Internat., Chgo., 1976-79; project engr. Goodman Equipment Corp., Chgo., 1979-84; project engr. Nabisco Brands, Inc., Chgo., 1984—. Roman Catholic. Avocations: racquetball, vintage automobiles. Office: Nabisco Brands Inc 7300 S Kedzie Ave Chicago IL 60629

DYRHAUG, KEVIN JOHN, financial planner, benefits consultant; b. LaCrosse, Wis., June 22, 1955; s. Dennis John and Juneal Elizabeth (Sammon) D. B.S.B.A., Creighton U., 1977; C.F.P., Coll. for Fin. Planning, Denver, 1983. Benefits asst. Towers, Perrin, Forster & Crosby, Mpls., 1977-79; benefits cons. Ind. Service Co., Inc., Albert Lea, Minn., 1979-83; sr. account mgr. Profl. Fin. Mgmt., Ltd., Mpls., 1983-85; v.p., stockholder Adminstrv. Resources, Inc., 1985—; benefits cons. Dyrhaug & Assocs., Mpls., 1979—. Republican. Roman Catholic. Home: 5356 71st Circle N Minneapolis MN 55429 Office: Adminstrv Resources Inc 900 2d Ave S Internat Centre Suite 300 Minneapolis MN 55402

DYSINGER, THOMAS EUGENE, lawyer; b. Tipp City, Ohio, Jan. 11, 1953; s. Ernest Eugene and Mary Louise (Wallen) D. B.A., Ohio State U., 1974, J.D., 1977. Bar: Ohio 1977, U.S. Dist. Ct. (so. dist.) Ohio 1977, U.S. Dist. Ct. (no. dist.) Ohio 1979. Assoc. Shulman, Furry, Hall & Hammond, Dayton, Ohio, 1977-82; sole practice, Tipp City, Ohio, 1982—. Asst. Scoutmaster Miami Valley council Boy Scouts Am., Kettering, Ohio, 1977-80; mem. Tipp City Planning Bd., 1981—; pres. Tipp City Mum Festival com., 1984-85. Mem. ABA, Ohio State Bar Assn., Dayton Bar Assn., Miami County Bar Assn., Tipp City C. of C. (2nd v.p. 1984—). Club: Tipp City Players. Lodge: Rotary. Avocations: Tennis; skiing; golf. Home: 326 W Main St Tipp City OH 45371 Office: 326 W Main St Tipp City OH 45371

DZIBINSKI, DUWAYNE MICHAEL, city official; b. Milw., Feb. 13, 1941; s. Michael Francis and Hattie (Jaskulski) D.; m. Barbara Sue Maeisch, July 18, 1964; 1 child, Jeffrey P. A.A. in Police Sci., Waukesha Inst., 1976; B.A. in Criminal Justice, Milton Coll., 1980. Lic. real estate broker; cert. tchr. Wis. Dep. sheriff Waukesha County, Waukesha, Wis., 1966-67; police lt. Muskego Police Dept., Wis., 1967-81; chief Police Hales Corners, Wis., 1981—. Contbr. articles to profl. jours. Mgr. softball team, Muskego, 1984. Recipient Police Officer of the Year award City of Muskego, 1972. Served with USAF, 1960-64. Mem. Milw. Chiefs Police Assn. (v.p. 1984—). Roman Catholic. Avocations: Sports; hunting; fishing. Home: W 175 S 7241 Schubring Dr Muskego WI 53150 Office: PO Box 399 5635 S New Berlin Rd Hales Corners WI 53130

DZIUBAN, STEVEN EDWIN, mining engineer; b. Wayne County, Mich., Feb. 27, 1951; s. Edwin S. and Henrietta A. (Wojtyniak) D. B.S. in Mining Engring., Mich. Tech. U., 1974. Registered profl. engr., Pa., Ky., Ind., Ill.; cert. asst. mine foreman, Ky.; cert. mine examiner, mine mgr., Ill. Project engr. Consolidation Coal Co., 1974, asst. mining engr. Harmar, Oakmont and Renton Mines, 1975, mining engr., 1976; resident engr. Pyro Mining Co., 1978, chief engr., 1978, resident engr., 1979; sr. prodn. engr. Old Ben Coal Co., Standard Oil-Ohio, 1980; sr. planning engr. Royal Land Co., Chgo., 1982-84; chief engr. Internat. Anthracite Corp., Valley View, Pa., 1984—. Mich. Vocat. Rehab. scholar, 1969-74. Mem. Soc. Mining Engrs., Nat. Soc. Profl. Engrs., Ill. Soc. Profl. Engrs. Republican. Roman Catholic. Club: Moose. Home: 1015 Donna Rd Orwigsburg PA 17961 Office: PO Box 546 Valley View PA 17983

DZIURMAN, JOHN JOSEPH, architect planner, educator; b. Hamtramck, Mich., July 5, 1941; s. John Leonard and Helen (Sklarski) D.; m. Katherine G. Rasegan, Oct. 3, 1964; children—Kimberly, Tiffany. B.Arch., Lawrence Inst. Tech., 1970; postgrad. U. Detroit, 1959-61. Registered architect, Mich. Architect, Meathe Kessler Assocs., Grosse Pointe, Mich., 1964-70; project designer Giffels Assocs., Detroit, 1970-74; v.p. Straub, VanDine, Dziurman Architects, Troy, Mich., 1974-79, Wade Trim Group, Plymouth, Mich., 1980—; pres. John Dziurman Assocs., Inc., Rochester, Mich., 1979—; adj. instr. Mich. State U., East Lansing, 1983—; lectr. in design Lawrence Inst. Tech., Southfield, Mich., 1970-75. Patentee in field. Mem. Downtown Devel. Authority, City of Rochester, 1983—. Recipient Alumni Achievement award Lawrence Inst. Tech., 1980. Mem. Engring. Soc. Detroit (Outstanding Young Engr. 1975), AIA (housing com. 1981—, treas. Detroit chpt. 1976-78, sec. 1980). Club: University (Detroit). Avocations: sketching; golfing; squash; carpentry. Office: John Dziurman Assocs Inc Architects/Planners 155 Romeo Rd Rochester MI 48063

EAGER, WILLIAM EARL, information systems corporation executive; b. Trenton, N.J., Dec. 22, 1946; s. Earl V. and Dorothy E. (Bowen) E.; m. Janice M. Kudlak, July 12, 1969; 1 child, Jason C. B.A., Lycoming Coll., 1968; M.B.A., Gannon U., 1977; postgrad. Kent State U., 1984—. Cert. data processing. Systems supr. Gen. Electric Co., Erie, Pa., 1969-72; sr. cons. Touche Ross & Co., Detroit, 1972-74; mgmt. info. systems dir. Limbach, Inc., Pitts., 1974-81; dir. systems GenCorp, Inc., Akron, Ohio, 1981—; pres., cons. W.E. Eager & Assocs., Hudson, Ohio, 1982—. Home: 2239 Edgeview Dr Hudson OH 44236 Office: GenCorp Inc 1 General St Akron OH 44329

EAGLE, DAVID WILLIAM, musicologist, flute educator; b. Crookston, Minn., Aug. 13, 1929; s. E. William and Almira Beatrice (Uggen) E. B.S. in Pharmacy, U. Minn., 1957, B.A., 1957, Ph.D. in Musicology, 1977. Author record notes for Quintessence and Pro Arte Records; flute instr. U. Minn., Mpls., 1977—. Mem. Upper Midwest Flute Assn. (dir.), Am. Legion (dir., mem. band), Am. Musicol. Soc., Coll. Music Soc., Soc. for Ethnomusicology, Nat. Flutist Assn., Evergreen Club. Contbr. articles in field to profl. jours. Home: 2904 W River Rd Minneapolis MN 55406 Office: 104 Scott Hall U Minn Minneapolis MN 55455

EAGLE, EDWARD, toxicologist; b. Balt., Nov. 27, 1908; s. Louis E. and Sadie (Kushnoy) E.; m. Mary Frances Rowe, Dec. 28, 1942; children—Nancy, Ellen, Margaret, Louis. A.B., Johns Hopkins U., 1929; M.S., U. Va., 1931; Ph.D. in Physiology, U. Chgo., 1940. Asst. in physiology U. Chgo., 1936-38, research asst., 1938-42; toxicologist, physiologist Swift & Co., Chgo., 1946-48, head div. toxicology, 1948-73; cons., Evanston, 1973—; mem. industry com. of food protection com. Food and Nutrition Bd., Nat. Acad. Scis., 1960-68, mem. industry liaison com., 1966-67. Contbr. numerous articles to sci. jours. Served to maj. USAAC, 1942-46. DuPont felow, 1929, 30. Mem. Am. Physiol. Soc., Soc. Toxicology, Am. Soc. Pharmacology, Soc. Exptl. Biology and Medicine, Am. Heart Assn. Council on Arteriosclerosis, Sigma Xi. Unitarian. Avocation: scientific history. Home: 2230 Asbury Ave Evanston IL 60201

EAGLE, RICHARD, steel company executive; b. Zion, Ill., Jan. 19, 1929; s. Alfred Pretty Voice and Nora (Eckels) E.; m. Normalee June Cook, Oct. 27, 1950; children—Richard Douglas, Ronn Thomas, Lynn Susan, Dougals Earl, Lisa Sue. Student Lake Forest Coll., Ill., 1948. With operating and constrn. dept. Cyclone Fence div. U.S. Steel Corp., Waukegan, Ill., 1948-55, salesman, Chgo., 1955-66, sales mgr.,Cleve., 1966-71, mgr. West coast, San Francisco, 1971-79; mgr. U.S. Steel Roof Deck, Birmingham, Ala., 1979-82; gen. mgr. Coatings and Coated Products div. U.S Steel, Chgo., 1982—. Served with U.S Army, 1951-53. Republican. Clubs: Relay House. Lodge: Masons. Home: 2900 Glenrose Dr Portage IN 46368 Office: 1701 E 122d St Chicago IL 60633

EAGLETON, THOMAS FRANCIS, U.S. senator, lawyer; b. St. Louis, Sept. 4, 1929; s. Mark David and Zitta Louise (Swanson) E.; B.A. cum laude, Amherst Coll., 1950; LL.B. cum laude, Harvard U., 1953; m. Barbara Ann Smith, Jan. 20, 1956; children—Terence, Christin. Admitted to Mo. bar, 1953; practiced in St. Louis, 1953—; past mem. firm Eagleton & Eagleton; circuit atty., St. Louis, 1957-60; became atty. gen., State of Mo., 1960; lt. gov. of Mo., 1964-68; U.S. senator from Mo., 1968—. Served with USNR, 1948-49. Office: 197 Dirksen Senate Office Bldg Washington DC 20510

EAKIN, THOMAS CAPPER, sports promotion executive; b. New Castle, Pa., Dec. 16, 1933; s. Frederick William and Beatrice (Capper) E.; B.A. in History, Denison U., 1956; m. Brenda Lee Andrews, Oct. 21, 1961; children—Thomas Andrews, Scott Frederick. Life ins. cons. Northwestern Mut. Life Ins. Co., Cleve., 1959-67; regional dir. sales Empire Life Ins. Co. Ohio, 1967-68; dist. mgr. Putman Pub. Co., Cleve., 1968-69; regional bus. mgr. Chilton Pub. Co., Cleve., 1969-70; dist. mgr. Hitchcock Pub. Co., Cleve., 1970-72; pres. TCE Enterprises, Shaker Heights, Ohio, 1973—; trustee Newcomerstown (Ohio) Sports Corp., 1975-80, Nat. Jr. Tennis League of Cleve., 1985-87; dir. New Hope Records, 1984—. Founder, nat. chmn. Cy Young Centennial, 1967, Cy Young Golf Invitational champion, 1967, 69, 70, 71, 72, 79; mem. adv. bd. Cleve. Indian Old Timers Com., 1966-67, Ohio Racquetball Assn., 1981-82, Sportsbeat, 1985—, Old Time Ball Players' Assn. of Wis., 1985— founder, pres. Golf Internat. 100 Club, Shaker Heights, 1970—, founder, pres. Ohio Baseball Hall of Fame, 1976—, Ohio Baseball Hall of Fame Celebration, 1977-79; Ohio Baseball Hall of Fame and Mus., 1980—; founder, chmn. Cleve. Phi Delta Theta Alumni Club Golf Invitational, 1970—, champion, 1970; founder chmn. Ohio Baseball Hall of Fame Golf Invitational, 1980—; hon. dir. Tuscarawas County (Ohio) Old Timers Baseball Assn., 1972—, commendation award, 1970; Ohio exec. sponsor chmn. World Golf Hall of Fame, Pinehurst, N.C., 1979—; fund rep. Boy Scouts Am., Cleve., 1959-60, United Appeal, 1959-63, Heart Fund, 1963-64; mem. Cleve. Council Corrections, 1971-73; mem. adv. bd. Cuyahoga Hills Boys Sch., Warrensville Heights, Ohio, 1971—, Camp Hope, Warrenville Twp., 1973—; founder, dir. TRY (Target/Reach Youth), 1971—, Interact Club Shaker Heights, 1971—; trustee Nat. Jr. Tennis League Cleve., 1985—; founder, pres., dir. Cy Young Mus., 1970-80; mem. exec. com. Tuscarawas County Am. Revolution Bicentennial Commn., 1974-76; bd. mem. Shaker Heights Youth Center, Inc., 1975; adv. bd. Fitness Evaluation Services, Inc., 1977-79, Portage County Sports Hall of Fame, 1983—; bd. dirs. Tuscarawas Valley Tourist Assn., 1979-81, Buckeye Tourist Assn., 1979-80; adv. bd. Interact Club of Twinsburg, Ohio, 1981—; bd. dirs. Greater Toledo Sports Hall of Fame, 1985—; hon. bd. dirs. Chautauqua Sports Hall of Fame, 1982—. Served with AUS, 1956-58. Recipient commendation awards Cy Young Centennial Com., 1967, Tuscarawas County C. of C., 1967, Sporting News, 1968, Gov. James A. Rhodes Ohio, 1968, 75, Gov. John J. Gilligan Ohio, 1972, 74, Newcomerstown C. of C., 1967, City of Springfield, Ohio, 1980, Toledo Recreation Dept. and Baseball Commn., 1984, N.C. Senate, 1984, Pa. Senate, 1984; Outstanding Contbn. to Baseball award baseball commr. William Eckert, 1967; Sport Service award Sport mag., 1969; Civic Service award Cuyahoga Hills Boys Sch., 1970; citation of merit La. Stadium and Expn. Dist., 1972; Presdl. commendation Richard M. Nixon, 1973, Gerald R. Ford, 1977; Disting. Service award Camp Hope, 1974; Founder's award Interact Club Shaker Heights, 1974; Proclamation award-Thomas C. Eakin Day, City of Cleve., Ohio, 1974, Toledo, 1984, London, Ont., Can., 1984, New Orleans, 1984, Salem, Ohio, 1985, Westlake, Ohio, 1985, Bay Village, Ohio, 1985, Vermilion, Ohio, 1985, Garfield Heights, Ohio, 1985, Eastlake, Ohio, 1985, Middleburg Heights, Ohio, 1985, Solon, Ohio, 1985, Mentor, Ohio, 1985, Cuyahoga Falls, Ohio, 1985, Stow, Ohio, 1985, Mantua, Ohio, 1985, Munroe Falls, Ohio, 1985, Lucas County, Ohio, 1985, Maumee, Ohio, 1985, Baton Rouge, 1985, Brecksville, Ohio, 1985, Summit County, Ohio, 1985; Gov.'s award for community action State of Ohio, 1974; award of achievement Ohio Assn. Hist. Socs., 1975; Chief Newawatowes award Newcomerstown C. of C., 1975; commendation Ohio Senate, 1976, 79, Ohio Ho. of Reps., 1978, Ohio Am. Revolution Bicentennial Adv. Commn., 1976, Toledo Recreation Dept. and Baseball Commn., 1984; cert. of merit Tuscarawas County Am. Revolution Bicentennial Commn., 1976, appreciation award, 1977; cert. of merit State of La., 1978; Ohio Gov.'s award, 1978; Founder's award TRY Target/Reach Youth, 1979; Appreciation award Am. Revolution Bicentennial Adminstrn. feature cover story personality award Amateur Athlete's World, 1982; Order of the Long Leaf Pine, State of N.C., 1984; honor resolution New Orleans City Council, 1984; honor tribute Premier of London, Ont., 1985; named hon. citizen City of New Orleans, 1978; named to Chautauqua Sports Hall of Fame, 1983; Shaker Heights Rotary Golf Invitational champion, 1966, 71, 73, 76, 81; Rotary Dist. 663 Golf champion, 1970; Jamestown, N.Y. Rotary Golf Tournament champion, 1985. Mem. Denison U. Cleve. Men's Club (v.p. 1964-65), Tuscarawas County Hist. Soc. (trustee 1978-81), Internat. Platform Assn., English Speaking Union, Shaker Hist. Soc. (trustee 1980-82), Phi Delta Theta (pres. Cleve. alumni club 1970, Appreciation award 1971, dir. 1971-75, exec. com. nat. Lou Gehrig award com. 1975—, Outstanding Alumnus award 1975, trustee Ohio Iota chpt. 1979-82). Baptist (mem. bd. 1966-69). Clubs: Rotary (Outstanding young Rotarian award, 1962, pres. Shaker Heights 1970-71, founder and chmn. club's Internat. student exchange program U.S. and Can. 1965-70, trustee V. Blakeman Qua Scholarship Fund 1972-73, founder, chmn. Henry G. Duchscherer Meml. award 1971—); Wahoo (dir. 1975-77); Executive (Woodmere, Ohio); PGA Nat. Golf (Palm Beach Gardens, Fla.); Legend Lake Golf (Chardon, Ohio); U.S. Tennis (Shaker Heights, Ohio). Address: 2729 Shelley Rd Shaker Heights OH 44122

EARHART, MICHAEL JON, pharmacist; b. Wichita, Kans., Nov. 29, 1945; s. Harold Wilson and Dorothy Lee (Yeager) E. B.S. in Pharmacy, U. Mo.-Kansas City, 1972; M.A. in Health Services Mgmt., Webster U., 1983. Registered pharmacist, Mo., Tex. Pharmacist, Deaconess Hosp., St. Louis, 1973-75, 76, asst. dir. pharmacy, 1976-77, dir. pharmacy, 1977-81, div. mgr.-pharmacy/IV therapy, 1981-85, dir. physician services, 1985—; pharmacist Valley Bapt. Hosp., Harlingen, Tex., 1975-76; dir. Network, St. Louis, 1984—; adj. clin. instr. pharmacy St. Louis Coll. Pharmacy, 1980—. Treas. Shaw/Garden/Central, Inc. Neighborhood Assn., St. Louis, 1984—. Served to USN, 1963-66. Mem. Am. Soc. Hosp. Pharmacists, St. Louis Soc. Hosp. Pharmacists, U. Mo.-Kansas City Alumni Assn. (life), Webster U. Alumni Assn. Republican. Lutheran. Avocations: art glass, camping. Home: 3857 Shaw Blvd Saint Louis MO 63110 Office: Deaconess Hosp 6150 Oakland Ave Saint Louis MO 63139

EARL, ANTHONY SCULLY, governor of Wisconsin; b. Lansing, Mich., Apr. 12, 1936; s. Russell K. and Ethlynne J. (Scully) E.; m. Sheila Rose Coyle, Aug. 11, 1962. B.A., Mich. State U., 1958; LL.D., U. Chgo., 1961. Bar: Wis. 1964. Asst. dist. atty. Marathon County (Wis.), Wausau, 1965-66; city atty. City of Wausau, 1966-69; mem. Wis. State Assembly, 1969-74; mem. fir Crooks, Low and Earl, 1969-74; sec. Wis. Dept. Adminstrn., Madison, 1974-75, Wis. Dept. Nat. Resources, 1975-80; v.p. Foley & Lardner, Madison, 1980-82; gov. State of Wis., Madison, 1983—. Served to lt. USN, 1962-65. Democrat. Roman Catholic.

EARLE, LOUIS BION, farm appraiser, former government official; b. Anselmo, Nebr., June 15, 1912; s. James Louis and Bertha C. (Vincent) E.; m. Francis Louise Young, Jan. 24, 1942; children—Stephan Earle, Linda Gregory, Kerry Earle. B.S., Kansas State U., 1934. Cert. Kans. appraiser. Conservation technician U.S. Soil and Conservation Service, Kans. and Colo., conservation supr., P.R., 1942-45, conservation supr., Wichita, Kans., 1945-67; assessor Sedgwick County (Kans.), 1967-77; prin. Louis B. Earle Assocs., Appraisers and Farm Sales, Wichita, 1977—. Former bd. dirs. Sedgwick County Mental Health Assn., United Way, Vol. Services Adv. Bd., Arkansas Ave. Homeowners Assn., Council of Sr. Citizens Clubs, Kans. Mental Health Assn., Wichita Zoo. Soc., Boy Scouts Am., Campfire Girls, Community Planning Council, Ret. Sr. Vol. Program, Adopt A Nursing Home Program; chmn. adv. bd. Salvation Army, 1978-79, Christmas program, 1981—, men's social service com., 1980—; class pres. Pleasant Valley United Methodist Ch., 1966, 72, 78, 79; mem. United Meth. Urban Ministries Bd., 1984; Republican precinct committeeman, 1970—. Recipient Disting. Service award United Way, 1961, 66, 75, 78, Meritorious Service to Kans. Agr. award Fed. Land Bank, 1967, Dr. Wright Conservation Meml. award, 1975, Fed. Cert. of Merit, U.S. Soil Conservation Service, 1966; named Fed. Civil Servant of Yr., Kiwanis, 1965. Mem. Soc. Rural Appraisers, Nat. Assn. Ret. Fed. Employees (pres. 1979-80), Wichita C. of C. (com. mem., chmn. Farm Family of Yr. program 1979—), Izaak Walton League, Tau Kappa Epsilon. Avocation: yard work. Home and Office: Louis B Earle Assocs Appraisers and Farm Sales 3220 Arkansas St Witchita KS 67204

EARLY, BERT HYLTON, lawyer, legal executive search consultant; b. Kimball, W.Va., July 17, 1922; s. Robert Terry and Sue Keister (Hylton) E.; student Marshall U., 1940-42; A.B., Duke U., 1946; J.D., Harvard U., 1949; m. Elizabeth Louise Henry, June 24, 1950; children—Bert Hylton, Robert Christian, Mark Randolph, Philip Henry, Peter St. Clair. Admitted to W.Va. bar, 1949, Ill. bar, 1963, Fla. bar, 1981; assoc. firm Fitzpatrick, Marshall, Huddleston & Bolen, Huntington, W.Va., 1949-57; instr. Marshall U., 1950-53; asst. counsel Island Creek Coal Co., 1957-60, asso. gen. counsel, 1960-62; dep. exec. dir. Am. Bar Assn., 1962-64, exec. dir., 1964-81; sr. v.p. Wells Internat., Chgo., 1981-83, pres., 1984—; mem. W.Va. Jud. Council, 1960-62; vice chmn. Conf. Nat. Orgns., 1971-73; mem. Task Force on Govtl. Regulation and Press Freedom, Twentieth Century Fund, 1971. Mem. Huntington City Council, 1961-62, Hinsdale Plan Commn., 1982—; bd. dirs. Huntington Public Library, 1951-60, Morris Meml. Hosp. Crippled Children, 1953-60, Huntington Galleries, 1961-62, W.Va. Tax Inst., 1961-62, Robert Crown Center for Health Edn., 1970-76, United Charities Chgo., 1972-80, Community Renewal Soc., 1965-76, Am. Bar Endowment, 1983—; trustee Davis and Elkins Coll., 1960-63; mem. vis. com. U. Chgo. Law Sch., 1975-78. Served to 1st lt., pilot, USAAC, 1943-45. Fellow Am. Bar Found. (life); mem. Am. Law Inst. (life), ABA (ho. of dels. 1958-59, 84— nat. chmn. Jr. Bar Conf. 1958), Internat. Bar Assn. (asst. sec.-gen. 1967-82), Inter-Am. Bar Assn. W.Va. Bar Assn., Chgo. Bar Assn., Legal Club Chgo., W.Va. State Bar (chmn. jr. sect. 1951), Fla. Bar, Am. Judicature Soc. (bd. dirs. 1982-84), Nat. Legal Aid and Defender Assn. Presbyterian. Clubs: University, Economic (Chgo.); Hinsdale (Ill.) Golf; Harvard (N.Y.C.); Metropolitan (Washington). Office: Three First National Plaza Suite 3900 Chicago IL 60602

EARLY, GERALD LEE, cardiovascular and thoracic surgeon, educator; b. St. Joseph, Mo., June 10, 1947; s. Abram Lee and Arline Joyce (Stein) E.; 1 dau., Jennifer Lynn. B.A., Central Methodist Coll., Fayette, Mo., 1969; M.D., U. Mo.-Kansas City, 1973; M.A., U. Mo.-Columbia, 1975. Diplomate Nat. Bd. Med. Examiners, 1974, Am. Bd. Surgery, 1980, Am. Bd. Thoracic Surgery, 1983. Intern, Kansas City Gen. Hosp. and Med. Ctr., 1973-74; resident in internal medicine Pensacola Ednl. Program, 1974-75; resident in surgery U. Mo.-Kansas City, 1976-79, in thoracic surgery Ohio State U., 1979-81; dir. dept. emergency medicine Pensacola (Fla.) Ednl. Program, 1975-76; dir. cardiovascular and thoracic surgery Truman Med. Ctr., Kansas City, Mo., 1982-83, also asst. prof. surgery U. Mo.-Kansas City, 1982—. Recipient Meritorious Service award West Fla. Heart Assn., 1976; named Surgery Resident of Yr., Truman Med. Ctr., 1978, 79; USPHS Reproductive Biology Tng. grantee, 1970-71. Mem. Jackson County Med. Soc., Mo. Med. Assn., AMA, Assn. Acad. Surgery, Kansas City Pulmonary Round Table. Methodist. Contbr. articles sci. jours. Office: 6700 Troost St 348 Rockhill Medical Bldg Kansas City MO 64131

EARLY, JAMES DAVID, life sciences educator; b. Kansas City, Mo., May 6, 1947; s. Forrest D. and Ruth G. (Slater) E. Student, Penn Valley Community Coll., Kansas City, 1965-67; B.S. in Biology, S.W. Mo. State U., 1971, M.A. in Biology, 1973. Teaching asst. S.W. Mo. State U., Springfield, 1972-73; instr. Metro Community Coll. Dist., Kansas City, 1973—; chmn. life scis. Penn Valley Community Coll., Kansas City, 1981—, assoc. dean occupational edn., 1985—, pres. faculty assn., 1980-81. Avocations: stained glass, flying. Office: Penn Valley Community Coll 3201 SW Throughway Kansas City MO 64111

EARP, BRENDA CAROL, medical technologist; b. Lafe, Ark., Aug. 25, 1946; d. A.G. Harrison and Clarice Beatrice (Harris) Earp; A.S., Mott Community Coll., 1966; A.B., U. Mich., 1969; cert. Hurley Med. Center Sch. Med. Technology, 1970. Lab. asst. Dr. F.W. Baske, Flint, Mich., 1966-68; substitute tchr. Flint Community Schs., 1969; med. technologist microchemistry lab. Hurley Med. Center, Flint, 1970—; lectr. in field. Vol. ARC. Named Hurley Med. Center Employee of Month, 1976, of Yr., 1977; Brenda Earp Day proclaimed by mayor of Flint, 1977. Mem. U. Mich. Alumni Assn., Hurley Med. Center Med. Technologist Orgn., Am. Soc. Clin. Pathologists. Democrat. Baptist. Contbr. articles to profl. jours. Home: 652 Vermilya Ave Flint MI 48507 Office: 1 Hurley Plaza Flint MI 48502

EASTBURN, RICHARD A., manufacturing company executive; b. West Chester, Pa., Jan. 16, 1934; s. Louis W. and Alma S. (Shellin) E.; B.A., Shelton Coll., 1956; M.S.T., N.Y. Theol. Sem., 1959; M.Ed., Temple U., 1970; M.B.A., Columbia U., 1979; m. Heidi Fritz, June 15, 1963; children—Karin J., R. Marc. Ordained to ministry Am. Baptist Conv., 1959; minister, Laurelton, N.J., 1959-61; dir adult programs Central YMCA, Phila., 1961-65; dir. Opportunities Industrialization Ctr., Phila., 1965-67; mgr. tng. and devel. Missile & Surface Radar div. RCA, Moorestown, N.J., 1967-68, mgr. mgmt. devel. govt. and comml. systems group, dir. mgmt. devel., 1969-71; group mgr. personnel for internat. field ops. Digital Equipment, Maynard, Mass., 1971-75; corp. dir. orgn. and mgmt. devel. Am. Standard, Inc., N.Y.C., 1975-79; corp. dir. mgmt. devel. edn. and staffing TRW, Inc., Cleve., 1979—; pres. Retirement Community Concepts, 1981—; producer, moderator Ask the Clergy, Sta. WIP, Phila., 1965-67. Bd. dirs. exec. program adv. bd. U. Ind.; bd. dirs. Burlington County Community Com., 1967-69. Recipient Disting. Community Service award Shelton Coll. Alumni, 1956; Dedicated Service award Phila. March of Progress, 1967. Mem. Am. Soc. Tng. and Devel. (dir., 1979-80), Orgn. Devel. Network. Mem. United Ch. Christ. Clubs: Chagrin Valley Athletic, A & A Sportsman. Home: 213 Monticello Dr Chagrin Falls OH 44022 Office: TRW Inc 1900 Richmond Rd Cleveland OH 44124

EASTERLING, RAYMOND WILLIAM, respiratory therapist, polysomnographer; b. Cin., Feb. 20, 1946; s. Raymond and Ruth Irene (Best) E.; m. Barbara Sue Denny, Mar. 10, 1973; children—Adam, Christopher. B.A. in Bus., U. Cin., 1970, B.S. in Biology, 1975; postgrad. Stanford U., 1984. Asst. dir. spl. diagnostic and therapeutic medicine Bethesda Hosp., Cin., 1975-77; dir. pulmonary dept. Mercy Hosp., Portsmouth, Ohio, 1977—; cons. Respiratory Health Affiliates, Columbus, Ohio, 1982—. Mem. Polysomnographic Tech., Respiratory Therapy Tech., Delta Tau Kappa, Sigma Chi. Republican. Presbyterian. Avocations: tennis; history; gardening. Home: 3003 N Hill Rd Portsmouth OH 45661 Office: Mercy Hosp 1248 Kinneys Ln Portsmouth OH 45662

EASTMAN, ALAN RICHARD, biochemistry educator, researcher; b. Ewell, Surrey, Eng., Oct. 16, 1949; came to U.S., 1976, permanent resident, 1979; s. Leonard Ernest and Edith Dorcas (Beakhust) E.; m. Teresa Rosamond Spoto, Feb. 19, 1982. B.Tech., Brunel U., London, 1972; Ph.D., London U., 1975. Research assoc. Chester Beatty Research Inst., London, 1975-76; research assoc. U. Vt., Burlington, 1976-78, research asst. prof., biochemistry, 1978-83; asst. prof. U. Nebr. Med. Ctr., Omaha, 1983-85, assoc. prof. Eppley Inst. Cancer Research with joint appt. in biochemistry, 1985—. Contbr. articles to sci. research publs. Recipient Jr. Faculty Research award Am. Cancer Soc., 1980-83, Research Career Devel. award NIH, 1983-88. Mem. Am. Assn. Cancer Research, Am. Soc. Biol. Chemists. Office: Eppley Inst Cancer Research U Nebr Med Ctr Omaha NE 68103

EATON, DAVID FOSTER, lawyer; b. Kansas City, Kans., Sept. 6, 1955; s. Merrill Thomas and Louise (Foster) E.; m. Margaret Mary Dorsey, Oct. 13, 1979; children—Abigail, Ann-Louise, Eric James. B.S., Ind. U., 1977; J.D., Creighton U., 1980. Bar: Nebr. 1980, U.S. Dist. Ct. Nebr. 1980, U.S. Ct. Mil. Appeals 1981, U.S. Ct. Appeals (8th cir.) 1984. Assoc. Gallup & Schaefer, Omaha, 1984—. Served to capt. USAF, 1980-84; capt. Res. Mem. Nebr. State Bar Assn., Omaha Bar Assn., Nat. Geog. Soc., Air Force Assn., Phi Alpha Delta. Republican. Home: 310 S 50th Ave Omaha NE 68132 Office: Gallup & Schaefer 1001 Farnam Omaha NE 68102

EBBEN, MARK ARTHUR, optometrist; b. Appleton, Wis., June 30, 1954; s. Edward Martin and Inez Harriet (Hendricks) E.; m. Mary Catherine Brittnacker, Sept. 30, 1983. B.S., Ill. Coll. Optometry, 1978, O.D., 1978. Practice medicine specializing in optometry, Kimberly, Wis., 1978-81, Kaukauna, Wis., 1981—; optometrist Menominee Indian Reservation, Keshena, Wis., 1979—. Pres. St. John's Parish Council, 1983-84. Mem. Am. Optometric Assn., Wis. Optometric Assn., Fox Valley Optometric Assn., Beta Sigma Kappa. Democrat. Roman Catholic. Club: Rotary (Kaukauna). Avocations: Cross country skiing; jogging; bicycling; fishing; bow hunting. Home: 530 N Lawe St Appleton WI 54911 Office: 120 E 2nd St Kaukauna WI 54130

EBBING, MICHAEL DANIEL, machine tool company executive; b. Detroit, Nov. 28, 1951; s. Daniel and Helen A. Ebbing. B.S., Eastern Mich. U., 1973. Store mgr. Don Thomas Sporthaus, Birmingham, Mich., 1973-75; asst. buyer J.L. Hudson, Detroit, 1975-76; prodn. control mgr. Detroit Edge Tool Co., Milw., 1979-82, sales mgr., Detroit, 1984—, sec., dir., 1985—. Roman Catholic. Avocations: skiing; sailing. Home: 5060 Buckingham Troy MI 48098 Office: Detroit Edge Tool Co 6570 E Nevada Detroit MI 48234

EBELING, GARY DAVID, pharmacist; b. Mason City, Iowa, Dec. 28, 1932; s. Fred Joseph and Evelyn Fay (Thompson) E.; m. Alice Marie Fitzgerald, Aug. 7, 1954; children—Sheree Ebeling Cran, Lori, Lisa, Sandra Ebeling Johnson, David, Michael. A.A., Mason City Jr. Coll., 1952; B.S. in Pharmacy, U. Iowa, 1955. Registered pharmacist, Iowa. Pharmacist, Pletch Drug, Waterloo, Iowa, 1957-58; owner, pharmacist Mac's Pharmacy, Waterloo, 1958-70, Humboldt Pharmacy (Iowa), 1970—; owner, operator Prescription Shop, Waterloo, 1961-70, Park Pharmacy, Humboldt, 1972—, Sheree's Hallmark Shop, Algona, Iowa, 1978—, Estherville, Iowa, 1979—, Humboldt, 1982—. Served to 2d lt. U.S. Army, 1955-57. Mem. Am. Pharm. Assn., Iowa Pharm. Assn., Black Hawk County Pharm. Assn. (pres. 1963), Humboldt C. of C. Roman Catholic. Clubs: Elks, KC. (Ft. Dodge). Home: 1110 7th Ave SW Humboldt IA 50548 Office: Park Pharmacy 1010 15th St N Humboldt IA 50548

EBELING, MELVIN EBELING, chemical company executive; b. Chgo., May 26, 1937; s. Edward Roudolf and Olive Ruth (Lewis) E.; m. Leslie Ruth Phinney, Apr. 7, 1960 (div. 1979); children—Kenneth, Cheryl; m. Darlene Barbara Florek, May 10, 1980. B.S. in Chemistry, Wheaton Coll., Ill., 1959; M.B.A. in Mktg., U. Chgo., 1967. Control chemist Am. Potash, West Chicago, Ill., 1959-60; chief application chemist Coleman div. Perkin Elmer Corp., Maywood, Ill., 1960-71; v.p. mktg. P-L Biochems., Milw., 1971-83; v.p. sales and mktg. Pandex Lab., Mundelein, Ill., 1983-84; dir. mktg. Pierce Chem. Co., Rockford, Ill., 1984—. Contbr. articles to profl. publs. Chmn. bd. trustees Villa Park Bible Ch., Ill., 1963-65. Mem. BioMed. Mktg. Assn., Am. Chem. Soc., No. Ill. Ad Council, Chgo. Chromatography Discussion Group. Avocations: automobile mechanics; cross country skiing; photography. Home: 5141 Camelot Ln Greenfield WI 53221 Office: Pierce Chem Co 3747 N Meridian Rd Rockford IL 61105

EBENHOLTZ, SHELDON MARSHAL, psychology educator, vision consultant; b. N.Y.C., Nov. 27, 1932; s. David and Sally (Werier) E.; m. Jean Miriam Cohen, Jan. 30, 1955; 1 son, Keith. B.S., CCNY, 1955; M.A., New Sch. Social Research, 1958, Ph.D., 1961. Asst. prof. Conn. Coll., New London, 1961-66; assoc. prof. U. Wis.-Madison, 1966-70, prof. psychology, 1970—. Mem. vision com. Nat. Acad. Sci./NRC, 1984—. Cons. editor Perception and Psychophysics, 1970—. Contbr. book chpts. and articles to prof. jours. Killam Sr. fellow, 1971; Spatial Orientation research grantee NSF, 1984; vision research grantee Nat. Eye Inst., 1984. Fellow AAAS, Am. Psychol. Assn., Am. Acad. Optometry; mem. Aerospace Med. Assn., Optical Soc. Am., Sierra Club. Avocations: hiking, backpacking. Home: 4810 Waukesha St Madison WI 53705 Office: U Wis Dept Psychology Madison WI 53706

EBERHARD, WILLIAM THOMAS, architect; b. St. Louis, Apr. 11, 1952; s. George Walter and Bettie Alma (Seilkop) E.; m. Cynthia Ann Hardy, Aug. 20, 1977 (div. 1981). B. Arch., U. Cin., 1976; postgrad. Archtl. Assn., Eondon, 1974. Registered architect Ohio, Mich., Pa., Fla., D.C. Vice pres. Visnapuu & Assocs. Inc., Cleve., 1972-82; prin., regional mgr. Oliver Design Group, Cleve., 1983—. Profl. team leader Inst. Urban Design, Cleve., 1983. Mem. AIA (chpt. sec. 1982-84), Nat. Trust for Hist. Preservation, Inst. Urban Design Am. Soc. Interior Designers (assoc.), Seminotic Soc. Am. (founding), Avocations: drawing; photography; tennis; snowmobiling; golf. Home: 12900 Lake Ave Lakewood OH 44107 Office: Oliver Design Group 1920 Huntington Bldg Cleveland OH 44115

EBERIUS, KLAUS OTTO, machine tool executive; b. Koethen, Germany, Feb. 13, 1940; s. Otto and Gertrud (Marx) E.; came to U.S., 1972; engring. degree Akademie of Engring., Cologne, Germany, 1967; m. Amei Brauns, Apr. 17, 1964; children—Edda, Susanne. Asst. plant mgr. Anton Piller Kg., Osterode, Germany, 1967-68; mgr. tng. center VDF Corp., Hannover, Germany, 1968-72; tech. services mgr. Upton, Bradeen & James, Sterling Heights, Mich., 1972-73, mgr. metal cutting div., 1973-76; v.p., gen. mgr. Unitec Nat. Co., Broadview, Ill., 1976-79; pres., dir. Uni-Sig Corp., 1979-82; corp. v.p. Oerlikon Motch Corp., 1983-84, corp. exec. v.p., 1984-85, pres., chief exec. officer, dir., 1985—; instr. programming night sch., Hannover. Recipient award NC-Research, 1969. Mem. Soc. Mfg. Engrs. Home: 7545 Muirwood Ct Chagrin Falls OH 44022 Office: 1250 E 222d St Cleveland OH 44117

EBERLY, CHARLES GEORGE, university administrator, educator; b. McComb, Ohio, Sept. 8, 1941; s. George Willis and Herma Elizabeth (Sower) E.; m. Sharon Rosalee Newcomer, June 21, 1964; children—Mary Barbara, Judith Elizabeth, Michael Charles. B.S. in Chemistry, Bowling Green State U., 1963; M.S. in Edn., Syracuse U., 1966; Ph.D. in Edn., Mich. State U., 1970. Acting asst. dean students Wilmington Coll., Ohio, summer 1964; instr. student personnel U. Wis.-Oshkosh, 1966-69; asst. prof. evaluation services Mich. State U., East Lansing, 1970-74, assoc. prof. undergrad. univ. div., 1974—, asst. to dir. admissions, 1981—; vis. instr. Mie U., Tsu, Japan, 1977-78. Author: Building and Maintaing the Chapter Library, 1970. Mem. zoning bd., Mason, Mich., 1970-71. Recipient Carter Ashton Jenkens award Sigma Phi Epsilon, 1964. Mem. Assn. for Measurement and Evalution in Counseling and Devel. (newsletter editor 1979-84, treas. 1984—), Mich. ACT Council (exec. council 1981—), Mich. Assn. for Measurement and Evaluation in Guidance (pres. 1984—), Mich. Personnel and Guidance Assn. (chmn. adminstrv. asst. evaluation com. 1984—, editor jour. 1985—), Am. Coll. Personnel Assn. (founder Commn. XVI 1979, dir. Commn. XVI 1979-82, profl. standards com. 1980-83), Am. Assn. Counseling and Devel., Nat. Council on Measurement in Edn., Am. Ednl. Research Assn., Nat. Assn. Acad. Affairs Adminstrs., Mich. Coll. Personnel Assn., Phi Delta Kappa, Sigma Phi Epsilon, Alpha Phi Omega, Phi Kappa Phi. Republican. Methodist. Avocations: racquetball; cycling; woodworking; music; little theatre. Home: 644 Joan Dr Mason MI 48854 Office: Mich State U 276 Adminstrn Bldg East Lansing MI 48824

EBERLY, WILLIAM ROBERT, biology educator; b. North Manchester, Ind., Oct. 4, 1926; s. John H. and Ollie M. (Heaston) E.; m. Eloise L. Whitehead, June 30, 1946; children—Diana Sue, Brenda Kay, Sandra Jo. B.A., Manchester Coll., 1948; M.S., Ind. U., 1955, Ph.D., 1958. Tchr. music and sci. Laketon and Somerset pub. schs., Wabash County, Ind., 1947-52; teaching asst. dept. zoology Ind. U., Bloomington, 1952-55; asst. prof. Manchester Coll., North Manchester, 1955-60, assoc. prof., 1960-67, prof. biology, 1967—, dir. Environ. Studies, 1971—; cons. Ind. Dept. Natural Resources, Indpls., 1968, 76-82; vis. scientist U. Uppsala Inst. Limnology, Sweden, 1963-64. Author: History of Church of the Brethren in Northwestern Ohio, 1982. Contbr. articles to profl. jours. Mem. Ind. Pesticide Rev. Com., Indpls., 1971-83. Named Sagamore of Wabash, Ind. Gov., 1983; Ind. scholar Indpls. Star newspaper, 1984. Fellow Ind. Acad. Sci. (founder/editor spl. monograph series of publs. 1968—, chmn. publs. com. 1977-80, pres. 1982, chmn. constn. rev. com. 1983—); mem. Am. Soc. Limnology and Oceanography, Am. Inst. Biol. Scis., Internat. Assn. Theoretical and Applied Limnology, Nat. Assn. Biology Tchrs., Izaak Walton League (charter mem., bd. dirs. Resource chpt. Ind. 1965—, pres. 1976—), Beta Beta Beta. Republican. Mem. Ch. of Brethren. Avocations: fishing; historical and genealogical research. Home: 304 Sunset Ct North Manchester IN 46962 Office: Dept Biology Manchester College North Manchester IN 46962

EBERSOLE, RONALD OTIS, hospital administrator; b. Wichita, Kans., June 25, 1943; s. Harvey Orrison and Dortha (Otis) E.; m. Rhoda Beth Bartz, Sept. 9, 1972; children—Catherine Emily, Jay William. A.B., Wichita State U., 1966; M.H.A., Washington U., St. Louis, 1969. Asst. adminstr. M.D. Anderson Hosp. and Tumor Inst., Houston, 1969-75; assoc. adminstr. St. Joseph Hosp., Mo., 1975-82; adminstr. Johnson County Meml. Hosp., Warrensburg, Mo., 1982-84; exec. dir. North Iowa Med. Ctr., Mason City, 1984—; mem. accreditation com. Mo. Hosp. Assn., 1982-84. Pres. bd. dirs. Northwest Mo. Health Edn. Ctr., St. Joseph, 1980-82; bd. dirs. Warrensburg unit Am. Heart Assn., 1982-84. Named Boss of Yr., Am. Bus. Women's Assn., Warrensburg, 1983. Mem. Am. Coll. Hosp. Adminstrs., Mason City C. of C. (mem. leadership devel. com. 1984, bd. dirs. 1985), Iowa Hosp. Assn. Council Profl. Affairs. Republican. Lutheran. Lodge: Rotary. Avocations: gardening; fishing; cooking. Home: 181 Parkridge Dr Mason City IA 50401 Office: North Iowa Med Ctr 910 N Eisenhower Ave Mason City IA 50401

EBERT, DOUGLAS EDWARD, lawyer; b. Marion, Ohio, Nov. 17, 1949; s. Edward E. and Janet L. (Cobourn) E.; m. Heather S. Hamilton, June 28, 1980. B.A., Ohio State U., 1972, J.D., 1976. Bar: Ohio 1976. Assoc. Conkle & Harris, Marion, 1976-79; ptnr. Conkle, Harris & Ebert, Marion, 1980-82; ptnr. Harris & Ebert, Marion, 1983—. Vice pres. Friends of Marion Pub. Library. Mem. Marion County Bar Assn., Ohio State Bar Assn., Order of Coif, Phi Beta Kappa, Pi Sigma Alpha. Office: Harris & Ebert 142 S Prospect St Marion OH 43302

EBERT, FLORENCE SONERIN, occupational health program planner, nurse; b. Chgo., May 16, 1924; d. Daniel and Julia (Wallis) Sonerin; m. Carl H. Ebert, Nov. 27, 1946; 1 dau., Regan. R.N., Ravenswood Hosp., Chgo., 1946; B.S., St. Joseph's Coll., 1982; postgrad. Triton Coll., Oakton Coll., U. Ill., Johns Hopkins U. Occupational health nurse Echlin Mfg. Co., Elk Grove

Village, Ill., 1959-60, A. B. Dick Co., Niles, Ill., 1960-62, Motorola, Inc., Chgo., 1962-69, Sargent-Welch Sci. Co., Skokie, Ill., 1969-78; corp. occupational health nurse Velsicol Chem. Corp., Chgo., 1978—; cons. mem. Cert. Bd. Hazard Control Mgmt., Bethesda, Md., 1983—. Contbr. articles on occupational health nursing to profl. jours. Vol. Muscular Dystrophy Assn., Chgo., 1970. Mem. Am. Bd. Cert. Occupational Health Nurses (founder), Ill. Occupational Health Nurses, Chgo. Assn. Occupational Health Nurses (editor 1981-84), Am. Assn. Occupational Health Nurses (con. 1983—). Office: Velsicol Chem Corp 341 E Ohio Chicago IL 60611

EBERT, REGAN DANIELLE, lawyer, educator; b. Chgo., June 13, 1954; d. Carl Henry and Florence (Sonerin) E.; m. Daniel Lee Balzano, July 13, 1981; 1 child, Daniel Carl. B.S., U. Ill., 1976, M.S., 1977; J.D., John Marshall Law Sch., Chgo., 1979. Bar: Ill. 1979, U.S. Dist. Ct. (no. dist.) Ill. 1979, U.S. Ct. Appeals (7th cir.) 1980, U.S. Dist. Ct. (no. dist.) Ill. Trial Bar 1983. Staff atty. City of Chgo., 1980; trial atty. Hartford Ins. Co., Chgo., 1980-84, Judge & Knight Ltd., Park Ridge, Ill., 1984, Carl H. Ebert & Assocs., Chgo., 1984—; prosecutor City of Park Ridge, 1984—; adj. faculty John Marshall Law Sch., 1980—. Legal advisor 41st Ward Democratic Orgn., Chgo., 1979—, precinct capt., 1977—. Grad. research asst. U. Ill., 1977; Ill. state scholar, 1972; mem. John Marshall Law Sch. Law Rev., 1977-79; recipient Order of John Marshall, 1979. Mem. ABA, Assn. Trial Lawyers Am., Ill. Bar Assn., Ill. Trial Lawyers Assn., Chgo. Bar Assn. Office: Carl H Ebert & Assocs 188 W Randolph Suite 926 Chicago IL 60601

EBERT, ROGER JOSEPH, film critic; b. Urbana, Ill., June 18, 1942; s. Walter H. and Annabel (Stumm) E.; B.S., U. Ill., 1964; postgrad. U. Cape Town (South Africa), 1965, U. Chgo., 1966-67. Staff writer Champaign-Urbana News Gazette, 1958-66; editor Daily Illini, 1963-64; film critic Chgo. Sun-Times, 1967—; co-host Sneak Previews, PBS, 1977-82, At the Movies, Syndicated TV program, 1982—; film critic Sta. WMAQ-TV, Chgo., 1980-83, WLS-TV, Chgo., 1984—; commentator Movie News, ABC-FM network, 1982-85; instr. Chgo. City Coll., 1967-68; lectr. fine arts U. Chgo. extension, 1969—; lectr. film Columbia Coll., Chgo., 1972-73, 76-77. Recipient award Chgo. Headline Club, 1963, Overseas Press Club award, 1963; Chgo. Newspaper Guild award, 1973; Pulitzer prize for disting. criticism, 1975; Chgo. Emmy award, 1979. Rotary fellow, 1965. Mem. Am. Newspaper Guild, Nat. Soc. Film Critics, U. Ill. Alumni Assn. (dir. 1975-77), Phi Delta Theta. Clubs: Arts, Cliff Dwellers (Chgo.). Author: An Illini Century, 1967; (screen play) Beyond the Valley of the Dolls, 1970; Beyond Narrative: The Future of the Feature Film, 1978; A Kiss is Still a Kiss, 1984; Roger Ebert's Movie Home Companion, 1985. Office: 401 N Wabash Ave Chicago IL 60611

EBERWEIN, JANE DONAHUE, English educator; b. Boston, Sept. 13, 1943; d. Joseph Daniel and Mary Leyden (O'Brien) Donahue; m. Robert T. Eberwein, July 10, 1971. A.B., Emmanuel Coll., 1965; Ph.D., Brown U., 1969. From asst. prof. to prof. English Oakland U., Rochester, Mich., 1969—. Author: Dickinson: Strategies of Limitation, 1985. Editor: Early American Poetry, 1978. Contbr. articles to profl. jours. Mem. MLA, Am. Studies Assn., Mich. Acad. Sci., Arts and Letters, Phi Beta Kappa. Home: 379 W Frank St Birmingham MI 48009 Office: Dept English Oakland U Rochester MI 48063

EBLE, JOHN NELSON, pathologist, oncology researcher; b. Madison, Wis., Sept. 15, 1951; s. John Nelson and Jane Mildred (Brewer) E.; Kathy Marie Stelter, Sept. 30, 1972 (div. 1983); children—Nicholas, Benjamin, Elizabeth; m. Rosemarie A. Heltsley, May 25, 1985. B.S., Ind. U., 1973, M.D., Ind. U.-Indpls., 1976. Diplomate in anat. and clin. pathology Am. Bd. Pathology. Resident in pathology Ind. U. Hosp., Indpls., 1980; asst. prof. pathology Ind. U.-Indpls., 1980-82, asst. prof. pathology and exptl. oncology, 1982-85, assoc. prof., 1985—; chief pathologist VA, Indpls., 1982—; cons. pathologist Hawley Army Hosp., Ft. Benjamin Harrison, Ind., 1984—; dep. coroner Marion County Coroner's Office, Ind. Contbr. articles to profl. jours. Fellow Coll. Am. Pathologists, Am. Soc. Clin. Pathologists; mem. AMA, Internat. Acad. Pathology. Office: Lab Service 113 Roudebush VA Med Ctr 1481 W 10th St Indianapolis IN 46202

EBLE, TIMOTHY EUGENE, lawyer; b. Evansville, Ind., Apr. 19, 1952; s. Roscoe Hendricks and Lucille (Brooks) E.; m. Elizabeth Jackson, Aug. 14, 1976; 1 child, Matthew Timothy. B.A., Ind. U., 1974; J.D., No. Ky. U., 1980. Bar: Ohio 1981, U.S. Dist. Ct. (so. dist.) Ohio 1981, U.S. Ct. Appeals (6th cir.) 1981, Ky. 1982, U.S. Tax Ct. 1982, U.S. Dist. Ct. (ea. and we. dists.) Ky. 1983, U.S. Ct. Claims 1983, U.S. Ct. Internat. Trade 1983, U.S. Supreme Ct. 1984. Staff atty. U.S. Ct. Appeals (6th cir.), Cin., 1981-83; atty. Robinson Arnzen, Parry & Wentz, Covington, Ky., 1983—. Mem. Assn. Trial Lawyers Am., Ohio State Bar Assn., ABA, Ky. Bar Assn., Cin. Bar Assn. (fed. cts. com., common pleas ct. com.). Lodge: Kiwanis. Home: 1427 Pape Ave Cincinnati OH 45215 Office: Robinson Arnzen Parry & Wentz PSC 600 Greenup Covington KY 41012

EBNER, JUDITH MARILYN, educational administrator; b. Grove City, Pa., Nov. 19, 1939; d. Emil Emanuel and Gladys Mary (Morton) E.; B.M., U. Mich., 1962, M.M., 1964, Ph.D., 1984; postgrad. Columbia U., 1963-72. Tchr. vocal music Frewsburg (N.Y.) Central Sch., 1964-65, East Williston (N.Y.) Public Schs., 1965-74; stock broker First Investors Corp., N.Y.C., 1973-75; tchr. vocal music Beecher Community Schs., Flint, Mich., 1975-79; staff assoc. Flint Community Schs., 1979—; lectr. U. Mich.-Flint, 1980. Mem. Greater Flint Fine Arts Council; mem. U. Mich. Regents-Alumni Scholarship Interview Com.; mem. Dailey Community Ednl. Council, Flint; mem. exec. bd. Flint Community Cultural Festivals, Inc.; past bd. dirs. East Williston Community Concert Assn.; mem. profl. devel. adv. council Genesee Intermediate Sch. Dist.; mem. Mich. state planning com. Inst. for Comprehensive Arts Planning; del. Mich. Women's Assembly III. Recipient Outstanding Tchr. award Beecher Community Schs., 1977. Mem. Am. Assn. Sch. Adminstrs., Assn. Supervision and Curriculum Devel., Council Basic Edn., Council Ednl. Facility Planners, Internat. Soc. Study Edn., Assn. Tchr. Educators, Music Educators Nat. Conf., Mich. Music Educators Assn. (dir.), Mich. Sch. Vocat. Assn. (bd. dirs.), Mich. Council Women in Ednl. Adminstrn. (treas.), Alliance for Arts Edn., Internat. Platform Assn., Phi Delta Kappa, Delta Kappa Gamma, Mu Phi Epsilon. Clubs: Zonta Internat., U. Mich. Alumni. Co-author music curriculum guides; contbr. articles to profl. jours. Home: 3601 Balfour Ct Apt 15 Flint MI 48507 Office: 924 E 6th St Flint MI 48503

EBRIGHT, RODERICK MELVILLE, advertising executive, athletic coach; b. Wooster, Ohio, Dec. 4, 1951; s. Melville Lloyd and Donna Mildred (Acker) E.; m. Lynn Boggs, May 24, 1975; children—Jonathan Melville, Frances Bernae. B.F.A., Bowling Green State U., 1974. Art dir. Hamilton Design, Columbus, Ohio, 1974-77; dir. advt. Sports Imports, Inc., Columbus, 1978—; head volleyball coach Grandview Heights High Sch., Columbus, 1982—. Team capt. Men's Intercollegiate Volleyball, Bowling Green, 1973. Mem. Ohio High Sch. Volleyball Coaches Assn. (pres. 1983—), U.S. Volleyball Assn. (bd. dirs. 1982—), Kappa Sigma, Delta Phi Delta (pres. 1972). Mem. United Ch. of Christ. Club: Westerville Volleyball (Ohio). Home: 3347 Colchester Rd Upper Arlington OH 43221 Office: Sports Imports Inc 2549 Westbelt Dr Columbus OH 43228

ECHOLS, M. EVELYN, travel consultant; b. LaSalle, Ill., Apr. 5, 1915; d. Francis Ira and Mary Irene (Coleman) Bassett; grad. Josephinum Acad., Chgo., 1931; m. David H. Echols, Aug. 31, 1951; children—Susan Echols O'Donnell, William. Pres., founder Internat. Travel Tng. Courses, Inc., Chgo., Los Angeles, San Francisco, Washington, 1962—; pres. Echols Internat. Hotel Schs.; ptnr. Internat. Travel Industry Cons., 1959—. Bd. dirs. U. Ill. Grad. Sch. Bus., Chgo. Conv. and Tourism Bur., Chgo. Better Bus. Bur., Mental Health Soc. Greater Chgo., United Cerebral Assn.; mem. Pres. Reagan's Adv. Com. for Women's Bus. Ownership; vice chmn. adv. bd. Northwestern Psychiat. Hosp.; trustee Mundelein Coll. Named Bus. Woman of Yr., Nat. Assn. Bus. Women, 1985; Woman Entrepreneur of Yr., Women Bus. Owners of N.Y. Mem. Chgo. Execs. Club (bd. dirs.), Acad. TV Arts and Scis., Soc. Am. Travel Agts., Chgo. Network, Com. of 200, Nat. Women's Forum. Club: 200 Club. Office: Time-Life Bldg 303 E Ohio St Chicago IL 60611

ECKARDT, ROBERT EDWARD, gerontologist, foundation official; b. N.Y.C., June 29, 1951; s. Robert Edward and Mary Lenore (Harvey) E.; m. Virginia A. Sheehan, Feb. 18, 1983; 1 child, Allison Lenore. B.A. with honors, Grinnell (Iowa) Coll., 1973; Thomas J. Watson fellow, Spain and Denmark, 1973-75; M.P.H. (Klare Meml. fellow 1976-77), U. Mich., 1977, cert. aging, 1977. Research asst. Mich. Dept. Pub. Health, 1976-77; planning asso. Fedn. Community Planning, Cleve., 1977-82; coordinator Long Term Care Gerontology Center, Cleve., 1979-82; program officer Cleve. Found., 1982—. Pew Meml. fellow in health policy U. Mich., 1984—. Mem. Am. Public Health Assn., Gerontol. Soc. Am., Ohio Public Health Assn., Grantmakers in Health, Grantmakers in Aging, Cleve. Orch. Pub. Relations Adv. Council, Phi Beta Kappa. Author monograph in field. Home: 26700 Midland Rd Bay Village OH 44140 Office: 1400 Hanna Bldg Cleveland OH 44115

ECKARDT, STEPHEN ROBERT, writer, human rights activist; b. Bethlehem, Pa., June 4, 1952; s. A. Roy and Alice (Lyons) E. B.A. in Psychology, U. Pa., 1974. Coordinator Polit. Rights Def. Fund, Phila., 1974-77; chmn. Socialist Workers Party, Phila, 1978-81, Gary, Ind., 1981-83; mgr. Militant Bookstore, Gary, Ind., 1981-83; cons. mem. Harper-Dean Def. Com., Gary, 1982—; organizing com. mem. UAW, East Greenville, Pa., 1973; union rep. Transport Workers Union, Phila., 1979. Contbr. articles to profl. jours. Founding mem. Nat. Student Coalition Against Racism, Boston, 1976; bd. dirs. U.S. Commn. for Justice to Latin Am. Polit. Prisoners, Phila., 1973-76, Hector Marroquin Def. Com., 1976-77; organizer Marie Head Mayor Campaign Com., Gary, Ind., 1982. Socialist. Home: 2529 N Talman Chicago IL 60647

ECKART, DENNIS EDWARD, Congressman; b. Euclid, Ohio, Apr. 6, 1950; s. Edward Joseph and Mary Delores (Luzar) E.; B.A., Xavier U., Cin., 1971; J.D., Cleve. Marshall Law Sch., 1974; m. Sandra J. Pestotnik, Jan. 24, 1975; 1 son, Edward John. Bar: Ohio 1974. Asst. county prosecutor Lake County, 1974; mem. Ohio Ho. of Reps. from 18th Dist., 1975-81, chmn. Cuyahoga County del., 1979-81; mem. 97th Congress from 22d Ohio Dist., 98th-99th congresses from 11th Ohio Dist. Democrat. Roman Catholic. Office: 1224 Longworth House Office Bldg House Office Bldg Washington DC 20515

ECKDAHL-SLEEGER, PATRICIA JOSEPHINE, hospital administrator, nursing educator, management consultant; b. Scottsbluff, Nebr., Mar. 30, 1939; d. Arthur Finguel and Evelyn Josephine (Ehn) Eckdahl; m. Donald Eugene Sleeger, June 4, 1961; children—Toni Rene, Jodi Lynn, Lori Ann. Diploma in nursing, West Nebr. Gen. Hosp., Scottsbluff, 1960; B.S. in Nursing, Idaho State U., 1974, postgrad., 1975-76; M.S. in Nursing Adminstrn., U. Colo., 1979. Staff nurse West Nebr. Gen. Hosp., Scottsbluff, 1978-79, 60; head nurse Platte County Meml. Hosp., Wheatland, Wyo., 1960-67, dir. nursing, 1967-68; successively student health nurse, instr., faculty coordinator West Nebr. Gen. Hosp. Sch. Nursing, Scottsbluff, 1968-73, 74-79; staff nurse St. Anthony Hosp., Pocatello, Idaho, 1973-74; dir. nursing St. Joseph Hosp., Marshfield, Wis., 1979-81; instr. Milton (Wis.) Coll., 1980-81; asst. adminstr. St. Vincent Hosp., Green Bay, Wis., 1981—; instr. U. Wis.-Green Bay, 1982—; bd. dirs. Green Bay Area Free Clinic, 1983; mem. adv. com 3-yr. Kellogg Project Midwest Alliance in Nursing; mem. commn. edn. Nebr. Nurses Assn., 1970's. Mem. Task Force Labor Relations Cath. Insts. Green Bay, 1983, Mayor's Commn. Status of Women, 1975, Title IX Commn., 1976, aux. scholarship com. St. Vincent Hosp., Green Bay; bd. dirs. Wells Scholarship Fund, 1982-83. Recipient Recognition award Nebr. Nurses, 1976, Spl. Recognition award, 1978. Mem. Am. Nurses Assn. (state del. Hawaii Conv. 1978), Wis. Soc. Nursing Service Adminstrs. (chairperson ad hoc com. on research), Am. Soc. Nursing Service Adminstrs., Cath. Hosp. Assn. Wis. (nursing, pub. policy coms.), Nat. League, Nursing, Green Bay Dist. Nurses Assn. (bd. dirs. 1983—), LWV, Sigma Theta Tau. Democrat. Home: 1316 Dancing Dunes Dr Green Bay WI 54304 Office: St Vincent Hosp 835 S Van Buren St Green Bay WI 54301

ECKERLINE, C(HARLES) AUSTIN, office products company executive; b. Poughkeepsie, N.Y., Apr. 9, 1922; s. William James and Katharine Austin E.; m. Eleanor Joan Buckley, Sept. 10, 1950; children—Charles A., Paul B., Mark D., Peter E., Katharine A. B.S., N.Y. State Coll. Forestry, 1947. Prodn. engr. Quincy Adams Yachts, Quincy, Mass., 1948-59; plant mgr. L.F. Deitenborn, Hartford, Conn., 1960-62; dir. wood use center U. Ky., Lexington, 1963-69; plant mgr. Conwed Corp., Ladysmith, Wis., 1970-80; v.p. prodn. and product devel. Advance Office Concepts, Inc., Shoreview, Minn., 1981—. Trustee, Rusk County Meml. Hosp., Ladysmith, 1975-82. Mem. Forest Products Research Soc. Roman Catholic. Avocations: skiing, sailing, fishing. Home: 2679 Sumac Ridge White Bear Lake MN 55110 Office: Advance Office Concepts Inc 507 Shoreview Park Rd Shireview MN 55112

ECKERT, LARY CORNELL, orchard executive; b. Belleville, Ill., Nov. 17, 1943; s. Curt Eugene and Ruth Adel (Staub) E.; m. Judith Gayle Lannert, July 10, 1965; children—Sarah, Jill, Chris. B.S. in Agrl. Econs., U. Ill., 1965; M.S. in Agrl. Econs., Oreg. State U.-Corvallis, 1967. Pres., chmn. Eckerts, Inc., Belleville, Ill., 1967—; v.p., chmn. Eckert Orchards, Belleville, 1967—; v.p., dir. Eckert Land Co., Belleville, 1969—; participant Ill. Agr. Leadership Found., Macomb, Ill., 1982-84; chmn. Ill. Apple & Peach Market Bd., Springfield, 1983-84; dir. South Pass Products, Carbondale, Ill. Mem. Internat. Apple Inst. (trustee 1981-83). Republican. Methodist. Club: Rotary (pres. 1979-80) (Belleville). Home: Rural Route 1 Millstadt IL 62260 Office: Eckert Orchards Inc Rural Route 5 Box 325 Belleville IL 62221

ECKLAR, LAURA RUTH, public relations executive; b. Berea, Ohio, Dec. 19, 1950; d. Lawrence Paul and Ruth Ann (Bebenroth) Stelter; m. George Patrick Ecklar, Sept. 2, 1972; 1 son, Trent Edward. B.S. in Journalism, Ohio U., 1972. Advt. saleswoman, feature writer, Cable TV Program mag., Worthington, Ohio, 1976-77; asst. pub. info. adminstr. Mid-Ohio Regional Planning Commn., Columbus, 1977-79, pub. info. adminstr., 1979-82; pub. info. officer Columbus pub. schs., 1982—. Publicity chmn. Snyder for Council com., 1981; trustee Columbus Area Leadership Program, 1981-84; mem. fin. devel. operating unit Ohio council Girl Scouts U.S.; active YWCA, Met. Women's Ctr., Mt. Carmel Hosp. Aux. Recipient Outstanding Employee award Mid-Ohio Regional Planning Commn., 1979. Mem. Pub. Relations Soc. Am., Central Ohio Pub. Relations Soc., Nat. Sch. Pub. Relations Assn. (pres. Ohio chpt. 1983-84), Nat. Assn. Regional Councils (award of excellence, 1981). Club: Met. (Columbus). Office: Columbus Public Schools 270 East State St Columbus OH 43215

ECKLER, JOHN ALFRED, lawyer; b. Elyria, Ohio, July 2, 1913; s. Frank Roy and Ida Jean (Phipps) E.; m. Mary Emily Rickey, Dec. 21, 1936; children—Rickey, Jenne, Molly. A.B., Ohio Wesleyan U., 1935; J.D., U. Chgo., 1939. Bar: Ill. 1939, Ohio 1945. With Gen. Electric Co., Schenectady, N.Y., 1935-36; assoc. Knapp, Allen and Cushing, Chgo., 1939-43; adminstrv. asst. to Senator John W. Bricker, Washington, 1947-49; assoc. firm Bricker and Eckler, 1946-53, ptnr., 1954—; mem. Ohio Bd. Bar Examiners, 1954-59; chmn. Nat. Conf. Bar Examiners, 1958—, chmn. standing com. on multi-state bar exam., 1968-74; chmn. Fed. Bar Exam. Com., 1975—. Contbr. articles U. Chgo. Law Rev., others. Pres. Upper Arlington Civic Assn., 1952; active United Appeals; bd. health City Upper Arlington, 1956-70; chmn. bd. trustees Ohio Wesleyan U., 1958—, World Neighbors, Inc., 1952—. Served to lt. USNR, World War II. Fellow Am. Bar Found., Ohio State Bar Found. (pres. 1977-79), Am. Coll. Trial Lawyers; mem. Am. Judicature Soc. (bd. dirs. 1977-79), ABA (chmn. spl. com. ct. congestion 1958-60, mem. ho. of dels. 1960-69, assembly del. to ho. of dels. 1977-82), Ohio Bar Assn. (Ohio Bar medal), Columbus Bar Assn. (pres. bd. govs.), Am. Legion, Ohio Wesleyan U. Alumni Assn. (pres. 1958-60), Order of Coif, Phi Beta Kappa, Omicron Delta Kappa, Dalta Sigma Rho, Phi Delta Theta. Methodist. Clubs: University, Scioto Country, Torch (pres. 1955), Kit Kat (pres. 1972-73). Lodges: Masons (33 degree), Rotary (bd. dirs.). Office: 100 E Broad St Columbus OH 43215

ECKRICH, DONALD, company executive; b. Fort Wayne, Ind., Sept. 6, 1924; m. Barbara Eckrich; children—Emily, George, Joseph, Ellen, James, Eleanor, Louise, Diane. B.B.A., U. Mich., 1948. Plant mgr. Peter Eckrich & Sons, Inc., Kalamazoo, 1958-62, corp. gen. mgr. ops., Fort Wayne, 1962-65, dir. ops., 1965-66, exec. v.p., 1966-69, pres., 1969-72, chmn. bd., chief exec. officer, 1972-75; exec. v.p. Beatrice Foods Co., Chgo., 1975-77, vice chmn., 1977-79, pres., chief operating officer, 1979-82; pres., chief exec. officer Central Soya Co., Inc., Fort Wayne, 1985—, dir., 1982—; dir. Gen. Telephone of Ind., Micro Data Base Systems, Lafayette, Ind., Harris-Kayot, Fort Wayne, Kanppen Milling Co., Augusta, Mich., Pioneer Hi-Bred Internat., Inc., Des Moines. Bd. dirs. St. Joseph Hosp., Fort Wayne Fine Arts, Cath. Social Services, Jr. Achievement, all Fort Wayne. Served with U.S. Army, 1943-45. Address: Central Soya 1300 Fort Wayne Nat Bank Bldg Fort Wayne IN 46802

ECKRICH, THOMAS, real estate developer; b. Dec. 10, 1937; m. Sally A. Eckrich; 5 children. B.S. in Bus. Adminstrn., Notre Dame U. With Peter Eckrich & Sons; with Northill Devel. Corp., Fort Wayne, Ind., pres.; dir. Lincoln Nat. Bank & Trust Co. Bd. dirs. Econ. Devel. Group, Fort Wayne-South Bend Cath. Diocesan Bd. Mem. Fort Wayne C. of C. (dir.), Apt. Assn. Ind., Young Pres. Orgn. Ind., Real Estate Securities and Syndication Inst. Address: Northill Devel Corp 609 E Cook Rd PO Box 5103 Fort Wayne IN 46825

EDDLEMAN, ROBERT LEROY, soil conservationist; b. Milltown, Ind., Feb. 18, 1938; s. Claude and Bertha Leola (Haub) E.; m. Patricia Mary French, Aug. 6, 1960; children—Mary Beth, Susan, Julie, Donna. B.S. in Agr., Purdue U., 1959; M.P.A., U. Okla., 1976. Dist. conservationist USDA, Soil Conservation Service, Terre Haute, Ind., 1964-68, area conservationist, Rensselaer, Ind., 1968-72, asst. state conservationist, Syracuse, N.Y., 1972-75, dep. state conservationist, Champaign, Ill., 1975-80; state conservationist USDA, Soil Conservation Service, Indpls., 1980—. Ofcl. referee U.S. Swimming, Ill., Ind., 1975—; com. mem. Ind. 4-H Found., 1983—, 4-H leader, 1963—. Served to capt. USAR, 1959-68. Mem. Soil Conservation Soc. Am. (pres. 1974). Roman Catholic. Lodge: Rotary. Avocations: golf, swimming official, photography. Home: 8729 Chapel Glen Dr Indianapolis IN 46234 Office: USDA Soil Conservation Service 5610 Crawfordsville Rd Indianapolis IN 46224

EDELEN, JOSEPH R., JR., librarian; b. Belleville, Ill., Sept. 5, 1944; s. Joseph R. and Marilyn Jane (Weber) E.; m. Mary Margaret Beaty, June 8, 1968; children—Audra, Anthony, Jarrod. B.A., St. Mary's Coll., Lebanon, Ky., 1966, St. Mary's U., San Antonio, 1967; M.L.S., Cath. U. Am., 1968. Cataloger I.D. Weeks Library U. S.D., Vermillion, 1968-69, bibliog. control librarian, 1969—; chmn. bd. trustees Vermillion Pub. Library, 1983—; chmn. S.D. State Library Bd., 1981—. Author Index S.D. State Publs., 1975—, Index S.D. Legis. Bills, 1982—. Contbr. articles to profl. jours. Mem. Mountain Plains Library Assn. (exec. sec. 1972—), S.D. Library Assn. (pres. 1984-85), ALA (various coms. 1975-82), Council Library Assn. Execs. Republican. Roman Catholic. Lodge: Rotary (pres. 1980-81). Avocations: farming, skiing, snowmobiling, racquetball. Home: 311 Canby St Vermillion SD 57069 Office: I D Weeks Library U S D Vermillion SD 57069

EDELNANT, JAY ALAN, theater educator, actor; b. Chgo., Mar. 5, 1948; s. Nathan and Eleanore Mae (Fishman) E.; m. Vicki Van Vark, Dec. 9, 1973; children—Noah Samuel, Julia Elizabeth. B.A., MacMurray Coll., 1970; M.A., Northwestern U., 1971, Ph.D., 1978. Assoc. prof. performance U. No. Iowa, Cedar Falls, 1981—; dir. theatre Theatre U. No. Iowa, Cedar Falls, 1981—; freelance actor Iowa, Ill., Wis.; freelance performance cons., Iowa, Ill., Wis.; dir. various plays, 1971—. Mem. Am. Theatre Assn., Speech Communication Assn., Mid-Am. Theatre Conf., Central States Speech Assn., Iowa Communication Assn. Office: Theatre U No IA Cedar Falls IA 50614-0371

EDELSON, ALVIN LEON, university media director, educator; b. Detroit, Nov. 3, 1931; s. Arthur and Bessie (Bender) E.; m. Joanna Grossman, Aug. 16, 1959; children—Julie, Karin, Andrew. B.S., Wayne State U., 1953, M.A., 1963, Ph.D., 1977. Tchr. Fitzgerald Schs., Warren, Mich., 1959-63; mktg. mgr. Mut. of N.Y., Detroit, 1963-70; prof., media dir. Wayne State U., Detroit, 1973—; owner, cons. JANKA Assoc., Huntington Woods, Mich., 1978—. Producer ednl. TV series numerous subjects. Producer, writer TV documentary Is My Baby Normal?, 1980 (Emmy nomination). Contbr. articles to profl. jours. Chmn. Policy Com. Berkley Schs., Mich., 1978-82, Cable TV Adv. Bd., Huntington Woods, 1981—; media cons. March of Dimes, Detroit, 1979-80; media com. Arthritis Found. Mich., Detroit, 1982—. Served with U.S. Army, 1953-55, Germany. Mem. Mich. Soc. Instructional Tech., AAUP, Am. Film Inst., Nat. Acad. TV Arts and Scis. Avocations: tennis, photography. Office: Wayne State U Detroit MI

EDELSTEIN, CELINA, biochemist, educator; b. Czestochowa, Poland, Dec. 3, 1938; came to U.S., 1948, naturalized, 1957; d. Jack Sophie (Zeid) Berkowitz; m. Barry Bernard Edelstein, June 25, 1960 (div. 1978); 1 child, Scott Andrew. B.A., NYU, 1960; postgrad. U. Chgo., 1974-76. Guest scientist U. de Bruxelles, Brussels, Belgium, 1968-70; sr. research technician U. Chgo., 1970-73, sr. scientist, 1973-79, research assoc., 1979-81, research assoc. and instr., 1981-83, research assoc. and asst. prof. biochemistry, 1983—. Author: Plasma Proteins, 1974, Handbook of Electrophoresis, 1980, Lipid-Protein Interactions, 1982, Handbook of HPLC, 1984. Fellow Am. Heart Assn.; mem. Am. Oil Chemists Soc., N.Y. Acad. Scis. Jewish. Avocations: computers, swimming. Office: U Chgo 5841 S Maryland Chicago IL 60637

EDEN, REBECCA PLOTKIN, nursing educator; b. Youngstown, Ohio, June 22, 1922; d. Benjamin L. and Frieda (Schwartz) Plotkin; children—Samuel W., David N., Sheryl R., Diane H. R.N., St. Luke's Hosp. Sch. Nursing, 1943; B.S.N., Case Western Res. U., 1949. Staff, head nurse St. Luke's Hosp., Cleve., 1943-44; staff nurse Mt. Sinai Hosp., Cleve., part-time 1944-46; instr. St. John's Hosp. Nursing, Cleve., 1949-50, Jane Addams Sch. Practical Nursing, Cleve., 1959-71, dir., 1971-85; ret., 1985; mem. Ohio Bd. Nursing Edn. and Nurse Registration, 1976-80, 81-85, pres., 1978-80; mem. com. Nat. Council State Bds. Nursing. Served with Nurse Corps, U.S. Army, 1944-46. Mem. Am. Vocat. Edn. Assn., Ohio Vocat. Edn. Assn., Nat. League Nursing, Ohio Student Fin. Aid Adminstrs., Midwest Student Fin. Aid Adminstrs., Nat. Assn. Practical Nurse Edn., Ohio Practical Nurse Educators Assn., Jewish War Vets Aux. (pres. 1962-64, 69-70). Democrat. Jewish. Club: ORT. Home: 3271 Warrensville Center Rd Apt 17D Shaker Heights OH 44122

EDEN, ROBERT ELWOOD, lawyer; b. Freeport, Ill., Mar. 8, 1947; s. Bert Richard and Glades Kathryn (Randecker) E.; m. Kathryn Sue Martin, Aug. 7, 1976; children—Angela, Rebecca, Andrew. B.A., Luther Coll., 1969; M.A., U. Iowa, 1976, J.D., 1979. Bar: Iowa 1979, Ill. 1979, U.S. Dist. Ct. (no. dist.) Ill. 1980. Tchr. Kee High Sch., Lansing, Iowa, 1969-75; tchr. supr. U. Iowa, Iowa City, 1975-76; assoc. Plager, Hasting & Krug, Freeport, Ill., 1979-83, dir., asst. sec., 1984—. Mem. Assn. Trial Lawyers Am., Ill. Trial Lawyers Assn., Iowa State Bar Assn., Ill. State Bar Assn., Stephenson County Bar Assn. (sec. 1980-81), Phi Delta Kappa. Lutheran. Club: Lena Bus. and Profl. (Ill.). Lodge: Lions. Home: 827 W Cleveland Freeport IL 61032 Office: Plager Hasting & Krug Ltd 10 N Galena Ave Freeport IL 61032

EDEWAARD, LAVERN D., mobile homes executive; b. Holland, Mich., Aug. 24, 1934; s. Menno and Julia (Hulst) E.; m. Carol G. Gort, Aug. 31, 1957; children—Steven, Jeffrey, Randal, James. A.B., Calvin Coll. Pharm. salesman Lederle, Pearl River, N.Y., 1956-60; ptnr. dry cleaners Hi-Lo, Holland, 1960-62; tchr. biology Holland High Sch., 1962-66; ptnr. mobile homes sales, mobile home parks Leisure Homes & Leisure Estates, 1966—. Editor: DeLiar, 1967-83; Tracker, 1979—. Republican. Mem. Christian Ch. Clubs: Holland Fish & Game (pres. 1978, 79), Mich. Safari (pres. 1982, 83), Safari Internat (Tucson, Ariz.) (v.p. 1984—, Presidents award 1982); Mich. United Conservation (Lansing, Nat. Home Builders; Steelheaders (St. Joe, Mich.). Avocation: hunting. Home: 75 E 33d St Holland MI 49423

EDGAR, ARLAN LEE, biology educator, researcher; b. Gatiot County, Mich., June 3, 1926; s. Sherman J. and Letha (Perdew) E.; m. Bonnie Jean Anderson, Mar. 30, 1952; children—Rosemary, Amy, Andrew. B.A., Alma Coll., 1949; M.A., U. Mich.-Ann Arbor, 1950, M.S., 1957, Ph.D., 1960. Instr., Alma Coll., 1950-51, asst. prof., 1953-58, assoc. prof., 1958-65, prof., 1965—, Charles Dana prof. biology, 1976-85; vis. prof. Mich. State U. Biol. Sta., summer, 1961, U. Mich. Biol. Sta., summer, 1965-75. Served with U.S. Army, 1951-53. Named Disting. Prof. of Yr., Alma Coll., 1981; recipient Citation for Scholarly Achievement, Mich. Acad. Scis., 1973. Mem. Am. Inst. Biol. Scis., Am. Microscopical Soc., Am. Arachnol. Soc., Mich. Acad. Sci. Arts and Letters (chmn. zoology sect. 1968), Sigma Xi (v.p., pres. Cen. Mich. chpt. 1964-65, 65-66, 66-67, 67-68, 83-85). Avocations: Photography; sailing; gardening; golf; fishing. Home: 602 Woodworth St Alma MI 48801 Office: Alma Coll West Superior St Alma MI 48801

EDGAR, JAMES ROBERT, secretary state Ill.; b. Vinita, Okla., July 22, 1946; s. Cecil E. and Elizabeth M. (Moore) E.; B.S., Eastern Ill. U., 1968; postgrad. U. Ill., 1968-69; m. Brenda M. Smith, 1967; children—James Bradley, Elizabeth Ann. Legis. intern with pres. pro tem Ill. Senate, 1968; key asst. to speaker Ill. Ho. of Reps., 1972-74; aide to pres. Ill. Senate, 1974; aide to Ill. Ho. Majority, 1976, mem. Ho., 1976-79; aide to gov. Ill., 1979-80; sec. of state Ill., 1980—. Republican precinct committeeman; treas. Coles County Rep. Com., 1974; mem. Ill. Ho. Rep. Campaign Com.; pres. Coles County Hist. Soc., 1976-79; dir. state services Nat. Conf. State Legislatures, 1975-76. Baptist. Office: State Capitol Room 213 Springfield IL 62706*

EDGELL, GEORGE PAUL, lawyer; b. Dallas, Mar. 9, 1937; s. George Paul and Sarah Elizabeth (McDonald) E.; B.S. in Aero. Engring., U. Ill., 1960; J.D.,

Georgetown U., 1967; M.B.A., Roosevelt U., 1983; m. Karin Jane Williams; 1 son, Scott Rickard. Admitted to Va. bar, 1967, D.C. bar, 1968, Ill. bar, 1980; patent examiner U.S. Patent Office, Washington, 1963-65; ptnr. firm Schuyler, Birch, McKie & Beckett, Washington, 1969-80, assoc., 1965-69; group patent counsel Gould Inc., Rolling Meadows, Ill., 1980—. Vol. tutor Hopkins Ho., 1968-69; officer St. Stephen's Dads' Club, 1975-77. Served with USMC, 1960-63. Mem. ABA, D.C., Ill., Va. bar assns., Am. Intellectual Property Law Assn., Licensing Execs. Soc. Republican. Presbyterian. Clubs: Army Navy Country, Meadow. Home: 5403 Chateau Dr Rolling Meadows IL 60008 Office: 10 Gould Center Rolling Meadows IL 60008

EDGERTON, F(REDRICK) VAN, college administrator; b. Allegan, Mich., Nov. 27, 1947; s. Fredrick G. and Gertrude (VandeBunte) E.; B.A., Alma Coll., 1974; M.S.A., Central Mich. U., 1982; m. Patricia Louise Dehne, Sept. 8, 1973. Asst dir. placement Alma (Mich.) Coll., 1975, coordinator practicums, 1975—, dir. placement, 1977—, asst. to v.p. for student life and career programs, 1982—. Bd. dirs. Alma Highland Festival and Games, 1979-83, pres., 1981-82; pres. bd. dirs. Mid-Mich. Community Action Council, 1982-84; mem. Greater Gratiot Devel., Inc., 1982—, CAPC Pvt. Industry Council, 1983—. Served with AUS, 1969-72. Decorated Bronze Star. Recipient Disting. Service award Jaycees, 1983. Mem. Mich. Coll. and Univ. Placement Assn. (pres. 1980-81), Midwest Coll. Placement Assn., Mich. Acad. Sci., Arts and Letters. Presbyterian. Club: Kiwanis (pres. 1982-83). Home: 229 Purdy Dr Alma MI 48801 Office: Alma Coll Alma MI 48801

EDGY, L. JAMES, JR., dance administrator; b. Augusta, Ga., May 26, 1936; s. Lester J. and Eleanor (Ware) E. B.A., Stetson U., 1958; M.A.T., Wesleyan U., 1962. Headmaster, Capital Day Sch., Frankfort, Ky., 1965-69; dir., asst. dir. Ky. Arts Commn., 1967-74; dir. Ohio Arts Council, 1974-77; dep. chmn. Nat. Endowment for the Arts, 1978-79; gen. mgr. Cin. Ballet, 1978—. Office: 1216 Central Pkwy Cincinnati OH 45210*

EDIGER, MARLOW, education educator; b. Inman, Kans., Oct. 10, 1927. B.S. in Edn., Kans. State Tchrs. Coll., 1958, M.S. in Edn., 1960; Ed.D., U. Denver, 1963. English tchr. Mennonite Sch., Jericho, 1952-53; tchr. English and geography, Ramallah, 1953-54; tchr. Countryside Sch., Lehigh, Kans., 1955-57; tchr., prin. Lincolnville Grade Sch., Kans., 1957-61; prof. edn. N.W. Mo. State U., Kirksville, 1962—; speaker in field; mem. editorial bd. Experiments in Edn. Jour., India, Jour. Karnataka State Edn. Fedn., India. Author: Relevancy in the Elementary Curriculum, 1975; The Elementary Curriculum, A Handbook, 1977; Social Studies Curriculum in the Elementary School, 2d edit., 1980; Language Arts Curriculum in the Elementary Sch., 1983. Contbr. articles to profl. jours. Mem. adv. council Himalayan Soc. Ednl. Research and Devel., India, Religion in the Schs. Mem. Nat. Council Soc. Studies (mem. adv. council rural schs. and the social studies), Mo. Council Social Studies, NEA, Phi Delta Kappa. Office: Northeast Mo State U Div Edn Kirksville MO 63501

EDISON, JULIAN, retail executive; m. Hope Rabb Edison; children—Mark R., Aaron. A.B., Harvard U., 1951, M.B.A., 1953. With Edison Bros. Stores, Inc., St. Louis, chmn. bd., 1974—; chmn. bd. Edison Bros. Shoe Stores, Inc., 1983—, pres., 1963-83; dir. Boatmen's Nat. Bank, St. Louis, Boatmen's Bancshares, Inc., Stop and Shop Cos., Inc. Pres. Assocs. of St. Louis U. Libraries, Inc., 1967-69; bd. dirs. Jewish Fedn. St. Louis, 1967-76, 78-80; mem. Pres.'s Council, St. Louis U., 1967—; co-chmn. Interracial Council for Bus. Opportunity of St. Louis, 1969-72; bd. trustees St. Louis Art Mus., 1969-75, KETC-TV, 1977-84; bd. dirs. Barnes Hosp., 1978—, John Burroughs Sch., 1978-84. Served with U.S. Army, 1953-55. Mem. Footwear Retailers Am. (pres. 1976-77), Am. Retail Fedn. (dir.). Address: 400 Washington Ave Saint Louis MO 63102

EDISON, ROBERT GAY, chem. products co. exec.; b. Chgo., June 14, 1928; s. Sylvan M. and Anita Gay (Gore) E.; B.S., Northwestern U., 1949; m. Joyce Lerner, Nov. 27, 1953; children—Pamela, Marcey, Steven. Vice pres. S.M. Edison Chem. Co., Chgo., 1949-52, exec. v.p., 1954-60; founder, pres. The Hosiery Mate Co., Chgo., 1960—, also dir.; dir. Kleen Chem. Mfg. Co., Hosiery Mate Co. Can. Ltd. Served with USN, 1952-54. Mem. Soc. Cosmetic Chemists. Home: 3032 University Ave Highland Park IL 60035 Office: 2501 N Sheffield Ave Chicago IL 60614

EDMISTON, CHARLES NATHAN, lawyer, educator; b. Shelbyville, Ill., Dec. 15, 1954; s. Robert Lee and Catherine Jean (Attebery) E.; m. Gretchen Elaine Bockhorst, May 21, 1977; children—Sarah, Benjamin. B.S. with honors, U. Ill., 1976; J.D. with honors, U. Iowa, 1979. Bar: Iowa 1980, Ill. 1980, U.S. Dist. Ct. (no. dist.) Iowa 1980, U.S. Dist.Ct. (so. dist.) Iowa 1980, U.S. Dist. Ct. (so. dist.) Ill. 1985. Assoc. Karr, Karr & Karr, P.C., Webster City, Iowa, 1980-82; asst. state's atty. Wayne county State's Atty.'s Office, Fairfield, Ill., 1982-84; sole practice, 1985—; bus. law Frontier Community Coll., Fairfield, Ill. Mem. ABA, Ill. State Bar Assn., Iowa Bar Assn., Wayne County Bar Assn., Assn. Trial Lawyers Am. Republican. Methodist. Lodge: Lions (treas. local club 1983—). Home: 4 Windsor Ln Fairfield IL 62837 Office: 106 NE 2d St PO Box 651 Fairfield IL 62837

EDMONDSON, JAMES WILLIAM (JAY), insurance company executive; b. Artesia, Calif., July 1, 1930; s. Edward Vernon and Doris Laverna (Hoisington) E.; m. Susanne Martin, Sept. 5, 1953; children—Susan and John. B.A., U. of Calif.-Berkeley, 1952. Vice pres. service and systems State Farm Mutual Auto Ins. Co., State Farm Fire and Casualty Ins. Co., State Farm Gen. Ins. Co., Bloomington, Ill., 1954—. Bd. dirs. United Way, McLean County, Ill., Bloomington-Normal Symphony; chmn. Human Relations Com., Normal, Ill., 1975-76. Mem. Soc. of C.P.C.U. Republican. Roman Catholic. Office: State Farm Ins Cos Suite 1 State Farm Plaza Bloomington IL 61701

EDMONDSON, LYNN ELLEN, physical therapist facility executive; b. Lodi, Calif., June 11, 1952; d. Leonard and Mildred Irene (Thompson) Preszler; divorced; 1 child, Matthew Armstrong. B.S. in Phys. Therapy, Long Beach State U., 1976. Lic. phys. therapist, Ohio, W.Va., Calif. Staff phys. therapist Dominques Valley Hosp., Compton, Calif., 1976-77; dir. phys. therapy Los Altos Hosp., Long Beach, Calif., 1977-79, Cerritos Gardens Hosp., Hawaiian Gardens, Calif., 1979-80, East Liverpool City Hosp., Ohio, 1980-85; contracted phys. therapist Ohio Valley Home Health Ctr., East Liverpool, 1980-85; pres. Edmondson Phys. Therapy, Inc., Youngstown, Ohio, 1985—; cons. arthritis patient edn. Ohio State Dept. Health, Columbus, 1985—; tchr., lectr. Compton Community Coll., Calif., 1977-78. Mem. com. patient care Cleve. Arthritis Found., 1984—; bd. dirs. Youngstown Arthritis found., 1984—. Ohio Dept. Health grantee, 1983-85. Mem. Am. Phys. Therapy Assn., Allied Health Profls. Arthritis Found., Bus. Profl. Women's Club (treas.). Democrat. Avocations: arts and crafts; reading; golf; bowling; skiing. Office: Edmondson Phys Therapy Inc 1745 Belmont Ave Youngstown OH 44501

EDMUNDS, PALMER DANIEL, lawyer, educator; b. Terre Haute, Ill., Oct. 29, 1890; s. Amos and Mary Ann (Campbell) E.; A.B., Knox Coll., 1912, LL.D., 1945; LL.B., Harvard U., 1915; LL.D., John Marshall Law Sch., 1973, Piedmont Coll., 1975; m. Margaret Burton, June 29, 1932 (dec. 1964); m. 2d, Sarah Shepard Brown, 1970. Admitted to Ill. bar, 1915, since practiced in Chgo.; dir., counsel Ill. Service Recognition Bd., 1922-25; mem. firm Dodd, Matheny & Edmunds, 1925-29; commr. Supreme Ct. Ill., 1929-32; mem. firm Dodd & Edmunds, Chgo., 1932-58; lectr. conflict of laws and Ill. practice John Marshall Law Sch., Chgo., 1926-58, prof. law, 1958—, lectr. fed. practice, 1938-58, dir. Lawyers Inst.; vis. prof. law Knox Coll., 1944-57; compliance commr. WPB and Civilian Prodn. Adminstrn., 1944-47; hearing commr. NPA, 1951-53. Charter mem. World Peace Through Law Center. Trustee John Marshall Law Sch. First lt. A.E.F., 1917-19; capt. O.R.C. Past comdr. Black Hawk Post, Am. Legion, Chgo., past historian Dept. of Ill. Mem. Am. Polit. Sci. Assn., Am. Acad. Polit. and Social Sci., Fgn. Policy Assn., Am., Ill., Chgo., Internat. bar assns., India Soc., Internat. Law, Ill. Hist. Soc., S.A.R., Nat. Sojourners, Am. Bantam Assn., Sebright Club Am., 40 and 8, Soc. of 28th Div., Com. for Continuation Congl. Christian Chs. U.S., Phi Gamma Delta, Delta Sigma Rho. Democrat. Conglist. Mason, Elk. Club: Harvard (Chgo.). Author: (with W. F. Dodd) Illinois Appellate Procedure, 1929; Edmunds Common Law Forms, 1931; Illinois Civil Practice Forms, 1923; Edmunds Federal Rules of Civil Procedure, 1938; Cyclopedia of Federal Procedure Forms, 1939; Law and Civilization, 1959; co-author Encyclopedia of Federal Procedure, 2d edit., 1944; Edmunds Conflict of Laws, 1948. Editor, compiler: Jones Illinois Statutes Annotated, vols. 18-22, 24. Home and Office: Gilman IL 60938

EDSON, ALLAN CURTIS, osteopathic allergist; b. Marinette, Wis., Feb. 14, 1943; s. Ervin Julius and Anita Wanda (Pearson) E.; m. Antoinette Czarnecki, Nov. 30, 1969; children—Allison, Angela, Andrea, Aaron, Amber. D.O., Kirksville Coll. Osteo. Medicine, 1976. Diplomate Am. Osteo. Bd. Gen. Practice. Intern Bay Osteo. Hosp., Bay City, Mich., 1976-77; practice osteo. medicine specializing in allergy, Milw., 1980—; preceptor in allergy Allergists S.C., Milw., 1982-83, pres., 1982—; mem. staff Good Samaritan Med. Ctr., Northwest Gen. Hosp.; med. dir. Physicians Weight Control System; pres. Econ. Research Assocs. Served to lt. M.C., USNR, 1972-79. Mem. Am. Osteo. Assn., Am. Osteo. Coll. Allergy and Immunology (cert.), Am. Coll. Gen. Practitioners. Republican. Mormon. Home: 8545 N Regent Rd Fox Point WI 53217 Office: 2040 W Wisconsin Ave Suite 327 Milwaukee WI 53233

EDSON, SANDRA JENE, professional association executive; b. Gothenburg, Nebr., May 10, 1948; d. Darwin Elmer and Eunice Eileen (Anderson) E. B.S. in Bus. Adminstrn., U. Denver, 1972. C.P.A. Colo. Ptnr., Thomas A. Ward & Co., Denver, 1972-80; v.p. Fleming Assocs., Denver, 1980-82; exec. dir. Am. Soc. for Quality Control, Milw., 1982—. Pres. Mental Health Assn. Colo., 1982; v.p. fin. devel. Mental Health Assn. Wis., 1984; bd. dirs. Nat. Mental Health Assn., Alexandria, Va., Mental Health Assn. Milwaukee County. Named Vol. of Yr., Mental Health Assn. Colo., 1977. Mem. Am. Soc. Assn. Execs. (com. mem. 1982—), Am. Inst. C.P.A.s, Colo. Soc. C.P.A.s, Council Engrng. and Sci. Soc. Execs. Republican. Office: American Soc for Quality Control Suite 700 230 W Wells St Milwaukee WI 53203

EDSON, WAYNE E., dentist, consultant; b. Marinette, Wis., July 4, 1947; s. E.J. Edson and Anita (Pearson) Edson Sebero; m. Linda Mary Hullison, Apr. 3, 1971; 1 child, William Earl. B.S., U. Wis.-Madison/Milw., 1973; D.D.S., Northwestern U., 1977. Pvt. dentist, Winnetka, Ill., 1982—. Pres. Kenilworth United Fund, 1983-84, bd. dirs., 1981—; com. mem. Kenilworth Baseball, 1978-83. Served with USN, 1965-72. Mem. Chgo. Dental Soc., Ill. State Dental Soc., ADA. Roman Catholic. Avocations: hunting; fishing. Clubs: John Evans of Northwestern U., G.V. Black Soc. of Northwestern U. Home: 624 Exmoor Rd Kenilworth IL 60043 Office: 22 Greenbay Rd Winnetka IL 60093

EDWARDS, ANDREW WALLACE, social work educator, clergyman; b. Danville, Ill., Dec. 16, 1946; s. Simeon and Edna (Henderson) E.; m. Anna Bell, Aug. 2, 1980; children—Andrew Wallace, Mark, Gregory. B.A. in Sociology, William Jewell Coll., 1969; M.S.W., U. Kans., 1971; Ph.D., Kans. State U., 1978; postgrad. Central Bapt. Theol. Sem., 1981, Ashland Theol. Sem., 1982—. Faculty Cleve. State U., 1982—, prof. social work, 1985—. Recipient civic community service awards. Mem Nat. Assn. Christian Social Workers, NAACP, Nat. Assn. Black Social Workers, Assn. Social and Behavioral Scientists, Nat. Acad. Counselors and Family Therapists. Baptist. Contbr. articles to profl. jours. Office: Cleve State U Dept Social Services Cleveland OH 44115

EDWARDS, CHARLES ARTHUR, fund raising consultant; b. Chgo., May 7, 1940; s. Arthur Lewis and Kathleen (McGinnis) E.; m. Sandra Rae Hughes, July 14, 1984; children by previous marriage—Valerie Kathleen, Jennifer Anne. A.B., U. Chgo., 1965. Asst. dir. devel. Smith Coll., Northampton, Mass., 1966-69, Conn. Coll., New London, 1969-71; dir. devel. and pub. affairs Wadsworth Atheneum, Hartford, Conn., 1971-78; dir. devel. Barnard Coll., N.Y.C., 1979-81; v.p. Charles R. Feldstein & Co., Chgo., 1982-84; pres. The Edwards Group, Hinsdale, Ill., 1984—. Contbr. articles to profl. jours. Mem. exec. com. Nat. Alumni Fund Bd., U. Chgo., 1975-77, Conn. Gov.'s Com. on Arts and Tourism, 1973-75; mem. Nat. Alumni Cabinet, U. Chgo., 1969-72; chmn. New Eng. Conf. Devel. Group, Am. Assn. Mus., 1977-78. Served with U.S. Army, 1958-62. Mem. Nat. Soc. Fund Raising Execs., Am. Assn. Mus., Art Mus. Devel. Assn. (pres. 1976-77), Intelligence Corps Assn. (hon. life), Newport Artillery Co. (hon.). Congregationalist. Office: Edwards Group PO Box 153 Hinsdale IL 60521

EDWARDS, CHARLES C., JR., newspaper publisher; b. Denver, Jan. 5, 1947; s. Charles C. and Sue Cowles (Kruidenier) E.; m. Harriet Hubbell, June 24, 1979; children—Hayley, Emily. B.A. in History, U. Colo., 1970; postgrad. Drake U., 1973. Advt. salesman Des Moines Register, 1970-74, news reporter, 1974-79, circulation dir., 1979-82, advt. dir., 1982-84, mktg. dir., 1984, v.p. pub., 1984—. Vice-pres. Des Moines Art Ctr., 1985; truste Gardner Cowles Found., Inc., Des Moines; bd. dirs. Iowa Meth. Med. Ctr.; past pres. Des Moines Met. Opera, Inc., Boys' and Girls' Club Des Moines. Served with Air N.G., 1970-76. Republican. Congregationalist. Avocations: running; tennis; golf. Office: Des Moines Register 715 Locust St Des Moines IA 50309

EDWARDS, CLIFFORD DUANE, English educator; b. Atwood, Kans., Jan. 20, 1934; s. Murray Frank and Maude Loretta (Ray) E.; m. Neva LouAnn Morgan, Aug. 28, 1954; children—Mark, Marilyn, Cecily. B.A., Fort Hays State U., 1958; M.A., U. Mich., 1959, Ed.D., 1963. Lectr. English, U. Mich., Ann Arbor, 1963; assoc. prof. Fort Hays State U., Hays, Kans., 1963-69, dir. composition, 1974-83, prof. English, 1974—, chmn. dept., 1983—; chmn. dept. English, prof. U. Wis.-Platteville, 1969-74. Author: Conrad Richter's Ohio Trilogy, 1970; also essays, revs. Mem. Kansas Commn. on Aerospace Edn., 1982—; mem. Airport Adv. Bd., Hays, 1982-85. Served with USAF, 1951-55. Woodrow Wilson fellow, 1958-59. Mem. Airplane Owners and Pilots Assn., Nat. Council Tchrs. English, Danforth Found. Assocs. Avocation: flying; playing guitar, banjo and piano in musical groups; folk music. Home: 2725 Willow St Hays KS 67601 Office: Dept English Fort Hays State Univ Hays KS 67601

EDWARDS, DAN HILTEN, educational administrator; b. Monmouth, Ill., Mar. 1, 1949; s. G. Roland and Alice (Hilten) E.; m. Lorene Singleton, Aug. 17, 1972 (div. 1985); children—Brittany, Aaron. A.A., S.E. Iowa State U., 1969; B.A., No. Ky. U., 1972; M.A., N.E. Mo. U., 1975; Ph.D., St. Louis U., 1984. Tchr. Cool Springs Jr. High Sch., O'Fallon, Mo., 1972-76; asst. prin. Fort Zumwalt High Sch., O'Fallon, 1976-77; asst. prin. Kirkwood High Sch., Mo., 1977-79, assoc. prin., 1979-81; prin. Nipher Middle Sch., Kirkwood, 1981—; computer dir. Kirkwood Schs., 1983—. Contbr. articles to ednl. jours. Bd. dirs. Progressive Youth Ctr., Town and Country, Mo., 1983. Mem. Nat. Middle Sch. Assn. (presenter 1982-84), Assn. for Supervision and Curriculum, Mo. State Middle Sch. Assn., St. Louis Metro Middle Sch. Assn. (conf. head 1984), Phi Delta Kappa. Presbyterian. Office: Nipher Middle Sch 700 S Kirkwood Rd Kirkwood MO 63122

EDWARDS, DENNIS GEORGE, tax accountant; b. Amery, Wis., Jan. 23, 1948; s. George A. and Virginia (Heibel) E.; m. Danette R. Cicchese, Mar. 29, 1969 (div. June 1975); Susan M. Bastian, Dec. 15, 1984; 1 child, Allison. A.A., Minn. Sch. Bus., 1971, Rice Lake Vocat. Sch., 1968. Acct. Computer Age Acctg., Rhinelander, Wis., 1971-72, Estabrooks Inc., Rhinelander, 1972-77; prin. Edwards Acctg., Rhinelander, 1977—. Served with USMC, 1968-70. Mem. Nat. Assn. Tax Practitioners, Ambassadors Assn., Jaycees (alumni, bd. dirs. 1978, pres., treas. 1972-82), Rhinelander League (treas. 1980). Republican. Roman Catholic. Clubs: Vadomers (Oceanside) (treas. 1969-70) Bus. (pres. 1966-68). Avocations: golf, softball, reading, drawing. Home: 404 Lincoln St Rhinelander WI 54501 Office: 404 Lincoln St Rhinelander WI 54501

EDWARDS, DORIS STECK, nursing educator; b. Montgomery County, Ohio, Dec. 27, 1944; d. Russell Luther and Elsie Elizabeth (Schumaker) Steck; m. Neil Kenneth Edwards, Sept. 17, 1966; children—Jeffrey Kenneth, Steven Donald. Diploma, Miami Valley Hosp. Sch. Nursing, 1965; B.S.N. summa cum laude, U. Cin., 1976, Ed.D., 1984; M.S., Wright State U., 1980. R.N., Ohio. Head nurse Dayton State Hosp. (Ohio), 1965-66; clinic nurse Hamilton County Ct., Cin., 1967-68; nursing instr. Jewish Hosp. Sch. Nursing, Cin., 1976-80; nursing instr. U. Cin., 1980-82, asst. prof. nursing, 1982—, Sophomore dept. chmn., 1983—, exec. com. Women's Studies Faculty, 1983—. Mem. Southwestern Ohio Nurses Assn. (dir. 1979-82, pres. 1982—, legis liaison 1982-83), Am. Nurses Assn., Council Nurse Researchers, Ohio Nurses Assn. (bd. dirs. 1983—, Mary/Hamer Greenwood award), Assembly of Nurse Educators (chmn.), Assembly of Nurse Researchers, Assn. Women Faculty U. Cin. (bd. dirs.), Sigma Theta Tau (region 4 coordinator), Kappa Delta Pi (region 4 coordinator). Pi, Phi Delta Kappa. Lutheran. Home: 7711 Shadow Hill Way Cincinnati OH 45242 Office: College of Nursing and Health U Cin ML 38 3110 Vine St Cincinnati OH 45221

EDWARDS, GEORGE CLIFTON, JR., federal judge. U.S. cir. judge U.S. Ct Appeals Sixth Cir., Ohio. Office: US Ct Appeals US Courthouse Cincinnati OH 45202*

EDWARDS, HENRY DEXTER, hospital and homes administrator; b. San Francisco, Aug. 2, 1938; s. Roy Waldrup and Ruby (Lee) E.; m. Beverlee Jean Salts, Oct. 10, 1964; children—Tara, Jason. B.A., San Francisco State Coll., 1964; M.A., Chico State Coll., 1970; Ed.D., Calif. Coast U., 1983. Teaching and adminstrv. credentials, Calif., N.D. Tchr., South San Francisco Unified Sch. Dist., 1964-66, Yuba City (Calif.) Unified Sch. Dist., 1966-70, prin., 1971-75; supt. Manzanita Sch. Dist., Gridley, Calif., 1970-71; prin. Western Placer Unified Sch. Dist., Lincoln, Calif., 1975-81; adminstr. Anne Carlsen Sch., Lutheran Hosps. and Homes Soc., Jamestown, N.D., 1981—; recreation dir. Brisbane Sch. Dist. (Calif.), 1958-62; chief negotiator Western Placer Unified Sch. Dist., 1981; state coop. dir. State of Calif., 1979-81; mem. curriculum and instrn. com. Assn. Calif. Sch. Adminstrs., 1971-75. Mem. Greater N.D. Assn.: State C. of C. (bd. dirs.). Author: History of Brisbane School District, 1970; Anne Carlsen School, 1983. Served with USN, 1962-64. Republican. Clubs: Lions, Elks, Masons, Rotary, Shrine (pres. Central Sacramento Valley 1972). Home: 1021 Eighth Ave NW Jamestown ND 58401 Office: Lutheran Hosps and Homes Soc Anne Carlsen Sch 301 7th Ave NW Jamestown ND 58401

EDWARDS, HERBERT, engineering company exec.; b. Cin., Mar. 13, 1934; s. William and Eloise (Beckman) E.; m. Loretta Young, Jan. 7, 1937; children—Darryl Edwards, Mark Edwards. Diploma, Withrow Coll., Cin., 1952; postgrad. Ohio U., 1955. Pres., DER-Tech., Cin., roofer Firestone, Indpls., 1985. Energy advisor Ky. Energy Cabinet, 1985. Mem. Assn. Engrs., Assn. MBE Contractors (asst. dir. 1985). Home: 7231 Reading Rd Cincinnati OH 45237

EDWARDS, HOMER FLOYD, JR., educator; b. Forsyth, Ga., June 25, 1918; s. Homer Floyd and Mary Beulah (Jay) E.; B.A., Emory U., 1947, M.A., 1948, Ph.D., 1964; m. Marjorie H. Duncan, Apr. 29, 1967; 1 son, Christopher B. Instr. classics Emory U., Atlanta, 1954-55, instr. French and German, Emory-at-Oxford, 1955-57; asst. prof. humanities Morehouse Coll., Atlanta, 1959-63, Wayne State U., Detroit, 1963-65; faculty, head dept. theoretical studies Cranbrook Acad. Art, Bloomfield Hills, Mich., 1967-75; asso. prof. humanities Wayne State U., 1965-80, prof., 1980—, chmn. dept. humanities, 1964-75; adj. prof. history U. Windsor (Ont., Can.), 1977-79; music critic Detroit Monitor, 1968—; dir. Passau-Augsburg program Mich. Consortium Medieval and Early Modern Studies, Detroit, 1977-82; dir. Consortium for Austro-Bavarian Studies, 1982—; asso. fellow U. Mich., 1978—. Served with AUS, 1941-45. Univ. fellow Emory U., 1958-59. Mem. AAUP, Am. Musicol. Soc., Am., Brit. socs. aesthetics, Assn. Gen. Studies, Coll. Art Assn., Mind Assn. (Eng.), Modern Lang. Assn., Am. Hist. Assn., Hist. Assn. (Eng.), Mich. Acad., Nat. Assn. Humanities Edn. Episcopalian. Clubs: Scarab; Faculty of Wayne State U. Home: 201 E Kirby St Apt 904 Detroit MI 48202

EDWARDS, HORACE BURTON, oil pipeline company executive; b. Tuscaloosa, Ala., May 20, 1925; s. Burton and A.B. (Bryant) E.; m. Patsy M. Carter, Sept. 11, 1948 (div.); children—Adrienne, Paul, David, Michael. B.S. in Naval Sci., Marquette U., 1947, B.S.M.E., 1948; M.B.A. in Fin. Mgmt, Iona Coll., 1972; L.D.H. (hon.), Tex. So. U., 1982. Registered prof. engr., Wis., Kans. Various engrng. positions Allis Chalmers, 1948-52, Gen. Motors, 1952-56, Conrac, 1956-63, Northrop, 1963-71; with Atlantic Richfield Co., 1967-80, mgr. planning/evaluation, N.Y.C., 1976-79, v.p. planning/control, Los Angeles, 1979-80; pres., chmn., chief exec. officer ARCO Pipe Line Co., Independence, Kans., 1980—; v.p., dir. Independence Industries, Inc., 1981—; mem. adv. bd. Energy Bur.; mem. adv. com. Energy and Environ. Law Sect., Nat. Bar Assn. Pres. bd. dirs. Jr. Achievement, Independence, 1980—; trustee Kans. Council Econ. Edn., Topeka, 1981—, Leadership Independence, 1984-85. Recipient Marquette U. Dist. Engrng. Alumnus award, 1984. Mem. Am. Petroleum Inst., Assn. Oil Pipelines (exec. com.), Am. Assn. Blacks in Energy (bd. dirs.), Kans. Chamber Commerce and Industry (trustee Leadership Kans. 1983, dir. 1983—). Clubs: Independence Country, Petroleum of Tulsa. Lodges: Rotary; Elks. Office: ARCO Pipe Line Co ARCO Bldg Independence KS 67301

EDWARDS, IAN KEITH, obstetrician, gynecologist, clinic director; b. Spartanburg, S.C., Mar. 2, 1926; s. James Smiley and Georgina (Waters) E.; A.B., Duke U., 1949, M.D., 1953; m. Glenda Melissa Joselyn, Dec. 27, 1968; children—Darien, Jennifer, Carol, Terry. Spl. study pediatrics St. Bartholomew's Hosp., London, 1952; resident in ob-gyn Grady Meml. Hosp., Atlanta, 1955-58; chief ob-gyn Valley Forge (Pa.) Army Hosp., 1958-61; practice medicine specializing in ob-gyn, Olney, Ill., 1969—; ptnr. Trover Clinic, Madisonville, Ky., 1961-68; ptnr. Weber Med. Clinic, Olney, 1969—, dir. dept. ob-gyn, 1970-74, 78—, chmn. bd. dirs., 1983—; chief of staff Hopkins County (Ky.) Hosp., 1967-68, Richland Meml. Hosp., Olney, 1974-76; clin. instr. ob-gyn U. Ky. Med. Ctr., Lexington, 1965-68; cons. Childbirth Edn. League. Mem. Found. com. Olney Central Coll. Served to capt. M.C., U.S. Army, 1954-55; Korea. Diplomate Am. Bd. Ob-Gyn. Fellow Am. Coll. Obstetricians and Gynecologists (exec. com. Ill. sect. dist. VI, mem. nat. mktg. com., del. to Am. Group Practice Assn.); mem. Phila. Obstet. Soc., S.E. Ill. Consortium Maternal and Fetal Welfare, Ill. Assn. Maternal and Child Health (bd. dirs.), Am. Acad. Med. Dirs., Am. Legion, VFW, AMA, Ill., Hopkins County (pres. 1968), Richland (pres. 1974-76) med. socs., Ill. Soc. Ob-Gyn. Democrat. Methodist. Contbr. articles to med. jours. Clubs: Lions, Kiwanis. Office: Weber Med Clinic 1200 N East St Olney IL 62450

EDWARDS, JOHN, human services agency administrator, consultant; b. Monticello, Fla., Aug. 31, 1946; s. Alexander and Alberta (Robinson) E.; m. Anna D. Bryant, children—Kimberly, Deborah, Chinyere, Courtney, Carrie, DeAnna. A.A., Suwanne River Jr. Coll., 1965; B.S., Fla. A&M U., 1967; M.Ed., U. Ill., 1971. Tchr., Loudoun County Sch. Bd., Leesburg, Va., 1967-68; organizer, planner Kankakeeland Community Action Program, Inc., Kankakee, Ill., 1968-69, early childhood edn. dir., 1969-70, 71-74, dep dir., 1974-77, acting exec. dir., 1977-79, exec. dir., 1979—. Exec. bd. Concerned Citizens Coalition, Kankakee, 1983—; chmn. bd. dirs. Martin De Porres Nursery, Kankakee, 1983—; trustee Ill. Health and Welfare Fund, chmn. energy com., 1980-83. Recipient Cert. of Recognition, Kankakee Sch. Dist. Ill, 1985; Cert. of Recognition Ill. Head Start-Day Care Assn., 1984. Mem. Ill. Community Action Assn., Nat. Community Action Exec. Dirs. Assn., Ill. Pub. Action Club (com. chmn. 1982—). Democrat. Mem. Disciples of Christ. Avocations: writing, jogging, softball. Office: Kankakeeland Community Action Program Inc 1309 E Court St Kankakee IL 60901

EDWARDS, KAREN LENORE, clinical, organizational and social psychologist, organization development consultant; b. Phila., Aug. 6, 1947; d. Reginald Clarence and Winifred Oretta (Morman) Edwards. B.S., Howard U., 1969, M.S., 1971; Ph.D., U. Cin., 1979. Instr. psychology Fed. City Coll., Washington, 1971-72; psychology asst. Montgomery County Children's Services Bd., Dayton, Ohio, 1974-75; internal orgn. devel. and affirmative action cons. Procter & Gamble Co., Cin., 1977-78; core faculty U. Without Walls, Cin., 1979-80; asst. prof. psychology, asst. dir. Multi-Ethnic Psychol. Services Ctr. U. Cin., 1980—; asst. prof. psychology Evening Coll. U. Cin.; cons. ednl., community orgns. Bd. dirs. Cin. Ctr. Devel. Disorders and Mental Health Services Northwest; active NAACP Women's Conf., 1981, Cin. Women's Conf., 1982. Mem. Am. Psychol. Assn., Assn. Black Psychologists, United Black Assn. Faculty, Adminstrs., Staff (v.p.), Soc. for Psychol. Study Social Issues, AAUP, Psi Chi, Alpha Sigma Lambda. Baptist. Club: Women's City (Cin.). Contbr. articles to profl. jours. Office: Dept Psychology U Cin 401-B Dyer Hall Cincinnati OH 45221

EDWARDS, LUCILLE CHRISTINE, mobile home park owner; b. Seneca, Kans., Feb. 26, 1920; d. Herman Henry and Emma Augusta (Hecht) Wiesedeppe; m. Frederick Ferdinand Filger, Aug. 12, 1942 (div.); 1 son, Dennis Lee; m. 2d, Harry Cornelius Edwards, Aug. 26, 1962. Student Burroughs Bus. Sch., 1939. Accounts payable clk. Montgomery Ward, Kansas City, Mo., 1938-40; with payroll dept. Kelly Field, San Antonio, 1940-41; bookkeeper H.D. Lee, Kansas City, Mo., 1941-45; prop. Denny's Cafe, Northmoor, Mo., 1945-50; founder, owner service sta., Northmoor, 1951—; founder, owner Lakeview Terrace, 1954—; ptnr. Clayco Bank, Claycoma, Mo., 1983—, also adv. dir.; dir. 1st Nat. Bank Gladstone, 1971-80, chmn., 1980—. Mem. zoning bd. City Northmoor (Mo.), 1960-62, councilwoman, 1962-68; campaign mgr. Charles Wheeler for Mayor, Kansas City, No., Mo., 1979; adv. bd. Maple Woods Community Coll., Kansas City, 1983. Mem. Kansas City Citizens Assocs. Democrat. Lodge: Eastern Star.

EDWARDS, MARGENE MAE, univ. records mgr.; b. Highland, Ill., June 3, 1931; d. Freemon H. and Cornelia (Schoeck) Schmidt; student So. Ill. U., 1968-70; m. Robert Miles Edwards, Jan. 22, 1949; children—Robert Miles,

Debra, Thomas, Demaris. Office mgr. Madison Service Co., Marine and Edwardsville, Ill., 1961-72; records mgr., micrographics So. Ill. U., Edwardsville, 1972—; cons. area records and micrographic services. Mem. Assn. Records Mgrs. and Adminstrs., Nat. Micrographics Assn. (treas. St. Louis chpt.). Office: So Ill U Box 11 Edwardsville IL 62026

EDWARDS, ROBERT HAZARD, college president; b. London, May 26, 1935; s. Arthur Robinson and Marjorie Hazard (Mayes) E.; A.B., Princeton U., 1957; B.A., Cambridge (Eng.) U., 1959, M.A. (hon.), 1977; LL.B., Harvard U., 1961; m. Ellen Ramsey Turnbull, Sept. 10, 1966; children—Elizabeth, Daphne, Nicholas. Admitted to Fed. bar, D.C., 1961; Ford Found. fellow in Africa, 1961-63; with UN polit. affairs Dept. State, 1963-65; with Ford Found., 1965-77, rep. for Pakistan, 1968-72, head Middle East and Africa, 1973-77; pres. Carleton Coll., Northfield, Minn., 1977—; dir. Great No. Ins. Co., First Nat. Bank of Mpls. Trustee Deerfield Acad., Sci. Mus of Minn., Carnegie Found. for Advancement of Teaching. Mem. Council Fgn. Relations. Office: Carleton College One N College St Northfield MN 55057

EELLS, WILLIAM HASTINGS, automobile company executive; b. Princeton, N.J., Mar. 30, 1924; s. Hastings and Amy (Titus) E.; B.A., Ohio Wesleyan U., 1946; M.A., Ohio State U., 1950; D.H.L. (hon.), Kent State U., 1983 D.Pub. Service, Bowling Green State U., 1983. Asst. to dir. Inst. Practical Politics, Ohio Wesleyan U., 1948-50, asst. dir., 1952-53, dir., 1953-57; instr. dept. polit. sci., 1952-59; instr. polit. sci. Mt. Union Coll., 1950-51; coordinator Atomic Devel. Activities, State of Ohio, 1957-59; Midwest regional mgr. civic and govtl. affairs Ford Motor Co., Columbus, 1959—. Mem. Ohio Gov.'s Cabinet, 1957-59; chmn. bd. Blue Cross of Northeast Ohio, 1967-72, Blossom Music Center, Cleve., 1968-76; chmn. bd. govs. Gov.'s Council on Rehab., 1966-68; mem. exec. com. Met. Opera's Nat. Council, 1967-81; pres. Nat. Council High Blood Pressure Research, 1974-79; chmn. Ohio Pub. Expenditure Council, 1981—, Ohio Adv. Council Coll. Prep. Edn., 1981—, Gov.'s Task Force on State Ops., 1984—; mem. Nat. Council on Arts, Nat. Endowment for Arts, 1976-82; bd. dirs. Am. Heart Assn., 1974-79, award for disting. service, 1979; trustee Cleve. Orch., 1964—, Ednl. TV, Cleve., 1965-75, Cleve. Playhouse, 1965—, Cleve. Ballet, Cleve. Zoo, Columbus Arts Council, Columbus Symphony, Columbus Assn. Performing Arts, 1980—, Cleve. Luth. Hosp.; bd. dirs. Columbus Mus. Art, 1982—, Opera/Columbus, 1984—, Columbus Ballet, 1985—. Recipient awards including USCG Distinguished award, 1965, Silver medal Royal Life Saving Soc., Ohio State U. Devel. award, 1967, Silver medal Japanese Red Cross Soc., award Ohio Arts Council, 1979, Ohio Theatre Alliance, 1981. Mem. SAR, Ohio C. of C. (v.p.), Ohio Mfrs. Assn. (trustee), N.J. Hist. Soc. (trustee 1983—), Soc. Cin., Pi Sigma Alpha, Pi Gamma Mu, Omicron Delta Kappa, Delta Tau Delta. Republican. Presbyn. Clubs: Princeton (N.Y.); Columbus, U. Columbus (pres.); Union (Cleve.); F Street (Washington). Author: Your Ohio Government, 1953, 6th edit., 1967. Contbr. articles to profl. publs. Home: 54 Elmwood Dr Delaware OH 43015 Office: 37 W Broad St Columbus OH 43215

EFFINGER, KATHARINA VIOLA, hosp. exec.; b. Milw., June 15, 1941; d. Charles William and Eleanora (Hauer) E.; student Ft. Wayne (Ind.) Luth. Sch. Nursing, 1959-61; B.A. in Behavior Scis., Nat. Coll. Edn., Evanston, Ill., 1981. Reservation supr. Braniff Internat., 1961-69; sales rep. United Gasket Corp., 1969-70; admitting mgr. MacNeal Meml. Hosp., Berwyn, Ill., 1970-73; bus. office mgr. Lake Forest (Ill.) Hosp., 1974-77; asst. v.p. fin. Victory Meml. Hosp., Waukegan, Ill., 1978—; adv. bd. Lake County Vocat. Center. Mem. Hosp. Fin. Mgmt. Assn., Nat. Assn. Patient Accounts Mgrs. Office: 1324 N Sheridan Rd Waukegan IL 60085

EFTEKHAR, KAMBIZ, management consultant; b. Tehran, Iran, Nov. 4, 1944; came to U.S., 1963; s. H.E. Amireddin Eftekhar and Vageeheh (Meghnot) Steele; m. Judith Laura Pashby, Dec. 7, 1970; children—Darius, Damien. B.S.E. in Aerospace Engring., U. Mich., 1968, M.S.E. in Fluid Dynamics, 1970, M.M. in Gen. Mgmt., 1976. Mktg. coordinator Reynold's Aluminum Co., Richmond, Va., 1970-73; product devel. engr. Ford Motor Co., Dearborn, Mich., 1973-76; sr. cons. Arthur Andersen & Co., Chgo., 1976-78; mgr. Kearney Mgmt. Cons. (A. T. Kearney Inc.), Chgo., 1978—. Mem. Am. Mgmt. Assn. Office: A T Kearney Inc 222 S Riverside Plaza Chicago IL 60606

EGAN, DONALD JOSEPH, optometric educator, optometrist; b. Bklyn., Mar. 19, 1948; s. Charles Robert and Margaret Jane (Parot) E.; m. Gillian Leslie Hollands, June 7, 1980; children—Jennifer Jay, Keltie Lynn. B.S., St. John's U., 1968; B.S. and O.D. in Optometry, Pa. Coll. Optometry, 1975. Lic. Optometrist, Mo., Mass., N.Y., Pa., Ont. Clin. supr. U. Waterloo, Ont., Can., 1975-81, lectr., 1981-82; asst. prof. U. Mo., St. Louis, 1982-83, dir. clinics, 1983—. Contbr. articles to profl. jours. Fellow Am. Acad. Optometry; mem. Assn. Contact Lens Educators, Mo. Optometric Assn., Am. Optometric Assn., St. Louis Optometric Assn., Assn. Optometric Educators, Beta Sigma Kappa. Home and Office: U Missouri-St Louis Sch Optometry 8001 Natural Bridge Rd Saint Louis MO

EGAN, JAMES J., mayor; married, 10 children. LL.B., St. Louis U. Bar: Mo. 1954, U.S. Supreme Ct. Claim rep. Am. Auto. Ins. Co.; legal counsel Painter's Local #1199; prosecuting atty., City of Florissant, city atty.; majistrate judge First Dist., St. Louis County; mayor City of Florissant, Mo., 1963—. Mem. Mo. Municipal League (pres.), St. Louis County Municipal League (pres.), Mayors of Large Cities in St. Louis County (pres.). Roman Catholic. Address: 955 Rue Saint Francois Florissant MO 63031

EGAN, KEITH JAMES, theology educator, college adminstrator, author; b. Pitts., Sept. 27, 1930; s. James Washington and Agnes Elizabeth (Shevlin) E.; m. Constance Kane, Aug. 8, 1976; children—Bridget G. R., Brendan K. K. B.A., Mt. Carmel Coll., 1952; M.A., Cath. U. Am., 1959; Ph.D., Cambridge U., Eng., 1965. Vice prin. Joliet Cath. High Sch., Ill., 1956-59; vis. prof. Pontifical Inst. Mediaeval Studies, Toronto, Ont., Can., 1965-67; pres. Mt. Carmel Coll., Niagara Falls, Ont., 1966-68; prof. theology Marquette U., Milw., 1968-83; adj. prof. theology U. Notre Dame, Ind., 1983—; chmn. religious studies St. Mary's Coll., Notre Dame, 1983—, co-dir. Ctr. for Spirituality, 1984—; co-dir. Inst. for Ecumenical Spiritual in Am., Evanston, Ill., 1970-80; mem. Carmelite Forum, Washington, 1982—. Author: What is Prayer, 1974. Contbr. articles to profl. jours. Marquette U. research grantee, 1972, 79, 80, 81, 82; Theologian in residence Ecumenical Lay Acad., Dubuque, Iowa, 1981; Dehon fellow Sacred Heart Sch. Theology, Hales Corners, Wis., 1983-84; Ecumenical Inst. Culture and Research fellow St. John's U., Collegeville, Minn., 1980-81. Mem. Am. Acad. Religion (consultation of spirituality 1983—), Medieval Acad. Am., Coll. Theol. Soc. Am. (nat. v.p. 1978-80), Am. Cath. Hist. Assn., Coll. Theology Soc. Democrat. Roman Catholic. Avocations: swimming; hiking. Office: St Mary's Coll Religious Studies Dept Notre Dame IN 46556

EGAN, TERRY MICHAEL, marketing executive; b. Campbell County, Ky., June 21, 1948; m. Marian Gayle Fromme, Oct. 25, 1975; children—Christopher, Patrick, Jonathan. B.A., Thomas More Coll., Covington, Ky., 1971; M.B.A., Xavier U., Cin., 1972. Acct. mgr. Quaker Oats Co., Cin., 1972-73; territory mgr. Baxter Travenol, Cin., 1973-74; product mgr. Kendall Co., Boston, 1974-80; mktg. dir. Patient Care System subs. Zimmer Co., Charlotte, N.C., 1980-81; v.p. mktg. Snyder Labs. subs. Zimmer Co., Dover, Ohio, 1981—. Mem. Am. Mktg. Assn. Republican. Roman Catholic. Lodge: Elks. Office: Snyder Labs Inc 200 W Ohio Ave Dover OH 44622

EGGEN, DAVID L., forester; b. Mpls., Dec. 26, 1934; s. Owen J. and Lorna (Juul) E.; m. Barbara Margaret Martin, Aug. 23, 1955; children—Dawn, Bryn, Starr, Erik, Leif, Joy. B.S., U. Minn., 1961. Dist. ranger U.S. Forest Service, Isabella, Minn., 1961-66; gen. mgr. J.C. Campbell Co., Two Harbors, Minn., 1966-71; pres. Arrowwood, Inc., Sturgeon Lake, Minn., 1971-76, Woodland Services, Inc., Moose Lake, Minn., 1976—. Inventor. Bd. dirs. West Side Ch., Kettle River, Minn., 1985—. Served with U.S. Army, 1955-58; Ger. Recipient Superior Accomplishment award U.S. Forest Service, 1964; U.S. Dept. Agr. research and devel. grantee. Mem. Assn. Cons. Foresters, Soc. Am. Foresters (dist. chair 1965), Minn. Assn. Cons. Foresters (chair 1984-85). Mem. Christian Ch. Avocations: skiing; photography. Home: Rt 1 Box 257 Moose Lake MN 55767

EGGLESON, ROBERT AAKER, public relations executive; b. Stoughton, Wis., Nov. 18, 1928; s. Anon Odegard and Caroline (Aaker) E.; m. Barbara Ann Krupnick, June 25, 1960; 1 dau., Karen Jean. B.A. in English, Luther Coll., 1950. Newspaper reporter, Iowa and Minn., 1950-57; pub. relations rep. Northwestern U., Evanston, Ill., 1957-59; div. publicist 3M Co., 1959-61; pub. relations asst. Internat. Minerals & Chem. Co., 1961-62; asst. to dir. pub. affairs Champion Papers Inc., 1962-66; pub. relations mgr. Welch Foods Inc., 1966-72; mfg. communications mgr. Internat. Harvester Co., 1972-83; pres. Robert Eggleson/Communications, 1983; dir. pub. affairs Black Hawk Coll., Moline, Ill., 1984—. Mem. long range task force United Way of Rock Island-Scott Counties. Served with U.S. Army, 1950-52. Mem. Iowa-Ill. Pub. Relations Council, Rock Island C. of C. (past dir.). Republican. Lodge: Rotary. Home: 9 Hawthorne Rd Rock Island IL 61201 Office: 6600 34th Ave Moline IL 61265

EHINGER, STANTON EXEL, cement plant executive; b. Adrian, Mich., Mar. 9, 1935; s. Exel Stanton and Lila Lucille (Konarski) E.; m. Barbara Joyce Steele, May 28, 1961; children—Sabrina, Todd, Kristina. B.S. in Mining Engring., Mich. Tech. U., 1957; postgrad., U. Utah, 1961-63. Engr. Kennecott Copper Corp., Salt Lake City, 1957-63; plant engr. Aetna Portland Cement Co., Essexville, Mich., 1964-66; plant engr. Dundee Cement Co., Clarksville, Mo., 1966-74, mgr. maintenance, engring., 1974-81, plant mgr., 1981—; instr. Holderbank Maintenance Courses, 1976-78. Contbr. articles to profl. jours. Mem. La. Sch. Bd., 1979—, pres., 1982; mem. La. C. of C., 1977—, pres., 1979, 82; adv. Pike & Lincoln County Voc. Sch., Eolia, Mo., 1978—; com. chmn. Troop 155, Great Rivers council Boy Scouts Am., 1980—. Served to 1st lt. U.S. Army, 1958-61. Mem. Mining Industry Council Mo. (bd. dirs., v.p. 1983—), Am. Mining Congress (mem. Western dist., bd. govs. 1983—), Am. Mgmt. Assn. (mgmt. course 1981), Bay City Jr. C. of C. (Mich.) (dir. 1965-66), Tau Beta Pi. Lodge: Lions (v.p. 1973). Avocations: investing; golf; skiing. Home: RR #1 Ladera Estates Louisiana MO 63353 Office: Dundee Cement Co PO Box 67 Clarksville MO 63336

EHLEN, JAMES KENNETH, II, student personnel professsional, consultant; b. Chgo., Feb. 21, 1957; s. James Kenneth and Ingeborg Hilda (Cannizzo) E. B.S. in Edn., Ill. State U., 1979, M.S., 1982. Cert. tchr., Ill. Educator of the deaf Richwoods High Sch., Peoria, Ill., 1979-81; residence hall coordinator Ill. State U., Normal, 1982-85, area coordinator, 1985—; cons. Ill. Tchrs. of Hearing Impaired, Schaumburg, 1985. Scout master Cornbelt council Boy Scouts Am., 1977-79. Mem. Am. Coll. Personnel Assn., Am. Assn. Counseling and Devel., Ill. Tchrs. of Hearing Impaired (regional rep. 1979-81). Roman Catholic. Avocations: running, biking, triathelons, cooking. Home and Office: 18 W Manchester Hall Normal IL 61761

EHLERS, THOMAS MARTIN, investments and retail consultant; b. Worthington, Minn., Feb. 6, 1937; s. Martin Andrew and Genevieve Ellen (Rust) E.; m. Sandra Joan McCartney, Apr. 12, 1964; children—Joseph, Genevieve, T. Michael. B.A., Hamline U., 1959; M.S.R., NYU, 1960. Exec. trainee Daytons, Mpls., 1960; v.p. Ehlers of Redwood Falls (Minn.), 1961-70, pres., 1971—; pres. Boxrud Bldg. Corp., 1985—; v.p. MGT Investment Corp. Bd. dirs. Minn. Episcopal Found. Home: 595 N Lake Spicer MN 56288 Office: 219 S Washington St Redwood Falls MN 56283

EHRESMANN, CURTIS RAY, educator; b. Ipswich, S.D. May 19, 1947; s. Harold Christian and Winniefred (Haar) E.; m. Coleen Rae Schaffer, June 6, 1970; children—Kari, Karl. B.A. in Elem. Edn., Huron Coll., 1969; M.A. in Elem. Edn., No. State Coll., 1979. Elem. tchr. Java Sch., S.D., 1969-70, Hosmer Sch., S.D., 1971-74, Watertown Sch., S.D., 1976—; claims adjuster Farmers Union Ins., Huron, S.D., 1974-76; athletic coach Java Schs., 1969-70, Hosmer Schs., 1971-74, Watertown Schs., 1976—. Staff sgt. USNG, 1970—. Mem. NEA, S.D. Edn. Assn., Watertown Edn. Assn. (pres. 1980-81). Democrat. Lutheran. Avocation: basketball and football officiating. Home: 1144 1st St NW Watertown SD 57201 Office: Grant Elementary Sch 612 3rd St NE Watertown SD 57201

EHRLICH, BURTON STANLEY, lawyer; b. Chgo., July 21, 1953; s. Sam A. and Tobie (Schwartz) E. B.A. with high honors, Northeastern Ill. U., 1974; M.B.A. with distinction, DePaul U., 1975; J.D. with high honors, IIT-Chicago-Kent, 1978; postgrad. LL.M. John Marshall Law Sch., 1978—. Bar: Ill. 1978, U.S. Dist. Ct. (no. dist.) Ill. 1978, U.S. Ct. Appeals (7th cir.) 1979, U.S. Ct. Customs and Patent Appeals 1980, U.S. Supreme Ct. 1980. Law clk. Burton R. Rosenberg, Chgo., 1975-78; assoc. Brezina & Lund, Chgo., 1979, Brezina & Buckingham, Chgo., 1979—; dir. various corps. Contbr. articles to profl. publs. Active Congl. elections. Mem. ABA, Ill. Bar Assn., Chgo. Bar Assn., Am. Judicature Soc., Delta Mu Delta (award Eta chpt.), B'nai Brith (various chpt. offices, awards), Econs. Club (award). Home: 1116 W 187th St Homewood IL 60430 Office: Brezina & Buckingham PC 135 S LaSalle St Chicago IL 60603

EHRLICH, CLARENCE EUGENE, physician, educator; b. Rosenberg, Tex., Oct. 19, 1938; s. Oscar Lee and Gertrude Gene (Walzel) E.; children—Tracey Janet, Bradlen Scott, Suzanne Margaret. B.A., U. Tex., 1961; M.D., Baylor Coll. Medicine, 1965. Diplomate Am. Bd. Ob-Gyn (mem. div. gynec. oncology 1982—, dir. 1985—). Intern, Hosp., 1965-66; resident Charity Hosp.-Tulane U., New Orleans, 1966-69; asst. prof. Ind. U., Indpls., 1973-77, assoc. prof., 1977-81, prof., chmn. ob/gyn dept., 1981—. Contbr. articles to profl. publs., chpts. in books. Served to major USAF, 1969-71. Grantee USPHS, 1975-78, Upjohn Co., 1976-81, Gynecol. Group, 1978-80, 80-84, Eli Lilly & Co., 1982-85. Mem. AAAS, Am. Assn. Cancer Research, Am. Coll. Obstetricians and Gynecologists, ACS, AMA, Am. Radium Soc., Am. Soc. Clin. Pharmacology and Therapeutics, Am. Soc. Parental and Enteral Nutrition, Am. Soc. Clin. Oncology, Am. Soc. Colposcopists and Colpomicroscopists, Assn. Profs. Gynecology and Obstetrics, Sigma Xi, others. Office: Ind U 926 W Michigan St Indianapolis IN 46223

EHRLICHER, EDWARD JOHN, personnel ofcl.; b. Chgo., Nov. 24, 1943; s. Frederick Erasmus and Rose Rita (Meyer) E.; A.A., Kennedy-King Jr. Coll., 1968; B.A., Roosevelt U., Chgo., 1972. Clk., supr., mgr. check processing div., personnel specialist LaSalle Nat. Bank, Chgo., 1967-74; personnel asst. Nystrom div. Carnation Co., Chgo., 1974-77, asst. personnel mgr., 1977—. Mem. Jane Addams Center Bd., Hull House Assn. Served with AUS, 1962-65. Mem. Am. Soc. Personnel Adminstrn. (accredited), Soc. Personnel Adminstr. Greater Chgo., N.W. Personnel Assn. Chgo. Home: 1405 W Edgewater Ave Apt 2 Chicago IL 60660 Office: 3333 N Elston Ave Chicago IL 60618

EHRMAN, CHAIM MEYER, marketing educator; b. Scranton, Pa., Sept. 3, 1947; s. Gaston and Esther (Horowitz) E.; m. Eva Darcy Glick, May 19, 1973; children—Rivka Laya Gitl, Deetsa Mindl, Sara Hadassa, Yaakov Zev. Student, Yeshiva S.R. Hirsch, N.Y.C., 1966-70; B.B.A., Baruch Coll., CUNY, 1970, M.B.A., 1973; M.S., Temple U., 1980; Ph.D. in Mktg. U. Pa., 1984. Ordained rabbi, 1970. Cert. tchr. math., N.Y. Editor, pub. Market Research Analyst, 1972-74; instr. Queensborough Community Coll., CUNY, Bayside, N.Y., 1974-75, Rutgers U., Camden, N.J., 1975-78, Pa. State U., Lima, 1978-81; grad. faculty Wharton Sch., U. Pa., Phila., 1981-83; prof. dept. mktg. U. Ill.-Chgo., 1983—. Grantee Ctr. Internat. Bus. Studies, U. Pa., 1981-83, Pepsico-Mktg. Dept., 1982-83; recipient Community Service award Young Israel Wynnefield, Phila., 1983. Mem. Am. Mktg. Assn., Am. Statis. Assn., Inst. Mgmt. Sci., Ops. research Soc. Am. Republican. Jewish. Avocations: playing violin; sailing; swimming. Home: 6735 N Richmond Chicago IL 60645 Office: U Ill Mktg Dept 601 S Morgan Chicago IL 60680

EHRMANN, PAUL ROBERT, osteopathic physician; b. Detroit, July 8, 1953; m. Robin S. Ehrmann. B.S. in Pharmacy, Wayne State U., 1976; D.O., Mich. State U., 1980. Pharmacist, Mich., 1976—; practice medicine specializing in osteo. medicine, Royal Oak, Mich., 1980—; dir. family practice program, mem. staff Bi County Community Hosp., Warren, Mich., Beaumont Hosp., Troy, Mich. Contbr. articles to medical jours. Physician leader Senior Citizens Activity Ctr., Royal Oak, 1982—. Mem. Am. Osteo. Assn., Mich. Osteo. Assn., Oakland County Osteo. Assn., Am. Osteo. Assn. Sports Medicine. Avocations: computers; all sports; physical fitness. Office: 2033 Crooks Royal Oak MI 48073

EIBERT, JOHN, chemist, chemical company executive, consultant; b. St. Louis, Sept. 18, 1918; s. John and Margaret (Mueller) E.; m. Johanne E. Freudenthal, Aug. 1, 1975; children—Rocky, Casandra, Gary, Mosette. B.S., Washington U., 1940, M.S., 1942, Ph.D., 1944. Analytical chemist Scullin Steel Co., St. Louis, 1942-43; lectr. physics Washington U., St. Louis, 1943-44; research chemist Pan Am. Corp., Tex. City, 1944-45, Anheuser-Busch Inc., St. Louis, 1945-46; sec. Sci. Assocs., St. Louis, 1946-60, pres., 1960—. Mem. Am. Chem. Soc., AAAS, Am. Inst. Chemists, N.Y. Acad. Sci., Inst. Food Tech., Nat. Soc. Profl. Engrs., Soc. Cosmetic Chemists, Sigma Xi, Alpha Chi Sigma, Tau Beta Pi, Phi Mu Epsilon. Club: Greenbriar Hills Country (St. Louis). Home: 1423 Jamaica Ct Saint Louis MO 63122 Office: Sci Assocs Inc 6200 S Lindbergh Blvd Saint Louis MO 63123

EICHELMAN, BURR SIMMONS, JR., psychiatrist, researcher, educator; b. Hinsdale, Ill., Mar. 20, 1943; s. Burr Simmons and Evelyn Cora (Budde) E.; children by previous marriage—Kathryn Elise, Burr Andrew; m. Anne del Carmen Gonzalez-Hartwig. S.B. with honors, U. Chgo., 1964, M.D., 1968, Ph.D. in Biopsychology, 1970. Diplomate Am. Bd. Psychiatry and Neurology. Pediatric intern U. Calif.-San Francisco, 1969-70; resident, then fellow in psychiatry Stanford U., Calif., 1972-75, Kennedy fellow in medicine, law and ethics, 1975-76; asst. prof. psychiatry U. Wis.-Madison, 1976-79, assoc. prof., 1979-84, prof., 1984—; chief psychiatry service, dir. lab. behavioral neurochemistry William S. Middleton Meml. VA Hosp., Madison, 1976—; cons. Mendota Mental Health Inst., Madison, 1984—. Co-editor: Terrorism and Interdisciplinary Perspectives, 1983. Contbr. chpts. to books, articles to profl. jours. Elder, Presbyn. Ch. Served to lt. comdr. USPHS, 1970-72. Recipient A.E. Bennett award Soc. Biol. Psychiatry, 1972; Westerman prize Am. Fedn. Clin. Research, 1976. Fellow Am. Psychiat. Assn. (Falk fellow 1973-75), Am. Psychol. Assn.; mem. Am. Coll. Neuropsychopharmacology (chmn. ethics com. 1985), Internat. Soc. Research on Aggression (co-chmn. ethics com. 1980—), Soc. Neurosci., Sigma Xi, Alpha Omega Alpha. Avocations: music (piano and voice); tennis; skiing. Office: William S Middleton Meml VA Hosp Psychiatry Service 2500 Overlook Terr Madison WI 53705

EICHENBERGER, JERRY ALAN, lawyer; b. Columbus, Ohio, Apr. 16, 1947; m. Candace R. Roberson, Jan. 17, 1971; 1 child, Sara Marie. B.S., Ohio State U., 1970; J.D., Capital U., 1975. Bar: Ohio 1975, U.S. Supreme Ct. 1978. Ptnr., Martin, Eichenberger & Baxter, Columbus, 1975—. Author: (mags.) Plane and Pilot News, 1983—. Maj. Civil Air Patrol. (chief check pilot 1980-84). Named Ky. Col., Commonwealth of Ky., 1972; mem. Lawyer-Pilots Bar Assn., ABA, Ohio State Bar Assn., Aviation Ins. Assn. Republican. Mem. Christian Ch. Lodges: Masons, Shriners. Avocations: Aviation; writing. Office: Martin Eichenberger & Baxter 6641 N High St Worthington OH 43085

EICHHORN, JACOB, chemical company executive; b. Sheboygan, Wis., Sept. 14, 1924; s. Jacob and Elizabeth (Strauch) E.; m. Mary Kay Winn, Dec. 27, 1959; children—Kurt, Eric, Karen. B.S. in Chem. Engring., U. Mich., 1946, M.S., 1947, Ph.D., 1950; P.M.D., Harvard U., 1968. Research engr. Dow Chem. Co., Midland, Mich., 1950-61, mgr. flex packaging tech. service and devel., 1961-66, mgr. spl. projects, packaging, 1966-71, ventures mgr. plastics, 1971-80, lab. dir., 1980-82, sr. project mgr., corp. research and devel., 1982—; grad. lectr. U. Mich., Ann Arbor, 1952-54; v.p., dir. Dolco Packaging Corp., Los Angeles, 1968-74. Contbr. articles to profl. jours. Contbr. chpt. to Industrial and Specialty Papers, 1968. Patentee in field. Mem. Am. Chem. Soc., Am. Inst. Chem. Engrs. (pres. local sect. 1957), TAPPI. Republican. Mem. United Ch. of Christ. Clubs: U. Mich. (v.p. 1963), Midland Country (Midland). Avocations: photography; golf; skiing. Home: 4501 Arbor Dr Midland MI 48640 Office: Dow Chemical Co Bldg 1702 Midland MI 48674

EICKMAN, JENNIFER LYNN, conference center manager, writer, artist; b. Urbana, Ill., Nov. 7, 1946; d. Marvin A. and Emma L. (Hartrick) Smith; B.F.A., U. Ill., 1967, postgrad. in Art History, 1967-70; m. Gary Edwin Eickman, June 9, 1968. Tchr., Univ. High Sch., Urbana, 1968, Champaign (Ill.) Public Schs., 1969-70; mem. faculty U. Ill., 1968-77, Richland Coll., Decatur, Ill., 1975-77; asst. to dir. of extension in visual arts U. Ill., 1969-70, asst. dir. Allerton House Conf. Center, 1974—; guest lectr., tchr. art workshops. Mem. Pacific Tropical Bot. Gardens, Defenders of Wildlife, Nat. Trust Hist. Preservation, Internat. Platform Assn., Kappa Alpha Theta. Staff writer Champaign-Urbana mag.; author articles on art history, music, edn. and natural history. Home: Gate House Allerton Park Monticello IL 61856 Office: Allerton House Allerton Park Monticello IL 61856

EIDELMAN, MARK, dentist; b. St. Louis, Apr. 6, 1947; s. Harry and Mildred (Fox) E. D.D.S., U. Mo.-Kansas City, 1972. Pvt. practice dentistry, St. Louis, 1972—; pres. Prepaid Preventive Dental Care Inc., St. Louis, 1982—, Dental Health Plan of Am., St. Louis, 1984—. Mem. Pierre Fauchard Acad., South County Dental Soc., ADA, Greater St. Louis Dental Soc., Mo. Dental Assn., Council for Competitive Economy (assoc.), Delta Sigma Delta. Avocations: Photography, electronics, bike riding. Address: 12579 Mason Forest St Saint Louis MO 63141

EIGEN, DARYL J., electrical engineer, psychologist; b. Milw., July 29, 1947; s. David J. and Pearl (Rice) E.; m. Carol A. Kois, Mar. 30, 1972; children—Tony, Molly. B.A., U. Wis.-Madison, 1972; M.S., Northwestern U., 1973, Ph.D., 1981. Teaching asst. U. Wis.-Milw., 1971-72, research asst., 1972-73; mem. tech. staff Bell Labs., Piscataway, N.J., 1973-75, Naperville, Ill., 1975-81, supr. tech. staff, 1981—, supr. system analysis and human factors group, 1981—. Served with USMC, 1966-68. Decorated Purple Heart. Recipient Chancellor's Office Scholarship, U. Wis.-Milw., 1970, Undergrad. Research award, 1971; NASA ann. research asst. grantee, 1972; Bell Labs. Doctoral Support Program, 1981. Mem. IEEE Communications Soc., IEEE Computer Soc., IEEE System Man and Cybernetics, Am. Psychol. Assn., Human Factors Soc., AAAS, Tau Beta Pi. Reviewer, System Man and Cybernetics, 1973-77, Bell System Tech. Jour., 1980—; contbr. articles in field to profl. jours. Home: 1541 Fender Rd Naperville IL 60540 Office: Naperville-Wheaton Rd Suite 4B-148 Naperville IL 60566

EIGHMEY, DOUGLAS JOSEPH, JR., hospital official; b. Cambridge, N.Y., Dec. 19, 1946; s. Douglas Joseph and Theresa E. (McGuire) E.; B.S. in Biology, SUNY, Cortland, 1968; M.P.H., U. Tenn., 1971; m. Karen S. Rife, Apr. 27, 1973; 1 child, Sarah Elizabeth. Public health cons. Ohio Dept. Health, Columbus, 1971-76, supr. cert. of need program Ohio Dept. Health, 1976-78; v.p. Central Ohio River Valley Assn., Cin., 1978-79, St. Francis-St. George Hosp., Inc., Cin., 1979-82; pres., adminstr. Huber Heights Health Services Inc. (Ohio), 1982-84; pres., v.p. Children's Med. Ctr., Dayton, Ohio. Recipient award USPHS, 1970. Mem. Am. Hosp. Assn., Ohio Hosp. Assn., Am. Coll. Hosp. Adminstrs., Ohio Hosp. Planning Assn. (dir.-at-large 1980-82, pres. elect 1985), Am. Soc. Hosp. Planning, Ohio Public Health Assn., Nat. Assn. Clock and Watch Collectors, St. Vincent DePaul Soc. Roman Catholic. Lodges: Rotary, Elks. Office: One Children's Plaza Dayton OH 45404

EILER, MARY ANN, association executive; b. Chgo., Oct. 10, 1940; d. Peter Nicholas and Marie (Giannini) E. B.A., Mundelein Coll., 1962; M.A., Loyola U., Chgo., 1962-64; M.A. in Linguistics, Northeastern Ill. U., 1971; Ph.D., Ill. Inst. Tech., 1979. Lang. cons., tchr. Lyons Twp. High Sch., LaGrange, Ill., 1964-81; project coordinator dept. data releases AMA, Chgo., 1982, asst. dir., 1983—; adj. lectr. linguistics Northeastern Ill. U., 1980; adj. lectr. tech. writing Coll. DuPage, Glen Ellyn, Ill., 1983—. Mem. Editorial bd. Tng. Today, 1983—, editor, 1985; contbr. articles to profl. jours. NDEA grantee, 1966 summer. Mem. Nat. Council Tchrs. English (curriculum evaluation com. 1981—), Soc. Tech. Communications, Am. Bus. Communications Assn., Assn. Computational Lingusitcs, Am. Med. Writers Assn. (cert. med. editor). Avocations: Italian; swimming; doll history; comparative religion. Home: 2914 N Mason St Chicago IL 60634 Office: AMA 535 N Dearborn St Chicago IL 60610

EILERS, JOHN WAGNER, JR., lawyer; b. Cin., Nov. 21, 1939; s. John Wagner and Mary (McEvilley) E.; m. Elizabeth Lamson, Aug. 16, 1969; children—Michael McE., Christopher R. B.A. in Econs., Marietta Coll., 1961; postgrad. Xavier Coll., 1961-62; J.D., Chase Coll. of Law, 1967. Bar: Ohio 1967, U.S. Dist. Ct. (so. dist.) Ohio 1968, U.S. Ct. Appeals (6th cir.) 1970, U.S. Supreme Ct. 1970, U.S. Tax Ct. 1980. Trust assoc. First Nat. Bank, Cin., 1962-65; tax law clk. Walker and Chatfield, Cin., 1965-68; asst. pros. atty. Hamilton County, Cin., 1968-69; assoc. Paxton and Seasongood, Cin., 1969-74; trust officer Fifth Third Bank, Cin., 1974-79; sole practice, Cin., 1979—; lectr. probate and tax law. Treas. Com. to Re-elect Judge Painter, Hamilton County, Ohio, 1984; vice chmn., treas. Ohio State League of Young Republicans, 1969-70; chmn. Hamilton County Young Republicans, 1968; mem. exec. com. Better Housing League, pres. 1982-84. Mem. Internat. Assn. Fin. Planning (pres. 1983-84), Ohio State Bar Assn. (dist. rep. probate bd. govs. 1983—), Cin. Bar Assn. (vice chmn. probate com.), ABA, Cincinnatus Assn., Wing and

Torch, Friendly Sons St. Patrick, Cowan Lake Sailing Assn. Republican. Roman Catholic. Avocation: sailing. Home: 1131 Beverly Hill Dr Cincinnati OH 45226 Office: John W Eilers Jr 511 Walnut St 2004 Dubois Tower Cincinnati OH 45202

EIMER, LAWRENCE LEE, educator; b. Lincoln, Ill., Sept. 8, 1951; s. Ralph F. and Joyce (Johnson) E.; m. Connie L. Kaiser, Aug. 11, 1973; children—Neil, Nicole. B.S. in Edn., Ill. State U., 1973. Tchr., United Twp. High Sch., East Moline, Ill., 1973-76; vocat. agr. and indsl. arts tchr. Easton (Ill.) High Sch., 1976—; advisor Future Farmers Am. Recipient Excellence in Teaching award Ill. Vocat. Agr. Tchrs. Assn., 1982. Mem. Ill. Vo-Ag. Tchrs. Assn. (sect. chmn.), Easton Edn. Assn. (past pres.), Ill. Edn. Assn., NEA, Am. Vocat. Assn. Roman Catholic. Lodge: Optimists. Home: Rt 1 Greenview IL 62642 Office: PO Box 8 Easton IL 62633

EINHORN, EDWARD (EDDIE) MARTIN, See *Who's Who in America*, 43rd edition.

EINODER, CAMILLE ELIZABETH, educator; b. Chgo., June 15, 1937; d. Isadore and Elizabeth T. (Czerwinski) Popowski; student Fox Bus. Coll., 1954; B.Ed. in Biology, Chgo. Tchrs. Coll., 1964; M.A. in Analytical Chemistry, Gov.'s State U., 1977; postgrad. in edn. and adminstrn. Roosevelt U.; m. Joseph X. Einoder, Aug. 5, 1978; children—Carl Frank, Mark Frank, Vivian Einoder, Joe Einoder, Tim Einoder, Sheila Einoder, Jude Einoder. Secretarial positions, Chgo., 1955-64; tchr. biology Chgo. Bd. Edn., 1964—, tchr. biology and agr., 1975-81, tchr. biology, agr. and chemistry, 1981—; human relations coordinator Morgan Park High Sch., Chgo., 1980—, tchr. biology Internat. Studies Sch., 1983—; career devel. cons. for agr. related curriculum. Bds. dirs., founding mem., author constn. Community Council, 1970—; bd. dirs., edn. cons. Neighborhood Council, 1974; rep. Chgo. Tchrs. Union, 1969. Mem. Phi Delta Kappa. Home: 10637 S Claremont St Chicago IL 60643 Office: 1744 W Pryor St Chicago IL 60643

EINSPAHR, DEAN WILLIAM, forest genetics researcher; b. Sioux City, Iowa, May 24, 1923; s. Benjamin William and Stella B. (McCrea) E.; m. Ann Elizabeth Stickrod, June 15, 1946; children—Larry William, DeAnn Elizabeth. B.S., Iowa State U., 1949, M.S., 1960, Ph.D., 1955. Research assoc. Gamble Bros., Inc., Montgomery, Ala., 1950-51; research fellow Iowa State U., Ames, 1952-55; research assoc. Inst. Paper Chemistry, Appleton, Wis., 1955-70, sr. research assoc., 1970—, div. dir., 1980—; adj. prof. forestry Mich. Tech. U., Houghton, 1982—; mem. research adv. com. Wis. Dept. Natural Resources, Madison, 1968-80. Contbr. articles to profl. jours. Served to 1st lt. USAF, 1942-46, PTO. Mem. Soc. Am. Foresters (chpt. chmn. 1980-82), TAPPI (chmn. research and devel. div. 1981-83; Service award 1983), Soil Sci. Soc. Am. Avocations: hunting, fishing, skiing. Home: 2808 Crestview Dr Appleton WI 54912 Office: Inst of Paper Chemistry E South River St Appleton WI 54912

EIS, LORYANN MALVINA, educator; b. Muscatine, Iowa, Apr. 3, 1938; d. Chester N. and Anna M. (Lenz) E. A.B., Augustana Coll., 1960; M.Ed., U. Ill., 1963; postgrad. Montclair State Coll., 1965-67, Indiana U. of Pa., 1968, U. Iowa, 1970, Western Ill. U., 1978-80. Circuit analysis engr. Automatic Electric Co., Northlake, Ill., 1960-61; math. tchr. Orion (Ill.) Community Sch. Dist., 1961-63; math. tchr., dept. chmn. United Twp. High Sch., East Moline, Ill., 1963—; lectr. Augustana Coll., Rock Island, Ill., 1982—. Bd. sec. Citizens to Preserve Black Hawk Park Found., 1977—; v.p. council Salem Lutheran Ch.; bd. dirs. Augustana Coll. Hist. Soc.; mem. Moline YWCA. Mem. NEA, Ill. Edn. Assn., Nat. Council Tchrs. of Math., Ill. Council Tchrs. of Math., Classroom Tchrs. Assn., Assn. Supervision and Curriculum Devel., Rock Island Scott Counties Sci. and Math. Tchrs. Assn., Women in Ednl. Adminstrn., AAUW (past state pres.; grantee 1975-76), Delta Kappa Gamma (state treas.), Am. Philatelic Soc., TransMiss. Philatelic Soc., Quad City Stamp Club. Republican. Cons. General Mathematics Textbook, 1978-79. Home: 2037 15th St Moline IL 61265 Office: 42nd Ave and Archer Dr East Moline IL 61244

EISENBACH, GEORGE WILLIAM, decorating products executive; b. Columbus, Ohio, Dec. 22, 1947; s. George Leroy and C. Jane (Wilson) E.; m. Marie Amelie Johnston, July 20, 1969; 1 child, G. David. Student Internat. Am. U., San Juan, P.R., 1970-71; B.S. in Bus. Adminstrn., Ohio State U., 1975. Region mgr. Am. Home Shield, Dublin, Calif., 1977-83; pres. Town & Country Paint 'n Paper, Inc., 1983—. Designer, project chmn. study seminar, Operation Threshold, 1977 (Ohio Jaycees Best Overall Drug and Alcohol Abuse Project of Yr., 1978); councilman City of Newark, Ohio, 1980-81; chmn. Licking County Young Republicans, 1982-83; county chmn. Clarence Brown for Gov., Licking County, 1983. Served with USN, 1967-71. Named Young Rep. of Yr., Licking County Young Reps., 1980. Mem. Nat. Decorating Products Assn., Newark Area C. of C. (bd. dirs. 1982-83), Newark Jaycees (pres. 1981-82, senator 1984). Lutheran. Home: 11 Wyoming St Newark OH 43055 Office: Town & Country Paint 'n Paper Inc 224 Granville St Newark OH 43055

EISENMAN, HARRY JAMES, III, historian, university adminstrator; b. Cleve., May 9, 1940; s. Harry James and Eleanor Violet (Warth) E.; m. Jean Ann Schnorbus, Aug. 26, 1967. B.S. in Engring. Sci., Case Inst. Tech., 1962; M.A., Case Western Res. U., 1964, Ph.D., 1967. Asst. prof. history U. Mo.-Rolla, 1967-70, assoc. prof., 1970—, chmn. dept. social scis., 1980-83, chmn. dept. history and polit. sci., 1983—. Contbr. articles to profl. jours. Grantee NEH, 1973, Mo. Dept. of Natural Resources, 1980, 83. Mem. Soc. for History of Tech., History of Sci. Soc., Orgn. Am. Historians. Methodist. Avocations: travel; gardening. Home: 911 W 12th St Rolla MO 65401 Office: U Missouri Rolla MO 65401

EISENMANN, DALE RICHARD, dental educator, administrator, researcher; b. Watseka, Ill., Jan. 13, 1941; s. Chris Robert and Lydia Rose (Koehl) E.; m. Judith Ann Feller, June 25, 1961; children—Bradley, Todd, Luann. D.D.S., U. Ill.-Chgo., 1965, Ph.D., 1968. USPHS trainee U. Ill. Coll. Dentistry, Chgo., 1965-68, asst. prof. to prof., 1968—, head dept. histology, 1973—, chmn. Coll. Dentistry Research Bd., 1978—. Contbr. chpts. Oral Histology-Development Structure and Function, 1980. Contbr. articles to profl. jours. Elder Apostolic Christian Ch. Am., Hillside, Ill., 1975—. Grantee NIH, 1984—. Mem. Internat. Assn. Dental Research, Am. Assn. Anatomists, Sigma Xi, Phi Kappa Phi. Republican. Avocation: Gardening. Home: 6913 Wilmette Darien IL 60559 Office: Univ Ill College Dentistry 801 S Paulina Chicago IL 60612

EISINGER, PETER K(ENDALL), political science educator; b. Ann Arbor, Mich., July 9, 1942; s. Chester E. and Marjorie (Kendall) E.; m. Erica Mendelson, Sept. 6, 1967; children—Jesse, Sarah. B.A., U. Mich., 1964, M.A., 1965; Ph.D., Yale U., 1969. Asst. aprof. polit. sci. U. Wis., Madison, 1969-74, assoc. prof., 1974-79, prof., 1979—; vis. lectr. U. Essex (Eng.), 1972-73; vis. prof. Columbia U., 1982-83; adj. scholar Joint Ctr. Polit. Studies, 1982—. Mem. Am. Polit. Sci. Assn. Author: The Patterns of Interracial Politics, 1976; American Politics: The People and the Polity, 1978; The Politics of Displacement, 1980; contbr. articles to profl. jours. Office: Dept Polit Sci U Wis Madison WI 53706*

EISSFELD, LOTHAR, pastry chef; b. Lobstadt, Saxony, Leipzig, Germany, Apr. 21, 1923; came to U.S., 1951; s. Herman Rudolph and Rosa Olga (Drexler) E.; m. Lillian Marie Heflin, June 27, 1953; children—Charlotta Louise, Michael August. Bakery/Pastry Chef (hon.), Grimma, Saxony, 1940. Ice cream and frozen dessert chef Hotel Sheraton-Gibson, Cin., 1951-59; owner, pastry chef Coll. Hill Bakery and Pastry Shop, Cin., 1959-70, European Pastries, Cin., 1970—. Served with German Army, World War II, prisoner of war. Recipient 1st Place awards Nat. Bakery Conv. Mem. Am. Retail Bakers Assn., Cin. Retail Bakers Assn., Kolping Soc., German Soc., Bavarian Soc. Cin. Home: 9169 Gila Dr Cincinnati OH 45239 Office: European Pastries 9035 Colerain Ave Cincinnati OH 45239

EITEL, ALTA WALKER, osteopathic physician and surgeon, educator, antique dealer; b. Mercer County, Mo., Oct. 3, 1911; d. William Madison and Adda May (Covey) Walker; m. Manuel M. Eitel, Apr. 8, 1950; children—Peggy Karen Eitel Mitchell, Manuel M., Elaine Riddle. B.S. in Edn., North East U., Kirksville, Mo., 1941; D.O., Kirksville Coll. Osteopathy and Surgery, 1950. Diplomate Am. Coll. Osteopathy and Surgery. Gen. practice osteo. medicine, Galt, Mo., 1950-73, Trenton, Mo., 1973—; chief of staff Wright Meml. Hosp., Trenton. Mem. Mo. Assn. Osteo. Physicians and Surgeons, North Central Osteo. Assn., Am. Osteo. Assn., AAUW, DAR. Republican. Baptist (tchr.). Contbr. articles to local newspapers. Office: 400 E 9th St Trenton MO 64683

EK, ALAN RYAN, forestry educator; b. Mpls., Sept. 5, 1942; s. Evert Curt and Margaret Helen (Ryan) E.; m. Carolyn Louise Anderson, June 26, 1964; children—Christine Louise, Karl Alan. B.S. in Forestry, U. Minn.-St. Paul, 1964, M.S., 1965; Ph.D., Oreg. State U., 1969. Research officer Can. Dept. Forestry and Rural Devel., Gt. Lakes Forest Research Ctr., Sault Ste. Marie, Ont., Can., 1966-69; asst., then assoc. prof. forestry U. Wis.-Madison, 1969-77; assoc. prof. Coll. Forestry, U. Minn., St. Paul, 1977-84, prof., head dept. forest resources, 1984—; dir. Forestronics, Inc., St. Paul, 1980—. Contbr. articles to profl. jours. Mem. Soc. Am. Foresters (editorial adv. bd. 1980-83, forest sci. and tech. bd. 1984), Biometric Soc., Am. Soc. Photogrammetry, Internat. Union Forestry Research Orgns. Lutheran. Avocations: fishing; hunting; weight lifting. Home: 4744 Kevin Ln Shoreview MN 55126 Office: Dept Forest Resources Univ Minn Saint Paul MN 55108

EKBLAD, GLENN STEPHEN, osteopathic physician, educator; b. Salt Lake City, May 24, 1949; s. Frank Sr. and Pearl (Harrison) E. B.S. magna cum laude, U. Utah, 1974, B.S. magna cum laude in Nursing, 1975; M.S. in Nursing, Yale U., 1977; D.O., Mich. State U., 1980; student USAF Flight Surgeons Sch., 1984. R.N., Utah. Medic, U.S. Army, Viet Nam, 1968-70; nurse technician U. Utah Med. Ctr., 1970-75; intern Detroit Osteo. Hosp., 1980-81; practice osteo. medicine specializing in emergency medicine Ferris State Coll., Big Rapids, Mich., 1981-82; emergency physician Mecosta County Community Hosp., Big Rapids, 1981-84, Detroit Receiving Hosp., 1984—; physician U.S. Air Force Res., Air N.G., Selfridge, Mich., 1981—; physician, pres. Disaster Response Systems, Big Rapids, 1983—; tchr. emergency medicine Am. Heart Assn. Cardiac Life Support. Served with USAF, 1981-83; to capt. Air N.G., 1981—. Decorated Bronze Star. Mem. Am. Coll. Emergency Physicians, Am. Coll. Gen. Practice, Am. Soc. Contemporary Medicine and Surgery, Am. Osteo. Assn., Res. Officers Assn., Phi Kappa Phi, Sigma Sigma Phi. Republican. Roman Catholic. Home: #809 Parkview Towers 27200 Parkview Blvd Warren MI 48092 Office: Detroit Receiving Hosp 4201 Saint Antoine Detroit MI 48201

EKHOLM, BRUCE PETER, biostatistician; b. Mpls., Nov. 1, 1956; s. Richard Ernest and Beverly Maxine (Carlson) E.; m. Julie Kay Hunnicutt, Sept. 14, 1985. B.A., St. Olaf Coll., 1978; M.S., U. Minn., 1980. Advanced biostatistician 3M/Riker Labs., Inc., St. Paul, 1981-84, sr. biostatistician, 1984—. Mem. Am. Statis. Assn. (chpt. sec.-treas. 1984-86), Biometrics Soc., Sigma Pi Sigma. Lutheran. Avocations: cross-country skiing; softball. Home: 4511 Audrey Ave E Inver Grove Heights MN 55075

EKIZIAN, JOHN, printing company executive; b. Evanston, Ill., June 21, 1933; s. Michael and Marie (Cherkezian) E.; m. Frances Laura Talerico, June 12, 1960; children—Sharon Marie, Michael John, Laura Lynn. B.A., Monmouth Coll., 1957. Prodn. operator Rand McNally, Skokie, Ill., 1957-60; purchasing agent CNA Ins., Chgo., 1960-63; salesman Speed-O-Lith Offset, Chgo., 1963—; pres., owner Pride in Graphics, Inc., Chgo., 1975—. Served with U.S. Army, 1953-55; Korea. Mem. Exec. Club of Chgo., Printing Industry of Ill. Clubs: Crystal Lake Country (pres. 1975-77), Biltmore Country (Barrington). Home: 325 S Valley Rd Barrington IL 60010

EKLUND, CLAUDIA RIETH, lawyer; b. Cleve., Nov. 9, 1951; s. Carlton E. and Mildred (Olson) R.; m. Paul D. Eklund, Dec. 16, 1978; children—Craig, Kristen. B.A., Cleve. State U., 1974; J.D., Cleve.-Marshall U., 1979. Bar: Ohio 1979, U.S. Dist. Ct. (no. dist.) Ohio 1981, U.S. Ct. Appeals (6th cir.) 1983. Assoc. Sindell, Lowe & Guidubaldi, Cleve., 1979—. Mem. Ohio State Bar Assn., Assn. Trial Lawyers Am., ABA, Greater Cleve. Bar Assn. Home: 585 Parkside Dr Bay Village OH 44140 Office: Sindell Lowe & Guidubaldi 910 Leader Bldg Cleveland OH 44114

EKLUND, DARREL LEE, statistician, data processing administrator; b. Miltonvale, Kans., July 28, 1942; s. Emery Paul and Cora Elizabeth (Rothfuss) E.; m. Phyllis Colleen Sprecker, Aug. 15, 1965; children—Kelly, Michelle, Melissa. A.A. in Math., Miltonvale Wesleyan Coll., 1962; B.S. in Math., Kans. State U., 1964, M.S. in Stats., 1966, Ph.D., in Stats., 1971. Survey statistician Nat. Ctr. Health Stats., Washington, 1966-68; asst. prof. stats., cons. U. Mo., Columbia, 1971-77; chief research and analysis sect. Kans. Dept. Health and Environment, Topeka, 1977-83, dir. office info. systems, 1983-84; water resource mgr. Kans. Water Office, Topeka, 1984—; adj. prof. stats. U. Kans., Lawrence, 1983—. Editor publs. for Kans. Dept. Health and Environment, 1977-83. Contbr. articles to profl. jours. Served to sr. asst. health service officer USPHS, 1966-68. Postdoctoral fellow U. Mo., 1971; NIH trainee 1964-66, 68-71. Avocation: fishing. Home: 1400 Caledon St Topeka KS 66611 Office: Kans Water Office 109 SW 9th St Topeka KS 66612

EKLUND-EASLEY, MOLLY SUE, lawyer; b. Benton Harbor, Mich., Aug. 17, 1953; d. Robert Gordon and Arlene Ann (Weinlander) Eklund; m. Herman Easley, Jr., July 18, 1981; 1 child, Rachel Nicole. B.A., Grand Valley State Coll., 1975; J.D. U. Detroit, 1979. Bar: Mich. 1979, U.S. Dist. Ct. (ea. dist.) Mich. 1979. Assoc., Stalburg, Fisher & Weberman, Detroit, 1979—. Mem. ABA, Women Lawyer's Assn. Mich., Assn. Trial Lawyers Am., Mich. Trial Lawyers Assn., Mich. Bar Assn. Lutheran. Office: Stalburg Fischer & Weberman 139 Cadillac Sq 5th Floor Detroit MI 48226

EKVALL, BERNT, dentist; b. Nora, Sweden, June 25, 1915; s. Johan Alexis and Elin Karolina (Persson) E.; L.D.S., U. Stockholm, 1944; D.D.S., U. Mich., 1951; m. Margit Andersson, June 23, 1940 (div. 1982); 1 dau., Lucie Margita. Came to U.S., 1949, naturalized, 1954. With Swedish Govt. Dental Services, 1943-45; pvt. practice dentistry Sweden, 1945-49, Clinton, Mich., 1951-52, Dearborn, 1951-55, 57-58, Detroit, 1958-81, St. Clair, Mich., 1981—; mem. staff River Dist. Hosp. Vice pres. Scandinavian Am. Republican Club, 1960-68, pres., 1968-72; treas. Rep. State Nationalities Council, 1971-73; Bd. dirs. Scandinavian Symphony Soc., 1961-72; bd. mgrs. Hannan br. YMCA, 1962—, chmn. Eastside br., 1976. Served to capt. AUS, 1955-57. Fellow Royal Soc. Health, Internat. Acad. Dentistry, Acad. Gen. Dentistry, Internat. Coll. Dentists, Am. Coll. Dentists; mem. Am., Mich. dental assns., Detroit Dist. Dental Soc., Detroit Dental Clinic Club (membership sec. 1972-73, sec. 1973-74, pres. 1975-76), Bunting Periodontal Study Club, Mich. Acad. Gen. Dentistry (sec. 1975-76, v.p. 1976-78, pres. 1978-80). Clubs: Prismatic Renaissance (Detroit); Grosse Pointe Hunt. Home: 1063 Woodbridge E Saint Clair Shores MI 48080 Office: 4150 S River Rd Saint Clair MI 48079

ELAM, JOHN CARLTON, lawyer; b. Fort Wayne, Ind., Mar. 6, 1924; s. Bernard C. and Eunice (Gawthrop) E.; m. Virginia Mayberry, July 14, 1945; children—Nancy Lee, Patricia Scott, Mary Jane, John William. B.A., U. Mich., 1948, J.D. with distinction, 1949. Bar: Mich. 1949, Ohio 1950. Assoc. Vorys, Sater, Seymour & Pease, Columbus, Ohio, 1949-54, ptnr., 1954—, presiding ptnr., 1968—. Trustee Columbus Coll. Art and Design, 1981—. Fellow Am. Coll. Trial Lawyers; mem. Ohio Bar Assn., ABA, Columbus Bar Assn., 6th Cir. Jud. Conf., Am. Judicature Soc. (dir. 1984—), U. Mich. Alumni Assn. Home: 5000 Squirrel Bend Columbus OH 43220 Office: Vorys Sater Seymour & Pease 52 E Gay St Columbus OH 43215

ELAM, MICHAEL HYDE, lawyer; b. Cambridge, Mass., Aug. 10, 1954; s. James L. and Sheila (Hyde) E.; m. Tracey Shafroth, Aug. 4, 1984. B.A., Macalester Coll., 1976; student Universite Libre de Bruxelles (Belgium), 1979; J.D., Ind. U., 1980. Bar: Ind. 1980, Ill. 1980, U.S. Dist. Ct. (so. dist.) Ind. Asst. instr. environ. law clinic Ind. U. Sch. Law, Bloomington, 1979-80; sr. atty. Comprehensive Environ. Response Compensation and Liability act, sect. chief, assoc. regional counsel U.S. EPA, Chgo., 1980—. Assoc. editor Ind. U. Sch. Law Interdisciplinary Law Jour., 1976. Recipient Spl. Achievement award EPA, 1982, 83. Mem. Environ. Law Inst. Ind. State Bar Assn., Ill. State Bar Assn., ABA, Phi Beta Kappa, Phi Delta Alpha. Republican. Home: 7580 Westfield Rd Indianapolis IN 46240 Office: US EPA Office of Regional Council 230 S Dearborn 5C-16 Chicago IL 60604

ELAM, RICK, accounting educator; b. Hannibal, Mo., Feb. 11, 1944; s. Albert Gray and Helene (Richards) E.; m. Karen J. Morgan, Nov. 19, 1979; 1 child, Paula. B.S., Culver-Stockton Coll., 1966; M.A., U. Mo., 1969, Ph.D., 1973. C.P.A., Mo. Teaching asst. U. Mo., Columbia, 1970-73, asst. prof. acctg., 1973-78, assoc. prof., 1978-83, prof., 1983—, dir. Sch. Accountancy, 1979—. Contbr. articles to profl. jours. Mem. Am. Acctg. Assn., Fin. Execs. Inst., Am. Inst. C.P.A.s, Mo. Soc. C.P.A.s, Fedn. Schs. of Accountancy (pres. 1985—), Beta Alpha Psi, Beta Gamma Sigma. Office: U Mo Sch Accountancy Columbia MO 65211

ELASH, DANIEL DAVID, clinical psychologist; b. Pitts., Sept. 30, 1946; s. Daniel and Margaret Cecilia (Tunney) E.; m. Sharon K. Rose, Aug. 18, 1976; children—Daniel, Gabriel, Nathan, Joshua, Matthew. B.S., Pa. State U., 1968; M.A., U. Kans., 1971, Ph.D., 1975. Psychologist, Wyandotte (Kans.) Mental Health and Guidance Ctr., 1973-74; pvt. practice with Charles L. Johnson, Ph.D., Kansas City, 1973-78; sr. research assoc. Greater Kansas City Mental Health Found., 1975-78; exec. dir. Interpersonal Systems, Kansas City, Mo., 1978—; cons. Greater Kansas City Mental Health Found., dept. plastic surgery Truman Med. Ctr., Kansas City, 1978-80; psychologist Prime Health, Kansas City, 1982—; lectr. U. Mo. Med. Sch., Kansas City, 1978-80; mem. staff St. Luke's Hosp., St. Mary's Hosp., Menorah Med. Ctr., Kansas City. Nat. bd. trustees Com. to Combat Huntington's Disease, 1975-77; community organizer Tribal Council Potawatomie Tribe, Mayetta, Kans., 1969-71. NIMH fellow, 1968-71. Mem. Am. Psychol. Assn., Mo. Psychol. Assn. Co-author: The Dynamics of Lawyering, 1983.

ELBERSON, ROBERT EVANS, food industry executive; b. Winston-Salem, N.C., Nov. 9, 1928; B.S. in Engring., Princeton U., 1950; M.B.A., Harvard U., 1952; m. Helen Hanes; children—Nancy Ann, Charles Evans II. Mgmt. trainee Hanes Hosiery Mills Co., Winston-Salem, 1954-56, office mgr., 1956-62, sec., 1959-62, v.p. mfg., 1962-65, mem. exec. com., dir., 1963-65, v.p. planning Hanes Corp. (merger Hanes Hosiery Mills Co. and P.H. Hanes Knitting Co.), 1965-68, pres. hosiery div., v.p. corp., 1968-72, pres., chief exec. officer, 1972-79, dir., 1972-79; exec. v.p. Sara Lee Corp. 1979-82, vice chmn., 1982-83, pres., chief operating officer, 1983—, dir., 1979—; dir. W.W. Grainger, Inc., Skokie, Ill., CBI Industries, Inc., Oak Brook, Ill. Chmn. bd. visitors Babcock Grad. Sch. Mgmt., Wake Forest U., Winston-Salem, 1977-83; trustee Salem Acad. and Coll., Winston-Salem, 1980—, Chgo. Mus. Sci. and Industry, 1984—. Served as lt. USAF, 1952-54. Home: Chicago IL Office: Sara Lee Corp 3 First National Plaza Chicago IL 60602

ELCIK, JOHN PAUL, IV, educator; b. Washington, May 3, 1952; s. John Paul Elcik III and Jacquiline Elcik Skillin; m. Pamela McClanahan, Nov. 3, 1979. A.A., Anne Arundel Community Coll.; B.A., U. Md., 1974; M.A., Ball State U., 1981, Ed.D., 1984. Asst. dir. enrollment services, acting registrar Tri-State U., Angola, Ind., 1978-82; doctoral fellow Ball State U., Muncie, Ind., 1982-84; dir. admissions Viterbo Coll., LaCrosse, Wis., 1984-85; v.p. human resource devel. Alpha Systems Resource, Inc., Shelbyville, Ind., 1985—. Mem. Nat. Assn. Coll. Admissions Counselors, Am. Assn. Coll. Registrars and Admissions Officers, Am. Assn. Adult and Continuing Edn., Am. Assn. Higher Edn., Nat. Assn. Student Personnel Adminstrs., LaCrosse C. of C. Lodges: Masons, Shriners. Avocation: personal computing. Home: 879 S Tompkins St Shelbyville IN 46176 Office: Alpha Systems Resource One Alpha Way Shelbyville IN 46176

ELDER, ALFRED OSCAR, financial services company executive; b. St. Paul, Minn., May 5, 1933; s. Alfred Oscar and Ruby (Sakavich) E.; m. Mary Ann Schemmel, Dec. 31, 1955; children—Kevin Andrew, Catherine Mary, Susan Marie, Teresa Marie, John Alfred. B.B.A., U. Minn.-Mpls., 1955; M.S., Am. Coll., Bryn Mawr, Pa., 1980. C.L.U.; chartered fin. cons. Spl. agt. Provident Mut. Life Ins., Mpls., 1958-70; pres. Chelsea Fin. Co., Mpls., 1970—; dir. EMS Inc., Mpls., Cytrol Inc., Mpls. Mem. adv. com. Senator Rudy Boschwitz, 1983—. Mem. Assn. Advanced Life Underwriters (assoc. v.p. 1972-73), Am. Soc. C.L.U.s, Nat. Assn. Life Underwriters, Minn. Assn. Life Underwriters, Mpls. Assn. Life Underwriters (pres. 1971-72), Republican. Roman Catholic. Home: 2909 Idaho Ave N Minneapolis MN 55427 Office: Chelsea Fin Corp Parkdale Plaza Suite 526 W 1660 Hwy 100 S Minneapolis MN 55416

ELDER, JAMES LANPHERE, lawyer; b. Hanover, Ill., Mar. 21, 1914; s. Frank Ray and Frances Mae (Lanphere) E.; m. Frances Emily Wagner, Jan. 27, 1950; children—James Lanphere, William Paddack, Suzanne DuVal. B.A., Hampden-Sydney Coll., 1936; LL.B., Harvard U., 1939. Bar: Pa. 1940, Ohio 1941. Assoc. Taft, Stettinius & Hollister, Cin., 1942-49; ptnr. Aug, Elder & Rielly, Cin., 1949-59, Nieman, Aug, Elder & Jacobs, Cin., 1959—; prof. Chase Coll. Law, Cin., 1952-60, Cin. Law Sch., 1961; lectr. Ohio Bar Legal Edn. Program. Author: Elder's Revision, Stearns on Suretyship, 1951. Founding mem. Greater Cin. Found., 1963, mem. distbn. com., 1963-75, chmn., 1969-70. Fellow Am. Bar Found., Ohio State Bar Found. (trustee 1980—, pres. 1985); mem. ABA, Ohio State Bar Assn. (exec. com. 1975-77), Cin. Bar Assn. (pres. 1966-67). Republican. Presbyterian. Clubs: University (bd, govs. 1960-66), Harvard (pres. 1979-80). Home: 5 Dexter Pl Cincinnati OH 45206 Office: Nieman Aug Elder & Jacobs 1000 Atlas Bank Bldg Cincinnati OH 45202

ELDER, KENNETH MATHEWS, lawyer; b. Springfield, Ohio, Feb. 16, 1953; s. Kenneth Wildman and Frances Dean (Mathews) E. B.A., Hanover Coll., 1975; J.D., U. Cin., 1978. Bar: Ohio 1978, U.S. Dist. Ct. (so. dist.) Ohio 1981. Assoc. Elder, Elder & Borley, Springfield, 1978-80; asst. pros. atty. Clark County Prosecutor's Office, Springfield, 1980-84; assoc. Elder, Borley & Roberts, Springfield, 1984-85; ptnr. Elder, Roberts & Elder, 1985—; dir. Madison Ave. Group Home, Inc., Springfield. Sec. bd. deacons Covenant Presbyn. Ch., Springfield, 1983—; pres. Vol. Service Bur., Springfield, 1985—. Mem. Ohio State Bar Assn., Springfield Bar and Law Library Assn., Springfield Jaycees. Republican. Office: Elder Roberts & Elder 330 M&M Bldg Springfield OH 45502

ELDRED, GRAIG EDWARD, physiologist; b. Pontiac, Mich., Nov. 28, 1949; s. Edward Ernest and Betty Ann (Greenough) E.; m. Barbara Jo Hoppe, Aug. 1, 1970; children—Mariah, Danielle. B.S., U. Mich., 1972; M.S., Mich State U., 1975, Ph.D., 1979. Research asst. Mich. State U., East Lansing, 1974-75, teaching asst., 1975-76, research asst., 1976-79; postdoctoral fellow U. Mo., Columbia, 1979-82, research asst. prof., 1982—; lectr. in field. Contbg. editor Jour. Investigative Ophthalmology and Visual Sci., 1983; Lipids, 1985. Contbr. articles to profl. jours. Foster parent Div. Family Services, East Lansing, 1977; attendant to handicapped Personal Friend orgn., Columbia, 1981; campaigner Democratic Orgn., Columbia, 1984; Recipient Research Service award Nat. Eye Inst., NIH, Columbia, 1980-82; grantee Nat. Soc. to Prevent Blindness, 1980-82, Nat. Inst. Aging, NIH, 1982-85. Mem. Assn. Research in Vision and Ophthalmology, Am. Aging Assn., N.Y. Acad. Scis., AAAS (reviewer jour. 1982—), Union Concerned Scientists (organizer Columbia chpt. 1984). Home: 1500 Richardson St Columbia MO 65201 Office: U Mo Sch Medicine Dept Opthalmology Mason Inst Ophthalmology Columbia MO 65212

ELEK, PATRICK WILLIAM, construction company executive; b. McKeesport, Pa., Dec. 14, 1953; s. John William and Mary Patricia (Kavanaugh) E.; m. Michele Marie Chanyi, July 12, 1975; children—Jared Michael, Amanda Lynn. Student public schs., Los Angeles and Munhall, Pa. Shift leader, VA, San Francisco, 1976-77; operating engr., foreman Asphalt Treatment Co., Emeryville, Calif., 1977; constrn. Malibu Grand Priz, Woodland Hills, Calif. 1977-80; project mgr. W-D Constrn. Co., Columbus, Ohio, 1981; constrn. engr. Caprice Constrn., Columbus, 1981-83; constrn. engr. Rax Restaurants, Inc., Columbus, 1983—. Served with USN, 1971-76; Vietnam. Named Ambassador of Good Will, Sec. State W.Va., 1984. Republican. Roman Catholic. Home: 3363 Edgebrook Dr Dublin OH 43017 Office: Rax Restaurants Inc 1266 Dublin Rd Columbus OH 43215

ELFRINK, NEIL MARTIN, geologist, cartographer; b. St. Louis, May 21, 1956; s. Theodore John and Ceceilia Augustus (Martin) E. B.S. in Geology, U. Mo., 1977. Geologist, Geol. Logging, Oklahoma City, Okla., 1977-79; cartogrpher DMA Aerospace Ctr., St. Louis, 1982—. Home: 6804 Fyler Ave Saint Louis MO 63139

ELIAS, JOHN SAMUEL, lawyer; b. Lawrence, Mass., May 2, 1951; s. Fred G. and Evon (Erban) E.; m. Cynthia Lee Eppley, Jan. 29, 1979; 1 child, Daniel John. A.B. summa cum laude, Dartmouth Coll., 1973; M.A., Oxford U., Eng., 1975; J.D., Harvard U., 1979; LL.M. in Taxation, NYU, 1982. Bar: Ill. 1979, Ohio 1980, U.S. Tax Ct. 1980, N.Y. 1981, Mass. 1982. Law clk. Ohio Supreme Ct., Columbus, 1979-81; assoc. Curtis, Mallet, & Prevost, N.Y.C., 1981, Goodwin, Proctor & Hoar, Boston, 1982-84; ptnr. Sutkowski & Washkuhn Assocs., Peoria, Ill., 1984—; lectr. Ill. Inst. Continuing Legal Edn., Springfield, 1984. Contbr. articles to legal jours. Recruiter Dartmouth Coll., Peoria, 1984. Dartmouth Coll. Reynolds Meml. scholar Oxford U., 1974. Mem. ABA, Ill. State Bar Assn., Peoria County Bar Assn., Phi Beta Kappa. Roman Catholic. Club: Peoria Country. Lodge: Rotary. Home: 1017 Greenfield Dr Peoria IL

61614 Office: Sutkowski & Washkuhn Assocs 560 Jefferson Bank Bldg Peoria IL 61602

ELICEIRI, GEORGE L., molecular biologist; b. Buenos Aires, Argentina, Oct. 27, 1939; came to U.S., 1961, naturalized, 1970; m. Ellen M. Enright, Nov. 12, 1966; children—Brian P., Kevin W., Dennis B. M.D., U. Buenos Aires, 1960; Ph.D. in Biochemistry, U. Okla., 1965. Postdoctoral fellow U. Chgo., 1965-67; research assoc. NYU, N.Y.C., 1967-68, instr., 1968-69; asst., then assoc. prof. St. Louis U. Med. Sch., 1969-76, prof., 1976—. Contbr. articles to profl. jours. Recipient Research Career Devel. award USPHS, 1972-77; USPHS fellow, 1967-69. Mem. Am. Soc. Biol. Chemists, Am. Soc. Cell Biology, Am. Assn. Pathologists. Office: Dept Pathology St Louis U Med Sch 1402 S Grand Blvd Saint Louis MO 63104

ELICK, RONALD LEE, electrical engineer; b. Lancaster, Ohio, Aug. 3, 1953; s. Jerry Lester and Shirley Louise (Thomas) E.; m. Mary Ann Kearns, Sept. 18, 1976; children—Michelle, Amanda. B.S. in Elec. Engring., U. Cin., 1977. Sales engr. Gen. Electric Co., Cin., 1977-84; sr. sales engr. ITRAN Corp., Cin., 1984—. Mem. Soc. Mfg. Engrs. Home: 5692 Lake Michigan Dr Fairfield OH 45014 Office: 270 Northland Blvd Suite 225 Cincinnati OH 45246

ELKHANIALY, HEKMAT ABDUL RAZEK, demographic cons.; b. Egypt, Dec. 17, 1935; came to U.S., 1961, naturalized, 1975; d. Abdul Razek Hussein and Nabiha Mursi (Kutb) E.; B. Commerce/Econs., Cairo U., 1959; Ph.D. in Sociology, U. Chgo., 1968; m. Chandra Kant Jha, Dec. 20, 1969; 1 dau., Lakshmi. Mem. faculty Roosevelt U., Chgo., 1968-75, asso. prof. sociology, 1973-75; demographic cons., Chgo., 1975—; research assoc. Population Research Ctr., U. Chgo., 1977-80; sec., treas. PSM Internat. Mem. Population Assn. Am., Am. Sociol. Assn., Chgo. Council Fgn. Relations. Contbr. articles to profl. jours. Home: 2800 N Lake Shore Dr Chicago IL 60657 Office: care PSM Internat Suite 1600 200 W Monroe St Chicago IL 60606

ELKINS, JAMES PAUL, physician; b. Lincoln, Nebr., Mar. 20, 1924; s. James Hill and Antonia (Wohler) E.; M.D., U. Va., 1947; m. May Hollingsworth Reynolds, June 15, 1946; children—Patricia May Elkins Riggs, Paulette Frances Elkins Phillips, James Barrington. Cert. Emergency Med. Services Commn. Intern, DePaul Hosp., Norfolk, Va., 1947-48; resident in ob-gyn Alexandria (Va.) Hosp., 1948-49, Franklin Sq. Hosp., Balt., 1949-50, St. Rita's Hosp., Lima, Ohio, 1950, Tripler Army Hosp., Honolulu, 1953-54; practice medicine specializing in ob-gyn, Indpls., 1954-73; chief ob-gyn St. Francis Hosp., Beech Grove, Ind., 1965-66; mem. teaching staff Gen. Hosp., Indpls., 1954-73; dep. coroner Marion County, 1965-74; med. cons. disability determination div. Ind. Rehab. Services; med. dir. Phys. Exams. Inc.; ringside physician Ind. State Boxing Commn., Indpls. Pal Club, Ind. Golden Gloves. Service chmn. Beech Grove unit Am. Cancer Soc. Served with AUS, 1949-54. Mem. Am. Coll. Ob-Gyn, AMA, Ind. State Med. Assn., Marion County Med. Soc., Indpls. Press Club (hon. life), Police League Ind., Fraternal Order Police, Nat. Sojourners, 500 Festival Assos., Police League Ind., Ind. Sports Corp. (charter gold mem.), U.S. Auto Club (life), Phi Chi. Clubs: Ind. Pacers Booster (charter), Thundering Herd (charter mem.). Lodges: Masons, Shriners (life). Home: 2045 Lick Creek Dr Indianapolis IN 46203 Office: 6th Floor Illinois Bldg 17 W Market St PO Box 7069 Indianapolis IN 46207

ELLEBRACHT, PAT, business administration educator; b. San Antonio, June 13, 1933; s. Irvin Louis and Ruby Lillian (Lindsay) E.; m. Eleanor Viola Kirks, Dec. 17, 1966; children—Rex Van, Elena Marie. B.B.A., Tex. Tech U., 1953, M.B.A., 1954. Indsl. relations analyst ARAMCO, Dhahran, Saudi Arabia, 1954-55; cost analyst Temco Aircraft, Dallas, 1956-57, Bert Fields, Inc., Dallas, 1957-59; instr. bus. adminstrn. Ark. State U., Jonesboro, 1959-67; asst. prof. NE Mo. State U., Kirksville, 1967—. Bd. dirs. Garrett Lake Homeowners Assn., 1982—, treas., 1983—. Mem. Delta Sigma Pi, Sigma Iota Epsilon, Pi Gamma Mu. Methodist. Avocations: collecting western art; reading. Home: 2505 S 1st St Box 347 Kirksville MO 63501 Office: NE Mo State U Violette Hall 119B Kirksville MO 63501

ELLERBRAKE, RICHARD PAUL, health care administrator, minister; b. Chgo., Dec. 14, 1933; s. George P. and Wilhelmina M. (Gluth) E.; m. Johann Lee Havenner, June 11, 1957; children—David (dec.), Stephen, Christopher, Laura (dec.). B.A., Elmhurst Coll. (Ill.), 1955; B.D., Eden Theol. Sem., Webster Groves, Mo., 1958; M.H.A., Washington U., St. Louis, 1964. Ordained to ministry United Ch. Christ, 1950. Chaplain St. Louis Juvenile Ct., Episcopal City Mission soc., 1957-58; pastor, dir. Back Bay Mission, Biloxi, Miss., 1958-62; exec. v.p. Deaconess Hosp., St. Louis, 1963-82; pres., chief exec. officer, 1982—; adj. faculty mem. Washington U. Sch. Medicine, St. Louis, 1971—; pres., chief exec. officer Deaconess Health Services Corp., St. Louis, 1982—, Deaconess Manor, St. Louis, 1982—, Deaconess Found., St. Louis, 1982—; dir. Group Health Plan, St. Louis, 1982—; dir. Central East Mo. Profl. Rev. Orgn., St. Louis, 1984—; pres. Council Health and Human Service Ministries, Lancaster, Pa., 1985—. Contbr. articles and poetry to profl. jours. Editor ch. denominational monthly jour. Chmn. United Way Health Services Div., St. Louis, 1984. Recipient Merit award Elmhurst Coll., 1982. Mem. Mo. Profl. Liability Ins. Assn. (bd. dirs. 1983—), Am. Protestant Health Assn. (bd. dirs. 1983—), Mo. Hosp. Assn. (bd. dirs. 1983—), Regional Transplant Assn. (bd. dirs. 1977—), Hosp. Assn. Met. St. Louis (bd. dirs. 1985—). Avocations: fishing, camping, gardening. Home: Old Enterprise Farms Ltd Route 2 Lebanon IL 62254 Office: Deaconess Health Services Corp 6150 Oakland Ave Saint Louis MO 63139

ELLERT, MARTHA SCHWANDT, physiologist, educator; b. Jersey City, Nov. 27, 1940; d. Harry Richard and Emily (Brando) Schwandt; m. William Sam Hunter, Aug. 3, 1972; children—Anthony Martin, William Fritsche. B.S., Barry Coll., 1962; Ph.D., U. Miami, Fla., 1967. Instr. physiology St. Louis U. Sch. Medicine, 1967-70, asst. prof., 1970-75, dir. summer program, 1971-75; assoc. prof. Sch. Medicine, So. Ill. U., Carbondale, 1975—, asst. dean for curriculum, 1981—. Precinct committeeman Democratic Party, Makanda, Ill., 1978—; pres. exec. bd. Carbondale New Sch., 1983-85; mem. exec. bd. Makanda Community Devel. Council, 1980-83, consumer adv. bd. Family Practice Ctr., Carbondale 1976-80. Mem. Am. Physiol. Soc., AAUP (nat. council 1976-79, chpt. pres. 1973-74, 79-80), Sigma Xi. Democrat. Mem. Christian Church. Avocations: singing; weightlifting; raising dairy goats. Home: High Pines RR 2 Box 4 Makanda IL 62958 Office: So Ill Univ Sch Medicine Carbondale IL 62901

ELLIE, YVONNE KISSINGER, principal; b. Wisconsin Rapids, Wis., Mar. 21, 1936; d. Alfred J. and Louise J. (Brockman) Kissinger; B.S., Coll. St. Teresa, 1958; M.S., U. Wis.-Stevens Point, 1978; postgrad. U. Wis.-Madison, 1979—; m. Gene C. Ellie, June 28, 1958; children—Gregory, Jean Marie, Katherine, Daniel, David, Brian. Tchr., Mpls. Pub. Schs., 1958, Lowell Sch., Moses Lake, Wash., 1958-59, Vesper Elem. Sch., Wisconsin Rapids, 1967-78, Mead, Howe, Woodside Schs., Wisconsin Rapids, 1978-79; adminstrv. intern Grove and Pitsch Elem. Sch., Wisconsin Rapids, 1979-80, prin., dir. community services, 1980—; mem. Wood County Environ. Edn. Com. Chmn. unified bargaining com. Central Wis. Uniserve Council, 1976-79. Mem. Wisconsin Rapids Tchrs. Assn. (pres. 1978-79), LWV, NEA, Wis. Edn. Assn. (council), Wisconsin Rapids Edn. Assn., Internat. Reading Assn., Wis. Reading Assn., Central Wis. Reading Assn., Wis. Community Edn. Assn., Nat. Assn. Elementary Prins., Assn. Wis. Sch. Adminstrs., Assn. Supervision and Curriculum Devel., Network Outcome Based Schs., Nat. Council Tchrs. of English, Wis. Math. Council, Phi Delta Kappa. Home: 990 1st Ave S Wisconsin Rapids WI 54494 Office: 2750 Lincoln St Wisconsin Rapids WI 54494

ELLIOT, DIANE ALYNN, dancer and choreographer, dance educator; b. Chgo., Apr. 25, 1949; d. Leonard and Florence (Asher) E. B.A., U. Mich., 1971. Dancer, Phyllis Lamhut Dance Co., N.Y.C., 1974-77; master tchr. Centre Nat. de Danse Contemporaine, Angers, France, 1979-80; artist in residence U. Minn., Mpls., 1981-82; ind. dance artist N.Y.C., Mpls., 1974—, Body Arts Network, Mpls., 1982—. Choreographer more than 30 works, most recently Todora, 1984. Sweet Honey, 1984, Florence's Dress, 1984. Contbr. articles to profl. jours. McKnight Found. fellow, 1983-84; Minn. State Arts Bd. fellow, 1983; Jerome Found. grantee, 1983. Mem. Minn. Ind. Choreographers Alliance (bd. dirs. 1984—). Jewish. Avocations: reading; running; writing songs and poetry.

ELLIOTT, BARBARA JEAN, librarian; b. Bluffton, Ind., Oct. 2, 1927; d. Dale A. and Gwendolyn I. (Long); m. Robert J. Elliott, June 13, 1949; 1 son, Michael Roger. B.S. with honors, Ind. U., 1949, M.L.S., 1979. Dir. tech. info. services uranium div. Mallinckrodt Chems., St. Louis, 1949-59; research librarian Petrolite Corp., Webster Groves, Mo., 1961-63; head tech. services St. Frances Coll., Ft. Wayne, Ind., 1974-76; asst. dir. Bluffton-Wells County Pub. Library, 1976—. Publicity chmn. TRIALSA Library Coop., Ft. Wayne, 1983—. Mem. ALA, Ind. Library Assn., LWV of Ind. (state sec. 1981-83, chmn. health care 1983—). Club: Bluffton Garden (v.p. 1983—), Bus. and Profl. Women (v.p. 1985—). Home: 6831 SE State Rd 116 Bluffton IN 46714 Office: Bluffton Wells County Pub Library 223 W Washington St Bluffton IN 46714

ELLIOTT, CAROL GEANNE, nursing educator; b. Sedalia, Mo., Nov. 2, 1938; d. James R. and Helen C. (Workover) Scott; grad. Penn Valley Coll., 1968; nurse anesthesia diploma U. Kans., 1973; B.A., Ottawa (Kans.) U., 1975; M.P.A., U. Kans., 1982, postgrad., 1982—; m. Robert Lee Elliott, Mar. 23, 1957; children—Kelly Ann, Michael, Kimberly Karol, Karen Kathleen. Asst. prof. Sch. Allied Health, U. Kans. Med. Center Campus, Kansas City, 1973—, chmn. dept. postgrad. edn. nurse anesthesia, 1973—; lectr. in field. Mem. Am. Nurses Assn., Am. Hosp. Assn., Am. Assn. Nurse Anesthetists, Mo. Assn. Nurse Anesthetists, Kans. Assn. Nurse Anesthetists, Internat. Anesthesia Research Soc., Assn. Operating Room Nurses, Allied Health Profls. Assn., Phi Theta Kappa, Pi Sigma Alpha. Contbr. articles on nurse anesthesia to profl. jours. Home: 14901 Rosehill Rd Olathe KS 66062 Office: Univ of Kansas 39th and Rainbow Kansas City KS 66103

ELLIOTT, DANA RAY, biology educator, consultant; b. Grain Valley, Mo., Feb. 7, 1945; s. Franklin Ellwood and Edna Mae (Rowe) E.; m. Cheryl Jeanne Boyd (div.); 1 child, Rebecca Leigh; m. Harriet Margaret Thompson, Mar. 17, 1978; children—Daniel Paul, Margaret Anne. B.A., William Jewell Coll., 1967; M.S., Central Mo. State U., 1971; Ph.D., U. Mo., 1981. Cert. secondary tchr., Mo. Pub. sch. tchr. Raytown Pub. Sch., Raytown, Mo., 1967-68, Kansas City Pub. Schs., Kansas City, Mo., 1971-72, Liberty Pub. Schs., Liberty, Mo., 1972-74; prof. Central Meth. Coll., Fayette, Mo., 1974—; cons., Fayette, 1981—. Contbr. articles to profl. jours. Canvasser, Area Common Fund, Fayette, 1983-84. Served with U.S. Army, 1968-70. Decorated Bronze Star with oak leaf cluster. Mem. Entomol. Soc. of Am., Ecol. Soc. Am., Central States Archaeol. Soc., Mo. Archaeol. Soc. (v.p. 1985-86), Mo. Acad. Sci. Democrat. Mem. Disciples of Christ Ch. Club: Round Table (Fayette, Mo.). Lodge: Optimist (Fayette). Avocations: Missouri Indian archaeology; paleontology; collecting insects; hunting; fishing. Home: 103 Lucky St Fayette MO 65248 Office: Dept Biology Central Methodist Coll Fayette MO 65248

ELLIOTT, DAVID LEROY, engineering educator; b. Cleve., May 29, 1932; s. Reed LeRoy and Roma Cyril (Benjamin) E.; m. Kiyoko Akaeda, Mar. 23, 1956 (div. 1980); children—Marguerite, Philip David; m. 2d Pauline Wei-Ying Tang, Oct. 31, 1984. B.A., Pomona Coll., 1953; M.A., U. So. Calif., 1959; Ph.D., UCLA, 1969. Registered profl. engr., Calif. Mathematician, U.S. Naval Ocean Systems Ctr., Pasadena, Calif., 1955-69; mem. faculty Washington U., St. Louis, 1971—, prof. math., 1980—. Contbr. articles to profl. jours. Assoc. editor Math. Systems Theory Jour., 1976—. Mem. adv. com. St. Louis Mus. Sci. and Natural History, 1984—. Fellow IEEE; Mem., Am. Math. Soc., Soc. Indsl. and Applied Maths., Math. Assn. Am. Democrat. Avocations: science fiction; computers. Home: 6600 Washington St Apt 8 University City MO 63130 Office: Washington U Dept Systems Sci and Math Box 1040 Saint Louis MO 63130

ELLIOTT, ESCALUS EMERT (CHIP), III, author; b. Franklin County, Ohio, June 21, 1945; s. Escalus Emert Jr. and Janet Patricia (Berry) E.; m. Francine Rasco, 1976. B.A. in Journalism and English, Ohio State U., 1968; student Stanford U., 1963-69, San Francisco State U., Reporter, asst. night city editor Columbus Dispatch, Ohio, 1964-68; police reporter San Francisco Chronicle, 1970-72. Author: Tomorrow Come Sunrise (Book of the Month Club selection), 1969. Pres., chmn. bd. trustees Beechwold-Clintonville Community Resource Ctr., Columbus. Avocations: antique motorcycles, sailing, cooking. Home: 110 Orchard Ln Columbus OH 43214

ELLIOTT, EVANGELINE WILSON, hospital official; b. Chgo., June 26, 1941; d. Jackie and Lillian Evelyn (Lowry) Wilson; L.P.N., Cabrini Sch. Practical Nursing, 1964-65; m. John Wallace Elliott, June 30, 1973; children—Louis, Chiquita. Nurse, Cook County Sch. of Nursing, Chgo., 1965-66, Med. Staffing for Nurses, Chgo., 1968-70, Alice Toch Registry for Nurses, Chgo., 1970-71; asst. supr. central service Columbus Hosp., Chgo., 1974-80; supr. central service Hosp. of Englewood, Chgo., 1980—. Mem. Am. Soc. for Central Service Personnel, Chgo. Assn. Hosp. Central Service Personnel. Roman Catholic. Home: 2909 N Sheridan Rd 1007 Chicago IL 60657 Office: Hosp of Englewood 6001 S Green St Chicago IL 60621

ELLIOTT, HOWARD, JR., gas distribution company executive; b. St. Louis, July 4, 1933; s. Howard and Ruth Ann (Thomas) E.; student Brown U., 1956; J.D., Washington U., 1962; m. Susan Jane Spoehrer, Sept. 2, 1961; children—Kathryn Spoehrer, Elizabeth Gray. Admitted to Mo. bar, 1962; assoc. firm Boyle, Priest, Elliott & Weakley, St. Louis, 1962-65, partner, 1965-67; commr. Mo. Pub. Service Commn., 1967-70; commr. U.S. Postal Rate Commn., 1970-73; assoc. gen. counsel Laclede Gas Co., St. Louis, 1973-77, v.p. adminstrn., 1977—. Mem. com. on electricity and nuclear energy Nat. Assn. Regulatory Utility Commrs., 1968-70, mem. exec. com., 1971-73. Charter mem. com. of 40 for Adoption of St. Louis and St. Louis County Jr. Coll. Dist., 1962. Served with U.S. Army, 1956-58. Mem. Am. Gas Assn., ABA, Mo. Bar, Fed. Bar Assn., Fed. Energy Bar Assn., Bar Assn. Met. St. Louis. Republican. Presbyterian. Clubs: Noonday, St. Louis County, Chevy Chase, Mo. Athletic. Home: 46 Clermont Ln Saint Louis MO 63124 Office: 720 Olive St Saint Louis MO 63101

ELLIOTT, JAMES LEE, educational administrator, educator; b. Detroit, Jan. 19, 1937; s. Percy Alexander and Lillian Kathryn (Davey) E.; m. Janet Louise Fisher, Sept. 29, 1959; children—Joan Lynn, John Lindsay. B.S., Alma Coll., 1958; M.Ed., Miami U., 1959; Ed.D., U. Ill., 1966; postgrad. Tchrs. Coll., Columbia U., 1981. Research asst. Miami U., Oxford, Ohio, 1958-59; tchr. chemistry Charles F. Brush High Sch., Cleve., 1959-63; research asst. U. Ill., Urbana, 1963-65; prin. Evanston (Ill.) Twp. High Sch., 1965-69; asst. supt. Lyons Twp. High Sch., LaGrange, Ill., 1969-80; supt. Pekin (Ill.) Pub. Schs., 1980—; prof. evening div. Roosevelt U., Chgo., 1967-69, extramural div. U. Ill., Urbana, 1977—. Sec. Pekin Community Concert Assn., 1983—; chairperson Pekin Cancer Crusade, 1983; bd. dirs. Pekin United Way, 1980—. Charles F. Kettering Found. fellow, 1967, 68, 73, 77. Mem. Am. Assn. Sch. Adminstrs., Ill. Assn. Sch. Adminstrs., Nat. Orgn. Legal Problems in Edn., Nat. Assn. Secondary Sch. Prins., Nat. Soc. for Study of Edn., Phi Delta Kappa, Pekin C. of C. (bd. dirs. 1980—). Home: 31 Olympia Fields Dr Pekin IL 61554

ELLIOTT, KAREN CASEY, publishing company executive; b. LaFayette, Ind., July 18, 1939; d. James Orlando and Thelma Bernice (Kirkpatrick) E.; m. William Joseph Hilty, Jan. 28, 1961 (divorced Apr. 1973); m. Joseph Mathew Casey, Oct. 2, 1982. B.S., Purdue U., 1962; M.A., U. Minn., 1975, Ph.D., 1979. Cert. elem. tchr., Ind., Minn. Elem. tchr. LaFayette Pub. Schs., Ind., 1962-64, St. Paul Pub. Schs., 1964-69; instr. U. Minn., Mpls., 1971-76; mng. editor Hazelden Found., Center City, Minn., 1979-80, mktg. mgr., 1981-83, div. dir., 1984—; cons. Minn. State Depts. Edn., St. Paul, 1977-79. Author: Each Day A New Beginning, 1982, The Promise of a New Day, 1983; The Love Book, 1985. Mem. Nat. Women's Polit. Caucus, 1984—, NOW, 1984—, Soc. Against Nuclear Expansion, 1984—, Am. Friends Soc., 1984—, Alcohol and Drug Problems Assn. Mem. Am. Booksellers Assn., Upper Midwest Booksellers Assn., Minn. Roundtable Assn. (v.p. 1984). Democrat. Roman Catholic. Avocations: participatory sports; cooking; reading.

ELLIOTT, MILDRED HENSLEY, hospital services administrator; b. Harlen County, Ky., Dec. 3, 1925; d. Lewis and Susie (Reed) Hensley; m. William M. Elliott, Dec. 5, 1965 (div.); children—Jerry L. Cowles, Carol Elaine Cowles Pelz. Student Sue Bennett Coll., London, Ky., 1941-45. Tchr. Knox County (Ky.) Bd. Edn., 1943-44; with security div. E. I. Dupont Co., Charlestown, Ind., 1952-57, Scotty's Markets, Louisville, 1947-52; exec. dir. environ. services, mgr. laudnry and linen services Meml. Hosp. of Floyd County, New Albany, Ind., 1959—; condr. in-service tng. programs; cons. Jefferson County Bd. Edn., Mary Kay Cosmetics. Chmn. Taxpayer's Action Group, Clark County, Ind., 1983; active Democrat Women's League. Named Laundry Mgr. of Yr., Ky. Laundry Assn., 1976. Mem. Nat. Bus. and Profl. Women's Club, Bus. and Profl. Women (rec. sec. Clarksville, Ind.), Nat. Laundry and Linen Assn., Ky. Blue Grass Laundry Assn., Nat. Housekeepers Assn. (pres. 1978-80, v.p. Ky. chpt. 1980-82). Baptist. Club: Women's. Contbr. articles to profl. jours. Office: 1850 State St New Albany IN 47150

ELLIOTT, PETER R., athletic organization executive; b. Bloomington, Ill., Sept. 29, 1926; s. Joseph Norman and Alice (Marquis) E.; s. Joan Connaught Slater; children—Bruce Norman, David Lawrence. B.A., U. Mich., 1949. Asst. football coach Oreg. State U., 1949-50, U. Okla., 1951-55; head football coach U. Nebr., 1956, U. Calif.-Berkeley, 1957-59, U. Ill., 1960-66; head football coach U. Miami (Fla.), 1973-74, dir. athletics, 1974-78; asst. football coach St. Louis Cardinals, 1978; exec. dir. Pro Football Hall of Fame, Canton, Ohio, 1979—. Served with USNR, 1944-45. Mem. Am. Football Coaches Assn. (Region 8 Coach of Yr. award 1958, Region 5 Coach of Yr. award 1963). Presbyterian. Home: 3003 Dunbarton St Canton OH 44708 Office: 2121 Harrison St Canton OH 44708*

ELLIOTT, ROBERT BURNETT, retired coal company executive; b. Roseburg, Oreg., Sept. 26, 1925; s. Archie Eli and Blanche Marie (Burnett) E.; m. Frances LeNore Moore, Jan. 11, 1947; children—Kathryn Lynn, Susan Lee, Robert Eugene. Student U. Oreg., 1945-47. Mgr. motion picture theatres, 1947-53; with Hanna Mining Co., Riddle, Oreg., 1956-77, supr. inventory control, until 1977; purchasing agt. Colowyo Coal Co., Meeker, Colo., 1977-80, purchasing mgr., 1980-84; dir. devel. Supreme Lodge, Loyal Order of Moose, Mooseheart, Ill., 1984—. Commr. Meeker Housing Authority, 1980-84. Served with U.S. Army, 1944-45. Mem. Nat. Assn. Purchasing Mgmt., Am. Prodn. and Inventory Control Soc. Republican. Episcopalian. Clubs: Lions, Masons, Shriners, Moose (internat. officer 1971-78, mem. supreme council, internat. bd. dirs. 1982-84). Home: 141 Whittington Course Saint Charles IL 60174

ELLIOTT, ROBERT GEORGE, land developer; b. Lansing, Mich., Feb. 10, 1929; s. Elmer Duane and Eleanor Ione (Stowe) E.; m. Nancy A. Marker, May 23, 1947; children—Bradford N., Stephanie L., Robert Scott. Student pub. schs., Okemos, Mich. Builder, Lansing, Mich., 1955-61; sales mgr. Am. Central Corp., Lansing, 1961-63; pres. Lake Tahoe Devel. Corp., Lansing, 1963-68, Moon Lake Resort Corp., Lansing, 1967-79, Guthrie Lakes Devel. Corp., Lansing, 1967-80, Bradford-Scott Corp., Lansing, 1980—; Served with U.S. Army, 1951-52. Mem. Lansing C. of C. Republican. Lutheran. Club: City of Lansing. Home: 2170 Longlief Trail Okemos MI 48864 Office: 835 Louisa Lansing MI 48910

ELLIOTT, ROBERT MICHAEL, physician executive; b. Lawton, Okla., Mar. 9, 1945; s. Robert B. and June C. (Waggener) E.; m. Jean Lynn Hansen, May 17, 1976; children—Michael, Susan, Kathleen. B.S., Johns Hopkins U., 1966; M.D., U. Nebr., 1970. Intern, Nebr. Meth. Hosp., Omaha, 1971; resident U. Iowa Hosps., Iowa City, 1972; founder, chief exec. officer Elliott & Jones (now Critical Care Med. Services, Ltd.), Chgo., 1972—; co-founder, pres. Correctional Health Services Ltd. of Chgo., 1981—; pres. Critical Care Inst., Chgo., 1980—; med. dir. Pontiac and Dwight (Ill.) Correctional Ctrs., 1982—; med. dir. emergency service St. Francis Hosp., Blue Island, Ill., 1979; v.p. Elliott Enterprises and Westside Realty Co., Omaha, 1965-70; physician mem. Illowa Health Planning Council, Quad Cities, 1973-76; instr. advanced cardiac life support Am. Heart Assn.; instr. advanced trauma life support ACS. Served to maj. M.C., U.S. Army, 1971-77. Fisons Pharms. grantee, 1971, 72. Mem. AMA (recipient Physicians Recognition award 1974, 77, 81), Am. Coll. Emergency Physicians, Acad. Family Practice, Am. Correctional Assn., Am. Correctional Health Services Assn., Soc. Tchrs. Family Medicine, Chgo. Med. Soc. Republican. Clubs: Mid-Am., Chgo. Yacht. Author: A Compendium on Emergency Medicine for Critical Care, 1977. Home: 614 Pine Ln Winnetka IL 60093 Office: 179 W Washington St Suite 1100 Chicago IL 60601

ELLIOTT, ROBERT WAYNE, JR., lawyer; b. Landstuhl, Fed. Republic Germany, Aug. 2, 1954; came to U.S., 1955, naturalized 1955; s. Robert W. and Helen Joyce (Morton) E. Ed. Am. Sch. Paris, 1968-71; B.S., Purdue U., 1975; J.D. summa cum laude, Ind. U., 1978. Bar: Ind. 1978, U.S. Dist. Ct. (so. dist.) Ind. 1978. Assoc. Ice, Miller, Donadio & Ryan, Indpls., 1978-80; atty. Eli Lilly & Co., Indpls., 1980-83 and Eli Lilly Internat., 1983-84; staff counsel Cardiac Pacemakers, Inc., St. Paul, 1984—. Mem. ABA, Order of Coif, Phi Kappa Phi, Alpha Phi Omega. Republican. Baptist. Avocations: stamp collecting, refinishing antiques, racquetball. Office: Cardiac Pacemakers Inc 4100 N Hamline Ave Saint Paul MN 55112

ELLIOTT, THOMAS CARLTON, investment adviser; b. Gary, Ind., Oct. 23, 1954; s. Frank Milton and Erma (Downs) E.; 1 dau., Antoinette Rene. B.S. in Bus. Adminstrn. and Econs., Culver-Stockton Coll., 1977. Mut. fund salesman Waddell & Reed, Highland, Ind., 1977-78; fin. counselor Urban League, Gary, 1978-80; investment adviser Lake Park Investments, Inc., Chgo., 1980—; cons. Small Stride Day Care Ctrs., Inc., Chgo., 1983—. Named Future Leader of Gary, 1979. Mem. Investment Analysts Soc. Chgo. (assoc.), Assn. M.B.A. Execs. Democrat. Home: 4800 S Lakeshore Dr Apt 2011 N Chicago IL 60615 Office: Lake Park Investments Inc 4800 S Lakeshore Suite 2011N Chicago IL

ELLIOTT, WILLIAM DOUGLAS, English educator, writer, academic administrator; b. Bemidji, Minn., Jan. 13, 1938; s. Alfred Marlyn and Lulu (Maynard) E.; m. Gwendolyn Warren, July 19, 1960; children—Sharon Elizabeth, Douglas Warren. B.A., Miami U., Oxford, Ohio, 1960; M.A., U. Mich., 1961, Ed.D. in English, 1967; M.F.A. in Creative Writing, U. Iowa, 1962. Teaching asst. in English, U. Mich., Ann Arbor, 1960-61, 63-64, teaching fellow in English, 1962-63; scholar in writing U. Iowa, 1961-62; instr. Muskingum Coll., New Concord, Ohio, 1964-65; instr. Washtenaw Community Coll., Ypsilanti, Mich., 1966-67; asst. prof. English Bemidji State U., 1967-68, assoc. prof., 1969-79, prof., 1980—, chmn. dept. English, 1983—; author: (criticism) Henry Handel Richardson, 1975, (novel) Blue River, 1978, (poetry) Fishing the Offshore Island, 1980, To Middle River, 1984; dir. Can. Studies Com.; dir. Upper Midwest Writers' Conf. Recipient Hopwood award in creative writing U. Mich., 1959-62, award in short fiction McKnight Found., 1968, award for distinction Best Am. Fiction, 1969, Research award Am. Philos. Soc., 1974; fellow Miami U., 1959-60, Minn. State Arts Bd., 1975; Can. embassy grantee, 1981, 83. Mem. MLA, Midwestern MLA, Associated Writing Programs, Internat. Council Can. Studies, Assn. Can. Studies, Assn. Commonwealth Studies in Can., Am. Assn. Can. Studies, World Lit. Written in English. Democrat. Methodist. Contbr. to lit. jours.

ELLIOTT, WILLIAM H(UECKEL), biochemistry educator; b. St. Louis, June 4, 1918; s. William Collins and Edna Agnes (Hueckel) E.; m. Dorothy E. Singer, Aug. 6, 1949; children—William J., Mary C. Elliott Welch, Martha A.Elliott Koehler, Robert J. B.S., St. Louis U., 1939, M.S., 1941, Ph.D., 1944. Research asst. Ind. U., Bloomington, 1944; instr. biochemistry St. Louis U., 1944-50, asst. prof., 1950-53, assoc. prof., 1953-59, prof., 1959—, prof. chemistry, 1977—. Contbr. articles to profl. jours. Mem. sci. and engring. com. Adv. to Regional Commerce and Growth Assn. St. Louis, 1975—. Fellow AAAS; mem. Am. Chem. Soc., Am. Soc. Biol. Chemists, Am. Soc. for Mass Spectrometry, Am. Soc. Study of Liver Diseases, Soc. Exptl. Biology and Medicine, Sigma Xi, Phi Beta Kappa. Roman Catholic. Avocations: music; photography; stamp collecting. Home: 6300 Tholozan Ave Saint Louis MO 63109 Office: St Louis U Sch Medicine Dept Biochemistry 1402 S Grand Blvd Saint Louis MO 63104

ELLIS, BURNETT ESTON, geology educator; b. Greenway, Ark., Nov. 11, 1921; s. Burnett Eston and Trella Lea (Sargent) E.; m. Jessie Bird Stark, Aug. 20, 1946; 1 child, Eston Burnett. A.B., U. Mo., 1944, M.A., 1948. Lab. asst. geology U. Mo., Columbia, 1946-48, instr. geology, 1949-74, assoc. prof., 1974—. Bd. dirs. Community Nursery Sch., Columbia, 1966—, pres., 1983. Served with M.C., U.S. Army, 1944-46; PTO. Mem. AAUP, AAAS, Geol. Soc. Am., Mo. Acad. Scis., Nat. Assn. Geology Tchrs. (pres. central sect. 1972), Assn. Mo. Geologists, Nat. Sci. Tchrs. Assn., Sigma Zeta. Home: 1106 Eastwood Circle Columbia MO 65201 Office: Columbia Coll 8th and Rogers Sts Columbia MO 65216

ELLIS, CHRISTINE DUBOULAY, ballet school administrator, educator; b. London, June 12; came to U.S., 1952; d. Guy George and Raby (Knox) DuBoulay; m. Richard John Ellis. Prin. dancer Internat. Ballet, London, 1942-45, Sadler's Wells Ballet Co. (now Royal Ballet), London, 1945-52; dir., tchr. Ellis-Duboulay Sch. of Ballet, Chgo., 1954—. Office: Ellis-Duboulay Sch Ballet 185 N Wabash Chicago IL 60601

ELLIS, DORSEY D., JR., financial executive; b. Cape Girardeau, Mo., May 18, 1938; s. Dorsey D. and Anne (Stanaland) E.; m. Sondra Wagner, Dec. 27, 1962; children—Laura Elizabeth, Geoffrey Earl. B.A., Maryville Coll., 1960; J.D., U. Chgo., 1963. Bar: N.Y. 1967, Iowa 1976, U.S. Ct. Appeals (2d cir.) 1967, U.S. Ct. Appeals (8th cir.) 1976. Assoc. firm Cravath, Swaine & Moore, N.Y.C., 1963-68; assoc. prof. U. Iowa, Iowa City, 1968-71, prof., 1971—, v.p.

fin. and univ. services, 1984—, spl. asst. to pres., 1974-75; vis. mem. sr. common room Mansfield Coll., Oxford U., Eng., 1972-73, 75; vis. prof. law Emory U., Atlanta, 1981-82. Contbr. articles to profl. jours. U. Chgo. Nat. Honor scholar, 1960-63, Joseph Henry Beale prize, 1961. Mem. ABA, Iowa Bar Assn., Selden Soc., Am. Econ. Assn., Order of Coif. Home: 428 Ferson Iowa City IA 52240 Office: Univ Iowa 101 Jessup Hall Iowa City IA 52242

ELLIS, JACK CLARE, theatre arts educator; b. Joliet, Ill., July 9, 1922; s. Louis Nyle and Anna Louise (Cary) E.; m. Mary Catherine Bent, Sept. 1, 1974; children—David Hodges, Cameron Cary. Student Wabash Coll., 1943; M.A., U. Chgo., 1948; Ed.D., Columbia U., 1955. Instr. English, Western Mich. U., Kalamazoo, 1948-50; audio-visual specialist Citizenship Edn. Project, N.Y.C., 1951-53; research assoc. Film Council Am., Evanston, Ill., 1953-56; from asst. prof. film to prof. film Northwestern U., Evanston, 1956—, chmn. dept. radio-TV film, 1980-85; vis. asst. prof. UCLA, 1959-60; vis. assoc. prof. TV, motion pictures, radio NYU, 1965-66; prof. radio, TV and film U. Tex., Austin, 1972-73; mem. U.S. del. UNESCO Internat. Meeting on Teaching Film and TV Appreciation, Oslo, Norway, 1962; mem. adv. com. Am. Council on Edn., 1964-66; mem. adv. film panel Ill. Arts Council, 1970-72; dir. NEH Summer Seminar on History of Film, 1979, 80. Author: A History of Film, 1979, rev. edit., 1985. Co-editor: Cinema Examined, 1982; mem. bd. editorial advs. History of Am. Cinema project, 1980—; editor Cinema Jour., 1976-82, adv. editor, 1982—. Adv., contbr. The International Dictionary of Films and Filmmakers (13 essays), 1984. Served with U.S. Army, 1943-46. Mem. Am. Fedn. Film Socs. (pres., chmn. bd. dirs., newsletter editor 1955-75), Soc. for Cinema Studies (pres., treas., councilman 1959—). Home: 2118 Asbury Ave Evanston IL 60201 Office: Dept Radio-TV Film Northwestern U 1905 Sheridan Rd Evanston IL 60201

ELLIS, JACK GRAVES, university administrator; b. Frankfort, Ky., May 14, 1934; s. Earl Graves and Sally Mae (True) E.; student Miami U., Oxford, Ohio, 1952-54; B.S., Ohio U., 1957; m. Dewana Sue Mathis, Jan. 16, 1960; children—Sallie Renee, Rebecca Suzanne, Patricia Leah, Joel Mathew. Credit analyst Atlantic Richfield Co., Los Angeles, 1957-58; systems analyst Remington Rand Corp., Los Angeles, 1958-59; dist. mgr. Speery Rand Corp., Pomona, Calif., 1959-60; mfg. rep. Pacific Bus. Interiors, Los Angeles, 1961-67; exec. dir. Ohio U. Alumni Assn., Athens, 1967-70, dir. devel., 1970-85, v.p. devel., 1985—; exec. dir. Ohio Univ. Fund, Inc., 1973—. Bd. dirs. Athens Concerned Citizens Against Drug Abuse, 1980—. Mem. Council Advancement and Support Edn. (dist. program chmn.), Ohio Assn. Devel. Officers, Athens C. of C. Republican. Methodist. Club: Rotary. Home: 17 Mulligan Rd Athens OH 45701 Office: Ohio Univ 305 McGuffey Hall Athens OH 45701

ELLIS, JOYCE ANN, nursing educator; b. Hammond, Ind., May 17, 1936; d. Samuel and Helen (Van Dreal) Hoekema; m. William Charles Ellis, Apr. 22, 1960; children—Christy Ann, Lawrence Charles. Diploma St. Margaret Hosp. Sch. Nursing, 1957; B.S.N., DePaul U., 1963, M.S., 1965; Ed.D., No. Ill. U., 1979. Staff nurse St. Margaret Hosp., Hammond, 1957-64; instr. nursing St. Margaret Sch. Nursing, 1958-66; asst. prof. psychiat. mental health nursing Purdue U., Hammond, 1966-69, assoc. prof., sect. chmn., program dir., 1968-73, prof., dept. chmn., 1973—; cons. numerous colls. and universities, 1974—; lectr. numerous workshops and univs., 1980—. Editor: Qualitative Nursing Research, 1984; Communications in Health Care, 1977. Contbr. articles to profl. jours. Mem. Lake Central Sch. Bd., 1972-76; adv. com. Northwest Ind. Home Health Services; chmn. Citizens Adv. Com., Purdue U., 1976—; bd. dirs. Community Health Assn., 1981—; div. bd. hosp. govs. Our Lady of Mercy Hosp., Dyer, Ind., 1983—. Recipient Disting. Service award, Purdue U., 1982, Outstanding Adminstr. award, Purdue U., 1983. Recipient numerous grants, 1965—. Mem. Am. Nurses Assn., Nat. League Nursing, St. Margaret Hosp. Alumni Assn. Avocations: coin and antique collecting. Home: 434 Pontiac Rd Schererville IN 46375 Office: Purdue U Calumet Dept Nursing Hammond IN 46323

ELLIS, LUCILLE LORRAINE LAUGHLIN (MRS. WALLACE IVERSON ELLIS), realtor; b. Solsberry, Ind., Sept. 22, 1914; d. Rutherford and Mabel (Ingles) Laughlin; student Ind. U., 1930-31, 60-61, Danville Central Normal, 1931-32; m. Wallace Iverson Ellis, July 28, 1931; children—Betty Lucille (Mrs. Timothy Wininger), Charles Robert, Mary (Mrs. Hane), Rebecca (Mrs. Maxwell-Slingsby-Davies). Tchr., LaCrosse Sch., Martinsville, Ind., 1932-33; partner Ellis Gen. Store, Springville, Ind., 1933-44; partner, mgr. Ellis Super Market, Bloomington, Ind., 1945-59; founder, owner Ellis Real Estate, Bloomington, 1960—; owner Bloomington Downtown Motel, 1973—. Den Mother White River council Boy Scouts Am., 1948-50; brownie leader Tulip Trace council Girl Scouts U.S.A., 1954-56. Patron Hoosier Art Salon, Indpls. Mem. Bloomington Bd. Realtors (sec.-treas. 1963-65), Ind. Real Estate Assn., Nat. Assn. Real Estate Bds., Bloomington C. of C. (bd. dirs., sec. exec. com. 1969-70), Ind. U. Alumni Assn. (life), Internat. Platform Assn., Motel Assn. Am., Nat. Brokers Council, Ind. U. Woodburn Guild (charter), Delta Sigma Kappa (life mem.; nat. treas. 1965-67, nat. v.p. 1967-69, nat. pres. 1969-71, chmn. bd. 1971-73). Clubs: Arganaut, Women's Dept. (Bloomington). Republican. Presbyn. Home: 835 Sheridan Rd Bloomington IN 47401 Office: 408 S Walnut St Bloomington IN 47401

ELLIS, MARY LOUISE, state official; b. Albert Lea, Minn., May 29, 1943; d. Stanley Orville and Neoma Lois (Guthier) Helgeson; m. Melvin Eugene Ellis, July 31, 1966; children—Christopher, Tracy. B.S. in Pharmacy, U. Iowa, 1966; M.Pub. Adminstrn., Iowa State U., 1982, postgrad., 1982-83. Faculty Duquesne U., Pitts., 1977; cons. in pharmacy, Colville, Wash., 1978-79; dir. pharmacy Mt. Carmel Hosp., Colville, 1978-79; clin. pharmacist Iowa Vets. Home, Marshalltown, Iowa, 1980-81; instr. Iowa Valley Community Coll., Marshalltown, 1981-83; dir. Iowa Dept. Substance Abuse, Des Moines, 1983—; adj. asst. prof. U. Iowa, Iowa City, 1984—. Mem. Iowa State Bd. Health, 1981-83, v.p., 1982-83; mem. adv. council Iowa Valley Community Coll., 1983—. Mem. Am. Pharm. Assn., Iowa Pharmacists Assn., Marshalltown Pharmacists Assn., AAUW, Alpha Xi Delta, Phi Kappa Phi, Pi Sigma Alpha. Republican. Home: 2801 Woodland Ave West Des Moines IA 50265 Office: Iowa Dept Substance Abuse 507 10th St Des Moines IA 50319

ELLIS, ROBERT GRISWOLD, engineering company executive; b. Kokomo, Ind., Dec. 28, 1908; s. Ernest Eli and Ethel (Griswold) E.; A.B., Ind. U., 1934; m. Rachel O. Burckey, Oct. 27, 1984. Mem. staff Ind. U., Bloomington, 1930-34; researcher Blackett-Sample-Hummert Inc., Chgo., 1934, asst. mgr. merchandising, 1935-36; prodn. mgr. Harvey & Howe, Inc., Chgo., 1936-37; dist. mgr. L.F. Grammes & Sons, Inc., Allentown, Pa., serving Chgo. and Midwest, 1937-45; with Ellis & Co., Chgo. and Park Ridge, Ill., 1945—, pres., chief engr., 1948—, mng. dir., chief engr. Ellis Internat. Co., Chgo. and Park Ridge, Ill., 1965—, chief engr. Ellis Engring. Co., Park Ridge, 1969—. Chmn. Citizens Com. for Cleaner and More Beautiful Park Ridge, 1957-60; trustee, treas. bd. dirs. 1st United Methodist Ch., Park Ridge, 1974-77. Recipient Civic Achievement award City of Park Ridge, 1959. Mem. Soc. Automotive Engrs., Armed Forces Communications and Electronics Assn. (life), Ind. U. Alumni Assn. (life), Quartermaster Assn. (pres. Chgo. chpt. 1957-58), Ind. Acad. Sci., Am. Powder Metallurgy Inst., Ill. Acad. Sci., Mfrs. Agts. Assn. Gt. Britain and Ireland, Internat. Union Comml. Agts. and Brokers, Am. Logistics Assn., Am. Soc. Metals, Indiana Soc. of Chgo. Republican. Clubs: Internat. Trade, Union League, Varsity (pres. Chgo. 1957), Ind. U. Alumni (pres. Chgo. 1956-57). Home: 643 Parkwood St Park Ridge IL 60068 Office: Box 344 306 Busse Hwy Park Ridge IL 60068

ELLIS, WILLIAM GRENVILLE, educational administrator, management consultant; b. Teaneck, N.J., Nov. 29, 1940; s. Grenville Brigham and Vivian Lilian (Breeze) E.; m. Nancy Elizabeth Kempton, 1963; children—William Grenville, Bradford Graham. B.S. in Bus. Adminstrn., Babson Coll., 1962; M.B.A., Suffolk U., 1963; Ed.M., Westfield State Coll., 1965; Ed.D., Pa. State U., 1968; MLE (Sears Roebuck Found. scholar), Harvard U., 1980; IAL, MIT, 1984. Asst. prof. bus. Rider Coll., 1968-69; div. dir., assoc. prof. Castleton State Coll., 1969-72; exec. v.p., prof. Coll. of St. Joseph the Provider, Rutland, Vt., 1972-73; acad. v.p., dean grad. sch. Thomas Coll., Waterville, Maine, 1973-82; pres. Wayland Acad., Beaver Dam, Wis., 1982—; corporator 1st Consumers Savs., 1974-81, Maine Savs., 1981-83; dir. Marine Bank. Auditor, Town of Castleton (Vt.), 1969-71; pres. Kennebec Valley Youth Hockey, Augusta, Maine, 1975-77. Named Cons. of Yr., SBA, 1975, 77; recipient Community Service award Rutland C. of C., 1973. Mem. Am. Psychol. Assn., Nat. Assn. Ind. Schs., Nat. Assn. Intercollegiate Athletics cert. of merit 1979), North Central Assn. Colls. and Secondary Schs., Wis. Assn. Ind. Schs. (pres. 1984-86), Ind. Schs. Assn. Central States, Beaver Dam C. of C. (pres.-elect 1985, pres. 1986), Cum Laude Soc., Alpha Chi, Pi Omega Pi, Alpha Delta Sigma, Delta Pi Epsilon, Phi Delta Kappa Clubs: Madison, Natanis, Old Hickory. Lodge: Rotary. Author: The Analysis and Attainment of Economic Stability, 1963; The Relationship of Related Work Experience to the Teaching Success of Beginning Teachers, 1968; contbr. numerous articles, abstracts to profl. publs. Home: 101 N University Ave Beaver Dam WI 53916 Office: Wayland Acad PO Box 398 Beaver Dam WI 53916

ELLISON, GERALD (GARY) L., advertising executive, entertainer; b. San Francisco, May 24, 1943; s. Olyn G. and Margaret (Gracey) E.; m. Janet A. Wulkan, July 26, 1969; children—Shannon, Mark. B.S., Southwest Mo. State U., 1966. Nightclub entertainer, U.S.A., 1965-72, concert entertainer, 1972—; pres. Gary Ellison Prodns. Inc., Springfield, Mo., 1972—. Cinematographer film: ECCO (Addy award), 1980; TV comml.: Ozark Mountain Country (Addy award), 1981. Pres., Friends of the Zoo, 1978-82, host and exec. producer Telethon, 1984; host Telethon, United Cerebral Palsy S.W. Mo., Springfield, 1980—; bd. dirs. Mus. of Ozarks History, 1985—. Named Mo.'s Ofcl. Ragtime Piano Player, 1973; Gary Ellison Day proclaimed by Gov. Mo., Mar. 3, 1984; recipient 1st Friend of the Sch. award, Springfield Sch. Bd., 1978; Entertainment citation Dept. Def., 1967. Mem. Springfield Assn. Musicians, Am. Advt. Fedn. (nat. govt. relations 1982, chmn. govt. relations 9th dist. 1981), Springfield Advt. Club (Ad Man of Yr., Silver medal 1980). Presbyterian (elder). Clubs: Twin Oaks Country (Springfield); Stockton Yacht (Mo.). Home: 4554 S Roanoke Springfield MO 65807 Office: Gary Ellison Prodns Inc 4564 S Campbell Springfield MO 65807

ELLISON, RICHARD HOWARD, personnel consultant; b. Ft. Wayne, Ind., Jan. 21, 1943; s. Paul F. and Julia Mae (Crabill) E.; m. Nancy Louise Hammond, Aug. 7, 1961; 1 child, Richard Howard. B.S. in Indsl. Mgmt., U. Akron, 1971. Sr. programmer B.F. Goodrich, Akron, 1962-72; project leader U. Akron, Ohio, 1972-75; pres. Sanford Rose & Assocs. (SRA), Youngstown, Ohio, 1975—; speaker Cert. personnel cons. Mem. Nat. Assn. Personnel Cons., N.E. Ohio Assn. Personnel Cons., Ohio Assn. Personnel Cons., Assn. Systems Mgmt. (sec. 1983-85), SRA Dirs. Assn. (sec. 1976-80, pres. 1980-81). Republican. Lodge: Jaycees (bd. dirs. 1975-76) (Akron). Avocations: art collecting; jogging; traveling. Office: SRA 400 Ohio One Bldg Youngstown OH 44503

ELLMANN, SHEILA FRENKEL, investment co. exec.; b. Detroit, June 8, 1931; d. Joseph and Rose (Neback) Frenkel; B.A. in English, U. Mich., 1953; m. William M. Ellmann, Nov. 1, 1953; children—Douglas Stanley, Carol Elizabeth, Robert Lawrence. Dir. Advance Glove Mfg. Co., Detroit, 1954-78; v.p. Frome Investment Co., Detroit, 1980—. Mem. U. Mich. Alumni Assn. Home: 28000 Weymouth St Farmington Hills MI 48018

ELLOS, WILLIAM JOSEPH, priest, philosophy educator; b. Ironwood, Mich., May 15, 1937; s. Simon Francis and Leone Elizabeth (La Fave) E. A.B., St. Louis U., 1961, M.A. in Philosophy, 1962, Ph.L. in Philosophy, 1962, S.T.L. in Theology, 1969, M.A. in Theology, 1970; postgrad. U. Wash., 1966-70; Ph.D. in Philosophy, Pontifical Gregorian U., Rome, 1975. Ordained priest Roman Catholic Ch., 1968. Asst. prof., chmn. dept. philosophy Gonzaga U., Spokane, Wash., 1976-80; asst. prof. Loyola U., Chgo., 1980-83, assoc. prof., 1983—, adj. assoc. prof., 1983—, grad. dir., 1984—; mem. Univ.-wide Com. Values and Ethics, Chgo.; mem. ethics com. VA Hines Hosp., Chgo., St. Mary Nazareth Hosp., Chgo. Author: Thomas Reid's Newtonian Realism, 1981. Contbr. articles to profl. jours. NEH grantee, 1980. Mem. Am. Philos. Assn., Am. Cath. Philos. Assn., Jesuit Philos. Assn., Soc. Health and Human Values, World Congress of Philosophy, Am. Soc. Law and Medicine, Hastings Ctr. Med. Ethics, Am. Acad. Religion, Inst. Ultimate Reality and Meaning. Avocations: music, backpacking. Home: Jesuit Residence Loyola U 6525 N Sheridan Rd Chicago IL 60626 Office: Loyola U of Chgo 6525 N Sheridan Rd Chicago IL 60626

ELMENDORF, HENRY J., auto agency executive; b. Sept. 28, 1922; married; children—Donna, Marcy. Student, St Louis U. With Jim Meagher Chevolet-Oldsmobile of St. Charles, Mo., sec.-treas.; dir. Mercantile Bank of St. Peters, Mo., Chmn. bd. St. Charles Visitor Info. Ctr., Crossroads Econ. Devel. Corp. of St. Charles County, Inc., Mo.-St. Louis Met. Airport Authority, Devel. council St. Joseph Health Ctr. of St. Charles and lay bd. dirs., Lindenwood Coll., St. Charles, St. Louis Symphony, St. Louis Regional Commerce and Growth Assn.; vice chmn. devel. council Archdiocese of St. Louis, Indsl. Devel. Authority of St. Charles County. Named Knight of Malta and Knight of Holy Sepulchre of Jerusalem, Roman Catholic Ch., named Man of the Year, St. Charles C. of C., 1964, 66. Mem. St. Charles C. of C. Lodge: Kiwanis (past pres.). Address: 902 Hawthorne Saint Charles MO 63301

ELMETS, HARRY BARNARD, osteopath, dermatologist; b. Des Moines, Apr. 22, 1920; s. William and Sara Charlotte (Ginsberg) E.; m. Charlotte Irene Musin, Dec. 9, 1945; children—Craig Allan, Steven Kent, Douglas Gregory. B.A., U. Iowa, 1942; D.O. with distinction, Coll. Osteo. Medicine and Surgery, Des Moines, 1946. Intern, Des Moines Gen. Hosp., 1946-47; resident in dermatology Coll. Osteo. Medicine, Des Moines, 1947-52; practice osteo. medicine specializing in dermatology, Des Moines, 1952—; mem. staff Iowa Methodist Med. Ctr., Iowa Lutheran Hosp., Broadlawns Polk County Med. Ctr., Mercy Hosp. Med. Ctr. Clin. prof. dermatology U. Osteo. Medicine and Health Scis., 1947—; vis. prof. dermatology Kirksville Coll. Osteo. Medicine; guest lectr. Coll. Medicine U. Iowa; cons. dermatology VA Med. Ctr., Knoxville, Iowa; mem. Iowa Task Force Venereal Disease. Trustee, bd. dirs. Coll. Osteo. Medicine and Surgery; co-chmn. Des Moines-Polk County Immunization Program; bd. dirs. Des Moines Ctr. Sci. and Industry. Recipient Alumnus Yr. award Coll. Osteo. Medicine and Surgery, 1980. Fellow Am. Osteo. Coll. Dermatology; mem. Am. Osteo. Coll. Dermatology (pres. 1963, 71), Am. Osteo. Bd. Dermatology (chmn. 1962—), Am. Osteo. Assn., Iowa Soc. Osteo. Physicians and Surgeons, Polk County Osteo. Assn. (past pres.), Iowa Acad. Sci., Am. Social Health Assn. (dir. 1968-77), Am. Venereal Disease Soc., Am. Acad. Dermatology, Iowa Dermatol. Soc., Missouri Valley Dermatol. Soc., Minn. Dermatol. Soc. Republican. Jewish. Clubs: Wakonda Country, Embassy (Des Moines); Masons, Shriners. Editorial referee Jour. Am. Osteo. Assn.; editorial bd. CUTIS, 1982—. Home: 4238 Park Hill Dr Des Moines IA 50312 Office: 1010 Midland Financial Bldg Des Moines IA 50309

EL-NAGGAR, AHMED SAMI, civil engineering educator, laboratory and global engineering executive; b. Egypt, Dec. 18, 1926; s. Ahmed Mohammad and Sanya (Hefny) El-N.; m. Janet Eileen Spinn, May 26, 1956; children—Tarik, Rhonda, Jilanne, Kareem. B.S.C.E., U. Cairo (Egypt), 1948; M.S.C.E., U. Calif.-Berkeley, 1951 Ph.D. in Environ. Engring., Purdue U., 1956. Registered profl. engr., Egypt, Ind., Ill. Asst. lectr. Engring. Coll., Cairo, 1949-50; teaching asst. U. Calif.-Berkeley, 1951-53; constrn. engr. C.E., U.S. Army, San Francisco, 1952-56; asst. prof. environ. engring. U. Alexandria, 1956-56; research assoc. Purdue U., 1956-59; design engr. Clyde E. Williams & Assocs., 1959-60; prof. environ. and civil engring. Valparaiso U. (Ind.), 1960—, also pres. No. Labs. and Engring., Inc., 1978—, Global Engring. & Testing Services, Inc., 1981—; cons. Met. San. Dist. Greater Chgo.; vis. prof. High Inst. Pub. Health, Alexandria, 1957-58, Ains Shams U., Cairo, 1958. WHO fellow in san. engring., 1958; recipient Egyptian Govt. award, 1948; NSF grantee, 1962-64, 66-68, 74, 77-79. Mem. Am. Soc. Engring. Edn., ASCE, Am. Water Works Assn., Am. Pub. Works Assn., AAAS, Water Pollution Control Fedn., Ind. Water Pollution Control Assn. (pres. 1970-71, award for outstanding paper 1965), Am. Water Resources Assn., Valparaiso C. of C., Sigma Xi, Chi Epsilon, Mu San, Tau Beta Pi. Lodge: Kiwanis (pres. 1969-70). Contbr. articles profl. jours.; patentee biol. reactor. Office: Valparaiso University Valparaiso IN 46383 also 2400 Cumberland Dr Valparaiso IN 46383

ELROD, ROBERT GRANT, lawyer; b. Indpls., Feb. 24, 1940; s. French McElroy and B. Burrlene (Holland) E.; B.A. with honors, DePauw U., 1962; J.D. cum laude, Harvard, 1965; m. Beverly Anne Wahl, Aug. 23, 1964; children—Franklin Matthew, Benjamin Grant, Jeremiah French, Jonathan Robert. Bar: Ind. 1965. Practice, Indpls.; assoc. firm Elrod, Taylor & Williams, 1965-66; ptnr. Elrod & Elrod, Indpls., 1967-79, Elrod, Elrod & Mascher, Indpls., 1980—; asst. county atty., Indpls., Marion County, Ind., 1967-68, county atty., 1969, asst. atty., city-county legal div., 1970-71, gen. counsel, city-county council, 1972—. Treas., Young Republicans Marion County, 1968-69, sr. v.p., 1969-71, pres., 1971-73; 11th dist. chmn. Ind. Young Rep. Fedn., 1971-74, nat. committeeman, 1975-77; del. Rep. State Conv., 1968, 70, 72, 74, 76, 78; precinct committeeman Rep. party, 1970-78, 84—, ward chmn., 1977-80. Recipient Outstanding Male Young Rep. award Ind., 1972, Marion County, 1974. Mem. Am., Ind. State (chmn. local govt. law sect. 1984), Johnson County, Indpls. bar assns., Am. Judicature Soc., Comml. Law League Am., Am. Acad. Hosp. Attys. Methodist. Mason. Clubs: Columbia (Indpls.); Valle Vista (Greenwood, Ind.). Home: 6730 S Arlington Ave Indianapolis IN 46237 Office: 803 First Ind Bldg Indianapolis IN 46204 also 310 Nat Bank of Greenwood Greenwood IN 46142

EL SAFFAR, RUTH SNODGRASS, educator; b. N.Y.C., June 12, 1941; d. John Tabb and Ruth (Wheelwright) Snodgrass; B.A., Colo. Coll., 1962; Ph.D., Johns Hopkins U., 1966; m. Zuhair M. El Saffar, Apr. 11, 1965; children—Ali, Dena, Amir. Instr. Spanish, Johns Hopkins U., 1963-65; instr. English, Univ. Coll. Baghdad, 1966-67; asst. prof. Spanish, U. Md., Balt. County, 1967-68; asst. prof. U. Ill., Chgo. Circle, 1968-73, asso. prof., 1973-78, prof., 1978-83, research prof. Spanish lit., 1983—; Nat. Endowment for Humanities summer seminar dir., 1979, 82. Woodrow Wilson fellow, 1962; Nat. Endowment for Humanities fellow, 1970-71; Guggenheim fellow, 1975-76; Am. Council Learned Socs. grantee, 1978; Newbery Library fellow, 1982. Mem. MLA (exec. council 1974-78), Am. Assn. Tchrs. Spanish and Portuguese, Midwest MLA, Cervantes Soc. Am. Author: Novel to Romance: A Study of Cervantes' Novelas Ejemplares, 1974; Distance and Control in Don Quixote, 1975; Cervantes' Casamiento engañoso and Coloquio de los perros, 1976; Beyond Fiction, 1984. Home: 7811 Greenfield River Forest IL 60305 Office Dept Spanish U Ill Chicago IL 60680

ELSBACH, HENRY GEORGE, pediatric dentistry educator, pediatric dentist; b. Hamburg, Germany, Dec. 3, 1931, came to U.S. in 1936, naturalized 1941; s. Kurt Joe and Hanna (Wolf) E.; m. Mary Janice Rheinkender, Oct. 20, 1973; children—Amelia, Theresa. B.S., U. So.Calif., 1956; D.D.S., Chgo. Coll. Dental Surgery, 1958; cert. pediatircs, State U. Iowa, 1960. Intern Michael Reese Hosp., Chgo., 1958-59; practice dentistry specializing in pediatric dentistry, Alton, Ill., 1960—; assoc prof. pediatric dentistry So. Ill. U., Alton, 1978—. Presenter numerous profl. confs., 1962—. Contbr. articles to profl. jours. Fellow Am. Acad. Pediatric Dentists; mem. ADA, Soc. Dentistry Children, Ill. State Dental Soc., Madison Dist. Dental Soc. (chmn. peer rev. 1980—), Madison County Econ. Opportunity Commn. (v.p. 1963), Greater St. Louis Health Systems Agy. Lodge: Rotary (pres. 1974). Home: 4308 Briar Cliff Dr Alton IL 62002 Office: 2305 State St Alton IL 62002

ELSBERND, HELEN AGNES, college dean; b. Calmar, Iowa, Jan. 15, 1938; d. Alois and Loretta (Kuennen) E.; B.A., Viterbo Coll., 1965; M.S., U. Ill., 1967, Ph.D., 1969; postgrad. Harvard U., 1979. Tchr., Sacred Heart Sch., Eau Claire, Wis., 1959-62; tchr. sci. and math. St. Francis High Sch., Provo, Utah, 1963-65; research fellow U. Ill., Urbana, 1966-69, summer 70-72, tchg. asst., 1968-69; mem. chemistry faculty Viterbo Coll., LaCrosse, Wis., 1969-75, dept. chairperson, 1970-75, acad. dean, 1976—, Title III Coordinator, 1975-76; vis. prof. U. Wis., Madison, 1975; cons. Regional Sem. Project, Milw., 1981. Contbr. articles to profl. jours. NIH, fellow, 1967-69; Bush Found. fellow, 1979; named Woman of Yr. Bus. and Profl. Women, 1984. Mem. Am. Assn. Higher Edn., Nat. Assn. Women Deans, Adminstrs., and Counselors, North Central Assn. Acad. Deans, Soc. Higher Edn., Greater LaCrosse C. of C. (bd. dirs. 1984—, ambassador 1982—, com. chmn. 1983—). Office: Viterbo Coll 815 S 9th St LaCrosse WI 54601

ELSTEIN, ARTHUR SHIRLE, psychologist, educator, consultant; b. Chgo., July 30, 1935; s. Aaron and Rae Esther (Glick) E.; m. Rochelle Sue Berger, June 19, 1960; children—Elana Judith, Aaron Solomon, David Jacob. B.A., U. Chgo., 1953, M.A., 1956, Ph.D., 1960. Diplomate Am. Bd. Psychology. Staff psychologist Presbyn. St. Luke's Hosp., Chgo., 1960-65; from clin. instr. to clin. asst. prof. psychiatry U. Ill., Chgo., 1960-65; staff psychologist Mass. Mental Health Ctr., 1965-68; research assoc. psychology Harvard Med. Sch., Cambridge, 1965-68; from assoc. prof. to prof. Office Med. Edn. Research and Devel., Mich. State U., East Lansing, 1968-84, acting dir., 1974-75, dir., 1976-79; prof. Ctr. for Ednl. Devel., U. Ill., Chgo., 1984—; vis. prof. med. edn. Hebrew U.-Hadassah Med. Sch., Jerusalem, 1973, 1984; vis. prof. dept. health services, mem. Ctr. for Analysis of Health Practices Harvard Sch. of Pub. Health, Cambridge, Mass., 1975-76; mem.-at-large Nat. Bd. Med. Examiners, Phila., 1984—; edn. adv. com. Nat. Fund for Med. Edn., Hartford, Conn., 1976-79; biomed. library rev. com. Nat. Library Medicine, Bethesda, Md., 1980-83; cons. Josiah Macy Jr. Found., N.Y.C., 1982-83. Author: (with others) Renal Function and Renal Failure, 1965, Clinical Decision Analysis, 1980; Medical Problem Solving, 1978; contbr. articles to profl. jours. Recipient Disting. Faculty award Mich. State U., 1982. Mem. Soc. Med. Decision Making (pres. 1981-82), Am. Edn. Research Assn. Office: Ctr for Ednl Devel 808 S Wood St Chicago IL 60612

ELSTER, TOBY, petroleum geologist, oil company executive, planning and financial consultant; b. Calipatria, Calif., Feb. 15, 1923; s. Jack and Pauline (Gelles) E.; m. Mary M. Benest, 1949 (div. 1975); children—Marc, Louis, Paulette; m. T. Alayne Corbell, Jan. 28, 1979. B.S. in Bus. Adminstrn., Wichita State U., 1948, B.A. in Geology, 1950. Staff geologist, Nat. Coop. Refining Assn., Wichita, 1953-55, Petroleum, Inc., Wichita, 1955-56; cons., Wichita, 1956-68, 70—; sr. v.p. exploration Acme Oil Corp., Wichita, 1968-70. Author articles. Wing comdr CAP, Wichita, 1968-70, mem. CAP, 1965—. Served to capt. USAFR, 1942-83. Mem. Soc. Ind. Profl. Earth Scientists (service award 1970, 72, chmn. Wichita chpt. 1970, nat. dir. 1971-72), Am. Assn. Petroleum Geologists, Kans. Geol. Soc., Soc. Exploration Geophysicists, Rocky Mountain Geol. Soc., Am. Arbitration Assn., Alumni Assn. Wichita State U. (life), VFW (life). Clubs: Petroleum, Cosmopolitan (Wichita). Lodges: Moose, Elks. Home: PO Box 18628 SE Station Wichita KS 67218-0628 Office: Pan-Western Petroleum Inc One Twenty Bldg 501 Wichita KS 67202

ELSWICK, JERRY CLARENCE, poet, pharmacist; b. Pike County, Ky., Oct. 19, 1931; s. John Robert and Carmen Forest (Maynard) E. B.S. in Pharmacy, Ohio State U., 1963. Registered pharmacist, Ohio. Pharmacist Gray Drug Fair div. of Sherwin Williams Co., Columbus, Ohio, 1963—. Author numerous poems. Patentee billiard cue with guide member, 1970. Served with U.S. Army, 1953-55. Mem. Am. Pharm. Assn., Ohio State Pharm. Assn., Acad. Am. Poets, Delta Phi Alpha. Democrat. Avocations: boating, swimming. Office: Gray Drug Fair 2772 Maysville Pike Zanesville OH 43701

ELVIN-LEWIS, MEMORY PATIENCE FREDRIKA, educator microbiology, researcher; b. Vancouver, B.C., Can., May 20, 1933; came to U.S. 1955; d. Richard James and May Winnifred (Foster) Elvin; m. Walter Hepworth Lewis, Feb. 2, 1957; children—Memoria Florence Richenda May Lewis, Walter Hepworth Jr. B.A. in Micro-Genetics, U. B.C., 1952; M.Sc. in Med. Microbiology, U. Pa., 1957; M.Sc. in Virology-Epidemiology, Baylor Med. Sch., 1960; Ph.D. in Med. Microbiology, U. Leeds, Eng., 1966. Bacteriologist Pearson Tb Hosp., Vancouver, B.C., 1953-55; research assoc. Stephen F. Austin U., Nacogdoches, Tex., 1960-62; instr. Washington U., St. Louis, 1966, asst. prof. botany, 1966-67, adj. prof. biology, 1980—, asst. prof. microbiology, 1967-70, assoc. prof., 1970-81, prof., 1981—. Co-author: Medical Botany 1977; contbr. chpts. to books. Mem. Internat. Assn. Dental Research (chmn. micro-immunology 1981-82), Am. Assn. Dental Schs. (chmn. Microbiology sect. 1973-74), Am. Soc. Microbiology, Nat. Council Internat. Health. Avocations: gourmet cooking; antique collecting. Home: 7915 Park Dr Saint Louis MO 63117 Office: Washington U Sch Dental Medicine 4559 Scott Ave Saint Louis MO 63110

ELWOOD, WILLIAM R., educator; b. Smith Center Kans., July 25, 1935; s. Cecil J. and Alice Naoma (Shook) E.; m. Margaret Mee Elwood, May 20, 1961 (div. 1979); children—Coleen, Molly, Simeon, Graham; m. Diane Hass, May 27, 1982. B.A., Western Wash. U., 1957, B.A. in Edn. 1957; M.A., State U. Iowa, 1961; Ph.D., U. Oreg., 1966. Tchr. high schs., 1957-62; lectr. Western Wash. U., Bellingham, Wash., 1962-63; prof. U. Wis.-Madison, 1967—. Fulbright Hays Fulbright grantee, 1966-67, 75-76. Mem. Am. Theatre Assn., Brecht Soc. Democrat. Avocations: piano, squash. Home: 4467 Crescent Rd Madison WI 53711 Office: 6173 Vilas Hall U Wis Madison WI 53706

ELY, WAYNE HARRISON, broadcast engr.; b. Alliance, Ohio, Aug. 31, 1933; s. Dwight Harrison and Mable Evellen (Jones) E.; student Mount Union Coll., 1955-56, Ohio U., 1956-62; m. Roslyn Rose Ambrose, June 14, 1964 (div. Nov. 2, 1981); children—Eric (dec.), Kevin, Gayle, Mitchell. Transmitter engr. Sta. WOUB-AM-FM, Ohio U., Athens, 1958-62; studio field engr. ABC, N.Y.C., 1962-66, 67-72; studio engr. CBS, N.Y.C., 1966-67; transmitter supr. Sta. WOUC-TV, Ohio U., Quaker City, 1972—; tchr. radio tech. Ohio U., Zanesville. Served with C.E., U.S. Army, 1952-54. Mem. Soc. Broadcast Engrs. (sr. broadcast engrs. cert.). Home: 3705 Woodland Dr Zanesville OH 43701 Office: WOUC-TV Route 3 Quaker City OH 43773

ELZINGA, RICHARD JOHN, entomologist, educator; b. Salt Lake City, Apr. 23, 1931; s. John and Hildur (Ekberg) E.; m. Agnes Lewis, Sept. 9, 1957; children—Mark Richard, Tanya Lynn, Jasmin, Nathan Eric, Natalie. B.S., U. Utah, 1955, M.S., 1956, Ph.D., 1960. Postdoctoral fellow U.S. Army Biol. Labs., Frederick, Md., 1960-61; from asst. prof. to prof. entomology Kans. State U., Manhattan, 1961—; prof. U. Minn., Lake Itasca, summers 1981-83. Author: Fundamentals of Entomology, 1977; Fundamentals of Entomology, 2d edit., 1981; also articles. Active Boy Scouts Am. Manhattan, 1961-84; bishop Mormon Ch., Manhattan, 1968-71; high council Topeka Kans. Stake, 1972-81. Served with U.S. Army, 1952-54. NSF grantee, 1962-69. Mem. Entomol. Soc. Am. (Teaching award 1980), Central States Entomol. Soc. (pres. 1965), Acarological Soc. Am., Sigma Xi, Phi Kappa Phi, Phi Sigma. Avocation: photography. Office: Kans State U Dept Entomology Manhattan KS 66506

EMAD, PARVIS, philosophy educator; b. Teheran, Iran, Sept. 4, 1935; s. Mostafa and Tahereh (Houman) E.; m. Gertrude Josepha Schindler, June 25, 1962; children—Mitra, Mona, Eric. Ph.D., U. Vienna, 1966. Mem. faculty De Paul U., Chgo., 1967—, prof., 1978—; dir. Collegium Phaenomenolgieum, 1984. Austrian Ministry of Culture scholar, 1963-66; grantee NEH, 1985. Mem. Soc. for Phenomenology and Existential Philosophy, Hegel Soc. Am., Conf. of Heidegger Scholars, Metaphys. Soc. Am. Author: Heidegger and the Phenomenology of Values, His Critique of Intentionality, 1981; contbr. revs., articles to profl. jours.; contbg. editor Philosophisches Literaturanzeiger; co-editor Heidegger Studies, 1985. Office: 2323 N Seminary Ave Chicago IL 60614

EMANUEL, JOSEPH TROY, JR., industrial engineering educator, consultant; b. El Paso, Tex., June 17, 1941; s. Joseph Troy and Fay (Culpepper) E.; m. Barbara Ann Kott, Aug., 1, 1970; children—Karen, Brian, Roger. B.S., U. N.Mex., 1963; M.S., Ohio State U., 1965, Ph.D., 1968. Research asst. Ohio State U., Columbus, 1963-67; asst. prof., then assoc. prof. Bradley U., Peoria, Ill., 1967—, chmn. dept. indsl. engring., 1975—; cons. Motorola Semi-condr. Products Div., 1973-74, Peoria Police Dept., 1976-78, Caterpillar Tractor Co., Peoria, 1978—. Contbr. articles to profl. jours. Recipient Putnam Award for Excellence in Teaching Bradley U., 1982. Mem. Inst. Indsl. Engrs. (chpt. pres. 1978-81), Human Factors Soc., Am. Soc. Engring. Educators (Dow Outstanding Young Engring. Faculty award 1978). Methodist. Avocations: basketball; bowling; scouting. Office: Coll of Engring and Tech Bradley U Peoria IL 61625

EMBREE, CHARLES MONROE, minister, development executive; b. Monroe County, Mo., May 26, 1935; s. Melvin R. and Dora E. (McGee) E.; m. Joyce L. Worner June 12, 1955; children—David E., Timothy C., Stephen M. B.A., Lincoln Christian Coll., 1958, M.A., 1967. Ordained to ministry, Christian Ch., 1958. Minister Akers Chapel Ch. of Christ, Plainville, Ill., 1958-63, minister Athens Christian Ch., Ill., 1963-69, First Christian Ch., Clarence, Mo., 1969-80; dir. devel. Central Christian Coll. of Bible, Moberly, Mo., 1980—, dir. 1970-80; pres., dir. Central Mo. Christian Evangelizers, Columbia, Mo., 1984—. Contbr. articles to profl. jours. Democrat. Avocation: photography. Home: Rt 3 Box 80-S Moberly MO 65270 Office: Central Christian Coll PO Box 70 Moberly MO 65270

EMDE, RICHARD K., insurance agent; b. Indpls., Sept. 21, 1938; s. Herman C. and Kathren (Devaney) E.; m. Doris Thompson, Sept. 9, 1961; children—Christine Louise, Gregg Alan. B.Sc., Ohio U., 1960. Chartered fin. cons. Agt., Union Central Life, Dayton, Ohio, 1962-71; asst. gen. agt. New Eng. Life, Dayton, 1971-72, gen. agt., St. Louis, 1972—, exec. com. gen. agts., 1984-85. Mem. Life Underwriters (bd. dirs. 1978-81), Chartered Life Underwriters, Million Dollar Round Table (life, gen. agts. mgmt. award), Gen. Agents Assn. (bd. dirs. 1981-83). Republican. Presbyterian. Office: New England Fin Services 999 Executive Pkwy St Louis MO 63141

EMDEN, NARVIN IRA, savings and loan executive, lawyer; b. Cin., Nov. 5, 1921; s. Leo and Elizabeth (Orlin) E.; m. Ruth Cohen, June 4, 1950; children—Lisa, Craig, Faith, Julie. B.B.A., U. Cin., 1948, J.D., 1949. Bar: Ohio. Dir. Foundation Savings & Loan Assn., Cin., 1948—, mng. officer, exec. v.p., 1949-79, pres., 1979—; dir. Savs. and Loan League S.W. Ohio, Cin., 1972-74, pres. bd. dirs., 1974; dir. Ohio Savs. and Loan League, Columbus, 1982—. Pres. Garfield Place Citizens Assn., Cin., 1972. Served with U.S. Army, 1942-46, PTO. Recipient Kovod award Jewish Community Ctr., Cin., 1961, Life Membership award, 1984. Mem. Ohio Bar Assn., Cin. Bar Assn. Jewish. Avocations: golf; tennis; swimming. Home: 3160 Longmeadow Ln Cincinnati OH 45236 Office: Foundation Savings & Loan Co 719 Vine St Cincinnati OH 45202

EMERING, EDWARD JOHN, insurance brokerage executive, actuary; b. N.Y.C., June 14, 1945; s. Edward John and Antoinette (Imperato) E.; m. Sandra Ann Troutmann, July 11, 1981; children—Whitney, Scott, Eric. B.A. in Econs., Seton Hall U., 1967; M.B.A. in Fin., U. Utah, 1970; M. Taxation, DePaul U., 1985. Enrolled actuary. Mgmt. trainee Prudential, Newark, 1970-72; sr. cons. Becker Co., East Orange, N.J., 1972-75; sr. actuary William Mercer Co., Detroit, 1976-77; mgr. Coopers & Lybrand, Chgo., 1977-79; ptnr. Touche Ross & Co., Chgo., 1979-85; sr. v.p. Johnson & Higgins, ins. and human resource cons., 1985—. Contbr. articles to publs. in field. Served to lt. USN, 1967-70. Decorated Navy Cross, Nat. Order (Republic of Vietnam); recipient hon. sci. award Bausch & Lomb, 1964. Fellow Am. Soc. Pension Actuaries; mem. Am. Acad. Actuaries, Internat. Actuarial Assn., Am. Mgmt. Assn., Chgo. Assn. Commerce and Industry. Club: East Bank (Chgo.). Office: Johnson & Higgins 101 N Wacker Dr Chicago IL 60606

EMERING, SANDRA ANN, actuary; b. Chgo., Sept. 12, 1949; d. Adrian Douglas and Marie (Wojnowiak) Troutman; m. Edward John Emering, July 11, 1981; 1 son, Daniel T. B.S. in Math., U. Ill., 1970. Enrolled actuary. Mgr. CNA Ins. Co., Chgo., 1970-75; pension actuary Reed Ramsey, Inc., Oakbrook, Ill., 1975-77, Kemper Life Ins. Co., Long Grove, Ill., 1977-78; actuary Karel & Assocs., Northbrook, Ill., 1979-80; pres. Consulting Actuarial Group, Northfield, 1981—. Adviser Northfield Community Ch., 1982. Mem. Am. Acad. Actuaries, Am. Soc. Pension Actuaries, Women in Mgmt., Nat. Assn. for Female Execs., Inc., Chgo. Council on Foreign Relations, Nat. Assn. of Women Bus. Owners, Smithsonian Assocs. Republican. Congregationalist. Clubs: Chgo. Actuarial, East Bank (Chgo.). Office: Cons Actuarial Group 778 Frontage Rd Northfield IL 60093

EMERSON, WILLIAM, congressman; b. St. Louis, Jan. 1, 1938; s. Norvell Preston and Marie (Reinemer) E.; B.A., Westminster Coll., Fulton, Mo., 1959; LL.B., U. Balt., 1964; m. Jo Ann Hermann, June 21, 1975; children—Victoria Marie, Katherine Rebekah; children by previous marriage—Elizabeth, Abigail. Spl. asst. to U.S. Rep. Robert F. Ellworth, 1961-65; adminstrv. asst. to U.S. Rep./Senator Charles McC. Mathias, Jr., 1965-70; dir. govt. relations Fairchild Industries, Germantown, Md., 1970-74; dir. public affairs Interstate Natural Gas Assn., 1974-75; exec. asst. to chmn. Fed. Election Commn., Washington, 1975; dir. fed. relations TRW Inc., Washington, 1975-79; pres. William Emerson & Assocs., govt. relations cons., De Soto, Mo., 1980; mem. 97th-99th Congresses from 10th Mo. Dist. Capt. USAF Res. Republican. Presbyterian. Home: 1310 Lexington Cape Girardeau MO 63701 Office: 418 Cannon Office Bldg Washington DC 20515

EMERSON VAN SCHAAK, GAIL, advertising executive; b. Milw., May 22, 1948; d. Grant Rife and Evangeline Adel (Bartels) Emerson; m. Harding Van Schaack, Sept. 20, 1975. J.B.A., U. Wis.-Madison, 1970, M.S., 1972. Editor, Miller Pub. Co., Mpls., 1974-76; coordinator telephone communications products div. 3M, St. Paul, 1976-79, sr. markets communications coordinator data recording products div., 1979-81, markets communications supr. med. products div., 1981—. Mem. Bus. Profl. Advt. Assn. (Oliver awards chmn. 1981). Avocations: cross-country skiing, canoeing. Office: Med Products Div 3M Bldg 224-55-01 St Paul MN 55144

EMERY, CHARLES CHRISTIAN, JR., hospital executive; b. Pitts., Oct. 11, 1946; s. Charles C. and Gloria V. (Nuttridge) E.; m. Nancy J. Falk, Nov. 5, 1966; children—Charles Christian III, Sandra J. B.S. in Mech. Engring., U. Pitts., 1968, M.S., 1973, M.B.A., 1982. Engr. Avco Lycoming, Bridgeport, Conn., 1968-69, Westinghouse, Pitts., 1969-70; systems mgr. U. Pitts., 1970-71; v.p. Monsour Hosp., Jeannette, Pa., 1971-73; assoc. exec. dir. St. Elizabeth Hosp., Youngstown, Ohio, 1973—; adj. faculty Youngstown State U., 1981—, Kent State U., Ohio, 1982—. Mem. Am. Coll. Hosp. Adminstrs., Healthcare Fin. Mgmt. Assn. Methodist. Clubs: Youngstown Country, Oak Tree Country (West Middlesex, Pa.). Office: St Elizabeth Hosp Med Ctr Park and Belmont Ave Youngstown OH 44501

EMERY, KATHLEEN LOUISE, insurance company executive, statistician; b. Toledo, Apr. 28, 1948; d. Arthur Bernard and Marie (Obarski) Szymanowski; m. Byron Elwyn Emery, Dec. 14, 1974. B.Edn., U. Toledo, 1970, M.Ed., 1974. Tchr. sci. and math. Toledo Bd. Edn., 1970-71; coll. adminstr. U. Toledo, 1971-77; statis. analyst Blue Cross of N.W. Ohio, Toledo, 1978-79, mgr. health econs., 1979-82, dir. health services, 1982-85; asst. v.p., 1985—; loaned exec. Bur. of Surveillance and Utilization Rev. Ohio Dept. Pub. Welfare, Columbus, 1984. Mem. Am. Statis. Assn., Am. Mgmt. Assn., Phi Kappa Phi. Club: Zonta. Avocations: dressage, horse training. Home: 2714 Barrington Dr Toledo OH 43606 Office: Blue Cross of NW Ohio 3737 Sylvania Ave Toledo OH 43656

EMERY, MARIE THERESE, association executive; b. St. Louis, Sept. 27, 1933; M.A., U. Detroit, 1955; M.A., Mich. State U., 1965, Ph.D., 1969. Leader, Siena Heights Coll. Lansing bd. Girl Scouts U.S., 1983; prin. St. Antoninius Sch., Cin., 1956-60; coordinator practice teaching programs Mich. State U., East Lansing, 1960-73; dept. head Gabriel High Sch., Lansing, Mich., 1960-73; dir. Mich. Fleet Safety Program, Mich. Dept. Budget and Mgmt., Lansing, 1974; cons. Motorcycle Safety Found., Washington, 1975; dir. Rose A. Clark Sch. at Lansing Ice Arena, 1975-78; exec. dir. Mich. Women For Hwy. Safety, East Lansing, 1973; Mich. rep. Hwy. Safety Leaders, 1973—. active in traffic safety, including coordinator task forces to solve traffic safety problems, organizer citizen's support for edn. in hwy. traffic safety. First aid instr. ARC. Recipient Profl. of Yr. award Mich. Safety Conf., 1979; award for Excellence, Exxon Corp., 1979, 80; citation for vol. services VFW, 1979; Disting. Achievement award Mich. Driver and Traffic Safety Edn. Assn., 1981, Diana award, 1982, grantee, 1973; Mich. Office Hwy. Safety Planning grantee, 1976, 79. Mem. NEA, 99's, Airplane Owners and Pilots Assn., Mich. Safety Conf., Adrian Dominican Community, Mich. Farm Bur., Mich. Women for Hwy. Safety. Democrat. Roman Catholic. Clubs: Zonta, Gruman Airplane. Author: Pedestrian Safety Guide, 1980; Mich. Women for Hwy. Safety Bull., 1973-84; Management Guide, 1982, Basic Computer Guide, 1983. Home: 3142 Lake Lansing Rd East Lansing MI 48823 Office: Room 66 Kellogg Center Hwy Traffic Safety Center Mich State U East Lansing MI 48824

EMINGER, ANDREA, pharmaceutical company advertising executive; b. Cleve., Jan. 16, 1949; d. Andrew Cyril and Helene Eleanor (Deutsch) Vidra; m. Ronald Clifford Eminger, Feb. 15, 1974; children—Kristina Leigh, Andrew Scott. B.A., Notre Dame Coll., Cleve., 1972. Advt. prodn. mgr. Cook United, Cleve., 1973-75, Wattenmaker Advt., Cleve., 1981-82, Gray Drug Fair, 1982—. Editor Euclid Presch. PTA newsletter, 1979-81. Mem. Advt. Prodn. Club, Internat. Plastic Modelers Soc. Democrat. Roman Catholic. Avocations: knitting; reading; carpentry; photography. Home: 85 E 280th St Euclid OH 44132 Office: Gray Drug Fair Inc 666 Euclid Ave Cleveland OH 44114

EMMENS, DAVID PECK, lawyer; b. Ashland, Ohio, Apr. 9, 1948; s. Merrill Lovering and Elizabeth Arlene (Peck) E.; A.B. cum laude, Kenyon Coll., 1970; J.D., Ohio State U., 1973. Bar: Ohio 1984. Sec. Shelby Printing Inc., Ohio, 1978—; v.p., gen. counsel IPBS Inc., Shelby, 1979—; sec. First Travel Service Inc., Worthington, Ohio, 1980-84; asst. gen. counsel Shelby Mut. Ins. Co., 1980—; sec. Travel Assoc. Inc., Columbus, Ohio, 1983-84; dir. Shelby Printing Inc. Pres. Richland Alt. Program, Mansfield, Ohio, 1980-83; dist. chmn. Johny Appleseed council Boy Scouts Am., 1981—. Mem. Ohio State Bar Assn. (bd. govs. corp. counsel sect. 1984—). Avocations: sailing, scuba diving, flying. Home: 645 Yale Dr Mansfield OH 44907 Office: Shelby Mut Ins Co 175 Mansfield Ave Shelby OH 44875

EMMERICH, JAMES CHARLES, athletic trainer, coach; b. New Ulm, Minn., Mar. 18, 1911; s. Charles and Bertha (Keckeisen) E. B.S., S.D. State Coll., 1940. Asso. prof. phys. edn., coach of track and field, also cross country, trainer S.D. State Coll. Brookings, 1940-60; phys. therapist Drs. Dooley Clinic, Pomona, Calif., 1962; vis. lectr. Eastern Mich. U., Ypsilanti, 1966, Calif. Western U., San Diego, 1968. Am. Specialist U.S.A. State Dept., 1961. Coach track and field; trainer, adminstrv. asst. Amateur Athletic Union of U.S.A., U.S. Olympic com., 1956—; state leader Pres.'s Council Phys. Fitness. Served with AUS, 1942-46. Named S.D. Coll. Coach of Year, 1954; elected to Helms Hall Track and Field Coaches Hall Fame, N. Central Collegiate Athletic Hall Fame, S.D. State U. Athletic Hall Fame, S.D. Sports Hall Fame, S.D. Cowboy and Western Heritage Hall of Fame; recipient Disting. Service award S.D. State U. Jackrabbit Club, 1977. Mem. Nat. Athletic Trainers Assn., Internat., U.S. track coaches assns., Assn. U.S. Army, Am. Legion, 40 and 8, DAV, S.D. State U. Alumni Assn. (charter mem. Campanile Soc. 1985), U.S. Olympic Soc., Brookings C. of C. (Community Service award 1981), S.D. High Sch. Activities Assn. (disting. service award 1982), Am. Turners, Blue Key, Phi Kappa Phi, Alpha Zeta, Pi Gamma Mu. Conglist. Clubs: Elks (Elk of Yr. award 1977, S.D. Elk of Yr. award 1983), Lions. Address: Gen Delivery Brookings SD 57006

EMMONS, LARRY LEON, city official, personnel consultant; b. Sublette, Ill., Apr. 17, 1941; s. Cecil Paul and Evelyn Elizabeth (Vivian) E.; m. Janet Sue Apland, Aug. 5, 1967. B.S. in Art Edn., Ill. State U., 1964; M.S. in Art Edn., No. Ill. U., 1974. Art tchr. Dist. 220, Polo, Ill., 1970-73; edn. specialist in art, Ill. Office Edn., Springfield, 1973-75; asst. prof. No. Ill. U., DeKalb, 1975-77; personnel mgr. E.D. Etnyre & Co., Oregon, Ill., 1978-82; personnel dir. City of Rockford, Ill., 1982—. Grant rev. panelist Ill. Arts Council, 1985—; bd. dirs., 2d v.p. Rockford Art Mus. 1985—; bd. dirs. ARTS, Inc., Rockford, 1983-85; co-chmn. civic div. United Way, Rockford, 1983-85; chmn. Arts Alliance Ogle County, Oregon, Ill., 1976-80. Served with USN, 1966-70. Recipient Cert. of Recognition, Am. Legion, 1981, Cert. of Commendation, Ill. Job Service, 1980-81. Mem. Am. Soc. Personnel Adminstrn., Rockford Area Personnel Assn., Nat. Pub. Employer Labor Relations Assn., Ill. Pub. Employer Labor Relations Assn., Internat. Assn. for Quality Circles, Ogle County Personnel Assn. (pres. Oregon 1981-82). Presbyterian. Club: Rotary. Avocations: building handcrafted sports cars; travel. Office: City of Rockford 425 E State St Rockford IL 61104

EMMONS, LILLIAN (LIN) M(ILLER), nutritionist, consultant; b. New Westminster, B.C., Can., Apr. 6, 1932; came to U.S., 1957, naturalized, 1963; d. Alfred and Kirstine Miller; m. Hamilton Emmons, Aug. 29, 1959; children—Robert, Lisa, Susie. B.Home Econs., U. B.C. (Can.), Vancouver, 1954; M.S. in Nutrition, U. Man. (Can.), 1957; Ph.D. in Nutrition, U. Minn., 1962; M.S. in Health Scis. Edn., Case Western Res. U., 1981, doctoral candidate in med. anthropology, 1982—. Teaching asst. in nutrition U. Man., U. Minn., 1955-58; therapeutic dietitian U. Sask. (Can.) Hosp., Saskatoon, Mt. Sinai Hosp., Mpls., Perth Amboy (N.J.) Hosp., 1956-65; sr. research assoc. Grad. Sch. Nutrition, Cornell U., Ithaca, N.Y., 1969-72; nutrition cons. Opinion Research Corp., Princeton, N.J., 1976—; nutritional cons. Comprehensive Psychiat. Services, Beachwood, Ohio, 1982—; cons. appetite disorders, health scis. edn. Bd. dirs. health systems agy. serving various counties, Ohio, 1976-82; mem. Ohio Health Coordinating Council. Gen. Foods Fund fellow, 1958-59. Mem. Soc. Nutrition Edn., Am. Dietetic Assn., Can. Dietetic Assn., Am. Anthropol. Assn., Soc. Med. Anthropology, Sigma Xi, Omicron Nu. Contbr. articles to profl. jours. Home: 2925 Broxton Rd Shaker Heights OH 44120 Office: Comprehensive Psychiat Services 24075 Commerce Park Rd Beachwood OH 44122

EMORD, DEBORAH SUSAN, nurse, artist; b. Brockton, Mass., Nov. 12, 1952; d. Ernest Alfred and Jeanette Alys (Walker) E. B.A., So. Ill. U.-Carbondale, 1974; Assoc. Degree in Nursing, Parkland Coll., 1983. R.N. Free lance artist, 1974—; artist, Cogitations, Gifford, Ill., 1983—; nurse Burnham Hosp., Champaign, Ill., 1983—, Carle Hosp., Urbana, Ill., 1984—. Artist and author children's books: Isabelle Pearl, 1981, Nathanael's Rainbow, 1982; artist polit. mag. Views, 1980. Mem. Alpha Omega. Roman Catholic. Home: 105 W Center St Gifford IL 61847 Office: Cogitations 106 S Main Ave Gifford IL 61847

EMPSON, CYNTHIA SUE, retail executive, nurse; b. Mpls., May 29, 1947; d. Charles and Mary Jane (Levernier) Wiersch; m. Charles Lee Empson, Oct. 8, 1970; children—Stacey Renee, Stepanie Lea. R.N., Mastin Sch. Nursing, Mobile, Ala., 1968. R.N. Charge nurse Research Hosp., Kansas Cit, Mo., 1968-70; nurse Raytown Clinic, Mo., 1970-72; mgr./buyer Mardee's Clothing Store, Independence, Kns., 1982-83, owner/buyer, 1983—; office nurse, Independence, 1972—. Mem. Riley PTA, Independence, 1974-82, pres., 1976-77; pres. PTA City Council, 1979-80; active Neewollah, Inc., Independence, 1975-82; chair comml. div. drive Community Chest, 1982, bd. dirs., 1984—; city chmn. Mental Health Fund Dr., 1979; mem. bd. Unified Sch. Dist. 446, 1983-84, pres., 1984—; bd. dirs. Tri County Spl. Edn. Coop., Independence, 1981—, v.p., 1982-83, pres., 1983—; mem. SEK Med. Aux., 1975—, pres., 1979-80; mem. SEK Lutherans Assn. Republican. Club: PEO (Independence). Avocations: tennis; reading. Home: PO Box 848 Independence KS 67301

EMRICK, CHARLES ROBERT, JR., lawyer; b. Lakewood, Ohio, Dec. 19, 1929; s. Charles R. and Mildred (Hart) E.; m. Lizabeth Keating; children—Charles R. III, Caroline K. B.S., Ohio U., 1951, M.S., 1952; J.D., Cleve. State U., 1958. Bar: Ohio 1958. Ptnr. Calfee, Halter & Griswold, Cleve., 1965—; lectr. U. Services Bus. Ctr., John Carroll U., 1970—; dir. Best Sand Co., Gt. Lakes Lithograph, Clamco Corp., Cleve. Motive Products, Inc., Hunter Mfg. Co., Ken-Mac Metals, Kirkwood Industries, S & H Industries, Somerset Techs., Inc., Wedron-Silica Sand Co. Former trustee, br. bd. chmn. YMCA; former officer, trustee Lake Erie Jr. Nature and Sci. Ctr.; former adj. prof. Baldwin Wallace U., Chartered Life Underwriters Assn.; former adj. lectr. Case Western Res. U.; trustee Rocky River Pub. Library, Cleve. Area Devel. Fin. Corp., Fairview Gen. Hosp.; prin. nat. policy adv. com. New Eng. Mut. Life Ins. Co.; mem. vis. com. Cleve. State Law Sch.; bd. dirs. N.E. chpt. Am. Cancer Soc. Republican. Methodist. Clubs: Westwood Country (sec., legal counsel), Union, Cleve. Yachting, The Clifton. Office: Calfee Halter & Griswold 1800 Central Nat Bank Bldg Cleveland OH 44114

EMRICK, DONALD DAY, chemist; b. Waynesfield, Ohio, Apr. 3, 1929; s. Ernest Harold and Nellie (Day) E.; B.S. cum laude, Miami U., Oxford, Ohio, 1951; M.S., Purdue U., 1954, Ph.D., 1956 Grad. teaching asst. Purdue U., Lafayette, Ind., 1951-55; with chem. and phys. research div. Standard Oil Co. Ohio, 1955-64, research asso., 1961-64; cons., sr. research chemist research dept. Nat. Cash Register Co., Dayton, Ohio, 1965-72, chem. cons., 1972—. Mem. AAAS, Am. Chem. Soc., Phi Beta Kappa, Sigma Xi. Patentee in Field. Contbr. articles to profl. jours. Home: 4240 Lesher Dr Kettering OH 45429

ENAS, GREGORY GEORGE, statistician, medical researcher; b. Berkeley, Calif., Mar. 7, 1956; s. Jeffrey George and Dorothy Marian (Gilmore) E. B.S., Biola Coll., 1978; Ph.D., Va. Commonwealth U., 1982. Sr. statistician Lilly Research Labs., Indpls., 1982—. Minister Agape Fellowship, Indpls., 1985. Mem. Am. Statis. Assn., Biometrics Soc., Soc. Clin. Trials, Sigma Xi (assoc.). Avocations: musical composition; performance. Home: 1222 N Central Ave Indianapolis IN 46202 Office: Lilly Corp Ctr MC730 22/3 Indianapolis IN 46285

ENDERS, GEORGE LEONHARD, JR., microbiologist; b. Glendale, N.Y., Nov. 13, 1945; s. George Leonhard and Mathilda (Novak) E.; m. Maria Guadalupe Villarreal, Aug. 9, 1969; children—Margaret Ann, George L., Katherine Patricia, Robert Charles, Steven James. B.A., Rutgers U., 1967; M.A., Immaculate Heart Coll., Los Angeles, 1971; Sc.D., U. Kans., 1974. Research assoc. Food Research Inst., Madison, Wis., 1974-77; research scientist Microbiology dept. Ames div. Miles Labs., Elkhart, Ind., 1977-79, immunology dept., 1979-80, sr. research scientist food microbiology and biotechnology, 1980-83, staff scientist dairy and agrl. fermentation research, 1984-85, sr. staff scientist dairy and agrl. fermentation research, 1985—. Contbr. articles to sci. jours. Treas., Old Mill Homeowners Assn., Elkhart, Ind., 1980—; cubmaster Boy Scouts Am., 1981-84. Recipient N.J. State Scholarship award, 1963-67, NIH Predoctoral award, 1971-74, Nat. Inst. Environ. Health Sci. Postdoctoral award, 1975-76. Mem. Am. Soc. Microbiology (pres. Ind. br. 1983-84, councillor 1984—), Inst. Food Microbiologists, Soc. Indsl. Microbiology, Am. Assn. Animal Sci. Roman Catholic. Avocations: Woodworking, swimming, sports. Home: 22797 Bainbridge Dr Elkhart IN 46514 Office: Miles Labs 1127 Myrtle St Elkhart IN 46515

ENDRES, JOSEPH GEORGE, food products company executive; b. Chgo., Aug. 15, 1932; s. Joseph and Johanna (Schranz) E.; m. Barbara Ruth Nehls, Sept. 7, 1959; children—Elizabeth, Joseph, Kurt. B.S. in Chem. Engring., U. Ill., 1955, Ph.D. in Food Sci., 1961. Research chemist Armour Co., Chgo., 1961-64, asst. dir. food research, 1964-70; v.p. CFS Continental Co., Chgo., 1970-72; dir. research Central Soya Co., Chgo., 1972-84, dir. corp. research, Ft. Wayne, Ind., 1984—; adj. prof. U. Ill., Urbana, 1975—. Contbr. chpts. to books, articles to profl. jours. Patentee food products and food engring. Active local Boy Scouts Am., 1973-78. Mem. Am. Oil Chemists Assn. (treas. 1971-73), Inst. Food Technologists. Republican. Office: Central Soya PO Box 1400 Fort Wayne IN 46801

ENDRES, RICHARD WILLIAM, administrator camp for handicapped, consultant; b. Faribault, Minn., Dec. 9, 1927; s. Raymond Godfrey and Marie (Savoie) E.; m. Jeanne Marie Christenson, Apr. 22, 1954; children—Deborah, Richard, Timothy, Patrick, Michael, Kyung, Jeffrey. B.A. in English, St. John's U., M.Ed. in Therapeutic Recreation, U. Minn. Recreation dir. Faribault State Hosp., 1950-60; patient program supr. Brainerd State Hosp., 1960-67; founder, dir. Camp Confidence, Brainard, 1967—; advisor, originator Camp Confidence Celebrity Classic, 1974—; advisor Camp Confidence Found., 1980—; chmn. child devel. com. Brainerd Community Coll., 1978—. Contbr. articles to profl. jours. Mem., chmn. St. Francis Parish Council, Brainerd, 1971-81; mem. Outstanding Citizen Yr. Com., Brainerd, 1975-82. Served to cpl. U.S. Army, 1950-52. Mem. AAHPERD, Am. Legion, Brainerd C. of C. Roman Catholic. Lodges: K.C., Eagles, Moose. Avocations: racquetball, golf, tennis, fishing, hunting, woodworking. Home: 407 N 2nd St Brainerd MN 56401 Office: Camp Confidence E Oak St Brainerd MN 56401

ENDRESS, JEFFREY CRAIG, lawyer; b. Cleve., June 26, 1954; s. Richard Roy and Judith Ann (Hacha) E.; m. Tina Ann Morris, Sept. 10, 1977; 1 child, Jason Edward. B.A., Ind. U., 1976; J.D. cum laude, Cleve.-Marshall U., 1980. Bar: Ohio 1980, U.S. Dist. Ct. (no. dist.) Ohio 1981. Ptnr. Endress & Endress, Cleve., 1980—. Mem. ABA, Ohio Bar Assn., Assn. Trial Lawyers Am. Methodist. Lodge: Kiwanis. Office: Endress & Endress 17119 Madison Ave Lakewood OH 44107

ENGEL, ALBERT J., federal judge. U.S. cir. judge U.S. Ct. Appeals Sixth Cir., Mich. Office: US Ct Appeals Federal Bldg Grand Rapids MI 49502*

ENGEL, DOUGLAS ARTHUR, accounting firm executive; b. Shawano, Wis., Sept. 16, 1950; s. Charles Arthur and Jermain (Schultz) E.; m. Linda Irene Hauk, Sept. 5, 1970; 1 child, Christopher. B.B.A., U. Wis.-Oshkosh, 1972. C.P.A., Wis. Staff acct. Deloitte Haskins & Sells, Milw. 1972-77, mgr., 1978-82, ptnr., 1983—. Moderator capital formation Gov.'s Conf. on Small Bus., 1980-81; treas. Lt. Gov. Russ Olson Reelection Campaign, 1982; co-treas. Kohler for Gov. Campaign, 1982. Mem. Wis. Assn. Mfg. and Commerce (mem. small bus. adv. council 1980-82), Ind. Bus. Assn., Wis. Venture Group, Nat. Assn. Accts. (treas. Milw. chpt. 1981-82, v.p. 1983-85, bd. dirs. 1978-85), Wis. Inst. C.P.A.s, Am. Inst. C.P.A.s. Republican. Methodist. Clubs: Tuckaway Country, Wisconsin. Avocations: golf, hunting, fishing, flying. Office: Deloitte Haskins & Sells 1920 Marine Plaza Milwaukee WI 53202

ENGEL, HOWARD ANDREW, insurance executive; b. Chgo., Nov. 13, 1932; s. Emanuel M. and Rose (Vein) L.; m. Sydney Ida Markel, Dec. 15, 1957; children—Mark Richard and Dean Kenneth. B.S.C., Roosevelt U., 1954. With estate planning dept. Conn. Gen., Chgo., 1957; claims supr. U.S. Fidelity & Guaranty Co., Chgo., 1957-62; account exec., mgr. employee benefits Assoc. Agys., Chgo.; mgr. State Mutual Life Assurance Co. Gen. Agy., Chgo., 1962-71; sr. v.p. Robert M. Schrayer Co. and RMSCO Mgmt. Services, Chgo., 1971-84; exec. v.p. Mesirow/Chas. U. Victor Ins. Services div. Mesirow Fin. Services, Inc., Chgo., 1984—. Served with U.S. Army, 1954-56. Office: Mesirow Chas U Victor Ins Services 350 N Clark St Chicago IL 60610

ENGEL, RICHARD CARL, JR., plastic packaging manufacturing executive, financial advisor; b. Manitowoc, Wis., May 2, 1942; s. Richard Carl and Sybil Elizabeth (Aulik) E.; m. Joan Marie Engel, Jan. 7, 1962; children—Rick, Corinna, Turk, Jason. B.B.A. in Acctg., U. Wis., 1964. C.P.A., Wis. Pub. acct. Ronald Mattox & Assocs., Madison, Wis., 1964-72; treas. and controller Placon Corp., Madison, 1972-75, v.p. fin. and treas., 1975—; pres. BonFaire Am., Inc., Madison, 1982—; dir. Instant Housing, Inc. Bd. dirs. Madison Civic Repertory Theatre; mem. Gov.'s Adv. Commn. Small Bus. Mem. Nat. Assn. Accts., Soc. Plastics Industry, Sales and Mktg. Execs., Wis. Inst. C.P.A.s. Club: Rotary. Patentee Blister Box Display Package, 1977. Home: 1107 Rutledge St Madison WI 53701 Office: 6096 McKee Rd Madison WI 53711

ENGELHARDT, DIANE MARY, light and power company official; b. Postville, Iowa, Sept. 9, 1956; d. Rachel Kathleen (Connor) E. B.A. in Criminal Justice Adminstrn., Mount Mercy Coll., 1978. Security supr. Duane Arnold Energy Ctr., Iowa Electric Light & Power Co., Cedar Rapids, Iowa, 1978—;

v.p. Hawkeye Security & Services, Cedar Rapids, 1982—. Mem. Am. Mgmt. Assn., Midwest Nuclear Security Assn. Roman Catholic. Avocations: boating, arts and crafts. Home: 1067 Juniper Dr SW Cedar Rapids IA 52404

ENGLAND, ROBERT CLEYTON, optometrist, contact lens accessory manufacturer; b. Columbus, Ohio, Jan. 30, 1941; s. Dennis Cleyton and Louella May (Rush) E.; m. Anne-Marie Baker, Sept. 18, 1964; children—Kirk Alan, Keith Andrew, Kristen Elaine. B.S. in Optometry, Ohio State U., Dr. Optometry, 1967. Diplomate Am. Bd. Optometry. Gen. practice optometry, Bellevue, Ohio, 1967-78, Zanesville, Ohio, 1978—; owner, mgr. Ophthalmic Arts Lab., Bellevue, 1972-74; pres. DMV Corp., Zanesville, 1977—; clin. instr. Ohio State U., Columbus, 1975-78. Patentee in field. Bd. dirs. St. John's Lutheran Zanesville, 1980—, Goodwill Industries, 1982—, YMCA, 1983—; pres. Samaritan Counseling Ctr., Zanesville, 1982-84; assoc. bd. dirs. Bethesda Hosp., Zanesville, 1983—. Mem. Ohio Optometric Assn. (sec. zone 5 1979—), Am. Optometric Assn. Republican. Lodges: Kiwanis (pres. Bellevue 1972), Rotary (pres. Zanesville 1983). Avocations: photography, flying, graphic art, canoeing, computer programming.

ENGLAND, ROBERT EUGENE, religion educator, minister; b. Bedford, Pa., June 30, 1941; s. John Clyde and Maxine Daisy (Price) E.; m. Marilyn Kay Hofacker, July 6, 1963; children—Joanna, Rebecca, Daniel, Robert, Kristin. Th.B., God's Bible Sch. and Coll., Cin., 1963; M.A., Cin. Bible Sem., 1984, postgrad., 1984—. Ordained to ministry Methodist Ch., 1974. Pastor, Wesleyan Meth. Ch., Murrysville, Pa., 1963-67, Beaver Falls, Pa., 1969-72, Limaville, Ohio, 1972-80; instr. Salem Bible Coll (Ohio), 1967-73, Allegheny Wesleyan Coll., Salem, 1973-80, God's Bible Sch. Coll., Cin., 1980—; dir., adviser Brinkhaven Enterprises, Inc., North Lawrence, Ohio, 1979—. Contbr. articles to religious publs. Mem. Wesleyan Theol. Soc. Avocation: Landscaping. Home: 1834 Josephine St Cincinnati OH 45219

ENGLE, MICHAEL JEAN, biochemist; b. St. Louis, Mar. 22, 1947; s. John Dauphin and Josephine Agnes (Colombini) E.; m. Jacquelyn Anne Textor, Sept. 3, 1983. A.B. in Biology, St. Louis U., 1969, Ph.D. in Biochemistry, 1976. Chemist Sigma Chem. Co., St. Louis, 1969-70; postdoctoral fellow, State U. Utrecht, The Netherlands, 1976-77, W. Alton Jones Cell Ctr., Lake Placid, N.Y., 1977-78; asst. scientist dept. pediatrics U. Wis.-Madison, 1978-83, assoc. scientist, 1983—; affiliate scientist Wis. Regional Primate Ctr., Madison, 1981—. Contbr. chpts. to books, articles to sci. jours. Served with U.S. Army, 1970-71. Recipient Research Career Devel. award Nat. Inst. Child Health and Human Devel., 1980-85; research grantee NIH, 1981-86, U. Wis. Med. Sch., 1984, Juvenile Diabetes Assn., 1979-81. Mem. Am. Soc. Biol. Chemists (assoc.), AAAS, Am. Oil Chemists Soc., Am. Chem. Soc. Roman Catholic. Avocations: cross-country skiing, woodworking, tennis, gardening, bird-watching. Office: Clin Scis Ctr H4-432 600 Highland Ave Madison WI 53792

ENGLEHART, DANIEL LEE, manufacturing company executive; b. Grove City, Pa., Jan. 10. 1952; s. William Allen and Joann (Latshaw) E.; m. Gail Ann Long, Aug. 4, 1972; children—Danelle Lynn, Joshua Michael. Student, Slippery Rock U. (Pa.), 1970-72. Fitter, G.A.T.X., Masury, Ohio, 1973-75, estimator inspector, 1975-76, foreman, 1977-79, lead foreman, 1979-80, gen. foreman, 1980-84; gen. mgr. Develco Tool and Stamping, Inc., Warren, Ohio, 1984—. Recipient Cert., Wis. Protective Coating Corp., 1980, Youngstown State U., 1981, G.A.T.X., 1982, Value Analysis Inc., 1982. Mem. Mahoning Valley Indsl. Mgmt. Assn., Am. Welding Soc. Avocations: Hunting, camping. Home: 340 N Maple St Mercer PA 16137 Office: Develco Tool and Stamping Inc 1000 University St NE Warren OH 44483

ENGLER, JOHN MATHIAS, state senator; b. Mt. Pleasant, Mich., Oct. 12, 1948; s. Mathias John and Agnes Marie (Neyer) E.; B.S. in Agrl. Econs., Mich. State U., 1971; J.D., Thomas M. Cooley Law Sch., 1981; m. Colleen House, Apr. 5, 1975. Mem. Mich. Ho. of Reps., 1971-78; mem. Mich. Senate, 1979—, Republican leader, 1983, majority leader, 1984—. Bd. dirs. Mich. State U. Agr. and Natural Resources Alumna; del. White House Conf. on Youth, 1972. Recipient Disting. Service to Agr. award Mich. Agr. Conf., 1974; named Legislator of Yr., Police Officers Assn. Mich., 1981; One of 5 Outstanding Young Men of Mich., Mich. Jaycees, 1983. Mem. Nat. Conf. State Legislators. Republican. Roman Catholic. Club: Detroit Economic. Office: Box 30036 State Capitol Lansing MI 48909

ENGLER, PHILIP, materials scientist; b. N.Y.C., Jan. 5, 1949; s. Samuel and Selma (Cohen) E.; m. Shelley Falb, July 7, 1973; children—Daniel, Seth. B.S., Cornell U., 1970; M.S., Northwestern U., 1972, Ph.D., 1978. Tech. service scientist Johnson & Johnson, Chgo., 1972-74; analytical scis. project leader Standard Oil Co. Ohio, Cleve., 1978-83, analytical scis. group leader, 1983—. Served to capt. USAR. Mem. Am. Chem. Soc., Soc. Plastics Engrs. (dir. engrng. properties and structures div. 1980-83), Sigma Xi, Tau Beta Pi, Acacia. Contbr. articles to tech. lit. Office: Sohio Research Center 4440 Warrensville Center Rd Cleveland OH 44128

ENGLEY, FRANK B., JR., microbiologist, educator; b. Wallingford, Conn., Oct. 26, 1919; s. Frank B. and Anne (Brown) E.; m. Beatrice Winslow Doak, June 26, 1948; children—Karen Winslow, Elizabeth Ann, Heather Cooke, Frank B. III. B.S., U. Conn., 1941; M.S., U. Pa., 1944, Ph.D., 1949; postgrad. Johns Hopkins U., 1946-47. Diplomate Am. Bd. Microbiology. Research technician Atwater Animal Disease Labs., Storrs, Conn., 1938-41; asst. instr. microbiology U. Pa. Sch. Medicine, 1941-44; research microbiologist U.S. Govt., 1946-50; assoc. prof. bacteriology and parasitology, cons. microbiologist Univ. Hosps., U. Tex. Med. Br., 1950-55; prof. microbiology, chmn. dept. U. Mo. Sch. Medicine, 1955-77, asst. dean, 1955-60, prof., acting chmn. dept. pub. health and preventive medicine, 1960-61; vis. prof. Lagos, Nigeria, 1974, Tripoli, Libya, 1979; cons. in field, 1954—; cons Armed Forces Epidemiological Bd.; mem. council Nat. Inst. Allergy and Infectious Diseases. . Served with AUS, 1944-46. Recipient Civil Service award, 1948; Osteon Faculty award U. Tex. Med. Br., 1954; Commonwealth Fund research and travel award, Switzerland, 1965-66; SAMA Faculty Teaching award, 1970; commendations U.S. Army, 1946, VA, NASA, 1977. Fellow AAAS, Am. Pub. Health Assn. (chmn. lab. sect. 1968, pres. Mo. br. 1964), Am. Acad. Microbiology; mem. Am. Soc. Microbiology (sec.-treas. Tex. 1953-55, pres. Mo. 1959), Research Soc. Am., AMA (affiliate), Royal Soc. Health, Am. Inst. Biol. Scis., AAUP, Soc. Exptl. Biology and Medicine, N.Y. Acad. Scis., Am. Assn. Med. Colls., Soc. Indsl. Microbiology, Assn. Advancement Med. Instrumentation, Inst. Environ. Scis., Conf. State and Provincial Lab. Dirs., Inst. Infectious Diseases, Assn. Practitioners Infection Control, Sigma Xi. Author: Pocket Reference Guide to Medical Microbiology, 1963; Persistence of Microorganisms, 1963; Advanced and Elementary Laboratory Manuals for Medical Microbiology, 1965; also numerous articles. Mem. editorial bd. Jour. Bacteriology, Health Lab. Sci., Cytobios and Microbios, Hygiene and Medizin (Germany). Home: 609 Westmount Ave Columbia MO 65203

ENGLISH, FLOYD LEROY, telecommunications executive; b. Nicolaus, Calif., June 10, 1934; s. Elvan Leroy and Louise (Corliss) E.; m. Wanda Parton, Sept. 8, 1955 (div. 1980); children—Roxane, Darryl; m. Elaine Ewell, July 3, 1981; 1 dau., Christine. A.B. in Physics, Calif. State U.-Chico, 1959; M.S., Ariz. State U., 1962, Ph.D., 1965. Div. supr. Sandia Labs., Albuquerque, 1965-73; gen. mgr. Rockwell Internat. Collins, Newport Beach, Calif., 1973-75; pres. Darcom, Albuquerque, 1975-79; cons., 1979-80; v.p. U.S. ops. Andrew Corp., Orland Park, Ill., 1980-82, pres., 1982-83, pres., chief exec. officer, 1983—, also dir. Served to 1st lt. U.S. Army, 1954-57. Mem. IEEE. Republican. Presbyterian. Avocations: flying; skiing. Office: Andrew Corp 10500 W 153d St Orland Park IL 60462

ENGLUND, JANET LYNN, lawyer; b. St. Paul, Nov. 17, 1953; d. Curtis John and Priscilla Ruth (Widen) E. B.A., Trinity Coll., 1975; J.D., Hamline U., 1978. Bar: Minn. 1979, U.S. Dist. Ct. Minn. 1979. Admitting clk. Luth. Deaconess Hosp., Mpls., 1975-76; law clk. O'Connor & Hannan, Mpls., 1978-79; assoc. Kuduk & Walling, Mpls., 1979-80; fin. analyst, atty. Fed. Land Bank, St. Paul, 1980-81, fin. services coordinator, 1981-82; fin. planning analyst, mgr. IDS/Am. Express, Mpls., 1982-83, regional mgr. fin., 1983-84, mgr. analysis plans devel., 1984-85, mgr. sales devel., 1985—; lectr. fin. planning, 1978—; sole practice law, Mpls., 1979—. Editor Hamline U. Law Rev. Contbr. articles to profl. jours. Vol., dist. coordinator United Way of Mpls., 1981-82, 71; musician local/regional chs., 1971—. Hamline U. Legal Research scholar, 1978. Mem. Christian Legal Soc., Cert. Fin. Planners, Internat. Assn. Fin. Planners, ABA, Ctr. for Law and Religious Freedom, Sigma Nu Phi. Republican. Baptist. Club: Christian Bus. Women's. Home: 5546 Donegal Dr Shoreview MN 55112 Office: IDS/Am Express IDS Tower Minneapolis MN 55402

ENGWALL, JAMES LARUE, health care services company executive, consultant; b. Chgo., Dec. 26, 1939; s. Harry Leonard and Violet Dorothy (Johnson) E.; m. Lola Mae Anderson, May 9, 1964; children—Bradley, Brent, Karna. B.A. in Econs., North Park Coll., 1963. Credit mgr., data processing mgr. Swedish Covenant Hosp., Chgo., 1963-67; data processing mgr., cost acct., budget dir. Swedish Hosp., Rockford, Ill., 1967-71; bus. mgr., news dir. Arctic Broadcasting, Inc., Nome, Alaska, 1971-80; risk mgr. Swedish-Am. Corp., Rockford, 1980—. Chmn., Collection Agy. Licensing Bd., Occupational Licensing div. Alaska Dept. Commerce and Econ. Devel., 1975-80; pres., treas., bd. dirs. Pub. Sch. Dist. Bd. Edn., Nome, 1975-80. Recipient Nat. Spot News Coverage award AP, 1974-75. Mem. Am. Soc. for Hosp. Risk Mgmt., Am. Hosp. Assn., Risk and Ins. Mgmt. Soc., Inc. (pres. chpt., speaker ann. confs.), Nat. Fire Protection Assn. Contbr. stories and photos to AP, CBS News; writer, producer, narrator 2 CBS Radio network shows (Dateline Am.); developer computerized systems in field. Home: 5008 David Dr Rockford IL 61108 Office: Swedish Am Corp 1400 Charles St Rockford IL 61101

ENKE, CHRISTIE GEORGE, chemistry educator, consultant; b. Mpls., July 8, 1933; s. Alvin Christie Enke and Mae Eileen (Ferris) Nichols; m. Mary Crane, June 23, 1956; children—Paul F., David M., Anne. B.A., Principia Coll., 1955; Ph.D., U. Ill., 1959. Instr., then asst. prof. Princeton U., 1959-66; assoc. prof., then prof. chemistry Mich. State U., East Lansing, 1966—. Author: Electronics and Instrumentation, 1982. Patentee in field. Sloane Found. fellow, 1969. Fellow AAAS, Am. Chem. Soc. (chmn. div. of computers; Chem. Instrumentation award 1974); mem. Am. Soc. Mass Spectrometry, IEEE. Episcopalian. Avocation: stained glass. Office: Mich State U Dept Chemistry East Lansing MI 48824

ENLUND, E. STANLEY, savings and loan association executive. Chmn., chief exec. officer, dir. First Fed. Savings and Loan Assn. of Chgo. Office: First Federal Savings and Loan Assn of Chgo One S Dearborn St Chicago IL 60603*

ENNEKING, RONALD LEO, finance executive, controller; b. Batesville, Ind., Apr. 7, 1953; s. Alphonse Arthur and Edna Marie (Flaspohler) E.; m. Sandra Kay Forsgren, Dec. 30, 1978; 1 son: Jason Michael. B.S. in Acctg. with distinction, Ind. U., 1975; postgrad. in mktg. Xavier U., 1979-84. C.P.A., Ind. Staff acct. Crowe Chizek & Co., C.P.A.s, Elkhart, Ind., 1975-77; treas., controller Elkhart Motor Car Co., Inc. (Ind.), 1977-78; fin. exec. Batesville Casket Co., Inc. (Ind.), 1978-83, controller, 1983-85, controller wood div., Nashua, N.H., 1985—. Pres. St. Louis Parish Bd. Edn., Batesville, 1983-84; house gov. Ind. U. Wright Quad-Lowe House, Bloomington, 1972-73. Mem. Nat. Assn. Accts., Ind. C.P.A. Soc. Democrat. Roman Catholic. Club: Hillcrest Golf and Country (Batesville).

ENNENBACH, JOSEPH PETER, lawyer; b. LaSalle, Ill., Sept. 12, 1948; s. Peter James and Marjorie Catherine (Scholle) E.; m. Maryann Fahlander, Oct. 16, 1982; 1 child, Laura. A.A., Ill. Valley Community Coll., 1968; B.S., U. Ill., 1970; J.D., John Marshall Law Sch., 1980. Bar: Ill. 1980. Asst. states atty. LaSalle County, Ottawa, Ill., 1980-84; ptnr. Gearhart & Ennenbach, LaSalle, 1984; sole practice law, La Salle, 1985—. Voting mem. Stage 212 Community Theater, LaSalle, 1974; bd. dirs. Easter Seal Soc. La Salle County, United Way of Ill. Valley, LaSalle. Mem. ABA, Ill. Bar Assn., LaSalle County Bar Assn. Republican. Roman Catholic. Home: 1204 Pike St Peru IL 61354 Office: 328 Bucklin LaSalle IL 61301

ENNIS, THOMAS MICHAEL, national health agency administrator; b. Morgantown, W.Va., Mar. 7, 1931; s. Thomas Edson and Violet Ruth (Nugent) E.; student W.Va. U., 1949-52; A.B., George Washington U., 1954; J.D., Georgetown U., 1960; m. Julia Marie Dorety, June 30, 1956; children—Thomas John, Robert Griswold (dec.). Subrogation-arbitration examiner Govt. Employees Ins. Co., Washington, 1956-59; asst., legis. analyst to v.p. pub. affairs Air Transport Assn. Am., Washington, 1959-60; dir. ann. support program George Washington U., 1960-63; nat. dir. devel. Project HOPE, People to People Health Found., Inc., Washington, 1963-66; nat. exec. dir. Epilepsy Found. Am., Washington, 1966-74; exec. dir. Clinton, Eaton, Ingham Community Mental Health Bd., 1974-83; nat. exec. dir. Alzheimer's Disease and Related Disorders Assn., Inc., Chgo., 1983—; clin. instr. dept. community medicine and internat. health Georgetown U. Sch. Medicine, 1967-74; adj. asso. prof. dept. psychiatry Coll. Medicine, Mich. State U., 1975—; lectr. Univ. Ctr. for Internat. Rehab., Mich. State U., 1977—; cons. health and med. founds., related orgns.; cons. Am. Health Found., 1967-69, Reston, Va.-Georgetown U. Health Planning Project, 1967-69; mem. adv. bd. Nat. Center for Law and Handicapped; advisor Nat. Reye's Syndrome Found.; mem. Pres.'s Com. on Employment Handicapped, Internat. Bur. Epilepsy, Nat. Com. for Research in Neurol. Disorders; mem. nat. adv. bd. Developmental Disabilities/Tech. Assistance System, U. N.C. Nat. del. trustee, v.p. Nat. Capitol Area chpt., bd. dirs., exec. com. Nat. Kidney Found., 1969—, pres., 1972—, nat. trustee, 1970-74; bd. dirs. Western Inst. Epilepsy, 1969-72, Nat. Assn. Pvt. Residential Facilities for Mentally Retarded, Epilepsy Found. Am.; bd. dirs., v.p. Epilepsy Center Mich.; bd. dirs., pres. Mich. Mid-South Health Systems Agy.; mem. nat. adv. bd. Handicapped Organized Women, Charlotte, N.C., 1984—; v.p. nat. bd. Nat. Assn. for the Accidentally Disabled, 1983—. World Rehab. Fund fellow, Norway, 1980. Mem. Nat. Rehab. Assn., Am. Public Health Assn., Nat. Epilepsy League (dir.), Mich. Assn. Community Mental Health Bd. Dirs. (pres.), AAAS, Phi Alpha Theta, Phi Kappa Psi. Contbr. articles on mental health and health care to profl. jours. Home: 726 W Junior Terr Chicago IL 60613 Office: Alzheimer's Disease and Related Disorders Assn Inc 70 E Lake St Chicago IL 60601

ENRIGHT, GARY JAMES, institute adminstrator; b. Mobridge, S.D., June 5, 1939; s. Thomas Abraham and Marie Gertrude (Scherer) E.; m. Constance Jeanette Ottum, Sept. 22, 1962 (div. 1980); children—Kim, Kathleen; m. Felice Stockert, June 5, 1982; stepchildren—Bradley, Michael, Patrick. News dir. KTIV-TV, Sioux City, Iowa, 1962-66; mgr. Market News Found., Sioux City, 1966-70; adminstrv. dir. S.D. Farm Bur., Huron, 1970-76; mgr. pub. affairs N.W. Pub. Service, Huron, 1976-82; pres. Insight Devel. Inst., Grand Forks, N.D., 1982—. Author: Leadership Communications, 1984. Author radio series. Recipient George Washington Honor medal Freedoms Found., 1978; Chem-Agra award Chem. Mfg. of Am., 1983. Mem. Nat. Speakers Assn., Nat. Assn. Farm Broadcasters, Grand Forks C. of C. (chmn. 1984-85). Republican. Roman Catholic. Lodge: Elks. Avocation: carving; reading; woodworking. Home: Rt 8 Box 4320 Rapid City SD 57702 Office: PO Box 5777 Rapid City SD 57709

ENSLEN, RICHARD ALAN, See *Who's Who in America,* 43rd edition.

ENTRIKEN, ROBERT KERSEY, JR., newspaper editor, motorsport writer; b. Houston, Feb. 13, 1941; s. Robert and Jean (Finch) (stepmother) E.; married, 1972; div., 1982; 1 child, Jean Louise. Student Sch. Journalism, U. Kans., 1961-69. Gen. assignment reporter Salina Jour., Kans., 1969-71, motorsport columnist, 1970-83, courts reporter, 1971-82, Sunday editor, 1972-75, spl. sects. editor, 1975—; sr. editor Sports Car Mag., Santa Ana, Calif., 1972—; motorsport columnist Motorsports Monthly, Tulsa, Okla., 1983—; operator Ikke Så Hurtig Racing. Served with USN, 1969-71, Guam. Mem. Am. Auto Racing Writers and Broadcasters Assn. (gen. v.p. 1982—, Midwest v.p. 1980-82), Sigma Delta Chi, Sports Car Club Am. (Best Story award 1972, 73, 76, 77, 78, 83, 84; Solo Cup nat. award 1981; Solo Driver of Yr. Wichita region 1976, 1982, Solo Champion, Kans. 1978, 84, Midwest div. 1984). Club: Tri-Rivers Running. Avocations: sport car racing; autocrossing; running; skiing. Home: 1513 Pershing Salina KS 67401 Office: The Salina Journal 333 S 4th PO Box 740 Salina KS 67402

ENYART, WILLIAM L., lawyer, educator; b. Pensacola, Fla., Sept. 22, 1949; s. William L. and Alta (Dallas) E.; m. Annette A. Eckert, Mar. 12, 1983; 1 child, James David. B.A. in Journalism and Polit. Sci., So. Ill. U., 1974, J.D., 1979. Bar: Ill. 1979, Mo. 1980, U.S. Dist. Ct. (so. dist.) Ill. 1979. Ptnr. Levy, Levy, & Enyart, Caseyville, Ill., 1979-83; sole practice, Belleville, Ill., 1983—; instr. bus. law Belleville Area Coll., 1980—. Committeeman, Monroe County Democratic Central Com., Waterloo, Ill., 1982-84. Served with USAF, 1969-73, USNG, 1982—. Mem. Assn. Trial Lawyers Am., Ill. State Bar Assn., St. Clair County Bar Assn., Mo. Bar Assn., N.G. Assn. of U.S. Clubs: Oak Hill Racquet, YMCA (Belleville); Monroe County Democrat (Waterloo). Lodges: Masons, Shriners. Home: 9 Oak Knoll Pl Belleville IL 62223 Office: 12 S Second St Belleville IL 62220

ENZLER, JEROME ANTHONY, museum director; b. Washington, Aug. 12, 1951; s. Clarence Joseph and Kathleen (Crowley) E.; m. Katherine Mary Fischer, Oct. 6, 1973; children—Rebekah, Jason, James, Elizabeth. B.A. in Acctg., Loras Coll., 1973; M.A. in Mus. Studies, SUNY-Cooperstown, 1979. Dir. of mus. Dubuque County Hist. Soc., Iowa, 1977—; co-founder Woodward Miss. Riverboat Mus., Dubuque, 1979. Roman Catholic. Lodge: Rotary. Office: Dubuque County Hist Soc PO Box 305 Dubuque IA 52001

EPPLEY, ROBERT JAMES, JR., municipal administrator; b. Youngstown, Ohio, Jan. 26, 1921; s. Robert J. and Louise Maguerite (Rose) E.; m. Joan Elaine Fortney, Dec. 27, 1942; children—Robert J. III, William L., Elaine L. Hand, John L. B.A., Ohio State U., 1942. City mgr. City Washington (Ohio), 1946-47; village mgr. Village of Greendale (Wis.), 1947-50; purchasing agt. Johnson Rubber Co., Middlefield, Ohio, 1951-57; village mgr. Village of Palatine, Ill., 1957-60; city mgr. City of Northlake, Ill., 1960-61; village mgr. Village of Lombard, Ill., 1961-63; exec. v.p. Homebuilders Assn. Chicagoland, Oak Brook, Ill., 1963-65; city mgr. City of Wheaton, Ill., 1965-71; village mgr. Village of Mt. Prospect, Ill., 1971-78, Village of Skokie, Ill., 1979—; council pres. City of Middlefield, 1951, mayor, 1952-54. Served to 1st lt. AUS, 1942-45; ETO. Mem. Ill. City Mgmt. Assn. (pres. 1970-71). Methodist. Lodges: Rotary (pres. Middlefield 1951-52), Shriners. Home: 8214 Laramie Ave Skokie IL 60077

EPPS, DAVID CURTIS, insurance association executive; b. Oklahoma City, Mar. 26, 1945; s. Curtis Howard and Marie (Jones) E.; m. Bonnie J. Clark, Feb. 23, 1980. B.A. in Bus. Adminstrn., Central Methodist Coll., 1967. Underwriter Fireman's Fund Ins. Co., St. Louis, 1970-75; loss control rep., 1975-78; risk mgmt. supr. City of Columbia (Mo.), 1978-81; exec. dir. Mo. Intergovtl. Risk Mgmt. Assn., Columbia, 1981—; v.p. assn., 1982-84, pres. pooling sect., 1983-84, bd. dirs. pooling sect., 1983—, all Pub. Risk and Ins. Mgmt. Assn. Active Citizens Com. for Right to Keep and Bear Arms, Columbia. Served to sgt. U.S. Army, 1968-70. Decorated Bronze Star, Air medal, Army Commendation medal; recipient Disting. Service award City of Columbia Fin. Dept., 1981. Mem. Am. Soc. Safety Engrs., Am. Pub. Power Assn. (risk mgmt. and ins. com. 1982—), Pub. Risk Ins. Mgmt. Assn., Internat. Platform Assn., Nat. Rifle Assn. Club: Columbia Ski. (bd. dirs.) Contbr. articles to profl. jours. Office: Mo Intergovtl Risk Mgmt Assn 310 Tiger Ln Columbia MO 65203

EPPS, ROBERT LYLE, state agency administrator; b. Harrisonville, Mo., Oct. 14, 1941; s. Robert Lyle and Charlotte Mary (Ely) E.; m. Anita Maxine Johnson; children—Renee Christine, Benjamin Robert. B.A., Washburn U., 1965; M.P.A., U. Kans., 1970; cert. health care adminstrn., U. Ala., 1972. Bus. mgr. Kans. Neurol. Inst., Topeka, 1972-74; sr. fiscal analyst Kans. State Legislature, Topeka, 1974-79; dir. planning Div. State Planning, Topeka, 1979-80; prin. budget analyst Div. Budget, State of Kans., Topeka, 1980-83, dir. adminstrn. dept. health and environment, Topeka, 1980—; cons. Nebr. Dept. Adminstrn., Lincoln, 1979-80. Author: (govt. report) Budget in Brief, 1982-83. Editor (govt. report) Kansas State Investment Practices, 1980. Treas. Shawnee County Mental Health Ctr., Topeka, 1983—; sec. Kans. Advocacy and Protective Services Inc., Manhattan, 1980—; chmn. Essex County Planning Commn., Westport, N.Y., 1971-72; bd. dirs. Adirondack Found., Westport, 1980-81. Mem. Am. Assn. Pub. Adminstrn. Republican. Episcopalian. Home: 1825 Webster Ave Topeka KS 66604 Office: Kans Dept Health and Environment Forbes Field Topeka KS 66620

EPSTEIN, GEORGE, computer science educator; b. Bayonne, N.J., July 4, 1934; s. Max and Frieda Ann (Barron) E.; m. Laraine Pat Lesser, Sept. 9, 1956; children—Mark, David, Elein. B.S., Calif. Inst. Tech., 1955; M.S., U. Ill.-Urbana, 1957; Ph.D., UCLA, 1959. Mem. tech. staff Hughes Aircraft Co., Culver City, Calif., 1957-59; staff scientist, project engr. ITT-Gilfallan, Van Nuys, Calif., 1959-72; prof. computer sci. Ind. U., Bloomington 1973—. Patentee in field (10); contbr. articles to profl. jours. Mem. Assn. Computing Machinery, Am. Math. Soc., Assn. Symbolic Logic. Office: Ind U Dept Computer Sci Bloomington IN 47405

EPSTEIN, MARVIN MORRIS, construction company executive; b. Cleve., June 2, 1928; s. Isadore Elchanan and Rose (Gevelber) E.; m. Lois M. DeSure, June 10, 1957; children—Deborah L. Epstein Merkin, David A. B.A. with honors, U. Mich., 1951; student Princeton U., 1952, Western Res. U., 1947-79. Reporter Cleve. Plain Dealer, 1951-52; editor AP, Columbus, Ohio, 1953-55, Times-Star, Cin., 1956-59; cons. Eden and Assocs., Cleve., 1959-60; dir. pub. relations The Austin Co., Cleve., 1961—. Contbr. articles to profl. jours. Active Greater Cleve. Growth Assn., 1975—; bd. overseers, vis. com. Case Western Res. U., Case Inst. Tech., Cleve., 1981. Served with U.S. Army, 1946-47. Recipient McNaught Gold medal for disting. journalism U. Mich., 1951. Mem. Soc. Profl. Journalists, U. Mich. Alumni Assn. (pres. 1975-76). Democrat. Jewish. Club: Mid-Day (Cleve.) Home: 4161 Hadleigh Rd University Heights OH 44118 Office: Austin Co 3650 Mayfield Rd Cleveland OH 44121

EPSTEIN, MAX, engineering educator, consultant; b. Lodz, Poland, Feb. 5, 1925; came to U.S., 1952, naturalized, 1958; s. Israel and Dola (Grad) E.; m. Judith Ray Slotnikoff, Sept. 10, 1963; children—Michael, David, Deborah. B.S., Israel Inst. Tech., 1952; M.S., Ill. Inst. Tech., 1955, Ph.D., 1963. Tool designer Folding Carrier Corp., Oklahoma City, 1952-53; engr. Admiral Corp., Chgo., 1953-54; instr. Ill. Inst. Tech., Chgo., 1954-58, sr. research engr. Research Inst., 1958-67; prof. Northwestern U., Evanston, Ill., 1967—; cons. Ill. Inst. Tech. Research Inst., 1967—; assoc. research staff Evanston Hosp., 1975—; v.p. Midwest Bio-laser Inst., Chgo., 1981—. Office: Northwestern U Tech Inst Evanston IL 60201

EPSTEIN, SIDNEY, moving and storage company executive; b. Stamford, Conn., Jan. 26, 1923; s. Max and Rae Epstein; m. Paula Goldenberg, Feb. 15, 1951; children—Ellen, Julie. Student pub. schs., Stamford. Vice pres. Neptune Worldwide Moving, Inc., New Rochelle, N.Y., until 1978; sr. v.p. Allied Van Lines, Inc., Broadview, Ill., 1978-79, pres., 1979—, also chief operating officer. Served with USAF, 1942-46. Mem. Conn. Warehousemen's Assn. (pres.), Household Goods Carriers Bur. (pres.), Am. Movers Conf. (exec. com.). Office: Allied Van Lines Inc 25th Ave and Roosevelt Rd Broadview IL 60153*

ERAZMUS, ROBERT FRANCIS, consumer electronics co. exec.; b. Chgo., May 12, 1942; s. Frank and Bernice (Wydra) E.; B.A., St. Mary's Coll., Winona, Minn., 1964; M.B.A., DePaul U., 1966; m. July 16, 1966; children—Marilou, Elizabeth, Susan. Teaching fellow DePaul U., 1964-66; instr. acctg. St. Mary's Coll., 1966-68; audit sr./mgr. Arthur Andersen & Co., Mpls., 1968-69, Chgo., 1969-73; controller Heizer Corp., Chgo., 1973-75; v.p. fin., treas. Internat. Jensen Inc., Schiller Park, Ill., 1975-80, pres., 1980—. Mem. Pres.'s Assn., Am. Inst. C.P.A.s, Ill. C.P.A. Soc. Club: Econ. of Chgo. Office: 4136 N United Pkwy Schiller Park IL 60176

ERB, RICHARD LOUIS LUNDIN, resort community hotel executive; b. Chgo., Dec. 23, 1929; s. Louis Henry and Miriam (Lundin) E.; B.A., U. Calif.-Berkeley, 1951, postgrad., 1952; student San Francisco Art Inst., 1956; m. Jean Elizabeth Easton, Mar. 14, 1959; children—John Richard, Elizabeth Anne, James Easton, Richard Louis. Asst. gen. mgr. Grand Teton Lodge Co., Jackson Hole, Wyo., 1954-62; mgr. Colter Bay Village, Grand Teton Nat. Park, Wyo., 1962-64, Mauna Kea Beach Hotel, Hawaii, 1964-66; v.p., gen. mgr. Caneel Bay Plantation, Inc., St. John, V.I., 1966-75; gen. mgr. Williamsburg (Va.) Inn, 1975-78; exec. v.p., gen. mgr. Seabrook Island Co., Johns Island, S.C., 1978-80; v.p., dir. hotels Sands Hotel and Casino, Inc., Atlantic City, 1980-82; chief operating officer Grand Traverse Resort, Grand Traverse Village, Mich., 1982—. Vice pres. V.I. Montessori Sch., 1969-71, bd. dirs., 1968-76; bd. dirs. Coll. of V.I., 1976-79; mem. adv. bd. U. S.C., 1978-80; vice chmn. Charleston (S.C.) Tourism Council, 1979-80; bd. dirs. Anaheim Conv. Bur., 1982, Grand Traverse Conv. and Visitors Bur., 1984—; mem. adv. bd. Northwestern Mich. Coll., 1983—, Munson Med. Ctr., 1984—, Traverse City Osteo. Hosp., 1984—; mem. Traverse City Area Indsl. Fund, 1983—; bd. dirs., U.S.-131 Area Devel. Assn., 1983—, Northwestern Mich. Symphony, 1984—, Traverse City Area C. of C., 1984—, mem. Gov.'s Communities of Econ. Excellence Commn., 1984—. Contbr. articles to trade jours. Served to lt., arty. U.S. Army, 1952-54. Mem. Am. Hotel and Motel Assn. (dir. 1975-77, Service Merit award 1976; trustee Ednl. Inst. 1977-83, exec. com. 1978-83), Caribbean Hotel Assn. (1st v.p. 1972-74, dir. 1970-76, hon. life mem. Extraordinary Service Merit award 1974), V.I. Hotel Assn. (pres. chmn. bd. 1971-76, Merit award 1973), Calif. Hotel Assn. (dir. 1982-83), Caribbean Travel Assn. (dir.

1972-74), Internat. Hotel Assn. (dir. 1971-73), S.C. Hotel Assn. (dir. 1978-83), Va. Hotel Assn., Williamsburg Hotel Assn. (dir. 1975-78), Atlantic City Hotel Assn., Mich. Lodging Assn. (dir. 1983—, chmn. edn. com. 1983-84), Traverse City Hotel/Motel Assn., Acme Businessmen's Assn., Atlantic City Casino Hotel Assn. (dir. 1980-82), Va., Charleston, Trident chambers commerce, Nat. Restaurant Assn., Beta Theta Pi. Congregationalist. Clubs: Tavern, Golden Horseshoe, German, Greate Bay, Grand Traverse Village, Seabrook Island, Kiawah Island. Lodge: Rotary. Address: Grand Traverse Resort Grand Traverse Village MI 49610

ERDEL, SALLY ELIZABETH, nurse; b. Peoria, Ill., Mar. 28, 1952; d. Robert William and Mary Maxine (Vick) Birky; m. Timothy Paul Erdel, Aug. 28, 1977; children—Sarah Beth, Rachel Elaine. A.A., Ft. Wayne Bible Coll., Ind., 1972; diploma West Suburban Hosp. Sch. Nursing, Oak Park, Ill., 1975; B.S. in Nursing, U. Ill. Med. Ctr., Chgo., 1977, M.S., 1980. Staff nurse, West Suburban Hosp., 1975-77; teaching asst. U. Ill. Med. Ctr., 1980; staff nurse Highland Park Hosp., Ill., 1981-82; staff nurse Carle Found. Hosp., Urbana, Ill., 1982—, seminar/workshop speaker, 1982—, clin. nurse specialist, 1985—. Mem. Am. Nurses Assn., Ill. Nurses Assn., Oncology Nurses Soc., Central Ill. Oncology Nurses (co-editor newsletter 1983—), Am. Soc. Psychoprophylactics in Obstetrics, East Central Ill. Research Network. Republican. Mennonite. Home: 2110 Orchard St #304 Urbana IL 61801

ERDMAN, LOWELL PAUL, civil engineer, land surveyor; b. Wesley, Iowa, Aug. 11, 1926; s. Paul William and Olive Jane (Stillwell) E.; m. Audrey Lucille Stephenson, Aug. 18, 1956; children—Lindsay, Paul, Jeffrey. B.S. in Civil Engring., Iowa State U., 1950. Profl. engr., Iowa, Minn., Wis.; registered land surveyor, Iowa, Wis. Inspector Iowa Hwy. Commn., Jefferson, 1950-52; field engr. Phillip Petroleum Co., Bartlesville, Okla., 1952-55; cons. engr. Erdman Engring., P.C., Decorah, Iowa, 1955—, pres., 1955—; city engr., Decorah, 1955—. Co-chmn. Brandstad for Gov. Com., Winneshiek County, 1982. Served with USAAF, 1945-46. Fellow ASCE; mem. Nat. Soc. Profl. Engrs., Iowa Engring Soc., Soc. Land Surveyors of Iowa. Republican. Lutheran. Club: Oneota Golf and Country. Avocations: Golf; bowling; fishing; fly tying. Home: 1303 Skyline Dr Decorah IA 52101 Office: Erdman Engring P C 405 College Dr Decorah IA 52101

ERDMANN, MARVIN ELMER, food company executive; b. Milw., July 1, 1930; s. Walter and Lenora E.; student public schs., Milw., m. Lois Jean Yellick, Apr. 14, 1951; children—Mark Karter, Scott Kevin, Kim Robin. With A&P Tea Co., Milw., 1944-60, dept. mgr., 1949-51, store mgr., 1953-60; store mgr. Paulus Foods, Cedarburg, Wis., 1960-63; with Super Valu Stores, Inc., 1963—, field supr., 1964-69, sales mgr., Mpls., 1969-74, retail ops. mgr., Mpls., 1974-77, pres. Bismarck (N.D.) div., 1977—; dir. Norwest Bank, Bismarck; lectr. bus. adminstrn. at high schs., colls. Chmn. fin. of expansion Good Shepherd Ch.; bd. regents Mary Coll.; pres. lay bd. St. Alexius Hosp. Served with U.S. Army, 1951-53. Decorated Bronze Star, Am. Spirit medal. Mem. N.D. Food Retailers Assn. (legis. cons.), Greater N.D. Assn. (speaker), Bismarck C. of C. (pres., dir., mem. exec. com., mem. indsl. com.). Republican. Lutheran. Clubs: Apple Creek Country, Supreme Ct. Racquetball. Home: 1217 Crestview Ln Bismarck ND 58501 Office: 707 Airport Rd Bismarck ND 58502

ERET, DONALD, state senator; Mem. Nebr. Senate, 1983—. Office: 712 Lincoln St Dorchester NE 68343*

ERICKSON, B. ARTHUR, science educator; b. Springfield, Mo., Nov. 26, 1934; s. James Henry and Mabel Francis (Brashears) E.; m. Mary Leota Pendegrass, June 6, 1958; children—Gregory Arthur, Susan Lynn. B.S., U. Mo., 1956, M.S., 1958, Ph.D., 1961. Research biochemist, research div. Procter and Gamble Co., Cin., 1961-68; asst. prof. chemistry Evangel Coll., Springfield, Mo., 1968-70, assoc. prof., 1970-76, prof., 1976—, chmn. dept. sci. and tech. 1972-77. Bd. dirs., Springfield Acad. Sci., S.W. Mo. Sci. Tchr's. Assn., Gen. Council Credit Union. Mem. Am. Chem. Soc. Republican. Mem. Assembly of God Ch. Lodge: Lions. Contbr. articles to profl. jours. Patentee in field. Home: 3541 S Dayton Springfield MO 65807 Office: Evangel Coll Springfield MO 65802

ERICKSON, BARBARA ANN, nurse, educator; b. Fairmont, W.Va., Dec. 28, 1936; d. John Joseph and Addie May (Carr) Erickson. B.S.N. cum laude, St. John Coll. of Cleve., 1962; M.S.N., Cath. U. Am., 1971. Staff nurse, head nurse, supr. St. Elizabeth Hosp., Youngstown, Ohio, 1962-65, nurse clinician, 1972-75; asst. head nurse Villa Maria Infirmary (Pa.), 1965-66, dir. nursing service, 1966-67; head nurse, supr. CCU, St. Joseph Hosp., Lorain, Ohio, 1967-69; instr. nursing Youngstown State U., 1971-76, asst. prof., 1976-78; cardiovascular clin. specialist Frank Tiberio, M.D., Inc., Youngstown, 1975—; clin. specialist Family Medicine Ctr. of St. Elizabeth Hosp. Med. Ctr., Youngstown, 1979-81; co-dir. Clin. Edn. Assocs., 1979—; clin. specialist Youngstown Hosp. Assn., 1981-84; asst. prof. nursing Youngstown State U., 1984—; cons. to film – Cardiac Auscultation –, 1978. Co-author: Problem Oriented Medical Record, 1973; Cardiac Auscultation, 1975; mem. editorial staff Dimensions of Critical Care Nursing, 1981-82, Heart and Lung-Jour. Critical Care, 1973-76; contbr. articles to profl. jours. Mem. Ohio Nurses Assn. (bd. dirs. dist. 3), Am. Assn. Critical Care Nurses (cert.), Sigma Theta Tau, Phi Kappa Phi. Democrat. Roman Catholic. Office: Youngstown State U Youngstown OH 44555

ERICKSON, CHARLES EDWARD, contractor; b. Chgo., June 19, 1944; s. Edward Charles and Phillis Edith (Weaire) E.; children—Caren, Edward, Christopher, Charles Edward, Jr. Mgr., Enco Gas, Chgo., 1961-66; foreman Skokie Lumber (Ill.), 1966—; pres. C.E. Erickson Constrn., Chgo., 1969—; v.p. Great Lakes Brush Co. Home: 750 Portwine Rd Riverwoods IL 60015 Office: CE Erickson 6417 N Ravenswood Ave Chicago IL 60626

ERICKSON, GARWOOD ELLIOTT, manufacturing company official; b. Little Silver, N.J., Jan. 8, 1946; s. Gustaf Walter and Martha Lake (Adams) E.; m. Carol Wyborski, July 21, 1973; 1 son, Christopher Lake. A.B., Dartmouth Coll., 1967; B.E., Thayer Sch. Engring., 1968, M.E., 1969; M.B.A., U. Mich., 1974. Systems analyst Ford Motor Co., Dearborn, Mich., 1969-72, unit supr., 1972-76, cons., 1976-78, sect. supr., 1978-82, mgr., 1982-83; corp. dir. mgmt. info. services Hoover Universal, Ann Arbor, Mich., 1983—. Sec., Trayer Lakes Community Assn., Ann Arbor, Mich., 1977. Advanced Research Projects Agy. fellow, 1967-69. Republican. Club: Dartmouth (pres. Ann Arbor 1982—). Office: Hoover Universal 825 Victors Way Ann Arbor MI 48109

ERICKSON, GUS T(HEODORE), pharmacist, store owner; b. Vermillion, S.D., June 15, 1940; s. Theodore G. and Johanna L. (Lucken) E.; m. Janet L. Jones, Aug. 17, 1963; children—Bradley, Brian. B.S. in Pharmacy, U. Iowa, 1962. Mgr. May Drug, Cedar Rapids, 1962-66, Superx Drug Co., Dallas, 1966; pharmacist, Vanderlinden Drug Co., Pella, Iowa, 1966; owner, pharmacist Erickson Pharmacy, Garner, Iowa, 1966—. Councilman City of Garner, 1977—. Mem. Iowa Pharmacists Assn. (registered pharmacist). Republican. Methodist. Home: 820 Division St Garner IA 50438

ERICKSON, HOWARD HUGH, veterinarian, physiology educator; b. Wahoo, Nebr., Mar. 16, 1936; s. Conrad and Laurene (Swanson) E.; m. Ann E. Nicolay, June 6, 1959; children—James, David. B.S., D.V.M., Kans. State U., 1959; Ph.D., Iowa State U., 1966. Commd. 1st lt., U.S. Air Force, 1959, advanced through grades to col., 1979; area veterinarian, U.K., 1960-63; vet. scientist Sch. Aerospace Medicine, Brooks AFB, Tex., 1966-75, dir. research and devel. aerospace med. div., 1975-81; prof. physiology Kans. State U., Manhattan, 1981—; clin. asst. prof. U. Tex. Health Sci. Ctr., San Antonio, 1972-81; vis. mem. grad. faculty Tex. A&M U., College Station, 1967-81; affiliate prof. Colo. State U., Fort Collins, 1970-75. Editor: Animal Pain, 1983. Contbr. articles to profl. jours. Recipient Alumni Achievement award Midland Luth. Coll., Fremont, Nebr., 1977. Fellow AAAS, Royal Soc. Health, Aerospace Med. Assn. (assoc.); mem. Am. Vet. Med. Assn. (chmn. council on research 1984), Am. Physiol. Soc. Republican. Lutheran. Optimists (Manhattan). Home: 2017 Arthur Dr Manhattan KS 66502 Office: Dept Anatomy and Physiology Coll Vet Medicine Kans State U Manhattan KS 66506

ERICKSON, JEANNE HOLLAND, pharmacist, business executive; b. Warroad, Minn., Nov. 17, 1921; d. Edward James and Henrietta (Berglund) Holland; m. Martin A. Erickson, June 21, 1941; children—Martin III, Kirk E., Marilyn J. Student Macalester Coll., 1939-40; B.S. in Pharmacy, U. Minn., 1946; postgrad. Cornell U., 1958. Registered pharmacist, Minn. Analyst Minn. Bd. Pharmacy, Mpls., 1943-46; pharmacist in charge Holland Pharmacy, Warroad, Minn., 1946-56, Heritage Pharmacy, Warroad, 1975—; staff pharmacist Olson Bros. Pharmacy, Edina, Minn., 1966-71; mgr. Rembrandt Pharmacy, Edina, 1971-75; mem. adv. com. Minn. Bd. Pharmacy, 1973; v.p. Warroad Heritage, Inc., retail sales-rental property, 1975—; pharmacy cons., mem. infection control com. Warroad Care Ctr., 1979—. Leader Girls Scouts U.S.A., Minn. and N.Y.; v.p. PTA, Wanaka, N.Y., 1962; dir. religious edn. Hamburg Schs. Release Time Edn., N.Y., 1963-66; crusade chmn. Erie County unit Am. Cancer Soc., Hamburg, 1965. Recipient Hall of Fame award Rembrandt Corp., Cert. of Appreciation Warroad Care Ctr., 1985. Mem. Am. Pharm. Assn., Nat. Assn. Retail Pharmacists, Am. Soc. Hosp. Pharmacists, Minn. Pharm. Assn. (del. 1972-74), Am. Legion Aux., U. Minn. Alumni. Lodge: Order of Eastern Star. Avocations: boating; swimming; music; flying. Office: Warroad Heritage Inc 321 E Lake St Warroad MN 56763

ERICKSON, JOHN DUFF, mining engineering educator; b. Crawford, Nebr., Apr. 1, 1933; s. Harold Edward and Ruth Isabel (Duff) E.; m. Janet Eileen Lind, Dec. 28, 1955; children—Gregory Duff, Sheryl Ann. B.S. in Mining Engring., S.D. Sch. Mines and Tech., 1955; M.S. in Indsl. Mgmt., MIT, 1965. Various positions in engring. and mgmt. Kennecott Co., Salt Lake City, 1955-69; sr. exec. Bougainville Copper Ltd., Papua, New Guinea, 1970-78; prof., head dept. mining engring. S.D. Sch. Mines and Tech., 1978—; exec. dir. S.D. Sch. Mines and Tech. Alumni Assn., 1984—. Served to capt. C.E., U.S. Army, 1956, 61-62. Sloan fellow MIT. Mem. Am. Inst. Mining Engrs. (past chmn. Black Hills sect.), S.D. Mining Assn. Republican. Club: Arrowhead Country (Rapid City, S.D.). Lodge: Elks. Contbr. articles to profl. jours. Office: SD Sch Mines and Tech Rapid City SD 57702

ERICKSON, KEVIN RODMAN, sheriff; b. Newberry, Mich., Oct. 29, 1957; s. Harold Lenard and Jacquelyn Muriel (Heath) E.; m. Kathy Rae Swanson, Mar. 31, 1979; 1 child, Douglas McKay. Assoc. in Law Enforcement, N.W. Mich. Coll., 1978. Park ranger State of Mich., Newberry, 1977; security agt. Giantway Inc., Traverse City, Mich., 1977-78; dep. sheriff Luce County, Newberry, 1978-80, sheriff, 1980—. Mem. gun bd. Luce County, Newberry, 1980—. Mem. Nat. Rifle Assn. (firearms instr. 1982—), Mich. Sheriff Assn., Nat. Sheriff Assn., Mich. Chiefs Police, Nat. Chiefs Police, Am. Police Hall of Fame (Outstanding Commendation 1981). Recipient J. Edgar Hoover Gold medal, 1984. Republican. Lutheran. Lodges: Masons. Avocations: pistol shooting; hunting; fishing; wood craft. Home: 106 Cherry Hill Dr Newberry MI 49868 Office: Luce County Sheriff Dept 411 W Harrie St Newberry MI 49868

ERICKSON, LARRY EUGENE, chemical engineering educator; b. Wahoo, Nebr., Oct. 8, 1938; s. Conrad Robert Nathaniel and Laurene Hanna (Swanson) E.; m. Laurel L. Livingston, May 31, 1981. B.S. in Chem. Engring., Kans. State U., 1960, Ph.D., 1964. Instr. chem. engring. Kans. State U., Manhattan, 1964-65, asst. prof., 1965-67, assoc. prof., 1968-72, prof., 1972—; NIH spl. research fellow U. Pa., Phila., 1967-68; vis. scientist MIT, Cambridge, Mass., 1975, USSR Acad. Scis., Pushchino, 1977-78. Contbr. articles to profl. jours. Pres. Lutheran Help Assn., Manhattan, 1984. Recipient Career Devel. award NIH, 1970-75; Prof. Baehr award Beta Sigma Psi, 1981. Mem. Am. Inst. Chem. Engrs., Am. Chem. Soc. (sec.-treas. chpt. 1983), Inst. Food Tech., Sigma Xi. Avocation: square dancing. Home: 408 Wickham Rd Manhattan KS 66502 Office: Kans State U Dept Chem Engring Durland Hall Manhattan KS 66506

ERICKSON, LEROY, state senator, farmer; b. DeLamere, N.D., May 15, 1926; s. Ed and Agnes (Martinson) E.; grad. high sch.; m. Lila Moxness, Nov. 10, 1946; children—Marsha Susag, Kim Mund. Rep. N.D. Legislature, 1967-68, 73-80, N.D. Senate, 1981-84; grain farmer, DeLamere. Del., N.D. Constnl. Conv., 1972; twp. supr., 1952-54; mem. County Sch. Reorgn. Bd., County Spl. Edn. Bd.; dir. S.E. Mental Health; active PTA, Farm Bur. Task Forces. Recipient Sparkplug award for communication for agr., 1981. Mem. Farm Bur., Internat. Flying Farmers, N.D. Stockmen's Assn. (legis. rep.), Aircraft Owners and Pilots Assn. Republican. Lutheran. Club: Milnor Satellite. Home and Office: Rural Route DeLamere ND 58022

ERICKSON, LUCERNE REDD, educational consultant; b. Buffalo, Feb. 12, 1923; d. Ernest Clarence and Arvilla Marian (Terwilliger) Redd; B.S., Ohio No. U., 1961; M.S., Ind. U., 1965, Ed.D., 1973; m. Omar Isadore Erickson, June 9, 1941; children—Omar Stephen, Karen Kjarista, Karl Dennis. Coordinator curriculum Allen County, Lima, Ohio, 1966-69; instr. Ohio State U., Lima, 1969-70; county curriculum coordinator Van Wert County, (Ohio), 1971-73; coordinator Auglaize County curriculum, Wapakoneta, Ohio, 1973-84; co-owner E & D Ednl. Providers, Lima, 1984—; instr. Findlay Coll., 1984—; mem. adv. bd. Area XI Back to Basics. Ednl. chmn. Shawnee United Meth. Ch., 1978, adminstrv. bd., 1978-80. Margaret Webb Blanton scholar Delta Kappa Gamma, 1970-71; Ind. U. grantee, 1970-71. Mem. AAUW (pres. Lima br. 1981-83), Ohio Sch. Suprs. Assn. (state pres. 1981), Ohio Assn. Sch. and Curriculum Developers, West Central Ohio Sch. Suprs. Republican. Club: Eastern Star. Home: 3140 Juliette St Lima OH 45805 Office: 3115 W Elm St Lima OH 45805

ERICKSON, RICK, educator, school counselor, coach; b. Chgo., Aug. 14, 1944; s. Bengt Ivar and Bridget (Moran) E.; m. Juliet Stoegerl, Oct. 13, 1979; children—Sean, Dan. B.S. in Psychology, Loyola U., Chgo., 1973, M.S. in Psychology, 1976; M.S., U. Wis.-Oshkosh, 1984. Dir., counselor South Chgo. Alcohol and Drug Abuse Clinic, Chgo., 1969-73; tchr., coach, counselor Willibrord Sch., Chgo., 1973-81; counselor, tchr., coach St. Mary's Springs High Sch., Fond du Lac, Wis., 1981—. Campaign mgr. Perkich for Senate, Ill., 1972; pres. North Fond du Lac Sch. Bd., 1982—. Mem. Wis. Coaching Assn. (Coach of Yr. Dist. 4 1984), Ill. Warrior Assn. (Basketball Hall of Fame 1984), Am. Psychol. Assn., Wis. Counselors Assn., Am. Counselors Assn. Nat. Fedn. Coaches. Roman Catholic. Home: 235 Broadway North Fond du Lac WI 54935

ERICKSON, ROBERT PORTER, genetics researcher, educator, clinician; b. Portland, Oreg., June 27, 1939; s. Harold M. and Marjorie S. (Porter) E.; m. Sandra De'Ath, June 20, 1964; children—Andrew Ian, Colin De'Ath, Tanya Nadene, Tracy Lynn, Michelle Lee, Christof Phillipe. B.A., Reed Coll., 1960; M.D., Stanford U., 1965. Diplomate Am. Bd. Pediatrics. Asst. prof. pediatrics U. Calif.-San Francisco Med. Sch., 1970-75; vis. scientist Institut Pasteur, Paris, 1975-76; assoc. prof. human genetics and pediatrics U. Mich., Ann Arbor, 1976-80, prof., 1980—, dir. div. pediatric genetics, 1985—; vis. scientist Imperial Cancer Research Fund, London, 1983-84. Editorial bd. Jour. Reproductive Immunology, 1978—, Dictionary of Laboratory Technology, 1983. Contbr. articles to sci. jours. Served with USPHS, 1967-69. Guggenheim fellow, Paris, 1975; Eleanor Roosevelt fellow, London, 1983; Fulbright grantee, London, 1983; NIH grantee, 1971—. Mem. Am. Soc. Human Genetics, Soc. Pediatric Research, Am. Soc. Cell Biology. Avocations: skiing; backpacking. Home: 2717 Kenilworth Ann Arbor MI 48104 Office: U Mich Ann Arbor MI 48109

ERICKSON, ROY FREDERICK, JR., hosp. adminstr.; b. Chgo., Aug. 16, 1928; s. Roy Frederick and Irene Elsa E.; B.S. in Bus. Adminstrn., Northwestern U., 1950, M.S. in Hosp. Adminstrn., 1956; m. Julia Ellen Raffington, Oct. 18, 1958; children—Elizabeth, Peter, Stephen. Asst. adminstr. Decatur (Ill.) Meml. Hosp., 1956-60; adminstr. Passavant Meml. Area Hosp., Jacksonville, Ill., 1960-64; adminstr. Blessing Hosp., Quincy, Ill., 1964-72; pres. Ball Meml. Hosp., Muncie, Ind., 1972—; adj. prof. physiology and health sci. Ball State U., 1979-81; mem. asso. faculty Muncie Center for Med. Edn.; mem. Central Ind. Health Systems Agy.-Area II Council; bd. dirs. Bi State Regional Med., 1969-72. Served with USAF, 1950-54. Mem. Am. Hosp. Assn., Ind. Hosp. Assn. (dir. 1976-82), Am. Coll. Hosp. Adminstrs., Am. Mgmt. Assn. Methodist. Club: Rotary. Home: 4201 University Ave Muncie IN 47304 Office: 2401 University Ave Muncie IN 47303

ERICKSON, SHARON K., investment broker, tax specialist; b. Mpls., Nov. 14, 1938; d. Ivar Carl and Beatrice Josephine (Wiberg) Erickson; B.A. in Sociology and Psychology, Macalester Coll., St. Paul, 1961; postgrad. in bus. U. Minn., NYU; div.; children—Kathleen Ann, Deborah Jean, Rebecca Joanne. Chief exec. officer Erickson Motor & Oil Co., Inc., Mpls., 1972—; pres., owner Kabobs, Inc., St. Paul and Edina, Minn., 1972-76; investment broker Prudential-Bache Securities, Inc., Mpls., 1977—; cons., seminar speaker in field. Founder Minn. chpt. Alliance Displaced Homemakers, also chmn., regional cons., 1974-77; nat. speaker, local officer, chmn. employment com. Mpls. chpt. NOW, 1972-76; founding mem., mem. steering com. Minn. Women's Polit. Caucus, 1971; Minn. rep. LWV, 1974-75; founder St. Croix Valley Human Rights Com., 1965; founder, pres. Horizon 100, 1981-82, bd. dirs., 1983; treas., mem. exec. com. Epilepsy Found. Minn., 1983—. Mem. Internat. Soc. Registered Reps., Am. Mgmt. Assn., Minn. Women Investment Brokers Assn., AMEX Club. Lutheran. Clubs: Greenway Athletic, Blaisdell Women's. Home: 9714 Brighton Ln Eden Prairie MN 55344 Office: 2020 IDS Tower Minneapolis MN 55402

ERICKSON, WALTER BRUCE, economist, educator; b. Chgo., Mar. 4, 1938; s. Clifford Eric and Mildred (Brinkmeier) E. B.A., Mich. State U., 1959, M.A., 1960, Ph.D., 1965. Asst. prof. mgmt., U. Minn., Mpls., 1966-70, assoc. prof., 1971-75, prof., 1975—, chmn. dept. mgmt., 1976-79; staff mem. antitrust and monopoly subcom. U.S. Senate, 1960-62; cons. antitrust cases. Author: Business and Government Enterprise, 1984; An Introduction to Contemporary Business, 4th edit., 1985. Contbr. articles to profl. jours. Mem. Am. Econ. Assn., Royal Econ. Soc. Home: 2849 35th Ave S Minneapolis MN 55406

ERICKSTAD, RALPH JOHN, state chief justice; b. Starkweather, N.D., Aug. 15, 1922; s. John T. and Anna L. Erickstad; student U. N.D., 1940-43; B.S. in Law, U. Minn., 1947, LL.B., 1949; m. Lois Katherine Jacobson, July 30, 1949; children—John Albert, Mark Anders. Admitted to N.D. bar, 1949; mem. firm Teigen & Erickstad, Devils Lake, N.D., 1950-54; police magistrate, Devils Lake, 1951-53; states atty., Ramsey County, 1953-57; mem. firm Erickstad & Foughty, 1954-62; asso. justice Supreme Ct. of N.D., Bismarck, 1963-73, chief justice, 1973—. Mem. Gov.'s Spl. Com. on Labor, 1960; past commr. Missouri Valley council Boy Scouts Am.; mem. N.D. Senate, 1957-62, asst. majority floor leader; chmn. bd. trustees Missouri Valley Family YMCA, 1966-77; mem. Task Force on Public Image of Cts., Williamsburg Conf. Recipient Silver Beaver award Boy Scouts Am., 1967; Sioux award U. N.D., 1973; 1st Disting. Service award Missouri Valley YMCA, 1978. Mem. Am., N.D., Burleigh County bar assns., Am. Judicature Soc., Am. Law Inst., Nat. Conf. Chief Justices (exec. council 1977-78, 80-82, 1st vice chmn. 1982-83, pres. 1983-84), Nat. Ctr. for State Cts. (pres. 1983-84). Republican. Lutheran. Club: Kiwanis. Office: Supreme Ct ND Capitol Bldg Bismarck ND 58505

ERICSON, RICHARD CHARLES, social service agency executive, consultant; b. St. Paul, June 21, 1933; s. Rolph Christopher and Sonia Margaret (Carlson) E.; m. Carol Joy Turnwall, Jan. 1, 1955; children—Lynn Ericson Starr, David Alan. B.A., Roosevelt U., 1959; M.A., U. Chgo., 1961. U.S. probation officer U.S. Probation Office, Chgo., 1960-61; juvenile probation officer Hennepin County Ct. Services, Mpls., 1961-62; asst. supr. Hennepin County Juvenile Detention Center, Mpls., 1962-63; asst. dir. Pres.'s Com. on Youth Crime, Charleston, W.Va., 1963-64; project coordinator parolee rehab. project Mpls. Rehab. Center, 1964-67; pres. Minn. Citizens Council on Crime and Justice, 1967—; trustee Klingberg Family Centers, New Britain, Conn., Sunny Ridge Family Center, Wheaton, Ill.; mem. Minn. Crime Victim and Witness Adv. Council; pres. Ericson Properties, Inc. Active Mpls. Soc. Fine Arts, Walker Art Center. Served with C.E., U.S. Army, 1954-56. Grantee in field. Mem. Nat. Council on Crime and Delinquency, Am. Correctional Assn. Presbyterian. Lodge: Rotary of Mpls. Contbr. articles on crime and justice to profl. jours. Home: 1235 Yale Pl 1308 Minneapolis MN 55403 Office: 1427 Washington Ave S Minneapolis MN 55454

ERICSON, RICHARD ERIC, economics educator, researcher; b. San Miguel, Mex., Mar. 25, 1949; s. Richard Joseph and Ruth Delafield (White) E.; m. Joann Carol Russell, Mar. 12, 1982; 1 child, Emily Ruth. B.S.F.S., Georgetown U., 1971; M.I.A., Columbia U., 1974; Ph.D. in Econs., U. Calif.-Berkeley, 1979. Instr. econs. Harvard U., Cambridge, Mass., 1978, asst. prof., 1979-83; vis. assoc. prof. Yale U., New Haven, 1983; vis. asst. prof. Northwestern U., Evanston, 1981, assoc. prof., 1983-85; assoc. prof. Harriman Inst., Columbia U., N.Y.C., 1985—. Contbr. articles to profl. jours. Grantee Fulbright Hays Com., 1977-78, NSF, 1980-83, 84-87. Mem. Am. Econ. Assn., Econometric Soc., Assn. Comparative Econ. Studies, Joint Com. for Soviet Studies, Phi Beta Kappa. Republican. Roman Catholic.

ERIKSEN, ROBERT LEE, chemical engineer; b. Carrington, N.D., Feb. 24, 1952; s. Bjerge and Hazel A. (Nelson) E. B.S. in Chem. Engring., U. N.D., 1974. Registered profl. engr., N.D., Wyo. Environ. control supr. Basin Electric Power Coop., Bismarck, N.D., 1978—, environ. control coordinator, 1977-78, chem. engr., 1974-77. Contbr. articles to profl. jours. Mem. Am. Inst. Chem. Engrs., Air Pollution Control Assn., Jaycees (state v.p. 1984-85, internat. senator 1981—). Republican. Methodist. Avocations: skiing; camping; canoeing; hunting. Home: 1026 S 3d St Apt 18 Bismarck ND 58501 Office: Basin Electric Power Coop 1717 E Interstate Ave Bismarck ND 58501

ERIKSEN, SUSAN ANN, data processing educator, consultant; b. Edgewood, Iowa, Sept. 17, 1939; d. Mike and Elinor May (Chapman) Yankey; m. William R. Lee, (div.); children—Mark L., Mona L., William J. Student Mason City Jr. Coll., 1957-59; B.S., Iowa State U., 1962, postgrad., 1968. Data processing instr. Des Moines Community Coll., Ankeny, 1971—; cons. CTI, Phoenix, 1981, Clay County, Spencer, Iowa, 1982, Prouty Co., Des Moines, 1984—, Bob Allen Cos., Des Moines, 1985—. Mem. Data Processing Mgmt. Assn., Assn. Systems Mgmt., AAUW (pres. 1972). Avocations: jogging; swimming; gardening. Home: 705 NW School St Ankeny IA 50021

ERIKSON, EVANS W., heavy machinery manufacturing executive. Chmn., chief exec. officer, dir. Sundstrand Corp., Rockford, Ill. Office: Sundstrand Corp 4751 Harrison Ave Box 7003 Rockford IL 61125*

ERIKSON, JAMES MEEGAN, computer company executive, consultant; b. N.Y.C., June 1, 1943; s. James Norton and Patricia Mary (Meegan) E.; m. Susan Lynch, Nov. 12, 1966; children—Patricia Mary, Dawn Kathleen. A.S., John Jay Coll., 1968; B.A., CUNY, 1969; M.B.A., Iona Grad. Sch. Bus., 1970; Ph.D., NYU, 1984. Dir. city ops. City of N.Y., 1964-74; assoc. prof. U. Balt., 1974-75; mgr. mktg. and sales Gen. Electric Co., N.Y., Washington and Va., 1975-80, mgr. govt. sales, Washington, 1980-82; v.p. central area United Info. Services, Chgo., 1982; exec. v.p. sales United Telecom Computer Group, Overland Park, Kans., 1982-84; pres. Aviation & Mgmt. Assocs., Inc., Jamaica, N.Y., 1984—; cons., advisor N.Y. Shut-In Soc., N.Y.C., 1965—; faculty reviewer Command and Gen. Staff Coll., U.S. Army, Ft. Leavenworth, Kans., 1978—; manuscript reviewer Little, Brown & Co., Boston, 1976-78. Advisor, Jr. Achievement, Lynchburg, Va., 1979; mem. adv. council Mayor's Woodside Task Force, Woodside, N.Y., 1975-79. Served to lt. col. U.S. Army, 1962-65. Forbes mag. scholar, 1967; recipient Excellent Police Citations, N.Y. Police Dept., 1964-70. Mem. Res. Officers Assn., Am. Soc. Indsl. Security, Nat. Assn. Flight Instrs., Airplane Owners and Pilots Assn. Republican. Roman Catholic. Clubs: Capitol Hill, Army and Navy (Washington); NYU, Wings (N.Y.C.). Home: 4800 W 87th St Prairie Village KS 66207 also Office: Aviation & Mgmt Assocs Inc John F Kennedy Internat Airport PO Box 30-707 Jamaica NY 11430

ERIKSSON, LARRY JOHN, company executive, electrical engineer; b. Milw., Feb. 12, 1945; s. Henry Charles and Frances (Bartol) E.; m. Karen Ruth Kroenke, Aug. 26, 1967; children—Mark Alan, Jodi Marie. B.S. in Elec. Engring., Northwestern U., 1967; M.S. in Elec. Engring., U. Minn., 1969; Ph.D. in Elec. Engring., U. Wis., Madison, 1985. Registered profl. engr., Wis. Research scientist Honeywell Corp., Hopkins, Minn., 1968-71; pres. Sonotek, New Berlin, Wis., 1971-72; acoustical engr. AMF/Harley-Davidson, Milw., 1972-73; v.p. research Nelson Industries, Stoughton, Wis., 1973—. Contbr. articles to profl. jours. Mem. IEEE (sr. mem.), Soc. Automotive Engrs. (Outstanding Younger Mem., 1977), Acoustical Soc. Am. (founder, service award 1983), ASME. Lodge: Rotary. Home: 5301 Greenbriar Ln Madison WI 53714 Office: Nelson Industries Inc Hwy 51 Stoughton WI 53714

ERKIS, RONALD SHELDON, orthodontist, educator; b. Columbus, Ohio, July 10, 1942; s. Donald and Sylvia (Hartman) E.; m. Joyce L. Mulford, Dec. 18, 1976; children—Todd, Andy, Brad. Student Ohio State U., 1960-63; D.D.S., Case Western Res. U., 1967; M.S. in Orthodontics, U. Pitts., 1974. Gen. practice dentistry, Columbus, Ohio, 1969-72; practice dentistry specializing in orthodontics, Columbus, 1974—; tchr. Ohio State U., Columbus Children's Hosp. Bd. dirs. Columbus Jewish Ctr.; past bd. dirs. Jewish Family Services. Served with Dental Corps, US Army, 1967-69. Recipient Koach leadership award Jewish Ctr., 1982. Mem. Columbus Dental Assn., Ohio Dental Soc., ADA, Am. Assn. Orthodontists, Central Ohio Orthodontic Study Club (pres.), Alpha Omega (past pres.). Home: 50 Ashbourne Columbus OH 43209 Office: 5350 E Main St Columbus OH 43213

ERLANDSON, ARVID LEONARD, microbiologist; b. Norway, Mich., Sept. 26, 1929; s. Arvid Leonard and Mildred Anna (Ahlich) E.; m. Grace Marie Collica, May 28, 1955; children—Paul Matthew, Kathryn Marie, Teresa Ann, Mark Arvid, Susan Diane. B.S., U. Mich., 1951, M.S., 1952, Ph.D., 1954. Research microbiologist Parke Davis & Co., Detroit, 1957-63; instr. microbiology U. Mich., Ann Arbor, 1963-64; asst. prof. Sch. Medicine, Marquette U., Milw., 1964-71; dir. microbiology Bronson Hosp., Kalamazoo, 1971—; cons. Upjohn Co., Kalamazoo, 1971—. Author, co-author publs. in sci. lit. Chmn. Kalamazoo County Com. for Infectious Disease Prevention, Edn. and Control, 1973-81. Served to lt. USN, 1954-57. Mem. Am. Soc. Microbiology, Mich. Soc. for Infection Control (pres. 1976-78), Am. Acad. Microbiology (cert. in pub. health and med. lab. microbiology), Nat. Registry Microbiologists, Sigma Xi, Phi Sigma. Roman Catholic. Avocations: golf; bowling. Home: 6340 Marlow Portage MI 49081 Office: Bronson Meth Hosp 252 E Lovell St Kalamazoo MI 49007

ERLENBORN, JOHN NEAL, lawyer, former congressman; b. Chgo., Feb. 8, 1927; s. John H. and Veronica M. (Moran) E.; student U. Notre Dame, 1944, U. Ill., 1945-46; J.D., Loyola U. (Chgo.), 1949; m. Dorothy C. Fisher, May 10, 1952; children—Debra Lynn, Paul Nelson, David John. Bar: Ill. 1949. Practice, Wheaton, Ill., 1949-50, mem. firm Erlenborn and Bauer, 1952-63, Erlenborn, Bauer, and Hotte, 1963-71; mem. 89th-97th Congresses from 14 Dist. Ill., and 98th Congress from 13th Dist. Ill., 1965-85; ptnr. Seyfarth, Shaw, Fairweather & Geraldson, Washington and Chgo., 1985—. Mem. Ill. Ho. of Reps., 1956-64; assistant states atty., DuPage County, Ill., 1950-52. Served with USNR, 1944-46. Mem. Am. Legion. Republican. Office: Seyfarth Shaw Fairweather & Geraldson 1111 19th St NW Washington DC 20036 also 55 E Monroe St Chicago IL 60603

ERNEST, ROBERT C., paper company executive; b. 1924; ed. U. Wis., M.I.T. With Kimberly-Clark Corp., 1952—, v.p. paper products, 1971, group v.p. fine paper and spltys. group, 1971, dir., 1971, exec. v.p., 1972, pres., 1978—, vice chmn., 1985—. Office: Kimberly Clark Corp 2100 Winchester Rd Neenah WI 54956

ERNSBERGER, DAVID JACQUES, psychologist, clergyman; b. Rochester, N.Y., Apr. 8, 1930; s. Paul Edgar and Helen (Jacques) E.; m. Deborah Scott, Aug. 29, 1953; children—Paul, Daniel, Gail. B.A., Wesleyan U., 1952; M.Div., Yale U., 1955; S.T.M., Union Theol. Sem., 1957; Ph.D., U. Tex.-Austin, 1976. Lic. cons. psychologist, Minn., 1980; ordained to ministry, Presbyn. Ch., 1956. Organizing minister Countryside Presbyn. Ch., Saginaw, Mich., 1955-62; minister Greenhills Community Ch., Cin., 1962-68, Covenant Presbyn. Ch., Springfield, Ohio, 1968-72; vis. prof. Austin Presbyn. Sem., 1972-75; minister Grace Presbyn. Ch., Mpls., 1975-83; staff psychologist Inst. for Psychol. Therapies, Mpls., 1977-84; dir., cons. Neighborhood Involvement Program, Mpls., 1976—; dir. Kiel Clin. of Mpls., 1985—. Mem. Am. Psychol. Assn., Minn. Psychol. Assn. Democrat. Presbyterian. Author: A Philosophy of Adult Christian Education, 1959; Education for Renewal, 1965. Home: 3921 Xerxes Ave S Minneapolis MN 55410 Office: 204 W Franklin Ave Minneapolis MN 55404

ERSKINE, CHARLENE G., psychologist, educator; b. Stoneham, Mass., Sept. 13, 1943; d. Ervin E. and Eleanor V. (Weston) Gloor; 1 child, Frederick T. Erskine IV. B.A., Atlantic Union Coll., 1966; M.Ed., Mass. State Coll., Fitchburg, 1971; Ph.D., U. Iowa, 1974. Clin. psychologist Creighton U., Omaha, 1974—, dir., adj. assoc. prof., 1978—; pvt. practice clin. psychology, Omaha, 1980—; mem. State Bd. Examiners, Nebr., 1984—. Mem. Nebr. Psychol. Assn. (sec.-treas. 1980-82), Am. Psychol. Assn., Nat. Registry Health Providers. Office: Creighton U California at 24th St Omaha NE 68178

ERWIN, CHESLEY PARA, JR., utility co. exec.; b. Milw., Apr. 6, 1953; s. Chesley Para and Constance June (Raab) E.; student Occidental Coll., 1971-72; A.B., Stanford U., 1974; M.A. in Public Policy and Adminstrn., U. Wis., Madison, 1976, M.S. in Bus., 1976, postgrad. in law; m. Karen Jane Leonard, Dec. 27, 1974. Intern, Bur. Fiscal Policy Planning and Analysis, Wis. Dept. Revenue, 1976; energy researcher energy systems and policy research group Inst. Environ. Studies, U. Wis., Madison, 1974-76; health planning analyst Wis. Dept. Health and Social Services, Madison, 1976-77; energy analyst Office State Planning and Energy, Wis. Dept. Adminstrn., Madison, 1977-78; govt. relations specialist Wis. Power & Light Co., Madison, 1978-81; regulatory affairs advisor, 1981-85, coordinator environ. regulation, 1985—. Mem. New Republican Conf. Wis., 1976—; coordinator Anderson for Pres., Dane County, Wis., 1979-80; alt. del. Rep. Nat. Conv., 1980; mem. Waukesha County Solid Waste Mgmt. Bd., 1982-85. Mem. Am. Econs. Assn., ABA (student div.), Am. Soc. Public Adminstrn., Chgo. Council Fgn. Relations, Oconomowoc Jaycees. Republican. Home: 820 Old Tower Rd Oconomowoc WI 53066 Office: PO Box 192 222 W Washington Ave Madison WI 53701

ERWIN, RAYMOND MAURICE, educator; b. Ames, Iowa, Dec. 8, 1924; s. Maurice Weir and Ruth (Martin) E.; m. Gloria Yvonne Crews, June 18, 1949; m. 2d, Marion Emma Schwarting, Oct. 14, 1972; stepchildren—George Ness, Cinda Sue Garske, Tammy McGlinnen. B.S., N.D. State U., 1948; B.S., U. Minn., 1954, M.A., 1971. Cert. vocat. agr., agribus. tchr., audio-visual dir. Minn. Vets. instl. on-farm instr. Minot (N.D.) State Coll., 1948-51; vocat. agr. instr. Stillwater (Minn.) High Sch., 1954—; agr. adv. Lam Dong province South Viet Nam, AID, 1966-67; freelance comml. photographer. Baytown twp. supr., Washington County, Minn., 1963-66. Served to col. USMCR, 1942-76. Sears Coll. scholar N.D. State U., 1942. Mem. Future Farmers of Am. (life alumni), Minn. Edn. Assn., NEA, Minn. Vocat. Agr. Instrs. Assn. (dist. dir., sec., editor Ag Man), Am. Vocat. Assn., Minn. Vocat. Assn., Marine Corps Assn., Marine Corps Res. Officers Assn., Res. Officers Assn. U.S., Ret. Officers Assn. U.S., Kappa Delta Pi, Alpha Zeta, Alpha Tau Alpha, Alpha Phi Gamma, Phi Delta Kappa. Republican. Methodist. Lodges: Elks, Eagles, Rotary. Contbr. articles to profl. jours. Home: 5225 Northbrook Blvd N Stillwater MN 55082 Office: 523 W Marsh St Stillwater MN 55082

ESCHBACH, JESSE ERNEST, federal judge; b. Warsaw, Ind., Oct. 26, 1920; s. Jesse Ernest and Mary W. (Stout) E.; B.S., Ind. U., 1943, J.D. with distinction (Hastings scholar), 1949; m. Sara Ann Walker, Mar. 15, 1947; children—Jesse Ernest III, Virginia. Admitted to Ind. bar, 1949; partner firm Graham, Rasor, Eschbach & Harris, Warsaw, 1949-62; city atty., Warsaw, 1952-53; dep. pros. atty. 54th Jud. Circuit Ct. Ind., 1952-54; judge U.S. Dist. Ct. No. Dist. Ind., 1962-74, chief judge, 1974-81; judge U.S. Ct. Appeals for 7th circuit, 1981—. Pres. Endicott Church Furniture, Inc., 1960-62; sec., gen. counsel Dalton Foundries, Inc., 1957-62. Trustee, Ind. U., 1965-70. Served with USNR, 1943-46. Recipient U.S. Law Week award, 1949. Mem. U.S. (labor relations com. 1960-62), Warsaw (pres. 1955-56) chambers commerce, Nat. Assn. Furniture Mfrs. (dir. 1962), Ind. Mfrs. Assn. (dir. 1962), Am., Ind. (bd. mgrs. 1953-54, ho. dels. 1950-60, 7th Circuit Fed. bar assns., Am. Judicature Soc., Order of Coif. Presbyterian. Rotarian (pres. Warsaw 1956-57). Editorial staff Ind. Law Jour., 1947-49. Office: Fed Bldg 1300 S Harrison Room 243 Fort Wayne IN 46802*

ESCHMAN, GARY LEE, software development company executive; b. West Point, Iowa, July 23, 1936; s. Omer D. and Evelyn M. (Wilson) E.; m. Dianne Meyer, Apr. 7, 1979. B.A., U. Iowa, 1959. Supt. Lowe-Eschman Constrn. Co., Marion, Iowa, 1961-66; mgr. New Eng. Life Co., Iowa City, 1966-74; salesman Marsh & McLennan, Iowa City, 1974-82; pres. Network Microdesigns Corp., Cedar Rapids, Iowa, 1982—. Served to 1st lt. U.S. Army, 1959-61. Avocations: photography; skiing; mountaineering; jogging. Home: 140 A Stewart Rd Iowa City IA 52240 Office: Network Microdesigns Corp 200 5th Ave SE Cedar Rapids IA 52401

ESCHMANN, JOEL EDWARD, equipment manufacturing corporation executive; b. Racine, Wis., Aug. 6, 1942; s. Edward and Lydia (Pribyl) E.; m. Nancy Gayle Hostad, Nov. 23, 1974 (div. Dec. 1984); children—Joellen, Sara. Assoc. in Math. and Physics, Gateway Inst., 1968. Mech. engr. Gould/Gettys Mfg. Co., Racine, 1963-80, Graham Co., Milw., 1980-83, Allen Bradley Co., Brown Deer, Wis., 1983—; instr. Milw. Sch. Engring., 1981-83. Mem. Internat. Electronics Packaging Soc., Am. Soc. Metals. Lutheran. Club: Lakeshore Repeater Assn. (Racine) (pres. 1976-79). Avocations: amateur radio; sailing; fishing. Home: 6964 Meadowdale Dr Hartford WI 53027 Office: Allen Bradley Co 8949 N Deerbrook Trail Brown Deer WI 53223

ESCURE, GENEVIEVE JEANNE, language educator; b. Perpignan, France, July 11, 1942; came to U.S., 1970; d. Pierre and Lucienne (Gasq) Escure; m. Jacques Soppelsa, Aug. 4, 1962 (div. 1969); 1 child, Muriel. Licence in English Lit., Sorbonne U., 1963, CAPES in English, 1967; M.A. in French Linguistics, Ind. U., 1973, M.A. in Gen. Linguistics, 1973, Ph.D. in Linguistics, 1975. Tchr. English Lycee, Paris, 1967-70; instr. French and linguistics Hollins Coll., Roanoke, Va., 1970-72; asst. prof. U. Minn., Mpls., 1974-80, assoc. prof. dept. English, 1980—; researcher in theoretical linguistics, sociolinguistics, 1978—. Contbr. articles to profl. jours., chpts. to books. IPES, Ministere de l'Education Nationale scholar, 1963-65; grantee Ford Found., 1971-72, U. Minn., 1978—. Mem. Linguistics Soc. Am. (local organizer 1975), Midwest MLA (chmn.), Can. Linguistic Assn., Soc. for Caribbean Linguistics, Societas Linguistica Europea. Avocations: scuba-diving; skiing, running; painting. Home: 161 Seymour Ave SE Minneapolis MN 55414 Office: Dept English U Minn 207 Church St SE Minneapolis MN 55455

ESHLEMAN, J. ROSS, sociology educator, author; b. Mt. Joy, Pa., Apr. 11, 1936; s. John E. and Ruth (Forney) E.; m. Janet W. Hershberger, May 31, 1958; children—Jill Renee, Sidney R. B.A., Manchester Coll., 1958; M.A., Ohio State U., 1960, Ph.D., 1963. Prof. sociology Western Mich. U., Kalamazoo, 1963-72; program mgr. NSF, Washington, 1972-73; prof. sociology Wayne State U., Detroit, 1973—, chmn. dept. sociology, 1973-83; Fulbright-Hays lectr. Philippine-Am. Edn. Found., Manila, 1968-69, 71; dir. Insts. in Sociology, NSF, Kalamazoo, 1966-72. Author: Sociology: An Introduction, 2d edit., 1985; The Family, 4th edit., 1985. Bd. dirs., exec. com. Oakland Family Services, Oakland County, Mich., 1981-86. Fulbright-Hays grantee, Washington, 1968-69, 71; NIMH fellow Ohio State U., Columbus, 1962. Mem. Am. Sociol. Assn. (sec. family div. 1982-85), Soc. for Study Social Problems (chmn. family div. 1981-83), Nat. Council Family Relations, Philippine Sociol. Soc., Sci. Edn. Consortium. Home: 6815 Orinoco Circle Birmingham MI 48010 Office: Wayne State U Dept Sociology Detroit MI 48202

ESMER, GERALD PETER, engineering executive; b. Chgo., Apr. 28, 1943; s. Peter and Lottie (Wojciechowski) E.; m. Suzanne K. Eastman, Sept. 16, 1964 (div. Oct. 1978); children—Rand M., Robert G., Gregory J. B.S.E.E. with honors, Mich. State U., 1965; M.S.E.E., Stanford U., 1966; student in systems enging. U. Pa., 1968-69; M.B.A. with distinction, U. Mich., 1981. Asst. elec. engr. Gen. Motors Corp., Saginaw, Mich., summers 1963, 64; mem. tech. staff Bell Telephone Labs., Whippany, N.J., summer 1965; chief enging. staff Gen. Electric Co., Valley Missiles & Space Div., Valley Forge, Pa., 1966-70; project engr. Systems Div., Bendix Corp., Ann Arbor, Mich., 1970-72; supr. Transport Systems Ops., Ford Motor Co., Dearborn, Mich., 1972-77, supr. Elec. and Electronics Div., 1977—. Patentee in field. Chmn. Green Oak Twp., South Lyon, Mich., 1974; bd. dirs. Georgetown Commons S. Condominium Assn., 1984-85. NSF fellow, 1965-66. Mem. Eta Kappa Nu, Tau Beta Pi, Beta Gamma Sigma. Club: Ann Arbor Ski. Avocations: skiing, tennis, racquetball, reading, computers. Home: 2832 Bombridge Ct Ann Arbor MI 48104 Office: Fort Motor Co Elec and Electronics Div C370 DPTC 17000 Rotunda Dr Dearborn MI 48121

ESPESETH, DONALD WILLIAM, hospital radiology administrator; b. Rice Lake, Wis., May 4, 1932; s. Robert E. and Mary (Willemssen) E.; m. Kathryn Ann Stafford, Sept. 7, 1957 (div.); children—Brady D., Lori Kay. Cert. Lawton Sch. Radiologic Tech., Beverly Hills, Calif., 1951. with Waukesha (Wis.) Meml. Hosp., 1955—, chief radiologic technologist until 1970, radiology adminstr., 1970—; mem. Waukesha County Health Systems Com.; corp. mem. Southeastern Wis. Health Systems Agy.; mem. Wis. Adv. Com. for Para-Med. Health Occupations, Wis. Bd. Vocat. Tech. Adult Edn.; chmn. radiology adminstrs. adv. com., mem. shared services com. Wis. Hosp. Purchasing, Inc.; mem. health-care team working with refugees in Indo-China, 1980; mem. China-U.S. Sci. Exchange (radiation adminstrn.). Served with USAF, 1951-55. Mem. Am. Soc. Radiologic Technologists, Wis. Soc. Radiologic Technologists (pres. 1975-76), Am. Hosp. Radiology Adminstrs., Radiology Adminstrs. Southeastern Wis. Home: 207 Coolidge Ave Waukesha WI 53186 Office: 725 American Ave Waukesha WI 53186

ESPOSITO, LOUIS JOSEPH, marketing executive, manufacturing consultant; b. Bklyn., Aug. 15, 1931; s. Louis J. and Mary E. (Ward) E.; m. Dolores E. Barry, Mar. 13, 1954 (dec. 1974); m. Elinor A. Amshey, Feb. 28, 1976; children—Edward L., Donna A., Barbara M. Shelton, Patricia E. B.M.E., Bklyn. Poly. Inst., 1953. Trainee Continental Can, Syracuse, N.Y., 1953-54; sales engr. Union Carbide Corp., Washington, 1956-63; sales mgr. Carbone Corp. U.S.A., Wilmington, Del., 1963-67; v.p. sales Norco Inc., Cleve., 1967-75; pres., chmn. bd. Eljay Assocs., Akron, Ohio, 1975—; chmn. bd. Spec Industries Inc., Akron, 1968—. Founder, pres. Devonshire Civic Assn., Wilmington, 1966; pres. Granger Lake Condo Assn., Medina, Ohio, 1984. Served to 1st lt. C.E., U.S. Army, 1954-56. Mem. Mfr. Agts. Nat. Assn. Republican. Roman Catholic. Avocations: photography; golf; sailing; tennis. Home: 171 Granger Rd 129 Medina OH 44256

ESPRIT, LEE GARLAND, JR., educator; b. Port Arthur, Tex., Nov. 17, 1936; s. Lee Garland and Velma (Linton) E.; m. Delores Ann Martin, Aug. 10, 1957; children—Sylvia, Lee, Michael, Anita, Karen, Reginald, Darryl, Jonathan, Velma, Bryan. B.S. in Edn., Prairie View (Tex.) A&M U., 1959; M.S. in Nat. Sci., Okla. State U.-Stillwater, 1969, Ed.D., 1971. Cert. life educator, Tex.; cert. jr. coll. pres., Calif., supr. biol. scis., Calif. Chmn., instr. edn. div. Wilberforce (Ohio) U., 1971-72; chmn. secondary edn. Central State U.-Wilberforce, 1972-77, assoc. prof., 1977-80, dir. field based experiences, 1980—, chmn. profl. edn. dept., 1980. Pres., Ohio Children's Mental Health Bd., 1981—, Ohio Human Relations Comm., NDEA fellow, 1971. Mem. NEA, Ohio Assn. Teaching Educators; Council Tchrs. Math and Sci., Ohio Edn. Assn., Dayton Urban League, NAACP, Higher Edn. Adv. Council, AAUP, Phi Delta Kappa, Kappa Alpha Psi, Delta Kappa Pi. Republican. Roman Catholic. Clubs: Town and Country, Promotion Art, Sci., Lit. Home: 1968 El Camino Dr Xenia OH 45385 Office: 143 Henderson Coll Educ Central State U Wilberforce OH 45384

ESSENBURG, SHERYL K(AE), lawyer; b. Charlevoix, Mich., Oct. 9, 1953; d. Theodore Lewis and Rotha June (Alofs) E.; m. David Leslie Ross, Sept. 2, 1978; 1 child, Sarah. B.A., Calvin Coll., 1975; J.D., U. Ill., 1978. Bar: Ill. 1978, U.S. Dist. Ct. (so. dist.) Ill. 1978. Staff atty. Nat. Ctr. for Youth Law, St. Louis, 1978; asst. atty. gen. Office of Ill. Atty. Gen., Springfield, Ill., 1978-81; asst. states atty. Sangamon County States Atty.'s Office, Springfield, 1981—. Author pamphlet: The Parent Pamphlet: Preventing Sexual Abuse of Children, 1982. Bd. dirs. Com. for Children, Springfield, 1981—. Mem. Ill. State Bar Assn., Sangamon County Bar Assn. Mem. Christian Ref. Ch. Home: 1737 S Whittier Ave Springfield IL 62704 Office: Sangamon County States Atty 8th and Monroe Sts Springfield IL 62701

ESSER, JOHN MICHAEL, bookseller; b. Milw., Dec. 13, 1940; s. John and Marian (Platta) Shuda E. B.S., Wis. State U.-Stevens Point, 1965; M.A., U. Wis.-Milw., 1973, M.L.S., 1975. Tchr. Parkview High Sch., Orfordville, Wis., 1965-67; tchr. East Troy High Sch., Wis., 1967-68; tchr. Kettle Moraine High Sch., Wales, Wis., 1968-84; co-owner, bookseller Constant Reader, Milw., 1969—. Roman Catholic. Avocation: book collecting. Home: 1901 N Prospect Ave Milwaukee WI 53202 Office: Constant Reader Bookshop 1625-27 E Irving Pl Milwaukee WI 53202

ESSEX, GRACE ANN, social service administrator; b. Gallipolis, Ohio, Nov. 29, 1951; d. Carl Cecil and Rachel Maxine (Folan) Miller; m. Richard Logan Essex, Sept. 1, 1973; 1 dau., Kelly Marie. B.S. with honors in Home Econs., Ohio U., 1974, M.S., 1978. Teaching cert. Ohio. Home econs. tchr. Athens (Ohio) High Sch., 1974-80; coordinator adolescent pregnancy program Tri-County JVS, 1980—; owner, operator Hocking Valley Day Sch., 1983—. Mem. Ohio Vocat. Assn., Home Econs. Bd., NEA, Ohio Edn. Assn., Child Conservation League. Mem. Christian Ch. Home: 6 Virginia Ln Athens OH 45701 Office: Route #1 Nelsonville OH 45764

ESSMAN, DENISE IRENE, marketing educator; b. Greenfield, Iowa, Mar. 31, 1948; d. Harold William and Eleanor Irene (Johnson) Bricker; m. Allen Kent Essman, June 1, 1968; children: Bradly Allen, Brady Kent, Barrett William. B.S., Iowa State U., 1973, postgrad., 1977-78; M.B.A., Drake U., 1980. Mktg. trainee The Bankers Life, Des Moines, 1975-76; v.p. mktg. Essman & Assocs., 1977—; instr. mktg. Iowa State U., Ames, 1978-79, 81-84; cons. Small Bus. Devel. Ctr., 1984—, instr. mktg. Drake U., Des Moines, 1984—; manuscript reviewer. Com. mem. Des Moines Art Ctr., 1975—. Mem. AAUP, Am. Mktg. Assn. (dir. 1983—, v.p. midwestern region 1983—85), Iowa Mktg. Assn. (dir. 1982-85, treas. 1979-80, v.p. 1980-81, pres. 1981-82), Life Office Mgmt. Assn., Alpha Mu Alpha (advisor). Democrat. Lutheran. Home: 3008 SW Thornton Ave Des Moines IA 50321

ESSNER, STEPHEN W. (STEPHEN WILLIAM STILGENBAUER), entertainer, stage director, choreographer; b. Tulsa, Mar. 5, 1952; s. Ned Thomas and Elizabeth Patricia (Wright) Stilgenbauer; m. Nancy Elizabeth Carroll, Nov. 18, 1978. B.A. in Theatre Arts, U. Cin., 1974, M.A. with honors, 1976. Appeared in dinner theatres, summer stock, indl. shows throughout U.S. including AT&T, Internat. Harvester, R.T. French, 1973-83; jingle singer, producer jingles, N.Y.C., 1978-82; choreographer Taft Broadcasting Theme Parks, various locations, 1977-83; appearances on TV. Mem. Actors Equity Assn.

ESTEP, ERNEST ROBERT, obstetrician and gynecologist; b. Tiffin, Ohio, Sept. 6, 1941; s. Wade Louis and Margaret C. (Wetzel) E.; m. Bonnie Lynn Cline, Aug. 9, 1964. B.S., Heidelberg Coll., 1963; M.D., Ohio State U., 1967. Intern, Akron (Ohio) City Hosp., 1967, resident in ob-gyn, 1970-74, chief resident, 1974; practice medicine specializing in ob-gyn, Greeley, Colo., 1974-76, Akron, Ohio, 1976—; active teaching staff Akron City Hosp. Served with Div. Indian Health, USPHS, 1968-70. Named Resident of Yr., Akron City Hosp., 1974. Fellow Am. Coll. Ob-Gyn.; mem. Am. Assn. Gynecologic Laparoscopists, AMA, Ohio State Med. Assn., Summit County Med. Assn. Republican. Lutheran. Club: Heidelberg Fellows (pres.). Contbr. article to profl. publ. Office: 733 W Market St Akron OH 44303

ETHEREDGE, FOREST DEROYCE, state legislator; b. Dallas, Oct. 21, 1929; s. Gilbert W. and Theta E. (Tate) E.; B.S., Va. Poly. Inst. and State U., 1951; M.S., U. Ill., 1953; postgrad. Northwestern U., 1953-55; Ph.D., Loyola U., Chgo., 1968; m. Joan Mary Horan, Apr. 30, 1955; children—Forest William, John Bede, Mary Faith, Brian Thomas, Regina Ann. Mem. faculty City Colls. of Chgo., 1955-65, chmn. dept. phys. sci., 1963-65; dean of instrn. Rock Valley Coll., Rockford, Ill., 1965-67, v.p., 1966-67; pres. McHenry County Coll., Crystal Lake, Ill., 1967-70, Waubonsee Community Coll., Sugar Grove, Ill., 1970-81; mem. Ill. Senate, 1981—; dir., sec. No. Ill. Public Telecommunication Corp., 1977-81; mem. Ill. Council Pub. Community Coll. Pres., 1967-81, chmn., 1971-72. Bd. dirs. Mercy Center for Health Care Services, 1972—, Aurora Community Concert Assn., 1974-80, Suburban Community Coll. TV Consortium, 1978-81; pres. Aurora (Ill.) United Way, 1979-81; mem. Citizens Ad. Council Dangerous Drugs Commn.; mem. Intergovtl. Coop. Commn.; mem. Sci. Adv. Council. Mem. Greater Aurora C. of C. (bd. dirs. 1978-82), Chgo. Met. Higher Edn. Council (dir. 1978-79), Sigma Xi, Phi Delta Kappa, Sigma Gamma Epsilon. Home: 843 W Hardin Ave Aurora IL 60506 Office: 52 W Downer Pl Aurora IL 60507

ETHERIDGE, MARGARET DWYER, medical center administrator; b. Atlanta, Jan. 5, 1938; d. Philip Fitzgerald and Mary Catharine (Dwyer) E.; m. Roy Charles McCracken, May 5, 1975; m. William Bertram Smitheram, Aug. 17, 1985. B.A., Emory U., 1960; M. Hosp. Adminstrn., Washington U., St. Louis, 1973. Registered record adminstr. Spl. asst. to dir. VA Med. Ctr., Roseburg, Oreg., 1973-74; hosp. adminstrn. specialist VA Central Office, Washington, 1974-76; asst. dir. trainee VA Med. Ctr., Phila., 1976; assoc. dir. VA Med. Ctr., Hampton, Va., 1976-80, Buffalo, N.Y., 1980-81; Presdl. exchange exec. Kimberly Clark Corp., Neenah, Wis. and Roswell, Ga., 1981-82; dir. VA Med. Ctr., Grand Island, Nebr., 1982—; instr. Cerritos Coll., Calif., 1969-70. Bd. dirs. Project 2M Coordinating Council, Inc., Grand Island, 1985—. Mem. Fed. Exec. Assn. Grand Island, Am. Coll. Healthcare Execs., Am. Hosp. Assn., Nebr. Hosp. Assn., Grand Island C. of C. (legis. affairs com. 1984-85, priorities com. 1984-85), Altrusa. Democrat. Roman Catholic. Club: Riverside Golf (Grand Island). Home: 2508 Apache Rd Grand Island NE 68801 Office: VA Med Ctr 2201 N Broadwell Ave Grand Island NE 68803

ETHERINGTON, RICHARD EARL, aeronautical engineer; b. Fredonia, Kans., Apr. 4, 1930; s. Alfred Earl and Jessie Marjorie (Elrod) E.; m. Mary Lou Allen, June 5, 1952; children—Glenn Allen, Charles Alfred, Richard Andrew. B.S. in Aero. Enging., Kans. U.-Lawrence, 1952. Registered profl. engr., Kans. Engr., Beech Aircraft Corp., Wichita, Kans., 1952-67; mgr. advance design Gates Lear Jet Corp., Wichita, Kans., 1967-73, program mgr., 1973-76, dir. tech. enging., 1976-81, dir. program mgmt., 1981-84, dir. tech., exptl. enging., 1984—. Assoc. fellow AIAA (chmn. gen. aviation system com. 1976-78); mem. Soc. Automotive Engrs. (chmn. bus. and utility aircraft com. 1979-81). Avocations: pilot pvt. planes; radio control model aircraft. Home: 4257 Janesville St Wichita KS 67220 Office: Gates Learjet Corp PO Box 7707 Wichita KS 67277

ETHIER, DOLORES OLSON, chemical engineering consultant; b. St. Paul, Aug. 6, 1924; d. Oscar Hilmer and Alice Augusta (Lindstrom) Olson; m. George Daniel Ethier, July 11, 1951. Student U. Minn., 1946; B.S., St. Cloud State Coll., 1948. Electrician, Northwest Airlines, St. Paul, 1942-42; with 3M Co., St. Paul, 1944-69, supr. 1952-69; sr. research assoc. H.B. Fuller Co., St. Paul, 1969-70; sr. chem. engr., prin. engr., supervising staff engr. Sperry Univac, St. Paul, 1973-80; product dir. membrane switches Dura Process Co., Mpls., 1980; research and devel. mgr. Press On Inc., Stillwater, Minn., 1980-82; pvt. practice cons., White Bear Lake, Minn., 1970—; expert witness various; Sci. Fair judge, St. Paul. Patentee in field. Recipient Highest Achievement award Dale Carnegie Course, 1965. Mem. Am. Chem. Soc., Fedn. Socs. for Coating Tech., Soc. Women Engrs. Republican. Mem. Convenant Ch. Club: Fleetwood Stamp. Home: 2187 Floral Dr White Bear Lake MN 55110 Office: Ethier Enterprises 2187 Floral Dr White Bear Lake MN 55110

ETIENNE, ANTHONY DOYLE, educational administrator; b. Mt. Pleasant, Ind., June 9, 1936; s. Oscar and M. Lettia (Cart) E.; m. Mary Susan Sherman, June 19, 1971; children—Anthony Erich, Patrick Kieran, Drew Stefan. B.A., St. Meinrad Coll., 1958; M.Ed., Spalding Coll., 1967; Ed.D., Ind. U., 1974. Tchr. Providence High Sch., Clarksville, Ind., 1962-67; Nat. Assn. Secondary Sch. Prins. intern Ritter High Sch., Indpls., 1967-68; supr., student tchr. Ind. U., Bloomington, 1970-71; guidance dir. Met. Sch. Dist., Wayne Twp., Indpls., 1971-74; asst. prin. Decatur Twp., Indpls., 1974-77, prin., 1978—; chmn. North Central Assn. Team, Indpls., 1982-84. Bd. dirs. Hill Valley Home Owners Assn., Indpls., 1982—; v.p. IDEA-Gifted and Talented Perry Twp., Indpls., 1983-84. Mem. Nat. Assn. Secondary Sch. Prins., Assn. Supervision and Curriculum Devel. Democrat. Roman Catholic. Lodge: Lions. Avocations: gardening; woodworking; golf. Home: 215 Val Del Ct Indianapolis IN 46227 Office: Decatur Central High Sch 5251 Kentucky Ave Indianapolis IN 46241

ETTER, EDITH FRANCES, educator; b. Plummer, Minn., Aug. 7, 1932; d. Fred Eugene and A. Katherine (Polson) Mykleby; m. Wallace Herman Etter, Aug. 28, 1954; 1 son, David Fred. B.S., Bemidji State U., 1963, postgrad. Elem. tchr. Aurora (Minn.) Public Schs., 1952-54, Mounds View (Minn.) Pub. Schs., 1954-55, St. Peter (Minn.) Pub. Schs., 1956-57, Pipestone (Minn.) Pub. Schs., 1957-61, Thief River Falls (Minn.) Pub. Schs., Minn., 1961—. Sunday Sch. tchr. Trinity Luth. Ch., 1962-69; den mother Cub Scouts, 1964-66; chmn. youth bd. Trinity Luth. Ch., 1967-69; youth bd. Thief River Falls Conf., 1967-79, No. Minn. Dist. Youth, 1968-79; Sunday sch. supt. Trinity Luth. Ch., 1972-75; human relations com. Thief River Falls Schs., 1972-73; city planning comm. Thief River Falls, 1980—. Recipient, Honor Roll Tchr. Yr. Minn., 1973; Outstanding Woman educator, 1978; commendation Outstanding Reading Council Activities, 1981. Mem. Thief River Falls Edn. Assn., Kramer-Brown Uniserv (chairperson 1980-81, chairperson Instrn. and Profl. Devel. Council 1975-81), Thief River Falls Edn. Assn. (TEPS chmn., 1962-63, v.p., 1964-66, program chmn., 1964-68, salary com., 1967-68, negotiating council, 1967-68, 69-70, 70-71, 74, 75, 79—, chmn. Improvement Instrn., 1967-69), Minn. Edn. Assn. (sec. resolutions com., 1973—, state instrn. and profl. devel. council, 1975—, chmn. tchr. ctr. instrn., 1978-81, chairperson women's caucus, 1979-81), NEA (del., 1967-69, 71-72, 76—, resolution com., 1976-80), AAUW, Assn. Supervision and Curriculum Devel., Thief River Falls Concert Assn., Internat. Reading Assn., Educators Exceptional Children, Assn. Classroom Tchrs. (div. pres. 1967-71, state pres., 1972-74, del., 1967-69, 71-72. Democrat. Lutheran. Lodge: Modern Woodmen. Home: 416 S Maple Thief River Falls MN 56701 Office: 1424 E Gulf Thief River Falls MN 56701

ETTINGER, JOSEPH ALAN, lawyer, educator; b. N.Y.C., July 21, 1931; s. Max and Frances E.; B.A., Tulane U., 1954, J.D. with honors, 1956; children—Amy Beth, Ellen Jane. Admitted to La. bar, 1956, Ill. bar, 1959; asst. corp. counsel City of Chgo., 1959-62; practiced in Chgo., 1962-73, 76—; sr. partner firm Ettinger & Schoenfield, Chgo., 1980—; asso. prof. law Chgo.-Kent Coll., 1973-76; chmn. Village of Olympia Fields (Ill.) Zoning Bd. Appeals, 1969-76; chmn. panel on corrections Welfare Council Met. Chgo., 1969-76. Served to capt., Judge Adv. Gen. Corps, U.S. Army, 1956-59. Recipient Service award Village of Olympia Fields, 1976. Mem. Chgo. Bar Assn., Assn. Criminal

Def. Lawyers (gov. 1970-72). Clubs: Ravisloe Country, Carlton Club. Contbr. articles to profl. publs. Office: 180 N La Salle St Chicago IL 60601

ETZEL, BARBARA COLEMAN, psychologist, educator; b. Pitts., Sept. 19, 1926; d. Walter T. and Ruth (Coleman) E.; A.A., Stephens Coll., 1946; B.S. in Psychology, Denison U., 1948; M.S., U. Miami (Fla.), 1950; Ph.D. in Exptl. Child Psychology, State U. Iowa, 1953. Staff psychologist Ohio State Bur. Juvenile Research, Columbus, 1953-54; asst. prof. psychology Fla. State U., Tallahassee, 1954-56; chief psychologist, child psychiatry U. Wash. Med. Sch., Seattle, 1956-61; asso. prof. psychology Western Wash. State U., Bellingham, 1961-65, dir. grad. program in psychology, 1963-65; spl. fellow sect. early learning and devel. NIMH, Bethesda, Md., 1965-66; asso. prof. dept. human devel. U. Kans., Lawrence, 1965-69, mem. grad. faculty, 1965—, prof. dept. human devel., 1969—, dir. Edna A. Hill Child Devel. Lab., 1965-72, dir. Kansas Center for Research in Early Childhood Edn., 1968-71, asso. dean Office of Research Adminstrn. and Grad. Sch., 1972-74, dir. John T. Stewart Children's Center, 1975-85; vis. prof. Universidad Central de Venezuela, Caracas, 1981-82; cons. Manchester Sch. Presch. Program, U. Mex., Mexico City, 1973-75, George Peabody Tchrs. Coll., 1978, St. Luke's Hosp., Kansas City, Mo., 1981—. Bd. dirs. Community Children's Center, Inc., 1968-71; trustee Center for Research, Inc., U. Kans., 1975-78. Elected to U. Kans. Women's Hall of Fame, 1975; Japan Soc. for Promotion for Sci. fellow, 1981. Fellow Am. Psychol. Assn.; mem. Soc. for Research in Child Devel., Midwestern Psychol. Assn., Am. Ednl. Research Assn., AAAS, AAUP, Southwestern Soc. for Research in Human Devel., Sigma Xi, Psi Chi, Pi Lambda Theta. Author: (with J.M. LeBlanc and D.M. Baer) New Developments in Behavioral Research, 1977; contbr. numerous articles on learning and human devel. to profl. publs.; editorial bd. Behavior Analyst, 1979—. Home: Woodsong at JB Ranch Rt 1 PO Box 82-E Oskaloosa KS 66066 Office: Dept of Human Development U Kans Lawrence KS 66045

ETZKORN, MERLE DEWEES, turbojet engine manufacturing company executive; b. St. Louis, Dec. 17, 1944; d. Merle Edward and Jeanette Margaret Dewees; m. Richard Dennis Etzkorn, June 19, 1965 (div. 1977); 1 son, Kurt Michael. Student, MacMurray Coll., 1964-65, Oakland Community Coll., 1974-76, U. Mich., 1977—. Customer service rep. Dow-Corning Corp., Farmington, Mich., 1974-75; adminstrv. trainee IBM, Detroit, 1975-76; adminstrv. asst. F & H Electronics, Dearborn, Mich., 1976-77; exec. asst. to chief operating officer Williams Internat., Walled Lake, Mich., 1977—. Mem. Nat. Assn. Exec. Secs., Am. Airlines Fair Ladies, Nat. Assn. Female Execs., Mensa. Republican. Roman Catholic.

EUBANKS, MARY, biologist, anthropologist; b. Hattiesburg, Miss., May 21, 1947; d. Michael Joseph and Nell Elizabeth (Bass) E.; m. Thomas Patrick Settlemyre, May 31, 1967 (div. 1973); children—Dealey; m. Edward James Dunn, Mar. 3, 1974 (div. 1983); children—Laura Louise, Edward Wilkes. B.A., U. N.C., 1970, M.A., 1973, Ph.D., 1977. Vis. scientist Harvard Bot. Mus., 1972; instr. U. N.C., Chapel Hill, 1975; research assoc. So. Meth. U., 1976-77, Tulane U. Middle Am. Research Inst., New Orleans, 1977-78, Vanderbilt U., Nashville, 1978-80; vis. scholar anthropology U. Cin., 1981-84; research assoc. biology Ind. U., Bloomington, 1984—; vis. asst. prof. crop sci. N.C. State U., 1981-82. Research Corp. grantee, 1971-72; Nat. Geog. Soc. grantee, 1975-76. Mem. Am. Anthrop. Assn., Soc. Am. Archaeology, Soc. Econ. Botany, AAAS, Sigma Xi. Contbr. articles on archaeology, genetics and ethnobotany to profl. jours. Office: Ind U 138 Jordan Hall Bloomington IN 47405 Office: Ind U 138 Jordan Hall Bloomington IN 47405

EUCHNER, EVERETT BRUCE, chemical company executive; b. Chgo., Jan. 9, 1924; s. Charles Andrew and Joan (Dienert) E.; B.S. in Chem. Engring., Purdue U., 1948; M.S. in Organic Chemistry, Case-Western Res. U., 1952; m. Patricia Enz, Aug. 21, 1948; children—Renee, Jenee, Elaine, Eric. With Glidden Coating and Resin, Cleve., 1948—, dir. polymer research, 1961-64, mgr. regional labs., 1964-65, dir. research center, 1965-75, v.p., dir. research and devel., 1976—. Bd. dirs. Community Chest, 1962-64; mem. Zoning Bd. Appeals, Avon Lake, Ohio, 1962-68; mem. Bldg. Code Bd. Appeals, Avon Lake, 1962-68. Served with USAAF, 1942-45. Decorated D.F.C. Mem. Am. Chem. Soc., Cleve. Engring. Soc., Soc. Plastics Industry, Fedn. Socs. Paint Tech., Indsl. Research Inst., AAAS, Sigma Xi. Office: 16651 Sprague Rd Strongsville OH 44136

EULL, JOEL ROY, concrete company executive, consultant; b. Mpls., Sept. 5, 1956; s. Earl Arnold and Clarine Jeanette (Roy) E.; m. Kim M. Kjellberg, June 14, 1980. Student North Hennepin Community Coll., 1981-83. Prodn. mgr. Eull Concrete Products, Monticello, Minn., 1974-79; v.p. Eull Concrete Products, Inc., Albertville, Minn., 1979-84, pres., 1984—; cons. concrete prodn. machinery Zenith Block Co., Mpls., 1985, Acme Brick, Dallas, 1985, Fleming Mfg., Cuba, Mo., 1982-84. Designer, fabricator automated precast concrete system, 1978, automated material storage and handling system, 1984. Campaign vol. Congressman Vin Weber, Wright County, Minn., 1980. Mem. Associated Gen. Contractors, Minn. Utility Contractors Assn. (directory com. 1985, membership com. 1985). Republican. Roman Catholic. Avocations: travel; golf; photography. Home: Route 3 Box 136 Monticello MN 55362 Office: Eull Concrete Products Inc 5836 Large Ave NE Albertville MN 55301

EUSTICE, BRADLEY MICHAEL, dental association administrator, consultant; b. Waseca, Minn., May 3, 1954; s. Donald Dean and Esther (Clayton) E.; m. Mary K. Sinner, June 16, 1979; children—Molly, Donald. B.A., St. Johns U., 1977; M.S.A., St. Michael's Coll., 1980. Home sch. liaison Apollo High Sch., St. Cloud, Minn., 1975-76; instr. English and religion, coach De LaSalle High Sch., Mpls., 1977-79; head football and ski coach St. Michael's Coll., Winooski, Vt., 1979-80; promotional cons. Princeton Industries, Evansville, Ind., 1981-82; instr. Coll. St. Benedict, St. Joseph, Minn., 1982-83; adminstr. Northway Dental Assn., St. Cloud, 1983—; cons. in field, 1981—. Bd. dirs. Mill Stream Arts Festival, St. Joseph, 1983-84. St. John's U. Acad. scholar. Mem. Nat. Dental Group Mgrs. Assn., State Dental Group Mgrs. Democrat. Roman Catholic. Clubs: Banshee Rugby Football, Eagles. Avocations: rugby, writing, wood carving, camping. Home: Rural Route 3 St Joseph MN 56374 Office: Northway Dental Assn 1500 Northway Dr St Cloud MN 56301

EVANGELISTA, RICHARD NICHOLAS, systems engineer; b. Chgo., Aug. 14, 1942; s. William J. and Julia A. (Schiavoni) E.; m. Mary C. Presto, Nov. 14, 1964; children—Lisa M., Laura L., Richard N. Jr. Student Wright Jr. Coll., Chgo., 1961, Northwestern U., 1963-64; DuPage Coll., 1981-87. Computer programmer Herst-Allen Co., Chgo., 1963-70, Lindberg Hevi-Duty Co., Chgo., 1970-71; systems supr. Litton Sweda Internat., Chgo., 1971-75; regional system mgr. Royal Bus. Systems, Chgo., 1975-80; sr. systems engr. Norand Corp., Chgo., 1980—. Avocations: golf, tennis, water sports. Home: 255 Lincoln Ct Wood Dale IL 60191 Office: Norand Corp 650 Woodfield Dr Suite 250 Schaumburg IL 60195

EVANS, ALAN LEE, psychologist; b. Hot Springs, S.D., Dec. 4, 1945; s. Aubra Milton and Elsie May (Young) E.; B.S., Colo. State U., 1968; M.A., Mich. State U., 1970, Ph.D., 1976. Three county coordinator Community Mental Health Child Abuse & Neglect Prevention Program, Lansing, Mich., 1974-76; vis. asst. prof. Oreg. State U., Corvallis, 1976-77; faculty mem. W.W. Knight family practice residency program Toledo Hosp., 1978-81; asst. prof. U. Toledo, 1977—; pvt. practice clin. psychology, Toledo, 1978—; clin. asst. prof. Med. Coll. Ohio, Toledo. Served to lt. USN, 1970-73. Mem. Am. Psychol. Assn., Psychologists in Family Medicine (nat. pres. 1981—). Democrat. Methodist. Author: Personality Characteristics of Child Abusing Mothers, 1981. Home: 17 Proctor Place Toledo OH 43610 Office: 4334 W Central Suite 217 Toledo OH 43615

EVANS, BILLY JOE, chemistry educator, consultant; b. Macon, Ga., Aug. 18, 1942; s. Will and Mildred (Owens) E.; m. Adye Bel Sampson, Aug. 31, 1963; children—William Joseph, Carole Elizabeth, Jesse Niles. B.Sc. summa cum laude in Chemistry, Morehouse Coll., Atlanta, 1959-63; Ph.D. in Chemistry, U. Chgo., 1968. Asst. prof. Howard U., Washington, 1969-70; asst. prof. chemistry U. Mich., Ann Arbor, 1970-73, assoc. prof., 1973-79, prof., 1979—; dir. Program Scholarly Research Urban/Minority High Sch. Students, Ann Arbor, 1980—, Comprehensive Studies Program, Ann Arbor, 1984—; cons. Nat. Bur. Standards, Washington, 1970-80, Ford Motor Co., Detroit, 1977, U.S. Geol. Survey, Washington, 1977—. Contbr. articles to profl. jours. Bd. dirs. Detroit Met. Sci. and Engring. Fair, 1983—; judge Southeastern Mich. Sci. and Engring. Fair, Ann Arbor, 1983—. Fellow Woodrow Wilson Found., 1963, Nat. Research Council Can., 1968-69, Alexander von Humboldt Found., 1977-78. Mem. U. Mich. Research Club (pres. 1984—), Am. Phys. Soc., Am. Chem. Soc., Minerol. Soc. Am., Am. Geophys. Union, Phi Beta Kappa. Club: Exchange (Ann Arbor). Home: 810 Oxford Rd Ann Arbor MI 48104 Office: U Mich Dept Chemistry 930 N University Ann Arbor MI 48104

EVANS, BRUCE HASELTON, art museum official; b. Rome, N.Y., Nov. 13, 1939; s. E. Arnold and Joan Sawyer (Haselton) E.; m. Margo Elizabeth Frey, July 14, 1962; children—Barton Haselton, Christopher Andrew. B.A., Amherst Coll., 1961; M.A., NYU, 1964. Asst. curator Dayton (Ohio) Art Inst., 1965-66, curator, 1967-68, chief curator, 1969-72, asst. dir., 1973-74, dir., 1975—; mem. adv. panels Nat. Endowment for Arts and Humanities, 1973—; v.p. Midwest Mus. Conf. Council; active Dayton River Corridor Design Rev. Com, Historic Architecture Com. Author: Fifty Treasures of the Dayton Art Institute, 1969; The Paintings of Jean-Leon Gerome, 1972; The Paintings of Edward Edmondson, 1972. Mem. Assn. Art Mus. Dirs., Ohio Mus. Assn. (trustee), Intermus. Conservation Assn. (pres.), Am. Assn. Mus., Internat. Council Mus. Office: Dayton Art Inst PO Box 941 Dayton OH 45401*

EVANS, COOPER, congressman; b. Cedar Rapids, Iowa, May 26, 1924; s. Thomas and Ora E.; m. Jean Marie Ruppelt, June 20, 1948; children—Jim, Charles. B.S., Iowa State U., 1949, M.S., 1955. Registered profl. engr., Iowa. With C.E. U.S., Army, 1949-65; dir. advanced manned lunar missions NASA, Washington, 1963-65; farmer, mng. ptnr., nr. Grundy Center, Iowa, 1965—; mem. Iowa Ho. of Reps., Des Moines, 1974-79, 98th-99th Congresses from 3d Iowa Dist. Served to lt. col., inf. U.S. Army, 1943-46. Decorated Army Commendation medal. Mem. Am. Legion. Republican. Methodist. Lodge: Rotary. Office: US Ho of Reps 127 Cannon House Office Bldg Washington DC 20515

EVANS, DAVID PAUL, marketing executive; b. Detroit, Aug. 7, 1922; s. Emerys Reese and Gladys Julia (Barns) E.; m. Lorraine Julia (DePiere) Evans, Apr. 25, 1945; children—David, Paul, Wayne Hubert. B.E.E., U. Mich., 1943. Gen. zone mgr. sales Ford Motor Co., Detroit, 1949-52, mgr. sales promotions, Dearborn, Mich., 1952-55, mgr. performance and economy engring., 1955-75; pres. Evans Sales & Mktg., Inc., Dearborn, 1975—; sales mgr. Ameritech Met. Communications Mobile Phone, Redford, Mich., 1984—; cons., 1981-84. Author: Performance and Economy, 1960. Bd. dirs. Sobriety House, Detroit, 1974-81, River Oaks Civic Assn., Dearborn, 1960-63; trustee Galloway Bosy Ranch of Minn., 1969-72. Served with USMC, 1942-46. Mem. U.S. Auto Club. Republican. Methodist. Avocation: flying. Home: 22176 Nona St Dearborn MI 48124 Office: Met Communications Ameritech 24350 Capitol Ave Redford MI 48239

EVANS, JAMES EDGAR, optometrist; b. Columbus, Ohio, Jan. 11, 1945; s. Addison Victor and Mary (Morgan) E.; m. Jan Lee Holmgren, June 3, 1972; children—Brian, Regin, Meghan. A.B., Ohio U., 1966; O.D., Ohio State U., 1970. Diplomate Nat. Bd. Examiners in Optometry; lic. optometrist Va., Ohio. Pvt. practice optometry, Wellston, Ohio; dir. Milton Banking Co., Wellston. Served to lt. USN, 1970-74, to maj. Air N.G. Mem. Am. Optometric Assn., Ohio Optometric Assn. (gov. zone 7 1976-80), Wellston Area C. of C. (bd. dirs. 1976-79). Presbyterian. Club: Lions. Lodges: Elks, Masons, Scottish Rite (32d degree), Shriners. Home: 554 Aaron Ave Jackson OH 45640 Office: 11 S Penn Ave Wellston OH 45692 also 107 S Market St McArthur OH 45651

EVANS, LANE, congressman; b. Rock Island, Ill., Aug. 4, 1951; s. Lee Herbert and Joyce (Saylor) E. B.A., Augustana Coll., 1974; J.D., Georgetown U., Washington, 1978. Bar: Ill. 1978. Atty., Western Ill. Legal Assistance, 1975-76, Community Legal Clinic, Rock Island, Ill., 1982-83; nat. staffer Harris for Pres., 1975-76, Kennedy for Pres., 1979-80; mem. 98th-99th Congresses from 17th Dist. Ill. Served with USMC, 1969-71. Recipient Community Service award AFL-CIO, 1979, NAACP, 1979. Mem. Vietnam Vets. Ill., Ill. Pub. Action Council, Marine Corps League, Am. Legion. Democrat. Roman Catholic. Office: 3917 16th St Moline IL 61265

EVANS, MALINDA MURPHEY, librarian; b. Bloomington, Ill., Sept. 11, 1935; d. Earl C. and Imogene (Swigart) Murphey; B.S. in L.S., Ill. State U., Normal, 1973; m. Donald Lee Evans, Apr. 25, 1976; children by previous marriage—Melanie, Laurie, Patrick. Librarian, Vespasian Warner Pub. Library, Clinton, Ill., 1973—; author weekly column Bookmarks, Clinton Daily Jour.; pub. sec. Jr. Mens Round Table, 1977. Mem. Central Ill. Tourism Council, 1983—. Mem. Am., Ill. (dir.-at-large jr. mems. round table), Am. Bus. Women's Assn. (sec. 1976, pres. 1977, Woman of Yr. 1977), Clinton C. of C. (pres. 1985). Methodist. Home: 40 Park Ln Clinton IL 61727 Office: 120 W Johnson St Clinton IL 61727

EVANS, MARTHA MACCHESNEY, educator; b. Chgo., Nov. 2, 1941; d. Luther Johnson and Harriet (MacChesney) E.; A.A., Kendall Jr. Coll., 1961; B.A., Roosevelt U., 1964; M.A., Northeastern Ill. U., 1974; cert. advanced study Nat. Coll. Edn., 1981; Ed.D., Vanderbilt U., 1986. Cert. master tchr., Ill. Tchr. lang. arts East Maine Jr. High Sch., Des Plaines, Ill., 1965-66; caseworker Cook County Dept. Public Aid, Chgo., 1966-67; tchr. English coordinated basic English program Farragut High Sch., Chgo., 1968-73, reading lab. dir., 1973-74, reading clinician Wells High Sch., Chgo., 1974-83, learning disabled tchr., 1983—, content area reading coordinator, 1984, lead tchr. degrees of reading power, 1984-85 mem. reading clinic adv. bd. Chgo. Bd. Edn., 1976-78. Chmn. membership com. 2d Unitarian Ch. Chgo., 1978-79, pres. Womans Group, 1979-80, chmn. involvement com., 1984-85 mem. adv. bd. Nat. Hydrocephalus Found., 1984—. Mem. Internat. Reading Assn. (presenter St. Louis regional conv. 1984, Minn. regional conv. 1985), Chgo. Area Reading Assn., Assn. Curriculum Devel., Assn. Children with Learning Disabilities, Phi Delta Kappa. Home: 1940 Sherman St Evanston IL 60201 Office: Wells High School 936 Ashland Ave Chicago IL 60622

EVANS, MAX WELLINGTON, educator; b. Norwich, Ohio, Mar. 26, 1927; s. John Sherman and Mary Janette (Hoon) E.; m. Kathleen May Briggs, June 4, 1955; children—Eric, Maureen, John. B.Sc., Ohio U., 1951; M.A., Ohio State U., 1956, Ph.D., 1961. Elem. tchr., prin., pub. schs., Bremen, Ohio, 1951-53; exec. head Clinton-Liberty Sch. Dist., Mt. Vernon, Ohio, 1953-55; prin., supt. Mt. Vernon City Schs., 1955-58; asst. supt. Marietta (Ohio) City Schs., 1961-64, supt., 1964-67; assoc. prof. ednl. adminstrn. Ohio U., Athens, 1967-79, prof., 1980—; chief-of-party Ohio U/US AID team in Botswana; head primary edn. U. Botswana cons. in field. Served with USN, 1945-46. Recipient Bd. Dirs. award Appalachina Ednl. Lab., 1982; Danforth/Nat. Acad. for Sch. Execs. fellow, 1975. Mem. Am. Assn. Sch. Adminstrs., Am. Assn. Sch. Personnel Adminstrs. (award of appreciation 1979), Nat. Conf. Profls. Ednl. Adminstrn. (pres. 1980), Buckeye Assn. Sch. Adminstrs., AAUP, Phi Delta Kappa. Methodist. Clubs: Kiwanis, Rotary. Author: Standards for School Personnel Administrators, 1978; Selecting and Evaluating the School Superintendent, 1981. Home: Dept State Gaborone Washington DC 20520 Office: McCracken Hall Ohio U Athens OH 45701

EVANS, MICHAEL ALLEN, toxicologist, educator; b. New Albany, Ind., Oct. 19, 1943; s. Robley W. and Ruth A. (Kimmell) E.; m. Michelle J. Ferguson, Dec. 30, 1973; children—Michael S., Cara L., Justin J. B.S. in Biology and Chemistry, St. Joseph Coll., Rensselaer, Ind., 1967; Ph.D. in Toxicology, Ind. U., 1974. Diplomate Am. Bd. Toxicology. Postdoctoral fellow Vanderbilt U., Nashville, 1974-76; asst. prof. U. Ill.-Chgo., 1976-82, assoc. prof., 1983—, assoc. dir. Toxicology Research Lab.; cons. Am. Inst. Drug Detection, Chgo., 1984—; adv. U.S. EPA, Washington, 1984—. Contbg. author books in field. Contbr. articles to profl. jours. Served to sr. sgt. U.S. Army, 1968-70, Vietnam. Grantee NIH. Fellow Am. Acad. Forensic Sci.; mem. Soc. Toxicology, (regional pres. 1980-82), Teratology Soc. Home: 411 Lenox St Oak Park IL 60302 Office: Dept Pharmacology U Ill 835 S Wolcott St Chicago IL 60612

EVANS, ROBERT EDWARD, recording company executive; b. Little Rock, Dec. 2, 1943; s. Robert Edward and Ida Vera (Thomas) E.; m. Doris, Dec. 23, 1972; children—April, Kim. Writer/singer Trevia Record Co., Detroit, 1972-73, Big Star Records, Detroit, 1973-75, D.T. Records, 1975-81, Liberty Records; owner, pres. April Records, 1981—, Funnwagon Music Co., 1983—; pub. relations dir. Renaissance Contemporary Music, Inc., 1980-81. Jehovah's Witness. Recorded album Shades of Love/Gold, 1981; recs. include: You Can't Stop Me From Loving You (included in Blues Archives, U. Miss. Ctr. Cultural Study 1983), The Ingredient of Love.

EVANS, ROBERT JAMES, artist; b. Chgo., May 2, 1944; s. Fred G. and Marion (Higgins) E.; m. Ruth C. Hendrick; children—Jennifer, James. B.S. in Edn., Northeast Mo. State U., 1967; M.F.A., So. Ill. U., 1971. Art tchr. Guthrie Ctr. Community Schs., Iowa, 1967-69; research asst. U. Art Galleries So. Ill. U., Carbondale, 1969-70; head art sect., curator art Ill. State Mus., Springfield, 1971-85; dir. Tarble Arts Ctr., Eastern Ill. U., Charleston, 1985—; chmn. dept. art Rockford Coll., Ill., 1985—; cons. various art orgns.; guest curator Lakeview Mus., Evanston Art Ctr.; adj. prof. Sangamon State U., 1973-80; visual arts adv. bd. Ill. Arts Council, 1974-76; adv. panel Archives of Am. Art, 1979—; fine arts rev. coms. Ill. Capital Devel. Bd., 1980—. Exhibited in shows at Zaks Gallery, Chgo., 1981, 84, also numerous other exhibits, catalogs and articles; represented in pub. and pvt. art collections. Va. Ctr. for Creative Arts fellow, 1972; recipient Best in show awards, Quincy Art Ctr., 1972, 78, Gov.'s Art award Ill. Arts Council, 1981. Mem. Am. Assn. Mus. Office: Rockford Coll Dept Art 5050 State St Rockford IL 61108-2393

EVANS, TERENCE THOMAS, See *Who's Who in America,* 43rd edition.

EVANS, TOMMY NICHOLAS, physician, educator; b. Batesville, Ark., Apr. 12, 1922; s. James Rufus and Carrye Mae (Goatcher) E.; m. Jessica Ray Osment, June 12, 1945; 1 dau., Laura Kathreen. A.A., Mars Hill Jr. Coll., 1940; student Duke U., 1940-41; A.B., Baylor U., 1942; M.D., Vanderbilt U., 1945. Intern, U. Mich. Hosp., 1945-46, asst. resident ob-gyn, 1948, resident, 1948-49, jr. clin. instr., 1949-50, sr. clin. instr., 1950-51, instr. ob-gyn, 1951-54, asst. prof., 1954-56, assoc. prof., 1956-60, prof., 1960-65; prof. ob-gyn, Wayne State U., 1965-83, dean Sch. Medicine, 1970-72, dir. C.S. Mott Ctr. Human Growth and Devel., 1973-83; prof., vice chmn., chief gynecology U. Colo., 1983—; sr. attending physician Hutzel Hosp., 1966-83, chief ob-gyn, 1966-82, vice chief of staff, 1967-70, chief of staff, 1970-74, trustee, 1975-78; teaching staff, surgeon Harper-Grace Hosps., 1965-83, chief gynecology Harper div., 1970-83, chief ob-gyn, 1975-83; chief gynecology, sr. attending physician Detroit Receiving Hosp., 1965-83; cons. pediatric surgery Children's Hosp.; cons. Sinai Hosp. William Beaumont Hosp., Wayne County Gen. Hosp.; past mem. med. adv. com. Detroit Med. Ctr. Corp. Bd. dirs. Alan Guttmacher Inst. Fellow Am. Assn. Ob-Gyn; mem. Am. Coll. Obstetricians and Gynecologists (past exec. bd., past pres.), ACS (adv. council ob-gyn credentials com. 1983—, bd. govs., 1982—), Am. Fedn. Clin. Research, Am. Fertility Soc., Am. Gynecol. Club (past pres.), Am. Gynecol. Soc. (past pres.), Am. Gynecol. and Obstetrical Soc. (council), AMA, Am. Med. Soc. Vienna, Am. Pub. Health Assn., Am. Soc. Andrology (exec. council), Am. Soc. Study Sterility, Anthony Wayne Soc., Assn. Profs. Ob-Gyn (past chmn. nominating com.), Central Assn. Ob-Gyn (past pres.), Charlie Flowers Ob-Gyn Soc., Chgo. Gynecol. Soc., Continental Gyneco. Soc., Detroit Acad. Medicine, Detroit Cancer Club (past mem. program com.), Engring. Soc. Detroit, Greater Detroit Area Hosp. Council Inc., Internat. Fedn. Ob-Gyn (exec. bd.), Internat. Soc. Advancement Humanistic Studies in Gynecology, Miami Obstet. and Gynecol. Soc., Mich. Assn. Retarded Children, Mich. Cancer Found. (trustee), Mich. Council Study of Abortion, Mich. Soc. Ob-Gyn (past pres.), Mich. State Med. Soc. (past exec. council), Mich. United Cerebral Palsy Assn., Norman F. Miller Gynecol. Soc., Ob-Gyn Soc. N.Y., Planned Parenthood League, Pan-Am. Med. Assn., Royal Soc. Medicine, Soc. Study of Reprodn., Soc. Ob-Gyn of Can., South Atlantic Assn. Ob-Gyn, numerous others. Republican. Presbyterian. Clubs: Country of Detroit, Detroit Athletic; Cosmos.

EVANS-O'CONNOR, KATHLEEN M., epidemiologist nurse, consultant; b. Evergreen Park, Ill., Mar. 14, 1941; d. James J. and Imelda J. (Scully) Evans; children—James P., M. Kate, J. Daniel. R.N., South Chicago Community Hosp. Sch. Nursing, 1962; B.S., St. Francis Coll., Joliet, 1976; postgrad. Roosevelt U., 1978-79, Harvard U., 1983. R.N., Ill. Staff nurse South Chicago Community Hosp., 1962-69; asst. head nurse emergency room Provident Meml. Hosp., El Paso, Tex., 1969-70; supr. R.E. Thomson Gen. Hosp., El Paso, 1970-71; dir. nursing, supr. nursing Mercy Ctr., Mercy Manor Facility, Aurora, Ill., 1971-72; charge nurse Brookwood Convalescent Ctr., Des Plaines, Ill., 1972-75; coordinator spl. projects Holy Family Hosp., Des Plaines, 1975-78, hosp. infection control coordinator, nurse epidemiologist, 1978—; tchr. Assoc. Practitioners in Infection Control, Chgo.; lectr. in field. Mem. Nat. League Nursing, Assn. Practitioners Infection Control, Chgo. Assn. Practitioners Infection Control (nominating com. 1981-83, edn. com. 1982), Am. Soc. Microbiologists, Ill. Soc. Microbiologists. Roman Catholic. Author in-house publs. Home: 9370 Hamilton Ct Des Plaines IL 60016 Office: Holy Family Hosp 100 N River Rd Des Plaines IL 60016

EVENBECK, SCOTT EDWARD, university official, psychologist; b. Findlay, Ohio, Aug. 14, 1946; s. Benjamin F. and Norma H. (Kelley) E.; m. Elizabeth Ann Jones, Aug. 14, 1970; 1 son, Benjamin F. III. A.B., Ind. U., 1968; M.A., U. N.C., Chapel Hill, 1971, Ph.D., 1972. Asst. prof. psychology Ind. U.-Purdue U., Indpls., 1972-76, asst. dean Purdue U. Sch. Sci., 1977-79, assoc. dean, 1979-80, assoc. dir. adminstrv. affairs, assoc. prof. psychology, 1976—, assoc. dir. adminstrv. affairs, 1980-85, dir. continuing studies, 1985—, also assoc. dean Ind. U. Sch. Continuing Studies, 1985—; bd. dirs. Parent Info. Resource Center, 1977—. Mem. exec. com., asst. treas., v.p., pres. Am. Lung Assn. Central Ind., bd. dirs., 1985—; bd. dirs. Christamore House, 1985—; sec. Indpls.-Scarborough Peace Games, 1977-80. USPHS trainee, 1968-72; Arthur R. Metz scholar Ind. U., 1964-68. Mem. Am. Psychol. Assn., Nat. Council Univ. Research Adminstrs. (mem. exec. com. 1979-80), Indpls. C. of C. (mem. exec. com. speaker's bur.). Republican. Episcopalian. Clubs: Kiwanis (Indpls.); Masons. Contbr. articles in field to profl. jours. Home: 1630 E 83d St Indianapolis IN 46240 Office: Adminstrn Bldg Ind U-Purdue U 355 N Lansing St Indianapolis IN 46202

EVERETT, RONALD EMERSON, government official; b. Columbus, Ohio, Jan. 4, 1937; s. John Carmen and Hermione Alicia (Lensner) E.; B.A., Ohio U., 1959; postgrad. Baldwin-Wallace Coll., 1962-63; grad. U.S. Army Command and Gen. Staff Coll., 1978, U.S. Army War Coll., 1984; cert. Inst. Cost Analysis, 1982; m. Nancy Helen Leibersberger, Aug. 10, 1963; children—Darryl William, Darlene Anne, John Lee. Reporter, Dun & Bradstreet, Cleve., 1960-66; program analyst Lewis Research Center, NASA, Cleve., 1967-70, contract price analyst and negotiator, 1970-85, chief contract support br., 1985—. Served with inf. U.S. Army, 1960; now col. USAR. Decorated Meritorious Service medal with two oak leaf clusters, Army Commendation medal with oak leaf cluster; recipient NASA Group Achievement awards, Sustained Superior Performance award, 1974, 80; cert. cost analyst. Mem. Assn. Govt. Accts., Res. Officers Assn., Internat. Platform Assn., Am. Def. Preparedness Assn., Assn. U.S. Army, Am. Security Council, Nat. Estimating Soc., Army War Coll. Found. Republican. Mem. Reformed Ch. in Am. Home: 27904 Blossom Blvd North Olmsted OH 44070 Office: 21000 Brookpark Rd Cleveland OH 44135

EVERHART, ROBERT (BOBBY WILLIAMS), entertainer, songwriter, recording artist; b. St. Edward, Nebr., June 16, 1936; s. Phillip McClelland and Martha Matilda (Meyer) Everhart. Student U. Nebr., 1959-62, Iowa Western Coll., 1976-78, U. Iowa, 1979-80. Pres., Royal Flair Music, BMI Pub., Council Bluffs, Iowa, 1974—; rec. artist Folkways Records, N.Y.C., Westwood Records, G.B., Folk Variety Records, Europe, Allied Records, Philippines, RCA Records, N.Z., internat. concert artist performing traditional Am. country and folk music; festival promotor Old-Time Country Music Contest and Pioneer Exposition, 1976-85; pres. Nat. Traditional Country Music Assn., Inc., 1982—; regular performer La. Hayride, 1985—. Served with USN, 1954-59. Mem. Great Plains Old Time Music Assn., Kans. Bluegrass Assn., Mo. Area Blue Grass Assn., Minn. Old Time Music Assn., Heart of the Ozarks Assn., Acad. Country Music, Nat. Bluegrass Assn., Ill. Traditional Country Music Assn., Tri-State Bluegrass Assn., Swallow Hill Music Assn., Ind. Friends of Country Music, Profl. Musicians Club of Iowa. Democrat. Lutheran. Club: Carribean. Editor, Tradition Country Music Mag., 1980—; author: Clara Bell, 1976; Hart's Bluff, 1977; (poetry) Silver Bullets, 1979; Savage Trumpet, 1980; Prairie Sunrise, 1982; Snoopy Goes to Mexico, 1983; (TV scripts) The Life of Jimmie Rodgers, 1984, Matecombe Treasure, 1984; recordings include: Let's Go, Dream Angel, She Sings Sad Songs, Love to Make Love, Bad Woman Blues. Address: 106 Navajo Lake Manawa Council Bluffs IA 51501

EVERS, LA FONDA A., library director; b. Randalia, Iowa, Feb. 13, 1931; d. William Donald and Loretta Caroline (Treager) Bronn; m. Wayne Leonard Evers, Mar. 22, 1949; children—Keith Wayne, Cheri Lynn. B.S., Eastern Ill. U., 1981; studied music with Allen Hancock, Santa Maria, Calif., 1968-70. Cert. social rehab. activity dir., social services dir. Social rehab. dir. Wil-Care Home, Wilmington, Ill., 1971-74; workshop tchr. Assn. Health Care, Chgo., 1974; social rehab. dir. Ill. Knights Templar, Paxton, 1975-79; activity therapist

Ford County Home, Paxton, 1979-81; dir. Paxton Carnegie Library, 1981—. Bd. dirs. Paxton Nursery Sch., 1983—; mem. welfare services com. and personnel adv. bd. Ford County (Ill.) Dept. Pub. Aid, 1984—. Mem. Lincoln Trails Library Assn. (sec. 1981-82, v.p. 1982-83, pres. elect 1985). Lutheran. Lodge: Order Eastern Star (officer Paxton 1978-81). Home: 1001 Park Terr Paxton IL 60957 Office: Paxton Carnegie Library 154 S Market Paxton IL 60957

EVERS, MARLYN SUE, pianist, educator, fast-food executive; b. Norton, Kans., July 1, 1934; d. Howard Gustav and Dorothy Ruth (Drummond) Butler; m. John Herman Evers, June 17, 1955; children—Pamela Sue, John Howard. B.A. in Music, U. Kans., 1973. Pianist, Dixieland Band, Kans. City, Kans., 1972-74; sole performer, 1967-74; keyboardist (piano, synthesizers) Providence Christian Band, 1979-83; pvt. piano tchr., 1967-74; v.p. Dairy Queen of Corpus Christi (Tex.). Trustee Lake Bluff (Ill.)/Chgo. Homes for Children, 1978-83; trustee Council Ministries, Libertyville (Ill.) United Meth. Ch., conf. del., 1978-81; vol. Winchester House, home for disabled and elderly, Lake County, Ill., 1975-83. Mem. Am. Musicol. Soc., Pi Kappa Lambda. Composer Songs. Home: 810 Hawthorne Ln Libertyville IL 60048

EWALD, CHRISTOPHER JOHN, architect; b. Toledo, Mar. 16, 1952; s. Alvin E. and Ruth (Thorton) E.; m. Vicki Lynn Whitescarver, Apr. 1, 1978; children—Katrina Renee, Melinda Ann. B.Arch., Kent State U., 1975. Student architect Bauer, Stark and Lashbrook, Toledo, 1971-75, architect-in-tng., 1975-78, architect, 1978, assoc., 1979-80, sr. assoc., 1980-83, prodn. dir., 1981-83; project mgr. SSOE, Inc., Toledo, 1983-85, assoc., 1985—. Mem. AIA (sec. Toledo chpt. 1982-83, v.p. 1984, pres. 1985), Architects Soc. Ohio (alt. dir. 1984-85). Lodge: Kiwanis (dir. 1984-85). Home: 3232 River Rd Toledo OH 43614

EWALD, HENRY THEODORE, JR., foundation executive; b. Detroit, Sept. 29, 1924; s. Henry T. and Oleta (Stiles) E.; m. Carolyn Davison Taylor, June 24, 1950; children—Wendy, Holly, Henry, John, Tracey, Kristi. B.A., Yale U., 1947; LL.B., Detroit Coll. Law, 1950. Bar: Mich. 1951. Pres. Ted Ewald Chevrolet Co., Detroit, 1958—; pres. H.T. Ewald Found., Grosse Pointe, Mich., 1954—. Bd. dirs. Franklin Wright Settlement, Detroit Ednl. TV-PBS. Recipient Northwood Inst. Dealer Edn. award 1973. Bd. dirs. Detroit Pistons, Hutzel Hosp. Clubs: University, Country of Detroit. Office: 15175 E Jefferson Grosse Pointe MI 48230

EWALD, RICHARD A., dentist; b. LaSalle, Ill., Oct. 1, 1934; m. Joretta E. Cheli, Aug. 24, 1956, children—Lynne, Greg, Lisa, Roger. Student U. Notre Dame, 1954; D.D.S., St. Louis U., 1958; postgrad., Coll. Physicians and Surgeons, San Francisco, 1963, U. Ill., 1969-71. Practice dentistry specializing in pedodontics, Sunnyvale, Calif., 1963-69, Elmhurst, Ill., 1970-71, Ottawa, Ill., 1971—; mem. staff Wheeler Hosp., Kaiser Hosp., Ill. State Pediatric Inst., El Camino Hosp., Ill. Research Edn. Hosp., Community Hosp.; guest lectr. dept. dental hygiene San Jose City Coll., Calif., 1965-69; instr. dept. pedodontics U. Ill.-Chgo., 1970-71, asst. prof., 1971-75; chmn. Children's Dental Health Edn., Calif.; adv. com. Dental Asst. Program, San Jose City Coll.; mem. dental panel Crippled Children Service, Calif.; pres. Santa Clara Valley Pedodontic Acad., Calif.; del. Calif. State Dental Conv., 1965, 69. chief cons. Pedodontic Splty. Exam., Ill. Contbr. articles to profl. jours. Served to capt. USAF, 1958-62. Mem. ADA, Calif. Dental Assn., Santa Clara Valley Dental Soc., Am. Acad. Pedodontics, Am. Soc. Dentistry for Children, Acad. Dentistry Handicapped, Ill. Valley Dental Soc. (chmn. dental health edn.), Ill. Soc. Dentistry for Children (exec. council), Ill. State Dental Soc., Ill. Acad. Pedodontics, Chgo. Dental Soc. (assoc.). Home: 105 Leland Ln Ottawa IL 61350 Office: 1704 Polaris Circle Ottawa IL 61350

EWART, (RALPH) BRADLEY, author; b. Mt. Pleasant, Iowa, Mar. 4, 1932; s. Samuel Roosevelt and Mary Virginia (Crane) E.; m. Mary Elisabeth Heim, Aug. 8, 1964. B.A., U. Iowa, 1956; M.A., Washington U., St. Louis, 1962, Ph.D., 1969. Tchr. various high schs., Ill., 1956-65; prof. botany, chmn. performing arts Northwest Mo. State U., Maryville, 1969-74; prof. botany Mo. Western State Coll., St. Joseph, 1974-78; gen. mgr. St. Joseph Symphony Soc., Mo., 1979-81; freelance writer, 1974—. Author: Chess: Man vs. Machine, 1980. Contbr. articles to various jours. Mem. Lee County Mcpl. Band, Ft. Myers, Fla., 1984. Served with U.S. Army, 1953-55. Recipient Eagle Scout award Boy Scouts Am., 1948; NSF fellow Washington U., 1960; NDEA fellow Washington U., 1966. Mem. U.S. Chess Fedn. (life, Golden Knights award 1969), Cape Coral Chess Club (Fla.). Avocations: bridge, music, travel, photography.

EWBANK, THOMAS PETERS, banker, lawyer; b. Indpls., Dec. 29, 1943; s. William Curtis and Maxine Stuart (Peters) E.; m. Alice Ann Shelton, June 8, 1968; children—William Curtis, Ann Shelton. Student Stanford U., 1961-62; A.B., Ind. U., 1965, J.D., 1969. Bar: Ind. 1969, U.S. Tax Ct., 1969, U.S. Dist. Ct. (so. dist.) Ind. 1969, U.S. Supreme Ct. 1974. Legis. asst. Ind. Legis. Council, 1966-67; estate and inheritance tax adminstr. Mchts. Nat. Bank, Indpls., 1967-69; assoc. Hilgedag, Johnson, Secrest and Murphy, Indpls., 1969-71; asst. gen. counsel Everett I. Brown Co., Indpls., 1971-72; with Mchts. Nat. Bank & Trust Co., Indpls., 1972—, successively probate adminstr., head probate div., head personnel account adminstrn. group in trust div., v.p. and sr. trust officer, sr. v.p., head trust and investment div. Asst. treas. Ruckelshaus for U.S. Senator Com., 1970; candidate for Ind. Legislature, 1970, 74. Fellow Ind. Bar Found.; mem. Estate Planning Council Indpls. (pres. 1982-83), Indpls. Bar Assn., Ind. Bar Assn., Indpls. Bar Found. (treas. 1976-81), Blue Key. Republican. Baptist. Clubs: Meridian Hills Country, Broadmoor Country, Riviera, Masons (Indpls.); Kiwanis Circle K Internat. (internat. trustee 1963-65, pres. 1964-65), Kiwanis of Indpls. (treas. 1980-81, 84-85 designated a maj. builder 1983). Contbr. articles to profl. jours. Home: 4516 Sylvan Rd Indianapolis IN 46208 Office: One Merchants Plaza Suite 600E Indianapolis IN 46255

EWING, RAYMOND PEYTON, ins. co. exec.; b. Hannibal, Mo., July 31, 1925; s. Larama Angelo and Winona Fern (Adams) E.; A.A., Hannibal La-Grange Coll., 1948; B.A., William Jewell Coll., 1949; M.A. in Humanities, U. Chgo., 1950; m. Audrey Jane Schulze, May 7, 1949; 1 dau., Jane Ann. Marketing mgmt. trainee Montgomery-Wards, Chgo., 1951-52; sr. editor Commerce Clearing House, Chgo., 1952-60; corp. communications dir. Allstate Ins. Cos. & Allstate Enterprises, Northbrook, Ill., 1960—, issues mgmt. dir., 1979—; pub. relations dir. Chicago Mag., 1966-67, book columnist, 1968-70; staff Book News Commentator, Sta. WRSV, Skokie, Ill., 1962-70; lectr. pub. relations. Mem. Winnetka (Ill.) Library Bd., 1969-70; pres. Skokie Valley United Crusade, 1964-65; bd. dirs. Suburban Community Chest Council, Onward Neighborhood House, Chgo., Kenilworth Inst.; mem. Pvt. Sector Foresight Task Force, 1982-83. Served with AUS, 1943-46; ETO. Mem. Pub. Relations Soc. of Am. (accredited; Silver Anvil awards for pub. affairs, 1970, 72, for fin. relations 1970, for bus. spl. events 1976, chmn. nat. pub. affairs sect. 1984), Publicity Club of Chgo. (v.p. 1967, bd. dirs. 1966-68; Golden Trumpet award for pub. affairs, 1969, 70, 72, 79, for fin. relations 1970), Insurers Public Relations Council (pres. 1980-81), Issues Mgmt. Assn. (co-founder, pres. 1981-83, chmn. 1983-84), Mensa, World Future Soc., U.S. Assn. for Club of Rome, Chgo. Poets and Writers Found. (pub. relations dir. 1966-67), Issues Mgmt. Cons. Group (pres.). Club: Union League (Chgo.). Author: Mark Twain's Steamboat Years, 1981; editor: Publicity Club of Chgo. Jour., 1971—; contbr. articles to mags. Office: Allstate Plaza Northbrook IL 60062

EXE, DAVID ALLEN, electrical engineer; b. Brookings, S.D., Jan. 29, 1942; s. Oscar Melvin and Irene Marie (Mattis) E.; m. Lynn Rae Roberts; children—Doreen Lea, Raena Lynn. B.S. Elec. Engring., S.D. State U., 1968; M.B.A., U. S.D., 1980; postgrad. Iowa State U., 1969-70, U. Idaho, 1978-80. Registered profl. engr., Idaho, Oreg., Minn., S.D., Wash., Wyo., Utah. Applications engr. Collins Radio, Cedar Rapids, Iowa, 1969-70; dist. engr. Bonneville Power Adminstrn., Idaho Falls, Idaho, 1970-77; instr. math U. S.D., Vermillion, 1977-78; chief exec. officer EXE Assocs., Idaho Falls, Idaho, 1978-83; agys. mgr. CPT Corp., Eden Prairie, Minn., 1983-85; owner, chief exec. officer Exe Inc., Eden Prairie, 1983—; chmn. bd. Applied Techs. Idaho, Idaho Falls, 1979—; chmn., chief exec. officer Azimuth Cons., Idaho Falls, 1979-81; v.p. D & B Constrn. Co., Idaho Falls, 1980-83. Mem. Eastern Idaho Council on Industry and Energy, 1979—. Served with USN, 1960-64. Mem. Am. Cons. Engrs., IEEE, Nat. Soc. Profl. Engrs., Nat. Contrcts Mgrs. Assn., IEEE Computer Soc., Mensa, Am. Legion. Lodges: Masons, Elks. Home: 18830 Partridge Circle Eden Prairie MN 55344

EXLEY, CHARLES ERROL, JR., manufacturing company executive; b. Detroit, Dec. 14, 1929; s. Charles Errol and Helen Margaret (Greenizen) E.; B.A., Wesleyan U., Middletown, Conn., 1952; M.B.A., Columbia U., 1954; m. Sara Elizabeth Yates, Feb. 1, 1952; children—Sarah Helen, Evelyn Victoria, Thomas Yates. With Burroughs Corp., 1954-76, exec. v.p. fin., dir., 1973-76; pres., dir., mem. exec. com. NCR Corp., Dayton, Ohio, 1976-83, pres., chief exec. officer, 1983-84, chmn. bd., pres., 1984—. Chmn. Dayton United Way campaign, 1982. Mem. Fin. Execs. Inst. Clubs: Grosse Pointe (Mich.); Dayton Racquet, Moraine Country (Dayton); Miami Valley Hunt & Polo; The Brook (N.Y.). Office: 1700 S Patterson Blvd Dayton OH 45479

EXON, J(OHN) JAMES, U.S. senator; b. Geddes, S.D., Aug. 9, 1921; s. John James and Luella (Johns) E.; student U. Omaha, 1939-41; m. Patricia Ann Pros, Sept. 18, 1943; children—Stephen James, Pamela Ann, Candace Lee. Mgr., Universal Finance Corp., Nebr., 1946-53; pres. Exon's, Inc., Lincoln, Nebr., 1954-71; gov. State of Nebr., 1971-79; U.S. Senator from Nebr., 1979—. Mem. exec. com. Nat. Govs. Conf., 1971, Democratic Govs. Conf., 1971, 74; vice chmn. Midwest Govs. Conf., 1973, chmn., 1974; co-chmn. Old West Reg. Commn., 1974-75; active state, local, nat. Dem. coms., 1952—; del. Dem. Nat. Conv., 1964, 68, 72, 76; Dem. nat. committeeman, 1968-71, 81—. Served with Signal Corps, AUS, 1942-45. Mem. Am. Legion, VFW. Clubs: Eagles, Elks, Optimists Internat. (past lt. gov. Nebr. dist.); Masons (32 deg.), Shriners. Office: SH-330 Hart Senate Office Bldg Washington DC 20510

EY, GARY VAN, state official; b. Lincoln, Ill., Mar. 12, 1947; s. Otto Henry and Edna Pauline (Rothwell) E.; m. Kittra Kae Werth, June 21, 1969; children—Mathew, Heather. B.B.A., U. N.Mex., 1969; M.A., Sangamon State U., 1977. Personnel mgr. various State of Ill. depts., Springfield, 1969-75, mgr. income tax div. Ill. Dept. Revenue, 1976-82, dep. dir. tax processing bur., 1982-85, exec. dep. dir., 1985—. Lutheran. Club: Railsplitter Sertoma (pres. 1984—). Avocations: running; racquetball, hunting; sailing; golf. Home: 3608 Bounty Circle Springfield IL 62707 Office: State of Ill Dept Revenue 101 W Jefferson St Springfield IL 62708

EYHUSEN, EDWARD ALLEN, lawyer; b. Springfield, Ohio, June 25, 1951; s. George R. and Elinore A. (Evans) E.; m. Cathy S. Johnson, Aug. 25, 1974 (div. Dec. 1983); m. Deidra D. Dixon, Apr. 11, 1985. B.A., Wittenberg U., 1973; J.D., Yale U., 1976. Bar: N.Y. 1977, Ohio 1985. Assoc. Chadbourne, Parke, Whiteside & Wolff, N.Y.C., 1976-83, Baker & Hostetler, Cleve., 1985—. Mem. ABA. Avocations: record collecting; guitar. Home: 25275 Shaker Blvd Beachwood OH 44122 Office: Baker & Hostetler 3200 Nat City Ctr Cleveland OH 44114

EYL, FREDERICK EUGENE (GENE), insurance agent; b. New Richmond, Ohio, Aug. 19, 1938; s. Eugene Joseph and Agnes (Ebaugh) E.; m. Barbara A. Beer, May 7, 1960; children—David E., Jeffrey S., Steven M. C.L.U., Am. Coll., Bryn Mawr, Pa., 1977. Agt., registered rep. Prudential Ins., Hamilton, Ohio, 1966—. Mem. parish council St. Peter's Ch., Hamilton, Ohio, 1977-83, 85-88. Mem. Hamilton Assn. Life Underwriters (instr. Life Underwriter Tng. Council 1982-84, bd. dirs. 1970-82, nat. quality award 1984). Roman Catholic. Club: Catham (Hamilton, Ohio) (pres. 1979-81). Lodge: KC. Home: 1180 Cleveland Ave Hamilton OH 45013

EYMAN, FRANCIS EARL, conservation official; b. St. Louis, June 25, 1925; s. Francis Earl and Harriette May (Dovey) E.; m. Willa Jean Williams, Oct. 18, 1958. Stock control staff United Wholesale Druggists, St. Louis, 1947-52; conservation agt. Mo. Dept. Conservation, Buffalo-Lamar-Springfield, 1952-67, conservation agt. supr., Jefferson City, 1967-77, asst. supt. edn., 1977—. Contbr. articles to profl. jours. Lobbyist Nat. Rifle Assn. Am.; bd. dirs. Mid-Mo. Conservation Fedn., 1979—; bd. dirs. Mo. Sport Shooting Assn., Jefferson City, 1972—, lobbyist, 1979—. Served with USN, 1943-45. Recipient Hon. Chpt. Farmer award Future Farmers of Am., 1962, Hon. State Farmer award, 1976; Coordinator of Yr. award Nat. Rifle Assn., 1983. Mem. North Am. Assn. Hunter Safety Coordinators (bd. dirs. 1972-81, Hunter Edn. Hall of Fame 1981), Soc. State Dirs. (com.), Am. Legion. Episcopalian. Lodges: Masons, Shriners. Avocations: handicapped program development; shooting sports. Home: 710 Stanford Jefferson City MO 65101 Office: Mo Dept Conservation 2901 N 10 Mile Dr Jefferson City MO 65101

EYNON, THOMAS GRANT, sociology educator; b. Evanston, Ill. Aug. 10, 1926; s. John and Ruth (Deal) E.; m. Janet Arstingstall, Nov. 24, 1956; children—James Walter, John Robert, Sarah Carolyn. B.Sc. in Psychology, Ohio State U., 1953, M.A. in Anthropology (Scott fellow), 1955, Ph.D. in Criminology and Sociology, 1959. Asst. prof. to assoc. prof. Ohio State U., 1959-68; prof. sociology So. Ill. U., 1968—; vis. prof. U. Stockholm, 1972, Nat. U. Ireland, Galway and Dublin, Queens U. Belfast, Oxford U., London Sch. Econs., U. Leeds, 1973, St. Lawrence U., 1962-70, U. Minn., 1970-75, Ill. Inst. Tech. Research Inst., 1974; dir. Social Sci. Research Bur., 1977-79; commr. Ill. Juvenile Justice Commn., 1983—; mem. Task Force on Prison Crowding, 1983-84. Chmn. adv. bd. Ill. Dept. Corrections, 1979—; chmn. Reading Is Fundamental Program, 1978—; mem. Gov.'s Task Force Mental Health, 1970-72. Served with USNR, 1944-51. Decorated Silver Star, Purple Heart, D.F.C. Methodist. Author: Offender Classification in the United States, 1976. Editor Sociol. Quar., 1981-84. Contbr. numerous articles and revs. to profl. jours., chpts. in books. Office: Dept of Sociology So Ill U Carbondale IL 62901

EYNON, THOMAS HENRY, broadcasting executive; speech educator; b. Providence, Sept. 30, 1928; s. Thomas Benjamin Eynon and Ivy Rita (Robertshaw) Dubrotsky; separated; children—Thomas Mark, Wendy, Marisa. B.A., Saginaw Valley State U., 1973; M.A., Central Mich. U., 1976. News anchorman Sta. WSUN-TV, St. Petersburg, Fla., 1953-55, Sta. KIVA-TV, Yuma, Ariz., 1955-56; news anchorman Sta. WNEM-TV, Saginaw, Mich., 1956-60, news dir., 1960-72, community affairs dir., 1972—; pres. Tom Eynon & Assocs., Saginaw, 1980—. Served with USAF, 1946-53. Recipient Sch. Bell award NEA, 1972, Addy award Flint Advt. Fedn., 1980, Addy award Advt. Fedn. Saginaw Valley; U. Chgo. fellow, 1982. Republican. Club: Elf Khurafeh. Lodges: Shriners, Masons. Avocation: golf. Home: 3114 Studor Saginaw MI 48602 Office: WNEM-TV 107 N Franklin Saginaw MI 48607

EYRES, JUDITH ANN, banker; b. Paterson, N.J., Mar. 30, 1955; d. Huburn Binney and Annamae (Memmelaar) E. B.A., Montclair State Coll., 1977; M.B.A., Fairleigh Dickinson U., 1979. Cert. systems profl. Comml. loan officer 1st Nat. Bank N.J., Totowa, 1976-81; ops. officer Marine Midland Bank, N.A., N.Y.C., 1981-82; asst. v.p. Marine Bank Springfield, Ill., 1982—. Mem. Spring Board, Council Arts, 1983-84; bd. dirs. Springfield Theatre Ctr.; vol. United Way, 1982—. Mem. Assn. Systems Mgmt. (pres.), Nat. Assn. Female Execs., Avocations: reading; travel; cooking. Home: 13 Whisperglen Ln Springfield IL 62704 Office: Marine Bank Springfield East Old State Capitol Plaza Springfield IL 62701

EZELL, CHARLES LAVERN, educational administrator, educator; b. Orient, Ill., Aug. 3, 1941; s. Glen L. and Pearl (Summers) E.; m. Judith A. Hoffard, May 12, 1962; children—Charles Kevin, Toni Renee. B.A. So. Ill. U., 1963, advanced cert., 1977; M.A., Duke U., 1968. Tchr. biology, chemistry various schs., Ill., 1963-74; prin. Hoopeston Jr. High Sch., Ill., 1974—. Mem. Grant Twp. Youth Commn., Hoopeston, 1975. Named Outstanding Young Educator, Jaycees, 1970; NSF scholar, 1965-69. Mem. NEA, Ill. Prins. Assn., Ill. Edn. Assn., Vermilion County Elem. Sch. Assn., Hoopeston Edn. Assn. (pres. 1971-72). Lodges: Rotary, Owls (pres. 1984—). Avocations: gardening, horseback riding, swimming. Home: 860 E Seminary Ave Hoopeston IL 60942 Office: Hoopeston-East Lynn Sch 615 E Orange St Hoopeston IL 60942

EZZAT, HAZEM A(HMED), research executive; b. Cairo, July 12, 1942; came to U.S., 1966, naturalized, 1978; s. Ahmed M. and Hanya A. (Safwat) E.; m. Shaza Abdelghaffar, Aug. 2, 1972; children—Jeneen H., Waleed H. B.Sc., U. Cairo, 1963; M.S., U. Wis., 1966, Ph.D., 1971. Project engr. Suez Canal Authority, Egypt, 1963-65; instr. faculty engring. Cairo U., 1965-66; research asst. U. Wis., Madison, 1966-70; with Gen. Motors Research Labs., Warren, Mich., 1970—, asst. head engring. mechanics dept., 1981-84, head power systems research dept., 1984—. Mem. ASME (Henry Hess award 1973), Soc. Automotive Engrs., Am. Acad. Mechanics, Engring. Soc. Detroit, Sigma Xi. Contbr. articles to profl. jours. Office: Gen Motors Research Labs Warren MI 48090

EZZO, FRANK RONALD, psychologist, consultant, educator; b. Cleve., Jan. 20, 1949; s. Frank and Molly (Babic) E.; m. Cynthia Marie Podmore, Jan. 15, 1972; children—Matthew, Melissa. B.A., U. Dayton, 1971; M.A., John Carroll U., 1976; Ph.D., Case Western Res. U., 1980. Lic. psychologist, Ohio Juvenile probation officer, supr. vol. in ct., and coordinator psychol. services Lake County (Ohio) Juvenile Ct., 1972-79; therapist and psychologist, Beech Brook, Cleve., 1979-82; dir. Ohio Residential Services, Ambulatory Health Care Clinic, North Royalton, 1982—; pvt. practice, Mentor, Ohio; tchr. Cuyahoga Community Coll.; v.p. Comprehensive Social Services; supervising psychologist Consumption Control Clinic. Bd. dirs. Assn. Juvenile Justice, Ohio. Mem. Am. Psychol. Assn., Ohio Psychol. Assn., Cleve. Psychol. Assn. Roman Catholic. Home: 2110 Kingsborough Painesville OH 44077 Office: 9040 Mentor Ave Mentor OH 44060

FAABORG, JOHN RAYNOR, ecology educator; b. Hampton, Iowa, Jan. 23, 1949; s. Rolfe Folmer and Darlene Margaret (Jergensen) F.; m. Judith Ann Schlezes, July 12, 1969 (div. 1977); children—Jason, Jodine; m. Janice Elaine Winters, June 7, 1980. B.S. in Fisheries and Wildlife, Iowa State U., 1971; Ph.D. in Ecology, Princeton U., 1975. Asst. prof. U. Mo., Columbia, 1975-81, assoc. prof., 1981—. Contbr. articles to profl. jours. Mem. Am. Ornithol. Union (elective), Wilson Ornithol. Soc., Cooper Ornithol. Soc. Home: Route 14 Box 13 Columbia MO 65202 Office: U Mo 110 Tucker Hall Columbia MO 65211

FAARLUND, JAN TERJE, linguistics and Norwegian studies educator; b. Hamar, Norway, May 3, 1943; came to U.S., 1983; s. Anners and Ruth (Haugen) F. Baccalaureat Eidsvoll Landsgymnas, Norway, 1962; Cand. mag., U. Oslo, Norway, 1968, 1974. Postdoctoral research U. Trondheim, Norway, 1974-79, assoc. prof., 1979, prof., 1981-83; vis. prof. U. Chgo., 1979-80, prof., 1983—; vis. scholar U. Cambridge, Eng., 1976, U. Reading, Eng., 1976-77; guest lectr. various univs. Scandinavia, Eng., U.S. Author: Verb og predikat, 1978; Norsk syntaks i funksjonelt perspektiv, 1980; Fra meining til ytring, 1982. Contbr. articles to profl. jours. Active various polit. orgns., Norway. Mem. Philol. Soc., Royal Norwegian Soc. Scis. and Letters, Norwegian Lang. Assn. Home: 5801 S Dorchester Ave Chicago IL 60637 Office: U Chgo 1010 E 59th St Chicago IL 60637

FABRICIUS, VALEDA CLAREEN, school administrator, nursing educator; b. Ellsworth, Kans., Sept. 10, 1940; d. Theodore Frederick and Clara Lydia (Weinhardt) Steinle; m. Edward Phil Fabricius, June 10, 1962 (div. 1973); children—Craig Philip, Sheri Kay. B.S., Ft. Hays State U., 1962; M. Nursing, Ind. U., 1966; cert. gerontology N. Tex. State U., 1980, Ph.D., 1982. Instr. Bartholomew County Hosp., Columbus, Ind., 1971-72; asst. prof. Ft. Hays State U., Kans., 1973-74; Tex. Woman's U., Denton, 1974-80; asst. prof. Minot State Coll., N.D., 1980-82, dean, 1982—; cons., expert witness Zuger & Bucklin, Bismarck, N.D., 1982-83. Contbr. articles to profl. jours. Bd. dirs. Minot chpt. ARC, 1983-85, Consortium on Gerontology, 1983-85; judge State Sci. Fair, Minot, 1984. Bush Found. grantee, 1983-84; Matthews fellow N. Tex. State U., 1979. Mem. N.D. State Nurses Assn. (treas. Dist. 2 1982-84, nominating com. 1984-85), Phi Delta Kappa, Sigma Theta Tau, Delta Kappa Gamma. Republican. Club: Quota Internat. Avocations: reading; camping; sewing; cooking; crafts; decorating. Home: 1245 15th Ave SW Minot ND 58701 Office: Minot State Coll Sch Nursing and Health Mgmt Scis 500 9th Ave NW Minot ND 58701

FACENTE, GARY, publisher; b. Teaneck, N.J., Aug. 3, 1944; s. Alfred A. and Pauline F.; B.A., MacMurray Coll., 1966; m. Jane Carlin, June 22, 1968; children—Blake Carlin, Brooke Lynn. Tchr., N.Y.C. Schs., 1966-67; research fellow U. Denver, 1967-68; asst. to mayor, N.Y.C., 1968-71; mktg. exec. McGraw-Hill Book Co., N.Y.C., 1971-75; gen. mgr. Follett Pub. Co., Chgo., 1975-80, v.p., editor-in-chief, 1980-82; dir. pub. ALA, Chgo., 1982—; adj. asst. prof. edn. Chgo. State U., 1976-77. Mem. Assn. Am. Pubs., Chgo. Press Club. Contbr. to Chgo. Sun Times. Home: 2818 Harrison St Evanston IL 60201 Office: ALA 50 E Huron Chicago IL 60611

FACEY, FEBES TAN, accounting educator, administrator, consultant; b. Philippines, Dec. 11; came to U.S., 1955, naturalized, 1968; d. Cayetano and Asuncion (Begk) Tan; m. Edward Crowell Facey, July 5, 1964; children—Edward Jr., Elizabeth. B. Comml. Sci., U. San Carlos, Philippines, 1954; M.B.A., Stanford U., 1957; Ph.D., NYU, 1964. C.P.A., Philippines. Controller La Perla Industries, Inc., Philippines, 1957-60; asst. prof. St. John's U., N.Y.C., 1964-68, 70-73; mgmt. cons. La Perla Industries, Inc., 1968-70; prof., chmn. acctg. dept. Hillsdale Coll., Mich., 1973—; vis. prof. Columbia U. Grad. Sch. Bus., N.Y.C., 1972; cons. AOC Internat., Kansas City, 1984. Fulbright scholar Stanford U.; Ford Found. grantee NYU; Lincoln Found. grantee NYU; named Prof. of Yr., Hillsdale Coll. Roman Catholic. Avocations: Cooking; advising students; photography. Home: 175 Oak St Hillsdale MI 49242 Office: Hillsdale Coll Hillsdale MI 49242

FACKLER, HELEN, nurse; b. Florence, Colo., May 18, 1940; d. John J. and Mary (Lave) Martinez; m. LeRoy Everett Fackler, May 30, 1974; children—Mark M., Sandra Garcia; 1 stepchild, Lisa Fackler. A.A., Kansas City Community Coll., Kans., 1976; B.A., Coll. of St. Francis, Joliet, Ill., 1985. Lic. psychol. technician, St. Mary's Hosp., Kansas City, Mo., 1970-76, staff nurse, 1976-77; staff nurse Providence-St. Margaret's Health Ctr., Kansas City, Kans., 1977-79, asst. head nurse, 1979-80, head nurse oncology, 1980—. Bd. dirs. Am. Cancer Soc., Kansas City, Kans., 1983—. Mem. Oncology Nurses Soc. Democrat. Office: Providence St Margaret's Health Ctr 8929 Parellel Pkwy Kansas City KS 66102

FAESSLER, EDWIN JOSEPH, management consultant; b. Cin., Nov. 27, 1944; s. Edwin C. and Rosemarie (Schlie) F.; B.A. in Psychology, U. Cin., 1967; M.S.W., Ohio State U., 1969; m. Deborah Braun, Nov. 25, 1978; children by previous marriage—Joseph Michael, Robert James. Clin. instr. psychiat. social work U. Cin., 1971-72; dir. therapeutic foster home project Children's Home of Cin., 1972-75; asst. prof. Edgecliff Coll., Cin., 1974-78, program dir. social work, 1975—; pres. Interpersonal Communication Assoc., Inc., Cin., 1977-79; adj. asst. prof. dept. social work U. Cin., 1978-79; dir. social service Jewish Hosp. Cin., 1977—; cons. to various schs., ch. groups and hosps., Cin. area, 1974—; Mem. human resources com. Gt. Rivers council Girl Scouts U.S., 1977—; pres. Norwood Bd. Health, 1977—; bd. dirs. Norwood Service League, mem. Bd. Mental Health Services of N. Central Hamilton County, 1981—. Mem. Cin. C. of C., Cin. Inst. Small Enterprise. Home: 5228 Parmalee Pl Cincinnati OH 45212 Office: 5258 Montgomery Rd Cincinnati OH 45212

FAGAN, JOHN PAUL, holding company executive; b. Yonkers, N.Y., Apr. 28, 1930; s. John J. and Winifred P. (Murray) F.; m. Theresa A. Kivion, Aug. 20, 1955; children—Robert, Nancy, Thomas. B.B.A., Pace Coll., 1962; grad. Advanced Mgmt. Program, Harvard U., 1973. Asst. treas. N.Y.C. R.R., 1953-68; asst. v.p. ICRR, Chgo., 1968-69; treas. IC Industries, Chgo., 1969-72, v.p., 1972-75, v.p. fin., treas., 1975-81, sr. v.p. fin., 1981-82, exec. v.p. fin., 1982—; dir. Philipsborn Equities, Inc., IC Leasing Co., H.F. Philipsborn & Co., Chgo. Bank Commerce, Evanston Group Cos., UMI Group, Inc. Bd. dirs. Better Bus. Bur., Chgo.; mem. adv. bd. Chgo. Catholic Charities; trustee Ill. Inst. Tech. Served with USMC, 1951-53. Mem. Newcomen Soc. Clubs: North Shore Country (Glenview, Ill.); Econs., Execs. of Chgo. Home: 1319 Southwind Dr Northbrook IL 60062 Office: 111 E Wacker Dr Chicago IL 60601

FAGERBERG, ROGER RICHARD, lawyer; b. Chgo., Dec. 11, 1935; s. Richard Emil and Evelyn (Thor); B.S. in Bus. Adminstrn., Washington U., St. Louis, 1958, J.D., 1961, postgrad. 1961-62; m. Virginia Fuller Vaughan, June 20, 1959; children—Steven Roger, Susan Vaughan, James Thor, Laura Craft. Grad. teaching asst. Washington U., St. Louis, 1961-62; admitted to Mo. bar, 1961, since practiced in St. Louis; asso. firm Rassieur, Long & Yawitz, 1962-64; partner firm Rassieur, Long, Yawitz & Schneider and predecessor firms, 1965—. Mem. exec. com. citizens' adv. council Pkwy. Sch. Dist., 1974—, pres.-elect, 1976-77, pres., 1977-78; bd. dirs. Parkway Residents Orgn., 1969—, v.p., 1970-73, pres., 1973—. Mem. Am., St. Louis bar assns., Mo. Bar, Christian Bus. Men's Com. (dir. 1975-78), Full Gospel Bus. Men's Fellowship, Order of Coif, Omicron Delta Kappa, Beta Gamma Sigma, Pi Sigma Alpha, Phi Eta Sigma, Phi Delta Phi, Kappa Sigma. Republican. Presbyterian (elder, congregation pres. 1968-70, 77-78, 83-84). Clubs: Kiwanis (dir. 1972-74, 76-79, 81-83, 84-85, v.p. 1978-79, 84-85), Masons, Shriners. Home: 13812 Clayton Rd Town and Country MO 63011 Office: 700 Boatmen's Tower Saint Louis MO 63102

FAGERLIND, MARVIN CARL, social work educator; b. Waterloo, Iowa, Apr. 6, 1951; s. Carl Lawrence and Mary Celeste (Thome) F.; m. Teresa Dorothy Herring, May 31, 1975; children—Matthew, Rachel. B.A., U. No. Iowa, 1973; M.S.W., St. Louis U., 1975. Assoc. prof. social work Loras Coll.,

Dubuque, Iowa, 1975—, faculty chmn., 1985—. Bd. dirs. Cath. Charities, Dubuque, 1982-83; chmn. United Way Services, Dubuque, 1985. Mem. Nat. Assn. Social Workers, Iowa Conf. Social Work Edn. (sec.-treas. 1982—), Phi Delta Kappa. Avocations: biking, camping. Home: 1764 Wood St Dubuque IA 52001 Office: Loras Coll Dubuque IA 52001

FAGG, GEORGE GARDNER, judge; b. Eldora, Iowa, Apr. 30, 1934; s. Ned and Arleene (Gardner) F.; m. Jane E. Wood, Aug. 19, 1956; children—Martha, Thomas, Ned, Susan, George, Sarah. B.S. in Bus. Adminstrn., Drake U., Des Moines, 1956, J.D., 1958. Bar: Iowa 1958. Ptnr., Cartwright, Druker, Ryden & Fagg, Marshalltown, Iowa, 1958-72; dist. judge State of Iowa, 1972-82; judge U.S. Ct. Appeals (8th cir.), Des Moines, 1982—; chmn. Com. on Iowa Uniform Jury Instrns., 1980-82; mem. adv. com. rules of civil procedure Iowa Supreme Ct., 1981-82; mem. faculty Nat. Jud. Coll., 1979. Former bd. dirs. Marshalltown United Campaign, Marshalltown YMCA. Mem. Am. Judicature Soc., ABA, Iowa Bar Assn., Order of Coif. Republican. Methodist. Office: 301 US Courthouse E 1st and Walnut Sts Des Moines IA 50309

FAHEY, RICHARD PAUL, lawyer; b. Oakland, Calif., Nov. 2, 1944; s. John Joseph and Helene Goldie (Whetstone) F.; m. Suzanne Dawson, June 8, 1968; children—Eamon, Aaron Chad. A.A., Merritt Coll., 1964; B.A., San Francisco State U., 1966; J.D., Northwestern U., 1971. Bar: N.Mex. 1971, U.S. Dist. Ct. N.Mex. 1972, U.S. Ct. Appeals (10th cir.) 1972, Ohio 1973, U.S. Dist. Ct. (no. and so. dists.) Ohio 1973, U.S. Supreme Court 1975. Vol. Peace Corps, Liberia, 1966-68; atty.-in-charge Dinebeiina Nahiilna Be Agaditahe, Shiprock, N.Mex., 1971-73; asst. atty. gen. State of Ohio, Columbus, 1973-76; ptnr. Fahey & Schraff, 1976-80, Sanford, Fisher, Fahey, Boyland & Schwarzwalder, 1980-84; of counsel Knepper, White, Arter & Hadden, 1984—; adj. prof. law Capital U., 1976—. Contbr. articles to profl. jours. Russell Sage Found. grantee, 1969. Mem. ABA, Ohio Bar Assn., N.Mex. Bar Assn., Columbus Bar Assn. Democrat. Unitarian. Home: 449 E Dominion Columbus OH 43214 Office: Knepper White Arter & Hadden 180 E Broad St Columbus OH 43215

FAHLGREN, JAMES WHITCOMB, plastics manufacturing company executive, lawyer; b. Rochester, Minn., June 27, 1938; s. Nels Oscar and Mary Cynthia (Whitcomb) F. B.A., Macalester Coll., 1960; LL.B. cum laude, U. Minn., 1963. Bar: Minn. 1963; U.S. Supreme Ct. 1978. Law clk. to justice Minn. Supreme Ct., St. Paul, 1963-64; trial atty. NLRB, Mpls., 1964-66; assoc. Maun, Hazel, & Green, St. Paul, 1966-71; ptnr. Fahlgren & Hartfeldt, St. Paul, 1971-78; pres. Dura-Process Co., Mpls., 1971—, Twin Cities Industries, Inc., Mpls., 1973—; adj. instr. law U. Minn., Mpls., 1968-73. Mem. editorial bd. Minn. Law Rev., 1961-63. Vol. atty. Ramsey County Legal Aid, St. Paul, 1969-78; mem. planning com. Minn. Zoo, St. Paul, 1968. Mem. ABA, Minn. Bar. Assn., Am. Mgmt. Assn. Methodist. Clubs: Minnesota, University, Town and Country (St. Paul). Home: 32 N Mississippi River Blvd Saint Paul MN 55104 Office: Dura-Process Co 4000 Winnetka Ave N Minneapolis MN 55427

FAHNER, HAROLD THOMAS, mktg. exec.; b. Detroit, Sept. 4, 1940; s. Harold L. and Beatrice H. (Craig) F.; B.S. in Econs., U. Detroit, 1962; m. Patricia A. Churchvara, Aug. 25, 1962; children—Michael, Janet Peter. With sales dept. Dun & Bradstreet, Inc., N.Y.C., 1963-67; mgr. sales tng. Blue Cross-Blue Shield, Detroit, 1967-70; mgr. sales, mgmt. tng. A. O. Smith Harvestore Products, Inc., Arlington Heights, Ill., 1970-76, dist. sales mgr., 1976-77, eastern regional mgr., 1977-79; mktg. cons., 1980-82; v.p. mktg. Neuero Corp., West Chicago, Ill., 1982—. mem. adv. bd. William Rainey Harper Coll.; instr. Internat. Sales Mgmt. Inst.; lectr. in field. Mem. Sales-Mktg. Execs. Assn. (v.p. Chgo.), Sales Mgmt. Execs. Inst. (Outstanding Performance award 1969-70), Am. Soc. Tng. and Devel., Pi Sigma Epsilon. Author: The Problem Solving Approach to Selling, 1975; The Sales Manager's Model Letter Book, 1976; Successful Sales Management, 1983. Home: 2319 Brighton Pl Arlington Heights IL 60004 Office: 1201 Hawthorne Ln West Chicago IL 60185

FAHNER, TYRONE CLARENCE, lawyer, former state atty. general; b. Detroit, Nov. 18, 1942; s. Warren George and Alma Fahner; B.A., U. Mich., 1965; J.D., Wayne State U., 1965; LL.M., Northwestern U., 1971; m. Anne Beauchamp, July 2, 1966; children—Margaret, Daniel, Molly. Admitted to Mich. bar, 1968, Ill. bar, 1969, Tex. bar 1984; mem. criminal def. litigation unit Northwestern U., 1969-71; asst. U.S. atty. for No. Dist. Ill., Chgo., 1971-75, dep. chief consumer fraud and civil rights, 1973-74, chief ofcl. corruption, 1974-75; mem. firm Freeman, Rothe, Freeman & Salzman, Chgo., 1975-77; dir. Ill. Dept. Law Enforcement, 1977-79; partner firm Mayer, Brown & Platt, Chgo., 1979-80, 83—; atty. gen. State of Ill., Springfield, 1980-83; instr. John Marshall Law Sch., 1973—. Ford Found. fellow, 1969-71. Mem. Am. Bar Assn., Ill. Bar Assn., Mich. Bar Assn., Chgo. Bar Assn., Tex. Bar Assn., Am. Judicature Soc., Nat. Assn. Attys. Gen. Republican. Lutheran. Office: Mayer Brown & Platt 231 S LaSalle St Room 1955 Chicago IL 60604

FAHRENHOLTZ, STEVEN KENNETH, applied statistician; b. Buffalo Ctr., Iowa, Feb. 25, 1956; s. Ervin John and Bethel Ann (Borchardt) F.; m. Marcey M. Mente, Sept. 10, 1977; children—Jenny Kae, Cale Dean. B.S. in Math., Mankato State U., 1978; M.S. in Stats., Iowa State U., 1980, Ph.D. in Stats., 1982. Indsl. statistician Pillsbury Co., Mpls., 1982—. Mem. Am. Statis. Assn. Avocation: racquetball. Home: 2831 Comstock Ln Plymouth MN 55447 Office: Pillsbury Co 311 2d St SE Minneapolis MN 55414

FAHRER, CLARE, lawyer; b. Wood County, Ohio, Feb. 28, 1914; s. Charles O. and Verna B. (Hatcher) F.; m. Marian Louise White, Apr. 7, 1939; 1 child, Sandra Kay Fahrer Moore. A.B., Defiance Coll., 1935; J.D., U. Cin., 1948. Bar: Ohio. Loss and claim supt. Home Ins. Co., Toledo, 1950-53, Cleve., 1953-57; ptnr. Longano, Papandreas, Fahrer & Marksz, Cleve., 1957—. Served with U.S. Army, 1943-45. Decorated Purple Heart. Mem. Ohio State Bar Assn., Cleve. Bar Assn., Order of Coif. Democrat. Presbyterian. Club: Columbia Hills Country (pres., historian 1970-85). Home: 24006 Bruce Rd Bay Village OH 44140 Office: Longano Papandreas Fahrer & Marksz 706 Citizens Bldg Cleveland OH 44140

FAILLA, PATRICIA MCCLEMENT, biomedical and environmental research administrator; b. N.Y.C., Dec. 22, 1925; s. Morgan Hall and Louise (Yandell) McClement; m. Gioacchino Failla, Jan. 22, 1949 (dec. 1961). A.B. in Physics cum laude, Barnard Coll., 1946; Ph.D. in Biophysics, Columbia U., 1958; M.B.A., U. Chgo., 1976. Asst. physicist N.Y.C. Dept. Hosps., 1946-48; research scientist Columbia U., N.Y.C., 1950-60; biophysicist Argonne Nat. Lab., Ill., 1960-71, asst. div. dir., 1971, asst. lab. dir., 1971-80, program coordinator, 1980—; mem. tech. electronic product radiation safety standards com., FDA-HHS, 1973-75; mem. biomed. research support program subs., NIH-HHS, 1978-82; chmn. radiation com. corp. of Marine Biology Lab., 1964. Contbr. articles to various jours. Mem. Com. of One Hundred, Hinsdale, Ill., 1976—. AEC predoctoral fellow Columbia U., 1948-50. Mem. Radiation Research Soc. (councilor 1976-79), Health Physics Soc., AAAS, Sigma Xi (bd. dirs. 1975-78, 80-83). Home: 301 Lake Hinsdale Dr Clarendon Hills IL 60514 Office: Argonne Nat Lab 9700 S Cass Ave Argonne IL 60439

FAIN, MIKE, lawyer; b. Miami, Fla., July 15, 1946; s. James Edward and Laura Bennett (Turner) F.; m. Catherine Amelia Smith, Mar. 29, 1969; children—Paul Augustus, James Marshall. B.S. in Polit. Sci., Yale U., 1968; J.D., U. Pa., 1972. Bar: Ohio 1973, U.S. Dist. Ct. (so. dist.) Ohio 1973, U.S. Ct. Appeals (6th cir.) 1980. Assoc. Estabrook, Finn & McKee, Dayton, Ohio, 1973-77; ptnr. Bogin & Patterson, Dayton, 1977—; bd. commrs. character and fitness Ohio Supreme Ct., 1979—. Chmn. various coms. Dayton United Way, 1983—; gen. counsel Montgomery County Democratic Com., Ohio, 1982—. Served with USNR, 1969-71. Recipient cert. of merit Epilepsy Found. Am., 1979. Mem. Dayton Bar Assn., Ohio State Bar Assn., ABA (jud. qualification and selection com. 1983—), Dayton Alumni Assn. (chmn. 1982). Methodist. Lodge: Kiwanis. Avocation: computer and non-computer simulations. Home: 110 Greenmount Blvd Dayton OH 45419 Office: Bogin & Patterson 131 N Ludlow St Dayton OH 45402

FAINGOLD, CARL LAWRENCE, pharmacologist, researcher; b. Chgo., Feb. 1, 1943; s. Charles and Ann Faingold; m. Carol Ann Baskin, June 21, 1964; children—Scott, Charles, Robert. B.S., U. Ill.-Chgo., 1965; Ph.D., Northwestern U., 1970. Postdoctoral fellow U. Mo., Columbia, 1970-72; asst. prof. pharmacology So. Ill. U., Springfield, 1972-76, assoc. prof., 1976—, acting chmn. dept., 1981-82. Contbr. articles to profl. jours. Grantee NIH, 1979-82, Deafness Research Found., 1985—, Am. Heart Assn., 1985—. Mem. Am. Soc. Exptl. Therapeutics, Soc. for Neurosci., Am. Epilepsy Soc., AAAS, N.Y. Acad. Sci., Sigma Xi. Home: 60 Danbury Dr Springfield IL 62704 Office: So Ill U Sch Medicine 801 Rutledge St Springfield IL 62708

FAIRCHILD, DAVID LAWRENCE, philosophy educator; b. Malden, Mass., Feb. 28, 1946; s. Lawrence Wahl and Margaret (Piper) F.; m. Janice Louise Miller, June 29, 1968; 1 child, Emily Meara. B.A., Purdue U., 1968; M.A., Northwestern U., 1970, P D., 1972; prof. Purdue U.-Ft. Wayne, Ind., 1971—. Author: Toward the Examined Life, 1983; Prolegomena to Methodology, 1978; Logic A First Course, 1976. Contbr. articles to profl. jours. Bd. dirs. United Way Allen County, Ft. Wayne, 1980—, United Cerebral Palsy, Ft. Wayne, 1977-79, Allen County Assn. for the Retarded, 1977-83. Mem. Philosophic Soc. for the Study of Sport (sec. treas. 1980-84), Am. Catholic Philos. Assn., Philosophy of Sci. Assn. Home: 604 W Oakdale Dr Ft Wayne IN 46807 Office: Philosophy Dept 2101 Coliseum Blvd Ft Wayne IN 46805

FAIRHURST, CHARLES, engineering educator, consultant; b. Widnes, Lancashire, Eng., Aug. 5, 1929; came to U.S., 1956, naturalized 1966; s. Richard Lowe and Josephine (Starkey) F.; m. Margaret Ann Lloyd, Sept. 7, 1957; children—Anne E., David L., Charles E., Catherine M., Hugh R., John P., Margaret M. B.Engring. with honors, Sheffield U., Eng., 1952, Ph.D., 1955. Mining engr. Nat. Coal Bd., Eng., 1958-56; research fellow mines and metallurgy U. Minn., 1956-57, asst. prof., 1957-61, assoc. prof. 1961-66, prof., 1966—, assoc. chmn. dept., 1966-68, chmn. dept., 1968-70, prof., dept. civil and mineral engring., 1970—, chmn. dept., 1972—, E.P. Pfleider prof. mining engring. and rock mechanics, 1983—; chmn. Nat. Acad. Sci.- NRC com on underground disposal mine surface wastes; mem. U.S. Nat. commn. on Rock Mechanics, 1972-74; chmn. program com. 3d Internat. Congress on Rock Mechanics, 1974; chmn. NSF com. on civil and environ. engrs., 1982-84. Editor: (with Springer) Rock Mechanics, 1970-78; (with Pergamon) Underground Space, 1974—, Internat. Jour. Rock Mechanics and Mining Sci., 1965—; editor procs. 5th Symposium on Rock Mechanics, 1964, 8th symposium on Rock Mechanics, 1967, (with S.L. Crouch) 16th Symposium on Rock Mechanics, 1973. Contbr. articles to profl. jours. Co-recipient Best Rock Mechanics Research Paper award Internat. Com. on Rock Mechanics, 1970, Pergamon medal Am. Underground Space Assn., spl. award for 25 yrs. disting. achievement U.S. Nat. Commn. Rock Mechanics, 1983. Mem. ASCE (com. rock mechanics 1978-80), AIME (com. rock mechanics 1973, outstanding achievement award in rock mechanics 1972), South African Inst. Mining and Metallurgy, Internat. Soc. Rock Mechanics, Royal Swedish Acad. Engring. Scis. (fgn.). Roman Catholic. Office: U Minn Dept Civil and Mineral Engring 500 Pillsbury Dr Minneapolis MN 55455-0220

FAISON, HAWTHORNE, educational administrator; b. Clinton, N.C., Aug. 31, 1933; s. Daniel and Dorothy (Boone) F.; children—Adria L., Allan B. D.Ed., U. Toledo, 1976. Adminstrv. intern, Toledo, 1969; curriculum specialist, Toledo, 1969; coordinator Tchr. Corps, Toledo, 1970-75; coordinator Met. League Multi Unit Schs., Toledo, 1971-74; prin. Toledo Pub. Schs., 1975-80, Sussex Sch., Shaker Heights, Ohio, 1980-83; exec. dir. instrnl. programs; Omaha, 1983-85; asst. supt. instructional programs and services Dayton City Schs., Ohio, 1985—. Mem. Nat. Assn. Elem. Sch. Prins., Assn. Supervision and Curriculum Devel., Phi Delta Kappa. Home: 4123 Indian Runn Dr #F Dayton OH 45415

FAJANS, STEFAN STANISLAUS, physician, educator; b. Munich, Germany, Mar. 15, 1918; came to U.S., 1936; s. Kasimir M. and Salomea (Kaplan) F.; m. Ruth Stine, Sept. 6, 1947; children—Peter S., John S. B.S., U. Mich., 1938, M.D., 1942. Diplomate Am. Bd. Internal Medicine. Intern, Mt. Sinai Hosp., N.Y.C., 1942-43; resident U. Mich. Hosp., Ann Arbor, 1947-49; instr. internal medicine U. Mich.-Ann Arbor, 1949-51, asst. prof., 1951-55, assoc. prof., 1955-61, prof. internal medicine, 1961—, chief Div. Endocrinology and Metabolism, 1973, dir. Mich. Diabetes Research and Tng. Ctr., 1977; sr. mem. Inst. Medicine, Nat. Acad. Sci. Contbr. numerous articles to med. jours., chpts. to books. Served to maj. AUS, 1943-46. Mem. Am. Diabetes Assn. (past pres.), Endocrine Soc. (past v.p.), ACP, Assn. Am. Physicians, Am. Soc. Clin. Investigation, Am. Fedn. Clin. Research, Central Soc. Clin. Research. Avocations: reading, music, skiing, tennis. Home: 2485 Devonshire Rd Ann Arbor MI 48104 Office: U Mich Hosps D4103 Med Profl Bldg Box 02 Ann Arbor MI 48109

FALK, MARSHALL ALLEN, physician; b. Chgo., May 23, 1929; s. Ben and Frances (Kamins) F.; B.S., Bradley U., 1950; M.S., U. Ill., 1952; M.D., Chgo. Med. Sch., 1956; m. Marilyn Levoff, June 15, 1952; children—Gayle Debra, Ben Scott. Intern, Cook County Hosp., Chgo., 1956-57; gen. practice medicine, Chgo., 1959-64, specializing in psychiatry, 1964—; mem. staff Edgewater Hosp., Chgo., St. Mary's of Nazareth Hosp.; prof., dep. chmn. psychiatry Chgo. Med. Sch.; dean Chgo. Med. Sch. U. Health Scis., 1974—, v.p., 1981—; mem. Ill. Hosp. Licensing Bd., 1981—; v.p. Ill. Council of Deans, 1979-81, pres., 1981-84. Mem. adv. com. to Commr. of Health, City of Chgo. Served to capt. AUS, 1957-59. Recipient Alumnus of Year award Chgo. Med. Sch., 1976. Diplomate Am. Bd. Psychiatry, 1969. Fellow Chgo. Inst. Medicine, Am. Psychiat. Assn., Am. Coll. Psychiatrists; mem. AMA, Chgo., Ill. (contbn. to edn. Silver Award 1968, chmn. council mental health 1971-74) med. socs., Ill. Psychiat. Soc. Author articles on med. econs., research and psychiat. drugs. Home: 3860 S Mission Hills Rd Northbrook IL 60062 Office: 3333 Greenbay Rd North Chicago IL 60064

FALK, MOWRY W., insurance company executive; b. Attleboro, Mass., Dec. 22, 1937; s. Merrill N. and Beatrice M. F.; m. Vicky J. France, May 26, 1984; children—Derrith Palmer, Susan Stanley, James Falk, Glenn Falk, Michael France, Mark France. With Tex. Instruments nuclear div. Attleboro, Mass., 1958-62; with John Hancock Mutual Life Ins. Co., 1962—, sales and sales mgmt. mktg. staff asst., Boston, 1971-73, retirement plan cons., 1973-79, asst. supt. gen. agys., met. N.Y. div., Wayne, Pa., 1979-81. Office: John Hancock Co Central Ill Fin Group Suite 730 124 SW Adams St Peoria IL 61602

FALKENHAIN, VERNON EDWARD, optometrist; b. Rosamond, Ill., May 11, 1937; s. Vernon Arthur and Virginia Louise (Davis) F.; m. Linda Lee Russell, June 4, 1960; children—Dina, Michael, David, Donna. Student U. Ill., 1955-57, S. Ill. U., 1957-58; O.D., So. Coll. Optometry, 1961. Practice optometry, Rolla, Mo., 1965—; visual cons. U.S. Geol. Survey, Rolla, 1972—, Schwitzer div. Wallace Mussy Corp., Rolla, 1970—. Served to 1st lt. U.S. Army, 1962-65. Recipient Vol. Actions award Pres. Reagan, 1985. Mem. Am. Optometric Assn., Vol. Optometric Service to Humanity (internat. pres. 1981-83), Mo. Optometric Assn. (trustee), Heart of Am. Contact Lens Soc. Rolla C. of C., Beta Sigma Kappa, Sigma Alpha Sigma, Theta Xi, Omega Delta. Roman Catholic. Lodges: Lions (bd. dirs. Eye Research Ctr. 1985—), Rotary, K.C. Avocations: photography, jogging. Home: Route 2 Westridge Estates Rolla MO 65401 Office: 1001 Pine St Rolla MO 65401

FALLER, SUSAN GROGAN, lawyer; b. Cin., Mar. 1, 1950; d. William M. and Jane (Eagen) Grogan; m. Kenneth R. Faller, June 8, 1973; children—Susan Elisabeth, Maura Christine. B.A., U. Cin., 1972; J.D., U. Mich., 1975. Bar: Ohio 1975, U.S. Dist. Ct. (so. dist.) Ohio 1975, U.S. Ct. Appeals (6th cir.) 1982, U.S. Ct. Claims 1982, U.S. Supreme Ct. 1982, U.S. Tax Ct. 1984. Assoc. Frost & Jacobs, Cin., 1975-82, ptnr. 1982—. Assoc. editor Mich. Law Rev., 1974-75. Contbg. author: LDRC 50-State Survey of Media Libel and Privacy Law, 1982—. Vice pres. Summit Alumni Council, Cin., 1982—, bd. dirs. 1983—; trustee Newman Found., Cin., 1980—, Catholic Social Service, Cin., 1984—. Mem. Fed. Bar Assn., ABA, Ohio Bar Assn., Cin. Bar Assn. (various coms.), Greater Cin. Bus. and Profl. Women's Club, Assn. Profl. Women, Greater Cin. Women Lawyer's Assn., U. Cin. Alumni Assn., U. Mich. Alumni Assn., Mortar Bd., Phi Beta Kappa, Theta Phi Alpha. Roman Catholic. Clubs: Leland Yacht (Mich.); Lawyers, College, Clifton Meadows (Cin.). Home: 5 Belsaw Pl Cincinnati OH 45220 Office: Frost & Jacobs 2500 Central Trust Ctr 201 E 5th St Cincinnati OH 45202

FALLEY, MARGARET DICKSON (MRS. GEORGE FREDERICK FALLEY), author, genealogist; b. Mpls., Nov. 8, 1898; d. George E. and Edith (Baker) Dickson; B.S., Northwestern U., 1920; m. George Frederick Falley, Mar. 10, 1921 (dec. 1962); children—Katharine (Mrs. Edward H. Bennett, Jr.), Margaret Jane (Mrs. Raymond M. Galt), Carol (Mrs. Warner G. Baird, Jr.), Priscilla (Mrs. Henry W. Apfelbach). Ann. lectr. to Am. Inst. Genealogy at Nat. Archives, Washington, 1955-60, Geneal. Inst. Samford U., Birmingham, Ala., 1967; participant Inst. Humanistic Studies, Aspen, Colo., 1967; geneal. lectr. state, tchr. hist. socs., clubs, orgns. Mem. exec. bd. library council Northwestern U., 1979—. Recipient Merit award Nat. Geneal. Soc., 1963; cert. of merit Nat. Library Ireland and Public Record Offices Dublin and Belfast, 1979. Fellow Am. Soc. Genealogists (v.p. 1962-63); mem. Harleian Soc. (London) (Am. rep. council), New Eng. Historic Geneal. Soc. (colonial mem.), mem. Northwestern U. Alumni Assn. (v.p. 1935-36), Northwestern U. Settlement Sr. Bd. (pres. 1945-46), Colonial Dames Am., DAR, Nat. Soc. Descs. Lords of Md. Manors, Daus. of Barons of Runnymeade, Kappa Kappa Gamma (Outstanding Alumnae award 1970). Methodist. Clubs: Union League (Chgo.); Glen View (Golf, Ill.); John Evans (founding mem.) (Northwestern U.). Author: Richard Falley and Some of His Descendants Including Grover Cleveland, 1952; Palmer Genealogy, Part I (English and Irish Ancestry of George Palmer), 1957; Irish and Scotch-Irish Ancestral Research, 2 vols., 1962; Baird-Green and Allied Families, Part II, 1976; contbr. articles to geneal. jours. Address: 1500 Sheridan Rd Wilmette IL 60091

FALLIS, JAMES EDWARD, II, recreation and physical education educator, coach; b. Darmstadt, Germany, Nov. 28, 1952; s. Archie Thomas and Karin Marie (Driver) F.; m. Anna Marie Czap, Aug. 28, 1976; children—Thomas Edward, Natalie Marie. B.A., Lake Superior State Coll., 1974; M.Ed., No. Mich. U., 1977. Cert. level III defensive tactics instr., Mich. Instr. Lake Superior State Coll., Sault Ste. Marie, Mich., 1974-81, asst. prof. recreation and phys. edn., 1981—, head wrestling coach, 1974—; developer wellness program for city police and U.S. Forest Service, Sault Stt. Marie, 1982. Dir. Eastern Upper Peninsula Spl. Olympics, 1982. Named to Nat. Assn. Inter-collegiate Athletics Hall of Fame, 1980; Gt. Lakes Intercollegiate Athletic Conf. Coach of Year, 1985; travelled to USSR for study in field, 1978. Mem. AAHPERD (life), Assn. Advancement of Health Edn., Assn. for Research, Adminstrn., Profl. Councils and Socs., Nat. Assn. Sport and Phys. Edn., Nat. Wrestling Coaches Assn. Roman Catholic. Club: Lions. Coached two teams to top ten place finishes. nat. competition, 1978, 82; coached 10 individual Nat. Collegiate All-Americans including 1 nat. champion. Office: Norris Center Lake Superior State Coll Sault Sainte Marie MI 49783

FALLON, JAMES, automobile company executive; b. Hamilton, Ont., Can., Feb. 6, 1940. B. Mech. Engring. Gen. Motors Inst., 1962. With Gen. Motors Corp., Oshawa Car Assembly Plant, 1962, jr. process engr., engr., 1964, sr. process engr., 1966, asst. supt., 1969, supt. mfg., 1974, gen. supt. mfg. engring., 1978, mgr. Oshawa Truck Plant, 1982, mgr. Truck & Bus, Roanoke, Ind. Address: General Motors Truck and Bus 1220 Lafayette Center Rd Roanoke IN 46783

FALLON, RICHARD HENRY, physician, health care administrator; b. Boston, Mar. 4, 1931; s. William T. and Mary V. (O'Donoughue) F.; m. Ann Giessow, June 28, 1957; children—Lynn, Brian, Malcolm, Duncan, Lara. B.S. in Biology, Boston Coll., 1952; M.D., Harvard U., 1956; M.A. in History, Washington U., 1974. Diplomate Am. Bd. Surgery. Intern, Barnes Hosp., St. Louis, 1956-57, resident, 1959-62; resident Boston City Hosp., 1957-59; practice medicine, St. Louis, 1964-79; pres. Physicians Multisplty. Group, St. Louis, 1979—, Maxicare Health Plan Mo., St. Louis, 1983—; asst. prof. Washington U. Med. Sch., St. Louis, 1964—; pres. St. Louis PSRO, 1973. Served to capt. USAF, 1962-64. Fellow Am. Coll. Surgeons; mem. Group Health Assn. (med. dirs. div.), St. Louis Met. Med. Soc. (councilor 1971-73, v.p. 1973), Mo. State Med. Soc. (councilor 1978-85), AMA, So. Med. Soc. Republican. Clubs: Univ. Racquet (St. Louis). Avocations: squash; sailing; Russian history. Home: 57 Berkshire St Louis MO 63117 Office: Physicians Multispecialty Group 3908 S Grand St Louis MO 63118

FALLON, ROBERT KYLE, university administrator; b. Springfield, Mass., May 31, 1950; s. Richard A. and Jean H. (King) F.; m. Susan Moore; children—Jennifer, Kyle. A.A., Onondaga Community Coll., 1970; B.S., Eastern N.Mex. U., 1973, M.A., 1974; doctoral candidate U. No. Colo., 1981-83. Hall dir. Eastern N.Mex. U., Portales, 1974-75; dir. student activities South Plains Coll., Levelland, Tex., 1975-80; hall dir. U. No. Colo., Greeley, 1980-83, adv. residence hall assoc., 1983; asst. dir. residential life U. Minn.-Morris, 1983—. Mem. Am. Coll. Personnel Assn. Avocations: running, swimming, golf. Home: 111 E 2d St Morris MN 56267 Office: U Minn Morris MN 56267

FALLS, ARTHUR GRANDPRÉ, physician, surgeon; b. Chgo., Dec. 25, 1901; s. William Arthur and Santalia Angelica (de GrandPré) F.; m. Lillian Steele Proctor, Dec. 1928; 1 child, Arthur GrandPré. Student Crane Jr. Coll., 1918-20; B.S. in Medicine, Northwestern U., 1924, M.D., 1925; postgrad. U. Chgo., U. Ill.-Chgo., Cook County Postgrad. Sch., NYU. Intern Kansas City Gen. Hosp., Mo., 1924-25; gen. practice medicine and surgery, Chgo., 1925—; mem. staff Provident Hosp.; faculty Postgrad. Sch. Tb, Chgo., 1939-44, Sch. Nursing, Provident Hosp., Chgo., 1960-65; founder, pres. Com. to End Discrimination in Chgo.'s Med. Instns.; founder, exec. vice chmn. Council for Equal Med. Opportunity; founder, pres. Council for Bio-Med. Careers; founder, chmn. Chgo. chpt. Med. Com. for Human Rights; mem. pub. health com. Commn. on Human Relations, City of Chgo.; mem. health com. Welfare Council Met. Chgo.; chmn. ann. health campaign Nat. Negro Bus. League. Editor Bull. Cook County Physicians Assn., 1930-32, 35-36; assoc. editor Interracial Rev., 1931-34, Bull. Interracial Commn. of Chgo., 1933-36; Chgo. editor Catholic Worker, 1935-38. Contbr. articles to various publs. Mem. exec. bd. Nat. Cath. Interracial Fedn., 1931-36, pres. Chgo. br., 1933-34; founder Chgo. Cath. Workers Credit Union, 1937, bd. dirs., 1950-53, pres., 1952-53; founder, chmn. Progress Devel. Corp., 1959. Recipient award for service in civil rights and liberties Kenwood-Ellis Community Ctr., 1957, Good Am. award Chgo. Com. of 100, 1963. Fellow Am. Coll. Chest Physicians, Am. Geriatrics Soc.; mem. ACLU, Chgo. Urban League, Nat. Urban League, NAACP, Ams. for Democratic Action, Am. Cath. Sociol. Soc. Roman Catholic. Avocations: gardening; traveling; photography; stamp collecting; coin collecting. Home: 4812 Fair Elms Ave Western Springs IL 60558 Office: 5050 S State St Chicago IL 60009

FALLS, ROBERT ARTHUR, theater director; b. Springfield, Ill., Mar. 2, 1954; s. Arthur Joseph and Nancy (Stribling) F. B.F.A., U. Ill., Urbana, 1976. Artistic dir. Wisdom Bridge Theatre, Chgo., 1977—. Office: Wisdom Bridge Theatre 1559 W Howard St Chicago IL 60626

FAN, LIANG-TSENG, chemical engineering educator; b. Yang Mei, Taiwan; came to U.S., 1952; naturalized, 1970. B.S. in Chem. Engring., Nat. Taiwan U., 1951; M.S. in Chem. Engring., Kans. State U., 1954; Ph.D., W.Va. U., 1957, M.S. in Math., 1958. Prodn. engr. Kaohsiung Agrl. Chem. Works, Taiwan, 1951-52; research specialist W.Va. U., Morgantown, 1954-58; instr., then asst., then assoc. prof. Kans. State U., Manhattan, 1958-63, prof., 1963—, chmn. dept., 1968—, univ. disting. prof., 1984—; vis. prof. Cambridge U., 1964, U. Sydney, Australia, 1979, East China Inst. Chem. Tech., 1980; cons. EPA, 1969-75; lectr. in field. Author: The Discrete Maximum Principle, 1964; The Continuous Maximum Principle, 1966; Flow Models for Chemical Reactors, 1975; Environmental Systems Engineering, 1977. Patentee in field. Recipient Kans. Power and Light Co. Professorship award Kans. State U., 1967-73, Disting. Grad Faculty award, 1972-73. Fellow AAAS, Am. Inst. Chem. Engring.; mem. Am. Chem. Soc., IEEE, Am. Soc. Engring. Edn., Soc. Chem. Engrs. (Japan), Soc. Engring. Scis. (founding), Am. Water Resources Assn., AAUP, Internat. Assn. Water Pollution Research, N.Y. Acad. Sci., Biomass Energy Inst., Internat. Ozone Inst., Profl. Engrs. Formosa. Office: Kansas State U Dept Chem Engring Manhattan KS 66506

FANDRICH, LLOYD LINCOLN, school administrator; b. Jamestown, N.D., Feb. 12, 1934; m. Ardith Schlenker, Aug. 5, 1960; children—Steven, Daniel, Sue Ann. B.S., Jamestown Coll., 1956; M.S., N.D. State U., 1965; Ed.S., U. S.D., 1978. Sch. supt., Drayton, N.D., 1965-68, Kenmare, N.D., 1968-70, Magnolia, Minn., 1970-74, Graceville, Minn., 1974-76, Humboldt St. Vincent, Minn., 1976-79; sch. adminstr. philos. testing program, Glenville, Minn., 1979—. Author: The Spirit of the Unknown Defender of Democracy, 1983. Active ARC, Boy Scouts Am., Northwest Region I, Fine Arts Council, Minn., 1976-77; chmn. Rock County Drug Council, Minn., 1971-74; Rock County Town Meeting, 1971-74; mem. Freborn County Chem. Adv. Bd., Minn., 1981—; adv. bd. Freeborn County Foster Care, 1980—, Minn. State Fair Commn. Pres. local ch. Am. Luth. Ch., 1984-85, nat. del., 1984. Charles F. Kettering fellow, Calif., Utah and Ga.; fellow NEH Inst., Brandeis U., 1985. Mem. Minn. Assn. of Sch. Adminstrs. (chmn. dist. 21), Tri County Conf. Minn. (chmn.), Am. Assn. Sch. Adminstrs. (evaluation com.), Am. Personnel and Guidance Assn. (nat. del.), No. Interscholastic Press Assn. (service to schs. award), Council Ednl. Facilities Planners N.D. High Sch. Activities Assn. (exec. com. dist. 10), Pemoina county Schoolmen's Assn. (chmn.). Lodges: Lions (treas. 1981-82) (Glenville), Rotary, Elks, Masons. Avocations: marquestary, sports. Home: 120 2d Ave SE Glenville MN 56036

FANKHAUSER, WILLIAM, JR., educational administrator; b. Humboldt, Nebr., Dec. 2, 1920; s. William and Pearl Viola (Kinter) F.; m. Willistine Marie Clark, June 21, 1950; children—William A., Suzanne M., Stuart L. B.A., Peru State Coll., 1942; M.E., U. Nebr., 1954, Ed.S., 1969; cert. in adminstrn. and supt. Nebr. State Dept. Edn., 1969. Prin., vocal instr. Sidney Pub. Sch., Nebr. 1956-62; music tchr. Gordon Pub. Schs., Nebr., 1953-56; supt., music dir. Honey Creek Consol. Schs., Salem, Nebr., 1951-53; music dir. Tabor Pub. Schs., Iowa, 1948-51; prin. Sidney Jr. High Sch., Nebr., 1962—. Elder, choir dir. Light Meml. Presbyterian Ch.; co-dir. Ft. Sidney Cols. Mem. Nat. Assn. Secondary Sch. Prins., Nebr. State Assn. Secondary Sch. Prins. (sec.), Western Nebr. Prins. Assn. (past pres.), Nebr. Sch. Masters Club, Nat. Edn. Assn. (life), Sidney Edn. Assn. (past pres.), Nebr. Music Educators Assn. (past state choral chmn.), Cheyenne C. of C. Republican. Lodges: Kiwanis, Masons, Shriners. Office: Sidney Jr High Sch 1122 19th St Sidney NE 69162

FANNON, COLIN JAMES, petroleum wax broker; b. Bournmouth, Eng., May 3, 1955; came to U.S., 1957; s. Robert and Dora K. (Thrasher) F. B.S., U. Wis.-Eau Claire, 1980. Quality assurance mgr. Aldrich Chem. Co., Milw., 1980-81; biologist Applied Biochemists, Mequon, Wis., 1981-82; petroleum wax broker Nat. Wax Co., Chgo., 1982—; mgr. Eschem, Inc., Chgo., 1982—; aquatic cons. Applied Biochemists, Inc., Mequon, 1981-82. Vol. Republican Re-election Com., Chgo., 1984. Mem. Am. Mgmt. Assn., Profl. Assn. Diving Instrs. Lutheran. Avocations: scuba diving; baseball; reading; traveling. Home: 170 N Old Rand Rd Lake Zurich IL 60047 Office: PO Box 549 Skokie IL 60076

FARBER, PAUL SIMON, chemical engineer; b. N.Y.C., Apr. 29, 1947; s. Lew and Gertrude (Hollander) F.; m. Judith Ann Bernfeld, July 27, 1969; children—David Aaron, James Benjamin. B.Ch.E., CCNY, 1968; M.S., U. Ill.-Chgo., 1980; postgrad. U. Cin., 1971-72. Registered profl. engr., Ohio, Ill. Tech. engr. Procter & Gamble, Cin., 1968-71; project mgr. Kintech Services, Inc., Cin., 1972-77; program mgr. Argonne Nat. Lab., Ill., 1977—; cons., prin. P. Farber & Assocs., Willowbrook, Ill., 1983—; cons. UN, 1985—; mem. Ohio Environ. Control Commn., 1972-73. Contbg. author: Energy Cost of Air Pollution Control, 1980; author: A Guidebook for Expansion Planning for Electrical Generation Systems, 1984. Twp. coordinator Simon for Senate, 1984; v.p. Congregation Etz Chaim, Lombard, Ill., 1980-82, trustee, 1982-85. Recipient letter of appreciation City Council Cin., 1973. Mem. Am. Inst. Chem. Engrs. (sect. chmn. 1975-76, cert. 1976), Air Pollution Control Assn. (div. chair 1982—, com. chair 1978-81; cert. 1981). Democrat. Jewish. Avocations: cooking; hiking; computers; gardening. Home: 7619 Virginia Ct Willowbrook IL 60514 Office: Argonne Nat Lab 9700 S Cass Ave Argonne IL 60439

FARBMAN, ALBERT IRVING, neurobiologist educator; b. Boston, Aug. 25, 1934; s. Benjamin and Pearl (Rickler) F.; m. Ruth Ellen Shacknow, Aug. 20, 1961 (div. 1978); children—Leon Edward, Caroline Barbara, Samuel Peter; m. Winifred Vanderwalker, Nov. 18, 1978. A.B., Harvard U., 1955, D.M.D., 1959; M.S., NYU, 1961, Ph.D., 1964. Instr. NYU, N.Y.C., 1962-64; asst. prof. Northwestern U., Evanston, Ill., 1964-67, assoc. prof., 1967-72, prof. neurobiology, 1972—; cons. NIH, Bethesda, Md., 1980-84. Contbr. articles to profl. jours. and chpts. to scholarly texts. NIH grantee. Mem. Soc. for Neurosci., European Chemoreception Research Orgn., Assn. Chemoreception Scis., Am. Assn. Anatomists, Am. Assn. Cell Biology, Soc. Devel. Biology, AAAS. Avocations: wine making, skiing. Home: 1203 Hinman St Evanston IL 60202 Office: Northwestern U 2153 Sheridan Rd Evanston IL 60201

FARE, CHARLEY EUGENE, construction company executive; b. Sheridan, Mich., June 1, 1948; s. Charles Fred and Geraldine Dorthey (Thompson) F.; student Montcalm Community Coll., 1967-68, Lansing Community Coll., 1982-83; children—Mark John, Steven Matthew. Owner, pres. Gene Fare Inc., Stanton, Mich., 1973-84, Fare Investment Co., 1975-84. Served with AUS, 1968-69. Home: 1117 Holland Rd Stanton MI 48888 Office: 611 E Walnut Stanton MI 48888

FAREED, AHMED ALI, university dean; b. Cairo, Sept. 27, 1932, came to U.S. 1961; s. Ali E. and Fayka M. (Yousef) F.; m. Houreya A. Abul-Kheir, Sept. 26, 1957, children—Dahlia, Tony-Khalid. B.A. with honors, Cairo U., 1953; gen. diploma Ein Shams U., Cairo, 1954, spl. diploma, 1959; Ph.D., U. Chgo., 1969. Tchr. Kobba Model Sch., Cairo, 1954-56; curriculum expert Ministry of Edn., Cairo, 1956-61; diagnostician U. Chgo., 1965-68; vis. prof. Northwestern U., Evanston, Ill., 1969; prof., chmn. Northeastern Ill. U., Chgo., 1968-79, dean Coll. Edn., 1979—; cons. sch. dists., Ill., 1967—; speaker, panelist profl. orgns., 1965—; ednl. planning expert Kuwait U., 1978; cons. Am. Islamic Coll., Chgo., 1983—. Author standardized silent reading tests, instructional resource units, resource units for elem. tchrs. Contbr. articles to profl. jours. Recipient Outstanding Dissertations in Reading award Internat. Reading Assn., 1970, Outstanding Contbn. Field of Vision award Coll. Optometrists in Vision Devel., 1974, Outstanding Educator Am. award Outstanding Educators of Am., Washington, 1975. Mem. Ill. Assn. Deans of Pub. Colls. Edn. (pres. 1983-84), Am. Assn. Colls. of Tchr. Edn., Am. Ednl. Research Assn., Tchr. Edn. Council State Colls. & Univs., Ill. Assn. Colls. of Tchr. Edn., Internat. Reading Assn. (commendation for excellent service 1981), Assn. Egyptian Am. Scholars, Phi Delta Kappa. Avocations: classical music; poetry. Office: Dean Coll Edn Northeastern Ill U 5500 N St Louis Ave Chicago IL 60625

FARHA, WILLIAM F., food company executive; b. Lebanon, Nov. 27, 1908, s. Farah Farris and Nahima (Salamy) F.; m. Victoria Barkett, Apr. 15, 1934; 1 child, William George. Grad. U.S. Indsl. Coll., 1948, Brooking Inst., 1968; LL.D., Hamilton State U., Ariz., 1973. Bd. dirs. NCCJ, Kans. Found. Blind; founder Antiochian Greek Orthodox Dioceses N.Am.; mem. bd. advisors Salvation Army; founder St. Jude Research Hosp., Tenn.; chmn. Wichita Police and Firemen Pension Plan; trustee Wichita Symphony Soc., others. Recipient Gold medallion Antiochian Patriarch Alexander of Damascus, Syria, 1952, Antiochian Gold medal Merit Antiochian Orthodox Christian Archdiocese N.Y., 1972. Mem. Wichita C. of C. (bd. dirs.), Lodge: Rotary. Home: 8630 Shannon Way Wichita KS 67206 Office: 2220 Somerset Wichita KS 67204

FARHADIEH, ROUYENTAN, research company executive, engineer; b. Tehran, Iran, Nov. 3, 1944; came to U.S., 1964; m. Tira Sorooshian, Jan., 1976; children—Piran, Paymon, Ashkan. B.S. with honors, U. Ariz., 1968; M.S., Stanford U., 1969; Ph.D., Northwestern U., 1974. Registered profl. engr., Ill. Asst. mech. engr. Stanford Linear Accelerator Ctr., Calif., 1969; postdoctoral fellow Argonne Nat. Lab, Ill., 1974-75, asst. mech. engr., 1975-79, mech. engr., 1979-84; pres. Sinex Co., Westmont, Ill., 1984—. Contbr. articles to profl. jours. Bd. dirs. ZAC, Chgo., 1982. Mem. ASME, Am. Nuclear Soc., Sigma Xi, Tau Beta Pi. Zoroastrian. Research in heat transfer, solar energy, melting and solidification. Office: Sinex Co PO Box 786 Westmont IL 60559

FARINA, LUCIANO FERNANDO, Italian language educator; b. Carate Brianza, Milan, Italy, Jan. 3, 1943, came to U.S., 1966, naturalized, 1981; s. Luigi and Maria (Caglio) F.; m. Claire M. Cormany, Jan. 22, 1982. B.S.T. in Theology, Cath. U. Am., 1970; M.A. in Italian Lit., Ohio State U., 1972, Ph.D. in Romance Linguistics, 1977; B.A. in Philosophy, PIME Classical Lyceum, Milan, 1963. Teaching asst. Ohio State U., 1970-76, instr., 1976-77, asst. prof., 1977-83, assoc. prof., 1983—, dir. Italian lang. programs, 1976—, research dir. computer applications in Italian, Instrn. and Research Computer Center, 1975—; cons. in field. Mem. Assn. Computers in Humanities, Assn. Computational Linguistics, Assn. Linguistic and Literary Computing, Società di Linguistica Italiana, Modern Lang. Assn., Am. Assn. Applied Linguistics. Author: Semantic Glossary of Luganese Statutes, 1983; contbr. articles to profl. jours. Home: 3590 Grafton Ave Columbus OH 43220 Office: 248 Cunz Hall 1841 Millikin Rd Columbus OH 43210 also Pyramid Service Corp 4530 Tetford Rd Columbus OH 43220

FARIS, JAMES VANNOY, cardiology educator, hospital executive; b. Indpls., July 18, 1943; s. Vannoy and Maudeline (Freeman) F.; m. Jacqueline Claire Bexell, July 1, 1978; children—Nathan James, Jamie Lynn, Jenna Claire. A.B., Ind. U., 1965, M.D., 1968. Diplomate Am. Bd. Internal Medicine, Am. Bd. Cardiology. Intern, resident Ind. U. Med. Ctr., Indpls., 1968-71, asst. prof. medicine, 1976-80, assoc. prof. medicine, radiology, 1980-84; chief of staff Richard L. Roudebush VA Med. Ctr., Indpls., 1983—. Served to maj. U.S. Army, 1971-73, Vietnam. Ind. Heart Assn. grantee. Fellow Am. Coll. Cardiology; mem. Ind. State Med. Assn., AMA, Alpha Epsilon Delta. Republican. Methodist. Avocations: snow skiing; tennis; water skiing. Office: 1481 W 18th St Indianapolis IN 46202

FARKAS, EMIL CARL, lawyer; b. Chgo., June 27, 1912; m. Elva J. Dahlstrand; children—Kenneth, Paul, Scott. A.B., Baldwin Wallace Coll., 1933; J.D., Western Res. Law Sch., 1938; postgrad. Georgetown U., 1941. Bar: Ohio 1938, U.S. Supreme Ct. 1970. Legis. analyst Legis. Reference Service, Library of Congress, Washington, 1940-42; rev. atty. NLRB, Washington, 1946-50, field atty., Detroit, 1950-54, supervising atty., 1954-55, asst. regional atty., 1955-62, regional atty., Cin., 1962-74, regional dir. region 9, 1974—; lectr. U. Cin., 1965-77, Ohio State U.; lectr. in field. Served to lt. comdr. USNR, 1942-46, PTO. Mem. Indsl. Relations Research Assn. (past pres. Cin. chpt.), Fed. Bar Assn. (past pres. Cin. chpt., bd. govs. labor law sect.), Ohio State Bar Assn. (bd. govs. labor law sect.), Cin. Bar Assn. (labor law sect.). Club: Lawyers' (chmn. fed. exec. bd.) (Cin.). Office: 3003 Fed Office Bldg 550 Main St Cincinnati OH 45202

FARKAS, NEIL JUAN, osteopathic physician, researcher; b. Detroit, May 16, 1952; s. Boris Jerry and Edith (Katanick) F. B.A. in Chemistry, Wayne State U., 1974, M.S. in Anatomy, 1975; D.O., Mich. State U., 1980. Intern, Garden City Hosp., 1980-81; practice osteo. medicine specializing in family practice, Royal Oak, Mich., 1983—; mem. staff Botsford Gen. Hosp., Farmington Hills, Mich.; cons. Cranbrook Inst. and Mus., Bloomfield, Mich.; lectr. in field. Wayne State U. Bd. Govs.' scholar and fellow, 1970-76. Mem. Am. Osteo. Assn., Phi Beta Kappa. Jewish. Research in neurosci.; described first reported cerebral multi-axonal nerve cells in mammals, 1978. Home: 30028 W Twelve Mile Rd Unit 36 Farmington Hills MI 48018 Office: 1228 Catalpa Royal Oak MI 48067

FARLEY, LLOYD EDWARD, educator; b. Nebr. Sand Hills nr. Broken Bow, Nebr., June 20, 1915; s. Arthur L. and Effie (Tyson) F.; A.B., Kearney State Coll., 1945; M.A., Stanford U., 1947, Ed.D., 1950; postgrad. U. Hawaii, U. Oreg., Princeton U.; Litt.D., William Woods Coll., 1982. Tchr. elem. and secondary schs., also adminstr., 1937-41, 47-51; ednl. specialist U.S. Govt., Washington, Anchorage, Edwards AFB, Calif., 1952-60; prof. edn. U. Alaska, Anchorage, 1960-64; Louis D. Beaumont Distinguished prof. edn., head div. social sci., Marshall faculty William Woods Coll., Fulton, Mo.; chmn. dept. edn. Westminster and William Woods Colls., Fulton, 1964-80, prof. edn. emeritus, 1980—; vis. prof. St. Cloud State U., summers 1968-72, Aeromed. Inst., FAA, 1980—. Served to maj. AUS, 1941-46. Named Hon. Tchr. Korea; recipient Centennial medal William Woods Coll. Mem. Mo. Tchrs. Assn., Nat. Assn. Tchr. Educators, Internat. Council on Edn. for Teaching, Phi Delta Kappa, Kappa Delta Pi (hon. mem., named Outstanding Educator). Methodist. Kiwanian. Address: 12 Tucker Ln Fulton MO 65251

FARMAKIS, GEORGE LEONARD, educator; b. Clarksburg, W.Va., June 30, 1925; s. Michael and Pipitsa (Roussopoulos) F.; B.A., Wayne State U., Detroit, 1949, M.S.Ed., 1950, M.A., 1966, Ph.D., 1971; M.A., U. Mich., 1978; postgrad. Columbia U., Yale U., Queens Coll. Tchr., audio-visual aids dir. Roseville (Mich.) Public Schs., 1951-57; tchr. Birmingham (Mich.) pub. schs., 1957-61; tchr. Highland Park (Mich.) Public Schs., 1961-70, resource specialist, 1971-84; computer sci. specialist, 1984—; instr. Highland Park Community Coll., 1966-68, Wayne County Community Coll., 1969-70; founder Ford Sch. Math. High Intensity Tutoring Program, 1971; chairperson Highland Park Sch. Dist. Curriculum Council and Profl. Staff Devel. Governing Bd., 1979-82; pres. Mich. Council for Social Studies, 1984-86; participant ESEA Title I/Nat. Diffusion Network. Served to cpl., USNG, 1948-51. Recipient spl. commendation Office of Edn., 1978. Mem. Mich. Assn. Supervision and Curriculum Devel., Am. Hist. Assn., Nat. Council Social Studies, Acad. Polit. Sci., Am. Philol. Assn., Assn. Supervision and Curriculum Devel. (bd. dirs. Mich. 1983—), Internat. Reading Assn., U. Mich. Alumni Assn., Wayne State U. Coll. Edn. Alumni Assn. (bd. dirs. 1985—), Internat. Platform Assn., Modern Greek Studies Assn., Nat. Assn. Adminstrs. State and Fed. Edn. Programs, Mich. Assn. Adminstrs. State and Fed. Edn. Programs Specialists, Mich. Reading Assn., Mich. Tchrs. Math., Phi Delta Kappa. Greek Orthodox. Co-author: Michigan School Finance Curriculum Guide. Contbr. poems to books of poetry, articles to Focus jour. Home: 752 Trombley Rd Grosse Pointe Park MI 48230 Office: 20 Bartlett St Highland Park MI 48230

FARNELL, ALAN STUART, lawyer; b. Hartford, Conn., Mar. 14, 1948; s. Denis Frank and Katherine Dorothy (Dettenborn) F.; m. Roberta Ann Arquilla, May 21, 1983; 1 child, Thomas Alan. B.A. with honors, Trinity Coll., 1970; J.D., Georgetown U., 1973. Bar: D.C. 1973, N.Y. 1975, Ill. 1980, U.S. Dist. Ct. (no. dist.) Ill. 1980, U.S. Ct. Appeals (7th cir.) 1980. Assoc. Kaye, Scholer, Fierman, Hayes & Handler, N.Y.C., 1973-79; assoc. Isham, Lincoln & Beale, Chgo., 1979-83, ptnr., 1983—; gen. counsel 1550 N. State Pkwy. Condominium Assn., Chgo., 1984—; gen. counsel, bd. govs. Ginger Creek Community Assn., Oak Brook, Ill., 1984—. Editor Georgetown Law Jour., 1972-73. Mem. ABA. Home: 31 Baybrook Ln Oak Brook IL 60521 Office: Isham Lincoln & Beale Three First Nat Plaza Chicago IL 60602

FARNER, PETER WORDEN, management consultant, venture consultant; b. South Bend, Ind., Apr. 21, 1954; s. James Edward and Maryanne (Worden) Harvey F.; m. Betsy J. Meyers, Oct. 18, 1980. B.A., Duke U., 1976; M.B.A., U. Mich., 1980. Pricing analyst Stroh Brewery Co., Detroit, 1977-79, corp. planning assoc. mgr., 1980-81, asst. to pres., 1981-82, brand dir., 1982-84; pres. Peter Worden & Co., 1984—. Republican. Club: Country of Detroit (Grosse Pointe, Mich.); Detroit. Home: 16899 Village Ln Grosse Pointe MI 48230 Office: Peter Worden & Co 345 Fisher Rd Grosse Pointe MI 48230

FARNHAM, GEORGE WILLIAM, state official; b. Pierre, S.D., July 9, 1944; s. George William and Marrilynn Faye (Everson) F.; m. Janith Faye Fritz, June 7, 1964; children—Jacquelynn Marie, Charles William. B.A., No. State Coll., Aberdeen, S.D., 1968. Systems analyst Info. Mgmt. Tech., Inc., Fargo, N.D., 1968-69; bus. mgr. St. Luke's Hosps., Fargo, 1969-74; agt. Prudential Ins., Fargo, 1975; adjuster Gen. Adjustment Bur., Bismarck, N.D., 1976-77; agy. mgr. Pierre Ins., 1978-79; div. dir. Motor Fuel Tax div. S.D. Dept Revenue, Pierre, 1979—. Dist. chmn. Sioux council Boy Scouts Am., Pierre, 1980-82; bd. dirs. Mountain Plains Regional Ctr. Multihandicapped Children, Denver, 1976-79, Pierre Econ. Devel. Corp., 1984. Recipient Dist. Merit award Boy Scouts Am., 1982, Silver Beaver award, 1985. Mem. Nat. Assn. Tax Adminstrs. (steering com., chmn. motor fuel tax sect. 1983-84). Republican. Lutheran. Club: Exchange of Pierre (chmn. youth com. 1981-82). Lodge: Elks (esquire 1981-82, chmn. youth com. 1980-82). Avocations: boating, hunting, golf. Home: 811 Sibert Pl Pierre SD 57501 Office: SD Dept Revenue 118 W Capital Ave Pierre SD 57501

FAROOQUI, AKHLAQ AHMED, biochemistry research scientist; b. Rampur, India, Aug. 10, 1946; came to U.S., 1977, permanent resident; s. Sharafyab Ahmed and Azaz Jahan (Bagum) F.; m. Tahira Khan, May 17, 1972; 1 child, Soofia. B.Sc. Agra U., India, 1966; M.Sc., Aligarh Muslim U., India, 1968, M.Philosophy, 1970, Ph.D., 1972. Research fellow Australian Nat. U., Canberra, 1972-75; postdoctoral fellow Centre de Neurochimie, Strasbourg, France, 1975-77; research assoc. U. Ga., Athens, 1977-82; research scientist Ohio State U., Columbus, 1983—. Editor book revs. Neurochem. Pathology, 1983—. Alzheimer's Disease and Related Disorders Assn. grantee, 1984. Mem. Soc. Biol. Chemists of India, Internat. Neurochem. Soc., Am. Soc. Biol. Chemists. Office: Ohio State U 1645 Neil Ave 214 Ham Hall Columbus OH 43210

FARQUHAR, ROBERT NICHOLS, lawyer; b. Dayton, Ohio, Apr. 23, 1936; s. Robert Lawrence and Mary Frances (Nichols) F.; A.B., Kenyon Coll., 1958; J.D., Cornell, 1961; m. Elizabeth Lynn Bryan, Aug. 29, 1959 (div. 1971); children—Robert Nichols, Laura Ann; m. 2d, Carol A. Smith, Dec. 27, 1975. Bar: Ohio 1961, U.S. Dist. Ct. 1962, U.S. Ct. Appeals 1966, U.S. Supreme Ct. 1978. Assoc. Altick & McDaniel, Dayton, 1961-69; ptnr. Gould, Bailey & Farquhar, and predecessor firms, Dayton, 1969-78, Brumbaugh, Corwin & Gould, Dayton, 1978-80, Altick & Corwin, 1981—; dir. ACB Am., Inc., Dayton. City atty., Centerville, Ohio, 1969—. Mem. Montgomery County Rep. Central Com., 1965-69, Exec. Com., 1968-69. Bd. dirs. Centerville Hist. Soc., 1971-75, pres., 1973-74; trustee Montgomery County Legal Aid Soc., 1972-76; trustee Dayton Law Library Assn., 1972—, pres., 1980—; mem. congressional screening com. U.S. Naval Acad., 1979—. Mem. ABA, Ohio Bar Assn. (chmn. legal ethics and profl. conduct com.), Dayton Bar Assn. (pres. 1984-85), Delta Phi, Phi Delta Phi. Episcopalian. Clubs: Dayton Bicycle, Dayton Lawyers. Home: 32 Williamsburg Ln Centerville OH 45459 Office: 1300 Talbott Tower Dayton OH 45402

FARRA, CHARLES RAYMOND, physician; b. Alexandria, Egypt, Nov. 29, 1929; came to U.S., 1962; s. Fadlalla and Chafika (Wakim) F.; m. Nadia Toutounji, Feb. 28, 1958; children—Charles, George, David. M.B., B.Ch., Ein Shams U., Cairo, 1953, D.L.O., 1955, D.S., 1959. Diplomate Am. Bd. Internal Medicine. Intern, resident Demerdash U. Hosp., Cairo, 1953-55, Cook County Hosp., Chgo., 1962-67; practice medicine, Riverside, Ill.; attending physician McNeal Meml. Hosp., Berwyn, Ill., 1967—; mem. courtesy staff Hinsdale Sanitarium, Ill., 1977—; clin. asst. prof. Abraham Lincoln Sch. Medicine, U. Ill.-Chgo., 1970—. Bd. dirs. Am. Lebanese League, Washington, 1978—. Mem. AMA, Chgo. Med. Soc., Ill. State Med. Soc. Republican. Avocations: history, classical music, travel, languages. Office: 3722 S Harlem Ave Riverside IL 60546

FARRAGUT-HEMPHILL, SANDRA, lawyer; b. Tampa, Fla., Dec. 9, 1953; d. William and Catherine (Singleton) Farragut; m. Ralph E Hemphill, Sept. 13, 1980; children—Ryan Jamal, Ashley Jahan. B.S., Spelman Coll., 1975; J.D., U. Fla., 1979. Bar: Mo. 1982, U.S. Dist. Ct. (ea. dist.) Mo. 1982. Law clk. Jacksonville Area Legal Aid, Inc., Fla., 1979-81; asst. prof. Edward Waters Coll., Jacksonville, 1981-82; staff atty. Legal Services of Eastern Mo., St. Louis, 1983—; asst. adj. prof. Sch. Law, St. Louis U., 1983—. Bd. dirs. Jacksonville Urban League, 1980-81, North Fla. council Camp Fire Girls Am., 1980-81, Children's Home Soc. Fla., Jacksonville, 1980-81, St. Louis Neighborhood Mediation Ctr., 1984. Council on Legal Edn. Opportunity grantee U. Fla., Gainesville, 1976-79; Earl Warren Scholar U. Fla., 1976-79, Fla. Bd. Regents grantee U. Fla., 1978-79; Reginald Herber Smith fellow, 1979-81. Mem. Met. Bar Assn. St. Louis, Mound City Bar Assn., Assn. Trial Lawyers Am., Alpha Kappa Alpha, Phi Alpha Delta. Office: Legal Services Eastern Mo Inc PO Box 4999A Field Sta Saint Louis MO 63108

FARRAN, DON WILSON, author; b. Rowan, Iowa, Mar. 24, 1902; s. John Simon and Charlotte (Duncan) F. Student U. Iowa, 1922-1923, Dartmouth Coll., 1942-43. Editor, Fed. Writers Project, Des Moines, 1937; state dir. Fed. Hist. Survey, Des Moines, 1937-38; regional dir. Fed. Theatre Service Bur., Chgo., 1938-39; nat. editor Fed. Am. Imprints Inventory, Chgo. and Washington, 1940-41, nat. dir., 1941-42; asst. nat. dir. Hist. Records Survey, 1941-42; commd. lt. U.S. Navy, 1942, advanced through grades to comdr., 1953; officer-in-charge motion picture prodn. for 13 allied nations; mem. offshore search and rescue team, World War II; writer/dir./producer films U.S. Navy, head worldwide motion picture prodn. Coast Guard, 1958-64; ret., 1964; author books: (with MaMurtrie) Wings for Words, 1940; Ballad of the Silver Ring, 1935; author plays: (with others) Off The Record, 1939; Broadway D., 1940; Pie in the Sky, 1939, Dirt; biographer of actor Richard Bennett, 1936; screenwriter 140 motion pictures for USN, USCG, State Dept., White House, 1942-64; writer screenplay The Seventh Fleet, 1956; contbr. numerous short stories, articles, poems to nat. mags.; cons. Iowa Bicentennial, 1976. Decorated Gen. Alfaro gold medal (Ecuador); recipient awards, including: First prize Liberty Mag. Short Story Contest, 1933, award Edinburgh Film Festival, 1959, Am. Film Festival, 1959, 1960, 1961, 1962, 1963, 1964. Fellow Internat. Soc. Biographers, Internat. Acad. Poets (Eng.); mem. Gypsey Lore Soc. Gt. Britain, Calif. Writers Club, Iowa Authors Club (pres. 1933, 1934), Screenwriters Guild Am., Am. Poetry Soc. (v.p. 1928-29). Home: Rowan IA 50470

FARRAND, ARCHIE FRANKLIN, engineering manager, consultant; b. Chester, Okla., July 7, 1937; s. Orville Franklan and Dora Marie (Thomas) F.; m. Shirley Ann Case, Sept. 4, 1964; children—David, Timmy, Arthur, Ray, Richard. B.S. in Petroleum Engring., Northwestern Coll. Allied Scis., 1982. Cons. Alpine Resources, Scotland, 1960-62; driller Johnson Drilling (Kans.), 1974-79; tester Bomin Testing, Liberal, Kans., 1979-80; engr. Milchem, Inc., Liberal, 1980, staff engr., 1981; area engr. Hughes Drilling, Okla., Kans. and Tex., 1981—; cons. drilling rigs. Mem. ARC, 1964-81. Served with USMC, 1955-60. Mem. Am. Petroleum Inst., Nat. Rifle Assn., VFW, Clubs: Mark 75, Fins and Feathers Sportsman. Republican. Home: 641 S Oklahoma Liberal KS 67901 Office: Hughes Drillings PO Box 1827 Liberal KS 67901

FARRELL, BRUCE JOSEPH, lawyer; b. Geneva, Ill., Nov. 4, 1949; s. Richard James and Vera Clare (Mealey) F.; m. Rita K. Bishop, Mar. 1, 1980. B.A., St. Procopius Coll., 1971; J.D., Lewis U., 1978, No. Ill. U., 1981. Bar: Ill. 1978, U.S. Dist. Ct. (no. dist.) Ill. 1978, U.S. Ct. Appeals (7th cir.) 1979, U.S. Supreme Ct. 1983. Sole practice, Westmont, Ill., 1978—. Served to sgt. USAF, 1971-75. Mem. Ill. Bar Assn., DuPage County Bar Assn. Republican. Roman Catholic. Office: 700 E Ogden Ave Suite 101 Westmont IL 60559

FARRELL, CLIFFORD MICHAEL, lawyer; b. Gallup, N.Mex., Jan. 17, 1956; s. Francis and Carolyn Louise (Evans) F.; m. Ariane Pinkerton, Nov. 10, 1984. B.A., Moravian Coll., 1978; J.D., Capital U., 1982. Bar: Ohio 1982, Pa. 1983, U.S. Dist. Ct. (we. dist.) Pa. 1983, U.S. Ct. Appeals (3d cir.) 1983, U.S. Dist. Ct. (so. dist.) Ohio 1984, U.S. Ct. Appeals (6th cir.) 1984. Staff atty. HHS, Columbus, Ohio, 1982-83; mem. firm Robert N. Peirce, Jr., P.C., Pitts., 1983-84, Barkan & Neff Co. L.P.A., Columbus, 1984—. Mem. ABA, Assn. Trial Lawyers Am., Ohio State Bar Assn., Ohio Acad. Trial Lawyers, Pa. Bar Assn., Allegheny County Bar Assn., Columbus Bar Assn. (common pleas ct. com., med. malpractice com.). Home: 4628 Winterset Dr Columbus OH 43220 Office: Barkan & Neff Co LPA 50 W Broad St Suite 1515 PO Box 1969 Columbus OH 43215

FARRELL, DAVID C., retail executive; b. 1933; grad. Antioch Coll., 1956. Pres., Kaufmann's, 1969-75; pres., chief operating officer May Dept. Stores, St. Louis, 1975-79, pres., chief exec. officer, 1979-85, chmn., chief exec. officer, 1985—, also dir. Office: May Dept Stores 611 Olive St Saint Louis MO 63101

FARRELL, JAMES L., JR., investment counselor, educator, financial executive; b. Farmington, Mo., May 11, 1937; s. James and Barbara (Ketter) F.; m. Cyrille Agnes McLaughlin, June 3, 1972; children—Barbara, Catherine, Jimmy. B.S., U. Notre Dame, 1959; M.B.A., Wharton Sch. Fin., 1962; Ph.D., NYU, 1972. Chartered fin. analyst. Investment analyst CNA Fin., Chgo., 1962-66; investment officer TIAA/CREF, N.Y.C., 1966-77; v.p. Citicorp., N.Y.C., 1977-80; chmn. MPT Assocs., N.Y.C., 1980—; chmn. Inst. for Quantitatives, N.Y.C., 1976—. Author: Guide to Portfolio Management, 1983. Contbr. articles to profl. jours. Served as capt. U.S. Army, 1959-67. Recipient Inst. Mgmt. Scis., Coll. Practice Mgmt. Scis. prize 1982. Fellow Fin. Analysts Fedn.; mem. Inst. Chartered Fin. Analysts. Republican. Roman Catholic. Avocations: bridge, tennis. Home: 8 Tamarack Pl Greenwich CT 06830 Office: MPT Assocs 600 Fifth Ave New York NY 10020

FARRELL, MARY LOU, business educator; b. Whittemore, Iowa, Aug. 20, 1947; d. Orville John and Alvina (Reding) Wagner; m. Dennis Michael Farrell, July 3, 1970; children—Janelle, Nicolle, Ian. B.S., Mt. Mercy Coll., 1969; M.A., U. Iowa, 1977. Educator/coordinator Clear Creek Community Schs., High Sch. Center, Tiffin, Iowa, 1969—. Mem. Iowa Edn. Assn., NEA, Clear Creek Tchrs. Assn., Nat. Bus. Edn. Assn., Iowa Bus. Edn. Assn., Am. Vocat. Assn., Am. Bus. Women's Assn., Multi-Occupations Coop. Coordinators of Iowa. Democrat. Roman Catholic. Home: 1511 Derwen St Iowa City IA 52244 Office: Clear Creek Community Schs Tiffin IA 52340

FARRELL, NEAL JOSEPH, banker; b. Bklyn., Aug. 31, 1932; s. Joseph D. and Gertrude B. (Behan) F.; B.A., Dartmouth Coll., 1954; grad. Advanced Mgmt. Program, Harvard U., 1970; m. Joan Pendergast, Aug. 13, 1955; children—Michael J., Daniel S., Patrick J., Nancy E. With Chase Manhattan Bank, N.Y.C., 1956-78, sr. v.p., 1971-78; pres., dir. Mercantile Trust Co. N.A., St. Louis, 1978—, chief exec. officer, 1983—; vice chmn., dir. Mercantile Bancorp. Inc. Bd. dirs. United Way St. Louis, Arts and Edn. Fund Greater St. Louis; trustee St. Louis U. St. Louis Children's Hosp., bd. dirs. St. Louis Regional Commerce and Growth Assn. Served to lt. (j.g.) USNR, 1954-56. Mem. Am. Bankers Assn., Assn. Rev. City Bankers. Clubs: Old Warson Country, St. Louis, Media (St. Louis); Log Cabin. Office: Mercantile Trust Co NA Mercantile Tower St Louis MO 63166

FARRELL, THOMAS NEELY, engineering corporation executive, pollution control consultant; b. Memphis, Tenn., Aug. 11, 1930; s. Edwin Thomas and Lois (Neely) F.; m. Mary Mathis, June 22, 1962; children—Michael Geren, John Neely. Student U. Tenn., 1952-55. Photographic technician U.S. Forest Service, 1955-58; mil. analyst U.S. Army Photo Interpretation Ctr., 1958-63; sr. intelligence analyst Nat. Photog. Interpretation Ctr., 1963-77; pres. DeVansco Inc., Fenton, Mich., 1977-79; gen. mgr. Vander Velden, Inc., Grand Blanc, Mich., 1979-80; pres. Xebex Engring. Corp., Fenton, 1980—; pres. Farrell Enterprises, Fenton, 1980—; cons. pollution control Gen. Motors, 1980—. Asst. scout master Tall Pines council Boy Scouts Am., Fenton, 1978-81; chmn. adminstrv. bd. Fenton United Meth. Ch., 1982-84; del. Mich. Republican. Conv., 1982-83. Served with USAF, 1948-52. Recipient Spl.

Service award Def. Intelligence Agy., 1965, Outstanding Performance awards, 1965, 68. Mem. Am. Soc. Photogrammetry, Air Pollution Control Assn., Sigma Nu. Lodge: Lions (sec. Fenton 1980-82, pres. 1985-86). Home: 337 W Caroline St Fenton MI 48430 Office: PO Box 189 Fenton MI 48430

FARRINGTON, HELEN AGNES, utility company executive; b. Queens, N.Y., Dec. 1, 1945; d. Joseph Christopher and Therese Marie (Breazzano) F. A.S., Interboro Inst., N.Y.C., 1965; A.A., Ohio State U., 1983, B.S., 1985. Mgmt. cert. U. Mich., 1980. With Ohio Power div. Am. Electric Power Co., Newark, Ohio, 1979—, now personnel mgr. Mem. Licking County Personnel Mgmt. Assn., Safety Council. Mem. adv. bd. Central Ohio Tech. Coll., Licking County Joint Vocat. Sch., Newark High Sch.; mem. Presdl. Task Force, 1983-84. Mem. Am. Soc. Profl. Female Execs., Nat. Assn. Female Execs., Licking County C. of C. Home: 1380 Londondale Pky C-1 Newark OH 43055

FARRIS, WILLIAM PETER, computer/sensors company executive; b. Chgo., May 9, 1952; s. Rolland F. and Mary Anne (Diemer) F.; m. Robbyn Lee Howell, Aug. 9, 1975; children—Michael William, Andrew Timothy. B.S. Mech. Engring., in Ind. Inst. Tech., 1974; M.B.A., Xavier U., 1981. Sales engr. Gen. Electric Co., 1974-77, sales specialist, Schenectady, 1977-78, generation sales engr., Cin., 1978-79; mgr. product devel. FMC Link-Belt, Lexington, Ky., 1979-80, mgr. mktg. devel., 1980-82, mgr. mktg. planning, Cedar Rapids, Iowa, 1982, mgr. product and resource planning, 1982; mgr. nat. accounts Accu-Ray Corp., Columbus, Ohio, 1983—. Named Peak Performer, Gen. Electric Co., 1975. Mem. Sigma Phi Epsilon (alumni bd. 1978-79). Democrat. Roman Catholic. Home: 792 McCall Ct Worthington OH 43085 Office: 650 Ackerman Rd Columbus OH 43202

FARUKI, CHARLES JOSEPH, lawyer; b. Bay Shore, N.Y., July 3, 1949; s. Mahmud Taji and Rita (Trownsell) F.; m. Nancy Louise Glock, June 5, 1971; children—Brian Andrew, Jason Allen, Charles Joseph. B.A. summa cum laude, U. Cin., 1971; J.D. cum laude, Ohio State U., 1973. Bar: Ohio 1974, U.S. Dist. Ct. (no. and so. dists.) Ohio 1975, U.S. Ct. Appeals (9th cir.) 1977, U.S. Tax Ct. 1977, U.S. Supreme Ct. 1977, U.S. Ct. Appeals (6th cir.) 1978, U.S. Dist. Ct. (no. dist.) Tex. 1979, U.S. Dist. Ct. (ea. dist.) Ky. 1982, U.S. Ct. Appeals (D.C. cir.) 1982, U.S. Ct. Customs and Patent Appeals 1982. Assoc. Smith & Schnacke, Dayton, Ohio, 1974-78, ptnr., 1979—, also dir. Contbr. articles in field. Served to capt. U.S. Army Res. Mem. ABA, Fed. Bar Assn. Ohio Bar Assn., Dayton Bar Assn. Avocation: numismatics. Home: 238 Greenmount Blvd Oakwood OH 45419 Office: Smith & Schnacke PO Box 1817 2000 Courthouse Plaza NE Dayton OH 45401

FASS, FRED WILLIAM ROBERT, geologist, consultant; b. Milw., Oct. 30, 1951; s. Fred William and Barbara Ann (Schwerdtmann) F. B.S., Mich. Tech. Univ., 1975; M.S. (grad. research asst.), Univ. Mo., Rolla, 1981. Temp. geologist Amoco Minerals Co., Englewood, Colo., 1978, Asarco, Inc., Knoxville, Tenn., 1979; geologist I Cities Service Co. Tulsa, 1981, geologist II, Oklahoma City, 1981-83; jr. processing geo-physicist Digicon Geophys. Corp., Oklahoma City, 1984; cons. geology, Milw., 1984—. Mem. AIME, Am. Assn. Petroleum Geologists, Oklahoma City Geol. Soc., Sigma Xi, Sigma Gamma Epsilon. Avocations: Rock and mineral collecting; singing; camping; canoeing; hiking. Home: 1654 E Newton Ave Milwaukee WI 53211

FASSER, WALTER BLANCHARD, JR., fluid power company executive, marketing executive; b. Springfield, Mass., June 27, 1937; s. Walter B. and Pauline A. (Marceau) F.; m. Cheryl Lynn Biskup, Dec. 20, 1980; 1 child, David Joseph; 1 child by previous marriage, Cynthia Ann. Cert. mfg. engr. Ops. mgr. Gen. Electric Co., 1955-69; salesman Bellows Internat., Peoria, Ill., 1969-73; sales mgr. Parker Hannifin Co., Cleve., 1973-79; gen. mgr. Alloy Engring., Berea, Ohio, 1979-82; v.p., gen. mgr. MacLean-Fogg-Flodar, Cleve., 1982-85; pres. I.C. Cons. Inc., Euclid, Ohio, 1985—; cons., Ill., Ohio, Ind., Pa., 1971—. Mem. Soc. Mfg. Engrs., Sliva Internat. Grads. Assn. (pres. 1983-84). Republican. Home: 13126 Tradewinds Dr Strongsville OH 44136 Office: IC Cons PO Box 17423 Euclid OH 44117

FASSLER, CRYSTAL G., marketing consultant; b. Marion, Ohio, Mar. 15, 1942; d. Lloyd C. and Iola M. (Runkle) Mahaffey; student public schs., Prospect, Ohio; m. Donald D. Fassler, May 6, 1960; 1 son, Curtis A. Media buyer H. Swink Advt., Marion, 1968-73; media buyer and planner Tracey Locke Advt., Columbus, Ohio, 1973-74, Lord, Sullivan & Yoder Advt., Marion, 1974-82; youth conselor State of Ohio Employment Services, Marion, 1982-83; nat. mktg. consultant WMRN-AM and FM, Marion, 1983-84, asst. gen. mgr., 1985—. Home: 1846 Smeltzer Rd Marion OH 43302 Office: 1330 N Main St Marion OH 43302

FAST, DELTON L., optometrist; b. Lamar, Mo., Sept. 9, 1950; s. Clarence Franklin and Lavena (Burke) F.; m. Deborah Joyce Gardner, Aug. 11, 1971; children—Allison, Jeremy, Eric. Student SW Mo. State U., 1968-71; O.P., So. Coll. Optometry, Memphis, 1975. Pvt. practice optometry, Nevada, Mo., 1975—; clin. assoc. Optometric Extension Program, 1976—. Mem. Am. Optometric Assn., Mo. Optometric Assn., SW Mo. Optometric Soc. (pres. 1981-82), Council on Sports Vision, Heart Am. Contact Lens Soc., Omega Delta. Baptist. Club: Country (Nevada) (pres. 1982-83). Lodge: Rotary. Avocations: gospel singing; golf; water skiing; camping. Home: Route 1 Box 162-A Nevada MO 64772 Office: 119 S Main Nevada MO 64772

FATH, DALE FREDERICK, optometrist; b. Marion, Ind., Aug. 2, 1949; s. Frederick Emmett and Evelyn Louise (Kelley) F.; m. Patty Jo Haynes, Jan. 6, 1973; 1 child, Lauren Marie. B.S., Ind. U., 1971, O.D., 1973; cert. concentrated ocular therapy Pa. Coll. Optometry, 1983. Optometrist assoc. Thomas W. Lantz, O.D., Goshen, Ind., 1973-74, Falls Optometric Clinic, Memomonee Falls, Wis., 1974-75; gen. practice optometry, Muncie, Ind., 1976-81; staff optometrist VA Med. Ctr., Ft. Wayne, Ind., 1981—; adj. assoc. prof. Ind. U. Sch. Optometry, Bloomington, 1982—; lectr. In-Service Nursing Instrn., 1984. Contbr. articles to profl. jours. Vol. ARC, Ft. Wayne, 1983-84. Mem. Am. Optometric Assn., Ind. Optometric Assn., Nat. Assn. VA Optometrists. Roman Catholic. Club: Ind. U. Varsity. Office: Ft Wayne VA Med Center 1600 Randalia Ave Fort Wayne IN 46805

FAUBER, BERNARD M., retail company executive; b. 1922; married. With K Mart Corp., 1942—, asst. mgr. So. region, 1961-65, exec. asst. to pres., 1965-66, Western regional mgr., 1966-77, v.p., 1968-77, sr. exec. v.p., chief adminstrv. officer, 1977-80, chmn., chief exec. officer, 1980—, also dir. Served with USN, 1941-45. Office: K Mart Corp 3100 W Big Beaver Troy MI 48084*

FAUCI, JAMES JOHN, pharmacist, administrator; b. Chgo., Sept. 13, 1957; s. John Jeremiah and Rose Marie (Marzullo) F.; m. Gail Marie Mark, Sept. 1, 1979; children—John Nicholas, Paul Anthony. B.S. in Pharmacy, Drake U., 1980. Lic. pharmacist, Iowa. Tech. pharmacist VA Hosp., Des Moines, 1978-80, staff pharmacist, 1980-82, Orange City Municipal Hosp., Iowa, 1982-84, dir. pharm. services, 1984—. State Ill. scholar, 1975. Mem. Am. Pharm. Assn. Iowa Pharmacists Assn. Avocations: collecting games, coaching youth soccer. Home: 508 Arizona Ave SW Orange City IA 51041 Office: Orange City Municipal Hosp 610 4th St NW Orange City IA 51041

FAUGHN, SHIRLEY JEAN, educational administrator, consultant; b. Paducah, Ky., July 15, 1953; d. Everett Leslie and Lalah (Sullivan) F. B.S. in Psychology and Social Work, Murray State U., 1975, M.A.Ed. in Guidance and Counseling, 1976. Resident dir. U. Wis.-River Falls, 1976-78; resident dir. coordinator U. Ill., Champaign-Urbana, 1978-81, area coordinator, 1978-83; assoc. dir. for residential life Mankato State U., Minn., 1983-85; guest instr. U. Ill., Mankato State U., 1982—; cons. Perkins Roost & Assocs., Grand Rapids, Mich., 1984—. Author (workbook) Getting Control: A Guide to Being an Effective Woman Manager and Respected Leader, 1984. Contbr. articles to profl. jours. Mem. Am. Assn. Counseling & Devel., Am. Coll. Personnel Assn., Assn. Coll. & Univ. Housing Officers, Nat. Assn. for Women Deans, Adminstrs., Counselors, Alpha Delta Mu, Psi Chi, Phi Delta Kappa, Kappa Delta Pi. Avocations: Bible study, aerobics, skiing, tennis, golf. Office: Dept Residential Life Box 30 Mankato State Univ Mankato MN 56001

FAULKNER, CHARLES BRIXEY, government official; lawyer; b. Springfield, Mo., Feb. 11, 1934; s. Charles Franklin and Josephine Frances (Brixey) F.; B.S., U. Ark., 1956; LL.B., U. Mo., 1960; m. Noralee Phariss, Dec. 29, 1956; children—Charlesa, Charles Byron. Admitted to Mo. bar, 1960, Fed. bar, 1962; partner Ratican & Faulkner, Aurora, Mo., 1960-71; legal adviser U.S. Bur. Prisons, U.S. Med. Center, Springfield, Mo., 1972; regional atty U.S. Bur. Prisons, Kansas City, Mo., 1974—; pros. and county atty., Lawrence County, Mo., 1961-70; city atty. Aurora, 1970-72, Marionville, Mo., 1961-72. Chmn. bd. dirs. A.R.C., Lawrence County, 1963-65. Served with 1st div., 26th Inf., AUS, 1956-57. Recipient Kansas City Trust award in estate planning, 1960. Mem. 39th Jud. Circuit Bar Assn. (v.p. 1966-70), Scabbard and Blade, Beta Gamma Sigma. Rotarian (dir. 1961-72). Editorial bd. Mo. Law Rev., 1958-60. Home: 312 S Elliott St Aurora MO 65605 Office: Air World Ctr 10920 Ambassador Dr Suite 2 Kansas City MO 64151

FAULKNER, EDWIN JEROME, insurance company executive; b. Lincoln, Nebr., July 5, 1911; s. Edwin Jerome and Leah (Meyer) F.; B.A., U. Nebr., 1932; M.B.A., U. Pa., 1934; m. Jean Rathburn, Sept. 27, 1933. With Woodmen Accident & Life Co., Lincoln, 1934—, successively claim auditor, v.p., 1934-38, pres., 1938-77, dir., 1938—, chmn. bd., chief exec. officer, 1977-84, hon. chmn. & exec. counsel, 1984—; pres., dir. Comml. Mut. Surety Co., 1938—; dir. Lincoln Tel. & Tel. Co., Universal Surety Co., Inland Ins. Co. Chmn. Health Ins. Council 1959-60. Chmn. Lincoln-Lancaster County Plan Commn., 1948-68; mem. medicare adv. com. Dept. Def., 1957-71; chmn., trustee Bryan Meml. Hosp.; trustee Doane Coll., Cooper Found., Lincoln Found., Nebraskans for Pub. TV; pres. Nebr. Hist. Soc.; chmn. U. Nebr. Found., Nebr. Council on Econ. Edn. Served from 2d lt. to lt. col. USAAF, 1942-45. Decorated Legion of Merit, recipient Distinguished Service award U. Nebr., 1957, Nebr. Builders award, 1979; Harold R. Gordon Meml. award Internat. Assn. Health Ins. Underwriters, 1955, Ins. Man of Year award Ins. Field, 1958, Exec. of Year award Am. Coll. Hosp. Adminstrs., 1971. Mem. Am. Coll. Life Underwriters (trustee), Health Ins. Assn. Am. (1st pres. 1956), Am. Legion, Am. Life Conv. (exec. com. 1961—, pres. 1966-67), Phi Beta Kappa, Phi Kappa Psi, Alpha Kappa Psi (hon.). Republican. Presbyterian. Lodges: Masons, Elks. Author: Accident and Health Insurance, 1940; Health Insurance, 1960; editor: Man's Quest for Security, 1966. Home: 4100 South St Lincoln NE 68506 Office: 1526 K St Lincoln NE 68508

FAULKNER, JAMES CHARLES, electrical contractor; b. Fairfax, Mo., Oct. 21, 1951; s. James Gerald and Eva Gertrude (McClaskey) F.; m. Katherine Dell Martin, Dec. 15, 1973; children—Joshua James, Renee Elizabeth. Student Universal Trade Sch., Omaha, 1969-70, Southwest Mo. State U., 1979. Electrician, B & N Cooling and Heating, Fairfax, Mo., 1970-71; electrician Polk County Elec. Co., Bolivar, Mo., 1971-79, ptnr., 1979—. Mem. Nat. Fedn. Ind. Bus., Bolivar C. of C. Mem. Christian Ch. Lodges: Optimists (Bolivar, Mo.); Masons (sec.). Home: Route 2 Bolivar MO 65613 Office: 116 S Market St Bolivar MO 65613

FAULKNER, THOMAS SAMUEL, agrl. educator; b. Carthage, Ill., Feb. 5, 1955; s. Melvin Adriph and Darlene (Smith) F. B.S., Western Ill. U., 1977. Tchr. agr., FFA adv. Union Community Unit #115, Oquawka, Ill., 1977—. Project leader 4-H. Mem. Ill. Assn. Vocat. Agr. Tchrs. (chmn. sect. 4), Union Fedn. Tchrs. (treas. local chpt.), Nat. Vocat. Agr. Tchrs. Assn. (state winner 1982), Ill. Vocat. Assn., Am. Vocat. Assn. Office: R R Biggsville IL 61418

FAULKNER, WILLIAM JOE, ophthalmologist; b. Dayton, Ky., Jan. 31, 1950; s. Joseph Stanley and Madrew Moran (Hendren) F.; m. Carol Marie Demos, Aug. 20, 1977; children—Daniel Jonathan, Sara Adele. B.A., Ohio Wesleyan U., 1972; M.D., U. Louisville, 1976; degree in Ophthalmology, U. Okla., 1980. Diplomate Am. Bd. Ophthalmology. Intern, Santa Clara Valley Med. Ctr., San Jose, Calif., 1976-77; cornea fellow Harvard U., 1980; practice medicine specializing in ophthalmology; ophthalmologist Cin. Eye Inst., 1980—. Contbr. articles to profl. jours. Mem. AMA, Ohio State Med. Assn., Acad. Medicine Cin., Cin. Soc. Ophthalmology, Keratorefractive Soc., Castroviejo Soc. Methodist. Avocations: skiing, running, golf. Office: Cincinnati Eye Inst 10496 Montgomery Rd Cincinnati OH 45242

FAUVER, VERNON ARTHUR, chemical engineer; b. Hammond, Ind., Mar. 25, 1928; s. Gale Vernon and Charlotte Irene (Guss) F.; m. Dorothy Ruth Faulstich, Dec. 23, 1947; children—John Vernon, Gayle Ellyn. B.S. in Chem. Engring., Purdue U., 1952, M.S. in Chem. Engring, 1953. Registered profl. engr., Mich. Chem. engr. Eastman Kodak Co., Rochester, N.Y., 1953, Dow Chem. U.S.A., Midland, Mich., 1954—. Bd. dirs. Chippewa Nature Ctr., Midland, Mich. 1981—, pres., 1985-86. Served with USN, 1946-48. Mem. Am. Inst. Chem. Engrs. (chmn. mid-Mich. sect. 1980), Am. Chem. Soc. (editorial adv. panel chemtech 1975-83, chmn. div. indsl. and engring. chemistry, 1973, disting. service award, 1974) Nat. Soc. Profl. Engrs. Avocations: nature study; photography. Office: Dow Chem USA Bldg 743 Midland MI 48667

FAVORS, ANITA RENEE NEAL, state government administrator, educator; b. Kansas City, Kans., Feb. 8, 1951; d. Abraham and Barbara Franklin (Fuller) N.; m. Wayman Walter Favors, Sept. 6, 1970; children—Jocelyn, Wayman, Jr., Ahmad Khalil. B.A. in Sociology, Park Coll., Parkville, Mo., 1977; M.A. in Pub. Adminstr., Central Mich. U., 1981. Dir. Area Agy. on Aging, Kansas City, Kans., 1973-82; asst. city adminstr. City of Kansas City, 1982-83; commr. adult services Kans. State Dept. Social and Rehab. Services, Topeka, 1983—; instr. Kansas City Community Coll., 1982—; mem. adv. bd. Washburn U., Topeka, 1984—, Kansas City Jr. League, 1982—. Author: Mental Health and the Elderly, 1982; (with others) The Dynamics of Aging, 1981, Older Women: Issues and Problems, 1983. Mem. Democracy, Inc., Kansas City, 1977—; commr. Kans. Commn. Civil Rights, Topeka, 1983—. Presdl. scholar Park Coll., 1977; named Black Woman of Distinction, Yates Br. YWCA, 1982; recipient In Service to Kans. award Panhellenic Council Kansas City, 1983. Mem. Women's C. of C. (bd. dirs. 1984—), LWV, Kans. Social Welfare Assn., Am. Pub. Welfare Assn., Mid Am. Congress on Aging (pres. 1981-82, bd. dirs.), Kans. Caucus on Black Aged (bd. dirs. 1982—). Democrat. Baptist. Club: Topeka Women's Network (treas. 1983-84). Avocation: reading. Office: Kans Dept Social and Rehab Services 2700 W 6th St Topeka KS 66109

FAWCETT, JAMES DAVIDSON, herpetologist, educator; b. New Plymouth, N.Z., Jan. 10, 1933; s. James and Edna Lola (Catterick) F.; B.Sc., U. N.Z., 1960; M.Sc., U. Auckland (N.Z.), 1964; Ph.D., U. Colo., 1975; m. Georgene Ellen Tyler, Dec. 21, 1968. Head dept. biology Kings Coll., Auckland, 1960; grad. demonstrator dept. zoology U. Auckland, 1961-62, sr. demonstrator, 1963-64; grad. asst. U. Colo., 1969-72; instr. biology U. Nebr., Omaha, 1972-75, asst. prof., 1975-81, asso. prof., 1981—. Recipient Great Tchr. award U. Nebr., 1981. Mem. Royal Soc. N.Z., N.Z. Assn. Scientists, Am. Soc. Zoologists, Soc. Systematic Zoology, Herpetologists League, Brit. Soc. Herpetologists, AAAS, Nebr. Herpetological Soc. (pres. 1979-80), Sigma Xi (pres. Omaha chpt. 1980-81), Phi Sigma. Contbr. articles to profl. jours. Home: 7305 Grant Omaha NE 68134 Office: Biology Dept U Nebr Omaha NE 68182

FAWCETT, RUTH HARWELL, educational administrator, speaker; b. Akron, Ohio, May 14, 1938; d. Robert Henley and Ruth Edna (Weyand) Harwell; m. William Henry Fawcett, May 2, 1957; children—April Christina, John Henry, Jennifer Elaine. B.S. in Edn., Lake Erie Coll., 1973, postgrad. 1978-79, Cleve. State U., 1977-78; M.Ed., John Carroll U., 1984. Elem. tchr. Willoughby, Ohio, 1973-80, 81-82, career edn. coordinator 3 dists., 1980-81; dir. Chpt. I Disadvantaged Pupil Program Fund Reading Program, Willoughby-Eastlake (Ohio) Schs., 1982—. Recipient Book Award for Writing Lakeland Coll., 1969; 1st place Ohio State Awards Program for Teaching Econs., 1980; Martha Holden Jennings grantee, 1980; Inst. for Ednl. Leadership fellow, 1983-84. Mem. Nat. Assn. Elem. Sch. Adminstrs., Ohio Assn. Elem. Sch. Adminstr., Internat. Reading Assn., Delta Kappa Gamma. Presbyterian. Clubs: Timberlake Women's, Royal Order of Tanstaafl. Editor newsletter; author tchrs. guides for films. Home: 2 Waban Dr Timberlake OH 44094 Office: 503 Vegas Dr Eastlake OH 44094

FAWELL, HARRIS W., congressman; b. West Chicago, Ill., March. 25, 1929; grad. North Central Coll., Ill.; JD., Chgo.-Kent Coll. Law, 1952. Bar: Ill. 1952, U.S. Dist. Ct. (no. dist.) Ill. 1983. Asst. state's atty. DuPage County, Ill., 1952-57; mem. Ill. State Senate, 1963-77; ptnr. Fawell James & Brooks, Napervile, Ill.; mem. 99th Congress from 13th Ill. Dist., mem. edn. and labor, sci. and tech. and aging coms. Mem. ABA, Sssn. Trial Lawyers Am., Am. Judicature Soc., Phi Alpha Delta. Republican. Office: 511 Cannon House Office Bldg Washington DC 20515*

FAYNOR, JOHN, manufacturing company executive; b. Auburn, N.Y., June 24, 1932; s. John and Anna (Mateyak) F.; m. Nola Jean Robbins, Dec. 29, 1951; children—Elizabeth, Margaret. B.S. in Mech. and Indsl. Engring., SUNY, 1960. Mgr. engring. services Gulf-Western, Union Springs, N.Y., 1960-67, plant mgr., Kitchener, Ont., 1967-70, plant mgr., Glasgow, Ky., 1970-74; v.p. mfg. Fusite/Emerson, Cin., 1975-76, exec. v.p. ops., 1976—. Contbr. articles to profl. jours. Served with USN, 1951-55, Korea. Recipient Ky. Colonel award Office of Gov. Glasgow, 1972. Mem. Auburn Jaycees. Republican. Club: Bobwhite (Claryville). Lodge: Rotary (chmn. 1972). Avocations: trap and skeet shooting, fishing, golf. Home: 8396 Holiday Hills Cincinnati OH 45230

FEATHERLY, ARDIE, publishing company executive; b. White Cloud, Mich.; d. Otis V. Stroud and Martha M. Lesley; m. Everard B. Featherly; children—Richard R., Connie S. Student Grand Rapids Jr. Coll., Mich., 1980-81. Supr. Computer Mgmt., Grand Rapids, Mich., 1962-65; supr. data entry Skeketees, Grand Rapids, 1965-72; supr. data entry Zondervan, Grand Rapids, 1972-83, office automation adminstr., 1983—. Mem. Assn. Systems Mgmt., Assn. Info. Systems Profls., Internat. Soc. Wang Users. Republican. Methodist. Home: 5056 Burlingame St SW Wyoming MI 49509 Office: Zondervan Corp 1415 Lake Dr SE Grand Rapids MI 49506

FEATHERSTONAUGH, HENRY GORDON, psychologist; b. San Diego, Nov. 11, 1917; s. Henry Stuart and Evelyn (Borrow) F.; B.S., U. Calif., Berkeley, 1939; M.S., Lehigh U., 1974; Ph.D., U. Mo., 1978; m. Nancy Ellen Couper, July 28, 1946; children—Wendy, Rusby. Chemist, H.J. Heinz Co., Berkeley, Calif., 1938-40; dist. mgr. Union Carbide Corp., N.Y.C., 1945-73; geriatric services coordinator The Center for Mental Health, Anderson, Ind., 1979-82; v.p., sec. Living Skills Inst., Inc., Indpls., 1982—; lectr. in field. Exec. bd. Madison County Council on Aging, 1979—. Served with U.S. Army, 1941-43, USAAF, 1943-45; ATO, CBI. Decorated Air medal with oak leaf cluster, D.F.C.; Lehigh U. teaching asst. and tuition grantee, 1972-73; U. Mo. research grantee, 1974-78; diplomate in profl. psychotherapy Internat. Acad. Profl. Counseling and Psychotherapy. Mem. Am. Psychol. Assn., Ind. Psychol. Assn., Gerontol. Soc. Am., Internat. Assn. Applied Psychology, Am. Assn. Sex Educators, Counselors and Therapists, Am. Chem. Soc., Internat. Platform Assn., Psi Chi, Phi Kappa Phi. Contbr. articles to profl. jours. Office: 8204 Westfield Blvd Indianapolis IN 46240

FEATHERSTONE, ROBERT PAUL, electrical engineer; b. Fergus Falls, Minn., Sept. 29, 1920; s. Harold Childe and Frances Katherine (Erickson) F.; m. Genevieve Ruth Kretschmar, Feb. 14, 1948; children—Ruth Lynn, Kathleen Ann, Carol Joann. B.E.E., U. Minn., 1942. Registered elec. engr., Minn. Elec. engr. Lightning and Transient Research Lab., Mpls., 1946-49; research assoc. physics dept. U. Minn., Mpls., 1949-67; vis. scientist European Org. for Nuclear Research, Geneva, Switzerland, 1967-68; elec. engr. Nat. Accelerator Lab., Batavia, Ill., 1968-69; v.p. Central Engring. Co., Mpls., 1969—. Served to capt. U.S. Army, 1942-46. PTO. Republican. Presbyterian. Home: 4933 3d Ave S Minneapolis MN 55409

FEBRES, YORK SERGIO, Spanish educator; b. Arequipa, Peru, Aug. 14, 1932; came to U.S., 1962; s. Flavio Roberto and Clodomira F.; m. Julie Marie Heilig, June 9, 1972; children—York Sergio, Gina, William. B.A., Nat. U. St. Agustin, Arequipa, 1954; M. in Spanish Am. Lit., U. Minn., 1970, Ph.D. in Spanish Am. Lit., 1975. Vis. prof. Gustavus Adolphus Coll., St. Peter, Minn., 1971-72; asst. prof. Coll. St. Catherine, St. Paul, 1972-80, assoc. prof. Spanish, 1981—; head Spanish dept., 1978-84; Coll. St. Catherine rep. Associated Colls. Twin Cities Latin Am. Studies, St. Paul, 1976—; advisor Student Project for Amity Among Nations, U. Minn., Mpls., 1976-78, Upper Midwest Assn. Intercultural Edn., St. Paul, 1980-82. Faculty devel. grantee Mpls. Found., 1981, Bush Found., Mpls., 1983, 85, NEH, 1983. Mem. Am. Assn. Tchrs. Spanish and Portuguese (v.p. Minn. chpt. 1975-76, pres. 1977-78), N. Central Council Latinamericanists (assoc. U. Wis.-Milw. chpt.). Club: Latin Am. (St. Paul) (pres. 1978-79). Avocations: classical music, stamp collecting; travel. Office: Coll St Catherine 2004 Randolph Ave Saint Paul MN 55105

FECHHEIMER, NATHAN S., dairy science educator, scientist; b. Cin., May 24, 1925; s. Marcus and Caroline (Freiberg) F.; m. Lotti Juras, Dec. 22, 1946; children—Jean, Marcus. B.Sc. in Agr., Ohio State U., 1949, M.Sc., 1950, Ph.D., 1957. Instr. Ohio State U., Columbus, 1952-57, asst. prof., 1957-61, assoc. prof., 1961-65, prof., 1965—; cons. Central Ohio Breeding Assn., Columbus, 1954-70, Am. Jersey Cattle Club, Columbus, 1978-82; bd. dirs. Ohio State U. Research Found., Columbus, 1974-77. Contbr. articles to profl. publs., chpts. to books. Served with USN, 1943-46, PTO. Fellow NATO, 1960, Ford Found., 1970, 78; recipient Meritorious Research award Gamma Sigma Delta, 1984. Fellow AAAS; mem. Am. Dairy Sci. Assn., AAUP (pres. chpt. 1964, pres. Ohio conf. 1965), Genetics Soc. Am., Soc. Study Fertility. Home: 114 S Broadleigh Rd Columbus OH 43209 Office: Ohio State U 2027 Coffey Rd Columbus OH 43210

FEDAN, STEPHEN ANTHONY, tool manufacturing company executive; b. New Kensington, Pa., Sept. 20, 1943; m. Mary Ellen Lavelle, Oct. 11, 1975. B.B.A. in Bus. Mgmt., Cleve. State U., 1966; M.B.A. in Systems Mgmt., Baldwin Wallace Coll., 1980. Cert. practitioner inventory mgmt. Mfg. supr. Gen. Motors Corp., Cleve., 1966-81; gen. supr. prodn. control Terex Corp., Hudson, Ohio, 1981-84; prodn. control mgr. Stanley Works-Mac Tools, Sabina, Ohio, 1984—. Served with U.S. Army, 1966-68. Mem. Am. Prodn. and Inventory Control Soc. Roman Catholic. Avocations: golf, jogging. Home: 5283 Pheasant Dr Orient OH 43146 Office: Mac Tools 197 Jefferson St Sabina OH 45169

FEDELL, JEAN MARIE, gemologist, jewelry appraiser, consultant; b. Neenah, Wis., Sept. 22, 1956; d. John Randolph and Arlene Ross (Jenzen) F. B.A., U. Wis.-Madison, 1979; postgrad. Gemological Inst. Am., 1980. Gemologist, colored stone buyer Ball Co., Chgo., 1980, ind. auditor of jewelry, 1981; pres. Nature's Art, Crystal Lake, Ill., 1984—; gemologist appraiser Bailey Banks and Biddle div. of Zale Corp., Schaumburg, Ill., 1980—. Leader Blackhawk council Girl Scouts U.S., 1978. Recipient Tech. Excellence award Bailey Banks and Biddle, 1985. Mem. Gemmological Assn. of Great Britain, Gemological Inst. Am., Smithsonian Assocs. Avocations: photography; needlework. Office: Bailey Banks and Biddle J308 Woodfield Mall Schaumburg IL 60195

FEDERWITZ, DUWAYNE, banker; b. Appleton, Wis., Feb. 8, 1943; s. Elmer Gustav and Dorothy (Schwalenberg) F.; m. Deidra Kinast, Aug. 12, 1967 (div. May 1977); children—Denise, Dennis, Dorie; m. Virginia Clara Topp, Nov. 27, 1977; children—Darla, Douglas. B.S. in Math. and Econs., Luther Coll., 1965. Loan officer Wis. Fin., Elkhorn, 1965-66, loan officer Fed. Land Bank, Appleton, Wis., 1966-69, br. mgr., 1969-84, acting pres., 1985—. Pres. Clintonville Bd. Edn., 1982; project leader Woodland Badgers 4H, Clintonville, 1982; treas. troop Fox River-Bay Lakes Council Boy Scouts Am., 1980. Mem. Future Farmers Am. Alumni Assn. Republican. Lutheran. Avocations: gardening; fishing. Home: Rt 1 Clintonville WI 54929

FEDI, PETER FRANCIS, dentistry educator; b. East Hampton, N.Y., Feb. 16, 1924; s. Peter and Rose (Sorce) F.; m. Ann Agnes Donnelly, Oct. 1, 1944; children—Bonnie, Peter F. III, Robert. D.D.S., U. Pa., 1946; M.Sc., Ohio State U., 1956. Diplomate Am. Bd. Periodontology. Practice dentistry, Southampton, N.Y., 1946-52; commd. lt. Dental Corps, U.S. Navy, 1952, advanced through grades to capt., 1963; chmn. dept. dentistry USS Yorktown, 1958-60; chmn. dept. periodontics U.S. Navy Dental Sch., Bethesda, Md., 1962-69; chmn. dental services U.S. Navy Hosp., Orlando, 1970-72; ret., 1972; Rinehart prof. U. Mo.-Kansas City Sch. Dentistry, 1972—, chmn. dept. periodontics, 1976-82, dir. clin. spltys. advanced edn. programs, 1982—; cons. periodontics VA Hosp., Leavenworth, Kans., 1972—. Author: The Periodontics Syllabus, 1985. Fellow Am. Coll. Dentists; mem. ADA (cons. Council on Dental Edn. 1982—), Am. Acad. Periodontology (chmn. subcom. on predoctoral edn. 1981—, mem. exec. council 1981-84), Midwest Soc. Periodontology, Am. Assn. Dental Schs. Republican. Roman Catholic. Home: 455 E Lakeshore Dr Lake Quivira KS 66106 Office: Univ Mo Sch Dentistry 650 E 25th St Kansas City KS 64108

FEDOR-JOSEPH, STEPHANIE RAE, counselor, total fitness educator; b. Milw., Jan. 9, 1956; d. Alexander Thomas Fedor; m. David Barry Joseph, June 6, 1982. B.S., U. Wis.-LaCrosse, 1977; M.S., U. Wis.-Madison, 1981. Job coach, asst. counselor LaCrosse Courthouse, Wis., 1976-77; counselor U. Wis.-Madison, 1979-84; fitness educator Harbor Athletic Club, Middleton, Wis., 1982-85; mktg. rep. Munz Corp., Madison, Wis., 1984-85; cons. total fitness edn. Gov.'s Council on Phys. Fitness and Health and Wis. Park and Recreation Assn., Madison/Appleton, 1984; stress mgmt. cons. U. Wis.-Madison, 1980-85, Family Health Plan, Health Maintenance Orgn., Milw., 1981; guest instr. U. Wis.-Madison, 1981; dancer, choreographer, tchr., performer Madison Jazz Dance Theatre, 1979-80; jazz dance instr. Kanopy Dance Theatre, 1981-82. Creator group program relaxation/dance exercise, 1981. Fitness educator vol.

Am. Heart Assn., Am. Cancer Soc., Madison, 1983; crisis phone vol., LaCrosse, Wis., 1977; CPR instr. ARC. U. Wis.-LaCrosse Alumni Assn. scholar, 1976-77. Mem. Am. Assn. Counseling and Devel., Am. Coll. Personnel Assn., Nat. Bd. Cert. Counselors, Inc. (counselor 1984—), Aerobics and Fitness Assn. Am. (cons. 1983—), Wis. Personnel and Guidance Assn., U. Wis.-Madison Student Personnel Assn. Club: Harbor Athletic (Middleton, Wis.) (fitness educator 1982—). Avocations: dance; artwork, sewing; cooking; swimming.

FEELY, RICHARD ALAN, physician, surgeon; b. Berwyn, Ill., Jan. 4, 1952; s. Daniel Richard and Donna Jean (LaCount) F.; m. Carol Anne Frieders, June 29, 1974; 1 son, Brad Richard. B.S., N.E. Mo. State U., 1974; D.O., Kirksville Coll. Osteo. Medicine, 1978. Diplomate Nat. Bd. Examiners Osteo. Physicians and Surgeons; cert. Nat. Assn. Disability Evaluating Physicians. Dir. osteo. manipulative medicine Good Samaritan Hosp., Tampa, Fla., 1979-80; physician Mauer Clinic, Zion, Ill., 1980-81; instr. Chgo. Coll. Osteo. Medicine, 1980-82, asst. prof., 1982-83, clin. asst. prof. osteo. medicine, 1983—; pres. Rhema Med. Assocs. Ltd., Chgo., 1985—. Sci. editor Cranial Acad. Newsletter, 1983—. Chmn. adminstrv. services commn. Santa Maria Del Popolo Ch., Mundelein, Ill., 1983. Mem. Sutherland Cranial Found. (faculty mem. 1982—), Cranial Acad. (trustee 1983—), Christian Med. Found. (regional v.p. 1983—), Christian Med. Soc., Am. Osteo. Assn., North Am. Acad. Manipulative Medicine, Am. Osteo. Acad. of Sports Medicine. Republican. Roman Catholic. Office: Rhema Med Assocs Ltd 46 E Oak St Suite 401 Chicago IL 60611

FEENEY, AGNES MARY, educator; b. Chgo., Dec. 5, 1933; d. Joseph Martin and Agnes Veronica (Whalen) F.; B.A. in Art, Rosary Coll., 1955; M.A., Pius XII Inst., Florence, Italy, 1956; postgrad. Art. Inst. Chgo., 1965-70, No. Ill. U., 1970-71, Concordia Coll., 1972-74, U. Ill., summer, 1964, Gonzaga U., 1966. With Marshall Field's, Chgo., 1952-56, Reuben Donnelley Pub. Co., Chgo., 1956-57; tchr. Sch. Dist. 88, Bellwood, Ill., 1957-58; tchr. Sch. Dist. 100, South Berwyn, Ill., 1958-63, tchr. gifted program, 1963-68, dir. gifted program, 1968-82, curriculum dir., 1981—; condr. workshops in field. Bd. dirs. No. Ill. Planning Commn. for Gifted Edn., 1980-82; mem. adv. council Area I-South Gifted Service Region, 1982—; mem. Morton Twp. Articulation Steering com., 1970-82, Morton Twp. Gifted Articulation Com., 1981-82; mem. adv. com. Morton Twp. Coll. for Kids, 1982, others. Mother Catherine Wall scholar, 1955; recipient Those Who Excel hon. mention award Sch. Adminstrs., 1982; Commitment to Excellence award Ill. State Gifted Conf., 1982. Mem. Assn. Supervision and Curriculum Devel., Ill. Assn. Supervision and Curriculum Devel., No. Ill. Planning Commn. for Gifted Educators. Roman Catholic. Contbr. articles to profl. jours.; author: (with John Leckel) The Great Chicago Melting Pot Cookbook, 1980; The Legendary Illinois Cookbook, 1982. Office: 26th and East Ave Curriculum Office Berwyn IL 60402

FEHR, RANDOLPH EUGENE, university business executive; b. Melrose Park, Ill., Jan. 19, 1943; s. Eugene Clayton and Bernice (Winehoff) F.; m. Jane Gillespie, May 9, 1964; children—Timothy Randolph, Robin Katharine. B.A., Park Coll., 1964; M.A., Central Mich. U., 1984. Credit analyst Phillips Petroleum Co., Kansas City, Mo., 1964-68; credit supr. Montgomery Ward Co., Merriam, Kans., 1968-71; corp. ops. mgr. Western Auto Supply, Kansas City, 1971-73; office mgr. Park Coll., Parkville, Mo., 1973-78; bus. mgr., treas. U. Dubuque, Iowa, 1978—. Mem. Nat. Assn. Coll. and Univ. Bus. Officers, Coll. and Univ. Personnel Assn., Presbyterian. Lodge: Rotary. Home: 5590 Barrington Dr Dubuque IA 52001 Office: U Dubuque 2000 University Ave Dubuque IA 52001

FEHRING, THOMAS H., utility company executive; b. Milw., Jan. 4, 1947; s. Jerome J. and Loretta M. (Kaltenbach) F.; m. Suzan M. Ogas, Aug. 29, 1970; children—Beth, Nicolas, Alicia. B.S.M.E., Marquette U., 1970, M.S.M.E., 1976. Registered mech. engr., Wis. Co-op engr. Ford Motor Co., Dearborn, Mich., 1967-69; project adminstr. Wis. Electric, Milw., 1970-81, sr. project engr., 1981-82; asst. mgr. corp. planning, 1982-83; asst. mgr. Oak Creek Power Plant, Milw., 1984-85, dir. fin. mgmt., 1985—. Editor: Mechanical Engineering A Century of Progress, 1980. Account exec. Milw. United Way, 1981. Served as staff sgt. USAR, 1970-76. Mem. ASME (bd. dirs., Centennial medallion 1980, chmn. 1981-82, history and heritage chmn. 1982—). Roman Catholic. Avocation: industrial archeology. Home: 4765 N Woodburn St Whitefish Bay WI 53211 Office: Wis Electric Power Co 231 W Michigan St Milwaukee WI 53281

FEIGHAN, EDWARD FARRELL, congressman, lawyer; b. Lakewood, Ohio, Oct. 22, 1947; s. Francis X. and Rosemary (Ling) F.; m. Nadine Hopwood; children—Lauren, David. B.A., Loyola U., New Orleans, 1969; J.D., Cleve. State U., 1978. Bar: Ohio 1979. Tchr., 1969-72; mem. Ohio Ho. of Reps., 1973-78; commr. Cuyahoga County (Ohio) 1979-82; mem. 98th Congress from 19th Dist. Ohio. Mem. Nat. Adv. Council Econ. Opportunity, 1978-80; mem. exec. com. Cuyahoga County Democratic Party. Mem. Cleve. Bar Assn., Cuyahoga County Bar Assn., Ohio Bar Assn., Citizens League, LWV. Office: 1223 Longworth Bldg Washington DC 20515

FEIKENS, JOHN, judge; b. Clifton, N.J., Dec. 3, 1917; s. Sipke and Corine (Wisse) F.; A.B., Calvin Coll., Grand Rapids, Mich., 1939; J.D., U. Mich., 1941; LL.D., U. Detroit, 1979, Detroit Coll. Law, 1981; m. Henriette Dorothy Schulthouse, Nov. 4, 1939; children—Jon, Susan Corine, Barbara Edith, Julie Anne, Robert H. Admitted to Mich. bar, 1942; gen. practice law, Detroit; judge U.S. Dist. Ct. Eastern Dist. Mich., 1960-61, 70—. Past co-chmn. Mich. Civil Rights Commn.; past chmn. Rep. State Central Com.; past mem. Rep. Nat. Com. Past bd. trustees Calvin Coll. Fellow Am. Coll. Trial Lawyers; mem. Am., Detroit (dir. 1962, past pres.) bar assns., State Bar Mich. (commr. 1965-71). Club: University of Michigan. Home: 10750 Koebbe Rd Manchester MI 48158 Office: Fed Bldg Detroit MI 48226

FEINBERG, HARVEY DAVID, advertising agency executive, public relations consultant, copy writer; b. Cleve., Mar. 3, 1922; s. Alfred Joseph and Mary F.; m. Audrey Lois Friedman, June 25, 1950; children—Steven Richard, Rachel Ann, Amy Marcia, Barbara Rose. B.B.A., Case Western Res. U., 1949. Exec. asst. to pres. of clothing mfg., 1950-52; advt. account exec. Robert Silverman Agy., Cleve., 1953-64; founder Ad-Vantages, Inc., Cleve., 1964—; co-founder, sec.-treas. Seven-Step, Inc., Cleve., 1985; pub. relations cons. City of Cleveland Heights, 1967-68, City of Cleve., 1970; producer audio/visual material for Cleve. Poison Ctr., 1967; pub. relations cons. Cleve. Mental Health Assn., 1968, Karamu Settlement House, 1968. Mem. bd. Edn. Cleveland Heights, 1972-80, pres., 1973, 74, 77, 79, negotiator affirmative action policy, author human relations policy; dist. chmn. University Heights Neighbors Watch; chmn. Save Our Schs. com., 1984. Served with USAAF, 1942-45. Named to Cleveland Heights High Sch. Disting. Alumni Hall of Fame, 1984; Citizen of Yr., University Heights, 1984. Mem. Cleve. Advt. Club, Ohio Sch. Bd. Assn., Nat. Sch. Bd. Assn. Lodge: Masons. Creator several audio/visual programs dealing with drugs and alcohol control. Home and office: 14449 E Carroll Blvd University Heights OH 44118

FEINBERG, RICHARD ALAN, consumer science educator, consultant; b. N.Y.C., June 12, 1950; s. Irving and Belle (Kolkowitz) F.; m. Fran Susan Jaffe, Jan. 21, 1973; 1 son, Seth Jason. B.A., SUNY-Buffalo, 1972; M.S., SUNY-Cortland, 1974; Ph.D., U. Okla., 1976. Asst. prof. psychology Ohio State U., 1976-78, Juniata Coll., Huntington, Pa., 1978-80; asst. prof. consumer scis., retailing and environ. analysis Purdue U., West Lafayette, Ind., 1980-85, assoc. prof. consumer and retailing, 1985—, dir. retail mgmt. internship program; research assoc. Purdue Retail Inst., 1980—. David Ross fellow, 1980; NIMH fellow, 1975; Purdue Agrl. Expt. Sta. grantee, 1981. Mem. Am. Psychol. Assn., AAAS, Assn. Coll. Profs. Textiles and Clothing. Contbr. articles in field to profl. jours. Office: Dept Consumer Scis and Retailing Purdue U West Lafayette IN 47907

FEINGOLD, MARCIA, mathematical sciences educator, statistician; b. N.Y.C., Apr. 13, 1932; d. George and Charlotte (Mirsky) G.; m. Eugene Neil, Mar. 26, 1960; children—Eleanor, Ruth Paula. A.B., Cornell U., 1953; M.A., U. Mich., 1978, Ph.D., 1983. Computer programmer Mpls.-Honeywell, Waltham, Mass., 1953-59; asst. mgr. service, 1959-60; asst. research mathematician U. Mich., Ann Arbor, 1960-62, research assoc., 1962-68; instr. Oakland U., Rochester, Mich., 1982-83, asst. prof. math. scis., 1983—. Contbr. articles to profl. jours. Health Services research fellow VA, Ann Arbor, 1981-82. Mem. Am. Statis. Assn. (treas. Ann Arbor chpt. 1982—). Home: 352 Hilldale Dr Ann Arbor MI 48105 Office: Dept Math Scis Oakland U Rochester MI 48063

FEINGOLD, RUSSELL DANA, state senator, lawyer; b. Janesville, Wis., Mar. 2, 1953; s. Leon and Sylvia (Binstock) F.; m. Susan Levine, Aug. 21, 1977; children—Jessica, Ellen. B.A. with honors, U. Wis.-Madison, 1975; postgrad. Magdalen Coll., Oxford U., 1975-77; J.D. with honors, Harvard U., 1979. Bar: Wis. 1979. Assoc., Foley & Lardner, Madison, 1979-82, LaFollette, Sinykin, Anderson & Munson, Madison, 1983—; mem. Wis. Senate, 1983—. Wis. Honors scholar, 1971; Rhodes scholar, 1975. Mem. Phi Beta Kappa. Democrat. Jewish. Office: Room 28 S PO Box 7882 Madison WI 53707

FEINHANDLER, HAROLD SAMUEL, ophthalmologist, medical educator; b. Ukraine, Sept. 24, 1908; came to U.S., 1921, naturalized, 1924; m. Helen W. Fenton, Feb. 21, 1954; children—Steven, Raymond, Michael. M.D., U. Ill.-Chgo., 1934. Diplomate Am. Bd. Ophthalmology. Intern Michael Reese Hosp., Chgo., 1934-35, resident, 1946-47, sr. attending ophthalmologist, 1948—, Mt. Sinai Hosp., Chgo., 1948—; prof. ophthalmology Chgo. Med. Sch., 1948-80; asst. prof. ophthalmology Rush Med. Coll., Chgo., 1978—; cons. Social Security Adminstrn., Chgo., 1978—. Served to capt. M.C., U.S. Army, 1945, ETO. Mem. AMA, Ill. Med. Soc., Chgo. Med. Soc., Am. Acad. Ophthalmology. Democrat. Jewish. Avocation: swimming. Home: 3518 Riverside Dr Wilmette IL 60091 Office: 111 N Wabash Ave Chicago IL 60602

FEINSILVER, DONALD LEE, psychiatrist; b. Bklyn., July 24, 1947; s. Albert and Mildred (Weissman) F. B.A., Alfred U., 1968; M.D., Autonomous U.-Guadalajara, Mexico, 1974. Diplomate Am. Bd. Psychiatry and Neurology. Intern in medicine L.I. Coll. Hosp., Bklyn., 1975-76; resident in psychiatry SUNY-Bklyn., 1977-78, chief resident, 1979; asst. prof. psychiatry and surgery Med. Coll. Wis., Milw., 1980-85, assoc. prof., 1985—; dir. psychiat. emergency service Milw. County Mental Health and Med. Complexes, 1980—. Contbr. articles to profl. jours.; editor: Crisis Psychiatry: Pros and Cons, 1982; mem. editorial bd. Psychiat. Medicine Jour., 1983—. Mem. Am. Psychiat. Assn., AMA, Am. Acad. Psychiatry and the Law, AAAS, Acad. Psychosomatic Medicine. Office: Med Coll Wis 8700 W Wisconsin Ave Milwaukee WI 53226

FEINWACHS, DAVID, association executive; b. St. Paul, Jan. 28, 1951; s. Henry and Klara (Post) F.; m. Deborah Louise Blehert, Dec. 21, 1975; children—Rebecca M., Sarah L. B.A., Macalester Coll., 1973; M.H.A., U. Minn., 1978, M.A., 1980; J.D., William Mitchell Coll. Law, 1980. Bar: Minn., 1980, U.S. Dist. Ct. Minn. 1980, U.S. Ct. Claims 1980, U.S. Tax Ct. 1980, U.S. Ct. Customs and Patent Appeals 1980, U.S. Ct. Mil. Appeals 1980, U.S. Ct. Appeals (8th cir.) 1980, U.S. Ct. Internat. Trade 1981, U.S. Supreme Ct. 1983. Adminstrv. trainee Hennepin County Med. Ctr., Mpls., 1975-76; adminstrv. resident Midway Hosp., St. Paul, 1977-78; corp. counsel Paster Enterprises, St. Paul, 1980-81; mgr. regulation Minn. Hosp. Assn., Mpls., 1981-82, v.p. planning and regulation, 1982-84, v.p., gen. counsel, 1984—; instr. in health law U. Minn., Mpls., 1982—. Mem. Assn. Trial Lawyers Am., Rho Chi, Alpha Kappa Delta. Home: 2261 Fairmont Saint Paul MN 55105 Office: Minn Hosp Assn 2221 University Ave Minneapolis MN 55414

FEIRER, JOHN LOUIS, technology educator; b. Menomonie, Wis., Mar. 14, 1915; s. John and Elizabeth Feirer; m. Jane Katrine Smith, Sept. 23, 1941; children—Mark David, Nina Marie. B.S., U. Wis.-Stout, 1936; M.S., U. Minn., 1938; Ed.D., U. Okla., 1946. Faculty mem. Western Mich. U., Kalamazoo, 1946—, prof. indsl. tech., 1946, head dept. indsl. tech. and edn., 1983—; cons., vis. prof. U. P.R., San Juan, 1965; cons. NASA, 1965-72; cons., field editor Charles A. Bennett Co., Inc., Peoria, Ill., 1966—; cons., vis. prof. U. Hawaii, Honolulu, 1955, 59-60; founder bd. dirs. Ctr. for Metric Edn., 1972-76. Exec. editor Indsl. Edn., mag., 1959—. Contbr. to Ency. Brit. Served to lt. USNR, 1942-46. Recipient Achievement Apollo award NASA, 1969, Disting. Achievement awards Edn. Press Assn. Am., 1975, 77; named Man of Yr. in Indsl. Edn., Internat. Indsl. Arts Assn., 1954, Disting. Faculty scholar Western Mich. U. Bd. Regents, 1982. Mem. AIAA (acad. fellows award 1985). Home: 3642 Woodcliff Dr Kalamazoo MI 49008 also: 201 Bermuda House 328 N Ocean Blvd Pompano Beach FL 33062 Office: Dept Indsl Tech and Edn 240 Moore Hall Western Michigan U Kalamazoo MI 49008

FEIT, JEROME ANTHONY, chemist; b. Chgo., Aug. 4, 1922; s. Aloysius J. and Barbara (Piper) F.; Student Northwestern U., 1942, Purdue U., 1943; B.S., Northwestern U., 1949; m. Genevieve Trella, June 14, 1947; children—Jerome Jeffrey, Antonia Camille (Mrs. Carl Paul Adducci), Lawrence Anthony. Cons. chemist, 1950: founded Jerome & Co., cosmetics co., 1959-65, pres., chmn. bd. Jerome Labs., Inc., Chgo., 1965—. Served with USAAF, 1942-46; ETO. Fellow Am. Inst. Chemists, Am. Chem. Soc., ASTM, Smithsonian Instn., Audubon Soc.; mem. Chgo. Perfumery, Soap and Extract Assn. (dir.), Soc. Cosmetic Chemists (chmn.), Ill. Mfrs. Assn., Chgo. Drug and Chem. Assn. Club: Variety of Ill. Patentee in field; musical composer under name Jerry Feit. Office: 95 E Bradrock Dr Des Plaines IL 60018

FEJÉR, PAUL HARALYI, design engineer; b. Gyoma, Hungary, Feb. 27, 1921; s. Lajos Haralyi Fejer and Laura (Varasdi) Persaits F.; B.S., Ludovica Academia, Budapest, Hungary, 1944; m. Maria Shylo-Wasylchenko, Nov. 16, 1946; children—Paul Haralyi, Alexandra Martha, Douglas Kay. Came to U.S., 1949, naturalized, 1955. Sr. product analyst Chrysler Corp., Highland Park, Mich., 1962-68; sr. design engr. Ford Motor Co., Mt. Clemens, Mich., 1968-83. Served to 2d lt. Hungarian Army, 1944-45. Recipient Gold medal Hungarian Arpad Acad. Scis., 1984. Mem. Macomb Electronics Assn. (treas. 1958), Indsl. Math. Soc. (treas. 1970-73, pres. 1985-86), Soc. Automotive Engrs., Soc. Plastic Engrs., Soc. Mfg. Engrs., Soc. Exptl. Stress Analysis. Author: Measuring Numbers System, 1975; Fundamentals of Dynamic Geometry: The Fejer Vector System, 1980; Time in Dynamic Geometry, 1984; Originator measuring numbers system for measuring continuous magnitudes, dynamic geometry, Fejer Vector system; pioneer new time theory. Home: 23 Lodewyck St Mount Clemens MI 48043

FELDESMAN, ABRAHAM, investment advisor; b. Kishineiv, USSR, May 24, 1937; came to U.S., 1966; s. Aaron and Reizel (Moreinis) F.; m. Carmela Shvedsky, Jan. 9, 1963 (div. Apr. 1975); 1 child, Shirley Sonia; m. Iris Lavy, Sept. 1983; 1 child, Karen Lidia. Student Hebrew U., 1963-65; B.B.A., Akron U., 1969, M.B.A., 1970. Jr. exec. El-Al Israel Airlines, Lod, Israel, 1965-66; tchr. Temple Israel, Akron, Ohio, 1967-69; portfolio mgr. Westfield Cos., Westfield Center, Ohio, 1969-74; pres., treas. AFA Fin., Cleve., 1974—. Governance mem. Dyke Coll., Cleve., 1981—; mem. endowment fund com. Jewish Community Fedn. Cleve. Served with Israeli Air Force, 1955-58. Mem. Midwest Pension Conf. (charter mem.), Fin. Analysts Fedn., Cleve. Soc. Security Analysts. Jewish. Clubs: Akron City; Mayfield Village Racquet (Ohio). Avocations: tennis; concerts; reading; films; theater. Home: 12611 Lake Shore Blvd Bratenahl OH 44108 Office: AFA Fin 525 Hanna Bldg Cleveland OH 44115

FELDMAN, EDGAR ALLAN, surgeon; b. Chgo., Apr. 16, 1936; s. Irving and Beatrice (Berg) F.; B.S., U. Ill., 1956, M.D., 1960; m. Ina Y. Scheckman, June 21, 1959; children—Robert A., Steven I., Susan L., Laura B. Resident in gen. surgery Brooke Gen. Hosp., Ft. Sam Houston, Tex., 1960-65, chief resident, 1964-65; chief of surgery Dewitt Army Hosp., Ft. Belvoir, Va., 1965-66; chief surgeon, army hosp., Ft. Carson Colo., 1966-68; surgeon 5th Inf. Div., Ft. Carson, Colo., 1968-69; attending surgeon Sherman Hosp., and St. Joseph Hosp., Elgin, Ill., 1969—, Suburban Med. Center, Hoffman Estates, Ill., Good Shepherd Hosp., Barrington, Ill.; cons. surgeon Geneva (Ill.) Community Hosp. Pres., Dist. Bd. Edn. Schaumburg (Ill.), 1974—; trustee Suburban Med. Center; bd. dirs. Crescent Counties Found. for Med. Care. Served with M.C., U.S. Army, 1960-69. Diplomate Am. Bd. Surgery. Fellow A.C.S., mem. Kane County (Ill.) Med. Soc. (dir. 1975—). Contbr. articles to surg. jours. Office: 1795 Grandstand Pl Elgin IL 60120

FELDMAN, HARRIS JOSEPH, radiologist, educator; b. Balt., Mar. 4, 1942; s. Charles William and Ruth (Emanuel) F.; A.B., Western Md. Coll., 1963; M.D., U. Md., 1967. Intern, Mercy Hosp., Balt., 1967-68; resident in radiology George Washington U. Hosp., Washington, 1968-71; staff radiologist U. Ill. Hosp., Chgo., 1973-77, Bethany Meth. Hosp., Chgo., 1977—, Walther Meml. Hosp., Chgo., 1977—; cons. radiologist Langley AFB Hosp., 1972-73; asst. prof. Abraham Lincoln Sch. Medicine, U. Ill., Chgo., 1974-77, clin. asst. prof., 1977—. Served with M.C., USN, 1971-73. Diplomate Am. Bd. Radiology. Mem. AMA, Ill., Chgo. med. socs., Am. Coll. Radiology, Ill., Chgo. radiol. socs., Radiol. Soc. N.Am. Home: 1339 N Dearborn St Chicago IL 60610 Office: 6450 N California Ave Chicago IL 60645

FELDMAN, TOBA JEANNE, lawyer; b. Chgo., June 13, 1946; d. Jack E. and Margaret Helen (Hirsch) F. B.A., U. Cin., 1968, J.D., 1977. Bar: Ohio 1977. Staff writer Jour. Herald, Dayton, Ohio, 1969-73; asst. atty. gen. State of Ohio, Columbus, 1977-84; office counsel Ohio Pub. Employee Retirement System, Columbus, 1984—; faculty Capital U., Columbus, 1983—. Mem. Ohio Bar Assn., Columbus Bar Assn., Women Lawyers Franklin County (pres. 1983-84). Office: Ohio Pub Employees Retirement System 277 E Town St Columbus OH 43215

FELIX-RETZKE, JO ANN, insurance agent, manager; b. Denver, Sept. 19, 1946; d. Marvin Carl and Lilliam May (Theisen) Jorgensen; m. Richard M. Felix, Jan. 29, 1966 (div. Sept. 1972); children—Tina Jo, Maria Ann, Trisha; m. George R. Retzke, Mar. 12, 1982. Student in bus. Barnes Coll., Denver, 1962-64. Lic. ins. agt., Iowa. Underwriter Equity Gen. Agts., Los Angeles, 1972-76; asst. v.p. Alexander & Alexander, Mpls., 1976-80; staff dir. ABA, Chgo., 1981-84; mgr. profl. assns. dept. Kirke-Van Orsdel Ins. Services, Des Moines, 1984—; cons. malpractice and mgmt.; instr. Ill. Inst. Tech. Kent Sch. Law, Chgo., 1983. Author: A Lawyer's Guide to Legal Malpractice Insurance 1982; (with D. N. Stern) A Practical Guide to Preventing Legal Malpractice, 1983; contbr. articles on legal malpractice to profl. jours. Mem. Nat. Assn. Realtors, Lake County Bd. Realtors, Ill. Assn. Realtors, Nat. Assn. Female Execs. Democrat. Roman Catholic. Author: Reducing Malpractice Exposures through Effective Docket Control, 1984. Home: 4010 Concord Plaza West Des Moines IA 50265 Office: 777 3d St Des Moines IA 50309

FELL, GEORGE STAFFORD, sales executive; b. Detroit, Oct. 10, 1934; s. Charles Leslie and Mary Alice (Stafford) F.; m. Frances Jean Hartman, Sept. 8, 1956; children—Charles, Cynthia, Curt. B.S. in Civil Engring., U. Mich., 1956. With Harnischfeger Corp., Milw., 1956—, sales engr., dist. mgr., regional sales mgr., 1975—. Lutheran. Lodge: Kiwanis (sec.-treas. 1972). Avocations: golfing, bowling, boating. Home: 245 Parkview Dr Avon Lake OH 44012 Office: Harnischfeger Corp PO Box 208 Avon Lake OH 44012

FELLAND, BRUCE GODFRED, investment company executive, mortgage broker, consultant; b. Madison, Wis., Dec. 30, 1942; s. Godfred Carl and Evelyn Elda (Kerlinski) F.; m. Inger Johanna Tjomsaas, July 7, 1968; children—James, Ruthann, Jason. Student AG Aviation Acad., 1967. Lic. real estate broker, Wis. Real estate broker, developer Exec. Mgmt., Inc., Madison, 1974-79; pres. Global Investors, Inc., Madison, 1979—; cons. to bowling industry, Wis., Fla. Named hon. lt. col. Ala. State Militia; former treas. Wis. Epilepsy Assn. Served with U.S. Army, 1963-64. Mem. Fla. Bowling Proprietors Assn. Democrat. Lutheran. Home: 148 E Prospect St Stoughton WI 53589 Office: Global Investors Inc 4610 Univ Ave Suite 1200 Madison WI 53705

FELLER, GENE PAUL, insurance agent; b. Chgo., Sept. 4, 1942; s. Harold Albert and Ann (Kersek) F.; m. Mary Margaret Radosh, Sept. 3, 1977; 1 son, Cameron Christian. B. Law Enforcement Columbia Pacific U., San Francisco, 1982, M.B.A., 1983, postgrad. in psychology, 1983-84; also various other courses, including Ind. U., 1961-62, 75, LaSalle Extension U., 1965-66, Purdue U., 1969, 70, 82, U. Ill., 1980, Am. Police Acad., 1982. Owner, operator engrng. co., Chgo., 1966-71; ind. contractor ins. agt. State Farm Ins. Co., Inc., Crown Point, Ind., 1971—; tchr. Life Underwriters Tng. Council; lectr. on bus., ins. Bd. dirs. Lake County Prosecutors Vehicle Theft Investigations Task Force, Lake County, Ind., 1979-81. Served to sgt. U.S. Army, 1964-66; Vietnam. Decorated Air medal, Army Commendation medal. Mem. Nat. Assn. Chiefs of Police, Ind. Sheriffs Assn., Am. Law Enforcement Officers Assn., Nat. Assn. Life Underwriters (Health Ins. Quality award 1981, 82, Leading Producers Round Table Bronze award 1982), Nat. Assn. Health Underwriters. Democrat. Baptist. Club: Crown Point Frat. Order of Police Contbr. article series to Lake County Star Newspaper. Home: 9634 Buchanan St Crown Point IN 46307 Office: 1312 N Main St Crown Point IN 46307

FELMLEE, CHERYL ANN, librarian; b. Dry Run, Pa., Feb. 25, 1955; d. Cecil Campbell and Geraldine (Book) Felmlee. B.A., Washington Bible Coll., 1977; M.A., No. Ill. U., 1984. Cataloging asst. Trinity Evang. Div. Sch., Deerfield, Ill., 1978-83, acquisitions and serials librarian, 1983—. Mem. ALA, Am. Theol. Library Assn., Assn. Christian Librarians, Am. Soc. Info. Sci., Chgo. Area Theol. Library Assn. Home: 208 Llewellyn Highwood IL 60040 Office: Rolfing Meml Library Trinity Evang Div Sch 2065 Half Day Rd Deerfield IL 60015

FELT, GREGORY MARK, transportation engineer; b. Mpls., Nov. 26, 1948; s. Raymond Oliver and Edna Marie (Leikham) F.; m. Linda Marie Niccum, June 28, 1968; children—Patience Janel, Heidi Marie, April Lynne. B.S. in Civil Engring., U. Minn., 19. Transp. project mgr. Minn. Dept. Transp., Oakdale, 1978-81, environ. engr., Golden Valley, 1981—. Served to 1st lt. U.S. Army, 1978—. U.S. Dept. Transp. Study grantee, 1975. Mem. Minn. Govt. Engring. Council, Air Pollution Control Assn. (Upper Midwest chpt.). Lutheran. Office: Minn Dept Transp 2055 Lilac Dr Golden Valley MN 55422

FELT, JULIA KAY, lawyer; b. Wooster, Ohio, Apr. 8, 1941; d. George Willard and Betty Virginia (Fishburn) F.; m. Lawrence Roger Van Til, May 31, 1969. B.A., Northwestern U., 1963; J.D., U. Mich., 1967. fund, 1984-86, Ohio 1967, Mich. 1968. Tchr. Triway Local High Schs., Wooster, Ohio, 1963-64; assoc. Dykema, Gossett, Spencer, Goodnow & Trigg, Detroit, 1967-75, ptnr., 1975—; adj. asst. prof. dept. community medicine Wayne State U., Detroit, 1974—. Contbr. articles to profl. jours., chpts. to books. Trustee Rehab. Inst., Detroit, 1971—, sec., 1974-77, vice chmn., 1978-83, chmn. bd., 1983-85; trustee Detroit Med. Ctr. Corp. 1984-85; bd. dirs. Travelers Aid Soc., Detroit, 1974—, v.p., 1978-81; adv. bd. United Found., Detroit, 1980, bd. dirs., 1981—; vis. com. U. Mich. Law Sch., Ann Arbor, 1972—, nat. vice chmn. law sch. fund, 1984-86, bd. dirs. Detroit Assn. U. Mich. Women, 1968-72, pres., 1971-72. Campbell Competition winner U. Mich. Law Sch., 1967; recipient Service award Mich. League Nursing, 1977. Mem. Am. Acad. Hosp. Attys. (pres. 1985-86, bd. dirs. 1980—, adv. com.), Mich. Soc. Hosp. Attys. (pres. 1975-76, bd. dirs. 1975-77), Cath. Health Assn. U.S. (legal services adv. com. 1980-84), ABA, Ohio State Bar Assn., State Bar Mich. (com. medicolegal problems 1973-81, adminstrv. rule making com. 1978-79, others), Am. Hosp. Assn., Detroit Bar Assn., Women Lawyers Mich., Am. Soc. Law and Medicine, Nat. Health Lawyers Assn. Presbyterian. Office: Dykema Gossett Spencer Goodnow & Trigg 35th Floor 400 Renaissance Ctr Detroit MI 48243

FELTEN, EDWARD JOSEPH, business executive, accountant; b. Manitowoc, Wis., July 7, 1938; s. Peter N. and Adela A. (Stein) F.; m. Catherine A. Poehling, June 16, 1962; children—Edward W., Anne C., Peter G., Mark D. B.A. magna cum laude in Acctg., U. Wis., 1960. Acct., Armour & Co., Sheboygan, Wis., 1960-65, controller div. sheepskin leather subs. Armour Leather Co., Boston, 1962-65; with Wis. Supply Corp., Madison, 1965—, pres., gen. mgr., 1977—; dir. Community Banks Inc., Madison, Bank of Shorewood Hills (Wis.), La Crosse Plumbing Supply Co., Eau Claire Plumbing Supply Co.; lectr. in field. Pres. adv. bd. Edgewood High Sch., Madison, 1981-82. Recipient Man of Achievement award State of Wis., 1976. Mem. Am. Supply Assn. (bd. dirs. 1980-81, 85-86), Mid. Am. Supply Assn. (pres. 1984-85), Plumbing Heating Cooling Council U.S.A. (bd. dirs. 1979—). Roman Catholic. Club: Nakena. Home: 5205 Whitcomb Dr Madison WI 53711 Office: 630 W Mifflin St PO Box 8124 Madison WI 53708

FELTHOUSE, TIMOTHY ROY, research chemist; b. Berkeley, Calif., Sept. 25, 1951; s. James Whitman and Patricia Mae (Avrit) F. B.S. magna cum laude, U. Pacific, 1973; Ph.D., U. Ill., 1978. NSF research participant Wash. State U., Pullman, 1972; research asst. U. Pacific, Stockton, Calif., 1973; grad. teaching, research asst. U. Ill., Urbana, 1973-78; research assoc. Tex. A&M U., College Station, 1978-80; sr. research chemist Monsanto Co., St. Louis, 1980-83, research specialist, 1983—. Contbr. articles on chemistry to profl. jours. Calif. State scholar, 1969-73. Mem. Am. Chem. Soc. (news editor St. Louis 1981-82, analytical div. undergrad. award 1972), N.Y. Acad. Scis., Catalysis Soc., Phi Kappa Phi, Sigma Xi, Phi Lambda Upsilon. Republican. Methodist. Club: Monsanto-Catalysis (chmn. 1982-83). Office: Monsanto Co 800 N Lindbergh Blvd Q3B Saint Louis MO 63167

FELTMANN, JOHN MEINRAD, former advt. and radio exec.; b. St. Louis, Jan. 30, 1910; s. Henry Conrad and Catherine (Lake) F.; certificate in commerce and finance St. Louis U., 1938; m. Adeline A. Fiedler, Nov. 25, 1944; children—John Thomas, Mary Anne Kenney, Robert Joseph, James Anthony (dec.). Clk., Nat. Telephone Directory Co., St. Louis, 1924-36, auditor, 1936-60; sec., dir. Von Hoffmann Corp., Union, N.J., 1947-60, treas., dir., 1960-67, v.p., treas., dir., 1967-69; dir. Von Hoffmann Press, Inc., St. Louis, 1947-69, treas., dir., 1960-69; treas. dir. Publishers Lithographers, Inc., St.

Louis, 1959-69; sec., treas. von Hoffmann Realty and Mortgage Corp., 1954-59; v.p., treas., dir. Victory Broadcasting Corp., Jacksonville, Fla., 1968-78, ret., 1978; v.p. treas. Nat. Telephone Directory Corp., Union, N.J., 1968-72, dir., 1968-83, exec. v.p., 1972-78, also cons.; dir. Mid-State Printing Co., Jefferson City, Mo., 1947-54. Sec., treas. George Von Hoffmann Found., 1954-59. Mem. Delta Sigma Pi, Roman Catholic. Club: Mo. Athletic. Home: 7250 Christopher Dr Saint Louis MO 63129

FELTON, JOHN RICHARD, economics educator, consultant; b. Toledo, March 25, 1917; s. Elmer Franklin and Georgia Hazel (Templeton) F.; m. Katherine Adele Lofgren, Jan. 25, 1947; children—James Lofgren, Joyce Adele. B.A., UCLA, 1939, M.A., 1941, Ph.D., 1961. Head food and distbn. sect. War Labor Bd., San Francisco, 1943-45; asst. prof. econs. San Diego State U., 1948-51; dir. Los Angeles br. Wage Stablzn. Bd., 1951-53; edn. dir. U.S. Naval Weapons Ctr., China Lake, Calif., 1953-62; prof. econs. U. Neb., Lincoln, 1962—; cons. Am. Tel. & Tel. Co., Omaha, 1984-85, Am. Freight System, Jefferson City, Mo., 1984, Conrail, Washington, 1982. Author: Economics of Freight Car Supply, 1978. Contbr. articles to profl. jours. Agrl. Exptl. Sta. fellow, 1979-82; Energy Research and Devel. Ctr. fellow, 1981; U.S. Naval Weapons Ctr. fellow, 1959-60. Mem. Am. Econs. Assn., Transp. Research Forum, Midwest Econs. Assn., Mo. Valley Econs. Assn. Democrat. Unitarian. Avocations: sailing, tennis, skiing. Home: 3481 Anaheim Dr Lincoln NE 68506 Office: U Nebr Dept Econs Lincoln NE 68588

FELTS, ROSEMARIE KOSCHEL, restaurant owner; b. Berlin, Nov. 29, 1934; came to U.S., 1954; d. Willi Johannes T. and Klara L. Hedwig (Frölich) Koschel; m. Jerry Lee Felts, Nov. 29, 1953; children—Michael Lee, Cynthia Yvonne, Marcus David. Student Free U. Berlin, 1951-54. Sec. to county surveyor, Huntington, Ind., 1973-77; bookstore mgr. Huntington Coll., 1977-85, union bldg. dir., 1982-85; owner The Provincial, Huntington, 1985—. Mem. Ind. Assn. Coll. Stores (sec. 1980-82), Am. Bus. Women's Assn. Republican. Avocations: cooking, reading, gardening, embroidery, writing.

FEMEA, PAUL LEROY, nursing educator; b. Altoona, Pa., Oct. 19, 1946; s. Paul L. and Virginia (Davis) F.; m. Edith Rupp, May 4, 1968; children—Tina, Misty. Diploma, Clearfield Hosp., 1967; B.S.N., Duquesne U., 1970; M.S.N., Cath. U., 1976, D.N.Sc., 1981. Staff nurse Altoona Hosp., Pa., 1967-68, Columbia Hosp., Wilkinsburg, Pa., 1968-69, Presbyn. Univ. Hosp., Pitts., 1969-70, Ind. U. Med. Ctr., Indpls., 1971-72, VA Med. Ctr., Washington, 1973-79; asst. prof. nursing Purdue U., West Lafayette, Ind., 1979—. Contbg. editor Nursing mag.; editorial rev. bd. Dimensions of Critical Care Nursing, Computers in Nursing; contbr. articles to profl. jours. Purdue U. summer faculty grantee, 1983, 84. Mem. Sigma Theta Tau. Baptist. Home: 1722 Mason Dixon Dr West Lafayette IN 47906 Office: Purdue U Sch Nursing West Lafayette IN 47907

FEMRITE, RODNEY LAWENNCE, pharmaceutical company executive, pharmacist; b. Jamestown, N.D., Apr. 30, 1943; s. Alfred Lawrence and Lillian Eileen (Boyd) F.; m. Pamela Kay Wiese, June 3, 1966; children—Darin, Sara, Chad. B.S. in Pharmacy, N.D. State U., 1966. Pharmacist, White Drug, Minot, N.D., 1966-70, store mgr., 1970-71; mfr.'s rep. Eli Lilly & Co., Sioux Falls, S.D., 1971—. Basketball coach Jr. Hi-Y YMCA, Sioux Falls, 1980-84, soccer coach Sioux Falls Soccer Assn., 1976-79. Mem. S.D. Soc. Hosp. Pharmacy (del. 1980-84), S.D. State Pharm. Assn. (Salesman of Yr. 1975, 78). Republican. Avocations: golf, tennis. Home: 2208 Tamarac Dr Sioux Falls SD 57103

FENICHEL, HENRY, physics educator; b. The Hague, Netherlands, Apr. 13, 1938; came to U.S., 1953, naturalized, 1958; s. Morris and Paula Fenichel; m. Diana Milgram, June 17, 1961; children—Joan, Debbie. B.S., Bklyn. Coll., 1960; M.S., Rutgers U., 1962, Ph.D., 1964. Asst. prof. physics U. Cin., 1965-69, assoc. prof., 1969-76, prof., 1976—. Contbr. articles to profl. jours. Mem. Am. Assn. Physics Tchrs., Am. Phys. Soc., Sigma Xi. Office: U Cin Dept Physics ML 11 Cincinnati OH 45221

FENNER, TIMOTHY DANIEL, lawyer; b. Eau Claire, Wis., Aug. 19, 1948; s. Daniel LaVerne and Audrey Jean (LaPage) F.; m. Patricia Marie Spanel, June 19, 1971. B.A., U. Wis.-Madison, 1970, J.D., 1972. Bar: Wis. 1972. Assoc. Brynelson, Herrick, Gehls & Bucaida, Madison, 1972-76, ptnr., 1977—. Author monthly column Ind. Ins. Agts. Wis. Mag., 1983—. Mem. pub. affairs com. Dane County, Madison, 1981—. Mem. ABA, State Bar Wis., Dane County Bar Assn., Phi Beta Kappa, Phi Kappa Phi, Phi Eta Sigma. Lutheran. Avocations: biking; swimming; reading. Office: Brynelson Herrick Gehl and Bucaida 123 W Washington Ave Madison WI 53703

FENNESSEY, JOHN FRANCIS, physician, lawyer; b. Boston, June 7, 1922; s. John Francis and Catharine Theresa (Whalen) F.; m. Anita Marie Palmer, May 26, 1951; children—Anita, John, Judith, Thomas. B.S., MIT, 1947; M.D., Tufts U., 1950; J.D., Wayne State U., 1972. Diplomate Am. Bd. Pathology. Intern Resident New Eng. Med. Ctr., Boston, 1950-53; chief lab. services Fort Carson Army Hosp., Colorado Springs, Colo., 1953-54; lab. dir. Deaconess Hosp., Detroit, 1955-78; pathologist Samaritan Health Ctr., Detroit, 1978—; mem. Mich. Bd. Medicine, 1978—. Fellow Am. Soc. Clin. Pathology, Coll. Am. Pathologists. Roman Catholic. Clubs: Detroit Yacht; Crescent Sail Yacht (Grosse Pointe, Mich.). Avocations: sailing. Home: 512 Rivard St Grosse Pointe MI 48230

FENSTER, LAURA, jewelry manufacturer's representative; b. N.Y.C., Aug. 14, 1932; d. Irving Israel and Fannie (Rosenbaum) Sternberg; m. Bernard Fenster, June 14, 1952; children—Frederic, Kenneth, Ivan. Mgr. order dept. Norman M. Morris Corp., N.Y.C., 1950-54; mgr. sales, buying Lipson Potter, Ltd., Highland Park, Ill., 1970-83; prin. Laura Fenster Enterprises, Higland Park, Ill., 1984—; rep. manufacturers of fine jewelry Eshel Jewelry Co., N.Y.C., 1984—, Sandy Baker Jewelry Co., N.Y.C., 1984—. Fundraiser Democratic Party, Highland Park, 1968-72. Jewish. Club: Women's Am. Ort. Lodge: Ctr. for Enriched Living. Avocations: boating; swimming; tennis; racquetball; aerobics. Office: PO Box 497 Highland Park IL 60035

FENTON, MARC IRA, lawyer; b. Chgo., July 8, 1953; s. Donald Raymond and Esther Alice (Cohen) F.; m. Ellen Desnet, June 15, 1980; children—Alison, Aaron. B.A., Loyola U., 1975; J.D., No. Ill. U., 1981. Bar: Ill. 1981, U.S. Dist. Ct. (no. dist.) Ill. 1981, U.S. Ct. Appeals (7th cir.) 1982. Asst. pub. defender Cook County, Ill., 1981-82; staff atty. Office of U.S. Trustee, U.S. Dept. Justice, Chgo., 1982-84; assoc. Berman, Fagel, Haber, Maragos & Abrams, Chgo., 1984—. Mem. ABA, Ill. Bar Assn., Comml. Law League, Chgo. Bar Assn. (bankruptcy sub-com). Jewish. Home: 313 Redwing Dr Deerfield IL 60015 Office: Berman Fagel et al 140 S Dearborn Suite 1400 Chicago IL 60603

FERDON, CLIFFORD WALTER, parapsychologist, consultant; b. Cin., July 3, 1927; s. Walter and Ida Mae (Jacobs) F.; (div.); children—Collette Yvonne Ferdon Witker, Clifford. C.B.S., Cin. Christian Coll., 1952; student Purdue U., 1962, U. Cin., 1957-58, Universal Life Inst., 1974-76, Life Dynamics Inst., 1974, Ferdon Inst., 1978-83. Prin. Clifford Ferdon Inc., Amelia, Ohio, 1980—; owner, dir. Ferdon Inst., investment think tank; cons., tchr. for religious community ctrs. Am. Parapsychol. Assn. research fellow, 1978—. Mem. Accredited Investors Assn., Universal Bd. Hypnotherapists. Club: Masons. Research in parapsychology, investments. Home: 484 Old State Route 74 Suite 309 Cincinnati OH 45244 Office: PO Box 223 Amelia OH 45102

FERGUSON, ADLAI CLEVELAND, broadcasting executive; b. Arthur, Ill., Jan. 14, 1919; s. Adlai Cleveland and Arlena (Jones) F.; m. Marjorie Virginia Weber, Oct. 6, 1942; children—Sandra L. Ferguson Wheeler, Karen A., Jan D. Ferguson Lange. Grad. Terre Haute Comml. Coll., 1938. Chmn. bd. Paris Broadcasting Corp., Stas. WPRS-WACF-FM, Paris, Ill., 1951—. Served as lt. USAF, 1942-45. Mem. Nat. Assn. Broadcasters, Nat. Radio Broadcaster's Assn., Ill. Broadcasters Assn., Ill. C. of C. Club: Paris. Lodge: Rotary. Home: 9 Janice Ave Paris IL 61944 Office: PO Box 398 Paris IL 61944

FERGUSON, ARDALE WESLEY, industrial supply company executive; b. Cedar Springs, Mich., Aug. 6, 1908; s. George Ardale and Alice Lucina (Andrus) F.; student pub. schs.; m. Hazel Frances Lokker, Oct. 28, 1931; children—Constance Ann (Mrs. Donald F. Klaasen), Mary Alice (Mrs. Robert A. Ritsema), Judy Kaye (Mrs. Charles Ruffino); m. G. Dolores Laker, Aug. 1976. Sales exec. John Deere Plow Co., Lansing, Mich., 1935-50; exec.-treas., mgr. Ferguson Welding Supply Co., Benton Harbor, Mich., 1950-76; sec.-treas. Lape Steel Stores, Inc., Benton Harbor, 1955-85; dir. Modern Light Metals, Inc. Mem. Benton Twp. Bd. Rev., 1963, Mich. Econ. Advancement Council, 1963-64; chmn. Mich. Hwy. Commn., 1964-68; pres. Twin Cities Community Chest, 1956. Treas. Mich. Republican Central Com., 1957-61; del. to Rep. Nat. Conv., 1960. Recipient award of spl. merit, Twin Cities Community Chest, 1956; named to Mich. Transp. Hall of Honor, 1984. Methodist. Clubs: St. Joseph-Benton Harbor Rotary (pres. 1960), Berrien Hills Country, Mountain Shadows Country, Peninsular. Home: 2609 Golfview Dr Apt 105 Troy MI 48084

FERGUSON, BOB LYNN, photographer; b. Seymour, Ind., Nov. 25, 1930; s. Clarence Roscoe and Ruby (Eller) F.; m. Ida Joan Goble, May 29, 1954; children—Brian Lynn, Jaffrey Wayne, Juli Joann, John David. Student Winnona Sch. Profl. Photography, 1975-79. Cert. profl. photographer. With Cosco, Columbus, Ind., 1956—, photog. supr., 1974—. Served with U.S. Army, 1951-53; Korea. Decorated Purple Heart. Mem. Profl. Photographers Am., Profl. Photographers Ind. Democrat. Home: Rural Route 1 Box 34 Freetown IN 47235 Office: 2525 State St Columbus IN 47201

FERGUSON, DENZIL M., osteopathic physician and surgeon; b. Terre Haute, Ind.; Sept. 21, 1946; s. D.M. and Eleanor (Thomas) F.; m. Robin Lynn Pentland, Nov. 26, 1977; 1 dau., Lindsey Nicole. B.S., Ind. State U., 1972; D.O., Kirksville Coll. Osteo. Medicine, 1976. Intern, Carson City (Mich.) Hosp., 1976-77; gen. practice osteo. medicine, Crystal, Mich., 1978—, Carson City, Mich., 1982—; mem. exec. com., intern tng. com. Carson City Hosp., 1979—, chmn. dept. obstetrics, 1979-83. Served with U.S. Army, 1966-69. Mem. Am. Osteo. Assn., Mich. Assn. Osteo. Physicians and Surgeons, Central Mich. Assn. Osteo. Physicians and Surgeons (pres. 1983-84). Democrat. Baptist. Club: Gratiot Country (Ithaca, Mich.). Home: 433 S 2d St Carson City MI 48811 Office: 122 Main St PO Box 232 Crystal MI 48818 also 321 E Maple St Carson City MI 48811

FERGUSON, DONALD JOHN, orthodontist, educator; b. Scotia, Calif., May 25, 1945; s. John Charles and Agnes Bregeta (Dahlberg) E.; m. Janet Ethyl Schmiege, July 30, 1977; children—Jon, Dana, Zachary. Student Humboldt State U., 1963-66; D.M.D., U. Oreg., 1970; cert. of residency Oakland Naval Hosp., 1971; cert. of orthodontics U. Pacific, 1976. Clin. instr. endodontics U. Pacific Sch. Dentistry, San Francisco, 1974, lectr. anatomy, orthodontics, 1976-77, research assoc., 1976-77; orthodontic dir. Mt. Zion Hosp., San Francisco, 1976-80, co-dir. craniofacial deformities team, 1976-80; assoc. dir. gen. practice residency program Highland Gen. Hosp., Oakland, Calif., 1980-82; orthodontic dir. Ctr. for Correction Dentofacial Deformities, San Francisco, 1980-82; assoc. prof. orthodontics Ind. U., Indpls., 1982-85; chmn. orthodontics Marquette U.-Sch. Dentistry, Milw., 1985—; cons. craniofacial anomalies team Ind. U. Med. Ctr., 1982-85, dir. surg. orthodontics Ind. U. Sch. Dentistry, 1982-85; cons. Wishard Mem. Hosp., Indpls., 1983-85; cons. VA Hosp., San Francisco, 1980-82. Author: Craniofacial Growth and Development, 1984. Served to lt. USN, 1970-73, Vietnam. Recipient Ann. Teaching award Mount Zion Hosp., 1978, Outstanding Achievement award in orthodontics and periodontics U. Oreg. Sch. Dentistry, 1970. Mem. Am. Assn. Dental Schs., ADA, Am. Assn. Orthodontists, Ind. Dental Assn., Great Lakes Soc. Orthodontists, Indpls. Dist. Dental Soc., Ind. Soc. Orthodontists, Edward H. Angle Soc. Orthodontists. Republican. Presbyterian. Avocations: sculpture; photography; horticulture; scuba diving; skiing. Office: Dept Orthodontics Marquette U Sch Dentistry 604 N 16th St Milwaukee WI 53233

FERGUSON, FRANCIS EUGENE, retired insurance company executive; b. Batavia, N.Y., Feb. 4, 1921; s. Harold M. and Florence F. (Munger) F.; B.S. in Agrl. Econs., Mich. State U., 1947, LL.D. (hon.), 1972; D.C.L. (hon.), Ripon Coll., 1978; LL.D. (hon.), Cardinal Stritch Coll., 1983; m. Patricia J. Reddy, Aug. 11, 1945; children—Susan L., Patricia A. Asst. sec.-treas. Nat. Farm Loan Assn., Lansing, Mich., 1947-48; appraiser Fed. Land Bank, St. Paul, 1948; extension specialist Mich. State U., 1951; with Northwestern Mut. Life Ins. Co., Milw., 1951—, v.p. mortgages, 1963-67, pres., 1967-80, chmn. bd., chief exec. officer, 1980-83, chmn. bd., 1983-85, also dir.; dir. Djinnii Industries, Inc., Dayton, Ohio, Green Bay Packaging, Inc. (Wis.), Ralston Purina Co., St. Louis, Rexnord, Inc., Milw., Singer Co., Stamford, Conn., WICOR and Wis. Gas Co., Milw.; trustee Northwestern Mut. Life. Served to capt. USAAF, World War II; Germany. Mem. Alpha Zeta. Republican. Clubs: Milw., Univ. Milw., Milw. Country.

FERGUSON, JOHN BOWIE, profl. hockey team exec.; b. Vancouver, B.C., Can., Sept. 5, 1938; s. John Bowie and Mary Stuart (Howie) F.; student public schs.; m. Joan Elizabeth Bate, Sept. 5, 1959; children—Christina, Catherine, John, Joanne. Profl. hockey player Montreal Canadiens, 1963-71; pres. now also v.p., gen. mgr. Winnipeg Jets, Nat. Hockey League. Address: Winnipeg Jets 15-1430 Maroons Rd Winnipeg MN R3G 0L5 Canada

FERGUSON, JOHN WAYNE, librarian; b. Ash Grove, Mo., Nov. 4, 1936; s. John William and Eula M. Ferguson; m. Nancy C. Southerland, Sept. 25, 1939; children—John Wayne, Mark, Steven. B.S., S.W. Mo. State Coll., Springfield, 1958; M.S. in Library Sci., Okla. U., 1962. Librarian, Springfield Pub. Library, 1952-64; asst. dir. Mid-Continent Pub. Library, Independence, Mo., 1964-81, dir. libraries, 1981—. Past pres. Independence YMCA; bd. dirs. Independence Hosp. and Sanitarium. Served to capt. F.A., U.S. Army, 1959-65. Mem. ALA, Mo. Library Assn. Lodge: Rotary (past pres.). Home: 3820 Stonewall Ct Independence MO 64055 Office: 15616 E 24 Hwy Independence MO 64050

FERGUSON, NANCY IVERS, lawyer, court referee; b. Huntington, W.Va., June 28, 1951; d. Ralph Earl and Merle (Hairston) Ivers; m. Gerald Paul Ferguson, Aug. 20, 1977. B.S. in Edn., Ohio State U., 1973; M.Ed., Xavier U., Cin., 1976; J.D., Capital U., 1979. Bar: Ohio 1980, U.S. Dist. Ct. (so. dist.) Ohio 1981. Hearing officer div. real estate Ohio Dept. Commerce, Columbus, 1979-80, staff atty. div. securities, Columbus, 1980-83; referee Franklin County Mcpl. Ct., Columbus, 1983—. Mem. Columbus Bar Assn., Ohio State Bar Assn., Women Lawyers Franklin County, German Village Soc. Republican. Presbyterian. Office: Franklin County Mcpl Ct 375 S High St Columbus OH 42306

FERGUSON, SUZANNE CAROL, English educator; b. East Stroudsburg, Pa., Aug. 13, 1939; s. Edwin Roy and Edna Mabel (Reeves) Butts; m. James H. Ferguson, May 29, 1960; 1 child, Cynthia Katherine Ferguson Heuschele. A.A., Va. Intermont Coll., 1958; B.A., Converse Coll., 1960; M.A., Vanderbilt U., 1961; Ph.D., Stanford U., 1966. Asst. prof. English, U. Calif.-Santa Barbara, 1966-71; assoc. prof. Ohio State U., Columbus, 1971-83; prof., chmn. dept. English, Wayne State U., Detroit, 1983—; vis. assoc. prof. Kenyon Coll., Gambier, Ohio, 1976. Author: The Poetry of Randall Jarrell, 1971. Editor: Critical Essays on Randall Jarrell, 1983; co-editor: Literature and the Visual Arts in Contemporary Soc., 1985. Contbr. articles to profl. jours. Trustee Erich Katz Meml. Fund, N.Y.C., 1983—. Woodrow Wilson, 1960-61; Stanford U. Wilson fellow, 1965-66; U. Calif. summer faculty fellow 1970. Mem. MLA, Am. Lit. Soc., Midwest Modern Lang. Assn., Virginia Woolf Soc., Am. Recorder Soc. (bd. dirs. 1980—). Democrat. Episcopalian. Avocations: performing early music Home: 1329 Berkshire Rd Grosse Pointe Park MI 48200

FERIN, MICHAEL JOHN, university official, fund raiser; b. Des Moines, July 16, 1940; s. Albert Joseph and Mary Frances (Macri) F.; m. Jane Lenore Leonard, Feb. 17, 1961; children—Mark A., Michelle R., Amy M. Student Loras Coll., 1958-59; B.A., Drake U., 1962, postgrad., 1962-64; postgrad. U. Wis.-Milw., 1967-68. Vice pres. devel. Beloit Coll., Wis., 1973-74, Ripon Coll., Wis., 1974-81; dir. devel. Purdue U., West Lafayette, Ind., 1982-83; v.p. devel., 1983-84; v.p. for advancement Wittenberg U., Springfield, Ohio, 1985—; cons. St. Edward's U., Austin, Tex., 1978, Milton Coll., Wis., 1979, Carroll Coll., Waukesha, Wis., 1983. Mem. Council for Advancement and Support of Edn. Home: 213 Cedar Hollow Ct West Lafayette IN 47906

FERLIS, NICHOLAS WILLIAM, investment executive; b. Kankakee, Ill., Sept. 17, 1947; s. William Nicholas and Magdeline Gail (Bogordos) F.; m. Sally Phillippi, Sept. 18, 1982. B.B.A., Loyola U., Chgo., 1970; M.B.A., Northwestern U., 1972. C.P.A., Ill.; registered investment advisors Registry Fin. Planners; registered securities broker dealer. Internal auditor Consol. Packaging Co., Chgo., 1968-70; sr. staff acct. Arthur Andersen & Co., Chgo., 1970-74; group controller Apeco Corp., Evanston, Ill., 1974-75; v.p. Fin. Services, Glenview, Ill., 1975-79; pres. Ferlis & Assocs., Des Plaines, Ill., 1979-82; pres. Equity Advisors, Inc., Northfield, Ill., 1982—. Mem. Am. Mgmt. Assn. (pres. club 1979—), Internat. Assn. Fin. Planners (nat. rev. com. 1983—), Am.Inst. C.P.A.s, Ill. Soc. C.P.A.s, N.Am. Assn. Securities Dealers. Republican. Greek Orthodox. Office: Equity Advisors Inc 790 Frontage Rd Northfield IL 60093

FERLO, JOSEPH ANTHONY, artistic director; b. Rome, N.Y., Nov. 30, 1959; s. Albert M. and Nathaline M. (Grasso) F.; m. Denise A. Bennett, July 19, 1982. B.A. in Am. Music Theatre, Oberlin Coll., 1981. Mng. artistic dir. Nettle Creek Players, Hagerstown, Ind., 1981—; program dir. First Christian Ch., New Castle, Ind., 1982-83; guest dir. Jay County Civic Theatre, Portland, Ind., 1983; artistic dir. New Castle Civic Theatre, 1982-84; featured soloist piano Young artists competition Utica Symphony Orch., N.Y., 1977. Music dir. First United Methodist Ch., Hagerstown, 1984—. Mem. Am. Theatre Assn., Hagerstown 1st Commerce Assn. Democrat. Lodges: Rotary, Masons. Avocations: piano, collecting baseball cards. Home: 203 N Elm St Hagerstown IN 47346 Address: Nettle Creek Players Inc PO Box 23 98 E Main St Hagerstown IN 47346

FERMIN, JOSE SIMON, mathematics educator; b. Anaco, Venezuela, Nov. 22, 1949; came to U.S., 1981; s. Simon Jose and Ana Josefina Alvarez; m. Juana Beltrana Andarcia, Dec. 28, 1974; 1 son, Jose Alberto Fermin Andarcia. B.E. in Math., Universidad de Oriente, Cumana, Venezuela, 1974; M.S. in Stats., Universidad de Los Andes, Merida, Venezuela, 1980. Instr. Instituto Universitario Politecnico de Guayana, Venezuela, 1975-77, Universidad de Los Andes, Merida, 1977-78; assoc. prof. math. Instituto Universitario de Technologia, Cumana, 1978-81; grad. teaching asst. stats. dept. Kans. State U., Manhattan, 1983—. Contbr. articles to profl. jours. Mem. Am. Statis. Assn. Avocations: reading; music; softball; baseball. Office: Dickens Hall Dept Stats Kansas State U Manhattan KS 66502

FERNANDES, BRISTON JOSEPH, social services administrator; b. Bombay, India, Nov. 4, 1941; came to U.S., 1973; s. John J. and Basilia (Pereira) F.; m. Melanie Bernadette Kirthisinghe, July 18, 1981; 1 dau., Melissa Bernadine. B.E., Tilak Coll., Pune, India, 1968; M.Ph., Colegio San Francisco de Borja, Barcelona, Spain, 1965; Th.M., Pontifical Athenaeum, Pune, 1972; M.A. in Couseling Psychology, Loyola U., Chgo., 1973-75. Tchr., St. Xavier's High Sch., Bombay, 1965-66; counselor St. Peter's Parish, Bombay, 1972-73; counseling psychologist Elgin Catholic Social Service (Ill.), 1976-80; exec. dir. McHenry County Cath. Social Service, Woodstock, Ill., 1980-83, Cath. Social Service Elgin, 1983—. Mem. Commn. for Justice and Peace, Cath. Diocese of Rockford (Ill.). Author articles, poetry. Democrat. Roman Catholic. Home: 8858 E Dee Rd Des Plaines IL 60016 Office: 566 Dundee Ave Elgin IL 60120

FERNANDEZ, LOUIS, See *Who's Who in America,* 43rd edition.

FERNANDEZ, RAMONA LOUISE, lawyer; b. Fredonia, Kans., Feb. 22, 1955; d. Louis and Josephine (Fernandez) F. B.A. with honors in Edn., U. Mich., 1977, J.D., 1980. Bar: Mich. 1980. U.S. Dist. Ct. (we. dist.) Mich. U.S. Ct. Appeals (6th cir.). Teaching fellow women and the law U. Mich., Ann Arbor, 1979-80; atty. Legal Aid S.W. Mich., Kalamazoo, 1980-82; assoc. Edward M. Welch, P.C., Battle Creek, Mich., 1982—. Dir. community edn., bd. dirs. Safe Place Shelter, Battle Creek, 1982-84; bd. dirs. Calhoun County Guardian Office, 1982-83; Calhoun County Dept. Soc. Services, Battle Creek, 1983—, Kimball Pines Nonprofit Housing, 1983—. Mem. State Bar Mich. Assn., Mich. Trial Lawyers Assn. Democrat. Office: 301 Peoples Savings Bldg 2 W Michigan Mall Battle Creek MI 49017

FERNAU, GEORGE ROBERT, trophy company executive; b. St. Louis, Jan. 4, 1940; s. George Lawrence and Margaret Catherine (Parks) F.; m. Lois Jean Hagedorn, Sept. 10, 1960; children—Jeanné, Lori, Gelnnon, Christopher. Student personnel adminstrn. St. Louis U., 1961, polit. sci. Florissant Valley Community Coll., Ferguson, Mo., 1971, econs., 1972. Pres., exec. dir. Futures of Am., Florissant, Mo., 1971—; writer McDonough Democrat., Bushnell, Ill., 1977—; pres. Maj. Ind. soccer Cons., Florissant, 1982—; mktg. rep. Atlas Travel Agy., Florissant, 1984—. Mem. youth bd. St. Vincent dePaul Soc., 1966. Named Man of Yr., Jaycees, 1974; recipient Community Service award Freedom Found., 1975, Disting. Service award Easter Seal Soc., 1976, Am. Legion, 1976, VFW, 1984. Roman Catholic. Avocations: soccer; public speaking, traveling.

FERNELIUS, W(ILLIS) CONARD, chemist, educator, researcher; b. Riverdale, Utah, Aug. 7, 1905; s. George T. and Lottie (Bowman) F.; m. Naomi Baker, Apr. 10, 1931; children—Nils C., Sigrid Fernelius Byers. Student Carnegie-Mellon U., 1922-24; B.A., Stanford U., 1926, M.A., 1927, Ph.D., 1928; D.Sc. (hon.), Franklin and Marshall U., 1959; D.Sc. (hon.), Kent State U., 1984. From instr. to prof. Ohio State U., Columbus, 1928-42; prof. Purdue U., West Lafayette, Ind., 1942-43, 46-47; lab. dir. Monsanto Co., Dayton, Ohio, 1943-46; chmn. chemistry dept. Syracuse U., N.Y., 1947-49; head chemistry dept. Pa. State U., University Park, 1949-60; assoc. dir. research Koppers Co., Inc., Monroeville, Pa., 1960-70; disting. prof. U. South Fla., Tampa, 1970-75; adj. prof. Kent State U., Ohio, 1975—; cons. various corps. and govt. agencies, 1939—. Author five textbooks in chemistry. Contbr. articles to profl. jours. Mem. editorial bds. various profl. jours., 1939—. Guggenheim fellow Oxford U., 1956-57; Fulbright fellow Cairo U., 1960. Fellow Am. Inst. Chemists (chmn. Pitts. chpt. 1970); mem. Am. Chem. Soc. (dir. 1951-59, various offices; Pitts. award, 1969, Patterson-Crane award Dayton and Columbus sects. 1981), Internat. Union Pure and Applied Chemistry (chmn. com. on nomenclature of inorganic chemistry, 1971-75, mem. interdivisional com. on nomenclature and symbols, 1971-75), Sigma Xi. Democrat. Mem. United Ch. Christ. Avocations: travel, photography, philately, genealogy. Home: 548 E Summit St Apt 103 Kent OH 44240 Office: Dept Chemistry Kent State Univ Kent OH 44242

FERNER, CLINTON ORAL, railroad executive; b. Oostburg, Wis., Nov. 23, 1927; s. Oral Thompson and Viola Henrietta (Quarnstrom) F.; m. Maureen Joan Browne, May 27, 1961; children—David Lawrence, Elizabeth Kay. B.S. in Econs., U. Wis., 1951. Clk. Green Bay and Western R.R., Wis., 1946-51; with Elgin, Joliet and Eastern R.R., Joliet, Ill., 1951-81, supt., 1959-78, gen. supt., 1978-81; asst. gen. mgr., then gen. mgr. Duluth, Missabe and Iron Range Ry. Co., Duluth, Minn., 1981—; chmn. AAR Operating Data Systems Commn., 1981. Mem. Munster Planning Commn., Ind., 1976-81; bd. dirs. N.E. Minn. Devel. Assn., Duluth, 1981—, Lake Superior Mus. Transp., Duluth, 1982—, pres., 1985—, Minn. Safety Council, St. Paul, 1982—, St. Luke's Hosp. Found., Duluth, 1982—, St. Luke's Hosp., Duluth, 1982—; campaign chmn. U.S. Savs. Bonds, Duluth-Superior, 1984-85; mem. Duluth Futures Task Force, Congl. Award Council, Duluth, 1984-85. Mem. AIME, Assn. R.R. Supts., Minn. R.R.s Assn. (bd. dirs.). Republican. Presbyterian. Clubs: Northland Country (Duluth), Kitchi Gammi. Lodges: Masons, Shriners. Home: 5200 London Rd Duluth MN 55804 Office: Duluth Missabe and Iron Range Ry Co 500 Missabe Bldg Duluth MN 55802

FERRANTE, DAVID ANTHONY, insurance executive; b. Oakland, Calif., Sept. 11, 1943; s. Edmund Salvatore and Myrtle (Sullivan) F.; m. Jacqueline Kay Peterson, July 27, 1962; children—David, Charles, Angela. A.A., Long Beach City Coll., 1964; B.S., Calif. State U.-Long Beach, 1967. Loss control mgr. State Compensation Ins. Fund, Los Angeles, 1967-75; dir. loss control Employee Benefits Ins. Co., Santa Monica, Calif., 1975-77, asst. mgr. NW div., 1977-79, v.p., div. mgr., 1979-82, pres. Midwest div., Chgo., 1982—. Mem. Am. Soc. Safety Engrs. Republican. Roman Catholic. Home: 258 Pebble Creek Dr Barrington IL 60010 Office: One Pierce Pl Itasca IL 60601

FERREE, JEREMIAH DAVID, educator; b. Anderson, Ind., Oct. 17, 1938; s. George M. and Mary C. (Stolsig) F.; m. Jacqueline K.; children—Sheri Lynn Strahan, Jill Annette, Bethany Dianne. B.A., Olivet Nazarene Coll., 1961; M.A., Mich. State U., 1967. Gen. laborer Meadow Gold Ice Cream, Kankakee, Ill., 1957-61; 6th grade tchr. Haviland Elem. Sch., Waterford Twp., Mich., 1961-62; tchr. French and English, Lincoln Jr. High Sch., Pontiac, Mich., 1962-74, tchr. English, Pontiac Central High Sch., 1974—; asst. football coach, 1974-79, volleyball coach, 1979-80, girls softball coach, 1983—. mem. curriculum com. for secondary English and fgn. lang. Pontiac Sch. Dist., 1967-72; sports ofcl. Mich. High Sch. Athletic Assn., 1969—. Playground supr. Pontiac Parks and Recreation, 1974-77; treas. Pontiac Ch. Softball League, 1973-79, dir., 1980-81. Mem. NEA, Assn. Supervision and Curriculum Devel., Council Basic Edn., Nat. Assn. Sports Ofcls., Mich. Edn. Assn., Pontiac Edn. Assn. Republican. Nazarene. Dir. music Lake Louise Ch. of Nazarene, Ortonville, Mich., 1982—; dist. dir. Vacation Bible Sch., Eastern Mich. Ch. of the Nazarene, 1979-82.

FERREIRA, JO ANN JEANETTE CHANOUX, computer center administrator; b. Melrose Park, Ill., Dec. 3, 1943; d. John W. and June B. Chanoux; B.S., Purdue U., 1965, M.S. (NSF fellow), 1969; m. G. Dodge Ferreira, Apr. 21, 1979. With systems devel. research IBM, San Jose, Calif., 1965-67; asst. dir. mgmt. info. systems edn. Union Carbide Corp., N.Y.C., 1969; mgmt. cons. Touche Ross & Co., N.Y.C., 1970-72, Peat Marwick Mitchell, N.Y.C., 1974-75; dir. corp. devel. strategy cons. A.T. Kearney-Mgmt. Cons., Chgo., 1975-83; dir. Computer Devel. Center, United Airlines, 1983—; lectr. Purdue U., 1969, 73-74; guest lectr. Northwestern U., 1981. Mem. Assn. for Corp. Growth (mergers and acquisitions profls.), Inst. Mgmt. Cons. (cert. mgmt. cons.), Am. Arbitration Assn. Phi Kappa Phi. Contbr. articles to profl. publs.; speaker various groups. Home: Rural Route 2 Box 110 Barrington Hills IL 60010 Office: PO Box 66100 Chicago IL 60666

FERRELL, BARBARA ANN, educator; b. Rochester, Pa., Jan. 1, 1941; d. Matt and Mary (Zapotocky) Fatur; m. C. Duane Ferrell, Aug. 24, 1963; children—Jennifer, Stephanie, Ryan. B.A., U. Pitts., 1962; Ed.M., U. Ariz., 1969. Tchr., Mt. Lebanon High Sch., Pitts., 1962-63, Amphitheater High Sch., Tucson, 1963-69, Jefferson Twp. High Sch., Oak Ridge, N.J., 1970-73; gifted tchr. Indian Trail Jr. High Sch., Olathe, Kans., 1981—. Past sec. Shawnee Hist. Soc. Named French Tchr. of the Yr., State of Ariz., 1969. Mem. Kans. Assn. Gifted, English Tchrs. Kans., Pi Lambda Theta, Delta Kappa Gamma. Republican. Roman Catholic. Club: Shawnee Welcome Wagon (past pres.). Home: 14016 W 69th St Shawnee KS 66216 Office: Indian Trail Jr High Sch 1440 E 151st St Olathe KS 66062

FERRELL, HERMAN LEE, physician; b. Forrest City, Ark., Aug. 12, 1951; s. George and Lonneva (Wade) F.; m. Jewelette Smith, Apr. 14, 1976; children—Kristin Marie, Alanna Karen. B.S. magna cum laude, U. Ark., 1973, M.D., 1975. Diplomate Am. Bd. Internal Medicine, Am. Bd. Pulmonary Medicine. Intern St. Louis U., 1975-76, resident in medicine, 1976-78, fellow in pulmonary medicine, 1978-80, instr., 1980-81, asst. prof. medicine, 1981-84, clin. asst. prof. medicine, 1984—; dir. respiratory therapy dept. Central Med. Ctr., St. Louis, 1979—, sec.-treas., 1985—. Fellow Am. Coll. Chest Physicians, AMA. Avocations: classical pianist; table tennis; swimming; tennis. Home: 862 Minarca Dr Des Peres MO 63131 Office: St Louis City Hosp 1515 Lafayette St Saint Louis MO 63104

FERRELL, JAMES EDWIN, oil company executive, utility company executive; b. Atchison, Kans., Oct. 17, 1939; s. Alfred C. and Mabel Anna (Samson) F.; m. Elizabeth J. Gillespie, May 10, 1959; children—Kathryn E., Sarah A. B.S. in Bus. Adminstrn., U. Kans., 1963. Pres., Ferrell Cos., Inc., Liberty, Mo., 1965—; chmn. chief exec. officer Gas Service Co., Kansas City, Mo., 1983—; dir. United Mo. Bancshares, Kansas City, Mo. Served with U.S. Army, 1963-65. Lutheran. Office: One Liberty Plaza Liberty MO 64068

FERRELL, LARRY HOWARD, lawyer; b. Cape Girardeau, Mo., Aug. 6, 1954; s. Bartley C. and Melba Louise (Kirkpatrick) F.; m. Patricia L. Ehlers, July 31, 1977; 1 child, Matthew Brian. B.A. in Polit. Sci., Southeast Mo. State U., 1976; J.D., U. Mo., 1980. Bar: Mo. 1980, U.S. Dist. Ct. (we. dist.) Mo. 1980, U.S. Dist. Ct. (ea. dist.) Mo. 1984. Asst. pros. atty., Jackson County, Kansas City, Mo., 1980-81, Cape Girardeau County, Mo., 1981-83, pros. atty., 1983—; instr. criminal evidence Southeast Mo. State U., Cape Girardeau, Mo., 1982-83; spl. instr. Mo. Dept. Pub. Safety, Cape Girardeau, 1982—. Bd. dirs. Cape County Maj. Case Squad, Cape Girardeau, 1983—, Cape Girardeau County Council on Child Abuse and Neglect, 1982—. Regents scholar S.E. Mo. State U., 1972, Earl E. Grambling scholar S.E. Mo. State U., 1973, 74, 75. Mem. ABA, Nat. Dist. Attys. Assn., Mo. Bar Assn. (criminal law and procedure com. 1983), Mo. Assn. Pros. Attys. (state treas. 1984), Mo. State Pros. Attys. Coordinators Tng. Council, Cape Girardeau County Bar Assn., Delta Theta Phi. Republican. Home: 2015 Bainbridge Rd Jackson MO 63755 Office: Pros Attys Office Courthouse Park Cape Girardeau MO 63701

FERRIELL, JEFFREY THOMAS, legal educator, consultant; b. Columbus, Ohio, Nov. 27, 1953; s. Merlin Thomas and Frances Loretta (Sponseller) F. B.S. in Edn., Ohio State U., 1975; J.D., Santa Clara U., 1978; LL.M., U. Ill., 1983. Bar: Calif. 1978. Law teaching fellow U. Ill., Champaign, 1978-79; vis. asst. prof. law U. Santa Clara, Calif., 1979; asst. prof. law Ohio No. U., Ada, 1979-82, assoc. prof. law, 1982-85, prof. law, 1985—. Author articles. Named Outstanding Grad., Law Sch. U. Santa Clara, 1978. Mem. ABA, Nat. Lawyers Guild. Home: PO Box 54 Ada OH 45810 Office: Ohio No U Ada OH 45810

FERRIS, RICHARD J., airline executive; b. Sacramento, 1936; B.S., Cornell U., 1962; postgrad. U. Wash. Grad. Sch. Bus. Staff analyst and restaurant mgr. Olympic Hotel, to 1971; gen. mgr. Savoy Plaza, Anchorage Westward Hotel, Continental Plaza Hotel, Carlton Hotel; project officer-new constrn. Western Internat. Hotels, to 1971; pres. carrier's food services div. United Air Lines, Chgo., 1971-75, sr. v.p. mktg., 1975-76, pres., 1976-79, chmn., chief exec. officer, dir., 1979—; dir. UAL, Inc., Western Internat. Hotels. Office: United Air Lines Inc PO Box 66100 Chicago IL 60666*

FERRY, JAMES ALLEN, electrostatics company executive; b. Roxbury, Wis., Sept. 9, 1937; s. Darwin J. and Eleanor J. (Irwin) F.; m. Karen A. Greenwood, Feb. 8, 1964; children—Thomas E., Jennifer J. B.S. in Physics, U. Wis., 1959, M.S. in Physics, 1962, Ph.D. in Physics, 1965. Research assoc. U. Wis., Madison, 1965-66; exec. v.p., chief operating officer Nat. Electrostatics Corp., Middleton, Wis., 1967—. Patentee in field. Mem. Am. Phys. Soc. Home: 6810 Forest Glade Ct Middleton WI 53562 Office: Nat Electrostatics Corp PO Box 310 Graber Rd Middleton WI 53562

FERSTENFELD, JULIAN ERWIN, internist, educator; b. Des Moines, Sept. 5, 1941; m. Sharon Rukas, Mar. 8, 1975; children—Megan Ann, Adam Justin. B.A., U. Iowa, 1963, M.D., 1966. Intern Milwaukee County Gen. Hosp., Milw., 1966-67, resident in internal medicine, 1969-71, fellow in infectious diseases, 1972-73; instr. internal medicine Med. Coll. Wis., Milw., 1974-75, asst. prof. medicine, 1975-78, asst. clin. prof. medicine and family practice, 1978-83, assoc. clin. prof. family practice and medicine, 1983—, internal medicine dir. Waukesha family practice residency, 1978—; practice medicine specializing in infectious diseases, Milw., 1974—; mem. staff Waukesha Meml. Hosp. (Wis.), West Allis Meml. Hosp. (Wis.), Elmbrook Meml. Hosp., Brookfield, Wis., Froedtert Meml. Hosp., Milw. Served as capt. M.C., U.S. Army, 1967-69; Korea. Fellow ACP; mem. Wis. Thoracic Soc., Am. Fedn. Clin. Research, Phi Beta Kappa. Contbr. articles, abstracts to profl. jours.

FESS, MARILYNN ELAINE EWING, occupational therapist; b. Casper, Wyo., June 20, 1944; d. Frederick Eugene and Norma Pence (Jarrett) Ewing; B.S., Ind. U., 1967, M.S., 1977; m. Stephen W. Fess, Nov. 26, 1966. Staff occupational therapist Marion County Gen. Hosp., Indpls., 1966-70; supr. phys. dysfunction unit, 1970-72; supr. adult occupational therapy Ind. U. Med. Center, Indpls., 1972-74, instr. occupational therapy curriculum, 1974-76; hand therapist Strickland & Steichen, M.D.'s, Inc., 1974-79; designer, developer, dir. hand therapy Hand Rehab. Center Ind., 1976-79; cons. hand rehab. and hand research, 1979—; cons. to hand surgeons various hosps. and nursing homes. Mem. exec. bd. Ind. Cerebral Vascular Accident Com., 1973-76. Mem. Am. Occupational Therapy Assn. (roster of fellows 1983, sec. orgn. affiliate pres. 1976-78), Am. Soc. Hand Therapists (founding, mem. at large exec. bd. 1978-79, sec. 1980-82), Ind. Occupational Therapy Assn. (sec. 1969-71, v.p. 1972-73, pres. 1974-76, hand therapy liaison to exec. bd. 1978—). Author: (with others) Hand Splinting Principles and Methods, 1980; mem. editorial rev. bd. Occupational Therapy Jour. Research, 1983-84, Am. Jour. Occupational Therapy, 1985—, also articles. Patentee externally powered hand orthosis. Office: 635 Eagle Creek Ct Zionsville IN 46077

FESTOFF, BARRY WILLIAM, neurologist, researcher, educator; b. N.Y.C., July 30, 1940; s. Emanuel Jacob and Ceil Ruth (Stein) F.; m. Shea Jane Gordon, Apr. 2, 1976: 1 child, Mara Alexsandra. B.A., U. Fla., 1962; M.D., U. Miami, 1966. Diplomate Am. Bd. Psychiatry and Neurology. Intern in medicine Duke U. Hosp., Durham, N.C., 1966-67; fellow in neurobiology Duke U. Med. Ctr., 1967-69; resident in neurology U. Miami Med. Ctr., Fla., 1969-71; clin. assoc. investigator in neurology NIH, Bethesda, Md., 1971-76; assoc. prof. neurology U. Kans. Med. Ctr., Kansas City, 1976-80, prof., 1980—; adj. prof. neurophysiology Antioch Coll., Balt., 1972-74; cons. neurology Nat. Navy Med. Ctr., Bethesda, 1973-76; chief neurology service, dir. neurobiology research lab. Kansas City VA Med. Ctr., Kans. U. Med. Ctr., 1976—. Contbr. articles to profl. jours. Med. adviser Muscular Dystrophy Assn. Clinic, Kans. U. Med. Ctr., 1977—; trustee Neurologic Psychiatry Research Treatment Found., Chgo., 1984—; mem. Contemporary Art Soc., Kansas City, 1978—. Served to comdr. USPHS, 1971-76. Research grantee Muscular Dystrophy Assn., 1977-82, 83-85, NIH, 1981-85, VA, 1976—; recipient research award Soc. Biol. Psychiatry, 1972; sr. fellow Fulbright Commn., Paris, 1984-85. Fellow Am. Acad. Neurology; mem. Am. Neurol. Assn., Am. Fedn. Clin. Research, Am. Soc. Biol. Chemists, Am. Soc. Clin. Investigation, Am. Soc. Neurosci. Democrat. Jewish. Avocation: darts. Home: 5155 Wornall Rd Kansas City MO 64112 Office: VA Med Ctr Neurology Service (127) 4801 Linwood Blvd Kansas City MO 64128

FETRIDGE, BONNIE-JEAN CLARK (MRS. WILLIAM HARRISON FETRIDGE), civic worker; b. Chgo., Feb. 3, 1915; d. Sheldon and Bonnie (Carrington) Clark; student Girls Latin Sch., Chgo., The Masters Sch., Dobbs Ferry, N.Y., Finch Coll., N.Y.C.; m. William Harrison Fetridge, June 27, 1941; children—Blakely (Mrs. Harvey H. Bundy III), Clark Worthington. Bd. dirs. region VII com. Girl Scouts U.S.A., 1939-43, mem. nat. program com., 1966-69, mem. nat. adv. council, 1972-85, mem. internat. commr.'s adv. panel, 1973-76, mem. Nat. Juliette Low Birthplace Com., 1966-69, region IV selections com., 1968-70; bd. dirs. Girl Scouts Chgo., 1936-51, 59-69, sec., 1936-38, v.p., 1946-49, 61-65, chmn. Juliette Low world friendship com., 1959-67, 71-72; mem. Friends of Our Cabana Com. World Assn. Girl Guides and Girl Scouts, London, Eng., 1969—, vice chmn., 1982—; asst. sec. Dartnell Corp., bus. pubs., Chgo., 1981—; bd. dirs. Jr. League of Chgo., 1937-40, Vis. Nurse Assn. of Chgo., 1951-58, 61-63, asst. treas., 1962-63; women's bd. dirs. Children's Meml. Hosp., 1946-50; founder mem., pres. Olave Baden-Powell Soc. of World Assn. Girl Guides and Girl Scouts, 1984—. Staff aide, ARC and Motor Corps, World War II. Vice pres. Latin Sch. Parents Council, 1952-54; bd. dirs. Latin Sch. Alumni Assn. 1964-69, Fidelitas Soc., 1979; women's bd. U.S.O., 1965-75, treas., 1969-71, v.p., 1971-73; women's service bd. Chgo. Area council Boy Scouts Am., 1964-70, mem.-at-large Nat. council, 1973-76, mem. nat. Exploring com., 1973-76; governing mem. Anti-Cruelty Soc. of Chgo.; assoc. Nat. Archives. Recipient Citation of Merit for community contbns. in field of human relations Sta. WAIT, Chgo., 1971; Baden-Powell fellow World Scout Found., Geneva, 1983. Mem. Nat. Soc. Colonial Dames Am. (Ill. bd. mgrs. 1962-65, 69-76, 78-82, v.p. 1970-72, corr. sec. 1978-80, 1st v.p. 1980—, state chmn. geneal. info. services com. 1972-76, hist. activities com. 1979-83, mus. house com. 1980-83, house gov. 1981-82), Youth for Understanding (couriers bicentennial project), English-Speaking Union, Chgo. Dobbs Alumnae Assn. (past pres.), Nat. Soc. DAR, Chgo. Geneal. Soc., Conn. Soc. Genealogists, New Eng. Historic Geneal. Soc., N.Y. Geneal. and Biog. Soc., Newberry Library Assos., Chgo. Hist. Soc. Guild. Republican. Episcopalian. Clubs: Casino, Saddle and Cycle, Woman's Athletic. Home: 2430 Lakeview Ave Chicago IL 60614

FETRIDGE, WILLIAM HARRISON, publisher; b. Chgo.; s. Matthew and Clara (Hall) F.; B.S., Northwestern U., 1929; LL.D., Central Mich. U., 1954; m. Bonnie Jean Clark, June 27, 1941; children—Blakely Fetridge Bundy, Clark Worthington. Asst. to dean Northwestern U., 1929-30; editor Trade Periodical Co., 1930-31, Chgo. Tribune, 1931-34, H. W. Kastor & Son, 1934-35, Roche, Williams & Cleary, Inc., 1935-42; mng. editor Republican mag., 1939-42; asst. to pres. Popular Mechanics mag., 1945-46, v.p., 1946; exec. v.p., 1953-59; v.p. Diamond T Motor Truck Co., Chgo., 1959-61; exec. v.p. Diamond T div. White Motor Co., 1961-65; pres. Dartnell Corp., Chgo., 1965-78, chmn. bd., 1978—; dir. Bank of Ravenswood. Pres., United Republican Fund Ill., 1967-73, 79-80, hon. pres., 1973-79; Rep. state fin. chmn., 1967-74; alt. del.-at-large Rep. Nat. Conv., 1956, del.-at-large, 1968; campaign mgr. Merriam for Mayor of Chgo., 1955; chmn. Midwest Vols. for Nixon, 1960; chmn. Nixon Recount Com., 1960, Rep. Forum, 1958-60; mem. Rep. Nat. Finance Com., 1968-73; trustee Lake Forest Coll., 1969-77, Am. Humanics Found., Jacques Holinger Meml. Assn.; pres. U.S. Found. Internat. Scouting, 1971-79, hon. chmn., 1979; vice chmn. World Scout Found., Geneva, 1978—; del. World Scout confs., Rhodes, Greece, 1963, Helsinki, Finland, 1969, Tokyo, 1971, Nairobi, Kenya, 1973, Denmark, 1975, Montreal, 1977, Detroit, 1983; past pres. bd. trustees Latin Sch. Chgo.; nat. v.p. Boy Scouts Am., 1958-76. Served as lt. comdr. USNR, 1942-45. Recipient Silver Buffalo, Silver Beaver and Silver Antelope awards Boy Scouts Am., also Disting. Eagle Scout award; Bronze Wolf, World Scout Bur., Nairobi, Kenya, 1973; Disting. Citizen's award St. Andrew Soc., 1980; Abraham Lincoln award United Rep. Fund, 1980. Mem. Navy League U.S. (past regional pres.; trustee Chgo. council), Soc. Midland Authors, Grand Priory Malta (chevalier), Sovereign Order St. John of Jerusalem, Beta Theta Pi. Clubs: Chgo., Union League, Saddle and Cycle, Casino (Chgo.); Chikaming Country; Rotary/One. Author: With Warm Regards, 1976; editor: The Navy Reader, 1943; The Second Navy Reader, 1944; American Political Almanac, 1950; The Republican Precinct Workers Manual, 1968. Home: 2430 Lakeview Ave Chicago IL 60614 Office: Dartnell Corp 4660 N Ravenswood Ave Chicago IL 60640

FETZER, JOHN EARL, business, baseball, broadcasting executive; b. Decatur, Ind., Mar. 25, 1901; s. John Adam and Della Frances (Winger) F.; student Purdue U., 1921; A.B., Andrews U., 1927, LL.D. (hon.), 1980; student U. Mich., 1929; LL.D. (hon.), Western Mich. U., 1958, Kalamazoo Coll., 1972, Andrews U., 1980; Litt.D. (hon.), Elizabethtown Coll., 1972; D.Eng. (hon.), Lawrence Inst. Tech., 1979; m. Rhea Maude Yeager, July 19, 1926. Owner, chmn. bd. Fetzer Broadcasting Co., 1930—, Fetzer TV Corp., Kalamazoo-Grand Rapids, Mich., 1970—, Cornhusker TV Corp., Lincoln, Nebr., 1953—; chmn. Detroit Tigers, Am. League Baseball Club, 1956—, Fetzer Music Corp., Fetzer TV, Inc., Cadillac, Mich., 1958-79, John E. Fetzer, Inc., 1968—; pres. Pro Am Sports System, Inc., 1983; dir. Domino's Pizza, Inc., 1983; dir. emeritus Am. Nat. Bank & Trust Co., Kalamazoo. Chmn., Maj. League TV Com., 1963-71. U.S. Censor of radio, 1944-45; reporting to Gen. Eisenhower, engaged in ETO radio studies in Eng., France, Russia, Germany, Italy and other European countries, 1945; fgn. corr. radio-TV-newspaper mission Europe and Middle East, 1952; mem. mission Radio Free Europe, Munich, Germany, and Austrian-Hungarian border, 1956; Broadcasters Mission to Latin-Am., Dept. State, 1962, Detroit Tiger Baseball tour of Japan, Okinawa, Korea, under auspices Dept. State, 1962; mem. A.P. tour Europe, 1966; Dept. State del. Japanese-U.S. TV Treaty, 1972; mem. adv. bd. N.Am. Service, Radio Diffusion Française, Paris, 1946-47. Trustee Kalamazoo Coll., 1954—. Recipient Broadcast Pioneers award, 1968; Disting. Service award Nat. Assn. Broadcasters, 1969; Mich. Frontiersman award, 1969; Fourth Estate award Am. Legion, 1972; citation Mich. Legislature, 1972; C. of C. Detroit Tiger 75th Anniversary award, 1976; Mich. Legis. citation, 1976; Nebr. Pub. TV citation, 1976; Summit award Detroit C. of C., 1977; Abe Lincoln Railsplitter award So. Bapt. Radio and TV Commn., 1979. Fellow Royal Soc. Arts London; mem. Nat. Assn. Broadcasters (chmn. TV bd. 1952), C. of C. (past pres.), Nat. Geneal. Soc., Acad. Polit. Sci., Am. Soc. Mil. Engrs., IEEE (life mem.), Internat. Radio and TV Execs. Soc., Broadcast Pioneers (19th Mike award to Sta. WKZO 1981), Alpha Kappa Psi. Presbyn. Mason (33 deg., Shriner), Elk. Clubs: Park, Kalamazoo Country (Kalamazoo); Economic, Detroit Athletic, Press, Detroit (Detroit); Tucson Country. Author: One Man's Family, 1964; The Men from Wengen and America's Agony, 1972. Contbr. Radio and Television Project, Columbia, 1953. Home: 2714 Clovelly Rd Kalamazoo MI 49008 Office: Kalamazoo MI 49008 also Tiger Stadium Detroit MI 48216

FEYERHERM, ARLIN MARTIN, statistics educator; b. West Point, Nebr., May 21, 1925; s. Fred William and Ida Augusta (Kuester) F.; m. Junavae Gail Henry, Aug. 25, 1951; children—Carol Ann, Joan Louise, Roger Arlin. Student Doane Coll., 1943-44; B.S., U. Minn., Mpls., 1946; M.S., State U. Iowa, 1948; Ph.D., Iowa State U., 1952. Asst. prof. math. Iowa State U., Ames, 1952-53; prof. stats. Kans. State U., Manhattan, 1953—. Contbr. articles to profl. jours. Served to lt. (j.g.) USN, 1943-46. Mem. Am. Statis. Assn., Inst. Math. Stats., Am. Soc. Agronomy. Lutheran. Home: 350 N Delaware St Manhattan KS 66502 Office: Dept Stats Dickens Halls Kans State U Manhattan KS 66506

FIALA, DAVID MARCUS, lawyer; b. Cleve., Aug. 1, 1946; s. Frank J. and Anna Mae (Phillips) F.; m. Maryanne E. McGowan, Jan. 4, 1969; 1 child, D. Michael. B.B.A., U. Cin., 1969; J.D., Chase Coll., No. Ky. State U., 1974. Bar: Ohio 1974, U.S. Dist. Ct. (so. dist.) Ohio 1974, U.S. Tax Ct. 1974. Assoc., Walker, Chatfield & Doan, Cin., 1974-78, ptnr., 1979—; lectr. Southwestern Ohio Tax Inst., 1978-79. Trustee, sec. Sta. WCET-TV, Cin., 1983, auction chmn., 1979; trustee Jr. Achievement Greater Cin., 1979—, Mental Health Services West, 1974-83, Contemporary Dance theatre, 1974-80. Mem. ABA, Ohio State Bar Assn., Cin. Bar Assn. Home: 5913 Quailhill Dr Cincinnati OH 45238 Office: Walker Chatfield & Doan 1900 Carew Tower Cincinnati OH 45202

FIALA, KENNETH R., savings and loan officer; b. Mar. 15, 1932; m. Joan Armbruster; children—Dick, Gretchen Ann. B.S.B.A., U. Mo.-Columbia, 1954. With Cornell & Co., C. I.A., St. Louis, Peat, Marwick, Mitchell & Co., St. Louis; with Community Fed. Savs. and Loan Assn., St. Louis, chmn. bd., chief exec. officer, 1984—; dir. Bank Bldg. Corp., Fed. Home Loan Bank Bd. of Des Moines; chmn. bd. Community Agy., Inc., Money Matic, Inc.. Pres. Am. Field Service, Ritenour Community chpt.; bd. dirs. Northwest br. St.Louis YMCA; mem. Met. bd. dirs. YMCA of Greater St. Louis; bd. trustees Williams Coll., Fulton, Mo.; exec. bd. St. Louis Area council Boy Scouts Am.; bd. trustees St. Louis Coll. Pharmacy; bd. dirs. St. Louis Regional Commerce and Growth Assn., Better Bus. Bur.; adv. bd. Salvation Army; mem. St. Louis County Bus. and Indsl. Devel. Commn. Mem. Fin. Mgrs. Soc. of Savs. Instns. (chpt. pres., nat. bd. govs.), St. Louis Savs. and Loan League (past pres.), Mo. Soc. C.P.A.'s, Am. Inst. C.P.A.'s, Kappa Sigma. Lodges: Rotary (past pres.), Masons, Shriner. Address: Community Federal Savings and Loan Assn #1 Community Federal Center Saint Louis MO 63131

FIALKOWSKI, CONRAD TIMOTHY, commercial artist; b. Chgo., June 30, 1938; s. Chester J. and Genevieve M. (Czaszewicz) F.; m. Carol J. Anderson, Nov. 3, 1962; children—Beth, Mark. Student, Art Inst. Chgo., 1956-57; B.A., U. Ill., 1961. Trainee, art supr. Foote, Cone & Belding, Chgo., 1961-69; assoc. creative dir., v.p. Earle Ludgin & Co., 1969-74; freelance art dir., 1974—. Office: c/o Daily Planet 401 N Michigan Ave Suite 3260 Chicago IL 60611

FICKLE, WILLIAM DICK, lawyer; b. Kansas City, Mo., Oct. 29, 1943; s. William and Elvarea (Dick) F.; B.A., Westminster Coll., Fulton, Mo., 1965; J.D., U. Mo., Columbia, 1969; m. Jane Thompson Jones, Nov. 29, 1969; children—Tara Elizabeth, William Dick. Admitted to Mo. bar, 1968; asso. firm James, McFarland, Trimble, Austin, North Kansas City, Mo., 1971-72; pros. atty. Platte County (Mo.), 1973-74; ptnr. Fickle & Hull, Platte City, Mo., 1973-74, Clevenger, Fickle & McGinness, Platte City, 1975—; chmn. bar ethics com. 6th Jud. Cir. Mem. Mo. Mo. Hos. Reps., 1974-79; bd. dirs. Eyebank of Kansas City, Mo., Home Health Services Clay-Platte and Jackson Counties. Served with U.S. Army, 1969-70. Decorated Legion of Honor; named Outstanding Young Man of Platte County, 1973. Mem. Mo. Bar, Platte County Bar Assn. (pres.). Democrat. Episcopalian. Clubs: Masons, Shriners, Jesters. Home: 7708 NW Mastern Kansas City MO 64152 Office: 204 Marshall Rd Platte City MO 64079

FIEBIG, JAMES ARTHUR, jeweler; b. Hillsdale, Mich., Oct. 3, 1956; s. Arthur Melvin and Ila Lavina (Armbruster) F.; m. JoAnn Gilchrist, Aug. 15, 1981; children—Chad Nettleman, Jared Arthur. B.A. in Music, U. Mich., 1978. Vice pres. Dan Yessian Assocs., Farmington Hills, Mich., 1977-79; mgr. Fiebig Jewelry, Sturgis, Mich., 1979—; consumer educator local high schs., 1980—. Mem. Sturgis Labor-Mgmt. Relations Bd., 1982-83; pres. Sturgis Council Arts, 1983; vice chmn. Downtown Devel. Authority, Sturgis, 1984. Mem. Downtown Sturgis Assn. (pres. 1980), Sturgis C. of C. (pres. 1984), Jewelers Am. Lutheran. Lodge: Rotary (sec. 1984-85). Avocations: music, family, racquetball. Office: Fiebig Jewelry 211 W Chicago St Sturgis MI 49091

FIEDLER, LEIGH ALLAN, mathematics and computer science educator; b. Moline, Ill., July 22, 1930; s. Leroy Charles and Blanche Emma (Curran) F.; m. Andree Mery Golaz, Nov. 15, 1958; children—Mark, Luc, Daniel, Stephan. A.A., Moline Community Coll., 1950; B.S., U. Ariz., 1952, M.A., 1959; Ph.D., U. Okla., 1969; postgrad. U. Colo., summer 1955, U. Geneva, Switzerland, 1971-72, Augustana Coll., fall 1984. Tchr. Marana High Sch., Ariz., 1955-57; mathematician, computer analyst Shell Oil Co., Los Angeles, 1958, Ctr. European Nuclear Research, Meryn, Switzerland, 1959-60; mathematician, computer cons. Deere and Co., Moline, 1963, 64, 65, 66; dean univ. parallel programs Black Hawk Coll., Moline, 1969-77, prof. math., 1960-69, 77—. Contbr. articles to profl. jours. Allocations com. United Way, Rock Island, Ill., 1972-73, 78; coach Moline Dads Club Baseball, 1968-81; ch. diaconate First Covenant Ch., Moline, 1968-71, 78-83; long range curriculum planning com. Moline Sch. Dist. 40, 1974-75. Ford Found. fellow, 1959-60; NSF fellow, 1965-66. Mem. Math. Assn. Am., Nat. Council Tchrs. Math., AAUP, Pi Mu Epsilon, Phi Delta Kappa (pres. 1979-80). Avocations: golf; travel; softball. Home: 3200 26th Ave Ct Moline IL 61265 Office: Black Hawk Coll 6600 34th Ave Moline IL 61265

FIELD, DAVID THOMAS, real estate developer, poet; b. Rochester, Minn., Sept. 19, 1946; s. M. Wayne and Phyllis Lorraine (Pesch) Bump; m. Diane Ellen Houkom, Feb. 13, 1984; 1 child, Jonathan Stanley Alexander. B.A. in Zoology, U. Minn-Duluth, 1968; postgrad. U Pa., 1971-72. Vice Pres. real estate ops. Rembrandt Enterprises, Inc., Edina, Minn., 1978—, also dir.; chief exec. officer Creative Energy Prodns. Inc., Mpls., 1981—, Enigma Images, Inc., Mpls., 1981—; sec. treas. Multi Dimensional Computer Services, Inc., Bloomington, Minn., 1982—; Author: David Field the Poems Collected, 1985. Served with U.S. Army, 1968-71. Mem. Nat. Orgn. Indsl. Office Parks, Edina C. of C. Republican. Home: 2457 Lyndale Ave S Minneapolis MN 55405 Office: Rembrandt Enterprises Inc 3434 Heritage Dr Edina MN 55435 also Address: Creative Energy Prodns Inc 2457 Lyndale Ave S Minneapolis MN 55405

FIELD, HAROLD GREGORY, lawyer; b. Chgo., Fb. 27, 1923; s. Harold Gregory and Catherine (Crowley) F.; m. Marilyn Daw, June 21, 1947 (div. July 1977); children—Lnda, Karen, Jennifer, Gregory; m. Nancy L. Kesecker, Sept. 30, 1977. B.S., Ariz. State U., 1948; LL.B., Chgo. Kent Coll. Law, 1952. Bar: Ill. 1953. Ptnr., Burek & Field, Wheaton, Ill., 1965—. Mem. Dist. 41 Bd. Edn., Glen Ellyn, Ill., 1960-65, chmn., 1965. Served with U.S. Army, 1942-45, ETO. Decorated Bronze Star. Fellow Am. Bar Found., Ill. Bar Found.; mem. Ill. Bar Assn. (bd. govs. 1983—), DuPage County Bar Assn. (pres. 1977-78, Man of Yr. 1982), ABA, Assn. Trial Lawyers Am., Ill. Trial Lawyers Assn., Am. Acad. Matrimonial Lawyers (chpt. pres.-elect 1983—, nat. bd. dirs. 1981—). Republican. Club: Naperville Country (pres. 1975-76) (Ill.). Avocations: golf; skiing; tennis; running. Home: 979 Creekside Circle Naperville IL 60540 Office: 100 N Hale St Wheaton IL 60187

FIELD, LARRY FRANCIS, lawyer, county prosecutor; b. Phila., June 15, 1942; s. Frank Sylvester and Lucille (Ward) F.; m. Tamara Myers, June 20, 1964; children—Sean, Nicholas. B.A., Georgetown U., 1964; M.A., Tufts U., 1965; Ph.D., Johns Hopkins U., 1968; J.D., U. Detroit, 1977. Bar: Mich. 1977. Tchr. Latin, U. Liggett's Sch. and Grosse Pointe, 1971-77; assoc. Casanova and Schwedler, Crystal Falls, Mich., 1978-82; county prosecutor County of Iron (Mich.), 1982—; instr. Gogebic Community College Extension Program, Iron River, Mich., 1978-82. Bd. dir. Hiawathaland council Boy Scouts Am.; mem. Timberland Chamber Players. Served to capt. U.S. Army, 1968-71; Vietnam. Woodrow Wilson fellow, 1964-65, Dissertation fellow, 1967-68. Mem. Mich. Bar Assn., Assn. Trial Lawyers Am., Am. Soc. for Legal History, Classical Soc. for the Middle West and South, VFW, Am. Legion. Democrat. Club: Kiwanis. Home: 730 Harrison Crystal Falls MI 49920 Office: Courthouse Crystal Falls MI 49920

FIELD, LARRY SCOTT, sales manager; b. Chgo., Oct. 22, 1954; s. Elmer and Frieda Field; m. Ellen B. Field, Dec. 22, 1984; B.A. in Englist, U. Ill.-Chgo. Cert. elem. tchr., Ill. Asst. mgr. David C. Cook Pub. Co., Elgin, Ill., 1980-82; regional sales mgr. Concordia Pub. House, St. Louis, 1982—. Vol. Kane County Emergency and Disaster Agy., Geneva, Ill., 1982. Avocations: amateur radio, photography. Home: 1002 Castilian Ct Apt B-209 Glenview IL 60025 Office: Concordia Pub House 3558 S Jefferson Ave Saint Louis MO 63118

FIELD, SAMUEL THOMAS, lawyer; b. Ann Arbor, Mich., May 3, 1952; s. Eugene and Ruby (Thomas) F.; m. Shon Oliver, Feb. 9, 1980. B. Gen. Studies with high distinction, U. Mich., 1974, J.D. with honors, 1977. Bar: N.Y. 1978, U.S. Dist. Ct. (so. dist.) N.Y. 1978, Mich. 1980, U.S. Dist. Ct. (we. dist.) Mich. 1980. Assoc. Casey, Lane & Mittendorf, N.Y.C., 1977-80; assoc. Field & Miller, P.C., Kalamazoo, 1980-81; prin. Field & Field, P.C., Kalamazoo, 1983—. Adviser Explorer div. Boy Scouts Am., 1983—. Mem. ABA, Assn. Trial Lawyers Am., State Bar Mich., Mich. Trial Lawyers Assn., Kalamazoo County Bar Assn., N.Y. Bar Assn. Office: Field & Field PC 248 W Michigan Ave Kalamazoo MI 49007

FIELDING, V(ELMA) JOYCE, educational administrator; b. Parsons, Kans., Mar. 22, 1933; d. Jack E. and Anna V. (Easterday) Newfield; m. Marvin R. Fielding, Mar. 22, 1955 (div. 1977); children—Steven, David Gregg, James, Jeri Bird; m. Darrell D. Kimball, June 26, 1981. A.A., Parsons Jr. Coll., 1954; B.S., Kans. State Coll., 1957, M.S., 1959; D.Edn., U. Mo., 1968. Cert. secondary tchr., Kansas. Counselor, tchr. Isabel Consol. Schs., Kans., 1959-63; counselor Labette County Consol. High Sch. Altamont, Kans., 1963-64; dean of students State Fair Community Coll., Sedalia, Mo., 1968—. Mem. Act Mo. (pres. adv. bd. 1977-78), Mo. Coll. Personnel Assn. (pres. 1975-77), Am. Vocat. Assn. (com. chmn. 1973-77), Am. Assn. Coll. Registrars and Admissions Officers, Mo. Assn. Coll. Registrars and Admissions Officers. Office: State Fair Community Coll 1900 Clarendon Rd Sedalia MO 65301

FIELDS, DEAN STANLEY, dentist; b. Detroit, May 31, 1931; s. Dean Stanley and Lenore Jeanette (Wolfe) F.; m. Suzanne Lee, Oct. 5, 1957; children—Jenifer, Dean S. III, Nancy. B.S. in Biology, U. Detroit, 1953; D.D.S., St. Louis U., 1957. Lic. dentist, Mich. Gen. practice dentistry, USAF, Tachikawa, Japan, 1957-60, Pontiac State Hosp., Mich., 1960-63, Rochester Hills, Mich., 1963—. Fellow Acad. Gen. Dentistry, Chgo., 1979, Am. Coll. Dentists, 1983, Internat. Coll. Dentists, 1984. Mem. ADA, Mich. Dental Assn., Oakland County Dental Soc. Roman Catholic. Home: 2419 Lost Tree Way Bloomfield Hills MI 48013

FIELDS, RICHARD DEAN, sales manager; b. Bedford, Ind., Apr. 23, 1946; s. Richard Austin and Hazel O. (Fletcher) F.; m. Jane Ann Kitterman, Aug. 22, 1970; 1 child, Spencer Austin. B.S., Ball State U., 1970. Salesman Indpls. Life Ins., 1970-73; asst. div. mgr. McFadden Sales, Columbus, Ohio, 1973-79; phone power cons., Ind. Bell Telephone, Indpls., 1979-80, account exec., 1980-84, sales-mgr., 1984—; cons. Gen. Bus. Services, 1983—. Contbr. articles to profl. jours. Bd. dirs. New World Chamber Orch. Served with U.S. Army, 1968-69, Vietnam. Republican. Methodist. Clubs: Optimist (event chmn. 1983), Pres.'s Achievers. Avocations: sailing, tennis, music. Home: 5350 N Capitol St Indianapolis IN 46208 Office: Ind Bell Telephone 240 N Meridian 800 Indianapolis IN 46204

FIELDS, ROBERT LYNN, hospital administrator; b. Dayton, Ohio, May 7, 1952; s. Robert James and Fannie Mae (Walker) F.; m. Stephanie Ann Hines, Apr. 7, 1955; children—Courtney Erin, Ashley Rian. B.A., Coll. of Wooster, 1974; student Inst. Fin. Edn., Sinclair Community Coll., 1975-86. Br. mgr. Household Finance Corp., Dayton, 1974-75; loan officer Gem Saving Assn., Dayton, 1975-77; patient accounts mgr. St. Elizabeth Med. Ctr., Dayton, 1977-81, Children's Hosp. Med. Ctr. of Akron, Ohio, 1981-84, Mich. Osteo. Med. Ctr., Detroit, 1984—. Mem. Am. Guild Patient Accounts Mgrs., Healthcare Fin. Mgmt. Assn., Kappa Alpha Psi. Presbyterian.

FIENUP, SPENCER RALPH, pharmacist; b. St. Louis, Jan. 19, 1956; s. Ralph Frederick and Bonnie Jean (Wheatly) F.; m.. Judith Carol Bothe, Apr. 10, 1982. B.S. in Pharmacy, St. Louis Coll. Pharmacy, 1979. Registered pharmacist, Mo. Pharmacist intern Bloemkers Drugs, St. Louis, 1973-79; pharmacist St. Louis State Hosp., 1979—; pharm. cons. in field. Mem. Am. Pharm. Assn., St. Louis Coll. Pharmacy Alumni Assn. Republican. Lutheran. Avocations: Skiing, water skiing, swimming, history, politics. Office: St Louis State Hosp 5400 Arsenal St Saint Louis MO 63139

FIETSAM, ROBERT CHARLES, accountant; b. Belleville, Ill., Oct. 18, 1927; s. Celsus J. and Viola (Ehret) F.; B.S., U. Ill., 1955; m. Miriam Runkwitz, Apr. 12, 1952; children—Robert C., Guy P., Nancy A., Lisa R. C.P.A., Mo., Ill. Claims adjuster Ely & Walker Dry Goods, St. Louis, 1947-48; accountant Price Waterhouse & Co., 1949-54; staff accountant J.W. Boyle & Co., East St. Louis, 1955-59; owner R.C. Fietsam, C.P.A., Belleville, Ill., 1959-68; mng. ptnr. R.C. Fietsam & Co. C.P.A.s, 1969—. Mem. Belle-Scott Com., 1979—; bd. dirs., pres. Belleville Center, Inc., 1980-81; mem. adv. bd. Masterworks Chorale, 1984—. Served with USAF, 1951-53. Mem. Ill. Soc. C.P.A. (pres. So. chpt., 1972-73, Mr. So. Chpt. award 1976, bd. dirs. Chgo. 1979-81, pub. service award 1982-83), Mo. Soc. C.P.A.s, Am. Inst. C.P.A.s (council 1981—), U. Ill. Alumni Assn. (life), U. Ill. Greater Belleville Illini Club (past pres.), Belleville C. of C. (pres. 1973-74), Belleville Jr. C. of C. (life, Key Man award 1959-60, Outstanding Citizen award 1976), Lambda Chi Alpha Alumnae Assn. Mem. United Ch. of Christ (pres. 1972-73). Elk, Moose. Clubs: St. Clair Country; Belleville Optimists (pres. 1979-80, disting. pres. award internat. orgn. 1979-80, Optimist of Yr., Belleville 1977, Ill. dist. 1980). Home: 23 Persimmon Ridge Dr Belleville IL 62223 Office: 325 W Main Belleville IL 62220

FIGHTMASTER, WALTER JOHN, college administrator; b. Barberton, Ohio, Dec. 14, 1930; s. Verderman Cantrill and Amanda (Stone) F.; B.S., U. Louisville, 1952, M.A., 1954; m. Sue N. Tabler, June 8, 1958. Cons. psychologist Kemper & Assos., Louisville, 1952-54; research psychologist George Washington U., Washington, 1957-58; sr. indsl. psychologist Martin Marietta Corp., Balt., 1958-59, Westinghouse Electric Corp., Balt., 1959-60; staff psychologist Bendix Corp., Ann Arbor, Mich., 1960-63; chief staff psychologist Ling-Temco-Vought, Inc., Warren, Mich., 1963-65; dir. community services Oakland Community Coll., Bloomfield Hills, Mich., 1965-68, exec. dir. of community services, 1968-71, provost Southeast campus, 1971—. Chartered com. mem. Oakland County Police Acad. Served to capt. USAF, 1954-57. Commd. col. Hon. Order Ky. Cols., 1966. Lic. psychologist, D.C., Mich. Mem. Am. Assn. Jr. Coll., AAAS, Am., Midwestern, D.C., Eastern, Mich. Ky. psychol. assns., U.S.A., Mich. adult edn. assns., Nat., Mich. assns. pub. sch. adult edn., NEA, Mich Soc. for Instrnl. Tech. (past pres.), Am. Assn. Community and Jr. Colls. (past dir.), Nat. Council Community Services (past sec. and pres.), Psi Chi. Home: 1442 Kings Cove Dr Rochester MI 48063 Office: Oakland Community Coll Southeast Campus System 739 S Washington St Royal Oak MI 48067

FIKSDAL, ALLEN JAMES, geologist; b. Seattle, Dec. 4, 1946; s. Aksel I. and Shirley (Bondimere) F.; m. Susan Reeves, Aug. 21, 1971; children—Mara, Alex. B.A., Western Wash. U., 1965; M.S., Portland State U., 1979. Geologist, Wash. Dept. Natural Resources, Olympia, 1972-81; sr. geologist Bechtel Co., Ann Arbor, Mich., 1981-84; project mgr. Applied Geotech., Inc., Bellevue, Wash., 1984—. Mem. Assn. Engring. Geologists.

FILIPPINE, EDWARD L., See *Who's Who in America,* 43rd edition.

FILLMAN, LEONARD NOEL, health care executive; b. Vinita, Okla., Feb. 13, 1941; s. Gettis I. and Charlotte M. (Parsons) F.; m. Jinnie Vee Wilson, Jan. 3, 1942; children—Kenneth, Terry, Sharon. B.S., So. Coll., 1963; M.B.A. in Health Services Mgmt., Century U., 1981. Adminstrv. dir. blood bank/immunology Hinsdale (Ill.) Med. Ctr., 1964-74; adminstrv. dir. lab. services Berrien Gen. Hosp., Berrien Center, Mich., 1974—, weekend hosp. adminstr.; univ. lectr. Active planning, participant local health fairs. Mem. Am. Coll. Hosp. Adminstrs., Am. Soc. Med. Tech. Seventh-Day Adventist. Home: Rt 1 PO Box 24 A Berrien Center MI 49102 Office: Berrien Gen Hosp 1250 Deans Hill Rd Berrien Center MI 49102

FILMON, GARY ALBERT, legislator, civil engineer; b. Winnipeg, Man., Can., Aug. 24, 1942; s. Albert and Anastasia (Doskocz) F.; m. Janice Clare Wainwright, 1963; children—Allison, David, Gregg, Susanna. B.Sc. in Civil Engring., U. Man., 1964, M.Sc., 1967. Registered profl. engr. Municipal design engr. Underwood McLellan and Assocs., Winnipeg, 1964-67, br. mgr., Brandon, Man., 1967-69; v.p. Success Bus. Coll., Winnipeg, 1969-71, pres., 1971-81. City councillor Queenston Ward, City of Winnipeg, 1975-77, Crescent Heights Ward, City of Winnipeg, 1977-79; mem. legis. assembly River Heights Constituency, Man., 1979-81, Tuxedo Constituency, Man., 1981—, minister consumer and corp. affairs and environment Man. Govt., 1981, leader of the opposition, 1983—; chmn. com. of works and ops. City of Winnipeg, 1977-79; dir. Winnipeg Jets Hockey Club, 1977-78. Mem. Assn. Profl. Engrs. (Providence of Man.), Assn. Can. Career Colls. (pres. 1974-75), U. Man. Alumni Assn. (pres. 1974-75). Progressive Conservative. Anglican. Office: Legis Assembly Province Of Manitoba Legislative Bldg Room 172 Winnipeg MB R3C OV8 Canada

FINCH, CHARLES RICHARD, chemical engineer; b. Memphis, Nov. 30, 1928; s. Charles Henry and Clara Gene (Kupperschmidt) F.; m. Shirley Rich Peery, Mar. 25, 1956; children—Valerie, Gregory, Steven, William. B.S. in Chem. Engring., U. Md., 1950, Ph.D., 1955. Registered profl. engr., Mich. Research assoc. Dow Chem. Co., Midland, Mich., 1956—. Contbr. articles to profl. jours. Served to 1st lt. USAF, 1954-56. Mem. Soc. Plastics Engrs. Republican. Lutheran. Avocations: gardening, camping. Home: 1280 E Chippewa Rd RR 12 Midland MI 48640 Office: Dow Chem Co 433 Bldg Midland MI 48640

FINCH, DAVID RICHARD, plastic surgeon; b. Kearny, N.J., Dec. 3, 1947; s. Charles Wesley and Fritzi (Wasserburger) F.; m. Susan Marie Drummond, May 20, 1972; children—Andrea Courtney, John Patrick. B.S., Ohio U., 1969; M.D., W.Va. U., 1973. Diplomate Am. Bd. Plastic Surgery. Intern, U. Wis., Madison, 1973-74, resident, 1974-78; practice medicine specializing plastic surgery, Appleton, Wis., 1978—. Fellow Am. Coll. Surgeons; mem. Am. Soc. Plastic and Reconstructive Surgeons, AMA (Physician's Recognition award), Wis. Soc. Plastic Surgeons, Midwest Soc. Plastic Surgeons. Republican. Avocations: Horseback riding; guitar playing. Office: David F Finch MD SC 1611 S Madison Appleton WI 54915

FINCH, HAROLD BERTRAM, JR., See *Who's Who in America,* 43rd edition.

FINCH, JUNE JOHNSON, educator; b. Chgo., June 6, 1927; d. Willard Thomas and Lucile Sarah (Adams) Johnson; m. William Hayes Finch, July 3, 1948; children—Lisa Lynnette, Tina Stephanie. Student Northwestern U., 1944; B.E., Chgo. State U., 1948; postgrad. DePaul U., 1953; M.A., Governors State U., 1977. Tchr., Hayes Sch., Chgo., 1948-53, Lewis Champlain Sch., Chgo., 1957-59, Dixon Sch., Chgo., 1959-70, Powell Sch., Chgo., 1973-76; math. lab. resource tchr., elem. math. tchr. tng. centers Chgo. Public Schs., 1970-73, coordinator living metric environment program, 1976-77, coordinator intensive math. improvement program, 1977—; instr. Loyola U., Chgo., summer 1972; cons. in field. Mem. Chatham-Avalon Community Council, Chgo.; active St. Monica's Guild, Social Service Guild. Named Tchr. of Yr., Dixon Sch., 1965, Outstanding Tchr., Powell Sch., 1978. Mem. Nat. Council Tchrs. of Math., Ill. Council Tchrs. of Math., Nat. Council Suprs. of Math., Chgo. Elem. Tchrs. of Math., Assn. for Supervision and Curriculum Devel., Met. Math. Club, Phi Delta Kappa, Delta Sigma Theta. Episcopalian. Clubs: Les Plus Belles, Paragons. Home: 8215 Saint Lawrence Ave Chicago IL 60619 Office: 1819 W Pershing Rd 6 Center SE Chicago IL 60609

FINCH, PEGGY ANNE, company executive, editor; b. Evergreen Park, Ill., Nov. 22, 1952; d. William Mathias and Ada Margaret (Ferguson) Schroeder; stepdau. Virginia Lee (Conn) Schroeder; m. Nathan Francis Finch, Nov. 20, 1982. Student Miami-Dade Coll., 1975-77. New accounts rep., sec. Comml. Bank, Miami, 1970-74; office mgr., adminstrv. asst. Conv. Contractors, Miami, 1974-80; office mgr., bookkeeper R. E. Alexander Ltd., Chgo., 1980-81; officer mgr., exec. sec. R. G. Ibbotson Assocs., Inc., Chgo., 1981-83, mktg. div. mgr., editor, 1983-84; mktg. support rep. J F M Bus. Systems, Inc., computer hardware and software vendor, Chgo., 1984—. Pres., founder South Suburban br. Am. Diabetes Assn., Flossmoor, Ill., 1982-83, chmn. Bike-A-Thon, Homewood, Ill., 1983; mem. pub. edn. com. Am. Diabetes Assn., No. Ill. affiliate, Chgo., 1983, mem. speakers bur. com., 1982—. Mem. Nat. Assn. Female Execs. Home: 1700 Forest Cove Dr Mount Pospect IL 60056 Office: J F M Business Systems Inc Merchandise Mart Suite 144 Chicago IL 60654

FINDL, JEFF DORE, petroleum geologist; b. Los Angeles, Feb. 18, 1956; s. Eugene and Dolores (Koppelman-Shindle) F. B.S. in Geology, Ohio State U., 1979. Analyst Core Lab., Inc., Wilmington, Calif., 1979; engring. geologist Found. Engring., Tarzana, Calif., 1979-81; head geologist Opex, Inc., Columbus, Ohio, 1981-82; ind. petroleum geologist, pres. J. F. Geology Co., Columbus, 1982—. Mem. Am. Assn. Petroleum Geologists, Ohio Oil and Gas Assn., Ohio Geol. Soc. Jewish. Avocations: jogging; skiing; guitar; travelling. Home and Office: 9 E Longview Ave Apt A Columbus OH 43202

FINE, HAROLD RONALD, government executive; b. Jordan Valley, Oreg., Jan. 31, 1933; s. Fredrick Harold and Elizabeth Mary Fine; m. Ree Edda Marie Fine, Dec. 15, 1962; children—Michael Joseph, Raymond K., LeAnna E., Lynna S. B.A., Coll. of Idaho, 1961; M.P.A., George Washington U., 1974, postgrad., 1983-84. C.P.A., Oreg.; With U.S. GAO, Seattle, 1961-69, staff mgr., 1969-72, asst. dir. personnel devel., 1972, asst. dir. Office of Staff Mgmt., 1973, asst. dir. field ops., 1975, asst. regional mgr., Washington and Cin., 1976-83; dir. program devel. div. Dept. Energy, Washington, 1983-84. Mem. Presdl. Adv. Com., 1981-82; mem. Congl. Adv. Com., 1979-83. Intergovtl. Affairs fellow, 1981-82. Mem. Am. Inst. C.P.A.s, Oreg. Soc. C.P.A.s, Am. Soc. Pub. Adminstrs., Assn. Govt. Accts., Am. Soc. C.P.A.s, Nat. Assn. Accts. Republican. Roman Catholic. Lodges: Rotary, Elks, Eagles. Office: 1000 Independence Ave Washington DC

FINEBERG, SAMUEL EDWIN, medical educator, researcher; b. Bridgeport, Conn., May 4, 1936; s. Gabriel and Sylvia (Zwerdling) F.; m. Naomi Esther Schwartz, Aug. 30, 1959; children—Rachel Judith, Samuel Abraham, Joshua Nathan. A.B., Dartmouth Coll., 1958; M.D., U. Vt., 1962. Diplomate Am. Bd. Internal Medicine. Intern, Hosp. U. Pa., Phila., 1962-63; resident in internal medicine Phila. Gen. Hosp., 1965-67; fellow in endocrinology John Hopkins U., Balt., 1967-68; fellow in endocrinology Boston U., 1968-70, instr., 1970-74, asst. prof., 1974-77; assoc. prof. Ind. U., Indpls., 1977-84, prof. medicine, 1984—. Contbr. articles to profl. jours. Treas. Bethel Zedeck, Indpls., 1983—. Served to capt. U.S. Army, 1962-65. Recipient Research and Devel. award Am. Diabetes Assn., 1974; NIH grantee, 1974-80. Fellow ACP; mem. So. Med. Assn., Am. Diabetes Assn. (pres. Ind. affiliate 1984-86), Endocrine Soc., Central Soc. Clin. Research, Am. Fedn. Clin. Research, Sigma Xi. Democrat. Jewish. Avocations: sailing, gardening, photography. Home: 7501 N Meridan St Indianapolis IN 46260 Office: Ind U Sch Medicine 1100 W Michigan Indianapolis IN 46202

FINEDORE, WILLIAM FRANCIS, SR., manufacturing company executive; b. Grand Rapids, Mich., Apr. 11, 1923; s. William and F. and Clara F.; m. Grace M. Brush, Apr. 28, 1952; children—William F., Thomas E., James G., Nancy C., Jeffrey P. Student pub. schs., Chgo. With mech. div. Kraft Foods, Morton Grove, Ill., 1945-62; from apprentice sheetmetal layout to leadman Dover div. Groen Mfg. Co., Elk Grove, Ill., 1962-72; from foreman to supt. custom div. Leedal Inc., Chgo., 1972-77; plant mgr. Bloomfield Indsl. div. Beatrice Foods, Chgo., 1977-78; dir. mfg., supt. custom div. Elkay Mfg. Co., Broadview, Ill., 1978—. Served with USMC, 1942-45. Recipient Ill. Swimming Assn. Swimming and Diving Ofcls. award, 1981; North Suburban YMCA Swim Coach award, 1973. Mem. Nat. Skeet Shooting Assn., Nat. Rifle Assn., Boat Owners Assn. U.S., Mfg. Mgrs. Assn. (past pres.), Republican. Roman Catholic. Clubs: Northbrook Sports, Gt. Lakes Cruising, Harbor Lite Yacht, Keymen's (pres. execs. Elkay Mfg. Co.). Home: 1850 Beechnut Rd Northbrook IL 60062 Office: 2700 S 17th Ave Broadview IL 60153

FINEFROCK, LAWRENCE CHARLES, retail furniture executive; b. Massillon, Ohio, May 31, 1947; s. Charles Raymond and Mary Elizabeth (Henrich) F.; m. Joan Elizabeth Forney, Mar. 20, 1971; children—Douglas, Kevin, Lauren. B.S. in Bus. Adminstrn., Georgetown U., 1969. Pres., C.O. Finefrock Co., Massillon, 1972—; dir. 1st Savs. and Loan Co., Massillon. Chmn. United Way Western Stark County, 1978; pres. bd. YMCA, Massillon, 1981-83; trustee Massillon Area Community Civic Trust Fund; chmn. bd. Better Bus. Bur. Stark County, 1984—. Served to lt. (j.g.) USNR, 1970-72. Mem. Interior Design Soc. (sec. local chpt. 1980-82), Nat. Home Furnishings Assn., Massillon C. of C. (pres. bd. 1976, J.S. Sanders award 1984). Republican. Roman Catholic. Avocations: tennis; volleyball.

FINESMITH, STEPHEN HARRIS, scientist, psychologist; b. N.Y.C., Nov. 7, 1934; s. Murray and Cele (Lerner) F.; B.B.A., Coll. City N.Y., 1955; postgrad. State U. N.Y. at Buffalo, 1955-59, 71-74, U. Wis., 1976-77, Wis. Sch. Profl. Psychology; m. Barbara Kaden, Aug. 28, 1955 (div. June 1977); children—Terri, Robin; m. Cher Halliday, Aug. 3, 1979 (div. Sept. 1979). Asso. scientist Systems Devel. Corp., Santa Monica, Cal., 1959-60; asst. prof. Rutgers U., New Brunswick, N.J., 1960-62; systems analyst Internat. Tel. & Tel. Co., Paramus, N.J., 1962-63; prin. systems design engr., head new techniques and systems group Univac div. Sperry Rand Corp., St. Paul, 1963-67; assoc. prof. U. So. Miss., Hattiesburg, 1967-68; assoc. prof. Mankato (Minn.) State Coll., 1968-71; prof. Governors State U., Park Forest South, Ill., 1971-72; pres., Serendipity Systems, Inc., Janesville, Wis., 1973-75, now chmn. bd.; prof., chmn. psychology dept. Milton (Wis.) Coll., 1972-76; asst. dir. Bur. Systems and Data Processing, Wis. Dept. Revenue, Madison, 1976-79; psychotherapist, communications therapist. Cons. In Mental Health, Janesville, 1973-74. Research scientist, human relations lab. cons., 1960—. Mem. Am. Psychol. Assn. (asso.), AAAS, Assn. Humanistic Psychology, Assn. for Computing Machinery. Club: Country (Lake Windsor, Wis.). Inventor bionic evolutionary adaptive stock trading system, 1964. Home: 222 Randolph Dr Apt 312A Madison WI 53717

FINK, JOHN PHILIP, magazine editor; b. Farmington, Ill., Mar. 15, 1926; s. Walter Philip and Alta Blanche (Payton) F.; m. Eloise Darlene Bradley, Aug. 8, 1949 (div.); children—Sara Elizabeth, Joel Bradley, Alison Erika. B.A., Millikin U., 1949; M.A., U. Ill.-Urbana, 1950; student U. Wis.-Madison, 1950-51. Reporter, City News Bur., Chgo., 1952-53; reporter, editor Chgo. Tribune, 1953-75, editor Tribune mag., 1963-75; exec. editor Regnery Pub., Chgo., 1975-77; editor Chicago mag., 1977—; instr. bus. writing Northwestern U. Evening Div., 1962-65, mag. writing Columbia Coll., Chgo., 1969-75. Served with USNR, 1944-46. Office: 303 E Wacker Dr Suite 800 Chicago IL 60601

FINK, KARL JULIUS, German language and literature educator, researcher; b. Delmont, S.D., Nov. 12, 1942; s. Emil Herman and Gertrude Luise (Grosz) F.; m. May 31, 1964; children—Charlie, Brian, Melissa. B.A., Wartburg Coll., 1964; M.A., U. Ariz., 1966; Ph.D., U. Ill., 1974. Cert. secondary sch. tchr., Iowa. Instr. Tex. Luther Coll., Seguin, 1966-67, Luther Coll., Decorah, Iowa, 1967-69; Fulbright tchr. Nicolaus Cusanus Gymnasium, Bonn, Fed. Republic Germany, 1969-70; vis. asst. prof. U. Ill., Urbana, 1974-77, So. Ill. U., Carbondale, 1977-78; asst. prof. U. Ky., Lexington, 1978-82; assoc. prof., chmn. German dept. St. Olaf Coll., Northfield, Minn., 1982—. Editor: The Quest for the New Science, 1979, Goethe as a Critic of Literature, 1984; corr. editor Eighteenth Century Life, 1983—. Contbr. articles on history of sci. and lit. to profl. jours. Recipient Grawemeyer award U. Louisville, 1979, Faculty Growth awards U. Ky., St. Olaf Coll., grantee Am. Philos. Soc., 1981. Mem. Am. Assn. German Tchrs., MLA, Am. Soc. Eighteenth Century Studies, German Soc. Eighteenth Century Research, Friends of Wolfenbuttel Library. Republican. Lutheran. Avocations: cross-country skiing; canoeing; cross-country bicycling. Home: 715 Orchard Place Northfield MN 55057 Office: St Olaf Coll Norhtfield MN 55057

FINKEL, BERNARD, public relations, fund-raising, and resource development executive, radio show host; b. Chgo., Nov. 12, 1926; s. Isadore and Sarah (Goldzweig) F.; m. Muriel Horwitz, Dec. 23, 1951; children—Phillip Stuart, Calvin Mandel, Norman Terry. Student Hebrew Theol. Coll., Chgo., 1939-44, Lewis Inst. Arts and Scis., Ill. Inst. Tech., Chgo., 1944-45, U. Ill.-Chgo., 1947-48; B.S. in Journalism, U. Ill., 1951. Reporter, rewriter Peacock Newspapers, Chgo., 1949, Defender Newspapers, Chgo., 1951, Chgo. North Side Newspapers, 1952; asst. dir. pub. relations Combined Jewish Appeal-Jewish Fedn. Met. Chgo., 1953; mng. editor Electric Appliance Service News, Chgo., 1954-57; asst. account exec. Burlingame-Grossman Advt., Chgo., 1957; account exec. Glassner & Assocs., Pub. Relations, Chgo., 1958-61; pub. relations cons. Bernard Finkel Assocs., Chgo., 1961—; dir. devel. and pub. relations Japanese Am. Service Com., Chgo., 1981—; owner, producer, host weekly radio show Jewish Community Hour, Sta. WONX-AM, Evanston, Ill. Author: Life and the World, 1947. Mem. pub. relations and youth commns. Village of Skokie, 1964-65; v.p., coach Boys Baseball, Skokie, 1963-67; mem. adv. bd., chmn. pub. relations Chgo. Area Career Conf., 1961-62; pres. Acad. Assocs. of Ida Crown Jewish Acad., Chgo., 1973-75; v.p. Hillel Torah North Suburban Day Sch., 1965-66, Congregation Or Torah, Skokie, 1970-71. Served with U.S. Army, 1945-46. Recipient awards for pub. service Jewish Community Hour, 1978, also awards Chgo. Rabbinical Council, Chgo. Bd. Rabbis, Council Traditional and Orthodox Synagogues of Greater Chgo., Midwest Region of Nat. Fedn. Jewish Men's Clubs, Israel Aliyah Ctr. of World Zionist Orgn., Religious Zionists of Chgo., B'nai B'rith Lodge of Survivors of Nazi Holocaust, others. Mem. Nat. Soc. Fund-Raising Execs., World Zionist Orgn., Pub. Relations Soc. Am., Publicity Club of Chgo. (profl. achievement awards). Lodges: B'nai B'rith. Home: 3300 Capitol St Skokie IL 60076 Office: 4427 N Clark St Chicago IL 60640

FINKELMEIER, PHILIP RENNER, lawyer; b. Cin., Sept. 5, 1914; s. Louis Philip and Lena (Renner) F.; m. Marion A. Oberling, June 24, 1936; children—Phyllis Ruth Finkelmeier Head, Robert Louis. J.D., Salmon P. Chase Law Sch., 1940. Bar: Ohio 1940, U.S. Dist. Ct. (so. dist.) Ohio 1949, U.S. Ct. Appeals (6th cir.) 1967, U.S. Supreme Ct. 1968. Dep., Indsl. Commn. Ohio, 1941-48; ptnr. Hoover, Beall & Eichel, Cin., 1948-58; sole practice, Cin., 1958-68; ptnr. Finkelmeier & Finkelmeier, Cin., 1968—; tchr. Chase Law Sch. Ruling elder Immanuel Presbyterian Ch. Mem. Ohio Bar Assn. (workers' compensation com.), ABA, Ohio Acad. Trial Lawyers, Assn. Trial Lawyers Am., Cin. Bar Assn. (workers' compensation com.). Club: Cincinnati. Lodges: Masons, Shriners. Home: 5300 Hamilton Ave #1700 Cincinnati OH 45224 Office: 524 Walnut St #808 Cincinnati OH 45202

FINKELSTEIN, LEO, JR., air force officer, communications specialist; b. Asheville, N.C., Aug. 24, 1946; s. Leo and Sylvia (Bein) F.; m. Phyllis Adele Baer, June 11, 1969. A.B., U. N.C., 1968; M.A., U. Tenn., 1969; Ph.D., Rensselaer Poly. Inst., 1978. Commd. 2d lt. U.S. Air Force, 1969, advanced through grades to lt. col., 1972; film producer, dir. Aerospace Audio Visual Service, Norton AFB, Calif., 1969-72; comdr. 601 Photo Flight, Korat, Thailand, 1972-73; assoc. prof. communication U.S. Air Force Acad., Colo., 1974-81; research asst. to comdr. Air Force Logistics Command, Wright Patterson AFB, Ohio, 1981; sci. research analyst Space Command, Peterson AFB, Colo. 1984-85, plans and programs specialist, 1985—. Contbr. articles to profl. jours. Decorated Bronze Star. Mem. Speech Communications Assn., Western Speech Communication Assn., Soc. Tech. Writers, Am. Radio Relay League. Jewish. Home: 385 Silver Spring Circle Colorado Springs CO 80919 Office: Space Command Peterson AFB CO 80914

FINKELSTEIN, RICHARD A., microbiologist, educator; b. N.Y.C., Mar. 5, 1930; m. Helen Rosenberg, Nov. 30, 1952; children—Sheryl, Mark, Laurie; m. Mary Boesman, June 20, 1976; 1 child, Sarina. B.S., U. Okla., 1950; M.A., U. Tex., 1952, Ph.D., 1955. Diplomate, Am. Bd. Microbiology. Teaching fellow, research scientist U. Tex., Austin, 1950-55; fellow in microbiology, instr. U. Tex. Southwestern Med. Sch., Dallas, 1955-58; chief bioassay sect. Walter Reed Army Inst. Research, Washington, 1958-64; dep. chief dept. Bacteriology and mycology U.S. Army Med. Component, SEATO Med. Research Lab., Bangkok, 1964-67; assoc. prof. dept. microbiology U. Tex. Southwestern Med. Sch., Dallas, 1967-79; prof., chmn. dept. microbiology Sch. Medicine, U. Mo., Columbia, 1979—; cons. and lectr. in field. Contbr. chpts. to books, articles to profl. jours. Mem. numerous editorial bds. profl. jours. including: Toxin Revs., 1981—. Patentee in field. Served with USAR, 1950-66. Recipient numerous awards for excellence in microbiology, most recent: named Hon. Prof., Free U. of Herborn, Fed. Republic Germany, 1984. Fellow Am. Acad. Microbiology, Infectious Diseases Soc. Am.; mem. Am. Assn. Immunologists, Soc. Gen. Microbiology, Am. Soc. Microbiology (pres. Tex. br. 1974-75, div. counselor 1985—), Pathol. Soc. Great Britain and Ireland, Sigma Xi. Address: M264 Med Scis Bldg U Mo Columbia MO 65211

FINKELSTEIN, STANLEY MICHAEL, engineering educator, research biomedical engineer; b. Bklyn., June 16, 1941. B.S. in Elec. Engring., Poly. Inst. Bklyn., 1962, M.S. in Elec. Engring., 1964, Ph.D. in Elec. Engring. and Systems Sci., 1969. Asst. prof. Poly. Inst. Bklyn., 1968-74, assoc. prof., 1974-77; assoc. prof. U. Minn., Mpls., 1977—; lectr. Mt. Sinai Sch. Medicine, N.Y.C.. Contbr. articles to profl. jours. Active High Sch. Curriculum Adv. Com., St. Louis Park, 1984-85, High Sch. Adv. Com., 1983-85, Scholarship Awards Com., 1983-85; NDEA grad. fellow, 1962-64; NSF faculty fellow in sci., 1975-77. Mem. Engring. Medicine and Biology Soc. (sr., vice chmn. 1984, chmn. 1985), Biomed. Engring. Soc. (sr.), N.Y. Acad. Scis., AAAS, Assn. Advancement Med. Instrumentation, Cardiovascular System Dynamics Soc., Acad. Clin. Lab. Physicians and Scientists, Sigma Xi. Avocations: hiking; biking; cross country skiing; jogging. Office: U Minn Dept Lab Medicine and Pathology Div Health Computer Scis Box 511 Mayo Bldg Minneapolis MN 55455

FINLEY, HAROLD MARSHALL, investment manager, financial author; b. McConnelsville, Ohio, Feb. 24, 1916; s. Harry M. and Kate Conklin (Cotton) F.; m. Jean Rowley, Sept. 19, 1943; 1 child, Robert W. B.S. cum laude, Northwestern U., 1933; B.D. cum laude, Chgo. Theol. Sem., 1944; LL.D. (hon.), Lincoln Meml. U., 1975. Vice-pres. Chgo. Title & Trust Co., 1963-76; sr. v.p. Burton J. Vincent, Chesley & Co., Chgo., 1976-84, Prescott, Ball & Turben, Chgo., 1984—; dir. Bank of Lockport, Ill., Desoto Securities Co., Chgo. Author: Everybody's Guide to the Stock Market, 1955; The Logical Approach to Successful Investing, 1970; columnist. Mem. High Sch. Bd., Lockport, 1961-64; trustee Alice Lloyd Coll., Pippa Passes, Ky., 1967—, Kobe Coll., Japan, 1976—, Chgo. Theol. Sem., 1977—, Lewis U., Lockport, 1978—, Lincoln Meml. U., Harrogate, Tenn., 1981—; bd. dirs. Boys' and Girls' Clubs of Chgo., 1977—; pres. Rotary Club of Chgo., 1978-79; chmn. Lockport Area Devel. Commn., 1982-85. Mem. Investment Analysts Soc. Chgo. (sec. 1959), Phi Beta Kappa, Delta Sigma Pi. Congregationalist. Club: U. Chgo. Home: 630 E 12th St Lockport IL 60441 Office: Prescott Ball & Turben 230 W Monroe St Chicago IL 60606

FINLEY, NICHOLAS FRANCIS, information systems professional; b. Chgo., Aug. 26, 1946; s. Nicholas F. and Laura H. (Busking) F.; m. Judith A. Kurtys, Nov. 22, 1965 (div. 1976); children—Sean Michael, Brian Edward; m.

Sandra L. Cormican, June 2, 1984. Assoc. in Computer Sci., Daly City Coll. Systems analyst John Nuveen & Co., Chgo., 1972-74; systems mgr. C.B.A., 1974-77; mgr. programming services Midas Muffler, 1977-80; dir. mgmt. info. systems Edward Hines Lumber Co., Chgo., 1981—. Served with U.S. Army, 1966-70. Decorated Army Commendation medal. Mem. Am. Mgmt. Assn., Assn. for Systems Mgmt. Republican. Avocations: oil painting; skiing; trap shooting; golf. Office: Edward Hines Lumber Co 2431 S Wolcott St Chicago IL 60608

FINN, MARY MURPHY, orchestra administrator; b. Phila., June 27, 1939; d. Albert Vincent and Mary Catherine (Martin) Murphy; B.A. in Art, Duchesne Coll., 1961; B.A. in Music, St. Mary's Coll., Omaha, 1962; children by previous marriage—Thomas Jerard, Mary Catherine. Tchr. instrumental music Council Bluffs (Iowa) Public Schs., 1961-63; asst. mgr. Omaha Symphony Orch., 1969-75; mgr. Nebr. Chamber Orch., Lincoln, 1975-77; exec. dir. Omaha Pops Orch., 1977—; free-lance comml. artist, 1957—; cons. computer programming, 1977—; systems analyst Automation Inc., 1979—; violinist Omaha Symphony Orch., Lincoln Symphony, Sioux City Symphony bd. dirs. Voices of Omaha; music contractor for Labor Unions' Septemberfest. Recipient Service awards Omaha Musicians Assn., 1977 through 1984; numerous scholarships. Mem. Am. Fedn. Musicians, Am. Symphony Orch. League, Chamber Music Players Am. Democrat. Roman Catholic. Contbr. articles to various publs. Home and Office: 5167 Jackson St Omaha NE 68106

FINN, MICHAEL STEPHEN, municipal utility executive; b. Princeton, Ill., Aug. 23, 1941; s. Eugene Calvin and Virginia (Maupin) F.; m. Maryann Catherine Frkol, June 15, 1974; children—Shelley Jean, Kristi Lynn, Joseph Michael, Eugene Stephen. B.S., Western Ill. U., 1963; Advanced Cert., Augustana Coll., Rock Island, Ill., 1964; Cert. Exec. Devel. Ctr., U. Ill., 1979. Speech therapist, audiologist Rock Falls Sch., Ill., 1964-66, Western Schs., Buda, Ill., 1966-68, Spring Valley Schs., Ill., 1968-78; asst. mgr. utilities City of Princeton, Ill., 1978-81, mgr. utilities, supt. water, 1981—; water utility cons., 1975-78. Co-publicity chmn. Princeton Homestead Festival, 1982-83; div. chmn. Bur. County United Way, 1983-84; mem. Princeton Econ. Devel. Bd., 1984; dist. com. Boy Scouts Am., 1982. Recipient award for outstanding leadership City of Princeton, 1982—. Mem. Am. Water Works Assn., Am. Pub. Power Assn., Ill. Mcpl. Utilities Assn. (bd. dirs., treas.), Ill. Mcpl. Electric Agy. (bd. dirs., treas.), Ill. Portable Water Supply Operation, Am. Mgmt. Assn. Roman Catholic. Clubs: Optimists, Newcomers. Avocations: amateur radio, golf, reading, stamp collecting. Home: 766 Anita Ln Princeton IL 61356 Office: Princeton Mcpl Utilities 2 S Main St Princeton IL 61356

FINNARN, THEODORE ORA, lawyer; b. Greenville, Ohio, Aug. 20, 1949; s. Theodore Lincoln and Jeannie (Kelman) F.; B.Ed., Miami U., 1972; J.D. cum laude, U. Toledo, 1976; m. Holly C. Bankson, Sept. 15, 1973; children—Shawn April, Theodore O., Thomas A. Acting dir. Preble County Community Action Com., 1973, program developer, 1972-73; chief agrl. engr. Finnarn Farms, Greenville, Ohio, 1976—; admitted to Ohio bar, 1976, U.S. Dist. Ct. So. Ohio bar, 1978; individual practice law, Greenville, 1976—; sec.-treas. Finnarn Devel. Corp., 1977—. Bd. dirs. Darke County Center for Arts; active Greenville Friends of the Library, 1977—; sec.-treas. Greenville Boys Clubs, Inc., 1977—. Mem. Assn. Trial Lawyers Am., Ohio Acad. Trial Lawyers, Am., Ohio, Darke County bar assns., Ohio Farmers Union, Darke County Farmers Union (sec.-treas.), Scribes, Phi Alpha Delta. Democrat. Presbyterian. Editor articles in legal jours. Home: 3060 US Rt 127S Greenville OH 45331 Office: 127 W 5th St Greenville OH 45331

FINNEGAN, THOMAS JOSEPH, lawyer; b. Chgo., Aug. 18, 1900; s. Thomas Harrison and Marie (Flanagan) F.; J.D., Chgo. Kent Coll. of Law, 1923; m. Hildreth Millslagel, July 1, 1933 (dec. Mar. 1977). Admitted to Ill. bar, 1923, and since practiced in Chicago; mem. firm Fithian, Spengler & Finnegan, 1935-51; mem. firm Korshak, Oppenheim & Finnegan, 1951—. Mem. ABA, Fed., Ill., Chgo. bar assns., Chgo. Law Inst., Phi Alpha Delta. Home: 5630 Sheridan Rd Chicago IL 60660 Office: 69 W Washington St Chicago IL 60602

FINNEY, FREDERICK MARSHALL, cost analyst, writer, educator; b. Troy, Ala., Nov. 18, 1941; s. Marshall and Lucille (Curtis) F.; m. Gladys Turner, July 1, 1972. B.A. in History, Wilberforce U., 1967; M.A. in Edn., Antioch Coll., 1969; M.S. in Econs., Wright State U., 1973; Ph.D. in Work Econs., U. Cin., 1980. Intern supr., asst. prof. edn. Antioch Grad. Sch., 1968-70; program analyst City of Dayton, Ohio, 1969-70, evaluation dir., 1970-76; numismatic writer, 1972—; prof. econs., bus. and polit. sci. U. Cin., Capital U., and Sinclair Community Coll., 1976-82; cost analyst U.S. Air Force, 1983; founder Econ. Research Ctr., Inc. and Confrontation/Change Rev.; authority on paper money of U.S. Contbr. over 300 articles to profl. publs. Editor and pub. Econ. Research Ctr. Revs., 1973. Office: Air Force Logistics Command Wright-Patterson AFB OH 45433

FINNEY, JOAN MARIE MCINROY, state treasurer of Kansas; b. Topeka, Feb. 12, 1925; d. Leonard L. and Mary M. (Sands) McInroy; B.A., Washburn U., Topeka, Kans.; m. Spencer W. Finney, Jr., July 24, 1957; children—Sally, Dick, Mary. Sec. Washington and Topeka offices U.S. Senator Frank Carlson, 1953-69; commr. elections Shawnee County, Kans., 1970-72; adminstrv. asst. to mayor of Topeka, 1973-74; treas. State of Kans., Topeka, 1974—. Pres., Girls' Club Topeka, 1981; mem. Kans. Young Dems.; mem. Nat. Human Rights Com. for POW-MIA's; mem. Mended Hearts, Inc. Mem. Kans. Women's Polit. Caucus, Am. Legion Aux., Nat. Assn. State Auditors, Comptrollers and Treas. (2d v.p.), Nat. Assn. State Treas., Nat. Assn. Unclaimed Property Adminstrs. (v.p.), Bus. and Profl. Women's Club (Woman of Yr. 1980), Sigma Alpha Iota. Democrat. Roman Catholic (bd. dirs. mem. fin. com.). Clubs: Century, Jeffersonian. Office: Office of State Treasurer 535 Kansas PO Box 737 Topeka KS 66603

FINNK, HOWARD, dental surgeon; b. Detroit, Aug. 31, 1946; s. William and Ethel (Etkin) F.; m. Lynn Rhoda Margolin, July 7, 1968; children—Amy, Steven. B.S. in Psychology, Wayne State U., 1968; D.D.S., U. Detroit, 1972. Substitute tchr. Detroit Pub. Schs., 1968-72; warehouseman Standard Electric Co., Pontiac, Mich., 1969; clk./carrier U.S. Post Office, Detroit, 1966-72; assoc. clinician to dentist, Birmingham, Mich., 1972, Redford, Mich., 1972-73; practice dental surgery, Warren, Mich., 1973—; clin. assoc. Macomb Project Dental Health, Mt. Clemens, Mich., 1974-81. Mem. ADA, Mich. Dental Assn., Detroit Dist. Dental Soc., Macomb Dental Soc., Alpha Omega (pres. 1971-72), Acad. Gen. Dentistry. Jewish. Office: 30050 Hoover Rd Warren MI 48093

FINSTAD, MARTIN M., ret. educator; b. Winger, Minn., Feb. 11, 1900; s. Martin and Martha (Lutness) F.; B.A., St. Olaf Coll., 1920; postgrad U. Minn., 1921-22; B.D., Chgo. Luth. Theol. Sem., 1934; M.A. in Edn., Northwestern U., 1936, M.A. in History and Social Studies, 1939, postgrad. 1944-45; M.Div., Luth. Sch. Theology, Chgo., 1972; m. Gertrude Gilbert, May 29, 1930 (dec.); m. 2d, Olga Winter Dicke, Sept. 9, 1978. Prin. Nelson (Minn.) Consol. Sch., 1920-21; supt. Montrose (Minn.) Pub. Schs., 1922-24; tchr. history Stillwater (Minn.) High Sch., 1924-31; instr. social studies Proviso Twp. High Sch., Maywood, Ill., 1934-65, instr. psychology evening sch., 1944-55. Pres. Maywood Pub. Library Bd., 1955-69; village clk., Maywood, 1961-69; active other civic affairs. Bd. dirs. Chgo. Luth. Theol. Sem., 1954-63. Served with U.S. Army, 1918. Recipient Churchman of Yr. award Ch. Fedn. Greater Chgo., 1958. Mem. Nat. Council for Social Studies, Adult Edn. Assn., ALA, Internat. Inst. Mcpl. Clks., NEA, Am. Legion (vice comdr. Ill. 1950-51), Ill. Tchrs. Assn. (dir. 1958-61), Phi Delta Kappa. Republican. Lutheran. Clubs: Masons (32 deg.), KT, Shriners. Contbr. articles to profl. jours. Home: 350 W Schaumburg Rd A352 Schaumburg IL 60194

FINSTER, MARK P., statistics educator; b. Milw., Oct. 27, 1948; s. Milton R. Finster and Eleonore B. (Worgull) Helvey. B.A., U. Wis.-Madison, 1970; Ph.D., U. Mich., 1976. Asst. prof. Cornell U., Ithaca, N.Y., 1976-79, Johns Hopkins U., Balt., 1979-80, U. Ky., Lexington, 1980-81, U. Wis.-Madison, 1981—. Author articles in field. NSF fellow, 1970-74, grantee, 1976-79; Horace H. Rackham grantee, 1973-76; Inst. Tech. Bandung grantee, Indonesia, 1980; Wis. Alumni Research Found. grantee, 1985. Mem. Am. Statis. Assn., Inst. Math. Stats., Am. Math. Soc. Avocations: dancing; mountaineering. Office: U Wis Commerce Bldg 1155 Observatory Dr Madison WI 53706

FIRENZE, LOUIS JOHN, business educator; b. Englewood, N.J., Apr. 17, 1948; s. Carmine Louis and Freda Ida (Hess) F.; m. Judith Suzanne Williams, Feb. 15, 1952; children—Michael Carmine, Beth Marie. B.S., Central Mich. U., 1970; M.B.A., 1972; Ph.D., Mich. State U., 1982. Time study mgmt. staff Ferro Mfg. Co., Mt. Pleasant, Mich., 1971-72; purchasing agt. Delta Strapping Industries, N.Y.C., 1973-74; assoc. prof. bus. Northwood Inst., Midland, Mich., 1974—, dir. bus. div., 1984—; cons. in external plans of study. Chmn. Isabella County Republican Com., 1981-82. Mem. Acad. Mgmt., Council Advancement Experiential Learning, Phi Delta Kappa, Sigma Iota Epsilon. Roman Catholic. Home: 468 W Remus Rd Mount Pleasant MI 48858 Office: Northwood Inst Midland MI 48640

FIRESTONE, RICHARD F., chemistry educator; b. Canton, Ohio, June 18, 1926; s. Lester Ellis and Elizabeth Mary (Corkran) F.; m. Olwen Margaret Huskins, Aug. 21, 1943; children—William, Mark, Robert. A.B., Oberlin Coll., 1950; Ph.D., U. Wis.-Madison, 1954. Research assoc. Argonne Nat. Lab., Ill., 1954-56; asst. prof. Western Res. U., Cleve., 1956-61; assoc. prof. Ohio State U., Columbus, 1961-67, prof. chemistry, 1967—. Served with USNR, 1944-46, PTO. Fellow AAAS; mem. Am. Chem. Soc., Am. Phys. Soc., AAUP, Sigma Xi. Unitarian. Office: Ohio State Univ 140 W 18th Ave Columbus OH 43210

FIRKINS, STEPHEN WILLIAM, educational administrator; b. Independence, Mo., Nov. 29, 1947; s. Lynn Wood and Margaret Louise (Arthur) F.; m. Kammeron Kay Carlton, Nov. 7, 1970; children—Stephanie Kay, JaLynn Chrystal. B.S. in Edn., Emporia State U., 1970, M.S. in Edn., 1980. Tchr. pub. high schs., Kans., 1971-76, 1978-80; asst. prin. Augusta Jr. High Sch., Kans., 1980-84; prin. Valley Falls High Sch., Kans., 1984—. Named Area Athletic Dir. of Yr. for jr. high schs. Kans. Athletic Dirs. Assn., 1983-84. Mem. Nat. Interscholastic Athletic Adminstrs. Assn., Nat. Assn. Secondary Sch. Prons., Nat. Assn. Student Activity Advisors, United Sch. Adminstrs. Kans., Kans. Assn. Secondary Sch. Prins. Republican. Mem. Christian Ch. Lodge: Lions. Avocations: jogging, bicycling. Office: Unified Sch Dist #338 601 Elm Valley Falls KS 66088

FISCH, JONATHAN ALAN, obstetrician, gynecologist; b. Indpls., Feb. 28, 1946; s. Charles and June (Spiegal) F.; m. Marcia Ellen Kusnitz, June 22, 1969; children—Stephen, Allison. B.A., Johns Hopkins U., 1968; M.D., Ind. U., 1972. Resident in Ob-Gyn, St. Vincent Hosp. and Med. Center, Indpls., 1972-77; practice medicine specializing in Ob-Gyn, Indpls., 1977—; clin. instr. Ob-Gyn, St. Vincent Hosp. and Med. Center. Active Pickwick Commons Civic Assn. Inland Contained Corp. scholar, 1968. Mem. Am. Coll. Obstetricians and Gynecologists, AMA, Ind. State Med. Assn., Marion County Med. Assn. Club: Broadmoor Country. Office: 8330 Naab Rd Suite 302 Indianapolis IN 46260

FISCHER, HOWARD DAVID, cell and molecular biologist; b. Melrose Park, Ill., May 24, 1955; s. Howard Bremer and Gertrude Hildegarde (Buch) F.; m. Eileen Maloney, June 3, 1978; 1 child, David Daniel. A.B., Wash. U., 1977, Ph.D., 1981. Research assoc. Wash. U., 1981-82; Searle Fund postdoctoral fellow Northwestern U., 1982; NIH postdoctoral fellow, 1983; research fellow Northwestern U., 1983-84; scientist Upjohn Co., Kalamazoo, 1984—, research scientist, 1985—; teaching asst. molecular cloning of eukaryotic genes Cold Spring Harbor Lab., N.Y., 1982. Contbr. articles (16) to profl. jours. Mem. AAAS, Phi Beta Kappa. Office: Upjohn Co 1400-89-1 Kalamazoo MI 49001

FISCHER, JACK LEE, architect; b. Appleton, Wis., Oct. 31, 1953; s. Milton J. and Erma I. (Springstroh) F.; m. Karen R. Adler, Jan. 2, 1982. Student U. Wis.-Stout, 1972-73; B.S., U. Wis.-Milw., 1976, M. Arch., 1978. Pres. Jack L. Fischer Constrn. Co., Appleton, 1970-75, Contemporary Dwellings, Inc., Appleton, 1976-81, Fischer Schutte & Jensen, Inc., Appleton, 1978-82; v.p., dir. Marathon Engrs., Architects, Planners, Inc., Menasha, Wis., 1982—. Prin. works include Earth Shelter Residence, Appleton (Nat. Design award 1979), Tenterasol I Residential Design, Mpls. (Nat. Design award 1979), Earth Shelter Residences, St. Paul (Earth Shelters award 1980). Mem. Am. Planning Assn. (charter 1978), AIA, Wis. Soc. Architects, C. of C., (planning com. 1980-83). Lutheran. Lodge: Elks. Avocations: scuba diving; skiing; nature enthusiast; drawing; boating. Home: 1821 N Blossom Dr Appleton WI 54914

FISCHER, KLAUS PAUL, heavy equipment manufacturing and construction company executive, lawyer; b. Peine, W.Ger., Feb. 6, 1947; came to U.S., 1951, naturalized, 1962; s. Max Paul and Elizabeth F.; m. Patricia Louise Crawley, Aug. 9, 1975; children—Douglas Paul, Jennifer Lynne. B.A. in Polit. Sci. cum laude, U. Akron, 1969, J.D., 1976. Bar: Ohio 1976, U.S. Dist. Ct. (no. dist.) Ohio 1978. Loss control rep. Fireman's Fund Ins. Co., Cleve., 1971-74; contract analyst, contracts-legal, fossil power div. Babcock & Wilcox, Barberton, Ohio, 1974-76, staff atty. legal dept., 1976-79, mgr. legal dept., indsl. and marine div., Canton, Ohio, 1979-83, regional mgr. corp. law dept. McDermott, Inc., Lynchburg, 1983—; adj. prof. grad. bus. program Lynchburg Coll., 1983—. Bd. dirs. Lynchburg Mental Health Assn. Served to 1st lt. AUS, 1971-72, Korea. Mem. Ohio State Bar Assn., VFW. Republican. Avocations: racquetball; swimming; jogging; hunting.

FISCHER, PATRICIA ANN, financial analyst; b. Enid, Okla., July 16, 1957; d. James R. and JoAnn (Wagner) F. B.A., U. Chgo., 1979; M.B.A., Loyola U., Chgo., 1984. Telecommunications analyst Carson Pirie Scott & Co., Chgo., 1982; research asst. Loyola U., Chgo., 1982-83; planning analyst Fed. Res. Bank, Chgo., 1983-85; sr. fin. analyst Fed. Res. Bank, Chgo., 1985—. Mem. Phi Beta Kappa, Beta Gamma Sigma. Office: Fed Res Bank 230 S LaSalle St 14th Floor Chicago IL 60690

FISCHER, PHYLLIS LENORE, animal rights activist, beauty shop executive; b. Parkersburg, W.Va., June 24, 1951; d. Robert Paul and June (Fultz) F.; m. Richard Morgan, May 1975; 1 son, Richard. B.S. summa cum laude, Ohio U., 1973. Founder, Writers for Animal Rights, Jonesboro, Tenn., 1978-83; founder, dir. Mobilization for Animals, Columbus, Ohio, 1981-84; founder Protect Our Earth's Treasures, Columbus, 1984-85; founder Care about the Strays, New Albany, Ohio, 1985—; speaker, media cons. several orgns., 1985—; mng. dir. Topcuts, Inc., Columbus, 1983—. Author numerous published poems. Editor Black Cat jour., 1975—. Avocations: writing; lecturing; rescuing stray animals. Home: PO Box 474 New Albany OH 43054

FISCHER, ROBBINS WARREN, oilseed industry consulting company executive; b. Turin, Iowa, Mar. 31, 1919; s. Lewis Warren and Edith (Robbins) F.; B.A., U. Colo., 1942, postgrad., Sch. Law, 1944-45 postgrad. Rutgers U., 1954; m. Jean Noreen Greenawalt, Apr. 10, 1943; children—Barbara Jean, Martha Lou, Dorothy Ellen. Co-owner, operator Fischer Farms, Turin, 1947-53; sales promotion mgr. Payway Feed Mills, Kansas City, Mo., 1953-55; regional sales mgr. Bristol Myers Co., Kansas City, 1956-58; campaign dir. Burrell, Inc., Kansas City, 1958-59; asst. to pres. Soybean Council Am., Waterloo, Iowa, 1960-63; pres. Soypro Internat., Inc., Cedar Falls, 1963—, Soypro of Iowa, Cedar Falls, 1973—, Internat. Bus. Assos., Cedar Falls, 1965—; v.p. Continental Soya, Manning, Iowa, 1973-81; chmn. bd., chief exec. officer Burst Products, Denison, Iowa, 1979-82; vice chmn. Iowa Farm Council, 1950-53; mem. Pres. Kennedy's Task Force on Internat. Trade in Agrl. Products, 1962, Pres. Reagan's Task Force on Internat. Agrl. Devel., 1982—; chmn. food and agr. com. Pres. Reagan's Task Force on Internat. Pvt. Enterprise, 1983-84; mem. Agribus. Devel. Council, 1982—, Agri-Tech. Com. on Oilseeds and Products, 1982—. Mem. Cedar Falls C. of C. (dir.), Inst. Food Technologists, Monona Harrison Flood Control Assn. (pres. 1951-54), Phi Beta Kappa, Delta Sigma Rho, Pi Gamma Mu. Congregationalist. Club: Des Moines. Lodges: Rotary, Masons. Home: 5614 University Ave Cedar Falls IA 50613 Office: 314 Main St Cedar Falls IA 50613

FISCHLER, BARBARA BRAND, library administrator, educator; b. Pitts., May 24, 1930; d. Carl Frederick and Emma Georgia (Piltz) Brand; m. Edward McGough, Aug. 15, 1953 (div. Dec. 1957); m. 2d Drake Anthony Fischler, June 3, 1961; 1 son, Owen Wesley. A.B. cum laude, Wilson Coll., 1952; M.M. with distinction, Ind. U., 1954, A.M. in Library Sci., 1964. Asst. reference librarian Ind. U., Bloomington, 1958-61, asst. librarian undergrad. library, 1961-63, acting librarian undergrad. library, 1963, part-time vis. and assoc. prof Sch. Library and Info. Sci., 1972—, counselor/coordinator, Indpls., 1974-82; circulation librarian Ind. U.-Purdue U. at Indpls., 1970-76, pub. services librarian univ. library-sci., engring. and tech. unit, 1976-81, acting dir. univ. libraries, 1981-82, dir. univ. libraries, 1982—; cons. in field. Contbr. articles to library jours. Vol. tchr. St. Thomas Aquinas Sch., Indpls., 1974-75; fund raiser Am. Cancer Soc., Indpls., 1975, Indpls. Mus. Art, 1971, Am. Heart Assn., 1985 mem. core com., program chairperson Ind. Gov.'s Conf. on Libraries and Info. Services, Indpls., 1976-78; bd. advisors N.Am. Wildlife Park Found.; bd. dirs. Historic Amusement Found Inc. Recipient Outstanding Service award Central Ind. Area Library Services Authority, 1979. Mem. ALA, Ind. Library Assn. (vice chmn. coll. and univ. div. 1976-77, chmn. 1977-78, vice chmn. library edn. div. 1980-81, chmn. 1981-82, treas. 1984—), Central Ind. Kennel Club (bd. dirs. 1985—), German Shepherd Dog Club of Central Ind. (sec. 1973-74, pres. 1978-79), Wabash Valley German Shepherd Dog Club (sec. 1980-81, 83-85, pres. 1982-83). Beta Phi Mu, Pi Kappa Lambda. Republican. Presbyterian. Club: Central Ind. Kennel (bd. dirs. 1985-87). Home: 4232 Central Ave Indianapolis IN 46205 Office: Univ Library Ind U-Purdue U at Indpls 815 W Michigan St Indianapolis IN 46202

FISH, CARLTON THOMAS, architect; b. Decatur, Ill., Nov. 24, 1945; s. Russel Allen and Mary Edith (Allen) F.; m. Merrilyn Kay Campbell, Aug. 20, 1966; children—Edith Lynn, Jason Lee. A.Arch., So. Ill. U., 1965; B.Arch., U. Okla., 1977, B.S. in Environ. Design, 1977. Registered architect Okla., Mo., Tenn., Tex., Ga., Ohio, Nat. Council Archtl. Registration Bds. Assoc. architect Locke Wright Foster, Architects, Oklahoma City, 1971-78; corp. architect Silver Dollar City, Inc., Marvel Cave Park, Mo., 1978—. Served with U.S. Army, 1967-71. Mem. AIA, Mo. Council Architects. Republican. Baptist. Architect of record for WhiteWater amusement parks, Branson, Mo., Oklahoma City, Grand Prairie, Tex., Garland, Tex., Marietta, Ga.

FISH, FEROL FREDRIC, scientist, research institute executive; b. East Chicago, Ind., Jan. 15, 1930; s. Ferol Fredric and Edna Mae (Arms) F.; m. Joline McVicker, June 6, 1956 (div. 1983); children—Ferol, Molly, Ruth, Hannah, Matthew; m. Lois Ann Stewart, May 21, 1983. B.S., Ind. U., 1955, M.A., 1957; Ph.D., Pa. State U., 1961. Geophys. investigator N.J. Zinc, Palmerton, Pa., 1960-63; sr. scientist Gen. Dynamics, Ft. Worth, 1963-64, McDonnell-Douglas, Santa Monica, Calif., 1964-68; mgr. applied physics Borg-Warner Research Ctr., Des Plaines, Ill., 1968-78; mgr. phys. sci. Gas Research Inst., Chgo., 1979—. Contbr. articles to profl. jours. Served with U.S. Army, 1948-51. NSF fellow, 1958-60. Mem. Am. Geophys. Union, Soc. Petroleum Engrs., Am. Inst. Chem. Engrs. Methodist. Home: 804 N Kaspar Arlington Heights IL 60004 Office: Gas Research Inst 8600 W Bryn Mawr Chicago IL 60631

FISH, JAMES STUART, advertising consultant, college dean; b. Mt. Pleasant, Iowa, Sept. 8, 1915; s. Don E. Fish and Avlerda B. (Osborn) Thompson; m. Dorothea June Merritt, Nov. 3, 1941; children—James Stuart, Richard Merritt, Nancy Osborn. B.A., U. Minn., 1937; postgrad. Northwestern U., 1937-38. With Gen. Mills, Inc., Mpls., 1938-79, v.p. advt. and mktg. services, 1953-79, sr. v.p. corp. communications, 1976-79; pres. Ad-Ventures in Wayzata, Minn., 1979—; dean grad. programs in bus. communications Coll. St. Thomas, St. Paul, 1983—; dir. Northwest Teleprodns., Mpls., Quantum, Inc., Mpls- Bd. dirs. Wayzata Crime Prevention Coalition, 1980—; pres., bd. dirs. Wayzata Hist. Soc., 1981—. Served to lt. USNR, 1943-46; PTO. Recipient AAF-Printer's Ink Silver medal Mpls. Ad Club, 1966; Disting. Alumnus award U. Minn., 1984, Outstanding Achievement award, 1984; named to Advt. Hall of Fame, 1984. Fellow Am. Acad. Advt.; mem. Am. Advt. Fedn. (chmn. bd. 1976- 77, bd. dirs.), Advt. Council (bd. dirs. 1970-79, bd. dirs. emeritus 1979—), Advt. Fedn. Minn. (pres. 1959-60, bd. dirs.), Advt. Research Found. (bd. dirs. 1960-63), Assn. Nat. Advertisers (bd. dirs. 1962-64). Republican. Congregationalist. Mpls. C. of C. (bd. dirs. 1977-79), Wayzata C. of C. (bd. dirs. 1981-84). Clubs: Wayzata Country (pres. 1962-63); Minneapolis, Skylight (Mpls.). Avocations: travel; sketching. Home: 19005 12th Ave N Plymouth MN 55447 Office: College St Thomas 2115 Summit Ave Saint Paul MN 55105

FISH, SHIRLEY WILSON, investment executive; b. Worthington, Minn., Mar. 15, 1936; d. Cecil Lloyd and Ruth Irene (Shore) Wilson; m. Merton Raymond Fish, June 7, 1964. B.B.A., U. Minn., 1958. Chartered fin. analyst. Economics research asst. Harris Trust & Savs. Bank, Chgo., 1958-64, security analysis research asst., 1966-77, investment portfolio mgt., v.p., 1977—. Mem. The Investment Analysts Soc. Chgo., D.A.R. Avocations: photography, bridge. Office: Harris Trust and Savs Bank 111 W Monroe St Chicago IL 60690

FISH, WILLIAM EDWARD, optometrist; b. Washington, Ind., Aug. 12, 1952; s. John W. and Alma (Sipes) F.; m. Mary L., June 26, 1976; children—Jessica L., Jennifer D. B.S., Ind. U., 1974, O.D., 1976. Gen. practice optometry, Gibson City, Ill., 1977—. Mem. Ill. Optometric Assn., East Central Optometric Soc. (pres. 1983—). Methodist. Lodge: Lions (bd. dirs. 1982-84). Avocation: organist. Home: 411 E 14th St Gibson City IL 60936 Office: 207 N Sangamon Ave Gibson City IL 60936

FISH, WILLIAM LEWIS, purchasing executive; b. Phila., Apr. 7, 1943; s. Charles Henry and Lillian (Scudder) F.; m. Karen L. Gardner, Nov. 27, 1982; children—Maurisa, Jacob; children by previous marriage—Jason, Michelle. B.S. in Bus. Adminstrn., Tri-State U., 1966. Foreman, Gen. Motors Co., Kokomo, Ind., 1966-67; buyer Diamond Shamrock, Painesville, Ohio, 1967-74; purchasing agt. Clow Co., Oskaloosa, Iowa, 1974-75, Elliott Co., Jeannette, Pa., 1975-77; mgr. purchasing Phelps Dodge Corp., Ft. Wayne, Ind., 1977—. Recipient Man of Yr. award Ft. Wayne Assn. Purchasing Mgmt., 1981-82. Mem. Nat. Assn. Purchasing Mgmt. (nat. v.p.), Ind. Minority Council (bd. dirs. 1980-83), Fort Wayne Minority Council (pres. 1981-83), Fort Wayne Purchasing Assn. (pres. 1981-83), Fort Wayne C. of C. Republican. Presbyterian. Club: Elks. Home: 3232 Simcoe Ct Fort Wayne IN 46815 Office: Phelps Dodge Magnet Wire Co PO Box 600 1302 E Creighton Ave Fort Wayne IN 46801

FISHER, CHARLES DONALD, oil company executive; b. Xenia, Ohio, June 15, 1937; s. Zebulon E. and Elizabeth (Weingart) F.; m. Judith Ann Parker, Sept. 18, 1965; children—Elizabeth Ann, Charles Parker, Dorothy Caroline. AB., Depauw U., 1959; Ph.D., U. Wash., 1964; M.B.A. Harvard U., 1969. Vice-pres. research and devel. Airwick Industries, Inc., Carlstadt, N.J., 1973-76; research dir. Church & Dwight, Inc., N.Y.C., 1976-77; v.p. research and devel. Van Straaten Chem. Co., Chgo., 1977-80, Viscosity Oil Co., Chgo., 1980—. Patentee in reaction mechanisms, polymers, surfactants, coatings. Corp. rep. Mus. Sci. and Industry, Chgo., 1984—. Rector scholar, 1955-59. Mem. Soc. Mfg. Engrs. (sr.), Am. Soc. Lubrication Engrs., Am. Chem. Soc., Sigma Xi, Phi Lambda Upsilon. Avocations: sailing; tennis; golf. Office: Viscosity Oil 3200 S Western Ave Chicago IL 60608

FISHER, CHARLES LEROY, sheet metal company executive; b. Peoria, Ill., Oct. 6, 1942; s. Charles James and Dorthy (Courson) F.; student Ill. Central Coll., 1967-68; cert. Bradley U., Peoria, 1971; m. Bonnie Louise Hudson, Feb. 22, 1977; children—Debbie, Tim, Jim, Tom, Jerry, Jeff. Sheetmetal worker Natkin & Co., Peoria, 1961-70, project engr., 1970-77; co-mgr. Allied Metal Craft Co., St. Paul, 1977-83; v.p., gen. mgr. Faircon Inc., New Brighton, Minn., 1983-84; pres., owner Pioneer Sheetmetal, Inc., St. Paul, 1984—. Life mem. Peoria Jaycees, pres., 1976-77, named outstanding state local pres., bd. dirs., 1974-75. Mem. ASHRAE (pres. elect 1983-84), Midway Civic C. of C. Republican. Lutheran. Clubs: Masons, Shriners, J.C.I. Senators. Home: 4303 Metcalf Dr Eagan MN 55122 Office: 1231 Pierce Butler Route Saint Paul MN 55104

FISHER, CHARLES THOMAS, III, banker; b. Detroit, Nov. 22, 1929; s. Charles Thomas, Jr. and Elizabeth Jane (Briggs) F.; A.B. in Econs., Georgetown U., 1951; M.B.A., Harvard, 1953; m. Margaret Elizabeth Keegin, June 18, 1952; children—Margaret Elizabeth Fisher Jones, Charles Thomas IV, Curtis William, Lawrence Peter II, Mary Florence. With Touche, Ross, Bailey & Smart, C.P.A.s, Detroit, 1953-58; asst. v.p. Nat. Bank Detroit, 1958-61, v.p., 1961-66, sr. v.p., 1966-69, exec. v.p., 1969-72, pres., chief adminstrv. officer, 1972—, also dir.; pres., dir. NBD Bancorp, Inc., 1973—, chmn., pres., 1982—; dir. Internat. Bank of Detroit, Detroit Edison Co., Hiram Walker-Resources, Ltd., Gen. Motors Corp., Am. Airlines. Mem. Mackinac Bridge Authority. Bd. dirs. Greater Detroit Area Hosp. Council. C.P.A., Mich. Mem. Assn. Res. City Bankers, Am. Inst. C.P.A.s, Mich. Assn. C.P.A.s. Republican. Roman Catholic. Clubs: Bloomfield Hills (Mich.) Country; Country of Detroit (Grosse Pointe); Detroit Athletic, Detroit, Yondotega (Detroit); Links (N.Y.C.). Office: National Bank Detroit Detroit MI 48232

FISHER, DAVID J., company executive; b. Boone, Iowa, Dec. 7, 1936; s. Harold L. and Alice (Judson) F.; m. Dorie Onthank, Sept. 10, 1962; children—Gregory Woods, Anne Katherine, Amy Milinda. B.S. in Econs., and Bus., Grinnell Coll., 1957; J.D., U. Iowa, 1962. Pres., chmn. Onthank Co., Des Moines, 1962—; dir. Employers Mutual Ins. Group, Des Moines, Kirke-Van Ursdel, Inc., Des Moines. Dir. YMCA Boys Home of Iowa, 1980—; pres. Des Moines Ballet Assn., 1984—, Ronald McDonald House, 1984—; mem. fin. steering com. Gov. Terry Branstad, Des Moines, 1981-84; Rep. com. chmn. Gov. Terry Branstad, 1985, Rep. fin. com. chmn. Senator Roger Jopson, 1984.

Presbyterian. Clubs: Des Moines (pres. 1985), Wakunda, Bohemian; Univ. Athletic (Iowa City). Home: 621 Glenview Dr Des Moines IA 50312 Office: PO Box 1462 Des Moines IA 50306

FISHER, ERMAN CALDWELL, corporate executive; b. Mt. Sterling, Ky., Oct. 10, 1923; s. Cato and Mattalean W. (Tyler) F.; cert. Highland Park Jr. Coll., 1947, Wayne State U., 1965, B.E. in Archtl. Engring., Detroit Inst. Tech., 1954; m. Ruby Nelson, June 28, 1947; children—Paul Cato, Nancy Carol. With Aero. Products, Inc., Detroit, 1943, Great Lakes Mut. Life Ins. Co., Detroit, 1946-48; prin. constrn. insp. City of Detroit Water Dept., 1948-68, supt. bldg. and grounds maintenance, 1968-74, supt. plant and mech. maintenance, 1974-75, mgr. plant, bldg. and mech. maintenance, 1975-77; dep. dir. Detroit Water and Sewage Dept., 1977-80, asst. dir. tech. support, 1980-81; dir. phys. plant Wayne State U., Detroit, 1980-83; gen. mgr. Central Installation Co., Fraser, Mich., 1984—. Bd. dirs. Shaw Coll., 1970-73; del. state conv. Republican party, 1954-55; now mem. Democratic State Central Com. Served with U.S. Army, 1943-46. Recipient Edward Dunbar Rich Service award, 1974. Mem. Am. Pub. Works Assn. (past pres. Inst. Bldgs. and Grounds 1977—, pres. Detroit Met. br.), Assn. Phys. Plant Adminstrs. Univs. and Colls., Phylon Soc. Wayne State U., NAACP (life), Am. Water Works Assn., Water Pollution Control Fedn., Engring. Soc. Detroit, Soc. Municipal Engrs., Mich. Assn. Phys. Plant Adminstrs. DAV (life), Alpha Phi Alpha. Club: Lions. Home: 17360 Rainbow Dr Lathrup Village MI 48076 Office: 16505 Thirteen Mile Rd Fraser MI 48026

FISHER, EUGENE, marketing executive; b. Chgo., Sept. 30, 1927; s. Morris and Sarah (Edelstein) F.; m. Joline Cobb, July 28, 1956; children—Robin Fisher Downing, Amy, Douglas. Ph.B., U. Chgo., 1945, M.B.A., 1948. Product mgr. Brunswick Corp., Skokie, Ill., 1955-59, group product mgr., 1959-63, product mktg. mgr., 1963-67, dir. mktg. planning, 1965-72, dir. corp. mktg. research, 1972—; mem. mktg. com. Nat. Bowling Council, 1975—; guest lectr. in field Mem. Am. Mktg. Assn., Conf. Bd. (research council), Phi Sigma Delta. Home: 1233 Elder Rd Homewood IL 60430 Office: Brunswick Corp One Brunswick Plaza Skokie IL 60077

FISHER, GENE LAWRENCE, financial executive; b. Chillicothe, Ill., Nov. 15, 1929; s. Lawrence Hubert and Alyce Anne (Neigemeyer) F.; m. Sandra Kay Burns, Sept. 19, 1959; children—Kyle Butler, Kelley Anne. B.S., U. Ill., 1957. Staff acct. Inland Container Corp., Indpls., 1957-63, mgr. corp. acctg., 1964-65, asst. corp. controller, 1966-78, dir. fin. systems, 1979—. Chmn. fin. com.-exec. com. Winona Meml. Hosp., Indpls., 1979-81, chmn. bd. dirs., 1982-83. Served wtih U.S. Army, 1951-53. Mem. Beta Alpha Psi, Sigma Iota Epsilon. Republican. Avocations: fishing, swimming. Home: 5427 Washington Blvd Indianapolis IN 46220 Office: Inland Container Corp 151 N Delaware St Indianapolis IN 46206

FISHER, JAMES HAROLD, geologist; b. Mayfield, Ky., Nov. 8, 1919; s. Clyde and Lillian (Smithson) F.; m. Anne Brown, June 5, 1943 (div. 1975); children—James M., John A., Jeanne A.; m. Normalee Waggoner, June 12, 1982. A.B. in History, U. Ill.-Urbana, 1943, B.S. in Geology, 1947, M.S., 1949, Ph.D., 1953. Cert. petroleum geologist, profl. geol. scientist. Geologist, Pure Oil Co., Casper, Wyo., 1948-51; asst. prof. U. Ill.-Urbana, 1952-55, U. Nebr., Lincoln, 1955-57; prof. Mich. State U., East Lansing, 1957—; cons. Contbr. articles to sci. jours. Served to capt. inf., U.S. Army, 1943-46; ETO. Shell Oil Co. fellow, 1952. Fellow Geol. Soc. Am., Am. Inst. Profl. Geologists; mem. Am. Assn. Petroleum Geologists (sect. pres. 1974-75), Mich. Basin Geol. Soc. (pres. 1961-62). Republican. Unitarian. Lodge: Elks. Avocation: photography. Home: 1175-F Arbor Dr East Lansing MI 48823 Office: Mich State U East Lansing MI 48824

FISHER, JAMES WILLIAM, bank executive; b. Detroit, Mar. 28, 1935; s. Joseph Sylvester and Agnes Ceclia (Brennan) F.; m. Mary Jo Statum, June 20, 1961 (dec.); children—Martha, Mary, Margaret, James; m. 2d, Barbara Ellen Somersall, July 3, 1970; 1 son, Jeffrey. B.S. in Acctg., U. Detroit, 1957. Mgr. cost acctg. and analysis Nat. Bank of Detroit, 1952-69; mgr. Comac, Bloomfield Hills, Mich., 1969-70; asst. v.p., sr. v.p. Community Nat. Bank of Pontiac (Mich.), 1970, exec., v.p., cashier, sr. exec. v.p., cashier, 1983, pres., 1983—; dir. Computer Communications Am., Detroit, 1978-83; mem. Pontiac Gen. Bldg. Authority, 1982-83. Pres., dir. United Way, Pontiac, 1979—; dir., trustee Mich. Cancer Found., Detroit, 1980-83; bd. dirs. YMCA, Pontiac, 1977-83, Clinton Valley Council Boy Scouts Am., Pontiac, 1979-83. Mem. Mich. Assn. Community Bankers (dir.), Bank Adminstrn. Inst. (dir.). Club: Pine Lake Country. Home: 4474 Cherrywood Ln Troy MI 48098

FISHER, JAN DAVID, business machines company official; b. Los Angeles, Feb. 2, 1942; s. Jerome Abraham and Betty Jean (Fisher) F.; m. Phyllis Jane Gross, Dec. 27, 1964; children—Joe Isaac, Jon Richard, Bunni Rochelle, Betty Jean, Robin Joelle, Simmi Ann. B.S.E.E., Purdue U., 1965. Systems engr. IBM, Wichita, Kans., 1965-74, plastic IMSR, 1974-75, market support rep., Rochester, Minn., 1975-77, product planner, 1977-85, architect-planner, 1985—. Author programs: Plastic Injection Molding, 1974; Discreet Production Monitoring, 1975. Pres., Southeastern Minn. Youth Orch., Rochester, 1982-84, B'nai Israel Synagogue, Rochester, 1981; post advisor Pine Island Explorer Post 69, Minn., 1980—. Served with Kans. N.G., 1967-73. Republican. Jewish. Lodge: Toastmasters (pres. 1981, Man of Yr. award 1984). Avocations: science fiction; camping. Address: Route 1 Box 533 Pine Island MN 55963

FISHER, JOANITA KANT, museum director, educator; b. Watertown, S.D., Jan. 4, 1947; d. Harlan Rudolph and Caroline Helen (Schaack) K.; m. Dean D. Fisher, Jan. 31, 1976; 1 child, Michelle Kant. B.S. in Sociology, U. S.D., 1972. Curator Kampeska Heritage Mus., Watertown, 1975-76, dir. 1982—; adj. instr. Mt. Marty Coll., Watertown, 1984—; appraiser Am. Indian art, Watertown, 1984—. Editor: Maggie: The Civil War Diary of Margaret Wylie Mellette, 1983; The Hutterite Cookbook, 1984; (with others) Archaeological Fieldnotes of W.H. Over, 1973, The Civil War Diary of Arthur C. Mellette, 1983. Pres. Concerned Citizens for Safe Energy, Britton, S.D., 1981. Grantee Burlington No. Found., 1984. Mem. Codington County Hist. Soc. (hon., life). Avocation: collecting antique Sioux Indian beadwork. Home: 405 NE 18th St Watertown SD 57201 Office: 27 1st Ave SE Watertown SD 57201

FISHER, JOANNE LOUISE, lawyer; b. Detroit, Dec. 13, 1949; d. Charles Eugene and Helen Ruth (Bluhm) F.; B.A., Oberlin Coll., 1972; J.D., Wayne State U., 1975. Admitted to Mich. bar, 1975; mem. firm Leonard C. Jaques, Detroit, 1976-78; asst. cashier, legal counsel Bank of Commonwealth, Detroit, 1978-79, asst. v.p., legal counsel, 1979-80; legal officer Mich. Nat. Bank Detroit, Clawson, 1980-83, asst. v.p., legal officer, 1983-84; staff counsel Mich. Nat. Corp., 1984—. Mem. Women Lawyers Assn. Mich. (corr. sec. 1981-82, treas. 1982-83), ABA, State Bar Mich., Detroit Bar Assn. Lutheran. Office: 1400 W Fourteen Mile Rd Clawson MI 48017

FISHER, JOHN EDWIN, insurance company executive; b. Portsmouth, Ohio, Oct. 26, 1929; s. Charles Hall and Bess (Swearingin) F.; student U. Colo., 1947-48, Ohio U., 1948-49, Franklin U., Columbus, Ohio, 1950-51; m. Eloise Lyon, Apr. 25, 1949. With Nationwide Mut. Ins. Co., Columbus, 1951—, v.p., office gen. chmn., 1970-72, pres., gen. mgr., dir., 1972-81; gen. chmn., chief exec. officer, 1981—; dir. Nationwide Mut. Fire Ins. Co., Nationwide Life Ins. Co., Nationwide Gen. Ins. Co.; chmn. Neckura-Neckermann Versicherungs A.G., Oberursel, Germany, 1976—; dir. Ohio Center Co. Chmn. Nationwide Found., 1981—; bd. dirs. Children's Hosp., pres. bd., 1984—. Mem. Chartered Property and Casualty Underwriters Assn., C.L.U. Soc., Assn. Ohio Life Ins. Cos. (past pres.), Ohio Ins. Inst. (pres. 1975-77), Nat. Assn. Ind. Insurers, Am. Risk and Ins. Assn., Griffith Ins. Found. (pres. 1978-80), Am. Inst. Property-Liability Underwriters (chmn. 1985—), Columbus C. of C. (chmn. 1982), Am. Council Life Ins. (bd. dirs.). Office: One Nationwide Plaza Columbus OH 43216

FISHER, JOHN WESLEY, II, manufacturing company executive; b. July 15, 1915; s. Arthur Justin and Rachel (Malott) F.; B.S., U. Tenn., 1938; M.B.A., Harvard, 1942; LL.D. (hon.), Ball State U., 1972, Butler U., 1977, DePauw U., 1981, Ind. U., 1985; m. Janice Kelsey Ball, Aug. 10, 1940; children—Joan C., Michael J., James A., Jeffrey E., Judith Fisher Musselman, John Wesley III, Jerrold M. Field sec. Delta Tau Delta Frat., Indpls., 1938-40; trainee, various mfg., sales and adminstrv. positions Ball Corp., Muncie, Ind., 1941-70, pres., chief exec. officer, 1970-78, chmn. bd., chief exec. officer, 1978-81, chmn. bd., 1981—, also dir.; dir. Ind. Bell Telephone Co., Ransburg Corp., Inland Steel Co., Chgo., Muncie Airport, Inc., Minnetrista Corp., Am. Nat. Bank & Trust Co., Muncie, Kindel Furniture Co., Grand Rapids, Mich.; partner Blackwood & Nichols Corp., Oklahoma City, bd. dirs. N.Y. Stock Exchange, 1981-84. State del. Republican Party Ind., 1950-70, mem. Rep. State Finance Com., 1952—, del. nat. conv., 1952, 54, 64, 68; trustee DePauw U.; bd. dirs. Ball Meml. Hosp., Ball Bros. Found. Mem. Glass Packaging Inst. (trustee 1962-68, pres. 1965-67), Ind. (dir. 1959—, pres. 1966-68), Muncie (past pres.) chambers commerce, Conf. Bd., N.A.M. (chmn. 1979-80, dir.), Grocery Mfrs. Am. (dir.), Delta Tau Delta. Republican. United Methodist. Clubs: Rotary (past pres.), Muncie, Delaware Country (Muncie); Indpls. Athletic, Columbia, Skyline (Indpls.); Metropolitan (Chgo.). Office: Ball Corp 345 S High St Muncie IN 47302

FISHER, JON HERBERT, chemical company executive; b. Wheeling, W. Va., May 14, 1947; s. Herbert Austin and Mary Melissa (Lewis) F.; m. Sarah May Lewis, Dec. 3, 1966; children—Jon Jeffrey, Matthew Austin. Student Ohio U., 1965-67; M.B.A., Case Western Res. U., 1982. With Harshaw Chem. Co., Cleve., 1970—, mgr., 1976-80, bus. mgr., 1980-81, dir., 1981-83; v.p., Harshaw Filtrol, Cleve., 1983—; dir. Harshaw Chem. BV, DeMeern, Holland, Harshaw Murata, Kobe, Japan, Harshaw Juarez, Mexico City, Harshaw Chem. Ltd., Daventry, Eng. Asst. scoutmaster Boy Scouts Am., Geneva, Ohio, 1971—. Mem. Dry Color Mfrs. Assn. (bd. dirs.), Chem. Market Research Assn., Cleve. Com. on Fgn. Relations. Office: Harshaw Filtrol Partnership 30100 Chagrin Blvd Cleveland OH 44124

FISHER, JON JAY, agronomist; b. Bismarck, N.D., July 14, 1953; s. John Harrison and Ruth Alberta (Marquardt) F.; m. Marlys Jane Naaden, June 1, 1979; children—Tara Suzanne, Janelle Kathryn. B.S. in Agr., N.D. State U., 1975, M.S., 1977. Teaching asst., lab. and field worker N.D. State U., 1971-75, grad. research asst. hybrid wheat program, 1975-77, area agronomist Coop. Extension Service, 1978—. Contbr. in field. Mem. Minot C. of C., Nat. Assn. County Agrl. Agts., Am. Soc. Agronomy, Crop Sci. Soc. Am., Weed Sci. Soc. Am., North Central Weed Control Conf., Blue Key, Epsilon Sigma Phi, Alpha Zeta. Home: 8 Fairway Minot ND 58701 Office: Route 3 Box 174 Minot ND 58701

FISHER, LESTER EMIL, zoo director; b. Chgo., Feb. 24, 1921; s. Louis and Elsie (Vodicka) F.; D.V.M., Iowa State U., 1943; m. Wendy Astley-Bell, Jan. 23, 1981; children—Jane Serrita, Katherine Clark. Mem. faculty animal care sect. Northwestern Med. Sch., Chgo., 1946-47; dir. Berwyn (Ill.) Animal Hosp., 1947-62; dir. Lincoln Park Zoo, Chgo., 1962—. Served with U.S. Army, 1943-46. Mem. Am. Assn. Zool. Parks and Aquariums (pres. 1971-72), Internat. Union Dirs. Zool. Gardens (pres. 1983—). Home: 3180 N Lake Shore Dr Chicago IL 60657 Office: 2200 N Cannon Dr Chicago IL 60614

FISHER, LLOYD EDISON, lawyer; b. Medina, Ohio, Oct. 23, 1923; s. LLoyd Edison and Wanda (White) F.; m. Twylla Dawn Peterson, Sept. 11, 1949; children—Karen S., Kirk P. B.S., Ohio State U., 1947, J.D., 1949. Bar: Ohio 1950. Practice law, Columbus, 1962—; mem. gen. hearing bd. Ohio Dept. Taxation, 1950-53; trust officer Huntington Nat. Bank, Columbus, 1953-62; ptnr. Alexander, Ebinger, Fisher, McAlister & Lawrence, Columbus, 1962—; adj. prof. law Ohio State U., 1967-69, 84—. Bd. dirs. Wesley Glen Retirement Center, 1974-80. Served to sgt. AUS, 1943-45. Felow Am. Coll. Probate Counsel; mem. ABA, Ohio Bar Assn., Columbus Bar Assn., Order of Coif. Methodist. Home: 611 Lummisford Ln N Columbus OH 43214 Office: 1 Riverside Plaza Columbus OH 43215

FISHER, MARJORIE HELEN, librarian; b. Losantville, Ind., Nov. 27, 1924; d. James Cleo and Isie May (Sutton) Hardwick; student Olivet Nazarene Coll., 1943-45; A.B., Ball State U., 1947; postgrad Ariz. State Tchrs. Coll., 1949, Ind. U., 1955, Ind. State U., 1957, Butler U., 1958; m. Delmar Fisher, Sept. 29, 1950; children—Deljon Ray, Madge Denise Fisher Gaines. Tchr., Superior (Ariz.) Elem. Schs., 1947-48, Yuma (Ariz.) schs., 1949-51; tchr. English, librarian Hamlet (Ind.) High Sch., 1952-56; dir. library services Plymouth (Ind.) Community Sch. Corp., 1957—; organizer Divine Heart Sem. Library, Donaldson, Ind., 1960. Mem. AAUW (sec. Plymouth br. 1979-80), NEA, Ind. State Tchrs. Assn., Assn. Ind. Media Educators. Co-author computer software program; contbr. articles to profl. jours. Home: 917 N Walnut St Plymouth IN 46563 Office: 810 N Randolph Plymouth IN 46563

FISHER, MICHEAL DUANE, data processing executive; b. Ft. Wayne, Ind., Dec. 9, 1952; m. Mary Jo Emerson, Aug. 26, 1978; 1 child, Christopher. Student computer tech. Purdue U., 1971-76. Cert. systems profl. (CSP); cert. info. systems auditor (CISA). Programmer trainee Midwestern United Life, Ft. Wayne, 1970-71; computer operator Peoples Trust Bank, 1971-72; ops. support mem. Essex Internat., 1972-74; supr. systems devel. Ft. Wayne Schs., 1974-82; mgr. computer audit assistance group Coopers & Lybrand, Ft. Wayne, 1982—; mem. IV Tech. Programming Curriculum Adv. Com., 1982—. Mem. Ft. Wayne Schs. Bus. Curriculum Adv. Com., 1982-84, Pleasant Twp. Adv. Com., 1979; pres. Branning Hills Community Assn., 1982, Pheasant Run Community Assn., 1978. Mem. Assn. Systems Mgmt. (pres. 1984—), EDP Auditors Assn. Avocations: golfing, sailing, skiing, reading. Home: 2238 Rosita Ct Fort Wayne IN 46815 Office: Coopers & Lybrand 490 Lincoln Bank Tower Fort Wayne IN 46802

FISHER, NEAL FLOYD, clergyman, educator; b. Wash., Ind., Apr. 4, 1936; s. Floyd Russell and Florence Alice (Williams) F.; m. Ila Alexander, Aug. 18, 1957; children—Edwin Kirk, Julia Bryn. A.B., DePauw U., 1957; M.Div., Boston U., 1960, Ph.D., 1966; L.H.D. (hon.) DePauw U., 1982. Ordained to ministry United Methodist Ch., 1958. Pastor First Meth. Ch., Revere, Mass., 1960-63, North Andover Mass., 1963-68; planning assoc. United Meth. Bd. Global Ministries, N.Y.C., 1968-73, dir. planning, 1973-77; pres., prof. theology and soc. Garrett-Evangelical Theol. Sem., 1980—; assoc. dean, asst. prof. theology and society Boston U., Mass., 1977-80. Author: From Slavery to Nationhood, 1977; The Parables of Jesus; Glimpses of the New Age, 1979; Context for Discovery, 1981. Mendenhall lectr. DePauw U., 1982, 83; Willson lectr., Nashville, 1983; Voigt lectr. McKendree Coll., 1984, Britt lectr. First United Meth. Ch., Honolulu, 1985; recipient Disting. Alumnus award Boston U. Sch. Theology, 1985. Mem. Assn. United Meth. Theol. Schs., United Meth. Ch. Bd. of Ordained Ministry North Central Jurisdiction. Univ. Senate of United Meth. Ch. Avocation: distance running. Office: Garrett-Evangelical Theol Sem 2121 Sheridan Rd Evanston IL 60201

FISHER, OSCAR JAMES, power engineer, manager technology company; b. Covert Mich., Sept. 18, 1921; s. Leon Meredith and Stella (Larrieu) F.; m. Olga Teliak, Aug. 23, 1947; children—Steven, Jeffrey, Christopher. B.S. in Chem. Engring., Ill. Inst. Tech., 1950. Service engr. Babcock & Wilcox, Midwest, 1950-59, new products engr., Barberton, Ohio, 1959-63, adminstrv. asst., 1963-70, indsl. engr., 1970-72, mgr. gen. tech., 1972—; dir., chmn. numerous engring., safety, energy and edn. coms. and councils. Contbr. articles to profl. jours. Served with USN, 1942-46. Fellow ASME (Centennial medal 1980); mem. Am. Welding Soc. Republican. Avocations: investing, travel. Home: 5694 Sherwood Forest Akron OH 44319 Office: McDermott/Babcock & Wilcox 20 S Van Buren Ave Barberton OH 44203

FISHER, WILL STRATTON, electrical engineer; b. Nashville, June 27, 1922; s. Will Stratton and Estelle (Carr) F.; B.S.E.E., Vanderbilt U., 1947; m. Patricia A. Fesco, Nov. 10, 1945; children—Patricia Jo, Will Stratton, Robert J. With Lighting Bus. Group, Gen. Elec. Co., Cleve., 1947—, mgr. advanced application engring., 1971-85, mgr. lighting edn., 1985—. Served to 1st lt. C.E., AUS, 1943-46. Registered profl. engr., Ohio. Fellow Illuminating Engring. Soc. N.Am. (pres. 1978-79, Disting. Service award 1980); mem. Internat. Commn. Illumination (U.S. expert on tech. com. 3.3, U.S. rep. to Div. 3), ASHRAE, IEEE. Methodist. Contbr. articles, papers to profl. jours. and symposia. Patentee Parabolic wedge louver; developer concepts for utilizing heat from lighting systems to heat bldgs.; designer calorimeter; developer procedure for calculating contbn. of lighting to heating of bldgs. Home: 120 Meadowhill Ln Moreland Hills OH 44022 Office: General Electric Co Nela Park Cleveland OH 44112

FISHER-MCCANNE, LYNN PATRICIA, psychologist; b. Glendale, Calif., May 7, 1949; d. Ernest and Gertrude Luli (Braun) Fisher; m. Thomas Robert McCanne, Dec. 28, 1974; 1 child, Robert William. B.A., Occidental Coll., 1970; M.A., Ohio State U., 1971, Ph.D., 1974. Registered psychologist and sch. psychologist, Ill. Psychologist DeKalb Spl. Edn. Assn., Ill., 1974-75; instr. spl. edn. dept. No. Ill. Univ., DeKalb, 1975, psychologist health service, 1975-81, psychologist counseling and student devel., 1981-84, assoc. dir., 1984—; cons. Genoa Sheltered Village, Ill., 1979-81, Woodstock Sheltered Village, Ill., 1977-79. Contbr. articles to profl. jours. Mem. Kishwaukee Symphony Orch., DeKalb, 1977—; bd. dirs. DeKalb County Villages, Ill., 1976-79. Mem. Am. Assn. Counseling and Devel., Am. Coll. Personnel Assn., Am. Psychol. Assn., Midwestern Psychol. Assn. Home: 631 Joanne Ln DeKalb IL 60115 Office: Counseling and Student Devel Ctr Northern Ill Univ DeKalb IL 60115

FISHER-MCPEAK, JANET, language educator; b. Midland, Mich., Sept. 17, 1953; d. Arthur J. and Bettie L. (Graves) Fisher; m. John David McPeak, Sept. 5, 1976. M.A. in French, Middlebury Coll., 1976, M.A. in German, 1979. Instr. French, German, Delta Coll., University Center, Mich., 1977—; instr. German, Saginaw Valley State Coll., University Center, 1981—; asst. dir. Internat. Long. Sch., Midland, Mich.; tech. German cons. Brown & Wilson Machine Co. Author: Street Survivial in France, En Garde. Mem. Am. Assn. Tchrs. German. German Cultural Service grantee, 1983, 84. Office: Delta Coll University Center MI 48710

FISHKIN, ARTHUR FREDERIC, biochemistry educator; b. N.Y.C., May 27, 1930; s. Sidney Leonard and Ruth (Schneiderman) F.; m. Jane Leslie, Sept. 9, 1956; children—Paul, Charles, James, Joel. A.B., Ind. U., 1951, A.M., 1953; Ph.D., U. Iowa, 1957. Assoc. S.W. Found., San Antonio, 1957-58; assoc. La. State U. Sch. Medicine, New Orleans, 1958-64; asst. prof. N.Mex. State U., Las Cruces, 1964-68; assoc. prof. biochemistry Creighton U., Omaha, 1968—. Contbr. articles to profl. jours. Mem. bd. Beth Israel Synagogue, Omaha, 1969-81. Mem. Am. Chem. Soc., Sigma Xi, Gamma Alpha, Alpha Chi Sigma, Phi Lambda Upsilon. Democrat. Jewish. Home: 5014 Hamilton St Omaha NE 68132 Office: Creighton U 2500 California St Omaha NE 68178

FISHLOVE, HOWARD IRWIN, novelty company executive; consultant, actor; b. Chgo., May 25, 1936; s. Irving Haim and Anna Mae F.; m. Hildegarde Lynn Webster, June 6, 1966; children—Thomas Irving, William Howard. B.F.A., Drake U., Des Moines, 1957, B.A., 1958; M.S., U. Wis., 1960. Office mgr. H. Fishlove & Co., Chgo., 1960-63, v.p., 1968-80, pres. and chief operating officer, 1980—; accounts mgr. Brunswick Corp., Chgo., 1963-68; cons.; tchr.; dir. H. Fishlove & Co. and Fishlove Mgmt. Corp. Pres. and treas. East Maine Dist. 63 Band Boosters Assn., Niles, Ill., 1979-83. Served with USAR, 1960-65. Recipient Clio award most humorous TV comml., 1980. Mem. Actors Equity Assn., Screen Actors Guild, AFTRA. Psi Chi, Theta Alpha Phi. Democrat. Jewish. Patentee in field. Office: H Fishlove & Co 720 N Franklin St Chicago IL 60610-3548

FISHMAN, DAVID LEON, cardiologist, educator; b. Chgo., Nov. 10, 1944; s. Jerry N. and Fanchon Pauline (Block) F.; m. Madelyn Levy, July 2, 1966 (div. Sept. 1979); children—Jennifer Mia, Zachary Michael. B.S. in Biology, Loyola U., Chgo., 1966, M.Sc. in Physiology, Stritch Sch. Medicine, 1978; M.D., U. Ill.-Chgo., 1970. Diplomate Am. Bd. Internal Medicine. Intern U. Ill. Affiliated Hosps., Chgo., 1970-71, resident, 1973-75; asst. in medicine U. Ill.-Chgo., 1970-71, instr. in medicine, 1973-75; instr. in internal medicine U. Nebr., Omaha, 1971-73; research fellow, trainee in cardiology Loyola U., Chgo., 1975-77, chief fellow in cardiology, 1976-77; clin. asst. prof. medicine, sect. cardiology, 1977—; attending physician St. Francis Hosp., Evanston, Ill., 1978—, Northwest Hosp., Chgo., 1978—, Bethesda Hosp., Chgo., 1980—, Forkosh Hosp., Chgo., 1981—; pvt. practice medicine specializing in cardiology; med. cons. Employers of Wausau; med. dir. Better Heart of Lake County (Ill.). Served as capt. M.C., U.S. Army, 1971-73. NIH grantee, 1975-78. Fellow Am. Heart Assn. Clin. Council, Am. Coll. Cardiology, ACP, Am. Coll. Chest Physicians; mem. Chgo. Med. Soc., Ill. State Med. Soc., AMA, AAAS, Am. Heart Assn., Chgo. Heart Assn., Alpha Omega Alpha. Jewish. Co-editor Ill. Med. Jour., 1977-78. Home: 9126 Ridgeway Skokie IL 60076

FISHMAN, MADELINE DOTTI, management consulting company executive, consultant; b. Chgo., Oct. 7, 1942; d. Martin and Anne (Sweet) Binder; m. Norton Lee Fishman, Apr. 7, 1963; children—Mark Nathan, Marla Susan. B.Ed., Nat. Coll. Edn., 1964, M.S., 1972. Tchr., Rochester Schs. (Minn.), 1963-64, Orange County Schs., Orlando, Fla., 1967-68; reading cons. Palatine Schs. (Ill.), 1972-73; instr. Parent Effective Tng., Wilmette, Ill., 1974-76, tchr. effective tng., 1974-76; pres. Profls. Diversified, Wilmette, Ill., 1976—; mgmt. cons. World Wide Diamonds Assn., Schaumburg, Ill., 1979—, Color Artistry, Dallas, 1983—; Pearl direct distbr. Amway Corp., Ada, Mich., 1976—. Author: Organic Gardening, 1975. Leader, Camp Fire Girls, Evanston, Ill., 1963, 75. Recipient Ednl. Scholarship, Nat. Coll. Edn., 1971. Mem. Kappa Delta Pi. Republican. Jewish.

FISK, CARLTON ERNEST, professional baseball player. Catcher Chgo. White Sox. Office: Chgo White Sox Comiskey Park Chicago IL 60616*

FISK, DAVID DUWAYNE, international development executive; b. Wabasha, Minn., Apr. 21, 1941; s. Myron Ellis and Anna (Kohn) F.; m. Marta Rosa Pina, Nov. 9, 1969; children—Kevin, Andrea. B.A., St. Mary's Coll., Winona, Minn., 1974. Dir. in country tng. U.S. Peace Corps, Santiago, Chile, 1967; dir. food and nutrition office AID, Santiago, 1968-75; dir. High/Scope Internat. Center, Ypsilanti, Mich., 1975-84; exec. dir. Fisk Assocs. Internat., Ypsilanti, 1984—; cons. child and family programs Govt. St. Kitts & Nevis, W.I., 1980—, Govt. of Ecuador, 1985—, also pvt. and vol. orgns. Contbr. articles to profl. jours. Bush Found. fellow, 1981; grantee UNICEF, U.S. State Dept., pvt. founds. Roman Catholic. Lodge: Rotary (chmn. internat. youth program 1981—). Home: 1402 W Cross St Ypsilanti MI 48197 Office: Fisk Assocs Internat 2796 Packard Rd Ann Arbor MI 48197

FISK, JEAN A., child devel. clinic adminstr.; b. Aberdeen, S.D., June 11, 1946; d. Darwin A. and Ardith (Severance) F.; B.S., U. Wis., Oshkosh, 1972; M.S.Ed., U. Wis., Whitewater, 1974; postgrad. Nat. Coll. Edn., Evanston, Ill., 1975, No. Colo. U., 1979. Supr., N.W. Spl. Edn. Dist., Freeport, Ill., 1972-73; cons. Racine County Spl. Edn., Union Grove, Wis., 1973-74; instr. Nat. Coll. Edn., 1974-77; founder, exec. dir. Chgo. Clinic for Child Devel., 1976—; in-service dir., cons. to schs. Recipient Title VI-D fellowship award, 1972. Mem. Assn. for Children with Learning Disabilities, Exec. Female Assn., Hyde Park Businessmen's Assn., Council for Exceptional Children. Christian. Club: Zonta. Author: EmH-SLD????, 1972; Handbook for Parents of Children with Learning Disabilities, 1973; Nonsense Syllables as an Aide to Teaching Reading, 1973. Office: 1525 E 53d St Chicago IL 60615

FISKE, DONALD WINSLOW, psychologist, educator; b. Lincoln, N.H., Aug. 27, 1916; s. Paul Southard and Ruth (Tufts) F.; m. Barbara Page, Sept. 10, 1938; children—Alan, Susan. A.B., Harvard U., 1937, A.M., 1939; Ph.D., U. Mich., 1948. Asst. project dir. U. Mich., Ann Arbor, 1946-48, instr., 1948; faculty U. Chgo., 1948—, prof. psychology, 1960—, dept. chmn., 1982-85. Author: (with S. Maddi) Functions of Varied Experience, 1961; Measuring the Concepts of Personality, 1971; (with S. Duncan Jr.) Face to Face Interactions, 1977; Strategies for Personality Research, 1978. Contbr. articles to profl. jours. Served to lt. comdr. USNR, 1942-46. Fellow AAAS; mem. Am. Psychol. Assn., Midwestern Psychol. Assn., Soc. Multivariate Exptl. Psychology. Club: Columbia Yacht. Avocation: sailing. Home: 5711 Blackstone Ave Chicago IL 60637 Office: U Chgo 5848 University Ave Chicago IL 60637

FITCHETT, VERNON HAROLD, physician, surgeon, educator; b. Grover, Colo., May 14, 1927; s. Harold Leroy and Mazie (Bengston) F.; m. Kathryn Hellen Mullin, Aug. 3, 1963; children—Michael, Elizabeth, Benjamin. B.S., Buena Vista Coll., 1949; M.D., U. Iowa, 1953. Diplomate Am. Bd. Surgery. Commd. officer U.S. Navy, 1956, advanced through grades to capt., intern U.S. Naval Hosp., Bremerton, Wash., 1953-54; resident VA Hosp., Portland, Oreg., 1955-56, U.S. Naval Hosp., St. Albans, N.Y., 1956-59; med. officer-in-charge USPHS, DaNang, Vietnam, 1964-65; chief surgery U.S. Navy, DaNang, 1968-69; chmn. dept. surgery Naval Hosp., Oakland, Calif., 1970-76; ret., 1976; mem. staff Jamestown Hosp., N.D., 1976—; asst. clin. prof. surgery N.D. Med. Sch., 1982—; chmn. bd. Jamestown Clinic, 1979-85; surg. cons. State Hosp., Jamestown, Ann Carlson Sch., 1976—. Author: War Surgery, 1971. Contbr. articles to profl. jours. Mem. exec. com. N.D. chpt. Am. Cancer Soc., 1979-84. Decorated Legion of Merit with Combat V. Fellow ACS (past pres. N.D. chpt.); mem. AMA, Pan Pacific Surg. Soc., Assn. Mil. Surgeons. Roman Catholic. Lodges: Eagles, Elks, K.C. Office: Dakota Clinic-Jamestown Box 951 Jamestown ND 58401

FITZ, RAYMOND L., university president, clergyman, electrical engineer; b. Akron, Ohio, Aug. 12, 1941; s. Raymond L. and Mary Fitz. B.S., in Elec. Engring., U. Dayton, 1964; M. S. in Elec. Engring., Poly. Inst. Bklyn., 1967, Ph.D. in Elec. Engring., 1969. Joined Society of Mary, Roman Catholic Ch.,

1960; instr. elec. engring. U. Dayton, Ohio, 1968-69, asst. prof., 1969-73, acting dir. engring. mgmt., 1974-75, assoc. prof. engring. mgmt., 1975-78, pres.-elect, 1978-79, pres., chief exec. officer, 1979—; exec. dir. Ctr. for Christian Renewal, Dayton, 1974-79; dir. Assn. Cath. Colls. and Univs., 1980—; trustee St. Mary's U., San Antonio, 1982—; mem. Bishops and Pres. Com.; mem. adv. council on peace and justice edn. Assn. Cath. Colls. and Univs.; chmn. bd. Inst. for Inter-Univ. Coop. Research, Washington, Author (with I. Cada): Recovery of Religious Life, 1975; author workbook, reports. Mem. North Central Evaluation Team Col. White High Sch., Dayton; process cons. Horizon 76, Dayton; chmn. Community Round Table; facilitator Montgomery County Charter Task Force, Dayton, 1982; chmn. Community Affairs Com., Dayton; mem. Miami Valley Research Found., Dayton; bd. dirs. CAD-CAM, Inc., Dayton, 1982—. Kettering Found. fellow, 1973-74. Mem. IEEE. Office: Univ of Dayton 300 College Park Dayton OH 45469

FITZGERALD, BRYAN THOMAS, physician; b. Beech Grove, Ind., Apr. 1, 1950; s. Bryan and Lorraine Elizabeth (Barrett) F., Jr.; m. Suse Ann Smith, June 5, 1971; children—Brett Eric, Erin Brooke. B.S., Ind. State U., 1972; D.O., Kirksville Coll. Osteo. Medicine, 1977. Staff physician, chief clin. services U.S. Air Force Clinic, Rickenbacker AFB, Ohio, 1978-80; staff physician dept. emergency medicine U.S. Air Force Med. Ctr., Wright Patterson AFB, Ohio, 1980-82; staff physician sect. emergency medicine Grandview Hosp., Dayton, Ohio, 1982—; adj. clin. staff Coll. Osteo. Medicine Ohio U.; med. advisor Mad River Twp. Emergency Med. Services, Montgomery County (Ohio). Served to capt. USAF, 1978-82. Mem. Am. Osteo. Assn., Ohio Osteo. Assn., Dayton Dist. Acad. Osteo. Medicine, Am. Coll. Osteo. Emergency Physicians. Lutheran. Club: Marinole (Kettering, Ohio). Office: Grandview Hosp Sect Emergency Medicine 405 Grand Ave Dayton OH 45433

FITZGERALD, FRANCIS JOHN, chemical company executive; b. Springfield, Ill., Oct. 25, 1927; s. Francis John and Mary Catherine (MacGraugh) F.; m. Patricia Ann Sullivan, June 10, 1950; children—Mickey, John, Terence, Tim, Moira, Kerry, Megan. B.S., U. Notre Dame, 1950. With Monsanto Co., St. Louis, 1951—, exec. v.p., 1980—; dir. Nat. Life of Vt. Bd. dirs. Catholic Charities of St. Louis, Glennon Children's Hosp., Newman Chapel Wash. U. Mem. NAM (dir.), U.S. C. of C. Roman Catholic. Clubs: Bellerive Country, Bogey. Office: Monsanto Co 800 N Lindbergh Blvd Saint Louis MO 63167

FITZGERALD, JAMES FRANCIS, cable TV executive; b. Janesville, Wis., Mar. 27, 1926; s. Michael Henry and Chloris lHelen (Beiter) F.; B.S., Notre Dame U., 1947; m. Marilyn Field Cullen, Aug. 1, 1950; children—Michael Dennis, Brian Nicholas, Marcia O'Loughlin, James Francis, Carolyn, Ellen Putnam. With Standard Oil Co. (Ind.), Milw., 1947-48; pres., F.W. Oil Co., Janesville, 1950-73; v.p. Creston Park Corp., 1957—; pres. Sunnyside, Inc., 1958—, Total TV, Inc., cable TV systems, Wis., 1965—; dir. 1st Nat. Bank; chmn. bd., pres. Milw. Profl. Sports and Services (Milw. Bucks). Bd. govs. NBA, also chmn. TV com.; chmn. Greater Milw. Open (P.G.A. Tournament), 1985. Served to lt. (j.g.) USNR, 1944-45, 51-52. Mem. Chief Execs. Forum, World Bus. Council, Wis. Petroleum Assn. (pres. 1961-62). Roman Catholic. Clubs: Janesville Country (past pres.), Milw. Athletic, Vintage (Indian Wells, Calif.); Castle Pines Golf (Castle Rock, Colo.). Home: 420 Oak Rd Janesville WI 53545 Office: PO Box 348 Janesville WI 53547

FITZGERALD, JOY BEVERLY, business executive, lawyer; b. Zearing, Iowa, Apr. 22, 1917; d. Seymour Robert and Jennie Blanche (Stevens) Hix; m. Craig William Fitzgerald, June 17, 1963. B.A., Morningside Coll., Sioux City, 1938; J.D., Drake U., 1941. Bar: Iowa 1941. Atty. Hers, Nevada, Iowa, 1941-44; spl. agent U.S. Dept. Agr., Chgo., 1944-49; interviewer Iowa Employment Security Commn., Amex, 1950-54, mgr., 1954-58; exec. sec. Iowa State Reciprocity Bd., Des Moines, 1958-71; pres. Joy B. Fitzgerald, Inc., Altoona, Iowa, 1971—; pres. Joy B. Fitzgerald Resident Agts., Inc., Altoona, 1983—; broadcaster Sta. WMAQ, Chgo., 1975—. Mem. motor carrier adv. com. U.S. Dept. Transp., 1982—. Name Iowa Lawyer Advocate of Yr. SBA, 1983. Mem. ABA, Ind. Trucker's Assn. (sec. Iowa div. 1975, nat. sec. 1972—). Democrat. Author: Overdrive Magazine, 1971—. Home: Rural Route Collins Iowa 50055

FITZGERALD, JOYCE LUCILLE, biologist, coal company official; b. Coshocton, Ohio, Mar. 9, 1947; d. Earl Lester and Doris Lucille (Lapp) F.; B.S. in Edn. and Biol. Scis., Ohio U., 1970, postgrad., 1971; postgrad. Ohio State U., 1972. Instr. biol. sci. Zanesville (Ohio) Public Schs., 1970-72; adminstrv. asst. Ohio Dept. Natural Resources, Columbus, 1972-73; adminstrv. dir. Boys, Inc., Columbus, 1973-74; biologist Skelly & Loy, Cons. Engrs., Harrisburg, Pa., 1975-76; adminstrv. chief Ohio EPA, Columbus, 1976-78; mgr. environ. affairs Ind. div. Peabody Coal Co., Evansville, 1978—. Mem. Ind. CAP (2d lt.), Evansville. Named Ohio Wildlife Conservationist of Yr., 1977; cert. wastewater operator, Ind.; cert. biologist U.S. Fish and Wildlife Service; lic. pvt. pilot FAA. Mem. Ind. Wildlife Soc., Ind. Water Resources Assn., Nat. Wildlife Fedn., Ind. Coal Inst., Women in Mining Inc. (officer), Ind. Sportsman Alliance. Office: Peabody Coal Co NW 1st St PO Box 1112 Evansville IN 47710

FITZGERALD, LAURINE ELISABETH, educational administrator; b. New London, Wis., Aug. 24, 1930; d. Thomas Francis and Laurine Isabelle (Branchflower) F. B.S., Northwestern U., 1952, M.A., 1953; Ph.D., Mich. State U., 1959. Diplomate Am. Bd. Vocat. Edn. Residence dir., social program coordinator Kendall Coll., Evanston, Ill., 1951-53; instr. Psycho-Ednl. Clinic, Northwestern U., Evanston, Ill., 1952-53; dir. Devel. Reading Lab., head resident dir., instr. English, Wis. State Coll., Whitewater, 1953-55; area dir., instr. ednl. psychology Ind. U., Bloomington, 1955-57; grad. asst. adminstrv. and ednl. services, Mich. State U., East Lansing, 1957-58, instr., 1958-59, assoc. prof. counseling, personnel services and ednl. psychology, 1963-68, asst. dean students, 1963-70, prof. adminstrn. and higher edn., 1968-74, asoc. dean students, dir. div. edn. and research, 1970-74; assoc. dean students, asst. prof. psychology and edn. U. Denver, 1959-62; asst. prof. counseling psychology, staff counselor Carnegie Found. Project, U. Minn., Mpls., 1962-63; dir. N.E. Wis. Coop. Regional Grad. Ctr., U. Wis.-Oshkosh, 1974-80, dean grad. sch., prof. counselor edn., 1974-85; dean, dir. Mansfield Campus, Ohio State U., 1985—. Contbr. chpts. to books, articles to profl. jours. Exec. bd. Girl Scouts Council. Mem. Council of Grad. Schs. in the U.S., Midwest Assn. Grad. Schs. (exec. com. 1978—), Am. Coll. Personnel Assn. (archivist 1982—), Am. Personnel and Guidance Assn., Am. Psychol. Assn., Am. Assn. Higher Edn., Am. Assn. Univ. Adminstrs., Nat. Assn. Women Deans, Adminstrs. and Counselors, Nat. Assn. Student Personnel Adminstrs., Nat. Council Adminstrv. Women in Edn., AAUP, Women's Equity Action League, AAUW, Bus. and Profl. Women's Clubs (pres. 1980-81), Zonta Internat., Lakelands Consortium in Support of the Arts, Beta Beta Beta, Alpha Lambda Delta, Psi Chi, Delta Kappa Gamma. Republican. Congregationalist. Home: 1430 Royal Dr Mansfield OH 44906 Office: Ohio State U 1680 University Dr Mansfield OH 44906

FITZGERALD, MICHAEL LEE, state government official; b. Marshalltown, Iowa, Nov. 29, 1951; s. James Martin and Clara Francis (Dankbar) F.; m. Sharon Lynn Wildman, Dec. 15, 1979; children—Ryan William, Erin Elizabeth. B.B.A., U. Iowa, 1974. Campaign mgr. Fitzgerald for Treas., 1974; market analyst Massey Ferguson, Inc., Des Moines, 1975-83; treas. State of Iowa, Des Moines, 1983—. Democrat. Roman Catholic. Home: 211 SW Caulder St Des Moines IA 50315 Office: State Capitol Des Moines IA 50319

FITZGERALD, PHYLLIS ANN, nursing educator; b. New Haven, Mar. 12, 1937; d. Edward and Florence Fitzgerald. B.S. in Nursing, St. Louis U., 1962; M.A. in Nursing, NYU, 1967; Ph.D. in Higher Edn., U. Ariz., 1982. Profl. nurse trainee NYU, 1966; instr. U. Hawaii, Honolulu, 1967-69; from instr. to asst. prof. nursing So. Conn. State Coll., New Haven, 1968-76; asst. prof. U. Ariz., Tucson, 1976-79; assoc. prof. U. Akron, Ohio, 1982—, asst. dean baccalaureate nursing program, 1982—. Contbr. articles to profl. publs., chpts. to book. Mem. Midwest Alliance Nursing, Nat. League Nursing, Assn. Air N.G. Nurses (bd. dirs. 1983—), Ohio Nurses Assn. (program chmn. local dist. 1984—, bd. dirs. 1985—), Sigma Theta Tau (2d v.p. Delta Omega chpt. 1984—). Roman Catholic. Avocations: walking, hiking, bowling, reading. Office: U Akron Coll Nursing Mary Gladwin Hall Akron OH 44325

FITZGERALD, ROBERT HANNON, JR., orthopedic surgeon; b. Denver, Aug. 25, 1942; s. Robert Hannon and Alyene (Webber) Fitzgerald Anderson; m. Lynda Lee Lang, Apr. 27, 1968 (div. 1984); children—Robert III, Shannon, Dennis, Katherine, Kelly; m. Jamie Kathleen Dent, Mar. 9, 1985; children—Steven, Brian, Steven. B.S., U. Notre Dame, 1963; M.D., U. Kans., 1967; M.S., U. Minn., 1974. Instr. orthopedic surgery Mayo Med. Sch., Rochester, Minn., 1974-77, cons. orthopedic surgery, 1974—, assoc. prof., 1982—; cons. Ctr. Disease Control, Atlanta, 1981—. Mem. bd. edn. St. John's Grade Sch./Jr. High Sch., Rochester, 1983—; mem. Bd. Devel. Mayo Clinic, 1984—; trustee Lourdes High Sch. Devel. Bd., Rochester, 1982—. Served to capt. USAF, 1968-70. Decorated Air Commendation medal; recipient Stinchfield award Hip Soc., 1984; Kappa Delta award for musculoskeletal research, 1983. Fellow Am. Acad. Orthopedic Surgeons; mem. Orthopedic Research Soc., AMA, Zumbro County Med. Soc., Min-Da-Man Orthopedic Soc., Minn. Orthopedic Soc., Am. Soc. Microbiology, N.Y. Acad. Scis., Surg. Infection Soc., Clin. Orthopaedic Soc., Internat. Soc. Orthopaedic spl. Surgery and Traumatology, Sigma Xi, Kappa Delta. Republican. Roman Catholic. Avocations: cross-country and downhill skiing; swimming; coaching children's sports. Home: 706 4th St SW Rochester MN 55902 Office: Mayo Clinic 200 1st St SW Rochester MN 55905

FITZ GERALD, THOMAS JOE, psychologist; b. Wichita, Kans., July 8, 1941; s. Thomas Michael and Pauline Gladys (Zink) F.; B.A., San Francisco State U., 1965; M.A., U. Utah, 1969, Ph.D., 1971. Dir. behavioral services programs VA Hosp., Topeka, 1971-73; pvt. practice as psychologist, Topeka, 1973-74, Prairie Village, Kans., 1974—; clin. instr. Menninger Sch. Psychiatry, Topeka, 1972-74; sec.-treas. Kans. Bd. Psychologist Examiners, 1976-79, 79-80, chmn., 1980—, chmn. psychology examining com.; mem. Behavioral Scis. Regulatory Bd., 1980-82; pres. Psychol. Services Corp., Prairie Village, 1974—. Mem. Gov.'s Commn. on Criminal Adminstrn., 1974-76; vice-chmn. Gov.'s Com. on Med. Assistance, 1978-80; mem. Mid-Am. Health Systems Agy., 1979-82. Served with USMCR, 1958-60. Mem. Kans. Psychol. Assn. (pres. 1980-81), Kans. Assn. Profl. Psychologists (pres. 1981-82, Outstanding Psychologist award 1979, 80, 81, 82), Greater Kansas City Soc. Clin. Hypnosis (pres. 1978—). Office: 2108 W 75th St Suite 400 Prairie Village KS 66208

FITZGERALD, THOMAS JOSEPH, clinical psychologist, consultant; b. St. Louis, Jan. 12, 1924; s. Michael and Alice (Power) F.; m. Margaret June Gretzer, Nov. 8, 1952; children—Thomas Joseph, Mary, Kathy, James. B.S., St. Louis U., 1950, M.S., 1953, Ph.D., 1968. Chief psychologist, exec. dir. Community Out-Patient Clinics, Iowa, 1953-55, exec. dir., Ill., 1964-69; chief service St. Louis City Child Guidance Clinic, 1971-76; coordinator Mo. Children's Mental Health Service, 1976-77; coordinator, cons. Ill. State Dept. Mental Health and Developmental Disabilities, Chester, 1978-82; pvt. practice clin. psychology, St. Louis, 1969—; sr. partner S.W. Ill. Therapy Clinic, O'Fallon, 1980—; asst. prof. Marillac Coll., 1970-74; lectr. So. Ill. U., Edwardsville, 1965—. Past chmn. Jennings Youth Commn.; mem. White House Conf. on Edn.; active St. Louis Mental Health Assn., Childrens Study Home. Served with USMC, 1942-45, USAFR, 1950-68. Mem. AAAS, Am. Psychoo. Assn., Orthopsychiat. Assn., Psychology-Law Assn., Assn. Children with Learning Disabilities, Nat. Soc. Autistic Citizens, Am. Legion, VFW, Ill. Psychol. Assn., Mo. Psychol. Assn., Sigma Xi. Club: Scott AFB Officers. Home: 8809 Shady Grove St Saint Louis MO 63136 Office: Paul Brown Bldg Suite 1500 818 Olive St Saint Louis MO 63101

FITZGERALD, WILLIAM ALLINGHAM, savings and loan association executive; b. Omaha, Nov. 18, 1937; s. William Frances and Mary (Allingham) F.; m. Barbara Ann Miskell, Aug. 20, 1960; children—Mary Colleen, Katherine Kara, William Tate. B.S.B.A. in Fin., Creighton U., 1959; grad. Savs. and Loan League exec. tng. program U. Ga., 1962, U. Ind., 1969. With Comml. Fed. Savs. & Loan Assn., Omaha, 1959—, v.p., asst. sec., 1963-68, exec. v.p., 1968-73, pres., 1974—; Trustee Ind. Coll. Found.; vice chmn. bd. dirs. Creighton U.; bd. dirs. Coll. of St. Mary, United Way of Midlands; trustee Archbishop's com. for ednl. devel. Roman Catholic Ch. Served to lt. Fin. Corps, U.S. Army. Clubs: Omaha Country, Kiewit Plaza. Lodge: Knights of Ak-Sar-Ben (gov.). Office: PO Box 1103 DTS Omaha NE 68101

FITZGERALD, WILLIAM FRANCIS, banker. Chmn. Commercial Fed. Savs. & Loan Assn., Omaha, Nebr., also dir. Office: Commercial Fed Savs & Loan Assn PO Box 1103 DTS Omaha NE 68101*

FITZHARRIS, JOSEPH CHARLES, history educator; b. Mpls., Oct. 12, 1946; s. Maurice E. and Gertrude I. (McBride) F.; m. Mary Helen Schreiner, Aug. 30, 1969; children—Scott J., Keith R. B.A., Coll. St. Thomas, 1968; M.A., U. Minn., 1969; Ph.D., U. Wis., 1975. Instr. history Coll. St. Thomas, St. Paul, part-time 1971-72, full-time 1972-75, asst. prof., 1975-81, assoc. prof., 1981—, acting chmn. history dept., 1982; research fellow in agrl. and applied econs. U. Minn., part-time 1972-75, research assoc., 1975-79, part-time 1979-80; project evaluator Minn. Humanities Com., 1979-80; reader advance placement Ednl. Testing Service; cons. Ramsey County Hist. Soc. Mem. Mpls. Aquatennial Parades Com., 1972—; mem. coordinating com. St. Paul Campus Ministry, 1975-77, vice chmn., 1977. Recipient Certs. Appreciation, Coll. St. Thomas, 1977, 81, medallion, 1982, grantee, 1982; Ford Found. fellow, 1970-71; grantee Rockefeller Found., 1972-75, U. Minn. Agrl. Expt. Sta., 1975-79. Mem. Orgn. Am. Historians, Econ. History Assn., Am. Econ. Assn. Roman Catholic. Contbr. articles to profl. jours. Home: 13645 Elkwood Dr Apple Valley MN 55124 Office: 434 O'Shaughnessy Edn Ctr Coll St Thomas 2115 Summit Ave Saint Paul MN 55105

FITZPATRICK, CHRISTINE MORRIS, former television executive; b. Steubenville, Ohio, June 10, 1920; d. Roy Elwood and Ruby Lorena (Mason) Morris; student U. Chgo., 1943-44, U. Ga., 1945-46; B.A., Roosevelt U., 1947; postgrad. Trinity Coll., Hartford, Conn., 1970; m. T. Mallary Fitzpatrick, Jr., Dec. 19, 1942; 1 son, Thomas Mallary III. Asso. dir. Joint Human Relations Project, City of Chgo., 1965-66; tchr. English, Austin Sch. for Girls, Hartford, 1966-70; promotion coordinator Conn. Pub. TV, Hartford, 1971-72, dir. community relations, 1972-73, v.p., 1973-77; pub. relations/pub. affairs cons. Commonwealth Edison Co., Chgo., 1977-79; dir. spl. events Chgo. Public TV, 1979-84; pres. New Eng. chpt. Am. Women in Radio and TV, 1976-77; v.p. Public Relations Clinic Chgo., 1980-81. Pres., Chgo. chpt. LWV, 1962-64, v.p. Hartford chpt., 1971-73; bd. advisers Greater Hartford Mag., 1975-77; bd. dirs. World Affairs Center, Hartford, 1975-77; mem. adv. council Am. Revolution Bicentennial Commn. Conn., 1975-77. Mem. Pub. Relations Soc. Am. (dir. Conn. Valley chpt. 1976-77), Chgo. Council Fgn. Relations, Chgo. Architecture Found., Art Inst. Chgo. Mem. United Ch. Christ. Club: Arts (Chgo.). Home: 2614 W Logan Blvd Chicago IL 60647

FITZPATRICK, JAMES A., insurance company executive; b. Dayton, Ohio, Mar. 10, 1940; s. James A. and Ruby J. Fitzpatrick; children—Debby, James A. Agt., then state mgr. Res. Life Ins. Co., Columbus, Ohio, 1964-70; trainer, then asst. agy. dir. Universal Guarantee Life Ins. Co., Columbus, 1970-74; state mgr. Columbia Ins. Co., Indpls., 1974-76; v.p. Greenfield Assos., Inc., Indpls., 1976-81, pres., 1981—; founder, 1977, since pres. Greenfield Fin. Corp., Indpls.; chmn. bd. Greenfield Life Ins. Co., 1980—; founder, pres. Am.-Way Ins., 1982—; co-founder, sec., dir. Universal Computer Corp., Carmel, Ind., 1982—; dir. Med. Investors, Inc. Vice pres. Coalition for Welfare Reform. Served with USMC, 1959-63. Registered health underwriter. Mem. Nat. Assn. Health Underwriters (regional v.p. 1979-80), Life Underwriters Assn., Indpls. C. of C. (dir.), Greenfield C. of C. (v.p.). Clubs: Elks, Masons, Sertoma, Rotary. Office: PO Box 7079 Hilton Head Island SC 29938

FITZPATRICK, JOHN JOSEPH, opthalmologist; b. Omaha, Sept. 25, 1935; s. James Joseph and Gladys (Reece) F.; m. Mary Kathryn Heine, June 17, 1961; children—Mary C., Jeanne M., Ellen M., Anne M., Elizabeth E., Thomas J. M.D., Creighton U., 1961. Intern St. Catherine's Hosp., Omaha, 1961-62; resident in ophthalmology U. Nebr. Sch. Medicine, Omaha, 1962-65; practice medicine specializing in ophthalmology, Omaha, 1967—; instr. ophthalmology Creighton U., Omaha, 1967—. Served as lt. comdr. USN, 1965-67. Mem. Am. Acad. Ophthalmology, Omaha Ophthal. Soc. Roman Catholic. Home: 2916 S 97th Ave Omaha NE 68124 Office: 2420 S 73d St Omaha NE 68124

FITZPATRICK, SEAN KEVIN, advertising executive; b. Atlanta, Sept. 28, 1941; s. John Joseph and Roxanne Fitzpatrick; m. Sue Ellen Fitzpatrick; children—Seamus, Liz, Samantha. B.A., Hamilton Coll., 1963. Newspaper reporter Bloomington Daily Herald (Ind.), 1963-65; v.p., exec. creative dir. J. Walter Thompson, N.Y.C., Toronto, Los Angeles, San Francisco, 1965-75; v.p. Bing Crosby Prodns., Hollywood, Calif., 1976-77; creative dir. Columbia Pictures, Burbank, Calif., 1977-78; sr. v.p., creative dir. Dancer Fitzgerald Sample, Torrance, Calif., 1978-83; exec. v.p., creative dir. Campbell-Ewald, Warren, Mich., 1983—. Developer final chpt. Walking Tall, 1976, The Great Santini, 1977. Recipient film, art and advt. awards; named one of Top 100 Creative People in Am., Ad Day, 1983. Mem. Am. Acad. Motion Picture Arts and Scis., Detroit Adcraft Club, Los Angeles Creative Club, ASCAP.

FIZZELL, JAMES ALFRED, horticulturist; b. Chgo., Nov. 5, 1935; s. James Albert and Gladys Muriel (Blankley) F.; m. Adrienne Jane Ashbaugh, Aug. 30, 1975; children—Michael D., Lori J., Susan E., John W. Lucas. B.S., U. Ill.-Urbana, 1957, M.S., 1962. Farm adviser U. Ill.-Champaign, 1957-64; hort. service mgr. Tectrol div. Whirlpool Corp., St. Joseph, Mich., 1964-65; pres., mgr. Lakeland Greenhouses, Berrien Center, Mich., 1965-66; developmental mgr. Monterey Greenhouse, Salinas, Calif., 1966-69; developmental mgr., dir. Colorado Roses, Inc. div., LaFayette, Colo., 1969-71; sr. extension adviser horticulture U. Ill.-Rolling Meadows, 1971—; sec. Ill. Aborist Certifying Bd., 1985; guest appearances radio and TV shows. Mem. Am. Soc. Hort. Sci., Ill. Arborist Assn., Midwest Assn. Golfcourse Supts., Garden Writers Assn. Am., Nat. Assn. County Agrl. Agts. (Disting Service award 1984), Sigma Xi, Pi Alpha Xi, Epsilon Sigma Phi, Gamma Sigma Delta. Contbr. numerous articles to hort. bulls., landscape mags., others. Home: 1124 Garden St Park Ridge IL 60068 Office: 4200 W Euclid Ave Rolling Meadows IL 60008

FIZZELL, ROBERT LESTER, assn. exec., educator; b. Chgo., Apr. 29, 1939; s. James Albert and Gladys Muriel (Blankley) F.; B.A., Beloit Coll., 1961; M.A.T., Northwestern U., 1966, Ph.D., 1975; m. Marjorie Ann Moss, June 11, 1960; children—Richard Allan, James Tobias, Ronald Lester. Tchr. social studies, track coach Niles Twp. High Sch., West Div., Skokie, Ill., 1966-73; program coordinator Niles Twp. Action Learning Center, Skokie, 1973-77; assoc. prof. ednl. founds. dept. Western Ill. U., 1977—; exec. dir. Ill. Community Edn. Assn., Macomb, 1980-82; exec. dir. Ill. Alternative Edn. Assn., 1981—; cons. ednl. program devel. and evaluation. Pres., Planning Consortium for Children's Services in Ill., 1979-81. Served with U.S. Army, 1961-64. Mem. Ill. Alternative Edn. Assn. (pres., founder 1979—), Ill. Community Edn. Assn., Assn. Supervision and Curriculum Devel., World Future Soc., Phi Delta Kappa. Author: The Schooling Style Inventory, 1978; The Truants Alternative Program: An Evaluation, 1978. Home: 1706 Riverview Dr Macomb IL 61455 Office: 80 Horrabin Hall Western Ill U Macomb IL 61455

FLADEN, TODD DOUGLAS, ophthalmologist; b. Akron, Ohio, Sept. 8, 1952; s. Jerome D. and Elaine (Sabetay) F.; m. Sharon Vogel, Dec. 19, 1976; children—Elliot, Seth. B.A. in Chemistry, Emory U., 1974; M.D., Ohio State U., 1977. Intern Riverside Hosp., Columbus, Ohio, 1978; resident Ohio State U. Hosp., Columbus, 1978-81; ophthalmologist, Canton, Ohio, 1981—. Fellow Am. Acad. Ophthalmology; mem. AMA. Republican. Jewish. Avocations: Computer science, skiing, golf. Home: 808 47th St NE Canton OH 44714 Office: 1330 Timken Mercy Dr NW Canton OH 44708

FLAGG, RENWOOD STANLEY, chiropractor; b. Bath, Maine, Mar. 15, 1903; s. Albert Emerson and Mary Jane (Collins) F.; m. Mary Faye Hoback, Apr. 4, 1928; 1 son, Renwood Carl. Grad. Palmer Coll. Chiropractic, Davenport, Iowa, 1928. Pvt. practice chiropractor, Rogers City, Mich., 1928—. Mem. Internat. Chiropractors Assn., Mich. Chiropractic Council (Humanitarian award 1980) Rogers City C. of C., Presque Isle Hist. Soc. Republican. Presbyterian. Clubs: Kiwanis (past pres.), Mason, Shriner, Order Eastern Star.

FLAHERTY, JOHN JOSEPH, quality assurance co. exec.; b. Chgo., July 24, 1932; s. Patrick J. and Mary B. F.; B.E.E., U. Ill., 1959; m. Norrine Grow, Nov. 20, 1954; children—John, Bridgette, George, Eileen, Daniel, Mary, Michael, Amy. Design engr. Admiral Corp., Chgo., 1959-60; project engr. Magnaflux Corp., Chgo., 1960-79, v.p., mgr. research and engring., 1979-84, v.p., mgr. mktg. and sales, 1984—. Served with AUS, 1951-53. Mem. Am. Soc. Non-Destructive Testing, IEEE, Am. Soc. Quality Control. Roman Catholic. Numerous patents, publs. on nondestructive testing, including med. ultrasonic; laser scanning. Home: 671 Grosvener Ln Elk Grove Village IL 60007 Office: 7300 W Lawrence Ave Chicago IL 60656

FLAHIFF, CARDINAL GEORGE BERNARD, retired archbishop; b. Paris, Ont., Can., Oct. 26, 1905; s. John James and Eleanor Rose (Fleming) F.; B.A., St. Michael's Coll., U. Toronto, 1926; student U. Strasbourg (France), 1930-31; Dipl. Archiviste-Paleographe, Ecole Nat. des Chartes, Paris, France, 1935; hon. degree in law U. Seattle, 1965, U. Notre Dame, 1969, U. Man., 1969, U. Windsor, 1970, U. Winnipeg, 1972, U. Toronto, 1972; S.T.D., Université Laval, Quebec, 1974, St. Bonaventure U., 1975, U. St. Thomas, Houston, 1977. Ordained priest Roman Catholic Ch., 1930; prof. medieval history Pontifical Inst. Medieval Studies and U. Toronto, 1935-54, sec. Inst., 1943-51; superior-gen. Basilian Fathers, 1954-61; archbishop of Winnipeg, Can., 1961-82; named to Coll. Cardinals, 1969; mem. Sacred Congregation for Religious, Sacred Congregation for Edn. Decorated companion Order Can., 1974. Office: 50 Stafford St Winnipeg MB R3M 2V7 Canada

FLANAGAN, EDWARD JOSEPH, chiropractor; b. Cleve., Feb. 13, 1931; s. Edward Joseph and Esther Mary (White) F.; student Kent State U., 1950-52; D. Chiropractic, Great Lake Coll. Chiropractic, 1961; postgrad. roentgenology Lincoln Chiropractic Coll., 1968-70; m. Betty Sue Boone, Apr. 24, 1954; children—Linda, Susan, June, Collette, Lori, Mary Lou, Eddie. Pvt. chiropractic practice, North Olmsted, Ohio, 1961—; lectr.; cons. x-ray specialist Assos. Diagnostic Center, Akron, Ohio; owner Lorain Chiropractic Center, Memphis Chiropractic Center. Served with USNR, 1952-54. Licensed mechanotherapist, Ohio. Diplomate Am. Bd. Chiropractic Roentgenology. Mem. Am., Ohio, Northeastern Ohio chiropractic assns. Contbr. articles to profl. jours. Home: 31686 Lake Rd Avon Lake OH 44012 Office: 27712 Lorain Ave North Olmsted OH 44070

FLANAGAN, JOSEPH PATRICK, advertising executive; b. Chgo., Jan. 6, 1938; s. C. Larkin and Helen Mary (Sullivan) F.; m. Charlotte Mary Stepan, Sept 9, 1961; children—Charlotte, Joseph, Michael, Larkin, Brian. B.A., Mich. State U., 1959; M.B.A., U. Chgo., 1961. Dist. sales mgr. Time mag., Pitts., 1961-69; gen. mgr. Ctr. Advanced Research in Design, Chgo., 1969-75; v.p., dir. client services Cohen and Greenbaum Advt., Chgo., 1975-77; sr. v.p., dir. Impact, The Promotion and Design Co., Foote, Cone & Belding, Chgo., 1977-85, pres., dir., 1985—. Mem. governing bd. Chgo. Symphony Orch., 1971—. Mem. Council of Sales Promotion Agys. (1st v.p., dir. 1983). Roman Catholic. Club: Exmoor Country. Home: 136 Chestnut St Winnetka IL 60093 Office: 401 N Michigan Ave Chicago IL 60611

FLANAGAN, ROBERT WILLIAM, environmental engineering firm executive; b. Melcher, Iowa, Oct. 18, 1925; s. Forest Delno and Minnie Augusta (Horstmann) F.; m. Mildred Ann Dennison, Aug. 16, 1946 (div. 1974); children—Ruth Ann, Kathleen Karen, Steven Patrick. B.S.M.E., Iowa State U., 1949. Registered profl. engr., Iowa. Engring. trainee RCA, Camden, N.J., 1950-51; sales engr. Carrier Corp., Chgo., 1951-54, application engr., Syracuse, 1954-55; sales engr. Condition Air Corp., Des Moines, 1955-57; cons. engr. Stevenson-Flanagan-Schilling, Des Moines, 1957-69; pres. Environ. Engring. Inc., Des Moines, 1969—; cons. and lectr. in field; participant to numerous profl. confs. Contbr. articles to profl. jours. Mem. Des Moines Met. Transit Authority, 1983—, numerous other civic orgns. Served to sgt. USAF, 1943-46, ETO. Fellow ASHRAE (Disting. Service award 1972, Disting. Pub. Service award 1972); mem. ASME, Engrs. Joint Council (Engr. of Distinction award). Republican. Methodist. Lodge: Shriners (trustee 1976-82). Avocations: hunting; backpacking; hiking. Home: 1527 Ashworth Rd West Des Moines IA 50265 Office: Environ Engring Inc 806 Locust 300 Des Moines IA 50309

FLANDERS, DWIGHT PRESCOTT, economist, retired educator; b. Rockford, Ill., Mar. 14, 1909; s. Daniel Bailey and Lulu Iona (Nichol) F.; B.A., U. Ill., 1931, M.A., 1937; postgrad. Beloit Coll., 1933-34; Ph.D., Yale U., 1939; m. Mildred Margaret Hutchison, Aug. 27, 1939; children—James Prescott, Thomas Addison. Instr. coll. algebra Burr Sch., Beloit (Wis.) Coll., 1933-34; instr. U.S. history secondary schs., Rockford, 1934-36; asst. prof. econs. and statistics Syracuse U., 1939-42; prof. econs. U. Ill., Urbana-Champaign, 1946-77, prof. emeritus, 1977—, chmn. masters research seminar, 1947-74. grad. adviser, 1949-75, prof. emeritus dept. family and consumer econs. Coll. of Agr., 1980—; cons. in field. Del., Hazen Nat. Conf. Religion and Edn., 1948. Pres. Three Lakes (Wis.) Waterfront Homeowners Assn., 1969-71, mem. ofcl. bd., 1971-83. Served with AUS, 1930, 42-46. Recipient Best Grad. Tchr. award Coll. Commerce, U. Ill., 1977. Mem. Am. Econ. Assn., Econometric Soc., Royal Econ. Soc., Phi Beta Kappa, Phi Kappa Phi, Alpha Kappa Psi, Beta Gamma Sigma (pres. U. Ill. chpt. 1959-60, historian 1960-77), Chi Beta, Chi Psi. Club: Yale (Chgo.). Asso. editor Current Econ. Comment, 1946-54. Author monographs, books; contbr. articles to profl. publs. Home: 719 S Foley Ave Champaign IL 61820 Office: Dept Econs U Ill Urbana IL 61801

FLANDREAU, LEE ROBERT, manufacturing executive; b. Boston, Mar. 17, 1936; s. Robert Leeds and Elizabeth Jane (Zoeller) F.; children—Cynthia Lee, Susan Elizabeth. A.B., Miami U., Oxford, Ohio, 1958. Pres. Signode Can. Inc., Signode Corp., 1973-75; v.p. internat. Signode Corp., 1976-82, exec. v.p. internat., 1982—. Clubs: Thorngate Country (Deerfield, Ill.); Mid-America (Chgo.). Office: 3600 W Lake Ave Glenview IL 60025

FLANIGAN, EVERETT, research and development scientist; b. Atlanta, Apr. 10, 1944; s. Jesse and Evelyn Louise (Wilson) F.; m. Annette Lipscomb, Aug. 31, 1968; children—Kyle, Ryan, Asa, Erika. B.S., Clark Coll., 1965; M.Sc., Howard U., 1970; Ph.D., Wash. U., 1971. Sr. research assoc. Brookhaven Nat. Lab., Upton, L.I., N.Y., 1971-74; research scientist Armour Pharm. Co., Kankakee, Ill., 1974-76, group head, 1976-78, sr. scientist devel., 1983—; vis. scientist Brookhaven Nat. Lab., Upton, 1974-75; sect. head Revlon Health Care R & D, Tuckahoe, N.Y., 1978-83; grant reviewer NSF, Washington, 1977-79-81. Contbr. articles to sci. jours. Pres., bd. dirs. Kankakeeland Community Action, 1977, 84; pres. NAACP, Kankakee, 1978; commr. Westchester-Putnam council Boy Scouts Am., 1980-83. Recipient Citation for service Kankakee Sch. Dist. III, 1978, Kankakeeland Community Action Program, 1979, Boy Scouts Am., 1983, Kankakee Jr. High Sch. students, 1985. Mem. Am. Chem. Soc., N.Y. Acad. Scis., AAAS. Lutheran. Avocations: music; piano; reading; running. Home: RD3 Box 37 Kankakee IL 60901 Office: Armour PO Box 511 Kankakee IL 60901

FLANIGAN, ROSEMARY, philosophy educator; b. Kansas City, Mo., Aug. 23, 1926, d. Thomas Allen and Marguerite (McDonald) F.; A.B., Coll. St. Teresa, Kansas City, Mo., 1947; M.A., St. Louis U., 1956, Ph.D., 1964. Asst. prof. Fontbonne Coll., St. Louis, 1964-67, assoc. prof., asst. dean, 1967-68; prof. Avila Coll., Kansas City, Mo., 1968-72, Rockhurst Coll., 1975—. Contbr. articles to profl. jours. Named Tchr. of Yr., Rockhurst Coll., 1976, 77, 80. Mem. Metaphys. Soc. Am., Kansas City Area Tchrs. of Philosophy, Alpha Sigma Nu. Avocations: reading, gardening. Office: Rockhurst Coll 5225 Troost Ave Kansas City MO 64110

FLANNERY, ROBERT JAMES, consulting laboratory executive; b. Chgo., Sept. 10, 1930; s. John Sarsfield and Lucille Marie (Thurnes) F.; m. June Bernadine Thorsen, Jan. 30, 1954; children—Kathleen A., Joan E. B.S., Loyola U.-Chgo., 1952; M.S., Wayne State U., 1954, Ph.D., 1958. With Amoco Oil Co., Chgo., 1958-70, project chemist through sect. leader, 1958-70; coordinator corp. research planning Standard Oil Co. Ind., Chgo., 1970-73, research assoc., 1976-80; v.p. Pure Culture Products Co., Chgo., 1970-76; cons. Bernard Wolnak and Assocs., Chgo., 1980-84; adminstrv. dir. BW BIOTEC, Inc., Chgo., 1984-85, v.p. adminstrn., 1985—. Pres. Arcadia Homeowners Assn., 1965-66; mem. Olympia Fields (Ill.) Planning Bd., 1966-69. Recipient IR-100 award Industrial Research Mag., 1966. Mem. The Electrochem. Soc. (chmn. Chgo. sect. 1970), Am. Chem. Soc., Inst. of Food Technologists, Sigma Xi. Club: IJP Choir. Contbr. articles in field to profl. publs. Patentee in electrochemistry, analytical chemistry, food. Home: 20341 Ithaca Rd Olympia Fields IL 60461

FLANNIGAN, ANTHONY MICHAEL, airline pilot; b. Chgo., Feb. 18, 1950; s. Terrence J. and Ann (Spada) F. A.Aviation Tech., So. Ill. U., 1970, B.B.S., 1972; M.S., 1975. Lic. pilot, FAA. Asst. chief flight instr. So. Ill. U., Carbondale, 1972-75, chief instrument flight instr., 1975-78; pilot United Airlines, Chgo., 1978-81, 83—; chief flight instr. So. Ill. U., Carbondale, 1981-83. Mem. Airline Pilots Assn., Univ. Aviation Assn. (dir. 1977-80), Nat. Bus. Aviation Assn. Home: 5942 N Ozanam Chicago IL 60631 Office: O'Hare Airport Chicago IL

FLATHOM, GLORIA JEAN, nurse, consultant; b. Beloit, Wis., June 3, 1945; d. Jesse Drell and Jennie (Hynek) Perkins; m. Daniel Flathom; children—Julie, Jill, Jason. A.A.S., Moraine Valley Community Coll., 1980; B.A., Trinity Christian Coll., Palos Heights, Ill., 1985. R.N. Adminstrv. asst. Gen. Telephone Co., Madison, 1967-68; nurse Christ Hosp., Oak Lawn, Ill., 1980—; nurse cons. Johnson & Johnson, Boston, 1983; research nurse Rush-Presbyn.-St. Lukes Med. Ctr., Chgo., 1983; office nurse, 1984-85. Vice pres. Am. Lutheran Ch. Women, Chgo., 1970-72, McKay Sch. PTA, Chgo., 1972-74; patron chmn. cotillion Christ Hosp. Aux., 1982. Ill. state scholar, 1983-85. Mem. Nurses Assn. Am. Coll. Ob-Gyn., Trinity Christian Coll. Alumni Assn.

FLAUGHER, JAMES HAROLD, optometrist; b. New Castle, Pa., Feb. 27, 1925; s. Riley Columbus and Rosetta (Potter) F. Student Riverside Jr. Coll., Calif., 1946-47; B.S., Westminster Coll., 1947-48; O.D., No. Ill. Coll. Optometry, 1948-50. Served with U.S. Army, 1943-46. Mem. Cedar Falls C. of C. Republican. Club: Beaver Hills Country. Lodges: Elks, Rotary. Avocations: golf, table tennis, dancing. Home: 1104 Oak Park Blvd Cedar Falls IA 50613 Office: 1001 W 23rd St Cedar Falls IA 50613

FLAUM, JOEL MARTIN, See *Who's Who in America,* 43rd edition.

FLEENER, CHARLES JOSEPH, history educator; b. New Orleans, Nov. 22, 1938; s. J. Edwin and Marguerite Louise (Borda) F.; m. Mary Denise Cleary, Aug. 26, 1967; children—Cristina Borda, Margarita Cleary. B.S., Georgetown U., 1960; Ph.D., U. Fla., 1969. Instr., St. Louis U., 1966-69; asst. prof. dept. history, 1969-74, assoc. prof. Latin Am. history, 1974—, chmn. dept., 1980-85, dir. pre-law program, 1985—. Mem. Am. Hist. Assn., Am. Cath. Hist. Assn., Conf. Latin Am. History, Latin Am. Studies Assn., Midwest Assn. Latin Am. Studies (pres. 1969-70). Roman Catholic. Author: The Guide to Latin American Paperback Literature, 1966; Religious and Cultural Factors in Latin America, 1970. Home: 6363 Waterman University City MO 63130 Office: Dept History XH-357 St Louis U Saint Louis MO 63103

FLEISCH, JEROME HERBERT, pharmacologist, research scientist; b. Bronx, N.Y., June 6, 1941; s. Wolf and Miriam (Glaser) F.; m. Marlene L. Cohen, Aug. 8, 1976; children—Abby Faye, Sheryl Brynne. B.S. in Pharmacy, Columbia U., 1963; Ph.D. in Pharmacology, Georgetown U., 1967. Research fellow Harvard Med. Sch., Boston, 1967-68; research assoc. NIH Nat. Heart and Lung Inst., Bethesda, Md., 1968-70, sr. staff fellow, 1970-74; sr. pharmacologist Lilly Research Labs., Indpls., 1974-77, research scientist, 1977-82, research assoc., 1982—. Contbr. articles to profl. jours. Patentee in field. Served to lt. comdr. USPHS, 1968-70. Mem. Am. Soc. Pharmacology Exptl. Therapeutics, Am. Acad. Allergy and Immunology, Collegium Internationale Allergologicum, Soc. Exptl. Biology and Medicine. Office: Lilly Research Labs Lilly Corp Ctr Indianapolis IN 46285

FLEISCHACKER, PAUL REECE, actuarial consultant; b. Des Moines, July 15, 1942; s. Henry J. and Mary M. (Haworth) F.; m. Brenda Lee Lavent, May 30, 1964; children—David, Michael, Melissa, Anita. B.S., Drake U., 1965. Cons. actuary George V. Stennes & Assocs., Mpls., 1965-70, v.p. and treas., 1973-78; actuary Western Life Ins. Co., St. Paul, 1970-73; prin. Towers, Perrin, Forster & Crosby, Mpls., 1978—. Cubmaster, Boy Scouts Am., Mpls., 1975; mem. bus. adminstrn. com. St. John the Baptist Ch., New Brighton, Minn., 1984—. Fellow Soc. Actuaries; mem. Am. Acad. Actuaries, Twin Cities Actuarial Club. Roman Catholic. Lodge: KC. Avocations: fishing; boating; skiing. Home: 2157 Lakebrook Dr New Brighton MN 55112 Office: 8300 Norman Center Dr Suite 600 Bloomington MN 55437

FLEISCHAUER, JOHN FREDERICK, English educator, college dean; b. Dayton, Ohio, Apr. 29, 1939; s. Paul J. and Ruth (Hedgcock) F.; m. Janet Elaine Patterson, June 17, 1961; children—John Eric, Marc Lawrence, Scott Christopher. B.A., Cornell U., 1961; M.A., Ohio State U., 1966, Ph.D., 1970. Teaching fellow Denison U., 1968-69; asst. prof. English, Ohio U.-Athens, 1970-74, dir. 100-level English, 1973-74; div. chmn., prof. English, Columbus Coll., 1974-81; prof. English, dean Coll., Mt. Union Coll., 1981—; cons., lectr. bus. communications faculty devel. programs, 1975—. Author: Writing Skills, 1978; contbr. articles to profl. jours. Vice-pres., bd. dirs. Columbus Symphony Orch., 1980. Served with USN, 1961-65. Ohio U. research grantee, 1973; NEH grantee, 1978. Mem. Am. Conf. Acad. Deans, East Central Coll. Consortium (dir. 1982—), Council Ind. Colls. Methodist. Lodge: Kiwanis Internat. (dir.). Avocations: choral music; hiking; canoeing; photography. Home: 1446 S Union Ave Alliance OH 44601 Office: Mt Union Coll 1972 Clark Ave Alliance OH 44601

FLEISCHMANN, ROBERT ALAN, school administrator; b. Chgo., June 12, 1951; s. Max Werner and Else (Koller) F.; m. Lisa Hope Shakman, Aug. 19, 1973; children—Michael, David, Lauren Lindsay. B.A.S. in Elem. Edn., Spl. Edn., No. Ill. U., 1973, M.A.S. in Ednl. Adminstrn., 1976; postgrad. Nat. Coll. Edn. Cert. tchr., adminstr., Ill. Tchr. Plato (Ill.) Center Elem. Sch., 1973-74; tchr. Armstrong Elem. Sch., Hoffman Estates, Ill., 1974-79, asst. prin., 1976-79; prin. Lily Lake Elem. Sch., Maple Park, Ill., 1979—, coordinator inservice negotiations, sub-head elem. curriculum, 1979—. Ill. State edn. grantee, 1979-83. Mem. Ill. Prins. Assn., Supervision and Curriculum Devel. Assn., Kane County Elem. Prins. Orgn., Nat. Assn. Elem. Prins. Jewish. Lodge: B'nai Brith. Author: Central's Kindergarten Curriculum Guide, 1980; Central's Reading Curriculum Guide, 1981. Home: 653 Leslie Ln Schaumburg IL 60194 Office: Rural Route 2 Rt 47 Maple Park IL 60151

FLEMING, ALFRED JOSEPH, lawyer; b. Youngstown, Ohio, May 3, 1947; s. Paul John and Helen (Baeszler) F.; m. Suzanne Helen Morrison; children—Kyra Marie, Alfred Joseph. Student, Miami U., Oxford, Ohio, 1966-67; B.A., Youngstown State U., 1970; J.D., U. Akron, 1975. Assoc. McLaughlin, DiBlasio & Harshman, Youngstown, 1975-79; counsel Cafaro Co., Youngstown, 1979—; lectr. Youngstown State U., 1977-78. Author U. Akron Law Rev. 1975. Bd. dirs. Internat. Inst., Youngstown, 1983; charter mem., incorporator N. Side Citizens, Youngstown, 1977. Recipient achievement award Lawyers Coop. Pub. Co., 1974. Democrat. Roman Catholic. Club: Chesterton (Youngstown). Home: 1874 Selma Ave Youngstown OH 44504 Office: PO Box 2186 2445 Belmont Ave Youngstown OH 44504

FLEMING, DAVID AVERY, internist; b. Moberly, Mo., May 9, 1948; s. Jacob William and Mary Louise (Maddox) F.; m. Carolyn Marlow, July 24, 1970; children—Amy, Brian. B.A., U. Mo., 1970, M.A., 1972, M.D., 1976. Diplomate Am. Bd. Internal Medicine. Resident internal medicine U. Mo., Columbia, 1976-79; chief resident in medicine Truman VA Hosp., Columbia, 1979-80; pres. Woodland Internist Group, Moberly, 1980—; mem. clin. staff Mo. U. Health Scis. Ctr., Columbia, 1980—; dir. City Bank & Trust Co., Moberly, 1984—. Mem. Child Protection Team-Family Services, Moberly, 1982—, adv. bd. Home Care of Mid Mo., Moberly, 1984—. Mem. AMA, ACP, Am. Soc. Internal Medicine (councilor Mo. chpt. 1982—). Lodge: Rotary. Home: 1432 Corinth Dr Moberly MO 65270 Office: 1513 Union Ave Moberly MO 65270

FLEMING, DOUGLAS G., former feed company executive; b. Harvey, Ill., Apr. 28, 1930; s. Harold L. and Genevieve (Hodges) F.; B.S., Mich. State U., 1954; m. Sara L. Waters, May 25, 1952; children—Christine J., James C. With Central Soya Co., 1954-85, asst. mgr. field ops., Ft. Wayne, Ind., 1963-65, v.p., dir. mktg., 1965-70, exec. v.p., 1970-76, pres., 1976-79, pres., chief exec. officer, 1980-85, also dir.; sr. advisor to postmaster gen. U.S. Postal Service, Washington, 1985—; dir. Tokheim Corp., Midwestern United Life Ins. Co., Arvin Industries. Bd. dirs. United Way Allen County. Served to 2d lt. AUS, 1951-53. Mem. Am. Feed Mfrs. Assn. Clubs: Ft. Wayne Country, Summit (Ft. Wayne). Home: 16817 Tonkel Rd Leo IN 46765 Office: US Post Office Hdqrs Washington DC

FLEMING, GEORGE ROBERT, psychologist; b. New Haven, July 24, 1947; s. George Robert and Susie Mae F.; B.A., Hillsdale Coll., 1969; M.A., Mich. State U., 1972, Ph.D., 1975; m. Belinda M. Walker, June 18, 1983. Dir., East N.Y. Mental Health Clinic Adult Day Treatment Program, N.Y.C., 1973-77; chmn. psychology dept. Malcolm-King Harlem Coll. Extension, N.Y.C., 1979, adj. prof., 1977-79; staff psychologist Bedford-Stuyvesant Community Mental Health Center, N.Y.C., 1977-79; cons. Detroit Public Schs., 1981-82, Centrax Diversified Services, 1977—, City of Detroit Comprehensive Youth Services Program, 1980-81; dir. Central City br. Children's Center, Detroit, 1979-81, Sacred Heart Women's Day Treatment Ctr., 1981-84, Total Health Care, Inc., 1982—, Greater Detroit Life Consultation Ctr., 1982-84, Detroit Osteo. Hosp., 1984—. NIMH fellow, 1974-75. Mem. Nat. Black Child Devel. Inst. (mem. steering com. met. Detroit 1981), Nat. Register Health Service Providers in Psychology, Am. Psychol. Assn., Assn. Black Psychologists, Am. Orthopsychiat. Assn., Internat. Neuropsychol. Soc., Mich. Psychol. Assn., Mich. Assn. Black Psychologists (chmn. 1981-82), Mich. Soc. Clin. Psychologists, Omicron Delta Kappa. Home and Office: 5019 1/2 Woodward Ave Detroit MI 48202

FLEMING, LIBBY KOMAIKO, dancer, choreographer; b. Chgo., June 30, 1949; d. Robert and Dorothy (Rice) Komaiko. B.A., Northeastern Ill. U., Chgo., 1978. Scholar, dancer José Greco Spanish Dance Co., U.S.A., 1968-69; dancer Lola Montes Spanish Dance Co., U.S.A., 1976; mem. faculty/dance program dept. music Northeastern Ill. U., Chgo., 1975—; founder, dir. Ensemble Español, Chgo., 1976—, Am. Spanish Dance Festival, 1980—. Choreographer: Ben Amor, 1980, Concerto in D., 1982-83; Era del Romance, 1983; Ilusiones, 1983; Canciones de García Lorca, 1983; Ecos de España, 1983; Noches en Los Jardines de España, 1984; El Albaicin, 1985; Memorias de Vidas Gitanas, 1985; numerous others. Recipient Lazo de Dama de la Orden de Isabel La Católica, Juan Carlos I, King of Spain, 1982; Alumni Merit award Northeastern Ill. U., 1983; NEA fellow, 1980, 83; Ill. Arts Council fellow, 1984; Chgo. Council Fine Arts fellow, 1985. Mem. Chgo. Dance Arts Coalition (bd. dirs. 1983—). Office: Ensemble Español 5500 N St Louis Ave Chicago IL 60625

FLEMING, MILO JOSEPH, lawyer; b. Roscoe, Ill., Jan. 4, 1911; s. John E. and Elizabeth (Shafer) F.; A.B., U. of Ill., 1933, LL.B., 1936; m. Dorothea H. Kunze, Aug. 15, 1942 (dec. 1944); m. 2d, Lucy Anna Russell, June 30, 1948; step-children—Michael Russell, Jo Ann Russell (Mrs. Clemens); 1 dau., Elizabeth Fleming Weber. Pvt. practice law, 1936-42, 58-59; mem. firm Pallissard and Fleming, Watseka, Ill., 1942-46, Pallissard, Fleming & Oram, 1946-58, Fleming & McGrew, 1960-76, Fleming, McGrew and Boyer, 1977, Fleming & Boyer, 1977-79, Fleming, Boyer & Strough, 1980-82, Fleming & Strough, 1982—; master in chancery, Iroquois County, Ill., 1943-44. City atty., Watseka, Ill., 1949-57, 61—, Gilman, Ill., 1966-69; village atty. Milford, Ill., 1942-70, Wellington, 1962-72, Woodland, 1958-79, Danforth, 1961-78, Crescent City, Martinton, Sheldon, 1946-79, Onarga, Cissna Park, 1977-82, Beaverville, Papineau; atty. Lake Iroquois Lot Owners Assn. and Central San. Dist.; asst. atty. gen. Iroquois County, 1964-69; pres. Iroquois County Devel. Corp., 1961-68; bd. dirs. Belmont Water Co., 1963-81, pres., 1976-81; farmer. Chmn., Iroquois County Universities Bond Issues Campaign, 1960; mem. State Employees Group Ins. Adv. Commn., Ill., 1975-78; trustee Welles Sch. Fund, Watseka, 1978—. Candidate, state rep., Apr. 1940; life mem. U. Ill. President's Council, 1979—. Recipient award of merit for indsl. relations Watseka Area C. of C., 1983. Mem. Am. (vice chmn. com. ordnances and adminstrv. regulations 1968-69, 73-75, chmn. 1969-72, 75-78, mem. council local govt. sect. 1976-79, mem. council sect. urban, state and local govt. law 1979-80), Ill., Iroquois County (pres. 1966-67) bar assns., Internat. Platform Assn., Smithsonian Instn., Phi Eta Sigma, Sigma Delta Kappa. Democrat. Methodist. Lodges: Masons (32 deg.), Shriners, Odd Fellows (mem. jud. and appeals com. Ill. 1960-62, grand warden Ill. 1962, dep. grand master 1963, grand master 1964; grand rep. 1966; trustee Old Folks Home, Mattoon, Ill., 1966-71, sec. bd. 1966-68, vice chmn. bd. 1970—, atty. 1966—; 2d v.p. No. Assn. in Ill. Odd Fellows and Rebekahs 1981, 1st v.p., 1982, pres. 1983, recipient Meritorious Service Jewel, Grand Encampment of Ill. 1980, elected grand sr. Warden Grand Encampment of Ill. 1984). Author: One Hundred Twenty-five Years of Odd Fellowship at Watseka, Illinois. Prepared Municipal Code for City of Watseka, 1953, 80, Milford, 1957, Martinton, 1960, Crescent City, 1960, Woodland, 1961, Cissna Park, 1961, Papineau, 1978. Home: 120 W Jefferson Ave Watseka IL 60970 Office: Fleming & Strough Odd Fellows Bldg 216 E Walnut St Watseka IL 60970

FLEMING, RICHARD JOSEPH, mathematics educator; b. Dexter, Iowa, July 26, 1938; s. Joseph Julius and Luthera Edna (Ribble) F.; m. Janet Su Cox, Aug. 20, 1960 (div. May 1982); children—Deborah Christine, Joseph Josh, Margaret Nell; m. Diane Kaye Lambart, Jan. 9, 1983. B.S. in Edn., N.W. Mo. State U., 1960; M.S., Fla. State U., 1962, Ph.D., 1965. Asst. prof. U. Mo., Columbia, 1965-71; assoc. prof. Memphis State U., 1971-80, prof. math., 1980-82; prof., chmn. dept. math. Central Mich. U., Mt. Pleasant, 1982—. Contbr. articles to profl. jours. Mem. Am. Math. Soc., Math. Assn. Am. Republican. Mem. Christian Ch. Avocations: reading; writing; sports officiating high sch. level. Home: 615 N Lansing St Mount Pleasant MI 48858 Office: Dept Mathematics Central Mich Univ Mount Pleasant MI 48858

FLEMING, RICHARD WILLIAM, food company executive; b. Evanston, Ill., Jan. 14, 1944; s. James Richard and Henrietta Louise (Koellmann) F.; m. Amber Yarde, Feb. 20, 1971. B.S., Bradley U., 1965; M.B.A., DePaul U., 1975. Mgmt. trainee Campbell Soup Co., Chgo., 1969-70, planning mgr., 1970-74; mgr. fin. planning Am. Hosp. Supply Corp., Evanston, Ill., 1974-76, mgr. comml. devel., 1976-78; dir. corp. planning Stokely-Van Camp, Inc., Indpls., 1978-80; dir. corp. planning Libby, McNeill & Libby, Inc., Chgo., 1980-82, v.p. fin. and planning, 1982—, also dir., mem. exec. com.; mem. fin. com. Nestle Enterprises, Inc. Served with USN, 1967-69. Mem. Nat. Assn. Food Processors, Fin. Execs. Inst., Beta Gamma Sigma, Delta Mu Delta. Republican. Home: 1052 W Inverlieth Rd Lake Forest IL 60045 Office: Libby McNeill & Libby Inc 200 S Michigan Ave Chicago IL 60604

FLESHER, ROBERT DANA, gas company official; b. Columbus, Ohio, Dec. 4, 1945; s. John Harvey and Virginia A. (Jackson) F.; m. Sondra K. Arkley, Oct. 16, 1976; 1 dau., Angela Lynn. Student Ohio State U., 1964-67. Sales, Central Ohio Welding (Airco), Columbus, 1971-74; distbn. mgr. Chemetron Corp., Columbus, 1974, Toledo, 1974-78; gen. mgr. fleet maintenance AGA Gas, Inc., Cleve., 1978—. Served in USNR, 1966-70. Recipient numerous awards in field. Mem. Am. Trucking Assns., Soc. Automotive Engrs., ASTM, Pvt. Truck Council, Pvt. Carrier Conf., Ohio Trucking Assn., Am. Mgmt. Assn. Roman Catholic. Club: Literary Guild. Home: 7440 Midland Rd Independence OH 44131 Office: 3300 Lakeside Ave Cleveland OH 44114

FLESSNER, BRUCE WILLIAM, management consultant; b. Lansing, Mich., July 14, 1953; s. Lloyd William and Winifred Marie (Beeman) F.; m. Melanie Vlaich, Aug. 10, 1975; 1 child, Lauren Blair Vlaich. B.S., Central Mich. U., 1976; M.P.A., Western Mich. U., 1978; postgrad. U. Minn., 1978-84. Dir. ann. giving Kalamazoo Coll., 1975-78; devel. officer U. Minn., Mpls., 1978-80, v.p., assoc. dir. U. Minn. Found., 1980-83; prin. Bentz, Whaley, Flessner & Assocs., Inc., Mpls., 1983—. Bd. dirs. Kalamazoo Alcohol and Drug Abuse Council, 1976-78, Mac Phail Ctr. for Arts, 1983—, Family Networks, 1983—; vice chmn. Kalamazoo County Democratic Party, 1976-78. Recipient key to City of Bay City, Mich., 1972. Mem. Nat. Assn. Fundraising Execs., Pub. Relations Soc. Am., Council Advancement and Support of Edn. Presbyterian. Office: Suite 559 6800 France Ave S SE Minneapolis MN 55435

FLETCHER, ALAN GORDON, university administrator, civil engineering educator; b. Gibson's Landing, B.C., Can., Jan. 2, 1925; came to U.S., 1959; s. William George and Florence Gertrude (Smith) F.; m. A. Irene Flynn, Aug. 6, 1949; children—Christopher Lee, Elizabeth Joan, Lynn Patricia, Anne Marie. B.A.Sc., U. B.C., Vancouver, 1948; M.S., Calif. Inst. Tech., 1952; Ph.D., Northwestern U., 1965. Registered profl. engr., B.C. Supr. hydroelectric planning B.C. Electric Co., Vancouver, 1948-59; asst. prof. civil engring. U. Idaho, Moscow, 1959-62; assoc. prof. U. Utah, Salt Lake City, 1964-69; prof. U. N.D., Grand Forks, 1969—, also dean Sch. Engring. and Mines. Bd. dirs., pres. YMCA, Vancouver, 1950-59; active Presbyn. chs., various locations. Walter P. Murphy fellow Northwestern U., 1962. Mem. ASCE, Am. Soc. Engring. Edn., Assn. Profl. Engrs. B.C., Nat. Soc. Profl. Engrs., N.D. Soc. Profl. Engrs. (Elwyn F. Chandler award 1981). Home: 3117 Olson Dr Grand Forks ND 58201 Office: Univ ND Sch Engring and Mines Grand Forks ND 58202

FLETCHER, DALE WESLEY, avian toxicologist, researcher; b. Waupaca, Wis., July 23, 1948; s. Myron James and Ethel May (Boutwell) F.; m. Philomena Catherine Czysen, June 22, 1968; children—Keith, Christopher. B.S. U. Wis.-Eau Claire, 1970, Chemist P & L Biochems., Milw., 1970-71; group leader Indsl. Bio-Test Labs., Neillsville, Wis., 1970-77, sect. head, 1977-79; pres. Bio-Life Assocs., Ltd., Neillsville, 1979—; tchr. Mem. Soc. Environ. Toxicology and Chemistry, Am. Chem. Soc., ASTM, Soc. Toxicology. Club: Marshfield Curling. Lodge: K.C. Contbr. articles to profl. jours. Home: 9889 W Ives St Marshfield WI 54449 Office: Bio-Life Assocs Rt 3 PO Box 156 Neillsville WI 54456

FLETCHER, EDWARD ABRAHAM, chemistry and mechanical engineering educator; b. Detroit, July 30, 1924; s. Morris H. and Lillian (Protes) F.; m. Roslyn Silber, June 15, 1948; children—Judith, Deborah, Carolyn. B.S., Wayne State U., 1948; Ph.D., Purdue U., 1952. Head propellant chemistry NASA, Cleve., 1952-59; faculty U. Minn., Mpls., 1959—, prof. mech. engring.; cons. NSF, Washington, 1982—. Contbr. articles to profl. jours. Patentee in field. Served with USNR, 1942-46. Mem. Combustion Inst. Avocation: skiing. Home: 3909 Beard Ave S Minneapolis MN 55410 Office: U Minn 111 Church St SE Minneapolis MN 55455

FLETCHER, JOHN A., zoo director; b. Burlington, Wash., May 7, 1919. B.S., U. Wash., 1946; postgrad. U. Minn., 1973-74. Keeper, Seattle Zoo, 1947-57; dir. Como Zoo, St. Paul, 1957—. Served with AUS, 1941-45. Fellow Am. Assn. Zool. Parks and Aquaria. Office: Como Zoo Midway Pkwy and Kaufman Dr Saint Paul MN 55103

FLETCHER, MARIA VALENA, physician; b. Manila, Philippines, Aug. 18, 1955; came to U.S., 1970; d. Dominador and Patria (Laserna) Valena; m. Jerry Herbert Fletcher, May 10, 1980. B.S., Ball State U., 1976; M.D., Ind. U.-Indpls., 1980. Family practice resident Ball Meml. Hosp., Muncie, Ind., 1980-81, St. Francis Hosp., Beech Grove, Ind., 1981-83; family physician People's Health Ctr, Indpls., 1983—; advisor Maternity Family League, Indpls., 1983—, Decatur Central High Sch., Health Careers, Indpls., 1983—. Mem. AMA, Am. Acad. Family Physicians. Roman Catholic. Clubs: Aerobic, Greater Indpls. Choral Co. Home: 8117 Teel Way Indianapolis IN 46256 Office: People's Health Ctr 2340 E 10th St Indianapolis IN 46201

FLETCHER, WALTER EUGENE, purchasing agent; b. Detroit, Mar. 23, 1942; s. Eugene Reed and Marguerite K. (Bibbens) F.; m. Sue Ann Tickner, June 14, 1968; 1 son, Andrew Reed. A.S., McHenry County Coll., Crystal Lake, Ill., 1982. Cert. purchasing mgr. Asst. buyer Acme Mfg. Co., Ferndale, Mich., 1972-73; buyer Ex-Cell-O Corp., Howell, Mich., 1974-79, purchasing agt., Mundelein, Ill., 1980—. Ctr. dir. Howell Jr. Achievement, 1975-79. Served to sgt. U.S. Army, 1964-70. Republican. Methodist. Lodge: Elks. Home: 512 Silbury Ct McHenry IL 60050 Office: Ex-Cell-O Corp 209 Tower Rd Mundelein IL 60060

FLIDER, FRANK STANLEY, manufacturing company executive; b. Chgo., July 20, 1929; s. James J. and Sophia H. (Kalda) F.; m. Frances T. Lysak, Feb. 6, 1954; children—Frank J., Robert F., Jeanine T. Student, U. Ill., 1948. Engr., advt. mgr. Heyer, Inc., Chgo., 1952-64; art dir., salesman Jet Press, Inc., Berkeley, Ill., 1964-66; chief engr. Copy-Rite Corp., Chgo., 1966-69; now v.p. engring. Justrite Mfg. Co., Mattoon, Ill. Served with USN, 1948-52. Mem. Soc. Fire Protection Engrs., Am. Soc. Safety Engrs., Soc. Mfg. Engrs., ASTM. Clubs: Golf and Country (Mattoon, Ill.), KC. Patentee in field. Home: 13 Doral Ct Rural Route 3 Mattoon IL 61938 Office: West Route 121 Mattoon IL 61938

FLINT, JAMES RICHARD, automotive company executive; b. Janesville, Wis., Apr. 13, 1947; s. Llewllyn Carrier and Lillian Suzanne (Hoppe) F.; m. Imedla Marie Henige, Oct. 26, 1968; children—Jeffrey Allen, Christopher Jonathon. B. of Indsl. Engring., Gen. Motors Inst., Flint, Mich., 1970. Mfg. supr. Chevrolet Saginaw Mfg., Mich., 1969-70, mgr. supr., 1972-73, inspection supr., 1973-76, mfg. engr., 1976; gen. supr. quality assurance Delco Moraine-Saginaw Mfg., 1977—. Vice pres. Sch. Bd., Birch Run, Mich., 1976-80; chmn. Birch Run Athletic Boosters Assn., 1984-85; pres. Parish Council Sacred Heart Ch., Birch Run, 1978-81. Served with U.S. Army, 1970-72. Republican. Roman Catholic. Club: Saginaw Indsl. Mgmt. (pres. 1982-84). Lodge: KC. Avocations: investing, travel, hunting. Home: 12587 Marshall Rd Birch Run MI 48415

FLISS, WILLIAM MICHAEL, financial executive; b. Milw.; s. Alfred Michael Fliss and Evelyn Augusta (Grams) Beyer; m. Patricia Ann Ligman, Oct. 28, 1972; children—Jeremy Scot, Noel Michael, Bryan Christopher. B.B.A., U. Wis. 1973. Fin. planning analyst Walker Mfg. Tenneco Automotive, Racine, Wis., 1979-80; mgr. Gen. Acctg. Perfex div. McQuay, Inc., Milw., 1980-81, asst. div. controller, 1981-82, div. controller, 1982-83; div. controller energy Systems and Services div., 1983-85; mgr. adminstrn. McQuay Services, Plymouth, Minn., 1985—; cons. small bus. systems, Milw., 1984—. Adv. Jr. Achievement, Racine, 1976-79; cubmaster Milwaukee County council Boy Scouts Am., Milw., 1983—. Mem. Nat. Assn. Accts., Am. Mgmt. Assn. Republican. Roman Catholic. Avocations: camping; golf; baseball coach. Home: 15620 49th Ave N Plymouth MN 55446 Office: McQuay Inc 13600 Industrial Park Blvd Plymouth MN 55441

FLORESTANO, DANA JOSEPH, architect; b. Indpls., May 2, 1945; s. Herbert Joseph and Myrtle Mae (Futch) F.; B. Arch., U. Notre Dame, 1968; m. Peggy Joy Larsen, June 6, 1969. Designer, draftsman Kennedy, Brown & Trueblood, architects, Indpls., 1965-69, Evans Woolen Assn., architects,

Indpls., 1966; designer, project capt. James Assos., architects and engrs., Indpls., 1969-71; architect, v.p. comml. projects Multi-Planners Inc., architects and engrs., 1972-73; pvt. practice architecture, Indpls., 1973—; pres. Florestano Corp., constrn. mgmt., Indpls., 1973—; co-founder, pres. Solargenics Natural Energy Corp., Indpls., 1975—; prof. archtl. and constrn. tech. Ind. U.-Purdue U. at Indpls.; instr. in field. Tech. adviser hist. architecture Indpls. Model Cities program, 1969-70; mem. Hist. Landmarks Found. Ind., 1970-72; chmn. Com. to Save Union Sta., 1970-71, founder, pres. Union Sta. Found. Inc., Indpls., 1971—. Recipient 2d design award Marble Inst. Am., 1967, 1st design award 19th Ann. Progressive Architecture Design awards, 1972; Design award for excellence in devel. Marriott Inn, Indpls., Met. Devel. Commn.-Office of Mayor, 1977; 1st place award design competition for Visitor's Info. Center, Cave Run, Lake, Ky., 1978; 2d design award 1st Ann. Qualified Remodeler, Nat. Competition for Best Rehab. Existing Structures in Am., 1979. Mem. U. Notre Dame Alumni Assn., Notre Dame Club Indpls., A.I.A. (nat. com. historic resources 1974—, commn. on community services, Speakers Bur. Indpls. chpt. 1976—), Ind. Soc. Architects (chmn. historic architecture com. 1970—), Constrn. Specifications Inst., Constrn. Mgrs. Assn. Ind. (incorporator, dir. 1976—). Home: 5697 N Broadway St Indianapolis IN 46220 Office: 6214 N Carrollton Ave Indianapolis IN 46220

FLOREY, FRANCIS GARY, mathematics educator; b. Pingree, N.D., Mar. 26, 1936; s. Guy Emmett and Marie (Hopland) F.; m. Maxine Rose Christensen, April 20, 1957; children—Kevin Lee, Todd Francis, Pamela Rae. B.S., Augustana Coll., Sioux Falls, S.D., 1958; M.A., U. Ill., 1962; postgrad. U. Mich., 1965-66; Ph.D., Ill. Inst. Tech., 1970. Tchr. math. Watertown Sr. High Sch., S.D., 1958-61; instr. math. Ill. State Normal U., 1962-65; asst. prof. U. Wis.-Superior, 1966-70, assoc. prof., 1970-79, prof. math., 1979—; vis. prof. Clemson U., 1982-83. Author: Elementary Linear Algebra with Applications, 1979. Mem. ch. council Concordia Luth. Ch., Superior, 1974. NSF faculty fellow, 1969. Mem. Math Assn. Am. (vice chmn. Wis. sect. 1975-76, chmn. 1976-77), Math. Soc. Am. Avocations: fishing; hunting; racquet ball. Home: 88 N 21st St E Superior WI 54880 Office: Dept Math Scis U Wis Superior WI 54880

FLORIAN, MARIANNA BOLOGNESI, civic worker; b. Chgo.; d. Giulio and Rose (Garibaldi) Bolognesi; B.A. cum laude, Barat Coll., 1940; postgrad. Moser Bus. Sch., 1941-42; m. Paul A. Florian III, June 4, 1949; children—Paul, Marina, Peter, Mark. Asst. credit mgr. Stella Cheese Co., Chgo., 1942-45; With ARC ETO Clubmobile Unit, 1945-47; mgr. Passavant Hosp. Gift Shop, 1947-49; pres., Jr. League Chgo., Inc., 1957-59; pres. woman's bd. Passavant Hosp., 1966-68; bd. dirs. Northwestern Meml. Hosp., 1974-81, mem. exec. com., 1974-79; pres. Women's Assn., Chgo. Symphony Orch., 1974-77; chmn. Guild Chgo. Hist. Soc., 1981-84; vice chmn. v.p., exec. com. Orchestral Assn., 1978—; mem. women's bd. Northwestern U.; mem. vis. com. dept. music U. Chgo., 1980—. Recipient Citizen Fellowship, Inst. Medicine Chgo., 1975. Clubs: Friday (pres. 1972-74), Contemporary; Winnetka Garden.

FLORY, JANET SIMS, interior designer; b. Ft. Sill, Okla., June 9, 1933; d. Howard and Sara (Harmon) Sims; m. James L. Flory, Feb. 25, 1984; children—(by previous marriage) Larry Edward, James Robert, John Michael, William Frederick; stepchildren—Suzanne Pagel, Jill Warner, Kimberly, Michael. B.A., Auburn U., 1952, M.A., 1954. Interior designer Norman's, Salisbury, N.C., 1964-72, Carole Fabrics, Augusta, Ga., 1975-77, Macy's, N.Y.C., 1981-82, Aero Drapery, Charlotte, N.C., 1982-83; coordinator of interior design Bowling Green State U., Ohio, 1984—. Mem. Am. Soc. Interior Designers, Am. Soc. Tng. and Devel., Assn. of U. Interior Designers, Nat. Assn. Female Execs. Republican. Lutheran. Avocations: gourmet cooking; tennis; music; reading. Home: 7130 Glenmore Lambertville MI 48144 Office: Bowling Green State U 1008 Adminstrn Bldg 12th Floor Bowling Green OH 43405

FLOWER, TERRENCE FREDERICK, physics educator, consultant; b. Chgo. Aug. 24, 1941; s. Adolph Frederick and Julianna Theresa (Pechereck) F.; m. Margaret Ann Van Stone, Sept. 4, 1965; children—Julie Ann, Charles Frederick. Student U. Chgo., 1959-60; B.S., USAF Acad., 1964; M.S., U. Wyo., 1974, Ph.D., 1977. Instr., test pilot USAF, Craig AFB, Ala., 1965-70; tchr. sci. Wheatland High Sch., Wyo., 1976-79; instr. math. Eastern Wyo. Coll., Torrington, 1979; aerospace instr. U. Wyo., Laramie, 1975-79; assoc. prof., dept chmn. physics Coll. St. Catherine, St. Paul, Minn., 1979—; dir. Aerospace Resource Center, Laramie, 1976-79; cons. Estes Industries, Penrose, Colo., 1979—. Contbr. articles to profl. jours. Bd. dirs. Tech. in Edn., North Central U.S., 1981—; mem. Sch. Bd., Hastings, Minn., 1983—; precinct chmn. Senate Dist.; treas. Republican Party, Dakota County, Minn., 1982—; regional dir. Aerospace CAP, North Central U.S., 1982—; vice chmn. 4-H Fedn., Dakota City, 1984—. Recipient Outstanding Instr. Pilot USAF, 1967, Faculty Teaching award, Coll. St. Catherine, 1983. Mem. Am. Assn. Physics Tchrs. Minn. Acad. Sci., Nat. Sci. Tchrs. Assn., Minn. Assn. Physics Tchrs., Am. Assn. Aerospace Educators. Republican. Roman Catholic. Clubs: Civil Air Patrol (St. Paul) (region dir. 1982—), Air Force Assn. Avocations: flying, fishing, hunting. Home: 13875 Mississippi Trail Hastings MN 55033 Office: Dept Physics Coll St Catherine 2004 Randolph Ave St Paul MN 55105

FLOWERS, LARRY LEE, fire chief, educator; b. Newark, Ohio, May 5, 1952; s. Roy Edwin and Ruth Ellen (Fairell) F.; m. Patty Ann Ball, May 8, 1971; children—Mandy Leigh, Kiley Ann. Student, Ohio Acad., 1973, Eastland Vocat., 1973, Ohio State U., 1972. Instr. emergency med. tech. State of Ohio, 1971-81, fire instr., 1972—, rescue instr., 1974—. Chmn. Groveport Human Needs Com., Ohio, 1979—; mem. Grade Sch. Adv. Bd., Canal Winchester, Ohio, 1982—, High Sch. Adv. Bd., Canal Winchester, 1984—. Mem. Franklin County Firefighters Assn., Ohio Fire Chiefs' Assn. (bd. dirs. 1983—), Internat. Fire Chiefs' Assn. Republican. Methodist. Avocations: boating, water skiing, swimming. Home: 216 Washington St Canal Winchester Ohio Office: Madison Twp Fire Dept 306 College St Groveport OH 43125

FLOYD, JOHN CLAIBORNE, JR., physician, medical educator; b. Olla, La., July 3, 1927; s. John Claiborne and Linnie Leora (Gibson) F.; m. Esther Louise Martin, Feb. 23, 1952; children—Esther Elizabeth, Jennifer Marie, John Claiborne III, Sara Melissa. B.S. in Chemistry, La. State U., 1949, M.D., 1954. Diplomate Am. Bd. Internal Medicine. Resident in internal medicine U. Mich., Ann Arbor, 1954-58, instr. internal medicine, 1958-59, 60-61, from instr. to prof. internal medicine, 1961—; instr. internal medicine La. State U., New Orleans, 1959-60; vis. physician Charity Hosp. La., New Orleans, 1959-60; cons. internal medicine VA Hosp., Ann Arbor, 1964-81, 85—, Wayne County Gen. Hosp., Westland, Mich., 1973—; assoc. dir. Mich. Diabetes Research Tng. Ctr., Ann Arbor, 1977—. Contbr. chpts. to books, articles to profl. jours. Served with USNR, 1945-46. Mem. Am. Diabetes Assn. (bd. dirs. 1974-80), Endocrine Soc., Central Soc. Clin. Research, Am. Fedn. Clin. Research, Sigma Xi, Alpha Omega Alpha. Baptist. Avocation: music. Office: U Mich Sch Medicine Dept Internal Medicine Univ Hosp Ann Arbor MI 48109

FLYNN, BARBARA BECHLER, operations management educator; b. Milw., Sept. 13, 1952; d. Harold Edgar and Jane (Johnson) Bechler; m. Edward James Flynn, Mar. 12, 1983. A.B., Ripon Coll., magna cum laude, 1974; M.B.A., Marquette U., 1981; D.B.A., Ind. U., 1984. Elem. tchr. Kewaskum Community Schs., Wis., 1974-75, Berlin Area Schs., Wis., 1975-79; research asst. Marquette U., Milw., 1979-81; assoc. instr. Ind. U., Bloomington, Ind., 1981-84, vis. asst. prof., 1984; asst. prof. La. State U., Baton Rouge, 1985—. Contbr. articles to profl. jours. Grad. fellow Marquette U., 1979-81, Ind. U., 1981-84; summer research grantee Ind. U., 1983, La. State U., 1985. Mem. Am. Inst. for Decision Scis., Inst. for Mgmt. Scis., Acad. Mgmt., Assn. for Systems Mgmt., Alpha Delta Pi. Episcopalian. Lodge: Job's Daus. Avocations: crafts; bicycling; reading; computers. Home: 1342 Beckenham Dr Baton Rouge LA 70808 Office: Louisiana State Univ Dept Quantitative Bus Analysis 3182 CEBA Bldg Baton Rouge LA 70803-6316

FLYNN, ROBERT ANTHONY, business executive; b. Chgo., May 20, 1931; s. Mortimer G. and Helen M. (Fisherkeller) F.; m. Mary Lou Ladley, June 23, 1962. B.S., U. Ill., 1957. Zone sales mgr. Top Value Enterprises, Dayton, Ohio, 1957-69; v.p. sales Nat. Research, Chgo., 1969-76; pres. M.L. Flynn & Assocs., Naperville, Ill., 1976—. Served with USN, 1950-54. Roman Catholic. Clubs: O'Leary's Upside-Down (Chgo.)(v.p. 1982-84), Town & Country Equestrian Assn. (Chgo.)(pres. 1969-70). Avocations: golf, woodworking. Home: 1 Canterbury Ct South Barrington IL 60010 Office: ML Flynn & Assocs 319 S Washington St Naperville IL 60540

FLYNN, ROBERT WOOD, exploration geologist; b. Poughkeepsie, N.Y., Feb. 2, 1957; s. Michael B. and M. Jean (Wood) F. B.S., U. Ky., 1981. Geologist C.G. Collins Oil Producer, Campbellsville, Ky., 1979-81; regional exploration mgr. Tamarack Petroleum Co., Evansville, Ind., 1982-85; pres. Explorafoil Consultants Co. Inc., Evansville, 1985—. Mem. Ky.-Ind. Geol. Soc., Am. Assn. Petroleum Geologists, Jaycees. Republican. Roman Catholic. Office: Explorafoil Cons Co Inc 2621 Stringtown Rd Evansville IN 47711

FOBES, LINDA PEERY, pharmaceutical company marketing executive, nutrition educator, consultant; b. Omaha, Apr. 7, 1943; d. James William and Rosalie Adele (Reinhardt) Peery; children—Robert, Katherine, Elizabeth. B.S. in Home Econs. with distinction, U. Minn., 1968, postgrad. in nutrition, 1967, M.P.H. in Nutrition, 1974. Therapeutic dietitian Abbott Hosp., Mpls., 1965-66, Mt. Sinai Hosp., Mpls., 1969-73; cons. nutritionist Doyle Pharm. Co. subs. Sandoz Nutrition Corp., Mpls., 1964-67, nutritionist, 1967-75, dir. nutrition, 1975-82, dir. mktg., 1982-85; program dir./instr. food service mgmt. course for dietetic assts. St. Paul ATVI; cons. dietetics to area nursing homes. Mem. exec. com., chairperson program com. People Inc., St. Paul; chairperson fundraising Parents Endeavor for Retarded Children, St. Paul, 1979—. Recipient North Star award U. Minn., 1964. Mem. Am. Dietetic Assn. (registered dietitian), Am. Soc. Parenteral and Enteral Nutrition, Am. Coll. Nutrition, Minn. Dietetic Assn., Twin City Dist. Dietetic Assn., Can. Dietetic Assn., Ont. Dietetic Assn., Minn. State Nutrition Council, Soc. Nutrition Edn., Am. Home Econs. Assn., Nutrition Today Soc., Home Economists in Bus., Hosp., Instl. Ednl. Food Service Soc., Mortar Bd., Sigma Epsilon Sigma, Omicron Nu, Kappa Kappa Gamma. Club: Horizon 100. Author various Doyle Pharm. Co. edn. and audio visual materials, 1969-82.

FOGAL, ROBERT EDWIN, college administrator; b. Norristown, Pa., Oct. 6, 1944; s. Lawrence Edwin and Jane Elizabeth (Thompson) F.; m. Nancy Jean Zaugg; children—Mark Andrew, Alicia Joanne. B.Mus., Heidelberg Coll., 1966; M.S.M., Union Theol. Sem., 1968; M.A., Ind. U., 1974, Ph.D., 1981. Tchr. Protestant Inst. for Advanced Theol. Studies, Buenos Aires, 1969-78; dir. devel. Lancaster Theol. Sem., Pa., 1979-82; dir. devel. Otterbein Coll., Westerville, Ohio, 1982-85, v.p. devel., 1985—; devel. rep. United Methodist Bd. Global Ministries, N.Y.C., 1973-75, 78-79; cons. Bd. Devel. Network, Columbus, Ohio, 1982—. Editor: A Brief History of Mercersburg, 1982. Contbr. articles to profl. jours. Bd. dirs. Westerville Fund, Ohio, 1983—. Mem. Am. Guild Organists, Soc. Ethnomusicology, Nat. Soc. Fund Raising Execs., Am. Folklore Soc., Council for Advancement and Support of Edn. Office: Otterbein Coll Westerville OH 43081

FOGEL, STEVEN TEDD, physician; b. St. Louis, July 7, 1950; s. Harry Y. and Evelyn F.; m. Connie Jean Eller, Dec. 21, 1973 (div. Mar. 1980); 1 dau., Melissa Shawn. A.B., Washington U., St. Louis, 1973; M.D., U. Mo., 1976. Diplomate Am. Bd. Ob-Gyn., Nat. Bd. Med. Examiners. Intern, Kansas City Gen. Hosp. (Mo.), 1976-77; resident dept. ob-gyn U. Mo.-Kansas City, 1976-79, chief resident, 1979-80; practice medicine specializing in ob-gyn, Kansas City, 1980—; coordinator resident physician teaching program in ob-gyn Menorah Med. Ctr., Kansas City. Mem. AMA, Mo. Med. Soc., Jackson County Med. Soc., Kansas City Gynecol. Soc., Am. Coll. Obstetricians and Gynecologists, Phi Beta Kappa. Jewish. Clubs: Indian Creek Racquet (Overland Park, Kans.). Lodge: B'nai B'rith. Contbr. article in field. Home: 2304 W 121st St Leawood KS 66209 Office: 6724 Troost St Suite 210 Kansas City MO 64131

FOGELMAN, AVRON, professional baseball executive. Co-owner, vice-chmn. Kansas City Royals. Office: Kansas City Royals PO Box 1969 Kansas City MO 64141*

FOGERTY, JAMES EDWARD, archivist, state official; b. Mpls., Jan. 26, 1945; s. Robert P. and Ralpha Chamberlain (James) F. B.A., Coll. St. Thomas, 1968; M.L.S., U. Minn., 1972. Regional ctrs. dir. Minn. Hist. Soc., St. Paul, 1972-76, field dir., 1976-79, dep. state archivist, 1979—; sec.-treas. Midwest Archives Conf., Chgo., 1977-81, pres., 1983-85. Editor: Oral History Collections of the Minnesota Historical Society, 1984; contbr. articles to Am. Archivist, Midwestern Archivist, History News, others. Mem. Soc. Am. Archivists, Oral History Assn., Midwest Archives Conf., Am. Assn. For State and Local History, Phi Alpha Theta. Avocations: hiking, canoeing, thoroughbred bloodlines research. Office: Minnesota Historical Society 1500 Mississippi St Saint Paul MN 55101

FOGERTY, ROBERT PAUL, historian; b. Elwood, Ind., Sept. 12, 1905; s. Michael Joseph and Antoinette Genevieve (Hueper) F.; A.B., U. Notre Dame, 1928; LL.B., St. Thomas Law Sch., 1933; M.A., U. Minn., 1936, Ph.D., 1942; D.H.L., Coll. St. Thomas, 1983; m. Ralpha Chamberlain James, June 22, 1943; children—James Edward, Mary Curran. Admitted to Minn. bar, 1934; instr., Coll. St. Thomas, 1928-36, asst. prof., 1936-42, prof. history, 1946-75, prof. emeritus, 1975—, dir. Div. Social Scis., 1957-75, chmn. dept. history, 1970-75; vis. prof. U. Minn., 1950, Macalester Coll., 1969; mem. Minn. State Rev. Bd. Nat. Register of Historic Places, 1970-83, participating mem. emeritus, 1983—, chmn., 1974-75; reviewer Div. Research Grants, NEH, 1976—. Mem. Gov.'s Commn. on Constl. Revision, Minn., 1950-51. Served to maj. USAAF, 1942-46. Mem. Am. Assn. Colls. for Tchr. Edn. (instl. rep. 1960-72), Am. Hist. Assn., Orgn. Am. Historians, Minn. Hist. Soc., Nat. Trust for Historic Preservation, Upper Midwest History Conf. (chmn. 1953-54, 62-63, sec. 1960-61), Coll. St. Thomas Alumni Assn., Notre Dame Alumni Assn. Roman Catholic. Author: The Law of Contracts in Colonial Massachusetts and Maryland Compared with English Common Law, 1936; An Institutional Study of the Territorial Courts in the Old Northwest, 1788-1848, 1942. Home: 1780 Hampshire Ave Saint Paul MN 55116 Office: Box 4158 Coll St Thomas Saint Paul MN 55105

FOGG, MONICA, artist, designer, educator; b. Belaire, Tex., Oct. 26, 1951; d. Donald Stockton and Frances (White) Fogg. B.A., Principia Coll., 1974; student Washington U., St. Louis, 1973. M.A. in Painting, St. Cloud State U., 1986. Instr. U. Minn., Mpls., 1980, 83, 85, Art Ctr. Edina, Minn., 1980—, Art Ctr. Minn., Minnetonka, 1980—, St. Cloud State U., Minn., 1984—; artist, designer, owner Fogg-Gerber Studio, Mpls., 1976—; speaker nat. conv. AIA, Mpls., 1981, AAUW, Mpls., 1978. Represented in permanent collections AMFAC, Gen. Mills Corp., Woodhill Country Club, Minn. Protective Life Ins. Co. Recipient merit award Minn. State Fair, 1978, 2d prize Minn. State Fair, 1977, design award Hammerhill Paper Co., 1974. Mem. MW Watercolor Soc. (merit award 1977), Northstar Watercolor Soc. (speaker, demonstrator 1977—, award of excellence 1977, 80, 82, 83, 2d place award 1979), Minn. Artists Assn. (excellence award 1982). Home: 5117 Washburn Ave S Minneapolis MN 55410 Office: Fogg-Gerber Studio 700 N Washington Ave Suite 324 Minneapolis MN 55401

FOGLAND, DANIEL WILLIAM, city official; b. North Platte, Nebr., May 13, 1953; s. Max Norman and Fern Pauline (Forsberg) F.; m. Christine Ann Cohagan, Aug. 28, 1976; children—Chad, Kylie. A.A., North Platte Jr. Coll., 1973; A.G.S., Mid-Plains Community Coll., 1977. Bldg. insp. City of North Platte (Nebr.), 1972-77; mgr. W.T. Krvelberg Co., North Platte, 1977-78; bldg. insp. City of Rapid City (S.D.), 1978-80; chief bldg. ofcl. City of Grand Island (Nebr.), 1980-84; pres. Copycat Instant Print, 1985—. Mem. Internat. Conf. Bldg. Ofcls., Nebraskaland Conf. Bldg. Ofcls. and Inspectors. Methodist. Home: 1519 W Division Grand Island NE 68801 Office: 1212 W 2d St Grand Island NE 68802

FOK, THOMAS DSO YUN, civil engineer, educator; b. Canton, China, July 1, 1921; s. D.H. and C. (Tse) F.; came to U.S., 1947, naturalized, 1956; B.Eng., Nat. Tung-Chi U., Szechuan, China, 1945; M.S., U. Ill., 1948; M.B.A. (Dr. Nadler Money Markteen scholar), NYU, 1950; Ph.D., Carnegie-Mellon U., 1956; m. Maria M.L. Liang, Sept. 18, 1949. Structural designer Lummus Co., N.Y.C., 1951-53; design engr. Richardson, Gordon & Assocs., cons. engrs., Pitts., 1956-58; assoc. prof. engring. Youngstown (Ohio) U., 1958-68, dir. Computing Center, 1963-67; ptnr. Cernica, Fok & Assocs., cons. engrs., Youngstown, 1958-64; prin. Thomas Fok & Assocs., cons. engrs., Youngstown, 1964-65; ptnr. Mosure-Fok & Syrakis Co., Ltd., cons. engrs., Youngstown, 1965-76; cons. engr. Mahoning County Engr., Ohio, 1960-65; pres. Computing-Systems & Tech., Youngstown, 1967-72; chmn. Thomas Fok and Assocs., Ltd., cons. engrs., Youngstown, 1977—. Trustee Pub. Library Youngstown and Mahoning County, 1973—; trustee Youngstown State U. 1975-84, chmn., 1981-83; trustee Youngstown State U. Found., 1975—. Recipient Walter E. and Caroline H. Watson Found. Disting. Prof.'s award Youngstown U., 1966. Registered profl. engr. N.Y., Pa., Ohio, Ill., Ky., Fla., W.Va., Ind., Md. Fellow ASCE (Br. Outstanding Engr. 1984); mem. Am. Concrete Inst., Internat. Assn. Bridge and Structural Engring., Am. Soc. Engring. Edn., Nat. Soc. Profl. Engrs., AAAS, Soc. Am. Mil. Engrs., Ohio, N.Y. acads. scis., Sigma Xi, Beta Gamma Sigma, Sigma Tau, Delta Pi Sigma. Rotarian. Contbr. articles to profl. jours. Home: 325 S Canfield-Niles Rd Youngstown OH 44515 Office: 3896 Mahoning Ave Youngstown OH 44515

FOLEY, ANNA BERNICE WILLIAMS (MRS. WARREN MASSEY FOLEY), former librarian, author; b. Wigginsville, Ohio, Nov. 20, 1902; d. Karl Howland and Bertye (Young) Williams; student U. Cin., 1920-24, Columbia, 1931, Nanking (China) Lang. Coll., 1926; Grad. Sch. cert. Jesus Coll., Oxford U., 1969; m. Warren Massey Foley, Feb. 25, 1924; children—Williams Massey, Karlanne (Mrs. William Scully Hauer). Radio commentator WKRC, Cin., 1934, WSAI, Cin., 1938; commentator WCPO-TV, Cin., 1939-44; lectr. fashions U. Cin. Evening Coll., 1941-44; spl. events coordinator Mabley & Carew Dept. Store, 1951-66; model McCall Patterns-Singer Sewing Machine Co., Moscow, USSR, 1957; dir. The Martha Kinney Cooper Ohioana Library Assn., Columbus, Ohio, 1966-77, also editor Quar. Mag., Yearbook, 1966-77 Author: (juvenile books) Star Stories (also in Chinese), Spaceships of the Ancients; Korean Legends, 1979; A Walk among the Clouds, 1980; Why The Cock Crows Three Times, 1980; The Gazelle and the Hunter, 1980; author weekly column Columbus Scene, in Forest Hills Jour., 1971-77. Lectr. creative writing; book reviewer Sunday Columbus Dispatch, 1967-77, The Asia Mail, 1976-77. Mem. lit. panel Ohio Arts Council, 1966-70; bd. dirs. Ohio Poetry Day, 1968-77. Recipient Valley Forge honor cert. Freedoms Found.; cert. Columbus Art League, 1976; named Hon. Citizen, City of Paris, 1951; named to Ohio Women's Hall of Fame, Columbus, 1982. Mem. English Speaking Union (br. pres. 1966-69), World Assn. Women Journalists and Writers, Ohio Press Women, Women in Communications (pres. 1973-74), Overseas Press Club of Am., MacDowell Soc., Nat. League Am. Pen Women, DAR, Sigma Delta Chi, Kappa Kappa Gamma (Achievement award 1974). Home: 10224 Linden Ln Overland Park KS 66207

FOLEY, EDMUND FRANCIS, physician; b. Chgo., Aug. 18, 1896; s. John B. and Margaret Francis (Burke) F.; B.S., U. Chgo., 1918; M.D., 1920; m. Ruth Allen Farnham, Oct. 14, 1933; children—Edmund Francis, Jr., Thomas Francis. Intern, Cook County Hosp., Chgo., 1920-21, resident, 1921-23; practice medicine specializing in internal medicine, Chgo., 1928-73; prof. medicine emeritus U. Ill. Coll. Medicine, Chgo., 1943-65; dean Cook County Grad. Sch., 1961-73; attending physician Cook County Hosp., Columbus Hosp., Research and Ednl. Hosp., U. Ill; chief of staff Cook County Hosp., 1952-62, Columbus Hosp., 1962-65; cons. in field. Recipient E.S. Hamilton Teaching award, 1970, Allen award U. Ill. 1949, 1954, 1960, 1963; trustee Hektorn Inst. Med. Research; Edmund F. Foley professional chair in internal medicine named for him. Fellow A.C.P.; mem. AMA, Ill., Chgo. med. socs., Am. Heart Assn., Central Soc. Clin. Research, Chgo. Soc. Internal Medicine, Inst. Medicine, Sigma Xi, Alpha Omega Alpha. Contbr. articles to profl. jours. Home: 720 St Andrews Ln Crystal Lake IL 60014

FOLEY, MICHAEL THOMAS, broadcast corporation executive; b. Piedmont, S.D., July 21, 1945; s. Peter Francis and Mary Kathryn (Brockhoff) F.; m. Marilyn Kathryn Etten, July 9, 1977; children—Michelle Kathryn, Matthew John. B.A. in Math. and Sociology, Black Hills State Coll., Spearfish, S.D., 1967; B.S. in Computer Sci., Nat. Coll. Bus., Rapid City, S.D., 1971. Instr. data processing Gates Coll., Waterloo, Iowa, 1971-72; systems analyst Blackhawk Broadcast Corp., Waterloo, 1973; systems engr. NCR Corp., Dayton, Ohio, 1974-78; dir. data processing Forward Communications Corp., Wausau, Wis., 1978-80, v.p. data communications, 1980—; cons. in field. Served with U.S. Army, 1969-70. Decorated Vietnam Cross Gallentry, Bronze Star, Air medals, and numerous commendations; recipient Letter of Commendation, NCR, 1976. Mem. Fedn. Computer Users, Computer User Group, Nat. Computer Graphics Assn. Roman Catholic. Designer, installer computerized broadcast systems, info. systems, and music libraries for various radio and TV stas. Home: 3707 Powers St Schofield WI 54476 Office: 1114 Grand Ave Wausau WI 54401

FOLK, EUGENE ROY, pediatric ophthalmologist, ophthalmology educator; b. Chgo., Sept. 7, 1924; s. Max Lyon and Martha R. (Rubin) F.; m. Miriam Gallman, Jan. 11, 1954; children—Andrea, Tina, Carla. B.S., U. Ill., 1948, 1950. Intern Cook County Hosp., Chgo., 1950-51; resident in ophthalmology Ill. Eye and Ear Infirmary, Chgo., 1951-54; from asst. prof. to prof. ophthalmology U. Ill., Chgo., 1954—; practice medicine specializing in ophthalmology, Skokie, Ill., 1960—. Author: Treatment of Strabismus, 1965. Contbr. articles to profl. jours and book. Served to 2d lt. U.S. Army, 1943-46. Mem. AMA, Chgo. Ophthal. Soc. (pres. 1974), Am. Acad. Ophthamology, Am. Assn. Pediatric Ophthamology and Strabismus (pres. 1984—). Home: 444 Lakeside Dr Glencoe IL 60022 Office: 64 Old Orchard Rd Skokie IL 60076

FOLK, ROGER MAURICE, laboratory director; b. Junction City, Ohio, May 10, 1936; s. Howard Mendelson and Helen Marie (Saffell) F.; B.Sc., Ohio State U., 1962, M.Sc., 1965, Ph.D., 1971; m. Marilyn Irene Cannon, June 24, 1956; children—Mark Leslie, Michael Roger, Diana Lynn. Technician, Battelle Columbus Lab., Columbus, Ohio, 1957-62, research biologist, 1962-71, mgr. toxicology, 1972-79; dir. environ. health lab. Monsanto Co., St. Louis, 1979—; adj. asst. prof. Ohio State U., 1973-79. Mem. AAAS, Am. Assn. for Lab. Animal Sci., Am. Coll. Toxicology, Soc. Toxicology, Sigma Xi, Phi Eta Sigma. Methodist. Contbr. articles to profl. jours.; reviewer Cancer Treatment Reports, 1975-79. Home: 750 Muir View Manchester MO 63011 Office: 645 S Newstead St Saint Louis MO 63110

FOLKENING, JAMES, state education official. Supr. Higher Edn. Mgmt. Services State of Mich., Lansing. Office: Higher Edn Mgmt Services PO Box 30009 Lansing MI 48909*

FOLKERT, DAVID FLOYD, holding company executive, lawyer; b. Holland, Mich., Jan. 14, 1948; s. Floyd J. and Janet (Sneller) F.; m. Carol Ruth Rycenga, June 12, 1970; children—Lucinda Lea, Todd David. B.A., Hope Coll., 1970; J.D., Valparaiso U., 1973. Bar: Mich. 1973. Ptnr. Marietti, Mullally, Grimm, & Folkert, Muskegon, Mich., 1978-79; gen. counsel Westran Corp., 1979-81, sec., 1981—, v.p., 1983—, also dir.; dir. Commonwealth Fin. Group, Inc., Grand Haven, Mich., Rycenga Homes, Inc., Spring Lake, Mich., Harbor Steel & Supply Corp., Muskegon, Western Packaging Corp., Grand Haven. Trustee Westran Found., 1983—; sec. Internat. Aid., Inc., 1980—. Mem. Mich. Bar Assn., Muskegon County Bar Assn. Republican. Home: 16139 Harbor View Dr Spring Lake MI 49456 Office: Westran Corp 1148 W Western Ave Muskegon MI 49443

FOLKERTS, BYRON LEE, manufacturing company executive; b. Great Bend, Kans., Dec. 6, 1953; s. Doyle Dean and Ina Lea (Minson) F.; student Barton County Community Coll., 1972-73. With Great Bend Mfg. Co. (Kans.), 1973—, purchasing agt., 1979-80, dir. purchasing, 1980-82; dir. purchasing Great Bend Industries, 1982—. Home: 3322 Broadway Great Bend KS 67530 Office: Rural Route 1 Box 106 Great Bend KS 67530

FOLKINS, LARRY DUANE, school administrator; b. Niangua, Mo., Apr. 14, 1934; m. Georgeanne J. Prewitt, 1958; children—Margery Ann, Mark Alexander, Michael Alan, Mary Allison. B.S. in Edn., Southwest Mo. State U., 1957; M.S., Central Mo. State U., 1960; Ph.D. in Edn., U. Mo., 1976. Cert. tchr., adminstr., Mo. Student minister Springfield (Mo.) dist. Methodist Ch., 1955-56; field rep. Southwest Mo. State U., Springfield, 1956-57; tchr. Raytown (Mo.) High Sch., 1958-60; counselor South Jr. High Sch., Raytown, 1960-61, asst. prin., 1961-65; prin. Pittman Hills Jr. High Sch., Raytown, 1965-68; dir. personnel services Springfield (Mo.) Pub. Schs., 1968-72, dir. secondary edn., 1972-77; supt. schs. Jefferson City (Mo.) Pub. Schs., 1977—. Mem. adminstrv. bd. Jefferson City First United Methodist Ch., 1979-80; bd. dirs. Jefferson City YMCA, 1978-83; bd. govs. Meml. Hosp., 1980-83; bd. dirs. United Way, 1978—, pres., 1982-83; bd. dirs. Lincoln U. Found., 1981-83, Mo. Council Econ. Edn., 1980. Mem. Mo. State Tchrs. Assn., Nat. Assn. Secondary Sch. Prins., Mo. Assn. Sch. Adminstrs., Am. Assn. Sch. Personnel Adminstrs., Am. Assn. Sch. Adminstrs., C. of C. (Springfield and Jefferson City sect. chmn.), Phi Delta Kappa Lodge: Rotary (treas., v.p.). Home: 615 Crest Dr Jefferson City MO 65101 Office: 315 E Dunkin Jefferson City MO 65101

FOLLANSBEE, DOROTHY L. (DOROTHY L. LELAND), publisher; b. St. Louis, Mar. 24, 1911; d. Robert Leathan and Minnie Cowden (Yowell) Lund; grad. Sarah Lawrence Coll., 1931; m. Austin Porter Leland, Apr. 24, 1935 (dec. 1975); children—Mary Talbot Leland MacCarthy, Austin Porter Jr. (dec.),

Irene Austin Leland Barzantny; m. 2d, Robert Kerr Follansbee, Oct. 20, 1979. Pres., Station List Publ. Co., St. Louis, 1975—; dir. Downtown St. Louis Inc. Hon. chmn. Old Post Office Landmark Com., 1975—; bd. dirs. Services Bur. St. Louis, 1943, pres., 1951; bd. dirs. Robert E. Lee Meml. Assn.; mem. St. Louis County Parks and Recreation Dept., 1969; bd. dirs. Stratford Hall, Va., 1953—, pres., 1967-70, treas., 1970—; bd. dirs. Historic Bldgs. Commn. St. Louis County, 1959-85, Mo. Hist. Soc., 1960-77, Mo. Mansion Preservation Com., 1975-80, Chatillon DeMenil House, 1977-79. Recipient Landmarks award Landmarks Assn. St. Louis, 1974; Pub. Service award GSA, 1978; Crowninshield award Nat. Trust for Hist Preservation, 1979. Mem. Colonial Dames Am., Episcopalian. Clubs: St. Louis Country, Fox Chapel Golf, Princeton of N.Y., St. Louis Jr. League. Home: 35 Pointer Ln St Louis MO 63124 also 1001 River Oaks Dr Pittsburgh PA 15215 Office: 1221 Locust St Saint Louis MO 63101

FOLLETT, MARY VIERLING, artist, art conservator, appraiser; b. Chgo., Feb. 9, 1917; d. Arthur Garfield and Grace May (Cummings) Vierling; student U. Southern Calif., 1932-34, grad. Acad. Profl. Art Conservators, 1975, Masters, 1978; m. Garth Benepe Follett, Feb. 16, 1945; 1 dau., Dawn Goshorn; 3 stepchildren. Exhibited in group shows Palette and Chisel Acad. Fine Arts, 1975, 76, 77, 78, Municipal Art League, 1972-78, others; represented in permanent collection Fla., Calif., Italy, others; owner, operator Paintin' Place, gallery, Oak Park, Ill., 1973—; dir. Palette and Chisel Acad. Fine Arts, Chgo., 1975-76. Vice pres. Oak Park LWV, 1952-54, welfare chmn., 1956-58; treas. Oak Park Council Internat. Affairs, 1962-74. Recipient Gold medal Palette and Chisel Acad. Fine Arts, 1976-77, 1st award Civics and Art Found. Union League Chgo., 1977. Mem. Oak Park River Forest Art League (v.p., dir. 1981-82), Pen Women Am., Municipal Art League Chgo., Art Inst. Assos. Oak Park and River Forest (women's bd. 1967—), Oak Park River Forest Hist. Soc. Club: 19th Century Women's. Home: 1440 Park Ave River Forest IL 60305 Office: 820 North Blvd Oak Park IL 60301

FOLLETT, ROBERT JOHN RICHARD, publisher; b. Oak Park, Ill., July 4, 1928; s. Dwight W. and Mildred (Johnson) F.; A.B., Brown U., 1950; postgrad. Columbia U., 1950-51; m. Nancy L. Crouthamel, Dec. 30, 1950; children—Brian L., Kathryn R., Jean A., Lisa W. Editor Follett Pub. Co., Chgo., 1951-55, sales mgr., 1955-58, gen. mgr. ednl. div., 1958-68, pres., 1968-78; pres. Follett Internat., 1972—; chmn., dir. Follett Corp., 1979—; pres. Follett Group, Inc.; v.p. United Learning Corp.; chmn. School Pubs., 1971-73; dir. Ednl. Systems Corp. Mem. Ill. Gov.'s Commn. on Schs., 1972; pres. Alpine Research Inst., 1968—; mem. Nat. Adv. Council on Edn. Statistics, 1975-77; chmn. Book Distbn. Task Force of Book Industry, 1978-82. Bd. dirs. Village Mgr. Assn., 1964-84, Community Found. Oak Park and River Forest, 1959—, Fund for Justice, 1974-77; trustee Inst. Ednl. Data Systems, 1965—; bd. dirs. Ctr. for Book Research, 1984—; mem. Ill. Republican State Central Com., 1982—. Served in AUS, 1951-53. Mem. Assn. Am. Pubs. (dir. 1972-79), Ill. C. of C. (chmn. edn. com. 1977-79), Chgo. Pubs. Assn. (pres. 1976—), Sierra Club. Clubs: Tower (Chgo.); River Forest Tennis. Author: Your Wonderful Body, 1961; What to Take Backpacking and Why, 1977; How to Keep Score in Business, 1978; The Financial Side of Book Publishing, 1982. Home: Oak Park IL 60302 also Shorewood Hills MI 49125 Office: 1000 W Washington Blvd Chicago IL 60607

FOLLIS, ELAINE RUSSELL, Biblical studies educator, Christian Science practitioner; b. Quincy, Mass., Jan. 28, 1944; d. George Stanley and Celia Russell (Joy) F. A.B. summa cum laude, Tufts U., 1965, B.D., 1968; Ph.D., Boston U., 1976. Asst. prof. religion Principia Coll., Elsah, Ill., 1974-79, assoc. prof., chmn. dept. religion, 1979-83, assoc. prof., chmn. div. humanities, 1983-85, prof., chmn. div. humanities, 1985—; editorial cons. Christian Sci. Pub. Soc., Boston, 1973—; vis. scholar Harvard Div. Sch., Cambridge, Mass., 1979; reviewer NEH, Washington, 1978-82; lectr. Bibl. studies Principia Coll. Patrons Assn., Elsah, Ill., St. Louis, 1978—. Author: David King of Israel, 1979; Convenant-A Biblical Guide, 1985. Editor: Directions in Biblical Hebrew Poetry, 1986. Contbr. articles to profl. jours. Second reader First Ch. of Christ, Scientist, Elsah, Ill., 1983-85, trustee, 1975-78. Mem. Soc. Bibl. Lit. (Bibl. Hebrew poetry sect. chmn. 1983-85), Phi Beta Kappa. Clubs: Nat. Early Am. Glass (Boston); Lockhaven Country (Alton, Ill.). Lodge: Order Eastern Star (worthy matron 1974). Home and Office: Principia Coll Dept Humanities Elsah IL 62028

FOLTS, JOHN DAVID, medical educator; b. LaCrosse, Wis., Dec. 11, 1938; s. David Karl and Marie E. (Johnson) F. B.S. in Elec. Engring., U. Wis., 1964, M.S. in Physiology, 1968, Ph.D. in Cardiovascular Physiology and Pathology, 1972. Asst. prof. medicine cardiovascular research lab. U. Wis.-Madison, 1972-78, assoc. prof., 1978-83, prof., 1984—; mem. research com. NIH, 1983-84. Grantee NIH, 1973-79, 83—, Am. Heart Assn., 1977-79, Wis. Heart Assn., 1975-76, 76-77, 81-82. Fellow Am. Coll. Cardiology, Am. Heart Assn. Council on Circulation; mem. Wis. Heart Assn. (research com. 1980—), IEEE (Bioengring. Group 1969—), Am. Physiol. Soc. (circulation group 1977—), Central Soc. Clin. Research, Internat. Cardiac Systems Dynamics Soc. (charter), Internat. Soc. Heart Research, Internat. Soc. Hemostasis and Thrombosis, N.Y. Acad. Scis., Sigma Xi. Lutheran. Contbr. 57 articles to profl. jours. Home: 2537 Chamberlain Ave Madison WI 53705 Office: Clin Scis Center Cardiology U Wis Med Sch HG Room 356 600 Highland Ave Madison WI 53792

FOLTZ, ROGER ERNEST, music educator; b. Wichita, Kans., June 10, 1950; s. Gordon Edward and Opal Isabel (Kehl) F. B.Mus., Wichita State U., 1972; M.Mus., U. Tex., 1973, Ph.D., 1977. Instr. music theory Temple U., Phila., 1974-77, U. Minn., Mpls., 1977-78; assoc. prof. music, chmn. dept. U. Nebr.-Omaha, 1978—. Co-author: Melodic Structures in Sight Reading, 1977; Sight Singing and Related Skills, 1974; Sight Singing: Melodic Structures in Functional Tonality, 1978; Sight Singing and Related Skills, 1973. Bd. dirs. Joslyn Chamber Series, 1978—. Mem. Coll. Music Soc. (bd. dirs. 1980-83, pres. Great Plains chpt. 1980-82), Soc. Music Theory, Nat. Assn. Schs. Music, Assn. Devel. Computer-Based Instructional Systems. Avocations: hiking, travel, cooking. Home: PO Box 3102 Omaha NE 68131 Office: U Nebr Dept Music 60th and Dodge Omaha NE 68182

FOLTZ, THOMAS JAMES, computer company executive; b. Indpls., May 18, 1946; s. James Gerald and Barbara Alice (Dickey) F.; B.S., Rose Hulman Inst. Tech., 1968, M.S., 1971; m. Evelyn Rebecca Wilkinson, Dec. 22, 1979. With NASA, Cape Canaveral, Fla., 1968; numerical analyst Gen. Motors, Indpls., 1969-70; sr. systems analyst Ind. Blue-Cross-Blue Shield, Indpls., 1970-77; sr. ops. cons. Ind. Bell Telephone, Indpls., 1977-79; pres., chief exec. officer Total Systems, Inc., Indpls., 1979—. Exec. dir. United Conservatives of Ind., 1977—; exec. bd. Christian Freedom Council, 1974-77; deacon E. 91st St. Christian Ch., Indpls., 1977—; campaign coordinator various candidates U.S. Senate and state office. Named Hon. Sec. of State, Ind., 1980. Mem. Creation Research Soc. Republican. Contbr. articles to profl. jours. Office: 7007 N Graham Rd PO Box 50159 Indianapolis IN 46250

FONDILLER, SHIRLEY HOPE ALPERIN, nurse, journalist, educator; b. Holyoke, Mass.; d. Samuel and Rose (Sobiloff) Alperin; grad. Beth Israel Hosp. Sch. Nursing, Boston; B.S., Tchrs. Coll. Columbia U., 1962, M.A., 1963, M.Ed., 1971, Ed.D., 1979; m. Harvey V. Fondiller, Dec. 27, 1957 (div. June 1984); 1 son, David Stewart. Staff asst. Am. Nurses Assn., N.Y.C., 1963-64, dir. ednl. adminstrs., cons. and tchrs. sect., 1964-66, coordinator Am. Nurses Assn.-Nat. League for Nursing careers program, 1967-70; coordinator clin. sessions Am. Nurses Assn., 1971-72, editor Am. Nurse, Kansas City, Mo., 1975-78; asso. prof., asst. to dean for spl. projects Rush-Presbyn.-St. Luke's Med. Center, 1979—. Mem. Kappa Delta pi, Sigma Theta Tau. Contbg. editor Am. Jour. Nursing, 1971-75; also books and articles. Home: 1550 N Lake Shore Dr Chicago IL 60610 Office: 1753 W Congress Pkwy Chicago IL 60612

FONG, NELSON CHU-CHUNG, statistical educator; b. Hong Kong, Dec. 17, 1943; came to U.S., 1964, naturalized, 1973; s. Yat-Shun and C.S. Fong; m. Janeta Kay Prior, June 7, 1970; children—Shun-Szu, Shun-Lee, Shun-Yenn, Shun-Bok, Shun-Loui, Shun-Ching. B.S. in Math., Harding U., 1967; M.S. in Math., Memphis State U., 1968; Ph.D. in Stats., U. Nebr., 1974. Prof. math. York Coll., Nebr., 1969-75, U. Maine, Presque, 1976-81; program developer Met. Tech. Coll., Omaha, 1975-76; assoc. prof. Seattle Pacific U., 1981-82, Kearney State Coll., Nebr., 1982-84, Creighton U., Omaha, 1984—; programmer Hydro-Resources Co., Grand Isle, Maine, 1978-80; adj. prof. U. So. Calif., Loring AFB, Maine, 1979-81; system analyst Kearney State Coll., 1983-84; speaker to meetings and convs. in field. Contbr. articles to profl. publs. Mem. SETA Program Com., Sinclair, Maine, 1976-79; interpreter Internat. Red Cross, Kearney, 1982-84; adviser Kearney State Christian Fellowship, 1983; bd. dirs. St. Lukes Good Samaritan Ctr., Kearney, 1984. Nat. Inst. Edn. grantee, 1980. Mem. Am. Statis. Assn., Am. Ednl. Research Assn. Republican. Avocation: data collecting. Home: 4110 Devenport St Omaha NE 68131 Office: Creighton U 24th and California Omaha NE 68100

FONSECA, EMMA HAIDEE, histotechnologist; b. Oriente, Cuba, Dec. 31, 1917; came to U.S., 1964, naturalized, 1971; d. Dalmiro Abel and Ana Marie (Zayas) Sanchez; B.A., B.S., Immaculada Coll., Havana, Cuba, 1936; D.Pharmacy, Havana U., 1939; m. German E. Fonseca, Dec. 25, 1939; children—Emma Julia, Enid. Asst. dir., then tech. dir. Linner Labs., Inc., Havana, 1939-62; with Miles Labs., Inc., Elkhart, Ind., 1964-82, asso. research toxicologist, 1970-75, supr. histology and toxicology dept., 1975-82. Mem. AAUW, Nat. Assn. Female Execs., Nat. Soc. Histotechnologists, Am. Soc. Med. Technologists. Roman Catholic. Home: 54637 Michael Dr Elkhart IN 46516 1127 Myrtle St Elkhart IN 46515

FOODEN, JACK, zoologist, zoology educator; b. Chgo., May 21, 1927; s. Philip Albert and Anna Ethel (Siegel) F.; m. Elizabeth Angelica Hicklin, June 29, 1950; children—Florence, Grace. M.A., U. Chgo., 1951; M.Ed., Chgo. Tchrs. Coll., 1956; Ph.D., U. Chgo., 1960. Tchr. Chgo. Bd. Edn., 1953-56; prof. zoology Chgo. State U., 1962-84; research assoc. Field Mus. Natural History, Chgo., 1964—. Contbr. articles to profl. jours. Served with U.S. Army, 1945-1946. Research grantee NIH, 1972-76; research fellow NIH, 1965-69, Indo-Am. fellow Council for Internat. Exchange of Scholars, 1979-80; research grantee Com. on Scholarly Exchange with People's Republic of China, 1985-86. Mem. AAAS, Am. Soc. Mammalogists, Bombay Natural History Soc., Internat. Primatol Soc., Soc. Systematic Zoology. Club: Kennicott (Chgo.) (pres. 1976-78). Office: Field Mus Natural History Div Mammals Roosevelt Rd and Lake Shore Dr Chicago IL 60605

FOOTE, PAUL SHELDON, business educator; b. Lansing, Mich., May 22, 1946; s. Harlon Sheldon and Frances Norene (Rotter) F.; B.B.A., U. Mich., 1967; M.B.A. (Loomis-Sayles fellow), Harvard U., 1971; advanced profl. cert. NYU, 1975; Ph.D., Mich. State U., 1983; m. Badri Seddigheh Hosseinian, Oct. 25, 1968; children—David, Sheila. Br. mgr., divisional mgr. Citibank, N.Y.C., Bombay, India and Beirut, Lebanon, 1972-74; mgr. planning and devel. Singer Co., Africa/Middle East, 1974-75; instr. U. Mich., Flint, 1978-79; lectr. acctg. Mich. State U., East Lansing, 1977; asst. prof. U. Windsor (Ont., Can.), 1979-81; assoc. prof. Saginaw Valley State Coll., University Center, Mich., 1981-82; asst. prof. Oakland U., Rochester, Mich., 1982-83; asst. prof. NYU, 1983—; founder, pres. The Computer Coop., Inc., 1981-82. Served to lt. AUS, 1968-69. Haskins and Sells Doctoral Consortium fellow, 1977. Mem. Am. Accounting Assn., Nat. Assn. Accountants, Internat. Platform Assn., Nat. Speakers Assn., Toastmasters Internat. Club: Circumnavigators. Home: 2795 Southwood East Lansing MI 48823 Office: Acctg Dept NYU 417 Tisch Hall New York NY 10003

FORAN, DAVID JOHN, public relations executive, consultant; b. Milw., July 15, 1937; s. George Robert and Kathleen Terese (Melchior) F.; m. Donna Rae Skovira, June 11, 1960; children—Christopher G., Patrick D., Anne K., Mary E., Timothy. B.S. in Journalism, Marquette U., 1959, postgrad. 1966-68. Reporter Catholic Herald Citizen, Milw., 1960, Milw. Jour., 1960-66; dir. news bur. Marquette U., Milw., 1966-74, assoc. dir. pub. relations, 1974-81, exec. dir., 1981—, instr. journalism, 1975-81; moderator TV program Sta. WTMJ, Milw., 1982-83. Past mem. bd. dirs. Wis. Heart Assn., past chmn. pub. relations com.; chmn. adv. com. Walnut Improvement Council, 1981—; mem. Human Relations Radio and TV Council of Milw., 1981—. Served with U.S. Army, 1959, 61-62. Mem. Soc. Profl. Journalists-Sigma Delta Chi (past pres., chmn., dir. Milw. chpt.), Council for Advancement and Support of Edn., Edn. Writers Assn., Milw. Pen and Mike Club. Roman Catholic. Club: Milw. Press. Home: 209 W Lexington Blvd Glendale WI 53217 Office: 1212 W Wisconsin Ave Milwaukee WI 53233

FORBES, FRED WILLIAM, architect, engineer; b. East Liverpool, Ohio, Aug. 21, 1936; s. Kenneth S. and Phylis C. F.; B.S. in Architecture, U. Cin., 1960, postgrad. in Civil Engring.; m. Carolyn Lee Eleyet, Dec. 27, 1969; children—Tallerie Bliss, Kendall Robert. Material research engr. U.S. Air Force Materials Lab., 1960-61, structural research engr. Flight Accessories Lab., 1961-63, tech. area mgr. Aero Propulsion Lab., 1964-67; prin. Fred W. Forbes, Architect, Xenia, Ohio, 1966-68; br. chief U.S. Air Force Aero Propulsion Lab., Wright Patterson AFB, Ohio, 1967-72, pres. Forbes and Huie, Xenia, 1968-73; pres. Forbes, Huie & Assos., Inc., Xenia, 1973-76; pres. Fred W. Forbes & Assos., Inc., Xenia, 1976—; instr. U. Dayton, 1963-64. Past pres. Xenia Area Living Arts Council. Recipient Exceptional Civilian Service award U.S. Air Force, 1966; Archtl. Award of Excellence for Moraine Civic Center, Masonry Inst., 1976, Archtl. Award of Merit for Xenia br. of 3d Nat. Bank, 1981 Excellence in Masonry, Spl. award for renovation Dayton Area Red Cross Bldg., 1982; Dayton City Beautiful award for Martin Electric Co., 1977; award of merit Greene County Mental Health Facility 1983. Fellow Brit. Interplanetary Soc.; mem. Greene County Profl. Engrs. Soc. (past pres.), Am. Astron. Soc. (past nat. dir.), AIA, Ohio Soc. Profl. Engrs. (Young Engrs. award 1970), Nat. Soc. Profl. Engrs. (top 5 Outstanding Young Engr. award 1972), Nat. Asbestos Contractors Assn. (assoc.), Xenia Area C. of C. (dir., v.p.), Theta Chi. Republican. Methodist. Contbr. 24 articles to profl. jours.; patentee in field. Office: 158 E Main St Xenia OH 45385 Home: 465 Lamplighter Pl Xenia OH 45385

FORD, ALFRED LEE, data processing consultant; b. Indpls., Nov. 29, 1950; s. William Ernest and Lena Mae (Gaines) F.; m. Inez Ethel Hayes, Aug. 22, 1970; children—Gayle Alfreda, Alfred L. A.A. in Applied Sci., Purdue U., 1977, B.S., 1978. Computer operator Chevrolet Motor Div., Indpls., 1973-78; supr. ops. Ind. Bell Telephone, Indpls., 1978-81, space planner, 1981-84, data processing cons., 1984—. Served to sgt. U.S. Army, 1970-73. Mem. Minorities in Engring., Indpls. Jaycees (bd. dirs. 1983). Democrat. Baptist. Lodges: Shriners (chief rabban 1985), Henry Rogan (sr. warden 1983-84). Avocations: basketball, bowling, computer programming. Office: Ind Bell Telephone Co Room 805 220 N Meridian St Indianapolis IN 46204

FORD, DAVID CLAYTON, lawyer; b. Hartford City, Ind., Mar. 3, 1949; s. Clayton I. and Barbara J. (McVicker) F.; m. Joyce Ann Bonjour, Aug. 22, 1970; children—Jeffrey David, Andrew Clayton. B.A. in Polit. Sci., Ind. U., 1973; J.D., Ind. U.-Indpls., 1976. Bar: Ind. 1975, U.S. Dist. Ct. (no. dist.) Ind. 1977, U.S. Dist. Ct. (so. dist.) Ind. 1976, U.S. Supreme Ct. 1983. City atty. City of Montpelier, Ind., 1977-79; town atty. Town of Shamrock Lakes, Ind., 1977—; chief dep. prosecutor, Blackford County, 1979; pros. atty. 71st Jud. Cir., Blackford County, Hartford City, Ind., 1983—. Dir. Blackford County Young Republicans, 1977-82, pres., 1977-78; chmn. Town of Shamrock Lakes Republican Com., 1983; vice-chmn. Blackford County Rep. Central Com., 1978-82; precinct committeeman Blackford County, Licking 7, 1980—; mem. Ind. 10th Congl. Dist. Rep. Caucus, 1978-82; U.S. Edn. Appeals Bd. mem. U.S. Dept. Edn., 1982—; Nat. Def. Execs. Res. 1983—; mem. bus. adv. com. to Congressman Dan Burton; chmn. bus., industries and devel. com. Ptnrs. of Ams., Ind. chpt., 1983—; mem. Blackford County Bd. Aviation Commrs., 1977-83, pres., 1979-83; bd. dirs. Dollars of Scholars, Blackford County, 1977—, v.p., 1977—; mem. St. John's-Riedman Meml. Sch. Bd., 1978-82, pres., 1978-82; mem. Blackford County Sheriff's Merit Bd., 1981-82. Named Man of Yr., Hartford City C. of C., 1978; Sagamore of the Wabash, Gov. Otis Bowen, 1978; Hon. Sec. of State, Edwin J. Simcox, 1981; participant Rotary group study exchange to São Paulo, Brazil, 1981; named Outstanding Young Man of Am., U.S. Jaycees, 1982. Mem. ABA, Assn. Trial Lawyers' Am., Ind. State Bar Assn., Blackford County Bar Assn., World Trade Club Ind., Mensa, Sigma Iota Epsilon. Home: 2776 S Angling Park Hartford City IN 47348 Office: Ford & Young 210 W Main St Hartford City IN 47348

FORD, DONALD JAMES, insurance company executive, lawyer; b. Marshfield, Oreg., Oct. 18, 1930; s. Austin John and Lillian Augusta (Rasmus) F.; m. Bonnie Lou Brackin, Aug. 13, 1955; children—Jennifer K. Ralston, Karen Jane, Andrea Jean. B.S., U. Oreg., 1952, J.D., 1956. Bar: Oreg. 1956, U.S. Dist. Ct. (Oreg.) 1957. Sole practice, McMinnville, Oreg., 1956-58, also dep. dist. atty.; with Allstate Ins. Co., 1958—, dist. claim mgr., casualty div., Salem, Oreg., 1967, div. claim mgr., Santa Ana, Calif., 1968; regional claim mgr., Menlo Park, Calif., 1968-69, Santa Ana, 1969-71, mng. claim atty., 1971-73, Midwest Zone claim mgr., Deerfield, Ill., 1973-74, gen. claim mgr., 1975, asst. v.p., 1975-81, claim v.p., 1981—; dir. Tech Cor, Inc. Bd. dirs. Ins. Arbitration Forums, Inter-Industry Conf. on Auto Collision Repair; Ins. Crime Prevention Inst.; chmn. bd. Nat. Auto Theft Bur.; vice chmn. Am. Ins. Assn. Index System; mem. arbitration com. Def. Research Inst. Served with U.S. Army, 1952-54. Mem. ABA, Oreg. Bar Assn., Internat. Assn. Ins. Counsel, Nat. Assn. Ind. Insurers (rep. to ABA nat. conf. lawyers, ins. cos. and adjusters), Fedn. Ins. Counsel, Phi Eta Sigma, Delta Tau Delta, Phi Delta Phi. Republican. Presbyterian. Contbr. article to profl. jours. Address: 912 Morningside Lake Forest IL 60045

FORD, FREDERICK ROSS, university official; b. Kentland, Ind., Mar. 25, 1936; s. Merl Jackson and Marie Jeanne (Ross) F.; m. Mary A. Harrison, May 31, 1959; children—Lynne Elizabeth, Steven Harrison, Katherine Jeannette. B.S. in Mech. Engring., Purdue U., 1958, M.S., 1959, Ph.D., 1963. Asst. to bus. mgr. Purdue U., West Lafayette, Ind., 1959-61, asst. to v.p., treas., 1961-65, asst. bus. mgr., 1965-69, bus. mgr., asst. treas., 1969-74, exec. v.p., treas., 1974—; dir. First Fed. Savs. & Loan, Lafayette, Circle Income Shares, Indpls.; trustee Tchrs. Ins. and Annuity Assn., N.Y.C., 1982—. Treas. capital funds found. United Way, Lafayette, 1984-85. Mem. Council on Govtl. Relations (bd. mgmt. 1984—), Nat. Assn. Coll. and Univ. Bus. Officers (bd. dirs. 1980-83, sec. 1982-83), Central Assn. Coll. and Univ. Bus. Officers (exec. com. 1976-81, pres. 1979-80), Lafayette C. of C. (pres. 1978-79; chmn. edn. relations com. 1984-85), Delta Upsilon. Republican. Presbyterian. Lodge: Rotary. Avocations: sailing; fishing. Home: 160 Creighton Rd West Lafayette IN 47906 Office: Purdue U West Lafayette IN 47907

FORD, LEE ELLEN, scientist, educator, lawyer; b. Auburn, Ind., June 16, 1917; d. Arthur W. and Geneva (Muhn) Ford; B.A., Wittenberg Coll., 1947; M.S., U. Minn., 1949; Ph.D., Iowa State Coll., 1952; J.D., U. Notre Dame, 1972. CPA auditing, 1934-44; assoc. prof. biology Gustavus Adolphus Coll., 1950-51, Anderson (Ind.) Coll., 1952-55; vis. prof. biology U. Alta. (Can.), Calgary, 1955-56; asso. prof. biology Pacific Luth. U., Parkland, Wash., 1956-62; prof. biology and cytogenetics Miss. State Coll. for Women, 1962-64; chief cytogeneticist Pacific N.W. Research Found., Seattle, 1964-65; dir. Canine Genetics Cons. Service, Parkland, 1963-69. Sponsor Companion Collies for the Adult, Jr. Blind, 1955-65; dir. Genetics Research Lab., Butler, Ind., 1955-75, cons. cytogenetics, 1969-75; legis. cons., 1970-79; dir. chromosome lab. Inst. Basic Research in Mental Retardation, S.I., 1968-69; exec. dir. Legis. Bur. U. Notre Dame Law Sch., also editor New Dimensions in Legislation, 1969; bd. dirs. Ind. Interreligious Com. on Human Equality, 1976-80; exec. asst. to Gov. Otis R. Bowen, Ind., 1973-75; dir. Ind. Commn. on Status Women, 1973-74; bd. dirs. Ind. Council Chs.; editor Ford Assos. pubs., 1972—; mem. Pres.'s Adv. Council on Drug Abuse, 1976-77. Admitted to Ind. bar, 1972. Adult counselor Girl Scouts U.S.A., 1934-40; bd. dirs. Ind. Task Force Women's Health, 1976-80; mem. exec. bd., bd. dirs. Ind.-Ky. Synod Lutheran Ch., 1972-78; mem. social services personnel bd.; mem. DeKalb County (Ind.) Sheriff's Merit Bd., 1983—; mem. Ind. Caucus for Animal Legislation and Leadership, 1984—. Mem. or ex-mem. AAUW, AAAS, Genetics Soc. Am., Am. Human Genetics Soc., Am. Genetic Assn., Am. Inst. Biol. Scis., Am. Soc. Zoologists, La., Miss., Ind., Iowa acads. sci., Bot. Soc. Am., Ecol. Soc. Am., Am. (dir.), Ind. (dir.), DeKalb County (dir.) bar assns., Humane Soc. U.S. (dir.), DeKalb County Humane Soc. (dir.), Ind. Fedn. Humane Socs. (dir. 1978-85), Nat. Assn. Women Lawyers (dir.), Bus. and Profl. Women's Club, Nat. Assn. Republican Women (dir.), Women's Equity Action League (dir.), Assn. So. Biologists, Phi Kappa Phi. Club: Altrusa. Editor: Breeder's Jour., 1958-63; numerous vols. on dog genetics and breeding, guide dogs for the blind. Contbr. over 1000 sci. and popular publs. on cytogenetics, dog breeding and legal topics; contbr. Am. Kennel Club Gazette, 1970-81, also others. Researcher in field. Home and Office: 824 E 7th St Auburn IN 46706

FORD, LINCOLN EDMOND, physician, physiologist, educator; b. Boston, May 14, 1938; s. Johns Berchmans and Mary Margaret (Clark) F.; m. Erica W. Roy, Feb. 24, 1973; children—Catherine L., Gretchen A., Vanessa E., Emily W. B.A., Harvard Coll., 1960, postgrad., 1960-61; M.D., U. Rochester, 1965. Rotating intern Bassett Hosp., Cooperstown, N.Y., 1965-66; staff assoc. NIH, Bethesda, Md., 1966-68; NIH research assoc. Peter Bent Brigham Hosp., Boston, 1968-70, resident, 1970-71; NIH research fellow U. Coll. London, 1971-74; assoc. prof. medicine U. Chgo., 1974—, Am. Heart Assn. established investigator U. Chgo., 1975-80. chmn. research council Chgo., Heart Assn., 1978-79. Adv. editor Jour. Muscle Research, 1979—; mem. editorial bd. Am. Jour. Physiology, 1981—, Circulation Research, 1983—. Contbr. numerous articles to profl. jours. Served with USPHS, 1966-68. Mem. Am. Physiol. Soc., Biophys. Soc., Soc. Gen. Physiologists. Clubs: Harvard (Boston); Quadrangle (Chgo.). Avocations: gardening; skiing. Home: 4949 S Woodlawn Ave Chicago IL 60615 Office: Box 249 Univ Chgo Hosps 950 E 59th St Chicago IL 60637

FORD, RICHARD EARL, plant pathology educator; b. Des Moines, May 25, 1933; s. Victor S. and Gertrude F. (Headlee) F.; m. Roberta Jean Essig, June 20, 1954; children—Nina Diane, Linda Marie, Kent Richard (dec.), Steven Earl. B.S., Iowa State U., 1956; M.S., Cornell U., 1959, Ph.D., 1961. Instr., Iowa State U., Ames, 1956; asst. prof. and research plant pathologist Oreg. State U., Corvallis, 1961-65; from assoc. prof. to prof. Iowa State U., Ames, 1965-72; prof., head dept. plant pathology U. Ill.-Urbana, 1972—; cons. Contbr. chpts. to books, articles to sci. jours. Mem. bd. edn. United Community Sch., Ames, 1970-73; active Yankee Ridge PTSA, Urbana, 1974-75; treas. Yankee Ridge Little League Baseball, 1975-77, Wesley Found., 1980—. Fulbright Disting. prof., Yugoslavia, 1978; Nat. Acad. Sci. India fellow, 1984. Mem. Am. Phytopath. Soc. (sec. 1971-74, pres. 1982-83), Intersoc. Consortium for Plant Protection (chmn. 1984), Am. Soc. Virologists (charter), AAAS, Am. Inst. Biol. Scis., Phi Kappa Phi, Alpha Zeta, Gamma Sigma Delta, Gamma Gamma, FarmHouse Fraternity (nat. pres. 1968-72; Master Builder of Men award 1978). Lodge: Lions (Urbana). Avocations: handball; bowling; skiing; golf; gardening. Home: 11 Persimmon Circle Urbana IL 61801 Office: Dept Plant Pathology U Ill Urbana IL 61801

FORD, SUSAN HELM, chemistry educator, researcher; b. New Castle, Ind., May 3, 1943; s. Charles and Inez Marie (Hinton) Heim; m. Richard Clay Ford, July 26, 1968; children—Matthew Clay, Rebecca Hope. B.S., U. Mich., 1965; Ph.D., U. Chgo., 1969. Postdoctoral fellow U. Chgo., 1969-71, research assoc., 1973-78; lectr. Kennedy King Coll., Chgo., 1972; lectr., asst. prof., Loyola U., Chgo., 1974-77; asst. prof., then assoc. prof. Chgo. State U., 1978—; adhoc cons. NIH, 1979—. Contbr. articles to profl. jours. Bd. dirs. Phoenix Sch., Chgo., 1978-82. NSF fellow, 1964-65; NIH grantee, 1965-69, 70-71. Mem. Am. Chem. Soc., Sigma Xi. Office: Chicago State U Dept Phys Scis 95th St at King Dr Chicago IL 60628

FORD, WILLIAM CLAY, automotive manufacturing executive, professional football team executive; b. Detroit, Mar. 14, 1925; s. Edsel Bryant and Eleanor (Clay) F.; B.S., Yale, 1949; m. Martha Firestone, June 21, 1947; children—Martha, Sheila, William Clay, Elizabeth. Sales and advt. staff Ford Motor Co., 1949, indsl. relations, labor negotiations with U.A.W., 1949, quality control mgr. gas turbine engines Lincoln-Mercury div., Dearborn, Mich., 1951, mgr. spl. product operations, 1952, v.p., 1953, gen. mgr. Continental div., 1954, group v.p. Lincoln and Continental divs., 1955, v.p. product design, 1956-80, vice chmn. bd., 1980—, also chmn. exec. com., dir. Pres., owner Det. Lions Profl. Football Club; chmn. Edison Inst.; trustee Eisenhower Med. Center, Thomas A. Edison Found.; bd. dirs. Nat. Tennis Hall of Fame, Boys Clubs Am. Mem. Soc. Automotive Engrs. (asso.), Automobile Old Timers, Econ. Club Detroit (dir.), Phelps Assn., Psi Upsilon. Club: Masons (K.T.), (Detroit). Office: Ford Motor Co Dearborn MI 48121 also care Detroit Lions 1200 Featherstone Rd Box 4200 Pontiac MI 48057

FORD, WILLIAM DAVID, Congressman; b. Detroit, Aug. 6, 1927; s. Robert H. and Jean B. Ford; student Wayne State U.; B.S., J.D., U. Denver; hon. doctorate Central Mich. U., Eastern Mich. U., Mich. State U., No. Mich. U., Grand Valley State Coll., U. Detroit, Wayne State U., Westfield (Mass.) State Coll.; children—William D., Margaret Helene, John Phillip. Practice law, 1952—; justice of peace, Taylor Twp., Mich., 1955-57; city atty. Melvindale (Mich.), 1957-59; twp. atty. Taylor, 1957-64; Mich. senator, 1963-64; mem. 89th-99th congresses from 15th Mich. Dist., mem. edn. and labor com., chmn. post office and civil service com., 1981—; chmn. subcom. post secondary edn. Com. Edn. and Labor; Nat. Democratic whip-at-large, 1975—; house rep. to White House Library Conf.; mem. Dem. Policy and Steering Com.; del. Mich. Constl. Conv., 1961-62. Served with USNR, 1944-46, USAF, 1950-57. Named Outstanding Young Man of Taylor, 1962. Mem. Downriver (pres. 1961-62), Mich., Am. bar assns., Taylor Jr. C. of C. (charter), Phi Delta Phi. Mem. United Ch. of Christ. Mason (33 deg., Shriner), Moose, Eagle, Rotarian. Home: Taylor MI 48180 Office: Cannon House Office Bldg Washington DC 20515

FOREMAN, JAMES LOUIS, judge; b. Metropolis, Ill., May 12, 1927; s. James C. and Anna Elizabeth (Henne) F.; B.S., U. Ill., 1950, J.D., 1952; m. Mabel Inez Dunn, June 16, 1948; children—Beth Foreman Banks, Rhonda Foreman Riepe, Nanette. Admitted to Ill. bar; individual practice law, Metropolis, Ill.; partner firm Chase and Foreman, Metropolis, until 1972; Ill. state's atty., Massac County; asst. atty. gen., State of Ill.; chief judge So. Dist. of Ill., East St. Louis, 1972—. Pres. Bd. of Edn., Metropolis. Served with USNR, 1945-46. Mem. Am. Bar Assn., Ill. State Bar Assn., Metropolis C. of C. (past pres.). Republican. Home: PO Box 866 Metropolis IL 62960 Office: PO Box 186 East St Louis IL 62202

FORGETTE, LISA KAY, data systems engineer; b. Detroit, Aug. 18, 1959; d. Eugene H. and Sarah Marie (Rogers) F. B.S., Central Mich. U., 1981. Process control programmer Gerber Products Co., Fremont, Mich., 1981-84, info. ctr. cons., 1984-85; systems engr. Electronic Data Systems, Bloomfield Hills, Mich., 1985—; tchr. Newaygo County Vocat. Sch., Fremont, 1982-84. Mem. Jaycee Women (treas. 1983-84), Rochester Jaycees (bd. dirs. 1985-86), Sigma Sigma Sigma, Kappa Mu Epsilon. Avocations: cross-stitch; bowling; golf; cross-country skiing; piano. Home: 87 Timberview Dr Apt 38 Rochester MI 48063 Office: Electronic Data Systems 6001 Adams Rd Bloomfield Hills MI 48013

FORMAN, FRANKLIN WOLD, fastener company executive; b. Sublette, Ill., Jan. 4, 1923; s. Frank Xavier and Gertrude Ethel (Wold) F.; m. Dorothy Louise Seiter, Apr. 10, 1970; m. Charlotte Mae Moser, May 12, 1944 (dec.); children—Charlyn, Franklin W., Eric, Konrad. Student Wheaton Coll., 1941-42; B.S.M.E., Tri-State U., 1946. Project methods and maintenance engr. Reynolds Wire Div., Dixon, Ill., 1950-57; mgr. plant engring. Barber-Colman Co., Rockford, Ill., 1957-74; mgr. plant engring. Am. Hoist, St. Paul, 1974-76; mgr. facilities and plant engring. Nat. Metalcrafters (formerly Nat. Lock Fasteners), Rockford, Ill., 1976—. Mem. Ill. Gov.'s Bd. Vocat. Edn., 1970-73; mem. Ill. State Grievance Bd., 1970-73. Precinct committeeman Republican party; advisor County Welfare Services; pres. PTA; chmn. Vocat. Sch. Adv. Bd.; trustee Rock Valley Coll. Served with USNR, 1942-45. Named Disting. Alumnus of Year, Tri-State U., 1968. Mem. Nat. Inst. Plant Engrs., C. of C. (edn. com.). Republican. Mem. Evangel. Free Ch. Am. Clubs: Masons. Home: 2212 Silverthorn Dr Rockford IL 61107 Office: 4500 Kishwaukee St Rockford IL 61101

FORMAN, JOEL, dentist; b. Detroit, Feb. 27, 1944; s. Samuel and Pauline (Blum) F.; m. Linda Sue Feldman, July 22, 1967; children—Seth, Adam, Jeremy. B.S., Wayne State U., 1965; D.D.S., U. Mich.-Ann Arbor, 1970. Assoc. prof. La. State U. Sch. Dentistry, New Orleans, 1972; pvt. practice dentistry, Taylor, Mich., 1972-74, Ferndale, Mich., 1974-78, Southfield, Mich., 1978—; dental cons. Kingswood Hosp., Ferndale, Mich., 1978—, Boys Republic, Southfield, Mich., 1981. Served to capt. AUS, 1970-72. Recipient U. Mich. Grant-in-Aid, 1969. Mem. Am. Dental Assn., Oakland County Dental Soc., Mich. State Dental Soc., Detroit Dist. Dental Soc., Alpha Omega. Avocations: Photography; skiing; traveling. Office: 20905 Greenfield St Suite 403 Southfield MI 48075

FORNATTO, ELIO JOSEPH, physician, educator; b. Turin, Italy, July 2, 1928; s. Mario G. and Julia (Stabio) F.; M.D., U. Turin, 1952; m. Mary Elizabeth Pearson, Dec. 17, 1960; children—Susan, Robert, Daniel. Came to U.S., 1953, naturalized, 1962. Intern Edgewater Hosp., Chicago, 1956-57; resident U. Illinois, 1953-56; practice medicine, specializing in otolaryngology, Elmhurst, Ill., 1958—; mem. staff Elmhurst Meml. Hosp.; clin. asst. prof. otolaryngology Stritch Sch. Medicine, Loyola U., 1967—; med. dir. Chgo. Eye, Ear, Nose and Throat Hosp., 1966-69; dir. laryngectomee program DuPage County chpt. Am. Cancer Soc., 1977—. Founding mem. Deafness Research Found. Diplomate Am. Bd. Otolaryngology. Mem. AMA, Ill. Med. Soc., Pan Am. Med. Assn., Am. Acad. Otolaryngologic Allergy, Am. Acad. Otolaryngology and Head and Neck Surgery. Home: 200 W Jackson St Elmhurst IL 60126 Office: 172 Schiller St Elmhurst IL 60126

FORNSHELL, DAVE LEE, educational broadcasting executive; b. Bluffton, July 9, 1937; s. Harold Christman and Mary Ann Elizabeth (Fox) F.; B.A., Ohio State U., 1959; m. Elizabeth Slagle Clinger, Nov. 11, 1978; 1 son, John David. Continuity dir. WTVN-TV, Columbus, Ohio, 1959-61; traffic dir., asst. program mgr. WOSU-TV, Columbus, 1961-69; ops. mgr. Md. Center for Pub. Broadcasting, Balt., 1969-70; exec. dir. Ohio Ednl. TV Network Commn., Columbus, 1970—; dir., mem. exec. com. Central Ednl. Network; exec. com. CEN Post-Secondary Edn. Council, Ohio Post-Secondary Telecommunications Council; pres. Ohio Radio Reading Services. Pres. Landings Residents Assn., 1973; active March of Dimes, 4-H. Served with USAF, 1961-62. Recipient award Dayton Fedn. Women's Clubs, 1974. Mem. N.G. Assn., Ohio State U. Alumni Assn., Nat. Acad. TV Arts and Scis. (2d v.p. Columbus 1968-69, gov. 1970—), Nat. Assn. TV Program Execs., Am. Assn. Higher Edn., Nat. Assn. Ednl. Broadcasters (chmn. state adminstrs. council), Health Scis. Communications Assn., Broadcast Pioneers, Am. Soc. Pub. Adminstrn., Alpha Epsilon Rho, Alpha Delta Sigma, Sigma Delta Chi. Clubs: Univ., Athletic (Columbus), Kiwanis. Home: 240 Larrimer Ave Worthington OH 43085 Office: 2470 N Star Rd Columbus OH 43221

FORREST, CLINTON RICHARD, industrial and construction equipment sales and service executive; b. Wellington, Kans., Jan. 30, 1950; s. Richard Sheridan and Wanda Merlene (Raine) F.; m. Julie Ann Drouhard, Feb. 28, 1970; children—Richard Sheridan, Kathleen Michelle, Weston Allen, Vashti Spring. Grad. Argonia high sch. Kans. Gen. mgr. Forrest Implement Co., Argonia, 1973-85; service mgr., shop foreman Berry Tractor and Equipment Co., Wichita, Kans., 1985—. Pres. Bd. Edn. USD 359, Argonia, 1979—. Served to sgt. U.S. Army, 1971-73. Recipient Commendation medal U.S. Army, 1973. Methodist. Lodge: Lions. Avocations: hunting, fishing, reading. Home: 205 E Walnut Argonia KS 67004 Office: Berry Tractor and Equipment Co Wichita KS

FORSBERG, EDWARD WILLIAM, SR., manufacturing company executive; b. Chgo., Nov. 30, 1945; s. Vernon Andrew and Virginia Ruth (Carlson) F.; m. Linda Carol Meents, Sept. 19, 1970; children—Edward William, Nelson Taylor. B.S.B.A., Northwestern U., 1969. C.P.A., Ill. Audit mgr. Price Waterhouse, Chgo., 1969-79; corp. dir. acctg. and fin. adminstrn. Fiat-Allis, Inc., Deerfield, Ill., 1979-81; v.p. fin. Ingrid, Ltd., North Chicago, Ill., 1981—, also dir. and officer various affiliated cos. Bd. dirs., v.p., treas. Glenkirk Assn. Retarded Citizens, Northbrook, Ill., 1980—. Mem. Am. Inst. C.P.A.s, Ill. C.P.A. Soc., Inst. Internal Auditors. Republican. Club: Kenilworth (bd. dirs. 1985—) (Ill.). Home: 521 Sheridan Rd Kenilworth IL 60043 Office: 3601 N Skokie Hwy North Chicago IL 60064

FORSLUND, ROBERT LEE, food company executive; b. Harcourt, Iowa, Apr. 9, 1938; s. Monrad William and Elsie Maye (Swanlund) F.; student Drake U., 1960; m. Mary Kay Wingert, June 2, 1962; children—Robert Lee, Kristen Kay. With George A. Hormel & Co., Austin, Minn., 1961—, mgr. licensing and joint venture ops., internat. div., 1979—; dir. Stefanutti/Hormel, Santo Domingo, Dominican Republic, Pure Foods Corp., Manila, Philippines, Hormel Ltd. (Japan), Vista Internat. Packaging, Kenosha, Wis. Served with U.S. Army, 1960-62. Republican. Presbyterian. Club: Austin Country. Home: 101 22d St NW Austin MN 55912 Office: 501 16th Ave NE Austin MN 55912

FORSMAN, SHIRLEY JEAN, nurse; b. Phila., Feb. 6, 1930; d. Hartley F. and Ellen T. (Carroll) Ness; A.A. in Nursing, Sacramento City Coll., 1966; B.S.N., Sacramento State Coll., 1971; M.A., Calif. State U., 1973; m. Willard John Forsman, June 18, 1949 (dec.); children—Daniel (dec.), John, Katie, Nancy. Staff nurse Kaiser Permanente Hosp., Sacramento, 1963-66; supervising head nurse psychiatry Eskaton Am. River Hosp., Carmichael, Calif., 1966-70, hosp. supr., 1970-71; dir. nursing edn. Golden Key Coll., Sacramento, 1971-74; dir. nursing services Douglas County Hosp., Alexandria, Minn., 1974-75; dir. public health Kandiyohi County Community Health Dept., Willmar, Minn., 1975-77; dir. nursing services Rice Meml. Hosp., Willmar, 1977-79; master staffing coordinator Roseville (Calif.) Community Hosp., 1979-80; instr. Am. River Coll., Sacramento, 1980-81; patient care coordinator Golden Valley Health Ctr. (Minn.), 1983—; dir. Beltrami County Nursing Service, Minn., 1985—; cons. Central Minn. Area Health Edn. Consortium, 1975—; mem. adv. com. to Lic. Practice Nurse Program, Minn.-Dakotas, 1974—; mem. Child Abuse Team, U. Minn. Continuing Edn. for R.N.s, 1978—; faculty/lectr. various schs., colls., instns., 1968—. HEW grantee, 1971. Mem. Am. Nurses Assn., Minn. Nurses Assn., Nat. Council Nursing Service Facilitators, Minn. State Council Nursing Service Adminstrs., Minn. Hosp. Assn. Area Nursing Service Adminstrs., AAUW, Am. Legion Aux. Clubs: Bus. and Profl. Women, Eagles Aux. Home: 1515 Calihan Ave NE Bemidji MN 56601

FORSYTHE, JAMES LEE, historian, university dean; b. Bransford, Tex., Dec. 18, 1934; s. Roy Theodore and Irma May (Smith) F.; B.S., N. Tex. State U., 1960, M.A., 1962; Ph.D. (fellow), U. N.Mex., 1971; m. Sherrill Kay Zartman, Aug. 10, 1956; children—James Lee, Garen David, Dana Sean. Transp. agt. Delta Air Lines, Dallas, 1952-62; asst. prof. history Ft. Hays (Kans.) State Coll. (now Ft. Hays State U.), 1963-68, asso. prof. history, 1968-71, prof., 1971—, chmn. dept. history, 1975-81, dean of grad. sch., 1981—; mem. Kans. Hist. Records Adv. Bd., 1976—; mem. Kans. State Historic Sites Bd. of Rev., 1980—; dir. Kans. Oral History Project, 1969—. Treas., Ellis County Young Democrats, 1966-70; Dem. precinct committeeman, 1974—. Served with Air N.G., 1953-55; U.S. Army, 1955-57. Recipient Disting. Alumni award Grapevine (Tex.) High Sch., 1970, named to Hall of Fame, 1983; Harry S. Truman Library Inst. Nat. and Internat. Affairs grantee, 1967, 72. Mem. Rocky Mountain Social Sci. Assn. (exec. council 1971-74), Western Social Sci. Assn. (pres. 1976-77), AAUP (pres. Kans. 1972-73), Kans. State Hist. Soc. (dir. 1977—), Kans. Com. Humanities (exec. com. 1975-81, chmn. 1981-82), Agrl. History Assn., Orgn. Am. Historians, So., N.Mex., Kans. (v.p. 1980-81, pres. 1982-83), Western hist. assns., Phi Alpha Theta, Pi Sigma Alpha, Phi Kappa Phi, Phi Delta Kappa. Baptist. Author: The First 75 Years: A History of Fort Hays State University, 1909-1977, 1977; contbr. articles to profl jours. Home: 2927 Walnut St Hays KS 67601 Office: Grad Sch Fort Hays State U 600 Park St Hays KS 67601-4099

FORSYTHE, STEVEN WILLIAM, agricultural educator; b. Killeen, Tex., Oct. 9, 1952; s. James V. and Elva E. (Whidden) F.; m. Cynthia Rose Bishop, Mar. 14, 1974; 1 dau., Mary Ellen. B.S., Tarleton State U., 1973; M.S., Okla. State U., 1979, Ed.D., 1981. Cert. tchr., Tex., 1973. Vocat. agrl. tchr., El Paso (Tex.) pub. schs., 1974-78; teaching assoc. Okla. State U., Stillwater, 1978-81; prof. agr. Mid-Am. Nazarene Coll., Olathe, Kans., 1981—. Nat. Feed Ingredients scholar, 1980. Mem. Am. Welding Soc., Am. Soc. Agrl. Engrs., Nat. Assn. Colls. Tchrs. of Agr., Am. Assn. Tchr. Educators in Agr. Mem. Ch. of the Nazarene. Contbr. articles to profl. jours.

FORTINI, JOHN LOUIS, communication corporation executive, lawyer; b. Chgo., Dec. 14, 1948; s. John Louis and Rosemary (Foy) F.; m. Patricia Smith, Feb. 7, 1970 (div. July 1983); children—Amanda, Laura, Sarah. A.B., Loyola U., Chgo., 1970; J.D. with distinction, U. Iowa, 1976. Bar: Iowa 1976, U.S. Dist. Ct. (no. dist.) Iowa 1976, U.S. Dist. Ct. (so. dist.) Ill. 1976, U.S. Ct. Appeals (8th cir.) 1976, U.S. Dist. Ct. (so. dist.) Iowa 1979, U.S. Tax Ct. 1979, U.S. Supreme Ct. 1979, Ill. 1981, U.S. Dist. Ct. (mid. dist.) Ill. 1981, Wis. 1981, U.S. Dist. Ct. (ea. and we. dists.) Wis. 1981, U.S. Ct. Appeals (7th cir.) 1981, Nebr. 1983, Pa. 1984, U.S. Dist. Ct. (mid. and we. dists.) Pa. 1984, U.S. Dist. Ct. (no. dist.) Ohio 1984, Ohio 1984, U.S. Ct. Appeals (2d and 6th cirs.) 1984. Law clk. U.S. Dist. Ct. (no. dist.) Iowa, Cedar Rapids, 1975; assoc. atty. Newport & Buzzell, Davenport, Iowa, 1976-77, gen. ptnr. Newport, Buzzell, Liebbe & Fortini, 1977-79, Newport, Fortini & Assocs., 1979-81; sr. atty. Gen. Telephone Co. Ill./Wis., Bloomington, Ill., 1981-83, assoc. gen. counsel, 1983, corp. sec. to bd. dirs., Gen. Telephone Co. Wis., Madison, 1982-83, state gen. counsel, sec. Gen. Telephone Co. Ohio/Pa., Marion, Ohio, 1983—; dir. Gen. Telephone Co. Ill. Employees Credit Union, Bloomington, 1982-83, vice chmn., 1983. Served to capt. AUS, 1970-73. Mem. ABA, Fed. Bar Assn., Iowa Bar Assns, Ill. Bar Assn., Wis. Bar Assn., Nebr. Bar Assn., Ohio Bar Assn., Pa. Bar Assn. Fed. Communications Bar Assn., Res. Officers Assn., Am. Assn. Individual Investors, Nat. Assn. Ind. Investment Clubs, Phi Delta Phi, Tau Kappa Epsilon. Roman Catholic. Avocations: running; coin collecting; reading; spectator sports. Home: 1055 Marseilles Dr Marion OH 43302 Office: Gen Telephone Co of Ohio/Pa 100 Executive Dr Marion OH 43302

FORTNEY, REX DUANE, judge. b. Van Wert, Ohio, Aug. 21, 1950; s. Morgan L. and Mary L. (Baker) F.; m. Beverly A. Hoover, June 12, 1976; children—Laura L., Ryan D. B.A., Bluffton Coll., 1972; J.D., Ohio No. U., 1975. Bar: Ohio 1975, U.S. Dist. Ct. (no. dist.) Ohio 1976, U.S. Ct. Appeals (6th cir.) 1981. Ptnr. Childs & Fortney, Van Wert, 1976-83, Zeigler & Fortney, 1983-84; dir. law City of Van Wert, 1980-83; judge probate div. Van Wert County Ct. of Common Pleas, 1985—. Bd. dirs. Van Wert Heart Assn., 1983—. Mem. Van Wert County Bar Assn. (pres. 1985—), Ohio State Bar Assn. Republican. Mem. United Ch. of Christ. Lodge: Kiwanis (v.p.). Avocations: photography; computers; jogging; reading. Home: 1026 Park St Van Wert OH 45891 Office: Ct of Common Pleas Courthouse Van Wert OH 45891

FOSHEIM, JON, justice S.D. Supreme Court; b. Howard, S.D., Jan. 25, 1923; s. Oscar A. and Margaret A.; student Gen. Beadle Coll., Madison, S.D., 1941-42; LL.B., U. S.D., 1946; m. Mary Lou Olson, Dec. 28, 1948; children—Patricia, Jon, Douglas, Peggy, Todd. Admitted to S.D. bar, 1946; practiced law, Huron, S.D., 1946-59; states atty. Beadle County (S.D.), 1951-55, dep. states atty., 1955-57; judge Circuit Ct., 1959-79, presiding judge, 1975-79; justice S.D. Supreme Ct., 1979—. Served with U.S. Army, 1942-43. Mem. Izaak Walton League, Am. Legion. Democrat. Roman Catholic. Office: Supreme Ct State Capitol Pierre SD 57501*

FOSHER, DONALD H., advertising company executive, inventor; b. St. Louis Mo., Jan. 6, 1935; s. Hobart L. and Alby U. (Andrews) F.; m. Charlotte B. Reich, Oct. 6, 1956 (div. Dec. 1976); 1 child, Carey B.; Janet L. Leiber, Dec. 31, 1977. B.S., in Bus. Adminstrn., Washington U., St. Louis Mo., 1956. Copywriter Gen. Am., St. Louis, Mo., 1956-59; art dir. Artcraft, St. Louis, 1959-67; creative dir. Frank Block Assocs., St. Louis, 1967-69; account exec. Vangard/Wells, Rich, Green, St. Louis, 1969-74; ptnr., v.p. Vinyard & Lee, St. Louis, 1974-77; sr. v.p., creative dir. Hughes Advt., St. Louis, 1977—; pres., owner Don Fosher, Inc., St. Louis, 1974—; co-owner Freelance Studios, Clayton, Mo., 1979—. Author: Art for Secondary Education, 1962. Contbr. articles on cuisine to popular mags. Patentee sports, medicine, mech. design. Advisor, St. Louis County Spl. Sch. Dist., 1966-76; bd. dirs. Vocat. Schs., St. Louis, 1969—; campaign designer St. Louis Better Bus. Bur., 1975, St. Louis Arts & Edn. Fund, 1984. Recipient Art Dir. of Yr. award Soc. Communications Arts, 1967; Venice Biennial, Internat. Congress Designers, 1966, Package Design award Am. Fishing Tackle Mfrs. Assn., 1981, numerous Creative awards Art Directors, 1959-1984. Mem. Internat. Congress Designers, Soc. Communications Arts (pres. 1966-67), Direct Mail Mktg. Assn., SAR. Mem. Christian Ch. Club: Glen Echo Country. Avocations: inventing, cooking, collecting primative art. Home: 7266 Creveling Dr University City MO 63130 Office: Hughes Advt Inc 130 S Bemiston Clayton MO 63105

FOSNIGHT, JOAN LADELLA, insurance company official; b. Ft. Wayne, Ind., Mar. 17, 1938; d. Paul Stoner and Lorene (King) Moore; m. Wallace Jay Fosnight, Aug. 30, 1958; children—Wendy Jo, Jonell Marie. B.S. in Edn., Ind. U., 1963. Work mgmt. cons. Lincoln Nat. Life, Ft. Wayne, 1979-81; mgr. productivity mgmt. Time Ins. Co., Milw., 1981—. Vice-pres., Channel 39 Pub. TV, Ft. Wayne, 1978-82; chmn. Adopt-A-Patient program Mental Health Assn., Ft. Wayne, 1978-82; pres. aux. Ft. Wayne Children's Zoo, 1979-80; pres. Civics, Inc., Ft. Wayne, 1980-81. Mem. Life Office Mgmt. Assn. (nat. productivity com.), Bus. and Profl. Women, LWV, AAUW. Lutheran. Home: 15370 Brojan Dr Elm Grove WI 53122 Office: 515 W Wells St Milwaukee WI 53201

FOSS, KARL ROBERT, income tax auditor; b. Madison, Wis., Aug. 26, 1938; s. Robert Henry and Ethel Caroline (Huston) F.; student U. Wis., 1956-59, 62; B.S., Madison Bus. Coll., 1961. Auditor Wis. Dept. Revenue, Madison, 1962—; owner, mgr. LIST, Middleton, Wis., 1968-76. Bd. dirs. Middleton Hist. Soc., 1976—, v.p., 1980; legis. adv. Old Car Hobby, 1971—. Co-recipient Spl. Interest Autos Appreciation award, 1971. Mem. Wis. Automobile Clubs in Assn. Inc. (co-founder 1971, pres. 1972-74, 77, 78, 80, v.p. 1975-76, 79, 85), Oldsmobile Club Am. (nat. dir. 1973—, treas. 1981—), Accounting and Mgmt. Assn. (treas. 1981—), Contemporary Hist. Vehicle Assn., Studebaker Drivers Club, Nash Car Club Am., Crosley Car Club, Antique Automobile Club Am., Model T Ford Am. Publisher: Suppliers List, 1968, Suppliers List Directory, 1969. Home: 1619 Middleton St Middleton WI 53562

FOSS, LUKAS, composer, conductor, musician; b. Berlin, Germany, Aug. 15, 1922; s. Martin and Hilde (Schindler) F.; student Paris Lycee Pasteur, 1932-37; grad. Curtis Inst. Music, 1940; spl. study Yale U., 1940-41; pupil of Paul Hindemith, Julius Herford, Serge Koussevitzky, Fritz Reiner, Isabelle Vengerova, Randal Thompson, Rosario Scalero, Felix Wolfes; 3 hon. doctorates; m.; 2 children. Came to U.S., 1937, naturalized, 1942. Former prof. UCLA in charge orch. and advanced composition; former condr., music dir. Buffalo Philharmonic; faculty Harvard U., 1970-71; prin. condr., mus. dir. Bklyn. Philharmonic, from 1971; now also music dir., condr. Milw. Symphony Orch.; composer, condr., pianist; orchestral compositions performed by many orchs.; best known works include (opera) The Jumping Frog; The Prairie; 3 string quartets; Song of Songs; Parable of Death, Griffelkin (opera in 3 acts); Psalms; Baroque Variations; Paradigm; Geod; Orpheus, Time-Cycle, Percussion Concerto, Echoi; American Cantata Thirteen Ways of Looking at a Blackbird, Round a Common Center, Solo Observed; piano pieces, ballets; works commd. by Kulas Found., League of Composers, Nat. Endowment for Arts, N.Y. Arts Council, NBS opera on TV, others. Guggenheim fellow, 1945; recipient N.Y. Critic Circle citation for Prairie, 1944, Soc. for Pub. Am. Music award for String Quarter in G, 1948; Rome prize, 1950; Horblit award for Piano concerto No. 2, 1951, Naumberg Rec. award for Song of Songs, 1957; Creative Music grant Inst. Arts and Letters, 1957; N.Y. Music Critics Circle award for Time-Cycle orch. songs, 1961, for Echoi, 1963; Ditson award for condr. who has done the most for Am. music, 1973; N.Y.C. award for spl. contbn. to arts, 1976; ASCAP award for adventurous programming, 1979; Creative Arts award Brandeis U., 1983; Gold Leaf for service to new music Am. Composers Alliance, 1983. Mem. Am. Acad. Arts and Letters. Address: care Milwaukee Symphony Orch 212 W Wisconsin Ave Milwaukee WI 53203 also Bklyn Philharmonic 30 Lafayette Ave Brooklyn NY 11217

FOSS, MARILYN, state official; b. Minot, N.D., Sept. 6, 1951; d. Baldwin Erwin and Shirley Rheeta (Hubbard) Martz; m. Mark Daniel Foss. B.A., U. N.D., 1973, J.D., 1978. Bar: N.D. 1978, Minn. 1979. Asst. cashier Bank N.D., Bismarck, 1978-79; staff counsel Mont. Dakota Utilities Co., Bismarck, 1979-81; asst. atty. gen. State of N.D., Bismarck, 1982-83; commr. N.D. State Dept. Banking and Fin. Inst., Bismarck, 1983—. Supervisory procedures com. Conf. State Bank Suprs., Washington, 1983—; govt. relations com. Nat. Assn. State Credit Union Suprs., Washington, 1984. Mem. N.D. State Bar Assn., Office: Dept Banking and Fin Inst State Capitol Bldg Bismarck ND 58505

FOST, NORMAN, pediatrician, educator; b. Newark, Jan. 6, 1939. A.B., Princeton U., 1960; M.D., Yale U., 1964; M.P.H., Harvard U., 1973. Diplomate Am. Bd. Pediatrics. Intern Johns Hopkins Hosp., Balt., 1964-65, resident in pediatrics, 1965-67, chief resident in pediatrics, 1969-71; asst. prof. pediatrics Johns Hopkins U., Balt., 1971-73; from asst. prof. to prof. pediatrics and history of medicine U. Wis.-Madison, 1973—, dir. program in med. ethics, 1973—. Contbr. numerous articles on ethical/legal issues in medicine, especially involving children, to profl. jours. Bd. dirs. Dane County Project for Prevention Child Abuse, Madison, 1982—. Served to maj. U.S. Army, 1967-69. Mem. Am. Acad. Pediatrics (com. on bioethics 1982—). Office: U Wis Dept Pediatrics 600 Highland Ave Madison WI 53792

FOSTER, DONALD LEROY, physics educator, university administrator; b. Portland, Oreg., Dec. 13, 1935; s. Raymond Leroy and Mae (McCrea) F.; m. Mary Sue Childers, Sept. 7, 1963; children—Andrew, Matthew. B.A., Reed Coll., 1957; Ph.D., U. Kans., 1968. Asst. prof. Wichita State U., Kans., 1966—. Mem. Am. Assn. Physics Tchrs., Am. Phys. Soc., Sigma Xi, Sigma Pi Sigma. Club: Ninnescah Yacht (Wichita). Avocations: sailing; printing; Home: 2520 N Roosevelt Wichita KS 67220 Office: Wichita State U #32 Wichita KS 67208

FOSTER, GREGORY ALAN, optometrist; b. Neillsville, Wis., Sept. 19, 1955; s. John Willard and Delores Grace (Schlager) F.; m. Linda Marie Anding, Dec. 6, 1975; children—Heather Tennille, Justin Tyler. B.S., Pacific U., 1978. O.D., 1980. Lic. optometrist, Wis. Optometrist, ptnr. Foster & Foster, Neillsville, 1980—; optometrist, Black River Falls, Wis., 1982—. Mem. Am. Optometric Assn., Wis. Optometric Assn. (dir. 1984—), Indianhead Optometric Assn. (pres. 1982), Neillsville C. of C. (bd. dirs. 1981-82), Beta Sigma Kappa. Republican. Roman Catholic. Lodge: Lions (sec. 1984—, bd. dirs. 1983-84). Avocations: cross country skiing, coin collecting. Home: Rte 4 Box 397 Neillsville WI 54456 Office: 446 Court St Neillsville WI 54456

FOSTER, JAMES FRANKLIN, sports management and marketing executive; b. Iowa M. (Egerer) F.; m. Susan Jane Salsi, July 19, 1976. B.G.S., U. Iowa, 1972; postgrad. U. Pa., 1982. Retail advt. specialist Maytag Co., Newton, Iowa, 1972-78; founder, gen. mgr. Iowa Nite Hawks AAA Pro Football Club, 1974-78; founder, dir. Am. Pro Football Tour of Europe, 1977, 79; promotion mgr. Nat. Football League Properties, Inc., N.Y.C., 1979-82; asst. gen. mgr. Ariz. Wranglers Pro Football Club, U.S. Football League, Phoenix, 1982-83; exec. v.p. Chgo. Blitz Pro Football Club, U.S. Football League, Chgo., 1983-84; founder, pres. Arena Sports Ventures Unltd., 1984—; v.p. Chgo. Sting Soccer Promotions/Burke Promotional Mktg. Inc., 1984—; cons. Minor League Pro Football Assn., Elmhurst, Ill., 1982—. Recipient Mktg. Excellence awards Nat. Football League Properties, Inc., 1981, 82; named Minor Pro Football Exec. of Yr., Pro Football Weekly, 1976, Gen. Mgr. of Yr., No. States AAA Football League All League Team, 1976; named to Minor Pro Football Hall of Fame, 1982. Mem. Iowa State Hist. Soc., Chgo. Jazz Inst., Antique and Classic Boat Soc., Boat Owners Assn. of U.S., Am. Mktg. Assn., Democrat. Methodist. Clubs: Nat. Lettermans; Illiana Traditional Jazz. Home: 3614 Walters Ave Northbrook IL 60062

FOSTER, JOHN WILLARD, optometrist; b. Black River Falls, Wis., Sept. 5, 1925; s. Leo W. and Martha (Dietsche) F.; student U. Minn., 1943-48; B.S., Pacific U., 1951, O.D., 1953; m. Dolores Schlaeger, Sept. 3, 1949; children—John, Jeffrey, Gregory, Gary, Mark. Practice optometry, Thorp, Wis., 1953-64, Owen, Wis., 1957-64, Neillsville, Wis., 1964—. Mem. Am. Optometric Found., Optometric Extension program. Mem. Am., Wis. optometric assns., Illuminating Engring. Soc. (asso.), Minn. Fedn. Engring. Socs., Blue Key, Omega Delta, Beta Sigma Kappa, K.C., Lion (pres., dir., chmn. visually handicapped children com.). Address: Box 31 Neillsville WI 54456

FOSTER, LEIGH CURTIS, electronics executive; b. Montreal, Aug. 24, 1925; came to U.S., 1943; s. John Stuart and Flora Marion (Curtis) F.; m. Anne Elizabeth Starke, Jan. 23, 1948; children—Karen Anne, John Curtis. B.Sc., McGill U., 1950; Ph.D., McGill U., 1956. Exec. v.p., gen. mgr. Zenith Radio Research Corp., Menlo Park, Calif., 1956-72; v.p., gen. mgr. Applied Tech., Sunnyvale, Calif., 1972-74; v.p. engring. Motorola, Inc., Schaumburg, Ill., 1974—; dir. Tegal Corp., Novato, Calif., 1977—. Patentee in field; contbr. articles to profl. jours. Mem. Gov.'s Sci. Adv. Bd., State of Ill., 1983—. Mem. IEEE, Am. Phys. Soc. Home: Rural Route 2 Middlebury Rd Barrington Hills IL 60010 Office: Motorola Corp 1303 E Algonquin Rd Schaumburg IL 60196

FOSTER, RICHARD LYNN, video company executive; b. Shawnee, Okla., Sept. 24, 1946; s. Richard Allen and Anita Maxine (Taylor) F.; m. Charlene Marie Czukas, Oct. 19, 1968 (div. 1974); m. Hollister Ann Olson, Mar. 6, 1975; 1 child, Richard Norman. Student Wichita State U., 1964-66, Marquette U., 1967, U. Minn., 1973-76, 80-81, Northwestern Electronics Inst., 1982-84. Dept. mgr. J.C. Penney Co., N.Y.C., 1967-73; regional mgr. Topps and Trousers, Inc., San Francisco, 1977-80; appraiser M.F. Bank & Co., Mpls., 1980-81; pres., owner High Tech. Video, Minnetonka, Minn., 1983—. Res. officer Minnetonka Police Dept., 1975; coach Little League Baseball. Recipient Crime Prevention award Gov.'s Commn. on Crime Prevention, 1976. Republican. Disciple of Christ. Home: 4200 Winchester Ct Minnetonka MN 55345 Office: High Tech Video 4200 Winchester Ct Minnetonka MN 55345

FOSTER, TORREY NORTON, business executive; b. St. Louis, Aug. 1, 1934; s. H. Torrey and Marjorie Helene (Capen) F.; m. Georgia Pierpont, June 11, 1960; children—Torrey Norton, Christopher Pierpont, Caroline Simmons, Harlan Stuart. A.B., Yale U., 1956; J.D., Washington U., 1961. Bar: Mo., 1961, Ohio, 1968, U.S. Supreme Ct., 1970. Assoc. counsel Armstrong, Teasdale, Kramer & Vaughan, St. Louis, 1961-68; assoc. gen. counsel Sherwin-Williams Co., Cleve., 1968-72, exec. asst. to v.p. internat. div., 1972-74, mng. dir., pres. Sherwin-Williams do Brasil, Sao Paulo, 1974-76, v.p. internat. div., Cleve., 1976-80; pres. Jotul U.S.A. Inc., Portland, Maine, 1980-82; v.p. internat. Ceilcote Co., Berea, Ohio, 1983—. Served to lt. USN, 1956-58. Mem. Ohio Bar Assn., Mo. Bar Assn. Republican. Episcopalian.

FOTOPOULOS, SOPHIA STATHOPOULOS, research scientist, administrator; b. Kansas City, Mo., Nov. 6, 1936; d. Marinos G. and Stauroula (Fotopoulos) Stathopoulos; m. Chris K. Fotopoulos, Aug. 27, 1963 (div.). B.A., U. Kans., 1958, M.A., 1964, Ph.D., 1970. Diplomate Behavioral Scis. Regulatory Bd. State of Kans., Council for Nat. Register of Health Service Providers. Research asst. U. Kans. Med. Ctr., Kansas City, 1958-61; research assoc. Inst. Community Studies, Kansas City, Mo., 1965-66; lectr. U. Kans., Lawrence, 1969-70; dir. Psychophysiology-Psychopharmacology Lab. Greater

Kansas City (Mo.) Mental Health Found., 1970-73; staff assoc. neuropsychophysiology Midwest Research Inst., Kansas City, Mo., 1974-75, head Psychophysiology Lab., 1975-77, assoc. dir. chem. scis. div., 1977-79, dir. life scis. dept., 1979—; adj. prof. U. Kans., Lawrence; spl. rev. com. Nat. Cancer Inst., 1978—; mem. adv. com. Am. Cancer Soc., 1982—; lectr. U. Mo.-Kansas City Sch. Medicine, 1970—. NIH research fellow, 1962-64, HHS research fellow, 1965-69; recipient Creative Scientist award Am. Inst. Research, 1971. Mem. Claude Bernard Soc., AAAS, N.Y. Acad. Scis., Biofeedback Soc. Am., Mo. Biofeedback Soc. (pres. 1979-80), Sigma Xi. Greek Orthodox. Clubs: Zonta (pres. KCII 1983—). Contbr. articles to profl. jours. Home: 495 Navajo W Lake Quivira KS 66106 Office: IIHS Suite 519 Parklawn Med Bldg 4620 JC Nichols Pkwy Kansas City MO 64110

FOULKE, EDWARD DOUGLAS, investment counselor; b. Webster Groves, Mo., Mar. 21, 1925; s. Ronald Edward and Mabel (Lacy) F.; m. Ramona Cornell, June 10, 1950; children—Caroline J. Foulke Wettersten, Katherine C., Douglas E (dec.). B.A., Principia Coll., Elsah, Ill., 1949; M.B.A., Harvard U., 1951. Chartered fin. analyst. Asst. to chmn. Consol. Foundries & Mfg. Co., Chgo., 1953-60; asst. v.p. Growth Research, Inc., Chgo., 1960-62; v.p. trust dept. Continental Ill. Nat. Bank & Trust Co., Chgo., 1962-84; v.p. Duff and Phelps, Inc., Chgo., 1984—. Pres. Family Service Ctr. Wilmette (Ill.), 1976-78; trustee Citizens Info. Service Ill., Chgo., 1966—, Meadville Theol. Sch., Chgo., 1966-74; dir. New Trier Twp. Mental Health Bd., Winnetka, Ill., 1979-83. Served with U.S. Army, 1943-46, ETO. Mem. Inst. Chartered Fin. Analysts, Investment Analysts Soc. Chgo. (bd. dirs. 1978-82). Clubs: Univ. (Chgo.); Mich. Shores (Wilmette). Office: Duff and Phelps Inc 55 E Monroe St Chicago IL 60603

FOURMY, SALLY YEARLING, fashion consulting and designing company executive; b. Columbus, Ohio, June 24, 1934; came to Can., 1967; d. Joseph Howard and Dorothy Gertrude (Huston) Yearling; m. Francois Paul Fourmy, Feb. 16, 1963 (div. 1981); children—Patrick René, Christian Stephen. Student Northwestern U., 1952-53; B.S. in Edn., Ohio State U., 1956; postgrad. U. Calif.-Berkeley, 1959, Columbia U. Tchrs. Coll., 1962-63. Asst. to fashion dir. Bloomingdale's, N.Y.C., 1956-57; tchr. pub. schs., Denver, 1957-58, San Francisco, 1958-61; flight attendant Pan Am. World Airways, 1961-62; tchr. pub. schs., N.Y.C., 1963; free-lance dir. of seminars for women in bus., Montreal, Que., Can., 1972-73; mem. fashion coordination faculty LaSalle Coll., Montreal, 1973; pres. Sally Fourmy and Assocs. Ltd., design, cons., mfr. corp. apparel, Toronto, Ont., Can., 1975—. Mem. Toronto Fashion Group. Mem. United Ch. of Christ. Uniforms designed for Four Seasons Olympic Hotel, Seattle (Hotel and Restaurants Internat. 1st Ann. Uniform Contest First Place award 1983). Home: 10 Heather St Toronto ON M4R 1Y3 Canada Office: 30 Duncan St 5th Floor Toronto ON M5V 2C2 Canada

FOUTY, MARVIN FRANCIS, land surveyor, land developer; b. Lansing, Mich., Oct. 5, 1936; s. John Watkins and Dorothy Marie (Sollid) F.; m. Margaret Ann Buxton, Jan. 5, 1957; children—Katherine, Elizabeth, Cynthia, Nancy. A.A. magna cum laude, Lansing Community Coll., 1964. Registered land surveyor, Mich., Ind. Technician Mich. Hwy. Dept., Lansing, 1960-65; jr. engr. City of East Lansing, Mich., 1965-71; surveyor Polaris Assocs., Inc., Lansing, 1971-74, Kyes Assocs., Inc., Okemos, Mich., 1974-77; owner, mgr. Fouty & Assocs., East Lansing, 1977—; v.p. Keystone Devel. Corp., Houghton Lake, Mich., 1978—; sec. Sandstone Devel. Corp., Okemos, 1983—. Fellow Mich. Soc. Registered Land Surveyors (pres. Central chpt. 1982, state bd. dirs. 1984—), Am. Congress Surveying and Mapping; mem. Mich. Assn. of Professions, Mensa, Phi Theta Kappa. Avocations: travel, computers. Home and Office: 717 Beech St East Lansing MI 48823

FOUTZ, HOMER EZRA, endodontist; b. Kansas City, Mo., Mar. 1, 1932; s. Homer Sylvanus and Margurite Saylor (Mohler) F.; m. Shirley Ann Rosenau, June 12, 1956 (dec. 1968); m. Cleo Elaine Cook, May 8, 1969; children—Kris Diane, Homer Paul. B.A., U. Kans., 1955; D.D.S., U. of Mo., 1960; postgrad. endodontia Loyola U., Temple U. and U. of Boston, 1965-71. Gen. practice dentistry, Colby, Kans. 1960-73; practice dentistry specializing in endodontics, Hays, Kans., 1973—; cons. Kans. Dental Bd., Topeka, 1978—; mem. exec. com. combined med.-dental staff St. Anthony and Hadley Hosps., Hays, 1983—; mem. dental adv. bd. Kans. Blue Cross-Blue Shield, Topeka, 1983—. Scoutmaster Coronado council Boy Scouts Am., Colby, 1961-71, Hays, 1979—, mem. exec. com., Salina, Kans., 1982—; elder Presbyterian Ch., Hays, 1972—. Mem. ADA, Kans. Dental Soc., Golden Belt Dental Soc. (past pres.), NW Dental Soc. (past pres.). Republican. Club: Smokey Hill Country (Hays) (pres. 1979-80). Lodge: Masons. Avocations: raising quarter horses; camping; fishing. Home: 3008 Tam O'Shanter Hays KS 67601 Office: PO Box 994 2501 Canterbury Rd Hays KS 67601

FOWLER, BERNARD JOHN, township official; b. Roscommon, Mich., Dec. 8, 1925; s. William John and Ella Leona F.; m. Patricia Arlene Stephan, June 28, 1952; children—Jeffrey William, Gail Ann Ney, Stuart John. Sales clk., grain mill operator Ohio Farm Bur., 1941-44; cloth cutter Wolverine Knitting Mills, Bay City, Mich., 1950-52; lodge caretaker McLouth Steel Corp., Trenton, Mich., 1952-55; owner, operator Edgewater on the AuSable, Grayling, Mich., 1955—; AuSable River fishing and hunting guide, 1946—; supr. Grayling Twp., Mich., 1961—. Mem. Republican Party Task Force. Served with USMC, 1944-46. Mem. Am. Legion, Mich. Twp. Assn. (pres. 1971, dir.), Mich. Assessors Assn. (dir.). Republican. Mem. Reorganized Ch. Jesus Christ of Latter-day Saints. Club: Booster (Grayling). Home: Route 2 Box 2333 Grayling MI 49738 Office: PO Box 521 Grayling MI 49738

FOWLER, DAVID WAYNE, architect; b. Omaha, Apr. 29, 1960; s. Robert Daryl and Donna Rae (Conger) F. B.S. in Archtl. Engring. Tech., U. Nebr., 1985. Mech. draftsman Matthew R. Reiser, P.E., Cons. Engr., Omaha, 1978-79; corp. mgr. archtl. engring. Richman Gordman Stores, Inc., Omaha, 1979—. Mem. Republican Nat. Com., 1984—; usher King of King's Luth. Ch., Omaha, 1984-85; vol. Easter Seal Soc. of Nebr. Telethon, Omaha, 1979; donor ARC 3 Gallon Club, Omaha, 1984; sponsor foster child Christian Children's Fund, Inc., Richmond, Va., 1981—. Recipient Archtl. award Met. Omaha Builders Assn., 1977. Home: 12441 Bel Dr Omaha NE 68144 Office: Richman Gordman Stores Inc 12100 W Center Rd Omaha NE 68144

FOWLER, DONN NORMAN, dentist; b. Denver, June 7, 1922; s. Roy Eugene and Vera Louise (Alderson) F.; B.S., Northwestern U., 1945, D.D.S., 1953; m. Charlotte Jean Goff, Mar. 18, 1944; children—Donna Jean (Mrs. Donald J. McLoughlin), Linda (Mrs. Malcolm Cardy), Charles R., Peter N., Paul R. Gen. practice dentistry, Glenview, Ill., 1953—; instr. Coll. Dentistry, Northwestern U., Chgo., 1953-55. Trustee, Kendall Coll., Evanston, Ill. Served to lt. (j.g.) USNR, 1943-46; PTO. Mem. Pierre Fauchard Acad., Acad. Gen. Dentistry, Am. Dental Assn., Chgo. Dental Soc., North Suburban Acad. Dental Research (past pres.), G.V. Black Soc., Glenview C. of C., Wis. Dental Study Club, Pi Kappa Alpha. Methodist (lay del. to ann. conf.). Lodge: Kiwanis. Home: 1548 Maple Ave Northbrook IL 60062 Office: 1765 River Dr Glenview IL 60025

FOWLER, DORA CAMACHO, association executive; b. Cali, Valle, Colombia, Mar. 19, 1934; came to U.S., 1951; d. Jorge Enrique and Aminta (Rincon) Camacho; m. George Barton Fowler, May 30, 1960; children—David Mark, DeeAnn Michelle, Dwight Matthew. B.A. with honors, Nat. Coll. Edn. Linguist UN Gen. Assembly, N.Y.C., 1955; headmistress Montessori Children's House, West Des Moines, Iowa, 1968-71; dir. Children's Ctr., Schaumburg, Ill., 1972-74; exec. dir. Elk Grove Twp. Community Day Care Ctr., Elk Grove Village, Ill., 1974-85; pres. Am. Assn. Exec. and Profl. Women, Palatine, Ill., 1983—; pres. Assocs. in Human Devel., Palatine, 1985—; gov. Benedictine Coll., Atchison, Kans., 1974—; mem. adv. bd. on day care Nat. Coll. Edn., Evanston, Ill., 1982—. Author: The Complete Book of Home Day Care, 1983; A Guide to Effective Administration in Day Care, 1983; editor The Tng. Ctr. nat. newsletter, 1981. Del., White House Conf. on Families, Chgo., Washington, 1980, Ill. Conf. on Children's Priorities for the 80's, Chgo., 1982. Mem. Nat. Assn. Edn. Young Children, Chgo. Assn. Edn. Young Children (exec. bd., sec. 1978-79), Day Care Action Council, N.W. Suburban Council Community Services (v.p. 1980-81), Sigma Alpha Iota (pres. 1969-70). Roman Catholic. Club: Altrusa (Arlington Heights, Ill.). Office: PO Box 256 Palatine IL 60078

FOWLER, GEORGE SELTON, JR., architect, writer, inventor; b. Chgo., Jan. 20, 1920; s. George Selton and Mabel Helena (Overton) F.; m. Yvonne Fern Grammer, Nov. 25, 1945; 1 child, Kim Ellyn. Cert. Hamilton Coll., 1944; B.S., Ill. Inst. Tech., 1949, postgrad. 1968; cert. Elec. Assn. Ill., 1976. Registered architect, Ill. Urban planner Chgo. Land Clearance Commn., 1949-50; liaison architect Chgo. Housing Authority, 1950-68, chief design-tech. div., 1968-80, dir. dept. engring., 1980-84; prin. George S. Fowler, Architect, Chgo., 1984—; cons. in field. Author: (text book study guide) Reinforced Concrete Design, 1959. Patentee. Served with C.E., U.S. Army, 1942-46. Recipient Citation for Residential Devel., Mayor Richard J. Daley, Chgo., 1960, Black Achievers of Industry Recognition award YMCA, Chgo., 1977; grantee Kappa Alpha Psi, 1936. Mem. Architects in Industry, Nat. Assn. Housing and Redevelopment Officials. Avocations: classic cars; classical music; jazz.

FOWLER, GLORIA R. VRIESMAN, medical group administrator; b. Muskegon, Mich., Feb. 20, 1933; d. Harry and Dena (Kuiper) Bultema; student Muskegon Community Coll., 1978; m. William H. Fowler, June 26, 1982; children—Robert, Laurel A. Hodgson, Lynn E. Caraway, Scott J., William Fowler, Robert Fowler, James Fowler, Barbara Rector. With various physicians Muskegon, Mich., 1952-69; with Muskegon Surg. Assocs., P.C., 1969—, adminstr., 1972—; guest instr. Muskegon Bus. Coll., 1978, 81. Fellow Am. Coll. Med. Group Adminstrs. (cert.), Med. Group Mgmt. Assn., Mich. Med. Group Mgmt. Assn. (sec. 1981-83, pres.-elect 1984—), Am. Mgmt. Assn. mem. Berean Ch. Home: 558 Airport Rd Muskegon MI 49441 Office: W Shore Profl Bldg 1560 E Sherman Blvd Muskegon MI 49444

FOWLER, JACK EDWARD, counselor; b. Columbus, Ind., Jan. 5, 1947; s. Lawrence Alfred and Norma Jean (Prall) F.; B.S., Purdue U., 1971, M.S., 1973; postgrad. Ind. State U., 1975—; m. Anna Mae Rains, June 6, 1970; children—Elizabeth Anne, Eric Wesley. Dir. Clark Residence Hall, Vincennes (Ind.) U., 1973-74, dir. housing, dir. Clark Hall, 1974-77, dir. Clark Residence Hall, 1977-78; counselor youth program, adult basic edn., 1978-79; command adminstrv. officer U.S. Army N.G., Terre Haute, Ind., 1980—. Served to capt. Army N.G., 1966—. Alumni scholar Purdue Alumni Assn., 1965; Ind. State U. grad. fellow, 1978, 79. Mem. Am. Personnel and Guidance Assn., Am. Coll. Personnel Assn., Assn. Coll. and Univ. Housing Officers (state rep. 1976-77), Assn. Supervision and Curriculum Devel., N.G. Assn. U.S., N.G. Assn. Ind., Assn. Purdue U. Counseling and Guidance Students, 38th Supply and Transport Bn. Officers Assn., Phi Delta Kappa. Democrat. Methodist. Home: Rural Route 2 Box 268 Vincennes IN 47591 Office: HQ 38th Supply and Transport Bn 3614 Maple Ave Terre Haute IN 47804

FOWLER, ROBERT E., JR., rubber and plastic products manufacturing company executive. Chmn., chief exec. officer, dir. Sundstrand Corp., Rockford, Ill. Office: Rubbermaid Inc 1147 Akron Rd Wooster OH 44691*

FOX, CHARLES D'ARCY, investment company executive; b. St. Louis, July 29, 1936; s. Charles Smith and Helen (D'Arcy) F.; student Brown U., 1954-59; m. Juanita Cox, Dec. 20, 1975; children—Amber, Carmen, Amanda, Samuel. With A.G. Edward & Sons, Inc., St. Louis, 1960—, mgr. Western region bond dept., 1962-65, research asso., 1965-66, corp. v.p., asst. sec., dir. tng. and registration, 1966—. Pres., fin. dir. Adult Edn. Council of Greater St. Louis, 1975—. Served with U.S. Army, 1959-60. Mem. Am. Soc. Training and Devel., Internat. Assn. Fin. Planners. Club: Racquet. Home: 16138 Chesterfield Lake Dr Chesterfield MO 63017 Office: 1 N Jefferson St Louis MO 63103

FOX, COTTRELL, insurance company executive; b. St. Louis, Apr. 16, 1946; s. A. Cottrell and Dorothy (Vernon) F.; m. Virginia Kay Hebeler, Sept. 15, 1979; B. Journalism, U. Mo., 1971, M. Journalism, 1972. Sr. mktg. rep. Aetna Casualty & Surety Co., St. Louis, 1973-76; mktg. mgr. J.W. Terrill, Inc., St. Louis, 1976-78, v.p., 1978—, prin., 1981—, exec. v.p., 1984—; regional rep. Aetna Life & Casualty Co. Gt. Performers Exec. Council, 1985. Served to sgt. USMC, 1966-68; S. Vietnam. Decorated three Purple Hearts, Navy Commendation medal; two Vietnamese Crosses Gallantry (Republic South Vietnam). Mem. St. Paul Ins. Co. Agts. Adv. Council (chmn. 1980-81), Comml. Union Ins. Cos. (chmn. 1983—, producer adv. panel), Ind. Ins. Agts. St. Louis Inc. (v.p. 1981-82, pres. 1983-84). Republican. Home: 217 New Salem Dr Creve Coeur MO 63141 Office: J W Terrill Inc 1982 Coucourse Dr Saint Louis MO 63146

FOX, DAN RAY, interior design director; b. Charles City, Iowa, May 6, 1935; s. Ray Alva and Myrtle Henrietta (Peterson) F.; m. Margaret Sodd, June 27, 1959; children—Girard Alexander, Gregory Winston. B.A. in Architecture, U. Minn., 1961. Interior designer Smiley & Assocs., Mpls., 1965-67; prin. interior designer Grover Dimond Assoc., St. Paul, 1967-69; dir. interior design Setter, Leach & Lindstrom, Mpls., 1969-73, Ellerbe Assoc., Bloomington, Minn., 1973—; adv. design bd. U. Minn., former instr. contract design. Chmn. bd. Bach Soc. Minn., 1962-63; chmn. music com. Center Arts Council, Walker Art Ctr., 1963-65. Mem. Am. Soc. Interior Designers, AIA. Episcopalian. Contbr. articles to profl. jours. Office: One Appletree Sq Bloomington MN 55420

FOX, KENNETH EUGENE, banker; b. Hamilton, Ohio, Sept. 11, 1936; s. Charles Kenneth and Francis Mae (Miller) F.; m. Belva Marie Brey, Oct. 6, 1957; children—Kenton P., Kevin E., Darrin K. Student Washburn U., 1955-56; cert. Grad. Sch. Banking, U. Wis., 1973. Vice pres. Rosedale State Bank, Kansas City, Kans., 1964-70; v.p. Commerce Bank of Moberly, Mo., 1970-74, pres., chmn. bd., 1976-80; exec. v.p. Commerce Bank of University City, Mo., 1974-75; sr. v.p. Commerce Bank of Kirkwood (Mo.), 1975-76; chmn. bd. Sedalia Merc. Bank & Trust Co. (Mo.), 1980—. Pres. Indsl. Devel. Authority, 1978-80; adv. bd. Moberly Jr. Coll., 1979; mem. Moberly Jr. Coll. Found., 1979, Regional Med. Ctr. Found., 1979; dist. fin. chmn. Chariton Valley dist. Boy Scouts Am., 1973-75; lay leader United Meth. Ch., 1978-79, 82-83, chmn. bd., 1972-74. Served to 1st lt. Army N.G., 1959-68. Mem. Am. Bankers Assn., Mo. Bankers Assn. (bank mgmt. com.), Moberly C. of C. (pres. and dir. 1978). Republican. Lodges: Rotary, Kiwanis. Home: Route 3 Box 298B Sedalia MO 65301 Office: 111 W 3d St Sedalia MO 65301

FOX, LAWRENCE MARTIN, veterinarian; b. Chgo., Feb. 26, 1946; s. Alexander Louis and Annette (Singer) F.; B.S., U. Ill., 1966, D.V.M., 1968; m. Carlina Mary Renzy, Mar. 18, 1967; children—Kevin Lawrence, Brandon Douglas, Robin Christopher. Practice vet. medicine, Chgo., 1970-72, River Grove, Ill., 1972—; dir. Elmwood-Grove Animal Hosp., Ltd., River Grove, 1972—; cons. on animal control Leyden Twp., Elmwood Park and Franklin Park, Ill., 1974—; treas., dir. Oak Park (Ill.) Village Humane Soc., 1974-76. Sec., Willard Sch. PTA, River Forest, Ill., 1978-79, v.p., 1979-80, pres., 1980-81; sec. River Forest Parental Music Assn., 1983-85; bd. mgrs. River Forest Schs., 1980; cubmaster Boy Scouts Am., River Forest, 1979-83, also Webelos leader, 1979-81. Served as capt. Vet. Corps, U.S. Army, 1968-70. Diplomate Am. Bd. Vet. Practitioners (chmn. Midwest cluster, pub. relations, continuing edn. coms.). Mem. AVMA, Ill. State, Chgo. (edn. com. 1981—, chmn. 1983—) vet. med. assns., Am. Animal Hosp. Assn., Vet. Inst. for Practitioners, Vet. Cancer Soc., Am. Assn. Feline Practitioners, Chgo. Zool. Soc., Chgo. Area Runners, Ground-Zero, Greenpeace, Mensa. Club: River Grove Lions (lion tamer, tail twister, dir. 1972—). Contbr. articles to profl. jours. Home: 1200 Franklin Ave River Forest IL 60305 Office: 8035 Grand Ave River Grove IL 60171

FOX, ROBERT DEAN, research agricultural engineer; b. Cass City, Mich., Oct. 26, 1936; s. Ronald Evans and Aletha Ruth (Morrish) F.; m. Marilynn Gail Trowbridge, Mar., 1966; children—Tracy, Leslie, Bambi, Sean, Andrew, Susan. B.S. in Agrl. Engring., Mich. State U., 1957, M.S., 1958, Ph.D., 1968. Instr. Mich. State U., East Lansing, 1963-64; agrl. engr. U.S. Dept. Agr., Wooster, Ohio, 1968—. Author research reports. Served to capt. USAF, 1958-63. Mem. Am. Soc. Agrl. Engrs. (com. chmn.), Am. Meteorol. Soc., Sigma Xi. Presbyterian. Club: Kiwanis (pres. Wooster 1985—). Avocations: Golf; Little League sports including soccer. Home: 1022 Quinby Ave Wooster OH 44691

FOX, SUSAN VALERIE, futures researcher, model; b. Waukegan, Ill., Aug. 13, 1948; d. Raymond James and Dorothy Evelyn (Chisholm) Proctor; m. Richard Kent Fox, Apr. 1, 1946; children—Michael Darin, Laura Evelyn. Profl. modeling cert. John Robert Powers, Chgo., 1983; student Coll. Lake County, Grayslake, Ill., 1973-81. Service mgr./bookkeeper National Co., Chgo., 1965-76; service mgr. A&P, Chgo., 1978-82; futures researcher MBH Commodities, Winnetka, Ill., 1980—; profl. model, 1983—; cons. Futures Symposium, Tucson, 1983—. Aerobic instr. Karcher Retirement Home, Waukegan, Ill. Recipient Tennis award Libertyville Park Dist. (Ill.), 1973; various Blue Ribbon/1st Place awards Libertyville Men's Garden Club, 1982, various rose growers awards, 1983. Mem. Am. Rose Soc., Northeastern Ill. Rose Growers, No. Ill. Rose Growers Assn., Am. Running and Fitness Assn. Republican. Office: MBH Commodity Advisors Inc PO Box 353 Winnetka IL 60093

FOX, WILLIAM KEITH DONALDSON, manufacturing company executive; b. Washington, Dec. 29, 1939; s. John Donaldson and Louise (Hancock) F.; m. Erika Schwenn, Feb. 12, 1962; children—Myles, Alison, Jennifer. B.A., Williams Coll., 1964; M.B.A., Rockhurst Coll., 1983. Mgmt. trainee, asst. br. mgr. C. V. Starr Co., N.Y.C., 1964-68; mktg. mgr. John Hancock Mut., Boston, 1968-71; sales and product mgr. Standard Havens, Inc., Kansas City, Mo., 1971-76, sr. v.p., 1976-82; pres. Standard Havens Research Corp., Kansas City, 1982—; adj. prof. mktg. Ottawa U., Kansas City, 1983—. Patentee in field. Pres., Bryant Sch. Fathers Club, Kansas City, 1976; chmn. Standard Havens United Fund Campaign, Kansas City, 1978; fund raiser Unitarian Ch., Kansas City, 1979. Recipient Cert. of Achievement, Kansas City Sch. Dist., 1979; Honorarium, McGraw-Hill, Inc., 1983; Cert. of Achievement, Stanford U., 1983. Mem. Air Pollution Control Assn., Am. Prodn. and Inventory Control Soc. Am. Mgmt. Assn., N.Am. Soc. Corp. Planning, Planning Execs. Inst., Phi Gamma Delta. Unitarian. Clubs: Woodside Racquet, Kansas City Blues Rugby (pres. 1976-77) (Kansas City, Mo.). Home: 214 W Concord Ave Kansas City MO 64112 Office: Standard Havens Research Corp 8800 E 63d St Kansas City MO 64133

FOX, WILLIAM RUSSELL, health care executive; b. Evanston, Ill., Dec. 2, 1955; s. John Raymond and Pearl Louise (Neumann) F.; m. Ellen Sue Gerhard, Sept. 19, 1981. B.A. in Biology/Econs., Luther Coll., 1977; M.H.A., Trinity U., 1979. Adminstrv. asst. Columbus/Cuneo/Cabrini Med. Ctr., Chgo., 1979-80, dir. mktg., 1980-82; dir. profl. services Chgo. Hosps. Universal Health Services, Inc., Chgo., 1982—; asst. adminstr. Bethesda Hosp., 1983—. Mem. Am. Hosp. Assn., Chgo. Area Hosp. Planning Assn., Am. Mktg. Assn., Health Execs. Forum Chgo., Alpha Phi Omega (life). Lutheran. Home: 130 E George St Apt 326 Bensenville IL 60106 Office: Universal Health Services 2451 W Howard Chicago IL 60645

FOX, YAKOV MICHAEL, lawyer, rabbi; b. Little Rock, May 23, 1954; s. Samuel and Miriam Fox; m. Chana Fox, Aug. 30, 1981. B.A., Northwestern U., 1976; student Hebrew Theol. Coll., 1972-81; J.D., John Marshall Law Sch., 1979. Bar: Ill. 1979, Fla. 1980, U.S. Dist. Ct. (no. dist.) Ill. 1982, U.S. Ct. Appeals (7th cir.) 1984, U.S. Supreme Ct. 1985. Ordained rabbi, 1981. Student extern Ill. Atty. Gen., Chgo., 1978; sole practice, Chgo., 1981-82; asst. pub. defender Cook County, Ill., 1982—, supervising atty. of pub. defender's probable cause unit, 1984—; sr. trial atty. in family custody unit, 1982-84. Book reviewer Chgo. Daily Law Bull., 1983—; mem. staff DePaul Tax Law Jour. Democratic precinct capt., Chgo., 1976—; mem. Civic Legis. Com., 1982—; mem. Northtown Community Council, 1982—. Mem. ABA, Ill. State Bar Assn., Chgo. Bar Assn., Decalogue Soc., Phi Eta Sigma. Home: 2952 W Birchwood Chicago IL 60645 Office: Pub Defender Juvenile Ct 1100 S Hamilton Chicago IL 60612

FOXEN, GENE LOUIS, insurance executive; b. Chgo., Mar. 28, 1936; adopted son Henry and Mary Foxen; student public schs.; children—Dan, Kathleen, Michael, Patricia, James, Karen. With New Eng. Life Ins. Co., 1957—, assoc. gen. agt., 1970-73, gen. agt., Chgo., 1973—. Cubmaster DuPage council Boy Scouts Am., 1963; Midwest regional dir. Adoptees Liberty Movement Assn. Served with USMC, 1954-57. Recipient life membership award Gen. Agents and Mgrs. Conf.; named as life mem. Hall of Fame, New Eng. Life Ins. Co., 1972, life mem. Million Dollar Round Table. C.L.U. Mem. Nat. Assn. Life Underwriters, Execs. Club Chgo., Gen. Agents and Mgrs. Assn., Am. Soc. C.L.U.'s (pres. Chgo. chpt. 1977-78, v.p. Midwest region 1981-82), Chgo. Estate Planning Council (pres. 1981-82), Am. Soc. Life Underwriters. Republican. Roman Catholic. Club: Metropolitan. Home: 1549 Mirror Lake Dr Naperville IL 60540 Office: 120 S Riverside Plaza Chicago IL 60606

FOXMAN, LORETTA DOROTHY, human resource consultant; b. Los Angeles, Sept. 4, 1939; d. Frederick and Helen (Goldberg) F.; m. Walter L. Polsky, Aug. 9, 1964; children—Michael William, Susan Jennifer. B.A., Calif. State U.-Los Angeles, 1963; M.A., Columbia U., 1964. Tchr., Culver City Unified Sch. Dist. (Calif.), 1964-68; asst. dir. St. Christopher Acad., Westfield, N.J., 1971-75; curriculum cons. Middlesex Community Coll. Daycare Ctr., Edison, N.J., 1973, Lakeview Montessori Acad., Summit, N.J., 1975; instr. Northwestern U., Evanston, Ill., 1982—; prin. Jack Dill Assocs., Chgo., 1976-81; exec. v.p. CAMBRIDGE Human Resource Group, Inc., Chgo., 1981—. Chmn. various coms. LWV, Cranford, N.J. and Glencoe, Ill., 1971—; mem. Ad Hoc Rent Control Com., 1973; chair adv. bd. Northwestern U. Program on Women, 1982—. Author: Resumes That Work: How to Sell Yourself on Paper, 1984; contbg. editor Personnel Jour.; contbr. several articles to profl. jours. Mem. AAUW, Am. Soc. Personnel Adminstrn. (Woman of Achievement award), Women in Mgmt. Home: 609 Drexel Ave Glencoe IL 60022 Office: Cambridge Human Resource Group Inc 1500 Skokie Blvd Suite 5 Northbrook IL 60062

FOXWORTH, MARY LOU, nursing educator, vocational educational consultant; b. Columbia, Mo., Dec. 12, 1923; d. Arthur Bryson and Ariel Inez (Gurley) Cline; m. Donald L. Foxworth, Dec. 29, 1951; children—Debbie Foxworth Robbe, Wendy Jean, Beth Foxworth Oberdick, Cindy Foxworth Spencer, Gary Scott. R.N., Jackson Meml. Hosp., Miami, Fla., 1946; B.S. in Nursing, U. Miami, 1951; M.A., U. Mich., 1961, postgrad. 1975-80; cert. Sch. Macrobiotics, Kuski Inst., 1984. Cert. vacat., continuing tchr. Coordinator sch. health River Rouge Pub. Schs., 1949-52; assoc. office mgr. Foxworth Ins. Agy., 1952-54; nursing instr. Mt. Carmel Sch. Nursing, 1954-57; nurse counselor Central High Sch., Flint, Mich., 1958-68; instr. nursing Mott Community Coll., Flint, 1968-70, instr macrobiotic disease prevention, adult edn. program, 1984-85; chmn. health occupations Genesee Area Skill Ctr., Flint, 1970—. Republican del. Flushing Twp. (Mich.), 1979-82. Fellow Am. Sch. Health Assn., Royal Soc. Health; mem. Mich. Coalition for Articulation Nursing Edn., Mich. Assn. Practical Nurse Educators (pres. 1980-82), Am. Vocat. Assn., Health Occupations Educators, Mich. Assn. Lic. Practical Nurses, Delta Kappa Gamma. Methodist. Created first high sch. to coll. practical nursing articulation program, 1972. Home: 8388 N Seymour Rd Flushing MI 48433 Office: Genesee Area Skill Ctr G-5081 Torrey Rd Flint MI 48507

FRACEK, EUGENE EDWARD, state educational adminstrator; b. Rosebud, S.D., Oct. 4, 1948; s. Raymond Alexander and Virginia (Pretty Voice Hawk) F.; m. Renee Tieszen, June 28, 1980; 1 child, Aaron Grant; m. Cynthia Lea Beckman, Dec. 18, 1971 (div. May 1980); 1 child, Nicolas Fracek. B.A., S.D. State U., 1971; M.A., U.S.D., 1980. Tchr. pub. schs. Rapid City, S.D., 1972-79; edn. rep. State of S.D., Pierre, 1979—; sec. credit com. Oahe Fed. Credit Union, Pierre, 1983—; extension instr. S.D. State U., Pierre, 1984, Black Hills State Coll., Pierre, 1984. Pres. Pierre Soccer Club, 1983—; active community theater Pierre Players. Mid Continent Regional Edn. Lab. fellow, 1980. Mem. Nat. Council Social Studies, Assn. Supervision and Curriculum Devel., S.D. Assn. Bilingual/Bicultural Edn. Avocations: singing; composing; guitar; soccer; home computer. Home: 316 N Madison Pierre SD 57501 Office: Instructional Services 700 N Illinois Pierre SD 57501

FRADE, PETER DANIEL, chemist; b. Highland Park, Mich., Sept. 3, 1946; s. Peter Nunes and Dorathea Grace (Gehrke) F.; B.S. in Chemistry, Wayne State U., 1968, M.S., 1971, Ph.D., 1978. Chemist, Henry Ford Hosp., Detroit, 1968-75, analytical chemist, toxicologist, dept. pathology, div. pharmacology and toxicology, 1975—; research assoc. in chemistry Wayne State U., Detroit, 1978-79; vis. scholar U. Mich., Ann Arbor, 1980-86. Recipient David F. Boltz Meml. award Wayne State U., 1977. Fellow Am. Inst. Chemists, Nat. Acad. Clin. Biochemistry, Assn. Clin. Scientists; mem. Fedn. Am. Scientists, Am. Chem. Soc., AAAS, IntraSci. Research Found., Soc. Applied Spectroscopy, Am. Assn. Clin. Chemistry, Assn. Analytical Chemists, N.Y. Acad. Scis., Am. Pharm. Assn., Acad. Pharm. Scis., Detroit Hist. Soc., Mich. Humane Soc., Am. Coll. Toxicology, Royal Soc. Chemistry (London), European Acad. Arts, Scis. and Humanities, Titanic Hist. Soc., Bibl. Archaeology Soc., Virgil Fox Soc., Founders Soc. Detroit Inst. Arts, Sigma Xi, Phi Lambda Upsilon, Alpha Chi Sigma. Lutheran. Club: U.S. Senatorial Faculty. Contbr. sci. articles to profl. jours. Office: Henry Ford Hosp 2799 W Grand Blvd Detroit MI 48202

FRAGEN, ROBERT JOSEPH, physician, anesthesiologist; b. Whiting, Ind., Jan. 18, 1935; s. Nathan and Ruth Sarah (Seitzick) F.; m. Joan Maureen Arenson, June 13, 1957; children—Daniel Scott, Kathleen Susan, Michael Philip, Patricia Beth. A.B., Ind. U., 1956; M.D., Ind. U.-Indpls., 1959. Diplomate Am. Bd. Anesthesiology. Dir. dept. anesthesia Ravenswood Hosp.,

Chgo., 1964-74; staff anesthesiologist Norhtwestern U., Chgo., 1974—. Contbr. articles to profl. jours. Served to lt. USN, 1962-64. Mem. Am. Soc. Anesthesiologists, Ill. Soc. Anesthesiologists, Chgo. Soc. Anesthesiologists, Internat. Anesthesia Research Soc., Sigma Xi. Jewish. Avocations: tennis, stamp collecting. Home: 1230 Lindenwood Dr Winnetka IL 60093 Office: Univ Med Sch Dept Anesthesia 303 E Superior St Room 360 Passavant Pavillion Chicago IL 60611

FRAIN, THOMAS WALTER, real estate development company executive; b. Muskegon, Mich., Jan. 18, 1948; s. Robert Roland and Shirley Mae (Dixon) F.; m. LeLanie Marie Root, May 6, 1970 (div. Dec. 1982); children—Heather, Tonya; m. Dorothy Mae Stoken, June 18, 1983; children—Michael, Jerome. B.A., Grand Rapids Jr. Coll., 1970; B.B.A., Grand Valley State U., 1973; diploma in real property adminstrn. Bldg. Owners and Mgrs. Inst., 1984. Cert. real property adminstr., Mich.; lic. builder, Mich. Acct., William P. DeLong & Co., Holland, Mich., 1973-76; pres., owner Foremost Real Estate subs. Foremost Corp. of Am., Grand Rapids, Mich., 1976—; v.p. Marriott Hotel, Grand Rapids, 1982—; dir. Access Control Systems, Grand Rapids, 1980—; pres. Exchequer Corp., Kalamazoo, Mich., 1981—. Prin. works include developing Centennial Park, Grand Rapids, 1976—. Served to sgt. U.S. Army, 1968-71. Mem. Soc. Real Property Adminstrs., Bldg. Owners and Mgrs. of Grand Rapids. Republican. Clubs: Charlevoix Athletic (treas. 1979-81), Meadowood Country. Avocations: golf; basketball; tennis; hunting; fishing; camping. Home: 1359 Northlawn NE Grand Rapids MI 49505 Office: Foremost Real Estate PO Box 2450 Grand Rapids MI 49501

FRAKER, JOHN RICHARD, engineering educator; b. Knoxville, Tenn., Dec. 20, 1934; s. J. Temple and Elsie Lee (Vineyard) F.; m. Martha Ann French, Aug. 28, 1954; children—John Temple, Rebecca Fraker Hadick, Jennifer Leeanna Fraker. B.S. in Indsl. Engring., U. Tenn.-Knoxville, 1956, M.S. in Indsl. Engring., 1965; Ph.D. in Engring. Mgmt., Clemson U., 1971. Registered profl. engr., Ohio. Mfg. engr. Westinghouse Electric Corp., Pitts., 1956-57; instr. Clemson U., 1965-72; assoc. prof. Western Carolina U., Cullowhee, N.C., 1972-75; prof., chmn. dept. engring. mgmt. and systems U. Dayton, 1975—. Contbr. numerous articles to profl. jours. Troop leader, mem. council Daniel Boone council Boy Scouts Am., 1965-75. Served to capt. U.S. Army, 1957-64. Ingalls Found. fellow U. Tenn., 1965; NSF fellow, Clemson U., 1965-66. Mem. IEEE Engring. Mgmt. Soc. (v.p. 1981-84, trustee, v.p. Engring. and Sci. Hall of Fame 1980—), Inst. Indsl. Engrs., Am. Soc. Engring. Edn. Republican. Methodist. Clubs: Kiwanis of Dayton (past pres.), Engineers of Dayton. Home: 1545 Langdon Dr Centerville OH 45459 Office: Dept Engineering Mgmt and Systems Sch Engring U Dayton Dayton OH 45469

FRAME, J. LEONARD, engineering company executive, retail company executive; b. Castle Rock, Minn., May 24, 1924; s. Leonard Alexander and Florence Emelina (Holt) F.; m. Dorothy Mae Gadde, May 27, 1944; children—Peggy, Susan, Douglas, Julie, Jennifer. B. in Aero. Engring., U. Minn., 1943. Flight test engr. Bell Aircraft Corp., Niagara Falls, N.Y., 1943-44, rocket research engr., 1946-47; flight test engr. NACA, Hampton, Va., 1944-45; flight test aide U.S. Army Air Corps., 1945-46; adminstrn. scientist U. Minn., Rosemount, 1947-52; pres. FluiDyne Engring. Corp., Mpls., 1952—; dir. Modern Controls Corp., Mpls., 1983—; pres., dir. Solarworks Plus, Inc., Mpls., 1977—. Chmn. Golden Valley Republican Party, Minn., 1970-72; elder Valley Community Presbyterian Ch., Golden Valley, 1958—. Recipient Outstanding Achievement award U. Minn. Alumni Assn. 1967. Mem. Am. Mgmt. Assn., AIAA, Presidents Assn., U. Minn. Inst. Tech. Alumni Assn. (bd. dirs., pres. 1964.). Clubs: Apollo (bd. dirs.), Minneapolis, Mpls. Athletic, Golden Valley Country. Avocations: choral music; tennis; fishing; hunting. Office: FluiDyne Engring Corp 5900 Olson Meml Hwy Minneapolis MN 55422

FRAME, VELMA ANITA WILLIAMS, retired counselor; b. Decatur County, Ind.; d. Frederick Virgil and Emma Flora (Robbins) Williams; B.S., Ball State U., 1935, M.A., 1949, postgrad., 1973; m. David C. Frame, June 29, 1946. Tchr. high sch., Yorktown, Ind., 1935-42, Daleville, Ind., 1951-59; counselor Central High Sch., Marion, Ind., 1959-62, Muncie (Ind.) Southside High Sch., 1962-71; counselor, dir. guidance high sch., Daleville, Ind., 1971-79. Mem. Am., Ind. (pres.) sch. counselors assns., Am., Ind., E. Central (pres.) personnel and guidance assns., Nat. Vocat. Guidance Assn., Ladies Golf Assn. of Valley View Golf Club (treas.). Democrat. Home: 307 Arch St Yorktown IN 47396

FRANCE, ERWIN ABNEY, management consulting firm executive; b. St. Louis, Oct. 26, 1938; s. Joseph L. and Inez (Jackson) F.; divorced; children—Mark Joseph, Eric Stephen. B.S., George Williams Coll., 1959; M.A., Loyola U., 1967; Ph.D., Union Grad. Sch., 1975. Dir. Com. on Youth Welfare, Chgo., 1959-65; dep. chief Ill. State Employment, Chgo., 1965-67; adminstrv. asst. to mayor City of Chgo., 1967-75; pres. Palmer, France & Assocs., Chgo., 1976—. Chmn. DuSable Mus. African Am. History, Chgo. Home: 6740 S Oglesby Chicago IL 60649 Office: Palmer France & Assocs Ltd One N LaSalle St Suite 2725 Chicago IL 60602

FRANCHOT, DOUGLAS WARNER, lawyer; b. Tulsa, Mar. 27, 1922; s. Douglas W. and Constance (Lippincott) F.; m. Janet L. Kerr, Oct. 21, 1944 (div. 1972); children—Douglas W., III, Peter VanR., Michael L., Jenny; m. Maryan Smagula, 1974. B.A., Yale U., 1945, J.D., 1949. Bar: R.I. 1950, Mich. 1963. Assoc., then ptnr. Hinckley, Allen, Salisbury & Parsons, Providence, 1949-62; sr. atty. Ford Mfg. Co., Dearborn, Mich., 1962-65; v.p., gen. counsel Bristol-Myers Co. subs., N.Y.C., 1965-75; assoc. gen. counsel Republic Steel Corp., Cleve., 1975—, v.p., gen. counsel, 1977-84; cons. LTV Steel Corp., Cleve., 1985—; of counsel Reminger & Reminger, Cleve., 1985—. Bd. dirs. Govtl. Research Inst., Cleve., 1978—; 1st v.p. Woodruff Hosp., Cleve., 1978—; sec., bd. trustees Cleve. Playhouse, 1984—. Served with USN, 1943-45. Mem. ABA, Assoc. Gen. Counsel, R.I. Bar Assn., Mich. Bar Assn., Ohio Bar Assn., Cleve. Bar Assn. Episcopalian. Clubs: Mayfield Country (Ohio); Cleve. Skating, Clevelander. Avocations: golfing, skiing, hunting, gardening. Home: 14707 Shaker Blvd Shaker Heights OH 44120 Office: Reminger & Reminger 300 Leader Bldg Cleveland OH 44114

FRANCIS, GORDON DEAN, physician; b. Bancroft, Nebr., Dec. 6, 1930; s. Marvin Bliss and Lillian Grace (Sleyba) F.; m. Harriette Salter, May 27, 1951; children—Michele Francis Stine, Rene F. Hinton, Mark Salter. A.B. U. Nebr., 1952; M.D. U. Nebr.-Omaha, 1955. Diplomate Am. Bd. Family Practice. Intern William Beaumont U.S. Army Gen. Hosp., El Paso, Tex., 1955-56; gen. practice medicine, Bellevue, Nebr., 1958-60, Arapahoe, Nebr., 1960-66, Grand Island, Nebr., 1966—. Served with U.S. Army, 1955-58; to comdr. USAFR. Fellow Am. Acad. Family Practice; mem. AMA, Nebr. Med. Assn., Hall County Med. Assn. (pres. 1978), Jaycees (Arapahoe pres. 1964-65, state v.p. 1965-66). Lodges: Lions, Masons. Republican. Presbyterian. Avocations: amateur radio, hunting, fishing. Home: 1743 Idlewood Ln Grand Island NE 68801 Office: 721 W 7th St Grand Island NE 68801-4221

FRANCKE, DANIEL WALTER, economist; b. Valentine, Nebr., Jan. 1, 1950; s. Daniel Walter and Monica Mary (Schubauer) F.; m. Marcia Ann Krienitz, Apr. 15, 1978; 1 child, Tara Ann. B.S. in Math., S.D. State U.-Brookings, 1972, M.S. in Econs., 1974. Economist, DPRA, Inc., Manhattan, Kans., 1974-77, assoc., 1977-80, sr. assoc., 1980—. Mem. Pi Gamma Mu. Roman Catholic. Club: Stagg Hill Golf (bd. dirs. 1981—) (Manhattan). Avocations: golf, travel. Office: DPRA Inc PO Box 727 200 Research Dr Manhattan KS 66502

FRANCOIS, GARY RAY, psychology educator; b. Centralia, Ill., May 18, 1937; s. Ray C. and Bonadean (Steward) F.; m. Lois Alice Paustian, Aug. 8, 1959 (dec. 1975); children—Mark, Scott, Todd, Dana; m. Martha Marie Giddings, June 7, 1975. B.A., Washington U., 1959, M.A., 1960; Ph.D., Tex. Christian U., 1963. Teaching fellow Tex. Christian U., Ft. Worth, 1961-63; instr. psychology Knox Coll., Galesburg, Ill., 1962-63, asst. prof., 1963-68, assoc. prof., 1968-80, prof., 1980—; cons. Galesburg Mental Health Ctr., 1979—. Contbr. articles to profl. jours. Bd. dirs. Western Ill. Family Planning, 1982—. Mem. Am. Psychol. Assn., Midwestern Psychol. Assn., Southwestern Psychol. Assn., So. Soc. Philosophy and Psychology, Sigma Xi. Democrat. Roman Catholic. Avocations: restoring old cars; radios. Home: 996 Bateman St Galesburg IL 61401 Office: Knox Coll Dept Psychology Galesburg IL 61401

FRANK, DAVID SCOTT, psychologist, educator; b. Chambersburg, Pa., Mar. 2, 1930; s. George A. and Elizabeth A. (Feldman) Trail; B.S., Shippensburg State Coll., 1954; M.Ed., Western Md. Coll., 1958; postgrad. U. Mo., Temple U.; Ed.D., W.Va. U., 1972; m. Doris Jean Witmer, Sept. 12, 1954 (div.); children—Kimberley Michelle, David Scott III; m. 2d, Luz Maria Latoni, June 24, 1968; stepchildren—James Brian, Edward Scott, Karen Irene. Tchr. area schs., Carlisle, Pa., 1954-58; guidance counselor, sch. psychologist No. Joint Schs., Dillsburg, Pa., 1958-64; pvt. practice as psychologist and counselor, 1958-68; assoc. prof. Shippensburg (Pa.) State Coll., 1965-67; asst. prof. edn. Purdue U., Westville, Ind., 1967-72; pres. David S. Frank Psychol. Services Inc., Michigan City, Ind., 1972—. Cons. Pa. Dept. Vocat. Rehab., 1958-68; vocat. expert Social Security Adminstrn., Bur. Hearings and Appeals, HEW, 1964—; psychologist LaPorte County Superior and Circuit Cts., 1970-75; psychologist drug abuse treatment program Ind. State Prison, 1975-78, clin. dir. therapeutic community tomorrows aspirations, 1976-78. Active LaPorte County Youth Service Bur., 1972-75, Meals on Wheels, 1973-77; mem. admission com. United Fund, 1972-78; bd. dirs. Family and Children's Service, Michigan City, Ind., 1968-77, No. Ind. Council Children with Learning Disabilities; bd. dirs. Michigan City Scholarship Found., 1975-81, pres., 1979. Served with USMC, 1949-52. Fellow Am. Bd. vocat. Experts (diplomate); mem. Am. Personnel and Guidance Assn., Nat. Vocat. Guidance Assn. (profl. mem.), Nat. Rehab. Assn., Nat. Rehab. Counseling Assn. (profl. mem.), Ind. Corrections Assn. (certificate of merit 1971), AAUP (pres. local chpt. 1969-71), Pa. Sch. Counselors Assn., Internat. Bd. on Counseling Services, Internat. Transactional Analysis Assn., Assn. Counselor Educators and Suprs., Nat. Assn. Disability Examiners, Wrestling Referees Assn. (pres. 1964-65), Mensa, Phi Delta Kappa. Presbyn. (deacon). Contbg. author: New Developments In Educating the Able, 1966. Home: 3207 Cleveland Ave Michigan City IN 46320 Office: David S Frank Psychol Services Inc Suite 356 Marquette Mall Michigan City IN 46360

FRANK, DONALD CLARENCE, lawyer; b. Saginaw, Mich., Dec. 31, 1949; s. Clarence William and Byatha Edna (Rice) F.; m. Nancy Ann Hulett, Aug. 18, 1979. Cert. Suficiencia en Lengua Espanola, U. Madrid, 1970; B.S., Mich. State U., 1972; J.D., Thomas M. Cooley Law Sch., 1980. Bars: Mich. 1981, U.S. Dist. Ct. (ea. and we. dists.) Mich. 1981, Ill. 1982. Owner/mgr. Frank's Flying Service, Mason, Mich., 1973-77, pres., 1977-81; sole practice, Lansing, Mich., 1981-83; ptnr. VendeBunte, Pratt & Frank, Lansing, 1983-84, Pratt & Frank, Lansing, 1984—. Mem. ABA, Lawyer-Pilots Bar Assn., Ingham County Bar Assn., Assn. Trial Lawyers Am., Mich. Trial Lawyers Assn., Ill. State Bar Assn., Aircraft Owners and Pilots Assn., Mich. Pilots and Owners Assn. Republican. Lutheran. Office: Pratt & Frank 3721 W Michigan Ave Suite 302 Lansing MI 48917

FRANK, JAMES HENRY, lawyer; b. Long Branch, N.J., Sept. 10, 1946; s. Clarence Ferdinand and Kathryn Elizabeth (Feeney) F.; m. Susan Gail Kempson, May 6, 1979. B.A., Rutgers U., 1974; J.D., Western State Coll. Law, Fullerton, Calif., 1978. Bar: Ind. 1978, U.S. Dist. Ct. (so. dist.) Ind. 1978, U.S. Ct. Appeals (7th cir.) 1980, U.S. Tax Ct. 1981. Sole practice, Indpls., 1978-83; of counsel Wunder & Hay, Indpls., 1983—; instr./lectr. in bus. law Marion Coll., Indpls., 1980—. Served to sgt. U.S. Army, 1964-67. Mem. Assn. Trial Lawyers Am., Ind. Trial Lawyers Assn., Ind. State Bar Assn., Indpls. Bar Assn. Republican. Roman Catholic. Office: 3824 N Georgetown Rd Indianapolis IN 46254

FRANK, JOHN V., investment advisor; b. Cleve., Oct. 14, 1936; s. Paul A. and Frances (Halbert) F. Student Babson Coll., 1956-57; B.B.A., U. Miami-Fla., 1960. Mgmt. trainee Nat. City Bank, Cleve., 1960-62; investment analyst officer First Nat. Bank, Akron, 1962-70, asst. trust officer, 1970-73, trust officer, 1973-80, v.p., trust officer, 1980-81; pres. Summit Capital Mgmt. Co., Akron, 1982—. Treas., Fairlawn Heights Assn., Inc., Akron, 1971—; pres. Ohio Ballet, 1973-74; trustee Howland Meml. Fund, Akron, 1974—; pres. Burton D. Morgan Found., Akron, 1977—; councilman City of Akron, 1978—; trustee Akron Art Mus., 1976-83, pres., 1979-81; trustee Akron City Hosp. Found., 1980-83. Served to 1st lt. USAR, 1963-69. Mem. Cleve. Soc. Security Analysts. Republican. Episcopalian. Clubs: Portage Country, Akron City; Hillsboro (Pompano Beach, Fla.). Avocation: art collecting. Address: Summit Capital Mgmt Co 2080 Stockbridge Rd Akron OH 44313

FRANK, MICHAEL ROBERT, record producer, artist manager; b. Pitts., May 5, 1949; s. Morton Frank and Agnes (Dodds) Kinard; m. Barbara Spring, Oct. 1985. B.A., Lehigh U., 1972; M.S.W., George Williams Coll., 1982. Owner, pres. Earwig Music Co., Chgo., 1978—; pres. The Traveling Blues Revue Inc., Chgo., 1985—. Producer record albums, 1979—. Mem. Nat. Assn. Ind. Record Distributors and Mfrs., M.S.W. Alumni Orgn. George Williams Coll., Delta Phi. Avocations: playing harmonica; travel; golf. Home and Office: 1818 W Pratt Ave Chicago IL 60626

FRANK, ROBERT E., hospital administrator; b. St. Louis, Nov. 30, 1926; m. Mary Catherine Frank; children—Michael, Nancy Frank Vahldieck. B.S. in Commerce, St. Louis U., 1950, M.A. in Hosp. Adminstrn., 1962. Asst. personnel dir. Gen. Cable Corp., 1950-53; personnel dir. DePaul Hosp., 1953-61; intern in hosp. adminstrn. Barnes Hosp., St. Louis, 1961-61, asst. dir., 1961-64, assoc. dir., 1964-65, acting dep. dir., 1965, dep. dir., 1965-66, acting dir., 1966, dir., 1966-73, pres., 1973—; lectr. Health Adminstrn. Program, Washington U. Sch. Medicine, St. Louis, 1963-66, asst. prof., 1966—. Bd. dirs. Blue Cross St. Louis, 1982-85, Health Care Network of St. Louis, 1979—, Washington U. Med. Ctr., 1983—, Family & Children's Service, 1985—. Mem. Hosp. Assn. Met. St. Louis (pres. 1971-73, dir. 1968-77, 79—), Mo. Hosp. Assn. (bd. trustees 1968-72, 80-83, mem. council on fin. 1983-85), Am. Coll. Hosp. Adminstrs., Am. Hosp. Assn. (council on fin. 1981-83), Assn. Am. Med. Colls. (adminstrv. bd. 1979-84). Home: 1525 Hampton Hall Dr Chesterfield MO 63017 Office: Barnes Hosp Barns Hosp Plaza Saint Louis MO 63110

FRANK, ROBERT NEIL, opthalmologist, vision research scientist, educator; b. Pitts., May 14, 1939; s. Stanton Harvey and Helen Ruth (Rosenbach) F.; m. Karni Warda Spitz; children—Stephen Emanuel, Ariel Ruth, Dale Michael, Gitta Naomi. A.B. summa cum laude, Harvard U., 1961; M.D., Yale U., 1966. Diplomate Am. Bd. Ophthalmology. Intern Grady Meml. Hosp., Altanta, 1966-67; fellow and resident in ophthalmology Johns Hopkins U., Balt., 1967-72; sr. staff ophthalmologist Nat. Eye Inst., NIH, Bethesda, Md., 1972-76; assoc. prof. ophthalmology Wayne State U., Detroit, 1976-80, prof., 1980—; cons. NIH, Nat. Eye Inst., Nat. Inst. Arthritis, Diabetes and Digestive Diseases and Kidney, Nat. Cancer Inst., VA; mem. adv. bd. Med. Sci. Juvenile Diabetes Found.; mem. steering com. Nat. Diabetes Research Interchange; cons. Nat. Diabetes Adv. Bd.; bd. dirs. Mich. Diabetes Assn. NIH grantee, 1976—. Mem. Am. Diabetes Assn., AMA, Am. Acad. Ophthalmology, AAAS, Assn. Research in Vision and Ophthalmology (Fight for Sight award 1977), So. Med. Assn., Mich. Med. Soc., Wayne County Med. Soc., Mich. Ophthal. Soc. Contbr. articles to profl. jours. Office: 3994 John R St Detroit MI 48201

FRANK, RONALD EDWARD, university dean, educator; b. Chgo., Sept. 15, 1933; s. Raymond and Ethel (Lundquist) F.; m. Iris Donner, June 14, 1958; children—Linda, Lauren, Kimberly. B.S.B.A., Northwestern U., Evanston (Ill.), 1955, M.B.A., 1956; Ph.D., U. Chgo., 1960. Instr. bus. stats. Northwestern U., 1956-57; asst. prof. bus. adminstrn. Harvard U., 1960-63; asst. prof. bus. adminstrn. Stanford U., 1963-65; assoc. prof. mktg. U. Pa., 1965-68, prof. mktg., 1968-84, chmn. dept., 1971-74, vice-dean, dir. research and Ph.D. programs, 1974-76, assoc. dean The Wharton Sch., 1981-83, cons. to provost on orgn. and mgmt. univ. research insts., 1983-84; prin. Mgmt. Analysis Ctr., 1977—; prof. mktg., dean Sch. Mgmt., Krannert Grad. Sch. Mgmt., Purdue U., 1984—; cons. numerous corps.; bd. dirs. Mgmt. Analysis Ctr., 1985—. Co-author: Quantitative Techniques in Marketing Analysis, 1962, Marketing: An Introductory Analysis, 1964, Computer Programs for the Analysis of Consumer Panel Data, 1965, Manager's Guide to Marketing Research, 1967, Quantitative Methods in Marketing, 1977; The Public's Use of Television, 1980; Audiences for Public Television, 1982. Contbr. articles to mktg., bus. jours. Mem. fin. com. bd. dirs. Home Hosp., Lafayette, 1985—. Mem. Am. Mktg. Assn., Am. Statis. Assn. (chmn. subsect. on mktg. 1975), Inst. Mgmt. Sci., Assn. Consumer Research, Am. Assn. Pub. Opinion Research, Consumer Research Inst. Republican. Home: 144 Creighton Rd West Lafayette IN 47906 Office: Purdue Univ Krannert Grad Sch Mgmt Krannert Bldg West Lafayette IN 47907

FRANK, ROY ROBERT, JR., land surveyor, educator; b. East St. Louis, Ill., Dec. 12, 1947; s. Roy Robert and Grace Bertha Olivia (Durrer) F.; m. Joan Ludene McKinnies, Aug. 29, 1980; children—Robert Roy, Mac Shane, Randy Ryan. B.A., So. Ill. U., 1970, M.S. in Edn. 1983. Registered land surveyor, Ill. Surveyor Luhr Bros. Constrn. Co., Columbia, Ill., 1966-69; chief survey crew R.A. Nack & Assocs., Inc., Carbondale, Ill., 1970-81; instr. dept. tech. So. Ill. U., Carbondale, 1981-83, asst. prof., 1983—; cons. King City Fed. Savs., Marion, Ill., 1982—, Century 21 Realty, Carterville and Marion, 1982—, Ozburn Agy., Murphysboro, Ill., 1983—. Bd. dirs., coach Tri C Little League, Carterville, 1982—; advisor John A Logan Coll., Carterville, 1976-78; asst. scoutmaster Egyptian council Boy Scouts Am., 1976. Mem. Ill. Registered Land Surveyors Assn. (edn. com. 1982—, legis. com. 1981—), Am. Congress Surveying and Mapping, Nat. Rifle Assn., Am. Soc. Engring. Educators, Phi Kappa Phi. Club: Crab Orchard Boat (Carterville). Avocations: reading, woodworking, fishing, hunting. Home: 408 James St Carterville IL 62918 Office: Dept Tech So Ill U Carbondale IL 62901

FRANK, RUBY MERINDA, employment agency executive; b. McClusky, N.D., June 28, 1920; d. John J. and Olise (Stromme) Hanson; student coll., Mankato, Minn., also Aurora (Ill.) Coll.; m. Robert G. Frank, Jan. 14, 1944 (dec. 1973); children—Gary Frank, Craig. Exec. sec., office mgr. Nat. Container Corp., Chgo., 1943-50; owner, operator Frank's Office & Employment Service, St. Charles, Ill., 1957—; dir. St. Charles Savs. & Loan Assn. Sec. bd. trustees Delnor Hosp., St. Charles, 1959-78, chmn. bd., 1985—, also life mem. Women's aux.; vice chmn. Kane County (Ill.) Republican Com., 1968-77; pres. Women's Rep. Club, 1969-77; adv. council Dellora A. Norris Cultural Arts Center; bd. govs. Luth. Social Service Baker Hotel; adv. bd. Aurora Coll.; chmn. bd. Delnor Hosp.; co-vice chmn. Delnor Community Health System. Recipient Exec. of Yr. award Fox Valley PSI; Charlemagne award for community service, 1982. Mem. St. Charles C. of C. (pres., dir. 1976-82), Kane-DuPage Personnel Assn. (v.p. 1971—), Nat., Ill. employment assns., Ill. Assn. Personnel Cons. (dir.), Women in Mgmt. Lutheran. Clubs: St. Charles Country; Execs. of Chgo. Contbr. weekly broadcast Sta. WGSB, 1970-80, WFXW weekly interview program. Home: 534 Longmeadow Circle Saint Charles IL 60174 Office: Arcada Theater Bldg 12 S 1st Ave Saint Charles IL 60174

FRANK, SANDRA KAYE, mathematics educator; b. Springfield Twp., Mich., June 11, 1941; d. Virgil Euleas and Dorothy Arliene (Wells) Noble; m. Joseph Frederic Frank, Aug. 1, 1970; 1 child, Joseph Lindbergh. B.A., Central Mich. U., 1963; M.A., U. Mont., 1967. Tchr. math. Dearborn Pub. Sch., Mich., 1963—, Edsel Ford High Sch., 1978—. Mem. Mich. Council Tchrs. Math., Mich. Assn. Computer Users and Learners. Clubs: Mich. Flyers, Ninety-Nines. Home: 21222 Audette St Dearborn MI 48124

FRANK, WILLIAM CHARLES, manufacturing company executive; b. Detroit, Mar. 17, 1940; s. Stanley Carl and Evelyn Ellen (Frank) F.; m. Kathleen MacDonald, Aug. 22, 1964; children—Kelly Suzanne, Wendy Michelle. B.S. in Elec. Engring., Wayne State U., 1963; A.M.P., Harvard Bus. Sch., 1983. Project engr. Cadillac Gage Co., Warren, Mich., 1964-69, sr. engr., 1969-73, devel. engring. mgr., 1973-77, gen. mgr. control systems div., 1977-78, exec. v.p., 1978-79, pres., 1979—; dir. Ash Stevens Inc., Detroit. Mem. Pvt. Industry Council, Macomb County, Mich., 1984. Mem. Assn. U.S. Army, U.S. Armor Assn., Am. Def. Preparedness Assn. (bd. dirs. Detroit chpt. 1983-84), Am. Mgmt. Assn., Engring. Soc. Detroit, Young Pres.'s Orgn. (sec. 1984—). Office: Cadillac Gage Co PO Box 1027 Warren MI 48090

FRANKE, BRUCE ALAN, surveyor, educator; b. Fort Wayne, Ind., May 19, 1951; s. Robert William and Mildred Louise (Keltsch) F.; m. Debra Kay Hoffman, June 3, 1978; children—Jennifer Elizabeth, Megan Mellisa. Assoc. in Applied Sci., Purdue U., 1972, B.S., 1973; M.Pub. Affairs, Ind. U., 1983. Asst. to v.p. Arlington Investment Corp., Fort Wayne, Ind., 1972; office mgr., party chief Walter J. David, land surveyor, 1972-78; instr. constrn. tech. Purdue U., Fort Wayne, Ind., 1978—. Chmn. Mayor's Floodplain Mgmt. Adv. Com., 1981—; chmn. Intergovtl. Flood Control Bd., 1982—; vice-chmn. Allen County Flood Control Bd., 1983—. Mem. Am. Congress Surveying and Mapping, Ind. Soc. Profl. Land Surveyors. Lutheran. Home: 1839 Vance Ave Fort Wayne IN 46805 Office: Purdue U Constrn Tech Dept 2101 Coliseum Blvd E Fort Wayne IN 46805

FRANKEL, KENNETH PAUL, lawyer; b. Elyria, Ohio, Nov. 12, 1950; s. Herman and Aileen (Cooperman) F.; m. Sarah Michelle Zadoff, Feb. 11, 1984. B.A., U. Pa., 1972, B.S. in Econs., 1972; J.D., George Washington U., 1975. Bar: Ohio 1975. Assoc., Smith & Smith, Avon Lake, Ohio, 1975—. Pres. Lorain County Child Guidance Ctr., Amherst, Ohio, 1979; pres. Temple B'nai Abraham, 1981-83. Mem. Ohio State Bar Assn., Lorain County Bar Assn. Democrat. Jewish. Lodge: B'nai B'rith. Home: 672 Washington Ave Elyria OH 44305 Office: Smith & Smith 110 Moore Rd Avon Lake OH 44012

FRANKEN, JAMES LESLIE, electrical contractor; b. Sioux Center, Iowa, Aug. 13, 1953; s. John A. and Darlene Faye (Sandbulte) F.; m. Nancy Ann Vanden Brink, July 20, 1974; children—Jaymi Noelle, Gabriel James. B.S., Northwestern Coll., Orange City, Iowa, 1975. Electrician, Interstates Electric & Engring. Co., Inc., Sioux Center, Iowa, 1966-76, v.p., 1976—, pres. IEEC Internat., Ltd., 1983—; mgr. Franken Manor, Sioux Center, 1974-78. Sec., 1st Reformed Ch., Sioux Center, 1980-82. Mem. Associated Builders and Contractors, Sioux Center C. of C. Republican. Office: 1520 Industrial Park Sioux Center IA 51250

FRANKEN, STEPHEN JAMES, data processing manager; b. Green Bay, Wis., Oct. 25, 1949; s. William Albert and Barbara Lucy (Hurley) F.; m. Mary Susan Delacenserie, May 22, 1971; children—Christina, Paul, Aimee, Erin. Cert. in data processing, Manpower Bus. Tng. Inst., Milw., 1970. Computer ops. mgr. Northeast Wis. Tech. Inst., Green Bay, Wis., 1972-78; cons. Computer Bus. Systems, Milw., 1978-80; data processing mgr. Howard Young Med., Woodruff, Wis., 1980—. Served with USMCR, 1967-73. Mem. Data Processing Mgmt. Assn. Roman Catholic. Avocations: Swimming, outdoor activities. Home: 9800 Wintergreen Dr Minocqua WI 54548 Office: Howard Young Med PO Box 470 Woodruff WI 54568

FRANKENA, KARL ROELOFS, lawyer; b. Ann Arbor, Mich., June 9, 1939; s. William K. and Sadie R. (Roelofs) F.; m. Gloria D. Sauer, June 4, 1966; children—Jason T., Lara K. B.A. with honors, U. Mich., 1961, LL.B., 1964. Bar: Mich. 1964. Law clk. Mich. Ct. Appeals, Lansing, 1965-66; assoc. Conlin, Kenney & Green, Ann Arbor, 1966-68; ptnr. Conlin, Conlin, McKenney & Philbrick, Ann Arbor, 1968—. Chmn. Ann Arbor Twp. Planning Commn., 1978-83; treas. Washtenaw Land Conservancy, Ann Arbor, 1978—. Mem. ABA, Washtenaw County Bar Assn., State Bar Mich. (council mem. young lawyers sect. 1966-70), Sierra Club (pres. Huron Valley Group 1968-70). Democrat. Mem. Christian Reformed Ch. Avocations: travelling; skiing; historic preservation. Home: 2600 Earhart Rd Ann Arbor MI 48105 Office: Conlin Conlin McKenney & Philbrick 700 City Center Bldg Ann Arbor MI 48104

FRANKENBERG, BRUCE LIND, investment banker; b. Medinah, Ohio, Feb. 21, 1955; s. Robert Curtis and Marjorie (Lind) F.; m. Kari Severson, Sept. 9, 1978; 1 child, Robert Reid. B.A., Vanderbilt U., 1977; M.B.A., U. Chgo., 1982. Account exec. Marsh & McLennan, Chgo., 1977-81, A.G. Becker Paribas, Chgo., 1982-84, Morgan Stanley, Chgo., 1984—; instr. Ins. Sch. Chgo., 1980-82. Pres. Shorely Woods Assn., 1980-81. Republican. Presbyterian. Clubs: Barrington Hills Country (Barrington); University (Chgo.). Home: 141 Coolidge Ave Barrington IL 60010 Office: Morgan Stanley & Co 115 S LaSalle St Chicago IL 60603

FRANKFORTER, WELDON DELOSS, museum director; b. Tobias, Nebr., May 1, 1920; s. Archie and Mary Ann (Schroder) F.; B.Sc., U. Nebr., 1944, M.Sc., 1949; m. Laura Glea Nicholas, Sept. 12, 1943; children—Mary Glea, Nicholas Dean, Gary Don, Matthew Jason, Lori Ann. Student asst., asso. curator vertebrate paleontology U. Nebr. State Mus., 1941-50; dir. Sanford Mus. and Planetarium, Cherokee, Iowa, 1951-62; asst. dir. Grand Rapids (Mich.) Public Mus., 1962-64, dir., 1965—; mem. Nat. Mus. Act adv. council Smithsonian Instn., 1971-76; adv. for Mich., Nat. Trust Historic Preservation, 1972-78, regional v.p., 1975-76; adv. council Mich. Hist. Preservation Act, 1971-78, chmn., 1975-78; mem. Kent County Council Historic Preservation, 1972—, pres., 1973-74; mrm. faculty Williamsburg Seminar, 1971-73; extension instr. Mich. State U., 1973-75; mem. Grand Rapids Hist. Commn., 1973—, Gerald R. Ford Presdl. Mus. Com., 1976—. Mem. Am. Assn. Museums (exec. bd. 1973-75, v.p. 1977-80, chmn. mus. services com. 1978-79), Midwest Museums Conf. (pres. 1966-67), Hist. Soc. Mich. (dir. 1970-76), Mich. Museums Assn., Am. Assn. State and Local History, AAAS, Geol. Soc. Am., Soc. Vertebrate Paleontology, Soc. Am. Archaeology, Mich. Archaeol. Soc., Mich. Acad. Scis., Arts and Letters, Iowa Acad. Scis., Nebr. Acad. Scis., Sigma Xi. Episcopalian. Clubs: Rotary, Torch. Author research papers in field. Home:

4856 Fuller Ave SE Grand Rapids MI 49508 Office: 54 Jefferson Ave SE Grand Rapids MI 49503

FRANKLIN, BENJAMIN BARNUM, dinner club executive; b. Topeka, Kans., Nov. 7, 1944; s. Charles Benjamin and Margaret Lavona (Barnum) F. B.A. in Speech, U. Colo., 1967. With Associated Clubs, Inc., Topeka, 1967—, v.p., 1972-83, pres., 1983—. Honoree, Benjamin Barnum Franklin Day, Lima, Ohio, June 11, 1983. Mem. Kans. Soc. Assn. Execs., Nat. Speakers Assn. (chmn. chpt. 1982-83), Internat. Platform Assn. (gov. 1975—), Am. Polar Soc., Topeka Sales and Mktg. Execs., Explorers Club. Republican. Presbyterian. Club: Adventurers (Chgo.). Lodge: Rotary (bd. dirs. 1975-78). Contbr. articles to profl. publs. Office: One Townsite Plaza Suite 315 Topeka KS 66603

FRANKLIN, CAROL SUSAN, anthropologist, educational administrator; b. Cleve., Feb. 5, 1953; d. Grant Lafayette and Frances (Mason) F. B.A. magna cum laude, Hiram Coll., Ohio, 1974; M.A. in Anthropology, U. Calif.-Berkeley, 1975, Ph.D., 1979. Research assoc. Coll. Urban Affairs, Cleve. State U., 1979-82, adj. prof. urban studies, 1980-82, vis. asst. prof. 1982; asst. dir. devel. edn. Cuyahoga Community Coll., Cleve., 1983—; cons., facilitator Cuyahoga Met. Housing Authority, Cleve., 1980-82; speaker in field. Mem. planning commn. Episcopal Diocese of Ohio. Nat. Fellowships Fund for Black Americans fellow, 1974-79; Inst. Race and Ethnic Relations, U. Calif.-Berkeley fellow, 1977-78. Mem. Soc. Urban Anthropology, Am. Anthrop. Assn., Am. Ethnol. Soc., Soc. Applied Anthropology, Pi Gamma Nu, Alpha Kappa Alpha (1st v.p. chpt. 1985—). Contbr. in field. Home: 3676 Avalon Rd Shaker Heights OH 44120

FRANKLIN, CHARLES CURTIS, business consultant; b. Colorado Springs, Colo., Mar. 16, 1932; s. William R. and Lilian P. (Jones) F.; m. Sandra Sue Smith, June 17, 1967; children—Bevin Duane, Brian Aaron. B.S.M.E., U. Wis., Madison, 1964; M.B.A., St. Ambrose Coll., 1982. Field service engr. The Marley Pump Co., Mission, Kans., 1964-66, product engring. mgr., 1966-69, quality control mgr., 1969-73, sales mgr. petroleum products, 1973-79, v.p. mktg., 1979-85. Served with USN, 1950-55. Mem. Petroleum Equipment Inst. Republican. Lutheran. Club: Davenport. Lodges: Masons, Shriners.

FRANKLIN, FREDERIC, dancer, choreographer. Founder, Mia Slavenska-Frederic Franklin Ballet, Monte Carlo, 1951; dir. Washington Ballet, 1956-61; artistic advisor Am. Ballet Theatre, Washington, 1965-75; co-artistic dir. Pitts. Ballet, 1975-77; choregrapher-in-residence Cin. Ballet, 1977—, also artistic dir. Dancer with Casino de Paris, 1931, Markova-Dolin Ballet, 1935, Ballet Russe de Monte Carlo, 1938-49 (ptnr. with Alexandra Danilova, Alicia Markova, Mia Slavenska), Ballet Russe de Monte Carlo (ptnr. with Maria Tallchief), 1954. Choreographer (Cin. Ballet) Swan Lake, Nutcracker, Coppelia, Aurora's Wedding, Les Sylphides, Giselle, Tribute, Frankie and Johnny, 1980-81, Billy Sunday, 1982-83, Poeme Lyrique, 1982-83, Le Beau Danube, 1984-85. Recipient Dance Mag. award, 1984, Laurence Olivier award for Best Choreographer of Yr., Soc. West End Theatres, London, 1984. Office: Cincinnati Ballet Co 1216 Central Pkwy Cincinnati OH 45210

FRANKLIN, FREDERICK RUSSELL, legal association executive; b. Berlin, Germany, Mar. 20, 1929; s. Ernest James and Frances (Price) F.; A.B., Ind. U., 1951, J.D. with high distinction, 1956; m. Barbara Ann Donovan, Jan. 26, 1952; children—Katherine Elizabeth, Frederick Russell. Bar: Ind. 1956. Trial atty. criminal div. and ct. of claims sect., civil div. U.S. Dept. Justice, Washington, 1956-60; gen. counsel Ind. State Bar Assn., Indpls., 1960-67; dir. continuing legal edn. for Ind., adj. prof. law Ind. U., Indpls., 1965-68; staff dir. profl. standards Am. Bar Assn., Chgo., 1968-70; exec. v.p. Nat. Attys. Title Assurance Fund, Inc., Indpls., 1970-72; staff dir. legal edn. and admissions to the bar Am. Bar Assn., Chgo., 1972—. Trustee, Olympia Fields (Ill.) United Methodist Ch., 1980-84; treas. bd. dirs. Olympia Fields Pub. Library, 1984—; mem. Olympia Fields Police Bd., 1983—. Served to capt. USAF, 1951-53. Mem. Am., Ind., Ill. bar assns., Fed. Bar Assn. (officer, found. bd. dirs. 1974—, historian 1979—, nat. council 1965—, nat. v.p. 1967-69, chpt. pres. 1965-66, chmn. admission to practice and recert. com. 1980-82, bd. dirs. Chgo. chpt. 1984—), Nat. Orgn. Bar Counsel (pres. 1967), Order of Coif, Phi Delta Phi. Kiwanian, Elk. Home: 3617 Parthenon Way Olympia Fields IL 60461 Office: 750 N Lake Shore Dr Chicago IL 60611

FRANKLIN, JOHN RICHARD, educational administrator; b. Milan, Mo., July 15, 1934; s. John Hartwell and Verda Lois (Pipes) F.; m. Mary Edith Cox, Apr. 11, 1958 (div. 1959); m. Joyce Ann Fishback, Jan. 14, 1961; children—James Clark, Elizabeth Ann. B.S. in Edn., Northeast Mo. State U., 1956; M.S. in Edn., U. Mo., 1963; postgrad. Central Mo. State U., 1971. Cert. secondary tchr., adminstr., Mo., Ill. Tchr. Novinger High Sch., Mo., 1955-56, Memphis High Sch., 1956-60, Churchill Jr. High Sch., Galesburg, Ill., 1960-61; tchr. Fort Osage Sr. High Sch., Independence, Mo., 1961-63, prin., 1963—. Served with U.S. Army, 1958-59. Mem. Community Edn. Assn. (v.p. 1967-68), Mo. State Tchrs. Assn., Mo. Assn. Secondary Sch. Prins. (Kansas City dist. rep. 1982—), West Central Mo. Prin. Assn. (v.p. 1965-66), Nat. Assn. Secondary Sch. Prins. Democrat. Presbyterian. Avocations: fishing, hunting, boating, bird watching. Home: 18005 Cheyenne Independence MO 64056 Office: Fort Osage Sr High Sch Rural Route 2 Box 928 Independence MO 64050

FRANKLIN, MARGARET LAVONA BARNUM (MRS. C. BENJAMIN FRANKLIN), civic leader; b. Caldwell, Kans., June 19, 1905; d. LeGrand Husted and Elva (Biddinger) Barnum; B.A., Washburn U., 1952; student Iowa State Tchrs. Coll., 1923-25, U. Iowa, 1937-38; m. C. Benjamin Franklin, Jan. 20, 1940 (dec. 1983); children—Margaret Lee (Mrs. Michael J. Felso), Benjamin Barnum. Tchr. pub. schs., Union, Iowa, 1925-27, Kearney, Nebr., 1927-28, Marshalltown, Iowa, 1928-40; advance rep. Chautauqua, summers 1926-30. Mem. Citizens Adv. Com., 1965-69; mem. Topeka Hosp. Aux.; bd. dirs. Topeka Pub. Library Found., 1984—. Recipient Waldo B. Heywood award Topeka Civic Theatre, 1967; named Outstanding Alpha Delta Pi Mother of Kans., 1971; Topeka Public Library award, 1977. Mem. DAR (state chmn. Museum 1968-71), AAUW, Topeka Art Guild, Topeka Civic Symphony Soc. (dir. 1952-57, Service Honor citation 1960), Doll Collectors Am., Marshalltown Community Theatre (pres. 1938-40), Topeka Pub. Library Bd. (trustee 1961-70, treas., 1962-65, chmn. 1965-67), Shawnee County Hist. Soc. (dir. 1963-75, sec. 1964-66), Nat. Multiple Sclerosis Soc. (dir. Kans. chpt. 1963-66), Stevengraph Collectors Assn., Friends of Topeka Public Library (dir. 1970-79, Disting. Service award 1980), P.E.O., Native Sons and Daus. Kans. (life), Topeka Stamp Club, Alpha Beta Gamma, Nonoso. Republican. Mem. Christian Ch. Clubs: Western Sorosis (pres. 1960-61), Minerva, Woman's (1st v.p. 1952-54, 2d v.p. 1984-85).

FRANKS, ALLAN DAVID, public relations executive, consultant; b. Cheyenne, Wyo., Nov. 14, 1943; s. Brooks Dudley and Victoria Mary (Florenz) F.; m. Marcia Lee Augenstein, Dec. 27, 1970; 1 child, Andrew Ryan. B.A. in Journalism, Ohio State U., 1971. Pub. info. officer Dept. Health, Columbus, Ohio, 1971-72; asst. dir. pub. info. Ohio EPA, Columbus, 1972-74, dir. pub. info., 1974—; pres. ADF Communications Inc., Columbus, 1982—. Served with U.S. Army, 1964-70. Non-elected state ofcl. USEPA region 5, 1976. Mem. Internat. Assn. Bus. Communicators, Nat. Environ. Communications Assn. (founder, pres. 1978-80). Avocations: photography; camping; skiing. Office: Ohio EPA PO Box 1049 361 E Broad St Columbus OH 43216

FRANKS, EDWIN CLARK, biology educator; b. Chagrin Falls, Ohio, Jan. 13, 1937; s. Elmer Clarence and Esther Marie (Scheetz) F.; m. Evelyn Christine Mayes, Sept. 11, 1958. B.Sc., Ohio State U., 1958, M.Sc., 1960, Ph.D., 1965. Biologist, Batelle Meml. Inst., Columbus, Ohio, 1958-61; trainee Pa. State U., State College, 1965-66; asst. prof. biology Western Ill. U., Macomb, 1966-70, assoc. prof., 1970-77, prof., 1977—. Contbr. articles to profl. jours. Mem. Am. Ornithologists Union, Wilson Ornithol. Soc., Inland Bird Banding Assn. (dir. 1984—), Phi Kappa Phi, Phi Eta Sigma, Gamma Sigma Delta. Avocation: birdwatching. Home: RD 1 Colchester IL 62326 Office: Western Ill U Biology Dept Macomb IL 61455

FRANKS, LAWRENCE ALBERT, machine tool company executive; b. Brimfield, Ind., Aug. 30, 1933; s. Newell Albert and Aletha Grace (Disler) F.; m. Patricia Ann Herbert, Sept. 5, 1953; children—Newell A. II, David L., Lee Ann. Student Olivet Coll., 1951-52; B.S. in Mech. Engring., Tri-State Coll., 1959. Mech. engr. Burr Oak Tool, Sturgis, Mich., 1959-63, v.p., 1963—; v.p., dir. Burr Oak Tool & Gauge, Sturgis, 1963—, Oak Products, Inc., Sturgis, 1978—, Oak Internat. Chem., Sturgis, 1976—. Patentee in field. Chmn. Sturgis Planning Bd., 1970-75; v.p., bd. dirs. Sturgis Improvement Assn., 1978—, Econ. Devel. Bd., 1978—; pres. Sturgis United Fund, 1968; trustee Tri-State U., Angola, Ind., 1984—; chmn. bd. trustees Methodist Ch., 1968-71; pres. Band and Orch. Parents, Sturgis, 1976-77. Named Disting. Alumnus, Tri-State U., 1981. Mem. Sturgis C. of C., (dir. 1963-64, 84—). Republican. Clubs: Klinger Lake Country, Tennis (pres. 1972). Lodge: Kiwanis (lt. gov. 1981). Home: 1105 Robin Hood Trail Sturgis MI 49091 Office: Burr Oak Tool & Gauge Co Inc Box 338 Sturgis MI 49091

FRANS, ROBERT DONALD, mechanical engineer, researcher; b. Auburn, Nebr., Aug. 13, 1924; s. Ruel Victor and Jessie Eleanor (Rebuck) F.; m. Deloris Mae Ridenour, June 8, 1947; children—Douglas R., Debra L. B.S., U. Nebr., 1950. Registered profl. engr., Wis. sr. process devel. engr. Allis Chalmers Corp., Milw., 1951-68; asst. to v.p. ops. Hanna Mining Co., Cleve., 1968-71, mgr. quality control, Hibbing, Minn., 1971-81, sr. process engr., Nashwauk, Minn., 1981-82, dir. research ops., 1982—. Contbr. articles to profl. jours. Patentee in field. Served with USAAF, 1943-46, PTO. Mem. Iron and Steel Soc., Soc. Mining Engrs., Pi Tau Sigma. Republican. Lodges: Shriners, Masons. Avocations: hunting; fishing; hiking. Office: Hanna Mining Co Research Ctr Box 67 Nashwauk MN 55769

FRANTA, WILLIAM ROY, former computer science educator, investment executive; b. St. Paul, May 21, 1942; s. Roy Andrew and Helen Aleta (Nicholson) F.; B.S., U. Minn., 1964, M.S., 1966, Ph.D., 1970. Asst. prof. computer sci. U. Minn., Mpls., 1970-76, assoc. prof., 1976-81, prof., 1981-84, assoc. dir. Univ. Computer Center, 1976-80, co-dir. Microelectronic and Info. Scis. Center, 1980-81, assoc. dir., 1981-82; mem. computer adv. com. Sci. Mus. Minn., 1981—; mem. tech. adv. com. 1st Midwest Capital Corp., 1981, v.p., 1978-83, pres., 1983-85; treas. ADC Telecommunications, 1985—. NSF grantee, 1979-81. Mem. IEEE, Inst. Mgmt. Scis., Assn. Computing Machinery. Author: The Process View of Simulation, 1977; (with I. Chlamtac) Local Networks: Motivation, Technology, Performance, 1981; (with others) Formal Methods of Program Verification and Specification, 1981; contbr. over 80 research papers in field. Office: 5501 Green Valley Dr Bloomington MN 55435

FRANTSVE, DENNIS JOHN, graphics company executive, educator, columnist; b. Chgo., Mar. 14, 1938; s. Carl Henning and Elizabeth Dorothy (Waldock) F.; m. Julieta Maria Chacon, Oct. 26, 1967; children—Lisa, Julie, Dennis. B.S. in Commerce, DePaul U., 1969. Cost acct. R.R. Donnelley & Sons Inc. Chgo., 1956-60; supr. Gregg Moore Co., Chgo., 1965-69; prodn. coordinator Regensteiner Press, Chgo., 1969-70; supr. Acme Press, Chgo., 1970-72; print buyer Beslow Assocs., Inc., Chgo., 1972-74; exec. v.p. Darby Graphics, Chgo., 1974—. Tchr., Printing Industry Ill. Assn., 1973—. Served with USAR, 1957-63. Honored at testimonial Internat. San. Supply Assn., 1979; recipient cert. of appreciation Printing Industry Ill. Assn., 1980. Mem. Internat. Assn. Bus. Communicators, Publ. Prodn. Club Chgo., Soc. Nat. Assn. Publs., Pan Am. Council, Park Ridge C. of C. (dir. 1980—; cert. of appreciation 1981). Clubs: Toastmasters (treas.) (Des Plaines, Ill.); N.W. Press (Chgo.). Author: Printing Production Management, 1983; columnist Am. Printer mag., 1976—. Home: 215 N Chester Ave Park Ridge IL 60068 Office: 4015 N Rockwell St Chicago IL 60618

FRANTZ, MICHAEL JENNINGS, lawyer; b. Piqua, Ohio, May 7, 1951; s. Richard Jennings and Harriet Rose (Simon) F.; m. Julia Ann Brunetto, June 16, 1973; children—Kathleen, Elizabeth, Michael Jennings, Joseph. B.A., U. Notre Dame, 1973; J.D., Georgetown U., 1976. Bar: Ohio 1976. Mem. Thompson, Hine & Flory, Cleve., 1976—; adj. lectr. labor law and indsl. relations Cleve. State U., 1982—. Trustee Hanna Perkins Sch., 1982—. Mem. ABA, Ohio Bar Assn., Greater Cleve. Bar Assn., Am. Soc. Hosp. Attys. Republican. Roman Catholic. Home: 31285 Kimberly Dr Bay Village OH 44140 Office: Thompson Hine & Flory 1100 National City Bank Bldg Cleveland OH 44114

FRANZ, JUDY ROSENBAUM, physics educator; b. Chgo., May 3, 1938; d. Eugene Joseph and Ruth (Comroe) R.; m. Frank Andrew Franz, July 11, 1959; 1 child, Eric Douglas. A.B., Cornell U., 1959; M.S., U. Ill., 1961, Ph.D., 1965. Research physicist IBM Research Lab., Zurich, Switzerland, 1965-67; asst. prof. Ind. U., Bloomington, 1968-74, assoc. prof., 1974-79, prof. physics, 1979—, assoc. dean Coll., 1980-82; vis. prof. Tech. U. Munich, W.Ger., 1978-79, Cornell U., Ithaca, N.Y., 1985—. Contbr. articles to profl. jours. Recipient Disting. Teaching award Ind. U., 1978; von Humboldt Found. research fellow, 1978-79; research grantee Research Corp., 1972-73, NSF, 1973-81, NATO, 1980-83. Fellow Am. Phys. Soc. (councilor 1984—, chmn. edn. com. 1983-85, exec. com. 1985); mem. AAAS, Assn. Women in Sci. (councilor 1981-83), Am. Assn. Physics Tchrs., AAUP, Phi Beta Kappa, Sigma Xi (pres. local chpt. 1981-82). Avocations: tennis; gardening. Home: 1900 Arden Dr Bloomington IN 47401 Office: Dept Physics Indiana U Bloomington IN 47405

FRANZBLAU, SANFORD ASHER, physician, medical educator; b. Ozone Park, N.Y., Mar. 15, 1918; s. Harris and Anna (Schwartz) F.; m. Eugenia Wysatt, Fe. 10, 1946; children—David, Anne, Daniel, Robert. B.A. in Chemistry with honors, U. Ill., 1939; M.S. in Biochemistry, U. Ill.-Chgo., 1942, Ph.D. in Cardiovascular Physiology, 1951, M.D. with honors, 1943. Diplomate Am. Bd. Internal Medicine. Intern, Mcpl. Contagious Disease Hosp., Chgo., 1943, St. Luke's Hosp., Chgo., 1943-44; resident U. Ill. Research Edn. Hosp., 1946-48, Ill. Neuropsychiat. Inst., fellow in neurology, 1948; clin. asst. dept. medicine, U. Ill., Chicago, 1946-48, clin. instr., 1948-53, clin. asst. prof., 1953-65, clin. assoc. prof., 1965-76, clin. prof., 1976—; practice medicine, specializing in internal medicine, Chgo., 1951—; mem. staff U. Ill. Hosps., 1953—, Luth. Gen. Hosp., Park Ridge, Ill., 1959—; mem. cons. staff Holy Family Hosp., Des Plaines, Ill., 1983—. Contbr. articles to med. jours. Active Boy Scouts Am.; bd. dirs. Tb Inst. Chgo. and Cook County. Served to capt. Med. Service Corps., AUS, 1944-46, ETO. Recipient Kellogg Found. award 1943. Fellow ACP; mem. Am. Fedn. Clin. Research (sr.), Am. Heart Assn., AMA, Chgo. Inst. Medicine, Chgo. Med. Soc., Ill. State Med. Soc. Lodge: Masons. Avocations: ham radio, sailing. Office: Maine-Ridge Med Assocs 9301 W Golf Rd Des Plaines IL 60016

FRANZMEIER, RONALD EDWIN, blood center administrator; b. Milw., Aug. 22, 1944; s. Edwin Lavern and Evelyn Mary (Houy) F. B.A., U. Wis.-Milw., 1968. With mktg. staff Manpower Inc., Milw., 1964-69, asst. to pres., 1970-76; sr. account exec. Zigman-Joseph-Skeen, Milw., 1977-80; dir. ops. Blood Ctr., Milw., 1980—; mem. nat. communications com. ARC, Washington, 1979—; mem. donor resources com. Council of Community Blood Ctrs., Washington, 1982—; mem. planning com. Am. Blood Commn., Washington, 1983—. Pres. Met.-Milw. Civic Alliance, 1984; pres. Milw. Mgmt. Support Orgn., 1983; chmn., bd. dirs. Greater Milw. chpt. ARC, 1984—; mem. steering council Action for Goals 2000-Milw., 1983—. Mem. Am. Assn. Blood Banks. Club: University (Milw.). Lodge: Rotary. Home: 7910 W Keefe Ave Milwaukee WI 53222 Office: Blood Ctr of Southeastern WI 1701 W Wisconsin Ave Milwaukee WI 53233

FRASCA, NEIL DONALD, pharmacist; b. Youngstown, Ohio, Oct. 17, 1942; s. Andrew Dan and Lucy (Nigro) F.; m. Angelina Marsilio, Nov. 5, 1966; children—Neil Daniel, Theresa Marie, Christine Louise. B.S. in Pharmacy, Ohio No. U., 1965; postgrad. bus. studies Youngstown State U., 1970-77. Asst. mgr. Thrift Drug Store, Canfield, Ohio, 1965-66, Niles, Ohio, 1966-67; pharmacist Youngstown Hosp., 1967-74; chief pharmacist Youngstown Hosp. Assn. North, 1974-78; pharmacist Youngstown Hosp. Assn. South, 1978—. Fin. sec. Austintown Band Parent Assn., Ohio, 1983-85, treas., 1985—. Mem. Ohio Pharm. Assn., Eastern Ohio Pharm. Assn., Soc. for Preservation and Encouragement of Barbershop Singing in Am. (treas. 1980—). Democrat. Roman Catholic. Avocations: piano; singing. Home: 2613 Birchwood Dr Youngstown OH 44515 Office: Youngstown Hosp Assn South Oak Hill Ave Youngstown OH 44501

FRASCH, JOSEPH FREDERICK, JR., lawyer, educator; b. Columbus, Ohio, Mar. 21, 1948; s. Joseph Frederick and Esther Lucille (Morehart) F.; m. Cheryl Sue Crawford, June 3, 1972. B.A., Capital U., 1970, J.D., 1974. Bar: Ohio 1974, U.S. Tax Ct. 1977, U.S. Supreme Ct. 1979. Assoc. Kenneth P. Bessey, Columbus, 1974-79; ptnr. Bessey & Frasch Co., L.P.A., Columbus, 1979—; adj. prof. Franklin U., Columbus, 1974—, gen. counsel, 1979—. Recipient Outstanding Educator of Yr. award Franklin U., 1983. Mem. ABA, Ohio State Bar Assn., Columbus Bar Assn., Nat. Assn. Coll. and Univ. Attys. Republican. Lutheran. Club: German Village Sertoma (pres. 1981-82). Office: Bessey & Frasch Co LPA 145 E Rich St 4th Floor Columbus OH 43215

FRASER, DONALD MACKAY, mayor, former congressman; b. Mpls., Feb. 20, 1924; s. Everett and Lois (MacKay) F.; B.A. cum laude, U. Minn., 1944, LL.B., 1948; m. Arvonne Skelton, June 30, 1950; children—Thomas Skelton, Mary MacKay, John DuFrene, Lois MacKay (dec.), Anna Tallman (dec.), Jean S. Admitted to Minn. bar, 1948; practice in Mpls., 1948-62; partner firm Lindquist, Fraser & Magnuson, and predecessors, 1950-62; mem. Minn. Senate, 1954-62, sec. Senate Liberal Caucus, 1955-62; mem. 88th-95th Congresses from 5th Dist. Minn., mem. internat. relations com., budget com., sec., whip, chmn. Dem. study group; mayor City of Mpls., 1980—; mem. study and rev. com. Dem. Caucus; congl. adviser U.S. del. to Law of Sea Conf., 1972-78, to UN Conf. on Disarmament, 1968-73, to UN Commn. on Human Rights, 1974; U.S. del. to 30th session UN Gen. Assembly, 1975, organizer regional presdl. candidate forums, 1975; mem. Commn. on Role and Future of Presdl. Primaries, 1976-77. Vice chmn., mem. bd. Mpls. Citizens Com. on Pub. Edn., 1950-54. Sec. Minn. del. Democratic Nat. Conv., 1960, mem. rules com., 1972, 76; chmn. Minn. Citizens for Kennedy, 1960; mem. platform com. Dem. Nat. Conv., 1964; chmn. commn. on party structure and del. selection Nat. Dem. Com., 1971-72, chmn. subcom. on internat. orgns.; nat. chmn. Dem. Conf., from 1976. Served as lt. (j.g.) USNR, 1944-46. Mem. Mpls. Fgn. Policy Assn. (pres. 1952-53), Citizens League Greater Mpls. (sec. 1951-54), Minn., Hennepin County bar assns., U. Minn. Law Alumni Assn. (dir. 1958-61, 79—), Ams. for Dem. Action (nat. pres. 1973-75), Univ. Dist. Improvement Assn. (pres.). Office: Office of the Mayor City Hall Minneapolis MN 55415*

FRASER, GEORGE C., sales executive; b. Bklyn., May 1, 1945; s. Walter F. and Ida F.; m. Nora J. Spencer, Sept. 7, 1973; children—George, Scott. Student NYU, 1963-66. Sales mgr. Ency. Brittannica Co., Cleve., 1968-70; pres. Black Ednl. Devel Co., Cleve., 1970-72; unit sales mgr. Procter & Gamble Co., Westlake, Ohio, 1972—. Exec. chmn. United Negro Coll. Fund Telethon, 1982-83; bd. dirs. Operation Alert; active Freedom Fund com., NAACP, Urban League Luncheon Com.; past bd. dirs. Ohio Jr. Olympics, Ohio Domestic Registry. Named Nat. Telethon Vol. of Yr., United Negro Coll. Fund, 1982, One of 84 Most Interesting People in Cleve. for 1984, Cleve. Mag. Mem. Black Profl. Assn. (trustee), Leadership Cleve. Clubs: Racqueteers Racquetball (pres.); Chippers Golf. Home: 24497 Hawthorne Dr Beachwood OH 44122 Office: Procter & Gamble 24650 Center Ridge Rd Westlake OH 44145

FRASIER, RALPH KENNEDY, banker; b. Winston-Salem, N.C., Sept. 16, 1938; s. Leroy Benjamin and Kathryn Oziebel (Kennedy) F.; m. Jeannine Marie Quick; children—Karen Denise, Gail Spaulding, Ralph K., Keith Lowery. Student U. N.C., 1955-58; B.S. in Commerce, N.C. Central U., 1960-62, J.D. magna cum laude, 1965. Vice-pres., gen. counsel Huntington Nat. Bank, Columbus, Ohio, 1975-76, sr. v.p., gen. counsel, 1976, sec., 1981-83, exec. v.p., gen. counsel, sec., cashier, 1983—; v.p., gen. counsel Huntington Bancshares Inc., Columbus, Ohio, 1976, sec., 1981—; v.p., asst. sec. Huntington Nat. Bank N.E. Ohio, Cleve., 1983-84; dir., sec. Huntington Mortgage Co., Columbus, Huntington Leasing Co., Columbus, Huntington Investment Mgmt. Co., Columbus, Scioto Life Ins. Co., Columbus, Huntington Co., Columbus, Seventeen Corp., Columbus, Huntington State Bank, Alexandria, Ohio, Huntington Bancshares Fin. Corp., Columbus; v.p., asst. sec. Union Capital Mgmt. Corp., Cleve., 1983—; v.p., asst. counsel The Wachovia Corp., Winston-Salem, N.C.; v.p., counsel Wachovia Bank and Trust Co., N.A., Winston-Salem, 1969-70, asst. v.p., 1968-69, asst. sec., 1966-68, legal asst., 1965-66.; mem. lawyers com. Assn. Bank Holding Co., 1981—. Sec. Family Services, Inc., Winston-Salem, 1966-71, 74, v.p., 1974, dir., 1966-74; vice-chmn. Winston-Salem Transit Authority, 1968-74, chmn., 1974-75; dir. Research for Advancement Personalities, Inc., Winston-Salem, 1968-71; treas. Forsyth Citizens Com. for an Adequate Justice Bldg., 1969; dir. Winston-Salem Citizens for Fair Housing, Inc., 1970-74, N.C. United Community Services, Inc., 1970-74; trustee Appalachian State U., Boone, N.C., 1973-83, sec., 1978-79, chmn. com.on student affairs, 1980-81, chmn. com. on acad. affairs, 1981-82; trustee Endowment Fund of Appalachian State U., 1973-83; mem. adv. council Winston-Salem/Forsyth County Sch. Bd., 1973-74; mem. Ohio Atty. Gen.'s Task Force on Minorities in Bus., 1977-78; mem. Mayor's Econ. Devel. Council, Columbus, 1980-82; trustee Edn. and Employment Commn. Franklin County, Ohio, 1981—, vice-chmn., 1981—; mem. community adv. council Office Minority Affairs, Ohio State U., Columbus, 1983—; mem. community adv. council Grad. Sch. Adminstrn., Capital U., Columbus, 1984—. Served with U.S. Army, 1958-60. Mem. ABA, Nat. Bar Assn., Ohio Bar Assn., Am. Corp. Counsel Assn. (bd. dirs. Columbus chpt. 1984—), N.C. Bar Assn. (com. on banking and corp. law 1970-76), Forsyth County Bar Assn., Columbus Bar Assn., Greater Winston-Salem C. of C. (mem. law enforcement commn. and consumer credit counseling commn. 1973), Am. Soc. Corp. Secs., Inc. Office: The Huntington Nat Bank 41 S High St PO Box 1558 Columbus OH 43260

FRAUENHOFFER, GAIL LYNNE, human resource executive; b. L.I., N.Y., Jan. 7, 1958. B.Bus. magna cum laude, Hofstra U., 1980. Trainee Gimbels, N.Y.C., 1980; asst. mgr. Lee Wards, subs. Gen. Mills, L.I., N.Y., 1980-81, retail personnel mgr., 1981-83, human resource mgr., tng. mgr., 1983—. Mem. Am. Mgmt. Assn., Assn. Tng. and Devel., Elgin C. of C., Beta Gamma Sigma, Omicron Delta Epsilon. Avocations: music; jogging; swimming; reading. Home: 1041 Perth Dr Schaumburg IL 60194 Office: 1200 St Charles St Elgin Il 60120

FRAZER, WENDY, nurse, physician's assistant; b. Steubenville, Ohio, June 3, 1943; d. Richard William and Mary Elizabeth (Sliday) F. R.N., Beaver Valley Gen. Hosp., New Brighton, Pa., 1964; A.A.S., Cuyahoga Community Coll., 1983. R.N., Ohio, Pa. Pediatrics nurse Cleve. Clinic Found., 1962-65; asst. head nurse Cardiovascular Lab., 1965-73; surg. nurse clinician cardiothoracic surgery Cleve. Clinic Found., 1978—; admissions officer Lakewood Hosp., 1984-85. Assoc. founder, counselor Inst. Creative Living, 1976-80. Mem. Nat. Acad. Physician Assts., Nat. Assn. Cardiovascular Physician Assts., Ohio Assn. Physician Assts., Cleve. Zool. Soc., Cleve. Mus. Art, Holden Arboretum, Nat. Geog. Soc., Smithsonian Soc. Republican. Baptist. Office: Cleveland Clinic Foundation 9500 Euclid St Cleveland OH 44106

FRAZIER, JIMMY LEON, physician; b. Beaumont, Tex., Aug. 29, 1939; s. Leon and Thelma (Cooper) F.; B.S., Tex. So. U., 1960; M.D., Meharry Med. Coll., 1967; m. Shirley Jolley, June 26, 1971; children—Keith, David, Andrea Nichole. Tchr. math. Beaumont (Tex.) Sch. Dist., 1960-63; aerospace engr. NASA, Houston, summer 1964; intern, Good Samaritan Hosp., Dayton, Ohio, 1967-68, resident in internal medicine, 1971-72; practice medicine specializing in family practice, Park DuValle Health Center, Louisville, 1968-69, Dayton, Ohio, 1972—; mem. staff Good Samaritan Hosp., St. Elizabeth Hosp., 1972—; mem. admission com. Wright State U. Med. Sch., Dayton, 1978-80. Served to maj. U.S. Army, 1969-71. Diplomate Am. Bd. Family Practice. Fellow Am. Acad. Family Physicians; mem. Gem City Med. Soc. (pres. 1976-78), AMA, Ohio Med. Soc., Nat. Med. Assn., Montgomery County Med. Assn., Alpha Phi Alpha. Methodist. Clubs: Dayton Selectmen, Dayton Racquet, Masons (Shriner). Home: 543 Valewood Ln Dayton OH 45406 Office: 1401 Salem Ave Dayton OH 45406

FRAZIER, TODD MEARL, health science adminstrator, epidemiologist; b. Lima, Ohio, Nov. 9, 1925; s. Todd M. and Gertrude (Blanks) F.; m. Barbara Welday, Sept. 28, 1946; children—Michael, Sarah, Nancy, David. A.B., Kenyon Coll., 1949; Sc.M., Johns Hopkins U., 1957. Dir. biostats. Balt. City Health, 1953-63; assoc. dir. planning and research D.C. Dept. Pub. Health, Washington, 1963-68; asst. dir. Harvard Ctr. Community Health and Med. Care, Harvard U., Boston, 1968-78; chief surveillance br. Nat. Inst. Occupational Safety and Health, Cin., 1978—; assoc. prof. Harvard Sch. Pub. Health, Boston, 1968-78; cons. WHO, Geneva, 1971-78. Served with USN, 1943-46, U.S. Army, 1950-51. Fellow Am. Pub. Health Assn.; mem. Sigma Xi. Home: 2164 Cablecar Ct Cincinnati OH 45244 Office: Robert A Taft Labs Nat Inst Occupational Safety and Health 4676 Columbia Pkwy R-17 Cincinnati OH 45226

FRECKA, JOHN ALLISON, steel co. exec., lawyer; b. Ironton, Ohio, Jan. 12, 1929; s. James Harold and Margaret Helene (Fowler) F.; B.S., Marshall U., 1950; J.D., Wayne State U., 1967; m. Lois Joann Williams, Sept. 23, 1950; children—Deborah, David, John, Mary Anne. Personnel mgr. Detroit Strip div. Cyclops Corp., Detroit, 1951-64, turn supt., 1964-68, gen. supt., 1969-73, gen. mgr., 1974-76; admitted to Mich. bar, 1967; v.p. Empire-Detroit Steel div. Cyclops Corp., Mansfield, Ohio, 1976-78, pres., 1979—. Mem. Mich. Bar Assn., Am. Iron and Steel Inst. Home: 2065 Matthes Dr Mansfield OH 44906 Office: 913 Bowman St Mansfield OH 44901

FREDEN, SHARON ELSIE, educational administrator; b. Watertown, S.D., Jan. 11, 1941; d. Harlon Arthur and Mildred Lillian (Jensen) Christman; m. Noble Everett Freden, July 3, 1973; 1 child, Anne Victoria. B.S., No. State Coll., Aberdeen, S.D., 1962; M.A., U. Iowa, 1966; Ed.D., U. Colo., 1973. Tchr. Manitowoc Pub. Schs., Wis., 1962-64, Boulder Valley Pub. Schs., Colo., 1966-70, K-12 lang. arts cons., 1970-72; cons. Colo. Dept. Edn., Denver, 1973-76, 77-80; ITV inservice coordinator Sta. KCPT Channel 19, Kansas City, Mo., 1980-81; dir. Kans. State Dept. Edn., Topeka, 1981-84, asst. commr., 1984—. Editor: Basic Skills: Promising Practices in Colorado, 1979; (with others) Pupil Progress in Colorado, 1978. Contbr. to books. Precinct com. chmn. Democratic Party, Broomfield, Colo., 1978. Hildegard Sweet Meml. scholar, 1972. Mem. Assn. Supervision and Curriculum Devel., Kans. Assn. Supervision and Curriculum Devel., United Sch. Adminstrs., Phi Delta Kappa. Home: 3711 SW 31st St Topeka KS 66614 Office: Kans State Dept Edn 120 E 10th Topeka KS 66612

FREDERICK, EDWARD CHARLES, university administrator; b. Mankato, Minn., Nov. 17, 1930; s. William H. and Wanda (MacNamara) F.; m. Shirley Lunkenheimer, Aug. 16, 1951; children—Bonita Frederick Treangen, Diane Frederick Labs, Donald, Kenneth, Karen Frederick Swenson. B.S. in Agrl. Edn., U. Minn., 1954, M.S. in Dairy Husbandry, 1955, Ph.D. in Anatomy and Physiology, 1957. Animal scientist, instr. Northwest Sch. and Expt. Sta. U. Minn., Crookston, 1958-64, supt. So. Sch. and Expt. Sta., Waseca, 1964-69, provost Tech. Coll., Waseca, 1969—; mem. Tech. Agrl. Edn. Study Team to Morocco, 1977. Contbr. articles to profl. jours. Bd. dirs. Bob Hodgson Student Loan Fund, 1971—, Minn. Agrl. Interpretive Ctr., 1978—. Recipient Alumni award 4-H, 1972. Mem. Am. Dairy Assn., Am. Soc. Animal Prodn., AAAS, Nat. Assn. Colls. and Tchrs. Agr. (pres. 1976-77), Am. Assn. Community and Jr. Colls., South Central Edn. Assn. (Disting. Service award 1971), Waseca Area C. of C. (bd. dirs. 1979), Phi Kappa Phi. Roman Catholic. Lodges: Rotary, K.C., Foresters. Home: Route 4 Box 32D Waseca MN 56093 Office: U Minn Tech Coll Waseca MN 56093

FREDERICKS, MARSHALL MAYNARD, sculptor; b. Rock Island, Ill., Jan. 31, 1908; s. Frank A. and Frances Margaret (Bragg) F.; student John Huntington Poly. Inst., Cleve.; grad. Cleve. Sch. Art, 1930; student Heimann Schule, Schwegerle Schule, Munich, Germany, Academie Scandinav, Paris, pvt. studios Rome and London, Carl Milles' Studio, Stockholm, Cranbrook Acad. Art, Bloomfield Hills, Mich.; recipient 3 hon. doctorates in fine arts; m. Rosalind Bell Cooke, Sept. 9, 1943; children—Carl Marshall and Christopher Matzen (twins), Frances Karen Bell, Rosalind Cooke, Suzanne Pelletreau. Faculty Cleve. Sch. Art, 1931, Cranbrook Acad. Art, Kingswood Sch., Cranbrook, 1932-42; Royal Danish consul Mich.; local, nat., internat. exhbns. art since 1928 include: Carnegie Inst., Cleve. Mus., Pa. Acad., Chgo. Art Inst., Whitney Mus., Detroit Art Inst., Denver Mus., Phila. Internat. Invitational, N.Y. World's Fair Am. Art Exhbn., Modern Sculpture Internat. Exhbn. Detroit, Internat. Sculpture Show Cranbrook Mus., AIA, Nat. Sculpture Soc., Archtl. League N.Y., Mich. Acad., Brussels, others; commns. include: N.Y. World's Fair Baboon Fountain, Levi Barbour Meml. Fountain, Rackham Meml. Bldg., Fort Street Sta., Vets. Meml. Bldg., Detroit; adminstrn. bldg., war meml. U. Mich., Louisville Courier-Jour. Bldg., Jefferson Sch., Wyandotte, Mich., Holy Ghost Sem., Ann Arbor, Mich., union bldg. Ohio State U., Ford Rotunda, Marc Joslyn Meml., Alvan Macauley Meml. City-County Bldg., Ford Auditorium, Detroit Zool. Garden, also the Indian River Shrine, State Dept. Fountain, Washington; Cleve. War Meml. Fountain, Milw. Pub. Mus. Sculpture, N.Y. World's Fair permanent sculpture, Fed. Bldg. sculpture, Cin., Community Nat. Bank, Pontiac, Mich., Sir Winston Churchill Meml., Freeport, Bahamas, Two Sister fountain, Cranbrook, Michigan, Dallas Library sculpture, Henry Ford Meml., Dearborn, Mich., fountain Oakland U., Rochester, Mich., Midland (Mich.) Center Arts, Crittenton Hosp., Rochester, Mich., Fgn. Ministry, Copenhagen, Hans Christian Anderson fountain, Skaelskor, Denmark, many others; portrait commns. include: Senator Arthur Vandenburg, Willard Dow, Midland, Mich., George G. Booth Meml., Cranbrook, Mrs. Horace Rackham Meml., Yoshita, Pres. John F. Kennedy, others; works included numerous museums, pvt., civic collections. Co-founder, dir. DIADEM Program for Internat. Exchange of Handicapped; trustee Am. Scandinavian Found., People-to-People Program; v.p. Rebild Nat. Park Soc.; v.p. Brookgreen Gardens; mem. internat. com. Internat. Ctr. for Disabled. Served with C.E., AUS, 1942-44, lt. col. 20th bomber command; 8th Air Force, Okinawa, 1944-45. Decorated knight 1st class Order of Dannebrog, 1963, 1971, comdr.'s cross, 1978; knight 1st class order St. Olav (Norway), 1972; recipient of 1st prize Cleve. Mus. Art, 1931; Anna Scripps Whitcomb prize Detroit Inst. Arts, 1938; 1st prize internat. exhbn. Dance Internat., Rockefeller Center, N.Y.C., 1st prize Barbour Meml. nat. competition, medal Mich. Inst. Architects, fine arts gold medal AIA, 1952, gold medal honor Mich. Acad. Arts, Letters, Sci., 1953; Archtl. League of New York; citation Am. Inst. Decorators, Nat. Soc. Crippled Children and Adults, State of Mich., U. Detroit. Henry Hering medal Nat. Sculpture Soc., 1972; Herbert Adams Meml. medal, 1982; Marshall Fredericks Day named in Detroit, 1972, in Birmingham, Mich., 1983; citation Gov. Mich., 1983; resolution Mich. State Legislature, 1983, numerous other U.S. and fgn. awards and decorations. Fellow Internat. Inst. Arts and Letters; mem. Mich. Soc. Architects, AIA, St. Dunstan's Dramatic Guild, Mich. Acad. Sci., Arts and Letters, C. of C., NAD, Am. Soc. Interior Design, Nat. Soc. Interior Designers, Nat. Sculpture Soc. (dir., medal of honor 1985), Beta Sigma Phi, Alpha Beta Delta. Clubs: Royal Swedish Yacht; Orchard Lake Country; Architectural League N.Y. (N.Y.C.) Prismatic (Detroit); Royal Norwegian Yacht; Royal Danish Yacht. Home: 440 Lake Park Dr Birmingham MI 48009 Studio: 4113 N Woodward Ave Royal Oak MI 48072 also East Long Lake Rd Bloomfield Hills MI 48072

FREDERICKSON, DENNIS RUSSEL, state senator, farmer; b. Morgan, Minn., July 27, 1939; s. Louis B. and Mary (Kragh) F.; m. Marjorie Davidson, July 15, 1961; children—Kari, Karl, Disa. B.S., U. Minn., 1961. Farmer, Morgan, Minn., 1967—; county commr. Redwood County, Redwood Falls, Minn., 1973-80; mem. Minn. Senate, 1981—. Served to lt. comdr. USN, 1962-67. Mem. Am. Soc. Agrl. Economists, Am. Soc. Animal Sci., Council for Agrl. Scis. and Techs. Ind. Republican. Presbyterian. Lodge: Lions (pres. Morgan, Minn.). Office: Minnesota Senate Room 145 State Office Bldg Saint Paul MN 55155

FREDETTE, ALAN LEE, international marketing company executive; b. Chgo., Aug. 27, 1938; s. Robert Lee and Margaret Lucille (Nichols) F.; m. Jean Marie Goulett, June 20, 1965; children—Michelle M., Andrew B., Scott M. B.S., Mich. State U., 1961; B.F.T., Am. Grad. Sch. Internat. Mgmt., 1966. Trainee, Ford Motor Co., Dearborn, Mich., 1961-62; space systems dir. TRW, Redondo Beach, Calif., 1962-65; internat. mktg. dir. Spalding Sporting Goods, Chicopee, Mass., 1966-71; v.p. ops. AMF Bowling Corp., Stamford, Conn., 1972-80; internat. sales mgr. Henny Penny Corp., Eaton, Ohio, 1980—. Recipient Key Employee award AMF Corp., 1976. Republican. Roman Catholic. Club: World Trade (Cin.). Avocations: Photography; sailing; golf. Home: 50 Walnut Ave Cincinnati OH 45215 Office: Henny Penny Corp Route 35 Eaton OH 45320

FREDMAN-(ZITLIN), SUSAN MIRIAM, interior designer; b. Chgo., Nov. 14, 1950; d. David Wolfe Fredman and Selma (Lobelson) Florio; B.S., Ill. State U., 1973. Display asst. Lane Bryant, Chgo., 1972-73, Lyttons, Chgo., 1973; asst. head visual merchandising Goldblatt's, Chgo., 1973-76; designer Advance Design Assocs., Chgo., 1976; prin. Susan Fredman & Assocs., Chgo., 1976—; dir. Seven-Thirty Network, 1980—. Mem. steering com. women in professions and trades Jewish United Fund, 1984—; mem. Hunger Project, Chgo., 1983; vol. Children's Meml. Hosp., Chgo., 1983; exec. com. audience devel. bd. Victory Gardens Theatre. Mem. Internat. Soc. Interior Designers (profl. mem., bd. dirs. 1984—). Club: East Bank (Chgo.).

FREDRICH, AUGUSTINE JOSEPH, civil engineer, educator; b. Little Rock, Sept. 12, 1939; s. Augustine Joseph and Barbara Mary (Strobel) F.; m. Cecelia Ann Waller, Sept. 1, 1962; children—Laura Ann, Augustine Joseph, Jr., Gregory Louis. B.S. in Civil Engring., U. Ark., 1962; M.S. in Civil Engring., Calif. State U.-Sacramento, 1972. Registered profl. engr., Calif. Hydraulic engr. U.S. Army Corps. Engrs., Little Rock, 1962-66, chief research br. Hydrologic Engring. Ctr., Davis, Calif., 1966-72, sr. policy analyst Office Chief of Engrs., Washington, 1973-76, dir. Inst. Water Resources, Ft. Belvoir, Va., 1976-79; prof. civil engring. U. So. Ind., Evansville, 1979—, dir. engring tech., 1981—; cons. UNESCO, Porto Alegre, Brazil, 1970. Contbr. articles to profl. jours. Bd. dirs. Evansville Port Authority, 1982; adv. bd. Evansville Environ. Protection Adminstrn., 1983; citizen rev. United Way Southwestern Ind., 1984. Congl. fellow Am. Polit. Sci. Assn., 1973. Mem. ASCE (tech. activities com. 1983-84). Democrat. Roman Catholic. Avocation: amateur youth soccer coach. Home: 1108 Glen Moor Ct Evansville IN 47715 Office: Ind State U Evansville 8600 University Blvd Evansville IN 47712

FREE, HELEN M., chemist, consultant; b. Pitts., Feb. 20, 1923; d. James Summerville and Daisy (Piper) Murray; m. Alfred H. Free, Oct. 8, 1947; children—Eric, Penny, Kurt, Jake, Bonnie, Nina. B.A. in Chemistry, Coll. of Wooster, Ohio, 1944; M.A. in Clin. Lab. Mgmt., Central Mich. U. Cert. clin. chemist Nat. Registry Clin. Chemists. Instr. continuing edn.-mgmt. Ind. U.-South Bend, 1975—; chemist Miles Labs., Elkhart, Ind., 1944-78, cons. chemist research products div., 1978-82, chemist, mgr., cons. Ames div. Miles Lab., 1982—. Author: (with others) Urodynamics and Urinalysis in Clinical Laboratory Practice, 1972, 76. Contbr. articles to profl. jours. Patentee in field. Women's chmn. Centennial of Elkhart, 1958. Recipient Disting. Alumni award Coll. of Wooster, 1980. Fellow AAAS, Am. Inst. Chemists (co-recipient Mosher award 1967); mem. Am. Chem. Soc. (chmn. women's continuing edn. and nominating com., council policy pub. affairs and budget, Service award local chpt. 1981, councilor; Garvan medal 1980), Am. Assn. for Clin. Chemistry (council, bd. dirs., nominating com. and pub. relations com., nat. membership chmn.), Am. Soc., Med. Tech. (chmn. assembly; Achievement award 1976), Iota Sigma Pi. Presbyterian. Lodge: Altrusa (pres. 1982-83, bd. dirs.). Home: 3752 E Jackson Blvd Elkhart IN 46516 Office: Ames Div Miles Labs PO Box 70 Elkhart IN 46515

FREE, WILLIAM NORRIS, academic administrator, English educator; b. Seaford, Del., Aug. 25, 1933; s. Louis Joseph and Mary Madeline (Marvel) F.; m. Anne M. Cahalane, Aug. 17, 1957; children—William Norris, Anne Rebecca, Daniel Louis. B.A., Yale U., 1955, Ph.D., 1961; M.A., Ind. U., 1957. Teaching asst. Ind. U., Bloomington, 1955-57, from instr. to asst. prof. English, 1959-66; assoc. prof. U. Toledo, Ohio, 1966-71, prof., 1971—, chmn. English dept., 1972-79, v.p. for acad. affairs, 1979—. Author: William Cowper, 1970. Contbr. articles to profl. jours. Mem. Toledo Arts Commn., 1980-82, Pvt. Industry Council, Toledo; bd. dirs. St. Angela Hall Sch., Toledo, 1969-75, St. Patrick of Heatherdowns, Toledo, 1973—. Served to capt. USAR. Univ. scholar Yale U., 1951-55; R.R. McCormick fellow, Yale U., 1957-59. Mem. Coll. English Assn. Ohio (pres. 1979-80). Roman Catholic Home: 4901 Eastwick Dr Toledo OH 43614 Office: U Toledo 2801 W Bancroft St Toledo OH 43606

FREED, CATHERINE CAROL MOORE, educator; b. Omaha, Dec. 27, 1925; d. Prentice Lauri and Henryetta (Banker) Moore; B.A., B.F.A., U. Tex., 1948; M.A., U. Kans., 1961; m. DeBow Freed, Sept. 10, 1949; 1 son, DeBow II. Mem. faculty St. Mary's Coll., Xavier, Kans., 1958-59, U. Kans., Lawrence, 1959-61, U. N.Mex., Albuquerque, 1961-65, Huntingdon Coll., Montgomery, Ala., 1965-67, Ladycliff Coll., Highland Falls, N.Y., 1967-69, No. Ohio U., Ada. Adviser, Albuquerque Sch. System on Gifted Child Edn., 1962-64; writer, producer film on purposes and objectives of PTA, 1964; elder United Presbyterian Ch. U.S.A., commr. 189th Gen. Assembly; moderator Gt. Rivers Presbytery, 1979; pres. Alliance Community Concert Assn., 1970-74; 1st v.p. Ada-Liberty United Way, 1981-83, pres., 1984, 85; pres. Ada-Lima chpt. Liturgical Art Guild Ohio, 1980-85. Mem. Speech Assn. Am., Nat. Council Tchrs. English, Daus. of U.S. Army (pres. chpt. Ft. Benning, Ga. 1954-55), Internat. Platform Assn., DAR, P.E.O., Mortar Bd., Phi Beta Kappa, Kappa Phi, Delta Sigma Rho, Pi Kappa Delta, Alpha Psi Omega, Alpha Delta Pi. Home: 115 W Lima Ave Ada OH 45810 Office: Ohio Northern U Ada OH 45810

FREED, DOUGLASS LYNN, artist, educator; b. Garden City, Kans., Dec. 24, 1944; s. Vernon Claude and Mary Maurine (Porter) F.; m. Nina Claire Misegadis, Dec. 18, 1965; children—Justin Garrett, Chad Aaron, Tiffany Bree, Damon Jared. B.F.A., Ft. Hays State U., 1967, M.A., 1968. Mem. faculty State Fair Community Coll., Sedalia, Mo., 1968—, chmn. dept. art. One-man shows include: Vorpal Gallery, N.Y.C., 1979, 80, 81, 82, 83, also others in San Francisco, 1982, Kansas City, Mo., 1983, St. Louis, 1984; exhibited in group shows throughout U.S.; represented in permanent collections: Mus. Art and Archeology of U. Mo., Meml. Union Collection of U. Mo.; rep. by Vorpal Gallery, N.Y.C., Greenberg Gallery, St. Louis, Batz/Lawrence Gallery, Kansas City, Mo., Zolla/Lieberman Gallery, Chgo.; Subject of profl. publs. Bd. dirs. Sedalia Arts Council, 1980—, Mo. Citizens for Arts, 1981-84, Liberty Ctr. for Performing Arts, Sedalia, 1984-86, Mo. Arts Council, 1984-87. Rotary Internat. fellow group study exchange, Italy, 1978; Mid Am. Arts Alliance grantee, 1980. Mem. Mo. Assn. Community Colls. Republican. Home: 1100 W 4th St Sedalia MO 65301 Office: Doug Freed Studio 110 E Main Sedalia MO 65301

FREED, GLENN STEPHEN, gastroenterologist; b. Phila., Feb. 23, 1952; s. Carl Robert and Sonia Lenore (Zubcov) F. Student Muhlenberg Coll., 1970-72; B.A., Temple U., 1974; D.O., Phila. Coll. Osteo. Medicine, 1978. Rotating intern Chgo. Osteo. Med. Ctr., 1978-79, resident in internal medicine, 1979-81; fellow in gastroenterology St. Louis U./St. Mary's Health Ctr., 1981-82, Loyola U. Med. Ctr., Chgo., 1982-83; practice osteo. medicine, specializing in internal medicine and gastroenterology, San Diego, 1983—; mem. staff Grossmont Hosp., Sharp Hosp., Alvarado Hosp., Hillside Hosp., Harborview Hosp.; asst. clin. prof. medicine Coll. Osteo. Medicine of Pacific. Mem. Am. Osteo. Assn., Am. Coll. Osteo. Internists, AMA, San Diego County Med. Soc., San Diego Osteo Med. Assn. (chmn.), Osteo. Physicians and Surgeons Calif, Am. Soc. Gastrointernal Endoscopy, Am. Cancer Soc. Office: 6336 Alvarado Ct Suite 3D San Diego CA 92120

FREED, JAMES MELVIN, zoology educator, family history researcher and publisher; b. Enid, Okla., Apr. 6, 1939; s. B. Leon and Ada Myrtle (Moyers) F.; m. Judith Vivian Miley, Aug. 16, 1969; children—Jana Loel, Jonathan David. B.S., McPherson Coll., 1961; M.S., U. Ill., 1963, Ph.D., 1969. Instr. biology Manchester Coll., North Manchester, Ind., 1963-65; prof. zoology Ohio Wesleyan U., Delaware, 1969—. Editor family newsletter. Contbr. articles to profl. jours. Fellow Ohio Acad. Sci. (dir. state sci. day State of Ohio 1980—); mem. Am. Soc. Zoology, Am. Soc. Human Genetics, AAAS. Democrat. United Methodist. Home: 218 W Fountain Ave Delaware OH 43015 Office: Ohio Wesleyan U Dept Zoology Delaware OH 43015

FREED, MARILYNNE MAUD, manufacturing company executive; b. Youngstown, Ohio, Sept. 18, 1949; d. Warren P. and Phyllis I. (Avery) F.; m. William E. Pastor, May 20, 1978; 1 child, Will A. Freed. B.S., Case Res. U., 1971. Acctg. mgr. TV and radio Sta. WFMJ, Youngstown, 1971-72; bus. mgr. Sta. WFLD-TV, Chgo., 1972-74; v.p., treas. Youngstown Steel and Alloy Corp., Canfield, Ohio, 1974-82; pres. Life-Time Truck Products Inc., Youngstown, 1982—; v.p., treas. Valley Truck and Trailer, Youngstown, 1979—. Choir dir. Ohltown United Meth. Ch., Youngstown, 1982—, bd. dirs., 1983—. Mem. Family Bus. Assn. N.E. Ohio (charter; bd. dirs., v.p. 1978-80) Pvt. Industry Council Mahoning County (chmn. 1980-83), Youngstown C. of C. (legis. com. 1982—). Republican. Office: 4300 Simon Rd PO Box 3346 Youngstown OH 44512

FREEDHEIM, DONALD KOPERLIK, psychology educator, clinical psychologist; b. Cleve., Aug. 31, 1932; s. Eugene H. and Mina K. Freedheim; m. Gerda Irene Kilian, Aug. 31, 1958; children—Amy Jean, Julie Kay, Sara Beth. A.B., Miami U., Oxford, Ohio, 1954; Ph.D., Duke U., 1960. Lic. psychologist, Ohio. Pvt. practice psychology, Cleve., 1963—; asst. prof. psychology Case Western Res. U., Cleve., 1965-69, assoc. prof., 1969—, clin. psychologist Mental Devel. Ctr., 1970-72, acting chmn. dept. psychology, 1970-72; staff psychologist Sonoma (Calif.) State Hosp., summer 1968; vis. assoc. prof. Tel Aviv U., 1974-75; mem. devel. behavioral scis. study sect. NIH, 1970-74; cons. in field. Trustee Montefiore Home, Cleveland Heights, 1964-69, 76—, Jewish Community Fedn., Cleve., 1971-74, 80—, Cleve. Jewish News, 1980—, Cleve. Internat. Program, 1979—; pres. Sheltered Adult Workshops, Inc., Cleve., 1980-83; vice chmn. child and youth panel United Way Services, Cleve., 1980—. Fellow Am. Psychol. Assn., Am. Orthopsychiat. Assn.; mem. Am. Assn. on Mental Deficiency, Sigma Xi, Psi Chi, Omicron Delta Kappa. Democrat. Jewish. Club: City (Cleve.). Contbr. chpt., articles to profl. pubs.; producer films on retardation, 1962, 66, 77; editor: Handbook for Volunteers for Mental Retarded (ARC), 1968; (with E. Walker) Newsletter Editors Manual (Am. Psychol. Assn.), 1974; editor Clin. Psychologist, 1966-69, Profl. Psychology, 1969-77, Psychotherapy, 1983—. Office: Dept Psychology Case Western Res U Cleveland OH 44106

FREEDMAN, BRUCE RICHARD, lawyer; b. Cleve., May 18, 1954; s. Harvey R. and Myrna L. (Boardman) F.; m. Laurel Lynch, Aug. 9, 1980; 1 child, Daniel. B.B.A., Miami U., Oxford, Ohio, 1976; J.D., Ohio State U., 1981. Bar: Ohio 1981, U.S. Dist. Ct. (no. dist.) Ohio 1982. Retailer exec. devel. program F. & R. Lazarus Dept. Stores, Columbus, Ohio, 1976-78; assoc. Jerome L. Holub & Assocs., Akron, Ohio, 1982—. Mem. Hospice Adv. Council of Summit County, Akron, 1984-85; mem. Summit County Mental Health Levy Steering Com., Akron, 1984-85; trustee Blick Clinic for Developmentally Disabled, Akron, 1984-86, treas., 1985. Robert K. Barton scholar Ohio State U., Columbus, 1979-81. Mem. ABA, Akron Bar Assn. (chmn. young lawyers sect. 1984-85, chmn. hospice lawyer program 1982-85, chmn. program and entertainment com. 1985), Assn. Trial Lawyers Am., Ohio State Bar Assn., Akron Bar Assn. (various coms.), Omicron Delta Kappa, Phi Alpha Delta (chpt. justice 1979-81). Home: 274 Kenilworth Dr Akron OH 44313 Office: Jerome L Holub & Assocs 1113 Centran Bldg Akron OH 44308

FREEDMAN, DAVID NOEL, clergyman, educator; b. N.Y.C., May 12, 1922; s. David and Beatrice (Goodman) F.; student CCNY, 1935-38; A.B., UCLA, 1939; Th.B., Princeton Theol. Sem., 1944; Ph.D. (William S. Rayner fellow) in Semitic Langs. and Lit., Johns Hopkins U., 1948; D.Litt. (hon.), U. of the Pacific, 1973; D.Sc. (hon.), Davis and Elkins Coll., 1974; m. Cornelia Anne Pryor, May 16, 1944; children—Meredith Anne, Nadezhda, David Micaiah, Jonathan Pryor. Ordained to ministry Presbyn. Ch., 1944; pastor Presbyn. Chs. in Acme and Deming, Wash., 1944-45; asst. instr. Johns Hopkins U., Balt., 1947-48; asst. prof. O.T., Western Theol. Sem., Pitts., 1948-51, prof. Hebrew and O.T., 1951-60; prof. Hebrew and O.T., Pitts. Theol. Sem. (successor to Western Theol. Sem.), 1960-61, James A. Kelso prof., 1961-64; prof. O.T., San Francisco Theol. Sem., 1964-70, dean of faculty, 1966-70, Gray prof. O.T. exegesis, 1970-71; prof. O.T., Grad. Theol. Union, Berkeley, Calif., 1964-71; prof. Bibl. studies U. Mich., Ann Arbor, 1971—, A.F. Thurnau prof. Bibl. studies, 1984—, dir. program on studies in religion, 1971—; Danforth vis. prof. Internat. Christian U., Tokyo, 1967; vis. prof. Hebrew U., Jerusalem, 1976-77, Macquarie U., North Ryde, New South Wales, Australia, 1980, Brigham Young U., Provo, Utah, 1981, 82, U. Queensland, St. Lucia, Brisbane, Australia, 1982, 84, Univ. Calif., San Diego, 1985; lectr.; cons. to Reader's Digest, Atlas of the Bible, 1979—, Funk & Wagnall Pub. Co., New Ency., 1979-83; tech. cons. to Milberg Productions, 1961—; ann. dir. Albright Inst. Archaeological Reserach, Jerusalem, 1969-70, 76-77; editorial cons. Macmillan Co., 1961-66; mem. task force on bibl. authority and interpretation United Presbyn. Ch. in U.S., 1979-82; vis. lectr. various colls. and sems., 1948—. Recipient Laymen's Nat. Bible Com. Ann. award, 1978; Guggenheim fellow, 1958-59. Mem. Am. Acad. Religion, Soc. Bibl. Lit. (pres. midwest br. 1964, nat. pres. 1976), Am. Schs. Oriental Research (v.p. for publs. 1974-82, editor Bull. 1974-78, editor Bibl. Archeologist 1975-82), Am. Oriental Soc., Am. Assn. Colls. (mem. commn. on religion in higher edn. 1974-76), Am. Archeol. Inst., U. Mich. Research Club, Bibl. Colloquium (sec. treas. 1958—), Explorers Club. Author books on Bible and Christianity, 1949—, including: (with Leona Running) William Foxwell Albright: Twentieth Century Genius, 1975; (with B. Mazar and G. Cornfeld) The Mountain of the Lord, 1975; (with W. Phillips) An Explorer's Life of Jesus, 1975; Pottery, Poetry, Prophecy, 1980; co-author: Commentary on Hosea, 1980; The Leviticus Scroll from Cave 11, 1985 contbr. numerous articles and Bibl. studies to scholarly jours.; editor-in-chief Anchor Bible Series, 1971—; co-editor Computer Bible Series, 1975—, Anchor Bible Series, 1956-71; editor Anchor Bible Dictionary. Home: PO Box 7434 Ann Arbor MI 48107 Office: Studies in Religion 445 W Engineering U Mich Ann Arbor MI 48109

FREEDMAN, JAMES OLIVER, university president, educator; b. Manchester, N.H., Sept. 21, 1935; A.B., Harvard U., 1957; LL.B., Yale U., 1962; M.A. (hon.), U. Pa., 1971. Bar: N.H., Pa., Iowa. Law clk. to Judge Thurgood Marshall, U.S. Ct. Appeals, 1962-63; assoc. firm Paul, Weiss, Rifkind, Wharton & Garrison, N.Y.C., 1963-64; asst. prof., assoc. prof. law U. Pa., 1964-69, prof., 1969-82, univ. ombudsman, 1973-76, dean Sch. Law, 1979-82; pres. U. Iowa, Iowa City, 1982—; cons. Adminstrv. Conf. U.S., 1968—, Office Fgn. Direct Investment, Dept. Commerce, 1969-70; vis. fellow Cambridge (Eng.) U., 1976-77; chmn. Pa. Legis. Reapportionment Commn., 1981. Author: Crisis and Legitimacy: The Administrative Process and American Government, 1978; contbr. articles to legal jours. NEH fellow, 1976-77. Mem. Am. Law Inst., Am. Arbitration Assn. Office: Office of Pres U Iowa Iowa City IA 52242*

FREEDMAN, ROBERT RUSSELL, psychology educator; b. Phila., Apr. 30, 1947; s. Bernard and Sarah (Lichtenstein) F.; m. Mary Ann Morris, July 12, 1981. B.A. in Psychology, U. Chgo., 1969; Ph.D., U. Mich., 1975. Lic. psychologist, Mich. Dir. behavioral medicine Lafayette Clinic, Detroit, 1975—; adj. asst. prof. psychology Wayne State U., Detroit, 1976-83, adj. assoc. prof. 1983—, adj. assoc. prof. psychiatry, 1983—; cons. Nat. Inst. Drug Abuse, Washington, 1976-78. Assoc. editor Biofeedback and Self-Regulation Jour., 1983—. Nat. Heart, Lung, Blood Inst. research grantee, 1980—. Mem. Soc. Behavioral Medicine (Pres.'s citation 1983), Soc. Psychophysiol. Research, Biofeedback Soc. Am. (publs. chmn. 1984—, Outstanding Paper award 1985), Assn. for Psychophysiol. Study Sleep, AAAS. Avocations: sailing, camping, music. Home: 605 Kellogg Ann Arbor MI 48105 Office: Lafayette Clinic 951 E Lafayette Detroit MI 48207

FREEMAN, DONALD MCKINLEY, political science educator; b. Asheville, N.C., Apr. 22, 1931; s. Major McKinley and Bertha Lee (Wright) F.; m. Ina Mae Benner, Sept. 1, 1955. B.A., Wake Forest Coll., 1954; M.A., U. R.I., 1955; Ph.D., U. N.C., 1964. Instr., Hollins Coll., Roanoke, Va., 1962-63; asst. prof. U. N.C., Charlotte, 1963-65; asst. prof. U. Ariz., Tucson, 1965-67, assoc. prof., 1967-69; prof. polit. sci., chmn. dept. U. West Fla., Pensacola, 1969-77; vis. prof. Tex. Technol. U., Lubbock, 1977-78; Igleheart prof. polit. sci. U. Evansville, Ind., 1978—; cons. Data Surveys, Phoenix, 1968-69, Ralph Rodes Assocs., Inc., New Harmony, Ind., 1983-84, Ctr. for Polit. Research, Riverside, Calif., 1984—; Fulbright sr. lectr. politics and fgn. policy Nat. U. Singapore, 1985-86. Author: (with Susan MacManus, Charles Bullock, III) Governing a Changing America, 1984. Co-editor: Political Parties and Political Behavior, 1966, 71; editor: Foundation of Political Science, 1977. Contbr. articles to profl. jours. Bd. dirs. Community Action Program, Evansville, 1978—, pres. bd., 1985—; mem. Evansville Mayor's Citizens Adv. Com. on Community Devel., 1978—; bd. dirs. Patchwork Central, Evansville, 1982—, pres. bd., 1984—. Nat. Conv. fellow Nat. Ctr. for Edn. in Politics, 1964; U. Ariz. Grad. Sch. Faculty research grantee, summer 1968, Nat. Assn. Broadcasters research grantee, 1970-71, S & H Found. grantee Lecture Series on Presidency, 1981-82. Mem. Am. Polit. Sci. Assn., Midwestern Polit. Sci. Assn., So. Polit. Sci. Assn., Am. Soc. for Pub. Adminstrn., Ind. Soc. for Pub. Adminstrn., Evansville Democrats for Better Govt. Presbyterian. Avocations: gardening; cooking; travelling. Home: 2317 E Michigan St Evansville IN 47711 Office: Dept Polit Sci Univ Evansville PO Box 329 Evansville IN 47702

FREEMAN, FRANK GEORGE, social history educator, research consultant; b. Ladysmith, Wis., Mar. 23, 1938; s. Francis G. and Eunice M. (Brand) F.; m. Theresa M. Schneider, Nov. 21, 1980; children—Mary, Ann Marie, Patrick, James, Margaret, Matthew. Prof. Am. history St. John's U., 1967; tchr. church history Sacred Heart Jr. High Sch., McAllen, Tex., 1967-70; tchr. local and Am. history St. Francis High Sch., St. Francis, S.D., 1970-78; research and labor studies United Auto Workers, Mishawaka, Ind., 1979-84; dir. Ednl. Programs and Services, South Bend, 1978—; cons. in field. Recipient Diocese of Ft. Wayne-South Bend, Ind. award 1980; St. George award, 1981. Mem. Am. Assn. Counseling and Devel., Am. Assn. State and Local History, Am. Personnel and Guidance Assn., Nat. Trust for Hist. Preservation, Nat. Mus. Assn., Catholic Coms. on Scouting. Democrat. Roman Catholic. Author: Modern Indian Psychology, 1969; Social Research and Urban Politics, 1970; Strength in Bargaining, 1977; A Short History of American Labor, 1980. Office: PO Box 4310 South Bend IN 46634

FREEMAN, NED LAVON, organization executive; b. Pittsfield, Ill., Dec. 12, 1942; s. Troy Manard and Grace Marie (Hendrickson) F.; m. Marjorie Ann Hayn, Aug. 31, 1963 (dec. 1977); 1 child, Debbra; m. Shirley Mae Worthington, Nov. 22, 1980; children—Lloyd Weber, Sarah. B.S., So. Ill. U., 1965; M.B.A., So. Ill. U.-Edwardsville, 1973. High sch. tchr. St. Louis County, Melvhille, Mo., 1965-67; tech. writer Universal Match Corp., Inc., St. Louis, 1967-75; dist. scout exec. Boy Scouts Am., Granite City, Ill., 1975-80, Hannibal, Mo., 1980—; cons. United Way, Hannibal, 1981-84; cons. to youth com. Mark Twain Sesquicentennial Commn., Hannibal, 1984—. Youth advisor Granite City C. of C., 1979-80. Recipient Eagle Scout award Boy Scouts Am., 1958, Vigil honor award Boy Scouts Am., 1961, hon. key to city Granite City, 1980; named Disting. Exec., Boy Scouts Am., 1978, 82, 84. Presbyterian. Lodge: Rotary (youth chmn. 1981-84). Avocations: photography, tropical fish. Home:

4300 Paris Gravel Rd Hannibal MO 63401 Office: Great Rivers Council Boy Scouts Am 1203 Fay St Columbia MO 65205

FREEMAN, PHILIP D., funeral director; b. Jefferson City, Mo., Aug. 3, 1953; s. Donald P. and Margaret G. (Clardy) F.; m. Amy D. Walz, June 28, 1975; children—Donald P., Ryan C. B.B.A., Columbia Coll., 1975. Lic. funeral dir., Mo. with Freeman Mortuary, Jefferson City, 1975—. Pres., Southside Bus. League, 1980; chmn. Jefferson City Parking and Traffic Authority; chmn. campaign United Way, Jefferson City, 1982, pres. bd. dirs., 1985; bd. dirs. Jefferson City celebrations, 1981-82. Mem. Mo. Funeral Dirs. Assn. (legis. com.), 5th Dist. Mo. Funeral Dirs. Assn., C. of C. (pres. 1983), Jaycees (Disting. Service award 1982). Lodge: Rotary (bd. dirs.). Home: 1324 Roseview Dr Jefferson City MO 65101 Office: Freeman Mortuary 915 Madison St Jefferson City MO 65101

FREEMAN, RICHARD DWAINE, clergyman; b. Stockton, Calif., May 6, 1945; s. Milford Dwaine and Shirley Jean (Bourn) F.; m. Vicki Ann Jarvis, May 23, 1970; 1 dau., Christina Lynn. A.A., McCook Jr. Coll., 1965; B.A., Hastings Coll., 1967; M.Div., United Theol. Sem., St. Paul, 1971; postgrad. McCormick Theol. Sem., 1981—. Ordained to ministry United Ch. of Christ, 1971; lic. instr. Parent Effectiveness Tng. Assoc. pastor Bath Community Ch., Akron, Ohio, 1971-72, 1st Congl. Ch., Grand Junction, Colo., 1972-73; sr. minister 1st Congl. Ch. Forest Glen, Chgo., 1974-80, St. Peter's United Ch. of Christ, Champaign, Ill., 1980—; cons. Christian Edn. Shared Approaches Ch. Sch. Curriculum; exec. sec. Chgo. Met. Assn. Ill. Conf. United Ch. of Christ, Chgo., 1978-80; on-site coordinator Nat. Gatherine United Ch. of Christ Clergy, 1978-81. Pres. Ill. Consortium on Govtl. Concerns, Springfield, 1982-84. Recipient Alfred and Catherine Cook Meml. award United Theol. Sem., 1971. Mem. Profl. Assn. Clergy Ill. Conf. of United Ch. of Christ (sec. 1975-79). Club: Kiwanis (lt. gov. Eastern Ill. Dist. 1978-79, dist. conv. chmn. 1979-80, dist. interclub chmn. 1981-82, dist. maj. emphasis chmn. 1982-83, dist. bull. editor 1983-84, pres. Forest Glen-Mayfair, Chgo. 1975-76). Home: 1003 S Russell St Champaign IL 61821 Office: St Peters United Ch of Christ 905 S Russell St Champaign IL 61821

FREEMAN, ROBERT ARNOLD, laboratory executive, consultant blood banking; b. Denver, Nov. 15, 1927; s. Siler Freeman and Ruth (Campbell) F.; m. Louise Marie Goetz, Oct. 30, 1982. B.S., Alma Coll., 1948; M.T., Wayne U., 1950, postgrad., 1951. Registered med. technologist. With ARC, St. Louis, 1955-66, asst. regional mgr., 1966; dep. adminstrv. dir. blood program ARC, Washington, 1967-72; sr. clin. research coordinator Travenol Labs., Deerfield, Ill., 1972-73, mgr. govt. ops., 1973-83, mgr. contract adminstrn. govt. ops. 1984—. Chmn. community health services ARC, Chgo., 1982—; commr. Deerfield Youth Baseball Assn., 1976-77. Editor: Camp Safety and Health Management, 1982. Pres., Holy Cross Ch. Parish, Deerfield, 1977; vice chmn. United Fund, 1964; vice chmn. St. Louis Archdiocese, 1963; Named Umpire of Yr., Deerfield Youth Baseball, 1979. Mem. Am. Assn. Blood Banks, Ill. Assn. Blood Banks (Merit award 1976). Home: 1305 Mulford St Evanston IL 60202 Office: Travenol Labs One Baxter Pky Deerfield IL 60015

FREEMAN, RONALD RAY, engineer; b. Lincoln, Ill., Aug. 19, 1940; s. Raymond L. and Mary E. (Conley) F.; m. Barbara A. Lueke, Sept. 19, 1964; children—Aimee, Michelle. Student Mich. Tech. U., 1964-66, U. Nebr., 1968, Met. Tech. Community Coll., 1983-84. Mgr. Northwestern Bell, Omaha, 1969-77; staff mgr. AT&T Corp. Hdqrs., Basking Ridge, N.J., 1977-79; sr. engr. Northwestern Bell Corp. Staff, Omaha, 1979—; cons. Personal Computer Support Group, Omaha, 1983—. Served with USAF, 1963-67. Mem. Telephone Pioneers Am., Am. Radio Relay League (life). Roman Catholic. Avocations: amateur radio; antique radio collecting. Office: Northwestern Bell Telephone Co 1314 Douglas on the Mall Omaha NE 68102

FREEMAN, WILLIAM MURIEL, clinical psychologist; b. French Lick, Ind., Oct. 13, 1932; s. William Stanford and Amanda Victoria (Fentress) F.; student U. Innsbruck (Austria), 1954-58; Ph.D. in Clin. Psychology, U. Louisville, 1972; m. Mary Colleen Welch, Dec. 27, 1968; children—Mary Michelle, Steven William. Clin. dir. Ky. Dept. Child Welfare Reception Center, Louisville, 1972-74, River Region Community Mental Health Center, 1974-76, Seven Counties Community Mental Health Center, 1976-78; pvt. practice clin. psychology Asso. Psychol. Services, Louisville, 1978—; cons. child protection bd. Floyd County Welfare, Ind. Mem. Am. Psychol. Assn., Ky. Psychol. Assn., Ind. Psychol. Assn., Assn. for Advancement of Psychology, Am. Soc. Clin. Hypnosis, Acad. of Psychosomatic Med. Republican. Roman Catholic. Contbr. articles to profl. publs. Office: Suite 1138 Medical Arts 1169 Eastern Pkwy Louisville KY 40217

FREERS, STEVEN GEORGE, lawyer; b. Indpls., Jan. 8, 1949; s. Howard P. and Eleanor (Reeder) F.; m. Christine Helena Lamos, Sept. 5, 1970; 3 children. J.D., Wayne State U., 1974. Bar: Mich. 1974. Ptnr. Binkowski & Freers, Warren, Mich., 1979—. Lodge: Elks (v.p. bldg. corp.) Home: 32749 Rugby Warren MI 48093 Office: Binkowski & Freers 28111 Hoover Ste 5A Warren MI 48093

FREESE, PAMELA COUILLARD, marketing communications executive; b. Bethleham, Pa., Feb. 22, 1951; d. Bruce Richard and Virginia Theresa (Angelucci) Couillard; m. Robert Paul Freese, Aug. 12, 1978; children—Benjamin Couillard, Stephanie Couillard. B.S., Kutztown State U., 1973; M.S., U. Rochester, 1977. Cert. art tchr., N.Y. Art tchr. Wilson Sch. Dist., Easton, Pa., 1973-74; artist, maxillofacial lab. technician Roswell Park Meml. Inst., Buffalo, 1974-76; head art, photography dept. SUNY-Batavia, 1978-80; mktg. communications exec. Orthopedic Products div. 3M Co., St. Paul, 1980—. Paraprofl. Washington County Sexual Assault Services, Minn., 1982—. Avocations: skiing; waterskiing; swimming; camping. Office: 3M Orthopedic Products Div 3M Ctr 225-5S-05 Saint Paul MN 55144

FREESE, ROBERTA GAIL, pharmaceutical service representative, pharmacist; b. Sedro Woolley, Wash., Sept. 6, 1941; d. Harold L. and Clara Belle (Pressentin) Dods; m. Robert Arthur Freese, July 17, 1962; children—Pamela, Jennifer, Stephanie. B.S. in Pharmacy, Wash. State U., 1966; student U. Tex., 1963-64. Registered pharmacist, Minn. Staff pharmacist Atkinsons, Jacksonville, Fla., 1966-68, Snyder Drug, Mpls., 1968-70, Danielson Med. Arts, Mpls., 1970-78; pharmacist, asst. mgr. Loop Pharmacy, Mpls., 1978-83; prof. service rep. Schering Labs., Mpls., 1983—. Mem. Am. Pharm. Assn., Schering Diamond 110 Club (pres. 1983; highest honor 1983), Minn. State Pharm. Assn., Lamba Kappa Sigma. Avocations: skiing, bridge, sailing.

FREESEN, O(SCAR) ROBERT, JR., construction executive; b. Naples, Ill., Sept. 2, 1925; s. Oscar Robert and Opal Mae (Haus) F.; m. Alice Jane Albright, Dec. 12, 1948; children—Oscar Robert III, Kerry Stuart, Matthew Sinclair, Guy Anthony. Student pub. schs., Bluffs, Ill. Ptnr. Freesen Bros., Inc., Bluffs, Ill., 1946-57, pres., 1957-72; ptnr. Heavy Equipment Hauling Co., Bluffs, 1965-70; chmn. bd. Freesen, Inc., Bluffs, 1972—; owner, operator live-stock and grain farms, 1962—; dir. Bank of Bluffs. Trustee McMurray Coll., Jacksonville, Ill., Grace United Methodist Ch., Jacksonville; bd. dirs. Salvation Army, Jacksonville, YMCA, Jacksonville, United Way Morgan County, Sch. Dist. 117, Jacksonville; exec. bd. Boy Scouts Am. Served with U.S. Army, 1944-45. Decorated Bronze Star (3), Purple Heart; recipient Silver Beaver award Boy Scouts Am., 1975; Service to Mankind award Sertoma Club, 1978; named Layman of Yr., Jacksonville YMCA 1977. Mem. Associated Gen. Contractors Ill., Jacksonville C. of C., Am. Legion. Republican. Lodges: Jacksonville Lions, Masons. Office: PO Box 277 Pearl St Bluffs IL 62621

FREHE, DONALD JOSEPH, broadcasting company executive; b. Chgo., Jan. 31, 1945; s. Daniel Joseph and Mary Alice (Tammone) F.; student Wright Jr. Coll.; m. Barbara Jean Ianello, Sept. 18, 1965; 1 son, Joseph James. Accountant, Sahara Coal Co., Chgo., 1964-67; Zenith Radio-Rauland Div., Melrose Park, Ill., 1967-68; v.p., treas. Bing Crosby Productions, Chgo., 1968-71; pres. Vipro Program Services, Chgo., 1971-83; v.p. Orion Pictures, Chgo., 1983—. Mem. River Grove and Elmwood Park (Ill.) Youth Commns., 1971—. Mem. Nat. Acad. TV Arts and Scis., Nat. Assn. TV Program Execs. Roman Catholic. Office: Orion Pictures 625 N Michigan Ave Chicago IL 60611

FREIBERG, RICHARD ALBERT, orthopaedic surgeon; b. Cin., Feb. 12, 1932; s. Joseph Albert and Louise R. (Rothenberg) F.; m. Betsy Ann Landau, June 20, 1958; children—Andrew, James Robert. A.B., Harvard U., 1953, M.D., 1957. Diplomate Am. Bd. Orthopaedic Surgery. Practice orthopaedic surgery Orthopaedic Offices, Inc., Cin., 1962—; dir. Orthopaedic Surgery Jewish Hosp., Cin., 1984—; assoc. clin. prof. U. Cin. Coll. Medicine, 1968—, asst. clin. prof. family medicine, Cin., 1980—. Contbr. articles to profl. jours. Mem. Am. Acad. Orthopaedic Surgeons, Forum Orthopaedic Club, Am. Rheumatism Soc., Arthritis Found. (bd. govs. Cin. chpt.), Clin. Orthopaedic Soc. Home: 7154 Knoll Rd Cincinnati OH 45237 Office: Orthopaedic Offices Inc 3120 Burnet Ave Cincinnati OH 45229

FREIBERGER, JAMES EVERETT, hospital administrator; b. Detroit, Oct. 26, 1928; s. Karl Franklin and Ann N. (Keseros) F.; children—Vicki L. Sizemore, James C., Tracy Alan. Student, Ohio State U., 1952-53, Burroughs Sch. of Data Processing, 1966-67. Registered ofcl. for football, baseball, Ohio High Sch. Athletic Assn., Nat. Collegiate Athletic Assn., Nat. Baseball Congress; With Mansfield Tire & Rubber Co. (Ohio), 1952-80, mgr. data processing ops., 1980; bus. office dir. Ashland Samaritan Hosp. (Ohio), 1981—. Sustaining mem. Republican Nat. Com. Served with USN, 1948-52. Mem. Am. Legion. Home: 682 Katherine Ave Apt A Ashland OH 44805 Office: Samaritan Hosp 1025 Center St Ashland OH 44805

FREIBURGER, KENNETH JOSEPH, JR., tool and manufacturing company executive; b. Kendallville, Ind., July 15, 1932; s. Kenneth Joseph and Ruth Harriet (Kraner) F.; m. Jane Corrine McKean, Dec. 11, 1971; children—K. Bruce, K. Bradley, Kevin J. (dec.). Student Purdue U., 1951-53, Ind. U.-Ft. Wayne, 1960-64. Ptnr., Acme Tool Co., 1953-59; process engr. Flint and Walling, 1959-62; engr. Kendick Mfg., 1962-64; pres., owner Noble Tool & Die, Inc., Kendallville, 1964-70, Kevco Tool & Mfg., Inc., Kendallville, 1971—. Mem. Kendallville C. of C., Soc. Mfg. Engrs. (cert. robotics engr.). Democrat. Methodist. Lodges: Elks, Moose. Patentee in field. Office: State Rd 3 North Kendallville IN 46755

FREIDHEIM, CYRUS F., JR., management consultant; b. Chgo., June 14, 1935; s. Cyrus F. and Eleanor Freidheim; B.S.Ch.E., U. Notre Dame, 1957; M.S.I.A., Carnegie Mellon U., 1963; m. Marguerite VandenBosch; children—Marguerite Lynn, Stephen Cyrus, Scott Jn. Plant mgr. Union Carbide Corp., Whiting, Ind., 1961; cons. Price Waterhouse, Chgo., 1962; fin. analyst Ford Motor Co., Dearborn, Mich., 1963-66; asso. Booz, Allen & Hamilton, Chgo., 1966-69, v.p., 1969-71, v.p. and mng. dir. S.Am., Sao Paulo, Brazil, 1971-74, exec. v.p. internat., Paris, 1974-79, pres. internat., N.Y.C., 1979-80, sr. v.p. and mng. dir., Chgo., 1980—, dir., 1976—. Trustee, Rush-Presbyn.-St. Luke's Med. Center, 1981—; mem. vis. com. Grad. Sch. Bus., U. Chgo., 1981—, also univ. vis. com. on public policy, 1982—; assoc. Northwestern U., 1981—; trustee Chgo. Symphony Orch., St. Ignatius Coll. Prep.; bd. dirs. Chgo. Central Area Com., Northwestern Library Council. Served as officer USN, 1957-61. Mem. Chgo. Council Fgn. Relations (bd. dirs.), Mid-Am. Com. Clubs: Chicago; Mid Day, Econ., Comml. (Chgo.); Stanwich (Greenwich, Conn.); Metropolitan (N.Y.C.). Home: 45 Indian Hill Rd Winnetka IL 60093 Office: Three First National Plaza Chicago IL 60602

FREIMUTH, MARC WILLIAM, lawyer; b. Duluth, Minn., Sept. 23, 1946; s. Edgar and Marcia (Zuckerman) F.; m. Sharon Rae Sager, Feb. 7, 1946; children—Ladeene Asher, Kyle Gregory, Joel Todd. B.A., U. Minn., 1968, J.D., 1971. Bar: Ohio, 1971. Assoc. Squire, Sanders, Dempsey, Cleve., 1971-78; sr. v.p., gen. counsel, sec. Ohio Savs. Fin. Corp., Cleve., 1978—; dir., sec. Superior Flux & Mfg. Co., Cleve., 1979—, Solid Sound Inc., Chgo., 1982—; dir. Sager Corp., Chgo., 1980—. Trustee Bur. Jewish Edn., Cleve., 1980—; pres., trustee The Agnon Sch., Cleve., 1984; trustee Park Synagogue, 1984—; chmn. allocations panel United Way, Cleve., 1984; mem. Greater Cleve. Growth Assn., Leadership Cleve., 1984. Mem. ABA, Ohio State Bar Assn., Greater Cleve. Bar Assn. Avocations: golf, tennis, softball. Office: Ohio Savs Fin Corp 1801 E 9th St Cleveland OH 44114

FREISE, EARL JEROME, university administrator, mechanical engineering educator; b. Chgo., Dec. 30, 1935; s. Otto H. and Mary A. (Hoffman) F.; m. Lenore A. Serpico, Dec. 27, 1959; children—Christopher E., Timothy P., Nora A., Lawrence M. B.S. in Metall. Engring., Ill. Inst. Tech., 1958; M.S. in Materials Sci., Northwestern U., 1959; Ph.D. in Metallurgy, U. Cambridge, Eng., 1962. From asst. prof. to assoc. prof. Northwestern U., Evanston, Ill., 1962-77; dir. research office, prof. mech. engring. U. N.D., Grand Forks, 1977-82; asst. vice chancellor research, prof. mech. engring. U. Nebr., Lincoln, 1982—. Contbr. articles to profl. jours. Fulbright fellow, 1959-61; recipient award for Excellence in Engring. Edn., Western Electric Co., 1971. Mem. Am. Soc. Metals (v.p., pres. Chgo. chpt. 1971-72), AIME, Am. Soc. Engring. Edn. (sec.-treas. Ill.-Ind. sect. 1963-64, 73-74), Soc. Univ. Patent Adminstrs., Nat. Council Univ. Research Adminstrs. (pres. 1984-85), Soc. Research Adminstrs. Office: U Nebr 414 Adminstrn Bldg Lincoln NE 68588

FREITAG, PHILIP CONLAN, optometrist; b. Sioux Falls, S.D., Jan. 22, 1924; s. Edward William and Mary Helena (Conlan) F.; m. Rosemary Louise Glennon, Nov. 12, 1949; children—Patricia, Terri, Virginia, William. Student Mont. State Coll., 1943; B.S., Coll. St. Thomas, 1946; O.D., No. Ill. Coll. of Optometry, 1949. Diplomate S.D. Bd. of Examiners in Optometry, 1950. Gen. practice optometry, Madison, S.D., 1951—. Chmn. Madison Housing and Redevel. Commn., 1968-82. Served with U.S. Army, 1943-46, ETO. Decorated Bronze Star; recipient HUD Regional Adminstr.'s Spl. Achievement award, 1983. Mem. S.D. Optometric Soc. (pres. 1983), S.D. Vol. Optometric Service to Humanity (pres. 1984—), North Central States Optometric Congress (bd. dirs. 1982-83), Madison C. of C. (Outstanding Service award 1970). Republican. Roman Catholic. Lodges: Kiwanis (pres. 1956), K.C. (Grand Knight 1957, S.D. State Dist. dep. 1959), Elks (Exaulted Ruler 1978, trustee 1979-82). Home: Route 1 Box 86 J Wentworth SD 57075 Office: Madison Vision Clinic PO Box A Madison SD 27042

FREITAS, JOHN EUGENE, nuclear medicine physician, internist; b. Detroit, June 1, 1945; s. Eugene Leo and Mary Elaine (Moriarty) F.; m. Mary Elizabeth Marra, June 27, 1970; children—Christopher, David. B.S., U. Notre Dame, 1967; M.D., U. Mich., 1971. Diplomate Am. Bd. Internal Medicine, Am. Bd. Nuclear Medicine. Intern then resident University Hosps., Ann Arbor, Mich., 1971-74; staff physician William Beaumont Hosp., Royal Oak, Mich., 1978—; pres. Mich. Coll. Nuclear Medicine Physicians, Royal Oak, 1983-84; clin. assoc. prof. U. Mich. Med. Sch., Ann Arbor, 1979—, Wayne State U. Med. Sch., Detroit, 1982—. Contbr. articles to profl. jours. Mem. Commn. Edn. St. Thomas Sch., Ann Arbor, 1982—; Served to lt. comdr. USNR, 1974-76. Univ. Hosps. fellow, 1976-78. Fellow ACP; mem. Soc. Nuclear Medicine, AMA, Am. Coll. Nuclear Physicians, Am. Thyroid Assn.; Sigma Xi, Alpha Omega Alpha, Alpha Epsilon Delta. Republican. Roman Catholic. Club: Notre Dame (bd. dirs. 1982—). Lodge: KC (grand knight 1983-85). Advocations: aviation sports. Home: 1459 Burgundy Ann Arbor MI 48105 Office: 3601 W 13 Mile Rd Royal Oak MI 48072

FRELAND, JAMES ISAAC, police chief; b. Cin., Mar. 19, 1950; s. Isaac T. and Martha L. (Blackwell) F.; m. Marianne Snider, Jan. 1977; children—Ann Marie, James Adam. Cert. FBI Nat. Acad., 1982; B.A. summa cum laude, Wilmington Coll., 1983; postgrad., Xavier U., 1983—. Police officer Woodlawn Police, Ohio, 1973-74, Springdale Police, Ohio, 1974-77, Police sgt., 1977-84, col., chief police, 1984—; adj. faculty mem. Wilmington Coll., Ohio, 1983. Served to sgt. USMC, 1969-71. Mem. FBI, Ohio Chief's Assn., Order of Ky. Cols. Baptist. Avocation: fitness. Office: Springdale Police Dept 12105 Lawnview Ave Springdale OH 45246

FRENCH, MARCUS EMMETT, mfg. co. exec.; b. Worcester, Mass., Jan. 21, 1929; s. Emmett A. and Marion A. (Brady) F.; B.S. in Chemistry, Holy Cross Coll., 1952, M.S. in Chemistry, 1953; postgrad. exec. devel. program Dartmouth Coll.; m. Mary M. Nugent, Sept. 25, 1954; children—Carol E. French Boyle, Margaret A., Marci M. Sect. leader Allied Chem. Corp., Buffalo, 1953-59; devel. chemist Hewitt Robbins Corp., Franklin, N.J., 1959-60; v.p. Gen. Foam div. Tenneco Chems., Inc., Hazleton, Pa., 1960-70; pres. Janesville Products unit AMCA Internat. Corp., Norwalk, Ohio, 1970—; dir. TWU Realty Co. Trustee, Textile Workers Pension Plan, Firelands Coll., Huron, Ohio. Served with U.S. Army, 1946-48. Mem. ASTM, Soc. Automotive Engrs., Soc. Plastics Engrs., Detroit Engring. Soc., Norwalk C. of C. (dir.). Clubs: K.C., Plumbrook Country; Renaissance (Detroit). Patentee on methods of urethane foam in U.S. and fgn. countries. Home: 6 Hillcrest Ct Milan OH 44846 Office: PO Box 349 Norwalk OH 44857

FRENCH, MARY LOU, optometrist; b. Evergreen Park, Ill., Sept. 11, 1950; d. Richard X. and Joan Marie (Landuyt) F.; m. Eric A. Lager, Oct. 15, 1977; children—Eric Andrew, Elizabeth Anne. Student, Loyola U., Chgo., 1968-73; B.S., Ill. Coll. of Optometry, 1975, O.D., 1977. Practice optometry, Olympia Fields, Ill., 1977-83, Orland Park, Ill., 1979—; vision cons. Tames, Inc., South Holland, Ill., 1979—. Trustee Palos Park Library Bd., Ill., 1978; bd. dirs. LaRabida Children's Hosp. Women's Bd., Chgo., 1983. Fellow Am. Acad. Optometry; mem. Ill. Optometric Assn., Am. Optometric Assn., AAUW (sec. Palos-Orland chpt. 1980-81), PEO. Avocations: golf; cross-country skiing; swimming. Office: 9031 W 151 St Orland Park IL 60462

FRENCH, ROBERT LEE, mgmt. cons.; b. Middletown, Mo., Dec. 18, 1929; s. Lee and Pearl Marie F.; B.S., U. Mo., 1951, M.S. in Bus. Adminstrn., 1951; m. Barbara Gail Burks, Sept. 17, 1950; children—Carol Jean, Cynthia Ann, James Robert, John Richard. Sr. indsl. engr. Chrysler Corp., Detroit, 1951-60; chief mng. engr. Boats div. Brunswick Corp., Warsaw, Ind., 1960-63; chief indsl. engr. Arnold Engring. div. Allegheny-Ludlum, Marengo, Ill., 1963-66; v.p., dir. Mfg. Household div. Hamilton-Cosco Inc., Columbus, Ind., 1966-70; v.p., gen. mgr. Buckeye Plastics div. Buckeye Internat., Columbus, Ohio, 1970-72; v.p., gen. mgr. Buckeye Ware Inc., Regal Ware Inc., Wooster, Ohio, 1972-74; pres. R.L. French & Co., Inc., South Bend, Ind., 1974—; chmn., chief exec. officer On-Line Data Inc., Mishawaka, Ind.; pres. Computerized Mfg. Mgmt. Corp., Medina, Ohio. Pres. Bartholomew County (Ind.) chpt. ARC, 1969. Found. for Youth, Wooster, Ohio, 1973. Served with USAF, 1950-51. Mem. Assn. Mgmt. Cons., Soc. Profl. Mgmt. Cons. Republican. Mem. Christian Ch. (Disciples of Christ). Home and Office: 1240 E Irvington St South Bend IN 46614

FRENGS, PHILIP JOSEPH, management company executive; b. San Mateo, Calif., June 14, 1951; s. Adolph Joseph and Margaret Susan (O'Donnell) F.; m. Mimi Scofield, Aug. 25, 1975; children—Kathryn Elizabeth, Meredith Jean. B.S. in Econs., UCLA, 1973. Sales rep. 3-M Co., Los Angeles, 1974-78; with Xerox Reprodn. Ctr., 1978-83, sales rep., Los Angeles, 1978-79, sales mgr., Dallas, 1979-81, ctr. mgr., Cleve., 1981-83; v.p. Pandick Facilities Mgmt., Inc., Los Angeles, 1983—. Named to Century Club, 3-M Co., 1977; Xerox Pres.'s Club, 1978, 79, Par Club, 1980, 81. Mem. Gyro Internat., Theta Delta Chi. Democrat. Roman Catholic. Club: Mayfield Country (Cleve.). Office: Pandick Facilities Mgmt Inc 444 S Flower St Los Angeles CA 90017

FRENKEL, NIZA BLUMA, virology educator; b. Tel-Aviv, Israel, June 3, 1947; came to U.S., 1968, naturalized, 1985; d. Haim and Shoshana Yair; m. Jacob Aaron Frenkel, Sept. 3, 1968; children—Orli Miriam, Tahl Ida. M.A., U. Chgo., 1970, Ph.D., 1972. Postdoctoral fellow Weizmann Inst., Rehovot, Israel, 1972-73; research assoc. U. Chgo., 1973-74, asst. prof., 1974-80, assoc. prof. molecular genetics and cell biology, 1981—. NSF grantee, 1979—; NIH grantee, 1975—. Mem. Am. Soc. Virology, Am. Soc. Microbiology. Office: U Chgo 910 E 58th St Chicago IL 60637

FRENZEL, BILL, congressman; b. St. Paul, July 31, 1928; s. Paul William and Paula (Schlegel) F.; B.A., Dartmouth Coll., 1950, M.B.A., 1951; m. Ruth Purdy, June 9, 1951; children—Deborah Anne, Pamela Ruth, Melissa Lee. With Mpls. Terminal Warehouse Co., 1954-69, mgr., 1957-60, pres., dir., 1960-69; mem. Minn. Legislature, 1962-70; mem. 92d-99th congresses from 3d Minn. Dist. Former mem. adv. council Minn. Dept. Employment Security. Served with USNR, 1951-54; Korea. Mem. Am. Legion, C. of C., Citizens League. Home: Golden Valley MN Office: 1026 Longworth House Office Bldg Washington DC 20515

FRERICKS, THOMAS ALFRED, lawyer; b. Marion, Ohio, Dec. 13, 1945; s. Theodore Paul and Dorothy Jane (Fetter) F.; m. Patricia Margaret Krzanowski, Nov. 6, 1971; children—Jeffrey, Joseph, Matthew. B.A., U. Notre Dame, 1968; J.D., Ohio State U., 1971. Bar: Ohio 1971, U.S. Dist. Ct. (no. dist.) Ohio 1977. Ptnr. Frericks & Howard Law Office, Marion, Ohio, 1971—. Articles editor Ohio State Law Jour., 1970-71. Bd. dirs. Palace Cultural Arts Assn., Marion, 1975—, pres., 1981-82; bd. dirs. Salvation Army Adv. Bd., Marion, 1977—; mem. Ohio Gov.'s Adv. Bd., Legal Services Corp., 1979-81. Mem. Marion County Bar Assn. (pres. 1984), Ohio State Bar Assn. (bd. govs. labor law sect. 1983—). Republican. Roman Catholic. Avocations: gardening, photography, sailing. Home: 1082 Hathaway Ln Marion OH 43302 Office: 152 E Center St Marion OH 43302

FRERICKS, TIMOTHY MATTHEW, lawyer; b. Marion, Ohio, June 5, 1949; s. Theodore Paul and Dorothy Jane (Fetter) F.; B.A., Notre Dame U., 1971; J.D., Ohio No. U., 1974. Bar: Ohio 1974. Ptnr. Frericks and Howard, Marion, 1974—. Contbr. articles to local newspaper. Bd. dirs. Marion Catholic High Sch., 1982—, Columbus Diocesan Schs., 1982—, Marion Cadets Drum and Bugle Corps, 1978—; pres. Marion County Republican Club, 1982; Rep. precinct capt., 1980—; founder Citizens for Responsible Govt., Marion, 1983—. Mem. Marion County Bar Assn. Lodges: Kiwanis (v.p. 1981), Optimists (chmn. community service 1975-82), K.C. Home: 2916 Neidhart Rd Marion OH 43302 Office: Frericks & Howard 152 E Center Marion OH 43302

FREUDENBERGER, JOHN EDWARD, manufacturing company executive; b. Chgo., Apr. 23, 1941; s. Joseph Edward and Mildred (Neilsen) F.; m. Terri Joy Weiland, Sept. 8, 1962; children—Tifinni J. (dec.), Tricia J., John Jr., Justin. B.S. in Mech. Engring., So. Ill. U., 1966. Process engr. Ford Motor Co., Indpls., 1966-68, design engr., Dearborn, Mich., 1968-70; chief engr. Powers and Sons, Montpelier, Ohio, 1970-80; pres., owner Indsl. Steering Products, Inc., Bryan, Ohio, 1980—, R.J. Flohr Co., 1985—. Pres., co-founder Nat. Reye's Syndrome Found., Bryan, 1974—. Served with USAR, 1963-73. Mem. Soc. Automobile Engrs., ASME, Methodist. Club: Rotary. Home: 924 Mayer St Bryan OH 43506 Office: 426 N Lewiw Bryan OH 43506

FREW, JAMES E., container manufacturing company executive. Pres., chief operating officer, dir. Stoned Container Corp., Chgo. Office: Rubbermaid Inc 1147 Akron Rd Wooster Stone Container Corp 360 N Michigan Ave Chicago IL 60601*

FREY, DONALD NELSON, manufacturing executive, engineer; b. St. Louis, Mar. 13, 1923; s. Muir Luken and Margaret Bryden (Nelson) F.; student Mich. State Coll., 1940-42; B.S., U. Mich., 1947, Ph.D., 1950, D.Sc. (hon.), 1965; D.Sc. (hon.), U. Mo., Rolla, 1966; children by previous marriage, Donald Nelson, Judith Kingsley, Margaret Bente, Catherine, Christopher, Elizabeth; m. 2d, Mary Elizabeth Cameron, June 30, 1971. Instr. metall. engring. U. Mich., 1949-50, asst. prof. chem. and metall. engring., 1950-51; research engr. Babcock & Wilcox Tube Co., Beaver Falls, Pa., 1951; various research positions Ford Motor Co., 1951-57, various engring. positions Ford div., 1958-61, product planning mgr., 1961-62, asst. gen. mgr. Ford div., 1962-65, gen. mgr., 1965-68, co. v.p., 1965-67, v.p. for product devel., 1967-68; pres. Gen. Cable Corp., N.Y.C., 1968-71; chmn. bd. Bell & Howell Co., Chgo., 1971—, pres., from 1973, also chief exec. officer; dir. Babcock & Wilcox Co., Cin. Milacron Inc., Spring Mills, Inc. Mem. devel. council U. Mich., from 1963; trustee Carnegie Found. for Advancement Teaching; bd. dirs. Childrens Meml. Hosp., Chgo., Lyric Opera, Chgo., Nat. Diabetes Assn. Served with AUS, 1943-46. Named Young Engr. of Yr., Engring. Soc. Detroit, 1953; recipient Russell Springer award Soc. Automotive Engrs., 1956; named Outstanding Alumni, Coll. Engring., U. Mich., 1957; Outstanding Young Man of Yr., Detroit Jr. Bd. Commerce, 1958. Mem. AIME (chmn. Detroit 1954; chmn., editor Nat Symposium on Sheet Steels 1956), Am. Soc. Metals, Nat. Acad. Engring. (mem. council 1972), ASME, Soc. Automotive Engrs. (vice chmn. Detroit 1958), Detroit Engring. Soc. (dir. from 1962), Elec. Mfrs. Club, N.Y. Council on Fgn. Relations, Sigma Xi, Phi Kappa Phi, Tau Beta Pi, Phi Delta Theta. Clubs: Chicago, Saddle and Cycle, Tavern (Chgo.). Office: Bell & Howell Corp 5215 Old Orchard Rd Skokie IL 60077*

FREY, GLENDA JOYCE, educator; b. Indpls., June 29, 1947; d. Oscar M. and Mary D. Butcher; m. Garry L. Frey, June 25, 1966; children—Laura Catherine, Mary Elizabeth. B.A., Purdue U., 1969; M.S., Ind. U., 1972; Adminstrv. Cert., Butler U., 1978. With Frankfort (Ind.) Sch. Bd., now prin. South Side Elem. Sch. Mem. Ind. Assn. Elem. Sch. Prins., Nat. Assn. Elem. Sch. Prins., Ind. Council Talented and Gifted Children, Ind. Council Internat. Reading Assn., Kappa Delta Pi, Kappa Kappa Kappa. Mem. United Ch. of Christ. Clubs: Frankfort Country Purdue of Clinton County (bd. dirs.). Home: RR4 Box 193 Frankfort IN 46041 Office: South Side Elementary School 1007 Alhambra Ave Frankfort IN 46041

FREY, H. GARRETT, stock broker; b. Cin., Dec. 2, 1938; s. John H. and Mary G. (Grever) F.; student U. Detroit, 1956-57, U. Cin., 1957-59, U. Miami, 1960-61; m. Mary Knollman, July 23, 1960; children—John, Robert, Meg,

Amy, Brad, Julie. Salesman, Verkamp Corp., Cin., 1958-60, Formica Corp., Cin., Miami, Fla., and Hartford, Conn., 1960-62; stockbroker Westheimer & Hayden Stone, Cin., 1962-64; stockbroker Harrison & Co., 1964-66, gen. partner, 1966-73, mng. partner, 1972-77; v.p. Bache Halsey Stuart Shields Inc., Cin., 1977-79; chmn. bd. Queen City Securities Corp., Cin., 1979—; dir. Broadcast Mgmt. Corp. Mem. investment com. Sisters of Charity, Cin., 1970; trustee, treas. St. Joseph Cemetery, Cin.; pres. Springer Ednl. Found.; v.p. Cath. Social Services of SW Ohio. Served with AUS, 1959. Named Big Brother of the Year, 1968. Mem. Cin. (v.p. 1970-72, trustee 1979—), N.Y., Am. stock exchanges, Purcell High Sch. Alumni (pres. 1972-73), Chgo. Bd. Options Exchange, Cath. Big Bros. Cin. (pres. 1966-67). Roman Catholic (council pres. 1971-72). Clubs: Cincinnati Stock and Bond (pres. 1969), Buckeye (pres. 1968-69). Home: 3660 Kroger Ave Cincinnati OH 45226 Office: 1500 Formica Bldg Cincinnati OH 45202

FREY, JOHN HATCHER, foundation executive; b. Holdrege, Nebr., Aug. 31, 1920; s. Omer Ray and Ida Elizabeth (Hatcher) F.; m. Marie Alda Furman, June 20, 1942; children—JoAnn Marie Hedges, Joy Theone Kinnan, John Omer, Jane Elizabeth Oliver. Student Lincoln Sch. Commerce, 1940-41; grad. Lincoln Aero. Inst., 1942; postgrad. Nebr. Wesleyan U., 1946-47. With First Nat. Bank, Grand Island, Nebr., 1942-43; owner, mgr. Credit Bur., Scottsbluff, Nebr., 1947-60; conf. treas., bus. mgr. Methodist Ch., Lincoln, Nebr., 1960-70; pres. Lincoln Found., 1970—; pres. L.L. Coryell and Son Park Founds.; mem. Scottsbluff City Council, 1958-59. Past pres. Scottsbluff County YMCA, Scottsbluff Kiwanis Camp; bd. dirs. Nebr. Wesleyan U., Lincoln Med. Edn. Found., Symphony Orchestra Assn.; bd. counsellors U. Nebr. Med. Ctr. Served with USAF, 1942-45. Recipient Disting. Service award YMCA, 1960; Disting. Service award Kiwanis Dist., 1970. Mem. Council Founds., Lincoln C. of C. (bd. dirs.). Methodist. Lodges: Masons, Shriner; Eastern Star. Home: Rt 9 7250 Revere Ln Lincoln NE 68506 Office: 215 Centennial Mall S Lincoln NE 68508

FREY, RONALD JAMES, motel executive; b. Minnesota City, Minn., Nov. 17, 1934; s. Felix Henry and Helen Marguerite (Strupp) F.; m. Melody Margaret Kafora, May 21, 1982; children by previous marriage—Susan, Michael; children—Laura, Karen. Student U. Ala., 1956-57, Upper Iowa U., 1974-75. Cert. property mgr. With Capri Motel, Niles, Ill., 1958-59; mgr. Niles Motel, 1959-61; gen. mgr. Adm. Oasis Motel, Morton Grove, Ill., 1961-65, MGM Motel, Morton Grove, 1965-73, Presdl. Inn, Lyons, Ill., 1973—. Mem. Morton Grove Aux. Police, 1963-67. Served to sgt., USAF, 1954-58. Mem. Motel Greeters of Am., Morton Grove C. of C. (pres. 1965-66, dir. 1963-65), Am. Legion, Frat. Order Police. Club: Yorktown Sertoma (dir.). Office: 3922 S Harlem Ave Lyons IL 60534

FREY, YVONNE AMAR, librarian; b. Chgo., Nov. 23, 1945; d. Wesley Francis and Yvonne Adele (Van Lent) Amar; m. Charles Jerry Frey, Sept. 20, 1975; 1 son, Benedict Francis Charles. A.B. with honors, Loyola U., Chgo., 1967; M.A., Johns Hopkins U., 1969; M.A. in Library Sci., Rosary Coll., 1981. Cert. tchr., Ill. Grad. asst. tchr. Johns Hopkins U., Balt., 1968-69; tchr. English, Montini High Sch., Lombard, Ill., 1970-73; instr. Western Ill. U., Macomb, 1973-78; antique dealer Frey's Tory Peddler, 1978—; instr. Bradley U. Peoria, Ill., 1981-82; supr. reference Ill. Valley Library System, Peoria, 1982-84; head children's room Peoria Pub. Library, 1985—. Contbr. articles and revs. to profl. jours. Woodrow Wilson scholar, 1968, Johns Hopkins U. scholar, 1968. Mem. ALA, Ill. Library Assn., Peoria Hist. Soc. (docent 1981—), Beta Phi Mu. Roman Catholic. Home: 6125 Fairlane Dr Peoria IL 61614

FRICK, JAMES WILLIAM, university administrator, consultant; b. New Bern, N.C., Aug. 5, 1924; s. Odo Aloysius and Mary Elizabeth (Cox) F.; m. Bonita Charlotte Torbert, Mar. 26, 1951 (div. 1984); children—Michael, Terence, Thomas, Theresa, Kathleen; m. Karen Ann Fogle, Oct. 13, 1984. B.S. in Commerce, U. Notre Dame, 1951, Ph.D. in Edn., 1973, LL.D., 1983. Project dir. U. Notre Dame, Ind., 1951-56, regional dir., 1956-61, exec. dir., 1961-65, v.p., 1965-83, asst. to pres., 1983—; pres. James W. Frick Assocs., Inc., South Bend, Ind., 1983—; chmn. exec. com. St. Joseph Bank and Trust, South Bend, 1968—; dir. W.R. Grace Co., Inc., N.Y.C., Magic Circle Energy Corp., Oklahoma City. Contbr. chpts. to books, articles to profl. jours. Chmn. United Way St. Joseph County, 1970, Project Future, South Bend, 1982; exec. com. Fin. Devel. Council Nat. Urban Coalition, Washington, 1975; nat. devel. council Assn. Am. Colls., Washington, 1978. Served to lt. (j.g.) USN, 1942-46. Recipient James E. Armstrong award U. Notre Dame, 1978; named Knight of Malta, Cath. Ch., 1981. Mem. Council Advancement and Support Edn. (pres. 1971-72, Ashmore award 1982), Assn. Governing Bds. (devel. adv. council 1982—), Phi Delta Kappa. Roman Catholic. Clubs: Marco Polo (N.Y.C.); Pith Helmet (Pomona, Calif.). Avocations: operas; symphonies; reading; historical novels; walking. Office: James W Frick Assocs Inc 888 St Joseph Bank Bldg South Bend IN 46601

FRIDLEY, RUSSELL WILLIAM, historian, association executive; b. Oelwein, Iowa, Mar. 21, 1928; s. Lloyd and Laura (Tift) F.; B.A., Grinnell Coll., 1950; M.A., Columbia, 1953; Litt.D., Concordia Coll., Moorhead, Minn., 1980; L.H.D., Gustavus Adolphus Coll., 1985; m. Metta Holtkamp, Feb. 26, 1954; children—Scott, Nancy, Jane, Susan, Elizabeth, Jennifer. Asst. dir. Minn. Hist. Soc., St. Paul, 1953-54, dir., 1954—; v.p. Grinnell (Iowa) Coll., 1966; state historic preservation officer, 1967—; vice chmn. Nat. Adv. Council on Hist. Preservation, 1967-70; mem. Nat. Mus. Act Adv. Council, 1976—; dir. div. edn. and pub. program Nat. Endowment for Humanities, 1968-69; chmn. Minn. Humanities Com., 1970—. Bd. dirs. Hubert H. Humphrey Inst. Public Affairs, 1979—, James J. Hill Reference Library, 1980—; trustee Charles A. Lindbergh Fund, 1981—, v.p., 1985—. Served with U.S. Army, 1946-48; PTO. Mem. Am. Assn. Mus. (dir. 1969-73), Am. Assn. State and Local History (pres. 1966-68), Nat. Conf. State Hist. Preservation Officers (v.p. 1977—). Author: Minnesota: A Students Guide to Localized History; The Uses of State and Local History; Historic Sites of North Dakota; Minnesota: A State That Works. Home: 740 Amber Dr Saint Paul MN 55126 Office: 690 Cedar St Saint Paul MN 55101

FRIEBERGER, M. DAVID, architect; b. St. Louis, June 5, 1945; s. Gordon August and Miriam Annette (Colvin) F.; m. Susan Marylyn Schwartz, Aug. 16, 1969; children—Sara Rachel, Lisa Joy. Student U. Mo., 1963-64, U. Mo.-St. Louis, 1965-68; student Washington U., St. Louis, 1964-65, B. Arch., 1985. Registered architect, Mo., Ill. Cub draftsman, team draftsman, then asst. project architect various firms, St. Louis, 1964-74; project architect HBE Corp., St. Louis, 1974—; land developer Olivette Exec. Office Park, 1981. Mem., past vice-chmn. Olivette Planning and Zoning Comm., Mo., 1977—. Jewish. Office: HBE Corp 11330 Olive St Rd Saint Louis MO 63141

FRIEDLAND, JOHN E., state senator; b. Elgin, Ill., Sept. 25, 1937; grad. Elgin Community Coll., Aurora Coll.; m. Marlene Diedrick; children—Linda, Renee, Susan. Former mem. Ill. Ho. of Reps.; now mem. Ill. Senate. Served with USN. Clubs: Masons, Shriners, Elks, Eagles. Address: Capitol Bldg Room 413 Springfield IL 62706

FRIEDMAN, BERNARD, pharmaceutical company executive, consultant; b. Rochester, N.Y., Apr. 2, 1926; s. Norman and Etta (Stein) F.; m. Katherine Lois Cohen, Dec. 24, 1950; children—Ellen Friedman Weinblatt, Tod Howard. Student U. Rochester, 1943-44, A.B. in Gen. Sci., 1948; student Stanford U., 1944-45; B.Sc. in Pharmacy, Ohio State U., 1951. Registered pharmacist, N.Y., Ohio. Pharmacist, v.p. Zell Prescription and Surg. Support Ctr., Columbus, Ohio, 1952-77, pres., chief exec. officer, 1977—, also dir.; cons. various nursing homes, Columbus. Past pres. Temple Israel Brotherhood; trustee Temple Israel; past pres. Jewish Community Blood Donor Council. Served with U.S. Army, 1944-46. Recipient Borden award, 1951. Fellow Am. Coll. Apothecaries; mem. Central Ohio Acad. Pharmacy, Ohio State Pharm. Assn., Am. Pharm. Assn., Nat. Assn. Retail Druggists. Clubs: Winding Hollow Country. Lodge: B'nai B'rith. Home: 168 S Merkle Rd Bexley OH 43209 Office: 226 E State St Columbus OH 43215

FRIEDMAN, CHARLES STUART, chem. co. exec.; b. Cleve., May 12, 1943; s. Armin Sam and Miriam F.; B.S., John Carroll U., 1965; M.S., Xavier U., 1969; m. Gail Rene Horwitz, July 23, 1967; 1 son, David. With Monsanto Research Corp., Miamisburg, Ohio, 1967-80, research group leader environ. analysis, Dayton, Ohio, 1980-82, environ. mgr., Miamisburg, Ohio, 1983—. Mem. Am. Chem. Soc. (chmn. public relations com. Dayton), DECUS Computer Soc., Internat. Platform Assn., Spectrum Assn. Gifted Edn. Contbr. articles to profl. jours. Office: Mound Rd Miamisburg OH 45342

FRIEDMAN, DEAN ALAN, advertising agency executive; b. Newark, Apr. 7, 1951; s. Daniel Alan and Rolla Joanne (Jacob) F.; B.G.S., U. Mich., 1973; student Lafayette Coll., 1971; m. Aviva Beth Sallen, Aug. 14, 1978; children—Ari Daniel, Joshua Sallen. Media buyer W. B. Doner & Co., Detroit, 1973-74, asst. account exec., Balt., 1974-75, account exec., Detroit, 1975-76, account mgr., 1976-78, account supr., 1979-81, v.p., account supr., 1981-84, v.p., mgmt. supr., 1984—, also dir.; ptnr. Oil Assocs. Investment Co., Southfield, Mich., 1973—, Proudfoot Farms, Birmingham, Mich., 1979—; dir. Lincoln Park One Hour Photography, Franklin Savs. & Loan Assn. Clubs: Adcraft of Detroit; Franklin Hills Country. Office: PO Box 422-A Detroit MI 48232

FRIEDMAN, JEROME, pharmacist; b. Columbus, Ohio, Oct. 10, 1943; s. Max Jack and Marjorie Lois (Grundstein) F.; m. Cheryl Ilene Lando, June 30, 1968; 1 child, Julie Beth. B.A. in Zoology, Ohio State U., 1965; B.S. in Pharmacy, 1969. Pharmacist, Ohio State U. Hosp., Columbus, 1969-72, Eastmoor Pharmacy, 1972-73; pharmacist, Westland Med. Pharmacy, Columbus, 1973—, pres., owner, 1979—. Trustee, Nat. Kidney Found Central Ohio, Columbus, 1981-84; bd. govs. Internat. B'nai B'rith Bowling Assn., 1982—, v.p., 1985—. Fellow Am. Coll. Apothecaries; mem. Nat. Assn. Retail Druggists, Ohio State Pharm. Assn., Central Ohio Acad. Pharmacy. Lodge: B'nai B'rith (pres. 1982-83). Avocations: Bowling, tennis, gardening, reading. Home: 345 S Cassingham Rd Columbus OH 43209 Office: Westland Med Pharmacy 455 Industrial Mile Rd Columbus OH 43228

FRIEDMAN, MARTIN, museum director; b. Pitts., Sept. 23, 1925; s. Israel and Etta (Louik) F.; student U. Pa., 1943-45; B.A., U. Wash., 1947; M.A., UCLA, 1949; postgrad. Columbia U., 1956-57, U. Minn., 1958-60; D.F.A. (hon.), Macalester Coll., Md. Inst. Coll. Art; L.H.D., Bates Coll. m. Mildred Shenberg, Sept. 3, 1949; children—Lise, Ceil, Zoe. Instr. art, curriculum cons. Los Angeles City Schs., 1949-56; instr. art UCLA, 1950-51; curator Walker Art Center, Mpls., 1958-60, dir., 1961—, organizer numerous exhbns.; commr. Am. Exhbn., Sao Paulo Bienal, 1963; co-chmn. mus. panel Nat. Endowment for Arts, 1977-78; mem. Nat. Collection of Fine Arts Commn., 1968-77; hon. mem. Nat. Mus. of Am. Art Commn.; mem. adv. com. Japan House Gallery Art; advisor Ind. Curators Inc.; mem. Nat. Council on Arts, 1978—. Author numerous exhbn. catalogues. Trustee Spring Hill Found., 1972-81; mem. adv. bd. on environ. planning Bur. Reclamation, 1956-68; mem. Commn. on Founds. and Pvt. Philanthropy, 1969-70. Served with USNR, 1943-46. Decorated officer des Arts et Lettres, French Ministry Culture, 1984; Bklyn. Mus. fellow, 1956-57; Belgian-Am. Ednl. Found. grantee, Brussels, 1957-58; fellow in Am. art U. Minn., 1959-60; Ford. Found. fellow, 1961-62; artist fellow Aspen Inst. for Humanistic Studies, 1980; Intellectual Interchange fellow, Japan, 1982. Mem. Assn. Art Mus. Dirs. (pres. 1978-79, trustee), Am. Fedn. Arts (trustee 1972-81), Coll. Art Assn. Am. (dir. 1973), Internat. Exhbns. Com., Clubs: Century Assn., Mpls. Office: Walker Art Center Vineland Pl Minneapolis MN 55403*

FRIEDMAN, NORMA SHEILA, social science and business educator; b. Springfield, Mass., May 17, 1954; d. Henry and Gladys May (Reiter) F. B.S., magna cum laude, U. Mass., 1976; M.Ed., Antioch U., 1978; postgrad. Columbia U. Exec. dir. Kulturama, Holyoke Arts Council (Mass.), 1976; asst. community rep. Mass. Office for Children, 1977; instr. continuing edn. div. U. Mass., Amherst, 1977-79; assoc. prof. social scis. and bus. Ind. Inst. Tech., Ft. Wayne, 1979—; assoc. faculty Ind. U., Purdue U.-Ft. Wayne, 1981—; cons. to social and cultural orgns. Recipient study award Project Adolescent Services, Ind. State U., 1979. Mem. Nat. Women's Studies Assn., Ind. Acad. Social Scis., Phi Kappa Phi, Alpha Lambda Delta. Democrat. Jewish. Office: 1600 E Washington St Suite 363A Fort Wayne IN 46803

FRIEDMAN, RICHARD CRAIG, lawyer, educator; b. St. Louis, Sept. 18, 1948; s. Maurice Louis and Hortense (Miller) F. B.A., Washington U., St. Louis, 1970, M.A., 1972, J.D., 1982. Bar: Mo. 1982, U.S. Dist. Ct. (ea. dist.) Mo. 1982, U.S. Ct. Appeals (8th cir.) 1982, Ill. 1983. Instr. U. Mo., St. Louis, 1973-78, acad. advisor, 1979; assoc. Goldstein & Price, St. Louis, 1982-83, Mann, Poger & Wittner, St. Louis, 1983—. Woodrow Wilson fellow, 1970. Mem. ABA, Ill. State Bar Assn., Bar. Assn. Met. St. Louis, Mo. Bar, Am. Philos. Assn., Phi Beta Kappa. Democrat. Jewish. Home: 942 Guelbreth Ln 304 Saint Louis MO 63141 Office: Mann Poger & Wittner PC 7711 Carondelet Suite 401 Saint Louis MO 63105

FRIEDRICH, CHARLES WILLIAM, industrial relations executive; b. Elgin, Ill., Aug. 30, 1943; s. Charles Kenneth and Veronica Elizabeth (Sharpe) F.; B.A., Parsons Coll., 1967; student Loras Coll., 1961-63; m. Janet Lee West, June 20, 1970; children—Joan Elizabeth, Charles Kenneth II. Salesman, Bendix Corp., South Bend, Ind., 1967; safety dir., asst. personnel mgr. Nat. Castings div. Midland Ross, Cicero, Ill., 1968-69; personnel mgr. Continental Tube Co. div. Hofmann Industries, Bellwood, Ill., 1969, asst. indsl. relations mgr., 1970, Midwest dir. indsl. relations Hofmann Industries, 1971-73; dir. indsl. relations, gen. mgr. Lemont Shipbuilding and Repair Co. (Ill.), 1973-75; indsl. relations exec. Modern Mgmt. Methods, Inc., Deerfield, Ill., 1975-77; pres. Standard Cons. Services Co., Inc., Hinsdale, Ill., 1977-83; dir. G.F. Marchant Co., Chgo., T. & H. Service Co., Oak Park, Ill. Pres., Burr Ridge (Ill.) Park Dist. Bd.; asst. scoutmaster Boy Scouts Am., 1982—; treas. Palisades Sch. Dist. Mem. Packard Automobile Classics Club (regent), Alpha Phi Omega. Club: K.C. (grand knight Mayslake council). Home: 10S431 Glenn Dr Burr Ridge IL 60521 Office: 15 W 700 Frontage Rd Suite 130 Hinsdale IL 60521

FRIEDRICH, MARILYN DALE, educator; b. Chgo., June 12, 1932; d. Arnold Alfred and Ruth Maria Johnson; m. Jerome William Friedrich, Feb. 14, 1952 (div.); children—Rochelle, Denise, Steven. Student Purdue U., 1951-52; B.A.E., U. Nev., 1955; postgrad. Ind. U., 1958-60, 82-84; M.A.E., Ball State U., 1962. Life cert. tchr., Ind. Recreation dir. Reno City Parks (Nev.), summer 1954; secondary tchr. Kokomo High Sch. (Ind.), 1956-65, cheerleader, block sponsor, 1956-65, 84—, Girls' Athletic Assn. sponsor, 1956-61, curriculum chmn., writer, 1966; recreation dir. Kokomo City Parks (Ind.), summers 1960-62; secondary tchr. Haworth High Sch., Kokomo, Ind., 1968-84, cheerleader, block sponsor, 1968-73, girls' tennis coach, 1975-84, swim meet dir., 1973-82; recreation dir. Crystal Beach Cottagers' Assn., Frankfort, Mich., summers 1963-82; dir., writer synchronized swim shows Internat. Aquatic Art Festival, 1959-68; mem. computer core com. Kokomo-Center Schs., 1983—. Mem. NEA, Ind. State Teachers' Assn., Kokomo Tchrs. Assn., Internat. Order Foresters, Delta Kappa Gamma, Psi Iota Xi. Mem. Disciples of Christ Ch. Club: Interracial. Office: Kokomo High Sch Downtown Campus 303 E Superior Kokomo IN 46901

FRIEDRICHS, NIELS GEORG, association executive; b. Luebeck, West Germany, Dec. 22, 1929; s. Peter H. and Gertrud (Hahn) F.; came to U.S., 1958; ed. Katharineum, Luebeck, 1949; m. Ilona Grund, Dec. 18, 1957; children—Kirsten, Dirk. Printer, Flint, Mich., 1959-61; salesman Lufthansa Airlines, Chgo., 1961-63; mng. dir. German Am. C. of C., Chgo., 1963—; lectr. in field. Vice chmn. Fgn. Trade Commrs. Group, Chgo. Recipient Order of Merit (Fed. Republic Germany), 1978. Mem. Internat. Bus. Council Midam., Chgo. Assn. Commerce and Industry, Assn. German Fgn. Chamber Mgrs. (Bonn, Germany), Chgo. Fgn. Trade Commn. Group. Lutheran. Clubs: Chgo. Athletic Assn., Execs., Lake Point Tower (Chgo.). Home: 515 Linden Ave Wilmette IL 60091 Office: 104 S Michigan Ave Suite 604 Chicago IL 60603

FRIEND, EDITH HAYWARD, practical nurse; b. Dadeville, Mo., Dec. 30, 1924; s. Homer Elsie and Cliffe Delina (Hawkins) Hayward; b. Trueman Eugene Friend, May 16, 1942; children—Judith Ann, Trudy Lynn, Jeanie Beth, Trueman Gregory. Student Southwest Mo. State Coll., 1942-45; L.P.N., Graff Vocat. Tech. Inst., 1971. Tchr. rural schs., Dadeville, 1942-45; nursing asst. Mo. State Chest Hosp., Mt. Vernon, Mo., 1969-70; practical nurse State Chest Hosp., Mt. Vernon, 1971-77, Cox Med. Center, Springfield, Mo., 1977-81, Dade County Nursing Home, Greenfield, Mo., 1981—. Democrat. Mem. Christian Ch. (Disciples of Christ). Clubs: Christian Women's Fellowship (Greenfield) (pres. 1968-69); Nursing Class (Mt. Vernon) (pres. 1970-71). Lodge: Eastern Star. Home: PO Box 67 Greenfield MO 65661

FRIEND, MICHAEL WAYNE, food microbiologist; b. Garrett, Ind., Jan. 7, 1950; s. Donald E. and Leanna May (Freeze) F.; m. Maureen Louise Loney, Aug. 17, 1974; children—Kathleen Marie, Julia Anne, David Michael. B.S., Purdue U., 1976, M.S., 1981. Cert. food, dairy and sanitation microbiologist. Chem. technician Peter Eckrich & Sons, Ft. Wayne, Ind., 1974-77, microbiol. technician, 1977-83; tech. service dir. Huntington Labs., Ind., 1983-84, market mgr., 1984—. Served with U.S. Army, 1969-71. Mem. Am. Soc. Microbiology, Internat. Assn. Milk, Food and Environ. Sanitarians. Republican. Roman Catholic. Avocations: reading; golf; bowling. Home: 6818 Bellefield Dr Fort Wayne IN 46815 Office: 970 E Tipton St Huntington IN 46750

FRIEND, ROBERT NATHAN, fin. counselor, economist; b. Chgo., Feb. 2, 1930; s. Karl D. and Marion (Wollenberger) F.; A.B., Grinnell Coll., 1951; M.S., Ill. Inst. Tech., 1953; m. Lee Baer, Aug. 12, 1979; children—Karen, Alan. With K. Friend & Co., Chgo., 1953—, v.p., early 1960's, 1st v.p., 1964—, dir. merger activities with Standard Oil Co. (Ind.), trustee employees' benefit trust, 1958—; active R. Friend Investments, registered investment counselors. Admissions cons. Grinnell Coll., Ill. Inst. Tech., 1968-70; alumni career counselor Ill. Inst. Tech. Fellow Econ. Edn. and Research Forum; Am. Finance Assn., So. Finance Assn., Southwestern Fin. Assn., Acad. Internat. Bus., Execs. Club Chgo., Am. Acad. Polit. and Social Sci., Am. Assn. Individual Investors (dir., contbg. editor jour.), Am. Assn. Commodity Traders, Vintage Soc., Renaissance Soc., Sarah Siddons Soc., Chgo. Hist. Soc., Art Inst. Chgo. (life), Newcomen Soc. N. Am., Chgo. Council Fgn. Relations, Am. Econ. Assn., Acad. Polit. Sci., Found. for Study of Cycles, Phi Kappa Phi. Clubs: Carlton, Yale. Home: 1209 N Astor St Chicago IL 60610 Office: 222 W Adams St Chicago IL 60606

FRIES, JAMES LAWRENCE, trade association executive; b. Wichita, Kans., Dec. 18, 1932; s. Leon and Edith (Gould) F.; m. June Elizabeth Fisher, Mar. 7, 1959; children—Thomas Blake, Dana Elizabeth. A.B., William Jewell Coll., Liberty, Mo., 1951-55. Asst. to nat. sales mgr. H.D. Lee Co., Kansas City, Mo., 1957-58; dir. pub. relations U. Kansas City, 1958-65; assoc. mgr. Livestock Mktg. Assn., Kansas City, 1967-71, gen. mgr., 1982—; exec. dir. Livestock Merchandising Inst., Kansas City, 1970—; dir. Meat Export Fedn., Denver, 1982—; chmn. Kansas City Commn. Agribus., Kansas City, 1981—. Served to 1st lt. USMC, 1955-57. Mem. Am. Soc. Assn. Execs., Kansas City C. of C. (agribus. council 1980—), Internat. Agribus. Club (pres. 1980—), Kappa Alpha. Republican. Club: Carriage (Kansas City). Home: 109 W 65th Terr Kansas City MO 64111 Office: Livestock Mktg Assn 301 E Armour Blvd Kansas City MO 64111

FRIES, VERNON JOHN, management consultant; b. Lorain, Ohio, Dec. 3, 1946; s. Vernon C. and Dolores A. (Ziegler) F.; m. Charlyn Vera Taylor, Aug. 28, 1970; children—Bryan James, Cynthia Maria, Susan Michelle. A.B., Lorain County Community Coll., 1970. Systems analyst Ohio Bell Telephone Co., Cleve., 1970-79; sr. cons. McDonnell Douglas, Cleve., 1979-83; mgmt. cons. Arthur Young & Co., Kansas City, Mo., 1983—. Served with USAF, 1964-68. Mem. Assn. Systems Mgmt., Phi Theta Kappa. Republican. Roman Catholic. Office: Arthur Young & Co 920 Main St Kansas City MO 64105

FRIESE, GEORGE RALPH, retail company executive. Pres., chief operating officer SCOA Industries Inc., Columbus, Ohio, also dir. Office: SCOA Industries Inc 33 N High St Columbus OH 43215*

FRIESEN, MILO EUGENE, manufacturing company executive, mechanical and electronic engineer; b. Sterling, Ill., Dec. 1, 1939; s. Andrew and Sarah Wilmina (Gudgel) F.; m. Phyllis June Cunningham, Aug. 23, 1958; children—David Eugene, William Joseph, Theresa Ann, Rita Kay, Richard Lee. B.S.E.E., Northrop U., 1966; postgrad. U. Ill., 1967-68. Chief engr. Penberthy Co., Prophetstown, Ill., 1970-71; prin. engr. Sundstrand Corp., Rockford, Ill., 1971-74, mktg. mgr., 1974-78; gen. mgr. Micro-Poise, Indpls., 1978-80; pres. Cybotech Corp., Indpls., 1980-82, chmn., 1980—; v.p. sci., tech. Ransburg Corp., Indpls., 1982—; Ransburg S.A., dir. Paris. Inventor device for aeration, 1970, submersible pump, 1970. Chmn. com. Corp. for Sci. and Tech., Indpls., 1983—; mem. policy com. Purdue U., West Lafayette, Ind., 1980—. Recipient Free Enterprise award Northrop U., 1982. Mem. ASME, Am. Welding Soc., Indsl. Robot Soc. Republican. Roman Catholic. Club: Carmel Racquet (Ind.). Avocations: tennis; sailing; chess; personal computer software. Home: 749 Ironwood Dr Carmel IN 46032 Office: Ransburg Corp 3939 W 56th St Indianapolis IN 46254

FRIESEN, STANLEY RICHARD, surgery educator, consultant; b. Rosthern, Sask., Can., Sept. 8, 1918; s. Dietrich F. and Margaret Friesen; m. Beth Hattan, 1942; children—Stanley Richard, Robert Hattan, Margaret Beth, Kathleen Sue. A.B., U. Kans., Lawrence, 1940; M.D., U. Kans. Med. Sch., Kansas City, 1943; Ph.D. in Surgery, U. Minn., 1948. Diplomate Am. Bd. Surgery. Intern, U. Minn., Mpls., 1943-44, resident, 1944-48; instr. surgery U. Minn. Grad. Sch., Mpls., 1948-49; asst. prof. surgery U. Kans. Med. Sch., Kansas City, 1949-52, assoc. prof., lectr. history of medicine, 1952-59, prof., lectr. history of medicine, 1959—, acting chmn. dept. surgery, 1970-71; cons., gen. surgeon VA Hosp., Kansas City, Mo., 1952—. Author, editor: Surgical Endocrinology, 1978. Co-editor: Current Surgical Management, I, 1957, II, 1965, III, 1966. Contbr. articles to med. publs., chpts. to books. Trustee St. Paul's Sch. Theology, Kansas City, Mo., 1970—, So. Meth. U., Dallas, 1953-56; mem. surgery test com. Nat. Bd. Med. Examiners, Phila., 1971-75. Recipient Disting. and Devoted Service award U. Kans. Sch. Medicine, 1975, Excellence in Teaching award, 1977; named Alumnus of Yr., U. Kans. Sch. Medicine, 1981, Friends U., 1982, U. Minn. Med. Sch., 1985. Fellow ACS; mem. Am. Assn. Endocrine Surgeons (pres. 1983-84), Am. Surg. Assn. (v.p. 1984-85), Soc. Clin. Surgery, Soc. Univ. Surgeons. Avocations: piano, photography. Office: U Kans Med Ctr Surgery Dept 39th and Rainbow Kansas City KS 66103

FRISCH, KURT CHARLES, educator, administrator; b. Vienna, Austria, Jan. 15, 1918; came to U.S., 1939; s. Jacob J. and Clara F. (Spondre) F.; m. Sally Sisson, Sept. 14, 1946; children—Leslie Frisch Nickerson, Kurt C. Jr., Robert J. M.A., U. Vienna, 1938; candidate Sc. Chim., U. Brussels (Belgium), 1939; M.A., Columbia U., 1941, Ph.D., 1944. Project leader Gen. Electric Co., Pittsfield, Mass., 1944-52; acting mgr. research E.F. Houghton & Co., Phila., 1952-56; dir. polymer research and devel. Wyandotte Chems. Corp., Mich., 1956-68; prof., dir. Polymer Inst., U. Detroit, 1968—; pres. Kurt C. Frisch, Inc., Grosse Ile, Mich., 1982—; dir. Polymetrics Corp., Monroe, Mich.; cons. various corps. Patentee in field. (50); author, co-author, editor 24 books. Contbr. articles to profl. jours. Recipient medal of merit German Foam Soc., 1981, medal of merit Brit. Rubber and Plastics Group, 1982; named to Polyurethane Hall of Fame, 1984; IR-100 award Indsl. Research Inst. Fellow Am. Inst. Chemists; mem. Soc. Plastics Industry (div. chmn.), Soc. Plastics Engrs., Am. Chem. Soc., Soc. Coating Tech. Republican. Episcopalian. Home: 17986 Parke Ln Grosse Ile MI 48138

FRISCHMEYER, LINDA ELIZABETH, lawyer; b. Carroll, Iowa, June 22, 1955; d. Lawrence Frederick and Irma Agnes (Schettler) F.; m. Joseph Anthony McCaffrey, July 10, 1982. B.A., St. Ambrose Coll., 1977; J.D., U. Iowa, 1981. Bar: Iowa 1981, Ill. 1981, U.S. Dist. Ct. (no. and so. dists.) Iowa 1982, U.S. Dist. Ct. (cen. dist.) Ill. 1982, U.S. Ct. Appeals (7th cir.) 1983. Assoc. planner Bi-State Met. Planning Com., Rock Island, Ill., 1976-78; research asst. U. Iowa, Iowa City, 1979-81; law clk. Iowa Dist. Ct., Davenport, Iowa, 1981-82; assoc. Katz, McAndrews, Durkee, Balch & Lefstein, P.C., Rock Island, 1982-85, mem. firm, 1985—. Mem. Zonta, Rock Island, 1983—, Quad-City Women's Network, Davenport, 1983—, United Way Planning Com., Rock Island, 1984—. Mem. Scott County Bar Assn. (com. chmn. 1983-84), Rock Island County Bar Assn. (by-laws com. 1984), Iowa Bar Assn., Ill. Bar Assn., ABA, Iowa Assn. Trial Lawyers, Ill. Worker's Compensation Lawyers Assn., Phi Alpha Delta, Phi Alpha Justice. Democrat. Roman Catholic. Office: Katz McAndrews Durkee Balch & Lefstein PC 1705 2d Ave Rock Island IL 61201

FRITSCHEN, ROBERT DAVID, educational administrator, animal science educator, researcher; b. Mitchell, S.D., Nov. 27, 1935; s. Andrew Carl and Matilda (Weihner) F.; m. Hazel LaVonne Robinson, May 3, 1958; children—Annette Andrea, Annita Kay. B.S., S.D. State U., 1961, M.S., 1963. Ext. livestock specialist U. Nebr. Northeast Sta., Concord, 1965-78, assoc. dir. Panhandle Sta., Scottsbluff, 1979-81, prof. animal sci., Lincoln, 1981-84, dir. Panhandle Research and Extension Ctr., Scottsbluff, 1984—. Contbr. articles to profl. jours. Mayor Village of Concord, Nebr., 1977-79. Recipient Superior Service award USDA, 1979, Outstanding Service to Nation's Swine Industry award Nat. Hog Farmer, 1981. Mem. Am. Soc. Animal Sci. (Disting. Service award 1979), Am. Registry Cert. Animal Scientists, Council Agrl. Sci. and Tech., Nebr. Council Pub. Relations for Agr., Gamma Sigma Delta. Lodge: Kiwanis. Avocations: history, travel, fishing. Home: 2305 17th St Gering NE 69341 Office: Univ Nebr Panhandle Research and Extension Ctr 4502 Ave I Scottsbluff NE 69361

FRITZ, HENRY EUGENE, American history educator; b. Garrison, Kans., June 20, 1927; s. Frank Alfred and Esther (Anderson) F.; m. Dolores Ileen Moeller, Sept. 3, 1950; children—Esther Anne, Malin Eugenia, Marie Louise. B.S., Bradley U., 1950, M.A., 1952; Ph.D. in History, U. Minn., 1957. Instr. history U. Wis.-Milw., 1956-58; asst. prof. St. Olaf Coll., Northfield, Minn., 1958-62, assoc. prof., 1962-68, prof. Am. history, 1968—, chmn. history, 1969-84, founder, dir. Am. minorities studies, 1970-72; faculty fellow Newberry Library, Chgo., 1968-69. Author: The Movement for Indian Assimilation, 1860-1890, 1963. Contbr. articles to profl. jours. Served with AUS, 1945-46, ETO. Louis and Maude Hill Fellow Hill Found., St. Paul, 1965. Mem. Orgn. Am. Historians (life), Am. Hist. Assn., Western History Assn. (life, chmn. local arrangements 24th ann. meeting 1984, mem. awards of merit com. 1981-84). Republican. Lutheran. Avocations: beef cattle; quarter horses; farming. Home: Rural Route 1 Box 281 Northfield MN 55057 Office: Dept History St Olaf Coll Northfield MN 55057

FRODEY, RAY CHARLES, baby food products company executive; b. Pitts., Sept. 6, 1923; s. Charles John and Carolyn Hartley (Mering) F.; m. Rosemary Hill, Apr. 18, 1944 (div. Dec. 1981); children—Carol, Christine, Michelle; m. Virginia Arlene Woodhouse, Jan. 9, 1982. B.S., MIT, 1948, M.S., 1949. Quality control chemist Gerber Products, Fremont, Mich., 1949-50, research chemist, 1950-53, research ops. coordinator, 1953-57, asst. to gen. mgr. ops. and controls, 1957-64, v.p. research and quality control, 1965—; dir. Tech S Corp., Washington, 1978—. Contbr. articles to profl. jours. City councilman City of Fremont, Mich., 1960-66, mayor pro tem, 1961-66; trustee Fremont Area Found., 1971-81. Served to 1st lt. U.S. Army, 1942-45. Mem. Inst. Food Tech. (com. chmn.), AAAS, Sigma Xi, Phi Tau Sigma, Fremont C. of C. Avocations: nature photography; ham radio; scuba; hiking; skiing. Office: Gerber Research Lab 445 State St Fremont MI 49412

FROILAND, SVEN GORDON, biologist; b. Astoria, S.D., May 4, 1922; B.S., S.D. State U., 1943; M.A., U. Colo., 1951, Ph.D., 1957; D.Hum. Luther Coll., 1978; married; 6 children. Mem. faculty Augustana Coll., Sioux Falls, S.D., 1946—, prof. biology, 1957—, chmn. dept., 1953-70, chmn. div. natural sci., 1959-76, dir. Center Western Studies, 1976—; dir. Black Hills Natural Sci. Field Sta., 1970-79; vis. scholar U. Ariz., 1970-71. Mem. AAAS, Ecol. Soc. Am., Am. Inst. Biol. Scis., Nat. Assn. Biology Tchrs., Soc. Study Evolution, Western History Assn. Address: Center Western Studies Augustana Coll 29th and S Summit Sioux Falls SD 57197

FROMAN, LAWRENCE MICHAEL, manufacturing company executive; b. Chgo., June 22, 1948; s. Rune G. and Pauline R. (Grillo) F.; m. Terry Kay Scheurmann, Sept. 30, 1973; children—Daniel J., Jane Elizabeth. B.S., Bradley U., 1971. Sales engr. Scam Instrument Corp., Skokie, Ill., 1971-75; product mgr. Riley Co., Skokie, 1975-80; sales mgr. U.S. Riley Corp., Skokie, 1980-82, gen. mgr., 1982—. Mem. Instrument Soc. Am. Republican. Roman Catholic. Avocations: Swimming; golf; softball; Little League coaching. Office: US Riley Corp 7401 N Hamlin Ave Skokie IL 60075

FROMME, RICHARD LEO, financial consultant; b. Jasper, Ind., Aug. 27, 1946; s. Andrew J. and Clarissa (Stenftenagle) F.; m. Jean F. Chamberlain, May 19, 1979; children—Mary Kathryn, Clarissa Sue. B.S. in Acctg., Ind. U.-Indpls., 1973. C.P.A. Provider auditor Ind. Blue Cross-Blue Shield, Indpls., 1973-75; chief acct. St. Elizabeth Hosp., Lafayette, Ind., 1976-79; dir. fiscal services Culver Union Hosp., Crawfordsville, Ind., 1979-81; fin. cons. Hosp. Bldg. & Equipment Co., St. Louis, 1981—. Served with U.S. Navy, 1966-70. Democrat. Roman Catholic. Office: Hospital Building & Equipment Co 11330 Olive St Rd Saint Louis MO 63141

FROMMER, GABRIEL PAUL, psychology educator, researcher; b. Budapest, Hungary, Apr. 27, 1936; came to U.S., 1941, naturalized, 1947; s. Joseph Charles and Magda (Lovas) F.; m. Sara Louse Hoskinson, June 14, 1958; children—Charles Paul, Joseph Arthur. B.A., Oberlin Coll., Ohio, 1957; Sc.M., Brown U., 1959, Ph.D., 1961. Sr. asst. scientist USPHS, Bethesda, Md., 1960-62; USPHS postdoctoral fellow Yale U., New Haven, 1962-64; from asst. prof. to prof. psychology Ind. U., Bloomington, 1964—; assoc. research scientist U. Mich., Ann Arbor, 1973-74, 75-76, USPHS spl. postdoctoral fellow, 1975-76. Mem. Soc. Neurosci., Am. Psychol. Assn., Midwestern Psychol. Assn., Psychonomic Soc., Sigma Xi. Office: Ind U Dept Psychology Bloomington IN 47405

FRONT, MARSHALL BERNARD, investment counselor; b. N.Y.C., Mar. 18, 1937; s. Leon and Sara (Seldner) F.; m. Carol Moss, Sept. 4, 1963 (div. Jan. 1983); m. Laura DeFerrari, Apr. 8, 1984; children—Jacqueline Ann, Christopher Ray, Stephanie Lynn. A.B., Columbia U., 1958, M.B.A., 1961. Mgmt. cons. Booz Allen & Hamilton, Chgo., 1962-65; investment counsel Stein Roe & Farnham, 1965—, also sr. ptnr., mem. exec. com.; pres. Stein Roe Total Return Fund, 1985—, Stein Roe Stock Fund, 1985—, Stein Roe Spl. Fund, 1985—. Bd. dirs. Leadership Council for Open Met. Communities, Chgo., 1979—; pres. Home Investment Fund, Chgo., 1975—; bd. visitors Columbia U., N.Y.C., 1983—; trustee Providence St. Mels High Sch., Chgo., 1984—. Served with USAR, 1962-63. Recipient Gold medal Columbia U. Alumni Fedn., 1983. Mem. Investment Analysts Soc., No-Load Mut. Fund Assn. (pres. 1983—), Am. Assn. Individual Dirs. (bd. dirs. 1982—). Clubs: Chicago, Mid-Day (Chgo.). Office: Stein Roe & Farnham One S Wacker Dr Chicago IL 60606

FROSCH, ROBERT ALAN, automotive company research executive; b. N.Y.C., May 22, 1928; s. Herman Louis and Rose (Bernfeld) F.; m. Jessica Rachael Denerstein, Dec. 22, 1957; children—Elizabeth Ann, Margery Ellen. A.B., Columbia U., 1947, M.S., 1949, Ph.D., 1952; D.Engring. (hon.), U. Miami, 1982, Mich. Tech. U., 1983. Research scientist, assoc. dir., dir. Hudson Labs., Columbia U., N.Y.C., 1951-63; dir. nuclear test detection Advanced Research Projects Agy., Dept. Def., Washington, 1963-65, dep. dir., 1965-66; assoc. sec. Navy for research and devel. Dept. Navy, Washington, 1966-73; asst. exec. dir. UN Environment Program, Nairobi, Kenya, 1973-75; assoc. dir. for applied oceanography Woods Hole Oceanographic Instn., Mass., 1975-77; adminstr. NASA, Washington, 1977-81; pres. Am. Assn. Engring. Socs., N.Y.C., 1981-82; v.p. in charge research labs. Gen. Motors Corp., Warren, Mich., 1982—. Patentee in field. Recipient Arthur S. Fleming award, 1966, U.S. Navy Disting. Pub. Service award, 1969, Def. Meritorious Civilian Service medal, 1973, Neptune award Am. Oceanic Orgn., 1973, Disting. Service medal NASA, 1981. Fellow AAAS, Acounstical Soc. Am., IEEE, AIAA, Am. Astronautical Soc. (John F. Kennedy Astronautical award 1981); mem. Nat. Acad. Engring., Am. Phys. Soc., Seismol. Soc. Am., Marine Tech. Soc., Soc. Naval Architects and Marine Engrs., Soc. Exploration Geophysicists (Spl. Commendation award 1981), Am. Geophys. Union, Soc. Automotive Engrs., Engring. Soc. Detroit. Clubs: Columbia of N.Y. (N.Y.C.); Cosmos (Washington). Home: 30495 Oakview Way Birmingham MI 48010 Office: Gen Motors Corp Research Labs Warren MI 48090-9055

FROST, GREGORY LYNN, judge; b. Newark, Ohio, Apr. 17, 1949; s. William Kenneth and Mildred Ellen (Swick) F.; m. Kathleen Schaller, May 27, 1972; children—Wesley Adam, Nicholas Brian, Andrew Gregory. B.A., Wittenberg U., 1971; J.D., Ohio No. U., 1974. Bar: Ohio 1974, U.S. Supreme Ct. 1979. Asst. Licking County prosecutor, Newark, Ohio, 1974-78; ptnr. Schaller, Frost & Hostetter, Newark, 1974-82; commn. clk. Heath' Civil Service Commn., Ohio, 1979-82; judge Licking County Mcpl. Ct., Newark, 1983—. Pres. exec. com. Licking County council Boy Scouts Am., 1985, mem. exec. com., 1980—, troop com. chmn., 1975—; bd. dirs. Licking Alcoholism Prevention Program, 1983—; county chmn. Licking County Heart Fund, 1981; mem. at large bd. dirs. Nat. Council Alcoholism, 1984-85; v.p. Symposiarchs Nat. Orgn., 1984-85; merit examiner for citizenship in community, nation, world and law Boy Scouts Am., 1976—; mem. Licking County Republican Exec. Com., 1975-82, ex-officio mem., 1983—; mem. Licking County Alcoholism Prevention Program, 1984—. Recipient Superior Jud. Conduct award Ohio Supreme Ct., 1983, Outstanding Young Man of Yr. award Jaycees, 1983, Service to Mankind award Moundbuilder's Sertoma Club, 1983, Disting. Service award Jaycee's, 1983, Wildlife award Ohio Dept. Natural Resources, 1984, Outstanding Service award Licking County Shrine Club, 1983-84, Cert. of Appreciation, Northwest Licking Kiwanis Club, 1983, Outstanding Community Service award Licking Alcoholism Prevention Program, 1984, Cert. of Appreciation, Buckeye Lake Fire Dept., 1984. Mem. Am. Judicature Soc., ABA, Ohio Jud. Conf., Ohio Mcpl. Judges Assn., Ohio State Bar Assn., Licking County Bar Assn., Newark Area C. of C., Ohio State Assn. Twp. Trustees and Clks. (hon.), Phi Mu Delta. Republican. Clubs: Teheran Grotto, Newark Rebounders, Newark Manennerchor, Big Red Touchdown, Symposiarchs, Ducks Unltd., Licking County Old Timers Athletic Assn. Lodges: Masons, Shriners, Elks, Moose, Rotary. Avocations: golf; fishing; swimming. Home: 229 Queens Dr N Newark OH 43055 Office: Licking County Mcpl Ct 40 W Main St Newark OH 43055

FROST, MARY KATHERINE, clinic executive; b. Windsor, Ont., Can., Nov. 13, 1928; came to U.S., 1951, naturalized, 1967; d. Philip Francis and Elizabeth Eppert; cert. in acctg. Windsor Bus. Coll., 1946; student Toronto Conservatory Music, 1946-47, Am. Inst. Banking, 1954-57; A.S., Wayne State U., 1967; m. William Max Frost, July 17, 1948; Teller, bookkeeper, asst. acct. Toronto Dominion Bank, Windsor, 1947-51; with Nat. Bank Detroit, 1951-54; mgr., customer relations officer City Nat. Bank Detroit, 1954-62; psychobiology research supr., adminstrv. asst. dept. mental health Lafayette Clinic, Detroit, 1964—; co-founder, coordinator, polysomnographer Lafayette Clinic Sleep Center, 1975—, lectr., 1978—. Mem. citizens adv. council Lafayette Clinic, chmn. membership, 1979-82, vice chmn., 1982—; bd. dirs. Travelers Aid Soc., 1973—, Casa Maria, 1974-81, Casgrain Hall, 1974—; trustee League Catholic Women, 1974—, mem. adv. bd., 1982—; co-founder Windsor Light Opera Co., 1948. Named Disting. Employee of 1981, Lafayette Clinic, 1982. Mem. Mich. State Employees Assn. (pres. mental health dept. Lafayette Clinic chpt. 1975-81), Assn. Polysomnography Technologists, Nat. Assn. Female Execs., Mich. Assn. Govt. Employees, Econ. Club Detroit, Internat. Platform Assn., Mich. Mental Health Soc., Project Hope League, Smithsonian Assocs. Republican. Clubs: Five o'Clock Forum, U. Detroit, U.S. Senatorial. Contbr. articles to profl. jours. Home: 1 Lafayette Plaisance Suite 1617 Detroit MI 48207 Office: Dept Psychobiology Lafayette Clinic 951 E Lafayette St Detroit MI 48207

FRUEHAUF, MARY LOUISE, medical records director; b. Superior, Wis., May 21, 1949; d. Richard P. and Evelyn M. (Lynch) Fruehauf. Student Superior State U., 1967-69; B.S. in Med. Records, Viterbo Coll., 1972. Cert. record adminstr. Asst. dir. med. records Broward Gen. Med. Ctr., Ft. Lauderdale, Fla., 1972-75; dir. med. records St. Elizabeth's Hosp., Appleton Wis., 1975-83; dir. med. records Mercy Hosp., Janesville, Wis., 1983—. Mem. Am. Med. Records Assn., Northeast Med. Record Assn., Madison Area Med. Record Assn., AAUW, Wis. Quality Assurance Profls., Blackhawk Jaycees. Home: 98 S Huron Dr Janesville WI 53545 Office: Mercy Hosp Janesville WI 53545

FRUTH, BERYL, family practice physician; b. Carey, Ohio, Mar. 27, 1952; d. Oscar W. and Alice (Arnett) Fruth. B.A. magna cum laude in Chemistry, Asbury Coll., 1973; M.D., Ohio State U., 1977. Intern, Grant Hosp., Columbus, Ohio, 1977-78, resident, 1978-79, chief resident, 1979-80; practice medicine specializing in family practice, Columbus, Ohio, 1980—; asst. dir. Family practice residency Grant Hosp., 1980-81. Contbr. Ohio State U. Med. Sch. Learning Module in Alcoholism, 1983-84. Lectr. Columbus Cancer Clinic, 1984. Named Alumna of Yr., Vanlue Sch. (Ohio). Fellow Am. Acad. Family Practice; mem. Am. Med. Women's Assn. Methodist. Office: 20 Governors Pl Columbus OH 43203

FRY, CHARLES GEORGE, theologian, educator; b. Piqua, Ohio, Aug. 15, 1936; s. Sylvan Jack and Lena Freda (Ehle) F.; B.A., Capital U., 1958; M.A., Ohio State U., 1961, Ph.D., 1965; B.D., Evang. Lutheran Theol. Sem., 1962, M.Div., 1977; D.Min., Winebrenner Theol. Sem., 1978. Ordained to ministry Lutheran Ch. U.S.A, 1963; pastor St. Mark's Luth. Ch. and Martin Luther Luth. Ch. (both Columbus, Ohio), 1961-62, 63-66; theologian-in-residence North Community Luth. Ch., Columbus, 1971-73; instr. Wittenberg U., 1962-63; instr. Capital U., 1963-75, asst. prof. history and religion, 1966-69, asso. prof., 1969-75; assoc. prof. hist. theology, dir. missions edn. Concordia Theol. Sem., Ft. Wayne, Ind., 1975-84; sr. minister First Congl. Ch., Detroit, 1984-85; Protestant chaplain St. Francis Coll., Fort Wayne, 1985—; vis. prof. Damavand Coll., Tehran, Iran, 1973-74, bd. dirs., 1976—; vis. prof. Reformed Bible Coll., 1975-79, Concordia Luth. Sem. at Brock U., summer 1977, St. Francis Coll., 1980—; bd. dirs. Samuel Zwemer Inst., 1978—; mem. Luth.-Baptist Dialogue team Luth. Ch. U.S.A.-World Bapt. Alliance, 1978-81; vis. theologian Luth. Ch. Nigeria, 1983, Luth. Ch. Venezuela, 1981, Nat. Presbyterian Ch. Mexico, 1977, 79, First Community Ch., Columbus, 1971-73; mem. N.Am. Laussane Com., 1977-78. Recipient Praestantia award Capital U., 1970, Concordia Hist. Inst. citation, 1977; Regional Council for Internat. Edn. research grantee, 1969. Mem. Am. Hist. Assn., Am. Acad. Religion, Middle East Studies Assn., Middle East Inst., Brit. Interplanetary Soc., Phi Alpha Theta. Democrat. Author books, including: Age of Lutheran Orthodoxy, 1979; Lutheranism in America, 1979; Islam, 1980, 2d edit., 1982; The Way, the Truth, the Life, 1982; Great Asian Religions, 1984. Home: 5020 Woodmark Dr Fort Wayne IN 46815 Office: Office Protestant Chaplain St Francis College 2701 Spring St Fort Wayne IN 46808

FRY, DONALD LEWIS, physiologist, researcher, educator; b. Des Moines, Dec. 29, 1924; s. Clair V. and Maudie (Long) F.; m. Virginia Milne, Sept. 13, 1947; children—Donald Stewart, Ronald Sinclair, Heather Elise, Laurel Virginia. M.D., Harvard U., 1949. Research fellow U. Minn. Hosp., Mpls., 1952-53; sr. asst. surgeon gen. NIH, Bethesda, Md., 1953-56, surgeon, 1956-57, sr. surgeon, 1957-61, med. dir., 1961-80; prof. physiology depts. medicine and pathology Ohio State U., Columbus, 1980—. Contbr. articles to jours., chpts. to books. Mem. AAAS, Am. Physiol. Soc. Am. Soc. Clin. Investigation, Biophys. Soc., Internat. Assn. for Math. Modelling, N.Y. Acad. Scis. Office: Ohio State U 2025 Wiseman Hall 400 W 12th Ave Columbus OH 43210

FRY, JEFFERY JOHN, SR., technical service technician; b. Granite City, Ill., Sept. 4, 1957; s. Thomas Charles and Gertrude (Fitzgerald) F.; m. Meta Ann Brandt, Aug. 28, 1976; children—Alicia Mae, Charles Martin. A.S., Kaskaskia Jr. Coll., 1977; B.A., Greenville Coll., 1980. Asst. mgr. Fry's Service Station, Sorento, Ill., 1977-80; material test operator Carlisle SynTec, Greenville, Ill., 1980-81, quality auditor, 1981-83, sr. tech. service technician, 1983—. Sunday Sch. Dir. Faith Chapel Bapt. Ch., Greenville, 1983, treas., 1984; adv. Greenville Jr. Achievement, 1982. Mem. Am. Soc. Quality Control, Quality Circles (sec. 1982-84), Tri Beta. Republican. Avocations: woodworking; antiques. Home: RR 2 Box 65A Sorento IL 62086 Office: Carlsile Syntec Systems Rt 127 & 40 Greenville IL 62246

FRY, J(OHAN) TRILBY, occupational therapist; b. Quincy, Mass., Apr. 27, 1937; d. Paul A. Gifford and Mary Gifford Blunt; A.A., Westbrook Coll., 1957; B.S. in Edn., Tufts U., 1960; M.A., Western Mich. U., 1971; children—Eluned, Erik, Kari. Staff occupational therapist hosps. in Mass. and Minn., 1961-63; tchr. applied arts and home mgmt. Skills Mpls. Soc. for Blind, 1964-68; supr. Minn. Services for Blind, St. Paul, 1968; tutor Kalamazoo Central High Sch., 1969; rehab. tchr. VA Hosp., West Haven, Conn., 1969; occupational therapist, ward supr. Gaylord Hosp., Wallingford, Conn., 1970-72; asst. prof. occupational therapy, clin. coordinator Quinnipiac Coll., 1972-79; asst. prof. occupational therapy U. N.D., Grand Forks, 1979-83; dir. occupational therapy Grafton State Sch., 1983—; sec. ann. meeting New Eng. Occupational Therapy Edn. Council, 1977, chmn. steering com., 1977, sec. steering com. 1978; presenter paper Internat. Conf. on Rural Rehab. Tech., 1984. Mem. N.D. Occupational Therapy Assn. (asst. editor newsletter 1979-84, chmn. com. on practice 1979-81, program chmn. 1980-82, pres. 1982-84, sec. 1984-86), Am. Occupational Therapy Assn. (rep. U. N.D. Commn. on Edn. 1980, rep. Commn. on Practice from N.D. 1980-81, mem. com. state assns. pres. 1982-84, state liaison commn. on practice 1983—), World Fedn. Occupational Therapy. Established formal techniques of daily living program for blinded vets. in VA system, 1969. Home: 1019 15th Ave S Grand Forks ND 58201 Office: Dept Occupational Therapy Grafton State Sch Grafton ND 58237

FRY, ROBERT WILLIAM, orthodontist; b. Independence, Mo., Apr. 23, 1948; s. Stanton and Marie (Jorgensen) F.; m. Mary Louise Stowell, Aug. 15, 1970; children—Jeremy Randall, Mary Whitney. B.S./A.A., Graceland Coll., Lamoni, Iowa, 1970; D.D.S., U. Mo.-Kansas City, 1973; M.S., U. N.C., 1977. Cert. fin. planner Coll. Fin. Planning, Denver, 1979. Gen. practice dentistry, U.S. Army, Fort Hood, Tex., 1973-75; practice dentistry specializing in orthodontics Radke and Fry, Overland Park, Kans., 1977—. Mem. Parks and Recreation Bd., Lenexa, Kans., 1979-80; vice chmn. Planning Commn., Lenexa, 1980-84; chmn. Leffel for Congress, Kans., 1984. Served to capt. USAR, 1973-75. Recipient Leadership Kans. award Kans. Assn. Commerce and Industry, 1984. Mem. ADA (del. 1983-84), Kans. Dental Assn. (del. 1979-82, chmn. publs. 1980-82, treas. 1982—), Am. Assn. Orthodontics, Kans. Orthodontics Soc. (assoc. editor jour. 1982-83), Assn. Fin. Planners, Lenexa C. of C. (pres. 1982). Republican. Mem. Reorganized Ch. Jesus Christ of Latterday Saints. Lodges: Rotary, Toastmasters. Home: 12340 Pflumm Rd Olathe KS 66062 Office: Drs Radke & Fry 5600 W 95th Overland Park KS 66207

FRY, ROY H(ENRY), librarian, educator; b. Seattle, June 16, 1931; s. Ray Edward and Fern Mildred (Harmon) F.; m. Joanne Mae Van de Guchte, Sept. 12, 1970; 1 dau., Andrea Joy. B.A. in Asian Studies, U. Wash., 1959, B.A. in Anthropology, 1959; M.A. in Library Sci., Western Mich. U., 1965; M.A. in Polit. Sci., Northeastern Ill. U., 1977; archives cert. U. Denver, 1970. Cert. tchr., Wash.; cert. pub. librarian, N.Y.; cert. Med. Library Assn. Librarian and audio-visual coordinator Zillah (Wash.) Pub. Schs., (Wash.), 1960-61; librarian Mark Morris High Sch., Longview, Wash., 1961-64; evening reference librarian Loyola U. of Chgo., 1965-67, head reference librarian, 1967-73, bibliog. services librarian, 1973-74, head circulation librarian, 1974-76, coordinator pub. services, 1976—, teaching asst. in anthropology, 1966-67, instr. sci. program for disadvantaged students, 1967, 68, univ. archivist, 1976-78, bibliographer for polit. sci., 1973—, instr. corr. study div., 1975—. Mem. Niles Twp. Regular Republican Orgn., Skokie, Ill., 1982—; mem. Skokie Caucus Party, 1981—; mem. Skokie Traffic Safety Commn., 1984—; election judge, Niles Twp., 1983—. Served with USNR, 1951-52. Mem. Nat. Librarians Assn. (founding mem., bd. dirs. 1975-76), Asian/Pacific Am. Librarians Assn. (founding mem.), Chgo. Area Theol. Librarians Assn., Pacific N.W. Library Assn., Chgo. Area Archivists (founding mem.), Midwest Archives Conf. (founding mem.), ALA, Assn. Coll. and Research Libraries, Ill. Prairie Path Assn., Skokie Hist. Soc., Nat. Cathedral Assn., Am. Legion, VFW, Pi Sigma Alpha. Republican. Episcopalian. Home: 10059 D Frontage Rd Skokie IL 60077 Office: EM Cudahy Meml Library Loyola Univ 6525 N Sheridan Rd Chicago IL 60626

FRY, WILLIAM ALLEN, English educator; b. Greenville, Ohio, Dec. 2, 1932; s. Walter Leonard and Grace Lucille (Moore) F.; m. Lura Jane McGarvey, June 6, 1953; children—Rebecca Lynne, Deborah Anne, Cynthia Lou, Katherine Joy. B.A., Wheaton Coll., Ill., 1955; M.A., Columbia U., 1966, Ph.D., 1973. Prof. English, Nyack Coll., N.Y., 1963-78, Taylor U., Upland, Ind., 1978—. Contbg. editor The Alliance Witness, Nyack, 1983—. Mem. Nat. Council Tchrs. English, Midwest Modern Lang. Assn., Conf. Christianity and Lit., Phi Delta Kappa. Christian and Missionary Alliance. Avocation: travel. Home: 502 Warkentin Ct Upland IN 46989 Office: Taylor U Upland IN 46989

FRYDENDALL, MERRILL JEAN, biology educator; b. Portis, Kans., Mar. 28, 1934; s. Milo Elgin and Bessie Bernetha (Goheen) F.; m. Karen Louise Laizure, Aug. 16, 1959; children—Edwin Gene, Laura Dawn. B.S., Ft. Hays State U., 1956, M.S., 1960; Ph.D., Utah State U., 1967. Tchr. biology Hays High Sch., Kans., 1956-57, 60-62; instr. biology Utah State U., Logan, 1965-66; assoc. prof. Mankato State U., Minn., 1966-73, prof. biology, 1973—; cons. Corps Engs. U.S. Army, 1973, 79. Regional cons. Future Farmers Am., Minn., 1968—; adult vol. Boy Scouts Am., Mankato, 1968—. Served with U.S. Army, 1957-59. Recipient Hon. State Farmer award Future Farmers Am., 1979; Outstanding Faculty award Mankato State U., 1980; NIH fellow, 1965, 66. Mem. Am. Ornithologists' Union, Minn. Ornithologists Union (pres. 1983, 84), Animal Behavior Soc., Cooper Ornithol. Soc., Minn. Acad. Sci. (ecology editor 1982—), Sigma Xi. Methodist. Avocations: birding; outdoor activities. Home: 136 Swiss St Mankato MN 56001 Office: Mankato State U Dept Biology Mankato MN 56001

FRYDENLUND, ARTHUR JORGEN, motel executive; b. nr. Buffalo, S.D., Aug. 16, 1907; s. Olaf and Ella (Halvorson) F.; student pub. schs.; m. Elaine A. Eyler, June 25, 1934; children—Gerald, John, Karen (Mrs. Gerald Bouzek), Jane (Mrs. Elliott Moore), Eric. Barber, Prairie du Chien, Wis., 1932-51; owner Motel Brisbois, Prairie du Chien, 1951—, Moto-Miter Co., Prairie du Chien, 1959—; dir. Hidden Valley-Nine County Tourist Promotion. City chmn. Heart Fund, Prairie du Chien, 1962; mem. adv. bd. Campion Jesuit High Sch., 1970—; mem. Father Marquette Tercentenary Com., 1972—; pres. Blackhawk Com., 1974—. Mem. County Bd. Suprs., chmn. health com., 1974—, mem. social services com. Bd. dirs. Indsl. Devel., 1952-63, pres., 1963—; trustee Meml. Hosp., 1957—; commr. transit com. Milw. R.R.; dir. 9 county tourist promotion Hidden Valley, 1979. Mem. Wis. Innkeepers (v.p. 1974—, bd. dirs.), Prairie du Chien C. of C. (pres. 1959, dir. 1952—, named Man of Yr. 1978), Gt. Fire Engine Race Am. (dir. 1972—). Methodist. Patentee in field. Home: 533 N Marquette Rd Prairie du Chien WI 53821

FRYE, CHARLES ISAAC, geologist, educator; b. Peterbrough, N.H., Dec. 15, 1935; s. Charles Haven and Nellie Elizabeth (Peters) F.; m. Linda Lou Rakow, June 7, 1965; children—Charles Erik, Robert William, Katherine Ann. B.A. in Geology, U. N.H., 1958; M.S., U. Mass., 1960; Ph.D., U. N.D., 1967. From asst. to prof., chmn. dept. Geology Muskingum Coll., New Concord, Ohio, 1965-78; cons. Charles I. Frye, Bexley, Ohio, 1979-80; assoc. prof. N.W. Mo. State U., Maryville, 1981—; cons. Ohio EPA, Columbus, 1972-79, Ohio Dept. Natural Resources, Columbus, 1979-80. Contbr. articles to profl. jours. Mem. Am. Inst. Profl. Geologists (cert.), Gemological Inst. Am. (cert.), Geol. Soc. Am., Am. Assn. Petroleum Geologists, Ohio Acad. Sci., Mo. Geologists Assn., Sigma Xi (past pres.), Sigma Gamma Epsilon. Unitarian. Lodge: Lions (past pres., bd. dirs.). Avocations: stamp collecting, fishing. Home: 212 North Ave Maryville MO 64468 Office: Geology Dept NW Mo State U Maryville MO 64468

FRYE, MYRON WILLIAM (MIKE), real estate company executive, appraiser; b. Richland Center, Wis., Oct. 27, 1934; s. Neil Dow and Agnes Sarah (Berberich) F.; m. Sharon-Lynn Rucinski, Nov. 24, 1962; 1 son, Randy. Student Mattison-Greenly Tech. Sch., 1960, Milw. Sch. Real Estate, 1966, Western Wis. Tech. Inst. LaCrosse, 1980, 82. Lic. real estate rep., appraiser, notary pub., Wis. Supt., plant mgr. Marten's Mfg. Inc. div. Foley Mfg., Richland Center, 1959-66; br. mgr. Tri County Fin., Elroy, Wis., 1967-70; pres., gen. mgr. Dairyland Auction Service Inc. & Gt. Rivers Realty, Elroy, 1970—; rep. Wilderness Log Homes; appraiser bank real estate and property. Club: Lions (Elroy). Home: PO Box 88 Kendall WI 54638 Office: Dairyland Auction Service Inc Gt Rivers Realty 118 S Main St Elroy WI 53929

FUCIK, MARGARET ANN, investment advisor; b. Evanston, Ill., Nov. 12, 1948; d. Edward Montford and Margaret (Reinig) F. B.A., U. Colo., 1970; M.B.A., U. Chgo., 1976. Mktg. analyst Quaker Oats Co., Chgo., 1973-75; investment advisor Stein Roe & Farnham, Chgo., 1976-81; investment advisor, Chgo., 1982—. Bd. dirs. YWCA Met. Chgo., 1982—, Alpha Phi Found., 1984—. Mem. U. Chgo. Women's Bus. Group. Office: 625 N Michigan Ave 500 Chicago IL 60611

FUERSTE, FREDERICK, physician, ophthalmologist; b. St. Louis, Dec. 9, 1921; s. Frederick and June (Brown) F.; m. Marion Skagen, Dec. 28, 1948; children—Nanette, Gretchen, Hunter, Rommel, Madelin, Garth. B.A., U. Iowa, 1953, M.D., 1945. Diplomate Am. Bd. Ophthalmology. Intern, Cook County Hosp., Chgo., 1945-46; resident Northwestern U. Med. Sch., Chgo., 1948-49, Milwaukee County Hosp., Wis., 1949-51; practice medicine specializing in ophthalmology, Dubuque, Iowa, 1953—; asst. in clin. ophthalmology eye dept. St. Louis City Hosp., 1952-53; asst. in clin. ophthalmology Washington U. Med. Sch., eye dept. McMillan Hosp., St. Louis, 1951-53. Served to lt. (j.g.) USNR, 1946-48. Mem. Dubuque County Med. Assn., Iowa Med. Assn., AMA, ACS, Am. Acad. Ophthalmology, Phi Beta Kappa, Alpha Omega Alpha. Home: 130 S Booth St Dubuque IA 52001 Office: 1400 Dodge St Dubuque IA 52001

FUHRBERG, CAROLYN ANN, pianist; b. Grand Island, Nebr., Aug. 4, 1931; d. Lawrence Edward and Ruth Marie (Lee) Baron; m. John Warwick Coons, June 9, 1951; children—Patricia Jean, Julie Lee, David, John. m. 2d, William Fuhrberg, July 16, 1971. B.Mus., Drake U., 1953; postgrad. Elmhurst Coll., 1969-70, Am. Conservatory, Chgo., 1968-69. Tchr. preparatory dept. Drake U., Des Moines, 1951-54; pvt. piano tchr., West Des Moines, Iowa, 1954-71, Columbus, Ohio, 1961-65, LaGrange Park, Ill., 1967—; tchr. Suzuki staff Wheaton (Ill.) Coll., 1977-83; concert pianist, 1969—. Recipient 2d pl. Composition Contest Iowa, 1951. Mem. Nat. Council Piano Tchrs., Ill. State Music Tchrs. Nat. Assn., Pi Kappa Lambda, Sigma Alpha Iota. Mem. Bible Ch. Home: 304 Richmond St Apt 1 La Grange Park IL 60525

FUHRER, LARRY, investment banker; b. Ft. Wayne, Ind., Sept. 23, 1939; s. Henry Roland and Wilhelmine Ellen (Kopp) F.; A.B., Taylor U., 1961; postgrad. No. Ill. U., 1965—; m. Linda Larsen, Dec. 31, 1962; 1 son, Lance. Exec. club dir. Youth for Christ, Miami, Fla., 1961; publs. mgr. Campus Life mag. Wheaton, Ill., 1962-65; asst. to pres. Youth for Christ Internat., Wheaton, 1965-66; asso. dir. devel. Ill. Inst. Tech., 1966-68; exec. asst. to pres. The Robert Johnston Corp., Los Angeles, Chgo., N.Y.C., 1968-69; pres. Compro, Inc.,

Glen Ellyn, Ill., 1966-72; chmn., pres. The Centre Capital Group Inc., Wheaton; pres. Killian Assocs. Inc., Wheaton, 1973-75; chmn. Equibanque Ltd., 1973-79; Chmn. Family Programming Inc., Rockford Equities Ltd., Rockford Prodns. Inc.; chmn. Fin. Services Group Ltd., Equity Realty Group Inc., Internat. Telemedia Ltd., Presdl. Services, Inc., Quadrus Media Ministry, Inc.; ednl. mgmt. cons. numerous pvt. colls. and sems. Bd. dirs. Chicagoland Youth for Christ. Mem. Am. Mgmt. Assn., Am. Inst. Mgmt. Cons.'s, DuPage Bd. Realtors, Nat., Ill. assns. realtors, Am. Mktg. Assn., Mortgage Bankers Assn. Presbyterian. Club: Union League (Chgo.). Home: 521 Iroquios Naperville IL 60540 Office: 226 E Roosevelt Rd Wheaton IL 60187

FUHRER, LINDA LARSEN, social worker; b. Bayonne, N.J., Aug. 29, 1940; d. Joseph Martin and Metha Kirsten (Sorensen) Larsen; student U. Aix-Marseile (France), 1960-61; A.B., Taylor U., 1962; M.S.W. (VA fellow 1963-64, NIMH grantee 1964-65), U. Ill., 1965; m. Larry R. Fuhrer, Dec. 31, 1962; 1 son, Lance. Social worker children's div. Cook County (Ill.) Dept. Public Aid, 1962-63; dir. camp for delinquent girls under auspices Gov. Ind., 1964, social worker Wheaton (Ill.) Public Schs., 1965-68; family counselor La Grange (Ill.) Family Services, 1968; instr. social work Wheaton Coll., 1969-70; social worker spl. project for disadvantaged, elem. schs. Naperville (Ill.) Schs., 1971-72; social worker Regional Program of Hearing Impaired Students, Hinsdale Twp. (Ill.) High Sch., 1975—; dir. Equity Realty Group, 1978-83; dir. Presdl. Services Inc., 1978—; pvt. practice social work, 1979—; founding bd. dirs. DuPage Pastoral Counseling Center, Glen Ellyn, Ill., 1975-78. Deacon, 1st Presbyn. Ch., Glen Ellyn, 1973-76; co-chmn. Wheaton Swim Team Parents Group, 1977-80; Class IV swim ofcl. AAU; bd. dirs. scholarship com. Longfellow Sch. PTA, Wheaton, 1976-77. Cert. social worker, Ill. Mem. Nat. Assn. Social Workers, NEA, Acad. Cert. Social Workers, Nat. Hearing Assn., Taylor U. Alumni Assn., Alpha Chi. Home: 521 Iroquois Ave Naperville IL 60540 Office: 226 E Roosevelt Rd Wheaton IL 60187

FULGHUM, DAVID ARLIN, truck manufacturing company executive; b. Mason City, Iowa, Oct. 9, 1945; s. Willard S. and Dorothy M. (Murren) F.; m. Brigid Murphy, Nov. 23, 1984; children—Katherine Brigid, Margaret Rebecca. B.S.A.E., Iowa State U., 1969; M.B.A., U. Chgo., 1974; P.M.D., Harvard U., 1981. Registered profl. engr., Ill.; C.P.A., Ill. Engr., Internat. Harvester Co., Chgo., 1969-77, controller strategic bus. unit, 1978-79, adminstrv. asst. to pres., 1980, mgr. agrl. tractors, 1981, mgr. worldwide prodn. programming, 1982-83, dir. prodn. programming and asset mgmt., 1983-85, mgr. market research and scheduling, 1985—; mem. engr. sub-com. Am. Nat. Standards Inst.; mem. safety standards devel. Consumer Product Safety Commn. Mem. Zoning Bd. Appeal, Indian Head Park. Mem. Am. Soc. Agrl. Engrs. Republican. Patentee in field. Home: 4131 Johnson Ave Western Spring IL 60558 Office: Internat Harvester Co 401 N Michigan Ave Chicago IL 60611

FULLER, BETTY WINN HAMILTON, writer, editor; b. Covington, Ky., Feb. 23, 1926; d. Jefferson Ogden and Elizabeth Ann (Winn) Hamilton; m. Samuel Ashby Fuller, June 10, 1948; children—Mary Cheryl Fuller Hargrove, Karen Elizabeth Fuller Wolfe, Deborah Ruth. B.S., U. Cin., 1948; M.S., Butler U., 1977. Children's library asst. Carmel Pub. Library, Ind., 1973-79; free-lance writer, Indpls.; editor: (health and edn.) Children's Better Health Inst., Benjamin Franklin Library and Med. Soc., Inc., 1979—, Jack and Jill Mag., Humpty Dumpty Mag., Turtle Mag., Child Life Mag., Children's Digest Mag., Children's Playmate Mag. Contbr. articles, poems, stories, book revs. to childrens' mags. Sec. Childrens. Bur. Aux., Indpls., 1960, Boys Club Aux., Indpls., 1964; pres. Ladywood Mothers Club, Indpls., 1966, St. Pius X Womens Club, Indpls., 1958; former bd. dirs. Indpls. Pub. Sch. Adv. council, Friends of Carmel Library, St. Luke Catholic Sch. Bd. Recipient Ednl. Journalism award Express, 1982. Mem. DAR (regent 1976-78, sec. 1984—), Soc. Profl. Journalists, Ednl. Press Assn. Am. Republican. Club: Meridian Hills Country. Office: Benjamin Franklin Literary and Med Soc 1100 Waterway Blvd Box 567 Indianapolis IN 46206

FULLER, DOROTHY WILKERSON, lawyer, consultant; b. Chgo., Sept. 3, 1946; d. Birl Floyd Madden and Aszie (Brown) Madden Simpson; m. Raymond Wilkerson, Aug. 18, 1961 (div. Jan. 1972); 1 child, Vicky; m. James Fuller, Jan. 22, 1975 (div. Apr. 1980). B.A., DePaul U., 1974, J.D., 1979. Bar: Ill. 1979, U.S. Dist. Ct. (no. dist.) Ill. 1980. Acct. Allied Radio, Chgo., 1962-68, Atlantic Richfield, Chgo., 1968-72; tchr. Chgo. Pub. Schs., 1974-80; asst. pub. defender Cook County Pub. Defender's Office, Chgo., 1980—; legal adviser 28th Ward alderman, Chgo., 1982-83. Chmn. prin's com. Suder Sch., Chgo., 1978, rec. sec. community council, 1979; adviser Westside People for Progress, Chgo., 1982. Recipient certs. merit Clemente High Sch. Bilingual Dept., Chgo., 1979, Kinsey Elem. Sch., Chgo., 1980, Kennedy High Sch., Chgo., 1980. Mem. Cook County Bar Assn. (bd. dirs. 1982-84, rec. sec. young lawyers sect. 1982-83, Merit award 1982), Am. Arbitration Assn., Nat. Assn. Criminal Def. Attys., Ill. State Bar Assn., Chgo. Bar Assn., ABA. Democrat. Methodist. Club: Brainstormers (Chgo.). Home: 533 N Ridgeway Ave Chicago IL 60624 Office: Pub Defender's Office 2650 S California Chicago IL 60608

FULLER, HARRY LAURENCE, oil company executive; b. Moline, Ill., Nov. 8, 1938; s. Marlin and Mary Helen (Ilsley) F.; m. Nancy Lawrence, Dec. 27, 1961; children—Kathleen, Laura, Randall. B.S. in Chem. Engring., Cornell U., 1961; J.D., DePaul U., 1965. Bar: Ill. 1965. With Standard Oil Co. and affiliates, 1961—, sales mgr., 1972-74, gen. mgr. supply, 1974-77, exec. v.p., Argo, 1977-78; pres. Amoco Oil Co., 1978—; exec. v.p. Standard Oil Co. of Ind., 1981-83, pres., 1983—. Mem. Ill. Bar Assn. Republican. Presbyterian. Clubs: Mid-Am., Chgo. Golf. Office: Amoco Corp 200 E Randolph St Chicago IL 60601*

FULLER, RAY WARD, biochemical pharmacologist, educator, consultant; b. Dongola, Ill., Dec. 16, 1935; s. Lloyd Myron and Wanda (Keller) F.; m. Bonnie Sue Brown, Dec. 22, 1956; children—Ray Ward II, Angela Lea. B.A., So. Ill. U., 1957, M.A., 1958; Ph.D., Purdue U., 1961. Dir. biochemistry research lab. Ft. Wayne State Hosp., Ind., 1961-63; with Lilly Research Labs., Eli Lilly and Co., Indpls., 1963—, head dept. metabolic research, 1968-71, research assoc., 1971-75, research advisor, 1976—; adj. assoc. prof. biochemistry Sch. Medicine, Ind. U., 1974-84, adj. prof. neurobiology, 1985—; vis. lectr. dept. nutrition and food sci. MIT, 1976—; cons. Pharm. Mfrs. Assn. Found., 1978-82, Nat. Inst. Drug Abuse, 1979, NIMH, 1980-84; mem. space motion sickness steering com. NASA, 1982—. Editorial bd. Circulation Research, 1973-79, Life Scis., 1975—, Jour. Neural Transmission, 1976—, Communications in Psychopharmacology, 1980, Jour. Pharmacology and Exptl. Therapeutics, 1981—, Biochem. Pharmacology, 1984—. Contbr. numerous chpts., articles to profl. publs. Patentee medicinal chemistry. Mem. Am. Soc. Biol. Chemists, Am. Soc. Neurochemistry, Am. Chem. Soc., Am. Soc. Pharmacology and Exptl. Therapeutics, Endocrine Soc., Soc. Neurosci., Internat. Soc. Neurochemistry, N.Y. Acad. Scis., AAAS. Home: 7844 Singleton Dr Indianapolis IN 46227 Office: Lilly Corp Ctr Lilly Research Labs Indianapolis IN 46285

FULLER, ROBERT HAROLD, mechanical engineer, consultant; b. Columbus, Ohio, July 1, 1941; s. Raymond Harold and Rhoda May (Hewitt) F.; m. Barbara Susan Steiner, May 1, 1965; children—James, Amy. B.S. in Mech. Engring., Ohio State U., 1964. Registered profl. engr., Ohio, N.Y. Engr. quality control Eastman Kodak Co., Rochester, N.Y., 1965-68; v.p. W.E. Monks & Co., Columbus, 1968-74; asst. dir. energy conservation Ohio State U., Columbus, 1974-78; pres. R.H. Fuller & Assocs. Inc., Columbus, 1979—; pres. Facility Mgmt. Services, Inc., Columbus, 1983—. Author: Energy Conservation Manual, 1975. Contbng. author Conserving Energy in Mechanical Systems, 1981. Contbr. articles to profl. jours. Recipient Disting. Service award Internat. Council Edn. Facility Planners, 1978. Mem. ASME, ASHRAE, Nat. Soc. Profl. Engrs., Am. Cons. Engrs. Council. Lutheran. Avocations: jogging, tennis, skiing. Home: 187 Riverview Park Dr Columbus OH 43214 Office: 2901 N High St Columbus OH 43202

FULTON, ELAINE, association executive, parliamentarian; b. Hunnewell, Mo., Apr. 12, 1928; d. Dennis Jefferson and Flora Opal (Barnes) Bailey; m. Irving Gerard Fulton, May 28, 1949; children—Nancy Elizabeth Fulton Beachner, Robert Dennis. Student in Acctg., Chillicothe Coll., Mo., 1946, Penn Valley Coll., Kansas City, Mo., 1975. Registered parliamentarian. Exec. sec. Nat. Assn. Parliamentarians, Kansas City, 1973—; parliamentarian Nat. Rural Elec. Assn., Washington, 1979—, Nat. Bds. Pharmacy, Chgo., 1979—, Nat. Pork Producers Council, Des Moines, 1980—. Author: (booklet) Sharpen Your Meeting Skills, 1983. Parliamentarian ch. groups, PTA, other local orgns., Kansas City area. Mem. Am. Soc. Assn. Execs. Republican. Clubs: Heart Am. Parliamentary (Kansas City) (pres. 1972-74); Santa Fe Trail Parliamentary (Independence, Mo.) (pres. 1971-73). Lodge: Eastern Star. Home: 4309 Crisp Ave Kansas City MO 64133 Office: Nat Assn Parliamentarians 3706 Broadway Suite 300 Kansas City MO 64111

FUNDERBURG, ROCHELLE ANN, lawyer; b. Lincoln, Ill., Sept. 14, 1956; d. Russell Edward and Judith Ann (Harnacke) F. B.S., U. Ill., 1978, J.D., 1981. Bar: Ill. 1981, U.S. Dist. Ct. (cen. dist.) Ill. 1981. Assoc. Craig & Craig, Mattoon, Ill., 1981—. Bd. dirs. Coles County Coalition Against Domestic Violence. Charles E. Merriam scholar U. Ill., Urbana-Champaign, 1978, 80. Mem. ABA, Coles county Bar Assn., Bus. and Profl. Women (chmn. fin. com. 1983, legis. com. 1984, Young Careerist award 1985), Phi Delta Phi. Lutheran. Home: 1405 1/2 Wabash St Mattoon IL 61938 Office: Craig & Craig 1807 Broadway Ave Mattoon IL 61938

FUNG, DANIEL YEE-CHAK, food microbiologist, food science educator; b. Hong Kong, China, May 15, 1942; came to U.S., 1965, naturalized, 1977; s. Francis K.K. Fung and Beatrice Iu-Yuk Wong; m. Catherine Lee, Feb. 17, 1968; 1 child, Francis Yein Chei. B.A., Internat. Christian U., Tokyo, Japan, 1965; M.S., U. N.C., 1967; Ph.D., Iowa State U., 1969. Asst. prof., asst. dir. adminstrn. Pa. State U., State Coll., 1969-78; from asst. prof. to assoc. prof. Kans. State U., Manhattan, 1978-85, prof., chmn. food sci., 1985—; cons. in field; lectr. sci. meetings fgn. countries. Contbr. articles to profl. jours. Composer of musical works. Tchr. Univ. for Man, Manhattan, 1980—; publicity chmn. Cub Scouts 273, Manhattan, 1982-84; mem. C.R.O.P. Hunger Awareness Group, Manhattan, 1982-84. USDA fellow, 1984-87; NSF grantee, 1982-84; recipient Faculty Service award Nat. Univ. Continued Edn. Assn., 1983, Profl. Achievement award Chinese Am. Food Assn., 1985. Mem. Kans. City Instn. Food Technologists (pres. 1982-84), Inst. Food Tech., Am. Soc. Microbiology, Sigma Xi (life), Gamma Sigma Delta (treas. 1982—). Lodge: Lions (pres. 1982-83). Avocations: pianist, chef, badminton. Home: 607 Houston St Manhattan KS 66502 Office: Kans State U Call Hall Manhattan KS 66506

FUNK, DAVID ALBERT, law educator; b. Wooster, Ohio, Apr. 22, 1927; s. Daniel Coyle and Elizabeth Mary (Reese) F.; children—Beverly Joan, Susan Elizabeth, John Ross, Carolyn Louise; m. 2d, Sandra Nadine Henselmeier, Oct. 2, 1976. Student U. Mo., 1945-46, Harvard Coll., 1946; B.A. in Econs., Coll. of Wooster, 1949; M.A., Ohio State U., 1968; J.D., Case Western Res. U., 1951, LL.M., 1972; LL.M. (Harlan Fiske Stone fellow), Columbia U., 1973. Bar: Ohio 1951, U.S. Ct. Appeals (6th cir.) 1970, U.S. Supreme Ct. 1971. Ptnr. Funk, Funk & Eberhart, Wooster, Ohio, 1951-72; vis. lectr. Coll. of Wooster, 1962-63; assoc. prof. law Ind. U. Sch. of Law, Indpls., 1973-76, prof., 1976—; dir. Juridical Sci. Inst., Indpls. Chmn. bd. trustees Wayne County Law Library Assn., 1956-71; mem. Permanent Jud. Commn., Synod of Ohio, United Presbyn. Ch. in the U.S., 1968. Served to seaman 1st class USNR, 1945-46. Recipient Am. Jurisprudence award in Comparative Law, Case Western Res. U., 1970. Mem. Assn. Am. Law Schs. (sec. comparative law sect. 1977-79, chmn. law and religion sect. 1977-81, sec., treas. law and soc. sci. sect. 1983-85), Am. Soc. Legal History, Law and Society Assn., Japanese-Am. Soc. for Legal Studies, Pi Sigma Alpha. Republican. Author: Oriental Jurisprudence, 1974; Group Dynamic Law, 1982; contbr. articles to profl. jours. Office: 735 W New York St Indianapolis IN 46202

FUNK, JAMES WILLIAM, JR., insurance agency administrator; b. Vincennes, Ind., May 31, 1947; s. James William and Elizabeth (Bauer) F.; B.A., Butler U., Indpls., 1969; m. Janis Burrell, Aug. 11, 1973; children—Christopher James, Kelly Elizabeth. Mem. campaign staff U.S. Senator Birch Bayh, Indpls., 1968; bus. cons. Dun & Bradstreet, Inc., Indpls., 1969-71; dir. ops. Terry Properties Inc., Springfield, Ill., 1971-72; personnel mgr. Am. Underwriters, Inc., Indpls., 1972-73, adminstrv. asst. to pres., 1973-75, asst. sec., 1975-78, v.p. public relations, 1978-79; adminstrv. mgr. Affiliated Agys., Inc., Indpls., 1979—. Sec., treas. Central N. Civic Assn., Indpls., 1976, pres., 1977-78. Mem. Ind. Soc. Chgo., Independent Ins. Agts. Ind. (chmn. legis com., mem. agy. co. relations com.), Profl. Ins. Agts. Ind. pres.-elect 1985—, chmn. legis. com., treas. polit. action com., bd. dirs. 1982-83), Indpls. Children's Mus., Indpls. Zool. Soc. Roman Catholic. Clubs: Preussian Benefit Soc., Heimaths Benefit Soc., K.C. Home: 6445 Spring Mill Rd Indianapolis IN 46260 Office: 8802 N Meridian St Suite 201 Indianapolis IN 46240

FUNK, JOHN WILLIAM, lawyer; b. Detroit, Apr. 6, 1937; s. Wilson S. and Myrtle Marquette (Johnston) F.; m. Carol Elaine Sutton, June 14, 1958 (div. Jan. 1979); children—Michael John, Steven John, David John, Susan Elizabeth; m. Helen Rebecca Kawalec, July 5, 1980. Student Gen. Motors Inst., 1955-57; B.B.A., U. Mich., 1959, M.B.A., 1962, J.D., 1962. Bar: N.Y. 1962. Assoc., Hodgson, Russ, Andrews, Woods & Goodyear, Buffalo, 1962-66; staff atty. Kroger Co., Cin., 1966-68; div. counsel Louise Allis div. Litton Industries, Milw., 1969-70, group counsel machine tool group, Hartford, Conn., 1970-71; gen. counsel Jeffrey Galion, Inc., Columbus, Ohio, 1972-73, v.p. internat. ops. Galion div. (merged with Dresser Industries, Inc.), 1973-77; gen. counsel and sec. Wendy's Internat., Inc., Dublin, Ohio, 1977—, exec. v.p., chief adminstrv. officer, sec., 1980—, dir., 1981—. Served with USAR, 1956-62. Mem. N.Y. State Bar Assn., Phi Kappa Phi. Roman Catholic. Clubs: University, Muirfield County (Columbus). Office: PO Box 256 Dublin OH 43017

FUNT, RICHARD CLAIR, horticulturist; b. Gettysburg, Pa., Feb. 13, 1946; s. Sterling Samuel and Dorothy Mildred (Guise) F.; m. Shirley May Fox, Sept. 6, 1969; children—Elizabeth Anne, Caroline Claire. B.S., Delaware Valley Coll., 1968; M.S., Pa. State U., 1971, Ph.D., 1974. Asst. prof., extension pomologist U. Md.-College Park, 1974-78, assoc. prof., extension pomologist, 1978; assoc. prof., extension horticulturist Ohio State U., Columbus, 1978—. Mem adminstrv. bd. United Methodist Ch., 1976-77, 81-83, pres. Men's Club, 1976-77, mem. council ministries, 1976-77. Served with U.S. Army, 1968-70. Decorated Bronze Star medal. Recipient Shepard award Am. Pomological Soc., 1977; C. K. Bay grantee, 1979-83. Mem. Sigma Xi, Gamma Sigma Delta, Phi Sigma, Phi Epsilon Phi, Epsilon Sigma Phi. Home: 1877 Stockwell Dr Columbus OH 43220 Office: 2001 Fyffe Ct Ohio State U Columbus OH 43210

FURCON, JOHN EDWARD, management and organizational psychologist, consultant; b. Chgo., Mar. 17, 1942; s. John F. and Lottie (Janik) F.; B.A., DePaul U., 1963, M.A., 1965; M.B.A., U. Chgo., 1970; m. Carolyn Ann Warden, Aug. 15, 1964; children—Juliana, Annalisa, Diana. With Human Resources Center (name formerly Indsl. Relations Center), U. Chgo., 1963-81, project dir., 1966-70, research psychologist, div. dir., 1970-81; with Chgo. div. Harbridge House, Inc., Northbrook, Ill., 1981—; mem. faculty Traffic Inst., Northwestern U., 1969—, DePaul U. Sch. for New Learning, 1974-82; cons. bus., ednl. and govt. orgns.; lectr. in field. Served to lt. AUS, 1963-65. Mem. Am. Psychol. Assn., Indsl. Psychology Assn. Chgo. (chmn. 1973-75), Internat. Assn. Chiefs of Police. Contbr. articles on personnel mgmt. and human resources planning to profl. jours. Office: Chgo Div Harbridge House Inc 2875 Milwaukee Ave Northbrook IL 60062

FUREY, PATRICK DENNIS, lawyer; b. Salmon, Idaho, June 7, 1954; s. Jack Bartlett and Nancy June (Stafford) F.; m. Ann Emilie Fredekind, July 9, 1977; 1 son, Rex Taylor. B.A. in English, U. Idaho, 1976, J.D., 1979. Bar: Idaho 1979, U.S. Dist. Ct. Idaho 1979, U.S. Ct. Appeals (9th cir.) 1984. Law clk. to chief justice Idaho Supreme Ct., Boise, 1979-80; law clk. to sr. dist. judge U.S. Dist. Ct. Idaho, Boise, 1980-81; assoc. Imhoff & Lynch, Boise, 1981-84, ptnr., 1984—. Recipient cert. of appreciation Idaho Supreme Ct., 1980; named to Outstanding Young Men Am., U.S. Jaycees, 1982, 84. Mem. Am. Judicature Soc., Idaho State Bar, Boise Bar Assn., Idaho Assn. Ins. Def. Counsel, Phi Alpha Delta. Republican. Episcopalian. Office: Imhoff & Lynch PO Box 739 Boise ID 83701

FURLAN, DANIEL JOSEPH, educator, coach; b. Chgo., Mar. 15, 1947; s. Joseph and Marie (Keblusek) F.; m. Nancee Marie Sondergaard, Aug. 9, 1980; 1 child, Jarred Daniel. B.S. in Edn., Eastern Ill. U., 1970; M.S. in Edn., Ind. U., 1974. Tchr., coach McHenry High Sch., Ill., 1970-71, Tri-State U., Angola, Ind., 1971-76, Joliet Jr. Coll., Ill., 1976—. Named to Swimming Hall of Fame Nat. Assn. Intercollegiate Athletics, 1980. Mem. Coll. Volleyball Coaches of Am., Nat. Jr. Coll. Athletic Assn. Volleyball Coaches Assn., North Central Community Coll. Conf. (Volleyball Coach of Yr. 1978, 79, 80, 81). Avocations: master's swimming; camping. Home: 5740 E Route 113 Coal City IL 60416 Office: Joliet Jr Coll 1216 Houbolt Joliet IL 60436

FURLAN, FRANK JACK, civil engineer; b. Waukegan, Ill., Oct. 13, 1929; s. Frank Matt and Antoinette Marie (Brence) F.; B.S.C.E., Chgo. Tech. Coll., 1953; m. Ione Carolyn Walenter, Oct. 18, 1952; children—Karen Marie, Diane Louise. Rodman, Gt. Lakes Naval Tng. Center, 1948-50; engr.-in-tng. William T. Hooper Engrs., Waukegan, 1952-53; surveyor, engr., jr. partner No. Ill. Survey Co., Waukegan, 1953-58, owner, operator, 1958—; city engr. City of North Chicago (Ill.), 1960—; village engr. Lindenhurst (Ill.), 1968—, Round Lake Park (Ill.), 1974—, Winthrop Harbor (Ill.), 1978, Mettawa (Ill.), 1978; interim city engr. City of Waukegan, 1977—; dir. Bank Waukegan. Supr., Lake County (Ill.) Bd., 1969-73. Served with USN, 1950-52. Mem. Nat. Soc. Profl. Engrs., Ill. Soc. Profl. Engrs., Am. Water Works Assn., ASTM, Ill. Profl. Engrs. Found. (founder mem.), Central States Water Pollution Control Assn., Soc. Am. Mil. Engrs., ASTM, Cons. Engrs. Council Ill., Council for Promotion of Profl. Employment Practices. Democrat. Roman Catholic. Clubs: Waukegan Yacht, Swedish Glee, Gaslight, Elks, Eagles. Home: 2632 E Bonnie Brook Ln Waukegan IL 60085 Office: 3233 W Grand Ave Suite-04 Waukegan IL 60085

FURLONG, PATRICK DAVID, administrator; b. Cleve., Sept. 27, 1948; s. Harold Joseph and Jean Ann (Blair) F.; B.A. magna cum laude, Lake Erie Coll., Painesville, Ohio, 1975. Staff psychometrist VA Med. Center, North Chicago, Ill., 1975-78; psychometrist Northwestern U. Med. Sch., Chgo., 1978-80; counselor/coordinator vets. affairs Columbia Coll., Chgo., 1980-81; assoc. coordinator internat. edn. Roosevelt U., Chgo., 1981-84; dir. accreditation Nat. Commn. on Correctional Health Care, Chgo., 1984—. Served with USN, 1967-71; Vietnam. Decorated Navy Achievement medal with combat V. Mem. N.Y. Acad. Scis., Am. Assn. for Counseling and Devel., Ill. Psychol. Assn., Psi Chi. Home: 1233 W Winnemac Chicago IL 60640

FURMAN, ANDREW RICHARD, sports executive; b. Bklyn., Dec. 16, 1949; s. Bernard and Ruth (Vilinsky) F.; m. Wendy Loney, Sept. 6, 1984. B.A., Hunter Coll., 1972. With sports dept. N.Y. Post, N.Y.C., 1972-73; sports pub. relations exec. St. Francis Coll., Bklyn., 1976-77, Oral Roberts U., Tulsa, 1978-79; dir. pub. relations Buffalo Raceway, Monticello Raceway, Lake Region Greyhound Park, Belmont, N.H., Latonia Race Course, Florence, Ky., 1981—. Mem. Baseball, Football, Basketball Writers' Assn., Turf Publicists. Lodges: Rotary, Lions. Office: Latonia Race Course PO Box 75007 Cincinnati OH 45275

FURMAN, JAMES MERLE, foundation administrator; b. Kansas City, Mo., Apr. 3, 1932; s. James Merle and Andrey Eldena (Phillips) F.; B.A., Ohio State U., 1954; LL.D. (hon.), Ill. Coll., 1976; L.H.D. (hon.), Nat. Coll. Edn., 1978, Govs. State U., 1981, Roosevelt U., 1984; Ed.D. (hon.), So. Ill. U., 1981; m. Carol Ann McGhee, June 10, 1977; children—Mark Carter, Douglas Walter. Research assoc. Ohio Legis. Service Commn., Columbus, 1955-61; dir. Community Research, Inc., Dayton, Ohio, 1962-64; exec. officer Ohio Bd. Regents, Columbus, 1964-70; dir., exec. coordinator Wash. State Council on Higher Edn., Olympia, 1970-74; exec. dir. Ill. Bd. Higher Edn., Springfield, 1975-80; v.p. MacArthur Found., Chgo., 1980-81, exec. v.p., 1981—; mem. exec. com. State Higher Edn. Planning Commns., U.S. Office Edn.; bd. advisors Fund for Improvement of Postsecondary Edn.; mem. student fin. assistance study group HEW. Trustee, Loyola U.; chmn. Gov.'s Commn. Tax Reform; mem. corp. adv. bd. U. Md., chmn. Midwest Panel White House Fellows; mem. higher edn. panel Carnegie Found.; mem. adv. panel Grad. Sch. Mgmt., Northwestern U. Mem. Edn. Commn. of States, Western Interstate Commn. on Higher Edn., State Higher Edn. Exec. Officers (pres. 1979-80), Nat. Center for Higher Edn. Mgmt. Systems (chmn.). Office: 140 S Dearborn St Suite 700 Chicago IL 60603

FURSTE, WESLEY LEONARD, II, surgeon; b. Cin., Apr. 19, 1915; s. Wesley Leonard and Alma (Deckebach) F.; A.B. cum laude, Harvard U., 1937, M.D., 1941; m. Leone James, Mar. 28, 1942; children—Nancy Dianne, Susan Deanne, Wesley Leonard III. Intern, Ohio State U. Hosp., Columbus, 1941-42; fellow surgery U. Cin., 1945-46; asst. surg. resident Cin. Gen. Hosp., 1946-49; sr. asst. surg. resident Ohio State U. Hosps., 1949-50, chief surg. resident, 1950-51; practice medicine specializing in surgery, Columbus, 1951—; instr. Ohio State U., 1951-54, clin. asst. prof. surgery, 1954-66, clin. asso. prof., 1969-74, clin. prof. surgery, 1974—; mem. surg. staffs Mt. Carmel, Children's, Grant, Univ., St. Anthony, Riverside, Meth. hosps. (all Columbus); surg. cons. Dayton (Ohio) VA Hosp., Columbus State Sch., Ohio State Penitentiary, Mercy Hosp., Columbus; regional adv. com. nat. blood program ARC, 1951-68, chmn., 1958-68; invited participant 2d Internat. Conf. on Tetanus, WHO, Bern, Switzerland, 1966, 3d Internat. Conf., Sao Paulo, Brazil, 1970, 5th Internat. Conf., Ronneby Brunn, Sweden, 1978, 6th Internat. Conf., Lyon, France, 1981, invited rapporteur 4th Internat. Conf., Dakar, Senegal, 1975; invited lectr. 7th Internat. Conf., Copanello, Italy, 1984; mem. med. adv. com. Medic Alert Found. Internat., 1971-73, 76—, bd. dirs. 1973-76; founder Digestive Disease Found. Mem. Ohio Motor Vehicle Med. Rev. Bd., 1965-67; bd. dirs. Am. Cancer Soc. Franklin County, pres., 1964-66. Served to maj., M.C., AUS, 1942-46; CBI. Recipient award for outstanding achievement in field of Clostridial infection Ohio State U., award for outstanding service to dept. surgery. Diplomate Am. Bd. Surgery. Mem. Central Surg. Assn., Soc. Surgery of Alimentary Tract, AAAS, ACS (chmn. Ohio com. trauma; gov.-at-large 1979-85; nat. subcom. prophylaxis against tetanus in wound mgmt., chmn. com. for selection Ohio Disting. Service award; Ohio adv. com.), Am. Assn. Surgery of Trauma, Ohio, Columbus (pres. 1983) surg. assns., AMA, Surg. Infection Soc., Am. Trauma Soc. (founding mem., dir.), Soc. Am. Gastrointestinal Endoscopic Surgeons, Shock Soc., Internat. Biliary Assn., Ohio Med. Assn., Acad. Medicine Columbus and Franklin County, Acad. Medicine Cin., Am. Public Health Assn., Am. Med. Writers Assn., Robert M. Zollinger Club, Mont Reid Grad. Surg. Soc., Am. Geriatrics Soc., N.Y. Acad. Scis., Assn. Physicians State of Ohio, Collegium Internationale Chirurgiae Digestivae, Assn. Am. Med. Colls., Internat. Brotherhood Magicians, Soc. Am. Magicians. Presbyterian. Clubs: Scioto Country, Ohio State Univ. Golf, Ohio State Faculty (Columbus); Univ. (Cin.); Harvard (Boston). Prime author: Tetanus A Team Disease; contbg. author: Advances in Military Medicine, 1948; Management of the Injured Patient; Conn's Current Diagnosis, Conn's Current Therapy, Current Emergency Therapy, Surg. Infectious Diseases, Current Therapy in Emergency Medicine; contbr. articles to profl. jours. Home: 3125 Bembridge Rd Columbus OH 43221 Office: 3545 Olentangy River Rd Columbus OH 43214

FYANS, LESLIE J., JR., clinical psychologist, researcher; b. Salt Lake City, Sept. 6, 1952; s. Leslie J. and Antoinette Marie (Picco) F.; m. Paula M. Peterson, May 18, 1974. B.A.Concordia Coll., Ann Arbor, Mich., 1973; M.A. in Psychology, U. Ill., 1975, Ph.D. in Psychology and Psychometrics, 1977. Cert. psychologist, Ill. Research fellow Inst. Child Behavior and Devel. U. Ill., Champaign; dir. testing program, research psychometrician Ill. Dept. Edn., Springfield, 1977-83; dir. Market Studies Ltd; chief exec. officer, cons. clin. psychologist Clin. Counseling Ltd., Springfield, 1983—; cons. in polit. polling to numerous polit. coms. Author: Achievement Motivation; Generalizability Theory, 1983; Productivity Theory, 1984; contbr. articles to profl. jours. Nat. Inst. Edn. grantee, 1975, 77, 80; U.S. Dept. Edn. grantee, 1979. Mem. Am. Bus. Club, Roman Cultural Soc. Lutheran Club: Sangamo (Springfield). Home: 1638 S Mac Arthur Blvd Springfield IL 62704

GAAR, NORMAN EDWARD, lawyer, former state senator; b. Kansas City, Mo., Sept. 29, 1929; s. William Edward and Lola Eugene (McKain) G.; student Baker U., 1947-49; A.B., U. Mich., 1955, J.D., 1956; m. Joanne M. Rupert, Aug. 1, 1953; children—Anne, James, William, John. Admitted to Mo. bar, 1957, Kans. bar, 1962, U.S. Supreme Ct. bar, 1969; asso. firm Stinson, Mag, Thomson, McEvers & Fizzell, Kansas City, 1956-59; partner firm Stinson, Mag & Fizzell, Kansas City, 1959-79; partner Gaar & Bell, Kansas City and St. Louis, Mo., Overland Park and Wichita, Kans., 1979—; mem. Kans. Senate, 1965-84, majority leader, 1976-80; dir., gen. counsel J.A. Tobin Constrn. Co., Kansas City, Kans.; mem. faculty N.Y. Practising Law Inst., 1969-74; adv. dir. Panel Pubs., Inc., N.Y.C. Mcpl. judge City of Westwood, Kans., 1959-63, mayor, 1963-65. Served with U.S. Navy, 1949-53. Decorated Air medal (2); named State of Kans. Disting. Citizen, 1962. Mem. Am. Bar Assn., Am. Judicature Assn., Nat. Conf. State Legislatures, Am. Radio Relay League, Antique Airplane Assn., Exptl. Aircraft Assn. Republican. Presbyterian. Clubs: Woodside Racquet, Brookridge Country. Office: 14 Corporate Woods 640 8717 W 110th St Overland Park KS 66210

GABRIEL, JOSEPH MARTIN, entrepreneur; b. Chgo., Jan. 27, 1927; s. Martin Joseph and Anna (Kohl) G.; m. Lillian Joyce Opie, May 8, 1958 (div. 1970); children—Mark John, Russel Knight, Loretta Lynn; m. Diane Lynn Horbacz, Nov. 23, 1972; 1 dau., Kerry Ann. Ph.B., U. Chgo., 1949. Asst. to pres. SMECO Industries, Inc., Chgo., 1958-60, exec. v.p., 1960-66, pres., chmn. bd., Willow Springs, Ill., 1966—; chmn. bd. Lippmann-Milw., Inc., Cudahy, Wis., Vira Corp., Burr Ridge, Ill. Served with inf. U.S. Army, 1945-46.

Methodist. Avocations: gardening; reading. Home: PO Box 222 Hinsdale IL 60521 Office: Vira Corp 8695 S Archer Ave Willow Springs IL 60480

GAETH, MATTHEW BEN, state senator; b. Oak Harbor, Ohio, June 1, 1921; s. Charles J. and Sophena (Millinger) G.; B.S. in Bus. Adminstrn., Bowling Green (Ohio) State U., 1943; m. Thelma D. John, Oct. 29, 1943; children—John, William, Gretchen. Service sta. operator, 1946-48; with vending bus., 1948-65; safety dir. City of Defiance (Ohio), 1962-65, mayor, 1965-74; mem. Ohio State Senate, 1975—. Republican fin. chmn. Defiance County, 1972-73; former pres. Defiance United Way. Served with USNR, 1943-45. Decorated Purple Heart; named Conservation Legislator of Yr., 1982. Mem. Ohio Mcpl. League (past pres.), Mayors Assn. Ohio (past pres.), Defiance Area C. of C., Am. Legion, VFW. Presbyterian. Clubs: Defiance Rotary, Elks, Eagles, Masons. Office: State house Columbus OH 43216*

GAGAS, ROBERT JOSEPH, toy company executive; b. Elizabeth, N.J., Jan. 22, 1933; s. Anthony Peter and Blanche Anne (Pasko) G.; m. Barbara Ann Crisler; children—Brian Anthony, Bradley Christopher. B.S. cum laude, Fairleigh-Dickinson U., 1970. Mgr. engring. Remco Corp., Harrison, N.J., 1968-72; mgr. engring. Aurora Corp., West Hampstead, L.I., 1972-75; dir. mfg. Conair Corp., Edison, N.J., 1975-77; dir. engring. Kenner Products, Cin., 1977-83, v.p. toy engring., 1983—. Served with U.S. Army, 1953-56. Roman Catholic. Avocations: fishing, chess, carpentry. Home: 7290 Kirby Dr Burlington KY 41005 Office: Kenner Products 1014 Vine St 10th Floor Cincinnati OH 45202

GAGE, ELLIOT HOWES, consulting engineer; b. Memphis, Jan. 27, 1923; s. Elliot Howes and Josephine Caroline (Giltner) G.; m. Margaret Mary Schroeder, Sept. 16, 1944; children—Elliot Howes, Margaret Mary, Anne Elizabeth, John Henry. B.S.M.E., Ill. Inst. Tech., 1944; J.D., DePaul U., 1951. Registered profl. engr., Ill. Engr. Internat. Harvester Co., Chgo., 1946-51, S.J. Reynolds Co., Inc., 1951-55; engr., v.p. Hunter Clark Vent Co., 1955-62, Alexander Gammie P & H, 1962-65; cons. engr., Chgo., 1966—; formulator, instr. Air Test and Balance Sch., Elmhurst, Ill., 1967-70; chmn. Constrn. Industry Affairs Com., Chgo., 1972—, Mech. Contractors Liaison Com., 1974-80; mem. profl. engr. exam. com. Ill. Dept. Edn. and Registration, 1980—. Designer Northern Home, 1981 (1st place energy conservation award 1981). Mem. planning commn. City of West Chicago, 1974-78, zoning appeals Bd., 1978-79. Served to ensign USN, 1941-46. Fellow Constrn. Specification Inst. (sec., dir. 1965-68, chmn. joint contracts document com. (1977—), Cons. Engrs. Council Ill. (v.p. 1973—), Am. Cons. Engrs. Council (past chmn. documents com.), Ill. Soc. Profl. Engrs., Nat. Soc. Profl. Engrs., ASHRAE (past. pres. Ill. chpt.), ASTM, Nat. Soc. Corrosion Engrs., Am. Arbitration Assn., Western Soc. Engrs., Am. Soc. Plumbing Engrs. Roman Catholic. Avocations: swimming; fishing; hunting; golf; tennis. Home and Office: 210 Chicago St West Chicago IL 60185

GAGE, JOHN MARSHALL, Bible company executive; b. Dallas, Jan. 11, 1937; s. John H. and Espicea (Ross) G.; m. Sonja, Aug. 21, 1960; children—J. David Gage, Michael B. B.S., Murray State U., 1960. Advt. mgr. Kirkbride Bible Co., Indpls., 1960-71, treas., 1972-81, exec. v.p., 1982—. Named Key Man Indpls. Jaycees, 1973. Mem. Evang. Christian Pubs. Assn. (treas., bd. dirs. 1979-81, 83—), Christian Booksellers Assn. Exhibitors Assn. (bd. dirs. 1982—). Republican. Mem. Christian Ch. (Disciples of Christ). Club: Indpls. Athletic. Lodge: Kiwanis (Indpls.). Avocations: jogging; squash; tennis. Home: 7359 N Chester Ave Indianapolis IN 46240 Office: B B Kirkbride Bible Co Inc PO Box 606 Indianapolis IN 46206

GAGE, THEODORE JUSTIN, journalist; b. Evanston, Ill., July 3, 1956; s. Edwin C. and Frances I. (Grange) G. B.S. in Journalism, Northwestern U., 1977, M.S. in Journalism, 1979. Freelance journalist, 1979—; sr. editor Cashflow mag.; feature articles in nat. and internat. newspapers, mags. including: Advt. Age, N.Y. Times, McGraw Hill World News, Time Inc. Publs., Chgo. Mag.; author monthly column: Capital Ideas, Cashflow mag., 1980—; contbr. short stories to publs., 1983—. Recipient Peter J. Lisagor award Soc. Profl. Journalists, 1978; Outstanding Sports Reporting award Ill. Gymnastic Coaches, 1980; Excellence in Writing award Am. Soc. Bus. Press Editors, 1983. Mem. Mensa, Mid-Am. Guitar Soc. (bd. dirs.).

GAGESCH, HILDA GERDA, health care adminstr.; b. Chgo., Oct. 3, 1926; s. Thomas L. and Sofia (Eckardt) G. B.A., Case Western Res./Ursuline Coll., 1979. X-ray technician Univ. Hosps. of Cleve., 1952-57, supr. div. coordinator program, 1965-67; asst. chief x-ray technician Childrens Hosp., Cin., 1957-59; chief x-ray technician Forest City Hosp., Cleve., 1958-65; dir. unit mgmt. Hillcrest Hosp., Cleve., 1967-77, dir. systems and ops., 1978-80, dir. div. profl. services, 1980-82, div. dir. patient and physician services, 1982—. Adviser explorer post Boy Scouts Am.; trustee Schnurmann House. Mem. N.E. Ohio Public Relations Assn. Clubs: Cleve. Hiking, Zonta (dir.). Home: 6809 Mayfield Rd Apt 1466 Mayfield Heights OH 44124 Office: 6780 Mayfield Rd Mayfield Heights OH 44124

GAGLIANO, BILL JOSEPH, lawyer; b. Cleve., July 6, 1955; s. Charles and Frances M. (Saracusa) G.; m. Lorraine Ruth Baumgardner, Sept. 4, 1982; 1 child, Margeaux Francesca. B.S.B.A., John Carroll U., 1977; J.D., Case Western Res. U., 1980. Bar: Ohio 1980, U.S. Dist. Ct. (no. dist.) Ohio 1981, U.S. Tax Ct. 1982, U.S. Ct. Appeals (6th cir.) 1984. Assoc. Gillombardo & Assocs., Cleve., 1980-83, Rosenzweig, Schulz & Gillombardo, Co., L.P.A., Cleve., 1983—. Head agt. John Carroll U. Alumni Fund, Cleve., 1980—; class agt. Case Western Res. U. Law Sch. Alumni Fund, Cleve., 1981; bd. dirs. Greater Cleve. chpt. ARC. Mem. Ohio Bar Assn., Assn. Trial Lawyers Am. Democrat. Roman Catholic. Home: 20288 Bonniebank Blvd Rocky River OH 44116 Office: Rosenzweig Schulz & Gillombardo Co LPA 700 Citizens Federal Tower Cleveland OH 44115

GAGNON, BERT CHARLES, wholesale company executive; b. Green Bay, Wis., July 17, 1948; s. Joseph A. and Annette P. (Gaie) G.; m. Lynn M. Krouth, Sept. 7, 1968; children—David C., Dawn M. A.A. in Acctg., Northeastern Wis. Tech. Inst., 1972. Storekeeper USCG, 1966-72; clk. sales Distbrs. Constrn. Supply and Equipment Inc., Green Bay, 1972-74, acct., treas., 1974-78, pres., 1978—; mng. ptnr. Three G & W Investments, 1979—; cons. Griffen Industries, Green Bay, 1980—. Mem. Ind. Bus. Assn. Wis. (com. unemployment 1984), Nat. Fedn. Ind. Bus. (com. 1980, designated Guardian Small Bus.) Republican. Roman Catholic. Avocations: racquetball, stock market, camping. Home: 444 Delwiche Rd Green Bay WI 54302 Office: Distributors Construction Supply 1654 Morrow St Green Bay WI 53405

GAGOSZ, BERNARD ARTHUR, diplomat; b. Val d'Or, Que., Can., Apr. 4, 1940; s. John and Emilia (Kostek) G.; came to U.S., 1983; m. Mary-Lou T. Wanamaker, May 9, 1964; children—Natalie Monique, Christopher B. Degree in Bus. Adminstrn. with honors, Sir Wilfred Laurier U., Waterloo, Ont., 1964; diploma Banff Sch. Advanced Mgmt., 1974. First sec. Can. Embassy, Brussels, Belgium, 1965-69, consul/sr. trade commr., Manila, Philippines, 1969-71, counsellor, Athens, Greece, 1971-76; dir. personnel Trade Commn. Service, Ottawa, Ont., Can., 1976-79; consul gen. Can. Consulate, Melbourne, Australia, 1979-83, Mpls., 1983—. Contbr. articles to internat. trade jours. Mem. Profl. Assn. Fgn. Service Officers. Clubs: Mpls., Minikahda (Mpls.). Lodge: Rotary. Avocations: sailing, scuba diving, skiing, tennis, golf. Office: Canadian Consulate General 15 S 5th St Minneapolis MN 55402

GAHN, DAVID KENTON, manufacturing company executive; b. Burlington, Iowa, May 16, 1952; s. Kenneth Harry and Marjorie Irene (Heckenberg) G.; m. Susan Diane Van Winkle, Oct. 10, 1981. A.S., S.E. Iowa Community Coll., 1972; B.B.A., U. Iowa, 1974; M.B.A., Coll. St. Thomas, 1984. Asst. mgr. Paul's Marina, Burlington, 1968-74; capt. charter yacht Bogey's Cove, Stillwater, Minn., 1974-78; mfg. mgr. Metro Hydraulics, Eden Prairie, Minn., 1978—; dir. QMRP User's Group, St. Paul. Mem. Am. Prodn. and Inventory Control Soc. Roman Catholic. Clubs: Century Boat (Albert Lea, Minn); Antique and Classic Boat (Mound, Minn.). Avocations: antique boat restoration; boating; water sports. Home: 4019 Kipling Ave S Edina MN 55416 Office: Metro Hydraulics 8001 Wallace Rd Eden Prairie MN 55344

GAINES, ERVIN JAMES, librarian; b. N.Y.C., Dec. 8, 1916; s. Ervin J. and Helen (Hennessy) G.; B.S., Columbia U., 1942, A.M., 1947, Ph.D., 1952; D.H.L. (hon.), Cleve. State U., 1983; m. Martha Zirbel, Feb. 11, 1938; children—Colleen Joy (Mrs. John Clark), Sanford Ervin. Instr., Columbia U., 1946-53; chief tng. Radio Liberation, 1953-56, Teleregister Corp., 1956-57; free-lance cons., 1957-58; asst. dir. Boston Pub. Library, 1958-64; dir. Mpls. Pub. Library, 1964-74, Cleve. Pub. Library, 1974—. Mem. ALA. Office: 325 Superior Ave Cleveland OH 44114

GAINES, JAMES DONALD, medical instrumentation company executive; b. Decatur, Miss., Jan. 11, 1936; s. James F. and Mary (Lee) G.; children—Donald Scott, Virginia Leigh. B.B.A., Memphis State U., 1960. Dist. sales mgr. Johnson & Johnson, Somerville, N.J., 1962-68; mktg. mgr. Sherwood Med. Co., St. Louis, 1971-75; dir. mktg. services Medtronics Co., Mpls., 1975-77; pres., chief operating officer Storz Instrument Co., St. Louis, 1977—; dir. Scherer Labs., M-F-G, Mercantile Commerce Co., SMR, Ergo Instruments Co., Leonhard Klein Co., Storz Instrument Co. Served with Air NG, 1960-66. Mem. Health Industry Mfs. Assn., St. Louis Regional Commerce and Growth Assn. Republican. Presbyterian. Clubs: St. Louis; Bellerive Country. Home: 14049 Baywood Villages Dr Saint Louis MO 63107 Office: 3365 Tree Court Industrial Blvd Saint Louis MO 63122

GAINES, MIRAH, management theory and marketing educator; b. Jersey City, Mar. 25, 1917; d. Morris and Ruth (Goldstein) G.; B.A., U. Chgo., 1935, M.B.A., 1937. Supr. R.R. Donnelley, Chgo., 1937-42; personnel dir. Wm. Shanhouse & Sons, Rockford, Ill., 1943-44; personnel mgr. 20th Century Glove and Safety Mfrs., 1944-46; asst. plant supr. Hoosier Factories, Michigan City, Ind., 1946-48; comptroller Proebsting-Taylor Ad Agency, 1956-61; ops. mgr. Associated Shops, Inc., 1967—; prof. bus. Richard J. Daley City Coll., Chgo., 1967—, acting acad. dean, 1972-73; instr., lectr. Elmhurst Coll., Ill., 1976—. Contbr. articles to profl. jours. Republican. Avocations: art, ballet, opera, writing. Home: 7990 Garfield Ave Burr Ridge IL 60521 Office: Chgo City Colls Daley Branch 7500 S Pulaski Rd Chicago IL 60521

GALANTE, LOUIS, municipal official. Fire chief, City of Chgo. Office: Chgo Fire Dept Office of the Fire Chief 121 N LaSalle St Chicago 60602*

GALASK, RUDOLPH PETER, obstetrician-gynecologist, educator; b. Fort Dodge, Iowa, Dec. 23, 1935; s. Peter Otto and Adeline Amelia (Maranesi) G.; m. Gloria Jean Vasti, June 19, 1965. B.A., Drake U., 1960; M.D., U. Iowa, 1964, M.S. in Microbiology, 1967. Diplomate Am. Bd. Ob-Gyn. Intern, Sacramento County Hosp., 1965; resident U. Iowa, Iowa City, 1967-70, asst. prof. ob-gyn, 1970-74, asst. prof. microbiology, 1973-74, assoc. prof. ob-gyn and microbiology, 1974-78, prof. ob-gyn and microbiology, 1978—. Examiner Am. Bd. Ob-Gyn. Sponsor Ducks Unltd., Isaac Walton League. Served with Air NG, 1956-64. Fellow Infectious Disease Soc. Am.; mem. Am. Coll. Ob-Gyn, Am. Gynecol. and Obstet. Soc., Soc. Gynecol. Investigation, Central Assn. Ob-Gyn, Infectious Disease Soc. Ob-Gyn (pres.), Am. Soc. Microbiology, Iowa Med. Soc., Johnson County Med. Soc., Iowa Ob-Gyn Soc., Sigma Xi. Author articles, book chpts., revs., abstracts. Home: 1824 Kathlin Dr Iowa City IA 52240 Office: University of Iowa Hospitals Dept Obstetrics and Gynecology Iowa City IA 52242

GALBRAITH, BRUCE W., educational administrator; b. Detroit, Apr. 4, 1940; s. Hugh T. and Sybil Louise (Cook) G.; m. Karen Anne Van Dam, Sept. 1, 1962; children—Michael, Elizabeth, Sarah. Mus.B., U. Mich., 1962, M.A. in Edn., 1963. Dir. bands Chelsea High Sch., Mich., 1964-68, asst. prin., 1968-69; mng. sec. Mich. Sch. Band and Orch. Assn., Ann Arbor, 1968-77; dir. arts acad. Interlochen Ctr. for Arts, Mich., 1977—, v.p., 1979—; mem. exec. com. Mich. Council for Arts, 1980—. Editor music jour. Mich. Sch. Band and Orch. Assn., 1969-77; music syllabus, 1971. Music adjudicator Performing Arts Abroad, U.S. and Europe, 1980—; co-chmn. stewardship com. Meth. Ch., Traverse City, Mich., 1982-83. Named Outstanding Educator, Jaycees, 1967; recipient Gov.'s award State of Mich., 1977; named Outstanding Mich. prin. Mich. Alliance for Arts in Edn., 1985. Mem. Ind. Schs. Assn. Central States (1st vice chmn. 1980—), Network Performing and Visual Arts Schs., (pres. 1985—), Assn. Ind. Mich. Schs. (pres. 1982- 84), Council Am. Pvt. Edn. (exemplary pvt. sch. award 1983-84), Interlochen C. of C. (v.p. 1984). Methodist. Lodge: Kiwanis. Avocations: music performance, sports. Home and Office: Interlochen Arts Acad Interlochen MI 49643

GALDA, MARIE ROSE, retired chemist, calculations and data processer; b. Omaha, May 14, 1923; d. Jaroslav and Anna (Skvor) G. B.A., U. Omaha, 1944. Technician, U. Nebr. Coll. Medicine, Omaha, 1943; sr. chem. analyst Cudahy Packing Co., Omaha, 1944-65; nuclear technician, chem. data processor Metabolic Research Unit Creighton U. Sch. Medicine, Omaha, 1965-84; retired. Chmn. task force for disabled Presbytery of Mo., River Valley, 1983; chmn. com. for disabled Presbyterian Metropolitan Ministries Omaha, 1984-85. Mem. Am. Chem. Soc. (emeritus), Am. Assn. for Women in Sci., Christian Bus. and Profl. Women (sec. Omaha 1971-73). Democrat. Club: Omaha Toastmistress (pres. 1976-77). Home: 726 N 91 Plaza 313 Omaha NE 68114

GALDIANO, JOSE M., educator, credit executive; b. Victoria, Tex., Oct. 6, 1925; s. Jose M. and Antonia (Lopez) G.; m. Betty Jane Reinwald, Oct. 30, 1948; children—David, Denise. B.A., U. Colo., 1961. Commd. Enlisted U.S. Air Force, 1943; advanced through grades to sr. master sgt., 1964; instr., 1943-59, edn. coordinator, Latin Am., 1959-61, Iran, 1962-63, sch. supt., Amarillo AFB, Tex., 1963-67; ret., 1967; dir. edn., research and pub. relations Am. Collectors Assn., Mpls., 1968-79; instr. mktg. Normandale Community Coll., Bloomington, Minn., 1973—; Owner Credit Humanics, Mpls., 1975—, seminar instr., 1975—, mgmt. cons., 1979—; owner, pres. Comml. Adjustment Corp., Mpls., 1982—. Contbr. articles to profl. jours. Decorated Air medal with 5 oak leaf clusters; recipient Silver Beaver award Boy Scouts Am., 1973. Mem. Sales and Mktg. Execs., Minn. Edn. Assn., NEA. Republican. Congregationalist. Lodge: Toastmasters. Home: 4617 York Ave S Minneapolis MN 55410 Office: Normandale Community Coll 9700 France Ave S Bloomington MN 55431

GALE, LARRY RICHARD, state conservation director; b. Newport, Ohio, Feb. 28, 1921; s. Larry Richard and Alice Elizabeth (Neptune) G.; m. Norma Eileen Schultheis, Apr. 24, 1942; children—Maureen Gale Hayes, Larry R., III. A.B. in Zoology, Ohio U., 1942, M.S. in Zoology, 1947. Biologist, wildlife extension agt. Ohio Conservation Dept., Columbus, Ohio, 1942, 47; biologist Ky. Fish-Wildlife Resources, Frankfort, Ky., 1947-49; game dir. Ky. Fish-Wildlife Resources, Frankfort, 1949-56; chief fish game div. Mo. Dept. Conservation, Jefferson City, 1957-64, asst., dep. dir., 1964-78, dir., 1979—. Contbr. numerous articles to various mags. Mem. Cole County Humane Soc., Jefferson City, Mo., 1980-85; chmn. United Way Mo. State Govt., Jefferson City, 1980; bd. govs. Meml. Hosp., Jefferson City, 1980-85. Recipient Silver Star medal USMC, 1944; Seth Gordon award Internat. Assn. Fish-Wildlife Agys., 1984. Mem. Internat. Assn. Fish-Wildlife Agys. (pres. 1980-81), Wildlife Soc., Am. Fisheries Soc., Am. Forestry Assn., S.E. Assn. Fish-Wildlife Agys. (pres. 1971-72), Assn. Midwest Fish-Wildlife Agys. (pres. 1983-84), Am. Legion, VFW. Democrat. Episcopalian. Office: Mo Dept Conservation PO Box 180 Jefferson City MO 65102

GALE, ROBERT HARRISON, JR., lawyer; b. Syracuse, Kans., Feb. 21, 1953; s. Robert H. and Avonne (Gould) G.; m. Linda C. Reitz, June 18, 1978; 1 child, Joshua Robert. B.S., U. Kans., 1975, J.D., 1978. Bar: Kans. 1978, U.S. Dist. Ct. Kans. 1978, U.S. Ct. Appeals (10th cir.) 1978. Asst. dist. atty. Johnson County, Olathe, Kans., 1978-79; Hamilton County atty. Syracuse, Kans., 1979-85; ptnr. Gale & Gale, Syracuse, 1983—; dir. First Nat. Bank, Syracuse, 1980-82; dir., pres. S.C.A.T., Inc., Syracuse, 1982-84. Precinct committeeman Democratic Party, Johnson County, Kans., 1978; elder First Presbyterian Ch., Syracuse, 1982—. Mem. Kans. Bar Assn., Kans. County and Dist. Attys. Assn., Nat. Dist. Attys. Assn., ABA, Hamilton C. of C. (bd. dirs. 1983-84). Lodges: Rotary, Moose. Home: 55 High Syracuse KS 67878 Office: Gale & Gale Box 906 Syracuse KS 67878

GALE, RUTH AMELIA, antiquarian book dealer, encyclopedia sales; b. Marshall County, Iowa, Jan. 30, 1917; d. Frank Edward Naumann and Ethel (White) N.; m. Theryl Henry Gale, Nov. 30, 1939; children—James, Frank, David, Jerry. Student, Grundy Ctr. Community Coll., 1934-35. Owner, mgr. Gale Books, Marshalltown, Iowa, 1960—; area mgr. World Book-Child Craft, Des Moines, 1968—. Mem. Democratic com., Marshalltown, 1976—; leader Marshall County 4-H program, 1962-82; tchr., youth leader Conrad Presbyterian Ch., Iowa, 1930-49. Recipient 20-Yr. award 4-H Orgn., 1982. Club: Goodwill (pres. 1983-84). Avocations: writing; decoupage; flower arranging; crafts. Home and Office: Gale Books Route 1 Box 61 Marshalltown IA 50158

GALE, STEVEN HERSHEL, college director; b. San Diego, Aug. 18, 1940; s. Norman Arthur and Mary Louise (Wilder) G.; m. Kathy L. L. Johnson, May 20, 1973; children—Shannon Erin, Ashley Alyssa, Kristin Heather. B.A., Duke U., 1963; M.A., UCLA, 1965; Ph.D., U. So. Calif., 1970. Reading asst. English, Los Angeles Met. Coll., 1965-66; teaching asst. U. So. Calif., 1966, instr., 1967-68; assoc. prof. UCLA, 1968-70; asst. prof. U. P.R., Rio Piedras, 1970-73; Fulbright prof. U. Liberia, Monrovia, 1973-74; assoc. prof. U. Fla., Gainesville, 1974-80; prof., head dept. English, Mo. So. State Coll., Joplin, 1980-84, dir. coll. honors program, 1984—; dir. Univ. Players, Monrovia Players; author lecture series Am. Film History for USIS, Liberia, 1974; spl. advisor Liberian Ministry Edn., 1973-74; cons. NEH, Fla. Fine Arts Council; participant confs., convs., seminars, also NEH Humanities Perspectives on Professions, USIS cultural exchange tour, India, 1964. Author: Butter's Going Up, 1977; Harold Pinter: An Annotated Bibliography, 1978; S. J. Perlman: An Annotated Bibliography, 1985; Harold Pinter: Critical Approaches, 1985; also short stories, dramas, poetry. Abstractor ann. Bibliography of the Theatre, Abstracts of English Studies. Series editor: Contemporary American and British Drama and Film. Guest editor Pacific Quar., 1985. Editor: Reading for Today's Writers, 1980. Contbr. articles to profl. jours. Reviewer, Garland Press, John Wiley & Sons, St. Martin's Press, Modern Drama, Pacific Quar., Harcourt, Brace, Jovanovich, Prentice-Hall, William C. Brown. Referee, Theatre Jour., Publs. of Mo. Philol. Assn., Studies in Am. Humor. Mem. alumni admissions com. Duke U.; judge Joplin Globe Regional Spelling Bee; sideline ofcl. Joplin Boys' Club Girls' Soccer; pres., adv. bd. dirs. Joplin-Nat. Affiliation for Literacy Advance, 1982—. Grantee U. P.R., 1971, 72, U. Fla. Humanities Council, 1975, 77; Danforth assoc., 1976—, grantee, 1982. Mem. MLA (dir. session grad. program and curriculum devel., Del. Assembly 1981-83, co-chmn. Assn. Depts. English Job Seekers Workshop 1981), Am. Theatre Assn. regional del. Univ. and Coll. Theatre Assn.), African Studies Ctr. (U. Fla.), AAUP, Am. Film Inst., So. Assn. Africanists, Fulbright Alumni Assn., Nat. Ret. Tchrs. Assn., Con. on Coll. Composition, Coll. Eng. Assn., Fla. Track Ofcls. Assn., Mid-Fla. Ofcls. Assn., Fla. High Sch. Activities Assn., Mo. State Tchrs. Assn., Am. Soc. Theatre Research, Chi Delta Pi. Home: Route 5 Box 490 Joplin MO 64801Office: Dept English Mo So State Coll Joplin MO 64801

GALEMORE, RONALD GENE, architect; b. Charleston, Mo., Jan. 25, 1943; s. Joe B. and Alma Elizabeth (Essary) G.; m. Carol Jane Bartholomew, June 27, 1965. B.S., Murray State U., 1968. Registered architect, Mo. Draftsman through sr. draftsman, job capt., project architect Buchmueller, Whitworth & Assocs., Sikeston, Mo., 1965-82; pvt. practice architecture, Sikeston, Mo., 1983—. Trustee First Baptist Ch. Mem. AIA, Mo. Council Architects, Architects So. Mo. Lodges: Shriners, Masons (past worshipful master, past trustee). Home: 311 Edmondson St Sikeston MO 63801

GALIGER, DOROTHY ANN, paper mill executive; b. Chgo., July 31, 1941; d. Selvian Anton and Victoria Louise (Bukovec) Krultz; m. Frank Everett Galiger, Jan. 28, 1961; children—James, Janet. B.S., Lake Forest Coll., 1964; M.B.A., U. Wis.-Oshkosh, 1977. Acct. McComb, Uphill & Pfeffer, C.P.A.s, Green Bay, Wis., 1972-74, Imperial, Inc., Green Bay, 1974-76; v.p. fin. U.S. Paper Mills Corp., De Pere, Wis., 1976—, also dir. Mem. Women In Mgmt., Inc. (bd. dirs. 1984), Women in Mgmt. (pres. chpt. 1983), Nat. Assn. Accts., AAUW, Nat. Assn. Female Execs. Baptist. Avocation: jogging. Home: 2521 Parkwood Dr Green Bay WI 54304 Office: US Paper Mills Corp 824 Fort Howard Ave De Pere WI 54115

GALIMORE, MICHAEL OLIVER, marketing communications company executive; b. Bloomington, Ind., June 15, 1947; s. Howard Fenwick and Donna (Patterson) G.; m. Kathryn Carol Kaser, Nov. 30, 1975; 1 child, Jonathan Michael. Student, Ind. U., 1966-68; B.A., Ambassador Coll., Pasadena, Calif., 1972. Art dir. White Arts, 1976-79; advt. mgr. Cook, Inc., Bloomington, 1979-80, graphics dir., 1980—. Graphic artist The Plain Truth mag., 1972. Recipient Recognition award for graphic arts excellence Consol. Papers, Inc., 1983. Mem. Ch. of God Seventh Day. Club: Ambassador Spokesman. Home: Route 1 Box 640 Spencer IN 47460 Office: Cook Inc 925 S Curry Pike Bloomington IN 47401

GALINDO, PETER ADON, insurance company executive; b. Rock Rapids, Iowa, May 18, 1945; s. Pete and Elizabeth Jean (Myhra) G.; m. Cathy Jo Ulven, Oct. 15, 1966; 1 son, Jason Peter. Student U. Calif.-Berkeley, 1967. Claims supr. S.D. Blueshield, Sioux Falls, 1968-70, mgr., 1971-74, dir., 1975-77, v.p., 1978-84, sr. v.p., 1984-85, exec. v.p., 1985—; lobbyist S.D. Blue Cross-Blue Shield, Pierre, 1973—; chmn. adv. com. Dakota State Coll. Bus. Sch., Madison, S.D., 1979-80. Chmn. Boy Scouts Scout-O-Rama, Sioux Falls, 1971; loaned exec. United Way, Sioux Falls, 1978; coach VFW Teenage Baseball, Sioux Falls, 1981-82; pres. Edison Jr. High PTA, Sioux Falls, 1982-83; bd. dirs. Food Service Ctr., 1984—, vice chmn., 1985—; chmn. Holiday Festival of Trees, S.D. Chpt. Am. Diabetes Assn., 1985—. Recipient Outstanding Service award Boy Scouts Am., 1971; Best TV campaign awards S.D. Advt. Fedn., 1974, 75; Spl. Vol. award United Way, 1978. Mem. S.D. Advt. Fedn., S.D. Press Assn. Republican. Roman Catholic. Home: 5501 W 52d St Sioux Falls SD 57106 Office: SD Blue Shield 1601 W Madison St Sioux Falls SD 57104

GALINIS, NORBERT MICHAEL, educational administrator; b. Detroit, Sept. 9, 1944; s. Charles Joseph and Marie Rita (Wojtczak) G. B.S., Western Mich. U., 1967; M.A., U. Mich., 1983, doctoral candidate, 1985—. Tchr. history Willow Run Community Schs., Ypsilanti, Mich., 1969-73, tchr. indsl. arts, 1973-80, ednl. asst. House B, Edmonson Middle Sch., 1980-83, tchr. microcomputer edn., 1984-86. Field sports dir. Boy Scouts Am., 1968-70, camp dir., 1971-74. Mem. NEA, Mich. Edn. Assn., Nat. Hist. Soc., Assn. Supervision and Curriculum Devel., Mich. Assn. Middle Sch. Educators, Mich. Assn. Computer Users in Learning, Nat. Council States on Inservice Edn., Internat. Council Computers in Edn., Pi Kappa Alpha (dist. pres. 1971-73 Disting. Service award 1972). Office: 1800 E Forest St Ypsilanti MI 48197

GALL, ELIZABETH BENSON, dating service executive; b. Williamson, W.Va., June 11, 1944; d. Thomas Jefferson Bluebaum and Ollie Mae (Moore) Bluebaum Walker; stepdau. Charles B. Walker; 1 child, Thomas Kontoleon. Ptnr., dir. Chicagoland Register, dating service, Chgo., 1974-84; cooking instr. Elizabeth Benson Internat. Cooking Lessons, 1978-84; owner Ethnic Party People Catering, 1981—, Phone-A-Friend Dating Service, Chgo., 1984—. Home and Office: 6314 N Troy St Chicago IL 60659

GALLAGHER, ANNETTE, nun, educator, librarian; b. Bevington, Iowa, Nov. 10, 1924; d. Thomas Francis and Mary Laura (Lickteig) G. A.A., Ottumwa Heights Coll., 1943; B.A., Marycrest Coll., 1948; M.A., Cath. U. Am., 1950; Ph.D., U. Ariz., 1970; M.A., U. Wis.-Madison, 1980. Joined Congregation of Sisters of Humility of Mary, Roman Catholic Ch., 1943. Tchr. St. Joseph Sch., Dunlap, Iowa, 1945-46; faculty Marycrest Coll., Davenport, Iowa, 1950—, reference librarian, 1973—. Bd. dirs. New Horizons of Faith, 1975—. Office: Marycrest Coll 1607 W 12th St Davenport IA 52804

GALLAGHER, DENNIS HUGH, TV, film and multi-media writer/producer/director; b. Chgo., May 2, 1936; s. Frederick Hugh and Mildred Agnes (Buescher) G.; student Wright Coll., 1954-56, Ill. Inst. Tech., 1956-57; B.Sc. in Physics, U. Ariz., 1966. Dir., Noble Planetarium and Obs., Ft. Worth Mus. Sci. and History, 1960-64; planetarium dir. Man. Mus. Man and Nature, Winnipeg, Can., 1966-70; pres. Omnitheatre Ltd., Winnipeg, 1970-72; pres. Gallagher & Assocs., Chgo., 1972-78, Internat. Travel Theatres, Chgo., 1978-81, Galaxy Prodns. Ltd., Chgo., 1981—; mem. faculty in astronomy and civil engring. U. Man., 1967-68; cons. edn., theater, 1967—. Served with USAR, 1959-65. Mem. Planetarium Assn. Can. (founding pres. 1968-69), Internat. Council Planetarium Execs., Am. Astron. Soc., Nat. Acad. TV Arts and Scis., Am. Soc. Tng. and Devel., Internat. TV Assn., Assn. Multi-Image, Chgo. Film Council. Author: North American Planetariums, 1966; Planetariums of the World, 1969; contbr. articles to profl. jours.; writer, producer, dir. multi-media road show: The Beginning & End of the World, 1972. Office: 5820 N Oriole St Chicago IL 60631

GALLAGHER, IDELLA JANE SMITH (MRS. DONALD A. GALLAGHER), foundation executive, author; b. Union City, N.J., Jan. 1, 1917; d. Fred J. and Louise (Stewart) S.; Ph.B., Marquette U., 1941, M.A., 1943, Ph.D., 1963; postgrad. U. Louvain, Belgium, U. Paris; m. Donald A. Gallagher, June 29, 1938; children—Paul B., Maria Noel. Lectr. philosophy Marquette U., 1943-52, 54-56; instr. philosophy Alverno Coll., Milw., 1956-58; asst. prof. philosophy Villanova U., 1958-62; asst. prof. philosophy Boston Coll., 1962-68, asso. prof., 1968-69; assoc. prof. philosophy U. Ottawa, 1969-71, prof., 1971-73; projects adminstr. DeRance Found., Milw., 1973-80, v.p., 1981—; vis. prof. philosophy Niagara U., 1976-81. Mem. Sudbury (Mass.) Com. for Human Rights, 1963-69; trustee Mt. Senario Coll., Ladysmith, Wis., 1976—. Recipient Sword and Shield award St. Louis U., Baguio City, Philippines, 1975. Mem. Metaphys. Soc. Am., Am. Cath. Philos. Assn. (exec. council 1967-69), Am. Soc. Aesthetics, Assn. Realistic Philosophy, AAUP, Brit. Soc. Aesthetics, Canadian Philos. Assn., Canadian Assn. U. Tchrs., Phi Alpha Theta, Phi Delta Gamma. Author: (with D. A. Gallagher) The Achievement of Jacques and Raissa Maritain, 1962; The Education of Man, 1962; (with D. A. Gallagher) A Maritain Reader, 1966; (with D.A. Gallagher) St. Augustine—The Catholic and Manichaean Ways of Life, 1966. Morality in Evolution: The Moral Philosophy of Henri Bergson, 1970. Gen. editor: Christian Culture and Philosophy Series, Bruce Pub. Co., 1965-68. Contbr. to New Cath. Ency., also articles to profl. jours. Home: 7714 W Wisconsin Ave Wauwatosa WI 53213 Office: DeRance Found 7700 W Bluemound Rd Milwaukee WI 53213

GALLAGHER, JAMES RICHARD, lawyer; b. Ironton, Ohio, Sept. 22, 1956; s. James R. and Margaret L. (Goydan) G. Student, Ohio U., Ironton, 1974-75; B.S. in Bus. Adminstrn., Miami U., Oxford, Ohio, 1978; J.D., Ohio State U., 1981. Bar: Ohio 1981, U.S. Dist. Ct. (so. dist.) Ohio 1982, U.S. Ct. Appeals (6th cir.). Assoc., then ptnr. Hamilton, Kramer, Myers & Cheek, Columbus, Ohio, 1981—. Recipient Am. Jurisprudence award Lawyers Coop. Pub. Co., 1980. Mem. ABA, Assn. Trial Lawyers Am., Ohio State Bar Assn., Columbus Bar Assn., Phi Alpha Delta (statewide coordinator 1984). Democrat. Roman Catholic. Home: 1046 Folkestone Rd Columbus OH 43220 Office: Hamilton Kramer Myers & Cheek 17 S High St Suite 920 Columbus OH 43215

GALLAGHER, KENT GREY, theatre arts educator; b. Oak Park, Ill., Nov. 9, 1933; s. Charles Joseph and Lucile Catherine Bianca (Nussle) G.; m. Sandra Rae Hamblin, Aug. 31, 1957 (div. 1975); children—Geoffrey Kent, Douglas Grey, Bradford Dean; m. Sonja Eileen Newland, Jan. 31, 1976; children—Justin Blake, Andrew Anthony. B.A., Carleton Coll., Northfield, Minn., 1957; M.A., Ind. U., 1960, Ph.D., 1962. Prof., dir. theatre Ball State U., Muncie, Ind., 1962-66; dir. theatre Wash. State U., Pullman, 1966-76, grants adminstr., 1973-75; chmn. theatre arts Tex. Christian U., Ft. Worth, 1976-80; chmn. theatre arts No. Ill. U., DeKalb, 1980-84, grants and devel. adminstr., 1984—; evaluator NEH, Washington, 1976-82; cons. N. Fort Worth Devel. Corp., 1977-80, Arts V, DeKalb, 1984—, Preserve the Egyptian Theatre Found., DeKalb, 1982-84. Author: Foreigner in American Drama, 1966; (film) The Bariloche Connection, 1979. Dir. numerous TV, film and stage prodns. Contbr. articles to profl. publs. Pres. ACLU, Pullman, 1968-70, bd. dirs., 1969-71. Prodn. cons. Ft. Worth Council Chs., 1976-80. Served with U.S. Army, 1953-55. Edwards fellow, 1961-62; Woodrow Wilson fellow, 1967; London prof. Northwest Interinstnl. Council, 1972; recipient Kennedy Ctr. Medallion, 1980. Mem. Am. Theatre Assn. (bd. dirs. 1968-76), Am. Coll. Theatre Festival (bd. dirs. 1972-76), Tex. Coll. Theatre Festival (bd. dirs. 1978-80), Northwest Drama Conf. (pres. 1973-74), Ill. Theatre Assn., Alpha Psi Omega. Mem. United Ch. Christ. Avocations: sailing, skiing. Home: 110 Thornbrook DeKalb IL 60115 Office: Coll Visual and Performing Arts No Ill U DeKalb IL 60115

GALLAGHER, MICHAEL TERRY, lawyer; b. Cedar Rapids, Iowa, Sept. 7, 1948. B.A., U. No. Iowa, 1970; J.D., U. Iowa, 1976. Bar: Iowa 1976, U.S. Dist. Ct. (no. and So. Dists.) Iowa 1976, U.S. Ct. Appeals (8th cir.) 1976. Assoc. Thoma, Schoethal, Davis, Hockenberg & Wine, Des Moines, 1976-78; mgr. labor relations Pickwick Internat., Inc., Mpls., 1978-80; dir. employee relations Cornelius Co., Anoka, Minn., 1980-82; mgr. labor relations Super Valu Stores, Inc., Eden Prairie, Minn., 1982—. Mng. editor Iowa Law Rev., 1976. Served with U.S. Army, 1970-73, Korea. Mem. ABA, Iowa State Bar Assn., Am. Soc. Personnel Adminstrs., Twin Cities Personnel Assn., Kappa Delta Pi. Democrat. Lutheran. Office: Super Valu Stores Inc PO Box 990 Minneapolis MN 55440

GALLAGHER, PAUL EVERETT, marketing company executive; b. Akron, Ohio, Mar. 5, 1950; s. Dominic and Berneda O. (Hanna) G.; m. Constance E. McCoy, Sept. 11, 1971; children—Kalle, Megan. B.S., U. Cin., 1976; M.B.A., Xavier U., 1977. C.P.A., Ohio. Asst. treas. Passpoint Corp., St. Louis, 1971-73; div. controller LCA/Whiteway, Cin., 1973-74; pvt. practice mgmt. cons., Cin., 1974-75; v.p. fin. and adminstrn. Stacey Mfg., Cin., 1975-78, mgmt. cons. Touche Ross & Co., Detroit, 1978—; pres. Mktg. Resources Co., Detroit, Acme Mills Co., Detroit. Mem. exec. com. Music Hall, Detroit; trustee Mich. Opera Theatre. Mem. Young Presidents Orgn. Clubs: D.A.C., Renaissance (Detroit). Office: 5151 Loraine St Detroit MI 48208

GALLANT, JENNIFER JUNG, media center administrator; b. Cleve., Sept. 26, 1951; d. Gan Lam and Helen Jung; m. Stephen Laurie Gallant, Apr. 23, 1983. B.A. in English, Case Western Res. U., 1973, M.L.S., 1974. Librarian, Rocky River High Sch. (Ohio), 1975-78, Cuyahoga County Pub. Library, Cleve., 1978—; dir. library Bay View Hosp., Bay Village, Ohio, 1979-81; dir. media ctr. St. John and West Shore Hosp., Westlake, Ohio, 1981—. Contbr. articles to Med. Newsletter Update, 1982-83. Chairperson alumni fund drive and telethon Case Western Res. U. Matthew A. Baxter Sch. of Info. Sci., Cleve., 1983-84, chairperson telethon drive, 1982-83. Recipient August Alpers award Case Western Res. U., 1974; H.W. Wilson scholar, 1974. Mem. ALA, Med. Library Assn., Med. Library Assn. of Northeast Ohio (v.p. 1983, pres. 1984), Ohio Ednl. Library Media Assn. (award 1974), Cleve. Area Met. Library Assn. (trustee 1985-87), Ohio Health Info. Orgn. (treas. 1986—), Phi Beta Kappa. Office: St John and West Shore Hosp 29000 Center Ridge Rd Westlake OH 44145

GALLATIN, HARLIE KAY, history educator; b. Meadville, Mo., Dec. 15, 1933; s. Harlie Campbell and Gladys Louise (Warren) G.; m. Nancy Mae Morgan, Aug. 5, 1954; children—Kaylene Louise Gallatin Cox, Rhonda Lee, Morgan Dean. B.A., William Jewell Coll., 1955; B.D., Central Bapt. Theol. Sem., 1959; M.A., Central Mo. State U., 1961; Ph.D., U. Ill., 1972. Grad. asst. Central Mo. State U., Warrensburg, 1960-61; instr. history Southwest Bapt. U., Bolivar, Mo., 1961-65, assoc. prof., 1967-73, prof., 1973—, dept. chmn., 1970—, dir. spl. studies, 1978—; grad. asst. U. Ill., Urbana, 1965-67. Commr., vice chmn. Mo. Bapt. Hist. Commn., Liberty, 1981—. Mem. Am. Hist. Assn., Assn. Ancient Historians, Am. Soc. Ch. History, Conf. on Faith and History. Baptist. Home: 121 W Keeling Place Bolivar MO 65613 Office: Southwest Bapt U History Dept 1601 S Springfield St Bolivar MO 65613

GALLE, WILLIAM JACOB, consultant; b. Dodge City, Kans., Sept. 29, 1921; s. Kurt R. and Louisa M. (Epp) G.; m. Geraldine M. Sey-Burgauer; children—Patricia, Carol, William K., Deborah, Robert E., Alan J. B.S. in Chem. Engring., Kans. State U., 1943; M.S., Purdue U., 1950. Registered profl. engr., Calif. Jr. chem. engr. Aluminum Co. Am., East St. Louis, Ill., 1943-44, 46-48; quality engr., statistician Armour & Co., Chgo., 1950-64; ops. research analyst Brunswick Corp., Chgo., 1964-69, John Morrell & Co., Chgo., 1969-75; tech. cons. W.A. Golomski & Assocs., Chgo., 1976—. Served to lt. (j.g.) USN, 1944-46, PTO. Mem. Am. Soc. Quality Control (sr. mem., div. chmn. 1984—), Am. Statis. Assn., Am. Prodn. and Inventory Control Soc. Presbyterian. Club: Toastmaster Internat. (pres. Park Forest, Ill. 1973). Avocations: music, pub. speaking, bridge. Home: 216 Washington St Park Forest IL 60466 Office: W A Golomski & Assocs 59 East Van Buren St Chicago IL 60605

GALLERO, JEFFERY ALAN, athletic coach; b. Pontiac, Mich., July 31, 1954; s. Florentine and Patricia Louise (Cooper) G.; m. Susan Carol Jeziorski, Apr. 28, 1978 (div.). Student Eastern Mich. U., 1972-73, Oakland Community Coll., 1974, U. Nev.-Reno, 1985. Lic. pvt. pilot. Asst. track coach Pontiac No. High Sch., 1973-77; head coach women's cross country, men's track, women's basketball Roeper City Country Sch., Bloomfield Hills, Mich., 1978-81; football coach Larson Middle Sch., Troy, Mich., 1982; head coach men and women track and field Rochester (Mich.) Adams High Sch., 1983; asst. track and cross country coach Southwestern Mich. Coll., Dowagiac, 1983-84; asst. coach Mich. Track Club; asst. meet dir. Nat. Jr. Coll. Marathon Championships, 1984; law clk. Harrison Law Offices, Dowagiac, 1983-84; asst. coach men's track and cross country U. Nev.-Reno, 1985—. Campaign vol. Waterford Democratic Club, 1983; mem. Pontiac PTA. Bd. regents scholar Eastern Mich. U., 1972-73. Mem. Track Athletics Congress, Nat. Jr. Coll. Coaches Assn., Mich. Interscholastic Track Coaches Assn. Roman Catholic. Home: 506 Jordon St Pontiac MI 48058

GALLIGAN, FRANK DANIEL, automotive parts company executive; b. Bronx, N.Y., Apr. 15, 1938; s. Frank A. and Mary G. (Moran) G.; B.S., U. Scranton, 1960; grad. exec. devel. program U. Ill., 1975; m. M. Elizabeth Jordan, Oct. 14, 1961; children—Michael F., Eileen M., Paul F. Vice pres. mktg. Toledo Tools Co., 1971-74; nat. sales mgr. AP Parts Co., Toledo, 1974-77; v.p. McQuay-Norris, Inc., St. Louis, 1977-84; exec. v.p., dir. Delta Inc. of Ark., Jonesboro, 1984—; v.p., dir. Delta Group Inc., 1984—. Pres., Brightwaters Acres Civic Assn., 1965-66; mem. bus. adv. com. Lucas County Port Authority, 1976-77. Mem. Automotive Parts and Accessories Assn., Automotive Service Industries Assn. (mem. young exec. nat. bd. dirs. 1977-78). Republican. Roman Catholic. Club: Glen Echo Country (bd. govs.) (St. Louis). Office: 4800 Krueger Dr Jonesboro AR 72401

GALLOWAY, JAMES ROBERT, educational administrator; b. Iroqois County, Ill., May 27, 1933; s. Harold Sherman and Beulah Florence (Nolan) G.; m. Mary Ann O'Malley, Sept. 3, 1955; children—Shawn Denise, Sheryl Deann. B.S. in Edn., Eastern Ill. U., 1958; M.S. in Ednl. Adminstrn., U. Ill.-Champaign, 1965. Tchr.-coordinator Coop. Edn., Sterling and Hoopeston, Ill., 1962-65; dir. vocat. edn. Whiteside Area Vocat. Center, Sterling, 1965-67; exec. dir. Denver Pub. Schs., 1967-69; dir. Program Approval and Evaluation, Div. Vocat. Edn., Ill. State Bd. Vocat. Edn. and Rehab., Springfield, 1969-76, now asst. state supt. Ill. State Bd. Edn., Springfield; vis. prof. So. Ill. U., Ill. State U., Eastern Ill. U.; cons. Nat. Inst. Edn., World Bank, Govt. of Jamaica. Served with USN, 1951-54. Recipient Disting. Alumni award Eastern Ill. U., 1980; named Outstanding Educator Denver, 1969. Mem. Am. Vocat. Assn., Nat. Assn. State Dirs. Vocat. Assn. (pres. 1982), Ill. Vocat. Assn., Ill. Council Local Adminstrs., Ill. Indsl. Edn. Assn., Ill. Guidance and Vocat. Services Assn., Nat. Guidance and Vocat. Services Assn., Nat. Council Local Adminstrs., Ill. Indsl. Edn. Assn., Ill. Employment and Tng. Council (exec. com.), Jr. C. of C., Nat. Assn. Pub. Continuing and Adult Edn., Epsilon Pi Tau. Contbr. articles on vocat. edn. to profl. jours. Home: 2112 Noble Ave Springfield IL 62704 Office: 100 N 1st St Springfield IL 62777

GALOFRE, ALBERTO, medical educator; b. Santiago, Chile, Dec. 10, 1937; came to U.S., 1973; naturalized, 1982; s. Estanislao and Margarita (Terrasa) G.; m. Nancy Kay Evert, June 23, 1968; children—Ana Margarita, Christine Elizabeth, Mary Kay. B.Sc., Catholic U. Chile, 1959; M.D. summa cum laude, U. Chile, 1962; M.Ed., U. Ill.-Urbana, 1974. Instr. pediatrics Catholic U., Santiago, 1963-70, asst. prof. pediatrics, 1970-73; asst. prof. pediatrics and human devel. Mich. State U., East Lansing, 1974-78; asst. prof. internal medicine St. Louis U., 1978-85, assoc. prof., 1985—, asst. dean curriculum Med. Sch., 1979-85, assoc. dean, 1985—; mem. adv. panel WHO, Geneva, 1980—; cons. med. edn. Panam. Health Orgn., Washington, 1975—; dir. pediatric research U. Chile, Santiago, 1964-72; mem. sci. adv. com. Latin Am. Ctr. Ednl. Tech. for Health Scis., Mexico City, 1979-81, Rio de Janeiro, Brazil, 1980-83. Contbr. chpts. to books, articles to med. jours. Nat. Fund Med. Edn. grantee, 1982-84; W.K. Kellogg fellow, 1967-68; USPHS fellow, 1974-75. Mem. ACP, Am. Ednl. Research Assn., Nat. Council Measurement in Edn., AAAS, Am. Pub. Health Assn., Am. Assn. Higher Edn. Avocations: nature photography; tennis; scuba; jogging. Office: Saint Louis U Sch Med 1402 S Grand LRC101 Saint Louis MO 63104

GALVAS, MARILYN DREW WELTY, social work administrator, language educator; b. Austin, Tex., May 7, 1946; d. John Allen and Marilyn Drew (Miller) Welty; m. Patrick Edward Galvas, June 5, 1971; children—Jason Michael, Jon Ryan. B.S., U. Tex., 1968; M.A., Ball State U., 1972; postgrad. Northeast Mo. State U., 1984—. Caseworker, Alcoholic Rehab. Center, Austin (Tex.) State Hosp., 1968-69; employment interviewer, test adminstr. Tex. Employment Commn., Austin, 1969; employment counselor Businessmen's Personnel Services, Inc., Dallas, 1977; tchr. Cedar Hill High Sch. (Tex.), 1977-78; adminstrv. asst. Secretaries of Dallas, Inc., 1978-79; sec. Rauscher Pierce Refsnes, Inc., Dallas, 1979-80; tchr. ESL, Travelers Aid Internat. Inst. (CETA), Cin., 1981; tchr. ESL ESL/Occupational Work Experience, Cin. pub. schs., 1981-82; rep. Episcopal Region S.W. Ohio, Refugee Resettlement Com., Cin., 1982-83, also sec. Consoritum of Services to Immigrants and Refugees, Cin., 1982-83; adj. instr. speech and communications Mountain View Coll., North Lake Coll., U. Tex.-Arlington, El Centro Coll., Sinclair Community Coll., Wright State U., Ball State U.; instr. Spanish, N.E. Mo. State U., Kirksville, 1984. Bd. dirs. Planned Parenthood; active Traveller's Community Theatre, Kirksville, 1983-84; vice chmn. Kirksville Betterment Council, 1984-85. Mem. Ohio TESOL, Am. Vocat. Assn., Ohio Vocat. Assn. Republican. Episcopalian. Clubs: KCOM/KOHC Wives, Sojourner's. Home: 701 E Harrison Kirksville MO 63501

GALVIN, ROBERT W., radio manufacturing executive; b. Marshfield, Wis., Oct. 9, 1922; student U. Notre Dame, U. Chgo.; LL.D. (hon.), Quincy Coll., St. Ambrose Coll., DePaul U., Ariz. State U. With Motorola, Inc., Chgo., 1940—, pres., 1956—, chmn. bd., chief exec. officer, 1964—, also dir. Bd. dirs. Jr. Achievement of Chgo.; chmn. bd. trustees Ill. Inst. Tech.; former mem. Pres.'s Commn. Internat. Trade and Investment; mem. Pres.'s Pvt. Sector Survey; chmn. Pres.'s Adv. Council on Pvt. Sector Initiatives; chmn. industry adv. com. to U.S. spl. rep. for trade negotiations. mem. 12 Fellows, trustee U. Notre Dame. Served with Signal Corps, AUS, World War II. Named Decision Maker of Yr., Chgo. Assn. Commerce and Industry-Am. Statis. Assn., 1973; recipient Golden Omega award, 1981; Washington award Western Soc. Engrs., 1984. Mem. Electronics Industries Assn. (pres. 1966, medal of Honor 1970, dir.). Office: Motorola Inc 1303 Algonquin Rd Schaumburg IL 60196

GAMBAL, DAVID, biochemistry educator, researcher; b. Old Forge, Pa., Dec. 16, 1931; s. Evan and Alice (Witiak) G.; m. Frances Anne Warfield, May 7, 1960; children—Mark, Scott, Todd. B.S., Pa. State U., 1953; M.S., Purdue U., 1955, Ph.D., 1957. Postdoctoral fellow Johns Hopkins U., Balt., 1957-59; asst. prof. Iowa State U., Ames, 1959-63, assoc. prof., 1963-65; assoc. prof. Creighton U., Omaha, 1965-67, prof., 1968—, chmn. biochemistry dept., 1976-79. Contbr. articles to profl. jours. NIH grantee; research fellow Purdue U.; recipient Golden Apple Teaching Award Am. Med. Student Assn., 1979. Mem. Am. Chem. Soc., AAAS, Soc. Exptl. Biology and Medicine, Sigma Xi, Alpha Chi Sigma, Phi Lambda Phi, Phi Kappa Phi. Republican. Episcopalian. Avocations: boating; waterskiing; scuba diving; cross-country skiing; fishing. Home: 5726 Willit St Omaha NE 68152 Office: Creighton U Sch Medicine 2500 California St Omaha NE 68178

GAMBHIR, SURINDER PAL, chemical engineer; b. Amritsar, India, Sept. 2, 1939; naturalized Am. citizen, 1973; m. Anu Soni, Oct. 11, 1968; children—Ajay, Anita, Sushma. B.S., Delhi U., 1962; M.S., Okla. State U., 1965. Registered profl. engr., Ill., Ala., Mich. Process/project engr. Horton Process Div., Oak Brook, Ill., 1966-70; process engr. Gillette Chem. Co., North Chicago, Ill., 1970-71, environ. engr. Ill. EPA, Chgo., 1971-76; program mgr. Ind. Pollution Control Gilbert Commonwealth, Jackson, Mich., 1977—. Mem. Ill. Commn. Atomic Energy, 1976-77; mem. nat. resources com. Mich. Mfrs. Assn., 1978. Recipient Cert. Appreciation, Nat. Plant Engring. Show, 1980. Mem. Am. Inst. Chem. Engrs., Water Pollution Control Fedn., Air Pollution Control Assn. Contbr. articles to profl. jours. Office: 209 E Washington St Jackson MI 49201

GAMBILL, BETHANY LUELLA, telephone company official; b. Painesville, Ohio, Oct. 12, 1953; s. Garfield and Shirley Mae (Jones) Johns; A.S. in Computer Programming, Inst. Computer Mgmt., Cleve., 1973; student Cuyahoga Community Coll., 1974, U. Akron, 1983, Kent State U., 1985; m. Stephen Carl Gambill, May 21, 1977. Bookkeeper, asst. to art dir. Revere Chem. Corp./Monroe Co., Solon, Ohio, 1973-75; with Alltel Corp., Twinsburg, Ohio, 1975—, transmission coordinator, 1976, toll coordinator, 1977-85, programmer, 1985—. Vol. ARC. Mem. Nat. Assn. Female Execs., Nat. Fedn. Bus. and Profl. Women (2d v.p. Tallmadge chpt. 1982-84, 1st v.p. 1984-86). Home: 95 N River Rd Munroe Falls OH 44262 Office: 2000 Highland Rd Twinsburg OH 44087

GAMBLE, SUE GIBBS, music educator; b. Evanston, Ill., Sept. 12, 1944; d. Thomas Parker and Jane (Miller) Gibbs; m. Edwin Walter Gamble, July 22, 1972 (div. May 1980). B.S., Pa. State U., 1966, M.Ed., 1971, D.Ed., 1978. Cert. music tchr., Pa. Choral dir. Bald Eagle Jr./Sr. High Sch., Wingate, Pa., 1966-74; music grad. teaching asst. Pa. State U., University Park, 1974-77; asst. prof. music Central Mich. U., Mt. Pleasant, 1978—, chmn. music dept., 1984—. Editor: The Vocal Performer, 1980; Listening Experiences, 1983. Mem. Music Educators Nat. Conf., Coll. Music Soc., Midwest Kodaly Music Edn. Assn. (exec. sec. Mt. Pleasant 1980-81), Mich. Music Edn. Assn. (dist. rep. Lansing 1981-82), Phi Kappa Phi, Phi Delta Kappa, Pi Lambda Theta. Club: Zonta Internat (Mt. Pleasant). Avocations: reading; needlepoint. Office: Music Dept Powers Music Bldg Central Michigan U Mount Pleasant MI 48859

GAMBLIN, RODGER LOTIS, research company executive; b. St. Louis, Sept. 18, 1932; s. Granville Lotis and Opal Ora (Taylor) G.; B.S., Princeton U., 1954, M.A., 1963, Ph.D., 1965; M.B.A., Wright State U., 1981; children—Anne W., Rodgers W.B., Lawrence R., Sarah A., Amanda T. Foreman, Phelps Dodge Co., Fort Wayne, Ind., 1954-55; research staff Princeton (N.J.) U., 1955-59; area mgr. IBM, Boulder, Colo., 1959-76; v.p. research and devel. Mead Corp., Dayton, Ohio, 1976-80, pres. Dayton Tinker Corp., 1980—; sec.-treas., dir. Bradford Chem. Corp.; dir. Yellow Springs Instrument Co. Mem. Am. Phys. Soc., AAAS, Mensa, Sigma Xi. Republican. Presbyterian. Patentee in field; contbr. articles to profl. jours. Home: 8 Springhouse Rd Dayton OH 45409 Office: Dayton Tinker Corp 143 Westpark Rd Dayton OH 45459

GAMOTA, GEORGE, university adminstrator, physics educator; b. Lviv, Western Ukraine, May 6, 1939; came to U.S., Aug. 1949; s. Bohdan and Olga (Prymak) G.; m. Christina S. Dawydowycz, Aug. 5, 1961; children—George, Daniel, Alexander. B.Physics, U. Minn., 1961, M.S., 1963; Ph.D. in Physics, U. Mich., 1966. Research asst., teaching asst. U. Minn., Mpls., 1959-63; research asst. U. Mich., Ann Arbor, 1963-66, research assoc., lectr., 1966-67; prof. physics, dir. Inst. Sci. and Tech., 1981—mem. tech. staff Bell Labs., Murray Hill, N.J., 1967-74; research specialist Office Undersec. Def., Research and Engring., Dept. Def., 1976-78, dir. research, 1978-81; mem. adv. Council Research, 1973-75, N.J. Gov.'s Commn. to Evaluate Capital Needs N.J., 1975; chmn., founder Sci. and Tech. Council for Congressman M. Rinaldo, 1974-75; exec. sec. Def. Sci. Bd. Study Fundamental Research in Univs., 1976; mem. Pres. Sci. Adv. Fed. Coordinating Council on Sci. and Engring. Tech., 1976-77; exec. sec. Def. Shale Oil Task Group, 1978; chmn. Def. Com. research, 1978; sr. corp. cons. Sci. Applications Internat. Corp., LaJolla, Calif., McLean, Va., 1981—; mem. adv. subcom. electronics NASA, 1972—, space systems and tech. adv. com., 1979—, research designee adv. com., 1983—, space commercialization com., 1984—; mem. adv. com. Mich. Econ. Devel. Authority, 1982—; mem. Task Force on Def. Requirements and Univ. Preparedness Assn. Am. Univs., 1981; mem. bd. advisors Nat. Coalition Sci. and Tech., 1981—; mem. NRC Office. Sci. and Engring. Personnel Adv. Panel to Assess the Quality of Scientists and Engrs. in Dept. Def. Labs., 1984—; bd. dirs. Mich. Tech. Council, 1981-84. Contbr. articles to profl. jours. Mem. Sr. Exec. Service Pres. Carter, 1979. Recipient Cert. of Appreciation, Presidential Mgmt. Interns, 1980; Meritorious Civilian Service medal U.S. Sec. Defense, Washington, 1981. Fellow Am. Phys. Soc. (mem. panel on pub. affairs 1981—), AAAS, Ukrainian Engrs. Soc. Am.; mem. IEEE (research and devel. com. 1979—), N.Y. Acad. Scis., Sigma Xi. Office: Inst Sci and Tech U Mich 2200 Bonisteel Blvd Ann Arbor MI 48109

GAMSKY, NEAL RICHARD, university administrator, psychology educator; b. Menasha, Wis., Feb. 17, 1931; s. Andrew P. and Lillian G.; m. Irene Janet Jimos, Aug. 16, 1956; children—Elizabeth, Patricia. B.S., U. Wis.-Madison, 1954, M.S., 1959, Ph.D., 1965. Counselor, Appleton Pub. Schs. (Wis.), 1959-62; ednl. and counseling cons. Wis. Div. Mental Hygiene, 1967. dir. ednl. services Wis. Diagnostic Center, Madison, 1962-67; dir. research pupil personnel services Coop. Edn. Service Agy., Waupan, Wis., 1967-70; dir. student counseling center Ill. State U., Normal, 1970-73, v.p. student affairs, prof. psychology, 1973—; Served with U.S. Army, 1954-56. Mem. Am. Psychol. Assn., Am. Assn. Counseling and Devel., Nat. Assn. Student Personnel Adminstrs., Am. Assn. Higher Edn., Am. Coll. Personnel Assn., Am. Orthopsychiat. Assn. Author: (with G.F. Farwell and B. Mathieu-Coughlan) The Counselor's Handbook, 1974; contbr. 26 articles in field to profl. jours. Office: 506 DeGarmo Hall Normal IL 61761

GANATRA, BHADRABALA BALVANT, neurologist, educator; b. Dar es Salaam, Tanzania, July 9, 1949; came to U.S., 1977; d. Keshavji Ramji and Shanta K. (Jasani) Tanna; m. Balvant Kurji Ganatra, May 1, 1976. Inter Sci., Elphinstone Coll., Bombay, India, 1969; M.D., Grant Med. Coll., Bombay, 1973. Diplomate Am. Bd. Internal Medicine, Am. Bd. Neurology. Intern, Hurley Med. Ctr., Flint, Mich., 1977; resident St. Louis U., 1979-82; asst. clin. prof. neurology Mich. State U., Lansing, 1982—. Mem. Am. Acad. Neurology. Home: 1146 Springbarrow Dr Flint MI 48504 Office: 3239 Beecher Rd Flint MI 48504

GANDHI, BHARAT R., construction company executive; b. India, Oct. 16, 1942; came to U.S., 1971; naturalized, 1979; s. Ramanlal and Shardaben (Sura) G.; m. Purnima Bharat, Dec. 25, 1966; children—Manish, Nisha. B.S. in Civil/Sanitary Engring., V.J.J. Inst., Bombay, India, 1964; postgrad. constrn. engring. U. Wis., 1971-72. Ptnr., v.p. constrn. co. in India; project mgr. Corbetta Constrn. Co. Des Plaines, Ill., 1972-75; project mgr. Pepper Constrn. Co., Schaumburg, Ill., 1975—, v.p. healthcare div., 1981-84, exec. v.p., 1984—. Contbg. author articles in field to profl. publs. Home: 2333 Sussex St Northbrook IL 60062 Office: Pepper Construction Co 643 N Orleans St Chicago IL 60610

GANDT, JEROME OTTO, dentist, health care administrator; b. Appleton, Wis., Aug. 28, 1930; s. Otto A. and Hedwig Cecelia (Hoppe) G.; children—Brian, Kathleen, Caroline. Student, Lawrence Coll., 1948-49; B.S., Marquette U., 1952, D.D.S., 1955. Lic. dentist, Wis. Pres., Valley Dental Assocs. Ltd., Green Bay, Wis., 1958—; pres., founder Wilderness Watch Inc., Green Bay, 1969—; chief exec. officer, v.p. Dental Group Ltd., Green Bay, 1980-83; v.p., Prepaid Profl. Services, Ltd., Green Bay, 1981—, also dir.; cons., plan dir. Prepaid Profl. Services Ltd., 1981—. Contbr. articles to profl. jours. Mem. adv. council Upper Mississippi River Basin Commn. Served to capt. USAF, 1955-57. Fellow Am. Endodontic Soc., Acad. Gen. Dentistry; mem. Am. Dental Assn., Chgo. Dental Soc., Wis. Dental Assn. Club: Sturgeon Bay Yacht. Avocations: sailing. Office: Valley Dental Assocs Ltd 1745 Dousman St Green Bay WI 54303

GANNON, RICHARD GALEN, state senator, rancher, farmer; b. Goodland, Kans., July 29, 1950; s. Bill Elmer and Geraldine Francis (Veselik) G.; m. Martha Ellen Nall, Nov. 26, 1976; 1 dau., Jessica Michelle. A.A., Colby Community Coll., 1970; B.S. in Edn., Kansas U., 1973. Vice-pres. Rocking Chair Farms Inc., Goodland, 1973—; mem. Kans. Senate, 1976—, minority whip, 1985—. Active 4-H, 1980—. Recipient citation Meritorious Service, Kans. Vets. World War I, 1978. Mem. Nat. Conf. State Legislatures, Midwestern Conf.-Council State Govts. (vice chmn. agr., food policy and nutrition com.), First Congressional Dist. Democrats, Acacia Frat. (dir. Kans. U. chpt. 1978—, pres. 1981—), Kans. U. Alumni Assn. (life). Democrat. Roman Catholic. Clubs: KC, Elks. Home: Route 3 Box 68 Goodland KS 67735 Office: State Capitol Topeka KS 66612

GANO, KENNETH REDMAN, JR., welding supply company executive, lawyer; b. Charleston, Ill., Mar. 11, 1952; s. Kenneth Redman Gano and Melba Maxine Gano Brown; m. Charlotte Amelia Carlet, May 21, 1983; 1 child, Jacob Redman. B.A., Eastern Ill. U., 1977; J.D., No. Ill. U., 1980. Bar: Ill. 1980, U.S. Dist. Ct. (cen. dist.) Ill. 1980. Assoc. Ron Tulin, Ltd., Charleston, 1980-82; ptnr. Newton & Gano, Charleston, 1982-84; mgr. Gano Welding Supply, Charleston, 1984—; instr. Lakeland Coll., Mattoon, Ill., 1980-82, Eastern Ill. U., Charleston, 1983. Active Coles-Moultrie Concerned Citizens, Charleston. Mem. Ill. Bar Assn., ABA, Ill. Trial Lawyers Assn., Coles-Cumberland Bar Assn. Office: Gano Welding Supply 320 Railroad St Charleston IL 61920

GANS, ERNA IRENE, printing co. exec.; b. Bielsko, Poland; d. Adolf and Rosa (Pelzman) Reicher; came to U.S., 1948, naturalized, 1953; B.A., Roosevelt U., 1971; M.A., Loyola U., Chgo., 1974; m. Henry Gans, Apr. 16, 1947; children—Alan, Howard. Asst. prof. dept. sociology Loyola U., Chgo., 1976; pres. Internat. Label & Printing Co., Bensenville, Ill., 1972—. Chmn., Skokie (Ill.) Youth Commn., 1968—; bd. govs. Israel Bond Orgn.; founder, chmn. Holocaust Meml. Found. Ill. Mem. Am. Sociol. Assn., Nat. Fedn. Ind. Bus., Am. Acad. Polit. and Social Sci. Democrat. Jewish. Clubs: B'nai B'rith (pres. 1976—). Home: 2812 Woodland Dr Northbrook IL 60062 Office: 810 Maple Lane Bensenville IL 60106

GANSEN, ADRIAN PETER, JR., dentist; b. Shawano, Wis., July 11, 1924; s. Adrian Peter and Eva Emma (Cattau) G.; m. Irene I. Kroening, Oct. 1, 1948 (dec. 1960); m. Janalee Gay Fellenz, June 16, 1962; children—Adrian P. III, Steven S. Schultz. D.D.S., Marquette U., 1951 Pvt. practice dentistry, Shawano, Wis., 1951—; cons. Delta Dental Plan of Wis., Stevens Point, 1981—. Patentee dressing for tooth dry socket, 1977. Pres. council Peace United Ch. Christ, Shawano, 1962. Served to lt. col. USAF, 1943-84. Fellow Internat. Coll. Dentists; mem. ADA, Shawano County Dental Soc. (pres. 1955, 57, 65, 72), Am. Acad. Orthodontics for Gen. Practice (pres. 1976-77), Fedn. Orthodontic

Assns. (pres. 1984—), Wis. Dental Assn., Piere Fauchard Acad., Omicron Kappa Upsilon, Shawano C. of C. (dir. 1968-71). Republican. Lodge: Am. Legion. Avocations: Hunting; fishing; skiing; boating; travel. Home: 136 Circle Dr Shawano WI 54166 Office: Gansen Dental Offices Ltd 312 W Green Bay St Box 7 Shawano WI 54166

GANSON, MICHAEL BLAINE, lawyer; b. Cin., May 23, 1952; s. Norman J. and Reva C. (Cirkin) G.; m. Ellen T. Bernstein, May 1, 1983; 1 child, Adam J. Student U. Cin., 1970, Ohio U., 1970-73; B.A., Ohio State U., 1974; J.D., Stetson U., 1978. Bar: Ohio 1978, Fla. 1978, U.S. Dist. Ct. (mid. dist.) Fla. 1978, U.S. Dist. Ct. (so. dist.) Ohio 1981, U.S. Supreme Ct. 1982. Law clerk to presiding justice U.S. Dist. Ct. (mid. dist.) Fla., Tampa, 1978; assoc. E.G. Boone, P.A., Venice, Fla., 1978-81, Nippert & Nippert, Cin., 1981-83; ptnr. Heuck & Ganson, Cin., 1983—. Trustee Asthma and Allergy Found. Am., Cin., 1982—, Big Bros./Big Sisters Assn., Cin., 1983-85, Adath Israel Men's Club, Cin., 1983-85, Jewish Nat. Fund, Cin., 1985. Mem. Ohio State Bar Assn., Cin. Bar Assn., Assn. Trial Lawyers Am., Ohio Acad. Trial Lawyers. Democrat. Jewish. Home: 8735 Tanager Woods Dr Cincinnati OH 45249 Office: Heuck & Ganson 1000 Atlas Bank Bldg 524 Walnut St Cincinnati OH 45202

GANSTER, DENNIS GEORGE, marketing executive; b. Pitts., Jan. 9, 1951; s. George S. and Theresa L. (Catanzaro) G.; m. Beverly J. Shelton, Aug. 8, 1975; children—Matthew, Andrew. B.S.I.E., U. Pitts., 1972; M.B.A., John Carroll U., 1980. Tech. rep. Comshare Inc., Pitts., 1972-73, mktg. rep., Cleve., 1973-74, dist. sales mgr., Cleve., 1974-80, area sales mgr., Cleve., 1980-81, profit planning mgr., Ann Arbor, Mich., 1981-82, dir. mktg., 1982—. Recipient President's award Comshare Inc., Ann Arbor, 1983. Mem. Planning Execs. Inst., Am. Mgmt. Assn., Mensa. Office: Comshare Inc PO Box 1588 Ann Arbor MI 48116

GANT, MARGARET DELGATTY, librarian; b. Flin Flon, Man., Can., Mar. 23, 1941; came to U.S., 1964; d. Clarence Robert Delgatty; m. Charles Francis Gant, Sept. 10, 1962; children—Francis (dec.), Elizabeth, Stephanie, Hilary. B.S. with honors, U. S.D., 1977; M.L.S., Emporia State U., 1982. Dir. Vermillion Pub. Library, S.D., 1973-76; librarian Holcomb Schs., Kans., 1979-81, United Sch. Dist. 457, Garden City, Kans., 1981—; chmn. Kans. Continuing Edn. Com., 1979-81; mem. Gov. Carlin's Network Bd., State of Kans., 1981-82. Columnist, Garden City Telegram. Contbr. articles to newspapers. Mem. ALA (cert.), Kans. Library Assn., Mountain Plains Library Assn., Am. Soc. Pub. Adminstrn., P.E.O. Roman Catholic. Home: 2004 Antelope Garden City KS 67846

GAPEN, DELORES KAYE, university library director; b. Mitchell, S.D., July 1, 1943. B.A. in Sociology, U. Washington, 1970, M.L.S., 1971. Gen. cataloger Coll. William and Mary Library, Williamsburg, Va., 1971-72; asst. head quick editing Ohio State U. Library, Columbus, 1972-74, quick editing head, 1974-77; asst. dir. tech. services Iowa State U. Library, Ames, 1977-81; dean of libraries U. Ala., University, 1981-84; dir. gen. library system U. Wis., Madison, 1984—. Contbr. articles to profl. jours. Mem. Online Computer Library Ctr. (trustee 1978—, exec. com. bd. trustees 1981-82, fin. com. 1982—), ALA, Wis. Library Assn., Ala. Library Assn., Southeastern Library Assn. Office: 360 Meml Library U Wis Madison 728 State St Madison WI 53706

GARB, ELLIOTT LAWRENCE, university administrator; b. Feb. 23, 1940; m. Frances Carrow; children—Micah, Sarah. B.A., Alma Coll., 1962; M.A., U. R.I., 1968; Ph.D., U. Iowa, 1980. Housing officer U. R.I., Kingston, 1965-68; dir. housing Moorhead State U., Minn., 1968-69, acting assoc. dean and dir. housing, 1969-70, assoc. dean, dir. housing, 1970-83; asst. chancellor for student affairs U. Wis., Eau Claire, 1983—. Contbr. articles to profl. jours. Mem. program and staff subcom. Ind. Sch. Dist. 152 Task Force, Moorhead, Minn., 1981, chmn. Title IX adv. bd., 1981-83; mem. City Joint Econ. Devel. and Mktg., Moorhead, 1982-83; mem. fund raising com. Eau Claire Regional Arts Council, 1984. Mem. Nat. Assn. Student Personnel Adminstrs., Am. Coll. Personnel Assn. Served with U.S. Army, 1963-65. Home: 1421 Jensen Rd Eau Claire WI 54701 Office: Univ Wis Schofield 240 Eau Claire WI 54701

GARBER, LAWRENCE LEE, chemistry educator; b. Goshen, Ind., July 4, 1942; s. Joseph Hess and Thelma M. (Hostetler) G.; m. Carolyn Mae Friedemann, Aug. 28, 1965; 1 child, Natalie Renee. B.A., Goshen Coll., 1963; Ph.D., Mich. State U., 1967. Asst. prof. Goshen Coll., 1968-69; assoc. prof. chemistry Ind. U.-South Bend, 1969—. Contbr. articles to sci. jours. Recipient Herman Lieber Disting. Teaching award Ind. U., 1980; Sigma Xi award, 1967. Mem. Am.Chem. Soc. (sect. chmn. 1982; Service award 1983, 84), AAAS, Ind. Acad. Sci., AAUP. Democrat. Lutheran. Avocations: hiking; mountain climbing; cross-country skiing. Home: 4022 Kennedy Dr South Bend IN 46614 Office: Indiana U 1700 Mishawaka Ave South Bend IN 46634

GARBER, SAMUEL B., lawyer, retail company executive; b. Chgo., Aug. 16, 1934; s. Morris and Yetta (Cohen) G.; children—Debra Lee, Diane Lori. J.D., U. Ill., 1958; M.B.A., U. Chgo., 1968. Bar: Ill., 1958; mem. firm Brown, Dashow and Langluttig, Chgo., 1960-62; corporate counsel Walgreen Co., 1962-69; v.p., gen. counsel, exec. asst. to the pres. Jewel Box Stores Corp., 1969-73; dir. legal affairs Stop & Shop Co., Inc., 1973-74; gen. counsel Goldblatt Bros., Inc., 1974-76; v.p., sec., gen. counsel Evans, Inc., 1976—; prof. bus. law DePaul U., 1975—. Served with U.S. Army, 1958-60. Mem. ABA, Nat. Retail Mchts. Assn., Ill. Retail Mchts. Assn. Clubs: Carlton, East Bank. Home: 320 Oakdale Chicago IL 60657 Office: Evans Inc 36 S State St Chicago IL 60603

GARBER, SANDRA LUCILLE, researcher in pathology; b. Chgo., June 12, 1942; d. Michael Herbert and Mildred Marie (Thorman) G. Ph.B., Northwestern U., 1975; Ph.D. Loyola U., Chgo., 1981. Postdoctoral fellow U. Pitts., 1981-83; sr. research assoc. U. Ill.-Chgo., 1983—. Contbr. articles to profl. jours. Mem. Am. Soc. Clin. Pathologists, AAAS, Am. Assn. Anatomists, Internat. Soc. Lymphology, Sigma Xi. Avocations: scuba diving, cross country skiing, tennis. Home: 2333 Cherry Ln Northbrook IL 60062 Office: U Ill-Chgo Dept Pathology PO Box 6998 Chgo IL 60680

GARBER, SHELDON, hospital executive; b. Mpls., July 21, 1920; s. Mitchell and Esther (Amdur) G.; B.A., U. Minn., 1942; postgrad. U. Chgo., 1952-53; m. Elizabeth Sargent Mason, May 16, 1949 (div. May 1983); children—Robert Michael, Daniel Mason, Sarah Sargent; m. Joellen Palmer Prullage, July 21, 1985. Reporter, editor U.P.I., Mpls., Chgo., Springfield, Ill., 1938-58; dir. media services U. Chgo., 1958-64; asso. dir. communication Blue Cross Assn., Chgo., 1964-69; exec. v.p. Charles R. Feldstein & Co., 1969-73; v.p. philanthropy and communication Rush-Presbyn.-St. Luke's Med. Center, Chgo., 1973—, sec. bd. trustees, 1976—; cons. Orthopaedic Research and Edn. Found., Chgo. Zool. Soc. (Brookfield Zoo), Dermatology Found., Commn. on Drug Safety, Great Books Found., Am. Assn. U. Programs in Hosp. Adminstrn., Am. Nurses Found., Sigma Theta Tau; mem. faculty Inst. on Indsl. and Tech. Communications, Colo. State U., Fort Collins, 1970. Adv. bd. Internat. Inst. Edn.; trustee Citizens Information Service, Northlight Theater, Evanston, Ill.; mem. bd. Nat. Soc. Fund Raisers, 1974-77. Served to 1st lt. C.E., AUS, 1942-46, 50-52. Fellow Royal Soc. Health (London); mem. Pub. Relations Soc. Am., Publicity Club Chgo., Am. Soc. Hosp. Pub. Relations Dirs., Am. Pub. Health Assn., AAAS, Nat. Assn. Sci. Writers, Am. Med. Writers Assn., Inst. Medicine Chgo., Chgo. Zoological Soc., Sigma Delta Chi. Club: Union League (Chgo.). Office: 1725 W Harrison Chicago IL 60612

GARBER, STANLEY LEE, physician, obstetrician-gynecologist; b. Dayton, Ohio, May 3, 1933; s. Paul Solomon and Edith Alvertia (Baker) G. B.S., U. Cin., 1955, M.D., 1959. Diplomate Am. Bd. Obstetricians and Gynecologists. Vice pres. South Dayton Ob-Gyn Assn., Ohio, 1964-82, pres., 1982—; assoc. clin. prof. Wright State Coll. Medicine, Dayton, 1975—. Fellow Am. College Obstetricians and Gynecologists. Republican. Mem. Ch. of Brethren. Avocations: concert piano playing; opera coaching; baseball. Home: 3119 Windingway Dayton OH 45419 Office: South Dayton Ob-Gyn Assn 529 E Stroop Rd Dayton OH 45429

GARBINSKI, RONALD ERNEST, journalist, marketing consultant; b. Detroit, Feb. 5, 1952; s. Ernest Henry and Jane (Wach) G. Student Eastern Mich. U., 1970-72; B.Journalism, U. Mo., 1974. Wire editor Adrian Daily Telegram, Mich., 1975; editor news, sports, bus. Observer and Eccentric Newspapers, Livonia, Mich., 1976-82; gen. mgr., exec. editor Huntington Publs., Detroit, 1982-84; editor in chief Mich. Bus. Mag., Southfield, 1984—; pres. Garbinski and Assocs. Mktg. Consultants, Birmingham, Mich., 1976—; real estate agt., Birmingham, 1981—. Herbert J. Davenport fellow U. Mo., 1979. Mem. First Soc. Detroit, Founders Soc. Detroit, Detroit Econ. Club, Soc. Profl. Journalists, Soc. Am. Bus. Econ. Writers, Assn. Area Bus. Publs., Kappa Tau Alpha. Roman Catholic. Clubs: Detroit Press, Downhill Freewheelers (pres. 1976-85). Avocations: bicycle touring, cross country skiing, bird watching, backpacking. Home: 1868 Yosemite Birmingham MI 48008 Office: Mich Bus Mag 302 Cranbrook Ctr Plaza 30161 Southfield Rd Southfield MI 48076

GARCIA, ABEL, investment company executive; b. San Antonio, Apr. 28, 1949; s. Max and Antonia (Hernandez) G.; m. Mary Theresa Bennett, Sept. 9, 1972; children—Aaron James, Theresa Ann. B.B.A., St. Mary's U., San Antonio, 1971; M.B.A., U. Pa., 1973. Jr. analyst Interfirst, Dallas, 1973-77; sr. planner Frito-Lay Co., Dallas, 1977-79; sr. sect. analyst USAA, San Antonio, 1979-81, Republic Bank, Dallas, 1981-83; portfolio mgr. Waddell & Reed, Inc., Kansas City, Mo., 1983—, v.p. United Funds, Inc., 1984—. Served to capt. USAR, 1971-79. Wharton Grad. scholar, 1971. Mem. Fin. Analyst Fedn. Republican. Roman Catholic. Avocations: racquetball; swimming. Office: Waddell & Reed Inc 2400 Pershing Rd PO Box 1343 Kansas City MO 64141

GARCÍA, AGUSTÍN G., lawyer; b. Chgo., Dec. 11, 1949; s. Agustin S. and Helena (Glazé) G.; m. Janet Irene Shaffer, Sept. 9, 1979; 1 child, Danielle. B.A., U. Ill.-Chgo., 1974; J.D., DePaul U., 1977. Bars: Ill. 1979, U.S. Dist. Ct. (no. dist.) Ill. 1979, U.S. Ct. Appeals (7th cir.) 1984. Hearings referee Ill. Dept. Labor, Chgo., 1977-79; staff atty. Office Hearings and Appeals, Soc. Security Adminstrn., Chgo., 1979-81; ptnr. Quiñones and García, Chgo., 1985—. Mem. ABA, Chgo. Bar Assn. (candidates and soc. security coms. 1982—, cert. of appreciation 1984), Ill. Bar Assn., Assn. Trial Lawyers Am., Nat. Orgn. Soc. Security Claimants Reps. Office: Quiñones and García 1200 N Ashland Ave Suite 500 Chicago IL 60622

GARCIA, JOSEPH E., accountant; b. Caibarien, Cuba, Mar. 1, 1945; came to U.S., 1958, naturalized, 1966; s. Enrique and Mirta (Gonzalez) G.; B.S., DePaul U., 1969; M.B.A. in Acctg., U. Miami, 1974. Reservation agt. TWA, Chgo., 1966-68; acctg. mgr. Burger King Corp., 1968-73, Mondex, Inc., 1973-77; asst. controller William M. Mercer, Inc., 1978-84. Mem. Nat. Assn. Accountants. Office: Allstate Ins Co Allstate Plaza Northbrook IL 60062

GARCIA, MARGARITA MARIA, advertising executive; b. Pinar del Rio, Cuba, Oct. 23, 1946; came to U.S., 1961; s. Rogelio Ernesto and Aurora Carmen (Martinez) G. B.A., Barat Coll. of Sacred Heart, 1967; M.S. in Journalism, Northwestern U., 1974. Asst. translator Rotary Internat., Evanston, Ill., 1968-70; acct. exec., copywriter O.M.A.R., Inc., Chgo., 1970-78, acct. supr., 1978-80, spl. asst. to pres., 1980-82, chief copywriter, 1980-82; pres. Hernandez & Garcia, Ltd., Chgo., 1983—; mem. editorial bd. New Guadalupe Shrine Soc., Chgo., 1977; writer 1st Hispanic-Am. Film Festival, Chgo., 1976; contbg. writer La Revista Mag., Chgo., 1979; writer, asst. producer Reporte TV Program, Chgo., 1979-80; copywriter Polit. Poster (Cert. of Excellence 1975). Writer, Com. Friends of Chgo. World's Fair 1992, 1982; mem. Hispanic cultural com. of women's bd. Art Inst. Chgo., 1981; state coordinator Com. Intellectuals for Freedom of Cuba, 1981-82; bd. dirs. Commerce Am. Credit Union. Recipient Cert. of Appreciation, Help for Guatemala Com., Chgo., 1976, Chgo. Internat. Film Festival, 1976; Pub. Service award Networking Together Host Com., Chgo., 1982; named Popularity Contest winner Buenos Dias Chgo. Radio Program, 1983. Mem. Cuban Nat. Journalists Assn., Cuban-Am. C. of C. (dir. 1979-80, 85; alt. deacon Chgo. United). Roman Catholic. Home: 7350 N Karlov Lincolnwood IL 60646

GARD, WILLIAM YOUNG, tooling manufacturing company executive; b. Detroit, June 10, 1927; s. Paul D. and Martha P. (Young) G.; B.S., Yale U., 1949; m. Nancy Frazer Pierson, Feb. 2, 1952; children—Elizabeth, Paul, Martha. Motor products salesman Sun Oil Co., Detroit, 1949-51; sales rep. Dura Corp., Detroit, 1952-67; pres. D & F Corp., Warren, Mich., 1968—. Bds. dirs. Univ.-Liggett Sch., 1971-77, Friends of Grosse Pointe Public Library, 1963-73, Grosse Pointe War Meml. Assn., 1970-73, Detroit Community Music Sch., 1982—; vestryman Christ Episcopal Ch., Grosse Pointe, 1970-73, 76-79. Served with USNR, 1945-46. Mem. Soc. Automotive Engrs., Econ. Club Detroit, Mich. Mfrs. Assn., Nat. Assn. Mfrs., Mich. Model Mfrs. Assn. Clubs: Detroit Athletic, County Club of Detroit. Home: 238 Dean Ln Grosse Pointe Farms MI 48236 Office: 11350 Kaltz Ave Warren MI 48089

GARDER, ARTHUR, mathematics educator; b. Kansas City, Mo., Dec. 17, 1925; s. Arthur O. and Ellen Elizabeth (Josephson) G.; m. Norma Jean Smith, Nov. 13, 1953; children—Douglas Arthur, Claire Elaine. A.A., Kansas City Jr. Coll., 1944; B.S., U. Chgo., 1948; M.A., Washington U., St. Louis, 1950, Ph.D., 1952. Research engr. United Gas Corp., Shreveport, La., 1952-54; mathematician IBM, N.Y.C., 1955-56; research engr. Humble Oil Co., Houston, 1956-64; assoc. prof. Washington U., St. Louis, 1964-66; assoc. prof., prof. math. So. Ill. U., Edwardsville, 1966—. Contbr. articles to profl. jours. Reviewer Math. Revs., 1964—. Served with USAAF, 1945-46. ETO. Mem. Soc. Indsl. and Applied Math., Math. Assn. Am. Home: 815 Harvard Dr Edwardsville IL 62025 Office: Dept Math So Ill U Edwardsville IL 62026

GARDINER, WAYNE JAY, advertising sales manager, novelist; b. Valentine, Nebr., Mar. 1, 1943; s. Lovel Jay and Evelyn Beatrice (De France) G.; m. Kathleen R. Poloway, Dec. 28, 1968; children—Heather Marie, Thomas Jay. B.S. in Edn., Chadron State Coll., 1965. With Chgo. Tribune Newspaper, 1968-81, staff mgr. mktg. services, 1978-81; mgr. midwest sales Food and Wine mag., Am. Express Pub. Co., Chgo., 1981—. Active Lions Club. Served with U.S. Army, 1965-68. Club: Agate of Chgo. Author: The Man on the Left, 1981. Home: 910 Harper Dr Algonquin IL 60102 Office: Food and Wine Mag 500 N Michigan Ave Suite 1520 Chicago IL 60611

GARDNER, CLIFFORD JAMES, JR., banker; b. Chgo., June 25, 1944; s. Clifford James and Mary Elizabeth (Hurley) G.; m. Renell Siemione, July 3, 1965; children—Lorraine, Brian. Student DePaul U., 1964-69. With Continental Ill. Nat. Bank, Chgo., 1962—, ops. mgr. Taipei br. (Taiwan), 1972-76, Paris br., 1976-79, mgr. letter of credit ops. div., Chgo., 1979-81, product mgr. trade fin. div., 1981—, v.p., 1984—. Lay zone minister United Methodist Ch., 1983—. Mem. Mid-Am. Council Internat. Banking (planning bd., 1982— chmn. letter of credit com. 1982-85, sec. 1985—). Home: 2018 Crown Point St Woodridge IL 60517 Office: Continental Ill Nat Bank 231 S LaSalle St Chicago IL 60697

GARDNER, DONALD JOSEPH, hospital personnel administrator; b. Buffalo, June 6, 1930; s. Randle Anthony and Bernadette Louise (Scherer) G.; m. Gertrude Johanna Thiessen, Oct. 27, 1956; children—Donald, John, Mary, Thomas, Paul, Matthew, Rachel, Loretta, Angela, Andrew. B.S.B.A., Washington U., St. Louis, 1956. Wage and salary analyst Barnes Hosp., St. Louis, 1962-66; asst. adminstr. personnel services St. Joseph Hosp., Kirkwood, Mo., 1966-73; dir. personnel Holy Family Hosp., Manitowoc, Wis., 1973-74; dir. personnel St. Anthony's Meml. Hosp., Effingham, Ill., 1975—; mem. rural health manpower resource and adv. com. So. Ill. U.; mem. Ill. Gov.'s Grievance Panel, 1983. Vice chmn. bd. dirs., v.p. St. Anthony's Meml. Hosp. Credit Union, 1976—; bd. dirs. Effingham County (Ill.) Right To Life, 1980—. Served with USN, 1951-55; Korea, China. Mem. So. Ill. Hosp. Personnel Assn. (pres. 1982-83), Am. Soc. Hosp. Personnel Adminstrn., Hosp. Personnel Dirs. Assn. Greater St. Louis (pres. 1969-70). Roman Catholic. Home: Rural Route 3 Box 109 Effingham IL 62401 Office: 503 N Maple St Effingham IL 62401

GARDNER, GARY EDWARD, manufacturing company executive; b. Chgo., Aug. 22, 1954; s. Edward George and Betty Ann (Gueno) G.; m. Denise Barnett, July 29, 1978; 1 son, Brandon Barnett. B.S., U. Ill.-Chgo., 1975; M.B.A., Northwestern U., 1980, J.D., 1980. Compounder, Soft Sheen Products Co., Chgo., 1971-75, mktg. dir., 1975-80, v.p., 1980-83, pres., 1983—; founder Shoptalk mag., 1980. Co-founder V.O.T.E. Community, Chgo., 1982. Mem. Am. Health and Beauty Aids Inst.

GARDNER, INEZ MARIE, lawyer; b. Chgo., Aug. 17, 1948; d. Albert Jerome and Marie (Richards) Bernard; m. Isacc Gardner, Jr., Aug. 17, 1974. B.S., Chgo. State Coll., 1969; J.D., DePaul U., 1973; LL.M., U. Ill., 1974. Bar: Ill. 1975. Asst. state's atty. Cook County, Ill., 1976-80; sole practice trial atty. I.M. Gardner, Ltd., Chgo., 1981—; mem. fed. trial bar No. Dist. Ill.; panel atty. Community Law Project, Cook County Bar Assn., 1983-84. U. Ill. grad. fellow, 1974. Mem. ABA, Ill. Bar Assn., Chgo. Bar Assn., Cook County Bar Assn. Office: I M Gardner Ltd 6708 S Prairie Ave Suite 1 Chicago IL 60637

GARDNER, JAMES ALEXANDER, history educator; b. Desloge, Mo., May 30, 1923; s. Alexander and Jessie Ann (Williams) G. B.S., Washington U., St. Louis, 1949, M.A., 1951, Ph.D., 1963. Tchr. Ritenour Sch. Dist., Overland, Mo., 1949-55; asst. prof. Lindenwood Coll., St. Charles, Mo., 1955-57; prof. history Flat River Jr. Coll., Mo., 1957-65; lectr. Washington U., Flat River, Mo., 1957-65; prof., chmn. dept. history Mineral Area Coll., Flat River, 1965—. Author: Lead King: Moses Austin, 1980. Served with AUS, 1943-46. Mem. Am. Hist. Assn., Western History Assn., Orgn. Am. Historians, Mo. Hist. Soc. Baptist. Avocation: creative writing. Home: 305 N Main St Desloge MO 63601 Office: Mineral Area Coll Old Hwy 67 Flat River MO 63601

GARDNER, JAMES RAYMOND, business executive, county official; b. Indpls., Dec. 24, 1920; s. Raymond and Flora (Eberhardt) G.; B.S., Purdue U., 1950; m. Viola M. Chandler, Sept. 7, 1952; 1 son, John S. Personnel rep., labor relations rep. Western Electric Co., 1952-64; clk.-treas. City of Lawrence, Ind., 1956-60; dep. commr. Ind. Revenue Dept., Indpls., 1964-68; pres. G & H Enterprises, Inc., Indpls., 1957-71, Gardner & Guidone, Inc., Indpls., 1965—; adminstr. Gov.'s Wage Stblzn. Bd.; treas., controller Marion County Health and Hosp. Corp., 1970-77; chief fin. officer Marion County Health Dept., 1978—; sec. Betatek, Inc., Indpls., 1981—. Pres. Lawrence Twp. Civic Assn., 1955-56; dist. commr. Boy Scouts Am., 1951-54; pres. Marion County Fair, 1976-79. Served with USMC, 1943-46. Mem. Ind. Soc. Pub. Accountants, Pi Kappa Alpha Home Assn. (pres. 1964-69, dir. 1960-75), Sagamore of Wabash, Pi Kappa Alpha, Alpha Phi Omega. Methodist (chmn. ofcl. bd.). Lodges: Masons, Rotary. Home: 7625 E 51st St Indianapolis IN 46226 Office: 222 E Ohio St Indianapolis IN 46204

GARDNER, JAMES WILBERT, real estate broker; b. Greenwood, Miss., Nov. 18, 1942; s. Johnny and Carrie B. (Moore) G.; m. Joanne Marie Garrard, Feb. 14, 1970; children—Vanessa, Amy, Kerry, Timothy. A.A., Triton Coll., 1979. Cert. real estate broker. Personnel supr. United Parcel Service, Chgo., 1962-75; owner Paramount Studio, Chgo., 1975-80; real estate broker, owner Mastermind Realty, Inc., Maywood, Ill., 1980—. Social worker St. James Ch., Maywood, Ill., 1980—; mem. Maywood Spl. Events Commn., 1982-85, Maywood Zoning and Planning Commn., 1983—; pres. 17th Ave. Block Club, Maywood, 1972—; mem. com. Boy Scouts Am., 1983—. Mem. Ill. Assn. Realtors(Bronze award 1983; Pres.'s Club). Roman Catholic. Home: 1419 S 17th Ave Maywood IL 60153 Office: 120 S 5th Ave Maywood IL 60153

GARDNER, JAY KENT, data processing executive; b. Davenport, Iowa, Mar. 29, 1947; s. Lowell Edmund and Louise Elizabeth (Eden) G.; m. Constance Jane Moe, July 23, 1973; children—Adam Jay, Joseph Paul, Anne Elizabeth, John Michael. A.S., Scott Community Coll., 1969; B.A., Govs. State U., Park Forest, Ill., 1983. Cert. data processing. Systems analyst Nat. Cash Register Corp., Davenport, Iowa, 1968-70, Northwest Bank, Davenport, 1970-75; ops. mgr. Fin. Industry Systems, Rock Island, Ill., 1975-79; v.p. data processing Microdata, Kankakee, Ill., 1979-83, Midwest Fin. Group, Peoria, Ill., 1984—; part-time instr. Kankakee Community Coll., 1980. Chmn., United Way Kankakee, 1981, 82; sustaining membership chmn. Kankakee Trails council Boy Scouts Am., 1983. Mem. Data Processing Mgmt. Assn. (v.p. 1978-80). Republican. Roman Catholic. Lodge: Kiwanis. Home: 1118 W Sleepy Hollow Ct Peoria IL 61615 Office: MFG Info Systems 1318 S Johanson Rd Bartonville IL 61607

GARDNER, JERRY DEAN, dental surgeon; b. Taylorville, Ill., Feb. 11, 1939; s. Lavern Y. and Helyn R. (Clements) G.; m. Judith M. Waud, June 17, 1961; children—Mark A., Jeffrey S., Jennifer A. B.S. U. Ill.-Chgo. 1961, D.D.S., 1964; M.S. Boston U., 1972. Diplomate Am. Bd. Prosthodontics. Commd. officer Dental Corps U.S. Air Force, 1964, advanced through grades to col.; gen. dental officer U.S. Air Force, 1964-72, prosthodontist, 1972-82, dir. dental services, 1982-85, command dental surgeon, 1985—; cons. to surgeon gen. U.S. Air Force, 1979—, cons. fixed prosthodontics, 1979-81. Decorated Bronze Star, Legion of Merit. Fellow Am. Coll. Prosthodontics, Internat. Coll. Dentistry; mem. ADA. Avocations: oil painting, fishing, collecting antiques. Home: 305 S Railway Ave Mascoutah IL 62258 Office: Scott AFB Dental Clinic Scott AFB IL 62225

GARDNER, JOHN CRAWFORD, newspaper publisher; b. Atlanta, Apr. 19, 1935; s. James Watts and Mary Jane (McCoy) G.; m. Ann Lindsay, Mar. 24, 1956; children—Ellen, Elizabeth, Paul, John, Matthew. B.S. in Journalism, Northwestern U., 1956; postgrad., Columbia U., 1957. Desk person AP, N.Y.C., 1956-57; reporter Charlotte Observer, N.C., 1957-59; reporter, editor, then pub. So. Illinoisean, Carbondale, 1959-83, pres. 1966-79; pub. Quad City Times, Davenport, Iowa, 1983—; dir. Lindsay-Schaab Newspapers Inc., Decatur. Bd. dirs. So. Ill., Inc., Carbondale, Ill., 1964-79, Quad Cities Devel. Group, Rock Island, Ill., 1985—; exec. com. Quad Cities United Way, Davenport, 1984—; mem. Ill. Humanities Council, Chgo., 1983. Mem. Inland Daily Press Assn. (news com.), Am. Soc. Newspaper Editors (edn. com.), Iowa Press Assn., Soc. Profl. Journalists, Davenport C. of C. (bd. dirs. 1984—). Episcopalian. Clubs: Davenport, Outing (Davenport). Home: 1016 Coffelt Ave Bettendorf IA 52722 Office: Quad City Times 124 E 2d St Davenport IA 52801

GARDNER, LARRY ALLAN, religion educator; b. Camden, Ohio, Aug. 24, 1929; s. Myron Alonzo G. B.A., Capital U., Columbus, 1951; M.Div., Evang. Luth. Theol. Sem., Columbus, 1955; Th.M., Princeton Theol. Sem., 1956; Th.D., Boston U., 1960; postgrad. Oxford U., Eng., 1968-69. Ordained to ministry Am. Luth. Ch., 1959. Instr. practical theology Evang. Luth. Theol. Sem., Columbus, Ohio, 1958-59; asst. prof. religion and psychology Capital U., Columbus, 1959-65, assoc. prof. religion, 1965-67, prof., 1967—, chmn. dept. religion and philosophy, 1982—; dean Regional Council for Internat. Edn. Summer Seminar in Japan, 1973, 75; mem. bd. publ. Am. Luth. Ch., 1978-84. Recipient Praestantia award for disting. teaching Capital U., Columbus, 1966, faculty growth award Am. Luth. Ch., 1968. Mem. Sex Info. and Edn. Council U.S. (profl. assoc.), Alpha Phi Omega. Avocations: sports photography; travel. Home: 911 Pleasant Ridge Ave Columbus OH 43209 Office: Capital U Columbus OH 43209

GARDNER, RICHARD ALLEN, mechanical engineering educator; b. Oak Park, Ill., Dec. 6, 1941; s. Edward M. and Helen R. G.; m. Sandra L. Jenkinson, June 13, 1964; children—Michael, Jennifer, Susan. B.S., Purdue U., 1963, M.S., 1965, Ph.D., 1969. Registered profl. engr., Mo., Mont. Asst. prof. Purdue U., West Lafayette, Ind., 1969; asst. prof. Washington U., St. Louis, 1969-75, assoc. prof. mech. engring., 1975—; assoc. prof. U. Wyo., Laramie, 1982-83; cons. engring. projects with various St. Louis cos., 1969—. Leader, Boy Scouts Am., 1978-81. Contbr. articles to profl. jours. Recipient Ralph R. Teetor teaching award, 1970. Mem. AIAA, ASME, Bioelectromagnetic Soc. Avocations: fishing; camping; woodworking. Office: Mechanical Engring Dept Campus Box 1185 Washington Univ Saint Louis MO 63130

GARDNER, STEVEN LESLIE, lawyer; b. Cleve., Nov. 4, 1950. B.S., Ohio State U., 1972, J.D., 1976; M.S.M., Case Western Res. U., 1973. Bar: Ohio 1976. Assoc., Zacks Luper & Wolinetz, Columbus, Ohio, 1976-77; asst. atty. gen. State of Ohio, Columbus, 1977-81; atty. Frost & Assocs., Columbus, 1981-84, McDonald, Hopkins & Hardy, Cleve., 1984—. Mem. Ohio Bar Assn., Cleve. Bar Assn., Cuyahoga County Bar Assn., Ohio Assn. Civil Trial Attys., Cleve. Acad. Trial Attys. Office: 1100 E Ohio Bldg Cleveland OH 44114

GARDNER, WILLIAM FREDERICK, professional baseball official; b. New London, Conn., July 19, 1927; s. Lesley B. and Eva M. (Maynard) G.; m. Barbara Carnaroli, July 18, 1952; children—Gwen Gardner Lakowsky, Shelly A., William Frederick. Student Chapman Tech. Sch., New London, 1943-45. Second baseman N.Y. Giants, 1954-55, Balt. Orioles, 1955-59, Washington Senators, 1960-61, N.Y. Yankees, 1961-62, Boston Red Sox, 1962-63; coach Boston Red Sox, 1965-66; mgr. minor leagues, 1967-76; coach Montreal Expos, 1977-78; mgr. minor leagues, 1979-80; coach Minn. Twins, Mpls., 1981, field mgr., 1981—. Served with U.S. Army, 1947-48. Democrat. Roman Catholic. Office: Hubert H Humphrey Metrodome 501 Chicago Ave S Minneapolis MN 55415

GARFIELD, JOAN BARBARA, mathematics/statistics educator; b. Milw., May 4, 1950; d. Sol L. and Amy L. (Nusbaum) G.; m. Michael G. Luxenberg, Aug. 17, 1980; children—Harlan Ross and Rebecca Ellen (twins). Student, U. Chgo., 1968; B.S., U. Wis., 1972; M.A., U. Minn., 1978, Ph.D., 1981. Asst. prof. math./stats. The Gen. Coll., U. Minn., Mpls., 1981—, coordinator research and evaluation, 1984—; created various tables on evaluations of coll. retention programs, 1979-82, 85. Mem. Am. Statis. Assn., Am. Assn. Higher Edn., Am. Ednl. Research Assn., Nat. Council Tchrs. Math. Jewish. Club:

Mpls. Twins Topics (research chmn. 1984—). Avocations: violinist/violist; participant in lit. group. Office: Div Sci Bus and Math 106 Nicholson Hall General College Univ Minnesota 216 Pillsbury Ave SE Minneapolis MN 55455

GARFIELD, JOEL FRANKLIN, life and health insurance agent; b. Detroit, May 15, 1944; s. Jack and Alyce H. (Pliss) G.; m. Linda Joyce Ferst, Aug. 11, 1969; children—Jennifer M., Marla L., Stephanie M., Lauren Andrea. Student U. Detroit, 1962-64, Mich. State U., 1964-65; B.A. in History, Grand Valley State Coll., Mich., 1967; M.A. in History, U. Detroit, 1969. Registered health underwriter; C.L.U.; lic. life ins. counselor. Sales rep. IBM Corp., 1969; ins. salesman Mass. Indemnity Ins. Co., 1970-72, Mass. Mut. Life Ins. Co., 1972-82; life and health ins. agt. Conn. Mut. Life Ins. Co., Southfield, Mich., 1982—; tchr. life underwriter tng. course; spl. cons. to Mich. Ins. Bur., 1982—. Vice pres. Met. Detroit B'nai B'rith Council, 1979-82, charge youth services appeal fundraising, 1980-81. Named Agt. of Month, Mass. Mut. Life Ins. Co., 1980; life and qualifying mem. Million Dollar Round Table, 1973—; fellow in history U. Detroit, 1968-69. Mem. Am. Soc. CLUs, Oakland County Estate Planning Council, Greater Detroit Assn. Life Underwriters (sec.), Mich. Assn. Life Underwriters, Nat. Assn. Life Underwriters (vice chmn. field practices), Mich. Assn. Life Ins. Counselors. Lodge: B'nai B'rith. Home: 20785 Winchester St Southfield MI 48076 Office: 3000 Town Center Suite 2400 Southfield MI 48075

GARFIELD, NANCY JANE, psychologist; b. N.Y.C., Oct. 24, 1947; d. William M. and Sue D. (Smalley) G.; m. Kenneth R. Softley. B.A., Parsons Coll., 1968; M.S., Western Ill. U., 1970; Ph.D., U. Mo., Columbia, 1975. Cert. psychologist, Kans. Counselor, career specialist Okla. State U., 1975-77; assoc. dean student life Wichita State U., 1977-80; staff psychologist Psychology Service VA Med. Ctr., Topeka, Kans., 1980—, dir. tng., 1981—; cons. Nat. Ctr. Career Research and Devel., Dept. Def., Columbus, Ohio, 1981-83; psychology rep. Kans. Behavioral Scis. Regulatory Bd., 1983—. Author: Career Exploration Groups, 1983. Assoc. editor Jour. Counseling and Devel., 1983—. Contbr. articles to profl. jours., chpts. to books. Bd. dirs. Kans. Med. Credit Union, Topeka, 1980-84. Mem. Am. Assn. Counseling and Devel. (bd. dirs.), Am. Coll. Personnel Assn. (senator, Presdl. Service award 1984), Am. Psychol. Assn. (site visitor 1982—), Kans. Psychol. Assn. Office: Psychology Service 116B 2200 Gage Blvd Topeka KS 66622

GARFIELD, ROBERT EARL, lawyer; b. Cleve., Sept. 23, 1937; s. Irwin Charles Garfield and Mathilda Rose; m. Joan Susan Ross, Mar. 24, 1963; children—Mark Clayton, Steven Matthew, Patricia Faith. B.A., Western Res. U., 1959; LL.B., Cornell U., 1962; LL.M., Georgetown U., 1969. Bar: Ohio 1962. Trial atty. Office Chief Counsel, IRS, Washington, 1963-68; assoc. Arter & Hadden, Cleve., 1968-69; ptnr. Hertz & Kates, Cleve., 1969-72, Chattman, Garfield, Friedlander & Paul, Cleve., 1973—. Bd. dirs., counsel Cleve. Childrens Mus., 1981. Served to capt. USAR, 1966-68. Mem. ABA, Ohio State Bar Assn., Cleve. Bar Assn., Cuyahoga Bar Assn. Democrat. Jewish. Club: Oakwood (Cleve. Heights). Avocations: golf; music; travel; history of WWII. Office: Chattman Garfield Friedlander & Paul 400 Engineers Bldg Cleveland OH 44114

GARGIULO, WILLIAM CARMINE, lawyer; b. Cleve., July 19, 1935; s. William A. and Marion R. (Sassane) G.; m. Sharon May Williams, Oct. 10, 1959; children—Susan R., Dawn M., Darrick W. A.B., Ohio U., 1957; postgrad., John Carroll U., 1960-63; J.D., Cleve. State U., 1969. Bar: Ohio 1969, U.S. Dist. Ct. Ohio 1970. Tchr., coach St. Joseph High Sch., Cleve., 1958-65; tchr. Wickliffe High Sch., Ohio, 1965-73; asst. county prosecutor and dir. Lake Geauga narcotic unit, Lake County Pros. Atty.'s Office, Painesville, Ohio, 1973-76; ptnr. Manley and Gargiulo, Willoughby, Ohio, from 1969; now sole practice, Eastlake, Ohio; pres. Export Cons., Inc., Cleve., 1964-66. Legal research writer Jefferson Ency. Contbr. articles to profl. jours. Served with USGGR, 1954-57. Mem. Ohio Bar Assn., Lake County Bar Assn. Democrat. Roman Catholic. Lodge: Rotary (pres. Wickliffe club 1982). Home: 29037 Homewood Dr Wickliffe OH 44092 Office: William C Gargiulo LPA 35550 Curtis Blvd 401 Eastlake OH 44094

GARLAND, CHARLES RALEIGH, music educator; b. Potter, Nebr., June 10, 1917; s. Charles Raleigh and Pearl (Finchum) G.; m. Shirley W. White, Sept. 9, 1945; 1 child, Susan. B.S., U. Ky., 1939; M.A., U. Iowa, 1942, Ph.D., 1945. Asst. prof. music Morningside Coll., Sioux City, Iowa, 1945-51; assoc. prof. U. Mo., Columbia, 1951-62; prof. Chgo. Mus. Coll., 1962—. Composer. Mem. AAUP, Music Tchrs. Nat. Assn., Phi Mu Alpha. Democrat. Methodist. Club: Cliff Dwellers (bd. dirs. 1982-85) (Chgo.). Avocation: jewelry making. Home: 828 W George St Chicago IL 60657 Office: 430 S Michigan Ave Chicago IL 60605

GARMER, WILLIAM ROBERT, lawyer; b. Balt., May 8, 1946; s. William M. and Grace (DeLane) G. B.A., U. Ky., 1968, J.D., 1975. Bar: Ky. 1975, U.S. Dist. Ct. (ea. dist.) Ky. 1977, U.S. Ct. Appeals (6th cir.) 1980, U.S. Supreme Ct. 1979. Law clk. to pres. justice U.S. Dist. Ct. (ea. dist.) Ky., Lexington, 1975-76; adj. prof. law litigation skills U. Ky. Law Sch., Lexington, 1981—; ptnr. Savage, Garmer & Elliott, P.S.C., Lexington, 1984—; mem. paralegal studies adv. counsel Midway Coll., 1983—; mem. faculty trial advocacy course, continuing legal edn. evidence seminar U. Ky. Law Sch., 1983, mem. faculty seminars on practice and procedure, 1984; mem. speedy trial com. U.S. Dist. Ct. (ea. dist.) Ky. Casenote editor St. Mary's Law Jour., 1975. Contbr. articles to profl. jours. Fayette county chmn. Harvey Sloane for Gov. Campaign, Lexington, 1979, 83; campaign chmn. Bill Lear for Legislature, Lexington, 1984. Served with USAF, 1969-73. Mem. ABA, Ky. Bar Assn. (com. on specialization and cert. 1982—), Fayette County Bar Assn., Ky. Acad. Trial Attys., Assn. Trial Lawyers Am., Phi Delta Phi. Democrat. Prebyterian. Office: Savage Garmer & Elliott PSC 300 W Short St Lexington KY 40507

GARMIRE, MARY JO, county library branch administrator; b. Bluffton, Ind., Dec. 12, 1954; d. Robert Hudson and Harriett Elizabeth (Heaney) Garmire. B.A. in Journalism, Central Mich. Univ., 1977; M.L.S., Univ. Mich., Ann Arbor, 1979. Cert. provisional tchr.; cert. librarian. Librarian, Mich. Audubon Soc., Mt. Pleasant, 1977-78; reference student asst. Central Mich. Univ. Library, Mt. Pleasant, 1976-78; library asst. Sturgis Pub. Library, Mich., 1979; asst. librarian Dorsch br. Monroe County Library System, Monroe, Mich., 1979-80, head librarian, 1980—. Pub. relations chmn. LWV, Monroe County, Mich., 1980-83, co-pres., 1981-82; sec. Michigan Audubon Soc., 1983-85. Mem. ALA, Mich. Library Assn., U. Mich. Alumnae, Beta Phi Mu. United Methodist. Avocations: Oboe; piano; calligraphy; refinishing furniture; needlecrafts. Office: Dorsch Meml Library 18 First St Monroe MI 48161

GARNER, JAMES PARENT, lawyer; b. Madison, Wis., Jan. 22, 1923; s. Harrison Levi and Mary (Parent) G.; m. Georgia Ann Trebilcock, Oct. 12, 1946; children—Gail G. Garner Resch, Ann G. Garner Catalano, Thomas W., Mary F. B.A., U. Wis.-Madison, 1947; LL.B., Harvard U., 1949. Assoc. Baker, Hostetler & Patterson, Cleve., 1949-58; ptnr. Baker & Hostetler, Cleve., 1959—. Served to capt. U.S. Army, 1943-46, PTO. Mem. ABA, Ohio Bar Assn., Cleve. Bar Assn. (trustee 1969-71), Selden Soc. Republican. Congregational. Clubs: Union (Cleve.); Harvard (N.Y.C.). Home: 31000 Shaker Blvd Pepper Pike OH 44124 Office: Baker & Hostetler 3100 Nat City Ctr Cleveland OH 44114

GARNER, LAFORREST DEAN, dental educator; b. Muskogee, Okla., Aug. 20, 1933; s. Sanford G. and Fannie (Thompson) G.; m. Alfreida Thomas, July 18, 1964; children—Deana Y., Thomas L., Sanford E. D.D.S., Ind. U., 1957, M.S.D., 1959; cert. orthodontics Ind. U., 1961. Diplomate Am. Bd. Orthodontics. Mem. faculty Sch. Dentistry Ind. U., Indpls., 1959—, assoc. prof. dentistry, 1967-70, prof., chmn. orthodontics dept., 1970—. Fellow Am. Coll. Dentists; mem. Am. Assn. Orthodontists, E.H. Angle Soc., Great Lakes Soc. Orthodontists, Internat. Assn. Dental Research, Am. Cleft Palate Assn., Ind. Dental Assn., Indpls. Dist. Dental Soc. Democrat. Presbyterian. Club: Nat. Boule (Indpls.). Contbr. articles to profl. jours. Home: 6245 Riverview Dr Indianapolis IN 46260 Office: 1121 W Michigan St Indianapolis IN 46202 also 2416 Capitol Ave N Indianapolis IN 46208

GARNER, LAWRENCE CRAIG, optometrist; b. Chgo., Mar. 20, 1951; s. Seymour and Maxine (Bender) G.; m. Patricia Anne Brousseau, Dec. 23, 1973; children—Carolyn Nicole, Stephen Wade. B.S., Ind. State U., 1973; D.Optometry, Ill. Coll. Optometry, 1977. Pvt. practice optometry, Garner Eye Care Assocs., Elk Grove Village, Ill., 1977—. Fellow Am. Acad. Optometry; mem. Ill Optometric Assn. (v.p. 1980—), Am. Optometric Assn., Elk Grove Village Jaycees. Republican. Jewish. Avocations: Golfing; hunting. Home: 1217 Tyburn Dr Schaumburg IL 60194 Office: Garner Eye Care Assocs 60 Turner Ave Elk Grove Village IL 60007

GARNER, ROYAL STANLEY, physician, flight surgeon; b. St. Louis, Mar. 11, 1940; s. Lynn Mason and Esther Vivian (Smith) G.; m. Mary Ellen Arrington, Mar. 30, 1968 (div. 1977) 1 dau., Darcy Paige; m. Karen Elizabeth Long, Feb. 11, 1977. A.B., Mo. U., 1963, M.D., 1968. Diplomate Am. Acad. Family Physicians. Intern U.S. Air Force, Wright-Patterson AFB, Ohio; commd. capt. U.S. Army, 1969, advanced through grades to lt. col., 1985; gen. practice medicine, Jefferson City, Mo., 1971—; med. dir. Westinghouse Electric, Jefferson City, 1972—; med. cons. Social Security Disability, Jefferson City, 1972—. Decorated Bronze Star, Air medal. Fellow Am. Acad. Family Physicians. Republican. Baptist. Avocations: railroading; fishing; flying. Home: 2025 Wendemere Ct Jefferson City MO 65101 Office: 1804 Southwest Blvd Jefferson City MO 65101

GARNER, STEPHEN FOSTER, tool company executive; b. Dayton, Ohio, Dec. 23, 1949; s. Joseph Marion and Janet Murray (Renaker) G.; B.S. in Physics, Ohio State U., 1972; M.B.A., Cornell U., Ithaca, N.Y., 1980. Asst. to v.p. eastern ops. Nuclear Engring Co., Inc. subs. Teledyne, Inc., Morehead, Ky., 1972-74, sales engr., Louisville, Ky., 1974-75; project engr., mgr. Protective Packaging, Inc. subs. Teledyne, Inc., Louisville, 1975-78; planning cons. Emerson Electric Co., St. Louis, 1980-82; dir. strategic planning Harris Calorific Co. subs. Emerson Electric, Cleve., 1982-83; dir. corp. planning Ridge Tool Co. subs. Emerson Electric, Elyria, Ohio, 1983—. Contbr. chpt. to book: Nuclear Power Waste Technology Transportation and Burial of Radioactive Waste, 1978. Mem. Ridge Tool Co. Mgmt. Club (v.p. 1984—), Health Physics Soc. (sec. Blue Grass chpt. 1974-75). Republican. Methodist. Club: Edgewater (Cleve.). Avocations: photography; competitive sailing; guitar; flute; wilderness backpacking. Home: 350 Bassett Rd Bay Village OH 44140 Office: Ridge Tool Co 400 Clark St Elyria OH 44036

GARNHOLZ, EDWARD WILLIAM, lawyer, arbitrator; b. St. Louis, Aug. 22, 1922; s. Edward S. and Marcella (Yochim) G.; m. Ivy Gall, July 24, 1948; children—Scott, Cynthia, Brant. B.S., B.A., Washington U., 1943, LL.B., 1947. Bar: Mo., 1947. Mem. Mo. Ho. of Reps., 1952-54; pros. atty., St. Louis County, 1955-58; sole practice, St. Louis, 1947—; mem. Bd. Election Commrs., St. Louis County, 1958-62; labor arbitrator Am. Arbitration Assn., 1977—, Fed. Mediation and Conciliation Service; atty. Scottish Rite, Mo., 1961—; gen. counsel Internat. Supreme Council, Order DeMolay, 1982—. Served as lt. USN, 1943-46. Mem. Mo. Bar Assn., St. Louis Met. Bar Assn., Indsl. Relations Research Assn., Am. Law Inst. Am. Arbitration Assn., Fed. Mediation Service. Lodges: Rotary, Masons. Home: 2323 Manor Grove Dr Chesterfield MO 63017 Office: 141 N Meramec Ave Ste 11 Clayton MO 63105

GAROFALO, VINCENT JAMES, teacher educator; b. Oneida, N.Y., July 6, 1939; s. Leonard John and Ethel Ida (Reick) G.; m. Patricia Sue Scheible, Jan. 15, 1966; children—Gianá, Leonardo, Giovanni, Prudence Keyes. B.A. in History, Albright Coll., 1961; M.A.T. in Social Studies, Colgate U., 1962; Ph.D. in Reading Edn., Syracuse U., 1969. Dir. Reading Ctr., Md. State Coll., Princess Anne, 1968-71; dir. spl edn. Clarksdale Pub. Sch., Miss., 1971-72; team leader Title I Standing Rock Sioux Tribe, Ft. Yates, N.D., 1972-74; dir. skills learning program U. Wis., Green Bay, 1974-77; dir. spl. services project SUNY, Plattsburg, 1977-79; chmn. edn. Aquinas Coll., Grand Rapids Mich., 1979—; dir. Migrant Research Project, Syracuse U., N.Y., 1968; coordinator and cons. to various confs. and tng. projects; 1968—; instr. COPE Montcalm Community Coll., 1980—. Contbr. articles to profl. jours. Presenter numerous workshops. Vol. U.S. Peace Corps, 1962-64. Mem. Congress of Racial Equality, Coll. KReading Assn., Internat. Reading Assn., Am. Assn. U. Profs., ACLU, Miss. Mental Health Assn., NEA, N.D. Edn., Assn., Alpha Psi Omega. Avocations: organic gardening; piano; classical and jazz music; hiking; reading. Office: Edn Dept Aquinas Coll 1607 Robinson Rd Grand Rapids MI 49506

GARRETT, CHARLES WESLEY, therapist and counselor; b. Gainesville, Tex., Apr. 17, 1923; s. Charles Ballard and Opal (Shaver) G.; B.A., So. Meth. U., 1943, B.D., 1946, M.A., 1948; Ph.D., N.Y. U., 1953; m. Avis Devon Bedford, Sept. 24, 1979; children—Susanna Wesley, Charles Davidson, Alice Frances, Thomas Ruston. Pvt. practice therapy, Prairie Village, Kans., 1970—; cons. Johnson County Dist. Cts., 1970—. Mem. Am. Psychol. Assn., Kans. Psychol. Assn. Research in geriatrics, conceptual models of health.

GARRETT, JOHN MICHAEL, ophthalmologist; b. Indpls., Sept. 29, 1948; s. Vernon and Patricia Garrett; m. Karen Ann Gookins; 1 child, Hillary Michele. B.S. in Zoology, Ind. U., 1970; M.D., Ind. U. Med. Sch., Indpls., 1973. Med. intern U. Fla., 1974, resident, 1975; resident in ophthalmology Med. Coll. Ga., 1975-77; fellow micro surgery Richard R. Schulze, M.D., Savannah, Ga., 1978; gen. practice ophthalmology, Iron Mountain, Mich., 1979—. Mem. Iron Mountain C. of C., Dickinson Iron County Med. Soc. (pres. 1982-83), Upper Peninsula Med. Soc. (pres. 1982-83), Mich. State Med. Soc., Am. Acad. Ophthalmology, Am. Intraocular Implant Soc., Outpatient Ophthalmic Surgery Soc. Roman Catholic. Club: Pine Grove Country. Lodge: Rotary. Avocations: water skiing; cross country skiing; golfing; tennis; flying. Home: W 9622 KO Swanson Dr Iron Mountain MI 49801 Office: 300 Commercial Bank Bldg Iron Mountain MI 49801

GARRETT, ROBERT DEAN, insurance company executive; b. Fairfield, Ill., Apr. 13, 1933; s. Roy Smith and Halene (Pickett) G.; student public schs., Carmi, Ill.; m. Peggy Jean Spence, Dec. 8, 1955; children—Daniel Bryant, Evelyn, Brenda, Ronald. With U.S. Post Office, Chgo., 1954-60, Gen. Telephone Co., So. Ill., 1960-67; agt. MFA Ins. Co., Mt. Carmel, Ill., 1967-70; with Fed. Kemper Ins. Co., Decatur, Ill., 1970—, v.p. adminstrn., 1977—. Bd. dirs. Jr. Achievement, Decatur, 1978-81; bd. dirs. Council of Community Services, Decatur, 1978—, pres., 1983-84; bd. dirs. Decatur Boys Club, 1979, pres., 1981-83. Served with USAF, 1950-54. Recipient Cert. in Gen. Ins., Ins. Inst. Am., 1975. Mem. Pvt. Industry Council (chmn. 1983-84), C. of C., Decatur Personnel Relations Assn. Home: 23 Oak Ridge Dr Decatur IL 62521 Office: 2001 E Mound Rd Decatur IL 62526

GARRETT, WILLIAM J., steel company executive; b. Muncie, Ind., July 7, 1936; s. Cletus Loren Garrett and Martha Sue (Turner) Stahl; m. Judith Ann Creviston, Aug. 3, 1955; children—Barbara, Beth, Bruce, Julie. Grad. Ironworker's Union, Indpls., 1959; student Ind. Bus. Co., Muncie, Ind., 1962-63, Ball State U., 1965-68. Steel fabricator, painter Creviston Steel Co., Inc., Cowan, Ind., 1955-57, steel fabricator, 1958-60, foreman erection crew, 1960-61, job supt., 1960-69, glass furnace rebuilder, 1969-70, gen. field supr., from 1970; now co-owner, pres. H.A.G. Steel Contractors, Inc., Muncie, Ind. Pres. Cowan Athletic Booster Club, Cowan Sch., 1975; pres. Monroe Community Sch. Bd., 1982-84, v.p., 1983. Republican. Methodist. Club: Murat Temple (Indpls.). Lodge: Masons. Avocation: private pilot. Home: RR #4 Box 272 Muncie IN 47302

GARRIS, MICHAEL JACK, lawyer; b. Ann Arbor, Mich., May 24, 1954; s. Jack John and Helen (Cazepis) G. B.A., U. Mich., 1976; J.D., Wayne State U., 1979. Bar: Mich. 1979, Fla. 1980, U.S. Dist. Ct. (ea. dist.) Mich. 1979. Ptnr. Garris, Garris & Garris, P.C., Ann Arbor, 1979—. Mem. Washtenaw County Trial Lawyers, Mich. Trial Lawyers Assn., Assn. Trial Lawyers Am.; ABA. Greek Orthodox. Office: Garris Garris & Garris PC 300 E Washington Ann Arbor MI 48104

GARRISON, EVE, artist; b. Boston, Apr. 22, 1908; d. Benjamin and Sadie Josephson; m. J.D. Garrison; 1 child, Virginia Garrison Dach. Student Art Inst. Chgo., Wayne State U., and others. One-man exhbns. include: Milw. Art Inst., 1955; Miami Mus. Modern Art, 1961, 65, 73; Denver Art Mus., Drian Galleries, London, 1968, 70-75; pub. collections include: Miami Met. Art Mus., Treasury Art Dept., Washington, Union League Chgo.; permanent collections include: Mt. Sinai Hosp., Chgo., 1971, Miami Mus. Modern Art, Fla., Streator Children's Ctr., Ill., 1973, Rehab. Inst. Chgo., 1974, Roosevelt U., Chgo., 1975, Presbyn. Hosp., Chgo., 1975, Michael Reese Hosp., Chgo., 1976, W. Suburban Hosp., 1979, Nat. Art Mus., Warsaw, Poland, 1979. Recipient Gold medal Figure Painting at Corcoran; 1st prize Union League Chgo., 1961. Address: 1410B Sherwin Chicago IL 60626

GARRISON, LARRY PAUL, international trade executive; b. San Angelo, Tex., July 31, 1945; s. Robert Allen Garrison and Dorothy Mae (Kelsall) Heitkotter; m. Carolyn Jean West, Apr. 2, 1977; children—Brianne, Kerry, Andrew. B.B.A., U. Minn., 1985. Asst. mgr. Moritani Am. Corp., Chgo., 1968-69; mgr. traffic and imports Reliance Trading Corp., Chgo., 1969-74; mgr. customs adminstrn. Control Data Corp., Mpls., 1974-79; pres. North Star World Trade Services, Mpls., 1979-84, Internat. Pursuits, Ltd., Mpls., 1985—; cons. Minn. Dept. Vocationsl Edn., St. Paul, 1984—; instr. St. Paul Tech. Vocational Inst., 1983-84. Mem. Econ. Devel. Commn., Burnsville, Minn., 1983—. Recipient Appreciation award City of Burnsville, 1984. Mem. Minn. World Trade Assn. (bd. dirs. 1984—, v.p. 1985), Nat. Customhouse Broker and Freight Assn. Am. Republican. Methodist. Avocations: music; travel; children. Office: International Pursuits Ltd 1408 Northland Ave Suite 306 Mendota Heights MN 55120

GARRITY, DENNIS G., lawyer; b. Green Bay, Wis., May 2, 1953; m. Mary Susan Fuhr, 1971; children—Nicole, Kristyn, Nathan. B.A., U. Wis.-Green Bay, 1974; J.D., U. Wis.-Madison, 1978. Bars: Wis. 1978, U.S. Dist. Ct. (ea. and we. dists.) Wis. 1978. Law clk. Wis. Circuit Ct. System, Brown County, 1976; law clk. Hanaway, Ross, Hanaway & Weidner, Green Bay, Wis., 1977, assoc., 1978-81; ptnr. Hanaway, Ross, Hanaway, Weidner & Garrity, S.C., Green Bay, 1982—. Mem. ABA, Assn. Trial Lawyers Am., Wis. Acad. Trial Lawyers, Brown County Bar Assn. Home: 722 Winding Trail Oneida WI 54155 Office: Hanaway Ross Hanaway Weidner & Garrity SC 414 E Walnut St Suite 201 Green Bay WI 54301

GARRITY, MICHAEL KELLY, physics educator, consultant; b. Austin, Minn., Sept. 1, 1942; s. George William and Marie Rose (Kelly) G.; m. Sandra L. Garrity; children—Nolan, Gwen, Brenden, Kelly, Shannon, Jon, Robert. B.S., St. John's U., 1964; M.S., Ariz. State U., 1965, Ph.D., 1968. Prof. physics St. Cloud State U., Minn., 1967—; postdoctoral fellow U. Minn., Mpls., 1973-74; radiation therapy cons. North Central Physics and Dosimetry, St. Paul, 1982—. Mem. Am. Assn. Physicists Medicine, Am. Assn. Physics Tchrs. Home: Route 5 East River Rd Saint Cloud MN 56301 Office: St Cloud State U Dept Physics Saint Cloud MN 56301

GARRITY, WILLIAM LAWRENCE, toy and game company executive; b. Woburn, Mass., Feb. 5, 1924; s. William Lawrence and Eunice (Jones) G.; m. Elizabeth Ann O'Neill, June 20, 1948 (div. 1975); children—William, Janice, Susan, Richard, David; m. Dolores Jean Tester, Jan. 20, 1978. A.B., Harvard U., 1950, M.B.A., 1952. Supr. mfg. research, sales Polaroid Corp., Cambridge, Mass., 1952-60, asst. nat. sales mgr., 1960-63; gen. mgr., v.p. Stancraft Products, Mpls., 1963-68; gen. mgr., v.p. Schaper Mfg. Co., Mpls., 1969-72, pres., chief exec. officer, 1972—. Patentee in field. Served with USAF, 1943-46. Republican. Clubs: Golden Valley Country (Mpls.); Harvard Varsity (Mass.). Home: 4641 Sunset Ridge Golden Valley MN 55416 Office: Schaper Mfg Co 9909 S Shore Dr Plymouth MN 55440

GARROW, DERINDA KYLE, nurse; b. Highland Park, Mich., Aug. 13, 1954; d. John Paul and Dorothy Marcellee (Wilkinson) Day; m. Donald Howard Garrow, Aug. 26, 1979; children—Heather Elayne, Joshua John. A.A.S. in Nursing with honors Delta Coll., 1982. R.N.; Mich. Asst. supr. Day's Adult Foster Care Home, Linwood, Mich., 1970-79; meter officer Bay City Police Dept., Mich., 1977-78; third shift charge nurse St. Mary's Hosp., Saginaw, Mich., 1982; ICU-CCU staff nurse Bay Med. Ctr., Bay City, 1982-84, emergency rm. staff nurse, 1984—. Twp. chmn. Com. to Elect Kevin Green Sheriff, Beaver Twp., Mich., 1980, Com. to Elect James Miner, Cir. Ct. Judge, Beaver Twp., 1980, Com. to Re-elect Kevin Green, Beaver Twp., 1984. Mem. Nat. Union Hosp. and Health Care Employees, Delta Coll. Student Nurses Assn. (v.p. 1980-81, pres. 1981-82), Phi Theta Kappa. Seventh-day Adventist. Home: 1835 S Eleven Mile Rd Auburn MI 48611 Office: Bay Med Ctr Emergency Rm 1900 Columbus Ave Bay City MI 48706

GARSON, WILLIAM J., writer, editor, historian; b. Hammond, Ind., May 1, 1917; s. John Soteriou and Helen Glenn (McKennan) G.; B.A., Milton Coll., 1939; postgrad. Grad. Sch. Bank Mktg., Northwestern U., 1968; m. Florence Rebecca Penstone, Sept. 21, 1974; children—Geneva Garson Swing, Gary William. Mng. editor, reporter, columnist Rockford (Ill.) Register-Republic, 1939-55; pub. relations dir. Sundstrand Corp., Rockford, 1956-65; community info. officer Rockford C. of C., 1965-66; mktg. dir. City Nat. Bank & Trust Co. Rockford, 1966-82; pub. relations cons. imagination plus, Rockford, 1955—. Bd. dirs. Tb Assn., Heart Assn., ARC, 1952-54; Recipient George Washington Honor medals Freedoms Found., 1965-66. Mem. Am. Interprofl. Inst. (local pres.), Rockford C. of C. (Community Service award 1952, dir.), Am. Inst. Banking, Bank Mktg. Assn., Internat. Assn. Bus. Communicators, Internat. Word Processing Assn., Rockford Hist. Soc. (pres., treas.). Methodist. Author: Daddy Wore An Apron, 1974; Brother Earth, 1975; The Knight on Broadway, 1978; also numerous short stories and articles; co-author: Political Primer, 1960; We The People..., 1976; Forest City Firelog, 1982; hist. cons. Wordprints in the Sands of Time, 1984—. Home: 3516 Meadow Ln Rockford IL 61107 Office: Box 3126 Rockford IL 61106

GARST, DAVID, agricultural company sales manager, consultant; b. Des Moines, Sept. 10, 1926; s. Roswell and Elizabeth Francis (Henak) G.; m. Georganne Orenstein; children—Samuel David, Sally Marilyn Haerr, James Morton. B.A., Stanford U., 1950. Ptnr., operator, Garst Co. Farms, Coon Rapids, Iowa, 1941-56; sales mgr. Garst Seed Co., Coon Rapids, 1956—; mem. presdl. mission for agrl. devel. to Central Am., Carribean, 1980. Mem. Nat. Agrl. Mktg. Assn., Am. Seed Trade Assn., U.S. Feed Grain Council, Am. Soc. Agrl. Cons. Served with U.S. Army, 1944-45. Democrat. Helped develop Acra-Plant planting concept; helped open trade with Eastern Europe, 1955-59. Home: 320 4th Ave Coon Rapids IA 50058 Office: Garst Seed Co 615 Main St Coon Rapids IA 50058

GARSTECKI, DEAN CLEMENS, audiologist, educator; b. Milw., Sept. 19, 1944; s. Clemens Jerome and Lonita Lucille (Kruszka) G.; m. Kathleen Rae Morrissey, June 1, 1968. B.S., Marquette U., 1967, M.S., 1969; Ph.D., U. Ill.-Champaign, 1974. Cert. speech pathology and audiology. Speech-lang. pathologist Milw. Pub. Schs., 1968-70; clin. supr. U. Ill.-Champaign, 1970-73; asst. prof. audiology U. Calif.-Santa Barbara, 1973-75; asst. prof. audiology Purdue U., 1975-78; assoc. prof., head audiology and hearing impairment Northwestern U., Evanston, Ill., 1978—. Profl. cons. VA Med. Ctr., North Chicago, Ill., 1981—; mem. edn. and tng. bd. Am. Speech-Lang.-Hearing Assn., 1983—; field reviewer U.S. Dept. Edn., 1983—. Contbr. articles to profl. jours. Mem. Chgo. Speech and Hearing Assn. (pres. 1983—), Ill. Speech and Hearing Assn. (chmn. audiology com. 1982—), Am. Speech-Lang.-Hearing Assn., Am. Auditory Soc., Acad. Rehabilitative Audiology, Sigma Xi. Democrat. Roman Catholic. Office: 2299 Sheridan Rd Evanston IL 60201

GARTENHAUS, SOLOMON, physicist, educator; b Kassel, Germany, Jan. 3, 1929; s. Leopolt and Hanna (Brandler) G.; m. Johanna Lore Weisz, Jan. 30, 1953; children—Michael M., Kevin M. B.S., U. Pa., 1951; M.S., U. Ill.-Urbana, 1953, Ph.D., 1955. Instr. Stanford U., Palo Alto, Calif., 1955-58; asst. prof. Purdue U., West Lafayette, Ind., 1958-61, assoc. prof., 1961-64, prof., 1964—, asst. grad. dean, 1972-77, sec. faculties, 1980—; dir., officer Advanced Research Corp., Atlanta, 1960-64; disting. vis. prof. U.S. Air Force Acad., Colorado Springs, 1977-78; dir. Purdue-Ind. U. Studienprogram, Hamburg, Fed. Republic Germany, 1979-80. Author: Elements of Plasma Physics, 1964; Physics Basic Principles, 1975; also articles. Vice chmn. West Lafayette Human Rights Commn., 1983; dir. Greater Lafayette Pub. Transp. Corp., 1984—. Fellow Am. Phys. Soc.; mem. AAUP (pres. state assn. 1983-84), Phi Beta Kappa. Democrat. Jewish. Club: Rotary. Home: 444 Littleton St West Lafayette IN 47906 Office: Purdue U Physics Dept West Lafayette IN 47907

GARTNER, W. JOSEPH, business executive; b. Chgo., Apr. 8, 1928; s. Andrew W. and Edith M. (Frame) G.; B.A., Knox Coll., 1950; postgrad. Northwestern U., 1954-60; m. Lois Ellen McQueen, Aug. 7, 1954; children—Lisa Dianne, Bryan Wright, Andrew Scott. Creative writer Montgomery Ward & Co., Chgo., 1953-58; planning and research mgr. Lions Internat., 1958-62; creative account supr. E.F. McDonald Co., 1962-63; dir. response advt. mgr. Encyclopaedia Britannica, 1964-68; creative dir. V.J. Giesler Co., 1968-74; founder, chmn., chief exec. officer Gartner & Assocs., Inc., 1974—. Served as officer U.S. Army, 1951-53; Korea. Mem. Nat. Soc. Fund Raising Execs. (dir. 1979—), Assn. for Children with Learning Disabilities (nat. pres. 1971-72), Ill. Assn. for Children with Learning Disabilities (pres. 1968-70), Direct Mktg. Assn., Direct Mktg. Creative Guild, Chgo. Assn. Direct Mktg., S.P.E.B.Q.S.A. Barbershop Quartet Soc. Congregationalist. Club: Cliff Dwellers (Chgo.). Lodge: Lions (pres. 1961-62) (Glen Ellyn, Ill.). Home: 406 Hill Ave Glen Ellyn IL 60137 Office: Gartner & Assocs Inc 2 N Riverside Plaza Suite 2400 Chicago IL 60606

GARTON, ROBERT DEAN, state senator; b. Chariton, Iowa, Aug. 18, 1933; s. Jesse Glenn and Ruth Irene (Wright) G.; B.S., Iowa State U., 1955; M.S., Cornell U., 1959; m. Barbara Hicks, June 17, 1955; children—Bradford, Brenda. Personnel rep. Cummins Engine Co., Columbus, Ind., 1959-61; owner Garton Assocs., mgmt. cons., Columbus, 1961—; mem. Ind. Senate, 1970—, minority caucus chmn., 1976—, 79, majority caucus chmn., 1979-81, pres. pro tempore, 1981—; chmn. Mid-West Conf. State Legislatures, Council State Govts., 1984—. Bd. dirs. Ind. Pub. Health Found., 1976—; chmn. Ind. Civil Rights Commn., 1969-70; mem. exec. com. Nat. Fedn. Young Republicans, 1966; bd. dirs. The Columbian Hist. Found., Inc., Ind. Econ. Devel. Council, Rural Water System, Columbus, 1969—. Served with USMCR, 1955-57. Named Hon. Citizen Iowa, 1962, Tenn., 1977; winner internat. speech contest Toastmasters, 1962; recipient Disting. Service award Jr. C. of C. Columbus, 1968, One of 5 Outstanding Young Men in Ind., 1968. Mem. Beta Theta Pi. Lodge: Rotary Office: 606 Franklin St Columbus IN 47201

GARTSIDE, PETER STUART, biostatistics educator; b. Oldham, Eng., Aug. 12, 1937; came to U.S., 1963, naturalized, 1969; s. Harry and Elsie (Burgess) G.; m. Marein Goosen, July 10, 1963; children—James, Paul, Elaine, Peter Jr., John, Jeanette. B.S., Brigham Young U., 1967, M.S., 1969; Ph.D., U. Calif.-Berkeley, 1976. Instr., Brigham Young Univ., Provo, Utah, 1966-69; trainee NIH Univ. Calif., Berkeley, 1969-72, statistician, 1972-73; asst. prof. biostats. Univ. Cin., 1973-78, assoc. prof. biostats., 1978—. Contbr. articles to profl. jours. Mem. Am. Statis. Assn. (mem. council 1981-83, pres. Cin. chpt. 1981-82), Biometric Soc., Phi Kappa Phi. Office: Univ Cin Med Ctr Cincinnati OH 45267

GARVER, THOMAS HASKELL, art museum director, writer, consultant; b. Duluth, Minn., Jan. 23, 1934; s. Harvie Adair and Margaret Hope (Foght) G.; m. Natasha Nicholson, Apr. 13, 1974. B.A., Haverford (Pa.) Coll., 1956; M.A., U. Minn., 1965; postgrad. Barnes Found., Merion, Pa., 1956, Mus. Mgmt. Inst., U. Calif.-Berkeley, 1979. Asst. to dir. Krannert Art Mus., U. Ill., Urbana, 1960-62; asst. dir. fine arts dept. Seattle World's Fair, 1962; asst. dir. Rose Art Mus., Brandeis U., Waltham, Mass., 1962-68; dir. Newport Harbor Art Mus., Newport Beach, Calif., 1968-72, 77-80; curator exhbns. Fine Arts Mus., San Francisco, 1972-77; dir. Madison (Wis.) Art Ctr., 1980—; panelist Nat. Endowment for Arts; mem. Newport Beach Art Commn., 1978-79, Madison Com. for the Arts; steering com. Western region Archives Am. Art, San Francisco, 1977-80. Mem. Art Mus. Assn. Am. (trustee 1970-72, 79-85, pres. 1970-71, 79-82), Internat. Inst. Conservation Hist. and Artistic Works (assoc.). Lodge: Rotary. Author: Twelve Photographers of the American Social Landscape, 1967; Just Before the War: Urban America from 1935-1941 As Seen by Photographers of the F.S.A., 1968; The Paintings of George Tooker, 1985; author exhbn. catalogues, including George Herms, 1978, 83, Nathan Oliveira, 1984. Office: 211 State St Madison WI 53703

GARVER, THOMAS K., industrial and research psychologist; b. Marion, Ohio, Dec. 29, 1938; s. Albert Asa and Dorothy Mae (Conklin) G.; m. Loretta E. Roloson, Jan. 9, 1966 (div. 1979); children—Lucreda E., Robin C. B.S. in Indsl. Psychology, Ohio State U., 1965; M.S., San Jose State Coll., 1967; postgrad. U. Akron, 1968-72, Ed.D. in ednl. adminstrn, 1978. Fireman, Erie Lackawanna R.R., Marion, 1960-65; research asst. Advanced System Design Devel. Lab., IBM, Los Gatos, Calif., 1966; asst. project dir. personnel research, U.S. Navy, San Diego, 1968; cons. program eval. and research, Akron, 1972-73; personnel analyst Akron CSC, 1973-75; assoc. coordinator, personnel devel., Firestone Tire and Rubber Co., 1979—. Served with USN, 1956-59. Mem. Am. Psychol. Assn., Am. Ednl. Research Assn., Phi Delta Kappa. Home: 144 7th St NE North Canton OH 44720 Office: 1200 Firestone Pkwy Personnel Devel Akron OH 44317

GARVEY, JOHN KINDEL, petroleum exploration company executive; b. Wichita, Kans., June 11, 1947; s. Willard White and Jean (Kindel) G.; m. Joan Ann Mirandy, Oct. 2, 1976 (div. 1980); m. Jane Mary O'Connor, Nov. 3, 1982; 1 child, John Robert. B.A., U. Kans., 1969; M.S.W., U. Denver, 1975, M. Pub. Adminstrn., 1976; M. in Pub. and Pvt. Mgmt., Yale U., 1979. Tchr., vol. VISTA, Peace Corps, Salt Lake City and Morocco, 1970-71; intern-analyst Congl. Budget Office, Washington, 1978; fin. analyst Overseas Pvt. Investment Corp., Washington, 1979-80; v.p. Amortibanc Investment Co., Wichita, 1981-82; pres. Global Resources, Wichita, 1982—, Spines-Garvey Exploration, Wichita, 1985—; pres., broker J.K. Garvey & Son., Wichita, 1984—; audit chmn. Garvey Industries, Wichita, 1983—, also dir.; project mgr. Kansas Showcase of Solar Homes, Wichita, 1983—. Del. White House Conf. on Youth, Estes Park, Colo., 1971; bd. dirs. Wichita Community Theater, 1982—; trustee Garvey Kans. Found., Wichita, 1982—; mem. Leadership Kans., 1982-83; trustee Plymouth Congl. Ch., Wichita, 1982—; mem. Gov.'s Task Force on Pre-sch. Handicapped Children, Kans., 1983-84; exec. com. Wichita Com. on Fgn. Relations, 1984—. Mem. Kans. Ind. Oil and Gas Assn., Nat. Assn. Realtors, Nat. Assn. Home Builders, Am. Solar Energy Soc., Beta Gamma Sigma, Sigma Iota Epsilon, Delta Upsilon. Lodge: Rotary. Home: 808 Brookfield Wichita KS 67206 Office: Global Resources/Garvey Industries 300 W Douglas #1000 Wichita KS 67202

GARVEY, OLIVE WHITE, investment company executive, civic worker; b. Arkansas City, Kans., July 15, 1893; d. Oliver Holmes and Caroline (Hill) White; m. Ray Hugh Garvey, July 8, 1916 (dec. June 1959); children—Willard White, James Sutherland, Ruth Garvey Fink, Olivia Garvey Lincoln. A.B., Washburn U., 1914; H.H.D., 1963; H.D., Friends U., Wichita, 1966; H.H.D., Wilson Coll., 1967; H.D. Letters, Okla. Christian Coll., 1970. Tchr. English, Augusta High Sch., Kans., 1914-16; chmn. bd., dir. Garvey, Inc., Wichita, 1959—, Garvey Ctr., Inc., 1966—, SRI Inc., Wichita, 1980—; pres., trustee Garvey Found., Garvey Family Found.; trustee Garvey Charitable Trusts. Bd. dirs., trustee Friends U., Wichita, 1961-76, chmn. 1974, hon chmn. 1974-84; bd. dirs., trustee Herbert Hoover Presdl. Library Assn., 1974—, Kans 4-H Found., Wichita, 1960—, Music Theatre Wichita, 1973—, Wichita Festival Com., Kans. Coliseum Bd., 1976; nat. bd. govs. Inst. Logopedics, 1970—. Author: The Obstacle Race, 1970; Produce or Starve, 1976; Once Upon A Family Tree, 1980; also plays, poems, articles. Recipient Salesman of Yr. award Sales and Mgmt. Execs., 1969; Brotherhood award NCCJ, 1969; Martin Palmer Humanitarian award Inst. Logopedics, 1970; Disting. Service award in Agr., Kans. State U., 1971; Over the Yrs. award Wichita C. of C., 1971, also Uncommon Citizen award, 1975; DAR Honor medal, 1983; Disting. Service citation Kans. U., 1983; named to 4H Hall of Fame, 1977; named Kansan of the Yr., 1984 Mem. Internat. Inst. Edn. (hon.), Wichita Met. Council, Nonoso, Nat. League Am. Pen Women (state pres. 1952), Kans. Authors Club (dist. pres.), PEO, Nat. Soc. Colonial Dames Am. (state pres. 1964), DAR, Jamestown Soc., Wichita Art Assn., AAUW, Delta Gamma, Phi Kappa Phi. Republican. Congregationalist. Clubs: Twentieth Century, Univ. Alumni and Faculty, Crestview Country. Home: Parklane Towers 5051 E Lincoln St Wichita KS 67218 Office: RH Garvey Bldg 300 W Douglas St Witchita KS 67202

GARVIN, GREGORY LLOYD, osteopathic physician; b. Davenport, Iowa, June 29, 1949; s. I. J. and Doris Juanita (Caulk) G.; m. Donna M. Norman, Dec. 28, 1973; children—Gregory, II, Gretchen, Andrew. Student St. Ambrose Coll., 1968; B.S., Tulane U., 1971; D.O., Kirksville Coll. Osteo. Medicine. Intern, Davenport (Iowa) Osteo. Hosp., 1976-78; resident in gen. pediatrics Normandy Osteo. Hosp., St. Louis, 1978; postdoctoral fellow in gen. and acute care pediatrics Cardinal Glennon Meml Hosp., St. Louis, 1979; practice osteo. medicine specializing in pediatrics, Davenport, 1979—; dir. Neonatal Intensive Care Nursery, St. Luke's Hosp., 1982-83; chmn. pediatrics Davenport Med. Ctr., 1979—; mem. staff Mercy Hosp. Mem. med. care evaluation com. Iowa Found. for Med. Care; past pres., bd. dirs. Community Health Care; past bd. dirs. Am. Cancer Soc. Recipient 1st place award Pediatric Residents Writing Contest, 1979. Mem. Scott County Med. Soc. (exec. com.), Scott County Osteo. Soc., Iowa Soc. Osteo. Physicians and Surgeons (membership chmn. 1981, trustee, mem. ho. of dels. 1981, 82, 83), Am. Osteo. Assn., Iowa Osteo. Med. Assn., Davenport Osteo. Hosp. Assn. (bd. dirs.), Miss. Valley Ind. Physicians Assn. (past pres., now chmn. utilization, bd. dirs.), Davenport C. of C. (chmn. edn. state legis. com.), Tri Beta, Sigma Chi. Republican. Methodist. Lodges: Kiwanis (Bettendorf), Masons. Mem. editorial bd. Hawkeye Osteo. Jour.

GARVIN, JOAN LA VONNE, educational administrator, educator; b. St. Peter, Minn., Mar. 6, 1936; d. Harold John and Pearl Verna (Wendelschafer) G.; B.S., Mankato State U., 1958, M.S., 1968. Tchr. pub. schs., Minn. and Calif., 1958-72; project dir. Bloomington (Minn.) Pub. Schs., 1972-76, instructional generalist, elem. schs., 1976-80, coordinator staff devel. programs, 1980—; cons. in health edn. field. Bd. dirs. Am. Lung Assn. Minn., 1983—; state rep. Trans-Nat. Golf Assn., 1975—. Recipient several state golf titles and awards, 1966—; Paul Schmidt award Minn. Assn. for Health, Phys. Edn., Recreation and Dance, 1978; Disting. Alumna Service award Mankato State U., 1983; Community Service award Am. Lung Assn. Minn., 1985; inducted into Athletic Hall of Fame, Mankato State U., 1980. Mem. Minn. Assn. for Supervision and Curriculum Devel. (bd. dirs. 1978-79), NEA, Minn. Edn. Assn., Nat. Staff Devel. Council, Minn. Women's Golf Assn. Mankato State U. Alumni Assn. (bd. dirs. 1985—), Delta Kappa Gamma, Phi Delta Kappa, Pi Lambda Theta. Mankato State U., Joan Garvin Sports Classic named after her, 1977—. Home: 8569 Dunkirk Ln Maple Grove MN 55369 Office: Bloomington Pub Schs 8900 Portland Ave S Bloomington MN 55420

GARY, EUGENE LEE, real estate company executive, consultant; b. Cleve., Apr. 6, 1929; s. David B. and Ruth I. (Levine) G.; m. Gerry Horowitz, Mar. 18, 1951 (div. 1977); children—Joel, H., Jamie S. B.C.S., Ohio State U., 1951. Owner, pres. Ohio Motor Sales, Lorain, 1951-78; sec.-treas. Shiff-Gary Inc., Lorain, 1979—; cons., officer Wedgewood Inc., G & S Inc., SSS & G Inc., Gary Enterprises. Active, Lorain Jewish Welfare. Mem. Lorain C. of C., Phi Sigma Delta (founder). Jewish. Clubs: Oak Hill Country (Lorain), Elks (Lorain), A.B.I. Men's.

GARY, ROBERT DALE, lawyer; b. Lorain, Ohio, June 4, 1941; s. David Bear and Ruth Ida (Levine) G.; m. Karen Miriam Schiller, Aug. 14, 1962; children—Wendy, Tracy. B.A., Western Res. U., 1963, J.D., 1966; LL.M., NYU, 1967. Bar: Ohio 1966, U.S. Supreme Ct. 1969, U.S. Tax Ct. 1969. Dep. chief for Ohio organized crime strike force U.S. Dept. Justice, Cleve., 1967-71; dir. Organized Crime Prevention Council, Columbus, Ohio, 1972-73; spl. asst. Gov. Ohio, Columbus, 1973-75; asst. prosecutor Lorain County, Ohio, 1975-80; sole practice, Lorain, Ohio, 1975—; instr. Western Res. U., Cleve., 1978, Lorain County Community Coll., Elyria, Ohio, 1979; lectr. Law Enforcement Officers Tng. Program, Ohio, 1979. Mem. 7 County Supermarket Settlement Com., Lorain, 1982-83; trustee Agudath Bnai Israel Synagogue, Lorain, 1984; chmn. Lorain County Blue Ribbon Com., Elyria, 1983-84. Recipient Spl. Achievement award U.S. Dept. Justice, 1971, Lorain County Commrs., 1982, 84. Mem. Lorain County Bar Assn., Ohio State Bar Assn. Democrat. Jewish. Avocations: Art appreciation, bicycling, skiing, golf. Home: 3716 Woodstock Lorain OH 44053 Office 446 Broadway Lorain OH 44052

GARZONETTI, JEFFREY ROCCO, probation officer; b. Chgo., June 25, 1953: s. Angelo Rocco and Emily Mary (Schmidt) G.; A.S. in Police Adminstrn., Triton Coll., 1974: student U. Ill., Chgo., 1975; B.A. in Polit. Sci., DePaul U., 1976, M.S. in Pub. Adminstrn./Mgmt. Scis., 1982. Desk officer Triton Coll. Police Dept., 1972-74; ramp service Flying Tiger Cargo Line, Chgo., 1974-75; clk., messenger Kirkland & Ellis, Chgo., 1975-76; bus operator Chgo. Transit Authority, summers 1975-76: adult probation officer Cook County, Chgo., 1977—; personal probation officer, investigator for Presiding Judge Dist. 4, Frank Barbaro, Criminal and Civil Div.; supr. Criminal Div. for Chief Judge Richard Fitzgerald. Founder Creative Impressions, 1982. Chmn. social com. young adult div. Joint Civic Com. of Italian Americans, 1977-78, pres., 1978—; precinct capt. 36th Ward Regular Democratic Orgn., 1972—. Served to comdr., 1st lt. CAP/USAF Aux. Lic. pilot. Mem. Airplane Owners and Pilots Assn., DePaul U. Alumni Assn., Roman Catholic (mem. Holy Cross Council). Lodge: K.C.

GASIOR, JOSEPH JOHN, lawyer, publisher; b. Chgo., May 10, 1918; s. John and Hattie (Wegrzyn) Gasiorek; m. Ruth M. Schuetz, Oct. 13, 1946; children—Laura, Janet, Barbara, Paul, John, Ralph. B.A., U. Chgo., 1939, J.D., 1942. Pres., chmn. bd. Ben Franklin Savs. & Loan, Oak Brook, Ill., 1945-82, Chgo. Law Book Co., 1945—; pres. Polish Am. Savs. and Loan League, Chgo., 1979. Mem. ABA, Chgo. Bar Assn., Am. Booksellers Assn. Republican. Roman Catholic. Avocations: reading; travel. Office: Chgo Law Book Co 4814 S Pulaski Rd Chicago IL 60632

GASIOR, WALTER DAVID, JR., law enforcement executive, consultant; b. Washington, Mar. 11, 1952; s. Walter David and Mary Alice (Mostoller) G.; m. Kathleen Ann Alt, Nov. 28, 1975; children—Rachel Maryanna, Matthew David. B.A., U. Notre Dame, 1974; M.S., Fla. State U., 1976. Cert. in Criminal Justice Planning. Criminal justice planner Crescent Region Criminal Justice Council, Geneva, Ill., 1976-77; program mgr. Crescent Criminal Justice Tng. and Edn. Project, Aurora, Ill., 1977-78; dir. planning and research Palatine Police Dept., Ill., 1978-82, dep. chief of police, 1982—; lectr. Northwestern U. Traffic Inst., Evanston, Ill., 1982—; cons. police exec. selection area municipalities, 1979—; faculty mem. Aurora U. Mgmt. Ctr., 1983—. Contbr. articles to profl. jours. Treas. Bridge Youth Services Palatine Twp., 1983-84, chmn., 1984-85; bd. dirs. Harper Coll. Criminal Justice Curriculum Adv. Bd., Palatine, 1983-85. Speaker White House Conf. on Productivity, Washington, Nat. Pub. Sector Productivity Conf., N.Y.C., 1983. Mem. Northwest Police Tng. Acad. (dir. 1981-84), Nat. Police Planners Assn. (conf. speaker 1983), North Suburban Police Chief Assn., Greater Cook County Police Capts. Assn. Roman Catholic. Club: Arlington Trotters Running. Avocations: running, handball, Am. Revolutionary history. Home: 451 E Colfax Palatine IL 60067 Office: Palatine Police Dept 200 E Wood St Palatine IL 60067

GASKILL, EDWARD LELAND, land surveyor; b. Akron, Ohio, Aug. 1, 1933; s. Elmer Edward and Mary Jane (West) G.; m. Gloria Moran, Jan. 30, 1954; children—Deanna Marie, Richard Edward, David Randal. Student U. Akron, 1975-76. Registered profl. surveyor. Civil designer Dalton, Dalton & Assocs., Akron, 1954-67; civil project mgr. Glaus Pyle DeHaven Co., Akron, 1967-69, Spagnuolo & Assocs., Akron, 1969-73; civil dept. head Forest City Dillon, Akron, 1973-74; pres., owner Gaskill & Assocs., Akron, 1974—; pres. Lakes Sr. Housing, Inc., Akron, 1977—. Mem. steering committeeman HUD A 95 Rev. Bd., Summit County, Ohio, 1978-83, U. Akron-Surveying Br., 1977—. Mem. Nat. Soc. Profl. Surveyors, Am. Congress Surveying and Mapping, Profl. Land Surveyors Ohio (cert.). Democrat. Roman Catholic. Lodge: Kiwanis Internat. (disting. pres. Portage Lakes club 1982-83, lt. gov. Ohio div. 1984-85). Avocations: golf; bowling; tennis. Home: 4237 Springdale Rd Uniontown OH 44685 Office: Gaskill & Assocs 2634 S Arlington Rd Akron OH 44319

GASKILL, REX WILLIAM, speech communication educator; b. Hutchinson, Kans., Dec. 21, 1942; s. Floyd Curtis and Nona Faye (Clemons) G.; m. Gayle Catherine Hubmer, Dec. 28, 1966 (div. Mar. 1984). A.A., Hutchinson Community Coll., 1962; B.A., Fort Hays Kans. State U., 1964; M.A., U. Nebr., 1970; Ph.D. candidate, U. Minn., 1972-76. Tchr., coach Omaha Pub. Schs., Nebr., 1964-69, Ind. State U., 1970-72; tchr. Midland Lutheran Coll., 1969-70, Wagner Coll., 1972-73; tchr. speech communication, adminstr. Normandale Coll., Bloomington, Minn., 1973—. Author: And Then There Were Nine, 1985. Mem. editorial bd. Soundings, 1983—. Mem. exec. com. Cathedral Ch. St. Mark, Mpls., 1979—; pres. Welles Meml. Inc. Found., 1980-81. Fellow Bush Found., 1982. Mem. Speech Communication Assn. (com. 1983), Am. Forensics Assn., Phi Rho Pi (v.p., exec. sec. 1979, Disting. Service award 1984). Episcopalian. Avocations: theatre; reading; disco dancing. Home: 735 E 16th St Apt 33 Minneapolis MN 55404 Office: Normandale Coll 9700 France Ave S Bloomington MN 55431

GASPAR, TIMOTHY MICHAEL, nurse, educator, consultant; b. Sioux Falls, S.D., Aug. 27, 1955; s. Michael Phillip and Madelyn Alice Gaspar; B.S. in Nursing, S.D. State U., 1977; M.S.N., U. Nebr., 1981. Asst. in nursing S.D. State U., Brookings, 1978-79, instr., 1981-84, asst. prof., 1984—; research assoc. U. Nebr., Omaha, 1980-81; nursing cons. Crowell Meml. Home, Blair, Nebr., 1980-81. Mem. Am. Nurses Assn., S.D. Nurses Assn., Midwest Nursing Research Soc., Oncology Nursing Soc. Home: 1438 7th St Brookings SD 57006 Office: South Dakota State University College of Nursing Box 2275A Brookings SD 57007

GASPER, DAVID ANTHONY, computer software executive; b. Dayton, Ohio, Aug. 14, 1956; s. William Bickford and Marie Elizabeth (Shroyer) G.; m. Nelda Christine Martinez, Mar. 17, 1979; 1 child, Laura Katherine. B.S., Wright State, 1978; M.B.A., U. Dayton, 1984. Programmer NCR, Dayton, Ohio, 1978-79; programmer-analyst Mead Corp., Dayton, 1979-80; systems analyst Source Data Systems, Dayton, 1980-83; pres. Gasper Corp., Dayton, 1983—. Vol. Bob Hipple Lab., Dayton, 1982—. Mem. Assn. Systems Mgmt. Roman Catholic. Avocation: basketball. Home: 1041 Yorkshire Pl Dayton OH 45419 Office: 28 E Rahn Rd Suite 114 Dayton OH 45429

GASSER, BRENT PADLEY, resort camp executive; b. Baraboo, Wis., June 23, 1956; s. David Lloyd and Elinore Doris Gasser. B.A., U. Wis., 1978. Ops. mgr. Yogi Bear's Jellystone Park, Wisconsin Dells, Wis., 1978—; supr., purchasing agt. Bear & Co., 1981-82; supr., retailer Happy Acres Grocery, 1981-82. Elder, United Presbyterian Ch., 1983—. Mem. Wis. Assn. Campground Owners (sec., dir. 1983-85), Wisconsin Dells C. of C. Home: PO Box 610 One Gasser Rd Lake Delton WI 53940 Office: Yogi Bear's Jellystone Park PO Box 510 Wisconsin Dells WI 53965

GASSMAN, MAX PAUL, mechanical engineer; b. Bonesteel, S.D., Sept. 1, 1930; s. Walter Ernest and Elizabeth (Schibli) G.; B.S. in Mech. Engring., S.D. Sch. Mines and Tech., 1956; M. Mech. Engring., Iowa State U., 1963; m. Gail Elizabeth Evans, Aug. 5, 1955; children—Paul Michael, Philip Walter. With John Deere Co., Waterloo, Iowa, 1956-85, sr. design engr., 1965-68, sr. design analyst, 1968-79, diagnostic coordinator, 1979-83; prof. mech. engring. Iowa State U., 1985—; v.p. John C. Rider & Assos., Inc., 1976-79. Cubmaster, Winnebago Council Boy Scouts Am., 1967-70, scoutmaster, 1970-74. Pres. bd. dirs. Splash Inc., 1970; pres. Lord of Life Luth. Ch., Waterloo. Served with USAF, 1948-52. Registered profl. engr., Iowa. Mem. Nat. Soc. Profl. Engrs. (chmn. Iowa sect. profl. engrs. in industry group), Iowa Engring. Soc. (pres. bd. dirs. N.E. Iowa 1971-72, Anson Marston award 1972), ASME (dir. 1971-72), Waterloo Tech. Soc. (chmn. tech. student activity com. 1970-71), Am. Soc. Agrl. Engrs. (vice chmn. T-5 computer com. 1983-84), Soc. Automotive Engrs. Club: John Deere Supervisors (Waterloo). Patentee in field. Home: 551 Alpine St Waterloo IA 50702 Office: Iowa State U Ames IA 50011

GASSMAN, MERRILL LOREN, biological sciences educator, consultant; b. Chgo., Feb. 10, 1943; s. Alfred Edward Gassman and Elvina (Chessen) Levin; m. beverly Sue Sacks, Sept. 3, 1967; children—Debra Eileen, Sharyl Jorene, Aaron Howard. S.B. in Biology, U. Chgo., 1964, S.M. in Botany, 1964-65, Ph.D. in Botany, 1965-67. Predoctoral fellow NASA, U. Chgo., 1964-67; postdoctoral fellow USPHS, Rockefeller U., 1967-68; guest investigator Rockefeller U., N.Y.C., 1967-68; research scientist Internat. Minerals, Libertyville, Ill., 1968-69; asst. prof. U. Ill., Chgo., 1969-75, assoc. prof., 1975-82, prof. biological sciences, 1982—; film cons. Coronet Films, Inc., Deerfield, Ill., 1973—; cons. textbook Wm. C. Brown Pub., Dubuque, Iowa, 1975, Scott, Foresman Co., Glenview, Ill., 1983. Contbr. chpts. to books and articles to reference jours. NSF grantee, 1972—. Mem. AAAS, Am. Soc. Plant Physiol., Am. Soc. for Photobiology (charter), Am. Soc. Biol. Chemists, Sigma Xi (sec. U. Ill.-Chgo. 1983-84, treas. 1984-86). Home: 3830 Knight St Glenview IL 60025 Office: U Ill PO Box 4348 Chicago IL 60680

GASSMANN, HENRY, insurance company executive; b. Olney, Ill., Nov. 8, 1927; s. Zean Goudy and Gertrude (Weber) G.; m. Patricia Louise Zuber, Feb. 11, 1956; children—Louis, Mary, Zean, James, John, Frank, Neal. B.S., U. Ill., 1949; M.B.A., U. Mich., 1950. With Zean Gassmann Co., Olney, Ill., 1950—, owner, 1981—; dir. Olney Trust Bank, Rich Land Bancorp. Mem. adv. bd. Ill. Dept. Ins., 1981—; mem. citizens com. U. Ill., 1958—; chmn. Richland County Republican Central Com., 1976—; chmn. 54th Rep. Legis. Dist., 1982—; chmn. 107th Rep. Rep. Dist., 1982—; v.p. Ill. Rep. County Chmns. Assn., 1982—; pres. Richland Heritage Found., 1984—. Served with USN, 1945-47. Mem. Ind. Ins. Agts. Am., Ind. Ins. Agts. Ill., Am. Legion. Republican. Roman Catholic. Club: Petroleum. Lodges: Rotary, Elks. Home: 316 N Elliott St Olney IL 62450 Office: 313 Whittle Ave Olney IL 62450

GAST, ROBERT GALE, agriculture educator/experiment station administrator; b. Philadelphia, Mo., July 28, 1931; s. Fred W. and Lolabel (McPike) G.; m. Mary Lou Parrish, June 6, 1954; children—Regina Rae, Roger Eugene, Kimberly Kay. B.S., U. Mo., 1953, M.S., 1956, Ph.D., 1959. Cert. profl. soil scientist. Asst. prof., assoc. prof. U. Tenn. AEC Agr. Research Lab., Oak Ridge, 1959-70; prof. soil sci. U. Minn., St. Paul, 1970-77; head dept. agronomy U. Nebr., Lincoln, 1977-83; dir. Agr. Expt. Sta., Mich. State U., East Lansing, 1983—. Editor: Jour. Environ. Quality, 1975-77. Served to 1st lt. USAF, 1953-55, Korea. Recipient Alumni award U. Mo., 1980. Fellow Am. Soc. Agronomy (pres.-elect 1986), Soil Sci. Soc. Am. (pres. 1982); mem. Clay Minerals Soc., AAAS, Sigma Xi. Presbyterian. Home: 2096 Belding Ct Okemos MI 48864 Office: Agr Expt Sta 109 Agr Hall Michigan State Univ East Lansing MI 48821

GASTMAN, IRVIN JOSEPH, physician, bio-medical physicist, consultant computer applications to medicine; b. N.Y.C., June 5, 1944; s. Adolph A. and Anna R. (Karp) G.; m. Eda Halpern, July 3, 1967; children—Brian Reuben, Rebecca Rachael, Michelle Ann. M.S. in Elec. Engring., CCNY, 1967; Ph.D. in Bio-Med. Physics, U. Mich., 1974; D.O., Mich. State U., 1977. Diplomate Nat. Bd. Med. Examiners; registered profl. engr., N.Y. Family practice medicine, Pontiac, Mich., 1976—; mem. faculty Mich. State U., 1974—; cons. various ins. groups. Bd. dirs. Jewish Community Center Mich.; trustee Holocost Meml. Center. NDEA fellow, 1966-68. Mem. Am. Osteo. Assn., Mich. Assn. Physicians & Surgeons, Oakland Osteo. Physicians & Surgeons. Contbr. articles to profl. jours. Patentee ultrasound field. Home: 1710 Morningside Way Bloomfield Hills MI 48013 Office: 3560 Pontiac Lake Rd Pontiac MI 48054

GASTON, HUGH PHILIP, marriage counselor, educator; b. St. Paul, Sept. 12, 1910; s. Hugh Philander and Gertrude (Heine) G.; B.A., U. Mich., 1937, M.A., 1941; postgrad. summers Northwestern U., 1938, Yale U., 1959; m. Charlotte E. Clarke, Oct. 1, 1945 (dec. 1960); children—Gertrude E. Gaston Crippen, George Hugh. Counselor, U. Mich., Ann Arbor, 1936; tchr., counselor W. K. Kellogg Found., Battle Creek, Mich., 1937-41; tchr. spl. edn., Detroit, 1941; instr. airplane wing contrn. Briggs Mfrs. Co., Detroit, 1942; psychologist VA, 1946-51; sr. staff asso. Sci. Research Asso., Chgo., 1951-55; marriage counselor Circuit Ct., Ann Arbor, 1955-60; pvt. practice marriage counseling, Ann Arbor, 1955—; former chief Guidance Center, U. Mich. and Mich. State U.; lectr., Eastern Mich. U., Ypsilanti, 1964-67, asst. prof., 1967-81; mem. Study Group for Health Care of Elderly, China, USSR, 1983. Acting postmaster, Ann Arbor, 1960-61. Chmn. Wolverine Boys State, Am. Legion, 1957-85; chmn. com. on Christian marriage Presbytery So. Mich., 1962-69; mem. exec. com., legis. agt., chmn. legis. com. Mich. Council Family Relations, 1972-74; bd. dirs. Internat. Parents Without Partners, 1968-69, 1st pres. Mich. chpt., 1961; bd. dirs. Ann Arbor Sr. Citizens, 1982-85, Washtenaw County Council Alcoholism, 1982-84. Served with U.S. Army, 1943-46. Decorated Purple Heart (2), Bronze Star; Medallion of Nice (France); named Citizen of Year, Am. Legion, 1968, Single Parent of Yr., 1978. Mem. Am. Assn. Marriage Counselors, Am. Personnel and Guidance Assn., Nat. Vocat. Guidance Assn., D.A.V. (past comdr.), Am. Soc. Tng. Dirs., Mich. Indsl. Tng. Council (charter), SAR (past pres.), U. Mich. Band Alumni Assn. (pres. 1957-58), Mil. Order Purple Heart (nat. exec. com. 1977-82, 1st comdr. chpt. 459 Mich., state comdr. Mich. 1984-85), Phi Delta Kappa (past pres. U. Mich.). Clubs: Rotary (Ann Arbor) Econ. Club of Detroit. Address: 1404 Cambridge Rd Ann Arbor MI 48104

GATES, CHARLES C., aircraft manufacturing company executive. Chmn., dir. Gates Lear jet Corp., Wichita, Kans. Office: Gates Lear jet Corp PO Box 7707 Wichita KS 67277*

GATES, JOHN EDWARD, English educator English; b. Chgo., Feb. 2, 1924; s. John Alexander and Nellie Mary (Sharar) G.; m. Marion McIntosh Thompson, Aug. 31, 1950; children—Elizabeth Thompson, William Sharar, Alan McIntosh. B.A., Maryville Coll., 1945; B.D., Yale U., 1949; S.T.M., Harvard U., 1953; Ph.D., Hartford Sem. Found., 1968. Tchr. Gerard Inst., Sidon, Lebanon, 1949-52; asst. editor G&C Merriam Co., Springfield, Mass., 1956-62; research assoc. Hartford Sem. Found., Conn., 1965-67; research assoc. U. Toronto, Ont., Can., 1968-70; prof. English, Ind. State U., Terre Haute, 1970—; dictionary cons. NEH, Washington, 1975—. Author: Analysis of Lexicographic Resources, 1972; co-editor: Papers on Lexicography in Honor of W.N. Cordell, 1979; editor: Dictionary of Idioms for the Deaf, 1966; contbr. articles to profl. jours. Served with USN, 1945-46. Mem. Linguistic Soc. Am., Ind. Council Tchrs. English, Dictionary Soc. N.Am. (pres. 1976-77, editor newsletter 1977—, sec./treas. 1977-85), Am. Dialect Soc. Presbyterian. Home: 330 S 22d St Terre Haute IN 47803 Office: Ind State U Dept English Terre Haute IN 47809

GATES, PATRICK THOMAS, educational administrator; b. Wichita, Kans., Jan. 12, 1945; s. Lewis Alvin Gates and Betty Elizabeth (Hilton) Keenan; m. Elizabeth Ellen Poston, June 30, 1970; 1 child, Christopher. B.A., Wichita State U., 1972, M.Ed., 1982. Tchr. Augusta High Sch., Kans., 1974-82; prin. Bluestem High Sch., Leon, Kans., 1982—. Sec./treas. South-Central Border League, Kans., 1983-84. Served to sgt. U.S. Army, 1963-67, Vietnam. Decorated Air medal with 14 oak leaf clusters. Mem. United Sch. Adminstrs.,

Nat. Assn. Secondary Sch. Prins., Kans. Assn. Secondary Sch. Prins., VFW. Democrat. Presbyterian. Avocation: mountain climbing. Office: Bluestem High Sch 500 Bluestem Dr Leon KS 67074

GATES, STEPHEN FRYE, lawyer; b. Clearwater, Fla., May 20, 1946; s. Orris Alison and Olga Betty (Frye) G.; m. Laura Daignault, June 10, 1972. B.A. in Econs., Yale U., 1968; J.D., Harvard U., 1972, M.B.A., 1972. Bar: Fla. 1973, Mass. 1973, Ill. 1977. Assoc. Choate Hall & Stewart, Boston, 1973-77; atty. Amoco Corp., Chgo., 1977-82, gen. atty., 1982—; dir. XMR Inc, Santa Clara, Calif. Knox fellow, 1972-73. Mem. ABA, Chgo. Bar Assn. Clubs: Univ. (Chgo.); Yale (N.Y.C.). Office: Amoco Corp 200 E Randolph Dr Chicago IL 60601

GATES, WILLIAM CYRIL, JR., museum curator, historian, author; b. North Syracuse, N.Y., Apr. 12, 1946; s. William C. and Alice Virginia (McCutcheon) G.; m. Harriet Ann, July 25, 1970; 1 child, Brian Joseph. A.A., Union Jr. Coll., Cranford, N.J., 1975; B.A., Kean Coll. of N.J., 1976; M.A., Wright State U., 1978. Asst. curator Mus. Early Trades and Crafts, Madison, N.J., 1975-78; curator Ohio Hist. Soc., Columbus, 1978-80, curator, adminstr. Mus. of Ceramics, East Liverpool, Ohio 1980—. Author: The City of Hills and Kilns: Life and Work in East Liverpool, Ohio, 1984; (with others) The East Liverpool Ohio Pottery District: Identification of Manufacturers and Marks, 1982. Served with U.S. Army, 1965-67. Mem. Am. Assn. for State and Local History, Am. Assn. of Museums, Orgn. Am. Historians, Ohio Acad. History. Roman Catholic. Lodge: Rotary (pres. 1983-84). Avocations: golf; racquetball; travel; photography. Office: Museum of Ceramics 400 East 5th St East Liverpool OH 43920

GATHERUM, PATRICIA BRANDLEY, public relations executive; b. Salt Lake City, Oct. 2, 1926; d. Ralph Canton and Nellie Emeline (Sutton) Brandley; m. Gordon Elwood Gatherum, July 31, 1947; children—Laurie Patricia, Mark Gordon, Kristin Lee. B.A., U. Utah, 1947; M.A., Ohio State U., 1980. Editorial asst. Miller Freeman Pubs., Seattle, 1947-49; librarian Ames Pub. Library, Iowa, 1964-69; chief reference librarian Ohio Hist. Soc., Columbus, 1969-74, devel./membership officer, 1974-79; community services mgr. Nationwide Ins., Columbus, Ohio, 1979—. Contbr. articles to profl. jours. Bd. dirs. Epilepsy Assn. Central Ohio. Democrat. Club: Columbus Met. (bd. dirs.). Avocations: reading; walking; cross-country skiing; jazz and classical music. Home: 5710 Strathmore Ln Dublin OH 43017 Office: Nationwide Ins Cos One Nationwide Plaza Columbus OH 43216

GATHMAN, JAMES DENIS, real estate investment company executive; b. Chgo., Dec. 23, 1941; s. James Arthur and Helen Mary (Konkolitz) B.; m. Julianne Clare Thompson; children—Alaina, Joseph, Matthew, Michael, Justin, Christopher. B.B.A. in Fin., Loyola u., 1963. Real estate appraiser Talman Fed. Savs. and Loan, Chgo., 1963-74; v.p., dir. Real Estate Research Corp., Chgo., 1974-83; 1st v.p. VMS Realty, Inc., Chgo., 1983—. Contbr. articles to profl. publs., chpts. to books. Mem. Am. Inst. Real Estate Appraisers, Soc. Real Estate Appraisers, Am. Arbitration Assn., Lambda Alpha. Roman Catholic. Home: 509 S Patton St Arlington Heights IL 60005 Office: VMS Realty Inc 8700 W Bryn Mawr St Chicago IL 60631

GATSON-BEY, HAROLD, electronics engineer; b. Hughes, Ark., July 1, 1941; s. Thomas and Lucille (Howard) G.; m. Ella Hennon, Sept. 15, 1972; children—Khaleel; m. Estella Dunlap, Nov. 28, 1963 (div. July 1972); children—Harold, Valorie, Dareck. A.S., Coyne Am., 1971; B.S.E.E., Chgo. Tech. U., 1975; M.B.A., Rosary Coll., 1983. Electronic engr. Victor Comptometer, Chgo., 1971-74; field service engr. Marquette Electronics, Milw., 1974-77; programmer C.P. Clare, Chgo., 1977-80; cons. CGA Computer Assn., Des Plaines, Ill., 1980-81; staff programmer Allstate, South Barrington, Ill., 1981—. Clubs: Internat. Toastmasters (South Barrington, Ill.); 1900 S 12th Ave Block (pres. 1980—) (Maywood, Ill.). Home: 1936 S 12th Ave Maywood IL 60153

GATTI, ROBERT MICHAEL, college dean; b. Indiana, Pa., Aug. 17, 1954; s. Joseph William and Lena (Ross) G.; m. Jackie Owen Faith, July 24, 1978; 1 child, Michael Ross. B.A., U. S.C., 1976; M.A., Ind. U. of Pa., 1978. Asst. dean student devel. Otterbein Coll., Westerville, Ohio, 1978-80, dir. campus ctr., 1980-82, dean student devel., 1982—. Pres., bd. dirs. Concord Counseling Ctr., Inc., Westerville, 1984-85; planning com. North Area Mental Health Bd., Columbus, Ohio, 1984; bd. dirs. Concord Counseling Ctr., 1984. Mem. Ohio Coll. Personnel Assn. (exec. com. govt. relations 1983-85, exec. com. at-large 1985—), Am. Coll. Personnel Assn., Assn. Fraternity Advisors. Republican. Roman Catholic. Avocations: golf; gardening. Office: Otterbein Coll Student Personnel Office Westerville OH 43081

GATTOZZI, ANGELO LUCIANO, engineer; b. Matrice, Campobasso, Italy, Dec. 12, 1947; s. Domenico Germano and Angiolina (Appugliese) G.; B.S., Case Western Res. U., 1971, M.S., 1975, Ph.D., 1978; accounting certificate John Carroll U., 1976. Grad. asst. Case Western Res. U., 1971-74; engr. Reliance Electric Co., Cleve., 1974-77, project mgr., 1977-80; pres. Tyler Power Systems, Inc., Mentor, Ohio, 1980—; instr. Cuyahoga Community Coll., Cleve., 1983—. C.P.A., Ohio. Mem. IEEE, Am. Inst. C.P.A.'s, Am. Mgmt. Assn., ASTM. Author: IEEE Industry Applications; IEEE Magnetics. Home: 2110 Apple Dr Euclid OH 44143 Office: 8648 Tyler Blvd Mentor OH 44060

GAUGHAN, NORBERT FELIX, bishop; b. Pitts., May 30, 1921; s. Thomas Leo and Martha (Paczkowska) G. M.A., St. Vincent Coll., 1944; Ph.D. in Philosophy, U. Pitts., 1963. Ordained priest Roman Catholic Ch., 1945; ordained titular bishop of Taraqua and aux. bishop of Greensburg (Pa.), 1975. Apptd. bishop of Gary, Ind., 1984—. Office: Diocese of Gary PO Box M-474 Gary IN 46401

GAUGHAN, PATRICK JOHN, real estate developer, property management executive; b. St. Paul, Aug. 11, 1931; s. Arthur Francis and Katherine Josephine (Landsberger) G.; m. Barbara Ann Houle, Aug. 21, 1954; children—Kathi, Kari, Maureen, Patrick Michael. Student U. Minn., 1949-50. With Dale/Selby Hardware, St. Paul, 1943-49, Thermo Co., St. Paul, 1949-51; with Fairbanks & Morse, St. Paul, 1951-52; salesman Endo Pharms., Mpls., 1952-69; pres. The Gaughan Cos., Coon Rapids, Minn., 1969—. Author/compiler: Cooking Your Catch, 1984. Recipient Americanism award Legion Club, 1977-78. Mem. Minn. Multi Housing Assn., St. Paul Builders Assn., Mpls. Builders Assn., Nat. Assn. Home Builders, Anoka C. of C. Republican. Roman Catholic. Clubs: Forest Hills Golf (bd. dirs.), Minn. Multi Housing Maxi (bd. dirs. 1975). Avocations: travel; fishing; tennis; boating. Office: The Gaughan Cos 299 Coon Rapids Blvd Coon Rapids MN 55433

GAUGHEN, FRANK XAVIER, JR., advertising executive; b. Cleve., Mar. 16, 1925; s. Frank X. and Jennie H. (DeMars) G.; m. Irene Heinselman, June 30, 1948; children—Frank X. III, John R., Kathleen F. A.B., Dartmouth Coll., 1946. Advt. sales mgr. Life Mag., Chgo., Pitts., Detroit, 1953-73; v.p., dir. client services Smy, Inc., Chgo., 1973—. Served with U.S. Army, 1943-46. Mem. Phi Kappa Psi. Club: The Tavern (Chgo.). Home: 525 Washington Ave Glencoe IL 60022 Office: 230 N Michigan Ave Chicago IL 60601

GAULDEN, DOROTHEA ELAINE, accountant, consultant; b. Havana, Ala., Mar. 30, 1939; d. F. U. and Anna Erin (Brown) Harris; m. Charles P. Gaulden, July 1, 1978; children by previous marriage—Crystal, Sharie. A.A.B., Youngstown State U., B.S. in Bus. Adminstrn.; M.B.A., St. Francis Coll. Acct., Packard Electric div. Gen. Motors Corp., Warren, Ohio, 1966-76; controller Prestolite Wire & Cable div. Eltra Corp., Port Huron, Mich., 1976-77; fin. analyst ITT Aerospace/Optical Div., Ft. Wayne, Ind., 1977-78, mgr. budgets, 1978-80, mgr. operational analysis, 1980-82, asst. comptroller, 1982—; part time instr. St. Francis Coll.; cons., guest speaker fin. workshops. Bd. dirs., fin. adviser YWCA; bds. dirs. United Way, Mental Health Assn. Mem. Nat. Assn. Black Accts., Nat. Assn. Accts., Nat. Assn. Female Execs., ITT Mgmt. Assn., Delta Sigma Theta (treas.). Democrat. Club: Links Inc. (treas.). Home: 5815 Oakfall Rd Fort Wayne IN 46825 Office: 3700 E Pontiac St Fort Wayne IN 46803

GAULT, GALE GEORGE, police officer; b. Akron, Ohio, July 4, 1947; s. Gale B. Gault and Alice (Langstaff) Sarkozi; m. Carol L. Inama, Aug. 8, 1970; children—Christi Lynn, Ryan Patrick. A.A.S. in Law Enforcement Tech., U. Akron, 1971, B.S., 1972; M.P.A., Kent State U., 1980; grad. FBI Nat. Acad. Watershed ranger City of Akron, 1967-72, watershed supr., 1972-75; police patrolman City of Tallmadge, Ohio, 1975-79, police sgt., 1979-82, chief of police, 1982—; instr. U. Akron, 1982—. Mem. Summit County Police Chiefs Assn. (pres. 1984—), Ohio Assn. Chiefs Police, Internat. Assn. Chiefs Police. Roman Catholic. Office: Tallmadge Police Dept 53 Northeast Ave Tallmadge OH 44278

GAULT, STANLEY CARLETON, See *Who's Who in America,* 43rd edition.

GAUTHIER, CLARENCE JOSEPH, utility executive; b. Houghton, Mich., Mar. 16, 1922; s. Clarence A. and Muriel V. (Beesley) G.; B.S.M.E., U. Ill., 1943; M.B.A., U. Chgo., 1960; m. Grayce N. Wicall, July 25, 1941; children—Joseph H., Nancy M. With Pub. Service Co. No. Ill., 1945-54; with No. Ill. Gas. Co., 1954—, v.p. fin., 1960-62, v.p. ops., 1962-64, exec. v.p., 1965-69, pres., 1969-76, chmn., 1971—, chief exec. officer, 1971-81, dir., 1965—; chmn., chief exec. officer, dir. NICOR Inc., 1976—; chmn., chief exec. officer, dir. all NICOR subs.; dir. GATX Corp., GDC, Inc., Cole-Taylor Fin. Group, AEGIS Ltd. (vice chmn. 1978—), Chgo. and North Western Transp. Co., CNW Corp., Nalco Chem. Co., Sun Electric Corp. Mem. pres.'s council U. Ill., 1978—; mem. Northwestern U. Assos., 1977—; bd. sponsors Evang. Hosp. Assn., Oak Brook, Ill., 1977—; chmn. devel. campaign Good Samaritan Hosp., Downers Grove, Ill., 1974-77; bd. dirs. Gas Research Inst., 1977-82. Trustee George Williams Coll., Downers Grove, 1968-77, Ill. Inst. Tech., 1976—, Ill. Inst. Tech. Research Inst., 1976-80, Council Energy Studies, 1977—; trustee Inst. Gas Tech., 1964-78, chmn. bd. trustees, 1976-78; bd. dirs. Mid-Am. chpt. ARC, 1962-78; trustee Met. Crusade of Mercy, Chgo., 1965-77; citizens bd. U. Chgo., 1972—. Served to capt., C.E., U.S. Army World War II; PTO. Decorated Silver Star, Bronze Star with V; recipient Distinguished Alumnus award Coll. Engring., U. Ill., 1971, Alumni Honor award, 1974; Loyalty award U. Ill. Alumni Assn., 1977; registered profl. engr., Ill. Mem. Am. (dir. 1970-76, chmn. bd. 1974-75, Distinguished Service award 1976), Midwest (dir. 1964-67), So. (dir. 1966-69) gas assns., Ind. Natural Gas Assn. Am. (dir. 1972-73), Chgo. Assn. Commerce and Industry (dir. 1966-71, 73-79), Ill. C. of C., Internat. Gas Union (council 1970-75, chmn. com. on gas utilization), AAAS, Am. Fin. Assn., Am. Mgmt. Assn., Pres.'s Assn., U. Chgo. Grad. Sch. Bus. Alumni Assn. (pres. 1964-65), U. Ill. Pres.'s Council, U. Ill. Found. (U. Ill. Coll. Engring. indsl. research adv. council 1978—), ME-IE Alumni Assn. (dir. 1973—, pres. 1976-77), Chgo. Council Fgn. Relations, Chgo. Com., Sigma Pi, Beta Gamma Sigma, Tau Nu Tau, Tau Beta Pi (Eminent Engr.), Pi Tau Sigma (hon. status). Clubs: Econ., Chgo., Comml., Mid-Am. (Chgo.); Butler Nat. Golf. Contbr. articles to profl. jours. Office: PO Box 200 Naperville IL 60566

GAVAN, JAMES ANDERSON, anthropology educator; b. Ludington, Mich., July 17, 1916; s. James Bartholomew and Mary (Anderson) G.; m. Dec. 17, 1945; children—Margaret Jean, James Charles. B.A. in Anthropology, U. Ariz., 1939, M.A. in Anthropology, U. Chgo. 1949, Ph.D. in Anthropology, 1953. Mem. staff Yerkes Labs. Primate Biology, Orange Park, Fla., 1950-53; from asst. prof. to assoc. prof. anatomy Med. Coll. S.C., Charleston, 1953-62; assoc. prof. anthropology and anatomy U. Fla. Gainesville, 1962-67; prof. anthropology U. Mo., Columbia, 1967—, dept. chmn., 1968-71, 75-78; mem. Dental Study Sect. NIH, 1970, 74, Anthropology Rev. Panel NSF, 1976-78, dept. anthropology rev. panel Ohio State U., Jan. 1979, dept. anthropology rev. panel U. Pa., Mar. 1979. Author: A Classification of the Order Primates, 1975; Paleoanthropology and Primate Evolution, 1977. Editor: The Non-Human Primates and Human Evolution, 1955; also articles. Served with U.S. Army, 1942-45, ETO. Decorated Purple Heart, Bronze Star. Fellow Am. Anthrop. Assn., AAAS; mem. Am. Assn. Phys. Anthropologists (exec. com. 1966-69, sec. treas. 1973-77, pres. 1977-79), Human Biology Council, Central States Anthrop. Soc., Sigma Xi. Roman Catholic. Home: Rt 1 Box 253 Clark MO 65243 Office: Dept Anthropology 210 Switzler Hall Univ Mo Columbia MO 65211

GAYDAR, LEONARD EDWARD, legal adminstrator; b. Cleve., May 7, 1935; s. Joseph John and Anna (Marchin) G.; m. Nancy Jean Domer, June 21, 1958; children—Kathleen Marie Gaydar Colson, Teresa Ann. B.F.A., Ohio U., 1957; M.S. in Edn., So. Ill. U., 1974; mil. edn. Highest Command and Gen. Staff Coll., 1978. Commd. 2d lt. U.S. Army, 1957, advanced through grades to lt. col., 1982; legal adminstr. Armstrong, Teasdale, Kramer & Vaughan, St. Louis, 1982—; instr. night sch. Washington U., St. Louis. Decorated Bronze Star with 2 oak leaf clusters, Legion of Merit, Bronze Star with two oak leaf clusters; Vietnamese Medal of Honor. Mem. ABA (econs. sect.), Assn. Legal Adminstrs. (pres. Gateway chpt.), Assn. Info. System Profls., Am. Mgmt. Assn., Am. Soc. Personnel Adminstrs., Ret. Officers Assn., Heritage Citizens Assn. (trustee). Roman Catholic. Avocations: basketball and football ofcl.; jogging; mil. history. Home: 1477 Gettysburg Landing Saint Charles MO 63303 Office: Armstrong Teasdale Kramer & Vaughan 611 Olive St Suite 1900 Saint Louis MO 63101

GAYLOR, ANNE NICOL, editor, foundation executive; b. Tomah, Wis., Nov. 25, 1926; d. Jason Theodore and Lucie Edna (Sowle) Nicol; m. Paul Joseph Gaylor, Jr., Dec. 29, 1949; children—Andrew, Ian Stuart, Annie Laurie, Jamie Lachlan. B.A., U. Wis., 1949. Founder Freedom from Religion Found., Madison, Wis., 1976, pres., 1978—; editor Freethought Today. Author: Abortion is a Blessing, 1975; Lead Us Not into Penn Station, 1983. Founder, adminstr. Women's Med. Fund, Inc., Madison, 1972, Zero Population Growth Referral Service, Madison, 1970; founder, pres. Protect Abortion Rights, Inc., Madison, 1978. founder Freedom from Religion Found., Madison, 1976. Recipient Achievement award Zero Population Growth, 1983; Humanist Heroine award Am. Humanist Assn., 1985. Home: 726 Miami Pass Madison WI Office: Freethought Today 30 W Mifflin St 801 Madison WI 53703

GAYTAN, NOE, manufacturing company executive; b. Lubbock, Tex., Oct. 12, 1944; s. Alvaro and Rafaela (Galvan) G.; m. Myra Lynn Jean, Apr. 26, 1966; children—Randy L., Christy M. Student, Lake Mich. Coll., Benton Harbor, Mich. Union official UAW, Saint Joseph, Mich., 1967-75; supr. Bendix Corp., Saint Joseph, 1975-77, indsl. relations sr., 1977-82; mgr. labor relations Bendix-Allied Corp., Saint Joseph, 1982—. Vice pres. Lakeview Credit Union, Saint Joseph, 1976—; bd. dirs. Berrien County Red Cross, Benton Harbor, 1979—. Mem. Lakeshore C. of C. (bd. dirs. 1982—). Club: Mgmt. (Saint Joseph) (bd. dirs. 1980-81). Home: 5773 Saint Joseph Ave Stevensville MI 49127 Office: Bendix-Allied Corp Red Arrow Hwy Saint Joseph MI 49085

GEAKE, RAYMOND ROBERT, state senator; b. Detroit, Oct. 26, 1936; s. Harry Nevill and Phyllis Rae (Fox) G.; B.S. in Spl. Edn., U. Mich., 1958, M.A. in Guidance and Counseling, 1959, Ph.D. in Edn. and Psychology, 1963; m. Carol Lynne Rens, June 9, 1962; children—Roger Rens, Tamara Lynne, William Rens. Coordinator child devel. research Edison Inst., Dearborn, Mich., 1962-66; dir. psychology dept. Plymouth (Mich.) State Home and Tng. Sch., Mich. Dept. Mental Health, 1966-69; pvt. practice ednl. psychology, Northville, Mich., 1969-72; mem. Mich. Ho. of Reps., 1973-76, Mich. Senate, 1977—; adj. asst. prof. edn./psychology dept. Madonna Coll., Livonia, Mich., 1984—. Trustee-at-large Schoolcraft Community Coll., 1969-72, chmn. bd. trustees, 1971-72; vice chmn. nat. adv. com. on mental health and illness of elderly HEW, 1976-77. Mem. N.E.A. (life), Mich. Soc. Geneal. Research. Republican. Rotarian. Co-author: Visual Tracking, a Self-instruction Workbook for Perceptual Skills in Reading, 1962. Office: Capitol Bldg Lansing MI 48901

GEALER, ROY LEE, chemical engineer; b. Detroit, Oct. 23, 1932; s. Joseph M. and Fannie E. (Atlivaick) G.; m. Norma Varnen, June 29, 1957; children—Charles A., Christine L. B.S. Ch.E., Wayne State U., 1954; M.S. Ch.E., U. Mich., 1955, Ph.D. in Chem. Engring., 1958. Research asst. U. Mich., Ann Arbor, 1954-58; research engr. Ethyl Corp., Ferndale, Mich., 1958-63; prin. research engr. Ford Motor Co., Dearborn, Mich., 1963—. Patentee in field. Mem. Am. Inst. Chem. Engrs., Am. Chem. Soc., Tau Beta Pi, Sigma Xi, Phi Lambda Upsilon. Avocations: sailing; home computers; science fiction. Office: Ford Motor Co Scientific Research Lab PO Box 2053 Room 3198 Dearborn MI 48121

GEDDES, BRUCE LEE, utility company official; b. East Cleveland, Ohio, July 7, 1947; s. Joseph and Minnie May (Madigan) G.; m. Jean McCraken Campbell, Oct. 16, 1971; children—Allison Jean, Susan Elizabeth. A.A. in Environ. Health Tech., U. Toledo. Cert. Nat. Registry Radiation Technologists. Chem. and radiation protection technician D.C. Cook Nuclear Power Sta., Bridgeman, Mich., 1973-76; nuclear quality assurance auditor, Toledo Edison, 1976—. Author: Ohio Jaycees Stress Management, 1983. Bd. dirs. St Thomas Aquinas Sch. Bd., Toledo, pres. 1984-85. Served to 1st class petty officer USN, 1965-73. Mem. Am. Soc. Quality Control, Jaycees Internat., Ohio Jaycees (pres. Oregon 1981-82, (Thiemeyer-Augustine award, 1983); U.S. Jaycees (Seiji Horiuchi award, 1983), Toledo Jaycees. Roman Catholic. Club. St. Thomas Holy Name (Toledo) (v.p. 1984-86). Avocations: bowling; boating. Home: 1902 Idaho St Toledo OH 43605

GEDGAUDAS, EUGENE, radiologist; b. Lithuania, Oct. 7, 1924; came to U.S., 1963, naturalized, 1968; M.D., U.Munich, 1948; married; children—Kristina, Nora, Sandra. Intern, St. Boniface Hosp., Winnipeg, Man., Can.; resident in radiology St. Boniface Hosp., Winnipeg, U. Minn., Hosp., Mpls.; chmn. cardiac unit, asso. radiologist St. Boniface Gen. Hosp., Winnipeg, 1958-63, also dir. dept. radiology Mericordia Gen. Hosp., Winnipeg; asst. prof. radiology U. Minn., Mpls., 1963-67, assoc. prof., 1967-69, prof., 1969—, head radiology, 1969—, chmn. council clin. scis. Med. Sch., 1975—. Diplomate Am. Bd. Radiology. Fellow Royal Coll. Physicians and Surgeons Can., Am. Coll. Radiology, Internat. Coll. Surgery; mem. AMA, Radiol. Soc. N.Am., Am. Roentgen Ray Soc. (pres. 1985), Minn. Radiology Soc. (past pres.), Minn. Acad. Medicine, Assn. Univ. Radiologists, Soc. Chmn. Acad. Radiology Depts. Contbr. articles to profl. jours. Home: 26 Evergreen Rd North Oaks St Paul MN 55110 Office: Box 292 Radiology 420 Delaware St SE Minneapolis MN 55455

GEE, DAVID ALAN, hospital administrator; b. Cambridge, Mass., Apr. 17, 1928; s. Harold F. and Thelma A. (Gilbert) G.; m. Lois Jean Ellis, Dec. 26, 1949 (dec. May 1969); children—Thomas H., John M., William M., Kimberley E.; m. Barbara Joan Singleton, Jan. 1, 1970. A.B., DePauw U., 1949; M.H.A., Washington U., St. Louis, 1951. Asst. dir. Jewish Hosp., St. Louis, 1951-63, pres., 1963—; mem. faculty Washington U. Sch. Medicine, 1957—. Contbr. chpts. to books, articles to profl. jours. Recipient Goldstein award Jewish Fedn. St. Louis, 1977; Disting. Service award Vaad Hoeir, 1978. Fellow Am. Coll. Hosp. Adminstrs. (regent 1977-80); mem. Am. Hosp. Assn. (bd. dirs. 1983—), Mo. Hosp. Assn. (chmn. 1976-78), Hosp. Assn. Met. St. Louis (chmn. 1966-68). Republican. Clubs: University, Washington U. Faculty (St. Louis). Home: 179 Riverbend Dr Chesterfield MO 63017 Office: 216 S Kingshwy Saint Louis MO 63110

GEE, GARY T., lawyer; b. Shenandoah, Iowa, Apr. 3, 1952; s. John W. and Marilynn (Taylor) G.; m. Patricia Otte, June 5, 1982; 1 child, Jasmyn Lynn. B.A. in Psychology, U. Iowa, 1974; J.D., Drake U., 1977. Bar: Iowa, Colo., U.S. Dist. Ct. (so. dist.) Iowa. County atty., Page County, Iowa, 1978; sole practice, Denver, 1979-80, Shenandoah, Iowa, 1980-83; ptnr. Gee & Gregg, Attys., Shenandoah, 1983—. Mem. Page County Bar Assn. (pres. 1982—), Fremont County Bar Assn. (pres. 1982-84), Am. Trial Lawyers Assn., SW Iowa Bar Assn., Iowa Bar Assn., Jaycees, Shendoah C. of C. Democrat. Presbyterian. Lodge: Elks. Office: Gee & Gregg Attys 112 S Elm St PO Box 177 Shenandoah IA 51601

GEE, ROBERT LEROY, dairy farmer; b. Moorhead, Minn., May 25, 1926; s. Milton W. and Hertha E. (Paschke) G.; m. Mae V. Erickson, June 18, 1953. B.S. in Agr., N.D. State U., 1951. With Clay County Extension Service, Moorhead, 1951-57; dairy farmer, Moorhead, 1957—. Mem. Clay-Cass Creamery, 1957—, pres., 1982—; Clay County rep. Red River Valley Devel. Assn., 1973—, Red River Valley Fair Bd., 1960—; appointed to Nat. Dairy Promotion and Research Bd., 1984. Served with USN, 1945-46. Mem. Minn. Milk Producers Assn. (treas.), Minn. Assn. Coop. Dairy Council (v.p. 1975-83). Republican. Mem. United Ch. of Christ. Club: Agassiz (pres. 1981-82).

GEEDING, PHILLIP WARREN, technical services veterinarian; b. Joplin, Mo., Dec. 19, 1949; s. George W. and Marjery K. (Bushner) G.; m. Ginger E. Shoemaker, Aug. 7, 1976; 1 child, Amy Antonia. Student Mo. So. State Coll., 1972; D.V.M., U. Mo., 1976. Herd health veterinarian Great Plains Ova Transplant, Ada, Okla., summer 1976; veterinarian Atchison Vet. Clinic, Kans., 1976; veterinarian, owner Larson Vet. Clinic, Pittsburg, Kans., 1976-79; relief veterinarian Vet. Relief Services, Atchison, 1979-80; veterinarian, owner Hillside Vet. Clinic, Atchison, 1980-81; tech. services staff veterinarian Boehringer-Ingelheim U.S.A. Animal Health Div., St. Joseph, Mo., 1981—. Mem. Am. Vet. Med. Assn., Am. Assn. Indsl. Veterinarians, Am. Assn. Bovine Practitioners, Kans. Vet. Med. Assn. Office: Boehringer Ingelheim USA 2621 N Belt Hwy St Joseph MO 64502

GEER, CHRISTOPHER, lawyer; b. Topeka, Kans., Nov. 2, 1948; s. Virgil Clyde and Margaretta (Liebrenz) G. B.S. in Edn., Ohio State U., 1977, J.D., Capital U., 1977. Bar: Ohio 1978, U.S. Dist. Ct. (so. dist.) Ohio 1979, U.S. Supreme Ct. 1982. Assoc. Matan, Rinehart & Smith, Columbus, Ohio, 1978-80; ptnr. Matan & Smith, Columbus, 1980—. Mem. Probate Reform Com., Franklin County, Ohio, 1983—. Mem. Columbus Bar Assn., Ohio State Bar Assn., Franklin County Trial Lawyers Assn., Assn. Trial Lawyers Am. Republican. Presbyterian. Home: 844 Old Farm Rd Columbus OH 43213 Office: Matan & Smith 261 S Front St Columbus OH 43215

GEER, THOMAS LEE, lawyer; b. Johnstown, Pa., Sept. 26, 1951; s. Frank Densmore, III, and Lillian Louise (Vivoda) G. B.A. cum laude, Boston U., 1973; J.D., U. Pitts., 1976; M.L.T., Georgetown U., 1978. Bar: Pa. 1978, U.S. dist. (ea. dist.) Mich. 1978, U.S. Tax Ct. 1978, Ohio 1982. Clk. NW Pa. Legal Services, Sharon, 1975; assoc. Silverstein & Mullins, Washington, 1976-78, Dykema, Gossett, Spencer, Goodnow & Trigg, Detroit, 1978-80, Keywell & Rosenfeld, Troy, Mich., 1980-81; ptnr. Carson, Vieweg, Geer & Smereck, Bloomfield Hills, Mich., 1981-82, Schwartz, Kelm, Warren & Rubenstein, Columbus, Ohio, 1982—; adj. prof. Walsh Coll., Troy, Mich., 1981, Franklin U., Columbus, 1983—. Author: 274-2nd T.M. Casualty Losses, 1979; 298-2nd T.M. Private Foundation-Definition & Classification, 1982; 337-2nd T.M. Exempt Organizations, 1984; author articles. Mem. ABA (chmn. continuing legal edn. subcom. tax acctg. problems com. 1981-82), Ohio State Bar Assn., Columbus Bar Assn. (chmn. task force on provision of legal services to nonprofit entities 1982-84). Home: 1991 Suffolk Rd Columbus OH 43221 Office: Schwartz Kelm Warren & Rubenstein 41 S High St Columbus OH 43215

GEETHA, RANGASWAMI, biostatistician; b. Manamadurai, Tamilnadu, India, Nov. 19, 1949; came to U.S., 1975; d. Agrapet Srinivasa and Thangam (Anantharamakrishnan) Rangaswami. B.A. with honors in Math., Lady Shri Ram Coll., New Delhi, 1969, M.A. in Math., 1971; M.Sc. in Stats., U. Alta., Edmonton, 1975; M.S. in Ops. Research, Mich. State U., 1979, Ph.D. in Stats., 1981. Grad. teaching asst. Mich. State U., East Lansing, 1975-81; asst. prof. Bowling Green State U., Ohio, 1981-84; research scientist, biostatistician Bristol-Myers, Evansville, Ind., 1984—; statis. cons. Computer Lab., Mich. State U., East Lansing, 1980-81; research project advisor Bowling Green State U., Ohio, 1982-83. Vol. Nat. ARC, Lansing, Mich., 1977-81, Friend A Friend Program, Evansville, Ind., 1984-85, Youth Crisis Bur., Evansville, 1984-85. Jr. research fellow Delhi U., India, 1972-73. Mem. Am. Statis. Assn., Am. Soc. Quality Control. Avocations: tennis; chess; volunteer work; traveling; photography. Home: 5599 Kenwood Dr Newburgh IN 47630 Office: Bristol Myers Pennsylvania Ave Evansville IN 47721

GEHLHAUSEN, TERRY CHARLES, physician; b. Ferdinand, Ind., Apr. 27, 1951; s. Charles Henry and Sylvia Mae (Fischer) G.; m. Nancy Elizabeth Perkins, July 27, 1974; 1 child, Nathan Charles. B.A. in Biology, U. Evansville, 1973; M.S. in Pharmacology, Ind. U., 1979; D.O., U. Health Scis. Coll. Osteo. Medicine, 1981. Intern, Normandy Hosp., St. Louis, 1981-82; gen. practice osteo. medicine, Oakland City, Ind., 1982—. Mem. Am. Osteo. Assn., Ind. Assn. Osteo. Physicians and Surgeons, Am. Coll. Gen. Practitioners. Lodges: Kiwanis, Eagles. Home: Route 3 Box 66D Oakland City IN 47660 Office: PO Box 266 Oakland City IN 47660

GEIER, GREGORY FRANCIS, pharmacist; b. Kansas City, Kans., May 28, 1958; s. Rupert Rudolph and Mary Helen (Sneller) G. B.S. in Pharmacy, U. Kans., 1981. Registered pharmacist, Kans., Mo. Pharmacist, asst. mgr. Treasury Drug, Olathe, Kans.; cons. pharmacist Regency Health Care Ctr., Olathe. Kappa Psi scholar, 1979. Mem. Kans. Pharmacists Assn., Phi Kappa Theta Alumni (pres. 1980, sec. bd. dirs. 1984—). Republican. Roman Catholic. Avocations: golf; weightlifting; tropical fish.

GEIER, JAMES AYLWARD DEVELIN, machine tools manufacturing company executive. Chmn., chief exec. officer Cin. Milacron Inc., also dir. Office: Cin Milacron 4701 Marburg Ave CIncinnati OH 45209*

GEIERSBACH, JOAN MARIE, communications specialist; b. Jackson, Mich., Jan. 28, 1955; d. Harold Arthur and Marilyn Ann (Kelly) G. A.A.,

Jackson Community Coll., 1975; B.A. summa cum laude in English, Albion Coll., 1977; postgrad. Ariz. State U., 1979. Tech. editor Gilbert and Commonwealth, Jackson, 1976-79, proposal coordinator, 1980-83, communications specialist, 1983—, bus. writing instr., 1984—; cons. in tech. writing and editing, Jackson, 1980—. Mem. Internat. Assn. Bus. Communicators, Nat. Assn. Female Execs., Mich. Lupus Found., Phi Beta Kappa. Lutheran. Avocations: sailing; charcoal sketching; photography. Home: 5917 Joymont Jackson MI 49201 Office: Gilbert and Commonwealth 209 E Washington Ave Jackson MI 49201

GEIGER, LEO, hospital administrator; b. Gladstone, N.D., Dec. 9, 1928; s. Peter and Tillie (Gieser) G.; m. Alvina Anderson, July 10, 1952; children—Marianne, Gregory, Edward. Cert. hosp. adminstrn., U. Minn., 1972. Adminstr. McIntosh County Meml. Hosp., Ashley, N.D., 1961-70, 1981—, St. Aloisius Hosp., Harvey, N.D., 1970-79; corp. adv. Sisters of Mary of the Presentation, Valley City, N.D., 1979-81; chmn. N.D. Hosp. Assn., 1975, trustee, 1971-81; del. Am. Hosp. Assn., Chgo., 1976-82. Mem. Am. Coll. Hosp. Adminstrs., Harvey C. of C. (bd. dirs. 1972-76), Ashley C. of C. (pres. 1985). Republican. Roman Catholic. Lodges: Lions, Kiwanis, Elks, Eagles. Home: Route 2 Ashley ND 58413 Office: McIntosh County Hosp ICF 612 N Center Ave Ashley ND 58413

GEIGER, MARY BARTON, real estate executive; b. Detroit, Oct. 28, 1933; d. Carl Osborn and Constance E. (Robertson) Barton; m. Paul Keith Geiger, Apr. 1956 (div. May 1982); children—Mary Louise, Catherine Elizabeth, William Barton, David Paul. B.A., U. Mich., 1955. Tchr. drama Cranbrook Theatre Sch., Bloomfield Hills, Mich., summers 1959-67; travel agt. Robert Davis Travel, Bloomfield Hills, 1972-74, Suburban Travel Service, Rochester, Mich., 1974-80; founder Dinner Theatre Co., 1975—; mgr. Barton Properties, Birmingham, Mich., 1980—. Mem. Jr. League Birmingham; vestryman Christ Episcopal Ch., Cranbrook, 1977-80. Mem. Am. Mgmt. Assn., Nat. Assn. Female Execs., Birmingham C. of C. Republican. Clubs: Birmingham Athletic; Village Woman's, Village (Bloomfield Hills). Office: 199 Pierce St Suite 202 Birmingham MI 48011

GEIGER, RONALD RAY, accountant, financial executive; b. Omaha, Dec. 2, 1949; s. Raymond A. and Twyla J. (Olson) G.; m. Wendy L. Wilson, Mar. 20, 1976; children—Matthew R., Laura L. B.S.B.A., U. Nebr., 1978. C.P.A., Nebr., Iowa. Auditor, Coopers and Lybrand, Omaha, 1978-81; controller Harker's Inc., LeMars, Iowa, 1981-84, treas., 1984—. Bd. dirs. Plymouth County Work Activity Ctr., LeMars, 1984. Served to petty officer 5 USN, 1970-75. Mem. Nebr. Soc. C.P.A.'s, Nat. Assn. Accts. (v.p. 1982—), Iowa Cash Mgmt. Assn. (sec. 1984—), LeMars C. of C. (v.p. 1984, pres.-elect. 1985). Lodge: Lions. Avocations: golf; softball; volleyball. Home: 530 1st Ave SW LeMars IA 51031 Office: Harker's Inc 527 8th Ave SW LeMars IA 51031

GEISBERGER, GEORGE BAHR, educator; b. Freeport, Ill., Jan. 21, 1935; s. August and Rose Anna (Bahr) G.; B.A., Rockford Coll., 1956, M.A., 1962; postgrad. U. Wis. Tchr., Harlem Jr. High Sch., Rockford, Ill., 1956, Union (Ill.) Sch., 1957-62; head tchr. Argyle Sch., Rockford, 1962-64; chmn. sociology dept., dir. field work placement program Milton (Wis.) Coll., 1964-70; program coordinator U. Wis. Extension, Madison, 1972-77; dir. Dept. Edn., Beloit (Wis.) Meml. Hosp., 1977-85; title search/cons. recreational devels., 1970-76. Sec.-treas. chpt. Muscular Dystrophy Assns. Am.; bd. dirs. Abaris Ctr. for the Chemically Dependent. Mem. AAUP, Am. Judicature Soc., Wis. Soc. for Health Manpower Edn. and Tng., Phi Delta Kappa. Home: PO Box 704 Rockford IL 61105

GEISENDORFER, JAMES VERNON, author; b. Brewster, Minn., Apr. 22, 1929; s. Victor H. and Anne B. (Johnson) G.; student Augustana Coll., 1950-51, Augsburg Coll., 1951-54, Orthodox Luth. Sem., 1954-55; B.A., U. Minn., 1960; LL.D., Burton Coll. and Sem., 1961; m. Esther Lillian Walker, Sept. 23, 1949; children—Jane, Karen, Lois. Grain buyer Pillsbury Mills, Inc., Worthington, Minn., 1947-48; hatchery acct., Worthington, 1949-50; night supr. Strutwear, Inc., Mpls., 1951-52; dispatcher Chgo. and North Western Ry., 1953-54; office mgr. Froedtert Malt Corp., Mpls., 1955-56, Nat. Automotive Parts Assn., 1957-60; sr. creative writer Brown & Bigelow, St. Paul, 1960-72; religious researcher, writer, 1972—; research cons. Inst. for the Study of Am. Religion; mem. panel of reference Chelston Bible Coll., New Milton, Eng.; mem. U.S. Congl. Adv. Bd., 1985. Recipient Amicus Poloniae medal Polish Ministry of Culture and Edn., 1969. Mem. Am. Acad. Religion, Acad. Ind. Scholars, Wis. Evang. Luth. Synod Hist. Inst., Augustana Hist. Soc., Wis. Acad. Scis., Arts and Letters, Can. Soc. Study of Religion, Aristotelian Soc. Lutheran. Author: (with J. Gordon Melton) A Directory of Religious Bodies in the United States, 1977; Religion in America, 1983; mem. editorial bd. Ency. of Am. Sect and Cult Leaders; contbr. articles to books and periodicals; cons. editor Directory of Religious Organizations in the United States, 1977. Address: 1001 Shawano Ave Green Bay WI 54303

GEISLER, DAVID ARTHUR, automobile museum executive; b. Pasadena, Calif., Sept. 28, 1937; s. Arthur John and Vivian C. (Petersen) G.; children—Vivian Carole, Patricia Lynn, Jennifer Marie, David Martin. B.S. in Edn., Concordia Coll., 1959; M.S. in Psychology, Oreg. State U., 1962. Coach, Zion Lutheran Sch., Corvallis, Oreg., 1959-62; pioneer, owner, mgr. Pioneer Automobile Museum, Murdo, S.D., 1970—; dealer Murdo Motor Co., 1962-84. Chmn. S.D. Tourism Bd., Pierre, 1980—; bd. dirs. S.D. State Chamber, 1981—; delegate Republican Nat. Conv., Dallas, 1984. Recipient 11 Disting. Dealer awards Ford Motor Co. Lutheran. Lodge: Lions (pres. 1964-66). Avocations: basketball coach; travel; toastmaster. Home: 404 E 2d St Murdo SD 57559 Office: Pioneer Auto Museum Murdo SD 57559

GEISS, JANICE M(ARIE), lawyer, educator; b. St. Louis, July 20, 1950; d. Frank W. and Marcella M. (Schmidt) Carney; m. John Robert Geiss, Dec. 22, 1972; children—Michael John, Jeffrey Phillip. B.S. in Nursing, St. Louis U., 1971, J.D., 1982; M.A. in Edn., Washington U., St. Louis, 1977. Bar; Mo. 1983, U.S. Ct. Appeals (8th cir.) 1983, U.S. Dist. Ct. (ea. dist.) Mo. 1984. Mem. nursing staff St. Mary's Health Ctr., St. Louis, 1972-82, coordinator nursing inservice edn., 1977-79, asst. dir. nursing, 1979-82; assoc. Klutho, Cody, Kilo and Flynn Attys., Inc., St. Louis, 1982—; adj. prof. health law Maryville Coll., St. Louis, 1983—; presenter health law seminars, 1983—. Mem. Am. Soc. Law and Medicine, Mo. Bar Assn., Met. Bar Assn. St. Louis, ABA, Assn. Trial Lawyers Am., Mo. Assn. Trial Attys. Home: 2928 Yale Blvd Saint Charles MO 63301 Office: Klutho Cody Kilo and Flyn Attys Inc 5840 Oakland Ave St Louis MO 63110

GELFAND, IVAN, investment adviser; b. Cleve., Mar. 29, 1927; s. Samuel and Sarah (Kruglin) G.; B.S., Miami U., 1950; postgrad Case-Western Res. U., 1951; grad. Columbia U. Bank Mgmt. Program, 1968; certificates Am. Inst. Banking; m. Suzanne Frank, Sept. 23, 1956; children—Dennis Scott, Andrew Steven. Accountant Central Nat. Bank of Cleve., 1950-53, v.p., mgr. bank and corp. investments, 1957-75; pres. Gelfand, Quinn & Assocs. Inc., 1975-79, chmn. bd., chief exec. officer, 1979-83; v.p., mng. dir. Prudential Bache Securities, Inc., 1983-85 pres. Ivan Gelfand & Assocs., Inc., 1985—; chief accountant Stars & Stripes newspaper, Darmstadt, Germany, 1953-55; account exec. Merrill Lynch, Pierce, Fenner & Smith, Inc., Cleve., 1955-57. Instr. investments Cleve. Bd. Edn. adult div., 1956-58, Am. Inst. Banking 1958-68; lectr. econs., instl. portfolio mgmt., 1972—; money market columnist Nat. Thrift News, 1977-78; TV and radio fin. commentator, 1984—; co-editor The Liquidity Portfolio Mgr., The Gelfand-Quinn Report, 1978-81, The Gelfand-Quinn Analysis-Money Market Techniques, 1981-84. Mem. Greater Cleve. Growth Assn., 1968—; mem. investment com. United Torch of Cleve., 1972-74; study-rev. team Lake Erie Regional Transp. Assn., 1973-77. mem. Cuyahoga County Republican Fin. Com., 1977-81; mem. Cuyahoga County Rep. Exec. Com., 1982—; mem. fin. com. and investment and bond com. Jewish Community Fedn., Cleve. trustee Mt. Sinai Med. Ctr., Cleve., 1983—. Served with AUS, 1945-47. Mem. Cleve. Soc. Security Analysts, Les Politiques. Clubs: Masons; Mid-Day, Commerce, Union (Cleve.); Oakwood, City, Citizens League. Guest money market columnist Nat. Thrift News, 1982—. Home: 2900 Alvord Pl Pepper Pike OH 44124 Office: 390 Statler Office Tower Cleveland OH 44115

GELFAND, MICHAEL JOSEPH, radiology educator; b. Detroit, Mar. 4, 1945; s. Jacob and Mildred (Weine) G.; m. Janelle Ann Magnuson, Mar. 24, 1973; children—Rebecca Ann, Karin Janelle. B.A., U. Mich., 1966; M.D., Stanford U., 1971. Diplomate Am. Bd. Pediatrics, Am. Bd. Nuclear Medicine. Intern, Children's Hosp., Cin., 1973-74, resident in pediatrics, 1974-75; resident in nuclear medicine U. Cin., 1975-77, asst. prof. pediatrics, 1978—, asst. prof. radiology, 1977-83, assoc. prof., 1983—; asst. attending radiologist Children's Hosp. Cin., 1978-79, attending radiologist, 1979—. Contbr. chpts. to books, articles to med. jours. Served with USPHS, 1971-73. Mem. Soc. Nuclear Medicine, Soc. Pediatric Radiology. Office: U Cin Cincinnati OH 45267

GELLER, ROBERT DENNIS, internist; b. N.Y.C., Apr. 5, 1941; s. Martin Max and Elvira Joan (Reich) G.; B.Met.E. cum laude, N.Y. U., 1962; M.D., Cornell U., 1966; m. Karen Hannk Greshes, Feb. 7, 1974; children—Meredith Anne, Evan Scott. Intern, Bellevue Hosp., N.Y.C., 1966-67, resident in medicine, 1967-68; resident in medicine North Shore U. Hosp., 1968-70; practice medicine specializing in internal medicine, cons. infectious disease, Manhasset, N.Y., 1972-77; practice medicine specializing in internal medicine, cons. infectious disease Freeport (Ill.) Clinic, S.C., 1977—, pres., chmn. bd., 1981—; pres. med. staff Freeport Meml. Hosp.; clin. asst. prof. medicine Cornell U.; mem. med. malpractice panel N.Y. State Supreme Ct., Mineola, 1976; peer rev. com., bd. dirs. No. Ill. Profl. Standards Rev. Orgn., Rockford, 1978. Served with USPHS, 1970-72. Diplomate Am. Bd. Internal Medicine. Fellow ACP; mem. Am. Heart Assn., Am. Soc. Microbiology, Am. Fedn. Clin. Research, AMA, Ill., Stephenson County med. socs. Contbr. articles on Coccidioidin skin test sensitivity to Am. Rev. Respiratory Diseases, 1972-73. Office: 1036 W Stephenson St Freeport IL 61032

GELLERSTEDT, MARIE ADA, manufacturing company executive; b. Davenport, Iowa, Oct. 19, 1926; d. Charles Beecher and Marie Elizabeth (Pasvogel) Kaufmann; m. Keith Orval Gellerstedt, Mar. 16, 1957; children—Lori Beth, Keith Todd, Jon Erik, Cory Andrew. B.A. in Bus. Adminstrn., Augustana Coll., 1950. Gen. mgr., pres. Nixalite Co. Am., East Moline, Ill., 1957—. Life mem. Moline St. High Sch. PTA, dir., 1973-76. Mem. Ill. Mfrs. Assn., Nat. Trade Show Exhibitors Assn., Internat. Exhibitors Assn., Nat. Pest Control Assn., Nat. Animal Damage Control Assn. Republican. Lutheran. Clubs: Zonta, Daus. of Mokanna, Zal Caldron, Daus. of the Nile.

GELLERT, EDWARD BRADFORD, III, architect, consultant; b. Norwalk, Conn., Aug. 19, 1954; s. Edward Bradford and Audrey Marie (Freese) G.; m. Juliet Pendleton Kostritsky, Dec. 21, 1980. B.A., Yale U., 1976; M.Arch., Columbia U., 1979; cert. Real Estate Inst., NYU, 1983, Nat. Council Archtl. Registration Bds. Registered architect, N.Y. Research asst. Regional Plan Assn., N.Y.C., 1977-78; architect Urban Devel. Authority, Colombo, Sri Lanka, 1979-80, Mullen Palandrani, N.Y.C., 1980-81, Cossutta & Assocs., N.Y.C., 1981-83; project architect Smotrich & Platt, N.Y.C., 1983-84, Teare Herman Gibans, Inc., Cleve., 1984-85, Dalton, Dalton, Newport/URS, Cleve., 1985—. Prin. works include Keuffner residence, Darien, Conn., 1982-83. Contbg. author: Cousteau Almanac of the Environment, 1981. Columbia U. Grad. Sch. Architecture and Planning William Kinne Fellows fellow, 1979; recipient 2d prize for fiction Atlantic Monthly, 1972. Mem. AIA (energy com. hist. preservation com.), Nat. Trust for Hist. Preservation. Democrat. Episcopalian. Club: Yale (N.Y.C.). Home: 3330 Maynard Rd Shaker Heights OH 44122 Office: URS/Dalton 3605 Warrensville Center Rd Shaker Heights OH 44122

GELLNER, CAROL ANN, educator; b. Wheeling, W.Va., June 19, 1950; d. Charles Herman and Helen June (Gantzer) G. B.A., West Liberty State Coll., 1971; M.Ed., Kent State U., 1975; postgrad. Miami U., Oxford, Ohio. Cert. vocat. educator and supr., supt., Ohio. Bus. edn. tchr. Yorkville (Ohio) High Sch., 1972; bus. edn. tchr. Wheeling Central High Sch., 1972-74; bus. edn. tchr. Belmont (Ohio) County Vocat. Sch., 1974-78; adj. faculty W.Va. No. Community Coll., Wheeling, 1974-78; CETA coordinator Belmont Vocat. Sch., 1978; ESEA project dir. Stark (Ohio) County Schs., 1978-79; instructional supr. Upper Valley Joint Vocat. Sch. Dis., Piqua, Ohio, 1979-83, equal employment opportunity, Title IX officer, 1979-83; vocat. dir. Greene Vocat. Sch., Xenia, Ohio, 1983—; cons. and lectr. in field. Vol., Am. Cancer Soc., 1981—. Mem. Am. Vocat. Assn., Ohio Vocat. Assn., Nat. Assn. Female Execs., Nat. Bus. Edn. Assn., Nat. Council Local Adminstrs., Ohio Bus. Tchrs. Assn., Ohio Vocat. Dirs. Assn., Bus. and Profl. Women, Phi Delta Kappa. Presbyterian. Author: (manual) Vocational Education for Exceptional Students, 1979; contbr. to profl. newsletter in field. Office: 2960 W Enon Dr Xenia OH 45385

GELPI, MICHAEL ANTHONY, venture capitalist; b. Columbus, Ohio, Dec. 28, 1940; s. Andre and Eleanor (Amorose) G. A.B., Georgetown U., 1962. Store mgr. Swan Cleaners, Columbus, 1964-65, dist. supr., 1965-68, v.p., 1968-76, exec. v.p., treas., 1976-81, also dir.; v.p. Rainbow Properties, Columbus, 1971-83, pres., 1983—; dir. Neoprobe Corp., Health Options. Trustee Am. Cancer Soc., 1978—, crusade chmn., 1979-84, 1st v.p., 1981-84, pres., 1984-85, chmn., 1985—, trustee Ohio div., 1984—, state spl. gifts chmn., 1984—, recipient Vol. of Yr. award, 1981; trustee Players Theatre of Columbus, 1981—, v.p., 1985—; trustee German Village Hist. Soc., 1980-81; trustee Central Ohio Radio Reading Service, 1982—, pres., 1983—; mem. Republican Fin. com., 1981—; trustee Town-Franklin Hist. Neighborhood Assn., 1979—, v.p., 1983; chmn. advance gifts Bishops Ann. Appeal, 1981—; bd. dirs. Human Rights Campaign Fund, 1985—. Served to 1st lt. U.S. Army, 1962-64. Roman Catholic. Clubs: Columbus, Athletic (Columbus). Office: The Gelpi Co 65 E State St Columbus OH 43215

GEMBOL, DOROTHY JANETTE, counselor; b. Key West, Fla., Nov. 30, 1950; d. Clovis I. and Dorothy R. (Hjort) Claxton; m. Robert V. Gembol, Aug. 24, 1974. A.A., Miami Dade Jr. Coll., with high honors, 1970; B.A. U. Fla., 1972; M.S., Kans. State U., 1974, Ph.D., 1981. Cert. counselor. Counselor, Drug/Alcohol Program, Ft. Riley, Kans., 1973, chief intake unit, 1973-74; counselor psychiat. ward Irwin Hosp., Ft. Riley, Kans., 1978-79; alcohol prevention coordinator Unified Sch. Dist. 383, Manhattan, Kans., 1981-84; intern Kans. State U. Counseling Ctr., Manhattan, 1984-85; v.p. Riley County Council Alcoholism and Drug Edn., 1981-84; mem. adv. bd. Fone Crisis Ctr., Manhattan, 1983—; adj. prof. dept. social work Kans. State U., 1982-84. Bd. dirs., treas. Teen Outreach, Inc., Manhattan, 1983-85. Served as 2d lt. WAC, 1971-74. Fla. Bd. Regents scholar, 1968-72. Mem. Am. Assn. Counseling and Devel., Am. Coll. Personnel Assn., Nat. Council Family Relations, Kans. Assn. Prevention Profls., Phi Delta Gamma. Avocations: tennis; bridge; computers; fishing; ornithology. Office: Kans State U Manhattan KS 66506

GEMIGNANI, MICHAEL CAESAR, dean, telecommunications educator, lawyer; b. Balt., Feb. 23, 1938; s. Hugo John and Dorothy (Karu) G.; m. Nilda Keller, June 30, 1962; children—Stephen, Susan. B.A., U. Rochester, 1962; M.S., U. Notre Dame, 1964, Ph.D., 1965; J.D., Ind. U.—Indpls., 1980. Asst. prof. math. SUNY, Buffalo, 1965-68; assoc. prof. Smith Coll., Northampton, Mass., 1968-72; prof., chmn. dept. math. sci. Ind. U., Indpls., 1972-81; dean, prof. Ball State U., Muncie, Ind., 1981—; cons. computer law, Muncie, 1980—; chmn. com. info. processing Ind. Corp. for Sci. & Tech., Indpls., 1983—. Author: Law and The Computer, 1981; Computer Law, 1985. Contbr. articles to profl. jours. Mem. Assn. Computing Machinery, Math. Assn. Am., ABA, Computer Law Assn., Sigma. Episcopalian. Avocation: Episcopal priest, music. Home: 3556 Johnson Circle Muncie IN 47304 Office: Ball State U NQ 112 Muncie IN 47306

GENDE, JOSEPH J(AMES), food service company executive, inventor; b. Rock Island, Ill., July 28, 1934; s. Joseph and Eva Theodora (Bawiec) G.; m. Irene Susan Most, July 21, 1962; children—Susan K., Theresa A., Joseph A., Mary M., Paul E. Student U. Ill., 1952-57, UCLA Extension, 1960-63. Mech. designer E. J. Kelly & Assocs., Los Angeles, 1959-61; project engr. Whittaker Corp., Los Angeles, 1961-70; pres. Sagemark Ltd., Moline, Ill., 1970—. Served with U.S. Army, 1957-59. Patentee spring mechanism, aerosol replacement. Mem. Nat. Restaurant Assn., Mississippi Valley Restaurant Assn., Nat. Assn. Ind. Businessmen, U.S. C. of C., Rock Island County C. of C. Roman Catholic. Club: Alleman Boosters (treas. 1976-77, v.p. 1980-81) (Rock Island, Ill.). Lodge: K.C. Home: 4311 7th Ave Moline IL 61265 Office: Hungry Hobo Div Sagemark Ltd 5306 23d Ave Moline IL 61265

GENEREAUX, DAVID WEEKS, international sales and marketing executive; b. Wilmington, Del., Mar. 9, 1942; s. Raymond P. and Helen (Millikin) G.; m. Donna Gundy, May 18, 1972; 1 child, Heather. B.S.B.A., U. Del., 1969. Sales rep. Eastman Kodak, Ft. Wayne, Ind., 1969-75; gen. mgr. Microcopy, Ft. Wayne, 1975-77; nat. sales mgr. Infodetics, Anaheim, Calif., 1977-79; sr. systems rep. A.B. Dick Co., Los Angeles, 1979-80; computer system sales PAC Corp., Los Angeles, 1980; sales mgr. energy mgmt. systems MCC Powers Co., Los Angeles, 1980-81; mgr. internat. sales Micron Corp., Iron Ridge, Wis., 1981-84; mgr. new product devel. Storage Technology, Longmont, Colo., 1984; dir. internat. mktg. Concept Pub. Systems, Beaver Dam, Wis., 1985—. Served with U.S. Army, 1965-67. Mem. Assn. Info. and Image Mgmt., Nat. Micrographics Assn., Internat. Image Mgmt. Congress. Republican. Episcopalian. Avocations: sailing; woodworking; travel. Home: 122 W Water St Beaver Dam WI 53916

GENETSKI, ROBERT JAMES, economist, bank executive; b. N.Y.C., Dec. 26, 1942; s. Alex and Helen Genetski. B.S., Eastern Ill. U., 1964; M.A., NYU, 1968, Ph.D., 1972. Tchr. English, St. Procopius Acad., Lisle, Ill., 1965-66; research analyst Nat. Econ. Research Assn., N.Y.C., 1967-68; lectr. econs. NYU, 1969-70; economic analyst Morgan Guaranty Trust, N.Y.C., 1969-71; sr. v.p., chief economist Harris Trust & Savs. Bank, Chgo., 1971—; lectr. bus. U. Chgo., 1973. Author: (with Beryl Sprinkel) Winning with Money, 1977. Chmn. ednl. com., mem. Sch. Bd. Dist. 25, West Chicago, Ill., 1973-79. Mem. Am. Statis. Assn., Am. Econ. Assn., Nat. Assn. Bus. Economists (econs. editor Newsletter 1978), Western Econ. Assn. Office: Harris Trust & Savings Bank PO Box 755-6E Chicago IL 60690

GENGLER, JOHN HILARY, principal; b. Dickinson, N.D., Apr. 25, 1939; s. John Frederick and Esther Scholastica (Hopfauf) G.; m. Mary Jean Amann, Mar. 27, 1967. A.A., Assumption Coll., 1959; B.S., Dickinson State Coll., 1962, B.A., 1962; student U. Iowa, 1972, U. N.D., 1967. Tchr. South Heart High Sch., N.D., 1962-64; devel. dir. Assumption Coll., Richardton, N.D., 1964-70; tchr., prin. Richardton High Sch., N.D., 1970—; mem. N.D. Postsecondary Edn. Commn., Bismarck, 1976-80. Editor: Law and Justice in North Dakota, 1977; Richardton—1883-1983, 1983; Sod House Times, 1984; (newspaper) The Richardton Merchant, 1965-75. Municipal judge City of Richardton, 1966-70; mem. Park Dist. Comn., Richardton, 1972-80, pres., 1980-82. Carnegie grant Carnegie Found., 1984-85. Mem. Nat. Assn. Secondary Sch. Prins., N.D. Assn. Secondary Sch. Prins. (pres. 1985—), Assn. for Supervision and Curriculum Devel., Nat. Council Tchrs. English. Nat. Council for Social Studies, Dickinson State Coll. Alumni Assn. (pres. 1981-82). Democrat. Roman Catholic. Club: Saddle (sec. 1973-78). Lodges: K.C. (Grand Knight 1970), Elks. Avocations: tenor soloist, oenalogist, reading, quarter horses. Home: PO Box 218 Richardton ND 58652 Office: Richardton High Sch Raider Rd Box 289 Richardton ND 58652

GENOVESI, ANTHONY DENNIS, geneticist, plant tissue culturist; b. Muskogee, Okla., June 20, 1944; s. Louis Antonio and Wilma Dell (Melton) G.; B.S., U. Tex.-Arlington, 1967; M.S., Tex. A&M U., 1975, Ph.D., 1978. Post doctoral fellow U. Ky., Lexington, 1978-81; cellular geneticist Dekalb-Pfizer Genetics, Dekalb, Ill., 1981—. Co-author several sci. publs. Served to capt. U.S. Army, 1967-70. Mem. Tissue Culture Assn., Internat. Assn. Plant Cell Tissue Cultures, Am. Soc. Agronomy, Sigma Xi, Phi Kappa Phi, Phi Sigma, Gamma Sigma Delta. Democrat. Baptist. Avocations: tropical fish, sports, jogging. Office: Dekalb-Pfizer Genetics 3100 Sycamore Rd Dekalb IL 60115

GENTILE, CHARLES R., lawyer; b. Omaha, Mar. 9, 1955; s. Samuel Richard and Rosemary (Traynor) G. B.A., U. Nebr., 1977; J.D., Creighton U., 1980. Bar: Nebr. 1980, U.S. Dist. Ct. Nebr. 1980, U.S. Ct. Appeals (8th cir.) 1980, U.S. Tax Ct. 1982. Assoc., Byrne & Randall, P.C., Omaha, 1980-83; prin. Byrne Rothery, Gentile & Blazek, P.C., Omaha, 1983; exec dir. Nebr. Commn. of Indsl. Relations, Lincoln, 1983—; sole practice, Omaha, 1983—; lectr. Nebr. Coll. Bus., Omaha 1980-84, U. Nebr., Omaha, 1981—. Mem. editorial staff Creighton Law Rev., 1979. Mem. ABA, Nebr. Bar Assn., Omaha Bar Assn., Phi Alpha Theta, Pi Sigma Theta. Republican. Office: Nebr Commn Indsl Relations 301 Centennial Mall S Lincoln NE 68509

GENTILE, RICHARD JOSEPH, geology educator, researcher; b. St. Louis, June 25, 1929; s. Richard and Anne L. (Kreji) G. B.A. in Geology, U. Mo.-Columbia, 1956, M.A. in Geology, 1958; Ph.D., U. Mo.-Rolla, 1965. Geologist Mo. Geol. Survey, Rolla, 1958-65, chief geologist (coal), 1965-66; asst. prof. U. Mo., Kansas City, 1966-70, assoc. prof., 1970-75, prof. geology, 1975—; cons. non-metallic mineral resources; faculty adv. U. Mo. student chpt. Am. Assn. Petroleum Geologists; lectr. various amateur geology clubs, Kansas City area. Author: Geology of the Belton Quadrangle, 1984. Contbr. articles on geology to profl. jours. Fellow Geol. Soc. Am.; mem. Nat. Assn. Geology Tchrs. (pres. Central sect. 1984-85), Soc. Engring. Geologists (pres. Kansas City/Omaha sect. 1979-81), Sigma Xi (sec., treas. Kansas City chpt. 1970-85; Cert. Recognition award 1981). Avocation: hiking. Home: 5401 Brookside Blvd Apt 300 Kansas City MO 64112 Office: Univ Mo Dept Geoscis 5100 Rockhill Rd Kansas City MO 64110

GENTILINI, JOSEPH MICHAEL, rehab. counselor; b. Columbus, Ohio, Aug. 22, 1948; s. Celso and Marie Elizabeth (Verhoff) G.; B.A. cum laude, Ohio Dominican Coll., 1970; M.A., Ohio State U., 1974; Ph.D., Ohio U., 1982. Cert. rehab. counselor. Tchr., Bishop Watterson High Sch., Columbus, 1970-71; rehab. counselor Ohio Rehab. Services Commn., Columbus, 1972—; instr. Ohio State U., 1982-83. Mem. Am. Personnel and Guidance Assn., Nat. Rehab. Assn. (bd. mem. Central Ohio chpt. 1975-77), Nat. Rehab. Counseling Assn. (bd. mem. Ohio chpt. 1982—), Am. Rehab. Counseling Assn., Phi Kappa Phi. Democrat. Roman Catholic. Home: 5000 Kings Highland Dr W #204 Columbus OH 43229

GENTRUP, SISTER CLARICE, nun, chaplain director, administrator; b. Beemer, Nebr., Dec. 5, 1937; s. Theodore Isadore and Theresa (Spenner) G. B.S. cum laude in Pharmacy, Creighton U., 1962; postgrad. Ministry Tng. Service, 1977-78. Chief pharmacist St. Mary Hosp., Columbus, Nebr., 1963-64; dir. pharmacy and administrn. St. Anthony Hosp., Denver, 1964-77; dir. formation Sisters St. Francis, Colorado Springs, Colo., 1978-79; asst. chaplain, St. Anthony Hosp., Denver, 1979-83; chaplain dir. St. Francis Med. Ctr., Grand Island, Nebr., 1983—; provincial councilor Sisters St. Francis, Colorado Springs, 1977—; del. to gen. chpt. Sisters St. Francis, Olpe, W.Ger., 1984. Bd. dir. Med. Ctr. Hosps., Colo. and Nebr., 1967—; mem. adv. bd. Erhard Seminar Tng., San Francisco, 1978-81; trustee Safehouse for Battered Women, Denver, 1982-83. Recipient Merck award Merck Sharp & Dohme, 1962; E.R. Squibb Pharmacy award, 1975. Mem. Sister of St. Francis, Nat. Assn. Catholic Chaplains. Democrat. Avocations: reading, music, waling. Office: St Francis Med Ctr 2620 W Faidley St Grand Island NE 68801

GENTRY, JOANNE MOSBAUGH, educator; b. Noblesville, Ind., Dec. 16, 1924; d. Harry and Lois (Tice) Mosbaugh; m. Neil R. Gentry, Sept. 25, 1943 (div.); children—John Michael, Sheryl Lynn. B.S., Ball State U., 1962, M.A., 1968; Ed.D., Ind. U., 1978. Tchr., elem., secondary, coll. and continuing edn. for adults, 1962-78; curriculum coordinator Wayne Twp. Elem. schs., Indpls., 1979—; cons. in field. Republican Precinct committeewoman, 1978-82. Recipient Delta Pi Epsilon Reward for Outstanding Research, Ball State U., 1968. Mem. Nat. Council Tchrs. Math., Internat. Reading Assn. (council treas.), Ind. U. Profl. Women, Ind. Assn. Supervision and Curriculum Devel.; Delta Pi Epsilon, Pi Lambda Theta, Phi Delta Kappa, Delta Theta Tau. Mem. Refuge Christian Ch. Contbr. articles to profl. jours. Home: 8393 Chapel Pines Dr Indianapolis IN 46234 Office: 1220 S High School Rd Indianapolis IN 46241

GENTRY, PATRICIA LOU, banker; b. Holland, Mich., July 22, 1948; d. Lester B. and C. Jane (Van Houten) Wiersma; m. Michael Lee Gentry, Sept. 24, 1983; stepchildren—Tara Leigh, Joel Travis. B.A., Hope Coll., 1970; diploma Sch. Bank Adminstrn., Madison, Wis., 1983. Tchr. math. Bethelehm Central Sch., Delmar, N.Y., 1970-72; with 1st Mich. Bank & Trust, Zeeland, Mich., 1972-81, asst. auditor, 1975-81; audit officer First Mich. Bank Corp., 1981—. Exec. bd. March of Dimes, Holland, 1977-84, sec., 1978, treas., 1979-81; bd. dirs Holland Community Theater, Inc., 1974—, pres., 1980-81. Zeeland Alumnus Grand Valley scholar, 1966-67; Hope Coll. scholar, 1969-70. Mem. Nat. Assn. Bank Women. Mem. Reformed Ch. Am. Avocations: theatre; reading; sewing; swimming. Office: 1st Mich Bank Corp PO Box 300 Zeeland MI 49464

GENTZ, TIMOTHY RAY, controller; b. Morrison, Ill., Oct. 28, 1949; s. Ray Gerald Gentz and Joan Allen (Layman) Johnson; m. Lesley L. Carpenter, July 25, 1970; 1 child, Lisha Alexandra. B.B.A., U. Iowa, 1977; M.B.A. candidate Mankato State U. C.P.A., Minn., Iowa. Audit staff Coopers & Lybrand, C.P.A.s, Chgo., 1977-79; sr. auditor, Mpls., 1979-80; fin. analyst Pickwick Internat., Mpls., 1980-81, acctg. mgr., 1981-83; asst. corp. controller Krelitz Industries, Mpls., 1983-84, corp. controller, 1984—. Served with U.S. Army, 1971-74; Korea. Mem. Am. Inst. C.P.A.s, Minn. Soc. C.P.A.s, Iowa Soc. C.P.A.s, Beta Alpha Psi (pres. 1977-78). Avocations: running, racquetball, weight lifting. Home: 9824 Upton Circle Bloomington MN 55431 Office: Krelitz Industries Inc 900 N 3rd St Minneapolis MN 55401

GEO-KARIS, ADELINE JAY, state senator; student Northwestern U., Mt. Holyoke Coll.; LL.B., DePaul U. Admitted to Ill. bar; founder Adeline J. Geo-Karis and Assos., Zion, Ill.; former mcpl., legis. atty. Mundelein, Ill., Vernon Hills, Ill., Libertyville (Ill.) Twp., Long Grove (Ill.) Sch. Dist.; justice of peace; former asst. state's atty.; former mem. Ill. Ho. of Reps.; mem. Ill. Senate, minority spokeswoman jud. com. Served to lt. comdr. USNR.; comdr. Res. ret. Recipient Americanism medal DAR; named Woman of Yr., Daus. of Penelope, Outstanding Legislator Ill. Fedn. Ind. Colls. and Univs., 1975-78, legis. award Ill. Assn. Park Dists., 1976. Sponsor Guilty but Mentally Ill Law. Office: State Capitol Springfield IL 62706

GEORGE, DONALD ELIAS, lawyer; b. Akron, Ohio, July 8, 1950; s. George John and Thelma Beatrice (Goforth) G.; m. Christine Kaderle Cirignano, May 1, 1982; 1 child, Michelle A. B.A., U. Akron, 1972, J.D., 1975. Bar: Ohio 1975, U.S. Dist. Ct (no. dist.) Ohio 1975, U.S. Supreme Ct. 1979, U.S. Ct. Appeals (6th cir.) 1985. Sole practice, Akron, 1975—; bankruptcy trustee, U.S. Bankruptcy Ct., Akron, 1975-78; arbitrator Am. Arbitration Assn., Cleve., 1976-79. Author: Israeli Occupation: International Law and Political Realities, 1979. Mem. Akron Regional Devel. Bd., 1984—, guest speaker Sta. WHLO, Steve Fullerton Show, Akron, 1979-80; mem. adv. com. to re-elect Judge Evan Reed, Akron, 1979; choir dir. St. George Orthodox Ch., 1969-75. Mem. ABA, Ohio State Bar Assn., Akron Bar Assn., Summit County Humane Soc., Akron Law Library Assn., Democrat. Avocation: Piano playing. Office: 572 W Market St Suite 11 Akron OH 44303

GEORGE, GARY RAYMOND, state senator; b. Milw., Mar. 8, 1954; s. Horace Raymond and Audrey C. (Chevalier) G.; B.B.A., U. Wis., 1976; J.D., Mich. Law Sch., 1979; m. Mary Cook, Aug. 26, 1978; 1 son, Alexander Raymond. With Tax Dept., Arthur Young & Co., Milw., 1979-81; Wis. State senator from 6th Senate Dist., Madison, 1981—. Democrat. Roman Catholic. Office: 319 S State Capitol Madison WI 53702

GEORGE, KENNETH FRANCIS, human resources development executive; b. Detroit, Oct. 14, 1935; s. Harold Joseph and Amelia Mary (Mowid) G.; m. Marion Ruth Baker, June 20, 1964; children—Theresa Marie, Steven Christopher, Karen Elizabeth. A.A., Macomb County Community Coll., 1964; B.A., Wayne State U., 1966; postgrad., 1966-67. Salesman Gen. Devel. Corp., Southfield, Mich., 1971-74, asst. sales mgr., 1982—; regional sales mgr. LaSalle Extension U., Chgo., 1974-77; salesman Deltona Corp., Detroit, 1977-82; pres. Opportunity Now, Warren, Mich., 1983—, radio and TV motivational speaker, 1982-84; instr. Chrysler Corp., Detroit, 1953-69; substitute tchr. Detroit Sch. System, 1970-71. Adviser Richard Sabaugh Mayoral Campaign, Warren, Mich., 1971. Named Number One Salesman, LaSalle Extension U., 1974-75, Deltona Corp., 1977-82, Gen. Devel. Corp., 1983. Republican. Roman Catholic. Home: 13002 Iowa St Warren MI 48093 Office: Opportunity Now Centerline MI 48015

GEORGE, MUMTAZ, physician; b. Baghdad, Iraq, Sept. 22, 1942; came to U.S., 1950, naturalized, 1955; s. John and Nora (Sharrak) G.; children—Jennifer, Matthew. Student Detroit Inst. Tech., 1960-61; B.S., Wayne State U., 1967; M.D., U. Granada, Spain, 1975. Resident in internal medicine Providence Hosp., Southfield, Mich., 1976-79, fellow in critical care, 1979-80; fellow in residence Rocky Mountain Poison Ctr., Denver, 1980; practice medicine specializing in internal medicine, 1980—; owner, dir. Farmington Urgent Care Ctr., Farmington Hills, Mich., 1982—; ptnr., owner Kingswood Urgent Med. Ctr., Bloomfield Hills, Mich., 1983—; emergency room physician Pontiac Gen. Hosp., Mich., 1981—, St. Mary's Hosp., Livonia, Mich., 1982—. Mem. AMA, Oakland County Med. Assn., Am. Coll. Emergency Physicians, Soc. Critical Care Medicine, Mich. State Med. Soc. Home: 34010 Ramble Hills Dr Farmington Hills MI 48018 Office: Farmington Urgent Care Ctr Suite F 23700 Orchard Lake Rd Farmington Hills MI 48024

GEORGE, W. JOYCE, nurse, educator; b. Liberal, Kans., Nov. 19, 1931; d. Claude William and Ida Almeda (Barrows) Holmes; children—Sanya R., Roxanne E. B.S.N., B.A., U. Kans. Med. Ctr., 1954; M.A. in Nursing, U. Iowa, 1963. R.N., Kans. Staff nurse, tchr., Kansas City, Mo. and Kansas City, Kans., 1958-65; asst. prof. nursing Kans. U. Med. Ctr., Kansas City, 1965-71; asst. prof. Avila Coll., Kansas City, Mo., 1974-76; dir. nursing Seward County Community Coll., Liberal, 1978—. Mem. Am. Nurses Assn., Nat. League for Nursing, Kans. Vocat. Assn., Kans. State Assoc. Degree Nurse Educators Council, Sigma Theta Tau. Home: 1110 N Holly Dr Liberal KS 67901 Office: Seward Coll PO Box 1137 Liberal KS 67901

GEORGE, WALLY NEWMAN, sheriff; b. Marshall, Mo., Nov. 4, 1945; s. Wallace Newman and Lucille (Ridge) G.; m. Joyce E. Newton, Mar. 8, 1974. Student high sch., Slater, Mo. Patrolman Slater Police Dept., Mo., 1967-69; radio dispatcher sheriff's dept., Marshall, Mo., 1970-73, civil paper server, 1973-74, road dep. sheriff, 1974-75, chief dep. sheriff, 1975-79; sheriff Saline County, Marshall, 1979—; adv. Law Enforcement Tng. Inst., Columbia, Mo., 1981—. Served with USN, 1963-66. Mem. Internat. Firearms Instrs. Inc., Nat. Rifle Assn. (life), Mo. Sheriffs Assn., Midwest Investigative Hypnosis Assn., VFW (life). Democratic. Methodist. Avocations: leather working; hand gun collecting; boating. Home: 358 S Salt Pond Box 613 Marshall MO 65340-0613 Office: Saline County Sheriffs Dept PO Box 366 Marshall MO 65340-0366

GEPHARDT, RICHARD ANDREW, congressman; b. St. Louis, Jan. 31, 1941; s. Louis Andrew and Loreen Estelle (Cassell) G.; B.S., Northwestern U., 1962; J.D., U. Mich., 1965; m. Jane Ann Byrnes, Aug. 13, 1966; children—Matthew, Christine, Katherine Hope. Admitted to Mo. bar, 1965; partner firm Thompson & Mitchell, St. Louis, 1965-76; alderman 14th ward, St. Louis, 1971-76; mem. 95th-98th Congresses from 3d Dist. Mo., 1977—, mem. Ways and Means com.; chmn. Ho. of Reps. Democratic Caucus. Pres., Children's United Research Effort, Inc., 1974-76; mem. devel. bd. St. Louis Children's Hosp., 1975-76; Democratic committeeman 14th ward St. Louis, 1968-71; bd. dirs. St. Louis council Boy Scouts Am., 1975—. Recipient Better Downtown award City of St. Louis, 1973; Disting. Service award St. Louis Jaycees, 1974. Mem. Mo. (chmn. young lawyers sect. 1972-73), St. Louis (chmn. young lawyers sect. 1971-72) bar assns., Am. Legion, Young Lawyer's Soc. (chmn. 1972-73). Clubs: Kiwanis, Mid-Town (St. Louis). Office: 1432 Longworth Office Bldg Washington DC 20515

GERALD, MICHAEL CHARLES, pharmacy educator, college dean; b. N.Y.C., Nov. 20, 1939; s. Tobias Gerson and Ruby Rose (Weinstock) G.; m. Gloria Elaine Gruber, Jan. 31, 1965; children—Marc Jonathan, Melissa Suzanne, B.S. in Pharmacy, Fordham U., 1961; Ph.D., Ind. U., 1968. Registered pharmacist, N.Y. Postdoctoral fellow USPHS, U. Chgo., 1968-69; asst. prof. Coll. Pharmacy Ohio State U., Columbus, 1969-74, assoc. prof., 1974-80, prof., 1980—, prof. and assoc. dean., 1984—; cons. WHO, Geneva, 1983-84; mem. adv. panel U.S. Pharmacopeia Com. Revision, Washington, 1980—. Author: Pharmacology: An Introduction to Drugs, 2d edit. 1981; Nursing Pharmacology and Therapeutics; (co-author) The Nurse's Guide to Drug Therapy: Drug Profiles for Patient Care, 1984. Editor: Instruction in Pharmacology: New Approaches and New Faces, 1979. Served to 1st lt. USAF, 1963-65. USPHS fellow Ind. U., 1965-68; Gustavus A. Pfeiffer Meml. fellow Am. Found. Pharm. Edn., 1983-84. Fellow Acad. Pharm. Scis. (sect. sec. 1975-77, sect. v.p. 1978-79); mem. Am. Assn. Colls. of Pharmacy (bd. dirs. 1980-82), Am. Soc. Pharmacology and Exptl. Therapeutics, N.Y. Acad. Scis., Soc. Neurosciences. Avocations: photography, reading, music. Home: 8379 Evangeline Dr Worthington OH 43085 Office: Coll Pharmacy Ohio State Univ 500 W 12th Ave Columbus OH 43210

GERBER, ANN JADE, editor, columnist, author; b. Chgo., Sept. 17, 1930; d. Benjamin James and Henrietta (Rabin) G.; m. Bernard James Kaplan, Apr. 23, 1966; children—Jeffrey, Blair. Student Wright Jr. Coll., Northwestern U., Mundelin U. Reporter, Lerner Newspapers, Chgo., 1945-46, assoc. editor, 1946-58, editor, 1958—; owner Panache Pub. Relations, Chgo., 1960-70; editor Tee Vee Guide, Chgo., 1955; pub. relations cons. Harlem-Irving Shopping Ctr., Chgo., 1955-56. Author: Chicago's Classiest Cuisine, 1983; Chicago's Sweet Tooth, 1985. Named Woman of Yr., Variety Club Women of Ill., 1982; recipient Editorial Excellence award Lerner Newspapers, 1982, hon. mention for columns, Ill. Press Assn., 1983. Jewish. Home: 5036 Fairview Ln Skokie IL 60077 Office: Lerner Newspapers 7519 N Ashland Ave Chicago IL 60625

GERBER, BERNARD CHARLES, surgeon; b. Aberdeen, S.D., Nov. 25, 1926; s. Henry Philip and Agnes M. (Egan) G.; m. Marcella Ann Aslesen, Sept. 15, 1951; children—Karen, Jean, Charles, Martin, Lawrence, Christopher. B.S., No. State Coll., Aberdeen, 1949; B.S. in Medicine, U. S.D., 1951; M.D., Northwestern U., 1953. Diplomate Am. Bd. Surgery. Resident in surgery Northwestern U., Chgo., 1954-58; assoc. chief surgeon Miners Meml. Hosp., Williamson, W.Va., 1958-60; practice medicine specializing in surgery, Aberdeen, 1960—. Contbr. articles to profl. jours. Pres. Aberdeen Sch. Bd., 1973-74; bd. dirs. N.E. Mental Health Ctr., Aberdeen, 1969—, N. Plains Hospice, Aberdeen, 1981—. Recipient Disting. Alumnus award No. State Coll., Aberdeen. Fellow ACS; mem. AMA, Western Surg. Assn., S.D. State Med. Assn. (councillor 1976-83). Roman Catholic. Avocations: photography; gardening; solar eclipses; travel. Home: 1821 Eisenhower Circle Aberdeen SD 57401 Office: Gerber Profl Assn 201 S Lloyd St Aberdeen SD 57401

GERBER, JEFFRY, lawyer; b. Glen Gardner, N.J., Oct. 4, 1943; s. Edwin Louis and Claire (Martin) G.; m. Mary Rose Sustersic, Aug. 24, 1980; children—Eric, Adam. B.S. in Mech. Engring., Stevens Inst. Tech., 1965; J.D., Boston U., 1972. Bar: Ohio 1972; registered profl. engr., Mass. Engr., Stone & Webster Corp., Boston, 1965-69; engr., computer analyst C.T. Main Corp., Boston, 1969-72; trial atty. Gallagher, Sharp et al, Cleve., 1972-76; sr. atty. Bendix Corp., Cleve., 1976-81; house counsel Donn Corp., Cleve., 1981-83; sole practice, Cleve., 1983-84; mem. Madorsky & Katz Co., L.P.A., Cleve., 1985—. Mem. Ohio Bar Assn., Mensa. Presbyterian. Avocations: skiing; sailing. Home: 1083 Pembrook Rd Cleveland Heights OH 44121

GERDE, PRISCILLA MURPHY, employee communications specialist; b. Indpls., Dec. 5, 1949; d. Moris Leon and Josephine (Clark) Murphy; B.A., Purdue U., 1972; postgrad. Ind.-Purdue U., Indpls., 1978; m. Carlyle Noyes Gerde, July 4, 1976. Dir. publs. Ind. Dept. Commerce, 1972-73; coordinator editorial services Eli Lilly & Co., 1973-76, dept. head employee communications, 1983—; sec. Eli Lilly & Co., Found., Indpls., 1976-83; Lilly sales rep., Pittsfield, Mass., 1979. Bd. dirs. Eli Lilly Fed. Credit Union, sec., 1980—; bd. dirs. Indpls. Civic Theatre, 1982—, Wilma Rudolph Found., 1982—, Christanore House, 1984—, Ind. Soc. to Prevent Blindness, 1983—. Named Outstanding Woman in Lafayette, Lafayette (Ind.) Bus. and Profl. Women, 1978. Home: Lakehurst Battle Ground IN 47920 Office: 307 E McCarty St Indianapolis IN 46285

GERDENICH, LINDA WESTRICH, dance educator, choreographer; b. Delphos, Ohio, May 23, 1942; d. Melvin F. and Adelia I. (Wehinger) Westrich; m. Maten G. Gerdenich, II, Aug. 8, 1964; children—Maten G., Wendy Kaye. B.A., Butler U., 1964; M.S., 1978. Mem. dance faculty Butler U., Indpl-., 1971—; artistic dir. Dancers Studio, Noblesville, Ind., 1972—; chair dance panel Ind. Arts Commn., 1981-84, mem. edn. panel, 1985—; v.p. Ind. Dance Alliance, 1981-83. Choreographer: (ballets) Dance Frivolities, Faux Pas - A Comedy, A Day in the Park. Sec., Forest Hill Sch. PTO, Noblesville, 1979. Recipient Cable award Delta Gamma, 1975. Mem. Nat. Soc. Arts and Letters (dance chair 1982-84), Sigma Rho Delta (nat. pres. 1983—). Republican. Roman Catholic. Avocations: skiing; water skiing; tennis; bicycling; collectibles. Home: 500 Tamarack Ln Noblesvile IN 46060 Office: Dancers Studio 121 S Harbour Dr Noblesvile IN 46060

GERDES, NEIL WAYNE, librarian, educator; b. Moline, Ill., Oct. 19, 1943; s. John Edward and Della Marie (Ferguson) G. A.B., U. Ill., 1965; S.T.B., Harvard U., 1968; M.A., Columbia U., 1971; A.M. in Library Sci., U. Chgo., 1975. Ordained to ministry Unitarian Universalist Assn., 1975. Copy chief Little, Brown, Inc., Boston, 1968-69; instr. Tuskegee Inst. (Ala.), 1969-71; editorial asst. Library Quar., Chgo., 1973-74; head librarian, prof. Meadville/-Lombard, Chgo., 1973—, Chgo. Theol. Sem., Chgo., 1980—; library program dir. Chgo. Cluster of Theol. Schs., 1977-80. Editor: Union List of Periodicals, 1979. Vice pres. Hyde Park Council of Chs. and Synagogues, Chgo., 1977—. Mem. ALA, Am. Theol. Library Assn., Chgo. Area Theol. Library Assn. (sec.), Phi Beta Kappa. Home: 1332 E 56th St Chicago IL 60637 Office: Meadville/-Lombard 5701 Woodlawn Chicago IL 60637

GERDING, PAUL SULLIVAN, lawyer; b. Chgo., Apr. 16, 1936; s. Julius Otto and Dorothy (Sullivan) G.; m. Ellen M. Rohde, June 23, 1962; children—Paul Sullivan, Keith, David. B.S. in Humanities, Loyola U., Chgo., 1957; J.D. with distinction, U. Mich., 1960. Bar: Ill. 1960, Ariz. 1978, U.S. Dist. Ct. (no. dist.) Ill. 1968, U.S. Ct. Appeals (7th cir.) 1968, U.S. Supreme Ct. 1968. Ptnr. Wilson & McIlvaine, Chgo., 1960-77, Adams, Fox, Marcus, Adelstein & Gerding, Chgo., 1978-83; asst. gen. counsel Travenol Labs., Inc., Deerfield, Ill., 1983—. Pres. Family Counseling Service, Glencoe, Ill., 1970, Glencoe Sch. Bd., 1978—; bd. dirs. Ill. div. Am. Cancer Soc., Chgo., 1970-84; chmn. bd. dirs. Chgo. unit Am. Cancer Soc., Chgo., 1979-81. Mem. Legal Club Chgo., Law Club Chgo. Roman Catholic. Club: Skokie Country (Ill.). Home: 537 Monroe Glencoe IL 60022 Office: Travenol Labs Inc 1 Baxter Pkwy Deerfield IL 60015

GERHARDT, JON STUART, mechanical engineer, engineering educator; b. Springfield, Ohio, June 5, 1943; s. Robert William and Mary Josephine (Jones) G.; m. Claudia Jay Sadler, Feb. 7, 1970; children—Kirsten Lea, Benjamin Luke. B.S.M.E., U. Cin., 1966, M.S.M.E., 1968, Ph.D., 1971. Registered profl. engr., Ohio. Asst. prof. U. N.C., Charlotte, 1971-73; project engr. Duff-Norton, Charlotte, 1973; sr. devel. engr. Gen. Tire and Rubber Co. (now GenCorp) Akron, Ohio, 1973-77, group leader, 1977-79, mgr. tech. staff devel., 1979-84, mgr. product engring., research ctr. adminstrn., 1984—; instr. U. Akron, 1976—. Mem. ASME (bd. dirs. 1981—), Akron Rubber Group, Soc. Automotive Engrs., Sigma Xi.

GERHARDT, RICHARD LEE, lawyer; b. Circleville, Ohio, Nov. 25, 1941; s. George Edward and Dorothy A. (Riegel) G.; m. Marie A. Baldwin, June 28, 1964; children—Kara, Richard Lee, II. B.A., Ohio No. U., 1963; J.D., Georgetown U., 1966. Bar: Ohio 1966, U.S. Dist. (so. dist.) Ohio 1969. Mayor, Circleville, 1968-72; pros. atty. Pickaway County, Circleville, 1972-76; sole practice law, Circleville, 1976—; spl. counsel Office Atty. Gen., State of Ohio, 1972—. Asst. contbg. editor: Ohio Prosecutor's Handbook, 1975. Mem. staff Sen. John Glenn Campaign, 1970-74, Pres. Carter Campaign, 1978, 80, v.p. Mondale Campaign, 1980; precinct committeeman Democratic Party, 1968-72, 80, 83, 84; campaign chmn. United Way Pickaway County, 1981. Recipient Am. Jurisprudence award Georgetown U. Law Ctr., 1968. Mem. Ohio Bar Assn., Pickaway County Bar Assn. Lodges: Masons, Shriners. Home: 527 Willow Ln Circleville OH 43113 Office: 143 W Franklin St Circleville OH 43113

GERIG, WESLEY LEE, minister, educator; b. Ft. Wayne, Ind., Sept. 17, 1930; s. Jared Franklin and Mildred Grace (Eicher) G.; m. Mary Carolyn Steiner, Aug. 21, 1952; children—Jeanne Marie, John Wesley, Jeffrey Lee, Jared Clayton. B.A., Ft. Wayne Bible Coll., 1951; postgrad. Ind. U., Ft. Wayne, summers 1948-51; M.Div., Fuller Theol. Sem., 1954, M.Th., 1956; postgrad U. London, 1959-62; Ph.D., U. Iowa, 1965. Ordained to ministry Missionary Ch., 1957. Asst. pastor, youth dir. Faith Missionary Ch., Pomona, Calif., 1951-55; grad. asst. Sch. Religion, U. Iowa, Iowa City, 1956-57; prof. Bible and theology, chmn. div. bibl. studies Ft. Wayne Bible Coll., 1957—; pastor Harvester Ave. Missionary Ch., Ft. Wayne; prof. bibl. lang. Winona Lake Sch. Theology, Ind., 1962-69; mem. constl. com. The Missionary Ch. Contbr. Zondervan Pictorial Ency. of the Bible, 1973. Mem. Evang. Theol. Soc. (chmn. MW dist. 1969-70), Nat. Assn. Evangelicals (mem. theol. commn.), Ind. State Tchrs. Religion, Am. Assn. Bible Colls. Republican. Avocations: trumpet playing; stamp collecting; ping pong. Home: 4030 S Wayne Ave Fort Wayne IN 46807 Office: Fort Wayne Bible Coll 1025 W Rudisill Blvd Fort Wayne IN 46807

GERLACH, FRANKLIN THEODORE, lawyer; b. Portsmouth, Ohio, Apr. 11, 1935; s. Albert T. and Nora Alice (Hayes), G.; m. Cynthia Ann Koehler, Aug. 1, 1958; children—Valarie, Philipp. B.B.A., U. Cin., 1958; M.P.A., Syracuse U., 1959; J.D., U. Cin., 1961. Bar: Ohio 1961, U.S. Dist. Ct. (so. dist.) Ohio 1969, U.S. Supreme Ct. 1971. Dir. Purchasing, Planning and Renewal, City of Portsmouth, 1961-62; city mgr., 1962-66; asst. dir. Ohio U., Portsmouth, 1966-68; sole practice, Portsmouth, 1968—; solicitor Village New Boston, Ohio, 1968-70; trustee Ohio Acad. Trial Lawyers, Columbus, Ohio, 1984—. Recipient Outstanding Young Man award (1 of 5) Ohio Jaycees, 1969, Portsmouth Jaycees, 1968. Mem. Portsmouth Law and Library Assn., Ohio Acad. Trial Lawyers, Assn. Trial Lawyers Am. Democrat. Lodges: Rotary; Elks. Avocation: antiques. Home: 1221 20th St Portsmouth OH 45662 Office: 1030 Kinneys Ln Portsmouth OH 45662

GERLACH, GARY GENE, publisher; b. Osage, Iowa, June 8, 1941; s. Gene Wayne and Norma Linda (Rosel) G.; m. Karen Ann Conner, June 21, 1980. B.A., U. Iowa, 1964; M.S., Columbia U., 1965; J.D., Harvard U., 1970, M.P.A., 1972. Bar: Iowa 1970, D.C. 1971, Mass. 1972. Reporter, copy editor Miami Herald, 1964; staff writer Nat. Observer, Washington, 1965-67; legal asst. to Commr. Nicholas Johnson, FCC, 1970-71; assoc. Arnold & Porter, Washington, 1972-74; exec. v.p., gen. counsel, dir. Des Moines Register and Tribune Co., 1974-82, exec. v.p., 1982—, pres., pub., 1982—. Trustee Civic Ctr. of Greater Des Moines, 1975—; bd. dirs. U. Iowa Found., Iowa City, 1978—; v.p. Des Moines Met. YMCA, 1979-81; pres. Des Moines Metro Opera, 1981. Mem. ABA, Am. Newspaper Pubs. Assn. (dir. press/bar com.). Lutheran. Clubs: Des Moines, Prairie, Harvard of N.Y. Home: 3314 John Lynde Rd Des Moines IA 50312 Office: 715 Locust St Des Moines IA 50309

GERLACH, WILLIAM EMBER, executive; b. Bay City, Mich., May 10, 1927; s. George Clayton and Lillian Mae (Sawden) G.; m. L. Eugenia Bowling, Oct. 28, 1946; children—Thomas Eugene, John William, James Walter, B.A., Mich. State U., 1949. Mgr. Aldrich Market, Lansing, Mich., 1950-53; ind. retail grocer, 1953-63; founder Check Reporting Services, Inc., Lansing, 1960—; condr. check cashing seminars Mich. Bankers Assn., Lansing Community Coll. Chmn. Caravan Circus, 1983, 84. Served with U.S. Army, 1946. Mem. Mich. Assn. Check Investigators, Nat. Fedn. Ind. Bus., Greater Lansing C. of C., Greater Lansing UN Assn., Lansing Council for the Arts. Baptist. Club: Mich. Conservation, Circus Fans Assn. Am. Lodges: Elks, Masons, Shriners. Office: Check Reporting Services Inc 5217 Lansing Rd Lansing MI 48917

GERLING, JOSEPH ANTHONY, lawyer; b. Dayton, Ohio, Feb. 25, 1952; s. Clarence Anthony and Betty Jane (Blue) G.; m. Janet Mary Cox, July 6, 1974; children—Anthony, Andrew, Christopher. B.S. in Chem. Engring., U. Notre Dame, 1974; J.D., Ohio State U., 1977. Bar: Ohio 1977. Research scientist Battelle Meml. Inst., Columbus, Ohio, 1974-77; assoc. Lurie Gifford & Davis, Columbus, 1977-78, Lane Alton & Horst, Columbus, 1978—. Mem. Columbus Def. Assn. (program chmn. 1984—). Club: Athletic of Columbus. Avocations: sports; basketball; softball; photography. Home: 463 E Como Ave Columbus OH 43202 Office: Lane Alton & Horst 155 E Broad St Columbus OH 43205

GERLINGS, EELCO DIRK, physician, physiologist, educator; b. Amsterdam, Holland, Mar. 27, 1936; came to U.S., 1970, naturalized, 1976; s. Pieter Godefridus and Fanny Paula (Kehlenbeck) G.; m. Birte Torp Petersen, July 7, 1962; children—Peter Dirk, Karla Johanna, Erik Eelco. M.D., U. Amsterdam, 1963, Ph.D., 1966. Bd. eligible Am. Bd. Internal Medicine. Wetenschappelyk medewerker U. Amsterdam, 1958-68; lector U. Utrecht, Holland, 1968-70; vis. asst. prof. U. Va., Charlottesville, 1967-68, asst. prof., 1970-71; pvt. practice internal medicine, Omaha, 1976—; assoc. prof. physiology, biophysics U. Nebr. Med. Ctr., Omaha, 1971—, clin. asst. prof. dept. internal medicine, 1976—. Grantee NIH, Am. Heart Assn. Mem. Assn. Computing Machinery (voting), Am. Physiol. Soc., Am. Soc. Internal Medicine, AMA, Am. Heart Assn. Republican. Lutheran. Avocations: computer applications in medicine; electronic design. Home: 8162 Spaulding St Omaha NE 68134 Office: 239 Doctors Bldg Omaha NE 68131

GERLT, JOSEPH LUTHER, utility executive; b. Avoca, Iowa, May 11, 1934; s. Joseph Henry and Elda Meta (Eckhoff) G.; m. Lavonne Faye Rock, Dec. 27, 1954; children—Connie Sue, Vicki Jo. B.C.E., Iowa State U., 1956. Registered profl. engr., Iowa; cert. water plant operator, Nebr. Asst. supt. water plants Met. Utilities, Omaha, 1964-66, asst. dir. Platte River plant, 1966-68, supt. Platte River plant, 1968, water supply engr., 1968-72, gen. supt. services, 1972-79, gen. supt. engring. and constrn., 1979—. Mem. Am. Water Works Assn. (pres. Nebr. chpt. 1982; Fuller award 1983), ASCE (pres. Nebr. chpt. 1970-71), Am. Gas Assn., Am. Pub. Works Assn., Midwest Gas Assn. Lodge: Kiwanis (pres. 1972-73, lt.-gov. 1975-76). Home: 7620 Davis Circle Omaha NE 68134 Office: Met Utilities Dist 1723 Harney St Omaha NE 68134

GERM, JOHN A., management consulting firm executive; b. Cleve., May 8, 1930; s. John A. and Doris Elizabeth (Taylor) G.; m. Shirley J. Oertel, June 30, 1956; children—Karen Brian, Lynn Walker. B.A., Case Western Res. U., 1956; M.B.A., U. Chgo., 1972. With mktg. dept. Standard Products, Cleve., 1955-60, Nalco Co., Chgo., 1960-67; dir. personnel Velsicol Chem. Co., 1967-69; prin. Cresap, McCormack & Paget, Chgo., 1969-75; v.p. Chi Systems, Ann Arbor, Mich., 1975-77, A.T. Kearney, Inc., Chgo., 1977-81; pres., dir. JNS Assocs., Inc., Naperville, Ill., 1981—; lectr. in field; dir. JNS Aviation Cons. Network Ltd. Served to sgt. USAF, 1949-53. Mem. Am. Mgmt. Assn., Am. Hosp. Assn., Am. Compensation Assn. Developed applied mgmt. programs. Office: JNS Assocs Inc 549 S Washington St Naperville IL 60540

GERMAINE, LEONARD MICHAEL, psychologist; b. Andover, Mass., July 28, 1953; s. Richard C. and Helen M. (Lustenberger) G. B.S., U. Lowell, 1975; M.A., Wayne State U., 1978, Ph.D., 1984. Lic. psychologist, Mich. Child care worker St. Ann's Home, Methuen Mass., 1970-75; supr. Vista Del Mar, Los Angeles, 1976; child care adminstr. Children's Home Detroit, Grosse Pointe, Mich., 1976-79; research assoc. Lafayette Clinic, Detroit, 1979—; psychotherapist. Wayne State U. grad. fellow, 1979-82. Mem. Am. Psychol. Assn., Soc. for Psychophysiological Research, Soc. Behavioral Medicine, Biofeedback Soc. Am., Psychologists Social Responsibity. Democrat. Unitarian. Clubs: The Tarrytown (N.Y.) Group; Civic (Detroit). Office: Lafayette Clinic 951 East LaFayette Blvd Detroit MI 48207

GERMANN, DAVID, publishing company executive; b. Springfield, Ohio, Sept. 22, 1943; s. Oswald Jacob and Helen Leora Germann. A.A., Am. Acad. Dramatic Arts, 1965; B.S., Wittenberg Coll., 1968; M.Ed., Wright State U., 1972. Tchr., Clark Tech. Coll., Springfield, Ohio, 1968-72, dir. pre-profl. edn., 1973-74, dir. pub. relations, 1974-77; asst. dir. admissions Wright State U., Dayton, Ohio, 1972-73; recruiting rep. Mead Corp., Dayton, 1977-79, mgr. coll. recruiting and relations, 1979-85; sr. cons. orgn. devel./tng. Mead Data Central, 1985—. Mem. adv. bd. Dayton Career Adv. Council, 1982—, Dayton Vocational Ednl. Adv. Bd., 1983-85; cons. United Way Mgmt. Assistance Program, Dayton, 1983—. Mem. Employment Mgmt. Assn., Coll. Placement Council. Republican. Lutheran. Avocations: golf, racquetball, investment real estate. Office: Mead Corp Courthouse Plaza NE Dayton OH 45463

GERMANN, RICHARD P(AUL), chemist, business executive; b. Ithaca, N.Y., Apr. 3, 1918; s. Frank E. E. and Martha Mary Marie (Knechtel) G.; B.A., Colo. U., 1939; student Western Res. U. (Naval Research fellow), 1941-43, Brown U., 1954; m. Malinda Jane Plietz, Dec. 11, 1942; 1 dau., Cheranne Lee. Chief analytical chemist Taylor Refining Co., Corpus Christi, 1943-44; research devel. chemist Calco Chem. div. Am. Cyanamid Co., 1944-52; devel. chemist charge pilot plant Alrose Chem. Co. div. Geigy Chem. Corp., 1952-55; new product devel. chemist, research div. W. R. Grace & Co., Clarksville, Md., 1955-60; chief chemist soap-cosmetic div. G.H. Packwood Mfg. Co., St. Louis, 1960-61; coordinator chem. product devel. Abbott Labs., North Chicago, Ill., 1961-71; internat. chem. cons. to mgmt., 1971-73; pres. Germann Internat. Ltd., 1973-82; pres. Ramtek Internat. Ltd., 1973—; real estate broker, 1972—. Rep. Am. Inst. Chemists to Joint Com. on Employment Practices, 1969-72. Vestryman, St. Paul's Episcopal Ch., Norwalk, Ohio, 1978-81, also chmn. adminstrn. and long range planning commn., 1980-81; trustee Services for the Aging, Inc., 1982—; chmn. nutritional council Ohio Dist. Five Area Agy. on Aging, 1983-84; sr. adv. Ohio Assn. Ctrs. for Sr. Citizens, Inc., 1982—; bd. dirs. Christie Lane Industries, 1981—. Fellow Am. Inst. Chemists (chmn. com. employment relations 1969—), Chem. Soc. (London), AAAS; mem. Am. Chem. Soc. (councilor 1971-73, chmn. membership com. chem. mktg. and econs. div. 1966-68, chmn. program com. 1968-69, del. at large for local sects. 1970-71, chmn. 1972-73; chmn. Chgo. program com. 1966-67, chmn. Chgo. endowment com. 1967-68, dir. Chgo. sect. 1968-72; chmn. awards com. 1972-73; sec. chem. mktg. and econs. group Chgo. sect. 1964-66, chmn. 1967-68), Internat. Sci. Found., Sci. Research Soc. Am., Comml. Chem. Devel. Assn. (chmn. program com. Chgo. conv. 1966, mem. fin. com. 1966-67, ad hoc com. of Comml. Chem. Devel. Assn.-Chem. Market Research Assn. 1968-69, co-chmn. pub. relations Denver conv. 1968, chmn. membership com. 1969-70), Chem. Market Research Assn. (mem. directory com. 1967-68, employment com. 1969-70), Midwest Planning Assn., Midwest Chem. Mktg. Assn., Internat. Platform Assn., Nat. Security Indsl. Assn. (Abbott Labs. rep. ocean sci. tech. com., maintenance adv. com., tng. adv. com. 1962-70), Water Pollution Control Fedn., Lake County Bd. Realtors, World Future Soc., Sigma Xi, Alpha Chi Sigma (chmn. profl. activities com. 1968-70, pres. Chgo. chpt. 1968-70). Clubs: Lions (sec. Allview, Md. 1956-57), Kiwanis, Masons, Rotary; Chemists (N.Y.C., Chgo.); Torch. Patentee in organic and pharm. field. Home and Office: 6 Vinewood Dr Norwalk OH 44857

GEROW, ROBERT KENT, former construction equipment distribution company executive, consultant; b. Bay City, Mich., Nov. 23, 1919; s. Lyman Claire and Alice Marie (Kent) G.; m. Betty Marie Cardenas, Jan. 9, 1942; children—Ronald K., David R., James D. Student Rose-Hulman Inst. Tech.,

1937-38, Ind. U., 1939-40. Draftsman, designer J.D. Adams Mfg. Co., Indpls., 1938-40, Victor div. RCA, Indpls., 1940-44; sales rep. Minn.-Honeywell, Indpls., 1946-47; v.p., gen. mgr. Reid Holcomb Co., Indpls., 1947-80. Bd. dirs. Angus-Scientech Edn. Found., Indpls., 1968—. Served with USN, 1944-46. Mem. Ind. Equipment Distbrs. Assn. (pres. 1968-69), Assn. Equipment Distbrs. (lt. dir. 1968-69, indsl. relations com. 1970). Presbyterian. Club: Scientech (pres. 1978). Lodge: Masons (pres. shrine chanters 1960). Avocations: woodworking; music; genealogy. Home: 134 E Brunswick Ave Indianapolis IN 46227

GERSHBEIN, LEON LEE, chemist; b. Chgo., Dec. 22, 1917; s. Meyer and Ida (Shutman) G.; m. Ruth Zelman, Sept. 30, 1956; children—Joel Dan, Marcia Renee, Carla Ann. S.B., U. Chgo., 1938, S.M., 1939; Ph.D.; Northwestern U., 1944. Research assoc. Northwestern U., Evanston, Ill., 1944-47; asst. prof. biochemistry U. Ill. Med. Sch., Chgo., 1947-53; assoc. prof. biology Ill. Inst. Tech., Chgo., 1953-57, adj. prof., 1957—; pres., dir. Northwest Inst. Med. Research, Chgo., 1957—; dir. labs. Northwest Hosp., Chgo., 1957—. U. Chgo. scholar, 1936-38; recipient Merit award Chgo. Chromatography Discussion Group, 1978; citations Ill. State Acad. Scis., 1975-79. Mem. Am. Chem. Soc., Am. Inst. Chemists, Am. Oil Chemists Soc., AAAS, Ill. Acad. Sci., Soc. Exptl. Biol. Medicine, Soc. Applied Spectroscopy, Am. Phys. Soc., Am. Fedn. Clin. Research, Am. Assn. Cancer Research, Contbr. numerous articles to profl. jours. Home: 2836 Birchwood Ave Wilmette IL 60091 Office: Northwest Inst for Medical Research 5645 West Addison St Chicago IL 60634

GERSHON, JERALD, chemical company executive; b. Kansas City, Mo., Jan. 16, 1924; s. Samuel and Ruth (Mnookin) G.; m. Hortense Joy Kahn, Mar. 9, 1946; children—Susan Jean Gershon Osman, Sharon Kay and Steven Alan (twins). B.S.B.A., Washington U., St. Louis, 1943. Pres. Modern Pharmacal Co., Kansas City, Mo., 1946-47, Vet Products Corp., Kansas City, Mo., 1974-75, Chem. Commodities, Inc., Olathe, Kans., 1955—. City chmn. Israel Bonds, Kansas City, 1976-81. Served to lt. USN, 1943-46; PTO. Mem. Am. Chem. Soc. Democrat. Jewish. Avocations: golf; tennis. Home: 2530 W 63d St Mission Hills KS 66208 Office: Chem Commodities 300-320 S Blake St Olathe KS 66061

GERSTEIN, KENNETH ALLAN, periodontist; b. Chgo., July 24, 1946; s. Kenneth Irwin Gerstein and Muriel June (Doonan) Welsh; m. Martha June Miller, June 22, 1971; children—Kimberly Inge, Kendra Leigh. B.S./D.D.S., U. Ill.-Chgo., cert. periodontics. Practice dentistry, specializing in periodontics, Champaign, Ill., 1978—; instr. Parkland Coll., Champaign, 1979—. Contbr. articles to profl. jours. Served to lt. comdr. USN, 1971-76. Recipient award Odontographic Soc. Chgo., 1971; Stanley D. Tylman award, Univ. award of Merit, Capt. Simon Kessler Meml. award U. Ill., 1971. Mem. ADA, Am. Acad. Periodontology, Midwest Soc. Periodontology, Western Soc. Periodontology, Ill. State Dental Soc., Illini Dist. Dental Soc., Omicron Kappa Upsilon. Avocations: golf; tennis; woodworking. Home: 1846 Maynard Lake Dr Champaign IL 61821 Office: 201 W Springfield #506 Champaign IL 61821

GERSTEIN, RONALD JAY, clinical psychologist; b. Chgo., July 13, 1945; s. Abe and Ida (Glass) G.; m. Joy Patricia Hawkes, June 26, 1976; 1 step-dau., Kathy. B.A., U. Ill.-Chgo., 1967; M.A., Roosevelt U., 1970. Staff psychologist-/instr. Mt. Sinai Hosp./Chgo. Med. Sch., 1969-70; psychologist II, Inst. for Juvenile Research, Chgo., 1970; staff psychologist St. Francis Hosp., Evanston, Ill., 1970-76; pvt. practice clin. psychology, Morton Grove, Ill., 1976-77; staff psychologist/supr. Proviso Family Services, Melrose Park, Ill., 1977-83; staff psychotherapist Inst. for Motivational Devel., Lombard, Ill., 1984—. Mem. Chgo. Musicians Union. Home: 9354 Shermer Rd Morton Grove IL 60053 Office: 2200 S Main St Lombard IL 60148

GERSTENBLITH, PATTY, lawyer, educator; b. Bklyn., July 24, 1950; d. Theodore A. and Evelyn (Zirinsky) G.; m. Samuel Neal Gordon, Jan. 29, 1977; 1 child, Jennifer Thea. A.B., Bryn Mawr Coll., 1971; A.M., Ph.D., Harvard U., 1977; J.D., Northwestern U., 1983. Bar: Ill. 1983, U.S. Dist. Ct. (no. dist.) Ill. 1984, U.S. Ct. Appeals (7th cir.) 1984. Lectr. archaeology Hebrew Union Coll.-Jewish Inst. Religion, Cin., 1977-80; postdoctoral fellow Cin. Art Mus., 1978-80; judicial clerk U.S. Ct. Appeals (7th cir.), Chgo., 1983-84; asst. prof. property law DePaul U. Coll. Law, Chgo., 1984—. Author: Levant at the Beginning of the Middle Bronze Age, 1983. Fellow Fulbright, 1975-76, Whiting, 1976-77; Am. Council Learned Socs. grantee, 1979-80. Mem. ABA, Ill. State Bar Assn., Archeol. Inst. Am. (pres. Cin. Soc. 1979-80). Home: 910 Sheridan Rd Wilmette IL 60091 Office: DePaul U Coll Law 25 E Jackson St Chicago IL 60604

GERSTNER, ROBERT WILLIAM, engineering educator; b. Chgo., Nov. 10, 1934; s. Robert Berty and Martha (Tuchelt) G.; B.S., Northwestern U., 1956, M.S., 1957, Ph.D., 1960; m. Elizabeth Willard, Feb. 8, 1958; children—Charles Willard, William Mark. Instr., Northwestern U., Evanston, Ill., 1957-59, research fellow 1959-60; asst. prof. U. Ill., Chgo., 1960-63, asso. prof., 1963-69, prof., 1969—; structural engr. cons., 1959—. Pres. Riverside Improvement Assn. Bd. dirs., v.p. Ravenswood Conservation Commn. Registered structural and profl. engr., Ill. Mem. ASCE, Am. Concrete Inst., Am. Soc. for Engring. Edn., AAUP, ACLU. Club: Belmont Yacht (rear commodore), Columbia Yacht. Contbr. articles to profl. jours. Home: 2628 Agatite St Chicago IL 60625

GERTNER, ABRAHAM, lawyer; b. Toronto, Ont., Can., Feb. 7, 1909; came to U.S., 1915, naturalized, 1922; s. Morris Hyman and Anna B. (Regenbogen) G.; m. Edythe Luper, Jan. 31, 1935; 1 child, Michael Harvey. B.A. with honors and high distinction, Ohio State U., 1929; M.A., Yale U., 1930, Ph.D. (Cowles fellow in Govt. 1930-32), 1934; J.D. summa cum laude, Ohio State U., 1935. Bar: Ohio 1935, U.S. Dist. Ct. (so. dist.) Ohio 1936, U.S. Ct. Appeals (6th cir.) 1983, U.S. Supreme Ct. 1959. Owner, operator A.B. Gertner Bar Rev. Sch., Columbus, Ohio, 1936-61; sole practice, Columbus, 1935-72; adminstrv. law judge Social Security Office Hearings and Appeals, Columbus, 1972-79; ptnr. Gertner & Gertner, Columbus, 1979—. Editor: Leading Cases in Ohio Law, 1935, 2d edit., 1939. Contbr. articles to law jours. Mem., founder Ohio Anti-Defamation League. Mem. ABA, Assn. Trial Lawyers Am. (hon.), Ohio Bar Assn., Columbus Bar Assn. (bd. govs. 1955-59), Order of Coif, Phi Beta Kappa, Tau Epsilon Rho (nat. pres. 1962). Jewish. Lodge: B'nai B'rith (pres. 1961). Home: 2753 Plymouth Ave Columbus OH 43209 Office: Gertner & Gertner 88 E Broad St Suite 1435 Columbus OH 43215

GERTNER, MICHAEL HARVEY, lawyer; b. Columbus, Ohio, Aug. 26, 1941; s. Abraham and Edythe Gertner. B.A. cum laude, Ohio State U., 1963, J.D., 1966. Bar: D.C. 1971, Ohio 1966, U.S. Dist. Ct. (D.C. dist.) 1971, U.S. Supreme Ct. 1971, U.S. Claims Ct. 1973, U.S. Tax Ct. 1973, U.S. Ct. Appeals (D.C. cir.) 1974, U.S. Dist. Ct. (so. dist.) Ohio 1979, U.S. Ct. Appeals (6th cir. and fed. cir.) 1983. Law clk. Ohio Supreme Ct., Columbus, 1966-68; legis. asst. to Sen. Wm. B. Saxbe, Washington, 1969-74; atty. advisor Office Atty. Gen., U.S. Dept. Justice, Washington, 1974; asst. U.S. atty, Washington, 1974-76; assoc. Vorys, Sater, Seymour & Pease, Columbus, 1977-79; ptnr. Gertner & Gertner, Columbus, 1979—. Mem. ABA, Ohio Bar Assn., Columbus Bar Assn., Fed. Bar Assn., Franklin County Trial Lawyers Assn., Phi Beta Kappa, Phi Eta Sigma, Eta Sigma Phi, Pi Sigma Alpha, Ohio Acad. Trial Lawyers, Assn. Trial Lawyers Am. Republican. Jewish. Home: 2753 Plymouth Ave Columbus OH 43209 Office: Gertner & Gertner 88 E Broad St Columbus OH 43215

GERTZ, ELMER, lawyer, author, educator; b. Chgo., Sept. 14, 1906; s. Morris and Grace (Grossman) G.; Ph.B., U. Chgo., 1928, J.D., 1930; m. Ceretta Samuels, Aug. 16, 1931 (dec.); children—Theodore, Margery Ann Hechtman; m. 2d, Mamie L. Friedman, June 21, 1959; 1 son, Jack M. Friedman. Admitted to Ill. bar, 1930, since practiced in Chgo.; formerly asso. firm McInerney, Epstein & Arvey, Chgo.; asst. to masters in chancery Jacob M. Arvey, Samuel B. Epstein, 1930-43; atty. for Nathan Leopold in successful parole procs., 1957-58; atty. various censorship litigations including Tropic of Cancer, 1961—; atty. for Jack Ruby in setting aside death sentence; counsel commn. to investigate disorders in Chgo. during spring, summer 1968; prof. John Marshall Law Sch., 1970—. Dir. pub. relations Ill. Police Assn., 1934; mem. exec. com. Ill. Com. Equal Job Opportunity; mem. nat., Chgo. adv. bd. commn. on law and social action Am. Jewish Congress; chmn. soldier vote com. Profl. and Bus. People, 1944; mem. law and order com. Chgo. Commn. on Human Relations, 1945—; v.p. Ill. Freedom to Read Com.; chmn. Vets. Housing Com., 1945-47; mem. Mayor's Housing Com., 1946-48, legal chmn., 1946-47; mem. Chgo. Com. on Housing Action, 1947-49; adv. com. Chief Justice Municipal Ct. Chgo., 1950-51; pres. Greater Chgo. council Am. Jewish Congress, 1959-63; del. 6th Ill. Constl. Conv., 1969-70, chmn. conv. Bill of Rights com., 1969-70; bd. dirs. Jackson Park Hosp.; exec. v.p. Blind Service Assn.; trustee Belefaire; nat. bd. trustees City of Hope. Recipient Golden Key award City of Hope, 1966; award Ill. div. A.C.L.U., 1963, 74, U. Chgo. Alumni Assn., 1959, State of Israel Prime Minister's medal, 1972; selected for Chicagoland honor roll Chgo. Council Against Discrimination, 1946, 47, Hadassah, 1975, Educator of Year award, 1975, numerous others. Mem. Pub. Housing Assn. (founder, counsel, pres. 1943-49), Civil War Round Table (founder, exec. com., pres., hon. life), Adult Edn. Council Chgo. (sec., pres.), Shaw Soc. (founder, pres., exhibit chmn. Shaw Centennial 1956, Darrow Centennial 1957), Am., Fed., Chgo. (chmn. legal edn. com. 1970-71, vice chmn. civil rights com. 1978-79, chmn. com. 1979-80) bar assns., Ill. State Bar Assn. (sect. council, individual rights and responsibilities sec. 1984-85), Bar Assn. 7th Circuit, Am. Judicature Soc., Decalogue Soc. Lawyers (mgr., pres., editor Jour.), First Amendment Lawyers Assn. (pres. 1978-79, chmn., 1979-80), Soc. Midland Authors (award 1969, sec. 1976, 1st award for body of writing 1984), Authors Guild, Appellate Lawyers Assn. Ill. Clubs: Chicago Literary (v.p. 1968-69, 1978-79, pres. 1979-80), Cliff Dwellers, City. Author: (with A.I. Tobin) Frank Harris: A Study in Black and White, 1931; The People vs. The Chicago Tribune, 1942; (play) Mrs. Bixby Gets a Letter, 1942; Joe Medill's War, 1946; American Ghettos, 1946; A Handful of Clients, 1965; Moment of Madness: The People vs. Jack Ruby, 1968; foreword The Tropic of Cancer On Trial, 1968; To Life (Friends of Lit. award), 1974; Short Stories of Frank Harris, 1975; Henry Miller: Years of Trial and Triumph: The Letters of Henry Miller and Elmer Gertz, 1978, German edit., 1980; Odyssey of a Barbarian, 1979; (with Joseph Pisciotte) Charter for a New Age, 1980; (with others) A Guide to Estate Planning, 1983; (with Edward Gilbreth) Quest for a Constitution, 1984; others. Contbr. to Henry Miller and the Critics, 1963, Mass Media and the Law, 1969; For the First Hours of Tomorrow, 1971; also articles in various periodicals and encys. Home: 6249 N Albany Ave Chicago IL 60659 Office: 315 S Plymouth Ct Chicago IL 60604*

GERTZ, THOMAS ERWIN, organization executive; b. Chgo., Dec. 4, 1944; s. Erwin August Henry and Camille Bertha (Eschenbach) G.; M. of Human Sexuality, Inst. Advanced Study of Human Sexuality, 1976, now postgrad. Adminstrv. asst. Midwest Population Center, Chgo., 1972-73; adminstrv. asst. Richard L. Bennett, M.D., Akron, Ohio, 1973-80; adminstrv. dir., sexologist Akron Forum, Inc., 1973-80; founder, pres. Thomas Gertz & Assos., Inc., 1980—, Akron Sex Forum, 1980—; mem. faculty Inst. Advanced Study of Human Sexuality, profl. sch., San Francisco, 1976-77. Past pres. Mattachine Midwest, Inc., Chgo.; bd. dirs. Akron Rape Crisis Center, sec., 1979, v.p., 1979-80, exec. com., 1980-81, mem. adv. bd., 1983—; trustee Mental Health Assn. Summit County, 1979-80. Mem. Am. Assn. Sex Educators, Counselors and Therapists (life, dir., treas. 1980-83, pres. elect 1983-84, pres. 1984-85, cert. sex educator, cert. sex therapist), Assn. Sexologists, Sex. Info. and Edn. Council of U.S., Soc. for Sci. Study of Sex, Inc., Am. Coll. Sexologists (cert.), Harry Benjamin Internat. Gender Dysphoria Assn., Inc. (charter), U.S. Consortium for Sexology (dir., treas. 1981—, conf. coordinator 1982-83). Home: 786 Hampton Ridge Dr PO Box 1803 Akron OH 44309 Office: 1653 Merriman Rd Suite 205 Akron OH 44313

GESINSKI, RAYMOND MARION, biological sciences corporation executive, emeritus educator; b. Monessen, Pa., July 16, 1932; s. Michael Anthony and Mary Magdelan (Turek) G.; m. Patricia Carolyn Payton, May 7, 1966. B.S., Kent State U., 1960, M.A., 1962, Ph.D., 1968. Instr., Kent State U., Ohio, 1962-68, asst. prof., 1968-72, assoc. prof., 1972-78, prof. biol. scis., 1978-85, prof. emeritus, 1985—; pres. Midwest Biol. Corp., 1985—; vis. scholar U. Del., Del. State Shellfish Commn., 1965; vis. scientist Manned Space Ctr., Preventive Medicine Div., Houston, 1971. Contbr. articles to profl. jours. Served with USN, 1952-56. Argonne Nat. Lab. fellow, 1970, 71; Sigma Xi exchange lectr., 1971; recipient Disting. Teaching award Tuscarawas County, Ohio, 1973, Kent State U. Alumni Assn., 1974. Fellow Ohio Acad. Sci. (v.p. med. scis. sect., exec. bd. 1985—); mem. N.Y. Acad. Sci., Fedn. Am. Soc. Exptl. Biology, AAAS, Am. Soc. Cell Biology, Internat. Exptl. Hematology Soc., Sigma Xi. Home: 2692 Woodward Rd Cuyahoga Falls OH 44221 Office: Biol Sci Dept Kent State Univ Kent OH 44242

GESS, LOWELL ARTHUR, ophthalmologist, minister, missionary; b. Paynesville, Minn., July 13, 1921; s. Arthur and Frances (Wolf) G.; m. Ruth Adabelle Bradley, Dec. 29, 1945; children—Timothy L., Mary R., Elizabeth A., John A., Paul R., Andrew D. B.A., MacAlester Coll., 1942; B.D., Evang. Theol. Sem., 1945; M.D. Washington U., St. Louis, 1951; L.H.D., Westmar Coll., 1985. Ordained to ministry Methodist Church, 1946. Intern Ancker Hosp., St. Paul, 1951-52; resident in ophthalmology U. Minn., Mpls., 1961-64; med. missionary Bd. Global Ministries, United Meth. Ch., 1952-67, 72-75; ophthalmologist Quain & Ramstad Clinic, Bismarck, N.D., 1967-72; vol. med. missionary, W. Africa, 3-4 months each year. Author numerous papers. Recipient Service to Mankind award Sertoma Service Club, 1977; Jackson Johnson scholar Washington U. Sch. Medicine, 1948. Mem. AMA, Acad. Ophthalmology, Am. Intraocular Implant Soc. Lodge: Lions (named hon. Lion 1979).

GESSLEY, GLEN ROYAL, park planning administrator; b. Hannibal, Mo., Mar. 9, 1951; s. Norman and Annabel Scott (Teeter) G.; m. Kristin Wassmuth, Feb. 14, 1981. B.S., Colo. State U., 1973. Long-range planner Mo. Dept. Natural Resources, Jefferson City, 1973-79, planning dir., 1979—; mem. Mo. Natural Areas com., Jefferson City, 1977—. Chmn. Holts Summit Planning and Zoning Comn., Mo., 1982; active Boy Scouts Am. Mem. Mo. Parks Assn. Mem. Disciples of Christ Ch. Lodges: Masons, Shriners. Avocations: making stained-glass windows; photography; woodworking. Home: Route 3 Box 227 Holts Summit MO 65043 Office: Dept Natural Resources PO Box 176 Jefferson City MO 65102

GETIS, ARTHUR, geography educator; b. Phila., July 6, 1934; s. Samuel J. and Sophie Z. Getis; m. Judith Miller Marckwardt, July 23, 1961; children—Hilary Hope, Victoria Lynn, Anne Patterson. B.S., Pa. State U., 1956, M.S., 1958; Ph.D., U. Wash.-Seattle, 1961. Asst. prof. Mich. State U., East Lansing, 1961-63; from asst. prof. to prof. Rutgers U., New Brunswick, N.J., 1963-77; vis. lectr. Bristol U., Eng., 1966-67, Princeton U., N.J., 1971-74; vis. scholar Cambridge U., Eng., 1982; prof., head dept. geography, dir. Sch. Social Scis. U. Ill., Urbana, 1977—; vis. scientist Assn. Am. Geographers, Washington, 1970-72. Co-author: Models of Spatial Processes, 1978; Geography, 1981; Human Geography, 1985; Point Patter Analysis, 1988. Active Zoning Bd. Appeals, Urbana, 1980-84; co-pres. Parent-Faculty Orgn., Univ. High Sch., Urbana, 1982-83. NSF research grantee, 1983-85. Mem. Assn. Am. Geographers (nominating com. 1971-72), Regional Sci. Assn. (pres. N.E. sect. 1973-74), Inst. Brit. Geographers, Nat. Council Geog. Edn., Assn. Japanese Geographers. Home: 309 W Indiana St Urbana IL 61801 Office: U Ill Dept Geography 607 S Mathews St Urbana IL 61801

GETTELFINGER, MICHAEL ALAN, optometrist, educator; b. New Albany, Ind., June 5, 1954; s. Irvin Charles and Geraldine Ruth (Scott) G.; m. Janet Lee Marie Madden, June 19, 1976; children—Megan Elaine, Paige Marie. B.S., Ind. U., 1975, O.D., 1978. Lic. optometrist, Ind. Practice optometry, New Albany, 1978—; adj. prof. biol. scis. Ind. U. S.E., 1982—. Chmn. programs and allocations Floyd County com. Metro United Way, Louisville, 1981-84. Fellow Am. Acad. Optometry; mem. Am. Optometric Assn., Ind. Optometric Assn. (pres. southeast soc. 1983-84). Lodge: Lions. Avocations: photomicrography. Office: 1501 State St New Albany IN 47150

GETZ, GODFREY SHALOM, pathology educator; b. Johannesburg, S. Africa, June 18, 1930; came to U.S., 1963; naturalized, 1971; s. Judah Nathan and Fay (Lakofski) G.; m. Millicent Lorraine Cohen; children—Edwin A., Andrew R., Keith S., Jonathan D. B.Sc., Witwatersrand U., Johannesburg, 1952, B.Sc. Hons. 1955, M.B., B.Ch., 1954; Ph.D., Oxford U., 1963. Lectr. Witwatersrand U., 1956, 59-63; Nuffield demonstrator Oxford U., Eng., 1956-59; research assoc. Harvard Med. Sch., Boston, 1963-64; asst. then assoc. prof. U. Chgo., 1964-72, prof., 1972—. Home: 5523 S Kimbark Ave Chicago IL 60637 Office: U Chgo 5841 S Maryland Chicago IL 60637

GETZENDANNER, SUSAN, See *Who's Who in America,* 43rd edition.

GEVERS, MARCIA BONITA, lawyer, lecturer, consultant; b. Mpls., Oct. 11, 1946; d. Sam and Bessie (Gottlieb) Fleisher; m. Michael A. Gevers, Sept. 13, 1970; children—Sarah Nichole, David Seth. B.A. Nat. Coll. Edn., 1968; M.A., N.E. Ill. U., 1973; J.D., DePaul U., 1980. Bar: Ill. 1980. Tchr., Chgo. Bd. Edn., Harris Sch., North Suburban Spl. Edn. Dist., Highland Park, Ill., 1968-73; legis. asst., campaign mgr. Ill. State Rep., Dolton, 1974-79; sole practice, Park Forest, Dolton, Ill.; cons. LWV, Chgo.; now ptnr. Getty and Gevers, Dolton. Producer, host cable TV show The Law and You, 1982-83. Bd. dirs. Park Forest Zoning Bd. Appeals, Fair Housing Rev. Bd., Housing Bd. Appeals, Equal Employment Opportunity Rev. Bd., 1975—; pres., bd. dirs. South Suburban Community Hebrew Day Sch., Olympia Fields, Ill., 1982—; bd. dirs. Congregation Beth Sholom Ch., Park Forest, 1980-82; pres. Ill. Women Polit. Caucus; mem. steering com. Nat. Women's Polit. Caucus, Washington; pres., founder Metro South Women's Polit. Caucus, Chgo. suburbs; alt. del. Dem. Nat. Conv., N.Y.C., 1980. Mem. ABA, Ill. State Bar Assn., South Suburban Bar Assn. (unauthorized practices com.), Chgo. Bar Assn., Am. Arbitration Assn. (arbitrator), Decalogue Soc. Lawyers, LWV. Lodges: Hadassah, B'nai B'rith Women. Office: Getty Gevers 15000 Dorchester Ave PO Box F Dolton IL 60419

GEYER, DOUGLAS WARREN, judge; b. Springfield, Ohio, Nov. 19, 1942; s. Warren William and Doris Irene (Rust) G.; m. Sharon Ann Ondrejka, June 24, 1978; children—Matthew, Molly. B.S., Ohio Northern U., 1965; J.D., Ohio No. Coll. Law, 1968. Bar: Ohio 1968, U.S. Dist. Ct. Ohio 1969, U.S. Supreme Ct. 1973. Ptnr. Jewett, West & Geyer, Springfield, Ohio, 1968-70; Juergens, Juergens & Geyer, 1970-75; asst. atty. gen. Ohio, 1969-75; judge, Springfield Mcpl. Ct., Ohio, 1975—, presiding judge, 1982—. Co-author: Insanity and Psycopathy, 1967. Recipient Outstanding and Excellent Jud. Service awards Supreme Ct. of Ohio, 1975-84, Stephen Curtis award, 1967. Mem. Am. Judges Assn., Ohio State Bar Assn., Ohio Jud. Coll., Ohio Mcpl. Judges Assn., Springfield-Clark County Bar Assn. Democrat. Lutheran. Home: 2025 Cheviot Hills Dr Springfield OH 45505 Office: Springfield Mcpl Ct Springfield OH 45501

GHANTOUS, ROBERT NICHOLAS, engineering company executive; b. Marj'oyoun, Lebanon, Mar. 23, 1939; s. Nicholas Simon and Saida (Bassit) G.; came to U.S., 1956, naturalized, 1964; student Toledo U., 1957-62; m. Patricia Ann Langer, Sept. 4, 1957; children—Robert Nicholas, Michael Eric, Tonya Sue. Lab. technician Maumee Chem. Co., Toledo, 1959, process engr., Cin., to 1965; instrument engr. Chem. & Indsl. Corp., Cin., 1965; with Devel. Cons.'s, Cin., 1965-69; sr. systems engr. Foxboro Co. (Mass.), 1969-70; engr., pres. Ghantous Corp., Cin., 1970—. Registered profl. engr. Ohio. Mem. Instrument Soc. Am., Nat. Soc. Profl. Engrs. Home: 767 Cedarhill Dr Cincinnati OH 45240 Office: 767 Cedarhill Dr Cincinnati OH 45240

GHERING, M(ARY) VIRGIL, nun, chemistry educator, librarian; b. Grand Rapids, Mich., July 18, 1910; d. Henry Christian and Frances Emily (Sharp) G. A.B., Central Mich. U., 1935; M.S., Marquette U., 1948; postgrad. Fordham U., 1957-60; Ph.D., St. Thomas Inst., 1968. Joined Sisters of St. Dominic, 1929. Tchr. Catholic Central High Sch., Grand Rapids, 1936-38, Maple Grove Pub. Schs., New Lothrop, Mich., 1943-49; asst. prof. chemistry Aquinas Coll., Grand Rapids, 1949-57, assoc. prof., 1957-61, prof., 1961-68, chmn. dept. phys. scis., 1959-63; librarian Grad. Sch. Sci. Research, St. Thomas Inst., Cin., 1968—. Telephone coordinator Common Cause, 2d Congl. Dist., Cin., 1973-83. NSF sci. faculty fellow; fellow St. Thomas Inst., 1963-68. Fellow Am. Inst. Chemists; mem. Am. Chem. Soc. Democrat. Home: Mercy Ctr 2335 Grandview Ave Cincinnati OH 45206 Office: St Thomas Inst 1842 Madison Rd Cincinnati OH 45206

GHETTI, BERNARDINO FRANCESCO, neuropathologist, researcher, educator; b. Pisa, Italy, Mar. 28, 1941; s. Getulio and Iris (Mugnetti) G.; came to U.S., 1970; m. Caterina Genovese, Oct. 8, 1966; children—Chiara, Simone. Doctorate in Medicine cum laude, U. Pisa (Italy), 1966. Diplomate Am. Bd. Pathology in Neuropathology. Intern, Hosp. S. Chiara, Pisa, Italy, 1965; postdoctoral fellow U. Pisa, 1966-70; research fellow in neuropathology Albert Einstein Coll. Medicine, Bronx, N.Y., 1970-73, resident and clin. fellow in pathology, 1973-75, in neuropathology, 1975-76; asst. prof. pathology Ind. U. Sch. Medicine, Indpls., 1976-77, asst. prof. pathology and psychiatry, 1977-78, assoc. prof., 1978-83, mem. grad. faculty, 1980—, prof., 1983—; mem. staff Ind. U. Hosp., Wishard Meml. Hosp. Mem. Am. Assn. Neuropathologists, Soc. for Neurosci., Assn. for Research in Nervous and Mental Diseases, Am. Soc. Cell Biology, Italian Soc. of Psychiatry Italian Soc. Neurology (neuropathology sect.), Sigma Xi. Roman Catholic. Contbr. numerous articles to profl. jours. and internat. publs.; research in neurobiology. Home: 1124 S Frederick Dr Indianapolis IN 46260 Office: Ind U Sch Medicine 635 Barnhill Rd Indianapolis IN 46223

GHOSH, SATYENDRA KUMAR, structural engineer, educator; b. Berhampore, W. Bengal, India, Sept. 17, 1945; came to U.S., 1975; s. Santosh Kumar and Sadhana (Bose) G.; m. Sumita Majumdar, July 4, 1973; children—Elka, Sourish. B.E., U. Calcutta, India, 1966; M.A.Sc., U. Waterloo, (Ont., Can.), 1969, Ph.D., 1972. Structural engr. Kuljian Corp., Calcutta, India, 1966-67; research and teaching asst. U. Waterloo, 1967-69; 70-72, postdoctoral fellow, 1973, research assoc., 1973, adj. prof., 1973-74; research and teaching asst. U. Pitts., 1969-70; structural engr. Portland Cement Assn., Skokie, Ill., 1974-75, sr. structural engr., 1975-80, prin. structural engr., 1980-83; assoc. prof. civil engring. U. Ill.-Chgo., 1984—; prin. Fintel Ghosh, Inc., Glenview, Ill., 1984—; ptnr. Elan Assocs., Waterloo, 1972-73; vis. lectr. dept. Materials Engring. U. Ill., Chgo., 1980, 82, 83. Treas. Ill. chpt. Assn. of Indians in Am., 1981-82, v.p., 1983-84. Recipient U. Calcutta Gold medal, 1966. Fellow Inst. of Engrs. India (Engring. Congress prize 1982); mem. Am. Concrete Inst., ASCE. Contbr. articles in field to profl. jours. Home: 1811 Cree Ln Mount Prospect IL 60056 Office: U Ill-Chgo Chicago IL 60680

GIANOS, JOHN GEORGE, chemical company executive; b. Chgo., Jan. 26, 1944; s. George John and Goldie (Schellin) G.; m. Kay Elaine Dunavant, Nov. 11, 1967; children—Paul John, Jennifer Lyn. B.S., Iowa State U., 1966. Patrolman, Chgo. Police Dept., 1966-69; sales rep. USS-Agri-Chems., Chicago Heights, Ill., 1969-74, chem. mktg. mgr., Rockford, Ill., 1974-79; regional mgr. Terra Chems., Inc., Sioux City, Iowa, 1979-84, gen. mgr. fertilizer mktg., 1984—. Chmn. citizens adv. com. Sioux City Police, 1979—; 1st v.p. Siouxland Crime Prevention Coalition, 1981—. Served with USAR. Mem. Nat. Fertilizer Solutions Assn., Mo. Agr. Council, Iowa Fertilizer and Chem. Assn., Beta Theta Pi. Advocations: showing and breeding Arabian horses; competitive running. Home: 3916 Military Rd Sioux City IA 51103 Office: Terra Chem Internat Inc PO Box 1828 Sioux City IA 51102

GIBALDI, ANDRE VINCENT, ostoepathic physician; b. Cleve., Jan. 1, 1933; s. Anthony and Elvira (Restifo) G. B.A., Case Western Res. U., 1957; D.O., Chgo. Coll. Osteo. Medicine, 1963. Lic. osteo. physician, Ohio, Fla., Colo., Wash., Wyo. Intern, Brentwood Hosp., Warrensville, Ohio, 1963-64; sole practice family medicine, Cleve., 1964-77; assoc. prof. family medicine Ohio U. Coll. Osteo. Medicine, Athens, 1977-78, prof., 1978—, dir. med. service clinics, 1978-81, chmn. dept. family medicine, 1977-81; mem. staff Brentwood Hosp., 1964-77, dir. med. edn., 1981—, clinic dir. Family Health Ctr., 1981—; mem. Ednl. Council on Osteo. Principles, 1977—; mem. cert. bd. Am. Osteo. Bd. Gen. Practitioners, 1972; chmn. student loan fund com. Nat. Osteo. Found., 1983; sec.-treas. Ohio Oste. Found., 1983; mem. panel HHS, 1982. Served to col. USAR, 1978—. Fellow Am. Coll. Gen. Practitioners of Osteo. Medicine and Surgery; mem. Ohio Osteo. Assn. (pres.-elect 1984), Am. Coll. Gen. Practitioners (state pres. 1983), Am. Osteo. Assn. (chmn. com.; del. 1977-85), Am. Acad. Osteopathy, others. Home: 3861 Sawbridge Dr Richfield OH 44286 Office: Brentwood Hosp 4110 Warrensville Center Rd Warrensville Heights OH 44122

GIBB, CLARK RAYMOND, mfrs. rep. co. exec.; b. Cottonwood, Minn., Sept. 5, 1914; s. Raymond J. and Huldah (Pettersen) G.; B.B.A., U. Minn., 1940; m. Margaret L. Foucault, June 30, 1954. Sales engr. Despatch Oven Co., Mpls., 1941; mem. prodn. control staff Gen. Mills, Mpls., 1941-42; owner Aurex Minn. Co., Mpls., 1946-51; partner A & G Chip Steak Co., Mankato, Minn., 1947-61; v.p. Chip Steak & Provision Co., Mankato, 1961-65, pres., owner, 1965—; pres. Clark R. Gibb Co., Mpls., 1952-79, GIBBCO Sci., Inc., 1974-79; owner Wooddale Farms, Yellow Medicine County, Minn.; developer ClarMar Woods, Washburn County, Wis., 1975—. Served with AUS, 1942-46, 51-52. Mem. U. Minn. Alumni Assn., Minn. Alumni Club, Electronic Reps. Assn. (chmn. bd., past pres.), Am. Legion, VFW. Republican. Presbyn. Elk. Clubs: Electronic VIP (past pres.), Mpls. Athletic, Minikahda (Mpls.). Home: 2020 Cedar Lake Blvd Minneapolis MN 55416 Office: 11100 Bren Rd W Minnetonka MN 55343

GIBBONS, CHARLES CREW, management consultant; b. Lost Springs, Wyo., June 21, 1916; s. Frank Eli and Alice Kathleen (Crew) G.; m. Wilma

Ruth Householder, Sept. 13, 1949; children—Betsy Gibbons Lindland, Jennifer Anne Lindland. B.S., Ohio U., 1937, M.A., 1938; Ph.D., Ohio State U., 1942. Dir. personnel research Owens Ill. Glass Co., Toledo, 1942-45; indsl. program dir. Upjohn Inst. for Employment Research, Kalamazoo, Mich., 1945-56, now vice chmn., adminstrv. cons. Upjohn Co., 1956-81, ret.; cons., speaker in field. Cons. Greater Kalamazoo United Way, Kalamazoo Forum. Fellow Am. Psychol. Assn. Methodist. Home: 223 E Ellis St PO Box 459 DeGraff OH 43318

GIBBONS, MRS. JOHN SHELDON (CELIA VICTORIA TOWNSEND), editor, publisher; b. Fargo, N.D.; d. Harry Alton and Helen (Haag) Townsend; student U. Minn., 1930-33; m. John Sheldon Gibbons, May 1, 1935; children—Mary Vee, John Townsend. Advt. mgr. Hotel Nicollet, Mpls., 1933-37; contbg. editor children's mags., 1935—; partner Youth Assos. Co., Mpls., 1942-65; pub. art dir. Mines and Escholier mags., 1954-65; founder Bull. Bd. Pictures, Inc., Mpls., 1954, pres., 1954—; founder Periodical Litho Art Co., Mpls., 1962, pres., 1962-65; artist Cath. Boy mag., 1938; chief photographer Cath. Miss mag., 1955. Mem. Women's aux. Mpls. Symphony Orch.; mem. Fort Lauderdale (Fla.) Art. Mus. Republican chairwoman Golden Valley, Minn., 1950; alternate del. Hennepin County Rep. Conv., 1962. Mem. Mpls. Inst. Arts, Internat. Inst., St. Paul Arts and Sci., Art Guild Boca Raton, Delta Zeta. Clubs: Woman's, Minikahda; Deerfield Beach Women's. Home: 1416 Alpine Pass Tyrol Hills Minneapolis MN 55416 Office: 1057 A-1-A Hillsboro Beach FL

GIBBONS, MARTIN EDWARD, pharmacist, healthcare administrator, consultant; b. Cin., Oct. 19, 1931; s. Edward and Martha Carol (Hirst) G.; m. Donna Estelle Tuggle, July 17, 1954; children—Lisa, David, Geoffrey. B.S. in Pharmacy, U. Cin., 1953; postgrad. U. Wash., 1954; M.H.A., Xavier U., 1982; grad. Air Command and Staff Coll. Air U., 1985. Registered pharmacist, Ohio. Owner, chief exec. officer Kinross Pharmacy, Cin., 1962-70; staff pharmacist Bethesda Hosp., Cin., 1970-72, supr. pharmacy, 1972-81, adminstrv. resident, 1981-82; med. info. system cons. Christ Hosp., Cin., 1983. Author: Bethesda Hospitals—Applied Management Studies, 1982. Bd. dirs. Dunham Complex, 1975-80. Served to lt. col. CAP, 1967—. Recipient Gill Robb Wilson award CAP, 1984, Comdr.'s Commendation award, 1982; Abbott Labs. grantee, 1954. Mem. Am. Coll. Hosp. Adminstrs., Tri State Health Adminstrs Forum, Greater Cin. Soc. Hosp. Pharmacists (treas. 1974-76), Cin. Coll. Pharmacy Alumni Assn. (pres. 1982-85), Xavier U. Alumni Assn. in Hosp. and Health Adminstrn., U. Cin. Alumni Senate, Appalachian Trail Conf., Nat. Muzzleloading Rifle Assn. Roman Catholic. Avocations: Ancient and medieval coins; wilderness backpacking; paleontology; archeology; photography. Home: 1113 Wing St Cincinnati OH 45204

GIBBONS, MARY CATHERINE, nursing education director; b. St. Louis, Aug. 7, 1944; d. John Patrick and Effie C. (Weber) G. B.S. in Nursing, St. Louis U., 1966, M.S. in Nursing of Children, 1971. Staff nurse St. Mary's Health Ctr., St. Louis, 1966-70, head nurse, 1970-71; instr. obstetrics nursing Jewish Hosp. Sch. Nursing, St. Louis, 1971-72; maternity coordinator Luth. Med. Ctr. Sch. Nursing, St. Louis, 1972-82, dir. nursing edn., 1982—; instr. continuing edn. programs. Bd. dirs. YWCA, St. Louis, 1984—. Recipient Humanitian award Hosp. Assn. St. Louis, 1983. Mem. Nat. League Nursing, Nurses Assn. of Am. Coll. Obstetricians and Gynecologists (chmn. Dist. VII 1982-83, Mo. sect. 1978-79), Assn. Female Execs., Sigma Theta Tau. Home: 10123 Mullally Dr Saint Louis MO 63123 Office: Luth Med Ctr Sch Nursing 3547 S Jefferson St Saint Louis MO 63118

GIBBS, CHARLES DANA, airline executive; b. Washington, June 22, 1939; s. Carlos Dana and Rose Mary (Wise) G.; children—Eric, Bradford, Melanie, Kurt. A.B. in Econs., Am. U., 1961. Air transport analyst Civil Aero. Bd., Washington, 1962-65; dir. route devel. Ozark Air Lines, Inc., St. Louis, 1966-73, v.p. route devel. 1974—. Avocation: travel; reading; phys. fitness. Home: 15061 Green Circle Dr Chesterfield MO 63017 Office: Ozark Air Lines Inc Box 10007 Saint Louis MO 63017

GIBBS, DONALD GARY, pipe manufacturing executive; b. Lawrence, Kans., Nov. 14, 1948; s. William Read and Mercedese (Muir) G.; m. Winona S. Jensen, Dec. 30, 1970; children—Roger Stuart, Curtis Andrew. B.S. in Bus. and Acctg., U. Kans., 1970. Acct. Builders Sand Co., Kansas City, Kans., 1970-73; sales rep. Millcon Corp., Wichita, Kans., 1973-75; br. mgr. Millcon Corp., 1975—, dir., 1981; dir., mem. exec. com. South Central Kans. Econ. Devel. Dist., 1979—, v.p., 1981-82, pres., 1982-83; mem. bd. examiners for mech. contractors, 1982—. Campaign dir. Gibbs for U.S. Senate, Kans. Republican Primary, 1978; campaign worker Bob Brown for City Commn., Wichita, 1979, coordinator, 1983; elder Covenant Presbyn. Ch., 1982—. Named Lambda Chi of Year, 1970. Mem. Assoc. Builders and Contractors (chpt. bd. dirs. 1982), Nat. Assn. Devel. Orgns. (bd. dirs., exec. com., treas.), Soc. Am. Mil. Engrs., Am. Concrete Pipe Assn., ASCE, Lambda Chi Alpha (Lambda Chi of Yr. 1970). Presbyterian. Home: RR 1 Box 222B Buhler KS 67522 Office: Millcon Corp 700 E 29th St N Wichita KS 67219

GIBBS, DORSIE JOE, botanist, executive; b. Ashland, Ky., Feb. 19, 1940; s. Dorsie Wilson and Frances Susan (Simpson) G.; m. Madalyn Jeanne Wiegman, Mar. 23, 1963; children—Kayla Dawn, April Renae. B.S. in Biology, Bethany Nazarene Coll., 1965. Ops. mgr. Stemen Labs., Visalia, Calif., 1965-67; botanist Internat. Biologicals Inc., Oklahoma City, 1967-72; owner, founder Aero-Allergen Labs., Carthage, Mo., 1972-80, exec. v.p., chief ops. officer subs. Pharmacia Diagnostics, Uppsala, Sweden, 1980-85; founder, pres. Pol-n-Fax Inc., Joplin, Mo., 1985—. Recipient Outstanding Alumni award Bethany Nazarene Coll., 1981. Republican. Inventor field vacuum for collecting pollens in large quantities; inventor methods for particle sizing and separation of pollens.

GIBBS, JOHN CLARK, psychology educator, consultant; b. Paterson, N.J., June 7, 1946; s. John Lowell and Ila Louise (Burns) G.; m. Valerie Viereck, Nov. 18, 1972; children—Valerie Sophia, Stephanie Anne, Jonathan Lowell. B.A., Princeton U., 1968; M.A., Harvard U., 1971, Ph.D., 1972. Instr. psychology dept. McMaster U., Hamilton, Ont., Can., 1973-75; research faculty mem. Harvard U. Grad. Sch. Edn., Cambridge, Mass., 1975-79; asst. prof. psychology Ohio State U., Columbus, 1979-84, assoc. prof., 1984—. Mem. adv. bd. Assn. for Moral Edn., 1982—. Served to capt. USAF, 1973. Can. Council Humanities and Social Scis. research grantee, 1974-75, NIMH grantee, 1980, 81-82; recipient William F. Milton Meml. Fund award, Harvard U., 1976-77. Mem. Am. Psychol. Assn., Jean Piaget Soc., Soc. for Research in Child Devel., Common Cause. Author: Social Intelligence, 1982; contbr. numerous chpts. to books, articles to profl. jours.; mem. editorial bd. Child Devel., 1982-83.

GIBSON, BENJAMIN F., See *Who's Who in America,* 43rd edition.

GIBSON, FRANK EVERETT, librarian; b. Des Moines, May 30, 1913; s. Frank Wesley and Maude Elizabeth (Trotter) G.; B.A., Drake U., 1948; B.S. in L.S., U. Minn., 1949, M.A., 1952; m. Bette J. Beckett, Dec. 15, 1935; 1 dau., Marianne. With Iowa Power & Light, Des Moines, 1932-42; asso. librarian U. Omaha, 1952-53; staff Omaha Pub. Library, 1953-83; ret., 1983. Served with AUS, 1942-46. Recipient Lura Hutchison award in library sci. U. Minn., 1949. Mem. ALA, Nebr. Library Assn. (pres. 1956-57), Phi Beta Kappa. Contbr. articles to profl. publs. Home: 12727 W Dodge Rd Apt 126C Omaha NE 68154

GIBSON, JAMES PATRICK, insurance company supervisor; b. Lawrenceville, Ill., Oct. 18, 1947; s. Chester William and Mary Catherine (Gootee) G.; m. Gertrude Ann Donahue, June 27, 1970; children—Sharon, David. Student Vincennes U., 1966. Clk. Golden Rule Ins. Co., Lawrenceville, Ill., 1965-67, mem. office mgr's. staff, 1970-73, procedures analyst, 1973-80, mem. data conversion team, 1980-83, tng. coordinator, 1983—. Served as sgt. U.S. Army, 1968-70, Vietnam. Fellow Life Office Mgmt. Assn. Lodge: Knights of Columbus (grand knight 1983, 84). Avocations: model railroading, photography. Office: Golden Rule Insurance 712 11th St Lawrenceville IL 62439

GIBSON, JOHN ROBERT, See *Who's Who in America,* 43rd edition.

GIBSON, LENORA JANE SPRINGER, occupational health nurse; b. Brownsvalley, Ind., Nov. 18, 1930; d. Ralph Leon and Helen Elnora (West) Springer; m. Kenton Glenn Gibson, Oct. 29, 1952; children—Kent Glenn, Dean Allen. Student Waynetown Sch., 1936-48; diploma, Home Hosp. Sch. Nursing, 1951. Cert. occupational health nurse. Surg. nurse Montgomery County Culver Union Hosp., Crawfordsville, Ind., 1951-52; occupational health nurse R.R. Donnelley & Sons, Crawfordsville, 1952-55; head nurse nursery Meth. Hosp., Inpls., 1958-59; staff Detroit Diesel Allison div. Gen. Motors Corp., Indpls., 1959-80, supr. nurses, 1981—. Recipient Occupational Health Nurse award Schering Corp., 1982. Fellow Ind. Acad. Occupational Health Nurses; mem. Mid-Ind. Assn. Occupational Health Nurses, Ind. Assn. Occupational Health Nurses (treas.), Am. Assn. Occupational Health Nurses. Baptist. Home: 3302 Shadow Brook Dr Indianapolis IN 46224 Office: General Motors Corp PO Box 894 Indianapolis IN 46206

GIBSON, LEONA (LEE) RUTH, medical society administrator; b. Columbia, Mo., Aug. 11, 1929; d. Raymon Henry and Mabel Virginia (Barnes) Keel; m. Willian Oscar Gibson, Jr., May 8, 1948 (div.); children—Linda Nadine Gibson Phillips, George William. Student U. Mo., 1947-48. Cert. profl. sec. Sec. to gen. mgr. Gen. Telephone Co. of Mid-West, Columbia, 1948-63; devel., owner, mgr. Lee Gibson Business Service, Columbia, 1963-84; owner, mgr. Office Plaza I Service Center, Columbia, 1984; exec. dir. Boone County Med. Soc., Columbia, 1984—; cons., tchr. adult edn. Chmn. fund raising Columbia Coll.; chmn. Bus. License Commn. City of Columbia. Mem. Profl. Assn. Secretarial Services, Columbia Northside Bus. Assn. (pres.), Profl. Secretaries Assn. (pres. chpt.), Columbia C. of C. (dir.). Republican. Lutheran. Club: Mo. State Genealogical Assn. (bd. dirs.). Office: 2100 I-70 Dr SW PO Box 658 Columbia MO 65205

GIBSON, ROBERT ALLEN, lawyer, real estate title insurance agent, construction company executive; b. Lancaster, Ky., Sept. 22, 1935; s. Russell Allen and Ora Lee (Bowlin) G.; m. Susan Posival (div.); children—Roger Allen, Judith Lee; m. Margaret Ann Caroselli. Student Norwood Inst. Tech.; cert. in mech. engring. Ohio Mech. Inst.; M.E., B.A., B.S.D., U. Cin., J.D., Chase Coll. Law. Bar: Ohio 1981, Ky. 1981, Fla. 1982. Asst. mgr. field services Cin. Milacron, 1964-70, mgr. field services, 1970-74, mgr. products safety and liability, 1974-81; chief exec. officer, chmn. Insured Land Title Agy., Cin., 1978—, also dir.; now ptnr. Caroselli & Gibson, Cin.; chief exec. officer Rob-Rae Constrn., Inc., Cin., 1982—, also dir.; chmn., dir. Robert A. Gibson Co., L.P.A., 1981—. Past pres. Ohio Mobile Home and Recreational Vehicle Assn., Cin. Milacron Winter Tennis League, Cin. Milacron Chess Club. Mem. Am. Lawyers Assn., ABA, Cin. Bar Assn. (environ. law com., products liability com.), Assn. Trial Lawyers Am., Ohio Land Title Assn. Republican. Home: 10558 Tanager Hills Dr Cincinnati OH 45249 Office: Caroselli & Gibson 125 E Court St Suite 1002 Cincinnati OH 45202

GIBSON, ROBERT PETER, hospital administrator; b. Pawtucket, R.I., Sept. 6, 1945; s. Foster Forrest and Laura Susan (Zakowski) G.; m. Jo Anne Passaggio, Jan. 6, 1968; children—Peter Scott, Amy Elizabeth, Matthew Patrick. B.A., U. Conn., 1967; M.H.A., Xavier U., 1975. Resident St. Francis Hosp., Cin., 1974-75; pres., adminstr. Fort Wayne State Hosp. and Tng. Center (Ind.), after 1975, now asst. supt. adminstr. Chmn. adult edn. Am. Cancer Soc.; bd. dirs. Health Systems Agy. Served to capt. USAF, 1967-72. Decorated Air Medals with clusters (4). Recipient Boss of Yr. award Am. Bus. Women's Assn., 1982. Mem. Am. Coll. Hosp. Adminstrs., Hosp. Fin. Mgmt. Assn., Am. Pub. Health Assn. Roman Catholic. Clubs: Kiwanis, Elks (Fort Wayne). Author: Relocation of Long Term Care Facility, microfilm, 1975. Home: 9108 Seawind Pl Fort Wayne IN 46804 Office: 4900 St Joe Rd Fort Wayne IN 46815

GIBSON, ROBERT RODNEY, finance executive, bank consultant; b. Athens, Ohio, Feb. 6, 1945; s. Robert Bradbury and Frances (Gilkey) G.; m. Anne Reed, Aug. 22, 1970; 1 child, Robin Elise. Student Ohio U., 1963-65, Franklin U., 1978. Regional dir. St. Jude Children's Hosp., Memphis, 1972-76; with Graham Ford Leasing, Columbus, Ohio, 1976-78; dir. leasing services Hills Leasing, Columbus, 1978-81; pres., founder Gibson Leasing Corp., Columbus, 1981—, BancNet Corp., Columbus, 1984—; bank cons. Deacon Overbrook Presbyterian Ch., Columbus, 1981-84. Served with USN, 1965-69. Recipient meritorious service award City of Columbus Div. Fire, 1978. Mem. Catrala, Central Ohio Sch. Diving (instr.). Republican. Avocations: scuba diving; power boating. Home: 4210 Reed Rd Upper Arlington OH 43220

GIBSON, WALTER SAMUEL, art history educator; b. Columbus, Ohio, Mar. 31, 1932; s. Walter Samuel and Grace Buena (Wheeler) G.; m. Sarah Ann Scott, Dec. 16, 1972. B.F.A. cum laude, Ohio State U., 1957, M.A., 1960; Ph.D., Harvard U., 1969. Asst. prof. Case Western Res. U., Cleve., 1966-71, assoc. prof., 1971-78, acting chmn., 1970-71, chmn., 1971-79, Andrew W. Mellon prof. humanities, 1978—. Served with U.S. Army, 1952-54. Fulbright scholar, 1960-61, 84; fellow Harvard U., 1964-66; Guggenheim fellow, 1978; grantee: NEH, Samuel H. Kress Found., Am. Council Learned Socs., 1975. Mem. Coll. Art Assn. Am., Internat. Ctr. Medieval Art, Medieval Acad. Am., Renaissance Soc. Am., Midwest Art History Soc., Historians of Netherlandish Art. Author: Hieronymus Bosch, 1973, German edit., 1974, Dutch edit., 1974; The Paintings of Cornelis Engebrechtsz, 1977; Bruegel, 1977, Dutch edit., 1977; Hieronymus Bosch: An Annotated Bibliography, 1983; contbr. numerous articles on art history to profl. jours. Office: Dept Art Mather House Case Western Res U Cleveland OH 44106

GIBSON, WILLIAM CHARLES, county government parks and recreation official; b. Midland, Mich., July 26, 1944; s. Harold David Gibson and Erma Elizabeth (Emmrich) Westfall; m. Karen Marie Jarmol, Oct. 5, 1974. Student Mich. Technol. U., 1962-63, U. Mich., 1963-65; B.S. with high honors, Mich. State U., 1972. Registered parks and recreation profl., Mich. Dir. parks and recreation City of Mason, Mich., 1972-74; supt. parks County of Midland, Midland, 1974-78, dept. dir. parks and recreation, 1978-83, dir. parks and recreation, 1983—. Chmn., County of Midland Employees Safety Com., 1983, 84; mem. Midland Found., 1984—, chmn. coms., 1985. Mich. Recreation and Parks Assn. scholar, 1971, 72. Mem. Nat. Recreation and Park Assn., Mich. Assn. County Park and Recreation Ofcls., Mich. Recreation and Park Assn. (park resources com. 1980—, chmn. 1982-83, bd. dirs. 1982-83, long range planning com. 1983—), Midland Area C. of C., Mich. State U. Coll. Agr. and Natural Resources Alumni Assn. (bd. dirs. 1985—), Alpha Zeta. Presbyterian. Avocations: golf; scuba diving; tennis; listening to music; woodworking. Home: 3712 Sharon Rd Midland MI 48640 Office: Midland County Dept County Devel 1270 James Savage Rd Midland MI 48640

GIDWITZ, RALPH W., ladder manufacturing company executive; b. Chgo., Feb. 11, 1936; s. Joseph Leon and Emily Rose (Klein) G.; separated; children—Teri Lynne, Linda Beth. A.A., Menlo Coll., 1955; B.A., Knox Coll., 1958; M.B.A., U. Chgo., 1974. Sales rep. Allied Corrugated Container Co., Detroit, 1961-65; staff mfg. asst. folding carton div. Consol. Packaging Corp., Chgo., 1965-66, asst. market research mgr., 1966-67, project mgr., 1967-69, buyer, 1969-71, purchasing agt., 1971-72, v.p. purchasing and transp., 1972-77; pres. Coster Corp., Chgo., 1974—, also dir.; sec., dir. ARESCO Mgmt., S.A., Nassau, Bahamas, 1973—; v.p., dir. Cam-AM Ltd., Curacao, Orion Travel Inc., 1976-84; pres., chief exec. officer Terlin Corp., 1978—; Rich Ladder Co., Carrollton, Ky., 1978-84; chmn. bd., chief exec. officer, 1984—; dir. Continental Materials Corp.; v.p., dir. LOM Holdings, Inc., 1984—; v.p., treas., stats. chmn. Am. Ladder Inst., 1982-84. Bd. dirs. Young People's div. Allied Jewish Campaign, 1962-65, v.p., 1964-65; bd. dirs. Young People's div. Jewish United Fund, Chgo., 1967-73, gen. campaign chmn. dir., 1970-71, pres. div., 1971-72, mem. steering com., 1976—; mem. pres.'s council Menlo Coll., Menlo Park, Calif., 1974-76; bd. dirs. Jewish Fedn. Met. Chgo., 1970-71, Jewish United Fund, Chgo., 1970-72. Served with U.S. Army, 1959-61. Mem. Chgo. Assn. Commerce and Industry, Am. Mgmt. Assn. Republican. Jewish. Clubs: Standard (Chgo.); Birchwood (Highland Park, Ill.). Office: Terlin Corp 325 N Wells St 3d Floor Chicago IL 60610

GIELEN, MICHAEL ANDREAS, conductor; b. Dresden, Germany, July 20, 1927; s. Josef and Rose (Steuermann) G.; student U. Dresden, 1936, U. Berlin, 1937, U. Vienna, 1940, Buenos Aires U., 1950; m. Helga Augsten, May 20, 1957; children—Claudia, Lucas. Coach, Teatro Colón, Buenos Aires, 1947-50; condr. Vienna State Opera, 1950-60, Stockholm Royal Opera, 1960-65; free lance condr., Cologne, Germany, 1965-68; mus. dir. Belgian Nat. Orch. Brussels, 1969-73; chief condr. Netherlands Opera, 1973-75; music dir., gen. mgr. Frankfurt (Germany) Opera House, 1977—; music dir. Cin. Symphony Orch., 1980—; guest condr. Washington Nat. Symphony, Chgo. Symphony, Pitts. Symphony, Minn. Orch., Detroit Symphony, N.Y. Philharm., Cleve. Orch. Composer: 4 Gedichte von Stefan George, 1958, Variations for 40 Instruments, 1959, Un dia Sobresale, 1963, die glocken sind auf falscher spur, 1969; Mitbestimmunes Modell, 1974; String Quartet, 1983. Office: Cin Symphony Orch 1241 Elm St Cincinnati OH 45210

GIER, RONALD, dental educator, dentist; b. Bloomington, Ind., Jan. 8, 1935; s. Herschel T. Gier and Wilma (Hobson) Alexander; m. Marjorie J. Matthews, Aug. 1948 (div. Nov. 1979); m. Patricia J., Dec. 23, 1982; children—Ronald E., Randall E., Richard E., Duane W., Kristi. B.S., Kans. State U., 1956; D.M.D., Washington U., St. Louis, 1959; M.S.D., Ind. U.-Indpls., 1967. Gen. practice dentistry, Manhattan, Kans., 1961-65, Bel Air Profl. Assocs., Overland Park, Kans., 1970—; prof., chmn. dept. oral diagnosis U. Mo.-Kansas City, 1967—. Author: (with others) Physical Evaluation of the Dental Patient, 1982. Served to capt. USNR, 1959—. Mem. Am. Acad. Oral Pathology, ADA, Orgn. Tchrs. Oral Diagnosis (pres. 1971-72), Internat. Assn. Dental Research, Am. Acad. Forensic Scis. Republican. Home: 8927 Sagamore Leawood KS 66206 Office: Sch Dentistry U Mo-Kansas City 650 E 25th St Kansas City MO 64108

GIERING, RICHARD HERBERT, computerized information systems co. exec.; b. Emmaus, Pa., Nov. 27, 1929; s. Harold Augustus and Marguerite (Bruder) G.; B.S. in Engring. and Math., U. Ariz., 1962; m. Carol Alice Scott, Aug. 16, 1959; children—Richard Herbert, Scott K. Joined U.S. Army, 1947, commd. 2d lt., 1963, advanced through grades to capt., 1965; sect. chief data processing Def. Intelligence Agy., Washington, 1965-67; ret., 1967; with Data Corp. (name changed to Mead Tech. Labs. 1968), Dayton, Ohio, 1967-77, v.p. tech. ops., 1970-71, dir. info. systems, 1971-77; pres., chief exec. officer DG Assos., Inc., 1974—; mng. partner Infotex Assos., 1977—; instr. data processing U. Ariz., Tucson, 1962-63. Mem. Assn. Computing Machinery, Am. Soc. Info. Scis. Inventor data/central (used to establish electronic newspaper libraries). Office: 1476 Route 725 Dayton OH 45459 Home: 5460 Royalwood St Box 2151 Dayton OH 45429

GIERKE, CRAIG SHERMAN, retail company executive; b. Escanaba, Mich., July 21, 1950; s. Sherman Gordon and Victoria Eulalia (Mroczkowski) G. B.A., Mich. Technol. U., Houghton, 1972. Dist. mgr. Am. Family Ins. Co., Escanaba, 1972-74; owner, founder G&R Contracting, Escanaba, 1974-75; mgr. retail store Radio Shack div. Tandy Corp., Ft. Worth, 1975-81, store group leader N.E. Wis. and Upper Mich., Escanaba, 1981—. Chmn. bd. govs. William Bonifas Fine Arts Center, 1979-81; mem. City of Escanaba Planning Commn., 1981—, chmn., 1984—; sec. Delta County Republican Com., 1978, treas., 1979; chmn. Delta County Milliken Re-election Com., 1978; chmn. 11th Congl. Dist. Reagen for Pres. Com., 1980; del. Rep. Nat. Conv., 1980. Recipient Achievement award City of Escanaba, 1981; Community Service Recognition award Delta County 4H Clubs. Roman Catholic. Lodges: Kiwanis (pres. 1983-84), Elks. Home: 929 Washington Ave Escanaba MI 49829 Office: 1019 Ludington St Escanaba MI 49829

GIERTZ, ROBERT WILLIAM, heavy equipment manufacturing company executive; b. Clifton, Ill., Mar. 24, 1925; s. William Chris and Emma Louise (Meyer) G.; B.S., U. Ill., 1950; postgrad. Mass. Inst. Tech., 1964; m. Vera Rosalie Herrmann, Nov. 30, 1946; children—Deborah Giertz Staack, Nancy Giertz Natvig, Norman, James, Julie Giertz Elias. Mech. engr. John Deere Waterloo Tractor Works of Deere & Co., Waterloo, Iowa, 1950-64, chief engr., 1964-67, gen. mgr., 1967-74, dir. mfg., Moline, Ill., 1974—; dir. Midwest Energy Co., Iowa Pub. Service Co., Nat. Bank of Waterloo, Iowa Nat. Bankshares Corp. Mem. Dist. Judicial Nominating Commn., 1969-75; mem. Waterloo Indsl. Devel. Assn., 1968-75; past mem. United Services of Black Hawk County. Trustee, Schoitz Meml. Hosp., 1968-74, Mt. Mercy Coll., Cedar Rapids, Iowa, 1979-82; bd. govs. Iowa Coll. Found., vice chmn., 1976, chmn., 1977; bd. govs. U. No. Iowa Found., pres. 1973-75; past dir. Waterloo Civic Found.; bd. dirs. Quad City World Affairs Council, pres., 1980-81. Served with USAF, 1946-47. Registered profl. engr., Ill. Mem. Soc. Automotive Engrs., Am. Soc. Agrl. Engrs., Am. Mgmt. Assn. Republican. Lutheran. Clubs: Crow Valley Golf, Symposium. Home: 2410 Eagle Circle Bettendorf IA 52722 Office: Deere & Co John Deere Rd Moline IL

GIERUT, CASIMIR FRANK, priest, researcher on social issues; b. Chgo., Feb. 25, 1919; s. John and Catherine (Falat) G. A.A.S., Lewis and Clark Coll., 1978; A.B. in Philosophy, Mt. Mary's Coll., Orchard Lake, Mich., 1944; B.A., So. Ill. U., 1976. Ordained priest Roman Catholic Ch., 1949; St. Patrick's Ch., Alton, Ill., 1949-54; asst. pastor Cathedral, Springfield, Ill., 1954-59, pastor St. Mary's Cath. Ch., Bunker Hill, Ill., 1959—; chmn. Nat. Com. Repeal for the Fed. Res. Act, Bunker Hill, 1972—, Pres. Citizens for Social Justice in Taxation, Bunker Hill. Author: Taxpayer's Message to Congress-Repeal the Federal Reserve Act-The Pandora's Box of Criminal Acts, 1984. Club: Legislative Research Assocs. Office: Nat Com Repeal Fed Res Act 300 S Putnam St Bunker Hill IL 62014

GIES, CAROL JEAN, public relations counselor; b. Detroit, Jan. 20, 1947; d. Stanley P. and Jean R. Homer; m. Craig M. Gies, Mar. 31, 1966; children—Jeffrey, Maureen. B.S., Wayne State U., 1971, M.A., 1972; M.B.A., Mich. State U., 1985. Pub. relations dir. Met. Detroit Conv. and Visitors Bur., 1973-78, v.p. civic affairs, 1979; exec. dir. host com. Republican Nat. Conv., 1980; exec. dir. Mich. Host Com. for Super Bowl XVI, 1982; sr. v.p. Anthony M. Franco, Inc., Detroit, 1982—. Communications chmn. United Found.; bd. dirs. Mich. Thanksgiving Day Parade Found. Recipient Gold Quill, Internat. Assn. Bus. Communicators, 1975; Mich. Embassy of Tourism award; named Woman of Wayne Headliner, 1980. Mem. Pub. Relations Soc. of Am. (Nat. Silver Anvil award, 3 dist. awards), Women in Communications (Clarion award). Roman Catholic. Office: 400 Renaissance Ctr Suite 600 Detroit MI 48243

GIFFEN, DANIEL H., lawyer; b. Zanesville, Ohio, Feb. 11, 1938; s. Harris MacArtor and Louise (Crawford) G.; A.B., Coll. William and Mary, 1960; M.A. in History of Art, U. Pa., 1963; Ph.D. in Am. Civilization, 1967; J.D., Case Western Res. U., 1973; m. Jane Louise Cayford, Nov. 23, 1963 (div. 1970); children—Sarah Louise, Thomas Harris; m. 2d, Linda S. Eastin, Aug. 19, 1972. Corp. asst. Lippincott Library, U. Pa., Phila., 1961-63; asso. curator La. State Mus., 1963-64; dir. N.H. Hist. Soc., Concord, 1964-69, also sec.; asst. dir. Arents Research Library, State U. N.Y., Syracuse, 1969-70; v.p. Village Press Publs., Inc., Concord, 1969-74; editor Walter H. Drane Co., Cleve., 1974-76; individual practice law, Cleve., asst. prof. Cleve. State U., 1976-79; asst. prof. Kent State U., 1980—, asst. dir. Sch. Family and Consumer Studies, 1982—. Vice pres. N.H. Antiquarian Soc. 1966-68, lectr. 1968; dir. Assn. Hist. Socs. N.H. 1967; mem. faculty Monadock (N.H.) Community Coll., 1968-69; life mem. pres.'s council Coll. William and Mary. Mem. Am., Ohio, Cleve. bar assns., Cleve. Restoration Soc., Am. Assn. Museums, Am. Assn. State and Local Historians, Nat. Trust, Soc. Am. Archivists, Soc. Archtl. Historians, Rushlight Club, Pewter Collectors Club. Author: Adventures in Vermont, 1969; Adventures in Maine, 1970; The New Hampshire Colony, 1970. Editor: Hist. N.H. mag. Contbr. profl. jours. Home: 2067 Ridgewood Rd Fairlawn Heights OH 44313 Office: Nixson Hall Kent State U Kent OH 44242

GIFFEY, DONALD F., agricultural cooperative executive. Pres., chief operating officer, chmn., dir. Harvest States Cooperatives, St. Paul, Minn. Office: Harvest States Cooperatives 1667 N Snelling Ave Saint Paul MN 55165*

GIGLEY, DAVID HARRY, business and office educator; b. Cin., May 21, 1946; s. John W. and Ruth B. (Ruehlwein) G.; m. Nancy Herriott, June 28, 1969; children—Christopher David, Gretchen, Meredith, Andrew David. B.S., U. Cin., 1969, M.Ed., 1971, A.B.D., 1982. Cert. tchr., Ohio. Tchr., coach Oak Hills Sch. Dist., Cin., 1969-71; asst. prof. secretarial sci. Rappahannock Community Coll., Glenns, Va., 1971-74; instr. secretarial tech. Prince George's Community Coll., Largo, Md., 1974-75; asst. prof. secretarial tech. No. Mont. Coll., Havre, 1975-76; realtor Flynn Realty, Havre, 1976-77; coordinator secretarial tech. Ohio U., Chillicothe, 1977—. Sec. Great Seal Recreational Assn., 1981—, Chillicothe City Little League, 1977—. Mem. Nat. Bus. Edn. Assn., Ohio Bus. Tchrs. Assn., Am. Vocat. Assn., Ohio Vocat. Assn., Delta Pi Epsilon. Lodge: Kiwanis (Chillicothe).

GILBERT, CLARENCE HARVEY, JR., educational administrator; b. San Diego, Mar. 3, 1947; s. Clarence Harvey and Ardith Corine (King) G.; m. Kathryn Jeanne Hogue, June 14, 1969 (div. Mar. 1985); children—Cori, Chris, Keri. A.A., Pratt Community Coll., 1967; B.A. in English and Journalism, Fort Hays State U., 1970; M.S. in Ednl. Adminstrn., Emporia State U., 1981; post grad. Okla. State U., 1984. Tchr. English and journalism, coach Iola High Sch., Kans., 1972-73; tchr. journalism, coach Hutchinson High Sch., Kans., 1973-78; tchr. English, coach F.L. Schlagle High Sch., Kansas City, Kans., 1978-81; bldg. prin. W. Elk Jr. Sr. High Sch., Howard, Kans., 1981-82, Udall Jr.-Sr. High Sch., Kans., 1983—; bldg. prin., acting supt. Unified Sch. Dest. 463, Udall, Kans., 1984-85; radio commentator Sta. KWHK, Hutchinson, Kans.,

1976-78. Author: (with others) Raymond Berry's Complete Guide to Coaching Pass Receivers, 1982; Raymond Berry's Complete Guide for Pass Receivers, 1982. Mem. Nat. Assn. Secondary Sch Prins., Kans. Assn. Secondary Sch. Prins., Assn. Supervision and Curriculum Devel., Kans. Assn. Sch. Adminstrs. Avocations: reading; writing; sports participation. Home: 301 S Blankenship Rd Apt 9 Udall KS 67146 Office: Udall High Sch 301 W 4th Udall KS 67146

GILBERT, ENID, pathologist, pathology and pediatrics educator; b. Sydney, New South Wales, Australia, May 31, 1927; came to U.S., 1952, naturalized, 1975; d. Christian Henry and Mabel (Milne) Fischer; m. James Bryson Gilbert, Aug. 12, 1954; children—Mary M., Elizabeth A., James C. (dec.), Jennifer E., Rebecca D. M.B.B.S., U. Sydney, 1950, M.D., 1983. Diplomate Am. Bd. Pediatrics, Am. Bd. Clin. Pathology, Am. Bd. Anat. Pathology. Intern, Children's Hosp., Boston; resident Children's Hosp., Phila., Children's Hosp., Washington, Brackenridge Hosp., Austin, Tex.; asst. prof. U. W.Va., 1963-67, assoc. prof., 1967-70; assoc. prof. pathology and pediatrics U. Wis.-Madison, 1970-71, prof., 1971—, dir. pediatric pathology, 1970—, dir. surg. pathology, 1975—. Author: Introduction to Pathology, 1978; also numerous chpts., articles. NIH grantee, 1978—. Mem. Am. Soc. Clin. Pathology, Soc. Pediatric Pathology, Internat. Acad. Pathology, Teratology Soc., Cardiovascular Soc. S.Am. (hon.). Republican. Episcopalian. Home: 6413 Landfall Dr Madison WI 53705 Office: U Wis Clin Sci Ctr E5/326 Madison WI 53792

GILBERT, KATHRYN A., association administrator; b. Detroit, Jan. 2, 1939; d. John Anthony and Lucille Marie (Migan) Schneider; div.; children—Peter, David, Robert, Richard. B.B.A., U. Detroit, 1981. Exec. dir. fin. Constrn. Assn. Mich., Detroit, 1976-82, mgr. edn., 1983; exec. dir. Oak County Bar Assn., Pontiac, Mich., 1984—. Mem. Am. Soc. Assn. Execs. (cert.), Mich. Soc. Asn. Execs. (bd. dirs. 1984—), Assn. Execs. Metro Detroit (pres. 1983-84, bd. dirs. 1978-84), Nat. Assn. Bar Execs. Office: Oakland County Bar Assn 1200 N Telegraph Suite 532 Pontiac MI 48053

GILBERT, PHYLLIS JO, dental assisting educator, consultant; b. Mpls., Jan. 25, 1944; d. Philip Rod and Josephine Elsie (Korinek) Wicklund; m. Richard Earl Gilbert, Sept. 17, 1966; children—Scott Richard, Nicole Susan. Cert. dental assisting, U. Minn., 1963; B.S. cum laude in Dental Assisting Edn., 1981. Cert. Dental Assisting Nat. Bd.; registered dental asst., Minn. Office dental asst., mgr. Ralph R. Nielson, Mpls., 1963-71; dental assisting instr. North Suburban Hennepin County Vocat. Sch., Mpls., 1971-73, Normandale Community Coll., Mpls., 1976-78; cons. Park Dental Health Ctrs. and freelance dental assisting instr., Mpls., 1981—; dir. Mpls. Vocat. Tech. Inst., China-U.S. Sci. Exchanges. Leader 1st dental assts. del. to China, 1982, 2d del., 1984. Mem. Mpls. Dental Soc., Minn. Dental Assts. Assn. (pres. 1984-86, achievement award 1981, 84), Am. Dental Assts. Assn. (outstanding article, most valuable state mem. 1982), Minn. Educators Dental Assts., Am. Needlepoint Guild, Minn. Alumni Club. Republican. Lutheran. Lodge: Order Eastern Star. Author curriculum for Mpls. Tech. Inst., 1982; contbr. articles to profl. jours. Home and Office: 3309 W 55th St Edina MN 55410

GILBERT, VINCENT NEWTON, publisher; b. Chgo., Dec. 7, 1955; s. Herman Cromwell and Ivy Newton (McAlpine) G.; m. Denise Sharon Rawlings, Aug. 15, 1982; 1 child, Diona Vinise. B.A. in Polit. Sci., Ind. U., 1978; J.D., John Marshall Law Sch., 1983. Dir., Maple Park Strong Ctr., Chgo., 1976; terr. mgr. Carnation Co., Chgo., 1978-81; sales dir. Path Press, Chgo., 1982—; exec. v.p. CDM Transp. Service, Inc., Chgo., 1984—. Speech writer Savage for Alderman campaign, Chgo., 1983; area coordinator Savage for Congress campaign, Chgo., 1982, Washington for Mayor campaign, Chgo., 1983. Mem. Student Bar Assn., Black Am. Law Student Assn. Methodist. Office: CDM Transp Services Inc 1402 W 103d St Chicago IL 60643

GILBERT, WILLIAM ALEX, manufacturing company executive; b. Granville, N.Y., Feb. 14, 1944; s. Nicholas and Helen (Zidovsky) G.; m. Helen Rose Reichl, Sept. 30, 1966; 1 son, Eric Nicholas. B.S., Boston Coll., 1966; M.B.A., Columbia U., 1969. Sales rep. Purex Corp., New Haven, 1966-67; bus. research analyst Monsanto Co., St. Louis, 1969-70; pres. Clean City Square Inc., St. Louis, 1970—, Upbeat, Inc., St. Louis, 1982—; dir. Boatmen's Bank of St. Louis County, St. Louis. Patentee in field. Trustee Forsyth Sch., St. Louis, 1984. Served with U.S. Army, 1967. Arthur D. Little, Inc. fellow, 1969. Mem. Am. Assn. Indsl. Mgmt., Nat. Exec. Council-Broadmoor. Home: 609 S Warson Rd Ladue MO 63124 Office: Clean City Squares Inc 315 W Pacific St Saint Louis MO 63119

GILBERT, WILLIAM CECIL, medical equipment company executive; b. Cloverport, Ky., May 17, 1945; s. William Earl and Margaret (Weatherholt) G.; B.A., Wayne State U., 1971; cert. in respiratory therapy U. Chgo., 1972; m. Joan Esche, Dec. 20, 1969; children—Kristopher, Nickolas. Supr. respiratory therapy Detroit Osteo. Hosp., 1966-71; dir. respiratory care service Mercy Hosp., Cadillac, Mich., 1971-75; chief exec. officer Pneumatology Assocs., Inc., Cadillac, 1975—; mem. Respiratory Therapy Nat. Bd., 1972—. Pres. N.W. chpt. Mich. Lung Assn., 1972, trustee, 1975—. Served with USAF, 1963-67. Registered respiratory therapist; cert. respiratory therapy technician. Mem. Am. Assn. Respiratory Therapy, Mich. Soc. Respiratory Therapy, Nat. Assn. Med. Equipment Suppliers. Republican. Episcopalian. Home: 210 Stimson St Cadillac MI 49601 Office: PO Box 283 Stimson St Cadillac MI 49601

GILBO, GERY OCTAVIUS, clinical therapist; b. Chgo., Aug. 4, 1950; s. James O. and Bette (Dennie) G.; B.A., Quincy Coll., 1972; M.A., Roosevelt U., 1976. Cert. Neuro-linguistic programming, cert. master programmer. Orderly, Little Co. of Mary Hosp., Evergreen Park, Ill., 1974-75, mental health technician/intern, 1975-77; assoc., cons. Palos Center for Individual and Family Counseling, Palos Heights, Ill., 1975-77; sr. staff mem., clin. coordinator Palos Neuropsychiatric Inst., Inc., Palos Heights, 1977—. Mem. Am. Psychol. Assn. (assoc.), Coordinating Council for Handicapped Children. Home: 14505 Central Ct Apt G2 Oak Forest IL 60452 Office: Palos Neuropsychiatric Institute Inc 7600 W College Dr Palos Heights IL 60463

GILBOA, NETTA, publishing company representative, sex researcher, lectr.; b. Israel, Jan. 5, 1958; came to U.S., 1960; d. Itzchak and Carolyn (Chiterer) G. B.A. in Journalism, SUNY-New Paltz, 1979; M.S. in Advt., Northwestern U., 1980, M.S. in Sociology, 1985. Instr. social scis. div. Coll. of Lake County, Grayslake, Ill., 1984-85; instr. dept. criminal justice Northeastern Ill. U., 1984-85; midwest sales rep. Wadsworth Inc., 1985—; lectr. on pornography to chs., women's groups, high schs. and profl. assns. in U.S. and Can. Editor: (slideshow) I Know It When I See It: Pornography, Eroticean and Sexual Deviance, 1978—. Pub. relations intern Planned Parenthood, New Paltz, 1978; advocate Women's Rape Crisis Ctr., New Paltz, 1979; mem. rape task force NOW, Evanston, 1979-80. Mem. Soc. Sci. Study of Sex, Popular Culture Assn., Am. Sociol. Assn., Women's Inst. for Freedom of the Press (assoc.), Soc. Study Social Problems. Home and Office: 2520 N Lincoln Ave #120 Chicago IL 60614

GILCHREST, THORNTON CHARLES, association executive; b. Evanston, Ill., Sept. 1, 1931; s. Charles Jewitt and Patricia (Thornton) Thornton; m. Barbara D. Dibbern, June 8, 1952; children—Margaret Mary Gilchrest Dulay, James Thornton. B.S., U. Ill., 1953. Cert. tchr. Tchr. pub. high sch., West Chicago, Ill., 1957; exec. dir. Plumbing-Heating-Cooling Bur., Chgo., 1958-64; asst. to pres. A.Y. McDonald Mfg., Dubuque, Iowa, 1964-68; exec. dir. Am. Supply Assn., Chgo., 1968-77, exec. v.p., 1977-82; exec. v.p. Nat. Safety Council, Chgo., 1982-83, pres., 1983—. Served with USN, 1953-55. Mem. Am. Soc. Assn. Execs., Chgo. Soc. Assn. Execs. Methodist. Club: University (Chgo.). Office: Nat Safety Council 444 N Michigan Ave Chicago IL 60611

GILDERSLEEVE, ROBERT EUGENE, medical center executive; b. Alton, Ill., Apr. 11, 1947; s. Alfred Lee and Mary Jane Gildersleeve; m. Darlene Gilyon; children—Kimberly, Mark, Desiree. B.S., So. Ill. U.-Edwardsville, 1974, M.A., 1976. Budget/cost acct. Jewish Hosp. St. Louis, 1974-77; controller St. Francis Hosp., Marceline, Mo., 1977-80; dir. fin. Audrain Med. Center, Mexico, Mo., 1980—. Treas., Disabled Handi-Shop of Mexico. Served to capt. AUS, 1967-71. Mem. Hosp. Fin. Mgmt. Assn. Republican. Roman Catholic. Club: Mexico Country. Home: 1788 Martin Pl Mexico MO 65265 Office: 620 E Monroe St Mexico MO 65265

GILES, CONRAD LESLIE, ophthalmic surgeon; b. N.Y.C., July 14, 1934; s. Irving Samuel Giles and Victoria Ampole; m. Marilyn Toby Schwartz, June 20, 1955 (div. 1978); children—Keith Martin, Suzanne Speer, Kevin William, Brian Alan; m. Lynda Fern Schenk, Nov. 26, 1978; stepchildren—Jared Schenk, Jamie Schenk. M.D., U. Mich., 1957, M.S., 1961. Diplomate Am. Bd. Ophthalmology. Clin. assoc. NIH, Bethesda, Md., 1961-63; clin. asst. prof. Wayne State U. Sch. Medicine, Detroit, 1965-72, clin. assoc. prof. ophthalmology, 1973—. Contbr. articles to med. jours. Vice Pres. Jewish Welfare Fedn., Detroit, 1981—. Fellow Am. Acad. Ophthalmology; mem. AMA, Mich. State Ophthal. Soc. Avocations: golf; tennis. Home: 6300 Westmoor St Birmingham MI 48010 Office: 4400 Town Ctr Southfield MI 48075

GILES, HOMER WAYNE, lawyer; b. Noble, Ohio, Nov. 9, 1919; s. Edwin Jay and Nola Blanche (Tillison) G.; A.B., Adelbert Coll., 1940; LL.B., Western Res. Law Sch., 1943, LL.M., 1959; m. Zola Ione Parke, Sept. 8, 1948; children—Jay, Janice, Keith, Tim, Gregory. Admitted to Ohio bar, 1943; mem. firm Davis & Young, Cleve., 1942-43, William I. Moon, Port Clinton, 1946-48; pres. Strabley Baking Co., Cleve., 1948-53; v.p. French Baking Co., Cleve., 1953-55; law clk. 8th Dist. Court Appeals, Cleve., 1955-58; partner Kuth & Giles, law firm 1958-68, Walter, Haverfield, Buescher & Chockley, 1968—; pres. Clinton Franklin Realty Co., Cleve., 1958—, Concepts Devel., Inc., 1980—; sec. Holiday Designs, Inc., Sebring, Ohio, 1964-82. Trustee, Teamster Local 52 Health and Welfare Fund, 1950-53; mem. Bakers Negotiating Exec. Com., 1951-53; troop com. chmn. Skyline council Boy Scouts Am., 1961-63. Trustee, Hiram House Camp, Florence Crittenton Home, 1965; chmn. bd. trustees Am. Econ. Found., 1973-80, chmn. exec. com., 1973-80. Served with AUS, 1943-46; ETO. Mem. ABA, World Law Assn. (founding), Am. Arbitration Assn. (nat. panel arbitrators), Com. on Econ. Reform and Edn. (life mem.), dir., sec. Inst. on Money and Inflation, Speakers Bur. Cleve. Sch. Levy, Citizens League (nationalities service com. 1965), Phils. Soc., Cleve. Hist. Soc., Delta Tau Delta, Delta Theta Phi. Unitarian (trustee 1965-68). Clubs: Cleveland Skating, Harvard Business. Editor: Banks Baldwin Ohio Legal Forms, 1962. Contbr. articles to profl. publs. Home: 2588 S Green Rd University Heights OH 44122 Office: 1215 Terminal Tower Cleveland OH 44113

GILFERT, JAMES CLARE, engineering educator, consultant; b. Tamaqua, Pa., June 21, 1927; s. Charles A. and Leah M. (Bensinger) G.; m. Sara Louise McCalmont, June 23, 1949; children—Susan, Ted, Charles. B.S., Antioch Coll., 1950; M.Sc., Ohio State U., 1951, Ph.D., 1957. Registered profl. engr., Ohio. Assoc. prof. dept. elec. engring. Ohio State U., 1957-67; cons., tech. specialist N.Am. Rockwell, 1961-67; faculty dept. elec. engring. Ohio U., Athens, 1967—, prof. elec. engring., 1969—; research contractor to Ohio Dept. Transp., 1975—; cons. Nat. Semiconductor Corp., 1977-78, Static Handling, Inc., 1982—; founder Athens Tech. Specialists, 1982—; vis. prof. Chubu Inst. Tech., Japan, 1973, 80. Served with USNR, 1945-46. Kettering fellow, 1950-51; Am. Council Edn. fellow, 1971-72; Japan Soc. Promotion Sci. vis. sr. researcher, 1980. Mem. IEEE, Sigma Xi, Sigma Pi Sigma, Eta Kappa Nu. Contbr. articles in field to profl. jours.; patentee in field. Home: S Canaan Rd Route 6 Box 194 Athens OH 45701 Office: Dept Elec and Computer Engring Ohio U Athens OH 45701

GILL, JOHN RAY, communications company executive; b. Milbank, S.D., Aug. 17, 1953; s. Ray Edwin and Margaret Irene (Steltz) G.; student Dakota Wesleyan U., 1971-73. Bookkeeper, Buford TV Inc., S.D., 1973-77, internal auditor, Tyler, Tex., 1977-80, asst. controller, 1980-81; controller Ind. Cablevision Corp., South Bend. 1981-83; controller CATV div. Buford TV Inc., 1983—. Mem. Data Processing Mgrs. Assn. Democrat. Methodist. Club: Mensa. Home: 4920 Thistle Dr Apt 179 Tyler TX 75703 Office: PO Box 9090 Tyler TX 75711

GILL, LYLE BENNETT, lawyer; b. Lincoln, Nebr., May 11, 1916; s. George Orville and Ruth (Bennett) G.; B.A., Swarthmore Coll., 1937; LL.B., Nebr. Coll. Law, 1940; m. Rita M. Cronin, Aug. 28, 1975; children by previous marriage—George, Valerie, Marguerite. Admitted to Nebr. bar, 1940; practice law, Fremont, 1945—; city atty. Fremont, 1959-62, 67—. Vice chmn. A.R.C., Dodge County, 1953-59. Chmn., Dodge County Republican Com., 1945-51. Served with USNR, 1942-45, 1951-52; lt. comdr. (ret.). Mem. Am., Nebr., Dodge County (pres. 1962) bar assns., Trial Lawyers Assn., V.F.W., Am. Legion. Episcopalian. Home: PO Box 642 Fremont NE 68025 Office: 505 Bldg Fremont NE 68025

GILL, SAFDAR ALI, civil engineer; b. Tharrawaddy, Burma, Nov. 21, 1931; came to U.S., 1965, naturalized, 1972; m. Habib Ali and Fatima Bibi G.; B.Sc. with honors, Govt. Coll. Engring. and Tech., Lahore, Pakistan, 1953; M.S., Northwestern U., 1962, Ph.D., 1970; m. Parveen Hira, Nov. 23, 1963; children—Kamran, Raheela, Aneela, Nabeela. Engr., Govt. of West Pakistan, Lahore, 1953-59, asst. dir. designs and research, 1959-61, 63-65; design engr. Kaiser Engrs., Chgo., 1962; design engr. Greeley & Hansen, Chgo., 1962-63, 65-70; sr. project engr. Soil Testing Services, Northbrook, Ill., 1970-71, asst. chief engr., 1972-75, chief engr., 1975—. Fulbright fellow, 1961-62. Fellow ASCE, Inst. Civil Engrs. (London); mem. Brit. Geotech. Soc., Structural Engrs. Assn. Ill. Muslim. Contbr. articles to profl. jours. Home: 9107 Samoset Skokie IL 60076 Office: 111 Pfingsten Rd Northbrook IL 60062

GILL, STEPHEN JOEL, counseling psychologist; b. Mpls., Feb. 2, 1947; s. Udell J. and Jessie Helen (Steinberg) G.; m. Nanette Sue Goodman, June 14, 1970. B.A., U. Minn., 1969; M.A., Northwestern U., 1974, Ph.D., 1976. Registered psychologist, Ill.; nat. cert. counselor. Mental health worker Chgo. Read Mental Health Ctr., 1970-72; grad. asst. Northwestern U., 1973-75, clin. supr., 1976; lectr. counseling U. Wis.-Milw., 1976-77; asst. prof. U. Mich., Ann Arbor, 1977-84; sr. assoc. Formative Evaluation Research Assocs., Ann Arbor, 1984—, cons., 1982-84. Mem. editorial bd. Jour. Specialists in Group Work, 1983-86. Contbr. articles to profl. jours. Chmn. youth com. Temple Beth Emeth, Ann Arbor, 1980. Grantee U. Mich., 1978, Nat. Inst. Edn., 1981. Mem. Am. Psychol. Assn., Am. Assn. Counseling and Devel., Assn. Specialists in Group Work, Mich. Coll. Personnel Assn. (pres. 1982-83), Mich. Assn. Specialists in Group Work (pres. 1983-84). Office: Formative Evaluation Research Assocs 218 N 4th Ave Ann Arbor MI 48104

GILLAHAN, ROBERT DUGAN, dentistry educator, administrator; b. Lawson, Mo., Sept. 25, 1926; s. William and Georgia (Roper) G.; m. Marjorie Louise Mossman, June 1, 1953; children—Sally, Sara, Susan. D.D.S., U. Mo.-Kansas City, 1952; diploma U. Mex., 1977, U. Paraguay, 1979. Licensed dentist, Kans., Mo. Gen. practice dentistry Lawrence, Kans., 1952-74; assoc. prof. U. Mo., Kansas City, 1974—, chmn. dept. occlusion, co-chmn. Tempro Mandibular Joint Clinic, 1979-85, dir. occlusion, 1979-85; lectr. U. Mex. Ptnrs. Am., Mexico City, Pueblo and Guadalahara, Mex., 1977-78, Paraguay, 1979, 81, 83; cons. Truman Hosp., Kansas City, 1980-85, Mercy Hosp., Kansas City, 1981-85. Author manual on occlusion, 1981. Contbr. articles to profl. jours. Chmn. bd. dirs. Achievement Place for Boys, Lawrence, 1966. Served to pvt. USAF, 1944-46. Mem. Ortho-occlusal Study Club (lectr., sec. 1979-80), 1st Dist. Dental Soc. (pres. 1961), Lawrence Dental Study Club (pres.), Oku (pres. 1982-83, Tchr. of Yr. 1962). Republican. Clubs: Lawrence Country (pres. 1956-57), Kansas U. Downtown Quarterback (pres. 1960-61) (Lawrence), Cosmopolitan (v.p. 1964-65). Avocations: woodworking, fishing, shooting, swimming. Office: U Mo Sch Dentistry 650 E 25th St Kansas City MO 64108

GILLANI, NOOR VELSHI, mechanical engineering and atmospheric sciences educator, researcher; b. Arusha, Tanzania, Mar. 8, 1944; came to U.S., 1963, naturalized, 1976; s. Noormohamed Velshi and Sherbanu (Kassam) G.; m. Mira Teresa Pershe, Aug. 13, 1971; children—Michael, Michelle, Nicole. GCE (Ord. Level), U. Oxford, Eng., 1960; GCE (Adv. Level), U. London, 1963; A.B. cum laude, Harvard U., 1967; M.S. in Mech. Engring., Washington U., St. Louis, 1969, D.Sc., 1974. Vis. scientist Stockholm U., 1977; research assoc. Washington U., St. Louis, 1975-76, research scientist, 1976-77, asst. prof., 1977-80, assoc. prof. 1981-84, prof. mech. engring., 1985—, faculty assoc. CAPITA, 1979—, dir. air quality spl. studies data ctr., 1981—; organizer NATO CCMS 15th internat. tech. meeting on air pollution modeling and its applications, St. Louis, Apr. 1985; presenter papers at tech. meetings. Author 2 chpts. in EPA Critical Assessment Document on Acid Deposition, 1984. Contbr. articles on superconductivity, bioengring., atmospheric scis. and air pollution to nat. and internat. profl. jours. Aga Khan scholar and travel grantee, 1961-63; Harvard Coll. scholar, 1963-67; grad. engring fellow Washington U., 1967-69; research assistantships NIH, EPA, 1971-74; research grantee EPA, 1978-85. Mem. N.Y. Acad. Scis., Air Pollution Control Assn., Am. Meteorol. Soc., Am. Chem. Soc., ASME. Club: Harvard (St. Louis). Avocations: music; racquetball; tennis. Home: 1455 Sycamore Manor Dr Chesterfield MO 63017 Office: Dept Mech Engring Washington U Box 1185 Saint Louis MO 63130

GILLER, RUTH EDNA, business association executive; b. Hampstead, London, Eng., Nov. 5, 1929; d. George and Judith (Gunzburg) Bradlaw; m. Marshall Giller, Jan. 27, 1952; children—Paul Bradlaw, Sara. Student London U., 1946-50. Mgr., Children's Zoo Festival of Britain, 1950-52; mgr. Better Bus. div. Cape Kennedy Area C. of C., 1967-72; mgr. Trade Practice div. Better Bus. Bur., Eastern Pa., Phila., 1972-78; mgr. Better Bus. Bur. Western Mich., Grand Rapids, 1979—. Mem. Scottish Israelite Soc., Soc. Consumer Affairs Profls., West Mich. Women Execs., Women in Communications. Democrat. Jewish. Club: Torch. Office: 620 Trust Bldg Grand Rapids MI 49503

GILLESPIE, ESTHER HOLBROOK, nursing care director; b. Madison County, Ill., Mar. 29, 1934; d. Orville and Ertrie E. (Fallin) Holbrook; m. Frank E. Gillespie, Aug. 26, 1956; children—Frank, Cassandra Funkhouser. Diploma, Alton Meml. Sch. Nursing, 1955; student Lewis and Clark Community Coll., 1975, Florissant Valley Community Coll., 1981, St. Louis U., 1983. R.N., Ill. cert. nurse adminstr. Staff nurse, Alton (Ill.) Mem. Hosp., 1955-56; nurse St. Joseph's Hosp., Alton, 1966-67, head nurse med. unit, 1967-68, inservice instr., 1968, asst. dir. nursing, 1968-78, dir. nursing care, 1978—. Mem. Ill. Soc. for Nurse Adminstrs. Office: St Joseph Hosp 915 E 5th St Alton IL 62002

GILLESPIE, HOUSTON OLIVER, JR., broadcasting executive; b. Nashville, Jan. 13, 1941; s. Houston Oliver and Mary Elizabeth (Haley) G.; m. Patricia Kirkland; children—David, Elizabeth. B.S., Western Ky. U., 1966; M.S., George Williams Coll., 1973. Dir. urban programs Nat. Park Service, U.S. Dept. Interior, Washington, 1965-74; exec. dir. Living History Farms Found., Des Moines, 1974-81; pres., gen. mgr. Quad-Cities Communications Corp., WQAD-TV, Moline, Ill., 1981—; adj. prof. Iowa State U., U. Minn. Pres. Iowa Travel Council; dir. Boy Scouts Am. Council, United Way, Quad Cities. Recipient Superior Performance Award, Nat. Park Service, 1970, Quad Cities Outstanding Citizen Award, Bethany Found., 1982. Mem. Iowa and Ill. Broadcasters Assn., Nat. Assn. Broadcasters, Assn. Broadcast Execs., NEA. Lutheran. Clubs: Minneapolis, Crow Valley Golf, Davenport. Contbr. numerous articles to nat. publs. Home: 901 Mississippi Ave Davenport IA 52803 Office: 3003 Park 16th St Moline IL 61265

GILLESPIE, JAMES LAURENCE, historian; b. Cleve., Apr. 5, 1946; s. James Joseph and Elizabeth A. M. (Koch) G.; A.B., Kenyon Coll., 1968; B.S. in Edn., Kent State U., 1973; M.A. (fellow), Princeton U., 1970, Ph.D. (fellow), 1973. Lectr., St. Mary's Coll. of Queen's U., Belfast, No. Ireland, 1971-72; asst. prof. Appalachian State U., Boone, N.C. 1974-75, Lakeland Community Coll., Mentor, Ohio, 1975-76, U. Minn., Duluth, 1976-77, Catawba Coll., Salisbury, N.C., 1977-81; vis. prof. U. Minn., Duluth, 1983-84; legal writer Squire, Sanders & Dempsey, Cleve., 1980-83; adj. prof. Ursuline Coll., 1985—; dean Griswold Inst., 1984—; reader on medieval English history for Albion publ., 1975—; mem. organizing com. Ohio Conf. Medieval Studies, 1975-76. Vestryman St. Paul's Episcopal Ch., Cleve., 1976-79; mem. exec. bd. Carolinas Symposium on Brit. Studies. Mem. Am., So. hist. assns., Cleve. Medieval Soc., Phi Beta Kappa, Kappa Delta Pi, Phi Alpha Theta. Author: A Series of Commentaries on the Sacraments, 1977; also articles; reviewer Library Jour. Home: 956 Roanoke Rd Cleveland Heights OH 44121 Office: Griswold Inst 6000 Memphis Ave Cleveland OH 44144

GILLESPIE, ROBERT W., multi-bank holding company executive. Chief executive officer Society Corp., Cleve. Office: Society Corp 127 Public Sq Cleveland OH 44114*

GILLESPIE, WILLIAM TYRONE, judge; b. Great Falls, Mont., Mar. 7, 1916; s. William G. and Alma (McBride) G.; A.B., J.D., D.C.L., Willamette U., 1939; LL.D., Hillsdale Coll., 1957; m. Eleanor Johnson, Aug. 31, 1941; 1 son, William Tyrone. Admitted to Oreg., Wash. bars, 1939, Mich. bar, 1948; spl. agt. FBI, 1939-42; partner Pope & Gillespie, Salem, Oreg., 1946-48; mem. legal dept. Dow Chem. Co., Midland, Mich., 1948-54, asst. to pres., 1954-66; partner firm Gillespie, Riecker & George, Midland, Mich., 1966-76; judge Mich. 42d Jud. Circuit, 1977—. Trustee Hillsdale Coll., 1957-72, chmn., 1972-75, chmn. emeritus, 1975—. Served from 2d lt. to lt. col. AUS, 1942-46. Mem. State Bar Mich., Oreg., Wash., Midland County (past pres.) bar assns., Am. Legion, Michigan C. of C. (v.p.), 40 and 8, Blue Key, Beta Theta Pi. Republican. Methodist. Clubs: Masons (33 deg.), Rotary. Home: 1200 W Sugnet Rd Midland MI 48640 Office: Courthouse Midland MI 48640

GILLET, ANDRE, food processing company executive. Chmn., chief exec., chief operating officer Internat. Mutlifoods Corp., Mpls., also dir. Office: Internat Multifoods Corp Mutlifoods Tower Box 2942 Minneapolis MN 55402*

GILLETT, RICHARD M., banker; b. Grand Rapids, Mich., 1923. Grad. U. Mich., 1944. With Old Kent Fin. Corp., Grand Rapids, now chmn. bd., dir.; chmn. bd. Old Kent Bank & Trust Co.; dir. Steketee Dept. Store, Ameritech, Consumers Power Co., Fed. Res. of Chgo. Ball Corp. Office: Old Kent Fin Corp 1 Vandenberg Center Grand Rapids MI 49503

GILLETTE, CAROL MAY, medical technologist; b. Cleve., Nov. 30, 1940; d. Henry Blair and Grayce Phare (Davidson) Hubble; m. Donald Alfred Gillette, Feb. 26, 1958; children—Catherine A., Anthony J., Lucia M., David G., Carroll D., Andrea J., Lisa M., Daniel A., Rosemary J. Assoc. in Sci., Flint Jr. Coll., 1960; B.A. in Biology, U. Mich.-Flint, 1963. With Fed. Dept. Store, 1958; lab. aide Flint Osteo. Hosp., 1960-61; intern in med. technology St. Joseph Hosp., Flint, 1961-62, 62-63, staff med. technologist, 1963—; staff lab. technologist Flint Gen. Hosp., 1961-62, 65-66; staff technologist Ballenger Hwy. Med. Lab. Clinic, Flint, part-time 1965-66; chief med. technologist Flint Med. X-Ray & Lab. Clinic, 1976—, microbiology technologist Flint Med. Clinic, 1984—; tutor students in field; tchr. piano. Vol. collector Cystic Fibrosis. Recipient 20 yr. service pin St. Joseph Hosp., 1983, Employee Suggestion award, 1983. Mem. Am. Soc. Clin. Pathologists (cert.), Mensa. Roman Catholic. Home: 9174 N Irish Rd Mount Morris MI 48458 Office: St Joseph Hosp 302 Kensington Ave Flint MI 48502

GILLEY, BARBARA KAY, optometrist; b. Kansas City, Mo., Dec. 22, 1955; d. Burl H. and Anna Sue (Horn) Gilley; m. Scott E. Foster, Jan. 12, 1979. Student Univ. Ark., Fayetteville, 1973-75; B.S. in Optometry, So. Coll. Optometry, Memphis, 1979. Registered optometrist, Mo., Tenn. Optometrist, Drs. Stringer, Friedman and Burke, Memphis, 1979-80, Dr. Charles Ingram, Memphis, 1980-82; pvt. practice, Raytown, Mo., 1984—. Mem. Tenn. Optometric Assn., Mo. Optometric Assn., Am. Optometric Assn. Republican. Mem. Assemblies of God. Avocations: Racquetball. Office: Barbara Gilley OD 5224 Blue Ridge Raytown MO 64133

GILLFILLAN, NANCY MILES, librarian; b. Robinson, Ill., Jan. 8, 1942; d. Halsey Lincoln Miles and Betty (Ingram) Miles Davenport; m. Richard Allen Gillfillan, June 9, 1963; 1 son: David Miles. B.A., U. Ill., 1964, M.S., 1966; student U. Denver, 1980. Reference librarian Kansas City Pub. Library (Mo.), 1964-66; instr., extended services librarian Ind. State U., Terre Haute, 1966-69; part-time instr. Ill. Valley Community Coll., Oglesby, Ill., 1977-80; owner, mgr. Book Barn, Walnut, Ill., 1980—. Contbr. articles to profl. jours.; author: Pocket Guide to Bureau County Authors, 1983. Vice pres. Bur. County Home Health Services Bd., 1979—. Mem. Ill. Homemakers Extension Fedn. (bd. dirs., editor newsletter 1977-80, state sec. exec. com. 1982—), Adult Edn. Assn. Ind. (exec. bd., co-editor newsletter), Assn. for Field Services in Tchr. Edn. (exec. bd. 1968-69), ALA. Republican. Methodist. Clubs: United Meth. Women, Ill. Fedn. Women's, Order Eastern Star. Address: Rural Route 1 Walnut IL 61376

GILLILAND, ROBERT EUGENE, consumers club executive; b. Van Wert, Ohio, Jan. 15, 1940; s. Eugene Joseph and Mary Evelyn (Nogel) G.; m. Carol Sue Baxter, July 11, 1959; children—Cynthia Sue, Brent Eugene. Student pub. schs., Van Wert. Agt., Western & So. Life Ins., Van Wert, 1964-66; state mgr. Nat. Heritage Mgmt. Corp., Cleve., 1967-76; gen. mgr. Jeffrey Martin Inc. DBA United Consumers Club, Country Club Hills, Ill., 1976-82, owner, chief exec. officer, 1982—; cons. United Consumers Club, Merrillville, Ind., 1977—. Served with USAF, 1958-64. Mem. United Consumers Club Dirs. Assn. (Dir. of Yr. 1979, Founders award 1983). Republican. Office: Jeffrey Martin Inc 4053 W 183d St Country Club Hills IL 60477

GILLILAND, ROY JUDSON, lawyer, judge; b. Jackson County, Ohio, Apr. 25, 1927; s. Roy Delbert and Mabel (Stephenson) G.; m. Karleene Mullen, Dec.

19, 1951; children—Kyle R., Arla L., Bret J. B.S. in Bus. Adminstrn., Ohio State U., 1950, J.D., 1952. Bar: Ohio 1952. Mem. staff Ohio Tax Dept., Columbus, 1952-55; prosecutor Jackson County, Ohio, 1957-63; mem. legis. State of Ohio, Columbus, 1963-67; probate judge Jackson County, 1967-73, county judge, 1973-78, municipal judge, 1978—; sole practice, Jackson County, 1955-67, 73-84; ptnr. Gilliland & Gilliland, 1984—; lectr. bus. law Ohio U., 1973—; solicitor Coalton Village, Ohio, 1955-67. Served to lt. comdr. USNR, 1945-75. Mem. Ohio State Bar Assn., Jackson County Bar Assn. Republican. Methodist. Lodge: Masons. Home: 347 S Penna Wellston OH 45692 Office: 23 E Broadway Wellston OH 45692

GILLIS, ALLEN DEAN, osteopathic physician; b. St. Joseph, Mo., Jan. 19, 1944; s. Dean Robert and Helen Marie (Browning) G.; m. Antoinette Finnell, Dec. 13, 1969; children—Heather Elizabeth, Paul David, Erica Mae, William Spencer. B.S. in Pharmacy, U. Mo., 1968; D.O., Kansas City Coll. Osteo. Medicine, 1976. Practice osteo. medicine Coffeyville Family Practice Clinic, P.A., Coffeyville, Kans., 1977—; chief of staff Coffeyville Meml. Hosp., 1983—. Bd. dirs. Kans. Found. for Med. Care, Topeka. Served with USAR, 1968-73. Mem. Am. Osteo. Assn., Kansas Osteo. Assn., Southeastern Kans. Osteo. Assn. (pres. 1982-83), Am. Diabetes Assn., Am. Heart Assn. Club: Mallard (Coffeyville). Lodge: Rotary. Home: 502 Centennial St Coffeyville KS 67337 Office: 209 7th St Coffeyville KS 67337

GILLUM, JACK DEAN, structural engineer; b. Salina, Kans., Nov. 21, 1928; s. Charles Z. and Lillian D. (Mulnix) G.; student Wichita U., 1946-47; B.S., U. Kans., 1950; m. Alice A. Reese, Dec. 1, 1951 (dec. July 1971); children—Jack A., Timothy, Richard, Traci, Charles, Chris; m. 2d, Judith L. Hoffmann, June 1, 1973. Designer, Stearn Roger, Denver, 1952-55; cons. engr. Jack D. Gillum & Assocs., Denver, 1955-69, Chgo., 1969-72, St. Louis, 1972-82; pres., chmn. bd. GCE Internat., Inc., St. Louis, 1982-85, KKBNA Unltd. Inc., St. Louis, 1985—; dir. Raptor Research & Rehab. Project. Mem. engring. adv. bd. Washington U., St. Louis. Active Boy Scouts Am. Served as lt. C.E., AUS, 1951-52; Korea. Recipient Spl. citation Am. Inst. Steel Constrn., 1975; 2d place award in engring. excellence Cons. Engring. Council Mo., 1975, engring excellence award, 1979; award of merit Structural Engrs. Assn. of Ill., 1981, 82; others; registered profl. engr., Calif., 30 other states. Mem. Nat. Soc. Profl. Engrs., ASCE, Prestressed Concrete Inst. (award 1975), Am. Concrete Inst., St. Louis Regional Commerce and Growth Assn. Christian Scientist. Clubs: Masons (32 deg.), Shriners. Home: 13682 Peacock Farm Rd Saint Louis MO 63131 Office: 100 N Broadway Saint Louis MO 63102

GILMAN, LEIGHTON CURTIS, communications executive; b. Cambridge, Mass., Apr. 15, 1931; s. George P. B. and Karen E. (Theller) G.; m. Audrey Knowles Gilman, Oct. 13, 1956; children—Scott, Gregg, Diane. B.A., U. N.H., 1954. News corr. AP, Boston Globe, Manchester Union-Leader, N.H., 1948-54; pub. relations mgr. So. New Eng. Telephone, New Haven, 1954-64, AT&T, N.Y.C., 1964-73; asst. v.p. pub. relations New Eng. Telephone, Boston, 1973-77; v.p. pub. relations Ohio Bell, Cleve., 1977-83; v.p. corp. communications Ameritech, Chgo., 1983—. Mem. Pub. Relations Soc. Am. Office: Ameritech 30 S Wacker Dr Chicago IL 60606

GILMAN, RICHARD JAY, accountant; b. Chgo., July 9, 1952; s. Marvin and Joyce Susan (Hoffman) G.; m. Helene Renee Rieger, Aug. 18, 1974; children—Jason Stuart, Jordan Elliott, Rachel Cari. A.A., Oakton Community Coll., 1972; B.S. in Mgmt., DePaul U., 1975, B.S. in Acctg., 1976. C.P.A., Ill. Acctg. ptnr. Kupferberg, Goldberg and Neimark, Chgo., 1976—. Exec. mem. Jewish United Fund. Mem. Ill. C.P.A. Soc., Am. Inst. C.P.A.s, Am. Mgmt. Assn., Am. Israeli C. of C. Democrat. Jewish. Home: 2517 Greenwood Glenview IL 60025

GILMOR, JANE ELLEN, artist, educator; b. Ames, Iowa, June 23, 1947; d. Fred Howard and Margery Ann (Maberry) F. B.S., Iowa State U., 1969; M.A.T., U. Iowa, 1973, M.A. in Painting, 1976, M.F.A. in Painting, 1977. Cert. secondary tchr., Iowa. Chmn. fine arts div., art instr. Regis High Sch., Cedar Rapids, Iowa, 1973-74; assoc. prof. art, chmn. dept. Mt. Mercy Coll., Cedar Rapids, 1974—, dir. McAuley Gallery, 1978-81; cons. Cedar Rapids Sch. Systems, 1979-83; lectr. in field. One woman and group shows include N.A.M.E. Gallery, Chgo., 1984, Renwick Gallery, Smithsonian Inst., Washington, 1981, Augustana Coll. Rock Island, Ill., 1980, Olbrick Gallery, Kassel, Germany, 1980, George Sand Gallery Los Angeles, 1977, Conn. Coll., New London, 1982, Birmingham Mullaly-Matisse Gallery, 1983, N.Y.C. FIT Galleries, 1980, Des Moines Hoover State Office Bldg, 1978. Bd. dirs. Cedar Rapids Mus. of Art, 1977-80. Recipient Art in Architecture Purchase award, Iowa Arts Council and NEA, 1978, 1st place award Nat. Exhibit Mullaly-Matisse Gallery, 1983. Mem. Coll. Art Assn., AAUP (v.p. Mt. Mercy chpt. 1977-79). Office: Mount Mercy Coll 1330 Elmhurst Ave NE Cedar Rapids IA 52402

GILMORE, HORACE WELDON, See *Who's Who in America,* 43rd edition.

GILMORE, JAMES STANLEY, JR., broadcasting executive; b. Kalamazoo, June 14, 1926; s. James Stanley and Ruth (McNair) G.; student Culver Mil. Acad., Western Mich. U., Kalamazoo Coll., 1945; Litt.D. (hon.), Nazareth Coll.; m. Diana Holdenreide Fell, May 21, 1949 (dec.); children—Bethany, Sydney, James Stanley III, Elizabeth, Ruth; m. Susan C. Maggio, Sept. 13, 1980. Owner, chmn. bd., chief exec. officer Jim Gilmore Enterprises, Gilmore Broadcasting Corp.; chmn. bd., pres. Continental Corp. Mich., Inc.; v.p. Jim Gilmore Cadillac-Pontiac Datsun Inc., Gilmore Racing Team, Inc., (A.J. Foyt, driver); v.p., chmn., pres. Continental Corp. Mich.; asst. sec., dir. Fabri-Kal Plastics Corp. Kalamazoo; ptnr. Greater Kalamazoo Sports, Inc. (hockey franchise), Kalamazoo Stadium Co.; owner Anthony Abraham Chevrolet, Miami, G.E.C. Ins. Co., Miami; dir., mem. trust com. First Am. Bank-Mich. N.A., Kalamazoo; dir. First Am. Bank Corp., William R. Biggs/Gilmore Assocs., Inc. presdl. advisor Republic Airlines. Mem. Pres.' Citizens Adv. Com. on Environmental Quality; mem., past chmn. Mich. Water Resources Commn.; mem. Mich. Gov.'s Forum; mem. nat. adv. cancer council HEW; mem. Nat. Assn. Broadcasters' adv. com. to Corp. for Pub. Broadcasting. Pres. Kalamazoo County Young Rep. Club, 1947-49; mayor, Kalamazoo, 1959-61; past mem. Kalamazoo County Bd. Suprs.; past chmn. Kalamazoo County Rep. Exec. Com.; del. Rep. Nat. Conv. Asso. bd. dirs. Boys Clubs Am.; bd. dirs., past chmn. Kalamazoo County chpt. A.R.C.; former chmn. bd. trustees Nazareth Coll.; trustee, mem. finance com. Greater Mich. Devel. Found.; mem., chmn. bldg. com. fund dr. Constance Brown Speech and Hearing Center; past trustee Kalamazoo Coll., mem. adv. group Center Urban Studies and Community Services; trustee past vice chmn. Kalamazoo Nature Center; mem. bldg. and exec. coms. Bronson Hosp., also chmn. ad hoc legis. com.; past trustee, past v.p. Mich. Found. for Arts, Detroit; life dir. Family Service Center Kalamazoo; mem. Mich. bd. dirs. Radio Free Europe; nat. sponsor Ducks Unlimited; life mem. March Dimes; chmn. spl. reorganizational com. United Fund; mem. fund raising com. Pres. Ford Library/Mus.; hon. trustee Mich. Alvin Bentley Charitable Found. Served with USAAF, 1943-46. Named Kalamazoo Young Man of 1960, One of Mich.'s 5 Young Men of 1960, hon. citizen of Houston and Indpls.; recipient Ann. Service to Mankind award Sertoma Club; Man of Yr. award Mich. Auto Racing Fan Club, Auto Racing Found. Frat.; honors Hoosier Racing Assn., Auto Racing Frat. Found., Inc., Milw. Mem. Kalamazoo County (past pres., past dir.; mem. exec. com. of indsl. devel. com.), Mich. (mem. law and order com.) chambers commerce, N.A.M., Mich. Acad. Sci., Arts and Letters. Episcopalian (mem. bd. diocese Western Mich., chmn. cathedral drive, mem. com. Bishop Whittemore Found.). Clubs: Capitol Hill (Washington); Park (past dir.) (Richland, Mich.); Mid-America (Chgo.); Otsego Ski (Gaylord, Mich.). Home: 1550 Long Rd Kalamazoo MI 49008 also 5040 Woodlawn Beach Gull Lake Hickory Corners MI 49060 also 15 Caloosa Rd Ocean Reef Club Key Largo FL also 25 Card Sound Ocean Reef Club Key Largo FL also Houseboat Islmorado FL Office: Jim Gilmore Enterprises 202 Mich Bldg Kalamazoo MI 49006

GILMORE, ROBERT EUGENE, earthmoving machinery manufacturing company executive; b. nr. Peoria, Ill., May 4, 1920; s. Myron E. and Lillian G. (Mallm) G.; grad. high sch.; m. Marguerite A. Best, May 1, 1948; children—Christine Ann, Scott Eugene. With Caterpillar Tractor Co., Peoria, 1938—, pres. Caterpillar France, Grenoble, 1963-68, gen. mgr. worldwide mfg. and facilities planning, 1968, gen. mgr. U.S. mfg. plants, 1968-69, v.p. U.S. mfg. plants, 1969-73, exec. v.p., 1973-77, pres., chief operating officer, 1977-85, also dir.; dir. Santa Fe So. Pacific Corp., Security Savs. & Loan Assn., Peoria. Served to 1st lt. USAAF, 1943-45; ETO. Decorated Air medal with 4 oak leaf clusters. Republican. Lutheran. Clubs: Peoria Country; Union League (Chgo.); Masons. Home: 7316 N Edgewild Dr Peoria IL 61614 Office: 100 NE Adams St Peoria IL 61629

GILMORE, ROGER, art school dean. Dean Sch. of the Art Inst. of Chgo. Office: Sch of the Art Inst of Chgo Columbus Dr at Jackson Blvd Chicago IL 60603*

GILMORE, WAYNE MERRILL, dentist; b. San Jose, Ill., Apr. 26, 1933; s. Carl Raymond and Gertrude Irene (Cogdal) G.; m. Lois Ann Schmaltz, May 22, 1954; children—William W., Kristin Leann, Gena Marie. B.A., Beloit Coll., 1955; B.S., U. Ill.-Chgo., 1957, D.D.S., 1959. Dental officer U.S. Air Force, Wichita Falls, Tex., 1959-61; practice gen. dentistry, Janesville, Wis., 1961—. Various offices YMCA, Janesville, 1964-78. Served to capt. USAF, 1959-61. Mem. ADA, Chgo. Dental Assn., Wis. Dental Soc., Rock County Dental Soc. (pres. 1970-71). Lutheran. Club: Ys Men (Janesville). Avocations: skiing; tennis. Home: 305 Apache Dr Janesville WI 53545 Office: 51 S River St Janesville WI 53545

GILPIN, JOHN STEPHEN, veterinarian; b. Kalamazoo, Aug. 30, 1941; s. Gerald Merle and Mildred Elaine (Davidson) G.; D.V.M., Purdue U., 1966. Veterinarian, Gateway Animal Hosp., Glendale, Calif., 1966-67. County Line Animal Hosp., La Habra, Calif., 1970-71, specializing in small animal practice, Highland Animal Hosp., Ind., 1971-85, Wabash Vet. Hosp., Ind., 1985—. Served to capt. U.S. Army, 1967-69; Vietnam. Deocrated Bronze Star. Mem. AVMA, Ind. (dir. 1982-85), Calumet Area (pres. 1981) vet. med. assns., Ind. Acad. Vet. Medicine, Delta Sigma Phi. Republican. Episcopalian. Club: Kiwanis Internat. Home: 1925 Vernon St Apt 5 Wabash IN 46992 Office: 1721 S Wabash St Wabash IN 46992

GILROY, JOHN, neurology educator; b. Newcastle-upon-Tyne, Eng., Mar. 29, 1925; came to U.S. 1958; s. William and Margaret Jane (Watson) G.; m. Betty Squire, April 19, 1962 (div. 1975); children—Ian Michael, Robin Paul, Wendy Allyson; m. Marcia Kollenberg, Dec. 20, 1975. M.B.B.S., U. Durham, Eng., 1948, M.D., 1957. Intern, Detroit Meml. Hosp., 1958-59, resident, 1959-60; resident Wayne State U., Detroit, 1960-63, instr. neurology, 1963-65, asst. prof., 1965-67, assoc. prof., 1967-68, prof., chmn. dept., 1968—. Author: Medical Neurology, 1968; Basic Neurology, 1982. Served with RAF, 1953-57. Fellow ACP, Royal Coll. Physicians (Can.), Detroit Acad. Medicine, Am. Heart Assn.; mem. Mich. Neurol. Assn. (pres. 1972), Detroit Med. Club (pres. 1985), Alpha Omega Alpha. Home: 25802 Franklin Park Dr Franklin MI 48025 Office: Dept of Neurology University Health Ctr 4201 St Antoine Detroit MI 48201

GILSON, M. DESALES, oil company official; b. Fremont, Ohio, Aug. 16, 1945; d. Richard C. and Mercedes C. (Ziebold) Grachek; student Bowling Green State U., 1964-66, Ursuline Coll., 1976-78, St. Mary-of-the-Woods Coll., 1978-79, Antioch Sch. Law, 1981; m. J. Richard Gilson, Jan. 31, 1970. Customer service rep. Toledo Edison Co., 1963-67; programmer Standard Oil Co. Ohio, Cleve., 1967-70, successively analyst, tng. coordinator, mgr. personnel devel. corp. adminstrn. employee relations, mgr. retail systems, from 1971, now mgr. retail credit and info systems; owner Ampersand & Friends, typesetters; Sumi painter; lectr. Trustee, Light. Recipient Woman of Achievement award YWCA, 1976. Mem. Assn. Humanistic Psychology, Am. Soc. Tng. and Devel. Club: Cleve. Women's City. Home: 3400 Wooster Rd Rocky River OH 44116 Office: 1228 State Office Bldg Cleveland OH 44115

GINDHART, MARY ELIZABETH, educational administrator; b. Phila., Nov. 7, 1937; d. Joseph Eugene and Beatrice Margaret (Mitchell) G. B.A., Holy Family Coll., 1959; M.A., Ind. U., 1967; M.A. in Religion, Athenaeum of Ohio, 1978. Tchr. Abraham Lincoln High Sch., Phila., 1959-61, Thomas Edison High Sch., Phila., 1963-64; adminstr. Grailville Ctr., Loveland, Ohio, 1966-72, 75-76, dir. career edn. project, 1977-81, devel. officer, 1982—; tutor, research officer James Cook U., Townsville, Australia, 1973-75; lay pastoral minister Archdiocese of Cin., 1978—; project dir., coordinator books on edn., history. Bd. dirs. Human Involvement Project, Inc., Cin., 1983—; chmn. allocations com. Community Chest, Cin., 1980-81; trustee Chatfield Coll., St. Martin, Ohio, 1975-77; sec. Townsville Welfare Council, 1973-74. Mem. Nat. Soc. Fund Raising Execs., The Grail, NOW. Home and Office: Grailville 932 O'Bannonville Rd Loveland OH 45140

GINIS, ASTERIOS MICHAEL, food scientist; b. Thessaloniki, Greece, Feb. 16, 1945; came to U.S., 1971, naturalized, 1981; s. Michael and Maria (Gouga) G.; m. Asimina Giannoulopoulou, June 12, 1971; 1 child, Michael. B.S. in Agr., Aristotelian U., Thessaloniki, 1968; M.S. in Food Sci., U. Wis., 1973, Ph.D. in Food Sci.-Biochemistry, 1976. Research asst. Cereal Research Inst., Thessaloniki, 1966-67, U. Wis., Madison, 1971-76; research and devel. mgr. Gen. Mills Inc., Mpls., 1976—. Mem. Am. Assn. Cereal Chemists, Inst. Food Technologists. Home: 10505 Co Rd 15 Plymouth MN 55441 Office: Gen Mills Inc 9000 Plymouth Ave N Minneapolis MN 55427

GINN, ROBERT MARTIN, See *Who's Who in America,* 43rd edition.

GINSBERG, BARRY HOWARD, physician, researcher; b. Bklyn., May 9, 1945; s. Emanuel and Ruth (Friedman) G.; m. Marjorie Ellen Kanef, Aug. 20, 1967; children—Susan, David. B.A., SUNY-Binghamton, 1965; Ph.D., Albert Einstein Coll., 1971, M.D., 1972. Intern Beth Israel Hosp., Boston, 1972-73, resident in internal medicine, 1973-74; fellow in endocrinology NIH, 1974-77; asst. prof. U. Iowa, Iowa City, 1977-82, assoc. prof. medicine, biochemistry, 1979—, assoc. dir. Diabetes-Endocrinology Research Ctr., 1982—, dir. 1984—; co-dir. Diabetes Control and Complications Trial, Iowa City, 1984—. Contbr. chpts. to profl. books. Served to comdr. USPHS, 1974-77. Mem. Am. Fedn. Clin. Research, Endocrine Soc., AAAS, Central Soc. Clin. Research, Am. Diabetes Assn. (pres. Iowa chpt. 1982-84, bd. dirs. 1982-85). Avocation: computer programming. Office: Dept Internal Medicine U Iowa 3E12 VAMC Iowa City IA 52240

GINSBERG, JANICE GORDON, marketing consultant, educator; b. Chgo., Feb. 13, 1950; d. David and Eunice (Wienshienk) Gordon; m. Marc David Ginsberg, Jan. 23, 1977; 1 son, Brian David. Grad. Engring. Inst., Northwestern U., 1966, B.S.J., 1971, M.B.A., 1973. With tennis mktg. dept. Wilson Sporting Goods Co., River Grove, Ill., 1973-76; advt. dir. Telemedia Inc., Chgo., 1976-78; sr. mgr. new products consumer products G.D. Searle Co., Skokie, Ill., 1978-82; mktg. cons., Wilmette, Ill., 1982—; prof. mktg. Kendall Coll., Evanston, Ill., 1982. Contbr. articles on marketing research to profl. jours. Recipient Outstanding award Ill. Acad. Sci., 1967; Best in Big Ten Univs. Journalism award, 1969; Outstanding Woman of Yr. award Northwestern U., 1968. Mem. Am. Mktg. Assn., Chgo. Mktg. Assn., Assn. M.B.A. Execs., Assn. Nat. Advertisers, Chgo. Heart Assn. Home: 312 Central Park Wilmette IL 60091

GIOIOSO, JOSEPH VINCENT, psychologist; b. Chgo., Mar. 6, 1939; s. Vincent James and Mary (Bonadonna) G.; B.A., DePaul U., 1962, M.A., 1963; Ph.D. summa cum laude, Ill. Inst. Tech., 1971; m. Gay Powers, Dec. 28, 1963; children—Joseph, Randy Marie, Danielle. Psychologist, Sch. Assn. for Spl. Edn. in DuPage County, Wheaton, Ill., 1964-67; pvt. practice as clin. psychologist, Chgo. and Downers Grove, Ill., 1966—; clin. psychologist J.J. McLaughlin, M.D., Profl. Corp., Chgo., 1970—. Founder dept. psychology Ill. Benedictine Coll., Lisle, 1968, chmn. dept. psychology, prof., dir. testing, 1968-71; cons. psychologist Chicago Ridge (Ill.) Sch. Dist. 127 1/2, 1973-76, Cath. Charities Counseling Service, Chgo., 1963-66, St. Laurence High Sch., Oak Lawn, Ill., 1963-64, Oak Lawn-Hometown Sch. Dist. No. 123, 1967-68, Addison (Ill.) Sch. Dist. 4, 1969-72; vis. prof. psychology Inst. Mgmt., Lisle, 1968-69, George Williams Coll., Downers Grove, 1970-71; chief psychologist Valley View Sch. Dist. 365U, Bolingbrook, Ill., 1971-73; dir. Pub. Program for Exceptional Children, Lisle, 1969-71; mem. Nat. Register Health Service Providers in Psychology, 1975—. Bd. dirs. Ray Graham Assn. for Handicapped, DuPage County, Ill., 1970-73; adv. bd. Care and Counseling Center DuPage County, 1977—. DePaul U. publ. grantee, 1959-61, Fitzgerald Bros. Found. grantee, 1969-71. Mem. Am., Midwestern, Ill. psychol. assns., Soc. Pediatric Psychology, AAAS, Alpha Phi Delta. Clubs: Lakeside Country (Downers Grove); Racquet (Hinsdale, Ill.). Author: Completion Intelligence Test, 1963; Children's Emotional Symptoms Inventory, 1979. Contbr. articles to profl. jours. Home: 6800 S Main St Downers Grove IL 60516 Office: 6800 S Main St Downers Grove IL 60516

GIORDANO, AUGUST THOMAS (GUS), choreographer, dancer, educator; b. St. Louis, July 10, 1923; s. Paul and Rose (Tedesco) G.; B.A., U. Mo., 1950; student Buckman Dancing Sch., St. Louis, 1932-40; m. Peggy Ann Thoelke, Oct. 14, 1950; children—Patrick Nelson, Marc August, Nan Elizabeth, Amy Paul. Dancer at Roxy Theater, N.Y.C., summers 1948-49; appeared as choreographer-dancer in On the Town, 1953; dancer-choreographer on Perry Como Show, 1954, Ed Sullivan Show, 1954, Colgate Comedy Hour, 1955; film conv. coordinator Film Council Am., 1953-56; propr., dir. Gus Giordano Dance Center, Evanston, Ill., 1953—, choreographer, 1953—; dir., choreographer Gus Giordano Jazz Dance Chicago Co., 1968—; choreographer Goodman Theatre, Chgo., 1978—, Sta. WTTW-TV, Chgo., 1968—, NBC, Chgo., 1969—, ABC-TV, Chgo., 1972-74; concert tours in U.S. and Europe, 1975—; producer various stage and indsl. shows, 1955—. Served with USMC, 1944-46. Recipient Emmy TV award, 1968, 75, 78, Dance Masters of Am. award, 1978, Outstanding Dancer award Boston Dance Masters, 1970, Chgo. Nat. Assn. Dance Tchrs. award, 1974, NET-TV Award of Excellence, 1969, Ill. Gov.'s award, 1971, Dance Educators Am. award, 1984, Focus on Arts award, 1985. Mem. Lambda Chi Alpha. Roman Catholic. Editor: Anthology of American Jazz Dance, 1976; originated the Giordano technique of jazz dance form. Home: 311 3d St Wilmette IL 60091 Office: 614 Davis St Evanston IL 60201

GIORDANO, PATRICK NELSON, lawyer, energy consultant; b. N.Y.C., Aug. 16, 1952; s. August Thomas and Margaret Ann (Thoelke) G.; m. Debra Anne Chalifoux, May 23, 1981. B.A., Tufts U., 1974; J.D., Lewis and Clark Coll., 1979. Bar: Ill., U.S. dist. ct. (no. dist.) Ill., U.S. Ct. Appeals (7th cir.). Supr. pub. utilities and transp. div. Cook County State's Atty's. Office, Chgo., 1980—; cons., expert witness Nev. Office Adv. for Customers of Pub. Utilities Nev., Reno, 1984, Utilities Div. Com. N.Mex. Legis., Santa Fe, 1982-83. Organizer, Congl. campaign, Skokie, Ill., 1974; mem. Big Bros. of Mass., Medford, 1971-74; mem. pub. issues com. Ctr. for Neighborhood Tech., Chgo., 1981—; active issue devel. campaign Daley for Mayor, Chgo., 1983; mem. Nat. Handball Team, Colorado Springs, Colo., 1983; researcher, lobbyist Common Cause, Portland, Oreg., 1979. Recipient bronze medal, team handball, Nat. Sports Festival, 1978, gold medal, 1979, silver medal, 1981. Mem. Ill. State Bar Assn. Democrat. Roman Catholic. Clubs: Covenant (spl. athletic mem.), Riviera 400 Health. Home: 714 Madison St Evanston IL 60202 Office: Cook County States Attys Office 500 Richard J Daley Ctr Chicago IL 60602

GIORGINI, ALDO, civil engineering educator; b. Voghera, Italy, Mar. 15, 1934; came to U.S. 1962; s. Adelmo and Pierina (Salvadeo) G.; m. Elena Belotti, June 21, 1964 (dec. Oct. 1977); children—Massimiliano, Flaviano. Dr.Ing., Politecnico di Torino (Italy), 1959; Ph.D., Colo. State U., 1966. Assoc. prof. hydraulics Politecnico di Torino, 1959-61; NATO researcher CISE, Segrate, Italy, 1961-62; fellow Nat. Ctr. for Atmospheric Research, Boulder, Colo., 1966-67; asst. prof. Sch. Civil Engring, Purdue U., West Lafayette, Ind., 1967-70, assoc. prof., 1970—. Bd. dirs. Lafayette Art Ctr., 1976-79; Opera De Lafayette, 1981. Recipient 1st place award Internat. Competition of Computer Art, Augsburgh, Germany, 1982; Purdue Research Found. grantee, 1968, 69, 71, 72; Office of Water Research and Tech. grantee, 1973-74, 83; Apple Found. grantee, 1981; Dept. Agr. grantee, 1980-83. Mem. AAAS, Soc. Indsl. and Applied Math. Contbr. articles to profl. jours.; art work exhibited in U.S., Europe, Japan. Home: 1137 Berkley Rd Lafayette IN 47904 Office: Sch Civil Engring Purdue U West Lafayette IN 47907

GIOVANNONI, ROBERT NICHOLAS, principal; b. Chgo., Sept. 14, 1947; s. Bruno C. and Angeline M. (Lucchesi) G. A.B. magna cum laude, Loyola U., Chgo., 1969, M.Ed., 1973; C.A.S., Harvard U., 1981. Cert. tchr. and adminstr., Ill., sch. adminstr., Chgo. Cath. Sch. Bd. Tchr., program dir. St. Patrick High Sch., Chgo., 1969-74; asst. gen. mgr. Grady Co., Chgo., 1974-75; asst. prin. and curriculum dir. Notre Dame High Sch., Chgo., 1975-80; prin. Harvard-St. George Sch., Chgo., 1981-83; prin. Immaculate Conception High Sch., Elmhurst, Ill., 1983—; ednl. and organizational cons. NSF fellow in comparative govt., 1969; NDEA fellow in govt., 1969. Mem. Assn. for Supervision and Curriculum Devel., Phi Delta Kappa. Roman Catholic. Club: Harvard (Chgo.) Co-author, I-Project: A Prospectus (monograph). Home: 1551 Monroe River Forest IL 60305 Office: 217 Cottage Hill Ave Elmhurst IL 60126

GIPPIN, ROBERT MALCOLM, lawyer; b. Cleve., Feb. 3, 1948; s. Morris and Helena (Weil) G.; m. Michelle Brudno, Mar. 28, 1969; children—Sarah, Joshua, Rebecca. A.B., Dartmouth Coll., 1969; J.D., Harvard U., 1973. Bar: Ohio 1973. Asst. to dir. Ohio Dept. Commerce, Columbus, 1973; exec. sec. Ohio Real Estate Commn., Columbus, 1974-75; prosecutor Municipal Ct., Cuyahoga Falls, Ohio, 1975; ptnr. Buckingham, Doolittle & Burroughs, Akron, Ohio, 1975—. Active exec. com. Summit County Democratic Party, Akron, 1976—; pres. Summit County Council, 1982-84. Mem. Akron Bar Assn., Ohio Bar Assn., Phi Beta Kappa. Jewish. Avocations: reading; tennis; cooking. Home: 737 Merriman Rd Akron OH 44303 Office: Buckingham Doolittle & Burroughs 50 S Main St PO Box 1500 Akron OH 44309

GIRARD, STEPHEN JOSEPH, telecommunications company executive; b. Phila., Dec. 29, 1948; s. Jean Louis and Harriet Frances (Westcott) G.; m. Martha Thompson Wright, Apr. 14, 1975 (div. Sept. 1979); 1 son, Thomas Michael. Student Marquette U., 1966-68, U. Wis.-Milw., 1968-70, U. Wis.-Madison, 1972-74; Assoc., Madison Area Tech., 1974. Cert. in data processing. Programmer, Cook Industries, Memphis, 1974-76; programmer analyst No. Telecom Inc., Mpls., 1976-79, project mgr., 1979—; cons. Automated Data Systems, Orlando, Fla., 1982—. Designer Omniword, 1979-80. Mem. Am. Mgmt. Assn., Assn. Info. Systems Profls. Club: Illuminati Loci (pres. 1984—) (Mpls.). Avocations: fishing; jazz; art; architectural history. Office: Northern Telecom Inc 9705 Data Park Minnetonka MN 55343

GISH, CHARLES WILLIS, public health administrator, dentistry educator; b. Camden, Ind. June 26, 1923; s. Floyd Milton and Thelma O. (Snider) G.; m. Treva B. Metsger, June 23, 1949; children—C. Bradley (dec.), Tracey Sue, Gail Lynn. Student Purdue U., 1942-43, U. Notre Dame, 1943-45; D.D.S. with honors, Ind. U., 1949, M.P.H., 1961. Regional dental cons. USPHS, San Francisco, 1952-54; asst. dir. dental health Ind. State Bd. Health, Indpls., 1955-62, dir., 1962—; prof. Ind. U. Sch. Dentistry, Indpls., 1977—. Contbr. articles to profl. jours. and books; speaker to city councils and dental organs., 1954—. Served to lt. USN, 1943-45, 52-54. Mem. Ind. Dental Assn. (v.p. 1972-73), Am. Dental Assn., Am. Assn. Pub. Health Dentistry (pres. 1969-70, disting. service award 1976), Assn. State and Territorial Dental Dirs. (pres. 1969-71), Ind. U. Dental Alumni (pres. 1975-76, disting. alumnus award 1981). Lodge: Masons. Avocations: sports of field and stream. Office: Ind State Bd Health 1330 W Michigan St Indianapolis IN 46206

GISH, EDWARD RUTLEDGE, physician; b. St. Louis, Sept. 5, 1908; s. Edward C. and Bessie (Rutledge) G.; A.B., Westminster Coll., 1930; M.D., St. Louis U., 1935, M.S., 1939; m. Miriam Schlicker, July 8, 1938; children—Ann Rutledge, Mary Priscilla. Intern, St. Louis U. Hosps., 1935-36; resident in surgery St. Mary's Group Hosps., St. Louis, 1936-39; pvt. practice medicine specializing in surgery, Fulton, Mo., 1946—; staff mem. Callaway Meml. Hosp., Fulton. Bd. dirs. Mo. Symphony Soc., pres., 1981; med. dir. Callaway County CD. Served from maj. to lt. col., AUS, 1943-46; lt. col. ret. Res. Hon. col. Gov.'s Staff Mo. Fellow ACS; mem. Royal Soc. London (affiliate), Internat. Coll. Surgeons, AMA, Mo., Callaway County med. socs., Mo. Red Poll Breeders Assn. (pres.), Am. Law Enforcement Officers Assn., Delta Tau Delta, Alpha Omega Alpha. Contbr. articles to profl. jours. Co-capt. U.S. team World Masters Cross-Country Ski Assn., 1985. Home: 7 W 10th St Fulton MO 65251 Office: 5 E 5th St Fulton MO 65251

GISSLER, SIGVARD (SIG) GUNNAR, JR., journalist; b. Chgo., July 2, 1935; s. Sigvard Gunnar and Louisa (Anderson) G.; B.A. in Am. Civilization, Lake Forest (Ill.) Coll., 1956; postgrad. Northwestern U., 1958-61; journalism fellow; Stanford U., 1975; m. Mary Catherine Engman, Oct. 23, 1954; children—Gary, Glenn, Gregory. News editor Libertyville (Ill.) Ind.-Register, 1958-59; exec. editor Waukegan (Ill.) News-Sun, 1963-67; editorial writer Milw. Jour., 1967-77, editorial page editor, 1977-84, assoc. editor, 1984-85, editor, 1985—; v.p., dir. Newspaper Inc. Recipient Disting. Service citation Lake Forest Coll., 1977. Mem. Am. Soc. Newspapers Assn. Home: 6021 N Kent St Whitefish Bay WI 53217 Office: 333 W State St Milwaukee WI 53201

GIVAN, RICHARD MARTIN, chief justice Ind. Supreme Ct.; b. Indpls., June 7, 1921; s. Clinton Hodell and Glee (Bowen) G.; LL.B., Ind. U., 1951; m. Pauline Marie Haggart, Feb. 28, 1945; children—Madalyn Givan Hesson, Sandra Givan Chenoweth, Patricia Givan Siwek, Elizabeth. Partner firm Givan & Givan, 1952-59, Bowen, Myers, Northam & Givan, 1959-69; pub. defender,

Ind., 1952-54; dep. atty. gen. State of Ind., 1954-65; dep. pros. atty., Marion County, Ind., 1965-67; mem. Ind. Ho. of Reps., 1967-68; judge Ind. Supreme Ct., 1969—. Served with USAAF, 1942-45. Mem. Am., Indpls., Ind. bar assns., Ind. Judges Assn., Ind. Soc. Chgo., Newcomen Soc. N.Am., Sigma Delta Kappa. Mem. Soc. of Friends. Clubs: Arabian Horse. Office: Office of the Chief Justice Indiana Supreme Ct Indianapolis IN 46204 Address: 6726 S White Lick Creek Rd Indianapolis IN 46231

GIVENS, CHARLENE KAY, wastewater superintendent; b. Lebanon, Ind., Oct. 6, 1947; d. John Robert and Anna Mildred (Bowers) Whittaker; m. Ralph A. Givens, June 19, 1969; children—Maria Lynn. B.A., Ind. U., 1969. Lab. technician City of Carmel, Ind., 1972-75; lab. technician City of Noblesville, Ind., 1975-82, supt. wastewater plant, 1982—; owner Wastewater Plant Cons., Noblesville, Ind., 1982—; program chmn. Ind. Vocat. Tech. Coll. pollution treatment, Indpls., 1983—. Named Businesswoman of Yr., Hamilton chpt. Am. Bus. Women's Assn., 1982. Mem. Am. Businesswomen's Assn. (pres. 1980-81), Central Ind. Operators Assn. (pres. 1983-84), Ind. Soc. Cert. Operators (sec.-treas.), Ind. Water Pollution Control Assn., Nat. Environ. Tng. Assn. Avocations: knitting; reading; antiques; exploring. Office: City of Noblesville WPCP 197 W Washington St Noblesville IN 46060

GIVENS, WILLIAM P., supermarket company executive. Chmn., dir. Marsh Supermarkets, Inc., Yorktown, Ind. Office: Marsh Supermarkets Inc Yorktown IN 47396*

GIVHAN, STEVEN ALLEN, engineering company executive; b. Chgo., Apr. 7, 1954; s. Claude Raymond and Christine E. (Jackson) G.; m. Octavia Walker, Jan. 3, 1982; children—Khaliah, Kevin. B.S. in Mech. Engring., U. Calif.-Santa Barbara, 1974; M.S., U. Hawaii, 1976; M.B.A. (hon.) Oxford U., Eng., 1981. Registered profl. engr., Ill., Calif., D.C. Mech. designer Sonicraft Inc., Chgo., 1980-82; pres. NDT 1 Inc., Chgo., 1982—; dir. Auburn Park Engelwood Local Devel. Corp. Patentee in field. Bd. dirs. Kennedy King Coll., Chgo., 1984; mem. Congl. Task Force, Chgo., 1984—. Served to lt. comdr. USN, 1973-79. Mem. ASME, Nat. Assn. Profl. Engrs., AAAS, Vietnam Vets. Roman Catholic. Avocations: golf, swimming, tennis, model railroading.

GIZYNSKI, MARTHA NOBLE, educator; b. Malden, Mass., Jan. 18, 1928; d. Royce Jennings and Ruth Lunt (Moulton) Noble; m. Waldemar Edmund Gizynski, Aug. 26, 1949; children—Elizabeth, Susan. B.A., Radcliffe Coll., 1949; M.S.W., U. Mich., 1967, Ph.D., 1971. Lectr. social work U. Mich., Ann Arbor, 1969-74, asst. prof., 1974-78, assoc. prof., 1978—; pvt. practice psychotherapy, Ann Arbor, 1980—. Mem. Nat. Assn. Social Workers, Am. Psychol. Assn. Home: 6478 Clark Lake Rd Jackson MI 49201 Office: U Mich 4060 Frieze Bldg Ann Arbor MI 49105

GLADNEY, LILLIE MAGGITT, business educator; b. Clarksdale, Miss., Oct. 2, 1946; d. Ed. and Bertha Lee (Jones) Maggitt; m. Mack Carl Gladney, July 16, 1974; 1 son, Lorenzo Carl. B.S., Miss. Valley State U., 1976; M. Ed., Wayne State U., 1980. Clk., typist Planning Research Center, Cape Canaveral, Fla., 1977-78, clk. bus. analyst, McDonnell Douglas, 1978; sec. Wayne State U., 1978-79; tchr. bus. edn. Luth. High Sch. West, Detroit, 1980—; asst. dir. Christian Edn. Supt. primary dept. Sunday Sch., Dexter Ave. Bapt. Ch., also pres. usher bd. 2. Mem. Am. Vocat. Assn. Baptist. Clubs: Miss. Valley State U. Alumni, Heroines of Jerico. Home: 15730 Braile St Detroit MI 48223

GLANERT, KAREN LOUISE, educator; b. Sheboygan, Wis., July 21, 1954; d. Alvin H. and Laverne E. (Haun) G. B.S. summa cum laude in Edn., U. Wis.-Whitewater, 1976, postgrad. Tchr., Lakeland (Wis.) Mfg. Co., 1972-76; instr. Sheboygan Pub. Schs., 1978—; counselor emotionally disturbed children; coach. Mem. Council Exceptional Children, Nat. Ret. Tchrs. Assn., Wis. Edn. Assn., Sheboygan Edn. Assn., PTA, Assn. Supervision and Curriculum Devel., Council Basic Edn., Luth. Women's League, Beta Sigma Phi. Lutheran. Home: 2427 Camelot Blvd Apt A Sheboygan WI 53081 Office: Farmsworth Middle Sch 1017 Union Ave Sheboygan WI 53081

GLASER, LOUIS FREDERICK, retail pharmacy executive; b. Clayton, Mo., Jan. 9, 1933; s. Morris and Edith (Katcher) G.; m. Ada Lee Hughes, July 16, 1967; children—Amy Sara, Robin Lee. Student, Rollins Coll., 1951-52; B.S., Washington U., St. Louis, 1957. With Medicare Pharmacies div. Glaser Drug Co., St. Louis, exec. v.p. Medicare-Glaser Corp., St. Louis, 1957—; dir. Landmark North County Bank & Trust Co. Trustee, St. Louis Coll. Pharmacy; 4th v.p., bd. dirs. St. Louis Assn. for Retarded Citizens; bd. dirs., treas. St. Louis Zoo Assn.; bd. dirs. v.p. St. Louis Jewish Hosp. Assocs. in Medicine; bd. dirs. mem. exec. com. St. Louis Holocaust Commn. Served with USMC, 1952-55. Mem. Nat. Assn. Chain Drug Stores, St. Louis Down Town, Inc. Republican. Jewish. Clubs: St. Louis, Racquet Ladue. Home: 4 Layton Terr Ladue MO 63124 Office: 2320 Schuetz Rd Saint Louis MO 63146

GLASER, THEODORE RICHARD, communications company executive; b. Chgo., Aug. 25, 1946; s. Edward Joseph and Joanne Mary G.; B.S., Loyola U., Chgo., 1972; m. Carolyn C. Martinkus, Apr. 26, 1969; children—Colleen, Teddy, Carrie. Nat. account mgr. AT&T Info. Systems (formerly Am. Bell Telephone Co.), Rolling Meadows, Ill. Served with USMC, 1966-72. Mem. Am. Mgmt. Assn., Internat. Air Freight Forwarding Assn. Roman Catholic. Club: KC (dist. dep. 1979). Developed Profile and Analysis of Air Freight Forwarding Industry, 1980-81. Home: 17401 S Oconto Tinley Park IL 60477 Office: 1 Crossroads of Commerce Room 600 Rolling Meadows IL 60008

GLASS, JAMES WILLIAM, theatre pipe organ installer; b. Oak Park, Ill., Dec. 13, 1946; s. Louis James and Grace Marie (Whaples) G.; B.S. in Elec. Engring., Ill. Inst. Tech., 1968. Electronic design engr. in data communications Gen. Telephone & Electronic Automatic Electric Labs., Inc., Northlake, Ill., 1968-72; self-employed as theatre pipe organ installer, Hinsdale, Ill., 1972—. Mem. Audio Engring. Soc., Am. Theatre Organ Soc., Owl Cinema Organ Guild (pres., chmn. bd. 1971—), Soc. Motion Picture and TV Engrs., Eta Kappa Nu. Home: 7823 Eleanor Clarendon Hills IL 60514 Office: 29 E 1st St Hinsdale IL 60521

GLASS, KENNETH EDWARD, material handling systems and wire and cable products executive; b. Ft. Thomas, Ky., Sept. 28, 1940; s. Clarence E. and Lucille (Garrison) G.; m. Nancy Romanek, May 9, 1964; children—Ryan, Lara. M.E., U. Cin., 1963, M.S., 1965, grad. student, 1967. With Allis Chalmers Mfg. Co., Cin. and Eng., 1963-73; v.p. mfg. Fiat Allis Contrn. Machinery, Inc., Chgo., 1973-75; pres. Perkins Diesel Corp., Canton, Ohio, 1975-77; pres., chief exec. officer Massey-Ferguson, Inc., Des Moines, 1978, v.p., gen. mgr. N. Am. ops. Massey Ferguson Ltd., Des Moines, 1978; chmn., pres., chief exec. officer Union Metal Mfg. Co., Canton, Ohio, 1979—; dir. Belden & Blake Oil Prodn., Inc. Trustee, Aultman Hosp. Mem. Young President's Orgn., ASME, Soc. Automotive Engrs. Patentee in field. Office: 111 2d St NW Canton OH 44702

GLASSER, JAMES J., leasing company executive; b. Chgo., June 5, 1934; s. Daniel D. and Sylvia G. Glasser, A.B., Yale U., 1955; J.D., Harvard U., 1958; m. Louise D. Rosenthal, Apr. 19, 1964; children—Mary, Emily, Daniel. Bar: Ill. 1968. Asst. states atty. Cook County (Ill.), 1958-61; mem. exec. staff GATX Corp., Chgo., 1961-69, pres., from 1974, chmn. bd., chief exec. officer, 1978—, also dir.; gen. mgr. Infilco Products Co., 1969-70; v.p. GATX Leasing Corp., San Francisco, 1970-71, pres., 1971-74; dir. Harris Trust & Savs. Bank, Mut. Trust Life Ins. Co., Oak Brook, Ill. Bd. trustees Northwestern Meml. Hosp., Chgo., Michael Reese Hosp. and Med. Center; sec. bd. trustees Chgo. Zool. Soc. Mem. Econ. Club Chgo., Chi Psi. Clubs: Casino, Chicago, Racquet, Tavern (Chgo.); Onwentsia, Winter (Lake Forest, Ill.); Lake Shore Country (Glencoe, Ill.). Office: GATX Corp 120 S Riverside Plaza Chicago IL 60606

GLASSMAN, BRIAN ASHER, lawyer; b. Washington, Aug. 3, 1955; s. Bernard Shalom and Audrey Ann (Lavine) G. Vis. student Brown U., 1975-76; B.A. with honors, Conn. Coll., 1977; J.D., Boston U., 1981. Bar: Ohio 1981, U.S. Dist. Ct. (no. dist.) Ohio 1981. Research asst. Nat. Consumer Law Ctr. Inc., Boston, 1978-80; intern Greater Boston Legal Services, 1980-81; staff atty. Legal Aid Soc. Cleve., 1981; mem. guardianship reform legis. com. Fedn. Community Planning Council on Older Persons, Cleve., spring 1983. Avocations: art; glassblowing; running; skiing; ice skating. Home: 2636 Queenston Rd Cleveland Heights OH 44118 Office: 5715 Woodland Ave Cleveland OH 44104

GLAUBER, ROBERT HASKELL, curator, author; b. N.Y.C., July 28, 1920; s. Lester and Lillian (Green) G. Student pub. schs. Editor, Alfred A. Knopf, Inc., N.Y.C., 1946-49, Decker Press, Prairie City, Ill., 1949-50; dir. pub. relations Nat. Assn. Bedding Mfrs., Chgo., 1951-58; writer pub. relations dept. Ill. Bell Telephone Co., Chgo., 1958-78, curator, 1958-78; curator AT&T, 1972-77; editor Beloit Poetry Jour., Wis., 1953-84; curator Union League Club, Chgo., 1982-84, First Ill. Bank, Evanston, 1981—, Sonnenschein Gallery, Lake Forest Coll., 1984—, Arthur Andersens' Co., Chgo., 1984—; writer art lit., lang. China and Japan, Ency. Brit. Jr., Chgo., 1965—; art critic Skyline, Art Scene, Chgo., 1967-75; instr. lit. Columbia Coll., Chgo., 1967-70; guest dir. Violence in Recent Am. Art, Mus. Contemporary Art, Chgo., 1968. Served with AUS, 1942-45. Recipient Chris award for documentary films Film Council Columbus, Ohio, 1962; writer Emmy-award- winning TV spls. Giants and the Common Man, 1968, From the Ashes, 1976. Contbr. articles to newspapers and lit. mags. Home: 424 Melrose St Chicago IL 60657

GLAUBERMAN, MURRAY, chemist, manufacturing company executive; b. Bloomfield, N.J., Dec. 27, 1927; s. Abe and Jean (Kass) G.; m. Lenore Marylin Sandler, Dec. 26, 1949; children—Stuart Craig, Jay D., Carol Glauberman Leaventon. B.S., MIT, 1948; student Inst. Paper Chemistry, Appleton, Wis., 1949-50. Chemist, Nopyron, Cambridge, Mass., 1949-50; plant mgr. Phipps Products, Richmond, Calif., 1950-51; gen. mgr. Kamen Soap Products, Barberton, Ohio, 1951-53; pres. Malco Products Inc., Barberton, 1953—. Trustee, Akron Jewish Ctr., 1964—, pres., 1972; trustee Akron Zool. Park, 1984; bd. dirs. Family Service Akron, 1984. Served with AUS, 1944-45. Mem. Chem. Specialties Mfrs. Assn. (bd. dirs. 1981-83, 1st vice chmn. 1984—). Avocation: wood carving. Office: Malco Products Inc 361 Fairview Ave Barberton OH 44203

GLAZER, SIDNEY, educator; b. Quincy, Mich., Nov. 1, 1905; s. Max and Mildred (Thal) G.; A.B., Wayne U., 1927; M.A., U. Mich., 1929, Ph.D., 1932. Asst. dept. history U. Mich., 1928-30; instr. Wayne State U., Detroit, 1930-37, asst. prof., 1937-48, asso. prof., 1948-55, prof., 1955—. Mem. Orgn. Am. Historians, Am., Mich. hist. socs., Econ. History Assn., A.A.U.P., Phi Beta Kappa. Author: (with M. M. Quaife) From Primitive Wilderness to Industrial Commonwealth, 1948; Industrial Detroit, 1951; The Middle West, 1962; Detroit: A Study in Urban Development, 1965. Contbr. articles to hist. revs. and mags.

GLAZER, STANFORD PAUL FRANK, restauranteur; b. Kansas City, Mo., Jan. 1, 1932; s. Jack and Ella (Gitterman) G.; m. Rita Ann Studna, July 1, 1951 (div. June 1968); children—Craig, Jeffery, Jack; m. Cheryl Anne Hurley Sheehan, Feb. 12, 1978. Grad. Kemper Mil. Sch., 1949. Pres., Royal Automotive Parts Co., 1958-61, Sav-On Stores, Inc., 1960-62, Mid-West Automobile Auction Corp., 1962-65; exec. v.p. Allied Material Equipment Corp., 1965-70; pres. Kansas City Arena, Ltd., 1970-74, Stanford Glazer & Assocs., 1978-81; chief exec. officer Stanford & Sons, Inc., Kansas City, Mo., 1976—, Stanford & Sons of St. Louis. Fellow Harry S. Truman Library. Served with M.C., U.S. Army, 1952-54. Recipient Epicurean award Carte Blanche, 1976, 77; Good Dining award Am. Diners Soc., 1977, 78; Silver Spoon award Outlook Mag., 1980. Mem. Nat. Restaurant Assn., Mo. Restaurant Assn. Jewish. Lodges: Masons, Shriners. Office: 504 Westport Rd Kansas City MO 64111

GLEASON, STEPHEN CHARLES, physician; b. Leon, Iowa, June 30, 1946; s. Charles Gerald and Ferne Louise (Pollard) G.; B.S., Iowa State U., 1971; D.Osteopathy, Coll. Osteo. Medicine and Surgery, 1974; m. Lisa Ann Corcoran, Aug. 22, 1981; children—Michael John, Timothy Charles, Christian Kelly, Sean Patrick. Resident in family practice, Meml. Med. Center, Corpus Christi, Tex., 1974-75; family practice medicine, West Des Moines, Iowa, 1975—; chmn. dept. family practice Mercy Hosp. Med. Center, Des Moines, 1979-83; med. dir. West Suburban Center, West Des Moines; pres. Talent Mgmt. Ltd., West Des Moines, 1979-80; dep. med. examiner, Polk County, Des Moines, 1976-82; chmn. bd. Valley Med. Services, P.C., adj. clin. prof. family practice Coll. Osteo. Medicine and Surgery, Des Moines, 1979—; regional med. adv. Emergency Med. Tng. Program Central Iowa, 1975-76; med. dir. emergency medicine, Clive, Iowa Fire Rescue, 1976-78, West Des Moines Fire Rescue, 1976-79; physician adv. Iowa Found. Med. Care, Profl. Standards Review Orgn., West Des Moines, 1978—; faculty instr. Iowa Heart Assn., Des Moines, 1978-80; mem. papal med. security team Pope John Paul's Am. Pilgrimage, 1979; mem. bishop's com. on health care Des Moines Diocese, 1982-83; med. dir. health and human services corp. Mercy Hosp. Med. Ctr., 1983, chief med. officer Mercy Med. Clinic System. Mem. nat. com. Republican party, 1978-79; mem. nat. Rep. Senatorial Com., U.S. Senatorial Club, 1979; bd. dirs. Mercy Health and Human Services, Our Primary Purpose, Inc.; mem. Iowa cares Med. Found. Diplomate Am. Bd. Family Practice. recipient Outstanding Young Iowan award, 1982. Mem. Am. Acad. Family Physicians, Am. Coll. Emergency Physicians, AMA, Iowa Acad. Sci., Iowa Med. Soc., Iowa Acad. Family Practice, Polk County Med. Soc., Sigma Alpha Epsilon, Sigma Sigma Phi. Democrat. Office: Valley West Mall Suite 106 West Des Moines IA 50265

GLEAVES, EARL WILLIAM, animal science educator; b. Miami, Okla., Apr. 3, 1930; s. Orville and Mattie L. (Able) G.; m. Lois D. Price, Dec. 30, 1950; children—Aloah, Kenneth, Dale. B.S., Okla. State U., 1953, M.S., 1961, Ph.D., 1965. Mgr., Williams Ranch, Santa Fe, 1953-56, Moneka Farm Stores, Parsons and Oswego, Kans., 1956-57; mem. faculty Okla. State U., Stillwater, 1962-63; mem. faculty U. Nebr., Lincoln, 1964—, prof. animal sci., poultry nutrition, 1973—. 4-H Club leader, 1965-75; active Partners of the Americas, 1979—. Ralston Purina Co. fellow, 1961; recipient Poultryman of Yr. award Nebr. Poultry Industries, 1971, Excellence in Programming award Nebr. Coop. Extension Service, 1979, Livestock Service award Walnut Grove Products, 1980. Mem. Poultry Sci. Assn. (Pfizer Extension award 1984), World Poultry Sci. Assn., Nebr. Coop. Extension Assn., Epsilon Sigma Phi, Gamma Sigma Delta (Extension award 1984). Democrat. Methodist. Contbr. numerous articles to profl. jours. Office: Dept Animal Sci 105 Mussehl Hall East Campus-U Nebr Lincoln NE 68583

GLEESON, LISA KRISTEN, communications company executive; b. Detroit, Mar. 3, 1953; d. Friedrich and Alice Newhall (Rutherford) Fiesselmann; m. Kevin Joseph Gleeson, Sept. 1, 1979. B.A., Mich. State U., 1975. Mgr., Mich. Bell Co., Detroit, 1976—. Founder, pres. Women in Mgmt. and Profl. Network, 1979-82; coordinator, recruiter Project Bus./Jr. Achievement, Southeastern Mich., 1979-83, bus. cons., 1978—. Named Citizen of Month, Mich. Bell Telephone Co., 1984. Mem. Nat. Assn. Credit Mgmt. (bd. dirs. 1985—). Club: Village (Bloomfield Hills, Mich.). Avocations: scuba diving; collecting art. Home: 334 Burtman Troy MI 48083

GLEICHMAN, JOHN ALAN, safety and security executive; b. Anthoney, Kans., Feb. 11, 1944; s. Charles William and Caroline Elizabeth (Emch) G.; m. Martha Jean Cannon, July 1, 1966; 1 son, John Alan Jr. B.S. in Bus. Mgmt., Kans. State Tchrs. Coll., 1966. Cert. hazard control mgr.; cert. safety profl. Office mgr. to asst. supt. Barton-Malow Co., Detroit, 1967-72, safety coordinator, 1972-76, corp. mgr. safety and security, 1976—; instr. U. Mich., Wayne State U., 1977-81; mem. constrn. safety standards commn. adv. com. for concrete constrn. and steel erection Bur. of Safety and Regulations, Mich. Dept. Labor, 1977—. Instr. multi media first aid ARC, 1976—; past trustee Apostolic Christian Ch., Livonia, Mich. Recipient Safety Achievement awards Mich. Mut. Ins. Co., 1979-83; Cameron award Constrn. sect. Indsl. div. Nat. Safety Conf., 1982. Mem. Mich. Safety Council (pres. 1984-85), Am. Soc. Safety Engrs. (pres. Detroit chpt. 1982; Safety Prof. of Yr. chpt. 1984) Nat. Safety Council (chmn. tech. rev. constrn. sect. indsl. div. 1980-84, chmn. standards com. indsl. div. 1983-85). Author: (with others) You, The National Safety Council, and Voluntary Standards, 1981. Office: PO Box 5200 Detroit MI 48235

GLENN, CLETA MAE, lawyer; b. Clinton, Ill., Sept. 24, 1921; d. John and Mattie Sylvester (Anderson) Glenn; B.S., U. Ill., 1947; J.D., DePaul U. Coll. Law, 1976; m. Rex Eugene Loggans, Sept. 3, 1948 (div.); 1 dau., Susan. Real estate builder, developer, 1959-69; communications dir. Transp. Research Center, Northwestern U., Evanston, Ill., 1969-72; admitted to Ill. bar, 1977; practice law, Chgo., 1977—; lectr. Assn. Trial Lawyers Am., John Marshall Law Sch. Served with U.S. Navy, 1943-59. Recipient Real Estate Humanitarian award Kislak Co., Miami, Fla., 1962. Mem. Am. Bar Assn. (com. chmn.), Ill. Bar Assn. (assembly rep., mem. standing com. on traffic laws and cts., family law sect. council), Chgo. Bar Assn., Assn. Trial Lawyers Am., Ill. Trial Lawyers Assn., Lex Leggio, Phi Alpha Delta. Editor: Collective Bargaining and Technological Change in American Transportation, 1979; contbr. articles to profl. publs. Home: 200 E Delaware Pl Chicago IL 60611 Office: 69 W Washington St Chicago IL 60602

GLENN, G(EORGE) DALE, educational administrator; b. Decker, Ind., Oct. 7, 1939; s. George Berry and Nola Marie (Hoffman) G.; m. Deborah Lynn Medenwald, Aug. 29, 1970; children—Darin, Shannon, Kevin. B.S. in Edn., Ind. U., 1962, M.S. in Edn., 1963, Ed.S., 1973, Ed.D., 1975. Tchr. Speedway High Sch., Indpls., 1962-70; basketball coach, asst. prin. Huntingburg High Sch., Ind., 1970-72; prin. Huntingburg Middle Sch., 1972-74, Univ. Middle Sch., Bloomington, Ind., 1975-83, Batchelor Middle Sch., Bloomington, 1983—; instr. Ind. U., Bloomington, 1976, 80. Author: History of IHSAA, 1976. Contbr. articles to ednl. jours. Mem. Nat. Assn. Secondary Sch. Prins., Ind. Secondary Sch. Adminstrs., Ind. U. Edn. Alumni Assn. (pres. 1981), Ind. U. Alumni Assn. (exec. council 1984-87), Monroe County Adminstrs. Assn., North Central Assn. Colls. and Schs. (Ind. state com.). Methodist. Avocations: traveling; reading; golf; tennis; jogging. Office: Batchelor Middle Sch 900 Gordon Pike Bloomington IN 47401

GLENN, JOHN HERSCHEL, JR., U.S. senator; b. Cambridge, Ohio, July 18, 1921; s. John Herschel and Clara (Sproat) G.; student Muskingum Coll., 1939, B.Sc., 1961; naval aviation cadet U. Iowa, 1942; grad. flight sch. Naval Air Tng. Center, Corpus Christi, Tex., 1943, Navy Test Pilot Tng. Sch., Patuxent River, Md., 1954; m. Anna Margaret Castor, Apr. 1943; children—Carolyn Ann, John David. Commd. 2d lt. USMC, 1943, advanced through grades to col.; assigned 4th Marine Aircraft Wing, Marshall Islands campaign, 1944, 9th Marine Aircraft Wing, 1945-46; with 1st Marine Aircraft Wing, North China Patrol, also Guam, 1947-48; flight instr. advanced flight tng., Corpus Christi, 1949-51; asst. G-2/G-3 Amphibious Warfare Sch., Quantico, Va., 1951; with Marine Fighter Squadron 311, exchange pilot 25th Fighter Squadron USAF, Korea, 1953; project officer fighter design br. Navy Bur. Aero., Washington, 1956-69; nonstop supersonic transcontinental Flight, July 16, 1957; astronaut Project Mercury, Manned Spacecraft Center NASA, 1959-64, pilot Mercury-Atlas 6, orbital space flight launched from Cape Canaveral, Fla., Feb., 1962; v.p. corp. devel. and dir. Royal Crown Cola Co., 1962-74; U.S. Senator from Ohio, 1975—. Trustee Muskingum Coll. Decorated D.F.C. (five), Air medal (18), Astronaut medal USMC, Navy unit commendation; Korean Presidential unit citation; Disting. Merit award Muskingum Coll.; Medal of Honor, N.Y.C. Mem. Soc. Exptl. Test Pilots, Internat. Acad. of Astronautics (hon.). Democrat. Presbyterian. Co-author: We Seven 1962. Author: P.S., I Listened to Your Heart Beat. Office: 503 Hart Office Bldg Washington DC 20510

GLENN, ROY JOHNSON, manufactured housing executive; b. Birmingham, Ala., Dec. 23, 1920; s. Willis and Maggie (Johnson) G.; student acctg. Massey Bus. Coll., 1938-39; student engring. Auburn U., 1941-42; m. Sammie Lee Spradling, Feb. 14, 1941; children—Ellen Glenn Andersen, Jerry Alan. Mold loftsman, Higgins Industries, New Orleans, 1943-44; partner Glenn Constrn. Co., Birmingham, Ala., 1946-50; profl. golfer, 1950-57; pres. Crab Orchard Golf Club, Inc., Carterville, Ill., 1958-63; sec., treas. Cavaness-Glenn-Storme, Inc., Carterville, 1964-75; pres. Glenn & Co., Inc., Carterville, 1963-76; sec. Component Building Systems, Inc., Carbondale, Ill., 1976—; ptnr. Roydon & Assocs., Carbondale, 1982—; owner Crest Builders Assocs., 1977—, Design Cons., 1983—; cons. various golf and country clubs; designer golf courses and bldgs. Bd. trustees John A. Logan Coll., 1968-70. Served with USN, 1944-46. Republican. Baptist. Home and Office: Route 2 Carbondale IL 62901

GLENNER, RICHARD ALLEN, dentist, dental historian; b. Chgo., Apr. 14, 1934; s. Robert Joseph and Vivian (Prosk) G.; B.S., Roosevelt U., 1955; B.S. in Dentistry, U. Ill., 1958, D.D.S., 1959; m. Dorothy Chapman, July 13, 1957; children—Mark Steven, Alison. Gen. practice dentistry, Chgo., 1962—; cons. on dental history to Smithsonian Instn., ADA, various corps., libraries, univs., museums, dental jours. Served to capt. AUS, 1960-62. Mem. Am. (monthly columnist Jour. ADA), Ill. dental assns., Chgo. Dental Soc., Assn. Mil. Surgeons U.S., Am. Acad. History of Dentistry (historian 1984, Hayden-Harris award 1983), Fed. Dentaire Internationale, Am. Med. Writers Assn., Alpha Omega. Author: The Dental Office: A Pictorial History; cons. editor A Bicentennial Salute to Am. Dentistry, 1976; contbr. articles on dental history to profl. jours. Home: 6715 N Lawndale Ave Lincolnwood IL 60645 Office: 3414 W Peterson Ave Chicago IL 60659

GLESNE, RONALD LEE, marketing executive; b. Elkader, Iowa, Mar. 29, 1935; s. Raymond Oliver and Myrtle (Josephine) G.; m. Gloria Elaine Lenning, Feb. 10, 1968; 1 dau., Michelle Marie. B.S.C., U. Iowa, 1957. Sales rep. Mobil Oil Co., Mpls., 1957-62; dist. sales mgr. Velie Sales Inc., Mpls., 1962-65; v.p., ptnr. G & D Sales, Inc., Mpls., 1965-71; v.p. Midwest Mktg., Inc., Mpls., 1971-75; pres. Glesne Sales Inc., Mpls., 1975—. Served with AUS, 1958-60. Mem. Sales & Mktg. Execs. (dir. 1979-80 Mpls.), Auto Booster Club, Auto Affiliated Reps. (dir. 1982-84), Auto Parts and Accessories Assn., N.W. Hardware Housewares Club. Republican. Lutheran. Clubs: Masons, Shriners. Home: 1470 Cherry Pl Orono MN 55364 Office: Glesne Sales Inc 2649 Louisiana Ave Minneapolis MN 55426

GLICK, CYNTHIA SUSAN, lawyer; b. Sturgis, Mich., Aug. 6, 1950; d. Elmer Joseph and Ruth Edna (McCally) G. A.B., Ind. U., 1972; J.D., Ind. U.-Inpls., 1978. Bar: Ind. 1978, U.S. Dist. Ct. (so. dist.) Ind. 1978, U.S. Dist. Ct. (no. dist.) Ind. 1981. Adminstrv. asst. Gov. Otis R. Bowen, Ind., 1973-76; law clk. Ind. Ct. Appeals, 1976-79; dep. pros. atty. 35th Jud. Cir., LaGrange County, Ind., 1980-82, pros. atty., 1983—. Campaign aide Ind. Republican State Central Com., Indpls., 1972-73. Named Hon. Speaker, Ind. Ho. of Reps., 1972, Sagamore of the Wabash, Gov. Ind., 1974. Fellow Ind. Bar Found.; mem. ABA, Am. Judicature Soc., Ind. State Bar Assn., LaGrange County Bar Assn. (pres. 1983—), DAR, Delta Zeta. Republican. Methodist. Lodge: Eastern Star. Home: 113 W Spring St LaGrange IN 46761 Office: 124 N Detroit St LaGrange IN 46761

GLICK, DAVID M., biochemist; b. San Francisco, Jan. 4, 1936; s. David and Ruth (Mueller) G.; m. Jacqueline Zwirn, Apr. 23, 1961; children—Daniel, Naomi, Noah. B.A., Oberlin Coll., 1957; Ph.D., Western Res. U., 1962. Research fellow Weizmann Inst. Sci., Rehovot, Israel, 1962, Kings Coll., London, 1963, Brookhaven Nat. Lab., Upton, N.Y., 1964-66; asst. prof. Med. Coll. Wis., Milw., 1966-72, assoc., 1972—; vis. prof. U. Libre, Brussels, 1973-74. Contbr. articles to profl. jours. Author self examination guide Biochemistry, 1975, 80, 83. Mem. Am. Chem. Soc., Biochem. Soc. (London), Am. Soc. Biol. Chemists. Jewish. Office: Med Coll Wis 8701 Watertown Plank Rd Milwaukee WI 53226

GLICK, MILTON DON, chemist, university administrator; b. Memphis, July 30, 1937; s. Lewis S. and Sylvia (Kleinman) G.; m. Peggy M., June 21, 1965; children—David, Sander. A.B. cum laude, Augustana Coll., 1959; Ph.D., U. Wis., 1965. Fellow, dept. chemistry Cornell U., Ithaca, N.Y., 1964-66; asst. prof. chemistry Wayne State U., Detroit, 1966-70, asso. prof., 1970-74, prof., 1974-83, chmn. dept., 1978-83; dean arts and sci. U. Mo.-Columbia, 1983—. Co-founder, pres. Congregation T'Chiyah, 1977-79. Mem. Am. Chem. Soc., Am. Crystallographic Assn. Contbr. articles in structural inorganic chemistry to profl. jours. Office: 210 Jesse Hall U Mo Columbia MO 65211

GLICK, WILLIAM LEVITT, automobile company executive; b. Bklyn., June 17, 1947; s. Norman and Edith Helen (Levitt) G.; divorced; children—Jason Lawrence, Lauren Michelle. B.S., U. Bridgeport (Conn.), 1968; postgrad. St. John's U., Fairleigh Dickinson U. Sr. acct. Peat, Marwick, Mitchell & Co., C.P.A.s, N.Y.C., 1969-72; regional mktg. mgr. N.E. region Ford div. Ford Motor Co., Detroit, 1972—; speaker in field. Mem. N.Y. Army N.G., 1968-73. Recipient Rotary award, 1978. Mem. Am. Inst. C.P.A.s, N.Y. State Soc. C.P.A.s. Office: Ford Motor Co 300 Renaissance Center Detroit MI 48243

GLICKMAN, DANIEL ROBERT, Congressman; b. Wichita, Kans., Nov. 24, 1944; B.A., U. Mich., 1966; J.D., George Washington U., 1969; m. Rhoda Yura, 1966; children—Jonathan, Amy. Practiced law, Washington; trial atty. SEC, 1969-70; partner firm Sargent, Klenda & Glickman, 1973-76; mem. 95th-98th congresses from 4th Kans. Dist., mem. agr. com., sci. and tech. com., judiciary com., chmn. subcom. on transp., aviation and materials. Mem. Wichita Sch. Bd., 1973-76, pres., 1975-76; active Arthritis Found., Big Bros.-Big Sisters. Democrat. Office: Room 2435 Rayburn House Office Bldg Washington DC 20515

GLIEBERMAN, HERBERT ALLEN, lawyer; b. Chgo., Dec. 6, 1930; s. Elmer and Jean (Gerber) G.; student U. Ill., 1947, Roosevelt U., 1948-50; J.D., Chgo. Kent Coll. Law, 1953; m. Evelyn Eraci, Nov. 26, 1936; children—Ronald, Gale, Joel. Admitted to Ill. bar, 1954; pvt. practice law, Chgo., 1954—; lectr. Chgo. Kent Coll. Law, Ill. Inst. Continuing Legal Edn. Trustee Chgo. Kent Coll. Law; bd. dirs. Chgo. Council on Alcoholism. Recipient certificates of appreciation Am. Acad. Matrimonial Lawyers, Ill. Bar Assn., 1967, Assn. Trial Lawyers Am., 1973, Ill. Trial Lawyers Assn., 1974, 83, 84, Decologue Soc., 1965, 66, 68. Mem. Am. Acad. Matrimonial Lawyers, Decologue Soc. Lawyers (bd. dirs.), Am., Ill., trial lawyers assns., Am., Ill., Chgo. bar assns. Jewish (pres. temple). Author: Some Syndromes of Love, 1965; Know Your Legal Rights, 1974; Confessions of A Divorce Lawyer; 1975; Closed Marriage, 1978; Four Weekends to an Ideal Marriage, 1981. Home: 180 E Pearson St Chicago IL 60611 Office: 19 S La Salle St Chicago IL 60603

GLINSKI, PATRICIA JANE, interior designer; b. Milw., Feb. 24, 1943; d. Edwin Frederick and Gertrude Carol (Anderson) Bandt; m. William Robert Glinski, Mar. 23, 1968; children—Gregory, Catherine, Mark, Elizabeth. B.S., U. Wis.-Madison, 1966. Interior designer Don Reppen & Assocs., Madison, Wis., 1965-68, Paul Albitz Studio, Inc., Mpls., 1968-70; owner, mgr. Glinski Design, Mpls. and Wausau, Wis., 1970-76; sr. office designer Wausau Ins. Cos., 1976-82; pres. GBI Group, Inc., Glinski Bus. Interiors, Wausau, 1982—; cons. Wausau Conservatory Music, 1984—. Pres. Wausau Symphony League, 1983-85; bd. dirs. Wausau Symphony, 1984-88. Mem. Inst. Bus. Designers (nat. trustee 1984-86), AAUW (cultural chair Wausau chpt. 1984—), Wausau C. of C. (chmn. beautification com. 1984—). Home: 7215 Wall St Schofield WI 54476 Office: GBI Group Inc 210 McClellan St Wausau WI 54401

GLOMMEN, HARVEY HAMILTON, social work consultant, counselor; b. Suttons Bay, Mich., Mar. 25, 1928; s. Lars Louis and Serena Sadie (Rorem) G.; B.A., Concordia Coll., 1953; postgrad. U. Minn., 1953-54, 60, 61, 62, U. Chgo., summer 1959; M.S.W., U. Mich., 1964; m. Ina Mae Wollertson, June 24, 1951; children—Brent, Barbara, Beth, Brenda. Social worker Hennepin and Anoka counties (Minn.) Welfare Bds., 1954-58; county welfare dir. Cottonwood County (Minn.) Welfare Dept., Windom, 1959-60; dir. Aitkin County (Minn.) Welfare Dept., Aitkin, 1960-63; tng. cons. for exec., supervisory tng. Minn. Dept. Pub. Welfare, St. Paul, 1964-65, supr. adoptions, 1965-66; dir. foster grandparents program Adminstrn. Aging, HEW, Washington, 1966-67; exec. dir. Minn. Assn. Retarded Citizens, Mpls., 1967-69; practice marriage and family counseling, cons. in human service, Mpls., 1972—; foster parent for mentally ill adults, 1975—; incorporator, pres. Our Place, emotionally disturbed facility, Blaine, 1977—; owner Circus Candy Co., Mpls., 1972—, 1048 87th Ave NE, Blaine, Minn., 1968—; instr. clock repair, St. Paul, 1981—. Mem. city charter commn., Blaine, 1974-82; chmn. Blaine City Charter Commn., 1976-79; mem. constn. commn. Minn. Dem.-Farmer-Labor Party, 1976-78, fin. dir. Minn. Senate Dist. 47, 1975-78, chmn., 1978-80; treas. Anoka County Assn. for Retarded Citizens, 1969-71, bd. dirs., 1969-72; bd. dirs., incorporator Anoka County Family Service Assn., 1970-72; incorporator, pres. Anoka County Mental Health Advocates Coalitions, 1982—; mem. Anoka County Health and Human Services Bd., 1983—; mem. Anoka County Mc Knight Mental Health Consortium, 1983—, chmn. residential services com., 1983—. Served to 1st lt. AUS, 1946-50; Germany. Minn. Tng. fellow, 1963. Mem. Minn., Nat. pub. health assns., Minn., Nat. vocat. rehab. assns., Nat. Assn. Watch and Clock Collectors, Minn. Watchmakers Assn. (bd. dirs. 1985—), Minn. Clockmakers (chmn. examining com. 1985—) Phi Kappa Phi. Democrat. Lutheran (youth bd. 1970-73, ch. council 1970-73, pres. congregation 1982-84). Home and office: 1048 87th Ave NE Blaine MN 55434

GLOU, RONALD STEPHEN, corporate environmental manager; b. Scranton, Pa., Oct. 4, 1938; s. Jack Carl and Cele (Isaac) G. B.S. in Chem. Engring., Pa. State U., 1960; M.S., U. N.C., 1968; Ph.D. in Environ. Sci., Marist U., 1971; J.D., NYU, 1975. Registered profl. engr., N.Y., Pa.; cert. indsl. hygienist, safety profl. Project officer Office Surgeon Gen. U.S. Army, Washington, 1963-66; regional indsl. hygienist IBM, Poughkeepsie, N.Y., 1968-75; dir. environ. health CNA Ins. Co., Chgo., 1975-77; corp. dir. environ. activities G.D. Searle Co., Skokie, Ill., 1977-80; corp. mgr. regulatory affairs Dart & Kraft, Inc., Northbrook, Ill., 1981—. USPHS grantee, 1966-68. Fellow Am. Indsl. Hygienist Assn., Am. Soc. Safety Engrs., Nat. Soc. Safety Mgrs.; mem. Air Pollution Control Assn., Am. Soc. Pub. Health. Avocations: tennis, running, cycling.

GLOVER, ROBERT EDWARD, ice cream mfg. co. exec.; b. Frankfort, Ind., Nov. 13, 1930; s. Foster Robert and Virginia Mary (Oldshoes) G.; B.S., U. Ark., 1952; m. Virginia M. Mann, Oct. 3, 1954; children—Robert Stephen, Thom Scott, Beth Marie. Pres., Glover's Ice Cream, Frankfort, Ind. Served with AUS, 1952-53. Mem. Sigma Chi. Clubs: Jesters, Masons, Shriners, Elks, Rotary, Moose, Symposiarchs, Country (Frankfort). Home: 609 Harvard Terr Frankfort IN 46041 Office: 705 W Clinton St Frankfort IN 46041

GLOYD, LAWRENCE EUGENE, hardware manufacturing company executive; b. Milan, Ind., Nov. 5, 1932; s. Oran C. and Ruth (Baylor) G.; m. Delma Lear, Sept. 10, 1955; children—Sheryl, Julia, Susan. B.A., Hanover Coll., 1954. Salesman, Amerock Corp., Rockford, Ill., 1961-68, regional sales mgr., 1968-69, dir. consumer products mktg., 1969-71, dir. merchandising, 1971-72, dir. mktg. and sales, 1972-73, v.p. mktg. and sales, 1973-81, exec. v.p., 1981-82, pres., gen. mgr., 1982—; v.p. Hardware Products Group, Anchor Hocking Corp., Lancaster, Ohio; dir. J.L. Clark Mfg. Co., Rockford, Ill., Am. Nat. Bank & Trust Co., Rockford, Ill., mem. Middle West adv. bd. Liberty Mut. Ins. Co. Bd. dirs. Russell R. Mueller-Retail Research Found., Council of 100; trustee Rockford Coll., Swedish Am. Corp. Served with AUS, 1954-56. Mem. Am. Hardware Mfrs. Assn. (bd. dirs.), Bldrs. Hardware Mfg. Assn., Hardware Group Assn., Ill. Mfg. Assn., NAM, Nat. Kitchen Cabinet Assn., Nat. Retail Hardware Assn., Nat. Wholesale Hardware Assn., Nat. Woodwork Mfg. Assn., Presidents Assn. Republican. Lodge: Masons. Home: 4979 Crofton Dr Rockford IL 61111 Office: PO Box 7018 4000 Auburn St Rockford IL 61125-7018

GLUECK, SIDNEY JOHN, ophthalmologist; b. Phila., Apr. 16, 1914; s. Samuel Jonathon and Anna (Fox) G.; m. Charlotte Ornsten, Nov. 8, 1959; children—David, Suzan. B.A., U. Pa., 1936; M.D., Sch. Medicine of Royal Colls., Edinburgh, Scotland, 1947. Diplomate Am. Bd. Ophthalmology. Intern Stobhill Hosp., Glasgow, Scotland, 1946-47; resident in ophthalmology Grad. Sch. Medicine, U. Pa., 1951-52, D.C. Gen. Hosp., 1953-55; gen. practice, Springfield, Ohio, 1947-51; practice medicine specializing in ophthalmology, Springfield; chmn. dept. ophthalmology Community Hosp., Springfield; mem. staff Greene Meml. Hosp., Xenia, Ohio; assoc. clin. prof. Wright State U. Sch. Medicine; cons. in field; mem. Oxford Ophthal. Congress, 1959. Contbr. articles to profl. jours. Pres. bd. trustees Ridgewood Sch., 1969-74; trustee Springfield Urban League, Fellow Am. Acad. Ophthalmology and Otolaryngology. Lodge: Lions. Office: 1525 Xenia Ave Yellow Springs OH 45387

GNAT, RAYMOND EARL, See *Who's Who in America*, 43rd edition.

GNAU, JOHN RUSSELL, JR., public relations executive; b. Detroit, Mar. 3, 1930; s. John Russell and Constance L. Gnau; Student in Journalism, U. Detroit, 1952; m. Margaret Maher, July 25, 1952; children—Kathleen, Russell, Michael, Margaret, Julie. With sales and promotion dept. Sta. WWJ-TV, Detroit, 1951-54; gen. agt. Ohio State Life and Columbus Mut. Ins. Co., 1954-68; v.p. Alexander Hamilton Life Ins. Co., Farmington, Mich., 1968-71; pres., chmn. bd. Gnau-Carter-Jacobsen, Washington, Detroit, Los Angeles, 1979—. State chmn. for Mich., Reagan campaign, 1976, 80, fin. chmn., 1984; mem. Oakland County (Mich.) Road Commn., 1972-84; trustee Bloomfield Twp., 1972-76. Named Man of Yr., Ohio State Life Ins. Co., 1967. Clubs: Detroit Athletic; Oakland Hills Country; Huron Hunting and Fishing. Address: 3894 Peabody Dr Bloomfield Hills MI 48013

GOBEILLE, WILLIAM PALMER, engineering and development administrator; b. Cin., Feb. 2, 1918; s. William Hugh and Gertrude (Palmer) G.; m. Catherine Ella O'Leary, Sept. 4, 1940; children—Nancy, Richard, Bette, Paul. B.S.M.E., Purdue U., 1940. Registered profl. engr., Ill. Sales engr. Union Spl. Machine, Chgo., 1940-42; chief engr. Ampco Metal Inc., Milw., 1942-45; works mgr. Cruver Mfg., Chgo., 1945-48; mgr. plastics div. Am. Motors Corp., Detroit, 1948-68; v.p. Sheller-Globe Corp., Toledo, 1968-83, cons., 1983—. Active PTA, Girl Scouts U.S.A., Boy Scouts Am., YMCA. Mem. Soc. Plastics Engrs. (dir., Man of Yr. 1972). Republican. Congregationalist. Club: Sylvania Country. Lodge: Shriners.

GOBER, MIKE, electronic cabinet company sales executive; b. Waukegan, Ill., Jan. 19, 1959; s. Miles Orval and Bernice (Bullock) G.; m. Wendi Lee Rymer, May 3, 1980; 1 child, Brandon Michael. A.A. in Bus., Coll. of Lake County, 1978. Sales mgr. Cabtron Systems Inc., Northbrook, Ill., 1977—. Mem. budget com. Second Bapt. Ch., Zion, Ill., 1982-83, trustee, 1984—. Republican. Baptist. Avocations: golf; racquet ball; bowling. Home: 41222 N Elizabeth Ave Zion IL 60099 Office: Cabtron Systems Inc 200 Anets Dr Northbrook IL 60002

GOBIN, SHAIRA, insurance company consultant; b. Guyana, July 13, 1950; came to U.S., 1974, naturalized, 1985; d. Wajid Ally and Azifan (Ally) Khan; m. Roy Tyrone Gobin, Sept. 8, 1973; children—Melissa, Allister. B.Sc. in Computer Sci and Math., U. Ill., 1977; M.S. in Stats., 1978. Teaching asst. U. Ill.-Chgo., 1977-78; programmer, analyst Jackson Park Hosp., Chgo., 1979-80; sr. cons. Blue Cross/Blue Shield, Chgo., 1980—. Mem. Assn. Systems Mgmt. Office: Blue Cross/Blue Shield Assn 676 N St Clair St Chicago IL 60611

GODDARD, JESSIE GRAY, school administrator, freelance writer; b. Bremerton, Wash., Dec. 19, 1913; d. Christian Carlos Breiland and Josie Amanda (Gray) B.; m. Cephas Jason Goddard, Aug. 17, 1942; children—Cephas Christian, Jeffrey Olaf, David Gray. Student U. Wash., 1930-34; B.S. in Edn., Minot State Coll., 1963-65; postgrad. Regis Coll. 1969, U. Minn., 1970, U. N.D., 1968-70. Reporter, writer for various newspapers, Wash., N.D., 1930—; tchr. Mandaree High Sch., N.D., 1965-67; grad. teaching asst. U. N.D., Grand Forks, 1968-71, instr. U. N.D.-Williston Ctr., 1972-75; mem. N.D. Humanities Council, 1979-84; county supt. schs. McKenzie County, Watford City, N.D., 1981—. Contbr. articles to profl. jours. Editor Jour. Flickertales, 1960s, Type Hi, 1960s; columnist Williston Daily Herald, 1976—. Fund solicitor Cancer Fund, McKenzie County; chmn. bd. McKenzie County Rural Library, Watford City, 1981—; sec. Helen Gough Scholarship Found., Watford City, 1981—, Tri-County Sch. Bds. Assn., 1981—. Recipient Outstanding Tchr. award Assn. Depts. English and MLA, 1969-70; Groundbreaking award Trenton Housing Project, N.D., 1976; 3d place award for book rev. N.D. Press Women, 1982, 2d place award for personal collection, 1983. Mem. N.D. Council Sch. Adminstrs., Young Citizens League (state bd. dirs. 1982—), State Dept. Pub. Instrn. (regional coordinator Chpt. I monitoring 1983—), N.D. Assn. County Supts. Republican. Presbyterian. Clubs: Nat. CowBelles, N.D. Press Women (dir. 1980-82), OX5 Aviation Pioneers. Lodge: Order Eastern Star (Worthy Matron 1965-66). Avocations: freelance writing and research; reading; travel. Office: McKenzie County Supt of Schs County Courthouse Watford City ND 58854

GODFREY, WILLIAM ASHLEY, ophthalmologist; b. Arkansas City, Kans., May 19, 1938; B.A., U. Kans.-Lawrence, 1961; M.D., U. Kans. Sch. Medicine, Kansas City, 1965. Diplomate Am. Bd. Ophthalmology. Intern, Tulane U., New Orleans, 1965-66; resident U. Kans. Sch. Medicine, 1968-71; research fellow U. Calif.-San Francisco, 1971-73; asst. prof., then assoc. prof. U. Kans. Sch. Medicine, 1973-84, prof. ophthalmology, 1984—; mem. staff St. Luke's Hosp., Kansas City, Mo., 1973—, Kansas U. Med. Ctr., Kansas City, 1973—; cons. Kansas City Vets Hosp., Mo., 1973—. Contbr. articles to profl. publs. Served with USAF, 1966-68. NIH fellow, 1971-73; fellow Am. Acad. Ophthalmology, (honor ward 1983), Am. Uveitis Soc., Am. Coll. Physicians. Mem. AMA, Am. Fedn. Clin. Research, Am. Rheumatism Assn., Assn. Research in Vision and Ophthalmology, Am. Math. Soc., Ocular Immunology and Microbiology Soc., Kansas City Soc. Ophthalmology, Kans. Med. Soc., Mo. Ophthalmology Soc., Jackson County Med. Soc., Wyandotte County Med. Soc., Johnson County Med Soc., Alpha Omega Alpha. Office: Curts Wurster & Godfrey 4320 Wornall Rd Kansas City MO 64111

GODLEW, CAROL LYNN, middle school administrator; b. Highland Park, Mich., Dec. 17, 1942; d. Leslie Kopplow and Elanora Katherine (Pfeffer) Walker; m. Dennis Allan Godlew, Dec. 16, 1961; children—Scott Allan, Cheryl Lynn. B.A., Western Mich. U., 1965, M.Edn. Leadership, 1980. Cert. secondary tchr., Mich. Tchr., Lawrence pub. schs., Mich., 1965-66, Bangor pub. schs., Mich., 1966-81; prin. Hartford pub. schs., Mich., 1981—. Recipient Freedoms Found. award Am. Legion Aux., Bangor, 1978. Mem. Mich. Assn. Secondary Sch. Prins., Prins. (Outstanding Secondary Sch. Prin. Center 7, 1984-85), Assn. Career Edn., Mich. Assn. Middle Sch. Educators. Republican. Congregationalist. Avocations: camping, travel, hand bells. Office: Hartford Middle Sch PO Box 158 Hartford MI 49057

GOEBEL, EDWARD JOHN, II, marketing executive; b. Indpls., Nov. 8, 1945; s. Edward John and Ruth C. (Hazelrigg) G.; m. Pamela Vandivort, July 19, 1980; children—Kip Andrew, Brad Christopher. B.S. in Pharmacy, Butler U., 1968. Registered pharmacist, Ind. With Eli Lilly & Co., Indpls., 1971-83; dir. mktg. Boehringer Mannheim Diagnostics, Indpls., 1983—. Mem. Am. Diabetes Assn., Am. Assn. Diabetic Nurse Educators, Am. Pharm. Assn. Republican. Home: 10619 Fall Creek Rd Indianapolis IN 46256

GOEBEL, JOAN MARY, physician, consultant; b. Marietta, Ohio, June 24, 1906; d. Joseph Sylvester and Augusta (Ryan) G. A.B., Trinity Coll., Washington, 1927; M.D., U. Mich., 1932. Diplomate Am. Bd. Anesthesiology. Intern, Hosp. for Women and Children, San Francisco, 1932-33; resident Inst. of Pa. Hosp., Phila., 1933-35; gen. practice medicine, 1935-40; resident in anesthesiology N.Y. Postgrad. Hosp., 1940-42; dir. dept. anesthesiology Deaconess Hosp., Evansville, Ind., 1943-45, St. Anthony's Hosp., St. Louis, 1945-62, dept. dir., 1951-60; with dept. anesthesia Lutheran Hosp. of St. Louis, 1962-72; med. cons. for natural family planning AWARE Ctr. of St. Louis, 1973—; instr., cons. Billings ovulation method of natural family planning. Recipient First Athena award Alumnae Council U. Mich., 1973. Mem. AMA, Am. Soc. Anesthesiologists, Mo. State Med. Soc., St. Louis Met. Med. Soc., LWV. Republican. Roman Catholic. Contbr. sect. to book in field. Home: 5128 Jamieson Ave Saint Louis MO 63109

GOETZ, ELIZABETH MOREY, psychology educator; b. Cin., Aug. 1, 1927; d. John Frederick and Jean White (McDowell) Morey; m. Raymond Goetz, Apr. 24, 1951; children—Raymond, Sibyl, Thomas, Victoria, Steven, Morey. B.A. in Sociology, Grinnell Coll., 1950; M.A. with honors, U. Kans., 1970, Ph.D. in Psychology, 1977. Teaching asst. dept. human devel. U. Kans., Lawrence, 1968-70, instr., 1969-74, tchr. tng. asst., 1970, asst. prof., 1974-78, assoc. prof., 1978-84, prof., 1985—; research cons., lab. supr., 1970—, dir. child devel. lab. dept. human devel., 1978—; cons. in field. Bd. dirs. U. Kans. Art Mus. Friends of Art, Nelson Gallery Friends of Art; pres. bd. dirs. Children's Learning Ctr., Lawrence, 1978-79. Mem. Internat. Reading Assn., Nat. Assn. Edn. of Young Children, Kans. Assn. Edn. of Young Children, Lawrence Assn. Edn. of Young Children, (pres. 1971-72), Am. Ednl. Research Assn., Assn. Early Childhood Tchr. Educators, Assn. Child Edn. Internat., Soc. Research in Child Devel., Am. Psychol. Assn., Council Exceptional Children, Assn. Behavior Analysis, Soc. Advancement Behavior Analysis. Contbr. chpts. to books and articles to profl. jours.; producer ednl. films. Home: 1500 Learned Lawrence KS 66044 Office: Haworth Hall U Kans Lawrence KS 66045

GOGGANS, LOUISE ELIZABETH, dietitian, nutrition consultant; b. Trenton, Ky., Mar. 8, 1934; d. Stonewall and Dorothy (Smith) Tyler; m. Otis Goggans, Jr., May 5, 1963; children—Gregory Tyler, Dorothy Victoria. A.B., Ind. U., 1956, M.S.Ed., 1969, D.M.S., 1982. Staff dietitian Hines (Ill.) VA Hosp., 1957; chief dietitian Highland Park (Ill.) Hosp., 1957-61; head therapeutic dietitian Marion County Gen. Hosp., Indpls., 1961-63; asst. chief dietitian Meth. Hosp., Indpls., 1963-68; nutritionist, adminstrv. asst. Vis. Nurses Assn., Indpls., 1968-73; dir. nutrition services Regenstrief Health Ctr., Wishard Meml. Hosp., Indpls., 1973—; vis. prof. Valparaiso U. Vol. Ind. Women's Prison; mem. parents com. Crossroads of Am. council Boy Scouts Am.; bd. dirs. Meals on Wheels, Craine House, Inc., Alpha Home Inc., mem. vol. action ctr. bd. United Way; mem. Ind. Adv. Council on Aging and Community Services. Recipient Ind. Disting. Citizen award Indpls. Bi-Centennial Com., 1976; Drum Major award Ind. Christian Leadership Council, 1981. Mem. Am. Dietetic Assn. (cert.), Ind. Dietetic Assn. (Lute Troutt fellow 1980), Central Dist. Dietetic Assn., Am. Diabetes Assn. (dir. Ind. affiliate), Am. Heart Assn. (program vol.), Home Econs. Alumni Ind. U. (dir.), NAACP, Urban League, Nat. Council Negro Women, Coalition 100 Black Women, Indpls. Zoo, Indpls. Children's Mus., Ind. Black Expo, Sigma Xi. Baptist. Contbr. articles to profl. jours. Home: 3321 N Keystone Ave Indianapolis IN 46218 Office: Wishard Meml Hosp 1001 W 10th St RHC Indianapolis IN 46202

GOGGIN, JOHN EDWARD, county official; b. Chgo., Oct. 20, 1923; s. John Patrick and Sara (McCabe) G.; student U. Ill., 1941-42, DePaul U., 1946-47; B.S.C., Chgo. Kent Coll. Law, 1953; m. Helen Marie McSweeney, Dec. 29, 1945; children—John, Michael, Terrence, Brian, Kevin, Trudi, Daniel. Personal bailiff to judge municipal ct., 1946-53; ins. broker, Chgo., 1950—; pub. relations mgr. Gen. Outdoor Advt., Chgo., 1953-56, regional dir., 1956-64; asso. clk. Circuit Ct. Cook County, Ill., 1965—; sec. GHJ Transport Co., 1956-60. Cons. advt. and pub. relations Cook County Democratic Central Com., 1965-72. Mem. pres. council St. Xavier's Coll. Trustee Ill. Benedictine Coll. Served to capt., AUS, 1943-46; CBI. Decorated Soldier's medal, Bronze Star with cluster, Combat Infantry Badge; knight comdr. Order St. Lazarus of Jerusalem, Knight Noble Co. of Rose. Mem. Inf. Assn., Mil. Order World Wars, Ill. Mfrs. Assn., Ill. Assn. Commerce, Chgo. Assn. Commerce and Industry (com. chmn. 1956-61), Am. Legion, Alpha Delta Phi, Phi Delta Theta. Clubs: Chgo. Athletic Assn., K.C., Federated Advertising (Chgo). Home: 7700 Augusta St River Forest IL 60305 Office: Daley Center Chicago IL 60602

GOGINSKY, DAVID PETER, compressor company executive; b. Chgo., Jan. 21, 1948; s. Peter Joseph and Helen Theresa (Bugajski) G.; m. Diane Francis Kovacik, Apr. 28, 1979. B.S. in Accounting, Ind. U., 1973; M.B.A., DePaul U., 1983. Sr. auditor Altschuler, Melvoin & Glasser, Chgo., 1974-78; mgmt. auditor, fin. analyst Clow Corp., Oak Brook, Ill., 1978-81; controller Manoir Internat., Inc., South Holland, Ill., 1981-83, v.p., controller, 1983—. Served with U.S. Army, 1969-71. Mem. Am. Mgmt. Assn., South Holland Businessmens Assn., South Suburban C. of C. Roman Catholic. Office: Manoir Internat Inc 450 W 169th St South Holland IL 60473

GOGOLA, JOSEPH L., insurance company executive; b. Kenosha, Wis., Jan. 26, 1948; s. Joseph L. and Ida Gogola; m. Bonnie K. Giannola, Aug. 18, 1973; children—Michael, Jaime, Brian. B.B.A., U. Wis., 1973, M.B.A., 1975. Bank examiner State of Wis., Madison, 1976-79; portfolio mgr. CUNA Mut. Ins. Soc., Madison, 1979—. Served with U.S. Army, 1968-70. Mem. Inst. Chartered Fin. Analysts, Fin. Analyst Fedn., Milw. Investment Analyst Soc. Office: CUNA Mut Ins Soc 5910 Mineral Point Rd PO Box 391 Madison WI 53701

GOHIL, PRATAP, podiatric physician and surgeon; b. Tanga, Tanzania, May 26, 1950; B.A., M.S., U. Mo., 1975, 76; D.P.M., Ohio Coll. Podiatric Medicine, 1980. Diplomate Am. Bd. Podiatric Surgery. Instr. biomechanics and orthopedics Ohio Coll. Podiatric Medicine, Cleve., 1977-81, research asst. anatomy, mem. research com., 1980-81; assoc. in podiatric medicine and surgery Ankle and Foot Clinic, Kokomo, Ind., 1981—; staff surgery dept. Univ. Heights Hosp., St. Francis Hosp., Indpls., St. Vincent's Hosp., Winona Hosp. Faculty advisor and clinician Kappa Rho Collective and Alpha Gamma Kappa, City of Cleve. Clinics, 1979-81; active Am. Diabetes Assn., ARC. Recipient Syntex award in dermatology, 1979. Fellow Am. Coll. Foot Surgeons (Dr. Kaplan award 1980); mem. Am. Podiatry Assn., Ind. Pub. Health Assn., Ohio Pub. Health Assn., Am. Pub. Health Assn., Am. Coll. Podopediatrics. Hindu. Author: (with Young and Clarke) Hypertensive Ischemic Ulcers of Legs, 1981; (with Young and Graham) Tension Fibrositis of the Legs, 1981. Office: 209 Freeway PO Box 3098 Kokomo IN 46902

GOHMANN, H. R., contractor; b. Louisville, Mar. 27, 1920; s. Herbert R. and Loula L. (Kaelin) G.; m. Josephine Ann Mirabile, Jan. 29, 1942 (div. Mar. 1975); children—Barton, Michael, Annette, Mary, John; m. Doris Mae Dugan, Jan. 26, 1985. B.C.E., U. Louisville, 1941. Civil engr. U.S. C.E., Louisville, 1941-42; constrn. supt. R.B. Tyler Co., Ky., Tenn., Fla. and Miss., 1946-52; owner Gohmann Co., Louisville, 1952-55, Gohmann Asphalt & Constrn., Clarksville, Ind., 1955—; dir. First Midwest Bank, New Albany, Ind. Served to lt. USN, 1942-46; PTO. Republican. Home: 2912 Victoria Dr Sellersburg IN 47172

GOLD, CLIFFORD DAVID, public relations executive; b. Pitts., Dec. 27, 1952; s. Harold Alvin and Thelma Ethel (Weinstein) G.; m. Julie Annette Siems, Nov. 8, 1975; 1 son, Jeffrey Joseph. B.A. in Journalism, Ohio State U., 1971-74. Asst. to pres. univ. relations U. Dubuque (Iowa), 1974-78; mgr. communications Blue Cross & Blue Shield of Iowa, Des Moines, 1978-80, dir. communications, 1980-82, dir. pub. relations, 1982—. Campaign promotions chmn. United Way of Greater Des Moines. Recipient Award of Excellence, Internat. Assn. Bus. Communicators, 1982, Council for Advancement and Support of Edn., 1977. Mem. Pub. Relations Soc. Am., Internat. Assn. Bus. Communicators. Jewish. Home: 516 NW Linden St Ankeny IA 50021 Office: 636 Grand Ave Des Moines IA 50307

GOLDBERG, HERBERT S(AM), academic administrator; b. N.Y.C., July 23, 1926; s. Murray and Bella (Rubin) G.; m. Helen S. Smilowitz, Dec. 26, 1948; children—Jacquelyn, Sheryl. B.S., St. John's U., 1948; M.A., U. Mo., 1950; Ph.D. Ohio State U., 1953. Diplomate Am. Bd. Med. Microbiology. Postdoctoral fellow Ohio State U., Columbus, 1953; from asst. prof. to assoc. prof. microbiology U. Mo., Columbia, 1953-57, prof., 1961-84, asst. dean, 1967-70, assoc. dean, 1970-83, assoc. v.p. research, 1985—; vis. prof. UCLA, 1984. Author: History of Medicine, 1963; Hippocrates, Father of Medicine, 1964; also numerous articles on microbiology research, 1955-85. Editor: Antibiotics: Their Chemistry and Non-Medical Uses, 1959. Served with USNR, 1944-46. Recipient pre-clin. teaching award Student AMA, U. Mo., 1963, Byler Adminstrv. award U. Mo., 1976; NIH grantee. Fellow Royal Soc. Medicine; mem. AAAS, Am. Soc. Microbiology, Soc. Research Adminstrn. Club: Chemist (N.Y.C.). Avocations: reading; fishing; cycling. Office: U Mo Columbia MO 65212

GOLDBERG, MARTIN STANFORD, lawyer; b. Youngstown, Ohio, July 11, 1924; s. George and Bee (Walker) G.; m. Donna Mae Lowry, Nov. 18, 1962; children—Jeffrey A., Jeralyn Goldberg Crawford. B.A., Ohio State U., 1952, J.D., 1952. Bar: Ohio 1952, Calif. 1981. Sole practice law, Youngstown, Ohio, 1952—. Served with USAF, 1941-45, PTO. Decorated D.F.C. Mem. ABA, Calif. Bar Assn., Mahoning County Bar Assn., Am. Trial Lawyers Assn. Republican. Jewish. Lodges: Masons, Lions. Avocations: Reading, writing, music. Home: 5750 Lockwood Blvd Youngstown OH 44512 Office: Martin S Goldberg Co LPA 20 1/2 W Boardman St Youngstown OH 44503

GOLDEN, JOHN TERENCE, lubrication engineering company technical and manufacturing administrator; b. Fort Wayne, Ind., Jan. 31, 1932; s. Thomas Francis Golden and Mary Elizabeth Jacquay. B.S. in Chemistry, U. Mich., 1953; M.Sc., Ohio State U., 1958, Ph.D., 1963. Research chemist Wyandotte Chem. Co., Mich., summer 1955; from research and teaching asst. to asst. instr. Ohio State U., Columbus, 1955-62; research chemist B.F. Goodrich Research Ctr., Brecksville, Ohio, 1962-63; index editor Chem. Abstracts Service, Columbus, 1963-64; tech. and mfg. mgr. Renite Co., Columbus, 1964—. Editor The Palatine Immigrant Jour., 1981—. Contbr. articles to profl. jours. Served with U.S. Army, 1953-55. Mem. Am. Chem. Soc. (past profl. relations chmn.), Am. Soc. Lubrications Engrs., AMVETS. Democrat. Roman Catholic. Clubs: Germania Singing and Sports (fin. sec. 1982, 83, 84), Shamrock. Avocations: genealogy, camping, travel. Home: 2609 Summit St Columbus OH 43202 Office: Renite Co 2500 E 5th Ave PO Box 19235 Columbus OH 43219

GOLDENHERSH, JOSEPH HERMAN, justice state supreme ct.; b. East St. Louis, Ill., Nov. 2, 1914; s. Benjamin and Bertha (Goldenberg) G.; LL.B., Washington U., St. Louis, 1935; LL.D. (hon.), John Marshall Law Sch., 1972; m. Maxyne Zelenka, June 18, 1939; children—Richard, Jerold. Admitted to Ill. bar, 1936; pvt. practice law, East St. Louis, 1936-64; judge Appellate Ct. Ill., 1964-70; justice Supreme Ct. Ill., 1970-78, 82—, chief justice, 1979-82. Chmn. Initial Gifts United Fund East St. Louis, 1952-53; dir. Mississippi Valley council Boy Scouts Am., 1952-58; pres. Jewish Fedn. So. Ill., 1949-51. Trustee emeritus Christian Welfare Hosp., East St. Louis. Mem. Appellate Judges Conf. (exec. com. 1969-70), East St. Louis (pres. 1962-63), Am., Ill. bar assns. Mason (33 deg., Shriner). Club: Missouri Athletic (St. Louis). Home: 7510 Claymont Ct Belleville IL 62223 Office: 6464 W Main St Suite 3A Belleville IL 62223

GOLDFARB, BERNARD SANFORD, lawyer; b. Cleve., Apr. 15, 1917; s. Harry and Esther (Lenson) G.; A.B., Adelbert Coll., Case Western Res. U., 1938, J.D., 1940; m. Barbara E. Brofman, Jan. 4, 1966; children—Meredith Stacy, Lauren Beth. Admitted to Ohio bar, 1940; practice law, Cleve., 1940—; partner firm Goldfarb & Reznick; spl. counsel to atty. gen. Ohio, 1950, 71-74. Mem. Ohio Commn. for Uniform Traffic Rules, 1973—. Served with USAAF, 1942-45. Mem. Am., Ohio, Cleve. bar assns. Contbr. articles to profl. jours. Home: 39 Pepper Creek Dr Pepper Pike OH 44124 Office: 1800 Illuminating Bldg 55 Public Sq Cleveland OH 44113

GOLDMAN, BETSY LEE, artist, writer; b. Chgo., Jan. 22, 1932; d. Max Arthur and Edith Elizabeth (Fischmann) Schein; m. Norman Louis Goldman, Dec. 19, 1954; children—Adam Scott, Amy Sue. Student, Sch. Art Inst. Chgo., 1938-39, Ray-Vogue Sch. Art, Chgo., 1943-44, Drake U., 1950-51, Meramec

Community Coll., St. Louis, 1977-78; student Lucile Leighton, John Kearney, Herbert Davidson. Art instr., Dekalb and Northbrook, Ill. and Chesterfield, Mo., 1954—. Exhibited in group shows at Des Moines Art Ctr., 1951, Acad. Profl. Artists, St. Louis, 1978, Foothills Art Ctr., Golden, Colo., 1979, Old Orchard Art Festival, Skokie, Ill., 1983—, North Shore Art League, Winnetka, Ill., 1972, San Diego Watercolor Soc. Internat., El Cajon, Calif., 1984, Art Inst. Chgo., 1974, 75, J. B. Speed Art Mus., Louisville, Galesburg Civic Art Ctr., Ill., 1983-85, numerous others. Represented in permanent collections at U. Mo. Sch. Edn., Kansas City, Kemper Group, Long Grove, Ill., AEtna Life and Casualty Ins. Co., Middletown, Conn., St. Joseph's Hosp., St. Charles, Mo., Capital Holding Corp., Louisville, numerous pvt. collections. Contbr., feature writer Am. Artist Mag., Draw Mag. Recipient award Internat. Soc. Artists, 1979, Old Orchard Art Festival, 1983, Art Happening, 1982, North Shore Art League, 1974, St. Louis Artists' Guild, 1980-84, Galex 19, 1985. Mem. St. Louis Artists' Guild, West County Artists' Assn., Women's Caucus for Art, Ky. Watercolor Soc., Am. Artists' Profl. League, Inc., Ga. Watercolor Soc. Home and Office: Chesterfield MO 63017

GOLDMAN, EDWARD ARON, rabbi, Rabbinic literature educator; b. Toledo, Mar. 25, 1941; s. Beryl Leonard and Ida Beatrice (Mostov) G.; m. Roanete B. Naamani, Dec. 18, 1966; children—Ariel, Dalia. A.B., Harvard Coll., 1963; M.A. in Hebrew Lit., Hebrew Union Coll., 1969, Ph.D., 1974. Ordained rabbi. Dir. B'nai B'rith Hillel Found., U. Cin., 1965-67; teaching fellow Hebrew Union Coll., Cin., 1969-72, mem. faculty, 1972—, asst. dean, 1981—. Editor: Jews in a Free Society: Challenges and Opportunities, 1978. Contbr. articles to profl. jours. Bd. dirs. Jewish Fedn. Cin., 1975-81, mem. allocations com., edn. div., 1975-81, chmn. subcom. on nat. and overseas allocations, 1978-79. Recipient Mother Hirsch Meml. prize Hebrew Union Coll., 1966, Simon Lazarus Meml. prize, 1969. Mem. Central Conf. Am. Rabbis, Nat. Assn. Profs. Hebrew (exec. council), Assn. for Jewish Studies, AAUP, Soc. Bibl. Lit. Avocations: playing piano and organ; listening to music. Office: Hebrew Union Coll 3101 Clifton Ave Cincinnati OH 45220

GOLDMAN, GERRY ALAN, construction and building products company executive; b. Los Angeles, Oct. 17, 1926; s. Martin and Sylvia Goldman; m. Marlene Diane Taylor, Sept. 22; children—Teri Lynn, Steven Michael, Tracy Kim, Martin Troy. Student, Los Angeles City Coll., 1946-48. Salesman, Whizzer Industries, Pontiac, Mich., 1947-52, mid-U.S.A. sales mgr., 1953-57, br. mgr., 1957-59; founder, pres. Builders Archtl. Products, Inc., Northbrook, Ill., 1960—, Gen. Constrn. Cons., Northbrook, 1965—. Precinct capt. Republican party, 1964-68. Served with USN, 1944-46. Recipient Distbr. Sales awards Wausau Metals Corp., 1974, 77, 79, 81. Mem. Am. Subcontractors Assn. (dir.), Constrn. Specifications Inst. (charter mem. suburban chpt.); assoc. mem. Builders Assn. Chgo., No. Ill. Indsl. Assn., Constrn. Specifications Inst. Home: 1060 Sanders Rd Northbrook IL 60062 Office: Builders Archtl Products Inc 425 Huehl Bldg 7 Northbrook IL 60062

GOLDMAN, LEON, dermatologist, laser surgeon, hospital administrator; b. Cin., Dec. 7, 1905; s. Abraham and Fannie (Friedman) G.; m. Belle Hurwitz, Aug. 23, 1936; children—John, Steve, Carol. M.D., U. Cin., 1929. Intern, U. Cin. Hosp., 1929-30, resident, 1930-36, chief resident, 1933-36; asst. prof. dermatology U. Cin., 1949-50, assoc. prof., 1950-51, prof., 1951-76, prof. emeritus, 1976—, dir. dermatology U. Cin. Med. Center, 1951-76, dir. laser lab., 1971-76; dir. Laser Treatment Ctr., Jewish Hosp. Cin., 1980—. Served with M.C., USAR, 1943. Recipient award for valuable service Laser Inst. Am., 1977, award for devel. laser medicine Internat. Soc. Laser Surgery, Tokyo, 1981, Finnerud award Dermatology Found., 1984, Xanor Gold medal, 1985; named Father of Laser Medicine, Opto-Elektronic Conf., Munich, W.Ger., 1979. Mem. Am. Dermatol. Assn., Am. Soc. Laser Medicine and Surgery (pres. 1979-80) W. D. Mark medal 1982), Soc. Investigative Dermatology, Am. Soc. Dermatol. Surgery, Internat. Confedn. Council Laser Medicine (pres. 1982—), Laser Industry Assn. Am. (Schawlow medal 1985), Alpha Omega Alpha. Jewish. Club: Losantiville. Author books, including: The Biomedical Laser; Applications of the Laser; Laser Medicine; contbr. numerous articles on dermatology and laser tech. to profl. jours., articles on history and art to sci. jours. Office: 711 Carew Tower Cincinnati OH 45202

GOLDSBOROUGH, ROBERT GERALD, editor; b. Chgo., Oct. 3, 1937; s. Robert Vincent and Wilma (Janak) G.; m. Janet Moore, Jan. 15, 1966; children—Suzanne Joy, Robert Michael, Colleen Marie, Bonnie Laura. B.S., Northwestern U., 1959, M.S., 1960. Reporter, Chgo. Tribune, 1960-61, copy editor, 1961-62, asst. mag. editor, TV mag. editor, 1962-72, Sunday editor, 1972-75, Sunday Mag. editor, 1975-82; exec. editor Advt. Age, Chgo., 1982—. Presbyterian. Clubs: Arts, Chicago Press (dir. 1982—). Office: Crain Communications 740 Rush St Chicago IL 60611

GOLDSTEIN, DAVID JOEL, medical genetics educator, physician; b. N.Y.C., June 25, 1947; s. Milton Sidney and Thelma (Weinman) G.; children—Benjamin, Philip. B.A., Franklin and Marshall Coll., 1969; M.D., U. Tenn.-Memphis, 1973, Ph.D., 1975. Diplomate Am. Bd. Med. Genetics. Resident in pediatrics Mayo Grad. Sch. Medicine, 1975-78; fellow in human genetics U. Pa., Phila., 1978-81; asst. prof. med. genetics Ind. U., Indpls., 1981—. Contbr. articles to med. jours. Asst. Democratic committeeman, Indpls., 1984. Recipient J. P. Quigley award. Mem. Am. Soc. Human Genetics, AAAS, Soc. Neurosci., Ind. Pub. Health Assn., Sigma Xi. Lodge: B'nai B'rith. Avocations: pen and ink sketching; racquetball; cooking. Office: Dept Med Genetics 702 Barnhill Dr RR 129 Indianapolis IN 46223

GOLDSTEIN, ERIC, mental health administrator; b. Boston, Apr. 8, 1946; s. George and Bertha Ann (Parker) G.; m. Ernestine Bakofen, Aug. 11, 1968; children—Jodi Heather, David Michael. B.S., L.I.U., 1970; Pharm.D., U. So. Calif., 1971, M.S., 1972. Asst. prof. pharmacy and psychiatry U. Fla. Colls. Pharmacy and Medicine, 1972-76; asst. prof. pharmacy, coordinator clin. edn. U. Mich. Coll. Pharmacy, Ann Arbor, 1976-78; dir. div. health care services Mich. Dept. Mental Health, Lansing, 1978—; asst. clin. prof. psychiatry Mich. State U. Coll. Human Medicine, Lansing, 1978—; cons. NIMH, 1976; mem. Consumer Adv. Bd., Mich. Delta Dental Corp., 1980. Mem. profl. bd. Shared Childbirth Assn. Lansing; mem. budget panel Capital Area United Way. VA postdoctoral tng. fellow. Mem. Am. Coll. Clin. Pharmacology, Am. Coll. Clin. Pharmacy, Am. Pub. Health Assn., Am. Soc. Hosp. Pharmacists, Rho Chi. Contbr. articles in field to profl. jours. Home: 425 Ardson Rd East Lansing MI 48823 Office: Dept Mental Health Lewis Cass Bldg Lansing MI 48926

GOLDSTEIN, RICHARD J., mechanical engineering educator; b. N.Y.C., Mar. 27, 1928; s. Henry and Rose (Steierman) G.; m. Anita Nancy Klein, Sept. 5, 1963; children—Arthur Sander, Jonathan Jacob, Benjamin Samuel, Naomi Sarith. B.M.E., Cornell U., 1948; M.S.M.E., U. Minn., 1950, M.S. in Physics, 1951, Ph.D. in Mech. Engring., 1959. Instr. U. Minn., 1948-51, instr., research fellow, 1956-58, mem. faculty, 1961—, prof. mech. engring., 1965—, dept. head, 1977—; research engr. Oak Ridge Nat. Lab., 1951-54; asst. prof. Brown U., 1959-61; cons. in field, 1956—; NSF sr. postdoctoral fellow, vis. prof. Cambridge U., 1971-72; chmn. Midwest Univ. Energy Consortium; chmn. Council on Energy Engring. Research. Served to 1st lt. U.S. Army, 1954-55. Honeywell fellow, 1955-57; NATO fellow, Paris, 1960-61; Lady Davis fellow, Technion, Israel, 1976; recipient NASA award for tech. innovation, 1977. Fellow ASME (v.p., Heat Transfer Meml. award 1978, Centennial medallion 1980); mem. Nat. Acad. Engring., Minn. Acad. Sci., Am. Soc. Engring. Edn., AAAS, Am. Phys. Soc., Nat. Acad. Engring., Sigma Xi, Pi Tau Sigma, Tau Beta Pi. Contbr. articles to tech. publs. Home: 520 Janalyn Circle Golden Valley MN 55416 Office: Dept Mech Engring 111 Church St SE Minneapolis MN 55455

GOLDSTEIN, SANDRA, consumer products importing company executive, designer and importer; b. Chgo., Dec. 7; d. Jack Julius and Esther Judith (Glickman) Gilbert; student U. Wis., U. Ill., Champaign-Urbana; m. Seymour Leo Goldstein, Aug. 12, 1951; 1 dau., Jennie S. Co-founder, sr. v.p., sales mgr. Jennie G. Sales Co., Inc., Lincolnwood, Ill., 1961—. Bd. dirs. Ill. Found. Dentistry for Handicapped. Mem. Nat. Assn. Convenience Stores, Nat. Oil Jobbers Assn., Ill. Petroleum Assn., Tex. Oil Marketers Assn., Intermountain Oil Jobbers Assn., Wis. Oil Jobbers Assn., Ind. Oil Jobbers Assn., Mich. Oil Jobbers Assn., Mo. Oil Jobbers Assn., Iowa Oil Jobbers Assn. Club: Carleton (Chgo.). Office: 3770 W Pratt Ave Lincolnwood IL 60645

GOLDSTEIN, STEVEN HAROLD, accountant; b. Indpls., Aug. 14, 1947; s. Louis and Gladys (Sachs) G.; m. Carol Diane Smith, June 14, 1970; 1 dau., Jamie. B.S., Ind. U., 1969, J.D., 1973. C.P.A., 1972. Bar: Ind. 1973. Staff acct. Katz Sapper & Miller, C.P.A.'s, Indpls., 1969-75; instr./Midwest supr. Becker CPA Rev. Course, Los Angeles, 1973-83; ptnr. Goldstein Brown & Co., Indpls., 1975-83, Goldstein Glanzman Brown Katzman & Frosch, Indpls., 1975-83; ptnr. Goldstein Swinford & Co., Indpls., 1985—; Chief exec. officer Pharm. Corp. Am., Indpls., 1984—; dir. Security Nat. Corp., Security Nat. of Ind., Inc., Security Nat. Life Ins., Conseco, Inc., Pharm. Corp. Am., Indy Graphics, Inc., The Gallows, Inc. Bd. dirs. Hooverwood, 1983—. Served with U.S. Army, 1968-70. Mem. Am. Inst. C.P.A.s, ABA, Ind. Bar Assn., Ind. Soc. C.P.A.s, Am. Assn. Attys. and C.P.A.s. Club: Broadmoor Country. Home: 1212 Kirkham Ln Indianapolis IN 46260 Office: 11611 N Meridian St Suite 750 Carmel IN 46032

GOLDSTEIN, WALTER ELLIOTT, pharmaceutical company executive; b. Chgo., Nov. 28, 1940; s. Henry H. and Dorothy (Davidson) G.; m. Paula G. Copen, Feb. 18, 1962; children—Susan, Marc. B.S. in Chem. Engring., Ill. Inst. Tech., 1961; M.B.A., Mich. State U., 1968; M.S. in Chem. Engring., U. Notre Dame, 1971, Ph.D., 1973. Registered profl. engr., Ind. Process devel. engr. Linde div. Union Carbide, Tonawanda, N.Y., 1961-64; with Miles Labs., Elkhart, Ind., 1964—, assoc. project engr., 1964-67, assoc. research scientist, 1967-72, research scientist, 1972-73, research supr., 1973-76, mgr. Chem. Engring. Research and Pilot Services, 1976-78, dir., 1978-82, v.p. research and devel., 1982—; adj. asst. prof. chem. engring. U. Notre Dame, 1975-76. Active in fund raising Am. Cancer Soc., Am. Heart Assn. Mem. Am. Inst. Chem. Engrs., Soc. Indsl. Microbiology, AAAS, Sigma Xi. Jewish. Club: B'nai B'rith (v.p.). Inventions and publs. in chem. engring. and biotech. field.

GOLDTHWAITE, MARY JANE, lawyer; b. Cleve., Jan. 3, 1947; d. Allen Benson and Margaret Goldthwaite. B.A., Smith Coll., 1969; J.D., Ohio State U., 1973. Bar: Ohio 1973, U.S. Dist. Ct. (so. dist.) Ohio, 1974. Assoc. Porter, Wright, Morris & Arthur, Columbus, Ohio, 1973-78, ptnr., 1979; v.p., gen. counsel, sec. ChemLawn Corp., Columbus, 1980—. Bd. dirs. Columbus U.S.A. Assn., 1983-84. Mem. ABA, Ohio State Bar Assn., Columbus Bar Assn., Am. Corp. Counsel Assn. (v.p. Columbus chpt. 1984—), Central Ohio Gen. Counsels Assn. (chmn. 1982—), Am. Soc. Corp. Secs. Office: ChemLawn Corp 8275 N High St Columbus OH 43085

GOLL, GEOFFREY STEVEN, lawyer; b. Columbus, Ohio, Feb. 2, 1944; s. Carl F. and Dru R. Goll; m. Kim Shauck. B.A., Denison U., 1966; J.D., Ohio State U., 1973. Bar: Ohio 1973, U.S. Dist. Ct. (no. dist.) Ohio 1974, U.S. Supreme Ct. 1980. Page, Ohio Ho. of Reps., 1972-73; asst. to pub. defender Columbiana County, Ohio, 1974-80; ptnr. Goll & Guehl, Salem, Ohio, 1982—. Legal advisor Parents without Ptnrs., 1976—; mem. exec. bd. Columbiana council Boy Scouts Am., 1978, mem. nat. council, 1981—, pres., 1984-85; mem. exec. bd. Mobile Meals of Salem, Inc., 1976—, v.p. 1979-81; mem. adv. bd. Salem Salvation Army, 1979-81, chmn., 1981; mem. exec. bd. Salem Area Indsl. Devel. Corp., 1980—, Columbiana County Port Authority, 1981—, Columbiana Bd. Elections, 1984—; vice chmn. Columbiana County Republican Central Com., 1977-84. Served to maj. USAFR, 1966—. Recipient District Merit award Boy Scouts Am., 1980, Silver Beaver award, 1984. Mem. ABA, Columbiana County Bar Assn. (sec.-treas. 1979—), Ohio State Bar Assn. (local com. 1980—), Columbiana County Mental Health Assn., Ohio State U. Alumni Assn. (trustee Columbiana County 1979-81, pres. 1984—), Salem C. of C. (bd. dirs. 1979, 81—, pres. 1984-85). Clubs: Sevakeen Country, Saxon. Lodges: Elks, Rotary (v.p. Salem club 1984). Avocations: golf; travel. Home: 1690 E State St Salem OH 44460 Office: Law Offices Goll & Guehl 657 E State St PO Box 558 Salem OH 44460

GOLLINGS, ROBERT HARRY, data processing consultant; b. Pitts., July 4, 1931; s. Chester Lyman and Lorena Elizabeth (Grady) G.; B.B.A., U. Pitts., 1953, M.B.A., 1961; postgrad. U. Ill., Chgo., 1979-80; m. Marilyn Campbell, Sept. 19, 1959 (dec. Apr. 1981); children—Anne, Graham. Systems analyst Westinghouse Electric Corp., Pitts., 1956-65; supr. systems and programming Joy Mfg. Co., Pitts. and Michigan City, Ind., 1965-67; project mgr. Standard Oil Co. (Ind.), 1967-75; project mgr., lead anlayst G.D. Searle & Co., Skokie, Ill., 1975-78; sr. mgr. Comsi, Inc., Oak Brook, Ill., 1978-79; coordinator mgmt. systems U. Ill., Chgo., 1979-80; data processing cons., owner RHG Systems, 1981-83; pres. Matrix Techs., Inc., Park Forest, Ill., 1983—; instr. Calumet Coll., Thornton Community Coll. Chmn., Parks and Recreation Bd., Park Forest, Ill., 1978-82; bd. dirs. Community Chest, Park Forest-Richton Park, 1973-82, pres., 1975; bd. dirs. South Suburban Symphony, 1975-78, Park Forest Symphony, 1978-83. Served to 1st lt. USAF, 1953-56; Korea. Mem. Assn. Systems Mgmt., Internat. Computer Consultants Assn. Republican. Presbyterian. Club: Chgo. Bus. Sch. Alumni Club of U. Pitts. (sec.). Home: 19 Dogwood St Park Forest IL 60466

GOLUB, EDWARD S., biological science educator, scientist; b. Chgo., Oct. 6, 1934; s. George Lion and Mildred (Mazer) G.; m. Rosalee Roman, Sept. 23, 1959 (div. 1974); children—Jonathan, Mark. B.S., Roosevelt U., 1956; M.S., Miami U., Oxford, Ohio, 1959; Ph.D., U. N.C., 1965. USPHS fellow Duke U., Durham, N.C., 1965, Scripps Clinic, La Jolla, Calif., 1966-68; prof. biol. scis. Purdue U., West Lafayette, Ind., 1968—; cons. NIH, Bethesda, Md., 1978-81; mem. adv. com. NCI, Bethesda, 1980; mem. adv. panel NSF, Washington, 1983—. Author: Cellular Basis of the Immune Response, 1976, 2d edit., 1981. Editor: Benchmark Papers in Immunology, 1980. Contbr. articles to profl. jours. Mem. Am. Assn. Immunologists, Brit. Soc. Immunology, Internat. Soc. Exptl. Hematology, Soc. Devel. Biology, History Sci. Soc., AAAS. Home: 902 N Chauncey St West Lafayette IN 47906 Office: Purdue Univ Dept Biol Scis Lilly Hall West Lafayette IN 47907

GONSER, STEPHEN GEORGE, travelogue film producer, lecturer; b. Marion, Ind., Sept. 30, 1945; s. Ralph Lloyd and Marjorie (Botkin) G.; m. Suzan Jo Scott, Dec. 28, 1968 (div. Sept. 17, 1984); children—Luke Mitchell, Joel Daniel; m. Rookmin Persaud, Nov. 29, 1984; 1 child, Ronnie. B.A. in Edn., Marion Coll., 1967; M.A. in Edn., Ball State U., 1971. Cert. elem. tchr., Ind. Tchr. Mississinewa Community Sch., Gas City, Ind., 1967-77; mgr. presentation services Bell Fibre Products, Marion, 1977-80; film producer, lectr. Windoes Travelogues, Grand Rapids, Mich., 1980—. Producer (film) Costa Rica: Gem of the Americas, 1984. Mem. Internat. Travel-Adventure Film Guild, Internat. Motion Picture and Lecturers Assn., Internat. Fedn. Travel Writers and Journalists. Republican. Lodge: Kiwanis. Avocations: mountain climbing, hiking, bicycling, golf, metal detecting. Home: 1131 E Taylor St Kokomo IN 46901 Office: Windoes Travelogues McKay Tower Suite 1326 146 Monroe Ctr NW Grand Rapids MI 49503

GONSER, THOMAS HOWARD, lawyer; b. Berkeley, Calif., May 8, 1938. A.A., U. Calif.-Berkeley, 1958, B.A. in Polit. Sci., 1960, J.D., 1965, postgrad., 1978. Bar: Calif. 1965, Idaho 1970. Atty., law dept. So Pacific Co., San Francisco, 1965-68; assoc. gen. counsel, asst. sec. Boise Cascade Corp., Idaho, 1969-81; exec. dir., chief operating officer ABA, Chgo., 1981—; lectr. in field. Mem. Nat. Conf. Bar Founds. (pres. 1979-82), Idaho Law Found. (pres. 1977-80), Internat. Bar Assn. (dep. sec. gen. 1982—), Inter-Am. Bar Assn. (asst. sec. gen. 1982). Office: ABA 750 N Lake Shore Dr Chicago IL 60611

GONZALEZ, DIANE KATHRYN, social worker; b. Cin., Aug. 20, 1947; d. Joseph Curtis and Kathryn Mary (Diskin) Gonzalez; B.A. in Social Work, U. Dayton, 1969; A.M. in Social Work, U. Chgo., 1973; m. Thomas Connolley Leibig, July 5, 1974; 1 dau., Abigail. Social worker Hamilton County Welfare Dept., Cin., 1969-71; social worker obstetrics dept. and prenatal clinic social service dept. St. Francis Hosp., Evanston, Ill., 1973-78; rap group leader Teen Scene, Planned Parenthood Assn., Chgo., part-time, 1979-80; social worker Chgo. Comprehensive Care Center, 1980—; chmn. adv. com. Evanston Continuing Edn. Center, 1978-80. Mem. landmark dist. com. Old Town Triangle, 1983—; co-chmn. Old Town Art Fair, 1984, gen. chmn., 1985. Cert. social worker, Ill. Mem. Nat. Assn. Social Workers, Acad. Cert. Social Workers. Roman Catholic. Home: 218 W Menomonee St Chicago IL 60614 Office: Chgo Comprehensive Care Center 3639 S Michigan Ave Chicago IL 60653

GOOD, J. PAUL, agricultural service administrator; b. Poland, Ohio, Feb. 24, 1930; s. Levi P. and Pauline Clara (Gould) G.; m. Patricia Sue Kohn, Aug. 21, 1960; children—Charlotte A., Jeffrey P. B.S., Juniata Coll., 1953. With Ford Motor Co., Cleve., 1957-58, Firestone Co., Cleve., 1958-59; owner Good Equipment Co., Youngstown, Ohio, 1959-63; exec. dir. Mahoning County Agrl. Stabilization and Conservation Service, Salem, Ohio, 1963—; dir. Springfield Twp. Ins., New Springfield, Ohio, 1972—. Mem. Mahoning County Bd. Edn., Youngstown, 1971—. Mem. Ch. of the Brethren. Lodges: Masons, Kiwanis (past sec., pres., lt. gov.). Address: 10159 Sharrott Rd North Lima OH 44452

GOOD, MARY LOWE, research center executive; b. Grapevine, Tex., June 20, 1931; d. John Willace and Winnie (Mercer) Lowe; m. Bill J. Good, May 15, 1952; children—Billy John, James Patrick. B.S., Ark. State Tchrs. Coll., 1950; M.S., U. Ark., 1953, Ph.D., 1955, LL.D. (hon.), 1979; D.Sc. (hon.), U. Ill.-Chgo., 1983, Clarkson Coll., 1984. Assoc. prof. chemistry La. State U., New Orleans, 1958-63; prof. chemistry U. New Orleans, 1963-74, Boyd prof. chemistry, 1974-78; Boyd prof. engring. research La. State U., Baton Rouge, 1978-80; v.p., dir. research Signal UOP Research Ctr., Inc., Des Plaines, Ill., 1980-85, pres., 1985—. Bd. dirs. Indsl. Research Inst., 1982—; trustee Renssalaer Poly. Inst., 1982—; mem. panel for materials sci. Nat. Bur. Standards, 1980—; mem. external adv. com. La. State U. Coll. Engring., 1980—; bd. dirs. Nat. Inst. for Petroleum and Energy Research, Bartlesville, Okla., 1984—; mem. Nat. Sci. Bd., 1980—; mem. adv. panel chemistry sect. NSF, 1972-76, sci. info. task force NSF, 1977; com. on medicinal chemistry NIH, 1972-76; mem. chemistry com. Brookhaven Nat. Lab., 1973-77; mem. Office Air Force Research, 1974-78. Author: Integrated Laboratory Sequence, Vol. III—Separations and Analysis, 1970. Contbr. chpts. to books, articles to profl. jours. Mem. Chgo. Mayor's Task Force on High Tech. and Devel., 1981-82. Recipient Disting. Alumni citation U. Ark., 1973; Scientist of Yr. award Indsl. Research and Devel. mag., 1982. Mem. Internat. Union Pure and Applied Chemistry (pres. inorganic div. 1981-85), Am. Chem. Soc. (soc. com. on chemistry/pub. affairs 1972-77; Garvan medal 1973, Herty medal Ga. sect. 1975, Outstanding Research-Teaching-Pub. Service award Fla. sect. 1979, chmn. bd. dirs. 1978, 80), Am. Inst. Chemists (Honor scroll La. chpt. 1974, Gold medal 1983), Nat. Acad. Scis. (panel sci. communications and nat. security 1983), Phi Beta Kappa (Disting. Alumnus 1972), Iota Sigma Pi (Agnes Faye Morgan award 1969), Delta Kappa Gamma (Tchr. of Yr. 1974). Club: Zonta (chmn. Amelia Earhart Fellowship com. 1978—). Avocations: canoeing; Scottish history. Home: 295 Park Dr Palatine IL 60067 Office: Signal Research Ctr 50 E Algonquin Rd Box 5016 Des Plaines IL 60017

GOOD, RONALD CHESTER, manufacturing company executive; b. Chgo., July 18, 1938; s. Michael and Rosie (Boch) G.; m. Mary B. Good, July 16, 1960; children—Michelle, Gerard. B.S., Loyola U. Chgo., 1966. Cost acct. Profexray div. Litton, Des Plaines, Ill., 1960-66; div. controller Halsam Corp. div. Milton Bradley, Chgo., 1966-67; with Ill. Tool Works, Chgo., 1967-71; gen. mgr., pres. Electro-Mel Industries, Hazelhurst, Wis., 1971—. Committeman, Vilas County Democratic Party, 1972. Lodges: Rotary, K.C. (Grand Knight 1984-85). Avocations: fishing; hunting; woodworking. Home: 8541 Parkview Minoqua WI 54548 Office: Electro-Mel PO Box 127 Hazelhurst WI 54548-00127

GOOD, SHELDON FRED, realtor; b. Chgo., June 4, 1933; s. Joseph and Sylvia (Schwartz) G.; student Drake U., 1951; B.B.A., U. Ill., 1955; m. Lois Kroll (dec. July 1985); children—Steven, Todd. Sales mgr. Baird & Warner Real Estate, Chgo., 1957-65; pres. Sheldon F. Good & Co. Realtors, Chgo., 1965—; guest lectr. Northwestern U., U. Chgo., U. Calif., Wharton Grad. Sch., U. Pa., Stanford U., Vanderbilt U., U. Ill.; staff instr. Central YMCA City Coll., Chgo.; cons. in field. Chmn. real estate divs. Chgo. Crusade Mercy, United Settlement Appeal, Chgo., YMCA Edn. Library Drive, Chgo., Chgo. Jewish United Fund. Bd. dirs. Child, Inc.; pres. Gastrointestinal Research Found., U. Chgo., 1979. Served with AUS, 1955-57. Recipient Levi Eshkol Premier medal State Israel, 1967, Crown of A Good Name award Jewish Nat. Fund, 1972; named one of 10 outstanding young men Chgo., 1968. Mem. Chgo. Real Estate Bd. (treas.), Nat. Assn. Real Estate Bds., Chgo. Better Bus. Bur., Chgo. Assn. Commerce and Industry, Alpha Epsilon Pi, Lambda Alpha, Omega Tau Rho. Club: Bryn Mawr Country (v.p.). Author: How to Sell Apartment Buildings; Techniques of Investment Property Exchanging; How to Lease Suburban Office Buildings; The Real Estate Auction as a Marketing Tool. Home: 180 E Pearson St Chicago IL 60611 Office: 11 N Wacker Dr Chicago IL 60606

GOOD, STEPHEN HANSCOM, college administrator, consultant; b. Columbus, Nebr., July 19, 1942; s. William Stanley and Cleora Eleanor (Hanscom) G.; m. Judith Ann Schroetlin, Sept 1, 1963; children—Jennifer, Catherine, William. B.A. with distinction, Nebr. Wesleyan U., 1964; M.A. U. Pitts., 1965, Ph.D., 1972. English instr. U. Nebr., Lincoln, 1966-68; prof., chmn. dept. English, Mt. St. Mary's Coll., Emmitsburg, Md., 1968-79; v.p. for acad. affairs Westmar Coll., Le Mars, Iowa, 1979-83; v.p. for acad. affairs Drury Coll., Springfield, Mo., 1983—; reader English composition test Ednl. Testing Service, Princeton, N.J., 1983—, cons. Council of Ind. Colls. Nat. Cons. Network, Washington, 1980—. Editor and introduction: The Virgin Unmask'd, 1975; A Treatise of the Hypochondriack and Hysterick Diseases, 1976; Free Thoughts on Religion, 1981: Mem. administrv. bd., lay leader Wesley United Meth. Ch., Springfield, 1983—; mem. adv. bd. S.W. Mo. Assn. Talented Gifted, Springfield, 1983—; mem. Springfield Commn. on Excellence in Ed., 1983—. Mem. AAUP, Am. Conf. Acad. Deans, Am. Assn. Higher Edn., East Central Conf. Am. Soc. for 18th Century Studies (pres. 1976-77). Avocations: tennis; reading; jogging. Home: 817 E Manchester Springfield MO 65807 Office: Drury Coll 900 N Benton Ave Springfield MO 65802

GOODENDAY, KENNETH BENJAMIN, marketing educator; b. London, July 28, 1930; s. Alexander and Minnie (Saunders) Goode; m. Lucy Sherman, Aug. 31, 1958. B.A. in English Lit., U. Calif.-Berkeley, 1972; M.B.A. in Fin. Eastern Mich. U., 1977. Product planning mgr. Burlington Industries, N.Y.C., 1953-63, Ernst Ties, San Francisco, 1965-68; ops. mgr. Paragon Resources, Warren, Mich., 1978-80; adj. prof. mktg. Eastern Mich. U., Ypsilanti, 1980-84, U. Toledo, 1984—. Office: U Toledo Dept Marketing 2801 W Bancroft Ave Toledo OH 43606

GOODFELLOW, ROBIN IRENE, surgeon; b. Xenia, Ohio, Apr. 14, 1945; d. Willis Douglas and Irene Linna (Kirkland) G. B.A. summa cum laude, Western Res. U., Cleve., 1967; M.D. cum laude, Harvard U., 1971. Diplomate Am. Bd. Surgery. Intern, resident Peter Bent Brigham Hosp., Boston, 1971-76; staff surgeon Boston U., 1976-80, asst. prof. surgery, 1977-80; practice medicine specializing in surgery, Jonesboro, La., 1980-81, Albion, Mich., 1984—. Bd. overseers Case Western Res. U., 1977-82. Fellow AAUW, 1970; mem. AMA, Phi Beta Kappa. Republican. Methodist.

GOODHEW, HOWARD RALPH, JR., wholesale executive; b. Manitowoc, Wis., Aug. 28, 1923; m. Marie Goodhew; 5 children. Grad. high sch. Various positions including credit mgr., br. store supr. Ridge Co., Inc., South Bend, Ind., 1940-46, sec., 1946-56, pres., 1956—; supt. South Bend Water Works, 1964-84, South Bend Utilities, 1966-68; dir. Nat. Bank & Trust Co., South Bend; sec., dir. H.J. Schrader Co., 1963-69, Grunow Authorized Service, Inc., 1966-69, pres. St. Joe Sales Co., 1949-55, P.B.M. Inc., 1968-79; chmn. bd. St. Joe Distbg. Co., 1984—. Mem. South Bend Crime Commn., 1974—; pres. Better Bus. Bur. South Bend-Mishawaka, 1961-62, 74-75; mem. adv. bd. Adrian Coll. Found., 1958-75; deacon 1st Presbyn. Ch., South Bend, 1963-66, trustee, 1967-76; bd. dirs. United Community Services of St. Joseph County, Inc., 1966-70; mem. bd. mgrs. community planning div. United Community Service, 1965-70; bd. dirs. Meml. Hosp. South Bend, 1969, chmn. bldg. com., 1960-72; bd. dirs. South Bend Community Sch. Corp., 1969-73, pres., 1971-72; mem. Ind. Wage Adjustment Bd., 1969-74; fin. chmn. Ind. Republican 3d Dist., 1964-70; fin. chmn. South Bend City Rep. Com., 1963, 67, St. Joseph County Rep. Com., 1964, 65, 70; mem. St. Joseph County Rep. Adv. Bd., 1964—; primary candidate for mayor of South Bend, 1963, 71; chmn. Local Property Tax Control Bd. Ind. State, 1982-84; pres. South Bend Middle Schs. Bldg. Corp., 1974-84, South Bend Pub. Library Leasing Corp., 1981-84. Brethern Care South Bend, Inc., 1974-83; numerous other civic activities. Served with U.S. Army, World War II. Decorated Bronze Star. Recipient GEORGE award Mishawaka Enterprise-Record newspaper, 1975; Rotary Community Service award, 1983. Mem. Automotive Service Industries Assn. South Bend-Mishawaka Area C. of C. (dir. 1968-84, v.p. 1970, 82). Club: Summit. Lodges: Rotary Eagles. Home: 2230 Topsfield Rd South Bend IN Office: 1535 S Main St South Bend IN 46613

GOODIN, EILEEN SUE, lawyer; b. Newark, Ohio, Jan. 29, 1955; d. Raymond L. and Joan (Green) G. B.A. cum laude, Kent State U., 1977; J.D., Ohio State U., 1980. Bar: Ohio 1980, U.S. Dist. Ct. (so. dist.) Ohio 1981, U.S. Ct. Appeals (6th cir.) 1981, U.S. Ct. Appeals (11th cir.) 1982. Law clk. Ohio Pub. Defender, Columbus, summer 1978; assoc. Barkan & Neff Co., L.P.A., Columbus, 1978-84, ptnr., 1984—. Assoc. adult Girl Scouts U.S.A., 1973—; active Friends of Library, Columbus, 1980—, Baseball Boosters Central Ohio, Columbus, 1982—, Nat. Orgn. Women, 1982—; life mem. Ohio State U. Alumni Assn., 1980—. Mem. ABA, Am. Trial Lawyers Assn., Ohio State Bar Assn., Columbus Bar Assn., Ohio Trial Lawyers Assn., Women Lawyers Franklin County. Democrat. Methodist. Home: 2908 Merrymount Ct Columbus OH 43232 Office: Barkan & Neff Co LPA 50 W Broad #1515 PO Box 1969 Columbus OH 43216

GOODKIN, MICHAEL JON, publishing company executive; b. N.Y.C., June 10, 1941; s. Harold and Rose (Mostkoff) G.; B.A., Harvard U., 1963; postgrad. U. Chgo. Bus. Sch., 1964; m. Helen Graham Fairbank, Oct. 1, 1971; children—Graham Laird, Nathalie Fairbank. Trainee, Random House, N.Y.C., 1964-65; asst. dir. Simulmatics, N.Y.C., 1966-67; account exec. World Book Ency., Inc., Chgo., 1967-70, research dir., 1970-73, v.p. mktg., 1973-76, v.p., gen. mgr., 1976-78, pres., chief operating officer World Book Ency. Inc., 1978—, chmn. bd., chief exec. officer, 1983—, also dir.; exec. v.p. World Book, Inc., 1978-84, pres., 1984—; pres. World Book Ins. Group, 1983—; exec. v.p., corp. dir. mktg. World Book Internat., Inc., 1983-84; pres. World Book Life Ins. Co., 1983, dir., 1982-83; dep. dir. World Book Pty. Ltd. (Australia), 1983—. Trustee, chmn. mktg. com. Art Inst. Chgo., 1975—, pres. aux. bd., 1975-77; mem. vis. com. visual arts U. Chgo.; bd. dirs. Chgo. Area Project, trustee, 1975; trustee Latin Sch. of Chgo., 1983—. Served with Army N.G., 1963-69. Mem. Direct Mktg. Assn. (trustee ednl. found. 1983, internat. steering com. 1983), Direct Selling Assn. (internat. com.), Chgo. Area Direct Mktg., Modern Poetry Assn. (trustee). Clubs: Racquet, Casino, Harvard (N.Y.C.); Harvard (Boston); Saddle and Cycle; Young Pres. Orgn. (Chgo. chpt.); Mchts. and Mfrs. Office: Room 510 Merchandise Mart Plaza Chicago IL 60654

GOODKIND, RICHARD JERRY, prosthodontist, educator; b. Bklyn., Oct. 5, 1937; s. Abraham I. and Adele (Bernstein) G.; m. Sondra H. Harrison, June 18, 1960; children—Risa, Ian. Student Columbia U., 1955-58; D.M.D. magna cum laude, Tufts U., 1962; M.S., U. Mich., 1964. From asst. prof. to prof. prosthodontics U. Minn., Mpls., 1966—; cons. ADA, 1983—, U.S. Navy, 1984, USPHS, 1978—. Co-author: Theory and Practice of Precision Attachment of Removable Partial Dentures, 1981. Contbr. articles to profl. jours. Served to capt. USAF, 1964-66. Diplomate Am. Bd. Prosthodontics. Fellow Midwest Acd. Prosthodontics (v.p. 1984), Am. Coll. Prosthodontists, Minn. Prosthodontic Soc.; mem. ADA. Avocations: fly fishing; painting; writing. Office: U Minn 515 Delaware SE Minneapolis MN 55455

GOODMAN, DONALD JOSEPH, dentist; b. Cleve., Aug. 14, 1922; s. Joseph Henry and Henrietta Inez (Mandel) G.; B.S., Adelbert Coll., 1943; D.D.S., Case-Western Reserve U., 1945; m. Dora May Hirsh, Sept. 18, 1947; children—Lynda (Mrs. Barry Allen Levin), Keith, Bruce; m. 2d, Ruth Jeanette Weber, May 1, 1974. Pvt. practice dentistry, Cleve., 1949—. Served with Dental Corps, USNR, 1946-48. Mem. Am. Acad. Gen. Dentistry, ADA Ohio State Dental Assn., Cleve. Dental Soc., Fedn. Dentaire Internationale, Cleve. Council on World Affairs, Greater Cleve. Growth Assn., Council of Smaller Enterprises, Phi Sigma Delta, Zeta Beta Tau, Alpha Omega. Clubs: Masons (32 deg.), Shriners. Home: 29099 Shaker Blvd Pepper Pike OH 44124 Office: 2031 W 25th St Cleveland OH 44113

GOODMAN, RICHARD M., lawyer; b. Detroit, Sept. 28, 1933; s. Ernest and Freda (Kesler) G.; children—Carlos, Alicia. B.A., U. Mich., 1955; J.D., U. Chgo., 1958. Bar: Mich. 1959, Calif. 1960, Colo. 1976. Atty., ptnr. Goodman, Eden, Millender, Goodman & Bedrosian, Detroit, 1958-76; atty., pres. Richard M. Goodman, P.C., Detroit, 1977—; lectr. Editor U. Chgo. Law Rev., 1957-58; contbr. articles to law jours. Mem. Assn. Trial Lawyers Am., Inner Circle of Advs. Office: Richard M Goodman P C 1394 E Jefferson St Detroit MI 48207

GOODMAN, TERRY LEE, lawyer; b. Canton, Ohio, Dec. 18, 1948; d. Harold Dwight and Valerie Florence (Pierson) G. B.A., Otterbein Coll., 1970; J.D., Ohio State U., 1973. Bar: Ohio 1973, U.S. Dist. Ct. (so. dist.) Ohio 1973, U.S. Ct. Appeals (6th cir.) 1974. Assoc. Brownfield, Bowen, Bally & Sturtz, Columbus, Ohio, 1973-77, ptnr., 1977-83; ptnr. Brownfield, Bally & Goodman, 1983-84; v.p., gen. counsel Buckeye Crude Exploration, Inc., 1984—. Trustee, Otterbein Coll., Westerville, Ohio, 1983—, mem. exec. bd., 1984—, chmn. facilities com., 1984-85, mem. student affairs com., 1985—. Mem. ABA, Ohio Bar Assn., Columbus Bar Assn. Republican. Lutheran. Avocation: travel. Office: Buckeye Crude Exploration Inc 5151 Reed Rd Suite 212 Columbus OH 43220

GOODRICH, DONALD W., utility company executive; b. Omaha, July 17, 1945; s. Donald W. and Dorothy (Chapman) G.; m. Marlys; children—Jeffrey W., John B., Naomi J. B.S., U. Nebr., 1974. Designer No. Natural Gas, Omaha, 1966-67; design engr. Gibbs, Hill, Durham & Richardson, Omaha, 1967-71; project engr. Gibbs & Hill, Omaha, 1971-78; ops. mgr. Commonwealth Electric Co., Aurora, Colo., 1978—. Served with USAR, 1972. Mem. Am. Assn. Cost Engrs. Republican. Roman Catholic.

GOODRICH, SARAH JANE, shopping center administrator; b. Fort Atkinson, Wis., Mar. 30, 1947; d. Robert Ellis and Agnes M. (Rude) G.; 1 child, Tyson Derek Navis. B.S., U. Wis.-Whitewater, 1970. Promotion mgr. Meml. Mall, Sheboygan, Wis., 1973-74; mktg. dir. Forest Mall, Fond du Lac, Wis., 1974-79, mgr. 1979—. Bd. dirs. Big Bros. and Big Sisters, Fond du Lac, 1984-87, Waubun council Girl Scouts U.S., 1981-83, Easter Seal Soc., Fond du Lac, 1977-80. Mem. Internat. Council Shopping Ctrs. (cert. mktg. dir. 1978, cert. shopping ctr. mgr. 1982). Lodge: Soroptimists (rec. sec. 1981-83). Avocations: Downhill skiing, boating, golfing, bridge. Office: Melvin Simon & Assocs Forest Mall 835 W Johnson St Fond du Lac WI 54935

GOODSTEIN-SHAPIRO, FLORENCE, artist, art historian; b. N.Y.C., July 22, 1931; d. Philip and Cecilia (Pletchnow) Goodstein; 1 child, Lisa Jean; m. John A. Walton, 1968. B.S. in Edn., CCNY, 1951; M.A., U. Minn., 1973. Book designer U. Chgo., 1953-54; art historian, tchr. Lakewood Coll., White Bear Lake, Minn., 1972-73; art historian, lectr. Minn. Inst. Fine Arts, Mpls., 1973-74; represented by Peter M. David Gallery, Mpls. Exhibited in group shows at Aspects Gallery, N.Y.C., 1963-65, Roko Gallery, 1962-64, Peter Cooper Gallery, 1967, Molly Barnes Gallery, Los Angeles, 1969, Juana Mordo Gallery, Madrid, 1968, Bonython Gallery, Australia, 1970, Los Angeles County Art Mus., 1969, Augsburg Coll. Gallery, 1971, U. Minn.-Duluth Tweed Gallery, 1971, Hamline U., 1976, Kiehle Gallery, St. Cloud, Minn., 1983, Peter M. David Gallery, Mpls., 1984. Recipient Excellence award Soc. Typographic Arts, 1954. Mem. Archeol. Inst., Minn. Inst. Arts. Home: 8066 Ruth St NE Minneapolis MN 55432 Studio: 25 University Ave SE Minneapolis MN 55414

GOODWIN, DAVID WILLIAM, educational administrator; b. Angola, Ind., Nov. 9, 1947; s. William C. and Janet L. (Mitchell) G. B.S. Ball State U., 1970, Ed.S., 1982; M.S., St. Francis Coll., Ft. Wayne, Ind., 1974. Tchr. Angola High Sch., 1970-77, Angola Middle Sch., 1977-80; prin. Winamac Middle Sch., Ind., 1980—. Active Pulaski County Mental Health Assn., Winamac, Pulaski County Arts Assn. Mem. Nat. Assn. Secondary Sch. Prins., Ind. Secondary Sch. Adminstrs., Ind. Assn. Elem. and Middle Sch. Prins., Phi Delta Kappa. Lodges: Masons, Shriners, Elks, Moose, Kiwanis. Office: Winamac Community Middle Sch 715 School Dr Winamac IN 46996

GOODWIN, DELLA MCGRAW, nurse, educator; b. Claremone, Okla., Nov. 21, 1931; d. James Edward and Allie Mae (Meadows) McGraw; m. Jesse F. Goodwin, Dec. 26, 1959; children—Gordon Francis, Paula Therese, Jesse Stephen. M.S. in Nursing, Wayne State U., 1962. R.N., Mich. Dir. nursing Blvd. Gen., Detroit, 1964-69; cons. Paramed., Detroit, 1969—; dean nursing and health Wayne County Community Coll., Detroit, 1970—; chmn. Detroit Substance Abuse Council, 1982—; pres. Health Systems Agy., Southeast Mich., 1979-81; lectr. in field. Author column. Mem. State Health Coordinating Council, Lansing, Mich., 1979; mem. Detroit Health Commn., 1982; mem. Drunk Driving Task Force, Lansing, 1982; mem. Womens Conf. Concerns, Detroit, 1984. Recipient Health Law award Detroit Coll. Law, 1980, Senate Concurrent resolution, Mich., 1982, Cert. Recognition Detroit Common Council, 1973, Headliners award Wayne State U., 1973. Mem. Am. Nurses Assn. (cabinet nursing edn. 1984—), Mich. Nurses Assn., Nat. League Nursing, Am. Soc. Allied Health Profls., United Community Services (v.p. 1983—), Delta Sigma Theta, Sigma Theta Tau. Democrat. Roman Catholic. Avocations: swimming, golf, photography. Home: 19214 Appoline St Detroit MI 48235 Office: Wayne County Community Coll 801 W Fort St Detroit MI 48235

GOODWIN, NORMAN J., state senator; b. Austin, Minn., Jan. 5, 1913; s. Nels and Nellie G.; B.S., U. Minn., 1936, M.S., 1945; m. Marion Blomgren, 1936; 3 children. Extension dir. Clinton County (Iowa), 1951-78; now mem. Iowa Senate. Recipient Bereford-Quaife award, 1967; Iowa Cattlemen's award, 1969; named hon. master pork producer, 1971; Liberty Bell award, 1975; R. K. Bliss extension citation, 1976. Mem. Iowa Assn. County Extension Service Dirs. (pres. 1965), Nat. Assn. Agrl. Agts. (pres. 1975), Farm Bur., Cattlemen's and Pork Producers Assn. Methodist. Clubs: Lions, Masons, Toastmasters. Office: State Senate Des Moines IA 50319*

GOODWIN, SALLY PETERSON, computer company executive; b. Memphis, Mar. 4, 1946; d. Harold Ray and Peggy Louise (Kelley) G.; m. Rex Lee Peterson, Sept. 4, 1967; 1 child, Christopher Ray. B.A., Phillips U., 1968; M.S., Kans. State U., 1971; postgrad. U. Wis.-Madison, 1971-76. Instr. U. Wis., LaCrosse, Wis., 1971-72; systems analyst State of Wis., Madison, 1972; instr. Madison Area Tech. Coll., 1972-78; cons. Intel Corp., 1979—; chief exec. officer Micro-Mgrs., Inc., Madison, 1980—. Author course Principles of Microprocessors, 1982; set cassette/book courses Software, Hardware Micro Concepts, 1984. Mem. Assn. Computing Machinery, Cardinal Key Pi Mu Epsilon, Beta Gamma Sigma. Clubs: Altrusa, Tempo. Avocations: Sports; travel; piano. Office: Micro Mgrs Inc 1435 E Main St Madison WI 53703

GOODWIN, THELMA LUCILLE, physical education educator, coach; b. Des Moines, Aug. 15, 1936; d. Lawrence Clark and Thelma Iona (Cross) Stoddard; m. Charles K. Goodwin, Dec. 31, 1962; children—Robin, Dawn. B.S. in Edn., Drake U., 1959; M.S. in Edn., 1965; cert. secondary prin. U. Des Moines, 1978. Tchr., Knoxville Schs. (Iowa), 1959-65; asst. prof. phys. edn. Central Coll., Pella, Iowa, 1965—, coach, 1971—. City recreation dir. Knoxville; chmn. Cancer Soc., Knoxville, 1971-77; mem. recreation commn., Knoxville, 1971-78; cons. for recreation programs, Knoxville, 1976. Mem. AAHPER. Home: 905 W Main St Knoxville IA 50138 Office: Central Coll Pella IA 50219

GOOR, IVAN W., tire and rubber company executive. Pres., dir. Cooper Tire and Rubber Co., Findlay, Ohio. Office: Cooper Tire and Rubber Co Lima and Western Aves Findlay OH 45840*

GOOTEE, THOMAS PAUL, computer software company executive; b. Jasper, Ind., Mar. 15, 1957; s. Thomas Herbert and Anne Marie (Dreifke) G. B.S.E.E., Purdue U., 1978. Research asst. Purdue U., 1979-80; engr. McDonnell Aircraft, St. Louis, 1980-84; owner, operator Gootee Automation, Hillsboro, Ill., 1984—. Contbr. articles to profl. jours. Mem. Tau Beta Pi, Theta Tau. Home: Route 2 Box 248 Hillsboro IL 62049 Office: Gootee Automation Route 2 Box 248 Hillsboro IL 62049

GOPALSAMI, NACHAPPA GOUNDER, electrical engineer; b. Karaipalayam, Tamilnadu, India, Apr. 3, 1948; s. K. and Thirumayi (Pappai) Nachappagounder; m. Chellam I. Chitra, Apr. 23, 1982; 1 child, Anand. B.S., Coimbatore Inst. Tech., India, 1970; M.S., P.S.G. Coll. Tech., 1973; Ph.D., U. Ill.-Chgo., 1981. Trainee, Malco, Mettur Dam, India, 1970; research scholar Indian Inst. Sci., 1973-76; research asst. U. Ill.-Chgo., 1976-79, teaching asst., 1979-80; cons. Argonne (Ill.) Nat. Lab., 1979, asst. elec. engr., 1980-84, elec. engr., 1984—. Mem. IEEE, Sigma Xi. Contbr. articles on control theory and instrumentation to sci. jours. Home: 8025 Janes Ave Apt G Woodridge IL 60517 Office: Argonne Nat Lab Bldg 308 9700 S Cass Ave Argonne IL 60439

GORALSKI, PATRICIA JEAN, lawyer; b. Paynesville, Minn., June 16, 1923; d. Arthur and Lillian Constance (Hanson) Schwarz; m. Edwin Anthony Goralski, Sept. 4, 1947. B.S., U. Minn., 1947, M.A., 1956, Ph.D., 1964, J.D., 1981. Bar: Minn. 1982, U.S. Dist. Ct. Minn. 1982, U.S. Ct. Appeals (8th cir.) 1983. Cert. elem. and secondary sch. tchr., Minn., Ill. Engring. aide U.S. Govt., 1943-45; with Maple Lake State Bank, Minn., 1941-42; teller First Nat. Bank Mpls., 1942; collateral evaluator Mdse. Nat. Bank, Chgo., 1951-52; tchr. Whittier Jr. High Sch., Lincoln, Nebr., 1948-51, Blackhawk Jr. High Sch., Park Forest, Ill., 1954-55, Stillwater Sr. High Sch., Minn., 1962-66; instr., supr. off campus student tchrs., coordinator off campus student tchrs. U. Minn. Coll. Edn., Mpls., 1955-62; developer, presenter workshops for various coll. faculty, state personnel, 1968-77; research coordinator Mpls. Pub. Schs., 1966-68; personnel adminstr. R.R. Donnelley and Sons Co., Chgo., 1953-54; dir. Professions Devel. Sect. Minn. State Dept. Edn., St. Paul, 1968-77; sole practice law, Mpls., 1981—. Author: Handbook for Student Teachers, Handbook for Supervising Teachers. Contbr. articles to profl. jours. Mem. ABA, Minn. State Bar Assn., Ramsey County Bar Assn., Minn. Trial Lawyers Assn., Assn. Trial Lawyers Am., Phi Beta Kappa, Phi Kappa Phi, Pi Lambda Theta. Office: Ste 300 Iris Park Pl 1885 University Ave Saint Paul MN 55119

GORCHOFF, C(HARLES) PHILLIP, insurance brokerage firm executive; b. Chgo., May 18, 1931; s. Albert, Sr. and Myrtina (Newman) G.; m. Barbara Schulman, Aug. 9, 1950; children—David, Lawrence, Debra, Donna. Student U. Ill., 1948-50. Ins. broker Gorchoff Ins. Agy., Chgo., 1950-69; account exec., producer Alexander & Alexander, Inc., Chgo., 1970-74, group v.p., 1975-77, prodn. mgr., 1978-80, dep. mng. v.p., 1981-82, mng. v.p., 1983—. Address: 615 Indian Hill Rd Deerfield IL 60015

GORCZYNSKI, RICHARD JOHN, pharmaceutical research manager; b. Rochester, N.Y., Mar. 24, 1948; s. Richard F. and Isabel (Chiapperinni) G.; children—Christopher, Melissa; m. Diane Lulofs, Oct. 19, 1984; stepchildren—Gregg, Caree. B.A. in Biol. Sci., Cornell U., 1970; Ph.D. in Physiology, U. Va., 1976. Research investigator Am. Critical Care, McGaw Park, Ill., 1976-78, sr. research investigator, 1978-80, group leader, 1980-83, sect. head, 1983—; editorial staff mem. Jour. Cardiovascular Pharmacology, Chgo.; 1984—; ad hoc reviewer Jour. Pharmacology and Exptl. Therapeutics, Microvascular Research, Am. Jour. Physiology. Contbr. articles to profl. jours. Speaker Cardiovascular Discussion Group, Skokie, Ill., 1982. Recipient Pres. award Am. Critical Care, 1979. Mem. AAAS, Internat. Soc. Heart Research, Am. Soc. Pharmacology and Therapeutics. Home: 3402 Chelmsford Dr Spring Grove IL 60081 Office: Am Critical Care 1600 Waukegan Rd McGaw Park IL 60085

GORD, MARY ANN SHERWIN, educator; b. Aurora, Ill., Jan. 20, 1948; d. Norman B. and Daisy Elsie (Miller) Sherwin; m. Robert Perry Stenfelt, Aug. 8, 1970 (dec. 1980); m. 2d, Robert Andrew Gord, July 14, 1983; stepchildren—Katherine Sue, Timothy Andrew. B.S. in Edn., No. Ill. U., 1970; M.S. in Edn., 1974; postgrad. U. Ill., 1975, U. Wis.-Superior, 1978, Nat. Coll. of Edn., 1982. Tchr. Greenman Sch., West Aurora, Ill., 1970-81, 83—; lang. arts resource tchr. Dist. 129, West Aurora, 1981-82; intermediate team tchr. Smith Sch., West Aurora, 1982-83; condr. in-service workshops on reading and writing edn. Recipient Book of Recognition, life membership, Nat. Council of PTA. Mem. Internat. Reading Assn., Ill. Reading Council, No. Ill. Reading Council, Fox Valley Reading Council (pres.), NEA, Ill. Edn. Assn., Aurora Edn. Assn. (West chpt.), Assn. for Supervision and Curriculum Devel., Nat. Council Tchrs. English, Alpha Delta Kappa (v.p.). Club: Hinckley Jr. Women's (pres.). Home: 321 Maple St Box 776 Hinckley IL 60520 Office: Greenman School 729 W Galena Blvd Aurora IL 60506

GORDIN, RICHARD DAVIS, former university athletic director, educator; b. South Charleston, Ohio, July 16, 1928; s. Edwin Ray and Mildred (Davis) G.; B.A., Ohio Wesleyan U., 1952; M.A., Ohio State U., 1954, Ph.D., 1967; m. Paula Alice Egan, July 23, 1949; children—Richard D. Jr., Robert H., Douglas P. Grad. asst. phys. edn. Ohio State U., 1953; dir. recreation United Cerebral Palsy, Columbus, Ohio, 1954; Instr. phys. edn. Ohio Wesleyan U., Delaware, 1954-59, asst. prof., 1959-67, asso. prof., 1967-71, prof., 1971—, dir. athletics, 1977-85, emeritus, 1985—; ednl. cons. Nat. Golf Found., 1966—; mem. parks recreation bd. City of Delaware, 1970-77, chmn., 1974. Recipient citation Delaware City Council, 1977; named to Golf Coaches Hall of Fame, 1980. Mem. U.S. Golf Assn. (mus. com. 1981), Golf Coaches Assn. Am. (pres. 1979-80, 81-82). Co-author: Golf Fundamentals, 1973. Editor: The Golf Coach's Guide, 1975. Home: 180 N Franklin St Delaware OH 43015 Office: Ohio Wesleyan Univ Delaware OH 43015

GORDON, ALAN MCINTOSH, hotel executive; b. Toronto, Ont., Can., Aug. 30, 1945; came to U.S., 1965; s. Edward Thomas Gordon and Norma (McIntosh) Stuart; m. Jerryl Linda Miller, Feb. 24, 1973; children—Rachel Sara, Alexander John. Hotelier diplomé Ecole Hotelieir de la Société Suisse des Hoteliers, Lausanne, Switzerland, 1968. Cert. hotel adminstr. Am. Hotel Mgmt. Assn., 1985. With Holiday Inns Inc., Freeport, Grand Bahamas, Memphis, 1969-74; resident mgr. Peabody Hotel, Memphis, 1974, Pick Motor Inn, Memphis, 1974-75; gen. mgr. Tiergarten Restaurant, Ft. Collins, Colo., 1976-77, Holiday Inn, Ft. Collins, 1977-78, Quality Inn Airport, Memphis, 1978-79, Roosevelt Hotel, Cedar Rapids, Iowa, 1981—; pres., dir. ops. Hammos Hotels, Nashville, 1979-81. Organizer, Republican Party, Fla., 1960-68, Iowa, 1984—; bd. dirs. Hawkeye Council Boy Scouts Am., 1981—, Cedar Rapids Conv. Bur., 1981—. Mem. Iowa Hotel Motel Assn. (bd. dirs. 1982—). Republican. Episcopalian. Lodges: Rotary, Shriners. Avocations: hunting; knifemaking; skiing. Home: 316 Day St NW Cedar Rapids IA 52405 Office: Roosevelt Hotel 200 1st Ave NE Cedar Rapids IA 52401

GORDON, BARBARA ANN, educator; b. Cin., Jan. 31, 1950; d. James Joseph and Rosemary Virginia (Kuderer) Papke; m. Robert Steward Gordon, Apr. 1973. A.B., Coll. Mt. St. Joseph-on-the-Ohio, 1972; M.Ed., Miami U., Oxford, Ohio, 1982. Tchr. English, St. Bernard Elmwood Place City Schs., 1972-80; tchr. jr. high lit. Ross Local Schs., Hamilton, Ohio, 1980—; cons. curriculum devel. Mem. Assn. for Supervision and Curriculum Devel., NEA, Ohio Edn. Assn. Roman Catholic.

GORDON, EDWARD, See *Who's Who in America,* 43rd edition.

GORDON, GRISELDA, university administrator; b. Battle Creek, Mich., Feb. 7, 1938; d. Edward and Teritha (Faulce) Daniel; m. Henry Gordon, Oct. 25, 1956; children—Cornell A., Gary L., Cheri A., Patrick H. B.S. magna cum laude, Western Mich. U., 1973, M.S. Adminstrn. in Higher Edn., 1980. Surg. nurse Borgess Hosp., Kalamazoo, 1958-66; attendent nurse Kalamazoo State Hosp., 1966-70; counselor trainer Coll. Gen. Studies, Western Mich. U., Kalamazoo, 1970-73, dir. Martin Luther King Jr. program, 1975-80, asst. to v.p. acad. affairs/dir. spl. programs, 1980—; supr. packaging dept. Peter Echrich & Co., Kalamazoo, 1974-75; lectr. in field. Mem. NAACP, AA Univ. Adminstrs., Nat. Assn. Female Execs., Nat. Consortium Black Profl. Devel. Home: 42818 N 30th St PawPaw MI 49079 Office: Western Mich U 2312 Adminstrn Bldg Kalamazoo MI 49008

GORDON, IRVING MARTIN, osteopathic physician; b. Canton, Ohio, Aug. 10, 1926; s. Harry and Sarah (Axelrod) G.; m. Roberta Levine, Feb. 12, 1956; children—Ellen, Nina, Bruce, Roger. B.A., Case Western Res. U., 1949; B.S., Kent State U., 1950; D.O., Chgo. Coll. Osteo. Medicine, 1954. Lic. osteo. physician, Ohio, S.C.; cert. in family practice Am. Bd. Gen. Practitioners in Osteo. Medicine and Surgery. Intern, Detroit Osteo. Hosp., 1954-55; locum tenens, Fort Lee, N.J., 1955-56; gen. practice osteo. medicine, Massillon, Ohio, 1957-63, Gordon & Sharkis, 1963-70, Gordon, Sharkis & Larusso, Inc., 1970-71; pres. Perry Family Practice Ctr., Inc., 4 physician group; gen. practice family medicine Perry Family Practice Ctr., Inc., Massillon, 1972-85; clin. asst. prof. family practice Ohio U. Coll. Osteo. Medicine, 1977—; lectr. Chgo. Coll. Osteo. Medicine, 1980, 81; lectr. Howard U. Hosp., Washington, and Grandview Hosp., Dayton, Ohio, Ohio U. Coll. Osteo. Medicine, 1984, Des Moines Gen. Hosp., 1984, Botsford Hosp., Farmington, Mich., 1985. Trustee Wooster Eight County Health Systems Agy. (Ohio), 1975-81; mem. pres.'s adv. bd. Stark Tech. Coll., Canton, 1980—, trustee, 1982; mem. annual fund-raising com. United Jewish Appeal, 1970—, fin. com. Temple Israel, 1979—; founding mem., trustee Doctors Hosp. Stark County (Ohio), 1963—, also mem. fin. com. Served to cpl. USAF, 1945-46. Fellow Am. Coll. Gen. Practice; mem. Am. Osteo. Assn., Akron-Canton Acad. Osteo. Medicine and Surgery (pres. 1974-75), Ohio Soc. Am. Coll. Gen. Practitioners Osteo. Medicine and Surgery (pres. 1981-82). Clubs: Catawba Island (Port Clinton, Ohio); Nat. Amateur Radio Relay League, Med. Amateur Radio Council (founding mem.), Am. Osteo. Med. Tennis Assn., Masons, Scottish Rite, Shriners. Home: 2915 Croydon Dr NW Canton OH 44718 Office: 4125 Lincoln Way E Massillon OH 44646

GORDON, L(ELAND) JAMES, lawyer; b. Phila., Mar. 17, 1927; s. Leland James and Doris Mellor (Gilbert) G.; m. Jane B.; children—James Douglas, Leslie Ann, John Scott. B.A., Denison U., 1950; J.D., Yale U., 1953. Bar: Ohio, U.S. Dist. Ct. (so. dist.) Ohio, U.S. Tax Ct., U.S. Supreme Ct. Assoc. E. Clark Morrow, Newark, Ohio, 1953-60; ptnr. Morrow & Gordon, Newark, 1960-70, Morrow, Gordon & Byrd, Newark, 1970—; dir. 70-37 Corp., Hebron, Ohio, Weakley Mfg. Co., Newark. Pres. bd. edn. Granville Exempted Village, Ohio, 1969-79, United Way of Licking County, Newark, 1972-74. Served as sgt. USAF, 1945-47. Fellow Am. Coll. Trial Lawyers, Am. Bar Found.; mem. ABA, Ohio State Bar Assn., Licking County Bar Assn. (pres. 1968), Newark Area C. of C. (treas. 1983-84). Democrat. Baptist. Club: Sumposiarchs (Newark) (pres. 1981-82). Lodge: Masons, Kiwanis (pres. 1965). Home: 732 Mount Parnasus Granville OH 43023 Office: 33 W Main St PO Box 4190 Newark OH 43055-8190

GORDON, LEWIS ALEXANDER, electronics executive; b. Milw., 4, 60121 s. Lewis Alexander and Verna Alma (Stocker) G.; B.S. in Mech. Engring., Purdue U., 1959; postgrad. RCA Insts., 1962, No. Ill. U., 1967-68; m. Frances Rita Dziadzio, June 4, 1960; children—Robert Alan, Richard Alan, Pamela Ann. Process engr. Ill. Tool Works, Elgin, 1959-63; chief engr. Norcon Electronics, Elgin, 1963-65; v.p. Midland Standard, Inc., Elgin, 1964-78, chmn. bd., 1967-78; pres., chief exec. officer Gt. Lakes Industries, Elgin, 1978—; del. Joint Electronics Industry Conf.; mem. adv. bd. Electronics mag., 1976—. Vice pres. bd. trustees Gail Borden Pub. Library Dist., 1971—, pres., bd. dirs. North Suburban Library System, 1971-74; mem. automation com. Ill. State Library, 1982—; bd. advisers Easter Seal Assn., Elgin, 1971-74; adv. bd. Elgin Community Coll., 1977—. Registered profl. engr., Ill., Mich., Wis. Mem. Ill. C. of C., Elgin Assn. Commerce, ALA, Ill. Library Assn. (automation com. 1975—), Ill. Council Library Systems Presidents (pres.), Ill. Library Trustee Assn. (bd. dirs. 1983—, pres. 1985—), Future Ill. Libraries Com., Exptl. Aircraft Assn., Future Ill. Libraries Com., Exptl. Soc. Profl. Engrs., Nat. Brit. Horological Inst., Kane County Farm Bur., Ill. Mfrs. Assn., Assn. Watch and Clock Collectors, Mensa, Agent-Aeronca Champion Club, Pi Tau Sigma. Lutheran. Contbr. articles to profl. jours. Patentee in field. Home: 705 Diane Ave Elgin IL 60120 Office: PO Box 783 Elgin IL 60121

GORDON, LONNY JOSEPH, choreographer, dance and fine arts educator; b. Edinburg, Tex.; s. Floyd Charles and Ruth Rebecca (Lee) G. B.F.A., U. Tex., 1965; M.F.A., U. Wis., 1967; D.F.A., Nishikawa Sch. of Classical Japanese Dance, Tokyo, 1980. Numerous teaching positions in the fine arts, 1964—, including: dir. Kinetic Art Theater, N.Y.C., 1970, Tokyo, 1971-72; dir. modern dance Jacobs Pillow, Lee, Mass., 1970; dir. So. Repertory Dance Theater, So. Ill. U., Carbondale, 1972-76; artist-in-residence Smith Coll., Northampton, Mass., 1975; grad. dir. dance U. Wis., Madison, 1976—; choreographer numerous dance works including Fleetings; cons. and lectr. in dance and fine arts to numerous profl. dance cos. and ednl. instns. Contbr. articles to profl. jours.; subject of numerous books and profl. works in dance. One man exhbn. watercolor paintings, collage and mixed media works. Grantee numerous profl. and ednl. instns., fellow Fulbright-Hays, 1967-69, NEA Choreographers, 1982-83. Mem. Fulbright Alumni Assn. Club: University Club (U. Wis.). Advocations: painting; writing; swimming; bodybuilding; gardening. Office: U Wis Lathrop Hall 1050 University Ave Madison WI 53706

GORDON, LOUIS EDWARD, hospital administrator; b. Jackson, Mich., Dec. 18, 1930; s. George Edward and Anna A. (Hansmann) G.; m. Shirley Winifred Bishop, Nov. 14, 1954; children—Jan Alyce, Jill Annette, Traci Lynn. B.A., Andrews U., 1952; M.A., Mich. State U., 1957. Adminstr., Battle Creek (Mich.) Sanitarium, 1961-67; chief party Liberian Nat. Med. Ctr. Project, Liberia, 1967-72; dir. Ind. Regional Med. Program, Indpls., 1972-73; dir. Kino Community Hosp., also dept. hosps. and nursing homes, Pima County, Tucson, 1973-78; adminstr. Bannock Regional Med. Ctr., Pocatello, Idaho, 1978-83; exec. v.p. Shawnee Mission Med. Ctr., Kans., 1983—; cons. Health Care Orgn. and Devel., AID; mem. faculty Idaho State U., Pocatello. Bd. dirs., v.p. Mountain States Shared Service Corp., 1978-83; city commr. City of Battle Creek; bd. dirs. Idaho Health Systems Agy., 1978-83; pres., founder Idaho Health Services Consortium, 1978-83; pres. South Ariz. Hosp. Council, 1976. Served with U.S. Army, 1952-54. Decorated Govt. of Liberia, 1973; recipient Unity for Service award Nat. Exchange Club, 1967, award U.S. Dept. State. Mem. Royal Soc. Health, Am. Coll. Hosp. Adminstrs., Am. Hosp. Assn., Am. Pub. Health Assn., Idaho Hosp. Assn. (dir. 1978-83), Idaho Hosp. Research and Edn. Found. (pres.), Internat. Fedn. Hosps. Lodges: Rotary, Masons, Shriners. Office: Shawnee Mission Med Ctr Shawnee Mission KS 66201

GORDON, MICHAEL DUANE, optometrist; b. Coffeyville, Kans., Apr. 14, 1949; s. Otho Wayne and Wilma Lea (Hodges) G.; B.S. cum laude, U. Houston, 1973, O.D. magna cum laude, 1973; m. Vicki Jo Baker, May 31, 1969; children—Kimberly Michelle, Ryan Michael, Nicole Tasha. Pvt. practice optometry, Wichita, Kans., 1973—, Derby, Kans., 1977—; optometric cons. VA Hosp., Wichita, 1975-84; v.p. Rota Enterprises, Inc., Derby, 1978-81, pres.,

1981—; cons. Winfield State Mental Hosp., 1980—; FDA clin. investigator for Cooper Labs., 1981—, for Baush & Lomb Soflens, 1981—. Mem. Coll. Optometrists in Vision Devel., Am. Optometric Assn., Optometric Extension Program Found., Inc., Kans. Optometric Assn., Wichita Optometric Soc., Derby C. of C., Derby Jaycees. Republican. Co-inventor, patentee motorized revolving visual exam. center; co-inventor Rota module. Home: 942 Brook Forest Rd Derby KS 67037 Office: 154 S Rock Rd Wichita KS 67207 also 248 Greenway St Derby KS 67037

GORDON, ROBERT JAY, lawyer; b. Pontiac, Mich., Dec. 22, 1949; s. Irving Edward and Bertha Mae (Finkelstein) G.; m. Barbara Lynn Tobias, June 25, 1972; children—Arianna Lea, Zachary Issac Eli. B.A. with honors, U. Mich., 1971; J.D. cum laude, Boston U., 1974. Bar: Mich. 1974. Assoc. Jaffe, Snider, Raitt & Hauer, P.C., Detroit, 1974-80, ptnr., 1980—. Vice-pres. Anti-Defamation League, Detroit, 1980—. Mem. ABA, Mich. Bar Assn. Jewish. Office: Jaffe Snider Raitt & Heuer PC 1800 First National Bldg Detroit MI 48226

GORDON, STUART, theater producer and director, playwright; b. Chgo., Aug. 11, 1947; s. Bernard Leo and Rosalie (Sabbath) G.; student U. Wis.; m. Carolyn Purdy, Dec. 20, 1968; 1 dau., Suzanna Katherine. Founder, producing dir. Organic Theater Co., Chgo., 1969—, dir. nat. TV show Bleacher Bums; dir. Broadway, off-Broadway, throughout U.S. and Europe. Former mem. bd. dirs. Ill. Arts Council. Recipient Emmy award for Bleacher Bums; Golden Hugo award for Bleacher Bums, Chgo. Internat. Film Festival; Joseph Jefferson awards for writing and directing. Mem. League Chgo. Theaters (dir.), Theater Communications Group (past dir.). Jewish. Office: 3319 N Clark St Chicago IL 60657*

GORDY, JACK LESTER, accountant, industrial engineer; b. Decatur, Ill., Jan. 16, 1936; s. Lester E. and Freida A. (Toole) G.; m. Darla Jean Lebo, Apr. 5, 1958 (dec. Nov. 3, 1979); children—Christine, Julia, Mary; m. Brenda L. Mathis, Sept. 30, 1981; children—Elizabeth, Kevin, Andrew, Amy. B.S., Millikin U., 1961. Clk. Wagner Castings, Decatur, 1959-61, foreman, 1961-64, supr. indsl. engring., 1964-81, mgr. indsl. engring., 1981-83, mgr. cost acctg., 1983—. Served with U.S. Army, 1956-58. Home: 3646 N Woodridge Dr Decatur IL 62526 Office: Wagner Castings Co 825 N Lowber Decatur IL 62525

GORE, CATHERINE ANN, social worker; b. Mullens, W.Va., Feb. 2, 1937; d. Bernard Joseph and Agnes Cecilia (Spradling) G.; B.A., Thomas More Coll., 1968; M.S.W., Ohio State U., 1971, M.A. in Pub. Adminstrn., 1983. Caseworker, Cath. Charities, Cin., 1967-69, 71-72; psychiat. social worker Mcpl. Ct. Psychiat. Clinic, Cin., 1973; instr. psychiat. social work, social work supr., Ct. Psychiat. Center, U. Cin., 1974-77, asst. prof. psychiat. social work, coordinator consultation services, 1978-80, grad. research and teaching assoc. Ohio State U., Columbus, 1981—; cons. Hamilton County Welfare Dept.; instr. No. Ky. U. Mem. Nat. Assn. Social Workers, Acad. Cert. Social Workers. Democrat. Roman Catholic. Home: 2599 Scioto View Ln Columbus OH 43221

GORELICK, PAUL A., osteopath; b. Bronx, N.Y., July 20, 1937; s. Benjamin and Martha (New) G.; m. Carol Sue Burrill, June 23, 1980; children—Renee, Scott, Michelle, Danielle. B.S., Wayne State U., 1961; D.O., Coll. Osteo. Medicine and Surgery, Des Moines, 1965. Cert. Nat. Bd. Osteo. Physicians and Surgeons. Chief resident Pontiac Osteo. Hosp., 1968; gen. practice internal medicine 1970—; mem. staff Lapeer (Mich.) County Gen. Hosp., 1970-83, now dir. nuclear medicine dept. Recipient Mosby Book award, 1965. Fellow Am. Coll. Osteo. Internists; mem. Am. Osteo. Assn., Mich. Assn. Osteo. Physicians and Surgeons, Lapeer County Osteo. Assn., Am. Soc. Nuclear Medicine, Franklin Mint Soc., N.R.A., Buffalo Bill Hist. Soc., Psi Sigma Alpha. Office: 1386 N Main St Lapeer MI 48446

GOREN, MICHAEL, lawyer, real estate invester; b. Haifa, Israel, Feb. 18, 1952; came to U.S., 1959, naturalized, 1965; s. Simon Leslie and Hilda (Feuerstein) G.; m. Sherry Ann Rotberg, July 3, 1979. B.A. in Econs. and History, Case Western Res. U., 1974, J.D., 1977. Bar: Ohio 1977, U.S. Dist. Ct. (no. dist.) Ohio 1977, U.S. Supreme Ct. 1983. Assoc. Dworken & Bernstein, Cleve., 1977-80; ptnr. Schmelzer & Goren, Cleve., 1980—, Phoenix Erie Devel. Co., Cleve., 1980—, Tanglewood Country Club, Cleve., 1982—. Pres. Lake County Mental Health Assn., Painesville, Ohio, 1979-80. Mem. Ohio State Bar Assn., Ohio Trial Attys. Assn. Home: 18534 Parkland Dr Shaker Heights OH 44122 Office: Schmelzer & Goren 1404 E 9th St Cleveland OH 44114

GORENCE, PATRICIA JOSETTA, lawyer; b. Sheboygan, Wis., Mar. 16, 1943; d. Joseph and Antonia (Marinsheck) G.; m. John Michael Bach, July 11, 1969; children—Amy Jane Bach, Mara Jo Bach, John Christopher Bach. B.A., Marquette U., 1965; M.A., U. Wis.-Madison, 1968, J.D. cum laude, 1977. Bar: Wis. 1977, U.S. Dist. Ct. (ea. and we. dists.) Wis. 1977, U.S. Ct. Appeals (7th cir.) 1979, U.S. Supreme Ct. 1980. Writer/researcher Alverno Coll., Milw., 1970-71; writer/editor Council on Urban Life, Milw., 1970-73; instr. Carroll Coll., Waukesha, Wis., 1973-74; law clk. U.S. Dist. Ct. (ea. dist.) Wis. 1977-79; asst. U.S. atty. Dept. Justice, Milw., 1979-85, 1st asst. U.S. atty., 1985—; vol. instr./adviser, trial advocacy course Law Sch., Marquette U., Milw., 1979—; mem. adv. com. on local ct. rules U.S. Dist. Ct. (ea. dist.) Wis. 1982—. Mem. Wis. state com. U.S. Commn. on Civil Rights, 1972—. Mem. State Bar Wis., Milw. Bar Assn. (asst. chairperson region 8 Nat. Moot Ct. Competition 1982), Assn. Women Lawyers. Roman Catholic. Home: 3028 N Hackett Ave Milwaukee WI 53211 Office: US Atty's Office 517 E Wisconsin Milwaukee WI 53202

GORKES, RICHARD EDWARD, JR., automotive executive, consultant; b. Abington, Pa., Sept. 1, 1952; s. Richard Edward and Janet (Volpe) G.; m. Susan Elaine Hirlehey, May 9, 1980; 1 dau., Laura Elaine Gorkes. B.S., Phila. Coll. Textiles and Sci., 1974. Asst. buyer The Pep Boys Co., Phila., 1974-77; dist. service mgr. Am. Motors Sales Corp., 1977-79; sr. owner relations mgr. Am. Motors Corp., Detroit, 1979-81, field service supr., Southfield, Mich., 1981-82, supr. warranty adminstrn., 1982—; cons. Farmington Hills (Mich.) Auto Brokerage, 1983—. Mem. Nat. Inst. Automotive Service Excellence, Aircraft Owners and Pilots Assn. Republican. Club: Gulf Sierra Aero (Pontiac, Mich.). Home: 25562 Briarwyke Dr Farmington Hills MI 48018 Office: 14250 Plymouth Rd Detroit MI 48232

GORMAN, CORNELIUS FRANCIS, JR., account manager; b. N.Y.C., Aug. 13, 1952; s. Cornelius Francis and Madonna I. (Riendeau) G.; B.S., Marquette U., 1974; m. Rita Elaine Iris, May 21, 1974; 1 son, Cornelius Francis. Sales rep. Robertson, Inc., Milw., 1975-76, Surg. div. Parke-Davis, Madison, Wis., 1976-77, IPCO Hosp. Supply, Chgo., 1977-78, Medi, Inc., Chgo., 1978-79; regional rep. William Harvey Research Corp., Detroit, 1979-85; account mgr. Laser Sonics, 1985—; system analyst Cordis Corp., 1981—. Roman Catholic. Home: 553 N Riverside Saint Clair MI 48079

GORMAN, ERIN ELIZABETH, securities company executive; b. Chgo., Sept. 4, 1952; d. James Joseph and Kathleen Anne (Egan) Martin. B.A., Clarke Coll., 1974. Mktg. assoc. Midwest Stock Exchange, Chgo., 1974-77, dir. broker mktg., 1977-78; v.p. mktg. John Nuveen & Co., Inc., Chgo., 1978—. Roman Catholic. Home: 1313 Ritchie Ct Chicago IL 60610 Office: John Nuveen & Co Inc 333 W Wacker Dr Chicago IL 60606

GORMAN, GERALD WARNER, lawyer; b. North Kansas City, Mo., May 30, 1933; s. William Shelton and Bessie (Warner) G.; A.B. cum laude, Harvard U., 1954, LL.B. magna cum laude, 1956; m. Anita Belle McPike, June 26, 1954; children—Guinevere Eve, Victoria Rose. Admitted to Mo. bar, 1956, since practiced in Kansas City; assoc. Dietrich, Davis, Dicus, Rowlands, Schmitt & Gorman, 1956-62, partner, 1963—; dir. Musser-Davis Land Co. Bd. govs. Citizens Assn. Kansas City, 1962—; trustee Harvard/Radcliffe Club Kansas City Endowment Fund, chmn. bd., 1977-83; trustee Kansas City Mus., 1967-82, Avondale Methodist Ch., 1969—, Citizens Bond Com. of Kansas City, 1973—; bd. dirs. Spofford Home for Children, 1972-77; chmn. 7th Jud. Circuit Citizens Com., 1983—. Served with AUS, 1956-58. Mem. Lawyers Assn. Kansas City (exec. com. 1968-71), Am., Mo., Kansas City, Clay County bar assns., Harvard Law Sch. Assn. Mo. (pres. 1973). Republican. Clubs: Harvard (pres. 1966), Univ., Kansas City, 611, Old Pike Country. Home: 917 E Vivion Rd Kansas City MO 64118 Office: 1700 City Center Sq Kansas City MO 64105

GORMAN, JOHN COURTNEY, orthodontist; b. Louisville, Dec. 7, 1935; s. Marion Archibald and Regina (Alcorn) G.; m. Faye Cozart, June 12, 1958; children—John Courtney, Edward Russell, Kathleen Ballatine. Student Northwestern U., 1953-55; D.M.D., U. Louisville, 1959; M.S., Washington U., St. Louis, 1963. Diplomate Am. Bd. Orthodontics. Dentist, Louisville, 1959-61; pvt. practice orthodontics, Marion, Ind., 1963—; bd. dirs. Fidelty Fed. Savs., Bank, Marion, 1978—. Contbr. articles to profl. jours. Bd. dirs. Tweed Found., Tucson, 1959-61, United Way of Grant County, Inc., Marion, 1973, 82; pres. Marion Area C. of C., 1973, Marion Devel. Corp., 1976, 77; elder Westminster Presbyn. Ch., Marion, 1968, 84. Served to lt. USNR, 1957-62. Fellow Am. Coll. Dentists, Internat. Coll. Dentists; mem. ADA, Ind. Dental Assn. (v.p. 1984—), Ind. Soc. Orthodontists (pres. 1978), Wabash Valley Dental Soc. (pres. 1969), Am. Assn. Orthodontists (del. 1985). Republican. Presbyterian. Clubs: Meshingomesia Country, Marion Mecca (pres. 1973). Home: 2407 Overlook Rd Marion IN 46952 Office: 444 Wabash Ave Marion IN 46952

GORMAN, JOHN JOSEPH, radio executive; b. Malden, Mass., May 7, 1950; s. John Joseph and Eugenia Josephine (Ignatowicz) G.; m. Mary Helen Nicholas. Student pub. schs., Boston. Contbg. editor Fusion Mag., Boston, 1968-69; program coordinator WNTN Radio, Newton, Mass., 1969-71; cons. Alternative Media, Inc., Cambridge, Mass., 1971-73; music dir. WMMS Radio, Cleve., 1973, program dir., 1973-83, ops. mgr., 1984—; ops. mgr. WHK, 1984—; founder, pres. John Gorman & Assocs., Media Cons., Inc., 1985—. Named Program Dir. of Yr., Malrite Communications Group, 1980, 83. Democrat. Roman Catholic. Office: WHK-WMMS Radio 1200 Statler Office Cleveland OH 44115 also 19754 Tanbark Strongsville OH 44136

GORMAN, JOSEPH TOLLE, lawyer, corporate executive; b. Rising Sun, Ind., Oct. 1, 1937; s. Burton William and Rebecca Evelyn (Tolle) G.; B.A., Kent State U., 1959; LL.B., Yale U., 1962; m. Margaret Mary Bustard, June 25, 1960; children—Joseph Tolle, Leslie L., Bradley G. Asso. firm Baker, Hostetler & Patterson, Cleve., 1962-68; counsel TRW, Inc., Cleve., 1968-70, corporate sec., 1970-72, 73-76, v.p., sr. counsel, 1972-75, v.p., gen. counsel, 1976-80, exec. v.p., 1980-85, pres., chief operating officer, 1985—; dir. Centran Corp., Central Nat. Bank. Trustee, Govtl. Research Inst., Cleve. Play House, Fedn. Community Planning, Univ. Circle, Inc.; mem. advisory com. program on urgent issues Law Sch., Yale U.; mem. exec. com. Center for Public Resources Project on Dispute Resolution, Leadership Cleve. Mem. Am., Ohio, Cleve. bar assns., Assn. Gen. Counsel, Am. Soc. Corporate Secs., U.S. C. of C. (chmn. corp. governance and policy com.). Clubs: Union; Pepper Pike, Country of Cleve. Office: TRW Inc 23555 Euclid Ave Cleveland OH 44117

GORMAN, PAUL JOSEPH, educator; b. Mitchell, S.D., June 29, 1946; s. Elmer E. and Celestine (Turnis) G.; m. Janice Miller, May 25, 1985; 1 child, Carma. B.S. in Agrl. Edn. S.D. State U., 1968; M.S., Mankato State U., 1977. Vocat. agr. instr. Central City, Iowa, 1968-71; farm mgmt. ops. instr. Northwest Iowa Tech. Coll., 1971-74; agri-bus. instr. Mankato (Minn.) Area Vocat. Tech. Inst., 1974—; sec., bd. dirs. Minnesota Valley Sch. Employees Fed. Credit Union. Vol. leader Divorce and Personal Growth Seminar; precinct del. Minn. Democratic Farmer-Labor Party county conv.; co-founder, bd. dirs. Minn. Earth Assn. Mem. NEA (del. 1985 conv. Washington), Minn. Vocat. Assn., Am. Vocat. Assn., Minn. Vocat. Agr. Instrs. Assn., Am. Vocat. Assn., Minn. Edn. Assn. Democrat. Contbr. articles to profl. jours. Developed successful alternative on-farm fuel energy project. Home: 1405 Lor Ray Dr North Mankato MN 56001 Office: 1920 Lee Blvd North Mankato MN 56001

GORMAN, THOMAS JOSEPH, educational administrator; b. Sidney, Nebr., May 12, 1942; s. Leo M. and Madeline E. (Zwickl) G.; m. Lynda H. Clonch; children—Patrick, Michael, Christopher. B.A., Chadron State Coll., 1964, B.S., 1965; M.S., Kearney State Coll., 1970. Cert. secondary tchr., Nebr. Tchr., coach Minden High Sch., Nebr., 1965-70; bus. instr. North Platte Jr. Coll., Nebr., 1970-75; dean community services Mid-Plains Community Coll., North Platte, 1975—; chmn. community service council Nebr. Community Colls., 1979-80. Bd. dirs. Sr. Vol. Program, North Platte, 1973—; co-chmn. Total Community Forum, North Platte, 1977. Mem. Adult and Continuing Edn. Assn. Nebr. (treas. 1978-80, outstanding adult educator award 1984), North Platte C. of C. (chmn. small bus. council 1984). Republican. Roman Catholic. Club: Buffalo Bill Sports Booster (North Platte) (bd. dirs. 1977-82). Lodge: Optimists (v.p. 1975-77, Key Man of Yr. 1980, Optimist of Yr. 1979), Elks. Avocations: golf, coaching baseball. Home: 1107 William Ct North Platte NE 69101 Office: Mid-Plains Community Coll Route 4 Box 1 North Platte NE 69101

GORNICK, ALAN LEWIS, lawyer, tax counsel; b. Leadville, Colo.; s. Mark and Anne (Grayhack) G.; A.B., Columbia U., 1935, LL.B., 1937; m. Ruth L. Willcockson, 1940 (dec.); children—Alan Lewis, Diana (Mrs. Lawrence J. Richard), Keith Hardin; m. Pauline Martoi, 1972. Admitted to N.Y. State bar, 1937; practiced with firm Baldwin, Todd & Young, N.Y.C., 1937-41; practiced with firm Milbank, Tweed, Hope & Hadley, 1941-47, mem. firm, 1947; assoc. counsel charge tax matters Ford Motor Co., Dearborn, Mich., 1947-49, dir. tax affairs, tax counsel, 1949-64; lectr. tax matters N.Y.U. Inst. on Fed. Taxation, 1947-49, ABA and Practising Law Inst. courses on fundamentals in fed. taxation, 1946-55, Am. Law Inst. courses in continuing legal edn., 1950; spl. lectr. sch. bus. adminstrn. U. Mich., 1949, 53; chmn. Otsego Ski Club-Hidden Valley, Inc., Gaylord, Mich., Perry-Davis, Inc.; pres. Meadowbrook Park Devel. Co.; pres. Bloomfield Center, Inc., Bloomfield Hills, Mich. Chmn. state and fed. tax coms.; mem. Mayor's Detroit Tomorrow Com., Citizens Adv. Com. on Taxation to Mich. Senate, Detroit Bd. Commerce; chmn. Mich. tax survey adv. com. Legis. Interim Tax and Revenue Study Com., 1951-53; chmn. Mich. State Aid Survey Com.; pres. Mich. Assn. Emotionally Disturbed Children, 1962; mem. exec. bd. adv. council Detroit area council Boy Scouts Am.; v.p., trustee Detroit chpt. Archives of Am. Art; v.p. Detroit Hist. Soc., 1980, pres., 1983; mem. Bd. Zoning Appeals, City of Bloomfield Hills, 1980—; mem. fin. com. Mich. Heart Assn. Recipient Gov.'s Spl. Award State of Colo., 1952; Disting. Alumni Accomplishment medal Columbia, 1947. Mem. Fed., Am. (mem. fed. tax com. 1954-56; chmn. subcom. on health and welfare plans, com. pension and profit sharing trusts, sect. taxation 1950, com. extra-territorial application of taxes 1951), Mich., Detroit, N.Y.C. (chmn. subcom. estate and gift taxes 1943-47) bar assns., Am. Law Inst., Tax Inst. Inc. (pres. 1954-55, dir. 1951), Nat. Tax Assn. (exec. com. 1954-56), Internat. Fiscal Assn. (council mem.; nat. reporter 6th Internat. Congress Fiscal Law, Brussels 1952), Internat. Law Assn., World Assn. Lawyers, U.S. C. of C. (mem. taxation com.), Assn. Ex-Mems. Squadron A., Nat. Fgn. Trade Council (mem. com. taxes 1950), Automobile Mfrs. Assn. (chmn. com. taxation 1961-63), Tax Exec. Inst. (pres. 1956-57), Fedn. Alumni Columbia (dir. 1946), Class of 1935, Columbia Coll. (permanent pres.), Supreme Ct. Hist. Soc. (founder mem.), N.Y. Adult Edn. Council, Inc. (dir. 1939-45), Phi Delta Phi. Clubs: Bloomfield Hills Country; Detroit, Detroit Athletic; University (Washington); Columbia University, Church (N.Y.C.); Lawyers (Univ. Mich.); Little (Gulfstream, Fla.); Columbia University Alumni of Mich. (pres. 1950). Author: Divorce, Separation and Estate Taxes, Estate Tax Handbook, 1952; Arrangements for Separation or Divorce, Handbook of Tax Techniques, 1952; Taxation of Partnerships, Estates and Trusts, rev. edit., 1952. Adv. editor Nat. Tax Jour., 1952. Contbr. articles tax matters to various law revs., profl. pubs. Home: PO Box J Bloomfield Hills MI 48013 Office: PO Box J 1565 Woodward Ave Suite 8 Bloomfield Hills MI 48013

GORSKE, ROBERT HERMAN, lawyer; b. Milw., June 8, 1932; s. Herman Albert and Lorraine (McDermott) G.; student Milw. State Tchrs. Coll., 1949-50; B.A. cum laude, Marquette U., 1953, J.D. magna cum laude, 1955; LL.M. (W.W. Cook fellow), U. Mich., 1959; m. Antonette Dujick, Aug. 28, 1954; 1 dau., Judith Mary (Mrs. Charles H. McMullen). Bar: Wis. 1955, D.C. 1968, U.S. Supreme Ct. 1970. Asso. Quarles, Spence & Quarles, Milw., 1955-56; atty. Allis-Chalmers Mfg. Co., West Allis, Wis., 1956-62; instr. law U. Mich. Law Sch., Ann Arbor, 1958-59; lectr. law Marquette U. Law Sch., 1963; assoc. Quarles, Herriott & Clemons, Milw., 1962-64; atty. Wis. Electric Power Co., Milw., 1964-67, gen. counsel, 1967—, v.p., 1970-72, 76—; mem. firm Quarles & Brady, Milw., 1972-76; dir. Wis. Natural Gas Co., Racine, Wis., Wis. Mich. Power Co., Appleton. Bd. dirs. Guadalupe Children's Med. Dental Clinic, Inc., Milw., 1976—. Mem. State Bar Wis., Am. Bar Assn., Edison Electric Inst. (vice chmn. legal com. 1975-77, chmn. 1977-79). Contbr. articles to profl. jours. Editor-in-chief Marquette Law Rev., 1954-55. Home: 12700 Stephen Pl Elm Grove WI 53122 Office: 231 W Michigan St Milwaukee WI 53203

GORSKI, PAMELA LEE, hospital administrator; b. Ancon, Panama Canal Zone, July 27, 1944; came to U.S., 1962; d. Walter Dean and Margaret Evelyn (Rutledge) Johnston; m. Damian John Gorski, Aug. 26, 1967; children—Jeffrey, Justin. B.S., Case Western Res. U., 1966, M.B.A., 1980. Adminstrv. asst. (1st woman) to mayor City of Lakewood, Ohio, 1978-80, personnel asst., 1980-81; planning asst. Lakewood Hosp., 1981-84, dir. planning and devel., 1984—. Vice pres. Lakewood Mcpl. Employees Fed. Credit Union, 1985—; commr. Lakewood Youth Softball Commn., 1985—; co-chmn. Lakewood Arts Festival, 1978—. Mem. Nat. Soc. Fund Raising Execs., Lakewood Pub. Relations Officers Assn. Republican. Home: 1063 Wilbert Rd Lakewood OH 44107 Office: Lakewood Hosp 14519 Detroit Ave Lakewood OH 44107

GORSKI, ROBERT VINCENT, financial executive; b. Chgo., June 29, 1951; s. Robert Charles and Dorothy Mary (Wojcik) G.; m. Nancy Ann Burnett, June 9, 1979; 1 child, Robert Andrew, B.S.A.B.A., John Carroll U., 1973; M.B.A., Loyola U., Chgo., 1979. C.P.A., Ill. Sr. acct. Ernst & Ernst, Chgo., 1973-76; sr. bus. analyst NW Industries, Chgo., 1976-79; project mgr. Baxter Travenol, Deerfield, Ill., 1979-81; mgr. planning Gould, Inc., Rolling Meadows, Ill., 1981-85, Household Internat., Prospect Heights, Ill., 1985—; dir. Pulaski Savs. & Loan Assn., Chgo. Mem. Am. Inst. C.P.A.s, Ill. C.P.A. Soc., Beta Gamma Sigma. Roman Catholic. Avocations: racquetball; golf; softball. Home: 101 Honeysuckle Ct Rolling Meadows IL 60008 Office: Household Internat 2700 Sanders Rd Prospect Heights IL 60070

GORSUCH, RICHARD HAROLD, power company executive; b. Columbus, Ohio, Dec. 22, 1939; s. Paul Douglas and Kathleen (Clawson) G.; m. Rita Elaine Zimmerman, Aug. 27, 1961 (dec. June 1973); children—Heidi, Hans; m. Sarah Elizabeth Rose; stepchildren—Joanna, Calvin. B.A., Otterbein Coll., 1961; postgrad. Franklin Law Sch., 1962-64. Claims mgr. suit unit Allstate Ins., Columbus, 1964-69; v.p. ins. div. Frank Gates Service Co., 1979-83; pres. Am. Mcpl. Power Ohio, Inc., Westerville, 1983—. Contbr. articles to profl. jours. Chmn. Westerville City Council, 1972-74, 80-81, Central Ohio Transit Authority, Columbus, 1981-82; pres. Amalthea Retirement Village, 1980-82. Served with U.S. Army, 1957-62. Named gov. Boys State, Am. Legion, 1956; named to Am. Legion Hall of Fame, 1983; recipient disting. service award Westerville Jaycees, 1972. Mem. Am. Pub. Power Assn. (com. 1983—). Lodges: Masons, Order Eastern Star. Office: Box 549 Westerville OH 43081

GORTNER, ROBERT VANDERBILT, management educator, administrator; b. Davidsville, Pa., Jan. 20, 1930; s. Maurice Rynerson and Ruth Runyan (Vanderbilt) G.; m. Aileen Melva Kraekel, Feb. 15, 1952 (dec. Apr. 1981); children—Deborah, Susan, William, David: m. 2d, Jane Elaine Le Master, May 22, 1982; stepchildren—Ted, Beth. B.S. in Commerce and Engring., M.B.A., Drexel U. Cert. mgmt. cons. Indsl. engr. Eastman Kodak Co. Rochester, N.Y., 1955-59; supt. Hercules, Inc., Rocky Hill, N.J., 1959-65; prodn. mgr. Polymer Corp., Reading, Pa., 1965-68; plant mgr. Thiokol Corp., Trenton, N.J., 1968-70; sr. mgr. (cons.) Price Waterhouse & Co., N.Y.C., 1970-80; assoc. prof., chmn. mgmt. dept. Taylor U., Upland, Ind., 1980—; adj. prof. Drexel U., Phila., 1963-65, Union Community Coll., Westfield, N.J., 1979-80, Rochester Inst. Tech., (N.Y.), 1958. Pres. PTA, Wyomissing Hills, Pa., 1967; supr. twp. Northampton Twp., Bucks County, Pa., 1963-65; coach and mgr. Little League and Babe Ruth Baseball, Lower Makefield, Pa. and Summit, N.J., 1968-80; bd. dirs. Jr. Achievement, Marion, Ind., 1981-83, Leadership/Grant County, Marion, 1983. Served as lt. USNR, 1952-55. Mem. Acad. Mgmt., Inst. Indsl. Engrs., Am. Prodn. and Inventory Control Soc., Inst. Mgmt. Cons., Blue Key, Phi Kappa Phi. Republican. Presbyterian. Lodge: Rotary (Marion, Ind.). Home: 9240 E 700S Upland IN 46989 Office: Taylor U Upland IN 46989

GOSNELL, WILLIAM HOOVER, optometrist; b. Bartlesville, Okla., Apr. 12, 1932; s. Walter Harold and Estella Mae (Dean) G.; m. Wanda Louise Orr, Apr. 8, 1951; children—William H. II, Gerald Robert. A.A., Central Christian Coll., 1952; B.S., No. Ill. Coll. Optometry, 1954, O.D., 1955. Lic. optometrist, Mo, Kans., Okla. Optometry officer U.S. Army, Tacoma, 1955-58; pvt. practice optometry, Independence, Mo., 1958—. Mem. Optometric Soc. Greater Kansas City (pres. 1971-72), Mo. Optometric Assn. (trustee), Am. Optometric Assn. Republican. Christian. Lodges: Lions (pres. 1963), Optimists (pres. 1976). Avocations: Duck hunting, fishing, photography. Home: 12214 E Oak Ridge Rd Independence MO 64052 Office: 10612 E 18th St Independence MO 65052

GOSSAIN, VED VYAS, medical educator; b. Jhang, India, Mar. 25, 1941; came to U.S., 1967; s. Bhagwan Dass and Rani (Virmani) G.; m. Veena Virmani, May 25, 1970; children—Anuja, Maneesh; m. 2d, Rama Dhamija, Aug. 24, 1979; 1 child, Vineeth. M.B.B.S., Med. Coll. Amritsar (India), 1963; M.D., All India Inst. Med. Scis., 1967. Diplomate Am. Bd. Internal Medicine. Intern V.J. Med. Coll. Hosp., Amritsar, India, 1963-64; clin. resident All India Inst. Med. Scis., New Delhi, 1965-67, vis. prof., 1979, 81; resident Springfield (Mass.) Hosp. Med. Ctr., 1967-70; clin. and research fellow endocrinology and metabolism U. Cin. Med. Ctr., 1970-72; research fellow endocrinology and metabolism Milw. County Gen. Hosp., 1972-73; mem. staff internal medicine VA Hosp., St. Louis, 1973-75, dir. endocrine metabolic clinic, 1973-75; asst. prof. internal medicine St. Louis U., 1973-75; asst. prof. internal medicine Coll. Human Medicine, Mich. State U., East Lansing, 1975-78, assoc. prof., 1978-82, prof., 1982—; vis. prof. Guy Hosp. Sch. Medicine, London, 1981; cons. in field. Fellow Royal Coll. Physicians Can., ACP, All India Inst. Diabetes; mem. Am. Fedn. Clin. Research, The Endocrine Soc., AAAS, Mich. State Med. Soc., Ingham County Med. Soc. Hindu. Contbr. articles to profl. jours.

GOSSER, JON WALTER, educator; b. Seattle, May 15, 1941; s. Lawrence and Ellinore (Jones) G.; B.S. cum laude, U. Wash., 1962, M.S., 1964, postgrad., 1964-65; postgrad. U. Kans., 1965-67. Reader in stats. U. Wash., Seattle, fellow research asst. in psychology, 1962-63, USPHS predoctoral research fellow NIMH, 1963-65; predoctoral trainee in ednl. research Bur. Child Research, U. Kans., Kansas City, 1965-66; tchr. psychology, logic and marriage and family relations Kansas City (Kans.) Community Jr. Coll., 1966-67; instr. psychology Delta Coll., University Center, Mich., 1967-69, asst. prof., 1970-75, asso. prof., 1975—, dir. Mid-Mich. Psychologist, Inc., 1973-76, 79-83, treas., 1978-83; bd. dirs., acting pres. Nat. Ednl. Network, Inc., 1982—. Mem. Data Processing Mgmt. Assn. (dir. 1971-73; individual performance award 1981), Am. Psychol. Assn., AAAS, AAUP (corr. sec. Delta chpt. 1969), Am. Ednl. Research Assn., Assn. Behavior Analysis, Mich. Acad. Sci., Arts and Letters, Internat. Soc. for Individual Instrn., Sigma Xi. Author: (with Harbans Lal) Research on Teaching Pharmacy: The Role of Student Ratings, 1968; A Computerized Method of Longitudinal Evaluation of Student Performance, 1969; Computerized Test Library, 1974; Longitudinal Evaluation and Improvement of Teaching: An Empirical Approach Based on Analysis of Student Behaviors, 1975; (with Packwood and Walters) The Effect of Repeated Testing on Long Term Retention and Generalization in a General Psychology Course, 1979. Home: 3200 Noeske St Midland MI 48640 Office: Delta Coll University Center MI 48710

GOSSETT, GLORIA JEAN, nurse, social worker; b. Urbana, Ohio, Oct. 7, 1953; d. Owen Edward and Goldie (Gardenhire) G.; m. Michael C. Rogan, Apr. 27, 1985. B.S. cum laude, Central State U., 1975; nursing diploma Community Hosp. Sch. Nursing, 1982. R.N., Ohio. Social field worker Greene County Commn. on Aging, Yellow Springs, Ohio, 1975; social worker Ohio Orphans Home, Xenia, 1976-77; staff nurse Community Hosp., Springfield, 1982—. Mem. Alpha Kappa Mu. Home: 2803 Oxford Dr Springfield OH 45506

GOTCH, LOU ANN MEYER, banker; b. Ft. Wayne, Ind., June 23, 1947; d. Donald LeRoy and Marjorie Ruth (Dyer) Meyer; m. John Raymond Gotch, Oct. 7, 1967; 1 child, Andrew John. Student, So. Ill. U., 1965-66, Am. Inst. Banking, 1979-81; cert. Sch. Bank Mktg., 1982. Teller Carbondale Savs. & Loan, Ill., 1974-76; customer service/advt. mgr. State Savs., Bowling Green, Ohio, 1976-78; mktg. asst. Pk. Nat. Bank, Newark, Ohio, 1978-79; dir. mktg. Central Trust Co., Newark, 1979-85; v.p. mktg. United Nat. Bank, Canton; Ohio, 1985—; cons. pub. speaking Bus. and Profl. women, Newark, 19; cons., mktg. Bldg. Better Bds., Newark, 1984. Newspaper columnist 1984-85. Loaned exec. United Way, Licking County, Ohio, 1978; bd. dirs. Am. Cancer Soc., Licking County, 1978-85, Named Outstanding Women of Am., 1983. Mem. Nat. Assn. Bank Women, Ohio Sch. Bank Mktg. Alumni Assn., C. of C. Licking County. Avocations: teaching aerobics, public speaking, music, Sunday Sch. Lit., sewing. Office: United Nat Bank PO Box 190 Canton OH 44701

GOTKIN, MICHAEL STANLEY, lawyer; b. Washington, Aug. 15, 1942; s. Charles and Florence (Rosenberg) G.; A.A., Montgomery Community Coll., 1962; B.S., Columbia U., 1964; J.D., Vanderbilt U., 1967; m. Diana Rubin, Aug. 22, 1964; children—Lisa, Steven. Admitted to D.C. bar, 1968, Tenn. bar, 1973; trial atty. Bur. Restraint of Trade, FTC, Washington, 1967-70; atty. H.J. Heinz Co., Pitts., 1970-73; partner firm Moseley & Gotkin, Nashville, 1973; atty. K.F.C. Corp., Louisville, 1974-75; v.p., gen. counsel Fairley Candy Co., Skokie, Ill., 1975—, also dir.; v.p., gen. counsel, dir. Taste-T-Sweets, Inc., Am.

Flexo Inc., Skokie, So. Spirits, Inc., Montgomery, Ala.; dir. Photo Express, Inc., Chgo. Mem. ABA, Am. Corp. Counsel Assn. (bd. dirs. Chgo. chpt.), D.C. Bar Assn., Tenn. Bar Assn., Montgomery Community Coll. Assn. (past pres.), Skokie C. of C. (pres., dir.), Columbia U. Alumni Assn., Candy Prodn. Club, Vanderbilt U. Alumni Assn. Clubs: Sportsman Country, B'nai B'rith. Office: 4820 Searle Pkwy Skokie IL 60077

GOTT, WESLEY ATLAS, art educator; b. Buffalo, Mar. 6, 1942; s. Raymond and Rowena (Pettitt) G.; m. Alice Blalock, May 26, 1972; children—Andrew, Deidre. B.S., S.W. Mo. State U., 1965; M.Ch.Music, Southwestern Theol. Sem., 1969; M.F.A., George Washington U., 1975. Tchr. ceramic classes Springfield Art Mus., Mo., 1964-66; minister of music Terrace Acres Bapt. Ch., Ft. Worth, Tex., 1966-70; minister music and youth First Bapt. Ch. Wheaton, Md., 1970-75; asst. prof. art S.W. Bapt. U., Bolivar, Mo., 1975-79, assoc. prof., chmn. dept. art, 1979—; judge art contests, 1978-84. Artist sculpture with lights, 1981-84. Mem. Coll. Art Assn. Am., Mid-Am. Coll. Art Assn., Smithsonian Assocs., Nat. Trust for Historic Preservation, Community Concert Assn., Alpha Gamma Theta, Phi Mu Alpha. Baptist. Avocations: hunting; fishing; boating; tennis; golf. Home: 127 W Maupin Bolivar MO 65613 Office: Southwest Bapt Univ 623 S Pike Bolivar MO 65613

GOTTLEABER, VERN H., osteopathic physician; b. Monticello, Iowa, Feb. 4, 1953; s. Harold Edward and Darlene Marie (Chapman) G.; m. Debra Ann Koselke, July 31, 1982. B.A. cum laude, Coe Coll., 1976; D.O., Coll. Osteo. Medicine and Surgery, Des Moines, 1981. Diplomate Nat. Bd. Osteo. Med. Examiners; cert. advanced cardiac life support. Staff, Mannabaro Luth. Hosp. (Madagascar) 1980-81; intern Waldo Gen. Hosp., Seattle, 1981-82; mem. Med. Assocs. of Maquoketa, P.C. (Iowa), 1982—; mem. staff Jackson County Pub. Hosp. Mem. Am. Osteo. Assn., Am. Coll. Gen. Practitioners, Wash. Osteo. Med. Assn., Iowa Soc. Osteo. Physicians and Surgeons, AMA, Iowa Med. Soc., Jackson County Med. Soc., Am. Osteo. Coll. Rheumatology, Am. Acad. Osteopathy, Iowa Acad. Family Physicians, Am. Acad. Family Physicians, World Med. Assn., Cornbelt Running Club, Road Runners Club Am., Phi Kappa Phi. Democrat. Lutheran. Home: 909 W Farmland Dr Maquoketa IA 52060 Office: 611 W Quarry St Maquoketa IA 52060

GOTTLIEB, MARVIN EMANUEL, psychiatrist; b. Cleve., Aug. 1, 1934; s. Ben Nathan and Sylvia (Horowitz) G.; m. Judith Balin, June 22, 1958 (div. 1981); children—Joel, Robert; m. Margaret R. Reissig, June 10, 1983. B.A., Case Western Res. U., 1956, M.D., 1961. Diplomate Am. Bd. Psychiatry and Neurology, 1968. Intern, Mt. Sinai Hosp., Cleve., 1961-62; resident in psychiatry U. Rochester (N.Y.), 1962-65; asst. chief outpatient service Fairhill Psychiat. Hosp., Cleve., 1967-68; asst. prof. Med. Coll. Toledo, 1968-70, assoc. prof., 1970—, dir. psychiat. residency, 1970—; pvt. practice, Cleve., 1967-68, Toledo, 1968—. Vice pres. Jewish Family Services Toledo, 1970. Served to lt. comdr. USNR, 1965-67; Viet Nam. Fellow Am. Psychiat. Assn., mem. Ohio Med. Assn., Toledo Lucas County Med. Assn., Am. Coll. Psychiatrists. Jewish. Lodge: B'nai B'rith (dir. 1981—). Co-editor Psychiatry Continuing Edn. Rev., 1973. Home: 5211 Saddle Creek Rd Toledo OH 43623 Office: Med Coll Ohio CS 10008 Toledo OH 43699

GOTTSCHALK, ALFRED, Biblical scholar, author, college president; b. Oberwesel Germany, Mar. 7, 1930; s. Max and Erna (Trum-Gerson) G.; came to U.S., 1939, naturalized, 1945; A.B., Bklyn. Coll., 1952; B. Hebrew Lit., Hebrew Union Coll., 1954, M.A. with honors, 1956; Ph.D., U. So. Calif., 1965, S.T.D. (hon.), 1968, LL.D. (hon.), 1976; D.Litt. (hon.), Dropsie U., 1974; D.R.E. (hon.), Loyola Marymount U., 1977; LL.D. (hon.), U. Cin., 1976, Xavier U., 1981; L.H.D. (hon.), Jewish Theol. Sem., 1971; L.H.D. (hon.), St. Thomas Inst., 1982; m. Deanna Zeff, Dec. 31, 1977; children by previous marriage—Marc Hillel, Rachel Lisa. Ordained rabbi, 1957; instr. Jewish history Hebrew Union Coll.-Jewish Inst. Religion, Cin., 1957-59, asst. prof. Bible, 1959-62, assoc. prof., 1962-65, prof., 1965—, pres., 1971—; acting dean Hebrew Union Coll., Los Angeles, 1958-59, dean, 1959-71; vis. prof. UCLA, 1966, 68, 70, 71; mem. exec. com. Central Conf. Am. Rabbis, 1971—. Mem. Pres. Johnson's Com. Equal Employment Opportunity, 1964-66, Calif. Gov.'s Poverty Support Corps Program, 1965-67, Los Angeles Mayor's Community Devel. Adv. Com., 1965-70; trustee Council Religious and Interreligious Affairs, 1975-78, Albright Inst. Archaeol. Research, 1973—, Union Am. Hebrew Congregations, 1972; mem. Pres.'s Commn. on the Holocaust, 1979-80; co-chmn. coordinating com. Holocaust Meml. Council, 1980—. Recipient Human Relations award Am. Jewish Com., 1971, Los Angeles City Council award, 1971, Tower of David award for Cultural Contbn. to Israel and Am., Israel Govt., 1972, Gold Medallion award Jewish Nat. Fund, 1972, Myrtle Wreath award Hadassah, 1977, Alumnus of Year award Bklyn. Coll., 1972, Man of Year award Boys High Sch. Alumni Assn., 1976; Nat. Educators award NCCJ, 1980; Guggenheim fellow, 1969, Smithsonian Inst. grantee, 1963, 67. Mem. NEA, Soc. Bibl. Lit. and Exegesis, Am. Philos. Soc., Am. Acad. Religion, Am. Assn. Higher Edn., World Union Jewish Studies, So. Calif. Jewish Hist. Soc. (hon. pres. 1972—), Jewish Publ. Soc. Am. (publs. com. 1975), Assn. Theol. Schs. (exec. com. 1974-76), World Union Progressive Judaism (v.p. 1973—), Israel Exploration Soc., N.Y. Bd. Rabbis (hon. v.p. 1972—), World Inst. Sephardic Studies, Synagogue Council Am. (policy planning inst.), World Zionist Orgn., Am. Assn. Pres. of Ind. Colls. and Univs., Am. Friends of Alliance Israelite Universelle (trustee 1972—), So. Calif. Assn. Liberal Rabbis (pres. 1965-66), Zionist Fedn. Am. (organizing pres. western region 1968), Zionist Orgn. Am. (Louis Dembitz Brandeis award 1977), Delta Sigma Rho. Contbr. articles to scholarly and popular jours.; editorial bd. Hebrew Union Coll. Ann.

GOTTSCHLICH, GARY WILLIAM, lawyer; b. Dayton, Ohio, Aug. 27, 1946; s. William Frederick and Rosemary Teresa (Heberle) G.; m. Sharon Melanie Plunkett, Oct. 7, 1978; children—David W., Andrew J., Thomas M. B.S., U. Dayton, 1968; cert., Univ. Coll., London, 1970; J.D., U. Notre Dame, 1971. Bar: Ohio 1971. Asst. pros. atty. Montgomery County, Dayton, 1971-73; assoc. Young, Pryor, Lynn & Jerardi, 1973-80, ptnr., 1980-84; ptnr. Louis & Froelich, Dayton, 1984—. Served to capt. USAR. Mem. ABA, Assn. Trial Lawyers Am., Ohio Bar Assn. (bd. govs. litigation sect.), Dayton Bar Assn. (treas. 1981-82). Roman Catholic. Avocations: golf; sailing. Home: 5260 Little Woods Ln Dayton OH 45429 Office: Louis & Froelich 1812 Kettering Tower Dayton OH 45423

GOUDY, JOSEPHINE GRAY, social worker; b. Des Moines, Nov. 30, 1925; d. Gerald William and Myrtle Maria (Brooks) Gray; B.A., State U. Iowa, 1953, M.S.W., 1966; m. John Winston Goudy, June 5, 1948; children—Tracy Jean, Paula Rae. Child welfare supr. Iowa Dept. Social Services, 1960-68; psychiat. social worker Community Mental Health Center Scott County (Iowa), 1966-71; social work instr. Palmer Jr. Coll., Davenport, Iowa, 1967-70; psychiat. social worker, chief social services Jacksonville (Ill.) State Mental Hosp., 1971-74; coordinator community mental health outpatient services McFarland Mental Health Center, Springfield, Ill., 1974; exec. dir. Macoupin County Mental Health Center, Carlinville, Ill., 1974—; chmn. Human Services Edn. Council, Springfield, 1979-81; past exec. Davenport Community Welfare Council. Mem. Nat. Assn. Social Workers (Social Worker of Yr. Central Ill. area 1983), Acad. Cert. Social Workers, Am. Personnel and Guidance Assn., AAUW (br. pres. 1964-66, mem. state bar 1966-68, br. grantee 1975), Internat. Fedn. U. Women, U. Iowa Alumni Assn., Bus. and Profl. Women (Woman of Yr. 1983), Delta Kappa Gamma. Republican. Methodist. Club: Carlinville Women's (pres. 1975-77). Home: 364 W Tremont St Waverly IL 62692 Office: 100 N Side Sq Carlinville IL 62626

GOUGH, RUTH RUUD, educational consultant; b. Long Beach, Calif., Dec. 12, 1952; d. Paul David and Virginia June (Bentley) Ruud; m. William Roger Gough, Aug. 19, 1979; 1 son, Mark Roger. B.A. in Sociology and Elem. Edn., Calif. State U., Long Beach, 1975; M.S. in Counseling and Guidance, Univ. Wis., Madison, 1978, Ph.D. in Ednl. Adminstrn., 1981. Cert. tchr. Tchr., Garfield Elem. Sch., Bell Gardens, Calif., 1976; house fellow, residence halls, U. Wis., Madison, 1976-77; intern Dean of Students Office, 1977-78, student orientation leader for new student services, summer 1979; tchr. adult edn. Madison Area Tech. Coll., 1978-81; cons. human devel., St. Paul, 1981—; researcher in field. Campaign worker Mondale/Ferraro Campaign, St. Paul. Villas scholar, 1980; Legis. appointment Univ. Wis. State Senator Krueger, 1976-81. Mem. Am. Coll. Personnel Assn., Am. Assn. Counseling and Devel., Pi Lambda Theta, Phi Kappa Phi. Mem. United Ch. Christ. Club: Mother's (St. Paul). Avocations: Traveling; sewing; baking; piano playing; painting. Home and Office: 2153 Eleanor Ave St Paul MN 55116

GOUKE, CECIL GRANVILLE, economist, educator; b. Bklyn., Dec. 5, 1928; s. Joseph and Etheline (Grant) G.; B.A., CCNY, 1956; M.A., N.Y. U., 1958, Ph.D., 1967; m. Mary Noel, June 19, 1964; 1 son, Cecil Granville. Instr. econs. Fisk U., 1958-60; asst. prof. Grambling Coll., 1962-64, asso. prof., 1964-67; prof., chmn. Hampton (Va.) Inst., 1967-73; prof. econs. Ohio State U., 1973—; vis. lectr. U. Wis., 1970; vis. asso. prof. UCLA, 1969; economist Fed. Res. Bank N.Y., 1972; cons. U.S. Treasury Dept., 1973. Served with U.S. Army, 1947-49, 50-51. Recipient Founders Day award N.Y. U., 1967; Fulbright scholar Internat. Exchange of Scholars, 1979-80. Mem. Am. Econ. Assn., Am. Fin. Assn., Am. Statis. Assn., Indsl. Relations Research Assn., Western Econ. Assn., Nat. Econ. Assn., Hampton NAACP (exec. bd. 1968-70), Phi Beta Sigma (pres. Beta Omicron Sigma chpt. 1977). Democrat. Episcopalian. Author: Amalgamated Clothing Workers of America, 1940-1966, 1972; asso. editor Jour. Behavioral and Social Scis., 1974—. Home: 1788 Kenwick Rd Columbus OH 43209 Office: Economics Dept Ohio State U Columbus OH 43210

GOULD, JANICE SANDRA, stockbroker; b. St. Louis, Dec. 20, 1942; d. Gilbrt Raymond and Frances Elizabeth (Ellingsworth) Caldwell; B.A., U. Iowa, 1967; student Simpson Coll., 1961-62, Drake U., summer 1974; children—Troy Bryan, Jonna Ryon. Med. sec., 1965-67; legal sec., 1967-68; real estate salesperson Las Vegas, 1973-75; stockbroker Dain Bosworth Inc., Des Moines, 1974-82, Edward D. Jones & Co., Ankeny, Iowa, 1982-83, R.G. Dickinson & Co., Des Moines, 1983—; owner pvt. bus., 1983—; substitute tchr. high sch., Las Vegas, 1973; condr. investment/market seminars. Mem. citizens ad hoc com. Law Sch. U. Nev. Las Vegas, pres., sec., organizer, lobbyist; mem. adv. bd. Bd. Regents Law Sch., also adv. bd. historian; bd. dirs. Clark County Central Republican Com., 1969-82, state conv. del., election bd. chm., state credential com.; mem. Warren County Rep. Central Com., 1979—, dist. conv. del., 1979—; state conv. del., 1979—; county conv. del., 1980, 82; pres. Tri T.A.G. parents gifted children; tchr. secondary level Sunday Sch. Mem. PEO (charter chpt. pres., state conv. del.), AAUW (state legis. chmn., del. nat. conv. 1975), U. Iowa Alumni Assn., Alpha Xi Delta. Clubs: Zonta (fin. com., advt. com. for projects, seminar speaker 1982), La. Sertoma. Home: 1307 E Detroit St Indianola IA 50125 Office: 200 Des Moines Bldg Des Moines IA 50308

GOULD, JOHN PHILIP, educator, university dean; b. Chgo., Jan. 19, 1939. S.B. with highest distinction, Northwestern U., 1960; M.B.A., U. Chgo., 1963, Ph.D., 1966. Instr. Grad. Sch. Bus., U. Chgo., 1965-66, asst. prof., 1966-69, assoc. prof., 1969-74, prof. econs., 1974—, dean, 1983—, dean, disting. service prof., 1984—; spl. asst. for econ. affairs Sec. of Labor, 1969-70; cons. econ. affairs to dir. Office Mgmt. and Budget, Exec. Office Pres., 1970; program leader on econs. of info. Gen. Electric Found. Program on Recent Devels. in Applied Econs., U. Chgo., 1975-82; cons. Chemetron Corp., 1971-78; expert witness in anti-trust cases and related cases U.S. Fed. Ct. and FTC, 1978-81. Author: (with Ferguson) Microeconomic Theory, 4th edit., 1975, Teoria Microeconomia, 1978, Microeconomic Theory, 5th edit., 1980; David-Bacon Act-The Economics of Prevailing Wage Laws, 1971; The Economics of the Davis-Bacon Act: An Analysis of Prevailing Wage Laws, 1980; referee Am. Econ. Rev., Bell Jour. Econs., Can. Jour. Econs., Econometrica, Econ. Inquiry, Jour. Econ. Theory, Jour. Bus., Jour. Fin., Jour. Fin. Econs., Jour. Am. Statis. Assn., Jour. Polit. Economy, Internat. Econ. Rev., Mgmt. Sci., Quarterly Jour. Econs., Rev. Econ. Studies; editor Jour. Bus., 1976-83; assoc. editor Jour. Fin. Econs., 1976-82, Jour. Acctg. and Econs., 1978-81. Contbr. articles to profl. jours. Recipient awards Am. Mktg. Assn., 1960, Wall Street Jour., 1960; Earhart fellow U. Chgo., 1962-64; grantee NSF, 1972-76, Mobil Found. faculty research grantee, 1976. Mem. Am. Econ. Assn., Econometric Soc., Western Econ. Assn., Beta Gamma Sigma. Office: Grad Sch Bus U Chgo 1101 E 58th St Chicago IL 60637

GOULD, PHILLIP L., civil engineering educator; b. Chgo., May 24, 1937; m. Deborah Paula Gould, Feb. 5, 1961. B.S., U. Ill., 1959, M.S., 1960; Ph.D., Nothwestern U., 1966. Registered profl. engr., Wis., Ill., Mo. Structural designer Skidmore, Owings & Merrill, Chgo., 1960-63; prin. structural engr. Westenhoff & Novick, Chgo., 1963-64; NASA trainee Northwestern U., Evanston, Ill., 1964-66; asst. prof. civil engring. Washington U., St. Louis, 1966-68, assoc. prof., 1968-74, prof., 1974-78, prof., dept. chmn., 1978—; cons. to numerous govt. and indsl. orgns., 1966—. Author: Static Analysis of Shells: A Unified Development of Surface Structures, 1977; (with S.A. Abu-Sitta) Dynamic Response of Structures to Wind and Earthquake Loading, 1980; Introduction to Linear Elasticity, 1984; Finite Element Analysis of Shells of Revolution, 1985. Editor: (with C.A. Brebbia and J. Munro) Environmental Forces on Engineering Structures, 1979; (with I. Mungan, W. Kratzig and U. Wittek) Natural Draught Cooling Towers, 1984. Served to 1st lt. U.S. Army, 1959-60, 63. Fellow ASCE; mem. Internat. Assn. for Shell Structures, Am. Soc. Engring. Edn., Am. Acad. Mechanics, Sigma Xi. Home: 102 Lake Forest Richmond Heights MO 63117 Office: Wash U Campus Box 1130 Saint Louis MO 63130

GOULD, TERRY ALLEN, lawyer, financial executive; b. St. Louis, Sept. 30, 1942; s. Courtney A. and Dorothy (Bitker) G.; B.S., Miami U., Oxford, Ohio, 1965; postgrad. Grad. Sch. Bus. Adminstrn., Washington U., St. Louis, 1966; J.D. cum laude, St. Louis U., 1981; m. Patricia Ann Wolf, July 21, 1968; children—Kristine Ann, Bradford Allen. Security analyst Merc. Trust Co., St. Louis, 1965-66; mgmt. trainee Misco-Shawnee, Inc., St. Louis, 1966-68, br. mgr., 1969-72, v.p., 1972-73, exec. v.p. adminstrn., 1973-78, sec./treas., 1975-78, dir., 1976-79; trustee Misco-Shawnee Profit Sharing Trust, 1975-78; v.p., dir. GORA Investment Co., St. Louis, 1975-78; gen. ptnr. Tera Investment Assocs., 1978—; sole practice law, 1981-85; of counsel Morganstern, Soraghan, Stockenberg, McKitrick & Spoeneman, 1985—; pres., dir. Tera Mgmt. Corp., 1980—; dir. Suburban Nat. Bank Elk Grove (Ill.), 1972-77. Mem. bd. mgrs., vice chmn. fin. com., mem. membership com., downtown br. Greater St. Louis YMCA, 1976-82; bd. dirs. Wis. Music Network, 1982—, Clef, Inc., 1982—, St. Louis Charitable Found., 1984—. Mem. ABA, Met. St. Louis Bar Assn. (chmn. real estate and devel. com. 1983-84, chmn. bus. law sect. 1985-86), Mo. Bar Assn., Delta Sigma Pi, Beta Theta Pi. Office: 2162 Pierre Laclede Ctr 7733 Forsyth Blvd Saint Louis MO 63105-1831

GOULD, WILLIAM R., photographic paper and chemistry company executive; m. Marian Gould; 3 children. Student, U. Calif. With DeKalb Ag Research, 1949-56; with Western Litho Plate, exec. v.p.; ptnr. Nat. Graphics, Inc., St. Louis, 1974—, pres. Chmn. Small Bus. Assn. adv. council; founding bd. dirs. Midcontinent Small Bus. United; bd. dirs. Regional Commerce and Growth Assn., chmn. small bus. council; del. White House Conf. on Sl. Bus., 1980, co-planner, 1983 and 84 for Mo. Conf. on Sml. Bus.; mem. Mo. Dist. Export Council of Commerce Dept. Club: World Trade. Lodge: Rotary. Address: 2711 Miami St Saint Louis MO 63118

GOULET, LEO DAVID, food manufacturing company executive; b. Colon, Panama, May 28, 1926; s. Arthur Wilfred and Mary Macel (Butler) G.; m. Carol Kenyon Ruoff, May 12, 1950; children—Beverly, Stephanie. B.S., U. Denver, 1949. Vice pres. for Latin Am., Gerber Products Co., Fremont, Mich., 1973-81, v.p., gen. mgr. gen. mdse., 1981-82, exec. v.p., gen. mgr., 1982-83, pres., chief operating officer, 1983—, also dir. Served with USN, 1944-46. Republican. Roman Catholic. Club: Ramshorn Country. Office: 445 State St Fremont MI 49412

GOULET, PETER GREGORY, business educator; b. Chgo., Nov. 24, 1944; s. George Alphonse and Sarabel (Williams) G.; m. Lynda Mary Lantz, Mar. 18, 1967; 1 dau., Meridith. B.A. with honors, Denison U., 1966; M.B.A., Ohio State U., 1967, Ph.D., 1970. Asst. prof. So. Ill. U., Edwardsville, 1970-71; asst. to the pres. ILC Products Co., Elkhart, Ind., 1972-74; asst. prof. bus. U. No. Iowa, Cedar Falls, 1974-77, assoc. prof., 1977—, head dept. mgmt., 1981-82. Author: Real Estate: A Value Approach, 1979; contbr. articles to profl. jours. Mem. Am. Fin. Assn., Fin. Mgmt. Assn., Phi Alpha Kappa. Avocations: electronics; bridge; reading. Home: 2718 Abraham Dr Cedar Falls IA 50613 Office: U No Iowa Sch Bus Cedar Falls IA 50614

GOVONI, JAMES DANIEL, dentist; b. Joliet, Ill., Nov. 2, 1945; s. Daniel J. and Sarah (Bright) G.; m. Jane E. Gage, June 17, 1972; children—Rebecca, Maria, Amanda, Gina. Diploma, Joliet Jr. Coll., 1963-65; student, Lewis Coll., 1965-66; B.S., No. Ill. U., 1966-67; D.D.S., Marquette U., 1971. Dental intern VA, Martinsburg, W.Va., 1971-73; practice medicine specializing in dentistry, Oxford, Wis., 1975—; cons. prisons, nursing homes. State of Ill. scholar, 1967-68. Mem. Tri-County Dental Soc., Nat. Hearing Aid Soc., Am. Acad. Orthodontics for Gen. Practitioners, Am. Dental Assoc., Phi Sigma, Psi Omega. Lutheran. Lodge: Lions (Oxford). Avocations: hunting; fishing; banjo; cross-country skiing; iceskating. Home: Route 1 Oxford WI 53952 Office: Crossroads Clinic Route 1 Oxford WI 53952

GOWER, RONALD ALLAN, English educator, administrator; b. St. Paul, Mar. 12, 1935; s. Allan Edgar and Lucile Katherine (Meyer) G.; m. Anne Marguerite Hocking, 1969; children—Owen, Hugh. B.A., Hamline U., 1957; B.S., Mankato State U., 1962, M.S., 1963; Ph.D., U. N.Mex., 1970. Tchr. Nicollet High Sch., Minn., 1963-65; prof. Mankato State U., Minn., 1965-68, 70—, chmn. English dept., 1983—; teaching asst. U. N.Mex., 1968-70. Author numerous poems and short stories. Editor Mag. Corresponder, 1983—. Contbr. articles to profl. jours. Bd. dirs. Dollars for Scholars, Good Thunder, Minn., 1983. Served to capt. U.S. Army, 1958-60. Fellow NDEA, 1970; grantee Mankato State U., 1973, 1978, Bush Found., 1982. Mem. Assn. Depts. English, English Alumni Bd., NEA, Associated Writing Programs, Phi Kappa Phi. Avocations: camping; hunting; fishing; skiing; tennis. Home: Route 2 Box 36 Good Thunder MN 56037 Office: Mankato State U Dept English Mankato MN 56001

GOYAL, ARVIND KUMAR, physician; b. Haryana, India, Sept. 30, 1948; came to U.S., 1972; s. Vishnu Kumar and Giriraj Kishori G.; B.Medicine and Surgery, Govt. Med. Coll., Patiala, Punjabi U., India, 1970; M.P.H., U. Ill., 1975; m. Renu, June 6, 1974; children—Sapna Arvind, Saya Arvind. Intern, Postgrad. Inst. Med. Edn. and Research, Chandigarh, India, 1970, resident in medicine, 1971, resident in surgery, 1971; resident in family practice Cook County Hosp., Chgo., 1972-75, chief resident, 1974-75, attending physician family practice residency program, 1975-76; clin. instr. family practice Abraham Lincoln Sch. Medicine and U. Ill., Chgo., 1976; family physician Comprehensive Med. Assos. and Cure Health Plan, Chgo., 1976; family practice, Arlington Heights and Rolling Meadows, Ill., 1976—; attending staff physician Northwest Community Hosp., Arlington Heights, 1977—, chmn. family practice, 1985—; attending staff Alexian Bros. Med. Center, Elk Grove Village, Ill., 1977—, Humana Hosp., Hoffman Estates, Ill., 1979-84; dir. family health ctr. Norwegian Am. Hosp., 1978-80. Served as capt. Indian Army, 1971-72. Diplomate Am. Bd. Family Practice, Am. Bd. Preventive Medicine. Fellow Am. Acad. Family Physicians, Am. Coll. Preventive Medicine; mem. AMA, Ill. Med. Soc., Chgo. Med. Soc., Am. Public Health Assn., Indian Med. Assn. Home: 550 E Alexandra Ct Itasca IL 60143 Office: 3407 Kirchoff Rd Rolling Meadows IL 60008

GOYAL, SATISH CHANDRA, engineering educator, consultant; b. Kasganj, Uttarpradesh, India, Sept. 10, 1921; came to U.S., 1979; s. Bankeylal and Ram Devi (Agrawal) Karriwale; m. Kunti Kumari, Jan. 16, 1941; children—Ashok Kumar, Sushma Rani, Arunkumar, Arvindkumar, Anand Kumar. B.Sc., Agra U., India, 1940; C.E., Thomason Coll. Civil Engring., Roorkee, U.P., India, 1943; M.S. in Civil Engring., U. Calif.-Berkeley, 1961. Engr. Pub. Works Dept. Govt., Agra, Gonda, Basti, U.P., India, 1943-47; lectr., reader Roorkee U., U.P., India, 1947-54; prof. structural engring. M.B.M. Engring. Coll., Jodhpur U., Rajasthan, India, 1954-63, 69-72, 77-79, dean engring., 1963-66, 1972-74; dean engring. Pant U., Pantnagar, U.P., India, 1966-69; vice-chancellor Jodhpur U., Rajasthan, 1974-77; prof. civil engring. Tri-State U., Angola, Ind., 1979—; cons. structural design work, U.S.A., India. Author: (with O.P. Tain) Manual of Estimating, 1954; (with S. Divakaran) Design of Structures in Structural Steel, 1961; (with B. C. Punmia) Theory of Structures and Strength of Materials, 1964; (with M. R. Sethia) Engineering Mechanics, 1977. Dir., chmn. Univ. Centre of Desert Studies, Jodhpur, 1976-77; dir. Rural Housing Wing, Govt. India, Jodhpur, 1977-79. Recipient citation Rajasthan Govt. India, 1962; exchange visitor to U.S.A., AID, 1960. Fellow ASCE, Instn. Engrs. India (chmn. Rajasthan Centre, Citation 1974), Indian Soc. Desert Tech. (pres. 1975-78); mem. ASME. Hindu. Lodge: Rotary. Avocations: yoga; reading; meditation. Home: 42451 Ravina Ct Northville MI 48167 also 1 Residency Rd Jodhpur 342001 India Office: Tri State U Dept Civil Engring Angola IN 46703

GRABINSKI, LAWRENCE AUGUST, electronics executive, designer; b. Chgo., Aug. 10, 1929; s. August Jerome and Pearl Josephine (Wanat) G.; m. Rita Ann Caddigan, Sept. 17, 1955 (div. Apr. 1973); children—Martin, Thomas. Student U. Md., 1950-52, Ill. Inst. Tech., 1952-54, Morraine Valley Coll., 1980. Quality control engr. Foote Bros., Chgo., 1952-55; designer W.L. Stennsgaard, Chgo., 1955-57; chief draftsman Klemp Corp., Chgo., 1957-65; structural designer Rippel Archt. Metals, Chgo., 1965-74; asst. div. mgr. Pullman Sheet Metal Co., Chgo., 1974-77; computer systems specialist Castle Engring. Co., Chgo., 1977—. Served with USAF, 1948-52, ETO. Mem. Am. Fedn. Musicians. Home: 7801 S Lotus Burbank IL 60459 Office: Castle Engring Co 3579 W Columbus Ave Chicago IL 60652

GRABLE, R(EGINALD) HAROLD, psychologist; b. Putnam County, Ind., Sept. 22, 1917; s. Reginald R. and Cecil Ruth (Jones) G.; A.B., U. Kans., 1938, tchr.'s diploma, 1940; M.A., U. Minn., 1949; m. Elizabeth Hannah Baird, Aug. 17, 1946; children—Celia, Nancy, Daniel. Group leader occupational coders Nat. Roster Sci. and Specialized Personnel, Washington, 1940-42; vocat. counselor U. Minn., Mpls., 1947; clin. psychologist trainee VA Hosp., St. Paul, 1947-49; chief clin. psychologist Willmar (Minn.) State Hosp., 1949-51, Winnebago (Wis.) State Hosp., 1951-61; clin. psychologist West Shore Mental Health Clinic (formerly Hackley Adult Mental Health Clinic), Muskegon, Mich., 1961-82; psychologist Kalamazoo Regional Psychiat. Hosp., 1983—; pvt. practice psychology, Willmar, Minn., 1949-51, Oshkosh, Wis., 1951-61, Spring Lake, Mich., 1961—; instr. extension div. U. Wis., 1956-61; mem. profl. adv. bd. Wis. Council Mentally Retarded Children, 1956-61. First aid instr. ARC, 1963-79; exec. bd. Grand Valley council (name now West Mich. Shores council) Boy Scouts Am., 1966-76, dist. chmn., 1968-70, commr., 1972—; various offices PTA, 1953-78; active Vols. in Probation; chmn. bd. Christian Ch. (Disciples of Christ), 1970-73. Served with AUS, 1942-46. Recipient Silver Beaver award Boy Scouts Am., 1981, Dist. Merit award, 1977; lic. psychologist, Mich. Mem. Am. Psychol. Assn., Mich. Assn. Children with Learning Disabilities. Contbr. articles to profl. jours. Home: 717 Summer St Spring Lake MI 49456

GRABOW, RAYMOND JOHN, mayor; b. Cleve., Jan. 27, 1932; s. Joseph Stanley and Frances (Kalata) G.; B.S. in Bus. Adminstrn., Kent State U., 1953; J.D., Western Res. U., 1958; m. Margaret Jean Knoll, Nov. 27, 1959; children—Rachel Jean, Ryan Joseph. Bar: Ohio 1958. Counsel, No. Ohio Petroleum Retailers Assn., Cleve., 1965—; counsel, trustee Alliance of Poles Fed. Credit Union, 1972, also gen. counsel Alliance of Poles of Am.; councilman City of Warrensville Heights (Ohio), 1962-68, mayor, 1969—; sec. Sam's Investment Inc. Cleve., 1965—, Atlas Sewer & Pipe Cleaning Corp., Cleve., 1962—, Wick Restaurant Inc., Cleve., 1962—, Ohio Awning Co., Space Comfort Co., Wagner Awning & Mfg. Co. Mem. exec. com. Democratic party Cuyahoga County, 1966—, precinct com., 1966-80; trustee Brentwood Hosp.; bd. dirs. Polonia Found. Recipient award Polonia Found., 1970, other groups. Mem. Ohio State, Cuyahoga County, Greater Cleve. bar assns., Nat. Advs. Soc., Am. Judicature Soc., Assn. Trial Lawyers Am., Ohio Trial Lawyers Assn., Am. Legion, PLAV Vets., Cath. War Vets., Cleve. Soc., Warrensville Heights C. of C. (trustee), Nat. League Cities, Ohio Assn. Pub. Safety Dirs., Mcpl. Treas. Assn., Ohio Service Dirs. Assn., Cuyahoga County Safety Dirs. Assn., Ohio Mayors Assn., Ohio Mcpl. League, numerous ethnic orgns. Lodge: Order of Alhambra. Home: 20114 Gladstone Rd Warrensville Heights OH 44122 Office: Suite 815 Superior Bldg Cleveland OH 44114

GRABOWSKI, TRENNA RAE, accountant; b. Centralia, Ill., Aug. 4, 1945; d. Ralph Moren and Imogene (Schafer) Wallace; m. Ronald Joseph Grabowski, Dec. 2, 1967; children—Paul Joseph, Elizabeth Martha. B.A., So. Ill. U., 1970; student Ind. U., 1968, 69, 73, U. Ill.-Urbana, 1981-82. C.P.A., Ill. Bus. mgr., controller Marshall Browning Hosp., DuQuoin, Ill., 1968-73; accountant, auditor Laventhol & Horwath, C.P.A.s, Carbondale, Ill., 1973-75; dir. fiscal services Washington County Hosp., Nashville, Ill., 1977-81; chief fiscal officer Grabowski Farms, 1975—; cons. agrl. fin., fin. mgmt., commodity mktg.; condr. seminars. Mem. Ill. State Extension adv. com. U. Ill.; trade and mktg. chmn. Ill. Women for Agr.; del. Agrl. Council Am. Mem. Am. Inst. C.P.A.s, Ill. C.P.A. Soc., Am. Agri-Women, Ill. Women for Agr., Bus. and Profl. Women, Hosp. Fin. Mgmt. Assn., Agrl. Council Am., Ill. Farm Bur., Beta Sigma Phi. Roman Catholic. Weekly columnist Ag Business/Your Business, Ill. Agri-News and Ind. Agri-News, others. Address: RR #1 DuBois IL 62831

GRADISON, WILLIS DAVID, JR., congressman; b. Cin., Dec. 28, 1928; s. Willis David and Dorothy (Benas) G.; A.B., Yale U., 1948; M.B.A., Harvard U., 1951, D.C.S., 1954; m. Helen Ann Martin, June 25, 1950 (div. 1975); children—Ellen, Anne, Margaret, Robin, Beth Maile Jo, Benjamin David; m.

2d, Heather Jane Stirton, Nov. 29, 1980. With W.D. Gradison & Co., Cin., 1949, gen. partner, 1958—; asst. to under sec. Treasury, Washington, 1953-55; asst. to sec. HEW, Washington, 1955-57; mem. 94th-99th congresses, Ohio, 2d dist.; mem. Cin. City Council, 1961-74, mayor, 1971. Republican. Home: 2027 Calvin Cliff Ln Cincinnati OH 45206 Office: 2311 Rayburn House Office Bldg Washington DC 20515*

GRADY, JOHN F., See *Who's Who in America,* 43rd edition.

GRAEBE, ANNETTE MULVANY, college administrator, educator; b. Benton, Ill., Feb. 11, 1943; d. Augusta (Magnabosco) Mulvany; m. William Fredrick Graebe, Jr., Feb. 23, 1974. B.S., So. Ill. U.-Carbondale, 1962, M.A., 1964. Research asst., speech instr. So. Ill. U.-Carbondale, 1962-64; chmn. speech and theater dept. McKendree Coll., Lebanon, Ill., 1964-68; dir. info. center, So. Ill. U., Edwardsville, 1968—, assoc. prof. speech communication, 1968—, mem. faculty bd. govs. Coordinator Edwardsville Autumn Festival Children. Recipient Ill. and U.S. Bicentennial Commn. citation, 1976, Council Advancement and Support of Edn. exceptional achievement community relations award, Washington, 1976, 77, 81, Toronto, Can., 1982; named Outstanding Faculty Adviser, Pub. Relations Soc. Am., 1982; Outstanding Faculty-Midwest, Pub. Relations Student Soc. Am., 1982; Woman of Year, Bus. and Profl. Women's Club, Edwardsville, 1983. Mem. Pub. Relations Soc. Am. (edn. chmn., chpt. adviser), Univ. Ambassadors (hon.), Pi Kappa Delta, Kappa Delta Pi, Zeta Phi Eta, Alpha Phi Omega. Contbr. articles to profl. jours. Office: Campus Box 15a So Ill U Edwardsville IL 62026

GRAEF, LUTHER WILLIAM, consulting civil engineer; b. Milw., Aug. 14, 1931; s. John and Pearl (Luther) G.; B.C.E., Marquette U., 1952; M.C.E., U. Wis., 1961; m. Lorraine Linnerud, Sept. 18, 1954; children—Ronald, Sharon, Gerald. Engr., C.W. Yoder & Assos., cons. engrs., Milw., 1956-61; partner Graef-Anhalt-Schloemer, cons. engrs., Milw., 1961—; chmn. bd. Graef Anhalt Schloemer Assos., Inc., Milw., 1967—; chmn. engr. adv. com. U. Wis., Milw., also U. Wis. extensions. Active Boy Scouts Am. Chmn. bd. assessment, City of Milw., 1962—. Served to 1st lt. AUS, 1953-56. Named Disting Marquette U. alumnus, 1982, Wis. Profl. Engr. of Yr., 1983. Mem. ASCE (sect. pres. 1968), Nat., Wis. socs. profl. engrs., Cons. Engrs. Council Wis. (pres. 1973-75), Engrs. Scientists Milw. (pres. 1975), Am. Legion, Marquette U. Alumni Assn., Tau Beta Pi, Pi Mu Epsilon, Chi Epsilon. Lutheran (pres. ch. council 1969). Home: 3788 S Massachusetts St Milwaukee WI 53220 Office: 6415 W Capitol Dr Milwaukee WI 53216

GRAF, MICHAEL, physician, publisher; b. Yugoslavia, Aug. 23, 1924; came to U.S., 1953; s. Leonid Ivan and Barbara D. (Brylkin) G.; m. Philomena Steigenberger, Aug. 28, 1953; children—Michael, Jr., Elisabeth, Mark, Tamara. M.D., Ludwig Maximillians Universitat, Munich, W.Ger., 1951, Ph.D., 1953. Intern, St. Mary's Hosp., Long Beach, Calif., 1953-54; resident in internal medicine Wayne (Mich.) County Gen. Hosp., 1956-59; pvt. practice specializing in internal medicine, Kalamazoo, 1960—; mem. staff Borgess Hosp., chief dept. medicine, 1973-74; pub., pres. Am. Acad. for Sci. Acupunture and Auricular Medicine. Fellow Am. Coll. of Chest Physicians; mem. AMA, Mich. Med. Soc., Kalamazoo Acad. of Medicine, Mich. Soc. Internal Medicine (regional trustee 1970-76). Republican. Russian Orthodox. Clubs: Crystal Lake Yacht, Crystal Downs Country (Frankfort, Mich.); Club: Shriners. Home: 3904 Bronson Blvd Kalamazoo MI 49008 Office: 1634 Gull Rd Kalamazoo MI 49001

GRAF, STEVEN ALLEN, chief of police; b. Toledo, Ohio, July 31, 1951; s. Richard A. and M. Lucille (Weaver) G.; m. Karen S. Beck, June 28, 1975; children—Linda K., Julie A. Student in Acctg., Bowling Green State U., 1969-72. Cert. peace officer, Ohio, Police officer Waterville Police Dept., Ohio, 1973-74, Grand Rapids Police Dept., Ohio, 1971-73, 74-76, Archbold Police Dept., Ohio, 1976; chief of police Weston Police Dept., Ohio, 1976—; sec.-treas. Weston Improvement Corp., 1984. Scoutmaster Toledo Area council Boy Scouts Am., Ohio, 1972-76, unit commr., Weston, 1981-84; asst. coordinator Wood County Arson Task Force, Bowling Green, 1984. Recipient Commendation award Am. Fedn. Police, 1976, Commendation, FBI, 1978, Commendation, Bowling Green Police, 1983. Mem. Internat. Assn. Chiefs of Police, Ohio Assn. Chiefs of Police (audit com. 1983, 84). Lutheran.

GRAFE, WARREN BLAIR, television executive; b. N.Y.C., June 22, 1954; s. Warren Edward and Maree Lee (Ahn) G.; m. Pamela Arden Rearick, Mar. 8, 1980 (div. 1982). Student Kendall Coll., 1974-75, U. Wis.-Platteville, 1975-76; B.A., Ind. U., 1979. Part-time announcer sta. WTTS-WGTC, Bloomington, Ind., 1978-79, sales rep., sta. WGTC-FM, 1979-80, account exec., coop. coordinator, 1980-84; nat. sales rep. Sta. WTTS-WGTC, 1984; account exec. Sta. KLFF-KMZK, Phoenix, 1985, Rita Sanders Advt. and Pub. Relations Agy., Inc., 1985—, Times Mirror Cable TV, Dimension Media Services, Am. Cable TV, 1985—. Home: 2146 W Isabella Ave #241 Mesa AZ 85202 Office: Times Mirror Cable TV of Ariz Dimension Media Services PO Box 37827 17602 N Black Canyon Hwy Suite 111 Phoenix AZ 85069

GRAFF, ARTHUR STEVEN, educational consultant; b. Highland, Ill., June 15, 1946; s. William Arthur and Roberta Pauline (Partridge) G.; m. Janet Marie Hall, Dec. 27, 1975; children—Geoffrey Hall, Hannah Marie. B.A., Coll. Wooster, 1968; M.A., Case Western Res. U., 1972; Ed.D., Columbia U., 1981. Asst. dir. admissions Coll. Wooster, Ohio, 1971-73, assoc. dir. admissions, 1973-79, instr. freshman studies, 1974-81, dir. Westminster House, 1977-79, dir. admissions planning and research, 1979-81; dir. admissions and guidance services Coll. Bd., Evanston, Ill., 1981—. Served with U.S. Army, 1968-70. Mem. Am. Assn. Counseling and Devel., Am. Coll. Personnel Assn., Nat. Assn. Coll. Admissions Counselors, Am. Assn. Coll. Registrars and Admissions Officers. Presbyterian. Avocations: singing; camping; tennis.

GRAFF, JOHN FREDERIC, insurance executive; b. Highland Park, Ill., Dec. 1, 1933; s. Karl Von and Bernice Mildred (Mattes) G.; B.A. in Econs., DePauw U., 1955; children—Barbara Lynn, Karen Sue; m. Mary Lynn Bjerke, Sept. 5, 1981; stepchildren—Charlene, Ericka. Agt., Provident Mut. Life Ins. Co., Chgo., 1958-61; mem. mgmt. devel. program, Phila., 1961-62, agy. mgr., Chgo., 1962-73; owner, propr. John F. Graff & Assocs., Chgo., 1973—; pres. United Corp. of Am., Inc., 1973—, Ill. Bus. Corp., 1976—. Past officer New Trier Republican Orgn.; past chmn. Village Party, Wilmette, Ill.; charter mem., pres. Greater Chgo. Ins. Council of City of Hope, 1980-84. Served to lt. (j.g.) USN, 1955-58. Named Ins. Man of Yr., City of Hope, 1978; C.L.U.; registered health underwriter Nat. Assn. Health Underwriters. Mem. Nat. Assn. Life Underwriters, Chgo. Estate Planning Council, Chgo. Assn. Life Underwriters (pres. 1975-76, Disting. Service award 1979), Chgo. Chpt. C.L.U.s (pres. 1976-77, Huebner Scholar-Disting. Service award 1979), Ill. Life Underwriters Assn. (pres. 1977-78), Chgo. Assn. Health Underwriters (dir. 1975—, Edward H. O'Connor Disting. Service award 1977), Chgo. Gen. Agts. and Mgrs. Assn. Republican. Methodist. Clubs: Univ. (Chgo.); Westmoreland Country. Contbr. articles to trade mags. Office: United Corp Am 223 W Jackson Blvd Suite 1108 Chicago IL 60606 Home: 843 Hibbard Rd Wilmette IL 60091

GRAFF, WILLIAM ARTHUR, glass technologist; b. Highland, Ill., Dec. 25, 1923; s. Arthur Oscar and Stella Emily (Koch) G.; m. Roberta Pauline Partrige, Apr. 7, 1945; children—Arthur, Steven, Trudy Ann. B.S., U. Ill., 1946, M.S., 1947, Ph.D., 1949. Research glass technologist, lamp glass dept. Gen. Electric Co., Cleve., 1949-57, research supr., Richmond Heights, Ohio, 1957-66, mgr. glass research, 1966-74, mgr. materials lab., 1974-80, mgr. engring. adminstrn., glass and metall. products dept., 1980—. Patentee in field. Mem. Am. Ceramic Soc., Am. Chem. Soc., Soc. Glass Tech., Deutsche Glastechnische Gesellschift, Sigma Xi. Presbyterian. Office: Gen Electric Co 24400 Highland Rd Richmond Heights OH 44143

GRAGG, DONALD EDWARD, county official; b. Wichita, Kans., Oct. 5, 1939; s. Farris G. and Velma Iclone (Fuson) G.; m. Rebecca Ann, Jan. 11, 1964; children—Gretchen, Donald Edward II. Student, Wichita State U., 1957-61. Account exec. Wheeler Kelly Hagny Investment Co., Wichita, Kans., 1961-79; county commr. First Dist. Sedgwick County, Wichita, 1979—, chmn. bd., 1981—. Chmn. Tri County Planning Com., 1981-82; bd. dirs. S.E. Kans. Econ. Devel. Commn., 1980—. Mem. Nat. Assn. Counties (vice chair energy policy), Am. Soc. Pub. Adminstrn., Wichita State U. Alumni Assn., Phi Delta Theta. Republican. Mem. Christian Ch. Clubs: Crestview Country, Petroleum, Mason. Home: 926 Lawrence Lane Wichita KS 67206 Office: Sedgwick County Court House 525 N Main St Suite 320 Wichita KS 67203

GRAHAM, A. RICHARD, engineering educator; b. Wichita, Kans., Aug. 5, 1934; s. Thomas James and Margaret Florence (Lyon) G.; m. L. Carol McWhorter, Dec. 28, 1962; children—Cara L., Evan T. B.S., Kans. State U., 1957, M.S., 1960; Ph.D., U. Iowa, 1966. Instr. mech. engring. U. Mo.-Rolla, 1960-63, U. Iowa, Iowa City, 1963-64; asst. prof. Wichita State U., Kans., 1965-68, assoc. prof., 1968-78, prof., chmn. dept. mech. engring., 1978-84, prof. mech. engring., assoc. dir. Ctr. for Productivity Enhancement, 1984—; dir. Foster Automated Systems Tech., Wichita. Author: An Introduction to Engineering Measurements, 1975. Contbr. articles to profl. jours. Mem. Energy Conservation Task Force, Wichita, 1975-79; mem. Energy Advising Bd., Wichita, 1980-83, chmn., 1982. NSF faculty fellow, 1964-65. Mem. ASME, Am. Soc. for Engring Edn. (chmn. div. experimentation and lab. oriented studies 1979-80, chmn. instrument div. 1982-83. chmn. midwest sect. 1984-85), Soc. Mfg. Engrs., Phi Kappa Phi, Pi Tau Sigma, Tau Beta Pi. Presbyterian. Avocations: gardening; wood working; model railroading. Home: 5722 E 10th St Wichita KS 67208 Office: Center for Productivity Enhancement Wichita State U Wichita KS 67208

GRAHAM, DAVID BOLDEN, food products executive; b. Miami Beach, Fla., Feb. 10, 1927; s. Robert Cabel and Bertha Eugenia (Hack) G.; m. Stuart Hill Smith, Sept. 1, 1956; children—Bird, Ellen, Darnall, Lamar, Lyle, Gerard, Barbara, David Bolden. Student Colegio de Bartolome, Bogota, Colombia, 1946; B.S., Georgetown U., 1949; postgrad. Harvard Bus. Sch., 1950. Pres. Graham Farms, Inc., Washington, Ind., 1950—, Graham Cheese Corp., Washington, 1950—; sec. Bal Harbour Square (Fla.), 1956-57, Graham Bros., Inc., Washington, 1950-72; chmn. Peoples Nat. Bank, Washington. Pres. Washington Planning Commn. Served to lt. col. USAF Res., 1949-77. Republican. Roman Catholic. Clubs: Columbia (Indpls.); Rotary (past pres.). Lodge: Elks. Contbr. articles on agr., transp., early fur traders to various publs. Home and Office: Graham Farms PO Box 391 Washington IN 47501

GRAHAM, DENNIS ALLEN, agricultural electronics company executive; b. Springfield, Ill., Aug. 24, 1950; s. John William and Marie Lavina (Neal) Graham Smallwood; m. Jill Johnetta Smith, July 14, 1969 (div. Jan. 1976); 1 son, Christopher William; m. Karen Sue Snyder, Nov. 22, 1978; stepchildren—Jill Lynn Whitler, Andrea Lynn Whitler. Student U. Ill., Urbana, 1968-69, Springfield Coll., Ill., 1969-70; B.A. in Math., Ill. Coll., 1973; M.A.B.A., Sangomon State U., 1981. Test technician DICKEY-john Corp., Auburn, Ill., 1969-70, test engr., 1970-72, product engr., 1972-79, OEM account rep., 1979—. Chmn. fin. com. Ch. of the Brethen, Virden, Ill., 1985, mem. 1983, 84; mgr. Pony League Baseball, Virden, 1982-83. Republican. Avocations: Golf; racquetball; smowmobiling; hunting. Home: 560 E Holden St Virden IL 62690 Office: DICKEY-john Corp Box 10 Auburn IL 62615

GRAHAM, JACK W., psychologist, educator; b. Kokomo, Ind., May 11, 1925; s. Ralph Waldo and Christine (Vickery) G.; m. Sofie B. Larson, June 16, 1953; children—Mark, Karen. A.B., DePauw U., 1946; M.A., U. Wis., 1949; Ph.D., Purdue U., 1951. Asst. in math. U. Wis., 1946-47; instr. in math. DePauw U., 1947-49; research asst. Purdue U., 1950-51; asst. prof. guidance So. Ill. U., Carbondale, 1951-54, assoc. prof. guidance and psychology, 1954-63; prof. guidance and ednl. psychology, 1963—, prof. higher edn., 1967—, dir. Counseling and Testing Ctr., 1951-64, dean students, 1964-67, assoc. dean Grad. Sch., 1974-79, chmn. dept. higher edn., 1983-85. Recipient Outstanding Service to Students award So. Ill. U., 1981. Mem. Ill. Coll. Personnel Assn. (pres. 1968-69), Am. Coll. Personnel Assn., Am. Personnel and Guidance Assn (mem. senate 1963-64), Phi Kappa Phi (pres. Carbondale chpt. 1978-79). Methodist. Club: Rotary. Contbr. articles to profl. jours. Home: 25 Hillcrest Dr Carbondale IL 62901 Office: Dept Ednl Adminstrn and Higher Edn So Ill U Carbondale IL 62901

GRAHAM, JAMES ARTHUR, manufacturing executive; b. McComas, W.Va., 1925. B.S. in Mech. Engring., W.Va. U., 1949. Corp. mgr. prodn. SKF Industries Inc., 1949-60; gen. mgr. bearings Bearing Co. Am. div. Fed. Mogul Bower Bearings, 1960-65; v.p. and group gen. mgr., v.p. and dir. mktg. and tech. devel. Standard Pressed Steel Co., 1965-71; pres. gen. indsl. group and automotive group Gulf & Western Industries Inc., 1972-80; corp. exec. v.p. and pres. auto and truck group Sheller-Globe Corp., Toledo, 1980-81, corp. exec., v.p. ops., 1981-82, pres., chief operating officer, 1982—. Served to lt. USAF, 1943-46. Office: Sheller-Globe Corp 1505 Jefferson Ave Toledo OH 43697

GRAHAM, RICHARD BRIAN HILL, investment banker, financial services executive, consultant; b. N.Y.C., June 29, 1956; s. Philip L. and Louise (Hill) G. B.A. magna cum laude with departmental honors, U. Pa., 1978; M.B.A., U. Chgo., 1981. Accounts analyst Elkins, Stroud Suplee & Co., Phila., 1978-79; assoc. corp. fin. Warburg Paribas Becker, N.Y.C., 1981; assoc. corp. fin. dept. Continental Ill. Nat. Bank and Trust Co. of Chgo., 1981—; v.p. Diversified Fin. Services Corp., Chgo., 1983—; fin. planner and cons. various profl. and service corps. Club: University. Office: 664 N Michigan Ave Chicago IL 60611

GRAHAM, ROBERT BRUCE, insurance company executive, fire chief; b. Evanston, Ill., Aug. 2, 1944; s. Robert L. and Marie A. (Rose) G.; m. Consuelo B. Brandon, Sept. 4, 1976; children—Robert Bruce, II, Ross B. B.S., No. Ill. U., 1966. Exec. v.p. Braniff Internat. Airlines, Dallas, 1966-71; pres. Graham Ins. Co., Skokie, Ill., 1971—; pres. Mut. Aid Box Alarm System, Waukegan, Ill., 1981—; mem. Gov.'s Task Force on Hazardous Materials. Bd. dirs. Lake County Heart Assn., Libertyville, Ill., 1983—; pres. Ill. St. Andrew Soc., North Riverside, Ill., 1984. Mem. Chartered Property Casuality Underwriter, Lake County Fire Chiefs (v.p.), Ill. Fire Chiefs, Internat. Fire Chiefs. Roman Catholic. Office: Graham Ins Agy Inc PO Box 3110 Skokie IL 60076

GRAHAM, ROBERT GRANT, business executive; b. Ottawa, Ont., Can., Apr. 8, 1931; s. Wilmer A. and Lylian (Wiltsie) G.; B.Comm., McGill U., 1952; m. Diane K. Wilson, May 28, 1953; children—Susan Diane, Bruce Wilson. Pres., chief exec. officer, dir. Inter-City Gas Corp., Winnipeg, Man., Can., MICC Investments Ltd., Toronto, Ont.; pres. Mortgage Ins. Co. Can.; chmn. bd. Winnipeg Jets Hockey Club, Roam Communications, KeepRite Inc. dir. mem. exec. com. Guaranty Trust Co. Can., Traders Group Ltd., Great-West Life Assurance Co., Can. Gen. Ins. Co.; dir. Fed. Industries Ltd., Moffat Communications Ltd., ICG Scotia Gas Ltd. Bd. dirs. Winnipeg Found. Mem. Conf. Bd. Can. (sr. mem., dir.). Office: 444 St Mary Ave Winnipeg MB R3C 3T7 Canada also Suite 16 1 Dundas St W PO Box 12 Toronto ON M5G 1Z3 Canada

GRAHAM, STEVE, zoo director; b. Waynesboro, Pa., Feb. 25, 1945; s. Donald Albert and Virginia Louise (Steck) G.; m. Karen Krabbenhoft, Dec. 27, 1984. B.S., Mt. St. Mary's Coll., 1971. Dir. Salisbury (Md.) Zoo, 1972-77; assoc. dir. Balt. Zoo, 1977-78, dir., 1978-82; dir. zool. parks City of Detroit, 1982—; adj. specialist Mich. State U. Mus.; adj. asst. prof. Wayne State U. Fellow Am. Assn. Zool. Parks and Aquariums. Author: (with Roger Caras) Amiable Little Beasts, 1980.

GRAHAM, WILLIAM B., pharmaceutical company executive; b. Chgo., July 14, 1911; s. William and Elizabeth (Burden) G.; S.B., cum laude, U. Chgo., 1932, J.D. cum laude, 1936; LL.D. (hon.), Carthage Coll., 1974, Lake Forest Coll., 1983; L.H.D., (hon.), Nat. Coll. Edn., 1983, St. Xavier Coll., 1983; m. Edna Kanaley, June 15, 1940 (dec.); children—Elizabeth Anne, Margaret (Mrs. Benson T. Caswell), Robert B., William J.; m. Catherine Gaubin, July 23, 1984. Admitted to Ill. bar, 1936; patent lawyer Dyrenforth, Lee, Chritton & Wiles, 1936-40; mem. Dawson & Ooms, 1940-45; v.p., mgr. Baxter Travenol Labs., Inc., Deerfield, Ill., 1945-53, pres., chief exec. officer, 1953-71, chmn. bd., chief exec. officer, 1971-80, chmn., 1980—, also dir.; dir., mem. exec. com. 1st Nat. Bank, Chgo.; dir., chmn. audit com. Northwest Industries; dir., chmn. compensation com. Deere & Co. Bd. dirs. Bot. Garden, Nat. Park Found.; bd. dirs., pres. Lyric Opera Chgo.; trustee Orchestral Assn., U. Chgo., Evanston Hosp.; mem. Nat. Council U.S. China Trade. Recipient Disting. Citizen award Ill. St. Andrew Soc., 1974; Decision Maker of Yr. award, 1974; Marketer of Yr. award Am. Mgmt. Assn., 1976; Chicagoan of Yr. award Chgo. Boys Club, 1981; award Nat. Kidney Found., 1981, recognition for pioneering health care products Health Industry Mfrs. Assn., 1981; named Weizmann Inst. professorial chair, 1978. Mem. Am. Pharm. Mfrs. Assn. (past pres., award for spl. distinction and leadership 1981), Ill. Mfrs. Assn. (dir., past pres.), Pharm. Mfrs. Assn. (dir., past chmn.), Phi Beta Kappa, Sigma Xi, Phi Delta Phi. Clubs: Chicago (past pres.), Commonwealth, Mid-America, Commercial, Indian Hill, Casino, Old Elm (Chgo.); University, Links (N.Y.C.). Home: 40 Devonshire Ln Kenilworth IL 60043 Office: One Baxter Pkwy Deerfield IL 60015

GRAHAM, WILLIAM QUENTIN, computer lessor; b. Ann Arbor, Mich., Jan. 17, 1944; s. William and Marie (MacGregor) G.; B.B.A., Eastern Mich. U., Ypsilanti, 1969; m. Susan H. Scheinker, Sept. 10, 1967; children—David Aaron, Robert Lewis, Alexandra Marie. Research asst. TRW, Los Angeles, 1965; field engr. IBM, Ann Arbor, 1966-69, salesman, Detroit, 1969-73; salesman Cambridge Memories, Inc., 1973-76; large computer specialist CMI Corp., Troy, Mich., 1976-81; lessor Meridian Leasing, Birmingham, Mich., 1981-84, Graham Wirt & Assocs., 1984—; data processing cons. and advisor. Mem. Zionist Orgn. Am. Mem. Detroit Soviet Jewry Com., Jewish Welfare Fedn. Clubs: Motor City Striders, Motor City Packards, B'nai B'rith. Home: 5709 Stonington Ct West Bloomington MI 48033 Office: 7001 Orchard Lake Rd West Bloomfield MI 48033

GRALL, RICHARD LAWRENCE, fire prevention officer; b. Antigo, Wis., Oct. 7, 1929; s. Frank James and Mary Anna (Wachal) G.; m. Clara L. Frankovich, Aug. 6, 1960; children—Linda, Loreen, Lawrence. Student pub. schs., Antigo, Wis. Firefighter, Rockford, Ill., 1958-68, driver engr., 1968-74, insp., investigator, 1974—, also fire prevention officer. Service with USN, 1950-54. Mem. Am. Soc. Safety Engrs., Ill. Fire Insps. Assn., Ill. Fireman's Assn., Ill. Assn. Fire Fighters. Home: 2015 Latham St Rockford IL 61103 Office: 204 S 1st St Rockford IL 61104

GRAMCZAK, MARY EULODIA, nun, college administrator; b. Chgo., July 21, 1928; d. Andrew and Catherine (Kucharczyk) G. Ph.B., DePaul U., 1957, M.Ed., 1963. Joined Congregation of Sisters of St. Felix, Roman Catholic Ch., 1947. Tchr. St. John of God Elem. Sch., Chgo., 1949-50, St. Helen Elem. Sch., 1950-56, St. Joseph High Sch., Chgo., 1957-62; tchr., counselor Good Counsel High Sch., Chgo., 1962-71; guidance dir. Providence High Sch., New Lenox, Ill., 1971-75; dean students, dir. fin. aid Felician Coll., Chgo., 1975—. Mem. Nat. Vocat. Guidance Assn., Am. Assn. Counseling and Devel., Am. Sch. Counselor Assn., Am. Coll. Personnel Assn., Ill. Guidance and Personnel Assn., Ill. Sch. Counselor Assn., Ill. Coll. Personnel Assn. Avocations: reading; puzzle solving. Home: 3800 W Peterson Ave Chicago IL 60659

GRAMDORF, MARILYN CAROL, nurse, accessory specialist; b. Watertown, Wis., Jan. 12, 1948; d. Harry Herman Joseph and Ruth Gertrude (Roth) G. Diploma in nursing Bellin Sch. Nursing, Green Bay, Wis., 1969; B.S., U. Wis.-Madison, 1981. Lic. nurse, Wis. Head nurse Bethesda Lutheran Home, Watertown, 1969-73, Lake Shore Manor, Madison, 1973-76; R.N. II, U. Wis. Hosp. and Clinic, Madison, 1976—; accessory specialist Home Interiors and Gifts, Madison, 1981—; sales person Tandy Leather Co., Madison, 1984—; union rep. United Profls. for Quality Health Care, Madison, 1980-82, lobbyist, 1980—; chart auditor Clin. Sci. Ctr., Madison, 1985—; speaker, com. mem. Spl. Concerns of Elderly, Pre-Operative Teaching Conf., 1985. Author: (with others) teaching booklet If You're Having Surgery, 1984. Recipient Five Yr. Service award Ctr. Clin. Sci., U. Hosp., Madison, 1981. Mem. Home Interiors and Gifts Assn., Wis. Alumni Assn. Mem. Evangelical Free Ch. Avocations: leather crafter; reading; writing; gardening; music. Home: 409 W Broadway Monona WI 53716 Office: Clin Sci Ctr D4-6 600 Highland Madison WI 53704

GRAMPP, GUSTAVO EDUARDO, agricultural equipment company executive; b. Cali, Colombia, Jan. 16, 1939; came to U.S., 1965, naturalized, 1971; s. Gustavo and Blanca (Lalinde) G.; m. Joan U. Loeb, Apr. 28, 1962; children—Gustavo E., Adriana R. B.S., Iowa State U., 1961; M.B.A., U. Iowa, 1970. Credit mgr. Agrocol s.a., Cali, 1962-66; internat. order clk. Deere & Co., Moline, Ill., 1966-72; internat. mktg. mgr. OPICO, Mobile, Ala., 1972-75; internat. sales mgr. Allis Chalmers, West Allis, Wis., 1975—; dir. Agrocol S.A., 1962-65, INCOLDA, 1964-65, Defensa Civil, 1964-65, Cali, Colombia. Defense chief Opus Dei, Cali, 1964. Republican. Roman Catholic. Clubs: Daniel Boone Conservation League (Hubertus, Wis.); Fletcher's gun (Waukesha, Wis.). Avocations: sailing; photography; hunting; target shooting. Office: Allis Chalmers Corp PO Box 512 Milwaukee WI 53201

GRAN, VIOLA MARGARET, real estate broker; b. LaCrosse, Wis.; d. Bernard George and Margaret Caroline (Cain) Kramer; student Wis. Sch. Real Estate, 1967; grad. Realtors Inst., Mpls., 1974; student U. Wis. Bus. and Mgmt. Extension, 1966, 73; m. James K. Gran, Sept. 16, 1937 (dec. Aug. 1977); 1 son, James B.; 1 stepson, Richard Oscar. Real estate broker, La Crosse, 1967—; owner, mgr. V. M. Gran Realty, La Crosse, 1967—, La Crescent, Minn., 1969—; owner, mgr. VMG Rentals and Advt., La Crosse, 1965—; instr. Wis. Sch. Real Estate, Milw., 1968—. Mem. Nat. Assn. Realtors, Wis., Minn. (state legis. com.), realtors assns., Greater LaCrosse, Southeastern Minn. bds. realtors, Realtors Nat. Mktg. Inst., LaCrosse, LaCrescent chambers commerce, Mississippi Valley Exchange (pres.), VFW Ladies Aux., Women of Moose (publicity chmn. La Crosse 1978-80). Methodist. Office: 1009 East Ave S LaCrosse WI 54601 also PO Box 135 LaCrescentia MN 55947

GRANBERG, KURT MICHAEL, lawyer; b. Breese, Ill., June 16, 1953; s. Marnen George and Agnes Mary (Vahlkamp) G. B.S., U. Ill.-Chgo., 1975; postgrad. Sangamon State U., 1975-76; J.D., Ill. Inst. Tech., 1980. Bar: Ill. 1980, U.S. Dist. Ct. (so. dist.) Ill. 1983. Legis. intern. Ill. Ho. of Reps., Springfield, 1975-76, mem. staff, 1975-77; assoc. James Donnewald Law Office, Breese, 1980-83; asst. pub. defender Clinton County, Ill., 1981-83; ptnr. Donnewald & Granberg, Breese, 1983—; spl. asst. atty. gen. State of Ill., Breese, 1983—; registered lobbyist, Breese, 1984—. Mem. fin. com. Ill. Inst. Tech.-Chgo. Kent. Sch. Law, 1979-80; Democratic precinct committeeman, Carlyle, Ill., 1982-84; mem. Clinton County Bd., Carlyle, 1984—, Carlyle Lake Adv. Com.; bd. dirs. Central Comprehensive Mental Health Ctr., Centralia, Ill., 1984—. Mem. Ill. Bar Assn., ABA, Clinton County Bar Assn., Jaycees, Carlyle Bus. and Profl. Assn., Sons of Am. Legion. Roman Catholic. Lodges: Lions, K.C., Optimists. Home: 1570 Clinton Carlyle IL 62231 Office: Donnewald & Granberg 550 N 2d St Box 57 Breese IL 62230

GRANDLE, RALPH WESLEY, manufacturing company executive; b. Chgo., May 28, 1936; s. William Raymond and Jessie Victoria (Anderson) G.; m. June Marlene King, Sept. 24, 1960; children—Patricia, Susan. B.S. in Indsl. Engring., Bradley U., 1958. Exec. v.p. Tricon Industries, Inc., Downers Grove, Ill., 1963—; mem. Ill. Gov.'s Conf. on Small Bus., Springfield, Ill., 1984. Bd. dirs. Indian Boundry YMCA, Downers Grove, 1969-84; pres. bd. dirs. Bradley U. Parents, Peoria, Ill., 1984—; bd. dirs., assoc. trustee Bradley U., 1974-84. Recipient Service to Youth award Indian Boundry YMCA, 1974. Mem. Inst. Indsl. Engring., Am. Soc. Quality Control, Downers Grove C. of C. (chmn. 1983-84). Republican. Baptist. Club: Oakbrook Executive Breakfast (Ill.). Avocations: water and snow skiing, basketball, softball, flying, boating. Home: 906 Central Ave Downers Grove IL 60516

GRANGER, WILLIAM WOODARD, JR., food company executive; b. Norfolk, Va., Mar. 10, 1919; s. William Woodard and Grace (Williams) G.; student Coll. William and Mary, 1938-40; m. Norma White, Sept. 7, 1946; children—Shirley W., Gail P., William Woodard III. With Norfolk Shipbldg. & Dry Dock Corp., 1940; with Beatrice Foods Co. (now Beatrice Cos., Inc.) and subs., 1946—, mgr. Meadow Gold Dairies, Inc., Pitts., 1963-66, regional v.p. Eastern region, 1966-76, pres. Internat. Foods div., Chgo., from 1976, sr. v.p., 1977, exec. v.p., 1977-83, vice chmn., 1983—, also dir. Served with AUS, 1942-45. Office: Beatrice Cos Inc 2 N La Salle St Chicago IL 60602

GRANLUND, WILLIAM HENRY, educational administrator; b. Chgo., Feb. 2, 1928; s. John Joseph and Marie Yvonne (Garratt) Byrns; m. Frances Jeanne Balbierz, June 10, 1950; children—David Michael, James Garratt. B.S., No. Mich. U., 1952; M.A., Central Mich. U., 1965. Instr. history Gaylord (Mich.) Schs., 1952-65, asst. prin. Gaylord High Sch., 1966-67, prin., 1967—. Chmn., Otsego County UN Com., 1960; mem. planning com. Otsego County Centennial, 1975. Served with AUS, 1946-48. Mem. Nat. Assn. Secondary Sch. Prins., Mich. Assn. Secondary Sch. Prins., Center II Prins., Otsego County Hist. Soc. (pres. 1967-69). Roman Catholic. Club: Optimist (v.p. 1983—). Avocations: Historical research, book collecting, rock collecting. Office: Gaylord High Sch 240 E 4th St Gaylord MI 49735

GRANNEMAN, GARY NORMAN, high technology executive, consultant; b. Clinton, Iowa, Oct. 9, 1944; s. Melvin A. and Mary Elizabeth (Rowe) G.; m. Marilyn J. Moore, Nov. 28, 1968; 1 son, Christopher N. Student Ind. U., 1962-66. Pres. Granneman Automotive Co., Indpls., 1973—, Granneman & Assocs., Inc., Indpls., 1973—; chmn. Granneman Internat., Indpls. and London, 1981—; v.p., sec.-treas. Am. Coating Labs., Inc., Indpls., 1983—; mktg. cons. internat. high tech. Chmn. Democrats For Lugar, Indpls., 1976; founder Ted Doesn't Either Com., Indpls., 1978, Com. for Multilateral Disarmament, Indpls., 1981, Com. for Soviet Disarmament, Indpls., 1983.

Mem. Family Support Ctr. Indpls. (founding). Republican. Unitarian. Club: Mackinac Family (pres. 1985). Home: 7206 Crest Ln Indianapolis IN 46256 Office: Granneman Internat PO Box 509244 Indianapolis IN 46250-9244

GRANT, ANETT D., communications executive; b. Montreal, Que., Can., May 25, 1950; d. Ralph and Mildred (Gussman) Drabinsky; m. Peter Williams Grant, Aug. 24, 1975. B.E., McGill U., 1971; M.F.A., U. Minn., 1975. Free-lance theater reviewer, nat. feature writer and community theater dir., 1975-79; pres. Exec. Speaking, Inc., Mpls., 1979—. Steel Co. Can. scholar, 1967; recipient Gardner Kneeland Meml. prize in English, McGill U., 1969; Que. Govt. Grad. scholar, 1971-73. Mem. Pub. Relations Soc. Am., Am. Soc. Tng. and Devel. Contbr. articles to profl. jours.; developer Core-Satellite Systems, 1982. Home: 5011 Colonial Dr Minneapolis MN 55416 Office: 960C Butler Sq Minneapolis MN 55416

GRANT, BUD, professional football coach. Head coach Minn. Vikings, NFL. Office: Minn Vikings 9520 Viking Dr Eden Prairie MN 55344*

GRANT, CHARLES TRUMAN, acquisitions and mergers, manufacturing and distributing executive; b. Chgo., Oct. 10, 1946; s. Charles H. and Mildred E. (Larrey) G.; B.A., DePaul U., Chgo., 1968, M.B.A. in Fin. and Acctg., 1975; 1 dau., Jordanna Lynne. Dir. internal audit, internat. dir. credit Rand McNally & Co., Skokie, Ill., 1973-75; cost and gen. acctg. mgr. V. Mueller div. Am. Hosp. Supply Corp., Chgo., 1971-73, corp. dir. acctg. and reporting Am. Hosp. Supply Corp., Evanston, 1975-77, officer and controller Am. Hosp. Supply div., McGaw Park, Ill., 1977-78; area v.p. ops. and adminstrn. Mead Corp., Hillside, Ill., 1978-80, pres. Ft. Dearborn Paper Co., Chgo., 1980-83; pres. The Guidance Concept Inc.; exec. v.p. Acquisition Mgmt., Inc., 1983-85; pres. Acquisition Mgmt./MidAm., Inc., 1985—; dir. CEDCO Capital, Inc. Lectr. Merit Youth Employment Council, 1976—; fin. adv. Jr. Achievement, 1971-75. Recipient Disting. Alumni award De Paul U., 1982; named Outstanding M.B.A. of Yr., 1982, Top Ten Bus. Profl. of Yr., 1982. Mem. Nat. Black M.B.A. Assn. (pres. 1981-83). Contbr. career articles to Ebony, Black Enterprise mag., Dollars and Sense mag., Crain's Chgo. Bus., Bus. and Soc. Rev., Bus. and Society Rev. Home: 2861 Shannon Ct Northbrook IL 60062

GRANT, HAROLD PETER, professional football coach; b. Superior, Wis., May 20, 1927; student U. Minn. Player, Mpls. Lakers, Nat. Basketball Assn., 1949-51, Phila. Eagles, NFL, 1951-52; player Winnipeg (Man., Can.) Profl. Football Team, 1953-54, head coach, 1957-66; head coach Minn. Vikings, NFL, 1968-84, 85—. Coach, Can. Football League championships, 1958-59, 61-62, Super Bowl IV, VIII, IX, XI. Address: Minn Vikings 9520 Viking Dr Eden Prairie MN 55344*

GRANT, HELEN KAY, occupational therapist, educator; b. Lima, Ohio, Nov. 6, 1937; d. Nye and Martha Lucille (Sherman) G. B.S., Ohio State U., 1959, M.S. in Anatomy, 1968, Ph.D., 1982. Registered occupational therapist, Ohio. Staff therapist Highland View Hosp., Cleve., 1959-62; chief occupational therapy Children's Hosp., Columbus, Ohio, 1962-64; faculty Ohio State U., Columbus, 1964-68, 70—, program dir., 1970—; dir. occupational therapy Univ. Hosp., Columbus, 1968-70. Recipient Life with Dignity award Heritage House, Columbus, 1981. Fellow Am. Occupational Therapy Assn. (chmn. Commn. on Edn. 1983—; service award 1981); mem. Ohio Occupational Therapy Assn. (pres. 1966-69, del. 1969-72; award of merit 1981), AMA (chmn. com. on allied health edn. and accreditation 1984—). Avocations: sailing; travel; needlework. Home: 207 Girard Rd Columbus OH 43214 Office: Ohio State Univ 1583 Perry St Columbus OH 43210

GRANT, LOIS MARGARET, architect; b. Peoria, Ill., June 8, 1937; d. Virgil Vesco and Esther Elizabeth (Lundberg) Grant; m. John Walter Voelpel, Aug. 16, 1958 (div. Jan. 10, 1983); children—Mark Alan, Diane Elizabeth; m. Keith F. Weiland, Aug. 24, 1985. B.S., U. Ill., 1959; B.S., Lawrence Inst. Tech., Southfield, Mich., 1979, B.Arch., 1980. Registered architect, Mich. Writer, researcher, Mike Whorf, Inc., Birmingham, Mich., 1970-73; behavioral analyst Exec. Cons. Service, Southfield, 1973-74; teaching asst. and slide curator Lawrence Inst. Tech. Sch. of Architecture, Southfield, 1976-78; archtl. asst. Minoru Yamasaki & Assocs., Inc., Troy, Mich., 1978-79; project designer Harley Ellington Pierce Yee Assocs., Southfield, 1980-85; project designer Stevens & Wilkinson, Atlanta, 1985—. Mem. AIA (Atlanta chpt., chmn. women in architecture com.).

GRANT, MICHAEL PETER, electrical engineer; b. Oshkosh, Wis., Feb. 26, 1936; s. Robert J. and Ione (Michelson) G.; B.S., Purdue U., 1957, M.S., 1958, Ph.D., 1964; m. Mary Susan Corcoran, September 2, 1961; children—James, Steven, Laura. With Westinghouse Research Labs., Pitts., summers 1953-57; mem. tech. staff Aerospace Corp., El Segundo, Calif., 1961; instr. elec. engring. Purdue U., 1958-64; sr. engr. Accu Ray Corp., Columbus, Ohio, 1964-67, mgr. advanced devel. and control systems, 1967-72, mgr. control and info. scis. div., 1972-74, asst. gen. mgr. indsl. systems div., 1974-76, mgr. system design, 1976—. Mem. IEEE, Sigma Xi, Eta Kappa Nu, Pi Mu Epsilon, Tau Beta Pi. Contbr. articles to profl. jours. Patentee in field of automation. Home: 4461 Sussex Dr Columbus OH 43220 Office: 650 Ackerman Rd Columbus OH 43202

GRANT, MICHELE BYRD, educator; b. Kansas City, Mo., Oct. 30, 1926; d. Ernest Louis and Violetta (Wallace) Byrd. B.S., Lincoln U., 1952; M.S. in Sci. Edn., U. Ill., 1955, advanced cert., 1964. Tchr., Unit 4, Champaign, Ill., 1956-66; tchr. sci. St. Louis Pub. Schs., 1966—, dept. head, 1978—, Mo. Outstanding Biology Tchrs. program dir., 1974—; participant NSF Summer Inst., CCNY, 1968-69; instr. Webster Coll. Upward Bound Program, 1969-70; judge Monsanto-St. Louis Post Dispatch Sci. Fair, 1970—. Mem. Cath. Sch. Bd., St. Louis, 1982-83; mem. life aux. Barnes Hosp., 1968—; trustee Meml. and Planned Funeral Soc., 1980. Recipient Mo. Outstanding Biology Tchr. award, Nat. Biology Tchrs. Assn., 1974. Mem. Nat. Sci. Tchrs. Assn., Nat. Assn. Biology Tchrs., Biology Tchrs. Assn., Mo. Sci. Tchrs. Assn., Mo. Acad. Sci., Assn. Supervision and Curriculum Devel., Kappa Delta Pi. Roman Catholic. Club: League of Women. Office: 3405 Bell Ave Saint Louis MO 63106

GRANT, STANLEY CAMERON, geologist, consultant, geotechnical manager; b. Cedar Rapids, Iowa, Apr. 21, 1931; s. Hobart McKinley and Elizabeth (Cameron) G.; m. Jeanne Stevens, June 26, 1954 (div. 1978); children—Laura, Stuart, Douglas; m. Norine Anne Kruse, Oct. 6, 1984. B.A. cum laude, Coe Coll., 1953; M.A., U. Wyo., 1955; Ph.D., U. Idaho, 1971. Registered profl. geologist. Petroleum geologist Standard Oil of Calif., Casper, Wyo., 1955; chief geologist Am. Nuclear, Riverton Wyo., 1955-56; served to maj. USAF, 1956-69; prof. U. No. Iowa, Cedar Falls, 1970-75; dir., state geologist Iowa Geol. Survey, Iowa City, 1975-80; geologist, ptnr. Grant Geol. Services, Independence, Kans., 1980—; engring. geologist Brice Petrides & Assoc., Waterloo, Iowa, 1972-75; science adv. to Gov., State of Iowa, Des Moines, 1975-80. Explorer scout leader Buffalo Trail council Boy Scouts Am., 1960-62; vice chmn. Nat. Gov.'s Council on Sci. Tech., Washington, 1977-78. Danforth Found. fellow, 1953-71; Freemont Energy Corp. grantee, 1968-69. Mem. Am. Assn. Petroleum Geologists, Am. Inst. Mining Engrs., Am. Inst. Profl. Geologists (pres. Kans. sect. 1985), Geol. Soc. Am., Iowa Acad. Sci. (dir., pres., 1976-82), Independence C. of C. Republican. Episcopalian. Lodge: Rotary (Outstanding Service award 1962). Home: 201 S 2d St Independence KS 67301 Office: Grant Geol Services 201 S 2d St PO Box 906 Independence KS 67301

GRANT, SUSAN HENNIGAN, lawyer; b. Highland Park, Mich., Jan. 18, 1948; d. Charles John and Irene (Thomas) Hennigan; m. A. Donald Grant, Oct. 6, 1973; B.A., Eastern Mich. U., 1969; M.A., Wayne State U., 1972, J.D., 1981. Bar: Mich. 1981, U.S. Dist. Ct. (we. dist.) Mich. 1981. Personnel adminstr. City of Clearwater, Fla., 1974-77; employment counselor State of Mich., White Cloud, 1978; instr. bus. law Ferris State Coll., Big Rapids, Mich., 1981-83; staff atty. Legal Aid Western Mich., Big Rapids, 1981-83, mng. atty., 1983—. Mem. ABA, Assn. Trial Lawyers Am., Mich. Trial Lawyers Assn., Women Lawyers Assn. Mich., Mecosta-Osceola Bar Assn. (v.p. 1984-85), AAUW (pres. Big Rapids br. 1983-85), ACLU. Lutheran. Office: Legal Aid Western Mich 124 S Michigan Big Rapids MI 49307

GRANZEIER, ROBERT WILLIAM, human services administrator; b. Cleve., Sept. 25, 1929; s. Phil and Elizabeth (Weisbarth) Hynes; m. Loudeen Mary Rant Oct. 12, 1957; 1 child, Mary Beth A. Farmer. B.A., Mich. State 1952. Exec. mgmt. trainee Sears Roebuck & Co., Saginaw, Mich., Chgo., 1954-59; sales mgr. Central Soya Co., Ft. Wayne, Ind., 1959-67; mgmt. exec. Ill. Dept. Rehab., Springfield, 1967-80, cabinet office dir., 1980-84; mgmt. exec. Ill. Dept. Mental Health, Springfield, 1984—; instr. Sangamon State U., Springfield, fall 1983; faculty Valpar Corp., Tucson, 1979-80; cons. instr. So. Ill. U. Rehab. Inst., Carbondale, 1974; cons. San Diego State U. Rehab. Inst., Spring 1982; commr. Commn. on Cert. Work Adjustment and Vocat. Evaluation Specialists, Washington, 1982-84; vice chmn. facilities com. Council State Adminstrn. Vocat. Rehab., Washington, 1982-84; mem. nat. adv. Menninger Found., Topeka, 1983—; bd. dirs. Electronic Industries Found., Washington, 1983. Served to 1st lt. U.S. Army, 1952-54, Korea. Recipient Disting. Service award Electronic Industries Found., Washington, 1983, Community Service award Chgo. Lighthouse for Blind, 1982, Spl. Recognition award Commn. Accreditation of Rehab. Facilities, Chgo., 1983. Mem. Nat. Rehab. Assn., VFW. Lodge: Elks. Avocations: Fishing, stained glass. Home: 1224 Wickford Dr Springfield IL 62704

GRAPES, DAVID GENE, theatre director, actor, administrator; b. Parkersburg, W.Va., Mar. 13, 1951; s. David G. and Nita Jean (Wagner) G. B.A., Glenville State U., 1972; M.F.A., U. N.C.-Greensboro, 1976; postgrad. W.Va. U., 1973-1974, Ind. State U., 1974. Dir. theatre Parkersburg Community Coll., 1976-78; mng. and artistic dir. Billings Studio Theatre, Mont., 1978-80, Madison Civic Repertory, Wis., 1980-81; mng. resident dir. Mule Barn Theatre, Tarkio, Mo., 1981-83; prof. theatre arts Tarkio Coll., 1981-83; assoc. dir. Kalamazoo Civic Players, 1983—; bd. dirs., theatre panel Mont. Arts Council, Wis. Arts Council, Mo. Arts Council; guest dir. prodns. Fort Wayne Civic, Theatre Memphis, Lincoln Community Playhouse, Roubidoux Resident Theatre, St. Joseph, Mo.; artistic dir. Shoestring Players, Parkersburg, summer 1978; Finale Stage Co., Billings, Mont., summer 1979-80; co-owner, dir. Depot Dinner Theatre, Billings, 1978-80; producing dir. Red Barn Theatre, Saugatuck, Mich., summer 1985. Author film revs. Kalamazoo Gazette, 1983—; TV film critic. Contbr. articles and photographs to profl. jours. Mem. Soc. Stage Dirs. and Choreographers, Am. Community Theatre Assn. (bd. dirs. 1980—), Wis. Community Theatre Assn. (pres. 1981), Am. Theatre Assn., Am. Film Inst., Community Theatre Assn. Mich., Alpha Psi Omega (pres. 1968-69). Avocations: Sports cars, travel; film criticism; chocolate. Home: 525 S Burdick #3802 Kalamazoo MI 49007 Office: Kalamazoo Civic Players 329 S Park St Kalamazoo MI 49007

GRASER, EARL JOHN, industrial designer; b. Toledo, Dec. 27, 1920; s. Ottomar S. and Irene Olga (Frommer) G.; m. Marianne Loveless, Nov. 19, 1942; 1 child, Cathy Ann. B.S., U. Cin., 1950. Assoc. Edwin W. Fuerst Indsl. Design, Toledo, 1947-50; v.p., assoc. Packaging and Product Devel. Inst., Cin., 1958-61; mgr. product devel. Olinkraft Inc. subs. Johns-Manville Corp., West Monroe, La., 1961-75, mgr. packaging systems div., 1975-77, dir. indsl. design, 1977-81, dir. indsl. design Manville Forest Products Corp., 1981-82; pres. Packaging and Product Devel. Assocs., Inc., Cin., 1982—. Contbr. articles to profl. jours. Patentee in field. Set design dir. Miss La. Pageant, 1974; flotilla comdr. USCG Aux., 1958-61; active Monroe Fine Arts Found., CAP, St. Francis Hosp., Bldg. Fund; bd. dirs. Monroe Little Theater. Served with USN, 1942-45. Recipient Inventor of Yr. award Olinkraft, Inc., 1971, Package of Yr. award Food and Drug Packaging mag., 1972, Set Design of Yr. award Strauss Playhouse, 1974. Mem. Packaging Inst. U.S.A., World Packaging Orgn., Am. Mgmt. Assn., Am. Soc. Innovators in Tech. (bd. dirs.), Am. Frozen Food Inst., Nat. Soft Drink Assn., Soc. Indsl. Designers, Nat. Assn. Awareness in Music, Aircraft Owners and Pilots Assn., Soc. Soft Drink Technologists, Alpha Sigma Phi. Republican. Roman Catholic. Club: Aero Nutz, Inc. Home: 6520 Apache Circle Cincinnati OH 45243

GRASHA, RUDOLPH MICHAEL, JR., sales executive; b. East Chicago, Ind., Nov. 11, 1947; s. Jacquelyn Clark, Sept. 23, 1979; children—Veronica, Ian Michael; children by previous marriage—Rudolph Michael III, Elizabeth Ann. B.A., Duquesne U., 1970; cert. in Advanced Mgmt., U. Chgo., 1982. Indsl. engr. U.S. Steel, Gary, Ind., 1974-79; sr. indsl. engr. Ingersoll Products, Chgo., 1979-81, supr. indsl. engring., 1981-82, mgr. engring., 1982-83, regional sales mgr., 1983—. Advisor Jr. Achievement, Gary, Ind., 1978. Served to capt. USAF, 1970-73. Recipient Scholarship, Duquesne U. Tamburitzans, Pitts., 1965; named Advisor of Yr., Jr. Achievement, Gary, 1978. Avocations: aviation; golf; football; semi-profl. music. Office: Ingersoll Products Corp 1000 W 120th St Chicago IL 60643

GRASSLEY, CHARLES E., U.S. Senator; b. New Hartford, Iowa, Sept. 17, 1933; m. Barbara Ann Speicher; children—Lee, Wendy, Robin Lynn., Michele Marie, Jay Charles. B.A., U. No. Iowa, 1955, M.A., 1956; postgrad., U. Iowa, 1957-58. Farmer; instr. polit. sci. Drake U., 1962, Charles City Community Coll., 1967-68; mem. Iowa Ho. of Reps., 1959-75, 94th-96th Congresses from 3d Iowa Dist., U.S. Senate from Iowa, 1980—. Mem. Am. Farm Bur., Iowa Hist. Soc., Pi Gamma Mu, Kappa Delta Pi. Baptist. Clubs: Masons, Order of Eastern Star. Office: Senate Office Bldg Washington DC 20510

GRAUERHOLZ, JAMES LESTER, bank executive; b. Kensington, Kans., Nov. 20, 1949; s. Lester Henry and Mildred (Hermanns) G.; m. Dianna Lynn Woods, Aug. 18, 1969; children—Bob, Julie, Mike. B.S., Kans. State U., 1971, M.S., 1983. v.p. Salina Prodn. Credit Assn., Kans., 1973-76; dir. tng. Fed. Intermediate Credit Bank, Wichita, Kans., 1976-79, asst. v.p., 1979-83; asst. v.p., supr. field Fed. Land Bank, Wichita, 1984—; v.p. Field Farm Credit Bank of Wichita, 1985—; cons. Farm Credit System, 1978-84. Author booklet The People in Farm Credit, 1978, Career Planning, 1982, Performance Objectives, 1983; Contbr. articles to profl. jours. Kans. chmn. Nat. All Breeds Jr. Dairy Show, Salina, 1975-76, Mid. Am. Agrl. Expn., Salina, 1975-76, United Way, 1976. Served to capt. U.S. Army, 1971-73. Mem. Am. Inst. Cooperation (vol. instr. 1981-82), Am. Soc. Adult Educators, Am. Soc. Personnel Adminstrs., Am. Mgmt. Assn., Am. Soc. Tng. and Devel., Adminstrv. Mgmt. Soc.; Phi Kappa Phi. Republican. Lutheran. Avocations: reading; astronomy; carpentry; music.

GRAVEREAU, VICTOR P., marketing cons., ret. educator; b. Thunder Bay, Ont., Can., Mar. 20, 1909; s. James and Malvina (Lemieux) G.; came to U.S., 1910, naturalized, 1934; B.A., Ohio Wesleyan U., 1936; M.A., Kent State U., 1943; M.B.A., Case Western Res. U., 1951; m. Mildred Irene Snyder, Aug. 11, 1934. Salesman, Motorists Mutual Ins. Co., Wooster, Ohio, 1936-37; tchr. of commerce Rittman (Ohio) High Sch., 1937-46; accountant Gerstenslager Co., Wooster, Ohio, 1944; asst. prof. commerce Kent (Ohio) State U., 1946-49, asso. prof. commerce, 1949-51, prof. marketing, 1951-76, prof. marketing emeritus, 1976—, coordinator coll. grad. program, 1957-60, asst. dean, 1960-61; partner Pfeiffer, Gravereau & Assos., Kent, 1954-63; dir., v.p. Clark Zimmerman & Assos., Inc., Cleve., 1971—. Recipient Pres.'s. medal Kent State U., 1977; Republic Steel Corp. Economics-in-Action fellow Case Western Res. U., 1964. Mem. Am. Mktg. Assn., Am. Acad. Advt., Nat. Assn. of Purchasing Mgmt. (faculty intern fellow 1962), Bus. Profl. Advt. Assn., Advt. Club Akron, Beta Gamma Sigma, Delta Sigma Pi, Delta Tau Delta, Kappa Delta Pi. Clubs: Masons, Kiwanis, Akron City. Author: Purchasing Management: Selected Readings, 1973; contbr. articles in field to profl. pubs.; mktg. scholarship Kent State U. established in his name, 1977. Home: 212 Elmwood Dr Kent OH 44240

GRAVES, GREGORY MICHAEL, air pollution control engineer; b. Sioux Falls, S.D., Jan. 20, 1958; s. Joseph John and Darlene (Thom) G.; m. Deanna Lynn Pryor, Sept. 15, 1979; 1 child, Jessica Nicole. B.S. in Mech. Engring., S.D. Sch. Mines and Tech., 1980; postgrad., 1980—. Asst. air quality engr. Burns & McDonnell, Kansas City, Mo., 1980-81; staff air quality engr., 1981-83, project air quality engr., 1984—. Mem. ASME, Air Pollution Control Assn. Democrat. Roman Catholic. Avocations: tennis; gardening. Home: 12508 Craig Grandview MO 64030 Office: Burns & McDonnell PO Box 173 Kansas City MO 64141

GRAVES, JAMES HENRY, psychiatry educator, physician; b. Herrin, Ill., Sept. 29, 1924; s. James Henry and Anna Joyce (Keaster) G.; m. Helen A. Mataya, June 26, 1949 (div. June 1984); children—Christina Adrienne, James Willis, John David Nicholas. B.S., Northwestern U., 1946, M.B., M.S., 1949, M.D., 1950. Diplomate Am. Bd. Psychiatry and Neurology. Intern, Charity Hosp., New Orleans, 1949-50; resident in psychiatry U.S. Air Force Med. Corp., 1950-53; chief women's div. Ypsilanti State Hosp., Mich., 1953-55; chief male service-psychiatry Detroit Receiving Hosp., 1955-58, dir. psychiatry, 1958-64; clin. assoc. prof. psychiatry Wayne State U. Coll. Medicine, Detroit, 1963—; practice medicine specializing in psychiatry, Ann Arbor, Mich., 1954-55, Detroit, 1955—; commr. mental health State of Mich., 1959-63; chmn. Pub. Policy Task Force on Mental Health, 1983-84. Mem. Med. Adv. Com. to Pres. Kennedy, 1960-61, Physicians for Social Responsibility, Detroit, 1983—. Served to capt. USAF, 1950-53. Fellow Am. Psychiat. Assn., Am. Pub. Health Assn., Am. Orthopsychiat. Assn.; mem. AMA, Mich. State Med. Soc., Wayne County Med. Soc., Mich. Psychiat. Soc. (councillor 1960-63, v.p. 1984-85, pres. elect 1985-86). Club: Cajal (Montreal, Que., Can.). Avocations: tennis; distance swimming; sailing; skiing. Home: 1738 Shore Club Dr Saint Clair Shores MI 48080 Office: 16980 Kercheval St Grosse Pointe MI 48230 also Dept Psychiatry Wayne State Univ College Medicine Detroit MI 48226

GRAVES, JON DAVID, lawyer; b. Newton, Kans., July 7, 1953; s. Waldo Edgar and Esta Ethyln (Killion) G.; m. Susan Lynn Spaulding, Dec. 19, 1975; 1 child, Kimberly Sue. B.A. in Bus. Adminstrn. and Econs., Bethel Coll., North Newton, Kans., 1975; postgrad. Wichita State U., 1975-76, 80-82; J.D., Washburn U., 1979. Bar: Kans. 1980, U.S. Dist. Ct. Kans. 1980. Assoc. Jerry L. Berg, P.A., Wichita, Kans., 1979-83; sole practice, Wichita, 1983—. Worker Robert Stephan for Atty. Gen. campaign, Topeka, 1978; mem. steering com. John Anderson for Pres. campaign, Wichita, 1980. Mem. Kans. Bar Assn., Wichita Bar Assn., Phi Delta Phi. Republican. Methodist. Home: 2832 S Mosley St Wichita KS 67216 Office: 940 N Main St Wichita KS 67203

GRAVES, VERNA LOUISE, educational consultant; b. Bowling Green, Ky., May 29, 1950; d. Basil and Jennie Ora (Maxey) Richardson. B.S., Ind. U., 1973, Ed.D., 1978; M.S., Ball State U., 1977. Tchr., Indpls. Pub. Schs., 1972-80; self-employed human relations, communications cons., Indpls., 1980—; cons. Perry Twp. Sch.; YWCA day camp dir., 1975; Indpls. Parks Dept. camp counselor, 1976. Mem. Assn. Supervision and Curriculum Devel., NEA, Phi Delta Kappa, Zeta Phi Beta. Democrat. Author: Human Relations Handbook for Indianapolis Public Schools, 1980. Office: 120 E Walnut St Indianapolis IN 46204

GRAY, DON NORMAN, chemist; b. Carlyle, Ill., July 28, 1931; s. Garold Norman and Mary Louisa (Shoupe) G.; B.S. in Chemistry, Colo. State U., 1953; Ph.D. in Chemistry, Colo. U., Boulder, 1956; m. Mary Kelly, Oct. 10, 1959; children—Christy Elizabeth, Andrew Kelly, Jane Moore. Faculty Denver U., staff Denver Research Inst., 1956-63; scientist Martin Marietta Aerospace, Balt., 1963-66; mgr. biotechnology and toxicology Owens-Illinois, Toledo, 1966—; pres. Shenandoah Research, Inc. Mem. Am. Chem. Soc., N.Y. Acad. Scis., Am. Soc. Artificial Internal Organs, Sigma Xi. Inventor Biobland plastics; contbr. writings to profl. publs.; patentee. Home: 5503 Brixton Dr Sylvania OH 43560

GRAY, FREDERICK CUMMINGS, lawyer; b. Des Moines, July 5, 1955; s. Donald Wayne and Nancy Morgan (Saar) G.; m. Deidre Pifer, July 26, 1980; 1 son, Whitney Alan. B.S., U. Wyo., 1977; J.D., Drake U., 1980. Bar: Iowa 1980, U.S. Dist. Ct. (so. dist.) Iowa 1980, U.S. Dist. Ct. (no. dist.) Iowa 1980, U.S. Ct. Appeals (8th cir.) 1980, Nebr. 1981, U.S. dist. Ct. Nebr. 1981, Fla. 1984. Assoc. Neiman, Neiman, Stone & Spellman, Des Moines, 1980-81; assoc. Warren Schrempp & Assocs., Omaha, 1981-82; ptnr. Schrempp, Hoagland & Gray, Omaha, 1983—. Mem. Assn. Trial Lawyers Am. Republican. Episcopalian. Home: 1314 S 138th St Omaha NE 68144 Office: Schrempp Hoagland & Gray 617 N 90th St Omaha NE 68114

GRAY, GARY WILLIAM, petroleum geologist; b. Glen Ridge, N.J., Aug. 22, 1951; s. Edward William and Ruth L. (Kauff) G.; m. Mary C. Meeker, Mar. 30, 1974; children—Elizabeth R., Carolyn M. B.A., Coll. Wooster, 1974; M.S., Ariz. State U., Tempe, 1977. Cert. profl. geologist, Ind. Staff geologist Lone Star Producing Co., Wooster, Ohio, 1974, Exxon Co. USA, Pensacola, Fla., and New Orleans, 1977-80; sr. geologist ANR Prodn. Co., Oklahoma City, Okla., 1980-81; exploration geologist Republic Resources, Oklahoma City, 1981-82; geol. cons., Oklahoma City, 1982-83; dist. geologist Carless Resources (formerly RSC Energy Corp.), New Philadelphia, Ohio, 1983—. Contbr. to book: Carbonate Rock Environments, 1977. Lectr. Wayne County pub. schs., Wooster, Ohio, 1984. Grantee Ohio Acad. Sci., 1973. Mem. Am. Assn. Petroleum Geologists (vis. petroleum geologist 1984, mem. com. on astrogeology 1984), Am. Inst. Profl. Geologists, Ohio Geol. Soc., No. Ohio Geol. Soc., Soc. Profl. Well Log Analysts. Republican. Lutheran. Office: Carless Resources Route 2 Box 2174 New Philadelphia OH 44663

GRAY, GEORGE MCBURNEY, clergyman, consultant psychologist; b. Belfast, No. Ireland, Oct. 12, 1941; came to U.S., 1970; s. Charles and Wilhemina (McBurney) G.; m. Christine Irvine, Aug. 20, 1966; children—George Andrew, Charis Mary. Student Bible Tng. Inst. Glasgow (Scotland), 1963-66; diploma in theology, U. London, 1966; Th.M., Luther Rice Sem., 1973, Th.D., 1974; D.Ministry in Psychology, Fuller Theol. Sem., 1979. Ordained to ministry Baptist Ch., 1966; pastor Patrick Baptist Ch., Glasgow, Scotland, 1966-70, United Baptist Ch., Milo, Maine, 1970-74, First Baptist Ch., Gloversville, N.Y., 1974-82, Kenwood Baptist Ch., Cin., 1982-85, Grace Bapt. Ch., Westchester, Ohio, 1985—; cons. family counselor, mental health. Am. Baptist Chs. scholar, Regents Coll., Oxford U., 1981. Mem. Am. Assn. Marriage and Family Therapists, Am. Psychol. Assn., Brit. Psychol. Soc., Am. Baptist Minister's Council. Contbr. articles to psychology, religious jours. Office: Grace Baptist Ch 7983 Cox Rd Westchester OH 45069

GRAY, GEORGIA NEESE, banker; b. Richland, Kans.; d. Albert and Ellen (O'Sullivan) Neese; A.B., Washburn Coll., 1921; D.B.A. (hon.), 1966; student Sargent's, 1921-22; L.H.D. (hon.), Russell Sage Coll., 1950; m. George M. Clark, Jan. 21, 1929; m. 2d, Andrew J. Gray, 1953. Began as actress, 1923; asst. cashier Richland State Bank, 1935-37, pres., 1937—; pres. Capital City State Bank & Trust Co., Topeka, 1964-74; dir. Capital City State Bank and Trust, Topeka; treas. of U.S., 1949-53; mem. Commn. Jud. Qualifications Supreme Ct. Kans. Del.-at-large nat. adv. com. SBA; Democratic nat. committeewoman, 1936-64; hon. chmn. Villages project C. of C. Bd. dirs. Kans. A.A.A., 1950—; bd. dirs., former chmn. Kans. div. Am. Cancer Soc.; mem. bd. exec. campaign and maj. gifts com. Georgetown U.; bd. dirs. Seven Steps Found., Harry S. Truman Library; chmn. Alpha Phi Found., 1962-63; mem. nat. bd. Women's Med. Coll. Pa.; chmn. bd. regents Washburn U., 1975—; mem. bd., treas. Sex Information and Edn. Council U.S.; mem. White House Com. on Aging. Recipient Disting. Alumni award Washburn U., 1950. Mem. Am. Bus. Women's Assn., Topeka C. of C., Met. Bus. and Profl. Women's Club, Women in Communications, Alpha Phi (nat. trustee), Alpha Phi Upsilon, Alpha Delta Kappa. Clubs: Soroptimist (hon. life), Met. Zonta, Topeka Country. Address: 2709 W 29 St Topeka KS 66614

GRAY, HANNA HOLBORN, university president; b. Heidelberg, Germany, Oct. 25, 1930; d. Hajo and Annemarie (Bettmann) Holborn; m. Charles Montgomery Gray, June 19, 1954. B.A., Bryn Mawr Coll., 1950; Fulbright scholar Oxford U., 1950-52; Ph.D., Harvard U., 1957; hon. degrees: M.A., Yale U., 1971; L.H.D., Grinnell Coll., Lawrence U., Denison U., 1974, Wheaton Coll., 1976, Marlboro Coll., 1979, Rikkyo U., 1979, Roosevelt U., 1980, Knox Coll., 1980, Thomas Jefferson U., 1981, Coe Coll., 1981, Duke U., 1982, Clark U., 1982, New Sch. for Social Research, 1982, Brandeis U., 1983, Colgate U., 1983, Wayne State U., 1984, Miami U., 1984, So. Methodist U., 1984, CUNY, 1985, U. Denver, 1985; Litt.D., Oxford U., 1979, St. Lawrence U., 1974, Coe Coll., 1981; H.H.D., St. Mary's Coll., 1974, Washington U., 1985; LL.D., Union Coll., 1975, Regis Coll., 1976, Dartmouth Coll., 1978, Trinity Coll., 1978, U. Bridgeport, 1978, Yale U., 1978, Dickinson Coll., 1979, Wittenberg U., 1979, Brown U., 1979, U. Rochester, 1980, U. Notre Dame, 1980, U. So. Calif., 1980, U. Mich., 1981, Princeton U., 1982, Georgetown U., 1983, Marquette U., 1984, W.Va. Wesleyan U., 1985, Hamilton Coll., 1985. Instr., Bryn Mawr (Pa.) Coll., 1953-54; teaching fellow Harvard U., 1955-57, instr., 1957-59, asst. prof., 1959-60, vis. lectr., 1963-64; asst. prof. U. Chgo., 1961-64, assoc. prof., 1964-72; dean, prof. Northwestern U., Evanston, Ill., 1972-74; provost, prof., history Yale U., 1974-78, acting pres., 1977-78; pres., prof. history U. Chgo., 1978—; dir. Cummins Engine Co., Morgan Guaranty Trust Co., J.P. Morgan & Co., Atlantic Richfield Co., Ameritech. Fellow Center for Advanced Study in Behavioral Scis., 1966-67, vis. scholar, 1970-71; hon. fellow St. Anne's Coll., Oxford U. Mem. Pulitzer Prize Bd.; bd. dirs. Andrew W. Mellon Found., Field Found. Ill., Nat. Humanities Center, Howard Hughes Med. Inst.; trustee Bryn Mawr Coll., Mayo Found., Brookings Instn., Mus. Sci. and Industry. U. Chgo. Newberry Library fellow, 1960-61; Phi Beta Kappa vis. scholar, 1971-72. Fellow Am. Acad. Arts and Scis.; mem. Renaissance Soc. Am., Chgo. Council Fgn. Relations (dir.), Am. Philos. Soc., Council Fgn. Relations, Nat. Acad. Edn., Phi Beta Kappa. Editor (with Charles Gray) Jour. Modern History, 1965-70; contbr. articles to profl. jours. Office: U Chgo 5801 Ellis Avenue Chicago IL 60637

GRAY, KENNETH J., U.S. congressman; b. West Frankfort, Ill., Nov. 14, 1924; m. Gwendolyn June Croslin; children—Diann, Rebecca, Jimmy. Student Army Advanced Sch., World War II. Engaged in automobile business; operated air service, Benton, Ill.; mem. 84th-93d Congresses; 99th Congress; pres. Ken Gray & Assocs., Bus. Cons.; owner Ken Gray's Antique Car Mus. Founder Walking Dog Found. for Blind, 1950; bd. dirs. Nat. Coal Mus. Served with USAAF, World War II. Mem. Am. Legion, Forty and Eight, VFW. Lodges: Elks, Kiwanis. Address: 2109 Rayburn House Office Bldg Washington DC 20515

GRAY, MARY JANE, curriculum and instruction planning educator; b. Cherokee, Iowa, B.E., Buena Vista Coll., 1955; M.Ed., Loyola U., 1962; Ph.D., U. Chgo., 1973. Cert. elem., secondary tchr., supr., adminstr., Ill., Iowa, Minn. Elem. and secondary tchr. various Ill., Iowa, Minn. schs., 1951-66; assoc. prof., chmn. dept. curriculum and instrn. Loyola U., Chgo., 1966—. Contbr. articles to profl. jours. LaVerne Noyes scholar, 1967-68. Mem. Internat. Reading Assn., Nat. Council Tchrs. of English, Assn. Supervision and Curriculum Devel., Coll. Instrs. of Reading Profls., Pi Lambda Theta. Roman Catholic. Avocations: reading, music. Office: Loyola U Chicago 820 N Michigan Ave Chicago IL 60611

GRAY, NANCY JEAN, communications specialist, consultant; b. Waterbury, Conn., Nov. 29, 1939; d. William Vernon and Mearl Lauretta (Smith) Sigmon; m. Carl L. Gray, Mar. 14, 1976; stepchildren—Steven, Cheryl. B.S., Manchester Coll., 1966; M.A., U. Dayton, 1984. Tchr. Beavercreek Schs., Dayton, Ohio, 1962, New Madison Schs., Ohio, 1965-72; communications specialist Good Samaritan Hosp. and Health Ctr., Dayton, 1972—; producer, host Room to Grow cable TV and FM radio show, 1981—; workshop presenter Samaritan Ctr. for Youth Resources, Dayton, 1972—; pres., founder Dayton Area Step-family Assn. Am., Inc., 1984—. Vol. social service worker Brethren Vol. Services, 1962-64. Mem. Ohio Speech Communication Assn., Am. Orthopsychiat. Assn., Sigma Phi Gamma (corr. sec. Kappa Beta chpt. 1984-85, service sec. 1985). Democrat. Methodist. Avocations: travel; photography; entertainment. Home: 405 Westview Pl Englewood OH 45322 Office: Samaritan Ctr for Youth Resources 5670 Philadelphia Dr Dayton OH 45415

GRAY, ROBERT, police sci. educator; b. Chgo., Sept. 5, 1935; m. Janet Eileen Johnson, June 25, 1960; children—Paul Robert, Julie Ann, James Thomas. A.A. in Law Enforcement, St. Joseph's Calumet Coll., Whiting, Ind., 1972, B.S. in Sociology, 1974; M.S. in Pub. Adminstrn., DePaul U., 1976; Ph.D. in Sociology, Calif. Coast U., 1978. Cost acct. Republic Steel Corp., Chgo., 1955-61; police officer Chgo. Police Dept., 1961-76; police sci. educator NE Wis. Tech. Inst., Green Bay, 1976—, also mem. ad hoc adv. bd. Served with U.S. Army, 1957-59. Recipient 7 dept. commendations Chgo. Police Dept., 1962-67. Mem. No. Wis. Tech. Inst. Tchrs. Assn. (v.p. 1979-80, pres. 1980-81), Bayland United Tchrs. Assn. (bd. dirs. 1980-81), Wis. Vocat. Assn. (bd. dirs. 1982-83). Democrat. Roman Catholic. Home: 600 E Longview Ave Green Bay WI 54301 Office: NE Wis Tech Inst Dept Police Sci 2740 W Mason St Green Bay WI 54303

GRAY, SANFORD DURHAM, educator; b. Kansas City, Mo., Mar. 3, 1929; s. William Clinton and Geneva (Durham) G.; B.A., U. Mo., 1951, M.A., 1954; m. Marie Isabel Correll, June 9, 1959 (div.); children—Sharon Marie, Martin Sanford, Clinton Bruce; m. 2d, Joan Frances McConville, June 27, 1970 (div.); children—Angela Nordica, Christopher Hansford; m. 3d, Marybeth Feehan, Mar. 3, 1979; children—Benjamin Oscar, Elizabeth Margaret. Rec. engr. Artist Rec. Studios, Kansas City, Mo., 1954; grad. asst. U. Mo., 1956-58; instr. UCLA, 1958-59; rec. engr. Calvin Prodns., Inc., 1960; instr., asst. prof. communication, dir. film prodn. U. S.D., Vermillion, 1960-80, 81—, acting chmn. mass communication dept., 1985—; vis. asst. prof. film, acting head film area U. Tex., Austin, 1980-81; owner Orpheus Records, Vermillion, 1957—. Recipient Calvin Notable film award, 1965; CINE Golden Eagle award, 1968; honors certificate Am. Film Festival, 1969. Mem. Internat. Platform Assn., Speech Communication Assn., Univ. Film and Video Assn. (dir.), Soc. Motion Picture and TV Engrs., AAUP, Sigma Phi Epsilon. Presbyterian. Clubs: Masons, Shriners. Author mystery novels. Designer electronic devices. Home: 323 N Pine St Vermillion SD 57069

GRAY, TED WARREN, educational administrator, financier; b. Vinita, Okla., Aug. 4, 1935; s. William Wilbur and Elta (Betts) G.; m. Sue Dudgeon, July 7, 1954; children—Kim, Tina, Tammy. A.A., Northeastern Okla. Jr. Coll., 1955; B.S., Kans. State Tchrs. Coll., 1957; M.S., Kans. State Coll., Pittsburg, 1957; postgrad. La. State U., 1958; Ed.D., U. Kans., 1969. Lic. sch. psychologist, Kans., 1961. Spl. edn. tchr. West Jr. High Sch., Kansas City, Mo., 1958-59; tchr./prin. N.W. Elem. Sch., Bonner Springs, Kans., 1959-60; supt. Linwood Schs. (Kans.), 1960-63; supr. Kans. Dept. Pub. Instrn., Topeka, 1963-64; dir. spl. edn. and diagnostic services Kansas City (Kans.) Pub. Schs., 1964-69; gen. dir. spl. services, dist. assn. supt. and area supt. Shawnee Mission Pub. Schs. (Kans.), 1969-79; adj. prof. U. Kans. and Kans. State U., 1977-78; supt. schs. Davenport Community Sch. Dist. (Iowa), 1979-86; pres. fin. mgmt. firm. Active Jr. Achievement, 1979-84, sec. bd., 1982-84; bd. dirs. ARC, 1980—; active Closeup Found. Mem. Am. Assn. Sch. Adminstrs., Iowa Assn. Sch. Adminstrs., PTA. Lodge: Rotary. Home and Office: Box 819 Grove OK 74344

GRAY, THOMAS WARREN, purchasing executive; b. Greenville, Miss., Mar. 16, 1948; s. Arthur L. and Fannie M. (Redmond) G.; m. Geraldine Johnson, Aug. 18, 1946; children—Keith, Brian. B.S., Tougaloo Coll., 1969; postgrad. Ind. Central U., 1980-82. Analytical chemist Internat. Harvester, Indpls., 1971-72, prodn. supr., 1972-76, process engr., 1976-79, EEO tng. supr., 1979-80, buyer components group, 1980-82, corporate buyer, Schaumburg, Ill., 1982—; sales advisor Jr. Achievement Central Ind., 1970-73; mem. adv. council Center Leadership Devel., Indpls., 1981-82; cons. Nat. Alliance Bus., Washington, 1983—. Mem. planning com. Washington Twp. Sch. System, Indpls., 1979-81; mem. child devel. com. Jewish Community Assn., Indpls., 1980-82; loaned exec. United Way of Greater Indpls., 1981; treas. Trinity Ch. Young Adult Task Force, Indpls., 1981-83. Served with U.S. Army, 1969-75. Recipient Acad. Scholarship, Tougaloo Coll., 1969; Disting. award Center for Leadership Devel., 1981. Mem. Am. Foundrymen Soc. (dir. Central Ind. 1978-81), Alpha Phi Alpha (Man of Yr. 1981). Methodist. Club: Jack and Jill Am. Home: 150 Brookside Dr Glendale Heights IL 60139 Office: Internat Harvester 600 Woodfield St Schaumburg IL 60196

GRAZIANO, CHARLES DOMINIC, pharmacist; b. Cariati, Italy, June 28, 1920; s. Frank Dominic and Marianna (Bambace) G.; student Dowling Jr. Coll., 1939, 40; B.S. in Pharmacy, Drake U., 1943; m. Corrine Rose Comito, Feb. 5, 1950; children—Craig Frank, Charles Dominic II, Marianne, Kimberly Rose, Mark, Suzanne. Pharamacist Kings Pharmacy, Des Moines, 1946-47; partner Bauder Pharmacy, Des Moines, 1948-61, owner, 1962—. Mem. Des Moines Art Center. Served with AUS, 1943-45; ETO. Decorated Bronze Star. Named Drake U. Parent of the Year, 1983-84. Mem. Des Moines C. of C., Nat. Assn. Retail Druggists, Iowa, Polk County pharm. assns., St. Vincent de Paul Soc., Am. Pharm. Assn., Phi Delta Chi. Roman Catholic. Office: 3802 Ingersoll Ave Des Moines IA 50312

GREASER, MARION LEWIS, biochemistry educator; b. Vinton, Iowa, Feb. 10, 1942; s. Lewis Levi and Elisabeth P. (Sage) G.; m. Marilyn Sue Pfister, June 12, 1965; children—Suzanne, Scott. B.S., Iowa State U., 1964; M.S., U. Wis., 1967, Ph.D., 1969. Postdoctoral fellow Boston Biomed. Research Found., 1968-71; asst. prof. U. Wis., Madison, 1971-73, assoc. prof., 1973-77, prof. 1977—. Contbr. articles to profl. jours. Recipient Disting. Research award, Am. Meat Sci. Assn., 1981; numerous researach grants, NIH, Am. Heart Assn. Mem. Biophys. Soc., Am. Soc. Biol. Chemists, Am. Meat Sci. Assn., Inst. Food Technologists, Am. Soc. Cell Biology. Christian Church. Avocations: photography; soccer. Address: Univ Wis 1805 Linden Dr Madison WI 53706

GREATHOUSE, FERN LUCILLE, social worker; b. Garden City, Kans., Nov. 15, 1924; d. Ralph Goodman and Viola Fern (Collins) Greathouse. B.A.E., Wichita State U., 1957. Lic. social worker, Kans. Tchr. Finney County (Kans.) Rural Schs., 1942-46; sec. 1st United Meth. Ch. Garden City, 1946-51; tchr. Shawnee Mission (Kans.) Pub. Schs., 1955-71; social worker Kans. Dept. Social and Rehab. Services, Garden City, 1971-78; dir. social services St. Catherine Hosp., Garden City, 1978—. Active LWV, Garden City Friends of the Zoo. Mem. Nat. Assn. Social Workers, Kans. Conf. on Social Welfare, Kans. Soc. Hosp. Social Work Dirs. (pres. Sunflower chpt. 1985—), Nat. Assn. Hosp. Social Work Dirs., Nat. Com. for Prevention Child Abuse, Kans. Com. for Prevention Child Abuse. Home: 901 Lyle Garden City KS 67846 Office: 608 N 5th St Garden City KS 67846

GREATON, KAREN MARGUERITE, jewelry store executive; b. St. Paul, Jan. 19, 1948; d. W. Eben and Geraldine Evelyn (Swanson) G.; m. Daniel Michial Hoverman, Nov. 14, 1974 (div. Jan. 1983); m. William Charles Gillespie, Mar. 24, 1984; 1 child, Robert Eben Greaton Gillespie. Student Patricia Stevens Sch. (now Lowthian Coll.), 1966-67, Gemol. Inst. Am. Mgr. Patricia Stevens Sch. (now Lowthian Coll.), Mpls., 1967-70; employment counselor Assoc. Clerical Specialists, Mpls., 1970-72; mgr., counselor Roth Young-Clerical div., Mpls., 1972-74; mgr. Greaton's Jewelers, Inc., New Richmond, Wis., 1975-84, pres., 1984—. Mem. New Richmond C. of C. (chmn. retail com. 1977, bd. dirs. 1977-79, Appreciation award 1979), Hist. Soc. New Richmond. Republican. Methodist. Lodge: Jobs Daus. (hon. queen 1965). Avocations: breeding Old English sheepdogs; aquariums; photography; aerobics; skiing. Home: 454 S Hill Dr New Richmond WI 54017 Office: Greatons Jewelers Inc 224 S Knowles Ave New Richmond WI 54017

GREAVES, ROBERT GEORGE, industrial engineer, computer software consultant; b. Oak Park, Ill., Dec. 31, 1924; s. Walter Martin Greaves and Florence (Gundstrom) Hill; m. Alison Janet Ash, June 9, 1962; children—Edmund Ash, Cordilia Ann. B.S. in Indsl. Engring., Ill. Inst. Tech., 1950; M.B.A., U. Chgo., 1966. Mfg. engr. S.A. Oakley Co., Chgo., 1950-51; sr. engr. R.R. Donnelley & Sons Co., Chgo., 1951—; software cons., Evanston, Ill., 1983—. Served with USN, 1943-46. Mem. Inst. Indsl. Engrs. (sr. mem.), Am. Statis. Assn. Episcopalian. Avocations: Personal computers, sailing. Home: 117 Custer Ave Evanston IL 60202 Office: RR Donnelley & Sons 350 E 22d St Chicago IL 60616

GREBENS, GEORGE, executive management consultant; b. June 12, 1943; m. Katherine Panon, Sept. 3, 1972; 1 dau., Alexandra. B.A. in European Studies, U. Montreal (Que., Can.), 1966; M.A. in Internat. Relations Mgmt., Mich. State U., 1968, Ph.D. in Internat. Relations and Sovietology, 1972. Instr., lectr. Oberlin Coll. (Ohio), 1970; asst. prof. European studies U. Ky., Lexington, 1972-74; asst. prof. Russian area studies Tex. A&M U., College Station, 1974-78; sr. lang. specialist data processing, contracts, mgmt. Fluor Engring., Houston, 1979-80; exec. cons. PCA/Internat. Airports Project, Riyadh, Saudi Arabia, 1980-83; directorate staff asst. at internat. airports, exec. planner ABCL/KKIA Riyadh, 1983-84; asst. to dir., planning cons. in industry and airports ATW, 1984—; directorate staff asst. Bechtel, Middle East, 1982-84. Author: Theory of Soviet Science, 1978; Before the Beginning, 1979; contbr. articles, 1975-78. Mich. State U. fellow, 1968-70. Mem. AAAS, Am. Mgmt. Assn. Home: 323 Franklin Blvd S804/K20 Chicago IL 60606

GREEN, ALLISON ANNE, educator; b. Flint, Mich., Oct. 5, 1936; d. Edwin Stanley and Ruth Allison (Simmons) James; m. Richard Gerring Green, Dec. 23, 1961 (div. Oct. 1969). B.A., Albion Coll., 1959; M.A., U. Mich., 1978. Cert. tchr., Mich. Tchr. phys. edn. Southwestern High Sch., Flint, 1959-62; tchr. math. Harry Hunt Jr. High Sch., Portsmouth, Va., 1962-63; receptionist Tempcon, Inc., Mpls., 1963-64; tchr. phys. edn. and math. Longfellow Jr. High Sch., Flint, 1964-81, tchr. math., 1981—; chmn. Intervention Team Sch. Improvement Project, 1984. Mem. Fair Winds council Girl Scouts U.S.A., 1943—, leader Lone Troop, Albion, Mich., 1957, sr. tchr. aide adviser, 1964-67; mem. Big Sisters Genesee and Lapeer Counties, 1964-68; mem. adminstrv. bd. Court St. United Methodist Ch.; treas. edn. work area, mission commn. United Meth. Women Soc. Christian Service (memorials chmn. 1985—, chmn. endeavor circle 1985). Mem. NEA, Mich. Edn. Assn., Mich. Assn. Mid. Sch. Educators, United Tchrs. Flint (bldg. rep.), Delta Kappa Gamma (treas. 1982—, profl. affairs chmn. 1978-80, legis. chmn. 1980-82), Alpha Xi Delta (pres. Flint. alumnae, v.p., treas., corp. pres. Albion Coll., alumnae dir. province 1972-77, Outstanding Sr. Albion Coll. 1959), Phi Delta Kappa (historian 1985), Embroiderers Guild Am. (sec. 1977-80, maps rep. 1980-82). Home: 824 Frost St Apt 2-B Flint MI 48504 Office: 1255 N Chevrolet Ave Flint MI 48504

GREEN, DAVID, manufacturing company executive; b. Chgo., Mar. 22, 1922; s. Harry B. and Carrie (Scheinbaum) G.; m. Mary I. Winton, June 15, 1951; children—Sara Edmond, Howard Benjamin, Jonathan Winton. B.A. in Econs., U. Chgo., 1942, M.A. in Social Scis., 1949. Mgr., Toy Co., Chgo., 1949-54; founder, pres. Quartet Mfg. Co., Chgo., 1954—; pres. Colleague, Inc., Booneville, Miss., 1967—; chmn. bd. and cons. DG Group, Chgo., 1977—. Spl. cons. to White House-Trade Expansion Act, Washington, 1962; chmn. Winnetka Caucus (Ill.), 1971; chmn. Ill. state Dan Walker for Gov., 1972, 76; spl. asst. to Gov. for intergovtl. relations, Ill., 1973-76. Served with U.S. Army, 1942-45; PTO. Mem. Nat. Office Products Assn., Wholesale Stationers' Assn. Clubs: Metropolitan (Chgo.); Pelican Bay (Naples, Fla.). Home: 969 Tower Manor Dr Winnetka IL 60093 also 6075 Pelican Bay Blvd Naples FL 33940 Office: Quartet Mfg Co 7131 N Ridgeway Ave Chicago IL 60645

GREEN, DAVID FERRELL, city official; b. Sioux Falls, S.D., Nov. 13, 1935; s. John C. and Mary A. (Meyer) G.; m. Renata M. Kappenman, Apr. 15, 1961; children—Tobin L., Anthony F., Thomas D. B.A. summa cum laude, Augustana Coll., Sioux Falls, 1980; postgrad. U. S.D., 1981—; grad. FBI Nat. Acad., 1972; Juvenile Officers Inst., 1966. Cert. police officer; cert. police firearms instr. Dispatch dept. mgr. Sioux Falls Argus Leader, S.D., 1954-58; with Sioux Falls Police Dept., 1958—, patrol officer, 1958-63, sgt., 1963-68, lt., 1968-71, capt., 1971-82, chief, 1982—; mem. NCIC Policy Bd. Justice Dept., Washington, 1976-78; mem. NCIC North Central Group, 1978—; vice chmn. Gov.'s Police Task Force S.D., 1979-81. Bd. dirs. Vol. Nat. Ctr. for Citizen Involvement, Washington, 1978-81, St. Therese Sch. Bd., Sioux Falls, pres., 1973-74; pres. Vol. Action Ctr., Sioux Falls, 1979-80. Served with USNR, 1953-61. Recipient J. Edgar Hoover award Justice Dept., 1972; Jaycees Officer Yr. award Sioux Falls Jaycees, 1972; named to Augustana Coll. Honor Soc., 1980. Mem. Fraternal Order of Police (trustee 1971-83, chmn. bd. trustees 1979-83, Outstanding Service award 1983), Am. Soc. Pub. Adminstrs., Internat. Assn. Police Chiefs, S.D. Police Chief's Assn., Tri-State Peace Officers Assn. (v.p. 1972-73), S.D. Peace Officers Assn. Republican. Roman Catholic. Clubs: Flatlander's Muzzle-Loading (Garretson, S.D. pres. 1980-82); Split-Rock Muzzle-Loading (Baltic, S.D.). Lodges: Elks, K.C. Office: Sioux Falls Police Dept 501 N Dakota Ave Sioux Falls SD 57104

GREEN, DAVID THOMAS, evangelist; b. N.Y.C., July 28, 1925; s. David and Sarah Louise (Oldham) G.; m. Arlene L. Cole, Feb. 14, 1983. D.D., God's Bible Sch. and Missionary Tng. Home, Cin., 1949. Evangelist, 1934—; home and fgn. missionary, 1949-64; radio and TV appearances, 1953-56; missionary to Am. Indians, 1954-67; pastoral counselor, Bible instr.; active various evangelistic assns.; locksmith, safe and alarm technician, security cons., 1980—; author, ghost writer, speaker in field. Served with AUS, 1946-47. Mem. Heavenly Host Missionary Baptist Assn., Noah's Ark Missionary Bapt. Assn., Nat. Locksmith Assn.

GREEN, (GEORGE) DALLAS, professional baseball team executive. Pres., gen. mgr. Chgo. Cubs. Office: Chgo Cubs Wrigley Field Clark & Addison Sts Chicago IL 60613*

GREEN, GEORGIA M., linguistics educator, consultant; b. Atlanta, Apr. 16, 1944; d. Lester Victor and Marjorie Mantel (Fishbein) Marks; m. Jerry Morgan; children—Robin, Dylan. A.B., U. Chgo., 1966, A.M., 1969, Ph.D., 1971. Asst. prof. U. Ill., Urbana, 1971-73, assoc. prof., 1973-85, prof., 1985—. Author: Semantics and Syntactic Regularity, 1974. Ctr. for Advanced Study in Behavoral Scis. fellow, 1978-79. Mem. Linguistic Soc. Am. (chmn. com. status of women 1979). Office: Dept Linguistics U Ill 707 S Mathews Urbana IL 61801

GREEN, HAROLD DANIEL, dentist; b. Scranton, Pa., Feb. 4, 1934; s. Harold Charles and Viola Mildred (Brown) G.; m. Cornelia Ann Ellis, Aug. 1, 1959; children—Scott Alan, Mary Ann. B.A., Beloit Coll. (Wis.), 1956; D.D.S., Northwestern U., 1960. Gen. practice dentistry, Beloit, Wis., 1964—; dir. Beloit Savs. Bank. Contbr. articles to profl. jours. Active Wis. div. Am. Cancer Soc., 1964-75; 1st pres., co-organizer Citizen's Council Against Crime, Beloit; past officer, chmn. membership Beloit YMCA; mem. adv. bd. Salvation Army; chmn. adminstrv. bd., chmn. Council of Ministries, First United Methodist Ch., Beloit. Recipient award for creativity in dentistry Johnson & Johnson Co., 1970; 3 citations for Community Service United Givers Fund, 1970-75; Disting. Sevice citation Greater Beloit Assn. Commerce. Fellow Acad. Gen. Dentistry, Internat. Coll. Dentists., Am. Acad. Dental Practice Adminstrn., mem. ADA (chmn. council on dental practice 1982-84), Wis. Dental Assn. (pres. 1979-80, trustee 1968-74), Wis. Dental Assn. Found., Rock County Dental Soc. (pres. 1976), Wis. Council of Professions (bd. dirs. 1974-80, pres. 1973-75), Chgo. Dental Soc., Greater Milw. Dental Assn., Fedn. Dentaire Internationale, Pierre Fauchard Acad., Am. Acad. History of Dentistry, Delta Sigma Delta. Avocations: cycling, golf, basketball, running, fishing. Home: 2207 Collingswood Dr Beloit WI 53511 Office: 419 Pleasant St Beloit WI 53511

GREEN, HARWOOD, quality assurance executive; b. Boston, Feb. 10, 1956; s. Victor J. and Shirley M. Green. B.A., Duke U., 1978; postgrad. bus. adminstrn. program Babson Coll., 1978-80. Quality control technologist New Eng. Nuclear, Billerica, Mass., 1974-77, spl. projects engr. quality assurance, 1978-79, process engring. supr., 1980; tech. rep. Gelman Scis., Ann Arbor, Mich., 1981, sr. tech. cons., 1982, mgr. corp. quality assurance, 1983—. Mem. Am. Mgmt. Assn., Internat. Soc. Pharm. Engrs., Parenteral Drug Assn., Am. Soc. Quality Control. Office: Gelman Scis 600 S Wagner Rd Ann Arbor MI 48106

GREEN, JACK ALLEN, lawyer; b. Detroit, Dec. 15, 1945; s. Martin and Frieda Francis (Freeman) G.; m. Pamela Arlene Stern; children—Marla Elizabeth, Carrie Lynn. B.B.A., U. Mich., 1967, J.D., 1970. Bar: Ohio 1970, Mass. 1984. Assoc. Schwartz & Schwartz, Columbus, Ohio, 1970-72; gen. counsel Prestolite Co., Toledo, 1972-83; v.p. legal Converse Inc., Wilmington, Mass., 1983—. Mem. Ohio State Bar Assn., Mass. Bar Assn., ABA. Avocations: skiing; tennis; running. Home: 6 Tallyho Ln Andover MA 01810 Office: Converse Inc 55 Fordham Rd Wilmington MA 01887

GREEN, JEROME KEITH, manufacturing executive; b. Highland Park, Ill., 1936. B.A., Dartmouth Coll., 1958, M.B.A., 1959; m. Kathy Jane Haefelin, June 26, 1965; children—Keith Edward, Julie Katherine. C.P.A., Ill. Sr. acct. Price Waterhouse & Co., 1960-64; with J.J. Case Co., Inc., Racine, Wis., 1964—, sr. v.p. fin. and corp. planning, 1975, sr. v.p. and gen. mgr. internat., 1975, group v.p. internat., 1975, exec. v.p. internat., 1976-78, pres., chief operating officer, 1978-79, pres., chief exec. officer, dir., 1979—; dir. First Wis. Bank of Racine, Poclain, S.A. Bd. dirs. Racine YMCA. Served with Adj. Gen. Corps, U.S. Army, 1959-60. Mem. Farm and Indsl. Equipment Inst. (dir.). Office: J I Case Co Inc 700 State St Racine WI 53404

GREEN, JERRY HOWARD, banker; b. Kansas City, Mo., June 10, 1930; s. Howard Jay and Selma (Stein) G.; B.A., Yale U., 1952; m. Betsy Bozarth, July 18, 1981. Pres., Union Chevrolet, 1955-69, Union Securities, Inc., Kansas City, Mo., 1969—, Mo. Banc-Mgmt., Inc., Kansas City; chmn. Stadium Bank, Kansas City, 1976—, Budget Rent-A-Car of Mo., Inc., 1961—, Budget Rent-A-Car of Memphis, Inc., Union Nat. Bank of Kansas City, 1983—; chmn., dir. Security Bank & Trust Co., Branson, Mo., 1979—; pres. Douglas County Bancshares, Kansas City, Taney County Bancorp., Kansas City, 1981—, Pembroke Bancshares, Kansas City, Mo., 1983—; chmn., dir. Citizens Bank, Ava, Mo., 1980—; dir. Churchill Records and Video, Inc., Tulsa, Stadium Bank, Kansas City. Bd. dirs. Boys' Clubs Kansas City, Jackson County Pension Plan Com. chmn. Yale Class of 1952 Reunion Gift. Served to 1st lt. USAF, 1952-55. Mem. Am. Bankers Assn., Yale Alumni Assn. (bd. dirs.). Republican. Clubs: Kansas City, Oakwood County, Saddle and Sirloin. Home: 6801 Belinder Mission Hills KS 66208 Office: 8959 East New Hwy 40 Kansas City MO 64129

GREEN, JOYCE, book pub. co. exec.; b. Taylorville, Ill., Oct. 22, 1928; d. Lynn and Vivian Coke (Richardson) Reinerd; A.A., Christian Coll., 1946; B.S., MacMurray Coll., 1948; m. Warren H. Green, Oct. 8, 1960. Asso. editor Warren H. Green, Inc., St. Louis, 1966-78, dir., 1978—; v.p. Visioneering Advt. Agy., 1972—; exec. sec. Affirmative Action Assn. Am., 1977—; pres. InterContinental Industries, Inc., 1980—; asst. to pres. Southeastern U., New Orleans, 1982—. Mem. Am. Soc. Profl. and Exec. Women, Direct Mktg. Club St. Louis, Arch Soc., Sangamon County Hist. Soc., Mo. Hist. Soc., Mo. Bot. Gardens, C. of C. Democrat. Methodist. Clubs: Jr. League, Clayton, Clayton Women's. Home: 12120 Hibler Dr Creve Coeur MO 63141 Office: 8356 Olive Blvd Saint Louis MO 63132

GREEN, MARY AGNES, hotel manager; b. Sullivan, Ind., July 1, 1915; d. Thomas Mann and Lora (Ridgeway) Durham; m. Robert Eugene Green, Oct. 9, 1937; children—Robert Durham, Thomas Eugene. Tchrs. cert. Ind. State Tchrs. Coll., 1934. Tchr. elementary sch., Graysville, Ind., 1934-37; clk. Soil Conservation Office, Sullivan, Ind., 1937-40; sec. and officer mgr. Green Constrn. Co., Oaktown, Ind., 1940-50; hotel mgr. Executive Inn, Vincennes, Ind., 1968—. Home: 604 State Rd 67 Vincennes IN 47591 Office: Executive Inn 1 Executive Blvd Vincennes IN 47591

GREEN, RALPH EMIL, trust company executive; b. Belleville, Ill., Feb. 20, 1923; s. John Fred and Edna Ida (Werner) G.; m. Elizabeth June Edmiston, Aug. 24, 1954; children—Ralph E., Elizabeth S. A.B., Washington U., St. Louis, 1949, J.D., 1950. Bar: Ill. 1951, U.S. Dist. Ct. (ea. dist.) Ill. 1953. Assoc. Strubinger, Tudor, Tombrink & Wion, St. Louis, 1952, Baker, Kagy & Wagner, East St. Louis, Ill., 1952-56; asst. trust officer to sr. v.p. Ill. State Trust Co., Belleville, 1956—. Served with U.S. Army, 1943-45. Decorated Purple Heart. Mem. VFW, DAV. Lodges: Masons, Elks. Home: 8 Country Club Pl Belleville IL 62223 Office: 222 E Main St PO Box 523 Belleville IL 62222

GREEN, RAYMOND ARTHUR, county official; b. Gary, Ind., Aug. 18, 1944; s. Harold and Clara (Taylor) G.; m. Lucile McConnell, June 18, 1971; children—Caleb, Adam. B.A. in Indsl. Engring., Ind. State U.-Terre Haute, 1966; B.A., U. Chgo.; postgrad. in law Cornell U. Engr., United Cons. Engrs., Indpls., 1979-81; asst. engr. Lake County Commr., 1981-85; chief dep. recorder County of Lake, Crown Point, Ind., 1985—; owner, trainer U.S. Trotting Assn., Columbus, Ohio. Democrat. Home: 1400 E 49th Ave Gary IN 46409 Office: Lake County Recorder 2293 N Main St Crown Point IN 46307

GREEN, RUTH MILTON, college administrator; b. Sioux City, Iowa, Feb. 29, 1924; d. John and Myrtle Alma (Phipps) Milton; student Morningside Coll., 1943-45; m. Robert Wood Green, Dec. 31, 1943; children—Robert William, Sandra Lou Green Montignani. Registrar, East High Sch., Sioux City, Iowa, 1943; acct. Buehler Bros., Iowa City, 1947-49; asst. dir. tchr. placement Morningside Coll., Sioux City, 1951-55, mem. staff registrar's office, 1960-65, asst. to registrar, 1965-70, dir. spl. project funding, 1971-81, dir. Title III Strengthening Devel. Institutions program, 1975-84; v.p. instl. research, planning and spl. projects, 1984—. Pres., First Congregational Ch., Sioux City, 1980; bd. dirs. Siouxland Mental Health Agy. Mem. Nat. Council Univ. Research Adminstrs., Nat. Assn. Title Three Adminstrs., Nat. Council Univ. Bus. Officers, LWV, Am. Assn. Higher Edn., Council Advancement and Support of Edn., World Future Soc. Democrat. Home: 3801 6th Ave Sioux City IA 51106 Office: Morningside Coll 1501 Morningside Ave Sioux City IA 51106

GREEN, RUTH NELDA (CUMMINGS), educator; b. Greenway, Ark., Aug. 25, 1928; d. William Harrison and Opal Lee (Davis) G.; B.S. in Edn., U. Omaha (now U. Nebr., Omaha), 1966, postgrad.; m. Robert C. Green, Jr., Apr. 22, 1951 (dec.); children—Dana Lynn Green Schrad, Lisa Jane Green Noon. Tchr., Public Schs. Greenway, 1948-51, Hancock County (Miss.), 1951-53, Bellevue (Nebr.), 1961—. Bd. govs. edn. com. Fontenelle Forest Nature Center. NSF scholar, 1968-73. Mem. Greater Nebr. Assn. Tchrs. of Sci. (v.p. 1984, pres. 1985), NEA, Nebr. Wildlife Assn., Nat. Audubon Soc. (Edn. award 1975), Omaha Audubon Soc., Bellevue Edn. Assn., Nebr. Edn. Assn., Inland Bird Banding Assn., Am. Birding Assn., Nebr. Ornithologists Union (state pres. 1984, state v.p. 1984—, bd. dirs.), Alpha Delta Kappa. Mem. Ch. of Christ. Columnist for Audubon Soc. Omaha Newsletter, Nebr. Ornithologists Union Newsletter. Home: 506 W 31st Ave Bellevue NE 68005 Office: 700 Galvin Rd Bellevue NE 68005

GREEN, THEOPHILUS EVANS, psychologist; b. Chgo., Sept. 2, 1945; s. William DeWitt and Naomi (Harper) G. B.S., Northwestern U., 1975; M.S. in Mktg. Communications, Roosevelt U., 1977; Psy.D., Ill. Sch. Psychology, 1982. Registered psychologist, Ill. Asst. editor Ebony and Jet mags., Chgo., 1970-73; pub. relations liaison Inst. Urban Life, Chgo., 1970-73; account exec. Ill. Bell Telephone Co., Chgo., 1977-78; sales mgr. Exxon Co., Chgo., 1978-79; with Edgewater-Uptown Community Mental Health Ctr., Chgo., 1976-77; psychology intern Forest Hosp., Des Plaines, Ill., 1980-81; staff cons. Ebony Mgmt. Assocs., Chgo., 1980-81; outpatient therapist Seven Springs, Des Plaines, Ill. 1981-82; clin. dir. Assoc. Psychol. Services, Chgo., 1982—; cons., tchr., speaker in field. Contbr. articles to profl. publs. Bd. dirs. Network for Youth Services. Served with USAF, 1965-68. Mem. Mental Health Assn. Greater Chgo., Am. Psychol. Assn., Chgo. Psychol. Assn., Assn. Black Psychologists, Ill. Group Psychotherapy Soc. Home: 4742 N Kenmore Ave 2d Floor Chicago IL 60604 Office: 53 W Jackson St Suite 1621 Chicago IL 60640

GREEN, WARREN HAROLD, publisher; b. Auburn, Ill., July 25, 1915; s. John Anderson Logan and Clara Christina (Wortman) G.; student Presbyn. Theol. Sem., 1933-34, Ill. Wesleyan U., 1934-36; B.M., Southwestern Conservatory, Dallas, 1938; M.M., St. Louis Conservatory, 1940, Ph.D., 1942; H.L.D., Southeastern U., New Orleans, 1981; L.L.D., Institut de Droit Practique, Limoges, France, 1983; Litt.D., Confederation Europeene de L'Ordre Judiciaire, France; D.D., Calif. Theol. Sem.; m. Joyce Reinerd, Oct. 8, 1960. Prof. voice, composition and aural theory St. Louis Conservatory, 1938-44; program dir. USO, Highland Park, Ill., Brownwood and Orange, Tex., Waukegan, Ill., 1944-46; community service specialist Rotary Internat., Chgo., 1946-47; editor in chief Charles C. Thomas, Pub., Springfield, Ill., 1947-66; pub., pres. Warren H. Green, Inc., St. Louis, 1966—; sec. John R. Davis Assos., Chgo., 1955—; exec. v.p. Visioneering Advt., St. Louis, 1966—; mng. dir. Publishers Service Center, St. Louis and Longview, Tex., 1967—; exec. dir. Affirmative Action Register, 1974—; pres. InterContinental Industries, Inc., 1976—, Southwestern Univ., New Orleans, 1982-83; cons. U.S. and European pubs., profl. socs.; lectr. med. pub. and Civil War. Mem. Mayor's Com. on Water Safety; mem. Met. St. Louis Art Mus., Mo. Bot. Gardens. Recipient Presdl. citation outstanding contbn. export expansion program U.S., 1973, awards AMA, Internat. Acad. Preventive Medicine. Mem. Civil War Round Table (v.p. 1969—), Am. Acad. Criminology, Am. Acad. Polit. and Social Sci., Am. Med. Pubs. Assn., Am. Judicature Soc., Am. Soc. Personnel Adminstrn., Direct Mktg. Club St. Louis, Great Plains Hist. Soc., Co. Mil. Historians, Am. Soc. Personnel Adminstrn., University City C. of C. (pres. 1979—). Clubs: Mo. Athletic, World Trade, Elks (St. Louis), Clayton, Media. Contbr. articles and books on Civil War history, writing and editing to profl. jours. Home: 12120 Hibler Dr Creve Coeur MO 63141 Office: 8356 Olive Blvd Saint Louis MO 63132

GREENBERG, DAVID BERNARD, engineering educator; b. Norfolk, Va., Nov. 2, 1928; s. Abraham David and Ida (Frenkil) G.; m. Helen Muriel Levine, Aug. 15, 1959 (div. Aug. 1980); children—Lisa, Jan, Jill. B.S. in Chem. Engrng., Carnegie Inst. Tech., 1952; M.S. in Chem. Engring., Johns Hopkins U., 1959; Ph.D., La. State U., 1964. Registered profl. engr., La. Process engr. U.S. Indsl. Chem. Co., Balt., 1952-55; project engr. FMC Corp., Balt., 1955-56; asst. prof. U.S. Naval Acad., Annapolis, Md., 1958-61; instr., asst. prof., assoc. prof., prof. La. State U., Baton Rouge, 1961-74; prof. chem. and nuclear engrng. U. Cin., 1974—, head dept., 1974-81; cons. Chem. Systems Lab., Dept. Army, Edgewood, Md., 1981-83, Burk & Assocs., New Orleans, 1970-78; program dir. engrng. div. NSF, Washington, 1972-73. Mem. Cin. Mayor's Energy Task Force, 1981—. Served to lt. USNR, 1947-52. ESSO research fellow, 1964-65, NSF, 1961. Fellow Am. Soc. for Laser Medicine and Surgery; mem. Am. Inst. Chem. Engrs., Am. Chem. Soc., Am. Soc. for Engring. Edn., Tau Beta Pi, Sigma Xi, Phi Lambda Upsilon. Jewish. Contbr. numerous articles on chem. engrng. to profl. jours. Home: 8591 Wyoming Club Dr Cincinnati OH 45215 Office: PO Box 21068 Cincinnati OH 45221

GREENBERG, EVA MUELLER, librarian; b. Vienna, Austria, July 19, 1929; came to U.S., 1939; d. Paul and Greta (Scheuer) Mueller; m. Nathan Abraham Greenberg, June 22, 1952; children—David Stephen, Judith Helen, Lisa Pauline. A.B., Harvard/Radcliffe Coll., 1951; M.L.S., Kent State U., 1975. Head reference McIntire Library, Zanesville, Ohio, 1978; with Lorain Pub. Library, Ohio, 1978-81; head reference Elyria Pub. Library, Ohio, 1981-82; reference librarian adult services Cuyahoga County Pub. Library, Strongsville, Ohio, 1983—. Contbr. articles to profl. jours. Mem. ALA, Ohio Library Assn. (coordinator community info. task force). Home: 34 S Cedar St Oberlin OH 44074 Office: Cuyahoga Public Library 13213 Pearl Rd Strongsville OH 44136

GREENBERG, MARTIN JAY, lawyer, educator, author; b. Milw., Aug. 5, 1945; s. Sol and Phyllis (Schunder) G.; m. Beverly L. Young, Apr. 29, 1969; children—Kari, Steven. B.S., U. Wis., 1967; J.D., Marquette U., 1971. Bar: Wis. 1971. Assoc. Hoyt, Greene & Meissner, Milw., 1971-74, Weiss, Steuer, Berzowski & Kriger, Milw., 1974-76; ptnr. Greenberg & Boxer, Milw., 1976-78; sole practice, Milw., 1978—; asst. prof. law Marquette U., Milw., 1976-79, adj. prof., 1979—; bd. dirs., pres. Law Projects, Inc.; mem. book revisions com. Wis. Real Estate Examining Bd., 1978—. Mem. brotherhood bd. Congregation Emanu-El B'ne Jeshurun, Milw., 1976-78, treas., 1979—; bd. dirs. Community Coordinated Child Care, Milw., 1976-77; mem. Shorewood (Wis.) Bd. Rev., 1977-81. Served with Wis. N.G., 1968-74. Morris Guten Vets. scholar, 1965; I.E. Goldberg scholar, 1966; Carnegie grantee, 1966; Wis. Student Assn. scholar, 1967; Thomas More scholar, 1969; Francis X. Swietlik scholar, 1971. Mem. ABA, Wis. Bar Assn., Milw. Bar Assn., Wis. Bar Found. (lectr. Project Inquiry 1980-81, Lawyer's Pro Bono Publico award 1978), Marquette U. Law Alumni Assn. (trustee), Jewish Vocat. Service (corp.), Woolsack Soc., Scribes, Tau Epsilon Rho (chancellor grad. chpt. 1972-73). Lodge: Masons. Author: Real Estate Practice, 1976, rev. edit., 1977; Wisconsin Real Estate, 1982; Mortgages and Real Estate Financing, 1982; editor Marquette Law Rev., 1969-71. Home: 9429 N Broadmoor Bayside WI 53217 Office: 1139 E Knapp St Milwaukee WI 53202

GREENBERG, MICHAEL ALAN, dermatologist; b. Chgo., Feb. 6, 1949; s. Max S. and Helen (Friedman) G.; m. Geri Ileen Pelunis, Apr. 16, 1970; children—Renee Michelle, Heidi Joy. A.B. in Biology, Case-Western Res. U., 1970; M.D., U. Ill.-Chgo., 1974. Diplomate Am. Bd. Dermatology. Intern, Luth. Gen. Hosp., Park Ridge, Ill., 1974-75; resident U. Ill. Hosp., Chgo., 1975-78; pres. Michael Greenberg, M.D., Ltd., Elk Grove Village, Ill., 1978—; bd. dirs. Alexian Bros. Ill., Elk Grove Village, 1984—. Contbr. chpt. to book: Adolescent Dermatology, 1978. Contbr. articles to profl. publs. Trustee Gus Giordano's Jazz Dance Chgo. Fellow Am. Acad. Dermatology, Am. Coll. Cryosurgery, Am. Acad. Skin Cancer (hon.); mem. AMA, Ill. State Med. Soc., Chgo. Med. Soc., Chgo. Dermatology Soc., Ill. Alumni Assn. (life mem.). Jewish. Clubs: Tower of Cornell U. (Ithaca, N.Y.). Avocations: classic ballet, jazz dance, collecting illuminated manuscripts and modern works of art. Office: Michael A Greenberg MD Ltd 850 Biesterfield Rd Elk Grove Village IL 60007

GREENBERG, NAT, See *Who's Who in America,* 43rd edition.

GREENBERG, PAUL, publishing company executive; b. Indpls., Aug. 4, 1921; s. Louis and Ida (Schwartz) G.; B.S., Purdue U., 1949; m. Janet Sussman, May 5, 1957; children—Beth, Amy. Research and devel. engr. Reilly Tar & Chem. Co., Indpls., 1949-51; with RCA, Indpls., 1951-75, gen. plant mgr., 1970-73, ops. mgr., 1973-75; dir. quality control Revlon, Inc., N.Y.C., 1958-59. group dir. ops. ITT Publ. Co., Indpls., 1976—. Served with USAF, 1942-46. Office: 4300 62d St W Indianapolis IN 46268*

GREENBLATT, DEANA CHARLENE, educator; b. Chgo., Mar. 13, 1948; d. Walter and Betty (Lamasky) Beisel; B.S. in Edn., Chgo. State U., 1969; M.A. in Guidance and Counseling, Roosevelt U., 1973; m. Mark Greenblatt, June 22, 1975. Tchr., counselor Chgo. Pub. Schs., 1969-75, City Colls. of Chgo. GED-TV, 1976; tchr. Columbus (Ohio) Pub. Schs., 1976—; participant learning exchange, Chgo. Active B'nai B'rith; vol. Right-to-Read, Columbus; mem. Community Learning Exchange, Columbus. Certified tchr. K-9, Ill., Ohio; certified personnel guidance, Ill., Ohio; certified Chgo. Bd. Edn. Mem. Am. Personnel and Guidance Assn. Democrat. Club: B'nai B'rith Women (chpt. v.p., co-chmn. Mothers Day flower sale). Home: 4083 Vineshire Dr Columbus OH 43227

GREENBLATT, MARK LEO, urban planner, lawyer; b. New Brighton, Pa., Mar. 9, 1947; s. Harry Abraham and Edna Bess (Rosenberg) G.; m. Deana Charlene Beisel, June 22, 1975. B.A., Mich. State U., 1968, postgrad., 1968-69; M.City Planning, U. Pa., 1971; J.D., Capital U., 1985. Asst. acct. Harry A. Greenblatt, New Brighton, Pa., 1971-72; planner Village of Arlington Heights (Ill.) Planning Dept., 1972-75; planner Allen L. Kracower & Asso., Des Plaines, Ill., 1975-76; planner Mid-Ohio Regional Planning Commn., Columbus, 1976-84. Served with U.S. Army, 1971, capt. Res. Richard King Mellon fellow, 1968-69. Mem. ABA, Am. Inst. Cert. Planners, Am. Planning Assn., Ohio Planning Conf. Jewish. Club: B'nai B'rith. Home: 4083 Vineshire Dr Columbus OH 43227

GREENBLATT, RUSSELL EDWARD, lawyer, consultant; b. Chgo., Jan. 7, 1952; s. Abraham Abel Greenblatt and Freda (Katz) Leader. B.S., Ind. U., 1973; J.D., Northwestern U., 1978. Bar: Ill. 1978, Calif. 1983, U.S. Dist. Ct. (no. dist.) Ill. 1979. Acct., Arthur Andersen & Co., Atlanta, 1973-75; atty.-advisor Office of Chief Counsel, IRS, Washington, 1978-80; cons. Russell E. Greenblatt Cons. Co., Newport Beach, Calif. and Chgo., 1982—; ptnr. Katten, Muchin, Zavis, Pearl & Galler, Chgo., 1980—; speaker fed. taxation NYU Inst., N.Y.C., 1982, U.S.C. Fed. Tax Inst., Los Angeles, 1984, 85; witness Ways and Means Com., U.S. Ho. Reps., Washington, 1984. Contbr. articles to profl. jours. Mem. ABA (sect. taxation), Ill. State Bar Assn. (sect. taxation). Office: Katten Muchin Zavis Pearl & Galler 525 W Monroe St Suite 1600 Chicago IL 60606

GREENE, ALLAN, association executive; b. N.Y.C., Sept. 5, 1944; s. George J. and Mildred G.; m. Sharon Linda Davis, Oct. 21, 1973; children—Brenda, Douglas. B.A., Queens Coll., 1965; M.S.W., Yeshiva U., 1967. Staff assoc. Assoc. YM-YWHAs of Greater N.Y., 1972-77; exec. dir. Jewish Community Ctr. of Palm Beaches, 1977-78; dir. planning and budgeting Jewish Fedn. of Omaha, 1978-82, exec. v.p., 1982—. Bd. dirs. Emmy Guiford Children's Theatre, Nebr. Jewish Hist. Soc. Mem. Jewish Community Orgn. Personnel Assn. Jewish. Lodge: Rotary. Office: 333 S 132d St Omaha NE 68154

GREENE, CHRISTOPHER LEE, construction company executive, estimator; b. Milw., Mar. 11, 1959; s. Lyle W. Greene; m. Maureen Therese Morrisey, Oct. 16, 1982; 1 son, Ryan Christopher. Student indsl. arts U. Wis.-Stout, 1977-78; student engrng. U. Wis.-Milw., 1978-80. Foreman Endurall Products, Glendale, Wis., 1977-80; ptnr., gen. mgr. L&R Builders, Milw., 1980-83; v.p. gen. mgmt. Lakeland Contractors, Glendale, 1983—. Patentee elec. toggle switch. Mem. Nat. Home Improvement Council, Assoc. Gen. Contractors. Roman Catholic. Avocations: raquetball; weightlifting; bicycling; children. Office: Lakeland Contractors 6748 N Sidney Pl Milwaukee WI 43209

GREENE, DARYLE EUGENE, animal nutritionist, feed company research executive; b. Garfield, Ark. June 27, 1932; s. Howard Lester and Mildred Louise (Patton) G.; m. Peggy Ann Patterson, June 6, 1954; children—Stephen, Teresa, Lisa, Janet. B.S.A., U. Ark., 1954, M.S., 1955; Ph.D., U. Ill., 1960. Mgr. turkey research Ralston Purina Co., St. Louis, 1960-64, dir. poultry research, 1966-75, dir. Chow research, 1975-83, v.p. Chow research, 1983—; assoc. prof. U. Ark., Fayetteville, 1964-65. Served to 1st lt. U.S. Army, 1955-57. Mem. Poultry Sci. Assn. (bd. dirs. 1970-72). World Poultry Sci. Assn., Am. Soc. Animal Sci. Methodist. Avocations: fishing; boating. Office: Ralston Purina Co Checkerboard Sq Saint Louis MO 63164

GREENE, ELLIN, library service educator; b. Elizabeth, N.J., Sept. 18, 1927; d. Charles M. and Dorothea (Hooton) Peterson. A.B., Rutgers U., 1953, M.L.S., 1957, Ed.D., 1979. Children's librarian Free Pub. Library, Elizabeth, 1953-57, specialist in group work with children, 1957-59; asst. group work specialist N.Y. Pub. Library, N.Y.C., 1959-64, supervising children's librarian, Bronx, 1964, asst. coordinator children's services, 1965-67; mem. adj. faculty Rutgers U. Grad. Sch. Library and Info. Studies, New Brunswick, N.J., 1968-79; vis. prof. Nat. Coll. Edn.-McGaw Grad. Sch., Chgo., 1976-77; dean students U. Chgo. Grad. Library Sch., 1980-82, 82—, assoc. prof., 1980-85; cons. library services to children, 1985—; vis. prof. U. Ill. Grad. Sch. Library and Info. Sci., 1979; mem. adv. com. N.Y. Pub. Library Early Childhood Resource & Info. Ctr., 1982—. Author: Recordings for Children, 1964; Stories; A List of Stories to Tell and to Read Aloud, 1965; Films for Children, 1966; (with Augusta Baker) Storytelling: Art and Technique, 1977; (with Madalynne Schoenfeld) A Multimedia Approach to Children's Literature, 1977. Co-author, contbr. to numerous ednl. books and profl. jours. Mem. nat. editorial bd. Arrow Book Club, 1975-85; adv. com. Bull. of Ctr. for Children's Books, 1980-85; editorial bd. The Library Quar., 1980-85; editorial council The Nat. Storytelling Jour., 1983—. Books for children include: The Pumpkin Giant, 1970; Princess Rosetta and the Popcorn Man, 1971; The Rat-Catcher's Daughter: A Collection of Stories by Laurence Housman, 1974; Clever Cooks, 1973, 1977; Midsummer Magic, 1977. Mem. ALA, Assn. Library Service to Children, Authors Guild Inc., Children's Lit. Assn., Friends of Internat. Bd. on Books for Young People, Internat. Research Soc. for Children's Lit., Nat. Assn. for the Preservation and Perpetuation of Storytelling, Nat. Council Tchrs. English, Rutgers Adv. Council on Children's Lit. Home and Office: 113 Chatham Ln Point Pleasant NJ 08742

GREENE, HARVEY MITCHELL, lawyer; b. Shelburn, Ind., Jan. 25, 1927; s. Guy Benton and Arslee (Mitchell) G.; student Butler U., 1947-49; LL.B., Ind. U. at Indpls., 1954; m. Charlotte Elizabeth Shook, Dec. 25, 1946 (dec. Nov. 1979); children—Cheryl Greene Palmer, Guy Frederick, Cynthia Diane Greene Dicken, Carole Dawn; m. 2d, Theda L. Poole, Oct. 25, 1980. Admitted to Ind. bar, 1954; ordained to ministry Primitive Bapt. Ch., 1959; dep. prosecutor Dearborn County, Ind., 1965-66; city atty., Aurora, Ind., 1960-63, 68-71; county atty. Dearborn County, 1977-80. Pres., Aurora High Sch. Booster's Club, 1964-70. Bd. dirs. Dearborn and Ohio Counties Humane Soc., 1971-72. Served with USAAF, 1945-47. Mem. Am. Bar Assn., Dearborn and Ohio Counties Bar Assn. (pres. 1961), Assn. Trial Lawyers Am. Club: Rotary (past pres.). Home: 110 Dawn Dr Aurora IN 47001 Office: 437 2d St Aurora IN 47001

GREENE, JAMES ALDEN, research director, consultant; b. Wilmington, Ohio, May 18, 1942; s. Robert Coate and Virginia Mae (Gray) G.; m. Barbara Carole Huse, Nov. 28, 1941; children—Heather Anastacia, Vanessa Oriana. B.S. in Chemistry, U. Cin., 1968, M.S. in Environ. Health, 1972. Chemist, Andrew Jergens Co., Cin., 1963-71, C.M. Bundy Co., Cin., 1971-72, Eli Lilly & Co. (Elizabeth Arden), Indpls., 1972-78; mgr. presonal care research and devel. Amway Corp., Ada, Mich., 1978-83; dir. research and devel. Vipont Labs., Inc., Ft. Collins, Colo., 1983—. Mem. Royal Soc. Health, AAAS, Ohio Acad. Sci., N.Y. Acad. Scis., Soc. Cosmetic Chemists, Am. Chem. Soc. Episcopalian. Patentee field of aqueous polymer nail coatings.

GREENE, JEFFERY DATE, sales engineer; b. Evanston, Ill., Sept. 26, 1953; s. Gordon Date and Jolene Harvey (Nelson) G.; B.A., U. Wyo., 1975. Purchasing agt. Butler Paper Co., Denver, 1975-77, sales rep., 1978-79; sr. sales rep. Johns Mansville Corp., Seattle, 1979-84, asst. dist. sales mgr., Oak Brook, Ill., 1984—. Mem. ASHRAE, Sigma Chi. Republican. Home: 15-085 Spring Rd #2C Oakbrook Terrace IL 60126 Office: Manville Corp 2222 Kensington Ct Oakbrook IL 60521

GREENE, MARY SNIDER, computer specialist; b. Memphis, Nov. 11, 1929; d. Luther Lonnie and Carolyn Gardner (Peterson) Snider; m. Fredericke Marshall Greene, Nov., 1959 (div.); 1 dau., Jeanie Carolyn Mercer. A.A., U. Md., 1975; B.S., SUNY, 1984. Cert. data processor. Computer programmer Dept. Army, Washington, 1959-61; comml. pilot flight instr., mgr. Giles County Mcpl. Airport, Pulaski, Tenn., 1961-64; computer specialist, Dept. Army Redstone (Ala.) Arsenal, 1964-69, Zweibruecken, Germany, 1969-75; with Acad. Computer Facility, U.S. Army Adminstrn. Ctr., 1975-79; dir. U.S. Army Info. Systems Command and info. mgmt. U.S. Army Soldier Support Ctr., Ft. Harrison, Ind., 1979-85; dir. U.S. Army Info. Systems Command, Ft. Harrison, 1985—. Recipient Dept. Army comdrs. award for civilian service, 1982. Mem. Federally Employed Women, Assn. Women in Computing. Presbyterian. Club: Sertoma. Office: US Army Soldier Support Center Dir Info Management Ft Harrison IN 46216

GREENE, ROBERT BERNARD, JR., journalist; b. Columbus, Ohio, Mar. 10, 1947; s. Robert Bernard and Phyllis Ann (Harmon) G.; m. Susan Bonnet Koebel, Feb. 13, 1971. B.J., Northwestern U., 1969. Reporter, Chgo. Sun-Times, 1969-71, columnist, 1971-78; syndicated columnist Field Newspaper Syndicate, 1976-78; columnist Chgo. Tribune, 1978—; contbg. editor Esquire mag., from 1980; commentator CBS TV and radio. Recipient award for best newspaper column in Ill., AP, 1975; award for best sustaining feature in Chgo., Chgo. Newspaper Guild, 1976; Nat. Headliner award for best newspaper column in U.S., 1977. Author: We Didn't Have None of Them Fat Funky Angels on the Wall of Heartbreak Hotel, 1971; Running: A Nixon-McGovern Campaign Journal, 1973; Billion Dollar Baby, 1974; Johnny Deadline, Reporter: The Best of Bob Greene, 1976; (with Paul Galloway) Bagtime, 1977; American Beat, 1983. Office: Chicago Tribune 435 N Michigan Ave Chicago IL 60611*

GREENFIELD, SEYMOUR, microbiologist, researcher; b. N.Y.C., Jan. 18, 1933; s. Harry and Rose (Arnstein) G.; m. Eudice Rachel Estreicher, Dec. 30, 1962; children—Jonathan Isaac, Chaviva Beth, Naftali Tzvi. B.A., Yeshiva U., 1955; M.A., Brandeis U., 1959; postgrad. Western Res. U., 1959-63; Ph.D., Pa. State U., 1970. Research asst. Case Western Res. U., Cleve., 1963-67; sr. biochemist, microbiologist New Eng. Nuclear Corp., Boston, 1970-77; biochemist, project mgr. Abbott Labs., North Chicago, Ill., 1977—. contbr. articles to profl. jours. NIH fellow, 1968. Mem. Am. Soc. Microbiology. Office: Abbott Labs Abbott Park North Chicago IL 60064

GREENGRASS, MARTIN JOSEPH, clinical psychologist; b. N.Y.C., Nov. 8, 1948; s. Isidore and Freda (Warszawska) G.; m. Judith Prizer, Oct. 28, 1973, children—Sara, Rachel. B.A., Brandeis U., 1970; M.A., U. Conn., 1974, Ph.D., 1976. Lic. clin. psychologist, Ind. Clin. psychologist Conn. Correctional Facility, Somers, 1976-77; chmn. dept. of psychology St. Francis Coll., Ft. Wayne, Ind., 1977-79; psychologist Park Center, Inc., 1979—; cons. mcpl. govt.; neuropsychology cons. Co-founder Alzheimers group, Ft. Wayne. NIMH fellow U. Conn., 1970. Mem. Am. Psychol. Assn., Ind. Psychol. Assn. (membership chmn. Div. II), Assn. of Children of Holocaust Survivors. Democrat. Jewish. Home: 5613 Albany Ct Fort Wayne IN 46815 Office: Park Center 909 E State Blvd Fort Wayne IN 46805

GREENLEE, THOMAS WRIGHT, chemist; b. Dayton, Ohio, Mar. 13, 1932; s. John McKinley and Lucia Walker (Wright) G.; m. Joanne Emidy, Oct. 10, 1964; children—Patrick, Kevin, Joel. A.B., U. Chgo., 1953; A.B., Northwestern U., 1955; Ph.D., Stanford U., 1959. Assoc. physicist and assoc. chemist Armour Research Found., Chgo., 1959-60; devel. chemist Aerojet-Gen. Corp., Sacramento, 1960-65, Dow Corning Corp., Midland, Mich., 1966-71; Angestellter in der Tatigkeit eines Studienrats, Schulbehorde der Freien Hansestadt, Bremen, W.Ger., 1971-73; sr. chemist Tremco Inc., Cleve., 1973—. Levehulme vis. fellow Trinity Coll., 1965-66. Mem. Am. Chem. Soc., AAAS, Phi Lambda Upsilon. Anglican Catholic. Lodge: Order of Scottish Clans. Patentee in field. Office: 10701 Shaker Blvd Cleveland OH 44104

GREENQUIST, ALFRED C., chemical company executive; b. Boston, June 4, 1944; s. Alfred N. and Lillian Elizabeth (Cedar) G.; m. Janet Irene Santos, Aug. 17, 1968; children—Jennifer Ann, Thomas Alfred. B.S., U. Mass., 1966; Ph.D., U. Del., 1971. Research fellow Harvard Med. Sch., Boston, 1970-72; assoc. research scientist U. Calif.-San Francisco, 1972-78; research scientist Ames div. Miles Labs., Elkart, Ind., 1979, supr., 1982-84, mgr., 1984—. Contbr. articles to profl. jours. Patentee in field. Damon Runyon fellow 1971. Mem. Am. Soc. Hematology, Am. Chem. Soc., Am. Assn. Clin. Chemistry, AAAS. Avocations: photography; tennis; cross country skiing; racquetball. Office: Miles Labs Ames Div 1127 Myrtle St Elkhart IN 46515

GREENSPAN, PETER BOGACH, physician; b. Bklyn., Sept. 12, 1954; s. Reynold Solomon and Lenore (Bogach) G.; divorced; children—David Benjamin, Aliya Rebecca. B.A., U. Mo., 1975; D.O., Chgo. Coll. Osteo. Medicine, 1980. Fellow osteo. medicine Chgo. Osteo. Med. Ctr., 1977-80, intern, 1980-81; resident ob-gyn Truman Med. Ctr., Kansas City, Mo., 1981-84, chief resident dept. ob-gyn, 1984-85; practice medicine specializing in ob-gyn, Independence, Mo., 1985—; docent dept. ob-gyn U. Mo.-Kansas City Sch. Medicine. Mem. Am. Coll. Obstetricians and Gynecologists. Jewish. Avocations: photography; coin collecting; antique medical books. Office: Hausheer Braby and Assocs 1515 W Truman Rd Suite 306 Independence MO 64050

GREENWOOD, RUSSELL LEE, electrical company executive; b. Peoria, Ill., Aug. 29, 1945; s. Lester Carl and Maxine Virginia (Wood) G.; m. June Audry Augnsinger, Dec. 3, 1984; children—Carl, Angela, Paulette, Loretta. Degree in Bus. magna cum laude, Ill. Central Coll., 1970. Prodn. control supr. Westinghouse, Peoria, Ill., 1964-70; material control mgr. Kiefer Electric, 1970-80; corp. ops. mgr. Kirby Risk, Lafayette, Ind., 1980-83; exec. v.p., gen. mgr. Interstate Electric Supply, Racine, Wis., 1983—. Mem. Internat. Material Mgrs. Soc., Adminstrv. Mgmt. Soc., Electric League of Milw., Nat. Assn. Elec. Distbrs. Republican. Methodist. Avocations: boating; golf; fishing; reading. Home: 6613 Green Ridge Racine WI 53406 Office: Interstate Electric Supply 2601 Lathrop Ave Racine WI 53405

GREENWOOD, SYLVIA RUTH, educator; b. Detroit, July 10, 1951; d. Lawson Cullen and Annie Alfreada (Smith) G. B.S., Central State U., 1973; postgrad. Wayne State U., 1977-79. Tchr., Detroit Bd. Edn., 1974—; producer Vol. Devel. of Youth Talent, Detroit, 1975—; mezzo soprano Brazeal Dennard Chorale, 1985—. Choir dir. Youth Second Grace Ch., Detroit, 1977-85, Broadstreet Presbyn. Ch., Detroit, 1985—. Named Outstanding Tchr. in Area D, Detroit Pub. Schs., 1985. Democrat. Methodist. Avocation: sewing.

GREER, JERRY LEE, college counselor; b. Sedalia, Mo., Oct. 19, 1938; s. Leonard L. and Mattie Ellen (Barnes) G.; m. Sylvia Kay Richardson, Aug. 2, 1959; children—Gay Lea Greer Wilson, Joy Beth. B.S. in Edn., Central Mo. State U., 1960; M.S., U. Ill., 1963. Cert. sch. psychol. examiner, Mo. Bus. tchr. Mehlville Sr. High Sch., St. Louis, 1960-62; counselor Raytown South Jr. High Sch., Mo., 1963-69; counselor State Fair Community Coll., Sedalia, 1969—. Pres. Pettis County R-XII Sch. Bd., Dresden, Mo., 1974-84; rep. committeeman Pettis County, 1978—; treas. Virginia Moore for Senate, Dist. 21, 1984; bd. dirs. Sedalia United Way, 1976. Mem. Mo. Assn. Community and Jr. Colls., Mo. Coll. Personnel Assn., Post Secondary Central Mo. Guidance Assn. (v.p. 1984), State Fair Community Coll. Faculty Assn. (sec.-treas. 1982), Republican. Methodist. Club: Choral Music Soc. (v.p. 1980-81). Avocations: jewelry making; fishing. Home: 90 Gottschalk Rd Sedalia MO 65301 Office: State Fair Community Coll 1900 Clarendon Rd Sedalia MO 65301

GREER-LARUE, CHERYL ANN, human resources executive; b. Harlan, Iowa, June 13, 1958; d. Merle E. Greer and Irene A. Greer Schmitz. B.A. in Bus. Adminstrn., U. N. Iowa, 1979; postgrad. in bus. Coll. St. Thomas. Sales adminstr. Investment Rarities, Minn., 1979-80; personnel mgr. Motherwell Controls, Minn., 1980-82; mgr. human resources Digigraphic Systems, Minn., 1982—. Mem. Twin City Personnel Assn., Twin West Chamber. Office: Digigraphic Systems 10273 Yellow Circle Dr Minnetonka MN 55343

GREGERSON, DALE SANNES, immunologist, educator; b. Seattle, May 10, 1949; s. William Arthur and Mildred Elaine (Sannes) G.; m. Claudette Kay Northway, Dec. 21, 1970 (div. Dec. 29, 1975); children—Marc Sannes, Brook Alexander. m. Eileen Frances Fogg, Sept. 1, 1976. B.A. in Biology, Luther Coll., 1971; Ph.D. in Immunology, U. B.C., Can., 1976. Postdoctoral trainee Yale U., 1976-78, asst. prof., 1978-83; asst. prof. U. Minn., Mpls., 1983—. Contbr. articles to profl. jours. James S. Adams research scholar 1983; NIH grantee, 1979—. Mem. AAAS, Assn. for Research in Vision and Ophthalmology. Democrat. Home: 228 Vincent Ave N Minneapolis MN 55405 Office: Dept Ophthalmology Univ Minnesota 516 Delaware St SE Minneapolis MN 55455

GREGG, ALVIS FORREST, profl. professional coach; b. Birthright, Tex., Oct. 18, 1933; B.S. in Phys. Edn., So. Methodist U., 1959. Player, Green Bay (Wis.) Packers, NFL, 1956, 58-70, Dallas Cowboys, 1971; asst. coach Green Bay Packers, 1969-70, San Diego Chargers, 1972-73; asst. coach, then head coach Cleve. Browns, 1974-77; head coach Toronto Argonauts, CFL, 1979, Cin. Bengals, NFL, 1980-83, Green Bay Packers, 1984—. Played in NFL Pro Bowl, 1960-64, 66-68, NFL Championship Game, 1960, 61, 62, 65-67, Super Bowl, 1966, 67, 71; coach Super Bowl team, 1981. Address: Green Bay Packers PO Box 10628 Green Bay WI 54307*

GREGORCY, JOHN RAYMOND, controls engineer, business executive; b. Rockford, Ill., Dec. 3, 1929; s. Stanley and Evelyn Alice; student in Indsl. Electronics, Memphis State U., 1948-52; m. Willie May Mickey, Aug. 12, 1950; children—Perry, Paul, Patricia, Pamela, Philip. Design engr. W.F. and John Barnes Co., Rockford, 1952-56; chief elec. engr. Ill. Water Treatment Co., Rockford, 1956-72; chief controls engr. Techni-Chem, Inc., Cherry Valley, Ill., 1972—, now v.p. Trustee, Techni-Chem, Inc. Pension Fund. Served with U.S. Navy, 1948-52. Recipient award Foxboro Instrument Sch., 1966. Mem. IEEE, Instrument Soc. Am., Rockford Engrng. Soc. Republican. Lutheran. Club: Rockford Hockey. Designer cobolt unit treatment, solid state ion exchange unit. Home: 912 Starview Dr Rockford IL 61108 Office: 6853 Indy Dr Belvidere IL 61008

GREGORY, DELLA ARLENE ARLEDGE, educator; b. Martinsville, Ohio, Oct. 6, 1938; d. George and Lucille Irene (Shiverdecker) Arledge; B.A., Ohio State U., 1959, M.A., 1977, doctoral candidate, U., 1979—; student Ohio Wesleyan U., summers 1969, 70, 72, 74, 75, 77, 78; m. James Andrew Gregory, Dec. 20, 1959; children—James Andrew, Julie Ann, Janis Arlene. Tchr., Delaware (Ohio) City Schs., 1960—; part-time communications instr. Marion Tech. Coll.; also ednl. cons. Mem. adv. bd. Help Anonymous, 1974-83; adv. 4-H Club, 1969—; adv. Am. Field Service, 1973-79, host mother, 1974-75; mem. edn. com. local Methodist ch., 1977-82; publicity coordinator Delaware Arts Festival, 1977-79; vol. family outreach program Juvenile Ct. Annie Webb Blanton scholar Delta Kappa Gamma, 1979-81, Louise And Marguerite Morse scholar, 1981; NEH grantee, 1983. Mem. United Teaching Profession, Ohio Council Tchrs. of English Lang. Arts (sec. 1973-76), Nat. Council Tchrs. of English (com. on poets in schs. 1974-76, judge writing awards 1975-79), Delaware City Tchrs. Assn. (pres. 1979-81, treas. 1981-85), AAUW (charter pres. Delaware br. 1965-67), Delta Kappa Gamma (pres. Iota chpt. 1982-84, mem. Alpha Delta state scholarship com.), Pi Lambda Theta. Contbr. articles to profl. jours. Home: 240 Homestead Ln Delaware OH 43015 Office: 289 Euclid Ave Delaware OH 43015

GREGORY, JAMES EDWARD, JR., university administrator; b. Springfield, Ohio, Oct. 13, 1948; s. James Edward and Elaine Montex (Jensen) G.; m. Marilyn Ann Adkins, Feb. 26, 1982. B.S. in Math., Ohio State U., Columbus, 1970; A.Sc., Clark Tech. Coll., Springfield, 1976. Systems mgr. Wittenberg U., Springfield, 1976-79, Clark Tech. Coll., Springfield, 1979—. Officer, diver Clark County Ohio Underwater Search and Recovery Team, Springfield, 1978—. Mem. Digital Equipment User's Soc. Clubs: Springfield Scuba (pres. 1980-82), Ski. Avocations: scuba diving, skiing, tennis, camping, canoeing. Home: 428 N Shaffer St Springfield OH 45504 Office: Clark Technical Coll 100 S Limestone St Springfield OH 45502

GREGORY, KEITH EDWARD, supervisory research geneticist; b. Franklin, N.C., Oct. 27, 1924; s. Parker and Leila (Woodard) G.; married, Nov. 17, 1951; children—Mark, Greta. B.S., N.C. State U., 1947; M.S., U. Nebr., 1949; Ph.D., U. Mo., 1951. Assoc. prof. Auburn U. (Ala.), 1951-55; investigations leader, beef cattle breeding research U.S. Dept. Agr., Lincoln, Nebr., 1955-66, dir. U.S. Meat Animal Research Ctr., Clay Center, Nebr., 1966-77, research geneticist (animal) 1977-84, research leader prodn. systems, 1984—; animal breeding and genetics, leader livestock devel. team USAID, Washington, 1963; cons. in field of animal prodn. research and devel. Contbr. articles to sci. and tech. jours. Fellow AAAS, Am. Soc. Animal Sci. (hon.); Mem. Am. Genetic Assn., Sigma Xi. Office: US Meat Animal Research Ctr PO Box 166 Clay Center NE 68933

GREGORY, STEVEN DALE, home intravenous therapy company executive; b. Joplin, Mo., Oct. 25, 1957; s. W. Dale and Anna L. (Moore) G.; m. Sheryl L. Latino, July 31, 1982. B.S. in Pharmacy, U. Mo.-Kansas City, 1980. Registered pharmacist, Mo. Staff pharmacist U. Mo. Med. Ctr., Columbia, 1980-82; clin. pharmacist Trinity Lutheran Hosp., Kansas City, Mo., 1982-84; adminstr. Home Med. Support Services, Inc., Kansas City, 1984—, chmn. adv. bd., 1984—. Mem. Am. Soc. Hosp. Pharmacists, Mo. Soc. Hosp. Pharmacists, Greater Kansas City Soc. Hosp. Pharmacists. Episcopalian. Avocations: golf, softball, scuba diving, real estate, reading. Home: 18 East 70th Terr Kansas City MO 64113 Office: 8355 Melrose Dr Lenexa KS 66214

GREIN, RICHARD FRANK, See *Who's Who in America,* 43rd edition.

GREINER, JACK VOLKER, physician, eye researcher, educator; b. Fountain Hill, Pa., Aug. 25, 1949; s. Harry Sandt and Vera Lilian G.; m. Cynthia Ann Mis, May 17, 1980. A.A., Valley Forge Mil. Acad., 1969; B.A., U. Vt., 1971; M.S. in Anatomy, Purdue U., 1973; Ph.D. in Anatomy, U. Toledo, 1974; D.O., Chgo. Coll. Osteo. Medicine, 1982. Research fellow in ophthalmology Howe Lab. Ophthalmology, Harvard U. Med. Sch., Mass. Eye and Ear Infirmary, Boston, 1974-76; research fellow in corneal and external diseases of eye Eye Research Inst. of Retina Found., Boston, 1976-78, adj. asst. scientist, 1978; research fellow in ophthalmology Harvard U. Med. Coll., 1976-78; research assoc. ophthalmology Eye and Ear Infirmary, U. Ill.-Chgo., 1979-81, research asst. prof. ophthalmology, 1981—; adj. asst. prof. ophthal. pathology Chgo. Coll. Osteo. Medicine, 1979-82, asst. prof. dept. pathology, 1982-83, assoc. prof., 1983—, co-dir. Eye Research Lab., 1980—; intern Cook County Hosp., Chgo., 1982-83. Served to capt., C.E., USAR, 1971-78. Fight for Sight grantee, 1980-82; Nat. Soc. to Prevent Blindness grantee, 1981; Nat. Eye Inst., NIH grantee, 1982—. Mem. Am. Assn. Anatomists, Assn. for Research in Vision and Ophthalmology, Contact Lens Assn. Ophthalmologists, Soc. for Exptl. Biology and Medicine, N.Y. Acad. Scis., AMA, Chgo. Med. Soc., Cook County Med. Soc., Am. Acad. Ophthalmology, Sigma Xi, Phi Kappa Phi, Sigma Sigma Phi. Contbr. chpts. to books, articles to profl. jours. Office: Chgo Osteopathic Hosp 5200 S Ellis Ave Chicago IL 60615 also Dept Ophthalmology U Ill Eye and Ear Infirmary 1855 W Taylor St Chicago IL 60612

GREINER, JOHN, land surveyor; b. St. Louis, Feb. 25, 1941; s. August Ernst and Clara Mathilda (Mohn) G.; m. Jacqueline Rita Brandhorst, Oct. 14, 1961; 1 son, James Michael. A.S., Purdue U., 1967; B.A., Coll. of Pacific, 1962. Lic. surveyor, Mo., Ill. Surveyor, Harrison and Assocs., St. Louis, 1955-63, Elbring Co., St. Louis, 1963-73; survey supr. Sterling Co., St. Louis, 1973-74; pres. F.P. Research Co., St. Louis, 1974—; v.p. PHG Inc., St. Louis, 1974—. Mem. Am. Congress of Surveying and Mapping, Southwest Ill. Land Surveyors. Republican. Lutheran. Clubs: Affton Athletic Assn. (Mo.) (v.p. 1978-80); Gateway Athletic League (St. Louis) (pres. 1981—). Lodge: Elks (Chaplain 1971-73). Home: 7823 Ravensridge Shrewsbury MO 63119 Office: PHG Inc 8615 Gravois St Louis MO 63123

GREJCZYK, DENNIS FRANCIS, marketing executive; b. Chgo., Oct. 9, 1943; s. Robert I. and Laura (Bawelkiewicz) G.; m. Diane Lynn Dufty, Oct. 21, 1966; children—Deborah Ann, Dennis F., Daniel B. Student Marquette U., 1980-82. Dist. sales mgr. Apeco, Cin., 1972-73; sales rep. W. H. Brady, Milw., 1973-74; regional sales mgr. Kroy, Detroit, 1974-77; br. gen. mgr. Savin, Detroit, 1977-78; gen. mktg. mgr. Sycom, Madison, Wis., 1978-83; v.p. mktg. Barber-Greene Info. Systems, Inc., Downers Grove, Ill., 1983-84; mgr. O.E.M. Mktg. Ryan-McFarland Corp., Chgo., 1984—. Pres., Parent Tchrs. Orgn., Canton, Mich., 1975. Served with USAF, 1961-65; ETO. Mem. Sales and Mktg. Execs., Am. Mgmt. Assn. Roman Catholic. Home: 423 Justine Ave Bolingbrook IL 60439 Office: Ryan-McFarland Corp 8600 W Bryn Mawr Suite 200N Chicago IL 60631

GREMMINGER, ROGER ANTHONY, physician; b. Campbellsport, Wis., Feb. 24, 1947; s. Paul Killian and Frances Josephine (Fox) G. B.S. in Math., Divine Word Coll. Sem., 1969; M.D., Med. Coll. Wis., 1976. Intern, St. Mary's Hosp., Milw., 1976-77, emergency physician, 1978—; staff mem. Brady E. Sexually Transmitted Disease Clinic, Milw., 1978—, med. dir., 1979-84; staff St. Joseph's Hosp., Milw., 1978—, St. Mary's Hosp., Racine, Wis., 1978-83; mem. staff St. Anthony's Hosp., Milw., 1983—, also med. dir. Herpes Health Ctr. Mem. Ad Hoc Task Force for Vaccination Strategies for Sexually Transmitted Hepatitis B, 1981-83. Active Am. Pub. Health Assn., Wis. Pub. Health Assn., Am. Venereal Disease Assn., Nat. Coalition of Gay Sexually Transmitted Disease Services, ACLU, Wis. Civil Liberties Union, Wis. Council of Human Concerns. Mem. AAAS. Democrat. Roman Catholic. Lectr. symposia, workshops.

GRENZEBACH, JOHN, consulting firm executive; b. Buffalo, Apr. 26, 1914; s. John Edward and Ida May (Linch) G.; m. Marilynn Clark, Oct. 27, 1939; children—John, Eric, Martin. Student pub. schs. Vice pres. Beaver Assocs., Chgo., 1950-61; pres. John Grenzebach & Assocs., Chgo., 1961-83, chmn., 1983—; chmn. Am. Assn. Fund Raising Counsel, N.Y.C., 1984—. Democrat. Clubs: Chicago, Whitehall, Carlton. Home: 230 Lake View Dr Anna Maria FL 33501 Office: John Grenzebach & Assocs 845 N Michigan Ave Chicago IL 60611

GRETICK, ANTHONY LOUIS, lawyer; b. Chgo., June 26, 1936; s. Anthony L. and Martha M. (Leinar) G.; m. Caroline Hogue, Dec. 30, 1955; children—Kirsten, David. A.B., Northwestern U., 1958, J.D., 1964. Bar: Ill. 1964, Ohio 1965, U.S. Supreme Ct. 1971. Assoc. Gebhard, Hogue, Dwyer & Wilson, 1964-67, ptnr., 1967-71; exec. asst. Atty. Gen. Ohio, 1971-72, also chief trial div. of spl. litigation sect.; ptnr. Hogue, Dwyer, Gretick, Bish & Lowe, Bryan, Ohio, 1972-82; ptnr. Gretick, Bish, Lowe & Roth, Bryan, 1982—; pros. atty., William County, Ohio, 1977—. Pres. Bryan Swim Team Assn., 1978; Gov.'s Commn. on Prison Crowding, 1984—. Served with USNR, 1958-75. Ohio Bar Found. fellow, 1982—; mem. Nat. Dist. Attys. Assn. (dir. 1984—), Ohio Pros. Attys. Assn. (dir. 1978—, pres. 1982). Home: 115 Deerfield Circle Bryan OH 43506 Office: 1210 W High St PO Box 486 Bryan OH 43506

GREYSON, JEROME, laboratory instrument manufacturing executive, chemical engineering consultant; b. N.Y.C., Nov. 7, 1927; s. Oscar and Pauline (Yagman) G.; m. Jacqueline Vis, July 27, 1957; children—Clifford, Ann, Paul. B.A., Hunter Coll., 1950; Ph.D., Pa. State U., 1956. Mem. tech. staff Bell Telephone Labs., Murray Hill, N.J., 1956-57, IBM Research, Yorktown Heights, N.Y., 1957-62; supr. physical chemistry Stauffer Chem. Co., Richmond, Calif., 1962-63; supr. contract research Rockwell Internat., Canoga Park, Calif., 1963-71; dir. blood chemistry Miles Labs., Inc., Elkhart, Ind., 1971-82; engring. dir. GCA Instrument and Equipment Group, Chgo., 1982—; owner, cons. J & J Assocs., Consulting Chemists, Chgo., 1982—; lectr. clin. chem. devels. various nat. and internat. confs. Contbr. numerous articles to sci. jours. Patentee device for measuring osmomality, reagent strips, suspension dewatering method. Served wtih USN, 1945-46, PTO. mem. Am. Chem. Soc., Am. Assn. Clin. Chemistry, Tissue Culture Assn., Instrument Soc. Am., Assn. Consulting Chemists and Chem. Engrs., Sigma Xi, Pi Mu Epsilon. Avocations: photography; microcumputer software devel.

GRIDER, JEAN CATHERINE, business educator, consultant; b. Leesburg, Ohio, Aug. 1, 1928; d. Frank C. Shope and Ida C. (Redmon) S.; m. Curtis Grider, Apr. 15, 1960 (div.), children—Pamela, Carla, Lisa, Paula. B.S. in Edn., Wilmington Coll., 1950; Ed.M., U. Cin., 1960, Cert., tchr. and supr. vocat. edn., Ohio. Tchr., Anderson Hich Sch., Cin., Xenia City and Western Brown High Schs., Mt. Orab, Ohio, and So. Joint Vocat. Sch., Georgetown, Ohio; adult supr. So. Hills Joint Vocat. Sch.; instr. So. State Community Coll., Sardinia, Ohio, U. Cin.; cons. to industry. Mem. AAUW, Delta Pi Epsilon, Delta Kappa Gamma. Methodist. Club: Order of Eastern Star.

GRIDLEY, JOHN WILLIS, JR., controller; b. Rochester, Minn., May 10, 1939; s. John Willis and Dorothy Janet (Root) G.; B.A., Hamline U., 1960; postgrad. Princeton U., 1961-62, Harvard U., 1973; m. Elizabeth Linda Lohn, Sept. 8, 1962; children—James, Janet, Richard. Securities analyst Value Line Investment Survey, N.Y.C., 1962-64; mgr. profit analysis Ford Motor Co., Dearborn, Mich., 1964-74; asst. controller Xerox Info. Products, El Segundo, Calif., 1974-76; controller TRW Energy Systems, Redondo Beach, Calif., 1976-79; v.p., controller McQuay-Perfex, Inc., Mpls., 1979-82, First Bank System Inc., Mpls., 1982—. Budget and taxation commr. City of Redondo Beach, 1976-80. Served with AUS, 1959. Mem. Fin. Execs. Inst. Republican. Congregationalist. Clubs: Harvard Bus. Sch. Minn., King Harbor Yacht, Mpls. Athletic. Lodges: Masons, Shriners. Home: 2537 Washburn Ave S Minneapolis MN 55416 Office: 1300 First Bank Pl E PO Box 522 Minneapolis MN 55480

GRIEM, J. MICHAEL, management consultant; b. San Francisco, Apr. 29, 1945; s. John Dyrsen and Gwendolyn (Pyeatt) G.; Sc.B.E. magna cum laude, Brown U., 1965, Sc.M.E., 1966; M.B.A., U.Chgo., 1968; m. Peggy Clarke, Sept. 16, 1967; children—John Michael, Marjorie Lynne. Sr. economist USPHS, 1968-70; assoc. to v.p., dir. Cresap, McCormick and Paget, Chgo., 1970-81, mng. partner subs. Cresap, McCormick and Paget do Brasil Servicos Ltda., 1978-81; v.p. A.T. Kearney, Chgo., 1981—, pres. Kearney; Health Services Cons., 1981—. Gov. Am. Soc. of Sao Paulo (Brazil), 1979-81. NDEA fellow, 1965-66; Ford Found. fellow, 1965, 67-68. Mem. Inst. Mgmt. Cons. (cert.), Am. Assn. Hosp. Cons., Sigma Xi, Tau Beta Pi, Beta Gamma Sigma. Republican. Presbyterian. Clubs: Exmoor Country; Atletico Sao Paulo; Brown U. (Chgo.). Home: 120 Indian Rd Lake Bluff IL 60044 Office: 222 S Riverside Plaza Chicago IL 60606

GRIEVE, BONNIE-JO MCLEAN, physician, medical geneticist; b. N.Y.C., Jan. 1, 1949; d. Jesse Terry and Josephine (Stanton) G.; B.S., Cornell U., 1969; M.D., U. Utah, 1973; M.S. in Med. Genetics, U. Wis., 1979. Intern, U. Wis., Madison, 1973-74, resident in pediatrics, 1974-76, Steifer Found. postdoctoral fellow in clin. genetics, 1976-78, NIH postdoctoral fellow in molecular genetics, 1978-79; asst. prof. human genetics and pediatrics Med. Coll. Va., Richmond, 1979-81; regional med. adv., mem. Nat. Ski Patrol Systems, 1976—. Diplomate Am. Bd. Pediatrics, Am. Bd. Med. Genetics. Fellow Am. Acad. Pediatrics; mem. AMA, Am. Med. Women's Assn., Am. Soc. Human Genetics, Med. Soc. Wis., Phi Kappa Phi, Alpha Lambda Delta. Office: Milw Med Clinic Milwaukee WI 53217

GRIEVE, PIERSON M., business executive, entrepreneur; b. Flint, Mich., Dec. 5, 1927; m. Florence R. Brogan, 1950; children—Margaret, Scott, Bruce. B.B.A., Northwestern U., 1950; postgrad. U. Minn., 1955-56. Staff engr. Caterpillar Tractor Co., 1950-52; mgmt. cons. A.T. Kearney & Co., 1952-55; pres. Rap-In-Wax, 1955-62; exec. AP Parts Corp., Toledo, 1962-67; pres., chief exec. officer Questor Corp., Toledo, 1967-81; cons., entrepreneur in venture capital, San Jose, Costa Rica, Jackson, Mich., 1981-82; chmn. Econs. Lab., Inc., St. Paul, 1982—. Mem. adv. council J.L. Kellogg Grad. Sch. Mgmt., Northwestern U.; bd. overseers Sch. Mgmt., U. Minn.; bd. dirs. Guthrie Theater, St. Paul Chamber Orch.; trustee Macalester Coll. Served with USN, 1945-46. Mem. Beta Gamma Sigma (dirs. table). Episcopalian. Clubs: St. Paul Athletic, Minnesota, Mpls.; Economic (N.Y.C.).

GRIFFIN, JAMES ANTHONY, bishop, lawyer; b. Fairview Park, Ohio, June 13, 1934; s. Thomas Anthony and Margaret Mary (Hanousek) G. B.A. in Philosophy, Borromeo Coll.; J.C.L., Pontifical Lateran U., Rome; J.D., Cleve. State U. Bar: Ohio. Ordained priest, Roman Catholic Ch., 1960; vicar gen. Cleve. Diocese, 1978, pastor St. William Parish, Cleve., 1978-79, aux. bishop Cleve. Diocese, 1979-83, bishop, Columbus Diocese, 1983—; mem. adv. bd. N.Am. Coll., Rome, 1980—; mem. adminstrv. com. Region VI, Nat. Conf. Cath. Bishops, 1984—, mem. liaison com. Leadership Conf. Women Religious, 1982—; chmn. ad hoc com. on Alienation, 1983—. Author: Sackcloth and Ashes, The Priestly Heart; co-author: Thoughts for Sowing, Thoughts for Our Times, Ashes From the Cathedral. Bd. dirs. Children's Hosp., Columbus, 1983—, United Way Franklin County, 1984—, Franklin County Alcoholism and Alcohol Abuse Program, 1983—, Pontifical Coll. Josephinum, Columbus, 1983—. Office: Chancery Diocese of Columbus 198 E Broad St Columbus OH 43215

GRIFFIN, JOSEPH LAWRENCE, transp. exec.; b. Utica, Miss., Sept. 5, 1951; s. Shallie, Jr., and Carrie B. (Lyle) G.; student U. Ill., 1969-71; cert. in transp. and traffic mgmt. Coll. Advanced Traffic, 1978; m. Rhonda Evans, July 28, 1970; children—Joel, Jerl, Rael, Marel. Supr. terminal ops. Consol. Rail Corp., Chgo., 1977-78, asst. terminal mgr., 1978-79; asst. terminal mgr. Pa. Truck Lines, Inc., Chgo., 1979-81; multimodal sales rep. Consol. Rail Corp., Chgo., 1981-83, multimodal sales mgr., Detroit, 1983-84, King of Prussia, Pa., 1984-85; pres. Griffin Transp. Services Inc., Chgo., 1985—; transp. cons., 1981—. Notary public. Mem. Intermodal Operating Com., Am. Mgmt. Assn., Piggyback Assn. Chgo., Detroit Intermodal Assn., Kappa Alpha Psi. Home: 7946 S Princeton Ave Chicago IL 60620 Office: 7946 S Princeton Ave Chicago IL 60620 also PO Box 3205 Southfield MI 48075

GRIFFIN, KENNETH ROLAND, manufacturing company executive; b. Muskegon, Mich., Mar. 21, 1941; s. Roland A. and Veronis (Heiss) G.; m. Linda L. Lewis, Feb. 3, 1967; children—Kendra, Kyle, Kip. B.S. in Bus. Adminstrn., Aquanis Coll., Grand Rapids, Mich., 1977. Sr. programmer, analyst Kaydon Corp., Muskegon, Mich., 1967-71, dir. systems, 1973—; data processing supr. C-E Tyler, Mentor, Ohio, 1971-73. Bd. dirs. Little League Baseball, Muskegon, 1977-79. Served with U.S. Navy, 1962-66. Avocations: hunting; fishing; golf. Home: 1575 Vesta St Muskegon MI 49445 Office: Kaydon Corp 2680 McCraken St Muskegon MI 49443

GRIFFIN, MARY VELMA SHOTWELL (MRS. JAMES LEONARD GRIFFIN), author; b. nr. Carrollton, O., Aug. 11, 1904; d. Winfield Scott and Eva Anaz (Smith) Shotwell; certificate elementary edn., Kent State U., 1925; m. James Leonard Griffin, Oct. 2, 1929. Accordionist, Radio Sta. WTAM, Cleve., 1926, Chatuauqua and Lyceum circuits, 1927-28, Accordion Gypsies, 1931-48, Ringling Bros.-Barnum and Bailey Circus, 1935-36; tchr. pub. schs., Ohio, 1922-65; ret., 1965; now free lance writer. Gray lady, ARC, 1967—; bd. dirs. Bell-Herron Scholarship Found., 1965—; pres. Carroll County Hist. Soc., 1965-67, dir., 1963—, curator, 1967—. Recipient Disting. Service award Jaycees, 1979. Mem. NEA, Carroll County Ret. Tchrs. Assn., Ohio, Carroll County (pres. 1964-65) edn. assns., Ohio Hist. Soc., Ohio, Carroll County geneal. socs., Ohioana Library Assn. (county chmn. 1958—). Republican. Presbyterian. Clubs: Rebekah, Order Eastern Star. Author: Fair Prize, 1956; Circus Daze, 1957; Mystery Mansion, 1958; numerous short stories pub. in popular mags. Home: 11 Arch St Dellroy OH 44620

GRIFFIN, MICHAEL JAMES, media design and production company executive; b. Valparaiso, Ind., Feb. 9, 1948; s. Charles F. and Pauline A. (Lungren) G.; m. Janet Kay Yudt, Feb. 12, 1972; children—Heather, Shannon, Shane, Tara, Nathan, Patrick, Eric. B.S. in Edn., Ind. U., 1971. Tchr., Fegley Middle Sch. Portage, Ind., 1971-73; copy dir. Whiteco & Assocs. Advt., 1973-74; founder, pres. Michaeljay Communications, Inc. (name now Griffin Media Design), Chesterton, Ind., 1975—; adj. lectr. Valparaiso U. Pres., bd. trustees Westchester Twp. Library; bd. dirs. Jackson/Liberty Sch. Bldg. Corp. Recipient William Randolph Hearst Journalism award Ind. U., 1970; Golden Drummer award Bldg. Supply News, 1979; U.S. Indsl. Film Festival awards, 1981, 83; Cert. of Craftsmanship, Internat. Film Festival, Salerno, Italy, 1983; Advt. Achievement award Fleet Owner Mag., 1981; Community Improvement award Westchester C. of C., 1981; Ernie Pyle scholar. Mem. Assn. for Multi-Image, Sigma Delta Chi. Roman Catholic. Writer, producer numerous film and audio-visual prodns. for bus., industry and edn. Home: 313 1300 N Chesterton IN 46304 Office: 802 Wabash Chesterton IN 46304

GRIFFIN, RICHARD EUGENE, osteopath, educator; b. Kansas City, Mo., Apr. 18, 1934; s. James Emmett and Angela Dorothea (Haas) G.; m. Grace Marie Daly, June 15, 1957; children—Kathleen, Richard, Jr. Student Rockhurst Coll., 1951-54; D.O., Kansas City Coll. Osteo. Medicine, 1958. Cert. in gen. practice and addictionology. Intern Lakeside Hosp., Kansas City, Mo., 1958-59; surgeon Fire Dept. Lakewood, Colo., 1961-66; asst. police surgeon, Jefferson County, Colo., 1961-66; gen. practice osteo. medicine, Denver, 1961-76, Kansas City, Mo., 1959-61; mem. detoxification unit staff Denver Gen. Hosp., 1971-73, asst. psysician jail ward, 1973-76; physician Denver County Jail, 1973-76; emergency room physician Rocky Mountain Hosp., Denver, 1970-76; physician adult medicine Eastside Neighborhood Health Ctr., Denver, 1973-76; lectr. in obstetrics Denver Police Acad., 1973-76; assoc. prof. dept. family medicine Coll. Osteo. Medicine, Mich. State U., 1976-78, prof. 1978—, acting chmn., 1981-82; dep. med. examiner Ingham County, Lansing, Mich., 1983-85; dir. Ingham Family Medicine Clinic, Ingham Med. Ctr., Lansing, 1976-78, Family Medicine Clinics, 1977-85; mem. council of deans prison health subcom. State of Mich., 1979-80, mem. formultaion com. Office of Health Care, Dept. of Corrections, 1981; dir. Family Practice Clinic State Prison So. Mich., 1979-81; physician substance abuse/alcoholism unit St. Lawrence Dimondale Ctr., 1983—; lectr., cons. in field. Lector, commentator, extraordinary minister Eucharist St. Thomas Aquinas Catholic Ch., East Lansing, Mich.; instr. C.C.D. program; team physician East Lansing Hockey Club. Fellow Am. Coll. Medicine; mem. Coll. Osteo. Medicine (active numerous coms.), Sons of Am. Revolution, Soc. Tchrs. in Family Medicine, Am. Osteo. Assn., Ingham County Assn. Osteo. Physicians and Surgeons, Mich. Assn. Osteo. Gen. Practitioners, Am. Correctional Health Services Assn., Psi Sigma Alpha. Lodge: KC. Avocation: woodworking. Office: B216 Fee Mich State U East Lansing MI 48824

GRIFFIN, RONALD CHARLES, law educator; b. Washington, Aug. 17, 1943; s. Roy John and Gwendolyn (Points) G.; m. Vicky Treadway, Nov. 26, 1967; children—David Ronald, Jason Roy, Meg Carrington. B.S., Hampton Inst., 1965; postgrad. Harvard U., summer 1965; J.D., Howard U., 1968; LL.M., U. Va., 1974. Bar: D.C. 1970, U.S. Supreme Ct. 1973. Asst. corp. counsel Govt. of D.C., 1970; asst. prof. law U. Oreg., 1974-78; assoc. prof. law Washburn U., Topeka, 1978-81, prof., 1981—; vis. prof. U. Notre Dame, 1981-82; dir. Council on Legal Ednl. Opportunity, Summer Inst., Great Plains Region, 1983; grievance examiner Midwest region EEOC, 1984-85. Served to capt. JAGC, U.S. Army, 1970-74. Rockefeller Found. grantee Howard U., 1965-68; fellow Parker Sch. Fgn. and Comparative Law, Columbia U., summer 1981; Kline sabbatical research and study, Japan, 1985. Mem. ABA. Contbr. articles to legal jours. Home: 2031 Bowman Ct Topeka KS 66604 Office: Sch Law Washburn U Topeka KS 66621

GRIFFIN, WILLIAM LESTER HADLEY, shoe company executive; b. Edwardsville, Ill., May 17, 1918; s. Ralph D. and Julia (Hadley) G.; A.B., Williams Coll., 1940; LL.B., Washington U., St. Louis, 1947; m. Phoebe M. Perry, Apr. 1, 1942; children—Dustin H. II, Lockwood Perry, Peter Burley. Bar: Mo. 1947. Counsel Wohl Shoe Co., St. Louis, 1947-51, asst. sec. treas., 1950-51; sec. Brown Shoe Co. (name changed to Brown Group, Inc. 1972), St. Louis, 1954-64, v.p., 1964-66, exec. v.p., 1966-68, pres., 1968-72, chief exec. officer, 1969-82, chmn. bd., 1972—, pres., 1972-79, chmn. exec. com., 1971, also dir.; dir., chmn. Fed. Res. Bank of St. Louis; dir. Gen. Am. Life Ins. Co., Owens-Corning Fiberglas Corp., Trans World Corp., TWA, Ralston Purina Co. Chmn. bd. trustees Washington U.; trustee Williams Coll., 1975-80; pres. St. Louis Symphony Soc., 1979-83, chmn. bd. dirs., 1983; bd. dirs. Govtl. Research Inst.; bd. dirs., mem. exec. com. Taxpayers Research Inst. of Mo.; pres. United Fund Greater St. Louis, 1973, campaign chmn., 1972; pres. Civic Progress, Inc., 1972-74. Served from ensign to lt. USNR, 1941-45; as lt. comdr., Korea, 1951-52. Mem. Am. Footwear Industries Assn. (past chmn.), Smithsonian Assocs. (chmn. nat. bd. dirs.). Republican. Home: Mason Rd Saint Louis MO 63131 Office: 8400 Maryland Ave Saint Louis MO 63105

GRIFFITH, CALVIN ROBERTSON, baseball club executive; b. Montreal, Que., Can., Dec. 1, 1911; s. James and Jane (Davies) Robertson; adopted by Clark C. Griffith, 1923; brought to U.S., 1921; ed. Staunton Mil. Acad., 1928-32, George Washington U., 1932-35; m. Natalie N. Niven, Feb. 1, 1940; children—Clark C., N. Corinne, Clare. Sec. Chattanooga Baseball Club, 1935-37, pres., 1937, mgr., 1937; pres., mgr., treas. Charlotte Club, 1938-41; v.p. Washington, Am. League Baseball Club, 1943-55, pres., 1955-61; pres. Minn. Twins, Am. League, 1961—, also chmn. bd.; v.p. Am. League Profl. Baseball; mem. planning com. Profl. Baseball, also rules com. Named Baseball exec. of Year, 1965. Mem. Am. Legion (v.p.). Presbyterian. Address: Hubert H Humphrey Metrodome 501 Chicago Ave S Minneapolis MN 55415*

GRIFFITH, CLEM WITHERS, consulting engineer, electrical engineer; b. Lodgepole, Nebr., July 8, 1917; s. Louie Eugene and Leola Elsie (Withers) G.; m. Alvina Frank, Oct. 23, 1943; children—Lucille, Louise. B.S.E.E., Colo. State U., 1939. Registered profl. engr., Kans., Okla. Design engr. Boeing Airplane Co., Wichita, Kans., 1942-46, Brink & Dunwoody, Iola, Kans., 1947-52; city engr. Iola, 1952-59; design engr. Brink & Dunwoody, 1959-74; v.p. Shetlar Griffith Shetlar, Iola, 1974—. Contbr. articles to profl. jours. Elder First Presbyn. Ch., Iola, 1960—. Served wtih USN, 1945-46. Mem. IEEE, Nat. Soc. Profl. Engrs., Kans. Engring. Soc. (sec. 1952-58, pres. 1958-59), Am. Water Works Assn., Kans. Rural Water Assn. Republican. Lodge: Rotary (bd. dirs. 1982—). Home: 209 S Oak St Iola KS 66749 Office: Shetlar Griffith Shetlar 216 N Jefferson Ave Iola KS 66749

GRIFFITH, DOUGLAS, research scientist; b. Paterson, N.J., May 6, 1946; s. Fred Gleason and Grace (Nilsson) G.; m. Kisoon Jung, Jan. 3, 1978. B.A. in Psychology with distinction, Ohio State U., 1967; M.S., U. Utah, 1972, Ph.D., 1974. Research asst. dept. psychology U. Utah, 1970-74, teaching assoc., 1974-77; research psychologist Army Research Inst., Ft. Hood, Tex., 1974-81; research scientist Environ. Research Inst. Mich., Ann Arbor, 1981—. Served with U.S. Army, 1968-70. Mem. Psychonomic Soc., Human Factors Soc., Am. Psychol. Assn., Am. Ednl. Research Assn., AAAS. Contbr. articles to profl. jours.

GRIFFITH, FRANK WELLS, utility company executive, b. Ft. Dodge, Iowa, July 1, 1921; s. Frank Whitcombe and Gladys (Wells) G.; B.S. in Gen. Engring., Iowa State U., 1947; student in utility mgmt. U. Mich. 1960; m. Betty Marie Harrelson, Sept. 12, 1945; children—Clark Wells, Steven Harrelson, Jon Lance. Gen. engr. U.S. Gypsum Co., Sweetwater, Tex., 1947-48; with Iowa Pub. Service Co., Sioux City, 1948—, asst. to pres., 1961-63, v.p. ops., 1963-65, exec. v.p., 1965-66, pres., chmn. bd., 1966—, also dir.; chmn. bd., Midwest Energy Co., Sioux City, 1984—; dir. Security Nat. Corp. Bd. dirs. Edison Electric Inst., 1970-85, vice chmn., 1980-81, chmn., 1981-82; bd. dirs. Electric Power Research Inst., 1981—, Electric Info. Council, 1983—; trustee Iowa Natural Heritage Found. Gen. chmn. United Fund, 1968; commr. Iowa Devel. Commn., 1970-76; mem. electric utility adv. com. U.S. Fed. Energy Office, 1975. Bd. dirs. Sioux City Symphony Assn., Sioux City Art Center, Siouxland Blood Bank; chmn. bd. trustees Westmar Coll., 1967-74. Served to maj. USAAF, 1941-45; CBI. Mem. ASME, Am., Midwest (chmn. 1971-72) gas assns., Nat. Assn. Electric Cos. (dir. 1974-77), North Central Electric Assn. (pres. 1969), Sioux City C. of C. Episcopalian (vestryman). Clubs: Sioux City Engrs., Sioux Racquet (Sioux City). Lodges: Masons, Shriners, Rotary. Home: 4019 Hiawatha W Sioux City IA 51104 Office: PO Box 778 Sioux City IA 51102

GRIFFITH, HARLEY JOSEPH, JR., educational administrator; b. Fowler, Ind., Sept. 26, 1928; s. Harley Joseph and Lee Etta (Nichols) G.; m. Carol Jean Cox, June 5, 1950; children—Karry Lane, Gregory Joe, Bradley Gene. B.S., Ind. Central U., 1950; M.S., Purdue U., 1954, Ph.D., 1967. Tchr., coach Goodland High Sch., Ind., 1950-55; prin. Chili High Sch., Ind., 1955-58; supt. North Miami Consolidated Sch. Dist., Denver, Ind., 1958-63; grad. asst. Purdue U., West Lafayette, Ind., 1963-64, conf. coordinator, 1964-65. Pres. Greater Lafayette Conf. and Visitors Bd., 1984-85. Mem. Ind. Assn. for Adult Continuing Edn., Nat. Univ. Continuing Edn. Assn. (Stanley C. Robinson Disting. Service award 1981), Greater Lafayette C. of C., Phi Delta Kappa. Republican. Methodist. Lodges: K.P., Masons, Rotary (pres. 1979-80, sec.

1980—, sec. found. 1980—). Home: 3527 Canterbury Dr Lafayette IN 47905 Office: Purdue U 116 Stewart Ctr West Lafayette IN 47907

GRIFFITH, LARRY BRUCE, college business manager; b. Youngstown, Ohio, Jan. 25, 1952; s. Wayne L. and Betty L. (Snyder) G.; m. Pamela Kay Richards, Aug. 18, 1973; children—Daniel Richard, Emily Lynn. B.S., Mt. Union Coll., 1974. C.P.A., Ohio. Audit Supr. Ernst & Whinney, Canton, Ohio, 1974-80; dir. fin. aid Mt. Union Coll., Alliance, Ohio, 1980-82, bus. mgr., 1982—. Bd. dirs. SBA Alliance C. of C., 1982—; bd. diaconal ministers United Methodist Ch., Canton, 1983—. Mem. Am. Inst. C.P.A.s, Ohio Soc. C.P.A.s, Nat. Assn. Coll. and Univ. Bus. Officers, Sigma Alpha Epsilon. Avocations: volleyball, golf, spectator sports, travel. Home: 1469 Robinwood Rd Alliance OH 44601 Office: Mount Union College 1972 Clark Ave Alliance OH 44601

GRIFFITH, MARIELLEN, psychologist; b. Newton, Kans., Mar. 28, 1935; d. Peter Simon and Mabel Bertha (Deschner) Shellenberger; m. David Scott Griffith, June 15, 1961; children—Scott Whittier, Jon Peter. B.A., Bethel Coll., 1958; 19; M.A., Ind. U., 1959; Ed.S. in Counseling and Psychometrics, Butler U., 1973; Ed.D. in Counseling Psychology, Ball State U., 1976. Cert. psychologist, Ind. Asst. prof. edn. Bluffton (Ohio) Coll., 1959-61; tchr. Indpls. Pub. Schs., 1968-70; sch. counselor Western Boone Corp., Thorntown, 1971-74; assoc. prof. counseling and psychometrics Butler U., Indpls., 1975—; cons. to bus. schs. Recipient Significant Concerns for Women in Humanistic Edn. award, Assn. Humanistic Edn. and Devel., 1980. Mem. Am. Psychol. Assn., Am. Assn. Counseling and Devel., Am. Assn. for Marriage and Family Therapy, AAUW. Author: (with P.R. Coleman) Beyond the Systems Approach to Family Therapy: An Ecological Perspective, 1981. Home: 5001 N Capital Indianapolis IN 46208 Office: 4600 Sunset Ave Indianapolis IN 46208

GRIFFITH, RICHARD GRANT, consulting petroleum geologist; b. Somerset, Pa., Aug. 30, 1927; s. Grant Jay and Sally Margaret (Rhoads) G.; m. Marjorie Helen Brown, Feb. 17, 1951; children—Patti Jo, Michael Richard. B.Sc. in Geology, Ohio State U., 1951. Registered land surveyor, Ohio. Surveyor-engr. Standard Oil Co. Ohio, Cleve., 1952-55; petroleum geologist Sohio Petroleum Co., Oklahoma City, 1955-60; chief geologist Algonquin Petroleum Co., Marion, Ohio, 1964-66; pres., cons. geologist Profl. Petroleum Services, Inc., Columbus, Ohio, 1966—; cons. geologist, various locations, 1960-64. Served with USN, 1946, PTO. Mem. Am. Assn. Petroleum Geologists, Am. Inst. Profl. Geologists, Ohio Geol. Soc., Oklahoma City Geol. Soc., Dallas Geol. Soc. Republican. Lutheran. Avocations: fishing; boating. Home: 2058 Springhill Dr Upper Arlington OH 43221 Office: Professional Petroleum Services Inc 2280 W Henderson Rd Suite 216 Columbus OH 43220

GRIFFITH, STEVEN JOHN, theater educator, theatre designer; b. St. Paul, Feb. 20, 1953; s. Harvey John and Deloris (Merzenich) G. A.B., Gustavus Adolphus Coll., 1975; M.F.A., U. Minn., 1977. Instr. theatre Agnes Scott Coll., Decatur, Ga., 1977-79; asst. prof. Gustavus Adolphus Coll., St. Peter, Minn., 1979—; designer Colo. Shakespeare Festival, Boulder, 1976, Performance Community, Chgo., 1984. Mem. Am. Theatre Assn., U.S. Inst. Theater Tech. Democrat. Lutheran. Home: Gustavus Adolphus Coll Box 1417 Saint Peter MN 56082 Office: Gustavus Adolphus Coll Theatre Dept Saint Peter MN 56082

GRIFFITHS, ALBERT OWEN, veterinarian, consultant; b. Talgarth, South Wales, Apr. 7, 1925; came to U.S., 1949, naturalized, 1956; s. John Pryce and Elizabeth (Williams) G.; m. Helen Irene Van Law, Aug. 30, 1952 (div. 1957); m. Suzanne Nichols, Sept. 2, 1962. B.S. in Vet. Medicine, U. Ill.-Urbana, 1954, D.V.M., 1956. Instr. Coll. Vet. Medicine U. Ill., Urbana, 1956-58; pvt. practice Crossroads Vet. Clinic and Hosp., Urbana, 1958—. Contbr. articles to profl. jours. Com. mem. Parkland Coll. Curriculum Devel., Champaign, 1973; chmn. Urban Chamber Environ. Com., Urbana, 1975; founder, pres. Champaign County Pet Animal Council, Urbana, 1977; commr. Gov.'s Small Bus. Adv. Com., Springfield, Ill., 1983—. Served with Royal Air Force, 1943-47. Recipient Merit awards Coll. Vet. Medicine Alumni Assn., 1982. Mem. Am. Vet. Med. Assn. (Ill. del.), Ill. State Vet. Med. Assn. (pres. 1980, Service, award 1978), Am. Animal Hosp. Assn., Brit. Small Animal Vet. Assn., Am. Soc. Vet. Ethology. Republican. Club: Am. Bus. Avocations: flying; trumpet; dancing. Office: Crossroads Vet Clinic and Hosp RR1 Box 134 Urbana IL 61801

GRIFFITHS, MARTHA WRIGHT, state lieutenant governor, lawyer; b. Pierce City, Mo.; Jan. 29, 1912; m. Hicks Griffiths, Dec. 25, 1934. B.A., U. Mo., J.D., U. Mich. Bar: Mich. 1941, U.S. Supreme Ct. 1955. Mem. Mich. Legislature, 1949-52; judge and recorder Detroit Recorder's Court, 1953, mem. Detroit Election Commn.; mem. Congress from 17th Mich. Dist.; sponsor Equal Rights Amendment, mem. Joint Econ. Com.; sole practice, Romeo, Mich., 1975-82; lt. gov. State Mich., 1982—; Affirmative Action Officer State Mich., permanent chmn. Mich. Equal Employment and Bus. Opportunity Council; past dir. Chrysler, Burroughs, Consumers Power, others. Office: Lt Governor State of Michigan Room #128 Capitol Bldg Lansing MI 48909

GRIFFITHS, ROBERT PENNELL, banker; b. Chgo., May 6, 1949; s. George Findley and Marion E. (Winterrowd) G.; m. Susan Hillman, Jan. 31, 1976. B.A., Amherst Coll., 1972; M.S. in Mgmt., Northwestern U., 1974. Comml. banking officer No. Trust Co., Chgo., 1978-80, 2d v.p., 1980-83, v.p., 1983-85; sr. v.p. comml. lending Unibanc Trust Co., Chgo., 1985—. Club: University (Chgo.). Home: 1100 Waveland Rd Lake Forest IL 60045 Office: Unibanc Trust Co Sears Tower Chicago IL 60606

GRIMES, HUGH GAVIN, physician; b. Chgo., Aug. 19, 1929; s. Andrew Thomas and Anna (Gavin) G.; student Loyola Acad., 1943-47, Loyola U., 1947-50; B.S., U. Ill., 1952, M.D., 1954; m. Rose Anne Leahy, Aug. 21, 1954; children—Hugh Gavin, Paula Anne, Daniel Joseph, Sarah L. Robey, Nancy Marie, Jennifer Diane. Intern St. Joseph Hosp., Chgo., 1954-55, resident ob-gyn, 1955-58; pvt. practice ob-gyn, Chgo., 1960—; lectr., asst. clin. prof. Stritch Sch. Medicine Loyola U., Chgo.; active staff St. Joseph Hosp., Chgo., also mem. exec. adv. bd., v.p. med. staff, 1977-78, pres. staff, 1979-80; asst. prof. clin. ob-gyn Northwestern U. Med. Sch., 1980—. Trustee, Regina Dominican High Sch. Served to capt. M.C., AUS, 1958-60. Diplomate Am. Bd. Ob-Gyn. Fellow Am. Coll. Ob-Gyn, Chgo. Gynecol. Soc.; mem. Am. Assn. Maternal and Infant Health, Am. Cancer Soc. (mem. profl. edn. com. Chgo. unit), Am. Fertility Soc., AMA, Ill., Chgo. med. socs., Cath. Physicians Guild, Assn. Am. Physicians and Surgeons, Am. Soc. Colposcopy and Colpomicroscopy, Am. Assn. Gynecologic Laparoscopists, Assn. Art Inst. Chgo., Assn. Field Mus., Assn. Smithsonian Instn., Pi Kappa Epsilon. Contbr. articles to profl. jours. Office: 7126 N Lincoln Ave Lincolnwood IL 60646 also 800 Austin St Suite 202 Evanston IL 60202 also 2800 Sheridan Rd Suite 404 Chicago IL 60657

GRIMLUND, PETER HANS, marketing product executive, microbiologist, medical technologist; b. Bellingham, Wash., Nov. 13, 1952; s. Arnold J. and Tora Gerda (Hansen) G.; m. Barbara Jean Moser, Dec. 27, 1975. B.S. in Microbiology, Colo. State U., 1975; Med. Tech., children's Orthopedic Hosp., 1976; M.B.A. in Mktg., 1984. Med. Tech., Group Health Coop. Hosp., Seattle, 1976-79; mem. sales, mktg. staff Cathra Internat., St. Paul, 1979-81; ops. Mgr. U. Minn. Hosps., Mpls., 1982-84; product mgr. Cerner Corp., Kansas City, Mo., 1985—; nat. maintenance subcom. chmn. MEDLAB Users Group, Salt Lake City, 1983-84. Mem. Am. Soc. Clin. Pathologists (cert.). Lutheran. Avocations: skiing; boating; golfing; reading; traveling. Home: 1505 Oregon Ave North Golden Valley MN 55427 Office: Cerner Corp 2800 Rockcreek Pkwy Suite 601 Kansas City MO 64117

GRIMM, LOUIS CHARLES, educational administrator; b. Muscatine, Iowa, Jan. 16, 1930; s. Louis and Dorothy Violet (Opel) B.; m. Shirley Louise Wagner, Nov. 24, 1961; children—Lori Louise, Suzanne Beth, Matthew Louis. A.A., Muscatine Jr. Coll. (Iowa), 1950; B.A., N.E.Mo. State U., Kirksville, Mo., 1952, B.S., 1952; M.A., U. Iowa, 1958. Tchr., coach Kahoka Pub. Sch. (Mo.), 1955-56, Pub. schs. Burlington, Iowa, 1956-66; prin., athletic dir. Lincoln Community Sch., Stanwood, Iowa, 1966-78, prin., asst. supt., 1978—; cons. in field. Mayor protem Stanwood City Council, 1975-81, 83—, chmn. Plan and Zone Commn., 1980—; mem. County Republican Com., Stanwood, 1983—. Served to sgt. U.S. Army, 1953-55. Mem. Nat. Assn. Secondary Sch. Prins., Nat. Edn. Assn. Republican. Methodist. Lodges: Masons, Shriners. Avocations: Umpiring; refereeing; track officiating, stamp collecting. Home: 201 N Ash Stanwood IA 52337 Office: Lincoln Community North St Stanwood IA 52337

GRIMM, ROBERT ARTHUR, chemical company executive; b. Two Rivers, Wis., July 25, 1937; s. Arthur Adolph and Lillian Ann (Zimmer) G.; m. Mary Catherine Schwinghamer, June 26, 1965; children—Ann, Therese, Christopher. B.S., U. Wis., 1959; Ph.D., Stanford U., 1963. Research chemist Archer Daniels Midland Co., Mpls., 1963-67, sr. research chemist, 1967-73, mgr. organic chemistry, 1973; sect. mgr. organic chemistry Ashland Chem., Columbus, Ohio, 1973-77, sect. mgr. organic ventures, 1977-80, research mgr. organic ventures, 1980-83, research mgr. new project generation, 1983—. Mem. Am. Chem. Soc., AAAS, Sigma Xi. Contbr. articles to profl. jours. Home: 1810 Ivanhoe Ct Columbus OH 43220 Office: Ashland Chem PO Box 2219 Columbus OH 43216

GRIMMER, MARGOT, dancer, choreographer; b. Chgo., Apr. 5, 1944; d. Vernon and Ann (Radville) Grimmer; student Lake Forest Coll., 1963, Northwestern U., 1964-68. Dancer, N.Y.C. Ballet prodn. of Nutcracker, Chgo., 1956-57, Kansas City Starlight Theater, 1958, St. Louis Mcpl. Theater, 1959, Chgo. Tent House-Music Theater, 1960-61, Lyric Opera Ballet, Chgo., 1961, 63-66, 68, Ballet Russe de Monte Carlo, N.Y.C., 1962, Ruth Page Internat. Ballet, Chgo., 1965-70; dancer-choreographer Am. Dance Co., Chgo., 1972—, artistic dir., 1972—; dancer, choreographer Bob Hope Show, Milw., 1975, Washington D.C. Bicentennial Performance, 1976, Woody Guthrie Benefit Concerts, 1976-77, Assyrian Cultural Found., Chgo., 1977-78; dir.-tchr. Am. Dance Sch., 1971—; appeared in TV commls. and indsl. films for Libbys Foods, Sears, Gen. Motors, others, 1963-84; soloist in ballet Repertory Workshop, CBS-TV, 1964, dance film Statics (Internat. Film award), 1967; soloist in concert Ravinia, 1973, Chgo. Council Fine Arts programs, 1978-84, U.S. Boating Indsl. Show tour, 1981-84, in film Risky Business, 1982; dance critic Mail-Advertiser Publs., 1980-82; host Spotlight cable TV program, 1984-85. Ill. Arts Council grantee, 1972-74, 78, Nat. Endowment for Arts grantee, 1973-74. Mem. Actors Equity Assn., Screen Actors Guild, Am. Guild Mus. Artists. Important works include ballets In-A-Gadda-Da-Vida, 1972, The Waste Land, 1973, Rachmaninoff: Theme and Variations, 1973, Le Baiser de la Fee and Sonata, 1974, Four Quartets, 1974, Am. Export, 1975, Earth, Wind and Fire, 1976, Blood, Sand and Empire, 1977, Disco Fever, 1978, Pax Romana, 1979, Xanadu, 1980, Vertigo, 1981, Cha! Cha! Suite, 1982, American Graffiti, 1983, Eye in the Sky, 1984, others. Office: 442 Central Ave Highland Park IL 60035

GRIMMET, ALEX J., educator, clergyman; b. McVeigh, Ky., July 17, 1928; s. Alex A. and Edna Mae (Boyd) G.; m. Lois Jean Carter, June 24, 1949; children—Larry Bruce, Raven Alexis. A.B., Ky. Christian Coll., 1949; M.Ed., U. Cin., 1964; postgrad. Washburn U., 1967, U. Cin., 1968-69, Georgetown U., 1968. Ordained to ministry Ch. of Christ, 1948. Elem. tchr. Highland County schs., Hillsboro, Ohio, 1957-62; tchr. math. Warren County, Morrow, Ohio, 1964-67; tchr. math. Lebanon High Sch., Ohio, 1967-85, head dept., 1969-84; minister Lerado Ch. of Christ; chmn. math. curriculum revision com. Lebanon City Schs., 1969-70, 82-85, chmn. competency based edn. program for math., 1982-85. Precinct exec. Democrats Hamilton County, Loveland, 1980—. Mem. NEA, Ohio Edn. Assn., Ohio Council Tchrs. Math. (dist. dir. 1981-84, v.p. 1984-87), Lebanon Tchrs. Assn. (mem. liaison com.). Club: Kiwanis (sec.-treas. 8th Ohio div.). Home: 848 Kenmar Dr Loveland OH 45140

GRIMMING, RONALD HENRY, law enforcement administrator; b. St. Louis, Dec. 16, 1944; s. Henry Louis and Evelyn (Stout) G.; m. Karen Lynn Hopfinger; children—Julie, Jodie, Todd, Brian, Jeffrey. A.A., Belleville Area Coll., 1964; B.A., So. Ill. U., 1967. Tchr. Landsdowne Jr. High Sch., East St. Louis, Ill., 1967-69, West Jr. High Sch., Belleville, Ill., 1969-70; spl. agt. Ill. Bur. Investigation, Belleville, 1970-78; spl. agt., comdr. Ill. Div. Criminal Investigation, Belleville, 1978-82, spl. agt. in charge, 1982-83, asst. dir., Springfield, Ill., 1983—. Recipient Ill. Govs. award, 1982. Mem. So. Ill. Police Chiefs Assn., Ill. Assn. Chiefs Police, Internat. Assn. Chiefs Police. Methodist. Home: 2 Teakwood Dr Belleville IL 62221 Office: Ill Div Criminal Investigation 500 Armory St Springfield IL 62706

GRIPP, MIRIAM LUCILLE, medical office administrator, radiology technician; b. Jamestown, N.Y., May 31, 1939; d. Everett Barry and Frances Mildred (Taylor) Eaton; m. William Arthur Gripp, Sept. 30, 1961; children—Cynthia Lane, Richard Eaton. Grad. Mt. Sinai Hosp. Sch. Radiology Technologists, 1959; student Western Res. U., 1958-61. X-ray technician to Drs. Krause, Lubert and Assocs., Inc., Cleveland Heights, 1959, office mgr., 1974, adminstr., University Heights, Ohio, 1979—. Mem. Am. Registry Radiologic Technologists (cert.), Am. Mgmt. Assn. Republican. Presbyterian. Club: Chagrin Valley (Ohio) Athletic. Office: 14100 Cedar Rd 250 University Heights OH 44121

GRISHAM, ARNOLD TERRY, banker; b. Chgo., Dec. 3, 1946; s. John Terry and Gladys (Holloway) G.; m. Jane Aleece Armstrong, Jan. 18, 1969; children—Kristine, Jonathan. B.S. in Mgmt., DePaul U., 1970; M.B.A. in Fin., 1973. Asst. cashier Central Nat. Bank, Chgo., 1972-75; 2d v.p. Continental Bank, Chgo., 1975-81; v.p. Wells Fargo Corporate Services, Chgo., 1981—. Vice chmn. Mercy Health Care and Rehab. Ctr., Homewood, Ill., 1982—; bd. dirs. Matteson Sch. Dist. 162, Ill., 1983—. Club: Chgo. Athletic Assn. Avocations: chess, jogging. Home: 20924 Corinth Road Olympia Fields IL 60461 Office: Wells Fargo Corporate Services Inc 55 W Monroe Suite 1100 Chicago IL 60603

GRISIM, WENDELL ROGER, golf club administrator; b. Mpls., Jan. 24, 1955; s. Roger Orlando and Hilda Fay (Montgomery) G. Asst. mgr. The Haberdashery Radisson Hotel, Mpls., 1975-77, mgr. The Lodge, 1977-78; gen. mgr. Estebans Mexican Restaurants, Inc., Mpls., 1978-81; asst. mgr. Mpls. Golf Club, St. Louis Park, 1981—. Mem. Am. Mgmt. Assn., Club Mgrs. Assn. Am. Democrat. Baptist. Home: 4149 Flag Ave N New Hope MN 55427 Office: Minneapolis Golf Club 2001 Flag Ave S Saint Louis Park MN 55426

GRISMORE, JOHN RICHARD, jeweler, watchmaker; b. Corydon, Iowa, Oct. 21, 1924; s. John Arthur and Jennie Gertrude (Bussey) G.; m. Virginia Lynn Rice, Dec. 30, 1947; children—John Richard, Jr., Carol Lynn. Student Bradley U., 1946-48. Lic. watchmaker. Ptnr. Grismore Jewelry, Centerville, Iowa, 1963—. Author poetry, short stories, genealogy. Pres. Community Club, Seymour, Iowa, 1956. Served with U.S. Army, 1943-46, ETO. Mem. C. of C. Methodist. Avocations: astronomy; archaeology; physics; anthropology; nature. Home: 1101 S 15th St Centerville IA 52544 Office: Grismore Jewelry 303 N 13th St Box 543 Centerville IA 52544

GRISWOLD, BERNARD LEE, research laboratory director; b. Hastings, Mich., Apr. 25, 1942; s. Kenneth Preston and Helen Grace (Hogan) G.; m. Mary Louise Gessner, Sept. 13, 1982. B.S., Iowa State U., 1964; M.S., U. Maine, 1966; Ph.D., U. Minn., 1970. Fishery biologist Nat. Marine Fisheries Service, Woods Hole, Mass., 1970-73; fishery biologist, leader Ohio Coop. Fishery Unit, Columbus, 1973-79; supr. Coop. Fish Units, U.S. Fish and Wildlife Service, Washington, 1979-83, dir. Great Lakes Fishery Lab., Ann Arbor, Mich., 1983—. Contbr. articles to various tech. jours. Tech. advisor on Indian treaty fishing rights U.S. Dist. Ct., Kalamazoo, Mich., 1983-84. Research grantee U.S. Soil Conservation Service, 1974-75, U.S. Fish and Wildlife Service, 1973-76, U.S. EPA, 1978-79. Mem. Am. Inst. Fishery Research Biologists (chmn. membership 1983-84), Am. Fishery Soc. (cert. fishery scientist, chmn. profl. cert. com.), Sigma Xi. Office: Great Lakes Fishery Laboratory 1451 Green Rd Ann Arbor MI 48105

GRISWOLD, KENNETH WALTER, educator; b. Joliet, Ill., Nov. 2, 1937; s. Robert P. and Louise A. (Kaatz) G.; B.S., Ill. State U., 1961; M.S., No. Ill. U., 1965; m. Carole Rockwood, Feb. 3, 1962; children—Stephen R., Kent R. Tchr., coach Reed-Custer High Sch., Braidwood, Ill., 1961-64; counselor Lockport (Ill.) Central High Sch., 1964-66, Santa Ana (Calif.) Unified and Jr. Coll. Dist., 1966-67; prof. Rock Valley Coll., Rockford, Ill., 1967—. Mem. Am. Assn. Counseling and Devel., Am. Psychol. Assn., Am. Coll. Personnel Assn., Internat. Soc. Sport Psychology. Republican. Episcopalian. Contbr. articles in field to profl. jours. Home: 3901 Spring Creek Rd Rockford IL 61111 Office: 3301 N Mulford Rd Rockford IL 61101

GROESCH, JOHN WILLIAM, JR., oil company executive; b. Seattle, Nov. 22, 1923; s. John William and Jeanette Morrison (Gilmur) G.; B.S. in Chem. Engring., U. Wash., 1944; m. Joyce Eugenia Schauble, Apr. 25, 1948; children—Sara, Mary, Andrew. Engr., Union Oil Co., Los Angeles, 1944-48, corp. economist, Los Angeles, 1948-56, chief statistician, 1956-62, mgr., 1962-68, mgr., Schaumburg, Ill., 1968—. Bd. dirs. Arlington Heights (Ill.) Boy Scouts Am., 1977—, v.p., 1982—; treas. Scout Cabin Found., Barrington, 1977—. Served with USN, 1944-47. Mem. West Coast Mktg. Research Council (chmn. 1969), Am. Petroleum Inst. (chmn. com. 1970-72). Lodge: Mason. Home: 17 Shady Ln Deer Park Barrington IL 60010 Office: 1650 E Golf Rd Schaumburg IL 60196

GROH, STANLEY ROBERT, educator; b. Melrose, Minn., July 15, 1920; s. Robert Carlyle and Mary Katherine (Barbellau) G.; m. Muriel Harriet LaCroix, Aug. 5, 1942; children—Sandra Lee Clark, Daphne Toshi, Stanley Robert (dec.). B.B.A., U. Pitts., 1957; M.Ed., Pa. State U., 1963. Counselor, Elgin (Ill.) Community Coll., 1965-67; dean student service Waubonsee Community Coll., Sugar Grove, Ill., 1967-78, v.p. planning and research, 1978-82, interim pres., 1981, dir. research, 1982-84; pres. Skyway Intercollegiate Athletic Conf. No. Ill., 1975-76. Pres. Two Rivers council Boy Scouts Am., St. Charles, Ill., 1980-82; mem. nat. council Boy Scouts Am., Dallas, 1980—; trustee Geneva (Ill.) Twp., 1978—; bd. dirs. Aurora (Ill.) YMCA, 1976-80; mem. Ill. Assn. Twp. Suprs. and Trustees, Springfield, 1978—. Served to lt. col. USAF, 1942-64. Recipient Silver Beaver award Boy Scouts Am., 1983. Mem. Nat. Assn. Student Personnel Adminstrs., Soc. Coll. and Univ. Planning, Am. Assn. Collegiate Registrars and Admissions Officers, Ill. Community Coll. and Midwest Research Orgn., Phi Delta Kappa. Republican. Lodge: Lions (pres. 1977-78) (Geneva, Ill.).

GROHOWSKI, FRANK, information industry executive; b. Wilkes-Barre, Pa., May 13, 1941; s. Frank John and Lottie (Emanski) Thomas G.; m. Marie L. Navazo, Jan. 7, 1977; children—Elizabeth, Frank. B.A., Queens Coll., 1963. Asst. advt. mgr. Barnes & Noble, N.Y.C., 1959-64; art dir., advt. mgr. Mills Music, N.Y.C., 1964-67; mgr. mfg. Holt, Rinehart & Winston, CBS, Inc., N.Y.C., 1967-78; v.p. prodn. div. Scott, Foresman & Co., Glenview, Ill., 1978-81; v.p. corp. ops. SFN Cos., Inc., Glenview, 1981—. Recipient Outstanding Achievement award CBS Pub. Group, 1978. Mem. Internat. Materials Mgmt. Soc., Am. Mgmt. Assn., Nat. Composition Assn., Assn. Am. Pubs., Purchasing Mgmt. Assn., Am. Prodn. and Inventory Control Soc., Nat. Council Phys. Distbn. Mgmt., Chgo. Book Clinic.

GRONLI, JOHN VICTOR, college administrator; b. Eshowe, South Africa, Sept. 11, 1932; s. John Einar and Marjorie Gellet (Hawker) G.; came to U.S., 1934, naturalized, 1937; B.A., U. Minn., 1953; M.Div., Luther Theol. Sem., 1958, D.Min., 1978; M.A., Pacific Luth. U., 1975; m. Jeanne Louise Ellertson, Sept. 15, 1952; children—Cheryl Marie Mundt, Deborah Raechel Hokanson, John Timothy, Peter Jonas, Daniel Reuben. Ordained to ministry, 1958; pastor Brocket-Lawton Luth. Parish, Brocket, N.D., 1958-61; Harlowton (Mont.) Luth. Parish, 1961-66; sr. pastor St. Luke's Luth. Ch., Shelby, Mont., 1966-75; missionary Paulinum Sem., Otjimbingwe, Namibia, 1975-76; dean, chmn. dept. philosophy and humanities Golden Valley Luth. Coll., Mpls., 1976-85; dir. Summer Inst. Pastoral Ministry, Mpls., 1980-85. Bd. dirs. Mont. Assn. Chs., 1973-75; sec. bd. for communications and mission support Am. Luth. Ch., 1973-75; mem. dist. council Rocky Mountain Dist., 1963-75, sec., 1963-70, mem. S.African affairs task force SEM Dist., 1978-79. Mem. personnel and guidance assns., Am., Minn. coll. personnel assns. Editor: Rocky Mountain Dist. Yearbook, 1963-70; Rocky Mountain Views, 1973-75; contbr. to Lutheran Standard, 1973-77; contbr. articles to religious jours. Home: 1321 Orkla Dr Minneapolis MN 55427

GROSCHEN, RALPH EDWARD, educator; b. Mpls., Aug. 2, 1945; s. William John and Katherine Julia (Ludwig) G.; m. Sandra Jo Scullen, June 19, 1970; children—Chad, Michelle, Alicia. B.S. in Agronomy, U. Minn., 1968, B.A. in Agr. Edn., 1975. Adult farm bus. mgmt. instr. Sch. Dist. 640, Wabasso, Minn., 1975-78; dist. sales mgr. Standard Chem. Mfg. Co., Omaha, 1978; cons., mgmt. tng. seminar leader Sandy Corp., Southfield, Mich., 1978-80; agr. resource mgmt. coordinator Hennepin Tech. Ctrs., Mpls., 1979—; cons. seminar leader Sandy Corp.; cons. writer Control Data Corp.; Chmn. Minn.-Grown Promotion Group, 1983-85. Served with U.S. Army, 1978-79. Decorated Bronze Star, Army Commendation medal. Mem. Minn. Vocat. Agr. Instr. Assn., Nat. Vocat. Agr. Instr. Assn. Contbr. articles to profl. jours. Home: 9240 Saint Croix Trail North Stillwater MN 55082 Office: 1820 N Xenium Ln Minneapolis MN 55441

GROSFELD, JAMES, real estate development company executive. Chmn., pres., chief exec. officer, dir. Pulte Home Corp., West Bloomfield, Mich. Office: Pulte Home Corp 6400 Farmington Rd West Bloomfield MI 48033*

GROSS, GARRETT JOHN, pharmacology educator; b. Britton, S.D., July 4, 1942; s. Maurice John and Frances Marie (Smith) G.; m. Carol Anne King, Mar. 31, 1967. B.S., S.D. State U., 1965, M.S., 1967; Ph.D., U. Utah, 1971. Instr. pharmacology Med. Coll. Wis., Milw., 1973-75, asst. prof., 1975-77, assoc. prof., 1977-80, prof., 1980—; cons. in field. Co-author: Modern Pharmacology, 1982. Deborah Heart Found. grantee, 1976; recipient Pharm. Mfrs. Found. Faculty Devel. award, 1975. Mem. Am. Soc. Pharmacology and Expl. Therapeutics, Internat. Soc. Heart Research. Methodist. Lodge: Masons. Avocations: golf; raquetball; jogging. Home: 1320 Fairhaven Blvd Elm Grove WI 53122 Office: Med Coll Wis 8701 W Watertown Plank Rd Milwaukee WI 53226

GROSS, KURTIS ROLAND, railroad conductor; b. Red Bud, Ill., Nov. 18, 1946; s. Thomas Felix and Ruth Dorothy (Runge) G.; m. Vickie Jean Rieckenberg, May 17, 1969; children—Tina Ruth, Natalie Jean. Grad. high sch., Chester, Ill. Brakeman, condr. Mo. Pacific R.R., Dupo, Ill., 1983—; dep. apiary insp. Beekeepers Assn., Sparta, Ill. Served with U.S. Army, 1966-68. Mem. Ill. State Beekeepers Assn. (dir., editor bi-monthly bull. 1980—), St. Clair Beekeepers Assn. (sec., editor monthly newsletter 1980—). Roman Catholic. Avocation: beekeeping. Home: 125 Fox Run Sparta IL 62286-1011

GROSS, MONICA IRENE, college administrator; b. Los Angeles, Mar. 23, 1924; d. Adam P. and Lena M. (Unruh) Dirks; m. Harold H. Gross, June 8, 1947; children—Camille, Cheryl, Cuyler. B.S., Bethel Coll., 1945. Editorial asst. McCormick Mathers Publishing Co., Wichita, Kans., 1945; sec. to pres. Bethel Coll., North Newton, Kans., 1945-47, dir. pub. info., editor Bethel Coll. Bull., 1965-80, dir. alumni, devel. records, 1980—. Mem. Am. Assn. Univ. Women (treas. 1976-80, historian 1981-82, program dir. 1982-83, chmn. edn. found. 1983-85). Mennonite. Club: Soroptimist (sec. 1981-83). Avocation: flower gardening. Home: 205 E 24th St North Newton KS 67117 Office: Bethel College 27th & College Ave North Newton KS 67117

GROSS, ROBERT ULSH, veterinarian; b. Russell, Kans., Dec. 11, 1929; s. Norman Joseph and Mary Eva (Cleveland) G.; m. Virginia Lee Sheppard, June 30, 1956; children—Thomas Andrew, Jennifer Leigh. B.S., Kans. State U., 1954, D.V.M., 1954. Gen. practice vet. medicine Gross Vet. Clinic, Virginia, Ill., 1954-66, Jacksonville, Ill., 1966—. Author: A Veterinarian's Limerick Book, 1979. Mem. AVMA. Club: Literary Union (Jacksonville). Lodge: Kiwanis. Avocations: writing; cooking; guitar; speaking. Home: 252 N Webster Ave Jacksonville IL 62650 Office: Gross Vet Clinic 1215 W Walnut St Jacksonville IL 62650

GROSS, STEVEN LANDERS, advertising agency executive; b. Watertown, N.Y., Dec. 3, 1946; s. Joseph B. and Bertha (Landers) G.; m. Mary Elizabeth Little, Apr. 13, 1983; 1 dau. by previous marriage, Lisa Joy. B.A., Ohio Wesleyan U., 1969; M.B.A., M. Internat. Affairs, Columbia U., 1972. Mktg. exec. Proctor & Gamble, Cin., 1972-74, Thomas J. Lipton, Englewood Cliffs, N.J., 1974-76, Gillette Co., Boston, 1976-78; agy. exec. Leber Katz & Ptnrs., N.Y.C., 1978-79; mktg. exec. Abbott Labs., North Chicago, Ill., 1979-83; sr. v.p., mgmt. supr. Bozell & Jacobs, Inc., Chgo., 1983—; adj. prof. Coll. of Lake County, Grayslake, Ill., 1980-82. Mem. Am. Mgmt. Assn., Omicron Delta Epsilon (pres. 1968-69), Kappa Sigma. Republican. Office: Bozell & Jacobs Inc 625 N Michigan Ave Chicago IL 60601

GROSS, THOMAS LESTER, obstetrician/gynecologist, researcher; b. Decatur, Ill., Aug. 17, 1945; s. Gilbert Wayne and Anna (Graham) G.; m. Judy Beth Osborn, Dec. 30, 1967; children—Elizabeth, Matthew, Joshua. B.A. in Chemistry, Bluffton (Ohio) Coll., 1967; M.D., U. Ill., 1971. Diplomate Am. Bd. Ob-Gyn, subsplty. maternal/fetal medicine. Intern and resident Akron (Ohio) Gen. Med. Ctr., 1973-77; fellow in maternal/fetal medicine Case Western Res. U., 1977-79; asst. to dir. perinatal clin. research ctr. Cleve. Met. Gen. Hosp., 1982—; asst. prof. ob-gyn Case Western Res. U., Cleve., 1977-85, assoc. prof. ob-gyn, 1985—. Mem. Physicians for Social Responsibility. Mem. Am. Coll. Obstetricians and Gynecologists (1st prize for research ann. clin. meeting 1984),

Soc. Gynecol. Investigation, Central Assn. Obstetricians and Gynecologists (Community Hosp. Research award 1981, Ann. Prize award for Research, 1982), Soc. Perinatal Obstetricians, Cleve. Ob-Gyn Soc. Contbr. numerous articles to sci. jours. Office: 3395 Scranton Rd Cleveland OH 44109

GROSS, WILLIS CHARLES, JR., dentist; b. St. Louis, June 3, 1924; s. Willis Charles and Mary Ida (Kelly) G.; A.A., Harris Jr. Coll., 1943; D.D.S., St. Louis U., 1946; postgrad. U. Detroit, 1952-53; m. Rosemarie Dorothy Horak, Feb. 14, 1948; 1 son, Alan Charles. Commd. 1st lt. Dental Corps, U.S. Army and USAF, 1946, advanced through grades to maj., 1952; ret., 1953; pvt. practice dentistry, Affton, Mo., 1954—; pres. Willis C. Gross Dental Assos.; v.p. C & W Gross Corp. Served with AUS, 1942-44. Fellow Acad. Gen. Dentistry, Royal Soc. Health (Eng.); mem. Am., Mo. dental assns., St. Louis Dental Soc., Concord Village Bus. Men's Assn., Am. Legion, V.F.W., Alpha Sigma Nu, Omicron Kappa Upsilon, Delta Sigma Delta (past pres., sec.-treas. St. Louis chpt.), Alpha Phi Omega. Republican. Mason (Shriner, chmn. temple med. staff, 32 deg.), Lion (pres. Concord Village 1965-66). Clubs: Liberty Country (dir.) (Horine, Mo.); Big Game Hunters (St. Louis). Home: 20 Dorclin Ln Saint Louis MO 63128 Office: 7 Concord Center Dr Saint Louis MO 63123

GROSSI, WILLIAM ANTHONY, lawyer; b. Chgo., June 8, 1953; s. Angelo Dominic and Anna Mary (La Mantia) G.; m. Monica Mary LaSusa, Mar. 10, 1979; 1 child, William Thomas. B.S., Marquette U., 1975; M.S., DePaul U., 1976; J.D., Ill. Inst. Tech. Chgo.-Kent Coll. Law, 1979. Bar: Ill. 1979, U.S. Dist. Ct. (no. dist.) Ill. 1979, U.S. Tax Ct. 1982; C.P.A., Tex. Estate tax atty. IRS, Chgo., 1979-82; tax atty. FMC Corp., Chgo., 1982—. Mem. ABA (sect. taxation), Ill. State Bar Assn., Am. Inst. C.P.A.s. Office: FMC Corp Tax Dept 200 E Randolph Dr Chicago IL 60601

GROSSKREUTZ, JOSEPH CHARLES, physicist, engineering researcher; b. Springfield, Mo., Jan. 5, 1922; s. Joseph Charles and Helen (Mobley) G.; m. Mary Catherine Schubel, Sept. 7, 1949; children—Cynthia Lee, Barbara Helen. B.S. in Math., Drury Coll., 1943; postgrad. U. Calif.-Berkeley, 1946-47; M.A., Washington U., St. Louis, 1948, Ph.D. in Physics, 1950. Research physicist Calif. Research Corp., La Habra, 1950-52; asst. prof. physics U. Tex.-Austin, 1952-56; research scientist Nuclear Physics Lab., Austin, 1952-56; sr. physicist Midwest Research Inst., Kansas City, Mo., 1956-59, prin. physicist, 1959-63, sr. adviser, 1963-67, prin. adviser, 1967-71; chief mech. properties sect. Nat. Bur. Standards, Washington, 1971-72; mgr. solar programs Black & Veatch Cons. Engrs., Kansas City, Mo., 1972-77, mgr. advanced tech. projects, 1979—; dir. research Solar Energy Research Inst., Golden, Colo., 1977-79; spl. cons. NATO, 1967. Served to lt. USN, 1943-46. Recipient Disting. Service award Drury Coll., 1959, Merit award ASTM, 1972; Washington U. fellow, 1948-49. Fellow Am. Phys. Soc., ASTM (dir. 1977-80); mem. Sigma Xi, Sigma Pi Sigma. Methodist. Contbr. physics and energy articles to profl. jours. Home: 4306 W 111th Terr Leawood KS 66211 Office: Black & Veatch PO Box 8405 Kansas City MO 64114

GROSSMAN, LISA ROBBIN, clinical psychologist, lawyer; b. Chgo., Jan. 22, 1952; d. Samuel R. and Sarah (Kruger) G. B.A. with highest distinction and departmental honors in Psychology, Northwestern U., 1974, J.D. cum laude, 1979, Ph.D., 1982. Bar: Ill. 1981; registered psychologist, Ill. Jud. intern, U.S. Supreme Ct., Washington, 1975; pre-doctoral psychology intern Michael Reese Hosp. and Med. Center, Chgo., 1979-80; therapist Homes for Children, Chgo., 1980-83; psychologist Psychiat. Inst., Cir. Ct. Cook County, Chgo., 1981—; invited participant workshop HHS, Rockville, Md., 1981. Contbr. articles to profl. jours. Mem. Am. Psychol. Assn., Ill. Psychol. Assn., Chgo. Assn. Psychoanalytic Psychologists (parliamentarian 1982), ABA, Ill. State Bar Assn., Chgo. Bar Assn., Mortar Bd., Phi Beta Kappa, Shi-Ai, Alpha Lambda Delta. Office Psychiat Inst Circuit Ct Cook County 2650 S California Ave Chicago IL 60608

GROSSMAN, MICHAEL, animal science educator; b. N.Y.C., Dec. 21, 1940; s. Benjamin Harry and Alice (Berkowitz) G.; m. Margaret Rosso, June 27, 1970; children—Aaron, Daniel. B.S., CCNY, 1962; M.S., Va. Polytech., 1965; Ph.D., Purdue U., 1969. From asst. prof. to prof. genetics U. Ill., Urbana, 1969—; vis. prof. Instituto Fitotechnia, Castelar, Argentina, summer 1970, Gadjah Mada Univ., Yogyakarta, Indonesia, fall 1974; research geneticist U.S. Dept. Agr. Beltsville, Md., 1979-80. Editor: Monograph in Theoretical and Applied Genetics. Contbr. articles to profl. jours. Recipient Danforth Found. Faculty Assoc., 1976—; AMOCO Found. Instructional award 1972. Mem. Am. Genetic Assn. (council 1979-83), Am. Dairy Sci. Assn., Am. Soc. Animal Sci., Genetics Soc. Am., Biometric Soc., AAAS. Avocations: music; reading; gardening. Office: 315 Animal Sci Lab 1207 W Gregory Dr Urbana IL 61801

GROSSMAN, MORTON SAMUEL, artist, art educator; b. N.Y.C., May 28, 1926; s. Edward S. and Rita (Cooperman) G.; m. Elaine M. Christeson; children—Philip, Inga, Neil. Student Art Students League, N.Y.C., 1944-47; B.A., Queens Coll., 1948. Assoc. prof. art SUNY-Buffalo, 1956-60; instr. Cleve. Inst. Art, 1961-64; asst. prof. art U. Md., College Park, 1964-69; prof. art Kent State U., Ohio, 1969—. One-man shows include Albright-Knox Gallery, Buffalo, Kansas City Art Inst., Pub. Archtl. Gallery, Wellington, N.Z., Phila. Art Alliance; represented in permanent collections Cleve. Mus. Art, Birmingham Mus. Art, Norfolk Mus. Art. Recipient Dana medal Pa. Acad. Arts., 1959, Gold medal Am. Watercolor Soc., First. prize Am. Drawing Biennial, 1954, award Hallmark Watercolor Internat., 1952; Tiffany Found. fellow. Home: 217 Crain Ave Kent OH 44240 Office: Sch Art Kent State U Kent OH 44242

GROSSMAN, N. BUD, rental transportation company executive. Chmn., cheif exec. officer, dir. Gelco Corp., Eden Prairie, Minn. Office: Gelco Corp One Gelco Dr Eden Prairie MN 55344*

GROTBERG, JAMES BERNARD, biomedical engineer, educator; b. Oak Park, Ill., July 22, 1950; s. John Edward and Edith (Henderson) Burchinal; m. Karen Faith Rubner, June 22, 1980. Ph.D., Johns Hopkins U., 1978; M.D., U. Chgo., 1980. Lic. physician, Ill. Asst. prof. Northwestern U., Evanston, Ill., 1980—. Contbr. articles to profl. jours. Recipient Achievement award Johns Hopkins U., 1973, New Investigator, NIH, 1983, Presl. Young Investigator, NSF, 1984. Mem. Am. Phys. Soc., Phi Beta Kappa, Taue Beta Pi. Office: Dept Engring Scis & Applied Math Technological Inst Northwestern Univ Evanston IL 60201

GROTBERG, JOHN E., U.S. congressman b. Winnebago, Minn., Mar. 21, 1925; s. Bernard G.; B.S., George Williams Coll., 1961; m. Jean Oswalt; children—Sandra Mae Grotberg Kistler, Karen Grotberg Weinberg, James Bernard; stepchildren—Melinda and Benjamin M. Oswalt. Farmer, N.D., 1942-44; theatrical and supper club entertainer and mgr., Fargo, Saint Louis, Mpls. and Chgo., 1944-47; mgr. YMCA Hotel Shop, 1948-49, 51, 59; dept. mgr. Montgomery Ward, Chgo., 1950; resident mgr. Pheasant Run Lodge, St. Charles, Ill., 1964-65; dir. public relations YMCA Hotel, Chgo., 1966-71; cons. to mgmt. Hotel Baker Retirement Home for Sr. Citizens, from 1972; corp. dir. fin. devel. YMCA Met. Chgo., 1966-71; rep. Ill. Gen. Assembly, 1973-76; mem. Ill. Senate, 1976-85, asst. Republican leader, 1981-85; mem. 99th Congress, 14th Ill. dist.; profl. singer and actor. Chmn. bd., lay leader Baker Meml. United Methodist Ch.; founder Fox Valley Hospice; former bd. dirs. St. Charles Community Chest; past pres. and bd. dirs. Playmakers, Inc.; founder St. Charles YMCA Indian Guides; Rep. precinct committeeman; past chmn. St. Charles Twp. Rep. Party; chmn. Kane County Rep. Central Com. Mem. Assn. Profl. Dirs. YMCA, Kappa Delta Pi. Clubs: Geneva Golf, Tower (Chgo.). Lodge: Rotary (Chgo.). Office: 515 Cannon House Office Bldg Washington DC 20515*

GROTE, JAMES ROBERT, college administrator, consultant; b. Hays, Kans., Mar. 14, 1945; s. Henry and Hilda Laurs (Roeder) G.; m. Linda M. Stephens, June 9, 1972; 1 son, Curtis James. B.S., U. Kans., 1967; M.S., Kans. State U., 1974, Ph.D., 1980. Instr., dept. head Norton (Kans.) Community Schs., 1968-73; dean community service Colby (Kans.) Community Coll., 1974-78, dean instl. advancement, 1983—; dean instrn. Fort Scott Community Coll. (Kans.), 1980-83; chmn. Western Kans. Community Service, Colby, 1976-77; tech. advisor Kans. 1202 Commn., Topeka, 1977-78; cons. Lake Region Community Coll., Devils Lake, N.D., 1979-80; sec. Kans. Council Deans of Ins., Topeka, 1981-82. Mem. Kans. State Bd. Nursing, Topeka, 1976-80. State Dept. Edn. grantee, Topeka, 1974-83. Mem. Am. Higher Edn. Assn., Am. Assn. Community and Jr. Colls., Am. Mgmt. Assn., Nat. Assn. Pub. Continuing and Adult Edn., Kans. Assn. Community Colls., Phi Delta Kappa. Democrat. Roman Catholic. Lodge: K.C. Home: 1785 Harvey St Colby KS 67701

GROTEFELD, MARK STEPHEN, lawyer; b. Chgo., Sept. 18, 1956; s. William Sven and June (Stewart) G.; m. Michele Miller, July 10, 1983. B.A., U. Ariz., 1978; cert. in internat. law U. Strasbourg, France, 1980; J.D., John Marshall Law Sch., 1981. Bar: Ill. 1981, Fla. 1982, U.S. Dist. Ct. (no. dist.) Ill. 1981. Assoc. W. S. Grotefeld & Assocs., Chgo., 1981—. Mem. Chgo. Bar Assn., Ill. Assn. Hosp. Attys., Assn. Trial Lawyers Am. Democrat. Club: Union League (Chgo.). Home: 552 W Roscoe Chicago IL 60657 Office: W S Grotefeld & Assocs PC 20 N Clark St Chicago IL 60602

GROTHMAN, JAMES RUSSELL, land surveyor; b. Portage, Wis., June 18, 1953; s. Byron G. and Audrey E. (Sherman) G.; m. Karen Ann Paske, Apr. 5, 1975; 1 child, Mariah Rae. A.S., Madison Area Tech. Coll., 1974. Registered land surveyor. Assoc., mgr. land surveying dept. Gen. Engring. Co., Inc., Portage, 1974—; mem. land surveying adv. com. Madison Area Tech. Coll., Wis., 1984—. Mem. Wis. Soc. Land Surveyors, Am. Congress Surveying and Mapping, Nat. Soc. Profl. Land Surveyors. Republican. Roman Catholic. Avocations: flying; racquetball. Home: 1122 W Plasant St Portage WI 53901 Office: Gen Engring 412 E Slifer St Portage WI 53901

GROTJAN, H(ARVEY) EDWARD, JR., physiologist, educator; b. Moberly, Mo., July 31, 1947; s. Harvey Edward and Pansy Juanita (Clanton) G.; m. E. Gayle Kothe, July 3, 1969. B.S., U. Mo., 1969, M.S., 1971; Ph.D., U. Kans., 1975. Postdoctoral fellow U. Tex, Houston, 1975-77, asst. prof., 1977-83; assoc. prof. U. S.D., Vermillion, 1983—. V.P. Concordia Lutheran Ch., Vermillion, 1984—. Recipient Research Service award NIH, Bethesda, Md., 1975-77; grantee NIH, Bethesda, 1977-84, Robert Welch Found., 1982-83. Mem. Endocrine Soc., Soc. Study Reproduction, AAAS, Am. Physiol. Soc., Sigma Xi. Lodge: Optimist. Avocation: computer programming. Home: 714 Brooks Dr Vermillion SD 57069 Office: Dept Physiology Pharmacology U SD Vermillion SD 57069

GROTZINGER, LAUREL ANN, educator; b. Truman, Minn., Apr. 15, 1935; d. Edward F. and Marian Gertrude (Greeley) G.; B.A., Carleton Coll., 1957; M.S., U. Ill., 1958, Ph.D., 1964. Instr., asst. librarian Ill. State U., 1958-62; asst. prof. Western Mich. U., Kalamazoo, 1964-66, asso. prof., 1966-68, prof., 1968—, asst. dir. Sch. Librarianship, 1965-72, dean/chief research officer Grad. Coll., 1979—, interim dir. Sch. Library and Info. Sci., 1982-85. Mem. ALA (sec.-treas. Library History Round Table 1973-74, chairperson 1984-85), Acad. Mgmt., Assn. Library and Info. Sci. Edn., Mich. Council Grad. Deans (chairperson 1983-84), Am. Assn. Higher Edn., Council Grad. Schs., Nat. Council Research Adminstrs., Soc. Research Adminstrs., Mich. Acad. Sci., Arts and Letters (mem. exec. com. 1980—, pres. 1983-85), AAUP (sec. W.M. chpt. 1968-70), Phi Beta Kappa (pres. Southwestern Mich. Assn. 1977-78), Beta Phi Mu (v.p., pres. Kappa chpt.), Pi Delta Epsilon, Delta Kappa Gamma, Alpha Beta Alpha. Author: The Power and the Dignity, Scarecrow, 1966; mem. editorial bd. Jour. Edn. for Librarianship, 1973-77, Dictionary Am. Library Biography, 1975-77; contbr. articles to profl. jours.; also monographs. Home: 2729 Mockingbird Dr Kalamazoo MI 49008

GROVE, HELEN HARRIET, historian, artist; b. South Bend, Ind.; d. Samuel Harold and LaVerne Mae (Drescher) Grove; grad. Bayle Sch. Design, Meinzinger Found., 1937-39, Washington U., 1940-42; spl. studies, Paris, France. Owner studios of historic research and illustration, St. Louis, Chgo., 1943—; dir. archives, bus. history research Sears, Roebuck & Co., 1951-67; com. missions art and research for Northwestern U., Chgo.-Sears Roebuck & Co. Home: 6326 N Clark St Chicago IL 60626 Studio: 6328 N Clark St Chicago IL 60626

GROVE, HENRY FREDERICK, III, prosthodontist, educator; b. Milw., Sept. 7, 1933; s. Henry F., Jr. and Eunice J. (De Groat) G.; m. Leslie Moberg, June 20, 1970; children—Sara, Daniel. B.A., Marquette U., 1953, D.D.S., 1959. Commd. 1st lt. U.S. Army, 1959, advanced through grades to col., 1975; dental officer, U.S.A., Europe, Vietnam, 1959-79; ret., 1979; instr. dentistry Marquette U., Milw., 1979—; cons. in field. Contbr. articles to Profl. jours. Coach, youth sports, Milw., 1980—. Mem. ADA, Am. Coll. Prosthodontics, Am. Prosthodontic Soc., Assn. Am. Dental Schs., Midwest Acad. Prosthodontics (sec.-treas. 1983—). Episcopalian. Avocations: skiing; running; swimming; tennis; woodworking. Office: Dept Removable Prosthodontics Marquette U Sch Dentistry 604 N 16th St Milwaukee WI 53233

GROVE, JACK FREDERICK, lawyer, educator; b. Hamilton, Ohio, Aug. 31, 1953; s. James Edward and Eleanor Katherine (Schlichter) G.; m. Susan Kathleen Flick, July 24, 1976; 1 child, Adam Nathaniel. B.S. in Agr., Ohio State U., 1975; J.D., U. Dayton, 1979. Bar: Ohio 1979, U.S. Dist. Ct. (so. dist.) Ohio 1979, U.S. Supreme Ct. 1984. Law clk. to Judge Fred B. Cramer, Hamilton, Ohio, 1979-80; asst. pros. atty. Butler County, Hamilton, 1980—; instr. fin. Miami U., Oxford, Ohio, 1981-84; ptnr. Grove & Matre, Fairfield, Ohio, 1979—; mem. adv. council Hamilton Tool Co., 1982—. Mem. exec. com. Butler County Republican party, Hamilton, Ohio, 1980-81. Mem. ABA, Ohio State Bar Assn., Butler County Bar Assn., Cin. Bar Assn., Gamma Sigma Delta. Republican. Clubs: New London Hills, Hamilton City; Sierra, Audubon Soc. Home: 1093 Davis Rd Hamilton OH 45013 Office: 1251 Nilles Rd Suite 10 Fairfield OH 45014

GROVE, WALTER HENRY, JR., collector's society administrator; b. Apr. 21, 1939; s. Walter H. and A. Marie (Fee) G.; m. Patricia C. Rossi, July 28, 1973; children—Marc, Scott, Heather. B.S. in Mgmt., Rutgers U., 1973. Supr. Westinghouse Electric Co., Trenton, N.J., 1969-73; program mgr. Franklin Mint Corp., Franklin Center, Pa., 1974-82; dir. program devel. Calhoun's Collector Soc., Mpls., 1982—. Mem. Imperial Hills Civic Assn., Plymouth, Minn. Served with Army N.G., 1959-66. Mem. Upper Midwest DMA Assn., Delta Sigma Pi. Home: 2200 Urbandale Ln Plymouth MN 55447

GROVER, HERBERT JOSEPH, educational administrator, educator; b. Fond du Lac, Wis., Feb. 5, 1937; s. Felix N. and Helen (Hardgrove) G.; m. Caroline Grover, July 3, 1965; children—John, Michael. Pat, Johanna, Caroline, Kristie, Mary, Herbert. B.A., St. Norbert Coll., DePere, Wis., 1959; M.A., Am. U., 1963; Ph.D., U. Wis., 1974, cert. in edn. adminstrn., 1974. Mem. Wis. Ho. of Reps., 1965-74, majority floor leader, 1971-72, mem. assembly edn. com., 1973-74; supt. schs. Niagara (Wis.) Schs., 1974-78, Monona (Wis.) Schs., 1978-81; supt. dept. pub. instrn. State of Wis., Madison, 1981—; mem. Edn. Commn. of States, Coll. Bd., Wis. Bd. Regents, Higher Edn. Aids Bd., State Bd. Vocat. Tech. and Adult Edn.; lectr., speaker in field. Contbr. in field. Recipient Disting. Service award Wis. Assn. Retarded Children, 1971; Alma Mater award St. Norbert Coll., 1981; Wis. Assn. Environ. Edn. award, 1983; Spl. Recognition award Am. Assn. Ednl. Service Agys.; Outstanding Ednl. Leadership award Coop. Ednl. Service Agy. #2 Dist. Adminstrs., 1983; Pub. Service award Wis. Sch. Safety Coordinators Assn., 1984; Pres.'s award Wis. Edn. Assn. Council, 1984; Disting. Leadership award Nat. Ctr. Health Edn., 1984; Outstanding Educator award Wis. Assn. Sch. Dist. Adminstrs., 1984; Disting. Friend of Edn. award Assn. Wis. Sch. Adminstrs., 1984. Mem. Council State Sch. Officers, Ctr. for Advancement of Sci. Edn., Wis. Assn. Sch. Dist. Adminstrs., Wis. Assn. Tchr. Educators, Wis. Assn. Sch. Bus. Ofcls., Wis. Juvenile Ct. Intake Assn., Wis. Sch. Counselors Assn., Wis. Acad. Scis., Arts and Letters, Wis. Assn. Supervision and Curriculum Devel., Phi Delta Kappa. Roman Catholic. Office: 125 S Webster St PO Box 7841 Madison WI 53707

GROVES, DELORES ELLIS, educational administrator; b. Shelby County, Ky., Jan. 29; d. David Irvin and Mary Eliza (Powell) Ellis; m. Robert Louis Graves, Sept. 29, 1957; children—Angela, Robin; m. Clyde Groves, Dec. 20, 1969. B.S., Spalding Coll., 1966; M.A., John Carroll U., 1972; postgrad. postgrad. Kent State U., Cleve. State U., Akron U. Tchr., pub. schs., Louisville, 1966-69, Cleve., 1970, Shaker Heights, Ohio, 1970-78; adminstr. pub. schs., Shaker Heights, 1978—, prin. elem. sch., 1980—. Mem. Assn. Supervision and Curriculum Devel., NAACP, Ohio Assn. Elem. Sch. Adminstrs., Nat. Assn. Elem. Sch. Prins., Nat. Alliance Black Educators, Ohio Alliance Black Educators, Shaker Heights Interest Group, Phi Delta Kappa, Delta Sigma Theta. Baptist. Democrat. Club: VIPS Social and Civic.

GROWE, JOAN ANDERSON, state official; b. Mpls., Sept. 28, 1935; d. Arthur F. and Lucille M. (Brown) Anderson; B.S., St. Cloud (Minn.) State U., 1956; cert. in Spl. Edn., U. Minn., 1964; children—Michael, Colleen, David, Patrick. Tchr., Bloomington (Minn.) Public Schs., 1956-58; tchr. exceptional children St. Paul Public Schs., 1964-65; tchr. spl. edn. St. Anthony (Minn.) Public Schs., 1965-66; mem. Minn. Ho. Reps., 1973-74; sec. state State of Minn., St. Paul, 1975—. Mem. Indianhead Council Boy Scouts Am., Minn. Assn. Retarded Citizens, Minn. Shares for Hunger, Urban Concerns, YWCA; mem. adv. bd. Fed. Elections Commn., State Bd. Investment. Recipient Minn. Sch. Bell award, 1977; YWCA award, 1978. Mem. Minn. LWV, AAUW, Minn. Women's Polit. Caucus, Women Against Mil. Madness, Minn. Econ. Roundtable, Citizens League, Democratic Statewide Elected Ofcls., Dem. Policy Commn., Common Cause, Nat. Assn. Secs. of State (pres. 1979-80), Bus. and Profl. Women's Club. Club: Zonta. Roman Catholic. Office: 180 State Office Bldg Saint Paul MN 55155

GRUENWALD, JAMES HOWARD, association executive, consultant; b. Cin., Aug. 30, 1949; s. Howard Francis and Geraldine Emma (Mueller) G. B.S., Xavier U., 1971. Cert. profl. in recreation and leisure service, Ill. Rep. pub. relations Catholic Youth Orgn., Cin., 1969-72; advtransp. sales rep. Spade Trucking Co., Cin., 1972-73; field rep. Ohio Dept. Transport, Columbus, 1973-76; editorial, sales rep. Cin. Suburban Newspaper, 1976-77; asst. devel. dir. Cin. Art Acad., 1977-79; nat. exec. dir. SAY SOCCER USA, Cin., 1979—; chmn. Buckeye Men's Baseball, Cin., 1982—; dir. Amateur Athletic Union, Indpls., 1983—; cert. trainer Am. Coaches Effectiveness Program, Champaign, Ill., 1983—. Author Jour. Nat. Recreation and Parks, 1983; Jour. Ohio Parks and Attractions, 1985. Editor jour. Touchline, 1980—. Candidate for city council City of St. Bernard, Ohio, 1977; mem. adv. bd. Church Parish, Cin., 1974-76. Recipient Exec. Dir. Service award SAY SOCCER USA, 1979. Mem. Cin. Assn. Execs., Nat. Council Youth Sports Dirs., Am. Soc. Assn. Execs., Nat. Recreation and Parks Assn., Soc. for Non Profits. Avocations: hiking; reading; writing; teaching; conducting workshops. Home: 610 E Mitchell Ave Cincinnati OH 45217 Office: SAY SOCCER USA 5945 Ridge Rd Cincinnati OH 45213

GRUNDLAND, PAUL, osteopathic surgeon; b. Miami Beach, Fla., Oct. 25, 1935; s. Max and Anne B. (Berenberg) G.; m. Jill Rifkin, Oct. 5, 1967; children—Dayna, Traci, Mark. B.A., U. Minn., 1958; D.O., Kirksville Coll. Osteopathy, 1966. Practice osteopathic medicine, Madison Heights, Mich., 1967—; asst. clin. prof. family medicine Mich. State U. Served with U.S. Army, 1958-62. Recipient Cert. Recognition Nat. Republican Congl. Com., 1982. Mem. Am. Osteo. Assn., Oakland County Osteopathy Soc., Am. Coll. Gen. Practitioners Osteopathy Medicine and Surgery. Republican. Jewish. Home: 3960 Nearbrook Dr Bloomfield Hills MI 48013 Office: 1385 E 12 Mile Rd Madison Heights MI 48071

GRUNLAN, STEPHEN ARTHUR, clergyman, educator; b. N.Y.C., Feb. 9, 1942; s. Magnus Arthur and Esther (Helliksen) G.; m. Sandra Jean Smits, Oct. 7, 1964; children—Stephen Arthur, Jaime C., Rebecca Sue. B.S., Nyack (N.Y.) Coll., 1970; M.A., Wheaton (Ill.) Coll., 1972; M.A., U. Ill., Chgo., 1976; D.Min., Luther Theol. Sem., St. Paul, 1981. Ordained to ministry Christian and Missionary Alliance, 1978; missionary Missionary Gospel Fellowship, Turlock, Calif., 1972-74; prof. Moody Bible Inst., Chgo., 1974-77, St. Paul Bible Coll., 1977-82; sr. pastor Minnetonka (Minn.) Community Ch., 1983—; prof. Northwestern Coll. and St. Paul Bible Coll., part-time, seminar leader pastoral tng. Served with U.S. Army, 1960-65. Mem. Christian Assn. Psychol. Studies, Christian Sociol. Soc. Author: (with Marvin Mayers) Cultural Anthropology: A Christian Perspective, 1979; (with Milton Reimer) Christian Perspectives on Sociology, 1982; (with Daniel Lambrides) Healing Relationships, 1983; Marriage and the Family: A Christian Perspective, 1984; Serving with Joy, 1985; also numerous articles. Office: Minnetonka Community Ch 13243 Minnetonka Dr Minnetonka MN 55343

GRUNOW, MILLIE HUST, librarian; b. Bedford County, Tenn., Oct. 16, 1931; d. William B. and Georgia Mae (Elkins) Hust; B.A., George Peabody Coll. Tchrs., Nashville, 1953, M.A. in Library Sci., 1955; m. Hubert L. Near, Aug. 13, 1955; children—Elizabeth Near Hanes, Katherine Near Baize, Margaret; m. 2d, Donald A. Grunow, Mar. 17, 1973. Head cataloging dept. W.Va. Inst. Tech., Montgomery, 1967-70; coordinator tech. services U. Evansville (Ind.), 1970-72; med. librarian Deaconess Hosp., Evansville, 1972—; exec. dir. Evansville Area Health Sci. Library Consortium, 1975-79, pres., 1981-83, state council rep. to regional council, 1981-84. Mem. Med. Library Assn., Greater Midwest Regional Med. Library Network, Ind. Health Scis. Librarians Assn., Evansville Area Health Sci. Library Consortium. Methodist. Home: 508 S Boeke Rd Evansville IN 47714 Office: 600 Mary St Evansville IN 47747

GRUTZMACHER, HAROLD MARTIN, JR., bookstore owner, writer; b. Chgo., Nov. 17, 1930; s. Harold Martin and Irene Evelyn (Kowalski) G.; m. Marjorie Sharlene Andersen, Nov. 5, 1955; children—Stephen, Sharon, Alison. B.A., Beloit Coll., 1952; M.A., Northwestern U., 1953, Ph.D., 1962. Asst. prof. Carthage Coll., Ill., 1958-60, Knox Coll., Galesburg, Ill., 1960-65; chmn. rhetoric Parsons Coll., Fairfield, Iowa, 1965-67; v.p. acad. affairs U. Tampa, Fla., 1967-70; dean students Beloit Coll., Wis., 1970-75; owner, mgr. Passtimes Books, Ephraim and Sister Bay, Wis., 1978—; book reviewer Chgo. Tribune, 1962-73, Tampa Tribune, 1967-70; poetry reviewer/editor Milw. Jour., 1980—. Author: A Giant of My World, 1960; Generations, 1983 (poetry). Editor: A Grace Samuelson Sampler, 1985; Young With Ephraim, 1985. Polit. reporter Door County Advocate, 1976-85. Served with U.S. Army, 1956-58. Mem. Wis. Regional Writers, Wis. Acad. Republican. Avocations: reading; sports reporting. Home: Box 153 Ephraim WI 54211 Office: Passtimes Books Box 153 Ephraim WI 54211

GRUYS, ROBERT IRVING, physician, surgeon; b. Silver Creek, Minn., Oct. 15, 1917; s. Herman and Dorothy (Vondergon) G.; m. Cornelia Mol, June 30, 1943 (div. 1976); children—Kathy, Robert, William, John. B.S., U. Minn., 1945, B.S. in Medicine, 1946, M.D., 1947. Rotating intern Wayne County Gen. Hosp., Detroit, 1949, Mpls. VA Hosp., 1958, 62; postgrad. Cook County Gen. Hosp., Chgo., 1957, 63, 64, Mayo Clinic, Rochester, Minn., 1949-58, U. Minn., 1958-68, 70-75; physician, surgeon Watkins Clinic, Wells, Minn., 1950-58, 63-67, 70-75, Ganado Presbyn. Hosp., Ariz., 1953-57, Southwest Clinic, Edina, Minn., part time, 1967-68, Chiayi Christian Hosp., Taiwan, 1968-70, Estes Park Med. Clinic, Colo., 1975-79, St. Cloud Va Med. Ctr., 1979—; mem. staff Wells Community Hosp., 1951-75, Meth. Hosp., Mpls., 1967-68, Mt. Sinai Hosp., Mpls., 1967-68, North Meml. Hosp., Mpls., 1967-76, Fairview Southdale Hosp., Mpls., 1967-68, Met. Med. Ctr., Mpls., 1967-76, Elizabeth Knutson Meml. Hosp., Estes Park, Colo., 1975-79, Weld County Gen. Hosp., Greeley, Colo., 1976-79, St. Cloud VA Med. Ctr., 1979—. Mem. Colo. State Med. Assn., Larimer County Med. Assn., Am. Soc. Abdominal Surgeons, Internat. Coll. Surgeons, Christian Med. Soc., AMA, Wayne County Med. Assn., Stearns-Benton County Med. Soc., Alpha Omega Alpha. Lutheran. Lodge: Masons. Avocations: flying country-western music. Home: PO Box 1817 Saint Cloud MN 56302-1817 Office: St Cloud VA Hosp 8th St Saint Cloud MN 56301

GRYTE, ROLF EDWARD, internist; b. Mpls., Mar. 8, 1945; s. Ralph Edward and Irene (Lindquist) G.; m. Diane Wedin, June 24, 1967 (div. Apr. 1971); m. Barbara Lee Deems, June 8, 1971; children—David, Kirsten, Kristofer. B.A., U. Minn., 1967; D.O., Kirksville Coll. Osteopathic Medicine, 1971. Diplomate Am. Osteopathic Bd. Internal Medicine. Intern Kirksville Osteopathic Hosp., Mo., 1971-72, resident in internal medicine, 1972-75, chief resident, 1974-75, assoc. prof. internal medicine, 1975-79, mem. clin. faculty, 1979—, hosp. epidemiologist, 1977-79; practice medicine specializing in internal medicine, Kirksville, 1979—; med. dir. inhalation therapy dept. Kirksville Osteopathic Hosp., 1975-80, Grim-Smith Hosp., Kirksville, 1979—, med. dir. pulmonary rehabilitation program, 1983—; black lung examiner Dept. Labor, Denver, 1983—; social security disability examiner, Jefferson City, Mo., 1975—. Med. dir. Planned Parenthood of Northeast Mo., Kirksville, 1972-82, chmn. med. adv. com., 1972—; mem. Great Lakes Region Med. Adv. Com. Planned Parenthood World Fedn., 1983—. Named Outstanding Prof., Kirksville Coll. Osteopathic Medicine sophomore class, 1979; Nat. Osteopathic Coll. scholar. Mem. Am. Coll. Internal Medicine, Am. Heart Assn., Mo. Thoracic Soc., Mo. Assn. Osteopathic Physicians and Surgeons, Northeast Mo. Osteopathic Assn., Sigma Sigma Phi, Psi Sigma Alpha. Republican. Lutheran. Clubs: Appaloosa Horse (Moscow, Ida.); Central Mo. Appaloosa Horse (Columbia) (pres. 1981—). Avocations: Appaloosa breeding farm; hunting; fishing. Home: RR 1 Kirksville MO 63501 Office: 1108 E Patterson Ste 2 Kirksville MO 63501

GSCHNEIDNER, KARL ALBERT, JR., metallurgy educator, editor; b. Detroit, Nov. 16, 1930; s. Karl and Eugenie (Zehetmair) G.; m. Melba E. Pickenpaugh, Nov. 4, 1957; children—Thomas, David, Edward, Kathryn. B.S., U. Detroit, 1952; Ph.D., Iowa State U., 1957. Mem. staff Los Alamos Sci. Lab., 1957-62, sect. chief, 1961-62; assoc. prof., metallurgist Iowa State U., Ames, 1963-67, prof., sr. metallurgist, 1967-79, Disting. prof., 1979—, dir. Rare-earth Info. Ctr., 1966—; vis. asst. prof. U. Ill., Urbana, 1962-63; vis. prof. U.

Calif.-San Diego, La Jolla, 1979-80. Editor: Handbook on the Physics and Chemistry of Rare Earths, 7 Vols., 1979-84; Industrial Application of Rare Earth Elements, 1981. Contbr. numerous chpts. to books and numerous articles to profl. jours. Recipient Outstanding Sci. Accomplishment in Metallurgy and Ceramics award U.S. Dept. Energy, 1982. Mem. Am. Chem. Soc., Am. Soc. Metals, Am. Crystallographic Assn., AIME (William Hume-Rothery award Metall. Soc. 1978), AAAS. Roman Catholic. Avocations: gardening; bicycling; photography. Office: Ames Lab Iowa State Univ Ames IA 50011

GSCHWIND, KAMIL STEPHAN, architect; b. Pilsen, Czechoslovakia, July 4, 1931; came to U.S., 1959; s. Otakar and Miloslava (Sammer) G.; m. Nancy Caroline Siska, Nov. 9, 1963; children—Colette Jane, Barbara Kathryn, Ingrid Elise. D. in Archtl. Engring., Tech. U., Prague, Czechoslovakia, 1955; M.Arch., Acad. Fine Arts, Prague, 1958. Registered architect, Ohio. Dir. design William Dorsky & Assocs., Cleve.; project architect Don Hisaka & Assocs., Cleve.; pres. Kamil S. Gschwind, Architect, Richmond Heights, Ohio, 1975—; vis. critic, lectr. Kent (Ohio) State U., 1970—. Mem. AIA, Architects Soc. Ohio. Clubs: Suburban Ski, Mayfield Village Racquet. Home: 26700 Loganberry Dr 114 Richmond Heights OH 44143 Office: 26700 Loganberry Dr 114 Richmond Heights OH 44143

GUAPPONE, WILLIAM JOSEPH, optometrist; b. Cin., June 14, 1956; s. William Anthony and Suzanne Marie (Legrand) G.; m. Mary Ann Mayer, Aug. 11, 1979; 1 child, Anne Marie. B.A. in English, U. Notre Dame, 1978; O.D., Ohio State U., 1982. Lic. optometrist, optometric pharmacologist, Ohio. Practice medicine specializing in optometry Gilman & Guappone, Optometrists, Inc., Cin., 1982—. Contbr. articles to profl. jours. Recipient Nikon Scholar award, 1979. Mem. Cin. Optometric Assn. (sec.-treas. 1984—), Beta Sigma Kappa. Club: Serra (Cin.). Lodge: K.C. (Cin.). Avocations: sports; music; arts. Office: 3411 Michigan Ave Cincinnati OH 45208

GUBANC, DAVID MICHAEL, environmental engineer, consultant; b. Toledo, Oct. 31, 1949; s. Robert David and Louise Marie (Soule) G.; m. Rosemary Ades, Aug. 4, 1973 (div. 1980); m. Phyllis Anne Hammer, Mar. 21, 1981. B.S. in Chem. Engring., Northwestern U., 1971; M.B.A., Cleve. State U., 1979; postgrad. Cleve. Marshall Coll. Law, 1982-84. Registered profl. engr., Ohio. Combustion technologist Republic Steel, Independence, Ohio, 1975-77, environ. engr., Cleve., 1977-82, asst. dir. environ. control, 1982-84; regional environ. engr. Chem. Waste Mgmt., Columbus, Ohio, 1984; sr. environ. engr. Gen. Electric Co., Worthington, Ohio, 1984—; environ. cons. Med. Incineration Service, Columbus, R&R Industries, Inc., Dayton, Ohio. Contbr. chpt. to book in field. Vice chmn. Parma Heights Planning Commn., Ohio, 1980-82; treas. senatorial campaign com., Parma Heights, 1980-84. Served to lt. USN, 1971-75. Am. Iron and Steel Inst. fellow, 1982-84. Mem. Am. Inst. Chem. Engrs., Ohio Mfrs. Assn. (com. on environ. 1978—), Water Mgmt. Assn. Ohio (trustee Columbus chpt. 1980—). Republican. Club: City (Cleve.). Lodge: Masons (sr. warden 1978—). Avocations: furniture finishing; polit. campaigns. Home: 184 Corbin's Hill Dr Dublin OH 43017 Office: General Electric Spl Materials Dept 6325 Huntley Rd Worthington 43085

GUBBE, LAWRENCE WILLIAM, engineering company executive, consultant; b. St. Paul, Feb. 22, 1944; s. Lawrence William and Myrtle Elizabeth (Houlistan) G.; m. Barbara Jean Bigelow, Sept. 27, 1966 (div. June 1982); children—Carol, Diane. B.C.E., U. Minn., 1966, M.S. in Civil Engring., 1969, Ph.D., 1973. Registered profl. engr., Minn., Wis., Mich., Wash. Engr. Barr Engring. Co., Mpls., 1966-73, project mgr., prin., 1973-80; owner, operator Project Engring. and Mgmt., Inc., Mpls., 1980—; mem. Task Com. Dam Safety Minn. Dept. Natural Resources, St. Paul, 1978. Author of several conf. papers. Recipient Engring. Excellance award Consulting Engrs. Council, 1977; official del. to China to exchange tech. info. and experience with Chinese mgrs. in gov. and ind., 1983. Mem. ASCE (A.P. Greensfielder prize 1979), Project Mgmt. Inst., Minn. Alumni Assn. (life mem.). Republican. Congregationalist. Avocations: sailing; tennis; cross country skiing; bicycling, theatre. Home and Office: 5552 Rowland Rd Minnetonka MN 55343

GUBBINS, JOSEPH XAVIER, educational administrator; b. Oak Park, Ill., Feb. 16, 1936; s. Joseph Xavier and Mae (Mullen) G.; m. Alice Teresa Doyle, Aug. 2, 1958 (div. Apr. 1980); children—Joseph Xavier, III, Colin John, Matthew Thomas, Paul Owen. B.A., DePaul U., 1958; M.A. with honors, Roosevelt U., 1977. Dean of students Marian Central High Sch., Woodstock, Ill., 1959-65; chmn. guidance dept., adminstr. St. Philip High Sch., Chgo., 1965-68; athletic dir., student dir. Eastridge High Sch., Kankakee, Ill., 1968-75; asst. prin. Zion Benton High Sch., Ill., 1978-80; prin. Reddick High Sch., Ill., 1980—, Essex Elem. Sch., Reddick, 1980—. Coordinator Jerry Joyce for Senator Ill. Campaign, Kankakee, 1972; Democratic candidate Kankakee County, 1975; appointee Ill. Project for Sch. Reform Com., 1984—. Recipient Outstanding Educator award State of Ill., 1973. Mem. Ill. Prins. Assn., Nat. Assn. Secondary Sch. Prins., Nat. Council English Tchrs., Ill. High Sch. Assn. (legis. commr., basketball adv. com.), Ill. Basketball Coaches Assn. Roman Catholic. Lodges: Moose, K.C. Avocations: golf; political history. Home: 1009 S Poplar St Kankakee IL 60901 Office: Reddick High Sch PO Box 67 Reddick IL 60961

GUBBINS, MICHAEL ANTHONY, corporate executive; b. Chgo., Dec. 6, 1950; s. George Phillip and Eve Ann (Panneck) G.; m. Jeanmarie Delegato, Aug. 24, 1973; children—Jessica, Anna, Kyle, Keith. B.S., St. Joseph's Coll., Rensselaer, Ind., 1972; M.S., George Williams Coll., Downers Grove, Ill., 1977. Mgr. personnel Midwest region reservation ctr. Holiday Inns, Inc., Oak Brook, Ill., 1975-78; orgn. devel. rep. Zurich Ins. Co., Chgo., 1978-80; dir. compensation G.A.T.X. Corp., Chgo., 1980—. Mem. adv. bd. DuPage Area Vocat. Ednl. Assn., Addison, Ill., 1975-78; co-pres. W. suburban adoptive parent orgn., 1981-82. Mem. Am. compensation Assn., Human Resource Mgmt. Assn. Chgo., Chgo. Compensation Assn. Democrat. Roman Catholic. Avocations: folk music; composing. Home: 1219 Mandel St Westchester IL 60153 Office: GATX Corp 120 S Riverside Plaza Chicago IL 60606

GUCKENBERGER, JANIS MELLENTHIN HUMMER, librarian; b. LaPorte, Ind., Apr. 22, 1948; d. Harold A. and Louise R. (Pfaffenbach) Mellenthin; m. James A. Hummer, Aug. 16, 1968 (div. 1980); children—Wendy D., Nick D.; m. Dale E. Guckenberger, July 21, 1984. A.B., Ind. U., 1971. M.L.S., 1976. Library asst. Prince Georges County Meml. Library System, Oxon Hill, Md., 1971-72; audio visual dir. LaPorter County Pub. Library (Ind.), 1980—. Pres. Ind. Library Film Service, Evansville, 1982-83; library rep. LaPorte Community Service, 1981—; chmn. needs assessment com. Community Ednl. TV Adv. Council, 1982-83. Named Outstanding Young Woman of Ind., 1983. Mem. ALA, Ind. Library Assn. Home: 4132 N Blueridge Dr LaPorte IN 46350 Office: LaPorte County Pub Library 904 Indiana Ave LaPorte IN 46350

GUERRA, VERA BELLE, nurse; b. Tyndall, S.D., Feb. 29, 1924; d. Floyd Arthur Ball and Ruth Ella (Kubrowitz) Graybill; m. Virgil Benjamin Guerra, Nov. 3, 1942; children—Kathleen, Lawrence, Jill, Jeanine. Lic. practical nurse, Omaha Pub. Sch. Practical Nursing, 1962; A.S., Coll. of St. Mary's, 1982. R.N., Nebr. Practical nurse Archbishop Bergan Mercy Hosp., Omaha, 1967-69, Univ. Med. Ctr., Omaha, 1970-82, staff nurse, 1983—. Recipient Commendation Univ. Med. Ctr. Hosp., 1976. Mem. Am. Nurses Assn. Democrat. Roman Catholic. Office: Univ Med Ctr 42d and Emilie Sts Omaha NE 68105

GUETH, THOMAS FRANKLIN, electrical engineer; b. Columbus, Ohio, Jan. 18, 1950; s. Clarence Francis and Jacqueline (Cummins) G.; B.S. in Elec. Engring., Ohio State U., 1973; B.S. in Engring. Mgmt., U. Evansville, 1979. Elec. engr. Warrick ops. Alcoa, Newburgh, Ind., 1974-77, sr. elec. engr., 1978-79; mgr. systems dept. Kinetic Systems Corp., Lockport, Ill., 1979-81, indsl. market dir., 1981-82, v.p. indsl. systems, 1982-83, pres. systems. tech. group., 1983-84; dir. computer engring. Multigraphics div. AM Internat., 1983-84, dir. elec. systems engring., 1984—; evening lectr. U. Evansville, 1979. Mem. IEEE, Instrument Soc. Am., Am. Mgmt. Assn., DECUS, Tau Beta Pi. Home: 812 Thornapple Dr Naperville IL 60540 Office: 1800 W Central Rd Mount Prospect IL 60056

GUFFEY, JAMES ROGER, bank executive, lawyer; b. Kingston, Mo., Sept. 11, 1929; s. John William and Elsie Mae (Palmer) G.; m. Sara Katherine Carmack, Feb. 7, 1959; children—James Michael, Sara Elizabeth. B.S., U. Mo., 1952, J.D., 1958; advanced mgmt. program Harvard U., 1974. Bar: Mo. 1958. Ptnr. Knipmeyer, McCann & Millett, Kansas City, Mo., 1958-64, Fallon, Guffey & Jenkins, Kansas City, 1965-68; gen. counsel Fed. Res. Bank, Kansas City, 1968-70, sr. v.p., 1970-76, pres., 1976—. Dir. St. Luke's Hosp., 1978—, Mo. U. Devel. Fund, 1980—, Jr. Achievement, 1982—, adv. com. U. Mo., Kansas City, 1979—; bd. regents Rockhurst Coll., 1980—; trustee Midwest Research Inst., 1985—. Served with U.S. Army, 1952-54, Germany. Recipient cert. of merit, U. Mo., 1980, Faculty Alumni award, U. Mo. Columbia Alumni Assn., 1981. Mem. Mo. Bar Assn. Episcopalian. Club: Mission Hills Country. Home: 72 LeMans Ct Shawnee Mission KS 66208 Office: Fed Res Bank Kansas City 925 Grand Ave Kansas City MO 64198

GUIDEBECK, RONALD PATRICK, plating company executive; b. Marquette, Mich., June 29, 1935; s. Avert Alexander and Helen Ria (Riopelle) G.; m. Catherine Mary Davis, Sept. 2, 1966; 1 dau., Caroen Marie. M.E., U. Toledo, 1959; postgrad. U. Mich., 1960. Foreman, lab. technician Clinton Engines (Mich.), 1957-62; buyer, sr. buyer Motor State Products, Ypsilanti, Mich., 1962-65; mgr. Gen. Plating Co., Detroit, 1965-72; gen. mgr. Indian Head div. Demco and Gen. Plating Co., 1972-76, pres. Chesapeake Industries, 1976-78; pres. Gen. Plating Co., Detroit, 1978—. Served with USAF, 1953-57. Named Div. Market Maker of Yr., Indian Head Corp., 1971. Mem. Electro Platers Soc., Soc. Mfr. Engrs. Republican. Roman Catholic. Clubs: Washtenaw Country, Moose (Ypsilanti). Office: 6547 St Paul St Detroit MI 48207

GUILFORD, HARRY GARRETT, biology educator; b. Madison, Wis., June 20, 1923; s. Harry Morrill and Irene (Garrett) G.; m. Vivian Grace Bull, June 16, 1948; children—Joan Ellen, Susan Marie. Ph.B., U. Wis., 1944, Ph.M., 1945, Ph.D., 1949. Grad. asst. U. Wis., Madison, 1944-49; assoc. prof. Mercer U., Macon, Ga., 1949-50; asst. prof. biology U. Wis., Green Bay, 1950-56, assoc. prof., 1956-63, prof., 1963—; chmn. dept. human biology, 1980-84. Contbr. articles to profl. jours. Mem. Am. Soc. Parasitologists, Soc. Protozoology, Am. Microscopical Soc., Wis. Acad. Sci. Arts and Letters, Sigma Xi. Congregationalist. Avocations: photography; hiking. Home: 2320 Hawthorne Pl Green Bay WI 54301 Office: Univ Wis Dept Human Biology Green Bay WI 54302

GUINN, CLYDE EDWARD, hotel manager; b. Tucson, Mar. 8, 1948; s. Evin Nickel and Eleanor (Bell) G.; m. Norma Luisette, July 3, 1982; 1 child, Gabriella. B.A., Athens Coll., 1971. Various mgmt. positions Marriott Hotels, Washington, Houston and New Orleans, 1972-79; dir. sales Adam's Mark, Houston, 1979-82; asst. v.p. sales and mktg. Adam's Mark Hotels, St. Louis, 1982; gen. mgr. Adam's Mark, Kansas City, Mo., 1982—; dir. Greater Kansas City Conv. and Visitors Bur., Mo., 1984—. Mem. Nat. Assn., Executive Club (assoc.), Nat. Restaurant Assn., Greater Washington Soc. Assn. Execs. (assoc.), Mo. Hotel Motel Assn. (bd. dirs. 1983—), Confrerie de la Chaine des Rotisseurs (charge'de missions). Republican. Presbyterian. Avocations: golf; enology. Home: 803 NE Panther Vallley Dr Lee's Summit MO 64063 Office: Adam's Mark 9103 E 39th St Kansas City MO 64133

GUINN, WILLIAM HARRY, city official; b. Joplin, Mo., May 21, 1931; s. William Irene and May Ellen (Campbell) G.; m. Doris Jean Highley, Sept. 30, 1952; children—William Harry, John Robert. Grad. Nat. Hazards Control Inst., 1978. Firefighter Joplin Fire Dept., 1953-57, engr., 1957-59, lt., 1959-63, tng. officer, 1963-71, insp., asst. chief, 1971-81, fire chief, 1981—; cons. Health Tank Testing, Whitefish Bay, Wis., 1983—, Ozark Gateway Fire Chief, Carthage, Mo., 1983—; adviser Fire Protection and Rescue Tech., Crowder Coll., Neosho, Mo., 1984. Author: In Case of Fire, 1983; Hazardous Materials Disaster Operation Plan, 1982. Active Toys for Tots, Joplin, chmn., 1982; officer Civil Def. Joplin, 1959-81; chmn. Mokan council Boy Scouts Am., Joplin, 1957. Recipient Outstanding Service award State of Mo., 1963, 1965. Mem. Ozark Gateway Fire Chief Assn. (v.p. 1983), Internat. Assn. Fire Chiefs, Nat. Fire Protection Assn., Mo. State Fire Chiefs Assn., Mo. Valley Fire Chiefs. Lodge: Scottish Rite (master 1975). Avocations: hunting, fishing. Home: 711 Moffet Joplin MO 64801 Office: 303 E 3d St Joplin MO 64801

GUINNUP, DAVID ROBERT, urban and regional planner; b. Marion, Ind., Jan. 4, 1948; s. Robert E. and Doris I. (Campbell) G.; m. Diana Louise Stone, Aug. 29, 1970. B.S. in Urban Planning, Ball State U., 1971; postgrad. Wright State U., 1981—. Planner, Henry-Hancock Community Action Program, Inc., New Castle, Ind., 1972-75; dir. Wyoming County (Pa.) Planning Commn., 1975-78; dir. Shelby County (Ohio) Regional Planning Commn., 1978-83; research grad. asst. dept. econs. Wright State U., 1983-85; econ. and planning cons., 1984—; planning cons. Mem. Am. Planning Assn., Am. Inst. Cert. Planners, Am. Soc. Pub. Adminstrn., Omicron Delta Epsilon, Theta Xi. Democrat. Lodge: Kiwanis (Sidney). Contbr. articles to profl. jours. Home: 1142 Evergreen Dr Sidney OH 45365

GUIO, MICHAEL VICTOR, Federal Bureau of Investigation agent; b. Indpls., Sept. 11, 1942; s. Victor Milton and Marian (Gearen) G.; m. Jean Marie Julian, Nov. 29, 1969; children—Michael Jason, Julian Matthew. B.A., Butler U., 1964. Spl. agt. FBI, Boston, 1968-69, N.Y.C., 1969-76, Gary, Ind., 1976-78, Indpls., 1978—; mem. organized crime com. FBI, Boston, N.Y.C., Gary, Indpls., 1969-76, organized and white collar crime com., 1976—. Contbr. articles to profl. jours., chpts. to books. Investigator Nat. Grant Child Abuse, Midwest Region, 1980-83. Served to lt. USNR, 1967. Republican. Presbyterian. Clubs: Indpls. Athletic (pres. men's swim 1984-85), Carmel Dads. Avocations: indoor and outdoor sports; creating stained glass windows and lamps. Office: FBI PO Box 1186 Indianapolis IN 46206

GULL, RANDALL LEIGH, educational systems company executive; b. Norfolk, Va., Dec. 13, 1948; s. Everett L. and Nina R. G.; m. Joan M.; 1 child, Sharon M. B.S. in Psychology, Old Dominion U., 1973, B.S. in Edn., 1973, M.A. in Adminstrv. Supervision, 1976. Cert. pub. sch. tchr., Va. Tchr., Norfolk Pub. Sch., Norfolk, Va., 1973-75, courseware specialist, 1975-79, supr., 1979-83; dir. Borg Warner Ednl. Systems, Mount Prospect, Ill., 1983—; speaker various groups. Contbr. articles to prof. jours. Served with USN, 1967-68. Recipient Meritorious Research award, Va. Ednl. Research Assn., 1977. Mem. Assn. Ednl. Data Systems (recipient outstanding educator 1981), Internat. Reading Assn., Nat. Council of Math. Tchrs., Assn. for Curriculim Devel. Home: 103 E Hintz Rd Arlington Heights IL 60004 Office: 800 E Business Center Dr Mount Prospect IL 60056

GULLEDGE, BILLY RAY, aero. engr.; b. Poplar Bluff, Mo., Aug. 25, 1947; s. Twedell Arvil and Virginia Genevieve (Campbell) G.; student Coll. of Sch. of Ozarks, 1965-67; A.A., Austin Peay State U., 1973; B.S., Embry-Riddle U., 19—; m. Brenda Diana Hill, June 2, 1968; children—Brian Dewayne, Piper Diana. Asst. mgr. trainee J.J. Newberry Co., Poplar Bluff, Mo., 1964-67; joined U.S. Army, 1967, advanced through grades to capt., 1971, ret., 1977; asso. Keele Realty, Poplar Bluff, 1977-79; regional mgr. United Nat. Life Ins. Co., Springfield, Ill., 1978; asso. Mattingly Realty, Florissant, Mo., 1979—; engr. product support planning McDonnell Aircraft Co., St. Louis, 1979—; grad. asst. instr. Dale Carnegie course, St. Louis. Vol. fireman Sch. of Ozarks, 1965-67; radiol. monitor instr., 1965-67. Decorated Bronze Star medal with oak leaf cluster, Meritorious Service medal, Air medal with 24 oak leaf clusters, Vietnamese Cross of Gallantry; recipient Flight Safety Achievement award U.S. Army Aviation Sch., 1971, Dale Carnegie Course Human Relations award, 1978. Travel-Study Club scholar, 1965-67. Licensed real estate and life ins. agt. Mo., radiol. monitoring instr., Mo. Mem. Aircraft Owners and Pilots Assn., AMVETS, Army Aviation Assn. Am. (local treas. 1974-75), Nat. Assn. Realtors, Ret. Officers Assn., Mo. Assn. Realtors, Florissant (Mo.) Jr. C. of C. (Springboard, Speak-up, Regional First-timer awards 1978). Clubs: Business; Library; Reading; United Nat. Presidents; Century. Home: 1950 Forest Haven Imperial MO 63052

GULLEKSON, EDWIN HENRY, JR., physician; b. Flint, Mich., May 14, 1935; s. Edwin Henry and Amy Marcella (Graves) G.; student Flint Community Coll., 1953-56; M.D., U. Mich., 1961; m. Rosemary Evelyn Leppien, May 5, 1968; children—Kathryn Dawn, Hans Edwin, Heidi M. Intern McLaren Gen. Hsop., Flint, 1961-62, resident, 1962-63; gen. practice medicine, Flint, 1963—; chief of staff McLaren Gen. Hosp., 1977-81; mem. staffs Hurley, St. Joseph, Genesee Meml. hosps. (all Flint). Served to capt. M.C., AUS, 1966-67. Upjohn Research grantee, 1958, 59, 60. Diplomate Am. Bd. Family Practice. Mem. Mich. Med. Soc., Genesee County Med. Soc. (pres. 1983-84), AMA, Am. Acad. Family Practice, Mich. Acad. Gen. Practice. Patentee surg. instrument. Home: 1721 Laurel Oak Dr Flint MI 48507 Office: 5031 Villa Linde Pkwy Flint MI 48504

GULLER, HAROLD, company executive; m. Mildred Bekow; 4 children. Student, Washington U. With Essex Industries, Inc., St. Louis, chmn. bd., chief exec. officer; chmn. bd., chief exec. officer Essex Cryogenics of Mo., Inc., Essex Fuel Systems, Inc., Essex Precision Controls, Inc., Essex Screw Products, Propellex Corp., Essex Fluid Controls Div.. Del., 1980 White House Conf. on Small Bus.; mem. Spl. Nat. Sml. Bus. and Innovation adv. task force; mem. 1984 Joint Civilian Orientation Conf., Washington; mem. Mo. Agrl. and Sml. Bus. Authority; bd. dirs. Am. Jewish Com., Arts and Edn. Council Greater St. Louis; pres. Central Agy. for Jewish Edn.; exec. com. Jewish Fedn. St. Louis; treas. March of Dimes Birth Defects Found.; pres. Solomon Schechter Day Sch. of St. Louis, others. Named Mo. Small Businessman of Year, U.S. Small Bus. Adminstrn., 1981, others. Mem. Air Force Assn., Am. Def. Preparedness Assn. (v.p.), Soc. Mfg. Engrs., Survival and Flight Equip. Assn., William Elliot Soc. of Washington U. Address: Essex Industries Inc 770 Gravois Ave Saint Louis MO 63123

GULLICK, THOMAS H., home health care administrator; b. Marshfield, Wis., July 16, 1949; s. Harold T. and Lenice M. (Swenson) G.; m. Susan Joan Fehrenbach, Nov. 25, 1972; 1 dau., Amy Sue. B.S., U. Wis.-LaCrosse, 1971, M.S., 1979; M.B.A., Western Colo. U., Grand Junction, 1983. Personnel adminstr. U.S. Air Force, 1972-76; county adminstr., clk. Juneau County, Mauston, Wis., 1976-80; asst. adminstr. St. Joseph's Hosp., Hillsboro, Wis., 1980-81; adminstr. VNA Home Care, Neenah, Wis., 1981—; VNA rep. Hospice of Neenah-Menasha. Blood chmn. ARC, Mauston, 1976-80; bd. dirs. Parkview Eldercare, Hillsboro, 1980—; loaned exec. United Way, Neenah, 1983. Recipient Meritorious Pub. Service award Am. Legion, 1977-78. Mem. Am. Coll. Health Care Adminstrs., Nat. Home Care Orgn., Wis. Home Care Orgn., U. Wis. Alumni Assn. Lodge: Rotary Internat. (dir. 1982-85, Rotarian of Yr. 1984). Home: 781 Manchester Rd Neenah WI 54956 Office: VNA Headquarters 406 E Wisconsin Ave Neenah WI 54956

GUMBERT, JACK LEE, surgeon; b. Ft. Wayne, Ind., July 14, 1934; s. Martin Fredrick and Beulah Faye (McClain) G.; B.A., Cin. U., 1957, M.D., 1961; m. Lois Irene Scheimann, June 15, 1957; children—Jack, Lori, Brad, Grant, Joseph. Intern, Marion County Gen. Hosp., Indpls., 1961-62, resident 1962-66; practice medicine specializing in surgery, Ft. Wayne, Ind., 1968—; staff surgeon Luth., St. Joseph hosps., Ft. Wayne, 1968—; chmn. surgery service Parkview Hosp., 1977—, also mem. bd. dirs.; asso. faculty mem. Ind. U. Sch. Medicine; chmn. Physicians Health Plan No. Ind. Bd. dirs. Ft. Wayne YMCA, UPD Inc., Dukes Day Inc., Allen County Bd. Health. Served to capt. M.C., U.S. Army, 1966-68. Decorated Bronze Star, Air medal (Vietnam); Army Commendation medal with oak leaf cluster; named to Ind. Basketball Hall of Fame, 1978. Diplomate Am. Bd. Surgery. Fellow ACS (bd. dirs. Ind. chpt.); mem. AMA, Ind. State, Ft. Wayne med. socs., Ind. State, Ft. Wayne (pres. 1978-79) surg. assns. Lutheran. Club: Pine Valley Country (pres. 1976-77). Contbr. articles to med. jours. Home: 10810 Old Colony Rd Fort Wayne IN 46825 Office: 5010 Riviera Ct Fort Wayne IN 46825

GUND, GEORGE, III, professional basketball team executive. Co-owner, co-chmn. bd. Cleve. Cavaliers, Richfield, Ohio. Office: Cleveland Cavaliers The Coliseum 2923 Streetsboro Rd Richfield OH 44286*

GUND, GORDON, professional basketball executive. Co-chmn., co-owner Cleve. Cavaliers. Office: Cleve Cavaliers The Coliseum 2923 Streetsboro Rd Richfield OH 44286*

GUNDERSON, STEVEN CRAIG, congressman; b. Eau Claire, Wis., May 10, 1951; B.A. in Polit. Sci., U. Wis., Madison, 1973; grad. Brown Sch. Broadcasting, 1974. Mem. Wis. Assembly, 1975-79; congl. legis. dir., 1979-80; mem. 97th-99th Congresses from 3d Dist. Wis. Republican. Lutheran. Club: Lions. Address: 227 Cannon House Office Bldg Washington DC 20515

GUNNER, MICHAEL THOMAS, lawyer; b. Toledo, Jan. 20, 1948; s. Dale Clare and Rosemary (Hennessy) G.; m. Barbara Patrice Jones, Aug. 10, 1974; children—Lora P., Michelle N. Student U. Detroit, 1966-68; B.A., U. Toledo, 1970, J.D. cum laude, 1973. Bar: Ohio, 1973, U.S. Dist. Ct. (so. dist.) Ohio, 1974, U.S. Ct. Appeals (6th cir.) 1975, U.S. Supreme Ct. 1976. Asst. atty. gen. Ohio Atty. Gen. Office, Columbus, 1973-74; pub. defender City of Dayton (Ohio), 1974-76; assoc. Snyder, Hochman & Rakay, Dayton, 1976-78; ptnr. Smith & Gunner, Hilliard, Ohio, 1978-84; sole practice Columbus, 1984—; instr. Sinclair Community Coll., Dayton, 1975-78. Articles editor U. Toledo Law Rev., 1973. village solicitor Village of Plain City, Ohio, 1979-83; asst. law dir. Village of Dublin, Ohio, 1978-84; hearing officer Ohio Dept. Health, Columbus, 1979—; advisor Arthritis Found. of Columbus, 1981-82. Mem. ABA, Columbus Bar Assn. (ethics com.), Dayton Bar Assn., Ohio State Bar Assn., Ohio Trial Lawyers Assn. Democrat. Roman Catholic. Club: Daybreakers (Dublin) (trustee 1984—). Lodge: Kiwanis. Avocations: numismatics; sports; reading; art appreciation. Office: 31 E Whittier St Columbus OH 43206

GUNTHER, ARTHUR G., restaurant franchise company executive. Pres., chief exec. officer, dir. Pizza Hut, Inc., Wichita, Kans. Office: Pizza Hut Inc 9111 E Douglas Wichita KS 67207*

GUNTHORP, JOHN DESBROW, printing executive; b. Evanston, Ill., Aug. 16, 1913; s. Walter John and Alice (Geddes) G.; m. Vera Hilda Anderson, Aug. 30, 1934 (dec. July 1976); 1 child, John D., Jr.; m. Nancy Jane Odh, May 27, 1977; stepchildren—Marion, Carolyn; 1 child, Scott. With Gunthorp-Warren Printing Co., Broadview, Ill., 1933—, chmn. bd., 1984—. Served with USN, 1942-45; PTO. Clubs: Execs. of Chgo., Econ. of Chgo.; Skokie Country (Glencoe, Ill.). Lodge: Mason. Avocations: golf; model railroading. Office: Gunthorp-Warren Printing Co Eisenhower Expressway and Gardner Rd Broadview IL 60153

GUNZBERG, GUY WALTER, apparel company executive; b. Buffalo, May 13, 1940; s. Arthur Samuel and Aline Marian (DuBin) G.; m. Joan Lubetkin, June 18, 1967; children—Adam Wile, Corey Alexander. B.A., Harvard U., 1963, M.B.A., 1968. Vol. tchr. Peace Corps, Malawi, 1963-66; sr. v.p. research and devel. M. Wile & Co., Inc., Buffalo, 1968-81; v.p. productivity improvement Hartmarx Corp., Chgo., 1981-83, v.p. info. services, 1983—; tech. program dir. Tailored Clothing Tech. Corp., 1980—. Mem. Am. Apparel Mfrs. Assn. Democrat. Jewish Avocations: photography; cabinet making; tennis; scuba diving. Office: Hartmarx Corp 101 N Wacker Dr Chicago IL 60606

GUPTA, SATYA PRAKASH, economics educator; b. India, July 4, 1931; came to U.S., 1968; s. Atma Ram and Sona Devi G.; m. Bhag Wanti, May 5, 1954; 1 child, Anuj Kumar. B.Sc., Agra (India) U., 1951, M.Sc., 1953; B.Ed., Jamia Millia Islamia, New Delhi, India, 1957; M.S., So. Ill. U., 1970, Ph.D., 1975. Sr. tchr. M.D. High Sch., Faridabad, Delhi, 1953-56; lectr. Bajoria Coll., Saharenpur, U.P., India, 1957-63; sr. tchr., head math. dept. Ministry of Edn., Addis Abada, Ethiopia, 1964-66; tchr. math. Miller Collegiate, Altona, Man., Can., 1966-68; teaching asst. So. Ill. U., Carbondale, 1969-74; research analyst Ill. Dept. Local Govt. Affairs, Springfield, 1975-76; assoc. prof. econs. Augsburg Coll., Mpls., 1976—. Danforth assoc., 1981—; Danforth Found. grantee, 1982; Am. Luth. Ch. faculty growth awardee, 1983. Mem. Am. Econ. Assn. Hindu. Contbr. articles to local newspaper; author book on solid geometry, 1963. Home: 7533 N Meadowood Ct Brooklyn Park MN 55444 Office: 731 21st Ave S Augsburg College Minneapolis MN 55454

GUPTA, SURENDRA KUMAR, chemical firm executive; b. Delhi, India, Apr. 5, 1938; came to U.S., 1963, naturalized, 1971; s. Bishan Chand and Devki G.; m. Karen Patricia Clarke, Oct. 12, 1968; children—Jay, Amanda. B.Sc. with honors, Delhi U., 1959, M.Sc., 1961; M.Tech., Indian Inst. Tech., Bombay, 1963; Ph.D., Wayne State U., 1968. Research assoc. Western Mich. U., Kalamazoo, 1968-73; indsl. postdoctoral fellow Starks Assocs., Buffalo, 1973-74; group leader New Eng. Nuclear Co., Boston, 1974-80, Pathfinder Labs., St. Louis, 1981-83; pres., chemist Am. Radiolabeled Chem., Inc., St. Louis, 1983—. Contbr. numerous articles to internat. sci. jours. Mem. Am. Chem. Soc. (chmn. pub. relations com. 1970-73). Hindu. Avocations: table tennis; stamp collecting; traveling. Home: 1539 Craig Rd Saint Louis MO 63146 Office: Am Radiolabeled Chem Inc 11612 Bowling Green Dr Saint Louis MO 63146

GUPTA, VIRENDRA PRAKASH, physicist; b. Moradabad, India, May 14, 1936; came to U.S., 1969, naturalized, 1976; s. Om Prakash and Godawari Devi (Agarwal) G.; m. Shakuntala Agarwal, May 19, 1962; 1 dau., Mini Gupta. B.Sc., M.Sc., Agra U. (India), 1959; Assoc., Saha Inst. Nuclear Physics, Calcutta U., India, 1960; M.S., Calgary U. (Can.), 1969; Ph.D., U. Calif., Riverside, 1974. Cert. healthcare safety profl. Sr. sci. officer Def. Research & Devel. Orgn., India, 1960-69; sr. lectr. in physics Maiduguri U., Nigeria, 1974-75; vis. prof. physics U. Cin., 1975-76; sr. applications programmer

Computervision Corp., Bedford, Mass., 1976-78; sr. research physicist U.S. Dept. Energy, Radiol. and Environ. Scis. Lab., Idaho Falls, Idaho, 1978-81; sci. specialist Idaho Nat. Engring. Lab., EG&G Idaho, Inc., Idaho Falls, 1982—; cons. in field, also mem. nat. sci. coms.; tech. expert Nat. Vol. Lab. Accreditation Program in Personnel Dosimetry. Mem. Am. Health Physics Soc. (membership com.), N.Y. Acad. Scis., Sigma Xi. Contbr. articles to profl. jours.; reviewer sci. jours. Office: PO Box 1625 Idaho Falls ID 83415

GUREVICH, YURI, computer scientist, logician, educator; b. Nikolayev, USSR, May 7, 1940; came to U.S., 1981; s. Shlomo and Dina Gurevich; m. Zoe Selezneva, Mar. 10, 1965; children—Hava, Naomi. M.S. in Math. and Computer Sci., Ural U., Sverdlovsk, USSR, 1962, Ph.D. in Math., 1964, D.Math., 1968. Programmer computing ctr., Ural U., Sverdlovsk, 1961-62, teaching asst math., 1962-64, asst. prof. math., 1964-66, assoc. prof., 1966-69; prof., chmn. computer sci. dept. Kuban U., Krasnodar, USSR, 1971-72; sr. sci. fellow computing ctr. Georgian Acad. Scis., Tbilisi, USSR, 1972-73; assoc. prof. math. Ben-Gurion U., Beer-Sheva, Israel, 1974-78, prof., 1978-82; prof. computer sci. U. Mich. Ann Arbor, 1982—; cons. USSR Transp. Ministry, 1962-72. Contbr. articles on math. and computer sci. to profl. jours. Office: U Mich Elec Engring and Computer Sci Dept Ann Arbor MI 48109

GURSIN, ALVIN VICTOR, orthodontist; b. Detroit, Dec. 7, 1930; s. Victor Z. and Alice L. (Krogul) G.; m. Doris M. Brien, June 27, 1959; children—Alvin V., Jr., Kevin J., Steve S. D.D.S., U. Detroit, 1956; M.S., Northwestern U., 1963; M.R.S.H. (hon.), Her Majesty, The Queen, London, 1959, F.R.S.H. (hon.), 1973. Practice dentistry specializing in orthodontics, Rochester, Mich. Contbr. articles to profl. jours. Chmn., Selective Service Commn., Mich., 1982—. Served to maj. USAF, 1956-61. Mem. Am. Assn. of Orthodontists, Am. Dental Assn., Great Lakes Soc. of Orthodontists, Mich. Soc. of Orthodontists, Oakland Dental Soc., Delta Sigma Delta, Omicron Kappa Upsilon. Roman Catholic. Lodge: Elks (Rochester). Avocations: fishing; hunting. Home: 1129 Main St Rochester MI 48063 Office: Alvin V Gursin DDS MS PC 412 Main St Rochester MI 48063

GURVICH, PHILIP BERNARD, publisher; b. N.Y.C., May 20, 1926; s. Philip and Marguerite Mary (Donnelly) G.; m. Bernice M. Hornstein, 1945 (div. 1971); children—Susan E., Martha J., Michael W.; m. June N. Busbridge, 1972; 1 son, Philip B. Student Bklyn. Coll., NYU; M.M.C., U. Western Ont. Mgr. internat. ops. Young & Rubicam, N.Y.C., 1956-60; v.p. mktg. Benson & Hedges, Montreal, Que., Can., 1964-70, Formosa Spring Breweries, Toronto, Ont., Can., 1970-71; pres. and pub. Can. Newspaper Services Internat. Ltd., Toronto, 1972—; sec., dir. Consol. Montclerg Mines Ltd. Served with AUS, 1944-46. Clubs: Toronto Press, Advt. and Sales Execs. Home: 85 Boulton Dr Toronto ON M4V 2V5 Canada Office: 66 Laird Dr Toronto ON M4G 3V1 Canada

GUSHLEFF, WILLIAM LEE, educator; b. Granite City, Ill., Sept. 21, 1939; s. William Naum and Berneice Lucretia (Ashley) G.; m. JoAnn Kathleen Buchek; 1 child, Christopher William. B.A., So. Ill. U., Edwardsville, 1964, M.S., 1974. Tchr., Madison Sch. Dist., Ill., 1964-66, Belleville Sch. Dist. 201, Ill., 1966—. Mem. Bd. Alderman Madison, 1972—; chmn. Bicentennial Commn., 1976. Served to 2d lt. Ill. Army NG, 1963-64. Mem. Ill. Fedn. Tchrs. (pres. 1976-80). Democrat. Presbyterian. Lodges: Lions (pres. 1973-74), Croation Frateral Union. Home: 1671 4th St Madison IL 62060 Office: Belleville Twp High Sch 201 2600 W Main St Belleville IL 62221

GUSTAFSON, BARBARA ANN HELTON, lawyer; b. Washington, Ill., Apr. 26, 1948; d. Joseph and Marilou (Buckles) Balogh; m. Lee Alan Gustafson, Dec. 20, 1969. B.Music, So. Ill. U., 1969; M.Mus. Edn., Vandercook Coll., 1972; J.D., U. Chgo., 1983. Bar: Ill. 1983. Tchr. music Harrison Sch., Wonderlake, Ill., 1969-72, Cook County Dist. 125, Alsip, Ill., 1972-73; dir. orch. Kankakee Dist. III, Ill., 1973-80; atty. MidCon Corp., Lombard, Ill., 1983—. Asst. dir. Kankakee Youth Symphony (Ill.), 1973-76; violinist Kankakee Orch., 1977-80; musician Kankakee Valley Theater, 1976-80. Mem. Ill. State Bar Assn., Chgo. Bar Assn., AAUW, Mu Phi Epsilon (treas. 1968-69). Lutheran. Home: 176 Hickory Creek Dr Frankfort IL 60423 Office: MidCon Corp 701 E 22nd St Lombard IL 60148

GUSTAFSON, LINDA CHANEY, educator, administrator; b. Washington, Feb. 7, 1947; d. James Louis and Louise (Bockelman) Chaney; m. Roger William Gustafson, Apr. 15, 1972. B.S., U. Md., 1970, M.L.S., 1973, Ed.D., 1982. Media specialist Howard County Pub. Schs., Columbia, Md., 1970-80; librarian Dixon (Ill.) Pub. Schs., 1980-84; prin. Neponset High Sch. (Ill.), 1985—. Treas. LWV, 1983—. Mem. NEA, Ill. Edn. Assn., Dixon Tchrs. Assn., Sauk Valley Reading Council, Bureau County Adminstrs. Assn., Ill. High Sch. Assn., Alpha Lambda Delta. Home: Hidden Lake Dr Princeton IL 61356

GUTERMUTH, SCOTT ALAN, accountant; b. South Bend, Ind., Nov. 24, 1953; s. Richard H. and Barbara Ann (Bracey) G.; B.S. in Bus., Ind. U., 1976; m. Susanne Pearson, May 10, 1980. With Coopers & Lybrand, Indpls., 1976-83, supervising auditor, 1980-83, audit mgr., 1983; controller Society Nat. Group, Indpls., 1983—; instr. Becker C.P.A. Rev. Course, 1980—. Adv., Jr. Achievement; mem. Marion County Republican Com., 1978—, Rep. Nat. Com., 1972—. C.P.A., Ind. Fellow Life Mgmt. Inst.; mem. Am. Inst. C.P.A.s, Nat. Assn. Accts., Ins. Acctg. and Statis. Assn., Ind. Assn. C.P.A.s (ins. com. 1984—), Life Mgmt. Inst. (assoc.). Methodist. Home: 7450 Glenview West Dr Indianapolis IN 46250 Office: 9101 Wesleyan Rd Indianapolis IN 46268

GUTHRIE, GEORGE RALPH, real estate corporation executive; b. Phila., Mar. 12, 1928; s. George Ralph and Myrtle (Robertson) G.; B.S. in Econs., U. Pa., 1948; m. Shirley B. Remmey; children—Mary Elizabeth, Brenda Ann. With I-T-E Imperial Corp., Phila., 1948-70, controller, fin. planner, 1960-68, treas., 1968-69, v.p. fin., 1969-70; pres. N.K. Winston Corp., N.Y.C., 1970-76; exec. v.p. Urban Investment and Devel. Co., Chgo., 1976-78, pres., 1978-82, chmn., 1982—; dir. Zenith Electronics Corp. Trustee Nat. Coll. Edn.; Luth. Social Services Ill., Pres.'s Council; bd. dirs. Augustana Coll., Jr. Achievement; chmn. fin. sect. United Way/Crusade Mercy; trustee Cornerstone Found.; bd. dirs. March of Dimes; assoc. trustee, pres.'s council U. Pa. Mem. Urban Land Inst., (vice chmn. urban devel. mixed-use council), Chgo. Assn. Commerce and Industry (bd. dirs.), Nat. Realty Com. (dir.), Fin. Execs. Inst. Republican. Clubs: Glen View, Jupiter Hills, Carlton (bd. govs.), Chicago, Economic. Office: 333 Wacker Dr Suite 2200 Chicago IL 60606

GUTHRIE, MYRNA JEAN, educator; b. Newton, Iowa, June 30, 1929; d. Frank Andrew and Hazel (Dolph) Guthrie; student Central Coll., 1947-49; B.A., Drake U., 1951, M.S., 1963. Child welfare worker State of Iowa, 1951-60; guidance counselor Newton Community Schs., 1960—, counselor Upward Bound, Central Coll., Pella, Iowa, 1967; cons. Jasper County Headstart program, 1968; coordinator Newton Achievement Motivation Project, 1971-72, Futures project Newton Community Sch., 1975. Past bd. dirs. Jasper County Community Action; past pres. RMR Soc.; past bd. dirs. Newton Community Orch; pres. Iowa Future Problem Bd. Recipient Maytag Found. Conv. award, 1965; named Nat. Future Problem Solving Coach of Yr., 1980. Mem. Internat. Platform Assn., Nat., Newton edn. assns., Am., Iowa personnel and guidance assns., Newton Bus. and Profl. Women's Club (past pres.), Jasper County Hist. Soc., Iowa Woman's Polit. Caucus, Newton Community Theater, Questers (past pres.), Alpha Xi Delta, Alpha Kappa Delta, Beta Sigma Phi. Republican. Methodist. Clubs: Soroptimist (past pres.) (Newton); Hazel Dell Acad., PEO. Co-pub. series Before the Colors Fade. Home: 326 E 4th St S Newton IA 50208

GUTHRIE, WILLIAM HARVEY, JR., advertising executive; b. Bartlesville, Okla., May 1, 1950; s. William Harvey and Martha (Rouse) G.; m. Susan Elizabeth Talley, Sept. 14, 1973; children—Rebekah Kendra, Andrew Downing. B.B.A., U. Kans.-Lawrence, 1972; M.B.A., Avila Coll., 1985. Sales rep. Baker & Taylor div. W.R. Grace Co., Somerville, N.J., 1973-75; sales rep. H. J. Heinz, Pitts., 1975-76; cons. Lawrence-Leiter Mgmt. Cons., Kansas City, Mo., 1976; account exec. Barickman Advt. div. Doyle, Dane, Bernbach, Kansas City, Mo., 1976-83; account supr. Bryan-Donald Advt., Kansas City, Mo., 1983—. Mem. Am. Mktg. Assn. (pres. chpt.), Bus.-Profl. Advt. Assn. Episcopalian. Home: 3524 Yale St Lawrence KS 66044 Office: 2345 Grand St Suite 2712 Kansas City MO 64108

GUTSCHE, CARL DAVID, chemistry educator; b. Oak Park, Ill., Mar. 21, 1921; s. Frank Carl and Vera Virginia (Mutchler) G.; m. Alice Eugenia Carr, June 4, 1944; children—Clara Jean, Betha Lynn, Christopher Glen. B.A., Oberlin Coll., 1943; Ph.D., U. Wis., 1947. Instr., Washington U., St. Louis, 1947-48, asst. prof., 1948-51, assoc. prof., 1951-59, prof., 1959—, dept. chmn. 1970-76; cons. Monsanto Co., St. Louis, 1957-79, Petrolite Corp., St. Louis, 1950—. Author: The Chemistry of Cabonyl Compounds, 1967; Fundamentals of Organic Chemistry, 1975; (with D. Redmore) Ring Expansion Reactions, 1968; also numerous articles to profl. jours. and books. Bd. dirs. Young Audiences (St. Louis Symphony), 1972-75, St. Louis Conservatory of Music, 1978-82. Guggenheim Found. fellow, 1981; recipient Founder's Day award Washington U., 1976. Fellow Royal Chem. Soc. Eng., AAAS; mem. Am. Chem. Soc. (mem. several nat. coms., St. Louis sect. award 1972), Phi Beta Kappa, Sigma Xi. Avocations: music; sailing; woodworking; reading. Home: 6933 Kingsbury Blvd University City MO 63130 Office: Dept Chemistry Washington Univ Saint Louis MO 63130

GUTSCHICK, RAYMOND CHARLES, geology educator, researcher, micro-paleontologist; b. Chgo., Oct. 3, 1913; s. Anthony William and Elizabeth (Bessie) (Kosatka) G.; m. Alice Edna Augusta Lude, July 2, 1939; children—Alice Antonette, Raal Emily. A.A., Morton Jr. Coll., 1934; B.S. in Engring. Physics, Univ. Ill., Urbana, 1938, M.S. in Geology, 1939, Ph.D. in Geology, 1942. Geologist, MOBIL-Magnolia Petroleum Co., Oklahoma City, 1943-45, ALCOA Alum. Ore Co., Rosiclare, Ill., 1942, 1946-47, Gulf Oil Co., Oklahoma City, 1947; asst. prof. dept. geology U. Notre Dame, Ind., 1947-50, assoc. prof., 1950-54, prof., 1954-79, dept. chmn., 1956-70, emeritus prof., cons., 1979—; geologist U.S. Geol. Survey, Denver, 1975—; cons. geologist Rogers Group, Inc., 1978—, Environment Service EIS, 1983—. Co-author geol. research: Redwall Limestone of N. Arizona, 1969; contbr., co-contbr. papers, articles to profl. jours. NSF grantee, 1954, 60; recipient ann. Teaching award U. Notre Dame, 1964; Neil A. Miner award Nat. Assn. Geology Tchrs., 1977. Fellow Geol. Soc. Am.; mem. Assn. Geol. Tchrs. (pres. 1952, 58), Am. Assn. Petroleum Geologists, Paleontol. Soc., Sigma Xi (pres. Notre Dame chpt. 1953). Independent Republican. Lutheran. Avocations: Photography; golf. Home: 53176 Oakmont West Dr South Bend IN 46637 Office: U Notre Dame Dept Earth Sciences Notre Dame IN 46556-1020

GUTSCHICK, WILLIAM CHARLES, retail corporation official; b. Chgo., Aug. 12, 1945; s. Lester Charles and Eileen May (Williams) G.; m. Nancy Michele Hobgood, June 29, 1968; children—Scott Charles, Brian William. B.S., No. Ill. U., 1967. Material control expediting supr. Zenith Radio Corp., Chgo., 1967-68, prodn. control systems analyst, 1968-69; sr. corp. methods and procedures analyst Walgreen Co., Deerfield, Ill., 1969-78, mgr. corp. methods and forms control, 1978—. Mem. council adv. bd. Boy Scouts Am., Arlington Heights, Ill., 1984—, dist. advancement chmn., 1982—, asst. council advancement chmn. N.W. Suburban Area, 1984—. Recipient Silver Tepee award Boy Scouts Am., 1983, Golden Tepee award, 1984, Dist. award of merit, 1985. Mem. Assn. Records Mgrs. and Adminstrs. (chmn. pub. relations, chmn. legis.), Assn. Systems Mgmt. (dir.), Nat. Micrographics Assn. Republican. Lutheran. Clubs: Young Couples Grace Lutheran Ch. (co-founder, dir. 1978-80). Home: 900 W Rand Rd B204 Arlington Heights IL 60004

GUTTERMAN, SAM, insurance company executive; b. Ravenna, Ohio, Dec. 19, 1947; s. Morris and Rebecca (Bazilan) G.; m. Judy Bard, Nov. 1979 (div. Aug. 1981). A.B., U. Mich., 1969, M.A.S., 1970. With CNA Ins. Cos., Chgo., 1970—, asst. v.p., actuary, 1982—. Mem. Chgo. Area Runners Assn. (treas. 1981-84, pres. 1984—), Am. Statistical Assn., Internat. Actuarial Assn. Soc. Ins. Research, World Future Soc., Soc. Actuaries (chmn. com. 1976—), Casualty Actuarial Soc., Am. Acad. Actuaries, Soc. Chartered Property and Casualty Underwriters, Am. Soc. Chartered Life Underwriters, Chgo. Actuarial Assn. (pres. 1983-84). Avocations: long-distance running; swimming; biking; skiing; reading. Home: 1500 N LaSalle St Chicago IL 60610 Office: CNA Ins Cos CNA Plaza Chicago IL 60685

GUTZMER, PETER ESMOND, lawyer; b. N.Y.C., Mar. 15, 1953; s. Alfred Albert and Catherine Viola (Ramshaw) G.; m. Lynn Carol Meyer, July 31, 1977. B.A., Boston U., 1976; J.D., John Marshall Law Sch., 1979. Bar: Ill. 1979, U.S. Dist. Ct. (no. dist.) Ill. 1979. Assoc. Ashcraft & Bridewell, Chgo., 1979-80; asst. sec., atty. Talman Home Fed. Savs. and Loan Assn., Chgo., 1980-85; gen. counsel Fed. Home Loan Bank of Chgo., 1985—. Mem. Lakeview Citizens Council, Chgo., 1976-80, Nat. Trust for Historic Preservation, Washington, D.C., 1977—, Rogers Park Community Council, Chgo., 1980—. Regents scholar N.Y. State, 1972. Mem. Chgo. Bar Assn., Ill. State Bar Assn., ABA. Episcopalian. Home: 1601 W Chase Ave Chicago IL 60626 Office: Fed Home Loan Bank 111 E Wacker Dr Suite 800 Chicago IL 60601

GUY, ERNEST THOMAS, association executive; b. Detroit, May 12, 1921; s. William G. and Anna (Utas) G.; B.A., Mich. State U., 1943; postgrad. U. Ga., 1946, U. Mich., 1948; m. Bernice Louise Smith, Mar. 8, 1945 (dec.); children—E. Timothy, Cynthia Louise. State coordinator vets. tng. Ga. Dept. Edn., Atlanta, 1946-47; mgr. sta. WATL, Atlanta, 1947-48; program dir. sta. WKNX, Saginaw, Mich., 1948-50; pub. relations dir. Mich. Heart Assn., Detroit, 1950-53, exec. dir., 1953-58; exec. dir. Tex. Heart Assn., Houston, 1958-68, Chgo. Med. Soc., 1968-69, Calif. Dental Assn., San Francisco, 1969-73, So. Calif. Dental Assn., Los Angeles, 1972-73, Unified Calif. Dental Assn., 1973-74, Am. Soc. Clin. Hypnosis, Des Plaines, Ill., 1974-75; dir. meetings Am. Bar Assn., Chgo., 1975—, project dir. ann. and midyr. meetings, 1984—; bd. dirs. Meeting Planners Internat.; mem. industry adv. bd. Meeting World, 1978-80. Mem. adv. com. Tex. Rehab. Assn. Faculty pub. health classes U. Mich., Ann Arbor, 1953-58; del. White House Conf. Edn., 1956; vice chmn. Fed. Service Campaign for Health Agys. in Tex., 1961-62; mem. governing council Soc. Heart Assns. Profl. Staff, 1959-62. Mem. Pres.'s Bicentennial Commn. Precinct worker Houston Republican Com.; mem. fin. com. George Bush for Pres. Campaign, 1978-80. Served to capt. AUS, 1943-46. Co-recipient Blakeslee award, 1953; recipient award of merit Mich. Heart Assn., 1958, Merit award Tex. Heart Assn., 1968, commendation award Calif. Dental Assn. Certified assn. exec. 1st class. Mem. Am. Soc. Assn. Execs., Am. Pub. Relations Soc., Nat. Assn. Parliamentarians, Profl. Conv. Mgmt. Assn., Internat. Platform Assn., Am. Assn. Dental Editors, Nat. Pub. Relations Council, Nat. Assn. Exhibit Mgrs., U.S. Parachute Assn. Republican. Episcopalian (lay reader). Contbr. numerous articles to profl. publs. Home: 930 N Northwest Hwy 202 Park Ridge IL 60068 Office: 750 N Lake Shore Dr Chicago IL 60611

GUY, JOHN EDWARD, lawyer; b. Danville, Ill., July 15, 1924; s. John Milton, Jr. and Beatrice (Marks) G.; Ph.B., U. Chgo., 1947; LL.B., J.D., John Marshall Law Sch., Chgo., 1951; m. Muriel Elaine Becking, Nov. 29, 1947; children—Randall Edward, Scott Evan, Carolyn Elizabeth. Bar: Ill. 1951, U.S. Supreme Ct., U.S. Dist. Ct. (no. dist.) Ill. Practice, Chgo., 1951—; partner Querrey, Harrow, Gulanick & Kennedy; lectr. continuing legal edn. programs. Active Civic Betterment Party, Village of Glen Ellyn, Ill., 1976-80; adult leader local Boy Scouts Am., 1971-72. Served with AUS, 1943-46. Recipient Order of Arrow, Boy Scouts Am., 1972. Mem. Soc. Hosp. Attys., Soc. Trial Lawyers, Appellate Lawyers Assn., Am. Judicature Soc., Am. Arbitration Assn., Ill. Bar Assn., Chgo. Bar Assn., Def. Research Inst. (chmn. practice and procedure com. 1983—), Ill. Def. Counsel (dir. 1972—, officer 1979-82, pres. 1982-83), Trial Lawyers Club Chgo. Author articles, monographs on surviving tort actions, punitive damages, distbn. tort damages, trial strategies, amicus curiae briefs. Office: 135 S LaSalle St Chicago IL 60603

GUY, JOHN MARTIN, lawyer; b. Detroit, July 16, 1929; s. Alvin W. and Ann G. (Martin) G.; B.S., Butler U., 1958; J.D., Ind. U., 1961; m. Norma J. Puterbaugh, Aug. 13, 1950; children—Janice Lynn, Robert John. Bar: Ind. 1962. Practice law, Monticello, 1962—; atty. firm Siferd, Guy, Christopher, Loy & Guy, 1962—; mem. Ind. Ho. of Reps., 1971-74, house majority leader, 1973-74; mem. Ind. Senate, 1977-84, majority leader, 1979-80; dir. State and Savs. Bank. Pros. atty. 39th Jud. Circuit, 1963-67. Pres. White County Mental Health Assn., 1965-68. Trustee Monticello-Union Twp. Library Bd., pres., 1970-71. Served with USAF, 1951-55. Named Outstanding Republican Freshman Ind. Ho. of Reps., 1971, Ind. Senate, 1977. Mem. Am., Ind., Monticello bar assns., Am. Judicature Soc., Am. Trial Lawyers Assn., Monticello C. of C. (pres. 1975—), Am. Legion. Clubs: Masons, Shriners, Elks, Moose. Home: 201 Western Heights Dr Monticello IN 47960 Office: 115 W Broadway Monticello IN 47960

GUY, RALPH B., JR., See *Who's Who in America,* 43rd edition.

GUY, ROXANNE JOSEPHINE, physician; b. Galesburg, Ill., Aug. 15, 1952; d. Robert Edward and Gertrude Josephine (Hoegg) Bowman; B.S., Ill. State U., 1974; postgrad. Salzburg Coll., 1973; M.D., So. Ill. U., 1977; m. Curtis Eguene Guy, May 17, 1980. Resident So. Ill. U. Sch. Medicine Affiliated Hosps., Springfield, 1977-81, chief resident gen. surgery, 1981-82, resident in plastic surgery, 1982, chief resident, 1983—. Diplomate Nat. Bd. Med. Examiners; Diplomate Am. Bd. Surgery, 1983. Mem. AMA, Am. Med. Women's Assn., Ill. State Med. Soc., Sangamon County Med. Soc., Sol. Ill. U. Sch. Medicine Alumni Soc. Methodist. Contbr. articles to profl. jours. Home: 2052 S Lincoln Ave Springfield IL 62704 Office: PO Box 3926 Room D334 Springfield IL 62708

GWIN, FRANCIS B., agricultural industry executive; b. 1921. Student Kans. State U., 1947. With Farmland Industries, Kansas City, Mo., 1954-59, now chmn. bd., dir.; gen. mgr. Farmway Coop., 1959—. Office: Farmland Industries Inc 3315 N Oak Trafficway Kansas City MO 64116

GWIN, ROBERT YOUNG, lawyer; b. Owensboro, Ky., Aug. 6, 1955; s. Robert Lee and Martha Nell (Bouche) G.; m. Ann Louise Visscher, Sept. 1, 1979; 1 son, Aaron Wallace. Student Ky. Wesleyan Coll., 1974-75; B.A., Ind. U., 1978; J.D., U. Ky., 1981. Bar: Ky. 1981, U.S. Dist. Ct. (we. dist.) Ky. 1981. Clk. firm Tarrant Combs & Bullitt, Lexington, Ky., 1979, Ky. Dept. Justice, Frankfort, 1980; assoc. Gwin, Iler, Waitman & Gwin, Owensboro, Ky., 1981-83, ptnr., 1983-84; assoc. Brown, Todd & Heyburn, Louisville, Ky., 1984—. Mem. Ky. Bar Assn., Jefferson County Bar Assn., Ky. Acad. Trial Attys., Order of Coif, Phi Beta Kappa. Office: Brown Todd & Heyburn 1600 Citizens Plaza Louisville KY 40202

GWINN, ROBERT P., electrical appliance manufacturing executive; b. Anderson, Ind., June 30, 1907; s. Marshall and Margaret (Cather) G.; Ph.B., U. Chgo., 1929; m. Nancy Flanders, Jan. 20, 1942; children—John Marshall, Richard Herbert. With Sunbeam Corp., Chgo., 1936—, successively in sales dept., asst. sales mgr., sales mgr., v.p. sales, 1936-55, pres., gen. mgr., dir., now chmn. bd., chief exec. officer; pres. Sunbeam Appliance Service Co., Chgo., 1952-82; chmn. bd., chief exec. officer Ency. Brit.; dir. Sunbeam Corp., Ltd. (Can., U.K., Argentina, Mex.); Continental Casualty Co., CNA Fin., Continental Assurance Co., Titan Oil Co., Exploration, Inc. Trustee Hanover Coll., U. Chgo., U. Chgo. Cancer Research Found. Mem. Alpha Sigma Phi. Clubs: Riverside Country (Ill.); Mid-Am., Wine and Food Soc., Chicago, Univ., Comml., Econ. (Chgo.); Confrerie des Chevaliers du Tastevin; Mill Reef. Home: 144 Fairbanks Rd Riverside IL 60546 Office: 5400 Roosevelt Rd Chicago IL 60650

GYURO, STEVEN JOHN, research administrator; b. Flint, Mich., June 3, 1934; s. Steven John and Helene Marie (Zsigray) G.; m. Jane Eilen Harmon, July 12, 1958; children—Steven T., Carolyn J., Robert M., Susan M. B.S., Ohio State U., 1957; M.A., 1964, Ph.D., 1969. Tchr., Columbus Pub. Sch., Ohio, 1957-67; research assoc. edn. Ohio State U., Columbus, 1967-69, assoc. dir. Nat. Ctr. Research Vocational Edn., 1972—; asst. prof. U. Ky., Lexington, 1969-71; coordinator product devel. Research Better Sch., Inc., Phila., 1971-72; gueat lectr. Temple U., Phila., 1972; asst. chmn. program Project Mgmt. Inst., Phila., 1972; invited guest editor Phi Delta Kappa, Bloomington, Ind., 1978; Co-author: Educational Project Management Instuuctional Ssytem, 1971. Contbr. chpt. to book. Vice pres. St. Andrew Bd. Edn., Columbus, 1968-69. Served to capt. U.S. Army, 1957-58. Mem. Am. Endl. Research Assn. (chmn. spl. interest group in research mgmt. 1981-84), Am. Vocational Assn., Phi Delta Kappa, Kappa Delta Pi, Omicron Tau Theta. Club: Leatherlips Yacht (Columbus). Avocations: sailing; racquetball; gardening; reading; soccer. Office: Nat Ctr Research Vocational Edn Ohio State U 1960 Kenny Rd Columbus OH 43210

HAACK, RICHARD WILSON, police officer; b. Chgo., July 7, 1935; s. Arthur Frank and Mildred Ann (Meyer) H.; m. Ruth Marie Tietz, May 27, 1972; children—Laura Marie, Karl Richard. Grad., Cook County (Ill.) Sheriff's Police Acad., 1967; A.S., Triton Coll., 1973; cert. Chgo. Police Acad., 1974; B.A., Lewis U., 1975; M.A., Northeastern Ill. U., 1979; B.S. in Bus. Adminstrn., Elmhurst Coll., 1982. Shipping clk. Am. Furniture Mart, Chgo., 1955-60; quality control insp. Nat. Can Co., Chgo., 1961-67; police officer Northlake Police Dept. (Ill.), 1967—, watch comdr. patrol div., 1978-85; realtor Internat. Realty World-Norton & Assocs., 1984—. Mem. Bill Bruce fundraising com. Aid Assn. Lutherans, Christ Evangelical Luth. Ch., Northlake, 1981-82, mem. Gala Variety Show, 1982, chmn. evang. bd., 1981-85, ch. rep. Internat. Luth. Laymen's League, 1984—, pub. relations dir., usher, 1973-85, dir. Project Compassion, 1983-85; ombudsman No. Ill. dist. Luth. Ch.-Mo. Synod, 1984-85; choir Apostles Luth. Ch., 1985—; active Oktoberfest, 1980—, chmn. entertainment, 1984—. Served with USMC, 1952-55. Recipient numerous letters of commendation, competitive shooting awards. Mem. Ill. Police Assn., Fraternal Order Police (sec.-treas. Perri-Nagle Meml. Lodge 18, 1977-85), St. Jude Police League, Nat. Police Officers Assn., Internat. Conf. Police Assn., German/Am. Police Assn. (bd. dirs. 1980—, Northeastern Ill. U. Alumni Assn. (bd. dirs. 1980—), Am. Polit. Sci. Assn., Nat. Rifle Assn., Schwaben Verein, N.W. Real Estate Bd., Leyden Real Estate Bd. (inner circle 1984—), Internat. Platform Assn., Realtors Polit. Action Com. Ill. (Inner Circle 1984—), Am. Legion. Republican. Club: Die Hard Cub Fans. Lodge: Moose. Contbr. law enforcement articles to profl. publs. Home: 244 E Palmer Ave Northlake IL 60164 Office: 55 E North Ave Northlake IL 60164

HAAG, ROBERT LEON, development company executive; b. N.Y.C., Sept. 23, 1926; s. Philip B. and Ida (Roth) H.; m. Sylvia M. Cohn, Dec. 22, 1951; children—Donna J., Philip R. Student Bklyn. Poly. Inst., 1943-44; B.S., NYU, 1950, postgrad., 1950-51. Salesman Jules Montenier & Co., N.Y.C., 1950, dist. sales mgr., Denver and Chgo., 1951; regional sales mgr. Leonard H. Lavin & Co., Chgo., 1951-54; nat. sales mgr. Alberto-Culver Co., Chgo., 1955-60, v.p. sales, 1960-66, group v.p. food div., 1966-70; pres. Robert L. Haag & Co., Chgo., 1970—; pres. Monroe Communications, Chgo., 1981—; co-founder, former dir. Alberto-Culver Co.; dir. Midas Internat., Calif. Dreamers, Inc., Shelby Williams Ind. Fine Arts Broadcasting, Banner Press, Albany Park Nat. Bank & Trust Co. Bd. dirs. Jewish Community Ctrs., 1972-81, Am. Jewish Com. Served to cpl. USAAF, 1945-46. Mem. Am.-Israel C. of C. (named Man of Yr. 1976, pres. 1977-79, bd. dirs. 1970—). Clubs: Standard (Chgo.), Internat. Chgo.; Hillcrest County (Long Grove, Ill.). Office: Robert L Haag & Co Monroe Communications 201 N Wells St Suite 1520 Chicago IL 60606

HAAPANEN, LAWRENCE WILLIAM, communication educator; b. Seattle, Apr. 24, 1945; s. Morris William and Helen Marie (Stearns) H.; m. Beverly Ann Biggi, Aug. 19, 1972; children—Laurell, Holly. B.A. in History, U. Wash., 1967; M.A. in Speech, Wash. State U., 1972, Ph.D. in Speech, 1974. Tchr. Neah-Kah-Nie High Sch., Rockaway, Oreg., 1974-76; asst. prof. Utah State U., Logan, 1976-81; assoc. prof., chmn. dept. communication Baker U., Baldwin City, Kans., 1981—. Contbr. chpt. to textbook. Del. State Democratic Conv., Salt Lake City, 1978. Served as capt. USAF, 1967-71. Decorated Air Force Commendation medal; summer fellow NEH, 1980. Mem. Speech Communication Assn. (chmn. commn. on govt. communication 1984-85), Central States Speech Assn., Am. Forensics Assn. Democrat. Lutheran. Avocation: genealogy. Home: 107 Dearborn St Baldwin City KS 66006 Office: Baker Univ Dept Communication 8th and Grove Sts Baldwin City KS 66006

HAAS, ERWIN, medical research administrator; b. Budapest, Hungary, Sept. 11, 1906; came to U.S., 1938, naturalized, 1945; m. Elisabeth Tysper; children—Wolfgang, Robert. Ph.D., U. Chgo., 1942. Asst. prof. exptl. pathology Western Res. U., 1945-46; asst. dir. Inst. Med. Research, Cedars of Lebanon Hosp., Los Angeles, 1946-53; dir. L.D. Beaumont Meml. Research Labs., Mt. Sinai Med. Ctr., Cleve., 1953—. Contbr. articles to profl. jours. NIH grantee, 1954-81. Mem. Am. Heart Assn., Council for High Blood Pressure Research, Internat. Soc. Hypertension Am. Chem. Soc. Home: 1081 Carver Rd Cleveland Heights OH 44112 Office: Dir LD Beaumont Meml Research Labs Mt Sinai Med Ctr University Circle Cleveland OH 44106

HAAS, KENNETH, symphony orchestra manager; b. Washington, July 8, 1943; s. Philip, Jr. and Eunice (Dillon) H.; m. Barbara Dooneief, Feb. 14, 1964; children—Elizabeth, Amanda. A.B., Columbia Coll., 1964. Asst. to mng. dir. N.Y. Philharm., 1966-70; asst. gen. mgr. Cleve. Orch., 1970-75, gen. mgr., 1976—; gen. mgr. Cin. Symphony Orch., 1975-76; co-chmn. orch. panel Nat. Endowment for Arts, 1982-85; chmn. challenge grant music panel, 1983—, co-chmn. music overview panel, 1983-85. Trustee, Cleve. Ballet, 1974-77; mem. music panel Ohio Arts Council, 1975-79, chmn. challenge grant panel, 1985—; trustee Laurel Sch., 1985—; adv. bd. Cleve. Inst. Music, 1985—; nat. adv. bd. Mandel Ctr. for Non-Profit Instns., Care Western Res. U., 1985—. Mem. Am. Symphony Orch. League (mem. recruitment com. Fellowship Program 1980—, bd. dirs. 1980-82), Mgrs. Major Orchs. U.S. and Can. (chmn. 1980-82). Office: 11001 Euclid Ave Severance Hall Cleveland OH 44106

HAAS, WILLIAM JAMES, educational administrator; b. Akron, Ohio, Jan. 20, 1943; s. William Luther and Laurel Jean (McLain) H.; m. Julie Ann Fennel, July 30, 1977; 1 child, Jeffrey John. B.A., U. Akron, 1965; M.A., U. Kans., 1969, Ed.D. with honors, 1974. Tchr., Wyandotte High Sch., Kansas City, Kans., 1969-74; teaching supr., U. Kans., Lawrence, 1973-74; asst. prin. Turner High Sch., Kansas City, 1974-79; prin. Pierson Jr. High Sch., Kansas City, 1979—. Contbr. articles to profl. jours. Mem. Task Force on Juvenile Crime, Kansas City, 1978. Served to capt. USAF, 1965-69. Mem. Nat. Assn. Secondary Sch. Prins., Phi Delta Kappa. Avocations: distance bicycling; model railroading; music; art. Home: 6233 Mission Rd Fairway KS 66205 Office: Pierson Jr High Sch 1800 S 55th St Kansas City KS 66106

HAASE, WILLIAM EDWARD, See *Who's Who in America,* 43rd edition.

HAAYEN, RICHARD JAN, insurance executive; b. Bklyn., June 30, 1924; s. Cornelius Marius and Cornelia Florence (Muskus) H.; B.Sc., Ohio State U., 1948; m. Marilyn Jean Messner, Aug. 30, 1946; children—Richard Jan, Peter Wyckoff, James Carell. With Allstate Ins. Co., 1950—, v.p. underwriting, 1969-75, exec. v.p., Northbrook, Ill., 1975-80, pres., 1980—, also dir.; chmn. Ins. Info. Inst., N.Y.C.; dir. Tech-Cor, Wheeling, Ill.; vice chmn. Ins. Inst. Am., Malvern, Pa. Bd. sponsors, Evang. Hosp. Assn. Mem. Nat. Assn. Ind. Insurers, Property Casualty Ins. Council, Phi Delta Theta. Republican. Club: Chgo. Union League. Home: 1410 Lake Shore Dr S Barrington IL 60010 Office: Allstate Ins Co Allstate Plaza Northbrook IL 60062

HABER, FRANKLIN BARRY, university administrator, accounting educator; b. Albany, N.Y., Jan. 14, 1933; s. Franklin Helmus and Elizabeth (Crone) H.; m. Marion E. Keene, June 29, 1958; children—Kimberly Jeanne, Matthew Barry. B.S., SUNY-Albany, 1959, M.S., 1962; Ph.D., Ariz. State U., 1973. C.P.A., S.D., Ind. Asst. to dean SUNY, Albany, N.Y., 1965-66, asst. dean, 1966-72; chmn. bus. adminstrn. Sioux Falls Coll., S.D., 1972-80; assoc. dean, prof. acctg. Valparaiso U., Ind., 1980-82, dean, prof. acctg., 1982—. Author (with others): Business and Consumer Arithmetic, 1981, College Business Mathematics, 1981, Accounting: Concepts, Procedures, and Applications-1st Yr. and Advanced, 1985. Dir. Greater Valparaiso C. of C., 1983—, Girls' Club, Sioux Falls, 1973-76; mem. Northwest Ind. Forum Inc., 1982—; charter dir. Children's Inn, Sioux Falls, 1978-80. Served to sgt. U.S. Air Force, 1952-56, Korea. Mem. Am. Inst. CPAs, Nat. Assn. Accts., Ind. CPA Soc., Am. Mgmt. Assn. Republican. Lutheran. Lodge: Rotary (dir. 1984—). Office: Valparaiso Univ Coll Bus Administration Valparaiso IN 46383

HABER, IRVING AARON, clinical psychologist, mental health administrator; b. Chgo., Feb. 5, 1926; s. Benjamin and Goldie (Kaplan) H.; m. Norma Joslove, July 4, 1962 (div.); 1 dau., Laura G. B.A., Roosevelt U., 1952, M.A., 1955; postgrad. Ill. Inst. Tech., 1956-60; Ph.D., Columbia Pacific U., 1983. Lic. psychologist, Ill., Pa.; registered Health Care Provider; cert. social worker, Ill. Psychology intern Ind. Central State Hosp., 1954-55; sr. psychologist Psychiat. Inst., Circuit Ct. Chgo., 1956-58, instr. Crane Jr. Coll., Chgo., 1958-61; psychologist and adminstrv. dir. inpatient ward, outpatient clinics Ill. Dept. Mental Health, Chgo., 1961—; cons. Circuit Ct. Chgo., 1958-61; indls. cons.; profl. cons. Rogers Park Mental Health Assn.; pvt. practice. Served with USAF, 1944-46. Mem. Am. Psychol. Assn., Ill. Psychol. Assn., Assn. Mental Health Adminstrs., Ill. Group Psychotherapy Assn. Office: 4201 N Oak Park Bldg B Chicago IL 60634 also 230 N Michigan Ave Suite 3701 Chicago IL 60601

HABER, LYN ROLAND, educator, researcher, photographer; b. Phila., Feb. 15, 1942; d. Bertram Frankel and Lucille (Ravner) Roland; m. Ralph Norman Haber, July 26, 1972; children—Sabrina, Rebecca. B.A., Brandeis U., 1963; M.A., U. Ill.-Chgo., 1984; M.A., U. Calif.-Berkeley, 1965, Ph.D., 1970. Cert. clin. competency in speech pathology, 1985. Teaching asst. U. Calif., Berkeley, 1965-68; asst. prof. Temple U., Phila., 1968-73; assoc. prof., research assoc. U. Rochester, N.Y., 1973-79; assoc. prof. edn. U. Ill., Chgo., 1979-80, adjunct assoc. prof. psychology, 1980—; speech therapist Chgo. Pub. Schs., 1984—; cons. in neurology V.A. Hosp., Canandaigua, N.Y., 1977-81, Ill. Inst. Devel. Disabilities, Chgo., 1980-81, Lovena Ohl Found., Scottsdale, Ariz., 1981—. Author: Vital English, 1977. Author Language Impairment Test, 1982. Contbr. articles to profl. jours. Photographer in mags. Am. Council for Learned Socs. grantee, 1967; foreign Service Inst. internship, 1966. Mem. Linguistic Soc. Am., Psychonomics Soc., Am. Speech-Language and Hearing Assn., Sigma Xi, Phi Beta Kappa. Avocation: backpacking. Office: Dept Psychology U Ill Chicago IL 60680

HABERLE, MARILYN JAYNE, pharmacist; b. Whiting, Ind., Feb. 5, 1932; d. John Earl and Julia (Janas) Springer; m. Joe E. Haberle, June 5, 1954. B.S. in Pharmacy, Purdue U., 1954. Registered pharmacist, Mo. Supr., pharmacist Mo. Baptist Hosp., St. Louis, 1966—. Mem. Am. Soc. Hosp. Pharmacists, St. Louis Hosp. Pharmacy Soc., Methodist Women's Assn., Gamma Circle, Profl. Frat. Assn. (pres.-elect 1978-79, pres. 1979-80), Alpha Delta Pi (pres. Lafayette Alumnae 1957-58), Lamda Kappa Sigma (ednl. trust bd., southern regional supr. 1972-74, grand pres. 1974-78, hon. advisor 1978—). Republican. Avocations: needlework; orchid culture; handcrafts.

HABERMAN, REX STANLEY, state senator, farm manager; b. Friend, Nebr., Jan. 23, 1924; m. Phyllis Kavan, Aug. 22, 1948; children—Mary Lou, George, Rex II, Phillip. Owner, operator 5 photog. studios, 1945-67; personnel dir. Nebr. Vets. Home, 1968-70; mgr. family farms, Imperial, Nebr., 1970—; mem. Nebr. Legislature, 1979—. Mem. Adams County Bd. Suprs., 1964-68, Imperial City Council, 1974-76; del. Republican Nat. Conv., 1976, 84; former state pres. Nebr. Jaycees; former chmn. Adams County Rep. Party, Chase County Rep. Party; former pres. Greater Nebr. Health Systems Agy.; exec. council Nebr. Episcopal Ch. Mem. Hastings C. of C. (dir.), Am. Legion, VFW. Clubs: Masons, Shriners, Elks, Eagles, Rotary. Office: State Capitol Lincoln NE 68509

HABERMAN, SHELBY JOEL, statistician, educator; b. Cin., May 4, 1947; s. Jack Leon and Miriam Leah (Langberg) H.; m. Elinor Penny Levine, Feb. 18, 1979; children—Shoshanah, Chasiah, Sarah. A.B. Princeton U., 1968; Ph.D., U. Chgo., 1970. Asst. prof. to prof. U. Chgo., 1970-82; prof. Hebrew U., Jerusalem, 1982-84; prof. stat. Northwestern U., Evanston, Ill., 1984—. Author: Analysis of Frequency Data, 1974; Analysis of Qualitative Data, Vol. I, 1978. Vol. II, 1979. Contbr. articles to profl. jours. Guggenheim fellow, 1977-78. Fellow Inst. Math. Stat. Am. Statis. Assn. Home: 2935 W North Shore Chicago IL 60645 Office: Dept Math Northwestern Univ 2033 Sheridan Rd Evanston IL 60201

HABLUTZEL, NANCY ZIMMERMAN, lawyer, educator; b. Chgo., Mar. 16, 1940; d. Arnold Fred Zimmerman and Maxine (Lewison) Zimmerman Goodman; m. Philip Norman Hablutzel, July 1, 1980; children—Margo Lynn, Robert Paul. B.S., Northwestern U., 1960; M.A., Northeastern Ill. U., 1972; J.D., Ill. Inst. Tech. Chgo.-Kent Coll. Law, 1980; Ph.D., Loyola U., Chgo., 1983. Bar: Ill. 1980, U.S. Dist. Ct. (no. dist.) Ill. 1980. Speech therapist various pub. schs. and hosps., Chgo. and St. Louis, 1960-63, 65-72; audiologist U. Chgo. Hosps., 1963-65; instr. spl. edn. Chgo. State U., 1972-76; asst. prof. Loyola U., Chgo., 1981—; adj. prof. Ill. Inst. Tech. Chgo.-Kent Coll. Law, 1982—; dir. and dir. legal services Legal Clinic for Disabled, Chgo., 1984—. Mem. Ill. Gov.'s Com. on Handicapped, 1972-75; mem. Council for Exceptional Children, faculty moderator student div., 1982—. Loyola-Mellon Found. grantee, 1983. Mem. ABA, Ill. Bar Assn., Chgo. Bar Assn. (exec. com. of corp. law com. 1984—), Am. Ednl. Research Assn. Republican. Home: 214 W Memomonee St Chicago IL 60614 Office: Loyola U Chicago 820 N Michigan Ave Chicago IL 60611

HACKEL, ALAN STUART, college administrator, educator; b. Delaware, Ohio, May 2, 1940; s. Morris Bernard and Celia (Brotkin) H.; m. Joan Karen Lieder, Aug. 11, 1963; children—Margo Joyce, Julie Beth. B.A., Western Res. U., 1962, M.A., 1964; Ph.D., Ohio State U., 1971. Edn. counselor Cleve. Coll., 1963-66; grad. asst., various positions Div. Continuing Edn., Ohio State U., Columbus, 1966-76, assoc. dir., acting asst. v.p. for continuing, edn. 1976-77; asst. prof., dean Coll. Continuing Studies, U. Nebr., Omaha, 1978—; instr. Peru State Coll., Nebr. 1983; courtesy appointments, U. Nebr., Omaha and Lincoln, 1985—. Pres. Central Ohio Assn. for Gifted, Columbus, 1976; v.p. Civic Assn., Columbus and Omaha, Nebr.; bd. dirs. Columbus United Way, Omaha, Jewish Community Ctr., Columbus and Omaha, Anti Defamation League, Omaha. Mem. Nat. U. Continuing Edn. Assn., Am. Soc. Tng. and Devel., Omaha C. of C. (central council exec. com.), Omicron Delta Kappa, Phi Delta Kappa. Democrat. Jewish. Avocations: golf; fishing; horticulture. Lodges: Kiwanis, B'nai B'rith (pres. 1974-76, dist. bd. mem. 1976), Zeta Beta Tau. Office U of Nebr at Omaha Coll Continuing Studies 1313 Farnam St Omaha NE 68182

HACKENBERG, DAVID ALAN, lawyer, city official; b. Phila., June 28, 1939; s. Melvin Bert and Ruth Lenore (Good) H.; m. Marilyn Adella Jones, Aug. 10, 1963; children—Alan David, Jill Marie. B.A., Heidelberg Coll., 1962; J.D., Ohio No. U., 1968. Bar: Ohio 1968. Ptnr. Hackenberg & Beutler, Findlay, Ohio, 1968—; dir. law City of Findlay, 1972—. Pres. Parent Tchr. Orgn., Central Jr. High Sch., Findlay, 1984-85. Mem. Ohio State Bar Assn., Findlay Hancock Bar Assn. (pres. 1982), N.W. Ohio Bar Assn., Ohio Mcpl. Attys. Assn., Ohio Land Title Assn. Republican. Methodist. Lodges: Elks, Masons. Avocations: golf; tennis; photography. Home: 1541 Marcelle Ave Findlay OH 45840 Office: Hackenberg & Beutler 215 W Main Cross Findlay OH 45840

HACKENBRACHT, PHILLIP DOUGLAS, agronomist; b. Coshocton, Ohio, Mar. 2, 1950; s. Charles Earl and Margaret Dewar (Shurtz) H.; B.S., Ohio State U., 1972. Lawn specialist, power crew chief Scotts Lawn Care Service, Columbus, Ohio, 1973-74; area supr. Perf-A-Lawn Corp., Columbus, 1975-76; agronomist Na-Chors Plant Food Co., Marion, Ohio, 1976-78; farmer, Coshocton, 1978—. Mem. Am. Soc. Agronomy, Nat. Wildlife Assn. Mem. United Ch. Christ. Club: Lions (1st v.p. 1982-83, pres. 1983-84). Home: 51300 CR 116 Fresno OH 43824 Office: 51001 CR 115 Coshocton OH 43812

HACKER, ELAINE MARY, physician; b. Clontarf, Minn., Feb. 24, 1925; d. George Henry and Emma Christine (Jansen) H.; m. Edward B. Mazzotta, June 21, 1955 (div. June 1974); children—Catherine, George. B.A., U. Minn., 1946, B.S., 1947, B.M., 1959, M.D., 1950. Diplomate Am. Bd. Ob-Gyn. from resident to chief resident Detroit Receiving Hosp., 1950-54; practice medicine specializing in ob-gyn, Detroit and Grosse Point, Mich., 1954-78; coordinator med. services Kans. Dept. Social and Rehab. Services, Topeka, 1978—. Fellow Am. Coll. Ob-Gyn. mem. AMA, Kans. Med. Soc., Shawnee County Med. Soc. Home: 3026 Quail Creek Topeka KS 66614 Office: Dept Social and Rehab. Services State Office Bldg Room 628 Topeka KS 66612

HACKETT, WILLIAM FRANZ, department store executive; b. Rochelle, Ill., July 14, 1939; s. Karl B. and Vera F. (Tousley) H.; m. Joanne M. Raddatz, June 27, 1970; 1 child, Carol. B.A. in Econs. and Bus. Adminstrn., Cornell Coll., Mount Vernon, Iowa, 1961. Banking trainee NW Bancorp., Owatonna, Minn., 1961-62; inspection and service analyst Sears Roebuck and Co., Mpls., 1965-66, catalog order buyer, 1966-73, Chgo., 1973-83, sr. catalog order buyer, Chgo., 1983—. Republican precinct chmn., Saint Louis Park, Minn., 1971-72; asst. Councilman's Reelection Campaign, Wheaton, Ill., 1982-83, campaign mgr., 1984-85; mem. housing commn. City of Wheaton, 1983—, liquor commn., 1985—, sch. bd. nominating com., 1983, 85. Served to 1st lt. U.S. Army, 1962-65. Methodist. Lodges: Masons, Kiwanis (pres. 1981-82). Avocations: reading; music; gardening; economics and finance; politics. Home: 911 Wakeman Ave Wheaton IL 60187

HACKL, DONALD JOHN, architect; b. Chgo., May 11, 1934; s. John Frank and Frieda Marie (Weichmann) H.; m. Bernardine Marie Becker, Sept. 29, 1962; children—Jeffrey Scott, Craig Michael, Cristina Lynn. B.Arch., U. Ill., 1957, M.S. in Arch., 1958. Architect, Comm, Comm & Moses, architects, Chgo., 1959-60, mechanics research div. Am. Machinery and Found., Niles, Ill., 1960-62; project architect Loebl Schlossman & Bennett, architects-engrs., Chgo., 1962-64; assoc. Loebl, Schlossman Bennett & Dart, Chgo., 1967—, ptnr., 1970—, exec. v.p., dir., 1974—; pres., dir. Loebl Schlossman & Hackl, 1975—, Dart-Hackl Internat. Ltd., 1975—; mem. com. to draft minimum design standards for design of detention facilities Ill. Dept. Pub. Safety, 1971; mem. Nat. Council Archtl. Registration Bds.; guest design critic dept. architecture U. Ill., 1975, 76, 81; guest lectr. U. Notre Dame, 1977, 78, 80, 82; cons. Pub. Service Adminstrn., Washington, 1974-76. Prin. works include: Samsonite Corp. Hdqrs., Denver, 1968, Water Tower Place, Chgo., 1974, HFC World Hdqrs. Northbrook, Ill., 1978, Square D Internat. Hdqrs., Palatine, Ill., 1978, Cancer Research Inst., King Faisal Specialist Hosp. and Research Ctr., Riyadh, Saudi Arabia, 1978, Allstate Ins. Co., South Barrington, Ill., 1981, Shriners Hosp. Crippled Children, Chgo., 1979, West Suburban Hosp., Oak Park, Ill., 1981, One Pierce Place, Itasca, Ill., 1984, Corp. Hdqrs., Commerce Clearing House, Riverwoods, Ill., 1985, Pepper Corp. Hdqrs., Chgo., 1985, Prudential Plaza, Chgo.; contbr. articles to profl. jours. Mem. Chgo. Met. Cancer Crusade, 1973; trustee West Suburban Hosp., Oak Park, Ill., 1983; bd. dirs. Chgo. Archtl. Assistance Ctr., 1982-85; trustee AIA Found., 1982-84. Fellow AIA (dir. 1981-84, documents bd. 1975-80, v.p. 1985, chmn. design commn. 1985; pres. Chgo. chpt. 1976-82; dir. Ill. council 1979-81, v.p. 1985, pres.-elect 1986); mem. Nat. Trust Hist. Preservation, Chgo. Bldg. Congress (v.p. 1982—, dir. 1978-79), Chgo. Assn. Commerce and Industry, Greater North Michigan Ave. Assn., Art Inst. Chgo. Roman Catholic. Clubs: Tavern, Carlton, Economic, Lake Zurich. Office: 845 N Michigan Ave Chicago IL 60611

HACKMAN, HELEN ANNA HENRIETTE, home economist; b. New Melle, Mo., Oct. 8, 1908; d. John Henry and Lydia Eliza (Meier) Hackman; A.B., Central Wesleyan Coll., Warrenton, Mo., 1929; B.S., U. Mo., 1942, postgrad., 1942; postgrad. U. Wis., 1934, U. Colo., 1953, 75, U. Ariz., 1975, 77. Prin., Wright City High Sch., 1929; home econs. tchr., Cape Girardeau, Mo., 1930-42; sr. extension adviser home econs. U. Ill., Pittsfield, 1942-78; sec. Pike County Health and Social Services Coordinating Com. Dietitian, buyer Oshkosh Wis. Camp Fire Girls Camp, summers 1935, 36, 37; sec.-treas. Western Ill. 4-H Camp Assn., 1952-54; mem. Western Ill. Fair Bd. Com., Griggsville, 1946—; v.p. Tri-county Assn. for Crippled, 1960—; tech. cons. White House Conf., 1960, 70; pres. Pike County Heart Assn., 1969, organizer Family Planning Centers, Diabetic and Blood Pressure Clinics, Pike County Health Dept., 1971; sec. Illini Hosp. Aux., 1978; Bd. dirs. Pike County Mental Health. Recipient Distinguished Service award Nat. Home Demonstration Agts. Assn., 1952; Meritorious Service award Heart Assn., 1960, 61. Mem. Ill. Home Advisers Assn. (sec. 1948), Nat. Assn. Extension Home Economists (3d v.p. 1951-53, pub. relations chmn. 1951-53), Am. Home Econs. Assn. (sec. Ill. nutrition com. 1967-69), Pittsfield Hist. Soc. Epsilon Sigma Phi (chief 1962), Gamma Sigma Delta. Clubs: Pittsfield Woman's (pres. 1979, 80, 81, 82), Pike County Bus. and Profl. (pres. 1970-71). Home: 230 S Illinois St Pittsfield IL 62363 Office: PO Box 227 Hwy 36 and 54th St E Pittsfield IL 62363

HACKNEY, ALLEN LEE, art educator, artist; b. Madison, Ind., Aug. 13, 1938; s. Oakley Lee and Juanita (Leach) H. B.S., Ind. State U., 1962, M.S., 1964. Tchr. art Vigo County Sch. Corp., Terre Haute, Ind., 1962—; with Gibson Enterprises. Recipient Outstanding Painting award Hoosier Salon, 1968, 75, Commemorative medal State of Ind., 1977, 78, other awards. Mem. Brown County Art Gallery Assn. (bd. dirs. 1984—), Nat. Soc. Painters in Casein and Acrylic, Ind. Realists Club (founder, pres.), Internat. Platform Assn. Democrat. Mormon. Lodges: Masons, Shriners. Avocations: golf; swimming, car restoring. Home Rural Route 21 Box 69 Oak Grove Terre Haute IN 47802

HACKNEY, HOWARD SMITH, county official; b. Clinton County, Ohio, May 20, 1910; s. Volcah Mann and Gusta Anna (Smith) H.; B.S. cum laude, Wilmington Coll., 1932; m. Lucille Morrow, June 28, 1933; children—Albert Morrow, Roderick Allen, Katherine Ann Becker. Farmer, Wilmington, Ohio; farm reporter Agrl. Adjustment Adminstrn., Wilmington, 1934-40, committeeman, 1940-52, office mgr., 1952—, county exec. dir. Agrl. Stblzn. and Conservation Service, 1961—. Treas., dir. Clinton County Community Action Council; treas. Clinton County Council Chs.; trustee mem. agrl. adv. com. Wilmington Coll.; trustee Clinton County Hist. Soc. Named to Ohio State Fair Hall of Fame, 1983. Mem. Nat. Assn. Stblzn. and Conservation Service Office Employees (awards 1970, state, regional legis. cons.), AAAS, Soil Conservation Soc. Am., Farmers Union, Ohio Duroc Breeders Assn. (pres., dir.), Ohio Acad. Sci., Ohio Acad. History, Ohio Hist. Soc., Grange, Ohio Southdown Breeders Assn., Clinton County Farm Bur. (sec., dir.), Clinton County Agrl. Soc. (treas., dir., award 1975), Clinton County Lamb and Fleece Improvement Assn. (dir.), Clinton County Hist. Soc. Republican. Quaker. Lodge: Masons. Home: 2003 Inwood Rd Wilmington OH 45177 Office: PO Box 509 24 Randolph St Wilmington OH 45177

HACKWORTHY, DAVID CHARLES, investment company executive; b. Milw., Aug. 26, 1938; s. Alan Charles and Theresa (Umhoefer) H.; m. Patricia Ann Kelly, May 13, 1961; children—David, Michael, Anne, Jennifer, James. B.A. in Econs., Lawrence U., 1960; postgrad. U. Wis., 1961-62. Security analyst First Nat. Bank, Mpls., 1961-65; with Robert W. Baird and Co., Madison, Wis., 1965—, resident mgr., 1980—, 1st v.p., 1980—, dir., 1985—; dir. Randall Bank, Univ. Book Store. Mem. fin. com. Madison Art Center, 1977—, bd. dirs., 1977-80, chmn., 1979-80; v.p. athletic assn. Edgewood High Sch. (Wis.), 1968-72, pres., 1972-75, 84-85, mem. adv. bd., 1972-82. Served with USCG, 1961-66. Republican. Roman Catholic. Mem. Lawrence U. Alumni Assn. (pres. 1981-83). Clubs: Madison (bd. dirs. 77), Nakoma Lodge: Rotary.

HADD, HARRY EARLE, biochemistry educator, medical researcher; b. Balt., Dec. 24, 1918; s. Marvin Lucius and Violet (French) H.; m. Mildred D'Agostino, Apr. 19, 1953; 1 child, Marc Harry. B.S., Purdue U., 1946; M.A., Temple U., 1949; Ph.D., Ind. U., Bloomington, 1964. Metabolic chemist Phila. Gen. Hosp., 1950-51; instr. Temple Univ. Hosp., Phila., 1951-57; scientist Worcester Found., Shrewsbury, Mass., 1957-60; research assoc. Ind. Univ. Med. Sch., Indpls., 1960-65; mem. faculty, 1965-77; mem. faculty Northwestern Ch. Med. Edn., Gary, 1977, assoc. prof. biochemistry, 1981—. Cons. Nat. Center Toxicological Research USPHS, 1977-81. Author: Conjugates and Steroid Hormones, 1969. Served with USAF, 1942-45. Grantee NIH, 1964-70, 73-75. Mem. Am. Chem. Soc., Endocrine Soc. Episcopalian. Home: 1606 Glenrose Ct Valparaiso IN 46383 Office: Northwest Center Med Edn 3400 Broadway Gary IN 46408

HADDAD, DELORRE SALEM, orthodontist; b. Canton, Ohio, Jan. 22, 1935; s. Tofy and Sumia (Rahal) H.; m. Lily Jean Baker, Mar. 18, 1956; children—Ellen Sue, David Delorre. Student Kent State U., 1953-56; D.D.S., Ohio State U., 1960, M.S., 1969. Practice dentistry specializing in orthodontics, Medina, Ohio, 1969—; del. China Am. Sci. and Tech. Exchange Group, 1984. Served to capt. USAF, 1960-62. Mem. ADA, Am. Assn. Orthodontists, Gt. Lakes Orthodontic Assn. Cleve. Orthodontic Assn., Cleve. Dental Soc., Akron Dental Soc., Medina County Dental Soc., EICO Study Club (sec. 1984—), Rocky Mountain Study Club. Republican. Methodist. Club: Ohio State U. Pres's. Avocations: golf; interior design; office planning.

HADDOCK, GERALD HUGH, geology educator; b. Neosho, Mo., Mar. 7, 1929; s. Hugh Ransom and Orpha Florene (Vaughan) H.; m. Faith Elizabeth Winsor, Aug. 23, 1960; children—Mary, Ralph, Frances. B.S. in Geology, Wheaton Coll., 1956; M.S. in Geology, Wash. State Coll., 1959; Ph.D. in Geology, U. Oreg., 1967. Instr. geology to prof. Wheaton Coll., Ill., 1959—. Instr. water safety Mid-Am. chpt. ARC, 1978—; instr. lifesaving YMCA, Glen Ellyn, Ill.; swimming referee U.S. Swimming Assn. Served with USN, 1948-52; Korea. Mem. Geol. Soc. Am., Mineral. Soc. Am., Soc. Econ. Paleontologists and Mineralogists, AAUP. Baptist. Club: Ryall Masters-Swim (Glen Ellyn). Home: 124 S Chase Wheaton IL 60187 Office: Dept Geology Wheaton Coll Wheaton IL 60187

HADGE, JACK, municipal government official; b. Wilson, N.C., Sept. 10, 1944; s. Jack and Effie (Nova) H.; m. Linda Burdick, Sept. 13, 1975. A.B., U. Calif.-Berkeley, 1966, M.B.A., 1968; M.A., U. Hartford, 1971. Prin. analyst City of Hartford, Ct., 1972-74; dir. Fin. Chapel Hill, N.C., 1974-75; budget adminstr. Howard County, Elliott City, Md., 1976-77; exec. dir., mgmt. and budget Bd. Edn. Newark, 1977-78; treas. City of Ocean City, N.J., 1979-83; mgr. City of Niles, Ill., 1983—. Mem. Internat. City Mgmt. Assn., Municipal Fin. Officers Assn. (mem. govtl. budgeting and mgmt. com., 1983—), Am. Soc. Pub. Adminstrs., Internat. Pesonnel Mgmt. Assn. Democrat. Episcopalian. Home: 8435 W Madison Dr Niles IL 60648 Office: Niles Municipal Administration Bldg 7601 Milwaukee Ave Niles IL 60648

HAEBERLE, WILLIAM LEROY, business educator, entrepreneur; b. Marion County, Ind., May 19, 1922; s. Louis Leroy and Marjorie Ellen (Jared) H.; B.S., Ind. U., 1943, M.B.A., 1947, D.B.A., 1952; m. Yvonne Carlton, June 17, 1947; children—Patricia, William C., David C. Faculty, Ind. U., Bloomington, 1946—, prof. mgmt., 1963—; chmn. bd. Gen. Ill. Investment Corp., 1949—, Century Petroleum Corp., 1957—, First Ind. Corp., 1972—, IDACO Oil & Gas Inc., 1984; pres., dir. 1st Ind. Securities Corp., 1973—, New Bus. Design, Inc., 1984—; dir. Innovest Group, Inc., Transactions Verifications Systems, Inc., Corp. Edn. Resources, High Plains Oil Corp., 1st Team Auctions, Inc.; pres., dir. Nat. Entrepreneurship Found., 1982—; dir. Ind. Inst. for New Bus. Ventures, Inc., 1983—. Served to capt. U.S. Army, 1943-46; lt. col. USAFR, 1947-82. Mem. Air Force Assn., Res. Officers Assn., Am. Legion, VFW, Sigma Alpha Epsilon. Clubs: Yale (N.Y.C.), Metropolitan (N.Y.C.). Home: 1213 S High St Bloomington IN 47401 Office: PO Box 5521 Bloomington IN 47402

HAEMIG, MARY JANE, lawyer; b. Mpls., Aug. 21, 1954; d. Ernest Albert and Jean Louise (Hafermann) Haemig. A.B., U. Minn., 1977; M.Theol. Studies, Harvard Div. Sch., 1981; J.D., Harvard U., 1981. Bar: Ill. 1981. Atty., Law Dept., Continental Ill. Nat. Bank & Trust Co. of Chgo., 1982—. German Acad. Exchange Service fellow, 1981-82. Mem. ABA, Ill. Bar Assn. Lutheran. Home: 415 W Fullerton Pkwy #605 Chicago IL 60614 Office: Law Dept Continental Ill Nat Bank 231 S LaSalle St Chicago IL 60697

HAENSCHEN, RODNEY JAMES, osteopathic physician; b. Jersey City, Aug. 31, 1946; s. Robert William and Mildred Catherine (Greenhalgh) H.; m. Judith Ann Gibson, Dec. 20, 1969; children—Eric, James. B.S., Fairleigh Dickinson U., 1968; D.O., Coll. Osteo. Medicine and Surgery, 1972. Intern, U.S. Army, Ft. Sam Houston, Tex., 1972-73; co-founder No. Ill. Emergency Physicians, Waukegan, Ill., 1975, dir., 1976—; co-designer, v.p. St. Therese Area Trauma Satellite, Lake Villa, Ill., 1980—; physician, dir. emergency services dept. St. Therese Hosp., Waukegan, Ill., 1982—. Served with U.S. Army, 1971-76. Fellow Am. Bd. Emergency Medicine. Mem. Am. Coll. Emergency Physicians, Am. Osteo. Assn. Office: Suite 325 Profl Office Bldg St Therese Med Park Waukegan IL 60085

HAERING, EDWIN RAYMOND, chemical engineering educator, consultant; b. Columbus, Ohio, Dec. 8, 1932; s. Edwin Jacob and Mary Mildred (Kunst) H.; m. Suzanne Rowe, June 9, 1956; children—Cynthia, David Arthur, Elizabeth. B. Chem. Engring., Ohio State U., 1956, M.S., 1956, Ph.D., 1966. Faculty, Ohio State U., Columbus, 1959—, assoc. prof., 1973-82, prof. chem. engring., 1982—, vice chmn. dept., 1974-76, chmn. dept., 1977-78; cons. in field, 1966—. Author: Laboratory Manual for Unit Operations Laboratory, 1980; also tech. articles. Served to lt. (j.g.) USNR, 1956-59. NROTC scholar, 1951-56, Dow Chem. Co. scholar, 1956; Koppers teaching fellow, 1962. Mem. Am. Inst. Chem. Engrs. (treas. Central Ohio sect. 1974-79), Am. Chem. Soc., Sigma Xi, Tau Beta Pi. Clubs: Ohio State Univ. Faculty, Scarlet and Gray, Columbus Maennerrhor Avocations: golf; gardening; sailing. Home: 8449 Riverside Dr Powell OH 43065 Office: Dept Chem Engring Ohio State Univ 140 W 19th Ave Columbus OH 43210

HAGAN, JOHN CHARLES, III, ophthalmologist; b. Mexico, Mo., Oct. 7, 1943; s. John Charles Hagan II and Cleta L. (Book) Neely; m. Rebecca Jane Chapman, July 15, 1967; children—Carol Ann, Catherine Elizabeth. B.A., U. Mo., 1965; M.D., Loyola U., Chgo., 1969. Diplomate Am. Bd. Ophthalmology. Intern Med. Coll. Wis., Milw., 1969-70; resident Emory U., Atlanta, 1972-75; practice medicine specializing in ophthalmology, North Kansas City, Mo., 1975—; cons. Am. Running and Phys. Fitness Assn., Washington, 1973—. Contbr. articles to med. jours. Served to capt. USAF, 1970-72. Fellow ACS; mem. Clay-Platte County Med. Assn. (pres. 1982), Kansas City Soc. Ophthalmology (Continuing Edn. award), AMA, Mo. Soc. Ophthalmology, Am. Intraocular Implant Soc. Avocations: marathons; triathalons; phys. fitness. Office: 2700 Hospital Dr North Kansas City MO 64116

HAGAN, MICHAEL FRANCIS, sales and marketing executive; b. St. Louis, Nov. 6, 1956; s. Russell M. and Helen M. (Hogan) H.; children—Erin M., Michael F., Jr. Student U. Wis., 1974-77. Pres., M.H. Market Devel. Co., Milw., 1973-74; ptnr. M&M Assocs., 1975-79; pres. Foticon Photog. Co., Milw., 1977-79; nat. mktg. dir. Solar Unltd. Inc., Huntsville, Ala., 1980-81; founder, pres., chmn. bd. Legal Guardian Am. Inc., Libertyville, Ill., 1981—. Youth del. Republican Nat. Conv., 1972. Home: 130 Midway Ln Vernon Hills IL 60061 Office: 1590 S Milwaukee Ave Suite 212 Libertyville IL 60048

HAGAN, PAUL WANDEL, educator, organist; b. Spencer County, Ind., Nov. 18, 1930; s. George Wandel and Cassie Alice (Byrne) H.; B. Music Edn. magna cum laude, U. Evansville, 1954; M.S., Ind. State U., 1955; M.S.T. cum laude, Sacred Heart Sch. Theology; Ph.D., Calif. U. Tchr., Ft. Wayne (Ind.)

Community Schs., 1963-76; organist St. Joseph Ch., 1968-76; prof. St. Francis Coll., Ind. U. Extension, Ft. Wayne. Recipient govt. grants to study music with M. Dupre, J. Langlais, A. Marchal, R. Falcinelli, F. Peeters, A. Heiller, M.C. Alain. Lodge: K.C. Composer: Psalm Chorale Preludes, 1970; Swedish Suite, 1975; Scottish Suite, 1975; Trois Petite Elegies, 1973; Sketches of Paris Churches, 1974; Apostolic Suite, 1976. Home: 1301 S Ruston Evansville IN 47714

HAGAN, RICHARD LEE, motor oil company sales executive; b. Aledo, Ill., May 13, 1943; s. Claude and Dagmar (Christianson) H.; m. Catherine Killgore, May 5, 1983. Student Iowa Wesleyan U., 1962. Salesman, unit mgr., dist. mgr., Purex Corp., Chgo., 1969-80; regional mgr. Gagliardi Bros., Subs. H.J. Heinz, Chgo., 1980-82, No Nonsense Fashions Inc., Chgo., 1982-83; mgr. dist. sales Burman Castrol Inc., West Chester, Ohio, 1983—, mgr. region, 1985—. Served to sgt. U.S. Army, 1964-66, Vietnam. Avocations: reading, jogging, racquetball, bridge. Home: 5767 McCarthy Ct West Chester OH 45069 Office: Burman Castrol Inc 6803 W 64th St Suite 226 Shawnee Mission KS 66202

HAGEBOECK, TERRY LEE, pharmacy educator; b. Richmond, Ind., Feb. 22, 1937; s. Robert Eugene and Florence Louise (Kares) H.; m. Frances Louise Russell, July 2, 1961; children—Charles R., Cynthia L. B.S. in Pharmacy, Butler U., 1959; M.S. in Pharmacy, Purdue U., 1976, Ph.D. in Pharmacy, 1981. Lic. pharmacist, Ind. Pharmacist, Keene Drug Co., Indpls., 1959-61; pharmacist, mgr. Mac's Pharmacy, Richmond, Ind., 1961-75; teaching asst. Purdue U., West Lafayette, Inc., 1975-77; asst. prof. Butler U., Indpls., 1977-83, assoc. prof., 1983—. Contbr. articles to profl. jours. Chmn. St. Marks' United Methodist Ch. Council Ministries, Carmel, Ind., 1983—; tchr. adult ch. sch. class, 1983—. Named Outstanding First Yr. Mem., Richmond Jaycees, 1963; named Outstanding Teaching Asst., Purdue U., 1977. Mem. Am. Pharm. Assn., Am. Assn. Coll. Pharmacy, Ind. Pharmacists Assn. (employee relations com.), Nat. Assn. Retail Pharmacists (nat. lectr. computer com.), Kappa Psi. Republican. Avocations: Photography; computer programming. Home: 595 Memory Ln Carmel IN 46032 Office: Butler U Coll Pharmacy 4600 Sunset Ave Indianapolis IN 46208

HAGEN, FLOYD WENDELL, aeronautical engineer; b. Montevideo, Minn., Mar. 31, 1937; s. Louis and Selma Clara (Moe) H.; m. Jacqueline Mary Wilson, May 18, 1960; children—Eric Louis, Pamela Ann, Kurt Robert, Mark Wendell. B.Aero. Engr., U. Minn., 1960. Mgr. engring. Rosemount, Inc., Eden Prairie, Minn., 1957—. Patentee in field. Council mem. Boy Scouts Am. Fellow AIAA (assoc., chmn., vice-chmn., sec., treas. 1980—, Young Engr. of Yr. 1972); mem. U. Minn. Alumni Assn. (bd. dirs. 1960—), Beta Theta Pi Alumni Soc. Republican. Lutheran. Lodge: Lions. Home: 15802 Cedar Ridge Rd Eden Prairie MN 55344 Office: Rosemount Inc 12001 W 78th St Eden Prairie MN 55344

HAGEN, ROY ROBERT, accountant; b. Racine, Wis., Feb. 13, 1947; s. Roy Alex and Elizabeth Mary (Gulyas) H.; m. Julie Frances Roberts, May 8, 1971; children—Robert, Brian, Kevin. B.B.A., Dominican Coll., Racine, 1969. Acct., Evoy & Kamschulte, Waukegan, Ill., 1968-69; cost acct. Rexnord, Milw., 1970-74; gen. acctg. supt. In-Sink-Erator, Racine, 1974-78, budget mgr., 1978-80, controller, 1980—. Treas. Racine Co-op Nursery Sch., 1978-79. Lutheran. Avocations: fishing; golf; bowling. Home: 5635 College Point Ct Racine WI 53402

HAGERSON, LAWRENCE JOHN, health agency executive, consultant; b. Lakewood, Ohio, Dec. 30, 1931; s. John Lawrence and Ruth Evelyn (Watson) H.; m. Shirley Lorraine Carter, July 2, 1955; children—Nancy Lynn, Tracy Ann, Laura Jane. B.S. in Econs., U. Pa., 1954, postgrad. in Economics, 1957-59. Cons. John Price Jones Co., N.Y.C., 1960-62, U.S Agy. for Internat. Devel. Southeast Asia, 1970-74; asst. to chancellor U. Calif., Santa Barbara, 1962-63, U. Mo., Kansas City, 1967-70; cons. Asia Found., Singapore, Malaysia, 1964-67; exec. v.p. Mid. Am. Health Edn. Consortium, Kansas City, 1970-78; dir. bus. and devel. Inst. Logopedics, Wichita, Kans., 1978—. Mem., officer Kans. City Civic Orchestra Bd., 1976-78; bd. dirs. Greater Kans. City Urban Coalition, 1969-70. Served to lt. USN, 1954-56. Mem. Nat. Soc. Fund Raising Execs. (chapter pres. elect, treas. 1984—). Republican. Presbyterian. Lodge: Kiwanis. Avocation: golf. Home: 7115 Chadowes Wichita KS 67206 Office: Inst Logopedics 2400 Jardine Dr Wichita KS 67219

HAGERTY, THOMAS PATRICK, county official; b. Cin., Jan. 26, 1954; s. Robert Anthony and Frances Elizabeth (Dierker) H.; m. Renee Elizabeth Hund, July 29, 1978 (div. 1982); 1 son, Sean Patrick; m. 2d, Alyson Jo Fleming, Sept. 17, 1983. B.A., Marquette U., 1976. Sales exec. Jack Winters, Inc., Waukegan, Ill., 1976-79; exec. dir. Lake/McHenry Law Enforcement Planning Commn., Waukegan, Ill., 1979-83; dir. Lake County Dept. Emergency and Pub. Safety Services, 1981-83; dir. Kenosha City/County Dept. Joint Services, 1981—. Mem. adv. bd. VA Hosp., 1980-82; mem. adv. com. law enforcement edn. Coll. of Lake County, 1980—. Mem. Internat. Assn. Police, Nat. Assn. Criminal Justice, Lake County Police Chiefs Assn., McHenry County Police Chiefs Assn., Ill. Assn. Chiefs of Police, Ill. Emergency Services Mgmt. Assn., U.S. Civil Def. Council. Roman Catholic. Home: 6618 43d Ave Kenosha WI 53140 Office: Kenosha City/County Joint Services 1000 55th St Kenosha WI 53140

HAGGARD, FORREST DELOSS, minister; b. Trumbull, Nebr., Apr. 21, 1925; s. Arthur McClellan and Grace (Hadley) H.; m. Eleanor V. Evans, June 13, 1946; children—Warren A., William D., Katherine A. A.B., Phillips U., 1948; M.Div., 1953, D.D. (hon.), 1967; M.A., U. Mo., 1960. Ordained to ministry Christian Ch., 1948; minister Overland Park (Kans.) Christian Ch., 1953—; pres. Kansas City Area Ministers Assn., 1959, Kans. Christian Ministers Assn., 1960; mem. adminstrn. com., gen. bd. Christian Ch., 1968-72; pres. World Conv. Chs. of Christ, 1975—; chmn. Grad. Sem. Council, Enid, Okla., 1970; pres. Nat. Evangelistic Assn., 1972. Pres., Johnson County (Kans.) Mental Health Assn., 1962-63; mem. council Boy Scouts Am., 1964-69; bd. dirs. Kans. Home for Aged, 1960-65, Kans. Children's Services League, 1964-69; pres., bd. dirs. Kans. Masonic Home, 1974-75; bd. dirs. Kans. Masonic Found., 1970—. Lodge: Masons (grand master Kans. Chaplain Gen. Grand chpt. Royal Arch Internat.), 1975—. Author: The Clergy and the Craft, 1970; contbr. articles to profl. jours. Office: 7600 W 75th St Overland Park KS 66024

HAGGH, RAYMOND HERBERT, music educator; b. Chgo., Sept. 4, 1920; s. Herbert Robert and Helen Gertrude (Dain) H.; m. Hilde Gertrud Wentzlaff-Eggebert, Jan. 16, 1949; children—Barbara Helen, Karen Elizabeth. Mus. B., Northwestern U., 1949, Mus.M., 1950; Ph.D., Ind. U., 1961. Assoc. prof. music Memphis State U., Tenn., 1950-60; prof. music U. Nebr., Lincoln, 1960—, assoc. dean, Coll. Arts and Sci., 1973-77, dir. Sch. Music, 1977-84. Translator: History of Music Theory, Books 1 and 11 (Hugo Riemann), 1962; School of Clavier Playing (D.G. Turk), 1982. Artists com. chair Lincoln Symphony Bd., Nebr., 1970-76; panel mem., reviewer Nebr. Arts Council, Omaha, 1976—; project reviewer Nat. Endowment Humanities, Washington, 1977—. Served to sgt. inf. U.S. Army, 1942-45; ETO. Tchr. grantee Danforth Found., 1955-56; fellow Ford Found., 1955-56, So. Fellowships Fund, 1959, Woods Found, 1968-69. Fellow Ctr. for Great Plains Studies (com. chmn. 1978—); mem. Am. Musicol. Soc., Phi Mu Alpha Sinfonia, Pi Kappa Lamda. Democrat. Lutheran. Avocations: reading, attending plays, concerts, films. Home: 4708 Kirkwood Dr Lincoln NE 68516 Office: Sch of Music Univ of Nebr WMB 368 Lincoln NE 68588

HAGGLUND, CLARANCE EDWARD, lawyer; b. Omaha, Feb. 17, 1927; s. Clarence Andrew and Esther (Kelle) H.; student Augustana Coll., 1946-47; B.A., U. S.D., 1949; LL.B., St. Paul Coll. Law, 1953; m. Dorothy Souser, Mar. 27, 1953; children—Laura, Bret; m. 2d, Merle Peterson, Oct. 28, 1972; 1 dau., Katherine. Admitted to Minn. bar, 1955, since practiced in Mpls.; partner firm Mordaunt, Walstad, Cousineau & Hagglund, 1960-63, Wiese, Cox & Hagglund, 1964-66, Hagglund & Johnson (all Mpls.), 1966-73, Clarance E. Hagglund P.A. and predecessor firm, 1973-84, Hagglund & Holmcren, 1984—. Sec., Southwest, Inc., 1961-68. Served to lt. comdr. USNR, 1945-46. Cert. civil trial specialist Nat. Bd. Trial Advocacy; diplomate Am. Bd. Profl. Liability Attys. Fellow Internat. Soc. Barristers; mem. Am., Minn. bar assns., Fedn. Ins. Counsel, Am. Judicature Soc., Res. Officers Assn., Toastmaster's Internat. (past chpt. pres.), Lawyer Pilots Bar Assn., U.S. Maritime Law Assn. (proctor), Trial Attys. Am., Delta Theta Phi, Pi Kappa Delta. Club: Ill. Athletic. Contbr. articles to profl. jours. Home: 3719 Xerxes Ave S Minneapolis MN 55410 Office: Lakeview Office Park 2622 W Lake St Minneapolis MN 55416

HAGUE, RICHARD NORRIS, architect; b. Chgo., Aug. 4, 1934; s. Howard B. and Harriet (Jones) H.; m. Gail L. Elwell, Mar. 24, 1960; children—Jonathan Norris, Mark Richard. B.A. in Architecture, U. Ill., 1959. Prin., Richard N. Hague, River Forest, Ill., 1961-63; with Hague-Richards Assocs. Ltd., Chgo., 1964—, v.p., 1966-69, pres., dir., 1969—. Mem. Frank Lloyd Wright Home and Studio Adv. Bd., Oak Park, 1983. Mem. Nat. Council Archtl. Registration Bds., AIA (Fall-Out Shelter Design award 1964), Scarab, Alpha Rho Chi. Republican. Presbyterian. Clubs: Tavern, Arts (Chgo.); Oak Park Country. Home: 1310 William St River Forest IL 60305 Office: Hague-Richards Assocs Ltd 153 W Ohio St Chicago IL 60610

HAHN, BENJAMIN DANIEL, health care executive; b. Embden, N.D., Oct. 24, 1932; s. Benjamin D. and Laura E. (Martin) H.; m. Eleanor B. Anseth, June 8, 1957; children—Lezlie, Deann Bobette, Lara, Amy. Staff acct. Broeker Hendrickson, Fargo, N.D., 1961-63; asst. adminstrn., controller N.D. State Hosp., Jamestown, 1963-74; pres. the Neuropsychiat. Inst., Fargo, 1974—; faculty Jamestown Coll., part-time, 1963-74. Bd. dirs. Bethany Home, Fargo, 1975-81, S.E. Mental Health Center, 1975-81. Served with U.S. Army, 1954-56. C.P.A., N.D. Am. Coll. Hosp. Adminstrs. fellow, 1976. Mem. Am. Inst. C.P.A.s, Med. Group Mgmt. Assn. Lutheran. Clubs: Elks, Fargo Country. Home: 21 35th Ave NE Fargo ND 58102 Office: 700 1st Ave Fargo ND 58102

HAHN, KANDRA, state official; b. Lincoln, Nebr., May 29, 1947; d. Kenneth Roy and Mildred Marie (Sedlacek) Bailey; m. Robert E. Hahn, Dec. 30, 1965 (div. 1967); 1 child, Kandalyn; m. Donald L. Hunter, June 6, 1976. B.A. in English, Nebr. Wesleyan U., 1970; M.B.A., U. Nebr., 1982. Reporter, Lincoln Jour., 1970-73; clk. Lancaster County Dist. Ct., Lincoln, 1974-82; media coordinator Kerrey for Gov. Campaign, 1982; dir. Nebr. Energy Office, Lincoln, 1983—. Office: Box 95085 Lincoln NE 68509

HAHN, RALPH CRANE, structural engineer, consultant; b. Springfield, Ill., Nov. 9, 1927; s. Lindsay Ralph and Amanda Louise (Crane) H., m. Jane Ann Stround, July 31, 1958; children—Lindsay Stroud, Charles Joseph, Alice Lou. B.S. in Civil Engring., U. Ill., 1951, M.S. in Structural Engring., 1952. Registered profl. engr., Ill. Civil engr., surveyor Chgo. Midland RR., Springfield, Ill., 1951; structural engr. Ill. Div. Hwys/Bridge, Springfield, 1952-61; founder, chief exec. officer Ralph Hahn & Assocs., Inc., Engrs., Architects, Cons., Springfield, 1961—. Sangamon County chmn. Percy for Gov., 1964, Ill. Youth for Nixon Com., 1968; trustee U. Ill., 1967—; mem. Ill. Adv. Council to Small Business, State Univs. Civil Service Merit Bd.; bd. dirs. Springfield Symphony Orch. Served with U.S. Army, 1947-47, 1952-54. Mem. Ill. Nat. Soc. of Profl. Engrs., Cons. Engrs. Council of Ill., Am. Cons. Engrs. Council, ASCE. Baptist. Club: Tavern (Chgo.) Lodges: Mason, Shriners. Home: 1111 Williams Blvd Springfield IL 62704 Office: Ralph Hahn Assocs 1320 S State St Springfield IL 62704

HAHN, RICHARD WAYNE, hospital administrator; b. Phillipsburg, N.J., June 12, 1942; s. Albert L. and Irene S. (Nagy) H.; m. Anne Lenora Waugh, Apr. 12, 1969; children—Gregory, Susan. B.S., Trinity U., San Antonio, 1964; M.H.A., U. Minn., 1970. Asst. adminstr. United Hosps., Newark, 1969-73, Mont. Deaconess Hosp., Great Falls, 1973-76; adminstr. Syosset Hosp., N.Y., 1976-78; exec. dir. Dunn Meml. Hosp., Bedford, Ind., 1978—; clinic adminstr. Mont. Air N.G., 1973-76, N.Y. Air N.G., 1976-78, Ind. Air N.G., 1978—. Elder, 1st Presbyn. Ch., Bedford, since 1984—. Served to maj. USAFR, 1973—. Decorated Bronze Star. Mem. Am. Coll. Hosp. Adminstrs. Republican. Lodge: Rotary (Bedford). Avocations: hunting; fishing; outdoor activities. Home: 435 Ravine Dr Bedford IN 47421 Office: Dunn Meml Hosp 1600 23d St Bedford IN 47421

HAHN, SALLY JO, lawyer; b. Detroit, Aug. 8, 1955; d. Gerald J. and Anneliese Traude (Rahn) H. B.S., Grand Valley State Coll., 1977; J.D., Antioch Sch. Law, Washington, 1982. Bar: Mich. 1982, U.S. Dist. Ct. (ea. dist.) Mich. 1983. Tech. writer Interstate Motor Freight System, Grand Rapids, Mich., 1977-79; law clk. U.S. Dist. Ct. (ea. dist.) Mich., Flint, 1982-83; staff atty. UAW-GM Legal Services Plan, Flint, 1983—. Contbr. to Abortion Law Reporter, 1980-82. Genesee County Democratic precinct del., Flint, 1984. Coll. honor scholar Grand Valley State Coll., Allendale, Mich., 1973-74, State of Mich. competitive scholar Grand Valley State Coll., 1973. Mem. Women Lawyers Assn. Mich., Mich. Trial Lawyers Assn., ACLU, NOW. Unitarian.

HAHN, WILLIAM FRANK, management and technical consultant, mechanical engineer; b. Holyoke, Mass., Nov. 16, 1940; s. Frank J. and Phyllis C. (Smith) H.; m. Marilyn E. Kleiber, Aug. 4, 1962; children—Karla Lyn, Douglas William, Gregory William. B.S.M.E., Valparaiso U., 1962; M.S.M.E., U. Ill., 1964, Ph.D., 1969. Instr., Valparaiso U. (Ind.), 1964-66; sr. project engr. Corning Glass Works (N.Y.), 1969-75; prin. Booz Allen & Hamilton, Cleve., 1975-83; owner, pres. Mfg. and Tech. Assocs., Inc., Cleve., 1983—. Mem. bd. ministers Christ Redeemer Lutheran Ch., Brecksville, Ohio, 1980-83. Mem. ASME, Soc. Mfg. Engrs., Robotics Internat., Illumination Engring. Soc. N.Am., Soc. Advancement Materials and Process Engring. Lodge: Rotary (pres. 1978-79) (Brecksville). Home: 10233 Log Cabin Ln Brecksville OH 49141 Office: Mfg & Tech Assocs Inc 5915 Schaaf Rd Cleveland OH 44131

HAIDLE, RUDY HENRY, chemist; b. Rochester, N.Y., Sept. 4, 1945; s. Rudolph Emil and Julianne (Banman) H. A.A.S., Rochester Inst. Tech., 1966, B.S., 1969; M.S., Cornell U., 1971. Trainee, Xerox Corp., Webster, N.Y., 1965-69; v.p. research and devel. Creative Plastics, Rochester, N.Y., 1971-72; mgr. electronics and machine shop Northwestern U., Chgo., 1972-75, analytical instrument specialist, Evanston, Ill., 1975—; cons. Fine Arts Research and Holographic Ctr., Chgo., 1979—, Columbia Coll., Chgo., 1979—; cons. in field of electronics, optics, med. application of lasers. Patentee in field (2). Contbr. articles to profl. jours. Recipient DuPont Teaching award, 1970. Mem. Am. Chem. Soc. (chpt. bd. dirs. 1978—), Analytical Lab. Mgrs. Assn. (founding mem., bd. dirs. 1979—, treas. 1979—), AAAS, Soc. Applied Spectroscopy (bd. dirs. 1981-83), Midwest Bio-laser Inst. Avocations: skiing; harmonica; orchids. Home: 1514 South Blvd Evanston IL 60202 Office: Northwestern U 2145 Sheridan Rd B107 Evanston IL 60201

HAIDLE, STANLEY JAMES, educational administrator, fund raising consultant; b. Eureka, S.D., June 14, 1949; s. Walter and Bertha (Will) H.; m. Ruth Ellen Keith, May 28, 1971; 1 child, Luke. B.A., Dakota Wesleyan U., Mitchell, S.D., 1971; M.Div., Asbury Sem., 1974, M.A. in Religion, 1975; D.Ministry, N.Am. Baptist Sem., 1983. Ordained deacon United Methodist Ch., 1974, elder, 1976. Pastor Onida and Agar United Meth. Chc., S.D., 1975-78; assoc. pastor 1st Meth. Ch., Huron, S.D., 1978-83; v.p. instl. advancement Dakota Wesleyan Univ., Mitchell, S.D., 1983—. Founder, chmn. bd. dirs. Blessing Ctr., Huron, S.D., 1979-83; founder, chmn. bd. trustees Mitchell Christian Edn. Assn., 1983. Republican. Lodge: Rotary. Avocations: hunting; fishing; camping; farming. Office: Dakota Wesleyan Univ University Ave Mitchell SD 57301

HAIGLER, HENRY JAMES, neuropharmacologist; b. Columbia, S.C., July 23, 1941; s. Harry D. and Evelyn (Talton) H.; m. E. Jean Smith, July 25, 1964; children—Henry James, Elizabeth Ashley. B.S., Wake Forest U., 1963; Ph.D., 1969. Postdoctoral fellow Mental Health Research Inst. Ann Arbor, Mich., 1969-71; research assoc. Yale U. Med. Sch., New Haven, 1971-74; asst., then assoc. prof. Emory U., Atlanta, 1974-83; sect. head G.D. Searle & Co., Skokie, Ill., 1983—; pres. Neuroscience, Atlanta, 1981-82. Deacon, Clairmont Presbyterian Ch., Atlanta, 1981-83. Mem. Soc. Neurosci., Am. Soc. Pharmacology and Exptl. Therapeutics, AAAS. Office: GD Searle & Co 4901 Searle Pkwy Skokie IL 60077

HAINES, GERRY P., optometrist; b. Unionville, Mo., July 13, 1940; s. Aaron W. and Lucille L. (Wells) H.; m. Janet M. Robb, Nov. 12, 1960; children—Beth A., Sheri L. A.A., Moline Community Coll., Ill., 1961; B.S., Ill. Coll. Optometry, Chgo., 1963, O.D., 1965. Optician Quad City Optical, Moline, Ill., 1957-61; pvt. practice optometry, Freeport, Ill., 1965—. Co-editor audio-cassette Wine Appreciation Course, 1984. Mem. Am. Optometric Assn., Ill. Optometric Assn., Soc. Wine Educators. Lodge: Kiwanis. Home: 1615 W Harrison St Freeport IL 61032 Office: 224 W Stephenson St Freeport IL 61032

HAINES, JAMES RICHARD, psychology educator; b. Topeka, Mar. 22, 1938; s. Walter Lawrence and Ruth Leota (Jackman) H.; m. Martha Elizabeth Guzman-Perry, May 26, 1960; children—Louise Anne, Laura Patricia. B.A. with honors, Washburn U., 1962; M.A., U. Kans., 1968, Ph.D., 1973. Research asst. Menninger Found., Topeka, 1959-65; asst. instr. Kans. U., Lawrence, 1965-68, teaching and research asst., 1968-70; lectr. Ind. U., South Bend, 1971-73, asst. prof., 1973-79, acting asst. dean faculties, 1974, acting dept. chmn., 1975, assoc. prof. psychology, 1979—, chmn. dept. psychology, 1983—; exec. v.p. Mgmt. Alternatives, Inc., Topeka, 1981-82. Contbr. articles in field to profl. jours. NDEA Title IV fellow Kans. State U., 1961; Residence Hall scholar U. Kans., 1957, Summerfield scholar, 1956, Putnam scholar, 1956; High Honors scholar Washburn U., 1956; Ind. U. grantee-in-aid, 1974, 76, 77, 84; faculty travel grantee, 1980, 84, 85. Mem. Am. Psychol. Assn., Nat. Assn. Jazz Educators, Am. Soc. Tng. and Devel., Music Educators Nat. Conf., Soc. Research in Music Edn., Nat. Collegiate Honors Council, Midwestern Psychol. Assn., Rocky Mountain Psychol. Assn., Sigma Xi, Phi Mu Alpha Sinfonia, Psi Chi, Alpha Chi Sigma. Home: 1616 Dorwood Dr South Bend IN 46617 Office: PO Box 7111 South Bend IN 46634

HAINES, JOHN ALDEN, lawyer; b. Merrill, Mich., July 26, 1934; s. John Alden and Pearl Ann (Bader) H.; m. Esther Catherine Mueller, Aug. 25, 1956; children—Kimberly Ann, Kathryn Sue, John Alden III. A.A., Bay City Jr. Coll., 1953; B.A., U. Mich., 1955; J.D., Detroit Coll., 1958. Bar: Mich., 1959. Sole practice law, Bridgeport, Mich., 1959-67; sr. ptnr. Haines & Marti, 1968—; justice of peace Bridgeport Twp., 1961-68. Pres., bd. dirs. Bridgeport Civic Assn., 1963, 1966; dist. chmn. Boy Scouts Am., Saginaw. 1969; county del. Saginaw Republican Party, 1964, 84. Mem. Saginaw Bar Assn. (sec. 1980-82, dir. 1983-85, v.p. 1985-86; Meritorious Service award, 1979, cert. commendation 1985), Mich. Bar Assn., Am. Judicature Soc., Bridgeport C. of C., (pres., dir. 1962-63), Delta Theta Phi. Lutheran. Clubs: Bridgeport Country, Bridgeport Gun. Avocations: golf, skiing. Home: 4030 Jordan Dr Saginaw MI 48601 Office: Haines & Marti 6221 Dixie Hwy Bridgeport MI 48722

HAINES, MICHAEL CURTIS, lawyer; b. Batavia, N.Y., Feb. 8, 1949; s. Paul R. and Dorothy G. (Ludington) H.; m. Patricia Yvonne Van Dyken, May 22, 1982; 1 child, Daniel Curtis. A.B., U. Mich., 1971, J.D., 1974. Bar: Mich. 1974, U.S. Dist. Ct. (we. dist.) Mich. 1974. Assoc., Mika Meyers Beckett & Jones, Grand Rapids, Mich., 1974-79, ptnr., 1980—; mem. city of Adrian Gas Rate Commn., Mich., 1983-84; mem. securities law adv. com. Mich. Bur. Corps. and Securities, 1977—; lectr. in field. Mem. ABA, State Bar Mich., Grand Rapids Bar Assn., Mich. Oil and Gas Assn. (chmn. legal and legis. com. 1977—), Phi Beta Kappa, Order of Coif. Republican. Mem. Reformed Ch. in Am. Office: Mika Meyers et al 500 Frey Bldg Grand Rapids MI 49503

HAINES, MICHAEL ROBERT, economist, educator; b. Chgo., Nov. 19, 1944; s. James Joshua and Anne Marie (Welch) H.; m. Patricia Caroline Foster, Aug. 19, 1967 (div. Jan. 1985); children—James, Margaret. B.A., Amherst Coll., 1967; M.A., U. Pa., 1968, Ph.D., 1971. Asst. prof. econs. Cornell U., Ithaca, N.Y., 1972-79; vis. lectr. econs. U. Pa., Phila., 1979, research assoc. prof. Sch. Pub. and Urban Policy, 1979-80; assoc. prof. econs. Wayne State U., Detroit, 1980—; cons. NIH, Bethesda, Md., 1980-84, The World Bank, Washington, 1983. Author: Economic-Demographic Interrelations in Developing Agricultural Regions, 1977; Fertility and Occupation, 1979. Contbr. articles to profl. jours. NIH grantee, 1974-77, 78-82. Mem. Internat. Union for Sci. Study Population, Econ. History Assn., Social Sci. History Assn. (bd. dirs. 1983—), Am. Econ. Assn., Population Assn. Am., Am. Statis. Assn. Episcopalian. Avocations: numismatics; wine; book collecting. Office: Wayne State U Dept Econs Detroit MI 48202

HAINES, PERRY VANSANT, cattle company executive; b. Middletown, Ohio, Mar. 14, 1944; s. John Percy and Pendery (Spear) H.; m. Sidonie Sexton, 1982. A.B., Princeton U., 1967; M.B.A., Harvard U., 1970. Research asst. Harvard U., 1970-71; cons. Boston Cons. Group, 1971-74; exec. v.p. Iowa Beef Processors, Dakota City, Nebr., 1974—; v.p. Occidental Petroleum, Los Angeles, 1981—. Served with USMCR, 1967-68. Office: PO Box 515 Dakota City NE 67831

HAIRSTON, HELEN COVINGTON, behavioral science educator; b. Jackson, Tenn., July 17, 1937; d. George E. Covington and M. Louise (Covington) Sutton; m. Raleigh D. Hairston, Dec. 22, 1962; children—John L., Karen N. B.A. in Sociology, Western Res. U., 1962, M.A., 1967; student Northwestern U., 1971, U. N.C., 1970. Asst. prof. sociology Catawba and Livingston Coll., Salisbury, N.C., 1968-71, Cuyahoga Community Coll., Parma, Ohio, 1971—; owner/dir. Writing Chores, Cleve., 1984—. Compiler/editor: Readings in Economic Society, 1983; Economic Issues and Consumer Skills: For Single Parents, 1985. Vol., Am. Cancer Soc., 1984; corr. sec. Jack and Jill Am., Inc., Cleve., 1984-85. Case Western Res. U. scholar, 1982; NSF grantee, 1970; NDEA grantee, 1971. Mem. Am. Sociol. Assn., Community Coll. Social Sci. Assn., Am. Mgmt. Assns., N. Central Sociol. Assn., Alpha Kappa Delta Educators Assn. Baptist. Mem. bd. Christian edn. Antioch Baptist Ch., 1981-83. Club: Social Sci. Book (Cleve.). Avocations: home computers; swimming; walking; old movies. Office: 11000 Pleasant Valley Rd Parma OH 44130

HAIRSTON, RUSSELL, city government administrator; b. Portsmouth, Ohio, Aug. 22, 1954; s. Harry Edward and Hortense Y. (Williams) H. A.A., Shawne State U., 1977; B.S., U. Cin., 1979, M.Planning, 1983. Social work counselor Scioto County United Way, Portsmouth, 1975-77; program adminstr. Scioto Community Action Inc., Portsmouth, 1977-79; planner Scioto County Employment, Portsmouth, 1979-81; grad. research asst. U. Cin., 1981-82; devel. specialist City of Cin., 1983—. U. Cin. scholar, 1978. Mem. Omicron Delta Kappa. Methodist. Avocations: racquetball; tennis; swimming. Home: 1753 Gilsey Ave #3 Cincinnati OH 45205 Office: Dept Neighborhood Housing and Conservation 415 W Court St Cincinnati OH 45203

HAISCH, LARRY DEAN, dental educator; b. Wayne, Nebr., May 8, 1943; s. Harold Leonard and Iola Maxine (Cogdill) H.; m. Jacqueline Kay Wilber, Aug. 28, 1965; children—Lisa Lynn, Scott David, Robyn Lea. Student Wayne State Coll., 1960-62; D.D.S., U. Nebr., 1967. Gen. practice dentistry, Grant, Nebr., 1969-79; instr. U. Nebr. Coll. Dentistry, Lincoln, 1979-83, asst. prof., 1983—; staff U. Nebr. Student Health Dental Clinic, Lincoln, 1980—; mem. adv. com. dept. of dental assisting, health occupation edn. Southeast Community Coll., Lincoln, 1982—; cons. in field. Contbr. articles to profl. jours. Mem. Grant Area Jaycees, 1970-79 (chpt. awards 1970, 71, 72). Served as capt. Dental Corps, USAF, 1967-69. Mem. ADA, Coll. Dentistry Alumni Assn. (dir. 1982—, pres. elect 1985), U. Nebr. Alumni Assn., Lincoln Dist. Dental Assn., Nebr. Dental Assn. (named Council Chmn. of Yr., 1984), Am. Assn. Dental Schs., Acad. Gen. Dentistry. Republican. Lutheran. Avocations: reading, spectator sports, boating. Office: U Nebr Med Ctr Coll Dentistry 40th and Holdrege St Lincoln NE 68583

HAISER, KARL FRANCIS, JR., accountant; b. Detroit, Dec. 5, 1942; s. Karl Francis and Mae Martha (Schram) H.; m. Linda Kay Clements, Nov. 18, 1967; children—Eric, Bryan, Justin. B.S., Ferris State Coll., 1965; M.B.A., Central Mich. U., 1967; diploma advanced acctg. Internat. Accts. Soc., 1973. C.P.A., Mich. Staff acct. Price Waterhouse & Co., C.P.A.s, 1966-71; asst. to controller Hygrade Food Products, Inc., Southfield, Mich., 1971-73; self-employed C.P.A., Grand Blanc, Mich., 1973—, mng. ptnr., 1983—; instr. Detroit Coll. Bus., 1983—; instr., advisor acctg. Mott Community Coll., 1983—. Twp. chmn. Planning Commn. and Bd. Appeals, 1974-76; cubmaster Boy Scouts Am.; founder Grand Blanc Jr. League Football. Served with USMC, 1967-69. Mem. Am. Inst. C.P.A.s, Mich. Assn. C.P.A.s, Pi Kappa Alpha. Republican. Lutheran. Home: 5186 Greenmeadows St Grand Blanc MI 48439 Office: 131 E Grand Blanc Rd Grand Blanc MI 48439

HAJJAR, LABIB ELIAS, restaurant company executive; b. Machgara, Lebanon, Dec. 17, 1951; came to U.S., 1970, naturalized, 1980; s. Elias Michael and Marie Hanna (Karam) H.; m. Karyn Labib Nichols, Sept. 3, 1978; children—Marie, Elias. B.S., Western Mich. U., 1974; M.B.A., U. Toledo, 1983. Founder, operator Beirut Bakery, Toledo, Ohio, 1974-80; founder, operator, pres. Beirut Restaurant, Toledo, 1977—; cons. U. Toledo Mgmt. Ctr., 1982-83. Mem. Assn. Self Employed, Assn. M.B.A. Execs. Avocations: tennis; backgammon; chess. Office: Beirut Inc 4082 Monroe Toledo OH 43606

HAKE, RANDALL JAMES, printing company executive; b. Sheboygan, Wis., May 13, 1940; s. Walter Victor and Elsa Emelia (Pinnecker) H.; m. Judith Faye Richter, Sept. 8, 1962; children—Trentan Forrest, Heidi Gretchen, Drew Randall, Tyler James. B.S. in Bus. Adminstrn., Northwestern U., 1962. With Diamond Printing Co., Inc., Sheboygan, 1962—, purchasing agt., 1962-64, office mgr., 1964-66, v.p., 1966-78, pres., 1978—. Pres., Sheboygan County March of Dimes, 1968-71; bd. dirs. Lutheran High Sch. Assn. Sheboygan County, 1978-80, John Michael Kohler Arts Ctr.; mem. St. John's Mil. Acad.

Parents Club, Delafield, Wis. Recipient cert. of appreciation Sheboygan County chpt. Nat. Found. March of Dimes, 1970, Disting. Vol. Leadership award, 1971; Very Important Parent award Trinity Luth. Sch., 1978. Mem. Travelers Protective Assn., United Comml. Travelers, Data Processing Mgmt. Assn., Northwestern U. Alumni Assn. (dir. 1978-83). Clubs: Pine Hills Country, Lions (dir. Sheboygan Evening Club 1965-75); Sports Core Tennis (Kohler, Wis.). Home: 3535 Meadowbrook Ln Sheboygan WI 53081 Office: 809 Wilson Ave Sheboygan WI 53081

HAKE, TIMOTHY LEO, company sales executive, consultant; b. Ft. Wayne, Ind., May 13, 1955; s. Joseph Henry and Rose Kathleen (Schenkel) H.; m. Karen Lynn Fosnaugh, Aug. 17, 1979; 1 child, Kelly Marie. Cert. Drake U. Law Sch., 1977; B.B.A., U. Notre Dame, 1977; M.B.A., St. Francis Coll., 1981. Mgr. Container Corp. Am., Ft. Wayne, 1977-79; v.p. sales Ayr-Way Industries, Kendallville, Ind., 1979-81; owner, pres. T. Hake & Assocs., Ft. Wayne, 1980-84; nat. sales mgr. Messenger/Dot Corp., Auburn, Ind., 1984-85, div. mgr., 1985—; cons. bd. dirs. KIP's Electronics, Ft. Wayne, 1980—; cons. mgmt. and fin. E&T Greenhouse, Ft. Wayne, 1984—. Active Small Bus. Communication Council, Ft. Wayne C. of C., 1983; founder, pres. Summit Future, Ft. Wayne, 1983. Republican. Roman Catholic. Clubs: Ft. Wayne Jaycees (dir. 1982-83), Notre Dame. Home: 6912 Ludwig Circle Ft Wayne IN 46825 Office: Messenger A Dot Group Co 318 E 7th St Auburn IN 46706

HAKE-GRIMWOOD, PATRICIA ANN, college administrator, counselor; b. Belleville, Ill., Dec. 12, 1951; d. Marshall N. and Margaret M. (Pals) Hake; m. Charles Gregory Grimwood, May 12, 1973. B.S. in Edn., Kans. State U., 1974, M.S., 1975. Dir. career, counseling and placement Marymount Coll., Salina, Kans., 1975-76, dir. counseling, 1976-84, title III coordinator, 1981—, asst. dean students, 1984—; counselor Luth. Social Service, Salina, 1977—; cons. Tabor Coll., Hillsboro, Kans., 1980, Salina Diocese, N.W. Kans., 1981-84, Asbury/St. John's Hosps., Salina, 1984—. Mem. Am. Assn. Counseling and Devel., Am. Mental Health Counselors Assn. (dist. coordinator 1981-84, regional rep. to bd. 1984-85), Kans. Mental Health Counselors Assn. (chair chartering com. 1980-81, pres. 1981-82), Kans. Coll. Personnel Assn. (pres. 1979-80), Kappa Delta Pi, Phi Delta Kappa, Phi Kappa Phi. Lutheran. Club: Literary of Salina. Avocations: reading; counted cross stitch; cooking; walking; home remodeling; antiquing. Office: Marymount Coll Salina KS 67401

HAKEL, EDWIN HENRY, clergyman; b. Silver Lake, Minn., June 2, 1909; s. Stephen and Emily (Zbitovsky) H.; student Macalester Coll., 1929, McPhail Sch. Music, Mpls., 1930-32, Mpls. Sch. Music, 1934-35, U. Minn., 1949, Western Pastor's Sch., 1956; m. Alice Vera Svihel, Aug. 16, 1946; adopted children—Pollyann, Richard. Ordained to ministry Congl. Ch., 1954; minister, St. Paul, 1945-54, Staples, Minn., 1954-60, 1st Congl. Ch., Sherburn, Minn., 1960-73, St. Matthew's United Ch. of Christ, Litchfield, Minn., 1973-81; dir. Oak Haven Retreat, Inc., Fairmont, Minn., 1981—. Tchr. Leadership Tng. Inst., 1961; registrar No. Pacific Assn. Congl. Chs., 1955-60, scribe Minn. Conf., 1961, youth adviser Southwestern Assn., 1962-63, registrar, 1962-63; registrar Southwestern Assn. United Ch. Christ, 1964, 65, 69, 70, 71; condr. Vesper Hour TV program, 1973-74; United Ch. of Christ rep. region Minn. Council Chs., 1976, 77, vice chmn. region 6E, also rep. theology of ecology com. Vice pres. Sherburn-Dunnell PTA, 1970, pres., 1971—; mem. Meeker County Community Adv. Council, 1976—; tenor Litchfield Area Male Chorus, v.p., 1976-77, pres., 1977—, also bd. dirs.; bd. dirs. Sherburn Civic and Commerce Assn., 1972-73; bd. dirs. Meeker County Concert Assn., 1976, 77; v.p. Meeker County unit Am. Cancer Soc., 1977—, pres.-elect 1978, pres., 1978-80; pres.-elect Meeker County Music and Arts Assn., 1978, pres., 1978-79. Served with AUS, 1942-45. Recipient Good Neighbor to NW award Radio Sta. WCCO, 1977; Certificate of Recognition for Bicentennial contbns. from Gov. Minn., 1977, Minn. Gov.'s cert. of commendation, 1980; Eastman Kodak scholar Photography Forum, 1983. Mem. Litchfield Area Ministerial Assn. (v.p. 1974-75, pres. 1975—, program com. 1978-79), Am. Legion (life mem. dist. 7; chaplain 4th dist. 1953-54, 71, chaplain 2d dist. 1972-73, chaplain 7th dist. 1976-79, state chaplain 1979—, Meritorious Service citation dist. 7, 1979), North Central Camera Club Council. Kiwanian (life mem., pres. elect Sherburn 1964, lt. gov. div. 2 Minn.-Dakotas dist. 1965, div. 5, 1977-79, v.p. Sherburn 1970, pres. 1971, dir. Litchfield 1974—, pub. relations chmn. 1975—). Clubs: Fairmont Camera (pres. 1966-67, 70-71; Gold Cup Trophy for color slide competition 1964-66, 70); Kiwanis of Fairmont (chmn. com. spiritual aims, spl. adv. to pres.; lt. gov. elect 1984-85). Address: Oak Haven Retreat Inc Route 3 Box 28K Fairmont MN 56031

HAKES, WANDA FAYE, nursing educator; b. Narka, Kans., Apr. 14, 1930; d. John and Margaret Elizabeth (Holan) Chaloupka; m. Lester B. Hakes, Sept. 16, 1951; children—Anita Lytle, Frederick, Daniel, Carol Rohlfing. R.N., St. Elizabeth Hosp. Sch. Nursing, 1950. R.N., Nebr., Kans. Charge nurse St. Elizabeth Hosp., Lincoln, Nebr., 1950; staff nurse St. Joseph Hosp., Concordia, Kans., 1952-58, Gelvin-Haughey Clinic, Concordia, 1958-65; supr. Mennonite Hosp., Beatrice, Nebr., 1966-72; nursing instr. S.E. Community Coll., Beatrice, 1972—. Mem. Beatrice Community Hosp. Devel. Council, 1981—. Mem. Nat. Vocat. Assn., Nebr. Vocat. Assn., S.E. Nebr. League Nursing (sec.), Nat. League Nursing, S.E. Community Coll. Beatrice Campus Faculty Assn., League Nursing and Vocat. Assn. Clubs: Beatrice Bus. and Profl. Women's, Order Eastern Star.

HAKIM, ALI HUSSEIN, export company executive, consultant; b. Mushref, Lebanon, Aug. 13, 1943; came to U.S., 1973; s. Hussein A. and Sabah (Wazni) H.; m. Raafat M. Siklawi, July 2, 1972; children—Hussein, Ronny, Sameer. B.S.B.A., Beirut U., 1970; postgrad. in acctg. Wayne State U., 1975; M.A. in Econs. and Politics, U. Detroit, 1980. Supr. Al-Mouharer Newspaper, Beirut, 1964-67; prin. Lebanese Soc. for Edn., Beirut, 1967-72; field services adviser Chrysler Corp., Detroit, 1973-75; owner, operator H & R Parking Co., Detroit, 1975-81; comptroller Met. Detroit Youth, 1979-82; pres. Gen. Bus. Corp., Detroit, 1982—, Hakim Export, Detroit, 1982—; cons. to trading and investment agys., Africa, Middle East; budget cons. Met. Detroit Youth Found., 1983—. Research on U.S./China trade relations, 1980, U.S. monetary policy, 1981, internat. mktg., 1983. Mem. Republican Presdl. Task Force, 1982—. Mem. Am. Mgmt. Assn., Acctg. Aid Soc. Club: Senatorial (Washington). Home: 35386 Indigo Dr Sterling Heights MI 48077

HAKKILA, LEON FRED, architect; b. Virginia, Minn., Oct. 22, 1945; s. Fred Leonard and Miriam Marie (Saari) H.; B.Arch., U. Minn., 1969, postgrad., 1970; m. Lonnie Kaye Dean, Aug. 10, 1968; 1 son, Bryan Lee. Staff architect, St. Paul Public Schs., 1970-72; supr. planning, 1972-74; chief architect Abe W. Mathews Engring. Co., Hibbing, Minn., 1974—. Counselor design Boy Scouts Am.; mem. Hibbing Planning Commn., 1975-82, chmn., 1977-81; chmn. Hibbing Bd. Variances and Appeals, 1977, 80, Downtown Devel. Authority, 1982—, Econ. Devel. Commn., 1983—. Served with AUS, 1970. Mem. Minn. Soc. AIA (pres. N.E. chpt. 1982, dir. 1982-83, exec. com. 1982), AIA, Constrn. Specification Inst., Houston C. of C. Lutheran. Club: Rotary (Hibbing). Home: 2035 E 31st St Hibbing MN 55746 Office: 555 W 27th St Hibbing MN 55746

HAKKINEN, RAIMO JAAKKO, aeronautical scientist; b. Helsinki, Finland, Feb. 26, 1926; s. Jalmari and Lyyli (Mattila) H.; diploma aero. engring., Helsinki U. Tech., 1948; M.S., Calif. Inst. Tech., 1950, Ph.D. cum laude, 1954; m. Pirkko Loyttyniemi, July 16, 1949; children—Bert, Mark. Came to U.S., 1949, naturalized, 1960. Head tech. office Finnish Aero. Assn., Helsinki, 1948; instr. engring Tampere Tech. Coll., 1949; design engr., aircraft div. Valmet Corp., Tampere, Finland, 1949; research asst. Calif. Inst. Tech., 1950-53; mem. research staff Mass. Inst. Tech., 1953-56; with Western div. McDonnell Douglas Astronautics Co., Santa Monica, Calif., 1956—, chief scientist phys. scis. dept., 1964-70, chief scientist flight scis. McDonnell Douglas Research Labs., St. Louis, 1970-82, dir. research, flight scis. 1982—. Lectr. engring. U. Calif. at Los Angeles, 1957-59; vis. assoc. prof. aeros and astronautics Mass. Inst. Tech., 1963-64. Served with Finnish Air Force, 1944. Fellow AIAA (mem. fluid dynamics com. 1969-71, honors and awards com. 1975-83, tech. activities com. 1975-78, dir. at large 1977-79); mem. Am. Phys. Soc., Assn. Caltech Alumni Assn., Sigma Xi. Contbr. articles to profl. jours. Home: 5 Old Colony Ln Saint Louis MO 63131 Office: PO Box 516 Saint Louis MO 63166

HALASZ, MARILYNN JEAN, cement association information services manager; b. Chgo., Nov. 12, 1937; d. Frank John and Vera Josephine (Staab) Macku; m. John Ernest Halasz, May 21, 1981. B.A., Rosary Coll., 1959; M.A.L.S., 1977; student foreign study, Univ. Coll., Oxford, Eng., 1971; M.A., DePaul U., 1972. Tchr. elem., secondary, and collegiate levels in English, sci. and math., 1959-77; cons. resource manual Ill. State Bd. Edn., Triton Coll., River Grove, Ill., 1975-76; sci. librarian John Crerar Library, Chgo., 1977-78; assoc. librarian Portland Cement Assn., Skokie, Ill., 1978, librarian, 1978-80, mgr. info. services sect., 1980—; cons. in field. Contbr. articles to profl. jours. Recipient grad. asst. award Dale Carnegie & Assocs., 1984. Mem. Spl. Libraries Assn. Roman Catholic. Club: Am. Assn. Univ. Women. Home: 514 S Garfield Ave Hinsdale IL 60521

HALBACH, RICHARD EDWARD, biomedical engineer, administrator; b. Milw., Feb. 19, 1947; s. Edward Anthony and Jane Elizabeth (Roth) H.; m. Linda Louise Pike, July 1, 1972; children—Sarah, Rebecca, David. B.S.E.E., Marquette U., 1970, Ph.D., 1977. Research assoc. Med. Coll. Wis., Milw., 1977-78, asst. prof. biomed. engring., 1978-84; dir. research and devel. Metriflow Inc., Milw., 1984—; specified profl. personal staff Milw. County Med. Complex, 1979-84. Vice-pres. Brookfield Jaycees, 1981, 82. Bacon fellow Marquette U., 1975. Mem. Bioelectromagnetics Soc., IEEE (sr. mem.). Office: Metriflow Inc 8702 W Watertown Plank Rd Milwaukee WI 53226

HALBEISEN, JOHN FRANCIS (JACK), industrial design consultant; b. Fremont, Ohio, Aug. 30, 1914; s. John Henry and Blanche Emma (Maillard) H.; m. Mary Louise Warnke, Jan. 14, 1939; children—John Francis Arthur, Eugene John, Mary Kay. Student, Toledo U., 1938-39, Cleve. Sch. Art, 1940-41, Wayne State U., 1943-45. Designer, Libbey Glass Co., Toledo, 1938-40, Gen. Motors, Detroit, 1940-45, Chrysler Corp., Highland Park, Mich., 1945-60; dir., design cons. Halbeisen Assocs., Dayton, 1960—. Patentee more than 90 devices in automotive technology. Holder 16 world records, Fedn. Aeronautique Internationale, Nat. Aeronautic Assn. as first man to fly east to west and west to east in an ultra-light aircraft. Mem. Am. Soc. Interior Designers (cons. designer, Design awards 1956, 58), Indsl. Designers Soc. Am. (cons.). Republican. Roman Catholic. Avocations: Flying; music; travel.

HALBERSTADT, KENNETH KEITH, ground support systems company executive; b. Champaign, Ill., Sept. 5, 1920; s. Harry B. and LaVerne Augusta (Moffett) H.; m. Hildred Marie Murphy, Aug. 27, 1966. Student U. Ill. Extension, 1939-41, Rock Island Arsenal, 1943, Ill. Inst. Tech., 1943. Engring. inspector U.S. Dept. War, Rockford, Ill., 1942-45; project engr. Barber Coleman Co., Rockford, 1945-64; with Modern Suspension Systems, Rockford, 1964—, now sales and mktg. mgr. Assoc. elder First Presbyterian Ch., Rockford, 1975-79. Mem. Am. Inst. Indsl. Engrs. (sec. and 2d v.p. Winnebago chpt. 1981-83). Republican. Lodges: Shriners; Masons, Moose. Avocations: golf; hunting; fishing; bird watching. Home: 4932 Fenwick Close Rockford IL 61111 Office: Modern Suspension Systems Inc 333 18th Ave Rockford IL 61108

HALBRITTER, TED LEROY, III, funeral director; b. Niles, Mich., Feb. 19, 1947; s. Ted L. and Ruthe E. (Montgomery) H.; m. Mary Jo Garritano, Aug. 8, 1970; children—Claire, Carrie. B.S., Mich. State U., 1969; Mortuary Sci. degree, Wayne State U., 1970. Ops. improvement analyst Am. Nat. Bank, Kalamazoo, Mich., 1970-72; co-owner, operator Halbritter Funeral Home, Niles, Mich., 1972—; tchr. seminars; dir. Am. Nat. Bank of Niles, N.A. Pres. Niles Sch. Bd., 1982-83; mem. Niles Econ. Devel. Found.; mem. adv. bd. Salvation Army; bd. dirs. WNIT Pub. TV, 1985—. Recipient Erikson Acctg. and Mgmt. award Wayne State U., 1970. Mem. Mich. Funeral Dirs. Assn. (dist. past pres.), C. of C. (pres. 1977). Club: Optimist (Niles). Editor pamphlet in field. Home: 552 Grant St Niles MI 49120 Office: 615 E Main St Niles MI 49120

HALCOMB, F. JOSEPH, III, physician executive; b. Scottsville, Ky., Mar. 27, 1951; s. F. Joseph, Jr. and Mariola (Shrewsbury) H.; m. Joan Marie Spears, June 1, 1974; children—Allison Archer, Alyssa Craig. B.S., U. Ky., 1974, M.D., 1978; M.S., MIT, 1980. Registered profl. engr., Ind.; diplomate Nat. Bd. Med. Examniners. Intern in internal medicine Albert B. Chandler Med. Ctr., Lexington, Ky., 1978-79; gen. practice medicine Halcomb and Oliver Clinic, Scottsville, 1979; postdoctoral research assoc. Mass. Gen. Hosp., Boston, 1979-80; assoc. med. dir. Zimmer, Inc. div. Bristol-Myers Corp., Warsaw, Ind., 1980-81, dir. new ventures, 1981-83, dir. new product devel., 1983-85, v.p. product devel., 1985—; industry rep. on orthopaedic and rehab. services panel FDA, 1985—; mem. Ky. Commn. on Alcohol and Drug Problems, 1974-75; mem. Contemporary Orthopaedics Surgeons Adv. Panel, 1983—. Contbr. sci. papers, articles to profl. publs. Patentee in field. Bd. dirs. Kosciusko Community YMCA, Warsaw, 1982, Employee Fed. Credit Union, Warsaw, 1982-83. Mem. AMA (Physician Recognition award 1982, 85), Med. Alumni Assn., Am. Acad. Med. Dirs., Am. Acad. Family Physicians, Nat. Soc. Profl. Engrs., Ind. State Med. Assn., Ind. Acad. Family Physicians, Ind. Soc. Profl. Engrs., Kosciusko County Med. Soc., Bioelec. Repair and Growth Soc., Sigma Alpha Epsilon (McChesney-Woodward Zeal award 1974), Mercedes-Benz Club Am. Presbyterian. Avocations: tennis; bicycling; photography; classic car restoration. Home: Route 7 Box 371-A Warsaw IN 46580 Office: Zimmer Inc PO Box 708 Warsaw IN 46580

HALDERMAN, ROBERT RICHARD, farm management company executive, realtor; b. Wabash, Ind., Jan. 28, 1936; s. Howard H. and Marie E. (Zahm) H.; m. Janet Elizabeth Squires, June 26, 1960; children—F. Howard, Richard. B.S. in Agr., Purdue U., 1958. Cert. real estate broker, Ind., Mich., Ohio, Ill., Ky. Farmer, Wabash, Ind., 1952-58; area mgr. Halderman Farm Mgmt. Service, Inc., Wabash, 1958-60, area mgr., v.p., 1960-64, pres., 1964—; incorporator, dir. Frances Slocum Bank, Wabash, 1963—. Bd. dirs. United Fund of Wabash County, 1970; elder, trustee, deacon Presbyterian Ch., Wabash, 1958—. Served to capt. U.S. Army, 1959. Recipient Disting. Service award Wabash Jaycees, 1970. Mem. Ind. Soc. Farm Mgrs. and Rural Appraisers (v.p. 1966, pres. 1967), Big Bros., Northfield Athletic Booster Club (pres. 1983, 84, 85). Republican. Club: Wabash Country (bd. dirs. 1970). Lodge: Kiwanis (pres. 1965), Masons, Shriners. Avocations: golf; skiing; boating. Home: PO Box 297 Wabash IN 46992 Office: Halderman Farm Mgmt Service Inc PO Box 297 Wabash IN 46992

HALE, EDWARD BOYD, physics educator; b. Washington, July 16, 1938; s. Charles Mansel and Annabel (Boyd) H.; m. Barbara Anne Nelson, May 30, 1963. B.S. in Elec. Engring., U. Md., 1960; Ph.D., Purdue U., 1968. Research assoc. U. Rochester, N.Y., 1968-69; asst. prof. U. Mo., Rolla, 1969-74, assoc. prof., 1974-80, prof. physics, sr. investigator Materials Research Ctr., 1980—. Contbr. articles, papers to profl. lit. Mem. Am. Phys. Soc., Am. Assn. Sci., Am. Vacuum Soc., Am. Assn. Physics Tchrs., Mo. Acad. Sci. (advisor prize winning physics students). Home: 611 W 9th St Rolla MO 65401 Office: Materials Research Ctr Univ Missouri Rolla MO 65401

HALE, LANNY BRYAN, ophthalmologist, educator; b. Malcomb, Ill., Oct. 3, 1948; s. Ross Junior and Maridonna (Hottel) H.; m. Anita Morrison, Sept. 2, 1967; children—Lindsay Erin, Brienne Marie. B.A., U. Wis.-Milw., 1971; M.D., Med. Coll. Wis., 1975. Diplomate Am. Bd. Ophthalmology. Intern Milw. County Med. Complex, 1975-76, resident Eye Inst., 1976-79; asst. clin. prof. ophthalmology Med. Coll. Wis., Milw., 1979—; practice medicine specializing in ophthalmology, Hales Corners, Wis., 1979—; mem. Sch. and Indsl. Eye Safety Com., Wis., 1982—. Chmn. Sightsaver Racquetball Tournament, Soc. To Prevent Blindness, 1981-83. Recipient Disting. Service award Soc. To Prevent Blindness, Physicians Recognition award AMA, 1982, 85. Chmn. council ministries Community United Methodist Ch., Elm Grove, Wis., 1982—. Mem. Am. Acad. Ophthalomlogy, Alpha Omega Alpha. Republican. Avocation: video and audio electronics. Home: 1065 Lone Tree Rd Elm Grove WI 53122 Office: 6080 S 108th St Hales Corners WI 53130 also 225 Eagle Lake Ave Mukwonago WI 53149

HALE, LAWRENCE CHARLES, specialty chemicals company executive; b. N.Y.C., June 9, 1947; s. Arthur H.; m. Pamella J. Epstein, Mar. 21, 1969; children—Victoria, Matthew. B.S. cum laude in Chem. Engring., U. Fla., 1969; M.B.A. magna cum laude, U. Fla., Newark, Del., 1973. Process engr., DuPont Co., Deepwater, N.J., 1969-73; engr. Betz Labs., Inc., Trevose, Pa., 1974-75, asst. mktg. mgr., 1975-76, mktg. mgr., 1976-80, area sales mgr., Griffith, Ind., 1980-82, dist. sales mgr., 1983-85; v.p. sales and mktg. Wright Chem. Corp., Schiller Park, Ill., 1985—. Contbr. articles to profl. jours. Bd. dirs. Jewish Community Ctr., Homewood, Ill., 1984. Mem. Am. Inst. Chem. Engrs. (pres. 1968-69), Nat. Assn. Corrosion Engrs., Am. Inst. Mech. Engrs., Western States Blast Furnace and Coke Producers, Sigma Tau. Republican. Club: Ravisloe Country (Homewood). Home: 20915 Cambridge Ln Olympia Fields IL 60461 Office: Wright Chem Corp 4328 N United Pkwy Schiller Park IL 60176

HALE, ROGER LOUCKS, manufacturing company executive; b. Plainfield, N.J., Dec. 13, 1934; s. Lloyd and Elizabeth (Adams) H.; m. Sandra Johnston, June 10, 1961; children—Jocelyn, Leslie, Nina. B.A., Brown U., 1956; M.B.A., Harvard U., 1961. With Tennant Co., Mpls., 1961—, v.p.-systems and corp. devel., 1965-67, v.p.-internat., 1972-75, pres., chief operating officer, 1975, pres., chief exec. officer, 1976—, also dir.; dir. Dayton Hudson, First Bank Mpls., Donaldson Co., St. Paul Cos. Sec. Democratic Party, Minn., 1968-70; pres., chmn. Walker Art Ctr., Mpls., 1975-78; chmn. Mayor's Employment Task Force, Mpls. Served to lt. (j.g.) USN, 1956-59. Congregationalist. Club: Mpls. Office: Tennant Co 701 N Lilac Dr Minneapolis MN 55440

HALE, S. EUGENE, manufacturing company executive; b. St. Louis, Aug. 7, 1946; s. Everett Monroe and Thelma Louise (Smith) H.; m. Donna L. Abeln, May 26, 1973; children—Darren Eugene, Matthew Bernard. B.A. in Math., U. Mo., 1969. Programmer, Banquet Foods, St. Louis, 1969-72; sr. programmer Blackburn Co., St. Louis, 1972-74, supr. data processing, 1974-79, application systems mgr., 1979—. Mem. Assn. Systems Mgmt. Roman Catholic. Avocations: golf; reading.

HALEY, GARY EUGENE, bank officer; b. Salem, Ind., Oct. 24, 1952; s. Isom T. and Thelma (Morris) H.; m. Victoria Louise Ford, July 1, 1978; children—Timothy, Gwendolen, Trevor, Alexander. B.S., Ball State U., 1974, M.A., 1979. Programmer analyst Gen. Telephone Electronics Data Services, Ft. Wayne, Ind., 1975-77; systems analyst Mchts. Nat. Bank, Indpls., 1977-78, Detroit Diesel Allison div. Gen. Motors Corp., Indpls., 1978-82; asst. v.p., sr. planning officer Am. Fletcher Nat. Bank, Indpls., 1982—. Mem. computer sci. adv. panel Ball State U., 1983—; mem. artificial intelligence com. Corp. for Sci. and Tech., Indpls., 1984—; lectr. Ind. U., Purdue U., Indpls., 1985—.

HALEY, JOHNETTA RANDOLPH, musician, educator, educational administrator; b. Alton, Ill., Mar. 19; d. John A. and Willye E. (Smith) Randolph; Mus.B. in Edn., Lincoln U., 1945; Mus.M., So. Ill. U., 1972; children—Karen, Michael. Vocal and gen. music tchr. Lincoln High Sch., E. St. Louis, Ill., 1945-48; vocal music tchr., choral dir. Turner Sch., Kirkwood, Mo., 1950-55; vocal and gen. music tchr. Nipher Jr. High Sch., Kirkwood, 1955-71; prof. music Sch. Fine Arts, So. Ill. U., Edwardsville, 1972—, dir. East St. Louis Campus, 1982—; adjudicator music festivals; area music cons. Ill. Office Edn., 1977-78; program specialist St. Louis Human Devel. Corp., 1968; interim exec. dir. St. Louis Council Black People, summer 1970. Bd. dirs. YWCA, 1975-80, Artist Presentation Soc., St. Louis, 1975, United Negro Coll. Fund, 1976-78; bd. curators Lincoln U., Jefferson City, Mo., 1974—, pres., 1978—; mem. Nat. Ministry on Urban Edn., Luth. Ch.-Mo. Synod, 1975-80; bd. dirs. Council Luth. Chs., Assn. of Governing Bds. of Univs. and Colls.; mem. adv. council Danforth Found. St. Louis Leadership Program, nat. chmn. Cleve. Job Corps, 1974-78. Recipient Disting. Citizen award St. Louis Argus Newspaper, 1970; Cotillion de Leon award for Outstanding Community Service, 1977; Disting. Alumnae award Lincoln U., 1977; Disting. Service award United Negro Coll. Fund, 1979, SCLC, 1981; Community Service award St. Louis Drifters, 1979; Disting. Service to Arts award Sigma Gamma Rho; named Duchess of Paducah, 1973; received Key to City, Gary, Ind., 1973. Mem. Council Luth. Chs., AAUP, Coll. Music Soc., Music Educators Nat. Conf., Ill. Music Educators Assn., Nat. Choral Dirs. Assn., Assn. Tchr. Educators, Midwest Kodaly Music Educators, Nat. Assn. Negro Musicians, Jack and Jill Inc., Friends of St. Louis Art Mus., Alpha Kappa Alpha, Mu Phi Epsilon, Pi Kappa Lambda. Lutheran. Clubs: Las Amigas Social. Home: 30 Plaza Sq Saint Louis MO 63103 Office: Box 20 B So Ill U Edwardsville IL 62026

HALICK, JOHN, physician; b. Detroit, Aug. 22, 1925; s. John Franklin and Stella (Bilek) H.; m. Muriel Sonja Krans, June 17, 1950. B.S. in Sci. and Math., U. Mich., 1946, M.D., 1950. Lic. physician, Mich. Intern, Detroit Receiving Hosp., 1950-51; gen. practice medicine, Greenville, Mich., 1953—; founding dir. Montcalm County Mental Health Ctr., 1965-76; mem., cons. West Mich. Comprehensive Health; emergency med. care com. Health Systems Agy., 1976-79, health facilities planning sect., 1976-83; chmn. Mich. Higher Edn. Facilities Commn. and Authority, 1972-83; mem. Mich. Post-secondary Council, 1974-80; pres. Smith Petroleum Internat. Mem. Greenville Sch. Bd., 1956-59; bd. dirs. World Affairs Council Western Mich., pres., 1985; bd. dirs. Inst. Emerging Technologies, Washington. Served to lt. (j.g.), U.S. Navy, 1951-53. Recipient Disting. Service award Assn. Ind. Colls. and U. Mich., 1978. Mem. AMA, Mich. Med. Soc., Am. Gerontol. Assn., Am. Assn. Higher Edn. Republican. Clubs: Peninsular (Grand Rapids, Mich.); French Soc. Mich. Office: 200 S Franklin St Greenville MI 48838

HALIKAS, JAMES ANASTASIO, medical educator, psychiatrist; b. Bklyn., Nov. 26, 1941; s. Peter Simon and Olga Peter (Vavayanni) H.; B.S. (N.Y. State Regents scholar), Bklyn. Coll., 1962; M.D., Duke U., 1966; m. Anna May Van Der Meulen, Aug. 20, 1967; children—Peter Christopher, Anna Catherine. Intern, Barnes Hosp., St. Louis, 1966-67; resident psychiatry Barnes/Renard hosps., Washington U. Sch. Medicine, St. Louis, 1967-70; research fellow alcoholism and drug abuse Sch. Medicine, Washington U., St. Louis, 1969-70, instr. psychiatry, 1970-72, asst. prof., 1972-77, mem. com. on admissions, 1975-77; asso. prof. psychiatry U. Louisville Sch. Medicine, 1978, dir. div. social and community psychiatry, 1978; assoc. prof. psychiatry Med. Coll. Wis., Milw., 1978-84, dir. div. alcoholism and chem. dependency, 1978-84, mem. human research rev. com., 1981-84; prof. psychiatry, dir. residency tng. in psychiatry U. Minn. Med. Sch., Mpls., 1984—; co-dir. chem. dependency treatment program U. Minn. Hosps. and Clinics, 1984—; asst. psychiatrist Barnes, Renard and Affiliated hosps., 1970-77; cons. Malcolm Bliss Mental Health Center, St. Louis, 1970-77; dir. psychiat. div. Webster Coll. Student Health Service, Webster Groves, Mo., 1973-75; dir. Grace Hill Settlement House Psychiatry Clinic, St. Louis, 1973-77; clin. instr. psychiatry dept. psychiatry Mo. Inst. Psychiatry, U. Mo., St. Louis, 1972-74; mem. profl. adv. com. Judevine Center for Autistic Children, St. Louis, 1975-77; psychiat. research cons. Reproductive Biology Research Found., Masters and Johnson Inst., St. Louis, 1975-77. Mem. Mo. Gov.'s Adv. Council on Alcoholism and Drug Abuse, 1974-75; exec. com. Drug and Substance Abuse Council Met. St. Louis, 1973-77, pres., 1971-72; chmn. Children's Mental Health Services Council Met. St. Louis, 1973-74; host KMOX-TV weekly TV series Trips - the Teenage Point of View about Drugs, spring-summer 1971; adviser on drug abuse St. Louis County Juvenile Ct., 1970-72; mem. adv. bd. Drug Crisis Intervention Unit, St. Louis, 1971-77; mem. St. Louis Youth Center profl. adv. com. Mo. Dept. Mental Health, 1977; adv. on drug abuse Drug Info. Center, St. Louis, 1970-74, Human Devel. Corp., St. Louis, 1970-73, Alliance for Regional Community Health, 1972-74; asso. psychiatrist, med. dir. for alcoholism services Jefferson County Alcoholism and Drug Abuse Center for Treatment and Research, Louisville, 1978; exec. and med. dir. River Region Mental Health-Mental Retardation Bd., Ky. Region VI Community Mental Health System, Louisville, 1978; dir. Wis. Alcoholism and Drug Abuse Research Inst., Milw., 1978-84; Sr. Scientist U. Wis., Milw., 1978-84; attending psychiatrist, dir. med. edn. DePaul Rehab. Hosp., Milw., 1978-84; dir. research and edn. in chem. dependency, sr. attending psychiatrist Milwaukee County Mental Health Complex, Milw., 1978-84, dir. psychiat. supervision div. long term care, 1983-84, dir. outpatient clinic, 1984, also chmn. or co-chmn. various cons.; sci. dir. DePaul Hosp. Found., Milw., 1978-84; assoc. psychiatrist U. Louisville Affiliated Hosps., 1978; attending psychiatrist Milw. Psychiat. Hosp., 1978-84, Columbia Hosp., Milw., 1980-84; attending psychiatrist U. Minn. Hosps. and Clinics, 1984—, Met. Med. Ctr., Mpls., 1985—; mem. planning com. Am. Med. Soc. on Alcoholism, 1977-78, mem. program com., 1983-84, chmn. com. on med. edn., 1981—, Wis. state chmn., 1979-84; psychiat. cons. Social Security Disability Determination Service, 1984—, Minn. Security Hosp., 1985—; mem. Wis. Alcohol and Drug Abuse Adv. Com., HHS, 1981-84; mem. Nat. Alcoholism Forum, 1978; co-chmn. clin. research task force Nat. Drug Abuse Conf., Seattle, 1978; mem. Mental Health Assn. Louisville, 1978, Louisville Council on Alcoholism, 1978; cons. Midwestern Area Alcohol Edn. and Tng. Program, 1976-77. Bd. dirs. Mental Health Assn. Met. St. Louis, 1973-77, chmn. St. Louis State Hosp. human research com., 1976-77; bd. dirs. Tellurian South Community, Inc., Madison, 1980—; mem. exec. council DePaul Rehab. Hosp., 1979-84; mem. med. appeals bd. Div. Motor Vehicles, State of Wis., 1980-84; mem. City of Mequon Bd. Appeals, 1980-84; mem. profl. adv. bd. Lactation Inst., Los Angeles, 1981—; also cons. Recipient NIMH Psychiatry Career Tchr. award in narcotics, drug abuse and alcoholism, 1972-75; diplomate Am. Bd. Psychiatry and Neurology, Nat. Bd. Med. Examiners. Mem. Am. Psychiat. Assn., Eastern Mo. Psychiat. Soc., Ky. Psychiat. Assn., Wis. Psychiat. Assn., Am. Psycho-Pathol. Assn., Assn. for Med. Edn. and Research in Substance Abuse, N.Y. Acad. Scis., AAAS, Ky. Med. Assn., Research Soc. on Alcoholism, Assn. for Acad. Psychiatry, Am. Acad. Clin. Psychiatrists (bd. dirs. 1984—, chmn. med. edn. com. 1984—), Kappa Nu. Greek Orthodox. Contbr. numerous articles to profl. jours. Home: 22 Hill Farm Circle North Oaks MN 55110 Office: Dept Psychiatry U Minn Med Sch Box 393 Univ Hosp Minneapolis MN 55455

HALL, BRUCE WARREN, banker; b. Dundee, Angus, Scotland, June 12, 1946; came to U.S., 1979, s. Charles Bruce Grant Clark and Shiela Doreen (Fennell) H.; m. Margaret Ann Lansdell, Sept. 16, 1967; children—Amanda June, Ian Grant. B.A. in Bus. Adminstrn., Capital U., 1982. Asst. comptroller Bank of Nova Scotia, Toronto, Ont., Can., 1974-76, rep., Cleve., 1979-83, sr. rep., 1983—; mgr. banking div. Bermuda Nat. Bank (affiliated with Bank N.S.), Hamilton, Bermuda, 1976-79. Trustee, treas. Canterbury Woods Rec. Assn., Inc., North Olmsted, Ohio, 1982—; com. mem. Cleve. World Trade Assn.; active Greater Cleve. Growth Assn., Cleve. Com. Fgn. Relations. Fellow Inst. Can. Bankers. Clubs: Clevelander; Pittsburgh. Avocations: Golf; fishing. Home: 4028 Fielding Dr North Olmsted OH 44070 Office: Bank of N S 1300 E 9th St #1006 Cleveland OH 44114

HALL, CHARLES RUDOLPH, financial services executive; b. Marysville, Kans., Nov. 7, 1929; s. Percy Allen and Zella (Yaussi) H.; B.S., U. Kans., 1951; postgrad. Northwestern U., 1955-57, U. Wis., 1961; m. Helen Persson, July 19, 1952; children—Charles Rudolph, Timothy P., Jeffrey P. With Continental Ill. Nat. Bank & Trust Co., Chgo., 1955-81, asst. cashier, 1957-61, 2d v.p. nat. div., 1961-64, v.p. nat. div. group G, 1964-68, v.p. personnel div., 1968-70, sr. v.p. adminstrv. services, 1970-71, exec. v.p., 1971-75, exec. v.p. trust and investment services, 1975-81; chmn. bd., chief exec. officer Rollins Burdick Hunter Co., 1981-83; mng. dir. Merrill Lynch Capital Markets, Chgo., 1984—. Asso. St. Luke's Presbyn. Hosp., Chgo., 1965-76; bd. dirs. United Way Met. Chgo., 1970-83; bd. dirs., chmn. fin. devel. Am. Diabetes Assn. Greater Chgo., 1976-80; mem. adv. bd. Citizenship Council Met. Chgo., 1973-80; mem. bus. adv. bd. Nat. Alliance Businessmen, 1973-78; bd. dirs., mem. audit com. Ravinia Festival Assn., 1976-78, mem. investment com., 1982—; chief crusader Crusade of Mercy, 1975-76; mem. program task force United Way Met. Chgo., 1976-82, mem. exec. com., 1977, chmn. personnel com., 1977; bd. dirs., v.p. John Crerar Library, 1977—; chmn. New Trier Twp. High Sch. Bd. Caucus, 1971-72. Served with USNR, 1951-54. Mem. Chgo. Council Fgn. Relations (com. (1974—), Ill. C. of C. and Industry (labor relations com. 1969-71), Phi Delta Theta, Alpha Kappa Psi, Omicron Delta Kappa. Mem. Glencoe Union Ch. (trustee). Clubs: Chicago, Mid Am., Carlton, Economic of Chicago; Skokie (Ill.) Country; Comml., Commonwealth, Lost Tree. Home: 800 Grove St Glencoe IL 60022 Office: 5500 Sears Tower Chicago IL 60606

HALL, CORNETT EUGENE, finance executive, electrical engineer, accounting and data processing educator; b. Liberal, Kans., Nov. 1, 1930; s. James Cornett and Ethel Marie (Kidd) C.; m. Wanda June Denney, Aug. 19, 1952; children—Gena Denise, Vance Eugene, Mark Denney, Wade Michael. B.S. in Bus. Adminstrn., Kans. U., 1953; B.S.E.E., Air Force Inst. Tech., 1961, M.S.E.E., 1966. Commd. officer U.S. Air Force, 1954, advanced through grades to lt. col.; ret., 1976; Comptroller Tradewind Industries, Inc., Liberal, 1977; instr., dir. occupational edn. Seward County Community Coll., Liberal, 1977-83; internal auditor First Nat. Bank, Liberal, 1983-84, v.p., 1984—. Contbr. articles to ednl. jours. Chmn. Liberal Airport Adv. Bd., 1979—; chmn. fund drive Seward County Community Coll. Devel. Found., Liberal, 1984; trustee Seward County Community Coll., 1985—; asst. treas. Pat Roberts for Congress Com., Liberal, 1985—; bd. dirs. Liberal High Sch. Booster Club., 1984—. Mem. N.Mex. Soc. of C.P.A.s, Liberal C. of C., Alpha Kappa Psi. Methodist. Club: Liberal Country. Lodge: Elks. Avocations: golf; tennis; woodworking. Home: 1909 N Webster Liberal KS 67901 Office: The First Nat Bank 324 N Kansas PO Box 1217 Liberal KS 67901

HALL, DAVID LESLIE, lawyer; b. Akron, Ohio, Oct. 12, 1940; s. LeRoy and Yutha Grace (Norman) H.; m. Linda Jean Kellough, June 12, 1965; children—Susan, Theresa. Student Syracuse U., 1959; B.A., Wilmington Coll., 1965; J.D, Case Western Res. U., 1968. Bar: Ohio 1968. Law clk. to presiding judge U.S. Dist. Ct., Cin., 1968-69; assoc. Pickrel, Schaeffer & Ebeling, Dayton, Ohio, 1969-76; ptnr. Hall & Dawson, Dayton, 1976-77; prin. David L. Hall & Assoc., Dayton, 1977—; dir. Bob Ross Buick, Inc., Centerville, Ohio, 1984—, Papco Corp., Centerville, 1983; gen. counsel South Suburban C. of C., Centerville, 1982—. Mem. Kettering Youth Commn., Ohio, 1975-76; pres. Legal Aid Soc., Dayton, 1980; vice chmn. Centerville Planning Commn., 1981; mem. Centerville-Washington Twp. Edn. Found., 1983; Centerville Charter Review Com., 1984. Served to airman 1st class USAF, 1958-63. Mem. ABA, Dayton Bar Assn., Ohio State Bar Assn., Greene County Bar Assn., Fed. Bar Assn., Phi Alpha Theta. Republican. Club: Dayton Optimists (pres. 1974-75). Lodge: Lions (dir. 1981—). Avocations: bridge; skiing; racquet sports; travel. Home: 1408 Streamside Dr Centerville OH 45459 Office: Slicer Hall & Slicer 1100 Hulman Bldg Dayton OH 45402

HALL, DAVID MELVIN, osteopathic cardiologist; b. Cincinnati, Iowa, Dec. 25, 1941; s. Melvin Eugene and Hazel Naomi (Inns) H.; m. Nancy Jo Kissinger, Aug. 21, 1965; children—David Anton, Damon Melvin, Diana Nicole. B.S. in Zoology Edn., Northeast Mo. State U., 1964; D.O., Kirksville Coll. Osteo. Medicine, 1968. Intern, Flint (Mich.) Osteo. Hosp., 1969-70; resident in internal medicine Kirksville (Mo.) Osteo. Hosp., 1969-72; cardiology fellow Chgo. Coll. Osteo. Medicine, 1978-80; gen. internist internal medicine dept. Kirksville Coll. Osteo. Medicine, 1972-73, asst. prof. medicine, 1972-73; practice osteo. internal medicine, Oklahoma City, 1973-78; chmn. dept. internal medicine Hillcrest Osteo. Hosp., Oklahoma City, 1977-78; attending cardiologist Coll. Osteo. Medicine and Surgery, Des Moines, 1980-82, assoc. prof. medicine, 1980-82; practice osteo. medicine specializing in cardiology, Des Moines, 1982—; mem. adj. faculty U. Osteo. Medicine and Health Scis., Des Moines, 1983-84; editor Hawkeye Osteo. Jour.; researcher pacemakers, anti-arrhythmic therapy. Mem. Am. Osteo. Assn., Am. Coll. Osteo. Internists, Iowa Heart Assn., Iowa Osteo. Med. Assn., Polk County Osteo. Med. Assn. (v.p.). Republican. Presbyterian. Contbr. articles to profl. jours. Home: 4209 Mary Lynn Dr Des Moines IA 50322 Office: 1440 E Grand St Des Moines IA 50316

HALL, DOROTHY MARIE REYNOLDS, educator; b. Columbus, Ohio, Dec. 22, 1925; d. Thomas Franklin and Nellie May (Nail) R.; student Ohio State U., 1973-79, Sinclair Community Coll., 1976; m. Grant Forest Hall; children—Stacy L., Cynthia Kay Hall Henderson, Mark Kevin. Dental asst. and office mgr., dental offices in Westerville, Ohio, 1954-68, Columbus, Ohio, 1968-70; dental asst., staff supr., clinic instr. Good Samaritan Dental Clinic, Columbus, 1970; instr., staff supr. Ohio State U. Coll. Dentistry, 1968-69; tchr. adult edn. Eastland Vocat. Center, Groveport, Ohio, 1972, instr. dental assisting, 1971—; examiner Ohio Commn. on Dental Testing, Inc., 1977-78, 81—; chief examiner Ohio Dental Assts. Commn. on Testing, Inc., 1978-81, trustee-dir. 1977-80, examiner, 1978-81, chief examiner, 1984—. Mem. Columbus Dental Assts. Soc. (pres. 1968-69, Dental Asst. of Yr. 1980), Ohio Dental Assts. Assn. (pres. 1978-79, 80-81), Am. Dental Assts. Assn. (cert., registered dental asst.), Eastland Edn. Assn., Ohio Edn. Assn., NEA, Eastland Vocat. Assn. (pres. 1981-82), Ohio Vocat. Assn., Am. Vocat. Assn., Nat. Ret. Tchrs. Assn. (life mem.). Mem. Reformed Ch. Am. Clubs: Order Eastern Star, Pythian Sisters (Westerville). Author profl. publs.; developer, artist: A Manual of Lesson Plans for the Ohio Adult Dental Assistant Programs, 1981. Home: 4676 Big Walnut Rd Galena OH 43021 Office: 4465 S Hamilton Rd Groveport OH 43125

HALL, EDWARD JAMES, JR., librarian; b. Boston, Mar. 31, 1935; s. Edward J. and Grace Marguerite (Phelps) H.; m. Margaret Jean Douglas, June 25, 1966; 1 child, Valerie Jean. A.B., Boston U., 1957; M.A.T., U. Vt.-Burlington, 1965; M.L.S., SUNY-Albany, 1973. Instr. Mount Wachusett Community Coll., Gardner, Mass., 1967-69; lectr. U. Cin., 1970-71; instr. State U. Coll., Plattsburg, 1971-72; librarian Kent State U., Ohio, 1973-77, asst. archivist, 1978-79, catalog librarian, 1979—. Contbr. articles to profl. jours. Bd. trustees Health Systems Agy-Summit and Portage County, Akron, Ohio, 1976-81, mem. exec. bd., 1979-81; mem. Akron Met. Areawide Transp. Systems, 1981—. Served to capt. U.S. Army, 1958-60, Germany. NDEA fellow, 1966-67. Mem. Am. Library Assn., No. Ohio Tech. Service Librarians, AAUP. Congregationalist. Club: Men's Garden (Kent). Lodge: Masons. Home: 635 Woodside Dr Kent OH 44240 Office: Kent State Univ Libraries Kent OH 44242

HALL, GLENN EUGENE, research engineer; b. Tiffin, Ohio, Apr. 21, 1931; s. Lester Calvin and Irene Elizabeth (Routzahn) H.; m. Sylvia Avila, July 15, 1984; children by previous marriage—Christine, Melissa. B.S. in Mech. Engring., Mich. State U., 1959, M.S. in Agrl. Engring., 1960, Ph.D., 1967. Asst. prof. Ohio Agr. Research and Devel. Ctr., Wooster, 1960-68, Agrl. Engring. Dept., U. Ill., Urbana, Ill., 1968-73; research engr. The Andersons, Maumee, Ohio, 1973—. Contbr. articles to profl. jours. Author: (C. W. Hall) Agricultural Engineering Index, 1961-70. Served with U.S. Army, 1954-56. Mem. Am. Soc. Agrl. Engrs., Am. Assn. Cereal Chemists, ASME, Republican. Lutheran. Avocations: woodworking; mechanical contraptions. reading. Home: 5453 Glenridge Apt 2 Toledo OH 43614 Office: The Andersons PO Box 119 Maumee OH 43537

HALL, HANSEL CRIMIEL, government official; b. Gary, Ind., Mar. 12, 1929; s. Alfred McKenzie and Grace Elizabeth (Crimiel) H. B.S., Ind. U., 1953; LL.B., Blackstone Sch. Law, 1982. Officer, IRS, 1959-64; gasoline service sta. operator, then realtor, Chgo., 1964-69; program specialist HUD, Chgo., 1969-73, dir. equal opportunity, St. Paul, 1973-75, dir. fair housing and equal opportunity, Indpls., from 1975; equal opportunity officer U.S. Fish and Wildlife Serivce, Twin Cities, Minn.; cons. in civil rights. Served with USAF, 1951-53; Korea. Mem. NAACP (Golden Heritage life mem.; pres. Minn.-Dakota State Conf.), Res. Officers Assn., Omega Psi Phi; mem. Am. Inst. Parliamentarians, Ind. U. Alumni Assn. Club: Toastmasters (past pres. Minnehaha chpt. 2563, past area gov.). Office: Fed Bldg Ft Snelling Twin Cities MN 55111

HALL, HAROLD ERNEST, English educator; b. Linden, Iowa, Jan. 26, 1924; s. Albert A. and Lois (Lisle) H.; m. Mary Jean Blair, Aug. 11, 1947; children—Linda Lois Hall Martin, Blair Alan. B.A., Simpson Coll., 1948; M.A., U. Pa. 1950, Ph.D., 1953. Asst. dir. pub. relations Simpson Coll., Indianola, Iowa, 1948; reporter Muscatine Jour., Iowa, 1951-52; instr. liberal studies Clarkson Coll., Potsdam, N.Y., 1952-53; assoc. prof. English, Nebr. Wesleyan U., Lincoln, 1953-59, prof., 1959—, head English dept., 1956—. Recipient Woods award Woods Charitable Fund, 1960, E.C. Ames Dist. Prof. award Bankers Life-Nebr., 1962-79. Mem. MLA, Nat. Council Tchrs. English, Am. Studies Assn., Nebr. Council Tchrs., English (pres. 1963-64), Am. Contract Bridge League (cert. dir. 1977—). Republican. Methodist. Home: 5235 Huntington Ave Lincoln NE 68504 Office: Nebr Wesleyan U Lincoln NE 68504

HALL, HELENE W., educator; b. Centralia, Ill., Sept. 17, 1926; d. James O. and Gladys (Hosman) Lawrence; B.S., Emporia State U., 1966, M.S., 1969, E.D.S., 1974; m. William E. Hall, June 27, 1948; children—Ronald William, Steven Charles, Jerry Victor. Sec., asst. to Medical Physicians & Dentists, Kansas City, Mo., 1966-69; tchr. Roosevelt Lab. High Sch., Emporia, Kans.; coordinator secondary sch. tchrs. Emporia State U., 1969-71, team leader Teacher Corps, 1971-73; instr., coordinator secretarial scis. Kansas City Community Coll., 1973—. Mem. Internat. Word Processing Assn., Nat. Bus. Edn. Assn., Am. Vocat. Assn., Kans. Vocat. Assn., Classroom Educators Adv. Com., Kans. Bus. Edn. Assn., Nat. Secretaries Assn., Office Edn. Assn., Assn. of Info. Systems Profls., Delta Pi Epsilon. Methodist. Home: 403 S 6th St Osage City KS 66523 Office: Kansas City Kansas Community College 7250 State Ave Kansas City KS 66112

HALL, HOWARD ERNEST, lawyer; b. Cleve., Oct. 4, 1945; s. Howard Leland and Edna Mae (Geiss) H.; m. Jamie L. Sundheimer, Sept. 21, 1968; children—Matthew Reed, Jennifer Kathleen, Michael John. B.S., Bowling Green State U., Ohio, 1967; J.D., U. Toledo, 1970. Bar: Ohio 1970; U.S. Dist. Ct. (no. dist.) Ohio 1972; U.S. Dist. Ct. (so. dist.) Ohio 1978. Sole practice, Parma, Ohio, 1970-72; assoc. Thomas E. Ray Law Office, Cardington, Ohio, 1972-74; ptnr. Ray & Hall, Cardington, 1974-80, Howard E. Hall Law Office, Cardington, 1980-84, Hall & Elkin, Cardington, 1985—; asst. prosecutor Morrow County, Ohio, 1977-82, prosecutor, 1985—; solicitor Village of Cardington, 1974-77, 83-85. Trustee Morrow County chpt. ARC, Mt. Gilead, Ohio, 1981—; pres. trustees Morrow County Council on Alcohol and Drugs, Inc., Mt. Gilead, 1982—. Mem. Am. Trial Lawyers Assn., ABA, Ohio State Bar Assn., Ohio Acad. Trial Lawyers, Morrow County Bar Assn. (pres. 1983-85). Republican. Methodist. Lodge: Rotary, Masons (master 1984-85). Avocations: Jogging; sports. Home: 2815 Twp Rd 167 Cardington OH 43315 Office: Hall & Elkin Law Office 126 E Main St Cardington OH 43338

HALL, JAMES JOSEPH, dentist; b. Kokomo, Ind., Mar. 8, 1931; s. Arol J. and Mary K. (Trayers) H.; m. Alice E. Harris, Sept. 3, 1955; children—Thomas A., Kathleen M. Hall Bernard. B.S., Ind. U., 1953; D.D.S., 1956. Intern Hines VA Hosp., Ill., 1956-57; practice dentistry, Indpls., 1960—. Served to capt. USAF, 1957-59. Master Acad. Gen. Dentistry, Ind. Acad. Gen. Dentistry (pres. 1985-86); mem. ADA, Ind. Dental Assn., Indpls. Dist. Dental Soc. Roman Catholic. Lodges: Lions (pres. 1970-71), K.C. Avocations: boating, sports. Office: 7172 N Keystone St Indianapolis IN 46240

HALL, JAMES RALPH, automotive parts company executive; b. Rockford, Ill., July 1, 1938; s. Robert Wade and Elaine (Shay) H.; m. Judith Porte, Dec. 23, 1967; children—James Robert, Emily Anne. B.S. in Mech. Engring., Gen. Motors Inst., 1961. Sr. research engr. Gen. Motors Corp., Detroit, 1961-64; chief engr. AP Parts Co., Toledo, 1964-72, v.p. engring., 1972-76, v.p. OEM sales, 1976-78, v.p. internat., 1978-81, sr. v.p. ops., 1981—. Patentee in field. Recipient Ora L. Pelton III award, 1956; Pullman award, 1958. Mem. Soc. Automotive Engrs., Fabricated Mfrs. Assn. (dir. 1983), Automotive Industry Action Group (dir. 1983), Phi Beta Tau. Republican. Club: Toledo Yacht. Home: 4356 Sadalia Rd Toledo OH 43623 Office: AP Parts Co One John Goerlich Sq Toledo OH 43694

HALL, JAMES ROBERT, educator; b. Salem, Ill., Dec. 24, 1947; s. James Wesley and Patricia Joyce (Ellis) H. B.S., U. Ill., 1970. Cert. secondary tchr., Ill. Tchr. Murphysboro High Sch., Ill., 1970—. Author, compiler: (tng. man.) Key Club Faculty Advisors, 1975. Sunday sch. tchr. United Methodist Ch., Murphysboro, 1973-76, youth dir., 1973-76, mem. council on ministries, 1984—, trustee, 1984—; founder, dir. Christian Lay Council Youth Coffeehouse, 1973-75; mem. Murphysboro Recreation Bd., 1974-76, pres. 1975-76; community ambassador So. Ill. 1984-85. U. Area Services, 1975—; bd. dirs. Murphysboro Heart Fund, 1973-76, co-chmn., 1975-76; chmn. Murphysboro Muscular Dystrophy Assn., 1971-74; counsellor Little Grassy Youth Ch. Camp, 1973; steering com. Murphysboro Apple Festival, 1975—, exec. com., 1983—; bd. dirs. Murphysboro United Way, 1978—, Murphysboro Sr. Citizens Council, 1980-83, Resource Reclamation, Inc., 1979—; vice chmn. Murphysboro Swimming Pool Project Commn., 1983-84, chmn., 1984—. Recipient Citizenship award Sta. WTAO Radio, 1983, 84, Ann. Community Service award Modern Woodmen Am., 1982, Citizen of Yr. award Murphysboro C. of C., 1984. Mem. NEA, Ill. Edn. Assn., Murphysboro Edn. Assn. Clubs: Key (advisor 1972—, adminstr. Ill.-Eastern Iowa dist. 1985—), Kiwanis (pres. 1977-78, lt. gov. dist. div. 1984-85, chmn. spl. club services Ill.-Eastern Iowa dist. 1984-85). Avocations: collecting books and plates; bowling; tennis. Home: 28 Candy Ln Murphysboro IL 62966 Office: Murphysboro High Sch 16th and Blackwood Dr Murphysboro IL 62966

HALL, JEFFREY LYNN, government official; b. Independence, Mo., Sept. 25, 1947; s. William H. and Margaret E. (Bales) H.; m. Brenda Marguerite Hall, July 30, 1978; children—Tracy Michelle, Jami Lynne, Bryan William, Todd Christopher. A.A.S., Longview Coll., 1978; B.S. in Data Processing, Avila Coll., 1980; M.A. in Bus. Adminstrn., Webster U., 1982. Cert. systems profl., 1985. Sr. programmer/analyst Ralston Purina Co., St. Louis, 1969-76; programmer/analyst Syscon, Inc., Edwardsville, Kans., 1977, Black & Veatch, Kansas City, Mo., 1977-80; systems analyst Iowa Beef Processors, Kansas City, 1981-83; project leader Adventist Health System, Overland Park, Kans., 1981-83; supr. systems and programming Water Dist. #1 Johnson County, Mission, Kans., 1983—; data processing instr. Nat. Coll., 1983—. Served with U.S. Army, 1966-68; Vietnam. Mem. Assn. Systems Mgmt. Seventh-day Adventist. Avocation: racquetball. Home: 8200 Evanston Raytown MO 64138 Office: Water Dist No 1 of Johnson County 5930 Beverly Mission KS 66202

HALL, JOHN HENRY, lawyer, historian educator; b. Mound Bayou, Miss., Nov. 7, 1932; s. John H. and Icey M. (Roundtree) H.; m. Katie B. Green, Aug. 15, 1957; children—Jacqueline D., Junifer D. B.S., Ind. U., 1970, M.S. in Edn., 1971, M.S. in Secondary Sch. Adminstrn., 72; J.D., Southland U., 1981; Ed.D., Loyola U., Chgo., 1986. Bar: Ind. 1983. Foreman U.S. Reduction Co., East Chgo. Ind., 1957-62, shift supt., 1962-68; tchr. Gary Community Schs., Ind., 1962-74, asst. prin., 1975-84; sole practice law, Gary, 1983—; prof. law, racism and social change Ind. U., Gary, 1984; legal resource Gary Community Sch. Corp., 1983-84. Article writer Blacks in World History Information Newspaper (edn. and Community Service award 1983), 1979—. Supporter Mayor Richard Gordon Hatcher, Gary, 1976-83; campaign mgr. Katie Hall State Rep., Indpls., 1976, Katie Hall Congress, Gary, 1984. Served with USAF, 1952-57. Mem. Gary Secondary Prins. Assn. (sec./treas. v.p., pres., Outstanding Leadership award 1982), ABA, Ind. Bar Assn., Gary Bar Assn., Hammond Bar Assn., Lake County Bar Assn., Phi Delta Kappa, Phi Alpha Delta. Democrat. Baptist. Lodge: Masons.

HALL, JON EM, oil company executive; b. Columbus, Ohio, July 6, 1956; s. John Milton and Ordena Hill (High) H.; m. Merri Lynn Pugh, May 20, 1978; children—Jessie, Jennifer, Ross. B.S. in Petroleum Engring., Marietta Coll., 1978; student Baldwin-Wallace Coll., 1984—. Registered profl. engr., Ohio. Petroleum engr. Amoco Prodn. Co., Brownfield, Tex., 1979-80, Houston, 1980-81, Atlas Energy Co., Warren, Ohio, 1981-83; asst. v.p., petroleum engr. Huntington Bank, Cleve., 1983-84; v.p. oil and gas ops. Royal Petroleum Properties, Inc., Cleve., 1984—; chief tech. adv. Hall Energy, Inc., Powell, Ohio, 1982—. Mem. Soc. Petroleum Engr. (bd. dirs. 1984—), Soc. Profl. Well Log Analysts (v.p. 1984—), Am. Assn. Petroleum Geologists, Ohio Oil and Gas Assn., Nat. Ohio Soc. Profl. Engrs. (cert. merit 1983). Republican. Methodist. Avocations: bowling; electric organ; sports. Lodge: Kiwanis. Home: 35454 Chesterfield Dr North Ridgeville OH 44039 Office: Royal Petroleum Properties Inc The Leader Bldg Suite 1010 Cleveland OH 44115

HALL, KATHLEEN JULIA, contractor, financial administrator; b. Detroit, Nov. 30, 1932; d. Daniel Joseph and Noreen Mary (O'Shea) O'Shea; m. Wendell George Hall, Sept. 20, 1969. Student Detroit Bus. Inst., 1954-57, Oakland Community Coll., 1980-81. Corp. staff Ex-Cello Corp., Detroit, 1964-69; staff asst. internat. div. Burroughs Corp., Detroit, 1969-77, Detroit Edison Co., 1979—; contractor VA, Detroit, 1983—. Vice-pres., Wensel Corp. to provide shelter for indigents, Detroit, 1982. Mem. Property Owners for Better Am. Living (sec. 1982—). Address: 2717 Ardmore St Royal Oak MI 48073

HALL, KAY MARGARET, nurse; b. Lima, Ohio, July 24, 1943; d. Harold Ray and Ruth (Gordon) H.; m. Robert G. Jarvis, Oct. 23, 1976 (div. 1983). Diploma Miami Valley Hosp. Sch. Nursing, Dayton, Ohio, 1965; student Wright State U., 1974-77, U. Dayton, 1971, Universidad Technologica De Santiago, Santo Domingo, Dominican Republic, 1984—. R.N., Ohio. Charge nurse recovery room Miami Valley Hosp., Dayton, 1965-66; indsl. nurse Harris Seybold Co., Dayton, 1966-68; office nurse to physician, Dayton, 1968-69, 80-82; coordinator nurse Mobile Unit Clinics, OEO, 1969-72; emergency nurse Kettering Med. Ctr., Ohio, 1972-80, radiology nurse, 1979-80. Author: (manual) Procedures for Nursing Care in Radiology, 1977. Big sister Big Bros.-Big Sisters, Dayton, 1979-83. Mem. Miami Valley Hosp. Sch. Nursing Alumni, Critical Care Nurses Dayton. Home: PO Box 1961 Kettering OH 45429

HALL, LEONARD ALLEN, lawyer; b. Kansas City, Kans., May 28, 1953; s. Richard Allen and Nancy (Meyer) H.; B.S. in Bus., Emporia State U., 1976; J.D., Washburn U., 1979. Bar: Kans. 1979. Sole practice, Olathe, Kans., 1979-80; asst. mcpl. counselor City of Olathe, 1980—. Chmn. volleyball Midwest Athletic Assn. for Deaf, Kansas City, Mo., 1984—. Named All-Am., U.S. Track and Field Fedn., 1976, Outstanding Male Athlete for Deaf, World Game for Deaf Tryouts, Washington, 1976. Mem. Johnson County Bar Assn., Kans. Bar Assn., Emporia State Alumni Assn, Am. Deaf Volleyball Assn. (pres. 1985). Republican. Methodist. Clubs: Belton Social (Mo.); Olathe for Deaf (v.p. 1981-83); Kansas City Racquetball for Deaf (Mo.) (chmn. 1982-84). Lodge: Masons. Office: City of Olathe PO Box 768 Olathe KS 66061

HALL, MARION TRUFANT, botanist, arboretum director; b. Gorman, Tex., Sept. 6, 1920; s. Frank Marion and Nora Gertrude (Wharton) H.; B.S., U. Okla., 1943, M.S., 1947; Ph.D. (Henrietta Heerman scholar 1951), Washington U., St. Louis, 1951; D.Sc. (hon.), North Central Coll., Ill., 1977; m. Virginia Riddle, Nov. 9, 1944; children—Susan, Alan Lee, John Lane. Ranger, Nat. Park Service, Dept. Interior, 1942; instr. botany U. Okla., 1946-47, curator Bebb Herbarium, 1949; field botanist, instr. Tex. Nature Camp, Nat. Audubon Soc., Kerrville, Tex., 1948; grad. asst. zoology, teaching fellow Washington U., 1948-50, spl. lectr. genetics and evolution Henry Shaw Sch. Botany, 1952; botanist Cranbrook Inst. Sci., Bloomfield Hills, Mich., 1950-56, acting dir., 1955-56; prof., head dept. botany Butler U., 1956-62; vis. prof. botany U. Okla., 1962, dir. Stovall Mus. Sci. and History, 1962-66; dir. Morton Arboretum, Lisle, Ill., 1966—; prof. botany, acting dir. U. Mich. Bot. Gardens, 1963-64; prof. horticulture U. Ill., Urbana; adj. prof. biology No. Ill. U. Cons. Mich. Dept. Conservation, Handbook Biol. Materials for Museums. Bd. dirs. Joyce Found., Chgo.; governing mem. Forest Found. DuPage County; mem. environ. concerns com. DuPage County Regional Planning Commn. Served to lt. (j.g.) USNR, 1943-45. NSF grantee; recipient Alumni award for achievement U. Okla., 1953. Fellow Ind. Acad. Sci., Cranbrook Inst. Sci.; mem. Am. Soc. Plant Taxonomists, Internat. Assn. Plant Taxonomists, Ecol. Soc. Am., Asa Gray Meml. Assn., Soc. Study Evolution, Mich. Natural Areas Council, Okla. Acad. Sci., Bot. Soc. Am., Mich. Bot. Club (past pres. Detroit), Phi Beta Kappa, Sigma Xi, Phi Sigma. Contbr. numerous research articles to profl. jours. Home: 3S751 Leask Ln Wheaton IL 60187 Office: Morton Arboretum Lisle IL 60532

HALL, REBECCA ANN, educator; b. Dayton, Ohio, July 27, 1940; s. Noel Gould and Anna Frances (Pyle) Easton; B.S., Wittenberg U., 1961; M.Ed., Miami U., Oxford, Ohio, 1964, Ph.D., 1982; m. Ted D. Hall, Dec. 21, 1963; 1 child, Robin Leigh. Tchr., counselor, public schs., Brookville, Ohio, 1961-63, Carlisle, Ohio, 1963-65, Centerville City Schs., 1965—. Mem., v.p. Clearcreek Bd. Edn., 1981-85. Mem. NEA, Ohio Edn. Assn., Nat. Bus. Edn. Assn., Ohio Bus. Tchrs. Assn., Am. Vocat. Assn., Ohio Vocat. Assn., Assn. Supervision and Curriculum Devel., Delta Pi Epsilon. Mem. United Ch. Christ. Author: A History of Springboro, Ohio, 1815-1965, 1965; Personal Typing, 1979; Gregg Typing Series 7, 1982, Series 8, 1986. Home: 9668 Quailwood Trail Spring Valley OH 45370 Office: Centerville City Schools 500 E Franklin St Centerville OH 45459

HALL, RICHARD DAVID, chemical engineer, environmental consultant; b. Newark, Ohio, Mar. 30, 1932; s. David William Martin and Freda Jane (Zinn) H.; m. Marjorie Elma Schultz, Sept. 16, 1956; children—Jeffrey William, Colleen Dawn. B.S. in Chem. Engring., Ohio State U., 1960. Registered profl. engr., Ohio, Ark., Del., Calif., Tex. Chem. engr. Hercules Powder Co., Parlin, N.J., 1960-61; research engr. Barnebey-Cheney Co., Columbus, Ohio, 1961-62; asst. engr. Ohio Dept. Health, Columbus, 1962-65; regional environ. control mgr., spl. projects mgr. Diamond Shamrock Corp., Cleve., 1965-80; mgr. environ. affairs B.F. Goodrich Chem. Co., Independence, Ohio, 1980-82; pres., chem. engr. Hall's Environ. Assistance Co., Inc., Parma Heights, Ohio, 1982—; mgr. environ. affairs Nat. Distillers & Chem. Co., 1985—; mem. air resources com. and water resources com. Chem. Mfrs. Assn., Washington, 1966-70; mem. chem. industry adv. com. Ohio River Valley Sanitation Compact, Cin., 1966-70. Author environ. statements for fed. and state legis. bodies. Water pollution analyst, author Cleve. Little Hoover Com., 1967. Served to sgt. U.S. Army, 1951-54, Korea. Mem. Am. Inst. Chem. Engrs., Water Pollution Control Fedn., Air Pollution Control Assn., Greater Cleve. Growth Assn. Lutheran. Lodge: Masons. Avocations: gardening, singing. Home: 6604 Loveland Miamiville Rd Loveland OH 45140 Office: Nat Distillers and Chem Co 11500 Northlake Dr PO Box 429550 Cincinnati OH 45249

HALL, RICHARD WILLIAM, hospital administrator; b. Jamestown, N.D., Oct. 7, 1935; s. Kenneth Rathman and Lona Adele (Donat)) H.; m. Geneal Evata Halverson, June 28, 1959; children—Julie Ann, Katherine, Kristin, Ken. B.B.A., Jamestown Coll., 1953; M.H.A., U. Minn., 1979. Mgr. Hall Hardware, Jamestown, 1956-59; mgr. bus. office Jamestown Hosp., 1959-63, asst. adminstr., 1963-69, adminstr., 1969-79, pres., 1979—. Mem. Jamestown City Council, 1961-75, pres. 1974-78. Named Outstanding Young Man, Jamestown Jaycees, 1966. Fellow Am. Coll. Hosp. Adminstrs. (regent N.D. 1981—), Healthcare Fin. Mgrs. Assn. (nat. bd. dirs. 1972-75, William Folmer award 1966, Robert H. Reeves award 1970, Fredrick Muncie award 1973), N.D. Hosp. Assn. (bd. dirs. 1982—). Republican. Lutheran. Lodge: Lions. Home: 515 1st Ave N Jamestown ND 58401 Office: Jamestown Hosp 419 5th St NE Jamestown ND 58401

HALL, ROBERT C., See *Who's Who in America,* 43rd edition.

HALL, TERRENCE LYON, lawyer; b. Jackson, Mich., Oct. 24, 1949; s. Kenneth F. and Jean (Lyon) H. B.A., Stanford U., 1972; J.D., Detroit Coll. Law, 1978. Bar: Mich. 1978, U.S. Dist. Ct. (ea. dist.) Mich. 1978, U.S. Ct. Appeals (6th cir.) 1982. Ptnr., Terrence L. Hall & John W. Isgrigg, P.C., Pontiac, Mich., 1978—. Sec., Oakland County Br. ACLU Mich., 1982—. Mem. Assn. Trial Lawyers Am., Mich. Bar Assn., Mich. Orgn. Social Security Claimants' Reps., Mich. Trial Lawyers Assn., Nat. Orgn. Social Security Claimants' Reps., Oakland County Bar Assn., Oakland Trial Lawyers' Assn. Unitarian. Office: 4519 Highland Rd Pontiac MI 48054

HALL, TONY P., congressman; b. Dayton, Ohio, Jan. 16, 1942; A.B., Denison U., 1964; m. Janet Dick, 1973; children—Jyl, Matthew. Mem. Ohio Ho. of Reps., 1969-72, Ohio Senate, 1973-78; mem. 96th-98th Congresses from 3d Dist. Ohio. Served with Peace Corps. Democrat. Club: Agonis. Office: 2448 Rayburn House Office Bldg Washington DC 20515

HALL, WILLIAM JOEL, civil engineering educator, consultant; b. Berkeley, Calif., Apr. 13, 1926; s. Eugene Raymond and Mary Frances Hall; m. Elaine Frances Thalman, Dec. 18, 1948; children—Martha Jane, James Frederick, Carolyn Marie. Student U. Calif.-Berkeley, 1943-44; B.S. in Civil Engring., U. Kans., 1948; M.S., U. Ill., Urbana, 1951, Ph.D., 1954. Registered profl. engr., Calif., Ill. Engr. Sohio Pipe Line Co., St. Louis, 1948-49; from asst. prof. to prof. civil engring. U. Ill., Urbana, 1954—, head dept. civil engring. Author: Brittle Fracture of Welded Plate, 1967, also chpts. in books, articles. Served with USNR, 1944-45. Recipient Huber Research award, 1963, Halliburton Engring. Edn. Leadership award, 1980, Nathan M. Newmark medal, 1984, Howard award, 1984. Fellow ASCE (chmn. structural div. 1973, chmn. tech. council lifeline earthquake engring. 1981), AAAS; mem. Seismological Soc. Am., others. Presbyterian. Home: 3105 Valley Brook Dr Champaign IL 61821 Office: U Ill Dept Civil Engring 1114 Newmark Civil Engring Lab 208 N Romine St Urbana IL 61801

HALL, WILLIAM PUDNEY, marketing executive; b. Montclair, N.J., June 20, 1923; s. Samuel Stickney and Charlotte (Pudney) H.; m. Ann Emerson, June 25, 1949; children—Stephen, Christopher, Jonathan, David, Elizabeth. A.B., Harvard Coll., 1947, M.B.A., 1948. Sales mgr. Greer Hydraulics Inc., Bklyn., 1948-51; ptnr. Duff, Anderson & Clark, Chgo., 1951-57; v.p. A.T. Kearney, Inc., Chgo., 1957-80; owner William P. Hall, Chgo., 1980-81; exec. v.p. Duff & Phelps Inc., Chgo., 1982—; dir. AEC Inc., Elk Grove Village, Ill., Gray Lyon Co., Chgo., Lindsay Brothers Inc., Milw. Bd. dirs. St. Leonard's House, Chgo.; active mem. Exec. Service Corps, Chgo., 1980—. Served to tech. sgt. U.S. Army, 1943-46, ETO. Fellow Fin. Analysts Fedn.; mem. Investment Analysts Soc. Chgo., Midwest Planning Assn., Harvard Bus. Sch. Club, Chgo., Harvard, N.Y.C., Chgo. (pres. 1979-80). Republican. Episcopalian. Clubs: Attic, Big Sand Lake (Phelps, Wis.) (pres. 1984-85); Skokie Country (Glencoe, Ill.). Home: 545 Greenwood Ave Glencoe IL 60022 Office: Duff and Phelps Inc 55 E Monroe St Chicago IL 60093

HALLAS, LAURENCE EDWARD, environmental microbiologist; b. Montgomery, Ala., Feb. 10, 1954; s. Gerald Edward and Ruth Linnea (Johnson) H.; m. Margaret Ellen Bergstein, July 30, 1978; children—Lorien Elizabeth, Matthew Laurence. B.A. with honors, Miami U., Oxford, Ohio, 1975; M.S., U. Cin., 1977; Ph.D., U. Md., 1981. Fellow, Cornell U., 1981-82; research specialist Monsanto Agrl. Co., St. Louis, 1982—. Miami U. fellow, 1974-75; Nat. Inst. Environ. Health Scis. toxicology tng. grantee, 1981-82. Mem. Am. Soc. Microbiology, Soc. Indsl. Microbiology, Sigma Xi. Lutheran. Contbr. articles to profl. jours. Home: 1350 Wakeshire Ter Ballwin MO 63011 Office: Monsanto Co T4G 800 N Lindbergh Blvd Saint Louis MO 63167

HALLBERG, TIMOTHY KREY, medical research technologist; b. Norfolk, Nebr., May 22, 1953; s. Harold and Elsie Clare (Krey) H.; children—Sarah K., Seth K. B.S. cum laude, Wayne State Coll., Nebr., 1974; M.S., U. Nebr., 1975. Research technologist U. Nebr. Med. Ctr., Omaha, 1974—. Contbr. articles to profl. jours. Republican. Lutheran. Office: U Nebr Med Ctr 42d and Dewey Sts Omaha NE 68105

HALLER, HAROLD S., statistical consultant; b. Pitts., Aug. 26, 1938; s. Harold Smith and Dorothy (Miller) H.; m. Gail Gerhart, Oct. 21, 1961; children—John Gerhart, Katherine Jean. B.S. in Engring. Physics, Lehigh U., 1961; M.A. in Math., Am. U., 1964; Ph.D. in Math./Stats., Case Inst. Tech., 1967. Project mgr. David Taylor Model Basin, Washington, 1961-64; mgr. stats./computer goup B.F. Goodrich Chem. Co., Avon Lake, Ohio, 1967-83; pres. Statis. Studies, Inc., Bay Village, Ohio, 1983—; adj. prof. Case Western Res. U., Cleve., 1968—; prin. Harold S. Haller Cons., Bay Village, 1974-82. Author workbook and articles in field. Sunday sch. tchr. Bay Village Presbyterian Ch., 1983. Mem. Am. Statis. Assn. Republican. Avocation: boating.

HALLER, ROBERT SPENCER, English educator; b. Washington, July 29, 1933, s. Mark Hughlin and Sarah Spencer (Gillogly) H.; m. Evelyn Harris, June 10, 1961; children—Scott Geoffrey, Charles Benet. B.A., Amherst Coll., 1955; M.A., Princeton U., 1958, Ph.D., 1960. Acting instr. English, U. Calif.-Santa Barbara, 1958-59; inst. English. U. Md., College Park, 1959-60, Emory U., Atlanta, 1960-61; asst. prof. English, U. Calif.-Berkeley, 1961-67; from asst. to assoc. prof. U. Nebr., Lincoln, 1967-72, prof., 1972—; chmn. Mid-Am. Linguistics Conf., Lincoln, 1978; bd. dirs. Nebr. Playwrights Project, Lincoln, 1984—. Editor: Achievement of Wallace Stevens, 1961; editor and translator: Literary Criticism of Dante Alighieri, 1974. Pres. Lincoln Fellowship of Chs., 1981; citizen adv. com. Dept. Corrections, Lincoln, 1980-83; bd. dirs. Nebraskans Against the Death Penalty, Lincoln, 1984—. NEH fellow, 1977. Mem. MLA, Medieval Acad. Am., Linguistic Soc. Am., AAUP (pres. 1977-78), Phi Beta Kappa (pres. Alpha of Nebr. 1982-83). Democrat. Roman Catholic. Avocation: tennis. Home: 1735 S 25th St Lincoln NE 68502 Office: U Nebr Lincoln NE 68588-0333

HALLIGAN, DWIGHT EUGENE, optometrist; b. Iona, S.D., June 2, 1931; s. Eugene and Mary Nora (Spreckles) H.; m. Barbara Jean Kunert, Aug. 13, 1955. B.S., Ill. Coll. Optometry, 1958, O.D., 1959. Gen. practice optometry, Eau Claire, Wis., 1959—; examiner U.S. Army, Eau Claire, 1968-69, Soc. Security Adminstrn., Eau Claire, 1980—, Served with USCG, 1952-55. Mem. Indianhead Optometric Soc. (pres. 1962-64), Wis. Optometric Assn. (bd. dirs. 1964-70), Am. Optometric Assn. (charter mem. contact lens sect.), U.S. Coast Guard Aux. (flotilla edn. officer 1980—). Lodges: Masons, Shriners. Avocations: pilot; renovating log cabin. Home: 1707 Hillsdale Rd Eau Claire WI 54703 Office: 605 Walker Ave Eau Claire WI 54701

HALLING, LEONARD WILLIAM, pathologist, laboratory administrator; b. Aurora, Ill., Apr. 1, 1927; s. Leonard Carl Gustave and Mildred Margaret (May) H.; m. Esther Suzanne Garon, May 18, 1957; children—Kevin Carl, Dale Brian, Julie Lynn. M.D., U. Vt., 1957. Diplomate Am. Bd. Pathology. Rotating intern Rose Hosp., Denver, 1957-58; resident in pathology Tripler Army Hosp., Honolulu, 1958-62; chief lab. Womack Army Hosp., Fayetteville, N.C., 1962-64; staff pathologist Armed Forces Inst. Pathology, Washington, 1965-67; dir. Hays Pathology Lab. (Kans.), 1967—; chief med. staff Hadley Regional Med. Ctr., Hays, 1972-73; pres. Kans. Found. Med. Care, Topeka, 1976. Bd. dirs. High Plains Edn. Consortium, Hays, 1975—; pres. Hays United Fund, 1976, Hays Arts Council, 1971. Fellow Coll. Am. Pathologists, Am. Soc. Clin. Pathologists; mem. Kans. Soc. Pathologists (past pres.). Republican. Presbyterian. Lodge: Rotary (pres. Hays 1978-79). Home: 3000 Tam O Shanter St Hays KS 67601 Office: Hays Pathology Labs PA 1300 E 13th St Hays KS 67601

HALLOCK, JOHN WALLACE, JR., lawyer, state representative; b. Ann Arbor, Mich., July 9, 1946; s. John W. and Gladys (Johnson) H.; m. Carol Horvath, Aug. 9, 1975; 2 sons, John W. III, Michael J. B.A., Loyola U., Chgo.; J.D., Chgo.-Kent Coll. Law. Bar: Ill., U.S. Supreme Ct., U.S. Ct. Appeals, U.S. Dist. Ct. Formerly chief counsel Ill. State Senate; ptnr. firm Smith, Hallock & Talley, Rockford, Ill.; rep. Ill. Gen. Assembly, 1979—. Recipient Best Feshman Rep. award Ill. Edn. Assn., 1979, Ill. Polit. Reporter, 1979; Man of Yr. award Ill. Young Rep. Orgn., 1979; Best Legislator award Ill. Nurses Assn., 1982, Landmarks Preservation Assn., 1983. Mem. ABA, Winnebago County Bar Assn. Roman Catholic. Lodge: KC. Office: 206 W State St Suite 607 Rockford IL 61101

HALLSTROM, CURTIS HOLGER, information scientist; b. Brook Park, Minn., Sept. 6, 1941; s. Holger Nels and Helen (Thorne) H.; m. Faye Dorothy Halverson, Aug. 10, 1963; children—Timothy, Jenifer, Leah. B.A., Bethel Coll., St. Paul, 1963; M.S., U. N.D., 1965, Ph.D. in Biochemistry, 1967. Sr. research food scientist Gen. Mills, Mpls., 1967-76, sr. research info. scientist, 1976-78, sect. leader tech. info. services, 1978-81, mgr. tech. info. services, 1981—. Contbr. articles to profl. jours. Patentee in field. Chmn. Elim Baptist Ch., Anoka, Minn., 1976-81. NIH fellow, 1963-67. Mem. Inst. Food Technologists, Am. Soc. Info. Scientists, Sigma Xi. Office: Gen Mills Inc 9000 Plymouth Ave N Minneapolis MN 55427

HALMAN, PAUL MARK, financial executive; b. Akron, Ohio, May 3, 1934; s. A. Paul and Ardella F. (Ford) H.; B.A., Houghton Coll., 1956; postgrad. (NSF grantee), Ohio U., summers, 1962, 63, 64; children—J. Mark, Lisa Jean, Pamela Sue. Youth dir. Sturgis (Mich.) Wesleyan Ch., 1956-57; dir. Christian edn. Central N.W. Presbyn. Ch., Detroit, 1958-59; dir. of devel., instr. Stony Brook (N.Y.) Sch., 1959-68; dir. alumni fund MacMurray Coll., Jacksonville, Ill., 1968-70; dir. trustee assos. Alma (Mich.) Coll., 1970-72; asst. to pres. First Dayton (Ohio) Corp., 1972-74; pres. Fin. Systems, Inc., Livonia, Mich., 1974—; dir. Hazen Corp., Mgmt. Systems, Inc. Republican. Clubs: Jaycees (dir. 1968), Kiwanis (pres. 1972). Home: PO Box 2782 Livonia MI 48151 Office: 27552 Schoolcraft St Livonia MI 48150

HALPERN, HENRY IRA, petroleum geochemist, researcher; b. N.Y.C., June 18, 1955; s. Bernard B. and Fay (Gorosh) H. B.S., Lafayette Coll., 1977; Ph.D., UCLA, 1981. Research assoc. UCLA, 1978-81; petroleum geochemist Standard Oil of Ohio, Cleve., 1981—. NSF grantee, 1976. Mem. Am. Assn. Petroleum Geologists, Am. Chem. Soc. (geochemistry div.). Republican. Jewish. Avocations: stock market, economics, antiques. Office: Standard Oil of Ohio 4440 Warrensville Ctr Rd Cleveland OH 44128-2837

HALPERN, JACK, scientist, educator; b. Tarnoruda, Poland, Jan. 19, 1925; came to U.S., 1962, naturalized U.S. citizen; s. Philip and Anna (Sass) H.; m. Helen Peritz, June 30, 1949; children—Janice Halpern Henry, Nina. B.Sc., McGill U., Montreal, 1946, Ph.D., 1949. Instr. U. B.C., 1950, prof. chemistry, 1961-62; prof. chemistry U. Chgo., 1962-71, Louis Block prof., 1972-84, Louis Block disting. service prof., 1984—; vis. prof. U. Minn., 1962, Harvard U., 1966-67, Calif. Inst. Tech., 1968-69, Princeton U., 1970-71, Max-Planck Institut fur Kohlenforschung, Mulheim, W. Ger., 1977, U. Copenhagen, 1978; guest scholar U. Kyoto (Japan), 1981; Firth vis. prof. Sheffield (Eng.) U., 1982; Werner lectr. U. Kans., 1982; Welch lectr. U. Tex., 1983; Kilpatrick lectr. Ill. Inst. Tech., 1984; Dow lectr. U. Ottawa, Ont., Can., 1985, numerous others; external sci. mem. Max-Planck-Inst. fur Kohlenforschung, 1983—; lectr. in field; mem. adv. panel for chemistry NSF, 1967-70; mem. chemistry vis. com. MIT, 1968-70; trustee and council Gordon Research Confs., 1968-70, chmn. conf. on inorganic chemistry, 1971; coordinator U.S.-USSR Joint Program in Catalysis by Coordination and Organometallic Compounds, 1972-77; mem. adv. panel on chemistry Argonne Nat. Lab., 1967-70; mem. medicinal chemistry study sect. NIH, 1975-78, chmn., 1976-78; mem. chemistry adv. council Princeton U., 1982—; mem. adv. com. Ency. Brit., 1985—. Recipient Am. Chem. Soc. award in inorganic Chemistry, 1968; Royal Chem. Soc. award, 1976; Alexander von Humboldt U.S. sr. scientist award, 1977; Richard Kokes award Johns Hopkins U., 1978; Sherman Fairchild Disting. Scholar award Calif. Inst. Tech., 1979; Am. Chem. Soc. award disting. service award, 1985. Nuffield Found. fellow, 1959-60; Alfred P. Sloan fellow, 1959-63. Fellow Chem. Inst. Can., Am. Acad. Arts and Scis., AAAS, N.Y. Acad. Scis., Royal Soc. London; mem. Nat. Acad. Scis., Am. Chem. Soc. (chmn. div. inorganic chemistry 1971, mem. petroleum research fund adv. bd. 1972-74); award inorganic chemistry 1968; Disting. Service award advancement inorganic chemistry 1985), Max-Planck Soc., Sigma Xi. Clubs: Quadrangle (Chgo.); Chemists (N.Y.C.) Editor: (with others) Collected Accounts of Transition Metal Chemistry, 1973, Vol. 2, 1977; co-editor: Oxford U. Press Internat. Series Monographs in Chemistry; assoc. editor Jour. Am. Chem. Soc., Inorganica Chimica Acta, 1969—; mem. editorial adv. bds. Jour. Catalysis, Jour. Coordination Chemistry, Inorganic Syntheses, Jour. Molecular Catalysis, Gazzetta Chimica Italiana, Organo Metallics, others; contbr. to Ency. Brit., also numerous articles to profl. jours. Office: Dept Chemistry Univ Chgo 5735 S Ellis Ave Chicago IL 60637

HALPERT, MARK HOWARD, medical products company executive; b. N.Y.C., July 1, 1948; s. Arthur Seymour and Gussie (Hartman) H.; m. Mira Rachel Stulberg, June 5, 1977; children—Andrew Victor, Julie Maiya. B.B.A., U. Mich., 1969, M.B.A., 1973. Fin./systems analyst Electronic Data Systems, N.Y.C., 1973-74; fin. supr. Ford Motor Co., Dearborn, Mich., 1974-77; fin. mgr. Airco, Montvale, N.J., 1977-78; asst. to v.p. mktg. and sales Ohio Med. Products div. Airco/BOC, Madison, Wis., 1978-79, gas mktg. mgr., 1979-80, gen. mgr. customer service, distbn. and gas mktg., 1980-81, v.p. fin., 1982—. Mem. task force for dist. atty., Madison. Mem. Inst. of Mgmt. Acctg., U. Mich. Alumni Assn. (pres. Madison chpt. 1983—). Office: 3030 Airco Dr Madison WI 53707

HALSEY, JAMES LEE, fire chief; b. Royal Oak, Mich., Apr. 2, 1940; s. William P. and Irmalee (Forester) H.; m. Charlotte R. Wieda, Nov. 26, 1966; children—Ann, John. Student in fire sci. Oakland Community Coll., 1970. Police officer Royal Oak Police Dept., 1961-63; fire marshal Troy Fire Dept., Mich, 1966-75, fire chief, 1975—. Served with U.S. Army, 1963-66. Named Outstanding Young Man, Troy Jaycees, 1974. Mem. Oakland County Fire Chiefs (pres. 1976), Southeastern Mich. Fire Chiefs (pres. 1984), Mich. Fire Chiefs Assn. (pres. 1984-85), Internat. Fire Chiefs Assn. (1st v.p. 1985—). Methodist. Lodges: Elks, Optimists. Avocations: golf; snow skiing. Office: 500 W Big Beaver Troy MI 48084

HALVERSON, GAYLON LEONARD, accounting educator, accountant; b. Decorah, Iowa, June 9, 1932; s. Leonard and Louise Rose (Swella) H.; m. Carmen Elaine Gabrielson, June 25, 1955; children—Michael, Kristi, Jon. B.A., Luther Coll., 1954; M.A., U. No. Iowa, 1963; D.B.A., Ind. U. 1968. C.P.A., Iowa. Tchr. high schs., Iowa, 1956-63; prof. acctg. U. No. Iowa, Cedar Falls, 1963—; owner, mgr. Halverson C.P.A. Firm, Cedar Falls, 1972—; edn. cons. McGladrey Hendrickson & Pullen, C.P.A., Davenport, Iowa, 1972-79; chmn. Iowa Bd. Acctg., 1983. Author: Basic 1040 Preparation, 1977. Served with U.S. Army, 1954-56. Recipient numerous educational awards. Mem. Am. Acctg. Assn., Am. Inst. C.P.A.s, Iowa Soc. C.P.A.s (pres. 1980). Nat. Assn. State Bds. Accountancy (bd. dirs. 1983-84). Republican. Lutheran. Club: Beaver Hills Country (bd. dirs. 1974-76, pres. 1976) (Cedar Falls). Avocations: golf, travel. Home: 2006 Rainbow Dr Cedar Falls IA 50613 Office: U No Iowa Cedar Falls IA 50614-0127

HALVERSON, RICHARD PAUL, trust company executive; b. Salt Lake City, Oct. 17, 1941; s. Lionel John and Anne Elizabeth (Linton) H.; m. Kathleen Taylor Ballstaedt, July 7, 1965; children—Kirsten, Bradley, Taylor, Ryan, Tanner, Kimberly, Blake. B.S., magna cum laude, U. Utah, 1966; M.B.A. with distinction, Harvard U., 1968. Vice pres. Waddell & Reed Inc., Kansas City, Mo., 1968-77; sr. v.p. First Trust St. Paul, 1977-80, exec. v.p., chief investment officer, 1980—. Author: Financial Freedom, 1982. Contbr. to Real Estate Handbook, Smart Money mag. Missionary, bishop, high councilman, counselor stake pres. Ch. of Jesus Christ Latter-day Saints, St. Paul, 1961—; bd. dirs. Heart Am. Boys Clubs, Kansas City, 1968-77, Washington County Devel. Learning Ctr., St. Paul, 1978-80; mem. exec. bd. Indianhead council Boy Scouts Am., 1980—. Baker scholar Harvard U.; recipient A. Van Biema award Nat. Comml. Fin. Conf., 1964; Surgeon award Indianhead council Boy Scouts Am., 1984. Mem. Fin. Analysts Fedn. (pres. Kansas City chpt. 1968—), Inst. Chartered Fin. Analysts, Fin. Planners Assn., Sigma Alpha Epsilon. Republican. Club: Harvard Bus. Sch. (Mpls.-St. Paul). Home: 7401 Pinehurst Ct Saint Paul MN 55109 Office: First Trust Saint Paul W 555 First Nat Bank Bldg Saint Paul MN 55101

HAM, GEORGE ELDON, soil microbiologist, educator; b. Ft. Dodge, Iowa, May 22, 1939; s. Eldon Henry and Thelma (Cran) H.; m. Alice Susan Bormann, Jan. 11, 1964; children—Philip, David, Steven. B.S., Iowa State U., 1961, M.S., 1963, Ph.D., 1967. Asst. prof. dept soil sci. U. Minn., St. Paul, 1967-71, assoc. prof., 1971-77, prof., 1977-80; prof., head dept. agronomy Kans. State U., Manhattan, 1980—; dir. Kans. Crop Improvement Assn., Manhattan, 1980—, Kans. Fertilizer and Chem. Inst., Hutchinson, 1980—, Kans. Crops and Soils Industry Council, Manhattan, 1982—; cons. Internat. Atomic Energy Agy., Vienna, Austria, 1973-79. Assoc. editor Agronomy Jour., 1979-84. Contbr. articles to profl. jours. Asst. scoutmaster Indianhead council Boy Scouts Am., St. Paul, 1977-80; pres. North Star Little League, St. Paul, 1979-80. Served to sgt. U.S. Army, 1963-69. Mem. Am. Soc. Agronomy, Crop Sci. Soc. Am., Soil Sci. Soc. Am., AAAS. Home: 2957 Nevada St Manhattan KS 66502

HAM, ROBERT NORRIS, choral director, educator; b. Logansport, Ind., Aug. 27, 1954; s. Robert S. and Lorraine (Broadwater) H.; m. Marilynn Joy McConnell, Aug. 20, 1977; 1 child, Norris Samuel. B.M.E., No. Mich. U., 1976, M.M.E., 1978. Music tchr. Brookwood High Sch., Ontario, Wis., 1977-79; asst. prof. music Friends Bible Coll., Haviland, Kans., 1979—, chmn. ch. music dept., 1979—, chmn. faculty, 1982-84, dir. community chorus, 1981-83. Chmn. music com. Haviland Friends Ch., 1979—. Named Prof. of Yr., Friends Bible Coll., 1982. Mem. Am. Choral Dirs. Assn. Mem. Soc. of Friends. Avocations: fishing; hunting; swimming; boating; coin collecting. Office: Friends Bible College Box 288 Haviland KS 67059

HAMBRIGHT, THEDA MACKIE, college administrator; b. Jackson, Miss., Apr. 3, 1919; d. James and Zelphia (Chambers) Mackie; m. Winford Hambright, Nov. 24, 1938; children—Winford P., Dianne Hambright Chenier. B.Edn., Pestalozzi Froebel Tchrs. Coll., 1960; M.S., Chgo State U., 1965; advanced grad. cert., U. Hartford, 1974. Cert. tchr. supervision Ill., 1965. Elem. tchr. Ill. dist. 152, Harvey, 1960-69; coll. counselor, Thornton Community Coll., South Holland, Ill., 1969-77, dean community services, 1977—. Active Urban League, NAACP, Nat. Assn. Ret. Fed. Workers, South Suburban Women's Network, Harvey Community; chmn. Econ. Devel. Assn. Cook County Named Tchr. of Year, Dist. 152, 1969; Counselor of Year, Thornton Community Coll. 1976. Mem. Ill. Assn. Continuing Edn., Assn. for Curriculum and Devel., Ill. Personnel and Guidance Assn., Delta Kappa Gamma. Democrat. Episcopalian. Theda Hambright scholarship/loan established Thornton Community Coll., 1982.

HAMEISTER, LAVON LOUETTA, social worker; b. Blairstown, Iowa, Nov. 27, 1922; d. George Frederick and Bertha (Anderson) Hameister; B.A., U. Iowa, 1944; postgrad. N.Y. Sch. Social Work, Columbia, 1945-46, U. Minn. Sch. Social Work, summer 1952; M.A., U. Chgo., 1959. Child welfare practitioner Fayette County Dept. Social Welfare, West Union, Iowa, 1946-56; dist. cons. services in child welfare and pub. assistance Iowa Dept. Social Welfare, Des Moines, 1956-58, dist. field rep., 1959-64, regional supr., 1964-65, supr., specialist supervision, adminstrn. Bur. Staff Devel., 1965-66, chief Bur. Staff Devel., 1966-68; chief div. staff devel. and tng. Office Dep. Commr., Iowa Dept. Social Services, 1968-72, asst. dir. Office Staff Devel., 1972-79, coordinator continuing edn., 1979—; farmer. Active in drive to remodel, enlarge Oelwein (Iowa) Mercy Hosp., 1952. Mem. Bus. and Profl. Women's Club (chpt. sec. 1950-52), Am. Assn. U. Women, Nat. Assn. Social Workers (chpt. sec.-elect 1958-59), Am. Pub. Welfare Assn., Iowa Welfare Assn., Acad. Cert. Social Workers. Lutheran. Home: 1800 Grand Ave West Des Moines IA 50265 Office: State Office Bldg Des Moines IA 50319

HAMEL, LOUIS REGINALD, systems analysis cons.; b. Lowell, Mass., July 23, 1945; s. Wilfred John and Angelina Lucienne (Paradis) H.; A.A., Kellogg Community Coll., 1978; m. Roi Anne Roberts, Mar. 24, 1967 (dec.); 1 dau., Felicia Antoinette; m. Anne Louise Staup, July 2, 1972; children—Shawna Michelle, Louis Reginald III. Retail mgr. Marshalls dept. Stores, Beverly, Mass., 1972-73; tech. service rep. Monarch Marking Systems, Framingham, Mass., 1973-74; employment specialist Dept. Labor, Battle Creek, Mich., 1977-78; v.p. corp. Keith Polygraph Cons. and Investigative Service, Inc., Battle Creek, Mich., 1978-79; systems analysis cons., 1975—; indsl. engr., engine components div. Eaton Corp., Battle Creek, Mich., 1979-82; tooling and process engr. Kelley Tech. Services, Battle Creek, Mich., Clark Equipment Inc., 1983-84; tooling and mfg. engr., mfg. mgr. Trans Guard Industries Inc., Angola, Ind., 1983-85. Mem. Calhoun County Com. on Employment of Handicapped, Battle Creek, Mich., 1977-78; mem. U.S. Congl. Adv. Bd. Served with USN, 1963-71; Vietnam. Recipient Services to Handicapped award Internat. Assn. Personnel in Employment Security, Mich. chpt., 1978. Mem. Nat. Geog. Soc., Mich. Assn. Concerned Vets. (dir.), Nat. Assn. Concerned Vets., VFW. Democrat. Roman Catholic. Home and Office: 12240 Assyria Rd Bellevue MI 49021

HAMERLINCK, FRANCIS PAUL, educational adminstrator; b. Minneota, Minn., Jan. 13, 1926; s. Charles Francis and Eliza Marie (Anseeuw) H.; m. Jeanette Branigan, Apr. 8, 1950; children—Barbara, Michael, Mark, Jeffrey. B.S., Bemidji State U., 1950, M.S., 1957; M.Ed., U. N.D., 1963. Cert. ednl. adminstr., Minn. Tchr., Clearbrook High Sch., Minn., 1950-58, Thief River Falls High Sch., Minn., 1958-59; adminstr. Sch. Dist. 564, Thief River Falls, 1960-74; prin. Lincoln Street High Sch., Thief River Falls, 1974-85; asst. supt. schs., Thief River Falls, 1985—. Mem. platform com. Minn. Republican Com., 1967. Served with USN, 1944-46. Kettering Found. fellow, 1981, 84. Mem. Nat. Assn. Sch. Prins. (activities com. 1978-79), Minn. Assn. Sch. Prins. (chmn. resolutions 1980-83), Minn. Edn. Assn. (pres. North div. 1965-67), Assn. Supervision and Curriculam Devel., North Central Assn., Am. Legion, Phi Delta Kappa. Lodge: Lions (pres. Thief River Falls 1969-70). Lutheran. Home: 1221 Edgewood Dr Thief River Falls MN 56701 Office: Lincoln Sr High Sch 1st and Knight Ave Thief River Falls MN 56701

HAMILTON, DAVID WENDELL, pathology assistant; b. Gregory, S.D., Feb. 20, 1953; s. Wendell Ralph and Doris Marie (Jacobson) H.; m. Priscilla Ann Boyer, Mar. 12, 1983. B.S. in Math., U. Nebr., 1979, M.B.A., 1984. Pathologist's asst. Pathology Med. Services, Lincoln, 1976—. Bd. dirs. Friendship Force, Lincoln; programmer Mayor's Com. of Internat. Visitors, Lincoln. Fellow Am. Assn. Pathologist Assts.; mem. Nat. Assn. Med. Examiners, Biol. Photographers Assn., Nat. Histology Assn. Democrat. Lutheran. Avocations: reading; antique clock repair; hunting; fishing. Home: 5950 Bartholomew Circle Lincoln NE 68512 Office: Pathology Med Services 100 N 56th Suite 203 Lincoln NE 68510

HAMILTON, LEE HERBERT, congressman; b. Daytona Beach, Fla., Apr. 20, 1931; m. Nancy Ann Nelson, Aug. 21, 1954; children—Tracy Lynn, Deborah Lee, Douglas Nelson. A.B., DePauw U., 1952; scholar, Goethe U., Frankfurt au Main, Germany, 1953; J.D., Ind. U., 1956. Mem. 89th-99th Congresses from 9th Dist. Ind.; vice chmn. congl. del. Interparliamentary Union, regional whip, mem. fgn. affairs com., chmn. subcom. on Europe and Middle East, chmn. subcom. on econ. goals and intergovtl. policy, mem. permanent select com. on intelligence, mem. joint econ. com. Office: 2187 Rayburn House Office Bldg Washington DC 20515*

HAMILTON, LOUIS GEORGE, lawyer; b. Phila., June 17, 1954; s. William Harry and Elizabeth (George) H.; m. Sheila Giles Kohrman, May 6, 1978. B.A. in Polit. Sci., U. Cin., 1976; J.D., No. Ky. U., 1982. Bar: Ohio 1982. Staff counsel Baldwin-United Corp., Cin., 1980-82; corp. atty. U.S. Shoe Corp., Cin., 1982—. Mem. Cin. Patent Law Assn. Republican. Roman Catholic. Home: 3369 Everson Ave Cincinnati OH 45209 Office: US Shoe Corp 1 Eastwood Dr Cincinnati OH 45227

HAMILTON, LYLE HOWARD, research scientist; b. Superior, Nebr., June 11, 1924. A.B., Williamette U., 1950; M.S., State U. Iowa, 1952; Ph.D., 1954. Adminstrv. asst. to dean U. Sask., Saskatoon, Can., 1956-57; chief physiol. sect. Research Service, VA Med. Ctr., Milw., 1957-61, acting assoc. chief staff, 1972-74, prin. scientist, 1961—. Co-author: (N.B. Slonim) Respiratory Physiology, 2d edit. 1971, 4th edit. 1981. Mem. Can. Physiol. Soc., Soc. Exptl. Biology and Medicine, Am. Coll. Sports Medicine, Am. Physiol. Soc., Am. Heart Assn. Home: 4905 W Wisconsin Ave Milwaukee WI 53208 Office: Research Service 151A VA Med Ctr 5000 W National Ave Milwaukee WI 53193

HAMILTON, MELVIN EUGENE, educational administrator; b. St. Louis, Dec. 24, 1940; s. Melvin and Aileen Virginia (Guess) H.; m. Claire Floretta McCoy, June 4, 1977; children—Michael E., Melissa A. B.A. in Elem. Edn., Harris Tchrs. Coll., 1962; M.Ed., U. Ill., 1967. Tchr. Vashon Elem. Ctr., Enright Middle Sch., St. Louis, 1962-71, adminstrv. asst. elem. and middle schs., 1971—, summer sch. tchr., 1968, 71, 76-79, prin. summer sch., 1974, 80, Clark Br. No. 1, 1976-77, substitute prin. Ford Middle Sch., 1981, tchr. adult edn., St. Louis, 1969-77, master tchr. Job developer and supr. YMCA Employment Program, 1969, 70; basketball coach Explorer Scouts, 1960; asst. baseball coach Olivette Athletic Assn., 1978; athletic dir., counselor YMCA, summers 1963, 64. Named Master Tchr. of Yr., 1976. Mem. Adminstrs. Assn. of St. Louis Pub. Schs., Am. Fedn. Sch. Adminstrs., Kappa Alpha Psi. Episcopalian. Home: 5264 Abington Rd Florissant MO 63033 Office: 1909 N Kingshighway Blvd Saint Louis MO 63113

HAMILTON, QUENTIN, ophthalmologist, otolaryngologist; b. Highland Park, Mich., Dec. 1, 1922; s. William and Edna R. (Hinder) H.; m. Josephine Janet Warner, Dec. 15, 1946; children—Gwendolyn Ann, William Warner, Gregory Charles. B.S., U. Mich., 1943, M.D., 1946. Diplomate Am. Bd. Ophthalmology, Am. Bd. Otolaryngology. Practice medicine specializing in eye, ear, nose and throat, Southfield, Mich., 1956—; chief dept. eye, ear, nose, throat Highland Park Hosp., 1960-70, Providence Hosp., Southfield, 1982; dir. Med. Eye Service Mich., 1982—. Served to capt. USAF, 1952-54. Mem. AMA, Mich. Med. Assn. (chmn. div. ophthalmology 1971), Oakland County Med. Assn., Mich. Ophthalmol. Club, Mich. Otolaryngol. Soc. Lodge: Kiwanis (treas. Highland Park 1960-62). Avocations: overseas medical work; stained glass; archeology; world travel. Office: 20905 Greenfield Southfield MI 48075

HAMILTON, RICHARD ALFRED, university administrator, educator; b. Pitts., Dec. 22, 1941; s. Robert Curtis and Dorothy Katherine (Sexauer) H.; B.A., Otterbein Coll., 1965; M.B.A., Bowling Green State U., 1968; D.Bus. Adminstrn. (Univ. fellow 1968-71, Marathon Oil Co. dissertation fellow 1972), Kent State U., 1973. Production rate analyst dept. indsl. engring. RCA, Findlay, Ohio, 1966-67; computer systems analyst dept. market research Marathon Oil Co., Findlay, 1967-68; teaching fellow Coll. Bus. Adminstrn. Kent State U., 1968-71; asso. prof. direct mktg. U. Mo., Kansas City, 1971—; pres. Mission Woods Cons., Inc.; cons. U.S. Senate Permanent Subcom. on Investigation, 1973-74, Midwest Research Inst. and Office of Tech. Assessment of U.S. Congress, 1974-75; speaker to profl. orgns. Mem. Am. Acad. Advt., Am. Inst. Decision Scis., Am. Mktg. Assn., Assn. M.B.A. Execs., Sales, Mktg. Execs., Beta Gamma Sigma. Methodist. Author: (with David R. Bywaters) How to Conduct Association Surveys, 1976; Tourism U.S.A.-Marketing Tourism, Vol. 3, 1978; rev. editor Akron Bus. and Econ. Rev., 1977—. Home: 5306 Mission Woods Rd Mission Woods KS 66205 Office: Sch Adminstrn U Mo Kansas City MO 64110

HAMILTON, RICHARD PARKER, clothing company executive; b. Worcester, Mass., Sept. 13, 1931; s. Ralph Ramsey and Doris Isabel (Waterhouse) H.; m. Nancy Marguerite Daniels, June 6, 1959; children—Jeffrey Richard, Jennifer Lynn, Kimberly Ann. B.B.A., U. Toledo, 1953; M.B.A., Ohio State U., 1954. With Florsheim Shoe Co., 1957-78, auditor, mgr. shoe shop, gen. mdse. mgr., regional sales mgr., v.p. and gen. mdse., mgr., pres. and chief exec. officer; chmn., chief exec. officer Hart Schaffner & Marx Retail Stores div. Hartmarx Corp., Chgo., 1978-80, pres., chief operating officer, 1981-84, chmn. bd., pres., chief exec. officer, 1985—. Mem. Better Bus. Bur. Met. Chgo., Ill. Council on Econ. Edn., U.S. Olympic Blue Ribbon Com. Served with U.S. Army, 1955-56. Congregationalist. Clubs: Chicago, Mid.-Am., Sunset Ridge Country. Office: Hartmarx Corp 101 N Wacker Dr Chicago IL 60606

HAMILTON, ROBERT APPLEBY, JR., insurance company executive; b. Boston, Feb. 20, 1940; s. Robert A. and Alice Margaret (Dowdall) H.; student Miami U. (Ohio), 1958-62; m. Ellen Kuhlen, Aug. 13, 1966; children—Jennifer, Robert Appleby, III, Elizabeth. With Travelers Ins. Co., Hartford, Conn., Portland, Maine and Phila., 1962-65; with New Eng. Mut. Life Ins. Co., various locations, 1965—, regional pension rep., Boston, 1968-71, regional mgr., Chgo., 1972-83, sr. pension cons., 1983—. Mem. Republican Town Com., Wenham, Mass., 1970-72, Milton Twp., Ill., 1973-75; mem. Wenham Water Commn., 1970-72. C.L.U.; chartered fin. cons. Mem. Midwest Pension Conf., Am. Soc. Pension Actuaries (assoc.), Am. Soc. C.L.U.s, Am. Assn. Fin. Planners, Profit Sharing Council Am., Chgo. Council Fgn. Relations, Alpha Epsilon Rho. Republican. Home: 2 S 110 Hamilton Ct Wheaton IL 60187 Office: 10 S Riverside Plaza Chicago IL 60606

HAMILTON, ROBERT OTTE, lawyer; b. Marysville, Ohio, July 27, 1927; s. George Robinson and Annette (Otte) H.; m. Phyllis Eileen Clark, Dec. 16, 1962; children—Nathan Clark, Scott Robert. A.B., Miami U., Oxford, Ohio, 1950; J.D., U. Mich., 1953. Bar: Ohio 1953, U.S. Supreme Ct. 1960. Sole practice, Marysville, 1953—; pros. atty. Union County, Ohio, 1957-65; city atty. City of Marysville, 1965-81. Mem. Union, Morrow and Delaware Mental Health Bd., 1957-72; pres. Marysville Jaycees, 1954; pres. Union County Hist. Assn., 1961-63; mem. Union County Republican Exec. Com., 1955-65, sec., 1955-60. Served with USN, 1945-46, to lt. (j.g.) USNR, 1946-66. Mem. ABA, Ohio State Bar Assn. (chmn. jr. bar sect. 1961, ho. of dels. 1976—, exec. com. 1983—), Union County Bar Assn. (pres. 1960), Ohio Acad. Trial Lawyers. Lodge: Masons. Home: 432 W 6th St Marysville OH 43040 Office: 116 S Court St Marysville OH 43040

HAMILTON, TED ALLEN, biostatistician; researcher; b. Niles, Mich., May 13, 1955; s. Harold Keith and Betty Lou (Knapp) H.; m. Jane Ann Long, Aug. 28, 1981. B.S. in Fisheries and Wildlife, Mich. State U., 1977; M.S. in Natural Resources, U. Mich., 1980, M.S. in Biostats., 1982. Fisheries biologist, statistician Ecol. Analysts, Inc., Northbrook, Ill., 1980-81; biostatistician, epidemiologist Ford Motor Co., Dearborn, Mich., 1982-83; coordinator, biostatistician dept. dermatology U. Mich. Hosp., Ann Arbor, 1983—. Mem. Am. Statis. Assn. Avocations: hiking, bird-watching, cooking, horticulture. Home: 3583 Pheasant Run Circle Apt 2 Ann Arbor MI 48104 Office: Dermatology Clin Research C2102 Outpatient Bldg Univ Mich Hosp Ann Arbor MI 48109

HAMILTON, VERA ELLEN, educator; b. Clark County, Ohio, Dec. 14, 1934; d. Elmer and Clarice Mildred (Schindler) Overholser; m. Carl R. Welty, Mar. 13, 1954 (div. June 1967); children—Garry Lynn, Keith Alan; m. 2d, Nelson C. Hamilton, Mar. 6, 1971. A.A. in Bus. Adminstrn., Bliss Coll., Columbus, Ohio, 1982; B.B.A. in Comml. Credit and Fin., Urbana (Ohio) Coll., 1984. Keypunch operator Hobart Mfg. Co., Troy, Ohio, 1959-61, Kissell Co., Springfield, Ohio, 1961-63, Ohio Steel Foundry, Springfield, 1963-64; keypunch operator, clk.-typist, accounts payable clk., export clk., cost clk., timekeeper, purchasing expeditor Internat. Harvester Co., Springfield, 1964-71; asst. to husband in body shop bus., Springfield, 1971-73; keypunch operator, census preparer Community Hosp., Springfield, Ohio, 1973-76; data entry operator State Automobile Ins. Co., Columbus, Ohio, 1976-79; payroll clk., sec., credit adminstr., credit supr. Air Conditioning div. Magic Chef, Columbus, 1979-84; instr. Bliss Coll., 1984—. Mem. Nat. Assn. Credit Mgrs., Air Conditioning and Refrigeration Inst., Houston Assn. Credit Mgmt., Nat. Assn. Female Execs., VFW Ladies Aux. Republican. Baptist. Home: 12 Hanford St Columbus OH 43206 Office: Bliss College 3770 N High St Columbus OH 43214

HAMILTON, WILLIAM FRANSIS SHANON, JR., club director; b. Mansfield, Ohio, Sept. 16, 1956; s. William Fransis and Mary Ellen (Orr) H.; m. Lisa Inara Cook, May 12, 1984; 1 dau., Jenifer Laurie. B.A., Baldwin-Wallace Coll., 1978. Asst. dir. Cleve. Police Athletic League, 1975-78; dep. corrections officer Cuyahoga County Sheriff's Dept., Cleve., 1978-84; tchr. Harding Jr. High Sch., Lakewood, Ohio, 1980-83; residential dir. Cleve. Job Corps, 1983-85; ctr. dir. Cleve. Boys and Girls Club, 1985—. Democrat. Lutheran. Home: 1818 Forestdale Ave Cleveland OH 44109 Office: Cleveland Boys and Girls Club 4600 Carnegie Ave Cleveland OH 44106

HAMLIN, ALLENE GAY, civic worker; b. Highland, Ill., May 11, 1946; d. Israel Benjamin and Margaret Virginia (Eckmann) Hiken; ed. schs. for visually handicapped, secretarial tng.; m. Leonard Albert Hamlin, Oct. 12, 1968; children—Eric Garrett, Stephen Wayne. Mem. adv. sch. bd. Sunnyside Sch., 1979-80; comdr. Red Wing chpt. DAV Aux., 1978-82, chaplain state dept., 1979-80, sr. vice comdr., 1977-78, publicity chmn. Minn. dept., 1978-79, patriotic instr. Minn. dept., 1980-81, patriotic instr. dept. Minn., 1981-82, adj. Red Wing chpt., 1982-84, recipient past comdrs. pin, 1979; transcriber Braille books. Republican. Home: 1527 Central Ave Red Wing MN 55066

HAMLIN, JANE GREENE, curriculum specialist; b. Washington, Nov. 26, 1934; d. Roosevelt Brown and Mildred Lola (Hendrix) Greene; B.S., Purdue U., 1956; M.Ed., Nat. Coll. Ed., 1975; m. Richard Peter Hamlin, Aug. 11, 1956; children—Diane, Peter, David, Andrea. Tchr., N.W. Suburban Spl. Edn. Orgn., Palatine, Ill., 1974-80; curriculum specialist Behavior Edn. Center, Wheeling, Ill., 1980—. Mem. Northfield Village Caucus, 1981-85. Office Supt. Public Instrn. fellow, 1974. Mem. Ill. Council Exceptional Children (govt. relations regional coordinator), Assn. Supervision and Curriculum Devel., NEA, Phi Delta Kappa, Phi Mu (nat. career devel. dir.). Republican. Mem. United Ch. of Christ. Office: 1001 W Dundee St Wheeling IL 60090

HAMLIN, RICHARD EUGENE, banker, former college president; b. Royal, Iowa, June 2, 1925; s. Fred E. and Nancy Jane (Schuetz) H.; student Drury Coll., 1943; B.S., George Williams Coll., 1949; M.A., U. Omaha, 1952; Ph.D., U. Nebr., 1956; m. C. Joan Dahl, Aug. 14, 1949; children—Robert E., Elizabeth Ann. Asst. camp dir., camp counselor, asst. youth sec. YMCA, 1946-49, exec. sec. South Omaha (Nebr.) YMCA, 1949-51, program sec., adult edn. dir., Omaha, 1951-53, assoc. dir. research nat. bd., 1953-61; pres. George Williams Coll., 1961-83; chmn., chief exec. officer Bank of Yorktown, Lombard, Ill., 1983—; tchr. summer confs. Am. Youth Found., summer sch. U. Omaha; chmn. bd., dir. Bank Yorktown, Lombard, Ill.; coord. human resources Cole/Taylor Fin. Group. Mem. Am. Psychol. Assn., Downers Grove C. of C. (chmn. bd. 1974-76), Fedn. Ind. Ill. Colls. and Univs. (chmn.), Alpha Omicron Alpha (past pres.). Congregationalist (lay moderator). Clubs: Economic, University (Chgo.); Butterfield Country (Oak Brook, Ill.). Author: Hi-Y Today, 1955; A New Look at YMCA Physical Education, 1957. Co-editor: YMCA Yearbook, 1958-61. Home: 3908 Forest Dr Downers Grove IL 60515 Office: Bank of Yorktown 1 Yorktown Ctr Lombard IL 60148

HAMM, VERNON LOUIS, JR., management and financial consultant; b. East St. Louis, Ill., Mar. 14, 1951; s. Vernon Louis and Colleen Ann Hamm; B.S., Murray (Ky.) State U., 1973; M.B.A., St. Louis U., 1975; postgrad. Stanford U., 1975. Jr. exec. corp. accounts Brown Group, Inc., St. Louis, 1973-75; group supr. APC Skills Co., Palm Beach, Fla., 1975-77; account mgr. Inst. Mgmt. Resources, Los Angeles, 1977-78; dir. mgmt. devel. Naus & Newlyn, Inc., Paoli, Pa., 1978-82; exec. v.p. Mgmt. Alternatives Ltd., 1982—; mgmt., fin. and energy cons., 1975—; dir. Psychosystems Mgmt. Corp., N.Y.C. Mem. Am. Soc. for Tng. and Devel., Am. Prodn. and Inventory Control Soc., Murray State U. Alumni Assn. Contbr. articles to profl. publs.

HAMMAN, KENNETH WILLIAM, educator, school administrator; b. Kalamazoo, Dec. 7, 1952; s. Lawrence Lloyd and Velnoe Marguarite (Welty) H.; m. Joan Etta Newhouse, Aug. 25, 1972; children—Jessica Dawn, Thea Grace. B.S., Eastern Mich. U., 1975, M.A., 1979. Cert. elem. tchr., Mich. Tchr.-coach Brighton Area Schs., Mich., 1975-79, asst. prin., 1979-1983, prin., 1983—; evaluator North Central Assn., Boulder, Colo., 1982—. Bd. dirs. PTA, Brighton, 1981—. Mem. Mich. Assn. Secondary Sch. Adminstrs., Nat. Assn. Secondary Sch. Adminstrs. Clubs: Breakfast Optimist (pres.), Brighton Elite Gourmet. Avocations: Alpine and nordic skiing; city league basketball. Office: Scranton Middle Sch 125 S Church Brighton MI 48116

HAMMANN, WILLIAM C., research chemist; b. Little Rock, Apr. 22, 1925; s. Arny H. and Wilma (Curl) H.; m. Audrey Kupperstein, Oct. 17, 1953; children—Mark, Joyce, Scott. Diploma, Little Rock Jr. Coll., 1943; B.Chemistry, U. Minn., 1948; Ph.D., U. Ill.-Urbana, 1951. Research chemist Monsanto Co., Dayton, Ohio, 1953-60, group leader, St. Louis, 1960-69, mgr. comml. devel., 1969-76, mgr. research and devel., 1976-80, dir. research and devel., 1980—. Patentee in field. Served with U.S. Army, 1943-46, ETO. Mem. Am. Chem. Soc., AAAS, Soc. Chem. Industry, Animal Health Inst., Sigma Xi. Home: 438 Fourwynd Dr Saint Louis MO 63141 Office: Monsanto 700 Chesterfield Village Pkwy Chesterfield MO 63198

HAMMEL, ERNEST MARTIN, health education administrator, educator; b. Ashtabula, Ohio, May 2, 1939; s. Eugene Christian and Etna Maria (Costas) H.; m. Martha Lorene Hertzer, Dec. 16, 1961; children—Eric John, James Martin. Student Hiram Coll., 1957-58; B.S., Heidelberg Coll., 1962; M.P.H., U. Mich., 1966, Ph.D., 1976. Sch. environ. health sanitarian Union County Health Dept., Marysville, Ohio, 1962-65; program planning specialist Mich. Commn. on Aging, Lansing, 1966-69; adminstr. local health dept. planning Mich. Dept. Pub. Health, Lansing, 1969-70; planning cons. Wayne County Health Dept., Eloise, Mich., 1970; program developer Mich. Assn. Regional Med. Programs, East Lansing, 1973-74, asst. dir. ops., 1975-76; exec. dir. Oakland Health Edn. Program, Rochester, Mich., 1976—; adj. prof., health care adminstrn. adviser Central Mich. U. Inst. for Personal and Career Devel., Mt. Pleasant, 1980—. Chmn. Oakland County Health Cable Communications Council, 1982-83; trustee Kenny Mich. Rehab. Found., Southfield, 1983—; mem. Republican City Com., Ann Arbor, Mich., 1972; troop com. chmn. Clinton Valley council Boy Scouts Am., 1981—. Behavioral Sci. fellow U. Mich., 1969-70, Behavioral Sci. Research fellow, 1971-72; grad. student Research grantee Rackham Sch. Grad. Studies, U. Mich., 1972; Pub. Health Service trainee U. Mich., 1965-66, 70-71, 72-73; contract Nat. Ctr. for Health Services Research and Devel., 1973. Mem. Assn. Am. Med. Colls., Am. Heart Assn., Am. Pub. Health Assn., Assn. Health Services Research, Assn. for Hosp. Med. Edn., Mich. Assn. for Med. Edn., Mich. Pub. Health Assn. U. Mich. Alumni Assn. Lutheran. Lodges: Masons, Shriners, Order of Eastern Star. Contbr. articles to profl. pubs. Editor several med. care orgn. publs. Office: Oakland Health Edn Program Varner House Adams at Butler Rochester MI 48063

HAMMER, JOHN HENRY, II, hospital administrator; b. Bartlesville, Okla., Dec. 27, 1943; s. John Henry and Lucy (Macias) H.; B.B.A., St. Joseph's Coll., 1966; student U. Md. (Europe), 1968-69; M.B.A., U. Ill., 1984; m. Michele Evano, June 27, 1970; children—John Henry, Erica. Project mgr. Econ. & Manpower Corp., N.Y.C., 1971-73; asst. dir. human resources St. Catherine Hosp., East Chicago, Ind., 1974-80, pres. Employees Credit Union, 1974-80; dir. personnel Lakeview Med. Center, Danville, Ill., 1980-84, v.p., 1984—. Chmn., De La Garza Career Center Program Com., 1974-80. Served to capt. USAF, 1967-71, to maj. USAFR. Mem. Ind. Soc. Hosp. Personnel Adminstrn. (chmn. 1976-77, dir. 1977-79, pres. 1979-80), Am. Soc. Hosp. Personnel Adminstrn., Central Ill. Soc. Hosp. Personnel Adminstrn. (pres. 1984), Am. Soc. Personnel Adminstrn. Roman Catholic. Home: 1324 N Walnut Ave Danville IL 61832 Office: 812 N Logan Ave Danville IL 61832

HAMMER, OSCAR LAWRENCE, II, pilot, computer consultant; b. St. Louis, Oct. 5, 1944; s. Oscar L. and Velma (Wood) H.; m. Mary Francis Feddersen (div.); children—Stephanie, Mary. Student Washington U. St. Louis, 1962-64; B.S.B.A. in Fin., Ind. U., 1967; postgrad. in urban studies St. Louis U., 1977. Fin. analyst Mellon Nat. Bank, Pitts., 1967-70; test pilot McDonnell Douglas, Long Beach, Calif., 1977-78; pilot U.S. Air Force, Dept. Def., St. Louis, 1970-76, Midway Airlines, Chgo., 1978—; pres. MicroLink Computers, Chgo.; chief exec. officer Old Halls Ferry Stables Ltd., St. Louis. Mem. sch. com. Lincoln Park Conservation Assn., Chgo. Served with USAF, 1970-75; Vietnam. Decorated Air medal, Meritorious Service medal, Air Force Commendation medal. Episcopalian. Club: Columbia Yacht. Exhibited photos at Old Town Art Fair, Chgo., 1980.

HAMMER, ROBERT EUGENE, psychologist; b. Faribault, Minn., Aug. 7, 1931; s. Rolf Walter and Verona (Bakken) H.; m. M. Kitti Nations, Apr. 30, 1967; children—Gregory Clay, Cynthia Beth. B.S. in Counseling Psychology, U. Houston, 1959, M.A., 1963; Ph.D. in Spl. Edn. Adminstrn., U. Iowa, 1970. Lic. psychologist, Iowa; cert. health service provider in psychology. Tchr. educable mentally retarded Houston Ind. Sch. Dist., 1961-63; testing supr. U. Houston Counseling Ctr., 1963-65; child psychologist Mental Health Inst., Independence, Iowa, 1965-67, dir. adolescent treatment unit, 1969-74, dir. psychol. services, 1969—; research dir. Iowa Div. State Mental Health Resources; pvt. practice counseling and cons. psychologist, 1974—. Bd. dirs. Iowa Nursing Found.; vol. fireman; moderator, asst. dir. men's choral group First Baptist Ch. Served with USAF, 1950-53. Mem. Am. Psychol. Assn., State Mental Health Dirs. Assn., Evaluation Network. Baptist. Lodges: Kiwanis, Masons. Contbr. articles to profl. jours. Home: PO Box 111 Independence IA 50644 Office: PO Box 111 Mental Health Inst Independence IA 50644

HAMMER, ROGER ALLEN, publishing executive; b. San Francisco, Nov. 11, 1934; s. Paul A. and Margaret J. (Lilly) H.; children—Calli, Stephen. A.A., U. Calif.-Berkeley, 1954; B.A., U. Minn., 1973. News editor Mobile (Ala.) Daily Press Register, 1959-66; bur. chief UPI, Montgomery, Ala., 1966-69; account exec. Carl Byoir & Assocs., N.Y.C., 1969-77; group mgr. pub. relations Honeywell, Mpls., 1977-80; editor Hammer News Service, editor, pub. The Place in The Woods, pres. Hammer Enterprise, Golden Valley, Minn., 1980—; adult edn. tchr. Bd. dirs. Ala. Open and Sr. Bowl tennis tournaments, 1964-65; community liaison minority projects, Honeywell, Mpls., 1975-77. Served with AUS, 1957-59. Mem. Pub. Relations Soc. Am. (accredited), U.S. Tennis Assn., Native Sons of Golden West, Soc. Profl. Journalists. Democrat. Roman Catholic. Club: Minn. Press. Author: Black America, American Woman, 1980; The People (Native Americans), 1981; Hispanic America, 1984. Office: 3900 Glenwood Ave Golden Valley MN 55422

HAMMER, SIGMUND IMMANUEL, retired geology and geophysics educator, consultant; b. Webster, S.D., Aug. 13, 1901; s. Ludvig Erikson and Laura Louise (Anderson) H.; m. Norma Lucille Johnson (dec. 1980); children—Sigmund Lewis, Mary Alice (dec.), John Phillip, Kirsten Norma Hammer Gardner, Paul Ludvig Norman, Laura Blanche Hammer Inglis (dec.), Douglas James, Ludvig Erikson; m. Doris E. Pullman Lomberg, 1985. Student Concordia Coll., 1919-21; B.A., St. Olaf Coll., 1924; Ph.D., U. Minn., 1929. Geophysicist, Gulf Oil Corp., Pitts., 1929-46, sect. head, 1946-67; lectr. U. Pitts., 1946-67, adj. mem. grad. faculty, 1963-67; prof. geology and geophysics, U. Wis., Madison, 1967-72, prof. emeritus, 1972—; cons. in exploration geophysics; exploration advisor United Nations Devel. Projects, Bolivia, 1972-75, Turkey, 1976-78; visiting prof. U. Mex., Mexico City, 1980, U. Minn., Duluth, 1981. Contbr. articles to profl. jours. Organizing chmn. French Cultural Ctr. Western Pa., (1965-67; chmn. Norwegian classroom com. U. Pitts., 1962-66; pres. Nationality Council, U. Pitts., 1966-67; organizing pres. Am. Scandinavian Found., Pitts. chpt. 1964-66, Madison chpt. 1970-71. Mem. Am. Physical Soc., Soc. Exploration Geophysicists (hon.), (v.p. 1950-51, pres. 1951-52), Am. Geophysical Union (fellow), Am. Assn. Petroleum Geologists. Republican. Club: Cosmos (Washington). Avocations: Norwegian and American heritage and culture. Home: 110 S Henry St Apt 406 Madison WI 53703 Office: U Wis Weeks Hall Geol Scis 1215 W Dayton St Madison WI 53706

HAMMES, RICHARD ROBERT, educator, researcher; b. Milw., Jan. 30, 1932; s. Henry Louis and Marvell (Flemming) H.; m. Sandra Lee Rubow, Aug. 16, 1958; children—Deborah, Susan, Richard, Robert, Mark. B.S., Wis. State Coll., 1954; M.S., U. Wis.-Milw., 1960; Ph.D., U. Wis., Madison, 1967. Asst. prof. Concordia Coll., Milw., 1962-64; prin. campus sch. U. Wis.-Oshkosh, 1967-70, dir. research, 1971-72, assoc. dean Coll. Edn., 1973-76, dir. tchr. corps project, 1978-82, prof., chmn. dept. human services and profl. leadership, 1982—; lectr. in field; cons. Wis. Sch. System, 1973—. Contbr. articles to profl. jours. Bd. dirs. Advocap, Oshkosh, 1982—. Served with U.S. Army, 1955-56. Recipient grants U. Wis., 1964-67, U.S. Dept. Edn., 1968, 70, 78-82, U. Wis. Faculty Devel. Bd., 1977, 83. Mem. Nat. Orgn. Legal Problems in Edn., Assn. Supr. and Curriculum Devel., Phi Delta Kappa. Lutheran. Home: 2470 Kingston Pl Oshkosh WI 54901 Office: Dept Human Services and Profl Leadership U Wis Coll Edn and Human Services 800 Algoma Blvd Oshkosh WI 54901

HAMMITT, FREDERICK GNICHTEL, mechanical engineering educator; b. Trenton, Sept. 25, 1923; s. Andrew Baker and Julia Stevenson (Gnichtel) H.; m. Barbara Ann Hill, June 11, 1949; children—Frederick, Harry, Jane. B.S. in Mech. Engring., Princeton U., 1944; M.S. in Mech. Engring., U. Pa., 1949; M.S. in Applied Mechanics, Stevens Inst., 1956; Ph.D. in Nuclear Engring., U. Mich., 1958. Registered profl. engr., N.J., Mich. Engr., John A. Roebling Sons Co., Trenton, 1946-48, Power Generators Ltd., Trenton, 1948-50; project engr. Reaction Motors Inc., Rockaway, N.J., 1950-53, Worthington Corp., Harrison, N.J., 1953-55; research assoc. U. Mich., Ann Arbor, 1955-57, assoc. research engr., 1957-59, assoc. prof., 1959-61, prof. nuclear engring., 1961-70, prof. mech. engring., 1965—, prof. in charge cavitation and multiphase Flow Lab., 1967—; vis. scholar Electricité de France, Paris, 1967, Societé Grenobloise Hydrauliques, Grenoble, France 1971; Fulbright sr. lectr. French Nuclear Lab., 1974; Polish Acad. Sci. lectr. Inst. Fluid Mechanics, Gdansk, 1976; lectr. on cavitation, China and Japan, 1982. Author: (with R.T. Knapp and J.W. Daily) Cavitation, 1970, Cavitation and Multiphase Flow Phenomena, 1980. Contbr. 400 articles and papers to profl. jours. Patentee in field. Served with USN, 1943-46. Fellow Instn. Mech. Engrs. (U.K.), ASME (past chmn. cavitation and fluids com., past chmn. S.E. Mich. sect., chmn. cavitation scale-effects com.), ASTM (past chmn. cavitation and liquid impingement com.); mem. Am. Nuclear Soc., Internat. Assn. Hydraulic Research, Phi Beta Kappa, Sigma Xi, Tau Beta Pi. Presbyterian. Home: 1306 Olivia Ave Ann Arbor MI 48104 Office: 312 Lay Automotive Lab North Campus U Mich Ann Arbor MI 48109

HAMMOND, DAVID CHRISTIAN, humanities educator; b. Chgo., June 23, 1951; s. Christopher David and Pauline Ermine (Crapple) H.; m. Carolyn Roberta Berg, Mar. 21, 1982; 1 child, Abigail Persephone. B.A., Kalamazoo Coll., 1973; student U. Strasbourg, 1971-72; M.A., U. Chgo., 1975, postgrad., 1976—. Instr., asst. prof. English, George Williams Coll., Downers Grove, Ill., 1978—, dir. Internat/Intercultural Studies program, 1982—. Editor Chgo. Rev. Author published poems. Mem. Gt. Lakes Rhetoric Assn., Nat. Council Tchrs. English. Home: 3043 N Kenmore St Chicago IL 60657 Office: George Williams Coll 555 31st St Downers Grove IL 60515

HAMMOND, ELIZABETH EOLYNE, lawyer; b. Detroit, Sept. 6, 1957; d. Harry Richard and Constance (Landen) H. B.A., Kent State U., 1979; J.D., U. Akron, 1983. Bar: Ohio 1983. Adminstr. Alside, Inc. subs. U.S. Steel Co., Akron, Ohio, 1980-82; mgr. Workers' Compensation Service Co., Cleve., 1982-84; assoc. Weltman, Weinberg & Assocs., LPA, Columbus, Ohio, 1985—; cons. in field. dir. Jem Products, Columbus. Adviser 4-H clubs, Ohio, 1977—. Mem. ABA, Ohio State Bar Assn., Assn. Trial Lawyers Am., Phi Alpha Delta (chpt. clk. 1980-81), Eta Sigma Phi (pres. chpt. 1978-79). Republican. Episcopalian. Home: 2563 N 4th St Columbus OH 43202 Office: Weltman Weinberg & Assocs LPA 527 S High St Columbus OH 43215

HAMMOND, GARY WRIGHT, lawyer; b. Youngstown, Ohio, Mar. 29, 1951; s. Robert Martin and Mary Carlton (Wright) H.; m. Terry Ellen Henry, Mar. 16, 1974; children—Carly Allison, Jonathan Henry. B.A., Miami U., 1974; J.D., Capital U., 1980. Bar: Ohio 1980, U.S. Dist. Ct. (so. dist.) Ohio 1981, U.S. Ct. Appeals (6th cir.) 1982. Counselor Butler County Youth Service, Hamilton, Ohio, 1974-76; Talbert House Bur., Cin., 1976-77; assoc. Graham, Dutro & Nemeth, Columbus, Ohio, 1980—. Mem. Ohio Bar Assn., Columbus Bar Assn., Columbus Def. Assn., Claims Club Columbus. Office: Graham Dutro & Nemeth 21 East Frankfort St Columbus OH 43206

HAMMOND, HAROLD LOGAN, pathology educator, oral pathologist; b. Hillsboro, Ill., Mar. 18, 1934; s. Harold Thomas and Lillian (Carlson) H.; m. Sharon Bunton, Aug. 1, 1954 (dec. 1974); 1 child, Connie; m. Pat J. Palmer, Aug. 1, 1985. Student Millikin U., 1953-57, Roosevelt U., Chgo., 1957-58; D.D.S., Loyola U., Chgo., 1962; M.S., U. Chgo., 1967. Diplomate Am. Bd. Oral Pathology. Intern, U. Chgo. Hosps., Chgo., 1962-63, resident, 1963-66, chief resident in oral pathology, 1966-67; asst. prof. oral pathology U. Iowa, Iowa City, 1967-72, assoc. prof., 1972-80, assoc. prof., dir. surg. oral pathology, 1980-83, prof., dir., 1983—; cons. pathologist Hosp. Gen. de Managua, Nicaragua, 1970—, VA Hosp., Iowa City, 1977—. Cons. editor: Revista de la Asociation de Nicaragua, 1970-71, Revista de la Federacion Odontologica de Centroamerica y Panama, 1971-77. Contbr. articles to sci. jours. Recipient Mosby Pub. Co. Scholarship award, 1962. Fellow AAAS, Am. Acad. Oral Pathology; mem. Am. Men and Women of Sci., N.Y. Acad. Scis., AAUP, Internat. Assn. Oral Pathologists, Internat. Assn. Dental Research. Avocation: collector antique clocks, gambling paraphernalia, slot machines, toys. Home: 1108 Weeber Circle Iowa City IA 52240 Office: Univ Iowa Dental Sci Bldg Iowa City IA 52242-0101

HAMMOND, JOHN LEROY, retail pharmacy excutive; b. Ft. Wayne, Ind., Dec. 12, 1948; s. John L. and Lila B. (Capatina) H.; m. Paula J. Parrish, Feb. 2, 1974; children—Rachel A., Brent J. B.S. in Pharmacy, Purdue U., 1971. Registered pharmacist, Ohio. Pharmacist Revco Drug Store, Sandusky, Ohio, 1971-73, pharmacist, mgr., 1973—. Active various coms. United Health Found., 1979-83; bd. dirs. Lorain County Kidney Found., 1984—. Mem. Lorain County Pharm. Assn. (pres. 1983-84). Republican. Methodist. Club: Lorain County Road Runners. Avocations: running, tennis, basketball, hiking, backpacking. Home: 358 Yale Ave Elyria OH 44035

HAMMOND, TOM EUGENE, lawyer; b. Kansas City, Kans., Apr. 15, 1954; s. James E. and Betty (Weiland) H.; m. Jennifer S. Mulford, Mar. 29, 1980; children—Thomas E., Lexi Diane. B.S., U. Kans., 1976; J.D., Washburn Law Sch., 1979. Bar: Kans. 1979, U.S. Dist. Ct. Kans. 1979, U.S. Ct. Appeals (10th cir.) 1982. Ptnr. Render and Kamas, Wichita, 1979—. Co-author Supplement to Kans. Workers Compensation Manual, 1984. Mem. ABA, Assn. Trial Lawyers Am., Kans. Bar Assn. (lectr. 1984), Kans. Trial Lawyers Assn. (bd. govs. 1983—). Democrat. Methodist. Home: 5904 Rockwood Wichita KS 67208 Office: PO Box 47370 700 Riverview Bldg Wichita KS 67201

HAMNER, RAY, city official, police chief; b. Evansville, Ind., Feb. 12, 1940; s. Lawrence Raeburn and Drusie Elizabeth (Brisby) H.; m. Eloise Mary Tompkins, June 6, 1964; children—Philip Ray, Douglas Ray. Student U. Evansville; grad. FBI Nat. Acad.; diploma in hazard device, Red Stone Arsenal, Huntsville, Ala., 1976. Chief of police Evansville Police Dept., Ind. Bd. dirs. Operation City Beautiful, Evansville, 1985. Served with USMC, 1958-63. Named Police Officer of Yr., Evansville Exchange Club, 1975. Mem. Fraternal Order of Police. Democrat. Roman Catholic. Lodges: Masons, Shriners. Office: Evansville Police Dept 15 NW 7th St Evansville In 47708

HAMPEL, CLIFFORD ALLEN, chemical engineer; b. Mpls., Mar. 15, 1912; s. Carl William and Gertrude (Allen) H.; m. Merrylyn E. Edmondson, June 7, 1935; 1 dau., Elizabeth Anne. B.S. in Chem. Engring., U. Minn., 1934. Research chemist Mathieson Alkali Works, Niagara Falls, N.Y., 1936-42; research chemist Diamond Alkali Co., Painesville, Ohio, 1942-43; research scientist SAM Labs., Manhattan Dist. Atom Bomb Project, Columbia U., N.Y.C., 1943-44; research chemist Minn. Mining & Mfg. Co., St. Paul, 1944-45; asst. chief chemist Cardox Corp., Chgo., 1945-46; chem. engr. Armour Research Found., Chgo., 1946-48, supr. inorganic tech., 1948-49, supr. extraction metallurgy, 1949-52; cons. chem. engr., Homewood, Ill., 1952-55;

chem. engr. Morton Salt Co., Chgo., 1953-55; mgr. chem. equipment div. Fansteel Metall. Corp., North Chicago, Ill., 1955-58; cons. chem. engr., Skokie, Ill., 1958—; guest lectr. Instituto Politecnico, Milan, Italy, 1950-51, mus. lecture series Mus. Sci. and Industry, Chgo., 1955; lectr. Chem. Inst. Can., 1957, 58. Mem. Mayor's Commn. for Nominations to Chgo. Bd. Edn., 1953-54. Awarded honor cert. for work on Manhattan Project, War Dept., Corps of Engrs., 1945. Mem. Am. Chem. Soc., AAAS, Am. Inst. Chemists (chmn. Chgo. chpt. 1955-56), Am. Soc. Metals, Electrochem. Soc. (bd. dirs. 1958-60, gen. chmn. 96th nat. meeting Chgo. 1949, chmn. indsl. electrolytic div. 1966-68), Chgo. Tech. Socs. Council (pres. 1953-54) (Award of Merit 1975), N.Y. Acad. Scis., Alpha Chi Sigma. Club: Chemists (N.Y.C.). Author chpt. on chlorine products Roger's Manual of Industrial Chemistry, 1942. Editor: Rare Metals Handbook, 1954, 2d edit., 1961; Ency. of Chemical Reactions, Vols. V-VIII; Periodic Table of Properties of the Elements, 1960-62; Ency. of Electrochemistry, 1964; Ency. of the Chemical Elements, 1967; (with Gessner G. Hawley) Ency. of Chemistry, 1973, Glossary of Chemical Terms, 1976, 2d edit., 1983; contbr. to encys., profl. jours. Address: 334 Red Bridge Rd Lake Zurich IL 60047

HAMPTON, ALFRED LOUIS, educational administrator; b. Phila., July 15, 1943; s. George Leroy and Ally Frances (Sims) H.; children—Alfred Louis, Arlan Lamont. B.A. in Math., Oakwood Coll., 1969; M.S. in Sci. Edn., U. Tenn., 1975. Supervising instr. math. Oakwood Acad., Huntsville, Ala., 1971-76; dir. minority engring. affairs U. Wis.-Madison, 1976—, cons. fin. aids com., 1976—, mem. coop. edn. com. Coll. Engring., 1981—, mem. scholarship com., 1980—; bd. dirs., lectr. Profl. Growth Inc., Madison, 1985—. Asst. scout leader Troop 80, Boy Scouts Am., Madison, 1985—; bd. dirs. Wis. Minority Suppliers Devel. Council, Madison, 1985—, Nat. Consortium for Grad. Degrees for Minorities in Engring., Notre Dame, Ind., 1983. Recipient Ednl. Leadership award Milw. Sch. Engring., 1984, Ednl. award Wis. Black Engring. Student Soc., Madison, 1981, 82, Faculty Appreciation award Council Black Profl. and Grad. Students, U. Wis.-Madison, 1985. Mem. Nat. Assn. Minority Engring. Program Adminstrs. (region C membership chmn. 1982-84, highest membership award 1983), Wis. Minority Engring. Council (co-founder, chairperson 1982—), Madison Urban League, NAACP (exec. com. 1985, Unsung Hero award 1982), Kappa Alpha Psi. Avocations: choral music, roller skating, basketball, jogging, cooking. Home: 5910 Spartan Dr Apt 3 McFarland WI 53558 Office: Coll Engring U Wis 1527 University Ave Madison WI 53706

HAMPTON, GLEN RICHARD, environmental engineer; b. Detroit, June 11, 1948; s. LaVerne P. and Virginia M. (Hubbard) H.; B.S. in Engring., Mich. Tech. U., 1973; m. Jane E. Fenlon, Jan. 30, 1981; children—Sarah Lynn, Melanie Anne. Project engr. Granger Engring., Inc., Cadillac, Mich., 1973-79; exec. v.p., dir. Chippewa Architects & Engrs., Inc., Kincheloe and St. Ignace, Mich., 1979-82; constrn. mgr. J.H. Granger and Assocs., Sault Ste. Marie, Mich., 1983—; cons. constrn. engring., environ. engring., civil engring., pollution control and solar energy. Registered profl. engr., Mich., Ky., Minn., Wis. Mem. Nat. Soc. Profl. Engrs., Mich. Soc. Profl. Engrs., ASCE (pres. N.W. Mich. chpt. 1980-82), Mich. Water Pollution Control Fedn., Mich. Soc. Civil Engrs., Nature Conservancy (dir. Mich. chpt.), Nat. Audubon Soc. Club: Kiwanis. Home: Route 2 Box 130 A Saint Ignace MI 49781 Office: Court St Sault Sainte Marie MI 49783

HAMPTON, RONALD KEITH, educator, science curriculum consultant; b. Houston, Mo., May 16, 1934; s. William Arthur and Mary Elizabeth (Houser) H.; m. Margaret Josephine Heriford, July 20, 1957; children—Kevin Keith, Ronda Rene. B.S., Samford U., 1956; M.A.T., Duke U., 1964. Cert. tchr., Mo. Tchr. sci. Licking Sch. Dist., Mo., 1956-68; tchr. sci., sci. coordinator Jennings Schs., Mo., 1968—; evaluation team mem. No. Central Coll. & U., 1974-85. Author: (with R. Crooks) Life Science Mastery Learning Curriculum, 1982. NSF fellow, 1959-70. Baptist. Avocations: outdoor recreation, fishing, hunting, camping, travel. Home: 1514 Sugargrove Ct Creve Coeur MO 63146

HAMRICH, ROBERT HERMAN, professional golfer, educator; b. Cleve., Oct. 8, 1928; s. Andrew and Mary (Gilch) H.; m. Dorothy Rose Hacker, Apr. 16, 1955; children—Robert, Deborah, Mark. Student Ohio State U., 1946-49, Okla. State U., 1969. Golf professional Fremont County Club (Ohio), 1955-58, Champaign County Club (Ill.), 1958-68, Mayfield County Club, Cleve., 1968-78, Nisseoquque County Club, L.I., N.Y., 1978-80; golf dir. Bob Hamrich Golf Schs., Cleve., 1981—. Contbr. articles to golf mags. Vice pres. Ill. Profl. Golf Assn., 1965-68; mem. exec. com. N. Ohio Profl. Golf Assn., 1970-77. Cert. master profl., Nat. Profl. Golf Assn., 1973; named Golf. Profl. of Yr., No. Ohio, 1974; Athletic Hall of Fame, Brush High Sch., Cleve., 1977. Mem. Profl. Golfers Assn. (v.p. sect.), Nat. Golf Found., Quarter Century Club (profl. golf assn.), Tournament Players Club, Western Golf Assn., Ohio State U. Varsity Club. Home: 2205 Halcyon Rd Cleveland OH 44122

HAMRICK, TERRY DANIEL, lawyer; b. Watseka, Ill., Apr. 27, 1950; s. Loren Herschel and Frieda Louise (Egolf) H. B.A., SUNY-Brockport, 1972; J.D. cum laude, Ind. U., 1980. Bar: Ill. 1981, Fla. 1982, U.S. Dist. Ct. (cen. dist.) Ill. 1982. With Peace Corps, 1972-74; assoc. Brock, Markwalder, Sunderland, Murphy, Spenn & Hamrick, Watseka, Ill., 1980-83, ptnr., 1983—. Bd. dirs. Iroquois Assn. Retarded Citizens, Watseka, 1983—. Mem. ABA, Ill. State Bar Assn., Iroquois County Bar Assn. (pres. 1984—), Fla. Bar. Lodge: Elks. Office: Brock Markwalder Sunderland Murphy Spenn & Hamrick PO Box 407 130 W Cherry St Watseka IL 60970

HANAWAY, DONALD JOHN, lawyer, state senator; b. Stevens Point, Wis., Dec. 25, 1933; s. John Leo and Agnes Marie (Flatley) H.; B.B.A., U. Wis., 1958, LL.B., 1961; m. JoAnn R. Gaskell, June 21, 1958; children—Patrick James, Mary Kathleen, Michael John, Maureen Megan. Bar: Wis. 1961. Asst. dist. atty. Brown County, Green Bay, Wis., 1963-64, spl. prosecutor, 1967-78; city atty. City of De Pere (Wis.), 1964-72, 76-79, mayor, 1972-74; mem. firm Condon, Hanaway & Wickert, Ltd., Green Bay, 1969-84; mem. firm Hanaway, Kuehne & Dietz, Green Bay, 1984—; mem. Wis. Senate, 1979—, asst. minority leader, 1981—. Active various local govtl., civic and parish coms. Served with U.S. Army, 1954-56. Mem. Wis. Bar Assn., Brown County Bar Assn., ABA, Wis. Acad. Trial Lawyers, Wis. Sch. Attys. Assn. (charter), De Pere C. of C. (exec. sec. 1964-69). Republican. Club: Optimist (charter) (De Pere). Office: PO Box 908 Green Bay WI 54305

HANCOCK, GEORGE LOUIS, JR., lawyer, army officer; b. Middletown, Ohio, June 8, 1953; s. George L. and Virginia (Ballard) H.; m. Dana R. Brennan, Sept. 2, 1978; 1 child, Ryan L. B.A., U. Ky., 1975; J.D., U. Toledo, 1978. Bar: Ohio 1979, U.S. Ct. Mil. Appeals 1979, U.S. Supreme Ct. 1982. Commd. capt. U.S. Army, 1979; trial def. counsel U.S. Army, Fort Knox, Ky., 1979-82, chief legal assistance officer, 1982-83, post judge advocate, Fort Detrick, Md., 1983—. Mem. Assn. Trial Lawyers Am. Democrat. Methodist.

HANCOCK, JAMES BEATY, interior designer; b. Hartford, Ky.; s. James Winfield Scott and Hettie Frances (Meadows) H.; B.A., Hardin-Simmons U., 1948, M.A., 1952. Head interior design dept. Thornton's, Abilene, Tex., 1945-54; interior designer The Halle Bros. Co., Cleve., 1954-55; v.p. Olympic Products, Cleve., 1955-56; mgr. interior designer Bell Drapery Shops of Ohio, Inc., Shaker Heights, 1957-78, v.p., 1979—; lectr. interior design, Abilene and Cleve.; works include 6 original murals Broadway Theater, Abilene, 1940, mural Skyline Outdoor Theatre, Abilene, 1950, cover designs for Isotopics mag., 1958-60. Served with AUS, 1942-46. Recipient 2d place award for oil painting West Tex. Expn., 1940, hon. mention, 1940. Mem. Abilene Mus. Fine Arts (charter). Home: 530 Sycamore Dr Cleveland OH 44132

HANCOCK, JOHN COULTER, telecommunications executive; b. Martinsville, Ind., Oct. 21, 1929; s. Floyd A. and Katherine (Coulter) H.; m. Betty Jane Holden, Feb. 6, 1949; children—Debbie, Dwight, Marilyn, Virginia. B.E.E., Purdue U., 1951, M.E.E., 1955, Ph.D., 1957. Engr., Naval Avionics Facility, Indpls., 1951-57; asst. prof. elec. engring. Purdue U., 1957-60, assoc. prof., 1960-63, prof., 1963-65, head Sch. Elec. Engring., 1965-72, dean Schs. Engring., 1972-84; exec. v.p., chief tech. officer United Telecommunications, Inc., Kansas City, Mo., 1984—; dir. Ctr. for Bus. Innovation, Kansas City, Mo., Hillenbrand Industries, Batesville, Ind., Ransburg Corp., Indpls., CTS Corp., Elkhart, Ind.; cons. NSF, 1984—. Author: An Introduction to the Principles of Communications Theory, 1961. Trustee, Midwest Research Inst., Kansas City, Mo. Fellow Am. Soc. Engring. Edn. (pres. 1983-84), IEEE, AAAS; mem. Nat. Acad. Engring., Sigma Xi, Eta Kappa Nu, Tau Beta Pi. Home: 803 W 48th St Apt 503 Kansas City MO 64112 Office: United Telecommunications Inc 2330 Johnson Dr Westwood KS 66205

HANCOCK, PATRICIA JEAN, body shop owner; b. Norfolk, Nebr., Oct. 18, 1945; d. John Joseph and Virginia Ruth (Simpson) Fagan, Jr.; m. Robert Dale Hancock, Mar. 1, 1965; 1 child, Jennifer Lynn. B.S. in Math., U. Nebr.-Lincoln, 1967, tchrs. cert., 1967, M.A. in Math., 1971. Tchr. math., Palmyra, Nebr., 1967-68; grad. asst. U. Nebr., Lincoln, 1968-69; tchr. math. Pound Jr. High, Lincoln, 1969-74; sec.-treas. Bob's Body Shop, Grand Island, Nebr. Bible sch. coordinator Trinity United Meth. Ch., 1983, 84, 85, mem. adminstrv. council ministries, 1984—; tchr. Soc. Collision Repair Specialists. Mem. Nebr. Auto Body Assn. (sec., newsletter editor, convention organizer 1981-83). Clubs: Riverside Golf (Grand Island) (treas., v.p. Ladies Golf Assn.). Avocations: golf; tennis; swimming; sewing; organ. Home: Route 1 Box 185 Cairo NE 68824 Office: Bob's Body Shop Inc 1800 W Lincoln Hwy Grand Island NE 68803

HAND, DIANE TELESCO, public relations executive; b. San Francisco, Oct. 4, 1946; d. Lee A. and Charlotte Umbreit Telesco; m. William Allen Hand, Jan. 19, 1968 (div. Aug. 1983). B.A., San Jose State U., 1967. Reporter, Santa Clara (Calif.) Jour., 1967-68, Seneca (S.C.) Jour., 1968-70; info. officer Va. Inst. Tech., Blacksburg, 1970-72, U.S. Dept. Agr., Washington, 1972-73; food editor The Times Mag., Army Times Pub. Co., Washington, 1973-76; communications specialist Dorn Communications, Mpls., 1976-82, account exec., 1982-83, account dir., 1983-84, v.p., 1984-85; account mgr. Fleishman-Hillard Inc., Kansas City, Mo.; cons. Va. Tech. Inst. Food Technologists Food Editors Conf., 1973-77. Mem. Nat. Fedn. Press Women (first place awards communications contest 1974, 75, 83), Pub. Relations Soc. Am., Press Women Minn. (founder, pres. 1977-79, Woman of Achievement 1982). Home: 13204 W 107th Ct Lenexa KS 66210 Office: One Crown Ctr 2400 Pershing Rd Kansas City MO 64108

HANDLER, ARLENE FRANCES, nurse; b. Chgo., Mar. 25, 1943; d. Hyman and Sophie (Twersky) Fridkin; m. Raymond Morton Handler, Dec. 7, 1962; children—Jonathan Alan, David Aaron, Deborah Lynn. Grad. Michael Reese Hosp. Sch. Nursing, Chgo., 1963; B.A. in Applied Behavioral Sci., Nat. Coll. Edn., 1981; B.S.N., U. Without Walls, Cin. R.N., Ill.; cert. sch. nurse, Ill. Staff nurse Michael Reese Psychiat. Hosp., Chgo., 1963-65; vol. nurse U.S. Air Force Hosp., Rantoul, Ill., 1965-67; staff nurse Lakeshore Psychiat. Hosp., Chgo., 1971; substitute sch. nurse Sch. Dist. 27, Northbrook, Ill., 1978—, Stevenson High Sch., Prairie View, Ill., 1982—, Hawthorne Sch., Vernon Hills, Ill., 1981—. Chmn. health and safety Sch. Dist. 27 PTA, Northbrook, 1974-78; co-chairperson screening com. Northbrook Caucus, 1976-78; mem., chairperson operation smoke detector Northbrook Safety Commn., 1977—; pres. Sch. Dist. 27 Council PTAs, Northbrook, 1978-80; v.p.-sch. Congregation Beth Shalom, Northbrook, 1981-83; vice chmn., chmn. by-laws Northbrook Plan Commn., 1982—. Co-honoree State of Israel Bonds, 1983. Mem. Michael Reese Nurses' Alumnae Assn., LWV. Home: 4022 Rutgers Ln Northbrook IL 60062

HANDLER, PAUL, physics educator; b. Newark, Apr. 24, 1929; s. Jacob and Yetta (Spector) H.; m. Ellen Oppenheimer; children—Ira, Harry, Lilly. M.S., U. Chgo., 1951, Ph.D., 1954. Mem. faculty U. Ill., Urbana, 1954—, assoc. prof. physics, 1960-64, prof., 1964—; cons. Gen. Motors, Warren, Mich., 1965-70; cons. long range weather. Contbr. articles to profl. jours. Mem. Am. Meteorol. Soc. Home: 706 W Oregon St Urbana IL 61801 Office: Dept Physics U Ill Urbana IL 61801

HANDLER, RAYMOND MORTON, dermatologist, educator; b. Chgo., Oct. 23, 1937; s. William and Pearl (Greenband) H.; m. Arlene Frances Fridkin, Dec. 8, 1962; children—Jonathan, David, Deborah. B.S. in Medicine, U. Ill.-Chgo., 1959, M.D., 1961. Diplomate Am. Bd. Dermatology. Intern Michael Reese Hosp., Chgo., 1961-62; resident in dermatology U. Ill. Hosp., Chgo., 1962-65; pvt. practice medicine specializing in dermatology, Des Plaines, Ill., 1967—; clin. instr. dermatology U. Ill., Chgo., 1967-72, clin. asst. prof., 1972-77, clin. assoc. prof. dermatology, 1977—; chmn. sect. dermatology Luth. Gen. Hosp., Park Ridge, Ill., 1981—. Contbr. articles to profl. jours. Mem. Bd. Edn., Sch. Dist. 27, Northbrook, Ill., 1977—, pres. 1983—, chmn. citizen's adv. council, 1974-77. Served to capt. USAF, 1965-67. Recipient State of Israel Bonds honor award Congregation Beth Shalom, 1982. Fellow Am. Acad. Dermatology, Acad. Psychosomatic Medicine; mem. Chgo. Detmatol. Soc., Dermatology Found., others. Home: 4022 Rutgers Ln Northbrook IL 60062 Office: 8780 Golf Rd Des Plaines IL 60016

HANDWERKER, A. M., transportation executive; b. Chgo., Mar. 15, 1928; s. Fred and Celia H.; m. Betty Jean Ellingson, Nov. 28, 1948; children—Michael L., Sharon J. Behtash, Nancy G. Karam, James A. B.S. in Indsl. Engring., Ill. Inst. Tech., 1950. With Chgo. & North Western Transp. Co., Chgo., 1950—, v.p. rates and divs., 1980-85, v.p. corp. analysis, 1985—. Author: (with others) A Guide to Railroad Cost Analysis, 1964. Chgo. Jaycees scholar Ill. Inst. Tech., 1946. Mem. Ops. Research Soc. Am., Inst. Mgmt. Sci., Soc. for Advancement Mgmt., Am. Ry. Engring. Assn., Cost Analysis Orgn., Am. Statis. Assn., Transp. Research Forum, Alpha Pi Mu. Republican. Methodist. Club: Union League (sr. counselor Civic and Arts Found. 1984—) (Chgo.). Avocations: tennis; hunting; traveling. Office: Chicago & North Western Transp Co One North Western Ctr 165 N Canal St Chicago IL 60606

HANEBORG, LARRY ROGER, beer distribution company executive, mechanical engineer; b. Denver, Sept. 16, 1944; s. Harold L. and Doris (Davidson) H.; m. Janice Higley, Aug. 28, 1965; children—Mark, Scott, Tad. B.S.M.E., Colo. State U., 1966. Indsl. engr., CF & I Steel Corp., Pueblo, Colo., 1966-69, asst. supt. mech. shops, 1969-77; pres. Coors Distbg., North Platte, Nebr., 1977—; Founder Youth basketball program, 1977, youth football program, 1980; pres. North Platte Little League, 1983-84; v.p. North Platte Indsl. Corp., 1977—; bd. dirs. Rough Riders Rodeo Assn., North Platte, 1982—, pres., 1985—. Recipient Life Mem. award Nebr. PTA, 1983; named Outstanding mem. Assn. Iron and Steel Engrs., 1975, Outstanding Coll. Supporter, Mid-Plains Coll., 1983. Mem. Negr. Beer Wholesalers Assn., Nat. Beer Wholesalers Assn., Ducks Unltd. (chpt. pres. 1979—), Nebr. Wildlife Protectors Assn. (bd. dirs. 1982—). Republican. Methodist. Lodges: Rotary (bd. dirs. 1983-85), Elks. Avocations: hunting, snow skiing, fishing, golf, basketball. Office: Coors Distbg North Platte 642 N Willow St North Platte NE 69101

HANENSON, IRWIN B., physician, educator; b. N.Y.C., Apr. 7, 1922; s. Millard and Pearl Beatrice (Lipskar) H.; m. Judith Adelson, June 12, 1949. B.S., NYU, 1942, M.D., 1946. Intern U.S. Naval Hosp., St. Albans, N.Y., 1946-47; resident VA Hosp., Bronx, N.Y., 1949-51; asst. prof. U. Cin. Med. Ctr., 1958-66, assoc. prof., 1967-74, prof. dept. pathology and medicine, 1974—, dir. clin. toxicology, 1971—, assoc. dir. lab. medicine, 1976-81, dir. quality assurance, 1980-84, asst. dean clin. and housestaff affairs, 1981-84. Author: Cardiac Diagnosis and Treatment, 1970. Editor: Quick Reference to Clinical Toxicology, 1980. Served to lt. (j.g.) USN, 1947-49, ETO. Mem. Am. Coll. Toxicology, Acad. Clin. Lab. Physicians and Scientists, Am. Fedn. Clin. Research, Soc. Exptl. Biology and Medicine, Am. Soc. Pharmacology and Exptl. Therapeutics, AAAS, Central Soc. Clin. Research, Phi Beta Kappa, Sigma Xi, Beta Lambda Sigma, Alpha Omega Alpha. Office: U Cin Med Ctr 231 Bethesda Ave Cincinnati OH 45267

HANGER, RICHARD B., banker; b. Detroit, Oct. 31, 1928; s. Orlando B. Hanger and Adelaide (Bush) Van Nice; m. Dorothy Greene, June 12, 1949; children—David, Melissa. Ins. broker Am. United Life and Midwest Insurors, Topeka, Kans., 1953-83; founder, dir., sr. v.p. Highland Park Bank and Trust, Topeka, 1965-82; pres. Highland Park Developers, Inc., Topeka, 1965—; founder, dir. North Plaza State Bank, Topeka, 1972-82; Trustee Doane Coll., Crete Nebr., 1968-72, Kans. Pub. Employees Retirement System, Topeka, 1969-77; mem. Econ. Adv. Council, Shawnee County, Topeka, 1984—; county commr. Shawnee County, 1961-69; bd. dirs. Shawnee County Family Service and Guidance Ctr., Topeka, 1980-83; commr. Kans. Fish and Game Commn., Pratt, Kans., 1981—. Mem. Nat. Wild Turkey Fedn., Ducks Unltd. Democrat. Congregationalist. Avocations: sports, developing natural habitat, sailing, scuba diving, flying. Home: 3575 Shoreline Dr Topeka KS 66605

HANGGI, GERALD ALBERT, JR., accountant; b. St Paul, May 28, 1944; s. Gerald Anthony and Bernice Susan (Leitner) H.; m. Sharyn Ann, Aug. 11, 1965; children—Gerald, Bradley. Ptnr., McGladrey Hendrickson & Pullen, St. Paul, 1964—. Mem. Minn. Soc. C.P.A.s, Am. Inst. C.P.A.s. Republican. Roman Catholic. Clubs: Minnesota (bd. govs. 1983—) (St. Paul); Dellwood Hills Golf. Home: 5 Eldorado Dr Dellwood MN 55110 Office: McGlandy Hendrickson Co 445 Minnesota St 1800 Town Sq Saint Paul MN 55101

HANIFAN, JAMES MARTIN, coach professional football team; b. Compton, Calif., Sept. 21, 1933; s. James and Bridget (O'Gorman) H.; B.A., U. Calif., Berkeley; m. Mariana Osuna, Dec. 26, 1958; children—Kathleen Marie, James Peter. Asst. football coach San Diego State U., 1972; asst. coach St. Louis Football Cardinals, 1973-78, head football coach, 1980—; asst. head coach San Diego Chargers, 1979. Served with U.S. Army, 1956-58. Named Asst. Football Coach of Yr., NFL, 1977. Republican. Roman Catholic. Office: 200 Stadium Plaza Saint Louis MO 63102

HANKET, MARK JOHN, lawyer; b. Cleve., Jan. 28, 1943; s. Laddie W. and Florence J. (Kubat) H.; m. Carole A. Dalpiaz, Sept. 14, 1968; children—Gregory, Jennifer, Sarah. A.B. magna cum laude, John Carroll U., 1965; J.D. cum laude, Ohio State U., 1968; M.B.A., Xavier U., 1977. Bar: Ohio 1968. Atty. Chemed Corp., Cin., 1973-77, asst. sec., 1977-82, sec., 1982-84, v.p., sec., 1984—. Com. chmn. Troop 850, Boy Scouts Am., 1984—. Served to capt. U.S. Army, 1968-73. Decorated Meritorious Service medal, Army Commendation medal with oak leaf cluster. Mem. ABA, Ohio Bar Assn. Office: Chemed Corp 1200 DuBois Tower Cincinnati OH 45202

HANKINS, EDWARD RAY, educational administrator; b. Burden, Kans., Mar. 19, 1933; s. Daniel Ray and Ruth Ellen (Woodruf) H.; m. Rose Marie Nichols, June 26, 1955; children—Kammi Marie, Ken Alan. B.S., Pitts. State U., 1958, M.S., 1974. Asst. prin. Abilene High Sch. (Kans.), 1974-77; spl. needs specialist State Dept. Edn., Topeka, Kans., 1977-79, accreditation specialist, 1979-81, research coordinating Unit, 1981-82, vocational edn. coordinator, 1982-84, edn. program specialist, 1984—. Served to cpl. U.S. Army, 1953-55. Named Outstanding Young Educator Jr. C. of C., 1967. Mem. Am. Vocat. Assn., Kans. Vocational Assn., Kans Council Vocational Adminstrn., Phi Delta Kappa. Methodist. Avocations: Tennis, Tennis instructing.

HANKINS, SWANETTA LYNN, nurse; b. Sycamore, Ill., Mar. 18, 1955; d. Oral Otto and Jean (Jacobs) Dodson; m. Eugene Franklin Hankins, June 12, 1971; children—Lena Kay, Katrina Gene, Twopony Joshua. L.P.N., Capital Area Sch. Practical Nursing, 1981. Lic. practical nurse St. John's Hosp., Springfield, Ill., 1981-84, Sheltered Village, Genoa, Ill., 1984—. Baptist.

HANKIS, ROY ALLEN, interior designer; b. Greenville, Mich., May 24, 1943; s. John LeRoy and Nila A. (Taylor) H.; interior design diploma Kendall Sch. Design, 1964; student Cranbrook Acad. Art, 1971. Dir. design, contract design firms, Grand Rapids and Detroit, Mich., 1964-73; owner, designer Roy Allen Hankis Interiors, Troy, Mich., 1974—; instr. interior design Henry Ford Community Coll., Dearborn, Mich., 1981—; trustee JONIRO Investment Co., Southfield, Mich., 1981—. Participating designer Detroit Symphony ASID Showhouse, Bloomfield Hills, Mich., 1985; designer Birmingham Jr. League-Mich. Design Ctr. Celebrity Room for Mich.'s first lady, 1985. Am. Soc. Interior Designers (dir. Mich. chpt. 1974), Christian Bus. Men's Com. Detroit. Baptist. Club: Rotary. Patentee. Home and Office: 5365 Breeze Hill Pl Troy MI 48098

HANKISON, JOHN ELLSWORTH, former transportation executive; b. Toledo, Ohio, Sept. 1, 1916; s. Otto Leroy and Lucy Sophia (Gabel) H.; m. Virginia Anastacia Werner, Apr. 11, 1942. Student, Ohio State U.; J.D., U. Toledo. Pres., chmn. bd. Midwest Haulers, Toledo, 1955-81; retired; dir. Ohio Citizens Bank. Bd. dirs. Toledo Humane Soc., 1965—. Republican. Roman Catholic. Club: Heather Downs Country (Toledo) (dir., sec., chmn. bd. 1955—). Avocations: boating; fly fishing; photography.

HANNA, JACK, zoo administrator; b. Knoxville, Tenn., Jan. 2, 1947; m. Suzanne Egli; children—Kathaleen, Suzanne, Julie. B.A. in bus., Muskingum Coll., 1969; Postgrad. U. Tenn., 1970; D.Sc. (hon.), Otterbein Coll., 1983. Curator Knoxville Zoo, Tenn., 1971-72; dir. Central Fla. Zoo, Sanford, 1973-75; v.p. Stan Brock Wilderness Adventureland, Fla., 1975-78; dir. Columbus Zoo, Powell, Ohio, 1978—. Chmn. Central Ohio chpt. Easter Seals, 1984—; pres. Leukemia Soc., 1984—; trustee Kiski Prep. Sch. Named Outstanding Young Citizen, Central Ohio Jaycees, 1979-80; recipient Disting. Service award Central Ohio Jaycees, 1980, Disting. Service award Muskingum Coll., 1981. Fellow Explorers Club; mem. Appalachian Zool. Soc. (hon. bd. dirs.), Am. Assn. Zool. Parks. Home: 8900 Turin Hill Ct N Dublin OH 43017 Office: Columbus Zool Gardens 9990 Riverside Dr PO Box 400 Powell OH 43065 0400

HANNA, RAYMOND WESLEY, osteopathic physician and surgeon; b. Kansas City, Mo., June 21, 1915; s. Raymond J. and Clara E. (Spence) H.; m. Peggy Jane Guffey, July 31, 1951; children—Ray, Michael, Marc, James, Peggy Jo. A.B., U. Kans., 1949; M.Sc., Ohio Christian U., 1954; D.O., U. Health Sci., Kansas City, Mo., 1955. Diplomate Am. Bd. Gen. Practice, 1970. Corp. physician Spear Constrn. Co., Independence, Mo., 1963—; plant physician Ford Motor Co., Claycomo, Mo., 1974-78; pres. Hanna Med. Corp., Independence, 1975—; dir. Hanna Corp., Independence; cons. HEW, 1960-75; dep. dir. Kansas City Med. Health Council, 1955-59; med. adv. Wash. State Disaster Medicine Com., 1964-66; cons. USPHS, 1960-70; founder gen. practice dept. Lakeside Hosp., Kansas City, 1962, chmn., 1963-70; v.p. Greater Kansas City Area Med. Council, 1978-79. Contbr. articles to med. jours. Mem. Raytown Sch. Bd., Mo., 1969-78; founder, mem. Cooperating Suburban Sch. Dist., Raytown, 1970; mem. Mo. State Higher Edn. Com., 1970-80; past-vice-chair dist. com. Boy Scouts Am.; mem. Jackson County Charter Transition Commn., Mo., 1971-72; mem. lay bd. Blue Ridge Methodist Ch.; chair Jackson County Assn. CD Com., 1955-58; vice-chair Mo. Gov.'s Med. CD Adv. Com., 1960-66; mem. Mo. Conservation of Natural Resources Com., 1968; bd. dirs. Drug Abuse Info. Ctr. Served to 1st lt. U.S. Army, 1941-46; PTO; to sr. surgeon USPHS, 1980. Recipient Pfizer award of Merit, U.S. CD Council, 1960; cited USPHS, 1967, Pres. U.S., 1968; Chancellor's medal U. Mo.-Kansas City, 1970. Fellow Am. Coll. Osteo. Gen. Practice, Am. Occupational Med. Assn.; mem. Jackson County Osteo. Med. Assn. (pres. 1978-79), Mo. Osteo. Assn., Am. Osteo. Assn. (chair com. disaster med. care 1960-68), Mo. State Osteo. Assn. (chair CD com. 1956-60), Great Plains Occupational Med. Assn. (pres. 1976-77), Res. Officers Assn., Commd. Officers Assn. USPHS. Republican. Lodges: Lions (pres. 1965) (Raytown); Masons (jr. warden 1948-49), Shriners (med. dir. 1975—). Avocations: golf; fly fishing; oil painting. Home: 207 Birch St Lee's Summit MO 64063 Office: Hanna Med Corp 10927 E 40 Hwy Independence MO 64055

HANNA, VICKI LYNNE, geologist, consultant; b. Noel, Mo., Jan. 26, 1953; d. John Paul and Shirley Jean (Goss) H. B.S., Pan-Am. U., 1975; student Bowling Green State U., 1980-81. Geologist, Mo. Dept. Natural Resources, Rolla, Mo., 1978-79; geologic asst. Weller & Bates, Edinburg, Tex., 1974-76, Bates & Rodgers, 1974-76; geology cons., Pineville, Mo., 1981—. Mem. Am. Assn. Petroleum Geologists, Soc. Econ. Paleontologists and Mineralogists, Assn. Women Geoscientists. Baha'i. Home: Box N Pineville MO 64856

HANNAGAN, ANGELA MARIE, educator; b. St. Louis, Dec. 21, 1917; d. Edward Michael and Helen A. (Piechowski) H.; B.A., Fontbonne Coll., 1940; postgrad. Northwestern U., 1942-43, Ind. U. N.W., summers 1969, 70, 71. Dir. public relations Fontbonne Coll., 1940-41; with Famour-Barr Co., 1941-42, Employers Mut. Ins. Co., 1942; tchr. English, East Lansing (Mich.) High Sch., 1943-44; tchr. English, Lew Wallace High Sch., Gary, Ind., 1944—, chmn. English dept., 1965—. Recipient Viola Briley award local 4 Am. Fedn. Tchrs., 1974; Outstanding Tchr. of Yr. award Lew Wallace High Sch., 1983. Mem. Nat. Council Tchrs. English (dir.), Ind. Council Tchrs. English (exec. bd. 1967—; E. H. Kemper McComb award 1981), Gary English Council (pres. 1960-61), Am. Fedn. Tchrs. (exec. bd. local 4, 1963—), Internat. Platform Assn., Fontbonne Coll. Alumnae Assn. (sec. 1940-42). Roman Catholic. Home: 430 S Grand Blvd Apt 415 Gary IN 46403 Office: Lew Wallace High Sch 415 W 45th Ave Gary IN 46408

HANNAH, JAMES BLAIN, lawyer; b. Mpls., Oct. 26, 1921; s. Hewitt Blain and Edna (Matre) H.; m. Rosemary Ethelyn Rathbun, Dec. 24, 1942; children—Holly Hannah Lewis, Duncan Rathbun. B.S. cum laude, Harvard U., 1942, J.D., 1948. Bar: Minn. 1948, U.S. Dist. Ct. Minn. 1948. Assoc. Synder, Gale, Hoke, Richards & Janes, Mpls., 1948-50; assoc. Mackall, Crounse & Moore, Mpls., 1950-59, ptnr., 1959—; dir. Day Devel. Co., Mpls., Nat. Realty Co., Mpls., Win Stephens Cos., Inc., Mpls. Chmn., campaign dir. March of Dimes, Nat. Found. Infantile Paralysis, Mpls., 1953-54; legal advisor, bd. dirs. Planned Parenthood of Minn., 1964-71; bd. dirs. Legal Aid Soc., Mpls., 1970-74, Citizens Com. on Pub. Edn., Mpls. Served to lt. USNR, 1942-46, PTO. Mem. Hennepin County Bar Assn., ABA, Minn. State Bar Assn., Am. Law Inst., Mpls. C. of C. (chmn. aviation com. 1957, Hundred Leaders of Tomorrow award 1953), Am. Legion. Unitarian. Clubs: Mpls., Minikahda, 5:55, Harvard (Mpls.) (pres. 1953). Avocations: skiing; sailing; tennis. Home: 7 E St Albans Rd Hopkins MN 55343 Office: Mackall Crounse & Moore 1600 TCF Tower Minneapolis MN 55402

HANNIBAL, GARY EUGENE, state senator, building contractor; b. Omaha, May 5, 1943; s. Russell L. and Lois (Campbell) H.; m. Mary Lou Hawk, 1963; children—Wendy, Amy, Sandy, Julie. Grad. U. Nebr.-Omaha, 1970. Real estate broker, Omaha, 1972—; pres. Hannibal Constrn., Inc., 1967—; mem. Nebr. Senate, 1983—. Pres., bd. dirs. South-S.W. YMCA. Mem. Nat. Assn. Home Builders, Nebr. Assn. Home Builders (dir.), Met. Omaha Builders Assn. (dir.), Omaha C. of C., Lambda Chi Alpha. Republican. Office: Dist 4 State Capitol Bldg Lincoln NE 68509

HANNIG, VIRGIL LEROY, healthcare executive; b Breese, Ill., Dec. 22, 1943; s. Paulie Frank and Gladys Marie (Kapp) H.; m. Virginia Frances Born, May 29, 1965; children—Laura, Tim. B.S., So. Ill. U. C.P.A., Ill. Controller, asst. treas. So. Ill. Health Services, Carbondale, 1972-75; controller Providence Hosp., Cin., 1975, Springfield Community Hosp., Ill., 1975-77; v.p. fin. St. Mary's Hosp., Kankakee, Ill., 1977-83; v.p. fin. HealthCor, Kankakee, 1983-84, sr. v.p., 1985—; pres. VentureCor, Inc., Kankakee, 1985—; dir. Kankakee County Catholic Credit Union. Bd. dirs. Kankakee chpt. ARC. Served with USAR, 1962-65. Fellow Healthcare Fin. Mgmt. Assn. (Robert J. McMahon award 1981, Robert H. Reeves award 1981, William G. Follmer award 1977; mem. Am. Coll. Hosp. Adminstrs., Am. Inst. C.P.A.s, Ill. Soc. C.P.A.s, Nat. Assn. Accts. Lodges: Rotary, Elks. Avocations: hunting, fishing, photography. Home: 1068 S Wildwood St Kankakee IL 60901

HANNON, NORMAN LESLIE, industrial management consultant; b. Ballymoney, No. Ireland, Dec. 31, 1923; came to U.S., 1963, naturalized, 1972; s. Arthur Gordon and Hilda Catherine Stewart-Moore (Denny) H.; B.S. in M.E., Queen's U., Belfast, No. Ireland, 1950; m. Patricia Ann Smale, June 2, 1951; children—Philip Leslie, Sarah-Louise, Michael John (dec.). Chief estimator British Tabulating Machines, No. Ireland, 1950-51; planning officer Hollerith Machines, South Africa, 1951-52; tech. sales engr. Babcock & Wilcox, South Africa, 1952-54; mgmt. cons. P.E. Cons. Group, London, 1954-63; supt. indsl. engring., adminstrn. mgr. Plastics and Fibers divs. Celanese Corp. U.S., Can., 1963-68; mgr. corp. devel. Forward Industries div. Will Ross, Inc., Kansas City, 1968-69; mgmt. cons. Richard Muther & Assos., Kansas City, Mo., 1969-72; dir. mgmt. services MAC Tools, Washington Ct. House, Ohio, 1972-73; dir. ops., mgr. adminstrn. and planning Gustin-Bacon div. Aeroquip Corp., Lawrence, Kans., 1973-77; v.p. Richard Muther & Assocs. Inc., Kansas City, Mo., 1977-83; sr. v.p., vice chmn. bd. Richard Muther & Assocs., Inc., 1983—. Served with RAF, 1942-46. Chartered Engr., U.K., Australia, South Africa, Can.; cert. mgmt. cons. Mem. Instn. Mech. Engrs. (U.K.), Inst. Prodn. Engrs. (U.K.), Inst. Mgmt. Cons. Home: 1219 W 27th St Lawrence KS 66046 Office: Richard Muther & Assos Inc 6155 Oak St Kansas City MO 64113

HANNON, STEVEN KEVIN, hospital administrator; b. Mpls., Jan. 10, 1951; s. Stanley Edward and Delores (O'Reilly) H.; m. Iris Perlene Custead, Feb. 20, 1982; 1 child, Timothy. B.A. in Hosp. and Bus. Adminstrn., Concordia Coll., 1973, B.A. in History and Polit. Sci., 1973; M.H.A., U. Minn., 1979. Resident Fairview Hosp., Mpls., 1973-74; cons. Hamilton Assocs., Mpls., 1974-77; assoc. adminstr. Huron Regional Med. Ctr., S.D., 1979-80; adminstr. Superior Meml. Hosp., Wis., 1980—; v.p. ops. Hosp. Mgmt. Profls. Mem. Am. Hosp. Assn., Am. Coll. Hosp. Adminstrs., Wis. Hosp. Assn., Hosp. Fin. Mgmt. Assn., Superior C. of C. Avocations: skiing; racquetball; hunting; fishing; running. Home: RR1 Box 177D Foxboro WI 54880 Office: Superior Meml Hosp 3500 Tower Ave Superior WI 54880

HANON, LILLIE EMMA, printing specialties company executive; b. Columbus, Ohio, May 28, 1916; d. Timothy and Martha E. (Menzel) Lehmann; m. Lowell Robert Hanon, Aug. 22, 1937 (dec. Jan. 1982); children—Lowell Robert, Kathleen Martha, Bruce Paul. B.S., U. Chgo., 1937. Cataloguer, Swift & Co., Chgo., 1937-38; librarian Enoch Pratt Free Library, Balt., 1938-41; office mgr. K & H Spltys. Co., Detroit, 1954-74, sec. corp., 1975—, dir., 1965—; librarian Detroit Pub. Library, 1941-42; dir. purchasing fiction Enoch Pratt Free Library, Balt., 1939-41, student trainee, 1938-39. Author: Vignettes of Europe and America, 1959; For Anybody's You, 1977. Mem. Phi Beta Kappa. Mem. United Ch. of Christ. Office: K & H Specialties Co 4520 W Warren St Detroit MI 48210

HANRAHAN, ROBERT PHILIP, township official; b. Chgo., Nov. 9, 1932; s. Robert Michael and Margaret Estelle (Connolly) H.; m. Theresa A. Ieraci, Nov. 25, 1954; 6 children. B.S., U. Notre Dame, 1955, M.A., 1957. Cert. Ill. Assessing Ofcl. Faculty U. Notre Dame, South Bend, Ind., 1955-57; tchr. Niles West High Sch., Skokie, Ill., 1962-83; Realtor Kruger Realtors, Skokie, 1962-77; assessor Niles Twp. (Ill.), 1977—. Chairperson Human Relations Commn. of Morton Grove (Ill.); mem. Morton Grove Traffic and Safety Commn. Named Outstanding Citizen of Yr., Morton Grove Youth Commn., 1979. Mem. Cook County Twp. Assessor's Assn. (bd. dirs.), Twp. Ofcls. Ill., Internat. Assn. Assessing Officers (presenter paper nat. conv. 1985), Nat. Monogram Club. Home: 8233 N Austin Ave Morton Grove IL 60053 Office: Niles Twp Assessor's Office 5255 Main St Skokie IL 60076

HANRATTY, THOMAS JOSEPH, chemical engineering educator; b. Phila., Nov. 9, 1926; s. John Joseph and Elizabeth Marie (O'Connor) H.; m. Joan Louise Hertel, Aug. 25, 1957; children—John, Vincent, Maria, Michael, Peter. B.Chem. Engring., Villanova U., 1947, Ph.D. (hon.), 1979; M.S., Ohio State U., 1950; Ph.D., Princeton U., 1953. With Fischer and Porter Co., Hatboro, Pa., 1947-48, Battelle Meml. Inst., Columbus, Ohio, 1948-50; engr. Rohm & Haas, Phila., summer 1951, Shell Devel. Co., Emeryville, Calif., summer 1954; asst. prof. chem. engring. U. Ill., Urbana, 1953-58, assoc. prof. chem. engring., 1958-64, prof. chem. engring., 1963—; vis. assoc. prof. Brown U., Providence, 1962-63; mem. U.S. Nat. Com. on Theoretical and Applied Mechanics; Shell disting. prof., 1981. Contbr. articles to profl. jours. Recipient Allan P. Colburn award, 1957; Disting. Engring. Alumnus award Ohio State U., 1984. Fellow Am. Acad. Mechanics, Am. Phys. Soc.; mem. Am. Soc. Engring. Edn. (Curtis W. McGraw award 1963, sr. research award 1979), Am. Inst. Chem. Engrs. (William H. Walker award 1964, Profl. Progress award 1967), Am. Chem. Soc. Roman Catholic. Club: Serra Internat. Home: 1019 W Charles St Champaign IL 61820 Office: 205 Roger Adams Lab U Ill 1209 W California Urbana IL 61801

HANSELL, EDGAR FRANK, lawyer; b. Leon, Iowa, Oct. 12, 1937; s. Edgar Noble and Celestia Delphine (Skinner) H.; A.A., Graceland Coll., 1957; B.B.A., U. Iowa, 1959, J.D., 1961; m. Phyllis Wray Silvey, June 24, 1961; children—John Joseph, Jordan Burke. Bar: Iowa 1961. Mem. firm Nyemaster, Goode, McLaughlin, Emery & O'Brien, P.C., Des Moines, 1964—, partner, 1968—; dir. Britt Tech. Corp. Bd. dirs. Des Moines Child Guidance Center, 1972-78, 81—, pres., 1977-78; bd. dirs. Child Guidance Found., 1983—; trustee Iowa Law Sch. Found., 1975—, pres., 1983—; bd. dirs. Des Moines Community Playhouse, Inc., 1982—. Served with USAF, 1961-64. Mem. Iowa Bar Assn. (pres. young lawyers sect. 1971-72, gov., 1971-72, 85—, mem. grievance commn. 1973-78, recipient Merit award young lawyers sect. 1977, chmn. corp. and bus. law com. 1979-85), ABA, Polk County Bar Assn. Mem. editorial adv. bd. Jour. Corp. Law, 1977—. Home: 4001 John Lynde Rd Des Moines IA 50312 Office: Nyemaster Goode McLaughlin Emery O'Brien Hubbell Bldg Des Moines IA 50309

HANSEN, BARBARA CALEEN, physiologist, psycholgist, university dean and official; b. Boston, Nov. 24, 1941; d. Reynold Lawrence and Dorothy (Richardson) Caleen; m. Kenneth Dale Hansen, Oct. 8, 1976; 1 child, David Scott. B.S., UCLA, 1964, M.S., 1965; Ph.D., U. Wash., 1971. Predoctoral fellow U. Pa. Inst. Neurosci., Phila., 1966-68; asst. and assoc. prof. U. Wash., Seattle, 1971-76; prof., assoc. dean U. Mich., Ann Arbor, 1977-82; assoc. v.p. research, grad. dean So. Ill. U., Carbondale, 1982—; mem. adv. com. to dir. NIH, Washington, 1979-83; mem. joint health policy com. Assn. Am. Univs., Nat. Assn. State Univs. and Land Grant Colls., Am. Council Edn., Washington, 1982—; mem. nutrition study sect. NIH, Washington, 1979—. Editor: Controversies in Obesity, 1983; Contbr. articles to profl. jours. chpt. to book. Mem. adv. com. Am. Bur. for Med. Advancement of China, N.Y.C., 1982—, Robert Wood Johnson Found., Princeton, N.J., 1982—. Fellow Am. Acad. Nursing; mem. Nat. Acad. Scis. Inst. Med., N.Am. Assn. Study Obesity (pres. 1984—), Am. Physiol. Soc., Am. Inst. Nutrition, Am. Soc. Clin. Nutrition, Phi Beta Kappa (Arthur Patch McKinley scholar 1964). Republican. Presbyterian. Home: 30 Meadowood Ln Carbondale IL 62901 Office: So Ill Univ Grad Sch Carbondale IL 62901

HANSEN, CARL R., management consultant, b. Chgo., May 2, 1926; s. Carl M. and Anna C. (Roge) H.; m. Christia Marie Loeser, Dec. 31, 1952; 1 son, Lothar. M.B.A., U. Chgo., 1954. Dir. market research Kitchens of Sara Lee, Deerfield, Ill.; dir. market research Earle Ludgin & Co., Chgo.; service v.p. Market Research Corp. Am., 1956-67; pres. Chgo. Assoc. Inc., 1967—. Chmn. Ill. adv. council SBA, 1973-74; mem. exec. com. Ill. Gov.'s Adv. Council, 1969-72; resident officer U.S. High Commn. Germany, 1949-52; vice chmn. Republican Central Com. Cook County; chmn. Young Rep. Orgn. Cook County, 1957-58, 12th Congl. Dist. Rep. Orgn., 1971-74, 78-82, Suburban Rep. Orgn., 1974-78, 82—; del. Rep. Nat. Conv., 1968, 84; chmn. Legis. Dist. Ill., 1964—; del. Rep. State Conv., 1962-84; Elk Grove Twp. Rep. committeeman, 1962—; pres. John Ericsson Rep. League Ill., 1975-76; Rep. presdl. elector Ill., 1972; mem. Cook County Bd. Commrs., 1970, 74—, Served to 1st lt. AUS, 1944-48, maj. Res. Mem. Am. Mktg. Assn., Am. Statis. Assn., Res. Officers Assn., Chgo. Hist. Soc., Am. Scandanavian Found., Am. Legion. Clubs: Danish, Norwegian, Swedish (Chgo.). Lodges: Lions, Masons, Shriners. Home: 110 S Edward St Mount Prospect IL 60056 Office: 109 N Dearborn Chicago IL 60602

HANSEN, CARL ROBERT, museum director; b. Chgo., Apr. 16, 1950; s. Robert Frank and Evelyn A. (Smith) H.; m. Arletta J. Reichard, Dec. 27, 1970; children—Bjorn, Kyle, Anne. B.A. with sr. acad. honors, Luther Coll., Decorah, Iowa, 1972; M.A., Mich. State U., 1980. Vol. Norwegian-Am. Mus., Decorah, 1970-72; dir. Frankenmuth Hist. Mus., Mich., 1972—; v.p. Midwest Mus. Conf., St. Louis, 1983-85. Contbr. articles to profl. publs. Mem. Saginaw County Hist. Dist. Commn., Mich., 1974-80; bd. dirs. Frankenmuth United Fund, 1984-85; speaker Hist. Soc. Mich., Ann Arbor, 1976-80. Mem. Mich. Mus. Assn. (pres. 1983-85), Am. Assn. Mus. (accreditation mem. 1982-85), Am. Assn. for State and Local History (program com. 1982-83), Frankenmuth Jaycees (treas. 1984-85). Lutheran. Avocations: cross country skiing, reading, wood working. Home: 9085 Lange Rd Birch Run MI 48415 Office: Frankenmuth Hist Museum 613 S Main St Frankenmuth MI 48734

HANSEN, DAVID WEARE, optometrist; b. Maryville, Mo., Apr. 11, 1945; s. Lester Weare and Gretchen (Hosman) H.; m. Linda Jean Kubina, July 24, 1971; children—John David, Stephanie Jean. B.S., U. Iowa, 1967; B.S. in Visual Sci., Ill. Coll. Optometry, 1969, O.D., 1971. Lic. optometrist, Iowa. Gen. practice optometry, Des Moines, 1971—; contact lens cons. CIBA Vision Care, Atlanta, 1984—; clin. contact lens researcher Bausch & Lomb, Wesley Jessen, Alcon, Syntex, Precision Cosmet, Vision Ease; also others. Contbr. articles to medical jours. Active Grace Lutheran Ch., Iowa Assn. of Children with Learning Disabilities, Des Moines Civic Ctr.; bd. dirs. Des Moines Ctr. Sci. and Industry, 1981—, pres., 1984—; chmn. exhibits com. Sci. Ctr. 1982—, mem. action council 1974—. Fellow Am. Acad. Optometry (pres. Edn. Commn. 1984—), Coll. Optometrists in Vision Devel.; mem. Am. Optometric Assn., Iowa Optometric Assn., Mid-Iowa Optometric Soc., Central Iowa Devel. Vision Group. Republican. Avocations: photography; swimming. Home: 3001 Sylvania Dr West Des Moines IA 50265 Office: Optometric Assocs of Des Moines 2182 82nd St Des Moines IA 50322

HANSEN, DONALD, optometrist; b. Davenport, Iowa, May 11, 1926; s. Henry O. and Stella M. Hansen; m. Constance Lorraine Wolf, Oct. 19, 1934; children—Leslie Christine Hansen-Newman, Todd Whitney. B.A. Coe Coll., Cedar Rapids, Iowa, 1948; B.S. and O.D., Chgo. Coll. Optometry, 1951. Practice optometry The Main Vision Clinic, Davenport, 1951—; founder U.S. Farmers Food Bank. Charter mem. fin. accountability com. Am. div. Christian Blind Mission; advisor, cons. Heritage Found., Washington. charter mem. bd. dirs. Olypiads of Knowledge. Fellow Am. Acad. Corrective Optometry; mem. Am. Optometric Assn., Iowa Optometric Assn., Am. Coll. Syntonic Optometry. Club: Rock Island Arsenal Golf. Lodges: Rotary, Lions. Author: Winding America's Mainspring with Prepaid Social Security; Free World Social Security Using Free Enterprise Educational Trust. Home: 1117 Eastmere Dr Bettendorf IA 52722 Office: 1923 Main St Davenport IA 52803

HANSEN, GLENN LEROY, dean, educational consultant; b. Hampton, Iowa, Nov. 17, 1933; s. Ernest H. and Marie (Nielsen) H.; m. Sherrill DeLane Paullus, Aug. 31, 1956; children—Scott C., Cara M. B.A., U. Northern Iowa, 1959, M.A., 1969; Ph.D., Texas A&M U., 1975. Tchr. Central High Sch., Davenport, Iowa, 1959-64; prof. U. Northern Iowa, Cedar Falls, Iowa, 1964—, dean Div. Continuing Edn., 1980—; cons., 1969—; chmn. Community Edn. Assn., Cedar Falls, Iowa, 1984—; treas. Quad Cities Grad. Study Center, Rock Island, Ill., 1984—. Served to sgt. U.S. Army, 1954-56, Germany. Recipient Profl. Devel. award U.S. Dept. Edn., 1973-74. Mem. Nat. U. Continuing Edn. Assn. (chmn. Region IV 1985—), Cedar Falls C. of C. Lutheran. Avocations: golf; fishing. Home: 1458 Laurel Circle Cedar Falls IA 50613 Office: U Northern Iowa Gilchrist Hall Cedar Falls IA 50614

HANSEN, GROVER J., savings and loan association executive; b. Chgo., Sept. 29, 1923; s. Aage and Johanne (Rasmussen) H.; B.S. in Edn., No. Ill. U., DeKalb, 1949; M.B.A., U. Chgo., 1956; grad. Advanced Mgmt. Program, Harvard U., 1970; m. Geraldine Jones, Oct. 9, 1965; children—Michael E., Debra E., Denyse A., Robert H., Charles R. Exec. sec., ednl. dir. Am. Inst. Banking, 1951-61; asst. dir. banking edn. com. Am. Bankers Assn., 1961-62; gen. mgr. Produce Reporter Co., Wheaton, Ill., 1962-66; with First Fed. Savs. and Loan Assn., Chgo., 1966—, sr. v.p., 1967-71, pres., chief adminstrv. officer, dir., 1971—, pres., chief operating officer, 1976—; dir. First Savs. Corp., First Fed. Savs. of Chgo. Found., Investors Mortgage Ins. Co., Ill. Power Co., chmn. bd. Savs. Place, Inc., Appraisal Services, Inc., First Fed. Agy.; pres., dir. First Savs. Investment Corp.; chmn. bd., chmn. exec. com., dir. Chgo. Area Renewal Effort Service Corp., 1972-76. Bd. dirs. Mid.-Am. chpt. ARC, from 1973, chmn., 1979-81; trustee Met. Crusade Mercy, 1976—, chief crusader bus. and profl. div., 1976-80; chief crusader United Way/Crusade of Mercy, from 1981; chmn. bd. Center Religion and Psychtherapy, Chgo., 1971-79; bd. dirs. Chgo. Theol. Sem., 1973-75, bd. assos., from 1980; chmn. devel. subcom. Cook County Econ. Devel. Adv. Com., 1977-79; bd. govs. Glenwood Sch. Boys, from 1974; bd. dirs. Ingalls Meml. Hosp., 1973-78; governing mem. Chgo. Symphony Orch., from 1980; mem. Cook County R.E. Tax Study Commn., 1977-79; vice chmn. spl. gifts campaign Chgo. YMCA, 1973-75; gen. fund dr. chmn. Chgo. Jr. Achievement, 1976. Served to lt. USAAF, 1942-45. Recipient Medal of Merit award from mayor of Chgo., 1976; Distinguished Service award Kiwanis Internat., 1977; Most Distinguished Alumni award No. Ill. U., 1977. Mem. Fed. Savs. and Loan Council Ill. (dir. 1977-79), Cook County Ins. Savs. Assns., Am. Inst. Banking (life), Am. Savs. and Loan Inst., Newcomen Soc. N.Am. Clubs: Union League (dir. 1973-80, 1st v.p. 1977-78, pres. 1978-80), Mid-Day, Econ., Harvard Bus. Sch. (Chgo.). Office: 1st Fed Savs & Loan Assn Chgo 1 S Dearborn St Chicago IL 60603 also PO Box 4444 Chicago IL 60680

HANSEN, JAMES OTTO, state educational administrator; b. Lead, S.D., Sept. 21, 1928; s. Harold J. and Lillian (Mattson) H.; B.S., Black Hills State Coll., 1952; M.A., U. No. Colo., 1956; Ed.D., U. S.D., 1968; m. Dora Laura Helmer, May 28, 1950; children—Linda Kay Hansen Whitney, Diana May Hansen Buseman, June Doreen. Tchr., prin. public schs., Philip, S.D., 1952-55; supt. schs., Wessington, S.D., 1956-60; supt. schs., Gregory, S.D., 1961-67; supt. schs., Madison, S.D., 1968-76; asst. supt. instrn. State of S.D., Pierre, 1976-77, dept. state supt., 1978-79, state supt. of elem. and secondary edn., 1979—; sec. S.D. Dept. Edn. and Cultural Affairs, 1985—. Served with USAF, 1946-49. Mem. NEA, Council Chief State Sch. Officers, Sch. Adminstrs. S.D. (Adminstr. of Yr., 1979), Phi Delta Kappa. Republican. Congregationalist. Clubs: Kiwanis, Rotary, Masons, Elks. Office: Kneip Bldg Pierre SD 57501

HANSEN, KATHRYN GERTRUDE, former state official, association editor; b. Gardner, Ill., May 24, 1912; d. Harry J. and Marguerite (Gaston) Hansen; B.S. with honors, U. Ill., 1934, M.S., 1936. Personnel asst. U. Ill., Urbana, 1945-46, supr. tng. and activities, 1946-47, personnel officer, instr. psychology, 1947-52, exec. sec. U. Civil Service System Ill., also sec. for merit bd., 1952-61, adminstrv. officer, sec. merit bd., 1961-68, dir. system, 1968-72; lay asst. firm Webber, Balbach, Theis and Follmer, P.C., Urbana, Ill., 1972-74. Bd. dirs. U. YWCA, 1952-55, chmn., 1954-55; bd. dirs. Champaign-Urbana Symphony, 1978-81. Mem. Coll. and Univ. Personnel Assn. (hon., life mem., editor Jour. 1955-73, Newsletter, Internat. pres. 1967-68), Annuitants Assn. State Univs. Retirement System Ill. (state sec.-treas. 1974-75), Pres.'s Council U. Ill. (life), U. Ill. Alumni Assn. (life), U. Ill. Found., Campus Round Table U. Ill., Nat. League Am. Pen Women, AAUW (state 1st v.p. 1958-60), Bus. and Profl. Women's Club, Champaign-Urbana Symphony Guild, Secretariat U. Ill. (life), Grundy County Hist. Soc., Delta Kappa Gamma (state pres. 1961-63), Phi Mu (life), Kappa Delta Pi, Kappa Tau Alpha. Presbyterian. Clubs: Monday Writers, Fortnightly (Champaign-Urbana). Lodge: Order Eastern Star. Author: (with others) A Plan of Position Classification for Colleges and Universities; A Classification Plan for Staff Positions at Colleges and Universities, 1968; Grundy-Corners, 1982; Sarah, A Documentary of Her Life and Times, 1984; editor: The Illini Worker, 1946-52; Campus Pathways, 1952-61; This is Your Civil Service Handbook, 1960-67; author, editor publs. on personnel practices. Home: 1004 E Harding Dr Apt 307 Urbana IL 61801

HANSEN, LOWELL C., II, lieutenant governor of South Dakota; b. Oct. 11, 1939; B.S. in Bus. Adminstrn., U. Nebr. Mem. S.D. Ho. of Reps., 1972-78, speaker pro tem, 1974, speaker, 1976; lt. gov. State of S.D., Pierre, 1979—. Mem. Sioux Falls Outstanding Young Man of Yr., 1972, Outstanding Young Man of Am., 1972. Mem. Sigma Alpha Epsilon. Republican. Office: Office of Lt Gov State Capitol Bldg Pierre SD 57501*

HANSEN, MARK BRIAN, systems analyst; b. Omaha, Aug. 2, 1957; s. Victor Albert and Phyllis Ruth (Pforr) H.; m. Kristin Lee Fellows, June 15, 1984. B.S. in Bus. Adminstrn., U. Nebr.-Omaha, 1981. Sr. systems designer Guarantee Mut. Life Ins. Co., Omaha, 1982—. Mem. Assn. for Systems Mgmt. (chmn. spl. projects/research). Lutheran. Home: 3529 N 57th St Omaha NE 68104 Office: Guarantee Mut Life Co 8721 Indian Hills Dr Omaha NE 68114

HANSEN, MICHAEL HILARY, veterinarian, consultant; b. Rockville, Minn., Nov. 26, 1931; s. Harry John and Mary Catherine (Krebsbach) H.; m. Mary Colleen Moran, Aug. 23, 1958; children—Pam, Paul, Jay, Greg, Jeff. B.S., U. Minn., 1955, D.V.M., 1957. Gen. practice vet. medicine Willmar Vet. Clinic, Minn., 1958-60; research veterinarian Land O'Lakes, Inc., Mpls., 1960-73; prodn. mgr. Koronis Mill, Paynesville, Minn., 1973-78; gen. mgr. Mill Farms, Paynesville, 1978-81; cons. Michael Hansen & Assocs., Paynesville, 1981—. Mem. AVMA, Minn. Vet. Med. Assn., Poultry Sci. Assn. Republican. Roman Catholic. Lodge: Lions. Office: Route 2 Box 310 Paynesville MN 56362

HANSEN, ROBERT SUTTLE, chemist; b. Salt Lake City, June 17, 1918; s. Charles Andrew and Bessie (Suttle) H.; m. Gilda Clementine Cappannari, Apr. 8, 1939; 1 son, Edward Charles. B.S., U. Mich., 1940, M.S., 1941, Ph.D., 1948; D.Sc., Lehigh U., 1978. Mem. faculty Iowa State U., Ames, 1948—, prof. chemistry, 1955—, chmn. chemistry dept., 1965-68, disting. prof. Coll. Sci. and Humanities, 1967—, with Ames Lab., 1948—, sr. chemist, 1955—, chief chemistry div., 1965-68, dir., 1968—; cons. Procter & Gamble Co., Union Carbide Corp.; mem. chemistry adv. panel NSF, 1971-75, materials research adv. panel, 1976-80; mem. Gov.'s Sci. Adv. Council, 1977—; vice chmn. Iowa Energy Policy Council, 1978—. Served with USAAF, 1942-46. Decorated Bronze Star; NSF sr. postdoctoral fellow, 1959-60. Fellow Iowa Acad. Sci. (Centennial citation 1975, disting. fellow 1982); mem. Am. Chem. Soc. (past sec. treas., chmn. div. colloid and surface chemistry; Kendall award 1966, Midwest award 1980), Am. Phys. Soc., AAAS, Internat. Union Pure and Applied Chemistry (titular mem. commn. on colloid and surface chemistry 1975-83). Assoc. editor Jour. Chem. Physics, 1981-83; contbr. articles to profl. jours. Home: 2030 McCarthy Rd Ames IA 50010 Office: Ames Lab Iowa State U Ames IA 50011

HANSEN, SCOTT EVAN, graphic designer; b. Albert Lea, Minn., May 25, 1958; s. Wayne Emmanuel and Gretchen Annette (Schiager) H. A.A., Alexandria Coll., 1978. Graphic designer Universal Cooperatives, Albert Lea, 1978-82; art dir. Scotsman Ice Systems, Albert Lea, 1983—. Mem. Nat. Mgmt. Assn., So. Minn. Charter of Printing House Craftsmen's Club. Republican. Lutheran. Avocations: golf; softball; basketball. Office: Scotsman Ice Systems 505 Front St Albert Lea MN 56007

HANSEN, WENDELL JAY, clergyman, gospel broadcaster; b. Waukegan, Ill., May 28, 1910; s. Christian Hans and Anna Sophia (Termansen) H.; m. Bertelle Kathryn Budman, Mar. 9, 1933 (dec. Jan. 6, 1956); 1 child, Sylvia Larson; m. 2d, Eunice Evaline Irvine, Nov. 2, 1957; 1 child, Dean. Grad. Cleve. Bible Coll., 1932; A.B., William Penn Coll., 1938; postgrad. Gletch Berg Skule, Switzerland, 1939; M.A., U. Iowa, 1940, Ph.D., 1947. Ordained to ministry Recorded Friends, 1936, Evang. Reformed Ch., 1944; pastor chs., Grinnell, Iowa, Mpls. and Iowa City, 1934-47; evangelist with talking and performing birds, 1946—, mgr. gospel radio stas. Two Rivers, Wis., Menomonie, Wis., Peru, Ind., Wabash, Ind., East St. Louis, Ill., Indpls., 1952—; pres., chmn. of bd. WESL Inc., East St. Louis, 1962—, cons. radio and TV, 1970—. Dir. St. Paul Inter-racial Work Camp, 1939; chmn. Minn. Joint Refuge Com., 1940-41. Recipient honor citation Nat. Assn. Broadcasters, 1980; Boss of Yr. award Hamilton County Broadcasters, 1979, award Boys Town, 1983, award Women of Faith, St. Louis, 1984. Mem. Internat. Platform Assn., Internat. Assn. Christian Magicians, Ind. Bird Fanciers, East St. Louis C. of C. (bd. dirs. 1981—), Pi Kappa Delta. Republican. Quaker. Club: Ind. Pigeon (best exotic bird award 1969, 75, 80). Lodge: Kiwanis. Contbr. articles to popular mags.

HANSON, ALLEN D., agricultural cooperative executive. Pres., gen. mgr. Harvest States Cooperatives, St. Paul, Minn. Office: Harvest States Cooperatives 1667 N Snelling Ave Saint Paul MN 55165*

HANSON, ARTHUR STUART, physician; b. Mpls., March 10, 1937; s. Arthur Emanuel and Francis Elenor (Larson) H.; m. Gail Joan Taylor, June 16, 1963; children—Marta Eileen, Peter Arthur. B.A., Darmouth Coll., 1959; M.D., U. Minn., 1963. Diplomate Am. Bd. Internal Medicine, Am. Bd. Pulmonary Disease. Staff physician Park Nicollet Med. Ctr., Mpls., 1971—, med. dir., 1975-82, v.p. legis. and community affairs, 1982—. Pres. and bd. chmn. Minn. Coalition for a Smoke Free Soc. 2000, 1984—; chmn. bd. Smoke Free Generation of Minn., 1984—. Recipient Community Service Recognition award Park Nicollet Med. Ctr., Mpls., 1984. Fellow Am. Coll. Chest Physicians; mem. ACP, AMA (alt. del.). Universalist. Avocations: basketball, gardening, running, travel. Office: Park Nicollet Med Ctr 5000 W 39th St Minneapolis MN 55416

HANSON, BRYANT R., hospital administrator; b. Price, Utah, Apr. 13, 1946; s. Rex R. and Christine (Passarella) H.; m. Annette Wilson, June 15, 1968; children—Tonya, Stephen. A.B. cum laude, Regis Coll., 1968; M.S. in Hosp. Adminstrn., Ohio State U., 1973. Asst. exec. dir. St. Francis Hosp., Blue Island, Ill., 1973-75, assoc. exec. dir., 1975-80, exec. dir., 1980—; preceptor Govs. State U., Park Forest, Ill., 1980—, Ohio State U., Columbus, 1980—. Bd. dirs. Family and Mental Health Cook County, Oak Lawn, 1976-85; mem. Blue Island Mayor's Adv. Com., 1980-85; hon. chmn. Los Amigos, Blue Island, 1982; bd. dirs. Community Fund South Cook County, 1978-80. Served with U.S. Army, 1968-71; Vietnam. Regis Coll. scholar, 1964-68; decorated Bronze Star. Mem. Blue Island C. of C. (bd. dirs. 1979-83), Am. Coll. Hosp. Adminstrs., Am. Acad. Med. Adminstrs., Ill. Hosp. Assn. (region pres. 1982-84), Cath. Hosp. Assn., Chgo. Conf. Cath. Hosps. (v.p. 1984). Roman Catholic. Lodges: Rotary (v.p. 1978-80), Deacons, K.C. (Blue Island). Avocations: golf; rose gardening. Home: 15304 Walnut Rd Oak Forest IL 60452 Office: St Francis Hosp 12935 S Gregory St Blue Island IL 60406

HANSON, ERNEST JEROME, neurosurgeon; b. Cheyenne, Wyo., Oct. 29, 1943; s. Ernest Jerome Sr. and Agnes Ann (Volk) H.; m. Mary Anne McElroy, June 23, 1966; children—Christopher, Elizabeth. B.S., U. N.D., 1965, B.A., 1967; M.D., U. Pa., 1969. Diplomate Am. Bd. Neurologic Surgery. Intern, Hosp. U. Pa., Phila., 1969-70; resident Mayo Clinic, Rochester, Minn., 1970-75; research assoc. Cerebrovascular Research Ctr., St. Mary's Hosp., Rochester, 1973-74; neurosurgeon Neurosci. Assn., Kansas City, Mo., 1975—; mem. staff St. Luke's Hosp., Kansas City, Children's Mercy Hosp., Providence-St. Margaret's Med. Ctr., Bethany Med. Ctr., Shawnee Mission Med. Ctr. Contbr. articles to profl. publs. Vice pres. St. Luke's Hosp. Found. for Med. Edn. and Research, Kansas City, 1985. Served to maj. USAR, 1970-77. Fellow Am. Heart Assn. (stroke council); mem. AMA, Mo. State Med. Soc., Jackson County Med. Soc. (treas.), Southwest Clin. Soc., Congress Neurol. Surgeons, Am. Assn. Neurol. Surgeons (cerebrovascular sect.), Mo. State Neurol. Soc. (pres. 1985—), Sigma Xi. Avocations: flying, sailing, skiing. Office: Neurosci Assocs 4320 Wornall Rd Suite 328 Kansas City MO 64111

HANSON, FRED T., lawyer; b. Wakefield, Nebr., Feb. 25, 1902; s. Peter H. and Hannah Ulrika (Anderson) H.; LL.B., U. Nebr., 1925; m. Helen Elizabeth

Haddock, Nov. 12, 1928; 1 son John Fredrik. Admitted to Nebr. bar, 1925, since in pvt. practice; probate judge, 1931-42, pros. atty., 1927-30, 51-54; spl. asst. to U.S. atty. gen., 1954-62; life mem. Nat. Conf. Commrs. Uniform State Laws from Nebr., com. on uniform probate code. Bd. dirs. Nebr. dist. Luth. Ch.-Mo. Synod, 1976-80. Served as capt. AUS, 1942-46. Mem. Am. Judicature Soc., Am. Coll. Probate Counsel (regent), Am., Nebr., local bar assns., Am. Legion. Office: 316 Norris Ave Mc Cook NE 69001

HANSON, GARY WAYNE, state senator, real estate broker; b. Sioux Falls, S.D., Apr. 20, 1950; s. Wendell Holmes and Helen Alberta (Brumbaugh) H.; m. Sandra Kay Fredricks, June 20, 1970; children—Alicia Jayne, Wayne Allan, Stacy Elizabeth. B.S., No. State Coll., Aberdeen, S.D., 1972. Owner, broker Hanson Realty, Sioux Falls, 1973—; expert witness real estate Circuit Ct. S.D., 1980—; appraiser, 1974—; mem. S.D. Senate, 1983—. Coach boys basketball, soccer, Sioux Falls, 1971—, girls basketball, soccer, volleyball, Sioux Falls, 1982—; mem. Nat. Republican Legislators Assn., Washington, Mem. Sioux Falls Bd. Realtors (bd. dirs. 1981-84, pres.-elect 1984-85), S.D. Legis. Affairs Com. Realtors, No. State Coll. Alumni Com. Methodist. Clubs: Jaycees (bd. dirs. 1975-76); Capitol (Pierre, S.D.). Office: Hanson Realty 705 S Minnesota Ave Sioux Falls SD 57102

HANSON, HARLAN LEE, manufacturing company executive; b. Hutchinson, Minn., July 27, 1939; s. Alvin R. and Lorraine (Block) H.; m. Marcia Kline Hanson, Feb. 24, 1980; children—Mark D., Scott E. B.S. in Bus. Adminstrn., Macalester Coll., 1961. Asst. buyer Dayton's, Mpls., 1961-63; mfrs. rep., prin. Mazie & Hanson, Mpls., 1963-73; v.p. mktg. Thermo-Serv, Inc., Anoka, Minn., 1973-80, exec. v.p., 1980-82, pres., 1982—, chmn. bd., 1982—; dir. Quest Co., Mpls. Pres. Am. Diabetes Assn. Minn., Mpls., 1979-80; chmn. bd. Am. Diabetes Assn., N.Y.C., 1981-83; fin. chmn. Minnetonka United Meth. Ch., Minn., 1983—. Recipient Legion of Honor, DeMolay Supreme Council, Kansas City, 1977; Diabetes and Youth award Am. Diabetes Assn., 1973, Charles Best medal, 1983. Republican. Methodist. Avocations: buying and selling businesses and real estate; golf; bridge. Home: 14200 Minnehaha Pl Wayzata MN 55391 Office: Thermo-Serv Inc 6th and Grant Sts Anoka MN 55303

HANSON, JERRY RANNEY, farmer; b. Monmouth, Ill., Aug. 1, 1924; s. Willard H. and Edna (Ranney) H.; m. Doris Johnson, Nov. 23, 1952; children—Bruce, Marc, Donna. Student Carl Sandburg Jr. Coll., Galesburg, Ill. Farmer, Monmouth 1938—. Mem. Warren Sch. Bd., Monmouth, 1956—, pres., 1978—; mem. Coldbrook Twp. Bd., Monmouth, 1975—; past bd. dirs. Trinity Lutheran Ch., Galesburg. Republican. Home: Rural Route 1 Monmouth IL 61462

HANSON, JOHN RICHARD, II, construction company executive; b. St. Louis, Oct. 19, 1940; s. Richard Gilbert Hanson and Gladys (Bolin) Hughes; m. Jeanette Marie Reitmeier, July 26, 1975; children—Lori, Jennifer, Richard, Lisa, Bryan. B.A., Washington U., St. Louis, 1962; M.B.A., Ga. So. U., Statesboro, 1972; M.A., Southeast Mo. State U.-Cape Girardeau, 1977. Commd. 2d lt. U.S. Army, 1962, advanced through grades to maj., 1971; served Vietnam, 1965-68; comdr., staff officer U.S. Army Aviation Sch., Savannah, Ga., 1969-71; acct. exec. Merrill Lynch, St. Louis, 1972-74; pres. Southeast Mo. Leasing, Cape Girardeau, 1974-76; dir. customer services Hart Schaffner & Marx, Chgo., 1976-80; dir., adminstr. Barrett Paving Materials, Chgo., 1980—. Commr., Village of Bloomingdale, Ill., 1982. Decorated Bronze Star. Lutheran. Home: 172 Hingham Ln Bloomingdale IL 60108 Office: Barrett Paving Materials Inc 11645 W Grand Ave Northlake IL 60164

HANSON, KENNETH HAMILTON, lawyer; b. Chgo., Sept. 10, 1919; s. Clinton H. and Della (Bonson) H.; student North Park Coll., 1939-40; B.S., Northwestern U., 1943, J.D., 1949; m. Elaine F. Bleck, May 19, 1951; children—Christine E., Karen D., Kenneth Hamilton. Admitted to Ill. bar, 1949; practiced law, Chgo., 1949-53; atty. bus. devel. dept. First Nat. Bank Chgo., 1953-61; trial atty. Antitrust div. U.S. Dept. Justice, Chgo., 1961-83; mem. firm Brace & O'Donnell, Chgo., 1983—. Served to lt. (j.g.) USNR, 1943-46. Mem. Ill. State Bar Assn., 7th Circuit Bar Assn., Am., Fed., Chgo. bar assns., Beta Theta Pi, Phi Delta Phi. Republican. Presbyn. Home: 955 Melody Rd Lake Forest IL 60045 Office: 333 S Michigan Ave Chicago IL 60604

HANSON, LEE EDWIN, university administrator; b. Lansing, Mich., Sept. 24, 1947; s. Leroy Edwin and Ida Mildred (Chandler) H.; m. Claire Lenore Huling, Jan. 11, 1973 (div. Sept. 1981). B.A., Northwestern U., 1968, M.A.T., 1970. Instr., Kendall Coll., Evanston, Ill., 1970; tchr. Dist. 111 Schs., Highland Park, Ill., 1970-71; dir. devel. services Northwestern U., Evanston, Ill., 1971-82; dir. devel. services Washington U., St. Louis, 1982—; cons. Rotary Internat. Found., Evanston, 1982, Case Western Res. U., Cleve., 1982-84. Mem. Council Advancement and Support Edn., Phi Delta Kappa. Republican. Home: 220 N Forsyth Blvd Clayton MO 63105 Office: Washington U Skinker and Lindell Blvds Saint Louis MO 63130

HANSON, MICHAEL LAWRENCE, labor union leader, construction equipment manufacturing company executive; b. Terre Haute, Ind., Mar. 1, 1942; s. Arnold Gilbert and Dorthy H.; foster s. Raymond and Annise Hirt; m. Dolores Ann Lanham, Mar. 11, 1967; children—Melinda Sue, William Eric. Student Ind. U., 1977-78. Cert. UAW. Lathe operator Ertels, Indpls., 1963-64; cleaner, installer Gen. Electric, Indpls., 1964; press operator Dormeyers, Rockville, Ind., 1965; with acids dept. P.R. Mallory, Greencastle, Ind., 1965-68; laborer J.I. Case Co., Terre Haute, 1975—; unionism lectr. Ind. State U. Vice pres. J.I. Case Co., chpt. UAW, 1976-77, pres., 1977-79; Labor rep., bd. dirs. Hamilton Mental Health Ctr., 1976-83; trustee, pres. J.I. Fed. Credit Union, 1975-76; pres. local PTO, 1979-80; active Wesley Chapel Methodist Ch., Berea Christian Ch., United Way Campaign, 1977; com. chmn. Wabash Valley council Boy Scouts Am., 1981—. Recipient certs. achievement and recognition Hamilton Ctr., Boy Scouts Am. Republican. Lodge: Masons. Avocations: hunting; swimming; bicycling; guns. Home: Route 17 Box 411 Brazil IN 47834 Office: J I Case Co PO Box 5215 Terre Haute IN 47805

HANSON, MONTE KENT, bookseller; b. Mexico, Mo., Jan. 11, 1955; s. Wilmer D. and Velma B. (Montague) H.; m. Glee Anne Brummitt, June 19, 1977; children—Josiah Kent, Lydia Michelle. B.S., Northeastern Mo. State U., 1977. Salesman, OCCO Feed Co., Oelwein, Iowa, 1973, dist. mgr., 1974-77; asst. mgr. K-Mart Corp., Mo., 1977-80; pres., gen. mgr. Faith Ctr., Kirksville, Mo., 1981—. Bd. dirs. Christian Life, Nazarene Ch., Mo., 1981, 82, 83. Named State Farmer, Future Farmers Am., Mo., 1973. Mem. Christian Booksellers Assn., Kirksville C. of C. (chmn. retail com. 1982), C. of C. U.S., Nat. Fedn. Ind. Bus. Repubican. Avocations: reading; Bible collecting; softball. Office: Faith Center 110 W Harrison St Kirksville MO 63501

HANSON, RICHARD LEON, music publisher; b. Bloomington, Ind., Oct. 19, 1946; s. Richard Arnold and Mary Ann (Fleener) H.; m. Sue Ann Harland, Oct. 27, 1964; 1 child, Christena L. Student Ind. U., 1964, 67. Pres. Ric Rac, Inc., Nashville, chmn. bd., 1985—, also pres. divs. Ric Rac Music, Rick Hanson Music, Ric Rac Records, Rick Hanson Prodns.; performer Rick Hanson Show, 1980—; mem. Bloomington Songwriters Workshop, 1980—; pub., composer numerous songs. Mem. United Brotherhood Carpenters and Joiners Am., Nashville Songwriters Assn., Country Music Assn. Am. Fedn. Musicians, ASCAP.

HANSON, ROBERT E., state government official. State treas. State of N.D., Bismarck. Office: Office of State Treasurer Capitol Bldg 3d Floor Bismarck ND 58505*

HANSSON, KELD, electronics company executive; b. Esbjerg, Denmark, Nov. 10, 1950; came to U.S., 1978, permanent resident, 1983; s. Erik and Inger H.; m. Julie Ann Smith, May 27, 1978. Student Aarhus (Denmark) Tech. Coll., 1968-69; cert. in elec. tech. Sonderborg Tech. Coll., Sonderborg, Denmark, 1970-74; student English Lang., Cambridge (Eng.) U., 1975-76. Technician Bang & Olufsen, Gloucester, Eng., 1975-76, service mgr., Brisbane, Australia, 1976-78, tech. mgr., Elk Grove Village, Ill., 1978—. Mem. Audio Engring. Soc. Home: 1010 N Plum Grove Rd Apt 201 Schaumburg IL 60195 Office: 1150 Feehanville Dr Mount Prospect IL 60056

HANSULD, ARTHUR MARR, educational administrator, musician; b. Newton, Iowa, July 15, 1942; s. George Arthur and SudieBelle (Marr) H.; m. Carol Jean Christiansen, Sept. 2, 1963; 1 child, Gregory Marr. B.A., U. No. Iowa, 1964; M.Mus., North Tex. State U., 1968; Ph.D., U. Miami, 1971. Cert. tchr., Iowa. Band, orch. dir. Dallas Pub. Schs., 1968-69; grad. fellow in music U. Miami, Fla., 1969-71; asst. prof. music Marietta Coll., Ohio, 1971-74; assoc. prof. Hiram Coll., Ohio, 1974-76; fine arts coordinator, dir. continuing edn. Iowa Western Community Coll., Council Bluffs, 1976—; mus. dir. Musick's Recreation, Council Bluffs, 1977—, Omaha Pops Orch., 1981—. Author: (method book) Rehearsal Method for Band, 1967. Bd. dirs. Omaha Symphony Guild, 1980—, Bluffs Arts Council, Council Bluffs, 1983—. Maytag scholar, 1960; NDEA fellow, 1970. Mem. Council Bluffs C. of C. (bus. council 1984—). Rep ublican. Universalist. Avocation: musical instrument making. Home: 12 Shady Ln Council Bluffs IA 51501 Office: Iowa Western Community Coll 2700 College Rd Council Bluffs IA 51502

HANTON, WILLIAM, law enforcement official. Police chief, City of Cleve. Office: Cleveland Police Dept Office of the Chief of Police Cleveland OH 44113*

HANUSCHAK, GEORGE ALAN, statistician; b. Youngstown, Ohio, Sept. 5, 1949; s. Mickey and Flora Jean (Popa) H.; m. Regina Marie Mazur, July 13, 1974; 1 child, John. B.A. in Math., Youngstown State U., 1971; M.S. in Stats., Ohio State U., 1973; postgrad. in mgmt. Cornell U., 1981. Teaching asst. Ohio state U., Columbus, 1971-73; math. statistician U.S. dept. Agr., Sacramento, 1973, Des Moines, 1973-75, Washington, 1975-80, supervisory math. statistician, 1981-84, supervisory agr. statistician, Columbus, 1984—; instr. stats. Des Moines Community Coll., 1974, U.S. Dept. Agr. Grad. Sch., Washington, 1978; agr. stats. cons. to UN and fgn. govts.; mem. Adminstr.'s Task Force on U.S. Dept. Agr. Crop Reporting Bd. Policies and Procedures, 1985. Contbr. articles to profl. publs. Recipient Adminstrs. Spl. Merit award for use of satellite data for crop estimation U.S. Dept. Agr. Statis. Reporting Service, 1980. Mem. Ohio State U. Alumni Assn., Ohio Agr. Mktg. Forum (treas. 1985), Am. Statis. Assn., Inst. Mgmt. Sci. Roman Catholic. Club: USDA (Columbus). Avocations: family activities, golf, bicycling, soccer, health spa. Home: 200 Buckeye Ct Westerville OH 43081 Office: US Dept Agr Fed Bldg 200 N High St Columbus OH 43215

HANZELY, STEPHEN, physics educator; b. Sátoraljajhely, Zemplén County, Hungary, Dec. 30, 1940; came to U.S., 1957; s. Stephen and Martha (Demien) H.; m. Brigitta Strammer, Aug. 25, 1962; children—Melinda, Erika. B.S., Kent State U., 1962; M.S., U. Toledo, 1964; M.S., N.Mex. State U., 1967, Ph.D., 1969. Asst. prof. physics Youngstown State U., Ohio, 1968-73, assoc. prof., 1973-79, prof., 1980—, chmn. dept. physics and astronomy, 1974-79; chmn. consumer adv. panel Ohio Edison Co., Youngstown, 1982—; mem. Youngstown Recycling Ctrs, Inc., 1980—. Named Disting. prof. Youngstown State U., 1981; recipient Faculty Service award Ohio Edn. Assn., 1981, Outstanding Professor, Youngstown State U., 1984-85; NSF summer workshop grantee, 1979, 80. Mem. Am. Phys. Soc., NEA, Am. Assn. Physics Tchrs., Sigma Xi. Roman Catholic. Avocations: sports; recycling. Office: Youngstown State U 410 Wick Ave Youngstown OH 44555

HAPPACH, BERNARD CHARLES, hospital management services administrator; b. Peoria, Ill., Oct. 3, 1930; s. Bernard Marius and Mildred Alma (Holliger) H.; B.S., Bradley U., 1955; m. Marlene R. Schroeder, Dec. 31, 1974; children—Rhonda, Karen, Tamara, Benjamin. Mgr., Comml. Credit Corp., Peoria, Ill., 1956-62; bus. mgr. St. Francis Hosp., Peoria, 1962-67; gen. credit mgr., corp. dir. patient accounts Sisters of the Third Order of St. Francis, Peoria, 1967—. Treas., Children's Center Tazewell County Inc. Served with USMC, 1947-51. Decorated Purple Heart; recipient Frederick T. Muncie Merit award, 1980. Nat. cert. mgr. of patient accounts, consumer credit exec. Mem. Nat. Hosp. Fin. Mgmt. Assn. (William G. Follmer merit award 1971, Robert A. Reeves merit award 1975, Robert M. McMahon achievement award 1975, life membership meritorious award 1978), Soc. Cert. Consumer Credit Execs., Ill. Assn. Hosp. Attys. Republican. Roman Catholic. Author: Collecting Receivables-How to get the Job Done, 1977; Managing Cash Flow, 1980; author articles. Home: 127 E Oakwood St Morton IL 61550 Office: 1124 N Berkeley Peoria IL 61603

HAQUE, MALIKA HAKIM, pediatrician; b. Madras, India; came to U.S., 1967; d. S. Abdul and Rahimunisa (Hussain) Hakim; M.B.B.S., Madras Med. Coll., 1967; m. C. Azeez ul Haque, Feb. 5, 1967; children—Kifizeba, Masarath Nashr, Asim Zayd. Rotating intern Miriam Hosp., Brown U., Providence, 1967-68; resident in pediatrics Children's Hosp., N.J. Coll. Medicine, 1968-70; fellow in devel. disabilities Ohio State U., 1970-71; acting chief pediatrics Nisonger Center, 1973-74; staff pediatrician Children and Youth Project, Children's Hosp., Columbus, Ohio, also clin. asst. prof. pediatrics Ohio State U., 1974-80; clin. asso. prof. pediatrics Ohio State U., 1981—; pediatrician in charge community pediatrics and adolescent services clinics Columbus Children's Hosp.; cons. Central Ohio Head Start Program, 1974-79. Mem. Republican Presdl. Task Force, 1982—, Nat. Rep. Senatorial Com., 1985—, U.S. Senatorial Club. Recipient Physician Recognition award AMA, 1971-86, Gold medals in surgery, radiology, pediatrics and ob/gyn; Presdl. medal of Merit, 1982; diplomate Am. Bd. Pediatrics. Fellow Am. Acad. Pediatrics; mem. Ambulatory Pediatric Assn., Central Ohio Pediatric Soc. Islam. Research on enuresis. Home: 5995 Forestview Dr Columbus OH 43213 Office: 700 Children's Dr Columbus OH 43205

HARB, JOSEPH MARSHALL, laboratory administrator, pediatric educator, researcher; b. Oakland, Calif., Dec. 20, 1938; m. Jacquelyn Heckert. B.S., Oglethorpe U., 1961; M.S., Tulane U., 1966, Ph.D., 1969. Mem. faculty dept. med. Tulane Med. Ctr., New Orleans, 1969-75; mem. faculty dept. pathology Wayne State Med. Ctr., Detroit, 1977-80; mem. faculty dept. anatomy U. Detroit, 1980; dir. electron microscopy program VA Med. Ctr., Allen Park, Mich., 1976-80, Milw. Children's Hosp., 1981—; mem. faculty dept. pediatrics Med. Coll. Wis., Milw., 1981—; electron microscopy tech. specialist Tulane U., New Orleans, 1963-69; cons. electron microscopy Delta Primate Ctr., New Orleans, 1965-66; doctorate staff Milw. Children's Hosp., 1981—. Contbr. articles to profl. jours. Research grantee NIH, 1984, Med. Coll. Wis., 1981, Milw. Children's Hosp., 1983. Mem. Electron Microscopy Soc. Am. (assoc. editor 1984—, bull. editor 1985), Am. Soc. Cell Biology, Midwest Soc. Electron Microscopists (pres. elect 1983-84, pres. 1984—, editor newsletter 1982-83). Avocations: tennis, golf, woodworking. Office: Dept Pediatrics Milwaukee Children's Hosp 1700 W Wisconsin Ave Milwaukee WI 53201

HARBERGER, ARNOLD CARL, economics educator; b. Newark, July 27, 1924; s. Ferdinand C. and Martha L. (Bucher) H.; m. Ana Beatriz Valjalo, Mar. 15, 1958; children—Paul Vincent, Carl David. Student Johns Hopkins U., 1941-43; M.A., U. Chgo., 1947, Ph.D., 1950; D.h.c., U. Tucuman, 1979. Asst. prof. polit. economy Johns Hopkins U., 1949-53, assoc. prof. econs., U. Chgo., 1953-59, prof., 1959—, chmn. dept., 1964-71, 75-80, Gustavus F. and Ann M. Swift Disting. Service prof., 1977—, dir. Ctr. Latin Am. Econs. Studies, 1965—; vis. prof. Ctr. Internat. Studies at MIT, New Delhi, India, 1961-62, Econ. Devel. Inst. IBRD, 1965, Harvard U., 1971-72, Princeton U., 1973-74; vis. prof. UCLA, 1983, 84, prof. econs., 1984—; cons. IMF, 1950, Pres.'s Materials Policy Commn., 1951-52, U.S. Dept. Treasury, 1961-75, Com. Econ. Devel., 1961-78, Planning Commn., India, 1961-62, 73, Pan Am. Union, 1962-76, Dept. State, 1962-76, Central Bank, Chile, 1965-70, Planning Dept., Panama, 1965-77, 84—, Columbia, 1969-71, Ford Found., 1967-77, Planning Commn., El Salvador, 1973-75, Budget and Planning Office, Uruguay, 1974-75, Can. Dept. Regional Econ. Expansion, 1975-77, Fin. Ministry, Bolivia, 1976, Mex., 1976—, Can. Dept. Employment and Migration, 1980-82, Indonesian Ministry Fin., 1981-82, Can. Dept. Fin., 1982-84, Chinese Ministry Fin., 1983, World Bank, 1984—. Author: Project Evaluation, 1972; Taxation and Welfare, 1973. Editor: Demand for Durable Goods, 1960; The Taxation of Income from Capital, 1968; Key Problems of Economic Policy in Latin America, 1970; World Economic Growth, 1984. Contbr. articles to profl. jours. and govt. publs. Served with AUS, 1943-46. Guggenheim fellow; Fulbright scholar; faculty research fellow Social Sci. Research Council; Ford Found. faculty research fellow, 1968-69. Fellow Econometric Soc., Am. Acad. Arts and Scis.; mem. Am. Econ. Assn. (mem. exec. com. 1970-72), Royal Econ. Soc., Nat. Tax Assn., Phi Beta Kappa. Home: 4840 S Greenwood Chicago IL 60615 Office: Dept Econs U Chicago 1126 E 59th St Chicago IL 60637

HARBICK, RICHARD LEONARD, university administrator; b. Shawano, Wis., May 31, 1930; s. Leonard Joseph and Della Emma (LeMay) H.; m. MaryAnn Phyllis Hoffmann, July 14, 1957; children—Timothy, Mark. B.S., No. Mich. U., 1957; postgrad. Harvard U., 1970, Ind. U., 1984. Account rep. Burroughs Corp., Peoria, Ill., 1957, WDMJ-TV, Marquette, Mich., 1957-59; retail store mgr. Montgomery Ward, Marquette, Mich., Houghton, Mich., Dubuque, Iowa, Kenosha, Wis., Monroe, Wis., 1959-66; dir. Univ. Ctr. and Bookstore, No. Mich. U., Marquette, 1966—; cons. Jansport, Inc., Appleton, Wis., 1985-86. Author video tng. film: College Store Merchandising, 1983. Personnel coordinator March of Dimes, Marquette, 1970-75. Recipient merchandising awards Montgomery Ward, 1961, 62, 66, Nat. Assn. Coll. Stores, 1968, 73, 74, 78, 80, 84. Mem. Mich. Assn. Coll. Stores (pres. 1972-73, trustee 1973-75), Nat. Assn. Coll. Stores (trustee 1985—), Assn. of Coll. Unions-Internat. Roman Catholic. Clubs: Exchange (bd. dirs. 1979-81, 84—), Investment (rec. ptnr. 1974, 80, 85) (Marquette). Avocations: skiing; jogging; hiking; woodworking; reading. Home: 1123 Presque Isle Ave Marquette MI 49855

HARBISON, STANLEY LINCOLN, social worker, religious counselor; b. Detroit, Jan. 30, 1937; s. Winfred A. and Ocie (Kelly) H.; m. Susan Winters, 1981; children—David L., Heather E. B.A. magna cum laude, Bethany Coll. (W.Va.), 1959; M.Div., Yale U., 1962; Ph.D., Vanderbilt U., 1975. Instr. history Eastern Mich. U., Ypsilanti, 1965-73, lectr. 1975, 78; lectr. social sci. Henry Ford Community Coll., Dearborn, Mich., 1973-78; instr. extension services U. Mich., Ann Arbor, 1975-76, nursing sch. research ethics com., 1979-80, lectr. religious studies, 1981; assoc. dir. Wesley Found., 1974-77; edn. dir. Ann Arbor West Side Meth. Ch., 1976-80; vol. services coordinator, caseworker Washtenaw County Juvenile Ct., Ann Arbor, 1979—; Mem. Ypsilanti City Council, 1977-80; exec. com. Southeast Mich. Council Govts., 1978—; legis. com. Mich. Mcpl. League, 1979-80; union mgmt. negotiating team Washtenaw County Govt.; chmn. Mental Health Edn. Task Force; bd. dirs. Ypsilanti Area Futures, Inc., sec. inter-govtl. relations task force, volunteerism task force; adv. bd. alcoholism therapy Beyer Hosp.; v.p. Friends in Deed Ministries; exec. bd. local NAACP; organizer, convener Ypsilanti Area Social Agys. Forum; founder, chmn. Ypsilanti Youth Supporters; adv. bd. Ypsilanti Pub. Schs.; del. Democratic State Conv.; elder, lay minister Christian Ch. (Disciples). Recipient Citizen of Yr. award Huron Valley chpt. Nat. Assn. Social Workers, 1982; So. Regional award scholar, 1959. Mem. Am. Acad. Religion, Am. Hist. Assn., Am. Soc. Ch. Hist., Am. Soc. Pub. Adminstrn., Nat. Council Crime and Delinquency, Beta Theta Pi. Author: The Social Gospel Career of Alva Wilmot Taylor, 1975. Contbr. articles on religious subjects to publs.; speaker local radio stas. Home: 1434 Collegewood Ypsilanti MI 48197 Office: 2270 Platt Rd Ann Arbor MI 48104

HARDEN, ANITA JOYCE, nurse; b. Jackson, Tenn., May 17, 1947; d. Percy Lawrence and Majorie (Robison) H.; B.S. in Nursing, Ind. U., 1968; M.S. in Nursing, Ind. U.-Purdue U., Indpls., 1973; 1 son, Brian Robison Weir. Staff nurse Indpls. hosps., 1968-71; instr. Ind. U. Sch. Nursing, 1973-75; dir. continuing care Gallahue Mental Health Center, Indpls., 1975-80; mgr. psychiatry Community Hosp., Indpls., 1980—; clin. asst. prof. Ind. U., 1977-82, clin. asso. prof., 1982—; clin. asso., trainer Suicide Prevention Service, Indpls., 1974-77; chmn. adv. bd. de-institutionalization project Central State Hosp., Indpls., 1978-79; mem. Ind. Council Community Mental Health Center, 1979-80. Recipient Outstanding Achievement in Professions award Center Leadership Devel., 1981. Mem. Ind. U. Alumni Assn., Christian Women's Fellowship, 500 Festival Assos., Coalition 100 Black Women (bd dirs.), Neal-Marshall Alumni Club, Alpha Kappa Alpha, Sigma Theta Tau, Chi Eta Phi. Mem. Christian Ch. (Disciples of Christ). Author articles in field. Home: 4057 Clarendon Rd Indianapolis IN 46208 Office: 1500 N Ritter Ave Indianapolis IN 46219

HARDEN, DANIEL ALEXANDER, JR., chemical engineer; b. Detroit, Nov. 9, 1946; s. Daniel Alexander Sr. and Jewell Mae (Pouncil) H. B.S. in Chem. Engring., Wayne State U., 1978, postgrad., 1982—. Engr. Exxon Co., USA, Linden, N.J., 1978-82; instr. Metro Youth Found., Detroit, 1984-85; supr. Hunter & Walker, Inc., Detroit, 1985—. Chmn. fund-raising com. to elect Clarence D. Green, Southfield, Mich., 1985. Served with U.S. Army, 1963-66, Vietnam. Mem. Engring. Soc. Detroit. Avocations: reading; marksmanship; music; modern art. Home: 3904 Mt Elliott St Detroit MI 48207 Office: Hunter and Walker Inc 9980 Erwin St Detroit MI 48234

HARDEN, NORMAN EUGENE, business services company executive; b. Fond du Lac, Wis., May 3, 1934; s. Russell J. and Norma (Mayer) H.; m. Sondra Willoughby, Dec. 23, 1976; children—Gary, Cheryl, Jeffrey. B.S. magna cum laude, Lawrence U., 1958. With A.C. Nielsen Co., 1958—, prodn. supr., Clinton, Iowa, 1958-60, gen. mgr., 1960-64, v.p., Denver and Boulder, Colo., 1964-68, exec. v.p., Northbrook, Ill., 1968-76; pres., 1976—. Trustee Lawrence U. Mem. Am. Mktg. Assn., Pres.'s Assn. Served with USAF, 1954-56. Clubs: Econ. (Chgo.); Biltmore Country. Office: AC Nielsen Co Nielsen Plaza Northbrook IL 60062

HARDER, ROBERT CLARENCE, state official; b. Horton, Kans., June 4, 1929; s. Clarence Leslie and Olympia (Kubik) H.; m. Dorothy Welty, July 31, 1953; children—Anne Harder Marley, James David. B.A., Baker U., 1951; Th.M., So. Meth. U., 1954; Th.D., Boston U., 1958; D.H.L. (hon.), Baker U., 1983. Ordained to ministry Methodist Ch., 1959. Pastor, East Topeka Meth. Ch., Kans., 1958-64; mem. Kans. Ho. of Reps., Topeka, 1961-67; research assoc. Menninger Found., Topeka, 1964-65; tech. assistance coordinator Office of Gov., Topeka, 1967-68; sec. Kans. Dept. Social and Rehab. Services, Topeka, 1969—; instr. Kans. U. Sch. of Social Welfare, 1969—. Bd. dirs. Topeka Day Care Assn., Topeka Assn. for Retarded Citizens, Kans. State Sec. Employment Rev. Bd.; trustee Baker U., Baldwin. Named Man of Yr., Midway Mag., Topeka Capital Jour., 1965; recipient The Romana Hood award Topeka Welfare Planning Council, 1965. Mem. Kans. Council on Social Welfare (cert. appreciation 1982), Am. Pub. Welfare Assn., Am. Soc. for Pub. Adminstrs. (Pub. Adminstr. Yr. Kans. chpt. 1980). Democrat. Avocations: woodcarving, reading. Office: Social and Rehab Services State Office Bldg Room 603-N Topeka KS 66612

HARDIN, CAROLYN MYRICK, physiology educator, researcher; b. New Albany, Ind., Dec. 31, 1929; d. James Madison and Olive Cleon (Venner) M. B.A., George Washington U., 1958, M.A., 1959, Ph.D., 1969. Trainee psychophysiol. lab. Perry Point (Md.) VA Hosp., 1959-61; psychology technician Salem (Va.) VA Hosp., 1962-64; fellow, trainee in physiology George Washington U. Med. Ctr., Washington, 1964-69; instr. Meharry Med. Coll., Nashville, 1969-70, asst. prof. psychiatry and pharmacology, 1970-75, assoc. prof., 1976; assoc. prof. physiology Palmer Coll. Chiropractic, Davenport, Iowa, 1977-81, prof, 1981—. Treas. Hawthorne Dr. Townhomes Assn., Bettendorf, Iowa, 1981-83; mem.-at-large adminstrv. bd. Broadview United Meth. Ch., Bettendorf, 1982—. Mem. Am. Physiol. Soc., Biophys. Soc., AAAS, Assn. Women in Sci., Iowa Acad. Sci., AAUP, Internat. Platform Assn., Sigma Xi. Democrat. Contbr. articles to profl. publs. Home: 2503 Hawthorne Dr Bettendorf IA 52722 Office: 1000 Brady St PO Box 2455 Davenport IA 52803

HARDIN, FRED A., transportation union executive; b. Greenville, S.C., Feb. 21, 1918; m. Eleanor Cady; children—Carol, Frederick, Jane. Brake operator So. Ry., Greenville, 1940-42, condr., 1942—; alternate v.p. Brotherhood Ry. Trains, Cleve., 1964-68, v.p., 1968-79; pres. United Transp. Union, Cleve., 1979, 1983—; chmn. Ry. Labor Exec. Assn., Washington, 1981-84. Bd. dirs. YMCA, Washington; mem. adv. council Am. Ditchley Found., N.Y.C., 1982. Democrat. Office: United Transp Union 14600 Detroit Ave Cleveland OH 44107

HARDING, CLIFFORD VINCENT, JR., ophthalmology educator, researcher; b. Cranston, R.I., Apr. 27, 1925; s. Clifford Vincent and Lillian May (Blinkhorn) H.; m. Drusilla Ruth Van Hoesen, June 12, 1948; children—Clifford Vincent III, Richard Haviland. A.B., Brown U., 1946; M.S., Yale U., 1948; Ph.D., U. Pa., 1950. Asst. prof. U. So. Calif., Los Angeles, 1952-54; assoc. prof. U. Pa., Phila., 1954-58; physiologist AEC, Washington, 1956-57; asst. prof., then assoc. prof. Columbia U. Coll. Physicians and Surgeons, N.Y.C., 1958-64; prof., chmn. biol. dept. Oakland U., Rochester, Mich., 1964-73; prof., dir. research Kresge Eye Inst. Wayne State U., Detroit, 1973—. U.S. editor Protoplasmatiologia, 1960-65; mem. editorial bd. Ophthalmic Research, 1975—. Contbr. articles to profl. publs., chpts. to books. recipient Career Devel. award NIH, 1963-64, Fight for Sight citation, 1982; Lalor fellow, 1958. Mem. Mich. Electron Microscopy Forum (pres. 1975-76), Assn. for Research in Vision and Ophthalmology, Internat. Soc. Eye Research, Am. Soc. Cell Biology, Internat. Soc. Cell Biology. Office: Kresge Eye Inst Wayne State U 540 E Canfield Detroit MI 48201

HARDISON, LESLIE C., chemical engineer; b. Chgo., Feb. 16, 1929; s. William L. and Lyda Sue (Sims) H.; m. Dolores Eleanor Wachdrof, June 14, 1952; children—William, John, Patricia, Susan, Janet, James, Paul. B.S. in

Mech. Engring., Ill. Inst. Tech., 1950. Registered profl. engr., Ill., Colo., Pa., Conn. Research engr. Ill. Inst. Tech. Research Inst., Chgo., 1950-53; chem. process engr. UOP, DesPlaines, Ill., 1953-63, dir. research and devel. Catalitic Combustion Co. div. UOP, Bloomer, Wis., 1963-66, tech. dir. Air Correction div. UOP, Darien, Conn., 1966-70; v.p., then pres. ARI Tech., Palatine, Ill., 1970—, chmn. bd., 1983—; chmn. bd. Nat. Seal Co., Palatine, 1979—. Contbr. articles to profl. publs. Patentee in field. Mem. Am. Inst. Chem. Engrs., Am. Chem. Soc., ASME. Republican. Home: 233 Apple Tree Ln Barrington IL 60010 Office: ARI Technologies 600 N 1st Bank Dr Palatine IL 60067

HARDT, VIRGINIA GAYLE, university administrator; b. Washington, Ind., Mar. 20, 1947; d. Arthur B. and Ethel V. (Holmes) Clarke; m. Herbert T. Hardt, June 14, 1970; 1 child, Adam Clarke. B.S., Ind. State U., 1969; M.S.E., U. Wis.-Oshkosh, 1982. Music tchr. West Bend Pub. Schs., Wis., 1969-70, South Hadley Pub. Schs., Mass., 1970-71, Sevastopol Schs., Sturgeon Bay, Wis., 1974-75; asst. circulation librarian Lawrence U., Appleton, Wis., 1977-79, dir. career planning and placement, 1979—. Mem. Wis. Career Planning and Placement Assn. (editor, chair publs. com. 1983—), Women in Mgmt. (state bd. dirs. 1984—, pres.-elect Valley chpt. 1985), Midwest Coll. Placement Assn. (conf. planning com. 1982-84), Am. Coll. Personnel Assn., Fox Valley Personnel Assn., Nat. Vocat. Guidance Assn., Am. Assn. Counseling and Devel. Office: PO Box 599 Appleton WI 54912

HARDWICK, PHILLIP KEITH, foundation executive, consultant; b. Richmond, Ind., Oct. 31, 1935; s. Herman Pearl and Emily cora (Richardson) H.; m. Patricia Ann Placke, Sept. 1, 1958 (div. 1976); children—Lucinda Kaye Hardwick Masterson, Phillip James; m. Karen Lynn Hickman, Nov. 20, 1976. B.S., Ind. U., 1959, M.S., 1963. Recreation assoc. Milw. Schs., 1959-61; supt. recreation Bloomington Parks, Ind., 1961-63; Indpls. Parks, 1963-67; campaign dir. United Way, Indpls., 1967-84; spl. asst. to pres. Marian Coll., Indpls., 1984-85; pres. Methodist Health Found., Indpls., 1985—; cons. P.K. Assocs., Indpls., 1983—. Bd. dirs. Indpls. Humane Soc., 1982—, Catholic Social Services, Indpls., 1985—. Recipient State High Sch. Football Official of Yr. award Ind. High Sch. Athletic Assn., 1985. Mem. Ind. Council Fund Raisers (bd. dirs. 1981-83, Profl. of Yr. award 1984). Republican. Lutheran. Clubs: Crooked Stick Golf, Speedway Golf (pres. 1982-84). Avocations: college and high school football official; golf. Home: 1074D Crooked Stick Ln Carmel IN 46032 Office: Meth Health Found 1812 N Meridian St Indianapolis IN 46202

HARDY, DOROTHY CARROLL, dean, consultant; b. Town Creek, Ala.; d. Odis Cal; divorced, 1956; 1 child, Althea J. Mootry. B.S., Ala. State U., 1956; M.Ed., Xavier U., 1960; Ed.D., U. Cin., 1976. Cert. tchr., Ohio. Asst. dean U. Cin., 1973-77; asst. prof. Kans. State U., Manhattan, 1979-80; pres. Cin. Life Adj. Inst., 1980-83, also dir.; commr. Ohio Dept. Mental Health, Columbus, 1983-84; dean student devel. services Southeast Mo. State U., Cape Girardeau, 1985—. Author: (poems) Peebles in the Pond. Editor Neighborhood Youth Corps News. Contbr. biog. sketches, articles to local newspapers, mags. Fundraiser Ohio Democratic party Citizens for Ohio, 1983; minority coordinator Citizens for Ohio for Issues 2 and 3; tng. vol. Gov. Richard F. Celeste campaign, Cin., 1982; tng. dir. Mondale/Ferraro presdl. campaign, 1984. Recipient Brodie Research award U. Cin., 1975, Outstanding Woman of 1981 Community Service award, NAACP, 1981; grantee U. Cin., 1974. Mem. Nat. Assn. Student Personnel Adminstrs. (chmn. 1981-83), Am. Assn. Counseling and Devel. (chmn. multicultural com. Nat. Conf. 1983), Omega Phi Psi. Baptist. Avocation: writing poetry, novels and articles. Home: 31 N Henderson Cape Girardeau MO 63701

HARDY, E. VERNEDA, nurse; b. Pinckneyville, Ill., Feb. 1, 1927; d. Roy Nesbitt and Etta Mae (McIlrath) Brown; 1 dau., Marvel Ann Hardy Donovan. Diploma, Christian Welfare Hosp. Sch. Nursing, 1948; B.S. in Occupational Edn., So. Ill. U. Carbondale, 1984. Nurse, Christian Welfare Hosp., East St. Louis, Ill., 1948-52, St. Mary's Hosp., East St. Louis, 1952-61; nurse Pinckneyville (Ill.) Community Hosp., 1961-66, operating room supr., 1966—. Mem. Assn. Operating Room Nurses. Republican. Baptist. Club: Pinckneyville Bus. Womens. Home: 605 Saint Louis St Pinckneyville IL 62274 Office: 101 N Walnut St Pinckneyville IL 62274

HARDY, H. GUY, lawyer; b. Bloomfield, Iowa, July 18, 1918; s. Rufus Guy and Mabel (Kenworthy) H.; student Bloomfield Jr. Coll., 1936-38, B.A., State U. Iowa, 1940, J.D. 1942; LL.M., Harvard, 1947; m. Dorothy Rice, Apr. 22, 1949; children—Susan (Mrs. Michael Doland), Barbara (Mrs. Samuel Maihack), Beverly (Mrs. Scott Montgomery), Richard, Nancy. Admitted to Iowa bar, 1942, Ohio bar, 1948; practiced in Cleve., 1947—; mem. firm McDonald, Hopkins & Hardy Co., Cleve., 1947—. Dir., sec. Am. Handling Equipment Co., Daniels Funeral Home, Inc., Jaquay Lake Park, Inc.; dir. Babcock's Schmid Assocs., Inc., H & H Data Products, Inc. Asst. area chmn. United Appeal, Cleve., 1966-67; bd. mgrs. West Shore YMCA, 1963-77; trustee Combined Health Fund Drive, Bay Village, Ohio, 1964-68, St. John West Shore Hosp., Bay Village Swimming Pool Inc.; councilman Bay Village, O., 1956-61, pres., 1960-61; mem. bd. edn., Bay Village, 1964-73, pres., 1968-70. Served to capt. CIC, AUS, 1942-46, 51. Recipient Extension award Lions Club, 1953. Mem. Am. Judicature Soc., Am., Ohio State, Cleve. bar assns., Order of Coif. Episcopalian (vestryman 1963-66). Lion. Home: 28334 Osborn Rd Bay Village OH 44140 Office: East Ohio Bldg Cleveland OH 44114

HARDY, MICHAEL LYNN, lawyer; b. St. Louis, Aug. 28, 1947; s. William Frost and Ruth (Shea) H.; m. Martha Bond, Sept. 2, 1972; children—Brian M., Kevin. A.B., John Carroll U., 1969; J.D., U. Mich., 1972. Bar: Ohio 1972. Assoc. Guren, Merritt, et al, Cleve., 1972-77, ptnr., 1977-84; ptnr. Thompson, Hine & Flory, Cleve., 1984—. Bd. advisors Harvard Environ. Law Rev., 1976-78. Served to capt. U.S. Army, 1969-74. Mem. Ohio State Bar Assn. (sec. environ. law com. 1983-84, vice-chmn. 1984—). Club: Canterbury Golf (Shaker Heights, Ohio). Home: 3330 Dorchester Rd Shaker Heights OH 44120 Office: Thompson Hine & Flory 1100 National City Bank Bldg Cleveland OH 44114

HARDY, NORMAN E. PETER, See *Who's Who in America,* 43rd edition.

HARDY, WILLIAM ROBINSON, lawyer; b. Cin., June 14, 1934; s. William B. and Chastine M. (Sprague) H.; m. Barbro Anita Medin, Oct. 11, 1964; children—Anita Christina, William Robinson. A.B., Princeton U., 1956; J.D., Harvard U., 1963. Bar: Ohio 1963, U.S. Supreme Ct. 1975. Analyst, Dept. Army, 1956-60; agt. New Eng. Mut. Life Ins. Co., 1956-63; assoc. Graydon, Head & Ritchey, Cin., 1963-68, ptnr., 1968—; mem. panel comml. and constrn. industry arbitrators Am. Arbitration Assn., 1972—; reporter joint com. for revision of rules of U.S. Dist. Ct. (so. dist.) Ohio, 1975, 80 83, co-chmn. arbitration tribunal, 1984—. Bd. dirs. Cin. Union Bethel, 1968—, pres., 1977-83; bd. dirs. Ohio Valley Goodwill Industries Rehab. Ctr., Cin., 1970—, pres., 1981—; mem. City of Cin. Bd. Bldg. Standards and Appeals, 1976—, vice chmn., 1983, chmn., 1983—. Served to capt. USAR, 1956-68. Recipient award of Merit, Ohio Legal Ctr. Inst., 1975, 76. Mem. ABA, Ohio Bar Assn., Cin. Bar Assn., Am. Judicature Soc., Assn. Trial Lawyers Am., Ohio Acad. Trial Lawyers, AAAS, 6th Circuit Jud. Conf. (life), Ohio Soc. Colonial Wars (gov. 1979), Phi Beta Kappa. Mem. Ch. of the Redeemer. Home: 1339 Michigan Ave Cincinnati OH 45208 Office: 1900 Fifth Third Ctr 511 Walnut St Cincinnati OH 45202

HARDYMON, MONICA ELLA, lawyer; b. Wilmington, Del., Feb. 20, 1954; d. Garnet Thomas and Cecelia Rebecca (Paul) Sleep; m. David Wayne Hardymon, Mar. 13, 1982. B.A., Am. U., 1975; J.D., Capital U., 1978; cert. Nat. Jud. Coll., 1979. Bar: Ohio 1978, U.S. Dist. Ct. (so. dist.) Ohio 1978. Legal writing adviser Capital U., Columbus, Ohio, 1976-77; law clk. Ohio Ct. Appeals, Columbus, 1977-79; atty. examiner Bd. Tax Appeals, Columbus, 1979—. Team mem. Upper Arlington Volleyball League, Ohio, 1980—; exercise instr. YMCA, Columbus, 1983—. Recipient cert. Order of Curia, 1978, cert. of appreciation YMCA, Columbus, 1984; named to Outstanding Young Women Am., U.S. Jaycees, 1984. Mem. Franklin County Women Lawyers Assn. Republican. Home: 3534 Redding Rd Columbus OH 43221 Office: Bd Tax Appeals 30 E Broad St Columbus OH 43215

HARGRAVE, HAROLD, retired educator; b. Boonville, Ind., June 10, 1908; s. Jacob Thurman and Dora (West) H.; B.S. in Edn., Oakland City Coll., 1930, LL.D., 1971; M.S. in Edn., Ind. U., 1936; m. Rowena Hullett, June 4, 1935; 1 dau., Ruth Ann. Began career as tchr. Crowe Sch., Ind., 1926-27, Kings (Ill.) Sch., 1930-31; tchr., guidance dir. pub. schs., LaPorte, Ind., 1931-56, prin., 1956-58, supt. schs., 1958-72; mem. faculty N.Y. U., 1947-49, Peabody Tchrs. Coll., 1948, Butler U., 1946-55. Pres. elect Ind. Pub. Sch. Study Council, 1971; spl. asst. to mayor 1972-80; sec. LaPorte Econ. Devel. Commn., 1972—; exec. com. Fairview Youth Treatment Center, 1973-78. Trustee Community Hosp., Roger Williams Found.; bd. dirs. Haven Hubbard Home for Ret., 1974-77, LaPorte Park Found., 1984—; trustee moderator, deacon First Baptist Ch. Mem. Am. Assn. Sch. Adminstrs., NEA, Ind. Assn. Pub. Sch. Supts. (v.p. 1967-68, pres. 1969-70), C. of C. (v.p. 1974-75), Phi Delta Kappa. Mason, Elk, Kiwanian (pres. 1945, lt. gov. 1947). Author: Extending Reading Skills, 1976. Home: 1808 Monroe St LaPorte IN 46350

HARGRAVE, SARAH QUESENBERRY, corporate foundation executive; b. Mt. Airy, N.C., Dec. 11, 1944; d. Teddie W. and Lois Knight (Slusher) Quesenberry Stout; student Radford Coll., 1963-64, Va. Poly. Inst. State U., 1964-67. Mgmt. trainee Thalhimer Bros. Dept. Store, Richmond, Va., 1967-68; Central Va. fashion and publicity dir. Sears Roebuck & Co., Richmond, 1968-73, nat. decorating sch. coordinator, Chgo., 1973-74, nat. dir. bus. and profl. women's programs, Chgo., 1974-76, v.p., treas., program dir. Sears-Roebuck Found., Chgo., 1976—, program mgr. corp. contbns. and memberships, 1981-84, dir. corp. mktg./pub. affairs, 1984—; bd. dirs. Am. Assembly Collegiate Schs. Bus., 1979-82, vis. com., 1979-82, fin. and audit com., 1980-82, mem. task force on doctoral supply and demand, 1980-82; mem. Com. for Equal Opportunity for Women, 1976-82, chmn., 1978-79, 80-81; mem. bus. adv. council Walter E. Heller Coll. Bus. Adminstrn., Roosevelt U., 1979-82, 85—. Co-dir. Ill. Internat. Women's Year Center, 1975. Named Outstanding Young Woman of Year, Ill., 1976; Woman of Achievement, State St. Bus. and Profl. Womans Club, 1978. Mem. Assn. Humanistic Psychology, Am. Home Econs. Assn., Nat. Fedn. Bus. and Profl. Women's Clubs, Eddystone Condominium Assn. (v.p. 1978—). Home: 421 W Melrose St Chicago IL 60657 Office: Sears-Roebuck Found Sears Tower Chicago IL 60684

HARING, DAVID ALVIN, manufacturing company executive; b. Akron, Ohio, Feb. 10, 1945; s. Stanley Alvin and Harriet Marie (Stark) H.; B.S., Baldwin-Wallace Coll., 1967; M.B.A., Ohio State U., 1973; m. Luella Mae Wiley, June 10, 1967; children—Douglas, Brian, Bradford. Programmer, systems analyst Chem. Abstracts Service, Columbus, Ohio, 1967-71; mgr. systems and programming Borden, Inc., Columbus, 1971-75; dir. mgmt. info. services Tremco, Inc., Cleve., 1975-77; dir. systems and data processing The Stouffer Corp., Cleve., 1977-80; v.p. mgmt. systems Hauserman, Inc. (formerly The E.F. Hauserman Co., Sunar Hauserman Co. and Sunar Ltd.), 1980—; track coach Solon (Ohio) High Sch., 1982-83, Gilmour Acad., 1984-85. Recipient Theodore O. Hoffman edn. grant Borden, Inc., 1973. Club: Cleve. Easy Striders Track (dir., head coach). Home: 6713 Duneden Ave Solon OH 44139 Office: 5711 Grant Ave Cleveland OH 44105

HARKIN, THOMAS RICHARD, U.S. Senator; b. Cumming, Iowa, Nov. 19, 1939; s. Patrick and Frances Harkin; B.S., Iowa State U., 1962; J.D., Catholic U. Am., 1972; m. Ruth Raduenz, July 6, 1968; children—Amy, Jenny. Bar: Iowa 1972. Mem. staff U.S. House Select Com. on U.S. Involvement in S.E. Asia, 1970; mem. 94th-98th Congresses from 5th Iowa Dist., mem. sci. and tech. com., agr. com.; mem. U.S. Senate from Iowa, 1985—, mem. appropriations com., agr. com. Served as lt. USN, 1962-67. Named Outstanding Young Alumnus, Iowa State U., 1974. Democrat. Home: Cumming IA 50061 Office: 317 Hart Bldg Washington DC 20510

HARKINS, JAMES LEONARD, JR., utility consultant, lawyer; b. Cleve., Aug. 2, 1929; s. James Leonard and Dorothy Sabrina (Wright) H. B.S., Western Res. U., 1951, LL.B., 1954. Bar: Ohio 1954, U.S. Supreme Ct. 1965. Traveling auditor. Gen. Electric Co., Cleve., 1956-58; comptroller Cleve. Utilities Dept., 1966-67; sr. budget analyst Cleve. Office of Budget, 1968-69; asst. dir. of law City of Cleve., 1970-78; self-employed utility cons., Shaker Heights, Ohio, 1979—. Served with U.S. Army, 1954-56. Mem. ABA, Ohio Bar Assn. Avocations: chess; duplicate bridge. Home and office: 18590 Parkland Dr Shaker Heights OH 44122

HARLAN, NORMAN RALPH, builder; b. Dayton, Ohio, Dec. 21, 1914; s. Joseph and Anna (Kaplan) H.; Indsl. Engring. degree U. Cin., 1937; m. Thelma Katz, Sept. 4, 1955; children—Leslie, Todd. Pres. Am. Constrn. Corp., Dayton, 1949—, Mainline Investment Corp., 1951—, Harlan, Inc., realtors; treas. Norman Estates, Inc. Mem. Dayton Real Estate Bd., Ohio Real Estate Assn., Nat. Assn. Real Estate Bds., C. of C., Pi Lambda Phi. Home: 303 Glenridge Rd Kettering OH 45429 Office: 2451 S Dixie Hwy Dayton OH 45409

HARLAND, MARY KATHRYN HOLTAN, business and economics educator; b. Forest City, Iowa, Mar. 3, 1946; d. Hans Oscar and Ruth (Hermanson) Holtan; m. Thomas Robert Harland, May 4, 1974. A.A., Waldorf Coll., Forest City, 1966; B.A., Wartburg Coll., Waverly, Iowa, 1969; M.A., Mankato State U. (Minn.), 1981. Instr., Chisago Lakes Area Schs., Minn., 1970-72, Albert Lea Area Vo-Tech Inst. (Minn.), 1977-80; asst. prof. bus. and econs. Waldorf Coll., 1980—; adj. faculty mem. Mankato State U., Minn., 1984; cons., lectr. in field. Author ednl. materials. Mem. Delta Pi Epsilon. Republican. Lutheran. Avocations: needlework, reading, bicycling. Home: RR 1 Box 44 Forest City IA 50436

HARMAN, DONALD LEE, nurse, educator; b. Titusville, Pa., Mar. 22, 1948; s. William Ceska and Eva Louise (Matha) H. B.S. in Edn., Edinboro Coll., 1970, M.S., 1972; A.A.S. in Nursing, Ohio U.-Zanesville, 1977. R.N., Ohio, Ill., Wis. Dir. out-patient services, Spencer Hosp., Meadville, Pa., 1974; in-service instr., Guernsey Meml. Hosp., Cambridge, Ohio, 1974-77; instr. in med., surg. and pediatric nursing Blessing Hosp., Quincy, Ill., 1977-79; pediatric staff nurse, Rush Presbyn. St. Luke's Hosp., Chgo., 1979; camp nurse Young Men's Jewish Council, Chgo., 1979; emergency room nurse Henrotin Hosp., Chgo., 1979, intervenous therapist, 1980; head instr. med. surg. nursing Madison (Wis.) Gen. Hosp. Sch. of Nursing, 1980-81, dir. nursing, edn., 1981—, v.p., bd. dirs. Common Health Co. Hon. bd. dirs. Colony Day Care. Recipient Copper Cup award, Madison Gen. Hosp., 1983. Mem. Am. Assembly for Men in Nursing, Am. Soc. Health, Edn. and Tng., Wis. Soc. for Health, Edn. and Tng., Nat. Assn. Orthopedic Nurses, Wis. Soc. for Nursing Service Adminstrs. Methodist.

HARMAN, JAMES RICHARD, structural engineer; b. Elkhart, Ind., May 3, 1952; s. John R. and Elizabeth (Crosier) H.; m. Christi J. Bock; children—Katie E., James J. B.C.E., Tufts U., 1974; M.B.A., Ind. U., 1978. Structural engr. U.S. Steel, Gary, Ind., 1975-81, environ. engr., 1981; project engr. Bock Industries, Elkhart, Ind., 1981-84, midd supt., 1984—. Advisor, Jr. Achievement, 1977-81; v.p. bd. dirs. Montessori Sch., Elkhart, 1984, pres. bd. dirs., 1984-85. Methodist. Office: 57540 State Rd 19 S Elkhart IN 46517

HARMON, DAVID ELMER, JR., oil company executive, consulting geologist; b. Kittanning, Pa., Aug. 12, 1932; s. David E. and Martha E. (Cochran) H.; m. Paula Ann Younker, Oct. 8, 1960; children—David Michael, Sabrina Marie, John Matthew Wills, Patrick Kevin, Paul Charles, Robert Jude. A.B. in Geology, Marietta Coll., 1954. Registered profl. engr., Ky., Ind. profl. land surveyor, Ind.; registered profl. geologist, Ga.; cert. petroleum geologist, Am. Inst. Profl. Geologists. Geologist, B.H. Putnam, Marietta, Ohio, 1954-58; chief geologist F.E. Moran Oil Co., Owensboro, Ky., 1958-64, cons., Louisville, Ky., 1964-67; chief engr. Jefferson Co., Louisville, 1967-69; chief geologist Guernsey Petroleum, Atlanta, 1969-72, cons., 1972-73; v.p. Johnston Petroleum Co., Cambridge, Ohio, 1973-75, O'Neal Petroleum Co., New Concord, Ohio, 1975-83; pres. Concord Energy, Inc., New Concord, 1983—, also dir.; cons. various cos. Pres., bd. dirs. East Muskingum Swimming Pool Assn., New Concord, 1976; dir. Southeastern Ohio Symphony Orch., New Concord, 1978. Served as sgt. U.S. Army, 1955-57. Fellow Geol. Soc. Am.; mem. Am. Assn. Petroleum Geologists (chmn. dist. 3 govt. affairs com.), Soc. Petroleum Engrs., Am. Inst. Profl. Geologists, Ohio Hist. Soc., Williamsburg Found. Roman Catholic. Clubs: Dunwoody Country (Atlanta), Zanesville Country (Ohio). Avocation: historical preservation. Lodge: K.C. Home: Morgan House Route 2 New Concord OH 43762 Office: Concord Energy Inc 22 W Main St New Concord OH 43762

HARMON, DOROTHY ANN, univ. adminstr.; b. El Paso, Tex., Aug. 1, 1924; d. Willis Wayne and Katie Irene (Jarrell) Ransom; B.A., Wichita State U., 1946; m. Francis E. Harmon, Aug. 23, 1948; children—Karen Lynn, Wayne Eugene. Field house mgr., Wichita (Kans.) State U., 1967-74, acad. coordinator athletic dept., 1968-74, asst. athletic dir., 1971-72, asso. dir. Marcus Center Continuing Edn., 1974—. Bd. dirs. Sr. Services, Inc., 1982; mem. planning div. United Way, 1977—; mem. planned giving ARC. Named to Shocker Hall of Fame, 1981. Mem. Nat. Assn. Edn. Secs. (state chmn. 1974-75), Kans. Assn. Edn. Secs. (fall workshop chmn. 1977), Wichita Assn. Edn. Secs. (bd. dirs.), Wichita State U. Alumni Assn. (bd. dirs.), Assn. Continuing Higher Edn., Am. Soc. Tng. and Devel., Alpha Chi Omega. Democrat. Methodist. Clubs: Wichita State U. Dames (2d v.p. 1982-83), Air Capital Track (bd. dirs.), Downtown Lioness (past pres.). Home: 2418 N Belmont St Wichita KS 67220 Office: Marcus Center Wichita State U Wichita KS 67208

HARMON, KEITH WELLINGTON, wildlife management specialist; b. Gary, Ind., Aug. 20, 1930; s. Clay W. and Virginia B. (Furr) H.; m. Marjorie A. Warren, Nov. 3, 1950 (div. 1976); children—Gareth Ann, David Gene, Margot Elizabeth; m. Constance M. Bowen, July 8, 1976. B.S., Mich. State U., 1959, M.S., 1965; Ph.D., Colo. State U., 1968. Conservation aide Mich. Div. Wildlife, Lansing, 1957-59; area game mgr. Minn. Div. Wildlife, Marshall, 1960-65; wildlife specialist N.D. State U., Fargo, 1967-70; field rep. Wildlife Mgmt. Inst., Firth, Nebr., 1970—; wildlife mgmt. cons., Firth, 1970—; chmn. habitat com. Miss. Flyway Council, Firth, 1970—. Contbr. numerous articles to pop. mags. and sci. jours. Served with USN, 1950-54. Recipient cert. appreciation Midwest Assn. Fish & Wildlife Agys., 1976. Mem. Wildlife Soc. (pres. N.D. chpt. 1969, Profl. award 1974), Nat. Wildlife Fedn., Nebr. Wildlife Fedn. Methodist. Club: Lincoln Gun (Nebr.) (bd. dirs. 1984—). Avocations: camping, hunting, skeet shooting. Home and Office: Wildlife Mgmt Inst Route 1 Box 122 Firth NE 68358

HARMON, WILLIAM LEWIS, JR., laser physicist; b. Grove City, Pa., Aug. 22, 1928; s. William Lewis and Alma Grace (Regnemer) H.; m. Naomi Ruth Leach, Feb. 19, 1955; children—William Lewis, Bruce Regnemer, Hawley Paris, Robyn Love. B.S., Ohio State U., 1949, M.S., 1955. Jr. physicist Communication and Navigation Lab., Wright-Patterson AFB, Ohio, 1949-55, sr. physicist Air Force Avionics Lab., 1955-66, 69—; sr. physicist Air Force Cloudcroft Electro-Optical Site, N.Mex., 1966-69. Contbr. articles to profl. jours. Trustee Greenwich Village Civic Orgn., Dayton, Ohio, 1960-62; host family Am. Field Service, 1980-81. Served with USAF, 1950-53. Mem. Dayton Chess Club (sec. 1978-79). Democrat. Methodist. Avocations: chess; traveling; swimming; hiking. Home: 5907 Rosebury Dr Huber Heights OH 45424 Office: Air Force Avionics Lab AFWAL/AARI Wright-Patterson AFB OH 45433

HARMS, MYRON LOUIS, mathematics and computer educator; b. Newton, Kans., Apr. 4, 1937; s. William and Marie L. Harms; m. Patricia Winifred Agger, Apr. 29, 1973; children—Brian, Joy. B.A., Bethel Coll., Newton, 1959; M.Ed., Tex. A&M U., 1966. Tchr. Eden Christian Coll., Niagara-on Lake, Ont., Can., 1959-60, Twillingate High Sch., Nfld., Can., 1960-61, Moeding Coll., Lobatse, Botswana, Africa, 1971-74; instr. Freeman Jr. Coll., S.D., 1961-71, asst. prof., 1974—. Mem. S.D. Council Tchrs. Math. Avocation: gardening. Home: 712 S Main St Freeman SD 57029 Office: Freeman Jr Coll 748 S Main St Freeman SD 57029

HARPER, ADA PATRICIA, radiologist; b. Port-of-Spain, Trinidad, Aug. 17, 1947; came to U.S., 1972; d. Oswald Emanuel and Cleopatra (Hall) Romilly; m. Noel Kennedy Harper, June 17, 1972; children—Melissa Stacia, Leah Kelly. M.B.B.S., U. W.I. Med. Sch., 1972. Diplomate Am. Bd. Radiology. Rotating intern Borgess Hosp., Kalamazoo, 1972-73; resident in diagnostic radiology Ind. U. Hosps., Indpls., 1973-76, staff, assoc. prof., 1976-82, clin. assoc. prof., 1982—; practice medicine, specializing in radiology Indpls. Breast Ctr., 1982—; also lectr. Research, publs. in field. Mem. Am. Coll. Radiology, AMA, Radiol. Soc. N. Am., Ind. Roentgen Soc. Episcopalian. Office: Indpls Breast Ctr 1950 W 86th St Indianapolis IN 46260

HARPER, CHARLES MICHEL, food company executive; b. Lansing, Mich., Sept. 26, 1927; s. Charles Frost and Alma (Michel) H.; B.S. in Mech. Engring., Purdue U., 1949; M.B.A., U. Chgo., 1950; m. Joan Frances Bruggema, June 24, 1950; children—Kathleen Harper Wenngatz, Carolyn Harper Wherry, Michel, Elizabeth Ann Harper Murphy. Sr. methods engr. Oldsmobile div. Gen. Motors Corp., Detroit, 1950-54; dir. indsl. engring. Pillsbury Co., Mpls., 1954-60, dir. engring., 1961-66, v.p. research, devel. and new products, 1965-70, group v.p. poultry and food service, 1970-74; exec. v.p., chief operating officer ConAgra Inc., Omaha, 1974-76, pres., chief exec. officer, 1976-81, chmn., chief exec. officer, 1981—, also dir.; dir. Valmont Industries, Northwestern Bell Telephone, InterNorth, Norwest Corp. Mem. council Village of Excelsior (Minn.), 1965-70, mayor, 1974; trustee Com. Econ. Devel.; bd. dirs. Joslyn Mus., Creighton U., Nebr. Ind. Coll. Found.; trustee Bishop Clarkson Meml. Hosp. Served with AUS, 1944-46. Mem. Grocery Mfrs. Am. (dir.), Greater Omaha C. of C. (chmn. 1979), Ak-Sar-Ben (gov.), Beta Theta Pi. Clubs: Omaha Country, Mpls. Office: ConAgra Ctr One Central Park Plaza Omaha NE 68102

HARPER, LINDA WALKER, lawyer; b. Davenport, Iowa, Dec. 14; d. Frank Barton and Golda (Schultz) Walker; m. Timothy W. Harper; 1 son, Jesse. B.S., U. Mich., 1978; J.D., Thomas Cooley Law Sch., Lansing, Mich., 1982. Bar: Mich. 1982, U.S. Dist. Ct. (ea. dist.) Mich. 1982. Vice pres. Twp. Zoning Bd., Gregory, Mich., 1977-81; law clk. Livingston County Cir. Ct., Mich., 1980-82; sole practice, Fowlerville, Mich., 1982—. Mem. ABA, Assn. Trial Lawyers Am., Women Lawyers Mich., Women Lawyers Livingston County. Republican. Home: Pinckney MI Office: 309 E Grand River Fowlerville MI 48836

HARPER, OLIVER WILLIAM, III, corporate plan consultant; b. Chgo., Nov. 25, 1953; s. Oliver William and Pauline W. (Simpson) H.; m. Patricia Ruth Hayes, Mar. 9, 1979; 1 son, Oliver William. B.A., U. Ill.-Chgo., 1978. Agt., Occidental Life of Calif., 1979; registered rep. Lincoln Nat. Life Ins. Co., Ft. Wayne, Ind., 1979-80; agt., registered rep. Penn Mut. Life Ins. Co., Phila., 1980-85; dir. employee benefit div. Penn Fin. Group, Chgo., 1981-85; ptnr., v.p. Corp. Plan Cons., Inc., 1985—. Assoc. bd. St. Edmund's Credit Union; co-chair bd. dirs. St. Edmund's Ch. Mem. Nat. Assn. Securities Dealers, Cert. Employee Benefit Specialists, Profl. Assn. Diving Instr., Notaries Assn. Ill., U. Ill. Alumni Assn., Underwater Explorers Soc. Episcopalian. Club: Masons.

HARPER, PATRICIA JANE LAMPITT, librarian, research analyst; b. Pekin, Ill., May 7, 1954; d. Edwin Andrew and Gwenda Lillian (Hibberd) Lampitt; m. Randall Lee Harper, Oct. 30, 1976 (div. Aug. 1980). B.S., U. Mo.-Columbia, 1976, M.A., 1982. Library asst. Daniel Boone Regional Library, Columbia, 1979-81, librarian, 1982; librarian/research analyst Sch. Family and Community Medicine/Behavioral Scis. U. Mo., Columbia, 1982-84, guest lectr. Sch. Library and Info. Sci., 1983; research cons. WIS-TV/PM Mag., Columbia, S.C., 1983; access services and reference librarian U. Mo.-Kansas City, 1984—. Author/editor: Marketing the Public Library, 1982; editor: Joint Practice: An Annotated Bibliography, 1983, Joint Practice in Pediatrics: An Annotated Bibliography, 1983; editor (with others) Membly-Peg, 1982-83; contbr. articles to profl. jours. Active campaign com. to Re-elect Temple Morgett, Columbia, 1978, campaign com. to elect Harriet Woods, Columbia, 1982. Recipient Delta Gamma Nat. Sorority Four Fold award, 1976; W.K. Kellogg Found., grantee, 1983. Mem. ALA, Mo. Library Assn., Friends of Pub. Library. Office: 5100 Rockhill Rd Kansas City MO 64110

HARPER, ROGER WESLEY, consumer products co. exec.; b. Youngstown, Ohio, July 11, 1933; s. Harry Edward and Helen Marjorie (Young) H.; B.A., Wittenberg U., 1956. Sales rep. Shell Oil Co., Cleve., 1958-62, Chicopee Mills, Inc., N.Y.C., 1962-64; sales rep. H.H. Cutler Co., Grand Rapids, Mich., 1964-68; exec. v.p. Scharp Contemporary, Inc., Columbus, Ohio, 1968-77, now dir.; chmn., pres. Am. Leather Village, Inc., Columbus, 1977—. Served with U.S. Army, 1956-58. Lutheran. Home: 622 Indian Mound Rd Columbus OH 43213 Office: 2163 S James Rd Columbus OH 43227

HARPER, WILLIAM VICTOR, statistician; b. Blue Island, Ill., July 17, 1949; s. Cecil Victor and Ila Lily (Adderson) H.; m. Lorraine Anne Harper, June 10, 1974. B.S. summa cum laude, Ohio State U., 1973, M.S., 1976, Ph.D., 1984. Statistician Ross Labs., Columbus, Ohio, 1976-77, mgr., 1977-78; research scientist Battelle Meml. Inst., Columbus, 1978-81, statistician, project mgr., 1981—. Contbr. articles to profl. jours. Served with USAF, 1967-71. Mem. Am Statis. Assn., Am. Soc. Quality Control, Assn. Computing Machinery, Materials Research Soc., Columbus Statis. Assn. (pres. 1982—). Presbyterian. Clubs: Running, Ski. Avocations: running; white water rafting; camping. Office: Battelle Project Mgmt Div 505 King Ave Columbus OH 43201

HARPOLE, JOHN ROBERT, dentist; b. Nebo, Ill., Aug. 29, 1939; s. John Hubert and Frances Marie (Lucht) H.; m. Sandra Kay Fansler, June 10, 1961; children—Lisa Ann, Steven Robert. Student Blackburn Coll., 1957-60; D.D.S.,

St. Louis, U., 1964. Asst. prof. dentistry So. Ill. U., Alton, 1976-79; clin. instr. St. Louis U., 1964-65; pvt. practice dentistry, Alton, 1965-66; mem. dental staff St. Louis Labor Health Inst., 1968—; Sec. troop com. St. Louis council Boy Scouts Am., 1979-83; mem. Republican Senatorial Club, 1982—; trustee Mo. Baptist Ch., St. Louis, 1976-82, chmn. bd. trustees, 1980-82; deacon Calvary Baptist Ch., Alton, deacon, 1970-84, chmn. bd. deacons, 1981-83. Mem. ADA, Mo. Dental Assn., Greater St. Louis Dental Soc. Avocations: hiking, coin and stamp collecting, reading. Home: 6740 Ryan Crest Florissant MO 63033 Office: St Louis Labor Health Inst 300 S Grand Saint Louis MO 63103

HARPST, JERRY ADAMS, biochemist, educator; b. Glasgow, Ky., Sept. 27, 1936; s. Harold Esslinger and Lena Brown (Adams) H.; m. Bethalee June Brandenberger, Dec. 30, 1961; children—Lisa Lynnelle, Tamara Lee. A.B., Wabash Coll., 1958; M.S., Yale U., 1960, Ph.D., 1962. Postdoctoral fellow U. Calif.-San Diego, La Jolla, 1962-64; asst. prof. Western Res. U., Cleve., 1965-71; vis. scientist Nat. Inst. Med. Research, Mill Hill, London, 1971-72; assoc. prof. Case Western Res. U., Cleve., 1971—; vis. assoc. prof. Oreg. State U., Corvallis, 1980-81. Contbr. profl. articles to jours. Am. Cyanamid research fellow, 1960-61; postdoctoral fellow USPHS, 1962-63, recipient Career Devel. award, 1967-77. Mem. Am. Chem. Soc., Am. Soc. Biol. Chemists, Biophys. Soc., Phi Beta Kappa. Democrat. Presbyterian. Avocations: backpacking, camping, tennis, squash. Home: 3077 Huntington Rd Shaker Heights OH 44120 Office: Dept Biochemistry Case Western Res U Cleveland OH 44106

HARRELL, JAMES THOMAS, business executive; b. Newport, Ky., Oct. 21, 1936; s. William Thomas and Stella May (Jones) H.; B.B.A., U. Cin., 1960; M.B.A., Xavier U., 1969; certificate in mgmt. acctg., 1977. With Miami Margarine Co., Cin., 1963—, asst. controller, 1977—. Served with U.S. Army, 1962-63. Mem. Nat. Assn. Accts., Delta Sigma Pi, Beta Alpha Psi. Episcopalian. Home: 3044 Carroll Ave Cincinnati OH 45248 Office: 5226 Vine St Cincinnati OH 45217

HARRELL, JOHN LIMPUS, fundraising consultant; b. Frankfort, Ind., May 9, 1918; s. Jesse Albert and Mildred Vale (Limpus) H.; A.B., Franklin Coll., 1940; M.A., Ohio State U., 1941; m. Helen Vernon Schumacher, Nov. 23, 1943; 1 dau., Helen F. Asst. dir. Duluth (Minn.) Community Fund, 1941-43; exec. sec. Community Chest and War Chest, Green Bay, Wis., 1943-46; exec. dir. Community Chest, Watertown, N.Y., 1946-50, Cedar Rapids, Iowa, 1950-54; exec. dir. United Way of Wyandotte County, Kans., 1954-79; ret., 1979; fundraising cons., 1980—. Med. field agt. SSS, 1943-46; treas. Kans. Conf. Social Welfare, 1964-66; mem. Human Relations Commn., Kansas City, 1966-75, vice chmn., 1970-71; mem. Manpower Planning Bd., City-County Consortia, 1975-79; mem. citizens adv. com. Kans. Dept. Social Rehab. Services, 1976-79; bd. dirs., cons. Econ. Opportunity Found., Inc., 1965-79. Recipient Silver Bow award, Boy Scouts Am., 1972, Com. award, YMCA, 1972, Service award United Way of Am., 1972; Service Appreciation award Econ. Opportunity Found., Inc., 1974, Founder's award, 1976; Community Services Adminstrn. Service award, 1980; Appreciation awards AFL-CIO Tri-County Labor Council Eastern Kans., 1979, Cath. Social Services, 1979; Charter Dir. Recognition award Kans. Citizens Council on Aging, 1980. Mem. Kappa Delta Rho. Republican. Baptist. Clubs: Rotary, Elks. Home: Rural Route 1 Box 194B Michigantown IN 46057

HARRELL, ROBERT LEWIS, fire chief; b. Sedalia, Mo., May 5, 1944; s. Clarence R. Ray and Ada M. (Carver) H.; m. Patricia Ann Carnes, June 5, 1965; 1 child, Amber Flame. Assoc. Sci. Penn Valley Community Coll., 1977. Platter Rivial Mfg. Co., Sedalia, Mo., 1962-70; firefighter City Sedalia, Mo., 1970-76; fire chief, City of Clinton, Mo., 1976—; vol. fireman Pettis County Vol. Fire Dept., Sedalia, 1967-76. Chmn. Henry County chpt. ARC, Clinton, 1980—; bd. dirs. Pettis County Muscular Dystrophy Assn., Sedalia, 1967-72; fund drive chmn. Muscular Dystrophy Assn., Kansas City chpt., Clinton, 1978-84. Served with U.S. Army, 1965-67. Mem. Internat. Assn. Fire Chiefs, Mo. Fire Chiefs, Mo. Firefighters Assn., Nat. Fire Protection Assn., Mo. Emergency Mgmt. Assn. Avocations: boating; fishing. Home: 1101 S Water Clinton MO 64735 Office: City Clinton Fire Dept 301 S Washington Clinton MO 64735

HARRELL, SAMUEL M., international grain company executive; b. Indpls., Jan. 4, 1931; s. Samuel Runnels and Mary (Evans) H.; ed. Groton Sch.; B.S. in Econs., Wharton Sch., U. Pa., 1953; m. Sally Bowers, Sept. 2, 1958; children—Samuel D., Holly Evans, Kevin Bowers, Karen Susan, Donald Runnels, Kenneth Macy. Chmn. bd., chief exec. officer, pres., treas. chmn. exec. com. Early & Daniel Industries; pres., chmn. bd., chmn. exec. com. Early & Daniel Co., Cin.; chmn. bd., chief exec. officer, chmn. exec. com. Tidewater Grain Co., Phila.; dir. Wainwright Bank & Trust Co., Wainright Abstract Co., Nat. Grain Trade Council, U.S. Feed Grains Council; mem. Chgo. Bd. Trade, St. Louis Mchts. Exchange, Mpls. Grain Exchange, Buffalo Corn Exchange. Bd. overseers Wharton Sch. Fin. and Commerce, U. Pa. Served with AUS, 1953-55. Mem. U. Pa. Alumni Assn. (past pres. Ind.), Terminal Elevator Grain Mchts. Assn. (dir.), Millers Nat. Fedn. (dir.), Assn. Operative Millers, Am. Soc. Bakery Engrs., Nat. Grain and Feed Dealers Assn. (dir.), N. Am. Grain Export Assn., Am. Finance Assn., Council on Fgn. Relations, Financial Execs. Inst., Delta Tau Delta (past pres. Ind. alumni). Presbyn. Mason (32 deg., Shriner), Rotarian. Clubs: Columbia, Indpls. Athletic, Woodstock, Traders Point Hunt, Dramatic, Players, Lambs (Indpls.); Racquet (Phila.); University (Washington); Les Ambassadors (London). Office: Early & Daniel Co 525 Carr St Cincinnati OH 45203

HARRIMAN, RICHARD LEE, educator; b. Independence, Mo., Sept. 10, 1932; s. Walter S. and M. Eloise (Faulkner) H.; A.B., William Jewell Coll., 1953, Litt.D. (hon.), 1983. M.A., Stanford U., 1959. Instr., asst. prof. English U. Dubuque, Iowa, 1960-62; asst. prof. English, William Jewell Coll., Liberty, Mo., 1962, acting head English dept., 1965-69, dir. fine arts program, 1965—, asso. prof., 1966—. Treas. Kansas City Arts Council, 1980, sec., 1981. Served from pvt. to cpl., AUS, 1953-55. Woodrow Wilson fellow, 1957. Mem. Shakespeare Assn. Am., MLA, Assn. Coll. Univ. and Community Arts Adminstrs. (nat. exec. bd. 1975-78), Nat. Council Tchrs. English, AAUP, Lambda Chi Alpha, Sigma Tau Delta, Alpha Psi Omega. Meth. Home: Route 5 Box 6 Liberty MO 64068

HARRINGTON, JEAN PATRICE, college president, nun; b. Denver, July 15, 1922; d. James M. and Katherine (Holland) H. B.A., Coll. Mt. St. Joseph, 1953; M.A., Creighton U., 1958; Ph.D., U. Colo., 1967; L.H.D. (hon.), Xavier U., Cin., 1983. Joined Sisters of Charity, Roman Catholic Ch., 1940. Prin. St. Rose of Lima, Denver, 1953-56; tchr. Cathedral High Sch., Denver, 1956-58, prin., 1958-64; provincial Sisters of Charity, Denver Province, 1969-76; pres. Coll. Mt. St. Joseph, Ohio, 1977—; dir. Cin. Bell, 1st Nat. Bank of Cin. Trustee Penrose Hosp., Colorado Springs, Colo., 1979—, Cin. Ctr. Econ. Edn., 1980—; pres. Conf. Small Pvt. Colls., 1984—; mem. Am. Council on Edn. Commn. on Adult Learning, 1983—. Named Woman of Yr., Cin. Enquirer, 1983, Outstanding Citizen, Pub. Relations Soc. Am., 1982, Career Woman of Achievement, YWCA, Cin., 1981. Mem. Assn. Cath. Colls. and Univs. (bd. dirs.), Assn. Ind. Colls. and Univs. Ohio (exec. com.), Council of Ind. Colls. (bd. dirs.), Greater Cin. Consortium Colls. and Univs. (exec. com.), Bus. and Profl. Women's Club Cin. (Disting. Bus. and Profl. Woman of Yr. 1982), Cin. C. of C. (blue chip task force). Club: Cin. Women's. Home and Office: Coll Mt St Joseph Mount Saint Joseph OH 45051

HARRINGTON, LARRY DAVID, educational administrator; b. Centerville, Iowa, Jan. 4, 1941; s. Orris More and Reta Avis (Moulton) H.; m. J. Ramona Howard, Aug. 19, 1962; children—Carol, Todd. B.S., Iowa State U., 1962, M.Ed., 1966; Ph.D., 1984. Cert. prof. tchr., Iowa. Tchr., coach Walnut Community Schs., Iowa, 1962-66; prin. Blakesburg Community Schs., Iowa, 1966-71, Boone Jr.-Sr. High Sch., Iowa, 1976—; asst. prin. Naperville Central High Sch., Ill., 1971-74, Naperville North High Sch., 1974-76. Mem. Ednl. Adminstrs. Iowa (dist. pres. 1984-85), Nat. Assn. Secondary Sch. Prins., Unified Iowa High Sch. Activities Fedn. (pres. 1985—). Methodist. Lodges: Lions (pres. Blakesburg 1970), Kiwanis (pres. Boone 1982), Masons. Avocations: golfing; bowling; archery. Office: Boone Jr-Sr High Sch 500 7th St Boone IA 50036

HARRINGTON, WARREN JOSEPH, steel company executive; b. Geneva, Ill., Oct. 19, 1951; s. Warren G. and Shirley (Wernes) H.; m. Carol Ann Kloubec, Aug. 19, 1972; 1 child, Jennifer Ruth. B.S. in Math., U. Ill., 1973; M.B.A., 1975. Sr. staff analyst U. Ill., Champaign, 1973-77; cons. Inland Steel Co., Chgo., 1977-78, sr. cons., 1978-80, mgr. systems, 1980—. Mem. Assn. Systems Mgmt., Steel Industry Systems Assn. Office: Inland Steel 30 W Monroe Chicago IL 60603

HARRIS, BART, photographer, director, producer; b. Chgo., Oct. 24, 1942; s. Jerome Herbert and Gussie (Frankel) H.; m. Andrea Ruth Sommers, Jan. 31, 1970; children—Aaron Matthew, Joel Wade. Student Roosevelt U., 1961-63. One man show: Pallas Gallery, Chgo., 1978; group shows include: Art Direction Mag. show, 1979, So. Ill. U., Chgo. Film Festival, 1981; represented in permanent collection Rochester Inst. Photography; owner Bart Harris Photography, Chgo., 1967—; lectr. in field; dir. and producer TV commls. Recipient numerous awards including: ADDY awards Best of Show, 1981; Chgo. Film Festival Silver Plaque, 1981, 82; Art Direction awards, 1980, 81, 83; Clio awards, 1983, 84. Mem. Advt. Photographers Assn. (bd. dirs.), Assn. Ind. Comml. Producers. Republican. Clubs: North Shore, Area Runners (Chgo.); Road Runners (N.Y.C.). Office: 70 W Hubbard St Suite 400 Chicago IL 60610

HARRIS, BERRY BENJAMIN, club business manager; b. Alton, Ill., July 28, 1929; s. Charles Wilkens and Anna Elizabeth (Holmes) H. Grad. high sch., Alton. Office clk. Meyer-Schmidt Co., Alton, 1947-51; office mgr. Dennis Bros., Inc., Alton, 1953-58; bus. mgr. Spaulding Club, Alton, 1958—. Democratic committeeman, Alton, 1953; mem. bd. suprs. Madison County, Edwardsville, Ill., 1967. Served as sgt. U.S. Army, 1951-53, Korea. Mem. Greater Alton C. of C., Ill. Police Assn., VFW, Am. Legion. Democrat. Roman Catholic. Lodge: K.C. (grand knight 1956-59). Home: 400 Mather St #5 Alton IL 62002 Office: Spaulding Club Assn 405 E 4th St Alton IL 62002

HARRIS, BOB FRANK, printing company executive; b. Evansville, Ind., Mar. 12, 1941; s. Thomas and Anna Martha (Schumacher) H.; m. Barbara Jean Harris, Aug. 14, 1965; children—Brian James, Brent Earl. B.S., Ind. State U., 1965, M.S., 1967. Tchr. Montgomery County schs., Rockville, Md., 1965-66, Evansville-Vanderburgh Schs., Evansville, Ind., 1967-80; pres. Graphic Supply of Evansville, Inc., 1980-85. Pres., Scott Twp. Civic Club, Evansville, 1974-76; tax adv. bd. Scott Twp., 1978-82; trustee, assessor Scott Twp., Vanderburgh, 1983—; mem. blood council ARC, Evansville, 1983—; pres. Scott Sch. PTA, 1982-85. Served with U.S. Army, 1960-63. Mem. NEA, Am. Indsl. Arts Assn., Ind. Indsl. Arts Assn., Phi Delta Kappa, Epsilon Pi Tau. Lodges: Masons, Shriners. Home: 1730 Montview Dr Evansville IN 47711 Office: Graphic Supply of Evansville Inc Rural Route #8 Box 168G Evansville IN 47711

HARRIS, CHARLES ALFRED, JR., professional placement firm executive; b. Towson, Md., June 8, 1932; s. Charles Alfred and Della (Deady) H.; m. Helen Ann Fenney, June 15, 1960 (div. 1979); children—Charles Alfred III, Debbie A., Cindy A.; m. Elizabeth Marie Brush, Feb. 21, 1980. B.B.A., John Hopkins U., 1954; M.B.A., U. Miami, 1957; Ph.D., Calif. U.-Santa Ana, 1982. Chief exec. officer Industries Internat., Inc., Thousands Oaks, Calif., 1960-65; v.p. divisional/corporate Litton Industries, Inc., Beverly Hills, Calif., 1965-70; pres., chief exec. officer Harris & Assocs., Hamilton, Ohio, 1970—. Author: Cost and Budget Manual, 1969; Emergency E.D.P. Preparedness Plan, 1979; Executive Data Processing Management Manual, 1978. Mem. Nat. Assn. Personnel Cons., Nat. Assn. Acctg., Am. Mgmt. Assn., Ohio Placement Service, Data Processing Mgmt. Assn., Hamilton C. of C., Alpha Delta Phi. Republican. Episcopalian. Lodges: Masons, Shriners, Elks, Kiwanis. Avocations: golf; tennis; boating; barbershop quartet singing. Home and Office: Harris & Assocs 229 Heaton St Hamilton OH 45011

HARRIS, CHARLIE, educational administrator; b. Hayneville, Ala., Aug. 26, 1940; s. Willie F. and Lucy B. (Campbell) H.; m. Eula S. Sims, June 12, 1971. B.S., Ala. State U., Montgomery, 1963; M.S., Va. State U., Petersburg, 1970; Ph.D., Mich. State U., 1976. Cert. supt., vocat. dir., tchr., Mo., Del., Ill., Mich. Mgmt. exec. Vault Service Co., Montgomery, Ala. 1965—; occupational tchr. Fredericksburg (Va.) Pub. Schs., 1966-71, Lansing (Mich.) Sch. Dist., 1971-77; vocat. adminstr. Newark (Del.) Sch. Dist., 1977-81, Spl. Sch. Dist. of St. Louis County, 1981—; cons. vocat. edn. and mgmt. Served with U.S. Army, 1963-65. Mem. Am. Mgmt. Assn., Am. Assn. Sch. Adminstrs., Am. Vocat. Assn., Nat. Council Local Adminstrs., Nat. Assn. Indsl. and Tech. Tchr. Educators, Assn. Supervision and Curriculum Devel., Council Basic Edn., Am. Council Indsl. Arts Tchr. Edn., Mo. Vocat. Spl. Need, Assn., NAACP. Democrat. Author: Competency-Based Education: What It Spells for Teachers and Students, 1980, and other. Home: 1504 Royal Crest Ct Chesterfield MO 63017 Office: 13480 S Outer Forty Chesterfield MO 63017

HARRIS, CLARA LOUISE TRINDLE, dietitian; b. Kingfisher, Okla., Mar. 16, 1928; d. Robert and Elva G. (Gosline) Trindle; B.S., Okla. State U., 1951; postgrad. Iowa State U., 1959; m. Clifford Charles Harris, June 20, 1954; children—Donna Kay, Clifford Charles. Dietetic intern St. Mary's Hosp., Rochester, Minn., 1951-52; staff dietitian VA Hosps., Muskogee, Okla., 1952-53; dietitian Okla. U. Med. Center, 1953-54, Okla. Bapt. Hosp., Muskogee, 1954, VA Hosp., Murfreesboro, Tenn., 1955-57, VA Hosp., Muskogee, Okla., 1957-67; chief dietitian, Fort Lyon, Colo., 1967-70; asst. chief dietitian VA, Lexington, Ky., 1970-72; chief dietitian VA, Chillicothe, Ohio, 1970-79; chief dietetic service VA Med. Center, Consol., Cleve., 1979—, dir. dietetic internship-coordinated master's degree program, 1979; asso. prof. nutrition Case Western Res. U., Cleve., 1979—; adv. Colo. S.E. Hosp. Instl. Edn. Food Service Soc., 1968-70; nutrition adv. Parent Child Care Center, Las Animas, Colo., 1968-70; cons. dietitian Weisbord County Meml. Hosp., Eads, Colo., St. Joseph of the Plains Hosp., Cheyenne Wells, Colo., 1968-70; cons. nutrition Title VII Program, Washington Court, Ohio, 1975-79. Registered dietitian. Mem. Am. Dietetic Assn., Am. Soc. Hosp. Food Service Adminstrs., Ohio Dietetic Assn., AAUW. Presbyterian. Club: Order Eastern Star. Home: 8607 Hinckley Circle Brecksville OH 44141 Office: 10000 Brecksville St Brecksville OH 44141

HARRIS, DEBORAH JEAN, psychometrician; b. Findlay, Ohio, Jan. 1, 1956; d. Wilbur Strode and Elaine Rosalie (Cervenka) H. B.S., Central Mich. U., 1977, M.A., 1979; Ph.D., U. Wis.-Madison, 1983. Tchr. math. Hinesville Middle Sch., Ga., 1977-78, Lincoln Jr. High Sch., Kenosha, Wis., 1979-80; lectr. ednl. stats. U. Wis.-Madison, 1982; postdoctoral assoc. U. Iowa, Iowa City, 1983-84; psychometrician Am. Coll. Testing Program, Iowa City, 1984—. WARF fellow, 1980-81, 81-82. Mem. Psychometric Soc., Am. Statis. Assn., Am. Ednl. Research Assn., Phi Kappa Phi. Democrat. Methodist. Office: Am Coll Testing Program Box 168 Iowa City IA 52243

HARRIS, DEBRA LYNNE, jewelry sales company executive; b. Columbus, Ohio, Oct. 26, 1956; d. Conrad London and Ruth Evelyn (Bergglas) H. B.S. in Bus., Ind. U., 1978. Founder, owner Gold Connection, Inc., Chgo., 1978—. Mem. Jewelers Bd. of Trade, Jewelers of Am.

HARRIS, DONNA ELAINE MEAKINS, principal; b. Austin, Minn., Nov. 15, 1937; d. Lloyd George and Doris DeSales (Duclos) Meakins; m. Robert Edward Harris, Feb. 13, 1956 (div.); children—Jean, David, Joan, Mark, Richard, Robert, Paul. A.A., Austin Community Coll., 1970; B.S., Winona State U., 1972, M.S., 1975, Ed. Specialist, 1978; Ed.D. in Ednl. Administrn., U. Wyo. With Mower County Christian Edn. Ctr., Austin, 1965-70, coordinator, dir. presch. program, 1968-70; tchr. Washington-Kosciusko Sch., Winona, Minn., 1972-75; tchr. Goodview Sch., Winona, 1975-77, asst. prin., 1976-77; tchr. Stockton Sch., Winona, 1977-78; elem. sch. prin. Hot Springs County, Wyo., 1978-81, Pine Bluffs, Wyo., 1981-83, Mankato, Minn., 1985—; asst. prof. edn. St. Mary's Coll., Winona, 1984-85. Bd. dirs. N.W. Child Devel. Ctr. Mem. Council Exceptional Children, Assn. Supervision and Curriculum Devel., Am. Assn. Pub. Health. Republican. Roman Catholic. Home: 562 W Wabasha St Winona MN 55987 Office: Washington Sch Mankato MN

HARRIS, FRANCES ALVORD (MRS. HUGH W. HARRIS), cons., retired radio-TV broadcaster; b. Detroit, Apr. 19, 1909; d. William Roy and Edith (Vosburgh) Alvord; A.B., Grinnell Coll., 1929; L.H.D. (hon.), Ferris State Coll., 1980; m. Hugh William Harris, Sept. 24, 1932; children—Patricia Anne (Mrs. Floyd A. Metz), Hugh William, Robert Alvord. With advt. dept. Himelhoch Bros. & Co., Detroit, 1929-31; broadcaster as Julia Hayes, Robert P. Gust Co., 1931-34; tng. and personnel dept. Ernst Kern Co., 1935-36; broadcaster as Nancy Dixon, Young & Rubicam, Inc., 1939-42; women's editor Sta. WWJ, Detroit, 1943-64, Sta. WWJ-TV, 1947-64, spl. features coordinator Sta. WWJ-TV-AM-FM, 1964-74; treas. I.C. Harris & Co., Detroit 1963-82, pres., chief exec. officer, 1982-84, chmn. bd., 1984-85. Mem. exec. bd. Wayne County chpt. Mich. Soc. for Mental Health, 1953-63; chmn. Mental Health Week, 1958-59; mem. Wayne County Commn. on Aging, 1975—, chmn., 1976-77; publicity com. YWCA, 1945, 2d v.p., 1963; mem. publicity com. Tri-County League for Nursing, 1956-61; publicity chmn. Met. Detroit YWCA Bd. Dirs., 1961-66, exec. com., 1962-67; campaign dist. chmn. United Found., 1959, unit chmn., 1960-61, chmn. speakers bur., 1974; exec. bd. United Found. Women's Orgn., 1962-64; governing bd. United Community Services Women's Com., 1961-66; bd. dirs. United Community Services, 1964-67; bd. dirs. Homemaker Service Met. Detroit, pres., 1969-70; bd. dirs. Vis. Nurse Assn., pres., 1974-76; bd. dirs. Camp Fire Girls of Detroit, mem. nat. council, 1967-72, mem. nat. bd., exec. com., 1970-72, pres., 1978-80; bd. dirs. Well Being Service Aging, 1969-74, Sr. Center, 1971-76, Friends Detroit Pub. library, 1972-77, Friends Children's Museum, 1972-74, 83—; trustee Detroit Com. Alcoholism, 1961-64; mem. Mayor's Com. for Freedom Festival, 1959, chmn. women's activities, 1965; mem. Mayor's Com. for UN Week, 1959; mem. Gov.'s Commn. Status of Women, 1962-69, Mich. State Women's Commn., 1969-77; mem. nat. council Homemaker Service, 1970-73; mem. adv. com. to trustees Grinnell Coll.; mem. bd. control Ferris State Coll., 1968-78; mem. def. adv. com. Women in the Services, 1970-73, chmn., 1973; program chmn. Met. Detroit YMCA, 1973-75; sec.-treas. Mich. Assn. Governing Bds. State Colls. and Univs., 1975, v.p., 1976-77, pres., 1977-78; bd. dirs. United Community Services, Detroit, 1983—, mem. assembly, 1984—. Recipient Grinnell Coll. Alumni award, 1959, Mental Health Soc. Mich. award, 1958, Theta Sigma Phi Headliner award for Mich., 1951, nat., 1952; Women's Advt. Club of Detroit Civic award, 1957; named Advt. Woman of Year, Detroit, 1958, 73, Soroptimist Woman of Year, 1965; Fran Harris Day in her honor, Detroit, 1960; Vol. State of Mich., 1975; Heart of Gold award, 1976; commendation service award Mich. Assn. Bus. Owners. Mem. Am. Women in Radio and TV (pres. Detroit chpt. 1957-58, gen. chmn. nat. conv. 1966, Outstanding Community Service award 1972), Women's Advt. Club of Detroit (pres. 1959-60, mem. bd. 1974-77), UN Assn. U.S.A. (dir. Detroit chpt. 1962-65, Mich. div. bd. 1963-65), Advt. Fedn. (nat. v.p. women's activities 1964-67), Nat. Fedn. Press Women (hon.), Women in Communications (pres. Detroit 1950-51; del. to Asian-Am. Women in Broadcasting Conf. 1966, nat. 1st v.p. 1968-71, nat. pres. 1971-73, chmn. Communications Conf. Ams., 1968, del. III World Congress Women Journalists 1973), Pi Epsilon Delta. Episcopalian (communications com. local congregation and Diocese of Mich. 1965-66). Club: Women's Econ. (charter mem.; dir. 1975—, membership chmn. 1975, program chmn. 1976, public relations co-chmn. 1977, treas. 1978, sec. 1979, 1st v.p. 1980, pres. 1981) (Detroit). Author, editor: Focus: Michigan Women, 1977. Home: 8120 E Jefferson Detroit MI 48214

HARRIS, GRENETTA MCKINSTRY, microbial geneticist; b. Birmingham, Ala., Oct. 10, 1947; d. Willie D. and Willie Gertrude McKinstry; A.B. cum laude, Biology, Stillman Coll., 1968; M.A. (NDEA fellow) in Microbiology, Ind. U., 1970; Ph.D., Ohio State U., 1979; 1 son, Robert L. Harris. Researcher, Eli Lilly Pharm. Co., Indpls., 1970-72; tech. asst. dept. microbiology Ohio State U., 1972-76, teaching asst., 1976-79; tutor European Molecular Biology Orgn., U. Erlangen-Nurnberg (W. Ger.), 1979; postdoctoral asso. Max Planck Inst. for Molecular Genetics, West Berlin, 1979, Ohio State U., 1979; microbial geneticist Abbott Labs., North Chicago, Ill., 1980—. Recipient Presdl. award, 1982. Mem. Am. Soc. for Microbiology, Assn. for Women in Sci., AAAS, N.Y. Acad. Scis., Am. Phytopath. Soc., Sigma Xi. Baptist. Contbr. articles on microbial genetics to sci. pubs. Home: 986 Peachtree Ct Vernon Hills IL 60061 Office: 1400 Sheridan Rd North Chicago IL 60064

HARRIS, HOWARD HUNTER, oil company executive, lawyer; b. Cushing, Okla., Dec. 7, 1924; s. Oscar Hunter and Gertie Lee (Stark) H.; m. Gwendolyne J. Moyers, Dec. 31, 1945; children—Howard Sidney, Rodney Craig. B.S. in Bus. Adminstrn., U. Okla., 1949, J.D., 1949; postgrad. in advanced mgmt., Stanford U., 1971. Bar: Okla. 1949, Ohio 1964. Assoc. Emery & Harris, Cushing and Stillwater, Okla., 1949-50; staff atty. Sun Oil Co., Tulsa, 1950-54; div. atty. Marathon Oil Co., Tulsa, 1954-63; staff atty. Marathon Internat. Oil Co., Findlay, Ohio, 1963-65; mgr. legal affairs Deutsche Marathon Petroleum GmbH, Frankfurt and Munich, 1965-70; mktg. atty., assoc. gen. counsel Marathon Oil Co., Findlay, 1970-74, v.p. corp. external affairs, 1974—. Served with AUS, 1943-45. Decorated Bronze star, 1944. Mem. Am. Petroleum Inst., ABA, Ohio State Bar Assn., Okla. Bar Assn., Findlay Bar Assn., Order of Coif, Beta Gamma Sigma. Club: Rotary. Lodge: Masons. Office: Marathon Oil Co 539 S Main St Findlay OH 45840

HARRIS, JAMES HENRY, JR., marketing analyst; b. Waukegan, Ill., Jan. 5, 1951; s. James H. and Bernice (Ervin) H.; m. Betty J. Olloway, Aug. 1, 1970. children—Earl, Ryan. Student So. Ill. U., 1969-71, Coll. Lake County, 1971-73; degree system engring. Honeywell Tech. Sch., 1978; degree applied behavior Nat. Coll. Edn., 1983. System engr. Honeywell Inc., Lincolnwood, Ill., 1974-76, sales engr., 1976-78, account mgr., 1978-82; account mgr. Bailey Controls, Lombard, Ill., 1982-83, nat. mktg. mgr., 1983—. Alderman, City of North Chicago; v.p. NAACP, 1977-78; bd. dirs. Lake County Urban League, 1971-81; precinct committeeman. Served with USMCR, 1971-77. Recipient Roadrunners Club award from Honeywell, 1977, Pres. Club. from Honeywell, 1980. Mem. Numerical Control Soc., Engring. Mgmt. Soc. Baptist. Home: 7141 Huntington Rd Hudson OH 44236 Office: 611 E Butterfield Rd Lombard IL 60145

HARRIS, JAMES HERMAN, pathologist, neuropathologist, consultant, educator; b. Fayetteville, Ga., Oct. 19, 1942; s. Frank J. and Gladys N. (White) H.; m. Judy K. Hutchinson, Jan. 30, 1965; children—Jeffrey William, John Michael, James Herman. B.S., Carson-Newman Coll., 1964; Ph.D., U. Tenn.-Memphis, 1969, M.D., 1972. Diplomate Am. Bd. Pathology; sub.-cert. in anatomic pathology and neuropathology. Resident and fellow N.Y.U.-Bellevue Med. Ctr., N.Y.C., 1973-75; adj. asst. prof. pathology N.Y. U., N.Y.C., 1975—; asst. prof. pathology and neuroscis. Med. Coll. Ohio, Toledo, 1975-78, assoc. prof., 1978-82, dir. neuropathology and electron microscopy lab., 1975-82; cons. Toledo Hosp., 1979-82, assoc. pathologist/neuropathologist, dir. electron microscopy pathology lab., 1983—, also mem. overview com.; cons. neuropathologist Mercy Hosp., 1976—, U. Mich. dept. pathology, 1984—; mem. AMA Physician Research and Evaluation Panel; mem. ednl. and profl. affairs comm., exec. council Acad. Medicine; mem. children's cancer study group Ohio State U. satellite; mem. adv. com. to Blue Cross, mem. task force on Cost Effectiveness N.E. Ohio; dir. PIE Mut. Ins. Co. Chmn. steering com. Pack 198, Boy Scouts Am.; chmn. fin. com., dir. bldg. fund campaign First Baptist Ch., Perrysburg, Ohio; faculty chmn. Med. Coll. Ohio United Way Campaign. Recipient Outstanding Tchr. award Med. Coll. Ohio, 1980; named to Outstanding Young Men Am., U.S. Jaycees, 1973; USPHS trainee, 1964-69, postdoctoral trainee, 1973-75; grantee Am. Cancer Soc., 1977-78, Warner Lambert Pharm. Co., 1978-79, Miniger Found., 1980. Mem. Am. Profl. Practice Assn., Lucas County Acad. Medicine (exec. council 1985—), Ohio State Med. Assn., Am. Assn. Neuropathologists (profl. affairs com., awards com., program com.), Internat. Acad. Pathologists, Ohio Soc. Pathologists, EM Soc. Am., Sigma Xi. Author med., sci. papers; reviewer Jour. Neuropathology and Exptl. Neurology. Home: 550 Oak Knoll Perrysburg OH 43551 Office: Dept Pathology 2142 N Cove Blvd Toledo OH 43606

HARRIS, JAMES HILTON, fire chief; b. Atlanta, June 12, 1919; s. Walton and Jewel Estelle (Snead) H.; m. Dreva Marie Blatt, Aug. 26, 1947; children—James Walton, Richard Lee, Donna Marie, Judy Kay. Student pub. schs., Akron, also Delehaney Fire Sci. Corr. Course. Grocery clk. Isaly Dairy Co., 1937-38; asst. mgr. Kroger Grocery, 1938-41; rubber worker B.F. Goodrich, 1946; firefighter Akron Fire Dept., 1946-52, lt., capt., 1952-58, dist. chief, dep. chief, 1970-81, fire chief, 1981—; fire sci. adv. Akron U. Served with U.S. Army, 1942-46; NATOUSA, ETO. Decorated Silver Star, 2 Bronze Stars, others. Mem. Internat. Fire Chiefs Assn., Ohio. Fire Chiefs Assn., Met. Fire Chiefs Assn., DAV, 62d Armored Field Arty. Bn. Assn. Mem. Ch. of Christ. Lodge: Masons. Office: 57 S Broadway Akron OH 44308*

HARRIS, JEAN NOTON, music educator; b. Monroe, Wis., Feb. 21, 1934; d. Albert Henry and Eunice Elizabeth (Edgerton) Noton; B.A., Monmouth (Ill.) Coll., 1955; M.S., U. Ill., 1975, adminstrv. cert., 1980, Ed.D., 1985; m. Laurence G. Landers, June 7, 1955; children—Theodore Scott, Thomas Warren, Philip John; m. Edward R. Harris, Nov. 27, 1981; stepchildren—Adrianne, Erica. Tchr. music schs. in Ill. and Fla., 1955-76; tchr. music Dist. 54, Schaumburg, Ill., from 1976. Named Outstanding Young Woman of Yr., Jaycee Wives, St. Charles, Mo., 1968. Mem. Music Educators Nat. Conf. (life) Ill. Music Educators Assn., NEA (life), Am. Choral Dirs. Assn., U. Ill. Alumni Assn. (life), Mortar Bd., Mensa, Sigma Omicron Mu. Mem. United Ch. Christ. Home: 914 Roxbury Ln Schaumburg IL 60194

HARRIS, JERALD DAVID, lawyer; b. Cin., July 14, 1947; s. Donald W. and Dorothy (Botwin) H.; m. Carol S. Fohlen, Mar. 25, 1972; children—Alyse,

Jeffrey, Danielle. B.A., Miami U., Oxford, Ohio, 1969; J.D., U. Cin., 1972. Bar: Ohio 1972, U.S. Dist. Ct. (so. dist.) Ohio 1972, U.S. Dist. Ct. (ea. dist.) Ky. 1978, U.S. Ct. Appeals (6th cir.) 1977, U.S. Supreme Ct. 1978. Assoc. Kondritzer, Gold & Frank, Cin., 1972-79; sole practice, Cin., 1979-81; sr. ptnr. Harris & Katz Co., L.P.A., Cin., 1982—. Author: Ohio Workers' Compensation Handbook, 1986. Mem. Assn. Trial Lawyers Am., Nat. Orgn. Social Security Claimants Reps. (Ohio state chmn. 1981-83), Am. Soc. Law and Medicine, Ohio State Bar Assn., Ohio Acad. Trial Lawyers (chmn. social security and adminstrv. law sect., regional coordinator workers' compensation com., service to legal profession award 1983), Cin. Bar Assn. (chmn. workers' compensation com.). Office: Harris & Katz Co LPA 36 E 4th St Suite 1212 Cincinnati OH 45202

HARRIS, JOHN MICHAEL, college administrator; b. Detroit, May 13, 1923; s. Arthur H. and Donna L. (Waddell) H.; m. Louise A. Reeder, July 3, 1948; children—Dean, Reed. B.A., Ohio State U., 1945. Gen. mgr. Toro Mfg. Co., Springfield, Ohio, 1959-69; sr. v.p., treas. Kissell Co., 1969-76; v.p. Urbana U., Ohio, 1976-79; dean Downtown Bus. Ctr., Clark Tech. Coll., Springfield, 1979—. Served with USNR, 1942-43. Mem. Downtown Springfield Assn. (pres. 1981—), Sigma Alpha Epsilon. Avocation: sailing. Home: 1901 Pembrook Rd Springfield OH 45504 Office: Clark Tech Coll Leffel Ln Springfield OH 45501

HARRIS, JOHN NEWTON, financial planning institution executive; b. International Falls, Minn., May 9, 1939; s. Elza Newton and Esther Viola (Freden) H.; m. Kathleen Joy Nelson, May 25, 1968; children—Julie, Ryan, Robert, Jeffrey. Student Va. Community Coll., Minn., 1958-60, U. Minn.-Duluth, 1960-61; M.S. in Fin. Sci., Am. Coll., 1979. C.L.U. Sales mgr. Collier, MacMillan, Mpls., 1962-63; mgr. Gt.-West Life Co., Mpls., 1963-70; v.p. IDS/Am. Express, Mpls., 1970—. Mem. Profl. Golf-Course Devel. Study Com., Brooklyn Park, Minn., 1973; chmn. Brooklyn Park Ind. Republicans, 1972-73; mem. Brooklyn Park Capital Long-Term Improvement Com., 1978-79. Fellow Life Office Mgmt. Assn.; mem. Chartered Fin. Cons. Lutheran. Home: 6724 80th Ave N Brooklyn Park MN 55474 Office: IDS/Am Express 400 IDS Tower Minneapolis MN 55474

HARRIS, JOSEPH BENJAMIN, dentist; b. Richmond, Va., June 8, 1920; s. Joseph Brown and Alice (Burrell) H.; B.S. summa cum laude, Va. Union U., 1949; D.D.S., Howard U., 1953; m. Pauline Elizabeth McKinney, June 19, 1955; children—Paula Jo, Joseph Carter, Joya Renee. Pvt. practice dentistry, Detroit, 1953—; dir. C.A. Howell & Co., mfr. and distbr. beauty supplies, 1967—, pres., chmn. bd., 1972—. Served with AUS, 1943-46. Recipient award Am. Soc. Dentistry for Children, 1953. Mem. Am., Nat., Wolverine, Mich., Detroit dental socs., Mich. Assn. Professions, Omicron Kappa Upsilon, Alpha Kappa Mu, Sigma Pi Phi, Omega Psi Phi. Home: 1190 W Boston Blvd Detroit MI 48202 Office: 2431 W Grand Blvd Detroit MI 48208

HARRIS, K. DAVID, justice Iowa Supreme Ct.; b. Jefferson, Iowa, July 29, 1927; s. Orville William and Jessie Heloise (Smart) H.; B.A., U. Iowa, 1949, J.D., 1951; m. Madonna Coyne, Sept. 4, 1948; children—Jane Harris Martino, Julie, Frederich. Admitted to Iowa bar, 1951; practiced law, Jefferson, 1951-62; county atty. Greene County (Iowa), 1958-62; judge 16th Jud. Dist. Iowa, 1962-72; justice Iowa Supreme Ct., 1972—. Served with inf. U.S. Army, 1945-46. Mem. Jefferson Bar Assn., Iowa Bar Assn., Am. Bar Assn. Republican. Roman Catholic. Contbr. poetry to mags. Office: Iowa Statehouse Des Moines IA 50319

HARRIS, MANKER RALPH, clergyman, state official; b. Englewood, Tenn., Apr. 29, 1933; s. John Riley and Sarah Elizabeth (Whitener) H.; m. Toni Camille Romano, Jan. 27, 1957; children—Desiree Camille, Sylvia Denise, Tamira Susan. B.A., Anderson Coll., 1957, B.D., M.Div., Anderson Sch. Theology, 1962. Ordained minister Ch. of God, 1962. Pastor Pennway Ch. of God, Lansing, Mich., 1962-66; assoc. exec. dir. Lansing Area Council of Chs., 1966; exec. dir. Decatur (Ill.) Area Council of Chs., 1966-69; dir. community affairs. Ill. Council of Chs., Cairo, 1969-71; exec. dir. East Side Housing, Econ. Devel. Corp., Decatur, 1972-76; records mgr. Office of Sec. of State, Springfield, Ill., 1977-78, 81—; dist. dir. U.S. Census Bur. for Central Ill., Springfield, 1979-80; instr., lectr. Pres. Fallingbroot Townhome Owners Assn.; bd. dirs. Wood Lake Assn. Recipient Human Relations award Human Relations Com. Decatur, 1968. Mem. Inst. Cert. Records Mgrs., Soc. Am. Archivists, Central Ill. Assn. Records Mgrs. and Adminstrs. (dir.), Nat. Assn. Records Mgrs. and Adminstrs., Ill. Fedn. Tchrs. Democrat. Author: Handbook manual on Records for Local Officals, 1983. Home: 12 Trailridge Ln Springfield IL 62704 Office: Archives Dept Sec State Office 1st Floor E Springfield IL 62756

HARRIS, MARCELLA H. EASON (MRS. HARLEY EUGENE HARRIS, social worker; b. Augusta, Ark., Apr. 19, 1925; d. William Harvey and Hazel Faye (Haraway) Eason; B.A., Wilberforce U., 1947; M.S.W., Loyola U., Chgo., 1961; M.Ed. in Health Occupations, U. Ill., 1979; m. Harley Eugene Harris, June 15, 1952. Child welfare worker Ill. Dept. Pub. Welfare, 1952-54, caseworker Family Consultation Service, 1954-64; clin. social worker Winnebago County Mental Health Clinic, Rockford, Ill., 1964—, now clin. mgr. sustaining care services Janet Wattles Mental Health Center. Mem. Rockford Bd. Edn., 1965—, sec., 1965-69; trustee Swedish Am. Hosp.; bd. dirs. Rockford Local Devel. Corp.; mem. Allen Chapel African Methodist Episcopal Ch. Recipient Francis Blair award Ill. Edn. Assn., 1970, Service above Self award Rockford Rotary Club, 1971. Mem. Nat. Assn. Social Workers (chpt. vice chmn. 1960-61), Ill. Welfare Assn., Acad. Certified Social Workers, Nat. Council Negro Women, Rockford Jr. League (hon.), AAUW, Nat. Registry Health Care Providers in Clin. Social Work, Delta Kappa Gamma (hon.), Alpha Kappa Alpha. Club: Taus Sevice. Home: Cloisters Apt 1665 2929 Sunnyside Dr Rockford IL 61111 Office: 1325 E State St Rockford IL 61108

HARRIS, MARY MCDONNELL, English educator; b. Carlisle, Pa., Feb. 28, 1945; d. Fred Vance and Lois (Eddy) McDonnell; m. Theodore Robert Harris III, Aug. 15, 1970; children—Joanne Jacobson, Rebecca Grace. A.B., Goucher Coll., 1967; M.Ed., Shippensburg State U., 1969; Ph.D., U. Pitts., 1974. Cert. elem. and secondary English tchr., Pa. Tchr. Carlisle Area Schs., 1969-70, Castle Shannon Schs., Pitts., 1970-72; mem. faculty Kans. State U., Manhattan, 1974—, head dept. curriculum and instrn., 1980—; writer United Methodist Pub. House, Nashville, 1969—. Author: (curriculum) Bible Studies for Methodist Children, 1980—. Contbr. articles to profl. jours. Chmn. bd. Kans. State U. Ecumenical Christian Ministries, 1984—; vice chmn. bd. Kans. Urban Edn. Ctr., Kansas City, 1983—; chmn. Kans. State U. Commn. on Status Women, Manhattan, 1979-81. Grantee Kans. Dept. Educ., 1982—, Women's Edn. Equity Act, Dept. Edn., 1984—; recipient Outstanding Teaching award Kansas State U., 1979. Mem. Kans. Assn. Colls. Tchr. Educ. (pres. 1977-80, sec.), Internat. Reading Assn. (com. chmn. 1981-83), Kans. Assn. for Curriculum and Supv. (higher edn. rep. 1982—), Nat. Council Tchrs. English, Phi Delta Kappa (pres. 1983-84, found. rep.). Democrat. Methodist. Avocation: child advocate. Home: 745 Elling Dr Manhattan KS 66502 Office: Kansas State Univ Bluemont 261 Manhattan KS 66506

HARRIS, MELVIN HERBERT, pharmacist; b. Winner S.D., May 28, 1945; s. Irene (Boerner) Vanneman; m. Barbara Jean Frey, Aug. 26, 1966; 1 child, Kristine. B.S., S.D. State U., 1969. Pharmacist Hartig Drug Co., Dubuque, Iowa, 1969-70, 1972-73, Disco Drug Co., Waverly, Iowa, 1973-74, Rohlf Meml Clinic, Waverly, 1974—; mem. pharmacy and therapeutics com. Waverly Hosp., Iowa, 1975—. Bd. dirs. United Way, Waverly, 1978-79. Served to 1st lt. U.S. Army, 1970-72. Mem. Am. Soc. Hosp Pharmacists, Am. Pharm. Assn., Iowa Pharmacists Assn., Am. Legion, AMVETS. Democrat. Methodist. Lodges: Masons (master 1982), Shriners. Avocations: car restoration; woodworking; electronics. Home: 725 2d Ave NE Waverly IA 50677 Office: Rohlf Meml Clinic 220 10th St SW Waverly IA 50677

HARRIS, NANCY SIMON, marketing executive; b. Cleve., Mar. 22, 1940; d. Seymour F. and Roslyn (Biel) Simon; m. H. Reed Harris, Aug. 1, 1963 (div. 1971); children—Jason Bennett, Julia. Student Colby Coll. for Women, 1960; E.D.P., J.L. Kellogg Grad. Sch. Mgmt., Northwestern U., 1982. Account exec. Martin E. Janis Co., Chgo., 1961-64; writer, producer Draper Daniels Advt., Chgo., 1977-80; mgr. mktg. services ICD/AV, Bell & Howell, Chgo., 1980—, dir. Ctr. Interactive Communications, 1982—; mktg. cons. charities. Mem. Spl. Events Com., State Ill., 1979-82. Bd. dirs. U. Chgo.-Lying In Hosp., Mt. Sinai Hosp., North Shore Art League, Democrat. Jewish. Club: East Bank. Patentee diet watch Skinny Time. Office 7100 N McCormick St Chicago IL 60645

HARRIS, NEISON, See *Who's Who in America,* 43rd edition.

HARRIS, PATRICIA ANNE, program analyst; b. Cleve., July 27, 1950; d. George Byron and Lillian Anne (Kippert) Srofe; A.A. cum laude, Anchorage Community Coll., 1979; children—Robert Alan, Mark Andrew, Gregory James. File clk. typist Alcan Aluminum, Warren, Ohio, 1968-69; sec. Manpower, Inc., St. Louis, 1969-70; sec. U.S. Air Force, Anchorage, 1970-73, adminstrv. systems mgr., 1977-79, chief systems mgmt. div., 1979-83, chief publs. and systems mgmt. div., 1983-84, program analyst, Wright-Patterson AFB, Ohio, 1984—, sec. IRS, Anchorage, 1973-75; supervisory clerical asst. Alaska Outer Continental Shelf Office, Anchorage, 1975-77. Recipient Outstanding Adminstrv. officer award U.S. Air Force, 1979; named Anchorage Fed. Employee of Yr., 1977. Mem. Am. Soc. Mil Comptrollers. Office: 2750 ABW/ACM Wright-Patterson AFB OH 45433

HARRIS, PHYLLIS IRENE, educator; b. Poplar Bluff, Mo., Aug. 10, 1927; d. Golly and Beulah Ruth (Tompkins) Hunter; m. Paul William Harris, May 27, 1950 (div. 1962); 1 son, Kevin Paul. B.S., Loyola U., Chgo., 1958; M.S., Chgo. State U., 1971, M.S., 1980; Ph.D., U. So. Ill., 1983. Tchr. mentally handicapped children Chgo. Pub. Schs., 1960—; tchr., counselor mentally handicapped adults Kennedy King Coll. Mem. Am. Fedn. Tchrs., NAACP, Council for Exceptional Children, Chgo. Assn. Retarded. Bahai. Home: 7729 S Cregier Ave Chicago IL 60649 Office: 6835 S Normal St Chicago IL 60621

HARRIS, RANDOLPH BURTON, lawyer; b. Highland Park, Ill., June 29, 1951; s. Robert Norman and Mildred (Burton) H.; m. Edith Boschwitz, May 28, 1978; 1 child, Abraham Nathan. A.B., Stanford U., 1973; J.D., Northwestern U., 1977; M.S. in Indsl. Relations, Cornell U., 1980. Bar: Oreg. 1978, Wis. 1980, U.S. Ct. Appeals (7th and 9th cirs.) 1978, U.S. Dist. Ct. Oreg. 1978, U.S. Dist. Ct. (ea. and we. dists.) Wis. 1980, U.S. Supreme Ct. 1984. Field rep. Oreg. Bur. Labor, Portland, 1975-77, conciliator, 1977-78; asst. atty. gen. Oreg. Dept. Justice, Portland, 1978-79; gen. counsel Pluswood Inc., Oshkosh, Wis., 1980—; Oreg. dir. civil rights Oreg. State Bar, Portland, 1978-79; mem. admissions com. Wis. State Bar, Madison, 1984-85, mem. products liability com., 1984-86. Bd. dirs. Wis. Med. Sch., Madison, 1983—, Temple B'Nai Israel, Oshkosh, 1982-84; mem. Am. Jewish Com. Mem. ABA (labor-spl. com. civil rights, litigation com.), Assn. Trial Lawyers Am. Lodge: B'Nai B'Rith. Home: 2242 White Swan Dr Oshkosh WI 54901 Office: Pluswood Inc PO Box 2248 Oshkosh WI 54903

HARRIS, R(AYMOND) WESLEY, business executive; b. Vinita, Okla., Feb. 17, 1940; s. Raymond N. and Ravanell A. (Pitts) H.; m. Renee E. LaFortune, June 2, 1962; children—Brian M., Daron J. B.S., Okla. State U., 1964, M.S. in Indsl. Engring. and Mgmt., 1965. Indsl. engr. E.I. duPont, Old Hickory, Tenn., 1965-68; with Hooker Chem. & Plastics Corp., Niagara Falls, N.Y., 1968-78, supt. plant services, 1973-74, project mgr. productivity improvement task force, 1974-75, corp. mgr. indsl. engring., 1975-78; v.p. Union Frondenberg U.S.A., Olney, Ill., 1978-84, pres., 1984—; v.p. B.U.A., Inc., Olney, 1978-84, pres., 1984—; pres., chief exec. officer Global Group Ltd., 1985—; dir. Richland Capital Group Inc., 1985—; cons. Weinmann Sports, Inc. Mem. planning and resource com. Olney Central Coll. Found., 1982, vice chmn. fin. com. and exec. com., 1983. Served to maj. USAFR, 1965—. Recipient Key to City of Olney, 1981, Congressman's award of Merit, 1981, Commendation award City of Olney, 1981. Mem. Am. Inst. Indsl. Engrs. (sec. chpt. 1974-75, pres. 1975-76, dir. 1976-77), Olney C. of C. (chmn. bus. and econ. devel. com. 1982-83), Alpha Pi Mu, Sigma Alpha Epsilon. Republican. Roman Catholic. Clubs: Petroleum, Richland County Country (dir. 1981—) (Olney). Lodges: Rotary, Elks. Home: 30 Willow Dr Olney IL 62450 Office: 1 Union Dr Olney IL 62450

HARRIS, RICHARD DELMAR, JR., retail company manager; b. Toledo, Aug. 7, 1955; s. Richard D. Harris and Helen Marie (Bobson) H. B.A. in Bus. Adminstrn., Morehouse Coll., 1979. Park supr. Toledo Dept. Natural Resources, summers 1972-76; home improvement salesman Colonial Builders, Toledo, summers 1977-78; 79-80; bus. coordinator Toledo Symphony Orch., 1981; asst. mgr. linens Lion Store Westgate, Toledo, 1981—. Prodn. supt. Jr. Achievement, Toledo, 1982-83; choreographer Mr. and Mrs. Coronation Ball ann. nat. convs., NAACP, 1978, 79, 80, 81; mem. Friendship Baptist Ch. Clubs: One Up, Inner Circle (Toledo). Avocations: singing; dancing; photography; producing; free-lance choreography. Home: 1422 Bell Ave Toledo OH 43607

HARRIS, RICHARD LEE, research chemist; b. Chgo., Nov. 1, 1934; s. Lee M. and Mae G. (Wood) H.; m. Carol S. Wahlstrom, June 11, 1957 (div. 1977); children—Jay, Susan; m. Elaine J. Polacek, Sept. 1, 1984; stepchildren—Pamela, Melissa. B.A. in Chemistry, North Central Coll., 1956; Ph.D. in Organic Chemistry, U. Ill., 1960. Chemist E.I. DuPont, Niagara Falls, N.Y., 1960-63, research chemist, Memphis, 1963-64; sr. research chemist Diamond Alkali, Painesville, Ohio, 1964-73; research mgr. Diamond Shamrock, Painesville, 1975-80, research specialist, 1980—. Patentee adhesives fields. Vice pres. Grand Island Jr. C. of C., N.Y., 1963. Mem. Am. Chem. Soc. Republican. Avocations: gardening, skiing. Home: 7897 Kellogg Creek Dr Mentor OH 44060 Office: Diamond Shamrock PO Box 191 Painesville OH 44077

HARRIS, ROBERT ALLISON, biochemistry educator; b. Boone, Iowa, Nov. 10, 1939; s. Arnold E. and Marie (Wilcox) H; m. Karen Kaye Dutton, Dec. 27, 1960; children—Kelly, Chris, Heidi, Shawn. B.S., Iowa State U., 1962; Ph.D., Purdue U., 1965. Asst. research prof. U. Wis., 1968-69; assoc. prof. Ind. U. Med. Sch., Indpls., 1970-75, prof. biochemistry, 1975—, assoc. chmn. dept., 1983—. Nat. Multiple Sclerosis Soc. fellow, 1966-68; established investigator Am. Heart Assn., 1969-74; recipient Disting. Teaching award AMOCO, 1981, Edward C. Moore Teaching award, 1985, Young Investigator award Ind. Diabetes Assn., 1977. Mem. Am. Soc. Biol. Chemists, Am. Oil Chemists Soc., Biochem. Soc., Am. Heart Assn., Am. Diabetic Assn., Am. Inst. Nutrition. Co-editor: Isolation, Characterization, and Use of Hepatocytes, 1983; contbr. articles to profl. jours. Office: Dept Biochemistry Ind Univ Sch Medicine Indianapolis IN 46223

HARRIS, RONALD LEE, technology company executive; b. Lincoln, Nebr., Aug. 1, 1942; s. Lewis Eldon and Antonia (Synovec) H.; m. Christine Marie Olson, June 19, 1965; children—Bretton, Jennifer. B.S., U. Nebr., 1965, M.B.A., 1968. Cert. adminstrv. mgr.; registered sanitarian. Vice chmn. chief exec. officer Harris Labs., Inc., Lincoln, 1969-74, pres., 1974-84; pres. Fin. Systems, Inc., Kearney, Nebr., 1982—; pres. Harris Tech. Group, Inc., Lincoln, 1984—; cons. R.B. Harris Co., Lincoln; dir. Harris Tech. Systems, Inc. Trustee, U. Nebr. Found., 1982-83; bd. dirs. Lincoln Found., 1984—. Mem. Am. Council Ind. Labs. (past pres.), Young Pres. Orgn., Adminstrv. Mgmt. Soc. (past pres.), Assoc. Industries Lincoln (past pres.), Lincoln C. of C. Republican. Methodist. Clubs: Adman's Gridiron, University. Avocations: golfing, boating, racquet ball. Home: 2215 The Knolls Lincoln NE 68512 Office: Harris Technology Group Inc 624 Peach St Box 80837 Lincoln NE 68501

HARRIS, RUTH ELLEN, learning therapist; b. Bklyn., Sept. 18, 1943; d. Maurice Daniel and Naomi K. (Kimball) H. B.S., U. Wis.-Milw., 1965, M.S. in Reading Disabilities, 1969; M.S. in Learning Disabilities, U. Minn., 1974; M.S. in Spl. Edn. Emotionally Disturbed, U. Wis.-Eau Claire, 1976. Elem. tchr. 4th grade Lake Bluff Elem. Sch., Shorewood, Wis., 1965-68; reading cons. transitional yr. program U. Wis.-Eau Claire, 1973-74; local interviewer Bush Found., Mpls., 1977—; sch. commr. Eau Claire Sch. Dist., 1971-86, v.p., 1973-76; dir., learning therapist N.W. Reading Clinic, Eau Claire, 1969—; organizer Vols. for Vision, Eau Claire Area Sch. Dist. Students, 1970-75; mem. profl. adv. bd. Wis. Assn. Children with Learning Disabilities, 1971-86; ednl. cons. in-service presentations on reading and learning disabilities, 1969—; organizer Vol. Tutoring Program, Sacred Heart Hosp. Psychiat. Ward, Eau Claire, Wis., 1974-75. Recipient Merit Tchr. award Shorewood Pub. Schs., 1966-67; Citation for Achievement and Recognition for Outstanding Leadership award State Wis. Jaycettes, 1975; Bush leadership fellow, 1975-77. Mem. Internat. Reading Assn., Assn. Children with Learning Disabilities, Eau Claire County Mental Health Assn. (Pres. 1974-75). Author: (with Mark Ozer) Problem Solving-The —What Works— Method for Educators, 1984; Dialogue of Education: Problem-Solving in Today's Schools. Office: 2712 Stein Blvd Eau Claire WI 54701

HARRIS, SHIRLEY G., personnel manager executive; b. Chgo., July 24, 1945; d. Henderson and Ruth (Johnson) Jackson; m. Arthur Lewis, May 3, 1968 (div.); children—Sam, Mike, LaChun. A.A., Malcolm X Coll., 1983; postgrad. Portland State U., 1975; postgrad. Nat. Coll. Edn., 1984—. Legal sec. Friedman Rochester, Chgo., 1974; clerical supr. Model Cities, Chgo. and Portland, Oreg., 1973-75; sec. Portland Met. Steering com., 1976-78; tchr. clerical Portland OIC, 1975-76; tchr. Yaun Youth Ctr., Portland, 1978-80; pres. Flexible Temps, Chgo., 1980—, cons., 1983—; cons. Personnel Plus, Chgo., 1983; typing tchr., Chgo., 1983; personnel recruiter, Chgo., 1974-75. Mem. Profls. Inc., Exec. Connections, Nat. Assn. Female Execs., MidAm. Mgmt. Assn. Democrat. Baptist. Clubs: Bus. Networking, Exec. Exchange (Chgo.). Office: Flexible Temps 323 S Franklin St 804 Chicago IL 60606

HARRIS, STEVEN DALE, oil company executive, lawyer; b. Findlay, Ohio, Oct. 13, 1949; s. Kenneth Dale and Charlotte Louise (Rosebrook) H.; m. Ann Geppert, July 20, 1974; children—Stefan Geppert, Eliot Kendall. Student Salzburg U. (Austria), 1970; B.A., Bowling Green State U., 1971; J.D., Capital U., 1975. Bar: Ohio 1975. Legis. dir. Ohio Republican Party, Columbus, 1972-75; adminstrv. asst. Ohio Dept. Devel., Columbus, 1975; gen. counsel Ohio Energy Agy., Columbus, 1975-77; dir. Kans. Energy Office, Topeka, 1977-79; mgr. govt. policy analysis Sun Gas Co., Dallas, 1979-81; v.p., gen. counsel, dir. Eagle Mountain Energy Corp., Reynoldsburg, Ohio, 1981—. Mem. Wichita Energy Commn., 1978, Interstate Oil Compact Commn., Oklahoma City, 1981; trustee Columbus E. Soccer Assn., 1984-85, v.p., 1985, coach, 1983-85. Mem. Ohio State Bar Assn., Columbus Bar Assn., Ohio Oil and Gas Assn., Ky. Oil and Gas Assn. Republican. Lutheran. Avocations: travel; photography; soccer; fishing. Office: Eagle Mountain Energy Corp 7626 E Main St Reynoldsburg OH 43068

HARRIS, SYDNEY JUSTIN, newspaper columnist; b. London, Sept. 14, 1917; student U. Chgo. and Central Coll., Chgo.; LL.D., Villa Maria Coll.; Litt.D., Schimer Coll.; D.H.L., Lenoir-Rhyne Coll.; m. Grace Miller (div. 1951); m. 2d, Patricia Roche, 1953; children—Carolyn (dec.), Michael, Barbara, David, Lindsay. Employed in various positions Chgo. Herald and Examiner, 1934-35, Chgo. Daily Times, 1936; editor Beacon Mag., Chgo., 1937-38; with public relations dept. legal div. City of Chgo., 1939-41; with Chgo. Daily News, 1941-78, drama critic and writer column Strictly Personal, syndicated in U.S. and Can. by Times of London Syndicate, 1944—, appearing in more than 200 newspapers; mem. faculty Univ. Coll., U. Chgo., from 1946; vis. scholar Lenoir-Rhyne Coll., Hickory, N.C., 1980-82; dir. Hickory Humanities Forum, Wildacres, N.C., 1981. Trustee Francis W. Parker Sch., Chgo. Recipient Ferguson award Friends of Lit., 1958; Brotherhood award NCCJ, 1968; Press award ACLU, 1980. Mem. Sigma Delta Chi. Clubs: Arts, Headline, Press. Author: Strictly Personal, 1953; A Majority of One, 1957; Last Things First, 1961; On the Contrary, 1964; Leaving the Surface, 1968; For the Time Being, 1972; The Authentic Person, 1972; Winners and Losers, 1973; The Best of Harris, 1975; Would You Believe?, 1979; Pieces of Eights, 1982. Mem. usage panel Am. Heritage Dictionary. Office: Chgo Sun-Times 401 N Wabash Ave Chicago IL 60611

HARRIS, THOMAS L., public relations executive; b. Dayton, Ohio, Apr. 18, 1931; s. James and Leona (Blum) H.; m. JoAnn Karch, Apr. 14, 1957; children—James, Theodore. B.A., U. Mich., 1953; M.A., U. Chgo., 1956. Vice pres. pub. relations Needham Harper & Steers, Chgo., 1967-72; exec. v.p. Daniel J. Edelman, Inc., Chgo., 1957-67; pres. Foote, Cone & Belding, Chgo., 1973-78; pres. Golin Harris Communications, Inc., Chgo., 1978—. Served with U.S. Army, 1953-55. Mem. Pub. Relations Soc. Am. Home: 556 Cherokee Highland Park IL 60035 Office: 500 N Michigan Ave Chicago IL 60611

HARRIS, THOMAS ROBERT, computer specialist; b. Milw., Apr. 1, 1952. B.S. in Math. and Physics, U. Wis.-Milw., 1976; postgrad. in engring. systems Marquette U., 1976-78. Plant mgr. Gehl's Guernsey Farms, Germantown, Wis., 1978; sci. programmer Weber N/C Systems, Wauwatosa, Wis., 1979; sci. programmer Environ. Research Ctr., Rexnord, Inc., Milw., 1979-80, computer specialist, project engr. Enviroenergy Tech. Ctr., 1981-83, computer project coordinator Sci. Systems Ctr., 1983-84, mgr. Sci. Systems Ctr., 1984—. Office: Rexnord Inc 5101 W Beloit Rd Milwaukee WI 53214

HARRIS, WENDELL BURKS, osteopathic physician; b. Brockton, Mass., Sept. 16, 1910; s. Charles Fisher and Emma Darling (Burks) H.; m. Helen Clareta Boulware, Sept. 4, 1951; children—Wendell Burks, Jr., Charles Boulware, Hobart Whitaker. M.D., Middlesex U., 1940; B.S., Morgan State, 1947; D.O., Coll. Osteopathic Medicine and Surgery, 1952. Intern Provident Hosp., Balt., 1940-42, resident, 1944-48; gen. practice osteopathic medicine, Flint, Mich., 1952—; mem. staff Flint Gen. Hosp., 1952—, sec., treas. profl. staff, 1958—; mem. Genesee County Bd. of Health, Flint, 1979—; world med. adv. bd. World Buying Council. Sec. Prismatic Images, Flint, 1980; ringside physician Police Athletic League, Flint, 1978. Life mem. Am. Osteopathic Assn.; mem. Mich. Assn. Osteopathic Physicians and Surgeons. Democrat. Baptist. Avocations: philatelist; coin collector. Home: 1632 Kensington Ave Flint MI 48503 Office: 416 E Pasadena Blvd Flint MI 48505

HARRIS, WILLIAM GERALD, psychology educator; b. Pitts., Oct. 13, 1950; s. Arthur Leonard and Lillian Annette (Porter) H.; m. Rochelle Minnie Grisom, Aug. 12, 1972; children—Hashim, Khalid. B.A., U. Rochester, 1972; M.S., U. Mass., 1975, Ph.D., 1980. Asst. prof. clin. psychology program Ill. Inst. Tech., Chgo., 1979—; dir. psychol. research Psych Systems, Inc., Balt., 1982. Mem. Am. Psychol. Assn., Midwest Psychol. Assn. Democrat. Author: (with Johnson, Johnson & Schuffert) New Approaches to Interpreting the MMPI, 1983. Office: Ill Inst Tech Center Dept Psychology Chicago IL 60616

HARRIS, WILLIAM HARMON, vocational educator; b. Belmont County, Ohio, Sept. 2, 1932; s. Jesse Edward and Lacy Lucile (Green) H.; m. Helen Jean Romshak, June 29, 1975; 1 dau., Jana Lee Ferrell. Student Ohio State U., 1970-73, Cleve. State U., 1973—. Service technician Bauer Ford Sales, Inc., Martins Ferry, Ohio, 1950-70, McCombs Gen. Motors and Chrysler, 1984—; instr. auto mechanics Belmont-Harrison Area Vocat. Sch., St. Clairsville, Ohio, 1970—. Recipient First Place award Nat. Ford Service Technician Contest, 1968, awards Ford Motor Co., 1969-70. Mem. Nat. Inst. Automotive Service Excellence, Nat. Assn. Trade and Indsl. Edn., NEA, Am. Vocat. Assn., Vocat. Indsl. Clubs Am., Ohio Edn. Assn., Eastern Ohio Tchrs. Assn., Belmont-Harrison Area Vocat. Sch. Edn. Assn., Nat. Automotive Service Council, Antomotive Service Council Ohio (affiliate), Nat. Muzzle Loading Rifle Assn., Harrison County Hist. Soc., Iota Lambda Sigma.

HARRIS-KINNEY, JANICE EVELYN, educational administrator, psychologist; b. Akron, Ohio, June 24, 1925; d. Howard Cleveland and Gladys Gertrude (Barnhart) Eckard; m. Fred Palfrey Harris, July 13, 1946; m. 2d, John Danford Kinney, Mar. 12, 1977. M.S., Akron U., 1952; postgrad. Ohio State U. Lic. psychologist, Ohio; cert. tchr., Ohio Spl. services adminstr. Bexley City Schs., Columbus, Ohio; spl. edn. cons. Worthington City Schs. Mem. Assn. for Supervision and Curriculum Devel., Ohio Psychology Assn., Ohio Sch. Psychology Assn. Republican. Methodist. Clubs: Worthington Music, Clintonville Women's, Columbus Women's Music. Home: 5657 Godown Rd Columbus OH 43220 Office: 752 High St Worthington OH 43085

HARRISON, DENNIS WAYNE, chemical engineer; b. Toledo, Jan. 21, 1949; s. Wayne Lowell and Violet Rose (Michalak) H.; m. Barbara Ann Henningsen, Apr. 22, 1972; children—Michelle, Scott. B.S. in Chem. Engring., Toledo U., 1971. Project engr. Prestolite, Toledo, 1972-73, plant resident engr., Oklahoma City, 1973-76; project engr. ESB, Inc., Cleve., 1976-77; quality assurance mgr. Prestolite, Toledo, 1977-80, dir. quality assurance, 1980—. Mem. Am. Soc. Quality Control (sr.), Soc. Automotive Engrs., Battery Council Internat., Toledo C. of C. Republican. Roman Catholic. Club: Topics Camera (pres. 1982, 83) (Toledo). Avocations: photography; woodworking. Home: 5436 Sugarmaple Ln Toledo OH 43623 Office: Prestolite 511 Hamilton St Toledo OH 43601

HARRISON, HERBERT PAUL, rancher; b. Meade, Kans., Aug. 29, 1926; s. Harry Martin and Ola Almyra (Borwn) H.; m. Lula Mae Billings, Oct. 18, 1947; children—Cyril Reed, Paul Barry, John Mark, William Eric, Leslie Ann, Kelly Brian, Nancy Lou. Student edn. Wichita U., 1950. Warehouse mgr. Hawk Pharmacy, Inc., Wichita, Kans., 1949-55; v.p., purchaser Hawk Pharmacy and Hawk Wholesale Drugs, Wichita, 1955-68, pres., gen. mgr., 1968-75; pres. Harrison Angus Ranch, Wichita, 1975—. Pres. Andover Sch. Bd. Edn., Kans., 1965-67, 82-83; trustee Andover Methodist Ch., 1965-70; Republican. Lodge: Kiwanis (pres. Andover 1970, 75). Avocations: fishing, hunting, coin collecting, woodworking. Home and office: 557 S 160th E Wichita KS 67230

HARRISON, JOSEPH WILLIAM, state senator; b. Chgo., Sept. 10, 1931; s. Roy J. and Gladys V. (Greenman) H.; B.S., U.S. Naval Acad., 1956; postgrad. Ind. U. Law Sch., 1968-70; m. Ann Hovey Gillespie, June 9, 1956; children—Holly Ann, Tracy Jeanne, Thomas Joseph, Amy Beth, Kitty Lynne, Christy Jayne. Asst. to pres. Harrison Steel Castings Co., Attica, Ind., 1960-64, sales research engr., 1964-66, asst. sec., 1966-69, sec., 1969-71, v.p., 1971-84, dir., 1968-84, mem. Ind. Senate, 1966—, majority leader, 1980—. Mem. Attica Consol. Sch. Bd., 1964-66, pres., 1966-67. Served with USN, 1956-60. Mem. Wabash Valley Assn., Am. Legion, Sigma Chi. Republican. Methodist. Lodges: Elks, Eagles. Home: 504 E Pike St Attica IN 47918 Office: PO Box 409 Attica IN 47918

HARRISON, LILLIAN MAY, retired college administrator, counselor, real estate broker; b. Detroit, Apr. 30, 1919; d. John and Beatrice Lillian (Bakeman) Bird; m. Thomas Samuel Harrison, Jr., Dec. 27, 1942; children—Irma Lois Doyle, T. Samuel III. B.A. in Social Sci., U. Mich., 1971, M.A. in Edn. Guidance and Counseling, 1973. Cert. nat. counselor. Sr. sec. U. Mich., Ann Arbor, 1965-77, program asst., 1977-79; career devel. coordinator, 1979-84; real estate broker Midwest Brokers Investment Co., Ann Arbor, 1965, 78—; counselor Ann Arbor Pub. Schs., 1975—; cons. U. Hosp., Ann Arbor, 1978, Albion Coll., Mich., 1983; sec.-treas. Consumers Realty, Inc., Ann Arbor, 1978—. Contbr. articles to profl. jours. Sec. PTA, Ann Arbor, 1952. Fellow U. Mich., 1972. Mem. Am. Assn. Counseling and Devel., Real Estate Alumni Mich., Washtenaw Counselors Assn., Mich. Personnel Guidance Assn. Methodist. Club: Twelve Plus. Avocations: walking; sleding; geneological research. Office: Midwest Brokers Investment Co 547 Detroit Ann Arbor MI 48104

HARRISON, MOSES WILLIS, state official; b. Lawrenceville, Va., Apr. 30, 1956; s. Moses and Annie (Willis) H. Student Howard U.; B.A., St. Paul Coll., 1980; postgrad. Va. State U., 1981—. Interpreter Nat. Trust, Washington, 1974-77; supr. U.S. Dept. Commerce, Petersburg, Va., 1980; fellow Va. State U., Petersburg, 1981-82; paralegal Va. Legal Aid, Emporia, 1981; adminstr. Mo. Dept. Natural Resources, Laclede, 1982-85. Recipient Disting. Alumni award Nat. Assn. Equal Opportunity in Higher Edn., 1985; NEH grantee, 1978. Mem. Am. Assn. State and Local History, Am. Assn. Mus. (mus. assessment program), Internat. Council Mus., Mo. Parks Assn., Nat. Trust for Historic Preservation, St. Paul Coll. Alumni Assn., NAACP, Alpha Phi Alpha. Baptist. Club: Toastmasters. Lodge: Lions.

HARRISON, WARREN CLAUDE, dentist; b. Greene, Iowa, July 11, 1924; s. Benjamin W. and Ruby N. (Shannon) H.; m. June J. Schwerdtfeler, Oct. 2, 1949; children—Scott M., Kevin C. B.A., Iowa State Tchrs. Coll., 1949; D.D.S., U. Iowa, 1958. Gen. practice dentistry, Mt. Vernon, Iowa, 1958—. Chmn. bd. Mount Vernon Community Sch., 1979-84. Served to cpl. USMC, 1942-46, PTO. Mem. ADA, Iowa State Dental Assn., Univ. Dental Assn. Lodge: Lions (pres. 1965). Avocations: golf; bowling; bridge; reading; woodworking. Home: 702 8th Ave N Mount Vernon IA 52314 Office: 108 1st St W Mount Vernon IA 52314

HART, ALAN, philosophy educator; b. Newark, May 13, 1933; s. Louis Sidney and Dorothy (Feins) H.; m. Judith Kerzner, July 14, 1957; children—Daniel, Jason. B.A., Syracuse U., 1954; M.A. in Philosophy, 1959; Ph.D. in Philosophy, U. Pa., 1965. Teaching fellow Syracuse U., 1958-59, U. Pa., 1959-62; asst. prof. Millersville State Coll., Pa., 1962-64, U. Conn., Storrs, 1964-68; vis. prof., acting chmn. Douglass Coll., Rutgers U., New Brunswick, N.J., 1968-69; program officer N.J. Dept. Higher Edn., Trenton, 1969-70; vis. lectr. Princeton U., N.J., 1970; prof. philosophy U. Akron, Ohio, 1970—. Author: Spinoza's Ethics Part I and II: A Platonic Commentary, 1983. Served to lt. (j.g.) USNR, 1954-57; comdr. Res. (ret.). N.Y. State Regents scholar, Albany, 1950; Syracuse U. scholar, 1950. Mem. Am. Philos. Assn., Soc. History Philosophy, Leibniz Soc. Am., Metaphys. Soc. Am. Home: 467 Malvern Rd Akron OH 44303 Office: Philosophy Dept U Akron Akron OH 44325

HART, DONALD WYMAN, police chief; b. Waverly, Ill., Oct. 7, 1937; s. Wyman John and Carrie O. (Knifley) H.; m. Joyce Eileen Madden, June 29, 1963; children—Mark Allen, Angela Eileen. Student Ill. Coll., 1956-58; A.A. in Law Enforcement Des Moines Area Community Coll., 1979, A.A. in Criminalistics, 1979; grad. Iowa Law Enforcement Acad., 1968. Patrolman Boone Police Dept., Iowa, 1963-67, sheriff's deputy, 1967-68, patrolman, 1968-70, sgt., 1970-76, police chief, 1976—. Chmn. Boone Community Betterment, 1984—; bd. dirs. Boone Community Contact Services, 1980—. Recipient Leadership award Gov. Iowa, 1984; Brown award Boone County Bd. Suprs., 1983. Mem. Iowa Police Assn., Iowa Chiefs Assn. Democrat. Episcopalian. Lodge: Rotary (pres.-elect 1985—). Home: 621 West 8th Boone IA 50036 Office: Police Dept 923 8th Boone IA 50036

HART, ELWOOD ROY, urban forest entomologist, researcher, educator; b. Sioux City, Iowa, Mar. 6, 1938; s. Roy Charles Hart and Ida Caroline (Cox) Young; m. Carole Ruth Nielsen, Aug. 13, 1960 (div. 1978); 1 child, Curtis Brian; m. Nancy Louise Fues, June 2, 1979. B.A., Cornell Coll., Mt. Vernon, Iowa, 1959; M.Ed., Tex. A&M U., 1965, Ph.D., 1972. Cert. forest entomologist. Sci. tchr. West Delaware Schs., Manchester, Iowa, 1961-64, Cedar Rapids Pub. Schs., Iowa, 1965-67; postdoctoral fellow Tex. A&M U., College Station, 1972-74; asst. prof. Iowa State U., Ames, 1974-78, assoc. prof. dept. entomology, 1978—. Author research articles. Peer group counselor and facilitator Youth and Shelter Services, Ames, 1980-83. Mem. Entomol. Soc. Am., Am. Registry Profl. Entomologists, Sigma Xi, Gamma Sigma Delta. Democrat. Lodge: Masons. Avocations: motorcycles, reading, firearms, skiing. Home: 1122 Johnson St Ames IA 50010 Office: Dept Entomology Iowa State U Ames IA 50011

HART, GILBERT ROGER, dentist, nutritionist; b. Waukegan, Ill., Nov. 13, 1947; s. Roger Warren and Violet Shirley (Halligan) H.; m. Nancy Jane Borus, Aug. 1, 1970; children—Christopher Scott, Kelly Jean. B.S. in Microbiology, San Diego State U., 1974, M.S. in Home Econ., 1976; D.M.D., Wash. U., 1982. Lectr. nutrition San Diego State U., 1977-78; instr. Grossmont Coll., San Diego, 1977-78; clin. asst. Wash. U., St. Louis, 1982—; practice medicine specializing in dentistry, St. Louis, 1982—. Served in U.S. Army, 1967-69, Vietnam. Recipient Pierre Fauchard Acad. award, 1982. Mem. ADA, AAAS, Am. Dietetics Assn., Acad. Gen. Dentistry. Republican. Baptist. Avocations: carving birds of nature; golf; racquetball; handball; cross country skiing. Office: 3720 Hampton Ave St Louis MO 63109

HART, JAMES HARLAN, emergency medicine physician; b. Hamilton County, Ill., Dec. 16, 1934; s. Gleason and Elizabeth Jane (Smith) H.; m. Sharon Lenore Darr, Sept. 20, 1937; m. 2d, Lora Rae Barnett, May 9, 1955; children—Shane, Kyle, Raelene. B.S., Southwestern State U., Weatherford, Okla., 1963; M.D., Okla. U., 1968. Intern, Mercy Hosp., Oklahoma City, 1968-69; resident in ob-gyn St. Anthony Hosp., Oklahoma City, 1969-72; practice medicine specializing in ob-gyn, Woodriver, Ill., 1972-77; emergency medicine physician St. Elizabeth Hosp., Danville, Ill., 1977-78, med. dir. emergency med. service, 1980—; practice medicine specializing in emergency medicine, Lincoln, Ill., 1977-80; med. dir. emergency med. technicians program; clin. assoc. prof. U. Ill. Med. Sch., Urbana. Served with U.S. Army, 1957-59. Mem. Am. Coll. Emergency Physicians, AMA, Ill. State Med. Soc., Vermillion County Med. Soc. Republican. Home: Rural Route 2 Williamsport IN 47993 Office: St Elizabeth Hosp 600 Sager Ave Danville IL 61832

HART, JAY ALBERT CHARLES, real estate broker; b. Rockford, Ill., Apr. 16, 1923; s. Jabez Waterman and Monty Evangeline (Burgin) H.; student U. Ill., 1941-42, U. Mo., 1942-43, U. Miami (Fla.), 1952-56, Rockford Coll., 1961-62; m. Marie D. Goetz, July 16, 1976; children—Dale M. (Mrs. Richard Peel Jr.), Jay C.H. Exec. v.p. Hart Oil Co., Rockford, 1947—; pres. Internat. Service Co., Pompano Beach, Fla., 1952-58; v.p. Ipsen Industries, Inc., Rockford, 1958-61; owner Hart Realtors, Rockford, 1961—; pres. Rock Cut Corp., 1978—; sec. Intra World, Inc., 1981-83; lectr. in field; trustee, sr. analyst Anchor Real Estate Investment Trust, Chgo., 1971-80. Dir. Winnebago County (Ill.) CD, 1975; dep. coordinator Winnebago County (Ill.) ESDA, 1976—. Chmn. Rock River chpt. ARC, 1973, nat. nominating com., 1971, disaster chmn. Illiana div., 1972-80; bd. counselors Rockford Coll., 1974-80; emergency coordinator 9th Naval dist. M.A.R.S., USN, 1960-68, civilian adv. council, 1968-78. Office mgr. Citizens for Eisenhower, Chgo., 1952. Served with USAAF, 1943-46. Mem. Rockford Air Guild (pres. 1974, 76-77), Tamaroa Watercolor Soc. (v.p. 1974-80), Rockford Art Guild Assn. (dir.), Exptl. Amateur Radio Soc. (pres. 1960-80), Internat. Council Shopping Centers, Nat. Assn. Real Estate Appraisers, Soc. Indsl. Realtors, Nat. Assn. Rev. Appraisers, Nat. Assn. Realtors, Phi Eta Sigma. Mason (Shriner). Clubs: Univ., City. Author: Real Estate Buyers and Sellers Guide, 1961. Paintings in pvt., pub. collections; illustrations in numerous publs. Home: 2406 E Lane Rockford IL 61107 Office: 3701 E State St Rockford IL 61108

HART, JEROME THOMAS, state senator; b. Saginaw, Mich., July 23, 1932. Sec.-treas. Quality Seal Oil Co., 1954-60; owner, operator Tiny Town Infant & Children Clothing, 1960. Exec. asst. to treas. State Mich., 1962-64; mem. Mich. Senate, 1964—, chmn. appropriations com., 1976-82, Democratic floor leader 1973-75. Treas. Saginaw County Dem. Com., Mich., 1956-60; pres. Saginaw County Dem. Club, 1958-60; mem. Dem. State Central Com., 1959-63, 8th Congl. Dist. chmn., 1962-64, re-elected 1974. Sec.-treas. Catholic Cemetery Commn., 1960-62.

HART, ROBERT FRANKLIN, statistical process control consultant, educator; b. Hinsdale, Ill., Dec. 2, 1930; s. Morris Broadway and Laura Louise (Miller) Wailes; m. Annamae Stack, May 19, 1953 (div. Dec. 20, 1981); m. Marilyn Klotnia, July 11, 1982; children—Robert, David, Laura, Linda. B.S. in Engring., U. Ill., 1949; M.S. in Engring. Ill. Inst. Tech., 1963, M.S. in Bus., 1982; Ph.D. in Engring., Northwestern U., 1966. Registered profl. engr., structural engr., Ill. Asst. chief engine design engr. electro-motive div. Gen. Motors, La Grange, Ill., 1961-80, mgr. statis. control, 1980-81; cons. Robert Hart & Assocs., Ltd., Oshkosh, Wis., 1981—; acad. specialist Coll. Bus., U. Wis.-Oshkosh, 1985—. Author: (with Marilyn Hart) Statistical Process Control Training Workbook, 1982. Mem. Am. Statis. Assn., Operation Research Soc. Am., Am. Soc. Quality Control, Tau Beta Pi, Sigma Tau, Chi Epsilon, Sigma Iota Epsion. Home: 816 Anchorage Ct Oshkosh WI 54901 Office Coll Bus U Wis Oshkosh WI 54901

HART, RUSSELL HOLIDAY, lawyer; b. Chgo., May 1, 1928; s. Russell Holiday and Allegra (Prince) H.; m. Mary Gehres, June 16, 1951; children—Holiday Hart McKiernan, Robert Russell, Andrew Richard. A.B., DePauw U., 1950; J.D., Ind. U., 1956. Bar: Ind. 1956. Ptnr., sr. ptnr. Stuart & Branignin, Lafayette, Ind., 1956—; lectr. Ind. Continuing Legal Edn. Forum; tchr. trial lawyers Nat. Inst. for Trial Advocacy. Served with U.S. Army, 1951-53. Fellow Am. Coll. Trial Lawyers, Am. Bar Found., Ind. Bar Found. (pres.-elect); mem. ABA, Ind. Bar Assn., Tippecanoe County Bar Assn., Ind. Def. Trial Counsel (diplomate). Office: Stuart & Branigin PO Box 1010 Lafayette IN 47902

HART, WILLIAM LEVATA, law enforcement official; b. Detroit, Jan. 17, 1924; s. Charles John and Gessener Mae (Brock) H.; student FBI Nat. Acad., 1972, Nat. Exec. Inst., 1977; B.S. in Criminal Justice, Wayne State U., 1977, M.Ed., 1978, D.Ednl. Sociology, 1981; m. Laura Elaine Johnson, Nov. 25, 1950; children—Cynthia Renee, Jennifer Lynn. Coal miner, Leechburg, Pa., 1940-43, 46-50; with Ford Motor Co., Detroit, 1950-52; with Detroit Police Dept., 1952—, insp., 1971-73, div. comdr., 1973-74, dep. chief hdqrs. bur., 1974-76, chief of police, 1976—; instr. criminal justice Wayne State U.; bd. dirs. Criminal Law Revision Com., from 1976; mem. U.S. Atty. Gen.'s Task Force on Violent Crime; chmn. bd. Criminal Justice Inst., Southeastern Mich., from 1978; mem. disaster adv. com. ARC; mem. Mich. Commn. on Criminal Justice; pres. Detroit Police Benefit and Protective Assn.; expert witness, juvenile justice subcom. Senate Judiciary Com. on Juvenile Justice and Deliquency Prevention. Mem. Detroit Mayor's Bus. and Labor Ad-Hoc Com.; chmn. Detroit United Fund Dr., 1978; bd. dirs. Boy Scouts Am., Boys Club Met. Detroit. Served with USN, 1943-46; PTO. Recipient Anthony Wayne award Wayne State U., 1979; Alumni award, 1979. Mem., Nat. Acad. Assn., Internat. Police Assn., Internat. Assn. Chiefs of Police, Mich. Assn. Chiefs of Police (chmn. crime prevention com., mem. subcom. on use of deadly force), Nat. Exec. Inst., Police Found., Am. Acad. Profl. Law Enforcement, Wayne County Assn. Chiefs of Police, Maj. City Chiefs of Police Assn., Police Exec. Research Forum, Nat. Orgn. Black Law Enforcement Execs. (exec. bd.), Wayne State Alumni Assn. Baptist. Club: Detroit Yacht. Lodge: Masons. Office: Detroit Police Dept 1300 Beaubien St Detroit MI 48226

HART, WILLIAM THOMAS, See *Who's Who in America,* 43rd edition.

HARTER, GARY RONALD, lawyer; b. Huntington, Ind., June 15, 1954; s. Harold Erwin and Geraldine S. (Shull) H.; m. Nancy Ruth Larson, Sept. 13, 1980; 1 child, Mark Larson. B.A., Valparaiso U., 1976; J.D., Ind. U.-Indpls., 1979. Bar: Mo. 1979, U.S. Dist. Ct. (ea. dist.) Mo. 1979, Ill. 1980, U.S. Dist. Ct. (so. dist.) Ill. 1980. Assoc. Lucas & Murphy, St. Louis, 1979-80; ptnr. Harter & Larson, Belleville, Ill., 1980—. Mng. editor Ind. Law Rev., Vol. 12, 1978, 79. Pres. Mascoutah Democratic Club, Ill., 1983-84; mem. St. Clair County Young Dems., Belleville, 1983—. Huntington County Bar Assn. Bicentennial law scholar, 1979; recipient Disting. Citizen cert. 375th Aeromed. Airlift Wing, Scott AFB, Ill., 1983. Mem. ABA, Mo. Bar Assn., St. Clair County Bar Assn., St. Louis Bar Assn., Assn. Trial Lawyers Am., Ill. Trial Lawyers Assn. (negligence com.), Mascoutah C. of C. (pres. 1984), St. Louis Soaring Assn. Lodge: Lions (sec. Mascoutah 1983). Home: 109 E Green Mascoutah IL 62258 Office: Harter & Larson 201 S Jackson Belleville IL 62221

HARTER, HARMAN LEON, mathematical statistician, writer, consultant; b. Keokuk, Iowa, Aug. 15, 1919; s. Harman Theodore and Mary Josie (Hough) H.; m. Alice Lauretta Madden, Oct. 23, 1943. B.A., Carthage Coll., 1940; M.A., U. Ill., 1941; Ph.D., Purdue U., 1949. Grad. asst. in math. U. Ill., Urbana, 1941-43; prof. physics Mo. Valley Coll., Marshall, Mo., 1943-44; instr. math. Purdue U., West Lafayette, Ind., 1946-48; asst. prof. math. Mich. State U., East Lansing, 1949-52; math. statistician Aero. Research and Flight Dynamics Labs., Wright-Patterson AFB, Ohio, 1952-78; research prof. math. and stats. Wright State U., Dayton, Ohio, 1979-84; dist. vis. prof. Air Force Inst. Tech., Wright Patterson AFB, Ohio, 1982-84; cons., writer, Dayton, 1979—; cons. U. Dayton Research Inst., Ohio, 1979-81; Author: New Tables of the Incomplete Gamma-Function Ratio, 1964; Order Statistics and Their Use in Testing and Estimation, Vol. 1, 1978, Vol. 2, 1983; The Chronological Annotated Bibliography of Order Statistics, 1978, 83. Editor: (with D.B. Owen) Selected Tables in Mathematical Statistics, Vols. 1-3, 1970-75. Served with USN, 1944-46. U. Ill. Carthage Coll. scholar, 1940-41; research fellow in math. Office Naval Research, West Lafayette, Ind., 1948-49. Fellow Am. Statis. Assn. (chpt. pres. 1954-55, sect. chmn. 1964), Inst. Math. Stats. (co-editor selected tables 1967-75); mem. Internat. Statis. Inst., Soc. Indsl. and Applied Math. (sect. pres. 1958-59; sec., treas. 1956-58), Math. Assn. Am., Ops. Research Soc. Am. Democrat. Mem. Christian Ch. Lodge: Masons. Avocations: bridge, baseball statistics. Home: 32 S Wright Ave Dayton OH 45403

HARTER, JAMES EDWARD, computer company executive, consultant; b. Wenona, Ill., July 10, 1954; s. Edward Clark and Mary (Harmon) H.; m. Paula Sheri Harris, Aug. 18, 1973. B.S. in Computer Sci., U. Ill., 1977. Mgr. Byte Shop, Champaign, Ill., 1977-81; sales support analyst Apple Computer, Chgo., 1981-83, sales support mgr., 1983-84, area service support mgr., 1984—. Mem. Data Processing Mgmt. Assn. (sec. 1979-81). Presbyterian. Avocations: music; golf. Office: Apple Computer 8700 W Bryn Mawr Chicago IL 60631

HART-GONZALEZ, LUCINDA, linguistics, sociology and anthropology educator; b. Mar. 31, 1950, d. Edward W. and Flori L. (Feder) H.; m. Cristian Gonzalez Valdiviezo; children—Ana Flor, Carla Mercedes. B.A. summa cum laude, U. Mass., 1975; M.S., Georgetown U., 1978, Ph.D., 1980. Cert. elem. tchr., Mass. Tchr. Harvard Yard Child Care Ctr., Cambridge, Mass., 1972-75; tchr. French, Boston Sch. Modern Langs., 1973-74; bilingual tchr. Boston Pub. Schs., 1975-76; freelance tech. translator, Boston, 1973-76; lectr-teaching asst. Georgetown U., Washington, 1976-81; asst. prof. dept. linguistics Oakland U., Rochester, Mich., 1981—; cons. Ministry Edn., Lima, Peru, Latin Am. Trade Specialists, Wyoming, Mich.; cons. grant proposal evaluation NSF, Washington. Contbr. articles to profl. jours. Mem. adv. bd. dirs. Lowry Early Childhood Ctr., Rochester, 1982-83. Grantee Oakland U., 1981, spl. project grantee, 1983; fellow Georgetown U., 1976-79. Mem. Latin Am. Indian Lits. Assn. (charter); mem. N.Y. Acad. Scis., Linguistic Soc. Am., Am. Anthrop. Assn. Office: Dept Linguistics Oakland U Rochester MI 48063

HARTHY, CHARLES OTIS, personnel executive; b. Hastings, Mich., July 15, 1937; s. Otis Clark and Vesta Clare (Reid) H.; m. Mary Lou White, Sept. 15, 1956; children—Jeffery D., Laura J., Paul S., Julie A., Linda M. B.S., Mich. State U., 1959. Asst. dir. indsl. relations Hastings Mfg., Mich., 1961-72; personnel mgr. Dake Corp., Grand Haven, Mich., 1972-79; personnel mgr. Zelenka Nursery, Grand Haven, 1979—. Author: Descendants of Philander Otis, 1962; Descendants of Jasper Reid, 1980; Descendants of Benjamin Harthy, 1979. Author, editor: Centennial History Hastings, 1971. Mem. Republican County Com., Hastings, Mich., 1968-70; spl. project mem. Econ. Devel. Com., Grand Haven, 1975-80; pres. Barry County Hist. Soc., 1968-71, life mem.; sec. Barry County Planning Com., Hastings, 1968. Mem. SAR (pres. 1971-72). Republican. Lodge: Masons (sr. warden 1985). Avocations: genealogy; travel; stamp collecting; photography. Home: 1629 Robbins Rd Grand Haven MI 49417 Office: John Zelenka Evergreen Nursery Inc 16127 Winans Grand Haven MI 49417

HARTICH, MARK DAVID, optometrist; b. Oceanside, Calif., Apr. 23, 1953; s. Jack Jacob and Ariel (Rockne) H. Student U. N.D., 1972-74; B.A. in Psychology, U. Minn., 1976; B.S. in Visual Sci., So. Calif. Coll. Optometry, 1978, O.D., 1981. Lic. optometrist, Minn., Calif. pvt. practice optometry, New Hope, Minn., 1981-82; optometrist Share Health Care Assn., Bloomington, Minn., 1982—; sect. chmn. Share Bloomington Clinic, 1982—. Mem. Am. Optometric Assn. Republican. Avocations: tennis, racketball, back packing, skiing, spelunking. Home: 16654 Terrey Pine Dr Eden Prairie MN 55344 Office: 7920 Cedar Ave S Bloomington MN 55344

HARTIGAN, JAMES J., airline executive; b. 1924. With United Air Lines Inc., Mt. Prospect, Ill., 1942—, asst. mgr. sales, 1961-63, sales mgr., 1963-67, asst. v.p. sales, 1967, v.p. passenger sales and services planning, 1968-71, v.p. system mktg., 1971-73, sr. v.p., gen. mgr. Western div. 1973-75, group v.p. opn. services, exec. v.p., 1975-81, pres., dir., 1981—. Served with USN, 1943-45. Office: United Air Lines Inc 1200 Algonquin Rd Mt Prospect IL 60007*

HARTIGAN, MARYELLEN, public relations executive; b. Evergreen Park, Ill., June 17, 1957; d. Edwin J. and Loretta J. (Przybylski) Kulakowski; m. James E. Hartigan, May 3, 1980. B.S. in Journalism, No. Ill. U., 1979. Mem. pub. relations staff Chgo. Met. United Way/Crusade of Mercy, 1979; advt. specialist Electro-Motive Div., Gen. Motors Corp., LaGrange, Ill., 1979-81, editor newsletter, 1980—, sr. sales promotion rep., 1981—. Trustee Chgo.-Cook County 4-H Found., 1984—; mem. communications com. Chgo. United Way Crusade of Mercy. Recipient award of merit Gen. Motors, 1983. Mem. Pub. Relations Soc. Am., Soc. Profl. Journalists, West Suburban C. of C. (dir. 1984—). Editor, Inside EMD newsletter, 1980—; co-editor Streamliner, 1981—. Office: 9301 55th St LaGrange IL 60525

HARTIGAN, NEIL F., state attorney general, former lt. gov. Ill.; b. Chgo.; grad. social scis. Georgetown U.; LL.B., Loyola U., Chgo.; LL.D. (hon.), Martin Luther King Coll., 1975; m. Marge Hartigan; children—John, Elizabeth, Laura, Bridget. Admitted to Ill. bar; formerly dep. adminstrv. officer City of Chgo.; legis. counsel City of Chgo. in Ill. 75th Gen. Assembly; then chief legal counsel Chgo. Park Dist.; lt. gov. State of Ill., 1972-77; pres., chief exec. officer Real Estate Research Corp., Chgo., 1977-79, dir., from 1977; head corp. affairs 1st Nat. Bank of Chgo., 1978-79, sr. v.p., area head Western hemisphere worldwide banking dept., 1979-82; now atty. gen. State of Ill.; Democratic committeeman 49th ward, Chgo., 1968-80; former lectr. John Marshall Law Sch., Chgo.; bd. regents, bd. dirs. Georgetown U.; vis. com. on public policy U. Chgo.; bd. dirs. Chgo. Conv. and Tourism Bur., TRUST, Inc.; co-chmn. Ill. Olympic Com.; exec. com. March of Dimes, chmn. Superwalk, 1978; active Am. Cancer Soc. fund drives. Named among Ten Outstanding Young Men of Yr., Chgo. Jr. C. of C., 1967, among 200 Future Leaders Am., Time mag.; hon. pres. Spanish-speaking div. Jr. C. of C., Chgo.; Mem. Nat. Conf. Lt. Govs. (chmn. 1976, regional vice chmn.), Midwest Conf. Attys. Gen. (chmn.), Dem. Adv. Council Elected Ofcls., Council State Govts. (exec. com.), Am. Bar Assn., Ill. Bar Assn., Chgo. Bar Assn., Chgo. Assn. Commerce and Industry, Nat. Council on Aging, Chgo. Council on Fgn. Relations, Young Pres.' Orgn. Clubs: Econ., Rotary, K.C., Irish Fellowship, Cook County Hundred. Office: Office of the Attorney General 500 South Second Springfield IL 62706

HARTITZ, JOACHIM ERNST, chemical engineer, scientist; b. Dessau, Germany, Aug. 11, 1929; came to U.S., 1965; s. Ernst Karl and Hedwig (Klockengiesser) H.; m. Armgard Erika Weigel, Oct. 28, 1958; children—Marcos Dominik, Raina Carlotta. Ing. Chem., Ohm-Poly., Nurenberg, Germany. Research engr. Bad. Anilin & Soda Fabrik, Ludwigshafen, Fed. Republic Germany, 1955-57; dep. mgr. Focke-Wulf Aircraft Co., Bremen, Fed. Republic Germany, 1957-59; plant mgr. Tubenplast S.A., Caracas, Venezuela, 1959-65; plant mgr. B.F. Goodrich Co., Ardee, Ireland, 1977-82, research fellow, Avon Lake, Ohio, 1965-77, 82—. Author: Polymer Engineering and Science, 1974. Patentee in field. Mem. Soc. Plastics Engrs. (sr.). Lodge: Masons. Home: 32833 Tanglewood Ct Avon Lake OH 44012 Office: BF Goodrich Chem Group Walker Rd Avon Lake OH 44012

HARTLEY, JAMES MICHAELIS, printing co. exec.; b. Indpls., Nov. 25, 1916; s. James Worth and Bertha S. (Beuke) H.; student Jordan Conservatory of Music, 1934-35, Ind. U., Purdue U., Franklin Coll.; m. E. Lea Cosby, July 30, 1944; children—Michael D., Brent S. With Arvin Industries, Inc., 1934-36; founder, pres. J. Hartley Co., Inc., Columbus, Ind., 1937—, treas., 1972—. Pres., Columbus Little Theatre, 1947-48; founding dir. Columbus Arts Guild, 1960-64, v.p., 1965-66, dir., 1971-74; musical dir., cellist Guild String Quartet, 1963-73; founding dir. Columbus Pro Musica, 1969-74; dir. Regional Arts Study Commn., 1971-74; v.p. Ind. Council Republican Workshops, 1965-69, pres., 1975-77; pres. Bartholomew County Republican Workshop, 1966-67. Served with USAAF, 1942-46. Mem. NAM, Nat. Fedn. Ind. Bus. Office: 101 N National Rd Columbus IN 47201

HARTLEY, WILLIAM DOUGLAS, art educator; b. Indpls., Nov. 24, 1921; s. James Worth and Bertha Sophia (Beuke) H.; m. Marucha del Socorro Trevino, Aug. 19, 1951; children—Gretel, Hetzal, Litzi. B.S., Ind. U., 1948, M.F.A., 1949; M.F.A., Kansas City Art Inst., 1951; Ph.D., NYU, 1971. Dir. art Pueblo High Sch., Colo., 1951-54; mem. faculty Ill. State U., Normal, 1954—, prof. art history, 1967—; art cons., 1959—. Author: The Search for Henry Cross, 1966; Things Invisible to See, 1979. Editor Alumni Bull., 1984—. Contbr. articles to profl. jours. Commd. sculptures include Arvin Inustries, Columbus, Ind., St. Matthew's Episcopal Ch., Bloomington, Ill., Adlai Stevenson Lecture Commn., Bloomington, Christ the King Episcopal Ch., Normal, Ill. Fellow Internat. Inst. Arts and Letters; mem. Midwestern Art History Soc. Republican. Episcopalian. Avocations: watercoloring painting; music; fiction writing. Home: 1001 S Fell Ave Normal IL 61761 Office: Art Dept Ill State U Normal IL 61761

HARTMAN, ALLEN ALBERT, real estate broker; b. Spades, Ind., May 12, 1936; s. August Henry and Hilda Cathrine (Brunsman) H.; m. Norma June Rouch; children—Diane Marie, Todd Anthony. Grad. high sch., Sunman, Ind. Lic. real estate broker, Ind. Warehouse ops. supr. Hillenbrand Industries, Batesville, Ind., 1958-76; broker, mgr. Grady Realtors, West Harrison, Ind., 1976—. Served with U.S. Army, 1954-58. Mem. Southeast Ind. Bd. Realtors (nominating chmn. 1984), No. Manchester Jaycees (pres. 1965). Democrat. Roman Catholic. Lodge: Kiwanis (pres. 1982). Avocation: golf. Home: RR4 Box 266 Batesville IN 47006 Office: Grady Realtors RR3 Box 107-1 W Harrison IN 47060

HARTMAN, EDWIN ALAN, psychology educator, consultant; b. Wisconsin Rapids, Wis., Oct. 15, 1944; s. Edwin John and Dorothy Marion (Polansky) H.; m. Diana Lynn Lindgren, Mar. 2, 1968; children—Elizabeth Ann, Amy Catherine. B.A., U. Wis.-Madison, 1968; M.A., Mich. State U., 1970, Ph.D., 1972. Research scientist Inst. Behavioral Research, Tex. Christian U., 1972-76; asst. prof. psychology and bus. adminstrn. U. Wis.-Oshkosh, 1976-79, assoc. prof. psychology and bus. adminstrn., 1979-83, acting asst. vice chancellor, 1984, prof., asst. dean Coll. Bus. Adminstrn., 1985—; cons. Air Can., Am. Airlines, Eastern Airlines, First Nat. Bank Ft. Worth, Ft. Worth Nat. Bank, Oshkosh Truck Corp., Thilmany Pulp and Paper, Rockwell Internat.-Oshkosh div., Winnebago County, Waushara County, Trinity Valley Mental Health Authority, Tarrant County (Tex.), Wis. Assn. Sch. Bds., AT&T, Braniff Airlines, Kaiser-Permanente Med. Care Program. NDEA grad. fellow, 1968-71; NIMH grantee, 1979-82; HEW grantee, 1974-75. Mem. Am. Psychol. Assn., Acad. Mgmt., Fox Valley Personnel Assn., Midwest Psychol. Assn., Sigma Xi, Psi Chi. Presenter numerous confs.; contbr. chpts. to books, articles to profl. jours. Home: 2745 Montclair Pl Oshkosh WI 54901 Office: Clow Faculty U Wis Oshkosh WI 54901

HARTMAN, JILL ANITA, software consultant, data entry operator; b. Columbia City, Ind., Oct. 23, 1955; d. Bill Junior and Barbara Ann (Kistler) Kessie; m. Timothy C. Hartman, Dec. 31, 1982. B.S. in Nursing, Goshen Coll., 1974. Cert. emergency med. technician. Nurses aide Millers Merry Manor, Columbia, City, 1976-77; lathe operator Bond-Flex Rubber Co., Columbia City, 1977-79; communications operator Whitley County Meml. Hosp., Ind.,

1979-82; clk.-typist Victor Temporary Services, Monroe, Mich., 1983-84; data entry operator Kelly Services, Monroe, 1984-85; owner, cons. Acronym Software, Monroe, 1985—. Vol. Whitley County Emergency Med. Services, 1979-82. Republican. Methodist. Avocations: reading; sewing; cooking; white-water rafting; cross-country skiing. Home and Office: Acronym Software 2870 2d St Suite DB Monroe MI 48161

HARTMANN, DONALD OTTO, SR., beverage corporation executive; b. St. Louis, Jan. 24, 1934; s. Otto Frederic and Mabel Lena (Schuessler) H.; B.S., U. Mo., 1963, M.Ed., 1964, Assoc. EED, 1966; m. Linda Lou Sparks, Sept. 8, 1962; children—Kimberly Lynn, Donald Otto, Jacqueline Marie, Michele Lee. Profl. scout exec. Boy Scouts Am., 1959-60; asst. prof. U. Mo., 1960-63; coordinator co-op. edn. Mo., 1963-67; dir. personnel, rehab. Goodwill Industries of Am., 1967-69; dir. forms mgmt., graphics communications, supply services Anheuser-Busch Cos., Inc., St. Louis, 1969—; tchr., counselor, cons. in graphic arts, forms design and mgmt., 1969—. Chmn. bd. Christian edn. United Ch. of Christ, St. Louis, 1974-77; bd. dirs. local bd. edn., 1972—, pres., 1973-76; active Boy Scouts Am., 1942—, Eagle Scout reviewer/presenter, 1960—; mem. community wide youth services panel United Way of St. Louis, 1970—; mem. White House Panel on Childhood Edn., Mo. Gov.'s Panel on Edn., 1977; active Lindbergh PTA, 1968—. Served with USN, 1953-59. Recipient Eagle Scout award Boy Scouts Am., 1952, Silver Explorer award, 1956, Silver Beaver award, 1985, Gt. Grant award, 1962, Regional Service award, 1973, Silver Beaver award; Outstanding Loaned Exec. award United Way, 1970, Community Service award Girl Scouts U.S.A. Mem. Am. Sch. Bds. Assn., Nat. Sch. Bds. Assn., Mo. Sch. Bds. Assn., St. Louis Suburban Sch. Bds. Assn., In-Plant Mgrs. Assn., Council of Reprographics Execs., Am. Mgmt. Assn., Nat. Eagle Scout Assn. (St. Louis area council 1982), Phi Delta Kappa, Sigma Phi Epsilon (alumni bd. pres. 1963-70). Home: 4824 Gatesbury Dr Saint Louis MO 63128 Office: Anehuser-Busch Companies Inc One Busch Pl Saint Louis MO 63118

HARTMANN, PAMELA JEANNE, telephone company executive; b. Muskegon, Mich., Nov. 5, 1952; d. DeVere Richardson and Patty Ellen (Pratt) Boyd; B.A., U. Mich., 1974, M.B.A., 1976; m. Michael W. Hartmann, June 9, 1973; 1 child, Elizabeth Boyd. Mcpl. bond underwriter, trader, portfolio analyst Nat. Bank of Detroit, 1976-80; mgr. pension fund, fin. mgr. Mich. Bell Telephone Co., Detroit, summer 1980, cash mgr., 1980-83, fin. mgr., 1983—. Chartered fin. analyst. Mem. Econ. Club Detroit, Fin. Analysts Soc. Detroit, Detroit Corp. Cash Mgmt. Assn. (program chmn. 1982-83, pres. 1983-84), Jr. League Detroit, Detroit Inst. Arts. Office: Mich Bell Telephone Co 444 Michigan Ave Room 1440 Detroit MI 48226

HARTMANN, RICHARD PAUL, accountant; b. Terre Haute, Ind., Sept. 4, 1934; s. Albert and Therese (Diekhoff) H.; m. Marcia Jean Von Blon, June 16, 1956; children—Richard P., Jeffrey B., Roger A. B.A., Capital U., 1956; student Officers Candidate Sch., Newport, R.I., 1956, U.S. Naval War Coll., 1969; postgrad. Xavier U., 1965-66, U. Dayton, 1967-68. C.P.A., Ohio, 1969. Sr. staff acct. Battelle & Battelle, C.P.A.s, Dayton, Ohio, 1960-69; owner, mgr. Richard P. Hartmann, C.P.A., Kettering, Ohio, 1970—. Mem. City Council Kettering, 1977—; mem. pres.'s council Capital U.; treas. Capital U. Alumni Bd., 1967-68. Served to capt. USNR, 1978—. Mem. Am. Inst. C.P.A.s, Ohio Soc. C.P.A.s, Kettering C. of C. (past pres.), Naval Inst., Nat. League Cities, Naval War Coll., Naval Res. Assn., U.S. Navy League. Republican. Lutheran. Club: Exchange (past pres.). Office: 3560 Marshall Rd Kettering OH 45429

HARTMANN, RONALD JOSEPH, pharmacist; b. Waconia, Minn., Jan. 10, 1946; s. Gilbert Joseph and Eva Verna (Gorski) H.; m. Mary Jean Moldestad, Feb. 12, 1947; children—Carey Ayn, Matthew Joseph. B.S., U. Minn., 1969. Registered pharmacist, Minn. Pharmacy intern Matson Drug Co., Waconia, 1966-69, Abbott Hosp., Mpls., 1968-69; hosp. pharmacist Rochester (Minn.) Methodist Hosp., 1969-81; dir. pharmacy Spring Valley (Minn.) Meml. Hosp., 1974-75; dir. pharmacy Olmsted Community Hosp., Rochester, 1975-78; cons. pharmacist Mayo Clinic, Rochester, 1979-81; dir. pharm. services St. Olaf Hosp., Austin, Minn., 1981-83; owner Mapleton Drug, Mapleton, Minn.; mem. adj. faculty U. Minn. Mem., officer Rochester Area Barbershop Chorus, 1970-81; active Boy Scouts Am.; mem. Mapleton Area Planning Team, 1985; bd. dirs. Mapleton Community Home, 1985. Recipient Outstanding Achievement award Rexall Co., 1969. Fellow Am. Soc. Cons. Pharmacists; mem. Am. Pharm. Assn., Minn. State Pharm. Assn. (bd. dirs. 1979-83), Am. Soc. Hosp. Pharmacists, Minn. Soc. Hosp. Pharmacists, So. Minn. Soc. Hosp. Pharmacists (pres. 1974), Mapleton Area C. of C. (v.p. 1985), Kappa Psi (Scholastic award 1968), Rho Chi. Roman Catholic. Club: Sertoma. Home: 503 1st Ave SE Mapleton MN 56065 Office: Mapleton Drug Box 414 Mapleton MN 56065

HARTMANN, WILLIAM MORRIS, physics educator; b. Elgin, Ill., July 28, 1939; s. Walter John and Marguerite (Weed) H.; m. Christine Ann Rein, June 24, 1967; children—Mitra, Daniel. B.S., Iowa State U., 1961; Ph.D., Oxford U., 1965. Research assoc. Argonne Nat. Lab., Ill., 1965-68; prof. physics Mich. State U., East Lansing, 1968—; hon. research assoc. Harvard U., 1976-77; acting dir. acoustics Institut de Recherche et Coordination Acoustique/Musique, Paris, 1981-82. Contbr. articles to profl. jours. Grantee NSF, 1971-81, NIH, 1981—. Fellow Acoustical Soc. Am. (chmn. tech. com. musical acoustics 1980-84). Home: 749 Beech St East Lansing MI 48823 Office: Dept Physics Mich State U East Lansing MI 48823

HARTNETT, JAMES PATRICK, engineering educator; b. Lynn, Mass., Mar. 19, 1924; s. James Patrick and Anna Elizabeth (Ryan) H.; m. Shirley Germaine Carlson, July 14, 1945 (div. 1969); children—James, David, Paul, Carla, Dennis; m. Edith Zubrin, Sept. 10, 1971. B.S. in Mech. Engring., Ill. Inst. Tech., 1947; M.S., MIT, 1948; Ph.D., U. Calif.-Berkeley, 1954. Engr. gas turbine div. Gen. Electric Co., 1948-49; research engr. U. Calif.-Berkeley, 1949-54; from asst. prof. to prof. mech. engring. U. Minn., 1954-61; H. Fletcher Brown prof. mech. engring., chmn. dept. U. Del., 1961-65; prof., head dept. energy engring. U. Ill., Chgo., 1965-74, dir. Energy Resources Ctr., 1974—; Guggenheim fellow, vis. prof. U. Tokyo, 1960; cons. ICA, Seoul, Korea, 1960; Fulbright lectr., cons. mech. engring. U. Alexandria, Egypt, 1961; sci. exchange visitor Romania, 1969; vis. prof. Israel Inst. Tech., 1971; cons. Asian Inst. Tech., Bangkok, 1977. Editor: Recent Advances in Heat and Mass Transfer, 1961; co-editor: Internat. Jour. Heat and Mass Transfer, 1960—, (with T.F. Irvine, Jr.) Advances in Heat Transfer, 1963—, Heat Transfer-Japanese Research, Soviet Research, 1971, Fluid Mechanics-Soviet Research, 1971, (with W.M. Rohsenow) Handbook of Heat Transfer, 1973, 2d edit. (with Rohsenow and Ganic), 1985. Contbr. articles on heat transfer, fluid mechanics, energy to tech. jours. Mem. organizing com. and sci. council Internat. Centre Heat and Mass Transfer, Belgrade, Yugoslavia, 1969—, Ill. Energy Resources Commn., 1974—; mem. sci. council Regional Ctr. for Energy, Heat and Mass Transfer for Asia and Pacific, 1976—. Recipient Profl. Achievement award Ill. Inst. Tech. Alumni Assn., 1977, Luikov medal Internat. Ctr. Heat and Mass Transfer, 1981. Fellow ASME (Meml. award Heat Transfer div. 1969); mem. AIAA, Am. Inst. Chem. Engring., Am. Soc. Engring. Edn., AAUP, AAAS, Sigma Xi, Tau Beta Pi, Pi Tau Sigma. Home: 200 E Delaware Chicago IL 60611 Office: Univ Ill Box 4348 Chicago IL 60680

HARTOONIAN, H. MICHAEL, educational administrator; b. Chgo., May 11, 1938; s. Michael M. and Rose (Alberty) H.; m. Nancy F. Kersten, Aug. 29, 1962; children—Christine Lee, Michael Lincoln. B.A., Lawrence U., 1960; M.A., U. Wis.-Madison, 1966, Ph.D. 1972. Tchr., dept. chair Pub. Schs., Omro, Wis., 1962-66; supr. social studies edn. Dept. Pub. Instrn., Madison, Wis., 1966—; prof., dir. social scis. U. Ariz., Tucson, 1973-74; adj. prof. U. Wis., Madison, 1972—; lectr., Marquette U., Milw., 1971-73; lectr. cons. Nat. Humanities Faculty, Concord, Mass., 1978—; ednl. cons. Panama Canal Zone, 1971. Co-author, editor: People and our Country, 1976, The Ethics of Education, 1977, Knowledge, Processes and Values in Social Education, 1977, Rethinking Social Education, 1985. Contbr. articles to profl. jours. Tchr. citizenship edn. Boy Scouts Am., Madison, Wis., 1981-84; council mem., v.p. St. Luke's Lutheran Ch., Middleton, Wis., 1980-83. Served to lt. USAF, 1960-62. Recipient State Service for Citizenship Edn. award Wis. Council for Social Studies, 1984; econ. and law edn. grantee U.S. Office Edn. and Dept. Edn., 1968-74. Mem. Educators of Social Responsibility (nat. adv. bd. 1984—), Nat. Council State Social Studies Specialists (pres. 1969-72), Social Sci. Edn. Consortium (bd. dirs. 1977-81, v.p., 1978-79), Nat. Council Social Studies (research and publs. bd. 1978-83, chair task force on future of orgn. 1984-85). Avocations: flying; running. Office: Wis Dept Pub Instrn 125 S Webster St Madison WI 53707

HARTSELL, ROBERT NEAL, fire department officer, safety instructor; b. Elmwood Park, Ill., Mar. 26, 1937; s. Ralph Miles and Mary Alice (Napier) H.; m. Joan Cunningham, Mar. 3, 1956; children—Terry Lynn Tammy Dawn, Toni Renee, Daniel Robert. A.S. in Fire Sci., Triton Coll., River Grove, Ill., 1980; B.S., So. Ill. U., 1982. Fire fighter Chgo. Fire Dept., 1962-72, fire lt. Fire Prevention Bur., 1972-73, co. officer, 1973—, fire capt., 1980—, comdg. officer air mask service; safety coordinator St. Joseph Hosp., 1979-83; fire safety instr. Mem. Republican Nat. Com. Served with USMC, 1954-57. Recipient commendations Chgo. Fire Dept., Mayor of Chgo., 1975, 1980. Mem. Internat. Soc. Fire Service Instrs., Fire Officers Assn., Am. Soc. Safety Engrs., Nat. Fire Protection Assn. Lodge: Internat. Order of Foresters. Home: 5525 N Nashville Ave Chicago IL 60656 Office: 558 W DeKoven St Chicago IL 60607

HARTSFIELD, PAULA KINDRICK, vocational home economics educator; b. Springfield, Mo., Apr. 12, 1954; d. Clarence Mitchell and Hilda N. (Nichols) Kindrick; m. George Thomas Hartsfield, May 1, 1982. B.S. in Edn., S.W. Mo. State U., 1976; M.S., Kans. State U., 1978. Cert. vocat. home econs. tchr., gen sci. tchr. vocat. dir. Sec. Ozark Empire Fair, Springfield, Mo., 1972-77; piano and flute tchr., Springfield, 1972-76; vocat. home econs. tchr. Monett Sch. Dist., Mo., 1976-78; consumer protection paralegal intern Mo. Atty. Gen., Jefferson City, Mo., 1978; Supr. home econs. edn. Mo. Dept. Elem. and Secondary Edn., Jefferson City, 1979-83, state dir. home econs. edn., 1983—; mem. home econs. adv. bd. Favorite Recipes Press, Nashville, 1983-85; proposal reader and ranker U.S. Office Consumer Edn., Washington, 1981; nat. bd. dirs. Future Homemakers Am., Washington, 1977-78. Contbr. articles to profl. jours. Treas. Capitol Area Chpt. March of Dimes, Jefferson City, 1982-83, exec. com. 1981-83, leader Mother's March, 1983-84; membership chairperson Capitol Women's Polit. Caucus, Jefferson City, 1982; trustee Caroline B. Ullman Student and Scholarship Fund Mo. PTA, 1983—. Recipient family econs. research assistantship Kans. State U., 1978, Disting. Service award Mo. Assn. Future Homemakers Am., 1984. Mem. Mo. Home Econs. Assn. (dist. H. pres. elect 1984-85, pres. 1985-86), Nat. Assn. Vocat. Home Econs. Tchrs. (state legis. contact person 1983-84), Am. Council Consumer Interests (state membership chmn. 1984-85), Am. Vocat. Assn., Bus. and Profl. Women's Club (1st v.p. Jefferson City chpt. 1983-84), Kappa Omicron Phi (nat. v.p. program 1984-85, chmn. membership 1985—, workshop leader Nat. Conclave, 1980). Democrat. Episcopalian. Club: Zonta (Jefferson City) (program com. mem. 1984—). Avocations: jogging, aerobic exercise classes, travel, reading. Home: 131 Forest Hill Ave Jefferson City MO 65101 Office: Dept Elementary and Secondary Edn 310 Chestnut St PO Box 480 Jefferson City MO 65102

HARTSMAN, ROBERT ALLAN, marketing executive; b. Milw., July 6, 1941; s. David and Bertha (Green) H.; m. Sharon Lynn Burton, May 20, 1978; 1 child from previous marriage, Scott Nelson. B.S., U. Wis.-Milw., 1964. Project leader Blue Cross Wis., 1972-77; sr. systems analyst Falk Corp., 1977-78; regional mktg. dir. Cap Gemini Dasd, Milw., 1978—. Patroller, Nat. Ski Patrol, Wis. and Mich., 1982—. Mem. Data Processing Mgmt. Assn., Assn. Systems Mgmt. Club: Optimist (chmn.). Avocations: skiing, boating, sports, cooking. Office: Cap Gemini Dasd 9045 N Deerwood Dr Brown Deer WI 53209

HARTSOOK, ROBERT FRANCIS, educational administrator; b. Eureka, Kans., July 12, 1948; s. Herbert Edwin and Beverly Mercia (James) H.; m. Elizabeth Drill, Oct. 24, 1981. B.A., Kans. State Coll., 1970, M.S., 1972; J.D., Washburn U., 1979. Vice pres. Colby Community Coll., Kans., 1972-76; exec. vice pres., chief exec. officer Kans. Engring. Soc., Inc., Topeka, 1978-82; v.p. Washburn U., Topeka, 1982-85, Wichita State U., Kans. 1985—. Bd. editors Washburn Law Jour. 1976-77, exec. editor, 1977-78. Commn. Kansas State Educ. Commn., Topeka, 1975-78; mem. adv. panel Gov.'s Commn. Criminal Admin., Topeka, 1975-78. Served with USNG, 1970-76. Danforth Found. fellow, summer 1973. Mem. Council for Advancement and Support of Educ. (most improved univ. 1983-84, exceptional achievement in fin. support 1983-84). Club: Topeka (pres. 1983-84). Home: 505 N Rock Rd Wichita KS 67206 Office: Wichita State U Wichita KS 67208

HARTUNG, RICHARD PENN, museum director; b. Columbus, Ohio, Jan. 31, 1938; s. Maurice Leslie and Gertrude (Penn) H.; m. Ilah M. Bjorklund, Aug. 27, 1960; children—Daniel Asher, Gregor Alan. Student Shimer Coll., 1953-56, Yale U. Sch. Architecture, 1956-57; B.A., U. Chgo., 1958. Adminstrn. asst. Philip Koenig, Architect, Chgo., 1956-61; dir. Rock County Hist. Soc., Janesville, Wis., 1964—; cons. hist. socs., pvt. corps., historic preservation commns., 1968—. Editor: Joseph Russell Jones, 1965; co-author, editor: Rock County Historic Sites and Buildings, 1976. Editor guidebooks, newsletters. Treas. Janesville Area Human Rights Council, 1965-70; sec. Rock Prairie Arts Council, Janesville, 1975-77; v.p. Downtown Mchts. Council, Janesville, 1981-84; pres. Rock County Tourism Council, Janesville, 1985—; bd. dirs. Campbell Ctr., Mt. Carroll, Ill., 1985—. Mem. Am. Assn. State and Local History, Wis. Fedn. Mus. (sec. 1984—), Nat. Trust Hist. Preservation. Congregationalist. Lodge: Rotary (sec. 1984—). Home: 121 S Academy St Janesville WI 53545 Office: Rock County Hist Soc PO Box 896 Janesville WI 53547

HARTUNG, ROLF, environmental toxicology educator, researcher, consultant; b. Bremen, Fed. Republic of Germany, Mar. 1, 1935; came to U.S., 1952, naturalized, 1958. B.S. in Wildlife Mgmt., U. Mich., 1960, M.W.M. in Wildlife Mgmt., 1962, Ph.D. in Wildlife Mgmt., 1964. Diplomate Am. Bd. Toxicology. Instr. in wildlife mgmt. U. Mich., Ann Arbor, 1963, lectr. in indsl. health, 1964, asst. prof. indsl. health, 1965-69, assoc. prof. environ. and indsl. health, 1969-73, prof. environ. toxicology, 1973—, chmn. toxicology program, 1974-80; com. or sub-com. mem. Nat. Acad. Scis., 1971-72, 79-82, Mich. Dept. Natural Resources, 1977-82; mem. Mich. Environ. Rev. Bd., 1982-85; mem. hazardous materials com. U.S. Congress Office Tech. Assessment, 1980-83; chmn. com. on environ. effects, transport and fate of sci. adv. bd. EPA, 1982-85, mem. exec. com. of sci. adv. bd., 1982-85. Editor, contbg. author: Environmental Mercury Contamination, 1972; assoc. editor Jour. Toxicology and Indsl. Health, 1984-85. Contbr. numerous chpts., articles to profl. publs. Recipient H. M. Wight award. U. Mich., 1963; NSF fellow, 1960-64. Mem. AAAS, Am. Indsl. Hygiene Assn., Mich. Indsl. Hygiene Assn., Soc. Environ. Toxicology and Chemistry, Soc. Toxicology, Wildlife Disease Assn., Wildlife Soc., Sigma Xi, Phi Sigma, Phi Kappa Phi. Home: 3125 Fernwood Ave Ann Arbor MI 48104 Office: U Mich Sch Pub Health Dept Environ and Indsl Health M7533 Ann Arbor MI 48109

HARTUNG, THEODORE EUGENE, food science educator, university dean; b. Denver, Jan. 28, 1929; s. Lothar and Lena (Ruedy) H.; m. D. Joann McKenney, June 10, 1951; children—Deborah, Robin, Christopher. B.S., Colo. State U., 1951, M.S., 1953; Ph.D., Purdue U., 1962. Instr., Colo. State U., Ft. Collins, 1951-53, extension specialist, 1953-60, assoc. prof., 1960-65; head food sci. dept. U. Nebr., Lincoln, 1965-72, assoc. dean, 1972-73, dean agr., 1973—; dir. Central Bapt. Theol. Sem., Kansas City, Kans., 1979—. Gen. Foods fellow Inst. Food Technologists, 1960. Mem. Poultry Sci. Assn., Inst. Food Technologists. Baptist. Avocations: reading, hiking. Home: 621 Redwood Dr Lincoln NE 68510 Office: Dean's Office Coll Agr Univ Nebr Lincoln NE 68583-0702

HARTY, KATHLEEN MARIE, educational administrator; b. Madison, Wis., Apr. 5, 1932; d. Thomas Monks and Katherine Mercedes (Keeley) Fahey; m. Charles Joseph Harty, Aug. 8, 1959 (div.); 1 son, Robert Thomas. B.Ed., U. Wis.-Whitewater, 1953, M.S., 1968; Ph.D., U. Wis.-Madison, 1975. Tchr. first grade Janesville (Wis.) Pub. Schs., Washington Sch., 1953-59; primary tchr. Madison (Wis.) Pub. Schs., 1961-66, reading cons., 1966-72, curriculum coordinator, 1973-74, elem. prin. Midvale Sch., 1974—; vis. lectr. U. Wis.-Madison, 1972-73. Bd. dirs. U. Wis.-Whitewater Found., 1978—. Recipient Wis. Prin. of Yr. award, 1983. Mem. Nat. Assn. Elem. Sch. Prins., Assn. Supervision and Curriculum Devel., Elem. Commn., Assn. Sch. Adminstrs., Madison Assn. Sch. Adminstrs., Madison Area Reading Council (past pres.), U. Wis.-Whitewater Alumni Assn. (nat. pres. 1978-80), Phi Delta Kappa, Delta Kappa Gamma. Roman Catholic. Club: Nakoma Golf (Madison, Wis.). Home: 5425 Irish Ln Madison WI 53711 Office: 502 Caromar Dr Madison WI 53711

HARTZELL, ROBERT LEROY, foods manufacturing executive; b. Barron, Wis., June 23, 1941; s. Raymond A. and Ruth (Schrader) H.; m. Mary C. Ladlie, Sept. 5, 1964; children—Christopher, Elizabeth. B.S., U. Wis., 1963. Mgr. sales and mdseing. Wilson and Co., 1963-70; pres. North Star Foods, Inc., St. Charles, Minn., 1971—, North Star Freight, St. Charles, 1975—; bd. dirs. Whitewater Marathon, St. Charles, 1984—. Office: North Star Foods Inc PO Box 587 St Charles MN 55972

HARTZMARK, LEE, investment banker; b. Cleve., Aug. 10, 1929; s. Joseph and Helen H.; m. Dolores Ringle, Aug. 10, 1950; children—Debby, Michael. B.A., U. Mich., 1951. Securities salesman Goodbody & Co., Cleve., 1951-62; co-mgr. Westheimer & Co., Cleve., 1962; pres. Hartzmark & Co., Inc., Cleve., mem. N.Y. Stock Exchange and Am. Stock Exchange, 1962-74; ptnr. Cowen & Co., Cleve., 1974-78; v.p. corp. fin. Midwest Thomson McKinnon Securities Inc., 1978—; pres. Hartzmark & Co., Hartzmark Option Mgmt. Co. Mem. Investment Bankers Assn. Bond Club, Jewish Community Fedn., Zeta Beta Tau. Republican. Jewish. Clubs: Oakwood Country, Cleve. Racquet; Boca West Country; U. Mich.; President's Club Mich. Lodge: B'nai B'rith. Home: 25022 Linksview Dr Boca Raton FL 33434 also: 19501 N Park Blvd Shaker Heights OH 44122 Office: 29529 Chagrin Blvd Pepper Pike OH 44122

HARVEY, EDWIN GORDON, lawyer; b. Muscatine, Iowa, June 4, 1958; s. Wilmer Gordon and Linnie Alice (Brown) H.; m. Terrie E. Drescher, July 28, 1979; 1 child, Sarah Elizabeth. B.A. in Polit. Sci. and Philosophy, N.E. Mo. State U., 1979; J.D., Washington U., St. Louis, 1982. Bar: Mo. 1982, Ill. 1982, U.S. Dist. Ct. (we. dist.) Mo. 1982, U.S. Dist. Ct. (ea. dist.) Mo. 1983, U.S. Ct. Appeals (8th cir.) 1983. Assoc. Coburn, Croft & Putzell, St. Louis, 1982—. Alderman, Lakeshire, Mo., 1983-85. Mem. Mo. Bar Assn., Bar Assn. Met. St. Louis. Office: Coburn Croft & Putzell 1 Mercantile Ctr Suite 2900 Saint Louis MO 63101

HARVEY, IRWIN M., carpet mill executive; b. Chgo., Apr. 24, 1931; s. Herman and Clara Smith (Pomerantz) H.; m. Marilyn G. Greenspahn, June 7, 1952; children—Beth I. Dorfman, Jill F., Gail L. B.S., Roosevelt U., 1952. Sales rep. Pinsky Floor Covering Co., Chgo., 1954-58; sales agt. Hyams & Harvey, Chgo., 1958-63; v.p., regional mgr. Evans & Black Carpet Mills, Elk Grove Village, Ill., 1963-67, v.p., dir. mktg., 1967-68; pres., chmn. Galaxy Carpet Mills, Inc., Elk Grove Village, Ill., 1968—. Mem. adv. bd. The Acad. Design Sch., Chgo., 1978—, Dallas Trade Mart, 1983—. Bd. dirs., mem. exec. com. Floor Covering Industry Found., 1980—. Served with AUS, 1952-54. Mem. Carpet and Rug Inst. (dir., exec. com. 1971—, past chmn.), Chgo. Floor Covering Assn. Jewish. Home: 868 Thackeray Dr Highland Park IL 60035 Office: 850 Arthur Ave Elk Grove Village IL 60007

HARVEY, JAMES, judge; b. Iron Mountain, Mich., July 4, 1922; s. Martin and Agnes (Thomas) H.; m. June Elizabeth Collins, 1948; children—Diane Elizabeth, Thomas Martin. Student U. Mich., 1940-43; LL.B., 1949. Bar: Mich. Assoc. firm Bauer & Williams, Mich., 1953-56; ptnr. firm Nash, Nash & Harvey, Mich., 1956-59, Smith, Brooker, Harvey & Cook, Mich., 1959-61; asst. city atty., Saginaw, Mich., 1949-53; mem. Saginaw City Council, 1955-57; mayor City of Saginaw, 1957-59; mem. U.S. Ho. of Reps from Mich., 1961-75; judge U.S. Dist. Ct., East Detroit, Mich., 1974—. Served to 2d lt. USAAF, 1943-45. Recipient Disting. Service award Jaycees, 1957; One of 5 Outstanding Young Men of Mich. award Mich. Jaycees, 1958; Boyd Cup, Outstanding Service to Community, 1956; Outstanding Native Son award, Rotary, Iron Mountain, Mich., 1973. Mem. ABA, Mich. Bar Assn. Republican. Presbyterian. Clubs: Germania; Congl. Country; Capitol Hill. Office: 6334 Golf Lakes Ct 214 Fed Bldg Bay City MI 48706*

HARVEY, KATHERINE ABLER, civic worker; b. Chgo., May 17, 1946; d. Julius and Elizabeth (Engelman) Abler; student La Sorbonne, Paris, 1965-66; A.A.S., Bennett Coll., 1968; m. Julian Whitcomb Harvey, Sept. 7, 1974. Asst. librarian McDermott, Will & Emery, Chgo., 1969-70; librarian Chapman & Cutler, Chgo., 1970-73, Coudert Freres, Paris, 1973-74; adviser, organizer library Lincoln Park Zool. Soc. and Zoo, Chgo., 1977-79, mem. soc.'s women's bd., 1976—, chmn. library com., 1977-79, sec., 1979-81, mem. exec. com., 1977—; mem. jr. bd. Alliance Francaise de Chgo., 1970-76, treas., mem. exec. com., 1971-73, 75-76, mem. women's bd., 1977-80; mem. Fred Harvey Fine Arts Found., 1976-78; hon. life mem. Chgo. Symphony Soc., 1975—; mem. Phillips Acad. Alumni Council, Andover, Mass., 1977-81, mem. acad.'s bicentennial celebration com. class celebration leader, 1978, co-chmn. for Chgo. acad.'s bicentennial campaign, 1977-79, mem. student affairs and admissions com., 1980-81; mem. aux. bd. Art Inst. Chgo., 1978—; mem. Know Your Chgo. com. U. Chgo. Extension, 1981-84; mem. guild Chgo. Hist. Soc., 1978—; mem. women's bd. Lyric Opera Chgo., 1979—, chmn. edn. com., 1980, mem. exec. com., 1980—, treas. women's bd., 1983-84; mem. women's bd. Northwestern Meml. Hosp., 1979—, treas., chmn. fin. com., 1981-84, mem. exec. com., 1981—; bd. dirs. Found. Art Scholarships, 1982-83; bd. dirs. Glen Ellyn (Ill.) Children's Chorus, 1983—, founding chmn. pres.'s com., 1983; mem. women's bd. Chgo. City Ballet, 1983-84. Mem. Antiquarian Soc. of Art Inst. Chgo. (life). Clubs: Arts of Chgo., Friday (corr. sec. 1981-83), Casino (gov. 1982—, sec. 1984—), Cliff Dwellers. Home: 1209 N Astor St Chicago IL 60610

HARVEY, LEAH STANTON, educational administrator; b. Mpls., Mar. 26, 1950; d. James M. and Geralda Eldena (Bofferding) Stanton; m. Robert Craig Fox, Aug. 17, 1978; children—Andrew Stanton Fox, Briana Leah Fox. B.A., U. Minn., 1971, M.A., 1976, Ph.D., 1978. Prof. Met. State U., St. Paul, 1975-84, acad. dean, 1984—; program evaluation cons. Minn. Ctr. Social Research, Mpls., 1980-83. Contbr. articles to profl. publs. Bd. dirs. HMO, Minn., 1982—. Mem. Interfaculty Orgn. (bd. dirs. 1980-84). Office: Met State U 7th and Robert Saint Paul MN 55101

HARVEY, LYNNE COOPER, broadcasting executive, civic worker; b. nr. St. Louis; d. William A. and Mattie (Kehr) Cooper; A.B., Washington U., St. Louis, 1939, M.A., 1940; m. Paul Harvey, June 4, 1940; 1 son, Paul Harvey Aurandt. Broadcaster ednl. program KXOK, St. Louis, 1940; broadcaster-writer women's news WAC Variety Show, Fort Custer, Mich., 1941-43; gen. mgr. Paul Harvey News, ABC, 1944—; pres. Paulynne Prodns., Ltd., Chgo., 1968—, exec. producer Paul Harvey Comments, 1968—; editor, compiler The Rest of the Story. Pres. woman's bd. Mental Health Assn. Greater Chgo., 1967-71, v.p. bd. dirs., 1966—; pres. woman's aux. Infant Welfare Soc. Chgo., 1969-71, bd. dirs., 1969—; mem. Salvation Army Woman's Adv. Bd., 1967; reception chmn. Community Lectures; Woman's com. Chgo. Symphony, 1972—; pres. Mothers Council, River Forest, 1961-62; charter bd. mem. Gottlieb Meml. Hosp., Melrose Park, Ill.; mem. adv. bd. Nat. Christian Heritage Found., 1964—; mem. woman's bd. Ravinia Festival, 1972—; trustee John Brown U., 1980—. Recipient Religious Heritage of Am. award, 1974. Mem. Phi Beta Kappa, Kappa Delta Pi, Phi Sigma Iota, Eta Sigma Phi. Clubs: Chicago Golf, Woman's Athletic, Nineteenth Century Woman's, Press (Chgo.); Oak Park Country. Home: 1035 Park Ave River Forest IL 60305 Office: Box 77 River Forest IL 60305

HARVEY, STUART CHARLES, computer services company executive; b. Chgo., Oct. 17, 1933; s. Charles Stuart and Helen Anna (Koessler) H.; m. Patricia Mary Van Der Bosch, Aug. 27, 1960; children—Stuart Charles Jr., Heather, Trish, Colleen, Michelle. B.S.E.E., MIT, 1956. Mktg. mgr. IBM, Memphis, 1967-70; dist. mgr. Martin Marietta Co., Chgo., 1970-72; regional mgr. Boeing Computer Services, Chgo., 1972-73; zone mgr. Pansophic Systems, Chgo., 1973-75; dir. mktg. nat. accounts Mead Data Central, Dayton, Ohio, 1975—. Founder, pres. Montessori Soc. Lake Forest, Ill., 1966. Mem. Sales and Mktg. Mgmt. Assn. Republican. Roman Catholic. Club: Metropolitan (Chgo.). Home: 255 Cold Spring Rd Barrington IL 60010 Office: Mead Data Central 9393 Springboro Pike Dayton OH 45402

HARVEY, WALTER ROBERT, dairy science educator; b. Tucumcari, N.Mex., June 19, 1919; s. Clarence Reed and Nora Lee (Burges) H.; m. Marie H. Zigler, Sept. 1, 1940; children—Robert Dale, Jerry Ray, Donna Marie. A.S., Cameron Coll., 1940; B.S., Okla. State U., 1942; M.S., Iowa State U., 1947, Ph.D., 1949. Instr. Iowa State U., 1947-49; assoc. prof. U. Idaho, 1950-54; biometrician Agrl. Research Service, U.S. Dept. Agr., Beltsville, Md., 1954-64; prof. dairy scis. Ohio State U., Columbus, 1964—; statis. cons., Columbus, 1970—. Editor in chief Jour. Animal Scis., 1972-75. Served to capt. U.S. Army, 1942-46. Am. Soc. Animal Sci. fellow, 82. Mem. Am. Soc. Animal Sci. (Animal Breeding award 1968), Am. Statis. Assn., Biometrics Soc., Am. Dairy Sci. Assn., Sigma Xi. Mem. Ch. of Christ. Avocations: golfing, hunting. Home: 4255 Mumford Dr Columbus OH 43220 Office: Dept Dairy Scis Ohio State Univ 2027 Coffey Rd Columbus OH 43210

HARWOOD, BRYAN SCOTT, construction company executive; b. Chgo., Oct. 22, 1956; s. Richard Pemberton and Vivian Clara (Depner) H. Student Chgo. Tech. Coll., Triton Coll., Real Estate Inst. Carpenter foreman Gustafson-Lindberg Co., Chgo., 1976-82; constrn. mgr. Bryce, Inc., Chgo., 1982—;

real estate devel. cons.; real estate salesman Supera Realty Co., Chgo. Mem. Friends of Downtown, Lincoln Park Conservation Assn., Chgo. Architecture Soc., Constrn. Specifications Inst. Democrat. Avocations: jazz dancing; yacht racing. Home and Office: 1823 Cleveland Chicago IL 60614

HARWOOD, FOREST HENRY, IV, marketing company executive; b. Evanston, Ill., July 17, 1944; s. Forest Henry and Martha May (Smith) H.; m. Georgene Tone, Oct. 30, 1968; children—Laura, Pamela. B.B.A., Ohio U., 1966; M.B.A., Loyola U., Chgo., 1969. Asst. product mgr. Dow Chem. Co., Midland, Mich., 1969-71; asst. product mgr. Am. Can Co., Greenwich, Conn., 1971-74; product mgr. Nestle Co., White Plains, N.Y., 1974-75, Standard Brands, Inc., N.Y.C., 1975-77; mgr. merchandising and sales promotion Jos. Schlitz Brewing Co., Milw., 1977-79; dir. mktg. Fleishman-Hillard Inc., St. Louis, 1979—. Mem. Promotional Mktg. Assn. Am. Republican. Presbyterian. Office: Fleishman-Hillard Inc 1 Memorial Dr Suite 600 Saint Louis MO 63102

HARWOOD, THOMAS RIEGEL, physician; b. Knoxville, Tenn., Dec. 9, 1926; s. Thomas E. and Grace D. (Thomas) H.; m. Phyllis Gail Bredthauer, Jan. 3, 1976; children—Joseph, Thomas, Shannon D. B.S., Georgetown U., 1949; M.D., Vanderbilt U., 1953. Intern, resident, Vanderbilt U. Hosp., Nashville, 1953-55; resident Med. Coll. Va. Hosp., Richmond, 1955-56; asst. in pathology Vanderbilt U., 1954-55; instr. pathology Med. Coll. Va., 1955-56, Northwestern U., Chgo., 1956-57, asst. prof. pathology, 1957-73, lectr. spl. course pathology of head and neck ann., otolaryngology dept., 1974—, assoc. prof. clin. pathology, 1973—; vis. lectr. pathology Ill. Coll. Podiatric Medicine, 1968-72; attending pathologist VA Research Hosp., Chgo., 1957-67; asst. pathologist Wesley Meml. Hosp., Chgo., 1958-59; pathologist, dir. labs. N.W. Community Hosp., Arlington Hts., Ill., 1959-68; dir. labs. Harwood Clin. Labs., 1962-68; assoc. chief lab. services VA Research Hosp., Chgo., 1969-73, chief clin. labs., 1971-73, acting chief, 1973-76, 80-81, pathologist, 1976—; med. dir. Blood Services of Chgo., 1973—; adj. med. staff Northwestern Meml. Hosp., 1980-82, assoc. attending staff, 1982—; lectr. in field. Contbr. articles to profl. jours. Fellow Am. Soc. Clin. Pathologists; mem. Ill. Med. Soc., Chgo. Pathol. Soc. (councilor 1974-82), Ill. Assn. Blood Banks (pres. 1979-80), Chgo. Med. Soc. (trustee 1983-84), Am. Assn. Pathologists, AMA, Am. Assn. Blood Banks, N.Y. Acad. Sci., AAAS. Home: 1142 Florimond Dr Elgin IL 60120 Office: Northwestern U McGaw Med Ctr 333 E Huron Chicago IL 60611

HASAN, A. RASHID, chemical engineering educator; b. Dhaka, Bangladesh, May 25, 1949; s. Abdul and Abeda (Khatun) Majid; m. Neelufar Rahman, Aug. 12, 1973; 1 child, Arshad. B.Sc.Eng., U. Engring. and Tech., Dacca, 1972; M.Sc., U. Waterloo, Ont., Can., 1975, Ph.D., 1979. Asst. prof. chem. engring. U. N.D., Grand Forks, 1979-84, assoc. prof., 1984—. Contbr. articles to profl. jours. Can. Commonwealth grantee, 1973-78. Mem. Soc. Petroleum Engrs., Am. Inst. Chem. Engrs., Sigma Xi. Avocations: bridge; ping pong. Home: 1338 Allwood Ct Grand Forks ND 58201 Office: Dept Chem Engring Univ ND Grand Forks ND 58202

HASBARGEN, ARTHUR, educator; b. Kankakee, Ill., Apr. 20, 1925; s. Arthur and Zelpha (Spence) H.; B.S., No. Ill. U., 1949; M.A., Mich. State U., 1950; Ed.D., U. Ill., 1969; m. Lorayne Raguse, Aug. 24, 1946; children—James, Janet, Karen, Nancy. Dir. student personnel N.D. State U., Fargo, 1950-52; head guidance Kankakee Sch. Dist. Ill., 1952-64; tchr., counselor Am. Dependents Sch., Stuttgart, Germany, 1959-60; dir. spl. edn. Kankakee State Hosp., 1964-66, dir. mental retardation div., 1968-71; dir. programs, Coldwater (Mich.) State Home and Tng. Sch., 1971-74; spl. edn. dept. Western Ill. U., Macomb, 1974—, prof.; cons. in field. Served with USAAF, 1943-46; ATO. U.S. Office Edn. fellow, 1966-68; Ill. Dept. Mental Health Employment Edn. grantee, 1966-68. Mem. Nat. Vocat. Guidance Assn., Am. Assn. Counseling and Devel., Council for Exceptional Children, Am. Assn. Mental Deficiency, Western Ill. Adminstrs. Round Table, Kappa Delta Pi, Phi Delta Kappa. Lutheran. Club: Kiwanis. Contbr. articles in field to profl. jours. Home: 813 Orchard Dr Macomb IL 61455 Office: 25C Horrabin Hall Western Ill Univ Macomb IL 61455

HASE, WILLIAM LOUIS, chemistry educator, researcher; b. Washington, Mo., Mar. 22, 1945; s. William Louis Hase and Leila June (Johnson) Myers; m. Betty Fern Criscuolo, June 11, 1967; 1 child, Heidi Joy. B.S. in Chemistry, U. Mo., 1967; Ph.D. in Phys. Chemistry, N.Mex. State U., 1970. Prof. chemistry Wayne State U., Detroit, 1973-83, 84—; program officer NSF, Washington, 1983-84. Contbr. chpts. to books, articles to profl. jours. Grantee NSF, Petroleum Research Fund. Mem. Am. Chem. Soc., Am. Phys. Soc. Home: 854 Cadieux Grosse Pointe MI 48230 Office: Chemistry Dept Wayne State U Detroit MI 48202

HASEL, GERHARD FRANZ, religion educator, researcher; b. Vienna, Austria, July 27, 1935; came to U.S., 1958, naturalized, 1964; s. Franz Joseph and Magdalena (Schroeter) H.; m. Hilde Schafer, June 11, 1961; children—Michael Gerald, Marlena Susan, Melissa Helen. Lic. Theol., Marienhohe Sem. (Germany), 1958; B.A., Atlantic Union Coll., 1959; M.A., Andrews U., 1960, B.D., 1962; Ph.D., Vanderbilt U., 1970. Ordained to ministry Seventh-day Adventist Ch., 1966, Minister So. New Eng. Conf., Boston, 1962-63; asst. prof. religion So. Coll., Collegedale, Tenn., 1963-67; prof. O.T. and Bibl. theology Andrews U., Berrien Springs, Mich., 1967—, chmn. O.T. dept., 1974-82, assoc. editor Sem. Studies, 1973—, dean Theol. Sem., 1982—. Author: The Remnant, 1972, Old Testament Theology, 1980, New Testament Theology, 1982, Jonah: Messenger of the Eleventh Hour, 1974, Understanding the Living Word of God, 1983, Interpreting the Bible Today, 1985. Contbr. articles to profl. jours., dictionaries, encys. Hillel grantee Vanderbilt U., 1968, Danforth tchr. grantee, 1968-70. Mem. Soc. Bibl. Lit., Internat. Soc. for Study of O.T., Am. Acad. Religion, Mich. Acad. Sci., Arts and Letters, Am. Schs. Oriental Research, Chgo. Soc. Bibl. Studies. Home: Rt 1 Box 496D Berrien Springs MI 49103 Office: Theol Sem Andrews U Berrien Springs MI 49104

HASELBY, RAY CLOYNE, internist, educator; b. Detroit, May 4, 1939; s. Cloyne and Grace Haselby; m. Connie F. Halberg, June 24, 1982; children—Lisa, Sam, Jessica, Emily, Cyrus. A.B., U. Mich., 1961; D.O., Chgo. Coll. Osteopathy, 1969. With Peace Corps, Colombia, 1961-63; intern Chgo. Coll. Osteopathy, 1969-70, Cleve. Clinic Found., 1970-71; resident in internal medicine Cleve. Clinic Found., 1971-72, resident in infectious disease, 1972-74; mem. staff infectious disease sect., dept. internal medicine Marshfield Clinic (Wis.), 1974—; clin. asst. prof. medicine U. Wis.-Marshfield, 1974—; La. State U. fellow in tropical medicine, 1969; chmn. infection control com. St. Josephs Hosp., Marshfield; dir. Marshfield Med. Found. Recipient Disting. Teaching award U. Wis. Med. Sch., 1978. Mem. Am. Osteo. Assn., Wis. Assn. Osteo. Physicians and Surgeons, Am. Soc. Microbiology, Infectious Disease Soc. Am. Contbr. articles to med. jours. Home: 1112 W State St Marshfield WI 54449 Office: Marshfield Clinic 1000 N Oak St Marshfield WI 54449

HASHMI, SAJJAD AHMAD, business educator, university dean; b. India, Dec. 20, 1933; m. Monica Ruggiero; children—Serena, Jason, Shawn, Michelle. B.A., U. Karachi, 1953, M.A., 1956; Ph.D., U. Pa., 1962. Lectr. Ohio State U., Columbus, 1962-64; asst. prof. Roosevelt U., Chgo., 1964-66; prof. Ball State U., Muncie, Ind., 1966-83, chmn. dept. fin., 1973-83; Jones disting. prof., dean Sch. Bus., Emporia State U., Kans., 1983—; cons. to profl. ins. agts., Indspl., Louisville, Springfield, Ill.; speaker to profl. groups, 1983-84; tech. advisor Ind. Arts Commn.; appeared on TV and radio programs, testified before N.Y. and Ind. legis. coms. Author: Insurance Is A Funny Business, 1972; Automobile Insurance, 1973; Contemporary Personal Finance, 1985. Contbr. articles, revs., monographs to profl. publs. Named Prof. Yr. Ball State U. Students, 1971, Outstanding Tchr. of Yr., Ball State U., 1970. Mem. Am. Risk and Ins. Assn., Western Risk and Ins. Assn., Midwest Fin. Assn., Fin. Mgt. Assn., Emporia C. of C., Beta Gamma Sigma, Sigma Iota Epsilon, Alpha Kappa Psi, Gamma Iota Epsilon, Phi Kappa Phi. Club: Emporia Country. Lodge: Rotary. Home: 1702 Coronado Ave Emporia KS 66801 Office: Emporia State U 1200 Commercial St Emporia KS 66801

HASKELL, ROBERT ELTON, charitable organization administrator; b. Rapid City, S.D., Feb. 4, 1934; s. Albert Elton and Thelma Josephine (Cook) H.; m. Sandi Jean Mains, May 14, 1952; children—Stephen, Terry, Roberta, Leslie. Pres. Rapid City United Way, S.D., 1960-64, 82-84; instnl. rep. Boy Scouts Am., Rapid City, 1960-64; pres. Lions Sight and Service Found., Sioux Falls, S.D., 1973-74, 85—. Pres. Rapid City PTA, 1962, Meth. Ch. Bd., Rapid City, 1971. Named to Library of Human Resources, Am. Bicentennial Inst., 1976. Mem. Rapid City C. of C. (bd. dirs. 1975), Rapid City Toastmasters, Nat. Rifle Assn. Republican. Lodges: Elks, Moose. Avocation: hunting. Home: 2703 Garden Ln Rapid City SD 57701 Office: BSR Distbn 2703 Garden Ln Rapid City SD 57701

HASKIN, GEORGE ROBERT, JR., insurance agency executive; b. Rockford, Ill., Aug. 12, 1943; s. George R. and Phyliss (Smith) H.; m. Linda Diane Meyer, Oct. 11, 1969; children—Angela A., David S., Aaron S. Student U. Minn., 1961-65, Dunwoody Inst. Mgr. Thorp Credit Co., Oelwein, Iowa, 1967-73, Gen. Fin. Co., Des Moines, 1973-79, Combined Ins. Co., Chgo., 1979-83; owner, mgr. Marquarot Haskin & Assocs., Norwalk, Iowa, 1983—. Vice pres. Young Democrat Club, Waterloo, Iowa, 1960-61; treas. Young Dem. Club, Mpls., 1962-63; treas. Republican Com., Oelwein, 1967-68. Served with U.S. Army, 1965-67. Mem. Jaycees (pres. Lakewood 1976-77, 79-80, state dir. 1977-78, dist. dir. Iowa 1980). Methodist. Lodges: Lions (pres. 1967-68), Elks (pres. 1968-69). Avocations: golf; fishing; bowling; collecting stamps and coins; softball. Home and Office: Marquardt Haskin & Assocs 9169 Oakwood St Norwalk IA 50211

HASLEY, JOHN HOEFFLER, urologist; b. Ft. Wayne, Ind., Apr. 28, 1938; s. Henry and Rosalie (Hoeffler) H.; m. Marilyn Rose Seyfert, June 15, 1963; children—Mary Suzanne, John Charles. B.S., U. Notre Dame, 1959; M.D., Georgetown U., 1963. Diplomate Am. Bd. Urology. Intern Henry Ford Hosp., Detroit, 1963-64, resident in surgery, 1966-70; practice medicine specializing in urol. surgery Northwest Ohio Urol. Scis., Inc., Toledo, 1971—; treas., bd. dirs. Northwest Physicians, Inc., Toledo, 1985—; dir. Health Benefits Mgmt. Ohio, Toledo. Bd. dirs. Physicians Med. Care Found. Toledo. Served to lt. M.C., USNR, 1964-66. Mem. AMA, Ohio State Med. Assn. (del. 1980—), Acad. Medicine Toledo (v.p. 1982), Am. Fertility Soc., Ohio Urol. Soc., Northwest Ohio Urol. Assn. Republican. Roman Catholic. Clubs: Toledo; University (Notre Dame, Ind.). Home: 5553 Sturbridge Rd Toledo OH 43623 Office: Northwest Ohio Urol Scis Inc 5930 Huntingfield Blvd Toledo OH 43615

HASLEY, MICHAEL JAMES, manufacturing company executive; b. Cedar Rapids, Iowa, Oct. 31, 1946; s. Earl Andrew and Leone Marie (Wall) H.; m. Janice Margaret Michalek, June 15, 1968; children—Lisa Marie, Kimberly Joy, Scott Michael, Lauren Margaret. B.S. in Econ., Regis Coll., 1968. Vice pres. Quality Control Corp., Chgo., 1975-80, exec. v.p., 1980-83, pres., dir., 1983—; dir., pres. Qualiseal Tech. Ltd., Chgo., 1984—. Mem. Olph Men's Ch. Club, Glenview, Ill., 1985; sec., treas. Harwood Heights Indsl. Assn., Ill., 1979, pres., 1980. Served to lt. USNR, 1968-71. Mem. Nat. Assn. Corp. Dirs., Pres.'s Forum, Pres.'s Council, Am. Mgmt. Assn., Midwest Indsl. Mgmt. Assn. Republican. Roman Catholic. Home: 1318 Pine St Glenview IL 60025

HASSAN, MOHAMMAD ZIA, management sciences educator; b. Gurgaon, India, Apr. 2, 1933; came to U.S., 1955, naturalized 1967; s. M. Ishar-Ul and Wilayat Hassan; m. Shakeela Z. Hassan, Dec. 18, 1959; children—Rubeena, Ayesha, Isra. B.S. in Mech. Engring., U. Punjab, Lahore, Pakistan, 1954; M.S. in Indsl. Engring., Ill. Inst. Tech., 1958, Ph.D., 1965. Registered profl. engr., Calif. From instr. to assoc. prof. Ill. Inst. Tech., Chgo., 1960-83, prof. mgmt. scis., 1983—, interim dean, 1982-83, assoc. dean Sch. Bus. Adminstrn., 1983—; mgmt. cons. Author: (with others) The Total Productivity Model, 1981; Basic Programs for Production and Operations Management, 1983. Bd. dirs. Muslim Community Ctr., Chgo., 1968-70; chmn. bd. trustees Islamic Found., Chgo., 1975—. Fellow Am. Soc. for Quality Control; mem. Am. Inst. Indsl. Engrs. (sr.), Inst. Mgmt. Sci., Ops. Research Soc. Am., AAUP. Sigma Xi, Tau Beta Pi, Alpha Pi Nu. Sigma Iota Epsilon. Home: 5633 S Woodlawn Ave Chicago IL 60637 Office: Ill Inst Tech Sch Bus Adminstrn 10 W 31st St Chicago IL 60616

HASSANEIN, KHATAB M., biostatistics educator, consultant; b. Cairo, Egypt, Dec. 18, 1926; s. Mohamed El-Leithy and Fairouza H. Ph.D., U. N.C., 1963. Asst. prof. biostats. U. N.C., Chapel Hill, 1962-63; mem. faculty U. Kans. Med. Ctr., Kansas City, 1967—, assoc. prof. biometry, 1969-72, prof. biometry, 1973—, chmn. dept. biometry, 1972—; cons. to various drug cos., 1970—. Contbr. articles to profl. jours. Recipient Dist. Teaching award U. Kans. Med. Ctr., 1981; FAO scholar, 1958. Mem. Am. Statis. Assn., Inst. Math. Stats., Biometrics Soc., Delta Omega, Sigma Xi. Home: 1900 W 56th St Shawnee Mission KS 66208 Office: Kans U Med Ctr Biometry Dept 39th and Rainbow Kansas City KS 66103

HASSANEIN, RUTH EVELYN STEPHENSON, research and statistics educator, consultant; b. Orangeburg, S.C., Jan. 19, 1936; d. Robert Edward and Jane Elizabeth (Ward) Stephenson; m. Khatab M. Hassanein, Dec. 31, 1964; 1 child, Sarah Jane. B.S., Duke U., 1957; M.S. in Pub. Health, U. N.C., 1962; Ph.D., U. Mo.-Kansas City, 1983. Asst. prof. biometry U. Kans., Kansas City, 1974-78, assoc. prof., 1978-85, prof., 1985—, assoc. dean allied health, 1984-85; pvt. practice statis. consulting. Contbr. articles to profl. jours. Recipient Angier Duke scholarship Duke U., 1953-56. Mem. Am. Statis. Assn., AAUP, Am. Assn. Adult and Continuing Edn., Sigma Xi, Phi Lambda Theta. Unity. Home: 1900 W 56th St Shawnee Mission KS 66208 Office: Kansas Univ Med Ctr Biometry 39th St and Rainbow St 3002 Hinch Hall Kansas City KS 66103

HASSELQUIST, MAYNARD BURTON, lawyer; b. Amador, Minn., July 1, 1919; s. Harry and Anna M. (Froberg) H.; B.S. in Law, U. Minn., 1941, LL.B., 1947; m. Lorraine Swenson, Nov. 20, 1984; children—Mark D., Peter L. Bar: Minn. 1948. Mem. tax dept. Gen. Mills, Inc., Mpls., 1947-53; sr. partner firm Dorsey & Whitney, Mpls., 1953—; dir. Graco Inc., Mpls., ADC Telecommunications, Inc., Mpls., Soprea, France, McLaughlin Gormley King Co., Mpls. Served with U.S. Navy, 1941-46. Decorated knight Order of North Star (Sweden). Mem. Am., Minn., Hennepin County, Internat. bar assns., Am. Soc. Internat. Law, Japan-Am. Soc. Minn. (past chmn.), Swedish Council Am. (dir.), Am. Swedish Inst. (dir.). Lutheran. Club: Minneapolis. Home: 2950 Dean Pkwy Minneapolis MN 55416 Office: 2200 First Bank Place E Minneapolis MN 55402

HASSETT, JACQUELYN ANN, nurse; b. La Crosse, Wis., Sept. 13, 1930; d. Frank Alois and Anne Helena (Milos) Spika; m. James John Hassett, Aug. 22, 1953; children—Barbara, Linda, Jean, Jane, Nancy, James David. Diploma in Nursing, St. Anthony de Padua Sch. Nursing, Chgo., 1951; B.S., Barat Coll., 1977; M.S., George Williams Coll., 1983. R.N., Ill., Wis. Operating room nurse VA Hosp., North Chicago, Ill., 1951-54; part-time nursing positions St. Therese Hosp., Waukegan, Ill., 1954-58, Johnson Motors, Waukegan, 1958-64, VA Hosp., North Chicago, Ill., 1964-71; dir. health services Coll. of Lake County, Grayslake, Ill., 1971—, co-chmn. Inst. Self-Study for Rehab. Act 1973, 1978. Mem. Project SUCCEED, No. Ill., 1980-81; com. mem. Health Systems Agy. Kane-Lake-McHenry Counties, 1978-80; vol. Lake County Cancer Soc., 1975—, Am. Heart Assn., 1975—; bd. dirs. Med. Service Adv. Com. Lake County Health Dept., 1980—. Recipient Appreciation cert. Lake County Bd. Commrs., 1978; Meritorious Service award Am. Heart Assn., 1979-82; Outstanding award No. Ill. Council on Alcoholism, 1982. Mem. Am. Coll. Health Assn. (council of dels. 1978-80, 83—), Mid-Am. Coll. Health Assn. (v.p. 1981-82, pres. 1983-84), No. Ill. Coll. Health Nurses Assn., Am. Legion Aux. Roman Catholic. Home: 42749 Washington St Winthrop Harbor IL 60096 Office: Coll of Lake County 19351 W Washington St Grayslake IL 60030

HASSLER, DONALD MACKEY, II, English language educator, writer; b. Akron, Ohio, Jan. 3, 1937; s. Donald Mackey and Frances Elizabeth (Parsons) H.; B.A. (Alfred P. Sloan scholar), Williams Coll., 1959; M.A. (Woodrow Wilson fellow), Columbia, 1960, Ph.D., 1967; m. Diana Cain, Oct. 8, 1960 (dec. Sept. 19, 1976); children—Donald, David; m. 2d, Sue Smith, Sept. 13, 1977; children—Shelly, Heather. Instr., U. Montreal, 1961-65; instr. English dept. Kent (Ohio) State U., 1965-67, asst. prof., 1967-71, assoc. prof., 1971-76, prof., 1977—, dir. exptl. coll., 1973-83, acting dean honors and exptl. coll., 1979-80. Co-chmn. Kent Am. Revolution Bicentennial Commn., 1974-77. Mem. Sci. Fiction Research Assn. (treas. 1983-84, pres. 1985-86), Phi Beta Kappa (chpt. pres. 1983-84). Presbyterian. (deacon 1971-74, elder 1974-77). Club: Kiwanis (dir. 1974-76). Author: Erasmus Darwin, 1974; The Comedian as the Letter D: Erasmus Darwin's Comic Materialism, 1973; Asimov's Golden Age: The Ordering of an Art, 1977; Hal Clement, 1982; Comic Tones in Science Fiction, 1982; Patterns of the Fantastic, 1983; Patterns of the Fantastic II, 1984; Death and the Serpent: Immortality in Science Fiction and Fantasy, 1985. Home: 1226 Woodhill Dr Kent OH 44240

HASTINGS, DAVID FRANK, biophysics educator, physiology researcher; b. Rochester, N.Y., Dec. 25, 1945; s. Frank Willard and Frances Smiley (Jones) H.; m. Martha Jean Oliphant, May 4, 1968; children—Brian, Alexander, Peter. B.A., Swarthmore Coll., 1968; Ph.D., Duke U., 1975. Research technician Duke Marine Lab., Beaufort, N.C., 1969-72; research assoc. U. Aarhus, Denmark, 1975-76, dept. biochemistry Duke U., Durham, N.C., 1976-77, Whitehead Med. Research Inst., Durham, N.C., 1977-78; asst. prof. U. S.D. Sch. Medicine, Vermillion, 1978—; vis. research scientist Duke Marine Lab., Beaufort, 1981. Contbr. articles to profl. jours. Mem. Biophys. Soc., AAAS, Am. Physiol. Soc., N.Y. Acad. Sci., S.D. Acad. Sci., Am. Friends Service Com. (mem. exec. com. North Central Region 1983—), Toastmasters (pres. Vermillion chpt. 1981-82, sec. 1982-83), Sigma Xi (pres. 1984-85). Avocations: canoeing; bicycling; hiking; running; radio controlled planes. Home: 112 Center St Vermillion SD 57069 Office: Dept Physiology and Pharmacology U South Dakota Sch Medicine Vermillion SD 57069

HASTINGS, GLEN RICHARD, II, hospital administrator, educator; b. Clovis, N.Mex., May 22, 1945; s. Glen Richard and Mary Evelyn (Milam) H.; m. Judith Ann Mitze, Oct. 1, 1967; children—Jay Dolphy, Katherine Ruth. B.S., U. Okla., 1967; M.B.A., Chapman Coll., 1975; M.H.A., U. Minn., 1977. Sports and gen. reporter Chickasha Daily Express, Okla., 1963-66; exec. dir., hosp. adminstr. St. Luke's Hosp., Kansas City, Mo., 1977—; asst. prof. Webster U., St. Louis, 1978—; clin. preceptor U. Minn., Mpls., 1980—; vice chmn. SLH Inc., Kansas City, 1984—; trustee Mo. Health Data Corp., 1985—. Author: Zero Based Budgeting, 1980; Product Line Management, 1985. Contbr. articles to profl. jours. Trustee Arthritis Found., Kansas City, 1978; mem. Mid Am. Com. Health Care Costs, Kansas City, 1980; bd. dirs. 1st Baptist Ch., Raytown, Mo., 1978; mem. Blue River Fin. Com., Lee Summit, Mo., 1984. Served to capt. USAF, 1967-75. Decorated Bronze Star. Recipient Pub. Health award Dept. Health, 1975. Mem. Am. Coll. Hosp. Adminstrs., Healthcare Fin. Mgmt. Assn., Am. Hosp. Assn., Kansas City Adminstrs. Assn., U. Minn. Alumni Assn. (preceptor 1977—), Kappa Alpha (sec. 1966-67). Lodge: Rotary. Avocations: personal computers; racquetball; basketball; tennis; golf. Home: 12012 E 56th Terr Kansas City MO 64133 Office: St Lukes Hosp Wornall & 44th Sts Kansas City MO 64133

HASTINGS, ROBERT EUGENE, city-county official; b. Council Bluffs, Iowa, June 17, 1932; s. Elmer Wayne and Lillian Irene (Potts) H.; student appraisal courses Omaha U., Iowa State U., Iowa Western Community Coll., 1967-78; m. Marcia Ann Martin, Aug. 2, 1969. Meter reader Council Bluffs Gas Co., 1950; clk. Milw. R.R., Council Bluffs, 1951-52; with Harding Cream Co., Omaha, 1952-54; clk. Safeway Stores, Council Bluffs, 1954-56; circulation mgr. World Herald Newspaper, Eastern Nebr., 1956-58; agt. Met. Life Ins., Omaha, 1958-59; asst. county assessor Pottawattamie County, Iowa, Council Bluffs, 1959-72; city assessor Council Bluffs, 1972-74; city-county assessor Pottawattamie County, 1974—. Taxation and fin. steering com. Nat. Assn. Counties, Washington, 1974-79; pres. C of C Cee Bees (Goodwill Ambassadors), 1978; county govt. lobbyist, 1974-75; mem. Iowa State Assessors Edn. Commn., 1983-85. Recipient ICA degree, Iowa Inst. Certified Assessors. Mem. Internat. Assn. Assessing Officers (CAE degree; contbr. report 1974; profl. admissions com. 1981—), Nat. Assn. Review Appraisers (C.R.A. degree), Iowa State Assn. Assessors, C. of C. (dir. 1975-77). Lutheran. Clubs: Kiwanis (pres. Downtown Council Bluffs 1976-77, On-To dist. Nebr.-Iowa Dist. conv. chmn. 1979, internat. conv. dist. chmn. 1983, club sec. 1983, lt. gov. div. 13, trustee Nebr.-Iowa Dist. 1981-82, dist. youth chmn. 1983-84, dist. community services chmn. 1985—). Home: 72 Bellevue Ave Council Bluffs IA 51501 Office: Court House PO Box 1076 Council Bluffs IA 51502

HASTINGS, WILLIAM CHARLES, state supreme ct. judge; b. Newman Grove, Nebr., Jan. 31, 1921; s. William C. and Margaret (Hansen) H.; B.Sc., U. Nebr., 1942, J.D., 1948; m. Julie Ann Simonson, Dec. 29, 1946; children—Pamela, Charles, Steven. Admitted to Nebr. bar, 1948; with FBI, 1942-43; mem. firm Chambers, Holland, Dudgeon & Hastings, Lincoln, 1948-65; judge 3d judicial dist. Nebr., Lincoln, 1965-79; judge Supreme Ct. Nebr., Lincoln, 1979—. Pres. Child Guidance Center, Lincoln, 1962, 63; v.p. Lincoln Community Council, 1968, 69; vice chmn. Antelope Valley Boy Scouts Am., Lincoln, 1968, 69. Pres. First Presbyn. Ch. Found., Lincoln, 1968—. Served with AUS, 1943-46. Mem. Am., Nebr., Lincoln bar assns., Neb. Dist. Judges Assn., Phi Delta Phi. Republican. Presbyterian (deacon, elder, trustee). Club: East Hills Country (pres. 1959-60). Home: 1544 S 58th St Lincoln NE 68506 Office: Nebr Supreme Ct State House Lincoln NE 68509

HASTY, ELVIRA FERNANDEZ, educator; b. Havana, Cuba, Nov. 29, 1946; came to U.S., 1961; d. Vicente and Dionisia (Zapatero) Fernandez; m. James H. Hasty, Jan. 30, 1971. B.A. in Chemistry, St. Mary Coll., 1969; M.S., U. Ill., 1971, Ph.D., 1974. Postdoctoral researcher Argonne Nat. Lab, Ill., 1974-75; instr. Harper Community Coll., Palatine, Ill., 1975-76; instr. U. Ill., Chgo., 1976-77; asst. prof. Mundelein Coll., Chgo., 1978-82, assoc. prof., 1982—, coordinator Women in Sci. Workshop, 1981—, subcom. chmn. new programs, courses curriculum, 1982—. Contbr. articles to profl. jours. Mem. Am. Chem. Soc., Kappa Gamma Pi. Avocations: photography; animal welfare, wildlife preservation, cooking.

HATCH, DALE, research scientist; b. Vernal, Utah, Oct. 14, 1944; s. David Milburn and Grace (Burke) H.; m. Cleone Wilson, Mar. 31, 1972; children—Jeffrey, Brian, Diana, Kimberly, Amy. Grad. with honors, Weltech Electronics Coll., 1963; A.A., Brigham Young U., 1968, A.S., 1971, B.S., 1973, M.S., 1974. Systems check-out rep. Kenway Engring. Inc., Salt Lake City, 1973-74; field elec. engr. Rohr Indsl. Systems, San Diego, 1974-75; indsl. engr. NCR Corp., San Diego, 1975-77; sr. electronics/software engr. Gen. Dynamics, San Diego, 1977-83, Battelle Meml. Inst., Columbus, Ohio, 1983—; instr. and cons. in field. Author: APT Systems and Numerical Control Programming, 1981. Asst. Scoutmastr Boy Scouts Am., 1974; rep. Utah State Republican Conv., 1972. Served with U.S. Army, 1968-70, Vietnam. Decorated Bronze Star. Mem. Soc. Packaging and Handling Engrs. (profl. cert.), Am. Inst. Indsl. Engrs., Nat. Mgmt. Assn. Mormon. Office: 505 King Ave Columbus OH 43201

HATCH, ROBERT WINSLOW, bakeries corporation executive; b. Hanover, N.H., Sept. 8, 1938; s. Winslow Roper and Dita Meiggs (Keith) H.; B.A., Dartmouth Coll., 1960, M.B.A., 1962; m. Nancy Packard Murphy, June 30, 1962; children—Kristin, Robert Winslow. Sales rep. Libby Glass Co., N.Y.C., 1961-62; research asst. Amos Tuck Sch., Hanover, 1962-63; with Gen. Mills, Inc., Mpls., 1963-84, product mgr., 1965-68, mktg. dir., 1968-71, exec. v.p. Gorton Corp., 1971-73, gen. mgr. protein div., 1973-75, gen. mgr. Golden Valley div., 1976, gen. mgr. Big G div., 1976-78, group v.p. splty. retailing, 1978-80, exec. v.p. splty. retailing, collectibles and furniture, 1980-84; dir. Leslie Paper Co. Pres. bd. East Side Neighborhood Services (Settlement House), 1980-84; exec. com. Mpls. Boys Club, 1978-84. Recipient Mpls. City Council's Com. on Urban Environment award, 1980. Republican. Presbyterian. Club: Calhoun Beach (pres. bd. govs. 1981-84), Kansas City, Carriage. Home: 601 W 55th St Kansas City MO 64113 Office: Interstate Bakeries 12 E Armour Blvd Kansas City MO 64111

HATCHER, RICHARD G., mayor; b. Michigan City, Ind., July 10, 1933; s. Carlton and Catherine H.; B.A., Ind. U.; J.D., Valparaiso U.; m. Ruthellyn; children—Ragen Heather, Rachelle Catherine. Admitted to Ind. bar, practiced in East Chicago; formerly dep. prosecutor Lake County (Ind.); councilman-at large Gary City Council, 1963-66; mayor of Gary, 1967—; v.p., mem. human resources com. U.S. Conf. Mayors, 1979-80, pres., 1980-81, also mem. exec. bd.; mem. steering com. human resources devel. Nat. League Cities, now chmn. com., also bd. dirs.; dir. Trans-Africa Corp. A founder Muigwithania, social and civic club, now v.p.; mem. Nat. Com. of Inquiry; chmn. edn. subcom. Ind. adv. com. U.S. Commn. Civil Rights; mem. exec. com. Nat. Urban Coalition; founder Nat. Black Caucus of Locally Elected Ofcls.; convenor Nat. Black Polit. Conv.; past pres. Nat. Conf. Democratic Mayors; mem. steering com. Nat. Black Assembly; mem. Ind. exec. bd. NAACP, legal adviser Gary chpt.; bd. dirs. Greater Gary United Fund; trustee, mem. adv. com. Gary Urban League; mem. adv. bd. Robert Woods Johnson Meml. Found.; chmn. Gary City Dem. Com.; mem. Ind. Dem. State Central Com.; mem. Nat. Dem. Com., from 1980; mem. U.S. Intergovernmental Adv. Commn. on Edn. to Sec. of Edn.; convenor Nat. Conf. on a Black Agenda for the 80's, 1980; chmn. bd. Trans-Africa. Mem. Am., Ind., Gary (exec. com.) bar assns., Gary Jaycees. Hall Address: City Hall 401 Broadway Gary IN 46402

HATCHER, THOMAS FOUNTAIN, mgmt. cons. co. exec.; b. Monroe, Mich., Dec. 26, 1931; s. Fountain H. and Cecilia E. (Boylan) H.; B.S., N.Y. U., 1968; m. Rosemary K. Downs, June 23, 1956; children—Mary Kathleen, Roberta Joan, Margaret Ann. With Equitable Life Assurance Soc., N.Y.C., 1955-71, mgr. learning systems, 1968-71; owner Thomas Hatcher Assos., Mpls., 1971-79; pres., owner Futures Unlimited, Inc., Mpls., 1979—. Mem. Nat. Speakers Assn., Am. Soc. Profl. Consultants. Roman Catholic. Author: The Definitive Guide to Long Range Planning, 1981. Home: 4916 W 82d St

Bloomington MN 55437 Office: Futures Unlimited Inc 5200 W 73d St Minneapolis MN 55435

HATHAWAY, KATHY R. MOORE, association administrator, editor; b. Sioux City, Iowa, Oct. 9, 1953; d. Harold W. and Marie E. (Karrer) Moore; m. Bruce A. Hathaway, Dec. 27, 1975 (div. Nov. 1982); 1 child, Tyler Daniel. B.A., U. S.D., 1975. Copywriter, Sta. KEZT, Ames, Iowa, 1976-79; pub. relations and sales mgr. Hot Line Inc., Ft. Dodge, Iowa, 1979-81; exec. mgr. Internat. Assn. Milk, Food and Environ. Sanitarians, Ames, 1981—. Mem. Nat. Assn. Female Execs. Lutheran. Avocations: writing fiction; promotional consulting. Home: 3408 Harcourt Dr Ames IA 50010 Office: Internat Assn Milk Food and Environ Sanitarians 502 E Lincoln Way Ames IA 50010

HATTERSLEY, ROBERT SHERWOOD, engineering manager; b. Dover, N.J., Sept. 4, 1931; s. William Joseph and Mabel Angela (Hall) H.; m. Jane Claire Williams, Aug. 22, 1958; children—Linda Jane, Robert Brent, Laura Beth. Registered profl. engr., Ohio, S.C. Engr. Procter & Gamble Co., Cin., 1957-61, group leader, 1961-66; plant engr., Quincy, Mass., 1966-73, sect. head, Cin., 1976—; ops. mgr. P & G de Mex., Mexico City, 1973-76. Author articles, reports. Served to 1st lt. C.E. USMC, 1954-57, Okinawa. Recipient medal Pi Tau Sigma, 1953. Mem. ASME (chmn. tech. and soc. div. 1983-85, nat. nominating com. 1982-85, issues mgmt. bd. 1983—), Nat. Soc. Profl. Engrs. (chpt. sec. 1983-84, chpt. pres. elect 1985-86). Avocation: amateur cabinet-maker. Home: 8722 Long Ln Cincinnati OH 45231 Office: Procter & Gamble Co 6060 Center Hill Rd Cincinnati OH 45224

HATTERY, JEFFREY LYNN, utility company executive; b. Dover, Ohio, Feb. 6, 1953; s. Jay Calvin and Ethel Marie (Lengler) H.; m. Luanne Elizabeth Merner, Oct. 9, 1982. B.A., Mt. Union Coll., 1975; postgrad. Cleve. State U., 1983—. C.P.A. Audit staff Meaden and Moore C.P.A., Cleve., 1975-78; sr. auditor Consol. Nat. Gas Co., Cleve., 1978-80; rate analyst East Ohio Gas Co., Cleve., 1980-84, mgr. reports and stats., 1984—. Mem. Am. Inst. C.P.A.s, Ohio Soc. C.P.A.s, Nat. Assn. Accts. Episcopalian. Avocations: bicycling; skiing. Office: East Ohio Gas Co 1717 E 9th St Cleveland OH 44114

HATTIS, ALBERT D., business executive, educator; b. Chgo., Oct. 12, 1929; s. Robert E. and Victoria C. (Kaufman) H.; B.S. with highest distinction, Northwestern U., 1948, postgrad. in bus. adminstrn., 1950, D.D. (hon.), 1968; m. Fern Hollobow; children—Kim Allyson, Kay Arlene Hattis Draper, John Elmore, Michael Allen, Sharon Beth. Vice-pres., sec.-treas. Robert E. Hattis Engrs., Inc., Hattis Service Co., Inc., Deerfield, Ill., 1950-73; co-mng. dir. Robert E. Hattis Engrs., Inc. AB, Robert E. Hattis Engrs., Inc. BV, 1950-73, all subs. White Motor Corp., 1966-70; trustee REH-HSC Profit Sharing & Retirement Trust, 1962-69; v.p., sec.-treas. Servbest Foods, Inc., Highland Park, Ill., 1973-78; v.p., sec.-treas., dir. W.D. Allen Mfg. Co., Sterling Products Co., Inc., Gearex Inc., Dinachrome, Inc., Fulton Machine Co., Inc., A.C. Equipment Co., 1978-80; v.p., sec.-treas. Prime Packing Co., Inc., Haitian Am. Meat and Provision Co., Spanish-Am. Foods, Inc., Packers Provision Co., Inc., Servbest Foods of P.R., Inc., 1973-78; pres., chief exec. officer Frigidmeats, Inc., Chgo., 1978-80; pres., dir. Gits Enterprises, Inc., 1978-80, Double K Bar J Ranch, Inc., 1968—; prof. bus., holder Schwan Endowed Chair for Free Enterprise, S.W. State U., Marshall, Minn., dir. Small Bus. Devel. Ctr., 1981—, S.W. Minn. Homegrown Economy Local Cooperation Office. Exec. dir. The Lambs, Inc., 1980-81; trustee Orphans of the Storm Found., 1972-74, Cobblers Found., 1972-74; mem. adv. bd. Northwestern Psychiat. Inst., 1972-74, Beta Gamma Sigma; bd. dirs. Marshall Industries Found.; chmn. Marshall Planning Commn., 1982-85. Served to capt. USAF, 1946-48, 50-52. Mem. Assn. Pvt. Enterprise Edn., Marshall Area C. of C. (bd. dirs.). Lodges: Lions, Rotary. Syndicated columnist, broadcaster Straight Talk, 700 newspapers, 400 radio stas. Home: 100 E Marshall Rd Marshall MN 56258 Office: A5321 Southwest State U Marshall MN 56258

HATTIS, FERN ELAINE, business executive, educator; b. Chgo., Apr. 4, 1939; d. Nathan Y. and Gertrude M. (Victorson) Ratner; m. Richard S. Hollobow, June 18, 1961 (dec. 1979); children—Michael, Sharon; m. Albert D. Hattis, Jan. 26, 1979; children—Kim, Kay, John. B.S. in Edn., Nat. Coll. Edn., Evanston, Ill., 1961. Cert. tchr., Ill., Minn. Tchr., Chgo. Bd. Edn., 1961-64; adminstrv. officer R.J. Olson & Co., Northbrook, Ill., 1976-78; pres. Fern Ltd., Marshall, Minn., 1981—. Commnr., Human Relations Commn., Marshall, Minn., 1982-84; dir. Lyon County Humane Soc., Marshall, 1982—; commnr. Housing Authority, Marshall, 1984—. Mem. Nat. Assn. Women Bus. Owners (bd. dirs. 1984—), Nat. Needlework Assn., Jewelers Assn. U.S., Minn. Jewelers Assn. Club: Courage Ctr. (Golden Valley, Minn.). Home: 100 E Marshall St Marshall MN 56258 Office: Fern Ltd Marshall MN 56258

HATTON, ROBERT WAYLAND, foreign language educator, writer, translator; b. Columbus, Ohio, Feb. 5, 1934; s. Wayland Charles and Ida Catherine (Eblin) H.; m. Marlene Ruth Tuller, June 25, 1954; children—Marc Emerson, Heidi Leigh, Kevin Robert. B.A., Capital U., Columbus, 1956; postgrad. Ohio State U., 1956-57, U. Madrid, Spain, 1957-58; M.A., Middlebury Coll., 1959. Cert. secondary edn. tchr., Ohio. Tchr. pub. schs., Columbus, 1958-60; rep. USIA, Bogota, Columbia, 1960-62; instr. Spanish lang. Ohio Wesleyan U., Delaware, Ohio, 1962-63; prof. Spanish lang. Capital U., 1963—; cons., interpreter, translator. Author: The Bullfight, 1974. Editor: Hombre Hispanico, 1970; Los Clarines del Miedo, 1971. Contbr. articles to profl. jours. Named Disting. Tchr., Capital U., 1969; grantee Capital U., Am. Luth. Ch., Binational Ctr. Mem. Am. Assn. Tchrs. of Spanish and Portuguese, Am. Council Teaching Fgn. Langs., Taurine Bibliophiles of Am., Midwest Assn. for Latin Am. Studies. Republican. Baptist. Avocations: bowling, book collecting, writing. Home: 6565 Calgary Ct Columbus OH 43229 Office: Dept Modern Langs Capital U Columbus OH 43209

HAUCK, JAMES NORMAN, biology and chemistry educator, counselor, educational consultant; b. Aberdeen, S.D., Feb. 12, 1936; s. Arnold and Luella Ann (Bullock) H.; m. Maxine Marie Feist, Apr. 27, 1973; children—Jennifer, Jeffrey. Student Northern State Coll., 1954-56; B.S. in Plant Pathology, S.D. State U., 1956-58; postgrad. Ind. U., 1958-60; teaching cert. St. Mary's U., 1964. Tchr. biology and chemistry Vianney High Sch., St. Louis, 1964-68; tchr. biology, botany and microbiology St. Louis Community Coll., 1968-70, tchr. biology and chemistry Roncalli High Sch., Aberdeen, S.D., 1971-72; counselor, asst. dir. River Park Alcohol Drug Center, Pierre, S.D., 1973-76; outreach counselor Capital Area Counseling Service, Pierre, 1976-78; sci. edn. dir. S.D. Div. Edn., Pierre, 1978—. Mem. Nat. Sci. Tchrs. Assn. (cert. of appreciation 1984), Council for State Sci. Suprs. Avocations: researching, gardening, fishing, cooking., reading. Office: Div Elem Secondary Edn 700 N Illinois Pierre SD 57501

HAUENSTEIN, HENRY WILLIAM, civil engineer; b. Cin., Apr. 23, 1924; s. Henry and Neva Blanche (Ivins) H.; m. Lucille Yeatts, May 2, 1947; children—Eric, Michael Lee, Susan Carol. B.S.C.E., U. Cin., 1948. Registered profl. engr., Ohio, Mich., N.C. Asst. engr. City of Cin., 1948-52; ptnr. Finkbeiner, Pettis & Strout Ltd., Toledo, 1952—; mem. adv. bd. Examiners Water and Wastewater Treatment Operators, Columbus, Ohio. Contbr. articles to profl. jours. Council mem., officer Grace Lutheran Ch., Toledo, 1959—. Served as sgt. U.S. Army, 1943-46. Fellow ASCE (Civil Engr. of Yr. award 1976); mem. Tech. Soc. Toledo (pres. 1978-79), Nat. Soc. Profl. Engrs. (trustee 1982-84), Am. Acad. Environ. Engrs. (diplomate), Am. Water Works Assn. Lodge: Rotary. Avocations: travel; photography; reading. Home: 5240 Carlingfort Dr Toledo OH 43623 Office: Finkbeiner Pettis & Strout Ltd 4405 Talmadge Rd Toledo OH 43623

HAUER, ANN, educator; b. Braddock, N.D., Sept. 19, 1942; d. Ray Joseph and Mildred Elizabeth (Kippes) Splonskowski; m. Jim Hauer, June 26, 1965; children—Todd, Missy. B.A., Mary Coll., 1969; M.A. in Ednl. Adminstrn., U. N.D., 1981. Cert. elem. prin. Elem. tchr. Richholt Sch., Bismarck, N.D., 1970-74, tchr., asst. prin., 1974-76; tchr. Roosevelt Sch., Bismarck, 1976—; elem. rep. Bismarck Pub. Schs. Curriculum Steering Com., developer curriculum metrics, nutrition, career edn. Tchr. rep. N.D. adv. bd. Project Wild. Mem. NEA, N.D. Edn. Assn., Bismarck Edn. Assn. (govt. relations com., elem. negotiator, profl. rights and responsibilities chmn., pres.), Phi Delta Kappa (v.p.), Delta Kappa Gamma. Roman Catholic. Clubs: Apple Creek Tennis League, Apple Creek Country. Lodge: Elks. Home: 2600 Mercury Ln Bismarck ND 58501 Office: 613 Ave B West Bismarck ND 58501

HAUFF, LAURA LYNN, computer specialist; b. Luverne, Minn., Apr. 7, 1955; d. Russell Cleon and Johanna Dorothy (Beyer) McClure; m. Peter John Hauff, Nov. 15, 1980. Grad. in computer programming Alexandria Vo-cat.-Tech. Coll. (Minn.), 1975. Programmer/analyst Tri-State Ins. Co., Luverne, 1975—. Mem. Ins. Inst. Am. Democrat. Lutheran. Home: PO Box 275 123 W Warren St Luverne MN 56156 Office: Tri-State Ins Co of Minn 1 Roundwind Rd Luverne MN 56156

HAUG, LARRY EDWARD, telecommunications company executive; b. Chgo., Apr. 4, 1951; s. Verne Peter and Florence (Jezischek) H. B.E.E. with honors, De Vry Inst. Tech., 1974; M.B.A., Roosevelt U., 1981. Engr., Automatic Electric Labs., Northlake, Ill., 1974-76, Motorola, Inc., Schaumburg, Ill., 1976-79, mktg. mgr., 1979-82, nat. acctg. mgr., 1982; pres., chief operating officer Celltech Communications Inc., Englewood, Colo., 1983—, also dir. Served with USNR, 1971-77. Lutheran. Home: 4145 Crimson Ct Hoffman Estates IL 60195 Office: Celltech Communications Inc 5500 S Syracuse Circle Englewood CO 80111

HAUGAN, HAROLD WALTER, plastics engr.; b. Stoughton, Wis., June 17, 1902; s. Paul Julius and Emma (Kildahl) H.; B.S., U. N.D., 1925, M.S., 1927; Ph.D., St. Andrews U., 1959. Adminstr. chemistry physics dept. York (Nebr.) Coll., 1939-41; instr. Eau Claire (Wis.) State Tchrs. Coll., 1941-43; research supr. U.S. ammunition plant, 1943-45; mem. research devel. staff Curtiss-Wright Research Lab., Cheektowaga, N.Y., 1945-47, Cornell U. Aero. Lab., 1947-49; devel. engr. Bell Aircraft Corp., 1949-54; prin. Harold Haugan Assos., Devel. Engrs., 1954-56; supr. plastics Mich. ordnance missile plant missile div. Chrysler Corp., 1956-63; plastics engr. space div. Chrysler Corp., New Orleans, 1963-68; promoter plastics edn. in schs. and libraries throughout U.S., 1968—; pioneer developer plastics for missiles and Saturn space boosters, 1947-68. Mem. Soc. Plastics Industry, Am. Chem. Soc., Am. Def. Preparedness Assn., AIAA, Ancient Astronaut Soc., Nat. Space Inst. Author tech. publs. in plastics engring. Home: 1396 Smith St Birmingham MI 48009

HAUGEN, ORRIN MILLARD, lawyer; b. Mpls., Aug. 1, 1927; s. Oscar M. and Emma (Moe) H.; B.S. in Chem. Engring., U. Minn., 1948, LL.B., 1951; m. Marilyn Dixon, June 17, 1950; children—Melissa, Kristen, Eric, Kimberly. Admitted to Minn. bar, 1951; patent lawyer Honeywell, Inc., Mpls., 1951-59, Univac div. Sperry Rand, 1959-63; pvt. practice specializing in patent law Haugen & Nikolai, P.A., Mpls., 1963—. Pres. Arrowhead Lake Improvement Assn., Inc., Mpls., 1958-79. Served with USN, 1945-46. Mem. Am., Minn. bar assns., Am. Patent Law Assn., Minn. Patent Law Assn., Minn. Trial Lawyers Assn., Minn. Acacia Alumni Assn., Inc. (pres. 1961-63), Acacia. Methodist. Club: Kiwanis. Home: 6612 Indian Hills Rd Edina MN 55435 Office: Internat Centre Minneapolis MN 55402

HAUGH, ROBERT JAMES, insurance company executive; b. Milw., Jan. 19, 1926; s. John J. and Adeline (Bolmes) H.; m. Mary Jane Botsch, Oct. 15, 1949; children—Jane, William, Nancy. Ph.B., Marquette U., 1946, J.D., 1948. With St. Paul Fire & Marine Ins. Co., 1948—, sr. v.p. ops., 1976-78, pres., 1978—, chief exec. officer from 1978, now chmn.; chmn., pres., chief exec. officer St. Paul Cos., Inc., 1984—; chmn. Underwriters Labs. Bd. dirs. ARC, St. Paul, Minn. Pub. Radio. Republican. Roman Catholic. Clubs: Minnesota, St. Paul Athletic. Office: St Paul Fire and Marine Ins Co 385 Washington St Saint Paul MN 55102*

HAUGHN, JAMES EUGENE, physician; b. Columbus, Ohio, Mar. 16, 1938; s. James Cyrus and Jeannetta Cora (Brown) H.; B.S. in Agr., Ohio State U., 1960; M.D., U. Louisville, 1967; m. Bonnie M. Grubb, June 14, 1959; children—James Eugene II, Elizabeth Anne, Ross Adam, David Noel. Intern Marion County Gen. Hosp., Indpls., 1967-68; gen. practice medicine, Tell City, Ind., 1970-77, Wabash, Ind., 1977—; mem. staff Wabash County Hosp., Wabash, Ind.; med. dir. Millers Manor, Wabash. Served with USAF, 1968-70; Vietnam. Diplomate Am. Bd. Family Practice. Fellow Am. Acad. Family Physicians; mem. Ind. Med. Assn., Wabash County Med. Soc., Phi Eta Sigma, Alpha Zeta. Club: Elks. Home: 654 W Hill St Wabash IN 46992 Office: 645 N Spring St Wabash IN 46992

HAUGHTON, VICTOR MELLET, radiology educator, researcher; b. Willimantic, Conn., July 9, 1939; s. Victor Mellet and Marion (Branch) H.; m. Kirsti Helene Staib, Aug. 20, 1965; children—Signe Helene, Karianne, Paul Victor. B.A. magna cum laude, Harvard Coll., 1961; M.D., Yale U., 1967. Diplomate Am. Bd. Radiology. Intern Tufts New Eng. Med. Ctr., Boston, 1967-68; resident in radiology Peter Bent Brigham Hosp., Boston, 1970-73; radiologist, neuroradiology chief Milw. County Med. Complex, 1974; radiology cons. VA Hosp., Wood, Wis., 1974; prof. radiology Med. Coll. Wis., Milw., 1981—, chief neuroradiology research, 1982—; mem. adv. bd. Gen. Electric Med. Systems, Waukesha, Wis., 1982—. Author: Computed Tomography of the Brain, 1979, Multiplanar Anatomy of the Head & Neck, 1980, CT of the Spine, 1982, 83. Served to lt. comdr. USPHS, 1968-70. Fellow NIH. Mem. Am. Soc. Neuroradiology (chmn. membership com. 1984), Am. Coll. Radiology, Radiol. Soc. N.Am. Episcopalian. Avocations: skiing; sailing. Office: Dept Radiology Froedtert Hosp 9200 W Wisconsin Ave Milwaukee WI 53226

HAUGTVEDT, CANDACE LOUISE, pharmacist; b. International Falls, Minn., July 10, 1959; d. John L. and Betty Jane (Thompson) Wenberg; m. Curtis Palmer Haugtvedt, Aug. 29, 1981. B.S., N.D. State U., 1982. Registered pharmacist, Mo., N.D. Pharmacy intern Falls Meml. Hosp., International Falls, 1980-81, City Drug Store, International Falls, 1980-81; pharmacist U. Mo. Hosp. and Clinics, Columbia, 1982—; part-time pharmacist Columbia Regional Hosp., 1984—, K-Mart, Columbia, 1983—. McKesson scholar, 1980; White Drug scholar, 1981. Mem. Mid-Mo. Soc. Hosp. Pharmacists, Am. Soc. Hosp. Pharmacists, Mo. Soc. Hosp. Pharmacists, Rho Chi, Kappa Epsilon (chpt. chaplain 1980-81). Democrat. Lutheran. Avocations: needlepoint; sewing; baking; gardening; golfing. Office: U Mo Hosp One Hospital Dr Rm 1E54 Columbia MO 65212

HAUKEDAHL, OREL ELDEN, ret. govt. ofcl.; b. Madison, Wis., May 12, 1907; s. Louis A. and Mina E. (Andrus) H.; B.S. in Elec. Engring., U. Wis., 1932; m. Ellen Sorensen, Sept. 1, 1951; children—Jane E., Brian L. Engr., Civil Works Adminstrn., Madison, 1933-34; works sec. Wis. Emergency Relief Adminstrn., 1934-35; area engr. Works Progress Adminstrn., 1935-41; asst. engr. Fed. Power Commn., Washington, 1941-42, asso. engr., Atlanta, 1942-46, supervising hydraulic engr. Chgo. Regional Office, 1946-53; engr. charge River Basin work Chgo. Fed. Power Commn., 1953-57, dep. regional engr., 1957-77; alternate Souris-Red-Rainy Basin Commn., 1967-73, Great Lakes Basin Commn., 1967-77, Mo. River Basin Commn. 1972-77, Upper Miss. River Basin Commn. 1972-77. Mem. coordinating com. on The Missouri River main stem reservoir operations, 1954-77. Served from lt. (j.g.) to lt. (s.g.), USNR, 1943-46. Mem. U. Wis. Alumni Assn., Am. Soc. Pub. Adminstrn. Lutheran. Mason, Moose. Home: 360 Neola Park Forest IL 60466

HAUMSCHILD, DANIEL JOHN, biomedical engineer; b. Arpin, Wis., Apr. 1, 1949; s. Lawrence John and Irene Regina (Meyer) H.; m. Carol Jean Fehrenbach, May 13, 1972; children—Tara, Eric, Sean. B.S., U. Wis., 1971; M.S., Iowa State U., 1979, Ph.D., 1981. Group leader Indsl. Biotest Labs., Neillsville, Wis., 1971-73; research fellow Mayo Clinic, Rochester, Minn., 1982-83; biomed. engr. TSI Inc., St. Paul, 1983—; cons. Renco Corp., Mpls., 1978-81. Mem. IEEE, Soc. Non-Invasive Vascular Tech., Am. Soc. Laser Medicine and Surgery. Avocations: hunting, fishing, woodworking. Home: 11950 Sycamore St NW Coon Rapids MN 55433 Office: TSI Inc PO Box 64394 500 Cardigan Rd St Paul MN 55164

HAUPT, HANS FRIEDRICH, data processing manager; b. Muhlhausen East-Prussia, Germany, Feb. 14, 1944; came to U.S., 1966, naturalized 1982; s. Hans Otto and Hedwig (Sintke) H.; m. Geraldine Louise Harman, Sept. 2, 1972. Certificat de l'Academie Commerciale, de l'Ecole des Hautes Etudes Commerciales, Paris, 1965; B.S., U. Md., 1969; M.S., Butler U., 1978. Programmer RCA, Indpls., 1969-72, analyst, 1972-76, adminstr., 1976-78; mgr. Boehringer Mannheim Corp., Indpls., 1978—. Coach Tabernacle Presbyn. Ch. League, Indpls., 1977-80. Mem. Am. Prodn. and Inventory Control Soc., Am. Mgmt. Assn., Omicron Delta Epsilon. Club: Indpls. Sailing. Avocations: sailing; model railroading; micro computers. Home: 4738 N Pennsylvania St Indianapolis IN Office: Boehringer Mannheim Corp 9115 Hague Rd Indianapolis IN 46256

HAUPT, SHIRLEY ELIASON, art educator, artist; b. Kanawha, Iowa, June 19, 1929; d. Olaf Clarence and Pearle Mae (Holbrock) Eliason; 1 child, George Holbrook Haupt. B.A. in Art Edn., Art Inst. Chgo., 1952; M.F.A., U. Iowa, 1954. Instr. U. Iowa, Iowa City, 1954-55; asst. curator prints Yale U. Art Gallery, New Haven, 1959-61; prof. art U. No. Iowa, Cedar Falls, 1966—, acting head dept. art, fall 1982, summer, 1975; numerous exhbns. Contbr. articles, poems, and illustrations to profl. jours. Del. State Democratic Conv., Des. Moines, 1972. Fulbright grantee, 1955-56, 56-57; U. No. Iowa Profl. Devel. Leave grantee, 1971-72, 81-82. Home: 803 Iowa Cedar Falls IA 50613

HAUPTMAN, JOHN LESLIE, lawyer; b. Bloomington, Ill., Feb. 19, 1953; s. Martin J. and Velma F. (Mullinax) H.; m. Deborah Kane, July 26, 1975; children—Elizabeth A., Katherine D. B.A., Western Ill. U., 1975; J.D., John Marshall Law Sch., Chgo., 1978. Bar: Ill. 1978, U.S. Dist. Ct. (no. dist.) Ill. 1980. Asst. state's atty. Whiteside County, Ill., Morrison, 1978-84; mem. firm Nelson, Kilgus, Richey and Tusek, Morrison, 1984—. Chmn. polit. campaign, Morrison, 1980; pres. Morrison Community Nursery Sch. Bd., 1983-84; sec.-treas. Morrison Community T-Ball League, 1984-85. Mem. Nat. Dist. Attys. Assn., Ill. Bar Assn., Whiteside County Bar Assn. (chmn. program com. 1982-83), Phi Delta Phi. Roman Catholic. Home: 500 S Cherry St Morrison IL 61270 Office: 209 E Main St Morrison IL 61270

HAUSAFUS, JOHN EARL, architect; b. Marshalltown, Iowa, Dec. 8, 1946; s. William Wayne and Margaret A. (Hastie) H.; m. Cheryl Ann Olmstead, May 26, 1973; children—Michael Todd, Tara Ann. A.S., Marshalltown Community Coll., 1970; B.Arch., Iowa State U., 1973. Archtl. draftsman Engelbrecht & Rice, Des Moines, 1973-75; asst. project architect Smith, Voorhees & Jensen, Des Moines, 1975-80; project architect J.E.H. Architects, Des Moines, 1980-84; architect FEH Assocs., Inc., Des Moines, 1985—. Mem. AIA, Constrn. Specifications Inst. (pres. Central Iowa chpt. 1984-86). Club: Bohemian. Home: 3700 Rollins Ave Des Moines IA 50312 Office: FEH Assocs Inc 1115 Midland Fin Bldg Des Moines IA 50309

HAUSER, ALEXIS, conductor; b. Vienna, Austria, May 25, 1947; s. Willy and Eleonore (Kern) H.; m. Nancy Lynn Fister, Sept. 5, 1981. Diploma Vienna Conservatory, 1968, Vienna Music Acad., 1970. Judge internat. competitions; lectr. Royal Conservatory, Toronto. Guest condr. Vienna Tonkunstler Orch., 1970-76; condr. Vienna Symphony Orch., 1973—; music dir. Orch. London (Ont., Can.), 1981—; condr. N.Y.C. Opera, Atlanta Symphony, Rochester Philharm., Belgrad Philharm., Orchestre Capitole de Toulouse (France), Montreal Symphony, Toronto Symphony, Vienna Chamber Orch., Winnipeg Symphony, Kansas City Philharm., Chgo. Grant Park Festival, 1983. Recipient Acad. prize Austrian Ministry Culture and Edn., 1970; Koussevitzky conducting prize Boston Symphony, 1974; Hans Swarowsky conducting prize Vienna Music Acad., 1977. Mem. Internat. Gustav Mahler Gesellschaft, Am. Mahler Soc. Office: 520 Wellington St London ON N6A 3P9 Canada

HAUSER, LES JOHN, health care public relations and marketing consultant; b. Peoria, Ill., May 3, 1946; s. Warren George and Ethel May (Widmer) H.; m. Sharon Ann Carius, June 28, 1969; children—Joshua, Kimberly. B.A. in English, Eureka Coll., 1969; M.S. in Mass Communications, Shippensburg State Coll., 1974. Communications coordinator, news editor Pa. Blue Shield Ins. Co., Camp Hill, 1973-75; mgr. pub. relations and advt. Del. Blue Cross/Blue Shield, Wilmington, 1975-76; dir. pub. relations Lansing (Mich.) Gen. Hosp., 1976-81; dir. community relations and devel. Mich. Hosp. Assn. Service Corp., Lansing, 1981-84; v.p. corp. planning and mktg. DePaul Health Ctr., St. Louis, 1984—; instr. Mich. State U., 1979-81, Lansing Community Coll., 1979; mem. pub. relations and mktg. com. Am. Osteo. Hosp. Assn., Chgo., 1979-80. Bd. dirs. Tri-County Emergency Med. Services Council, Lansing, 1979-81; mem. pub. relations adv. com. to pres. Wayne State U., Detroit, 1980-81. Served with U.S. Army, 1969-73. Named Outstanding Young Alumnus Eureka Coll., 1982. Mem. Acad. Hosp. Pub. Relations and Mktg. (MacEachern award 1978), Mich. Hosp. Pub. Relations Assn. (2 awards of achievement 1978), Pub. Relations Soc. Am. (founder, accredited, 1st pres. 1983), Am. Soc. Hosp. Pub. Relations, Am. Mktg. Assn. Methodist. Contbr. articles on to profl. jours. Home: 45 Kelly Leaf Dr Saint Charles MO 63303

HAUSER, LYNN ELIZABETH, eye surgeon; b. Cleve., Apr. 11, 1951; d. Cavour Herman and Ruth Natalie (Lageman) H.; B.S. in Medicine, Northwestern U., 1974, M.D., 1976; m. Neil L. Ross, June 20, 1975; children—Michael Hauser Ross, Benjamin Hauser Ross. Resident in ophthalmology Northwestern U., 1976-80; practice medicine specializing in cataract surgery, Dekalb, Ill., 1980—; clin. asst. prof. ophthalmology U. Ill., Chgo.; lectr. in ophthalmology Northwestern U.; project ophthalmologist Nat. Eye Inst. Early Treatment Diabetic Retinopathy Study, 1982. Diplomate Am. Bd. Ophthalmology. Fellow ACS, Am. Acad. Ophthalmology, mem. AMA, Dekalb County Med. Soc., Ill. Assn. Ophthalmology, Ill. Med. Soc., LWV. Office: 8 Health Services Dr Suite 2 DeKalb IL 60115

HAUSLER, RUDOLF HEINRICH, research chemist; b. Zurich, Switzerland, Apr. 9, 1934; s. Robert Ruppert and Elsa (Figi) H.; came to U.S., 1963, naturalized, 1969; diploma chem. engring., Swiss Fed. Inst. Tech., Zurich, 1958, D.Tech.Scis., 1961; m. Barbara Louise Corsaw, Feb. 5, 1972; 1 dau., Natasha Louise. Research chemist, project leader Battelle Meml. Inst., Geneva, 1961-63; research chemist, research assoc. Universal Oil Products Co., Des Plaines, Ill., 1963-76; tech. dir. Gordon Lab., Inc., Great Bend, Kans., 1976-79; sr. research chemist Tretolite div. Petolite Corp., St. Louis, 1979—; lectr. in field. Registered profl. engr., Calif. Mem. Electrochem. Soc. (chmn. Chgo. sect. 1967-68, councilor 1972—), Nat. Assn. Corrosion Engrs. (chmn. Chgo. sect. 1974-75), Chgo. Tech. Socs. Council (chmn. 1974-75), Am. Chem. Soc., Am. Soc. Metals. Unitarian-Universalist. Author, patentee in field. Office: 369 Marshall Ave St Louis MO 63119

HAUWILLER, ROBERT PAUL, university administrator; b. St. Paul, June 24, 1934; s. Paul Heliodore and Bertha Elizabeth (Sherman) H.; B.S., St. Mary's Coll., Minn., 1956; M.S., U. Notre Dame, 1962; D.P.A., Nova U., 1985; m. Mary Agnes Walsh, Aug. 15, 1970. High sch. tchr., Ill., 1956-63; asst. prof. math., registrar Lewis U., Romeoville, Ill., 1963-68; asst. registrar Chgo. State U., 1968-70, dir. instl. research and univ. relations, 1976—, acting v.p. adminstrv. affairs, 1979; dir. admissions and records, prof. math. Governors State U., University Park, Ill., 1968-76. NSF grantee, 1960-61. Mem. Am. Math. Assn., Phi Delta Kappa. Roman Catholic. Club: K.C. (4 deg.). Home: 15016 Castlebar Orland Park IL 60462 Office: Chicago State Univ 95th St and King Dr Chicago IL 60628

HAVEL, HENRY ACKEN, chemist; b. Palmerton, Pa., May 23, 1954; s. Charles Jerome and Janet (Acken) H.; m. Mary Patricia Stickelmeyer, Oct. 24, 1980. B.S., U. Rochester, 1976; Ph.D., U. Minn., 1981. Research scientist Upjohn Co., Kalamazoo, Mich., 1981—. Mem. Am. Chem. Soc., Am. Phys. Soc., Biophys. Soc., Coblentz Soc. Avocation: tennis. Home: 2775 Brahms Ave Kalamazoo MI 49002 Office: Upjohn Co 7000 Portage Rd Kalamazoo MI 49001

HAVEN, CARL OLE, hospital administrator; b. Detroit, July 13, 1940; s. Thomas Kenneth and Marion Lucile (Reading) H.; student Albion Coll., 1958-62; A.B., Wayne State U., 1968, M.A., 1976; postgrad. U. Mich., 1977; m. Patty Ann Foor, Aug. 3, 1975; children—Leslie, Brianne, Kathryn. With St. Joseph Mercy Hosp., Pontiac, Mich., 1956-57; operating technician, Grace Hosp., Detroit, 1960-61, adminstrv. resident, 1969-70, adminstrv. asst., 1970; emergency room, River Dist. Hosp., St. Clair, Mich., 1967; asst. hosp. dir., Harper-Grace Hosp., Detroit, 1971-81; dir. mgmt. Samaritan Health Center, Sisters of Mercy Health Corp., 1981-84; dir. mktg. A. Kuhlman & Co., Detroit, 1984—; pres. Pre-Paid Med. Legal Services, Inc.; cons. systems analysis and design for med. care delivery, Dominican Republic, 1977; profl. cons.; chmn. affiliated med. residency program, Wayne State U., 1973; chmn. fin. com. Associated Hosps. Processing Facility Corp., 1972; med. edn. com., Met. NW Detroit Hosp. Corp., 1978; cons. Mosman Electronics Inc. Com. chmn. Explorers Council 262, Dist. 13, Boy Scouts Am. Served with M.C., U.S. Army, 1962-65. Fellow Am. Coll. Hosp. Adminstrs.; mem. Am., Mich. (shared services com. 1978) Hosp. Assns., Greater Detroit Area Hosp. Council, Hosp. Fin. Mgmt. Assn. (advanced mem.), Alpha Kappa Delta. Contbr. articles to profl. hosp., med. jours. Home: 7800 Platt Rd Saline MI 48176 Office: 3939 Wooward Ave Detroit MI 48201

HAVENER, WILLIAM HENRY, ophthalmologist, educator; b. Portsmouth, Ohio, June 2, 1924; s. Gilbert and Laura (Braunlin) H.; m. Phyllis Johnson, Jan. 26, 1946; children—Michael, Mark, Ann, Gail, John, Amy, Neal. B.A., Wooster Coll., 1944, D.Sc. (hon.), 1982; M.D., Western Res. U., 1948; postgrad. in ophthalmology Harvard U., 1950-51; M.S. in Ophthalmology, U. Mich., 1953. Diplomate Am. Bd. Ophthalmology (examiner). Intern in medicine Univ. Hosps. Cleve., 1948-50; med. cons. in neuropsychiatry Cleve.

State Receiving Hosp., 1950; resident in ophthalmology U. Mich., Ann Arbor, 1951-53; asst. prof. ophthalmology Ohio State U., Columbus, 1954-56, assoc. prof., 1956-59, prof., 1959—, acting chmn. dept. ophthalmology, 1956-59, chmn. dept. ophthalmology, 1959-61, 72—. Author books, including: Ocular Pharmacology, 5th edit., 1983; Synopsis of Ophthalmology, 6th edit.; also numerous articles. Editorial bd. Jour. Continuing Edn. in Family Medicine, Medfact. Producer movies, TV tape. Named Prof. of Yr., Ohio State U. Coll. Medicine Class of 1978, Pre-clin. Prof. of Yr., Ohio State U. Coll. Medicine Class of 1979, Hon. Dir., Ohio Soc. for Prevention Blindness; recipient Pre-clin. Teaching award Ohio State U. Coll. Medicine Class of 1980, Founders' award Ohio affiliate Nat. Soc. to Prevent Blindness. Fellow Am. Acad. Ophthalmology and Otolaryngology; mem. Assn. Univ. Profs. Ophthalmology, Am. Assn. Ophthalmology, Assn. Research in Ophthalmology, Ohio Ophthalmol. Soc., Franklin County Acad. Medicine, Ohio State Med. Assn., AMA, Phi Beta Kappa, Alpha Omega Alpha. Home: 1859 Bedford Rd Columbus OH 43210 Office: 456 Clinic Dr Columbus OH 43210

HAVENOR, ROY DUANE, funeral executive; b. Eleva, Wis., Mar. 5, 1920; s. Harvey and Cora (Skogstad) H.; m. Myrtle Olson, June 4, 1944 (dec. Dec. 1953); 1 child, Linda Rae; m. Pauline Borchers, July 25, 1959; 1 child, Scott David. M.S., U. Minn., 1942. Dir., owner Havenor Funeral Chapel, White Bear Lake, Minn., 1952—. Bd. dirs. Am. Cancer Soc., St. Paul, 1957-64, YMCA, St. Paul, 1969-75. Served to lt. USNR, 1942-46, PTO. Mem. Minn. Funeral Dirs. Assn. (bd. dirs. 1979-81, now sec., treas.). Republican. Lutheran. Lodges: Rotary (pres. 1983-84, presdl. citation award, 1984), Lions (chmn. various coms.), Masons, Shriners. Avocations: golfing; fishing; boating. Home: 4531 Lincoln Ave White Bear Lake MN 55110 Office: 4531 Lincoln Ave White Bear Lake MN 55110

HAVENS, JOHN FRANKLIN, See *Who's Who in America,* 43rd edition.

HAVERLAND, ELOISE KEPPEL, airlines executive; b. Pittston, Pa., Apr. 22, 1942; d. Henry Robert and Edna Louise (Keppel) Carichner; B.A., U. R.I., 1964; M.A., U. Chgo., 1978; children—Lisa, Bradley. With Personnel Devel., Inc., Palatine, Ill., 1972-77, Spiegel, Inc., Oak Brook, Ill., 1978-79; mgr. tng. and devel. Sun Elec. Corp., Crystal Lake, Ill., 1979-82, United Airlines, 1982—; tchr. women's program Harper Coll., Palatine; founder, pres. Nat. Network of Women in Sales. Mem. Am. Soc. Tng. and Devel., Ill. Soc. Tng. and Devel., Chgo. Sales Trainers Assn. Home: 338 N Benton St Palatine IL 60067 Office: PO Box 66100 EXOTD Chicago IL 60666

HAVERS, ROBERT WILLIAM, auctioneer, consultant, appraiser; b. Onaway, Mich., May 3, 1953; s. William John and Eleanor (Booth) H.; m. Susan Kaye Simpson, Aug. 6, 1977; 1 son, Jason Robert. Student Mo. Auction Sch., Saginaw Bus. Inst., Am. Mgmt. Assn. Lic. auction cons., appraiser. Auctioneer Cummins Auction Co., Omaha, Nebr., 1981; franchisee United Auctioneers, Omaha, 1982-84; owner, pres. Bob Havers, Auctioneers, Midland, Mich., 1977—; lectr. Central Mich. U., Mt. Pleasant, 1982; cons. Randy Garner, Auctioneers, Fairfield, Ohio, 1982—; ran benefit auction Scottish Rite, Kansas City, Mo., 1979. Author Procalamtion Nat. Auctioneers Week, 1980, 84. Named largest auction ever conducted in Midland County Midland Daily News, 1982, largest auction ever conducted in Presquele Isle County Cheboygan Buyers Guide, 1983; recipient Cert. Appreciation Trout Unlimited, 1982-85. Mem. Nat. Auctioneers Assn., Am. Entrepreneurs Assn., Smithsonian Inst., Am. Auction Inst. Democrat. Baptist. Club: Eagles. Avocations: country and bluegrass music, leathercraft. Home: 700 E Haley St Midland MI 48640 Office: Bob Havers Auctioneers 700 E Haley St Midland MI 48640

HAVERTY, HAROLD V., printing company executive. Pres., dir. De Luxe Check Printers, Inc., St. Paul, Minn. Office: De Luxe Check Printers Inc 1080 W County Rd F Saint Paul MN 55112*

HAVIGHURST, BRUCE JAMES, lawyer; b. Cleve., Dec. 8, 1937; s. James Winfred and Helen Rennyson (Beetham) H.; m. Barbara Jean Corell, Oct. 1, 1966; children—Bryan James, Lauren Corell. A.B., Amherst Coll., 1959; J.D. Harvard U., 1963. Bar: Ohio 1964. Assoc. Jones, Day, Reavis & Pogue, Cleve., 1964-68; prof. law U. Va. Charlottesville, 1968; assoc. Jones, Day, Reavis & Pogue, Cleve., 1969-85, sr. atty., 1985—. Contbr. articles to profl. jours. Mem. Ohio Bar Assn., Cleve. Bar Assn., Harvard Law Sch. Assn. (treas. 1974-78); Phi Beta Kappa. Democrat. Congregationalist. Club: Cleve. Skating (Shaker Heights, Ohio). Avocations: Baseball, postal chess, classical music, mathematics, reading. Home: 20861 Byron Rd Shaker Heights OH 44122 Office: 1700 Huntington Bldg Cleveland OH 44115

HAVILL, DIANA, university cardiology program administrator; b. Chgo., Dec. 19, 1943; d. Russell and Clara (Zaloudek) H. Owner, mgr. Olympia Inc., Crete, Ill., 1961-66; clin. coordinator U. Chgo., Ill., 1965-68; cardiology adminstr. U. Chgo., 1969—; fiscal adminstrv. cons. NIH, Bethesda, Md., 1970—; research adminstrv. cons. in pvt. practice, Chgo., 1970—. Mem. Adminstrs. Internal Medicine. Club: Zonta Internat. (sec. 1982—) (Chgo.). Avocations: horseback riding; hiking; swimming. Home: 5712 S Kenwood Chicago IL 60637 Office: U Chgo 950 E 59th St Box 423 Chicago IL 60637

HAWBECKER, BYRON LEON, chemistry educator; b. Freeport, Ill., Oct. 2. 1935; s. Merle R. and Cora G. (Stauffer) H.; m. Anita M. Luxmore, June 24, 1961; children—Denise E., Melissa S. B.A., Manchester Coll., 1957; M.S., U. Ariz., 1962; Ph.D., Kent State U., 1968. Research chemist A.E. Staley Mfg. Co., Decatur, Ill., 1958, 62-63; asst. prof. Monmonth Coll., Ill., 1961-62; dept. chmn., prof. chemistry Ohio No. U., Ada, 1963—; lectr. Kent State U., Ohio, 1966-67. Contbr. articles to profl. jours. Mem. Ada Edn. Council, 1978—. Fellow NSF, 1959, Continental Oil, 1960-61, DuPont Chem. Co., 1966-67; recipient Central Ohio Heart Found. research award, 1968-74. Mem. Am. Chem. Soc. (chmn. N.W. Central Ohio sect. 1985), Sigma Xi (pres. 1977-78). Baptist. Avocations: athletics; music; writing. Home: 605 Conley Ave Ada OH 45810 Office: Ohio No U Ada OH 45810

HAWERCHUK, DALE, professional hockey player. Ctr., Winnipeg Jets. Office: Winnipeg Jets 15-1430 Maroons Rd Winnipeg MB R3G OL5 Canada

HAWES-DAVIS, DENZIL JEROME, radiologist; b. Topeka, Feb. 23, 1940; s. Denzil J. and Ida Hawes-Davis; m. LuNell McGee, Aug. 25, 1965; children—Douglas, Dana. Student, Central Meth. Coll., 1957-60; B.A., U. Dubuque, 1961; D.O., Kirksville Coll. Osteo. Medicine, 1968. Intern, resident Normandy Osteo. Hosp., St. Louis, 1968-72; staff radiologist Charles E. Still Hosp., Jefferson City, Mo., 1972—, vice chmn. dept., dir. dept. diagnostic ultrasound and vascular labs., 1976—, med. dir. Sch. Radiologic Tech., 1976-85; chief radiologist Mid-Mo. Med. Found., 1981-82; cons. St. Mary's Hosp., Meml. Hosp. Contbr. articles to profl. jours. Active Mo. div. Am. Cancer Soc., 1974-79, chmn. edn. com., 1978-79, v.p. Mo. div., 1976-77. Recipient Mead Johnson award in radiology, 1971. Mem. Jefferson City C. of C., Am. Osteo. Coll. Radiology, Soc. Nuclear Medicine, Radiol. Soc. N.Am., Soc. Non-Invasive Vascular Tech., Am. Inst. Ultrasound in Medicine. Republican. Baptist. Lodges: Lions, Masons.

HAWK, ROBERT NEIL, college official; b. Athens, Ohio, Sept. 9, 1947; s. Robert O. and Charlotte Marie (Addis) H.; m. Connie Sue Cain, Sept. 3, 1966; children—Wendi Sue, Christopher Neil. B.B.A., Ohio U., 1969. Mgmt. trainee Hobart Mfg. Co., Troy, Ohio, 1969-70; acct. Ohio U., Athens, 1970-76; v.p. fin., treas. Shawnee State Community Coll., Portsmouth, Ohio, 1976—. Bd. dirs. Valley Local Sch. System, Lucasville, Ohio, 1981—; mem. solicitor United Way, Portsmouth, 1983. Mem. Nat. Assn. Coll. and Univ. Bus. Officers, Central Assn. Coll. and Univ. Ofcls., Ohio Assn. Coll. and Univ. Ofcls. (pres. 1984-85), Ohio Tech. and Community Coll. Assn. (pres. 1981-82), Nat. Assn. Ednl. Buyers, Coll. and Univ. Personnel Assn., Retail Mchts. Assn., Order Ky. Cols. Club: Valley Athletic Boosters (Lucasville). Lodges: Elks, Lions (charter mem. Lucasville, bd. dirs.). Avocations: golf, tennis, hunting, racquetball. Office: Shawnee State Community Coll 940 2d St Portsmouth OH 45662

HAWK, ROBERT STEVEN, library administrator; b. Athens, Ohio, June 6, 1949; s. John Paul and Mary Lois (Briggs) H.; m. Constance Lyne Jodoin, June 16, 1979. B.S., Wright State U., 1971; M.S. in Library Sci., U. Ky., 1974. Library asst. Dayton and Montgomery County Pub. Library, Dayton, Ohio, 1972-73; project dir. Miami Valley Library Orgn., Dayton, 1974-76; library devel. cons. State Library of Ohio, Columbus, 1976-77; librarian, asst. dir. main library Akron-Summit County Pub. Library, 1977-79, librarian, asst. dir. brs., 1979-80, librarian, dir., 1980—; host, writer Cable TV program INFOCUS, 1982-83; mem. Gov.'s Pub. Library Fin. and Support Com., Columbus, 1983—, Ohio Multiple Interlibrary Coop. Com., 1980-81, Library and Info. Services to Citizens of Ohio Implementation Adv. Com., Columbus, 1983, Kent State U. Sch. Library Sci. Adv. Com., 1980—, U. Akron Continuing Edn. and Pub. Service Adv. Com., 1981—. Mem. Ohio Library Assn. (bd. dirs. 1983-85, v.p./pres.-elect 1985-86), ALA, Beta Phi Mu. Methodist. Clubs: Akron Torch, U. Akron Hilltopper. Lodge: Akron Kiwanis. Home: 311 Merriman Rd Akron OH 44303-1553 Office: 55 S Main St Akron OH 44326

HAWK, THOMAS WILLIAM, air force officer; b. Lock Haven, Pa., Sept. 30, 1942; s. Paul William and Helen Rebecca (Glossner) H.; m. Sandra Jean Ungard, Aug. 22, 1964 (div. 1973); 1 child, Joanne C.; m. Barbara Ann Woodward, June 16, 1974; children—Julie B. Moore, Jeffrey P. Moore, Gregory T. Hawk. B.S. in Secondary Edn., Lock Haven U. (Pa.), 1964; M.P.A., Golden Gate U., 1976. Commd. 2d lt. Air Force, 1964, advanced through grades to lt. col., 1980; combat aircrew 13th Air Force, Clark Air Force Base, PI, 1971-72, dir. flight simulator, 509th Bomb Wing, Pease Air Force Base, N.H., 1972-76, DLA flight test dir. Hayes Internat. Co., Birmingham, Ala., 1976-80, edn. with industry Martin-Marietta Co., Orlando, Fla., 1980-81, dir. mfg. quality assurance Wright Patterson Air Force Base, Ohio, 1981—, Aero Equipment Program Office, 1983—. Mem. Air Force Assn., Nat., Contract Mgmt. Assn., Def. Systems Mgmt. Coll. Alumni Assn. Republican. Roman Catholic. Avocations: Restoration of antique player piano, hunting, fishing. Home: 122 Buckeye Circle Wright Patterson Air Force Base OH 45433

HAWKINS, ARTHUR MICHAEL, automotive executive; b. St. Catharines, Ont., Canada, Sept. 22, 1942; s. William Thomas and Mary Ann (Deneka) H.; m. Linda Jane Dunning, Dec. 23, 1970; children—William Robert, Tracey Michelle, Michael John, Samantha Jane. B.S. in Indsl. Engring., Windsor Coll. of Engring., 1965; M.B.A., Mich. State U., 1982. Vice pres. mfg. Monroe Auto Equipment Co., Monroe, Mich., 1979-80, v.p. ops., 1980-82; sr. v.p. ops. Tenneco Automotive, Bannockburn, Ill., 1982-83; sr. v.p., gen. mgr. Walker Mfg. Co., Racine, Wis., group exec. I.T.T. Automotive Products Worldwide, Bloomfield Hills, Mich., 1984—; pres., chief exec. officer Exide Corp., Horsham, Pa. Mem. Am. Mgmt. Assn., Soc. Automotive Engrs., Beta Gamma Sigma. Republican. Presbyterian. Home: 1530 Surria Ct Bloomfield Hills MI 48013 Office: ITT APWW 505 N Woodward Bloomfield Hills MI 48013

HAWKINS, EDWARD JACKSON, lawyer; b. Fall River, Mass., June 24, 1927; s. Edward Jackson and Harriet (Sherman) H.; m. Barbara Anne Rollo, July 6, 1957; children—Daniel, George, Robert, Harriet. Grad. Phillips Acad., Andover, Mass., 1945; A.B. summa cum laude, Princeton U., 1950; L.L.B. magna cum laude, Harvard U., 1953. Bar: Ohio 1954. Mem. firm Squire, Sanders & Dempsey, Cleve., 1953-78; chief tax counsel U.S. Senate Fin. Com., Washington, 1979-80, minority tax counsel, 1981; adminstr. tax and employee benefits group Squire, Sanders & Dempsey, 1982—; gen. chmn. Cleve. Tax Inst., 1969. Contbr. articles to profl. jours. Mem. alumni council Phillips Acad., Andover, Mass., 1967-70. Mem. ABA (council mem. tax sect. 1982-85), Ohio State Bar, Cleve. Bar Assn., Princeton Alumni Assn., of No. Ohio (pres. 1966-68), Phillips Acad. Alumni Assn. of Clev. (pres. 1970-72). Served with U.S. Army, 1945-46. Democrat. Episcopalian. Club: City of Cleve.; Quadrangle (Princeton, N.J.). Home: 19800 Marchmont Rd Shaker Heights OH 44122 Office: Squire Sanders & Dempsey 1800 Huntington Bldg Cleveland OH 44115

HAWKINS, LAWRENCE CHARLES, administrator, management consultant; b. Greenville County, S.C., Mar. 20, 1919; s. Wayman and Etta (Brockman) H.; m. Earline Thompson, Apr. 29, 1943; children—Lawrence Charles, Wendell Earl. B.A., U. Cin., 1941, B.Ed., 1942, M.Ed., 1951, Ed.D., 1970; Assoc. Degree (hon.), Wilmington Coll., 1979. Cert. sch. supt., Ohio. Elem./secondary tchr. Cin. Pub. Schs., 1945-52, sch. prin./dir., 1952-67, asst. supt., 1967-69; dean U. Cin., 1969-75, v.p., 1975-77, sr. v.p., 1977-83; vis. asst. prof. Eastern Mich. U., Ypsilanti, summers 1955-60; v.p. Cincinnatus Assn., 1971—; bd. dirs. Wilmington (Ohio) Coll., 1980—; trustee Children's Home of Cin., 1978—; pres., chief exec. officer Omni-Man, Inc., 1964-66. Bd. dirs. Bethesda Hosp., Cin., 1980—; vice chmn. Greater Cin. TV Ednl. Found., WCET-TV, 1983; Co-chmn. Cin. area NCCJ 1980—. Served to lt. USAAF, 1943-45. Recipient award of Merit, Cin. Area United Appeal, 1955, 73, cert. Pres.'s Council on Youth Opportunity, 1968, City Cin., 1968. Mem. NEA (life), Nat. Congress Parents and Tchrs. (hon. life; chmn. com.), Phi Delta Kappa, Kappa Delta Pi, Kappa Alpha Psi, Sigma Pi Phi.

HAWKINS, RALPH G(ERALD), university media administrator; b. Lilbourn, Mo., June 12, 1930; s. Ralph N. and Marguriete (Landreum) H.; m. Dorothy Case, Aug. 6, 1955; children—Randy, Kim, Michael, Christopher. B.S.M.A. Kans. State Coll., 1958, M.S. in Edn., 1967; Ed.D., U. Ark., 1979. Lab. asst. Kans. State Coll., 1955-58; photo and editor, newspaper, Portageville, Mo., 1959-61; editor, pub. weekly newspapers, Clarkton and Gideon, Mo., 1962-64; dir. photography Kans. State Coll., Pittsburg, 1965-67; dir. graphics No. Ill. U., DeKalb, 1967-69; dir. ednl. media S.W. Mo. State U., Springfield, 1969—, assoc. prof. secondary edn., 1969—, supr. Media Ctr., 1983—. Deacon Presbyterian Ch., Springfield; mem. adv. bd. Springfield Cable TV. Served with USAF, 1951-55; Korea. Mem. Assn. Ednl. Communications Tech., Mo. Assn. Ednl. Tech., Phi Delta Kappa, Tau Kappa Epsilon. Democrat. Club: Univ. (pres.) (Springfield). Lodge: Kiwanis. Author multi-media show: Ed Media 2001, 1978. Home: 2020 S Oak Grove Springfield MO 65804 Office: SW Mo State U 901 S National Springfield MO 65804

HAWKINS, ROBERT EUGENE, wildlife materials company executive; b. Ft. Cobb, Okla., July 29, 1933; s. John Melvin and Ethel Lee Hawkins; m. Linda Lou Mize, June 2, 1956; children—Camille, Tim, Stacy, Robert. B.S., Tex. A&M U., 1962; M.S., So. Ill. U., 1967. Clk. Red River Arsenal, Texarkana, Tex., 1952-57; ecologist U.S. Forest Service, Andalusia, Ala., 1962-63; grad. asst. So. Ill. U., Carbondale, 1963-65; researcher Ill. Natural History Survey, Urbana, 1965-67; staff asst. So. Ill. U., 1967-73; owner Wildlife Materials, Inc., Carbondale, 1970—. Contbr. articles to profl. jours. Bd. dirs. Carbondale Jr. Sports, 1980, Carbondale High Sch. Athletic Boosters, 1983; vol. football coach Carbondale Community High Sch., 1982-83. Mem. Nat. Wildlife Soc., Ill. Wildlife Soc. Avocations: photography; travel; real estate. R R 1 Box 375 Carbondale IL 62901 Office: Wildlife Materials Inc R R 1 Box 427A Carbondale IL 62901

HAWKINS, ROBERT LYON, JR., chem. co. exec.; b. Cleve., Apr. 2, 1922; s. Robert Lyon and Catherine (Hanselman) H.; B.S. in Chem. Engring., Case Inst. Tech., 1947, M.S. in Indsl. Chemistry, 1956; m. Patricia O'Callaghan Boswell, Nov. 9, 1968; children—Robert Lyon III, Anne S., John W.; stepchildren—William O. Boswell, James T. Boswell. Paint chemist Empire Varnish Co. (name changed to Waterlox Chem. & Coatings Corp., 1967), Cleve., 1947-50, asso. tech. dir., 1950-56, corp. sec., 1950-60, exec. v.p., 1956-61, chmn. bd., chief exec. officer, 1961-—. Bd. dirs. Cleve. Paint-Up Clean-Up Fix-Up Campaign, 1961-62. Served to 1st lt., USAF, 1942-46. Fellow Am. Inst. Chemists; mem. A.A.A.S., Am. Chem. Soc., Am. Mgmt. Assn., Cleve. Paint Varnish and Lacquer Assn. (pres. 1961-62, exec. bd. 1970-71), Cleve. Soc. Paint Tech. (exec. com. 1968-71), Citizens League Cleve., Cleve. Art Mus., Mus. Natural Hist., Alpha Chi Sigma, Beta Theta Pi. Clubs: Hermit (dir. 1976-79) (Cleve.); Mayfield Country. Patentee in field. Home: 10000 Lake Shore Blvd Bratenahl Cleveland OH 44108 Office: 9808 Meech Ave Cleveland OH 44105

HAWKINS, WALTER LENELL, manufacturing engineer; b. Louisburg, N.C., May 2, 1948; s. Leonard Marion and Ruth (Yarborough) H.; m. Charlene Ashe, Aug. 26, 1978; children—Brandon Lenell Ashe, Justin Cameron Ash. B.S.M.E., N.C. A&T State U., 1970; M.B.A., Xavier U., 1976; postgrad. U. Cin., 1979. Engr. Gen. Motors Corp., Warren, Mich., 1969; field engr. Dow Chem. Co., Wayne, Mich., 1970; program engr. Gen. Electric, Cin., 1970-71; project mgr. Procter and Gamble, Cin., 1971—, computer integrated mfg. and robotics resource, 1983—. Bd. dirs. Big Bros./Sisters Greater Cin., 1973—. Recipient Ten Yr. award Big Bros./Sisters of Cin., 1983. Fellow Computer Mus.; mem. Soc. Mfg. Engrs., Robotics Internat., ASME, Engring. Soc. Cin. Baptist. Avocations: reading; specialized current events collection; bowling; exercising. Home: 1880 Fullerton Dr Cincinnati OH 45240 Office: Procter and Gamble Co 5204 Spring Grove Ave Cincinnati OH 45217

HAWKINSON-HICKEY, MARILYN BETH, sales executive; b. St. Paul, Oct. 2, 1954; d. Warren Sterling and Lorraine Elizabeth (Stegner) H.; m. Wayne Monroe Hickey, Nov. 7, 1981. B.S. with honors in Med. Tech., 1976. Employment cons. upper midwest, St. Paul, 1975; med. technologist U. Minn. Hosps., Mpls., 1976-78; tech. specialist Technicon Instruments, Cin., 1978-81, area sales mgr. diagnostics, 1981-82, regional sales mgr. diagnostics, Chgo., 1983-85, regional sales mgr. chemistry instruments, 1985—. Mem. Am. Soc. Clin. Pathologist (cert. med. technologist), Am. Assn. Clin. Chemists. Republican. Avocations: snow skiing, water skiing, swimming, bowling, piano.

HAWKS, TERRY FOSTER, optometrist; b. El Dorado, Kans., Jan. 13, 1950; s. Andrew J. and Juanita (Foster) H.; m. Teresa Lynne Gann, Aug. 22, 1971; 1 child, Ryan Matthew. A.A., Butler County Jr. Coll., 1970; B.S., U. Houston, 1974, O.D., 1974. Gen. practice optometry, Overland Park, Kans., 1974—; cons. sports vision Am. Optometric Assn. Nat. Sports Fest. Indpls., 1982. Contbr. articles to profl. jours. and mags. Recipient Optometric Recognition award Am. Optometric Assn., 1984. Mem. Kans. Optometric Assn. (chmn. pub. info. com. 1977-82, pres. elect 1984, pres. 1985-86), Greater Kansas City Optometric Soc. (bd. dirs. 1979-80), Heart of Am. Contact Lens Soc. (arrangements chmn. 1983—), Methodist. Club: Half Time Investment (Overland Park). Lodge: Optimist. Avocations: skiing, scuba diving, sports. Home: 13293 W 112 Terrace Overland Park KS 66210 Office: 5600 W 95th St Suite 204 Overland Park KS 66207

HAWLEY, SANDRA SUE, electrical engineer; b. Spirit Lake, Iowa, May 7, 1948; d. Byrnard Leroy and Dorothy Virginia (Fischbeck) Smith; m. Michael John Hawley, June 7, 1970; 1 child, Alexander Tristin. B.S. in Elec. Engring., U. Dayton, 1981; B.S. in Math. and Statistics, Iowa State U., 1970; M.S. in Statistics, U. Del., 1975. Research analyst State of Wis., Madison, 1970-71; research asst. Del. State Coll., Dover, 1972-73; asst. prof. math. and statistics Wesley Coll., Dover, 1974-81, chmn. dept. math. and computer sci., 1978-80; elec. engr. Control Data Corp., Bloomington, Minn., 1982-85; sr. elec. engr. Custom Integrated Circuits, 1985—. Elder, Presbyterian Ch. U.S.A., 1975—, mem. session Oak Grove Presbyn. Ch., Bloomington, 1985—. NSF scholar U. Dayton, 1981. Mem. IEEE, Assn. Women in Sci., Am. Statis. Assn., Sigma Delta Epsilon. Home: 7724 W 85th St Circle Bloomington MN 55438 Office: Custom Integrated Circuits 5353 Wayzata Blvd Minneapolis MN 55416

HAWN, WILLIAM FRANCIS, ophthalmologist; b. Fargo, N.D., Dec. 14, 1950; s. Hugh William and Vera Francis (Goulet) H.; m. Vicki Lyn Nissen, Dec. 18, 1976; children—Kimberly, Mark, Matthew. B.S., St. John's U., 1973; B.S. in Medicine, U. N.D., 1975; M.D., U. Nebr.-Omaha, 1977. Lic. ophthalmologist, Wis. Intern Univ. Hosps., Omaha, 1977-78; resident Mayo Clinic, Rochester, Minn., 1978-81; practice medicine specializing in ophthalmology, Eau Claire, Wis., 1981—. Fellow Am. Acad. Ophthalmology; mem. AMA, Wis. State Med. Soc., Tri County Med. Soc., State Ophthalmology. Republican. Roman Catholic. Avocations: skiing; boating; swimming; golf; tennis. Office: Med Eye Clinic Eau Claire 745 Kenney Ave Eau Claire WI 54701

HAWTHORNE, DOUGLAS LAWSON, banker; b. Chgo.; s. Francis R. and Dorothea (Lawson) H.; m. Sarah J. Archibald, Apr. 15, 1967; 1 child, Bryan Douglas. B.A., Wabash Coll., 1963; postgrad. NYU Grad. Sch. Bus., 1963-69. Mgmt. trainee Irving Trust Co., N.Y.C., 1963-67; corp. credit mgr. CBS, N.Y.C., 1967-69; pres., v.p., treas. Careers, Inc., N.Y.C., 1969-71; with Third Nat. Bank and Trust Co., Dayton, Ohio, 1971—, dir. research/planning, 1971-74, v.p. corp. devel., 1974-75, sr. v.p., 1975-78, exec. v.p., 1978-82; pres., chief operating officer, 1982-84, pres., chief exec. officer, 1984-85, chmn. bd., chief exec. officer, 1985—, also dir.; dir., treas. MedAm. Health Systems Corp., Dayton, 1984-85, chmn. bd. MedAm. Mgmt. Services, Inc., Dayton, 1984—. Trustee Dayton Art Inst. Dayton C. of C. (trustee, exec. com. 1984—), Young Pres. Orgn., Phi Gamma Delta. Clubs: Racquet (Dayton), Moraine Country. Office: The Third Nat Bank & Trust Co 34 N Main St Dayton OH 45402

HAWTHORNE, FRANK WALKER, JR., foundation researcher; b. Lansing, Mich., Jan. 30, 1954; s. Frank Walker and June Marie (Caldwell) H.; m. Dottie M. Dilts, May 15, 1982. B.A., Western Mich. U., 1979, M.S., 1981. Prospect research assoc. RMH Found., Rochester, Minn., 1982—. Mem. Rochester Human Rights Commn., 1985—, Minn. Episcopal Peace Commn, 1983—. Mem. Minn. Prospect Research Assn. (v.p. 1984—). Mem. Democratic Farm Labor Party. Avocations: reading; watercolors; cross country skiing. Home: 427 6th St SW Rochester MN 55902 Office: RMH Found 201 W Center St Rochester MN 55902

HAY, CHARLES DAVID, dentist; b. Terre Haute, Ind., May 21, 1936; s. Charles Alexander and Ruth Justus (Denehie) H.; m. Marcelyn Sue Conrad, Aug. 5, 1960; children—Bradley David, Kathryn Ann. B.S., Ind. U., 1958, D.D.S., 1961. Pres., W.I.D.S., Terre Haute, Ind., 1971-72; pvt. practice dentistry, Rosedale, Ind., 1961—. Vice-chmn. Parke County Health Bd., 1978—; pres. Rosedale Community Civic Club, 1964. Mem ADA, Ind. Dental Assn., Western Ind. Dental Soc. Nat. Forensic League, Audubon Soc., Sierra Club, Am. Forestry Assn., Kappa Delta Rho, Psi Omega. Republican. Club: Elks. Avocations: Photography, whitewater rafting. Address: PO Box 215 Rosedale IN 47874

HAY, DAVID MCKECHNIE, religious studies educator; b. Fargo, N.D., Sept. 19, 1935; s. Donald Gordon and Esther Lillian (McKechnie) H.; m. Mary Campbell Carmichael, June 30, 1961; children—Mary Cameron, Michael David. B.A., Duke U., 1957; B.D., Yale U., 1960, Ph.D., 1965. Ordained to ministry Presbyterian Ch., 1966. Asst. prof. religion Princeton Sem., N.J., 1964-71; asst. prof. Coe Coll., Cedar Rapids, Iowa, 1971-85, prof., 1983—. Author: Glory At The Right Hand, 1973. Contbr. articles to profl. jours. Adv. bd. Mercy Spiritual Ctr., Cedar Rapids, 1984—. Named to Joseph E. McCabe Chair of Religion Coe Coll., 1983. Mem. Soc. Bibl. Lit., Studiorum Novi Testamenti Societas, Inst. Antiquity and Christianity (assoc.). Democrat. Avocation: musical composition. Home: 240 25th St Dr SE Cedar Rapids IA 52403 Office: Coe Coll Cedar Rapids IA 52402

HAY, ROBERT PETTUS, history educator; b. Eagleville, Tenn., Oct. 23, 1941; s. Ira James and Alice Elizabeth (Pettus) H.; m. Carla Jean Humphrey, Dec. 31, 1966. B.S., Middle Tenn. State U., Murfreesboro, 1962; Ph.D., U. Ky., 1967. Instr. history Middle Tenn. State U., summer 1964; lectr. history U. Ky., 1966-67; asst. prof. history Marquette U., Milw., 1967-71, assoc. prof., 1971—, asst. chmn. dept., 1975, chmn. dept., dir. grad. study, 1975-79. Assoc. history editor USA Today, 1980—; contbr. numerous articles and revs. to hist., popular and profl. jours. Mem. Milw. County Zool. Soc., Milw. Art Mus., Friends of Milw. County Pub. Mus., Tenn. State Mus. Assn.; life mem. Pres.'s Council Marquette U., U. Ky. Fellows. Commd. Ky. col., 1980; Woodrow Wilson fellow, 1962-63, 65-66; NDEA fellow, 1962-65; Nat. Endowment Humanities fellow, 1969-70. Mem. Orgn. Am. Historians (life), So. Hist. Assn. (life), Soc. Historians Early Am. Rep. (life), Tenn. Hist. Soc. (life), Am. Cath. Hist. Assn. (life), Milw. County Hist. Soc. (life), Ky. Hist. Soc. (life), Filson Club (life), Am. Hist. Assn., Milw. Met. Historians Assn., Wis. Assn. Promotion of History, AAUP. Democrat. Roman Catholic. Home: 2146 Laura Ln Waukesha WI 53186 Office: Dept History Marquette U Milwaukee WI 53233

HAY, WILLIAM WALTER, civil engineering educator, consultant; b. Bay City, Mich., Dec. 10, 1908; s. William K. and Addelaide Belle (Kyler) H.; m. Mary Clark Hubley, Feb. 20, 1943; children—William Walter, Mary Elisabeth. B.S., Carnegie-Mellon U., 1931; M.S., U. Ill., 1948; Mgmt. engr. Carnegie-Mellon U., 1948; Ph.D., U. Ill. 1956. Registered profl. engr., Ill. Survey engr., track supr. various U.S. railroads, 1934-43; supt. maintenance of way U.S. Mil. Ry. Service, ETO, 1943-45; chief engr. Korean ry. U.S. Mil. Govt. in Korea, Seoul, 1945-46; asst. prof. to prof. ry. civil engring. U. Ill., Urbana, 1947-77, prof. emeritus, 1977—; mem. Profl. Engrs. Examining Com., State Ill., 1959-68; railroad cons. to govts. and bus., U.S. Africa, Can., Venezuela, 1950—. Author: Railroad Engineering, 1953, rev. edit., 1982; An Introduction to Transportation Engineering, 1961; rev. edit., 1977. Served to lt. col. U.S. Army, 1943-46, ETO, Korea. Recipient Alumni Merit award Carnegie-Mellon U., 1979. Mem. Am. Ry. Engring. Assn. (hon. mem., dir. 1957-60), Roadmasters and Maintenance of Way Assn. (dir. 1974-77), Sigma Xi, Chi Epsilon, Tau Beta Pi. Avocations: reading; music; gardening; current events. Office: U Ill 1308 W Green St Urbana IL 61801

HAYASHIDA, FRANK, educator, writer; b. Artesia, Calif., Feb. 9, 1933; s. Tamehachi and Chiya (Furuta) H. A.A., Wilson Coll., Chgo., 1955; M.A., Ind. State Coll., 1960; B.Ed. with honors, Chgo. State Coll., 1958; postgrad. Ind. U., 1960-62. Tchr., Ind. State Coll., Terre Haute, 1958-59; dir. student activities Wilson Coll., Chgo., 1962-71, adminstrv. asst., 1967-73; dean planning and ops. Kennedy-King Coll., Chgo., 1973-81, mem. faculty, 1981—; tech. dir. White Barn Theatre, Terre Haute, 1955; asst. dir. TV Variety Hour, Seoul, Korea,

1971; tech. dir. Shawnee Summer Theatre of Greene County, Inc., Bloomfield, Ind., 1960-81, assoc. producer, 1967-81, producer-dir., 1981—, bd. dirs., 1967—, sec. bd., 1967-77, sec.-treas., 1977—; mem. faculty Shawnee Sch. Speech and Dramatic Arts, 1960-78, dean, 1979—; mem. exec. bd. Sta. WKKC-FM, 1984; producer radio spots. Co-author: Communication through Speaking, 1983; also articles. Adapter radio and theatre scripts. Mem. Japanese-Am. Citizens League, Chgo., 1983; coordinator VISTA and Peace Corps activities, Chgo., 1971-72; cons. Project Share, Chgo., 1973. Served with U.S. Army, 1953-55; Korea. John Hay Whitney fellow; Lucile Gafford scholar. Mem. Am. Theatre Assn., Am. Film Inst., Phi Theta Kappa, Phi Beta Lambda, Theta Alpha Phi, Kappa Delta Phi. Office: 6904 S Harvard Ave Chicago IL 60621

HAYDEN, CARLA DIANE, librarian; b. Tallahassee, Fla., Aug. 10, 1952; d. Bruce Kenard and Colleen (Dowling) H. B.A., Roosevelt U., 1973; M.A., U. Chgo., 1977. Children's librarian Chgo. Pub. Library, 1973-79, young adult services coordinator, 1979-81; library services coordinator Mus. Sci. and Industry, Chgo., 1982—. Recipient Humanitarian award Fred Hampton Scholarship, Chgo., 1979; YMCA Black Achievers award, 1984. Mem. ALA, Assn. Library Service to Children (editor newsletter), Childrens Reading Roundtable, Spl. Libraries Assn., Ill. Library Assn. Office: Mus Sci and Industry 57th St and Lake Shore Dr Chicago IL 60637

HAYDEN, RONALD RAY, land surveyor; b. Prairie Du Chien, Wis., Jan. 25, 1952; s. Ray Daverne and Darlene Marie (Turk) H.; m. Carol Sue Paulson, June 19, 1971; children—Robbie Ray, Steven Elden. Student Western Wis. Tech. Inst., 1970-71, Rice Lake Vo-Tech., 1971-72. Registered land surveyor, Wis.; cert. soil tester, Wis. Land surveyor Davy Engrng. Co., La Crosse, Wis., 1974-77, Lampman & Assocs., Viroqua, Wis., 1977-79; land surveyor, owner Hayden Land Surveying Co., Soldiers Grove, Wis., 1979—; county surveyor Crawford County, Prairie Du Chien, 1979—. Contbr. articles to profl. jours. Mem. Gays Mills First Responders, Wis., 1983—, N. Crawford Rescue Squad, Soldiers Grove, 1983—. Served with U.S. Army, 1972-75. Mem. Am. Congress on Surveying and Mapping, Nat. Soc. Profl. Surveyors, Wis. County Surveyors Assn. (dir. 1980—), Wis. Soc. Land Surveyors (we. chpt.), Nat. Rifle Assn., Am. Legion. Lutheran. Avocations: hunting; fishing; camping; canoeing. Home and office: RFD 1 PO Box 138 Soldiers Grove WI 54655

HAYDOCK, WALTER JAMES, banker; b. Chgo., Dec. 14, 1947; s. Joseph Albert and Lillian V. (Adeszko) H.; student Harvard Bus. Coll., 1969-71, Daily Coll., 1971-73; B.S. in Acctg., DePaul U., 1976; m. Bonnie Jean Thompson, Aug. 22, 1970; children—Nicole Lynn, Matthew Michael. Computer operator, jr. programmer Pepper Constrn. Co., Chgo., 1972-73; input analyst Continental Bank, Chgo., 1973-76, data control supr., 1976-79, corporate fixed asset adminstr., 1979-83, properties systems analyst, 1983—; partner Day's End Motel, Wisconsin Dells, Wis., 1977—. Mem. Wis. Innkeepers Assn., Wisconsin Dells C. of C. Home: 6054 Rob Roy Dr Oak Forest IL 60452 Office: Continental Bank 231 S LaSalle St Chicago IL 60693

HAYES, ARTHUR CHESTER, safety cons., state legislator; b. Ft. Wayne, Ind., Aug. 24, 1918; s. Walter F. and Marie P. (Hardesty) H.; B.S., Ind. U., 1948; m. Miriam E. Peck, Feb. 1, 1946 (dec. Nov. 1968); children—Arthur C., Bethany M., Gayle W. Crosby. Sales corr. Magnavox Corporation, 1948-54; supr. Budget State Hwy. Dept., 1954-58; owner Vernors Bottling Co., Ft. Wayne, 1959-63; became dist. mgr. Colonial Life & Accident Ins. Co., 1963; mem. Ind. Ho. of Reps., 1963-72, 77—, ho. mem. Ind. Statutory com. on Commn. on Protection and Advocacy for Developmentally Disabled, 1977-78; safety cons. Chmn. Interstate Cooperation Com., Recodification of Cities and Towns Commn.; mem. Sesquicentennial Commn.; chmn. speakers bur. Ind. Am. Revolution Bicentennial Commn.; mem. Ind. Am. Negro Emancipation Centennial Commn. Served with AUS, 1941-45. Mem. Ft. Wayne C. of C., Am. Legion. Clubs: Ft. Wayne Civitan (pres. 1963-68; lt. gov. Midwest 1967). Home: 2001 Oakland St Fort Wayne IN 46808 Office: State House Bldg Indianapolis IN 46204

HAYES, CHARLES A., Congressman; b. Cairo, Ill., Feb. 17, 1918; widower; children—Barbara Delaney, Charlene Smith. Internat. v.p., dir. Region #12 United Food & Comml. Workers Internat. Union, AFL-CIO & CLC, 1968-83; mem. 98th-99th Congresses from Ill. 1st Dist.; dist. dir. Dist. #1 UPWA, 1954-68; field rep., exec. v.p. Coalition Black Trade Unionists; v.p. Ill. State AFL-CIO, Operation PUSH, Chgo.; exec. bd. Chgo. Urban League; mem. Ill. State Commn. Labor Laws. Office: Room 1028 Longworth House Office Bldg Washington DC 20515*

HAYES, CHARLES EDWARD, newspaper editor; b. Evanston, Ill., Mar. 13, 1931; s. Chester K. and Dorothy (Wilger) H.; B.S., Wittenberg U., 1953; M.S. in Journalism, Northwestern U., 1955. With Paddock Publs., Inc., Arlington Heights, Ill., 1954-75, newspaper series on social problems, 1958-75, exec. editor, 1960-68, editor-in-chief, 1968-75, v.p., 1970-75, publisher, 1971-75; v.p., editor Area Publs. Corp., Hinsdale, Ill., 1975-82; editorial bd. Chgo. Tribune, 1982—. Mem. adv. com. Suburban Press Found., Inc., Chgo., 1967-69; v.p. Opportunity Council Inc., 1958-59, pres., 1959-60. Chmn. bd. dirs. Salvation Army Community Counselling Center, 1971-75, mem. 1968—; bd. dirs. Salvation Army Family Service, 1978—, vice chmn., 1979—; mem. Ill. Health Facilities Authority, 1973-82. Recipient Instrument Peace award Christian Family Movement, 1960; named Arlington Heights Jr. C. of C. Man of Year, 1964. Mem. Chgo. Press Club, Suburban Press Club (pres. 1980-81), Chgo. Headline Club (pres. 1969-70), Soc. Profl. Journalists-Sigma Delta Chi, Chgo. Press Veterans Assn., League United Latin Am. Citizens (hon.), Blue Key, Kappa Phi Kappa, Pi Delta Epsilon, Phi Kappa Psi. Contbr. monographs and articles to various publs. Office: 435 N Michigan Ave Chicago IL 60611

HAYES, COY DENVERT, packaging company executive; b. Middlesboro, Ky., Aug. 23, 1928; s. Samuel and Rutha Edward (Drummonds) H.; m. Wanda Joyce McBee, May 24, 1947; 1 child, Arlene Nancy Hayes Willis. B.B.A., East Mich. U., 1967. Quality control supr. Consol. Paper Co., Monroe, Mich., 1964-65; paper mill chemist Union Camp Corp., Monroe, 1966-68; plant mgr. Sonoco Products Co., Rockton, Ill., 1968-72, midwest region mgr., 1972-73, so. region mgr., Hartsville, S.C., 1973-76, dir. mfg. services, Hartsville, 1976-81; prodn. mgr. Alton Packaging, Corp., Ill., 1981-84, gen. mgr., 1984—. Mem. TAPPI, Paper Industry Mgmt. Assn. Republican. Avocations: photography, golf, woodworking. Home: 1601 Biscay Dr Godfrey IL 62035 Office: Alton Packaging Corp 10 Cut St Alton IL 62002

HAYES, DAVID JOHN, elec. component manufacturing company marketing executive; b. Indpls., July 30, 1943; s. Alfred Henry and Jean Alexander (Morrison) H.; A.B., Boston U., 1965; M.B.A., Cornell U., 1967. Mgmt. trainee Westinghouse Broadcasting Co., Chgo., 1967-68, Norwalk, Conn., 1968, Boston, 1968-71; nat. sales rep. NBC, Chgo., 1971-72; pres. Dana Enterprises, Chgo., 1972-75; v.p. mktg. Micron Industries Corp., Stone Park, Ill., 1975—; dir. Haybec Enterprises, Inc., New Orleans Hotel Corp. Mem. Assn. M.B.A. Execs., Execs. Club Chgo., Salesmen with A Purpose (internat. v.p. 1980-81, Ill. pres. 1981-82), Ill. State Hist. Soc. (chmn. com. hist. markers 1980). Mem. Christian Ch. Clubs: Boston U. Chgo., Cornell Bus. Sch. Contbr. articles to Adminstrv. Sci. Quar. Office: 1830 N 32d Ave Stone Park IL 60165 Home: 156 N Brainard Ave La Grange IL 60525

HAYES, DAVID JOHN ARTHUR, JR., lawyer, bar association administrator; b. Chgo., July 30, 1929; s. David J.A. and Lucille M. (Johnson) H.; A.B., Harvard, 1952; LL.B., Chgo.-Kent Coll. Law, 1961; m. Anne Huston, Feb. 23, 1963; children—David J.A. III, Cary H. Admitted to Ill. bar, 1961; asst. sec., trust officer First Nat. Bank of Evanston (Ill.), 1962-63; gen. counsel Ill. State Bar Assn., 1963-66; asst. dir. Am. Bar Assn., 1966-68, div. dir., 1968-69, asst. exec. dir., 1969—; exec. dir. Naval Res. Lawyers Assn., 1971-75; asst. sec. Internat. Bar Assn., 1978-80; capt. JAGC, USNR. Fellow Am. Bar Found.; mem. Chgo. Bar Assn. (various coms.), Ill. Bar Assn. assembly rep. 1972-76), Nat. Orgn. Bar Counsel (pres. 1967), Inter-Am. Bar Assn. (asst. sec. 1984—), Phi Alpha Delta. Contbr. to profl. jours. Home: 908 Pontiac Rd Wilmette IL 60091 Office: 750 N Lake Shore Dr Chicago IL 60611

HAYES, GARY JOHN, information services executive; b. Chgo., Feb. 17, 1950; s. George Alphonse and Sophie (Michalowski) H.; m. Marsha Ann Telchuk, Oct. 2, 1971. B.S., U. Ill., 1972. Research analyst U. Ill., 1972-74; systems analyst Cenco, Inc., Chgo., 1974-77; sr. system analyst Pullman, Inc., Chgo., 1977-83; dir. tech. services AMA, Chgo., 1977—; dir. Rosebrook, Inc.; tchr. Chgo. and Lake County Jr. Colls., 1977-80; cons. AMA, GTE. Ill. state scholar, 1968-72. Mem. Assn. Computing Machinery, AMA, Data Processing Mgmt. Assn., Am. Assn. Med. Soc. Execs. Republican. Roman Catholic. Author: The Computer in Your Life, 1982. Home: 1307 N Cedar Lake Rd Round Lake Beach IL 60073 Office: 535 N Dearborn St Chicago IL 60610

HAYES, RONALD DEAN, law enforcement officer, limousine service executive; b. Moline, Ill., Jan. 16, 1943; s. James Albert and Margaret (Bardoel) H.; m. Barbara Ann Peugh; m. Deborah Sue Gillworth; 1 son, Jason Dean. Student Blackhawk Coll. Patrolman, Moline Police Dept., 1972-78, sergeant, 1978—; founder, pres. W. & H. Limo Service, Inc., Moline, 1977-84; Jason Limousine Service, Inc., Moline, 1984—. Treas. Moline Police Benevolent Assn., 1972-76. Served to sergeant U.S. Army, 1963-66, Vietnam. Mem. Am. Legion, Ill. Police Assn., Fraternal Order of Police, Univ. Ill. Police Inst. Alumni Assn. Baptist. Lodges: Elks, Masons. Avocations: combat shooting; coin collecting. Home: 3817 16th Ave Moline IL 61265 Office: Moline Police Dept 1630 8th Ave Moline IL 61265

HAYES, SONDRA ELAINE, educator; b. Indpls., Jan. 21, 1947; d. Bennie Ernest and Eva Mae James; div.; children—Sonya Nicole, Paul Vernon, II. B.S., Ind. U., 1968; M.S., Butler U., 1974. Chmn. fgn. lang. dept. Northwest High Sch., Indpls. Pub. Schs., 1968—; pres., dir. La Casita de los Ninos, Inc., Internat. Human Devel. Corp. Violinist, Butler Symphony Orch. Mem. Am. Assn. Tchrs. Spanish and Portuguese, Assn. Supervision and Curriculum Devel., Smithsonian Assocs., Ind. Assn. Adminstrs. and Sch. Counselors, Ind. Fgn. Lang. Tchrs. Assn.

HAYES, WALTER JOHN, data processing executive; b. N.Y.C., July 18, 1938; s. John C. and Mary (Mazgulski) Hayes; m. Dorothy Louise Hayes, Aug. 16, 1964; children—Walter, Daniel, Susan, Sarah. B.S. in Math., St. John's Coll., 1960, postgrad. 1960-62, 65-66, Athens Coll., 1967-68. Programmer/systems analyst Sperry Gyroscope Co., Lake Success, N.Y., 1963-66; sr. systems analyst/supr. Sperry Rand Space Support, Huntsville, Ala., 1966-68, info. systems mgr., 1968-69; regional data center mgr. Figgie Systems Mgmt. Group, Willoughby, Ohio, 1969-74, mgr. adminstrn., 1974-79, pres., 1979—; participant CAD/CAM Adv. Com., 1980—, Info. Resources Steering Com., 1981—, others; cons. in field. Mem. Figgie Polit. Action Com., 1981—, St. Anselm's Parish Council, Chesterland, Ohio, 1982—; bd. dirs. Fairmount Ctr., Russell, Ohio, 1985—. Served with USNG, 1955-61. Mem. Am. Prodn. and Inventory Control Soc., Assn. Data Processing Service Orgns. Republican. Roman Catholic. Club: Quail Hollow. Home: 8680 Camelot Dr Chesterland OH 44026 Office: Figgie Systems Mgmt Group 4420 Sherwin Rd Willoughby OH 44094

HAYMONS, DAN LESTER, JR., hospital administrator; b. Lumber City, Ga., Nov. 20, 1936; s. Dan Lester and Amanda (Grace) H.; m. Bettye Lynn Manner, Mar. 28, 1964; children—Lesley Lynn, Christopher Daniel. B.A., Valdosta State Coll., 1958; M.H.A., U. Minn., 1963. Adminstrv. resident Bapt. Meml. Hosp., Memphis, 1962-63, adminstrv. asst., 1963-65; asst. adminstr. Erlanger Med. Ctr., Chattanooga, 1965-69; assoc. adminstr. St. Dominic Hosp., Jackson, Miss., 1969-72; adminstr., chief exec. officer Union Med. Ctr., El Dorado, Ark., 1972-79; pres., chief exec. officer N. Kansas City Hosp., 1979—; dir. Boatman's North Hills Bank, 1981—. Contbr. articles to profl. jours. Bd. dirs. Am. Cancer Soc., Northland unit, Kansas City, 1981—, pres., 1981-83; bd. dirs. Vis. Nurse Assn. Kansas City, 1980-84; mem. J.C. Penney Golden Rule Award Com., 1983-84. Served to lt. USN, 1958-61. USPHS traineeship, 1962. Mem. Am. Coll. Hosp. Adminstrs. (fellow), Kansas City Area Hosp. Assn. (dir. 1980- 84). Episcopalian. Clubs: Kansas City, Old Pike. Home: 500 NW Briarcliff Extension Kansas City MO 64116 Office: North Kansas City Hosp 2800 Hospital Dr North Kansas City MO 64116

HAYNE, LONNIE RAY, state official; b. Star, Nebr., Sept. 18, 1940; s. Ralph and Ethel (Herman) H.; m. Gloria Pedersen, June 22, 1963; children—Lisa, Vicki. B.S., Dana Coll., 1962; M.A., U. Nebr., 1964. Mgmt. intern AEC, Las Vegas, Nev., 1964-65, procurement specialist, 1965; budget analyst Wis. Dept. Adminstrn., Madison, 1965-68, fed. aid analyst, 1968-70, budget dir., 1970-79; fiscal supr., Wis. Dept. Pub. Instrn., 1979—. Pres. Friends of Music, Stoughton, Wis., 1984—; treas. adult chpt. Am. Field Service, Stoughton, 1984—. Johnson fellow, 1962; recipient Wall Street Jour. award, 1962. Mem. Am. Soc. Pub. Adminstrn. (treas. 1976-80), Assn. Career Employees. Republican. Lutheran. Avocations: school government, lay church work. Home: 2536 Ridgetop Rd Stoughton WI 53589 Office: Dept Pub Instrn PO Box 7841 Madison WI 53707

HAYNES, FRANK MAURICE, business executive; b. Kansas City, Mo., June 1, 1935; s. William John and Marguerite Ida (Brown) H.; B.B.A., U. Colo., 1958; M.B.A. with honors, Roosevelt U., 1974; postgrad. Sch. Mgmt. Northwestern U., 1974-75; m. Arlene Claire Kidd, June 25, 1966; children—Jonathan Frank and Elizabeth Arlene (twins). Owner, operator Frank M. Haynes Ins. Agy., Chgo., 1960-65; pres. Employees Union Health & Welfare Agy., Inc., Chgo., 1965-72; cons. pension, health and welfare plans, Chgo., 1972-75; exec. v.p. W.J. Haynes & Co., Inc., Chgo., 1975-80, pres., 1980—. Served with U.S. Army, 1958-59. Recipient Wall St. Jour. award, 1974; certificate of merit Prudential Ins. Co., 1964; C.L.U. Mem. Am. Risk and Ins. Assn., Am. Soc. C.L.U.s, Internat. Found. Employee Benefit Plans, Beta Gamma Sigma. Home: 427 Sheridan Rd Kenilworth IL 60043 Office: 7045 N Western Ave Chicago IL 60645

HAYNES, JEAN REED, lawyer; b. Miami, Fla., Apr. 6, 1949; d. Oswald Birnam and Arleen (Weidman) Dow; m. William Rutherford Reed, Apr. 15, 1974 (div. Sept. 1981); m. Thomas Beranek Haynes, Aug. 7, 1982. A.B. with honors, Pembroke Coll., 1971; M.A., Brown U., 1971; J.D., U. Chgo., 1981. Bar: Ill. 1981, U.S. Dist. Ct. (no. dist.) Ill. 1983, U.S. Ct. Appeals (7th cir.) 1982. Tchr. grades 1-4 Abbie Tuller Sch., Providence, 1971-72; tchr./facilitator St. Mary's Acad., Riverside, R.I., 1972-74; tchr./head lower sch. St. Francis Sch., Goshen, Ky., 1974-78; law clk. U.S. Ct. Appeals (7th cir.), Chgo., 1981-83; assoc. Kirkland & Ellis, Chgo., 1983—. Sustaining fellow Art Inst. Chgo., 1982—. Mem. ABA, Chgo. Bar Assn., Ill. Bar Assn. (life), Am. Judicature Soc. Home: 505 N Lake Shore Dr #3112 Chicago IL 60611 Office: Kirkland & Ellis 200 E Randolph Dr Chicago IL 60601

HAYNES, MARY KATHERINE, nurse; b. Butler County, Mo., Oct. 2, 1931; d. Hershel Evert and Eva Mae (Hester) Heifner; cert. with highest honors, L P N Sch. Nursing, Poplar Bluff, Mo., 1960; R.N. with highest honors, Three Rivers Community Coll., 1973; B.Health Sci., Stevens Coll., Columbia, Mo., 1978; m. Robert W. Haynes, Aug. 14, 1948; children—Janice Haynes Thurman, Robert Randall. Nurse, Poplar Bluff Hosp., 1957-79, dir. nursing, 1974-79, nurse epidemiologist, 1975-79; adminstr. nursing service Richland Meml. Hosp., Olney, Ill., 1979-80, asso. adminstr., 1980—. Active PTA, 1958-70; troop leader Cotton Boll council Girl Scouts U.S.A., 1960-66; parliamentarian Democratic Woman's Club, 1962-65; instr. CPR, Mo. Heart Assn.; bd. advisers Three Rivers Community Coll. Sch. Nursing; mem. area project rev. com., bd. selection Comprehensive Health Planning Council of So. Ill. Southeastern Lung Assn. grantee, 1977. Mem. Assn. Practitioners of Infection Control, Assn. Infection Control Nurses. Club: Altrusa (dir. 1978). Home: 800 N Boone St Olney IL 62450 Office: 800 N Locust St Olney IL 62450

HAYS, ANTHONY LYNN, broadcasting executive; b. Washington Court House, Ohio; Jan. 28, 1954; s. Roger Lynn and Doris Lou (Brown) H.; m. Linda Susan Varney, Oct. 12, 1979; 1 child, Ashley Lynn. Grad. Internat. Broadcasting Sch., Dayton, Ohio, 1975. Announcer, Sta. WCHO, Washington Court House, 1975-76, salesman, 1978-80, gen. mgr., 1984—; announcer, salesman Stas. WVAK/WUME, Paoli, Ind., 1976-78; sales mgr. Sta. WBEX, Chillicothe, Ohio, 1980-84. Mem. Ross County Republican Promotion Com., Chillicothe, 1984. Mem. Washington Court House C. of C. Methodist. Lodge: Rotary. Avocations: fishing; genealogy; gardening and landscaping. Home: 5402 Plantation Pl New Holland OH 43145 Office: Sta WCHO 1535 N North St Washington Court House OH 43160

HAYS, BRADLEY GENE, bakery supply company executive; b. DeKalb, Ill., Jan. 6, 1957; s. William Gene and Joan Ellen (Spitz) H.; m. Kristine Ellen Tellison, Dec. 17, 1976; children—Michele Joan, Andrea Jane, Jennifer Jean. Student Kishwaukee Jr. Coll., 1974-76; grad. Am. Inst. Baking, Chgo., 1976. Blending delivery salesman Chgo. Hol'n One Donut Co., 1974-76, sales mgr., 1976-78, exec., 1978-80, ops. mgr., 1980-82, pres., 1982—. Chmn. bldg. and grounds com. First Ch. of Christ Scientist, DeKalb. Republican. Home: 312 George St Sycamore IL 60178 Office: PO Box 217 Waterman IL 60556

HAYS, L. CRANDALL, brokerage executive; b. Billings, Mont., July 9, 1938; s. Leonard C. and Grace M. (Chamberlin) H.; m. Brenda P. Ammons, June 2, 1963; children—Leonard, Natalie, Brandon. B.S. in Mech. Engrng., U. N.Mex., 1960; M.B.A., Stanford U., 1965. Chartered fin. analyst. Analyst, Prudential Ins. Co. Am., Newark, also Cin., 1965-67, Newton & Co., Milw., 1968-70; 1st v.p., dir. research Robert W. Baird & Co., Inc., Milw., 1970—, also dir. Coach amateur soccer team, Mequon, Wis., 1976—; active local Boy Scouts Am., 1977—; bd. dirs. Milw. Community Devel. Corp., 1980—. Served to lt. comdr. USN, 1960-63. Mem. Milw. Fin. Analysts Soc., Fin. Analysts Fedn. Clubs: Ozaukee Country, Milw. Curling (Mequon). Avocations: golf, hunting, fishing. Office: Robert W Baird & Co Inc 777 E Wisconsin Ave Milwaukee WI 53202

HAYS, WILLIAM FRANCIS, physician; b. Herrin, Ill., May 28, 1947; s. Morris Henry and Lela Evelyn (Misker) H.; m. Sue Ellen Eichhorn, July 11, 1970 (div. 1983); children—Kelly, Karen; m. Pamala Kay Holder, Oct. 1, 1983. B.A., So. Ill. U., 1970; M.D., Northwestern U., 1977. Diplomate Am. Bd. Family Practice. Resident U. Ill.-Meth. Med. Ctr., Peoria, 1977-80; family practice, Herrin, Ill., 1980—; mem. staff Herrin Hosp., v.p., 1983—; clin. asst. prof. family practice So. Ill. U. Sch. Medicine, 1982—. Fellow Am. Acad. Family Practice; mem. Ill. State Med. Soc. Methodist. Clubs: Elks. Office: 315 S 14th St Herrin IL 62948

HAYWARD, RICHARD ALDEN, city manager; b. Bakersfield, Calif., Nov. 4, 1952; s. Richard Bascommand Priscilla Elisabeth (Lane) H.; m. Rosalyn Kay Burkhart, May 21, 1977; 1 child, Richard David. B.A., Windham Coll., 1973; M.A., U. Toronto, 1975; M.P.A., U. Wyo., 1978. Adminstrv. asst. City of Gillette, Wyo., 1978-80, asst. to city adminstr., 1980-81, asst. city adminstr., 1981-82; city mgr. City of Napoleon, Ohio, 1982—. Bd. dirs. Henry County Sr. Ctr., 1982; mem. Pvt. Industry Council, 1983; trustee Napoleon Downtown Revitalization Corp., 1984. Recipient Small Employer of Yr. award, Govs. Commn. Handicapped, 1980. Mem. U.S. Fencing Assn. (exec. com. Wyo. div.), Internat. City Mgr. Assn., Ohio City Mgmt. Assn., Am. Soc. Pub. Adminstrs., Am. Pub. Works Assn. Presbyterian. Club: Optimists Internat. Avocations: geology; gemology; fencing; camping. Office: City of Napoleon 255 W Riverview St Napoleon OH 43545

HAYWOOD, CHARLES RICHARD, JR., food company executive; b. St. Louis, May 8, 1940; s. Charles Richard and Doris Louise (Korhammer) H.; m. Judith Ann Vaccaro, Aug. 17, 1963; children—Cheryl Lynn, Susan Marie. B.S., S.E. Mo. State U., 1963; M.B.A., U. Mo.-St. Louis, 1972. Programmer analyst Anheuser-Busch Cos., St. Louis, 1963-68, fin. analyst, 1968-70, sr. fin. analyst, 1970-71, mgr. ops. research, 1971-72, asst. to pres., 1973-75, mgr. fin. planning, 1976-77, mgr. info. services, 1977—. Officer Townsend, Kirby Jr. High Sch., Florissant, Mo., 1975—, Hazelwood High Sch., 1975—, Hazelwood PTA Council, 1975—, Spanish Lake Republican Club, 1974; dir. Paddock Forest Residents Assn., 1976—. Mem. Ops. Research Soc. Am. Home: 12931 Dunstone Dr Florissant MO 63033 Office: Anheuser-Busch Cos Inc One Busch Place Saint Louis MO 63118

HAYWOOD, MATILDA ANNA LAURA, educator; b. Ann Arbor, Mich., May 13, 1945; d. Lattimore David and Sarah Mae (Ford) H.; 1 dau., Fredericka. B.S. in Bus. Adminstrn., Roosevelt U., 1976; M.S. in Mktg. Communications, 1978. Cert. bus. educator. Instr. bus. communications Bryant & Stratton Bus. Sch., Chgo., 1972-73; tng. specialist, bus. edn. instr., project records analyst Chgo. City Colls., 1973-77; bus. communications instr. Chgo. Bd. Edn., 1976-81; labor market cons. James Lowery Cons., Chgo., 1979-80; instr. bus., music, Black history, dir. prodns. Evanston Twp. High Sch. (Ill.), 1981—; cons. U. Ill.-Chgo., summer 1983; v.p. ops. Search for Truth, Inc., Chgo., 1968—, also asst. editor. Author: Influence of African Culture on American Music, 1979 (Outstanding music and narrative 1980); writer, arranger choral ensemble arrangement: Razzmatazz, 1980 (Merit award 1982); author: Using Music to Teach Writing, 1984. Publicity agt. Nat. Assn. Media Women, Chgo., 1977-79; dir. research Community Cable Com., Chgo., 1981-82; charter mem. Roosevelt Alumni Council on Admissions, Chgo., 1983; dep./insp. Cook County Sheriff's Dept., 1972—. Recipient award for Outstanding and Dedicated Service, Nat. Assn. Media Women, 1978; City of Chgo. scholar, 1963. Mem. Nat. Assn. Media Women (publicity dir. 1977-79), Broadcast Music, Inc. (affiliated writer), Am. Assn. Individual Investors, Am. Fedn. Musicians, Chgo. Tchrs. Union, Internat. Jazz World Fedn. Democrat.

HAZEL, GERALD VERNON, trust officer; b. Stony Ridge, Ohio, Feb. 26, 1931; s. Wayne and Clarice (Bihn) H.; m. Loujean Marie Metzger, June 7, 1952; children—Elizabeth, Katherine. B.B.A., U. Toledo, 1952; postgrad. in bank mgmt. Rutgers U., 1964. Vice pres. Ohio Citizens Bank, Toledo, Ohio, 1956—; pres. bd. dirs. Delphos Quarries Co., Ohio, 1984—; sec. bd. dirs. Greenway Co., Toledo, 1979—. Pres., Toledo Dental Dispensary, 1972-82, Toledo Rose Soc., 1981-82, Luth. Social Services, 1979-80; treas. Toledo Soc. for Blind, 1984—. Served to capt., USN, 1952-75. Mem. Toledo Estate Planning Council, Am. Inst. Banking, Toledo C. of C., Toledo Sales and Mktg. Execs., Bank Mktg. Assn. Republican. Lutheran. Club: Glass Center Coin (treas.). Lodges: Masons, Kiwanis (pres. 1977-78). Avocations: golf; gardening; coin collecting. Home: 407 W Front St Perrysburg OH 43551 Office: Ohio Citizens Bank 405 Madison Ave Toledo OH 43603

HAZELTON, LUCY REED, advt. exec., writer; b. St. Louis, Sept. 9, 1929; d. Ferdinand Maximillian and Elizabeth Emily (Benson) Schaeffer; student Washington U., St. Louis, 1947-48, St. Louis U., 1954-56, U. Colo., summer, 1968, U. Houston, summer, 1971; m. Burton W. Hazelton, Feb. 15, 1958 (dec.); children—Terence G. Reed (dec.), Deborah Lucy Reed, Ellen Frisch. Writer and artist for ednl. programming Webster Pub. Co., Crestwood, Mo., 1962-63, Scharr Printers, St. Louis, 1966-67; advt. writer Christian Bd. Publs., St. Louis, 1967-69; mgr. advt. and pub. relations A.G. Edwards & Sons, Inc., St. Louis, 1969—. Bd. dirs. Poetry Center Inc. of St. Louis, v.p., 1975-80, pres., 1980—. Recipient Marianne Moore award, 1977, Merit award Fin. World Mag., 1973-77, Fin. World Merit award, 1973-79. Mem. Acad. Am. Poets, St. Louis Writers Guild (treas. 1975), Advt. Fedn. St. Louis, Women in Communications, Advt. Prodn. Club of St. Louis. Author: (book of poetry) Three Circles and the Princess, 1976; Eros/Agape, 1979; (verse plays) The Still Point (E. Oscar Thalinger award), 1965; The River Laughs, 1966. Contbr. poetry to various lit. mags.; columnist St. Louis Arts Mag. Home: 668 Kirkshire Dr Kirkwood MO 63122 Office: 1 N Jefferson Saint Louis MO 63103

HAZENFIELD, HUGH NORMAN, surgeon; b. Indpls., May 6, 1942; s. Harold Henry and Pearle Esther (Attig) H.; m. Barbara Lynn Shellabarger; Aug. 15, 1964; children—Anthony Michael, Andrew Bradley. B.A., U. Chgo., 1964, M.D., 1968. Diplomate Am. Bd. Otolaryngology. Chmn., div. otolaryngology Cook County Hosp., 1975-79, assoc. med. dir., 1978-79; chmn., div. otolaryngology Michael Reese Hosp., Chgo., 1979-84; attending surgeon Children's Meml. Hosp., Chgo., 1976—; cons. Larabida Hosp., Chgo., 1984—. Contbr. articles to med. jours. Mem. bd. St. Mary's Sch., Evanston, Ill., 1981-84. Served with USN, 1969-71. Fellow Am. Acad. Otolaryngology, ACS, Pan Am. Oto-Rhino-Laryngology, Chgo. Laryngological and Otological Soc. Avocations: computer science; sailing; classical music. Home: 314 Lake St Evanston IL 60201 Office: Michael Reese Hosp and Medical Ctr Lake Shore Dr at 31st St Chicago IL 60616

HAZLETON, BART COLIN, instruments manufacturing company executive; b. Phila., Feb. 20, 1939; s. Samuel Houston and Sara (Frances) H.; m. Ann Carroll, Mar. 18, 1967; children—Tracy, Christopher. B.A., U. Mich., 1962; German Lang. diploma Goethe Inst. (W.Ger.). With 3M Co., 1969-79, regional sales mgr. traffic control products dept., St. Paul, 1971-76, nat. sales mgr. visual products div., St. Paul, 1976-79; pres. Bison Instruments Inc., Mpls., 1979—, also dir.; dir. Midwest China Ctr., Mpls. Soccer coach Burnsville Athletic Assn. (Minn.), 1977-82; pres. Home Owners Assn., Burnsville, 1981-83; active local Boy Scouts Am. Served as lt. USN, 1963-67. Named Regional Salesman of Yr., visual products div. 3M Co., 1969, 70. Mem. Soc. Engrng. Geophysicists (affiliate), Am. Electronics Assn. (chmn. capital caucus com.). Avocations: tennis, skiing, fishing, running. Home: 2804 Bryce Ct Burnsville MN 55337 Office: Bison Instruments Inc 5708 W 36th St Minneapolis MN 55416

HAZZARD, ROBERT CHARLES, osteopathic physician, surgeon, consultant; b. Grand Rapids, Mich., Sept. 7, 1935; s. John William and Lucille Adel (Gaudio) H.; m. Mary Louise Hamlin, Apr. 26, 1974; children—Anne, Kristen, AnnMary. B.S., Aquinas Coll., 1963; D.O., Chgo. Coll. Osteo. Medicine, 1971. Intern, Grand Rapids Osteo. Hosp., 1972; gen. practice osteo. medicine, Saranac, Mich.; assoc. prof. clin. medicine Mich. State U. Coll. Osteo.

Medicine; cons. aerospace medicine. Bd. dirs. YMCA; leadership mem. Boy Scouts Am. Served with USN, 1954-58; USNR, 1979-81. Mem. Am. Osteo. Assn., Mich. Osteo. Assn., Wayne County Osteo. Assn., Aerospace Med. Assn., Am. Coll. Gen. Practitioners. Roman Catholic. Club: Peninsular. Lodge: Elks. Address: 4550 S Morrison Lake Rd Saranac MI 48881

HEACOX, JOHN LARRY, educator; b. Sikeston, Mo., Oct. 4, 1946; s. Eual W. and Lillas Geneva (Triplett) H.; m. Cathy Jean Rabaduex, Aug. 30, 1969; children—Kristopher, Bradley, Jeffrey. B.S. in Edn., Southeast Mo. U., 1968; M.Ed., Central Mo. U., 1982. Tchr., coordinator mktg. Sikeston (Mo.) Sr. High Sch., 1968—. First v.p. Three Rivers Muscular Dystrophy Assn., 1982-83; deacon, tchr. Sikeston 1st Baptist Ch.; recreation dir. for youth, Sikeston, Mo., summers, 1980—; pres. Dist. 12 Distributive Edn., 1985-86; bd. dirs. Little Piece of Heaven youth home. Recipient Outstanding Service awards Muscular Dystrophy Assn., 1980-83. Coach of Yr., 1976. Mem. Am. Vocat. Assn., Mo. Vocat. Assn., Mo. Tchrs. Assn., Nat. Assn. Ditributive Edn. Tchrs. Baptist. Club: Distributive Edn. of Am. Office: 200 S Pine St Sikeston MO 63801

HEAD, THOMAS FRANKLIN, consulting petroleum geologist; b. San Angelo, Tex., May 12, 1914; s. Thomas Hanson and Nettie Kathryn (Griffin) H.; m. Bonnie Jean Harrison, Aug. 12, 1943; children—Thomas Harrison, Lisa Ann, William Alan. B.Sc., U. Tex.-Austin, 1940, M.A., 1948. Cert. petroleum geologist. Field surveyor Petty Geol. Engring. Co., San Antonio, 1940-41, computer operator, 1946-47; dist. geologist Marathon Oil Co., West Tex., Can., 1948-66; div. mgr. exploration Pennzoil Co., Can., U.S., 1966-79; cons. geologist, Hebron, Nebr., 1979-84; assoc. cons. Backlund Engring., Omaha, 1984—; guest lectr. Marietta Coll., Ohio, 1977. Served to capt. USAF, 1941-46. Mem. Am. Assn. Petroleum Geologists. Republican. Episcopalian. Lodge: Rotary (pres. 1984-85). Avocations: golf; racquetball; travel. Home: 825 Union Ave Hebron NE 68370

HEADLEE, WILLIAM HUGH, emeritus educator; b. Morristown, Ind., June 15, 1907; s. Walter C. and Nellie Ann (Adams) H.; A.B., Earlham Coll., 1929; M.S. (Rockefeller Found. fellow), U. Ill., 1933; Ph.D. (Rockefeller Found. fellow), Tulane U., 1935; cert. of proficiency in tropical and mil. medicine Army Med. Sch., 1943; m. Gabrielle Mills, Aug. 4, 1937; children—Joan (Mrs. Charles Barrett Bowden), Anne. Instr. biology Am. U., Cairo, Egypt, 1929-31; research asst. internat. health div. Rockefeller Found., Cairo, 1930-32; asst. prin. Friendsville Acad., Tenn., 1933-34; instr. biology Purdue U., 1935-42, asst. prof. zoology, 1942-43; asst. prof. parasitic diseases Ind. U. Sch. Medicine, Indpls., 1943-46, asso. prof., 1946-53, prof. Grad. Sch., 1953-77, prof. emeritus, 1977—, parliamentarian of faculty, 1973-75, sec., 1973-74, exec. sec., 1974-75; dir. Parasitology Diagnostic Lab., Ind. U. Med. Ctr., 1943-57; cons. parasitologist dept. dermatology Indpls. Gen. Hosp., 1946-57; mem. faculty council Ind. U.-Purdue U.-Indpls., 1973-75, chmn. faculty bd. rev., 1974-75; chmn. dept. biology Nat. Pedagogic Inst., Caracas, Venezuela, 1937-38; sr. scientist USPHS Res., 1953-71; attache, med. parasitologist U.S. ops. mission Fgn. Ops. Adminstrn., Am. embassy, Bangkok, 1953-55; vis. prof. med. parasitology Sch. of Medicine, Chulalongkorn U. and Thailand Sch. Public Health, Bangkok, 1953-55; U.S. del. to 9th Pacific Sci. Congress, Bangkok, 1957; coordinator, dir. Ind. U.-AID, Pakistan Project to develop Jinnah Postgrad. Med. Center, 1957-66; asso. dir. Div. Allied Health Scis., Ind. U. Sch. Medicine, 1968; cons. epidemiologist Ind. Regional Med. Program, 1969-77. Bd. dirs. Central Ind. Council on Aging, 1979-82, mem. nominating com., 1979, long range planning com., 1979—; mem. Older Hoosiers Assembly of Commn. on Aging of State of Ind., 1977—, mem. aging network legis. com., steering com., 1978—; mem. Mayor's Adv. Com. on Aging and the Aged, Indpls., 1978-81; bd. dirs. Marion County Council on Aging, 1978-81; adv. council Ind. U. Center on Aging and Aged. Recipient Arts and Humanities award Shelbyville (Ind.) Rotary Club, 1980; John and Mary Markle Found. fellow, 1943, 44. Emeritus fellow AAAS (life, council 1957-62), Ind. Acad. Sci. (exec. com. 1944, chmn. zoology sect. 1944, mem. membership com. 1950-60, fellows com. 1972-77), Royal Soc. Tropical Medicine and Hygiene; emeritus mem. AAUP (sec.-treas. Ind. Conf. 1972-73, pres. 1974-75, Disting. Mem. award 1976), Am. Soc. Parasitologists (sr.; com. on hon. and emeritus mems. 1967), Am. Soc. Tropical Medicine and Hygiene (emeritus; program com. 1959, 60, nominating com. 1971), Sigma Xi (emeritus); mem. Soc. Internat. Devel., Internat. Coll. Tropical Medicine, Nat. Council on Aging, Nat. Ret. Tchrs. Assn., Ret. Profs. Ind., Soc. Ret. Execs., Am. Assn. Ret. Persons, Ind. Partners of Ams. (dir. 1978—), Tulane U. Med. Alumni Assn. (life mem.), Phi Sigma. Unitarian (bd. trustees 1953, 70-73, chmn. nominating com. 1970-71). Clubs: Ind. U. Emeritus, Earlham Coll. Emeritus. Contbr. numerous articles on epidemiology of parasite infections, med. edn., higher edn. to profl. jours., also poems and miscellaneous articles, manuals. Home: 762 N Riley Ave Indianapolis IN 46201

HEADLEY, KATHRYN WILMA, educator; b. Grand Rapids, Mich., Mar. 10, 1940; d. William L. and Kathryn (Mekkes) H. B.A., Hope Coll., 1967; M.Ed., Grand Valley Coll., 1981. Cert. tchr., Mich. Missionary, Reformed Ch. in Am., N.Y.C., summers, 1959-64; various ch. positions Ottawa Reformed Ch., West Olive, Mich., 1956—, Bible day camp dir., 1979—; tchr. English and phys. edn. Jenison Pub. Schs. (Mich.), 1967—, head coach girls basketball, volleyball, 1967-78, head coach girls track, softball, 1967-73, head coach girls bowling, 1973-78, class advisor, 1983—, numerous other sch. activities. coach girls soccer, basketball, Borculo Christian Sch., Mich., 1981—. Bd. dirs. Ottawa County Tchrs. Credit Union, Grand Haven, Mich., 1978—, v.p., 1984—. Mem. Mich. Edn. Assn. (rep.), NEA, Jenison Edn. Assn. (rep.), Mich. High Sch. Athletic Assn. (ofcl.), Hope Coll. Alumni Assn., Mich. Christian Endeavor Bd. (various offices), Delta Kappa Gamma (corr. sec. 1982—, various offices). Mem. Reformed Ch. in Am. Home: 9111 96th Ave Rural Route 1 Zeeland MI 49464 Office: Jenison Pub Schs 2140 Bauer Rd Jenison MI 49428

HEADLEY, LOUIS ALAN, hotel deskman, actor, poet; b. Ft. Sill, Okla.; s. Harry and Rachael Elizabeth (Patterson) H. Student, Chgo. Acad., 1949-51, Actors Co., 1950, Sch. of Radio Technique, 1952. Actor, many stage and screen plays; poet; impressionist; writer; soloist; deskman Phelps Townhouse, Cin., 1977—; dir., writer YMCA Hotel, Chgo., 1949-51. Served with USN, 1941-44, PTO. Mem. AFTRA, Screen Actors Guild. Home: 506 E Fourth St Cincinnati OH 45202

HEADRICK, JOHN ANDERSON, physician; b. Arbyrd, Mo., July 25, 1931; s. Elmer A. and Opal Marie (Shands) H.; A.B. with honors, Washington U., St. Louis, 1954, M.D., 1958; m. Barbara Ruth Hammond, June 9, 1956; children—John Anderson, Dean A. Intern, St. Luke's Hosp., St. Louis, 1958-59, resident, 1959-62; practice medicine, specializing in internal medicine, St. Louis, 1964-75; v.p. med. affairs Christian Hosps. N.E.-N.W., St. Louis, 1975—; mem. exec. com. Christian Hosp. N.W., 1969, asso. chief staff, 1974, chief staff, 1975; instr. clin. medicine Washington U. Sch. Medicine, St. Louis, 1964-68; cons. cardiology Service Mil. Acad. Bds., 1962-64; mem. adv. bd. Mo. Bapt. Hosp., 1970-75. Bd. mgrs. North County YMCA, St. Louis, 1976—; mem. adv. bd. St. Louis Jr. Coll. Dist., 1964-67. Served with U.S. Army, 1962-64. Diplomate Am. Bd. Internal Medicine. Mem. A.C.P., Am. Soc. Internal Medicine, AMA, Am. Acad. Med. Dirs., Mo. Med. Assn., St. Louis Met. Med. Soc., N.Y. Acad. Scis., AAAS, Inst. for Critical Care Medicine, Soc. for Critical Care Medicine, Am. Coll. Physician Execs. Lodge: Florissant Rotary. Home: 24 Lourdes Ct Lake Saint Louis MO 63367 Office: 11133 Dunn Rd Saint Louis MO 63136

HEALD, RAYMOND RUSSELL, educator, journalist; b. Kalamazoo, Jan. 14, 1940; s. James Russell and Marie Frances (Weyland) H.; m. Eleanor O'Neill, Aug. 5, 1969. B.S., U. Mich., 1963; M.S. in Chemistry, Simmons Coll., 1970. Cert. secondary tchr., Mich. Chemistry tchr. Royal Oak Pub. Schs., Mich., 1963—, head sci. dept., 1978—; wine columnist Ann Arbor News, Mich., 1982—; staff writer Practical Winery, San Rafael, Calif., 1983—. Contbr. chemistry articles to profl. jours. Recipient Internat. Italian Wine Journalism award, 1984. Mem. Nat. Sci. Tchrs. Assn., NEA, Mich. Edn. Assn., Royal Oak Edn. Assn., Soc. Wine Educators, Am. Wine Soc. (v.p. 1978—), Les Amis du Vin. Presbyterian. Avocations: wine writing; wine education; golf. Home: 3222 Vinsetta Blvd Royal Oak MI 48073 Office: Royal Oak Public Schs 1123 Lexington Blvd Royal Oak MI 48073

HEALY, THOMAS MARTIN, manufacturing company executive; b. Milw., May 9, 1921; s. Thomas and Helen (Galewski) H.; m. Ruth Marcella Johnson, Jan. 30, 1943; children—Kathleen Healy Brey, Maureen Ann Warzon, Timothy James, Eileen Marie, Daniel Michael. Student Milw. Area Tech. Sch., 1945-48; student U. Wisc., 1948-49. Draftsman, Norberg Mfg., Milw., 1946-50; designer Allis-Chalmers Co., Milw., 1950-52; engring. rep. Oilgear Co., Milw., 1952-59; mgr. Houston office, 1959-63, mgr. speciality sales, 1963-73, mgr. corp. devel., 1973-83, v.p. corp. devel., 1984—, also dir. Mem. Campaigner Rep. Nat. Com. Served as non-commissioned officer USN, 1943-45, PTO. Mem. Nat. Assn. Mfrs. (nat. com.), Am. Mgmt. Assn., World Future Soc., Roman Catholic. Avocations: travel, philosophy, bus. and profl. ethics. Office: The Oilgear Co 2300 S 51st St Milwaukee WI 53219

HEANEY, GERALD WILLIAM, U.S. judge; b. Goodhue, Minn., Jan. 29, 1918; s. William J. and Johanna (Ryan) H.; student St. Thomas Coll., 1935-37; B.S.L., U. Minn., 1939, LL.B., 1941; m. Eleanor R. Schmitt, Dec. 1, 1945; children—William M., Carol J. Admitted to Minn. bar, 1941; lawyer securities div. Dept. of Commerce Minn., 1941-42; mem. firm Lewis, Hammer, Heaney, Weyl & Halverson, Duluth, 1946-66; judge 8th Jud. Circuit, U.S. Court Appeals, 1966—. Mem. Dem. Nat. Com. from Minn., 1955. Bd. regents U. Minn., 1964-65. Served from pvt. to capt., AUS, 1942-46. Mem. Am., Minn. bar assns. Roman Catholic. Office: US Court of Appeals Duluth MN 55802*

HEARD, WILLIAM ROBERT, insurance company executive; b. Indpls., Apr. 25, 1925; s. French and Estelle (Austin) H.; student Ind. U.; m. Virginia Ann Patrick, Feb. 6, 1951; children—Cynthia Ann, William Robert, II. With Grain Dealers Mut. Ins. Co., 1948, exec. v.p., Indpls., 1978-79, pres., chief exec. officer, dir., 1979—; pres., chief exec. officer, dir. Companion Ins. Co., 1979—; vice chmn., dir. Alliance Am. Insurers; chmn., exec. com. IRM; pres., dir. Grain Dealers Mut. Agy., Inc.; chmn. bd. 15 N. Broadway Corp. Served with USNR, 1942-46. Mem. Assn. Mill and Elevator Ins. Cos. (chmn., dir.), Ins. Inst. Ind. (dir., exec. com.), Mut. Reins. Bur. (dir., exec. com.), Better Bus. Bur. (dir.), Excess of Loss Assn. (vice chmn., dir.), Sales and Mktg. Execs. Indpls. (past pres.), Sales and Mktg. Execs. Internat. (past dir.), Fla. 1752 Club (past pres.), Ind. Insurors Assn. (dir.), Hoosierland Rating Bur. (dir.), Ind. Mill and Elevator Rating Bur. (dir.), Ins. Claims Service (dir.), Property Loss Research Bur. (dir., chmn.), Mill and Elevator Rating Bur. (dir.), Mill and Elevator Fire Prevention Bur. (dir.), Econ. Club of Indpls., Am. Legion, Hon. Order Ky. Cols., Pi Sigma Epsilon. Club: Indpl. Skyline. Office: 1752 N Meridian St Indianapolis IN 46202

HEATH, GEORGE FREMONT, business executive, rancher; b. St. Louis, Aug. 15, 1907; s. George Baldwin and Jennie Bell (Jones) H.; B.S. in Civil Engring., Mo. Sch. Mines, 1930; LL.B., Benton Coll. Law, 1936; m. Frances Jackson; children—Susan, Sarah, George Fremont. Engr., James A. Hooke & Assos., St. Louis, 1930-34; sales engr., asst. sales mgr. Laclede Steel Co., St. Louis, 1934-40; sales mgr. Cleve. Worm & Gear Corp., Farval Corp., Cleve., 1940-46; owner Geo. F. Heath Co., Inc., St. Louis, 1946—; pres. Continental Pump Co., Lancer Equipment Co., Heartland, Inc., House of Heath, Inc., Vari-Master, Inc., Fremont Investments, Inc.; breeder Polled Hereford cattle on Hickory Heath Ranch, 1946—. Mem. St. Louis C. of C., Theta Tau, Sigma Nu. Republican. Clubs: Engineers, World Trade (St. Louis). Home: Route 3 Box 103 Warrenton MO 63383 Office: 11811 Westline Industrial Dr Saint Louis MO 63146

HEATH, MARIWYN DWYER, legislative issues cons.; b. Chgo., May 1, 1935; d. Thomas Leo and Winifred (Brennan) Dwyer; B.J., U. Mo., 1956; m. Eugene R. Heath, Sept. 3, 1956; children—Philip Clayton, Jeffrey Thomas. Mng. editor Chemung Valley Reporter, Horseheads, N.Y., 1956-57; self-employed freelance writer, platform speaker, editor Tech. Transls., Dayton, Ohio, 1966—; cons. Internat. Women's Commn., 1975-76; ERA coordinator Nat. Fedn. Bus. and Profl. Women's Clubs, 1974-82; mem. polit. and mgmt. coms. ERAmerica, 1976-82, exec. dir., 1982—; mem. Gov. Ohio Task Force Credit for Women, 1973; mem. Midwest regional adv. com. SBA, 1976-82; chmn. Ohio Coalition ERA Implementation, 1974-75. Bd. dirs. Dayton YWCA, 1968-74. Recipient various service awards; named One of 10 Outstanding Women of World, Soroptimist Internat., 1982. Mem. AAUW (dir. Dayton 1965-72; Woman of Year award Dayton 1974), Nat. Fedn. Bus. and Profl. Women's Clubs (pres. Dayton 1967-69, Ohio 1976-77; Woman of Year award Dayton 1974, Ohio 1974), Ohio Women (v.p. 1983—), Assn. Women Execs., Women in Communications. Republican. Roman Catholic. Address: 10 Wisteria Dr Dayton OH 45419

HEATHERLY, JAMES PATRICK, retail company executive; b. Chgo., Feb. 10, 1949; s. William A. and Annamae (Breslin) H.; B.A. in English, DePaul U., 1977, M.B.A. in Mktg., 1980, postgrad. in computer scis.; m. Nona Mangrum, Aug. 16, 1980; children—James, Wendy Melissa, Sean Michael, Scott Owen. Account exec. Ill. Bell Tel., Chgo., 1969-79; communications cons. Omni Group, Chgo., 1979-80; communications cons. Robert Donahue & Assos., Oakbrook, Ill., 1980-81; dir. corp. communications Carson Pirie Scott & Co., Chgo., 1981-83; bus., systems mgr. Montgomery Ward, Chgo., 1983-84; corporate telecommunications network mgr., 1984—; assoc. dir. telecommunications program. DePaul U., Chgo. Author: Telecommunications Management: A Practical Approach, 1986. Contbr. articles to profl. jours. Active Oak Forest Baseball Assn. (award 1983-84); mem. Chgo. Council on Foreign Relations. Mem. Chgo. Indsl. Communications Assn., Am. Mktg. Assn. (award 1982), Am. Mgmt. Assn., Internat. Communications Assn. (mem. seminar/conv. coms.). Roman Catholic. Office: One Montgomery Ward Plaza Chicago IL 60671

HEATHERSON, DAN MAURICE, mfg. co. exec.; b. La Porte, Ind., Feb. 4, 1947; s. Hugh Maurice and Florence Evelyn (Brady) H.; B.S. in Indsl. Mgmt., Purdue U., 1970; m. Patricia Louise Fogarty, Sept. 2, 1967; children—Jacqueline Anne, Danny Maurice, Michele Lee. Sect. indsl. engr. Colgate-Palmolive Co., Jeffersonville, Ind., 1970-71; sr. indsl. engr. AC Spark Plug div. Gen. Motors Corp., Flint, Mich., 1971-73; sr. indsl. engr. Joy Mfg. Co., Michigan City, Ind., 1974-76, mgr. mfg. engring., 1978-79, mgr. prodn. planning, 1979-82, mgr. prodn. planning and control, 1982-83, mgr. mfg. engring., 1983—; prodn. mgr. Penn Athletic Products Co., Phoenix, 1976-78. Founder, bd. dirs. Greater La Porte (Ind.) Pop Warner Football Assn., Inc., also head coach; past pres. Lake Porter Pop Warner Football Conf.; head coach La Porte Babe Ruth Baseball. Served with USMC, 1968. Mem. Am. Prodn. and Inventory Control Soc., Nat. Mgmt. Assn. (dir. 1979-80). Roman Catholic. Club: Elks. Home: 403 Sunrise Blvd La Porte IN 46350 Office: 900 Woodland Ave Michigan City IN 46360

HEATON, CHARLES LLOYD, dermatologist, educator; b. Bryan, Tex., May 8, 1935; s. Homer Lloyd and Bessie Blanton (Sharp) H.; B.S., Tex. A&M U., 1957; M.D., Baylor U., 1961; M.A. (hon.), U. Pa., 1973. Intern, Jefferson Davis Hosp., Houston, 1961-62; resident Baylor U., 1962-65; sr. attending physician Phila. Gen. Hosp., 1965-69, chief of service, 1970-77; mem. dept. dermatology U. Pa. Sch. Medicine 66-78; asso. prof. dermatology U. Pa., 1973-78; assoc. prof. dermatology U. Cin., 1978-85, prof., 1985—. Served to lt. comdr. USPHS, 1965-67. Diplomate Am. Bd. Dermatology. Fellow Coll. Physicians of Phila., ACP; mem. AMA, Soc. Investigative Dermatology, Am. Venereal Disease Assn., Am. Dermatol. Assn., Cin. Dermatol. Soc. Author: Audiovisual Course in Venereal Disease, 1972; Chancroid: Current Therapy, 1975; (with D.M. Pillsbury) Manual of Dermatology, 1980; contbr. papers to profl. jours. Home: 5534 E Galbraith Rd Apt 25 Cincinnati OH 45236 Office: U Cin Coll Medicine Dept Dermatology 231 Bethesda Ave Cincinnati OH 45267

HEATON, JAMES WARDEN, management company executive; b. Clarksburg, W.Va., Jan. 21, 1952; s. Hiram Hayward and Rose Marie (Bramer) H.; m. Linda Marie Kline, Apr. 11, 1973; children—Robert D., Mary R., Joseph D. Officer Massillon Police Dept., Ohio, 1980-83, chief exec. officer, pres. Harrington & Rhodes, Massillon, 1983—; chmn. bd. Becker Mgmt. Inc., Massillon. Founder internat. police liaison team in Europe, 1977-79, Bowerston Police Dept., Ohio, 1980; co-founder United Vietnam Vets. Inc., Stark County, Ohio, 1982, exec. dir. Ohio Mil. Mus., 1984-85; mem. steering com. Ohio N.G. Territorial Militia Mus., 1984-85; founder Stark County Polit. Action Com., Massillon, 1984. Served as sgt. U.S. Army, 1972-80. Mem. Fraternal Order Police, Am. Fedn. Police, Am. Assn. Fin. Profls., Police Patrol Officers Assn. (pres.), Ohio Soc. Mil. History (co-founder), VFW, Am. Vets.(steering com.). Republican. Baptist. Home: 601 Amherst St SW Navarre OH 44662 Office: Becker Mgmt Assocs Inc 316 Lincoln Way E Massillon OH 44646

HEATON, MONICA BAYER, communications executive; b. Louisville, Mar. 5, 1951; d. Ralph Joseph and Catherine Anna (Hanley) Bayer; m. Gary Howard Heaton, Oct. 8, 1977; children—Margeaux, Meredith. B.A., U. Iowa, 1973. Reporter, Times, Hammond, Ind., 1973, Herald-News, Joliet, Ill., 1973-74; city editor Compass, Hammond, 1974-75; asst. city editor Jour.-Register, Springfield, Ill., 1975-77; regional copy chief Globe-Democrat, St. Louis, 1978-80; dir. pub. relations Catholic Health Assn. U.S., St. Louis, 1980—. Recipient first place award Internat. Assn. Firefighters media awards, 1977. Mem. Women in Communications, Inc. (outstanding sr. 1973, founding pres. Springfield chpt. 1977), Pub. Relations Soc. Am., Internat. Assn. Bus. Communicators (Gold Quill 1984), Am. Soc. Assn. Execs., Religious Pub. Relations Council (award of excellence 1984), Kappa Tau Alpha. Office: Cath Health Assn US 4455 Woodson Rd Saint Louis MO 63134

HEAVEN, DONALD LEE, research administrator; b. Grand Rapids, Mich., Apr. 4, 1942; s. Milton Leroy and Ethlyn (Wride) H.; m. Mary Kay Scripps, Sept. 15, 1962; children—Gail S., Gerald L., Douglas J., Joy A. B.S. in Bus. Adminstrn., Aquinas Coll., 1976; student Hiram Coll., 1960-61. Accounts payable supr. Interstate Motor Freight, Grand Rapids, Mich., 1962-65; accounts payable supr. Lear Jet, Grand Rapids, 1966-67; cost acct. Attwood Corp., Lowell, Mich., 1967-69; research cost analyst Gerber Products Co., Fremont, Mich., 1969-72, mgr. research adminstrn., 1972—. Bd. dirs. Stage Door Players, Fremont, Mich., 1977—. Mem. Soc. Research Adminstrs. Republican. Presbyterian. Lodges: Lions (pres.), Masons (sr. deacon). Home: 6823 Groesbeck Hesperia MI 49421 Office: Gerber Products Co 445 State St Fremont MI 49412

HEAVENRICH, HERBERT SAMUEL, management consultant; b. Omaha, Nebr., Oct. 13, 1922; s. Herbert Samuel and Sadie (Kirschbraun) H.; B.S.E., U. Mich., 1943; M.B.A., U. Chgo., 1953; postgrad. U. Wis., 1967-69; m. Jill Sherry, Apr. 26, 1954; children—Hope, Amy, Hollis, Avery, Adam. Research asst. Bemis Found., M.I.T., Cambridge, 1946-48; with HUD, Washington, 1950-52; builder, Milw., 1952-54; asst. to pres. Am. Houses Inc., N.Y.C., 1954-56; v.p., dir. Mortgage Assos., Inc., Milw., 1957-66; program dir. Big 10 Univ. Consortium on Pub. Policy, Econ. Growth & Tech., Madison, Wis., 1966-68; dir. city planning City of Milw., 1968-75; v.p. Anderson/Roethle Inc., Milw., 1975—; dir., owner Heavenrich & Co., Inc., 1980—. Bd. dirs. Milw. Mental Health Cons., Inc., 1980—; bd. dirs., treas. Milw. Urban League, 1960-66; pres. Republican Workshop of Wis., 1960-64. Served as lt. (j.g.) USNR, 1944-46. Bemis Found. grantee, 1949. Mem. Inst. Mgmt. Cons. Jewish. Club: Univ. (Milw.). Contbr. articles to profl. jours. Home: 2443 N Wahl Ave Milwaukee WI 53211 Office: 811 E Wisconsin Ave Milwaukee WI 53202

HEAVILIN, JOHN KEITH, clergyman, educator; b. Marion, Ind., Feb. 7, 1929; s. McClellan Warren and Vera (Foster) H.; m. Beulah Mae Butcher, Aug. 12, 1952; children—Keetha Denise Heavilin Broyles, Pamela Rachelle Heavilin Holloway. A.B. magna cum laude, Marion Coll., 1951, Th.B., 1952; M.A. magna cum laude, 1982; post-grad. U. Wis., 1952-55, U. Wis.-Superior, 1957-58. Ordained to ministry Wesleyan Ch., 1954. Tchr. various high schs., Wis., 1952-72; pastor Wesleyan Ch., Wesleyan Ch., Springbrook, Wis., 1952-59, Spooner, Wis., 1955-59, Hayward, Wis., 1959-65, Wisconsin Rapids, Wis., 1965-72; pres. youth Wis. Dist. Wesleyan Ch., 1953-56, asst. supt., 1960-68, supt., 1970-77; trustee Marion Coll. Ind., 1970-77, 80, assoc. Instl. Advancement, 1977—. Editor monthly newsletter Wis. Wesleyan, 1959-70, quar. bull. The Triangle, 1980—, Marion Coll. jour., 1950-51. Mem. Assn. Instl. Advancement Officers, Ind. Council Advancement and Support Edn., Marion Area Ministerial Assn. Avocations: Gardening, hand bell player, reading, writing. Home: 4012 S Adams St Marion IN 46953 Office: Marion Colle 4201 S Washington St Marion IN 46953

HEBBRING, JUDITH BEVERLY, association executive, magazine editor; b. Chgo., May 3, 1944; d. Andrew Leroy and Ingeborg (Brehm) Smith; m. Vernon Edward Stratton, Feb. 28, 1965; children—Cinthy, Sheri, Vernon; m. Kelly Joseph Hebbring, July 7, 1977 (dec. 1984). Mgr. Custer County (S.D.) C. of C., 1976-77; sec.-treas. Nat. Buffalo Assn., Custer, S.D., 1977-78, exec. dir., editor Buffalo mag., 1978—. Recipient Theodore Roosevelt Conservation award Old West Trail Found., 1980. Mem. U.S. Animal Health Assn., Custer C. of C. (bd. dirs.), Bus. and Profl. Women (chmn. county-level polit. campaign 1982). Republican. Author: Buffalo Cookbook, 1981; co-author: Buffalo Management and Marketing, 1983; contbr. articles on buffalo management-husbandry to newspapers and profl. jours. Home: PO Box 223 Pierre SD 57501 Office: 10 E Main St Fort Pierre SD 57532

HEBDA, CYNTHIA RUTA, hospital personnel administrator; b. Jamestown, N.Y., Apr. 14, 1956; d. J. Arthur and Alma (Vacietis) Aizkalns; m. Lawrence John Hebda, June 17, 1978. B.A. in Mass Communications, Purdue U., 1978. Personnel asst. Lutheran Hosp., Moline, Ill., 1978-80, dir. human resources, 1980—, facilitator quality circle program, 1982—, coordinator employee assistance program, 1984—; tchr. motivational dynamics, 1980—; instr. classes on union activity and the law. Mem. adv. bd. St. Ambrose Coll., Davenport, Iowa, 1980-81; mem. planning and allocations com. United Way, 1982; mem. grievance panel for employees State of Ill.; mem. speakers bur. Lutheran Health Care Found. Mem. Am. Soc. Hosp. Personnel Adminstrn., Purdue Alumni Assn., Phi Mu, Delta Epsilon. Office: Lutheran Hosp 501 10th Ave Moline IL 61265

HEBERT, MARY OLIVIA, librarian; b. St. Louis, Nov. 11, 1921; d. Arthur Frederick and Clara Marie (Golden) Meyer; certificate librarianship, Washington U., St. Louis, 1972; m. N. Hal Hebert, Sept. 9, 1943 (dec. Mar. 1969); children—Olivia, Stephen, Christina, Deborah, Beth, John, James. Secretarial positions in advt., 1942-43; v.p. Hebert Advt. Co., 1955-66; adminstrv. asst. communications Blue Cross, St. Louis, 1966-69, librarian, 1969—. Mem. Spl. Libraries Assn. (pres. St. Louis Metro chpt. 1984), St. Louis Med. Librarians. Roman Catholic. Office: 4444 Forest Park Blvd Saint Louis MO 63108

HECK, GRACE FERN, lawyer; b. Tremont City, Ohio, Nov. 13, 1905; d. Thomas J. and Mary Etta (Maxson) H.; m. Leo H. Faust, May 25, 1977. B.A. cum laude, Ohio State U., 1928, J.D. summa cum laude, 1930. Bar: Ohio 1930, U.S. Dist. Ct. (so. dist.) Ohio 1932; U.S. Supreme Ct. 1960. Researcher, Nat. Commn. Law Observance and Enforcement, U.S. Dist. Ct. (so. dist.) Ohio, 1930-31, Ohio Judicial Council and Law Inst. Johns Hopkins U., 1931-32; prosecuting atty. Champaign County, Urbana, Ohio, 1933-37; sole practice, Urbana, 1937-43, 73-85, Springfield, 1943-73; mcpl. judge Champaign County, 1954-58. Exec. sec. War Price and Rationing Bd., Urbana, 1941-43; bd. trustees Spring Grove Cemetery Assn., 1954—; sec. bd. trustees Magnetic Springs Found., Ohio, 1957-62; pres. Ohio State U., Coll. Law Alumni Assn., Columbus, 1971-72; mem. Nat. Council Coll. Law, Ohio State U. Columbus, 1971—. Recipient Disting. Service award Ohio State U., 1971. Mem. Ohio State Bar Assn. (com. mem.), Champaign County Bar and Law Library Assn. (pres. 1965), Springfield Bar and Law library Assn. (sec. 1946-59, pres. 1963), ABA, Ohio State U. Alumni Assn. (2d v.p. 1956-58, adv. bd. 1962-73, Alumni Centennial award 1970, Order of Coif, Phi Beta Kappa, Zeta Tau Alpha, Kappa Beta Pi, Delta Theta Tau (nat. v.p. 1940-41, nat. pres. 1941-42, bd. trustees 1942-45). Democrat. Methodist. Clubs: Springfield Country (Ohio); Troy Country (Ohio); Altrusa. Lodge: Order of Eastern Star. Avocations: fishing; hunting; travel; photography; gravestone rubbings. Home: 134 W Church St Urbana OH 43078

HECKADON, ROBERT GORDON, plastic surgeon; b. Brantford, Ont., Can., Jan. 30, 1933; s. Frederick Gordon and Laura (Penrose) H.; B.A., U. Western Ont., 1954, M.D., 1960; postgrad. U. Toronto, 1960-66, U. Vienna, 1966; m. Camilla Joyce Russell, July 11, 1959; children—David, Louise, Peter, William, Barbara. Intern, Toronto Gen. Hosp., 1960-61; asst. resident Toronto Western Hosp., 1961, Toronto Wellesley Hosp., 1962, Toronto Gen. Hosp., 1962-63; resident in plastic surgery St. Michael's Hosp., Toronto, 1963, Toronto Western Hosp., 1964, Toronto Gen. Hosp., 1964, Toronto Hosp. for Sick Children, 1965; asst. resident orthopedics Toronto East Gen. Hosp., 1965-66; practice medicine specializing in plastic surgery, Windsor, Ont., Can., 1966—; chief med. staff Hotel Dieu; mem. staff Grace Hosp., Met. Hosp. (all Windsor). Served with RCAF, 1951-56. Fellow A.C.S.; mem. Canadian Med. Assn., Ont. Med. Assn., Essex County Med. Assn., Windsor Acad. Surgery, Royal Coll. Physicians and Surgeons, Can. Soc. Plastic Surgeons. Home: 882 Eastlawn St Windsor ON N8S 3H7 Canada Office: 1086 Ouellette Ave Suite 301 Windsor ON Canada

HECKEL, RICHARD WAYNE, metallurgical engineering educator, consultant; b. Pitts., Jan. 25, 1934; s. Ralph Clyde and Esther Vera (Zoerb) H.; m. Peggy Ann Simmons, Jan. 3, 1959; children—Scott Alan, Laura Ann Heckel Rowe. B.S. in Met.E., Carnegie-Mellon U., 1955, M.S., 1958, Ph.D., 1959. Sr. research metall. engr. DuPont, Wilmington, Del., 1959-63; prof. Drexel U., Phila., 1963-71; prof., head dept. metall. and materials sci. Carnegie-Mellon U., Pitts., 1971-76; prof. Mich. Tech. U., Houghton, 1976—; cons. to numerous firms. Contbr. articles to profl. jours. Served to 1st lt. U.S. Army, 1959-60. Recipient Lindback Teaching award Drexel U., 1969; Bradley Stoughton

Young Tchr. of Metall. award Am. Soc. for Metals, 1968; Ednl. Achievement award Phila. chpt. Am. Soc. for Metals, 1970; Adams Meml. Membership award Am. Welding Soc., 1967. Fellow Am. Soc. for Metals; mem. Metals Soc. (Eng.), AAAS, Am. Soc. for Engring. Edn., Metall. Soc. of AIME, Am. Powder Metall. Inst., Nat. Rifle Assn. Republican. Methodist. Club: Great Lakes Cruising (Chgo.). Avocations: Boating; fishing. Home: 1281 Hickory Ln Houghton MI 49931 Office: Mich Tech U Houghton MI 49931

HEDBERG, PAUL CLIFFORD, radio station executive; b. Cokato, Minn., May 28, 1939; s. Clifford L. and Florence (Erenberg) H.; student Hamline U., 1959-60, U. Minn., 1960-62; m. Juliet Ann Schubert, Dec. 30, 1962; children—Mark, Ann. Program dir. radio sta. KRIB, Mason City, Ia., 1957-58, radio sta. WMIN, Mpls., 1959; staff announcer Time-Life broadcast WTCN AM-TV, Mpls., 1959-61, Crowell Collier broadcast radio sta. KDWB, St. Paul, 1961-62; founder, pres. KBEW Radio Blue Earth (Minn.), 1963-81, KQAD Radio AM, KLQL-FM, LuVerne, Minn., 1971—; pres. Sta. KMRS-AM and KKOK-FM, Morris, Minn., 1971—; founder, pres. Blue Earth Cablevision Inc., 1973-82, Courtney Clifford Inc., advt. rep., Mpls., 1977-80; founder, owner Market Quoters, Inc., Blue Earth, 1974—; pres., owner KEEZ-FM, Mankato, Minn., 1977—; founder, v.p. Complete Commodity Options, Mpls., 1980—; founder, pres. Campus Radio Co., Sta. KUOO-FM, Spirit Lake, Iowa, 1983, Motion-Graphics Group, 1983; pres. Musicman Broadcasting Inc., River City Broadcasting Inc., stas. KLSS and KLSS-FM, Mason City, Iowa, 1984—. dir. First Nat. Bank, Blue Earth. Bd. dirs. Minn. Good Roads, v.p., 1976-79, pres., 1979; bd. dirs. Blue Earth Indsl. Service Corp., pres., 1970-76. Served with USCGR, 1962-70. Recipient Distinguished Service award Blue Earth Jaycees, 1971. Mem. Minn. A.P. Broadcasters (pres. 1966, dir. 1976-79), Blue Earth C. of C. (Leadership Recognition award 1967, pres. 1967), Minn. Broadcasters Assn. (pres. 1983-84), Nat. Assn. Broadcasters (dir.), Iowa-Great Lakes C. of C. (dir. 1985—), Iowa Great Lakes Indsl. Commn. (dir. 1985—), Minn. Press Council, Iowa Gt. Lakes C. of C. (bd. dirs.). Lutheran. Lodges: Masons, Shriners, Kiwanis. Home: RR Box 9379 Spirit Lake IA 51360 Office: KUOO Radio Bldg Hwy 9 W PO Box 528 Spirit Lake IA 51360

HEDGCOCK, WILLIAM ROBERT, superintendent schools; b. Paris, Ill., Sept. 3, 1928; s. John Harrison and Virginia (McCaskill) H.; m. Naomi Ruth Harner, May 10, 1953; children—David, Ronald, Todd. B.S., U. Ill., 1951, M.Ed., 1952; postgrad. Ill. State U., 1967-70. Tchr. Rantoul High Sch., Ill., 1959-67; prin. Wapella High Sch., Ill., 1967-82; supt. Wapella Unit Dist., 1982—. Scoutmaster Arrowhead council Boy Scouts Am., 1951-52, 55-67; dir. Clinton Barbershop Chorus, Ill., 1969-78; choir dir. Clinton Presbyterian Ch., 1978—; bd. dirs. DeWitt County Red Cross Bd., Clinton, 1983—. Recipient 20 Yr. Scouter Key award Boy Scouts Am., 1966. Mem. Nat. Assn. Secondary Sch. Prins., Ill. Prins. Assn., Ill. Assn. Sch. Adminstrs. Republican. Presbyterian. Clubs: Soc. for Preservation and Encouragement of Barbershop Quartet Singing in Am. (Urbana, Clinton) (pres. 1962—), Gideons Internat. (Clinton) (sec. 1983—). Lodges: Masons (Jr. Warden 1956—). Served to cpl. U.S. Army, 1952-54. Avocations: barbershop quartet singing.

HEDGE, CYNTHIA ANN, lawyer; b. LaPorte, Ind., June 7, 1952; d. John S. and Edith Rae (Badkey) H. A.B., Ind. U., 1975; J.D., Valparaiso U., 1978. Bar: Ind. 1978, U.S. Dist Ct. (no. dist., so. dist.) Ind. 1978. Staff writer Ind. Dept. Commerce, Indpls., 1975; pub. relations asst. Ravinia Festival, Chgo., 1976; free-lance writer, LaPorte County, Ind., 1978—; dep. pros. atty. LaPorte County, 1978—; sole practice, Michigan City, Ind., 1978—; dir. Michiana Industries, LaPorte County. Chairperson, Child Abuse Adv. Team, LaPorte County, 1982—; mem. bd. Bethany Lutheran Ch., LaPorte, 1982—. Mem. ABA, Ind. Bar Assn., LaPorte County Bar Assn., Michigan City Bar Assn., Christian Legal Soc., Ind. U. Alumni Assn., AAUW. Home: 2912 N Regal Dr LaPorte IN 46350 Office: 601 Franklin Sq Michigan City IN 46360

HEDGEPETH, ROYSTER CROMWELL, fund raising executive; b. Oxford, N.C., Dec. 5, 1944; s. Oliver Cromwell and Helen Lippard (Royster) H.; m. Virgie Mae Duffer, June 10, 1967; children—Ryan Chadler, Stefanie Janel. B.A., Wake Forest Coll., 1967; M.Ed., U. Fla., 1968; Ph.D., Cornell U., 1974. Cert. personnel counselor. Dir. counseling and career planning Hampden-Sydney Coll. (Va.), 1973-76, dir. devel., 1976-77; v.p. instl. advancement Meredith Coll., Raleigh, N.C., 1977-80; dir. devel. U. Ill. Found., Urbana, 1980—; chmn. CASE-Dist. 5, Gt. Lakes Dist., 1984, mem. commn. on dist. relations, Washington, 1983—; trainer CASE, Washington, 1983-84; cons. YMCA, IDF, WEF, Champaign, Ill.; seminar leader. Editor: Vaspa Interchange, 1974-76. Mem. Washington Sch. Found., Champaign, 1983; vol. Champaign Unit 4 Schs., 1983, Emmanuel Episcopal Ch., Champaign, 1981—. Served with U.S. Army, 1969-71. NDEA fellow, 1968; recipient Currin award Wake Forest Coll., 1967. Mem. Council for Advancement and Support of Edn., Am. Mgmt. Assn., Phi Kappa Phi, Phi Delta Kappa. Clubs: Champaign Country; University (Chgo.). Office: U Ill Found 224 Illini Union 1401 W Green St Urbana IL 61801

HEDGES, MARK STEPHEN, clinical psychologist; b. Chgo., Feb. 15, 1950; s. Norman T. and Doris Mae (Walters) H.; B.S., Purdue U., 1972; M.A., U. S.D., 1974, Ph.D., 1977; m. Janice Finnie, Aug. 16, 1975; children—Anna, Miriam. Psychology intern Western Mo. Mental Health Center, Kansas City, 1975-76; coordinator children and adolescent services, psychologist Northeastern Mental Health Center, Aberdeen, S.D., 1977—. Mem. exec. bd. New Beginning Center, 1978—. Mem. Am. Psychol. Assn., Phi Beta Kappa, Psi Chi, Phi Kappa Phi. Methodist. Club: Cosmopolitan. Office: Northeastern Mental Health Center 703 3d Ave SE Aberdeen SD 57401

HEDKE, DENNIS EUGENE, geologist; b. Manhattan, Kans., Oct. 1, 1952; s. Edward Arnold and Ethel Mary (Scott) H.; m. Annette Beame, Aug. 1, 1981; 1 child, Reasha. B.S. in Geophysics, Kans. State U., 1976; M.S. in Materials Sci. and Engring., U. Va., 1979. Cert. profl. geol. scientist. Ind. geologist, Manhattan, 1976-77; staff geologist Inter-Am. Energy Corp., Miami, Fla., 1979-80; hydrogeologist Applied Environ. Services, Miami, 1980-82; exploration mgr. Edco Drilling Co., El Dorado, Kans., 1982—. Mem. Am. Assn. Petroleum Geologists, Am. Inst. Profl. Geologists, Kans. Geol. Soc. Avocations: carpentry; auto mechanics. Home: 8910 E Parkmont Dr Wichita KS 67207

HEDRICH, WILLIAM CLIFFORD, photographer; b. Chgo., June 21, 1912; s. Theodore Louis and Anna Sophia (Knudsen) H.; student U. Ill., 1930-31, Inst. Design, Chgo., 1945-46, U.S. Army Motion Picture Sch., London, 1943; m. Te'a Dora Kre'mer, June 3, 1942; children—Ronald Ted, Paul Scott, Sandi Ann. Partner Hedrich-Blessing Studio, Chgo., 1931-46; chmn. bd. Hedrich-Blessing Ltd., Chgo., 1946-84, also dir.; photographer architecture and interiors, 1931—; one man shows Eastman House Photog. Exhibit, 1981, John Weber Gallery, N.Y.C., 1981; group shows with Hedrich-Blessing, Mich. Sq. Rotunda, Chgo., 1935, Offices Perkins & Will, Chgo., 1967, Archtl. Photographers Am. exhibits, 1946-62, AIA Exhibit, 1978-79, Art Inst. Chgo., 1983, Archicenter (AIA), Chgo., 1983; also represented in permanent collections, including Carnegie Inst. Museum Art; photographs include: Falling Water, a widely pub. archtl. photograph; owner, Hedrich-Blessing Island Homes, St. Maarten, N.A., 1970—; dir. Oyster Pond Devel. Corp., St. Maarten, N.A. Bd. dirs. Golden Sect. Soc., Boy Scouts Am., 1922-25. Served with U.S. Army, 1942-45. Decorated Bronze Star; recipient Gold medal award AIA, 1967, Archtl. Photographers Invitational award Pitts. Plate Glass, 1973, also other awards; named to Photography Hall of Fame, Santa Barbara, Calif., 1978. Mem. Profl. Photographers Am., Chgo. Photog. Guild. Lutheran. Club: South End Gun (Granville, Ill.). Contbr. articles to publs. Office: 11 W Illinois St Chicago IL 60010

HEDRICK, FRANK EDGAR, aircraft company executive; b. Paola, Kans., June 20, 1910; s. Melvin Earl and Hulda Catherine (Mellor) H.; m. Harriet Elizabeth Miller, Sept. 17, 1949; D.B.A. (hons.), Southwestern Coll., 1975. Sales mgr. E.S. Cowie Electric Co., Wichita, Kans., 1935-40; sales mgr. Beech Aircraft Corp., Wichita, 1940-60, asst. to gen. mgr., 1940-45, v.p., coordinator, 1945-60, exec. v.p., 1960-68, pres., 1968-81, vice chmn. bd., chmn. exec. com., 1981-82, dir., chmn. fin. com. and bus. cons., 1982-83, dir. Beech Aircraft and chmn. fin. com., 1983—; dir., mem. fin. com. Raytheon Co.; pres. Hedrick Investments, Inc., 1982—. Mem. Gov.'s Task Force on Effective Mgmt., 1976; pres. Beech Aircraft Found. Named Gen. Aviation Man of Yr., 1976; recipient Golden Plate award Am. Acad. Achievement, 1976; Disting. Donor award Kans. Ind. Coll. Fund, 1982. Mem. Conquistadores del Cielo. Republican. Clubs: Crestview, Wichita Country; Burning Tree (Washington); Garden of Gods (Colorado Springs, Colo.); Cherry Hills Country (Denver).

HEDRICK, ROSS MELVIN, research chemist; b. West Salem, Ill., Apr. 27, 1921; s. Ross Vernon and Nellie Lucinda (Markman) H.; m. Alice Jean Yates, Oct. 8, 1949; children—Robert Melvin, Charles Vernon, Steven Thomas. B.S., U. Ill., 1943; A.M., Ind. U., 1944, Ph.D., 1947. Research chemist Monsanto Co., Dayton, Ohio, 1947-52, group leader, 1952-63; fellow Monsanto Co., St. Louis, 1963-69, sr. fellow, 1969-72, disting. fellow, 1972—. Patentee polymers. Mem. Am. Chem. Soc., AAAS. Avocations: photography; traveling; reading; hiking. Office: Monsanto Co 800 N Lindbergh St Louis MO 63167

HEDSTROM, CHARLES EARL, broadcaster; b. Manistee, Mich., May 13, 1929; s. Carl Erland and Hazel Pearl (Hicking) H.; m. Nancy Martha Leet; children—Charles E., Pamela N. Student Central Mich. U., 1947-49; B.A., Mich. State U., 1956. Dir./producer, ops. dir. NBC, Chgo. and N.Y.C., 1958-60; nat. sales mgr. Nutronics, Chgo., 1956-58; southeastern sales mgr. McGavrin-Guild Co., N.Y.C. and Atlanta, 1960-63; with Avco Corp., Chgo., 1963-69; owner, operator Manistee Radio Corp. (Mich.), 1969—, Coast Broadcasting Corp., Bradenton and Sarasota, Fla., 1982—. Served with U.S. Army, 1950-52. Recipient Dirs. award NBC, 1959. Mem. Nat. Assn. Broadcasters, Radio Advt. Bur. Methodist. Lodges: Masons, Shriners, Elks. Office: 59 Maple St Manistee MI 59660

HEEB, CAMILLE STOREY, physician, educator; b. Brookfield, Mo., May 26, 1944; d. Kenneth Paul and Virginia May (Bailey) Storey; children—Marsha, Sarah. B.A. in Sociology with honors, U. Kans., 1966, M.S. in Spl. Edn., 1967, M.D., 1979. Corrective reading tchr., Chandler, Ariz., 1968-69; ednl. diagnostician Dept. Spl. Edn., Abilene, Tex., 1970-72; staff mem. dept. spl. edn. U. Kans., Lawrence, 1974-76, sponsor student chpt. Council for Exceptional Children; intern and pediatric resident U. Kans. Med. Center, 1979-81; pediatric resident Children's Mercy Hosp., Kansas City, Mo., 1981-82; staff physician Kans. Neurol. Inst., Topeka, 1982-84; pvt. practice, Topeka, Kans., 1984—. U.S. Office Edn./Bur. Handicapped fellow in spl. edn., 1966-67; U. Buffalo research grantee, 1968; recipient Daniel C. Darrow award; Paul Gyorgy award La Leche League. Mem. Council for Exceptional Children, Am. Assn. for Edn. Severely and Prodoundly Handicapped, PEO, AMA, Am. Acad. Pediatrics, Phi Beta Phi. Author: An Oral Language Development Program for the Educable Mentally Retarded, 1969. Home: 3120 W 15th St Topeka KS 66604

HEERMANS, THOMAS WILLISON, industrial designer, design consultant; b. Milw., Apr. 24, 1926; s. Thomas Minton and Vera Rose (Baxter) H.; m. Elizabeth Hobson, June 24, 1950; children—Jill Marie, Thomas Minton, Jody Lynn, Janice Ann, Joy Elizabeth. B.S. in Design, U. Mich., 1961. Project engr. Argus Cameras, Inc., Ann Arbor, Mich., 1952-62; design engr. Hamilton Beach, Racine, Wis., 1962-64; mgr. product planning Ekco Housewares Co., Franklin Park, Ill., 1964-67; dir. indsl. design Regal Ware, Inc., Kewaskum, Wis., 1967—. Patentee in field. Served with USN, 1944-46. Mem. Color Mktg. Group (chairholder 1977—), Soc. Glass Decorators, Assn. Home Appliance Mfrs. (portable appliance engring. com. 1972—). Republican. Episcopalian. Avocations: Fresh water aquarist; audiophile; 35mm photography. Home: 258 Lincoln Dr S West Bend WI 53095 Office: Regal Ware Inc 1675 Reigle Dr Kewaskum WI 53040

HEEZEN, JAY ALLEN, veterinarian, farmer; b. Plankinton, S.D., May 23, 1944; s. Arie Merle and Jesse Evelyn (Harman) H.; m. Darlene E. Bloch, Aug. 29, 1970 (div. Dec. 1979); children—Jon, Jason; m. 2d, Phyllis Kay DeBoer, Jan. 13, 1981; children—Jay, Julie, Jennifer. B.S., U. Minn., 1966, D.V.M., 1968. Veterinarian, Vietnam, 1969-70; pvt. practice veterinary medicine, Plankinton, 1970—. Chmn. Plankinton Sch. Bd. Served to capt. U.S. Army, 1968-70. Bd. dirs. Plankinton Pub. Sch., 1982—. Mem. AVMA, S.D. Vet. Med. Assn., U.S. Assn. Sheep and Goat Practioners, VFW. Democrat. Methodist (tchr. Sunday sch.).

HEFFERN, GORDON E., bank holding company executive; b. 1924. B.S., U. Va., 1949. Pres., chief exec. officer Society Corp., Cleveland, 1974-83, chief operating officer, from 1974, chmn. bd., 1983—, also dir.; chmn. bd., chief operating officer Society Nat. Bank, Cleve. Served with USN. Office: Society Corp 127 Public Square Cleveland OH 44114*

HEFFERNAN, NATHAN STEWART, chief state justice; b. Frederic, Wis., Aug. 6, 1920; s. Jesse Eugene and Pearl Eva (Kaump) H.; B.A., U. Wis., 1942, LL.B., 1948; postgrad. Harvard Bus. Sch., 1943-44; m. Dorothy Hillemann, Apr. 27, 1946; children—Katie Heffernan Thomas, Michael, Thomas. Bar: Wis. 1948. Assoc., Schubring, Ryan, Peterson & Sutherland, Madison, 1948-49; counsel Wis. League Municipalities, 1949; research asst. to Gov. Wis., 1949; pvt. practice law, Sheboygan, Wis., 1949-59; ptnr. Buchen & Heffernan, 1951-59; asst. dist. atty. Sheboygan County (Wis.), 1951-53; city atty. Sheboygan, 1953-59; dep. atty. gen. Wis., 1959-61; U.S. atty. Western Dist. Wis., Madison, 1962-64; justice Wis. Supreme Ct., 1964-83, chief justice, 1983—. Lectr. municipal corps. U. Wis., Law Sch., 1961-64, lectr. appellate procedure and practice, 1971—, faculty, appellate judges seminar, NYU, 1972—; chmn. Wis. Appellate Practice and Procedures Com., 1975-76. Gen. chmn. Wis. Democratic Conv., 1960, 61; former mem. bd. Meth. Hosp., Madison; trustee U. Wis. Meml. Union, Wis. State Library; bd. visitors U. Wis. Law Sch., chmn., 1973-76; mem. U. Wis. Found.; chmn. Wis. chpt. NCCJ, recipient Disting. Service award, 1967; mem. exec. com. Four Lakes council Boy Scouts Am.; Served to lt. USNR, 1942-46. Fellow Am. Bar Found.; mem. City Attys. Assn. (past pres.), ABA (spl. com. state-fed. jurisdiction; mem. com. improvement appellate teaching skills in law schs.), Wis. Bar Assn., Dane County Bar Assn., Sheboygan County Bar Assn., VFW, Wis. Hist. Soc. (curator), Am. Legion, Am. Judicature Soc. (dir., program chmn.), Am. Law Inst., Inst. Jud. Adminstrn., Council State Ct. Reps. of Nat. Center for State Cts. (chmn. council 1977), Order of Coif, Iron Cross, Phi Delta Phi, Phi Kappa Phi. Congregationalist (past deacon). Home: 17 Thorstein Veblen Pl Madison WI 53705 Office: Supreme Ct Capitol Bldg Madison WI 53702

HEFFNER, SUZANNE ELIZABETH, public relations executive; b. Chgo., Nov. 17, 1941; d. Henry Edward and Lillian Elizabeth (Ferguson) H.; children—Robin E. Hackenbruch, Michelle D. Hackenbruch. Student Upsala Coll., 1959-63. Editorial assoc. Griswold-Eshleman, Cleve., 1963-65; v.p. Press Relations, Glen Ellyn, Ill., 1974-80; mktg. dir. Crawford Savs., Chgo., 1980-82; pub. relations dir. Pathway Fin., Chgo., 1982—; Mem. Wheaton-Warrenville High Sch. Parent Adv. Com., 1980-83. Recipient Eagle award and certs. of excellence Chgo. Fin. Advertisers, 1979, cert. of excellence, 1982; Advt. award Savs. Instns. of Am., 1982. Home: 2S723 Winchester Circle Warrenville IL 60555 Office: 100 N State St Chicago IL 60602

HEFLIN, FREDERICK REEVES, printing company executive, accountant, teacher; b. Clarksburg, W.Va., Oct. 2, 1935; s. William Claire and Ethel Bertha (Coughanor) H.; m. Eleanor Queen, Aug. 31, 1957; children—Frederick Reeves, Douglas Miller, David Franklin. B.A., W.Va. U., 1958; M.B.A., Xavier U., 1973. Bus. exec. Procter & Gamble Co., Cin., 1960-83; pres., bus. exec. F. R. Heflin Inc., Cin., 1984—, also pub. acct. Pres., New Richmond Exempted Village Sch. Dist., Ohio, 1982, bd. edn., 1980-83. Precinct chmn. Clermont County Republican Party, Ohio, 1985. Served to capt. USAF, 1958-60. Mem. Pub. Accts. Soc. Ohio (lic. publ. acct.), Sigma Chi. Methodist. Lodges: Kiwanis, Masons. Avocations: numismatics; golf; sports. Home: 2915 Pond Run Ln New Richmond OH 45157 Office: F R Heflin Inc 921 Ohio Pike Cincinnati OH 45245

HEFLIN, LELAND EARL, bearing mfr.; b. Bolckow, Mo., Jan. 4, 1946; s. William Earl and Cleta Marie (Stuart) H.; student N.W. Mo. State U., 1963-65; B.S. in Bus. Adminstrn., U. Mo., Columbia, 1968, M.A. in Acctg., 1971; m. Barbara Sue Gilbert, May 19, 1968; children—Mark Alan, Matthew Lee. Supervisory acct. Peat, Marwick, Mitchell & Co., Richmond, Va., and Indpls., 1971-76; controller Park 100 Devel. Co., Indpls., 1976-77; v.p., treas. Waldemar Industries, Inc., Indpls., 1977—, also pres., dir. Terrecorp, Indpls., 1980—; former mem. faculty U. Richmond, Va. Commonwealth U., Butler U. Served with USMC, 1968-69. Mem. Am. Inst. C.P.A.s, Am. Mgmt. Assn., Soc. Mfg. Engrs. Republican. Methodist. Home: 6265 N Chester Ave Indianapolis IN 46220 Office: 5455 W 86th St Indianapolis IN 46268

HEFNER, ELROY M., state legislator; b. Coleridge, Nebr., Dec. 12, 1923; grad. high sch.; m. Carol Rae Wilms, June 12, 1949; children—William, Douglas, Cynthia. Pres., part owner Hefner Oil & Feed Co.; mem. Nebr. Legislature, 1976, 80—. Former Mem. Coleridge Sch. Bd.; former mayor, Coleridge; former mem. Coleridge Fire Dept. Mem. Am. Legion, Nebr. Petroleum Marketers, VFW. Club: Coleridge Comml. (past pres.). Home: Box 36 Coleridge NE 68727*

HEFT, JAMES LEWIS, theology educator; b. Cleve., Feb. 20, 1943; s. Berl Ramsey and Hazel Mary (Miller) H. B.A. in Philosophy, U. Dayton, 1965, B.S. in Edn., 1966; M.A. in Theology, U. Toronto, 1971, Ph.D. in Hist. Theology, 1977. Prof. theology U. Dayton, Ohio, chmn. religious studies dept., 1983—; lectr. Contbr. numerous articles to profl. jours. Trustee U. Dayton, 1970-77. U. Toronto scholar, 1969-77; recipient Excellence in Teaching award U. Dayton, 1983. Mem. Coll. Theology Soc., Catholic Theol. Soc. Am., Mariological Soc. Am. Roman Catholic. Avocations: theatre; basketball. Home: 300 College Park Dr Alumni Hall Community Dayton OH 45469 Office: U Dayton 300 College Park Dayton OH 45469

HEGARTY, MARY FRANCES, lawyer; b. Chgo., Dec. 19, 1950; d. James E. and Frances M. (King) H. B.A., DePaul U., Chgo., 1972, J.D., 1975. Bar: Ill. 1975, U.S. Dist. Ct. 1975, Fed. Trial Bar 1984. Ptnr. firm Lannon & Hegarty, Park Ridge, Ill., 1975-80; sole practice, Park Ridge, 1980—. Mem. fin. com.'s revenue study com. Chgo. City Council, 1983-84; bd. dirs. Legal Assistance Found. Chgo.; pres. Historic Pullman Found., Inc., 1984-85; mem. City of Chgo. Sole Source Rev. Bd., 1984—; v.p. Ill. Women's Agenda, 1984-85. Mem. Ill. Bar Assn., Women's Bar Assn. Ill. (pres. 1983-84), Chgo. Bar Assn., N.W. Suburban Bar Assn. Democrat. Roman Catholic. Club: Chicago Athletic; Park Ridge Women Entrepreneurs. Office: 22 S Washington St Suite 105 Park Ridge IL 60068

HEGGERS, JOHN PAUL, educator, microbiologist, retired army officer; b. Bklyn., Feb. 8, 1933; s. John and May (Hass) H.; B.A. in Bacteriology, Mont. State U., 1958; M.S. in Microbiology, U. Md., 1965; Ph.D. in Bacteriology and Pub. Health, Wash. State U., 1972; m. Rosemarie Niklas, July 30, 1977; children—Arn M., Ronald R., Laurel M., Gary R., Renee L., Annette M. Med. technologist U.S. Naval Hosp., St. Albans, N.Y., 1951-53; bacteriologist Hahnemann Hosp., Worcester, Mass., 1958-59; commd. 2d lt. U.S. Army, 1959, advanced through grades to lt. col., 1975; mem. staff dept. bacteriology 1st U.S. Army Med. Lab., N.Y.C., 1959-60; chief clin. lab. U.S. Army Hosp., Verdun, France, 1960-63; chief virology and rickettsiology div. dept. microbiology 3d U.S. Army Med. Lab., Ft. McPherson, Ga., 1965-66; chief diagnostic bacteriology 9th Med. Lab., Saigon, Vietnam, 1966-67; chief microbiology div. dept. pathology Brooke Gen. Hosp., Ft. Sam Houston, Tex., 1967-69; lab. scis. officer Office Surgeon Gen., Washington, 1972-74; microbiologist spl. mycobacterial disease br. div. geog. pathology Armed Forces Inst. Pathology, Washington, 1973, spl. asst. to dir., 1973-74; chief clin. research lab. clin. research service Madigan Army Med. Center, Tacoma, 1974-76, asst. chief clin. investigation service, 1976-77; ret., 1977; assoc. prof. dept. surgery U. Chgo., 1977-80, prof., 1980-83; prof., dir. research Wayne State U. dept. surgery, div. plastic and reconstructive surgery, 1983—, assoc. dept. immunology and microbiology, 1984—; instr. bacteriology Basic Lab. Sch., Ft. McPherson, 1965-66; chmn. dept. microbiology U.S. Army Sch. Med. Tech., Ft. Sam Houston, 1967-69; instr. bacteriology eve. div. San Antonio Jr. Coll., 1969; instr. immunology, parasitology and mycology Clover Park Vocat. Tech. Inst., 1976-77. Decorated Bronze Star; Legion of Merit; recipient certificate of appreciation A.C.S., 1969, Armed Forces Inst. Pathology, 1974; Valley Forge Honor certificate Freedoms Found., 1974; Fisher award in med. tech. Am. Med. Technologists, 1968, 82; Gerard B. Lambert award, 1973; diplomate Am. Bd. Bioanalysis. Fellow Am. Acad. Microbiology, Royal Soc. Tropical Medicine and Hygiene, Am. Geriatrics Soc., Am. Soc. Plastic and Reconstructive Surgery (asso.; Ednl. Found. Research award 1978); mem. Nat. Registry Microbiologists (chmn. exec. council 1976-79, exam. proctor 1985—), Am. Soc. Microbiology (chmn. com. tellers 1974-75), Wash. State Soc. Am. Med. Technologists (pres. 1975-77), Wash. Soc. Med. Tech. (chmn. sect. microbiology sci. assembly, dir. 1975-77), Assn. Mil. Surgeons U.S., Am. Soc. Clin. Pathologists (asso.), Am. Med. Technologists (disting. achievement award 1975, exceptional merit award 1976, Technologist of Yr. award 1983 nat. dir. 1979-80, nat. sec. 1980-82, nat. v.p. 1982—), Am. Burn Assn. (President's award 1981), Plastic Surgery Research Council, Ill. State Soc. Med. Technologists (v.p. 1979-84), N.Y. Acad. Sci., Sigma Xi. Elk. Author: Current Problems in Surgery, 1973. Contbr. articles to profl. jours. Contbg. editor Jour. Am. Med. Tech., 1972-83. Home: 701 Berkshire Grosse Pointe Park MI 48230 Office: Univ Health Ctr Dept Surgery 4201 St Antoine Detroit MI 48201

HEGYI, DOUGLAS FRANK, otorhinolaryngologist, plastic surgeon; b. Aurora, Ill., Mar. 13, 1945; s. Frank Julius and Grace Irene (Dziewior) H.; children—Justin Douglas, Jeffrey Douglas. Diploma Chgo. City Coll., 1968; B.S. in Psychology, Ill. Inst. Tech., 1971; D.O., Chgo. Coll. Osteo. Medicine, 1976. Diplomate Am. Bd. Osteo. Opthalmology and Otorhinolaryngology. Intern, Mt. Clemens Gen. Hosp., (Mich.), 1976-77; resident in otorhinolaryngology and oro-facial plastic surgery, Pontiac Osteo. Hosp., Mich., 1977-80; staff physician, treas. dept. opthalmology and otorhinolaryngology, 1980—, mem. teaching staff, 1980—; staff physician, sect. chief otorhinolaryngology Lapeer County Gen. Hosp., Mich., 1980—; cons. staff Almont Community Hosp., Mich., asst. clin. prof. otorhinolaryngology Mich. State U., Coll. Osteo. Medicine, 1980—. Recipient Cert. of Appreciation, Am. Cancer Soc., 1976. Fellow Am. Acad. Otolaryngology, Skin Cancer Found. (hon.). mem. Atlas Club (life, Cert. for Outstanding Service and Dedication 1976), Chgo. Coll. Osteo. Medicine Alumni Assn., Am. Osteo. Assn., Osteo. Coll. Ophthalmology and Otorhinolaryngology, Mich. Assn. Osteo. Physicians and Surgeons, Oakland County Osteo. Assn., Lapeer County Osteo. Assn., Am. Acad. Facial Plastic and Reconstructive Surgery. Roman Catholic. Lodges: Masons, York Rite, Scottish Rite, DeMolay. Office: 701 Pontiac State Bank Bldg Pontiac MI 48058

HEHN, LORNE FREDERICK, agricultrual association executive; b. Markinch, Sask., Can., July 16, 1936; s. Fredrick and Bertha (Selzer) H.; m. Beth Smoothy, Nov. 10, 1962; children—Jeff, Pam. B.S. in Agr., U. Sask. Farmer, Markinch, 1959-81; insp. Agr. Can., Sask., 1958-63 part-time; pres. United Grain Growers Ltd., Winnipeg, Man., Can., 1981—; also dir.; mem. Mgmt. Com. United Oilseed Products, Lloydminster, Alta., 1981—; dir. Can. Grains Council, 1982—; mem. Nat. Action Com. on Soils Conservation, Ottawa, Ont., 1984—. Mem. Agrl. Inst. Can., Man. Inst. Agrologists. Clubs: Manitoba, Winnipeg Winter. Office: United Grain Growers Ltd 433 Main St Winnipeg MB R3C 3A7 Canada

HEIDE, RICHARD THOMAS, lawyer; b. Lafayette, Ind., Feb. 2, 1931; s. Richard Jacob and Virginia Louise (Wells) H.; m. Evelyn Mae Thomas, Jan. 25, 1958; 1 son, Richard Wayne. B.S., Purdue U., 1957; L.L.B., Ind. U., 1960. Bar: Ind. 1961. Sole practice, Lafayette, Ind., 1962-72; ptnr. Heide & Gambs, Lafayette, 1972-74, Heide Gambs & Mucker, Lafayette, 1974—. Chmn. Tippecanoe Democratic Central Com. Served with USN, 1951-55. Mem. ABA, Tippecanoe Bar Assn., 7th Circuit Bar Assn., Ind. Bar Assn. Mem. United Ch. of Christ. Clubs: Country (Lafayette), Grotto, Uptowners, Old Hickory. Lodges: Masons, Elks, Eagles, Moose.

HEIDEL, CHARLES MACLEISH, See *Who's Who in America,* 43rd edition.

HEIDELOFF, WILLIAM R., savings and loan association executive; b. Cleve., May 18, 1940; s. Henry William and Louise Anna (Braatz) H.; m. Marla K. Wise, June 8, 1963; children—Eric, Elizabeth, Gretchen. B.B.A., Wittenberg U., 1962; postgrad. Case Western Res. U., 1963-65. Asst. auditing mgr. May Co., Cleve., 1962-63; controller, asst. controller Marble-Imperial Furniture Co. div. Dictaphone Corp., Cleve., 1963-69; asst. to pres. William H. Sullivan, Inc., Cleve., 1969; planning mgr. diversification U.S. Plywood div. Champion Internat., N.Y.C., 1969-71; v.p., mng. officer Broadco Inc. and Broadview Service corp. subs. Broadview Fin. Corp. and Broadview Savs. & Loan Co., 1971-74, v.p. Broadview Fin. Corp., 1974-80, v.p., dir., 1980-82, pres., dir., 1982—; sr. v.p. Broadview Savs. and Loan Co., 1975-78, exec. v.p., 1978-80, exec. v.p., chief operating officer, dir., 1980-82, pres., chief operating officer, dir., 1982—; dir. Chgo. Title Ins. Co., Taylor Chair Co. Trustee, past vice-chmn. loan com. Cleve. Action to Support Housing, 1978—; team capt. Cleve. Campaign for Wittenberg U., 1980; team capt., sustaining fund campaign Cleve. Orch., 1979-80; team capt. United Way Campaign, 1980-81; trustee, mem. fin. and grant coms. Cuyahoga County Hosp. Found. Inc., 1981-82. Served with USCGR, 1962-68. Mem. Ohio League Savs. Assns. (service corp. com. 1980—), U.S. League Savs. Assns. (investments and mortgage lending com. 1980—), Bldg. Owners and Mgrs. Assn., Cleve. Area Bd. Realtors, Mortgage Bankers Assn., Greater Cleve. Growth Assn., Lakewood Hist. Soc. (treas. 1980-81, trustee 1976-81). Presbyterian (deacon 1976-82). Clubs: Cleveland Athletic, Mid-Day, River Oaks Racquet, Westwood Country. Office: Broadview Fin Corp 6000 Rockside Woods Cleveland OH 44131

HEIDOLPH, JOHANN (HANS), small appliance manufacturing executive; b. Nuernberg, W.Ger., May 8, 1927; s. Johann Georg and Sabine Barbara (Stengel) H.; m. Marietta Greisbacher, Dec. 10, 1957; children—Christina Sabine, Karin, Vera Helga. Dipl. Ing. Maschinenbau, Technische Hochschule, Munich, 1953. Cert. tool and diemaker; registered profl. engr., Ont. Apprentice, Hans Heidolph Metallwarenfabrik, Schwabach, Germany, 1945-47, Metallwerke Diehl, Nuernberg, 1947-48, 51, AB Svenska Metallverken, Vasteras, Sweden, 1951, Terni Societaper L'Industria e L'Ellettriciti, Italy, 1952; owner soldering tin and aluminum die casting firm, Schwabach, 1949-54, Uffing, Upper Bavaria, 1951-54; pres. Caframo, Ltd., Wiarton, Ont., Can., 1954—; co-owner Heidolph KG, W.Ger. Served with German Navy, 1944-45. Mem. Profl. Engrs. Ont., Comml. Travellers Assn. Can. Lutheran. Holder German patent. Home: 115 Airport Rd PO Box 475 Wiarton ON N0H 2T0 Canada Office: 116 Airport Rd PO Box 70 Wiarton ON N0H 2T0 Canada

HEIDRICK, GARDNER WILSON, management consultant; b. Clarion, Pa., Oct. 7, 1911; s. R. Emmet and Helen (Wilson) H.; B.S. in Banking and Finance, U. Ill., 1935; m. Marian Eileen Lindsay, Feb. 19, 1937; children—Gardner Wilson, Robert L. Indsl. dist. sales mgr. Scott Paper Co., Phila., 1935-42; dir. personnel Farmland Industries, Kansas City, Mo., 1942-51; assoc. Booz, Allen & Hamilton, Chgo., 1951-53; co-founder, ptnr. Heidrick & Struggles, Inc., Chgo., 1953-82; co-founder, chmn. Heidrick Ptnrs., Chgo., 1982—; dir. Keller-Taylor Corp. Bd. dirs. Internat. Exec. Service Corps, Keller Grad. Sch. Mgmt.; bd. dirs. U. Ill. Found. Served with USNR, 1945-46. Recipient Pres.'s award U. Ill. Found., 1979. Mem. U. Ill. Alumni Assn. (past pres., Nat. Achievement award 1980), U.S., Am., Ill. srs. golf assns., Phi Kappa Sigma. Clubs: Chicago, Tower (Chgo.); Hinsdale (Ill.). Golf (past pres.); University (N.Y.C.); Country of Fla., Ocean (Delray Beach). Home: 101 S County Line Rd Hinsdale IL 60521 Office: 20 N Wacker Dr Chicago IL 60606

HEIGAARD, WILLIAM STEVEN, state senator, lawyer; b. Gardar, N.D. May 18, 1938; s. Oliver and Laufey (Erickson) H.; m. Paula Geston, 1960; children—Jody, Rebecca, Sara. B.A., U. N.D., 1961, J.D., 1967. Bar: N.D. 1967. Asst. atty. gen., Bismarck, N.D., 1967-68; state's atty., Cavalier County, N.D., 1970-75; mem. N.D. Ho. of Reps., 1980-81, N.D. State Senate, 1981—, minority leader. Served to 1st lt. U.S. Army, 1962-64. Mem. Am. Legion, Phi Delta Phi. Democrat. Lutheran. Lodges: Eagles, Elks. Office: PO Box 151 Langdon ND 58249

HEILMANN, MICHAEL GERD, lawyer; b. Berlin, Germany, Mar. 11, 1953; came to U.S., 1960; s. Gerhard Max and Ruth Hedwig (Ebeling) H.; m. Farrel Briggs, Aug. 4, 1984. A.B., U. Mich., 1975; J.D., U. Detroit, 1981. Bar: Mich. 1981. Fla. 1982, U.S. Dist. Ct. (ea. dist.) Mich. 1981. Assoc. Lppatin, Miller et al, Detroit, 1981—. Exec. dir. Livonia Bicentennial Com., 1975-76; adminstrv. asst. to U.S. Senator Donald W. Rieble, Jr., Mich., 1976-78. Mem. Am. Trial Lawyers Assn., ABA, Mich. Trial Lawyers Assn. Democrat. Lutheran. Office: 547 E Jefferson St Detroit MI 48226

HEIMERICKS, GARY W., state official; b. Jefferson City, Mo., Feb. 17, 1951; d. Robert E. and Frances Ann (Rackers) H.; m. Belinda Kay Heimericks, May 26, 1973; children—Gary Christopher, Kimberly Kay. B.S., Lincoln U., 1973; M.S., U. Mo.-Columbia, 1977. Fiscal grants specialist Div. Planning and Budget, Mo. Dept. Social Services, Jefferson City, 1975-78, adminstrv. officer, 1978-81, dir. fin., 1981-85; dep. dir. Mo. Div. Med. Services, 1985—; mgmt. cons. U. Mo., 1981. Coordinator blood drive ARC, Holts Summit, 1979-84; pres. North Sch. PTO, 1986. Mem. Nat. Conf. State Human Services Fin. Officers (regional bd. dirs. 1982-84), Am. Soc. Public Adminstrn., Assn. Govt. Accts. Roman Catholic. Lodge: Lions (sec. 1980-81). Home: RR 2 Box 27 Holts Summit MO 65043 Office: Dept Social Services Broadway State Office Bldg Jefferson City Mo 65101

HEIN, RONALD REED, lawyer; b. Seneca, Kans., Nov. 7, 1949; s. Henry Allan and Evelyn K. (Price) H.; B.A. summa cum laude, Washburn U., 1971, J.D., 1974; m. Linda S. Davis, May 26, 1979; children—Derek, Jennifer. Exec. dir. Associated Students of Kans., Topeka, 1973-74; asst. city atty., City of Topeka, 1974-76; mem. firm Sloan, Listrom, Eisenbarth, Sloan and Glassman, Topeka, 1976-79; devel. coordinator St. Francis Hosp. and Med. Center, Topeka, 1979-83; mem. Hiatt & Carpenter, Chartered, Topeka, 1983—; mem. Kans. State Ho. of Reps., 1975-77; mem. Kans. State Senate, 1977-84. Bd. trustees Kans. Nurses Found. Mem. ABA, Washburn U. Alumni (bd. dirs.), Phi Alpha Delta, Phi Kappa Phi, Phi Delta Theta. Republican. Episcopalian. Office: 627 S Topeka Blvd Topeka KS 66603

HEINEMAN, BEN WALTER, business executive, lawyer; b. Wausau, Wis., Feb. 10, 1914; s. Walter Ben and Elsie Brunswick (Deutsch) H.; student U. Mich., 1930-33; LL.B., Northwestern U., 1936; LL.D. (hon.), Lawrence Coll., 1959, Lake Forest Coll., 1966, Northwestern U., 1967; m. Natalie Goldstein, Apr. 17, 1935; children—Martha Heineman Pieper, Ben Walter. Bar: Ill. 1936. Pvt. practice law and govt. service, Chgo., Washington, Algiers, 1936-56; chmn. bd. dirs. Four Wheel Drive Auto Co., 1954-57; chmn., chief exec. officer N.W. Industries, Inc., 1968-85; chmn. C. & N.W. Ry. Co., 1956-72; dir., mem. exec. com. 1st Nat. Bank, Chgo.; mem. orgn. com. First Chgo. Corp. Chmn., White House Conf. to Fulfill These Rights, 1966, Pres.'s Task Force on Govt. Orgn., 1966-67, Pres.'s Commn. Income Maintenance Programs, 1967-69. Life trustee U. Chgo.; chmn. Ill. Bd. Higher Edn., 1962-69; trustee, mem. investment com. Savs. and Profit Sharing Fund of Sears Roebuck Employees, 1966-71; vis. com. dept. econs. Harvard, 1965-71; trustee, mem. exec. com., chmn. audit com. Rockefeller Found., 1972-78; life bd. dirs. Lyric Opera, Chgo.; trustee Orchestral Assn., Chgo.; sustaining fellow Art Inst. Chgo. Fellow Am. Bar Found. (life), Am. Bar Assn., Am. Acad. Arts and Scis.; mem. Am. Law Inst. (life), Ill., Chgo. bar assns., Order of Coif, Phi Delta Phi (hon.). Clubs: Ephraim (Wis.) Yacht; Mid-America, Chicago, Casino, Commonwealth, Wayfarers, Economic, Standard, Quadrangle, Executives, Commercial, Chicago Yacht (Chgo.); Metropolitan, Carlton. Home: 180 E Pearson St Chicago IL 60611 Office: 6300 Sears Tower Chicago IL 60606

HEINEMANN, CHARLES ALAN, health care consultant, educator; b. Mpls., June 8, 1941; s. Elvin Frederick and Marguerite Florence (Witte) H.; m. Barbara Joann Perso, Nov. 6, 1965; 1 child, Andrew Charles. B.A., U. Minn., 1964, M. Hosp. Adminstrn., 1966. Adminstrv. resident St. Luke's Hosp., Milw., 1965-66; asst. adminstr., Union Hosp., Lynn, Mass., 1966-69; cons. Hamilton Assocs., Mpls., 1969-71, dir. systems group, 1971—, prin., 1980—; mem. adv. group U.S. Dept. Health & Human Services, Washington, 1983; adj. instr. U. Minn., Mpls., 1969—; lectr. U. Wis., Eau Claire, 1979—. Author (unit lesson) Facility Development for Independent Study Program Hosp. Adminstrs., U. Minn., 1971—. Co-chmn. Greater Lynn Mental Health Assn., Mass., 1967-69; cubmaster Viking Council Boy Scouts Am., Mpls., 1982-83. Mem. Am. Hosp. Assn., Am. Coll. Hosp. Adminstrs.; fellow Am. Assn. Healthcare Cons. (cert.; bd. dirs. 1983—; chmn. elect bd. dirs.). Republican. Mem. Christian Ch. Avocations: travel; photography; boating; fishing. Office: Hamilton Assocs Inc 2021 E Hennepin Ste 450 Minneapolis MN 55413

HEINOLD, HAROLD JOSEPH, livestock and commodities broker; b. Porter County, Ind., Aug. 9, 1919; s. Joseph and Martha (Luthi) H.; m. Margaret Louise Yergler, Dec. 5, 1948; children—Donna Jean, Ann Louise. D.Agr. (hon.), Purdue U., 1981. Grain and livestock farmer, Kouts, Ind. 1940-54; founder, pres. Heinold Hog Market, Inc., Kouts, 1950—, chief exec. officer, chmn. bd., 1976—; founder, pres. Heinold Commodities, Inc., Kouts, 1967—, chief exec. officer, chmn. bd., 1976—; founder, pres. Heinold Cattle Market, Inc., 1969—; lectr. in field; dir. No. Ind. Bank, Midwestern United Life Ins. Co. Recipient cert. distinction Purdue Agr. Alumni, 1979; meritorious service award Ind. Pork Producers, 1981; industry award Ill. Pork Producers, 1976. Mem. Kouts C. of C., Future Farmers Am. (hon.), Livestock Merchandising Inst. (trustee), Ind. Livestock Mktg. Assn., Nat. Cattlemen's Assn. Home and Office: PO Box 375 Kouts IN 46347

HEINRICHS, MARY ANN, university dean; b. Toledo, Mar. 28, 1930; m. Paul Warren Heinrichs, Jan. 26, 1952; children—Paul, John, Nancy, James. Ph.D., U. Toledo, 1973. Prof. English, U. Toledo, Ohio, 1965-77, dean, 1977—. Contbr. articles to profl. jours.; editor: Listening Post Jour., 1985. Mem. Community Planning Council Research Project Employed Women, Ohio, 1982-84; mem. Council Family Violence, Toledo, 1981—; com. chmn. St. Joseph Sch. Bd., Toledo, 1976-79. Recipient Outstanding Scholarship award U. Toledo, 1965; AAUW scholar, 1984. Mem. Internat. Tech. Communications Soc. (chmn. 1979-80), Internat. Listening Assn. (presenter), Pi Lambda Theta (chpt. pres. and del. 1974-76), Phi Kappa Phi (chpt. pres. and del. 1969), AAUW (corp. rep. 1978-84). Roman Catholic. Lodge: Zonta. Avocations: hiking. Office: U Toledo 2801 W Bancroft Toledo OH 43606

HEINS, SHARON SZEWC, patent agent, researcher; b. Saginaw, Mich., Sept. 17, 1956; d. John Floyd and Marle Ann (Rusin) Szewc; m. Donald Edward Heins, Feb. 23, 1979. A.A.S. in Indsl. Chemistry, Ferris State Coll., 1976; B.S. in Chemistry, Saginaw Valley State Coll., 1981; M.B.A., Central Mich. U., 1983; student Thomas M. Cooley Law Sch., 1983—. Bar: U.S. Patent Office, 1981. Lab technician Dow Corning Corp., Midland, Mich., 1976-80, patent agt., 1980-83, researcher environ. law, 1984-85; cons., patent agt. Dow Chem. Co., Midland, 1984—. Mem. Am. Chem. Soc. (patent div.), ABA (student div.), Mich. Bar Assn. (student div.), Saginaw Valley Patent Law Assn. Home: 310 E Meadowbrook Midland MI 48640

HEINTZELMAN, ROSS GARFIELD, state ofcl.; b. Greensburg, Pa., Jan. 2, 1917; s. Ross Garfield and Bertha Lee (Acklin) H.; B.S., Ohio State U., 1948, M.A., 1950; m. Margery Isabel Major, Mar. 17, 1945; children—Christian Lee, Diane Kay. Supr. evaluation programs Timken Co., Canton, Ohio, 1960-73, engr., 1936-60; chief labor relations State Inter-govtl. Personnel Adminstrn., Columbus, 1973-74; adminstrv. staff asst. Indsl. Commn. Ohio, Columbus, 1974—; cons. personnel relations. Councilman, Canton, Ohio, 1957-69; mem. Ohio Ho. of Reps., 1969-72. Served with USAAF, 1943-46. Recipient awards Am. Econ. Found., Polit. Sci. Acad., Police Boys Club, YMCA, Ohio Ednl. Assn.; Canton Tchrs. Man of Year award 1972; Appreciation award Ednl. Community Northeastern Ohio; Canton City Schs. award; Ohio Dental Assn. award; Mayor's citation. Home: 206 Grandview Ave NW Canton OH 44708 Office: Ross Heintzelman Cons Public Affairs 206 Grandview Ave NW Canton OH 44708

HEINZ, EDWARD N., JR., mfg. co. exec.; b. Chgo., Nov. 27, 1914; s. Edward N. and Adeline (Kelly) H.; B.S. in Chem. Engring., Ill. Inst. Tech., 1937; m. Laurette F. Higgins, Oct. 22, 1943; children—Edward, Raymond, James, Pamela, Laurette, Joan, Mary Jayne. Vice pres., dir. Food Materials Corp., Chgo., 1937-67; pres., dir. Bell Flavors and Fragrances, Inc., Northbrook, Ill., 1967—. Served with U.S. Army, 1943-46. Mem. Flavor and Extract Mfrs. Assn. U.S. (past pres.), Am. Assn. Candy Technologists (past pres.), Serra Club Chgo. (past pres.), Am. Chem. Soc., Inst. Food Technologists, Am. Assn. Cereal Chemists. Clubs: N. Shore Country (Glenview, Ill.); JOM Country (Palm Beach, Fla.). Home: 22 Meadowview Dr Winnetka IL 60093 Office: 500 Academy Dr Northbrook IL 60062

HEIPLE, JAMES DEE, judge; b. Peoria, Ill., Sept. 13, 1933; s. Rae Crane and Harriet (Birkett) H.; B.S., Bradley U., 1955; J.D., U. Louisville, 1957; Certificate in Internat. Law, City of London Coll., 1967; grad. Nat. Coll. State Judiciary, 1971; m. Virginia Kerswill, July 28, 1956; children—Jeremy Hans, Jonathan James, Rachel Duffield. Bar: Ill. 1957, Ky. 1958, U.S. Supreme Ct. 1962; partner Heiple and Heiple, Pekin, Ill., 1957-70; circuit judge Ill., 10th Circuit 1970-80; justice Ill. Appellate Ct., 1980—, presiding justice, 1985—. Vice pres., dir. Washington State Bank (Ill.), 1959-66; dir. Gridley State Bank (Ill.), 1958-59; village atty., Tremont, Ill., 1961-66, Mackinaw, Ill., 1961-66; asst. pub. defender Tazewell County, 1967-70., legal clerk Ill. Appellate Ct., 1968-70. Chmn. Tazewell County Heart Fund, 1960. Pub. Adminstr. Tazewell County, Ill., 1959-61; sec. Tazewell County Republican Central Com. 1966-70; mem. Pekin Sch. Bd., 1970; mem. Ill. Supreme Ct. Com. on Profl. Responsibility, 1978—. Recipient certificate Freedoms Found., 1975, George Washington honor medal, 1976. Mem. Ky., Ill. (chmn. legal edn. com. 1972-74, chmn. jud. sect. 1976-77, chmn. Bench and Bar Council 1984-85), Tazewell County (pres. 1967-68) bar assns., Ill. Judges Assn. (pres. 1978-79), Ky., Ill., Pa. hist. socs., Nat. Rifle Assn., S.A.R., Delta Theta Phi, Sigma Nu, Pi Kappa Delta. Methodist. Clubs: Filson; Union League (Chgo.). Lodge: Masons. Office: 524 Court St Pekin IL 61554

HEISLER, HAROLD REINHART, mgmt. cons.; b. Chgo.; s. Harold Reinhart and Beulah Mary (Schade) H.; B.M.E., U. Ill., 1954. Mgmt. cons. Ill. Power Co., Decatur, 1954—, mem. Nuclear Power Group, Inc., Argonne (Ill.) Nat. Lab., 1955-57; chmn. fossil fuel com., West Central region FPC, Chgo., 1966-68; chmn. evaluation com. Coal Gasification Group, Inc., 1971-75; chmn. Decatur Marine Inc., 1964-66; dir. Indsl. Water Supply Co., Robinson, Ill., 1975-77; pub. speaker in field; mem. Ill. Gov.'s Fuel and Energy Bd., 1970, Ill. Commerce Commn. Fuel and Energy Bd., 1971-75, Ill. Energy Resources Commn. Coal Study Panel, 1976-79, evaluation com. of kilngas process, 1976-80; mem. power plant productivity com. Ill. Commerce Commn., 1977-79; mem. com. on nuclear power plant constrn. Inst. Nuclear Power Ops. Mem. ASME, Nat., Ill. socs. profl. engrs., U. Ill. Alumni Assn., Sigma Phi Delta. Conceptual designer power plant sites and recreational lakes, Baldwin and Clinton, Ill. Home: 1375 W Main St Decatur IL 62522 Office: 500 S 27th St Decatur IL 62525

HELBERT, JAMES RAYMOND, biochemist; b. Miles City, Mont., Aug. 4, 1918; s. Lu Roy and Maude Mae (Stevenson) H.; B.A. cum laude, St. John's U., Collegeville, Minn., 1947; M.S., Marquette U., 1958; Ph.D., Northwestern U., 1963; m. Bernice Cyganiak, July 9, 1949; children—Gregory, Helen, John, Monica. Chemist. Orthmann Labs., Inc., Milw., 1947-51; research chemist Red Star Yeast and Products Co., Milw., 1951-58; research biochemist, geriatrics research project VA Hosp., Downey, Ill., 1958-62, acting chief, 1962-63; research asso. div. clin. hematology dept. medicine Michael Reese Hosp. & Med. Center, Chgo., 1963-67; supr. biochem. and microbiol. research Miller Brewing Co., Milw., 1967-76; mgr. microbiol. research and adminstrv. affairs, 1976-85, ret., 1985; research asso. Marquette U., 1954-58; lectr. dept. biology Ill. Inst. Tech., Chgo., 1966; asst. prof. biochemistry Northwestern U., 1967-73; guest lectr. microbial biochemistry U. Wis., Milw., 1970. NIH fellow, 1960-63. Fellow Am. Inst. Chemists; mem. Am. Statis. Assn., Am. Chem. Soc., AAAS, Inst. Food Technologists, Am. Soc. Brewing Chemists. Roman Catholic. Clubs: Swedish Glee of Waukegan; Eagles. Contbr. in field. Office: PO Box 330 Milwaukee WI 53201

HELFER, HERMAN HYMAN, glass co. exec.; b. Chgo., Dec. 6, 1919; s. Harry and Sarah (Kurlansky) H.; student Herzl Jr. Coll., 1941; cert. U. Ill. Coll. Pharmacy, 1946; B.S. in Mktg., Roosevelt U., 1973, M.B.A., 1977; m. Frieda Hershkopf, Nov. 16, 1947; children—Joel, Harvey, Gail. With Novelty Glass & Mirror Co., Chgo., 1946—, gen. mgr., sec.-treas., 1960—; pres. Columbia Glass Co., Chgo., 1969—; pres. Energipane Insulating Glass Corp.; sec.-treas. Temper-Pane Inc.; pres. Insulating Glass Ednl. Inst., 1980-81, seminar chmn., Chgo., 1981. Instr., Boys State, Springfield, Ill., 1966; chmn. Glazier's Pension and Welfare Funds, Chgo., 1969-73; div. exec. com. Jewish United Fund, 1981. Served with USAAF, 1943-46. Recipient Dealer of Yr. award Glass Digest, 1979. Mem. Am. Legion (post comdr. 1967-68), Assn. Glazing Contractors (pres. 1957-73), Nat. Glass Dealers Assn. (exec. com., pres. 1979-80, rep. to Consumer Safety Products Commn.), Flat Glass Mktg. Assn. (dir.), Nat. Assn. Store Fixture Mfrs. (asso.), Sealed Insulating Glass Mfrs. Assn. Jewish (sec., treas. synagogue). Lodges: B'nai B'rith, Masons, Shriners. Contbr. articles to trade publs. Home: 8937 Forest View Rd Evanston IL 60203 Office: 4716 W Lake St Chicago IL 60644

HELGERSON, JOHN WALTER, lawyer; b. Cleve., Aug. 27, 1938; s. Floyd G. and Evelyn Ann (Wilder) H.; m. Dorothy Elizabeth Hart, Dec. 5, 1984, children from previous marriage—Heidi Wilder, Holly Ward. A.B., Wittenberg U., 1960; J.D., Yale U., 1963. Bar: Ohio 1963. Assoc., Porter Wright Morris & Arthur, Columbus, Ohio, 1963-68, ptnr., 1968—; dir. Bry-Air, Inc., Sunbury, Ohio, Mid-Ohio Coca-Cola, Newark, Richardson/Smith, Worthington, Ohio. Chmn., Family Counseling and Crittendon Services, Columbus, 1979-80; chmn. lawyers div. United Way, 1979. Served to capt. USAR, 1963-70. Mem. ABA, Ohio State Bar Assn., Columbus Bar Assn., (chmn. bus. law com. 1976-77). Republican. Unitarian. Clubs: Capital, University, Met. (Columbus).Avocations: sailing; scuba diving. Home: 1467 Lakeshore Dr Columbus OH 43204 Office: Porter Wright et al 41 S High St Columbus OH 43215

HELLEKANT, GORAN, educator; b. Malmo, Sweden, Apr. 28, 1936; s. Bengt and Rut H.; children—Charlotte, Peter, Monika, Bo. Ph.D., Royal Vet. Coll., Sweden, 1965, D.V.M., 1966. Postdoctoral fellow MIT, Boston, 1966-67; asst. prof. Royal Vet. Coll., Stockholm, Sweden, 1967-72, prof., 1972-78; dir. research Nat. Def. Inst., Stockholm, 1978-79; prof. U. Wis.-Madison, 1979—. Contbr. articles to sci. jours. Avocations: Oil painting, sailing, skiing, hiking, soaring, diving, skating, running. Office: U Wis 1655 Linden Dr Madison WI 53706

HELLER, ALBERTO, hospital administrator; b. Lima, Peru, Apr. 16, 1926; came to U.S., 1960, naturalized, 1965; s. Alberto S. and Isabel V. (Sotomayor) H.; m. Betsy Merino de Zela, Oct. 27, 1982; children by previous marriage—Luis Alberto, Raul Percy, Roberto Julio, Anne Isabelle. B.A., Cath. U., Lima, 1954, M.B.A., 1955, C.P.A., 1957. Owner, Heller & Assocs., C.P.A.s, Lima, 1957-60; rec. sec. Mun. La. Merced, 1945-48; mgr. acctg. dept. San Miguel S.A., Lima, 1949-52; asst. dir. Ministry Commerce and Industry, Lima, 1952-54; fin. dir., treas. Dofisa, Lima, 1955-56; exec. v.p. H.F. Gamarra S.A., Huacho, Peru, 1957-60; chief acct. Sun Electric Corp., Chgo., 1960-64; auditor Laventhol & Horwath, Chgo., 1964-65; asst. controller St. Francis Hosp., Evanston, Ill., 1967-69; dir. bus. ops. and controller Holy Family Hosp., Des Plaines, Ill., 1969-71, v.p. fin. and profl. services, 1971-79, v.p. fin. and planning, 1979-81, sr. v.p. fin., 1981—. Bd. dirs. Peruvian Arts Soc., Chgo., 1982, pres., 1969, 72, 81; chmn. clean community system Des Plaines City Commn., 1983—; bd. dirs. United Way Des Plaines, 1977-80; chmn. Des Plaines chpt. Am. Cancer Soc., 1978-80, treas., 1976-78; bd. dirs. Sacred Heart of Mary High Sch., Rolling Meadows, Ill., 1980—, Des Plaines Hist. Soc., 1983—. Served to lt. Peruvian Armed Forces. Mem. Hosp. Fin. Mgmt. Assn., Am. Coll. Hosp. Adminstrs., Ill. Notary Assn., Soc. Hosp. Planning, Fin. Execs. Inst., Des Plaines C. of C. (dir. 1978-81). Republican. Clubs: Rolling Green Country (pres.). Lodge: Lions. Home: 109 Michael Manor Glenview IL 60025 Office: 100 N River Rd Des Plaines IL 60016

HELLER, CHARLES ANDREW, JR., electric utilities co. exec.; b. Teaneck, N.J., Mar. 18, 1929; s. Charles Andrew and Lillian Laura (Reuter) H.; B.A., Rutgers U., 1951; M.B.A., U. Pa., 1956; M.S. (Alfred P. Sloan fellow), M.I.T., 1966; m. Helen Johansen, July 19, 1952; children—Charles Andrew, Janice Maria, Richard Craig. With Am. Electric Power Service Corp., N.Y.C., 1956-63; with Ohio Power Co., Canton, 1963-68, 70—, v.p., 1974-76, exec. v.p., 1976-81, chief operating officer, 1976—, pres., 1981—; exec. asst. Wheeling Electric Co. (W.Va.), 1968-70; exec. v.p., dir. Ohio Electric Co.; v.p., dir. Cardinal Operating Co., Central Coal Co., Central Ohio Coal Co., Central Operating Co., So. Ohio Coal Co., Windsor Power House Coal Co., 1976—; v.p. Beech Bottom Power Co., Inc., Franklin Real Estate Co., 1976—; v.p. Ind. Franklin Realty, Inc., 1979—; dir. Ohio Electric Utility Inst., 1976—, pres., 1978—; dir. Central Trust Co. Northeastern Ohio, 1975—. Mem. Council for Reorganization of Ohio State Govt., 1967; dir. Canton Welfare Found., 1975-78; mem. Malone Coll. Adv. Bd., 1976—. Served to capt., USAF, 1951-53. Republican. Lutheran. Clubs: Rotary, Canton, Brookside Country, Columbus Athletic, Elks. Office: 301 Cleveland Ave SW Canton OH 44701

HELLER, DICK DANIEL, JR., newspaper publisher; b. Decatur, Ind., May 22, 1929; s. Dick Daniel and Martha Delilah (Grant) H.; m. E. Jane Drew, Mar. 23, 1957; 1 child, Thomas Calvin. Student Ind. U., 1947-50, 54, U. Md., Augsburg, Germany, 1952-53; A.B., Syracuse U., 1956; postgrad. Ball State U., 1958-59, St. Francis Coll., 1964. Pres. Decatur Pub. Co., Ind., 1958—. Author: History of the Indiana Democratic Editorial Association, 1962. Editor: History of Adams County, Indiana, 1980. Editor newsletters: The Cardinal, 1979-84; The Craigellachie, 1980—. Historian, Adams County, 1980—; dir. Ind. Hist. Soc., 1982—, bd. dirs. genealogy sect. 1975—; chmn. Adams County-Decatur Sesquicentennial Com., 1984-86. Served as cpl. U.S. Army, 1951-54. Named Sagamore of Wabash, gov. of Ind., 1963, Ky. Col., gov. Ky., 1969; recipient End-to-End award Appalachian Trail Assn., 1973, Disting. Citizenship award Decatur Elks, 1975-76. Mem. Ind. Dem. Edn. Assn. (pres. 1965), Inland Daily Press Assn., Hoosier State Press Assn., UPI, Mid-Am. Press Inst., Decatur Trail Club (pres. 1984—). German Heritage Soc. (bd. dirs. Ind. chpt. 1984—). Avocations: bird watching; stamp collecting; genealogy; hiking. Home: Rural Route 3 Box 3 Decatur IN 46733-2703 Office: Decatur Pub Co Inc 141 S 2d St Decatur IN 46733-1688

HELLER, FREDERICK, mining company executive; b. Detroit, May 6, 1932; s. Robert and Lois Mouch H.; B.A., Harvard U., 1954; m. Barbara Ann McGreevy, Nov. 22, 1979; children—Thomas M., John G., Cynthia R. With Hanna Mining Co., 1957—, v.p. sales, 1973-76, sr. v.p. sales and transp., Cleve., 1976-81, sr. v.p. mktg., 1981-84, sr. v.p. sales and mktg., 1984—. Trustee, mem. fin. com. McGregor Home, 1978—. Served with U.S. Army, 1954-56. Mem. Ferroalloys Assn. (dir.), Am. Iron and Steel Inst., Am. Mining Congress, Am. Iron Ore Assn., Soc. Mining Engrs. Republican. Episcopalian. Clubs: Union, Kirtland Country, Pepper Pike, Tavern, Duquesne. Home: 2942 Fontenay Rd Shaker Heights OH 44120 Office: 100 Erieview Plaza Cleveland OH 44114

HELLER, JOACHIM, health service manager, nurse, educator; b. Berlin, Oct. 11, 1938; s. Guenter and Hedwig (Ritter) came to U.S., 1951; m. Marlies Gerda Gollnau, Apr. 29, 1960; children—David, Brian. L.P.N., Milw. Area Tech. Coll., 1964, R.N., 1977; postgrad. U. Wis.-Milw., 1977-79; B.S. in Nursing, Milton Coll., Wis., 1979; M.S. in Adminstrn. Leadership, U. Wis.-Milw., 1981, Ph.D. in Health Service Mgmt., 1982. Registered nurse, Wis.; registered emergency med. technician, Wis.; cert. edn. specialist, Wis. Surg. technician Misericordia Hosp., Milw., 1960-64; pub. health nurse Vis. Nurse Assn., Milw., 1964-66; staff nurse various hosps. and nursing homes, Milw., 1966-79; faculty, mgr. psychiat. unit Milw. County Mental Health Complex, 1979-83; health service and tng. mgr. House of Correction, Milwaukee County, 1983—; program evaluator, 1979—; cons. legal nursing intervention, 1981—. CPR affiliate faculty Wis. Heart Assn., 1980—; CPR instr. trainer Wis. Red Cross, 1984—. Served with USMC, 1957-59. Mem. Nat. League of Nursing, Wis. League of Nursing, Am. Heart Assn., Wis. Heart Assn. (co-editor Heartbeat), Wis. Correctional Health Assn. (v.p. 1984—), Am. Correctional Assn., Wis. Correctional Assn., Milwaukee County Mental Health Task Force. Author: Program Evaluation, 1982; Disturbed Behavior Intervention, 1982. Contbr. articles in field to local profl. jours. Home: 3901 W Oklahoma Ave Milwaukee WI 53215

HELLER, PHILIP HENRI, physician; b. Des Plaines, Ill., Feb. 6, 1919; s. William Frederick and Magdalene (Henschel) H.; A.B., U. Neb., 1941; M.D. Northwestern U., 1945; m. Ruth Wark, Apr. 28, 1945; children—Jeanne, Philip Henri, Nancy, Patricia, Mary. Intern, St. Lukes Hosp., Chgo., 1944-45; asso. staff St. Francis Hosp., Evanston, Ill., 1946-53; attending staff, staff officer Resurrection Hosp., Chgo., 1952-64, asso. dir. family practice residency program, 1978—; attending staff Luth. Gen. Hosp., Park Ridge, Ill., 1959-78, hon. staff, 1978—, v.p., 1970-71, chmn. div. family practice and dir. Family Practice Center and residency program, 1972-77; attending staff Holy Family Hosp., Des Plaines, Ill., 1960-74; asst. prof. Sch. Medicine, U. Ill. Pres., Des Plaines Bd. Health, 1949-63. Served to lt. comdr. USNR, 1945-46, 54-56. Diplomate Am. Bd. Family Practice. Fellow Am. Acad. Family Physicians; mem. Chgo. Med. Soc. (council mem. 1963-71, pres. Irving Park br. 1969-70), Ill. Acad. Family Physicians (pres. North Suburban br. 1959-60), Ill. Med. Soc., AMA, Soc. Tchrs. Family Medicine, Phi Rho Sigma. Congregationalist. Mason. Home: 2400 Windsor Mall Apt 1J Park Ridge IL 60068 Office: Resurrection Hosp 7447 W Talcott Ave Chicago IL 60631

HELLKAMP, LAWRENCE EDWARD, hospital administrator, management consultant; b. Cin., June 12, 1934; s. Edward Bernard and Elizabeth Catherine (Wuest) H.; m. Gale Sylvia Harrison, Sept. 27, 1952; children—Christine Zabechi, Leo, Martin, Stephen, Philip, Thomas, Alexis, Paul; m. 2d, Rita Victoria Andrews, May 27, 1977; children—Lori, Sarah. Cert., Good Samaritan Hosp. Sch. Radiol. Tech., Cin., 1958; student No. Ky. State Coll., 1973. Chief technologist Good Samaritan Hosp., Cin., 1958-66; br. mgr. Westinghouse X-Ray Co., Cin., 1966-68; adminstrv. asst. radiology Jewish Hosp. Cin., 1968-73, adminstrv. dir. radiologic services, 1974—, asst. v.p., 1983—; tech. adminstr. Duke U., Durham, N.C., 1973-74; owner, dir. Practical Mgmt. Services, Cin., 1980—; v.p., chmn. bd. Technician Services, Roanoke, Va., 1983—. Served with USN, 1952-60. Mem. Am. Soc. Radiologic Technologist, (cert.), Am. Hosp. Radiology Adminstrs. Inc., Soc. Radiologic Engring. Contbr. articles to profl. jours. Home: 8 Funston Ln Cincinnati OH 45218 Office: Jewish Hosp of Cincinnati 3200 Burnett Ave Cincinnati OH 45229

HELLYER, CLEMENT DAVID, writer, editor, bookseller; b. Glendale, Calif., Aug. 15, 1914; s. Clement David and Frances Edna (Dodge) H.; m. Gertrude Gloria Phillips, Sept. 8, 1939; children—Gloria Penrose, David Phillips, John Christian. B.A., Principia Coll., Ill., 1936; M.S., Columbia U., 1938; postgrad. U. Fla., 1950-52. Reporter, San Diego Union Tribune, 1939-41; pub. relations dir. San Diego C. of C., 1941-43; civilian aerial navigator USN, 1943-45; prof. journalism San Diego State Coll., 1947-49; dir. Centro Cultural Costarricense-Norteamericano, San Jose, Costa Rica, 1949-50; asst. dir. Sch. Inter-Am. Studies, U. Fla., 1950-52; vis. lectr. U.S. journalism Dept. State program leaders and specialists exchange, Latin Am., 1952; Latin Am. editor

San Diego Union, 1953-60; freelance writer, Sao Paulo and Rio de Janeiro, Brazil, 1960-64; writer/lectr. Latin Am. affairs, 1950—; U.S. del. Jose Toribio Medina Centenary, Santiago, Chile, 1952; editor, pub. South Pacific Mail, Santiago, 1964-66; editorial dir. Sta. KOGO-Radio/TV, San Diego, 1966-69; univ. editor, pub. affairs officer U. Calif.-San Diego, 1969-74, lectr., 1969-75; owner Five Quail Books, Spring Grove, Minn., 1978—; cons. editor Western Recreational Publs., Inc., San Diego, 1980—. Author: (with Charles Mattingly) American Air Navigator, 1946, Story of the U.S. Border Patrol, 1963, Making Money with Words, 1981. Contbr. articles to newspapers, jours. Recipient Maria Moors Cabot award Columbia U., 1959; 1st prize editorial competition Radio and TV News Dirs. Assn., 1968. Republican. Avocations: trout fishing; philately. Home: PO Box 278 Spring Grove MN 55974

HELMER, JAMES BURDETTE, JR., lawyer; b. Piqua, Ohio, May 20, 1950; s. James Burdett Helmer and Elizabeth (Moore) Wagner; m. Deborah Jean Jones, June 26, 1976. B.A., Denison U., 1972; J.D., U. Cin., 1975. Bar: Ohio 1975, U.S. Dist. Ct. (so. dist.) Ohio, 1975, U.S. Ct. Appeals (6th cir.) 1978, U.S. Dist. Ct. (ea. dist.) Ky. 1979, U.S. Supreme Ct. 1979, U.S. Ct. Claims 1981, U.S. Dist. Ct. (no. dist.) Ohio 1981, U.S. Dist. Ct. (ea. dist.) Wis., 1982. Law clerk Judge Timothy S. Hogan, Cin., 1975-77; assoc. John A. Lloyd, Jr., Cin., 1977-80, Sherman E. Unger, Cin., 1980-81; ptnr. Kohn & Helmer, Cin., 1981-83; sole practice, Cin., 1983—; charter mem. Arbitration Council of U.S. Dist. Ct. So. Dist. Ohio, 1984; Editor-in-chief U. Cin. Law Rev., 1974-75. Named Master of the Bench Cin. Inns of Ct., 1984. Mem. Fed. Bar Assn., Ohio Bar Assn., Cin. Bar Assn., ABA, D.C. Bar Assn., Scribes, Order of Coif. Republican. Methodist. Home: 4437 Edenton Lane Cincinnati OH 45242 Office: 2305 Central Trust Tower 1 W 4th St Cincinnati OH 45202

HELMS, JOSEPH HENRY, librarian; b. Jackson, Mich., Jan. 4, 1948; s. Leo Joseph and Lucille Catherine (Radkey) H. A.A., Jackson Community Coll., 1970; B.S., No. Mich. U., 1972; M.S., Butler U., 1977; M.L.S., Ind. State U., 1981. Tchr. lang. arts St. Gabriel Sch., Indpls., 1973-76; bookmobile librarian Knox County Pub. Library, Vincennes, Ind., 1976-78, adult services librarian, 1978-82; reference librarian Vincennes U. (Ind.), 1982—. Mem. ALA, Ind. Library Assn. Roman Catholic. Office: Shake Library Vincennes U Vincennes IN 47591

HELRICH, CARL SANFRID, JR., physicist, educator; b. Everett, Mass., Sept. 12, 1941; s. Carl Sanfrid and Anna Brita (Ohman) H.; m. Betty Jane Weaver, Aug. 26, 1967; children—Carl Svante, David Clinton. B.S., Case Inst. Tech., 1963; Ph.D., Northwestern U.-Evanston, Ill., 1969. Asst. prof. aerospace engring. U. Tenn. Space Inst., Tullahoma, 1969-71; scientist Kernforschungsanlage, Jülich, Germany, 1971-74, guest scientist, 1982-83; assoc. prof., dept. chmn. Bethel Coll., North Newton, Kans., 1976-85; prof. physics Goshen Coll., Ind., 1985—. fellow Am. Soc. Engring. Edn., NASA Flight Ctr., Huntsville, Ala., 1971. Contbr. articles to profl. jours. Lay pastor, tchr. New Creation Fellowship Mennonite Ch., Newton, Kansas, 1978-85. Mem. Am. Physical Soc., Kans. Acad. Sci., Fed. Am. Scientists, N.Y. Acad. Scis., Sigma Xi (assoc.). Democrat. Home: 618 S 3d St Goshen IN 46526 Office: Dept Physics Goshen Coll Goshen IN 46526

HELSEL, JAMES RICHARD, construction company executive; b. Gary, Ind., Sept. 16, 1939; s. Homer Leo and Dovie Marie (Potts) H.; m. Judy Sue Smallfield, Sept. 30, 1961; children—James Kip, Kristie Sue. Student Ind. U., Purdue U. Lic. real estate salesman, Ind. Draftsman, Henderlong Lumber Co., Crown Point, Ind., 1956-58; draftsman and field supr. Nolan & Clark Architects, Crown Point, 1959-62; multi-family designer Mid-Am. Homes, Inc., Merrillville, Ind., 1963-64; office and project mgr. Mirich Constrn. Corp., Merrillville, 1965-78; constrn. mgr. Triangle Constrn. Inc., Merrillville, 1978—. Mem. Home Builders Assn. Republican. Methodist. Avocations: architectural designing of custom homes; handball; boating. Home: 715 S East St Crown Point IN 46307 Office: Triangle Constrn Inc 8695 Broadway Merrillville IN 46410

HELSEL, JESS F., metallurgical company executive; b. Deerfield, Ohio, Dec. 22, 1924; s. Jesse A. and Alice Agnes (Bruey) H.; student Kent State U., Akron U., Earlham Coll.; m. Barbara Jene Ebert, Mar. 1, 1947; children—Peter Fredrich, Jessica Jane, Leslie Alison. Supts., Wel-Met Co., Kent, Ohio, 1946-51, plant mgr., Salem, Ind., 1951-55; sales mgr. Ferraloy Co., Salem, 1955-57, pres., 1957-70; gen. mgr. powder metal products div. Gould, Inc., Salem, 1970-73, dir. bus. devel., 1973; pres. Helsel Metall. Co., Campbellsburg, Ind., 1974—, also dir.; pres., dir. Hel-Met, Inc., Helsel Metall. Internat. Corp. Chmn. bd. trustees Ind. Vocat. and Tech. Coll.; bd. dirs., exec. com. Found. Ivy Tech., also chmn. state bd. trustees; chmn. Ind. Small Bus. Council. Served with USMRC, 1942-45. Decorated Purple Heart; named Hoosier Assoc. Mem. Soc. Automotive Engrs., Soc. Mfg. Engrs., Am. Soc. Metals, Am. Powder Metal Inst., Am. Ordnance Assn., Powder Metallurgy Parts Assn. (pres. 1965-67), Metal Powder Industries Fedn. (pres. 1967-69), Ind. State C. of C. (dir.). Ind. Appaloosa Assn., Appaloosa Horse Club, Hoosier Horse Council. Republican. Home: RFD 3 Salem IN 47167 Office: Box 68 State Rd 60W Campbellsburg IN 47108

HELTNE, PAUL GREGORY, museum administrator, environmental consultant; b. Lake Mills, Iowa, July 4, 1941; s. Palmer Tilford and Grace Catherine (Hanson) H.; children—Lisa, Christian. B.A., Luther Coll., 1962; Ph.D., U. Chgo., 1970. Asst. prof. Johns Hopkins Med. Sch., Balt., 1970-82; dir. Chgo. Acad. Scis., 1982—; cons. WHO (PAHO), Washington, 1976-82, Am. Petroleum Inst., Washington, 1983—. Editor, author: Neotropical Primates: and Conservation: Status, 1976, The Lion-tailed Macaque, 1985; assoc. editor-in-chief GROWTH jour., 1978—. Trustee Balt. Zool. Soc., 1972-82; mem. council Resurrection Lutheran Ch., Chgo., 1985—. Mem. Am. Assn. Museums, Assn. Sci. Mus. Dirs., AAAS, Am. Primatological Assn., Internat. Primatology Soc., Am. Zool. Soc., Soc. Study of Evolution, Systematic Zoology Soc. Office: Chgo Acad Scis 2001 N Clark St Chicago IL 60614

HELTON, WENDY (WINIFRED WENDOLYN HARRISON), state ofcl.; b. Lexington, Ky., Sept. 6, 1941; d. Damon Wilson and Helen Evelyn (Tuttle) Harrison; B.S., Western Ky. U., 1963; M.A., Ind. U., 1970. Tchr., Huntingberg (Ind.) High Schs., 1963-65, New Albany-Floyd County Consol. Schs., Floyd Knobs and Georgetown, Ind., 1965-68, Ellettsville (Ind.) High Sch., 1968-69, Ripley (W.Va.) High Sch., 1970, Ravenswood (W.Va.) High Sch., 1970-73; state FHA/HERO advisor Ind. Dept. Pub. Instrn., Div. Vocat. Edn., Indpls., 1973-75, state cons. Home Econs. Edn., 1975-80; state coordinator civil rights guidelines Ind. State Bd. Vocat. Tech. Edn., Indpls., 1980-81, state coordinator for reduction of sex bias, 1981—. Membership on adv. com. on sex discrimination Ind. Civil Rights Commn., 1981—; mem. N. Central Evaluation teams, 1975-81; bd. dirs. Big Sisters Greater Indpls.; dist. advisor Future Homemakers of Am., Ind., 1968-70. Recipient Ind. Hon. Membership FHA award, Ind. Assn. Future Homemakers of Am., 1975; Ind. U./Purdue U. fellow, 1975; Purdue U. grantee, 1978; Big Sister of Yr., 1983. Mem. Ind. U. Home Econs. Alumni Assn. (treas.-sec. 1974, treas. 1981-82), Am. Vocat. Assn., Ind. Vocat. Assn., Ind. Council Vocat. Adminstrs., Vocat. Edn. Equity Council, Nat. Assn. Female Execs., Ind. Vocat. Home Econs. Assn., Ind. Employment and Tng. Assn. Presbyterian. Home: 5658 N Broadway Indianapolis IN 46220 Office: 17 W Market St Room 401 Indianapolis IN 46204

HEMBEL, ALAN GEORGE, life insurance company executive, real estate consultant; b. West Bend, Wis., Sept. 6, 1946; s. George Benjamin and Fern Louise (Resch) H.; m. Carmen Gran Kelsey, Jan. 22, 1972 (dec. 1985); children—Benjamin Alan, Sara Ann Louise. B.B.A. with honors, U. Wis., 1971, M.S. in Real Estate, 1974. With CUNA Mut. Ins. Group, Madison, Wis., 1974—, real estate adminstr., 1974-78, asst. v.p. real estate mgmt., 1978—; instr. U. Wis. Extension, 1976—; cons. in field. Served to capt., field arty. USAR, 1973—. Fellow Life Office Mgmt. Inst.; C.L.U. Republican. Lutheran. Home: 5308 Scenic Ridge Trail Middleton WI 53562 Office: CUNA Mut Ins Group PO Box 391 Madison WI 53701

HEMBROUGH, BETTY LOU, university official, counselor; b. Jacksonville, Ill., Oct. 11, 1929; d. Wallace Trabue and Dorothy Lawrence (Black) Hembrough; A.B., U. Ill., 1951, postgrad., 1953, 61-67; Ed.M., Colo. State U., 1952; postgrad. Washington U., 1960-61, UCLA, 1955. Grad. counselor Colo. State U., 1951-52; head resident counselor, asst. to dean U. Kans., 1953-57; counselor Vocat. Counseling Service of Greater St. Louis, 1957-61; asst. to dean of women U. Ill. at Urbana, 1961-65, asst. dean of students, 1965—, dir. Office of Women's Resources and Services, 1975—. Mem. edn. com. Ill. Commn. on Status of Women, 1976—; adv. com. on women's studies program Parkland Coll., 1972-75; bd. dirs. East Central Ill. Health Systems Agy., 1980—, chmn. plan devel. com., 1982—. Mem. Adult Edn. Assn. U.S., Am. Assn. Higher Edn., AAAS, Am. Ednl. Research Assn., AAUW, Am. Assn. Counseling and Devel., Am. Coll. Personnel Assn., Nat. Vocat. Guidance Assn., Nat. Assn. Women Deans, Adminstrs. and Counselors (dir. inst. speakers and cons. 1976-80, chmn. publs. com. 1980-82), Nat. Council on Family Relations, Univ. and Coll. Women Ill., Ill. Hist. Soc., Sierra Club, Nat. Wildlife Fedn., Nat. Audubon Soc. Author: (with Miriam A. Shelden) The Student Wife and the Married Woman Student: Their Educational Needs, Desires and Backgrounds, 1964. Editor: Focus on Women: Yesterday, Today and Tomorrow, 1974. Contbr. articles to profl. jours. Home: PO Box 2407 Sta A Champaign IL 61820 Office: 346 Student Services 610 E John St Champaign IL 61820

HEMINGER, EDWIN LLOYD, newspaper publisher; b. Findlay, Ohio, July 30, 1926; s. Russell Lowell and Golda (McClelland) H.; m. Barbara Jo Rieck, Sept. 20, 1952; children—Karl Loyd, Margaret Ann Heminger Gordon, Kurt Frederick. B.A., Ohio Wesleyan U., 1948; M.S., Northwestern U., 1952; D. Jour. (hon.), Bethany Coll., 1980. Field sec. Delta Tau Delta, Indpls., 1948-49; asst. bus. mgr. Courier, Findlay, Ohio, 1952-59, pub., 1965—; v.p. Findlay Pub. Co., 1959-83, pres., 1983—, also dir.; pres. White River Broadcasting Co. Inc., 1983—; dir. AP, 1985—; dir. First Nat. Bank of Findlay, Celina Fin. Corp., Celina Mut. Ins. Co., Nat. Mut. Ins. Co., Nat. Gas & Oil Co., AP, 1985—, Warren Tool Corp. Pres., Findlay YMCA, 1965-67, United Way of Hancock County, 1969-70, Hancock Community Found., 1970-72, Hancock Hist. Mus. Assn., 1970—; mem. Constl. Revision Commn., State of Ohio, 1970-77. Served with USNR, 1944-45, 50-51. Mem. Am. Newspaper Pubs. Assn. (dir. 1980—), Am. Newspaper Pubs. Assn. Found. (vice chmn. 1985—), Ohio Newspaper Assn. (dir. 1979—), Newspaper Advt. Bur. (dir. 1980—), State of Ohio Newspapers Found. (pres. 1979-80), Soc. Profl. Journalists, Nat. Press Club, Toledo Press Club, Inland Daily Press Assn. (pres. 1981), Ohio C. of C. (chmn. bd. 1977-79), Nat. Interfraternity Conf. (dir. 1978—, v.p. 1985), Delta Tau Delta (nat. pres. 1972-74). Trustee, Findlay Coll., 1976—, Ohio Wesleyan U., 1977-85. Republican. Methodist. Clubs: Rotary, Findlay Country; Mid-Ocean (Bermuda); Belmont Country (Perrysburg, Ohio). Lodge: Elks.

HEMMER, JEROME OLIVER, insurance executive; b. Belleville, Ill., July 27, 1932; s. Nicholas and Loretta (Fournie) H.; m. Lois L. Burke, Oct. 15, 1955; children—David, Robert, William, Jeffrey, Nancy. B.B.A., So. Ill. U., 1957. Real estate broker Hemmer Agy., Belleville, 1957-67; stockbroker Mid-Am. Bd., Belleville, 1967-71; broker, owner Hemmer Ins. Agy., Belleville, 1971—; pres. Belleville Bd. Realtors, 1966; mem. gen. agts. council Life Investors Inc., Cedar Rapids, Iowa, 1975-80. Pres. United Youth Belleville, 1965, 69; pres. bd. YMCA S.W. Ill., 1975, 1983-84; mem. Belleville Zoning Bd., 1981—; pres. Holy Name Soc., St. Henry's Catholic Ch., Belleville, 1984—. Served to sgt. USMC, 1951-53, Korea. Lodge: Optimists (bd. dirs.). Avocation: basketball. Home: 21 Fourscore Dr Belleville IL 62223 Office: Box 512 Belleville IL 62223

HEMMING, JOHN PARR, optometrist, educator; b. Pontiac, Mich., Apr. 25, 1954; s. John Henry, Jr. and Shirley Jean (Wing) H.; m. Maureen Gibson, Feb. 8, 1980; children—Christi Marie, Cori Ann. Student Wayne State U., 1972-74, Ferris State Coll., 1974-75; O.D., Ferris Coll. Optometry, 1979. Cert. optometric clin. assoc. Optometrist, Lansing Ophthalmology, P.C., Mich., 1979-80; assoc. D.M. Burnett, O.D., Grand Ledge, Mich., 1979-80; clin. assoc. Ferris Coll. Optometry, Big Rapids, Mich., 1979—; ptnr. Burnett & Hemming, Grand Ledge and Lake Odessa, Mich., 1981—; cons., speaker in field. Mem. Am. Optometric Assn., Mich. Optometric Assn., Central Mich. Optometric Soc. (v.p.), Mich. Assn. Professions, Ferris State Coll. Alumni Assn. (v.p.), Lake Odessa C. of C. Episcopalian. Club: Lake Odessa Men's Softball. Lodge: Lions (Lake Odessa) (bd. dirs.). Office: 1038 4th Ave PO Box 516 Lake Odessa MI 48849

HEMOND, ROLAND, See *Who's Who in America,* 43rd edition.

HEMPHILL, HORACE DAVID, museum official; b. Edmonton, Alta., Can., May 25, 1933; s. David Hill and Louis (Warren) H. m. Maureen L. Miller, Apr. 7, 1958; children—Carol Ann, James David, Donald Ross, Susan Leslie. B.A., U. B.C., 1956; M.Ed., U. Alta., 1966, Ph.D. (Queen Elizabeth scholar), 1968. Tchr. high schs., B.C., Can., 1958-62; vice prin. West Vancouver (B.C.) Secondary Sch., 1962-65, dir. research Man. (Can.) Dept. Edn., 1968-70; mng. dir. Man. Mus. of Man and Nature, Winnipeg, Man., 1971-79, exec. dir., 1979—; pres. Hemphill Assocs., Winnipeg, 1980—; hon. prof. U. Winnipeg, 1972. Mem. exec. com. Man. Heart Found., 1973-78; bd. dirs. Winnipeg Social Planning Council, 1974-81. Mem. Mus. Dirs. Can. (chmn. council assocs.), Can. Mus. Assn., Man. Ednl. Research Council, Assn. Man. Mus., Beta Theta Pi. Office: 190 Rupert Ave Winnipeg MB R3B ON2 Canada*

HEMPHILL, ROBERT JULES, mechanical engineer; b. Oak Park, Ill., Nov. 1, 1941; s. William Taylor and Luella Eileen (Evans) H.; m. Lora Lee Wagner, Aug. 25, 1962; children—Todd, Mark, Scott. B.S., Purdue U., 1963. Product engr., Sears Roebuck & Co., Chgo., 1964-73, sales engr., 1973-78, buyer, 1978-80; mgr. appliances and space conditioning Gas Research Inst., Chgo., 1980—; chmn. steering com. Gas Appliance Tech. Center, Cleve., 1983—. Contbr. articles to profl. jours. Mem. Am. Soc. Heating, Refrigeration & Air Conditioning, Gas Engrs. Soc. Methodist. Avocations: boating, water sports. Office: Gas Research Inst 8600 W Bryn Mawr Ave Chicago IL 60631

HENDEE, SHELLBY LANE, radio executive; b. Lincoln, Nebr., July 22, 1948; s. Harland Aubrey and Sylvia Burdeen (Janecek) H.; m. Laura Louise Neemann, Aug. 21, 1949; children—Troy, Nathan. B.A. in Polit. Sci., John J. Pershing Coll., 1970. Vice pres. ops. Sta. KWBE/KMAZ, Beatrice, Nebr., 1967-80; pres. Sta. KMRN, Cameron, Mo., 1980—. Bd. dirs. Flying Conestogas, Beatrice United Way. Served U.S. Army N.G., 1970-76. Recipient Outstanding Service award Distributive Edn. Clubs. Am., 1975; Dist. Honor award Beatrice Sertoma Club, 1980; named Boss of Yr., Am. Bus. Women's Assn., 1982. Mem. Mo. Broadcasters Assn., Cameron C. of C. (bd. dirs.), Am. Legion. Clubs: Shriners, Rotary, Sertoma, Sportsmanship, Manson, Elks. Home: 323 S Elm Cameron MO 64429 Office: Hwy 69 S Cameron MO 64229

HENDERSON, CHERYL BROWN, educational and image consultant; b. Topeka, Kans., Dec. 20, 1950; d. Oliver Leon and Leda Marie (Williams-Montgomery) B.; m. Larry Dean Henderson, Aug. 5, 1972; 1 son, Christopher. B.S., Baker U., 1972; M.S., Emporia State U., 1976. Tchr., Topeka (Kans.) Elem. Schs., 1972-76, guidance counselor, 1976-79, parent edn. instr., 1977-79; vocat. edn. program specialist Kans. Dept. Edn., Topeka, 1979—; cons. ednl. and image, Brown & Brown Assocs., Topeka, Kans., 1984—; cons. Emporia State U., 1976, N.E. Region, Community Relations div. U.S. Dept. Justice, 1984. Pres.-elect Girls Club of Topeka, 1982—; commnr. Topeka Mayor's Commn. on Status of Women, 1983—; v.p., bd. dirs. Nat. Displaced Homemakers, 1982—. Mem. Kans. Assn. Counseling and Devel. (com. chmn. 1983—), Am. Vocat. Assn., Am. Assn. Counseling and Devel., Kans. Vocat. Assn., Kans. Assn. Career Edn. (co-founder), Alpha Kappa Alpha. Democrat. Methodist. Club: Jack & Jill. Avocations: Sewing, reading, traveling. Office: Kans Dept Edn 120 E 10th St Topeka KS 66612

HENDERSON, EUGENE LEROY, lawyer; b. Columbus, Ind., July 21, 1925; s. Harry E. and Verna (Guffey) H.; m. Mary Louise Beatty, Sept. 6, 1948; children—Andrew, Joseph, Carrie Henderson Walkup. B.A., Franklin Coll., 1950; J.D., Harvard U., 1953. Bar: Ind. 1953. Assoc. firm Baker & Daniels, Inpls., 1953-59, ptnr., 1959-65; sr. ptnr. Henderson Daily Withrow & DeVoe, Indpls., 1965—; dir. Hurco Mfg. Co., Inc., Paper Art Co., Maplehurst Farms, Inc., Advanced Mktg. Systems Corp., The Hoosier Group, Inc.; sec. Ind. Fin. Investors, Inc. Trustee, Franklin Coll., Lacy Found., Indpls., 1983—; v.p. Hoosier Art Salon; bd. dirs. Indpls. Boys' Club. Served with U.S. Mcht. Marines, 1943-44, AUS, 1944-46. Mem. Indpls. Bar Assn., Ind. Bar Assn., ABA, Internat. Law Assn., Indpls. Mus. Art. Democrat. Clubs: Contemporary, Indpls. Athletic, Meridian Hills Country, Skyline. Home: 6225 Sunset Ln Indianapolis IN 46260 Office: 2450 One Indiana Sq Indianapolis IN 46204

HENDERSON, FRANK ELLIS, justice state supreme court; b. Miller, S.D., Apr. 7, 1928; s. Frank Ellis and Hilda (Bogstad) H.; LL.B., U. S.D., Vermillion, 1951; cert. Nat. Jud. Coll., Reno, 1976, 78, 79, N.Y. U., 1980; m. Norma Jean Johnson, Dec. 27, 1956; children—Frank Ellis III, Kimberly Jo, Andrea Lynn, Patrick Hayes, Eric Peter, John Paul, Anastasia Marie, Matthew Joel. Admitted to S.D. bar, 1951, to practice before U.S. Dist. Ct. S.D., 1953; individual practice law, 1953-74; Circuit Ct. judge, 1975-78; justice S.D. Supreme Ct., Pierre, 1979—; U.S. commr., 1963-64. Mem. S.D. State Senate, 1965-66, 69-70. Served to 1st lt. inf., AUS, 1951-53; Korea. Mem. Pennington County Bar Assn., S.D. Bar Assn., Am. Legion, VFW, DAV (past state judge adv., post comdr.). Republican. Roman Catholic. Office: State Capitol Pierre SD 57501*

HENDERSON, GERALDINE JONES, school district library administrator; b. Chgo., Nov. 3, 1931; d. Robert David and Marie (Palasz) Jones; m. Clyde Dwight Henderson, Aug. 17, 1955; children—Jill Marie, Mark David. B.S. in Edn., So. Ill. U., 1949-52, M.S., 1955; M.A., Rosary Coll., 1964. Tchr. social studies Park Forest Schs. (Ill.), 1952-53; tchr. history Carbondale High Sch. (Ill.), 1953-55; speech therapist Hillside Elem. Sch. (Ill.), 1955-57; tchr. history, speech coordinator Downers Grove High Sch. (Ill.), 1957-60; tchr. history Naperville High Sch. (Ill.), 1960-61; head librarian Northwest High Sch., House Springs, Mo., 1972-76, Kirkwood High Sch. (Mo.), 1976-77; media specialist Title IVB program for non-pub. schs. Central Midwest Regional Ednl. Lab., St. Louis, 1978; dir. libraries Waterloo Community Unit Sch. Dist. 5 (Ill.), 1979—. Author, narrator video prodn. for Midwest Bapt. Gen. Conf., Christian Education: Lesson Preparation Goals, 1981. Tchr., coordinator ch. sch. Emmaus Bapt. Ch., Ballwin, Mo., 1981-83. Mem. ALA. Republican. Home: 408 Brass Lamp Dr Ballwin MO 63011 Office: Library Services Waterloo Community Unit Sch Dist 5 Bellefontaine Dr Waterloo IL 62298

HENDERSON, HAROLD RICHARD, mechanical engineer; b. Winchester, Ind., June 9, 1927; s. Harold Kenneth and Helen Marie (Shaw) H.; m. Carole Beth Bender, Nov. 17, 1969; children—John Richard, Marilyn Ann Henderson Alexander, Scott Kenneth. B.S. in Mech. Engring., Tri-State Coll., Angola, Ind., 1949. Registered profl. engr., Ohio. Vice pres. engring. Lancaster Engring. (Ohio), 1953-59; v.p. engring. Arcair Co., Lancaster, 1959-78, v.p. ops., 1978—; dir. Gorsuch Enterprises, Lancaster, 1980—. Patentee in field. Ch. bd. dirs. Jr. Achievement Fairfield County, Lancaster, 1962; leader Central Ohio council Boy Scouts Am., 1963. Served with USNR, 1944-46. Mem. Nat. Welding Soc., Nat. Mgmt. Assn. (Silver Knight Mgmt. award 1982), Am. Soc. Testing Materials. Republican. Presbyterian. Lodge: Rotary. Avocations: Private pilot, stained glass. Home: 152 Lenwood Dr Lancaster OH 43130 Office: Arcair Co 3010 N Memorial Dr Lancaster OH 42130

HENDERSON, JAMES ALAN, engine company executive; b. South Bend, Ind., July 26, 1934; s. John William and Norma (Wilson) H.; A.B., Princeton U., 1956; Baker scholar, Harvard U., 1961-63; m. Mary Evelyn Kriner, June 20, 1959; children—James Alan, John Stuart, Jeffrey Todd, Amy Brenton. With Scott Foresman & Co., Chgo., 1962; staff mem. Am. Research & Devel. Corp., Boston, 1963; faculty Harvard Bus. Sch., 1963; asst. to chmn. Cummins Engine Co., Inc., Columbus, Ind., 1964-65, v.p. mgmt. devel., 1965-69, v.p. personnel, 1969-70, v.p. ops., 1970-71, exec. v.p., 1971-75, exec. v.p., 1975-77, chief operating officer, 1975—, pres., 1977—, also dir.; dir. Cummins Engine Found., Ind. Bell Telephone Co., Indpls., Inland Steel Co., Chgo., Hayes-Albion Corp., Jackson, Mich. Pres., Jr. Achievement, Columbus, 1967-69; gen. chmn. Bartholomew County United Fund Campaign, 1970; pres. Hoosier Hills council Boy Scouts Am., 1970-72, Culver Legion, Culver Alumni Assn., 1971-72; mem. selection com. Rockefeller Pub. Service awards, 1978-79; Co-mgr. Rockefeller for Pres. Campaign, 1968; trustee Princeton U.; bd. dirs. Culver Ednl. Found., Heritage Fund of Bartholomew County, Inc. Served to lt. USNR, 1956-61. Mem. NAM (dir.), Columbus Area C. of C. (pres. 1973, adv. com. 1974). Presbyterian (elder). Author: Creative Collective Bargaining, 1965. Office: PO Box 3005 Columbia IN 47201*

HENDERSON, JAMES WILLIAM, JR., state natural resource administrator, lecturer, consultant; b. New Castle, Ky., June 28, 1931; s. James William and Sadie (Barnes) H.; m. Carma Dellia McCann, Mar. 17, 1960; children—Steven B., Karen Leslie, David Keith. B.S., Ky. State U., 1954; M.S.P.H., U. Ky., 1958; M.P.H.A., U. Mich., 1970, Ph.D., 1975. Cert. tchr., Ohio, Mich., Ky. Sanitarian I, Phila. Health Dept., 1959-62; sanitarian II, then III, Macomb County (Mich.) Health Dept., 1962-65; instr. environ. health, cons. to dept. student health Howard U., Washington, 1965-69; program dir. Washtenaw County (Mich.) Health Dept., 1970-81, chief sanitarian, 1982—; vis. lectr. Eastern Mich. U. Mem. Ann Arbor (Mich.) Draft Bd., 1971-76; pres. Parent Tchrs. Student Orgn., Claque Jr. High Sch., Ann Arbor, 1979; mem. exec. bd. Wolverine council Boy Scouts Am., 1980—. Served to cpl. U.S. Army, 1955-59. Ky. State U. scholar, 1950-54; U. Mich. Sch. Pub. Health trainee, 1969. Mem. Nat. Assn. Sanitarians (registered sanitarian; Presdl. citation 1967), Am. Pub. Health Assn., Mich. Environ. Health Assn., Mich. Pub. Health Assn., NAACP., Omega Psi Phi. Republican. Club: Rotary (Ann Arbor). Home: 2636 Prairie Ann Arbor MI 48105 Office: 608 W Allegan St Lansing MI 48909

HENDERSON, NORMAN LEE, photogrammetrist, engineer, surveyor; b. Erie, Pa., Oct. 18, 1925; s. Clyde Samuel and Bessie Ruth (Prindle) H.; m. Marjorie Holden, 1948 (div. 1963); children—Sharon Henderson Bauer, Lorraine Henderson Skinner, Susan.; m. Dorothy Taylor, Nov. 18, 1963. B.S. in Civil Engring., Syracuse U., 1951. Registered civil engr., surveyor, photogrammetric engr., Ohio. Photogrammetrist U.S. Geol. Survey, Washington, 1951-52; design engr. Ohio Hwy. Dept., Columbus, 1952-57; photogrammetry dir. Photronix Inc., Columbus, 1957-60; owner, pres. Henderson Aerial Surveys, Inc., Columbus, 1960—. Chmn. Scioto Valley council Boy Scouts Am., 1984—. Served with USAAF, 1944-46. Fellow Am. Congress Surveying and Mapping; mem. Am. Soc. Photogrammetry (bd. dirs. 1972, 80-82, 85—), Mgmt. Assn. Photogrammetric Surveyors (pres. 1973). Republican. Presbyterian. Club: Muirfield Golf (Dublin, Ohio). Lodge: Rotary (pres. 1983). Avocations: reading, collecting World War II books, swimming, golfing, piano. Home: 8614 Dornoch Ct Dublin OH 43017 Office: Henderson Aerial Surveys Inc 5125 W Broad St Columbus OH 43228

HENDERSON, RITA EVELYN, county official; b. Belcourt, N.D., Aug. 11, 1929; d. Joseph David and Mary Angeline (Herman) LaVerdure; m. George L. Lizotte, Jan. 21, 1946 (div.); children—George S., Lyman David; m. 2d, Alvy R. Henderson, Sept. 27, 1951. Student Belcourt Community Coll. (N.D.), 1978-79. Bookkeeper, sec. J.C. Penney, Wahpeton, N.D., 1948-50, Canfields, 1950-51; mgr. family farm, 1951-80; bookkeeper Rolette County Sr. Meals and Services, Rolla, N.D., 1980-82, project dir., 1982—. Mem. Rolette County Community Task Force; mem. Rolette County Bldg. Com.; v.p. Rolette County Council on Aging; bd. dirs. Region III Council on Aging, N.E. Health and Wellness; mem. N.D. Funding Task Force, 1985. Grantee Burlington No. Found., 1983; N.D. Community Found., 1983, World Relief Fund, 1984, Nat. Luth. Indian Bd., 1984, 85, William Randolph Hearst Found., 1985, N.D. Hwy. Dept., 1985. Mem. N.D. Project Dirs. Assn., Rolla Hosp. Aux. Democrat. Presbyterian. Lodges: Rebekah, Odd Fellows.

HENDERSON, ROSEMARY, librarian; b. Coffyville, Kans., July 15, 1936; d. Ray Aubrey and Irene Ora (Maxwell) Neale; A.A., Stephens Coll., 1956; B.S., Tex. Wesleyan Coll., 1959; M.L.S., Kans. State Tchrs. Coll., 1967; Ed.D., U. Kans., 1976; m. Vance John Henderson, Mar. 9, 1957 (div.); 1 dau., Jennifer Ann. Asst. prof. librarianship U. N.D., Grand Forks, 1967-68; dir. learning resources Coffeyville Community Jr. Coll., 1968—; cons.-evaluator North Central Assn. Schs. and Colls. Mem. ALA (chmn. community jr. coll. sect. 1975-76, sect. archivist, historian 1978—, membership promotion task force 1978-81, nominating com. 1979, membership com. 1981-83), Kans. (sec. 1972-74, mem. council 1970-74, 78—, pres. elect pres. coll. and univ. libraries sect. 1981-83), Mountain Plains (chmn. coll. and univ. sect. 1973-74) library assns. Reviewer, Library Jour., 1970-74, Am. Reference Books Annual-Libraries Unltd., 1974-80. Home: 1206 West 5th St Coffeyville KS 67337 Office: Coffeyville Community Jr Coll Coffeyville KS 67337

HENDERSON, ROSS, business administration educator; b. Winnipeg, Man., Can., Aug. 5, 1928; s. Douglas Dudgeon and Annie Colville (Douglas) H.; m. Jeanette Kirk, Oct. 10, 1953; children—Scott Douglas, Craig Alexander, Eric Grant. B.Sc.M.E., U. Manitoba, 1955; M.B.A., Harvard U., 1957; Ph.D. in Bus., U. Western Ont., Can., 1975. Registered profl. engr., Man. Prin. Ross Henderson Ins. Co., Winnipeg, 1950-66; analyst U.S. Steel Co., Cleve., 1958-60; pres. Damascus Steel Products Ltd., Winnipeg, 1960-65; asst. gen. mgr. Dosco Steel Ltd., Montreal Works, Montreal, Que., Can., 1965-68; prof. bus. adminstrn. U. Man., Winnipeg, 1968—. Author: Plant Startup Productivity, 1975. Contbr. articles to profl. jours. Recipient Gov. Gen.'s medal, 1945; George F. Baker scholar, 1956; recipient Stanton award for Teaching Excellence, U. Man., 1977. Mem. Assn. Profl. Engrs. Man., Am. Soc. Quality Control; fellow Fin. Analysts Fedn. Avocations: running; swimming. Office: U Man Dept Bus Adminstrn Winnipeg MB R3T 2N2 Canada

HENDERSON, THOMAS LEE, psychologist; b. Lone Pine, Calif., Aug. 12, 1941; s. Thomas A. and Pauline G. (Lyon) H.; B.S., Ind. U., 1963, M.A.T., 1965, Ph.D. (teaching fellow 1969-72), 1972; m. Sandra Kidd, July 24, 1965;

1 dau., Leigh Anne. Tchr., Shortridge High Sch., Indpls., 1965-69; asst. mgr. Kidd Ins. Agencies, Brazil, Ind., 1969-70; community mental health worker Katherine Hamilton Mental Health Center, Terre Haute, Ind., 1972-73, staff psychologist, supr. Clay County Program, Brazil, 1973-74; chief psychologist, program dir., dir. tng. Hamilton Mental Health Center, 1974—; mem. faculty Ind. State U., 1972—, adj. asst. prof., 1974—; cons. Gibault Sch. Boys. Chmn. Clay County Young Republicans, 1977—, Red Cross Safety Com., 1960—. Named Outstanding Young Rep. in Clay County, 1978. Mem. Am. Assn. Marriage and Family Therapy, Am. Psychol. Assn., Ind. Psychol. Assn., Am. Assn. Marriage and Family Therapy (clin. and approved supr.), Phi Delta Kappa, Pi Gamma Mu, Kappa Delta Pi. Republican. Presbyterian. Club: Elks. Author papers in field. Home: Rural Route 11 Box 93 Forest Manor Brazil IN 47834 Office: 1206 E National Ave Brazil IN 47834

HENDERSON, TOM MACK, surveyor; b. Omaha, Apr. 23, 1949; s. Robert Mack and Betty Laurene (Horner) H.; m. Susan S. Fish, Sept. 16, 1972; children—Erin Nicole, Andrew George. B.A. in Govt., Ohio U., 1971. Registered profl. surveyor, Ohio; lic. land surveyor, W. Va. Rodman, chmn., party chief Robert C. Vernon Inc., Marietta, Ohio, 1976-79; surveyor engring. div. City of Parkersburg, W. Va., 1979—. Coordinator city employees United Fund Drive, Parkersburg, 1984. Mem. Am. Congress Surveying Mapping, Profl. Land Surveyors Ohio, W. Va. Assn. Land Surveyors (bd. dirs. 1983—, pres.-elect 1985). Avocations: hiking, skiing, computing. Home: Route 1 Box 316 Fleming OH 45729 Office: City Parkersburg PO Box 1627 Parkersburg WV 26101

HENDREN, GARY GENE, mathematics educator; b. Bethany, Mo., Feb. 15, 1939; s. Dwight Lyle and Helen Irene (Beeks) H.; m. Lonna Sharon McComas, Aug. 30, 1959 (div. Feb. 17, 1977); children—Sheri Ann, Jana Beth; m. Lynda Rose Lederman, Dec. 4, 1981. B.S. in Edn., NE Mo. State U., 1962, M.A. in Edn., 1966. Math. tchr. Riverview Gardens Sch. Dist., St. Louis County, Mo., 1962-68; math. tchr. Parkway Sch. Dist., Chesterfield, Mo., 1968—, athletic coordinator, 1977—; off-campus instr. NE Mo. State U., St. Charles, Mo., 1968—; speaker math. and athletic confs. Named Outstanding Young Educator, Mo. Jaycees, 1972; recipient Pillar of Parkway award Parkway Sch. Dist., 1978, Faculty Dedication award Parkway Central High Sch., 1982. Mem. NEA (del. convs. 1978-80), Mo. Edn. Assn. (del. convs. 1978-79), Parkway Edn. Assn. (treas. 1976-77), Nat. Council Tchrs. Math. (local com. chmn. for confs. in St. Louis), Mo. Council Tchrs. Math. (pres. 1980-81, editor Math. Problems page 1981—), Ill. Council Tchrs. Math., Math. Club Greater St. Louis (pres. 1975-76), Mo. Interscholastic Athletic Adminstrs. Assn., Nat. Interscholastic Athletic Adminstrs. Assn., Greater St. Louis Stamp Club (jr. club advisor 1979—), Pi Mu Epsilon. Methodist. Avocation: philately. Office: Parkway Central High Sch 369 N Woods Mill Rd Chesterfield MO 63017

HENDREN, JAMES ANDREW, real estate broker, farmer; b. Moberly, Mo., Jan. 22, 1948; s. William Ashford and Dorothy Louise (Sears) H.; m. Connie Bell, Oct. 1, 1966; children—Andrew Quenten, Brett Cavender, Luke Robert. Student Moberly Jr. Coll., 1967; B.S., U. Mo., 1970, M.S., 1975. Regional supr. N.E. Mo., Nat. Farmers Orgn., Corning, Iowa, 1970-74; assoc. mgr., farm loan officer Fed. Land Bank, Hannibal, Mo., 1976-78; mgr. Mo. real estate and farm loans Bell Investment Co., Burlington, Iowa, 1978-82; owner, mgr., broker, loan officer Jim Hendren Real Estate, Columbia, Mo., 1982—; instr. Hannibal LaGrange Coll., 1977. U. Mo. grantee, 1974. Mem. Mo. Soc. Farm Mgrs. and Rural Appraisers. Baptist. Clubs: Columbia Soccer (dir. 1982—), Optimist (v.p. 1982—). Home: 1939 Hayselton Jefferson City MO 65101

HENDRICKS, LEWIS TALBOT, forest products educator, consultant; b. Rome, N.Y., July 3, 1940; s. Clarence Murray and Thola P. (Brinkman) H.; m. Suzanne Haskins Rose, Aug. 25, 1962; children—Wendy, Heather. B.S., SUNY-Syracuse, 1961, M.S. in Wood Products Engring., 1962; Ph.D. in Forest Products, Mich. State U., 1967. Wood products technologist U.S. Dept. Agr. Forest Service, Duluth, Minn., 1964-67; asst. prof. forest products U. Minn.-St. Paul, 1967-71, assoc. prof., 1971-76, prof., 1976—, extension specialist; dir. Woodcraft Industries, St. Cloud, Minn.; forest products cons. Mem. Gov.'s Task Force value added wood products, 1981—. SBA grantee, 1982, 83. Mem. Forest Products Research Soc., Sigma Xi, Epsilon Sigma Phi, Gamma Sigma Delta. Methodist. Contbr. articles to profl. jours. Office: 206 Kaufert Lab 2004 Folwell Univ Minn Saint Paul MN 55108

HENDRICKSON, GARY LEE, computer software consultant; b. Burlington, Vt., Oct. 17, 1944; s. Robert Rexford and Dorothy Mae (Ouimette) H.; m. Sharon Anne Britt, Jan. 13, 1966 (div.); children—Dana Michelle, Heather Lynn, Laura Brooke; m. Martha Fairchild Rech, July 16, 1984. Analyst, programmer U.S.S. Agri-Chem., Atlanta, 1964-66; analyst, programmer Tupperware, Orlando, Fla., 1966-68; analyst, programmer Fla. Software, 1968-69; sr. analyst Martin Marietta, Washington, 1969-71; sr. cons. Whiteside & Assocs., N.Y.C., 1971-77; pres. Cash Mgmt. Systems, Boca Raton, Fla., 1977—. Recipient NROTC scholarship U.S. Navy, Atlanta, 1962. Democrat. Mem. Pentacostal Ch. Designer, author computer software: standard cost, ledger, accounts receivable, automatic cash application systems. Office: Cash Mgmt Systems Inc PO Box 29-4323 Boca Raton FL 33429

HENDRICKSON, JAMES ROBERT, mechanical engineer; b. Scottsbluff, Nebr., Oct. 9, 1954; s. James Vinton and Mary Virginia (Malm) H.; m. Pamela Sue Groskopf, July 24, 1974; children—Ryan James, Megan Sue. A.S., Nebr. Western Coll., 1974; B.S. in Mech. Engring., U. Nebr., 1976. Registered profl. engr., Nebr., Wyo. Project engr. Norden Labs., Lincoln, Nebr., 1975-77; mech. engr. Nebr. Pub. Power, Columbus, 1977-78, planning engr., Scottsbluff, 1978—. Mem. ASME, ASHRAE, Nat. Soc. Profl. Engrs. Democrat. Roman Catholic. Avocation: computers. Home: 1608 Ave P Scottsbluff NE 69361 Office: Nebr Pub Power Dist PO Box 241 Scottsbluff NE 69361

HENDRICKSON, LAWRENCE HILL, insurance company executive; b. Mpls., May 3, 1939; s. Laurence Jacob and Alocoque Loretta (Tierney) H.; m. Yvonne Janice Gulbro, (div. 1978); children—Laurie A., L. Gordon, Lisa K.; m. 2d Karen Lynne Sparks, May 14, 1983. B.A., U. Minn., 1961. Ins. salesman Sunlife Can. Ins. Co., Mpls., 1960-63; sales mgr. Am. Plan Life Ins. Co., Mpls., 1963-65; ptnr. Hendrickson-Karvonen & Assoc., Mpls., 1965-68; life ins. cons. Nordstrom-Larpenteur Agy., Inc., Mpls., 1968-71; exec. v.p., v.p. Minn.-Tex. Land and Cattle Balanced Fin. Planning, Inc., Mpls., 1971-81; mem. Pres.'s council Alexander Hamilton Life Ins. Co., 1982-85; pres. Lar-Mel Cons. Group, Inc., 1984—; owner L.H. Hendrickson & Co., Mpls., 1981—; dir. Investment Corp. Am., Phila., 1974-78. Author: The Salary Continuation Plan, 1983; The Key Executive Plan, 1984. Named to All Stars, Western State Life Ins. Co., 1968-85, Man of Yr., Western States Life Ins. Co., 1968, 71, 73, 75, 79, 84; recipient Nat. Quality award Nat. Assn. Life Underwriters, 1972-84. Mem. Million Dollar Round Table, Top of the Table, Nat. Assn. Life Underwriters (nat. sales achievement award 1976-84). Republican. Roman Catholic. Clubs: Decathlon Athletic (Bloomington, Minn.); Hazeltine Golf (Chaska, Minn.); Missions Hills Golf (Palm Springs, Calif.). Avocations: squash, golf. Home: 4790 Baycliffe Rd S Excelsior MN 55331 Office: L H Hendrickson & Co 140 3600 W 80th St Bloomington MN 55431

HENDRIKSE, RANDALL DON, computer company executive, consultant; b. Sheboygan, Wis., Oct. 12, 1949; s. John D. and Jeanette (Van Houten) H.; m. Kathleen Joyce Fieldhouse, Aug. 22, 1970; children—Christopher Michael, Timothy John. Student Calvin Coll., 1967-70; Assoc., Davenport Coll., 1970. Rate clk. Chair City Motor Express, Sheboygan, 1971-72, mgr. claims, 1972-76, mgr. data processing, 1976-82, Transpo Services, Sheboygan, 1982-84; pres., owner Accutech Computer Systems Ltd. U.S.A., Sheboygan, 1985—; cons. Software PM, Sheboygan, 1984-85; mem. adv. com. data processing Lakeshore Tech. Inst., Cleveland, Wis., 1984—. Elder, Christian Ref. Ch., Sheboygan, 1983—; announcer religious broadcasting, Sheboygan, 1973—; youth leader Cadets, Sheboygan, 1982—. Republican.

HENDRIX, THOMAS CLAGETT, government official; b. Miraj, India, Sept. 3, 1920; s. Everett Jehu and Minnie Kate (Clagett) H.; came to U.S., 1924; B.A., Hastings Coll., 1942; J.D., Northwestern U., 1947; m. Carol Arden Crumpacker, Sept. 3, 1946 (div. Aug. 1966); children—Walker, Sarah, Anne, Kari; m. 2d, Dona Mae Farber, Oct. 2, 1981 (div. July 1982). Admitted to Mo. bar, 1948, Ill. bar, 1947; practice law, Kansas City, Mo., 1948-53; exec. sec. J.P. Hillelson, U.S. Congressman, Washington, 1953; legal asst., to chmn. NLRB, 1954-55, field atty., St. Louis, 1955-57, regional atty., Kansas City, Mo., 1957-69, regional dir., 1969—. Served wtih USAAF, 1942-45. Home: 10439 Ash St Overland Park KS 66207 Office: Suite 616 Two Gateway Center 4th and State St Kansas City KS 66101

HENKE, ROBERT JOHN, lawyer, engineer; b. Chgo., Oct. 13, 1934; s. Raymond Anthony and May Dorothy (Driscoll) H.; m. Mary Gabrielle Handrigan, June 18, 1960; children—Robert Joseph, Ann Marie. B.S.E.E., U. Ill., 1956; M.B.A., U. Chgo., 1964; J.D., No. Ill. U., 1979. Bar: Ill. 1980, Wis. 1980, U.S. Dist. Ct. (no. dist.) Ill. 1980, U.S. Dist. Ct. (we. and ea. dists.) Wis. 1980, U.S. Supreme Ct. 1984; registered profl. engr., Ill., Wis. Asst. dist. atty. Door County, Wis., 1981, ct. commr., 1981-82; sole practice, Door County, 1981-84, Lake County, Ill., 1984—; dir. Scand, Door County. Vice chmn. Door County Bd. Adjustment, 1983-84; atty. coach Wis. Bar Found. High Sch. Moot Ct. Competition, Door County, 1984. Served with USAR, 1958-63. Mwm. Wis. State Bar Assn., Door Kewaunee Bar Assn. (pres. 1983-84), Ill. State Bar Assn., Chgo. Bar Assn., Lake County Bar Assn., Am. Judicature Soc., Ill. Soc. Profl. Engrs., Assn. Trial Lawyers Am., IEEE, Wis. Soc. Profl. Engrs., Nat. Soc. Profl. Engrs. Roman Catholic. Home: 835 D Country Club Dr Libertyville IL 60048

HENKE, STEVEN JOHN, chemical company executive; b. Beatrice, Nebr., July 11, 1948; s. Gaylord George and Hilda Marie H. B.S., U. Nebr., 1970; M.B.A., Loyola U., Chgo., 1976; m. Janice Jo Barringer, Oct. 12, 1973. Research engr. Amoco Chems., Naperville, Ill., 1970-76, research supr., 1977—; tchr. plastics program Coll. DuPage, 1978-83, mem. plastics adv. bd., 1978-83. Recipient William Heusel award U. Nebr., 1966. Mem. Am. Ofcls. Assn., Soc. Advancement Materials Process Engring., Soc. Plastics Engrs., Internat. Motor Sports Assn. Ill. High Sch. Assn. Recognized Football Ofcls., Phi Eta Sigma. Lutheran. Home: 6713 Cherry Tree Woodridge IL 60517 Office: Warrenville Rd Naperville IL 60566

HENKEL, OTTO FREDERICK, JR., telephone company executive; b. Phila., May 25, 1955; s. Otto Frederick and Jean C. (Wadley) H.; m. Cynthia Ann Krieg, June 17, 1978. B.S. in Agr., Ohio State U., 1976, B.S. in Bus. Adminstrn., 1977. C.P.A., Ohio, Fla.; cert. internal auditor. Staff auditor Alexander Grant & Co., Dayton, Ohio, 1977-78, staff auditor, Cin., 1978-79; internal auditor Cin. Bell, Inc., Cin., 1980-83, corp. tax and acctg. researcher and planner, 1983—. Pres. Ross Citizens for a Better Community (Ohio), 1980-81; bd. dirs. Future Pioneers, Cin., 1983-84, treas. 1984-85. Mem. Inst. Internal Auditors (pres. 1984-85, v.p. 1983-84, treas. 1982-83, mem. internat. com. on membership, 1984-85, bd. govs. 1985-86), Inst. Mgmt. Acctg., Nat. Assn. Accts. (dir. 1981-83, sec. 1983-84, v.p. 1984-85, del. Ohio Council 1983-84, dir. Ohio Council 1984-86), Ohio Soc. C.P.A.s, Fla. Soc. C.P.A.'s, Am. Inst. C.P.A.s, Ky. Soc. C.P.A.s. Republican. Methodist. Home: PO Box 2847 Cincinnati OH 45201 Office: Cin Bell Inc 102-778 PO Box 2301 Cincinnati OH 45201

HENLEY, TERRY LEW, computer company executive; b. Seymour, Ind., Nov. 10, 1940; s. Ray C. and Barbara Marie (Cockerham) H.; B.S., Tri-State U., 1961; M.B.A., Loyola U., 1980, Psy.D., 1982; m. Martha L. Gill, Mar. 26, 1961; children—Barron Keith, Troy Grayson. Research and devel. engr. Halogens Research Lab., Dow Chem. Co., Midland, Mich., 1961-63, lead process engr., polymer plant, Bay City, Mich., 1964, supt. bromide-bromate plants, Midland, 1964-68; nat. sales mgr. Ryan Industries, Louisville, 1968-70; internat. sales mgr. Chemineer, Inc., Dayton, Ohio, 1970-77; cons. mktg., Xenia, Ohio, 1977-78; pres. Computer Guidance, Inc., Vandalia, Ohio, 1978—. Mem. Internat. Graphoanalysis Soc., Am. Inst. Chem. Engrs., Am. Mgmt. Assn., Med. Group Mgmt. Assn., Ohio Handwriting Analysts Assn., Soc. Integration Graphology. Author: Chemical Engineering, 1976. Contbr. articles in field to profl. jours. Home: 1167 Highview Dr Beavercreek OH 45385 Office: Computer Guidance Inc 601 W National Rd Vandalia OH 45377

HENLINE, FLORENCE, pianist; b. Ft. Wayne, Ind.; d. Samuel and Caroline Dorothy (Mollet) Henline; B.M., Chgo. Musical Coll., 1928; m. Milson Jezek, Sept. 2, 1936. Made first concert appearance at age of 13; appeared with Ill. Symphony and Grant Park Orchs., Chgo. Women's Symphony (ofcl. pianist); accompanist; staff pianist, NBC network, 1930-32; pianist, soloist Chgo. Symphony String Ensemble, 1946-56, Chgo. Pops Symphonette; solo concert engagements in Chgo. and throughout U.S.; soloist Indpls. Symphony String Ensemble, 1970, West Side Symphony Chgo.; presenter-performer works of Chgo. composers for Internat. Soc. Contemporary Music, 1960-61; artist faculty mem. Chgo. Conservatory Coll., 1959—. Judge piano solo contest auditions 35th Ann. Chicagoland Music Festival, 1964, soloists Ann. Young Judea Symphony Orch., 1965, 67. Fellow Internat. Inst. Arts and Letters (life); mem. Chgo. Artists Assn., Lake View Mus. Soc., Musicians' Club of Women, Alliance Francaise (Chgo.), Ill. Opera Guild, Art Inst. Chgo., Mu Phi Epsilon (soloist internat. conv. 1972). Club: Cordon. Home: 9715 S Vanderpoel Ave Chicago IL 60643

HENNENBERG, MICHAEL CHAIM, lawyer; b. Wieden, Germany, Sept. 23, 1948; came to U.S., 1949, naturalized, 1955; s. Jacob and Hildegard (Hohenleitner) H.; m. Susan Spitz, Mar. 7, 1982; 1 child, Julia Esther. B.S., Ohio State U., 1970; J.D., Cleve. State U., 1974. Bar: Ohio 1974, U.S. Dist. Ct. (no. dist.) Ohio 1974, U.S. Ct. Appeals (6th cir.) 1977, U.S. Supreme Ct. 1978. Legal intern Pub. Defender's Office Legal Aid, Cleve., 1973-74; ptnr. Greene & Hennenberg Co., L.P.A., Cleve., 1974—. Contbr. articles to profl. jours. Panel chmn. Cuyahoga County Common Pleas Ct. Arbitration Commn., 1974—; bd. dirs. Hebrew Free Loan Assn., 1979-83; active Citizens League Greater Cleve., City Club Cleve.; assoc. chmn. atty.'s div. ann. fundraising drive Jewish Community Fedn., mem. long-range planning task force Holocaust commemoration ann. meeting com.; mem. new leadership div. Israel Bonds, Cleve. Recipient New Life award Israel Bonds, Cleve., 1982. Mem. Ohio State Bar Assn., Cuyahoga County Bar Assn., Assn. Trial Lawyers Am., Nat. Assn. Criminal Def. Lawyers, Cuyahoga Criminal Def. Lawyers Assn. (bd. dirs. 1983—), ABA, Bar Assn. Greater Cleve., Am. Judicature Soc., Cleve. Acad. Trial Attys., Ohio Acad. Trial Lawyers, Nat. Bd. Trial Advocacy. Home: 29200 Shaker Blvd Pepper Pike OH 44114 Office: Greene & Hennenberg Co LPA 801 Bond Ct Bldg Cleveland OH 44114

HENNESSY, HAROLD RICHARD, physician; b. Two Harbors, Minn., Aug. 12, 1903; s. Maurice Alexander and Sarah Maude (Ousman) H.; B.A., Carleton Coll., 1926; B.S., U. Minn., 1930, M.B., 1930, M.D., 1931; cert. in public health U. Calif.-Berkeley, 1939; grad. U.S. Army Sch. of Mil. Govt., 1943; postgrad. U. Va., 1943; m. Helen Adele Lounsberry, July 24, 1930; children—Helen V., Irene E., Harold Richard, Marjorie J. Lic. physician, Minn., Calif., Ill. Intern, Calif. Lutheran Hosp., Los Angeles, 1930-31; resident Los Angeles City Health Dept., 1931-32; practice gen. medicine, Los Angeles, 1932-33; organizer, dir. Sutter-Yuba Bi-County Health Unit, Yuba City and Marysville, Calif., 1939; commd. 1st lt., M.C., U.S. Army, 1930, advanced through grades to col., 1946; chief med. unit instrs. sect. 9th Corps Area Presidio of San Francisco, 1940-41; chief indsl. med. officer Hdqrs. 9th Service Command, Salt Lake City, 1942-43; chief public health officer Hdqrs. Communications Zone G-5, ETOUSA, Hdqrs. SHAEF, 1944; chief public health officer Office of Surgeon, 15th U.S. Army, Belgium and Germany, 1945; cons. to surgeon gen. U.S. Army, 1947-52; cons. Office of Surgeon, 5th U.S. Army, 1962, ret., 1963; pvt. practice public health cons., Park Ridge and Winnetka, Ill., now Highwood, Ill.; mem. staff AMA, 1946-48; asst. sec. Council Indsl. Health, exec. officer com. profl. relations ACS, 1949-66. Decorated Bronze Star (U.S.); knight Order of Public Health (France); officer Order of Orange-Nassau with swords (Netherlands); Commemorative War Cross (Yugoslavia); recipient certs. of appreciation U.S. Army; hon. Ky. col., 1960; hon. mem. Indian Council, Clinton, Okla., named Chief White Arrow, 1960; named Hon. Citizen State of Tex., 1961, Hon. Col., Ala. State Militia, 1965, Hon. Adm. Tex. Navy, 1966; recipient Letter of Commendation, Pres. Harry S. Truman, 1971; Physician Recognition award AMA, 1980, 83; others. Fellow Am. Public Health Assn., Am. Assn. Indsl. Physicians and Surgeons; mem. Am. Assn. Sr. Physicians, Internat. Health Soc. (founder, 1st pres. 1949), Ret. Officers Assn. (Long Timers award 1983), Res. Officers Assn., Assn. Mil. Surgeons U.S., Fifty Yr. Club Am. Medicine, Mil. Order World Wars (mem. Silver Star roll Chgo. chpt.), Order of Lafayette (charter), Phi Beta Pi. Republican. Clubs: Officers (Ft. Sheridan, Ill.); Masons (Two Harbors, Minn.). Author geneal. books; contbr. articles to profl. jours. Home and Office: 616 Sheridan Rd Apt 4-B Highwood IL 60040

HENNESSY, TIMOTHY LEROY, mechanical engineer; b. Chicago Heights, Ill., Feb. 26, 1956; s. LeRoy Dennis and Jacqueline Agnes (Rogina) H.; m. Renee Ann Wroblewski, Oct. 21, 1978. B.S. in Mechanical Engring., U. Ill., 1978. Engr. Johnson & Johnson Products Co., Chgo., 1978-79, maintenance supr., 1979-80; maintenance supr. Personal Products Co., Wilmington, Ill., 1980-82, maintenance engr., 1982-83, project engr., 1983-84, facilities engr., maintenance mgr., 1984—. Named Supr. of Yr., Johnson & Johnson, Inc., 1980. Mem. Ill. Soc. Profl. Engrs., Pi Tau Sigma. Roman Catholic. Home: 15036 81st Ave Orland Park IL 60462 Office: Personal Products Co Kankakee River Rd Wilmington IL 60481

HENNEY, MAC LEE, lawyer; b. Columbus, Ohio, May 25, 1915; s. John Langford Wolbach and Ruth Oleta (Wilson) H.; m. Judith Ann Kauffman, May 29, 1947; children—Scott K., Cynthia Lee Henney Ayers, Deborah Lou Henney Crall, Christina Ann. J.D., Ohio State U., 1937. Bar: Ohio 1937. Sole practice, Columbus, Ohio, 1937-42; 1st officer Pan Am. Airways, Miami, Fla., 1942-46; mem. firm Henney & Walcutt, Columbus, 1946-60, Henney & Shaefer, 1960-70, White, Rankin, Henry, Morse & Mann, Columbus, 1970-85, White & Rankin, L.P.A., Columbus, 1985—; corp. sec. Ohio Bar Title Ins. Co., 1955—. Contbr. articles to profl. jours. Fellow Ohio State Bar Found.; mem. ABA, Ohio Bar Assn., Columbus Bar Assn. Republican. Episcopalian. Lodge: Optimists. Avocations: sailing; flying. Home: 2840 Canterbury Rd Columbus OH 43221 Office: White Rankin Co LPA 175 S Third St Room 900 Columbus OH 43215

HENNING, THOMAS KEITH, educational administrator; b. Fond du Lac, Wis., Apr. 10, 1941; s. Lester L. and Ruth E. (Strong) H.; m. Sandra Marie Gross, Aug. 8, 1964; children—Joie Danielle, Lynn Denise, John Thomas, LeeAnn Rose. B.S., Wis. State Coll.-Oshkosh, 1963; M.S., Wis. State U.-Superior, 1971; postgrad. U. Wis.-Superior, 1979. English tchr. Marinette High Sch., Wis., 1963-66, Slinger High Sch., Wis., 1966-75; prin. Augusta High Sch., Wis., 1975-78, Northwestern High Sch., Maple, Wis., 1978—; mem. state supt.'s adv. council on tchr. edn. and cert., Madison, Wis., 1984—. Pres. Immaculate Conception Parish Council, West Bend, Wis., 1974—; chmn. constn. com. St. Anthony Parish, Augusta, Wis., 1977; sec. adv. com. Chem. Dependence Services, Superior, 1982-84. Mem. Assn. Wis. Sch. Adminstrs. (bd. dirs. 1979-81, cert. 1981), Nat. Assn. Secondary Sch. Prins., Superior C. of C., Midwest High Sch. Ski Assn. (founder, exec. sec. 1972-75), Phi Delta Kappa. Lodge: K.C. Avocation: jogging. Home: 6012 Baxter Ave Superior WI 54880 Office: Northwestern High Sch PO Box 188 Maple WI

HENNING, WILLIAM CLIFFORD, cemetery consulting company executive; b. Kalamazoo, Oct. 21, 1918; s. Russell and Dott Lois (Stauffer) H.; B.A., Albion Coll. (Mich.), 1940; postgrad. Northwestern U. Law Sch., 1940-42, U. Mich. Law Sch., summer 1941; m. Charlotte Conrad, Sept. 14, 1946; children—Peggy J. Henning Berlin, Helen L. Henning Boddy. Sec., Sycamore (Ill.) C. of C., 1945-46; exec. sec. Allegheny County Funeral Dirs. Assn., Pitts., 1946-48, Am. Cemetery Assn., Columbus, Ohio, 1948-56; owner, pres. Am. Cemetery Cons., Inc., Springfield, Ohio, 1961—; sec., treas., gen. mgr. Rose Hill Burial Park, Springfield, Ohio, 1956-76. County chmn. United Appeals Fund, 1962; bd. dirs., 1964-67; moderator Snowhill United Ch. Christ, Springfield, 1958-60. Served to 1st lt. USAAF, 1943-45; PTO. Decorated Air medal with 2 oak leaf clusters. Mem. Am., Central Ohio (pres. 1958), cemetery assns., Ohio Assn. Cemetery Supts. and Ofcls. (pres. 1960), Am. Soc. Profl. Cons. Republican. Club: Springfield Lit. (pres. 1984). Lodges: Eagles, Kiwanis (pres. Springfield 1963), Masons. Contbr. articles to profl. jours. Home and Office: 6319 Plateau Dr Springfield OH 45502

HENRY, ALICE KATHERINE, lawyer; b. Lowville, N.Y., July 9, 1936. B.B.A., Case Western Res. U., 1958; J.D., Cleve. Marshall U., 1965. Bar: Ohio 1965, U.S. Dist. Ct. Ohio, U.S. Supreme Ct. 1969. Sole practice, Cleve., 1965—. Address: 5767 Mayfield Rd #21 Cleveland OH 44124

HENRY, BRUCE EDWARD, city official, educator, management consultant; b. Cin., Apr. 26, 1952; s. Talmage Reed and Evelyn Louise (Hines) H.; m. Arlene Karen Schwiermann, Aug. 25, 1973; children—Jill Michelle, Brett Edward. B.A., U. Cin., 1974, M.P.A., 1975. Cert. peace officer, Ohio. Planning intern Ohio-Ky.-Ind. Regional Council Govts., Cin., 1974-75; asst. county adminstr. Clermont County, Batavia, Ohio, 1975-76, county adminstr., 1976-79; dir. mgmt. services Santoro Engring. Co., Batavia, 1979-81; instr. Am. govt. U. Cin., Batavia, 1979—; dir. pub. safety City of Blue Ash, Ohio, 1981—; chmn. bd. Clermont Met. Housing Authority, Batavia; dir. Clerrenton Corp., Maineville, Ohio. Various polit. positions, Clermont County, 1970-75; mem. exec. bd. Clermont County Youth Services Bur., 1973-75; mem. Clermont County Youth Devel. Council, 1975-77, Clermont County League Women Voters, 1975-79, Fed. exec. Bd.: Intergovtl. Affairs, 1978-79, Clermont Met. Housing Authority, 1979—, Gov.'s Law Enforcement Liaison Com., 1984—; Clermont County rep., mem. various coms. Cin. Community Action Commn. Bd., 1976-77; mem. ednl. goal com. West Clermont Sch. Dist., 1975-77; mem. adv. com. Clermont County Family Services, 1976-79; vol. trustee, exec. com. alternate Ohio-Ky.-Ind. Regional Council Govts., 1976-78; trustee, Greater Community Chest and Council, 1983-85; chmn. Clermont County Community Chest, 1983-84; instr. Great Oaks Police Acad., 1983—; mem. search com. for health commr. Hamilton County Bd. Health, 1984. Recipient Am. Legion medal for Americanism, 1970, leadership awards Greater Cin. Community Chest and Council, 1980, 84, Campaign Vol. award Greater Cin. Community Chest and Council, 1981, planning award Greater Cin. Community Chest and Council, 1981-82; scholarship U. Cin., 1970-74, grad. scholar, teaching asst. U. Cin., 1974-75. Mem. Ohio Assn. Pub. Safety Dirs. (pres. 1985-86), Ohio Assn. Chiefs Police, Internat. City Mgmt. Assn., Am. Soc. Pub. Adminstrn., Internat. Personnel Mgmt. Assn., Greater Cin. City Mgmt. Assn., Fraternal Order Police Assocs., Omicron Delta Kappa. Methodist. Lodge: Kiwanis (sec. 1984). Avocations: hunting; fishing; camping. Office: City of Blue Ash 4343 Cooper Rd Blue Ash OH 45242

HENRY, EDWARD FRANK, computer accounting service company executive; b. East Cleveland, Ohio, Mar. 18, 1923; s. Edward Emerson and Mildred Adella (Kulow) H.; B.B.A., Dyke Coll., 1948; student Cleve. Inst. Music, 1972; m. Nicole Annette Peth, June 18, 1977. Internal auditor E.F. Hauserman Co., 1948-51; office mgr. Frank C. Grismer Co., 1951-52; Broadway Buick Co., 1952-55; treas. Commerce Ford Sales Co., 1955-65; nat. mgr. Auto Acctg. div. United Data Processing Co., Cin., 1966-68; v.p. Auto Data Systems Co., Cleve., 1968-70; pres. Profl. Mgmt. Computer Systems, Inc., Cleve., 1970—, Computer Ease, Small Bus. Computer Ctrs. div. Profl. Mgmt. Computer Systems, Inc., 1985—. Charter pres. No. Ohio Council Little Theatres, 1954-56; founder, artistic and mng. dir. Exptl. Theatre, Cleve., 1959-63; dramatic dir. various community theatres, 1955-65; actor Cleve. Playhouse, 1961-63; bd. dirs. Cleve. Philharmonic Orch., 1972-73. Served with USAAF, 1943-46; CBI. Notary public. Mem. Am. Mgmt. Assn., Nat. Assn. Accountants, Mil. Order World Wars, Heroes of '76, Ky. Cols. Republican. Presbyterian. Clubs: Rotary, Acacia Country, Hermit, Univ., Cleve. Grays, Deep Springs Trout, Nat. Sojourners (Nat. Pres.'s cert. 1977-78), Masons (33d degree), DeMolay (Legion of Honor 1970), K.T., Shriners (dramatic dir.), Jesters (dir. 1981), Grotto, Kachina. Author booklet. Home: 666 Echo Dr Gates Mills OH 44040 Office: 19701 S Miles Ave Cleveland OH 44128

HENRY, EDWIN D., educational administrator; b. Oklahoma City, Sept. 28, 1930; s. Howard E. and Opal R. (DeBoard) H.; m. Peggy A. McMartin, May 7, 1954; children—Angela Kay, Debra Ann. B.S. in Edn., Pittsburg State U., 1960, M.S. in Edn., 1964; postgrad. Emporia State U., 1968-70, Kans. State U., 1976, Pittsburg State U., 1983-84. Tchr. Osborne High Sch., Kans., 1960-62; tchr., coordinator Ottawa High Sch., Kans., 1962-64, Topeka High Sch., 1964-65; Manpower Devel. Tng. Act coordinator State Dept. Edn., Phoenix, 1965-66; tchr., coordinator Seaman High Sch., Topeka, 1966-72; edn. program specialist indsl. edn. Kans. Dept. Edn., Topeka, 1972—; pres. Kans. Indsl. Tchr. Edn. Council, Topeka, 1978-79. Contbr. edn. articles to profl. jours. Served with U.S. Army, 1951-54. Mem. Vocat. Indsl. Clubs Am. (hon. life, bd. dirs. 1979-83, pres. 1981-82), Nat. Assn. State Suprs. Trade and Indsl. Edn. (pres. 1982-84, past pres. plaque 1984), Kans. Assn. Vocat. Indsl. Clubs Am. (bd. dirs. 1969-72, state dir. 1974-76, service award 1972), Kans. Vocat. Assn., Seaman Unified Sch. Dist. (outstanding service award 1972), Am. Legion. Avocations: woodworking; crafts. Home: 499 Lakeshore Dr Route 1 Ozawkie KS 66070 Office: Kans State Dept Edn 120 E 10th St Topeka KS 66612

HENRY, GORDON HOWARD, university administrator; b. Westhope, N.D., Sept. 9, 1940; s. Howard Irving and Arline (Convis) H.; m, Patricia Ann O'Brien, June 23, 1962; children—David, Judith, Michael. B.S., Minot State Coll., 1962; M.S., U. N.D., 1966, Ed.D., 1970. Tchr., coach Tioga High Sch., N.D., 1962-65; asst. prof. counseling U. N.D., Grand Forks, 1971—, asst. dean of men, 1970-73, assoc. dean of students, 1973-84, Student Union dir., 1977-78, 80-84, v.p. student affairs, 1984—; chmn. United Ministries N.D., 1975-79, treas., 1980—; bd. dirs. Wesley Ctr. Found., Grand Forks, 1973—. Bd. dirs. Urban Devel. Com., Grand Forks, 1977-78; chmn. United Ministries in Higher Edn., N.D., 1977-79; bds. dirs. Grand Forks Communiversity, 1980-83; loaned exec. United Way Campaign, Grand Forks, 1985. Recipient Charles Debruyn

Kops award U. N.D. Alumni Assn., 1977. Mem. Am. Personnel and Guidance Assn., Am. Coll. and Personnel Assn., N.D. Personnel Deans (pres. 1976, 80), Phi Delta Kappa. Democrat. Methodist. Avocations: basketball; golf; softball; travel; people. Home: 3627 10th Ave N Grand Forks ND 58201 Office: Vice Pres Student Affairs Univ ND Grand Forks ND 58201

HENRY, JAMES E., industrial engineer; b. Irvine, Ky., Mar. 14, 1942; s. Beverly B. and Hoyte Mae (Tipton) H.; m. Lucille Mullins, Aug. 12, 1978; children—Gregory, Teresa, Michael, Matthew. Indsl. engr. NCR Co., Dayton, Ohio, 1967-72, Springfield, Ohio, 1972-77; mgr. indsl. engring. Internt. Harvester Co., Fort Wayne, Ind., 1977-78, div. indsl. engr., 1978-79, mgr. indsl. engring., Chgo., 1979-82, corp. sr. indsl. engr., 1982-84, productivity mgr., 1984—. Home: 215 Winston Dr Bolingbrook IL 60439 Office: 401 N Michigan Ave Chicago IL 60611

HENRY, KATHLEEN MARIE, international marketing director; b. Stillwater, Okla., Sept. 24, 1950; d. Irl Wayne and Hulda Mary (Duncan) Henry; B.S., Central State U. (Okla.), 1972. Community relations dir./account exec. Lowe Runkle Advt., Oklahoma City, 1972-74, account coordinator, 1975; sales promotion cons. McDonald's Corp., Houston, 1974; regional advt. supr. McDonald's Southfield (Mich.), 1975, regional advt. mgr., 1976-78, local store mktg. mgr., Oak Brook, Ill., 1978-80, staff dir., store mktg./sales promotion, 1980-82, home office dir. store mktg./sales promotion, 1982-83, dir. nat. sales promotion, 1983-84, internat. mktg. dir., 1984—. Publicity chmn. Keep Okla. Beautiful, 1973-74; publicity chmn. Muscular Dystrophy Assn. Am., Okla. chpt., 1973-74; bd. dirs. Southfield Arts Council, 1976-78. Recipient Pres.'s award, McDonald's Corp., 1978; Chgo. YWCA Leadership award, 1978; Disting. Former Student award, Central State U., 1979, Outstanding Sr. Woman, 1972, Outstanding Greek Woman, 1972. Mem. Central State U. Alumni Assn. (dir. 1974), Nat. Assn. Female Execs., Women's Advt. Club Chgo., Sigma Kappa. Home: 6386 Kindling Ct Lisle IL 60532 Office: McDonalds Plaza Oak Brook IL 60521

HENRY, PAMELA JANE, pharmacist; b. Greenville, Ohio, Nov. 3, 1954; d. John Harry and Juanita M. (Grilliot) H. B.S. in Pharmacy, Ohio No. U., 1978. Registered pharmacist, Ohio. Staff pharmacist Children's Med. Ctr., Dayton, Ohio, 1978-79; asst. mgr. Super X Drugs, Greenville, Ohio, 1979-84, Revco, Greenville, 1984—. Mem. Am. Pharm. Assn., Ohio Pharm. Assn., Kappa Epsilon, Alpha Omicron Pi. Roman Catholic. Avocations: music; travel; collecting. Home: 134 W Harmon Dr Greenville OH 45331 Office: Revco DS 534 S Broadway Greenville OH 45331

HENRY, PAUL BRENTWOOD, U.S. congressman; b. Chgo., July 9, 1942; s. Carl F. and H.I. (Bender) H.; B.A., Wheaton Coll., 1963; M.A. (fellow), Duke U., 1968, Ph.D., 1970; m. Karen Anne Borthistle, Aug. 28, 1965; children—Kara Elizabeth, Jordan Mark, Megan Anne. Vol. in U.S. Peace Corps, Liberia, 1963-64, Ethiopia, 1964-65; legis. asst. to Congressman John B. Anderson, 1968-69; instr. polit. sci. Duke U., Durham, N.C., 1969-70, assoc. prof. Calvin Coll., Grand Rapids, Mich., 1970-78; state legislator Mich. Ho. of Reps., 1979-82, asst. minority floor leader, 1979-82; mem. Mich. Senate, 1983-85; mem. 99th U.S. Congress, 5th Mich. dist. Mem. Mich. State Bd. of Edn., 1975-78; Kent County (Mich.) Republican chmn., 1975-76. Mem. Am. Polit. Sci. Assn. Republican. Mem. Christian Reformed Ch. Author: Politics for Evangelicals, 1974; (with Stephen V. Monsma) The Dynamics of the American Political System, 1970. Office: 502 Cannon House Office Bldg Washington DC 20515*

HENRY, THOMAS MITCHELL, lawyer, educator; b. Peoria, Ill., May 24, 1953; s. Warren Eugene and Alice Virginia (Tuttle) H.; m. Sandra Jane Perry, Oct. 6, 1979; 1 child, Jonathan Thompson. B.S., Ill. State U., 1975; J.D., So. Ill. U., 1978. Bar: Ill. 1978, U.S. Dist. Ct. (cen. dist.) Ill. 1978, U.S. Ct. Appeals (7th cir.) 1978. Assoc. W. D. Dersch, Peoria, 1978-81; ptnr. Henry & Henry Attys. at Law, Peoria, 1981—; adj. instr. bus. law Ill. Central Coll., 1981-84. Moderator Plymouth Congl. Ch., Chillicothe, Ill., 1981-83, chmn. refugee com., mem. mission com., 1981-84; pres. bd. dirs. Peoria Friendship House Christian Service, 1982-84. Mem. ABA, Ill. State Bar Assn., Peoria County Bar Assn. (civil practice coms., legal med. relations com.), Northside Businessmens Assn. (v.p. 1982-83). Mem. United Ch. of Christ. Office: Henry & Henry Attys at Law First Nat Bank Bldg Suite 1002 Peoria IL 61602

HENRY, VAUGHN WILLIAM, animal science educator; b. Jacksonville, Ill., Sept. 2, 1951; s. William D. and Ferol (Vaughn) H.; m. June A. Brown, Dec. 9, 1982; 1 dau., Julie Lynne. B.S., U. Ill., 1973, M.S., 1974. Horseshoer, Springfield, Ill., 1969-74; instr. animal sci. Colby Coll., Kans., 1974—, chmn. agr. dept., 1977—; farm mgr. Prairie View Stud, Colby, 1976-80; farm cons., 1974—; comml. pilot, co-owner Heliservices, Inc. Contbr. articles to profl. jours. Mem. Am. Soc. Animal Scientists, Am. Registry Cert. Animal Scientists. Avocations: airplane and helicopter flying; metal working. Office: Colby Community Coll 1255 S Range St Colby KS 67701

HENRY, WILLIAM C., lawyer; b. Cleve., Mar. 19, 1955; s. William W. and Marcella Frances (Beatty) H. B.A., St. Louis U., 1976; J.D., U. Akron, 1979; diploma Air and Space Law, McGill U., 1984. Bar: Ohio 1981, U.S. Dist. Ct. (no. dist.) Ohio 1981, Ill. 1982, U.S. Dist. Ct. (so. dist.) Ohio 1983, U.S. Ct. Appeals (6th cir.) 1983, U.S. Dist. Ct. (so. dist.) Ill. 1985. Sole practice, Cleve., 1981-83; staff atty. SE Ohio Legal Services, Chillicothe, 1983-84; assoc. Rick Reed, P.C., Belleville, Ill., 1984; staff atty. Hyatt Legal Services, Fairview Heights, Ill., 1985—. Mem. Ohio Bar Assn., Ill. Bar Assn., Phi Alpha Delta, Alpha Sigma Nu. Republican. Jewish. Office: Hyatt Legal Services 22 Cross Roads Ctr Fairview Heights IL 62208

HENSLER, VICKI SANDRA, personnel management consultant, career consultant; b. Cleve., March 7, 1946; d. Arthur Bennett and Marilyn Vivian (Brauer) Fine; m. Paul Michael Dorner, June 11, 1966 (div. 1975); children—James Hugh, David Paul; m. Guy Jack Hensler, July 16, 1976. B.S., U. Ill., 1968, M.A., 1977, Ph.D., 1985. Pres. Career Ctr., Inc., Champaign, Ill., 1974—; instr. Parkland Coll., Champaign, 1984—; prin., cons. Profl. Personnel Mgmt., Champaign, 1984—; v.p. Downtown Electric, Inc., Urbana, Ill., 1984—; cons. Marine Am. Nat. Bank, Champaign, Franchise Mgmt. Systems, Inc., Champaign. Author: Journal of Parks and Recreation, 1966. Mem. Better Housing Com., Champaign, 1975; sec., bd. dirs. Ill. Adult and Continuing Edn. Assn., 1975-77; Mem. Am. Assn. Counseling and Devel., Am. Vocat. Assn., Am. Vocat. Rehab. Assn., Assn. Measurement and Evaluation, Nat. Employment Counselors Assn., Vocat. Guidance Assn., Champaign C. of C. (spl. projects com. mem. 1982—), Phi Delta Kappa. Republican. Jewish. Club: Executive (Champaign). Avocations: writing; teaching. Home: 3306 Stoneybrook Champaign IL 61821 Office: Round Barn Sta PO Box 6105 Champaign IL 61821

HENSLEY, MAUDELINE AUDREY CHILTON, educator; b. Eminence, Mo., June 25, 1919; d. James Thomas and Eva Leona (Cox) Deatherage; m. Paul Gordon Chilton, Apr. 19, 1938 (dec.); children—James Paul and Elizabeth Carol; m. 2d, Jesse K. Hensley, Mar. 29, 1979. B.A., Nat. Coll. Edn., Chgo., 1958; M.A., Roosevelt U., Chgo., 1963; Ed.S. in Spl. Edn., So. Ill. U., Edwardsville, 1970. Tchr. rural schs., Mo., 1935-45, Am. Army Sch., Yokohama, Japan, 1945-48, pub. schs., Burlington, Iowa, 1949-52; curriculum specialist Park Forest, Ill., 1952-63; learning disabilities program supr. Granite City, Ill., 1963-79; dir. spl. edn. Rolla, Mo., 1979—. Mem. Council for Exceptional Children, Assn. Children with Learning Disabilities, Mo. State Tchrs. Assn. Clubs: Officers' Wives, Country. Democrat. Home: 812-A Wakefield Rolla MO 65401 Office: 6th and Main St Rolla MO 65401

HENSON, PAUL HARRY, telecommunications executive; b. Bennet, Nebr., July 22, 1925; s. Harry Elmer and Mae Vincent (Schoenthal) H.; B.S.E.E., U. Nebr., 1948, M.S.E.E., 1950, D.H.L. (hon.), 1983; m. Betty Lorene Roeder, Aug. 2, 1946; children—Susan Henson Flury, Lizbeth Henson Barelli. Engr., chief engr. Lincoln Tel.&Tel. Co., Lincoln, Nebr., 1945-59; v.p. United Telecommunications, Inc., Kansas City, Mo., 1959-60, exec. v.p., 1960-64, pres., 1964-66, chmn. bd., 1966—; dir. Armco, Inc., Duke Power Co., Williams Co.; mem. Nat. Security Telecommunications Adv. Com. Trustee, Nat. Legal Center for Public Interest; hon. consul for Sweden. Served with USAAF, 1942-45. Mem. Nat. Soc. Profl. Engrs., NAM, U.S. C. of C., Kansas City C. of C., IEEE, U.S. Ind. Telephone Assn. (dir. 1960-76), Armed Forces Communications and Electronics Assn., Sigma Xi, Eta Kappa Nu, Sigma Tau, Kappa Sigma. Republican. Clubs: River, Kansas City, Kansas City Country, Mission Hills Country, Chicago, Burning Tree, Castle Pines, El Dorado, Masons, Shriners. Office: PO Box 11315 Kansas City MO 64112

HENTHORNE, MARJORIE LUCILLE, designer, children's games manufacturing executive; b. Osawatomie, Kans., May 16, 1921; d. Benjamin F. and Mabel L. Emerson (Sturges) Henthorne; grad. Kansas City (Mo.) Jr. Coll., 1939; student Kansas City (Mo.) Art Inst., 1940-41, William and Mary Profl. Inst., Richmond, Va., 1942-43, King-Smith Sch., Washington, 1944-46; m. Huston Burns McClurc, June 28, 1947; 1 dau., Jeanne Emerson. Free-lance fashion designer, 1939—; Washington corr. Kansas City Star; chief French Lend Lease Control Office, Washington, 1943-45; aide to U.S. senator William F. Knowland of Calif., 1945-47; with Times-Harold News, Washington, 1947; propr., designer J.M.H. Products, Kansas City, Mo., 1975—. Fin. and publicity chmn. We the Women of Hawaii, 1953-54. Mem. Kansas City Women's C. of C., Columbia Arts Club Washington, Hist. Soc. State of Mo., Westport Hist. Soc., Polit. Study Club Alumni Assn., Federated Women's Club. Mem. Christian Ch. Patentee games for children, designs. Address: 133 N Lawn St Kansas City MO 64123

HEPPERMANN, BERDELL JOHN, JR., printing company executive; b. St. Peters, Mo., Mar. 11, 1934; s. Berdell John and Loyola Ann (Doll) H.; m. Margie Ann Kohnen, June 16, 1956; children—John, Jeffrey, Jeannie, Timothy, Marla. Student U. Mo.-Rolla, 1955, Washington U., St. Louis, 1956-58. Design draftsman McDonnell Aircraft, St. Louis, 1956-58; mgr. Crest Bowl, Florissant, Mo., 1958-66; pres. Kimbell Printing & Stationary Co., Florissant, 1967—; ptnr. Kim-Hep, Florissant, 1979—, Old Mische Ranch, Warrenton, Mo., 1970—. Bd. dirs. Florissant Valley Sheltered Workshop, 1960—, North County YMCA, Florissant, 1978—. Served with USN, 1952-54. Mem. Nat. Office Products Assn. (lt. gov. dist. 12 1983-84), Am. Legion, Ducks Unltd., Florissant C. of C. (bd. dirs., officer, Outstanding Bus. Person award 1983). Roman Catholic. Lodges: Optimists (Florissant) (pres., lt. gov.), Rotary (pres.-elect.), K.C. Avocations: hunting; gardening. Home: 14707 Sinks Rd Florissant MO 63034 Office: Kimbell Printing & Stationery 865 Rue St Francois Florissant MO 63031

HEPPNER, PUNCKY PAUL, psychology educator; b. Bismarck, N.D., Feb. 24, 1951; s. Cornelius and Katie (Stoppler) H.; m. Mary Jean Soehren, June 9, 1973. B.S., U. Minn., 1973; M.A., U. Nebr., 1975, Ph.D., 1979. Grad. asst. U. Nebr., Lincoln, 1973-78; counseling intern Colo. State U., Fort Collins, 1978-79; asst. prof. psychology U. Mo., Columbia, 1979-84, assoc. prof., 1984—. Life-lines editor Jour Counseling and Devel., 1984—. Contbr. articles to profl. jours. Research fellow U. Mo., 1982; Fulbright scholar, 1985. Mem. Am. Psychol. Assn., Am. Assn. Counseling and Devel., Am. Coll. Personnel Assn. (bd. dirs. commn. VII 1981-84). Avocations: Landscaping, gourmet cooking, brewing beer, hiking, traveling. Home: 113 Westridge Dr Columbia MO 65203 Office: U MO Psychology Dept 210 McAlester Hall Columbia MO 65211

HERBERT, EDWARD FRANKLIN, public relations executive; b. N.Y.C., Jan. 30, 1946; s. H. Robert and Florence (Bender) H.; m. Rhonda J. Scharf, Aug. 20, 1967; children—Jason Dean and Heather Ann (twins). B.S. in Communications, Syracuse U., 1967, M.S., 1969. Assoc. dir. pub. relations Am. Optometric Assn., Washington, 1971; community relations specialist Gen. Electric Co., Columbia, Md., 1971-73, pub. relations account supr., 1973-75; dir. pub. affairs Nat. Consumer Fin. Assn., Washington, 1975-78; regional dir. pub. relations Montgomery Ward Co., Balt., 1978-80, fin. info. services dir., Chgo., 1980-81, internal communications dir., 1981-82, corp. communications dir., 1982-83; regional dir. pub. relations MCI Communications Corp., Chgo., 1983-84; dir. communications MCI Midwest, MCI Telecommunications Corp., 1985—; adj. instr. Onondaga Community Coll. Served with U.S. Army, 1969-71. Mem. Pub. Relations Soc. Am., Chgo. Press Club, Sigma Tau Rho. Home: 830 Timber Hill Rd Highland Park IL 60035 Office: 225 N Michigan Ave Suite 1900 Chicago IL 60601

HERBERT, JOHN DAVID, laywer; b. Columbus, Ohio, Sept. 8, 1930; s. Thomas John and Jeannette Helen (Judson) H.; m. Joan Hoiles, Dec. 16, 1955 (div. Aug. 1973); m. F. Marlene Hense, Oct. 20, 1973; children—John D. Jr., Kathleen Granger, Martha Owens, Megan Hayden, Susan Herbert. B.A., Princeton U., 1952; J.D., U. Mich., 1957. Bar: Ohio 1957. Treas., State of Ohio, Columbus, 1962-71; v.p. Assocs. Corp. of N.A., South Bend, Ind., 1972-74; corp. atty., sec. Ace Doran Hauling & Rigging Co., Cin., 1974—. Del., Republican Nat. Conv., 1964, 68. Served to capt. U.S. Army N.G., 1952-54. Baptist. Home: 10145 Leacrest Rd Cincinnati OH 45215 Office: Ace Doran Hauling & Rigging Co 1601 Blue Rock St Cincinnati OH 45223

HERBISON, PRISCILLA JOAN, social work educator, consultant; b. Mpls., Sept. 13, 1943; d. Charles W. and Vonda C. (Rogers) H. B.A., Coll. St. Catherine, St. Paul, 1965; M.S.W., U. Ill.-Urbana, 1969; J.D., U. Minn., 1982. Bar: Minn. 1983; cert. Acad. Cert. Social Workers. Social worker Catholic Social Service, St. Paul, 1965-67, Cath. Welfare Service, Mpls., 1969-71; prof. social work U. W.Va., 1971-74; prof., dir. social work program St. Cloud (Minn.) State U., 1974—, chmn. dept. sociology, anthropology and social work, 1985—; cons., researcher in law; staff aide to speaker of Ill. Ho. of Reps., 1968-69; founder, dir. early childhood ctrs. in rural Appalachia, 1971-72. Fairchild fellow, 1980. Mem. Acad. Cert. Social Workers, Nat. Assn. Social Workers, ABA, Christian Legal Soc., Lawyers Guild of St. Thomas More, Conf. Social Work Edn., Delta Theta Phi. Roman Catholic. Home: 1077 Sibley Memorial Hwy #500 Saint Paul MN 55118 Office: 329-A Stewart Hall Saint Cloud State U Saint Cloud MN 56301

HERD, HAROLD S., state justice; b. Comanche County, Kans., June 13, 1918; A.B., Washburn U., Topeka, 1940, J.D., 1942; m. Margaret Zoe Rich; 6 children. Admitted to Kans. bar, 1943; practiced in Coldwater, Kans., 1946-79; atty. Comanche County 1954-58; justice Supreme Ct. Kans., 1979—. Past pres. Gyp Hills Devel. Com.; past chmn. Kans. Com. Humanities, 1980; mayor of Coldwater, 1950-54; mem. Kans. Senate 36th Dist., 1964-72, minority leader, 1968-72. Served with USNR, 1943-46. Mem. Kans. Bar Assn. (exec. council), Am. Legion (past post comdr.), VFW (past post comdr.), Phi Delta Theta. Presbyterian. Clubs: Lions (past pres., zone chmn.), Shriners. Office: Kans Jud Center Topeka KS 66612*

HERENDEEN, STEVEN JOE, educator; b. Kendallville, Ind., Mar. 8, 1947; s. Ervin Eugene and Josephine May (Kurtz) H.; m. Linda Jane Wyckoff, June 20, 1969; children—Sara Leslie, John Steven. A.S., Ind.-Purdue U., Ft. Wayne, 1978, 79; B.S., Purdue U., 1980; M.S.Ed., Ind. U., 1982. Dispatcher, ops. mgr. Transport Motor Express, FTW, Ft. Wayne, Ind., 1970-74, Werner Continental, Ft. Wayne, 1974; v.p. Diversified Tool Services, Ashley, Ind., 1977-83; dir. purchasing and material control Reliable Tool & Machine, Kendallville, 1974-85; pres. Quintessential Investment Group; asst. prof. Ind.-Purdue U., Ft. Wayne, 1985—; tax cons., 1985—. Served with U.S. Army, 1967-69. Mem. Am. Soc. Testing and Devel., Northeastern Ind. Mgmt. Club. Democrat. Lodges: Masons, Shriners, Elks. Home: Rural Route 2 Fairbanks Rd Kendallville IN 46755 Office: 2101 Coleiseum Blvd Fort Wayne IN 46755

HERINGTON, LEIGH ELLSWORTH, lawyer; b. Rochester, N.Y., Aug. 8, 1945; s. Donald G. and Ethel (Buck) H.; m. Anita Dixon, Dec. 12, 1970; children—Laurie, Tanya. A.A.S., Alfred State Coll., 1965; B.B.A., Kent State U., 1967, M.B.A., 1971; J.D., U. Akron, 1976. Bar: Ohio 1976. Asst. sports info. dir. Kent State U., Ohio, 1969-70, asst. coordinator internal communications, 1970-71, asst. dir. alumni relations, 1971-72; dir. pub. relations Walsh Coll., Canton, Ohio, 1972-73; dir. communications Hiram Coll., Ohio, 1973-77; sole practice, Aurora, Ohio, 1977-78; ptnr. Christley, Minton, Herington, Pierce & Silver, Aurora, 1978—; instr. law Hiram Coll., 1978—. Pres. Crestwood Bd. Edn., Portage County, Ohio, 1981, Portage County United Way, 1984; chmn. crusade Am. Cancer Soc., Portage County. Served with U.S. Army, 1968-69. Recipient Pres.'s award Portage County United Way, 1983; named Alumnus of Yr., Kent State U. Bus. Coll., 1984. Mem. ABA, Ohio State Bar Assn., Portage County Bar Assn., Ohio Council Sch. Bd. Attys., Pub. Relations Soc. Am. Democrat. Club: Aurora-Streetsboro (charter). Lodge: Rotary. Home: 1495 Lake Martin Dr Kent OH 44240 Office: Christley Minton Herington Pierce & Silver 14 New Hudson Rd Aurora OH 44202

HERMAN, AUBREY, planning executive, fundraising executive, consultant; b. Toronto, Ont., Can., Jan. 15, 1949; s. Irving I. and Dorothy (Camozene) H.; m. Arlene S. Topol, Feb. 17, 1972; children—Michelle, Suzanne. A.B., U. Mo., 1972; M.S.W., Washington U., 1973. Dir., Camp Sabra, Rocky Mount, Mo., 1976-79; asst. exec. dir. Jewish Community Ctrs. Assn., St. Louis, 1979-82; assoc. exec. dir. Jewish Fedn. of St. Louis, 1982—; instr. Washington U. Sch. Social Work, 1984. Bd. dirs. Vols. in Probation and Parole, St. Louis, 1981-85; cons. Jr. League St. Louis, 1981-82, Nat. Council Jewish Women, St. Louis, 1982. Recipient Grad. Studies award Jewish Welfare Bd., 1972-73, Vol. award, State of Mo. Citizens Adv. Bd., 1983. Mem. Assn. Jewish Communal Workers, Am. Camping Assn. Social Democrat. Lodge: Lions (Eldon, Mo.). Office: 12 Millstone Campus Dr St Louis MO 63146

HERMAN, JANET ROSALYN, theatre executive director; historical facility manager; b. Youngstown, Ohio, Feb. 15, 1953; d. Paul Lee and Barbara Jane (Rosenblum) H. B.F.A., Kent State U., 1976; postgrad. Ariz. State U., 1981. Adminstrv. asst. Kent Acting and Touring Co., Ohio, 1974-78; social worker Children's Services, Akron, Ohio, 1976-78; sec. Thomas Temporaries, Phoenix, Ariz., 1978-80; box office mgr. Ohio Showboat Drama, Marietta, 1978, 1981, pub. relations, 1981-83, exec. dir., 1983—; asst. dir. Parkersburg Actors' Guild, W. Va., 1981-84; promotions dept. Marietta Chorale, 1983-84; mem. ad hoc com. Office Travel and Tourism, Columbus, Ohio, 1984. Mem. Tourist and Conv. Bur., Marietta, 1981—; play therapy dir. Children's Services Bd., Washington County, Ohio, 1982—; com. mem. Ohio River Sternwheel Festival, Marietta, 1984—; advisor Temple B'nai Israel Youth Group, Parkersburg, 1982—. Recipient Arthur awards Youngstown Playhouse, 1968, 1969, 1970, 1971; Spl. Creative Tchr. award Phoenix/Mesa bds. edn., 1980, 1981; yearly arts grantee Ohio Arts Council, 1981, 1982, 1983, 1984; Promotions grantee Office/Travel & Tourism, 1984. Mem. Ohio Theatre Alliance, Southeastern Theatre Conf., Am. Theatre Assn., Am. Sternwheel Assn., Nat. Trust Hist. Preservation. Democrat. Jewish. Clubs: Phoenix Children's Theatre (bd. dirs. 1979-81); Junior Bd. (pres. 1970-71) (Youngstown). Lodge: B'nai B'rith (youth pres. 1969-70). Avocations: reading; attending movies; working with children. Home: 284-G Ridgewood Dr Marietta OH 45750 Office: Ohio Showboat Drama Inc 237 Front St PO Box 572 Marietta OH 45750

HERMAN, ROBERT DEAN, public administration educator, researcher; b. Harper, Kans., Jan. 6, 1946; s. Floyd Everett and Lois Virginia (Drake) H.; m. Charlotte Marion Davis, Aug. 22, 1971. B.A., Kans. State U., 1968; M.S., Cornell U., 1971, Ph.D., 1976. Asst. prof. U. Mo., Kansas City, 1972-77, assoc. prof. orgnl. behavior and community psychology 1977—. Contbr. chpts. to books, articles to profl. jours. Active Kansas City Consensus, 1984—; pres. Ctr. Developmentally Disabled, Kansas City, 1985—. Mem. Am. Soc. Pub. Adminstrn., Assn. Voluntary Action Scholars, Am. Sociol. Assn. Avocations: racquetball; music; travel.

HERMANEK, DONALD JOHN, marketing consultant; b. Oak Park, Ill., Sept. 7, 1948; s. Rudolph Joseph and Helen Marie (Kodat) H. B.S., U. Ill., 1970; postgrad. Loyola U., Chgo., 1970; grad. Advanced Mgmt. Program, Harvard U. Grad. Sch. Bus., 1980. Mktg. rep. IBM, Chgo., 1972-75, mktg. mgr., 1975-76, nat. account mgr., 1976-80; Midwest regional mgr. McGraw Hill Co., Rolling Meadows, Ill., 1980-81; v.p. mktg. J.M. Boros & Assocs. Ltd., Chgo., 1981—; mktg. cons., human resource cons. Served with AUS, 1970-71. Mem. Am. Mktg. Assn., Am. Mgmt. Assn., U.S. Auto Club. Roman Catholic. Club: Abbey Yacht (past vice commodore) (Lake Geneva, Wis.). Home: 1709 Lakecliffe Dr #D Wheaton IL 60187 Office: 208 S LaSalle St #1733 Chicago IL 60604

HERMANIES, JOHN HANS, lawyer; b. Cin., Aug. 19, 1922; s. John and Lucia (Eckstein) H.; m. Dorothy Jean Steinbrecher, Jan. 3, 1953. A.B., Pa. State U., 1944; J.D., U. Cin., 1948. Bar: Ohio 1948. Atty., Indsl. Commn. Ohio, 1948-50; asst. atty. gen. State of Ohio, 1951-57; asst. to gov. State of Ohio, 1957-59; practice, Cin., 1959—; now ptnr. Beall, Hermanies & Bortz; mem. Ohio State Bd. Bar Examiners, 1963-68; commr. on grievances and discipline Ohio Supreme Ct., 1976-82. Mem. Southwest Ohio Regional Transit Authority, 1973-76; trustee U. Cin., 1977-82; chmn. Hamilton County (Ohio) Republican Exec. Com., 1974-86. Served with USMC, World War II. Mem. ABA, Ohio State Bar Assn., Cin. Bar. Assn., Ohio State Bar Found., Ohio Acad. Trial Lawyers, Am. Judicature Soc. Clubs: Bankers, Queen City. Home: 2110 Columbia Pkwy Cincinnati OH 45202 Office: 36 E 4th St Suite 630 Cincinnati OH 45202

HERMANN, DONALD HAROLD JAMES, lawyer, educator; b. Southgate, Ky., Apr. 6, 1943; s. Albert Joseph and Helen Marie (Snow) H.; A.B. (George E. Gamble Honors scholar), Stanford U., 1965; J.D. (John Noble fellow), Columbia U., 1968; LL.M. (Law and Humanities fellow), Harvard U., 1974; M.A. (Grad. fellow), Northwestern U., 1979, Ph.D., 1981. Mem. staff, directorate of devel. plans Dept. Def., 1964-65, Legis. Drafting Research Fund, Columbia U., 1966-68; admitted to Ariz. bar, 1968, Wash. bar, 1969, Ky. bar, 1971, Ill. bar, 1972, U.S. Supreme Ct. bar, 1974; mem. faculty U. Wash., Seattle, 1968-71, U. Ky., Lexington, 1971-72; mem. faculty DePaul U., Chgo., 1972—, prof. law, 1973—, prof. law and philosophy, 1983—, dir. acad. programs and interdisciplinary study, 1975-76, asso. dean, 1975-78; fellow law and humanities Harvard U., 1973-74; vis. prof. Washington U., St. Louis, 1974, U. Brazilia, 1976; lectr. law Sch. Edn., Northwestern U., 1974-76, Am. Law and Soc. Found., 1975—, Christ Coll., Cambridge U., 1977; fellow in law and econs. U. Rochester, 1974; lectr. dept. philosophy Northwestern U., 1978-81; fellow law and econs. U. Chgo., 1975-76; lectr. Instituto Superiore Internazionale Di Science Criminali, Italy, 1978—; Nat. Endowment Humanities fellow UCLA, 1979, Cornell U., 1982; Law and Humanities fellow Stanford U., 1981; U.S. Jud. fellow U.S. Supreme Ct., 1983-84. Bd. dirs. Council for Legal Edn. Opportunity, Ohio Valley Consortium, 1972, Ill. Bar Automated Research Corp., 1975—, Criminal Law Consortium Cook County, 1977-80; cons. A Federacao de Comercia de Estado de Sao Paulo, Brazil; cons. Ctr. Law Focused Edn., Chgo., 1974-78; reporter Ill. Jud. Conf., 1972—; cons. Adminstrv. Office of Ill. Cts., 1974—. Nat. Endowment for Humanities fellow, 1978, 81, 82, 83. Mem. ABA, Ill., Chgo. bar assns., Am. Law Inst., Am. Acad. Polit. and Social Sci., Soc. Phenomenology and Existential Philosophy, Am. Soc. Polit. and Legal Philosophy, Am. Judicature Soc., Am. Philos. Assn., Internat. Assn. Philosophy of Law and Social Philosophy, Soc. Writers on Legal Subjects, Soc. Am. Law Tchrs., Am. Assn. Law Schs. (del., sect. chmn.), Chgo. Hist. Preservation Soc., Evanston Hist. Soc., Art Inst. Chgo., Northwestern Alumni Assn., Signet Soc. (Harvard). Episcopalian. Clubs: Hasty Pudding (Harvard); Univ., Quadrangle (Chgo.); Univ. (Evanston). Home: 1243 Forest Ave Evanston IL 60202 Office: DePaul U Coll Law 25 E Jackson St Chicago IL 60604

HERMANN, GARY, grocery store owner; b. Kansas City, Kans., Oct. 3, 1951; s. Paul William and Ruth Elizabeth (Scherman) H.; m. Judith Anne Jaskot, May 26, 1973; children—Thomas Michael, Steven Andrew. B.S., S.W. Mo. State U., 1973. Sec./treas. Paul's Market, Inc., Eldon, Mo., 1973—; gen. ptnr. Shores Plaza Co., Eldon, 1978—; realtor assoc. Gattermeir & Co. Mem. Nat. Fedn. Ind. Bus., Eldon C. of C., Sigma Chi. Roman Catholic. Lodge: Lions. Home: PO Box 233 Lake Ozark MO 65049 Office: PO Box 266 Eldon MO 65026

HERMANN, MARY KEVIN HOWARD, nurse, educator; b. St. Lawrence, Ky., Oct. 26, 1934; d. Charles Kevin and Mary M. Howard; R.N., St. Mary's Sch. of Nursing, Evansville, Ind., 1955; B.S. cum laude in Nursing, U. Evansville, 1970, M.A., 1972, M.S. in Nursing, 1974; Ed.D., Ind. U., 1984; m. Robert R. Hermann, Feb. 2, 1957; children—Michael R. (dec.), Barbara K., Leah M., Daniel J. Staff nurse St. Mary's Med. Center, Evansville, Ind., 1955-56, head nurse, 1956-58, asst. dir. nursing service, 1965-68; instr. nursing U. Evansville, 1970-73, asst. prof., 1973-76, assoc. prof., 1976-84, prof., 1984—, asst. dean baccalaureate program, 1974-80. Mem. adv. com. Am. Heart Assn. Program, Evansville, 1981. Mem. Am. Nurses Assn., Ind. Nurses Assn. (co-chmn. commn. on edn., chmn. task force on competencies, dir., dir. dist. 4 1982-84), Am. Assn. Critical Care Nurses. Home: 8011 Maple Ln Newburgh IN 47630 Office: 1800 Lincoln Ave Evansville IN 47702

HERNANDEZ, WILLIE (GUILLERMO HERNANDEZ VILLANUEVA), professional baseball player. Pitcher Detroit Tigers. Recipient Am. League Cy Young Meml. award, 1984. Office: Detroit Tigers Tiger Stadium Detroit MI 48216*

HERNANDEZ NIETO, HECTOR, philosophy and Spanish literature educator, researcher; b. Irapuato, Mex., Apr. 19, 1929; came to U.S. 1968, naturalized 1982; s. Santiago Hernandez and Felicitas Nieto; m. Maria Del Carmen Arcay, June 23, 1979; 1 child, Angelica Rocio. Baccalaureate, U. St. Thomas, Rome, 1959, Licenciate, 1960, Doctorate in Philosophy, 1964; M.A. in Classics, U. Ill., 1971, Ph.D. in Spanish, 1975. Dean students, prof. Colegio del Esp.S., Calahorra, Spain, 1960-62; prof. philosophy Instituto Superior de Estudios Eclesiasticos, Tlalpam, Mex., 1965-68; asst. prof. U. Ill., Chgo., 1972-77; chairperson Chgo. State U., 1977-83, prof., 1982—; founder Confedn. Latin Am. Students, Chgo., 1972, Spanish Club, Chgo., 1982. Author: Las raices metafisicas de la logica, 1971. Contbr. articles to profl. jours. Recipient Tchr. of Yr. award Chgo. State U., 1978, Outstanding Faculty award Chgo. State U., 1981. Roman Catholic. Avocations: computers, photography, short stories. Home: 706 W Chicago Ave East Chicago IN 46312 Office: Chgo State U C-301 95th at King Dr Chicago IL 60628

HERNDON, (MARTI) MARGARET LOUISE, health system administrator; b. Columbus, Ga., Dec. 11, 1956; d. George Washington and Cora Feild (Anthony) H. Student Wesleyan Coll., 1974-76; B.S. in Health Systems, Ga. Inst. Tech., 1981. Youth dir. United Methodist Ch., Irwinton, Ga., 1976; staff mgmt. engr. Evangelical Health Systems, Oak Brook, Ill., 1980-85, sr. mgmt. engr., 1985—. Tchr. mentally and physically handicapped Ch. of the Exceptional, Macon, Ga., 1974-75; vol. Family Consultation Services, Atlanta, 1979-80; active Calvary Temple Assembly of God, Naperville, Ill., 1982—. Wesleyan scholar. Mem. Hosp. Mgmt. Systems Soc. (v.p. programs Atlanta chpt. 1978-80, v.p. membership Chgo. chpt. 1983-84), Chgo. Health Execs. Forum. Avocations: breeding Maltese dogs. Office: Evangel Health Systems 2025 Windsor Dr Oak Brook IL 60521

HERR, DEAN MARTIN, technical writer; b. Battle Creek, Mich., Aug. 17, 1955; s. Martin Lee and Carol Ellen (Horton) H. B.S. in Math., Mich. Tech. U., 1978, B.S. in Physics, 1981. Tech. writer Control Data Corp., Arden Hills, Minn., 1978-80, 81-83, Zycad Corp., Arden Hills, 1983—. Author and editor: Zycad Intermediate Form Tool Kit, 1984; ZIF Reference Manual, 1985. Mem. Mpls. Writers' Workshop, 1982. Mem. Am. Phys. Soc., Soc. of Mayflower Descs. in Minn. Republican. Baptist. Club: Mini-Unit (Mpls.). Home: 1360 Terrace Dr Apt 103 Roseville MN 55113 Office: Zycad Corp 3499 Lexington Ave N PO Box 12828 Saint Paul MN 55112

HERRICK, CLAY, JR., civic worker, retired advertising executive; b. Cleveland Heights, Ohio, Dec. 15, 1911; s. C. Clay and Alice Mabel (Meriam) H.; B.A. Adelbert Coll. of Western Res. U., 1934; diploma John Huntington Poly. Inst.; m. Ruth Eleanor Penty, Apr. 27, 1935; children—Clay Herrick III, Jill. Pub. relations dir. General Tire & Rubber Co., Akron, 1940-45; creative dir. JP Smith creative printers for Eastman Kodak, Rochester, 1945-48; account exec. Fuller, Smith & Ross, Inc., 1948-58; v.p. Carpenter, Lamb & Herrick, Inc., 1958-64, pres., 1964-73; sr. v.p. Watts, Lamp, Kenyon & Herrick Inc., 1973-74, ret., 1974; pres. Western Res. Press, Inc., 1973-78; instr. graphics Cleve. State U., 1968—; originator, 1st chmn. Cleve. Printing Week celebrations, 1953 seminar leader In-Plant Printing Mgmt. Assn., 1978. Pres., Early Settlers Assn.; chmn. Cleve. Landmark Commn.; v.p. Shaker Landmarks Commn.; chmn. Cleve. Hall Fame Commn.; v.p. Cleve. Bicentennial Commn.; pres. univ. alumni council Western Res. U.; fund chmn. Cleve. Ch. Fedn.; scoutmaster, cubmaster Boy Scouts Am.; active PTA; trustee YMCA, Shauffler div. Defiance Coll.; pub. relations bd. United Appeal; chmn. task force Cleve. Ambassadors, 1978; mem. public relations com. ARC Centennial, 1981; v.p. Cleve. Sr. Council, 1981-82, pres., 1985-86; deacon, trustee Fairmount Presbyn. Ch., Shaker Heights, Ohio; trustee Cleanland Rapid Recovery, 1983—; mem. Univ. Circle Council, 1982—; mem. Warehouse Dist. and Rivers Bend Parks Corp. Named Cleve. Graphic Arts Man of Year, 1965; elected to Graphic Arts Hall of Distinction, 1977; recipient Heritage award New Eng. Soc., 1978; elected to Disting. Alumni Hall of Fame, Cleveland Heights High Sch., 1981, Cleve. Advt. Club Hall of Fame, 1981. Mem. Nat. Cartoonists Soc., Am. Assn. Advt. Agys. (chmn.), New Eng. Soc. (pres., named Man of Yr. 1977), Cleve. Cultural Gardens Fedn. (v.p., exec. sec.), Shaker Hist. Soc. (pres.). Cleve. Ad Club (v.p.), Founders and Patriots Am. (Ohio gov., lt. gov. nat. soc.), Fine Arts Assn. (trustee), Am. Advt. Fedn. (dist gov., named Advt. Man of Year 1974), Intercomm Communications Group (1st pres.), Cleve. Growth Assn. (speakers bur. 1980—), Cleve. Graphic Arts Council (organizer, pres., exec. sec. 1981—), Adelbert Alumni Assn. Western Res. U. (pres.), SAR (past pres., sec.-treas. 1974-84, chaplain 1985—), Soc. Boonesboro, Order Ky. Cols., Sons and Daus. Pilgrims, Jamestowne Soc., Cleve. Sr. Council pres. 1985-86, Cleve. Restoration Soc. (sec. 1981—), Delta Upsilon, Sigma Delta Chi, Delta Sigma Rho, Pi Epsilon Delta. Clubs: Toastmasters Internat. (hon. life), Cheshire Cheese (past pres. 4 times). Lodge: Rotary. Author: But It's So, 1934; Cleveland's Rich Heritage, 1975; Gags in Rhyme, 1983; Cleveland Landmarks, 1985; author monthly feature Cleveland Landmarks in Properties Mag., 1977—. Editor, pub. Graphic Artisan; editor Pioneer, others. Home: 16315 Fernway Rd Shaker Heights OH 44120

HERRICK, KENNETH GILBERT, See *Who's Who in America,* 43rd edition.

HERRING, HAZEL MARIE, civic worker; b. Queen City, Tex., Dec. 9, 1922; d. Charles Alfred And Gladys Mildred (Hunt) Jackson; m. Jack Herman Herring, Feb. 5, 1943; children—Judith Ann, David Robert. Student Tex. U. Arts and Industries, 1939-41. Chief dep. county clk. Willacy County, Raymondville, Tex., 1941-43; acct. Brown Express, Harlingen and Austin, Tex., 1943-48; sec. Hon. Menton J. Murray, Tex. Ho. of Reps., Austin, 1949, Tex. Hwy. Dept., Austin, 1950. Author: Hancock County Government, 1972. Council mem. Nat. Arboretum Adv. Council, Washington, 1984—; com. mem. Assoc. Country Women of the World, London, 1984—; com. mem. Archer M. Huntington Art Gallery, U. Tex., Austin, 1984—. Named Most Outstanding Mem. in Ohio, Woman's Nat. Farm and Garden Assn., 1976; Hazel J. Herring Civic Improvement award, 1983. Republican. Presbyterian. Clubs: Friends of Old Mill Stream (pres. 1974-75), Town and Campus (pres. 1976-78), Woman's Nat. Farm and Garden Assn. (pres. 1982-84). Avocations: gardening; travel; flower arrangements.

HERRMANN, ARTHUR DOMINEY, banker; b. Louisville, Sept. 29, 1926; s. Arthur Chester and Mattie Belle (Dominey) H.; m. Lucy Kindred, Apr. 7, 1951; children—Lucy Wharton, Anne Dominey, Martha Kindred. B.A., Ohio State U., 1947, J.D., 1949; postgrad. Rutgers U., 1956. Bar: Ohio 1950. Practiced in Columbus, Ohio, 1950; asst. trust officer Huntington Nat. Bank, Columbus, 1951-56, trust officer, 1956-63, v.p., 1963-67, sr. v.p., 1967-69, exec. v.p., 1969-72, pres., chief exec. officer, 1972-75, also dir.; exec. v.p., sec. Huntington Bancshares, Inc., 1966-70, pres., 1974-81, chief exec. officer, 1975-81, vice chmn., 1974-79, chmn., 1980-81, also dir.; chmn., chief exec. officer, dir. BancOhio Nat. Bank, 1981—, former pres.; dir. N.Am. Broadcasting Co. Pres., trustee Mt. Carmel Hosps., 1974-76; trustee Columbus Mus. Fine Art, 1974—, v.p., 1979—; trustee Ohio Dominican Coll., 1978—; bd. dirs. Columbus Conv. Bur. Mem. Columbus Retail Mchts. Assn. (treas., dir. 1966—), Ohio Bankers Assn., Columbus Bar Assn., Sigma Chi, Phi Delta Phi. Clubs: Columbus, Scioto Country, City (Columbus). Lodge: Masons. Office: BancOhio Nat Bank 155 E Broad St Columbus OH 43265*

HERRMANN, THOMAS ANTHONY, civil engineer; b. St. Louis, Oct. 30, 1928; s. Anthony E. and Susan K. (Shinker) H.; B.S.C.E., Mo. Sch. Mines, Rolla, 1950; cert. USPHS, Cin., 1966; diploma U.S. Army Command and Gen. Staff Coll., 1978; m. Mary M. Finan, Apr. 7, 1951; children—John T., Marguerite A. Field engr. Sverdrup & Parcel, Inc., St. Louis, 1950-52; design engr. Russell & Axon, Inc., St. Louis, 1952-56; profl. engr. Williamson & Assos., St. Louis, 1956-66; v.p./mgr. civil, environ. div. Zurheide-Herrmann, Inc., St. Louis, 1966—. Served to col. C.E. USAR, 1950—. Registered profl. engr., 10 states; registered land surveyor, Mo. Mem. Nat. Soc. Profl. Engrs. (nat. dir.), Mo. Soc. Profl. Engrs. (pres. 1979-80, pres. St. Louis chpt. 1969-70, St. Louis Young Engr. of Yr. 1963, St. Louis Outstanding Engr. in Pvt. Practice 1980, St. Louis Engr. of Yr. 1981), Cons. Engrs. Council, ASCE, Am. Pub. Works Assn., Am. Water Works Assn. (Disting. Service ciation 1977), U. Mo. at Rolla Acad. Civil Engrs., Water Pollution Control Fedn., Mo. Water and Sewerage Conf., Soc. Am. Mil. Engrs., Res. Officers Assn., Chi Epsilon. Office: 4333 W Clayton Ave Saint Louis MO 63110

HERRMANN, WYATT D., radio program director; b. Freeport, Ill., Nov. 14, 1956; s. Wayne E. and Arline L. (Rutter) H. Diploma Broadcasting Career Acad., Milw., 1975. Announcer Sta. WACI-FM, Freeport, 1974-77, Sta. WFRL - AM and FM, Freeport, 1977-79, program dir. stas. WFRL-AM and WXXQ-FM, Freeport, 1980-85; announcer, engr. Sta. KLSS-KSMN, Mason City, Iowa, 1979-80; program. dir. Sta. WFPS-FM, Freeport, 1985—. Republican. Methodist. Avocations: music; record collecting; bowling; softball; volleyball. Home: 516 S Carroll Freeport IL 61032 Office: WFPS Radio Box 701 5817 US Hwy 20 W Freeport IL 61032

HERROLD, ANNE MARIE, pharmacist, research chemist; b. Anderson, Ind., Feb. 21, 1950; d. Walter Joseph and Esther Lillian (Seipel) Brewster; m. Robert Earl Herrold, Aug. 7, 1971; children—Amy Anne, Joseph Alden. B.S. in Pharmacy, Purdue U., 1973; M.B.A., Ind. U., Indpls., 1981. Registered pharmacist, Ind. Research chemist Eli Lilly & Co., Indpls., 1973-80. Patentee Sunscreen composition, 1981, cosmetic cream formulation, 1981, cosmetic lotion formulation, 1981, skin cell renewal regime, 1981, sensitive skin care regime, 1983, cosmetic cream formulation, 1983. Mem. Am. Pharm. Assn., Kappa Epsilon (sec. 1972-73; named Outstanding Woman Pharmacy Graduate 1973), Tri Kappa. Republican. Lutheran. Avocations: reading; playing organ; cooking. Home: 121 Westbourne Dr Brownsburg IN 46112

HERRON, DONALD PATRICK, lawyer, psychologist; b. Springfield, Ill. Feb. 6, 1954; s. Donald Franklin and Patricia Ann (Flynn) H.; m. Kristine Lydia Gish, Aug. 7, 1976. B.A. in Psychology and Sociology, U. Mo.-Kansas City, 1976, M.S. in Psychology, 1978, J.D., 1981. Bar: Mo. 1981, U.S. Dist. Ct. (we. dist.) Mo. 1981. Counselor, Johnson County Mental Retardation Ctr., Kans., 1976-77; lectr. in psychology, acad. adviser U. Mo.-Kansas City, 1977-80; assoc. Morris and Foust, Kansas City, 1981-85; ptnr. Herron and Lewis, Kansas City, 1985—; cons. psychology, Kansas City, 1978—. Author profl. papers in psychology. Mem. ABA (litigation sect.), Mo. Bar Assn., Kansas City Bar Assn., Assn. Trial Lawyers Am., Mo. Trial Lawyers Assn., Nat. Assn. For Behavior Analysis, AAAS, Phi Delta Phi, Phi Kappa Phi, Psi Chi. Roman Catholic. Home: 8549 Wedd Overland Park KS 66212 Office: Herron and Lewis PO Box 2326 Rivergate Business Ctr Kansas City MO 64142

HERRON, MICHAEL DEAN, communications company executive; b. Cardington, Ohio, May 7, 1949; s. Walter Dean and Ruthella Grace (Heacock) H.; m. Dorothy Leah Keim, June 21, 1969; children—Jeffrey Michael, Gregory Andrew, Lisa Renee. B.B.A. cum laude, Kent State U., 1971; student Asbury Coll., 1967-68. With Gen. Telephone Co. Ohio, Marion, 1971-80, tng. coordinator, 1972-78, staffing and devel. mgr., 1978-80; mngt. devel. dir. GTE Directories Corp., Des Plaines, Ill., 1980—. Div. chmn. ann. fin. campaign Boy Scouts Am., 1980-82; elder Trinity Bapt. Ch., Wheaton, Ill., 1983. Lillian E. James scholar, 1967. Mem. Beta Gamma Sigma. Republican. Office: 1865 Miner St Des Plaines IL 60016

HERSCHER, WALTER RAY, educator; b. Niles, Mich., Apr. 5, 1946; s. Frederick Leonard and Cecile Lillian (Burkybile) H.; m. Susan Kay Arnold, June 12, 1976; children—Anne Marie, Brian Craig. B.A., Kalamazoo Coll., 1966; M.A., U. Notre Dame, 1968; postgrad. U. Okla., 1968-70, U. Wis.-Oshkosh, 1979—. Asst. mgr. SAGA Food Service, Kalamazoo Coll. and Nazareth Coll., Kalamazoo, Mich., 1971-73; social studies tchr. Appleton (Wis.) Pub. Schs., 1973—, head social studies dept., 1980-84, cross country coach Appleton West High Sch., 1973—; instr. U. Wis.-Fox Valley Ctr., Appleton, 1979-81, Lakeland Coll., 1985—. Treas., Methodist Ch. Kum Dubls, 1982-83. Stone scholar Kalamazoo Coll., 1963-66; Hearst fellow U. Notre Dame, 1966-67. Mem. Nat. Council Social Studies, Assn. Supervision and Curriculum Devel., Conf. Group Central European History, Wis. Council Social Studies, French Hist. Soc., Wis. Cross County Coaches Assn., Kappa Delta Pi. Methodist. Club: Pace Setters. Home: 1341 W Cloverdale Dr Appleton WI 54914 Office: 610 N Badger St Appleton WI 54914

HERSH, HERBERT NORMAN, chemist; b. Bklyn., Feb. 6, 1923; s. Abraham and Anna (Castle) H.; m. Blanche Glassman, Mar. 21, 1948; children—Joan, Jeff, Mark. Ph.D., Ohio State U., 1950. Aero. Scientist NASA, Cleve., 1950-53; scientist, research devel. mgr. Zenith Radio Corp., Glenview, Ill., 1954-78; systems analyst Argonne Nat. Lab., Ill., 1978—; cons. Timex Corp., Danbury, Conn., 1978. Patentee in field. Contbr. articles to profl. jours. Editor various chpts. in books, 1978—. Fellow Am. Phys. Soc.; mem. Am. Chem. Soc., Electrochem. Soc. Home: 706 W Buena Ave Chicago IL 60613

HERSH, LESLIE JANET, chemist; b. Phila., Aug. 16, 1947; d. Leslie Earl and Lillian Katherine (Klass) Small; m. David A. Hersh; 1 child, Patricia Lynn. B.S. with honors, Albright Coll., 1969; M.S., Purdue U., 1970. Chemist, Sugar Beet Products Co., Saginaw, Mich., 1981—. Formulator cosmetic products. Mem. adminstrv. bd. First United Methodist Ch., Saginaw, 1980. Mem. Am. Chem. Soc. (cert.), Soc. Cosmetic Chemists, United Methodist Women (bd. dirs. Saginaw 1978-80). Avocation: fishing. Home: 211 Winthrop Saginaw MI 48603 Office: Sugar Beet Products Co 302 Waller St Saginaw MI 48602

HERSHEWAY, CHARLES EUGENE, marketing executive; b. Chgo., Apr. 23, 1933; s. Louis and Jean (Manfre) H.; student U. Ill., 1951-53; B.S., Northwestern U., 1959; m. Shirley Leyendecker, Jan. 19, 1957; children—Deborah Lynn, Louise Jeffrey; m. 2d, Priscilla Karas, Dec. 1, 1974. Editorial dir. Nat. Research Bur., Chgo., 1958-62; promotion mgr. Advt. Publs., Inc., Chgo., 1962-64; advt. mgr. Pfaelzer Bros. div. Armour Co., Chgo., 1964-67, mktg. mgr., 1967-70, sales mgr., 1970, v.p. mktg., 1970-74; pres. United Am. Food Processors Gourmet Fare, 1974-76, Mail Market Makers, Inc., Clarendon Hills, Ill., 1976-79; v.p. Lerner Scott Corp., 1979-84; v.p. mktg. Allen Bros., 1984—; mktg. cons., 1984—. Mem. Percy for Gov. Finance Com., 1965. Served with USMCR, 1952-54, USN, 1954-58. Mem. Mail Advt. Club Chgo., Chgo. Federated Advt., Premium Industry Club, Sales Promotion Execs., Mail Advt. Author: NRB Retail Advt. and Sales Promotion Manual, vol. I, 1960, vol. II, 1961, vol. III, 1962; M.P. Brown Collection Letter Manual, 1961; Nat. Research Bur. Discount Store Manual, 1961. Contbr. articles to profl. jours. Home and office: 1450 Golden Bell Ct Downers Grove IL 60515

HERSHKOWITZ, NOAH, physicist, educator; b. Bklyn., Aug. 16, 1941; s. Abraham Louis and Sushie H.; m. Rosalyn Russ, Aug., 19, 1962; children—Elaine, Debra. B.S. in Physics, Union Coll., 1962; Ph.D., Johns Hopkins U., 1966. Instr. Johns Hopkins U., Balt., 1966-67; from asst. to prof. U. Iowa, Iowa City, 1967-81; prof. U. Wis., Madison, 1981—; vis. assoc. prof. UCLA, 1974-75; vis. prof. U. Colo., Boulder, 1980-81; cons. Lawrence Livermore Nat. Lab., Livermore, Calif., 1979-82, Argonne Nat. Lab., Ill., 1983—; dir. Phaedrus Tandem Mirror Expt. Contbr. articles to profl. jours. Assoc. editor jour. Physics of Fluids, 1981-83. Fellow Am. Phys. Soc.; mem. IEEE (sr.), Univ. Fusion Assn. (pres. 1985—); Phi Beta Kappa, Sigma Xi. Office: Dept Nuclear Engrng U Wis 1500 Johnson Dr Madison WI 53706

HERSZDORFER, PIERRE JACQUES, banker; b. Marseille, France, Apr. 20, 1939; s. Julius and Paula (Roniger) H.; came to U.S., 1955, naturalized, 1960; B.S., NYU, 1968; student Am. Inst. Banking; m. Doris Buntin, Dec. 24, 1968 (div. 1979). Mem. staff auditing dept. Irving Trust Co., N.Y.C., 1960-68; mem. staff comptroller's div. Citibank, N.Y.C., 1968-71; v.p. internat. div. Hartford Nat. Bank & Trust Co. (Conn.), 1971-79; v.p. Credit Agricole br. Caisse Nationale de Credit Agricole Paris, 1979-81; v.p. Union Commerce Bank Cleve., 1981; v.p., mgr. internat. banking dept. Norwest Bank Des Moines, N.A., 1981-84; v.p., mgr. internat. banking div. Mchts. Nat. Bank, Cedar Rapids, Iowa, 1984—; dir. Des Moines Fgn. Trade Zone Corp.; lectr. Des Moines Area Community Coll.; past mem. faculty dept. bus. careers Manchester (Conn.) Community Coll. Mem. adv. bd. Des Moines Area Community Coll. Internat. Trade Studies; mem. Iowa Dist. Export Council; adv. bd. Ctr. Indsl. Research and Service, Iowa State U., Ames; past chmn. fraud detection and safeguard com. Council Internat. Banking. Served with U.S. Army Res., 1959-65. Mem. Greater Des Moines C. of C., Des Moines World Trade Council, Des Moines Com. Fgn. Relations, Internat. Trade Bur., Cedar Falls-NE Iowa Internat. Trade Council, Davenport (Iowa)-Ill. Internat. Trade Assn., Sioux City-Siouxland Internat. Trade Assn., Robert Morris Assocs., Des Moines Art Ctr., Cedar Rapids Mus. Art, NYU Alumni Assn. Club: Embassy (Des Moines). Office: Cedar River Tower Cedar Rapids IA 52401

HERTEL, DENNIS MARK, lawyer, congressman; b. Detroit, Dec. 7, 1948; s. John and Marie (Kaufmann) H., Jr.; B.A. cum laude, Eastern Mich. U., 1971; J.D., Wayne State U., 1974; m. Cynthia S. Grosscup, 1971; children—Heather, Heidi, Katie. Former tchr. Detroit Public Schs.; admitted to Mich. bar, 1975; mem. Mich. Ho. of Reps., 1975-80; mem. 97th-99th congresses from 14th Dist. of Mich.; intern Office Atty. Gen., State of Mich.; aide to Ernest Browne, Detroit City Council. Head field staff for 14th dist. campaign activities Mich. Democratic Com. Mem. Mich. Bar Assn. Roman Catholic. Club: St. Matthews Men's. Office: 218 Cannon House Office Bldg Washington DC 20515*

HERTEL, JAMES ROBERT, insurance agency executive; b. Grand Rapids, Mich., June 7, 1929; s. George William and Kathryn Iris (Beukema) H.; m. Wilma Lucille Bylsma, Nov. 21, 1952; children—Jack Robert, Jane Ellen, Carol Ann. A.B., Calvin Coll., 1951. Salesman, Wurzburg Co., Grand Rapids, Mich., 1954-55; account exec. A. W. Hertel Agy., Holland, Mich., 1955-59; pres. James Hertel Agy., Fremont, Mich., 1959—; dir., sec. Old State Bank of Fremont (Mich.), 1971—. Pres., Fremont Indsl. Devel. Corp., 1976—; pres. Fremont Econ. Devel. Corp., 1983. Served with AUS, 1951-54. Mem. Profl. Agts. Assn., Ins. Agts. Assn. Republican. Christian Reformed. Club: Rotary. Home: 3522 Ramshorn Dr Fremont MI 49412 Office: James Hertel Agy Inc 6 E Main St Box A Fremont MI 49412

HERTZ, KARL VICTOR, educational administrator; b. Indpls., Oct. 19, 1936; s. Victor Peter and Mary Martha (Hockensmith) H.; m. Carol Sue Gruber, Dec. 28, 1957; children—Karen Ann, Michael Karl, Sarah Jane. B.A., Marian Coll., 1961; M.S., Butler U., 1964; Ed.D., Ind. U., 1973. Cert. tchr., sch. adminstr., Ind.,-Ill., Wis. Tchr. English pub. schs., Indpls., 1960-63, chmn. English dept. Brebeuf High Sch., 1963-68, asst. prin., 1968-70, prin. 1970-73; prin., lectr. Lab. Sch., U. Chgo., 1973-75; prin. pub. sch., Munster, Ind., 1975-79; dir. secondary edn. Neenah Joint Sch. Dist., Wis., 1979-81, asst. supt., 1981-85; supt. Mequon-Thiensville Sch. Dist., Wis., 1985—. cons. to sch. dists. Bd. dirs. Jr. Achievement, Big Sisters. Recipient citation City of Indpls., 1973; citation Jesuit Secondary Edn. Assn., 1973; citation Bd. Dirs. Marian Coll.; Inst. Devel. Ednl. Activities fellow. Mem. Am. Assn. Sch. Adminstrs., Assn. Supervision and Curriculum Devel., Nat. Assn. Secondary Sch. Prins. Club: Rotary (Neenah). Contbr. articles to profl. jours. Office: 5000 Mequon Rd Mequon WI 53092

HERZIG, DAVID JACOB, pharmaceutical company licensing director, immunopharmacologist; b. Cleve., Dec. 13, 1936; s. Marvin Laurence and Lillian Gertrude (Blaine) H.; m. Phyllis Glicksberg, Sept. 2, 1962; children—Michael, Pamela, Roberta, Karen. B.A., Oberlin Coll., 1958; Ph.D. in Chemistry, U. Cin., 1963. Vis. scientist NIH, Bethesda, Md., 1963-65, staff fellow, 1965-67; sr. research assoc. N.Y.U. Sch. Medicine, N.Y.C., 1967-68, Warner, Lambert, Parke-Davis Co., Ann Arbor, Mich., 1968-77, dir. immunopharmacology, 1977-81, dir. sci. devel., 1981—. Contbr. articles to profl. jours. Fellow NSF, Damon Runyon Memorial Fund. Mem. AAAS, Am. Soc. Pharmacology and Exptl. Therapeutics, Am. Acad. Allergy Immunology, N.Y. Acad. Scis., Sigma Xi. Club: N.Y. Fencers (bd. dirs. 1970-77). Avocations: squash; fencing; furniture building. Home: 3540 Windemere Dr Ann Arbor MI 48105 Office: Warner Lambert Parke-Davis 2800 Plymouth Rd Ann Arbor MI 48105

HERZOG, DORREL NORMAN ELVERT (WHITEY HERZOG), See *Who's Who in America,* 43rd edition.

HERZOG, GODOFREDO MAX, physician; b. Chemnitz, Germany, Jan. 12, 1931; s. Heinrich and Louise (Gittler) H.; came to U.S., 1950, naturalized, 1960; B.S., La. State U., 1953; M.D., Washington U., St. Louis, 1957; m. Eva R. Muller, Sept. 2, 1956; children—Jacques A., Patricia M., Elsa M. Intern, Jewish Hosp., St. Louis, 1957-58, Sch. Aerospace Medicine, San Antonio, Tex., 1960; resident in surgery Jewish Hosp., Cin., 1958-59; resident in ob-gyn Jewish Hosp., St. Louis, 1964-67; instr. ob-gyn Washington U., St. Louis, 1967—; practice medicine, specializing in ob-gyn, St. Louis, 1967—; sr. med. cons. Premenstrual Program Ctr., St. Louis; gynecol. cons. med. laser program DePaul Hosp., St. Louis; cons. in field. Med. adviser, bd. dirs. Life Seekers, Planned Parenthood, Abortion Rights Alliance; mem. Hispanic Leadership Conf., St. Louis. Served to capt. M.C., USAF, 1959-64. Diplomate Nat. Bd. Med. Examiners, Am. Bd. Ob-Gyn. Fellow Am. Coll. Ob-Gyn; mem. AMA, St. Louis County Med. Soc., Pan Am., Israel, Mo. med. assns., Mo., St. Louis gynecol. socs., Am. Soc. Gynecol. Laparoscopists, Am. Fertility Soc. Jewish. Contbr. articles to profl. publs. Home: 9 Wendover St Saint Louis MO 63124 Office: 77 Westport Plaza Dr Suite 265 Saint Louis MO 63141

HESBURGH, THEODORE MARTIN, clergyman, university president; b. Syracuse, N.Y., May 25, 1917; s. Theodore Bernard and Anne Marie (Murphy) H.; student U. Notre Dame, 1934-37; Ph.B., Gregorian U., 1939; postgrad. Holy Cross Coll., Washington, 1940-43; S.T.D., Cath. U. Am., 1945; 96 hon. degrees. Entered Order of Congregation of Holy Cross, 1934; ordained priest Roman Catholic Ch., 1943. Chaplain Nat. Tng. Sch. for Boys, Washington, 1943-44; vets. chaplain U. Notre Dame, 1945-47, asst. prof. religion, 1945-48, head dept., 1948-49, exec. v.p., 1949-52, pres., 1952—; chmn. Bus.-Higher Edn. Forum. Former mem. and chmn. U.S. Commn. on Civil Rights; former trustee Carnegie Fund for Advancement of Teaching; former Carnegie Commn. on Future of Higher Edn.; trustee and chmn. Rockefeller Found.; former mem. Presdl. Clemency Bd., Nat. Sci. Bd.; U.S. ambassador UN Conf. on Sci. and Tech. for Devel., 1979; former chmn. U.S. Select Commn. on Immigration and Refugee Policy; mem. Pontifical Council for Culture, Trilateral Commn., U.S. Holocaust Meml. Council; mem. Am. Com. East-West Accord; trustee Overseas Devel. Council; mem. Commn. on U.S.-Latin Am. Relations; co-chmn. Citizens Com. for Immigration Reform. Recipient numerous awards including U.S. Medal of Freedom, 1964; 100 hon. degrees. Meiklejohn award AAUP, 1970; Alexis de Tocqueville award. Mem. Am. Acad. Arts and Scis., Am. Philos. Soc., Nat. Acad. Edn., Nat. Acad. Scis. (hon.), Council on Fgn. Relations. Author: God and the World of Man, 1950; Patterns for Educational Growth, 1958; Thoughts for Our Times, 1962; More Thoughts for Our Times, 1965; Still More Thoughts for Our Times, 1966; Thoughts IV, 1968; Thoughts V, 1969; The Humane Imperative: A Challenge for the Year 2000, 1974; Three Bicentennial Addresses, 1976; The Hesburgh Papers: Higher Values in Higher Edn., 1979. Home: U Notre Dame Notre Dame IN 46556

HESS, BARTLETT LEONARD, clergyman; b. Spokane, Wash., Dec. 27, 1910; s. John Leonard and Jessie (Bartlett) H.; B.A., Park Coll., 1931, M.A. (fellow in history 1931-34), U. Kan., 1932, Ph.D., 1934; B.D., McCormick Theol. Sem., 1936; m. Margaret Young Johnston, July 31, 1937; children—Daniel Bartlett, Deborah Margaret, John Howard and Janet Elizabeth (twins). Ordained to ministry Presbyn. Ch., 1936; pastor Effingham, Kan., 1932-34, Chgo., 1935-42, Cicero, Ill., 1942-56, Ward Meml. Presbyn. Ch., Detroit, 1956-68, Ward, Presbyn. Ch., Livonia, Mich., 1968-80, Presbyn. Ch., 1980—. Tchr. ch. history, bible Detroit Bible Coll., 1956—, bd. dirs., 1956—; minister radio sta. WHFC, Chgo., 1942-50, WMUZ-FM, Detroit, 1958-68, 78—, WOMC-FM, 1971-72, WBFG-FM, 1972—; missioner to Philippines, United Presbyn. Ch. U.S.A., 1961; mem. Joint Com. on Presbyn. Union, 1980; adviser Mich. Synod council United Presbyn. Ch.; mem. com. Billy Graham Crusade for S.E. Mich., 1976; mem. adminstrv. com. Evang. Presbyn. Ch., 1980—. Mem. Organizer Friendship and Service Com. for Refugees, Chgo., 1940. Bd. dirs. Beacon Neighborhood House, Chgo., 1945-52, Presbyns. United for Bibl. Concerns, 1975-80; pres. bd. dirs. Peniel Community Center, Chicago, 1945-52. Named Pastor of Year, Mid-Am. Sunday Sch. Assn., 1974; recipient Service to Youth award Detroit Met. Youth for Christ, 1979. Mem. Cicero Ministers Council (pres. 1951), Phi Beta Kappa, Phi Delta Kappa. Author: (with Margaret Johnston Hess) How To Have A Giving Church, 1974; (with M.J. Hess) The Power of a Loving Church, 1977, How Does Your Marriage Grow, 1982, Never Say Old, 1984; contbr. articles in field to profl. jours. Traveled in Europe, 1939, 52, 55, 68; also in Greece, Turkey, Lebanon, Syria, Egypt, Israel, Iraq; condr. tour of Middle East and Mediterranean countries, 1965, 67, 73, 74, 76, 78, 80, China and Far East, 1982; missioner, India, 1981. Home: 16845 Riverside Dr Livonia MI 48154 Office: 17000 Farmington Rd Livonia MI 48154

HESS, JOHN, JR., physician; b. Hospers, Iowa, Dec. 20, 1916; s. John and Emma (Ehlenfeldt) H.; m. Veronica Ann Lindsey, June 21, 1942; children—John, Michael, Ann, Patrick. B.S., U. Iowa, 1939, M.D., 1941. Diplomate Am. Bd. Family Practice. Intern, Broadlawns Polk County Hosp., Des Moines, 1941-42, resident, 45; practice medicine, Des Moines, 1946-75; mem. staff Meth., Mercy, Luth. and Broadlawns hosps., asst. prof. family medicine U. Iowa, Iowa City, 1975—. Bd. dirs. Iowa Found. for Med. Care, 1977—. Served to maj. U.S. Army, 1942-46. Fellow Am. Acad. Family Physicians; mem. AMA, Iowa Acad. Family Physicians, Iowa Med. Soc., Polk County Med. Soc. Home: 4315 Greenwood Dr Des Moines IA 50312 Office: Broadlawns Med Ctr 18th and Hickman Rd Des Moines IA 50314

HESS, MARGARET JOHNSTON, religious writer, educator; b. Ames, Iowa, Feb. 22, 1915; d. Howard Wright and Jane Edith (Stevenson) Johnston; B.A., Coe Coll., 1937; m. Bartlett Leonard Hess, July 31, 1937; children—Daniel, Deborah, John, Janet. Bible tchr. Community Bible Classes Ward Presbyn. Ch., Livonia, Mich., 1959—, Christ Ch. Cranbrook (Episcopal), Bloomfield Hills, Mich., 1980—. Author: (with B.L. Hess) How to Have a Giving Church, 1974, The Power of a Loving Church, 1977; Love Knows No Barriers, 1979; Esther: Courage in Crisis, 1980; Unconventional Women, 1981; How Does Your Marriage Grow?, 1983; Never Say Old, 1984; contbr. articles to religious jours. Home: 16845 Riverside Dr Livonia MI 48154

HESSE, CAROLYN SUE, lawyer; b. Belleville, Ill., Jan. 12, 1949; d. Ralph H. Hesse and Marilyn J. (Midgley) Hesse Dierkes; m. William H. Hallenbeck. B.S., U. Ill., 1971, M.S., U. Ill.-Chgo., 1977; J.D., DePaul U., 1983. Bar: Ill.

1983, U.S. Dist. Ct. (no. dist.) Ill. 1983. Research assoc. U. Ill., Chgo., 1974-77; tech. adviser Ill. Pollution Control Bd., Chgo., 1977-80; environ. scientist U.S. EPA, Chgo., 1980-83; assoc. Pretzel & Stouffer, Chartered, Chgo., 1983—. Contbr. articles on environ. sci. to profl. jours. Mem. Chgo. Bar Assn., Ill. State Bar Assn., Air Pollution Control Assn. Office: Pretzel & Stouffer Chartered One S Wacker Dr Ste 2500 Chicago IL

HESSEL, TODD JAMES, pharmacist; b. Green Bay, Wis., Aug. 13, 1956; s. James Joseph and Darlene Ann (Keyes) H.; m. Christina Marie Thomson, Sept. 5, 1981; 1 child, Jessica Ann. B.S. in Pharmacy, St. Louis Coll. Pharmacy, 1981; postgrad., U. Mo., 1974-77. Registered pharmacist, Mo. Pharmacist Cardinal Glennon Hosp., St. Louis, 1981; DePaul Health Ctr., St. Louis, 1981—. Mem. Mo. Soc. Hosp. Pharmacists. Roman Catholic. Avocations: soccer, water skiing. Home: 524 Chele Dr St Charles MO 63303 Office: 12303 De Paul Dr Bridgeton MO 63044

HESSER, JAMES CRAIG, petroleum refinery executive; b. Wheeling, W. Va., Mar. 10, 1942; s. James M. and Helen Anne (Ruppin) H.; m. Susan Jane Flaum, Nov. 22, 1960; children—Catherine and David. Student, Antioch Coll., 1960-63; B.S. in Chem. Engring., U. Kans., 1965; M.B.A., Pepperdine U., 1980. Tech. rep., cons. UOP Process Div., Des. Plaines, Ill., 1965-76; ops. supt. Pacific Refinery Co., Hercules Calif., 1976-80, Belgische Petroleum Raff, Antwerp, Belgium, 1980-81; mgr. refining projects Coastal Corp., Houston, 1981-84, dir. refining, 1985—; refinery mgr. Derby Refining Co., Wichita, Kansas, 1984-85.

HESSION, ANNE MARIE, pharmacist; b. Pitts., Jan. 22, 1958; d. Charles Urban and Aurora Teresa (Cortes) Lux; m. Paul Charles Hession, June 11, 1983. B.S. in Pharmacy, Purdue U., 1981. Staff pharmacist Luth. Hosp., Ft. Wayne, Ind., 1981-82; asst. mgr. Arth Drugs, West Lafayette, Ind., 1982-84; staff pharmacist St. Francis Med. Ctr., Trenton, N.J., 1985—. Sec. Am. Cancer Soc., Lafayette, Ind., 1982-83, v.p., 1983-84. Mem. Am. Pharm. Assn., Ind. Pharmacists Assn., N.J. Pharmacists Assn., Alpha Delta Pi. Roman Catholic. Avocations: running; knitting; camping; basket-weaving; reading.

HESSLER, DALLAS DAN, osteopathic physician; b. Commercial Point, Ohio, Dec. 31, 1944; s. Dan Walter and Helen (Delores) H.; m. Marli Elizabeth Hessler, June 28, 1969; children—Dallas Dan, Kohli Elizabeth. B.A., Capital U., Columbus, Ohio, 1966; M.Div., Trinity Sem., Columbus, 1971; D.O., Kirksville Coll. Osteo. Medicine, Mo., 1975. Diplomate Am. Bd. Med. Examiners. Gen. practice osteo. medicine Grove City Med. Ctr., Ohio; gen. ptnr. Diagnostic X-Ray and Monitor Services, Grove City; mem. staff Grant Hosp.; chmn. dept osteo. principles and practice Doctors Hosp.; clin. faculty Ohio U. Coll. Osteo Med.; chief exec. officer, prin. Dallas Dan Hessler Co., Grove City. Contbr. articles to med. jours. Mem. Am. Coll. Osteo. Emergency Physicians (charter), Am. Coll. Gen. Practice (cert.), Am. Osteo. Assn., Am. Acad. Osteo. Republican. Lutheran. Avocations: snow skiing; water skiing; racquetball. Office: 3636 Broadway Grove City OH 43123

HESTAD, BJORN MARK, metal distributing company executive; b. Evanston, Ill., May 31, 1926; s. Hilmar and Anna (Aagaard) H.; student Ill. Inst. Tech., 1947; m. Florence Anne Ragusi, May 1, 1948; children—Marsha Anne Hestad Chastain, Patricia Lynn Krueger, Peter Mark. Sales corr., Shakeproof, Inc., Chgo., 1947-50; indsl. buyer Crescent Industries, Inc., Chgo., 1950-51; purchasing agt. Switchcraft, Inc., Chgo., 1951-73, materials mgr., 1973-74, dir. purchasing, 1974-77; pres. Tool King, Inc., Wheeling, Ill., 1977—; pres. H & H Enterprises of Northfield. Mgr. youth orgns. Northfield Jr. Hockey Club, 1968-71, Winnfield Hockey Club, 1972-73; bus. mgr. West Hockey Club, 1973-74. Served as cpl. USAAF, 1944-46. Mem. Tool and Die Inst., Sons of Norway. Republican. Mem. United Ch. Christ. Clubs: Waukegan Yacht, Lions. Home: 850 Happ Rd Northfield IL 60093 Office: Tool King Inc 275 Larkin Dr Wheeling IL 60090

HESTAND, NANCY LEE, physician; b. Columbus, Ohio, Jan. 17, 1950; d. Gerald Beverly and Shirley Mary (Fritsch) Davis; m. Harold Edgar Hestand, Oct. 6, 1973; children—Robert Wade, Jennifer Lynn, William Thomas. B.S. cum laude, Ohio State U., 1971; M.D., 1974. Diplomate Am. Bd. Pediatrics. Intern, resident Columbus Children's Hosp., 1974-76, fellow in ambulatory pediatrics, 1976-78; practice medicine specializing in pediatrics, Columbus, 1978—; mem. adv. bd. Columbus City Health Dept., 1980—. Mem. Central Ohio Pediatrics Soc. (health fair task force 1983—). Republican. Congregationalist. Office: 50 Old Village Rd Columbus OH 43228

HETER, JOHN ROBERT, educator; b. Bellevue, Ohio, Mar. 31, 1929; s. Hayes John and Mildred Bernice (Heffner) H.; m. Janice Marie Kaufman, June 12, 1955. B.S., Heidelberg Coll., 1951; M.A., Ohio U., 1954; Ed.D., Case Western Res. U., 1965. Asst. dir. admissions Heidelberg Coll., Tiffin, Ohio, 1951-53; tchr., asst. prin. Bellevue High Sch., Ohio, 1954-59; prin. Rittman High Sch., Ohio, 1959-66, Berea High Sch., Ohio, 1966-69; chmn. div. edn. Baldwin-Wallace Coll., Berea, 1973-84, prof. edn., 1969—. Contbr. articles to profl. jours. Mem. Nat. Assn. Secondary Sch. Prins., Ohio Assn. Pvt. Colls. for Tchr. Edn. (exec. com.), Assn. for Supervision and Curriculum Devel., NEA, Ohio Edn. Assn., Assn. Tchr. Educators, Am. Assn. Sch. Adminstrs., Kappa Delta Pi, Phi Delta Kappa. Presbyterian. Office: Baldwin-Wallace Coll 275 Eastland Rd Berea OH 44017

HETSKO, CYRIL MICHAEL, physician; b. Montclair, N.J., May 25, 1942; s. Cyril Francis and Josephine (Stein) H.; B.A., Amherst Coll., 1964; M.D., U. Rochester, 1968. Intern, U. Wis. Hosps., Madison, 1968-69, resident in internal medicine, 1969-72, clin. assoc. prof. medicine U. Wis., 1975—; practice internal medicine Dean Med. Ctr., Madison, 1975—, dir. Dean Care HMO, Inc., 1983—; chmn. dept. medicine St. Mary's Hosp. Med. Ctr., Madison, 1985—. Served to maj. M.C., AUS, 1972-75. Diplomate Nat. Bd. Med. Examiners, Am. Bd. Internal Medicine. Mem. AMA (alt. del. 1983—), Am. Soc. Internal Medicine, Am. Soc. Microbiology, Am. Thoracic Soc., Assn. Mil. Surgeons U.S., State Med. Soc. Wis. (Councillor 1979-81, dir. 1981—), Dane County Med. Soc. (chmn. com. on prepaid health plans 1977-82; Pres.'s award 1981), Wis. Soc. Internal Medicine (councillor 1981—), N.Y. Acad. Scis., New Eng. Soc. in City N.Y., Nat. Found. for Infectious Disease, Madison Acad. Medicine. Club: Madison. Home: 1114 Sherman Ave Madison WI 53703 Office: Dean Med Ctr 1313 Fish Hatchery Rd Madison WI 53715

HEUER, RONALD EUGENE, tunneling geotechnical consultant, civil engineer, engineering geologist; b. Pontiac, Ill., Apr. 7, 1940; s. George Ernest and Rosemary (Quinn) H.; m. Debra Lynn Virgens, May 8, 1981; children by previous marriage—Janna Leigh, Garrick Todd. B.S. in Civil Engring., U. Ill., 1963, M.S. in Geology, 1965, Ph.D. in Civil Engring., 1971. Registered engr., Calif., Ill., Va., N.Y. Sr. engr., geologist, A.A. Mathews Inc., Arcadia, Calif., 1969-73, Rockville, Md., 1973-74; sr. engr., geologist, Foster Miller Assocs., Alexandria, Va., 1974-75; geotech. cons., Champaign, Ill., 1975—; assoc. prof. civil engring. U. Ill., Urbana-Champaign, 1975-78; mem. Nat. Com. Tunneling Tech., NSF, 1973—, Nat. Com. Rock Mechanics, 1975-78. Contbr. papers to profl. publs. and confs. Recipient Bronze Tablet, U. Ill., 1963; NSF fellow, 1963-64. Mem. ASCE, Assn. Engring. Geologists, Am. Arbitration Assn. Clubs: Nat. Rifle Assn., League Am. Wheelmen. Avocations: Bicycle touring; photography; firearms.

HEUSINKVELD, EDWIN DAVID, college dean: b. Clinton, Iowa, Aug. 21, 1927; s. Edwin David and Rose Viola (Anderson) H.; m. Helen Joan Rod, June 8, 1957; children—David Scott, John Eric, Mark Stephen. B.A., Wheaton Coll. 1949; M.A., U. Iowa, 1957, Ph.D., 1964. Asst. counselor to men U. Iowa, Iowa City, 1956-59; asst. dean students Ferris State Coll., Big Rapids, Mich., 1959-66; dean students Wittenberg U., Springfield, Ohio, 1966-80, Grand View Coll., Des Moines, 1980—. Bd. dirs. Des Moines Choral Soc., Iowa, 1981, Convalescent Home for Children, Des Moines, 1981, Community Telephone Counseling, Inc., Des Moines, 1983. Served with USN, 1951-54. Mem. Nat. Assn. Student Personnel Adminstrs., Iowa Student Personnel Assn., Am. Coll. Personnel Assn., Am. Assn. Higher Edn. Lutheran.

HEWITT, JAMES WATT, lawyer; b. Hastings, Nebr., Dec. 25, 1932; s. Roscoe Stanley and Willa Manners (Watt) H.; student Hastings Coll., 1950-52; B.S., U. Nebr., 1954, J.D., 1956; m. Marjorie Ruth Barrett, Aug. 8, 1954; children—Mary Janet, William Edward, John Charles, Martha Ann. Bar: Nebr. 1956. Practice, Hastings, 1956-57, Lincoln, Nebr., 1960-61; v.p., gen. counsel Nebco, Inc., Lincoln, 1961—; vis. lectr. U. Nebr. Coll. Law, 1970-71; adj. fellow univ. studies U. Nebr., 1978—; dir. Gateway Bank, Lincoln. Mem. state exec. com. Republican party, 1967-70, mem. state central com., 1967-70, legis. chmn., 1968-70. Bd. dirs. Lincoln Child Guidance Center, 1969-72, pres., 1972; bd. dirs. Lincoln Community Playhouse, 1967-73, pres., 1972-73; trustee Bryan Meml. Hosp., Lincoln, 1968-74, 76-82, chmn., 1972-74; trustee U. Nebr. Found., 1979—. Served to capt. USAF, 1957-60. Mem. Am. (Nebr. state del. 1972-80, bd. govs. 1981-83), Nebr. State (chmn. ins. com. 1972-76, chmn. pub. relations com. 1982-84, pres. 1985-86), Fed., Lincoln bar assns., Newcomen Soc., Am., Nebr., Lincoln rose socs., Round Table, Beta Theta Pi, Phi Delta Phi. Congregationalist. Mason (Shriner). Clubs: University, Country of Lincoln (Lincoln). Home: 2990 Sheridan Blvd Lincoln NE 68502 Office: 1815 Y St Lincoln NE 68501

HEWITT, PATRICIA WIMAN, agriculturalist; b. Chgo., Jan. 17, 1925; d. Charles Deere and Pattie (Southall) Wiman; student Conn. Coll. for Women, 1942-44, U. Calif. at Santa Barbara, 1944-45, George Washington U., 1946-47; m. William Alexander Hewitt, Jan. 3, 1948; children—Anna Hewitt Wolfe, Adrienne Hewitt-Beer, Alexander Southall. Asst. to mgr. Midvale Farms Corp., Tucson, 1945-47, dir., sec., 1945-80, half owner, 1963-80; owner, mgr. Friendship Farms, East Moline, Ill., 1955—; owner, joint mgr. Camelot Vineyards, Rutherford, Calif., 1960—. Equestrian coach Japanese Self Def. Forces, 1967-68. Mem. Jr. League, San Francisco, 1951—; asst. to field dir. A.R.C., San Francisco, 1944-45, service cons., 1950-54; bd. dirs. YWCA, San Francisco, 1951-52, Moline Welfare Agy., 1959-69; governing mem. Arabian Horse Club Registry Am., 1963-64; trustee, pres.'s council Marycrest Coll., Davenport, Iowa, 1969-73; v.p. U.S. Modern Pentathlon Assn., 1971-76; mem. U.S. Olympic Games Com., 1970-76; mem. nat. bd. advisers Nat. Assn. for Retarded Children, 1967-73; mem. Ill.-Iowa Assn. for Children with Specific Learning Problems, 1970-79; mem. Ill. State Adv. Council Edn. Handicapped Children, 1973-75; mem. exec. com. Nat. Reading Council, 1970-72; trustee Charles Deere Wiman Meml. Trust, Morris Animal Found., Lincoln Acad. of Ill., Rock Island Franciscan Hosp., Knox Coll., Galesburg, Ill., 1975—; chmn. bd. trustees Butterworth Meml. Trust, 1963-82; trustee Arabian Horse Owners Found., 1961-73, mem. adv. bd., 1973—; mem. women's bd. Field Mus. Natural History, Chgo., 1972—; bd. dirs. Family YMCA, Rock Island, 1975-79; mem. service council United Way Rock Island, Ill. and Scott County, Iowa, 1973-76; governing life mem. Art Inst. Chgo., 1972—; mem. Nat. Com. on U.S.-China Relations, 1974—, Ill. Racing Bd., 1973-77, Nat. Assn. State Racing Commrs., 1973-77; mem. nat. bd. dirs. U.S. Equestrian Team, 1977—; mem. citizens com. U. Ill., 1974-77, animal sci. adv. com. Coll. Agr., 1974-77; mem. mental health adv. com. Rock Island County Pub. Health Bd., 1974-82; mem. adv. bd. Assn. for Retarded Children and Adults Rock Island County, 1972—; mem. corp. vis. com. for dept. psychology M.I.T., 1977—; mem. nat. com. Brandywine Conservancy. Mem. Internat. Arabian Horse Assn. (dir. 1964-67), Grayson Found., Arabian Horse Racing Assn., Am. Horse Show Assn. (life, mem. drugs and medications com.), Nat. Hunter and Jumper Assn. (div.). Episcopalian. Clubs: Santa Barbara Yacht; Arts (Chgo.). Home: 38th St and Blackhawk Rd Rock Island IL 61201 Office: Friendship Farms Rural Route 2 Box 612 East Moline IL 61244

HEWITT, THOMAS EDWARD, financial executive; b. West Lafayette, Ind., Sept. 7, 1939; s. Ernest Edward and Katherine (Thelen) H.; B.A., Dartmouth Coll., 1961, M.B.A., 1962; m. Jeraldine Lee Spurgeon, June 16, 1962; children—Debora Lynn, Laura Jean, Gregory Spurgeon. Staff acct. Ernst & Whinney, Chgo., 1966-67, acct. in charge, 1967, sr. acct., 1967-69; controller Thorne United Inc., Addison, Ill., 1969-70, sec.-treas., 1970; supr. Ernst & Whinney, Chgo., 1971-76; controller Waterloo (Iowa) Industries, Inc., 1976-79, v.p. fin., 1979—. Treas., Salvation Army, Waterloo, 1977-78, 80-82, Cedar Valley United Way, 1983-85; assoc. campaign chmn. United Way of Black Hawk County, 1981, 82; spl. project chmn. Chgo. Jaycees, 1969; trustee Westminster United Presbyterian Ch., 1984-85, vice-chmn., 1985. Served to capt. USMC, 1962-66. Named to Pres.'s Honor Club, Beatrice Foods Co., 1980; NROTC regular scholar, 1957-62; C.P.A., Ill. Mem. Am. Inst. C.P.A.s, Nat. Assn. Accts., Am. Mgmt. Assn. Club: Sunnyside Country (treas. 1984, pres. 1985). Lodge: Elks. Home: 1105 Prospect Blvd Waterloo IA 50701 Office: 999 Home Plaza Waterloo IA 50701

HEYDARI, MIR NASSIR, economist, engineer, educator, consultant, researcher; b. Tehran, Iran, Apr. 19, 1953; s. Abolghassem and Monir (Kazerounian) H.; m. Linda Garcia, Mar. 10, 1978. B.S. in Mining Engring., U. Tehran, 1974; M.S. in Mining Engring., Colo. Sch. Mines, 1978, Ph.D. in Mineral Econs., 1981, M.B.A., 1985. Registered profl. engr., Wis., Colo. Mining engr. BAFG and ANGURAN Mining Cos., Tehran, Iran, 1972-74; mining engr. Penarroya Mining and Metall. Co., Largentiere, France, 1975; research assoc. Excavation Engring. and Earth Mechanics Inst., Golden, Colo., 1976-78; project supr., prin. mining engr., fossil fuels tech. group Sci. Applications Inc., Golden, 1978-81; prin. mining engr., mining and metall. div. Ralph M. Parsons Co., Pasadena, Calif., 1982; asst. prof. mining engring. Coll. Engring., U. Wis.-Platteville, 1982—; dir. Techno-Search Internat., Golden; cons. U.S. Bur. Mines, mineral industry. Recipient Ralph M. Parsons cert. of achievement, 1982; grantee U.S. Bur. Mines, 1976—. Mem. Soc. Mining Engrs., AIME, Am. Assn. Cost Engrs. Contbr. articles to profl. jours. Home: 960 Stonebridge Rd Apt 3 Platteville WI 53818 Office: Coll Engring Univ Wis Platteville WI 53818

HEYDE, DENNIS LEE, travel agent, nursing home administrator; b. Chippewa Falls, Wis., Apr. 11, 1949; s. Lymann Alfred and Agnes Ruth (Thon) H.; m. Carol Jean Rowan, Nov. 21, 1970; children—Eric, April, Anne. B.B.A., U. Wis.-Eau Claire, 1972; cert. in health care acctg., U. Wis., 1980. Cert. nursing home adminstr., Wis., 1979. Asst. bus. office mgr. St. Joseph's Hosp., Chippewa Falls, 1969-74; controller Winona (Minn.) Gen. Hosp. Assn., 1974-76; dir. fin. St. Joseph's Hosp., Chippewa Falls, 1976-81; pres., adminstr. Eagleton Nursing Home, Bloomer, Wis., 1979—, also owner, operator Chippewa Valley Travel Service, Chippewa Falls, 1981—; pres. Chippewa Valley Travel Service, Inc. Treas., dir. Chippewa Area United Way.; dir., chmn. fin. com. Chippewa Valley Family YMCA; adv. com. St. Joseph's Hosp. Served with U.S. Army N.G., 1972-78. Recipient Crusade award Am. Cancer Soc., 1982, Gold award Chippewa Area United Way, 1979. Mem. Healthcare Fin. Mgmt. Assn. (past pres., William C. Follmer Merit award for service 1981, Robert H. Reeves award 1984), Chippewa County Health Planning Forum (pres. 1982), Am. Coll. Health Care Adminstrs., Wis. Hosp. Assn. Roman Catholic (pres. parish council). Clubs: Chippewa Falls Kiwanis (past pres.), United Comml. Travelers (exec. bd.), Elks (past chaplain). Home: 1877 Mansfield St Chippewa Falls WI 54729 Office: 110 N Bridge St Chippewa Falls WI 54729

HIBBE, DOUGLAS WARREN, association executive; b. Jersey City, Apr. 11, 1921; s. Elmer Herman and Bertha Catherine (Rogers) H.; m. Eleanor Alicia Bory, Feb. 20, 1943; children—Sharyn, Craig, Jill. B.S., NYU, 1948, J.D., 1951; postgrad. Army Lang. Sch., Monterey, Calif., 1962. Clk., Dun & Bradstreet, Inc., N.Y.C., 1945-46; ins. clk. Royal Liverpool Group, N.Y.C., 1946-48; ins. underwriter Phoenix London Group, N.Y.C., 1949-51; spl. agt. FBI, Washington, and various locations, 1951-77; legis. counsel Nat. Fraternal Congress Am., Chgo., 1979—. Served with USMC, 1941-45; ETO, PTO. Recipient Meritorious awards FBI, 1955, 61, 62. Mem. Assn. Fraternal Benefit Counsel, Soc. Former Spl. Agts. FBI, Phi Delta Phi. Republican. Home: 130 S Ellsworth St Naperville IL 60540 Office: Nat Fraternal Congress Am 230 W Monroe St Suite 720 Chicago IL 60606

HICKEY, M. JOE, college dean, retired naval officer; b. Armington, Ill., Sept. 15, 1933; s. Karle Merton and Edna Elizabeth (Kistler) H.; m. Norma Deane Neth, Oct. 31, 1959 (div. 1964). B.S., George Washington U., 1975; M.S., Western Ill. U., 1978. Enlisted U.S. Navy, 1956, commd. ensign, 1966, advanced through grades to lt. comdr., 1974, ret., 1977; div. chmn. allied health Nat. Coll., Rapid City, S.D., 1979-80; sr. program dir. Robert Morris Coll., Carthage, Ill., 1980-83, dean of students, 1983—. Mem. Carthage C. of C., Am. Assn. Med. Assts. (on-site visitor 1980—), Ret. Officers Assn. Republican. Avocations: Civil war history; antiques; general and herb gardening; pioneer skills. Home: 410 N Madison Carthage IL 62321 Office: Robert Morris Coll College Ave Carthage IL 62321

HICKMAN, DAVID MICHAEL, paper tableware manufacturing company executive; b. Salem, Oreg., Dec. 11, 1942; s. Vernon Combs and Margaret Irene (Copley) H.; student public schs.; m. Karen Joyce Cox, Aug. 24, 1968; children—Sean Michael, Shannon Lee. Terr. mgr. Brown & Williamson Tobacco Co., 1964-66, Gibson Greeting Cards, Inc., 1966-69; chain drug specialist Coty, Inc., 1970-73; pres., owner Expressions, Seattle, 1973-75; v.p. sales Paper Art Co., Inc., Indpls., 1975-78, exec. v.p., 1978—; pres., owner Paper Artery Co., Inc., 1979—, Shaniko Mktg. Co., 1978—, Paper Art Co., Inc., 1983—. Served with U.S. Army, 1960-63. Republican. Presbyterian. Home: 9202 Behner Brook Dr Indianapolis IN 46250 Office: 3500 N Arlington Ave Indianapolis IN 46218

HICKMAN, LESTER ANSLEY, educator, administrator; b. St. Clair Twp., Ohio, Apr. 5, 1927; s. James Harvey and Nannie Ola (Robinson) H.; m. Elaine Taylor, Aug. 19, 1950; children—Philip Jeffrey, David Kim, Timothy Craig, Elizabeth Ann. B.S. in Edn., Geneva Coll., 1954; M.S., U. Pitts., 1956; postgrad. U. Toledo, 1972, Ed.D., 1978. Tchr., Highlandtown (Ohio), 1951-54; prin. Beaver (Ohio) Local Schs., 1954-56; supt. Hopedale (Ohio) Local Schs., 1956-60; dir. Colegio Americano para Varones, Barranquilla, Colombia, 1960-65; prin. East Liverpool (Ohio) Sch., 1965-67, tchr., 1976—; prin. Greenford (Ohio) High Sch., 1967-69; supr. Millcreek-West Unity Sch. Dist., Ohio, 1969-73; chmn. edn. dept. Roberts Wesleyan Coll., 1973-76. Served with U.S. Army, 1945-47. Mem. NEA (life), Phi Delta Kappa. Presbyterian (elder). Author: A Study of the Effect of the Exemplary Center for Reading Instruction Program on Reading Scores, 1978. Home: 47458 Bell School Rd East Liverpool OH 43920 Office: W 8th St East Liverpool OH 43920

HICKMAN, ROBERT JOHN, JR., home furnishings manufacturing company executive, mail order company executive; b. Phila., May 21, 1946; s. Robert John Hickman and Dorothy Kamm. A.A., Fashion Inst. Tech., 1970. Asst. sales mgr. M. Lowenstein & Sons, N.Y.C., 1967-70, regional sales mgr., Chgo., 1970-78; v.p. sales Angwell Corp., Chgo., 1978-81; v.p., gen. mgr. Purofied Chgo., 1981-84; v.p., nat. sales mgr. Purofied Down, 1985—; ptnr., dir. Dreamy Down Fashions, Elmhurst, Ill., 1982—, Black Sheep, Chgo., 1976-78. Patentee hangwell hook. Party chmn. Young Republicans, Chgo., 1972; pres. Canyon Inc., 1979-81. Served with USN, 1964-66. Mem. English Speaking Union, Council Fgn. Relations. Roman Catholic. Clubs: Inner Circle (pres. Chgo. 1980-82), Lake Shore (bd. dirs. Chgo. 1974-80), Columbia Yacht. Home: 6325 N. Sheridan Chicago IL 60660 Office: Purofied Down Products 45 W 24th St Chicago IL 60616

HICKOK, DAVID KEITH, pediatrician, educator; b. Kalamazoo, Mich., Aug. 4, 1936; s. Keith and Laura L (Lane) H.; m. Rhea Marie Crandall, Nov. 30, 1957 (div. June 1982); children—Michael David, Mark Allen, Steven Edward, Robert Blair; m. Marlene Diane Myers, Dec. 18, 1982; 1 child, Kathryn Lynne. B.S., Mich. State U., 1958; M.D., U. Mich., 1962. Diplomate Am. Bd. Pediatrics. Intern Bronson Methodist Hosp., Kalamazoo, 1962-63, resident in pediatrics, 1963-64; resident Univ. Hosp., Ann Arbor, Mich., 1964-66; practice medicine specializing in pediatrics, Kalamazoo, 1968-82; asst. dir. Southwestern Mich. Area Health Edn. Ctr., Kalamazoo, 1982—; asst. prof. pediatrics and human devel. Coll. of Human Medicine, Mich. State U., 1982—. Dist. chmn. Southwest Mich. council Boy Scouts Am., 1968—; bd. dirs. Family Health Ctr., Kalamazoo, 1970-74. Served to capt. U.S. Army, 1966-68. Recipient Dist. Award of Merit, Boy Scouts Am., 1980, Silver Beaver award, 1982. Fellow Am. Acad. Pediatrics; mem. Western Mich. Pediatric Soc., Mich. State Med. Soc., Kalamazoo Acad. Medicine. Mem. Ch. Reformed. Lodge: Rotary. Avocation: scouting. Office: Southwestern Mich Area Health Edn Ctr 64 E Bronson Med Ctr 252 E Lovell St Kalamazoo MI 49007

HICKROD, GEORGE ALAN, educational adminstration educator; b. Fort Branch, Ind., May 16, 1930; s. Hershell Roy and Bernice Ethel (Karnes) H.; m. Lucy Jen Huang, June 17, 1964; 1 stepson, Goren Wallis Liu. A.B., Wabash Coll., 1954; M.A., Harvard U., 1955; Ph.D., Harvard U., 1966. Asst. prof. ednl. and social scis. Muskingum Coll., 1962-67; assoc. prof. ednl. adminstrn. Ill. State U., Normal, 1967-71, prof., 1971-83, disting. prof., 1983—, dir. Ctr. for Study Ednl. Fin., 1974—. Contbr. articles on ednl. fin. to profl. jours., chpts. to books. Served with USMC, 1950-52, Korea. State of Ill. and U.S. Govt. grantee. Mem. Am. Edn. Fin. Assn. (v.p. 1983-84, pres. 1984-85). Democrat. Unitarian. Clubs: Scottish-Am. Soc. Central Ill. (past chief), Clan Wallace Internat. Lodges: Masons, Elks. Avocations: history; genealogy; travel; cooking. Home: 2 Turner Rd Normal IL 61761

HICKS, JAMES THOMAS, physician, lawyer; b. Brownsville, Pa., June 5, 1924; s. Thomas and Florence Julia (O'Donnell) H.; B.S., U. Pitts., 1945, A.B., 1946, M.S., 1946; Ph.D., George Washington U., 1950; M.D., U. Ark., 1956; J.D., DePaul U., 1975; m. Ellen Elliott, Aug. 25, 1950; children—Ellen, Mary Jo. Intern USPHS, Balt., 1958-60; resident VA Hosp., Pitts., 1958-60; admitted to Ill. bar, 1977, U.S. Ct. of Appeals, 1977, Pa. bar, 1977 U.S. Supreme Ct. Bar, 1980; practice medicine specializing in forensic and legal medicine, River Forest, Ill., 1964—; dir. labs. Oak Park (Ill.) Hosp., 1964—; pres. Oakton Service Corp., 1968—; Oakton Service Corp. of Pa. Served with USPHS, 1956-57. Fellow Nat. Cancer Inst., 1949-50. Fellow ACP, Internat. Coll. Surgeons; mem. AMA, ABA, Ill. Bar Assn., Pa. Bar Assn., Assn. Am. Trial Lawyers, Am. Assn. Hosp. Lawyers, Sigma Xi. Clubs: Univ., Whitehall, Oak Park Country, Carlton. Contbg. editor Hosp. Formulary Mgmt., 1966-70. Home: 7980 W Chicago Ave River Forest IL 60305 Office: 520 Maple Ave Oak Park IL 60304

HICKS, JUDITH EILEEN, nursing administrator; b. Chgo., Jan. 1, 1947; d. John Patrick and Mary Ann (Clifford) Rohan; m. Laurence Joseph Hicks, Nov. 22, 1969; 1 dau., Colleen Driscoll. B.S. in Nursing, St. Xavier Coll., Chgo., 1969; M.S. in Nursing, U. Ill.-Chgo., 1975. Staff nurse Mercy Hosp., Chgo., 1969-70, nursing supr., 1970-73; cons. continuing edn. Ill. Nurses Assn., Chgo., 1974-75; dir. obstetrics and gynecology nursing Northwestern Meml. Hosp., Chgo., 1975-81; v.p. nursing Children's Meml. Hosp., Chgo., 1981—; dir. Near North Health Corp., Chgo., 1982—. Mem. Ill. Hosp. Assn. (chmn. Council on Nursing 1982-83), Inst. Medicine, Am. Soc. Nursing Adminstrs., Women's Health Exec. Network (pres. 1984). Roman Catholic. Home: 2206 Beechwood St Wilmette IL 60091 Office: Children's Meml Hosp 2300 Childrens Plaza Chicago IL 60614

HICKS, JUDITH KAE, educator; b. Grundy Center, Iowa, Feb. 2, 1940; d. Bertram Lyle and Victoria Marie (Smith) Robinson; m. John Richard Hicks, June 15, 1969; children—Jeremy Robinson, Sarah Elizabeth. B.A. in History, Wartburg Coll., 1963; student Colo. State Coll., 1960-61. History tchr. Nokomis Community Dist. 22 (Ill.), 1963-67, 68-69; social studies tchr. Greenview Sch. System (Ill.), 1967-68; tchr. history Webber Twp. High Sch., Bluford, Ill., 1978—; trustee Egyptian Area Schs. Employees Benefit Trust, 1983-85. Mem. AAUW, NEA, Ill. Edn. Assn., Webber Secondary Edn. Assn. (pres. 1983-84), Webber Twp. Edn. Assn. (pres. 1984-85). Methodist. Club: PEO. Home: 1806 Pace Ave Mount Vernon IL 62864 Office: Webber Twp High Sch S Main St Bluford IL 62814

HICKS, SAMUEL IRVING, teacher educator; b. Stormville, N.Y., Apr. 4, 1902; s. Irving J. and Elizabeth (Tripp) H.; A.B., U. Mich., 1924; M.A., Columbia, 1927; Ed.D., Columbia U., 1947; postgrad. N.Y. U., 1931-33; m. Margaret Anderson, Jan. 7, 1924; children—Eleanor (Mrs. Peter Werenfels), Virginia (Mrs. John Karl). Tchr., Boyne City (Mich.) High Sch., 1924-26; prin. jr. and sr. high sch., Dobbs Ferry, N.Y., 1926-29; supt. schs., Central Park, N.Y., 1929-32, Pearl River, N.Y., 1932-58; coordinator services to adminstrs. citizenship edn. project Columbia U., 1954-56; prof. edn. Ohio U., Athens, 1958—, dir. Center for Ednl. Research and Service, 1960-66, coordinator ednl. placement, 1972—; dir. Inst. Edn., Ahmadu Bello U., Nigeria, 1966-70; exec. sec. SEOKWA Council Adminstrv. Leadership, 1972—. Mem. Am. Ednl. Research Assn., N.Y. State Ednl. Research Assn. (past pres.), Am. Assn. Sch. Adminstrs., Nat. Conf. Profs. Ednl. Adminstrn., Comparative and Internat. Edn. Soc., Assn. Sch. Bus. Ofcls., Am. Ednl. Fin. Assn., AAUP, Kappa Delta Pi, Phi Kappa Phi Phi Delta Kappa. Clubs: Athens Rotary, Rotary (Zaria, Nigeria), Pearl River (past pres.). Home: 48 Briarwood Dr Athens OH 45701 Office: Lindley Hall Ohio University Athens OH 45701

HICKS, WILLIAM SEWARD, educator; b. Rochester, N.Y., Oct. 10, 1944; s. Charles R. and Ruth F. (Muller) H.; m. Charlotte Ann McVay, Aug. 27, 1966; 1 dau., Stephanie Frances. B.A. in Communication Edn., Purdue U., 1967, M.S. in Ednl. Adminstrn., 1974. Cert. tchr., Ind. Tchr., adminstr. Howe (Ind.) Mil. Sch., 1967—; mem. North Central Evaluation Team Steering Com., 1980-81; co-host Nat. Speech Tournament, Indpls., 1975, parliamentarian 1980, 83; gen. mgr. Sta. WHWE-FM, Howe Mil. Sch., 1970—. Pres. La Grange County Area Plan Commn., 1977-82; sec. Bd. Zoning Appeals, 1977-82, pres., 1983; mem. Lima Parent Adv. Com., bd. dirs. Howe Coop. Nursery Sch., 1978-80; chmn. adminstrv. bd. Howe United Methodist Church. Recipient numerous forensic awards; named to Ind. Speech Hall of Fame. Mem. Am.

Camping Assn., Ind. Camping Assn., Journalism Edn. Assn., Soc. Profl. Journalists Ind. Assn. Sch. Broadcasters, Speech Communication Assn., Ind. High Sch. Forensic Assn. (exec. sec. 1973—), Ind. Secondary Sch. Adminstrs. Assn., Ind. Speech Assn., Nat. Forensic League (dist. chmn.), Nat. Univ. Continuing Edn. Assn., Am. Inst. Parliamentarians, Ind. Planning Assn., Nat. Assn., Sports Ofcls., Nat. Fedn. Interscholastic Ofcls. Assn., Nat. Fedn. Interscholastic Coaches Assn., Ind. High Sch. Athletic Assn., Ind. Student Edn. Assn. (pres. 1966-67), Purdue U. Alumni Assn. (life), Ind. Tennis Coaches Assn., Alpha Phi Omega, Phi Delta Kappa. Republican. Lodge: Howe Lions (pres. 1973). Office: Box 247 Howe IN 46746

HIEBEL, JOANN HELEN, advertising agency executive; b. Hinckley, Minn., Dec. 7, 1936; d. Joseph Nicholas and Lillian Anna (Korbel) Williams; m. Kenneth John Hiebel, Sept. 5, 1959 (div. Apr. 1981); children—Caroline Kathleen, Michael John. Student Coll. of St. Benedict; B.A., U. Minn., 1958. Adminstrv. asst. Admiral-Merchants, St. Paul, 1958-63; tchr. piano, Mpls., 1964-74; adminstrv. asst. Minn. Opera Co., St. Paul, 1974-77; advt. assoc. Coulter & Assocs., Mpls., 1977-79; mgr. pub. relations Profl. Instruments, Mpls., 1979-81; owner, pres. chief exec. officer Jo Ann Hiebel & Assocs., Mpls., 1981—; exec. dir. Minn. Tooling and Machining Assn., 1981—; advt. rep. and pub. assoc. Bolger Publs., Mpls., 1982-85. Bd. dirs. Exec. Manor Condominium Assn., Mpls., 1980-81, Kidney Found. of Upper Midwest, St. Paul, 1983—; del. Minn. Conf. on Small Bus., Mpls., 1981; mem. Mrs. Jaycees, St. Anthony, Minn., 1963-70. Mem. Nat. Assn. Women Bus. Owners, Advt. Fedn. Minn., Sales and Mktg. Execs.-Mpls., Minn. Soc. Assn. Execs., Minn. Assn. Commerce and Industry, Gamma Phi Beta. Republican. Home: 1235 Yale Pl Minneapolis MN 55403 Office: JoAnn Hiebel & Assocs Inc 6700 Excelsior Blvd Minneapolis MN 55426

HIEBER, BARBARA ELIZABETH, railroad executive; b. East Chicago, Ind., Jan. 30, 1939; d. Fred H. and Barbara V. (Jankauskas) H.; divorced; children—Susan Poloncak Wilk, Steven Michael Poloncak. Cert. transp. mgmt. Calumet Coll., 1974; cert. advtg. studies Northwestern U., 1983; now student in bus. adminstrn. DePaul U. Mech. draftsman Combustion Engring., Inc., East Chicago, Ind., 1957-60; engring. technician Gen Am. Transp. Group, Hammond, Ind., 1961-63, Pullman Standard Co., Hammond, 1970-71, McKee-Berger-Manueto, Chgo., 1971-72; asst. to sales and traffic mgr. Chem. Haulers, Hammond, 1972-73; traffic and transp. generalist Am. Maize, Hammond, 1973-74, Ind. Harbor Belt RR, Hammond, 1974-78, Santa Fe Ry., Chgo., 1978-79; acct. Advt. Direction Inc., Chgo., 1979, specialty advt. coordinator, 1979-83; cost and research analyst Santa Fe Ry., Chgo., 1983—. Fellow Am. Assn. Advt. Agys.; mem. Women's Advt. Club Chgo. (chmn. ethics legis. com. 1982-85), Cost Analysis Orgn. Assn. Am. R.R., Transp. Research Forum, Women's Transp. Assn. Avocations: fishing; writing; architecture; gardening; cooking. Home: 277 Stony Island Calumet City IL 60409 Office: Santa Fe Railway 224 S Michigan Chicago IL 60604

HIEBERT, ELIZABETH BLAKE (MRS. HOMER L. HIEBERT), civic worker; b. Mpls., July 18, 1910; d. Henry Seavey and Grace (Riebeth) Blake; student Washburn U., 1926-30; B.S., U. Tex. 1933; m. Homer L. Hiebert, Aug. 29, 1935; children—Grace Elizabeth (Mrs. John E. Beam), Mary Sue (Mrs. Donald Wester), John Blake, Henry Leonard, David Mark. Free lance writer. Sec. Topeka Regional Sci. Fair, 1958-60, mem. bd., 1964—; mem. bd. Topeka Welfare Planning Council, 1958-62, YWCA, 1962—, Kans. Council Children and Youth; water safety instr., swimming instr. for handicapped; active Campfire Girls, Nat. Trust for Historic Preservation, Internat. Oceanographic Found., People-to-People, Nat. Council on Aging, Shawnee County Advocacy Council on Aging; Fellow Harry S. Truman Library Inst.; mem. bd. Can Help; mem. Topeka Friends of Zoo, Friends of Topeka Library, YMCA, Friends of John F. Kennedy Center Performing Arts, Los Angeles Internat. Fern Soc., Nat. League Am. Pen Women (pres. Topeka), AAAS, D.A.R., Daus. Am. Colonists (mem. bd.), Colo. Hist. Soc., AAUW (bd. mem. 1944-62, 65—, v.p.), New Eng. Women, Washburn U. Alumni Assn., Nat. Wildlife Fedn., Nat. Assn. Mature People, Nat. Ret. Tchrs. Assn., Am. Assn. Museums, Minn. Hist. Soc., Sci. Mus. of Minn., AMA Aux., Internat. Sr. Olympic Assn., Spencer Mus. Art of U. Kans., Kans. Hist. Soc., N.E. Hist. and Geneol. Soc., Tex. U. Alumni, Am. Home Econs. Assn., Shawnee County Med. Aux. (past pres.), Nat. Audubon Soc., Internat. Platform Assn., Topeka Civic Symphony, Met. Mus. Art, P.E.O. (past local pres. coop. bd.), Topeka Art Guild, Nat. Soc. Ancient and Hon. Arty., Cousteau Soc., Shawnee County Hist. Soc. (dir.), Oceanic Soc., Exec. Female, Delta Kappa Gamma, Delta Gamma. Republican. Methodist. Clubs: Capitol Hill, Knife and Fork. Editor children's page Household mag., 1934-39. Home: 1517 Randolph Topeka KS 66604

HIEBERT, NANCY BRAMLEY, county official; b. Hutchinson, Kans., Dec. 4, 1941; d. Harold Leslie and Lois Daile (Kitch) Bramley; B.S. in Nursing, U. Kans., 1963, M.S. in Ednl. Psychology and Research, 1977, Ph.D. in Ednl. Psychology and Research, 1982; m. John Blake Hiebert, Aug. 25, 1962; children—Eric Blake, Rebecca Joan. Staff nurse U. Kans. Med. Center, 1962-63, nursing instr., 1963-65, 68; sch. nurse Shawnee Mission (Kans.) High Sch., 1965-67; nursing instr. new parent edn. Research Hosp. and Med. Center, 1970; Montessori presch. tchr. Johnson County Presch. and Kindergarten, 1971-73; teaching asst. dept. ednl. psychology and research U. Kans., 1976, grad. asst. Emily Taylor Women's Resource Center, 1978-80, vis. fellow Research Inst. Women's Public Lives, 1980-81; field coordinator Watkins campaign 3d Congl. Dist. Kans., 1980; dir. Century Club Builders' campaign Kans. Democratic Com., 1982; commr. Douglas County, Lawrence, Kans., 1983—; project asst. Title IX Equity Workshop Project Region VI, 1977. Chmn. com. on women Kans. div. AAUW, 1979-82, mem. nat. com. on women, 1980-81; conv. adviser Intercollegiate Assn. Women Students, 1979, 80; co-chmn. steering com. UN Mid-Decade Conf. for Women Region VII, 1980; co-chmn. steering com. Kans. Women's Connection, 1981-82; chmn. Kans. Women's Polit. Caucus, 1981-82; fin. council Kans. Democratic Com.; vice chmn. Local Elected Ofcl. Bd., Job Tng. Partnership Act Program, S.D.A. II; mem. Victory Club Douglas County Dem. Party, Dem. Nat. Women's Council, 1983, Dem. Kans. Women's Council, 1983, Kans. Children and Youth Adv. Com., 1981—, Kans. Tax Rev. Commn., 1983-85. Named Outstanding Woman Staff Mem., U. Kans. Women's Recognition Com., 1979; vis. fellow Research Inst. Women's Public Lives, 1980-81. Mem. Nat. Assn. Women Deans, Adminstrs. and Counselors (exec. bd. 1981-82, Ruth Strang Research award 1981), Nat. Women's Polit. Caucus, Phi Delta Kappa, Pi Lambda Theta, Sigma Theta Tau. Home: 1521 Stratford Rd Lawrence KS 66044 Office: PO Box 1914 Topeka KS 66601

HIEGEL, JERRY M., food company executive; b. Davenport, Iowa, 1927; B.S., St. Ambrose Coll., 1949; M.B.A., U. Wis., 1950; married. With Des Moines Register, 1946; with Oscar Mayer & Co. Inc., Madison, Wis., 1946—, asst. v.p. and gen sales mgr. Western div., 1962-66, v.p. sales, 1966-70, v.p. mktg., 1970-71, group v.p., 1971-73, exec. v.p., 1973-77, pres., 1977-85, chief exec. officer, 1980—, chmn., 1985—, also dir. Served with USN, 1945-46. Office: 910 Mayer Ave PO Box 7188 Madison WI 53707*

HIEU, NGUYEN-TRUNG, social science educator, voluntary agency executive; b. Nghe-An, Viet Nam, Dec. 15, 1946; came to U.S., 1974, naturalized, 1980; s. Ngoc-Duc and Thu-Ba (Nguyen) N.; B.A., U. Saigon, 1970; M.A., Govs. State U., 1975, 76, 77, 78; M.Ed., Loyola U., Chgo., 1979, Ed.D., 1985; C.A.S., U. Chgo., 1980; Ph.D., Heed U., 1981. Tchr., Viet Nam Ministry Edn., Saigon, 1966-67; tng. officer U.S. AID, Viet Nam, 1968-69; instr. Nat. Sch. Social Work, Viet Nam, 1970-74; tchr. counselor Jones Community Ctr., Inc., Ill., 1974-75; counselor Catholic Charities, Lombard, Ill., 1975-76; tchr. Chgo. Bd. Edn., 1977—; instr. Nat. Coll. Edn., Chgo., 1979—; founder, pres. NghiaSinh Internat., Saigon, Chgo., 1963—; exec. dir. Social Service Ctr., Saigon, 1968-70; prin. NghiaViet High Sch., Saigon, 1971-74; exec. dir. Vietnamese Community for Human Devel. Inc., Chgo., 1976-80. Author: English-Vietnamese Idioms, 1977, 2d edit., 1981; Nineteen Songs for Love and Peace, 1974; English-Vietnamese Social Science Concepts, 1972. Editor: Lien-Nghia News, 1963—. Mem. Ill. Bilingual Adv. Council, Chgo., 1978-82, Asian Am. Adv. Council to Gov. Ill., 1983—; dir. Access, Inc., Chgo., 1979-84; sponsor more than 1,000 refugees, Chgo., 1975-84. Recipient Nat. Medal of Youth, 1969, Nat. Medal of Edn., 1970, Nat. Medal of Social Service, 1971, Nat. Medal of Labor, 1972; Edn. award Ill. Bd. Edn., 1979; Citizen of Yr. award Chgo. Citizenship Council, 1981; Pres.'s Vol. award White House, 1983-84. Mem. Nat. Assn. Vietnam-Am. Edn., Asian Am. Educators, Ill. Bilingual Edn. Assn., Chgo. Bilingual Educators Assn., Chgo. Citizenship Council. Office: Nat Coll Edn 18 S Michigan Ave Chicago IL 60603

HIGGINBOTHAM, SUZANNE GUGE, human resource consultant; b. St. Louis, Oct. 16, 1926; d. Lee Brown and Louise Suzanne (Reitz) Guge; m. William H. Higginbotham, Oct. 4, 1970; m. Carl H. Koch, Jan. 18, 1951 (div. June 1969); 1 stepchild, Patricia Koch. Student Washington U., 1955-59. Personnel mgr. Safeco Ins. Co., St. Louis, 1954-69; dir. personnel Volkswagen Ins. Co., St. Louis, 1969-76, Swank Motion Pictures, St. Louis, 1976-77; exec. dir. YWCA Met. St. Louis, 1977-85; mem. faculty Creative Problem Solving Inst., State Coll., Buffalo, 1971—; mem. adv. com. Project Search, St. Louis, 1981-85. Contbr. articles to ins. and personnel jours. Bd. dirs. Confluence, Citizens Action Group, St. Louis, 1983—. Mem. Indsl. Relations Assn., Ins. Women St. Louis (pres. 1964-65), Personnel Assn. Greater St. Louis (pres. 1979-80), Personnel Assn. Greater St. Louis (bd. dirs. 1969-84), Group Action Council Greater St. Louis (chmn. 1968), Women's Info. Network, St. Louis Forum Exec. Women's Network. Republican. Home: 890 Judson Manor Dr Saint Louis MO 63141

HIGGINS, ANDREW JACKSON, state justice; b. Platte City, Mo., June 21, 1921; A.B., Central Coll., 1943; LL.B., Washington U., St. Louis, 1948; m. Laura Jo-An Brown, Oct. 30, 1948; 2 children. Admitted to Mo. Bar, 1948; practice in Platte City, 1948-60; former pros. atty. Platte County; judge Mo. Jud. Circuit 6th Dist., 1960-64; commr. Supreme Ct. Mo., 1964-79, justice, 1979—. Former Mayor Platte City; bd. curators Central Methodist Coll., from 1977; mem. nat. awards jury Freedoms Found. Valley Forge, 1976. Served with USNR, 1942-46. Recipient Dist. Alumni award Central Meth. Coll., 1973. Mem. Am. Bar Assn., Mo. Bar Assn., VFW, Alumni Assn. Central Meth. Coll. (pres. 1978), Sigma Alpha Epsilon, Delta Theta Phi. Mem. Christian Ch. (Disciples of Christ). Address: Supreme Ct Mo Supreme Ct Mo Jefferson City MO 65101*

HIGGINS, FRANCIS EDWARD, educator; b. Chgo., Nov. 29, 1935; s. Frank Edward and and Mary Alyce (Fahey) H.; B.S., Loyola U., Chgo., 1959, M.A., 1964; postgrad. Exeter Coll., Oxford (Eng.) U., 1962, Am. U. Beirut, 1966, McGill U., Montreal, Que., Can., 1967; adminstrn. cert. St. Xavier Coll., 1971; Ed.D., U. Sarasota, 1977. Tchr., Washington Jr. High Sch., Chicago Heights, Ill., 1959; tchr. Chgo. Vocat. High Sch., 1960-68, dept. chmn., 1964; asst. prof. social sci. Moraine Valley Community Coll., 1968-69; tchr. history Hillcrest High Sch., Country Club Hills, Ill., 1969—; instr. nursing continuing edn. St. Francis Coll., 1978—. Mem. pres.'s council St. Xavier Coll., 1978—; mem. St. Germaine Sch. Bd., 1972-73, St. Alexander Sch. Bd., 1978-84; active Chgo. council Boy Scouts Am., 1969-77, asst. dist. commr., 1971-75, mem. dist. scout com., 1976-77; co-historian Palos Heights Silver Jubilee Com., 1984. Recipient Disting. Service award Chgo. council Boy Scouts Am., 1974; Brit. Univ. scholar, 1962; Fulbright fellow, summer 1966; English Speaking Union fellow, 1967. Mem. Ill. Hist. Soc., Del. Hist. Soc., Am. Cath. Hist. Soc., Nat. Council Social Studies, Ill. Council Social Studies, Nat. Curriculum and Supervisory Assn., Ill. Supervisory Assn., Ill. Assn. Supervision and Curriculum Devel. (editorial rev. bd. Jour. 1984-86), Chgo. Hist. Soc., Nat. Hist. Soc., Brit. Hist. Assn., Brit. Hist. Assn., Nat. Soc. Study Edn., Phi Delta Kappa, Phi Gamma Mu. Republican. Roman Catholic. Contbr. revs. to Am. Cath. Hist. Jour., History Tchr. Jour. Home: 7660 W 131st St Palos Heights IL 60463 Office: Hillcrest High Sch 175th and Pulaski Rd Country Club Hills IL 60477

HIGGINS, JAMES J., packaging company executive; b. Massillon, Ohio, May 15, 1920; s. John P. and Stella M. (Worth) H.; m. Gloria L. Pepoon, Aug. 20, 1949; children—Bruce J., Keith W., Anita L., Suzanne M. B. Chem. Engring., Ohio State U., 1942; M.S., Lawrence Coll., 1948, Ph.D., 1951. Chem. engr. Fox River Paper Co., Appleton, Wis., 1946, Union Bag & Paper Co., Savannah, Ga., 1947; chemist Morris Paper Mills, 1948; devel. chemist Ohio Boxboard Co., Rittman, 1950-54; paper mill supt. Packaging Corp. Am., Rittman, 1954-57, research group leader, research and devel. mgr., 1958-61, dir. tech. services and environ. control, Grand Rapids, Mich., 1961—. Patentee packaging. Contbr. writings to publs. in field. Served to capt. C.E. U.S. Army, 1942-46. Fellow Am. Inst. Chemists; mem. TAPPI, AAAS, Am. Inst. Chem. Engrs., N.Y. Acad. Scis. Home: 2035 Wilshire Dr SE East Grand Rapids MI 49506 Office: Packaging Corp Am 3251 Chicago Dr SW Grandville MI 49418

HIGGINS, ROBERT ARTHUR, electrical engineer, educator, consultant; b. Watertown, S.D., Sept. 5, 1924; s. Arthur C. and Nicoline (Huseth) H.; m. Barbara Jeanne Fagerlie, 1958; children—Patricia Suzanne, Daniel Alfred, Steven Robert. B.E.E. with honors, U. Minn., 1948; M.S.E.E., U. Wis., 1964; Ph.D. in Elec. Engring., U. Mo., 1969. Registered profl. engr. Engr., Schlumberger Well Survey Corp., Tex., 1948-57; research technologist Mobil Research and Devel. Corp., Tex., 1958-61; research engr. United Aircraft Research Labs., Conn., 1965; staff specialist Remote Sensing Inst., S.D., 1969-71; asst. prof. elec. engring. S.D. State U., 1969-74, assoc. dir. Engring. Expt. Sta., 1973-77, prof. elec. engring., 1974-79, cons. Control Data Corp., 1977-80, Mankato State U., 1980; prin. engr. Sperry Univac, 1981—; prof. elec. engring. St. Cloud State U., Minn., 1985—; cons. Lawrence Livermore Lab., 1971-73, U.S. Air Force Office Sci. Research, Fla., 1976; project dir., cons. NSF, 1973-80. Bd. dirs. Eden Prairie Bd. Edn. (Minn.), 1982-85. Served with Combat Engrs., AUS, 1943-46. NASA fellow, 1966-68; NSF grantee, 1966, 72, 74, AEC grantee, 1971-73; Office Water Resources Research grantee, 1971-74. Mem. IEEE (sr.), Sigma Xi. Lutheran. Contbr. articles to profl. jours. Patentee in field. Home: 11260 Windrow Dr Eden Prairie MN 55344 Office: Dept Elec Engring St Cloud State U Saint Cloud MN 56301

HIGH, DOROTHY HELEN FRANK, city recreation administrator; b. Lincoln, Nebr., Feb 3, 1935; d. Theodore Ludwig and Lillian Winifred (Schellberg) F.; m. Duane High, Nov. 18, 1955; children—Ted Frank, Catherine Nadine. B.S. in Edn., U. Nebr., 1956; M.S. in Edn., Chadron State Coll., 1967. Instr. phys. edn. Lincoln Pub. Schs., Nebr., 1956-58, Alliance City Schs., Nebr., 1964-67, Scottsbluff Pub. Schs., Nebr., 1967-69, Hiram Scott Coll., Scottsbluff, 1969-71; asst. prof. edn., Tarkio Coll., Mo., 1971; recreation supr. City of Scottsbluff, 1973—. Mem. adv. bd. Nebr. Council Ednl. TV, Lincoln, 1968-70, Nebr. Dept. Edn., 1970; bd. dirs. Southeast Recreation Ctr., Scottsbluff, 1975-80, Jaycee Sr. Ctr., Scottsbluff, 1978-82; mem. adv. bd. Foster Grandparent Program, Scottsbluff, 1983—. Mem. Am. Assn. Leisure and Recreation (pres.-elect 1985-86, pres. 1986-87), Am. Alliance Health, Phys. Edn., Recreation and Dance (pres. central dist. 1982-84, Honor award 1975), Nebr. Assn. Health, Phys. Edn., Recreation and Dance (pres. 1972-73, Honor award 1970), Western Gerontol. Soc. Republican. Lutheran. Club: Soroptimist Internat. of Scotts Bluff County (pres. 1978-79). Avocations: tennis; swimming. Home: 2210 7th Ave Scottsbluff NE 69361 Office: City of Scottsbluff 1818 Ave A Scottsbluff NE 69361

HILBISH, BARBARA SMITH, singer, actress, voice educator; b. Canton, Ohio, July 27, 1928; d. Ellsworth Price and Mary Ernestine (Strock) Smith; B.M., Westminster Choir Coll., 1950, M.M., 1958; m. Thomas Hilbish, July 2, 1950; children—Catherine Hilbish McNeela, Jennifer Sabina. Dir. choirs Trenton (N.J.) State Home for Girls, 1950-51; voice tchr., Ann Arbor, Mich., 1955—; vis. lectr. voice U. Mich., Ann Arbor, 1966; voice tchr. Nat. Music Camp, Interlochen, Mich., 1966-82, 74-82; soloist 1st Presbyterian Ch., Ann Arbor, 1969-75; soloist Phila. Orchestra, Detroit Symphony, 1971; lectr. voice Siena Heights Coll., Adrian, Mich., 1983—. Active Jr. League, Canton, 1950. Mem. Nat. Assn. Tchrs. Singing, Ann Arbor Civic Theatre, Saline Area Players, St. Andrew's Players, Sigma Alpha Iota. Republican. Home: 2189 S 7th St Ann Arbor MI 48103

HILBURG, ALAN JAY, public relations executive, marketing consultant; b. N.Y.C., May 7, 1948; m. Gail Lynn Bialek, June 6, 1976. B.F.A., N.Y. Inst. Tech., 1970. Publicity mgr. NBC-TV, N.Y.C., 1970-74; communications and mktg. dir. Jr. Achievement, N.Y.C., 1974-76; v.p. mktg. Michaels-Stern, N.Y.C., 1976-77; v.p., gen. mgr. Burson-Marsteller, Cleve., 1977—; cons. Nat. Inst. Dental Research, Washington, 1980, Nat. Cancer Inst., Washington, 1982-83; vis. instr. Ohio U., Athens, 1982-83. Co-chmn. Young Republicans, N.Y.C., 1976; chmn. long range planning mktg. subcom. United Way, Cleve., 1983. Recipient Clio awards, 1979, 81. Mem. Pub. Relations Soc. Am. (chmn. found. com. 1982-83), Nat. Acad. TV Arts and Scis. Republican. Clubs: City, University (Cleveland). Home: 101 Manorbrook Dr Chagrin Falls OH 44022 Office: Burson-Marsteller 3690 Orange Pl Beachwood OH 44122

HILDRETH, PATRICIA YVONNE, accounting executive; b. Clinton, Ind., Mar. 15, 1934; d. Leonard Adam and Wilma Vivian (Scifres) Prulhiere; m. James A. Hildreth, Jan. 20, 1954; children—John Alan, Patti Virginia, David Michael, Brian Spencer. Student Jackson Community Coll., 1974-80, Eastern Mich. U., 1980-81. Sales clk. Yeager Co., Akron, Ohio, 1951-52; acctg. clk. B.F. Goodrich Co., Akron, 1952-54; owner bookkeeping firm P.Y. Hildreth, Akron, 1965-72; owner Jackson Small Bus. Service (Mich.), 1972—; cons. in field. Millage campaign chmn. Jackson Pub. Sch., 1977, mem. various coms., 1972-81; active Girl Scouts U.S.A., Akron and Jackson; pres. PTA, Akron, 1968-70; treas. Jackson Med. Ctr. Inc., 1980-82; Mem. Ind. Accts. Assn. of Mich. (edn. com. 1983-84). Republican. Mem. Ch. of Christ. Office: Jackson Small Bus Service 2300 W Michigan Ave Jackson MI 49201

HILER, JOHN PATRICK, congressman; b. Chgo., Apr. 24, 1953; s. Robert J. and Fran Hiler; m. Catherine Sands, 1984. B.A., Williams Coll., 1975; M.B.A., U. Chgo., 1977; LL.D. (hon.), Tri State U., 1984. Mktg. dir. Charles O. Hiler and Son, Inc., also Accurate Castings, Inc., La Porte, Ind., 1977-81; mem. 97th-99th Congresses from 3d Dist. of Ind. Del., Ind. Republican Conv., 1978, 80, Rep. Nat. Conv., 1984; chmn. La Porte Rep. City Com., 1979; del. White House Conf. on Small Bus., 1980; trustee La Lumiere Sch., La Porte. Mem. La Porte C. of C. Roman Catholic. Office: 407 Cannon House Office Bldg Washington DC 20515*

HILGART, ARTHUR A., JR., pharmaceutical company executive; b. Chgo., Mar. 6, 1936; s. Arthur and Naomi (Nelson) H.; m. Carolyn Charleston, June 15, 1957; children—John Arthur, Joshua Carl. A.B., Shimer Coll., 1953; M.B.A., U. Chgo., 1955. With The Upjohn Co., Kalamazoo, Mich., 1957—, exec. dir. corp. planning and devel. 1982—; guest lectr. Kalamazoo Coll. Western Mich. U. Pres., Reproductive Health Care Ctr./Planned Parenthood; pres. Kalamazoo Civic Players; founding bd. dirs. ACLU of Western Mich.; past pres. Kalamazoo Council on Human Relations. Mem. Am. Econ. Assn., AAAS, Soc. Long-Range Planning (London). Home: 1801 Evanston Kalamazoo MI 49008 Office: The Upjohn Co Kalamazoo MI 49008

HILKE, EILEEN VERONICA, educator; b. Milw., Sept. 23, 1950; d. Arthur and Dorothy (Ingich) Gehlen; m. Thomas Hilke, July 13, 1974. B.S., U. Wis.-Eau Claire, 1972; M.Ed., Marquette U., 1977; Ph.D., U. Wis.-Milw., 1983. Tchr. elem. sch., Sheboygan Falls, Wis., 1972-77; assoc. prof. Lakeland Coll., Sheboygan, 1977—, chmn. dept. edn. and psychology, 1978—, chmn. div. social sci., 1981—. Bd. dirs. Mental Health Assn. Recipient Citizenship award DAR; Delta Kappa Gamma scholar. Mem. Interlake Reading Assn. (pres., program chmn.), Wis. Reading Assn. (dir.), Internat. Reading Assn. (sect. leader Great Lakes region), Wis. Ednl. Research Assn., Assn. for Supervision and Curriculum Devel., Wis. Math. Council, NEA, Northeastern Wis. Edn. Assn. (v.p.), Wis. Council for Social Studies (dir.), Wis. Assn. Colls. Tchr. Edn. (pres., exec. bd.), AAUW, Am. Personnel and Guidance Assn., Phi Delta Kappa (pres., dir., historian), Delta Kappa Gamma (rec. sec., exec. bd.). Author: Elementary Education as a Profession, 1981; contbr. articles to profl. jours. Office: Lakeland Coll Sheboygan WI 53081

HILL, ALVIN, digital equipment company executive; b. Moultrie, Ga., Feb. 3, 1940; s. Berry and Elizabeth H.; m. Maude E. Simmons, Apr. 14, 1979. Student Phila. Wireless Tech. Inst., 1962-64, U. Pa., 1966, Rider Coll., 1975. Customs engr. IBM, Phila., 1963-67; field engr. RCA, Riverton, N.J., 1967-70, Control Data Corp., Phila., 1970-72; product support mgr. Digital Equipment Corp., Rolling Meadows, Ill., 1972-83, br. mgr., Schaumburg, Ill., 1983—. Served with USN, 1957-62. Mem. Am. Mgmt. Assn., Assn. Field Service Mgrs. Democrat. Baptist. Lodge: Masons. Home: 333 Clearwater Ln Schaumburg IL 60194 Office: 1207 E Remington Rd Schaumburg IL 60195

HILL, ARTHUR CYRUS, history educator, consultant, researcher; b. Cowan, Tenn., Nov. 5, 1918; s. Arthur A. and Alice Ann (Allen) H.; m. Belvia Oneal Brasier, Sept. 21, 1941; 1 son, Bernard Cyrus. B.A., U. Minn., 1960, M.A., 1968, Ph.D., 1982. Ry. mail clk. U.S. Post Office Dept., St. Paul, 1949-60; social worker, Mpls., 1960-65; area rep. Job Corps, Mpls., 1965-68; prof. social sci. Mpls. Community Coll., 1968—; mem. faculty Minn. Met. State U., St. Paul. Mem. Minn. Bd. on Aging, 1983. Nat. Found. for the Humanities grantee, 1972, Duke U. summer seminar, 1974. Mem. Sociologists of Minn., Assn. for Study of Afro-Am. Life and History, Midwest Latin Ams. for the Study of Latin-Am. History, Midwest Polit. Sci. Assn., Alpha Phi Alpha. Mem. Democratic Farmer Labor Party. Mem. African Methodist Episcopal Ch. Home: 1615 127th Ave NW Coon Rapids MN 55433 Office: Mpls Community Coll 1501 Hennepin Ave Minneapolis MN 55403

HILL, CHARLES GRAHAM, JR., chemical engineering educator; b. Elmira, N.Y., July 28, 1937; s. Charles Graham and Ethel Mayburn (Pfleegor) H.; m. Katharine Mertice Koon, July 11, 1964; children—Elizabeth, Deborah, Cynthia. B.S., MIT, 1959, M.S., 1960, Sc.D., 1964. Asst. prof. MIT, Cambridge, 1964-65; asst. prof. U. Wis., Madison, 1967-71, assoc. prof., 1971-76, prof. chem. engring., 1976—; cons. A.D. Little, Cambridge, 1964-65, Joseph Schlitz Brewing Co., Milw., 1973-76, Nat. Bur. Standards, 1979—. Author: Introduction to Chemical Engineering Kinetics and Reactor Design, 1977. Contbr. articles to profl. jours. Served to capt. U.S. Army, 1965-67. Gen. Motors Nat. scholar, 1955-59; NSF fellow, 1959-62; Ford Found. fellow, 1964-65. Mem. Am. Inst. Chem. Engrs., AAAS, Am. Chem. Soc., Sigma Xi, Tau Beta Pi, Phi Lambda Upsilon. Republican. Presbyterian. Avocations: Sailing; coaching softball. Home: 2241 Fox Ave Madison WI 53711 Office: Dept Chem Engring U Wis 1415 Johnson Dr Madison WI 53706

HILL, DONAL DEAN, osteopathic physician; b. Fairfield, Iowa, Aug. 16, 1953; s. Gerald R. and Nada Lavelle (Hanna) H.; m. Mary Mieko Williams, Apr. 9, 1977; 1 dau., Heather Ellen. B.S. cum laude, Iowa Wesleyan Coll., 1976; D.O. with honors, U. Osteo. Medicine and Health Scis., Des Moines, 1979. Intern, Des Moines Gen. Hosp., 1979-80; ptnr. Med. Arts Clinic, Fairfield, Iowa, 1980—; mem. staff U. Osteo. Medicine and Health Scis., Des Moines, 1981-82; vice chmn. staff Jefferson County Hosp., 1983, chief of med. staff, 1984; mem. Pub. Health Adv. Bd. Mem. fin. comm. 1st Bapt. Ch. Recipient Outstanding Freshman award Iowa Wesleyan Coll., 1977; Charles Reed award U. Osteo. Medicine and Health Scis., 1979. Mem. Iowa Med. Soc., Iowa Osteo. Med. Soc., Am. Osteo. Assn., Osteo. Nat. Alumni Assn., Iowa Acad. Osteopathy, Jefferson County Med. Soc. (vice chmn.), S.E. Iowa Osteo. Med. Soc. (pres.), Iota Phi (hon.), Beta Beta Beta Soc. Republican. Clubs: Rotary Golf, Country (Fairfield). Home: 401 Heatherwood Circle Fairfield IA 52556 Office: Medical Arts Clinic 408 S Maple Fairfield IA 52556

HILL, JUDITH, broadcast sales executive; publishing executive; b. Chgo., Nov. 15, 1946; d. Gustave Paul and Elsie Sophia (Mutschler) Bade; m. Rodney Arthur Hill, Jan. 5, 1981 (div.); children—Elisabeth, Katharine. B.S. in Edn., Ill. Tchrs. Coll., 1967. Media rep. Leo Burnett Co., Chgo., 1968-72; sales rep. Westinghouse Broadcasting, Chgo., 1972-80, Midwest sales mgr., 1980—; v.p., treas. North Coast Inc., Chgo., 1981—. Republican. Lutheran. Office: 625 N Michigan Ave Suite 300 Chicago IL 60611

HILL, LEE EARL, marketing communications company executive; b. Chgo., July 22, 1937; s. Robert Edward and Priscilla Jewel (Brown) H.; m. Joyce A. Bergstrom, Feb. 4, 1956 (div. 1971); children—Donna, Michael, Richard; m. 2d, Cindy J. Weis, Jan. 8, 1983. B.S., U. Ill., 1961. Vice pres. Leo Burnett Co., Inc., Chgo., 1961-70; owner, pres. Lee Hill, Inc., 1970—. Office: Lee Hill Inc 25 E Superior St Chicago IL 60611

HILL, LLOYD LESTER, JR., health care executive; b. Nacagdoches, Tex., Jan. 8, 1944; s. Lloyd Lester and Ruby (Murchison) H.; m. Carol Ann London, Dec. 20, 1964; children—Ronald Lloyd, Brandt Lloyd; m. Sueann Staggs, June 25, 1978; 1 son, Joshua Lloyd. Student psychology N. Tex. State U., 1962-65; student U. Tex., 1965-67, Columbia U., 1980—; M.B.A., Rockhurst Coll., 1985. Dist. sales mgr. Marion Health and Safety div. Marion Labs., Dallas and Los Angeles, 1969-74, regional sales mgr., Chgo., 1974-76, mgr. new bus. devel., Kansas City, 1976-77, dir. sales, 1977-79; regional mgr. Norton SPD, Cranston, R.I., 1979-80; sr. v.p. Kimberly Services Inc., Kansas City, Kans., 1980—, dir., 1982—; cons. Carlton Mgmt. Inc., Kansas City, Mo., 1981—. Vice pres. adminstrn., organizer Santa Fe Blazers Swim Team, Overland Park, Kans., 1976-78. Mem. Home Health Supplemental Staffing Assn. Republican. Methodist. Office: Kimberly Services Inc 8500 W 110th Overland Park KS 66210

HILL, PATRICIA JO, media specialist, educator; b. Muncie, Ind., Oct. 28, 1944; d. Frederic Burnside and Elizabeth Becom (Zaring) Harbottle; m. Charles Francis Hill; 1 son, Thomas Frederic. B.S., Ball State U., 1964, M.A., 1978, Ed.S., 1981. Instr., head immunology dept. Ball Meml. Hosp., Muncie, Ind., 1963-74; tchr. emotionally disturbed Indpls. Pub. Schs., 1974-75, lead tchr. severe/profound mentally retarded, 1979-84; media specialist in spl. edn., 1985—; cons. Prescription Learning Corp., 1975-76. Dir. pub. edn. Am. Cancer

Soc., Lawrence Twp., Indpls.; Ind. vol. rep. Fed. Transp. and Archtl. Barriers Bd. NSF grantee, 1961; Shroyer scholar Mchts. Nat. Bank Muncie, 1972; Indpls. Pub. Schs. scholar, 1981. Mem. Council Vols. and Orgns. for Handicapped, Assn. Behavioral Analysts, Council Exceptional Children (tech. and media div.), Assn. Supervision and Curriculum Devel. Methodist. Home: 7330 Scarborough Blvd E Indianapolis IN 46256 Office: 3650 Cold Spring Rd Indianapolis IN 46222

HILL, ROBERT ARLEN, architect; b. Denver, Apr. 29, 1937; s. Wilfred Garland and Blanche Ann (Barada) H.; m. Gigi Lauridson, Dec. 21, 1968; children—Karen, Jeffrey. B.Arch., Iowa State U., 1961. Cert. architect, Nebr. Project architect Leo A. Daly Co., Omaha, 1961-68; v.p. Hellmuth Obata & Kassabaum, St. Louis, 1968—. Vice chmn., sec. Brentwood Planning and Zoning Bd., 1978—. Served to cpl. Army N.G., 1961-65. Mem. AIA, Phi Kappa Psi. Republican. Mem. United Ch. of Christ. Lodge: Lions. Home: 1931 Parkridge St Brentwood MO 63144 Office: 100 N Broadway St Saint Louis MO 63102

HILL, ROBERT MASON, lawyer; b. Excelsior Springs, Mo., July 16, 1947; s. Wilson D. and Betty J. (Rodgers) H.; m. Stephanie Marie Hamann, Dec. 3, 1982; m. Sharon L. Cahill, Aug. 25, 1969 (div. Oct. 1982); children—Andrea A., Caroline Wilson. B.A., U. Mo., 1969, J.D., 1971. Bar: Mo. 1972. Ptnr., Hill & Lehnen and predecessor firms, Richmond, Mo., 1972—; dir. Am. Bank of Richmond. Writer case notes Mo. Law Rev., 1970-71. Bd. dirs. Ray County Indsl. Devel. Corp., Richmond. Mem. ABA, Mo. Bar Assn., Ray County Bar Assn. Democrat. Presbyterian. Lodges: Kiwanis (pres. 1975-76), Masons, Shriners. Home: Route 1 Richmond MO 64085 Office: Hill & Lehnen 103 W Main St Richmond MO 64085

HILL, ROGER EARL, osteopathic physician; b. Kansas City, Mo., Oct. 7, 1953; s. Wilbur Thomas and Mary Sibyl (Green) H. Student William Jewell Coll., 1972-75; D.O., Kirksville Coll. Osteo. Medicine, 1979. Intern, Normandy Osteo. Hosps., St. Louis, 1977-80; practice osteo. medicine in family practice, Liberty (Mo.) Family Med. Services, 1980—. Bd. dirs. Liberty Sympony Orch.; mem. William Jewell Fine Arts Guild; deacon, soloist, Sunday Sch. tchr. Second Bapt. Ch., Liberty; tenor Kansas City Community Opera Co., Inc.; lead roles include Carman, LaBoheme, Faust, Rigoletto; performed sacred concerts throughout Mo. Mem. Mo. Assn. Osteo. Physicians and Surgeons (legis. com.), West Dist. Osteo. Assn. (sec.), Am. Osteo. Assn., Am. Coll. Gen Practioners. Office: Liberty Family Med Services Westowne 6 Liberty MO 64068

HILL, THOMAS MALLORY, accounting firm executive; b. Chgo., July 27, 1955; s. Thomas Lewis and Alma Louise (Davis) H.; m. Janice, Dec. 15, 1979. B.S. in Mgmt. Econs., Elmhurst Coll., 1977. Budget auditor analyst Ill. Toll Hwy., Oakbrook, Ill., 1977-79; corp. acct. Swift & Co., Chgo., 1979-82; dist. mgr. A.L. Williams, Inc., Chgo., 1983—; chief exec. officer King, Dill & Mallory, Chgo., 1982—; cons. Accounters Community Ctr., Chgo., 1983—; tax advisor DiCom Systems, Inc., Chgo., 1983—; tax advisor ins. King, Dill & Mallory, Chgo., 1982—; fin. cons. 79th St. Ch. Christ, Chgo., 1981—, Personal work dir., 1983—. Campaign mgr. Citizens for Foster, State Rep., Chgo., 1979; food pantry dir. Chgo. Chs. Christ, 1979. Democrat. Mem. Ch. of Christ. Office: King Dill & Mallory Financial Acctg Services 2600 S Michigan Ave Chicago IL 60616

HILL, W. CLAYTON, management consultant; b. New Hampton, Mo., Sept. 24, 1916; s. Charles A. and Elva E. (Riggins) H.; B.S. in Bus. Adminstrn., U. Mo., 1937; m. Dorothy L. Crosby, Aug. 24, 1938; children—Charles W., Douglas L. Acct., Gen. Elec. Co., Bridgeport, Conn., 1937-41; sales mgmt. IBM Corp., 1941-50; asst. to pres. Gen. Elec. X-Ray Corp., Milw., 1950-53; v.p. Hotpoint Co. div. Gen. Elec. Co., Chgo., 1953-57; cons., mgr. planning Gen. Elec. Co., N.Y.C., 1957-62; dir. planning Am. Can Co., 1962-64; mgmt. cons. C. Hill Assocs., Greenwich, Conn., 1964-80, Prairie Village, Kans., 1980—; instr. Marquette U., 1950-53; cons. RCA Corp., Sperry Co., Ford Motor Co., Pet, Inc., Gen. Elec. Co., Monsanto Co., H&R Block, Inc., Farmland Industries, Inc., United Telecommunications, Inc., others. Pres. King Merritt Community, Inc.; mem. adv. council Bus. Sch., U.Mo., City of Prairie Village. Served with Signal Corps, AUS, 1943-46. Decorated Army Commendation Medal. Mem. Am. Mktg. Assn., Nat. Assn. Accts., Sales Exec. Club N.Y.C., U. Mo.-Kansas City Bus. Sch. Alumni Assn. (pres.). Office: 8713 Catalina Dr Prairie Village KS 66207

HILLE, MICHAEL JOHN, library director; b. Shawano, Wis., Dec. 23, 1943; s. Arthur Fred and Ruth Roselyn (Redmann) H.; m. Marilyn Lou Mueller, Sept. 18, 1976; children—Jason, Lisamarie. B.S., U. Wis.-Oshkosh, 1965; M.S., U. Milw., 1971. Head librarian West Milw. High Sch., 1965-73, Nathan Hale High Sch., West Allis, Wis., 1973-74; dir. Shawano City-County Library, Wis., 1974—; adv. com. Nicolet Library System. Bd. dirs. Shawano County Hist. Soc., 1975—. Mem. Wis. Library Assn., Wis. Audio-Visual Circuit (bd. dirs. 1983—). Republican. Lutheran. Lodge: Rotary. Avocations: tennis, reading, painting, basketball, gardening. Home: Route 1 Pine Rd Cecil WI 54111 Office: Shawano City-County Library 728 S Sawyer St Shawano WI 54166

HILLIS, ELWOOD HAYNES, congressman; b. Kokomo, Ind., Mar. 6, 1926; s. Glen R. and Bernice (Haynes) H.; B.S., Ind. U., 1949, J.D., 1952; m. Carol Hoyne, June 12, 1949; children—Jeffrey H., Gary L., Bradley R. Admitted to Ind. bar, 1952; mem. Ind. Ho. of Reps., 1967-69; mem. 92d to 99th Congresses from 5th Ind. Dist. Pres. Elwood Haynes Meml. Charitable Trust; Howard County United Fund, 1969. Served with USAAF, 1944-46; ETO. Mem. ABA Ind., Howard County (past pres.) bar assns., Am. Legion, VFW. Presbyterian. Lodges: Rotary, Elks, Masons, Shriners. Office: 2336 Rayburn House Office Bldg Washington DC 20515

HILLMAN, DOUGLAS WOODRUFF, federal judge; b. Grand Rapids, Mich., Feb. 15, 1922; s. Lemuel Serrell and Dorothy (Woodruff) H.; A.B., U. Mich., 1946, LL.B., 1948; m. Sally Jones, Sept. 13, 1944; children—Drusilla W., Clayton D. Bar: Mich. 1948, U.S. Supreme Ct. 1967. Assoc., Lilly, Luyendyk & Snyder, Grand Rapids, 1948-53; partner firm Luyendyk, Hainer, Hillman, Karr & Dutcher, Grand Rapids, 1953-65, Hillman, Baxter & Hammond, 1965-79; U.S. dist. judge, Western Dist. Mich., Grand Rapids, 1979—; instr. Nat. Inst. Trial Advocacy, Boulder, Colo. Chmn., Grand Rapids Human Relations Commn., 1963-66; chmn. bd. trustees Fountain St. Ch., 1970-72; pres. Family Service Assn., 1967. Served as pilot USAAF, 1943-45. Decorated D.F.C., Air medal. Recipient Annual Civil Liberties award ACLU, 1970. Mem. ABA, Mich. Bar Assn., Grand Rapids Bar Assn. (pres. 1963), Am. Coll. Trial Lawyers (Mich. chmn. 1979), 6th Circuit Jud. Conf. (life), Internat. Acad. Trial Lawyers, Fedn. Ins. Counsel, Internat. Assn. Ins. Counsel, Internat. Soc. Barristers (pres. 1977-78), Nat. Bd. Trial Advocacy. Clubs: M (U. Mich.); University (Grand Rapids), Torch. Lodge: Rotary. Office: 110 Michigan St NW 682 Grand Rapids MI 49503

HILLMAN, STANLEY ERIC GORDON, retired business executive, company director; b. London, Oct. 13, 1911; s. Percy Thomas and Margaret Eleanor Fanny (Lee) H.; ed. Holyrood Sch., also Tonbridge Sch., Eng.; m. May Irene Noon, May 2, 1947; children—Susan Ann, Deborah Ann, Katherine Ann. Came to U.S., 1951, naturalized, 1957. With British-Am. Tobacco Co., Ltd., London and Shanghai, 1933-47; dir. Hillman & Co., Ltd., Cosmos Trading Co., FED Inc., U.S.A., Airmotive Supplies Co. Ltd., Hong Kong, 1947-52; v.p. Gen. Dynamics Corp., 1953-61; v.p., group exec. Am. Machine & Foundry Co., 1962-65; v.p., dir. Gen. Am. Transp. Corp., 1965-67; vice chmn., pres., dir. IC Industries, 1968-78; chmn., chief exec. officer Ill. Central Gulf R.R., 1976-78; bankruptcy trustee Chgo., Milw., St. Paul R.R., 1978-79; dir. SFN Cos., Bandag Corp., Avco Corp., Axia Corp., Bell & Howell Co., Cooper Industries, Consol. Rail Corp.; trustee Gen. Growth Properties. Clubs: Mid-Am., Chicago, Onwentsia, Royal Poinciana. Home: 533 N Mayflower Rd Lake Forest IL 60045

HILLMER, ROBERT RONALD, advertising agency executive; b. Jefferson, Iowa, June 21, 1923; s. Oscar F. and Florence W. (McMechan) H.; m. Carol J. Bassindale, Sept. 1, 1951; children—Nancy Carol, Robert Andrew, Paul Clifford. Student Kansas City Art Inst., Chgo. Acad. Fine Arts, Art Inst. of Chgo. Staff artist Simmons Co., Chgo., 1949-53; staff artist, art dir. Brady Co., Appleton, Wis., 1953-64; art dir., v.p. creative group head Hoffman-York, Milw., 1964-79; v.p. exec. art dir. R. L. Meyer Advt. Co., Milw., 1979-83; v.p., creative dir. Ken Schmidt Co., 1983—. Pres. men's internat. club YMCA, Appleton, Wis., 1961-62. Served with AUS, 1943-45. Decorated Purple Heart; recipient Gold medals Art Dirs. Club of Wis., 1968, 69, 70, 72, Silver medals, 197-, 72, 73. Mem. Illustrators and Designers of Milw. (pres. 1968), Milw. Advt. Club (awards 1968-83).

HILPERT, BRUNETTE KATHLEEN POWERS (MRS. ELMER ERNEST HILPERT), civic worker; b. Baton Rouge; d. Edward Oliver and Orvilla (Nettles) Powers; A.B., La. State U., 1930, B.S. in L.S., 1933; postgrad. Columbia, 1937; m. Elmer Ernest Hilpert, Aug. 1, 1938; children—Margaret Ray, Elmer Ernest II (dec.). Cataloguer, La. State U. Library, Baton Rouge, 1930-36, La. State U. Law Sch. Library, 1936-38; librarian Washington U. Law Sch. Library, St. Louis, 1940-42; reference librarian Washington U. Library, 1952-54; mem. women's adv. bd. Continental Bank & Trust Co., 1970-80. Drive capt. United Fund, St. Louis, 1956; del. White House Conf. on Edn., St. Louis, 1962, White House Conf. on Domestic and Econ. Affairs, 1975. Trustee John Burroughs Sch., 1959-63; bd. dirs. Grace Hill Settlement House, 1957-63, v.p., 1960-62; bd. dirs. Internat. Inst., 1964-68; exec. com., bd. dirs. Arts and Edn. Council, 1967—; bd. dirs. Miss. River Festival, 1969-75, Community Music Sch., 1972-74, Community Assn. Schs. for Arts, 1974-77, Artist Presentation Soc., 1974-77, Little Symphony Concerts Assn., 1975-78; exec. com., bd. dirs. Dance Concert Soc., 1977-80, St. Louis Conservatory and Schs. for Arts, 1977—; bd. dirs. St. Louis String Quartet, 1971-77, pres., 1975-79; bd. dirs. Neighborhood Health Center, 1964-67, sec., 1964-66; pres. Womens Assn. St. Louis Symphony Soc., 1969-71, dir., 1957—; exec. com., bd. dirs. St. Louis Symphony Soc., 1969—, St. Louis Inst. Music, 1971-74; exec. com. CASA Aux., also v.p., bd. dirs., 1978—; bd. dirs. Dance Concert Soc. Troup, 1979-80; bd. dirs. women's bd. Bethesda Gen. Hosp. Recipient Woman of Achievement award St. Louis Globe Democrat, 1967. Mem. Nat. Soc. Arts and Letters (dir. 1964-65), Delta Zeta. Republican. Presbyn. Clubs: Wednesday (rec. sec. 1963-64), University. Home: 630 Francis Pl Saint Louis MO 63105

HILTON, STANLEY WILLIAM, JR., theatrical manager, director; b. Phila., Mar. 24; s. Stanley William and Jennie (Parsons) H.; B.A., Fisk U., 1959; postgrad. Temple U.; m. Inge Himmersbach, Dec. 1962; 1 child, Richard H. Office mgr., resource cons., social worker Cook County Dept. Pub. Aid, Chgo., 1961-70; coordinator, ednl. and vocat. counselor Community Coll. Dist., San Francisco, 1971-74; co. mgr. prodn. Hair, Chgo., 1968, San Francisco, 1969; mgr. Orpheum Theatre, San Francisco, 1970; co. mgr. prodns. No Place To Be Somebody, 1971, My Fair Lady, 1973, San Francisco, Jesus Christ Superstar, 1973, Winner Take All, Los Angeles, 1976, Eleanor, Chgo., 1976; gen. mgr. Street Dreams, Chgo., 1982; dir. park and theatre ops. Art Park, Lewiston, N.Y., 1974; exec. dir. Blackstone Theatre, Chgo., 1974—; bd. dirs. The Ctrs. for New Horizons, Chgo., 1976-79, The Acad., Art, Music, Dance, Theatre, Chgo., 1980-84. Mem. Assn. Theatrical Press Agts. and Mgrs. Home: 1540 N State Pkwy Chicago IL 60610 Office: 60 E Balbo St Chicago IL 60605

HIMMELSBACH, LORETTA ANN, organization executive; b. LaCrosse, Wis., Apr. 5, 1954; d. W.A. and Rosemary (Cuff) H. Student, U. Vienna, Austria, 1974-75; B.A., Bradley U., 1975; postgrad. U. Wis.-Milw., 1980-81. Field dir. Singing Sands council Girl Scouts U.S.A., South Bend, Ind., 1976-78, tng. and program dir., Great Blue Heron Girl Scouts, Waukesha, Wis., 1978-81; dir. field services Bluebonnet council Girl Scouts U.S.A., Waco, Tex., 1981-83, exec. dir. Land of Lincoln Girl Scout council, Springfield, Ill., 1983—; internat. program liaison Central Coll., Pella, Iowa, 1985—. Editor vol. manuals, 1979-80. Mem. Women-In-Mgmt., Assn. Girl Scout Exec. Staff, Am. Soc. Tng. and Devel. Roman Catholic. Avocations: travel; skiing; sewing; photography. Office: Land of Lincoln Girl Scout Council 730 E Vine St Springfield IL 62703

HINCKLEY, CHARLES CLARENCE, See *Who's Who in America,* 43rd edition.

HINDEN, RICHARD ADAM, lawyer; b. N.Y.C., Oct. 7, 1954; s. Joshua and Florence (Bagary) H.; m. Barbara Anne Katz, Dec. 23, 1978; children—Scott, Kathryn. B.A., SUNY-Binghamton, 1975; J.D., George Washington U., 1978. Bar: D.C. 1978, Ill. 1980, U.S. Dist. Ct. D.C. 1979, U.S. Ct. Appeals (D.C. cir.) 1979. Assoc. Santarelli & Gimer, Washington, 1978-80; staff counsel Michael Reese Hosp., Chgo., 1980-84; assoc. Siegan, Barbakoff, Gomberg, Gordon & Elden, Chgo., 1984-85, Altheimer & Gray Chgo., 1985; spl. counsel Lieberman Geriatric Ctr., Skokie, Ill., 1983—. Bd. dirs. Young Men's Jewish Council, Chgo., 1982—. Mem. ABA, Am. Soc. Hosp. Attys., Nat. Health Lawyers Assn., Chgo. Bar Assn., D.C. Bar. Office: Altheimer & Gray 333 W Wacker Dr Chicago IL 60606

HINDO, WALID AFRAM, radiology educator, oncologist; b. Baghdad, Iraq, Oct. 4, 1940; s. Afram Paul and Laila Farid (Meshaka) H.; came to U.S., 1966, naturalized, 1976; m. Fawzia Hanna Batti, Apr. 20, 1965; children—Happy, Rana, Patricia, Heather, Brian. M.B., Ch.B., Baghdad U. Coll. Medicine, 1964. Diplomate Am. Bd. Radiology. Instr. radiology Rush Med. Coll., Chgo., 1971-72; asst. prof. Northwestern U., Chgo., 1972-75; assoc. prof. medicine and radiology Chgo. Med. Sch., 1975-80, prof., chmn. dept. radiology, 1980—; cons. to Ill. Cancer Council; bd. dirs. Lake County div. Am. Cancer Soc., 1975-80. Served to lt., M.C., Iraq Army, 1965-66. Named Prof. of Yr., Chgo. Med. Sch., 1981, 82, 83. Mem. Am. Coll. Radiology, Am. Soc. Acad. Radiologists, Am. Soc. Therapeutic Radiologists. Republican. Roman Catholic. Contbr. articles on cancer treatment to profl. jours. Office: Dept Radiology Chicago Medical School 3333 Greenbay Rd North Chicago IL 60064

HINE, HENRY BOARDMAN, lawyer; b. Glen Ridge, N.J., July 10, 1951; s. Edward Kirtland Hine and Betty (Hulburd) Hine Alderson; m. Cynthia Bradley, July 7, 1979; children—Anna, Charles. B.S. in Bus., U. Colo., 1978, B.S. in Pharmacy, 1978; M.B.A., St. Louis U., 1983, J.D., 1983. Bar: Mo. 1983, U.S. Dist. Ct. (ea. and we. dists.) Mo. 1983. Founder, owner, operator Beaver Creek Lumber, Boulder, Colo., 1973; founder, owner, operator Jane Murry Prodns., Inc., Boulder, 1976, also dir.; intern in pharmacy Drug Fair, Inc., Denver, 1978-79; law clk. Harry J. Sterling, P.C., Fairview Heights, Ill., 1982; sole practice, Clayton, Mo., 1983-84; ptnr. Roberts, Clayton and Hine, Clayton, 1984—. Editor, contbg. author: Pharmacy Law Bibliography, 1982. Founder Parent Network, Clayton, 1983, Glen Ridge Parents Against Drug Abuse, Clayton, 1983; town coordinator The Chem. People, Clayton, 1983; chmn. Mo. Fedn. Parents for Drug Free Youth, Jefferson City, Mo., 1984—; bd. dirs., 1983-84; bd. dirs. St. Elizabeth Adult Day Care Ctr. St. Louis, 1984—. Recipient James Hartly Beal award Am. Soc. Pharmacy Law, 1982. Mem. ABA, Mo. Bar Assn., Nat. Health Lawyers Assn., Am. Pharmacists Assn. (Nat. Achievement award 1977), Mo. Pharmacists Assn., St. Louis Pharmacists Assn. (bd. dirs.), Republican. Episcopalian. Office: 201 S Central Ave Suite 200 Clayton MO 63105

HINER, MARJORIE LOU, trucking company executive; b. Crawfordsville, Ind., June 5, 1944; d. Isaac Edwin and Dortha Eileen (Odell) Hoss; B.S., Ball State U., 1966, M.A., 1970; m. Homer F. Hiner, July 14, 1972; children—Richard, David, Marcy. Tchr., Maconaquah High Sch., Bunker Hill, Ind., 1966-67; substitute tchr. various schs., 1970-73; with Hiner Transport, Inc., Huntington, Ind., 1973—, owner, sec.-treas. bd. dirs., 1973—; bookkeeper, dir. Hiner Mgmt. Services, Inc. Bd. dirs. Huntington County United Way, Huntington Meml. Hosp. Found., mem. adv. bd. Salvation Army. Mem. Nat. Assn. Female Execs., Am. Bus. Women's Assn. Mem. Ind. Motor Truck Assn., Huntington C. of C., South Side Bus. Assn., Ball State U. Alumni Assn., Psi Iota Xi, Alpha Phi. Republican. Home: 1979N-600W Andrews IN 46702 Office: PO Box 621 Huntington IN 46750

HINES, CURTIS LEE, educational administrator; b. Decatur, Ill., Apr. 3, 1945; s. Sylvester and Nobie (Hempstead) H.; m. Lexanna Marie Johnson, Aug. 18, 1968 (div. 1974); m. Elinor Diane Ellis, July 25, 1978; children—Rayna Lynn, Shayla Ann. B.S. in Edn., N.E. Mo. State U., 1969, M.S. in Edn. Counseling, 1970. Cert. ednl. counselor, sch. adminstr., Ill. Tchr. driver edn. Eastridge High Sch., Kankakee, Ill., 1969-70, counselor, 1970-74, head wrestling coach, 1969-74; counselor Dept. Pub. Aid, Kankakee, 1972; part-time instr. psychology, sociology, polit. sci., health Kankakee Community Coll., 1972-74; dean of students Evanston (Ill.) Twp. High Sch., 1974-80, dean bldg. services, 1980—; div. mgr. A. L. Williams & Assocs., Atlanta, Ga., 1981—. Founder, past pres., mem. exec. bd. Concerned Blacks for Sch. and Community Improvement, Evanston; life mem. NAACP, mem. exec. bd. North Shore br., 1977-81, chmn. edn. com., 1977-79; mem. Chgo. chpt. People United to Save Humanity, 1980—. Mem. Ill. Edn. Assn., NEA, Am. Personnel and Guidance Assn., Ill. Personnel and Guidance Assn., Nat. Alliance Black Sch. Educators (local sch. commn. task force), Phi Delta Kappa, Kappa Delta Pi., Omega Psi Phi. Baptist. Home: 3437 Stonegate Rd Waukegan IL 60087 Office: Evanston Twp High Sch 1600 Dodge St Evanston IL 60201 also A L Williams Co 750 Arthur St Elk Grove Village IL 60007

HINES, THOMAS ALLEN, financial manager, consultant; b. Hammond, Ind., Sept. 17, 1948; s. Robert Orin and Elizabeth Anne (Mazur) H.; m. Donna Jean Excell, June 1969 (div. Oct. 1975); 1 dau., Kristen Irene; m. 2d, Rhonda Jill Stephens, Feb. 25, 1976; children—Partick Allen, Justin Peter. Student, Ind. U., Gary, 1972-75; B.S. in Bus., Oakwood Mgmt. Tng. Program, 1982. Staff auditor, Homer J. Russel & Co., Dolton, Ill., 1971-72; controller Lakeshore Foods Corp., Michigan City, Ind., 1972-78; controller Assn. for the Disabled of Elkhart County, Elkhart, Ind., 1978-83; pres. Thomas A. Hines Fin. Mgmt., Inc., Elkhart, 1978—; exec. v.p. Streamline Mgmt. Assocs., 1983—; ptnr. H & H Investments, Elkhart, 1981—, Just Imports, Warsaw, Ind., 1983—; dir. Lee H. Barth, Inc., No. Ind. Energy Mgmt., Inc., 1976—. Vol., Michiana Shore Fire Dept., 1976-79; pres. Porter Assn. of Concerned Citizens, 1979-83; regional v.p. Mich. Lakes & Streams Assn., 1980—. Served with USN, 1968-72. Mem. Nat. Assn. of Home Builders, Elkhart Assn. of Home Builders, Delta Sigma Pi. Republican. Episcopalian. Office: 363 S Elkhart Ave Elkhart IN 46515

HINK, JANICE JULE, elementary educator, counselor; b. Detroit, July 27, 1947; d. Metro Terry and Mary Ann (Kuhary) LaPay; m. Walter Thomas Hink, III, Mar. 1, 1975 (div.). Ed.B., Wayne State U., 1969, Ed.M., 1972, Ed.D., 1983. Tchr., Van Buren (Mich.) pub. schs., Detroit pub. schs.; supr. student tchrs. U. Mich.; dist. chmn. curriculum com.; writing cons. various schs. Mem. adv. bd. Wayne County Community Coll. Recipient Spl. Recognition award Project S.C.O.R.E., 1981. Mem. Am. Research Assn., Van Buren Edn. Assn., Mich. Edn. Assn., NEA, Wayne State U. Alumni Assn. Roman Catholic. Home: 45460 Lilac Ln Belleville MI 48111 Office: 13770 Haggerty Rd Belleville MI 48111

HINKLE, BENNY STEWART, food company executive; b. Blackstar, Ky., May 5, 1942; s. Everett Discel and Mabel Bell (Young) H.; m. Marlene Mary Reichert, July 12, 1966; 1 dau., Dawn Michelle. A.S., Sinclair Coll., 1967; Comml. Pilot, Burnside Ott Aviation Sch., Ft. Lauderdale, 1967. With Dayton Tire & Rubber (Ohio), 1964-67; pilot Burnside-Ott, Ft. Lauderdale, 1967-69; pilot, ins. sales CUNA Mut. Ins., Madison, Wis., 1969-81; pres. L. J. Products Co., Dayton, Ohio, 1981—; cons. L. J. Products, Dayton, 1981—. Served with USAF, 1960-64. Church of God. Home: 1378 Wilhelmina Dr Vandalia OH 45377 Office: L J Products Co 921 Bridge St Dayton OH 45407

HINKLE, ROBERT DOUGLAS, naturalist, educator; b. Hillsdale, Mich., June 23, 1946; s. Kennedy J. and Marcele Erma (Summers) H. B.S., Mich. State U., 1969, M.S., 1971, Ph.D., 1976. Staff naturalist Woldumar Nature Ctr., Lansing, Mich., 1969-75; instr. environ. studies Mich. State U., East Lansing, 1974-76, asst. prof., 1976-78; asst. prof. Johnson (Vt.) State Coll., 1978-82, chmn. dept. environ. studies, 1980-82; chief naturalist Cleve. Metroparks, 1982—; cons. East Lansing Pub. Schs., 1973, Johnson Pub. Schs., 1981-82. Author, editor lab. manual Supplementary Materials for Environmental Education, 1975; author monthly column on environment, 1982—. Recipient Excellence in Undergrad. Teaching award Mich. State U., 1975. Mem. Assn. Interpretive Naturalists (dep. dir. region 8), Mich. Environ. Edn. Assn. (bd. dirs. 1976-82), The Wildlife Soc., AAAS, Am. Soc. Mammalogists, Beta Beta Beta, Alpha Zeta. Home: 9756 Eastland Rd Strongsville OH 44136 Office: Cleveland Metroparks 4101 Fulton Pkwy Cleveland OH 44144

HINMAN, MYRA MAHLOW, English literature educator; b. Saginaw County, Mich., Jan. 11, 1926; d. Henry and Cynthia (Mims) Mahlow; B.S., Columbia U., 1946; M.A., U. Fla., 1954, Ph.D., 1959; m. George E. Olstead, 1948 (div. 1967); 1 son, Christopher Eric; m. 2d, Charlton Hinman, 1968 (dec. 1977); 1 stepdau., Barbara. Asst. prof. Memphis State U., 1959-61; instr. English lit. U. Kans., Lawrence, 1961-63, asst. prof., 1963-68, asso. prof., 1968—. Travel grantee Am. Council Learned Socs., 1966. Mem. MLA, Internat. Arthurian Soc., Shakespeare Assn. Am., U. Va. Bibliog. Soc., S. Atlantic Modern Lang. Assn., United Burmese Cat Fanciers, Am. Shorthair Cat Assn., Phi Kappa Phi. Asst. editor: Hinman Text, Complete Works of Shakespeare. Contbr. articles to profl. jours. Home: 1932 Maine St Lawrence KS 66046 Office: Wescoe Hall Univ Kans Lawrence KS 66044

HINNRICHS-DAHMS, HOLLY BETH, educator; b. Milw., Oct. 31, 1945; d. Helmut Ferdinand and Rae W. (Beebe) H.; m. Raymond H. Dahms, June 11, 1983 (dec. Oct. 2, 1983). Student U. Wis.-Milw., 1963-64, 66, 79—, Chapman Coll., 1965, 67, Internat. Coll. Copenhagen, summer 1968, Temple U., summer 1970, B.A., Alverno Coll., 1971; postgrad. Marylhurst Coll., 1972, Chapman Coll. World Campus Afloat, summers 1973, 74, Inst. Shipboard Edn., 1978, 79. Vice pres. Hinnrichs Inc., Germantown, Wis., 1964-72; tchr. Germantown Recreation Dept., 1965; coach Milw. Recreation Dept., 1966-67; rep. for Wis., Chapman Coll., Orange, Calif., 1967; clk. Stein Drug Co., Menomonee Falls, Wis., 1967-72; tchr. Milw. area Catholic Schs., 1967-72, 83—; asst. mgr. Original Cookie Co. (Mother Hubbard's) Cookie Store, Northridge Mall, Milw., 1977-84, deli dept. Sav-U-Warehouse, 1984—; substitute tchr. pub. schs. Milw. area, 1975-80; tchr. Indian Community Sch., Milw., 1971-72, Martin Luther King Sch., 1973-74, Crossroads Acad., Milw., 1974-75, Harambee Community Sch., 1980-83; Midwest rep. World Explorer Cruises, 1978—. Mem. Internat. Inst. Milw. Friends of Museum, Alpha Theta Epsilon. Christian Scientist. Traveled 63 countries; contbr. articles on travel to various publs. Home: W140 N9766 Hwy 145 Germantown WI 53022

HINTON, DAVID BRUCE, investment broker; b. Marshalltown, Iowa, Apr. 21, 1950; s. Cecil Marion and Dorothy Elizabeth (Kanzok) H.; m. Mary Claire Pleiss, Aug. 21, 1971; 1 dau., Alexandra Friederike. Student, Heidelberg, W.Ger., 1970-71; B.A., Drake U., 1972; M.A., U. Iowa, 1974. Registered rep. R.G. Dickinson & Co., Des Moines, 1976-77; asst. v.p. Piper Jaffray & Hopwood, Des Moines, 1977-83; v.p. mktg. R.G. Dickinson & Co., Des Moines, 1983—; lectr. univs. in Germany, 1974-76. Mem. Iowa Devel. Commn., 1982—; chmn. Des Moines Com. Fgn. Relations, 1978—; exec. com. Des Moines Bur. Econ. Devel., 1982—. Mem. Iowa Investment Bankers Assn., Securities Industry Assn. (govt. relations com.), Soc. for Iowa's Future (founding chair), World Future Soc. Republican. Unitarian. Club: Des Moines. Author: The Films of Leni Riefenstahl, 1978; A Place to Grow: Revitalizing Iowa's Economy, 1983. Home: 1617 Buffalo Rd West Des Moines IA 50265 Office: 200 Des Moines Bldg Des Moines IA 50308

HIPPS, DONNA MARIE (MRS. ROBERT O. HIPPS), media director; b. Waterloo, Iowa, May 18, 1925; d. George Fred and Mamie Jean (Livingston) Westlic; B.S., Iowa State U., 1946; M.A., U. Minn., 1963; m. Robert O. Hipps, Aug. 9, 1946; children—Alan, Margaret Hipps Peters, James. Tchr. pub. schs., Iowa, 1946-48; teaching asst. Univ. High Sch., U. Minn., Mpls., 1960-63; librarian Lincoln High Sch., Bloomington, Minn., 1963-70; library specialist Jefferson High Sch., Bloomington, 1970-74, dir. resource center, 1974-75, media dir., 1975—. Mem. Am. Fedn. Tchrs., NEA, LWV (state treas. 1958-59, dir. Edina 1955-58), Am. Field Service, AAUW, Sigma Kappa, Beta Phi Mu. Methodist. Home: 6604 Dakota Trail Edina MN 55435 Office: 4001 W 102d St Bloomington MN 55431

HIRN, DORIS DREYER, health services administrator; b. N.Y.C., Dec. 3, 1933; d. James M. and Dorothy Van Nostrand (Young) Dreyer; student Colby Jr. Coll., 1951-52, Hofstra U., 1953-56, Northwestern U., 1972-74; m. John D. Hirn, Oct. 27, 1956; children—Deborah Lynn, Robert William. Asst. to adminstr. Albany (N.Y.) Med. Coll., 1962-64; propr., dir. Hickory Hill Camp, Galena, Ill., 1965-72; v.p. Home Health Service of Chgo. North Inc., 1972-74; pres., adminstr. Suburban Home Health Service, Inc., Des Plaines, Ill., 1974—; pres. Hickory Hill Mgmt. Corp., 1977—; dir. Serengeti Prodns., 1979—. Bd. dirs. Nat. Health Delivery Systems, 1973—, Fox Valley council Girl Scouts U.S., 1965-70. Served with USN, 1951-53. Mem. Am. Fedn. Home Health Agys., Chgo. Home Care Assn. Ill. Council Home Health Agys. (bd. dirs.), Internat. Film Producers Assn., Am. Camping Assn. (dir. Chgo. chpt. 1968-70) Nat. Assn. Home Care. Republican. Club: Chicago Yacht. Home: 1 E Schiller Chicago IL 60610 Office: 2250 E Devon Ave Des Plaines IL 60018

HIRSCH, NORMA JEAN, neonatologist; b. Charles City, Iowa, Aug. 2, 1944; d. Milton Charles and Dorothy Leona (Lacour) H. B.S., Iowa State U., 1966; M.D., U. Iowa, 1970. Diplomate Am. Bd. Pediatrics. Intern pediatrics Children Med. Ctr., Dallas, 1970-71, resident, 1971-73; fellow in pediatrics Ind. U., Indpls., 1973-74; asst. prof. pediatrics U. Tex., Dallas, 1974-75; fellow Baylor Coll. Medicine, Houston, 1975-77; neonatologist, clin. asst. prof. Baylor U. Med. Ctr., 1977-79, Newborn Care Cons., P.C., U. Iowa, Des Moines, 1979—; med. dir. Variety Club Newborn Intensive Care Nursery, 1981—. Bd. dirs. Sherman Hill Assn., 1983—. Fellow Am. Acad. Pediatrics; mem. AMA, Am. Med. Womens Assn., Iowa Med. Soc., Polk County Med. Soc.

Republican. Lutheran. Club: Embassy. Office: Newborn Care Cons PC PO Box 4566 Des Moines IA 50306

HIRSCHEL, LIESELOTTE ANNE, dentist, writer; b. Breslau, Germany, Apr. 17, 1926; came to U.S. 1949, naturalized 1952; d. Richard F. and Alice (Isaac) E.; m. John U. Hirschel, Dec. 16, 1948; children—Anthony G., Alison E. L.D.S., Royal Coll. Surgeons, Eng., 1948; B.D.S., U. London, 1949; D.D.S., U. Mich., 1952. Dental officer Middlesex County Council, Eng., 1948-49; dentist City Detroit Health Dept., 1952-53; gen. practice dentistry, Detroit, 1953-66, Southfield, Mich., 1966—. Contbg. editor Medical Abstracts Newsletter, 1984—; contbr. articles to mags. Florence Huson scholar U. Mich., 1951-52. Fellow Royal Soc. Health; mem. ADA, Mich. Dental Assn., Oakland County Dental Soc., Am. Med. Writers Assn. Avocations: Book collecting, travel, antiques. Home: 20120 Ledgestone Dr Southfield MI 48076

HIRSCHMAN, MARTIN ABRAHAM, lawyer; b. Bklyn. Dec. 22, 1949; s. Ira Mark and Marion S. (Ginsberg) H.; m. Marcia Carol Abramson, May 16, 1971; children—Samuel, Jennifer, Daniel. B.A., U. Mich., 1972; J.D., Wayne State U., 1979. Bars: Mich. 1979, U.S. Dist. Ct. (ea. dist.) Mich. 1979, U.S. Ct. Appeals (6th cir.) 1984. Investigator-writer Ralph Nader Congress Project, Washington, 1972; reporter, editor AP, Detroit, 1972-76; assoc. Hurwitz & Karp, P.C., Dearborn Heights, Mich., 1979-84, ptnr. Hurtwitz, Karp, Hirschman & Wallack, 1984—; mem. civil liberties com. State Bar Mich., 1981—, vol. investigator, 1984—. Am. Jurisprudence award Bancroft Whitney Co. and Lawyer's Co-op Pub. Co., 1979. Mem. Assn. Trial Lawyers Am., Mich. Trial Lawyers Assn. Club: Am. Contract Bridge League. Home: 21729 Virginia St Southfield MI 48076 Office: Hurwitz Karp Hirschman & Wallach 8283 N Telegraph St Dearborn Heights MI 48127

HIRSCHMAN, SHERMAN JOSEPH, lawyer, accountant, educator; b. Detroit, May 11, 1935; s. Samuel and Anna (Maxmen) H.; m. Audrey Hecker, 1959; children—Samuel, Shari. B.S., Wayne State U., 1956, J.D., 1959, LL.M., 1968. Bar: Mich. 1959, Fla. 1983, Wis. 1984; C.P.A., Mich., Fla.; cert. tax lawyer, Fla. Practice, Mich., 1959—; instr. comml. law Detroit Coll. Bus., 1971—. Served with U.S. Army Res., 1959-62. Mem. Mich. Bar Assn., Fla. Bar Assn., Wis. Bar Assn. Home: 6127 Ledgeway Dr West Bloomfield MI 48033 Office: 29870 Middlebelt St Farmington Hills MI 48018

HIRST, LAWRENCE WILLIAM, ophthalmologist; b. Brisbane, Australia; Dec. 3, 1945; came to U.S., 1976; s. Paul and Fritzi Hirst; m. Christina Elizabeth McIvor, Dec. 5, 1969; children—Julian, Angela, Caroline, Tanya. MBBS with honors, U. Queensland, 1969, M.D., 1983; D.O., U. Melbourne, Australia, 1974; M.P.H., Johns Hopkins U., 1981. Diplomate Am. Bd. Ophthalmology. Intern Princess Alexandra Hosp., Brisbane; resident Royal Victorian Eye and Ear Hosp., Melbourne; instr. ophthalmology Johns Hopkins Hosp., Balt., 1978, asst. dir. Wilmer Inst., 1978, asst. dir. cornea service, 1978-79; dir. Bethesda Eye Inst., St. Louis U., 1984, chmn. dept. ophthalmology, 1984—. Author: Sights and Sounds Ocular and Periocular Trauma, 1984; Sights and Sounds Ocular and Periocular Infection, 1984. Mem. med. adv. bd. ARC. Mem. St. Louis Ophthal. Soc., Mo. Ophthal. Soc., AMA, Am. Acad. Ophthalmology and Otolaryngology. Home: 6344 Wydown Blvd Saint Louis MO 63105 Office: Bethesda Eye Inst St Louis U 3655 Vista Ave Saint Louis MO 63110

HITCHBORN, CHARLES D., automobile company executive; b. Kansas City, Mo., Oct. 8, 1930; s. Wilbur A. and Lois R. (Farrington) H.; m. Joan M. Hunter, July 29, 1952; children—Sherri D. Scadlock, Scott A. Student, U. Minn., 1966, U. Wis.-Madison, 1967. Sgt., Police Dept., City of Henderson, Las Vegas, Nev., 1957-59; security supr. Gen. Motors Corp., Kansas City, Mo., 1959-66; supr. Ford Motor Co., Kansas City, 1966-81, employee involvement coordinator, 1981—; lectr. in field. Served to sgt. USMC, 1948, 57. Decorated Bronze Star, Purple Heart (3). Mem. Chosin Few, Purple Heart Soc., 1st Marine Div. Assn., Internat. Quality Circles, Mich. Quality Worklife Council. Republican. Club: Chiefs (Kansas City). Lodges: Masons, Shriners. Avocations: Snowmobiling, hunting, fishing, needlepoint, photography. Home: 4229 N Hardesty Kansas City MO 64117 Office: Ford Motor Co Kansas City Assembly Plant PO Box 11009 Kansas City MO 64119

HJELMFELT, ALLEN TALBERT, JR., civil engineer; b. Holdrege, Nebr., Oct. 21, 1937; s. Allen Talbert and Doris Bertha (Hauber) H.; m. Barbara Joan Herron, June 10, 1962 (div. Jan. 1979); m. Marian Park, Aug. 6, 1980; children—Allen Talbert III, Eric, Allison, Joel. B.S. in Civil Engring., Kans. State U., 1959; M.S. in Engring. Mechanics, U. Kans., 1961; Ph.D. in Civil Engring., Northwestern U., 1965. Registered profl. engr., Mo. Devel. engr. Union Carbide Co., Oak Ridge, 1962-63; research engr. Northwestern U., Evanston, Ill., 1963-65; prof. civil engring. U. Mo., Columbia, 1965-78; research hydraulic engr. U.S. Dept. Agr., Agrl. Research Service, Columbia, 1978—; cons. Mineracao Vera Cruz, Belem, Para, Brazil, 1976. Author: Hydrology for Engineers and Planners, 1975. Contbr. articles to profl. jours. Mem. ASCE (J.C. Stevens award 1983), Am. Geophys. Union, Internat. Assn. Hydraulic Research, AAAS, Am. Water Resources Assn., Chi Epsilon. Home: 1004 Maplewood St Columbia MO 65203 Office: US Dept Agr Agrl Research Service 207 Bus Loop 70E Columbia MO 65203

HO, CHO-YEN, physical science researcher, scientific research administrator; b. Guiping, Guangxi, China, Aug. 11, 1928; s. Yu-Chih and Tsui-Chen (Huang) H.; M.S. in Mech. Engring., U. Ky., 1960; Ph.D., Purdue U., 1964; m. Nancy Yang Wang, June 1, 1963; children—Chris Meichung W., Chester Meihua W. Asst. sr. researcher Thermophys. Properties Research Center, Purdue U., West Lafayette, Ind., 1964-69, head reference data div., 1967—, assoc. sr. researcher, 1969-74, asst. dir. research Center for Info. and Numerical Data Analysis and Synthesis, 1973-82, sr. researcher, 1974—, interim dir., 1981-82, dir., 1982—; dir. Thermophys. and Electronic Properties Info. Analysis Ctr., U.S. Dept. Def., 1982—; indexer Applied Mechanics Revs., 1967-72; bd. govs., treas. Internat. Thermal Conductivity Confs., 1973—, co-chmn., 1968; instr. NSF short course Pa. State U., 1973; lectr. seminar and workshop Engring. Joint Council, U. Ill., 1975. Recipient Thermal Conductivity Achievement award Internat. Thermal Conductivity Confs., 1981. Mem. Am. Phys. Soc., ASME (mem. standing com. on thermophys. properties, reviewer Jour. Heat Transfer 1968—), AAAS, Am. Soc. Metals, ASTM, Tech. Transfer Soc., IEEE, Internat. Platform Assn., Sigma Xi, Pi Tau Sigma. Author, co-author 7 reference books, numerous articles on thermophysics, thermophys., elec. properties of materials, solar energy and thermoelectric power generation and conversion; tech. series editor Thermophys. Properties of Matter, 1969—; co-editor 22 reference books; co-editor McGraw-Hill/CINDAS Data Series on Material Properties, 1981—; editorial bd. Internat. Jour. Thermophysics, 1983—. Office: Center for Info and Numerical Data Analysis and Synthesis Purdue Univ 2595 Yeager Rd W Lafayette IN 47906

HO, JAMES CHIEN-MING, science educator; b. Kiengsu, China, July 31, 1937; came to U.S., 1961, naturalized, 1972; s. Jungsiao and Jing Po (Huang) H.; m. Lydia S. Hsu, Aug. 8, 1964; children—Claudia, Marilyn. B.S. in Chem. Engring., Nat. Taiwan U., Taipei, 1959; M.S. in Chemistry, Univ. Calif.-Berkeley, 1963, Ph.D. in Chemistry, 1966. Research fellow Lawrence Radiation Lab., Berkeley, Calif., 1966-67; sr. scientist Battelle Meml. Inst., Columbus, Ohio, 1967-71; assoc. prof. physics Wichita State U., Kans., 1971-76, prof., 1976—, joint prof. physics and chemistry, 1985—; sr. resident research assoc. Nat. Research Council, Dayton, Ohio, 1972, 1973, 1975; vis. prof. Chemistry Univ. Calif.-Berkeley, 1977-78. Contbr. articles to profl. jours. Pres. Wichita Asian Assn., 1981-82; chmn. bd. dirs. Wichita Indo-chinese Center, 1983-84; mem. Community Task Force, Wichita, 1982—; adv. com. Targeted Assistance, Wichita, 1983—; bd. dirs. South Central Kans. Econ. Devel. Dist., 1985—. Recipient 10 Who Care award KAKE TV, 1984. Mem. Am. Phys. Soc., Am. Chem. Soc., ASTM, AAAS, Sigma Xi. Office: Wichita State U Physics Dept Wichita KS 67208

HO, LYDIA SU-YONG, chemist; b. China, Dec. 16, 1939; came to U.S., 1962; d. Yu-Hwa and Ai-Hsueh (Lin) Hsu; m. James C. Ho, Aug. 8, 1964; children—Claudia, Marilyn. B.S. in Chem. Engring., Nat. Taiwan U., Taipei, 1961; M.S. in Chemistry, U. Calif.-Berkeley, 1964, Ph.D. in Nutritional Scis., 1967. Asst. editor Chem. Abstracts Services, Columbus, Ohio, 1967-70; clin. chemist St. Francis Hosp., Wichita, Kans., 1974-78; research assoc. U. Kans. Sch. Medicine-Wichita, 1980—. Contbr. articles on chemistry and endocrinology to profl. jours. Mem. Am. Chem. Soc., Am. Soc. Med. Tech., Am. Soc. Clin. Pathologists. Office: Dept Internal Medicine U Kans Sch Medicine 1001 N Minneapolis Wichita KS 67214

HO, PATRICK Y., electric company executive; b. Shanghai, China, Apr. 23, 1940; came to U.S., 1963, naturalized, 1974; s. Charles L. and Grace Z. Ho; m. Vicky Yue, Dec. 27, 1969; children—Cheryl J., Stacey J. M.S.E., Purdue U., 1965, Ph.D., 1969. Registered mech. engr., Ariz. Supr. acoustics Airesearch Garrett, Phoenix, 1969-77; mgr. engine systems acoustics Gen. Electric, Cin., 1977—; adj. assoc. prof. U. Cin., 1978. Inventor in field. Mem. ASME, AIAA. Avocation: tennis. Home: 6408 Commanche Dr West Chester OH 45069

HO, ROBERT EN MING, physician; b. Honolulu, Nov. 13, 1942; s. Donald Tet En Ho and Violette (Weeks) Gould; m. Edie Olsen, June 27, 1964; children—Lisa, Amy. B.S. cum laude, Mich. State U., 1964; M.D., Wayne State U., 1968. Diplomate Am. Bd. Neurol. Surgery. Surg. intern Detroit Gen. Hosp., 1968-69, surg. resident, 1969-70, neurosurg. resident, 1972-76; microsurg. fellow Neurochirurgische Universtatskilinik, Zurich, Switzerland, 1976; instr. dept. neurosurgery Wayne State U., Detroit, 1977-79, dir. dept. neurosurgery Gertrude Levin Pain Clinic, 1977-80, asst. prof., 1979-84, chief neurosurg. services Health Care Inst., 1979-84, founder, dir. Microneurosurg. Lab., 1977—; dir. neuroscis. intensive care unit Harper Hosp., Detroit, 1980-84; mem. audit com. Detroit Gen. Hosp., 1977-80, mem. med. device com., 1977-80, mem. credentials com., 1978—; sec., treas. Detroit Neurosurg. Acad. Program Com., 1978-84; mem. emergency room com. Harper Hosp., 1980—, neuroscis. intensive care unit com., 1980-84; dir. Oakland-Macomb PPO. Presenter of numerous exhibits, profl. papers; organizer numerous med. meetings.; lectr. in field. Contbr. articles to profl. jours. Served with U.S. Army, 1970-72, Vietnam. Recipient Intern of Yr. award Detroit Gen. Hosp., 1969. Mem. AMA, ACS, Congress Neurol. Surgeons, Detroit Neurosurg. Acad., Mich. Assn. Neurol. Surgeons (sec.-treas. 1979-82, v.p. 1982-84, pres. 1984—), Mich. State Med. Soc., Oakland County Med. Soc., Wayne County Med. Soc., Internat. Coll. Surgeons (U.S. sect.), Am. Assn. Neurol. Surgeons (spinal disorders sect. 1981, cerebrovascular surgery sect.). Office: 44199 Dequindre Rd Suite 212 Troy MI 48098

HO, TERRY JAUSHONG, physician; researcher; b. Shin-chu, Taiwan, Feb. 16, 1939; came to U.S., 1970, naturalized, 1975; s. Tein-chen and Fong (Chen) H.; m. Gloria Lomero Reyes, May 17, 1973; 5 children. B. Eng., Cheng-Kung U., Tainan, Taiwan, 1962, M.D., 1969. Diplomate Am. Bd. Ob-Gyn. Intern Elizabeth Gen. Hosp., N.J., 1970-71; resident in ob-gyn N.J. Med. Sch., Newark, 1971-75; practice medicine specializing in ob-gyn Greene County Hosp., Linton, Ind., 1975-77, Union Hosp., Regional Hosp., Terre Haute, Ind., 1977—; instr. N.J. Med. Sch., 1974-75; chmn. dept. ob-gyn Greene County Hosp., 1975-77, dept. ob-gyn, Regional Hosp., 1982-83; assoc. faculty Ind. U. Sch. Medicine, Indpls., 1979. Fellow A.C.S., Am. Coll. Obstetricians, Gynecologists; mem. Am. Fertility Soc., Vigo County Med. Soc., AMA. Avocations: oil painting. Home: PO Box 508 Riley IN 47871 Office: 1724 W 7th St Terre Haute IN 47804

HOAG, JAMES DAVID, safety executive; b. Downers Grove, Ill., July 14, 1924; s. Carroll I. and Goldie E. (Curry) H.; student Purdue U., 1946-49; B.S., N.Y. U., 1951; postgrad. La. State U., 1957; m. Angeline F. Freskos, Jan. 19, 1945; children—David, Dean, Kim, Daniel, Carol. Safety engr. Liberty Mut. Ins. Co., Chgo., 1949-50, Armed Forces Spl. Weapons Project, Albuquerque, 1950-52, U.S. Naval Ordnance Plant, Macon, Ga., 1952-56; safety supr. Kaiser Aluminum Corp., Baton Rouge, 1956-58; mgr. occupational safety and health Union Electric Co., St. Louis, 1960—; lectr. Washington U; v.p. Mo. Safety Council, St. Louis Safety Council. Pres. Kirkwood Theatre Guild. Served to 1st lt. USAAF, 1942-45. Decorated Air Medal with 5 oak leaf clusters. Recipient Louis H. Antoine award, 1979; profl. engr., Calif. Fellow Am. Soc. Safety Engrs. (safety profl. of year region IV, 1980, nat. pres. 1982-83); mem. Edison Electric Inst. (chmn. codes and standards exec. adv. com.), ASTM (com.), Profl. Photographers Am. Greek Orthodox. Club: Masons. Home: 1170 Glenway Dr Glendale MO 63122 Office: 1901 Gratiot St Saint Louis MO 63166

HOAGENSON, CONNIE LOU, practical nurse educator; b. Independence, Mo., Dec. 14, 1937; d. Kenneth John and Annabell (Bly) Smith Mosley; m. Evan Walter Seedorf, July 20, 1958 (div. Apr. 1970); m. Richard Eugene Hoagenson, Dec. 28, 1970; 1 son, Lloyd Walter. B.S., Coll. St. Francis, Joliet, Ill., 1982; R.N., Research Hosp., Kansas City, Mo., 1958. Cert. tchr., Mo. Inservice coordinator Jackson County Hosp., Kansas City, 1966-68; inservice instr. St. Joseph Hosp., Kansas City, 1968-70; surg. nurse Independence Sanitarium, 1970-71; instr. surg. technologists Health Occupations, Independence, 1971-81, instr. practical nurses, 1981—, coordinator daily activities, 1981—; author poetry. Mem. nurture com. Lutheran Ch. Mo. Synod, St. Louis, 1982—; tchr. midweek sch. St. Paul's Luth. Ch., Independence, 1981—; mem. Kansas City ARC, 1958—; bd. dirs. Beautiful Savior Home, Belton, Mo., 1980-82. Mem. Mo. State Assn. Health Occupation Educators (pres. elect 1984), Mo. Vocat. Assn. Democrat. Home: 1417 Millburn St Independence MO 64056 Office: Health Occupations 1509 W Truman St Independence MO 64050

HOAGLAND, JAMES LEE, See *Who's Who in America,* 43rd edition.

HOARD, ANN, court clerk; b. Georgiana, Ala., Nov. 7; d. Jimmy and Lena (Singer) Baggett; m. Gus Hoard, Jr., Jan. 12, 1951; children—Howard Dwayne, Stanley Marlon, Anita Elaine. A.A., Sinclair Community Coll., 1983. Health technician Blairwood Sch., Dayton, Ohio, 1963-64; procurement clk.-typist Wright-Patterson AFB, Fairborn, Ohio, 1966-68; dep. clk. Common Pleas Court, Dayton, 1968—. Contbr. articles to profl. jours. Active Women's Assn., Trinity United Presbyterian Ch., Dayton, Democratic Club. Recipient Woman of Influence award Great Lakes Region Internat. Toastmistress Club, Cleve., 1978. Mem. Nat. Assn. Female Execs., Iota Phi Lambda. Club: Jet Aire. Avocations: sewing; writing; traveling.

HOARD, MARTHA LEE, nurse, educator, administrator; b. Williams, Ariz., Feb. 22, 1925; d. Charles Walter and Ernestena (Busse) Rhyan; m. Harold N. Hoard, July 23, 1945 (dec. 1982); children—E. Gerry, Jeffrey S. Diploma in nursing Los Angeles County Med. Ctr. Sch. Nursing, 1947; B.A. in Nursing Edn., Calif. State U.-San Francisco 1951; M.A. in Edn., Stanford U., 1952; postgrad. U. Calif.-Berkeley, 1968-69, Calif. Coast U., 1983—. R.N., Calif., Iowa; life teaching credential. Head nurse Spadra State Hosp. (Calif.), 1947; office nurse, Pomona, Calif., 1947-48; head nurse Outpatient Clinic and Hosp., Pomona, 1948-49; staff nurse Stanford U. Hosp., San Francisco, 1948-51; camp nurse Thousand Pines Camp, Crestline, Calif., summers 1950-52; dir. nursing edn. Sioux Valley Hosp., Sioux Falls, S.D., 1952-54, dir. sch. nursing and nursing services, 1954-60; charge nurse/supr. Immanuel Hosp., Mankato, Minn., 1960; instr., coordinator Mankato U., 1960-62; dir. nurses Flandreau Mcpl. Hosp. (S.D.), 1962-63; instr. Pasadena City Coll., 1963-64; instr. Fresno City Coll., 1964-65, dir. nursing edn., 1965-75, program dir. respiratory therapy, 1968-75, dir. emeritus nursing, 1975—; facilitator continuing edn. for nurses, Iowa Central Community Coll., Ft. Dodge, 1979-81; accreditation visitor Calif. Bd. Nursing, 1970; mem. adv. com. Calif. San Joaquin Valley Health Consortium, 1970-75; mem. Calif. Western Council on Higher Edn. for Nurses, 1965-75. Contbr. articles to profl. jours. Sec., Pocahontas County Bd. Health, Iowa, 1979—; mem. career edn. council, Rolfe Community Sch., council, 1980—; sec. bd. trustees, ch. treas. Presbyn. Ch., Rolfe, Iowa, 1981-84; sec. Pocahontas County Homemaker Home Health Aide Adminstrv. Bd., 1983—; chmn. Rolfe Ambulance Service Bd., 1980-82, numerous others. Mem. Nat. League Nursing, Am. Nurses Assn., Los Angeles County Med. Ctr. Nurses Alumni Assn., P.E.O., AAUW, Sioux Valley Hosp Sch. Nursing Alumni Assn. (hon.), numerous others. Clubs: Zonta, Newcomers, Tuesday, Sorosis (pres. 1978-80), Soroptomist. Address: 505 Locust St Rolfe IA 50581

HOBBS, DEAN GLENN, marine transportation manager, marine master pilot; b. Ann Arbor, Mich., Mar. 11, 1954; s. Charles R. and Zelma D. Spaulding; m. Brenda Jo Goldammer, Apr. 2, 1977; children—Annette Camelia, Cortney Jo. A.A.S., Gt. Lakes Maritime Acad., 1976; student Thornton Community Coll., 1980, Regents Coll. Cadet, U.S. Steel Corp. Gt. Lakes Fleet, 1974, Amoco Oil Co., Gt. Lakes, 1975; 1st class tanker pilot Amoco Oil Co., Gt. Lakes Ops., 1976-79, master tanker pilot, 1979, coordinator marine services, Whiting, Ind., 1980-81, supr. ops. marine, 1981-84, supt. Marine ops., 1985—; instr. Gt. Lakes Maritime Acad., 1979. Bd. visitors Gt. Lakes Maritime Acad., also bd. dirs. Alumni Assn. Mem. Internat. Ship Master's Assn., Soc. Naval Architects and Marine Engrs., Profl. Mariners Assn., U.S. Naval Inst. Club: Propellor (Chgo.). Office: Amoco Transport Co Riley Rd East Chicago IN 46312

HOBBS, JAMES CALVIN, communications exec.; b. Harlingen, Tex., May 1, 1938; s. Edward and Bessie Mae (Jackson) H.; student N.Mex. State U., 1955-57; B.J., U. Mo., 1959, B.A. in Math, 1961, M.A. in Journalism, 1961; m. Marijo Caposell, July 11, 1970; children—Rachel Elizabeth, Jared Charles. Publs. editor Trane Co., La Crosse, Wis., 1962-65; publicist Dow Corning Corp., Midland, Mich., 1965-68; account exec., account supr. Ketchum, McLeod & Grove, Pitts., 1968-72; exec. v.p. Dave Brown & Assos., Inc., Oakbrook, Ill., 1972—. Served with M.P., U.S. Army, 1962. Recipient Golden Quill award Pitts. Communications Assn., 1971. Mem. Soc. Tech. Communicators (chmn. Pitts. 1971-72), Nat. Agrl. Mktg. Assn., Public Relations Soc. Am., Am. Med. Writers Assn., Chgo. Headline Club, Agrl. Relations Council, Am. Agrl. Editors Assn., Profl. Photographers Am., Kappa Tau, Phi Alpha Mu, Sigma Alpha Epsilon, Sigma Delta Chi. Presbyterian. Club: Elks. Contbr. articles to profl. jours. Home: 3026 W 76th St Woodridge IL 60517 Office: 900 Jorie St Suite 70 Oakbrook IL 60521

HOBEN, WILLIAM JOSEPH, university dean; b. Hardinsburg, Ky., May 19, 1927; s. William Joseph and Maud H. (Smith) H. B.S., U. Dayton, 1950; M.B.A., Xavier U., 1960. C.P.A., Ohio. Sr. acct. David E. Flagel & Co., Dayton, Ohio, 1952-57; asst. prof. U. Dayton, 1957-59, assoc. prof., asst. dean, 1959-62, acting dean, 1962-63, dean Sch. Bus. Adminstrn., 1963—; dir. Catholic Telegraph Register, MAP, Inc., Tech., Inc. Pres. and chmn. bd. Teach Fund, Inc., 1960; bd. dirs. S.W. Ohio chpt. NCCJ, 1965—; trustee Sinclair Community Coll., 1974-80. Served with USNR, World War II, Korean. Mem. Nat. Assn. Accts., Nat. Bus. Tchrs. Assn., Ohio Bus. Tchrs. Assn., Inst. Internat. Auditors, Am. Mgmt. Assn., Dayton C. of C., Lima C. of C., Columbus C. of C., Ohio Inst. C.P.A.s (dir., com. chmn. Dayton 1960), Alpha Kappa Psi. Roman Catholic. Clubs: Bicycle, Racquet, Rotary (Dayton). Office: U Dayton 300 College Park Dayton OH 45469

HOCHBERG, KENNETH J., mathematics educator; b. N.Y.C., July 26, 1950; s. Jona F. and Berta (Rapp) H.; m. Shifra Stollman, Dec. 19, 1971; children—Yael Vered, Sarit Dina, Yonit, Alyssa. B.A. summa cum laude, Yeshiva U., 1971; M.S. in Math., N.Y.U., 1973, Ph.D. in Math., 1976. Lectr. NYU, 1974-75; instr., asst. prof. Brooklyn Coll., 1974-76; asst. prof. Carleton U., Ottawa, Ont., Can., 1976-78, Northwestern U., Evanston, Ill., 1978; asst. prof. Case Western Res. U., Cleve., 1978-82, assoc. prof. math., 1982—; reviewer NSF, Washington, 1978—. Contbr. articles to profl. jours. Trustee Hillel Northeast Ohio, Cleve., 1981—. Research grantee NSF, 1978-81, NIH, 1980-83, NSF, 1984-87. Mem. Am. Math. Soc., Inst. Math. Stats. Avocations: gardening, swimming, chess, reading. Office: Case Western Reserve U Dept Math & Stats Cleveland OH 44106

HOCHSTEDLER, ELLEN, criminal justice educator, researcher; b. Angola, Ind., Oct. 20, 1952; s. Richard McLouth and Winona (Fields) H. A.B., Ind. U., 1973; M.A. in Criminal Justice, SUNY-Albany, 1976, Ph.D. in Criminal Justice, 1980. Asst. prof. criminal justice U. Wis.-Milw., 1979-84, assoc. prof., 1984—, dir. Ctr. for Advanced Studies in Human Services, 1984—; cons. Police Found., Washington, 1981-82; manuscript reviewer Holt, Rinehart & Winston, N.Y.C., 1984. Editor: Corporations as Criminals, 1984. Contbr. articles and chpts. to profl. publs. Mem. Task Force on Human Services and Law, Milw., 1983—; bd. dirs. Milw. chpt. Wis. Civil Liberties Union, 1984—. Mem. Acad. Criminal Justice Scis. (program com. 1983), Am. Soc. Criminology, Law and Soc. Assn. Office: Univ Wis-Milw PO Box 786 Milwaukee WI 53201

HOCHWALD, WERNER, economist, educator; b. Berlin, Germany, Jan. 21, 1910; s. Moritz and Elsa (Stahl) H.; grad. U. Berlin, 1932; Ph.D., Washington U., 1944; m. Hilde Landenberger, Jan. 28, 1938 (dec. June 1958); children—Miriam Ruth, Eve Fay. Came to U.S., 1938, naturalized, 1944. Counsel, Com. on Aid and Reconstrn., Berlin, 1933-38; accountant, St. Louis, 1938-42; instr. Army Specialized Tng. Program, 1942-44; instr. econs., Wash. U., St. Louis, 1944-47, successively asst. and assoc. prof., chmn. dept., prof., 1950-63, Tileston prof. polit. economy, 1963—; Kennedy Disting. prof. econs. U. of South, 1981-83; cons., U.S. Office Edn., 1967—; dir. Internat. Econ. Research, 1950-55; lectr. Army Fin. Sch., 1950-52; cons. Fed. Res. Bank St. Louis, 1947-58. Mem. Citizens' Budget Com., St. Louis, 1957. Mem. Nat. Planning Assn. (dir. study local impacts fgn. trade), Am. Econ. Assn., Indsl. Relations Research Assn., Econometric Soc., Am. Statis. Assn. (nat. council 1950-52), Econ. History Assn., Am. Farm Econ. Assn., So. (pres. 1966-67). Midwest econ. assns., Conf. Research Income and Wealth, Internat. Assn. Research in Income and Wealth, Nat. Acad. Scis. (hwy. research bd. 1961-64). Author: Local Impact of Foreign Trade, 1960; Essays in Southern Economic Development, 1964; An Economist's Image of History, 1968; The Idea of Progress, 1973. Contbg. author various books, profl. jours., Ency. of Econs. Editor: Design of Regional Accounts, 1961. Home: 6910 Cornell Ave Saint Louis MO 63130 Office: Washington U Saint Louis MO 63130

HOCKEIMER, HENRY ERIC, aerospace company executive; b. Winzig, Germany, Apr. 3, 1920; s. Erich and Gertrude (Masur) H.; came to U.S., 1946, naturalized, 1951; student RCA Insts., 1946-47, electronics and bus. mgmt. NYU, 1948-51; m. Margaret Feeny, May 26, 1956; children—Ellen Patricia, Henry Eric. With Philco-Ford Corp., Phila., 1947—, gen. mgr. communications and tech. services div., 1962-63, corp. v.p., 1963-72, v.p., gen. mgr. refrigeration products div., Connersville, Ind., 1972-75; pres. Ford Aerospace & Communications Corp., Dearborn, Mich., 1975-85, ret., bd. dir., cons.; v.p. Ford Motor Co., 1981-85; cons. U.S. Info Agy. Mem. Franklin Inst., Am. Ordnance Assn., Nat. Security Indsl. Assn., Soc. Automotive Engrs., Am. Def. Preparedness Assn., Assn. U.S. Army, Air Force Assn., Navy League U.S. Clubs: Renaissance, Fairlane, Amelia Plantation. Home: 50 Harlan Dr Bloomfield Hills MI 48013 Office: 300 Renaissance Center PO Box 43342 Detroit MI 48243

HOCKENBERG, HARLAN DAVID, lawyer; b. Des Moines, July 1, 1927; s. Leonard C. and Estyre M. (Zalk) H.; B.A., U. Iowa, 1949, J.D., 1952; m. Dorothy A. Arkin, June 3, 1953; children—Marni Lynn Vrona, Thomas Leonard, Edward Arkin. Bar: Iowa 1952. Assoc. Abramson & Myers, Des Moines, 1952-58; mem. firm Abramson, Myers & Hockenberg, Des Moines, 1958-64; sr. ptnr. firm Davis, Hockenberg, Wine, Brown & Koehn, and predecessor, Des Moines, 1964—; dir. West Des Moines (Iowa) State Bank. Pres., Des Moines Jewish Social Service Agy., 1958-60; mem. Internat. Relations and Nat. Security Adv. Council, Republican Nat. Com., 1978; chmn. Council of Jewish Fedns., Small Cities Com., 1970-71; regional v.p., mem. exec. com. Am. Israel Pub. Affairs Com.; pres. Willkie House Inc., Des Moines, 1965-66, Des Moines Jewish Welfare Fedn., 1973-74. Served with USNR, 1945-46. Mem. Des Moines C. of C. (chmn. Bur. Econ. Devel. 1979, 80, bd. dirs., 1st vice chmn.), Delta Sigma Rho, Omicron Delta Kappa, Phi Epsilon Pi. Republican. Clubs: Des Moines, Pioneer, Wakonda. Home: 2880 Grand Ave Des Moines IA 50312 Office: Davis Hockenberg Wine Brown & Koehn 2300 Financial Center Des Moines IA 50309

HOCKETT, MARCIA EILEEN, nurse, cardiovascular clinical nurse specialist; b. Dayton, Ohio, Jan. 10, 1948; d. Howard, Sr., and Mary Louise (Jennings) Dozier; m. Clarence Hockett, Jr., Sept., 16, 1967. A.S., Sinclair Community Coll., 1975; B.S. in Nursing, Miami U.-Oxford, Ohio, 1981; M.S., Ohio State U., 1982. Claims clerical Social Security Adminstrn., Dayton, Ohio, 1966-68, Lumberton, N.C., 1969; ward sec. VA Hosp., Dayton, 1969-70, outpatient dental clk., 1970-74, staff nurse intensive care, 1975-83, cardiovascular clin. nurse specialist, 1983—. Investigator/author research studies, 1982, 83. Vol., ARC, Dayton, 1983; mem. Cardiac Rehab. Task Force, Dayton, 1983. Grad. Traineeship grantee, Ohio State U., 1982. Mem. Am. Assn. Critical Care Nurses (pub. affairs com. 1983—), Ohio Nurses Assn., Am. Heart Assn., Cardiovascular Council on Nursing, Sigma Theta Tau. Democrat. Baptist. Home: 5268 Torch Ln Dayton OH 45427 Office: VA Med Center 4100 W 3d St Dayton OH 45428

HODA, QAMRUL, physician; b. Jamshedpur, India, Feb. 2, 1942; came to U.S., 1969; s. Syed Anwarul and Ummatuz (Zohra) H.; I. Sci., St. Xavier's Coll., Ranchi, India, 1960; M.B.B.S., P.W. Med. Coll., Patna, India, 1965; M.D. in Pediatrics, Patna U., 1968; m. Nikhat Bano, June 14, 1972; children—Syed Tanveer, Tasnim. Intern, St. Joseph Mercy Hosp., Pontiac, Mich., 1969-70, now staff mem.; resident in pediatrics, Pontiac Gen. Hosp., 1970-72, now staff mem., cons. in pediatric nephrology, 1975—; resident Hosp. for Sick Children, Toronto, Ont., Can., 1972-73; teaching fellow in nephrology and ambulatory pediatrics Wayne County Gen. Hosp., Pontiac, 1974-75; pvt. practice medicine specializing in pediatrics and pediatric nephrology, Pontiac, 1975—. Fellow Am. Acad. Pediatrics; mem. Mich. Med. Soc., Oakland County Med. Soc., Detroit Pediatric Soc. Office: 185 Elizabeth Lake Rd Pontiac MI 48053

HODAPP, LEROY CHARLES, bishop; b. Seymour, Ind., Nov. 11, 1923; s. Linden Charles and Mary Marguerite (Miller) H.; m. Polly Anne Martin, June 12, 1947; children—Anne Lynn Hodapp Gates, Nancy Ellen Hodapp Wichman. A.B., U. Evansville, 1944, D.D., 1961; B.D., Drew Theol. Sem., Madison, N.J., 1947; L.H.D., Ill. Wesleyan U., 1977; D.D., McKendree Coll., 1948, Wiley Coll., 1980. Ordained to ministry Methodist Ch., 1947. Pastor chs. in Ind., 1947-65; supt. Bloomington (Ind.) Dist. Meth. Ch., 1965-67, Indpls. West Dist., 1967-68, Indpls. N.E. Dist., 1968-70, dir. South Ind. Conf. Council, 1970-76; bishop Ill. area United Meth. Ch., Springfield, from 1970; pres. United Meth. Gen. Bd. Ch. and Soc., from 1980; now bishop No. Ind. and So. Ind. areas United Meth. Ch. Co-editor: Change in the Small Community, 1967. Democrat. Office: PO Box 869 Marion IN 46952

HODEL, MERLE ALVIN, airline executive, flight educator, captain; b. Roanoke, Ill., Mar. 25, 1941; s. Alvin Amos and Emma (Fanny), H.; m. Gayle Ann Tanner, June 10, 1967; children—Martin Merle, Michelle D. B.S., So. Ill. U., 1967, M.S. in Edn., 1972. Chief pilot, chief flight instr. Airgo, Inc., Carbondale, Ill. 1968-70, asst. mgr. flying, capt., dispatcher, Air Ill., Inc., Carbondale, 1970-77; pilot Mobil Corp., Chgo., 1977-79; flight mgr., check airman, ground sch. instr., capt., Midway Airlines, Chgo., 1979—; bd. dir. Coll. DuPage Travel & Tourism Dept., Glen Ellyn, Ill., 1984—. Mem. Am. Biog. Inst. Research Assn., Aerospace Edn. Assn., Am. Soc. Aerospace Edn., Pilots Internat. Assn., Nat. Aeronautics Assn., Aircraft Owners and Pilots Assn., Seaplane Pilots Assn., Phi Delta Kappa. Republican. Avocation: computing. Home: 6028 Ridgeway Drive Woodridge IL 60517 Office: Midway Airlines 5700 S Cicero Ave Chicago IL 60638

HODES, BARBARA, organization consultant; b. Chgo., Nov. 30, 1941; d. David and Tybe (Ziff) Zisook; B.S., Northwestern U., 1962; m. Scott Hodes, Dec. 19, 1961 (div. 1977); children—Brian, Valery. Partner Just Causes, cons.not-for-profit orgns., Chgo., 1978—; Chgo. cons. Population Resource Center, 1978-82. Woman's bd. dirs. Mus. Contemporary Art; bd. dirs., vice chmn. Med. Research Inst. Council, Michael Reese Med. Center; bd. dirs., chmn. Midwest Women's Center; trustee Francis W. Parker Sch. Office: Just Causes 1405 N Dearborn Pkwy Chicago IL 60610

HODGE, ROBERT DOUGLAS, educational administrator; b. Spokane, Wash., Feb. 14, 1951; s. Harold Etzel and Doris Elizabeth (Halloway) H.; m. Susan Ellen Marshall, July 1, 1972; children—Elesha Joy, Bethany Faith. B.A., Wash. State U., 1973; M.B.A., Eastern Wash. U., 1976. Cert. info. systems auditor, systems profl. Electronic data processing auditor Fidelity Bank, Spokane, Wash., 1973-80; data processing mgr. Lincoln Bank, Spokane, 1981-82; dir. info. services Taylor U., Upland, Ind., 1982—; cons. Soft Sell, Spokane, 1977-82; cons. Computing Assistance Program, Upland, 1982—. Contbr. articles to profl. jours. Tchr., treas. local chs., Spokane, Upland. Mem. Data Processing Mgrs. Assn., Christian Ministries Mgmt. Assn., Assn. Systems Mgmt. Republican. Avocations: tennis, amateur radio. Office: Taylor U Reade Ave Upland IN 46989

HODGE, VICTOR A(NTHONY), lawyer; b. Louisville, Apr. 4, 1947; s. Lester D. and Bridget T. (DeGeorge) H.; m. Barbara A. Downs, June 24, 1967; children—James Eric, Jill Marie. B.A. in Chemistry, Bellarmine Coll.; J.D. cum laude, U. Dayton. Bar: Ohio 1981, Fla. 1982. Forensic chemist Sanford Crime Lab., Fla., 1974-75, Miami Valley Regional Crime Lab., Dayton, Ohio, 1973-74, 75-80; assoc. Brannon & Cox Law Offices, Dayton, 1981-83; sole practice, Dayton, 1983—. Youth sports coach Merlin Heights Baseball Assn., Dayton. Served to sgt. U.S. Army, 1969-71. Mem. Ohio State Bar Assn., Dayton Bar Assn., Fla. Bar Assn., Assn. Trial Lawyers Am., Am Legion. Democrat. Roman Catholic. Office: 1510 First Nat Plaza Dayton OH 45402

HODGEN, EARL WAYNE, communications company executive, electrical engineer; b. Tulsa, Okla., July 15, 1942; s. Clayton Robert and Annabelle Kathryn (Wilson) H.; m. Carol Louise Zick, Dec. 31, 1978; children—Mathew Earl, Kathryn Kay, Kandall Joy. B.S. in Math., Tulsa U., 1967, B.S. in E.E., 1968; M.A. in Mgmt., Webster U., Webster Groves, Mo., 1984. Registered profl. engr., Okla., Mo. Devel. engr. Electro-Chem Lab, Tulsa, 1967-68; dist. mgr. Southwestern Bell Telephone Co., St. Louis, 1968—. Mem. IEEE, Soc. Profl. Engrs. Home: 2085 Pohlman Florissant MO 63033 Office: Southwestern Bell Telephone Co 1010 Pine St Room 2004 Saint Louis MO 63101

HODGES, ALBERT WILLFRED, retired music educator; b. Greensburg, Kans., Aug. 1, 1914; s. Albert Alton and Allatha Rebecca (Baer) H.; m. Ruby Winifred Dunlap, June 10, 1942; children—Woodrow Joe, Donald Albert. Mus.B., Southwestern Coll., 1936; Grad. Army Music Sch., Washington, 1943; M.Music Edn., U. No. Colo., 1957; postgrad. U. Ky., 1967-68. Music tchr., band dir. Kans. pub. schs., 1936-41; dir. Air Force Band, 1943-46; band dir. pvt. lesson instr. Kearney, Nebr. pub. schs., 1946-54; dir. bands, music edn. Southwestern Coll., Winfield, Kans., 1955-73; dir. music therapy State Hosp. Tng. Ctr., Winfield, 1973-78; pvt. tchr. instrumental lessons, 1978—; ret., 1978; adjudicator music contests Kans., Okla., Mo. and Nebr. pub. schs., 1946—; clinician music, bands, Kans., Okla. and Nebr. pub. schs., 1946—. Mem. Winfield Oratoria Soc., 1955—, pres., 1978—. Mem. Music Educators Nat. Conf., Kans. Music Educators Assn. (Hall of Fame 1976), Coll. Band Dirs. Nat. Assn. (chmn. Kans. State sect. 1957-73), Am. Legion, Phi Mu Alpha Sinfonia, Phi Beta Mu (nat. com rules and by-laws). Republican. Methodist. Lodge: Lions. Avocations: handicrafts; sports. Home: 1513 Olive Winfield KS 67156

HODGES, JAMES TROY, mfg. co. exec.; b. Chgo., Dec. 5, 1949; s. Troy Manual and Peggy Ann (White) H.; student Baylor U., Waco, Tex., 1967-70; B.A., U. Ill., 1971; postgrad. U. Louisville, 1973-75; m. Pamela Sue Vance, Dec. 19, 1970; children—Rebekah Lea, James Thomas, Joseph Adam. Systems programmer City of Louisville, 1971-72; systems analyst Liberty Nat. Bank, Louisville, 1972-73; computer center mgr. Med. Sch. U. Louisville, 1973-75; pres. Bloodstock Computers Services, Lexington, Ky., 1975-79; devel. mgr. Merrell Dow Pharm. Inc., Cin., 1979—. Deacon, budget dir. First Baptist Ch. of Anderson Hills, Cin. Mem. Digital Equipment Computer Users Soc., Assn. Computing Machinery, Assn. Timesharing Users, Am. Nat. Standard Inst. Republican. Home: 537 N Revere St Cincinnati OH 45230 Office: 2110 E Glabraith Rd Cincinnati OH 45215

HODGES, SIDNEY EDWARD, physics educator; b. Booneville, Miss., Feb. 11, 1924; s. James L. and Mildred (Murphy) H.; m. Francoise Novailletas, Oct. 2, 1942 (dec. 1981); children—Philippe, Annette, Sean, Chadwick, Angela; m. 2d Linda Susan Neal, Nov. 2, 1981. B.S. in Elec. Engring., So. Meth. U., 1949; M.S. in Physics, East Tex. State U., 1950; Ph.D., Tex. A&M U., 1958. Asst. prof. physics East Tex. State U., Commerce, 1950-58; faculty Stephen F. Austin State Coll., Nacogdoches, Tex., 1958-65; prof., head dept. physics Howard Payne U., Brownwood, Tex., 1965-67; prof. S.E. Mo. State U., Cape Girardeau, 1967—. Served with USAAF, 1942-45. Named Outstanding Educator of Am., Southeast Mo. State U., 1969, 70. Mem. Sigma Xi, Sigma Pi Sigma. Baptist. Lodge: Optimists. Avocations: cabinet making; camping. Home: 1615 Themio Cape Girardeau MO 63701 Office: SE Mo State U Cape Girardeau MO 63701

HODGKISS, ELEANOR B., day care center administrator; b. Cleve., July 17, 1917; d. William J. and Marjorie (Geer) Butler; m. James A. Hodgkiss, Feb. 16, 1942 (dec. 1969); children—Judith E., Margaret A. B.A. magna cum laude, Baldwin Wallace Coll., Berea, Ohio, 1981. Tchr., Westlake (Ohio) Coop. Nursery Sch., 1954-59, dir., 1959-69; adminstr. Cleve. Christian Day Care Ctr., 1969—. Mem. adv. com. Cuyahoga Community Coll.-Cleve., Cleve. Day Care; mem. Protective Service Consortium, Cleve. Recipient Continuing Edn. award Baldwin Wallace Coll. Student Assn., 1981. Mem. Cleve. Assn. for Edn. Young Children, Midwest Assn. for Edn. Young Children, Chi Psi, Beta Upsilon. Republican. Congregationalist. Created Hodgkiss self-concept scale for children, 1967. Office: Cleveland Christian Day Care Center 11401 Lorain Ave Cleveland OH 44111

HODGSON, GARY FRANCIS, educational administrator; b. Cadillac, Mich., July 24, 1941; s. Myles Wesley Hodgson and Beatrice Otilia (Denzel) Budnick; m. Johanna Wilhelmina Keur, Aug. 27, 1966; children—Jennifer, Elizabeth. B.S., Western Mich. U., 1964, postgrad., 1977-78; M.Ed., Kent State U., 1972; postgrad., Mich. State U., 1983—. Cert. secondary prin., Mich. Dir., tchr. Dawntreader Alternative High Sch., Kalamazoo, 1972-74; career edn. cons. Kent Intermediate Sch. Dist., Grand Rapids, Mich., 1974-75; alternative edn. tchr. East Kentwood High Sch., Mich., 1975-78; asst. prin. West Ottawa High Sch., Holland, Mich., 1978-80; prin. West Ottawa Middle Sch., Holland, 1980—; career edn. cons., Hastings, Mich., 1975-79; middle schs. cons., Holland, 1981—; career edn. instr. Western Mich. U., Kalamazoo, 1976. Contbg. editor: Career Education Resource Guide, 1975. Designer mentorship program, 1983. Mem. exec. council Hope Ch., Holland, 1981—; mem. Holland Area Arts Council, 1981—. Recipient Cert. of Appreciation, Mich. State Bd. Edn., 1984, Excellence in Edn. award U.S. Dept. Edn., 1983; Profl. Devel. Consortium grantee, 1981, 82, 85. Mem. Mich. Assn. of Academically Talented, Ottawa County Middle Level Educators (chmn. 1983), Nat. Assn. Secondary Prins., Mich. Assn. Secondary Prins., Assn. for Supervision of Curriculum Devel., Nat. Middle Sch. Assn., Ottawa Area Sch. Adminstrs., (Common Cause). Mem. Reformed Ch. Am. Lodge: Exchange Club. Avocations: travel, reading, racquetball. Office: West Ottawa Middle Sch 2700 140th Ave Holland MI 49423

HODJAT, YAHYA, metallurgist; b. Tehran, Iran, Aug. 8, 1950; came to U.S., 1977; s. Javad and Robabeh (Fayaz) H.; m. Patricia Anne Gray, Dec. 17, 1980. B.S., Arya-Mehr U., Tehran, Iran, 1972; M.S., Ohio State U., 1978, Ph.D., 1981. Engr. trainee August Thyssen Corp., Oberhausen, W. Ger., 1974-75; project mgr. Pahlavi Steel Corp., Ahwaz, Iran, 1975-77; grad. research assoc. Ohio State U., Columbus, 1977-81; dir. ops. Intercontinental Metals, Miami, 1981-82; research scientist The Standard Oil Co., Cleve., 1982-83; metall. specialist Dyneer Corp., Bloomfield Hills, Mich., 1983—; cons. Intercontinental Metals Corp., Miami, 1978-80. Asst. inventor Pyro-Technique Silver Refining, 1980. Served to lt. Iranian Imperial Army, 1972-74. Mem. AIME, Am. Soc. Metals, Am. Foundrymen's Soc., Alpha Sigma Mu. Home: 45200 Keding St Apt 304 Utica MI 48087 Office: Dyneer Corp 1133 W Long Lake Rd Bloomfield Hills MI 48013

HODSON, CONNIE JEAN, computer educator; b. Grinnell, Iowa, May 4, 1946; d. Rolland Everett and Mary Louise (Hensley) Doty; m. John Howell Hodson, Feb. 18, 1967; children—Mary, Jo. B.A., U. No. Iowa, 1968; M.S., Emporia State U., 1982. Tchr. gifted Flint Hills Spl. Edn. Coop, Emporia, Kans., 1979-80; coordinator gifted 3 Lakes Spl. Edn. Coop, Waverly, Kans., 1980-83; computer tchr. Allen County Community Coll., Iola, Kans., 1982-83; lectr. Emporia State U., summers 1982-84; computer tchr. Moraine Valley Community Coll., Palos Hills, Ill., 1983—; coordinator gifted, computers River Forest Pub. Schs., Ill., 1984—. Mem. Nat. Assn. Gifted Children, Assn. for Edn. Data Systems, NEA, Kans. Gifted, Talented, Creative Assn. Methodist. Avocation: leather work. Office: Willard Sch 1250 Ashland Ave River Forest IL 60305

HOEB, WILLIAM RALPH, JR., machine tool company executive; b. Cin., Aug. 7, 1941; s. William Ralph and Charlotte Marie (Bittner) H.; m. Karen Diane Bennett, Aug. 24, 1963. B.S. in Design, U. Cin., 1964. Advt. prodn. mgr. Cin. Milacron, 1964-68, graphic services mgr., 1968-81, mgr. ednl. relations and media devel., 1981—. Dist. chmn. Boy Scouts Am., Dan Beard Council, Cin., 1982-83; publicity chmn. Hyde Park Community United Methodist Ch., Cin., 1976-81; active United Appeal campaign, Cin., 1975—. Recipient Eagle Scout award Boy Scouts Am., 1956, Silver Explorer award, 1956, Order of the Arrow. Mem. Ohio Coop. Edn. Assn. (pres. 1984-85, Outstanding employer mem. of yr. 1982-83, 83-84), Midwest Coop. Edn. Assn. (treas. 1983-84), Coop. Edn. Assn., Inc. (employer rep. 1983—, bd. dirs.), Southland Hall Assn. (Pi Kappa Alpha Cin. Alumni Orgn., named Mr. Alpha Xi 1982). Republican. Lodge: Rotary. Home: 3035 Portsmouth Ave Cincinnati OH 45208

HOEFS, PAUL THEODORE, II, rancher; b. Wood Lake, Nebr., Nov. 30, 1926; s. Paul A. and Margaret (Roberts) H.; m. Patricia Anderson; children—Paul, Sheri, Mary, Jan, Bonnie, John, Patricia, Jim, Mark. Aerobatic and spray pilot; pvt. practive farming, Wood Lake, Nebr.; past pres., dir. Fed. Land Bank Assn., Valentine, Nebr. Mem. Wood Lake Vol. Fire Dept., 1972-76; mem. Class 6 Sch. Bd., Wood Lake; pres. Wood Lake Sch. Dist. 7; dir. Sch. Dist. 195; pres. Cherry County (Nebr.) Hosp. Bd., also pres. Found.; bd. dirs. Greater Nebr. Health System Agy.; trustee Sacred Heart Ch. Mem. Nebr. Stock Growers Assn. (past chmn.), Nat. Cattle Assn. (dir.), Aircraft Owners and Pilots Assn., S.D. Stock Growers Assn., Farm Bur., Sandhills Cattle Assn., Livestock Merchandising Inst. (trustee). Club: KC. Address: Skull Lake Ranch PO Box 727 Wood Lake NE 69221

HOEL, ROGER SATRANG, conductor; b. Chgo., Oct. 30, 1938; s. Bjarna and Ninnia Olga (Huggenvik) H.; m. Donna Ruth Harms, May 20, 1961; children—Elizabeth Ann, Gregory Roger. B.S., St. Olaf Coll., 1960; M.S., U. Minn., 1963; M.A., Cornell U., 1966; B.A., Augsburg Coll., 1973. Asst. Conductor St. Paul Civic Orch., 1964-68, St. Paul Chamber Orch., 1966-69; assoc. conductor Bloomington Symphony Orch., Minn., 1966-70; music dir., conductor Apollo Male Chorus, Mpls., 1977—; music dir., prin. conductor, founder Minnetonka Orchestral Assn., Minn., 1974—; minister music Edgewater Emmanuel Ch., 1966—; founder Minnetonka Symphony Orch., 1974, Minnetonka Children's Choir, 1976, Minnetonka Chorale, 1976, Minnetonka Chamber Orch., 1976, Minnetonka Civic Orch., 1976, Minnetonka Sr. Chorale, 1980, Minnetonka Youth Orch., 1980. Mem. fine arts com. Hopkins Sch. Dist., 1982-84, curriculum council, 1984; bd. dirs. Hopkins Assn. Children with Learning Disabilities, 1977. Recipient Citizen of Yr. award Minnetonka C. of C., 1977, Master Tchr. award Hopkins Sch. Dist., 1979, 2d place award Am. Choral Festival, Mpls., 1981, 2d prize Internat. Music Eisteddfod, Llangollen, Wales, 1982. Mem. Nat. Com. on Male Choruses, Nat. Com. on Children's Choirs, Internat. Children's Choir Assn., Conductor's Guild, Nat. Assn. Tchrs. of Singing, Bach Soc. (bd. dirs. 1984). Lutheran. Club: Evergreen (Mpls.). Avocations: Lincoln history; skiing; running. Home: 5216 Mayview Rd Minnetonka MN 55345 Office: Minnetonka Orchestral Assn 1001 Hwy 7 Minnetonka MN 55343

HOELLRICH, GENE RICHARD, lawyer, judge; b. Defiance, Ohio, Sept. 26, 1946; s. George R. and Laverne (Rohn) H.; m. Patricia C. Maddy, Aug. 15, 1968; children—Caroline, Garth, Abraham. B.A., Ohio State U., 1968, J.D., 1971. Bar: Ohio 1971. Assoc., Smith & Schnacke, Dayton, Ohio, 1971; assoc. Brumbaugh Law, Greenville, Ohio, 1972-75, ptnr., 1974-80; sole practice, Greenville, 1980—; county judge Darke County (Ohio), 1982—. Contbr. articles to profl. jours. Served to 1st lt. U.S. Army, 1972. Recipient scholar award Ohio State U., 1970. Mem. Darke County Bar Assn. (pres. 1978-79), Ohio Bar Assn., Order of Coif. Republican. Lutheran. Lodge: Lions. Avocations: Woodworking; bow hunting; snowmobiling. Home: 7947 Martz Rd Versailles OH 45380 Office: 213 Walnut St Greenville OH 45331

HOERNEMAN, CALVIN A., JR., educator; b. Youngstown, Ohio, Sept. 30, 1940; s. Calvin A. and Lucille A. (Leiss) H.; B.A., Bethany Coll., 1962; M.A., Mich. State U., 1964; m. Cheryl L. Morand, Aug. 10, 1973; children—David, Jennifer, Christina. Mem. faculty Delta Coll., University Center, Mich., 1966—, prof. econs., 1976—; syndicated wine columnist Wine and Spirits Buying Guide, Mich. Beverage News, Ariz. Beverage Guide, 1977—; cons. Prentice-Hall, Acad. Press, Goodyear Pub. Recipient Recognition award AAUP, 1972; Bergstein award Delta Coll. Grad. Class, 1972. Mem. Am. Econ. Assn., Midwest Econ. Assn., AAUP, Wine Educators Soc. Author: Poverty, Wealth and Income Distribution, 1969; co-author: —Caper— Principles of Economics Software Study Guide; contbr. articles to various publs. Home: 5712 Lamplighter Ln Midland MI 48640 Office: Delta Coll University Center MI 48710

HOESSLE, CHARLES HERMAN, zoo director; b. St. Louis, Mar. 20, 1931; m. Marilyn Mueller, Jan. 5, 1952; children—Maureen, Kirk, Tracy, Bradley. A.A., Harris Tchrs. Coll., St. Louis, 1951; student Am. Assn. Zool. Parks and Aquariums Zoo Mgmt. Sch., 1976-77. Reptile keeper St. Louis Zoo, 1963-64, asst. curator, 1964-68, curator reptiles, curator edn., 1968-69, gen. curator, dep. dir., 1969-82, dir. zoo, 1982—; adj. asst. prof. dept. biology St. Louis U. State chmn. UN Day, 1982; chmn. Reptile Study Merit Badge Counselors. Served with U.S. Army, 1952-54. Mem. Am. Assn. Zool. Parks and Aquariums, St. Louis Naturalists Club, Internat. Union Dirs. Zool. Gardens. Lodge: Rotary. Office: St Louis Zool Park Forest Park Saint Louis MO 63110

HOEY, RITA MARIE, public relations executive; b. Chgo., Nov. 4, 1950; d. Louis D. and Edith M. (Finnemann) Hoey; m. Joseph John Dragonette, Sept. 4, 1982. B.A. in English and History, No. Ill. U., 1972. Asst. dir. Nat. Assn. Housing and Human Devel., Chgo., 1975; public relations account exec. Weber Cohn & Riley, Chgo., 1975-76; publicity coordinator U.S. Gypsum Co., Chgo., 1976-77; with Daniel J. Edelman, Inc., Chgo., 1977-84, sr. v.p., 1981-84; exec. v.p. Dragonette, Inc., Chgo., 1984—. Mem. Pub. Relations Soc. Am., Women in Communications. Clubs: Chgo. Press, Young Execs. Home: 3416 S Cherry Valley Woodstock IL 60098 Office: 233 N Michigan Ave #1607 Chicago IL 60601

HOFERT, JOHN FREDERICK, biochemistry educator, researcher; b. Oak Park, Ill., Oct. 13, 1935; s. Oscar Andrew and Esther May (Bruns) H.; m. Priscilla Jane Bomberger, June 23, 1962; children—Daniel, Andrew. B.A., North Central Coll., 1957; M.S., Mich. State U., 1959; Ph.D., U. Wis.-Madison, 1963. Research fellow Albert Einstein Coll. Medicine, N.Y.C., 1963-65, instr., 1965-66; asst. prof. U. Nebr. Coll. Medicine, Omaha, 1966-71, assoc. prof., 1971—. Contbr. articles to profl. jours. Mem. Urban League Nebr., NAACP. Grantee NSF, 1968, USPHS, 1968, 1979, Damon Ranyon Meml. Found., 1971, Am. Diabetes Assn., 1975. Mem. AAAS, Endocrine Soc., Am. Soc. Biol. Chemists, Sigma Xi. Baha'i Faith. Club: Book Fellows (Council Bluffs). Avocation: tennis. Home: 2225 Rodney St Council Bluffs IA 51501 Office: U Nebr Dept Biochemistry 42d and Dewey Sts Omaha NE 68105

HOFFA, GERALD ALAN, sheriff; b. Greencastle, Ind., May 12, 1950; s. Gordan Cleve and Ronella Jeanne (Hurst) H.; m. Julie Jean Fisher, Sept. 6, 1969; children—Lori Rose, Travis Joseph. Student, Ind. State U., 1968-69, 1978-79. Cert. police officer. Dep. sheriff Putnam County Sheriff Dept., Greencastle, 1972-77, sheriff, 1983—; town marshal Cloverdale Town, Ind., 1978-83; bd. dirs. Putnam County Family Support Services, Greencastle, 1985—. Served to sgt. U.S. Army, 1970-71, Korea. Mem. Ind. Sheriffs Assn., Fraternal Order Police (pres. 1976-78). Democrat. Avocations: softball, golf. Home: 123 W Washington Greencastle IN 46135 Office: Putnam County Sheriff Dept 123 W Washington Greencastle IN 46135

HOFFA, HOWARD ALLEN, osteopathic physician; b. Detroit, Oct. 3, 1927; s. Leolan William and Pearl Cheseley (Foster) H.; m. Jo Ann Brockfeld, June 13, 1954; children—Jennifer Brush, Scott. A.B., U. Mich., 1950; D.O., Kirksville Coll. Osteo. Medicine, 1955. Intern, Still Hosp., Jefferson City, Mo., 1955-56; pvt. practice family and gen. osteo. medicine, Stover, Mo., 1956—; pres. bd. Golden Age Nursing Home, Stover Indsl. Devel. Corp.; sec., internal medicine com. Bothwell Hosp., Sedalia, Mo. Served with U.S. Army, 1945-46. Mem. Am. Osteo. Assn., Mo. Assn. Osteo. Physicians and Surgeons, Am. Coll. Gen. Practitioners Osteo. Medicine. Democrat. Methodist. Club: Lions. Home: Missouri Ave Stover MO 65078 Office: 2d and Oak Stat Box D Stover MO 65078

HOFFHEIMER, DANIEL JOSEPH, lawyer; b. Cin., Dec. 28, 1950; s. Harry Max and Charlotte (O'Brien) H.; m. Sara Wood Elder, May 9, 1970 (div. 1979) 1 child, Rebecca Anne; m. Penny Friedman, June 7, 1981; 1 child, Rachel Friedman. A.B. cum laude, Harvard Coll., 1973; J.D., U. Va., 1976. Bar: Ohio 1976, U.S. Dist. Ct. (so. dist.) Ohio 1976, U.S. Ct. Appeals (6th cir.) 1977, U.S. Supreme Ct. 1980. Assoc., Taft, Stettinius & Hollister, Cin., 1976-84, ptnr., 1984—; lectr. law Coll. Law, U. Cin., 1981-83. Co-author: Practitioners' Handbook Ohio First District Court of Appeals, 1984; Practitioners Handbook U.S. 6th Circuit Court of Appeals, 1984. Contbr. articles to profl. jours. Mem. Cin. Symphony Bus. Relations Com., 1977—; mem. Adv. Bd. for Consumer Protection, Cin., 1978-80; trustee Cin. Chamber Orch., 1977-80, Seven Hills Schs., Cin., 1980—, Internat. Visitors Ctr., Cin., 1980-84. Named Outstanding Young Man, U.S. Jaycees, 1984. Mem. ABA, Fed. Bar Assn. (asst. sec. 1983, treas. 1984), Ohio State Bar Assn., Cin. Bar Assn. Democrat. Clubs: Harvard of Cin. (dir. 1980—, v.p., 1983—). Avocations: Music; tennis; collections. Home: 1125 Edwards Rd Cincinnati OH 45208 Office: Taft Stettinius & Hollister 1800 First Nat Bank Ctr Cincinnati OH 45202

HOFFMAN, SISTER ANNE LUCY, librarian; b. Prairie du Chien, Wis., May 29, 1921; d. William Stanislaus and Anna Kingery (Fagan) H. B.A., Mt. Mary Coll., Milw., 1945; M.A. in L.S., Rosary Coll., River Forest, Ill., 1954. Life cert. secondary sch. educator, Wis.; joined Religious Congregation of Sch. Sisters of Notre Dame, 1941. Tchr., McDonell High Sch., Chippewa Falls, Wis., 1943-51, Sacred Heart High Sch., Laurium, Mich., 1951-52, St. Anthony High Sch., Detroit, 1952-53, Columbus High Sch., Marshfield, Wis., 1953-62; librarian Mt. Mary Coll., Milw., 1962-65, asst. librarian, 1971-77, dir. of library, 1977—; dir. library Notre Dame of the Lake campus Mt. Mary Coll., Mequon, Wis., 1965-68; tchr. Latin and English, St. Mary's High Sch., Burlington, Wis., 1968-71. Recipient vol. service citation Inner City Council on Alcoholism, Inc., 1977. Mem. ALA, Wis. Library Assn., Wis. Acad. Library Assn., Cath. Library Assn., Wis. Cath. Library Assn. (mem. exec. bd.; coordinator ann. conf. 1967, 83, 84), Nat. Right to Life Assn., Wis. Assn. Ind. Colls. and Univs. Librarians, Bookfellows of Milw. Roman Catholic. Home: 2900 N Menomonee River Pkwy Milwaukee WI 53222 Office: Mount Mary College 2900 N Menomonee River Pkwy Milwaukee WI 53222

HOFFMAN, CLYDE HARRIS, dean technical institute; b. Jamestown, N.D., Mar. 24, 1925; s. Clarence William and Ada Catherine (Gensrich) H.; B.S.E.E., U. N.D., 1950; M.S.E.E., U. Notre Dame, 1952, Ph.D. in Applied Mechanics, 1962; m. Betty Myra Ledingham, May 29, 1950. Instr. elec. engring. U. Notre Dame, 1951-52, asst. prof., 1953-62; project engr. Jack & Heintz, Inc., Cleve., 1952-53; asso. prof. elec. engring. Ill. Inst. Tech., Chgo., 1962-70, also head elec. engring. dept. Kabul (Afghanistan) U., 1966-68; mgr. IIT/TV Instructional Television Network, 1968-70; tng. mgr. Page Communications Engrs. INTS Program, Tehran, 1970-72; dir. tech. and vocat. tng. Harza Engring. Co., Chgo., 1972-73; 1st officer, program specialist UNESCO, Paris, 1973-78; mgr. transit communications systems IIT Research Inst., Chgo., 1978-80; dean acad. affairs DeVry Inst. Tech., Chgo., 1980—; evaluation panels undergrad. sci. instructional equipment program NSF, 1963-65; mem. Nat. Acad. Scis. adv. com. to electronics instrumentation div. Nat. Bur. Standards, 1965-68; mem. Nat. Def. Exec. Res., U.S. Dept. Transp. trustee Nat. Electronics Conf., Inc. Sustaining mem. Republican Nat. Com.; mem. nat. adv. bd. Am. Security Council. Served with inf. AUS, 1943-46; ETO, PTO. Decorated Bronze Star; registered profl. engr., Ill., Ind., Calif. Mem. Instrument Soc. Am. (sr. mem., governing bd. 1964-65, v.p. Chgo. sect. 1980-81), IEEE (sr.), Am. Def. Preparedness Assn. (life), DAV (life), Nat. Rifle Assn. (life), Nat. Assn. Watch and Clock Collectors, Am. Soc. Tng. and Devel., Am. Legion, Inst. Radio Engrs. (chmn. South Bend sect. 1960-61), IEEE (exec. com. Chgo. 1964-65), Am. Ordnance Assn., AAAS, ASME, Assn. Computing Machinery, Am. Soc. Engring. Edn., Nat. Electronics Conf. (dir. 1957-64), Art Inst. Chgo. Republican. Club: Elks. Contbr. numerous articles to profl. jours. Home: 184 Cascade Dr Indian Head Park IL 60525 Office: 3300 N Campbell St Chicago IL 60618

HOFFMAN, ELLEN BARKER, baking company executive; b. La Harpe, Kans., Oct. 12, 1920; d. Otis Earl and Gertrude Ellen (Jones) Barker; student Clark's Bus. Coll., Topeka, 1938, U. Kansas City Night Sch., 1947-48; m. Donald D. Hoffman, June 8, 1968. Continuity dir. KMBC-TV, Kansas City, Mo., 1955-58; set dir. Calvin Prodns., film producers, Kansas City, 1958-67; with Interstate Brands Corp., wholesale bakers, Kansas City, 1967—, dir. pub. and consumer communications, 1975-85, dir. corp. communications, 1985—. Mem. Am. Bakers Assn. (pub. relations com. 1977), Pub. Relations Soc. Am. (dir. Kansas City chpt. 1977-80). Democrat. Episcopalian. Home: 6325 W 52d St Mission KS 66202

HOFFMAN, GEORGE WILLIAM, accountant; b. Waukegan, Ill., Nov. 19, 1939; s. Edward Richard and Anna Marie (Titus) H.; B.A. in Bus. Adminstrn., Lake Forest (Ill.) Coll., 1962; m. Janet L. Rowe, Aug. 22, 1974; 2 sons, Peter William, George William, 2 daus. Sr. accountant Price Waterhouse & Co., Inc., 1962-66; mem. treas.'s staff United Greenfield Corp., 1966-68; chief fin. officer, sec., dir. J.W. Johnson & Co., 1968-70; treas. Morse/Diesel, Inc., Chgo., 1970-76; mng. partner G. W. Hoffman & Co. P.C., Chgo., 1976-82; chmn. bd. dirs. GWH, Inc., 1976—; dir., v.p., sec., treas. Maple Jackson Assos. Inc.; chmn., pres., treas. GWH Leasing Inc., GWH Mchts. Inc., GWH Realty Co.; chmn., pres. GWH Devel. Corp., GWH Fin. Cons. Corp., Fircon Assocs., Inc., George William Hoffman P.C., 1982—; sec.-treas. Design Forum, Ltd. Served with USAR, 1957-65. C.P.A., Ill. Mem. Am. Inst. C.P.A.s, Ill. Soc. C.P.A.s. Clubs: Met., Young Execs. (Chgo.). Home: 3100 N Sheridan Rd Chicago IL 60657

HOFFMAN, HERBERT AUGUST, city administrator; b. Elgin, Ill., May 16, 1912; s. John and Anna (Natz) H.; m. Olga Elena Schoster, June 13, 1939; children—Charles, Myrna, John. B.S. in Metallurgy, Mo. Sch. Mines, 1934. Mill foreman Inca Mining Co., Tirapata, Peru, 1934-36; mill supt. No. Peru Mining Co., Trujillo, 1936-45; mill supt. St. Joe Lead Co., Bonne Terre, Mo., 1945-62, research cons., 1962-68, div. supt., 1968-77; city adminstr. City of Desloge, Mo., 1979—; cons. S & S Engrs., Archtl. Services, Desloge, 1977-79. City councilman City of Desloge, 1955-68. Recipient 110 Percent award Radio Sta Krei, Farmington, Mo., 1983. Mem. Desloge C. of C. (pres. 1983-85, Citizen of Yr. 1982). Republican. Lutheran. Club: Engineers (Rivermines, Mo.)

(pres. 1958-59). Avocation: photography. Home: 111 N 6th St Desloge MO 63601 Office: Desloge C of C 209 N Main St Desloge MO 63601

HOFFMAN, JAMES PAUL, lawyer; b. Waterloo, Iowa, Sept. 7, 1943; s. James A. and Luella M. (Prokosch) H.; B.A., U. No. Ia., 1966; J.D., U. Ia., 1967; 1 dau., Tiffany Christine. Admitted to Ia. bar, 1967, since practiced in Keokuk; sr. partner firm Frazier and Hoffman, after 1967; now sr. partner firm James P. Hoffman. Lee County atty., 1973-74. Chmn. bd. HRW, Ltd.; dir. KEOWA Broadcasting, Inc. Co-Chmn. Am. Citizenship Program, 1969—; chmn. legal div. United Fund, 1968-72. Bd. dirs. Keokuk Art Center, Lee County Assn. Retarded Children, 1972, Vis. Nurses Assn., 1968-71. Mem. Iowa, Lee County bar assns., Am. Judicature Soc., Am. Trial Lawyers Assn., Jaycees (pres. 1971). Democrat. Club: Keokuk Country (pres. 1973—), Am. Inst. Hypnosis, Ill. Trial Lawyers Assn., Iowa Trial Lawyers Assn., Iowa Inst. Hypnosis (pres.). Home: Middle Rd Keokuk IA 52632 Office: Middle Rd Keokuk IA 52632-1066

HOFFMAN, JAMES SIMON, engineering educator; b. St. Paul, April 2, 1933; s. Simon J. and Agnes M. (Lammers) H.; m. Marilyn A. Zink, June 17, 1955; children—Stephen J., Gregg A., Ann Marie, Paul D. B.C.E., N.D. State U., 1955. Engr. Iowa Hwy. Commn., Ames, 1955-58, programmer, 1958-60, dir. data processing, 1960-67; systems engr. IBM, Austin, Tex., 1967-72, mktg. rep., Chgo., 1972-74, sr. instr., 1974—. Served to capt. U.S. Army, 1955-64. Mem. Phi Kappa Phi, Tau Beta Phi. Roman Catholic. Lodge: K.C. (grand knight 1966-67). Avocation: photography. Office: IBM One IBM Plaza Chicago IL 60611

HOFFMAN, JOHN HARRY, lawyer, accountant; b. Chgo., June 18, 1913; s. Dave and Rose (Gewirtzman) H.; J.D., John Marshall Law Sch., 1938; m. Gwen Zollo, Dec. 30, 1949; children—Alana Sue Glickson, Edward Jay, Gayle Beth Hoffman Olsen. Bar: Ill. 1938, U.S. Supreme Ct. 1956. Practice law, Chgo., 1938—; propr. John H. Hoffman & Co., 1952—, ptnr., 1966—; pres. John H. Hoffman, P.C., 1972. C.P.A., Ill. Mem. Am., Ill., Chgo. bar assns., Decalogue Soc., Am. Inst. C.P.A.s, Ill. Soc. C.P.A.s. Clubs: Covenant (Chgo.); Twin Orchard Country. Lodges: Masons (32d degree), Shriners, B'nai B'rith. Office: 221 N LaSalle St Chicago IL 60601

HOFFMAN, LORRIE LAWRENCE, airline computer analyst; b. Chgo., July 3, 1952; d. Richard Owen and Esther (May) Lawrence; m. Kevin Lynn Hoffman, May 24, 1975. B.S., Western Ill. U., 1973; M.S., U. Ill., 1975; M.S., U. Iowa, 1980, Ph.D., 1981. Instr. bus. stats. Western Ill. U., 1976-78; systems analyst Trans World Airlines, Kansas City, Mo., 1981-83; design analyst United Airlines, Chgo., 1983—. HEW Spirit grantee, 1977. Mem. Am. Statis. Assn. Avocation: travel. Home: 1509 S Redwood Ave Mount Prospect IL 60056 Office: United Airlines Dept EXOKC PO Box 66100 Chicago IL 60666

HOFFMAN, MARK LESLIE, lawyer, film maker; b. Cleve., Jan. 12, 1952; s. Nathan Norman and Sally (Coleman) H. B.A. with spl. honors, George Washington U., 1973; J.D., Case Western Res. U., 1976, Ph.D., 1978. Bar: Ohio 1976, D.C. 1978, U.S. Dist. Ct. (no. dist.) Ohio 1976, U.S. Tax Ct. 1979, U.S. Ct. Appeals (6th cir.) 1981, U.S. Supreme Ct. 1981. Assoc. Hoffman & Foote, Shaker Heights, Ohio, 1976-83, ptnr., 1983—; pres. Advocate Films, Inc. Shaker Heights, 1978—; acting judge Cleveland Heights Mcpl. Ct., Ohio, 1983—. Mem. Assn. Trial Lawyers Am. (sustaining), Ohio State Bar Assn., Greater Cleve. Bar Assn., Ohio Acad. Trial Lawyers, Cleve. Acad. Trial Lawyers. Office: Hoffman & Foote 20133 Farnsleigh Rd Shaker Heights OH 44122

HOFFMAN, MARY CATHERINE, nurse anesthetist; b. Winamac, Ind., July 14, 1923; d. Harmon William Whitney and Dessie Maude (Neely) H.; R.N., Methodist Hosp., Indpls., 1945; cert. obstet. analgesia and anesthesia, Johns Hopkins Hosp., 1949, grad. U. Hosp. of Cleve. Sch. Anesthesia, 1952; Staff nurse Meth. Hosp., 1945-49; research asst., then staff anesthetist Johns Hopkins Hosp., 1949-62; staff anesthetist Meth. Hosp., 1962-64, U. Chgo. Hosps., 1964-66; chief nurse anesthetist Paris (Ill.) Community Hosp., 1966-80; staff anesthetist Hendricks County Hosp., Danville, Ind., Ball Meml. Hosp., Muncie, Ind., 1981—; instr.-trainer CPR, 1975-81; mem. Terr. 08 CPR Coordinating Com., 1975-80. Mem. Am. Assn. Nurse Anesthetists, Am. Heart Assn., Ind. Fedn. Bus. and Profl. Women's Clubs (Ill. dist. chmn. 1977-78, state found. chmn. 1978-79; found. award 1979). Republican. Presbyterian. Home: 1700 N Maddox Dr Muncie IN 47304 Office: Ball Meml Hosp 2401 University Ave Muncie IN 47303

HOFFMAN, MARY MARGARET (PEG), university administrator, home economist; b. Pontiac, Ill., Oct. 4, 1931; d. Louis M. and Veronica M. (Winslow) H. B.S., Ill. State U., 1953; M.S., Purdue U., 1962. Home econs. tchr., Herscher, Ill., 1953-54, 55-59, Sycamore, Ill., 1957-60; county home econs. adv. U. Ill.-Urbana, 1960-62, state 4-H specialist internat. programs, 1962-69, asst. program leader spl. programs, 1969-72, spl. programs instr., 1972-78, regional dir. Coop. Extension Service, 1978—. Author teaching aids and pamphlets. Organist, St. Anne Roman Catholic Ch., Dixon, Ill., 1984—. Mem. Ill. Home Econs. Assn. (pres. 1981-82; Outstanding Home Economist 1984), Am. Home Econs. Assn. (v.p. internal relations 1983-85), Ill. IFYE Assn. (pres. 1957), AAUW, Am. Bus. Women's Assn., Gamma Sigma Delta, Omicron Nu, Kappa Omicron Phi. Avocations: music; sewing; reading. Office: U Ill Coop Extension Service 140 S Peoria Ave Dixon IL 61021

HOFFMAN, PAUL ALLEN, optometrist; b. Covington, Ky., Nov. 7, 1949; s. Roger Owen and Shirley Louise (Tieman) H.; m. Andrea Lee Engle, Sept. 8, 1973; children—Wendy, Jody, Douglas. B.S., Ohio State U., 1972, O.D., 1974. Pvt. practice optometry, Zanesville, Ohio, 1977—; clinic cons. Ohio State U. Coll. Optometry, Columbus, 1977-79. Profl. div. co-chmn. United Way, Zanesville, Ohio, 1982. Served to lt. USN, 1974-77. Mem. Am. Optometric Assn., Ohio Optometric Assn., Mideastern Ohio Optometric Assn. (lt. gov. 1983-85), Zanesville Jaycees. Club: Lions (pres. 1980-81). Avocations: bowling, soccer, volleyball, gardening. Home: 3230 Lakewood Dr Zanesville OH 43701 Office: 2577 Maysville Pike Zanesville OH 43701

HOFFMAN, WILLIAM KENNETH, obstetrician, gynecologist; b. Milw., Jan. 18, 1924; s. William Richard and Marian (Riegler) H.; student U. Wis., 1942-43; student U. Pa., 1943-44, postgrad, 1954-55; M.D., Marquette U., 1947; m. Peggy Folsom, July 28, 1952; children—Janet Susan, Ann Elizabeth. Intern, Columbia Hosp., 1947-48, resident in obstetrics and gynecology, 1948-49, mem. staff, 1949—; preceptor R.E. McDonald, M.D., Milw., 1949-50; resident in ob-gyn U. Chgo., 1950-51; practice medicine specializing in ob-gyn, Milw., 1955-74; mem. staff, Columbia Hosp.; dir. health service U. Wis.-Milw., 1974—, cons. Sch. Nursing, 1976-77, clin. assoc. prof., 1979—, vice chmn., mem. instl. rev. bd., 1976—, mem. instl. safety and health com., 1981—, chmn., 1984—. Mem. Am. Coll. Ob-Gyn, Am. Coll. Health Assn., Am. Coll. Sports Medicine, Milw. Acad. Medicine, N.Y. Acad. Scis., Royal Soc. Medicine, Am. Cancer Soc. (public edn. com. Milw. div., bd. dirs. 1983—). Home: 4629 N Murray Ave Milwaukee WI 53211

HOFMAN, CORNELIUS ADRIANUS, economics educator; b. Rotterdam, Netherlands, Aug. 4, 1932; came to U.S., 1937, naturalized, 1946; s. John Betting and Klazina (Kome) H.; m. Elaine Venna Davis, Dec. 14, 1956; children—Catherina Venna, John Betting, Casie Elaine, Cornelius Adrianus II. B.S. in Econs., U. Utah, 1957, Ph.D., 1964. Teaching asst. U. Utah, Salt Lake City, 1958-60; from instr. to asst. prof. econs. Idaho State U., Pocatello, 1960-65, assoc. prof., 1969-70, prof., 1970—, acting chmn. dept. econs., 1962-63, chmn., 1974—, acting assoc. dean Coll. Liberal Arts, 1974-75; assoc. prof. Utah State U., Logan, 1965-67; assoc. prof. Middle Tenn. State U., Murfreesboro, 1967-69, chmn. dept. econs., 1967-69; cons. revenue and taxation com. Idaho State Legislature, 1963, 65; mem. market research team R.I.T.A. Project, Rio Grande del Norte, Brazil for AID, owner, developer Gen. Econ. Cons., 1970—, co-ptnr., 1976—; cons. on income taxation Gov. of Idaho, 1971, cons. on property taxation, 1972, advisor on implementation of one percent initiative, 1978; research reporter Joint Fin.-Appropriations Com., Idaho, 1971, 1973; econ. research cons. Idaho State Dept. Edn., 1977-78, Gov.'s Tax Force on Taxation; invited speaker Annual Conf., Idaho Pub. Health Assn. Editor: Rendezvous, Journal of Arts and Letters, 1970-73. Contbr. articles and reports to profl. publs. Served with USAF, 1950-51. Mem. Am. Econ. Assn., Nat. Tax Assn. (standing com. 1969-72, 1977-80), Western Econ. Assn., Idaho Council on Econ. Edn., Beta Gamma Sigma.

HOFMAN, LEONARD J., clergyman. Stated clk. Christian Reformed Ch. N.Am., Grand Rapids, Mich. Office: Christian Reformed Ch NAm 2850 Kalamazoo Ave SE Grand Rapids MI 49560*

HOFMEISTER, BARBARA JEAN, practical nursing school administrator, home health agency executive; b. Bay City, Mich., Dec. 4, 1947; d. Alfred and Eleanor Augusta (Bublitz) Dinsmore; m. John Earl Hofmeister, Feb. 14, 1970 (div. July 1982); 1 child, Heidi Joy. Diploma Grace Hosp. Sch. Nursing, 1969; B.S., Central Mich. U., 1976; M.S., U. Detroit, 1978. Staff nurse Children's Hosp., Detroit, 1969-70, Oakwood Hosp., Dearborn Mich., 1969-70, St. Luke's Hosp., Saginaw, 1972-73; charge nurse Saginaw Gen. Hosp., 1970-72; instr. practical nursing Bay City Practical Nurse Ctr., Mich., 1973-78, dir., 1979—; instr. allied health Delta Coll., University Ctr., Mich., 1978-79; instr. med.-surg., team leading nursing Mid-Mich. Community Coll., Harrison, 1979. Juvenile probation officer Vol. Action, Bay City, 1977-79. Mem. Am. Nurses Assn. (bd. dirs. 1984—), Nat. League for Nursing, Mich. League for Nursing (bd. dirs. 1983—), Am. Heart Assn. (recording sec. 1983—), Bay City Assn. Sch. Adminstrs., Ladies Aid Soc. St. James Lutheran Ch., Altar Guild, Women's Aux. Home Builders Assn. Bay County. Republican. Lodges: North Eastern Rosarian Soc. (pres. 1983—), Zonta Internat. Avocations: rose culture; swimming; cross-country skiing; reading; sewing. Office: 312 S DeWitt St Bay City MI 48706

HOFRICHTER, DAVID ALAN, international management consulting firm executive; b. Lakewood, Ohio, July 10, 1948; s. David Christian and Virginia Amelia (Rickley) H.; m. Carol Ann Rybak, May 15, 1971; children—Kristin Ann, Matthew David. B.A., Baldwin-Wallace Coll., 1970; M.A., Duquesne U., 1972, Ph.D., 1976. Assoc., Hay Assocs., Pitts., 1977-78, prin., 1978-80, dir. orgn. and manpower services, 1980-81, gen. mgr., Cin., 1981—, ptnr., gen. mgr., 1983-85, v.p., gen. mgr., 1985—. Mem. Am. Psychol. Assn., Am. Soc. Cons. Mgmt. Engrs., Pa. Psychol. Assn. Republican. Roman Catholic. Home: 11660 Cedarview Dr Cincinnati OH 45242 Office: 425 Walnut St Suite 2110 Cincinnati OH 45202

HOFSTAD, RALPH PARKER, agricultural cooperative executive; b. Phila., Nov. 14, 1923; s. Ottar and Amelia (Davis) H.; student Hamline U., 1942-43, Gustavus Adolphus Coll., 1943-44, Northwestern U., 1944, U. Minn., 1946-47; B.B.A., Northwestern U., 1948; m. Adeline Smedstad, June 14, 1947; children—Diane (Mrs. Roger Dunker), Barbara (Mrs. Dan McClanahan), James, Ron, Tom, Susan. Accountant F S Services, Bloomington, Ill., 1948-51, mgmt. ops., 1953-65; pres. Farmers Regional Coop (Felco), Ft. Dodge, Iowa, 1965-70; sr. v.p. Agrl. Services, Land O' Lakes Inc., Ft. Dodge, 1970—, pres. Land O' Lakes Inc., Mpls., 1974—; dir. Hon Industries, Muscatine, Iowa, Control Data Corp., Mpls., United Central Bancshares, Des Moines. Bd. dirs. Nat. Council Farmer Coops., Washington, 1973—, Goodwill Industries Am., 1977—; trustee Hamline U., St. Paul, U. Minn. Found., St. Paul. Served with USNR, 1943-46. Mem. Grocery Mfrs. Am. (dir. 1983—). Methodist. Home: 8621 Basswood Rd Eden Prairie MN 55344 Office: Land O'Lakes Inc PO Box 116 Minneapolis MN 55440

HOGAN, ARTHUR MUIR, retailing consultant; b. Kansas City, Mo., Feb. 16, 1949; s. Arthur Muir and Ruth Madeline (Jordan) H.; m. Sharon Kay Sondergaard, June 20, 1981. A.B., William Jewell Coll., 1971; postgrad. U. Nebr., 1985. Vol. Am. Peace Corps, Bihar, India, 1971-72; asst. mgr. K-Mart Corp., 1972-83, store mgr., 1978-83; dir. retail ops. H. W. Mangelsen & Sons, Omaha, 1983-84, dir. sales, 1984-85; gen. mgr. Grandmother's Restraunts, Omaha, 1985—; cons. Retailers' Cons. Services, Omaha, 1985—. Dir. South Locust Bus. Improvement Bd., Grand Island, Nebr., 1980. Recipient Spl. Recognition award NASA, Warrensburg, Mo., 1967, Master Retailers award K-Mart Corp., Grand Island, 1980. Mem. Am. Mgmt. Assn., Omaha C. of C. Republican. Methodist. Club: Cosmopolitan Internat. (Omaha). Avocations: golf; fishing; gardening; music. Home: 820 S 90th St Omaha NE 68114

HOGAN, MARK JAMES, clinical pharmacist, pharmaceutical firm executive; b. Bloomington, Ill., July 2, 1956; s. James F. and Evelyn H.; m. Denise M. Deluca, May 4, 1984. B.S. in Pharmacy, St. Louis Coll. Pharmacy, 1979; Pharm.D., U. Cin., 1981. Registered pharmacist Ohio, Mich., Mo. Resident Univ. Cin. Hosps., 1979-81; clin. coordinator Harper-Grace Hosps., Detroit, 1981-82, asst. corp. dir., 1982-84; mgr. research and devel. Profl. Drug Systems, St. Louis, 1984—; adj. asst. prof. Wayne State U. 1982-84; computer cons. MegaSource, Detroit, 1983-84; staff cons. dept. medicine Faith Hosp., St. Louis, 1984—. Assoc. editor: Evaluations of Drug Interactions, 1985; author, editor company and hosp. publs. Contbr. chpts. in books, columns to profl. publs. Instr. basic life support Am. Heart Assn., 1978-82. Recipient Upjohn Pharmacy Achievement award St. Louis Coll. Pharmacy, 1979, Mckesson Robbins award, 1979; cert. of recognition Student Am. Pharm. Assn., 1979. Mem. Am. Pharm. Assn., Am. Soc. Hosp. Pharmacists, Mensa, Rho Chi. Office: Profl Drug Systems 2388 Schuetz Rd St Louis MO 63146

HOGER, DAVID EDWIN, manufacturing company executive; b. Paw Paw, Mich., Oct. 31, 1936; s. Wayne Edwin and Harriet Jane (Wiersba) H.; m. Phyllis Joan Johnson, Aug., 1956 (div. Feb. 1972); children—Bradley Jon, Wendy Sue; m. Sandra Jayne Ignatz, Mar. 23, 1972; children—Jill Marie, Heather Leigh. Student Western Mich. U., Kalamazoo Coll. Prodn. mgr. A. F. Murch Corp., Paw Paw, Mich., 1965-70; gen. mgr. Jessco Inc., Dowagiac, Mich., 1970-72; plant mgr. Richardson Homes, Waco, Tex., 1972-75; gen. mgr., v.p. Jessco, Inc., Dowagiac, 1975—; group v.p. Jessco div. Rospatch Corp., 1980—; v.p. Tiffin Enterprise subs. Rospatch Corp., Tiffin, Ohio, 1984—. Trustee Village of Paw Paw, Mich., 1964-69, pres., 1969-71; supr. Silver Creek Twp., Dowagiac, 1978-81; trustee, pres., sec. Dowagiac Union Sch. Dist., 1981—; bd. dirs. Cass County United Way, 1981—. Republican. Methodist. Lodges: Lions (treas. Paw Paw 1965), Rotary. Avocations: fishing; wood working. Home: 514 Green St Dowagiac MI 49047 Office: Jessco Div Rospatch Corp 202 Spaulding St Dowagiac MI 49047

HOGINS, MILDRED HOLDAR, medical technologist; b. Russelville, Ark., Jan. 18, 1939; d. Luther and Francess Eythl (Briscoe) Holdar; cert. in med. tech. Hillcrest Med. Center, Tulsa, 1963; B.S. in Biology, U. Mo., Kansas City, 1969; M.A. in Mgmt. and Supervision, Central Mich. U., 1976; m. Albert A Gumbs, Jr.; 1 son by previous marriage, Mark H. Med. technologist St. Joseph Hosp., Tucson, 1964-66; bacteriologist Providence Hosp., Anchorage, Alaska, 1966-67; med. technologist St. Margaret Hosp., Kansas City, Kans., 1967-68, Providence Hosp., Kansas City, Kans., 1969-71; edn. coordinator Sch. Med. Tech., also asst. chief med. technologist Providence-St. Margaret Health Center, Kansas City, Kans., 1971-76, chief med. technologist, 1976—. Bd. dirs. Mill Creek Run Home Owners Assn., 1979-82, 85—, Plaza Acad., Kansas City, Mo., 1982-84. Mem. Clin. Lab. Mgrs. Assn. (bd. dirs. Kansas city chpt. 1985—), Am. Soc. Microbiology, Nat. Assn. Female Execs., Am. Soc. Clin. Pathologists, Kans. Soc. Med. Tech. (conv. chmn. 1975), Greater Kansas City Soc. Med. Tech. (treas. 1980), U. Mo. Kansas City Alumni Assn., Central Mich. U. Alumni Assn., AAUW, Mensa (bd. dirs. Mid-Am. 1983—). Home: 14076 W 88th Terr Lenexa KS 66215 Office: 8929 Parallel Pkwy Kansas City KS 66112

HOHENDORF, ROBERT ARTHUR, optometrist; b. Grand Rapids, Mich., Aug. 8, 1948; s. Harold C. and Francis Loraine (Judson) H.; m. Susan L. Hackett, Oct. 25, 1969; children—Chad William, Jenni Loraine. O.D., Ill. Coll. Optometry, Chgo., 1975. Pvt. practice optometry, Grand Rapids, Mich., 1975—; cons. Lowell Sch. Dist., Mich., 1979-81, Kent County Head Start, Grand Rapids, Mich., 1984—; assoc. state dir. Optometric Extension Program, 1982, Coll. Optometrists in Vision Devel., 1982. Cons. editor Internat. Corr. Soc. Optometrists, 1980-82; corr. editor Visual Perspective, 1981. Bd. dirs. Assn. for Blind, Grand Rapids, Mich., 1978-80; enucleist Mich. Eye Bank, Grand Rapids, 1983—. Served with U.S. Army, 1969-71. Mem. Am. Optometric Assn., Mich. Optometric Assn. (co-chmn. 1982—), Western Mich. Optometric Assn. (pres. 1977-80, sec. 1984-85), Am. Legion. Republican. Roman Catholic. Lodge: Lions (pres.). Avocations: philately, HO trains, gardening. Home: 3977 Maple St SW Grandville MI 49418 Office: South Kent Profl Bldg 4364 S Division St Grand Rapids MI 49508

HOHENSTEIN, ALAN RAYMOND, appraisal and valuation consultant; b. Mpls., Nov. 11, 1936; s. Gilbert Wyle and Alice Ann (Delaney) H.; m. Shirley Dianne Culton, Apr. 4, 1970 (div. 1980); children—Jeffrey Owen, Steven Francis. Student St. Cloud State U., 1955-59. Exec. v.p. Premium Corp., Mpls., 1965; v.p. fin. D.I. Leasing Corp., Mpls., 1968-70; asst. investment mgr. Prudential Ins. Co., 1971-73; v.p. Affiliated Leasing Corp., Madison, Wis., 1973-74; regional v.p. Marshall and Stevens, Inc., Mpls., 1975—; v.p. Affiliated Leasing Corp., Madison, Wis., 1973-74. Spl. advisor U.S. Congl. Adv. Bd. Served with U.S. Army, 1959-61. Mem. Nat. Assn. Accts. Episcopalian. Club: Wayzata Yacht. Home: 5104 W 70th St Edina MN 55435 Office: 12 S 6th St Suite 930 Minneapolis MN 55402

HOHENSTEIN, JAMES BRYAN, architect, graphic designer; b. Lincoln, Nebr., Aug. 7, 1948; s. William Nels and Lillian Sarah (Hunt) H.; B.Arch., U. Nebr. at Lincoln, 1972; m. Donna Rae Gruenemeier, Dec. 27, 1969; children—Heather Suzanne, James Bryan. Design architect Reynolds, Smith & Hills, Tampa, Fla., 1972-73, Bahr, Hanna, Vermeer & Haecker, Omaha, 1973-75, Henningson, Durham & Richardson, Omaha, 1975-81; head designer med. architecture Kirkham & Michael Assos., 1981-84; design mgr. Henningson Durham & Richardson, Omaha, 1984—; contbg. illustrator The Landmark mag.; partner Hohenstein-Dance Studio, graphic and photographic design. Recipient Asso. Arts award AIA, 1976. Mem. Nebr. Soc., AIA. Club: Ak-Sar-Ben.

HOJNACKI, JOHN CHARLES, county data processing official; b. Toledo, Ohio, July 18, 1951; s. Stanley Joseph and Kathleen Anne (Flaherty) H.; m. Jill Joanne Wolf, July 30, 1982. Assoc., Owens Tech. Coll., 1979. Sr. operator Nat. Family Opinion, Toledo, Ohio, 1978-79; programmer analyst Lucas County Data Processing, Toledo, 1979-82, dir., 1982—; mem. steering com. N.W. Ohio Regional Users Group, Toledo, 1984—. Served with USCG, 1970-74. Mem. Am. Mgmt. Assn. Democrat. Roman Catholic. Avocations: running, scuba diving. Office: Lucas County Data Processing Ctr 1 Government Ctr Toledo OH 43604-2243

HOJNACKI, MICHAEL JOHN, advertising agency executive; b. Chgo., May 13, 1950; s. Matthew F. and Genevieve (Blaszak) H.; m. Marisue Scafidi, Aug. 14, 1971. B.F.A., Sch. of Art Inst. Chgo., 1973; student U. Ill., 1968-70. Owner, The Natural Union, Union Pier, Mich., 1975, Rainbow Gardens, Bridgman, Mich., 1976; v.p., corp. mgr. Sawyer Products (Mich.), 1977; pres. Artistic Energy Group/Madmoney, Union Pier, 1979—. Mem. Soc. Mfg. Engrs., Harbor County C. of C. Democrat. Roman Catholic. Address: 9843 Greenwood Ave PO Box 191 Union Pier MI 49129

HOJNACKI, WILLIAM PAUL, university administrator, political scientist, public and environmental affairs educator; b. South Bend, Ind., May 17, 1942; s. Henry Joseph and Helen Ethel (Bryant) H.; m. Sandra Kenney, June 17, 1967; children—Philip, Elaine. B.S. in Polit. Sci., Western Mich. U., 1966; M.A. in Govt. and Internat. Relations, U. Notre Dame, 1970, Ph.D. in Govt. and Internat. Relations, 1977. Tchr. South Bend Community Schs., 1966-68; asst. dir. South Bend Human Rights Com., 1968-69; dir. field service U.S. Congressman J. Brademas, Ind., 1970-74; dir. Dept. Human Services and Econ. Devel., City of South Bend, 1974-76; dir. Govt. Affairs Nat. Ctr. Law and Handicapped, South Bend, 1976-77; faculty Ind. U.-South Bend, 1977—, dir. Sch. Pub. and Environ. Affairs, 1983—; dir. Mich. Urban Obs., Ind. U., 1980-83. Editor: Politics and Pub. Policy in Indiana, 1983. Candidate for Ind. Ho. of Reps. from St. Joseph County, 1970; pres. Vol. Action Ctr., St. Joseph County, 1980; chmn. edn. div. United Way Campaign, St. Joseph County, 1983. Internat. Inst. Pub. Mgmt. fellow, Nigeria, 1982; Ind. U., U.S. Dept. Transp. Research grantee, 1978-84. Mem. Ind. Polit. Sci. Assn. (bd. dirs. 1982-85), Ind. Acad. Social Sci. (bd. dirs. 1980-83), Am. Soc. Pub. Adminstrn., Am. Polit. Sci. Assn., Urban Affairs Assn., Polish Bus. and Profl. Assn. Avocations: fishing, cooking, hiking. Office: Ind U 1700 Mishawaka Ave South Bend IN 46634

HOLAN, DAVID H., service company executive; b. Burlington, Vt., Aug. 26, 1943; s. Arnold and Irene (Carter) H.; student Tarkio Coll., Loyola U., 1961-63; m. Hildene King, Dec. 29, 1964; children—Jodi Lynn, Scott Harold. Pres., Crystal Tips of No. Ill., Chgo., 1974—, Iceman's Ice Co., 1976—, Crystal Tips of Ill., Inc., 1981—; pres. Sani-Serv of Ill., Ice Dispensers, Inc., 1981—, David Holan & Co., Inc., 1982—; v.p. Charter Beer of Am., 1973-81, 1140 Corp., 1978-81, Charter Imports, 1979—; pres. Phoenix Vending Co., 1983—, Blue Island Distbrs., Inc., 1983—. Mem. scholarship screening com. Nat. Italian Am. Sports Hall of Fame, 1983; bd. dirs. Tarkio Coll.; mem. Ill. Commn. for Econ. Devel.; treas. Epilepsy Found. Am. Mem. Associated Beer Distbrs. Ill. (trustee ins. and service bd. 1981—). Contbr. articles to profl. publs. Office: 9126 Medill Franklin Park IL

HOLBROOK, LANNY ROBERT, lawyer, investor; b. Covington, Ky., Oct. 1, 1946; s. Raymond and Marcella (Hilgefort) H.; m. Nancy Ann Kummler, Nov. 6, 1971; children—Jebedia, Zachary. B.A., Thomas More Coll., 1968; J.D., U. Cin., 1971. Bar: Ohio. Assoc., Keating, Muething & Klekamp, Cin., 1971-81; sole practice, Cin., 1981—. Contbr. articles to profl. jours. Chmn. Kenton County Democratic Com., 1980; campaign chmn. John Y. Brown for Gov., Ky., 1979; chmn. Ky. Workers' Compensation Bd., Lexington, 1983—. Served with USNR. Mem. Cin. Bar Assn., Kenton County Bar Assn., Ohio State Bar Assn. Roman Catholic. Avocations: golf; basketball; politics. Office: Lanny R Holbrook & Assocs 1 E 4th St 16th Floor Cincinnati OH 45202

HOLCOMB, DAVID NELSON, food company executive, chemist; b. Sioux City, Iowa, Sept. 12, 1936; s. Hollis Nelson and Kathryn June (Bieg) H.; m. Doris Marie Kenner, May 1, 1965; children—Timothy D., Mark D., Samuel D., Kathryn M. B.S., U. Nebr., 1958; Ph.D., U. Ill., 1962; M.B.A., Roosevelt U., 1977. Postdoctoral fellow U. Calif.-Berkeley, 1962-64; research scientist U.S. Dept. Agr., Phila., 1964-66; with Kraft, Inc. Research and Devel., Glenview, Ill., 1966—, group leader phys. chemistry, 1970-80, mgr. basic food sci. lab., 1980—; adj. prof. bus. Roosevelt U., Chgo., 1978—; adj. prof. chemistry Ill. Inst. Tech., Chgo., 1984—. Editor: Studies of Food Microstructure, 1981; Food Microstructure Jour., 1982—. Mem. adv. bd. Truman Coll., Chgo., 1982-84; precinct capt. Maine-Niles Twp. Republican Orgns. (Ill.), 1966—; bd. dirs. Ill. J.E.T.S., Champaign, 1983-84. Regents scholar U. Nebr., 1958-60; NSF fellow, 1962-64. Mem. AAAS, Am. Chem. Soc., Chgo. Chemists Club (pres. 1983-84), Am. Oil Chemists Soc. (co-chmn. short courses 1982—), Inst. Food Tech. Republican. Lutheran. Avocation: dealing in used books. Home: 8615 Callie Ave Morton Grove IL 60053 Office: Kraft Inc Research & Devel 801 Waukegan Rd Glenview IL 60025

HOLDEMAN, ROBERT LEWIS, II, architect, artist; b. Elkhart, Ind., June 11, 1941; s. Robert Lewis and Saritea (Lorenz) H.; m. Jane Day, Aug. 22, 1964; children—Robert Scott, John Edward. B.S. in Architecture, U. Cin., 1965. Assoc., Field, Graheck, Bell & Kline, Traverse City, Mich., 1965-70, David L. Stiffler, Traverse City, 1970-75; prin. Architecture/Artistry/Interiors Inc., Traverse City, 1975—; ptnr. Welch, Holdeman Studio (stained glass). Mem. AIA, Mich. Soc. Architects, Mich. Soc. Artists and Craftsmen, Internat. Soc. Artists. Methodist. Creator stained glass windows: St. Francis Church, TBA Credit Unions, Hagerty Ins. Agy. (all Traverse City), many residences; bronze sculpture, Munson Med. Center. Home: 2629 Nelson Rd Traverse City MI 49684 Office: 924 E 8th St Traverse City MI 49684

HOLDER, BILLY GENE, telephone engineer; b. Braymer, Mo., Nov. 3, 1946; s. Oral Eugene and Ruby Lee (McBee) H.; m. Marlys Kay Hilyard, Sept. 13, 1973; children—Brian, Tonya, Scott. Student, Kans. State Coll., Pittsburg, 1964-67, Rockhurst Coll., Kansas City, Mo., 1971-72. With Southwestern Bell, Kansas City, Mo., 1966—, telephone engr., 1969—. Alderman City of Belton, Mo., 1975-77, mayor, 1977-81; mem. Belton Sch. Bd., 1981-84, pres., 1984—. Served with USNG, 1966-72. Mem. Soc. Telephone Engrs., Belton C. of C. (Pub. Service award 1980), Little Blue Sewer Dist. (bd. dirs. 1977-81), Mo. Mcpl. League (bd. dirs. West Gate chpt. 1981), Cass County League Cities (v.p. 1980-81), Am. Legion. Methodist. Avocations: fishing; golf. Home: 1105 S Cleveland St Belton MO 64012 Office: Southwestern Bell Telephone 1101 McGee Room 522 Kansas City MO 64106

HOLDT, ROY HOWARD, manufacturing executive; b. Edgewood, Md., Nov. 19, 1920; s. Jacob S. and Francis (Hansen) H.; student Dyke Bus. Coll., 1941, Cleve. State U., 1947; children—Linda Holdt Greene, Douglas M. With Lake Erie Chem. Co., Cleve., 1938-40, Apex Elec. Mfg. Co., 1941-56; div. controller White Consol. Industries, Inc., Cleve., 1956-58, corp. controller, 1958-61, v.p., controller, 1961-64, v.p. fin., 1964-67, sr. v.p., 1967-69, exec. v.p., dir., 1969-72, pres., chief operating officer, 1972-76, chmn., chief exec. officer, 1976—; dir. Ameritrust Co., Cleve. Electric Illuminating Co., Email Ltd., Midland Ross Corp., LTV Corp. Mem. bd. Fairview Gen. Hosp., Cleve. State U. Devel. Found., Cleve. Found., Playhouse Sq. Found.; trustee Dyke Coll. Served with AUS, 1942-45. Mem. Greater Cleve. Growth Assn. (dir.). Clubs: Pepper Pike (Ohio); Ohio State U. Presidents; Westwood Country; Clevelander, Cleve. Atheletic, Mid-Day, The 50, Clifton, Country, Union (Cleve.); Duquesne (Pitts.). Office: White Consol Industries 11770 Berea Rd Cleveland OH 44111

HOLE, FLOYD MARVIN, vocational education educator; b. Crawfordsville, Ind., Feb. 14, 1935; s. Virgil Wesley and Lucy Fern (Weikel) H.; B.S., No. Ariz. U., 1957, M.S. in Biology, 1964; Ed.D., Ariz. State U., 1968; Ed.S., U. No. Colo., 1981; m. Wanda Ruth Clements, Jan. 25, 1957; children—Marva Ruth, Carl Earl, Zetta Chesney. Med. lab., x-ray technologist Flagstaff (Ariz.) Hosp., 1961-63; med., surg. lab. equipment salesman Southwestern Surg. Supply, Phoenix, 1964-66; dir. edn. Am. Protestant Hosp. Assn., Chgo., 1970-71; asst. prof. edn. Idaho State Univ., Pocatello, 1972-74; asst. adminstrv. dean Ill. Valley Community Coll., Oglesby, 1968-69; asst. prof. vocat. edn. Pa. State U., State College, 1975-78; lectr. adult edn., health occupations edn. and vocat. edn., dept. adminstrv. leadership U. Wis.-Milw., 1978—. Sec., treas. Townjacks, 1961-63; dir. Ariz. All-Stars, 1961-63. Served with U.S. Army, 1957-59. Recipient Leadership award Adult Edn. Assn. U.S.A. 1978; Leadership award Assn. Health Occupations Tchr. Educators, 1979, 80, 81, 82. Mem. Assn. Health Occupations Tchr. Educators (exec. com., treas.), Commn. Prof. Adult Edn., Am. Assn. Adult and Continuing Edn., Am. Vocat. Assn., Am. Soc. Healthcare Edn. and Tng., Am. Soc. Allied Health Professions, AAAS, Ariz.-Nev. Acad. Sci., Blue Key, Phi Delta Kappa, Beta Beta Beta, Iota Lambda Sigma. Home: 1315 E Elmdale Ct #304 Shorewood WI 53211 Office: 653 Enderis Univ Wis Milwaukee WI 53201

HOLIDAY, HARRY, JR., steel company executive; b. Pitts., July 2, 1923; s. Harry and Charlotte Poe (Rutherford) H.; B.S. in Metall. Engring. with honors, U. Mich., 1949; m. Kathlyn Collins Watson, Sept. 6, 1947; children—Edith Elizabeth, Harry III, Albert Logan II. Spl. assignment metall. engring. adminstrn. Armco Steel Corp., Middletown, Ohio, 1949-55, asst. to supt. blast furnace, Hamilton, Ohio, 1955-57, supt. blast furnace, 1957-59, asst. gen. supt. steel plant, Middletown, 1959-64, gen. supt. steel plant, 1964-66, dir. raw materials, 1966-67, v.p. steel ops., 1967-69, exec. v.p. steel, 1969-74, pres., 1974-79, chief exec. officer, 1979-85, chmn., 1985—, also dir.; dir. Allis-Chalmers Corp., Asarco Corp., Nat. Cash Register. Pres., Middletown YMCA, 1955-58; pres. Moundbuilders Area council Boy Scouts Am., 1963-67. Served to capt. AUS, 1943-46. Mem. Am. Inst. Metall. Engrs. (recipient J.E. Johnson, Jr. Blast Furnace award), Am., Internat. iron and steel insts., Tau Beta Pi, Psi Upsilon. Office: Armco Inc 703 Curtis St Middletown OH 45043*

HOLIGA, LUDOMIL ANDREW, metall. engr.; b. Dayton, Ohio, Dec. 7, 1920; s. Andrew and Antonia Margaret (Sefcek) H.; Engr. asso., Sinclair Coll., 1948; B.Sc., Calgary Coll. Tech., 1974, M.M.E., 1975; m. Aryetta Lillian Mernedakis, Feb. 6, 1960; children—David, Carol, Millard, Timothy, Michael. Engr. designer Wright Patterson AFB, Ohio, 1941-54; contract designer Product Design Services, Inc., Dayton, Ohio, 1955-60; with Dayton Progress Corp., 1961—, dir. corp. devel., 1972-73, dir. research and tech. edn., 1974—. Served with USAAF, 1942-45, AUS, 1951-52. Certified mfg. engr. Mem. Soc. Mfg. Engrs. (chmn. standards com. 1963-72), Ohio Research and Devel. Found., Foremans Club, Am. Metal Stamping Assn. Lutheran. Research on cutting clearances for perforating metals in stamping dies. Home: 2025 Oak Tree Dr E Kettering OH 45440 Office: 500 Progress Rd Dayton OH 45449

HOLLAND, PATRICIA MARCUS, lawyer; b. Pitts., July 29, 1952; d. E. Robert and Betty (Rosenfield) Marcus; m. Joel B. Holland, May 29, 1977. B.A. in History and Polit. Sci., U. Rochester, 1974; J.D., Case Western Res. U., 1977. Summer assoc. Jones, Day, Reavis & Pogue, Cleve., 1976; assoc. Schiff, Hardin & Waite, Chgo., 1977-82; assoc. Benesch, Friedlander, Coplan & Aronoff, Cleve., 1982-84, ptnr., 1984—. Mem. community relations com., strategic planning com., community housing com. Jewish Community Fedn. Cleve., 1984. Mem. ABA, Ohio Bar Assn., Cleve. Bar Assn., Order of Coif. Office: Benesch Friedlander Coplan & Aronoff 850 Euclid Ave Cleveland OH 44114

HOLLAND, ROBERT JAMES, lawyer; b. Dayton, Ohio, Jan. 8, 1936; s. John Edward and Alma Naomi (Himes) H.; m. Barbara Jane Drake, Aug. 27, 1960; children—Robert, Jr., Duncan, Wendolyn, Justin. B.A., Yale U., 1958; J.D., Ohio State Law. Sch., 1963. Bar: Ohio 1963, U.S. Supreme Ct. 1972. Assoc. Chester & Rose, Columbus, 1963-67; gen. counsel Banc Ohio Corp., Columbus, 1967-71; city atty. Upper Arlington, Ohio, 1976—; ptnr. Bodiker & Holland, Columbus, 1971—; gen. counsel Mid-Ohio Regional Planning Commn., Columbus, 1971—; gen. counsel, bd. dirs. Servinat., Inc., N.Y.C., 1976—. Co-author: Ohio Taxation; Truth in Lending, 1969. Mem. Med-Ohio Regional Planning Commn., Columbus, 1970-71; pres., bd. dirs. Central Ohio Transit Authority, Columbus, 1971-74; bd. dirs. Wellington Sch., Columbus, 1979—. Served to lt. USNR, 1958-60. Named to Ten Outstanding Men, Columbus Jaycees, 1970. Mem. ABA, Ohio State Bar Assn., Columbus Bar Assn. (chmn. Law Insts. com. 1968-70, chmn. unauthorized practice 1973-74, mem. ethics com. 1973-77). Clubs: Athletic, Scioto, Internat. Food and Wine Soc. Home: 4837 Slate Run Ct Upper Arlington OH 43220 Office: Bodiker & Holland 150 E Broad St Columbus OH 43215

HOLLAND, W(ILBUR) CHARLES, mathematics educator; b. Parkersburg, W.Va., Feb. 24, 1935; s. Wilbur C(harles) and Ada Irene (Morehead) H.; m. Claudia Octavia Brown, June 1, 1955; children—Eric C., Paul K., Claudia A., Rebecca W., David M. B.S., Tulane U., 1957, M.S., 1959, Ph.D., 1961. NATO fellow U. Tuebingen, W.Ger., 1961-62; instr. U. Chgo., 1962-64; faculty U. Wis., Madison, 1964-72, prof. math., 1971-72; prof. math. Bowling Green State U., Ohio, 1972—, chmn. dept. math., stats., 1981-83; vis. prof. Simon Fraser U., Vancouver, B.C. Can., 1983-84. Contbr. articles to profl. jours. Named Outstanding Tchr., Wis. Student Assn., 1969, Kappa Mu Epsilon-Bowling Green State U., 1975; NSF research grantee, 1964-73. Mem. Am. Math. Soc., Math. Assn. Am., French Assn. for Ordered Algebra (hon.), Phi Beta Kappa (v.p. Bowling Green State U. chpt. 1984). Presbyterian. Avocations: barbershop quartet singing; stamp collecting. Office: Dept Math and Statistics Bowling Green State Univ Bowling Green OH 43403

HOLLANDER, DORIS A., psychologist, consultant, businesswoman; b. St. Louis, Oct. 13, 1941; d. Samuel and Rose (Heller) H.; B.A., Washington U., 1964; M.A. with distinction, DePaul U., 1972; Ph.D., Loyola U., 1979; m. Jerrold Blumoff, June 9, 1963; children—Sam, Rebecca. Caseworker, Mo. Div. Welfare, St. Louis, 1964-65; research asso. Inst. Juvenile Research, Chgo., 1967-68; instr. ednl. psychology Loyola U., Chgo., 1973-74; psychologist, program developer Women's Achievement Program, Hammond, Ind., 1976-78; pres. Whole Food & Grain Depot, Oak Park, Ill., 1972-78; asst. prof. psychology Webster Coll., St. Louis, 1979-83, co-chmn. psychology, sociology and anthropology, dir. adult learner project; pres. New Options, Inc., organizational and career cons., St. Louis, 1983—. Editor Mo. Psychologist, 1984—. Exec. v.p., program chmn. Oak Park Mental Health Bd., 1976-79. Mem. Assn. Community Mental Health Authorities Ill. (del.), Am. Psychol. Assn., Midwest Psychol. Assn., Southeastern Psychol. Assn., Mo. Psychol. Assn. (chmn. women's issues com. 1983-84, sec. 1985-87), St. Louis Network Women Psychologists (coordinator 1982-84), St. Louis Psychol. Assn., Soc. Psychologists in Mgmt., Soc. St. Louis Psychologists (program chmn. 1983-84, pres. 1985—), Am. Ednl. Research Assn., Am. Assn. Counseling and Devel. Home: 6330 Alexander Dr Saint Louis MO 63105 Office: 8600 Delmar Blvd Saint Louis MO 63124

HOLLATZ, EDWIN ARTHUR, communications educator, consultant; b. Chgo., May 31, 1930; s. Edwin Arthur and Charlotte Elvira (Potter) H.; m. Joanne Amabel Simon, Aug. 6, 1960; children—Cheryl Anne, Celia Marie. B.A., Bob Jones U., 1952; M.A., Northwestern U., 1955, Ph.D., 1965. Prof. communications Wheaton Coll., Ill., 1954—, chmn. dept., 1966—; prof. speech Ill. Benedictine Coll., Lisle, Ill., 1969—; vis. prof. speech Trinity Christian Coll., Palos Heights, Ill., 1969-70; cons. Monarch Life Ins. Co., Chgo., 1959-60; TV panelist Nat. Broadcasting Co., Chgo., 1954-60. Author: College Literary Societies, 1965. Contbr. articles on speech and communications to profl. jours. Vice-pres. Friends of Library, Wheaton, Ill., 1955-61. Mem. Speech Communications Assn. Am. Am. Forensic Assn., Ill. Speech Assn. (editor 1960-64), Chgo. Area Forensics Assn. (exec. sec. 1955-64), Pi Kappa Delta (gov. 1966-68, 78-80). Avocations: sailing, gardening, travel. Home: 919 Santa Rosa Wheaton IL 60187 Office: Dept Communications Wheaton Coll Wheaton IL 60187

HOLLENBAUGH, FLORENCE ALMA, nurse, consultant; b. Lakewood, Ohio, Mar. 1, 1929; d. Melvin A. and Dorothy F. (Geiger) Heidloff; m. William J. Hollenbaugh, Feb. 11, 1955 (dec. Apr. 1981); 1 son, William. Student Western Res. U. Sch. Nursing, Cleve., 1946-50; cert. U. So. Calif. Sch. Pub. Adminstrn., 1956; student Harvard Med. Sch., 1977, 79, 81, 83, 84. R.N., Ohio. Head nurse Univ. Hosps., Cleve., 1950; clin. instr. Vis. Nurse Assn., Cleve., 1951-52; police officer, Lakewood, 1954-58; pub. health nurse Medina County (Ohio), 1958-61; inservice educator Lodi (Ohio) Community Hosp., 1961-76; nurse epidemiologist S.W. Gen. Hosp., Middleburg Heights, Ohio, 1976—; guest lectr. Cleve. State U., Kent State U., Baldwin-Wallace Coll. Mem. Army emergency relief com. ARC. Midpark Homeowners Assn. Served to 1st lt. Nurse Corps, U.S. Army, 1952-54. Stuart Pharms. grantee, 1981. Mem. Assn. for Practitioners Infection Control (pres. chpt. 1980, chmn. bd. 1981, 82, nat. adv. com.), Assn. Hosp. Risk Mgrs., Assn. Advancement Med. Instrumentation, Medina County Nurses Assn. (pres.), Pentagon Council Hosp. Inservice Edn. (chmn.), Akron Hosp. Assn. (edn. com.), Am. Soc. Hosp. Engrs., Res. Officers Assn., Am. Legion. Republican. Mem. United Ch. of Christ. Clubs: Women's Fellowship (Middleburg Heights); Lake Erie Sci. Ctr. (Bay Village, Ohio). Contbr. articles to profl. jours. Home: 15264 Hemlock Ln Middleburg Heights OH 44130 Office: Southwest Gen Hosp 18697 E Bagley Rd Middleburg Heights OH 44130

HOLLENHORST, ROBERT WILLIAM, SR., retired physician, ophthalmologist, consultant; b. St. Cloud, Minn., Aug. 12, 1913; s. John and Josephine (Meinz) H.; m. Alice Cecilia Nolan, June 17, 1939; children—Robert W. Jr., Michael J., Mary E., John T., Mark T., James N., Kathleen E., Thomas M., Stephen E. Student, St. Cloud State U., 1931-33, St. John's U., 1933-35; B.S., U. Minn., 1940; M.B., 1940, M.D., 1941, M.S. in Ophthalmology, 1948. Diplomate Am. Bd. Ophthalmology (bd. dirs. 1968-80). Med. and surg. intern Abbott Hosp., Mpls. 1940, Ancker Hosp., St. Paul, Minn., 1940-41; resident in ophthalmology Mayo Clinic, Rochester, Minn., 1946-48, ophthal. cons., 1949-79, ret., 1979; cons. in ophthalmology Minn. State Services for Blind and Visually Handicapped, 1962—. Contbr. over 90 articles to profl. jours. Mem. Am. Acad. Ophthalmology (Guest of Hon. 1980, 1st v.p. 1977), Am. Ophthal. Soc. (v.p., then pres. 1980-82, sec.-treas. 1972-80), Minn. Acad. Ophthalmology and Otolaryngology (pres. 1961-62), Served to maj. M.C., U.S. Army, 1941-46, PTO. Roman Catholic. Avocations: tennis, golf, boating, gourmet cooking. Home: 625 19th St NW Apt 300 Rochester MN 55901 Office: Mayo Clinic Rochester MN 55901

HOLLER, HARRIS WILLIAM, investigative agency executive; b. Drayton, N.D., Oct. 13, 1917; s. William Heinrich and Winifred Viola (Southard) H.; m. Jeanne Anne Bradley, Aug. 15, 1942; children—Michael, Gregory, Bonnie, Byron, Denise, Joseph, John, James. A.A., Mpls. Community Coll., 1981. With Mpls. Police Dept., 1962-82, fingerprint examiner, photographer identification div., 1970-82, lt. investigator, supr. div., 1976-82; pres. Assocs. for Identification, Mpls., 1982—. Served to lt. USNR, 1942-45. Mem. Soaring Soc. Am. (state gov.), Minn. Soaring Club (flight instr. 1960-80), Exptl. Aircraft Assn., Internat. Assn. for Identification. Lodges: Masons, Shriners. Home: 3901 Harriet Ave Minneapolis MN 55409

HOLLEY, JOHN MAYER, printing company executive; b. Denver, July 10, 1913; s. Harold H. and Carolyn (Volk) H.; m. Marguerite Elderkin, Sept. 23, 1949; children—Deborah, John Mayer II. Student indsl. engring. Carnegie Tech. Inst., 1931-35. Founder, pres., chmn. Graphic Forms, Inc., Nevada, Iowa, 1947—. Served to comdr. USN, 1942-45. Mem. Nat. Bus. Forms Assn., Internat. Bus. Forms Industries. Clubs: Rotary, Masons, Shriners. Home: 50 Meadow Ln Nevada IA 50201 Office: PO Box 468 Nevada IA 50201

HOLLIDAY, MARK RANSOM, fire chief; b. Lansing, Mich., Dec. 22, 1930; s. Mark A. and Gladys May (Ransom) H.; m. Anna J. Carmody, May 17, 1952; children—Jeffrey, Debra, Bruce, John. A.A., Lansing Community Coll., 1981. Cert. U.S. Fire Acad.-Arson Investigation. Firefighter, 1955—; with Lansing Fire Dept., 1965—, engr., 1967-72, chief, 1982—; mem. Internat. Assn. Arson Investigation, 1973—. Local developer arson team concept, 1975. Served with U.S. Army, 1951-53. Roman Catholic. Lodge: Kiwanis. Office: Lansing Fire Dept 120 E Shiawassee St Lansing MI 48933

HOLLIS, BRUCE WARREN, experimental nutritionist, industrial consultant; b. Elyria, Ohio, May 29, 1951; s. Warren Eugene and Evelyn Katherine (Jabbusch) H.; m. Betsy Eberle Yount, Aug. 16, 1980. B.S., Ohio State U., 1973, M.S., 1976; Ph.D., U. Guelph, Ont., 1979. Postdoctoral fellow Case Western Res. U., Cleve., 1979-82, asst. prof. nutrition, 1982—. Med. researcher, indsl. cons. Contbr. chpts. to books, articles to sci. jours. Recipient NIH awards, 1980, 82. Mem. Endocrine Soc., Am. Soc. Bone and Mineral Research, Am. Inst. Nutrition, Sigma Xi. Republican. Home: 4931 N Barton Rd North Ridgeville OH 44039 Office: Dept Nutrition Case Western Res U Cleveland OH 44106

HOLLIS, HAROLD BINKLEY, insurance company executive; b. Princeton, Ind., July 18, 1906; s. John S. and Jessie B. (Binkley) H.; B.S., Purdue U., 1928; m. Martha Jane Gehlman, Oct. 15, 1937; children—Richard, John, Barbara Hollis McWalter, Kenneth L. and Nancy J. Hollis Huston (twins). Engr., Ill. Hwy. Dept., Paris, 1928, bridge engr., Springfield, 1931-42; civil engr. Mo. Pacific R.R., Nevada, Mo., 1929; purchasing agt. Remington Rand Co., Springfield, Ill., 1942-45; owner ins. agy., Springfield, 1945-73; pres. Hollis-Neff-Bomke Ins., Inc., Springfield, 1973—; ptnr. Koke Mill Subdiv. Mgr. baseball team Little League, 1952-54, Pony League, Colt League, 1954-56. Clubs: Masons, Shriners, Springfield Purdue Alumni (pres. 1937-38, 41-42, 49-50, 83-84). Home: 1305 Wood Mill Dr Springfield IL 62707 Office: 1001 W Lawrence St Springfield IL 62704

HOLLIS, LUTHER RAY, training instructor, consultant; b. River Rouge, Mich., Dec. 30, 1949; s. Luther and Adel (Jones) H.; m. Debra Fay Devold, Aug. 27, 1969; children—Anthony, Felicia, Cassandra. Student Wayne State U., 1980-82; Assoc. B.A., Highland Park Community Coll., 19—; B. Gen. Studies, Oakland U., 1978. Supr. Fisher Body Fleetwood, Detroit, 1974-75, gen. supr., 1976-77; gen. supr. Fisher Body Pontiac, Mich., 1977-80, supr., Detroit, 1980-83; tng. program instr. assembly div. Gen. Motors, Orion, Pontiac, 1983—; chief cons. D&L Research Mktg., Southfield, Mich., 1983—. Author supr. tng. manual, 1975. Served with USN, 1969-73. Mem. Econ. Club Detroit. Democrat. Baptist. Office: GMAD Orion 4555 Giddings Rd Pontiac MI 48056

HOLLMAN, RICHARD MARTIN, glass company executive; b. Ft. Wayne, Ind., May 19, 1932; s. Harold and Alma F. (Burger) H.; m. Virginia M. Sonne, July 18, 1959; children—Michael, Kathleen, Anne, Robert, Mark, Beth Ann. B.S. in Civil Engring., Valparaiso U., 1954. Engr. City Glass Splty. Inc., Ft. Wayne, 1957-63, v.p., 1963-73, pres. 1973—. Pres. Concordia High Sch., Ft. Wayne, 1979—, Luth. Elem. Sch., Ft. Wayne, 1971-74. Served with U.S. Army, 1955-56. Recipient Stained Glass award Ind. Architects Assn. 1964. Mem. Stained Glass Assn. Am., Ft. Wayne Home Builders Assn., Ft. Wayne Contractors Assn. Lutheran. Lodge: Kiwanis (bd. dirs. 1974-76). Avocation: music. Home: 918 Aylesford Dr Fort Wayne IN 46819 Office: City Glass Speciality Inc 2124 S Calhoun St Fort Wayne IN 46804

HOLLON, TED GEORGE, pension fund administrator, corporate financial officer; b. Los Angeles, Apr. 15, 1949; s. George Odea and Addie Mae (Tallman) H.; m. Pam Deene, Sept. 25, 1969 (div. 1977); m. 2d, Kathryn Joanne Knopps, Sept. 16, 1978; children—Mike George, Nicole Marie. Student Kans. State Coll., 1967-70. Controller, office mgr. Canteen Corp., Kansas City, Mo., St. Louis, Milw., 1970-78; controller, mgr. food service Automatique, Kansas City, 1978-79; asst. adminstrv. mgr. Building Trades Pension Fund, Milw., 1979—; exec. v.p., chief fin. officer Lee Jost and Assocs. Inc., Milw., 1981—, Benefit Plan Adminstrn. of Wis. Inc., Milw., 1981—. Mem. Internat. Found. Employee Benefits. Republican. Roman Catholic. Home: 13065 Marquette New Berlin WI 53151 Office: Benefit Plan Adminstrn 2625 N Mayfair Rd Milwaukee WI 53226

HOLLORAN, CECILIA MUELLER, shoe company executive; advertising educator; b. St. Louis, Dec. 9, 1930; d. Anthony Louis Jungman and Ann Marie (Schnalzer) Jungman Mueller; m. Mark Richard Holloran, July 23, 1959 (div.); children—Michael Stephen Murdoch, Cara Lyn Schlotter, Cecilia Elizabeth. Student, Hadley Tech. Sch., 1949, Mo. U., 1954, Washington U.-St. Louis, 1957-59; B.A., St. Louis U., 1984, cert. mktg., 1985. Pres., House of Holloran, Inc., St. Louis, 1963-65; advt. mgr. Weiss-Neuman Shoe Co., St. Louis, 1965-71; art dir. Venture, St. Louis, 1971-72, Famous-Barr, St. Louis, 1972-80; dir. advt. Boston Stores, Ft. Smith, Ark., 1980-81; dir. advt. Tober Industries, Inc., St. Louis, 1981—; instr. St. Louis Community Coll., 1971-80; cons. Expertise, St. Louis, 1978-80. Author poetry, 1949. Vice-chmn. Democratic Party Nat. Campaign, St. Louis, 1960; hdqrs. mgr. Dem. Party State/Senatorial, St. Louis, 1962; hdqr. mgr. Dem. Party City/Mayoral, St. Louis, 1964; area chmn. Easter Seal Soc.-March of Dimes, St. Louis, 1963-64, 1st prize, 1949. Recipient Restoration/renovation award Dutchtown Assn., 1979, Tower Grove Bank, 1978. Mem. Retail Advt. Conf. (awards 3), Nat. Assn. Female Execs., Internat. Press Assn. Roman Catholic. Clubs: Advt. II, Press (St. Louis). Office: Tober Industries Inc 1520 Washington Ave Saint Louis MO 63103

HOLLOWAY, DONALD PHILLIP, librarian; b. Akron, Ohio, Feb. 18, 1928; s. Harold Shane and Dorothy Gayle (Ryder) H.; B.S. in Commerce, Ohio U., Athens, 1950; J.D., U. Akron, 1955; M.A., Kent State U., 1962. Title examiner Bankers Guarantee Title & Trust Co., Akron, 1950-54; acct. Robinson Clay Product Co., Akron, 1955-60; librarian Akron-Summit Pub. Library, 1962-69, head fine arts and music div., 1969-71, sr. librarian, 1972-82. Payroll treas. Akron Symphony Orch., 1957-61; treas. Friends Library Akron and Summit County, 1970-72. Mem. Music Library Assn., Am., Ohio, Akron bar assns., Ohio Library Assn., ALA, Nat. Trust for Historic Preservation, Internat. Soc. Archtl. Historians, Coll. Art Assn. Republican. Episcopalian. Club: Nat. Lawyers (Washington), Internat. Platform Assn. Home: 601 Nome Ave Akron OH 44320

HOLLOWAY, LAWRENCE MILTON, osteopathic physician; b. Kirksville, Mo., Sept. 8, 1913; s. Edward Lee and Vetta (Elmore) H.; student Kirksville Bus. Coll., 1933, NE Mo. U., 1933-36; D.O., Kirksville Coll. Osteopathy and Surgery, 1940; M.D., U. Santo Tomas, 1951; m. Roena Jane Williams, Dec. 24, 1935; children—Lawrence Milton, Lynette Jane. Intern, A.S.O. Hosp., Kirksville, 1939-40, Detroit Osteo. Hosp., 1940-42; gen. practice osteo. medicine, Byron, Mich., 1940-56, specializing in endocrinology, Flint, Mich., 1956—; examining physician Am. Pres. Life Ins. Co.; fellow in surgery Am. Coll. Osteo. Physicians and Surgeons, Byron, 1940-56; instr. Physiol. Chemistry Lab., Kirksville Coll. Osteopathy and Surgery, 1938-40; founder, chief surgeon, chief staff Lawrence Osteo. Hosp., Byron, 1942-56; dir., bus. mgr. L. M. Holloway Clinic; plastic and cosmetic surgeon Flint Gen. Hosp. Pres., L.M. Holloway Mfg. Co., Byron, 1944-47; v.p. Owosso Finance Co. (Mich.), 1952-56, pres., 1956—; adv. bd. Hamilton Internat. Life Ins. Co. Physician, Byron High Sch., 1940-54. Adviser Swartz Creek chpt. Boy Scouts Am.; sec. Orgn. for World Wide Postgrad. Study. Fellow Am. Soc. Clin. Hypnosis (life); mem. Am. (life mem.), Genesee County (life mem.) osteo. assns., Mich. Assn. Osteo. Physicians and Surgeons, Am. Coll. Osteo. Surgeons (life mem.), Am. Soc. Endocrinology and Nutrition, Am. Soc. Clin. Arthritis, Kirksville Osteo. Alumni Assn., Future Farmers Am. (life), Psi Sigma Alpha. Lodges: Masons (32 deg., life mem.), Shriners, Elks, 750 (pres. Mich. chpt. 1958-59, 61, 64-66). Home: 10283 Corunna Rd Swartz Creek MI 48473 Office: G 5200 Corunna Rd Flint MI 48504

HOLLY, JOHN, producing director, stage manager, actor; b. St. Louis, May 6, 1944; s. Jack Edwin and Harriet (Shellenberger) Williamson; m. Roseann Dezember, Dec. 22, 1967; children—Holly, Robin, Jacki. B.A. in Drama, Ariz. State U., 1966. Actor, stage mgr., dir., various theatre and TV prodns., 1963-72; prodn. stage mgr. Theatre Now, Inc., N.Y.C., 1972-74; gen. mgr. Music Theatre of Wichita, Kans., 1974-79, producing dir., 1979—; artistic dir. Wichita Children's Theatre, 1977-84; v.p., dir. Marketing Concepts, Inc., N.Y.C.; prodn. mgr. Wichita Symphony Soc.; guest prof., dir. Wichita State U., 1975-82; TV prodn. specialist U.S. Army, 1969-71. Vice pres. Conv. and Visitors Bur. Wichita, 1983-84; profl. chmn. Assn. Kans. Theatre, 1976-79; dir. Wichita Arts Council, 1979-84. Named to Outstanding Young Men Am. Nat. Jaycees, 1977; recipient Am. Spirit Honor medal Arms Service, 1970. Mem. Actors Equity Assn., Internat. Alliance Theatrical Stage Employees, Am. Theatre Assn., Bobkats Internat. (pres. 1976—), Theatre Communications Group (assoc.), Wichita C. of C. Republican. Office: Music Theatre of Wichita 225 W Douglas St Wichita KS 67202

HOLM, ROGER HERBERT, purchasing executive; b. New London, Minn., Aug. 6, 1930; s. Herbert A. and Ruth O. (Olson) H.; m. Eleanor E. Stuneck, Aug. 12, 1961; children—Michael Stephanie, Mary. Student pub. schs., New London. With Assoc. Loan Co., Mpls., 1960-63; asst. mgr. Northtown Fin. Co., Mpls., 1963-66; bus. mgr. Unity Med. Ctr., Fridley, Minn., 1966-73, dir. materials mgmt., 1973—. Mem. Healthcare Materials Mgmt. Soc., Upper Midwest Hosp. Purchasing Assn. (pres. 1983), Twin City Purchasing Mgmt. Assn., Minn. Assn. for Hosp. Safety and Security, Hosp. Fin. Mgmt. Assn. (pres. 1972-73). Roman Catholic. Home: 502 5 1/2 St Elk River MN 55330 Office: Unity Med Ctr 550 Osborne Rd Fridley MN 55432

HOLMAN, DENNIS RAY, pharmaceutical production manager; b. Beatrice, Nebr., Apr. 11, 1947; s. Clarence Woodford Holman and Ethel Elizabeth (Remmenga) H.; m. Carolyn Leah Gerner, Apr. 22, 1967; children—Lance Arling, Janel Anne. Student U. Nebr., 1981-83. With Barker Shoe Store, Lincoln, 1963-65, Control Data Corp., Lincoln, 1966; equipment operator Norden Labs., Lincoln, 1967-71, prodn. supr., 1971-78, dept. mgr., 1978—. Active Immanuel Lutheran Ch., Lincoln, local Boy Scouts Am. Served with USNG, 1965-71. Democrat. Avocations: gardening; animals; home handyman projects; camping. Office: Norden Labs 601 W Cornhusker St Lincoln NE 68521

HOLMAN, JAMES LEWIS, financial and management consultant; b. Chgo., Oct. 27, 1926; s. James Louis and Lillian Marie (Walton) H.; B.S. in Econs. and Mgmt., U. Ill., Urbana, 1950, postgrad., 1950; postgrad. Northwestern U., 1954-55; m. Elizabeth Ann Owens, June 18, 1948 (div. 1982); children—Craig Stewart, Tracy Lynn, Mark Andrew; m. 2d, Geraldine Ann Wilson, Dec. 26, 1982. Traveling auditor, then statistician, asst. controller parent buying dept. Sears, Roebuck & Co., Chgo., 1951-54; asst. to sec.-treas. Hanover Securities Co., Chgo., 1954-65; fin. analyst Hales & Hunter Co., Chgo., 1965; mgmt. controller Harry F. Chaddick Assos., Inc., Chgo., 1965-66; asst. to controller chem. ops. div. Montgomery Ward & Co. Inc., Chgo., 1966-68; controller Henrotin Hosp., Chgo., 1968; bus. mgr. Julian, Dye, Javid, Hunter & Najafi, Associated, Chgo., 1968-81; compensation and benefits mgr. Baha'i Nat. Ctr., Wilmette, Ill., 1981—; cons., dir., sec.-treas. Comprehensive Resources Ltd., Glenview, Wheaton, Ill. and Walnut Creek, Calif., 1982—; dir. Medtran, Inc. Sec., B.R. Ryall YMCA, Glen Ellyn, Ill., 1974-76, bd. dirs., 1968-78; trustee Gary Meml. United Methodist Ch., Wheaton, Ill., 1961-69, 74-77, Goodwill Industries Chgo., 1978-79; bd. dirs. DuPage (Ill.) Symphony, 1954-58, treas., 1955-58. Served with USN, 1944-46. Scholarship Nat. Music Camp, Interlochen, Mich., 1944. Mem. Hosp. Fin. Mgmt. Assn. Baha'i. Clubs: Kiwanis (dir. Chgo. 1956-60, bd. dirs. youth found. dir. 1957-60, pres. 1958-60). Office: 2 Wheaton Center Suite 1009 Wheaton IL 60187

HOLMAN, PAUL CAMERON, college administrator, consultant; b. Morris, Ill., Dec. 1, 1930; s. Jennings O. and Florence J. (Cameron) H. B.S., Ill. State U., 1956, M.S., 1957; M.N.S., Ariz. State U., 1964; Ph.D., Mich. State U., 1965. Tchr., Flint Pub. Schs., Mich., 1957-68; assoc. dir. Wis. State U., Research Consortium, Stevens Point, 1968-69; dir. instnl. research SUNY-Oneonta, 1969-72; dir. mgmt. info. and instnl. research U. Wis.-Stevens Point, 1972-80; dean computing, planning, research, registration and records, grants Niagara County Community Coll., Sanborn, N.Y., 1980-83; sr. univ. adminisr. King Saud U., Riyadh, Saudi Arabia, 1983-84; v.p. bus. and fin. Jackson Community Coll., Mich., 1984—; cons. in field. Contbr. articles to profl. jours. Served with U.S. Army, 1948-52. Decorated Silver Star, Purple Heart; Indsl. Mut. Assn. fellow, 1958; NSF fellow, 1959-62. Mem. Mich. Coll. Bus. Officers Assn., Assn. Instnl. Research, Soc. Coll. and Univ. Planning, Nat. Council Research and Planning, Am. Ednl. Research Assn. Avocations: music; theater; art; computers. Home: 4641 Westbrook Dr Jackson MI 49201 Office: Jackson Community Coll 2111 Emmons Rd Jackson MI 49201

HOLMAN, WILLIAM BAKER, surgeon, coroner; b. Norwalk, Ohio, Mar. 22, 1925; s. Merlin Earl and Rowena (Baker) H.; m. Jane Elizabeth Henderson, June 24, 1951; children—Craig W., Mark E., John S. B.S., Capital U., 1946; M.D., Jefferson Med. Coll., 1950. Intern, St. Luke's Hosp., Cleve., 1950-51, resident in gen. surgery, 1951-52, 55-57; practice medicine specializing in surgery, Norwalk, 1957—; coroner Huron County, Norwalk, 1962—. Bd. dirs. REMSNO, Toledo, 1974—, Norwalk Profl. Colony, 1983—; mem. exec. com. Huron County Republican Com., Norwalk, 1980. Served to 1st lt. U.S. Army, 1952-54; Korea. Fellow ACS; mem. AMA, Ohio State Med. Assn., Huron County Med. Soc. (pres. 1978), Ohio State Coroners Assn., Nat. Assn. Med. Examiners. Lutheran. Avocations: boating; photography; stamp collecting; gun collecting. Home: 39 Warren Dr Norwalk OH 44857 Office: 257 Benedict Ave Norwalk OH 44857

HOLMBERG, JOYCE, state senator; b. Rockford, Ill., July 19, 1930. B.A., No. Ill. U., 1952; M.A., Alfred Adler Inst., 1979. Parent coordinator Rockford Pub. Schs., 1973-82; instr. Rock Valley Coll., Rockford; mem. Ill. Senate, 1983—. Democrat. Office: 825 N Main St Rockford IL 61103

HOLMBERG, MARY LOU, nurse college administrator; b. Panama, Iowa, Oct. 29, 1930; d. Isadore M. and Helen (Gubbels) Schwery; m. James J. Holmberg, Oct. 2, 1954; children—James J., Mark J., Mary Jane, Holly. Diploma Mercy Sch. Nursing, 1951; B.S. in Nursing, Creighton U., 1954; M.A., Kearney State Coll., 1978. Staff nurse Mercy Hosp., Council Bluffs, Iowa, 1951-52, Children's Hosp., Omaha, 1952; nursing instr. Mercy Hosp. Sch. Nursing, Council Bluffs, 1952-55; dir. nursing edn. Platte Coll., Columbus, Nebr., 1969—. Bd. dirs. Nebr. State Bd. Nursing, Lincoln, 1981—. Named Nurse of Yr., Creighton U., 1983; recipient faculty award of yr. Nebr. Community Colls., 1984. Mem. Nebr. League for Nursing (bd. dirs. 1980-84), Sigma Theta Tau. Roman Catholic. Avocations: sewing, art, nature. Home: 4809 Country Club Dr Columbus NE 68601 Office: Platte Coll Box 1027 Columbus NE 68601

HOLMER, CURTIS IVAR, engineering company executive, consultant; b. Floral Park, N.Y., Nov. 14, 1942; s. Curt I. and Mary A. (Andersen) H.; m. M. Kathleen Matteson, Nov. 28, 1964; children—Curt I., Cynthia. B.S. in Physics, Rensselaer Poly. Inst., 1964, postgrad., 1965-66; M.S. in Physics, John Carroll U., 1969; postgrad., MIT, 1971-72. Physicist U.S. Plywood Corp., Brewster, N.Y., 1964-66; project engr. Lord Mfg. Co., Erie, Pa., 1966-69; supervisory cons. Bolt, Beranek & Newman, Inc., Cambridge, Mass., 1969-73; mech. engr. U.S. Nat. Bur. Standards, Washington, 1973-76; v.p., div. mgr. noise control tech. div. Underwater Systems, Inc., Rockville, Md., 1976-81; mgr. noise control engring. E-A-R div. Cabot Corp., Indpls., 1981—. Contbr. articles to profl. jours., also book chpt. Mem. Inst. Noise Control Engring. (bd. dirs. 1978-82, bd. examiners 1974-76), AIAA, Acoustical Soc. Am., ASTM. Avocation: flying. Office: E-A-R Div Cabot Corp 7911 Zionsville Rd Indianapolis IN 46268

HOLMES, ALLEN CORNELIUS, lawyer; b. Cin., May 27, 1920; s. Guy E. and Mary M. (Taylor) H.; m. Louise M.E. Quirk, Sept. 2, 1944; children—William Paul, Peter Allen, Thomas Taylor, Douglas Quirk. A.B., U. Cin., 1941; J.D., U. Mich., 1944; LL.D. (hon.), John Carroll U., 1985. Bar: Ohio 1944, D.C. 1976. Assoc. Jones, Day, Reavis & Pogue, Cleve., 1944-54, ptnr., 1954—, mng. ptnr., Cleve., 1974-85, nat. mng. ptnr., 1974-85; dir. Diamond Shamrock Corp., Dallas, Sherwin-Williams Co., Cleve., Nat. City Bank, Cleve., Nat. City Corp., Cleve. Bd. dirs. Kaiser Found Hosp., Oakland, Calif.; trustee Univ. Circle, Inc., Cleve., 1975—, Univ. Hosps. Cleve., 1983—; chmn. Cleve. Cultural Resources Study Commn., 1980—; chmn. edn. com. Greater Cleve. Roundtable, 1983; trustee Case Western Res. U., Cleve., chmn., 1983—; chmn. Greater Cleve. Growth Assn., 1984. Named Harvard Bus. Sch. Statesman of Yr, 1982; recipient Charles Eisenman award Jewish Community Fedn., 1983. Mem. ABA (past chmn. antitrust sect.), Ohio State Bar Assn., Greater Cleve. Bar Assn., Assn. Bar City N.Y., Am. Law Inst., D.C. Bar Assn. Clubs: Union of Cleve., 50 of Cleve.; Chagrin Valley Hunt, Tavern, Pepper Pike Country, Clevelander; Metropolitan (Washington); Links (N.Y.C.). Avocations: gourmet food and wine. Home: II Bratenahl Pl Apt 6BC Bratenahl OH 44108 Office: Jones Day Reavis & Pogue 1700 Huntington Bldg Cleveland OH 44115

HOLMES, CHARLES BROOKS, engineering company executive; b. Mpls., Dec. 30, 1938; s. Benton Harger and Florence Lorain (Cavanagh) H.; m. Joan Marie Roddy, Aug. 22, 1959; children—Beverly, Becky, Beth. Student U. Minn., 1959-60. Pres. Vector Engring., Chaska, Minn. Republican. Lutheran. Club: Rotary (bd. dirs., sec., treas. Chaska 1983). Home: 15005 County Rd 41 Cologne MN 55322 Office: Vector Engring Corp 331 Lake Hazeltine Dr Chaska MN 55318

HOLMES, DAVID VALENTINE, art educator, painter, sculptor; b. Newark, N.Y., Nov. 27, 1945; s. Raynor M. and Dorothy (Valentine) H.; m. Cathleen Schober, Mar. 17, 1975; children—Joshua, Raena. B.F.A. cum laude, Tyler Sch. Art, 1968; M.F.A., U. Wis.-Madison, 1972; student Temple U., Rome, 1966-67. Art tchr. for mentally retarded N.Y. State Dept. Mental Hygiene, Newark, 1968-70; artist-in-residence for pub. schs. Nat. Endowment for Arts grant, Madison, 1972-74; asst. prof. art U. Wis.-Milw., 1974-76; assoc. prof. U. Wis.-Parkside, Kenosha, 1977—. One man shows include U. Wis., Campuses, Marshfield, 1976, River Falls, 1979, Green Bay, 1981, Whitewater, 1982, Burpee Art Mus., Rockford, Ill., 1976, Kohler Arts Ctr., Sheboygan, Wis., 1977, Madison Art Ctr., 1977, Wustum Mus. of Art, Racine, Wis., 1979, Bergstrom Art Ctr., Neenah, Wis., 1980, Rahr-West Mus. Art, Manitowoc, Wis., 1981, Carthage Coll., Kenosha, 1981, Kent State U., Ohio, 1983, Northwestern U., Evanston, Ill., 1983, Ind. State U.-Terre Haute, 1983; exhibited in group shows at Kohler Arts Ctr., 1975, 76, 78, 79, 80, 84, Milw. Art Mus., 1975, 77, 78, 79, 80, Chgo. Art. Inst., 1975, Smithsonian Inst., 1979, 81, 82, Higbee Co. Auditorim, Cleve., 1982 (Best of Show), Am. Craft Mus., N.Y., 1979, represented in permanent collections Milw. Art Mus., Kohler Art. Ctr., Madison Art Ctr., U. Wis., Alverno Coll., Kent State U. Fellow in crafts Nat. Endowment for Arts, 1976-77. Mem. Coll. Art Assn. Am. Episcopalian. Avocation: Hiking. Home: 1428 S Wisconsin Ave Racine WI 53403 Office: U Wis Parkside Box 2000 Kenosha WI 53141

HOLMES, HOWARD SUMNER, executive; b. Chelsea, Mich., July 24, 1913; s. Howard Samuel and Mabel Irene (White) H.; m. Mary Ernestine Blodgett, June 12, 1943; children—Howard, Christine, Kathryn, William, Andrea. Student Princeton U., 1932; B.S. in Mech. Engring., U. Mich., 1937; D.Sci. in Bus. Adminstrn. (hon.), Cleary Coll., 1983. Pres., dir. Chelsea Milling Co. (Mich.), from 1946; v.p., dir. C&C Carton Co., Marshall, Mich., from 1972; dir. Domino's Pizza Co., Ann Arbor, Mich.; dir., exec. com. Millers Nat. Ins. Co., Chgo.; exec. bd., treas. Wheat Industry Council, Washington, 1980—. Mem. div. bd. Catherine McAuley Health Ctr., Ann Arbor; chmn. devel. council St. Joseph Mercy Hosp.; bd. dirs. devel. council U. Mich.; trustee Portage council Boy Scouts Am. Mem. Millers Nat. Fedn. (exec. com., former bd. chmn.), Mich. Millers Assn. (pres.), Tau Beta Phi, Alpha Delta Phi. Republican. Congregationalist. Clubs: Princeton (N.Y.), Athletic (Detroit), University (Chgo.), Barton Hills Country (Ann Arbor), Masons. Home: 175 Underdown Rd Ann Arbor MI 48105

HOLMES, JAMES MICHAEL, business executive; b. Luverne, Ala., Mar. 8, 1942; s. James F. and Helen (Mount) H.; m. Shirley Russell, May 25, 1963; children—Jennifer Jyll, Russell Michael. B.S., Troy State U., 1964. Sales trainee Ralston Purina Co., Montgomery, Ala., 1965-70; sales rep. DeKalb AgResearch, Montgomery, 1970-72, dist. mgr., York, Pa., 1972-75, regional mgr., DeKalb, Ill., 1975-79, gen. mgr. poultry div., 1979-83; v.p., gen. mgr. Warren's Turf Inc., Crystal Lake, Ill., 1983—; dir. Gortie Labs. Internat., Austin, Tex. Contbr. articles to profl. jours. Mem. Republican Nat. Com., Washington, 1983—; bd. dirs. St. Paul's Episcopal Ch., mem. bishops com., 1981; coach Soccer League, DeKalb, 1981-83; participant Harvard Agribus. Leaders Conf., Boston, 1983. Mem. Am. Sod Producers Assn., Golf Course Supt. Assn. Club: Sycamore Sportsman. Avocations: Jogging; road racing; camping; boating; fishing.

HOLMES, MELISSA ANN, vocational association administrator; b. Durham, N.C., Mar. 10, 1947; d. Austin and Gilda Ola (Gainer) Sampson; m. Larry Wayne Armstrong, Mar. 21, 1975 (dec. 1981); 1 son, Nicholas; m. Glenn Holmes, Nov. 19, 1982. B.S. in Adminstrn. Justice, Wichita State U., 1978. Ops. clk. Boeing, Wichita, Kans., 1974-76; teller Kans. State Bank & Trust, Wichita, 1977-78; minority recruiter Big Bros. and Big Sisters of Sedgwick County, Kans., 1978-82; exec. dir. 1st Nat. Black Hist. Soc. Kans., Wichita, 1982-83, Work Options for Women, Wichita, 1984—. Mem. Jr. League of Wichita, 1985—; bd. dirs. YWCA of Wichita, 1978-84; 1st v.p. Commn. Status of Women, 1983—; mem. adv. council Kans. Arts Commn., Topeka, 1985—; bd. dirs. Youth Devel. Services, Wichita, 1983—. Recipient Community Service award NAACP, 1985. Mem. Nat. Soc. Fund Raising Execs., Nat. Assn. Women Bus. Owners, Positive Black Networking (pres. 1983-85), Alpha Kappa Alpha. Democrat. Methodist. Avocations: counted cross stitch; bonsai culture. Home: 1455 N Ash St Wichita KS 67214 Office: Work Option for Women 1611 N Mosley St Wichita KS 67214

HOLMES, RICHARD WINN, state ofcl.; b. Wichita, Kans., Feb. 23, 1923; B.S., Kans. State U., 1950; J.D., Washburn U., Topeka, 1953. Admitted to Kans. bar, 1953; individual practice law, Wichita, 1953-77; judge Wichita Mcpl. Ct., 1959-61; instr. bus. law Wichita State U., 1959-60; justice Kans. Supreme Ct., 1977—. Mem. Kans. Bar Assn., Wichita Bar Assn., Topeka Bar Assn., Am. Judges Assn. (founder 1959, bd. govs. 1980—). Office: Kansas Judicial Center Topeka KS 66612

HOLMES, ROBERT EDWARD, state justice; b. Columbus, Ohio, Nov. 14, 1922; s. Harry B. and Nora (Birney) H.; A.B., Ohio U., 1943, LL.B., 1949; children—Robert E., H. Barclay. Admitted to Ohio bar; individual practice law, Columbus, 1949-69; mem. Ohio Ho. of Reps., Columbus, 1960-69; judge 10th Dist. Ct. Appeals, Columbus 1969-78; justice Supreme Ct. Ohio, Columbus, 1978—. Bd. dirs. Boy Scouts Am., Salvation Army, Pilot Dogs, Inc., Columbus. Served with USN. Mem. Nat. Council Internat. Programs (past pres.), ABA, Ohio Bar Assn., Columbus Bar Assn. Clubs: Agonis, Charity Newsies, Athletic. Lodge: Kiwanis. Office: 30 E Broad St Columbus OH 43215*

HOLMES, THOMAS JAMES, JR., medicinal chemistry educator; b. Braddock, Pa., Sept. 13, 1948; s. Thomas James and Elizabeth (Barsic) H.; m. Alyce Marie Chuba, Aug. 7, 1971; children—Thomas, Ana, James. B.S. in Pharmacy, Duquesne U., 1971; Ph.D., in Medicinal Chemistry, U. Mich., 1975. Registered pharmacist, Pa. Research assoc. U. Chgo., 1975-78; research scientist Ortho Pharm. Corp., Raritan, N.J., 1978-80; asst. prof. medicinal chemistry U. Minn., Mpls., 1980—; cons. Sar Tec Corp., Anoka, Minn., 1983—. Contbr. articles on protein modification and anti-arthritic drug action to profl. jours. Cub Scout den leader Indianhead council Boy Scouts Am., 1984—. Recipient New Investigator award NIH, 1981; named Tchr. of Yr., Coll. Pharmacy, 1984. Mem. Am. Chem. Soc. (div. medicinal chemistry, membership com. 1984-85), Am. Assn. of Colls. of Pharmacy. Roman Catholic. Avocations: record collecting, intramural basketball. Home: 2350 Carter Ave St Paul MN 55108 Office: Coll Pharmacy U Minn Minneapolis MN 55455

HOLOHAN, O. J., industrial and interior designer; b. Detroit, Sept. 18, 1936; s. James Frances and Ernestine Flora (Neumann) H.; degree in Indsl. Designs and Interiors, Cleve. Inst. Art, 1961; m. Laurinda Anne Loewe, Oct. 25, 1969; children—Eric James, Shauna Lynn, Brian James. Illustrator to Pres. D. Eisenhower, 1957-58; art dir. TV sta., Washington, 1958-59; dir. design O.J.K. Designers div. F.W. Roberts, Cleve., 1962-67; pres. O.J. Holohan Assocs., Inc., Burton, Ohio, 1967—, Inarco, Twinsburg, Ohio, 1984—; judge design juries. Served with U.S. Army, 1957-59. Recipient Merit award Nat. Stationary and Office Equipment Assn., 1962; Design award 2d place Nat. Office Furniture Assn., 1963; Design award, 1965; 1st and 2nd place awards Office Interior Design Mag., 1965; hon. mention award S.M. Hexter Co., 1975. Mem. Inst. Bus. Designers (founding, award for lounge group 1982-83), Zool. Assn. Am., Nat. Office Furniture Assn. Home: 2 Serenity Pk 12175 Snow Rd Burton OH 44021 Office: 1 Serenity Pk 12175 Snow Rd Burton OH 44021

HOLSCHUH, JOHN DAVID, judge; b. Ironton, Ohio, Oct. 12, 1926; s. Edward A. and Helen (Ebert) H.; B.A., Miami U., 1948; J.D., U. Cin., 1951; m. Carol Stouder, Aug. 13, 1927; 1 son, John David. Bar: Ohio 1951. Law clk. U.S. Dist. Ct. judge, 1952-54; mem. firm Alexander, Ebinger, Holschuh, Fisher & McAlister, Columbus, Ohio, 1954-80; judge U.S. Dist. Ct. So. Dist. Ohio, 1980—; adj. prof. law Coll. Law, Ohio State U., 1970. Chmn. bd. commrs. on character and fitness Supreme Ct. of Ohio, Pres. bd. dirs. Neighborhood House, 1969-70. Fellow Am. Coll. Trial Lawyers; mem. Order of Coif, Phi Beta Kappa, Omicron Delta Kappa. Office: 85 Marconi Blvd Columbus OH 43215*

HOLSINGER, PAMELA JO, campus activities director; b. Midland, Mich., Nov. 27, 1959; d. Carl Dee and Mary Lou (Zimmerle) H. A.A., Delta Coll., 1979; B.A., Mich. State U., 1981, M.A., 1983. Asst. to dir. student activities Delta Coll., University City, Mich., 1978-80; grad. adviser Mich. State U., East Lansing, 1981-83; residence life coordinator Coll. St. Thomas, St. Paul, 1983-84, dir. campus activities, 1984—. Mem. com. Aquatennial Planning Com., Mpls., 1985. Profl. Womens Assn. scholar, 1978; named Vol. of Month, Big Sisters, 1983. Mem. Nat. Assn. Campus Activities (bd. dirs. 1981-83, coordinator 1985), Am. Coll. Personnel Assn., Nat. Assn. Student Personnel Adminstrs., St. Thomas Women's Assn. Mem. Ch. of Nazarene. Avocations: travel, camping. Office: Coll St Thomas PO 4024 2115 Summit Ave Saint Paul MN 55105

HOLST, KENT R., utility company executive; b. Waterloo, Iowa, Nov. 30, 1938; s. Raymond Alfred and Edna B. (Petersen) H.; m. Judith Ann Wood, June 6, 1959; children—Carri Lynn, Jodi Lynn. B.A., Iowa State U., 1962. Pres., Ray Holst, Inc., Traer, Iowa, 1969—; gen. mgr. Traer Mcpl. Utilities, 1982—; dir. Iowa-Nebr. Farm Equipment Dealers Assn., Des Moines, 1977-84, pres., 1984. Scoutmaster, Tall Corn area council Boy Scouts Am., 1963-68; vol. fireman Traer Fire Dept., 1963—; pres. Traer Devel. Corp., 1984—. Mem. Gamma Sigma Delta. Methodist. Avocations: skiing; scuba diving; golf. Office: Traer Municipal Utilities 649 2nd St Traer IA 50675

HOLTER, ARLEN ROLF, cardiothoracic surgeon; b. Sullivan's Island, S.C., Feb. 1, 1946; s. Arne and Helen (Soderberg) H.; m. Elizabeth Anne Reid, Nov. 9, 1974; children—Matthew Arlen, Peter Reid, Andrew Douglas. B.S., Stanford U., 1968; M.S., U. Chgo., 1971, M.D., 1973. Diplomate Am. Bd. Thoracic Surgery; Am. Bd. Surgery. Intern in surgery Mass. Gen. Hosp., Boston, 1973-74, resident in surgery, 1974-78; sr. registrar in cardiac surgery Southampton Chest Hosp., Eng., 1978; resident in cardiac surgery Yale U., New Haven, 1978-80; practice medicine specializing in cardiothoracic surgery, Mpls., 1980—; instr. surgery Yale U., 1979-80. Contbr. articles to profl. jours. Recipient Franklin McLean research award U. Chgo., 1973. Fellow ACS, Am. Coll. Cardiology, Am. Coll. Chest Physicians; mem. Soc. Thoracic Surgeons, Pan Pacific Sur. Soc. Lutheran. Avocations: marathon running; skiing; photography. Office: Cardiothoracic Cons PA 6545 France Ave S Minneapolis MN 55435

HOLTER, MARVIN ROSENKRANTZ, physicist; b. Fairport, N.Y., July 4, 1922; m. Frances Elizabeth Jenkins, July 15, 1956; children—Christine E., Ann F. B.S., U. Mich., 1949, M.S. in Math., 1951, M.S. in Physics, 1958. Mem. faculty U. Mich., Ann Arbor, 1950—, prof. remote sensing Sch. Natural Resources, 1968-70, dep. dir. Willow Run Labs., 1972-73, exec. v.p. Environ. Research Inst. Mich., 1973—; chief earth observations div. Manned Spacecraft Ctr., NASA, Houston, 1970-71; assoc. prof. U. Toledo, 1956-57. Author: (with others) Fundamentals of Infrared Technology, 1962; Remote Sensing, 1970. Contbr. articles to profl. jours. Recipient Exceptional Sci. Achievement award NASA, 1973, William T. Pecora award Dept. Interior-NASA, 1976, Exceptional Civilian Service award Dept Air Force, 1979. Mem. Am. Soc. Photogrammetry (autometrics award 1966, photog. interpretation award 1969), Sci. Research Club U. Mich., Sigma Xi. Clubs: Explorers, Cosmos. Avocations: amateur radio, photography, history, gardening. Home: 493 Orchard Hill Dr Ann Arbor MI 48104 Office: Environ Research Inst Mich PO Box 8618 Ann Arbor MI 48107

HOLTKAMP, DORSEY EMIL, medical research scientist; b. New Knoxville, Ohio, May 28, 1919; s. Emil H. and Caroline E. (Meckstroth) H.; student Ohio State U., 1937-39; A.B., U. Colo., 1945, M.S., 1949, Ph.D., 1951, med. student, 2 1/2 yrs.; m. Marianne Church Johnson, Mar. 20, 1942 (dec. May 1956); 1 son, Kurt Lee; m. 2d, Marie P. Bahm Roberts, Dec. 20, 1957 (dec. Apr. 1982); stepchildren—Charles Timothy Roberts, Michael John Roberts. Teaching asst. in biochemistry, research asst. in biology U. Colo., 1945-46; grad. scholar (univ. fellow) U. Colo. Sch. Medicine, 1946, asst. in biochemistry, 1947-48, research fellow in biochemistry, 1948-51; sr. research scientist Biochemistry sect. Smith, Kline & French Labs., Phila., 1951-57, endocrine-metabolic group leader, 1957-58; head endocrinology dept. Merrell-Nat. Labs. div. Richardson-Merrell, Inc., Cin., 1958-70, group dir. endocrine clin. research, med. research dept., 1970-81; group dir. endocrinology, med. research dept. Merrell Dow Pharms. subs. Dow Chem. Co., 1981—. Fellow AAAS, Am. Inst. Chemists; mem. Am. Soc. Clin. Pharm. and Therapeutics, Endocrine Soc., Am. Fertility Soc., Am. Chem. Soc., Am. Soc. Pharmacology and Exptl. Therapeutics, N.Y., Ohio acads. scis., Soc. Exptl. Biology and Medicine, Reticuloendothelial Soc., Am. Inst. Biol. Scis., AMA (affiliate), Sigma Xi, Nu Sigma Nu. Republican. Presbyterian. Contbr. articles to sci. publs.; patentee on various phases endocrinology, pharmacology, tumor metabolism, fertility-sterility control, biochemistry, teratology, inflammation and nutrition. Research and devel. new drugs. Home: 9464 Bluewing Terr Cincinnati OH 45241 Office: 2110 E Galbraith Rd Cincinnati OH 45215

HOLTON, EARL D., retail company executive; b. 1934. With Meijer, Inc., Grand Rapids, Mich., 1952—, former v.p., exec. v.p., now pres., dir. Office: Meijer Inc 2727 Walker Ave NW Grand Rapids MI 49501*

HOLTSBERRY, ALBERT WALTER, retail store executive; b. Licking County, Ohio, Sept. 29, 1935; s. E. Frederick and Vina L. (Hartman) H.; m. Barbara J. Ramsey, Oct. 2, 1959 (div. 1977); children—Frederick W., Theresa L. Erickson; m. Melynda Rockey, Mar. 9, 1978. Student, Ohio U., 1953-54, Ohio State U., 1963-65. Sr. systems analyst Shoe Corp. Am., Columbus, Ohio, 1964-67; sr. systems analyst Am. Standard, Columbus, 1967-68, mgr. systems and data processing 1968-70; mgr. systems and data processing Big Bear Stores, Columbus, 1970-82, asst. dir. mgmt. info. systems, 1982—. Mem. Assn. Systems mgmt. (chpt. pres. 1971-72, div. dir. 1972-75, internat. merit award 1973, chpt. service award 1974, internat. achievement award 1982). Avocations: Motorcycle touring; tournament bridge. Home: 4788 CrazyHorse Ln Westerville OH 43081 Office: Big Bear Stores Co 770 W Goodale Blvd Columbus OH 43212

HOLTZ, GLENN EDWARD, band instrument manufacturing executive; b. Detroit, Jan. 15, 1938; s. Edward Christian and Evelyn Adele (Priehs) Foutz H.; m. Mary Eleanor Russell, Nov. 25, 1981; children by previous marriage—Robert, Kimberly, Rene, Letitia, Kimberly, Pamela. B. Mus. Edn., U. Mich., 1960, M. Mus. Edn., 1964; cons. motivation student Personnel Dynamics, Mpls., 1980. Mus. tchr. Middleville High Sch. (Mich.), 1960-62; dist. mgr. Selmer Co., Elkhart, Ind., 1965-74, sales mgr., 1974-76; pres. Knapp Mus. Co., Grand Rapids, Mich., 1976-80; v.p. mktg. sales Gemeinhardt/CBS, Elkhart, 1981-83, gen. mgr., 1983—, also v.p. CBS Columbia Music Div.; seminar leader Sch. Band Movement Phase II Gemeinhardt, Elkhart, 1982-83. Dist. gov. Lion's Internat., Jackson, Lansing, Battle Creek, Mich., 1970-71; pres. Middleville Bd. Edn., 1964-73. Recipient Disting. award Lion's Internat., Mich., 1971. Republican. Office: Gemeinhardt PO Box 788 Elkhart IN 46515

HOLTZINGER, JOHN IRVIN, realty company executive; b. Goshen, Ind., July 25, 1942; s. Irvin C. and Mary Ellen (Diveley) H.; student Goshen Coll., 1960-62; B.S. in Bus., Ind. U., 1965; m. Connie Rae Spindler, Nov. 23, 1967; children—John Todd, Nicole Marie, Bianca Jean, Celeste Rae. Fin. auditor Arthur Young & Co., Chgo., 1964-71; corp. controller Corterra Corp., Chgo., 1972-73; Midwestern U.S. controller Centennial Industries, Chgo., 1974; advisor to Arthur Rubloff, Arthur Rubloff Co., Chgo., 1975-82; treas. Jack Winters Group, Hinsdale, Ill., 1982—. C.P.A., Ind. Mem. Am. Inst. C.P.A.'s, Ind. Assn. C.P.A.'s, Internat. Council Shopping Centers. Lutheran. Home: 7220 W 138th Pl Cedar Lake IN 46303 Office: 244 E Ogden Ave Hinsdale IL 60521

HOLVICK, OLAF, II, computer cons. co. exec.; b. Long Beach, Calif., June 16, 1946; s. Olaf and Elaine Margaret (Klarr) H.; B.S. in Bus. Adminstrn., Babson Coll., 1968; children—Lindsay Fisher, Tara Fisher. Mktg. rep. Statis. Analyst Corp., Detroit, 1968-69; mktg. analyst Nat. Bank of Detroit, 1969; group sales mgr. Pathfinder Internat., Detroit, 1969-70; nat. account exec. R.L. Polk & Co., Taylor, Mich., 1970-75; Eastern regional mgr. Cutler-Williams, Inc., Dearborn, Mich., 1975-78; pres. Holvick Corp., Detroit, 1978—; dir. Interface Systems, Inc., Ann Arbor, Mich., 1972-75. Mem. Econ. Club Detroit. Republican. Roman Catholic. Clubs: Country of Detroit, Detroit Athletic, Detroit Racquet, Racquet of Chgo. Office: 400 Renaissance Center Suite 2760 Detroit MI 48243

HOLZ, HARRY GEORGE, lawyer; b. Milw., Sept. 13, 1934; s. Harry Carl and Emma Louise (Hinz) H.; B.S., Marquette U., 1956, LL.B., 1958; LL.M., Northwestern U., 1960; m. Nancy L. Heiser, May 12, 1962; children—Pamela Gretchen, Bradley Eric, Erika Lynn. Admitted to Wis. bar, 1958, Ill. bar, 1960; asso. firm Sidley & Austin, Chgo., 1959-60; partner firm Quarles & Brady, Milw., 1968—; teaching fellow Northwestern U. Sch. Law, 1958-59; lectr. U. Wis. Law Sch., 1971-74; adj. prof. Marquette U. Law Sch., 1975-85; faculty mem. Wis. Bar ATS-CLE Program on Anti-Trust Law, 1975—; bd. dirs. Corp. Practice Inst., dir., lectr. continuing legal edn. programs, 1977-78. Bd. visitors Marquette U. Sch. Law, 1978. Mem. Am. Bar Assn., State Bar Wis. (sec. corp. banking and bus. law sect. 1976-77, chmn. 1978-79, dir. 1978-83), Milw. Bar Assn., Bar Assn. 7th Fed. Circuit, Woolsack Soc. of Marquette U. Sch. Law, Beta Gamma Sigma. Lutheran. Clubs: Milw. Athletic; Western Racquet. Editor-in-chief, Marquette Law Rev., 1957-58. Home: 1720 Village Green Ct Elm Grove WI 53122 Office: 780 N Water St Milwaukee WI 53202

HOLZ, MICHAEL HAROLD, lawyer; b. Dayton, Ohio, Apr. 10, 1942; s. Harold L. and Norma (Montgomery) H.; m. Tanya Noffsinger, July 22, 1972 (div. Jan. 1983). B.A., Wittenberg U., 1964; J.D., U. Cin., 1967; M.B.A., U. Dayton, 1979. Bar: Ohio 1968, U.S. Tax Ct. 1975, U.S. Dist. Ct. 1971. Legal dep. probate Montgomery County, Dayton, 1971-73; asst. pros. atty. Greene County, Xenia, Ohio, 1973; sole practice, Dayton, 1974—. Mem. Democratic Central Com., 1972-84. Served with U.S. Army, 1968-70; Vietnam. ACLU (dir.), Dayton Bar Assn. (ethics com.), Ohio Bar Assn., VFW, Mensa. Episcopalian. Home: 737 Wilmington Ave 1 Dayton OH 45420

HOLZER, RICHARD JEAN, lawyer; b. Easton, Pa., Jan. 31, 1940; s. J. A. and Ann C. (Carta) H.; B.A., Gettysburg Coll., 1961; M.B.A., U. Dayton, 1971; student N.Y. U., 1968-69; J.D., Salmon P. Chase Coll. Law, No. Ky. State U., 1975; m. Charlotte L. Branson, Aug. 15, 1964; children—Richard Jean, C. Christopher. Field rep. INA, Pitts., 1961-66; asso. R. D. Griewahn & Assos., Erie, Pa., 1966-68; mgr. compensation and benefits Curtis-Wright Corp., Woodridge, N.J., 1968-69; mgr. personnel services, McCall Printing Co., Dayton, 1969-70; labor relations adminstr. City of Dayton, 1970-75; admitted to Ohio bar, 1975; atty. pub. sector labor and corp. law, ptnr. Pickrel, Schaeffer and Ebeling, Dayton, 1975—; law dir. City of Englewood (Ohio); asst. prof. U. Dayton, 1976-77, Wright State U., 1979-80. Com. chmn. Montgomery County Personnel Task Force, 1979—; soccer coach Northmont Bd. Edn., 1983—. Served with U.S. Army, 1962-64. Recipient Book award for labor law No. Ky. State U. Mem. Am. Soc. Personnel Adminstrs., Nat. Pub. Employers Labor Relations Assn., Ohio Pub. Employers Labor Relations Assn., Ohio League Mcpl. Attys., Ohio Council Sch. Bd. Attys., Ohio State Bar Assn., Fed. Bar Assn., Dayton Bar Assn., Scabbard and Blade, Phi Alpha Delta, Lambda Chi Alpha. Lutheran (council 1976—, pres. council 1978-79). Home: 10887 Putnam Rd Englewood OH 45322 Office: 2700 Kettering Tower Dayton OH 45423

HOLZHAUSEN, LYNNE MARIE, pharmaceutical company toxicologist; b. Greenfield, Ind., Nov. 14, 1954; d. Clyde Edward and Helen Elizabeth (Burns) Holzhausen. B.S. in Biology, Marian Coll., 1977; M.S., Purdue Univ., Indpls., 1984. Lab. techician Hancock Meml. Hosp., Greenfield, Ind., 1974-77 (part-time); research assoc. VA Med. Ctr., Indpls., 1977-80; toxicologist Eli Lilly and Co., Indpls., 1980—. Author, co-author sci. abstracts. Active Am. Diabetes Assn., Indpls., 1980-85. Mem. Nat. Audubon Soc., Sierra Club (Indpls.). Roman Catholic. Avocations: music; piano and voice; hiking; camping. Home: 60 N Routiers St Indianapolis IN 46219 Office: Eli Lilly and Co Toxicology Dept PO Box 708 Greenfield IN 46140

HOMAN, GERLOF, pharmaceutical company executive; b. Bandung, Indonesia, Feb. 10, 1930; came to U.S., 1973; s. Freerk Hinrik and Joan (Groosjohan) H.; Ph.D. in Organic Chemistry, U. Amsterdam, 1952, M.Clin. Pharmacy, 1961; m. Siekelina Rogaar, Oct. 10, 1955; children—Irma, Astrid, Floris, Paul. Plant mgr. Vitamin D Factories, Weesp, Netherlands, 1956-59; plant mgr. pharm. cos., Holland, India, 1960-63, 63-68, gen. pharm. mgr., 1968-72; gen. mgr. K-V Pharm. Co., St. Louis, 1973-75; dir. research and devel. Cartrix, Brentwood, Mo., 1975—, now v.p. research and devel. Survival Tech. Inc. Mem. Pharm. Mfrs. Assn., Assn. Clin. Pharms. Royal Dutch Soc. Chemistry, Parenteral Drug Assn. Author books in field. Patentee in field. Home: 748 Elkington St Louis MO 63132 Office: Survival Tech Inc 2615S Hanley Saint Louis MO 63144

HOMANDBERG, GENE ALVIN, biochemist; b. Inwood, Iowa, June 7, 1950; s. Alvin Arne and Darleen Winnifred (Keith) H. B.S., U. S.D., 1972, Ph.D., 1976. Undergrad. research asst. biochemistry dept. U. S.D., 1969-72, grad. research asst., 1972-76, teaching asst. biochemistry, 1973-74, postdoctoral research assoc., 1976; NIH trainee, 1972-73; postdoctoral research assoc. Purdue U., West Lafayette, Ind., 1976-78; postdoctoral fellow Lab. Chem. Biology, Nat. Inst. Arthritis, Metabolism and Digestive Diseases, NIH, Bethesda, Md., 1978-80; cancer research scientist II dept. molecular biology Roswell Park Meml. Inst., Buffalo, 1980-81; asst. scientist dept. medicine Mt. Sinai Med. Ctr., Milw., 1981—. Asst. prof. U. Wis. Med. Sch., Milw., 1981-85, assoc. prof., 1985—. Grantee Nat. Heart and Lung Inst., 1983-85. Mem. Am. Chem. Soc., AAAS, Am. Soc. Biol. Chemists, Am. Heart Assn., Sigma Xi. Democrat. Lutheran. Contbr. articles to biochem. jours. Home: 9000 N 75th St Milwaukee WI 53223 Office: 850 N 12th St Milwaukee WI 53233

HOMBURG, HAROLD NORMAN, constrn. co. exec.; b. Sun Prairie, Wis., Feb. 25, 1928; s. Chris Frederick and Anita Martha (Kassabaum) H.; student public schs., Sun Prairie and Madison, Wis.; m. Shirley Landsness, June 23, 1951; children—Annette Mae, Chris Adolph, Andrew Gilbert. Truck driver Madison Sand & Gravel Co., 1944-50; with L.S. Lunder Co., Madison, 1952-71, supt., 1960-65, asst. sec., 1965-71; pres. Homburg-Olp Constrn. Co. Inc., Monona, Wis., 1971—, Homburg Equipment Co. Monona Plumbing; partner Madison Rock & Sand Co., Homburg Farms; dir. Monona Grove State Bank. Served with U.S. Army, 1950-52. Mem. Asso. Gen. Contractors, East Side Businessman's Assn., Wis. Corn Growers Assn., Monona Jaycees (hon. life), Historic Blooming Grove Hist. Soc. Club: Four Lakes Yacht. Home: 4621 Tonyawatha Trail Monona WI 53716 Office: 100 E Broadway Monona WI 53716

HOMBURGER, THOMAS CHARLES, lawyer; b. Buffalo, Sept. 16, 1941; s. Adolf and Charlotte E. (Stern) H.; m. Louise Paula Shemin, June 6, 1965; children—Jennifer Anne, Richard Ephraim, Kathryn Lee. B.A., Columbia Coll., 1963; LL.B., Columbia U., 1966. Bar: Ill. 1966. Ptnr. law firm Sonnenschein Carlin Nath & Rosenthal, Chgo., 1966—. Contbr. articles to law jours. Mem. Glencoe (Ill.) Bd. Edn., 1984—. Mem. Chgo. Bar Assn. (chmn. real property law com. 1984-85), Chgo. Mortgage Attys. Assn., Am. Coll. Real Estate Lawyers. Clubs: Standard, Metropolitan; Law. Home: 123 Euclid Ave Glencoe IL 60022 Office: Sonnenschein Carlin Nath & Rosenthal 8000 Sears Tower Chicago IL 60606

HOMMER, CARL CHARLES, computer information services educator, consultant; b. Muskegon, Mich., June 19, 1932; s. Carl Charles and Uleutherius (Nevins) H.; m. Agnes May Howard, Dec. 29, 1956; children—Shawn Michael, Barbara Ann, Pamela Marle, Ann Marie. Assoc., Muskegon Community Coll., 1958; B.S., Central Mich. U., 1959; postgrad. U. Mich., 1960-61, Andrews U., 1984. Sr. works study engr. Chevrolet. Flint, Mich., 1961-66; project leader J.I. Case, Racine, Wisc., 1967-70; materials mgr. Applied Power Inc., Menonominee Falls, Wis., 1970-74, King Selly Thermos, Kendallville, Ind., 1974; mgr. systems and program Joy Mfg. Co., Michigan City, Ind., 1975-80; cons., 1982—; asst. prof. computer info. services Purdue U., Westville, Ind., 1980—; cons. InterRoyal, Michigan City, 1980-81, Jones Interprises, LaPorte, Ind., 1984—. Pres., Lake Fenton Bd. Edn., Fenton, Mich., 1965, Am. Field Services, LaPorte, Ind., 1978-79. Served to s/sgt. USAF, 1951-55. Mem. Data Processing Mgmt. Assn. Roman Catholic. Lodge: Elks. Avocations: fishing, hunting, cross country skiing. Home: 314 Bordeaux LaPorte IN 46350 Office: Purdue U North Central Hwy 421 Westville IN 46391

HOMSI, RATEB K., physician; b. Damascus, Syria, Mar. 1, 1929; came to U.S., 1955, naturalized, 1964; s. Khaled M. and Munira (Nahas) H.; m. Laura Jean Morgan, Sept. 3, 1958; children—Terence, Ray, Kenneth. B.S., Coll. Scis., Damascus, 1947; M.D., Coll. Medicine, Damascus, 1953. Diplomate Am. Bd. Surgery. Intern, Huron Road Hosp., Cleve., 1955-56; resident St. Vincent's Hosp., Jacksonville, Fla., 1957-60; gen. surgeon Community Meml. Hosp., Cheboygan, Mich., 1963-68, chmn. dept. surgery, 1968-84, med. dir., 1983—. Fellow Am. Soc. Abdominal Surgeons, Internat. Coll. Surgeons; mem. Mich. State Med. Soc., AMA, Assn. Arab-Am. Univ. Grads., Nat. Arab Am. Assn. Avocations: Golf, bridge. Home: 457 Foote Rd Cheboygan MI 49721 Office: Community Meml Hosp 802 S Main St PO Box 99 Cheboygan MI 49721

HONG, CAROL ANN, microbiologist; b. Altoona, Pa., Oct. 9, 1942; d. John Irwin and Lela Frances (Miller) Kleffman; B.A., Miami U., Oxford, Ohio, 1964; M.B.A., Cleve. State U., 1981; m. Philip Fernandez Ma, Sept. 15, 1965; 1 child, Michael; m. Jong Kyu Hong, Aug. 14, 1978; 1 child, Elizabeth. Teller, Akron (Ohio) Nat Bank, summers 1960-64; vol. Peace Corps, tchr. sci., math. and English, Philippines, 1964-66; bacteriology technologist Case Western Res. U. Hosps., Cleve., 1966; med. technologist, adminstrv. supr. microbiology, mgr. lab. services Cleve. Clinic Found., 1966—, sec. subcom. infectious diseases, 1974-79, mem. safety com., 1978—, chmn. hazardous waste subcom., 1978-81, mem. ops. group, 1981-82, adv. council, 1983—, vice chmn., 1985, lab. medicine safety officer, 1983—. Registered med. technologist, registered specialist in microbiology Am. Soc. Clin. Pathologists. Mem. AAUW (chmn. hospitality 1975-77, dir. 1977-79), Am. Soc. Clin. Pathologists (council on microbiology 1977-83), Cuyahoga Women's Polit. Caucus, Am. Soc. Microbiology, Assn. for Practitioners in Infection Control (pres. Greater Cleve. chpt. 1975-76, 76-77, dir. 1975-78, chmn. nominating com. 1977, mem. bylaws com. 1980, chmn. 1981-84), South Central Assn. for Clin. Microbiology (sec. 1975, dir. area 1976-77, chmn. nominating com. 1977-80, chmn. awards com. 1979-80, membership chmn. 1981, pres. 1984, bd. dirs. 1985, chmn. nominations com. 1985), Clin. Lab. and Mgmt. Assn. (pres. Cleve. chpt. 1975-76), Nat. Assn. Female Execs., Assn. M.B.A. Execs., Mensa, NOW. Lodge: Order of Eastern Star. Editorial bd. Med. Group Mgmt. Assn., Lab. Medicine, 1978-82. Contbr. articles to profl. publs. Home: 374 Karen Dr Chardon OH 44024 Office: 9500 Euclid Ave Cleveland OH 44106

HONIG, LAWRENCE EDWARD, retail company executive; b. Spartanburg, S.C., Jan. 19, 1948; s. O. Charles and Jean Gates (Davis) H.; m. Ellen Stokes, Aug. 7, 1971; children—Charles Edward, Ellenor Jackson. B.A., B.S., Washington and Lee U., 1970; M.A., U. Tex., 1972; M.B.A., Harvard U., 1975. Assoc., Loeb, Rhoades & Co., N.Y.C., 1972-73; prin. McKinsey & Co., Inc., Chgo., 1975-82; exec. v.p. May Dept. Stores Co., St. Louis, 1982—. Trustee St. Louis Art Mus. Served to capt. U.S. Army, 1971-72. Mem. Sigma Delta Chi, Kappa Tau Alpha. Episcopalian. Author: John Henry Brown, 1972. Home: 8 Ridgewood Rd Saint Louis MO 63124 Office: May Dept Stores Co 611 Olive St Saint Louis MO 63101

HONKE, SUE ANN, financial executive; b. Flint, Mich., Feb. 4, 1948; d. Ivan L. and Frances E. Tuttle; grad. Victor Bus. Sch., 1969; student U. Mich., 1970-73; m. Alfred A. Honke, June 27, 1981; children—Victoria Sue, Byron D. Med. sec. Univ. Hosp., 1966-69; adminstrv. asst. Inland Scholtz Modular Housing, 1971-72; adminstr., acct. Washtenaw County Rd. Commn., 1972-76; office mgr. Moehrle, Inc., Ann Arbor, Mich., 1976-79; fin. mgr. Lovejoy Tiffany & Assocs., Inc., Ann Arbor, 1979-80, dir. fin. and adminstrn., 1980-83, v.p., gen. mgr., 1983—. Mem. Nat. Assn. Female Execs., Nat. Assn. Accts., Am. Mgmt. Assn., Credit Women Internat. Office: Lovejoy Tiffany & Assocs Box 8259 Ann Arbor MI 48107

HOOD, LESLIE LYNN, publishing executive; b. Indpls., June 24, 1948; s. John Marquis and Gloria (Bennett) H.; m. Jean Marie Rawlings, Dec. 12, 1969; children—Derek, Heath, Brecka, Shamene. B.S., Mo. Valley Coll., 1970. Student personnel adminstr. Mo. Valley Coll., Marshall, 1969-71; dist. dir. Crossroads of Am. council Boy Scouts Am., Indpls., 1971-74, fin. dir. Don Beard council, Cin., 1974-83; v.p. Lay Leadership Internat., Christian lit. pub. co., Fairfield, Ohio, 1983—; pres. C.C.S. Consultants, Cin., 1980—; bd. dirs. Santa Marie Neighborhood, Cin., 1976-80, H.I.P. Inc., Cin., 1977-79. Author: Financing Local Institutions, 1981; Baptist Church in Scouting, 1983. Pres., Kansas City Council Higher Edn., 1969. Mem. Nat. Soc. Fund Raising Execs. (cert.; Honors scholar 1983; mem. exec. bd. 1980—), Cin. Soc. Fund Raisers, Advt. Council. Republican. Mem. Assemblies of God. Clubs: Hamilton (Ohio); Kiwanis (Cin.). Lodge: Elks. Avocations: hiking; camping; canoeing. Home: 5841 Gilmore Dr Fairfield OH 45014 Office: Lay Leadership Internat 1267 Hicks Blvd Fairfield OH 45014

HOOPER, JAMES MURRAY, service association executive; b. Waco, Tex., Jan. 4, 1928; s. Murray Robertson and Ersey (Cawthon) H.; m. Lorraine Marian Voehl, Mar. 9, 1967; children—William David, John Charles, Walter Brooks, Paul Ryan. B.Arch., Tex. Tech U., 1953. Vol., staff positions Peace Corps, Bolivia, Guatemala, Colombia, 1962-69; dir. Brazil, Rio de Janeiro, 1969-71; owner N.Mex. Office Supply Co., Santa Fe, 1971-72; adminstrv. officer Ohio Dept. Fin., Columbus, 1972-76; exec. dir. Sertoma Internat., Kansas City, Mo., 1976—. Served with USN, 1946-48. Mem. Am. Soc. Assn. Execs., Mid Am. Soc. Assn. Execs. Club: Sertoma (Kansas City, Mo.). Office: Sertoma International 1912 E Meyer Blvd Kansas City MO 64132

HOOPES, PHILLIP CARL, ophthalmologist; b. Provo, Utah, June 17, 1948; s. Preston Baker and Norma Rider (Holman) H.; m. Marilyn Margaret Lott, June 4, 1970; children—Phillip, Scott, Matthew, Janelle, Kimberly, Jeremy. B.S., U. Mo., 1972; M.S., Wake Forest U., 1974; M.D., Bowman Gray Sch. Medicine, 1976. Diplomate Am. Bd. Ophthalmology. Intern Bapt. Meml. Hosp., Winston-Salem, N.C., 1976-77; resident U. Iowa, Iowa City, 1979-82; asst. Harvard Med. Sch., Boston, 1983-84; practice medicine specializing in ophthalmology, Eye Cons., Inc., Kansas City, Mo., 1984—. Author: Suffer the Little Children, 1979; Cataracts-A Guide for Patients, 1985. Fellow Am. Acad. Ophthalmology; mem. AMA, Kerato-Refractive Soc., Am. Intra-Ocular Inplant Soc. Republican. Mormon. Office: Eye Cons Inc 2900 Baltimore Kansas City MO 64108

HOOPMAN, HAROLD DEWAINE, oil company executive; b. Lucas, Kans., July 22, 1920; s. Ira William and Mary B. (Dorman) H.; B.S. in M.E., U. Wyo., 1942; postgrad. Harvard U., 1964; LL.D. (hon.) Marietta Coll., 1979; L.H.D. (hon.), Eastern Ill. U., 1982; m. Eleanor Gessner, July 6, 1946; children—Judith Kristin Hoopman Hains, David W., Michael J. Test engr. Wright Aero. Co., Patterson, N.J., 1942-43; with Marathon Oil Co., 1946-84, v.p. internat. div., Findlay, Ohio, 1962-67, asst. to pres., 1967-68, v.p. prodn., 1968-69, v.p. mktg. U.S., 1969-72, pres., 1972-84, chief exec. officer, 1975-84; vice chmn., dir. U.S. Steel Corp.; dir. Pitts. Nat. Bank, PNC Fin. Corp., Am. Petroleum Inst. Served with USNR, 1943-46. Mem. Soc. Petroleum Engrs.

HOORNBEEK, LYNDA RUTH COUCH, librarian, educator; b. Springfield, Ill., July 12, 1933; d. Willard Lee and Mabel Magdalene (Forberg) Couch; m. Louis Arthur Hoornbeek, Nov. 9, 1957; children—John Arthur, David William, Mark Benjamin. B.A. in Sociology, U. Ill., 1955; M.Ed., Cornell U., 1956; M.L.S., U. So. Calif., Los Angeles, 1973. Cert. tchr. Ill., N.Y. Tchr. elem. sch. North Haven (Conn.) Pub. Schs., 1956-57; library adminstr. Winfield (Ill.) Pub. Library, 1974-77; interim library adminstr. Bloomingdale (Ill.) Pub. Library, 1977-78; ref. librarian Franklin Park (Ill.) Pub. Library, 1978-83; state literacy dir. program Literacy Vols. of Ill., Chgo., 1983—; research coordinator Ill. Literacy Council, Office of Sec. State, 1984—. Bd. dirs. YWCA, Pitts., 1957—. YWCA fellow 1954; Ford Found. fellow, 1955-56; U. Ill. scholar, 1951-55. Mem. Mortar Bd., Calif. Library Assn., Ill. Library Assn., ALA, AAUW, LWV, Beta Phi Mu, Pi Lambda Theta, Alpha Phi. Congregationalist. Home: 351 N Park Blvd Glen Ellyn IL 60137 Office: Literacy Vols of Ill 207 S Wabash 8th Floor Chicago IL 60604

HOOVER, CHARLES M., appliance manufacturing company executive. Chmn. Roper Corp., Kankakee, Ill., also dir. Office: Roper Corp 1905 W Court St Kankakee IL 60901*

HOOVER, DELANO C., accounting executive; b. Hamilton, Ohio, Aug. 21, 1945; s. Charles and Geneva (Winkle) H.; m. Patty J. Keller, Apr. 15, 1967; children—DeLana Rene, Monica Jo, Stacey Lynn. B.S. in Bus. magna cum laude, Miami U., Oxford, Ohio, 1969. C.P.A., Ohio. Staff acct. Coopers & Lybrand, Dayton, Cin., 1969-75; ptnr. Hoover & Roberts Inc., Eaton, Ohio, 1975—. Vice mayor Eaton City Council, 1981—. Served with USN, 1963-66. Recipient Haskins & Sells Found award, 1968. Mem. Am. Inst. C.P.A.s, Ohio Soc. C.P.A.s. Republican. Methodist. Club: Eaton Country (treas. 1979—). Lodge: Rotary (sec. 1978-82, pres. 1982-83). Avocations: fishing, boating, woodworking. Home: 221 S Maple St Eaton OH 45320 Office: 121 N Barron St Eaton OH 45320

HOOVER, EARL REESE, savings association executive, lawyer; b. Dayton, Ohio, Nov. 19, 1904; s. John Jacob and Flora Maude (Brosier) H.; m. Alice Lorene Propst, Dec. 18, 1931; 1 child, Richard Wilson. A.B., Otterbein Coll., 1926, LL.D., 1955; J.D., Harvard U., 1929; LL.D., Salem Coll., 1961. Asst. atty. gen. State of Ohio, Columbus, 1930-31, 32; assoc. Mooney, Hahn, Loeser, Keough & Beam, Cleve., 1933-46; sole practice, Cleve., 1946-50; instr. bus. Fenn Coll. (now Cleve. State U.), 1950-51; law dir. Town of Aurora, Ohio, 1949-50; judge Common Pleas Ct. of Cuyahoga County, Cleve., 1951-69; sr. v.p. Shaker Savs. Assn., Shaker Heights, Ohio, 1969-80, mem. adv. bd. dirs., 1977-80; sr. v.p. Ohio Savs. Assn., 1980—; guest speaker numerous clubs, assns. Author: Cradle of Greatness: National and World Achievements of Ohio's Western Reserve, 1977. Bd. dirs. Cleve. Law Library, 1942-54, Citizens Bur., 1945-53; bd. dirs. Cleve. Roundtable of NCCJ, 1946-52, mem. exec. com., 1950-52, treas., 1950-52, chmn. food industry com Cleve. Health Council, 1942-46; trustee, mem. exec. com. Nationalities Services Ctr., 1953-56; mem. Cleve. Landmarks Commn., 1974- 82; exec. bd. dirs. Greater Cleve. Bicentennial Commn., 1975-76; trustee Cleve. Masonic Library Assn., 1973-83; chmn. pub. relations com. Anti-Tv League of Cleve. and Cuyahoga County, Cleve., 1963-65; trustee Otterbein Coll., 1935-60, chmn. alumni relations and publicity com. of bd. trustees, 1945-60; mem. men's com. Cleve. Playhouse, 1950-57; bd. dirs. Neighborhood Settlement Assn., 1951-58; exec. bd. dirs. Greater Cleve. council Boy Scouts Am., 1956-59, chmn. council's Ct. of Honor, 1949-55, chmn. Newton D. Baker Dist., 1956-59, rep. to Nat. Council, 1957; bd. dir. Cleve. Ch. Fedn., 1955-58, Western Res. Hist. Soc., 1968—, Shaker Hist. Soc., 1969-81, v.p., 1970-71; bd. dirs. Religious Heritage of Am., 1958-59; v.p. Ripon Club (Rep. Club), 1949; mem. exec. Cleve. Civil War Round Table, 1969-70. Named Father of Hall of Fame Otterbein Coll., 1968; recipient Disting. Alumnus award Alumni Assn. of Otterbein Coll., 1970, award for Outstanding Service to Scouting Boy Scouts Am., Southwest Dist., 1972. Mem. Bar Assn. Greater Cleve., Cleve. Bar Assn. (rep. to Council of Dels. of Ohio State Bar Assn. 1937-38, chmn. coms.), Ohio State Bar Assn. (chmn. coms.), Cuyahoga County Bar Assn., Early Settlers Assn. of Western Res. (pres. 1971-72, bd. dirs. 1967—, mem. com. establishing Hall of Fame 1971), Harvard Alumni Assn. of Cleve., Harvard Law Sch. Alumni Assn., Otterbein Coll. Alumni Assn. (nat. pres.). Mem. United Ch. of Christ. Clubs: City (v.p. 1948, bd. dirs. 1946-48), Cleve. Shrine Luncheon (pres. 1959, bd. dirs. 1957-59), Cleve. Advt., Hundred Club (pres. 1938), Republic (bd. dirs. 1940-41, 44-48, pres. 1947). Lodges: Rotary (chmn. projects, emcee civic luncheons), Kiwanis of Cleve. (bd. dirs. Found. 1963-66, v.p. 1965-66), Masons, Shriners, Jesters. Home: 3356 Grenway Rd Shaker Heights OH 44122 Office: Ohio Savs Assn 13109 Shaker Sq Cleveland OH 44120

HOOVER, GLENN EDWARD, educational administrator; b. Lamar, Mo., May 17, 1944; s. Glenn O. and Margarite Nadine (Evilsizer) H.; m. Susan Verneille Schrock, Mar. 4, 1967; children—Laura Susan, Elisabeth Sarah. B.S., Southwest Mo. State U., 1966, M.S., 1970; Ed.S., U. Ark., 1977, Ed.D., 1980. Tchr. history Strafford Sch., Mo., 1969-70; prin. secondary sch. Niangua Sch., Mo., 1970-77, Fair Play Sch., Mo., 1978-80, Niangua Sch., 1980-81, Galena Sch., Mo., 1983—. Mem. Mo. State Tchrs. Assn., Southwest Prins. Assn. Republican. Baptist. Lodges: Elks, Masons, Eagles. Avocations: fishing, golf. Home: 1114 W Morningside Springfield MO 65807 Office: Galena High Sch PO Box 286 Galena MO 65656

HOOVER, HARRY ALLEN, state aeronautics official; b. Franklin, Pa., Aug. 16, 1932; s. Henry A. and Elizabeth (Scott) H.; m. Katherine Jensen, July 12, 1958; children—Elizabeth, Sarah. B.S. in Indsl. Engring., Iowa State U., 1955; B.S. in Aero. Engring., U.S. Naval Postgrad. Sch., 1962, M.S. in Elec. Engring., 1963. Lic. comml. and instrument pilot. Combustion engr. Gen. Motors Corp., Indpls., 1954; commd. officer U.S. Navy, 1955, advanced through grades to capt., pilot, various locations, ret., 1979; dir. aeronautics State of Iowa, Des Moines, 1979—. Decorated Legion of Merit, U.S. Air Force, 1976, Navy Commendation medal 1973; recipient Meritorious Service award Dept. Def., 1970. Mem. AIAA, Aerospace Edn. Council of Iowa, Nat. Assn. State Aviation Ofcls. (bd. dirs. 1981-83, 1984-85), Navy League (v.p. 1984-85). Republican. Methodist. Lodge: Rotary. Avocations: woodworking, antique automobiles, fishing, hunting, boating. Home: 2816 Watrous Ave Des Moines IO 50321 Office: Aeronautics Div Iowa Dept Transp Des Moines Airport Des Moines IO 50321

HOOVER, RICHARD LEE, physical therapist; b. Middleford, Ind., Feb. 24, 1941; s. Charles James and Vera Louise Hoover; m. Alice A. Berninger, Aug. 2, 1964; children—Betsy, Jennifer. B.S., Ball State U., 1963, M.S., 1965; cert. phys. therapist Ohio State U., 1964. Asst. prof. Ball State U., Muncie, Ind., 1963-67, Northwestern U., Evanston, 1967-72; edn. coordinator Cramer Products, Gardner, Kans., 1972-74; owner, pres. Phys. Therapy Services, Schaumburg, Ill., 1972—; athletic trainer Chgo. Sting; cons. Chgo. Bulls, Chgo. Cubs. Mem. Am. Phys. Therapy Assn., Nat. Athletic Trainers Assn., Am. Coll. Sports Medicine. Republican. Presbyterian. Clubs: Red Cloud, Christian Athletics. Editor: Athletic Tng.; author tng. texts. Home: 636 N Dunton Arlington Heights IL 60004 Office: 1100 Woodfield Rd Suite 109 Schaumburg IL 60195

HOOVER, THOMAS WAYNE, security equipment company executive; b. Chgo., Dec. 27, 1936; s. Joseph Wayne and Eileen Cecelia H.; A.B. in Econs., Loyola U., Chgo., 1969; children—Thomas Wayne, Caroline M., David M., Matthew R., Mark J. Sales and mktg. ofcl. Belden Corp., Chgo., 1963-69; sales and mgmt. ofcl. Diebold, Inc., Chgo., 1969-75; pres. Ill. Nat. Safe Corp., River Forest, 1975—. Served with USAF, 1956-59. Mem. Nat. Ind. Bank Equipment Suppliers Assn. Republican. Roman Catholic. Club: Union League (Chgo.). Office: 7308 Central St River Forest IL 60305

HOPCRAFT, DAVID L., journalist; b. Cleve., Feb. 15, 1944; s. Lester and Betty Kathrine (Coopland) H.; B.A. in Journalism, Ohio State U., 1967; children—Michael, David Stephen. Reporter, Dayton (Ohio) Jour. Herald, 1967-69; mem. staff Cleve. Plain Dealer, 1969—, Columbus (Ohio) bur. chief, now exec. editor; mem. vis. com. social and behavioral scis. Coll. Arts and Scis., Cleve. State U. Recipient Outstanding Govt. Reporting award AP Ohio; Disting. Reporting Public Affairs award Am. Polit. Sci. Assn. Mem. AP Mng. Editors Assn., Am. Soc. Newspaper Editors. Office: 1801 Superior Ave Cleveland OH 44114

HOPE, KENNETH WEAVER, foundation administrator; b. N.Y.C., Nov. 4, 1947; s. Quentin Manning and Nathalie May (Weaver) H.; m. Cheryl Zimmermann, June 27, 1970; children—Nathaniel, Trevor. B.S., U. Wis., 1970; M.A., Ind. U., 1973, Ph.D., 1975. Lectr. English, U. de Dijon, France, 1974-76; substitute tchr. Chgo. pub. schs., 1976-77; vis. asst. prof. Ind. U., Bloomington, 1977-78; adminstrv. asst. Bradford Exchange, Niles, Ill., 1978-80; asst. dir. MacArthur Found., Northbrook, Ill., 1980-82, acting dir., Chgo., 1982-84, dir. MacArthur Fellows Program, 1984—; dance panel Nat. Endowment for Arts, Washington, 1983; selection judge Coro Found., St. Louis, 1984-85. Author: An Introduction to Film: Textbook for Comparative Literature, 1978, 2d edit., 1984. Home: 1120 Midway Northbrook IL 60062 Office: MacArthur Found 140 S Dearborn Suite 700 Chicago IL 60603

HOPEN, DIANNE BROWN, French educator, educational administrator; b. St. Paul, Dec. 30, 1947; d. Maurice Leander and Ann Edith (Kell) Brown; m. Allan Nels Hopen, Aug. 16, 1969. B.S. in Edn., U. Minn., 1969, M.A. in Edn., 1980; cert. of participation Universite Catholique d'Angers (France), 1978. Teaching cert., Minn. Tchr. French and Am. history St. Paul Pub. Schs., 1969—; dean French Lang. Village Programs, Concordia Coll., Moorhead, Minn., 1972—, dir. French Mini Programs, 1973-80, dir. French Tchr. Immersion Experiences, 1973—, tchr./counselor Mpls. Pub. Schs. Lang. Camp, summers 1970, 71; group leader student trips to France, Intercultural Student Experiences, 1973—; French tchr. Twin City Inst. for Talented Youth, summers 1970, 71; Fulbright exchange tchr., France, 1985; mem. Com. of 11, Minn. Dept. Edn., 1975-78, trainer, 1978. Recipient 4 mini grants, St. Paul Pub. Schs., 1972-75; Julius Braufman award for excellence in edn. Minn. Bus. Found., 1984; named Tchr. of Excellence, Minn. Tchr. of Yr. Com., 1976. Mem. Am. Assn. Tchrs. of French (regional rep. to nat. exec. council for Mid-Central U.S. 1982—), Minn. Council on Teaching Fgn. Langs., Am. Council on Teaching Fgn. Langs. Author: Un Nouveau Jour., 1973; Leader's Handbook for Mini Programs, 1976; co-author: French Language Village Instruction Program, 1982; editor: Les Chansons du Lac du Bois (French songbook), 1982, Activity and Sport Instruction Program: Guidebook for Counselors, 1982, Medical Care Manual, 1983, Counselor Handbook, 1983, Dean's Handbook, 1983. Home: 250 Edgewood Ln West Saint Paul MN 55118 Office: Humboldt Secondary Complex 30 E Baker St Saint Paul MN 55107

HOPKINS, CURTIS RAY, conservation organization executive, wildlife consultant; b. Hattiesburg, Miss., Apr. 27, 1948; s. James Ray and Ann (King) H.; m. Sharon Kay Johnson, Aug. 19, 1967; children—Shannon Marie, Elizabeth Ann. B.S. in Forestry, Miss. State U., 1971, M.S. in Wildlife Ecology, 1973; Ph.D. in Wildlife Sci., Tex. A & M U., 1981. Cert. wildlife biologist. Asst. ranger U.S. Forest Service, Rolling Fork, Miss., 1972-74, wildlife biologist, 1974-75, wildlife biologist, Wiggins, Miss., 1975-77; instr. Tex. A & M U., College Station, 1978, research asst., 1979-81; regional dir. Ducks Unltd., Inc., Grenada, Miss., 1981—; sec. Miss. Sandhill Crane Team, U.S. Fish and Wildlife Service, Wiggins, 1974-77. Author, co-author sci. publs. on wildlife. Mem. Wildlife Soc. (pres. Miss. chpt. 1975-77), Soc. Am. Foresters (chmn. wildlife and fish ecology group 1977-79), Zi Sigma Pi. Roman Catholic. Home: Route 3 Box 81C Grenada MS 38901

HOPKINS, DIANNE MCAFEE, school library media administrator, consultant; b. Houston, Dec. 30, 1944; d. DeWitt Talmadge and Valda Lois (Baker) McAfee; m. Dale William Hopkins, July 7, 1982; children—Brent William, Scott McAfee. B.A., Fisk U., 1966; M.L.S., Atlanta U., 1967; Ed.S., Western Mich. U., 1973; Ph.D., U. Wis.-Madison, 1981. Sch. librarian Houston Ind. Sch. Dist., 1967-71; sch. library specialist Mich. Dept. of Edn., Lansing, Mich., 1972-73; library media specialist West Bloomfield Sch. Dist., Orchard Lake, Mich., 1973-74; library media cons. U. Mich., Ann Arbor, 1974-77; bur. dir. Wis. Dept. of Pub. Instrn., Madison, Wis., 1977—. Contbr. articles to profl. jours., also chpt. in book. Chmn. outreach bd. First Baptist Ch., Madison, 1981, pulpit com., 1982, chmn. bd. edn., 1982. Mem. ALA (governance council 1981-86), Assn. Edn. Commn. Tech. (bd. dirs. 1982-85), Wis. Intellectual Freedom Coalition (exec. com. 1984), Wis. Sch. Library Media Assn. (liaison 1977—), Wis. Ednl. Media Assn. Baptist. Club: Links, Inc. (Wis.). Avocations: piano; reading; cross stitchery; movies; museums. Home: 501 Meadowlark Dr Madison WI 53714 Office: Dept Pub Instrn 125 S Webster Box 7841 Madison WI 53707

HOPKINS, EDWARD DONALD, business executive; b. Little Rock, Apr. 16, 1937; s. Edward J. and Mildred I. Hopkins; m. Dawn Dee Fritz, May 20, 1965; children—Mark Edward, Scott Edward, Paige Noel. B.S., U.S. Air Force Acad., 1960; M.Aerospace Mgmt., U. So. Calif., 1966. Commd. 2d lt. U.S. Air Force, 1956, advanced through grades to capt., 1964; ret., 1967; unit mgr. Gen. Electric Co., Cin., 1967-70; v.p. mktg. Tri City Builders, Cin., 1971; group v.p. Roch Instrument Systems, Inc., Rochester, N.Y., 1972-74; dir. hermetic motors Gould Inc., St. Louis, 1974-75, v.p., gen. mgr. Powder Metal Parts div., Salem, Ind., 1976-77, pres., gen. mgr. Indsl. Battery div., Langhorne, Pa., 1977-80; pres., gen. mgr. Consumer div. Sherwin-Williams Co., Cleve., 1980-83, group v.p. parent co., 1983; pres., dir. Interlake Inc., Oak Brook, Ill., 1983—. Office: Interlake Inc 2015 Spring Rd Oak Brook IL 60521

HOPKINS, HAROLD A., clergyman. Bishop, Episcopal Ch., Fargo, N.D. Office: 809 8th Ave S Fargo ND 58102*

HOPKINS, MARTHA JEAN, production company executive; b. Chgo., Dec. 17, 1940; .. John L. and Idamae (Humiston) H.; B.A., Denison U., 1962; M.Ed., Nat. Coll. Edn., 1966, postgrad. Northwestern U. Staff editor Laidlaw Bros., River Forest, Ill., 1970-74; project dir. Ency. Brit. Ednl. Corp., Chgo., 1974-77, sr. producer, 1977-79, dir. prodn. planning and research, 1979-83, dir. planning and research, 1983—; guest speaker Columbia Coll.; cons. Sadlier Pubs. Mem. Assn. Supervision and Curriculum Devel., Internat. Reading Assn., Nat. Council Tchrs. English Nat. Council Social Studies, Nat. Council Tchrs. Math., AAAS, Assn. Ednl. Data Systems, Nat. Sci. Tchrs. Assn., Am. Soc. Tng. and Devel., Chgo. Council Fgn. Relations. Clubs: Sierra, Canyon. Author/producer: Open Box: Ideas for Creative Expression, 1977; That's Fantastic!, 1978; That's Incredible!, 1979; A Likely Story (Learning Filmstrip of Yr. award, Design '75 award), 1979. Home: 4300 N Marine Dr Chicago IL 60613 Office: 425 N Michigan Ave Chicago IL 60611

HOPKINS, SHEILA MARIE, pharmacy supervisor; b. Mpls., Sept. 24, 1954; m. Larry I. Hopkins, Oct. 2, 1982. B.S. in Pharmacy, Drake U., 1976; M.B.A., Ill. Benedictine Coll., 1985. Registered pharmacist, Ill. Pharmacist St. Mary's Hosp., Galesburg, Ill., 1976-78; pharmacist Good Samaritan Hosp., Downers Grove, Ill., 1978-81, pharmacy supr., 1981—. Mem. Am. Pharm. Assn., Am. Soc. Hosp. Pharmacists, No. Ill. Council of Hosp. Pharmacists, Lambda Kappa Sigma. Avocations: sports; family and outdoor activities; cooking; crafts.

HOPKINS, WILLARD GEORGE, health care administrator; b. Balt., Mar. 30, 1940; s. George Conrad and Laura Elizabeth (Elwell) H.; m. Valerie Jewell Hopkins, June 22, 1963; children—Michelle Marie, Tiffany Lynn. B.S. in Civil Engring., U. Md., 1963, M.H.A., Cornell U., 1969, M.B.A., 1969. Cons., Arthur Young & Co. San Francisco, 1969-74, health cons., practice dir., 1974-76, dir. health care, cons. practice dir., Washington, 1976-78; health cons., practice dir. Booz Allen & Hamilton, Washington 1977-79; exec. v.p. Scottsdale Meml. Hosp., Ariz., Scottsdale Meml. Health Service Co., 1979-83; exec. dir. Mednet/Euclid Clinic Found., Ohio, 1983—. Served with USPHS, 1963-69. Fellow Am. Coll. Hosp. Adminstrs., Soc. Advanced Med. Systems; mem. N.Am. Soc. Corp. Planning, Am. Health Planning Assn., NAM, Assn. Univ. Programs in Health Adminstrn., Comprehensive Health Planning Assn. Contra Costa County (bd. dirs. 1973-77). Mem. editorial adv. bd. Am. Jour. Health Planning, 1976-79. Presbyterian. Lodge: Rotary. Home: 110 Stonewood Dr Morland Hills OH 44022 Office: 18599 Lake Shore Blvd Euclid OH 18599

HOPPE, LESLIE JOHN, educator; b. Chgo., Sept. 22, 1944; s. Daniel John and Florence Martha (Kapuscinski) H. B.A., St. Francis Coll., 1967; M.A., Aquinas Inst., 1971; Ph.D., Northwestern U., 1978. Ordained priest, Roman Cath. Ch., 1971. Instr. St. Mary's High Sch., Burlington, Wis., 1971-73; asst. prof. Aquinas Inst., Dubuque, 1976-79; assoc. prof. St. Mary of Lake Sem., Mundelein, Ill., 1979-81; asst. prof. bibl. studies Cath. Theol. Union, Chgo., 1981—; bus. mgr. Bibl. Research, Chgo., 1982—; dept. chmn. Cath. Theol. Union, 1983-85; assoc. editor The Bible Today, Collegeville, Minn., 1981—. Author: Joshua Judges, 1982; What are They Saying, 1984. Contbr. articles to profl. jours. Mem. Cath. Bibl. Assn. (consultor), Soc. Bible. Lit., Chgo. Soc. Bibl. Research, Am. Schs. Oriental Research, Nat. Assn. Profs. Hebrew. Democrat. Club: Northwestern U. Lodge: K.C. Avocation: stamp collecting. Office: Cath Theol Union 5401 S Cornell Ave Chicago IL 60615

HOPPER, GORDON LEWIS, pub. relations counselor; b. Olney, Ill., Oct. 22, 1921; s. Lewis Dee and Barbara (Johnson) H.; m. Dorothy McKee, Apr. 14, 1946; children—Laura, Julia, Catherine, Barbara, Mary, James. B.A., Ill. Wesleyan U., 1946; LL.B., Lincoln Coll. Law, 1953. Info. rep. State of Ill., 1947-52; pub. relations dir. MacMurray Coll., 1952-54, Ill. Republican State Central Com., 1954; mgr. Marshall Mitchell Advt. and Printing, 1955-59; promotion dir. Downtown St. Louis, Inc., 1959-63, exec. dir., 1963-70; exec. dir. Environ. Planning Assn. Colorado Springs, 1970-75; mng. dir. BHN Pub. Relations, St. Louis, 1976—; instr. pub. relations Webster U., 1976-77; dir. Batz Hodgson Neuwoehner Inc. Chmn. pub. relations St. Louis March of Dimes, 1983—; mem. mktg. com. Downtown St. Louis Inc.; mem. Colorado Springs Charter Rev. Commn., 1975. Served with USNR, World War II. Mem. Pub. Relations Soc. Am., Internat. Downtown Execs. Assn. (past pres.). Republican. United Methodist. Clubs: Media; St. Louis Press. Author: Organization, Functions and Financing of Downtown Associations, 1973, 75. Home: 300 Holloway Rd Ballwin MO 63011 Office: 910 N 11th St Saint Louis MO 63101

HOPPERT, EARL W(ILLIAM), clergyman, educator; b. Duluth, Minn., Nov. 14, 1939; s. Glenn A. and Margaret J. (Server) H.; m. Candice N. Leuthold, Dec. 26, 1974; children—Lesley, Kelly. A.A. with honors, N.D. State Sch. Sci., 1959; B.A. magna cum laude, Yankton Coll., 1961; M.Div., Andover Newton Theol. Sch., 1965; postgrad. Trinity Coll., Glasgow U., 1965-68; D.Min. in Pastoral Care and Counseling, Christian Theol. Sem., Indpls., 1982. Ordained to ministry United Ch. Christ, 1965. Asst. pastor The Tron Ch., Balornock, Glasgow, Scotland, 1967-68; pastor 1st Congl. Ch., Eastlake, Colo., 1968-72, United Ch. Christ Westminster (Colo.), 1968-72; chaplain resident Methodist Hosp., Rochester, Minn., 1972-73; chaplain intern/resident St. Luke's Hosp., Milw., 1973-75; chaplain educator Central State Hosp., Indpls., 1975—, head dept. pastoral care, 1975—, founder, chmn. patient advocacy com., 1979-84; clin. pastoral edn. supr., mem. faculty Christian Theol. Sem., Indpls., 1976—, counselor Pastoral Counseling Services, 1980—. Leader Kick the Habit Clinics, Wis. Lung Assn., 1974-75. Turner fellow, 1965; Ind. Dept. Mental Health grantee, 1976-82; recipient numerous scholarships; recipient Dist. Service award DeMolay. Mem. Assn. Clin. Pastoral Edn. (cert. chaplain supr.; life mem.), Am. Assn. Pastoral Counselors (cert.), Internat. Preview Soc. Lodge: Masons. Contbr. to profl. publs. Home: 9001 Caminito Ct Indianapolis IN 46234 Office: 3000 W Washington St Indianapolis IN 46222

HOPPES, GARY JON, vocational educator; b. Davenport, Iowa, Oct. 9, 1946; s. James William and Viola Pearl (Johnson) H.; B.A. in Indsl. Edn., U. No. Iowa, 1973; M.S. in Indsl. Vocat./Tech. Edn., Iowa State U., 1976. Instr., coordinator vocat. programs Lakenheath Am. High Sch., RAF Lakenheath, Eng., 1973-74; tech. writer, tng. dept. Cherry Burrell Co., Cedar Rapids, Iowa, 1974-75; grad. research asst., spl. needs Iowa State U., 1975; program coordinator Alternative Edn. Ctr., Marion (Iowa) Ind. Sch., 1976-78; instr., coordinator collision repair program Kirkwood Community Coll., 1978—; vocat. cons. to trade and indsl. programs. Served with USN, 1965-69; Vietnam. Decorated service medal with 5 Bronze Stars, Navy Achievement medal; recipient Order of Arrow award Boy Scouts Am., 1961, Life Scout award, 1963. Mem. Council Vocat. Edn., Am. Vocat. Assn., Iowa Vocat. Assn., Nat. Assn. Indsl. and Tech. Tchr. Educators, Epsilon Pi Tau. Lutheran. Club: Vocat. Indsl. Clubs Am. Author: Working Papers Special Needs Population, 1976; The Administrator's Role in Establishing and Maintaining A Vocational Cooperative Education Program, 1976; Photojournalism, A Guide, 1978. Home: Ely Paddocks Route 1 Ely IA 52227 Office: 6301 Kirkwood Blvd Linn Hall 113 Cedar Rapids IA 52406

HOPPING, EARLE ALBERT, executive placement counselor; b. Glen Cove, N.Y., July 6, 1943; s. Earle Albert and Mary Rita (McLaughlin) H.; m. Judith Ann Streit, Nov. 15, 1964 (div. 1974); m. Doreen Joyce Moore, May 31, 1975; children—Michael, Billi, Lori, Lucy, Kathleen, Molly, Todd. B.S. in Elec. Engring., Milw. Sch. Engring., 1969; M.B.A., N.D. State U., 1983. fed. acct. rep. Control Data Corp., Washington, 1969-72; field rep. Neca, Chgo., 1972; asst. mgr., tng. dir. Dakotas chpt., Neca, Fargo, N.D., 1972-85; pres. Dunhill of Fargo, Inc., N.D., 1985—; cons. in field. Mem. State Bd. Adv. Com. for Vocat. Edn., N.D., 1975-78; mem. Job Service Adv. Com., N.D., 1980-83. Served with USN, 1960-64. Recipient Spl. Recognition award U.S. Dept. Labor, 1977. Mem. IEEE, Illuminating Engring. Soc. (pres. Red River chpt. 1975-76), N.D. Safety Council (pres. 1978-80, chmn. bd. dirs. 1980-81), Am. Legion. Republican. Lutheran. Lodges: Elks, Eagles, Optimist. Avocations: golf; bowling; computers. Home: 1215 S 15th St Moorhead MN 56560 Office: Dunhill of Fargo Inc 51 Broadway Suite 604 Fargo ND 58102

HOPSON, THERESA MAE, educator; b. Sanford, Fla., Mar. 1, 1945; d. Henry Reynold and Annie Mae (Davis) Garrett; B.S., Eastern Mich. U., 1967, M.S., 1970; Ph.D., U. Mich., 1981; m. Robert Louis Hopson, Aug. 27, 1966; 1 dau., Gwendolyn Denise. Tchr., Jackson (Mich.) Pub. Schs., 1967-68, Ann Arbor (Mich.) Pub. Schs., 1968-69, 71—; grad. intern Inkster (Mich.) Child Devel. Ctr., 1969-70. HEW Early Childhood fellow, 1969-70. Mem. NEA, Ann Arbor Edn. Assn. (lang. arts rep., chair retirement com., tchr. evaluation com., others), Mich. Edn. Assn., World Orgn. Early Childhood Edn., Assn. Curriculum and Supervision, Am. Bus. Women's Assn., Internat. Platform Assn., Phi Delta Kappa, Beta Sigma Phi. Democrat. Eckankar. Home: 1835 Franklin Ct N Ann Arbor MI 48103 Office: Carpenter Sch 4250 Central Blvd Ann Arbor MI 48104

HORAL, TIMOTHY THOMAS, plastics manager; b. Detroit, July 31, 1949; s. Thomas James and Shirley Ann (Bednarski) H.; m. Patrice Joann Downey, May 5, 1978; 1 son, Thomas James. A.S., Mich. State U., 1969, B.S., 1972. Jr. buyer Firestone Indsl. Products, Wash., Mich., 1972-75, buyer, 1975-82; gen. mgr. Alko Products Inc., Fraser, Mich., 1982—. Affiliate mem. Soc. Plastic Engrs. Roman Catholic. Club: Corvette of Mich. (Dearborn). Office: Al-Ko Products Inc 34155 Riviera Dr Fraser MI 48026

HORBELT, DOUGLAS VINCENT, physician, educator; b. N.Y.C., Jan. 2, 1947; s. Vincent and Kathryn (Kost) H.; B.A. with honors, U. Tex., Austin, 1969; M.D., U. Tex., Galveston, 1972; m. Patricia Ann Butschek, June 10, 1972; children—Robert, Christopher. Resident in ob-gyn, Wesley Med. Center, Wichita, Kans., 1972-75, asst. dir. ob-gyn edn., 1975-80; asst. prof. ob-gyn U. Kans. Sch. Medicine, 1975-80, assoc. prof. ob-gyn, 1980—; dir. div. gynecology, 1982—; practice medicine specializing in ob-gyn, Wichita, 1975-80; fellow in gynecol. oncology M.D. Anderson Hosp., Houston, 1980-82. Recipient Thor Jager, M.D. award, 1978; diplomate Am. Bd. Ob-Gyn. Fellow Am. Coll. Obstetricians and Gynecologists; mem. Central Assn. Obstetricians and Gynecologists, Assn. Profs. Gynecology and Obstetrics, AMA, Kans. Med. Soc., Med. Soc. Sedgwick County. Contbr. articles to med. jours. Office: 3243 E Murdock Level A Wichita KS 67214

HORBERG, KURT JOHN, lawyer; b. Galesburg, Ill., Feb. 6, 1952; s. Robert John and Lois Ione (Gustus) H.; m. Jane Ruth Bailey, Nov. 4, 1978 (div. 1981). B.A. with honors, Augustana U., 1974; J.D. with honors, John Marshall U., 1977. Bar: Ill. 1977, U.S. Dist. Ct. (so. dist.) Ill. 1977. Ptnr. Telleen, Telleen, Braendle & Horberg, Cambridge, Ill., 1978—. Bd. dirs. Augustana Coll., Rock Island, Ill., 1982-85, Moline Luth. Hosp. Found. (Ill.), 1983-87, Cambridge Rotary Club, 1983-86. Mem. ABA, Ill. State Bar Assn., Am. Judicature Soc., Ill. Trial Lawyers Assn. Republican. Lutheran. Home: 222 S Ridge Cambridge IL 61238 Office: Telleen Telleen Braendle & Horberg 124 W Exchange Cambridge IL 61238

HORICK, PAUL JOSEPH, geologist; b. LaGrange, Ill., May 6, 1922; s. Paul Joseph and Margaret Carr (Faulds) H.; m. Claudia Jan Ringgenberg, Aug. 16, 1958; children—Joan E., Jonathan P. B.A., Augustana Coll., 1945; M.S., U. Iowa, 1948. Geologist Iowa Geol. Survey, Iowa City, 1948—, chief groundwater, 1971-76, sr. groundwater geologist, 1977—. Author: Water Resources of Iowa, 1970; Minerals of Iowa, 1973; also book chpt. Recipient Disting. Service award State of Iowa, 1981. Fellow Iowa Acad. Sci. (chmn. geol. sect. 1969); mem. Am. Assn. Petroleum Geologists (communicator govt. affairs 1974—, Disting. Service award 1984), Nat. Waterwell Assn. (chmn. state regulatory ofcls. 1984), Iowa Groundwater Assn. (editor 1984—), Geol. Soc. Iowa (registered profl. geologist), Sigma Xi. Republican. Lutheran. Lodge: Kiwanis (editor 1981—). Avocations: photography, reading, gardening, travel, stamps. Office: Iowa Geol Survey 123 N Capitol St Iowa City IA 52242

HORMOZI, HORMOZ, chemical engineer; b. Kermanshah, Iran, July 19, 1936; came to U.S., 1959; s. Abbass and Moneer (Golestani) H.; m. Nahid Afshar, Dec. 23, 1976; 1 child, Shirin Moneer. B.S. in Chem. Engring., Ariz. State U., 1964; M.B.A., Mankato State U., 1979. Registered profl. engr., Tex. Plant Low density polyeth supr. Dow Chem. Co., Freeport, Tex., 1964-66, engr., 1966-70; low density polyeth supt. No. Petrochem. Co., Morris, Ill., 1970-75, plant mgr., Mankato, Minn., 1975-79, Streamwood, Ill., 1979—. Active Heart Fund, 1968; bd. dirs. Streamwood chpt. Am. Cancer Soc., 1981—; active mem. People to People Internat., 1962—. Recipient Mayor's award Lake Jackson, 1969. Mem. Soc. Plastics Engrs. (dir. 1980—), Streamwood C. of C. (dir. 1981—). Baha'i. Home: 1010 Douglas Rd Elgin IL 60120 Office: 601 E Lake St Streamwood IL 60103

HORN, THOMAS RON, safety engineer; b. Chgo., Nov. 29, 1950; s. Herbert Richard and Jeanett Ann (Scherrer) H. A.A., Broward Jr. Coll., 1971; B.S., No. Ill. U., 1975, M.S., 1976. Registered advanced safety profl. engr., Ill. Safety technician Tex. Eastern Transmission, Houston, 1977; loss control rep. Continental Ins. Co., Chgo., 1978-79; fire staff cons. Kemper Group, Chgo., 1979-80; safety dir. Jellissa Corp., Chgo., 1980-83; loss control cons. Tel-Mack Services, 1984—; instr. defensive driving, 1st aid, CPR. Mem. Am. Soc. Safety Engrs., Soc. Fire Protection Engrs. Democrat. Roman Catholic. Club: Chgo. Lions Rugby Football.

HORNSBY, EUNICE ELLEN, university administrator; b. San Diego, June 5, 1955; d. Henry Claude and Philomena Loretta (Casper) H. B.A., Calif. State U.-Chico, 1979; M.A., Ohio State U., 1982. Asst. residence hall dir. Ohio State U., Columbus, 1980-81, career exploration assoc., 1981-82, residence hall dir., 1982-84; area coordinator U. Ill., Urbana-Champaign, 1984—; instr. career devel. Ohio State U., Columbus, 1981, assertion trainer, 1981; counselor Regional Alcoholism Ctr., Columbus, 1981-82. Troop leader Girl Scouts U.S.A., Riverside, Calif., 1973, 74; mem. Champaign-Urbana Women's Network, 1984; bd. dirs. YWCA of U. Ill. Recipient Outstanding Achievement award residence life Ohio State U., Columbus, 1984. Mem. Am. Coll. Personnel Assn. (outstanding new profl. 1984), Am. Assn. Counseling and Devel., Nat. Assn. Student Personnel Adminstrs. Avocations: furniture refinishing; antique collecting and restoration; camping. Office: Florida Ave Residence Halls 1001 W College Ct Urbana IL 61801

HORNY, KAREN LOUISE, library administrator; b. Highland Park, Ill., Apr. 22, 1943; d. Hugo O. and Margaret L. (Bailey) H. A.B. in French Lit. magna cum laude with honors, Brown U., 1965; M.L.S., U. Mich., 1966. Asst. core librarian Northwestern U., Evanston, Ill., 1966-68, head core collection, 1968-71, asst. univ. librarian for tech. services, 1971—; mem. adv. council U. Ill. Grad. Sch. Library Sci., 1975-77. Bd. editors Jour. Acad. Librarianship, 1978-81. Contbr. articles to profl. jours. Recipient Disting. Alumnus award U. Mich., 1983. Mem. ALA (council 1983—, div. pres. 1980-81, chmn. div. 1973-74, 76-78), Ill. Library Assn. (coms.), Freedom to Read Found., Phi Beta Kappa, Phi Kappa Phi, Beta Phi Mu. Episcopalian. Club: Brown Univ. (Chgo.). Home: 1915 Sherman Ave Evanston IL 60201 Office: Northwestern U Library Evanston IL 60201

HOROWITZ, JOEL LAWRENCE, geography and economics educator, consultant; b. Pasadena, Calif., May 2, 1941; s. Norman Harold and Pearl (Shykin) H.; m. Susan Murray McCartney, Oct. 24, 1970; 1 child, Katharine Ann. B.S., Stanford U., 1962; Ph.D., Cornell U., 1967. Mem. tech. staff Research Analysis Corp., McLean, Va., 1967-71; sr. ops. research analyst EPA, Washington, 1971-82; professorial lectr. George Washington U., Washington, 1972-82; vis. assoc. prof. MIT, Cambridge, 1978-79; assoc. prof. U. Iowa, Iowa City, 1982—; cons. Energy & Environ. Analysis, Inc., Arlington, Va., 1983, Tenneco, Inc., Houston, 1983-84, Cambridge Systematics, Inc., Mass., 1984; treas. Policies & Strategies, Inc., Iowa City, 1982—. Author: Air Quality Analysis for Urban Transportation Planning, 1982. Contbr. articles to profl. jours. Grantee EPA, 1983, U.S. Dept. Transp., 1983, 84. Mem. editorial adv. bd. Transp. Research, 1979—. NSF fellow, 1962-67. Mem. Am. Econ. Assn., Econometric Soc., Assn. Am. Geographers (editorial adv. bd. annals 1985—), Transp. Research Bd., Regional Sci. Assn., AAAS, Inst. Mgmt. Scis, Phi Beta Kappa. Office: Dept Geography U Iowa Iowa City IA 52242

HOROWITZ, SUSAN ALISON, data services company executive; b. Amsterdam, N.Y., May 16, 1946; d. Bernard and Helen Belle (Goldmeer) H.; B.A., Wheaton Coll., 1968; M.S., SUNY-Albany, 1969; Ed.D., Ind. U., 1982. Dir. fin. aid No. Essex Community Coll., Haverhill, Mass., 1969-76; coordinator fin. aid Mass. Bd. Higher Edn., Boston, 1976-77; asst. to chancellor, 1976-77; exec. dir. Tng. & Ednl. Data Services, Indpls., 1980—; resident staff trainer Inst. Fin. Aid Adminstrn., Bentley Coll., 1979-80, Southeastern Mass. U., 1977-78; cons. Mansfield Beaty Coll., Wilfred Beauty Coll., Boston, 1975-77. Author: Rationale for Colleges for Women, 1981; contbr. articles to profl. jours. Mem. adv. com. Permanent Charities Fund Boston, 1974-77. Raleigh W. Homstedt fellow Ind. U., 1979-80. Mem. Ind. and Indpls. Econ. Forum, Ind. C. of C., Indpls. C. of C., Assn. Computer Career Info. Systems, (chmn. publs. com. 1982—), Ind. Occupational Info. Com., Nat. Assn. Student Fin. Aid Adminstrs., Coll. Scholarship Service Assembly. Democrat. Jewish. Home: 3242 Braeside Dr Bloomington IN 47401 Office: Tng and Ednl Data Service Inc 150 W Market St Suite 503 Indianapolis IN 46204

HORSEFIELD, DAVID REID, environmental engineer; b. Oak Park, Ill., Jan. 24, 1931; s. Raymond Ernest and Ellen (Crawford) H.; m. Rigmor Wienke, Feb. 16, 1957; children—Steven Reid, Robert David; m. 2 Joan Betty Weber, Nov. 11, 1972. B.S. in Civil Engring., U. Mass., 1952; M.S. in San. Engring., U. Mich., 1956. Registered profl. engr., N.Y., 19 other states. Engr., Camp Dresser & McKee, Boston, 1960-69, v.p., 1970-72, dir., sr. v.p., ptnr., Boston and Milw., 1972-82, sr. tech. cons., Milw., 1982—; cons. environ. engr., Mequon, Wis., 1982—; dir. Warzyn Engring., Inc., Madison, Wis. Vice pres.-ch. council, 1978-83; mem. Luther Manor Aux., 1983. Served to 1st lt. USAF, 1952-54; Korea. Recipient Service award Water Pollution Control Fedn., 1981; U. Mass. Engring. Alumni Assn. award, 1976; san. sect. award Boston Soc. Civil Engrs., 1969, Desmond Fitzgerald award, 1969. Fellow ASCE; mem. Am. Acad. Environ. Engrs. (trustee 1976-78), Water Pollution Control Fedn. (dir. 1981-83), Am. Water Works Assn. Republican. Lutheran. Contbr. articles to profl. jours.; developed total solids mgmt. plan for Milw. Met. Sewerage Dist., 1978.

HORSLEY, JACK EVERETT, lawyer; b. Sioux City, Iowa, Dec. 12, 1915; s. Charles E. and Edith V. (Timms) H.; A.B., U. Ill., 1937, LL.B., 1939, J.D., 1965; m. Sallie Kelley, June 12, 1939 (dec.); children—Pamela, Charles Edward; m. 2d, Bertha J. Newland, Feb. 24, 1950 (dec.); m. 3d, Mary Jane Moran, Jan. 20, 1973; 1 dau., Sharon. Admitted to Ill. bar, 1939, since practiced law in Mattoon, Ill.; sr. counsel Craig & Craig, attys. for Ill. Central Gulf R.R. Co., C. & E.I. R.R. Co., Penn Central R.R. Co., Internat. Harvester Co. and other cos.; legal counsel St. John's Luth. Ch., Mattoon; specializes in defensive trial work; vice chmn. bd., dir. Central Nat. Bank, 1976—; mem. lawyers adv. council U. Ill. Law Forum, 1960-63; lectr. Practising Law Inst., N.Y.C., 1967-73, Ct. Practice Inst., Chgo., 1974—, U. Mich. Coll. Law Inst. Continuing Legal Edn., 1968; vis. lectr. Duquesne Coll., Pitts., 1970, chmn. rev. com. Ill. Supreme Ct. Disciplinary Commn., 1973-76. Pres. bd. edn. Sch. Dist. 100, 1946-48; bd. dirs. Moore Heart Research Found., 1969—; narrator Poetry Interludes, WLBH-FM. Served with J.A.G.D., A.C., 1942-46; disch. as lt. col. Fellow Am. Coll. Trial Lawyers; mem. ABA, Ill. (mem. exec. council ins. law 1961-63, lectr. ins. law course for attys. 1962, 64, 65, Disting. Service award selection com. 1982-83), Coles-Cumberland (v.p. 1968-69, pres. 1969-70, chmn. jud. inquiry com. 1976—, chmn. meml. com. 1984—, mem. membership com. 1984—) bar assns., Assn. Bar City N.Y. (non-resident mem. emeritus), Am. Arbitration Assn. (nat. panel arbitrators), U. Ill. Law Alumni Assn. (pres.), Ill. Def. Counsel Assn. (dir. 1966-67, pres. 1967-68), Soc. Trial Lawyers (chmn. profl. activities 1960-61; dir. 1961-62), Adelphic Debating, Assn. Ins. Attys., Internat. Assn. Ins. Counsel (membership com. 1966-67), Am. Judicature Soc., Appellate Lawyers Assn., Scribe, Delta Phi (mem. exec. com. Alumni Assn. 1960-61), Sigma Delta Kappa. Republican. Mason (32 deg.). Author: Trial Lawyer's Manual, 1967; Voir Dire Examinations and Opening Statements, 1968; Current Development in Products Liability Law, 1969; Illinois Civil Practice and Procedure (textbook), 1970; The Medical Expert Witness, 1973; The Doctor and the Law, 1975; The Doctor and Family Law, 1975; The Doctor and Business Law, 1976; The Doctor and Medical Law, 1977; contbr. chpt. to Forensic Sciences, 1983, 2d edit., 1985. Contbr. Ill. Bar Jour., Def. Law Jour.; contbr. jury instructions and special defenses articles Fedn. of Ins. Council Quar. and Ill. Law Forum, 1958; cons., contbr. Med. Econs., 1969—; legal cons. Mast-Head, 1972—; contbr. RN Mag., 1976—. Home: 50 Elm Ridge Mattoon IL 61938 Office: 1807 Broadway Mattoon IL 61938

HORSTMAN, CAROL BELLHOUSE, lawyer; b. Brantford, Ont., Can., Oct. 14, 1953; came to U.S., 1960, naturalized, 1980; d. Gerald LaVerne and Irma (Vansickle) Bellhouse; m. James K. Horstman, July 2, 1980; children—Whitney Sarah, Michael Andrew. B.A., Wesleyan U., 1976; J.D., Washington U., St. Louis, 1980. Bars: Ill. 1981, U.S. Dist. Ct. (cen. dist.) Ill. 1981. Assoc., Costello, Young & Metnik, Springfield, Ill., 1980-82; sole practice, Springfield, 1982-84, 85—; ptnr. Horstman & Speta, P.C., Springfield, 1984-85. Mem. ABA, Ill. Bar Assn., Sangamon County Bar Assn., Ill. Trial Lawyers Assn. Club: Toastmasters. Office: 1205 S 1st St Springfield IL 62704

HORTON, JOHN EDWARD, periodontist, educator; b. Brockton, Mass., Dec. 30, 1930; s. Harold Ellsworth and Anita Helen (Samuelson) H.; children—John Edward, Janet Elaine, James Elliot, Jeffrey Eugene, Joseph Everett. B.S., Providence Coll., 1952; D.M.D., Tufts U., 1957; M.S.D., Baylor U., 1965; M.A., George Washington U., 1978. Commd. 1st lt. U.S. Army, 1957, advanced through grades to col., 1972; cons. to surgeon, Europe, 1967-70; guest scientist dept. immunology Nat. Inst. Dental Research, Bethseda, Md., 1970-73; chief depts. microbiology and immunology Inst. Dental Research U.S. Army, 1973-77; ret., 1977; lectr. Johns Hopkins U. Sch. Pub. Health, 1975-79; asst. professorial lectr. George Washington U., 1972-74, assoc. professorial lectr., 1974-76, professorial lectr., 1976-77; assoc. prof., chmn., program dir. dept. periodontology Harvard U. Sch. Dental Medicine, 1977-81; prof., chmn., program dir. dept. Periodontology Ohio State U. Coll. Dentistry, Columbus, 1981—; cons. VA Med. Ctr., West Roxbury and Brockton, Mass., 1978-81; cons. div. research grants NIH, 1973—, VA Out-Patient Ctr., Columbus, U.S. Air Force Med. Ctr., Wright Patterson AFB, U.S. Army Inst. Dental Research. Decorated Commendation medal, Meritorious Service medal, Legion Merit. Fellow AAAS, Am. Pub. Health Assn., Internat. Coll. Dentists, Royal Soc. Health; mem. Omicron Kappa Upsilon, Phi Delta Kappa, Sigma Xi. Editor: Mechanisms of Localized Bone Loss, 1978; contbr. numerous articles to profl. publs. Office: Ohio State University Coll of Dentistry Dept Periodontology 305 W 12th Ave Columbus OH 43210

HORTON, JOSEPH JULIAN, JR., educator; b. Memphis, Nov. 7, 1936; s. Joseph Julian and Nina (Williams) H.; A.A., Lon Morris Jr. Coll., 1955; B.A., N.Mex. State U., 1958; M.A., So. Meth. U., 1965, Ph.D., 1968; postgrad. (research fellow) Harvard U., 1970-71; m. Linda Anne Langley, May 30, 1964; children—Joseph Julian, Anne Adele, David Douglas. Claims examiner Social Security Adminstrn., Kansas City, Mo., 1958-60, claims authorizer, 1960-61; with FDIC, Washington, 1967-71, fin. economist, 1967-69, coordinator merger analysis, 1969-71; prof., chmn. dept. econs. and bus. Slippery Rock State Coll. (Pa.), 1971-81; vis. fin. economist Fed. Home Loan Bank Bd., Washington, 1978-79; prof., chmn. commerce div. Bellarmine (Ky.) Coll., 1981-82, dean W. Fielding Rubel Sch. Bus., 1982—; asst. prof. George Washington U., Washington, 1968-69, U. Md., College Park, 1969-70; pres. Pa. Conf. Economists. Ford Found. dissertation fellow, 1966-67; NSF grad. fellow, 1964-66; Bank Adminstrn. Inst. Clarence Lichtfeldt fellow, 1981; recipient Cokesbury award So. Meth. U., 1965. Mem. Am. Econ. Assn., Am. Fin. Assn., N. Am. Econs. and Fin. Assn. (dir., v.p.), Eastern Econ. Assn. (v.p.). Bd. editors Eastern Econ. Jour.; contbr. to profl. jours.

HORTON, RICHARD ADAM, nature center executive, environmental educator; b. Cleve., May 14, 1943; s. Adam Morrow and Florence Adelia (Gratz) H.; m. Ruth Ellen Lambert, Aug. 10, 1968 (div. Oct. 1979); children—Brian Richard, Chad Alan; m. Karen Kay Rosengarten, Aug. 22, 1980; 1 child, Megan Rose. B.A., Hiram Coll., 1965; M.Ed., Kent State U., 1968; postgrad. Gestalt Inst. of Cleve., 1973-75, Inst. for Earth Edn., 1977-84. Cert. tchr. high sch., Ohio. Tchr. sci. Warrensville Jr. High Sch., Warrensville Heights, Ohio, 1965-68, chmn. dept. sci., 1966-68; tchr. sci. University Sch. for Boys, Shaker Heights, Ohio, 1968-75, dir. lower sch. sci., 1970-75; summer naturalist Shaker Lakes Regional Nature Ctr., 1971, 74, 75, dir., 1975—; coordinator Ohio Valley Region/Inst. for Earth Edn., Warrenville, Ill., 1981—. Author sci. programs, family camp programs. Mem. task force Presbytery of the Western Res., Cleve., 1983-84; dir., program designer/All-Church Camp, Forest Hill Ch., Cleveland Heights, Ohio, 1982, 83, 84; mem. citizens adv. com. City of Shaker Heights planning com., 1980; mem. Joint Com. on Doan Brook Watershed, Cleve., 1975—, chmn., 1978-79. Mem. Inst. for Earth Edn. (assoc.), Nat. Sci. Tchrs. Assn., Natural Sci. for Youth Found., Northeast Ohio Inter-Mus. Council (vice chmn. 1979-83), Ohio Mus. Assn. (treas. 1980-83), Cleve. Regional Council of Sci. Tchrs., Phi Delta Kappa, Beta Beta Beta. Democrat. Presbyterian. Club: Group Couples (Cleveland Heights). Avocations: gardening; creating backyard wildlife habitats; cooking; cross-country skiing. Office: Shaker Lakes Regional Nature Ctr 2600 S Park Blvd Cleveland OH 44120

HORTON, WILLIAM HOWARD, lawyer; b. Detroit, June 13, 1954; s. Max Milan and Della Francis (DeRight) H.; m. Denise Maria Roualet, Aug. 9, 1980; 1 child, Jennifer Maria. B.A., Oakland U., 1976; J.D., Detroit Coll. Law, 1980. Bar: Mich. 1980, U.S. Dist. Ct. (ea. dist.) Mich. 1980, U.S. Dist. Ct. (we. dist.) Mich. 1984. Assoc. Talpos, Arnold & Rooyakker, P.C., Troy, Mich., 1980-83, Cook, Pringle, Simonsen & Goetz, P.C., Birmingham, Mich., 1983—. Contbr. chpt. to book, articles to profl. jours. Mem. Oakland U. Alumni Assn. (bd. dirs. 1981—), ABA, Mich. State Bar Assn., Oakland County Bar Assn., Assn. Trial Lawyers Am., Nat. Health Lawyers Assn. Office: Cook Pringle Simonsen & Goetz PC 1400 N Woodward Suite 101 Birmingham MI 48011

HORVATH, HELEN ELIZABETH, ballet school administrator; b. Cleve., Aug. 17, 1923; d. Julius and Clara (Boros) Nagy; m. Ernest Horvath, June 20, 1942; children—Ernie William, James Gerard, Deborah Marie. Student Cleve. pub. schs. Direct sales rep., mgr., ednl. dir. World Gift, Inc. and Decorama, Inc., Dallas, 1947-55; sec. to tax atty. Carling Brewing Co., Cleve., 1957-71; exec. adminstr. Sch. of Cleve. Ballet, also co.-mgr. Cleve. Ballet, 1972—; cons. to ballet schs. and cos. Mem. Cleve. Ballet Council, Ladies Aux. Club: Women's City (Cleve.). Office: 1375 Euclid Ave Suite 110 Cleveland OH 44115

HORWITZ, DAVID LARRY, health care executive, researcher, educator; b. Chgo., July 13, 1942; s. Milton Woodrow and Dorothy (Glass) H.; m. Gloria Jean Madian, June 20, 1965; children—Karen, Laura. A.B., Harvard U., 1963; M.D., U. Chgo., 1967, Ph.D., 1968. Diplomate Am. Bd. Internal Medicine. Resident in internal medicine U. Chgo. Hosp., 1971-72; fellow in endocrinology U. Chgo., 1972-74, asst. prof., 1974-79; assoc. prof. U. Ill.-Chgo., 1979—; med. dir. Travenol Labs., Inc., Deerfield, Ill., 1982—. Contbr. articles to profl. jours. Bd. dirs. No. Ill. affiliate Am. Diabetes Assn., 1976—. Served to comdr. USNR, 1969-71. Recipient Research and Devel. award Am. Diabetes Assn., 1974-76; Outstanding Young Citizen of Chgo. award Chgo. Jr. C. of C., 1976; Outstanding Young Citizen Ill. award Ill. Jaycees, 1977. Fellow ACP; mem. Endocrine Soc., Am. Thyroid Assn., Am. Assn. Clin. Nutrition. Office: Travenol Labs Inc 1425 Lake Cook Rd Deerfield IL 60015

HORWITZ, MICHAEL ROGER, children's home administrator, psychotherapist; b. Washington, Dec. 21, 1944; s. Bernard Herman and Margaret Helen (Carey) H.; m. Michele McKeen, Nov. 25, 1978; children—Alexander, Joshua, Nathaniel. B.A., U. Md., 1967; M.A., U. Chgo., 1972. Exec. dir. Family Service Assn., Dundee, Ill., 1972-74, Larkin Home for Children, Elgin, Ill., 1974—; psychotherapist Family Service Assn. Elgin, 1975-84, Barry Rabin, M.D. & Assocs., Elgin, 1984—. Mem. White House Conf. on Children, Chgo., 1980; bd. dirs. Elgin Area YMCA, 1982-83; trustees Elgin Community Coll., 1983—. Served with U.S. Army, 1968-70. HEW scholar, 1970-72. Mem. Nat. Assn. Social Workers, Acad. Cert. Social Workers, Register Clin. Social Workers. Jewish. Lodge: Rotary. Avocations: running, reading. Office: Larkin Home for Children 1212 Larkin Ave Elgin IL 60120

HORWITZ, MIRIAM R(ACHEL), lawyer; b. Joliet, Ill., Nov. 4, 1953; d. Philip H. and Jeanette (Adelston) H. B.A., Northwestern U., 1975; J.D., Northeastern U., 1978. Bar: Wis. 1978, U.S. Dist. Ct. (ea. and we. dists.) Wis. 1978, Ill. 1979, U.S. Ct. Appeals (7th cir.) 1979. Staff atty. Legal Aid Soc. Milw., 1978-79; assoc. Zubrensky, Padden, Graf & Maloney, Milw., 1979-84, ptnr., 1984—. Bd. dirs. Inner City Devel. Project, Milw., 1982. Mem. State Bar Wis., Milw. Bar Assn., Milw. Young Lawyers Assn. Jewish. Home: 929 N Astor St Milwaukee WI 53202 Office: Zubrensky Padden Graf & Maloney 828 N Broadway Milwaukee WI 53202

HORWITZ, ROBERT HENRY, political science educator; b. El Paso, Tex., Sept. 3, 1923; s. David and Louise (Mendelsohn) H.; B.A., Amherst Coll., 1949; M.A., U. Hawaii, 1950; Ph.D., U. Chgo., 1954; m. Noreen Margaret Surti, Jan. 1948; children—Susheila Louise, David D. Asst. prof., researcher U. Hawaii, 1948-51; research asst. com. for study citizenship edn. U. Chgo., 1953-55; from asst. prof. to prof. polit. sci. Mich. State U., 1956-66; prof. polit. sci., chmn. dept. Kenyon Coll., Gambier, Ohio, 1966-73, dir. Public Affairs Conf. Ctr., 1976-78. Served with AUS, 1942-46; ETO, PTO. Decorated Bronze Star, Combat Inf. badge. Fellow Emil Schwarzhaupt Found., 1953-55, Rockefeller Found., 1959, Ford Found., 1956-58, Nat. Endowment Humanities, 1973-76. Mem. AAUP, Am. Polit. Sci. Assn., Am. Soc. Polit. and Legal Philosophy. Jewish. Co-author: John Locke's Questions Concerning the Law of Nature, 1984; editor: The Moral Foundations of the American Republic, 1977; contbr. to profl. publs. Home: 214 Kokosing Dr Gambier OH 43022 Office: Dept Polit Sci Kenyon Coll Gambier OH 43022

HOSCHEIT, CHARLES EDWARD, park district administrator; b. Peru, Ill., Dec. 16, 1935; s. Charles M. Hoscheit; m. Nancy Sabotta, Aug. 16, 1958; children—Laura, Becky, Charles. B.S., Ill. State U., 1958; M.S., U. Ill., 1974. Tchr., coach Lockport (Ill.) West High Sch., 1962-65; exec. dir. Lockport Township Park Dist., 1965-77; exec. dir. Fox Valley (Ill.) Park Dist., Aurora, 1977—; guest tchr. U. Ill., Moraine Valley Coll. Chmn., United Way, 1982; mem. Aurora Planning Commn., 1982; chmn. Tomahawk Boy Scouts Am. Council, 1972-73; dir. Will County (Ill.) Historic Preservation Council, 1974-77. Decorated U.S. Gold Medal, 1976, 82. Mem. Ill. Park and Recreation Assn. (pres. finance sect. 1981), Nat. Park and Recreation Assn., Ill. Assn. Park Dists., Midwest Inst. Park Execs., South Suburban Parks and Recreation Assn. (pres. 1976). Club: Toastmasters. Lodges: Lions (pres. Lockport 1977), Moose, Elks. Author: Lockport Township Park & Recreation Plans, 1969. Home: 2535 Amy Ln Aurora IL 60506 Office: 712 S River St Aurora IL 60506

HOSE, JOHN EMIL, micrographic company executive, laser printing consultant; b. St. Louis, July 4, 1938; s. John H. and Viola M. (Lang) H.; m. Donna Marlene Handshy, Sept. 19, 1959; children—John Henry, Brian Paul. Student U. Mo., 1957, So. Ill. U., 1958-61. Salesman SCM Corp., St. Louis, 1964-68; br. mgr. Computer Micro Services, St. Louis, 1968-72; dir. mktg. Computer Microdata, St. Louis, 1972-75; pres. Custom Micrographics, St. Louis, 1975—; dir. Price Photocopy Products, St. Louis. Organizer Mehlville Oakville Boosters, St. Louis, 1982. Served with U.S. Army, 1957-63. Recipient award of spl. merit Mehlville R-9 Sch. Dist., 1982. Mem. Assn. Systems Mgmt. (treas. 1979, sec. 1980), Assn. Info. and Image Mgmt., XPLOR (mem. steering com.). Presbyterian. Avocation: golf. Home: 4527 Towne Centre Ct Saint Louis MO 63128 Office: Custom Micrographics Inc 2676 Metro Blvd Saint Louis MO 63043

HOSEK, WILLIAM RANDOLPH, economics educator; b. N.Y.C., Jan. 11, 1937; s. William and Mary Hosek; m. Jeanette McGregor, Sept. 18, 1960; children—Sibyl, Marissa. B.A., U. Calif.-Santa Barbara, 1964, Ph.D., 1967. Faculty, U. N.H., Durham, 1967-78, prof. econs., 1976-78; prof. econs. U. Nebr., Omaha, 1978—. Author: Macroeconomic Theory, 1975; Monetary Theory, Policy and Financial Markets, 1977; also articles. Grad. fellow U.S. Dept. Edn., 1964-67; research fellow U. N.H., 1970, U. Nebr., 1981. Mem. Am. Econ. Assn., Am. Fin. Assn., Nat. Assn. Bus. Economists. Republican. Presbyterian. Avocation: golf. Office: Dept Econs U Nebr Omaha NE 68182-0048

HOSFORD, KARL REYNOLD, state government official; b. Lansing, Mich., Jan. 11, 1940; s. Reynold W. and Dorothy L. (Griffin) H.; m. Mary Serene Qualman, Dec. 28, 1962; children—Amy Elizabeth, Michael Karl. B.S. in Land Planning, Mich. State U., 1962, Ph.D. in Resource Devel., 1978; M.S. in Urban Planning, Wayne State U., 1966. Registered profl. community planner, Mich. Assoc. planner Macomb County Planning Commn., Mount Clemens, Mich., 1965-66, Tri County Regional Planning Commn., Lansing, Mich., 1966-68; water resources planner Mich. Water Resources Commn., Lansing, 1968-73, chief office land use, 1973-76, chief div. land resource programs, 1976—; sec. Mich. Interdepartmental Com. on Land and Water Resources, 1970-73; co-chmn. joint Fed. and State Great Lakes Policies, Plans, Procedures and Instnl. Arrangements Study Group of Great Lakes Basin Commn., 1971-73; mem. Social Scis. and Legal Aspects Com., Great Lakes research Adv. Bd., Internat. Joint Commn., 1973; state evaluator Nat. Water Assessment Handbook, 1975; dept. Nat. Resources' rep. state Soil Conservation Com., 1978—. Editor: Michigan Planning News, 1970-76; supr., editor Info. Brochure, Mich.'s Coastal Mgmt. Program, 1978, Mich.'s Land Use Program, 1974. Contbr. articles to profl. publs. Guest lectr. at numerous univs. and civic orgns. on resource mgmt. issues; bd. dirs. Okemos Community Athletic Assn., Mich.; coach Greater Lansing Area Hockey Assn.; mem. Big Bros. Am. Recipient Spl. Conservation award Mich. United Conservation Clubs, 1983. Mem. Mich. Soc. Planning Officials (cert. service 1979, exec. dir. 1970-76, bd. dirs. 1976-79, program adminstr. Mich.'s mgmt. plan for St. Clair flats 1980, Mich.'s coastal coal storage plan 1981; program adminstr. visual improvement plan for downriver community 1981, linked river front parks project 1981, honor awards, 1980, 81, 82). Club: Capitol City Old Car. Avocations: historical research; antique firearms; Model A Fords; hunting; fishing. Office: Mich Dept Nat Resources PO Box 30028 Lansing MI 48909

HOSHOUR, THOMAS EUGENE, osteopathic physician; b. Dayton, Ohio, Mar. 9, 1945; s. Thomas Edward and Bernice Louella (Jarvis) H.; m. Barbara Collene Neff, Sept. 17, 1967 (div.); 1 dau., Deborah Collene. A.B. in Chemistry, Ind. U., 1968; postgrad. in biochemistry Ind. U. Sch. Medicine, 1968-69; D.O. with honors, Chgo. Coll. Osteo. Medicine, 1973. Diplomate Nat. Bd. Elaminers for Osteo. Physicians and Surgeons; lic. osteo. physician, Ind., Fla., Mich. Intern, Garden City Hosp. (Mich.), 1973-74; emergency room physician various hosps., Detroit and Jacksonville, Fla., 1974-76; house physician, dir. emergency room Westview Osteo. Med. Hosp., Indpls., 1976-77; gen. practice osteo. medicine, Indpls., 1977—; mem. staff Winona Meml. Hosp., Meth. Hosp.; lectr. in field. Assoc. mem. Nat. Republican Congl. Com., 1983—; mem. Rep. Nat. Com., 1983—; dep. constable Marion County Small Claims Ct. (Ind.); hon. dep. sheriff Marion County Sheriff's Dept. Mem. Salvation Army, Smithsonian Assocs., Am. Mus. Nat. History, Ind. State Police Alliance, Police Athletic League, Ind. Sheriffs Assn., Ind. U. Alumni Assn., AMA, Am. Coll. Gen. Practitioners in Osteo. Medicine and Surgery, Ind. U. Assn. Applied Chemists, Am. Chem. Soc., Am. Coll. Emergency Physicians, Ind. Assn. Osteo. Physicians, Chgo. Coll. Osteo. Medicine Alumni Assn., Am. Osteo. Assn., Wyoming Antelope Hunters Protective Assn., Sigma Sigma Phi, Iota Tau Sigma. Episcopalian. Home and Office: 824 E 28th St Indianapolis IN 46205

HOSKINS, JOHN HOWARD, urologist, educator; b. Breckenridge, Minn., Mar. 18, 1934; s. James Howard and Ruth (Johanson) H.; m. Nancy Weih, Aug. 3, 1959; children—William, James, Laura, Sara. B.A. in History, U. Iowa, 1956; M.D., Temple U., 1961. Diplomate Am. Bd. Urology. Resident, U. Minn., 1966; practice medicine specializing in urology, Urology Specialists, Sioux Falls, 1968—; sect. head urology Sch. Med., U. S.D., 1977—. Fellow ACS; mem. Fertility Soc., AMA. Methodist. Lodge: Rotary. Avocations: tennis, skiing. Office: Urology Specialists Chartered 1200 S Euclid Ave Sioux Falls SD

HOSKINS, WILLIAM KELLER, pharmaceutical company executive, lawyer; b. Cin., Feb. 22, 1935; s. John Hobart and Gertrude Louise (Keller) H.; m. Elizabeth Ann Grimm, Aug. 5, 1961; children—Bruce, Andrew, John, Elizabeth, Allison. B.A., Yale U., 1956; LL.B., Harvard U., 1962. Bar: Ohio 1962, N.Y. 1982, Mo. 1984. Assoc., Frost & Jacobs, Cin., 1962-68; gen. counsel Drackett Co., Cin., 1968-71, v.p., gen. counsel, 1971-81; assoc. gen. counsel Bristol Myers Co., N.Y.C., 1981, spl. counsel, 1982; v.p., gen. counsel, sec. Marion Labs, Kansas City, Mo., 1982—; chmn. Chem. Specialties Mfg. Assn., 1982. Sec., treas. Mid-Am. Com. on Sound Govt, Lake Quivira, Kans., 1982—; mem. Hamilton County Republican Central Com., Ohio, 1970-81. Mem. ABA, Mo. Bar Assn., Cin. Bar Assn. Roman Catholic. Home: 570 Mohawk W Lake Quivira KS 66106 Office: Marion Labs Inc 9221 Ward Pkwy Kansas City MO 64114

HOSS, RICHARD W., interstate transportation company executive; b. Cambridge, Mass., 1938. B.B.A., U. Mass., 1962. With Roadway Express Inc., Akron, Ohio, 1962—, terminal mgr., 1964-69, dist. mgr., 1969-73, v.p. northeastern div., 1973-76, v.p. so. div., 1976-79, v.p. ops., 1979-81, exec. v.p. ops., 1981, pres., dir., 1982—. Office: Roadway Express Inc 1077 Gorge Blvd PO Box 471 Akron OH 44309*

HOSTETTER, HAROLD VICTOR, union official; b. Coshocton, Ohio, May 7, 1928; s. Wilbert B. and Minnie Ellen (Emler) H.; m. Lily Ruth Patterson, June 9, 1945 (div. 1981); m. 2d, Wilma Jean Sharrer, Nov. 16, 1981; children—Patricia Ellen, Derek William. Student pub. schs., West Lafayette, Ohio. Tool and diemaker Steel Ceilings, Inc., Coshocton, 1946-63; dist. dir. Internat. Assn. Machinists Dist. 28, Zanesville, Ohio, 1963—; v.p. Ohio State Machinists, Columbus, 1974—, Ohio AFL-CIO, Columbus, 1978—; nat. planner Machinists Non-Partisan Polit. League, Washington, 1980—. Bd. dirs. Goodwill Industries, Zanesville, 1976-80. Democrat. Methodist. Lodges: Elks, Masons (master 1961), Order Eastern Star, Moose. Home: 5445 Heritage Dr Nashport OH 43830 Office: Internat Assn Machinists Dist 28 1526 Bluff Zanesville OH 43701

HOTCHKISS, EUGENE, III, See *Who's Who in America*, 43rd edition.

HOTTLE, DARRELL RIZER, judge; b. Hillsboro, Ohio, Sept. 13, 1918; s. George Emmitt and Alice Reverda (Bishop) H.; m. Catherine Carpenter, Nov. 15, 1947; children—Kay, Larry. B.A., Ohio State U., 1940; LL.B., Western Res. U., 1947. Bar: Ohio 1947. Pros. atty. Highland County, Ohio, Hillsboro, 1949-52; solicitor City of Hillsboro, Ohio, 1950; judge Highland County Common Pleas Ct., Hillsboro, Ohio, 1955—. Contbr. articles to legal jours. Chmn. Highland County Democratic Exec. Com., 1952-54; trustee Otterbein Home, Lebanon, Ohio. Recipient Silver Beaver award Central Ohio council Boy Scouts Am., 1967. Mem. ABA, Ohio State Bar Assn. (exec. com.), Am. Judicature Soc., Highland County Bar Assn. (past pres.). Democrat. Methodist (lay leader 1968-75, conf. 1971). Club: Rotary. Lodges: Masons (master 1976, 33 deg.), Elks (exalted ruler 1957). Home: 335 W Walnut St Hillsboro OH 45133 Office: PO Box 805 Hillsboro OH 45133

HOUCHINS, RODNEY T., personnel director, educator; b. Toledo, Aug. 24, 1940; s. Herman and Irene (Toth) H.; m. Marsha L. Schwan (div. 1972); children—Rebecca Lynn, Rodney Matthew; m. Margaret Ruth Brandeberry, Aug. 7, 1972; stepchildren—Deborah Jo, James Wesley. Grad. Toledo Police Acad., 1968; student Mary Manse Coll., 1969-71; A.B. in Bus., Davis Jr. Coll., 1976; B.A. in Gen. Mgmt., Siena Heights Coll., 1982; M.Ed., Bowling Green State U., 1984. Accredited sr. profl. in human resources. Patrolman, Toledo Police Dept., 1964-71; chief security officer Owens-Ill., Inc., Toledo, 1971-73; chief dispatcher Bellevue Trucking Co., Inc., Holland, Ohio, from 1973, supt., to 1976; personnel mgr. Essex-United Tech., Carey, Ohio, 1976-77; indsl. relations mgr. Crown Cork & Seal Co., Inc., Perrysburg, Ohio, 1977-80; personnel dir. metal container group Ball Corp., Findlay, Ohio, 1980—; tchr. self-esteem and motivation programs for learning disabilities students. Pres. Hancock County (Ohio) Coordinating Council; bd. dirs. Salvation Army; pres. Hancock County Safety Council; chmn. speakers bur. Hancock County Litter Bd.; chmn. personnel com. Big Bros./Big Sisters; trustee Hancock County Mental Health Soc.; chmn. Findlay (Ohio) City Sch. Trades and Indsl. Council; mem. adv. bd. Project P.I.P.E. (Parental Intervention/Parental Edn.); mem. disaster services team ARC. Served with USN, 1958-61. Recipient spl. citation ARC, 1982; Profl. Achievement and Contbn. award Hancock County Litter Bd., 1982; Red Apple award Findlay Schs., 1983; named Civitan Citizen of Yr., 1984. Mem. Am. Soc. Personnel Adminstrs., Hancock County C. of C. (chmn. edn. com.), Epsilon Pi Tau. Republican. Methodist. Lodges: Kiwanis (dir.) (Findlay); Odd Fellows. Home: 613 Lafayette Blvd Bowling Green OH 43402 Office: 12340 Allen Twp 99 E Findlay OH 45840

HOUGH, FREDERICK JOHN, II, chiropractic coll. ofcl.; b. Chgo., Sept. 14, 1936; s. Frederick John and Eleanora Francis (Cyra) H.; A.A., Coll. of DuPage, 1975; B.A., Elmhurst Coll., 1976; m. Lorraine Sacher, July 3, 1957; children—Frederick, Michael, Neil, Linda, Laura. Cost acct. Wilson Sporting Goods Co., 1957-58; office mgr. Howell Tractor and Equipment Co., 1958-60; pres. Great Lakes Sci. Corp., Lombard, Ill., 1960-74; comptroller, mem. faculty Nat. Coll. Chiropractic, Lombard, 1974—; instr. investing, fin., bus. and law, 1974—; lectr., bus. and investment adv., 1974—. Served with USMC, 1954-57. Lic. real estate broker, Ill., Wis. Mem. Adminstrv. Mgmt. Soc., 1st Marine Brigade, Fleet Marine Force, VFW (chpt. treas.), Delta Mu Delta. Republican. Methodist. Club: Ill. Athletic. Author: Investing and Financing, 1980. Home: 326 S Monterey St Villa Park IL 60181 Office: Nat Coll Chiropractic 200 E Roosevelt Rd Lombard IL 60148

HOUGH, JANE RUTH ELDER, soprano, educator; b. Tacoma, Wash., May 22, 1923; d. Roger Emerson and Mabel (Bradway) Elder; m. Eldred Wilson Hough, Dec. 28, 1948; children—Christine Elizabeth Hough Smith, Phyllis Jane, Roger Eldred, Carl Emerson. B.S. in Physics, U.Wash., 1945; B.A. in Music, Occidental Coll., 1946; M.L.S., U. Maine, 1975; M.M.Ed. in Music, Miss. State U., 1982. Mathematician, U.S. Govt. Army Ordnance, Los Angeles, 1946-49; soprano, symphony chorus, Los Angeles, 1946-48, Opera Theater, U. Maine, Orono, 1975, Bangor Community Theater (Maine), 1976; soloist Symphony Chorus, Starkville, Miss., 1976-82; operatic soprano Midland Repertory Players, Alton, Ill., 1983—; instr. singing, Carrollton, Ill., 1982—. Mem. Nat. Assn. Tchrs. of Singing, ALA, Sigma Alpha Iota Alumnae (treas. Tulsa 1951-52, organizer, 1st pres. Austin, Tex. 1959-61, Sword of Honor 1960), P.E.O. (1st pres. chpt. KZ Carbondale, Ill. 1967-69), AAUW, DAR, Alpha Omicron Pi. Methodist. Club: Nocturne Music (pres. 1979-81). Home: PO Box 90 Carrollton IL 62016

HOUGHTON, MATTHEW AMOS, JR., sports medicine physician, educator, family physician; b. Detroit, May 17, 1942; s. Matthew Amos and Jane Elizabeth (Hunter) H.; m. Barbara Ann Beckett, Oct. 2, 1971. A.B., Olivet Coll., 1965; D.O., Kirksville Coll. Osteo. Medicine, 1969. Intern, Riverside Osteo. Hosp., Trenton, Mich., 1969-70; editor Propellor Mag., 1970-71; practice medicine specializing in family medicine, Empire, Mich., 1971—; med. dir. Northwestern Mich. Sports Medicine Clinic, Traverse City, 1978—; mem. Mich. Council Phys. Fitness, 1982—; mem. staff Traverse City Osteo. Hosp.; asst. clin. prof. Mich. State U. Coll. Osteo. Medicine; med. examiner Leelanau County (Mich.); med. and safety dir. Am. Power Boat Assn. Recipient Boating Safety award Caesars Marine Acad., 1982; Mich. Joint Legislature commendation for sports medicine, 1980; named Disting. Alumnus, Olivet Coll., 1983. Mem. Am. Osteo. Assn., Am. Osteo. Acad. Sports Medicine (founder mem., Sports Medicine Physician of Yr. 1979), Spirit of Detroit Assn. Republican. Episcopalian. Author: History of Unlimited Hydroplane Racing, 1965; County Medical Examiner's Manual, 1976; Medical Manual of Am. Power Boat Assn., 1981; contbr. articles to profl. jours. Office: PO Box 255 Fisher Profl Bldg Empire MI 49630

HOUK, IRENE MILLER, dentist; b. Columbiana, Ohio, Aug. 1, 1921; d. Josiah Ellsworth and Ada Isophene (Rupert) Miller; m. George Albertus Houk, Mar. 23, 1949; children—Martha Helle, George. D.D.S., U. Pitts., 1944. Lic. dentist, Ohio. Gen. practice dentistry, Poland, Ohio. Sunday sch. tchr. 1st Presbyterian Ch., Columbiana, 1935-49, Emmanuel Lutheran Ch., New Springfield, Ohio, 1951—; Bd. dirs. Springfield Local Sch., New Middletown, Ohio, 1960-81, past v.p., past pres.; bd. dirs. Wittenberg U., 1962-70. Mem. ADA, Ohio Dental Assn., Corydon Palmer Dental Soc.

HOUK, JAMES MOULTON, landscape architect; b. Limestone, Maine, Feb. 1, 1956; s. John Moulton and Mary Elsie (Erler) H. B.S. in Landscape Architecture, Ohio State U., 1979. Registered landscape architect, Ohio, Ky., S.C., Fla. Designer, Housels Landscaping Inc., Temperence, Mich., 1977; designer Scruggs & Hammond, Inc., Columbus, 1978-79; landscape architect, site planner Design Enterprise, Ltd., Columbus, Ohio, 1979-81; sr. landscape architect, project mgr. Bohm-NBBJ, Inc., Columbus, 1981—; vis. lectr. Mich. State U.; vis. critic, lectr. Ohio State U. Chmn. Com. for Visibility of Landscape Architecture in Ohio. Mem. Am. Soc. Landscape Architects (mem. exec. com. Ohio chpt.), Landscape architect Riverfront Park, Columbus, Seabrook Island, S.C., other projects throughout Ohio, Ky., Ind., S.C. Home: 1357 W 6th Ave Columbus OH 43212 Office: 55 Nationwide Blvd Columbus OH 43215

HOULE, DAVID ECKHARDT, restaurant executive; b. Chgo., July 3, 1948; s. Cyril Orvin and Bettie Eckhardt H. B.A. in Fine Arts, Syracuse U., 1969. With systems office U. Chgo. Library, 1969-72; with Ward-Griffith Newspapers, 1974-76; account exec. NBC-TV, 1976-78; sr. account exec. CBS-TV, Chgo., 1978-81; dir. sales Warner Amex Satellite Entertainment Co., Chgo., 1981-84; v.p. advt. sales MTV Networks Inc., 1984-85; chmn. bd., chief exec. officer Mama Mia! Pasta Franchise Corp., 1985—. Office: Mama Mia! Pasta Franchise Corp 205 W Wacker Dr Suite 508 Chicago IL 60606

HOULE, WILLIAM JOHN, Indian reservation official; b. Knife River, Minn., Aug. 22; s. George and Nancy (Laundry) H.; m. Francis Mary Benick (div.); children—Lorraine, Briana, Lenore, Brenda. Student spl. courses U. Minn.-Duluth, Bemidji State U., Black River Coll. Home and sch. coordinator, Cloquet, Minn., 1965-66; with div. edn. Coll. St. Scholastica, 1966-68; rep. Brookston dist., 1968-70; chmn. Fond du Lac Reservation Bus. Com., Cloquet, 1971—; mem. Nat. Indian Gaming Task Force. Mem. Gt. Lakes Indian Fisheries Commn., Minn. Gov.'s Commn. on Human Rights; active Democratic-Farmer-Labor Party. Served with USN, 1950-56; Korea. Mem. Nat. Tribal Chairmen's Assn. (tribal exec. council), Nat. Congress Am. Indians, Four State Inter-Tribal Council, United No. Sportsmen, Lake Superior Trolling Assn., Gt. Lakes Steelhead Assn. Office: 105 University Rd Cloquet MN 55720*

HOUPIS, CONSTANTINE HARRY, electrical engineering educator; b. Lowell, Mass., June 16, 1922; s. Harry John and Metaxia (Gourokous) H.; student Wayne U., 1941-43; B.S., U. Ill., 1947, M.S., 1948; postgrad. Ohio State U., 1952-56; Ph.D., U. Wyo., 1971; m. Mary Stephens, Aug. 28, 1960; children—Harry C., Angella S. Spl. research asst. U. Ill., 1947-48; devel. elec. engr. Babcock & Wilcox Co., Alliance, Ohio, 1948-49; instr. elec. engring. Wayne State U., 1949-51; prin. elec. engr. Battelle Meml. Inst., Columbus, Ohio, 1951-52; prof. elec. engring. Air Force Inst. Tech., Wright-Patterson AFB, Ohio, 1952—; guest lectr. Nat. Tech. U. Athens, 1958, U. Patras, 1983 Weizmann Inst. Sci., 1983; cons. Air Force Flight Dynamics Lab. Served with AUS, 1943-46. Recipient Outstanding Engr. award Dayton area Nat. Engrs. Week, 1962. Mem. IEEE, Am. Soc. Engring. Edn., Am. Hellenic Edn. Progressive Assn., Tau Beta Pi, Eta Kappa Nu, Sigma Chi. Mem. Greek Orthodox Ch. Author: (with J.J. D'Azzo) Feedback Control System Analysis and Synthesis, 1960, 2d edit., 1966; Principles of Electrical Engineering: Electric Circuits, Electronics, Energy Conversion, Control Systems Computers, 1968; Linear Control Systems Analysis and Design: Conventional and Modern, 1975, 2d edit., 1981; (with J. Lubelfeld) Outline of Pulse Circuits; (with G.B. Lamont) Digital Control Systems: Theory Software, Hardware, 1985; also articles on automatic controls in profl. jours. U.S., Eng., Greece. Home: 1125 Brittany Hills Dr Centerville OH 45459 Office: Air Force Inst Tech Wright-Patterson AFB OH 45433

HOUSE, CHARLES BREWER, JR., college president, educator; b. Galesburg, Ill., June 24, 1927; s. Charles Brewer and Sarah Marguerite (Ostrander) H.; m. M. June Hornby, Apr. 9, 1950; children—Charles, David, Stephen, James, Robert. B.S., U. Nebr., 1949; M.Div., Princeton Theol. Sem., 1955; Ph.D., Mich. State U., 1975. Ordained to ministry Presbyterian Ch. Assoc. pastor Westminster Presbyn. Ch., Grand Rapids, Mich., 1955-58; asst. prof. religion and chaplain Alma Coll., Mich., 1958-64; vis. prof. humanities U. Nigeria, Nuskka, 1964-67; lectr. humanities Mich. State U., East Lansing, 1967-69; exec. asst. to pres. Central Mich. U., Mount Pleasant, 1969-82; pres. Valley City State Coll., N.D., 1982—; mem. Synod Adv. Council on Presbyn. Colls., Bloomington, Mich., 1983—; Mich. Council for Humanities, East Lansing, 1973-78. Served to lt. USN, 1945-52, PTO. Mem. Valley City C. of C. (dir. 1982), Sigma Iota Epsilon, Phi Delta Kappa. Lodges: Rotary, Elks, Eagles. Avocations: sailing; cross country skiing; backpacking; wood carving; music. Home: 159 Viking Dr Valley City ND 58072

HOUSE, DARLENE LOU ARTHURNETT, advertising copywriter, consultant; b. Detroit, Mar. 18, 1958; d. David Louis and Allean (Hines) House. B.A. in Communications, Mich. State U., 1979. Research asst. Mich. State U. Coll. Urban Devel., East Lansing, 1977; asst. to producer Sta. WKAR-TV, East Lansing, 1978; market surveyor Mich. Interviews, Lansing, 1979; telephone campaign caller Mich. State U. Devel. Fund, East Lansing, 1979; sales promotion asst. Aeroquip Corp., Jackson, Mich., 1979-82; account adminstr. Ross Roy, Inc., Detroit, 1983—; pub. relations officer Amvets Aux. Post #55, Detroit, 1975-76; cons. and liaison Mich. State U. All Campus Radio Bd., 1975-77. Contbr. articles to mags. Intern, State Rep. Larry E. Burkhalter, Lansing, 1978, State Senator Jackie Vaughn, III, Lansing, 1979; mem. friends of Detroit Pub. Library, Founders Soc. Detroit Inst. Arts, YWCA Met. Detroit. Mem. Women in Communications, Inc. (communicator of Yr. 1982, chmn. award com., publicity com. chmn. 1982), Sigma Gamma Rho (advisor Gamma Omega chpt. 1980-82, pub. relations officer and historian 1983-84), DAZS Coalition of Black Greek Women (social chair, publicity coordinator 1984), LWV, Mich. State U. Alumni Assn., Nat. Wildlife Fedn. Democrat. Baptist. Clubs: Nat. Pan-Hellenic Council (corr. sec., Greek week liaison 1978-79) (East Lansing); Allstates (corr. sec., program chmn. 1982—), Adcraft (Detroit). Home: 5811 Loraine St Detroit MI 48208

HOUSEHOLDER, TIMOTHY PAUL, insurance company executive; b. Los Angeles, May 31, 1949; s. Edgar Sayles and Mary Doris (Hudson) H.; m. Carolyn Ann Brode, Feb. 22, 1975. B.A., U. Wis.-Oshkosh, 1970. Adjuster, Kemper Group, Mt. Prospect, Ill., 1972-75, supr., 1975-76, div. adjuster, Long Grove, Ill., 1976-77, div. examiner, 1977-81, home office gen. adjuster, 1981—. Recipient Excellence in Managerial Edn. award Am. Ins. Assn. Mem. Western Loss Assn. (bd. dirs. 1979-81). Lutheran. Avocation: Woodworking. Office: Kemper Ins Route 22 Long Grove IL 60049

HOUSEMAN, GERALD L., political science educator, writer; b. Marshalltown, Iowa, Apr. 12, 1935; s. Lawrence D. and Mary N. (Smith) H.; m. Penelope Lyon, Feb. 11, 1961; children—Christopher, Elisabeth, Victoria. B.A., Calif. State U.-Hayward, 1965, M.A., 1967; Ph.D., U. Ill., 1971. Asst. prof. polit. sci. Ind. U., Fort Wayne, 1971-76, assoc. prof., 1976-82, prof., 1982—; vis. prof. Brock U., St. Catharines, Can., summer 1970, New Coll., Durham, Eng., 1975-76, Calif. State Polytech. U., San Luis Obispo, 1983-84. Mem. Transit Authority Bd., Ft. Wayne, 1973-75; city plan commr., 1982-83; active ACLU, Anti-Defamation League. Served with USMC, 1954-57. Grantee NSF, 1970, Ford Found., 1973, 74, NEH, 1977-78; Ind. U. fellow, 1973, 74, 77. Mem. Am. Polit. Sci. Assn. (seminar grantee 1980, 81), Caucus for a New Polit. Sci. Jewish. Author: (with H. Mark Roelofs) The American Political System, 1983; G. D. H. Cole, 1979; The Right of Mobility, 1979; City of the Right: Urban Applications of American Political Thought, 1982.

HOUSER, JON PETER, chiropractor; b. Bklyn., Aug. 27, 1929; s. Floyd Malachi and Dolly (Samish) H.; student Purdue U., 1953-55; D. Chiropractics, Lincoln Chiropractic Coll., 1956; m. Donna R. Youngberg, Dec. 28, 1968; children—Jon Peter, Jennifer Rae, Joi Lynn, Jessica Ruth, Tania Marina. Extern, Spears Chiropractic Hosp., Denver, 1956-57; dir. Palmer Chiropractic Clinic, Harvey, Ill., 1957—; co-dir. Oak Forest Chiropractic Clinic (Ill.), 1981—; mem., sec. chiropractic staff Janse Chiropractic Center, 1982-84, also mem. exec. rev. bd. Exec. bd. trustees Nat. Coll. Chiropractic, 1982-84, planning and devel. com., 1983-84, council alumni affairs and devel., 1983-85, pres.'s adv. panel, 1983-84, chmn. student liaison com., 1983-85. Served with USAF, 1948-52. Diplomate Nat. Chiropractic Bd. Mem. Am., Ill., Chgo. (pres.) chiropractic socs., Am. Acupuncture Soc., Lincoln Chiropractic Coll. Alumni Assn. (pres., dir.), Nat. Coll. Chiropractic Alumni Assn. (pres., dir. 1983—). Council on Roentgenology, Am. Legion (post comdr. 1979-85; life), VFW. Clubs: Masons, Shriners. Home: Box 184 Rural Route 1 Monee IL 60449 Office: 15412 Turlington St Harvey IL 60426 also 5149 W 159th St Oak Forest IL 60452

HOUSER, MARTHA JEAN, author, educator; b. Detroit, Apr. 20, 1928; d. Philip Leonard and Rose (Meszaros) Tucker; m. Mortimer Clarke Houser, Sept. 3, 1947; children—Leonard Paul, Rosemary Houser Taylor, Julia Houser Cassidy. B.S. cum laude, Kent State U., 1971, M.Ed., 1975. Pvt. piano and organ tchr., Oreg. and Ohio, 1950-65; tchr. La Brae Local Schs., Leavittsburg, Ohio, 1966-81, reading specialist Bascom Elem. Sch., 1974—; Right to Read dir., La Brae Local Schs., Ohio Dept. Edn., 1979-81. Mem. council on ministries, adminstrv. bd. Grace United Meth. Ch. Annie Webb Blanton grad. scholar Delta Kappa Gamma, 1973; Ohio Dept. Edn. Tchr. grantee, 1980. Mem. Trumbull Area Reading Assn., NEA, AAUW, Music Tchrs. Nat. Assn., Delta Kappa Gamma, Kappa Delta Pi. Clubs: Amateur Radio Relay League

(Warren, Ohio); East Ohio Lapidary Assn. Home: 2700 Heather Ln NW Warren OH 44485

HOUSER, RICHARD LYNN, banker; b. Butler, Ind., June 9, 1947; s. Frank F. and Viola M. (Hose) H.; m. Patty Jo Hudson, Oct. 31, 1968; (div. Nov. 1978); children—Tammy V., Richard Dean; m. Joyce E. Dunlap, Nov. 18, 1978. Student St. Francis Coll., Ind., 1964-65, Ind. U., 1970-75. Mgr., Am. Credit Corp., Charlotte, N.C., 1970-74; sr. v.p. Citizens Nat. Bank, Columbia City, Ind., 1974—; owner, operator H & B Bookstore, Columbia City, 1982—. Contbr. poetry to anthologies. Mem. exec. com. Ft. Wayne Credit Bur., Ind., 1981—; bd. dirs. Ft. Wayne Better Bus. Bur., 1980—; pres. Columbia City .Civic Theatre, 1981-82; bd. dirs. Jr. Achievement, 1975-83. Served with USMC, 1965-69, Vietnam. Mem. Robert Morris Assocs., No. Ind. Bankers Assn., Ind. Bankers Assn., Am. Bankers Assn., Assn. Profl. Poets, Nat. Manufactured Housing Assn., Columbia City C. of C. (bd. dirs. 1976-82, pres. 1978-80). Clubs: Poetry (Columbia City); Elks Country (Fort Wayne); Orchard Ridge Country. Lodge: Elks. Avocations: reading; computers; golf; basketball. Office: PO Box 510 Columbia City IN 46725

HOUSTON, WILLIAM ROBERT MONTGOMERY, ophthalmic surgeon; b. Mansfield, Ohio, Nov. 13, 1922; s. William T. and Frances (Hursh) H.; B.A., Oberlin Coll., 1944; M.D., Western Res. U., 1948; m. Marguerite LaBau Browne, Apr. 25, 1968; children—William Erling Tenney, Marguerite Elisabeth LaBau, Selby Cabot Truitt Vanderbilt. Intern, Meth. Hosp. Bklyn., 1948-49, Ill. Eye and Ear Infirmary, Chgo., 1949-50; resident N.Y. Eye and Ear Infirmary, 1950-52; practice medicine specializing in ophthalmic surgery, Mansfield, 1952—; mem. staffs Mansfield Gen. Hosp., Peoples Hosp., Mansfield, N.Y. U. Bellevue Med. Center, N.Y.C.; assoc. prof. clin. ophthalmology N.Y. U. Sch. Medicine. Pres. Mansfield Symphony Soc., 1965-68, Mansfield Civic Music Assn., 1965; mem. Mansfield City Sch. Bd., 1962-65, v.p., 1965. Served to capt. M.C. USAF, 1952-55. Diplomate Am. Bd. Ophthalmology. Recipient Honor award Acad. Ophthalmology. Fellow Internat. Coll. Surgeons; mem. SAR (color guard 1961-71), Ohio Hist. Soc. (life), Western Res. Hist. Soc. (life fellow), N.Y. Geneal. and Biog. Soc. (life), Ohio Geneal. Soc. (trustee 1955—). Editor, Ohio Records and Pioneers Families, 1970—. Address: 456 Park Ave W Mansfield OH 44906

HOUSTON, WILLIE WALTER, JR., biology educator, developmental cell biologist, researcher; b. Cedartown, Ga., Sept. 14, 1951; s. Willie Walter and Lois Lee (Richardson) H. B.S., Morehouse Coll., 1974; M.S., Atlanta U., 1976, Ph.D., 1981. Grad. teaching asst. Clark Coll., Atlanta, 1978-79; lectr. Spelman Coll., Atlanta, 1979; instr. Ky. State U., Frankfort, 1979-80; asst. prof. biology Central State U., Wilberforce, Ohio, 1980—, Minority Access to Research Careers faculty mem., 1983—; mem. Jack and Jill faculty, Wilberforce, 1983; vis. prof. Wright State U., Dayton, Ohio, 1980-82. Tchr., supt. Middle Run Baptist Ch., Xenia, Ohio, 1980-84; tchr. Mt. Enon Missionary Bapt. Ch., Dayton, summer 1984—; charter mem. Ellis Island Centennial Commn., 1984. Mem. Nat. Inst. Sci., Midwestern Developmental Biology Soc., Smithsonian Institution, Central State U. Biol. Soc., AAUP, NAACP, Internat. Platform Assn., Beta Beta Beta, Beta Kappa Chi, Alpha Phi Alpha. Democrat. Avocations: reading; auto collection; antique collecting. Home: 1000 Frederick Dr Xenia OH 45385 Office: Dept Biology Central State U Wilberforce OH 45384

HOUT, MARK MOUTRAY, optometrist; b. Highland Park, Ill., Nov. 14, 1925; s. Wesley Karl and Florence Irene (Moutray) H.; m. Esther Frances Galbraith, Sept. 1, 1956; 1 child, Lisa Marie. O.D., No. Ill. Coll. Optometry, 1948. Sole practice optometry, Winnetka, Ill., 1949-51, Highwood, Ill., 1951—. Mem. Highwood C. of C. (pres. 1972, 78). Republican. United Ch. Christ. Club: Deerfield Band (publicity 1975—). Lodge: Rotary (pres. 1972-73) (Deerfield, Ill.). Home: 857 Rosemary Terr Deerfield IL 60015 Office: 410 Green Bay Rd Highwood IL 60040

HOUTS, W. WALLACE, educator, real estate consultant; b. Rockford, Iowa, Oct. 30, 1927; s. John Max and Caroline (Talbot) H.; m. Beverly Swahn, Aug. 2, 1953; children—Robert, Mary Jane, Richard, Charles, Chris. B.A., Iowa Wesleyan Coll., 1950; M.A., State U. Iowa, 1951. Cert. tchr., Minn. Art supr. Omaha Pub. Schs., 1951-53; art tchr. Richfield Pub. Schs., Minn., 1953-84; investment cons. Ebbco Co., Mpls., 1964—. Dist. commr. Viking council Boy Scouts Am., Mpls., 1977-79, dist. chmn., 1982—, nat. jamboree leader, 1973, 77, 81. Served as cpl. U.S. Army, 1946-47. Recipient Award of Merit, Miniwicota Dist. Boy Scouts Am., 1973, Scouter of Yr. Award 1984, Silver Beaver award Viking council Boy Scouts Am., 1975. Mem. Richfield Fedn. Tchrs., Minn. Fedn. Tchrs., Am. Fedn. Tchrs., Minn. Art Educators Assn., Kappa Pi, Sigma Phi Epsilon. Republican. Methodist. Avocations: photography; sports; calligraphy. Home: 10210 Parkview Circle Bloomington MN 55431 Office: Ebbco Co Suite 688 4940 Viking Dr Edina MN 55435

HOVDESTAD, GARY DENNIS, accountant; b. Minot, N.D., June 24, 1942; s. Joe Allen and Ellen (Jonason) H.; m. Carol Joan Ramsay, Aug. 11, 1962; children—Pamela, Jodi, Brent. B.A. cum laude, Minot State Coll., 1963. C.P.A., N.D. Acct., office mgr. Brady, Martz & Assocs., Minot, 1963—, Pres., bd. dirs. First Lutheran Ch.; bd. dirs. Minot State Coll., First Luth. Found. Mem. Am. Inst. C.P.A.s., N.D. Soc. C.P.A.s, (bd. dirs. Chpt. pres. 1984-85), Minot State Coll. Alumni Assn. Lodge: Elks. Office: Brady Martz & Assocs PC 24 West Central Ave Minot ND 58701

HOWARD, ALAN JAY, legal educator; b. Washington, Mar. 25, 1947; s. Charles and Rose Beneck (Goldberg) H.; m. Lynn Sherry Propper, Mar. 16, 1980. B.S., Cornell U., 1969; J.D., U. Chgo., 1972. Bar: Ill., D.C., U.S. Supreme Ct. Assoc. Sidley & Austin, Chgo., 1973-75; adminstr. legis. research div. Inst. Govt., U. Ga., Athens, 1975-77; prof. law St. Louis U., 1977—. Contbr. articles to legal jours. Bd. dirs. Am. Jewish Congress, 1980—, mem. Nat. Commn. Law and Social Action, 1982-84; bd. dirs. ACLU, 1980-82. Recipient Best Teaching award St. Louis U. Law Sch., 1980. Mem. ABA, Ill. Bar Assn. Home: 7117 Maryland Ave University City MO 63130 Office: Saint Louis Univ Law Sch 3700 Lindell Blvd Saint Louis MO 63108

HOWARD, ALICE LAVERNE, bank executive; b. Blythesville, Ark., Apr. 4, 1943; d. Luther M. and Alice R. (Kinnision) Ford; Student, U. St. Louis, 1970—. Ops. officer - administrv. asst. Centerre Bank, St. Louis, 1977-80, dir. ops. tng., 1979-80, asst. v.p. mgr. domestic wire Ctr., 1980-81, asst. v.p., mgr., domestic ops., 1981-82, v.p., mgr. Air Transport Assn. of Am. dept., 1982-82, v.p., mgr. administrv. services div., 1983—; Officer, Santa's Helpers, St. Louis, 1972—. Recipient Leadership award YWCA, Metro St. Louis, 1984. Mem. Am. Inst Banking (dir. St. Louis chpt. 1984-86). Avocations: Reading, walking, water sports. Home: 1612 Forestedge Dr Saint Louis MO 63138 Office: Centerre Bank N A 1 Centerre Plaza Saint Louis MO 63101

HOWARD, DAVID MORRIS, missionary; b. Phila., Jan. 28, 1928; s. Philip E. Jr. and Katharine (Gillingham) H.; m. Phyllis Gibson, July 1, 1950; children—David, Stephen, Karen Elisabeth, Michael. A.B., Wheaton Coll., 1949, M.A. in Theology, 1952; LL.D., Geneva Coll., 1974; L.H.D., Taylor U., 1978. Ordained to ministry, 1952; asst. gen. dir. Latin Am. Mission, Colombia S.Am., Costa Rica, C.Am., 1953-68; missions dir. Inter-Varsity Christian Fellowship, Madison, Wis., 1968-76, asst. to pres., 1976-77; dir. Urbana Student Missionary Convs., 1973, 76; dir. Consultation on World Evangelization, Pattaya, Thailand, 1977-80; gen. dir. World Evangel. Fellowship, Wheaton, Ill., 1982—. Author: Hammered as Gold, 1969, reprinted as The Costly Harvest, 1975; Student Power in World Missions, 1979; How Come, God?, 1972, By the Power of the Holy Spirit, 1973; Words of Fire, Rivers of Tears, 1976, The Great Commission for Today, 1976. Bd. dirs. Am. Leprosy Mission; trustee Latin Am. Mission, Wheaton Coll. Home: 823 Anchor Ct Bartlett IL 60103 Office: World Evangel Fellowship PO Box WEF Wheaton IL 60189

HOWARD, EDWARD ALLEN, library administrator, consultant; b. Erlanger, Ky., May 10, 1931; s. William Edward and Betty (Smiley) H.; m. Phyllis Forster Vincent, May 16, 1959; children—Randall, Kim. B.A., U. Louisville, 1953; M.S., U. Ill., 1956. Cert. librarian I, Ind. Research asst. U. Ill., Urbana, 1954-56; head fine arts div. Topeka Pub. Library, 1956-58; city librarian Free Pub. Library, Lawrence, Kans., 1958-62; dir. Evansville-Vanderburgh County Pub. Library, Ind., 1962—; cons. Kans. State Library, Topeka, 1954-62; del. OCLC, Inc., Columbus, Ohio, 1979-83; cons. Pub. Library, Newburgh, Ind., 1983-84, New Castle, Ind., 1985—. Bd. dirs. Harmonie Assocs., New Harmony, Ind., 1980-84; mem. Mayor's Energy Conservation Com., Evansville, 1980, Center City Inc., Evansville, 1984. Recipient Disting. Service award Area Reading Council, Evansville, 1971; Cert. of Recognition, Office of Edn., HEW, Washington, 1975; Commendation, Office of Gov., Indpls., 1979; Award of Excellence, Pub. Library Friends, Evansville, 1983. Mem. ALA, Kans. Library Assn. (pres. 1961), Ind. Library Assn. (pres. 1972), Ind. Coop. Library Services Authority (pres. 1978), Adminstrs. Larger Pub. Libraries in Ind. Republican. Unitarian. Lodge: Kiwanis (pres. 1977-78). Office: Evansville-Vanderburgh County Pub Library 22 SE Fifth St Evansville IN 47708

HOWARD, GERALD LEE, manufacturing company executive; b. Mankato, Kans., Apr. 15, 1934; s. Wilbur Frank and Elsie Marie (Parsons) H.; B.A.A., Kans. State U., 1960; m. Donna Lee Power, Oct. 2, 1955; children—Pamela Sue, Steven Ray. Salesman, Holiday Shoe Store, Phillipsburg, Kans., 1955-57; auditor, tax acct. Kennedy & Coe, C.P.A., Salina, Kans., 1960-63; treas., controller Wenger Mfg., Inc., Sabetha, Kans., 1963—. Treas., Sabetha Community Hosp.; past lay leader, fin. com. Methodist Ch., Sabetha, Kans. Served with U.S. Army, 1953-55. Clubs: Lions (past sec.-treas.), Country (mem. bd.) (Sabetha, Kans.); Safari Internat. (Tucson); Game Conservation Internat. Home: 206 Harrison St Box 182 Sabetha KS 66534 Office: Wenger Mfg Inc 714 Main St Sabetha KS 66534

HOWARD, JERRY ARTHUR, children's home executive, consultant; b. Huntington, Ind., Oct. 13, 1940; s. Arthur W. and Esta G. (Herrmann) H.; m. Wanda Lee James, June 17, 1962; children—Jonathan A., James T. B.S., Greenville Coll., 1962; M.S., Purdue U., 1965, Ph.D., 1974. Tchr. jr. high sch. Carroll Consol. Sch., Flora, Ind., 1962-65; prin. Culver (Ind.) Schs., 1965-69; NDEA fellow Purdue U., West Lafayette, Ind., 1970-72; prin. North Miami Sch. Corp., Denver, Ind., 1972-73; asst. dir. stewardship dept. Free Meth. World Hdqrs., Winona Lake, Ind., 1974-79; dir. devel. Salem Children's Home, Flanagan, Ill., 1979—; guest instr. Greenville Coll., Ill., 1983, Huntington Coll., Ind., 1984; cons. Ont. Conf., Free Meth. Ch., Toronto, Ont., Can., 1974; chmn. audio/visual com. Free Meth. World Conv., 1978-79; ch. chmn. Hope Fellowship Evang. Mennonite, Wabash, Ind., 1983—; cons. estate planning Evang. Mennonite Conf., Ft. Wayne, Ind., 1979—. Contbr. articles to profl. jours. Named Hon. Farmer North Miami chpt. Future Farmers Am., 1973; NDEA fellow Purdue U., 1970. Mem. Am. Mgmt. Assn., Christian Stewardship Council, Phi Delta Kappa, Phi Alpha Theta. Republican. Mennonite. Home: Box 252 Rural Route 1 Akron IN 46910

HOWARD, LAURENCE EDWARD, judge; b. Ionia, Mich., Feb. 15, 1934; s. Leo Eugene and Marian Louise (Burtch) H.; m. Marilyn Teresa Howard, Aug. 23, 1958; children—Michael, Timothy, Nancy, Thomas. B.S. in Mktg., U. Notre Dame, 1958, J.D., 1961. Bar: Mich. Asst. city atty. City of Grand Rapids (Mich.), 1962-64; sole practice, Grand Rapids, 1964-76; U.S. bankruptcy judge Western Dist. Mich., Grand Rapids, 1976—. Democratic candidate for U.S. Congress, 1968. Served with U.S. Army, 1954-56. Mem. ABA, Mich. Bar Assn., Grand Rapids Bar Assn., Nat. Conf. Bankruptcy Judges. Office: 766 Federal Bldg 110 Michigan St NW Grand Rapids MI 49506

HOWARD, WILLIAM HERBERT, lawyer; b. Cin., June 27, 1953; s. Victor Jack and Dolores (Reiter) H.; m. Sara Conners Thomas, July 24, 1982; 1 dau., Claire Fontaine. B.A., Case Western Res. U., 1975, J.D. 1978. Bar: Ohio 1978, U.S. Dist. Ct. (so. dist.) Ohio 1978, U.S. Ct. Appeals (6th cir.) 1979. Law clk. U.S. Dist. Ct. (so. dist.) Ohio, Cin., 1978-80; assoc. Estabrook, Finn & McKee, Dayton, Ohio, 1980-83, Porter, Wright, Morris & Arthur, Dayton, 1983—. Mem. ABA, Ohio Bar Assn., Dayton Bar Assn., Cin. Bar Assn. Republican. Roman Catholic. Lodge: Optimists. Home: 235 Greenmount Blvd Dayton OH 45419 Office: Porter Wright Morris & Arthur 2100 First Nat Bank Bldg PO Box 1805 Dayton OH 45401

HOWARD, WILLIAM TERRY, dairy science educator; b. Pueblo, Calif., Apr. 14, 1936; s. George Charles and Mary Neola (Gause) H.; m. Karen Jane Boning, Apr. 24, 1960; children—Steven Louis, Matthew Charles, Rachel Elizabeth. B.S., U. Nebr., 1958, M.S., 1964; Ph.D., Purdue U., 1967. Instr. U. Nebr., Lincoln, 1959-64; research assoc. Purdue U., Lafayette, Ind., 1964-66; prof. dairy sci. U. Wis.-Madison, 1966—; nutrition cons. U.S. AID, Washington, 1977-80. Contbr. papers to profl. publs. Trustee St. Colletta Sch., Jefferson, Wis., 1976-82, 83—. Mem. Am. Dairy Sci. Assn. (extension com. 1982—), Holstein Assn. Am. (internat nutrition com. 1980—). Lutheran. Lodge: Kiwanis (bd. dirs. 1981-84). Home: 442 Agnes Dr Madison WI 53711

HOWDER, DELORIS JEAN, designer, manufacturer; b. Muscotah, Kans., Dec. 28, 1926; d. Ernest Oscer and Lona Ethel (Wiley) Hollenbeck; student Nat. Sch. Dress Design, 1953-54; m. Wilbern B. Obbards; 1 son, Glen Alan; m. 2d, Richard Joseph Howder, Jan. 29, 1968. With Horton Garment Co. (Kans.), 1948-54; with Paramount Studios, Hollywood, Calif., 1955; owner, designer Deloris Square Dance Dresses, Long Beach, Calif., Springfield, Mo., Seligman, Mo. and Horton, 1957—. Mem. Horton C. of C. (mem. arts and crafts show com. 1979, mem. arts, crafts and flea market 1983-84), Nat. Costume Assn., Parents Without Partners (editor newsletter 1979-82, N.E. Kans. chpt. 1071 membership dir. 1982-83). Office: 847 Central Horton KS 66439

HOWE, GARY LEWIS, innovation education company president; b. Highland Park, Mich., Jan. 2, 1942; s. Harold A. and Peggy Margaret (Christensen) Krueger; m. Marion K. Dukes, Mar. 9, 1963; children—Christine, James, Deborah, Vicky Lynn. Student Vocat. Tech. Sch., St. Paul, Mpls. and Mankato, 1961-82. Pres., gen. contractor Total Home Service, Mpls., 1972-74; application engr. Midtex Inc., Mankato, Minn., 1974-75; sales rep., trainer Curtis Indsl., Inc., Mankato, 1975-79; pres., co-founder research devel., dir. Future Tech., Inc., Mankato, 1979-82; pres. CEO Inno-Tech Internat., Mankato, 1982-83; pres., chief exec. officer Inno-Media Corp., Mankato, 1983—; educator Minn. Entrepreneurs Club, Mpls., 1983—; program dir. Minn. Inventors Tech. Transfer Commn. Workshops, Mpls., 1981—. Mem. Mankato C. of C. (mem. Conv. Visitor's Bur. 1982—). Author: (coursebook) Introduction to Innovation, 1984; Patentee Solar D Icer, 1984 Editor Gateways newsletter for inventors and innovators. Home: 230 10th Ave S Minneapolis MN 55415

HOWE, JOHN KINGMAN, sales and marketing executive; b. Everett, Wash., Nov. 7, 1945; s. John Cutler and Nancy Carpenter (Kingman) H.; m. Loretta Kerr, Aug. 27, 1966; children—Steven Cutler, Nancy Kingman. Student Ohio State U., 1963-65. Field technician Data Corp., Dayton, Ohio, 1965-66; letter carrier U.S. Post Office, Dayton, 1966; v.p., sales rep. E.S. Klosterman Co., Dayton, 1966-72; v.p. sales, dir. Springfield Binder Corp., Ohio, 1981-84, pres., chief exec. officer, 1984—; pres., chief exec. officer, dir. The John K. Howe Co., Dayton, Ohio, 1972—; pres., dir. Cutler-Kingman, Inc., Dayton, 1979—; gen. ptnr. H&B Enterprises, Dayton, 1977—, Design Investment Properties, Dayton, 1979—, BMR Properties, Ltd., Dayton, 1979-82; adminstr. John K. Howe Co./Profit Sharing, Dayton, 1973—, John K. Howe Co./Pension Plan, 1976—. Pres. South Dixie Bus. Assn., Kettering, Ohio, 1978-82. Mem. Dayton C. of C. Republican. Presbyterian. Home: 628 Cushing Ave Dayton OH 45429 Office: John K Howe Co Inc 2435 S Dixie Ave Dayton OH 45409-1897

HOWE, RICHARD RAY, lawyer; b. Decatur, Ill., Aug. 23, 1932; s. Elbert Davis and Marie (Harris) H.; A.B., U. Mo., 1954, J.D., 1959; m. Elaine Bondurant, Apr. 17, 1954; children—Richard R., Scott W., Dale A., Tracy. Admitted to Mo. bar, 1959, since practiced in Canton. Mem. Canton Bd. Edn., 1962-68, sec., 1962-67, v.p., 1967-68. Pros. atty. Lewis County (Mo.), 1969-72; commr., also chmn. Commn. to Reapportion Mo. Legislature, 1971. Mem., vice chmn. Mo. Commn. on Human Rights, 1974-76. Chmn., Republican Central Com. Lewis County, 1971-76, 79—; chmn. 9th Congl. Dist. Rep. Com., 1974-76. Trustee Canton Pub. Library, 1961-70. Served with USAF, 1955-57. Mem. Am. Bar Assn., Assn. Trial Lawyers Am., Am. Judicature Soc., Alpha Tau Omega, Phi Alpha Delta. Mason, Kiwanian. Home: Rural Route 2 Canton MO 63435 Office: 436 Lewis St Canton MO 63435

HOWE, STANLEY MERRILL, manufacturing company executive; b. Muscatine, Iowa, Feb. 5, 1924; s. Merrill Y. and Thelma F. (Corriell) H.; B.S., Iowa State U., 1946; M.B.A. (Gerard Swope fellow), Harvard U., 1948; m. Helen Jensen, Mar. 29, 1953; children—Thomas, Janet, Steven, James. Production engr. HON Industries, Muscatine, Iowa, 1948-54, v.p. production, 1954-61, exec. v.p., 1961-64, pres., 1964—, chmn. bd., 1984—, also dir.; chmn. bd. Holga Metal Products Corp., Murphy-Miller Co., Corry Jamestown Corp.; pres. Prime-Mover Co.; chmn. Hiebert, Inc., Heatilator, Inc.; dir. Rolscreen Co. Trustee Iowa Wesleyan Coll.; mem. Muscatine Community Health Found. Mem. NAM (bd. dirs.), Iowa Assn. Bus. and Industry, Am. Mgmt. Assn. Methodist. Clubs: Rotary, Elks, 33. Home: 1124 Oakland Dr Muscatine IA 52761 Office: 414 E 3d St Muscatine IA 52761

HOWELL, HONOR SHARON, minister; b. Seguin, Tex, Oct. 12, 1947; d. Joe Milam and Mary Elizabeth (McKay) H. B.A., Austin Coll., 1970; M.Div., St. Paul Sch. Theology, 1973. Youth minister Key Meml. United Methodist Ch., Sherman, Tex., 1969-71, Second Presbyterian Ch., Kansas City, Mo., 1971-72; pastor Edwardsville United Meth. Ch., Kans., 1972-75; assoc. program dir. Council on Ministries, Topeka, 1975-80; v.p. St. Paul Sch. Theology, Kansas City, Mo., 1980-85; sr. pastor St. Mark United Meth. Ch., Overland Park, Kans., 1985—; pres. Commn. on Status and Role of Women in United Meth. Ch., Evanston, Ill., 1984—; chmn. personnel com. Council on Ministries, Topeka, Kans., 1984—. Mem. NOW, ACLU, Christian Educators Fellowship, Nat. Assn. Female Execs., Smithsonian Assocs., Internat. Assn. Women Ministers. Democrat. Home: 6600 Reeds Dr Mission KS 66202 Office: St Mark United Meth Ch 6422 Santa Fe Dr Overland Park KS 66202

HOWELL, ORVIE LEON, geologist; b. Wichita, Kans., Sept. 4, 1931; s. Orville Clements and Hettie-Elizabeth (Brock) H.; divorced; children—Dale, Richard, Susan, Sally. B.S. in Geology, Wichita State U., 1954. Geologist, Lion Oil Co., Wichita, Kans., 1954-58; dist. geologist Lario Oil and Gas Co., Wichita, 1958-63, gen. mgr. Hinkle Oil Co., Wichita, 1973—. Fund raiser United Way, Wichita, 1970-83; sec. adv. com. dept. geology Wichita State U., 1983—. Mem. Am. Assn. Petroleum Geologists (speaker 1969-70, co-editor jour. 1969-70), Kans. Geol. Soc. (pres. 1968-69), N.Mex. Geol. Soc., Am. Inst. Profl. Geologists, Rocky Mountain Assn. Geologists, Kans. Ind. Oil and Gas Assn. Republican. Methodist. Clubs: Tallgrass Country, Crestview Country, Petroleum (Wichita). Avocations: Flying, travel. Home: 9031 Lakepoint Dr Wichita KS 67226 Office: Hinkle Oil Co 1016 Union Ctr Wichita KS 67202

HOWELL, WILLIAM KENNETH, manufacturing company executive; b. Radford, Va., May 22, 1930; s. Elbert Franklin and Hattie Lou (Holiday) H.; B.A. in Bus. Adminstrn., U. Richmond, 1953; m. Barbara Williams, Sept. 5, 1953; children—Dean, Spencer. With Philip Morris Co., 1955—, with C.A. Tabacalera Nacional, Venezuelan affiliate, to 1967, regional v.p. Phillip Morris Internat., Latin Am., 1967, corp. v.p. Philip Morris Inc., 1975—, pres., dir. Miller Brewing Co. subs., Milw., 1972—; dir. Philip Morris Inc.; 1st exec. in residence U. Richmond; dir. First Wis. Nat. Bank, Milw. Bd. dirs. St. Mary's Hosp., Milw., Boy Scouts Milw., Jr. Achievement Southeastern Wis.; mem. Greater Milw. Com.; mem. adv. council U. Wis., Milw. Sch. Bus. Adminstrn. with USMC, 1953-55. Clubs: Milw. Country, Univ., Wis., Johns Island. Office: 3939 W Highland Blvd Milwaukee WI 53201

HOWELLS, ROBERT ARTHER, scientist; b. Cleve., Feb. 4, 1948; s. Robert Maxwell and Arlene Betty (Mountcastle) H.; m. Mary Therese Miller, Jan. 23, 1971. B.S., Ohio State U., 1970; M.A., U. Dayton, 1974; Ph.D., Purdue U., 1983. Product specialist Dann Co., Cleve., 1970-72; research asst. U. Dayton, 1972-74; adminstr., instr. Purdue U., 1974-83; contract cons. Delco Electronics div. Gen. Motors Corp., Kokomo, Ind., 1983-84; corp. chief scientist Def. System Corp., Escondido, Calif., 1984-85; prin. scientist Calspan Corp., Buffalo, 1985—. Editor: Readings in Psychology, 1981. Contbr. articles to profl. jours. and chpts. to books. Mem. coll. adv. bd. Dushkin Pub. Group, 1976-82. Purdue U. research fellow, 1979; U. Dayton research fellow, 1974. Mem. Assn. Old Crows, Human Factors Soc., Soc. Math. Psychology, Gt. Pyrenees Club of Am., Sigma Xi. Avocations: photography, clock restoration, woodworking. Home: 5285 Little Woods Ln Dayton OH 45429 Office: Arvin/Calspan Corp 1769 Springfield St Dayton OH 45403

HOWLAND, JOHN GORDON BROWN, publisher; b. Norfolk, Va., Nov. 26, 1942; s. John B. and Diana L. (Gray) H.; m. Karen H. Chastain, Feb. 17, 1968; children—John Paul, Nicholas Chastain. B.S., U.S. Naval Acad., 1964; M.B.A., NYU, 1972. Corp. banking officer Citibank, N.Y.C., 1969-72; asst. treas. Am. Hosp. Supply Corp., Evanston, Ill., 1972-74; treas. CF Industries, Chgo., 1974-75; fin. cons., Chgo., 1975-76; treas. Skil Corp., Chgo., 1977-79; founder, pub. Cashflow Mag., Glenview, Ill., 1979—. Chmn. fin. com. Sch. Dist. 34, 1978; founder Glenview Soccer Program (AYSO), 1982; mem. Nat. bd. dirs. Am. Youth Soccer Orgn., 1985—. Served to lt. USN, 1964-69; Vietnam. Mem. Nat. Corp. Cash Mgmt. Assn. (founder), Fin. Execs. Inst. Club: Rotary (Glenview). Office: 1807 Glenview Rd Suite 205 Glenview IL 60025

HOWLETT, ROBERT GLASGOW, lawyer; b. Bay City, Mich., Nov. 10, 1906; s. Lewis Glasgow and Anne Lucille (Hurst) H.; B.S., Northwestern U., 1929, J.D., 1932; m. Barbara Withey, Sept. 19, 1936; children—Eleanor Howlett Burton, Craig G., Douglas W. Bar: Ill. 1932, N.Y. 1940, D.C. 1944, Mich. 1947, Tenn. 1947. Mem. Varnum Riddering, Schmidt & Howlett, Grand Rapids, 1949-83, of counsel, 1983—; mem. Mich. Employment Relations Commn., 1963-76, chmn., 1964-76; chmn. Fed. Service Impasses Panel, 1976-78, 82-84, Mem., 1984—; mem. Fgn. Service Impasse Disputes Panel, 1976-78, 81—; industry mem. shipbldg. commn. Nat. War Labor Bd., 1963-65; spl. asst. atty. gen., dept. aeronautics State of Mich., 1957-61; vis. prof. Mich. State U., East Lansing, 1972, 75. Chmn. Kent County Rep. Com., 1956-61; del. Rep. Nat. Conv., 1960. Mem. Am., Grand Rapids (pres. 1962-63) bar assns., State Bar Mich., Nat. Acad. Arbitrators, Indsl. Relations Research Assn. (pres. Detroit chpt. 1978-79), Soc. Profls. in Dispute Resolution (pres. 1974-75), Assn. Labor Relations Agys. (pres. 1977-78). Clubs: Kent Country, Peninsular (Grand Rapids). Contbr. articles to profl. jours. Home: 2910 Oak Hollow Dr SE Grand Rapids MI 49506 Office: Suite 800 171 Mouroett W Grand Rapids MI 49503

HOWSAM, ROBERT LEE, SR., professional baseball team executive. Pres., chief exec. officer Cin. Reds. Office: Cin Reds 100 Riverfront Stadium Cincinnati OH 45202*

HOWSE, CARL STANLEY, real estate management executive, property manager; b. Pulaski, Tenn., May 30, 1937; s. Theodore Roosevelt and Annie Dee (Payne) H.; m. Mamie Jane Sherman; children—Christopher Stanley, Talitha, Beverly Ann. Student LaSalle U. Extension, 1968-70. Rail tract layer Republic Steel Corp., Cleve., 1955-56; parts correlator White Motor Co., Cleve., 1962-69; Salesman Interstate Brands Corp., Cleve., 1969-70, Birkett Williams Ford, Cleve., 1969; master sales Cenral Chevrolet, Inc., Cleve., 1969; master sales Grabski Ford Sales, Cleve., 1969; discount mortgage broker AAA Mortgage, N.Y.C., 1982; assoc. fin. broker Hempel Fin. Corp., Los Angeles, 1982; co-broker/finder Calif. Fin. Planning Assocs., N.Y.C., 1982; pres., chief exec. officer C.S. Howse, Inc., Cleve., 1982—, also chmn. bd. Sr. deacon E. 116th St. Ch. of God in Christ; active Urban League, Friends of Cleve. Pub. Library, Friends of Warrensville Community Library, Boy Scouts Am. Mem. NAACP, Am. Mgmt. Assn., Apt. and Homeowners Assn. NE Ohio, Nat. Apts. Assn., Am. Assn. Individual Investors, Nat. Assn. Fin. Cons. Office: PO Box 5812 Cleveland OH 44101

HOWSER, RICHARD ALTON, baseball manager; b. Miami, Fla., May 14, 1937; B.S. in Edn., Fla. State U. Baseball player Kansas City Athletics, 1961-63, Cleve. Indians, 1963-66, N.Y. Yankees, 1967-68; mem. Am. League All-Star team, 1961, 63; coach N.Y. Yankees, 1969-78, mgr., 1980; baseball coach Fla. State U., Tallahassee, 1979; mgr. Kansas City Royals, 1981—. Office: Kansas City Royals Harry S Truman Sports Complex PO Box 1969 Kansas City MO 64141*

HOXTELL, EUGENE ORVILLE, dermatologist; b. Fargo, N.D., Aug. 21, 1944; s. Orville Theodore and Emma Emelia (Leininger) H.; m. Sharron Lee Johnson, Dec. 16, 1967; children—Jeffrey, Kirsten. B.S., U. Minn., 1967, M.D., 1969, M.S., 1976. Diplomate Am. Bd. Dermatology, Am. Bd. Dermatopathology. Staff dermatology Central Plains Clinic, Sioux Falls, S.D., 1976-82; practice medicine specializing in dermatology Dermatology Assocs., Sioux Falls, 1982—; cons. VA Hosp., Sioux Falls, 1976—. Contbr. articles to profl. jours. Pack leader Webelos, Boy Scouts Am., Sioux Falls, 1983. Served to maj. USAF, 1971-73. Fellow Am. Acad. Dermatology, Am. Soc. Dermatopathology, Am. Soc. Dermatologic Surgery; mem. AMA, Soc. Investigation Dermatology. Republican. Lutheran. Avocations: sailing, flying, photography. Home: 3812 Birchwood Ave Sioux Falls SD 57103 Office: Dermatology Assocs 1201 S Euclid St Sioux Falls SD 57105

HOXWORTH, GERALD MONROE, radiologist; b. Arbyrd, Mo., Mar. 24, 1927; s. Lewis D. and Della (Pollock) H.; m. Frances Lea Hardy, Feb. 1, 1950; children—Gregory N., Karen H. Rice, Deborah Ann, Dan Hardy. A.B.,

Central Methodist Coll., Mo., 1949; B.S. Medicine, U. Mo., 1952; M.D., Washington U., St. Louis, 1954. Diplomate Am. Bd. Radiology. Intern, U. Colo. Med. Sch., Denver 1954-55; resident in radiology U. Mo. Med. Ctr., Columbia, 1971-74, clin. assoc. prof. radiology, 1974-83; gen. practice medicine, Cape Girardeau, Mo., 1956-71; chmn. dept. med. imaging Audrain Med. Ctr., Mexico, Mo., 1974—, pres. med. staff, 1983—. Served with USNR, 1944-46. Mem. Am. Coll. Radiology, Mo. Med. Assn., AMA, So. Med. Assn. Unitarian. Avocations: farming, reading. Office: Audrain Med Ctr 620 E Monroe St Mexico MO 65265

HOYLAND, JANET LOUISE, government official; b. Kansas City, Mo., July 21, 1940; d. Robert J. and Dora Louise (Worley) H.; B.A., Carleton Coll., 1962; postgrad. in music (Mu Phi Epsilon scholar 1966) U. Mo. at Kansas City, 1964-67; M.L.A., So. Meth. U., 1979. Policy writer Lynn Ins. Co., Kansas City, 1963-64; music librarian U. Mo. at Kansas City, 1966-68; benefit authorizer Social Security Adminstrn., Kansas City, Mo., 1969-75, tech. specialist, 1976-79, claims authorizer, 1980—; piano tchr. Leta Wallace Piano Studio, Kansas City, 1963, 68; piano accompanist Barn Players, Overland Park, Kans., 1972-75, Off Broadway Dinner Playhouse, Inc., Kansas City, 1973, Resident Theatre, Kansas City, 1979. Co-chmn. Project Equality work area, 1971; work area chmn. on ecumenism Council on Ministries, 1969-70; sec. fair housing action com. Council on Religion and Race, Kansas City, 1968; active ward and precinct work Democratic Com. for County Progress, 1968; chairperson administrv. bd. United Methodist Ch., Kansas City, Mo., 1983—. Mem. Women's Div. Kansas City Philharmonic, Friends of Art Kansas City, Fellowship House Assn. Kansas City, Internat. Platform Assn., Kansas City Mus. Club (chmn. composition dept. 1967-68), Mu Phi Epsilon (v.p. Kansas City 1968, sec. 1971, pres. 1975-76), Pi Kappa Lambda. Methodist. Home: 7115 Grand St Kansas City MO 64114

HOYT, DON, SR., association executive; b. North Adams, Mich., Mar. 28, 1930; s. George Washington and Frances (Monroe) H.; m. Dorothy Hess, Mar. 7, 1947 (div. Oct. 1952); m. Ella Mae Lake, Dec. 20, 1952; children—Peggy, Jerry, Linus, Don Jr., Becky, Barbara. Pres. Nat. Trappers Assn., Bloomington, Ill., 1977—. Home: 15412 Tau Rd Marshall MI 49068 Office: Box 3667 216 N Center St Bloomington IL 61701

HOYT, RICHARD COMSTOCK, econs. consulting co. exec.; b. St. Paul, Sept. 30, 1939; s. Charles Richardson and Minnie (Comstock) H.; B.S., Kans. State U., 1961; M.S., U. Minn., 1968, Ph.D., 1972; m. Ingrid Langensiepen, Oct. 24, 1964; children—Monika Anna, Derek Richard. Milling engr. Tennant & Hoyt Co., Lake City Minn., 1971-72, pres., 1972; research asst. U. Minn., 1968-71; pres. Analytics, Inc., Excelsior, Minn., 1973—; lectr. in field. Served with C.E., U.S. Army, 1962-65. Mem. Am. Econ. Assn., Am. Agrl. Econ. Assn., Mgmt. Sci. Assn. Republican. Contbr. articles in field to profl. jours. Home: 5975 Ridge Rd Excelsior MN 55331 Office: 464 2d St Excelsior MN 55331

HRACHOVINA, FREDERICK VINCENT, osteopathic physician and surgeon; b. St. Paul, Sept. 2, 1926; s. Vincent Frank and Beatrice (Funda) H.; B.A. in Chemistry, Macalester Coll., 1948; D.O., Kirksville (Mo.) Coll. Osteopathic Medicine, 1956; m. Joan Halverson, July 2, 1955. Chemist, Twin City area, 1948-51; intern Clare (Mich.) Gen. Osteo. Hosp., 1956-57; pvt. practice, Mpls., 1957—; founder Physicians Placement Service, 1975—. Smith, Kline & French Labs. grantee, 1973. Mem. Am. Osteo. Medicine (council fed. health programs, drug enforcement adminstrn. prescribers working com. 1974-75), Minn. Med. Soc. (pres. 1965-66, exec. dir. 1966-74, pub. relations dir. 1974-75), Assn. Osteo. State Exec. Dirs. (pres. 1970-71, dir. 1971-74), Am. Coll. Gen. Practitioners Osteo. Medicine and Surgery (lectr. Mo. soc.), Am. Acad. Osteopathy, Fla. Acad. Osteopathy, Am. Assn. Sr. Physicians, Fla. Osteo. Med. Assn., Internat. Congress Osteo. Medicine (adminstrv. staff, lectr. Brussels, Belgium 1984), Am. Blood Resources Assn., Minn. Gymnastic Assn. (founder 1962-72), Twin City Model A Ford Club. Mason (Shriner). Clubs: Breakfast, Optimist (dir. Mpls. 1959-62, 69-72, pres. 1970-71, gen. chmn. floor exercise gymnastic program 1959-65), Antique Auto Am., Minn. Car, Classic Car Am. (membership chmn. Minn. Region 1977, sec. 1978), Cadillac La Salle (founder, treas. North Star Region 1978-83), Pierce Arrow Soc. (founder Midwest region 1983, dir., treas. 1983—), Masons, Shrine Author: Microscopic Anatomy, 1952; Methods of Development for New Osteopathic Medical Colleges in the Next Millennium, 1977. Contbr. articles to profl. jours. Home: 3655 47th Ave S Minneapolis MN 55406 Office: 202 Inland Bldg 1000 2d Ave S Minneapolis MN 55403

HRASTICH, THOMAS ANTHONY, chemical engineer; b. St. Louis, Nov. 25, 1943; s. Anthony Christian and Amy Louise (Heege) H.; B.S. in Chem. Engring., U. Mo., Rolla, 1965; postgrad. U. Mo., Columbia, 1965-68, Jacksonville (Ala.) State U., 1971-72, St. John's U., 1972-73; children—Jeffrey, Thomas. Asst. plant mgr. BASF Wyandotte Corp., Troy, Mich., 1974-75, plant mgr., 1975-79, sr. project engr., 1979-80; ops. mgr. Motor Oils Refining Co., 1980—. Served to capt. U.S. Army, 1968-73, to maj. USAR. Decorated Bronze star, Air Medals. Mem. Am. Chem. Soc., Am. Inst. Chem. Engrs., AAAS. Office: 7601 W 47th St McCook IL 60525

HRBEK, GEORGE WILLIAM, electrical engineer, electronics company executive; b. Oak Park, Ill., Dec. 27, 1927; s. George and Emily (Knourek) H.; m. Geraldine Barbara Shaw, June 27, 1953; children—George M., William D., Barbara K. B.S.E.E., Ill. Inst. Tech., 1953; M.S.E.E., Northwestern U., 1964. Engr., Sperry Gyroscope Co., Great Neck, N.Y., 1953-54; mgr. electron device research Zenith Radio Corp., Chgo., 1956-77, dir. video engring., Glenview, Ill., 1980—; mgr. mfg. research Motorola, Inc., Schaumburg, Ill., 1977-79; mgr. research Ardev Inc., Palo Alto, Calif., 1979-80; tech. speaker in field. Served with U.S. Army, 1954-56. Mem. IEEE (sr.), Sigma Xi, Eta Kappa Nu Assn. Republican. Roman Catholic. Club: Yacht (Milw.). Contbr. articles in field to tech. publs. Patentee in field. Home: Arlington Heights IL 60004 Office: Zenith Electronics Corp 1000 Milwaukee Ave Glenview IL 60025

HRINKO, DANIEL DEAN, clinical counselor; b. Springfield, Ohio, Dec. 14, 1955; s. Peter and Jean Ayr (Wallace) H.; m. Lisa Marie Rykowski, Oct. 23, 1976; children—Peter Daniel, Matthew David. B.A., Muskingum Coll., 1976; M.A., Ball State U., 1977. Cottage therapist Oesterlen Services for Youth Ctr., Springfield, Ohio, 1978-79; dir. day treatment Dayton (Ohio) Youth Drug Program, 1980-82; pvt. practice adolescent and family counseling, Springfield, Ohio, 1982-84; dir. assessment Alcohol and Drug Council Clark County, 1984—; cons. agys. Vol., Springfield Fire Dept., 1978—. Mem. Am. Psychol. Assn. Lutheran. Lodge: Masons (past master). Address: 3643 Troy Rd Springfield OH 45504

HRINKO, JEAN AYR, educator; b. Goes, Ohio, Mar. 20, 1923; B.S. in Elementary Edn., Wittenberg Coll., Springfield, Ohio, 1968; postgrad. in spl. edn. U. Dayton, Kent (Ohio) State U.; married; 1 child. Tchr., Mad-River Green Sch., Enon, Ohio, 1964-68; tchr. Springfield Pub. Sch., 1968—; mem. Ohio Low Incidence Curriculum Com. Vol. info. desk Mercy and Community hosps., also St. John's Convalescent Home, Springfield. Mem. Civic Opera Guild, 1974—. Recipient Tchr. of Yr. award, 1982. Mem. NEA, Ohio Edn. Assn., Springfield Tchrs. Assn. Ohio Deaf Tchrs. Assn., Quota Internat. for Deaf, Theta Phi Gamma, Alpha Iota. Jennings scholar, 1970-71. Certified, Ohio; specialist in field of hearing impaired, educable mentally retarded. Home: 3641 Troy Rd Springfield OH 45504 Office: 1600 N Limestone St Springfield OH 45506

HRISTOVSKI, BLAGOJE, lithographer; b. Bitola, Yugoslavia, July 30, 1947; s. Iliya and Christina Hristovski; m. Ilona Bata, June 14, 1969; children—Dennis, Angela. Cameraman, Jack Berger Ltd., 1967-70; foreman Litho Color Services, Winnipeg, Man., Can., 1970-72; pres. GB Graphics Ltd., Winnipeg, 1972—, gen. mgr., 1983—. Office: GB Graphics Ltd 250 Saulteaux Crescent Winnipeg MB R3J 3T2 Canada

HRUBAN, ZDENEK, pathology educator; b. Prerov, Czechoslovakia, June 15, 1921; came to U.S., 1951, naturalized, 1957; s. Jaroslav and Aloisie (Rieger) H.; m. Jarmila S. Stanek, Aug. 27, 1955; children—Paul Y., Ralph H., Diana J. Candidate medicine U. Rostock, Germany, 1943; M.U.C., Charles U., 1948; M.D., U. Chgo., 1956, Ph.D., 1963. Diplomate Am. Bd. Pathology. Intern Presbyn. Hosp., Chgo., 1956-57; resident U. Chgo., 1957-60, instr. pathology, 1960-63, asst. prof., 1963-67, assoc. prof., 1967-73, prof., 1973—. Author: (with M. Rechcigl) Microbodies and Related Particles, 1969. Mem. Am. Soc. Cell Biology, Am. Assn. Study Liver Diseases, Am. Assn. Pathologists, Electron Microscopy Soc. Am., Sigma Xi, Alpha Omega Alpha. Unitarian. Home: 1460 E 56th St Chicago IL 60637 Office: U Chgo Dept Pathology 5841 S Maryland Ave Chicago IL 60637

HRUBY, PAUL, educational administrator; b. Chgo., May 31, 1935; s. Peter and Jennie (Sima) H.; m. Joan Pyskacek, Jan. 26, 1963; children—Jennifer Lynn, Jean Kristin. B.S., Mich. State U., 1959; M.S., No. Ill. U., 1970. Phys. edn. tchr. Lincoln Jr. High Sch., 1966-78, asst. prin., 1976-78; prin. Custer Elem. Sch., Berwyn, Ill., 1978—; coach hockey Fenwick High Sch., Oak Park, Ill., part-time, 1966-72; mgr. ice skating rink Ridgeland Commons, Oak Park, 1962-65. Mem. Am. Assn. Curriculum Dirs., Internat. Reading Assn., Ill. Prins. Assn. Lodges: Berwyn Kiwanis (past pres.), Zobak of Antioch (pres.). Home: 2531 S Wesley Berwyn IL 60402 Office: 1427 S Oak Park Berwyn IL 60402

HRUSHESKY, WILLIAM JOHN MICHAEL, internist, oncologist, chronobiologist, inventor, educator; b. Poughkeepsie, N.Y., Nov. 9, 1947; s. William Michael and Mary Margaget (Burns) H.; m. Patricia A. Wood, June 28, 1983. B.A. with honors, Syracuse U., 1969; M.D., U. Buffalo, 1973. Diplomate Am. Bd. Internal Medicine, Am. Bd. Med. Oncology. Assoc. cancer scientist Roswell Park Meml. Hosp., Buffalo, 1971-73; fellow Johns Hopkins U., Balt., 1973-74; intern Balt. City Hosp., 1973-74; clin. assoc. Nat. Cancer Inst. NIH, Bethesda, Md., 1974-76; resident U. Minn.-Mpls., 1976-78, asst. prof., 1979—; cons. various tech. med. sci. instrument cos., 1982—; pres., chmn. Sine o graph Corp., Mpls., 1984—; pres., chmn., founder Info-Med Corp., 1985—. Editor: Practical Application of Chronbiology in Cancer Medicine, Pantentee in field. Contbr. articles to profl. jours. Adv. to special asst. to gov., St. Paul, 1984. Served to lt. comdr. USPHS, 1975-76. Grantee Union Internationale Centre le Cancer, India, 1979, NIH, 1982—, Nat. Cancer Inst., 1982—, various instrumentation pharmaceutical corps., 1984. Mem. Internat. Soc. Chronobiology, Am. Soc. Clin. Oncology, Am. Assn. Cancer Research, Am. Fedn. Clin. Research, ACP. Club: Calhoun Beach (Mpls.) Avocations; running, squash player, painter, public communication scientific concepts. Home: 3123 James Ave S Minneapolis MN 55408 Office: U Minn Box 414 Mayo Meml Bldg 420 Delaward St Minneapolis MN 55455

HSIUNG, HANSEN MAXWELL, research scientist; b. Han Kow, Hu-Pei, Republic of China, May 12, 1947; came to U.S., 1970, permanent resident, 1982; s. Sow-Tsow and Wei-Mei Chia H.; m. Ling-Ann Wei, Jan. 29, 1972; children—Amy W., Wayne. B.S. in Chemistry, Nat. Taiwan U., Taipei, 1969; M.S. in Biochemistry, U. Ill.-Urbana, 1972, Ph.D. in Organic Chemistry, 1975. Research assoc. Nat. Research Council of Can., Ottawa, Ont., 1977-80; sr. biologist Eli Lilly & Co., Indpls., 1980—. Mem. AAAS. Home: 108 W 88th St Indianapolis IN 46260 Office: Lilly Corp Ctr 307 E McCarty St Indianapolis IN 46285

HSU, CHIN-FEI, statistician, researcher; g. Taipei, Taiwan, Republic China, Oct. 29, 1947; came to U.S., 1972; s. Gin-Shyang and Yueh-Yuen H.; m. Chi Yin Huang, June 20, 1974; children—Josephine, Peter. B.S., Nat. Taiwan U., 1972; M.S., U. N.C., 1975, Ph.D., 1977. Research asst. U. N.C., Chapel Hill, 1972-77; assoc. profl. scientist, in stats. Ill. State Water Survey, Champaign, 1977-82, profl. scientist, 1982—. Contbr. articles to profl. jours. Pres. Central Ill. Osborne User Group, Champaign, 1982-83. NSF grantee, 1981-83; U.S. Geol. Survey grantee, 1984-85. Mem. Inst. Math. Stats., Am. Statis. Assn., Am. Meteorol. Soc., Sigma Xi. Avocations: micro-computers, camping. Office: Ill State Water Survey 2204 Griffith Dr Champaign IL 61820

HSU, DER-ANN, statistician, financial researcher; b. Canton, Peoples Republic of China, Dec. 9, 1943; s. Jen-Lin and Su-Yun (Lee) Hsu; m. Jane C. Hsu, July 27, 1974; children—Patricia, Andrew. B.A. in Econs., Nat. Taiwan U., Tapei, 1965; Ph.D. in Bus. Statistics, U. Wis., Madison, 1973. Research asst. prof. Princeton U., N.J., 1974-77; asst. prof. U. Wis., Milw., 1977-79, assos. prof., 1979-83, prof. statistics and finance, 1983—; cons. U.S. Fed. Aviation Adminstrn., Atlantic City, N.J., 1977—. Contbr. articles to profl. jours. Recipient Outstanding Research award Sch. Bus. Adminstrn., U. Wis., 1984; Research Com. award Grad. Sch., U. Wis., 1985. Fellow Royal Inst. Nav., Royal Statis. Soc.; mem. Am. Statis. Assn., Inst. Mgmt. Scis., Am. Finance Assn. Avocation: violin. Home: 9218 N 60th St Milwaukee WI 53223 Office: Sch of Bus Adminstrn U Wis PO Box 742 Milwaukee WI 53201

HSU, HSI FAN, medical educator; b. Huangyan, China, Mar. 9, 1906; came to U.S., 1954, naturalized, 1963; s. Cai Cheng and Xiao Mei (Wang) H.; m. Shu Ying Li, Apr. 18, 1954; children—Tung Mei, Tung Wen, Tung Tai, Tong Xu. B.S., Amoy U. (China), 1929; D.Sc., U. Neuchatel (Switzerland), 1935; M.D., U. Phillipines, 1949. Prof., head biology dept. China U., Beijing, 1936-41; chief parasitology lab. Chinese NIH, Nanking, 1948-49; prof., head zoology dept. Nat. Taiwan U., Taipei, 1949-54; asst. prof. preventive medicine U. Iowa, Iowa City, 1954-58, assoc. prof., 1958-61, prof., 1961-74, prof. emeritus, 1974—. Contbr. articles to profl. jours. Recipient Sci. Research prize China Found., 1939. Mem. emeritus AMA, Am. Acad. Allergy, Am. Soc. Tropical Medicine & Hygiene, Am. Assn. Immunologists, Am. Soc. Parasitologists. Home: 1512 Derwen Dr Iowa City IA 52240 Office: Dept Preventive Medicine Univ Iowa Iowa City IA 52242

HSU, SHU YING, medical educator; b. Beijing, China, Aug. 26, 1920; came to U.S., 1952, naturalized, 1961; m. Hsi Fan, Apr. 18, 1954; 1 child, Tung Mei. B.S., Nat. Peking Normal U., China, 1940; Ph.D. in Preventive Medicine, U. Iowa, 1957. Asst. prof., head Nat. Sheyang Med. Coll., China, 1947-48; assoc. prof., then prof. Nat. Taiwan U., Taipei, Republic of China, 1949-52; research assoc. Harvard Sch. Pub. Health, Boston, 1953-54; asst. prof. dept. preventive medicine U. Iowa, Iowa City, 1957-63, assoc. prof., 1963-73, prof., 1973—. Developer vaccine against schistosomiasis. Recipient Sci. Research award Taiwan, 1953. Fellow Royal Soc. Tropical Medicine and Hygiene, Am. Soc. Parasitologists, AAAS. Home: 1512 Derwen Dr Iowa City IA 52242 Office: U Iowa Dept Preventive Medicine and Environ Health Iowa City IA 52242

HU, CAN BEVEN, chemist; b. Taipei, Taiwan, Oct. 31, 1949; came to U.S., 1975; s. Der-Chang and Shen-Chi Hu; m. Li-Wen Yu, Nov. 24, 1982; 1 child, Alexander. B.S., Nat. Taiwan U., 1972; M.S., U. Ky., 1976, Ph.D., MIT, 1980. Polymer scientist Thoratec Labs. Corp., Berkeley, Calif., 1980-83; staff scientist Procter & Gamble Co., Cin., 1983-84; research assoc. Deseret polymer research Warner-Lambert, Dayton, Ohio, 1984—. Whitaker Health Scis. fellow, 1978-80. Mem. Am. Chem. Soc., Soc. Plastics Engrs., Sigma Xi. Mem. Christian Ch. Contbr. articles on polymer science to jours. Home: 1076 Beryl Trail Dayton OH 45459 Office: PO Box 1285 11125 Yankee St Dayton OH 45401

HU, STEPHEN NAI-KAI, statistician, researcher; b. Nanking, China, Dec. 6, 1933; came to U.S., 1957; s. Mai and Su-lian (Wu) H.; m. Louisa Shu-fong Lee, Sept. 6, 1969; 1 child, Nancy. B.A., Nat. Taiwan U., 1955; M.S., U. Tenn., 1958; Ph.D., U. N.C., 1966. Instr. Western Carolina Coll., Cullowhee, N.C., 1964-67; asst. prof. U. Detroit, 1967-74; statistician Mich. Dept. Transp., Lansing, 1976—. Mem. Am. Statis. Assn. Home: 3854 New Salem Circle Okemos MI 48864

HUANG, CHENG-CHER, physics educator; b. Taipei, Taiwan, May 25, 1947; came to U.S., 1970, naturalized, 1980; s. Yung-Lang and Sui (Chu) H.; m. Tsuey Chung, Sept. 10, 1972; children—Andrew, Benjamin. B.S., Nat. Taiwan U., 1969; Ph.D., U. Pa., 1975. Research assoc. U. Ill.-Urbana, 1975-77; asst. prof. U. Minn.-Mpls., 1977-82; assoc. prof., 1982—; vis. prof., cons. 3M Research Ctr., St. Paul, 1983—. Grantee Dept. Energy, 1978-81, NSF, 1981—, 3M, 1983—. Mem. Am. Phys. Soc. Avocations: tennis, volleyball. Office: Dept Physics U Minn 116 Church St SE Minneapolis MN 55455

HUANG, PEIR KUEN, chemical engineer; b. Taiwan, Jan. 29, 1942; s. Su Tou and Ye Yi (yen) H.; m. Chung Yuan Liu, Jan. 12, 1973; 2 sons, Kenny C., Andy P. B.S., Taiwan Cheng Kung U., 1966; M.S., Pa. State U., 1973, Ph.D., 1976. Plant shift supr. Taiwan Fertilizer Co., 1967-71; research asst. Pa. State U., 1971-76; chem. engr. Owens-Ill. Inc., Toledo, 1976-79; energy chief of council Econ. Planning and Devel., Taiwan, 1979-81; project supr. Owens-Ill. Inc., Toledo, 1981—. Cons. indsl. energy conservation. Vice-pres., Chinese Student Assn., Pa. State U., 1973-76. Served in Taiwan Army, 1966-67. Mem. Am. Inst. Chem. Engrs., Am. Ceramic Soc., Soc. Plastics Engrs., Sigma Xi, Phi Lambda Upsilon. Contbr. articles to profl. jours. Home: 5806 Pinecroft Dr Toledo OH 43615 Office: 1 Seagate Toledo OH 43666

HUBBARD, DELORES LABELLE, telecommunication technician; b. Ottawa, Kans., Nov. 10, 1938; d. Francis Henry and Alice Ruby (Alcorn) H. Daugherty, B.A. with honors in Biology, U. Kans., 1973; postgrad. (NIH trainee, USPHS grantee) in radiation biophysics, 1973-75. Chief nuclear med. tech., instr. dept. radiology Kans. U. Med. Center, Kansas City, 1960-67; instr., tech. program coordinator Nuclear Medicine Inst., Cleve., 1967-70; research asst. U. Kans., Lawrence, 1970-71, 73; nuclear medicine technician Meml. Hosp., Topeka, 1974-75, VA Center, Leavenworth, Kans., 1975-77; telecommunication technician ARCO Pipeline Co., Independence, Kans., 1979—; mem. guest faculty Cuyahoga Community Coll., Cleve., 1969-70; cons., lectr. nuclear medicine. Mem. Am. Registry Radiologic Technologists, Soc. Nuclear Medicine (asso.), Am. Soc. Clin. Pathologists. Home: 205 SW 16th St Seminole TX 79360 Office: ARCO Place Independence KS 67301

HUBBARD, DONNIE LLOYD, publishing company executive, consultant; b. Newton, N.C., Apr. 18, 1944; s. Charles Clarence and Hazel Verona (Bandy) H.; m. Carolyn Lee Estes, Aug. 1, 1967 (div. Jan. 1984); 1 son, Edwin Lloyd. B.A., Wake Forest U., 1966; M.S., U. Balt., 1975; M.Ed., Coppin State Coll., 1976. Sr. resident agt. FBI, Wilmington, Del., 1978; security mgr. Summa Corp., Las Vegas, Nev., 1979; security dir. Playboy Enterprises, Chgo., 1979-82, v.p. adminstrn. and security, 1982—; mng. dir. Playboy (Bahamas) Ltd., Nassau, 1981—; cons. Hubbard Assocs., Lake Forest, Ill., 1982—. Asst. chmn. crime prevention com. Chgo. Assn. Commerce and Industry. Served to 1st lt. U.S. Army, 1966-68; ETO. Mem. Soc. Former Spl. Agts. FBI, Am. Soc. Indsl. Security. Republican. Presbyterian. Office: Playboy Enterprises Inc 919 N Michigan Ave Chicago IL 60611

HUBBARD, FRANCIS ALLEY, English educator, consultant; b. Orange, N.J., Nov. 24, 1944; s. Edwin Schuyler and Frances Joyce (Peloubet) H.; m. Julie Lynnette Smith, Feb. 11, 1976; children—Jonathan, Elizabeth, Hannah. B.A., Amherst Coll., 1966; M.A., U. Calif.-Berkeley, 1970, Ph.D. in English and Linguistics, 1978. Instr., dir. freshman English, U. Wis.-Madison, 1974-76; asst. prof., coordinator composition Calif. State U.-Sacramento, 1976-81; asst. prof. U. Wis.-Milw., 1981-85; assoc. prof. English, Cleve. State U., 1985—; dir. Milw. Area Writing Project, 1983-85. Author: Theories of Action in Conrad, 1984. Contbr. articles to profl. jours. Mem. Modern Lang. Assn., Midwest Modern Lang. Assn. Office: Dept English Cleve State U Cleveland OH 44115

HUBBARD, JOHN BRUCE, industrial commercial realtor, photographer; b. Detroit, May 18, 1945; s. Roger C. and Mary Jane (Batchelor) H.; m. Kathy L. Smith, Jan. 6, 1983; 1 son, John Bruce. B.S., Babson Coll., 1970; B.A. in Photography, Brooks Inst., 1971; postgrad. U. Colo., 1971-72. With Hubbard Assocs., Troy, Mich., 1969-81, 82—, pres. Hubbard Energy Systems, Inc., Mt. Clemens, Mich., 1982—, Hubbard Mining, Inc., Wilkes-Barre, Pa., 1980—; photog. portrait artist, Chgo., 1973-83, Detroit, 1963-83, Miami, Fla., 1971-83, Palm Beach, Fla., 1971-83; lectr. in photog. field, 1971-77. Recipient Artist of Yr. award Nat. Portrait Artists, 1965; Artist of Yr. award Founders Soc., 1973. Mem. Profl. Photographers Am., Detroit Plumbing and Heating Assn., Solid Fuel Assn. Am. Clubs: Indidan Creek Country, Surf (Miami); Univ. (Detroit). Contbr. photog. works to profl. publs. Home: PO Box 1216 Birmingham MI 48012 (winter) 61 Camden Ct Bal Harbour FL 33154 Office: 36549 Gratiot Ave Mount Clemens MI 48043

HUBBARD, LINCOLN BEALS, medical physicist, consultant; b. Hawkesbury, Ont., Can., Sept. 8, 1940; s. Carroll Chauncey and Mary Lunn (Beals) H.; came to U.S., 1957; m. Nancy Ann Krieger, Apr. 3, 1961; children—Jill, Katrina. B.S. in Physics, U. N.H., 1961; Ph.D., MIT, 1967. Diplomate Am. Bd. Radiology; cert. health physicist Am. Bd. Health Physics. Postdoctoral appointee Argonne Nat. Lab., 1966-68; asst. prof. math. and physics Knoxville Coll. (Tenn.), 1968-70; asst. prof. physics Furman U., Greenville, S.C., 1970-74; chief physicist Mt. Sinai Hosp., Chgo., 1974-75, Cook County Hosp., Chgo., 1975—; ptnr. Fields, Griffith, Hubbard & Assocs., 1978—. Mem. Am. Assn. Physicists in Medicine, Am. Coll. Radiology, Am. Phys. Soc. Author: (with S.S. Stefani) Mathematics for Technologists, 1979, (with G. B. Greenfield) Computers in Radiology, 1984. Home: 4113 West End Rd Downers Grove IL 60515 Office: PO Box 367 Hines IL 60141

HUBBELL, JAMES WINDSOR, JR., See *Who's Who in America,* 43rd edition.

HUBBS, MARGUERITE ELIZABETH BOYD, vocational educator; b. Carlsbad, N.Mex., Sept. 7, 1946; d. Hiley Thompson and Bernice Marguerite (Fanning) B.; m. Thomas Michael Hubbs, Aug. 6, 1939; 1 son, Brian Allan Croxdale. B.S., S.W. Mo. State U., 1968; M.S., Pittsburg State U., 1977, prin. cert., 1979; Ph.D., U. Mo.-Columbia, 1983. Secondary lang. arts and social studies tchr., Springfield, Dallas, Webb City, and Joplin, Mo., 1968-76; lang. arts and math. assessment coordinator Joplin R-VIII Sch. Dist. (Mo.), 1977-80, alternative sch. dir., 1978-80; research asst. U. Mo.-Columbia, 1980-81, coordinator vocat. equity project, 1981—; tech. writer Columbia Pub. Schs., 1981. Peabody scholar, U. Mo.-Columbia, 1982. Mem. AAUW, Am. Vocat. Assn., Am. Soc. Tng. and Devel., Nat. Employment and Tng. Assn., Mo. Vocat. Assn., Phi Delta Kappa. Democrat. Author: (with John W. Schell) Missouri Skill Center Evaluation Instrument, 1981; (with Kathy M. Shaffer) Employing Nontraditional Students, 1982. Office: 10 Indsl Edn Bldg U Mo Columbia MO 65211

HUBBS, RONALD M., retired insurance company executive; b. Silverton, Oreg., Apr. 27, 1908; s. George W. and Ethel (Burch) H.; B.A., U. Oreg.; LL.D. (hon.), William Mitchell Coll. Law, Macalester Coll. H.L.D., (hon.), Carleton Coll., m. Margaret S. Jamie, Sept. 9, 1935; 1 son, George J. With St. Paul Fire & Marine Ins. Co., 1936-77, asst. to pres., 1948-52, v.p., 1952-59, exec. v.p., 1959-63; pres., chief exec., 1963-68, chmn., 1968-73; pres., chief exec. officer St. Paul Cos., Inc., 1968-73, chmn., 1973-77; past dir. Western Life Ins. Co., chmn. Toro Credit Co.; past chmn. AFIA Worldwide Ins. Past bd. dirs. Minn. Council on Econ. Edn.; bd. dirs., founding trustee Twin Cities Pub. TV Corp.; trustee James H. Hill Reference Library; bd. dirs. emeritus William Mitchell Coll. Law; trustee Coll. St. Thomas, Carleton Coll.; chmn. bd. trustees F.R. Bigelow Found.; past trustee, past chmn. Ins. Inst. Am.; mem., past chmn. pres.'s council St. Catherine's Coll.; gov. Internat. Inst. Seminars, Inc.; bd. dirs. Charles Lindbergh Fund, Cath. Digest; bd. overseers U. Minn. Sch. Mgmt.; bd. dirs. Inst. Philos. Research; trustee St. Paul Found., North Star Found.; bd. overseers Hill Monastic Manuscript Library and Univ. Without Walls; trustee Sci. Mus. Minn. elector Ins. Hall Fame. Served from 1st lt. to col. AUS, World War II. Decorated Legion of Merit; recipient St. Thomas Aquinas medal Coll. St. Thomas; creative leadership in adult edn. award MACAE; Life-long learning award Met. State U.; Disting. Community Builder award Indianhead council Boy Scouts Am.; King's medal Carl XVI Gustaf of Sweden; Disting. Service award Minn. Humanities Commn.; others. Mem. Am. Inst. Property and Liability Underwriters (past chmn., trustee), Orgn. Am. Historians, Minn. Hist. Soc. (past pres.), Co. Mil. Historians, Sherlock Holmes Soc. of London, Orchid Soc., Alpha Tau Omega, Phi Delta Phi, Scabbard and Blade, Friars, Beta Gamma Sigma. Episcopalian (past trustee diocese Minn.). Club: Minn. (past pres.). Home: 689 W Wentworth Ave #102 Saint Paul MN 55118 Office: 385 Washington St Saint Paul MN 55102

HUBEL, KENNETH ANDREW, medical educator; b. N.Y.C., Nov. 11, 1927; s. G. Andrew and Madeline Barbara (Rudinger) H.; m. Janis Greer, May 19, 1957; children—Wendy, Nancy, Adam. A.B., U. Rochester, 1950; M.D., Cornell U., 1954. Resident in medicine SUNY-Syracuse, 1954-56, 59-60; assoc. med. dir. Bristol Labs., Syracuse, 1956-59; assoc. in physiology George Washington U., Washington, 1960-62; asst. prof. then assoc. prof. medicine U. Iowa, Iowa City, 1962-74, prof., 1974—. Mem. editorial bd. Am. Jour. Physiology, 1982-85. Served with USNR, 1945-46. NIH grantee, 1965—. Fellow ACP; mem. Am. Physiol. Soc., Gastroenterology Research Group, Central Soc. Clin. Research, Democrat. Unitarian. Avocations: jazz alto saxophone; photography; bicycling. Office: Univ Hosp U Iowa Iowa City IA 52242

HUBER, JOAN NANCY, college dean; b. Bluffton, Ohio, Oct. 17, 1925; d. Lawrence Lester and Hallie (Althaus) H.; m. Anton Rytina, July 1946 (div. 1969); children—Nancy, Steven; m. William Humbert Form, Feb. 1971. B.A., Pa. State U., 1945; M.A., Western Mich. U., 1963; Ph.D., Mich. State U., 1967. Vis. asst. prof. sociology U. Notre Dame, 1967-69, asst. prof., 1969-71; Successively asst. prof., assoc. prof., prof. U. Ill., Urbana, 1971-83, dir. women's studies, 1978-80, head dept. sociology, 1979-83; dean Coll. Social and Behavioral Sci. Ohio State U., Columbus, 1984—; mem. program in sociology NSF, Washington, 1977-80. Author: (with William Form) Income and

Ideology, 1973. Editor: (with Paul Chalfant) Sociology of American Poverty, 1974; Changing Women in a Changing Society, 1973; (with W.G. Spitze) Sex Stratification: Children, Housework and Jobs, 1983. NSF grantee, 1978-81. Mem. Am. Sociol. Assn. (mem. council 1975-78, v.p. 1980-83), Midwest Sociol. Soc. (pres. 1978-81), North Central Sociol. Soc. (treas. 1970-73), Soc. Study Social Problems (v.p. 1976-79). Episcopalian. Home: 1439 London Dr Columbus OH 43221 Office: Coll Social and Behavioral Sci 164 W 17th Ave Columbus OH 43210

HUBIN, WILBERT NORMAN, physics educator; b. Crosby, Minn., Apr. 28, 1938; s. Edwin Gustav and Elizabeth (Wall) H. B.S., Wheaton Coll., 1960; M.S., U. Ill., 1962, Ph.D., 1969. Asst. prof. physics Kent State U., Ohio, 1966-77, assoc. prof., 1977-83, prof., 1983—. Author: Basic Programming for Scientists and Engineers, 1978. Contbr. articles to profl. jours. Mem. Am. Phys. Soc., Am. Assn. Physics Tchrs., AIAA, Exptl. Aircraft Assn., Aerobatic Club Am., Sigma Xi, Sigma Pi Sigma. Avocation: flying experimental aircraft. Home: 719 Cuyahoga St Kent OH 44240 Office: Kent State U Smith Hall Kent OH 44242

HUCKE, MICHAEL RAY, accountant; b. Dayton, Ohio, Apr. 29, 1942; s. Melvin Louis and Edythe Evangeline (Lisk) H.; m. Jeanette Yingling, June 8, 1963; children—John, Elizabeth, Timothy. B.S., Capital U., 1964; M.A., Wichita State U., 1966; postgrad. Okla. State U. Asst. prof. acctg. Carroll Coll., Waukesha, Wis.; fin. specialist Gen. Electric Co., Milw., 1975-77; mgr. fin. planning NCR, Dayton, Ohio, 1977-83; owner Hucke Acctg. Services, Dayton, 1983—. Chmn. bd. dirs. Wernle Children's Home, Richmond, Ind., 1985-86; pres. Epiphany Luth. Ch., Centerville, Ohio, 1984. Mem. Nat. Assn. Accts. (Mem. of Yr. 1977), Inst. Mgmt. Acctg., Nat. Assn. Tax Practitioners. Republican. Lutheran. Home: 621 Yeoman Ct West Carrollton OH 45449 Office: Hucke Acctg Services 3578 Kettering Blvd Suite 300 Dayton OH 45439

HUDDLESTON, GEORGE RICHMOND, JR., chemical engineer; b. Sandersville, Miss., Oct. 7, 1921; s. George R. and Pauline (Miller) H.; m. Opha Griffin, Oct. 31, 1942 (dec. 1976); 1 child, Particia Joan Huddleston Heege; m. Eileen M. Shaveyco, Dec. 16, 1977. B.S. in Chem. Engring., Miss. State U., 1943; M.S. in Chem. Engring., La. State U., 1949, Ph.D. in Phys. Organics, 1960. With Copolymer Rubber and Chem. Co., Baton Rouge, 1943-70, research mgr., 1961-66, tech. supt., 1968-70; research and devel. fellow B.F. Goodrich Co., Avon Lake, Ohio, 1970—, Patentee in field. Served to lt. (j.g.) USNR, 1944-46. Recipient Outstanding Tech. Achievement award Cleve. sect. Am. Inst. Chem. Engrs., 1982, Tech. Recognition award B.F. Goodrich Tech. Ctr., 1982. Mem. Am. Chem. Soc. (rubber div.), Akron Rubber Group, So. Rubber Group (chmn. 1971-72). Democrat. Avocations: golf, bowling. Home: 4031 Woodstock Dr Lorain OH 44053 Office: BF Goodrich Co PO Box 122 Avon Lake OH 44012

HUDDLESTON, MARLA LERNER, statistician; b. Chgo., Oct. 24, 1954; d. Gerald and Leah (Miller) Lerner; m. Rodney Kurt Huddleston, May 24, 1975; 1 child, Alice Rachel. B.S. in Stats., U. Ill.-Urbana, 1975; M.S. in Stats., U. Ill.-Chgo., 1976; postgrad. U. Chgo., 1982—. Statistician, U.S. R.R. Retirement Bd., Chgo., 1977-81, supervisory statistician, 1981-84, chief benefit and employment analysis, 1984—. Contbr. to fed. agy. publs. Mem. Am. Statis. Assn., Fed. Mgr.'s Assn. Avocations: tennis, reading. Office: US RR Retirement Bd 844 N Rush St Chicago IL 60611

HUDDLESTON, SHARON, physical education educator, consultant; b. Texarkana, Tex., Aug. 28, 1945; d. Clovis and Bertha Faye (Shannon) H. B.S., Stephen F. Austin U., 1968, M.S., 1969; Ph.D., U. Iowa, 1981. Instr., coach Midwestern U., Wichita Falls, Tex., 1969-70, Stephen F. Austin U., Nacagdoches, Tex., 1970-72; coach U. Wis., Madison, 1972-73; grad. teaching and research asst. U. Iowa, Iowa City, 1978-80; asst. prof. phys. edn. U. No. Iowa, Cedar Falls, 1973—, sport psychology cons., 1981—; self def. cons. Sexual Assault Intervention Ctr., Waterloo, Iowa, 1983—. Recipient Laura Tuttle Meml. Grad. award U. Iowa, Iowa City, 1979, Sims Riddle award, 1980. Mem. AAHPER and Dance, NEA, N.Am. Soc. Psychology Sport and Phys. Activity, Iowa State Edn. Assn., Iowa Assn. Health, Phys. Edn., Recreation and Dance (research chmn. 1984-86). Democrat. Office: East Gymnasium U No Iowa Cedar Falls IA 50614

HUDIK, MARTIN FRANCIS, hospital administrator, educator, consultant; b. Chgo., Mar. 27, 1949; s. Joseph and Rose (Ricker) H. B.S. in Mech. and Aerospace Engring., Ill. Inst. Tech., 1971; B.P.A., Jackson State U., 1974; M.B.A., Loyola U., Chgo., 1975; postgrad. U. Sarasota, 1975-76. Cert. health care safety mgr., hazard control mgr., hazardous materials mgr.; cert. police and security firearms instr., Ill. and Nat. Rifle Assn. With Ill. Masonic Med. Ctr., Chgo., 1969—, dir. risk mgmt., 1974-79, asst. adminstr., 1979—; lt. tng. div. Cicero (Ill.) Police Dept., part-time 1971—; instr. Nat. Safety Council Safety Tng. Inst., Chgo., 1977—; cons. mem. Council Tech. Users Consumer Products, Underwriters Labs., Chgo., 1978—; instr., lt. U.S. Def. Civil Preparedness Agy. Staff Coll., Battlecreek, Mich., 1977—. Pres. sch. bd. Mary Queen of Heaven Sch., Cicero, 1977-79, 84—; pres. Mary Queen of Heaven Ch. Council, 1979-81, 83—; pres. I.M.M.C. Employee Club, 1983-84. Ill. State scholar, 1969-71. Mem. Am. Coll. Hosp. Adminstrs., Am. Soc. Hosp. Risk Mgmt., Nat. Fire Protection Assn., Am. Soc. Safety Engrs., Am. Soc. Law and Medicine, Ill. Hosp. Security and Safety Assn. (co-founder 1976, founding pres. 1976-77, hon. dir. 1977-82), Cath. Alumni Club Chgo. (bd. dirs. 1983-84), Mensa, Pi Tau Sigma, Tau Beta Pi, Alpha Sigma Nu. Republican. Roman Catholic. Lodges: KC (Cardinal council); (Cicero); Masons. Office: 836 W Wellington Ave Chicago IL 60657

HUDNUT, WILLIAM HERBERT, III, mayor, former congressman, univ. adminstr.; b. Cin., Oct. 17, 1932; s. William H. and Elizabeth (Kilborne) H.; A.B. magna cum laude, Princeton U., 1954; B.D. summa cum laude, Union Theol. Sem., 1957; D.D., Hanover Coll., 1967, Wabash Coll., 1969; D.Litt., Ind. Central U., 1981; LL.D., Butler U., 1980, Anderson Coll., 1982, Franklin Coll., 1983; m. Susan Greer Rice, Dec. 14, 1974; children by previous marriage—Michael, Laura, Timothy, William H. IV, Theodore. Ordained to ministry Presbyn. Ch., 1957; asst. minister Westminster Ch., Buffalo, 1957-60; pastor 1st Ch., Annapolis, Md., 1960-63, 2d Ch., Indpls., 1963-72; mem. 93d Congress from 11th Ind. Dist.; dir. dept. community affairs Ind. Central U., Indpls., 1975; mayor, Indpls., 1976—. Pres., Anne Arundel County Mental Health Assn., 1961-63, Marion County Mental Health Assn., 1965-67, Westminster Found. Purdue U., 1967-72; mem. Central Area council Boy Scouts Am. (1964-72); mem. bd. Safety Indpls., 1971. Bd. dirs. Goodwill Industries; bd. dirs. Nat. League of Cities, 1977—, pres., 1981; trustee Ind. Central U., 1976—, Ptnrs. for Livable Places, 1982—; pres. bd. trustees Darrow Sch., 1965-75; bd. dirs. U.S. Conf. Mayors, 1984—, also mem. adv. bd.; pres. Ind. Assn. Cities and Towns, 1979, Ind. Rep. Mayors Assn., 1980; mem. Pres.'s Task Force on Federalism, 1981-82, Adv. Commn. Intergovtl. Affairs, 1984—. Recipient travelling fellowship Union Theol. Sem., 1957. Mem. Phi Beta Kappa. Presbyn. Republican. Clubs: Indpls. Columbia, Woodstock, Princeton. Editor: Union Sem. Quar. Rev., 1956-57. Home: 722 Pine Dr Indianapolis IN 46240 Office: City County Bldg 200 E Washington St Indianapolis IN 46240

HUDSON, CELESTE NUTTING, educator, reading clinic administrator, consultant; b. Nashville, Sept. 18, 1927; d. John Winthrop Chandler and Hilda Bass (Alexander) Nutting; m. Frank Alden Hudson III, Dec. 30, 1948 (dec.); children—Frank Alden IV, Jo Ann Hudson Algermissen, Celeste Jane Hudson Hayes, John Winthrop Nutting. B.S., Oreg. Coll. Edn., 1952; M.S., So. Ill. U., 1963, Ph.D., 1973. Cert. tchr., Tenn., Oreg., Mo., Iowa. Tchr. pub. schs., Crossville, Tenn., 1949-51, Salem, Oreg., 1952-53, West Walnut Manor and Jennings, Mo., 1953-54, Normandy Sch. Dist., St. Louis County, Mo., 1954-66; reading coordinator Sikeston (Mo.) Pub. Schs., 1966-71; traveling cons. Ednl. Devel. Labs., Huntington, N.Y., 1970-71; mem. clin. staff So. Ill. U. Reading Ctr., 1972; asst. prof. edn. St. Ambrose Coll., 1972-75, U. Tenn.-Chattanooga, 1975-76; project dir. Learning Skills Ctr., St. Ambrose Coll., 1976-80, asst. prof. edn., 1976-78, assoc. prof., 1979—, dir. elem. edn., 1972-75, 76-83, chmn. dept. edn., 1980-84, div. chair, 1984—, dir. Reading Clinic, 76—; cons. reading. Mem. Kimberly Village Bd., Davenport, Iowa, 1979-83. Mem. Assn. Supervision and Curriculum Devel., Internat. Reading Assn. (Scott County council), Am. Assn. Colls. Tchr. Edn., Assn. Tchr. Educators, New Eng. Women (pres.), Women in Ednl. Adminstrn., DAR, United Daus. Confederacy, Alpha Delta Kappa (pres. chpt.), Kappa Delta Pi, Phi Delta Kappa. Methodist. Author Sikeston Schs. handbook for remedial reading, 1967; Cognitive Listening and the Reading of Second Grade Children, 1973. Office: Saint Ambrose Coll Davenport IA 52806

HUDSON, DENNIS LEE, lawyer, government official; b. St. Louis, Jan. 5, 1936; s. Lewis Jefferson and Helen Mabel (Buchanan) H.; m. Linda Kay Adamson; children—Karen Marie, Karla Sue. B.A., U. Ill., 1958; J.D., John Marshall Law Sch., 1972. Bar: Ill. 1972, U.S Dist. Ct. (so. dist.) Ill. 1972, U.S. Dist. Ct. (no. dist.) Ill. 1972. Insp., IRS, Chgo., 1962-72; spl. agt. GSA, Chgo., 1972-78, spl. agt.-in-charge, 1978-83, regional insp. gen., 1983—; supervisory spl. agt., Dept Justice-GSA Task Force, Washington, 1978. Bd. govs. Theatre Western Springs, Ill., 1978-81; deacon Grace Lutheran Ch., LaGrange, Ill., 1977-81. Served with U.S. Army, 1959-61. John N. Jewett scholar, 1972. Mem. ABA, Ill. Bar Assn., Assn. Fed. Investigators. Home: PO Box 113 Western Springs IL 60558 Office: Office Insp Gen GSA Suite 408 230 S Dearborn St Chicago IL 60604

HUDSON, HAROLD DON, veterinarian; b. Audrain County, Mo., Nov. 22, 1943; s. Harold F. and Greta Arlene (Boyd) H.; A.A., Hannibal (Mo.) La Grange Coll., 1963; B.S., U. Mo., 1967, D.V.M., 1970; m. Carole Jacqueline Spence, Aug. 30, 1964; children—Dale Brent, Kim Marie. Asso. Clarinda (Iowa) Vet. Clinic, 1970-71, Bethany (Mo.) Vet. Clinic, 1971-72, Vet. Clinic, Mexico, Mo., 1972—. Mem. AVMA, Mo. Vet. Med. Assn., Am. Assn. Bovine Practitioners, Am. Assn. Swine Practitioners. Baptist. Home: 933 Emmons St Mexico MO 65265 Office: 1624 Hwy 54 E Mexico MO 65265

HUDSON, JOHNETTA, educational administrator; b. Gary, Ind., Oct. 2, 1947; d. John Walton and Geraldine (Gatlin) H. B.A., Ky. State U., 1969; M.A., U. Nebr., 1972; Ed.S., Ind. State U., 1978, Ph.D., 1980. Cert. pub. sch. adminstr., Ind. Tchr. Gary Community Schs., Ind., 1969-78, Latin Am. Family Edn. Program, Gary, Ind., 1975-78; asst. prin. LaSalle High Sch., South Bend, Ind., 1980-83, prin., 1983—; cons. Boys Club of Am., N.Y.C., 1984—. Sec., bd. dirs. YMCA Community Services Br., South Bend, 1981—; v.p., bd. dirs. Black Community Scholarship Found., South Bend, 1983—; mem. Jr. League of South Bend, 1984—. Recipient Cert. of Appreciation U.S. Air Force, Honorable Achievement in Community Service Ind. Black EXPO; named Woman of Yr., Bus. and Profl. Women's Orgn. South Bend. Mem. AAUW (legis. dir. 1983-84), South Bend Prins. Assn., Northwest Ind. Prins. Assn., Assn. Supervision Curriculum Devel., Nat. Assn. Secondary Sch. Prins., Delta Sigma Theta. Democrat. Methodist. Avocations: traveling; bowling; crocheting; cross country skiing; reading. Home: 51821 Trowbridge Ln South Bend IN 46637 Office: LaSalle High School 2701 W Elwood Ave South Bend IN 46628

HUDSON, MICHAEL LYNDELL, training and development company executive; b. Detroit, Feb. 17, 1950; s. Henderson and Myrtle Doris (Robinson) H.; A.A., Lansing Community Coll., 1976; B.S., SUNY-Albany, 1979; M. Mgmt., Aquinas Coll., 1981; M.L.E., Harvard U., 1983; m. Julia F. Walker, July 11, 1970; children—Kandyce Michelle, Michael Askyya; m. Ranita Griffin. With Exec. Systems, Inc., Lawrenceville, Ill., 1970-71; owner Maiden Voyage Enterprises, Lansing, Mich., 1970-72; adminstr. CCCDA, Lansing, 1972-74; pres., sr. cons. People Growth Systems, 1974—; instr. mgmt. Lansing Community Coll., 1982—. Treas., Forest View Sch. Parent Tchr. Orgn., 1981—; bd. dirs. New Birth Ctr., Clinton, Eaton, Ingham Community Mental Health Ctr., 1983—. Mem. Am. Mgmt. Assn., Am. Mktg. Assn., Am. Soc. Tng. and Devel. Home and Office: 900 Long Blvd #442 Lansing MI 48910

HUDSON, MICHAEL WESLEY, banker; b. Lafayette, Ind., Sept. 23, 1945; s. Wesley Talmadge and Anna Ruth (Hurn) H.; m. Linda Louise Mathis, Sept. 25, 1965; children—Clinton Michael, Sherry Ann. Grad. Am. Inst. Banking, 1971; student Purdue U., 1977-78. Br. mgr., officer Purdue Nat. Bank, Lafayette, 1967-78; v.p. State Bank Oxford (Ind.), 1978—. Pres., Warren County Young Democrats, 1975—; del. Ind. Dem. Conv., 1976; trustee Adams Twp., 1975-82; sec. treas. Pine Village Fire Dept.; mem. Warren County Sheriff Merit Bd. Served with U.S. Army, 1965-67. Mem. Am. Inst. Banking. Roman Catholic. Lodge: Lions. Home: RR 1 Box 116 Pine Village IN 47975 Office: 100 S Justus St Oxford IN 47971

HUDSON, ROBERT PAUL, medical educator; b. Kansas City, Kans., Feb. 23, 1926; s. Chester Lloyd and Jean (Emerson) H.; m. Olive Jean Grimes, Aug. 1, 1948 (div. 1963); children—Robert E., Donald K., Timothy M.; m. Martha Isabelle Holter, July 10, 1965; children—Stephen, Laurel. B.A., U. Kans., 1949; M.D., 1952; M.A., Johns Hopkins U., 1966. Instr., U. Kans.-Kansas City, 1958-59, assoc. in medicine, 1959-63, asst. prof., 1964-68, assoc. prof., 1968—, prof., chmn. history of medicine, 1968—. Author: Disease and its Control, 1983. Contbr. articles to profl. jours. mem. editorial bd. Bull. History of Medicine, Balt., 1981—. Served to 1st lt. U.S. Army, 1953-55. Fellow ACP; mem. Am. Assn. for History of Medicine (pres. 1984—), Am. Osler Soc. (bd. govs.). Home: 12925 Frontier Rd Olathe KS 66061 Office: Kans U Med Ctr 39th and Rainbow Kansas City KS 66103

HUDSPETH, DONNA GALASSI, psychologist, educator; b. Springfield, Ill.; d. Vincent and Mary Elizabeth (Foykier) Galassi; m. Lionel M. Hudspeth, July 23, 1970. A.A., Springfield (Ill.) Coll., 1963; B.A., Ill. Coll., 1965; M.A., Bradley U., 1967; postgrad. in psychology U. Ill., 1972. Lic. psychologist, Ill.; cert. sch. psychologist, Ill. Instr. psychology Lincoln Land Coll., Springfield, Ill., 1969-76, Sangamon State U., Springfield, 1967-83; clin. psychologist Baumann Clinic, Springfield, 1976-80; psychologist Springfield pub. schs., 1967—; psychologist Psychol. Assocs., Springfield, 1980-85; pvt. practice Centrum Psychol., 1985—; cons. Hope Sch., 1982—; mem. Ill. Status Offenders Bd. Mem. Am. Psychol. Assn., Ill. Psychol. Assn., Nat. Health Service Providers, Springfield Edn. Assn. (officer), NEA, Ill. Edn. Assn., Women in Healthcare, Springfield Art Assn., Women in Mgmt., Women in Healthcare Women's Profl. Orgn. Springfield. Roman Catholic. Office: 319 E Madison Suite D Springfield IL 62703

HUEBNER, DONALD FRANK, financial executive; b. New London, Wis., Oct. 24, 1925; s. Frank E. and Erna E. (Gorges) H.; m. Nancy Minor Stearns, Nov. 28, 1953; children—Donald Frank, Jr., Barry Carpenter, Orrin John, Scott Stearns, Christopher James, Heidi Gersdorf, Rebecca McLean, Mary-Esther. B.B.A., U. Wis.-Madison, 1950. Auditor Ernst & Ernst, C.P.A.s, Chgo., 1950-53, Curtis W. Catron, C.P.A., Chgo., 1953-64; comptroller, sec. Great Lakes Terminal and Transport, Chgo., 1964-74; acctg. mgr. Allied Van Lines, Broadview, Ill., 1974-75; controller Active Elec. Supply Co., Chgo., 1975—, treas., 1982—. Sec. Arts Guild, Arlington Heights, Ill., 1977-80. Served with USNR, 1944-46, PTO. Mem. Newcomen Soc. Am., Beta Gamm Sigma. Republican. Lutheran. Avocations: collecting antiques, geneology, singing. Home: 1104 Linden Ln Mt Prospect IL 60056 Office: Active Elec Supply Co 4240 W Lawrence Ave Chicago IL 60630

HUENEFELD, WESLEY CARL, agricultural conservationist; b. Aurora, Nebr., Aug. 19, 1909; s. Carl Henry and Grace Leon (Davis) H.; m. Beth Iova Stilgebouer, Aug. 14, 1938 (dec. 1976); children—Ann, Arthur, Ethel, Lynn, Patricia; m. Emma Louise Yerkes, Aug. 25, 1978. B.A., U. Nebr., 1935. Farmer, Aurora, Nebr., 1938-85; conservationist, historian, mus. builder County Nebr. Centennial Com., Hamilton County, Nebr., 1965; pres. Hamilton County Hist. Soc., Aurora, Nebr., 1965-85; planner Plainsman Mus., Aurora, 1976—. Designer, planter Nebs. Tree Farm Conservation Tree Farm, 1959; designer, dir. Plainsman Mus., Plainsman Agr. Mus., 1972-85; landscape architect Aurora Pub. Schs., mus., pub. bldgs., 1959-85. Sec. Hamilton County Fair Bd., 1955-63; county chmn. Hamilton County Am. Bicentennial Com., Hamilton County, Nebr., 1976; dir., planner Prodn. Hist. Murals and Celestial Scene in Plainsman Mus., 1974-80. Recipient A. E. Sheldon award Nebr. State Hist. Soc., Lincoln, 1977; named Neb. Outstanding Tree Planter, Neb. Forestry Dept., Nebr. Dept. Forestry, Wildlife and Fisheries, 1979; recipient Silver Tree Farm cert. Nebr. Tree Farm Program and Am. Forestry Inst., 1985. Republican.

HUESER, ROBERTA JEAN, city official; b. Dallas, Iowa, Oct. 3, 1932; d. Carl Robert and Lucille Julia (Logue) Wheeler; student Wayne (Nebr.) State Coll., Colo. State Coll., Greeley, Northwestern Coll., Orange City, Iowa; m. William Joseph Hueser, June 1, 1956; children—Kyle Robert, Jon William. Sch. tchr. in Iowa, 1953-63; city clk. George (Iowa), 1977—. Chmn. bd. George Bicentennial Mus., 1976-84; adv. bd. George Good Samaritan Center, 1978-85; chmn. George Centennial Celebration; treas. bd. dirs. Evergreen Lawn Cemetery. Mem. Lyon County Mcpl. League (sec.-treas. 1977-78, 84-85). Democrat. Mem. Ch. of Christ. Club: Facts and Fun (pres. 1978-80). Co-author: In and Around George 1872-1912. Home: 209 W Ohio Ave George IA 51237 Office: City Hall 120 1/2 S Main St George IA 51237

HUFF, C(LARENCE) RONALD, public administration and sociology educator; b. Covington, Ky., Nov. 10, 1945; s. Nathaniel Warren G. and Irene Opal (Mills) H.; m. Patricia Ann Plankenhorn, June 15, 1968; children—Tamara Lynn, Tiffany Dawn. B.A., Capital U., 1968; M.S.W., U. Mich., 1970; Ph.D., Ohio State U., 1974. Social worker Franklin County Children's Services, Columbus, Ohio, 1968; social work intern Pontiac (Mich.) State Hosp. and Family Service Met. Detroit, 1969-70; dir. psychiat. social work Lima (Ohio) State Hosp., 1970-71; psychiat. social worker Northwest Community Mental Health Ctr., Lima, 1971-72; grad. teaching assoc. Dept. Sociology, Ohio State U., 1972-74; asst. prof. social ecology U. Calif.-Irvine, 1974-76; asst. prof. sociology Purdue U., 1976-79; assoc. prof. pub. adminstrn. and sociology, dir. program for study of crime and delinquency Ohio State U.-Columbus, 1979—; cons. ABA, Bur. Justice Stats., Nat. Inst. Justice, Nat. Inst. Corrections, Nat. Inst. Juvenile Justice and Delinquency Prevention, others. Recipient Nat. Security award Mershon Found., 1980; prize New Eng. Sch. Law, 1981; Outstanding Teaching award, 1985; ABA grantee, 1974-77; Purdue U. grantee, 1978; Dept. Justice grantee, 1978-79; Ohio Dept. Mental Health grantee, 1982-83, 84-85. Fellow Western Soc. Criminology; mem. Acad. Criminal Justice Scis., AAUP, ABA, Am. Correctional Assn., Am. Soc. Pub. Adminstrn., Am. Soc. Criminology (exec. bd.), Am. Sociol. Assn., Internat. Sociol. Assn., Nat. Council on Crime and Delinquency, Phi Kappa Phi. Author: The Mad, the Bad and the Different: Essays in Honor of Simon Dinitz, 1981; Attorneys as Activists: Evaluating the American Bar Association's BASICS Program, 1979; Contemporary Corrections: Social Control and Conflict, 1977; Planning Correctional Reform, 1975; others; contbr. articles to profl. jours., chpts. to books. Home: 1825 Snouffer Rd Worthington OH 43085 Office: Ohio State U 202C Hagerty Hall 1775 College Rd Columbus OH 43210

HUFF, DENNIS LEE, banker; b. Elkhart, Ind., June 14, 1947; s. Bernard B. and Rachel E. (Fike) H. B.Music cum laude, North Central Coll., 1969; M.Music, DePauw U., 1971. From teller to asst. v.p. Midwest Commerce Banking Co., Elkhart, 1971-83; asst. v.p. Valley Am. Bank, South Bend, Ind., 1983—. Organist/choirmaster Castle United Methodist Ch., Elkhart, 1971-83; organist Central Christian Ch., Elkhart, 1983—. Mem. Am. Guild Organists (chpt. bd. dirs. and officer 1978-82), Assn. Systems Mgmt., No. Ind. PC Users Group. Club: Elkhart Vintage Auto. Avocations: classic cars; philately; syngraphy photography; home computers. Home: 809 Hiawatha Dr Elkhart IN 46517 Office: Valley Am Bank PO Box 328 South Bend IN 46624

HUFF, JAMES ELI, chemical engineer; b. Moscow, Idaho, Apr. 7, 1928; s. Laurence Edwin and Ruth Barbara (Harris) H.; m. Florence Mae Dudginski, Feb. 14, 1953 (div. 1964); children—Joan Clarice, Laurence Franklin, James Eli II; m. Janice Ann Helle, Nov. 18, 1967; children—Kimberly Jean, Randal Martin. B.S.C.E., U. Idaho, 1950; D.Engring. in Chem. Engring., Yale U., 1957. Registered profl. engr., Mich. Research engr. Dow Chem. Co., Midland, Mich., 1955-68; process engr., 1958-80, assoc. processing cons., 1980—; chmn. adv. and ad hoc coms. Design Inst. for Emergency Relief Systems, N.Y.C., 1968-84, chmn. tech. com. Users Group, 1984—. Contbr. articles to profl. jours. Co-inventor ethylcinnamic acid process, 1958. Mem. advancement com. Chippewa dist. Boy Scouts Am., 1967-82. Fellow Am. Inst. Chem. Engrs. (chmn. Mid-Mich. sect. 1971-72, named Engr. of Yr. 1978); mem. Sigma Xi (chmn. Midland br. 1963). Republican. Methodist. Avocations: auto mechanics, music, theater, handicrafts. Home: 1204 Sylvan Ln Midland MI 48640 Office: Dow Chem USA Process Engring Dept 566 Building Midland MI 48640

HUFF, RICHARD WRIGHT, veterinarian, researcher, inventor; b. Detroit, Aug. 26, 1930; s. Sidney Wright and Marian Elizabeth (Garlick) H.; m. Michaleen Ann Telep, Sept. 15, 1956; children—Janice, Richard Wright, Linda. B.S., Albion Coll., 1952; D.V.M., Mich. State U., 1956. Intern, Angell Meml. Animal Hosp., Boston, 1956-57; practice vet. medicine specializing in small animal ophthalmology, gen. surgery, reproductive physiology and sterility, Birmingham, Mich., 1957-69, Detroit, 1969-77, Beverly Hills, Mich., 1977—; mem. staff Gasow Vet. Hosp., Birmingham, 1957-66, Deporre Vet. Hosp., Birmingham, 1966-69, Huff Vet. Hosp., Detroit, 1969-77; mem. staff Beverly Hills Vet. Assocs., 1977—, pres., 1977—; lectr. continuing edn. meetings for veterinarians; cons., lectr. to nat. canine and feline breed clubs. Recipient Eagle Scout award Boy Scouts Am., 1944, Spl. Service award Terrier Club Mich., 1976. Mem. AVMA, Am. Animal Hosp. Assn., Oakland County Vet. Med. Assn. (pres. 1958-60), Mich. Vet. Med. Assn. (pres. 1975-76, Profl. Service award 1967), Orthopedic Soc. Am., S.E. Mich. Vet. Med. Assn. (pres. 1966—, Outstanding Clin. Practice award 1978), Am. Soc. Vet. Ophthalmology (pres. 1965-66). Republican. Episcopalian. Inventor intraocular silastic prosthesis for dogs, vaginal speculum for dogs; originator central vet. hosp. theory, pregnancy mgmt. program for canines. Home: 32420 E Lady Birmingham MI 48010 Office: 32831 Southfield Beverly Hills MI 48009

HUFF, ROBERT B., manufacturing executive; b. Evanston, Ill., 1941; B.B.A., U. Hawaii, 1965; M.B.A., Harvard, 1968. With Bell & Howell Co., 1965—, v.p. subs. Calhoun Co., 1968, gen. mgr. video div., 1969, adminstrv. asst. to pres., 1970, asst. to pres., 1972, corp. v.p., dir. corp. planning, 1973, pres. consumer group, 1974, corp. v.p., pres. micro-imagery group, 1977, sr. v.p., 1978, exec. v.p., 1980, pres., chief operating officer, 1981—. Address: Bell & Howell Co 5215 Old Orchard Rd Skokie IL 60077-1076

HUFF, WILLIAM E., refining company executive. Pres., dir. Rock Island Refining Corp., Indpls. Office: Rock Island Refining Corp PO Box 68007 Indianapolis IN 46268*

HUFFAKER, WILLIAM HAROLD, plastic surgeon; b. Ft. Madison, Iowa, Dec. 4, 1944; s. Willie Elmo and Clara Belle (Burrus) H.; m. Elizabeth May Weiter, June 10, 1967; children—Stephanie Leigh, Jennifer Lynn, William Harold Jr. A.B., U. Kans., 1966, M.D., 1970. Diplomate Am. Bd. Surgery, Am. Bd. Plastic Surgery. Straight surg. intern U. Ala., Birmingham, 1970-71; asst. resident in surgery U. Va., Charlottesville, 1971-72, 74-75; resident in otolaryngology U.S. Army Womack Army Hosp., Ft. Bragg, N.C., 1972-74; chief resident in surgery Roanoke Meml. Hosp., Va., 1975-76; resident in plastic surgery Barnes Hosp.-Washington U., St. Louis, 1976-78; plastic surgeon Plastic Surgery Cons., Ltd., St. Louis, 1978—, also dir. Mem. adminstrv. bd. Salem in Ladue United Methodist Ch., St. Louis, 1977-84, council of ministry, 1981-84. Served to maj. U.S. Army, 1972-74. Fellow ACS; mem. Am. Soc. Plastic and Reconstructive Surgeons, Am. Assn. Hand Surgery, Lipolysis Soc. N.Am., St. Louis Surg. Soc., St. Louis Met. Med. Soc. (councilor 1983—), AMA. Avocations: wood carving, swimming, tennis. Office: Plastic Surgery Cons Ltd 224 S Woods Mill Rd Saint Louis MO 63017

HUFFMAN, BETTY COZETTA HOOPES, college official, microbiology and immunology educator; b. Columbus, Ohio, Oct. 3, 1929; d. Harry Allen and Hazel DeMeryl (Hastings) H.; m. Randall Logus Huffman, Mar. 24, 1951; children—Lee Meryl, Mark Randall, Vi Ann. B.S., Ohio State U., 1951, M.A., 1981. Cert. med. technologist. Microbiologist Marion Gen. Hosp., Ohio, 1957-67; tchr. Spanish and biology River Valley High Sch., Marion, 1967-73; dir. med. lab. tech. Marion Tech. Coll., 1973—; cons. med. lab. tech. Stautzenberger Coll., Toledo, 1982, Washington Tech. Coll., Marietta, Ohio, 1982; chmn. accreditation team Nat. Accrediting Agy. for Clin. Lab. Scis., Mt. Aloysius Coll., 1983, mem. accreditation team, Somerset Community Coll., 1982. Named hon. Ky. Col. Mem. Am. Soc. Med. Technologists, Am. Soc. Clin. Pathologists, Ohio Soc. Med. Technologists (chair edn. 1982-83, moderator 1982-83), North Central Soc. Med. Technologists (contact 1978-80), Ohio Assn. Two-Yr. Colls. Republican. Lodge: Order Eastern Star. Avocations: photography, exercise, traveling, creative writing. Office: Marion Tech Coll 1465 Mount Vernon Ave Marion OH 43302

HUFFMAN, CARL EDWARD, JR., professional speaker, management trainer; b. Indpls., July 29, 1937; s. Carl Edward and Marie G. (Bolinger) H.; m. Judith A. Koziol, Mar. 10, 1973; children—Carl Edward, Natalie Ann Marie. B.A. in Speech and Theatre, Ind. U., 1975. Dist. mgr. McLean Employees. Credit Union, Winston-Salem, N.C., 1964-67; medicare-medicaid coordinator Ind. Blue Cross, Indpls., 1967-75; dist. mgr. Wis. PSRO, Madison, 1975-77; exec. dir. Ind. PSRO, Indpls., 1977-78; chief exec. officer MESA, Buffalo Grove, Ill., 1978-81; pres. Huffman Enterprises, Elgin, Ill., 1981—; instr. Am. Mgmt. Assn., N.Y.C., 1980—. Author: The Quick Fix, 1985, also article. Pres. St. Mary's Sch. Edn. Com., Elgin, 1984-85. Recipient Award for Excellence, Univ. Forum, Ind. U., Indpls., 1974; winner 1st pl. oratory Univ. Forum Ind. U.-Purdue U., Indpls., 1974. Mem. Nat. Speakers Assn. (pres. elect Ill. chpt. 1985), Ill. Tng. and Devel. Assn. (chmn. 1983), Chgo. Sales and Tng. Assn. Republican. Roman Catholic. Clubs: Toastmasters (pres. Schaumburg, Ill. 1981-82, award 1967), Jaycees (v.p. Indpls. 1964-67). Avocations: Camping; travel. Home: 358 Shiloh Ct Elgin IL 60120 Office: Huffman Enterprises Inc PO Box 1311 Elgin IL 60121

HUFFMAN, GARY NEIL, sales executive; real estate investor; b. Indpls., Apr. 6, 1954; s. Raymond Ross and Kathryn Jeanne (Henderson) H.; m. Mary Ann Myer, June 4, 1976; 1 child, Aaron Marshal. B.S. in Mgmt., Purdue U., 1976, M.B.A., Ind. U., 1982. Dist. mgr. Delco Electronics div. Gen. Motors Corp., Miami, Fla., 1976-79, profl. employment rep., Kokomo, Ind., 1979-80, Gen. Motors fellow, 1980-82, prodn. supr., 1981, fin. analyst, 1982-83, sr. sales engr., 1983-85, accounts mgr., 1985—; cons. Country Cottage Assocs., Kokomo, 1984—; gen. ptnr. Cambridge Pl. Assocs., Kokomo, 1984—. Mem. campaign cabinet United Way, Kokomo, 1984—; student adv. Jr. Achievement, Kokomo, 1982-83; team capt. YMCA Fund Drive, Kokomo, 1982-83, sect. mgr., 1984; block capt. Old Silk Stocking Neighborhood Assn., Kokomo, 1981-84. Recipient Thomas Arkle Clark Province award Alpha Tau Omega, 1976. Mem. M.B.A. Assn. (life), South Fla. Purdue Alumni Club (pres. 1977-79), Kokomo Purdue Alumni Club (v.p. 1983—), Detroit Purdue Alumni Club. Republican. Presbyterian. Avocations: restoring Victorian homes and antique furniture, golf, basketball, sports, mystery novels, studying politics. Home: 107 Rayson Northville MI 48167 Office: Delco Electronics New Center One Suite 535 PO Box 33119 Detroit MI 48232

HUFFMAN, H. ARLENE, banker; b. Paxton, Ill., June 18, 1933; d. Edward V. and Mabel R. (Johnson) Bankson; m. Richard M. Huffman, Nov. 25, 1953; children—Melinda Huffman Etter, Mark, David. Student Ind. Bus. Coll. With Community State Bank, Royal Center, Ind., 1969—, asst. cashier, 1969-75, asst. trust officer, 1975-78, ins. dept. mgr., 1978—. Helper for elderly Helping Hands, Royal Center; past pres. Progressive Club, Royal Center. Mem. Ind. Agts. Assn. Office: Community State Bank 101 Chicago St Royal Center IN 46978

HUFFMAN, RAYMOND C., manufacturing company executive; b. Columbus, Ohio, May 21, 1949; s. Walter O. and Jean Marie (Murphy) H.; m. Donna M. Curran, Sept. 30, 1950; 1 son, Todd Curran. B.S.B.A. in Acctg., Franklin U., 1975. Acct. Edmund M. Kagay, C.P.A., 1973-75; controller Precision Products Co., 1975-76; sec., treas. Argus Mfg. Co., Groveport, Ohio, 1976-78, pres., chmn. bd., 1978—. Served with USMC, 1969-75. Mem. Nat. Small Bus. Govt. Contractors Assn. (sec. 1982—), Columbus C. of C., Numeric Control Soc., Nat. Tooling and Machining Assn., Farm Equipment Mfg. Assn. Roman Catholic. Club: Presidents-Ohio State U. Copyright quality control systems, mfg. software. Office: 4445 Marketing Pl Groveport OH 43125

HUGGINS, CHARLES BRENTON, physician; b. Halifax, N.S., Can., Sept. 22, 1901; s. Charles Edward and Bessie (Spencer) H.; B.A., Acadia U., 1920, D.Sc., 1946; M.D., Harvard, 1924; M.Sc., Yale, 1947; D.Sc., Washington U., St. Louis, 1950, Leeds U., 1953, Turin U., 1957; Sigillum Magnum, Bologna U., 1964; D.Sc., Trinity Coll., 1965, Wales, 1967, U. Mich., 1968, Med. Coll. Ohio, 1973, Gustavus Adolphus Coll., 1975, Wilmington Coll., 1980, U. Louisville, 1980; LL.D., U. Aberdeen, 1966; D.P. S., George Washington U., 1967; LL.D. (hon.), York U. (Can.); hon. doctorate, U. Calif. at Berkeley, 1968; m. Margaret Wellman, July 29, 1927; children—Charles Edward, Emily Wellman (Mrs. Fine). Intern in surgery U. Mich., 1924-26, instr. surgery, 1926-27; instr. surgery U. Chgo., 1927-29, asst. prof., 1929-33, asso. prof., 1933-36, prof. surgery, 1936—, dir. Ben May Lab. for Cancer Research, 1951-69, William B. Ogden Distinguished Service prof., 1962; Macewan lectureship U. Glasgow, 1958; Chancellor Acadia U., Wolfville, N.S., 1972-79. Trustee Worcester Found. Exptl. Biology; hon. trustee Jackson Lab., Bar Harbor, Maine; bd. govs. Weizmann Inst. Sci., Rehovot, Israel. Recipient Charles L. Meyer award for cancer research Nat. Acad. Sci., 1943; Am. Urol. Assn. award for research on male genital tract, 1948; Francis Amory award for cancer research, 1948; AMA gold medals for research, 1936, 1940; Société Internationale d'Urologie, 1948; Am. Cancer Soc. award, 1953; Bertner award M.D. Anderson Hosp., 1953; award Am. Pharm. Mfrs. Assn., 1953; Gold medal Am. Assn. Genito-Urinary Surgeons, 1955; Borden award Assn. Am. Med. Colls., 1955; Cartwright medal Columbia U., 1975; decorated Order Pour le Merite, Germany, 1958, Order of The Sun, Peru, 1961; recipient Comfort Crookshank award Middlesex Hosp., London, 1957; Charles Mickel fellow Toronto U., 1958; Cameron prize Edinburg U., 1958; Valentine prize N.Y. Acad. Medicine, 1962; Hunter award Am. Therapeutic Soc., 1962; Lasker award for med. research, 1963; Gold medal for research Rudolf Virchow Soc., 1964, Passano award, 1965; Ramon Guiteras medal and award Am. Urol. Assn., 1966; Centennial medal Acadia U., 1967; Bigelow medal Boston Surgical Soc., 1967; Nobel prize for physiology and medicine, 1966; James Ewing Soc. award, 1975, others. Fellow A.C.S. (hon.), Royal Coll. Physicians (London), Royal Coll. Physicians, Royal Coll. Surgeons (Edinburgh; hon.), Royal Coll. Surgeons (Can.; hon.); mem. Am. Philos. Soc., Nat. Acad. Scis., Canadian Med. Assn. (hon.), Am. Assn. Cancer Research (hon.), Alpha Omega Alpha. Office: 5842 S Maryland Chicago IL 60637

HUGHES, BARBARA ANN LEROY, association executive; b. Mich. City, Ind., Feb. 22, 1932; d. Archibald Francis and Virgie Elizabeth (Matzke) LeRoy; m. Robert Jon Hughes, June 25, 1955; children—Elizabeth Ann Hitomi, Clare Frances, William LeRoy. B.S. in Chemistry, Purdue U., 1954; postgrad., 1954-55, 75-80. Chemist Pillsbury Co., Mpls., 1955-56; editor, reporter Sun Newspaper, Mpls., 1965-71; environ. program dir. Am. Lung Assn. Hennepin County, Mpls., 1973-82, exec. dir. St. Paul, 1983—. Editor Clean Air Newsletter, 1973—; contbr. to Congl. report, 1980. Chmn. trustees Anoka County Library, Blaine, Minn., 1962-65; chmn. Fridley Cable TV Adv. Bd., Minn., 1972-77, 81—; chmn. KUOM Radio Adv. Bd., 1980—; mem. Environ. Quality Bd., St. Paul, 1983—. Named Fridley Sun Woman of Yr. Fridley Sun Newspaper, 1972; recipient Outstanding Service award Minn. Library Assn., 1973; Pub. Citizen award Minn. Pub. Interest Research Group, 1982. Mem. Minn. Pub. Health Assn., Upper Midwest Air Pollution Control Assn. (pres. 1977), Congress Lung Assn. Staff (com. chmn. 1975-80). Democratic. Unitarian. Club: Sierra (Mpls.). Avocations: reading; skiing; theater; fishing. Home: 548 Rice Creek Terr Fridley MN 55432 Office: Am Lung Assn Ramsey County 614 Portland Ave Saint Paul MN 55102

HUGHES, GARY JOSEPH, school administrator; b. Flint, Mich., Aug. 25, 1948; s. Christopher John and Mary Josephine (King) H.; m. Frances Eleanora Schauf, Aug. 18, 1972. B.A., Marquette U., 1970; M.A., Central Mich. U., 1971; M.B.A., Wayne State U., 1975; Ed.D, Internat. U., St. Louis, 1984. Cert. secondary tchr., Mich. Guidance counselor Lake Orion Schs., Mich., 1973-75, guidance dir., 1975-79, basketball coach, 1973-79; high sch. adminstr., Allegan Schs., Mich., 1979-80, Lawton Pub. Schs., Mich., 1980-81; prin., curriculum dir. Goodrich Area Schs., Mich., 1981—; cons., Grand Blanc, Mich., 1984. Author: Impact of Role of Spouse, 1984. Contbr. articles to profl. jours. Inst. Edn. Leadership fellow 1984—. Mem. Jaycees, Genesee 8 Conf. (pres. 1984—), Southwestern Athletic Conf. (pres. 1980-81), Adminstrv. Council Internat. U., Oakland Personnel and Guidance Assn. (Recognition award 1979), Phi Delta Kappa (Recognition award 1984). Roman Catholic. Avocations: sports; woodworking. Home: 5594 Old Franklin Grand Blanc MI 48439 Office: Goodrich Area Schs 8029 S Gale Goodrich MI 48438

HUGHES, GERALD EDWIN, medical education administrator; b. Kansas City, Mo., July 16, 1921; s. Gerald Edwin and Elizabeth Yeatman (Smith) H.; m. Mary Ellen Atkinson, Sept. 5, 1945; children—Alan Atkinson, William Brian, Cathy Ann. B.S. in Medicine, Mo. U., 1943; M.D., Washington U., 1944. Diplomate Am. Bd. Pediatrics. Intern St. Louis City Hosp., 1944-45, resident, 1948-49; resident St. Louis Children's Hosp., 1947-48; practice medicine specializing in pediatrics, Kansas City, Mo., 1949-67; sec. for meetings Am. Acad. Pediatrics, Evanston, Ill., 1967-73, dir. continuing med. edn., 1973-83, dir. dept. edn., Elk Grove Village, Ill., 1983-85, sec., 1973—. Served to capt. U.S. Army, 1945-47. Fellow Am. Acad. of Pediatrics; mem. AMA, Ill. State Med. Soc., Chgo. Med. Soc., Alliance for Continuing Med. Edn., Profl. Conv. Mgrs. Assn. Office: Am Acad Pediatrics 141 NW Point Rd Box 927 Elk Grove Village IL 60007

HUGHES, HOWARD BOS, photographer; b. Chgo., Oct. 2, 1938; s. William B. and Wilhelmina (Bos) H.; m. Lynn Edith Bukoll, Aug. 10, 1963; children—Heather, Kelly. B.A., Hope Coll., 1961; B.F.A., Art Inst. Chgo., 1980. With Am. Oil Co., Chgo., 1961-65; registered rep. Wayne Hummer & Co., Chgo., 1965-70; asst. v.p. Palatine Nat. Bank, Ill., 1970-72; prin. Howard B. Hughes Photography, Palatine, 1972—. Bd. govs. Lutheran Social Services, Chgo., 1980—; Republican precinct capt., Palatine, 1975—; treas. United Luth. Ch., Oak Park, Ill., 1966-68. Recipient 1st pl. photo award 7th Internat. Human Unity Conf., 1980. Mem. Profl. Photographers Am., Beta Theta Pi. Republican. Club: Medinah Country (Ill.) (photographer 1980—). Avocations: golf; running. Home: 1791 Prestwick Dr Inverness IL 60067

HUGHES, JEROME MICHAEL, state senator, consultant; b. St. Paul, Oct. 1, 1929; s. Michael Joseph and Mary (Malloy) H.; m. Audrey M. Lackner, Aug. 11, 1951; children—Bernadine, Timothy, Kathleen, Rosemarie, Margaret, John. B.A., Coll. St. Thomas, 1951; M.A., U. Minn., 1958; Ed.D., Wayne State U., 1970. Tchr., Shakopee, Minn., 1951-53; tchr. St. Paul schs., 1953-61, counselor, 1963-66, research asst., 1966-67, edn. cons., 1968—; community faculty mem. Minn. Met. State Coll., 1973-74; hon. postdoctoral fellow, seminar leader U. Minn., 1980-81; mem. Minn. Senate, 1966—, chmn. edn. com., 1937-82, chmn. elections and ethics com., 1983—, pres. senate, 1983—. Mem. Minn. State Community Edn. Adv. Council, 1971-78, Edn. Commn. of the States, 1973, Nat. Community Edn. Adv. Council, 1980-83; bd. dirs. State Legis. Leaders Found., 1983—; mem. Nat. Conf. of State Legis.-State/Fed. Assembly, Leadership Mtgs. Recipient Cert. of Meritorious Service, St. Paul Counselor's Assn., 1967; Disting. Service award Jaycees, 1967, Minn. Elem. Sch. Prins. Assn., 1982, Minn. Community Edn. Assn., 1984; Penell award Minn. Fedn. Tchrs.; Community Educator of Yr. award Minn. Community Edn. Assn., 1975; Friend of 4H award, 1979; Eddy award Council on Quality Edn., 1981; Cert. of Appreciation, Alliance for Arts in Edn., Minn. Assn. Retarded Citizens, 1983, Agrl. Extension Service, U. Minn., 1984, Minn. State U. Students Assn. NDEA fellow U. Minn., 1961-62; Mott fellow, 1967-68; Bush summer fellow Sch. Law, U. Calif.-Berkeley, 1975; Disting. Policy fellow Inst. for Ednl. Leadership, George Washington U., 1977-78. Mem. Phi Delta Kappa. Democrat. Roman Catholic. Home: 1978 Payne Ave Saint Paul MN 55117 Office: Minn Senate 328 State Capitol Saint Paul MN 55155

HUGHES, LARRY NEAL, environmental engineer; b. West Plains, Mo., Aug. 19, 1941; s. Wilbur Emerson and Ruby Bernice (Johnson) H.; m. Carolyn Sue Mason, Mar. 22, 1968; children—John Thomas, Amanda Christine. B.S.C.E., Bradley U., 1964; M.S. in Pub. Health Engring., U. Hawaii, 1967. Registered profl. engr., Fla., Ill.; cert. sewage treatment works operator, class 1, Ill. E.P.A. Civil engr. Dept. Transportation, Peoria, Ill., 1964-65; asst. dir. waste treatment facilities Greater Peoria San. Dist., 1967-70, dir. waste treatment facilities, 1970—. Contbr. articles to profl. jours. Roundtable commr. staff W.D. Boyce Council Boy Scouts Am., Peoria, 1981-83, cubmaster, 1981-83, scouting coordinator, 1983—, asst. cubmaster, 1980-81. Recipient Scouter's Tng. award, Woodbadge award, Eagle Scout award, all Boy Scouts Am. Mem. ASCE, Water Pollution Control Fedn. (Hatfield award 1985), Ill. Assn. Water Pollution Control Operators (1st v.p. 1985—), Ill. Water Pollution Control Assn., Central States Water Pollution Control Assn. (operating award 1974). Clubs: Ducks Unlimited; National Rifle Assn.; Bass Anglers Sportsman Soc., Pi Kappa Alpha. Avocations: hunting; fishing; hiking; camping. Office: 2322 S Darst St Peoria IL 61607

HUGHES, MARGARET CYRENA, ret. assn. exec.; b. Springfield, Ill.; d. Thomas Patrick and Elizabeth (Donelan) H.; student Springfield Jr. Coll., U. Ill. Campaign chmn. Community Fund Assn., 1947-51; exec. dir. Sangamon County Tb Assn., Springfield, 1951-70, Lincoln Land Tb and Respiratory Disease Assn., 1970-76. Pres. Friends of Library, 1956; mem. com. Sangamon County Council Social Agys., 1940-41; pres. Ill. State Assn. Women's Divs. Chambers of Commerce; bd. dirs., sec.-treas. Springfield Safety Council, 1978—, trustee, 1976; bd. dirs. Sangamon County Mental Health, 1948-53, Ret. Sr. Vol. Program (R.S.V.P.), Sr. Citizens of Sangamon County; Cath. adv. com. Girl Scouts, 1946-51, nat. resettlement adv. com. 1948-53; bd. dirs. St. John's Sanitorium Aux. Recipient Pro Ecclesia at Pontifice medal. Mem. Assn. Commerce and Industry (pres. women's div. 1961-62), Ill. C. of C. (v.p. women's div.), Ill. Conf. Tb Workers (pres. 1961-62), Dioceasen Council Cath. Women (past pres.; dir.), Nat. Council Cath. Women (past provincial dir.; chmn. youth com. 1944-51), Louise de Marillac Guild, Sacred Heart Acad. Alumni Assn. (past pres.), Cathedral Altar Soc. (pres. 1956-57), Symphony Guild. Clubs: Zonta (pres. Springfield 1962, area dist. dir. 1963-64); Cotarle (dir. 1943-44); Springfield Women's (dir., chmn. safety com., v.p. 1971—, pres. 1973-75). Home: 417 E Canedy St Springfield IL 62703

HUGHES, RONALD MELVIN, oil company executive; b. Sandusky, Ohio, Oct. 18, 1945; s. Melvin A. and Ruth Ilene (Rinkel) H.; m. Rebecca Kay Sole, Jan. 31, 1970 (div. June 1982); children—Jason Scott, Brian Ross. B.B.A., Kent State U., 1968; M.B.A., Youngstown State U., 1977. Restaurant mgr. Interstate United, Sandusky, Ohio, 1967; with Standard Oil Co., Cleve., 1968-75, real estate developer, Youngstown, Ohio, 1975-77, mgr. distbn. ctr., Lima, Ohio, 1977—. Served with USN, 1968-72. Mem. Nat. Mgmt. Assn., Sohio-Lima Mgmt. Club, Petroleum Packaging Inst. Republican. Lutheran. Clubs: Sertoma, Sherwood Park Community (bd. dirs.), Sandusky Ski, Brand Lakes Fishing (Wapakoneta, Ohio). Avocations: fishing, hunting, skiing, boating, tennis. Home: 1624 Victoria Ln Lima OH 45805 Office: Standard Oil Co 1000 Hanthorn Rd Lima OH 45804

HUGHES, SUSAN LANE, social worker, health services researcher, gerontologist; b. Boston, Feb. 2, 1943; d. John Joseph and Agnes Thomasine (Lane) Mooney; m. Edward F.X. Hughes, Feb. 11, 1967; children—Edward Francis, John Patrick, Dempsey Lane. B.A., Manhattanville Coll., Purchase, N.Y., 1964; M.S.W., Simmons Coll., Boston, 1966; D.S.W., Columbia U., 1981. Social worker Mass. Gen. Hosp., Boston, 1966-67, Presbyn. Hosp., N.Y.C., 1967-69, 70-74; Project dir. Ctr. for Health Services Research, Northwestern U., Evanston, Ill., 1977-81, program dir., 1981—; research cons. Five Hosp. Homebound Program, Chgo., 1977—, Am. Found. for Blind, N.Y.C., 1976-77; mem. com. to plan maj. study of nat. long-term care policies Inst. Medicine, 1985. Contbr. articles to profl. publs., chpts. to books. Mem. nursing home adv. council Office of Ill. Atty. Gen., Chgo., 1984—, Adv. Com. for Maturing Adult, Chgo. Health Dept., 1984—. Kellogg Found. fellow, 1979. Mem. Am. Pub. Health Assn., Assn. Health Services Research, Gerontol. Soc. Am. Democrat. Roman Catholic. Avocations: swimming, sailing, gardening, mystery reading. Home: 810 Lincoln St Evanston IL 60201 Office: Northwestern U Ctr Health Services and Policy Research 629 Noyes St Evanston IL 60201

HUGHES, WILLIAM OWEN, accountant; b. Garden City, Kans., Oct. 13, 1914; s. John Perry and Leona (Green) H.; m. Zola Andrews, July 4, 1937; children—Steven Perry, B. Acctg., Park Coll., Denver, 1936; cert. in acctg. Northwestern U., 1947. Acct., dist. mgr. Internat. Harvester, Chgo., 1940-72; acct., mgr. Andrews Bus. Services, Kansas City, Mo., 1972-79; acctg. exec. Internat. Exec. Service Corp., Stamford, Conn., 1980—. Recipient Service to Country award Internat. Exec. Service Corps, 1980-81. Mem. Nat. Soc. Pub. Accts., Nat. Assn. Tax Cons. (dir. 1971-83), Overland Park C. of C., Nat. Model R.R. Assn. Methodist. Home: 9816 Horton Dr Overland Park KS 66207

HUGHEY, MICHAEL JOHN, obstetrician-gynecologist; b. Chgo., July 2, 1948; s. Merle Stanley and Elaine (Cartmel) H.; m. Kathleen Bailey, June 18, 1977; 1 child, Andrew Bailey. A.B., Princeton U., 1970; M.D., Loyola U., Chgo., 1974. Diplomate Am. Bd. Ob-Gyn. Intern, Evanston Hosp., Ill., 1974-75; resident in ob-gyn, Northwestern U., Chgo., 1974-78; instr. ob-gyn, 1978-80, asst. prof., 1980—; obstetrician North Care Med. Group, Evanston, Ill., 1978—, chmn. dept. ob-gyn, 1981—, v.p., 1981—, also dir. Author: The Complete Guide To Pregnancy, 1984. Contbr. articles to profl. jours. Ruling elder First Presbyterian Ch. Wilmette, Ill., 1983—. Fellow Am. Coll. Obstetricians and Gynecologists; mem. AMA, Chgo. Med. Soc., Ill. State Med. Soc., Am. Inst. Ultrasound in Medicine. Club: Mich. Shores (Wilmette). Office: North Care Med Group 500 Davis St Evanston IL 60201

HUGHSON, DEAN DAYTON, food processing company executive; b. Braymer, Mo., Apr. 30, 1951; s. Berlyn Dean and Patricia Ann (Collins) H.; m. Susan Doris Waldbaum, Dec. 31, 1978; children—Rachel Lynn, Joshua Daniel, Elizabeth Michele. A.A., Met. Community Coll., 1972; B.A., U. Mo., 1977. Social worker City of Kansas City, Mo., 1970-72, Salvation Army, Kansas City, Mo., 1973-74; edn. dir. So. Ariz. Alcoholism Council, Tucson, 1975; pres. N.E.W.S. Neighborhood House, Kansas City, Mo., 1973-75, edn. program dir. N.E.W.S., 1976; alcoholism counselor Immanuel Hosp., Omaha, 1977-78; salesman Waldbaum Co., Wakefield, Nebr., 1979-83, v.p., 1984—; dir. Southeast Poultry Export Council, Atlanta. Author Foolkiller newspaper, 1975. Bd. dirs. Shaire Zion Synagogue, Sioux City, Iowa, 1983-84; campaign mgr. Dodge County Clerk of Court incumbent, Fremont, Nebr., 1978. Democrat. Jewish. Club: Bubba Consciousness Found. (Winnipeg, Can.) (pres. 1975). Avocations: reading; travel; charitable organizations. Home: 3812 Jones Sioux City IA 51104 Office: Milton G Waldbaum Co 501 N Main Wakefield NE 68784

HUHEEY, MARILYN JANE, ophthalmologist; b. Cin., Aug. 31, 1935; d. George Mercer and Mary Jane (Weaver) H.; B.S. in Math., Ohio U., Athens, 1958; M.S. in Physiology, U. Okla., 1966; M.D., U. Ky., 1970. Tchr. math. James Ford Rhodes High Sch., Cleve., 1956-58; biostatistician Nat. Jewish Hosp., Denver, 1958-60; life sci. engr. Stanley Aviation Corp., Denver, 1960-63, N.Am. Aviation Co., Los Angeles, 1963-67; intern U. Ky. Hosp., 1970-71; emergency room physician Jewish Hosp., Mercy Hosp., Bethesda Hosp. (all Cin.), 1971-72; ship's doctor, 1972; resident in ophthalmology Ohio State U. Hosp., Columbus, 1972-75; practice medicine specializing in ophthalmology, Columbus, 1975—; mem. staff Univ. Hosp., Grant Hosp., St. Anthony Hosp., 1975-79; clin. asst. prof. Ohio State U. Med. Sch., 1976-84, clin. assoc. prof., 1985—, dir. course ophthalmologic receptionist/aides, 1976; Dem. candidate for Ohio Senate, 1982. Diplomate Am. Bd. Ophthalmology. Fellow Am. Acad. Ophthalmology; mem. AAUP, Am. Assn. Ophthalmologists, Ohio Ophthalmol. Soc. (bd. govs. 1984—, del. to Ohio State Med. Assn. 1984—), Franklin County Acad. Medicine (profl. relations com. 1979-82, legis. com. 1981—, edn. and program com. 1981—, chmn. 1982-85), Ohio Soc. Prevent Blindness (chmn. med. adv. bd. 1978-80), Ohio State Med. Assn. (dr.-nurse liaison com. 1983—), Columbus EENT Soc., LWV, Columbus Council World Affairs, Columbus Bus. and Profl. Women's Club, Columbus C. of C., Grandview Area Bus. Assn., Federated Dem. Women of Ohio, Columbus Area Women's Polit. Caucus, Phi Mu. Clubs: Columbus Met. (forum com. 1982—, fundraising com. 1983-84), Mercedes Benz (dir. 1981-83), Zonta, Herb Soc. (program com. 1984—, chmn. internat. com. 1983). Home: 2396 Northwest Blvd Columbus OH 43221 Office: 1275 Olentangy River Rd Columbus OH 43212

HUITEMA, BRADLEY EUGENE, psychologist, design consultant, educator; b. Hammond, Ind., July 28, 1938; s. Roy and Doris (Yeater) H.; m. Kathryn Ann Brock, Sept. 2, 1961 (div.); children—Craig Bradley, Laura Lynn. B.A., So. Ill. U., 1961; M.A., Western Mich. U., 1962; Ph.D., Colo. State U., 1968. Research prof., Oreg. State System of Higher Edn., Monmouth, 1967-68; prof. psychology, Western Mich. U., Kalamazoo, 1968—; research design cons. Anova Research, Inc. Research psychologist U.S. Army, 1962-64. Mem. Am. Psychol. Assn., AAAS, Am. Statis. Assn., Soc. of Behavioral Medicine. Author: The Analysis of Covariance and Alternatives, 1980. Home: 113 Braemar Ln Kalamazoo MI 49007 Office: Psychology Dept Western Mich U Kalamazoo MI 49008

HUIZENGA, DONALD LEE, manufacturing company executive; b. Muskegon, Mich., Nov. 8, 1946; s. Donald Irving and Anita J. (Wraalstad) H.; B.S., Drake U., 1968; m. Alice Jane Petersen, Aug. 23, 1968; children—Jason Donn, Jaime Lynn. With Old Kent Bank & Trust, Grand Rapids, Mich., 1968-77, v.p. trust ops., 1976-77; pres. Cedar Springs Castings, Inc. (Mich.), 1977—; mem. govt. adv. council Gulf Oil, 1982—. Bd. dirs. Grand Rapids (Mich.) chpt. Am. Cancer Soc., 1975-77; adv. bd. Sch. Engring., Western Mich. U. Served with U.S. Army, 1968-70, USAR, 1970-74. Mem. Cedar Springs C. of C. (bd. dirs. 1980—, Citizen of Yr. 1982), Foundry Assn. Mich. (bd. dirs. 1979—, pres. 1984-85), Am. Inst. Banking (pres. 1976-77), Am. Foundrymens Soc. Republican. Lutheran. Clubs: Rotary (bd. dirs. 1980—, pres. Cedar Springs 1982-83), Lions (pres. 1972-73); Grand Rapids Econs. Office: 69 W Maple St Cedar Springs MI 49319

HULBERT, FRANCIS LOSSING, association executive; b. Fairport, Ohio, Mar. 25, 1911; s. Wade Oakley and Berta (Burgess) H.; m. Margaret Catherine Rentenbach, May 12, 1939; children—James R., Gerald W., Janet M. B.S., U. Mich., 1935. Sales engr. W. A. Dalee, Detroit, 1936-42; flight test engr. Ford Motor Co., Ypsilanti, Mich., 1942-44, Power Equipment Co., Detroit, 1944-47; engring. supr. Square D Co., Detroit, Cedar Rapids, Iowa, 1947-76; chpt. officer, dist. rep. Service Corps Ret. Execs., Cedar Rapids, Iowa, 1976—. Inventor compensator, 1955. Mem. Air Pollution Bd. Rev., Cedar Rapids, Iowa, 1974—; trustee Fire Dist. 2, Bertram Twp., Linn County, 1973-82. Mem. UN Assn. (pres. 1980-82), Am. Assn. Ret. Persons (pres. 1978-80. Republican. Unitarian. Avocations: camping; travel.

HULESCH, WILLIAM STANLEY, physician; b. Cleve., Apr. 28, 1946; s. Stanley and Beatrice R. (Suchma) H.; B.S., U. Dayton, 1968; M.D., Loyola U., Chgo., 1972; m. Jane S. Liebel, Aug. 9, 1969. Resident in family practice MacNeal Hosp., Berwyn, Ill., 1972-75; practice medicine specializing in family practice, Downers Grove, Ill., 1975—; clin. assoc. prof. U. Ill.; past chmn. family practice dept. Good Samaritan Hosp.; past chmn. family practice dept. Hinsdale Hosp.; mem. faculty George Williams Coll., Hinsdale Hosp. Family Practice Residency; pres. D.G. Family Practice, H.S.M. Inc. Advisor, Downers Grove Sch. System, Hinsdale Sch. System. Diplomate Am. Bd. Family Practice, Nat. Bd. Med. Examiners. Fellow Am. Acad. Family Physicians (by-laws com.); mem. AMA (Physicians Recognition award), Ill. Acad. Family Physicians (dir., chpt. pres., chmn. bd.), Alpha Epsilon Delta. Republican. Editorial research bd. Sports Medicine. Office: 6800 Main St Downers Grove IL 60515

HULL, LOIS ANN, hosp. social service ofcl.; b. Detroit, Aug. 12, 1932; d. Joseph Guy and Cora Blanche (Daoust) Winefordner; student Black Hawk Jr. Coll., 1967-70; B.A., Marycrest Coll., 1972; M.S.W., U. Iowa, 1975; m. Ward Kenneth Hull, Aug. 11, 1951; children—Richard, Randall, Russell, Daniel, Jonathan. Dir. social services Hammond Henry Dist. Hosp., Geneseo, Ill., 1972—; instr. biofeedback Black Hawk Jr. Coll., Moline, Ill., part-time, 1980-82; mental health and social work counselor fields of alcohol and drug abuse. Treas. Henry County Mental Health Assn., 1973-75; founding bd. Growth Incorp Day Care, 1972-73, Marriage and Family Counseling, Geneseo, 1973-80; bd. dirs. Clinic on Alcohol and Drugs, 1977-78; founding bd., v.p. Good Shepherd Found., 1978-83; founding bd. dirs. N.W. chpt. Am. Cancer Soc., 1983—; pres. Jr. Women's Club, Geneseo, 1966-67. Cert. alcoholism counselor, Ill. Mem. Nat. Assn. Social Workers (certified), Ill. Alcohol and Drug Dependence Assn., Ill. Welfare Assn., Ill. Biofeedback Soc., Am. Assn. Biofeedback Clinicians (bd. dirs. 1985—; cert.), Am. Hosp. Assn. of Social Work Dirs. (chpt. pres. 1985—), Internat. Platform Assn. Roman Catholic. Home: Rural Route 4 Geneseo IL 61254 Office: Hammond Henry Dist Hospital 210 W Elk St Geneseo IL 61254

HULL, ROGER HAROLD, college president, lawyer, educator; b. N.Y.C., June 18, 1942; s. Max and Magda (Stern) H.; m. Anne E. Dyson, July 4, 1980. A.B. cum laude, Dartmouth Coll., 1964; LL.B., Yale U., 1967; LL.M., U. Va., 1972, S.J.D., 1974. Bar: N.Y. 1968. Assoc., White & Case, N.Y.C., 1967-71; spl. counsel to Linwood Holton, Gov. Va., Richmond, 1971-74; spl. asst. to chmn. and dep. staff dir. Nat. Security Council, Interag. Task Force on Law of the Sea, 1974-76; v.p. devel. Syracuse U., N.Y., 1976-79, v.p. devel. and planning, 1979-81, adj. prof. law, 1976-81; pres. Beloit Coll., Wis., 1981—; mem. U.S. del. Law of the Sea Conf., Caracas, Geneva, N.Y.C., 1974-76. Author: The Irish Triangle, 1976; co-author: Law and Vietnam, 1968; contbr. articles to profl. publs. Mem. bd. visitors Coll. William and Mary, Williamsburg, Va., 1970-74, Assn. Governing Bds. Pub. Instns. Task Force, 1975; bd. dirs. Heritage Bank-Beloit, 1984. Mem. N.Y. Bar, Chgo. Council on Fgn. Relations, ABA, Am. Soc. Internat. Law, Young Pres. Orgn. Clubs: Univ. (Chgo.); Country (Beloit, Wis.). Office: Beloit College 700 College St Beloit WI 53511

HULL, TIMOTHY JEROME, manufacturing company marketing executive; b. Springfield, Ohio, July 8, 1951; s. Robert Dean and Jeanne Marie (Casey) H.; m. Susan C. Waite, July 1, 1972; children—Christopher, John. B.S. cum laude, Wright State U., 1973, M.Ed., 1975. Tchr. art pub. schs., Xenia, Ohio, 1973-81; tech. writer, illustrator Tech. Illustrations & Publs. Service, Inc., Springfield, Ohio, 1979-81; sales promotion specialist Fluids Handling Div., Robbins & Myers, Inc., 1981-83, mgr. advt. and sales promotion, 1983—. Mem. Springfield Mktg. and Advt. Council (v.p. 1983-84), Dayton Advt. Club. Democrat. Home: 4406 Middle Urbana Rd Urbana OH 43078 Office: Robbins & Myers Inc 1345 Lagonda Ave Box 960 Springfield OH 45501

HULLIN, SUSAN LEE, public relations executive; b. Walla Walla, Wash., May 22, 1944; d. Edward D. and Wilberta M. (Kirkman) Kanz; m. Tod Robert Hullin, May 6, 1967. B.A. in Polit. Sci., U. Wash., 1966. Exec. asst. to chmn. Garfinckel's, Washington, 1977-81; press relations/spl. events coordinator Emporium-Capwell, San Francisco, 1981-83; sr. account supr. Hill and Knowlton, Chgo., 1983—. Mem. San Francisco Symphony 500 Arts Council of Eureka Coll., Ill., bd. dirs. Hist. Alexandria Found.; jr. bd. dirs. Infant Welfare Soc. of Evanston. Mem. Pub. Relations Soc. Am. (accredited), San Francisco Bay Area Publicity Club, Fashion Group Jr. League of Chgo. Republican. Presbyterian. Clubs: Commonwealth of Calif., Press of San Francisco (bd. dirs. 1983-84). Army-Navy Country (Arlington, Va.). Home: 634 Foster St Evanston IL 60201 Office: 111 E Wacker Dr Chicago IL 60601

HULLIN, TOD ROBERT, business executive; b. Seattle, May 28, 1943; s. Jack Elmer and Floretta Elizabeth (Light) H.; B.A. in Bus. Adminstrn., U. Wash., 1966; m. Susan Lee Kanz, May 6, 1967; Staff asst. domestic council White House, Washington, 1973-74, asso. dir. domestic council for housing and community devel., 1974-76; prin. dep. asst. sec. def. for public affairs, Washington, 1976-77; v.p. Interstate Gen. Corp., St. Charles, Md., 1977-83; pres. Interstate Condominiums, Inc., 1981-83; v.p. communications/pub. affairs G.D. Searle Pharms., Skokie, Ill., 1983—. Served to 1st lt. U.S. Army, 1967-69. Decorated Army Commendation medal; recipient Sec. of Def. award for outstanding public service, 1977. Mem. Nat. Assn. Home Builders, Urban Land Inst., Greater Washington Bd. Trade, U. Wash. Alumni Assn. (pres. San Francisco Bay Area club 1982-83), Eureka (Ill.) Coll. Council Arts, Sigma Nu. Republican. Presbyterian. Club: Army Navy Country (Arlington, Va.). Home: 634 Foster St Evanston IL 60201 Office: GD Searle Pharmaceutical 4930 Oakton Skokie IL 60076

HULLINGER, CRAIG HARLAN, city planner; b. Brookings, S.D., Dec. 1, 1947; s. Clifford Harlan and Louise Edna (Liffengren) H.; m. Joyce Schaller (div. 1982); children—Clint, Bret. B.A., Govs. State U., 1975, M.A., 1976; postgrad. U. Ill., 1980. Exec. dir. Will County Planning Dept., Joliet, Ill., 1973-77; planner, acting mgr. City of Park Forest South, Ill., 1977-78; chief devel. Prairie Devel. Ltd., Crete, Ill., 1978-80; pres. Planning Devel. Services, Chgo., 1980—; cons. to cities in Ind., Ill. and Mich., 1978—. Candidate, Will County Bd., Frankfort, Ill., 1979, precinct committeeman, 1980. Served to lt. col. USMC, 1966-71, Vietnam. Recipient Navy Commendation medal. Mem. Am. Inst. Cert. Planners, Am. Planning Assn., Misericordia Parents Assn. (chmn. ways and means com. 1981-83), Marine Corps Res. Officers Assn. (sec. 1983-84). Lutheran. Clubs: Plank Rd. Trail (Park Forest) (bd. dirs. 1984—); Friends of Parks (Chgo.).

HULLVERSON, JAMES EVERETT, JR., lawyer, educator; b. St. Louis, Sept. 20, 1953; s. James Everett and Shirley (Shaughnessey) H.; m. Laure Albers Bauer, Oct. 7, 1977; children—Everett James, Leigh Bauer. B.A., Yale U., 1975; J.D. cum laude, St. Louis U., 1978. Bar: Mo. 1978, U.S. Dist. Ct. (ea. dist.) Mo. 1978, Ill. 1979, U.S. Supreme Ct. 1981, U.S. Ct. Appeals (8th cir.) 1983; diplomate Am. Bd. Profl. Liability Attys.; cert. civil trial adv. Nat. Bd. Trial Advocacy. Ptnr. Hullverson, Hullverson & Frank, Inc., St. Louis, 1978—; adj. assoc. prof. law St. Louis U., 1983—; faculty Nat. Coll. Advocacy, 1983, 85; lectr. in field. Contbr. chpts. to books; author seminar program. Active Attys. Motivated for Mo. Mem. Assn. Trial Lawyers Am., Ill. Trial Lawyers Assn., Mo. Assn. Trial Attys., Mo. Bar Assn., Am. Soc. Law and Medicine. Roman Catholic. Clubs: Mo. Athletic, St. Louis Masters Swim, Yale (St. Louis). Home: 7937 Teasdale Ct University City MO 63130 Office: Hullverson Hullverson & Frank Inc 1010 Market Saint Louis MO 63101

HULSTRAND, DONALD MAYNARD, bishop; b. Parkers Prairie, Minn., Apr. 16, 1927; s. Aaron Emmanuel H. and Selma Avendla (Liljegren) H.; m. Marjorie Richter, June 11, 1948; children—Katherine Ann, Charles John. B.A. summa cum laude, Macalester Coll., 1950; B.D., Kenyon Coll., 1953; M.Div., Colgate-Rochester Theol. Sem., 1974. Ordained priest Episcopal Ch., 1953, consecrated bishop, 1982. Vicar St. John's Episcopal Ch., Worthington, Minn., 1953-57; rector Grace Meml. Ch., Wabasha, Minn., 1957-62, St. Mark's Episcopal Ch., Canton, Ohio, 1962-68, St. Paul's Episcopal Ch., Duluth, Minn., 1969-75; assoc. rector St. Andrew's Episcopal Ch., Kansas City, Mo., 1968-69; exec. dir. Anglican Fellowship of Prayer, 1975-79; rector Trinity Episcopal Ch., Greenley, Colo., 1979-82; bishop Episcopal Diocese of Springfield, Ill., 1982; exec. bd. Episcopal Radio (TV Found.), Atlanta, 1982—, Anglican Fellowship of Prayer, Winter Park, Fla., 1968—; adv. bd. Episcopal Boys' Homes, Salinas, Kans., 1983—; com. of execs. Ill. Conf. Chs., 1982—; mem. House of Bishops, 1982—, Minn. Standing Com., 1970-73; chmn. Minn. Examining Chaplains, 1954-61; chaplain Pewsaction Fellowships U.S.A., 1983—; advisor Diocesan Youth of Minn., 1956-60. Author: The Praying Church, 1978, And God Shall Wipe Away All Tears, 1968, Intercessory Prayer, 1972, Upper Room Dialogues, 1980. Bd. dirs. Sr. Citizens Housing, Duluth, 1972-75, St. Luke's Hosp., Duluth, 1969-75; pres. Low-Rent Housing Project, Greenley, 1979-82. Served with USNR, 1945-46. Recipient Disting. Service award Young Life Minn., 1974; named hon. canon Diocese of Ohio, Cleve., 1967. Mem. Pi Phi Epsilon. Lodge: Rotary. Office: Episcopal Diocese of Springfield 821 S 2d St Springfield IL 62704

HULTGREN, DENNIS EUGENE, farmer; b. Union County, S.D., Mar. 19, 1929; s. John Alfred and Esther Marie (Johnson) H.; grad. high sch.; m. Nelda Ethelyn Olson, Aug. 3, 1957; children—Nancy Hultgren Klemme, Jean Hultgren Doty, Jahn Dennis, Ruth Dorothy Hultgren Henneman. Farmer, Union County, 1953—; commr., chmn. Union County Planning and Zoning Bd., 1972-83; mem. bd. bylaw revision Union County Electric Co., 1983-85. Pres. bd. Union Creek Cemetery, 1958—; pres. bd. mgrs. Union-Sayles Watershed Dist., 1965-70. Treas., Sioux Valley Twp., Union County, 1980—; treas., bd. dirs. W. Union Sch., 1957-67; chmn. Union County Sch. Bd., 1961-68; pres. Alcester (S.D.) Sch. Bd., 1970-77; chmn. Alcester PTA, 1967-68; mem. tech. bd. rev. Southeastern Council Govts., Sioux Falls, S.D., 1976-77; bd. dirs. Siouxland Interstate Met. Planning Council, Sioux City, Iowa, 1977-83, sec. council ofcls., 1978-83; bd. dirs. Old Opera House Community Theater, Akron, Iowa, Akron Area Action Assn., 1983-85, 1983-84, Akron Devel. Corp., 1985—; Republican precinct committeeman, 1970—; mem. Union County Rep. Central Com., 1970—. Served with AUS, 1951-53; Korea. Decorated Combat Inf. badge; recipient Best Actor award Old Opera House Community Theatre, 1976, award for outstanding dedication and service, 1984; Sioux City Siouxland Disting. Citizen award Siouxland Interstate Met. Planning Council, 1983; Jefferson award for outstanding pub. service Sta. KELO-TV, 1985; Outstanding Community Service award Lions Internat., 1985. Mem. Farm Bur., Farmers Union, S.D. Livestock Feeders Assn., Nat. Cattlemen's Assn., Associated Sch. Bds. S.D. (Merit award 1976), Am. Legion (exec. bd. Akron 1978—, comdr. Akron 1980-81, historian 1981—, trustee 1983—), VFW. Lutheran (mem. bd. 1967-70, 82-84, lay chmn. 1970, 82—chmn. centennial com. 1974). Address: Hulteboda Farm Box 147 Route 2 Akron IA 51001

HULTGREN, LENNART SVEN, engineering educator; b. Ludvika, Sweden, Mar. 18, 1950; came to U.S., 1974; s. Sven Olof and Beerie Lilian (Eriksson) H.; m. Azam Ahmadi-Moghadam, 1983. B.S. in Engring. Physics, Uppsala U., 1973; M.S. in Aero. and Astronautical Engring., M.I.T., 1975, PH.D., 1978. Research engr. Aero. Research Inst. of Sweden, Stockholm, 1973-74; research asst. MIT, Cambridge, 1974-78, postdoctoral assoc., 1978-79; vis. asst. prof. Ill. Inst. Tech., Chgo., 1979-80, asst. prof., 1980-85, assoc. prof., 1985—; cons. Aero. Research Inst. of Sweden, Stockholm. Mem. Am. Phys. Soc. (fluid dynamics div.), AIAA, Am. Acad. Mechanics, Sigma Xi. Office: 3300 S Federal St Chicago IL 60616

HUMAY, PRISCILLA MARIE, artist, illustrator, writer; b. Chgo., June 8, 1942; d. Francis Joseph and Helen Barbara (Balun) Humay; m. Ralph Lepore, 1962 (dec. 1965); 1 dau., Michele; m. Chester Louis Witek, 1967 (div. 1973); 1 son, Anton; m. John Louis, July 5, 1975 (separated 1984); children—Priscilla, Demetrios. B.F.A., Art Inst. Chgo., 1969; M.S. in Visual Design, Inst. Design, Ill. Inst. Tech., 1971; postgrad. Charles U., Prague, Czechoslovakia, 1972, 73. Tchr., Deerpath Art League, Lake Forest, Ill., 1983—, Jewish Cultural Ctrs., Chgo., 1971; lectr. Willowbrook High Sch., 1971, Oakton Community Coll., Morton Grove, Ill., 1974, Govs. State U., Park Forest, Ill., 1974; gallery co-dir. ARC Gallery and Ednl. Found., Chgo., 1978-79; gallery co-dir., art festival coordinator, bd. dirs. Alumni Assn. Sch. of Art Inst. Chgo., 1975, 76; med. illustrator, graphic designer, visual designer, illustrator, 1973—; solo exhibits include Oak Park, 1967, Gallery at Garrett at Northwestern U., 1975, ARC Gallery, 1974, 76, Illini Union Gallery, U. Ill., Champaign-Urbana, 1978; participant group exhibits, also juried exhibit Films by Women 1974, Mus. of Art Inst. Chgo.; works represented in collections of Main Bank of Chgo., Household Internat. Corp., Citizens Bank of Waukegan, pvt. collections, U.S., W.Ger., Holland, Czechoslovakia; juror for animated film Chgo. Internat. Film Festival, 1978. Pres. Lake Forest-Lake Bluff Jr. Women, 1981-82; founder, dir. Lake Forest-Lake Bluff Concerned Citizens for Peace, 1982, 83; chmn. of events Art for Nuclear Weapons Freeze at Richard Gray Gallery, Chgo., 1983; pres. Lake Bluff-Lake Forest Com. of Arden Shore Assn. Home for Boys, 1982; pres. Arden Shore Assn. Home for Boys, 1983, 84; treas. bd. Deerpath Art League, 1983, 84; chair Art for a Nuclear Weapons Freeze, Gray Gallery, Chgo., 1983. Recipient cert. of merit Chgo. Internat. Film Festival, 1971, jury award Evanston (Ill.) Art Festival, 1971, purchase awards Citizens Bank of Waukegan, 1982, Household Internat. Corp. Collection, 1982, 2d place graphics award Fall Festival Deerpath Art League, Lake Forest, 1982, 1st place graphics award, 1983. Mem. AAUW. Home and office: 381 Pierce Ct Vernon Hills IL 60061

HUMBLE, JIMMY LOGAN, transportation company road engineer; b. Columbia, Ky., Dec. 6, 1944; s. William Rymon and Maxine (Brockman) H. B.S. in Elem. Edn., Western Ky. U., 1972. Field reporter Adair County, Columbia, 1963-66; surveyor Agr. Stabilization Com., Muskingum County Edn. Dept., Zanesville, Ohio, 1966-73; road engr. ARA/Smith's, Columbus, Ohio, 1974—; trustee Teamster's Local 413, Columbus, 1983-85. Mem. Fraternal Order Police, Smithsonian Instn., Regenerative Agr. Assn., Pub. Library Columbus and Franklin County (fellow). Democrat. Methodist. Clubs: Ohio Auto, Centurian (Columbus); 4-H (Columbia); Future Farmers Am. Sentinel. Avocations: reading; travel; writing. Home: 351 Garden Heights Ave PO Box 28014 Columbus OH 43228 Office: ARA/Smith's 2625 Westbelt Dr Columbus OH 43228

HUME, HORACE DELBERT, manufacturing company executive; b. Endeavor, Wis., Aug. 15, 1898; s. James Samuel and Lydia Alberta (Sawyer) H.; student pub. schs.; m. Minnie L. Harlan, June 2, 1926 (dec. May 1972); 1 son, James; m. 2d, Sarah D. Lyles Rood, Apr. 6, 1973. Stockman and farmer, 1917-19; with automobile retail business, Garfield, Wash., 1920-21, partner and asst. mgr., 1921-27; automobile and farm machine retailer, Garfield, partner, mgr., 1928-35, gen. mgr. Hume-Love Co., Garfield, 1931-35, pres., 1935-57; partner, gen. mgr. H.D. Hume Co., Mendota, Ill., 1944-52; pres. H.D. Hume Co., Inc., 1952—; partner Hume and Hume, 1952-72; pres. Hume Products Corp., 1953—; pres., dir. Hume-Fry Co., Garden City, Kans., 1955-73; dir. Granberry Products, Inc., Eagle River, Wis. Mayor, Garfield, Wash., 1938-40. Bd. dirs. Mendota Hosp. Found., 1949-73, pres., 1949-54; bd. dirs. Mendota Swimming Pool Assn.; mem. City Planning Commn., 1953-72, chmn., 1953-69; mem. Regional Planning Commn., LaSalle County, Ill., 1965-73, chmn., 1965-71; mem. Schs. Central Com., 1953—, LaSalle County Zoning Commn., 1966—, LaSalle County Care and Treatment Bd., 1970-73; chmn. Mendota Watershed Com., 1967-73. Mem. Am. Soc. Agrl. Engrs., Eagle River (Wis.) C. of C. (pres., dir. 1962-63), Mendota C. of C. (pres. 1948-49, dir. 1946-49, Community Service award 1972). Republican. Presbyterian (elder). Clubs: Kiwanis (pres. 1953, dir. 1954), Masons, Shriners, Order Eastern Star, Elks; Lakes (Sun City, Ariz.). Patentee in various fields. Home: 709 Carolyn St PO Box 279 Mendota IL 61342 Office: 1701 1st Ave Mendota IL 61342

HUME, JOSEPH RANDY, physiologist, pharmacologist, educator; b. Great Falls, Mont., Apr. 3, 1947; s. Joseph William and Laura Jean (Stuart) H.; m. Karen Lynne Bennett, Sept. 22, 1974; children—Ryan Joseph, Eric Christopher. B.A., U. Tex., 1969; Ph.D., U. Calif., 1979. Postdoctoral fellow U. Tex. Med. Br., Galveston, 1979-81, research asst. prof. physiology and biophysics, 1981-82; asst. prof. Mich. State U., East Lansing, 1982—. NSF fellow, 1979, NIH fellow, 1980; grantee NIH, 1982—, Mich. Heart Assn., 1983—. Mem. Biophys. Soc., Soc. Gen. Physiologists. Home: 4353 Tacoma Circle Okemos MI 48864 Office: Mich State U Dept Pharmacology and Toxicology East Lansing MI 48864

HUME, ROBERT DOUGLAS, microbiologist; b. Ann Arbor, Mich., Sept. 16, 1952; s. Robert Lee and Marbeth Joy (Hansel) H. B.S. in Microbiology, Ohio State U., 1974; M.S. in Microbiology, U. Dayton, 1978; Ph.D. in Microbiology, Bowling Green State U., 1983. Cert. profl. microbiologist. Bacteriologist, Ohio State U. Hosps., Columbus, Ohio, 1974-75; virologist Ohio Dept. Health, Columbus, 1978-79; research assoc. Med. Coll. Ohio, Toledo, 1980-81; instr. Bowling Green State U., Ohio, 1981; research assoc. N.Am. Sci. Assocs., Northwood, Ohio, 1981-84, mgr. microbiology, 1984—. Contbr. articles to profl. jours. Med. Coll. Ohio research grantee, 1980-81; grad. research fellow U. Dayton, 1976. Mem. Am. Soc. Microbiology. Avocations: photography, weightlifting, scuba diving. Home: 750 9th St Apt C Bowling Green OH 43402 Office: NAm Sci Assocs 2261 Tracy Rd Northwood OH 43619

HUMITA, TIBERIUS TED, educator; b. Clui, Romania, Dec. 20, 1913; s. Teodor and Teodosia (Abrudan) H.; student U. Bucharest (Romania), 1937-39, U. Rome (Italy), 1946-50; B.A., Wayne State U., 1958, M.A. in Polit. Sci., Tchrs. Coll., 1960, secondary teaching certificate, 1961; m. Sophie Kisch, Sept. 20, 1954. Came to U.S., 1951, naturalized, 1956. Sec., v.p. Romanian Polit. Refugee Welfare Com., Rome, Italy, 1948-50; worker, timekeeper, payroll clk. Chrysler Corp., Highland Park, Mich., 1951-60; tchr. fgn. langs. Detroit Pub. Schs., 1961—. Corr., Romanian News America, Cleve., 1964—. Romanian cons. Greater Detroit Ethnic Group Project, 1968—. Candidate, Mich. Constl. Conv., 1961; chmn. Romanian sect. nationalites div. Mich. Democratic Com., 1960—, v.p., 1965-66, treas., 1968—. Contbg. mem. Iulia Maniu Found., N.Y., 1965—. Served to 1st lt. Romanian Army, 1939-40; polit. prisoner, Buchenwald, Germany, 1942-44. Recipient Service award Nationalites div. Mich. Dem. Com., 1967; M. Banciu award Romanian of Year, 1978; Aron Cotrus award, 1979; Fonds European Secour Etud. Etranger, Switzerland scholar, 1949-50; Nat. Def. Edn. Act grantee N.Y. State U., 1963; Fed. grantee, P.R., 1966. Mem. Internat., Am. polit. sci. assns., Am. Fedn. Tchrs., Am. Acad. Polit. and Social Sci., Mich. Fgn. Lang. Assn., Am. Council Fgn. Lang. Tchrs. Editor Bull. Romanian Am. Nat. Com., Detroit, 1958-63; dir. sci. book exhibit Internat. Congress Dialectology. Louvain, Belgium, 1960. Home: 16424 Lincoln St East Detroit MI 48021

HUMKE, RAMON, telecommunication company executive. Pres., dir. Indiana Bell Telephone Co., Indpls. Office: Indiana Bell Telephone Co 240 N Meridian St Indianapolis IN 46204*

HUMLICEK, BERNIE LOUIS, data processing manager; b. David City, Nebr., Apr. 14, 1957; s. Bernard Anton and Marcella (Slavik) H.; m. Denise M. Doerneman, June 19, 1982. A.A.S., Southeast Community Coll., 1976-77. Programmer trainee Union Ins. Co., Lincoln, Nebr., 1977-78, programmer analyst, 1978-79, programming mgr., 1979-82, mgr. data processing, 1982—. Mem., Nat. Taxpayers Union, Washington, 1984. Mem. Data Processing Mgmt. Assn., Assn. Systems Mgmt., Internat. Soc. Wang Users, Omaha Area VS Users Group. Democrat. Roman Catholic. Avocations: Walking, reading, bicycling. Office: Union Ins Co 14th and Q St Lincoln NE 68501

HUMPHREY, DORIS DAVENPORT, business educator; b. Woodbury, Tenn., June 3, 1943; d. Luther and Gladys (Alexander) Davenport; m. John Sparkman Humphrey, Sept. 15, 1941; children—Heather, Holly. B.S., Middle Tenn. State U., 1965; M.B.E., Ga. State U., 1972, Ed.S., 1977; Ph.D., Ga. State U., 1983. Sec., coordinator creative services, asst. to pres. Noble-Dury & Assocs., Nashville, 1965-69; asst. account exec. McCann-Erickson & Assocs., Atlanta, 1969-70; adj. and full-time instr. DeKalb Community Coll., 1970-79; coordinator internship program Raymond Walters Coll., U. Cin., 1980-83, chmn. dept. office adminstrn., 1981—; lectr. in field; curriculum cons. Mem. Nat. Bus. Edn. Assn., North Central Bus. Edn. Assn., S.W. Ohio Word Processing Assn., Delta Pi Epsilon. Methodist. Author: Northside Medical Center, P.C.—The Medical Secretary, 1980; The Contemporary Medical Office-A Reference Manual, 1986. Office: 955 Plainfield Rd Cincinnati OH 45236

HUMPHREY, HUBERT HORATIO, III, attorney general of Minnesota; b. Mpls., June 26, 1942; s. Hubert Horatio and Muriel F. (Buck) H.; B.A., Am. U., 1965; J.D., U. Minn., 1969; m. Nancy Lee Jeffrey, 1963; children—Florence Christine, Pamela Katherine, Hubert Horatio IV. Admitted to Minn. bar, practiced law; mem. Minn. Senate, 1973-83; atty. gen. State of Minn., 1983—. Del. state conv. Democratic-Farmer-Labor party, 1970, nat. conv., 1980, 84. Mem. Am., Minn. bar assns. Club: Optimists. Office: Room 102 Capitol Bldg Aurora Ave Saint Paul MN 55155

HUMPHREYS, JAMES BURNHAM, hospital administrator; b. Fulton, Mo., July 25, 1943; s. James Carroll and Mary Thelma (Burnham) H.; m. Emily Elaine Earl, Oct. 2, 1971; children—Erica, James Burnham II. B.A., Westminster Coll., 1963; M.S., Trinity U., San Antonio, 1969. Adminstrv. resident Meml. Hosp., Lufkin, Tex., 1967-68, asst. adminstr., 1968-69; with St. Lukes Hosps., St. Louis, 1969—, assoc. adminstr., 1974-78, v.p. ops., 1978-84, v.p. adminstrn., 1984—; mem. adj. faculty Washington U., 1976—. Served to 1st lt. AUS, 1964-66 Fellow Am. Coll. Hosp. Adminstrs.; mem. Am. Mgmt. Assn., Am. Hosp. Assn., Hosp. Assn. Met. St. Louis. Democrat. Presbyterian. Home: 507 Bambury Way Kirkwood MO 63122 Office: 232 S Woods Mill Rd Saint Louis MO 63017

HUMPHRIES, BEVERLY NELL (MRS. DONALD R. HUMPHRIES), librarian; b. Gatesville, Tex., July 3, 1930; d. E.B. and Nora H. (Nelson) Harris; A.A., Clifton Jr. Coll., 1946-48; B.S., N. Tex. State U., 1950; M.S., So. Ill. U., 1971; m. Donald R. Humphries, May 27, 1951; children—Brett, Joel. Elem. tchr. Balmorhea (Tex.) Pub. Schs., 1948-49; res. librarian Tex. Technol. U., Lubbock, 1950-51; elem. tchr. Fairbanks (Alaska) Sch. Dist., 1952-54; serials and documents librarian Tex. A. and M. U., College Station, 1954-57; periodicals librarian Davenport (Iowa) Pub. Library, 1957-59; librarian Monticello Coll., Godfrey, Ill., 1965-71, Lewis and Clark Community Coll., Godfrey, 1971—. Bd. dirs. Greater Alton Concert Assn., 1968-80. Mem. Am., Ill. library assns. Club: Zonta. Home: Godfrey IL 62035 Office: Lewis and Clark Community College Godfrey IL 62035

HUNDER, GENE GERALD, physician; b. Lake City, Minn., Feb. 7, 1932; s. Tilman James and Melita Henrietta (Bremer) H.; m. Janet Gretchen Hunt, July 26, 1956; children—Heidi, Jennifer, Gregory, Grant, Naomi, Stephanie. Student, St. Olaf Coll., 1950-52; B.A., U. Minn.-Mpls., 1954, M.D., 1958, M.S., 1963. Diplomate Am. Bd. Internal Medicine. Intern, Strong Meml. Hosp., Rochester, N.Y., 1958-59, resident, 1959-61; resident Mayo Clinic, Rochester, Minn., 1961-64; instr. internal medicine Mayo Grad. Sch., Rochester, Minn., 1966-67, asst. prof. internal medicine, 1968-73, assoc. prof., 1973-78, prof., 1978—, full mem. internal medicine, 1981—, cons. internal medicine and rheumatology, prof. internal medicine Mayo Clinic, Mayo Found., 1978—, head sect. rheumatology Mayo Clinic, 1976-81, chmn. rheumatology research com., 1976-81, chmn. clin. investigator tng. program Mayo Grad. Sch., 1981-84. Co-author: Physical Examination of the Joints, 1978; Editor: Rheumatology, 1978; Assoc. editor: Jour. Lab. and Clin. Medicine, 1979-81. Mem. editorial bd. Jour. Arthritis and Rheumatism, 1973-83, Jour. Rheumatology, 1982—, Jour. Musculoskeletal Medicine, 1983—. Contbr. numerous sci. articles to med. jours. Mem. ho. dels. Arthritis Found., Atlanta, 1980-83, trustee, 1985—; mem. exec. com. Minn. Arthritis Found., Mpls., 1984—. Philip Showalter Hench lectr. Ariz. Med. Soc., Phoenix, 1965; Charles W. Thomas lectr. Med. Coll. Va., Charlottesville, 1979; Carl Pearson lectr. Los Angeles County Med. Assn., 1983. Nu Sigma Nu scholar, 1955; Minn. Med. Found. acad. scholar, 1955; Fellow ACP (pres. Minn. chpt. 1985—); mem. AMA, Am. Assn. Immunologists, Am. Fedn. Clin. Research, AAAS, Cen. Clin. Research Club, Cen. Soc. Clin. Research (mem. program com.), Am. Soc. Clin. Rheumatology (pres.), Am. Rheumatism Assn. (mem. exec. com. 1976—), Phi Beta Kappa, Alpha Omega Alpha. Republican. Lutheran. Home: 1305 Folwell Dr SW Rochester MN 55902 Office: Mayo Clinic 200 1st St SW Rochester MN 55905

HUNGER, J. DAVID, business educator; b. New Kensington, Pa., May 17, 1941; s. Jackson Steele and Elizabeth (Carey) H.; m. Betty Johnson, Aug. 2, 1969; children—Karen, Susan, Laura, Merry. B.A. Bowling Green (Ohio) State U., 1963; M.B.A., Ohio State U., 1966, Ph.D., 1973. Selling supr. Lazarus Dept. Store, Columbus, Ohio, 1965-66; brand asst. Procter and Gamble Co., Cin., 1968-69; asst. dir. grad. bus. programs Ohio State U., Columbus, 1970-72; instr. Baldwin-Wallace Coll., Berea, Ohio, 1972-73; prof. U. Va., Charlottesville, 1973-82; mgmt. area coordinator Sch. Bus., Iowa State U., Ames, 1983-84; assoc. prof. Coll. Bus. 1983—; cons. to bus., fed. and state agys. Served to capt. Mil. Intelligence, U.S. Army, 1966-68. Decorated Bronze Star. Mem. Acad. Mgmt., Case Research Assn., Midwest Case Writers, Strategic Mgmt. Soc. Author: Strategic Management and Business Policy (with T.L. Wheelen), 1983, An Assessment of Undergraduate Business Education in the U.S., 1980, Strategic Management, 1984; contbr. articles to pubs. Home: 1620 Buchanan Dr Ames IA 50010 Office: 300 Carver Hall Iowa State U Ames IA 50011

HUNT, DENNIS DWANE, college administrator; b. July 8, 1948; s. Dwane D. and Pauline C. (Arnett) H.; m. Linda Sue Hemmerick, Dec. 28, 1968; children—Jessica, Nathaniel, Nicholas, Joseph. B.A., Ohio No. U., 1970; M.A., Miami U., Oxford, Ohio, 1972. Dir. corp. and found. relations Ohio No. U., Ada, 1977-79; asst. v.p. devel. Nebr. Wesleyan U., Lincoln, 1979-84; v.p. devel. and coll. relations Simpson Coll., Indianola, Iowa, 1984—. Mem. Council for Advancement and Support Edn. Avocations: golf; antique collecting. Home: 1300 N C St Indianola IA 50125 Office: Simpson Coll Office Devel and Coll Relations 701 N C St Indianola IA 50125

HUNT, GRACE MENDENHALL, artist; b. Cin., Oct. 21, 1915; d. Graham Putnam and Frances Carisle (Mendenhall) H. B.A., Vassar Coll., 1937; student Cin. Art Acad., 1938-40. Portrait painter; one-woman shows include: Woman's Exchange, 1954, Univ. Club, 1962; portraits exhibited in Mich., Ind., N.J., Conn., Okla., Ky. and Washington. Mem. Cin. Woman's Art Club (past treas.), Profl. Artists Cin. (past treas.), Woman's Art Club Cin. Coll. Art. Republican. Roman Catholic. Home and Office: 164 Glenmary Ave Cincinnati OH 45220

HUNT, JAMES ROBERT, librarian; b. West Brownsville, Pa., May 5, 1925; s. James Clarence and Jesse (Sharp) H.; Ph.B., U. Detroit, 1951, M.A. in Polit. Sci., 1955; M.A. in L.S., U. Mich., 1959; m. Gloria Solli, June 26, 1954; children—Christopher James, Màrya Madeline, Megan Maura, Shelagh Maureen, Matthew Becket, Deirdre Mór. Co-mgr. Madonna Book Shop, Detroit, 1951-56; bookmobile librarian Wayne County (Mich.) Library, 1956-57, adminstrv. asst. to librarian, 1958-60, head central services, 1960-62; asst. state librarian Mich. State Library, Lansing, 1962-64; state librarian, asst. supt. library services Hawaii Dept. Edn., Honolulu, 1964-70, acting dep. supt. edn., 1970-71, state librarian, 1971; dir. Pub. Library Cin. and Hamilton County (Ohio), 1971—. Mem. library tech. com. Lansing Community Coll.; chmn. Hawaii Gov's. Com. State Library Resources, 1964; adv. com. U. Hawaii Grad. Library Sch., 1962—; mem. Gov.'s Com. on Hawaiian Textbook Materials, 1971; mem. adv. com. Continuation of Library Planning and Evaluation Inst., Ohio State U., 1972-73; mem. State Bd. Library Examiners, 1971. Mem. ALA (life mem.; v.p. Assn. State Library Agys. 1971-72, pres. 1972-73), Mich. Library Assn. (chmn. library adminstrn. sect. 1961-62), Hawaii Library Assn. (ALA rep. 1964-68), Ohio Library Assn. (life mem.), Hawaiian Hist. Soc. (dir.), Friends of Library, Cin. Hist. Soc. (mem. bd. 1972), Mcdowell Soc., Am. Soc. Pub. Adminstrn. (sec. Honolulu chpt. 1966—). Contbr. articles to profl. publs. Office: 800 Vine St Cincinnati OH 45202

HUNT, JOHN ROBERT, mathematics educator; b. Highland Park, Ill., June 25, 1945; s. Cloyce Lynn and Eugenia MaryLouise (Flori) H.; m. Lynn Arleen Wescott, Jan. 27, 1968; children—William, Susan. B.S., U. Ill., Urbana, 1967, M.S., 1968; D.Arts, U. No. Colo., 1980. Mem. faculty Wis. State U.-Platteville, 1968-70; mem. faculty U. Wis.-Stout, Menomonie, Wis., 1970—, assoc. prof. math., chmn. dept. math., 1980—. Cons. Pubs. Rev., 1983—. Curriculum Devel. grantee U. Wis.-Stout, 1983; U. Wis. System faculty devel. grantee, 1985. Mem. Math. Assn. Am. (dept. rep. 1981—). Home: 1414 River Heights Rd Menomonie WI 54751 Office: U Wis-Stout SW125 Jarvis Hall Menomonie WI 54751

HUNT, LAMAR, professional football team executive; b. 1933; grad. So. Meth. U.; m. Norma Hunt; children—Lamar, Sharon, Clark. Founder, pres. Kansas City Cheifs of Nat. Football League, 1959—; founder, pres. Am. Football League, 1959 (became Am. Football Conf. Nat. Football League 1970), pres. Am. Football Conf., 1970; pres. Kansas City Chiefs to 1977, chmn., 1977—; dir. Great Midwest Corp., Interstate Securities, Traders' Nat. Bank. Bd. dirs. Profl. Football Hall of Fame, Canton Ohio. Named Salesman of Year, Kansas City Advt. and Sales Execs Club, 1963, Southwesterner of Year, Tex. Sportswriters Assn., 1969. Address: care Kansas City Chiefs One Arrowhead Dr Kansas City MO 64129*

HUNT, MARK ALAN, museum executive; b. Topeka, Kans., May 21, 1949; s. Ira B. and Marjorie May (McConnell) H.; B.A. (Wiseman scholar, Washburn scholar), Washburn U., 1971; M.A., Cooperstown Grad. Programs, 1982; m. Cynthia E. Rush, Feb. 21, 1976; children—Alexander Rush, Alice Claire. Cert. Mus. Mgmt. Inst., 1983. Nat. Endowment for Humanities intern Am. Assn. State Local History, 1974-75; mus. dir. Plymouth (Mich.) Hist. Mus., 1976; curator exhibits Kans. State Hist. Soc., Topeka, 1976, asst. mus. dir., 1976-79, dir. State Hist. Mus., 1979—; cons. Menninger Found., 1980; faculty mem. summer inst. Pub. History Program, U. Calif., Santa Barbara, 1980. Recipient God and Country award, Boy Scouts Am., 1962, Eagle award, 1963; Clark fellow, 1973-74; recipient membership award Am. Assn. for State and Local History, 1977. Mem. Am. Assn. for State and Local History (nat. edn. com. 1981-84, state membership chmn. 1976-85), Mt. Plains Mus. Assn. (dir., Kans. rep. 1977), Kans. Mus. Assn. (pres. 1978-80), Am. Assn. Mus., Kans. State Hist. Soc., Kappa Sigma. Republican. Methodist. Contbr. articles to profl. jours. Office: 6425 SW 6th St Topeka KS 66615

HUNT, MARK EARL, publishing company executive; b. Detroit, Feb. 1, 1951; s. Keith Lynn and Gladys Mae (Schriemer) H.; m. Marian Eileen Bier, May 8, 1976; children—Jedediah, Austin. B.A., Mich. State U., 1974; M.Div., Trinity Evang. Div. Sch., Deerfield, Ill., 1978. Editor, Inter Varsity Press, Downers Grove, Ill., 1975-78; pastoral assoc. Huron Hills Baptist Ch., Ann Arbor, Mich., 1979; asst. dir. Cedar Campus, Cedarville, Mich., 1979-81; acad. book mktg. mgr. Zondervan, Grand Rapids, Mich., 1981-82, asst. mng. editor acad. books, 1982-83, database pub. mgr., 1983—. Editor: Hymns II, 1976; Carols, 1978. Mem. Assn. Systems Mgmt. Episcopalian. Avocations: sailing, ornithology. Office: Zondervan Corp 1415 Lake Dr SE Grand Rapids MI 49506

HUNT, ROBERT STEPHEN, transportation executive; b. St. Petersburg, Fla., June 8, 1948; s. John Kenneth and Georgia (Davis) H.; m. Ann Lee Francis, May 29, 1976; 1 child, Stephen Andrew. Student U. Ill., 1966-67, Parkland Jr. Coll., 1970-72. Ops. mgr. Stahly Truck City, Champaign, Ill., 1970-78; pres. RH Ford Trucks, Urbana, Ill., 1978-79; corp. fleet maintenance mgr. Super Valu Stores, Inc., Mpls., 1979—; bd. dirs. Nat. Automotive Inst. Service Excellence, Washington, 1984—. Contbr. articles on fleet mgmt. to profl. jours. Served with U.S. Army, 1967-69, Vietnam. Decorated Silver Star, Purple Heart with 2 clusters. Mem. Soc. Automotive Engrs., The Maintenance Council (vice chmn. 1981—), Pvt. Truck Council (com. mem. 1982—). Republican. Methodist. Club: Mpls. Computer Group. Lodge: VFW. Avocation: golf. Home: 6333 Markwood Dr Crystal MN 55427 Office: Super Valu Stores Inc PO Box 990 Minneapolis MN 55440

HUNT, ROBERT WAYNE, manufacturing company executive; b. Tipton County, Ind., May 28, 1940; s. Wayne G. Hunt and Janet Marie (Harris) Messick; m. Sandra Jean Kuhlman, June 22, 1963; children—Rhonda Jean, Jeffrey Robert. B.S. in Bus. Adminstrn., U. Evansville, 1963. Sr. mktg. exec. Ford Motor Co., Phila., 1965-71; dir. adminstrn., personnel W.E. Walker Co., Jackson, Miss., 1971-73; plant mgr. Northwest Industries, Jackson, 1973-80; asst. v.p. mfg., UNR-Leavitt Co., Chgo., 1980-81, v.p. mfg., 1981-82, v.p. ops., 1982—; chmn. energy Miss. Mfrs. Assn., Jackson, 1979-80. Dist. commr., Boy Scouts Am., Canton, Ohio, 1969. Recipient Outstanding Leadership award Internat. Brotherhood Elec. Workers, Jackson, 1980. Mem. Am. Mgmt. Assn. Republican. Methodist. Home: 1831 Wingate Ln Wheaton IL 60187 Office: UNR Leavitt 1717 W 115th St Chicago IL 60643

HUNT, ROGER SCHERMERHORN, hospital administrator; b. White Plaines, N.Y., Mar. 7, 1943; s. Charles Howland and Mildred Russell (Schermerhorn) H.; B.A., DePauw U., 1965; M.B.A., George Washington U., 1968; m. Mary Adams Libby, June 19, 1965; children—Christina, David. Adminstrv. resident Lankenau Hosp., Phila., 1966-68; asst. adminstr. Hahnemann Med. Coll. and Hosp., Phila., 1968-71, hosp. dir., 1971-74, assoc. v.p., hosp. adminstr., 1974-77; dir. Ind. U. Hosps., Indpls., 1977-84; pres. Luth. Gen. Hosp., Park Ridge, Ill., 1984—; pres. United Hosp. Services, Inc., 1979-81, dir., 1977-84; chmn. Alliance of Indpls. Hosps., 1981, dir., 1979-84; bd. trustees, sec.-treas. Delaware Valley Hosp. Laundry, 1969-77; bd. trustees Nat. Benefit Fund of Nat. Union Hosp. and Health Care Employees, 1973-77, Phila. Blood Center, 1972-74; assoc. prof. hosp. adminstrn. Ind. U. Sch. Medicine, 1977-84. Vice chmn. Pa. Emergency Health Services Council, 1975-77; pres. Chester County Emergency Med. Service Council, 1971-77; v.p. Wayne Area Jr. C. of C., 1969-70, pres., 1970-71, state dir., 1971-72. Fellow Inst. Medicine of Chgo., Am. Coll. Hosp. Adminstrs. (Postgrad. tng. award 1968, regent for Ind. 1984): mem. Am. Hosp. Assn., Ill. Hosp. Assn., Chgo. Hosp. Council. Office: Lutheran Gen Hosp 1775 Dempster St Park Ridge IL 60068

HUNTER, ANN GAIL, librarian; b. Milw., Nov. 8, 1949; d. Elmer Lester Herbert and Elizabeth Renatta (Bovee) Zaeske. B.A., U. Wis.-Madison, 1971, M.A., 1972. Asst. librarian U. Wis.-Wausau, 1972-73; cataloger, librarian MacMurray Coll., Jacksonville, Ill., 1973-76; corp. librarian Anheuser-Busch Co., Inc., St. Louis, 1976—; facilitator Anheuser-Busch Quality Circle, St. Louis, 1984—. Mem. Spl. Libraries Assn. (network liaison 1981-83, chmn. employment com., 1983-84, chmn. hospitality com. 1984-85), St. Louis Regular Library Network, AAUW (editor jour. 1981-84, scholar 1984). Avocation: stamp collecting. Office: Anheuser-Busch Co Inc One Busch Pl Saint Louis MO 63118

HUNTER, CHRISTOPHER B., lawyer; b. Jacksonville, Ill., Jan. 28, 1953; s. James G. and Mary Ann (Grubb) H.; m. Ann G. Zaeske, May 21, 1977 (div.). B.A., MacMurray Coll., 1975; J.D., St. Louis U., 1978. Bars: Ill. 1978, U.S. Dist. Ct. (so. dist.) Ill. 1979, Mo. 1979, U.S. Dist. Ct. (ea. dist.) 1979, U.S. Ct. Appeals (7th cir.) 1980, U.S. Ct. Appeals (8th cir.) 1980, U.S. Tax Ct. 1985. Atty., Land of Lincoln Legal Assistance, Alton, Ill., 1977-81; assoc. Farrell & Long, P.C., Godfrey Ill., 1981—. Mem. Saukee Area council Boy Scouts Am. Recipient Order of Arrow, Boy Scouts Am., 1967. Mem. ABA, Ill. Bar Assn., Am. Trial Lawyers Assn., Alton-Wood River Bar Assn. (sec. 1981-82), Phi Alpha Delta (local treas. 1981—). Republican. Roman Catholic. Home: 11051 Mollerus Dr Saint Louis MO 63138 Office: Farrell & Long PC 1310 W Delmar St Godfrey IL 62035

HUNTER, DONALD H., state justice; b. Anderson, Ind., Oct. 21, 1911; LL.B., Lincoln Law Sch., 1937. Admitted to Ind. bar, 1941; practice law, LaGrange, Ind., 1946-48; dep. hearing examiner Ind. Public Service Commn.; judge LaGrange Circuit Ct., 1948-62; judge Ind., Appellate Ct. 1963-66, then chief justice ct.; acting presiding judge Ct. of Appeals, 2nd Dist., Ind., acting chief justice of Ct.; justice Ind. Supreme Ct., 1967—, now sr. justice; mem. Ind. Jud. Council on Legal Edn. and Competence at the Bar, 1976—; chmn. Lake County Jud. Nominating Commn., 1973-76; jud. mem. Com. for Revision of Adoption Laws, Adv. Com. on Probation and Parole for Ind. Citizens Council; vol. instr. Ind. State Police Acad., Bloomington, 1972-74; guest lectr. various civic orgns. and legal assns.; mem. Constl. Revision Commn., 1967-71; chmn. com. creating disciplinary commn. financed by attys., 1970-71. Mem. Ind. Ho. of Reps., 1943-44. Served with inf., U.S. Army, 1943-46; ETO. Decorated Bronze Star, Purple Heart; Belgique Fouragere; named a Sagamore of the Wabash, 1976. Mem. Ind. State Bar Assn., Madison County Bar Assn., Ind. Council of Freedoms Found. (mem. Distinguished awards jury 1967-68, 70-72), VFW, Am. Legion, Ind. Sheriffs Assn. (hon. life), Phi Delta Phi (hon. mem.), Phi Alpha Delta (hon. mem.), Tau Kappa Epsilon. Methodist. Club: Masons. Home: 1719 Costello Dr Anderson IN 46011 Office: Supreme Ct Room 304 State House Indianapolis IN 46204

HUNTER, DOUGLAS LEE, elevator company executive; b. Greeley, Colo., May 3, 1948; s. Delmer Eural and Helen Converse (Haines) H.; m. Janet Lee Snook, May 26, 1970; children—Darin Douglas, Joel Christopher, Eric Andrew, Jennifer Lee. Student Phillips U., Enid, Okla., 1966-70; B.A. cum laude, Sioux Falls Coll., 1979; postgrad. N.Am. Bapt. Sem., Sioux Falls, 1977-79. Elevator constructor Carter Elevator Co., Inc., Sioux Falls, S.D., 1971-72, rep., 1972-74, controller, 1974-78, sec.-treas., 1978-82, v.p., 1982—; ptnr. Lifters Ltd., Sioux Falls, S.D., 1984—. Creator, editor: Body Building Manual for the Christian Church in the Upper Midwest, 1983. Mem. gen. bd. Christian Ch. (Disciples of Christ), Indpls., 1984-88; mem. regional bd. Christian Ch. in the Upper Midwest, Des Moines, 1985—; bd. dirs. Glory House, Sioux Falls, 1983—; teaching leader Bible Study Fellowship, Sioux Falls, 1981—. Named Outstanding Young Religious Leader, Jaycees, Sioux Falls, 1974. Mem. Nat. Assn. Elevator Contractors, Constrn. Specifications Inst., Christian Businessmen's Com. U.S.A. Republican. Club: Rotary. Avocations: golf; tennis; reading; music. Home: 1605 Shafer Dr Sioux Falls SD 57103 Office: Carter Elevator Co Inc 2504 S Duluth Ave Sioux Falls SD 57105

HUNTER, EARLE LESLIE, III, association executive; b. Juneau, Alaska, Nov. 23, 1929; s. Earle and Mary Uinta (Kirk) H.; m. Helen Doreen Dawson, Jan. 19, 1954; children—Barbara, James, Robert. B.S., Ill. Coll. Optometry, Chgo., 1956, O.D., 1957. Practice optometry, Juneau, 1957-59, McMinnville, Oreg., 1959-71; dir. clinics Pacific U., Forest Grove, Oreg., 1971-74; dir. primary care Am. Optometric Assn., St. Louis, 1974-78, asst. exec. dir., 1978-84, interim exec. dir., 1984—; mem. Z.80 com. Am. Nat. Standards Inst., 1974—. Contbr. articles to profl. jours. County chmn. various gubernatorial campaigns; vice chmn. Oreg. Health Commn., 1971-74. Served as cpl. U.S. Army, 1951-54. Named Optometrist of Yr., Oreg. Optometric Assn., 1971, Jr. Citizen of Yr., Jaycees, McMinnville, Oreg., 1961. Fellow Am. Acad. Optometry, Am. Pub. Health Assn.; mem. Optical Soc. Am., St. Louis Soc. Assn. Execs. (pres. 1983-84), Am. Soc. Assn. Execs. (com. 1981-84), Tomb and Key, Beta Sigma Kappa. Republican. Episcopalian. Clubs: University (St. Louis), Michelbook Country (McMinnville, Oreg.). Lodges: Masons, Elks. Avocation: sailing. Home: 213 Orchard St Webster Groves MO 63119 Office: Am Optometric Assn 243 N Lindbergh Blvd Saint Louis MO 63141

HUNTER, HARLEN CHARLES, orthopedic surgeon; b. Estherville, Iowa, Sept. 23, 1940; s. Roy Harold and Helen Iola (King) H.; m. JoAnn Wilson, June 30, 1962; children—Harlen Todd, Juliann Kristin. B.A., Drake U., 1962; D.O., Coll. Osteo. Medicine and Surgery, Des Moines, 1967. Diplomate Am. Osteo. Bd. Orthopedic Surgery. Intern Normandy Osteo. Hosp., St. Louis, 1967-68, resident in orthopedics, 1968-72, chmn. dept. orthopedics, 1976-77; founder, orthopedic surgeon Mid-States Orthopedic Sports Medicine Clinics of Am., Ltd. (St. Louis Orthopedic Sports Medicine Clinic and Iowa Orthopedic Sports Medicine Clinic, Urbandale), 1977—; mem. staff Normandy Osteo. Hosp., St. Louis, St. Peters Community Hosp. (Mo.), Des Moines Gen. Osteo. Hosp.; orthopedic cons., team physician to high schs.; mem. med. adv. bd. Mo. Athletic Activities Assn.; cons. sports medicine Sports St. Louis newspaper; founder Ann. Sports Medicine Clinic for Trainers and Coaches; lectr. various social, profl. orgns.; adj. clin. assoc. prof. Coll. Osteo. Surgery, Des Moines; orthopedic surgeon Iowa State Boys Basketball Tournament, 1966-85. Contbr. articles to profl. publs. Recipient Clinic Speaker award Iowa High Sch. Baseball Coaches Assn., 1982, 83. Fellow Am. Coll. Osteo. Surgeons, Am. Osteo. Acad. Orthopedics (past chmn. com. on athletic injuries); mem. Am. Osteo. Assn., Mo. Assn. Osteo. Physicians and Surgeons, Am. Coll. Sports Medicine, Am. Orthopedic Soc. Sports Medicine (del. sports medicine exchange program to China 1985), AMA, St. Louis Met. Med. Assn. Republican. Methodist. Lodges: Masons (Des Moines); Shriners. Home: 1230 Walnut Hill Farm Chesterfield MO 63017 Office: Saint Louis Orthopedic Sports Medicine Clinic 14377 Woodlake Chesterfield MO 63017 also Iowa Orthopedic Sports Medicine Clinic 2330 NW 106th St Suite 311 Urbandale IA 50322

HUNTER, JAMES EUGENE, optometrist, educator; b. Ft. Wayne, Ind., Oct. 17, 1950; s. Sherwood Eugene and Faye (Elliott) H.; m. Linda Kay Yager, Aug. 26, 1972; children—Barton, Curtis, Nicholas. Student U. Ill., 1969-71; B.A., Ind. U., 1972, O.D., 1976. Clinic dir. Ind. U. Eye. Clinic, Indpls., 1976—; gen. practice optometry, Indpls. and Franklin, Ind., 1977—; cons. med. staff Citizens Ambulatory Health Ctr., Indpls., 1981—; continuing med. edn. lectr. and in-service trainer for Am. Optometric Assn., Ind. Optometric Assn., Am. Acad. Optometry, Ind. U., Indpls., 1976—. Author ednl. video tapes on eye care Ophthalmic Video Edn., 1984. Contbr. articles to profl. jours. Fellow Am. Acad. Optometry; mem. Am. Optometric Assn., Ind. Optometric Assn. (pres's. citation, 1983). Lodge: Rotary. Office: 950 N Illinois St Indianapolis IN 46204

HUNTER, JOSEPH EDWARD, musician, consultant; b. Jackson, Tenn., Nov. 19, 1927; s. John G. and Vada Idona (Dreke) H.; m. Mable Daisy Miller, June 15, 1957 (div.); children—Joseph Jr., Michelle Dana. Student Lane Coll., U. Detroit, Detroit Inst. Tech. Profl. pianist, 1956-59; pianist, arranger, band leader Motown Record Corp., Detroit, 1959-61; band leader with Jackie Wilson, 1961; musical dir. Pied Piper records, 1967-68; musical dir. cons. Brohun Pub., 1968—; cons. various chs., rec. artists and firms. Served with USAF, 1946-49. Recipient awards Black Music Found., Upper Room, Mother Waddles' Perpetual Mission. Mem. Nat. Com. for Rec. Arts, Detroit Fedn. Musicians. Lodge: Masons. Composer numerous published songs. Office: 19935 Orleans Detroit MI 48203

HUNTER, LANE WILLIAM, sales executive; b. Chgo., June 23, 1952; s. Robert William and Mattie Lee (Thomas) H.; student Elmhurst Coll., 1971-72, Trinity Christian Coll., 1972-73; grad. in history Moraine Valley Coll., 1973-74; children—Jason Erik, Michelle Noel. With Stone Container Corp., Chgo., 1971—, asst. sales service mgr., 1976, sales rep., 1976-79, field sales mgr., 1979-80, gen. sales mgr., 1980—. Mem. Clay County Devel. Com. Nat. Merit scholar, 1970-73; Ill. State scholar, 1970-73. Mem. Am. Mgmt. Assn., Internat. Platform Assn., Liberty Hills Assn. Clubs: Chgo. Health, K.C. Home: Route 5 Box 36H Liberty MO 64068 Office: 933 S Kent Liberty MO 64068

HUNTER, ROBERT TYLER, investment management company executive; b. Peoria, Ill., Jan. 14, 1943; s. Thomas Oakford and Joan (Sargent) H.; m. Mary Michelle Tyrrell, June 12, 1965. A.B., Harvard U., 1965. Pres. First Union Trust Co., Kansas City, Mo., 1973-81; sr. v.p., trust div. mgr. Centerre Bank, Kansas City, 1981-84; v.p., mgr. client services and mktg. DST Systems, Inc., Kansas City, 1984-85; v.p. mktg. Waddell & Read Asset Mgmt. Co., Kansas City, 1985— Treas. M.S. Soc., Mission, Kans.; bd. dirs. Boys and Girls Club, Kansas City; trustee Menorah Hosp. Found., Kansas City; bd. govs. Kansas City Philharmonic Assn.; bd. dirs., com. chmn. Kansas City Youth Symphony. Fellow Fin. Analyst Fedn.; mem. Fin. Analyst Soc. Kansas City, Corp. Fiduciaries Soc. of Kansas City (past pres.), Estate Planning Assn. Republican. Roman Catholic. Clubs: Harvard/Radcliffe (pres. 1983-85); Kansas City Rcquet (Merriam, Kans.). Avocations: tennis; swimming; reading; coaching. Home: 8215 Noland Rd Lenexa KS 66215 Office: Waddell & Reed Asset Mgmt Co 2400 Pershing Rd Kansas City MO 64108

HUNTRESS, BETTY ANN, former music store propr.; b. Poughkeepsie, N.Y., Apr. 29, 1932; d. Emmett Slater and Catherine V. (Kihlmire) Brundage; B.A., Cornell U., 1954; m. Arnold Ray Huntress, June 26, 1954; children—Catherine, Michael, Carol, Alan. Tchr. high sch., Bordentown, N.J., 1954-55; part-time asst. to prof. Delta Coll., Northwood Inst., Midland, Mich., 1958-71; part-time tchr. Midland Pub. Schs., 1968-79; owner, mgr. The Music Stand, Midland, 1979-82. Bd. dirs. Midland Center for Arts, 1978—; v.p. MCFTA (Arts Center), 1980—; mem. charter bd. mgrs. Matrix Midland Ann. Arts and Sci. Festival, 1977-80; cons. Girl Scouts Am., 1964-76; mem. Mich. Internat. Council, 1975-76. named (with husband) Midland Musician of Yr., 1977. Mem. Music Soc. Midland Center for Arts (dir. 1971—, chmn. 1976-79), AAUW (dir. 1962-73, pres. 1971-73, mem. Mich. state div. bd. 1973-75, 1st v.p. Mich. state div. 1983—, outstanding woman as agt. of change award 1977, fellowship grant named in her honor 1976), Midland Symphony League Soc. (2d v.p.), LWV, Community Concert Soc., Kappa Delta Epsilon, Pi Lambda Theta, Alpha Xi Delta. Republican. Presbyterian. Home: 5316 Sunset Dr Midland MI 48640 Office: 6 Ashman Circle Midland MI 48640

HURAND, GARY JAY, franchise executive; b. Flint, Mich., Oct. 26, 1946; s. Arthur and Bess H.; m. Carol Levine, May 17, 1970; children—Joshua, Sara. B.S., Mich. State U., 1969. Dir. ops. and mgmt. Diversified, Inc., Flint, 1969-70, v.p., 1971; v.p. Dawn Donut Systems, Inc., Flint, 1970-71, pres., 1971—; v.p. Flint Motor Inn, 1971—; dir. So. Pride, Burlington, N.C. Mem. Flint C. of C., Mich. State U. Alumnae (life), Sales and Mktg. Execs. Flint, Young Pres. Orgn. Jewish. Home: 2040 Walden Ct Flint MI 48504 Office: G-4300 W Pierson Rd Flint MI 48504

HURL, RODNEY BECK, physician; b. Shelby, Ohio, Feb. 25, 1930; s. Robert Davis and Esther Helen (Beck) H.; B.S., Bethany (W.Va.) Coll., 1951; M.D., Temple U., 1955; m. Judith Rothrock, July 17, 1955; children—Megan, Marcy, Jeffrey. Rotating intern Mt. Carmel Hosp., Columbus, Ohio, 1955-56, resident in family practice, 1959; practice medicine specializing in family practice, Marysville, Ohio, 1959—; pres. R.B. Hurl M.D. Inc., 1970—; mem. staff Meml. Hosp., Marysville, Riverside Meth. Hosp., Columbus; pres., dir. Marysville Rest Homes, Mildon Park Assos. Inc.; dir. Marysville Newspapers Inc., Mid-Ohio Corp. Trustee Bethany (W.Va.) Coll., 1971—, chmn. devel. com., 1974—, also mem., sec. exec. com., mem. nominating com.; mem. Union County Mental Health Bd., 1970-80, pres., 1978-80; pres. Marysville City Parks and Recreation Commn., 1974-78. Served to capt. M.C., USAF, 1956-58. Recipient Outstanding Alumni Service award Bethany Coll., 1978; diplomate Am. Acad. Family Practice. Mem. AMA, Am. Acad. Family Practice, Ohio Med. Assn., Ohio Acad. Family Practice, Central Ohio Acad. Family Practice (dir. 1979-80), Union County Med. Assn. Republican. Lutheran. Club: Masons. Home: 381 Hickory Dr Marysville OH 43040 Office: 211 Stocksdale Dr Marysville OH 43040

HURLEY, JAMES TILDEN, clinical psychologist; b. Charleston, W.Va., Nov. 10, 1947; s. Winfred Lee and Imogene (Hendricks) H. Ed.D. in Counseling Psychology, U. Mo., 1981. Lic. psychologist, Mo.; diplomate Am. Acad. Behavioral Medicine. Psychologist Mo. Vocat. Rehab. Dept., St. Louis, 1973-81; psychologist Spl. Sch. Dist. St. Louis County, 1981-82; clin. dir. Inst. for Motivational Devel., St. Louis, 1982—. Mem. Am. Psychol. Assn., Mo. Psychol. Assn., Soc. St. Louis Psychologists, Am. Acad. Behavioral Medicine, Hon. Order Ky. Cols. Republican. Baptist. Home: 3704 Diamond Head Dr Saint Louis MO 63125 Office: Inst Motivational Devel 950 Francis Pl Suite 206 Clayton MO 63105

HURT, FLOYD ROBERT, corporation official, farmer; b. Belfield, N.D., Jan. 24, 1936; s. Louis James and Gladys Cecile (Owen) H.; m. Muriel Ethel Brown, Jan. 17, 1958; children—Floyd Robert, Linda Kay. Student schs. Belfield, N.D. Roughneck, Rutledge Drilling Co., 1959-62; driller, Noble Drilling Co., 1962-65; roustabout Amerada Corp., 1965-67; lease foreman Amerada-Hess Corp., Belfield, 1967-71, field maintenance supr., 1971-73, area supt., 1973-80, dist. supt., 1980—, asst. producer tng. films. City council mem. South Heart, N.D., police commr., 1978—; elder United Presbyterian Ch., Belfield. Served with USAF, 1955-59. Recipient Safety award Noble Drilling Co., 1965. Lodges: Masons, Shriners, Order Eastern Star (past patron, Elks, Eagles, Royal Arch Masons. (temple comdr.).

HURT, NATHAN HAMPTON, JR., mechanical engineer; b. Clifton, Mo., June 7, 1921; s. Nathan Hampton Sr. and Mary Lillian (Mayo) H.; m. LuCretia Ann Cutler, Feb. 16, 1946 (dec. 1980); children—Steven Eugene, Mark Lindsay; m. Karin Elisabeth Feuerstein, Aug. 30, 1980; stepchildren—Audrey Barbara Swanson, Christine Yvonne Reed, Nikki Alexandra Tuttle. Student in mech. engring. Mont. Sch. Mines, 1944, U. So. Calif., 1944-46; B.S. in Mech. Engring., U. Colo., 1947. Engr. Goodyear Tire and Rubber Co., Akron, Ohio, 1947-52, mgr. chem. plants engring., Brasil and Logan, Ohio, 1956-68; supt. plant engring. Goodyear Atomic Corp., Piketon, Ohio, 1952-56, mgr. plant engring., 1968-72, dep. gen. mgr., 1972-77, gen. mgr., 1977-85, pres., 1985—. Mem. Chief Logan council Boy Scouts Am., 1970-80; bd. dirs. Ross County Med. Ctr., Chillicothe, Ohio, 1974. Mem. Chillicothe C. of C., Waverly C. of C., Jackson C. of C., Portsmouth C. of C., ASME (v.p. 1984), Am. Inst. Chem. Engrs., Am. Soc. Engring. Mgmt., Atomic Indsl. Forum. Lodge: Rotary. Avocations: golf, racquetball, snow skiing. Home: 95 Woodland Dr Waverly OH 45690 Office: Goodyear Atomic Corp PO Box 628 Piketon OH 45661

HURT, WESLEY ROBERT, anthropology educator; b. Albuquerque, Sept. 20, 1917; s. Wesley Rosecrans and Amy (Passmore) H.; m. Mary Catherine Darden, Feb. 30, 1948; children—Stephen Donald, Rosalind, Teresa. B.A., U. N.Mex., 1938, M.A., 1942; Ph.D., U. Mich., 1952. Dir. mus., faculty U. S.D., Vermillion, 1949-63, prof. anthropology, 1949-63; prof. anthropology Ind. U., Bloomington, 1963—, dir. mus., 1963-83. Author: (with William E. Lass) Frontier Photographer, 1956; Sioux Indians, 1973; Sambaquis of Brazil, 1974; El Abra Rockshelters, 1976. NSF archeol. research grantee, Colombia, S.Am., 1959, Brazil, S.Am., 1966, 84. Mem. Soc. Am. Archaeology, Sociedade de Arqueologia Brasileira, Sigma Xi. Avocations: photography, sailing. Home: 120 Concord Rd Bloomington IN 47401 Office: Dept Anthropology Rawles Hall 108 Indiana U Bloomington IN 47405

HURTEAU, WILLIAM JAMES, hospital administrator, consultant; b. Iowa City, Iowa, June 14, 1943; s. William Winfield and Francis (Walling) H.; m. Peggie Jean Craig, May 27, 1980; children—Melissa, William F. B.S. in Bus. Mgmt., Ind. U., 1968; M.H.A., Washington U., 1971. Facility planner Health Planning Council, Omaha, 1971-73; asst. adminstr. Lutheran Med. Ctr., Omaha, 1973-74, Mercy Hosp., Des Moines, 1974-78; assoc. adminstr. Lapeer County Hosp., Mich., 1978-80; adminstr. Mason Dist. Hosp., Havana, Ill., 1980—; cons. small rural hosps., Ill., Ind., 1984, Am. Hosp. Assn., Chgo., 1984. Contbr. articles to profl. jours. Bd. dirs. Methodist Ch., Havana, 1982, Art Council, Havana, 1984. Served with U.S. Army, 1968-73. Mem. Am. Coll. Hosp. Adminstrs., Ill. Hosp. Assn. (various positions 1981—), C. of C. Lodge: Rotary (pres. 1980—). Avocations: collecting toy trains, hunting. Home: 226 N Orange St Havana IL 62644 Office: Mason Dist Hosp 520 E Franklin St PO Box 529 Havana IL 62644

HURTER, ARTHUR PATRICK, JR., economist, educator; b. Chgo., Jan. 29; s. Arthur P. and Lillian T. (Thums) H.; m. Florence Evalyn Kays; children—Patricia Lyn, Arthur Earl. B.S. in Chem. Engring., Northwestern U., M.S. in Chem. Engring., Ph.D. in Econs. Chem. engr. Zonlite Research Lab., Evanston, Ill., 1957-58; assoc. dir. Research Transp. Ctr., Northwestern U., 1963-65, asst. prof. dept. Indsl. Engring. and Mgmt. Scis. Tech. Inst., 1962-66, prof., 1970—, chmn., 1969—, assoc. prof. fin. Grad. Sch. Mgmt., 1969-70, prof., 1970—; cons. U. Chgo., ESCOR, Sears Roebuck & Co., Standard Oil of Ind., Ill.; bd. dirs. Ill. Environ. Health Research Ctr., 1972-77; mem. com. Sci., Tech. Adv., Ill. Inst. Nat. Resources, 1980—. Pres. Council St. Scholastica High Sch., 1972—; elder Granville Ave. Presbyn Ch., 1976—. Resources for the Future grantee, 1964; Office of Naval Research grantee, 1965; Social Sci. Research Council dissertation fellow; NSF grantee. Mem. Am. Econ. Assn., Regional Sci. Assn., Ops. Research Soc. Am., Inst. Mgmt. Scis., Phi Lambda Upsilon, Sigma Xi, Tau Beta Pi. Author: The Economics of Private Truck Transportation, 1965; contbr. articles to profl. jours. Office: 1505 W Norwood Chicago IL 60660

HUSAR, JOHN PAUL, newspaper columnist; b. Chgo., Jan. 29, 1937; s. John Z. and Kathryn (Kanupke) H.; A.A., Dodge City Coll., 1958; B.S. in Journalism, U. Kans., 1962; m. Louise Kay Lewis, Dec. 28, 1963; children—Kathryn, Laura. Reporter, Clovis (N.Mex.) News-Jour., 1960; night wire editor Okinawa Morning Star, 1961; city editor Pasadena (Tex.) Daily Citizen, 1962; bus. editor Topeka Capital-Jour., 1963; regional news editor Wichita (Kans.) Beacon, 1963-65; sports columnist and writer Chgo. Tribune, 1966—. Chmn., Village of Willow Springs (Ill.) Zoning Commn., 1975-77; mem. Ill. Forestry Adv. Com., 1981-82; mem. adv. com. Ill.-Mich. Canal Nat. Heritage Corridor, 1982. Served with U.S. Army, 1960-62. Recipient 1st pl. award in sportswriting Ill. UPI, 1977, Ill. AP, 1984; 1st pl. award in feature writing Bowling mag., 1979; environ. reporting award Chgo. Audubon Soc., 1979; Disting. Alumnus award Dodge City Coll., 1983; 2d pl. award for public service reporting Ill. AP, 1980, 2d pl. award for sports column writing, 1981; spl. writing award Chgo. Tribune, 1980; Jacob A. Riis award Friends of Parks, 1981. Mem. Golf Writers Assn. Am. (dir.), Baseball Writers Assn. Am., Phi Kappa Theta. Office: 435 N Michigan Ave Chicago IL 60611

HUSARIK, ERNEST A., ednl. adminstr.; b. Gary, Ind., July 2, 1941; married, 2 children. B.A. in History, Olivet Nazarene Coll., Kankakee, Ill., 1963; M.S. in Ednl. Adminstrn., No. Ill. U., DeKalb, 1966; Ph.D. in Ednl. Adminstrn. and Curriculum Devel., Ohio State U., Columbus, 1973; m. Elizabeth Ann Bonnette; children—Jennifer, Amy. Supt., Ontario (Ohio) Pub. Schs., 1973-75; supt. Euclid (Ohio) Pub. Schs., 1975—; adj. prof. Grad. Sch., Cleve. State U.; chmn. Cuyahoga Spl. Edn. Service Center, 1978. Sec., trustee Euclid Devel. Corp.; mem. adv. bd. Cleve. Ednl. Devel. Ctr.; mem. donor com. ARC; mem. alumni adv. council Ohio State U. Mem. Euclid Gen. Hosp. Assn., Am., Buckeye (dir.) assns. sch. adminstrs., Nat., Ohio assns. supervision and curriculum devel., Greater Cleve. Sch. Supts. Assn. (past pres.), Mid-Am. Assn. Sch. Supts., Euclid C. of C. (past pres.), Olivet Nazarene Coll. Alumni Assn. (past mem. alumni bd. dirs.), Phi Delta Kappa (past chpt. pres.), Sigma Tau Delta. Club: Kiwanis (pres.) (Euclid). Contbr. articles in field to profl. jours. Home: 25600 Breckenridge Dr Euclid OH 44117 Office: 651 E 222 St Euclid OH 44123

HUSBAND, RICHARD LORIN, SR., business executive; b. Spencer, Iowa, July 28, 1931; s. Ross Twetten and Frances Estelle (Hall) H.; A.A., Rochester State Community Coll., 1953; A.B., U. Minn., 1954; m. Darlene Joyce Granberg, 1954; children—Richard Lorin, Thomas Ross and Mark Thurston (twins), Julia Lynn, Susan Elizabeth. Pres., Orlen Ross Inc., Rochester, Minn., 1962—; partner The Gallery, European antiques, china, gifts, Rochester, 1968—, Millenium III, home furnishings, Rochester, 1975—. Active Episcopal Diocese of Minn., 1951-52, 58—, nat. dept., 1969-73, alt. dept., 1973-75; trustee Seabury Western Theol. Sem., 1975—, exec. com., 1976—, 2d v.p., 1983—; founder Rochester Arts Council, Rochester PTA Community Coll. Scholarship Program, H.D. Mayo Meml. Lecture in Theology, others; pres. Olmsted County (Minn.) Hist. Soc., 1976-77; bd. dirs. Rochester Symphony Orch., Choral, Opera, 1970-78, pres., 1974-75; del. Olmsted County Republican Com., 1974-82; mem. exec. council Minn. Hist. Soc., 1984—. Recipient Disting. Service award Rochester Jaycees, 1965, Fifty Mem. award YMCA, 1968, award for Minn. Bicentennial, Gov. Minn., 1976; named 1 of Minn's, 10 Outstanding Young Men, Minn. Jaycees, 1966, Disting. Christian Service award Seabury Western Sem. Mem. Minn. Home Furnishings Assn. (pres. 1976-79, trustee 1968—), First Dist. Hist. Assembly Minn. (pres. 1969-71), Minn. Retail Fedn. (trustee 1972—), Olmsted County Archeology Soc. (founder), Rochester Civil War Roundtable (founder), Rochester Revolutionary War Roundtable (founder), Rochester Arts Council (founder), Am., Nat. (charter), Minn., Norwegian/Am. hist. socs., Minn. Archeology Soc., Am. Assn. State and Local History, U. Minn. Alumni Assn. (life), U. Minn. Alumni Club (charter) Rochester C. of C., Alpha Delta Phi Alumni Assn., Soc. Mayflower Descs. (trustee Minn., under dep. gov. 1983—), SAR (Minn. pres. 1980-82), Descs. Colonial Clergy, Sons Union Vets of Civil War, Minn. Territorial Pioneers (trustee 1978—, pres. 1981-84), Soc. Archtl. Historians. Clubs: Rotary (historian 1980-82) (Rochester); Sertoma (Austin) (founder). Public speaker. Home: 1820 26th St NW Rochester MN 55901 Office: Orlen Ross Inc 105 N Broadway Rochester MN 55904

HUSBAND, WILLIAM SWIRE, computer industry executive; b. Hinsdale, Ill., Dec. 18, 1939; s. William Thompson and Arlene Martha (Frey) H.; m. Janet Lee, Nov. 26, 1965; children—Scott, Andrea. B.S., Iowa State U., 1962. Mktg. rep. IBM, San Francisco, 1966-70; dist. mktg. mgr. DPF, Des Plaines, Ill., 1971-78; v.p. Celtic Computer Investment Co., Palatine, Ill., 1978; pres. 20th Century Systems, Inc., Palatine, 1978—. Author: Computer Acquisition and Disposition Planning, 5th edit., 1985. Active Palatine Boys' Baseball, 1978-85. Served to lt. (j.g.) USN, 1962-66. Republican. Presbyterian. Office: 20th Century Systems Inc 330 W Colfax Ave Palatine IL 60067

HUSK, DONALD ESTEL, state official Indiana; b. Oakland City, Ind., Dec. 10, 1925; s. George Raymond and Hazel Rita (Ashley) H.; grad. high sch.; m. Velma Cunningham, June 7, 1946; children—Robert, Mark. With Hoosier Cardinal, Inc., Evansville, Ind., 1949; asst. cashier English State Bank (Ind.), 1946; with Ind. Dept. Financial Instns., 1953—, sr. examiner, 1958-70, supr. div. banks and trust cos., Indpls., 1970—. Served with USNR, 1943-46. Certified fin. examiner. Mem. Hist. Record Assn., Soc. Fin. Examiners. Clubs: Masons, Plainfield Optimists. Home: 424 Wayside Dr Plainfield IN 46168 Office: 1024 State Office Bldg Indianapolis IN 46204

HUSMAN, LOIS ARLENE, psychotherapist; b. Chgo., July 24, 1937; s. Nathan H. and Harriet (Bernstein) Schwartz; m. David L. Husman, Jan. 23, 1957 (div. Mar. 1969); children—Melinda, Lori. Student Northwestern U., 1954-57; B.G.S., Roosevelt U., 1972; M.S.W., U. Ill., 1974. Social worker A.E.R.O. spl. edn. sch., 1974-79; psychotherapist in pvt. practice, Chgo., 1979—. Mem. Chgo. Symphony Orch. Assn., Art Inst. Chgo., Chgo. Council Fgn. Relations, Nat. Assn. Social Workers, Am. Orthopsychiat. Assn. Home: 1430 Astor St Apt 10-C Chicago IL 60610 Office: 111 N Wabash St #1202 Chicago IL 60602

HUSS, ALLAN MICHAEL, lawyer; b. Chgo., Sept. 29, 1949; s. Henry A. and Emily (Rosenheim) H.; m. Sandra Joyce Cohn, Aug. 16, 1970; 1 dau., Leah E. B.S., Mich. State U., 1970; J.D., U. Cin., 1973. Bar: Ohio 1973, Mich. 1982. Staff atty. U.S. Fed. Trade Commn., Cleve., 1973-81; sr. staff counsel Chrysler Corp., Detroit, 1982—. Mem. ABA, Ohio Bar Assn., Mich. Bar Assn., Greater Cleve. Bar Assn. Avocation: Computer programming. Home: 5049 Langlewood Dr West Bloomfield MI 48033 Office: Chrysler Corp PO Box 1919 Detroit MI 48288

HUSS, EDWARD HARRY, JR., metallurgist; b. New Brunswick, N.J., Sept. 22, 1925; s. Edward Harry and Margaret (Hauth) H.; student U. Wis., 1945-46, Georgetown U., 1945-46, Iowa State. Tchrs. Coll., 1949; children—Joseph Edward, James Harold. Chemist, John Deere Waterloo (Iowa) Tractor Wks., 1948-50; metallurgist Viking Pump Co., Cedar Falls, Iowa, 1950-66, 67—, metallurgist, dept. head, 1956—; metallurgist Doerfer Engring., Cedar Falls, 1966-67; cons. in field; lectr. in field. Pres. bd. AMVET Home, Cedar Falls, Iowa, 1955. Served with U.S. Maritime Service 1942-43, U.S. Army, 1943-46. Decorated Bronze Star medal, Purple Heart. Mem. ASTM, Am. Soc. for Metals, Am. Foundrymans Soc., Smithsonian Inst., Metal Treating Inst., Am. Soc. Mil. Engrs. Am. Olympic Com., Am. Legion, VFW, AMVETS. Republican. Anglican. Club: Masons. Contbr. articles to profl. jours. Home: 904 W 10th St Cedar Falls IA 50613 Office: 4th and State St Cedar Falls IA 50613

HUSTAD, THOMAS PEGG, marketing educator; b. Mpls., June 15, 1945; s. Thomas Earl Pegg and John Charles and Dorothy Helen (Anderson) H.; B.S. in Elec. Engring., Purdue U., 1967, M.S. in Indsl. Mgmt., 1969, Ph.D. in Mktg., 1973; m. Sherry Ann Thomas, Jan. 30, 1971; children—Kathleen, John. Vis. asst. prof. Purdue U., West Lafayette, Ind., 1971-72; asst. prof. Faculty of Adminstrv. Studies, York U., Toronto, 1972-74, assoc. prof., 1974-76, asso. prof., mktg. area coordinator, 1976-77; asso. prof. mktg. Sch. Bus., Ind. U., Bloomington-Indpls., 1977-82, prof., 1982—, chmn. M.B.A. program, 1984—, program chmn. Ind. U. Ann. Bus. Conf., 1983, 84, exec. dir. Ind. U. Internat. Bus. Forum; cons. N. Am. corps., Can. Govt.; condr. seminars for U.S., Can. and Venezuelan industry. Mem. Am. Mktg. Assn. (award 1973), Assn. Consumer Research, Product Devel. and Mgmt. Assn. (program chmn. 3d ann. conf., v.p. confs. 1979, pres. elect 1980, pres. 1981, dir. 1982-83, chmn. publ. com. 1983—, sec./treas. 1984—), Ancient and Hon. Arty. Co. Mass., Internat. Assn. Jazz Record Collectors, Phi Eta Sigma, Tau Beta Pi, Beta Gamma Sigma. Author: Approaches to the Teaching of Product Development and Management, 1977; founder, editor: Jour. Product Innovation Mgmt.; contbr. articles to books and profl. jours. Home: 8931 Butternut Ct Indianapolis IN 46260 Office: Sch Business Indiana U Bloomington IN 47405

HUSTED, STEWART WINTHROP, business educator; b. Roanoke, Va., Oct. 22, 1946; s. John Edwin and Katheryn (Stewart) H.; m. Kathleen Lixey, May 6, 1947; 1 son, Ryan Winthrop. B.S., Va. Poly. Inst. and State U., 1968; M.Ed., U. Ga., 1972; Ph.D., Mich. State U., 1977. Trainee, Macy-Davison's Dept. Stores, Atlanta, 1967, Heironomus Dept. Stores, Roanoke, Va., 1967; distributive edn. coordinator Towers High Sch., Decatur, Ga., 1972-75; vocat. counselor Lansing (Mich.) Community Coll., 1975-76; prof. bus. Ind. State U., Terre Haute, 1976—; Ind. Dept. Pub. Instrn. rep. to Interstate Distributive Edn. Curriculum Consortium, 1978-85, also trustee. Bd. dirs., treas. Big Bros./Big Sisters, 1977-80. Served to maj. USAR, 1968—. Decorated Army Commendation medal. EPDA Nat. fellow U.S. Office Edn., 1975-76; Epsilon Delta Epsilon Nat. Research award, 1978. Mem. Am. Vocat. Assn., Am. Soc. Tng. and Devel., Midwest Mktg. Assn., Mktg. Edn. Assn., Delta Pi Epsilon, Beta Gamma Sigma. Methodist. Author: (with Sam Certo and Max Douglas) Business, 1984; (with Ralph Mason, Pat Rath.) Marketing Practices and Principles, 1986; contbr. articles to profl. jours.

HUTCHENS, JIM PAUL, sales executive; b. Paducah, Ky., Dec. 13, 1945; s. Joe and Mary Louise (Weatherford) H.; m. Pamela Paul Keith, Jan. 17, 1967 (div. Apr. 1969); 1 child, Cynthia Lynn; m. Shirrin Kay Lamb, July 25, 1969. Grad. high sch. Sales rep. B. Burdett Oxygen Co., Indpls., 1968-70, br. mgr., 1970-75; area mgr. Burdox Inc., Louisville and Indpls., 1975-80; ter. mgr. AGA Burdox, Inc., Cin., 1980-85; regional sales mgr. AGA Gas Inc., Dayton, Ohio, 1985—; adv. cons. Ivy Tech. Sch., Jeffersonville, Ind., 1976-78, Louisville Sch. System, 1976-77. Mem. adv. bd. Louisville C. of C., 1976. Mem. Am. Welding Soc. Republican. Mem. Assemblies of God Ch. Lodges: Kiwanis, Masons (jr. deacon 1978-79). Club: Blue Knights (Middletown, Ohio). Avocations: motorcycle touring; bowling; camping; tennis; reading. Office: AGA Gas 3300 Lakeside Ave Cleveland OH 44114

HUTCHENS, ROBERT ARTHUR, lawyer; b. New Albany, Ind., Apr. 14, 1951; s. Marvin Samuel and Ruth Joyce (Kraus) H.; m. Debra Lynn Alcorn, Jan. 12, 1974; children—Christopher Robert, Alison Marie, Jeffrey Allen. A.B., Wabash Coll., 1973; M.B.A., Butler U., 1976; J.D., Ind. U.-Indpls., 1980. Bar: Ind. 1980, U.S. Dist. Ct. (so. dist.) Ind. 1980, U.S. Tax Ct. 1980. Assoc. Patrick, Gabbert, Wilkinson, Goeller & Modesitt, Terre Haute, Ind., 1980-81; ptnr. Wilson Hutchens & Reese and predecessor Wilson & Hutchens, Greencastle, Ind., 1981—. Mem. ABA, Ind. State Bar Assn., Indpls. Bar Assn., Putnam County Bar Assn. Home: 604 Brentfield Ct Greencastle IN 46135 Office: Wilson Hutchens & Reese 16 S Jackson St Greencastle IN 46135

HUTCHENS, ROBERT DOUGLAS, physical chemist, consultant; b. Dayton, Ohio, Dec. 11, 1946; s. David Dale and Mary Frances H.; m. Joyce Elaine Herbst, Oct. 27, 1973; children—Kenneth James, Brian Douglas. Student, Washington & Lee U., 1964-66; B.S. in Chemistry, U. Mich., 1968; Ph.D., U. Pitts., 1972. Engr., Air Force Materials Lab., Wright-Patterson AFB, Ohio, 1976-79; mgr. materials devel. Raytheon Co., Waltham, Mass., 1979-82; prin. sr. engr. Universal Tech. Corp., Dayton, Ohio, 1982-84; with Gen. Research Corp., Dayton, 1984—; cons. electronics. Served to 1st lt. USAF, 1972-75. Named Engr. of Year, Air Force Materials Lab., 1979; NASA fellow, 1969, Andrew Mellon fellow, 1971. Mem. Sigma Xi. Presbyterian. Contbr. articles to profl. jours. Home: 8844 Rooks Mill Ln Centerville OH 45459 Office: 5200 Springfield Pike Dayton OH 45431

HUTCHESON, ROBERT WEBER, lawyer; b. Evanston, Ill., July 9, 1950; s. Allen Carrington and Anne Therese (Weber) H.; m. Jane Chenoweth Borah, June 5, 1976; 1 son, Matthew Borah. B.A., Duke U., 1972; J.D., So. Meth. U., 1975. Bar: Ohio 1975. Assoc., R.B. Brewer Law Office, Xenia, Ohio, 1975-76; pub. defender Greene County, Ohio, 1976-77; assoc. Wead & Aultman, Xenia, 1979-83, Smith & Pendry, 1984—; referee Greene County Juvenile Ct., 1977—. Mem. Ohio Bar Assn., Greene County Bar Assn., Republican. Avocations: Amateur boxing; running; professional modeling. Home: 550 Waynesville-Jamestown Rd Xenia OH 45385 Office: Smith & Pendry 133 E Market St Xenia OH 45385

HUTCHESON, SUSANNA KAYE, insurance executive, business writer; b. ElDorado, Kans., Jan. 8, 1944; d. Harold G. and E. Irene (Wedding) H.; student Butler County Community Coll., 1970-71, Kans. U., 1966-67. Soc. writer Joplin (Mo.) Globe, 1973; writer Antioch (Calif.) Daily Ledger, 1974; advt. mgr. Mulvane (Kans.) News, 1976—, columnist Points to Ponder, 1976—; freelance writer, Speciality Salesman Mag., Am. Salesman, Salesman's Opportunity, others, 1967—; pres. SKAY Features, 1977—, Skay Enterprises, Inc., 1977—; owner Hutcheson Ins. Agy., 1983—; gen. agt. Howard Life Ins. Co., Lakewood, Colo.; editor Altoona (Kans.) Tribune, 1977—; owner Park City (Kans.) Press, 1977—; ins. agt. Bankers Life & Casualty Co., Chgo., 1979—. Mem. Bus. and Profl. Women, Authors Guild, Author League Am., Assoc. Bus. Writers Am., NOW; Nat. Assn. Exec. Women, Women in Energy. Republican. Home: 2228 S Oliver #106 PO Box 1583 Wichita KS 67218

HUTCHINS, DONALD BYRON, tire company executive; b. Toledo, July 27, 1948; s. Donald Byron and Camilla Jane (Omey) H.; m. Jill Janice Rood, Aug. 23, 1969; children—Jennifer, Samantha. B.A., U. Mich., 1970, M.B.A., 1973. C.P.A., Mich., Ohio. Sr. auditor Coopers & Lybrand, Detroit, 1974-76, audit supr., 1976-78, audit mgr., 1978-81, lead mgr. Emerging Bus. Sect., 1978-81; mgr. fin. reporting Firestone Tire & Rubber Co., Akron, Ohio, 1981-83, asst. controller, 1983—. Membership recruiter Jr. Achievement, Detroit, 1979. Mem. Nat. Assn. Accts. (dir. community affairs 1983-84), Am. Inst. C.P.A.s, Mich. Assn. C.P.A.s, Ohio Soc. C.P.A.s (mem. industry liaison com. 1982). Episcopalian. Club: University (Detroit). Contbr. internal pubs. Office: Firestone Tire & Rubber Co 1200 Firestone Pkwy Akron OH 44317

HUTCHINS, WILLIAM BILL, state senator; b. Guthrie County, Iowa, Mar. 21, 1931; s. Jack and Hazel H.; grad. high sch.; m. JoAnn Reser, 1955; 4 children. Mem. Iowa Ho. of Reps., 1973-76, Iowa Senate, 1976—, asst. minority leader, 1979-80, 81, 82, asst. majority leader, 1983, 84, 85, 86. Mem. Vol. Fire Dept., 1963-81. Mem. C. of C., Am. Legion. Methodist. Democrat. Club: Lions. Home: 306 S Divison Audubon IA 50025 Office: State Senate Des Moines IA 50319

HUTCHINSON, DUANE DOUGLAS, storyteller, writer, clergyman; b. Elgin, Nebr., June 16, 1929; s. William Clyde and Eva Susan (Martin) H.; m. Marilyn Ann Burton, Sept. 3, 1950; children—Stephen Kent, James Wesley. B.A. in Edn., Kearney State Coll., 1953; Th.M., Perkins Sch. Theology, So. Meth. U., 1956; postgrad. U. Chgo., 1956-57; M.A. in English, U. Nebr., 1979. Ordained to ministry United Methodist Ch., 1954; cert. pub. sch. tchr., Nebr. Pastor, Chester and Hubbell, Nebr., 1957-61; teaching fellow Centennial Coll., U. Nebr., 1979-81; campus minister U. Nebr., 1961-79; travelling storyteller Nebr. Arts Council and Iowa Arts Council, 1979—; condr. writing and storytelling workshops. Author: Doc Graham: Sandhills Doctor, 1970; Exon: Biography of a Governor, 1973; Images of Mary, 1971; Savidge Brothers: Sandhills Aviators, 1982; Storytelling Tips: How to Love, Learn and Relate a Story, 1983. County del. Democratic party; past pres. local chpt. UN Assn. Mem. Nat. Assn. Preservation and Perpetuation of Storytelling, Nebr. Library Assn., Nat. Council Tchrs. English. Home: 3445 Touzalin Ave Lincoln NE 68507

HUTCHINSON, GRACE ANN, physical education instructor; b. Sandusky, Ohio, May 13, 1949; d. John Oscar and Martha Louise (Olcott) H. Student Hope Coll., 1967-68; B.S.E., No. Ill. U., 1972; postgrad. So. Ill. U., 1972-73, postgrad. Bowling Green U., 1978-80. Cert. tchr., Ohio. Program dir. Plymouth Shore, Lakeside, Ohio, 1968-72; grad. asst. Southern Ill. U., Carbondale, 1972; phys. edn. instr. Joliet Twp. Schs. (Ill.), 1973-76; phys. edn. instr. Norwalk City Schs. (Ohio), 1977—; coach, counselor Ohio Northern U. Volleyball Camp, Ada, 1982—; speaker at confs. Named Coach of All-Star Match Crestview Booster Club, Ashland, Ohio, 1983; named Coach of All-Star Match Ont. Booster Club, Mansfield, Ohio, 1983, Dist. 6AA Coach of Year, 1984, AA Coach of Yr.-All-State Hon. Mention, 1983, 84. Mem. NEA, Ohio Assn. Health Phys. Edn. Dance, Nat. Volleyball Coaches Assn., Ohio High Sch Volleyball Coaches Assn. (Dist. 6 rep. 1983-85, Dist. 6 pres. 1984-85), Ohio Edn. Assn. (state assn. v.p. 1985-86; pres. 1987-88). Republican. Office: Norwalk High Sch 80 E Main St Norwalk OH 44857

HUTCHINSON, MICHAEL CLARK, lawyer; b. Quincy, Mass. Feb. 25, 1953; s. William Thomas and Marguerite J. (Gunning) H. B.A. cum laude, Bowdoin Coll., 1975; J.D., cum laude, Suffolk U., 1979. Bar: Minn. 1980, U.S. Dist. Ct. Minn. 1980. Law clk. Seventh Jud. Dist. Ct., Moorhead, Minn., 1979-81; asst. county atty. Clay County Atty.'s Office, Moorhead, 1981-83; assoc. Clinton & O'Gorman P.A., Cottage Grove, Minn., 1983—. Mem. Minn. State Bar Assn., Minn. State Bar Assn. (real estate, criminal law sect.), Washington County Bar Assn. Roman Catholic. Lodge: Lions (pres. local club 1982-83). Office: Clinton & O'Gorman PA 7200 80th St S Cottage Grove MN 55016

HUTCHISON, CATHLEEN SMITH, instructional technologist; b. Detroit, June 6, 1949; d. Joseph Donald and Lola Mae (Smith) H.; m. Larry George Fichtner, May 3, 1970 (div. Nov. 1982); 1 son, Erik Matthew Hutchison Fichtner. B.A. in Art History, U. Mich., 1970; M.Ed., Wayne State U., 1982. Various positions with Lee Wards, Taylor, Mich., 1976-78, Chrysler Learning, Detroit, 1978-81; mgr. tng. and devel. Botsford Gen. Hosp., Farmington, Mich., 1981-84; instructional designer Gen. Motors Mktg. Ednl. Services, 1984—. Cons. in field. Mem. Nat. Soc. Performance and Instrn., Mich. Soc. Instrnl. Tech. (pres. 1985-86), Internat. Bd. Standards for Tng., Performance and Instrn. Profls. (bd. dirs.), Am. Soc. Tng. and Devel., World Future Soc. Club: Detroit Yacht. Office: 1700 W 3d Ave Flint MI 48502

HUTCHISON, STANLEY PHILIP, insurance executive, lawyer; b. Joliet, Ill., Nov. 22, 1923; s. Stuart Philip and Verna (Kinzer) H.; B.S., Northwestern U., 1947; LL.B., Kent Coll. Law, 1951; m. Helen Jane Rush, July 25, 1945; children—Norman, Elizabeth. Bar: Ill. 1951. Legal asst. Washington Nat. Ins. Co., Evanston, 1947-51, asst. counsel, 1951-55, asst. gen. counsel, 1955-58, asso. gen. counsel, 1958-60, gen. counsel, 1960-63, v.p., gen. counsel, dir., 1963-66, exec. v.p., gen. counsel, dir., 1966-67, exec. v.p., gen. counsel, sec., dir., 1967-70, chmn. exec. com., 1970-73, vice chmn. bd., 1974-75, chmn. bd., chief exec. officer, 1976—; pres. Wash. Nat. Corp., 1970—, chief exec. officer, 1978—, chmn., 1983—; dir. Anchor Nat. Life Ins. Co., Anchor Nat. Financial Services, Inc., Washington Nat. Devel. Co. Served to lt. (j.g.) USNR, 1942-46. Mem. Ill., Evanston (pres. 1973-74) chambers commerce, Am., Ill. bar assns., Assn. Life Ins. Counsel, Am. Council Life Ins. (dir. 1977—), Ill. Life Ins. Council (dir. 1978—), Ins. Econs. Soc. Am. (dir. 1977—). Home: 830 Heather Way Winnetka IL 60093 Office: 1630 Chicago Ave Evanston IL 60201

HUTJENS, MICHAEL FRANCIS, dairy scientist, educator; b. Green Bay, Wis., Nov. 21, 1945; s. Anthony C. and Catherine (O'Neil) H.; m. Carol Ann Seidl, Aug. 24, 1968; children—Christopher, Michelle, Melissa, Matthew. B.S., U. Wis.-Madison, 1967, M.S., 1969, Ph.D., 1971. Extension dairy specialist U. Minn.-St. Paul, 1971-79, U. Ill.-Urbana, 1979—; cons. Borden Co., Seoul, Korea, 1982, 84, 85, Mex. Holstein Assn., 1985, Am. Soybean Assn., Dublin, Ireland, 1979-81; writer Hoard's Dairyman, Ft. Atkinson, Wis., 1971—. Editor: Ill. Dairy Report, ann. report, 1980-85. Served with U.S. Army, 1968-74. Recipient Young Extension award Midwest Animal Sci. Soc., 1984. Mem. Am. Dairy Sci Assn. (DeLaval Nat. Dairy Extension award 1985), Am. Soc. Animal Sci., Council Agrl. Sci. Tech., Alpha Zeta, Gamma Sigma Delta. Roman Catholic. Lodge: K.C. Home: 9 Hale Haven Ct Savoy IL 61874 Office: U Ill 315 ASL 1207 W Gregory Dr Urbana IL 61801

HUTSEN, SIDNEY RANDOLPH, marketing executive; b. Indpls., Mar. 25, 1947; s. Sidney Earl and Martha Louise (Hill) H. Grad. Wabash Coll., 1969. Founder, pres. Exec. Mktg. Assocs., Indpls., 1970—; co-founder, pres. Exec. Mktg. Group Ltd., Indpls., 1981—; pres. Worldwide Mktg. Coop., 1982—; dir. world mktg. ops. Olde World, Inc.; dir. Exec. Mktg. Group Computer Corp. Co-founder, dir., chmn. bd. Legacy Internat., Inc., 1983—; bd. dirs. Olde Worlde Reps. Assn., 1977—, pres., 1982; past pres. Midwest Field Mgrs. Assn. Mem. Nat. Fedn. Ind. Bus., U.S. C. of C. Clubs: Grandview Yacht, Racquet Four Country, Country Squire Lakes Community, Toastmasters (past pres.). Lodge: Kiwanis. Office: 5204 Granite Ct E Indianapolis IN 46227 also 4211 Main St High Point NC 27261

HUTSON, JEFFREY WOODWARD, lawyer; b. New London, Conn., July 19, 1941; s. John Jenkins and Kathryn Barbara (Himberg) H.; m. Susan Office, Nov. 25, 1967; children—Elizabeth Kathryn, Anne Louise. A.B., U. Mich., 1963, LL.B., 1966. Bar: Ohio 1966, Hawaii 1970. Assoc. Lane, Alton & Horst, Columbus, Ohio, 1966-74, ptnr., 1974—. Served to lt. comdr. USN, 1967-71. Fellow Am. Coll. Trial Lawyers; mem. ABA, Ohio Bar Assn., Ohio Assn. Civil Trial Attys., Columbus Bar Assn., Internat. Assn. Ins. Counsel. Republican. Episcopalian. Clubs: Scioto Country, Athletic. Avocations: competitive running; cross country skiing; reading; music. Office: Lane Alton & Horst 155 E Broad St Columbus OH 43215

HUTT, HARRY ELMORE, professional basketball executive; b. Gloversville, N.Y., July 15, 1942; s. Herschel Harry and Valentine Melinda (Bohall) H.; m. Nancy Sergent, June 22, 1963; children—Shawna, Allyson, Vicki. B.A., Roberts Wesleyan Coll., 1965; postgrad. Brockport State Coll., 1965-66, Mich. State U., 1969-71; M.Ed., SUNY-Buffalo, 1976. Cert. tchr., N.Y. Sports info. dir., asst. basketball coach Roberts Wesleyan Coll., Rochester, N.Y., 1965-68, Spring Arbor Coll. (Mich.), 1969-74; asst. basketball coach SUNY-Buffalo, 1974-76; dir. promotions and group sales Buffalo Braves, 1977-78; dir. Basketball Prospect Info. Service, Buffalo, 1976-77; v.p. mktg. and broadcasting Detroit Pistons, 1978—; cons., lectr. in field. Named to Roberts Wesleyan Coll. Sports Hall of Fame, 1983. Mem. Adcraft Club of Detroit, Detroit Producers Assn., U.S. Basketball Writers Assn., Nat. Assn. Basketball Coaches, Coll. Sports Info. Dirs. Assn. (Basketball Brochure award 1965), Nat. Assn. Intercollegiate Athletics, Sports Info. Dirs. Assn. (Basketball Brochure award 1970). Republican. Methodist. Author: The Origin and Analysis of the Passing Game Offense in Basketball, 1975. Producer basketball film.

HUTT, MAX LEWIS, psychology educator, psychotherapist, consultant; b. N.Y.C., Sept. 13, 1908; s. Israel and Pauline Hutt; m. Anne Gromet, Feb. 4, 1933. A.B., CCNY, 1928, M.S., 1930; postgrad. Columbia U., 1930-33; Litt.D. (hon.), Nova U., 1983. Diplomate Am. Bd. Profl. Psychology; lic. psychologist, Mich. Instr. CCNY, 1928-41, head ednl. clinic, 1938-41, dir. child consultation clinic, 1941-43; sr. instr. clin. psychology to chief clin. psychology Surgeon Gen.'s Office, U.S. Army, 1943-46; lectr. Columbia U., 1946; prof., dir. Ph.D. program in clin. psychology U. Mich., 1947-60; pvt. practice clin. psychology, cons., Ann Arbor, Mich., 1960-68, 73—; prof., dir. psychology clinic U. Detroit, 1968-73, dir. Psychotherapy Inst., 1969-73; cons. to surgeon gen. U.S. Army, pub. sch. systems, various psychol. clinics, Ypsilanti State Hosp., U. Mich. Hosp., Mich. Dept. Mental Health. Named One of Top Living Psychologists, Ency. Psychology, 1984. Fellow Am. Psychol. Assn. (council mem., offered 1st postdoctoral program in clin. psychology, selected one of top 20 psychologists 1953), Mich. Psychol. Assn., AAUP, Mich. Soc. Cons. Psychologists, Soc. for Study Social Issues, Psychologists League (pres.), Mich. Assn. Projective Techniques (pres.). Jewish. Author: The Hutt Adaptation of the Bender-Gestalt Test, 4 edits., 3 fgn. transls., 1960-79; The Mentally Retarded Child, 4 eds., 1958-79; Patterns of Abnormal Behavior, 1957; The Child: Development and Adjustment (also fgn. transl.), 1959; Psychology: The Science of Interpersonal Behavior, 1966; An Atlas for the Hutt Adaptation of the Bender-Gestalt Test, 1970; The Science of Behavior, 2d ed., 1971; Psychosynthesis, 1977; adv. editor Jour. Projective Techniques; contbr. numerous research and profl. articles to profl. jours., ednl. and psychol. ency.; contbr. chpts. to psychology textbooks. Home: 21 Regent Dr Ann Arbor MI 48104 Office: 555 E William St Suite 24D Ann Arbor MI 48104

HUTTON, EDWARD LUKE, corporate executive; b. Bedford, Ind., May 5, 1919; s. Fred and Margaret (Drehobl) H.; B.S. with distinction, Ind. U., 1940, M.S. with distinction, 1941; m. Kathryn Jane Alexander, Dec. 22, 1942; children—Edward Alexander, Thomas Charles, Jane Clarke. Dep. dir. Joint Export/Import Agy., Berlin, 1946-48; v.p., dir. World Commerce Corp., N.Y.C., 1948-51; asst. v.p. W.R. Grace & Co., N.Y.C., 1951-53, cons., 1960-65, exec. v.p., gen. mgr. DuBois Chem. div., 1965-66, group exec. Splty. Products Group, v.p. parent co., 1966-68, exec. v.p. parent co., 1968-71; cons. in internat. trade and fin., 1953-58; fin. v.p., exec. v.p. Ward Industries, 1958-59; pres., chief exec. officer Chemed Corp., 1971—; also dir.; chmn. Omnicare, Inc., 1981—, also dir.; chmn. Roto Rooter, Inc., 1984—, also dir.; dir. Am. States Ins. Co., Nurotoco Inc., Vestal Labs., Inc., Herman's Sporting Goods, Inc., Vestal Internat. Ltd., DuBois Germany, El Torito Restaurants, Inc., Nat. San. Supply Co. Former trustee Village of Bronxville, Millikin U.; mem. governing bd. acad. freedom fund AAUP, 1958—; co-chmn., mem. exec. com., mem. subcom. President's Pvt. Sector Survey on Cost Control. Served from pvt. to 1st lt. AUS, 1943-46. Mem. Dirs. Table, Newcomen Soc., Internat. Platform Assn., Beta Gamma Sigma. Methodist. Clubs: Downtown Assn., Economics, University (N.Y.C.); Queen City, Bankers (Cin.). Home: 6680 Miralake Dr Cincinnati OH 45243 also Harris Rd East Orleans MA 02643 Office: 1200 DuBois Tower Cincinnati OH 45202

HUTTON-SEREDA, SHERYL LOUISE, association official; b. Cleve., Dec. 3, 1946; d. Murray Eugene and Marion Louise Garnett; B.S. in Biochemistry and Nutrients, U. Nebr., 1970. Assoc. producer Sta. WKYC-TV, NBC, Cleve., 1971-78; sales rep. Chase Bag Co., Chagrin Falls, Ohio, 1978-79; pub. relations dir. City of Cleveland Heights (Ohio), 1979-83; dir. communications Greater Cleve. Hosp. Assn., 1983—. Spl. edn. adv. council Shaker Heights (Ohio) Bd. Edn. Recipient Gavel award ABA, 1976; CINE award Council Internat. Non-theatrical Events, 1976; award of appreciation Cleve. Home and Flower Show, 1981. Mem. Pub. Relations Soc. Am. Home: 2671 Haddam Rd Shaker Heights OH 44120

HUTZELL, ROBERT RAYMOND, clinical psychologist; b. Des Moines, Dec. 6, 1948; s. Robert Roy and Dorothy Mae (Oldham) H.; m. Vicki Lynn Shinn, Aug. 31, 1969; children—Daisy Lynn, Angela Kathreen. B.S. with honors and distinction, U. Iowa, 1971; M.S., Fla. State U., 1973, Ph.D., 1975. Diplomate Inst. Logotherapy, regional dir., 1984—. Trainee, intern Southeastern U.S., VA, 1972-75; clin. psychologist VA, Biloxi, Miss., 1975-76, Knoxville, Iowa, 1976—; dir. psychol. services Mater Clinic, Knoxville, 1983—; adj. faculty U. Iowa, Iowa City, 1978-83. Recipient Performance award VA, 1978, 81-85. Mem. Am. Psychol. Assn. (Psychologists in Pub. Service cert. of recognition 1983), Midwestern Psychol. Assn., Southeastern Psychol. Assn., Iowa Psychol. Assn., Nat. Orgn. VA Psychologists (newsletter editor 1984—, cert. of recognition 1985), Iowa Nut Tree Growers Assn. Methodist. Editor, The Iowa Psychologist, 1978—. Researcher, contbr. book chpts. and articles to profl. jours. Home: Drawer 112 Knoxville IA 50138 Office: VA Med Center Knoxville IA 50138

HUYER, TOM, steel company executive; b. Eindhoven, Netherlands; s. Herman D. and Ina H.; m. Diane L. Kinsey, June 22, 1968; children—Robert Mark, Jamie Lynn, Matthew Tom. B.A., Hope Coll., 1969; M.B.A., Loyola U., 1973. C.P.A. Mo., Ill. Div. controller Chemetron Corp., Chgo., 1969-75; dir. planning Iowa Beef, Dakota City, Iowa, 1976-77; dir. planning Victor Bus. Products, Chgo., 1977-78; controller Internat. Harvester, Dusseldorf, W. Ger., 1978-80, Granite City Steel (Ill.), 1980—. Steel fellow Am. Iron & Steel Inst., Washington, 1982—. Treas. Tri-City YMCA, 1983-84; bd. dirs. Tri-City Red Cross, 1982-83; mem. Leadership St. Louis, 1983-84. Mem. Am. Inst. C.P.A.s, Ill. Soc. C.P.A.s, Mo. Soc. C.P.A.s, Nat. Assn. Accts., Planning Execs. Inst., Tri-City C. of C. (dir. 1983-84). Home: 15550 Highcroft Chesterfield MO 63017 Office: Granite City Steel 20th & State St Granite City IL 62040

HWANG, KAO, retired pharmacologist; b. Changsha, Hunan, China, Apr. 3, 1916; came to U.S., 1945, naturalized, 1957; s. Hung Hsi and Tsung Su (Hsu) H.; m. Sheila Ning-Tso Chen, July 17, 1948; children—Leila, Miriam, Catherine, Jason Kao. M.D., Hunan Yale Med. Coll., Kweiyang, China, 1940; M.S., U. Ill.-Chgo., 1947, Ph.D., 1953. Mem. faculty Hunan Yale Med. Coll., 1940-45; instr. Nat. Tsing-Hua U., 1945; fellow Mayo Found., 1945-46; faculty U. Ill. Med. Sch., 1946-61, asst. prof. dept. clin. sci., 1958-61; sr. pharmacologist Abbott Labs., North Chicago, Ill., 1950-67, group leader, 1957-61, sect. head, 1961-73, dept. pharmacology research fellow, 1972-75, sci. coordinator div. pharmacology and medicinal chemistry, sr. investigator, 1976-79; adj. assoc. prof. pharmacology U. Health Scis., The Chgo. Med. Sch., North Chicago, 1979-85, now ret. Mem. AAAS, Am. Soc. Pharmacology and Exptl. Therapeutics, Am. Soc. Microbiology, Am. Soc. Clin. Pharmacology and Therapeutics, Am. Soc. Nephrology, Am. Gastroenterol. Assn., Sigma Xi. Contbr. numerous articles to profl. jours. Home: 418-A Andover Dr Clearbrook Cranbury NJ 08512

HWANG, SUN-TAK, chemical engineering educator; b. Choong Buk, Korea, June 24, 1935; came to U.S., 1960, naturalized, 1972; s. Kyu-Yong and Jae-Hung (Song) H.; m. Soon Choi, June 15, 1963; children—Linda, Helen. B.S., Seoul Nat. U., 1958; M.S., U. Iowa, 1962, Ph.D., 1965. Instr. U. Iowa, Iowa City, 1964-65, asst. prof. chem. engring., 1966-69, assoc. prof., 1969-73, prof., 1973-82, dept. chmn., 1982; prof., head dept. chem. engring. U. Cin., 1982—, dir. Ctr. of Excellence in Membrane Tech., 1984—; engr. Mobil Oil Corp., Dallas, 1965-66. Mem. Am. Chem. Soc., Am. Inst. Chem. Engrs., Am. Soc. Engring. Edn., AAAS, AAUP, Sigma Xi, Phi Lambda Upsilon, Tau Beta Pi. Home: 9880 Humphrey Rd Cincinnati OH 45242 Office: U Cin ML 171 Cincinnati OH 45221

HYATT, GERHARDT WILFRED, clergyman, army officer; b. Melfort, Sask., Can., July 1, 1916; came to U.S., 1939; s. Francis William and Mary Elizabeth (Faber) H.; m. Elda Rosa Nueller, Mar. 8, 1947; children—Ruth Hannah Hyatt Heffron, Matthew Leavenworth. B.A., Concordia Sem., 1944; M.A., George Washington U., 1964; hon. D.D., Concordia Sem., 1969; hon. D.H.L., Tarkio U., 1973. Enlisted in U.S. Army, 1945, advanced through ranks to maj. gen., 1971; mil. chaplain, 1945-70; chief chaplains, Washington, 1971-75, retired, 1975; pres. Concordia Coll., St. Paul, 1976-83; v.p. Luth. Ch.-Mo. Synod, St. Louis, 1983—. Pres., Mill Creek Pk. Civic Assn., No. Va., 1962; v.p. St. Paul Midway Civic and Commerce Assn., 1983. Decorated medals and decorations (17) U.S. Army; recipient Golden Rule award N.Y. Police Dept., 1973; 4 Chaplains award B'nai Brith Goldman Chpt., 1969; Mem. Luth. Edn. Assn. N. Am. (dir., pres. 1981-82), Mil. Chaplain Assn. (dir.). Avocations: tennis, woodwork. Home: 10637 Hackberry #3 St Louis MO 63128 Office: Internat Hdqrs Luth Ch-Mo Synod 1333 S Kirkwood Rd St Louis MO 63122

HYATT, HUDSON, retired lawyer; b. Cleve., Jan. 1, 1914; s. Harry Cleve and Rose Evelyn (Miller) H.; A.B. cum laude, Adelbert Coll., Western Res. U., 1937, LL.B., 1939; m. Helen Fulmor, Feb. 3, 1940; children—David Hudson, Margaret (Mrs. Ross J. Dixon), Nancy, Shirley. Admitted to Ohio bar, 1939; asso. Davis & Young, 1939-40; adjudicator Social Security Bd., 1940-42; law clk. U.S. Dist. Ct., 1942-44; atty. Erie R.R. Co., 1946-52; practiced in Cleve., 1952-54; regional atty. SBA, Cleve., 1954-63, asst. regional counsel, 1963-66, dist. atty., 1966-71, dist. counsel, 1971-77; lectr. law Coll. Law, Cleve. State U., 1976. Pres., Cleve. Masonic Employment Bur., 1960-63, 1969-70, v.p., 1963-69; pres. Greater Cleve. Vets. Council, 1952-53; bd. control Cleve. Freedom Council, 1961—. Trustee C.L. Jack Meml. Fund, Shaker Masonic Bldg. Assn.; trustee Cleveland Heights Local Devel. Corp., pres., 1981, v.p., 1980, 82. Served from ensign to lt (j.g.), USNR, 1944-46. Mem. Fed. Bar Assn. (1st v.p. Cleve. chpt. 1965-66, pres. Cleve. chpt. 1966-67), ABA (chmn. small bus. com. 1965-69), Cleve. Cuyahoga County Bar Assn. (editorial bd. bull. 1962-73; chmn. editoral com. 1965-66; contbg. editor 1979-81), S.A.R., Am. Legion, V.F.W. (nat. judge adv. gen. 1947-48). Clubs: Masons, Shriners, Ripon. Contbg. editor Baldwin's Ohio Legal Forms, 1963, 70, 73, Baldwin's Kentucky Legal Forms, 1963; Carroll and Whiteside's, Forms for Commercial Transactions, 1963. Home: 2648 Euclid Heights Blvd Cleveland Heights OH 44106

HYATTE, REGINALD LEE, French educator; b. LaPorte, Ind., May 9, 1943; s. Merrill S. and Mary M. (Perky) H.; m. Maryse I. Ponchard, Aug. 14, 1982. B.A., Ind. U., 1965, M.A., 1966; Ph.D., U. Pa., 1971. Instr. French, Bowling Green State U., Ohio, 1970-71; asst. prof. Valley Forge Mil. Acad., Wayne, Pa., 1976-79; asst. prof., dept. chmn. Ripon Coll., Wis., 1979—. Author: Laughter for the Devil, 1983; contbr. articles to profl. jours. Mem. Midwest Modern Lang. Assn. Office: Ripon Coll French Dept 300 Seward St Ripon WI 54971

HYDE, ALAN LITCHFIELD, lawyer; b. Akron, Ohio, Nov. 4, 1928; s. Howard Linton and Katharine Pennington (Litchfield) H.; m. Charlotte Griffin Ross, July 10, 1954; children—Elizabeth, Pamela. A.B., Amherst Coll., 1950; J.D., Harvard U., 1953. Bar: Ohio 1953. Assoc., Thompson, Hine, and Flory, Cleve., 1953-64, ptnr., 1964—. Contbr. articles to profl. jours. Trustee, Planned Parenthood Greater Cleve., Inc., 1960-79, 80-81, pres., 1977-79; sec., gen. counsel Greater Cleve. Growth Assn., 1972-74, dir. 1974-80, 82—; trustee Cleve. World Trade Assn., 1978-81; exec. com. Cleve. Council World Affairs, 1980-83. Mem. Cleve. Bar Assn., Ohio State Bar Assn., ABA (mem. corp., banking and bus. law and internat. law sects., inter-Am. law com., Mex. com.), Inter-Am. Bar Assn. (mem. council, com. Latin Am. devel. and integration law), Internat. Bar Assn., Greater Cleve. Internat. Lawyers Group (pres.). Republican. Episcopalian. Office: Thompson Hine and Flory 1100 Nat City Bank Bldg Cleveland OH 44114

HYDE, HENRY JOHN, lawyer, congressman; b. Chgo., Apr. 18, 1924; s. Henry Clay and Monica Therese (Kelly) H.; student Duke U., 1943-44; B.S., Georgetown U., 1947; J.D., Loyola U., Chgo., 1949; m. Jeanne M. Simpson, Nov. 8, 1947; children—Henry J., Robert, Laura, Anthony. Admitted to Ill. bar; mem. Ill. Ho. of Reps., 1967-74, majority leader, 1971-72; mem. 94th to 98th Congresses from 6th Ill. Dist. Served with USNR, World War II; comdr. Res., ret. Mem. ABA, Ill., Chgo. bar assns. Office: 2104 Rayburn Bldg Washington DC 20515

HYDE, JANET SHIBLEY, psychology educator; b. Akron, Ohio, Aug. 17, 1948; d. Grant O. and Dorothy Mae (Reavy) Shibley; m. Clark Hyde, June 2, 1969; children—Margaret, Luke. B.A., Oberlin Coll., 1969; Ph.D., U. Calif.-Berkeley, 1972. Asst. prof. psychology Bowling Green State U., Ohio, 1972-76, assoc. prof. psychology, 1976-79; assoc. prof. psychology Denison U., Granville, Ohio, 1979-83, prof. psychology, 1983—. Author: Half the Human Experience: The Psychology of Women, 1976; Understanding Human Sexuality, 1979; also articles. Fellow Am. Psychol. Assn.; mem. Soc. Sci. Study Sex, Soc. Research Child Devel., Am. Assn. Sex Educators, Counselors and Therapists. Democrat. Episcopalian. Home: 98 W Central Ave Delaware OH 43015 Office: Denison U Psychology Dept Granville OH 43023

HYDE, LAWRENCE HENRY, JR., automotive company exec.; b. Cambridge, Mass., July 10, 1924; s. Lawrence Henry and Catherine I. (McMahon) H.; m. Lois A. Crehan, May 31, 1947; children—Abigail Ellen, Lawrence Henry III. A.B., Harvard U., 1946, M.B.A., 1947. With Ford Motor Co., 1947-65, dir. internat. purchasing office, 1960-62; v.p., gen. mgr. consumer products div. Philco Corp. div. Ford Motor Co., 1962-64; with Harris Corp., 1965-73, dir. internat. ops., 1965-69, group v.p. internat., 1969-73; with Am. Motors, Detroit, 1974-83, v.p. internat. 1974-77, group v.p. car and jeep vehicles, 1977-79, group v.p. internat., pres. Am. Gen. Corp., 1979-81, exec. v.p., pres., 1982-83, pres., 1983—; with LTV Corp., 1983—; dir. Harris Graphics Corp. Trustee Am. U., Cairo. Office: PO Box 3330 Livonia MI 48151

HYERS, THOMAS MORGAN, physician, biomedical researcher; b. Jacksonville, Fla., June 16, 1943; s. John and Joan (Clemens) H.; m. Elizabeth Mclean, June 12, 1965; children—Justin, Adam. B.S., Duke U., 1964, M.D., 1968. Diplomate Am. Bd. Internal Medicine, Am. Bd. Pulmonary Diseases. Intern in medicine Cleve. Met. Gen. Hosp., 1968-69; asst. chief Nat. Blood Resource Br., Nat. Heart, Lung and Blood Inst., NIH, 1971-72, pulmonary disease adv. com., 1983—; resident in medicine U. Wash., Seattle, 1972-74; chief resident, instr. medicine, 1974-75; fellow in pulmonary diseases U. Colo. Health Scis. Ctr., Denver, 1975-76, research fellow Cardiovascular Pulmonary Research Lab., 1976-77, asst. prof. medicine, staff physician respiratory care, assoc. investigator, 1977-82; research assoc. Denver VA Med. Ctr., 1979-82; assoc. prof. medicine, dir. div. pulmonary diseases St. Louis U. Med. Ctr., 1982-85, prof. medicine, 1985—; dir. NIH Specialized Ctr. Research in Adult Respiratory Failure, 1983—. Contbr. articles to profl. jours. Served to comdr. USPHS, 1969-71. Named hon. Ky. col. grantee NIH, Nat. Heart, Lung and Blood Inst. Fellow ACP, Am. Coll. Chest Physicians; mem. Am. Heart Assn. (mem. councils on thrombosis and cardiopulmonary disease), Internat. Soc. Thrombosis and Haemostasis, Am. Lung Assn. (Eastern Mo. chpt.), Am. Fedn. Clin. Research, Am. Physiol. Soc., Western Soc. Clin. Investigation, Am. Thoracic Soc., Phi Beta Kappa. Office: Pulmonary Div St Louis U Sch Medicine 1325 S Grand Blvd Saint Louis MO 63104

HYLAND, JOHN C., civic leader. Exec. v.p. Door County C. of C., Sturgeon Bay, Wis. Office: Door County C of C 6443 Green Bay Rd PO Box 219 Sturgeon Bay WI 54235*

HYLTON, TERRIE ELLERY, union executive; b. Detroit, Sept. 22, 1955; d. George Leroy and Hannah Belle (Mack) Ellery; m. Kenneth Niles Hylton Jr., 1 child, Kenneth Niles III. B.A. with honors, Wayne State U., 1975, M.A., 1984. Asst. juvenile ct. officer State of Mich., Detroit, 1978-79; counselor Wayne State U., 1979-80; admissions coordinator Detroit Inst. Tech., 1980-81; placement dir. Internat. Transp. Inst., Dearborn, Mich., 1981-82; program coordinator Mich. State AFL-CIO, Detroit, 1984—. Mem. Theatre Hospitality Enterprise, Detroit, 1980, editor newsletter, 1982, 83; vice chmn. Friends of Detroit Youtheatre, 1984, chmn., 1985; Democratic precinct del., Detroit, 1984. Mem. Am. Assn. Counseling and Devel., Nat. Employment Counselors Assn., Am. Coll. Personnel Assn., Assn. Specialists in Group Work, Founders Soc. Detroit Inst. Arts. Avocations: traveling; reading. Office: HCREP AFL-CIO 2550 W Grand Blvd Detroit MI 48208

HYNDMAN, ROBERT C., chemical company executive. Pres., chief operating officer, dir. Morton Thiokol, Inc., Chgo. Office: Morton Thiokol Inc 110 N Wacker Dr Chicago IL 60606*

HYSLOP, DAVID JOHNSON, arts administrator; b. Schenectady, June 27, 1942; s. Moses McDickens and Annie (Johnson) H.; B.S. in Music Edn., Ithaca Coll., 1965; m. Sandra Wheeler, June 25, 1978; children—Kristopher Jae, Alexander; stepchildren—Marc Langhammer, Monica Langhammer. Elem. sch. vocal music supr., Elmira Heights, N.Y., 1965-66; mgr. Elmira Symphony Choral Soc., 1966; asst. mng. dir. Minn. Orch., Mpls., 1966-72; gen. mgr. Oreg. Symphony Orch., Portland, 1972-78; exec. dir. St. Louis Symphony Soc., 1978—. Trustee, Nat. Com. on Symphony Orch. Support; bd. dirs. St. Louis Conservatory and Schs. for Arts, Portland State U., Chamber Music N.W.; bd. dirs. Am. Symphony Orch. League, also chmn. maj. mgrs. lobbyist Com. for Arts in Mo. Martha Baird Rockefeller grantee, 1966. Mem. Am. Symphony Orch. League. Clubs: Mo. Athletic, Univ. (St. Louis). Home: 7131 Pershing Saint Louis MO 63130 Office: 718 N Grand St Saint Louis MO 63103

IACCHEO, ARMAND RICHARD, meteorology executive, consultant; b. N.Y.C., Apr. 24, 1923; s. Armand and Anne Aurora (DiPietro) I.; m. Carole Armanda Soi, Mar. 30, 1946; children—Sandra Ann Iaccheo Lord, Karen E. Iaccheo Joest. Student, U. Calif.-Berkeley, 1941-42; degree in meteorology USAAF-TTC, 1943 B.S. in Natural Sci., Washington U., St. Louis, 1952. Cert. cons. meteorologist. Spl. Services meteorologist U.S. Weather Bur., 1949-52; research meteorologist, 1947-48; v.p. Weather Corp. Am., 1952-68, v.p., gen. mgr., St. Louis, 1970—; dir. environ. info. services Travelers Research Ctr., Hartford, Conn., 1969; cons. Served to capt. USAAF, 1942-46; ETO. Mem. Am. Meteorol. Soc., Nat. Council Indsl. Meteorologists (pres.-elect), Mo. Council Meteorol. Edn. and Research, Am. Meteorol. Soc. (chmn. St. Louis chpt. 1954, 61, Seal of Approval for radio weather broadcasting), Washington U. Alumni Assn. Office: Weather Corp of America 5 American Industrial Dr Saint Louis MO 63043

IACOBELLI, JOHN LOUIS, economist; b. Cleve., Dec. 24, 1931; s. Joseph and Theresa (Caporaso) I.; B.S., Kent State U., 1955, M.A., 1965; Ph.D., U. Tex., Austin, 1969; m. Eleanor M. Mandala, Sept. 3, 1956; children—Joseph, Andrew, Christopher. Sr. sales rep., ter. mgr. NCR, Cleve., 1957-64; asst. prof. labor and indsl. relations Cleve. State U., 1968-71, asso. prof. mgmt. and labor, 1971-76; prof. econs. Wright State U., 1976-78, chmn. dept., 1976-78; pres. Delphi Assocs., Inc., Cleve., 1972-75; economist, spl. rep. Columbus Mut. and other life ins. cos., Cleve., 1980—; v.p. Advance Planning Concepts, Inc., 1983—; registered rep. Integrated Resources Equity Corp., 1983-85, Lowry Fin. Services Corp., 1985—; cons. in field. Mem. legacy and planned giving com. Am. Cancer Soc.; mem. fin. com. St. Bartholomew's Ch. Served with U.S. Army, 1955-57. U.S. Dept. Labor grantee, 1967-68; HUD and Nat. League of Cities grantee, 1973-74. Mem. Am. Econ. Assn., Indsl. Relations Research Assn., Acad. Mgmt., Internat. Assn. Fin. Planners, Christian Family Movement, Delta Sigma Pi. Contbr. articles to profl. jours. Home: 19953 Idlewood Trail Strongsville OH 44136 Office: 6659 Pearl Rd Cleveland OH 44130

IACOCCA, LIDO ANTHONY (LEE), automotive company executive; b. Allentown, Pa., Oct. 15, 1924; s. Nicola and Antoinette (Perrotto) I; B.S., Lehigh U., 1945; M.E., Princeton U., 1946; m. Mary McCleary, Sept. 29, 1956 (dec.); children—Kathryn Lisa, Lia Antoinette. With Ford Motor Co., Dearborn, Mich., 1946-78, successively mem. field sales staff, various merchandising and tng. activities, asst. dirs. sales mgr., Phila., dist. sales mgr., Washington, 1946-56, truck mktg. mgr. div. office, 1956-57, car mktg. mgr., 1957-60, vehicle market mgr., 1960, v.p. Ford Motor Co., gen. mgr. Ford div., 1960-65, v.p. car and truck group, 1965-67, exec. v.p. of co., 1967-68, pres. of co., 1970-78, also pres. Ford N. Am. automobile ops.; pres., chief operating officer Chrysler Corp., Highland Park, Mich., 1978-79, chmn. bd., chief exec. officer, 1979—. Author: Iacocca: An Autobiography, 1984. Chmn. Statue of Liberty-Ellis Island Centennial Commn. Wallace Meml. fellow Princeton U. Mem. Tau Beta Pi. Club: Detroit Athletic. Office: Chrysler Corp 12000 Lynn Townsend Dr Highland Park MI 48231*

IANNACCONE, PHILIP MONROE, pathology educator; b. Syracuse, N.Y., May 3, 1948; s. Judith Ann Woznek, June 27, 1970; children—Philip, James, Stephen. B.Sc., Syracuse U., 1968; B.Sc. in Forestry, SUNY-Syracuse, 1968, M.D., 1972; Ph.D., U. Oxford, 1977. Diplomate Am. Bd. Pathology. Intern, SUNY Upstate Med. Ctr., Syracuse, 1972-73; resident Columbia U. Coll. Phys. and Surg., 1973-74; asst. prof. U. Calif.-San Diego, 1978-79, Northwestern U. Med. Sch., Chgo., 1979—. Contbr. articles to profl. jours. Mem. Internat. Acad. Pathologists, Am. Assn. Pathologists, Am. Assn. Cancer Research, AAAS, Am. Soc. Cell Biologists. Avocations: Skiing, photography, antiques. Office: Northwestern Univ Med Sch 303 E Chicago Ave Chicago IL 60611

IANNOLI, JOSEPH JOHN, JR., university development executive; b. Worcester, Mass., Oct. 28, 1939; s. Joseph John and Alice Bernadette (Moore) I.; A.B., Franklin and Marshall Coll., 1962; M.A., Syracuse U., 1967; m. Gail V. Cummings, Oct. 21, 1972; children—Juliet, Christopher. Devel. officer Franklin & Marshall Coll., Lancaster, Pa., 1965-68; asso. dir. med. devel. U. Miami, 1968-70; asst. dir., cons. Am. Bankers Assn., Washington, 1970-74, Marts & Lundy, Inc., N.Y.C., 1974-78; dir. capital support U. Hartford, Conn., 1978-82; v.p. devel. Ripon (Wis.) Coll., 1982—; sr. cons. J.M. Lord & Assos.; lectr. in field. Bd. dirs. Wau-Bun council Girl Scouts U.S.A. Recipient Samuel McDonald Humanitarian award, 1958. Cert. fund raising exec. Mem. Nat. Soc. Fund Raising Execs., Council for Advancement and Support of Edn., Fund Raising Inst., Bushnell Meml. Steering Com. Office: Box 248 Ripon Coll Ripon WI 54971

ICARD, LARRY DENNIS, social work educator, consultant; b. Lenoir, N.C., Aug. 4, 1949; s. Fred C. and Lorean M. (Thomas) I. B.A. in Sociology, Johnson C. Smith U., Charlotte, N.C., 1972; M.S.W., W.Va. U., 1975. Intern in social work N.C. Dept. Pub. Welfare, Charlotte, 1971; dir. minority recruitment Dis-Tran Personnel, Garland, Tex., 1972; pub. welfare worker Tex. Dept. Pub. Welfare, 1973; instr. dept. sociology and social work U. Wis.-Superior, 1976; asst. prof. social work Sch. Social Work, W.Va. U., Morgantown, 1976-80; asst. prof. Sch. Social Work, U. Cin., 1980—, chmn. baccalaureate social work program, 1980—; cons. organizational devel. Vice pres. Cin. Mental Health Assn., 1982—; trustee Humans United for Better Services Inc., Cin. Mem. Nat. Assn. Black Social Workers, Council Social Work Edn. Research in mental health. Office: Sch Social Work U Cin Cincinnati OH 45221

ICHNIOWSKI, THADDEUS CASIMIR, chemistry educator; b. Balt., June 1, 1933; s. Stanley Ferdinand and Stella Carolina (Mackowski) I.; m. Joan Pierce, July 25, 1959; children—Mary E., Isabelle A., Katherine L., Rebecca J. B.S., Washington Coll., 1955; M.S., Purdue U., Ph.D., 1961. Prof. chemistry Ill. State U., Normal, 1960—; vis. prof. Dow Chem. Co., Midland, Mich., 1980-81; speaker on careers in chemistry and coop. edn. Contbr. articles to profl. jours. Bd. dirs. Bloomington-Normal Pub. Transp. System, Ill., 1972-77; pres. Central Ill. Downs Syndrome Orgn., Bloomington and Normal, 1983. Served with U.S. Army, 1955-57. Mem. Am. Chem. Soc. (spl. intern 1978), Nat. Soc. Internship and Exptl. Edn., Midwest Coop. Edn. Assn., Ill. Acad. Scis. Republican. Roman Catholic. Avocations: travel, music. Home: 900 Randall Dr Normal IL 61761 Office: Ill State U Chemistry Dept Normal IL 61761

ICKOWICZ, GARY PEARCY, sales consultant, buyer, broker auto leasing; b. Toronto, Ont., Can., July 23, 1954; s. Joseph and Rose (Miller) I.; m. Gloria R. Levy. Student Ohio State U., 1972-75; A. Bus. Mgmt., Cuyahoga Community Coll., Cleve., 1983; student Ursuline Coll., Cleve., 1985—. Asst. mgr. Mogol's Mens Wear, Columbus, Ohio, 1975-76; mgmt. trainee Schottenstein's, Columbus, 1976-78; mgr. men's clothing Value City, Indpls., 1978-79; sales mgr., buyer J. Ickowicz Fur Salon, Inc., Cleve., 1979-84; sales cons. Allied Lighting Services Inc., Beachwood, Ohio, 1984—, sales mgr., Solon, Ohio, 1984—. Mem. Jewish Big Bro. Assn.; coach Tris Speaker Little League; active Ohio State Rep. campaign. Mem. Cleve. Fur Inst. Democrat. Jewish. Lodge: Masons. Home: 2049 S Green Rd South Euclid OH 44121 Office: PO Box 22903 Beachwood OH 44122

IDDINGS, ROGER GRIFFITH, college administrator, educator; b. Madison, Ind., June 4, 1930; s. Forrest and Cleta (Griffith) I.; m. Joy Lucelia Woods, Apr. 5, 1953; children—Pamela Joy, Roger Keith. B.A., Hanover Coll., 1952; M.Ed., Wayne State U., 1960; Ph.D., Ohio State U., 1966. Tchr. math. and sci. Edsel Ford High Sch., Dearborn, Mich., 1955-64; from instr. to prof. Wright State U., Dayton, Ohio, 1964—, dir. undergrad. studies, 1968-70, assoc. dean, 1970-73, dean, 1973—; vis. prof. Ohio State U., Columbus, summer 1967, Western Mich. U., Kalamazoo, summer 1968; cons. Ohio Dept. Edn., Columbus, 1975—. Author monograph: Memorandum to Faculty, 1977; Support of Teacher Education, 1978; contbr. articles to profl. jours. Active Montgomery County Adult Probationary Adv. Com., Dayton. Served with U.S. Army, 1952-54. Decorated Commendation medal U.S. Army, 1954; recipient Recognition of Service award state and profl. orgns. Mem. Tchr. Edn. Council State Colls. and Univs. (treas. 1982—, rep.). Baptist. Avocations: woodworking; reading; music; church work. Home: 1850 Stonewood Dr Dayton OH 45432 Office: Wright State U Coll Edn and Human Services 228 Millett Hall Dayton OH 45435

IDLEMAN, KENNETH DARRELL, college president; b. Champaign, Ill., Aug. 18, 1947; s. Kenneth F. and Lois R. (Collins) I.; m. Kaylene Ruth Conover, Aug. 17, 1968; children—Karissa Marie, Kyle David, Kamille Joy. A.B., Lincoln Christian Coll., Ill., 1969; M.Div., Lincoln Christian Sem., 1973. Ordained to ministry Christian Ch., 1968. Pastor, Broadwell Christian Ch., Ill., 1968-70, Mt. Pulaski Christian Ch., Ill., 1970-72; adminstr. Lincoln Christian Coll., 1972-73; prof. Ozark Bible Coll., Joplin, Mo., 1973-77, v.p., 1977-79, pres., 1979—, trustee, 1979—; bd. dirs. Am. Rehab. Ministry, Joplin, 1979-81, Christ in Youth, Joplin, 1980-82. Republican. Office: 1111 N Main St Joplin MO 64801

IDOL-MAESTAS, LORNA JEANNE, researcher, teacher educator; b. Glenwood Springs, Colo., Mar. 7, 1947; d. Loren Ellis and Lana (Gregory) Idol; m. Ricardo Timoteo Maestas, Mar. 7, 1978; 1 child, Paz Timoteo. Student U. Denver, 1965-67; B.S. in Edn., U. Nev., 1969, M.Ed. (fellow), 1974; Ph.D. in Edn., U. N.Mex., 1979. Cert. spl. edn. tchr., Nev. Counselor Wiltwyke Sch. for Boys, Ossining, N.Y., summer 1970; supr. tchr. Student Teaching Program, Dept. Spl. Edn., U. Nev., Reno, 1970-74; tchr. Washoe County Sch. Dist. Vets. Meml. Elem. Sch., Reno, 1970-74; grad. asst. spl. edn. U. N.Mex., Albuquerque, 1975, field supr. Spl. Edn., 1977-78, instr., 1976-78; tchr., lang. acquisition Albuquerque Pub. Schs., 1976; grad. intern Lovelace-Bataan Clinic Albuquerque, 1976; vis. lectr., coordinator Resource/Cons. Tchr. Program, Dept. Spl. Edn., U. Ill., Urbana, 1979—, dir. Lab. for Reading Improvement, Ctr. for Study of Reading, 1985—, instr. grad. courses; cons. pub. sch. inservice tchr. edn.; statis. analysis cons. Mem. com. for Rights of Exceptional Children, N.Mex., 1976-78; mem. ch. soc. com. 1st United Meth. Ch., 1981—. Recipient Scholars' Travel award U. Ill., 1981, 83, 84. Outstanding Presentation award Internat. Council for Exceptional Children, 1981. Mem. Council Exceptional Children (rep. to bd. govs. of tchr. edn. div. 1984—), Council Children with Learning Disabilities. Democrat. Methodist. Author: Special Educators Consultation Handbook, 1983. Editorial bd. Jour. Tchr. Edn. and Spl. Edn., 1984—. Contbr. articles to profl. jours. Home: 1807 Coventry Dr Champaign IL 61821 Office: 1310 S 6th St Suite 288 Edn Bldg Champaign IL 61820

IFFRIG, GREG FRANK, biologist; b. St. Louis, Aug. 30, 1954; s. Charles Frank and Mary Madeline (Hughes) I.; m. Lynn Katherine Rothermich, Nov. 24, 1984. B.S., Southwest Mo. State U., 1976; M.S., U. Mo., 1978. Natural areas coordinator Mo. Dept. Natural Resources, Jefferson City, Mo., 1979—. Author: (with others) Directory of Missouri Natural Areas, 1985. Editor, founder: Natural Areas Jour. 1981—. Tech. editor: Terrestrial Natural Communities of Missouri, 1985. Contbr. articles to profl. jours. Recipient Congressional Record-Interior Com. Recognition of Leadership U.S. Senate, 1984; Edward K. Love fellow, 1978; U.S. State Dept. grantee, 1982. Mem. Natural Areas Assn. (bd. dirs. 1981—), Mo. Acad. Scis., Mo. Native Plant Soc., The Nature Conservancy (bd. dirs. Mo. chpt. 1979—, chmn. stewardship com. 1982—). Democrat. Roman Catholic. Club: Sierra (bd. dirs. Ozark chpt. 1980-84, sec. 1980-81, Sierran of the Yr. 1983). Avocations: bicycle touring; landscape photography; travel; mountaineering. Home: Route 2 Box 357 Ashland MO 65010 Office: Mo Dept Natural Resources PO Box 176 Jefferson City MO 65102

IGASAKI, MASAO, JR., utility company executive; b. Los Angeles, May 24, 1925; s. Masao and Aiko (Kamayatsu) I.; m. Grace Kushino, June 5, 1948; children—David, Paul. B.S. in Bus. Adminstrn., Northwestern U., 1949; M.B.A., U. Chgo., 1963. C.P.A., Ill. With Peoples Gas Light & Coke Co., Chgo., 1949—, asst. v.p., 1970-76, asst. v.p., controller, 1976-77, v.p., controller, 1977-81, v.p., 1981—; v.p., controller Peoples Energy Corp., Chgo., 1981—. Scoutmaster N.W. Council Boy Scouts Am., 1964-67; trustee Mt. Sinai Hosp., Chgo., 1980—; bd. dirs. Civic Fedn., Chgo., 1982—; bd. govs. Chgo. Heart Assn., 1984—. Served with AUS, 1944-46. Mem. United Ch. of Christ. Clubs: Economic, Univ. Home: 247 E Chestnut St Apt 1201 Chicago IL 60611 Office: Peoples Gas Light & Coke Co 122 S Michigan Ave Chicago IL 60603

IGWEBUIKE, KATHLEEN OBEAGELI, health educator, nurse; b. Nigeria, Jan. 10, 1941; came to U.S., 1973; d. Anthony Nkakwa and Eunice M. Obinwa; m. Godwin Chike Igwebuike, Sept. 22, 1962; children—Eboh, Alvin, Leo, John, Ada, Uche. Diploma of Midwifery, St. Theresa Sch. Nursing, Nigeria, 1959; diploma of Food Hygiene, Coll. Distributive Trades, London, 1963; R.N., U. Toledo, 1976, B.S. in Community Health, 1977, M.Ed., 1980. Lab. asst. U. Toledo, 1974-76; social worker Toledo Clinic, 1977-83; nurse Toledo Health and Retiree Extended Care Center, 1977—; pediatric unit coordinator St. Theresa's Hosp., Nsukka, Nigeria, 1959; mid-wife coordinator Ngwo Maternity Home (Nigeria), 1960; project dir. and founder Kwashiorkor Clinic, Mbaise, Nigeria, 1968-70; cons. Health Clinics Internat., Toledo. Mem. Royal Soc. Health (London), Am. Sch. Health Assn., Ohio Sickle Cell Affected Families Assn., U. Toledo Alumni Assn. Roman Catholic. Home: 1142 W Woodruff Toledo OH 43606 also PO Box 11 Nsukka Anambra State Nigeria

IHLANFELDT, WILLIAM, university administrator, consultant; b. Belleville, Ill., Dec. 12, 1936; s. Raymond William and Olivia Anna (Boycourt) I.; m. D. Jeannine Huguelet, May 7, 1978; children—Troy, Kimberly, Holly. B.S., Ill. Wesleyan U., 1959, LL.D., 1980; M.A., Northwestern U., 1963, Ph.D., 1970. Adminstr., Monticello Coll., Godfrey, Ill., 1959-60; tchr., coach Rich Twp. High Sch., Park Forest, Olympia Fields, Ill., 1960-64; dir. fin. aid Northwestern U., Evanston, Ill., 1964-67, dean admission and fin. aid, 1973-78, v.p. instnl. relations, dean admissions, 1978—; chmn. pub. policy Consortium Financing Higher Edn., Cambridge, Mass., 1979-83; chmn. Fedn. Ill. Ind. Colls. and Univs., Springfield, 1981-83; vice chmn. Econ. Devel. Corp., 1983—; mem. exec. com. Student Loan Mktg. Assn., Washington, 1975—; cons. in field. Author: Achieving Optimal Enrollments and Tuition Revenues, 1980; contbr. chpts. to books, articles to profl. publs. Founder, Northwestern U. Chgo. Action Project, Evanston, 1966, Evanston/Univ. Research Park, 1984; co-author Ill. Ind. Higher Edn. Loan Authority, Northbrook, Ill., 1981. Wieboldt Found. grantee, 1966, 67, 68. Mem. Am. Assn. Higher Edn., Coll. Entrance Exam. Bd. (service award 1978), Phi Delta Kappa. Club: Indian Hill (Winnetka, Ill.). Avocations: tennis, skiing. Office: Northwestern Univ 633 Clark St Evanston IL 60201

IHLE, HERBERT DUANE, food company executive; b. Ames, Iowa, July 8, 1939; s. Joe and Martha Marie (Larson) I.; m. Catherine Eileen Klein, Dec. 27, 1959; children—Brenda Kirsten, Valerie Anne, Michael David. A.A., Waldorf Jr. Coll., Forest City, Iowa, 1959; B.A., Concordia Coll., Moorhead, Minn., 1961; M.S., U. Minn., 1963. Dir. fin. planning Pillsbury Co., Mpls., 1976-78, sr. v.p. fin. Burger King, 1979-80, v.p. fin. foods, 1980-81, v.p., controller, 1981-82, exec. v.p., chief fin. officer Burger King, 1982-83, sr. v.p., controller, 1983—; dir. Burger King Corp., Miami, Fla., Pillsbury Commodity Services, Chgo. Mem. Fin. Execs. Inst. (com. on copr. reporting). Republican. Lutheran. Clubs: Mpls., Mpls. Athletic. Avocation: tennis. Home: 6208 Fox Meadow Ln Edina MN 55436 Office: Pillsbury Co 200 S 6th St MS 4057 Minneapolis MN 55402

ILGES, HERMAN JOHN, industrial engineer; b. St. Louis, Aug. 29, 1932; s. Herman John and Florence Emma (Buerk) I.; m. Henrietta Elizabeth Risse, Nov. 27, 1952; children—Herman, Theodore, Daniel, Margaret, Henry, David. B.S. in Indsl. Engring., Washington U.-St. Louis, 1963. Indsl. engr. Mo. Pacific R.R., 1963-65, Gen. Steel Co., Granite City, Ill., 1965-66; indsl. engr., mgr.

quality control Olin Corp., East Alton, Ill., 1966-70; indsl. engr. Maloney Electric Co., St. Louis, 1970-71; plant supt. Incarnate Word Hosp., St. Louis, 1971—. Served with U.S. Army, 1953-55. Mem. Am. Inst. Plant Engrs., (cert.), Hosp. Engr. Maintenance Assn., Am. Soc. Hosp. Engring of Am. Hosp. Assn., Nat. Rifle Assn.

ILITCH, MICHAEL, professional sports team executive. Owner Detroit Red Wings, hockey team. Office: Detroit Red Wings 600 Civic Center Dr Detroit MI 48226*

ILORETA, ALFREDO T., urologist; b. Sinait, Philippines, Dec. 9, 1947; s. Basilio and Hipolita (Tabutol) I.; m. Maria Delia Calo; children—Alfred Marc, Francis, Joseph. B.S., Far Eastern U., Manila, 1966; M.D. cum laude, U. Santo Tomas, Manila, 1971. Rotating intern St. Thomas Hosp., Akron, Ohio, 1972-73, resident in surgery, 1973-74; resident in surgery St. Luke's Hosp., Bethlehem, Pa., 1974-75; resident in urology Albert Einstein Coll. Medicine, Bronx, N.Y., 1975-79, Sloan-Kettering Meml. Cancer Ctr., N.Y.C., 1978; practice medicine specializing in urology, Topeka, Kans., 1979—; chief of urology VA Med. Ctr.; staff urologist Topeka Urology Clinic, 1982—. Contbr. articles to profl. jours. Mem. Am. Urological Assn., Am. Soc. Clin. Urologists. Home: 6950 SW 33d St Topeka KS 66614 Office: 1516 W 6th St Topeka KS 66606

ILTIS, JOHN FREDERIC, advertising-public relations company executive; b. Chgo., Dec. 14, 1940; s. Frederic and Alice Henrietta (Nachman) I.; student Lincoln Coll., 1962; A.A., Bradley U., 1964; m. Gillian Ann Cane, Nov. 20, 1976; children—Claire Alexandra, Annika Leigh. Advt., pub. relations asst. Balaban & Katz Theatres, Chgo., 1965-68; midwest dir. advt., pub. relations Universal Pictures, Chgo., 1968-69, field ops. dir., N.Y.C., 1969-70; owner, operator film prodn. and mktg. co., London, 1971-73; pres. John Iltis Assocs., entertainment, advt. and pub. relations, Chgo., 1973—; instr. pub. relations Columbia Coll., Chgo. Bd. dirs. Variety Club Ill., Lawyers for the Creative Arts, Film Ctr. of Art Inst. of Chgo.; mem. vis. bd. dirs. DePaul Goodman Sch. Drama. Served with U.S. Army, 1964. Mem. Publicity Club Chgo., Chgo. TV Acad., Publicists Guild. Home: 3844 N Kenmore Chicago IL 60613 Office: 666 N Lake Shore Dr Chicago IL 60611

IMBROGNO, EUGENE FRANCIS, restaurant company executive; b. Montgomery, W.Va., Dec. 1, 1946; s. Eugene F. and Alice Josephine (Winkiewicz) I.; m. June Ann Paxton, Dec. 28, 1967; children—Christopher, Jason. B.S. in Bus. Adminstrn., W.Va. U., 1968, M.B.A., 1969. Market researcher Gen. Mills, Inc., Mpls., 1969-71; dir. New Concept devel. retail stores Borden, Inc., Columbus, Ohio, 1971-74; pres. Wendy's of W.Va., Inc., Charleston, 1974-78; v.p. product research and devel. Wendy's Internat., Inc., Dublin, Ohio, 1979-81; sr. v.p. Sisters Internat., Inc., Westerville, Ohio, 1981—; dir. Stanley Steemer Internat., Dublin. Bd. dirs. W.Va. U. Found., Morgantown. Roman Catholic. Home: 850 Bluffview Dr Worthington OH 43085 Office: 167 S State St Westerville OH 43081

IMGRUND, RICHARD EDWARD, corporate executive; b. Johnstown, Pa., June 25, 1931; s. Dominic Edward and Gladys Mary (Werner) I.; m. Victoria Mary Alexander, June 19, 1954; children—Richard, Edward, Dorothy, Theodore, Alexandra. B.S. in Bus. Adminstrn., Duquesne U., 1953. Prodn. foreman Continental Co., Three Rivers, Mich., 1959-64, systems analyst, 1964-73; dir. data processing Armstrong Internat., Three Rivers, 1973—. Treas., St. Joseph County Republican Com., Three Rivers, 1978—; bd. dirs. Three Rivers Hosp., 1973-80, pres., 1976-80. Served to 1st lt. USAF, 1954-59. Mem. Assn. Systems Mgmt. (pres. 1971-72, div. dir. 1972-74, Achievement prize, 1981, cert. systems profl.). Republican. Roman Catholic. Lodge: Elks. Avocations: canoeing, square dancing. Home: 501 E Hoffman St Three Rivers MI 49093 Office: Armstrong Internat 816 Maple St Three Rivers MI 49093

IMMER, BERYLE JEAN, nurse; b. Oklahoma City, Mar. 25, 1937; d. George Guy and Blanche Ermal (Garrett) Clesson; m. Robert Glenn Immer, June 23, 1962; children—Joy Lynn, Michael Guy, Steven Frederick. Diploma in Nursing, Independence Sanitarium and Hosp. Sch. Nursing, 1959; A.A., Graceland Coll., 1959; B.S. in Nursing, U. Colo., 1961; M.Ed., U. Mo.-Columbia, 1981. Pub. health nurse Graham County Health Dept. Safford, Ariz., 1961-62; nursing instr. Independence Sanitarium Hosp. Sch. Nursing, Mo., 1965-67; pub. health nurse City Health Dept., Independence, 1967-68; instr., coordinator Kansas City Sch. Dist., Mo., 1978-81; coordinator adult health occupations programs Independence Sch. Dist., 1981—; mem. program of practical nursing task force Mo. Council Practical Nursing Educators, 1984—; expert witness on nursing edn. Mo. House Com., 1983. Bd. dirs., sec. Center Place Credit Union, 1982—; bldg. com. Gudgell Park Congregation, Reorganized Ch. of Jesus Christ of Latter Day Saints, 1983—, organ com., 1984. Mem. Nat. League Nursing, Am. Vocat. Assn., Mo. Vocat. Assn., Mo. Project Aware, Practical Nurse Educators of Mo. Avocations: piano; organ; painting. Office: Independence Sch Dist Adult Health Occupations Program 1509 W Truman Rd Independence MO 64050

IMMKE, KEITH HENRY, lawyer; b. Peoria, Ill., Jan. 18, 1953; s. Francis William and Pearl Lenora (Kime) I. B.A., U. Ill., 1975; J.D., So. Ill. U., 1978. Bars: Ill. 1978, U.S. Dist. Ct. (so. and ea. dists.) Ill. 1979. Assoc. Lawrence E. Johnson & Assocs., Champaign, Ill., 1979—. Mem. ABA, Ill. State Bar Assn., Phi Kappa Phi, Pi Sigma Alpha, Phi Alpha Delta. Office: Lawrence E Johnson & Assocs 202 W Hill St Champaign IL 61820

IMREDY, STEPHEN ALMOS, electronics and computer services company executive; b. Gyula, Hungary, May 2, 1936; came to U.S., 1957, naturalized, 1962; s. Denis Stephen Imredy and Clara (Jantsovits) Kendi; m. Diane Cooper Sawyer, Nov. 6, 1958; children—Annemarie, Jennifer. B.A. in Internat. Relations, U. Denver, 1962; B.Fgn.Trade, Am. Grad. Sch. Internat. Mgmt., 1963. Sales mgr. Far East, Cummins Engine Co., Inc., Columbus, Ind., 1968-72, dir. internat. parts sales, 1972-73; dir. internat. mktg. group Cin. Milacron, Inc., Cin., 1973-77; pres. internat. Mfg. Data Systems, Ann Arbor, Mich., 1977-83; pres. controls and data systems div. White Consol. Industries, Inc., Cleve., 1983-84; exec. v.p. Hunkar Labs., Inc., Cin., 1984—, also dir., 1980—; dir. Encode Tech., Inc., Nashua, N.H., 1984—. Mem. steering com. Tech. Internat. Council, Ann Arbor, 1983. Mem. Am. Mgmt. Assn. Republican. Roman Catholic. Clubs: Barton Hills Country, Travis Pointe Country (Ann Arbor). Avocations: stamp and coin collections; swimming; bridge. Office: Hunkar Labs Inc 7007 Valley Ave Cincinnati OH 45244

INATOME, RICK, retail computer company executive; b. Detroit, July 27, 1953; s. Joseph T. and Atsuko Nan (Kumagai) I.; B.A. in Econs., Mich. State U., 1976; m. Joyce Helene Kitchen, Aug. 18, 1979; children—Dania Lynn, Evan Richard, Blake Everett. Vice pres., gen. mgr., founder Computer Mart, Inc., Clawson, Mich., 1976-85, pres., chief exec. officer, 1985—; lectr., cons. computers; instr. Marygrove Coll., Macomb Community Coll. Mem. Engring. Soc. Detroit, Am. Mgmt. Assn., ACM, Phi Delta Theta. Office: 1800 W Maple Rd Troy MI 48084

INBODY, MELVIN ROBERT, automotive executive; b. Findlay, Ohio, July 20, 1922; s. George Washington and Bertha (Powell) I.; m. Elizabeth Ann Kresser, June 26, 1945; children—Steven, Gregory, Amy, Emily. Student Findlay Coll., Ohio, 1940-42. Sales mgr. Ohio Automotive Supply Co., Findlay, Marion, Fostoria, 1945-56; self-employed cons. sales engr., 1956-58; pres. Centerline Steering Axle Div., Paul M. Gillmor Co., Findlay, 1958-61; pres. Centerline Steering Safety Axle Corp., Findlay, 1973—; exec. v.p., gen. mgr. Diversified Interest, Inc., Findlay, 1961-73. Exec. com. Hancock County Republican Party. Served to tech. sgt. USAF, 1942-45; ETO. Decorated Air Medal with 3 Oak Leaf Clusters, Purple Heart, Campaign commendations. Methodist. Clubs: Am. Ex-prisoners War, Inc. (Grand Prairie, Tex.), Am. Ex-Prisoners of War (dir. NW Central Ohio chpt.) Mil. Order Purple Heart Ohio (Americanism officer), Mil. Order Purple Heart Findlay (sr. vice comdr.), DAV, Am. Legion, Caterpillar Internat. Patentee improvements in controlled steering stability, brakes and wheel design; pioneer centerline steering safety axles for surface vehicles, conceived sci. test performance data used by fed. testing agys.; contbr. tech. articles on hwy. safety improvement to govt. agys., U. S. Army, research insts. publs. Home: 712 Franklin Ave Findlay OH 45840 Office: Danmar Profl Bldg Suite 7 233 S Main St Findlay OH 45840

INCH, MORRIS ALTON, theology educator; b. Wytopitlock, Maine, Oct. 21, 1925; s. Clarence Sherwin and Blanche (Mix) I.; m. Joan Dryden Parker, Dec. 16, 1950; children—Deborah, Lois, Thomas, Joel, Mark. A.B., Houghton Coll., 1949; M.Div., Gordon Div. Sch., 1951; Ph.D., Boston U., 1955. Pastor Am. Bapt. Chs., South Boston and Somerville, Mass., 1951-60; faculty, dean of students, acad. dean Gordon Coll., Wenham, Mass., 1955-62; prof. theology, chmn. dept. div. Wheaton Coll., Ill., 1962—. Author: Psychology in the Psalms, 1969; Christianity Without Walls, 1972; Paced By God, 1973; Celebrating Jesus as Lord, 1975, Understanding Bible Prophecy, 1977; The Evangelical Challenge, 1978; My Servant Job, 1979; Doing Theology Across Cultures, 1982; Saga of the Spirit: A Biblical, Systematic and Historical Theology of the Holy Spirit, 1985; editor: (with Samuel Schultz) Interpreting the Word of God, 1976; (with C.H. Bullock) The Literature and Meaning of the Scripture, 1981; (with R. Youngblood) The Living and Active Word of God, 1983. Contbr. articles to profl. jours. Mem. Coll. Theology Soc., Evang. Theol. Soc. Avocations: tennis; swimming; jogging. Office: Wheaton Coll Wheaton IL 60187

INFIELD, MARTHEA MAE, mental health service executive; b. Cleve., Dec. 31, 1929; d. Neil Edward and Freda Margaret (Schray) Bowler; m. Dwight Hosak Infield, Nov. 14, 1953; children—Susan, Dwight David, Donald, Elisabeth. B.B.A., Fenn Coll., 1952; M.S., Case Western Res. U., 1970. Asst. to overseas div. mgr. Goodyear Tire & Rubber, Akron, Ohio, 1953-54; social worker Lucas County Welfare Dept., Toledo, 1964-65; social worker protective services Cuyahoga County Welfare Dept., Cleve., 1967-68; crisis counselor Crisis Intervention Team, Cleve., 1970-72, coordinator, 1972-74, exec. dir. CIT Mental Health Services, 1974—. Republican. Presbyterian. Home: 8381 Celianna Strongsville OH 44136 Office: CIT Mental Health Services 2177 S Taylor Rd University Heights OH 44118

INGEBRITSEN, JEFFREY CHARLES, lawyer; b. Madison, Wis., Oct. 18, 1955; s. Charles Roger Ingebritsen and Carol Lucia (Knoke) Bender; m. Barbara June Black, May 21, 1983. B.S. in Criminal Justice/Corrections, U. Wis.-Platteville, 1977; J.D., Marquette U., 1980. Bar: Wis. 1980, U.S. Dist. Ct. (we. and ea. dists.) Wis. 1980. Assoc., Hamilton & Mueller, S.C., Dodgeville, Wis., 1980-81; ptnr. Knoke & Ingebritsen, Monroe, Wis., 1981—. Mem. ABA, State of Wis. Bar, Acad. Trial Lawyers Am., Wis. Acad. Trial Lawyers, Green County Bar Assn. (sec. 1983-84), Monroe Jaycees (pres. 1984-85). Republican. Methodist. Club: Monroe City Band. Home: 1705 28th Ave Monroe WI 53566 Office: Knoke & Ingebritsen 1904 10th St Monroe WI 53566

INGERSOLL, CHARLES CARVER, hospital administrator; b. Cedar Rapids, Iowa, Mar. 22, 1922; s. Charles Otto and Mabel Annetta (Carver) I.; m. Jane Weeks, June 30, 1946; children—Scott C., Barbara J., Nanette Ingersoll Hartman, Martin G. B.S. in Commerce, U. Iowa, 1943; M.H.A., Washington U., St. Louis, 1951. Asst. supt. U. Iowa Hosps. and Clinics, Iowa City, 1951-64; exec. dir. Broadlawns Med. Ctr., Des Moines, 1964—; mem. Des Moines Hosp. Council, 1964—; dir. Health Planning Council Central Iowa, 1966-72; mem. Iowa Hosp. Research and Edn. Found. Bd., 1968—, pres., 1971-75; mem. Iowa Hosp. Licensing Bd., 1968-80; mem. adv. com. Iowa-S.D. Blue Cross, 1970-80. Served to capt. U.S. Army, 1943-46; ETO. Decorated Bronze Star (2), Purple Heart. Mem. Iowa Hosp. Assn. (dir. 1966-78, pres. 1970-71), Am. Hosp. Assn. (del. 1971-78, trustee 1979-82), Am. Coll. Hosp. Adminstrs., Am. Hosp. Assn. Home: 1201 21st St West Des Moines IA 50265 Office: Broadlawns Med Ctr 18th St and Hickman Rd Des Moines IA 50314

INGERSOLL, JOHN THOMAS, manufacturing company executive; b. Huntington, W.Va., July 14, 1939; s. John Fredrick and Glenn Claire (Pirrung) I.; m. Martha Mae Miller, Jan. 23, 1960; children—Cynthia Claire, Catherine Elizabeth, Laura Ellen. B.B.A.; student Marshall U., 1957-62, Toledo U., 1965, UCLA, 1968, Purdue U., 1970, Northwestern U., 1985. With Owens-Ill., Inc., Toledo, Ohio, 1964—, dir. corp. staff adminstrn., 1975-78, v.p., dir. total compensation, 1978-85, v.p. exec. compensation and succession planning, 1985—; dir. planning and program control HUD, Washington, 1971-72. Chmn. Toledo Area Govtl. Research Assn. Studies, 1976-78; elder Glendale Presbyterian Ch., 1979—. Served to 1st lt. U.S. Army, 1962-64. Mem. Vanderbilt Group, Presdl. Interchange Exec. Assn. (Outstanding Achievement award 1972), Am. Compensation Assn., Sigma Alpha Epsilon. Presbyn. Home: 4838 Eastwick Dr Toledo OH 43614 Office: Owens-Ill Inc One Sea Gate St Toledo OH 43666

INGLE, CLYDE, state education official. Exec. dir. Higher Edn. Coordinating Bd., State of Minn., St. Paul. Office: Higher Edn Coordinating Bd Suite 400 Capitol Square Bldg 550 Cedar St Saint Paul MN 55101*

INGLE, JAMES HOBART, engineering technician; b. Dayton, Ohio, Nov. 30, 1951; s. Hobart Baird and Helen Elizabeth (Miller) I. A.A.S., Mich. Technol. U., 1972; postgrad. Bay-de-Noc Community Coll., Escanaba, Mich., 1973. Cert. engring. technician Nat. Inst. Cert. in Engring. Technologies. Mem. survey crew Davis Surveying, Escanaba, summers 1970-71, survey crew chief, 1972-73; survey crew chief, constrn. insp. Coleman Engring. Co., Escanaba, 1974-75; hwy. constrn. insp. Mich. Dept. Transp., Crystal Falls, 1975; constrn. insp. Soil Testing Services, Inc. (now STS Cons. Ltd.), Marquette, Mich., 1976—, also office mgr., sr. engring. technician. Mem. Am. Soc. Cert. Engring. Technicians, Mich. Technol. U. Alumni Assn., Marquette Jaycees (dir. 1977-79, treas. 1978-79, community action v.p. 1979-80, pres. 1980-81, chmn. 1981-82), Mich. Jaycees (region instnl. coordinator 1983-84, region 1 dir. 1984-85 dist. B dir. 1982-83). Club: Mich. Technol. U. Huskies (Houghton). Home: Star Route Box 447 Gwinn MI 49841 Office: 1909 Enterprise St Marquette MI 49855

INGRAHAM, VIVIAN JUNE LOWELL, employment specialist; b. Omaha, June 1, 1922; d. John Calvert and Pearl Mabel (Whitscell) Lowell; student schs. Omaha; Edwin L. Ingraham, 1948; children—Richard D., Leroy Lowell, John Edwin, Jeffrey Scott; m. 2d, Clarence Parson, Sept. 7, 1969. Supr. customer service Met. Utilities Dist., 1940-46; news reporter sta. KBON, Omaha, 1962-67; med. transcriber VA Hosp., Omaha, 1971-73; exec. dir. Gt. Plains Council Girl Scouts U.S.A., Omaha, 1973-75; job developer City of Omaha, 1976-81; employment coordinator CETA, Iowa, 1981-83; employment specialist Crawford Rehab. Services, Omaha, 1983—. Exec. com. Mid-Am. Council Boy Scouts Am., 1960—, Fontenelle Dist. Boy Scouts Am., 1958-76; youth coordinator Douglas County ARC, 1965-70; dist. II dir. Nebr. State PTA, 1964-68; v.p. Omaha PTA Council, 1966-68; pres. Walnut Hill Sch. PTA, 1958-60, Monroe Sch., 1965-67, Fontenelle Schs., 1962-64; dist. del. Rep. party; state PTA hon. life mem. Recipient hon. nat. life PTA award, 1972, Good Neighbor award Ak-Sar-Ben, 1970, Brotherhood Week-Good Neighbor award NCCJ, 1967, service award ARC, 1968-71; nat. officer (Stewards) Nat. Presbyn. Mariners, 1960-66; hon. adm. Nebr. Navy; Outstanding Citizen award Omaha Public Schs. Mem. Profl. Assn. Girl Scout Execs. Presbyterian. Panelist: Discrimination and Its Effect on Children, 1970; author booklet: A Look at PTA, 1966; contbr. articles to religious mags. Office: Crawford Rehab Services 511 N 87th St Omaha NE 68114

INGRAM, CHEYRL DELORES, public defender; b. Jackson, Tenn., Dec. 10, 1953; d. Walter James and Geneva (Davis) Johnson; m. Donald Eugene Ingram, Aug. 24, 1974; 1 child, Matthew Andre. B.A., U. Wis.-Madison, 1974; J.D., John Marshall Law Sch., 1978. Bar: Ill. 1979, U.S. Dist. Ct. (no. dist.) 1979. Asst. pub. defender Cook County, Chgo., 1979—. Democrat. Baptist. Office: Cook County Public Defenders 1100 S Hamilton Chicago IL 60612

INGRAM, DAVID CHRISTOPHER, physicist; material scientist; b. Nottingham, Eng., Sept. 9, 1953; came to U.S., 1982; s. Eric and Dorothy Mary (Armstrong) I.; m. Angela Mary Cross, Mar. 31, 1979; children—Paul Francis, Mark Edward, Elizabeth Mary. B.Sc., Salford U., Eng., 1975, M.Sc., 1976, Ph.D., 1980. Research fellow Salford U., 1978-82; sr. scientist Universal Energy Systems, Dayton, Ohio, 1982—. Mem. London Inst. Physics, London Inst. Elec. Engrs., Materials Research Soc., Am. Phys. Soc. Mem. Ch. of Eng. Avocations: reading, walking, fishing, cooking. Home: 239 Northwood Dr Yellow Springs OH 45387 Office: Universal Energy Systems Inc 4401 Dayton Xenia Rd Dayton OH 45432

INGRAM, LOIS SWINTON, pharmacist; b. Galesburg, Ill., Oct. 13, 1934; d. Wayne and Hope Gurnee (Giddings) Swinton; B.S., St. Louis Coll. Pharmacy, 1963; M.A., Webster U., 1985; m. William Ingram, Mar. 21, 1954; children—Susan, William Scott. Pharmacist, Bakers Rexall Drug Store, Keokuk, Iowa, 1963-69; dir. pharacy Graham Hosp., Keokuk, 1969-74; pharmacist Osco Drug Store, Keokuk, 1974-75; dir. pharmacy St. Lukes Hosp. West, Chesterfield, Mo., 1975—. Mem. Am. Soc. Hosp. Pharmacists, Mo. Soc. Hosp. Pharmacists, St. Louis Soc. Hosp. Pharmacists. Republican. Episcopalian. Home: 710 Wild Walnut St Manchester MO 63011 Office: 232 Woodsmill Rd Chesterfield MO 63017

INGRAM, TERRENCE NEALE, insurance agent; b. Shullsburg, Wis., Nov. 21, 1939; s. Forrest R. and Ida D. (Fiedler) I.; m. Nancy June Fleming Laun, May 30, 1981. B.S., U. Wis.-Platteville, 1961. Instr. physics and math. U. Wis., Platteville, 1961-64; Bald Eagle researcher, 1964-65; bird instr. Wis. Audubon Camp, 1964-65; tchr. high sch., Mauston, Wis., 1965-66, Cuba City, Wis., 1966-67; instr. physics U. Wis., Platteville, 1967-68; tchr. high sch., Harvard, Ill., 1968-70; field underwriter N.Y. Life Ins. Co., 1970-84; ind. agent, 1984—; founder, pres., exec. dir. Eagle Valley Environmentalists, 1972-84, The Eagle Found., 1984—. Bd. dirs. North Central Audubon Council, 1966-70; bd. dirs. Ill. Audubon Soc., 1963-70, v.p., 1970. Recipient Honor Roll award Izaak Walton League Am., 1976; Sol Feinstone Environ. award SUNY-Syracuse, 1979; Protector of Environment award Chgo. Audubon Soc., 1981. Mem. Assn. Life Underwriters, Wis. Acad. Sci., Northwest Ill. Guernsey Assn. (pres. 1982—), Inland Bird Banding Assn. (pres. 1983—). Republican. Editor: Bird Banding News, 1961-65. Coordinator: No. Am. Bird Bander, 1984—. Home: 8384 N Broadway Apple River IL 61001 Office: 300 Hickory St Apple River IL 61001

INKS, GERALD DUANE, television station engineer; b. Dayton, Ohio, Sept. 4, 1961; s. Duane G. Inks and Martha Lynn (Winfrey) Ridge. Assoc. Sci. in Elec. Engring. Tech., Purdue U., 1981; student Ind. U./Purdue U.-Indpls., 1982—. Studio engr. Neon Cornfield Rec. Studios, Indpls., 1978, Frontier Studios, Indpls., 1979; salesman Radio Shack, Indpls., summer 1981; TV engr. WISH-TV, Indpls., 1982—. Investigator, Castreton Fire Dept., Indpls., 1982—, capt. fire prevention, 1983—; spl. dep. Marion County Sheriff's Dept., Indpls., 1984—. Hoosier scholar State of Ind., 1979. Mem. Marion County Vol. Firemen's Assn., Marion County Dep. Sheriff's Lodge, Indpls. Repeater Assn., Internat. Thespian Soc. (pres. 1977). Methodist. Avocations: airplane pilot; computers; electronics; amateur radio. Home: Apt B 7154 Whitestone Rd Indianapolis IN 46256 Office: WISH-TV 1950 N Meridian Indianapolis IN 46220

INMAN, LYDIA LUCILLE, retired university dean; b. Collins, Iowa, June 28, 1918; d. Stephen Wall and Florence Iva (Dickson) I. B.S., Iowa State U., 1940, M.S., 1950; Ph.D., U. Minn., 1963. Tchr. home econs. secondary schs., Iowa, Ill., 1940-48; research fellow, instr. dept. household equipment Iowa State U., Ames. 1948-51, asst. prof., 1955-57, assoc. prof., 1957-65, prof., 1965-73, chmn., 1963-66, coordinator resident instrn., 1966-73; vis. instr. dept. home mgmt. Mich. State U., East Lansing, 1951; assoc. prof. dept. household sci. Okla. A&M U., Stillwater, 1951-55; head div. home econs. Northeast Mo. State U., Kirksville, 1973-83, acting dean grad. studies, 1975, dean grad. studies, 1975-83; cons. U. Ariz., 1962. Recipient merit award Dairy Council Greater Kansas City, 1977; General Foods Fund fellow, 1959-60. Mem. Internat. Fedn. Home Econs., Am. Home Econs. Assn., Assn. Adminstrs. Home Econs., Mo. Home Econs. Assn., Am. Vocat. Assn., Mo. Vocat. Assn., Nat. Council Adminstrs. Home Econs., Nat. Assn. Post Secondary Adult Vocat. Home Econs., Mo. State Tchrs. Assn., AAUW, Omicron Nu, Pi Lambda Theta, Delta Kappa Gamma, Sigma Delta Epsilon, Kappa Omicron Phi, Phi Upsilon Omicron, Phi Kappa Phi. Republican. Mormon. Club: Quota Internat. Co-author: (with F. Ehrenkranz) Equipment in the Home, 1973; contbr. articles to profl. jours.

INOKUTI, MITIO, physicist; b. Tokyo, Japan, July 6, 1933; came to U.S., 1962; s. Haruhisa and Takako (Kure) I.; m. Makiko Omori, Mar. 12, 1960; 1 child, Mika. B.S., U. Tokyo, 1956, M.S., 1958, Ph.D., 1962. Instr., U. Tokyo, 1961-64; research assoc. Northwestern U., Evanston, Ill., 1962-63, Argonne Nat. Lab., Ill., 1963-65, physicist, 1965-73, sr. physicist, 1973—; vis. fellow U. Colo., 1970; vis. prof. U. Tokyo, 1978, Odense U., Denmark, 1980; mem. Internat. Commn. on Radiation Units and Measurements, 1985—. Contbr. articles to profl. jours. Fellow Am. Phys. Soc., Inst. Physics (London); mem. Radiation Research Soc. (assoc. editor 1975-77, councilor 1978-80), Phys. Soc. Japan. Club: Internat. House of Japan (Tokyo). Avocation: reading. Home: 6481 Blackhawk Tr La Grange IL 60525 Office: Argonne Nat Lab 9700 S Cass Ave Argonne IL 60439

INSLEY, RICHARD WALLACE, lawyer; business executive; b. Tampa, Fla., Sept. 27, 1918; s. Levin Irving and Sadie Bell (Waddell) I.; m. Eleanor Jane Robinson, Oct. 22, 1945; children—Glen Thomas, Anne Insley McCausland. A.B., Trinity Coll., Hartford, Conn., 1946; J.D., U. Va., 1970; M.B.A., Harvard U., 1948. Bar: Mich. 1956. Mem. Richard W. Insley, Atty.-at-Law, St. Joseph, Mich., 1950—; pres. Southwestern Developers Inc., St. Joseph, 1960—, also dir.; pres. Whinco Inc., Pizza Hut franchisee, St. Joseph, 1969—, also dir.; v.p., sec. Jan Barb, Inc., Holiday Inn franchisee, St. Joseph, 1970—, also dir. Trustee Barat Coll., Lake Forest, Ill., 1972-82; mem. U.S. Senate Bus. Adv. Bd., Washington. Served to lt. USN, 1942-45. Decorated Silver Star. Mem. ABA, Mich. State Bar Assn., Berrien County Bar Assn. Republican. Episcopalian. Clubs: Point O'Woods Country, Berrien Hills Country (Benton Harbor, Mich.). Home: 278 Ridgeway Saint Joseph MI 49085 Office: 421 Main St Saint Joseph MI 49085

INZETTA, MARK STEPHEN, lawyer; b. N.Y.C., Apr. 14, 1956; s. James William and Rose Delores (Cirnigliaro) I.; m. Amy Marie Elbert, June 25, 1977; children—Michelle, Margot. B.B.A. summa cum laude, U. Cin., 1977; J.D., U. Akron, 1980. Bar: Ohio 1980, U.S. Dist. Ct. (no. dist.) Ohio 1980. Legal intern City of Canton, Ohio, 1979-80; assoc. W.J. Ross Co. L.P.A., Canton, 1980-84; real estate staff atty. Wendy's Internat. Inc., Columbus, Ohio, 1984—; instr. real estate law Stark Tech. Coll., Canton, 1983. Case and comment editor: Akron Law Rev., 1979-80. Chmn. campaign Earle Wise Appellate Judge, North Canton, Ohio, 1982. Recipient Am. Jurisprudence award Lawyers Coop. Pub. Co., 1978; Dir. of Yr. award North Canton Jaycees, 1982, Presdl. award of honor, 1984; Dist. Dir. award of honor, Ohio Jaycees, 1984. Mem. ABA, Ohio Bar Assn., North Canton Jaycees (bd. dirs. 1981-82, v.p. 1982-83, pres. 1983-84), North Canton C. of C. (bd. dirs. 1983-84), Brookside Village Civic Assn. (bd. dirs. 1985—). Democrat. Roman Catholic. Home: 1584 Sandy Side Dr Worthington OH 43085 Office: Wendy's Internat Inc 4288 W Dublin-Granville Rd Dublin OH 43017

IONASESCU, VICTOR VINTILA, neurologist, geneticist, researcher; b. Bucharest, Romania, Oct. 23, 1926; came to U.S., 1968, naturalized, 1976; s. George and Victoria (Papaianopol) I.; m. Rebeca Kahane, Apr. 19, 1951; children—Ani, Rodica. M.D., Med. Sch., Romania, 1951; Ph.D. U. Bucharest, 1956. Diplomate Romanian Bd. Neurology. Resident in neurology Neurol. Inst., Bucharest, 1951-56, asst. prof., 1956-57, 59-60, assoc. prof., 1960-67; neurochemistry fellow U. Rome, Italy, 1958; genetics fellow Inst. Genetics, Geneva, Switzerland, 1968; research prof. dept. pediatrics U. Iowa, Iowa City, 1968-72, assoc. prof., 1972-76, prof., dir. neuromuscular program, 1976—. Author: Temporal Lobe Epilepsy (research award 1957), 1957; Biochemical Disorders in Neurological Diseases (spl. mention award 1967), 1967; Genetics in Neurology, 1983; also numerous articles. NIH research grantee, 1970-85; Muscular Dystrophy Assn. research grantee, 1975-85; recipient teaching award U. Iowa, 1976. Mem. World Fedn. Neurology, Soc. Exptl. Biology and Medicine, Am. Acad. Cerebral Palsy, Am. Soc. Human Genetics, Am. Acad. Neurology, Child Neurology Soc. Greek Orthodox. Avocations: chamber and symphonic music, mountain hiking, jogging. Home: 1144 Melrose Ave Iowa City IA 52240 Office: Univ Hosps Dept Pediatrics Iowa City IA 52242

IORIO, RALPH ARTHUR, automotive company executive; b. Rochester, N.Y., Nov. 21, 1925; s. Andrew and Theresa (Civitillo) I.; m. Ann Marie Ferrante, Sept. 12, 1953; children—Kathleen, Alice, Robert. B.E.E., Villanova U., 1950. Supt. prodn. engring. Rochester (N.Y.) Products div. Gen. Motors, 1963-67; v.p. engring. ITT Higbie Mfg. Co., Rochester, Mich., 1967-73, v.p. ops., 1973-75, exec. v.p., 1975-81, pres., 1981—; instr. electronics Rochester Inst. Tech. (N.Y.), 1963-66. Trustee, Henry Ford Satellite Hosp., Sterling Heights, Mich. Served with USN, 1944-46. Mem. Engring. Soc. Detroit. Roman Catholic. Home: 574 Overbrook Rd Bloomfield Hills MI 48013 Office: Higbie Mfg Co 4th and Water Sts Rochester MI 48463

IPINA, JORGE MARIO, state official; b. Sucre, Bolivia, Jan. 27, 1940; s. Domingo D. and Rosa Teolinda (Melgar) I.; m. Christine M. Nowicki, Sept. 9, 1983. B. Humanities, U. St. Francis Xavier, Sucre, 1958; B.A., Dominican Coll., 1966; M.A., U. Notre Dame, 1968, M.B.A., 1974; M.P.A., Western Mich. U., 1978. Lic. real estate salesman, Mich. Market research analyst Wolverine World Wide, Rockford, Mich., 1968-72, mgr. mktg. research, 1972-76; mgr. research and data systems Mich. Dept. Mgmt. and Budget, Lansing, 1976-78; chief grants and contracts Bur. Community Services, Lansing, 1978-79; contract officer Mich. Dept. Labor, Lansing, 1979—. Mem. Mayor's Hispanic Council, Lansing, 1983—; chmn. bd. Renacimento Publs.,

Inc., 1982—; pres., bd. dirs. Mich. Hispanic Democrats, 1982—; mem. Ingham County Dems. Exec. Com., 1982—. Recipient Leadership award AID, 1965. Mem. Inst. Mgmt. Acctg., Am. Econ. Assn., Western Mich. U. Alumni Assn., U. Notre Dame Alumni Assn. Roman Catholic. Co-author: Benefit-Cost Analysis of Low Income Weatherization Programs in Michigan, 1983. Home: 910 Little Hill Ct Rochester MI 48063 Office: 7150 Harris Dr State Secondary Complex Lansing MI 48909

IRBY, TERRY RENEE, adult education administrator; b. New Orleans, May 23, 1949; d. John Duddley and Alice Pearl (Leonard) McEwen; m. Harry J. Irby, Aug. 22, 1970; children—Harry Vincent, James Courtland, Traci Donayle. B.S. in Edn., So. Ill. U., 1970, M.S. in Rehab. Counseling, 1973, Ph.D. in Edn., 1978. Tchr., A.D. Marshall Sch., Joliet, Ill., 1970-71; counselor Office of Off Campus Housing, So. Ill. U., 1971-73, counselor Counseling Ctr., 1972-73, admissions coordinator Med. Sch., 1973-78; asst. dir. acad. and health affairs Ill. Bd. Higher Edn., Springfield, 1978-81; asst. dean, dir. office student services U. Ill. Coll. Nursing, 1981-82; evaluator AMA, 1979—, Ill. State Bd. Edn., 1980—, Nat. Accrediting Commn. of Cosmetology Arts and Scis., 1980—; mem. Gov.'s Task Force of Voluntary Citizen Participation, 1981. Vice-pres. LWV, Springfield, 1980-81. Nat. Edn. Policy Fellows program fellow, 1979-80. Mem. Am. Personnel and Guidance Assn., AAUW, Nat. Assn. Women Deans and Counselors, Alpha Kappa Alpha. Baptist. Author: Craigs New Haircut, 1969, Renee and the Devil, 1969; contbr. poetry and essays. Home: 511 Wheeler Ave Joliet IL 60436

IRELAND, DENNIS, optometrist; b. Minot, N.D., Oct. 13, 1946; s. Harold and Jeanette (Evans) I.; m. Susan Lee Cesaro, Dec. 21, 1974; children—Jonathan Brooks, Lauren Blythe. B.S. in Biology, U. N.D., 1964-68; B.S. in Visual Sci., Ill. Coll. Optometry, 1973, also O.D.; M.Edn., Loyola U., 1978. Lic. optometrist Ill. Gen. practice optometry, Melrose Park, Ill. 1973—, Palos Heights, Ill., 1973—; clin. asst. prof. Ill. Coll. Optometry, Chgo., 1977—, mem. optometric extension program; also dir. devel. vision clinic. Contbr. articles to profl. jours. Bd. dirs. Christopher House Settlement House, Chgo., 1973-79, treas., 1973-75, v.p., 1975-77, pres., 1977-79; co-dir. Olivett-DePaul Tutoring Program, 1974-77; bd. dirs. United Christian Community Services, 1977-79. Mem. Ill. Optometric Assn., Am. Optometric Assn., Phi Delta Kappa. Presbyterian. Avocations: photography; music; reading. Home: 6317 Elmorro Ln Oak Forest IL 60452 Office: 6420 W 127th St Palos Heights IL 60463 also 154 Broadway Melrose Park IL 60160

IRELAND, JAMES JOSEPH, physiologist, educator, researcher; b. Clarksville, Tenn., June 30, 1947; s. William James and Mabel Viola (Cherry) I.; divorced; children—John Patrick, Amy Elizabeth. B.S., Austin Peay Coll., 1969; Ph.D., U. Tenn., 1975. Postdoctoral fellow U. Mich., Ann Arbor, 1975-77; assoc. prof. reproductive physiology Mich. State U., East Lansing, 1977—; cons. Fertility Research Products, Los Angeles, 1984—. Contbr. over 55 articles to sci. jours. Served to sgt. U.S. Army, 1969-71. Grantee NSF, 1978-81, Nat. Inst. Child Health and Human Devel., 1978-81. Mem. Am. Assn. Animal Scientists, Soc. Study of Reproduction. Avocation: sports. Office: Mich State U Dept Animal Sci East Lansing MI 48823

IRISH, GARY GENE, health systems administrator; b. Lancaster, Wis., Sept. 17, 1951; s. Clyde Gene and Florence Adele (Haudenshield) I.; m. Karen L. Seinhart, Aug. 18, 1974. B.A., Andrews U., 1973; M.P.H., Loma Linda U., 1975; M.B.A., UCLA, 1980. Asst. health planner Inland Counties Comprehensive Health Planning Council, San Bernardino, Calif., 1975; adminstrv. resident Corona (Calif.) Community Hosp., 1976; health planner Inland Counties Health Systems Agy., Riverside, Calif., 1977-78; dir. resource mgmt. and planning Loma Linda U. Med. Ctr., 1978-82; exec. dir. Loma Linda Gyn-Ob Med. Group, 1982-83; asst. v.p. Adventist Health System/North, Hinsdale, Ill., 1983-85, v.p., 1985—. Mem. Am. Mktg. Assn., Am. Hosp. Assn., Hosp. Mgmt. Systems Soc., Hosp. Planning Soc., Med. Group Mgmt. Assn. Home: 540 W 81st St Burr Ridge IL 60521 Office: 15 Salt Creek Ln Hinsdale IL 60522

IRISH, LEON EUGENE, lawyer, educator; b. Superior, Wis., June 19, 1938; s. Edward Eugene and Phyllis Ione (Johnson) I.; m. Carolyn Tanner, Aug. 6, 1960; children—Stephen, Jessica, Thomas, Emily. B.A. in History, Stanford U., 1960; J.D., U. Mich., 1964; D.Philosophy in Law, Oxford U., Eng., 1973. Law clk. to Assoc. Justice Byron R. White, U.S. Supreme Ct., 1967; cons. Office Fgn. Direct Investments, Dept. Commerce, 1967-68; spl. rep. sec. def. 7th session 3d UN Conf. Law of Sea; mem. firm Caplin & Drysdale, Washington, 1968-73, ptnr., 1973-85; prof. law U. Mich. Law Sch., Ann Arbor, 1985—; adj. prof. Georgetown U. Law Ctr., 1975-85; visitors com. U. Mich. Law Sch.; bd. dirs., chmn. exec. com. Vols. Tech. Assistance. Contbr. articles to legal jours. Mem. Council Fgn. Relations, Am. Law Inst., ABA, D.C. Bar Assn. Democrat. Episcopalian. Home: 1075 Cedar Bend Dr Ann Arbor MI 48105 Office: Hutchins Hall U Mich Law Sch Ann Arbor MI 48104

IRONS, WILLIAM GEORGE, anthropology educator; b. Garrett, Ind., Dec. 25, 1933; s. George Randall and Eva Aileen (Veazey) I.; m. Marjorie Sue Rogasner, Nov. 4, 1972; children—Julia Rogasner, Marybeth Rogasner. B.A., U. Mich., 1960, M.A., 1963, Ph.D., 1969; postgrad. London Sch. Econs., 1964-65. With Army Corps of Engrs., 1956-58; asst. prof. social relations Johns Hopkins U., 1969-74; asst. prof. anthropology Pa. State U., 1974-78; assoc. prof. anthropology Northwestern U., Evanston, Ill., 1978-83, prof., 1983—; cons. Nat. Geog. Soc., NSF, AAAS, Social Sci. Research Council, Time-Life Books, U. Wash. Press, Random House, Worth Pubs., Rutgers U. Press, U. Tex. Press, Pelenum Press, Oxford U. Press; bd. dirs. Am. Inst. Iranian Studies. Served with AUS, 1954-56. Grantee NSF, 1973, 76, 82, Ford Found., 1974, Harry Frank Guggenheim Found., 1976, 77. Fellow AAAS, Am. Anthrop. Assn., Royal Anthrop. Inst.; mem. Assocs. in Current Anthropology, Animal Behavior Soc., Internat. Soc. Human Ethology, Am. Inst. Iranian Studies, Brit. Inst. Persian Studies, Phi Kappa Phi. Author: The Yomut Turkmen, 1975; Perspectives on Nomadism, 1972; Evolutionary Biology and Human Social Behavior, 1979; mem. bd. editors Ethology and Sociobiology. Research on Turkmen of Iran, human sociobiology. Home: 2604 Payne St Evanston IL 60201 Office: 2006 Sheridan Rd Evanston IL 60201

IRSAY, JAMES, professional football team executive. Gen. mgr. Indpls. Colts. Office: Indpls Colts PO Box 20000 Indianapolis IN 46220*

IRSAY, ROBERT, professional football team executive. Pres., treas. Indpls. Colts. Office: Indpls Colts PO Box 20000 Indianapolis IN 46220*

IRSCH, CAROLYN RUTH, personnel executive; b. Chgo., Dec. 31, 1953; d. Paul Edward and Adele Loraine (Schultz) I.; m. Kenneth Edward Condy, Nov. 15, 1980. B.A. in Psychology, U. Ill., 1976. Office mgr. Greyhound Personnel, Chgo., 1976; personnel rep. Stewart-Warner, Chgo., 1976-79; supr. compensation ITT, Des Plaines, Ill., 1979-81; supr. personnel Long John Silvers, Des Plaines, 1981; mgr. employment and compensation Ben Franklin Stores div. Household Merchandising Inc., Des Plaines, 1981—. Mem. personnel com. Chgo. YWCA, 1983-84. Mem. Am. Soc. Personnel Adminstrs., Women in Mgmt., Internat. Assn. Personnel Women, Nat. Assn. Female Execs., Women's Ednl. Service Assn. Club: Des Plaines Toastmasters (ednl. v.p.). Color analyst, beauty-control. Home: 4234 W Nelson St Chicago IL 60641 Office: Ben Franklin Stores div Household Merchandising Inc 1700 S Wolf St Des Plaines IL 60018

IRSFELD, JAMES HEROLD, pharmacist; b. Wadena, Minn., Jan. 1, 1937; s. Paul Lambert and Irene (Peterson) I.; m. Mary Louise Skwiera, June 17, 1961; children—Thomas James, Steven Paul. B.S. in Pharmacy, N.D. State U., 1962. Pharmacist White Drug Enterprises, Jamestown, N.D., 1962-64, chief pharmacist, Dickinson, N.D., 1964-65, chief pharmacist, asst. mgr., 1965-82; owner, pharmacist Irsfeld Pharmacy, Dickinson, 1982—; pres. N.D. Bd. of Pharmacy, 1983-84, dir., 1980—. Bd. dirs. United Way of Dickinson, sec. 1974. Served with U.S. Army, 1955-58. Mem. N.D. Pharm. Assn. (dir. 1978-80), Southwestern Dist. Pharm. Assn. (pres. 1976). Roman Catholic. Lodges: K.C., Elks. Avocations: hunting; gardening. Home: 1042 4th Ave West Dickinson ND 58601 Office: Irsfeld Pharmacy 33 9th St West Dickinson ND 58601

IRVINE, JOHN ALEXANDER, lawyer; b. Sault Ste. Marie, Ont. Can., Aug. 10, 1947; s. Alexander and Ruth Catherine (Woolrich) I.; m. Jacquelyn Louise Church, June 13, 1970 (div. 1980); children—John Alexander, Allison Brooks; m. Lynda Kaye Myska Jenkins, May 24, 1981; 1 child, James Woolrich. B.S., Auburn U., 1969; J.D., Memphis State U., 1972. Bar: Tenn. 1972, Ohio 1982, Tex. 1985. Law clk. U.S. Dist. Ct. (we. dist.) Tenn., 1972-73; asst. dist. atty. gen. 15th Jud. Cir. Tenn., 1973-78; assoc. Glankler, Brown, Gilliland, Chase, Robinson and Raines, Memphis, 1978-81; asst. gen. counsel Mead Corp., Dayton, Ohio, 1981-84; ptnr. Porter & Clements, Houston, 1984—. Bd. dirs. Make-A-Wish Found. Tex. Gulf Coast, 1985—. Mem. ABA, Tenn. Bar Assn., Ohio Bar Assn., Memphis and Shelby County Bar Assn., Tex. Bar Assn., Houston Bar Assn., Dayton Bar Assn., Memphis State U. Law Sch. Alumnae Assn. (pres. 1975-76, 77-78), U.S. C. of C. (Council on Antitrust Policy 1983—). Republican. Presbyterian. Clubs: Phoenix (bd. dirs. 1977-78), Houston Met. Racquet, Heritage, Briar, Forum. Avocations: sports; travel; reading; painting. Office: Porter & Clements 3500 Republic Bank Ctr Houston TX 77002

IRVINE, MAGNUS KEITH, publishing company executive; b. Ipswich, Suffolk, Eng., Aug. 7, 1924; came to U.S., 1952; s. Frederick Robert and Dorothy Stuart Campbell (Gilchrist) I.; m. Marie Aline Hekimian, Apr. 9, 1949; children—Mary Lilian, Marie Dominique, Madeline Maya, John David. Student U. Manchester (Eng.), 1941-42, U. London, 1942, U. Edinburgh (Scotland), 1946-47, The Sorbonne, Paris, 1947-48. Asst. to state dir. Am. Found. for Polit. Edn., N.Y.C., 1956-58; research dir. Ghana Mission to UN, N.Y.C., 1958-69; prin. editor geography Ency. Brit., Chgo., 1969-73; gen. editor encys. Scholarly Press Inc., St. Clair Shores, Mich., 1973-75; pres. Reference Publs. Inc., Algonac, Mich., 1975—. Served with Brit. Royal Navy, 1943-46. Mem. Detroit Book Soc. Roman Catholic. Author: The Rise of the Colored Races, 1970; gen. editor: Encyclopaedia of Indians of North America, 1974-75, Encyclopaedia Africana Dictionary of African Biography, 1977; contbr. articles to numerous encys.

IRVINE, SHARON LOUISE, lawyer; b. St. Paul, May 2, 1941; d. Erwin Thomas and Ruth Sophia (Kennebeck) Smith; m. Stanley Gray Irvine, June 29, 1963. B.A., U. Chgo., 1963, M.A. in L.S., 1976; J.D., Ill. Inst. Tech.-Chgo. Kent Coll. Law, 1979. Bar: Ill. 1979. Res. librarian U. Chgo., 1965-68, circulation res. librarian, 1968-73; corp. librarian Kraft, Inc., Glenview, Ill., 1974-77, adminstrv. asst., 1977-79, atty., 1979-82, gen. atty., 1982—. Ill. Inst. Tech.-Chgo.-Kent scholar, 1978-79. Mem. ABA, Ill. Bar Assn., Chgo. Bar Assn. Roman Catholic. Home: 801 W Newport Chicago IL 60657 Office: Kraft Inc 1 Kraft Ct Glenview IL 60025

IRVING, EVELYN UHRHAN, retired language educator, consultant; b. Buffalo, Feb. 14, 1919; d. Charles Ludwig and Anna Clarissa (Hauer) Uhrhan; m. Thomas Ballantine Irving, June 30, 1961; stepchildren—Diana McClellan, Lillian de Vides, Nicholas M. B.A., Fla. State U., 1941, M.A., 1947; Ph.D., U. Ill., 1950. Instr. dept. physics Ind. U., Bloomington, 1943-44, instr. math., 1946-47; head fgn. langs. dept., prof. Spanish, French, S.D. State U., 1950-61; prof. Spanish Macalester Coll., St. Paul, 1963-65, North Central Coll., Naperville, Ill., 1965-67, U. Guelph, Ont., Can., 1967-69; cons., vis. prof. Spanish Carson-Newman Coll., Jefferson City, Tenn., 1969-71; vis. prof. French Maryville Coll., Tenn., 1971-72; assoc. prof., then prof. Spanish, English as 2d lang., Tenn. Technol. U., Cookeville, 1975-81, emeritus, 1981—; vis. prof. Universidad de las Americas, Cholula, Mex., 1985; cons. Am. Islamic Coll., Chgo., 1982—. Co-author: Let's Learn the Spanish Language-Aprendamos la lengua espanola, 1975; contbg. author: Descriptive Studies In Spanish Grammar, 1954, Short Stories of Rafaela Contreras de Dario, 1965. Grantee Social Sci. Research Council, 1962-63. Mem. Am. Assn. Tchrs. Spanish and Portuguese (emeritus), Linguistic Soc. Am. (emeritus), Instituto Internacional de Literatura Iberoamericana, Asociacion Internacional de Hispanistas, Internat. Assn. Learning Labs. (pres. 1969-71), Internat. Assn. Audio-Visual Methods, Phi Beta Kappa, Phi Kappa Phi, Sigma Delta Pi, Pi Delta Phi, Delta Kappa Gamma, Pi Gamma Mu, Phi Sigma Iota. Christian Scientist. Avocations: reading; travel; classical music; photography. Home: 2508 Glen Elm Dr NE Cedar Rapids IA 52402 Office: Am Islamic Coll 640 W Irving Park Rd Chicago IL 60613

IRWIN, DOUGLAS HINKLE, oral-maxillo facial surgeon, educator; b. Kansas City, Mo., Aug. 23, 1927; s. Douglas Hinkle and Virginia (Towell) I.; m. Beverly Sue Bennett, Oct. 29, 1978; children—Amanda, Douglas, Jennifer, Diane, John. D.D.S., U. Mo.-Kansas City, 1951; M.S. in Dentistry, Northwestern U., 1955; D.D.S. (hon.), U. Mexico, Mexico City, 1958. Diplomate Am. Assn. Oral and Maxillo-facial Surgeons. Oral surgeon Adminstrv. Command, Great Lakes, Ill., 1951; resident U. Kans., Kansas City, 1952-53; prof. Gen. Hosp., Kansas City, Mo., 1957, U. Kans., Kansas City, 1960—; chief dental service St. Mary's Hosp., Kansas City, Mo., 1978-82. Author: Reattachment Gingival Tissue, 1955. Chmn. United Funds, Prairie Village, Kans., 1960. Served to lt. USN, 1955-57. Mem. Internat. Soc. Oral/Maxillo-facial Surgeons, Midwest Soc. Oral and Maxillo-facial Surgeons (pres. 1973-74), Kansas City Soc. Oral Surgeons (pres. 1969-70), 5th Dist. Dental Soc. (pres. 1963-64), Jackson County Med. Soc., Pierre Fauchard Internat. (hon.), Dental Abstracts (pres. 1960-61). Republican. Avocations: fly fishing; skiing; gardening; jogging. Home: 818 W 56th St Kansas City MO 64113 Office: 4140 W 71st St Prairie Village KS 66208

IRWIN, RICHARD LOREN, association executive; b. Los Angeles, Dec. 8, 1924; s. Loren Wilson and Letty Elizabeth (Tate) I.; m. Letty Elizabeth Sutton, Dec. 15, 1945; children—Martha Jean, Carol Ann. Student Lockyear's Bus. Coll., 1942-43, 46-48. Cert. assn. exec. Am. Soc. Assn. Execs. Mgr. machine acctg. dept. U.O. Colson Co., Paris, Ill., 1949-55; founder Nat. Machine Assts. Assn. (now Data Processing Mgmt. Assn.), 1951, Internat. pres., 1954-55, exec. sec., 1955-60; adminstrv. dir. Am. Optometric Assn., St. Louis, 1960-62; exec. dir. Assn. Systems Mgmt., Cleve., 1962—. Served with USNR, 1943-46. Mem. Am. Soc. Assn. Execs., U.S. C. of C., Data Processing Mgmt. Assn. (life, pres. 1954-55). Republican. Presbyterian. Clubs: Am. Legion. Lodges: Masons, Shriners, Elks, Moose. Home: 156 Sunset Dr Berea OH 44017 Office: Assn for Systems Mgmt 24587 Bagley Rd Cleveland OH 44138

ISAAC, MARGRETHE GLORIA, educator; b. Chgo., May 6, 1927; d. Merle J. and Margrethe D. (Lehmann) Isaac; B.Ed., Chgo. Tchrs. Coll., 1947; M.A., Northwestern U., 1950, Ph.D., 1962. Tchr., Chgo. Pub. Schs., 1947-58; instr. TV Tchrs. Coll., WGN-TV, Chgo., 1958-59; asst. prof. Chgo. Tchrs. Coll., 1959-61; asso. prof. Northeastern Ill. U., Chgo., 1961—, asso. chmn. dept. early childhood edn., 1968-71, 73-80, chmn., 1980-83; vis. faculty Northwestern U., summer 1964. Mem. exec. com. Elem. Sch. sect. Nat. Safety Council, 1972-81, vice-chmn., 1975-76, chmn., 1976-77, mem. exec. com. Sch. and Coll. div., 1976-81, bd. dirs., 1977-80, Outstanding Service award, 1977; book reviewer Ill. Reading Service, 1971-76; advisory com. Child Safety Club, 1977—. Mem. Chgo. Public Schs. Kindergarten-Primary Assn. (pres. 1954-56), Ill. Edn. Assn. (pres. Chgo. div. 1964-65, Disting. Service award 1967), Ill. Assn. Higher Edn. (pres. 1968-69), Assn. Childhood Edn. Internat., (chmn. various coms. 1954—, v.p. Chgo. area br. 1973-77), NEA, AAUP, AAUW, Assn. Tchr. Educators, Nat. Assn. Edn. Young Children, Alpha Delta Kappa (pres. Ill. Alpha Epsilon chpt. 1957-59, Ill. historian 1958-60, Ill. rec. sec. 1964-66), Pi Lambda Theta (rec. sec. Alpha Zeta chpt. 1965-67, corr. sec. Chgo. area chpt. 1973-77, pres. Chgo. area chpt. 1977-81), Delta Kappa Gamma (chpt. music chmn. 1972-76), Phi Delta Kappa (chpt. historian 1977-79). Research on profl. problems of beginning tchrs. Home: 700 Victoria Rd Des Plaines IL 60016 Office: Dept Earl Childhood Edn Northeastern Ill U Bryn Mawr at Saint Louis Ave Chicago IL 60625

ISAACS, BURTON EDWARD, lawyer; b. Detroit, Dec. 4, 1934; s. Louis and Ethel (Kramer) I.; m. Sandra Zager, Mar. 20, 1958 (div. 1978); children—Ellen, Craig; m. Judith Roselle Lipson, Nov. 23, 1979. Student Wayne State U., 1953-56; LL.B., Detroit Coll. Law, 1959. Bar: Mich. 1959. With IRS, Detroit, 1958-66; revenue officer, estate tax atty. trust dept. Nat. Bank of Detroit, 1967-69; prin. Rubenstein, Isaacs, Lax & Bordman, Southfield, Mich., 1969—. Mem. ABA (real property, probate and trust, tax and econs. sects.), State Bar of Mich. (council legal econs. sect.). Office: 17220 W Twelve Mile Rd Suite 200 Southfield MI 48076

ISAACS, KENNETH S(IDNEY), psychoanalyst, educator; b. Mpls., Apr. 7, 1920; s. Mark William and Sophia (Rau) I.; B.A., U. Minn. 1944; Ph.D., U. Chgo., 1956; postgrad. Inst. Psychoanalysis, 1957-63; m. Ruth Elizabeth Johnson, Feb. 21, 1950 (dec. 1967); m. 2d, Adele Rella Bodroghy, May 17, 1969; children—Jonathan, James; step-children—John, Curtis, Peter and Edward Meissner. Intern, Worcester (Mass.) State Hosp., 1947-48; trainee VA Hosp., Chgo., 1948-50; chief psychologist-outpatient clinic system Ill. Dept. Pub. Welfare, 1949-56; research assoc. (assoc. prof.) U. Ill. Med. Sch., Chgo., 1956-63; practice psychoanalysis, Evanston, Ill., 1960—; supr. psychiat. residency program Evanston Hosp., Northwestern U., 1972—; pres. Chgo. Ctr. Psychoanalytic Psychology, 1984-85; cons. schs., hosps., clinics, pvt. practitioners. Served with AUS, 1943-45; ETO. Mem. Am. Psychol. Assn. (bd. dirs. div. psychoanalysis 1978-85, pres. sect. psychoanalyst practitioners 1985-86), AAAS, Chgo. Psychoanalytic Soc., N.Y. Acad. Sci., Chgo. Assn. Psychoanalytic Psychology (pres. 1984-85), Sigma Xi. Contbr. articles to profl. publs. Office: 636 Church St Evanston IL 60201

ISAACSON, CLIFFORD EDWIN, minister; b. Floodwood, Minn., May 17, 1934; s. Richard Emil Isaacson and Allie Marie (Nissila) Isaacson Thomas; m. Kathleen Mae Myre, Apr. 18, 1953; children—Duane, Mary, Shirley, Linda, Kevin. B.A., Northwestern Coll., Mpls., 1958; B.Div., U. Dubuque, 1961. pastor United Presbyterian Ch., Waukon, Iowa., 1961-64, United Presbyn. Ch., Keokuk, Iowa, 1964-70; assoc. pastor First United Methodist Ch., Clinton, Iowa, 1970-72; pastor First United Meth. Ch., Ida Grove, Iowa, 1972-79; Algona, Iowa, 1979—; facilitator Large Ch. Pastors Fellowship, Spencer, Iowa. Pres., bd. dirs. Northwest Iowa Mental Health, Ida Grove, 1978; v.p. Algona Area Substance Prevention, 1984. Mem. Algona Area Clergy Assn. (pres. 1983), Mensa. Democrat. Lodge: Kiwanis. Avocation: Counseling. Home: 20 Oakridge Dr Algona IA 50511 Office: First United Meth Ch 201 E Nebraska St Algona IA 50511

ISBELL, KAREN JUNE, consultant; b. Mountain Home, Ark., June 22, 1950; d. Henry H. and Alice I. Isbell (Phipps) I. B.S. in Psychology and Journalism, Murray State U., 1973. Editor empolyee publs. Mallinckrodt, Inc., 1973-77; asst. dir. pub. relations St. Louis Bi-State chpt. ARC, 1977-81, dir. pub. relations, 1981-84; account exec. UniCom Corp. Vol. counselor Reproductive Health Services, 1973-84; bd. dirs. Mo. Nat. Abortion Rights Action League, 1980—. Recipient Flair award, local advt. fedn., 1978, 81, 82, 83; named Leader in Communications, St. Louis YWCA. Mem. Am. Mktg. Assn., Internat. Assn. Bus. Communications (awards 1980, 81, 82, 83, dir. St. Louis chpt. 1977—), Pub. Relations Soc. Am. Office: UniCom Corp 505 S Ewing Ave Saint Louis MO 63103

ISETTS, BRIAN JOHN, pharmaceutical clinical scientist, pharmacist; b. Kenosha, Wis., Nov. 28, 1955; s. Roger Frederick and Dorothy Mae (Hoff) I.; student U. Wis.-Milw., 1973-74; B.S. in Pharmacy, U. Wis.-Madison, 1979; Ph.D. in Pharmacy Adminstrn., U. Minn., 1985. Registered pharmacist, Wis., Minn. Assembly messenger Wis. State Capitol, Madison, 1975-79; pharmacist, intern St. Catherine's Hosp., Kenosha, Wis., 1979-80; pharmacist Corner Drug Store, Dodgeville, Wis., 1980-81, Kadela Pharmacy, St. Paul, 1982-84; guest worker FDA, Rockville, Md., 1983; pharm. clin. scientist Coll. of Pharmacy, Mpls., 1981—. Community presentor Drug Talk, Inc., Mpls., 1983-84; Talkline expert Radio station KTIS phone in program, Roseville, Minn., 1984—; presentor Pharmacists Against Drug Abuse, St. Paul, 1984—. Kellog Found. fellow, U. Minn., 1981. Mem. Am. Pharm. Assn., Am. Soc. for Pharmacy Law, Am. Pub. Health Assn., Am. Soc. of Law and Medicine, Wis. Pharm. Assn. (asst. adminstrv. coordinator, 1980), Wis. Student Am. Pharm. Assn. (legis. chmn. 1978-79), Rho Chi (academic excellence award, 1982). Democrat. Catholic. Avocations: manage and coach young men and adults at all levels of baseball and basketball. Home: 110 1st Ave NE #905 Minneapolis MN 55413 Office: U of Minn Coll of Pharmacy 308 Harvard St SE Minneapolis MN 55455

ISIP, CONSOLITO MONTEMAYOR, accountant; b. Manila, Philippines, Aug. 10, 1935; came to U.S., 1968, naturalized, 1973; s. Eugenio and Alejandra (Montemayor) I.; m. Araceli Pascual, Sept. 25, 1966; children—Michael, Peter. B.S. in Bus. Adminstrn., U. of East, 1958. C.P.A., Philippines. Acct. Foamtex Mfg. Corp., Philippines, 1960-68; pvt. practice acctg., Philippines, 1966-68; with Work Wear Corp., Inc., Cleve., 1968—, mgr. gen. acctg. Mem. Nat. Assn. Accts. Avocations: fishing; basketball; reading. Home: 6224 S Perkins Rd Bedford Heights OH 44146

ISOME, MARI ELLEN, educator; b. Cin., Mar. 1, 1954; d. Charles and Nina Mae Isome. B.S. in Edn., U. Cin., 1976, M.Ed. in Guidance and Counseling, 1979, Ed.D. in Ednl. Adminstrn., 1983. Cert. spl. edn., counseling, prin., adminstr., supr., Ohio. Spl. edn. tchr. Princeton High Sch., Cin., 1976-80, learning disabilities resource tchr., 1980-83; guidance counselor Princeton Jr. High Sch., 1983—. Mem. Assn. for Supervision and Curriculum Devel., Council for Exceptional Children, Ohio Assn. of Children with Learning Disabilities, Ohio Sch. Counselors Assn., Ohio Edn. Assn., The Women's Network, Phi Delta Kappa. Home: 1508 Elizabeth Pl Apt 2 Cincinnati OH 45237 Office: Princeton Jr High Sch 11157 Chester Rd Cincinnati OH 45246

ISRAEL, HOWARD STANLEY, steel company executive; b. Cleve., Aug. 14, 1931; s. Jacob and Gertrude Rosalind (Ausdeutcher) I.; m. Lois Joy Eppstein, Sept. 9, 1956; children—Patricia Jo, Michael Alan. B.S., Ohio State U., 1953. With Consumers Steel Products Co., Cleve., 1953-56, 59-75, mng. ptnr., 1969-75; founder, owner, pres. Tunbridge Steel Co., Cleve., 1976—. Trustee, bd. dirs., v.p. fgn. affairs Cleve. chpt. Am. Jewish Com.; mem. Greater Cleve. Growth Assn., ACLU, Youth Inst. for Peace, Cleve. Mus. Art, Musical Arts Assn., Anti-Defamation League, Smithsonian Instn.; mem. Republican Nat. Com., Am. Israel Pub. Affairs Com., Beachwood Arts Council, Am. Com. for Weizman Inst., Zionist Orgn. Am., Simon Wiesenthal Ctr., Friends of Beachwood Library; George Bush for Pres. campaign worker. Served with U.S. Army, 1956-58. Jewish. Clubs: Temple Men's, B'Nai B'Rith (Cleve.).

ISSENDORF-BROWN, CLEO ELSIE, health care educator, nurse; b. Lake City, Minn., Jan. 23, 1945; d. Herman John and Irene Amelia (Brunkow) Issendorf; m. Richard Knight Brown, Aug. 30, 1980. R.N./B.S., Coll. St. Thomas, 1963, M.A. in Curriculum Instrn. Cert. CPR instr./trainer. Nurse, U. Minn. Hosps. and Clinics, St. Paul, 1966-68, head nurse, 1968-76, health care educator, staff devel., 1976-83, community services coordinator, 1983—. Cons. in field. Recipient Service award U. Minn. Hosp. and Clinic. Mem. Am. Soc. Healthcare Edn. and Tng. (nat. bd. dirs., Nat. Service award), Minn. Hosp. Assn. (cert. of appreciation Minn. chpt.). Home: 416 Van Buren Ave S Edina MN 55343 Office: 3300 University Ave Minneapolis MN 55414

ISTERABADI, SAIB, thoracic surgeon; b. Baghdad, Iraq, Sept. 18, 1934; came to U.S., 1966, naturalized, 1970; s. Abdul Wahab and Rahma (Najar) I.; m. Siobhan McCarthy, May 19, 1966. MB.Ch.B., Royal Coll. Medicine, Baghdad, 1957; fellow Royal Coll. Surgeons, Edinburgh, Scotland, 1964, Royal Coll. Surgeons, Glasgow, Scotland, 1965. Diplomate Am. Bd. Surgery, Am. Bd. Thoracic Surgery. Surgeon, Cambridge City Hosp., Mass., 1975-76, Hills and Dales Hosp., Cass City, Mich., 1976, Marlette Community Hosp., Mich., 1976-84; thoracic surgeon Henry Ford Hosp., Detroit, 1984—. Fellow Am. Coll. of Chest Physicians; mem. Soc. of N.Am. Pacing and Electrophysiology, Am. Thoracic Soc., AMA, AM. Soc. Abdominal Surgeons. Republican. Home: 1850 Boyne Rd PO Box 278 Marlette MI 48453

ITIN, TIMOTHY SEAN, financial company executive; b. Apr. 29, 1958. B.A. in Econs., Dartmouth Coll., 1981. Account exec. TWI Internat. Inc., 1981, profl. snow ski racer Rocky Mountain Pro Tour, 1981-82; sales mgr. Cropchem. Mfg. Co., Calif., 1982; profl. snow ski racer Rocky Mountain and Pro Ski Internat. Tours., 1982-83; account exec. Montgomery Securities, 1983—; v.p. Rocky Mountain Pro Tour Racers Council. Mem. Profl. Ski Racers Assn. (bd.). Home: 4831 Old Orchard Trail Orchard Lake MI 48033

ITON, LENNOX ELROY, research chemist; b. St. Vincent, W.I., Jan. 3, 1949; s. Maurice and Cynthia Elsa (Iton) Matthews; came to U.S., 1970; m. Jacqueline Rae Wallace, July 27, 1980; 1 son, Blair; 1 stepdau., Nicole Lynn. B.Sc. with 1st class honors, McGill U., 1970; Ph.D. in Chemistry, Princeton U., 1976. Postdoctoral appointee Argonne Nat. Lab. (Ill.), 1975-77, asst. chemist, 1978-82, chemist, 1982—. Contbr. numerous tech. articles to research jours. Mem. Chgo. Council Fgn. Relations. Mem. Am. Chem. Soc., Am. Phys. Soc., AAAS, Internat. Soc. Magnetic Resonance, Sigma Xi. Office: Argonne Nat Lab 9700 Cass Ave Argonne IL 60439

IVENS, VIRGINIA RUTH, educator; b. Decatur, Ill., July 27, 1922; d. John Raymond and Dessie Lenora (Underwood) I. B.S., U. Ill., 1950. Tracer blueprints Caterpillar Mil. Engine Co., Decatur, 1941-45; mem. faculty Coll. Veterinary Medicine, U. Ill., Urbana, 1950—, asso. prof. veterinary parasitology, 1979—, chmn. curriculum com. dept. veterinary pathobiology, 1976-78; chmn. 9th Ann. Conf. Coccidiosis, 1972. Mem. Am. Soc. Parasitologists (transl. com. 1963-71, 80-83), Soc. Protozoologist, Am. Inst. Biol. Scis., Entomol. Soc. Am., League Women Voters, Sigma Xi, Phi Zeta. Translator Russian articles on parasitology; contbr. articles to profl. jours. and co-author three monographs; sr. author: Principal Parasites of Domestic Animals in the

U.S., 1978, 81. Home: 608 S Edwin St Champaign IL 61820 Office: 2603 Veterinary Medicine Basic Sci Bldg U Ill 2001 S Lincoln Ave Urbana IL 61801

IVERSON, JANICE, nun, physical education and cardiac rehabilitation educator; b. Miranda, S.D., Mar. 3, 1941; s. Marvin W. and Viola D. (Gebhart) I. Teaching cert. Mt. Marty Coll., 1961, B.A., 1968; postgrad. Dickinson State Coll., spring 1968; M.S., S.D. State U., 1972, postgrad., 1974-75; M.S., Va. Poly. Inst. and State U., 1981. Joined Benedictine Sisters, Roman Catholic Ch., 1959; tchr. fourth grade St. Joseph's Cath. Sch., Piere, S.D., 1962-63, elem. grades St. Mary's Cath. Sch., Aberdeen, S.D., 1963-67; tchr. 5th and 6th grades, phys. educator all grades, high sch. girl's basketball coach, girl's dorm matron St. Mary's Grade and High Sch., Richardton, N.D., 1967-70; phys. educator, coach, adviser fgn. students Harmony Hill High Sch., Watertown, S.D., 1970-74; phys. educator, tchr. religion grade 6, tchr. math. grades 5 and 6, boy's basketball coach grades 5 through 8, Cath. sch., Richardton, 1975-76; asst. prof. phys. edn., head women's volleyball coach, asst. women's basketball coach Mary Coll., Bismark, N.D., 1976-77; athletic dir., tchr. phys. edn. and health grades 9 to 12, head women's volleyball coach, asst. women's basketball coach, head maintenance personnel Sacred Heart High Sch., East Grand Forks, N.D., 1977-78; phys. educator elem. grades, tchr. religion grades 5 and 6, tchr. mat grades 4 through 6, boys' basketball coach St. Bernard's Indian Mission Sch., Ft. Yates, N.D., 1978-79; intern, exercise technician dept. health, phys. edn. and recreation Va. Poly. Inst. and State U., Blacksburg, 1980; grad. student intern St. Catherine Hosp. Rehab. Ctr., East Chicago, Ind., 1981; instr. in health, phys. edn. and recreation, head women's softball coach S.D. State U., Brookings, 1981-83, instr. in health, phys. edn. and recreation, dir. cardiac rehab. program, phase II and III, 1983—; speaker on cardiac rehab. and phys. fitness to various civic orgns. Tennis Singles and Doubles City champion Watertown (S.D.) Recreation Dept., 1973; named Most Valuable Softball Player, Clark (S.D.) Invitation 8 Team Tournament, 1973. Mem. AAHPERD, Am. Coll. Sport's Medicine, Am. Volkssport Assn. Democrat. Home: Benedictine Sisters Mother of God Priory Watertown SD 57201 also 602 3d St Brookings SD 57006 Office: 261 Health Phys Edn Recreation Ctr SD State U Brookings SD 57007

IVKOVICH, RONALD SAMUEL, food industry executive; b. McKeesport, Pa., July 23, 1938; s. Samuel and Rose Marie (Kasunic) I.; m. Janice Murphy, June 15, 1963; children—Jill Michele, Cheryl Lynn, Kevin Ronald. B.S., Cornell U., 1961, M.S., 1962. Sales rep. Campbell Sales Co., Syracuse, N.Y., 1965-66, dist. sales supr., Boston, 1966-67; asst. mgr. food service systems Campbell Soup Co., Camden, N.J., 1967-68; v.p. food service div. P&C Food Markets, Syracuse, 1968-75; corp. dir. purchasing I.U. Internat. Viands Corp., Charlotte, N.C., 1975-76, pres. I.U. Internat. Clark & Lewis, Jacksonville, Fla., 1976-78; pres. Redi Froz Inc. div. Scot Lad Foods, South Bend, Ind., 1978-81; v.p. Simon Bros. Inc., South Bend, 1981—. Bd. dirs. Millhouse Children's Assn., 1982—. Served with AUS, 1962-64. Mem. Midwest Frozen Assn., Cornell Hotel Assn. Home: 52091 Farmington Square Rd Granger IN 46530 Office: Simon Bros Inc 1901 N Bendix Dr South Bend IN 46628

IVORY, GOLDIE LEE, social worker, educator; b. Chgo., Apr. 19, 1926; d. Percey Carr and Edna M. (Scott) Carr Williams; B.S., Ind. U., 1949; M.A., U. Notre Dame, 1956; M.S.W., Ind. U.-Purdue U., Indpls., 1977; m. Sam Ivory, Aug. 7, 1947; children—Kenneth L., Kevin D. Juvenile probation officer St. Joseph County Juvenile Probation Dept., South Bend, Ind., 1949-56, intake supr., 1956-59; chief probation officer South Bend City Ct., 1959; psychiat. social worker Beatty Meml. Hosp., Westville, Ind., 1960; instr. sociology Ind. U., South Bend, 1960-67; relocation rep. Urban Redevel. Commn., South Bend, 1960-62; social worker Elkhart (Ind.) Community Schs., 1962-66, supr. social services, 1966-69, dir. human relations, 1970—; mem. faculty Goshen (Ind.) Coll., 1971—, asst. prof. social work, 1971-81, adj. prof. social work, 1981—; pvt. practice social work, Ivory Caring Corner, 1981—; workshop cons. human social services; instr. sociology and social work St. Mary's Coll., 1967-69, dir. Upward Bound program, 1970; guest lectr. dept. sociology U. Swaziland, 1983. Recipient Human Service award Acad. Human Services, 1974-75, Merit award Indpls. Public Schs. Dept. Social Work, 1977; plaque for community services Mayor of Elkhart, 1981; Black Achiever award in edn. Ind. Black Expo, 1983; State chpt. Delta Kappa Gamma scholar, 1969-70. Registered clin. Social worker. Mem. Nat. Assn. Social Workers, Nat. Assn. Black Social Workers, Acad. Cert. Social Workers, Delta Kappa Gamma, Delta Sigma Theta. Methodist. Club: Altrusa. Author articles in field. Home: 1309 E Bissell St South Bend IN 46617 Office: 2720 California Rd Elkhart IN 46514

IVY, CONWAY GAYLE, paint company executive; b. Houston, July 8, 1941; s. John Smith and Caro (Gayle) I.; student U. Chgo., 1959-62; B.S. in Natural Scis., Shimer Coll., 1964; postgrad. U. Tex., 1964-65; M.B.A., U. Chgo., 1968, M.A. in Econs., 1972, postgrad. 1972-74; m. Diane Ellen Cole, May 25, 1973; children—Brice McPherson, Elizabeth Cole. Geol. asst. John S. Ivy, Houston, 1965-72; securities analyst Halsey Stuart & Co. and successor Bache & Co., Chgo., 1973-74, Winmill Securities Inc., Chgo., 1974; econ. and fin. cons., Chgo., 1974-75; dir. corp. planning Gould Inc., Rolling Meadows, Ill., 1975-79; v.p. corp. planning and devel. Sherwin-Williams Co., Cleve., 1979—; pres. Ivy Minerals Inc., Boise, Idaho, 1978—; dir. Ariz. Hillside Mining Co. Trustee Cleve. Inst. Music, 1983—. Mem. Am. Econs. Assn., N.Y. Acad. Scis., Phi Gamma Delta. Republican. Author of numerous analytical reports for brokerage industry. Office: Sherwin-Williams Co 101 Prospect Ave NW Cleveland OH 44115

IWANSKI, LEONARD JOSEPH, journalist; b. Oswego, N.Y., Apr. 9, 1950; s. Edward Francis and Ruth Mary (Heilig) I.; m. Nancy Charlene Tarnavsky, Dec. 20, 1974. B.A. in English Lit., LeMoyne Coll., 1972; postgrad. in communication, U. N.D., 1972-74. news dir. Sta. KNOX, Sta. KYTN-FM, Grand Forks, N.D., 1974-81; news dir. Sta. WDAY-AM-FM, Fargo, N.D., 1981-82; reporter, legis. corr., day editor AP, Bismarck, N.D., 1982—; guest lectr. U. N.D. Recipient Best Radio Editorial award, Northwest Broadcast News Assn., 1980. Mem. Radio-TV News Dirs. Assn., N.D. AP Broadcasters (pres. 1978-79, numerous awards), Sigma Delta Chi. Roman Catholic. Editor: North Dakota Broadcasting Stations and CATVs, 1977, 1978. Home: 1839 Allison Dr Apt 4 Bismarck ND 58501 Office: AP PO Box 1018 Bismarck ND 58502

IYER, SRINIVASA LEKSHMINARAYANAN, civil engineering educator; b. Kerala, India, Nov. 11, 1933; s. A. Lekshminarayana and Kumari I.; m. Sarada S. Iyer, May 10, 1962; children—Kumari, Lekshminarayanan. B.S. in Civil Engring., Coll. of Engring., Trivandrum, India, 1956, M.S. in Civil Engring., 1960; Ph.D., S.D. Sch. Mines and Tech., 1974. Registered profl. engr., S.D. Lectr., Coll. Engring., Trivandrum, India, 1957-63, asst. prof., 1963-71, prof. civil engring., 1971-72; asst. prof. civil engring. S.D. Sch. Mines and Tech., Rapid City, S.D., 1974-78, assoc. prof., 1978-82, prof., 1978—; participant seminars and workshops; engring. cons. S.D. Cement Plant; research cons. Celanese Corp., summer 1981. Recipient Control Data Corp. Tech. Transfer award, 1983. Mem. ASTM (faculty intern Phila. 1980, C-16 com. 1980), Nat. Soc. Profl. Engrs., Am. Concrete Inst. (participant seminars), ASCE (pres. S.D. sect.), Sigma Xi. Hindu. Contbr. articles on civil engring. to profl. jours. Home: 2506 Junction Dr Rapid City SD 57701 Office: 500 E St Joe St Rapid City SD 57701

JABLONKA, GLEN EDWIN, engineer; b. Milw., May 22, 1948; s. Edwin Herbert and Ruth Rosetta (Suess) J.; m. Roxanne Florence Ruh, Dec. 27, 1969; children—Melissa, Jonathan. B.S. in Mech. Engring., U. Wis., 1971. Registered profl. engr., Wis., Pa. Assoc. engr. Westinghouse Elec. Corp., Lester, Pa., 1971-73, sr. engr., East Pittsburgh, Pa., 1974-79; project engr. Briggs & Stratton Corp., Milw., 1973-74; sr. engr. Wis. Power & Light Co., Madison, 1979—, instr. engring. econs., 1982—; guest lectr. Argonne Nat. Lab., Ill., 1984—. Contbr. sect. to handbook, articles to publs. Developer SEROP evaluation technique and computer program. Bd. deacons and mem. ch. council Grace Luth. Ch., Madison, 1980—. Mem. IEEE (sr.), ASME, Nat. Soc. Profl. Engrs., Phi Kappa Phi, Tau Beta Pi, Pi Tau Sigma. Avocations: reading, music, foreign langs., sports. Office: Wis Power and Light Co 222 W Washington Ave Madison WI 53703

JACHNA, JOSEPH DAVID, photographer; b. Chgo., Sept. 12, 1935; m. Virginia Kemper, 1962; children—Timothy, Heidi, Jody. B.S. in Art Edn., Ill. Inst. Tech., 1958, M.S., 1961. Photo-technician Eastman Kodak Labs., Chgo., 1954; photographer's asst. DeSort Comml. Photo-Illustration Studio, Chgo., 1956-58; instr. photography Inst. Design, Ill. Inst. Tech., 1961-69, U. Ill.-Chgo., 1969—; free-lance photographer, Chgo., 1961—. One-man shows Art Inst. Chgo., 1961, St. Mary's Coll., Notre Dame (Ind.), 1963, U. Ill.-Chgo., 1965, 77, Lighfall Gallery, Evanston Art Ctr. (Ill.), 1970, Afterimage Gallery, Dallas, 1975, U. Notre Dame, 1975, Visual Studies Workshop Gallery, Rochester, N.Y., 1979, Chgo. Ctr. for Contemporary Photography, 1980, Focus Gallery, San Francisco, 1981, Perihelion Gallery, Milw., 1981; group shows include Art Inst. Chgo., 1963, U. Nebr., Lincoln, 1966, DeCordova Mus., Lincoln, Mass., 1967, MIT, Cambridge, 1968, Walker Art Center, Mpls., 1973, Renaissance Soc. Gallery, U. Chgo., 1975, Mus. Contemporary Art, Chgo., 1977, Mus. Fine Arts, Houston, 1977, Mus. Art, R.I. Sch. Design, 1978, Carpenter Ctr. for Visual Arts, Harvard U., Cambridge, Mass., 1981; represented in permanent collections Mus. Modern Art, N.Y.C., Internat. Mus. Photography, George Eastman House, Rochester, MIT, Art Inst. Chgo., Exchange Nat. Bank, Chgo., Mus. Contemporary Art, Chgo., Ctr. for Photog. Studies, Louisville, U. Kans. Art Mus., Lawrence, Ctr. for Creative Photography, U. Ariz., Tucson, Friends of Photography, Carmel, Calif. Grantee Ferguson Found., Friends of Photography, 1973, Nat. Endowment for Arts, 1976, Ill. Arts Council, 1979; Guggenheim fellow, 1980. Office: 5707 W 89th Pl Oak Lawn IL 60453 also Edwynn Houk Gallery 233 E Ontario St Chicago IL 60610

JACISIN, JOHN JAMES, psychiatrist; b. Ironwood, Mich., June 30, 1942; s. Frank Anthony and Amelia Lucy J.; m. Hoa Thi Hyunh, Feb. 27, 1971; children—Ann, Tina, Kim. Student Mich. Tech. U., 1960-61; B.S. in Psychology, U. Mich., 1964, M.D., 1968. Diplomate Am. Bd. Psychiatry and Neurology. Intern, Mt. Carmel Hosp., Columbus, Ohio, 1968-69; resident in psychiatry U., Mich., Ann Arbor, 1971-74; dir. inpatient psychiatry Riverwood Community Mental Health Ctr., St. Joseph, Mich., 1974-75; dir. psychiat. inpatient services Henry Ford Hosp., Detroit, 1975-81, acting dept. chmn., 1976-77, dir. psychiat. residency tng. program., 1977—, vice chmn. staff, 1984—, dir. psychiat. services Fairlane Ctr., 1981-84; clin. instr. U. Mich. Med. Sch., 1977—. Served to capt. USAF, 1969-71. Decorated Bronze star. Mem. Am. Psychiat. Assn., Mich. Psychiat. Soc., AMA, Am. Coll. Psychiatrists, Assn. Gen. Hosp. Psychiatrists, Wayne County Med. Soc., Am. Assn. Dirs. Psychiat. Residency Programs. Office: Henry Ford Hosp Detroit MI 48202

JACKARD, CHARLES ROY, JR., educational administrator; b. Berger, Tex., Apr. 5, 1936; s. Charles Roy and Lou Belle (Rutledge) J.; m. Judith A. Emerson, Sept. 1959 (div. Nov. 1984); children—Jane, Jeff, Jill. B.S., Kans. State Coll., 1959, M.S., 1961; Ed.D., Ariz. State U., 1972. Tchr., coach, Oil Hill, Kans., 1957-58, Newton, Kans., 1959-60, Odessa, Mo., 1961-62, El Dorado, Kans., 1962-68; dir. phys. edn. YMCA, Pittsburg, Kans.; asst. basketball coach Kans. State Coll., 1960-61; counselor, basketball coach Sunnyslope High Sch., Phoenix, 1968-72; grad. faculty Emporia State Coll., Ottawa U., U. Mo., Kansas City area, 1972—; dir. guidance-career edn. Shawnee Mission Pub. Schs., Kans., 1972-76, prin., dir. alternative edn. program, 1976—; owner, cons. J.F. Assocs., Mission, Kans., 1982—. Author: People are People, 1978; (workbook) Commandments for Communicating, 1983; also booklet and articles. Mem. Kans. State PTA (hon. life), Adult Edn. Assn. U.S., Kans. Northeast Guidance Assn., Kans. Vocat. Guidance Assn., Kans. Personnel and Guidance Assn., Shawnee Mission Adminstrs. Assn., Phi Alpha Theta. Republican. Baptist. Home: 5064 Clark Dr Shawnee Mission KS 66205 Office: Alternative Edn Program Shawnee Mission Pub Schs 5900 Lamar Rd Mission KS 66202

JACKOWSKI, KAROL ANN, college dean; b. East Chicago, Ind., Dec. 10, 1946; d. Henry Victor and Shirley Rita (Barrios) J. B.A., St. Mary's Coll., Ind., 1969; M.A., U. Notre Dame, 1973; doctoral candidate NYU, 1981—. Counselor, tchr. St. Joseph High Sch., South Bend, Ind., 1969-71; dean of students Bishop Noll High Sch., Hammond, Ind., 1971-72; campus minister St. Mary's Coll., Notre Dame, Ind., 1973-77, residence hall dir., 1977-80, dir. residence life housing, 1978-83, dean student affairs, 1983—, dir. alcohol edn., 1979-81. Author cookbooks: Let the Good Times Roll, 1980; Home on the Range, 1982. Named Outstanding Christian Woman, South Bend YWCA, 1981. Mem. Nat. Assn. Women Deans and Counselors, Nat. Assn. Student Personnel Adminstrs., Am. Assn. Counseling and Devel., Am. Assn. Higher Edn. Democrat. Roman Catholic. Avocations: writing; fishing; tap dancing; cooking; jogging. Office: St Mary's Coll 179 Lemans Hall Notre Dame IN 46616

JACKSON, A(MOS) HENRY, electronic data processing specialist, computer systems educator; b. Mt. Orab, Ohio, July 3, 1944; s. J(ohn) Pierce and Ocie Rebecca (Howlette) J. B.S., SW Mo. State U., Springfield, 1975. Programmer, Fasco Industries, Eldon, Mo., 1975-76, Rowlette and Assos. Acctg. Services, Eldon, 1976; programmer EDP coordination Office of Adminstrn., State of Mo., Jefferson City, 1976-78; programmer, analyst info. systems div. Mo. Dept. Revenue, Jefferson City, 1979—. Served with U.S. Army, 1965-68; ETO. Mem. Adminstrv. Mgmt. Soc., Pi Omega Pi. Mem. Ch. of God. Home: Route 1 Holt's Summit MO 65043 Office: Info Systems Div Mo Dept Revenue Harry S Truman Bldg Jefferson City MO 65105

JACKSON, CHARLES EUGENE, physician, human genetics researcher; b. Bluffton, Ind., Aug. 18, 1923; s. Charles Spurgeon and Lois Marie (Kyle) J.; m. Norma Lea Wampler, Jan. 23, 1947; children—Penny Rupley, Janice Byrd, Jeffrey A. A.B., Ind. U., 1944, M.D., 1946. Diplomate Am. Bd. Internal Medicine, Am. Bd. Med. Genetics in clin. genetics. Intern Scott & White Hosp., Temple, Tex., 1946-47; fellow in medicine Tulane U., New Orleans, 1949-51; internal medicine staff, dir. clin. research Caylor Nickel Clinic, Bluffton, Ind., 1951-70; internal medicine staff and chief clin. genetics div. Henry Ford Hosp., Detroit, 1970—; research assoc. dept. med. genetics, clin. prof. medicine U. Mich., Ann Arbor, 1970—. Contbr. articles to profl. jours. Served to maj. U.S. Army, 1942-51. NIH grantee 1957—. Fellow ACP (state councillor 1983—); mem. Central Soc. Clin. Research, Endocrine Soc. Republican. Methodist. Home: 1711 E Jefferson Grosse Pointe MI Office: Henry Ford Hosp 24055 E Jefferson Saint Clair Shores MI 48080

JACKSON, CURTIS MAITLAND, metallurgical engineer; b. N.Y.C., Apr. 20, 1933; s. Maitland Shaw and Janet Haughs (Dunbar) J.; B.S. in Metall. Engring., NYU, 1954; M.S., Ohio State U., Columbus, 1959, Ph.D. (Battelle staff fellow), 1966; m. Cordelia Ann Shupe, July 6, 1957; children—Carol Elizabeth, David Curtis. Prin. metall. engr. Columbus div. Battelle Meml. Inst., 1954-61, project leader, 1961-67, assoc. chief specialty alloys, 1967-77, assoc. mgr. phys. and applied metallurgy, 1977—. Mem. troop com. Boy Scouts Am., 1975—, asst. scoutmaster, 1978—; advisor Order of DeMolay, 1954-57, 78—; mem. ch. ofcl. bd. Meth. Ch., 1957-66. Registered profl. engr., Ohio; recipient IR-100 award Indsl. Research Mag., 1976, cert. of appreciation Soc. Mfg. Engrs., 1977; Legion of Honor, Order of DeMolay, 1978. Mem. Wire Found. (dir. 1974—), Wire Assn. Internat. (v.p. 1973-76, pres. 1976-77, dir. 1970-78, Mordica Meml. award 1977, J. Edward Donnellan award 1978, meritorious tech. paper award 1981), N.Y. U. Metall. Alumni Assn. (pres. 1966-68), Am. Inst. Mining, Metall. and Petroleum Engrs. (chmn. Ohio Valley sect. 1964-66, chmn. North Central region 1965-66), Am. Soc. Metals, Am. Vacuum Soc., N.Y. U., Ohio State U. alumni assns., Sigma Xi, Alpha Sigma Mu, Phi Lambda Upsilon. Club: NYU. Chmn. bd. Wire Jour., 1976-77, dir., 1973-78. Contbr. tech. articles profl. jours. Research on metall. tech. Home: 5088 Dalmeny Ct Columbus OH 43220 Office: 505 King Ave Columbus OH 43201

JACKSON, DAVID LAWRENCE, state official, medical educator; b. Morrisville, Vt., Oct. 27, 1939; s. Wallace R. and Helen (Suitor) J.; m. Doty J. Small, July 9, 1966; children—Elizabeth, Helen, Lawrence. B.A., Johns Hopkins U., 1961, Ph.D. with distinction, 1966, M.D., 1968. Intern dept. medicine Johns Hopkins U. Hosp., Balt., 1968-69, resident in medicine and neurology, 1971-73, 74-75; White House fellow U.S. EPA, Washington, 1973-74; prof. dept. medicine and neurology Case Western Res. U., Cleve., 1975-83; dir. Ohio Dept. Health, Columbus, 1983—; dir. Ctr. Critically Ill, Univ. Hosp., Cleve., 1979-83. Contbr. articles to profl. jours. Del. Democratic Nat. Conv., 1980; exec. com. Cuyahoga County Dem. Party, 1982—; bd. dirs. Cleve. Heights Dems., 1982-83. Served to lt. comdr. USN, 1969-71. Named Tchr. of Yr., dept. medicine Case Western Res. U., 1975; Nat. Endowment Humanities fellow, 1981. Fellow ACP; mem. Pan Am. Med. Soc., Undersea Med. Soc., Soc. Critical Care Medicine; mem. Am. Acad. Neurology (assoc., ethics com. 1982—), Phi Beta Kappa, Alpha Omega Alpha. Episcopalian. Avocations: tennis; basketball. Home: 1591 Fishinger Rd Upper Arlington OH 43221 Office: Ohio Dept Health Office of Dir 246 N High St Columbus OH 43215

JACKSON, ERIC FLYNN, state corrections agt., divorce mediator, counselor; b. Mt. Clemens, Mich., Jan. 12, 1948; s. Robert and Adaline (Harris) J.; m. Vicki Renee Whitsett, Oct. 1977; 1 child, Zenas Whitsett. A.A., Macomb Community Coll., 1973; B.A., Wayne State U., 1976, M.A. in Counseling, 1980; postgrad. in bus. adminstrn., Détre U., 1982—. Student recruiter, vet. counselor Macomb Community Coll., Warren, Mich., 1971-73; child care worker, group therapist Macomb County Juvenile Ct., Mt. Clemens, 1972-78; youth counselor Macomb County Community Services, Mt. Clemens, 1979-81, employment counselor, 1981-83; employment counselor Macomb/St. Clair county Job Tng., Mt. Clemens, 1983-84; parole agt. Mich. State Dept. Corrections, Mt. Clemens, 1984—; treas. Northeast Interfaith Ct. Racial Justice, Warren, 1979-85. Bd. dirs. Democratic Dist. Com., Mt. Clemens, 1983-85. Served with U.S. Army, 1969-71. Mem. Am. Guidance Counseling Assn., Am. Correctional Assn. Methodist. Avocations: chess; basketball; sailing. Home: 22615 Thomson St Mount Clemens MI 48043 Office: Mich State Dept Corrections 76 S Gratiot St Mount Clemens MI 48043

JACKSON, ERNEST HARDING, genealogist, publisher; b. Pollard, Ark., Oct. 13, 1920; s. James William and Minnie Mae (Holcomb) J.; student Harvard U., 1940-41; B.A., U. Albuquerque, 1954; M.A., U. N.Mex., 1955; m. Anna Amalia Hofflund, Aug. 5, 1951. Enlisted U.S. Air Force, 1942, advanced through grades to chief warrant officer, 1968; 35 combat missions, ETO, World War II; assigned to Berlin Air Lift, 1949-50, Spl. Weapons Command, 1951-56; staff supply officer 11th Air Div., Alaskan Air Command, 1956-60; supply officer SAC bases, 1960-68; ret., 1968; asst. prof. English, Rock Valley Jr. Coll., Rockford, Ill., 1968-74. Decorated Air medal with silver and bronze oak leaf clusters, Purple Heart. Mem. Nat. Geneal. Soc., Ill. Geneal. Soc., North Central Ill. Geneal. Soc. (charter mem., pres.), SAR (treas. Ill. soc.), Phi Delta Kappa. Pub.: Jacksoniana - A Jackson Family Newsletter, 1977; compiler: Marriages of Union County, Illinois, 1818-1880, 1977; compiler, pub.: Federal Census of Union County, Illinois, 1820-1880, 1978; editor: Combined Atlases of Winnebago County, Illinois, 1981; 1840 Federal Census, Winnebago County, Illinois, 1983; 1860 Federal Census, Winnebago County, Illinois, 1983. Home and Office: 730 Parker Woods Dr Rockford IL 61102

JACKSON, HAROLD EDWARD, JR., physicist; b. Pitts., Jan. 5, 1933; s. Harold Edward and Theodora Dagmar (Johnson) J.; m. Sally Ann Moseley, June 7, 1958; children—Mark Edward, Matthew Owen, Kimberly Lynn. B.A., Princeton U., 1954; Ph.D., Cornell U., 1959. Asst. physicist Argonne Nat. Lab., Ill., 1959-62, physicist, 1962-73, sr. physicist, 1973—, research project dir., 1981-83; vis. scientist Centre d'Etudes Nucleaires de Saclay, 1965-67, Accelerateur Lineaire de Saclay, 1975-76; mem. U.S. Nuclear Data Com., 1967-77, sec., 1972-73, chmn., 1973-74; U.S. rep. nuclear data com. Nuclear Energy Agy., 1972-77; chmn. LAMPF LEP Working Group, 1976-77, bd. dirs., 1979-83, chmn., 1982-83; nat. adv. bd. U.S. Nat. Electron Accelerator Lab.; collaborateur Estranger Inst. de Resherche Fondamentale, Saclay, 1984-85. Contbr. articles to profl. jours. Mem. Am. Phys. Soc., AAAS. Home: 58 Harris Ave Clarendon Hills IL 60514 Office: Physics Div Argonne Nat Lab Argonne IL 60439

JACKSON, IAN THOMAS, plastic surgeon; b. Glasgow, Scotland, Dec. 24, 1934; s. Thomas John and Alice (Gould) J.; m. Marjorie Dalrymple, June 27, 1959; children—Linda Anne Marjorie, Susan Patricia, Sarah Elizabeth, Andrew Hamilton, David Santoya. M.B.Ch.B., U. Glasgow, 1959. Intern Glasgow Royal Infirmary, Scotland, 1959-60, resident, 1961-71; resident Canniesburn Hosp., Glasgow; cons. plastic surgery, Glasgow, 1972-78; prof. plastic surgery Mayo Clinic, Rochester, Minn., 1978—, head plastic surgery sect., 1981—. Author: Basic Principles of Plastic Surgery and Burns, 1975; Atlas of Craniofacial Maxillary Surgery, 1982; Facial Flap Surgery, 1985. Editor: Recent Advances in Plastic Surgery, Vol. II, 1981, Vol. III, 1985; Mem. Skoog Soc. Plastic Surgery (pres.), Minn. Acad. Plastic Surgery (pres.-elect), Am. Soc. Plastic Surgery, Am. Assn. Plastic Surgery, Am. Soc. Aesthetic Surgery, Brit. Soc. Plastic Surgery, Can. Soc. Plastic Surgery, S. African Soc. Plastic Surgery, Cleft Palate Assn., Internat. Soc. Craniofacial Surgery. Avocations: downhill skiing, tennis. Office: Mayo Clinic Plastic Surgery Dept 200 1st St SW Rochester MN 55906

JACKSON, ISAIAH, conductor; b. Richmond, Va., Jan. 22, 1945; s. Isaiah Allen Jr. and Alma Alverta (Norris) J.; m. Helen Tuntland, Aug. 6, 1977; children—Benjamin, Katharine. B.A. cum laude, Harvard U., 1966; M.A., Stanford U., 1967; M.S., Juilliard Sch., 1969, D.M.A., 1973. Founder, condr. Juilliard String Ensemble, N.Y.C., 1970-71; asst. condr. Am. Symphony, N.Y.C., 1970-71; asst. condr. Balt. Symphony, 1971-73; assoc. condr. Rochester Philharm. Orch., N.Y., 1973—; music dir. Flint Symphony Orch., Mich., 1982—; guest condr. Boston Pops, Cleve. Orch., Detroit Symphony, N.Y. Philharm., Los Angeles Philharm. Recipient First Gov.'s awards for Arts in Va., 1979. Home: 615 E 2d St Flint MI 48503 Office: Flint Symphony Orch 1025 E Kearsley St Flint MI 48503

JACKSON, JAMES AVELON, JR., criminal justice educator; b. Granite City, Ill., June 5, 1942; s. James Avelon and Ruby Cleona (Lee) J.; B.S., So. Ill. U., 1970; M.A., Sangamon State U., Springfield, Ill., 1973; postgrad. St. Louis U.; children—James Avelon, Jay Allen. Juvenile officer Madison County Sheriff's Office, Edwardsville, Ill., 1970-73; dir., instr. law enforcement program Muscatine (Iowa) Community Coll., 1973-75; asst. prof. Minot (N.D.) State Coll., 1975-76; dir. Inst. for Adminstrn. of Justice McKendree Coll., Lebanon, Ill., 1976-78; coordinator criminal justice and community service programs Southeastern Community Coll., West Burlington, Iowa, 1979-81; assoc. prof., chmn. dept. criminal justice St. Louis Community Coll. at Forest Park, 1981—. Named Tchr. of Yr. St. Louis Community Coll. at Forest Park, 1982-83, 1983-84, 85. Mem. Am. Assn. Univ. Adminstrs., Acad. Criminal Justice Scis., Iowa Criminal Justice Educators Assn. (pres. 1981), Ill. Assn. Criminal Justice Scientists, Midwestern Assn. Criminal Justice Educators (exec. com.), So. Ill. Criminal Justice Educators Assn. (founder), Ill. Community Edn. Assn., Am. Soc. Criminologists, Anglo-Am. Acad., Lambda Alpha Epsilon. Home: 327 E Schuetz Lebanon IL 62254 Office: St Louis Community Coll at Forest Park Saint Louis MO 63110

JACKSON, JAMES SIDNEY, psychology educator, social science researcher; b. Detroit, July 30, 1944; s. Peter James Jackson and Johnnie Mae (Wilson) Jackson Taylor; m. Toni Claudette Antonucci, Dec. 1, 1979; children—Arian Marie, Kendra Rose. B.S., Mich. State U., 1966; M.A., U. Toledo, 1970; Ph.D., Wayne State U., 1972. Probation counselor Lucas County Ct., Toledo, 1967-68; asst. prof. psychology U. Mich., Ann Arbor, 1971-76, assoc. prof., 1977—. Bd. dirs. Pub. Commn. on Mental Health, Washington, 1978-84. Named to Outstanding Young Men of Yr., U.S. Jaycees, 1972; recipient Faculty Achievement award U. Mich., 1976. Mem. Am. Psychol. Assn. (policy and planning bd. 1981-85, contbr. to Psychology in Pub. Interest 1983), Nat. Assn. Black Psychologists (chmn. 1974-75), Assn. Advancement Psychology (chmn. 1978-80), Nat. Acad. Scis. (com. on black Ams.), Alpha Phi Alpha (pres. Mich. State U. chpt. 1965-66). Avocations: skiing; jogging; bridge. Office: Inst Social Research U Mich 429 Thompson Ann Arbor MI 48106

JACKSON, JERRY LEE, stockbroker; b. Mason City, Iowa, Feb. 7, 1936; s. Fred Lester and Marguerite (Arnold) J.; m. Karen Sue Twito; children—Kimberlee Jo, Todd Jerome, Jerry Lee. Student, Iowa State U., 1954-56; N.Y. Inst. Finance, 1965. Stockbroker Bosworth Sullivan, Denver, 1965-69, McDonnell & Co., Denver, 1969, Shearson Hammil & Co., Denver, 1969-71, Hanifen Imhoff, Denver, 1971-73, Birr Wilson, Kalispell, Mont., 1973-74; stockbroker, v.p., br. mgr., D.A. Davidson, Williston, N.D., 1974—. Exec. council Dist 1, N.D. Republican Party, 1984—; bd. dirs. Crimestoppers, 1984—. Mem. C. of C. (contact club). Lutheran. Lodges: Lions, Shriners. Home: 424 21st St E Williston ND 58801 Office: DA Davidson Box 1566 Williston ND 58801

JACKSON, JERRY STEPHEN, podiatrist; b. Talcott, W.Va., July 29, 1944; s. James Elex and Marie Jackson; m. Katherine Loraine Bradley, Nov. 27, 1963; children—Kelli, Jami, Jerry Stephen. Student W.Va. State Coll., 1962-65; B.S. in Chemistry, Cleve. State U., 1973; D.P.M., Ohio Coll. Podiatric Medicine, 1978. Lic. podiatrist, Kans., Mo. Computer machinist, Cleve., 1965-71; chemist Ceilcote Co., Cleve., 1972-73; resident in podiatry surgery VA Med. Ctr., Leavenworth, Kans., 1978-79; practice poditary specializing in podiatric surgery and gen. practice, Leavenworth, 1979—; mem. staff Horton (Kans.) Community Hosp., Jefferson County Meml. Hosp., Winchester, Kans. Ohio Coll. Podiatric Medicine scholar, 1974-78. Fellow Am. Assn. Hosp. Podiatrists, Am. Soc. Podiatric Dermatology; mem. Am. Podiatry Assn., Kans. Podiatry Assn. (sec.), Am. Acad. Ambulatory Foot Surgeons (diplomate), Am. Analgesia Assn. (diplomate), Leavenworth C. of C. Lutheran. Club: Kiwanis. Home: Rural Route 2 Box 137 H Leavenworth KS 66048 Office: 113 Delaware Suite D Leavenworth KS 66048

JACKSON, JESSE LOUIS, clergyman, activist civic leader; b. Greenville, N.C., Oct. 8, 1941; s. Charles Henry and Helen Jackson; student U. Ill., 1959-60; B.A. in Sociology, A. and T. Coll. N.C., 1964; postgrad. Chgo. Theol. Sem., D.D. (hon.); hon. degrees Pepperdine U., Oberlin U., Oral Roberts U., U. R.I., Georgetown U., Howard U., numerous others; m. Jacqueline Lavinia Brown, 1964; children—Saniita, Jesse Louis, Jonathan Luther, Yusef DuBois, Jacqueline Lavinia. Ordained to ministry Baptist Ch., 1968; founder (with others) Operation Breadbasket joint project SCLC, Co-ordinating Council Community Orgns., Chgo., 1966, nat. dir., 1966-71; founder, exec. dir. Operation PUSH (People United to Save Humanity), Chgo., 1971—. Active Black Coalition for United Community Action, 1969; Democratic nominee for Pres. U.S., 1984. Recipient Presdl. award Nat. Med. Assn., 1969; Humanitarian Father of Year award Nat. Father's Day Com., 1971. Address: 930 E 50th St Chicago IL 60615

JACKSON, KIMBERLY ANTCLIFF, lawyer; b. Lebanon, Ind., May 11, 1955; d. Clifford G. and Char (Kincaid) Antcliff. B.A., DePauw U., 1977; J.D., Ind. U.-Indpls., 1980. Bar: Ind. 1980, U.S. Dist. Ct. (so. dist.) Ind. 1980. Ptnr. Antcliff & Antcliff, Greenwood, Ind., 1980-84; sole practice, Riley, Ind., 1984—. Mem. Ind. Bar Assn., Johnson County Bar, Terre Haute Bar. Democrat. Office: PO Box 701 Hwy 46 E Riley IN 47871

JACKSON, LOUISE ANNE, lawyer; b. Bowling Green, Ohio, July 27, 1948; d. John Edward and Patricia Anne (Messmer) J.; B.B.A., Bowling Green State U., 1970; M.B.A., U. Colo., 1971; J.D., U. Toledo, 1976. Bar: Ohio 1977; C.P.A. Ohio. Sr. staff acct. Arthur Young and Co., Toledo, 1972-75; ptnr. Marshall & Melhorn, Toledo, 1976-85; sole practice, Toledo, 1985—. Mem. ABA, Toledo Bar Assn., Ohio Soc. C.P.A.'s (sec. 1983-84, bd. dirs. 1982-83). Club: Zonta of Toledo (treas. 1978-79, v.p. 1981-82, pres. 1982-83).

JACKSON, MARION THOMAS, life science educator; b. Versailles, Ind., Aug. 19, 1933; s. Marshall Marion and Stella Edith (Fox) J.; m. Gloria E. Doctor, Oct. 22, 1955 (div. Aug. 1984). B.S., Purdue U., 1961, Ph.D., 1964. Asst. prof., then assoc. prof. life scis. Ind. State U., Terre Haute, 1964-71, prof., 1971—. Editor Procs. Ind. Acad. Sci., 1969-74. Contbr. articles to profl. jours. Served with USN, 1953-55. Ind. Acad. Sci. fellow, 1975. Mem. Ecol. Soc. Am., Nature Conservancy (chmn. 1974-79, Oak Leaf award 1981), Audubon Soc. (life), Wilderness Soc. (life), Sigma Xi. Lutheran. Avocations: photography, woodworking. Office: Ind State U Dept Life Sci Terre Haute IN 47809

JACKSON, MYRON ANDRE, cellular communications company executive; b. Southern Pines, N.C., Jan. 29, 1956; s. Ernest Hallowed and Alice Dolly (Gregory) J. Assoc. in Elec. Tech., United Elec. Inst. Sr. elec. technician Motorola, Inc., Schaumburg, Ill., 1975-77, prodn. supr., 1977-78, sr. tech. supr. cellular products, 1978-83, prodn. mgr., 1983—, tech. recruiter, 1977—; instr. electronics Harper Coll., Palatine, Ill., 1982-83. Inventor Pulsar Terminal Test Card, 1977. Mem. NAACP. Club: Motorola Radio (v.p. 1981-82) (Schaumburg, Ill.). Home: 1772 Gilberto St Glendale Heights IL 60139 Office: Motorola Inc 1301 E Algonquin Rd F-41 Schaumburg IL 60196

JACKSON, RAY FRANCIS, JR., statistician; b. Toronto, Ohio, May 18, 1928; s. Ray Francis and Mary Ellen (Arehart) J.; Student Coll. of Steubenville, 1947-50; B.S., Bethany Coll., 1951. Sr. math. statistician Monsanto Research Corp., Miamisburg, Ohio, 1956—. Served with USAF, 1951-55. Mem. Am. Soc. Quality Control, Am. Statis Assn. Republican. Presbyterian. Lodge: Masons. Home: 531 Belmonte Park N Apt 206 Dayton OH 45405 Office: Monsanto Research Corp Mound Rd Miamisburg OH 45342

JACKSON, REGINALD SHERMAN, JR., lawyer; b. Toledo, Ohio, Oct. 8, 1946; s. Reginald Sherman and Frances (Holland) J.; m. Joanne Marie Warren, Aug. 31, 1968; children—Reginald Sherman III, Michael W., Adam H. B.A., Ohio State U., 1968, J.D., 1971. Bar: Ohio 1971. Mem. Fuller, Henry, Hodge & Snyder, Toledo, 1971-76; asst. U.S. atty. no. dist. Ohio, U.S. Dept. Justice, 1976-78; mem. Connelly, Soutar & Jackson, 1978—; adj. prof. U. Toledo, 1976—. Trustee Toledo Boy's Club, 1981—. Mem. ABA, Ohio Bar Assn., Toledo Bar Assn. Club: Toledo Country (trustee 1981—). Lodge: Rotary. Home: 2907 River Rd Maumee OH 43537 Office: Connelly Soutar & Jackson 2100 Ohio Citizens Bank Bldg Toledo OH 43604

JACKSON, ROBERT FRANKLIN, general and vascular surgeon; b. Logan, W.Va., May 27, 1938; s. Kinner F. and Lahoma (Jimison) J.; m. Margaret Tatem, Apr. 3, 1959; children—Robert Franklin, Thomas Logan, Susan Elizabeth. B.A., Taylor U., 1961; M.D., Ind. U. Sch. Medicine, Indpls., 1966. Diplomate Am. Bd. Surgery. Resident in surgery, Miami Valley Hosp., Dayton, Ohio, 1967-71; practice medicine specializing in general and vascular surgery, Surgeons, Inc., Marion, Ind., 1973—; dir. Vascular Lab., Marion Gen. Hosp., 1980—. Contbr. articles to med. jours. Mem. commn. Overseas Missions, Evang. Mennonite Ch. Served to maj. U.S. Army, 1971-73. Decorated Bronze Star medal. Recipient Disting. Alumnus of Yr. award Taylor U., Disting. Parent of Yr. award, 1983. Fellow ACS, Soc. Abdominal Surgeons, Internat. Coll. Surgeons; mem. Christian Businessmens Assn., Christian Med. Soc. Mennonite. Club: Rotary. Avocations: Equestrian sports, fox hunting, golfing. Office: 500 Wabash Ave Marion IN 46952

JACKSON, ROBERT HENRY, physician, medical administrator; b. Norwalk, Ohio, Oct. 5, 1922; s. Samuel Lloyd and Mona Mae (Zuelch) J.; m. Ann Elisabeth Dornback, Sept. 20, 1958; 1 child, Ann Dornback. B.S., Western Res. U., 1947; M.D., U. Heidelberg, Fed. Republic of Germany, 1953. Rotating intern St. Luke's Hosp., Cleve., 1953-54; fellow in Urology Mayo Clinic, Rochester, Minn., 1954-55; asst. surg. resident Luth. Hosp., Cleve., 1955-56, Perusse Traumatic Surg. Clinic, Chgo., 1956-57; gen. chmn. Internat. Congress on Neoplastic Diseases, Heidelberg, Fed. Republic Germany, 1973. Author: Joseph Colt Bloodgood: Cancer Pioneer, 1971. Mem. Presdl. Task Force, Washington, 1984—, Senatorial Com., Washington, 1984—; mem. Nat. Commn. on Health Manpower, Washington, 1965—. Served to brig. gen. U.S. Army, ETO. Named hon. prof. internat. affairs, recipient Jacob Gould Schurman plaque Cornell U., 1961; U. Heidelberg New Univ. dedicated in his honor. Mem. Mayo Clinic Alumni Assn., AMA (founder sect. neoplastic diseases 1971), Am. Assn. Study Neoplastic Diseases (exec. sec. 1960-73, pres. 1974), Assn. U.S. Army, Res. Officers Assn. (honor roll 1955—), Cleve. Grays, World Med. Assn., Deutsche Medizinische Gesellschaft Von Chgo., Ohio State Med. Assn., Cleve. Acad. Medicine, VFW, U. Heidelberg Med. Alumni in U.S.A., Am. Legion. Club: Cercle D'Etudes sur la Bataille des Ardennes. Avocations: military, woodworking, fishing, boating. Home: 10607 Miles Ave Cleveland OH 44105

JACKSON, ROBERT LORING, educator, academic administrator; b. Mitchell, S.D., June 8, 1926; s. Olin DeBuhr and Edna Anna (Hanson) J.; m. Helen M. Baker, June 2, 1951; children—Charles Olin, Catherine Lynne, Cynthia Helen. B.S., Hamline U., 1950; M.A., U. Minn., 1959; Ph.D., 1965. Tchr. math. and sci., pub. schs., Heron Lake, Minn., 1950-52; tchr. math. Lakewood (Colo.) Sr. High Sch., 1952-53, Nouassuer Air Force Sch. Casablanca, Morocco, 1953-54, Baumholder (Germany) Elem. Sch., 1954-55, U. Minn. Univ. Lab. Sch., Mpls., 1955-60; asst. prof. sci. and math. edn. U. Minn., Mpls., 1965-66, assoc. prof., 1966-70, prof., 1970—, head sci. and math. edn., 1980-84, assoc. chmn., dir. undergrad. studies, curriculum and instrn., 1984—; vis. prof. Hamline U., St. Paul, 1958, Mont. State U., Bozeman, 1981, Bethel Coll., St. Paul, 1981, No. Mich. U., Marquette, 1983-84; cons. math. Minn. Dept. edn., St. Paul, 1960-62. Bd. dirs. Minn. Chorale, Mpls., 1973—, pres., 1978-80. Served to pvt. inf. U.S. Army, 1944-46. Decorated Purple Heart; recipient Disting. Teaching award Coll. Edn., U. Minn., 1984. Mem. Minn. Council Tchrs. Math., Nat. Council Tchrs. Math., Council Diagnostic and Prescriptive Math., Internat. Group for Psychology of Math. Edn. Methodist. Co-author book/man. series: Laboratory Mathematics, 1975-76. Home: 2710 N Dale St Apt 101 Roseville MN 55113 Office: 230 Peik Hall U Minn Minneapolis MN 55455

JACKSON, WILLIAM BRUCE, biology educator; b. Milw., Sept. 10, 1926; s. Walter Raleigh and Dorothy (Greene) J.; m. Shirley Jean Slentz, Sept. 6, 1952; children—Beth, Mark, Craig. B.A., U. Wis.-Madison, 1948, M.A., 1949; Sc.D., Johns Hopkins U., 1952. Biologist, Am. Mus. Natural History, C.Z., 1952 NRC, U.S. Trust Ter., 1955-57; sr. asst. scientist USPHS, Atlanta, 1952-55; from asst. prof. to prof. biol. scis. Bowling Green State U., Ohio, 1957-84, Univ. prof., 1981—, emeritus, 1985—, dir. Environ. Studies Ctr., Ctr. Environ. Research, 1970-84; pres. Rodent Mgmt. Inc., 1982—; pres. Biocenotics, Inc., 1985—; sec. Internat. Pest Mgmt. Cons.; cons. WHO, FAO of UN, Rockefeller Found. Editor conf. procs. Contbr. articles to profl. publs. Served to lt. USPHS, 1952-55. Recipient S.S. Casper Disting. Faculty award Bowling Green State U., 1968, Disting. Service award Health Planning Assn., 1980, Ann. Educator award Ohio Alliance Environ. Edn., 1983. Fellow Ohio Acad. Sci. (v.p.), AAAS; mem. ASTM (com. chmn.), Sigma Xi, Omicron Delta Kappa (Man of Yr. 1985), Pi Chi Omega (exec. dir. 1980—). Home: 315 Donbar Dr Bowling Green OH 43402 Office: Bowling Green State U Dept Biol Scis Bowling Green OH 43403

JACKSON, WILLIAM GENE, computer company executive; b. Opelika, Ala., Nov. 22, 1946; s. John Willis and Lucy (Jackson) J.; m. Cornelia Turner, Aug. 17, 1969; children—Verzelia Yvett, Gena Nichole, William Gene. B.S. in Mgmt. and Mktg., Syracuse U., 1979, A.A.S. in Mgmt., 1976; postgrad. Pace U. With IBM, 1966—, customer engr. Huntsville, Ala., 1966-72, sr. customer engr., Atlanta, 1972-73, field mgr., Miami, Fla., 1973-75, eastern region ops. analyst Harrison, N.Y., 1975-76, br. mgr., N.Y.C., 1976, region ops. mgr. region 3, Montvale, N.J., 1977-78, employee relations program mgr. personnel, office products div. hdqrs., Franklin Lakes, N.J., 1979, adminstrv. asst. to dir. ops. west, office products div. hdqrs., Franklin Lakes, 1980, IBM corp. service staff, Armonk, N.Y., 1981-82, adminstrv. asst. to pres. customer service div., Franklin Lakes, 1983, region mgr. customer service div., region 7, Southfield, Mich., 1983-84, dir. service support Nat. Service div. Region 6, 1984—. Bd. dirs. spl. affairs Jaycees, Wanaque, N.J., 1978-79. Mem. Am. Mgmt. Assn. Home: 25220 Witherspoon Rd Farmington Hills MI 48018 Office: IBM-NSD Region 6 27800 Northwestern Hwy Southfield MI 48086

JACKY, RICHARD CHARLES, dentist; b. Walla Walla, Wash., June 30, 1935; s. Carl Frederick and Charlotte Mae Danner J.; m. Betty Jean Fields, Sept. 4, 1981; children—Leesa, Tina. B.S., Wash. State U., 1957; D.D.S., Washington U., St. Louis, 1961. Practice dentistry, St. Louis, 1961—; dir. Normandy Bank, St. Louis, 1974—; v.p. Jala Investment Corp., St. Louis, 1966-83. Mem. Am. Dental Assn., Greater St. Louis Dental Assn., Mo. State Dental Assn., Greater North St. Louis Dental Assn. Republican. Roman Catholic. Lodges: Rotary (past pres.), Elks. Home: 5 Manor Ln Ferguson MO 63135 Office: 10 Adams Ave Ferguson MO 63135

JACOB, MARY JANE, curator; b. N.Y.C., Jan. 5, 1952; d. Elmer J. and Catherine (Marino) J.; m. Russell L. Lewis. B.F.A., U. Fla., 1973; M.A. in Art History, U. Mich., 1976. Assoc. curator modern art Detroit Inst. of Arts, Mich., 1978-80; curator Mus. of Contemporary Art, Chgo., 1980-83, chief curator, 1983—. Author: (with others) The Rouge: The Image of Industry in Art of Charles Sheeler and Diego Rivera, 1978; also exhbn. catalogues. Contbg. author: The Amazing Decade: Women and Performance Art 1970-1980, 1983; Studies in Dade and Surrealism, 1985. Contbr. articles and essays to profl. jours. Office: Mus of Contemporary Art 237 E Ontario St Chicago IL 60611

JACOB, RICHARD JOSEPH, rubber and plastic manufacturing company executive; b. Detroit, July 25, 1919; s. Ben B. and Nettie (Byron) J.; m. Louise Marks, Apr. 2, 1949; children—Patricia Josephine, Arnold Marks. Student Butler U., 1938-39, Miami U., 1940-41. Exec. Mfg. Engring. Co., Detroit, 1945-46; exec. v.p., pres. Cadillac Plastics & Chem. Co., Detroit, 1945-65, dir., 1945—; exec. v.p. Dayco Corp., Dayton, Ohio, 1965-68, pres., 1968-73, chmn. bd., chief exec. officer, 1971—, also dir.; dir. Elder-Beerman Stores Corp., Dayton, Fla. Leasing & Capital Corp., Mich. Nat. Corp., Bloomfield Hills, Bank One, Dayton, Mich. Bank Detroit. Mem. adv. bd. Kettering (Ohio) Med. Ctr.; hon. trustee Childrens Med. Ctr., U. Dayton; bd. overseers Hebrew Union Coll. Cin.; life mem. bd. dirs. Brandeis U. Mem. Rubber Mfrs. Assn. (dir.), Dayton Area C. of C., Soc. Plastics Industry, Soc. Plastic Engrs. Clubs: Standard-City (past pres., dir.) Renaissance (dir.) (Detroit); Hundred (chmn., Racquet, Meadowbrook Country, Miami Valley Skeet (Dayton); Palm Beach (Fla.) Country; Ocean Reef (Key Largo, Fla.); Moraine Country (Kettering, Ohio); Franklin Hills Country (Franklin, Mich.); Harmonie (N.Y.C.); Muirfield Village Golf (Dublin, Ohio). Office: Dayco Corp Dayton OH 45401

JACOBI, ROGER EDGAR, arts executive, music educator; b. Saginaw, Mich., Apr. 7, 1924; s. Andrew E. and Olga C. (Schnell) J.; m. Mary Jane Stephans, Aug. 13, 1949; children—Richard William, Martha Jacobi Nale. Mus.B., U. Mich., 1948, Mus.M., 1951; Mus.D. (hon.), Albion Coll., 1980. Cert. tchr., Mich. Tchr. music Ann Arbor (Mich.) Pub. Schs., 1948-56, music dept. chmn., 1959-68; lectr. music U. Mich., Ann Arbor, 1957-59, asst. prof., 1959-63, assoc. prof., 1963-66, prof., 1966—, asst. dean, 1968-71, assoc. dean, 1971; personnel dir., sec. bd. Interlochen Ctr. for Arts, 1956-59, pres., 1971—; cons. Ford Found. Young Composers Project, 1960-62, Juilliard Repertory Project, 1965-67; chmn. music com. Arts Recognition Talent Search Project, Ednl. Testing Service, 1979-80. Named honored alumnus U. Mich. Sch. Music, 1981. Mem. Am. Council Arts, Am. Fedn. Musicians, Am. Sch. Band Dirs. Assn., Coll. Music Soc., Econ. Club Detroit, Internat. Soc. Performing Arts Adminstrs., Music Educators Nat. Conf. (bd. dirs. 1964-68), Music Industry Council, Nat. Assn. Schs. Music, Nat. Fedn. Music Clubs (presdl. citation 1981), Nat. Music Council, Delta Omicron (patron), Phi Mu Alpha Sinfonia. Lutheran. Lodge: Traverse City Rotary (pres. 1982-83, trustee Rotary Charities 1982-83). Author: (with Emil Holtz) Teaching Band Instruments to Beginners, 1966; contbr. articles to profl. jours.

JACOBS, ANDREW, JR., congressman; b. Indpls., Feb. 24, 1932; s. Andrew and Joyce (Wellborn) J.; B.S., Ind. U., 1955, LL.B., 1958. Practiced law in Indpls., 1958-65, 73-74; mem. 89th to 92d, 94th to 99th congresses from 10th Ind. dist. Mem. Ind. Ho. of Reps., 1959. Served with inf. USMCR, 1950-52; Korea. Mem. Am. Legion, Indpls. Bar Assn. Democrat. Office: 1533 Longworth Office Bldg Washington DC 20515

JACOBS, BRUCE EDWARD, management consultant; b. St. Louis, Mar. 27, 1952; s. Robert A. and Sara Lee (Brown) J.; m. Linda C. Schneider, May 26, 1973; children—Robert R., Nicholas C., Luke E., B.S., Washington U., 1976. Indsl. engr. Granite City Steel Co. (Ill.), 1974-75; project engr. Emerson Electric Co., St. Louis, 1976-77, sr. project engr., 1977-78; dir. mfg. Schlueter Mfg. Co., St. Louis, 1978-79; prin. White Haven Cons. Group, St. Louis, 1979-83; supr. cons. Fox & Co., St. Louis, 1983—; cons. St. Louis Zoo, 1975-76, Mo. Goodwill Industries, 1976-79; lectr. in field. Patentee in field. Mem. Inst. Mgmt. Cons., Am. Inst. Indsl. Engrs. (Region XI dir., pres. 1980, 1st place award in community affairs 1980, chpt. award of excellence 1980). Republican. Roman Catholic. Home: 6909 Dartmouth St Saint Louis MO 63130 Office: Fox and Co 720 Olive St Saint Louis MO 63101

JACOBS, DAVID R., JR., epidemiology educator; b. Bklyn., Apr. 16, 1945; m. Margaret Ruth Prosnit Sept. 1, 1968 (div.); children—Stephen, Theodore, Adam. Student Bucknell U., 1962-65; B.S. in Math., Hofstra U., 1966; Ph.D. in Math. Stats., John Hopkins U., 1971; postgrad. Cambridge U., Eng., 1969. Asst. prof. probability, stats., numerical analysis, Towson State Coll., Balt., 1970-71; lectr. John Hopkins U., Balt., 1971; asst. prof. epidemiology and biostats., U. Md., 1971-72, asst. prof. social and preventive medicine, 1972-74; asst. prof. biometry U. Minn., Mpls., 1974-79, dir. data processing ctr. lab. of physiol. hygiene, 1974-83, dir. biometrics sect. div. epidemiology, 1983—, assoc. prof. epidemiology, 1979—, mem. adv. com. health scis. computer service ctr., 1979-80, univ. computer ctr., 1980—, adviser grad. faculty, students, research tng., gen. courses in biometry and epidemiology U. Minn.; expert statis. witness in jud. procs., 1973-74; researcher in field. Mem. editorial bd. Jour. Chronic Diseases, 1976-83, Preventive Medicine, 1978—, Am. Statistician, 1980, Am. Jour. Epidemiology, 1980—, Psychophysiology, 1981, Israel Jour. of Med. Scis., 1981, Arteriosclerosis, 1982, Archives of Internal Medicine, 1982, Chest, 1983. Recipient Research Career Devel. award NIH, 1977-82. Fellow Am. Coll. Epidemiology, Am. Heart Assn. (council of cardiovascular epidemiology); mem. Minn. Affiliate of Am. Heart Assn. (chmn. Mpls. community program com. 1978-80), Am. Statis. Assn., Internat. Soc. and Fedn. of Cardiology (sci. council on epidemiology and prevention). Minn. Pub. Health Assn., Soc. for Epidemiol. Research, Soc. for Clin. Trials. Office: Div Epidemiology U Minn Stadium Gate 27 611 Beacon St SE Minneapolis MN 55455

JACOBS, DAVID SAMUEL, physician, pathologist; b. Detroit, Nov. 7, 1931; s. Harry L. and Rae (Goldman) J.; m. Judy Jacobs, Aug. 16, 1957; children—Diane Sue, Daniel Harry, Thomas Dale, Jonathan Todd. B.S. with distinction, U. Mich., 1953, M.D., 1956. Diplomate Am. Bd. Pathology, Intern, then resident U. Mich., Ann Arbor, 1956-62; resident Mt. Sinai Hosp., Chgo., 1962-63; pathologist Menorah Med. Ctr., Kansas City, Mo., 1963-65; vice chmn. Providence Hosp., Kansas City, Kans., 1964-65, pathologist, dir. labs., 1965-71; pathologist, dir. of labs. Providence-St. Margaret Health Ctr., Kansas City, Kans., 1971—; pres. Pathologists, Chartered, Shawnee Mission, Kans., 1971—; cons. VA Hosp., Leavenworth, Kans., 1972-82; clin. prof. U. Kans. Med. Ctr., Kansas City, 1979, U. Mo.-Kansas City Sch. Medicine, 1978. Author lab. manuals. Contbr. articles to profl. jours. Served as capt. U.S. Army, 1958-60. Fellow ACP, Coll. Am. Pathologists; mem. Am. Soc. Clin. Pathologists, Internat. Acad. Pathology, AMA, Kans. Med. Soc., Am. Assn. Blood Banks, Kansas City Soc. Pathologists, Kans. Soc. Pathologists (pres. 1978-79). Home: 6621 Overhill Rd Shawnee Mission KS 66208 Office: Lab Providence-St Margaret Health Ctr 8929 Parallel Pkwy Kansas City KS 66112

JACOBS, DENNIS ROGER, educational adminstrator; b. Pontiac, Mich., Oct. 3, 1949; s. Roger Earl and Maxine Elizabeth (Hotchkiss) J. B.A., U. Mich., 1971; M.Ed., Wayne State U., 1976. Community edn. intern Eastern Mich. U., 1978-79; tchr. alternative edn./adult edn. Brandon Sch. Dist., Ortonville, Mich., 1973-78, dir. Northwest Oakland Adult Basic Edn. Consortium, 1978-79, dir. adult and community edn., 1979-83; cons., presenter Oakland U., World Future Soc. Edn. Sect., Salt Lake City, 1981—. Chmn., Brandon-Groveland Area Youth Assistance Council, 1979-81; vice-chmn. Brandon-Groveland-Ortonville Joint Recreation Commn., 1980-81, chmn. 1981—; commr. Brandon-Groveland-Ortonville Cable TV Commn., 1982—; vice-chmn. Clinton Valley Citizens Adv. Council, 1981-82, North Oakland Life Enrichment Coalition, 1978—. Recipient Outstanding Achievement award Oakland Schs. Community Adminstrs., 1981-82; Outstanding Leadership award Brandon-Groveland Area Youth Assistance, 1981. Mem. Nat. Community Edn. Assn., Nat. Assn. Pub. Continuing and Adult Edn., Assn. Supervision and Curriculum Devel., Nat. Recreation and Parks Assn., Mich. Assn. Pub. Adult and Community Edn., Mich. Community Sch. Edn. Assn., Mich. Assn. Ednl. Options, Mich. Sch. Pub. Relations Assn., Mich. Recreation and Parks Assn. Home: 2629 Lakeview Dr Ortonville MI 48462 Office: 1025 Ortonville Rd Ortonville MI 48462

JACOBS, DONALD GUSTAVUS, clergyman; b. Chelsea, Mass., Aug. 24, 1916; s. Burchell Gustavus and Melissa Jane (VanDerZee) J.; m. Maxine Lanell Sides, June 11, 1942; children—Donald Albert, Burchell Lewis. A.B., Wilberforce U., 1939; B.D., Payne Theol. Sem., 1943; postgrad. Bucknell U., 1943-44, Duquesne Coll., 1946-47, Oberlin Sch. Theology, 1950-52; D.D. (hon.), Payne Sem., 1955; LL.D., Monrovia Coll., 1957, Edward Waters Coll., 1965. Ordained to ministry African Methodist Episcopal Ch., 1940. Pastor, African Methodist Episcopal chs., Pa. and Ohio, 1940—; exec. dir. Interch. Council Greater Cleve., 1968-82, gen. minister, 1983—; nat. dir. Ptnrs. in Ecumenism, Nat. Council Chs., N.Y.C., 1981—; tchr. Cleve. Theology Ctr., Ashland Coll., 1972-81. Sec., Wilberforce Bd. Trustees (Ohio); co-chmn. Stokes for Mayor Com., 1965, Operation Black Unity, 1969. Mem. Cleve. Ministerial Assn. (pres. 1961), NAACP (pres. Cleve. chpt. 1964-66), Nat. Assn. Ecumenical Staff, Cleve. Urban League, Connectional Council A.M.E. Ch. Democrat. Office: 475 Riverside Dr Room 870 New York NY 10115

JACOBS, DONALD SEYLER, ophthalmic surgeon; b. Cin., Nov. 20, 1945; s. Donald L. and Dorothy I. (Seyler) J.; m. Lynn Wilson Patterson, June 5, 1971; children—Donald P., Stephanie A. A.B., Cornell U., 1968; M.D., Johns Hopkins, 1972. Diplomate Am. Bd. Ophthalmology. Intern U. Cin. Med. Ctr., 1973; resident Eye and Ear Infirmary, U. Ill., Chgo., 1976; staff ophthalmologist U.S. Naval Regional Med. Ctr., Charleston, S.C., 1976-78; assoc., ophthalmic surgeon Eye Cons. of Cin., Inc., 1978—; mem. attending staff Christ Hosp., Cin., 1978—, Deaconess Hosp., Cin., 1978—. Served to lt. comdr. USNR, 1976-78. Fellow Am. Acad. Ophthalmology. Republican. Episcopalian. Club: Cin. Country. Office: Eye Cons Cin Inc 2123 Auburn Ave Suite 404 Cincinnati OH 45219

JACOBS, FRANCIS ALBIN, biochemistry educator; b. Mpls., Feb. 23, 1918; s. Anthony and Agnes Ann (Stejskal) J.; m. Dorothy Margaret Caldwell, June 5, 1953; children—Christopher, Gregory, Paula, Margaret John. B.S., Regis Coll., 1939; postgrad. U. Denver, 1939-41; Ph.D., St. Louis U., 1949. Postdoctoral fellow Nat. Cancer Inst., Bethesda, Md., 1949, 50; instr. physiol. chemistry U. Pitts. Sch. Medicine, 1951-52, asst. prof., 1952-54; asst. prof. biochemistry U. N.D. Sch. Medicine, Grand Forks, 1954-56, assoc. prof., 1956-64, prof., 1964—; research dir., supr. Nat. Sci. Research Participation Program in Biochemistry, 1959-63; advisor directorate for sci. edn. NSF. Mem. Bishop's Council, Diocese of Fargo, N.D., 1979-82, 82—. St. Louis U. fellow, 1941-49. Fellow AAAS, N.D. Acad. Sci. (editor 1967, 68); mem. Am. Soc. Biol. Chemists, Am. Inst. Nutrition, Soc. Exptl. Biology and Medicine, Am Chem. Soc., AMA, Sigma Xi (pres. chpt. 1965-66, Faculty award for outstanding sci. research U. N.D. chpt. 1982), Alpha Sigma Nu, Phi Lambda Upsilon. Roman Catholic. Contbr. articles to profl. jours. Home: 1525 Robertson Ct Grand Forks ND 58201 Office: Biochemistry and Molecular Biology U ND Sch Medicine Grand Forks ND 58202

JACOBS, LAURIE ALICE, insurance agency owner; b. Kenosha, Wis., Nov. 24, 1943; d. Steven and Irma Mabel (Rich) Jacobs. Student Carthage Coll., 1962-65. Lic. property and casualty, life health ins. agent, Wis. Sec. Steven Jacobs Agy., Kenosha, Wis., 1965, ind. ins. agent, 1974-79, owner Jacobs, Ins., Kenosha, 1979—; pres. Ins. Women of Kenosha, 1968, 70, 83. Pres., Kenosha County council Girl Scouts U.S.A., 1978-82; bd. dirs. Trinity Luth. Ch., Kenosha, 1974-78; div. chmn. United Way of Kenosha County, 1980-82. Recipient Lamb award Luth. Council of Am., N.Y.C., 1980; named Ins. Woman of Yr. Kenosha Assn. Ins. Women, 1968. Mem. Nat. Assn. Ins. Women, Ind. Ins. Agts. of Am.

JACOBS, LEO EDWARD, business exec.; b. Chgo., Feb. 15, 1893; s. David and Paulina (Robinson) J.; ed. public schs.; m. Harriet H. McKeon, Sept. 19, 1922; 1 dau., Nancy H. Jacobs Botbyl. Vice pres. Charles H. Besly Co., Chgo., 1907-1948; pres. Titan Abrasives, Chgo., 1948-71, ret., 1971. Mem. Soc. Mfg. Engrs. (life). Died Aug. 15, 1981. Home: 14994 Bignell Dr Grand Haven MI 49417

JACOBS, LESLIE WILLIAM, lawyer; b. Akron, Ohio, Dec. 5, 1944; s. Leslie Wilson and Louise Francis (Walker) J.; m. Laurie Stuart Hutchinson, July 12, 1962; children—Leslie James II, Andrew Wilson, Walker Fulton. Student Denison U., 1962-63; B.S., Northwestern U., 1965; J.D., Harvard U., 1968. Bar: Ohio 1968, D.C. 1980, U.S. Supreme Ct. 1971. Law clerk to chief justice Ohio Supreme Ct., Columbus, 1968-69; assoc. Thompson, Hine and Flory, Cleve., 1969-76, ptnr., 1976—; chmn. bd. Ohio Law Abstract Pub. Co., Columbus, 1984—. Contbr. articles to profl. jours. Trustee Citizens League Greater Cleve., 1972-78, Cleve. Ctr. Econ. Edn., 1984—; chmn. Citizens Adv. Bd. Juvenile Ct., 1978-81; pres. Juvenile Fund, Cleve., 1978-84. Served to lt. comdr. USNR, 1967-76. Fellow Am. Bar Found., Ohio State Bar Found.; mem. Ohio State Bar Assn. (exec. com. 1983—, pres.-elect 1985—), Cleve. Bar Assn. (trustee 1983-85). Republican. Presbyterian. Clubs: Chagrin Valley Hunt (Gates Mills, Ohio); Internat. (Washington); Harvard (N.Y.C.). Home: 18900 S Woodland Rd Shaker Heights OH 44122 Office: Thompson Hine & Flory 1100 Nat City Bank Bldg Cleveland OH 44114

JACOBS, LINDA LEE, hospital administrator; b. Lincoln, Nebr., Apr. 18, 1949; d. Jacob and Darleen Rose (Worster) J.; B.S. U. Nebr., 1971. Gastrointestinal asst. Bryan Meml. Hosp., Lincoln, Nebr., 1972-78, chief gastrointestinal asst., 1978-81, supr. gastronintestinal lab., 1981—, mem. employee adv. com., 1973-74; dir. Jacobs Constrn. Co., Inc., Lincoln. Active Vols. in Probation. Mem. Nat. Soc. Gastrointestinal Assts. (pres. 1980-81, chmn. nominating com. 1981-82, ex officio dir. at large 1981—, editor jour. 1981—), Nat. Assn. Female Execs., Am. Soc. Tng. and Devel., Am. Legion Aux., Gamma Phi Beta (corp. bd., pres. 1983-85). Home: 2624 Austin Dr Lincoln NE 68506 Office: 4848 Sumner St Lincoln NE 68506

JACOBS, LOUIS SULLIVAN, architect, engr., planner; s. Morris and Mary Jacobs; B.S. in Architecture and City Planning, Armour Inst. Tech., 1940; M.S. in Indsl. Engring., Ill. Inst. Tech., 1952, Ph.D. in Indsl. Engring., 1958; Sc.D. in Safety, Ind. No. U., 1972, Ph.D. in Human Engring., 1974; M.S. in Profl. Mgmt., 1980. Pres., Louis S. Jacobs & Assos., Architects, Engrs. and Planners, Chgo., 1946—; prof. archtl. engring. Loop Coll., Chgo., 1967—, coordinator engring., archtl. and tech. services dept. Pub. Service Inst., 1967-75, dept. applied sci., 1975—; prof. indsl. engring. Ill. Inst. Tech., 1948-58, 67; prof. architecture U. Ill., Chgo., 1967; prof. engring. Chgo. Citywide Coll., 1980. Bd. dirs. Old Town Boys Club, 1951—; trustee Chgo. Sch. Architecture Found., 1967. Served as lt. USN, 1942-46. Recipient award of merit Office CD, State of Ill., 1957; citation Gov. State of Ill., Office Emergency Services, 1964; citation for Outstanding public services Office of Pres. U.S., U.S. Emergency Resources Bd., 1967; registered profl. engr., Ill., Del., Calif.; registered indsl. engr., safety engr., mfg. engr., Calif.; registered architect, Ill.; cert. in materials handling, materials mgmt., indsl. hygiene. Fellow Am. Soc. Registered Architects, Nat. Soc. Profl. Engrs.; mem. AIA, Ill. Soc. Architects (dir. 1976-78 v.p. 1978-80, pres. 1980-82), Ill. Soc. Profl. Engrs. (v.p. 1976-83), System Safety Soc. (pres. 1980—), ASCE, Western Soc. Engrs. (life), Am. Soc. Mil. Engrs., Am. Soc. Safety Engrs., Internat. Materials Mgmt. Soc., Am. Inst. Indsl. Engrs., Soc. for Gen. Systems Research, Standards Engring. Soc., Soc. Mfg. Engrs., Vets. Safety, Constrn. Safety Assn. Am. (v.p. 1976—), Am. Soc. Environ. Engrs. (diplomate), Nat. Safety Mgmt. Soc., Nat. Assn. Fire Investigators, Nat. Fire Protection Assn., Nat. Safety Council, Mil. Order World Wars, Naval Order U.S., Res. Officers Assn., Tau Beta Pi, Sigma Iota Epsilon, Alpha Phi Mu, Tau Epsilon Phi. Editor: Vector, 1968. Office: 2605 W Pratt Blvd Chicago IL 60645

JACOBS, MARTIN DAVID, chiropractor; b. Dorchester, Wis., Sept. 25, 1922; s. Martin and Rose (Scrivanie) J.; m. Dolores M. Beyerl, Sept. 2, 1947; children—Maureen, Bruce, Terry Ann, Colette, Kristen, Gregory, Pamela. M.T., Century Coll. Med. Tech, 1941; Dr.Chiropractic, Los Angeles Coll. Chiropractic, 1948. Licensed med. technologist, Wis. Chiropractor, Evanston (Ill.) Assoc. Hosp., 1940-41, Lincoln Coll. Chiropractic, Indpls., 1943-45, Los Angeles Coll. Chiropractic, 1946-48; indsl. relations chmn. Wis. Chiropractic Assn., 1976-78; pvt. practice chiropractic, Marshfield, Wis., 1948—; cons. Weyerhaeuser Co., Marshfield, Wis., 1977—, Wis. Chiropractic Assn., others; lectr. in field. Mem. Marshfield Safety Com., 1970-82. Served with USN, 1941-43. Mem. Am. Chiropractic Assn. (pres.'s award 1981-82), Wis. Chiropractic Assn. (pres.'s award 1980-81, 81-82), Am. Med. Writers Assn. Republican. Clubs: Holy Name Soc., K.C. Contbr. articles to profl. jours. Office: 112 E 16th St Marshfield WI 54449

JACOBS, NAOMI RAE, librarian; b. Mpls.; d. Maurice and Bess (Douglas) Jacobs. B.A., Mich. State U., 1967; M.L.S., U. Mich., 1969. Reference librarian Hackley Pub. Library, Muskegon, Mich., 1969-70; librarian Undergrad. Library, Mich. State U.-East Lansing, 1970-72; serial bibliographer Wright State U. Library, Dayton, Ohio, 1972-73; tech. services librarian Jackson County Library, Jackson, Mich., 1973-74; acquisitions coordinator Nat. Ctr. Clearinghouse, Nat. Ctr. Research in Vocat. Edn., 1979-81; librarian Research Library, Nat. Ctr. for Research in Vocat. Edn., Ohio State U., Columbus, 1981—, acquisitions coordinator Erik Clearinghouse for Adult, Career, and Voc. Edn., 1983—. Mem. Palace Theatre Vols., Players Theatre Vols., Mershon Auditorium Vols., Ohio State U. Theatre Dept. Vols., WOSU Radio-TV Friends Orgn., Assn. Records Mgrs. and Adminstrs., Worthington Arts Council, Ohio Hist. Soc., Citizens Humane Action, Moblzn. for Animals Columbus Symphony Women's Orgn., Franklin County Library Assn., Acad. Library Assn. Ohio, Spl. Libraries Assn., Columbus Assn. for Performing Arts, Clubs: Altrusa International, Ohio State U Faculty Women's. Orgn., Franklin County Library Assn., Office: 1960 Kenny Rd Columbus OH 43210

JACOBS, RICHARD DEARBORN, consulting engineer; b. Detroit, July 6, 1920; s. Richard Dearborn and Mattie Phoebe (Cobleigh) J.; B.S., U. Mich., 1944; m. Mary Lou Hammel, Sept. 16, 1971 (div.); children—Richard, Margaret, Paul, Linden, Susan. Engr., Detroit Diesel Engine div. Gen. Motors, 1946-51; mgr. indsl. and marine engine div. Reo Motors, Inc., Lansing, Mich., 1951-54; chief engr. Kennedy Marine Engine Co., Biloxi, Miss., 1955-59; marine sales mgr. Nordberg Mfg. Co., Milw., 1959-69; marine sales mgr. Fairbanks Morse Engine div. Colt Industries, Beloit, Wis., 1969-81; pres. R.D. Jacobs & Assocs., cons. engrs., naval architects and marine engrs., Roscoe, Ill., 1981—. Served with AUS, 1944-46. Registered profl. engr., Ill., Mich., Wis., Miss. Mem. Soc. Naval Architects and Marine Engrs. (chmn. sect. 1979-80), Soc. Automotive Engrs., Am. Soc. Naval Engrs., Soc. Am. Mil. Engrs., Soc. Marine Cons., ASTM, Permanent Internat. Assn. Nav. Congresses, Navy League U.S., Assn. U.S. Army, Propeller Club U.S. Unitarian. Clubs: Country (Beloit); Rockford Polo, Masons. Home: 228 Summit St Poplar Grove IL 61065 Office: 11405 Main St Roscoe IL 61073

JACOBS, ROSEMARIE, clinical laboratory Manager; b. Lincoln, Nebr., Oct. 25, 1943; d. Jacob, Jr., and Darleen Rose (Worster) J.; B.S., U. Nebr., 1965; children—Michael Jacob and Douglas Henry Schwabauer. Staff med. technologist Shawnee Mission (Kans.) Hosp., 1965-66, Pediatric Profl. Assn., Shawnee Mission, 1971-73, Shawnee Mission Med. Center, 1976-77, lab. mgr., 1977—; v.p. Cons./Trainers S.W., 1982-83, pres., 1983-84, bd. dirs., 1982-84, interne mem., 1983-84, editor Newsloop, 1982—; dir. Jacobs Constrn. Co., Inc., Kansas City Milk Bank. Internal coordinator United Way campaign, 1980, 81; adminstrv. bd. Valley View United Methodist Ch., 1981-83, chair work area on worship, mem. Council on Ministries, 1981-83; pres. Shawnee Mission Women's Chorale, 1974-76; mem. Dimensions Unltd. Profl. adv. panel MLO. Cert. Am. Soc. Clin. Pathologists, Nat. Cert. Agy. Mem. Cons./Trainers S.W., Am. Soc. Med. Technologists, Kans. Soc. Med. Technologists, Clin. Lab. Mgmt. Assn., Am. Soc. Clin. Pathologists (affiliate), Kansas City Lab. Mgrs. Assn., AAUW, Shawnee Mission Med. Ctr. Aux., Nat. Assn. Female Execs., U. Nebr. Alumnae Assn., Alpha Xi Delta. Office: Shawnee Mission Medical Center 74th and Grandview Sts Shawnee Mission KS 66201

JACOBS, TAD BRADLEY, physician; b. Youngstown, Ohio, Apr. 12, 1953; s. Lamont Benton Jr. and Mildred Jane (Freed) J.; m. Kathy Louise Iott, Sept. 5, 1976; children—Kristin Erica, Brandon Christopher, Collin James. Student Westminster Coll., 1971-73; B.S., Youngstown State, 1973-75; D.O., Coll. Osteo. Medicine and Surgery, 1978-81. Intern Parkview Hosp., Toledo, Ohio, 1981-82; staff physician Flandreau Clinic, S.D., 1982—, owner, pres., 1982—; chief of staff Flandreau Mcpl. Hosp., 1983—; coroner Moody County, S.D., 1983—. Com. chmn. Troop 62 Boy Scouts Am., Flandreau, 1984-85; mem. Moody County Ambulance Bd., Flandreau, 1983—. Mem. Am. Osteo. Assn., Am. Acad. Family Physicians, S.D. State Med. Assn. (pres. 3d dist. 1985). Methodist. Lodge: Kiwanis. Avocations: hunting, horses, antiques. Home: 207 E Broad St Flandreau SD 57028 Office: Flandreau Clinic 309 N Prairie Flandreau SD

JACOBSEN, ERIC KASNER, consulting engineer; b. N.Y.C., July 21, 1932; s. Henry and Caroline (Kasner) J.; B.S.C.E., U. Iowa, 1956; m. Dorothy H. Caldwell, Mar. 30, 1957; 1 son, Steven. Structural engr. Stanley Engring. Co., Muscatine, Iowa, 1956-59; asso. dept. mgr. R. W. Booker & Assos., St. Louis, 1959-63; plant mgr. Tri-Cities Terminal div. Nat. Marine Service, Inc., Granite City, Ill., 1963-65; sr. engr. Monsanto Co., 1965-69; chief structural engr. Weitz-Hettalsater Engrs., Kansas City, 1969-72; supr. structural and archtl. engring. Austin Co., Cleve., 1972-78; mgr. Engring. Mining and Metals div., 1978—; cons. engr. structural and archtl. engring., 1960—; owner/mgr. Jacobsen Farms. Recipient Eagle Scout award Boy Scouts Am., 1951; registered profl. engr., Ill., N.Y., Iowa, Mo., Wis. Mem. ASCE, ASME, Cleve. Engring. Soc., Chi Epsilon. Presbyterian. Home: 16 Louise Dr Chagrin Falls OH 44022 Office: 3700 Mayfield Rd Cleveland OH 44121

JACOBSEN, NEIL SOREN, university administrator; b. Waterloo, Iowa, June 13, 1930; s. Soren M. and Lillian R. (Edwards) J.; m. Ruth Ann Stewart, Sept. 13, 1954; children—Teresa, Dennis, Linda. B.S., U. Iowa, 1952; M.S., U. Denver, 1956; Ph.D., Okla. State U., 1965; postdoctoral student U. Mass., 1964-66. High sch. tchr., Hawthorne, Calif., 1957-59, Whittier, Calif., 1959-62; assoc. v.p., dean N.D. State U., Fargo, 1966—. Author articles. Chmn. bd. Prairie Pub. TV, Fargo, 1974-79; Bd. dirs. N.D. Econ. Edn. Council, 1984—. Served to 2d lt. U.S. Army, 1952-54, Korea. NSF fellow, 1962; NIH fellow, 1963, 64; Eagles Club grantee, 1968. Mem. Am. Assn. Higher Edn. Republican. Lodge: Kiwanis (Fargo). Avocations: woodworking; fishing; gardening. Home: 1112 6th St S Fargo ND 58103 Office: ND State U Fargo ND 58105

JACOBSEN, THOMAS WINFIELD, manufacturing executive; b. Mpls., June 15, 1924; s. Oscar C. and Marguerite C. (Moon) J.; m. Ruth Marie Doyle, July 7, 1951; children—Daniel Thomas, Christopher Scott. B.A., U. Minn., 1950. Office mgr. Security Envelope Co., Mpls., 1951-55; v.p., gen. mgr. Tension Envelope Corp., Mpls., 1955—. Coordinator Mpls. Aquatennial Assocs., 1964-68. Served with USAAF, 1943-46; PTO. Mem. Mpls. Jaycees (1st v.p. 1960-61; Outstanding Dir. 1962), Mpls. Sales and Mktg. Execs. (Man of Yr. 1972; pres. 1973-74), Envelope Mfrs. Assn., U. Minn. Alumni Assn., Mpls. C. of C. Republican. Lodge: Rotary (sec. 1981-82) (Mpls.). Avocations: music; golf. Home: 5616 Bernard Pl Edina MN 55436 Office: Tension Envelope Corp 129 N 2d St Minneapolis MN 55401

JACOBSON, DONALD PAUL WHITFIELD, advertising agency executive; b. Springfield, Mass., July 13, 1953; s. William Norman and Shirley May (Kingsbury) J.; m. Pamela Jean Whitfield, Dec. 29, 1976; children—James, Katherine. B.A. in History, Northwestern U., 1975. Reporter, editor City News Bur., Chgo., 1976; editor Sandy Corp., Southfield, Mich., 1977; advt. coordinator Toyota Indsl. Trucks USA Inc., Carson, Calif., 1977-78, advt. mgr., 1978-81, market planning mgr., 1981; market planning mgr. Komatsu Fork Lift USA Inc., La Mirada, Calif., 1981-83; account exec. Robert McKim & Co., Inc., 1984; account mgr., asst. to pres. Ladd-Wells Advt. Agy., Chgo., 1984—. Contbr. articles to trade jours. Mem. Bus. Profl. Advt. Assn. Democrat. Club: Advt. of Los Angeles. Home: 3854 Fairview Ave Downers Grove IL 60515 Office: 211 W Wacker Dr Chicago IL 60606

JACOBSON, EARL JAMES, lawyer, tax leasing executive; b. Chgo., May 10, 1940; s. Benjamin L. and Mary (Urman) J.; m. Donna Jean Breen, Mar. 5, 1983; children—Joan, John. B.A., U. Ill., 1961; M.B.A., U. Chgo., 1963; J.D., Loyola U., Chgo., 1980. Bar: Ill. 1980, U.S. Dist. Ct. (no. dist.) Ill. 1980, U.S. Ct. Internat. Trade 1980, U.S. Ct. Customs and Patent Appeals 1980. Indsl. salesman Honeywell, Xerox, Chgo., 1964-67; dir. mktg. Mastech Computer, Chgo., 1967-71, Datronic Rental Co., Chgo., 1971-81; v.p. Dearborn Computer Co., Park Ridge, Ill., 1981-82; sr. syndication officer Seattle 1st Nat. Bank, Schaumburg, Ill., 1982-83; v.p. fin. and syndication Hartford Fin. Services, Inverness, Ill., 1983-85; v.p. corp. fin. and corp. counsel Lease Investment Corp., Chgo., 1985—; dir., gen. counsel Info. Systems, Arlington Heights, Ill., 1st Securities, Inc., Chgo., Citifirst, Inc., Chgo. Served with USAF, 1963-69. Mem. ABA, Nat. Assn. Securities Dealers, Equipment Syndication Assn., Ill. State Bar Assn., Chgo. Bar Assn. Club: 20 Plus (Chgo.) (pres. 1980-82). Home: 2517 Crawford Evanston IL 60201 Office: Lease Investment Corp 3 Illinois Ctr 13th Floor Chicago IL 60601

JACOBSON, EUGENE DONALD, physician, educational administrator; b. Bridgeport, Conn., Feb. 19, 1930; s. Morris and Mary (Mendelsohn) J.; m. Laura Kathryn Osborn, June 9, 1973; children—Laura Ellen, Susan Ruth, Morris David, Daniel Frederick, Miriam Louise. B.A., Wesleyan U., Middletown, Conn., 1951; M.D., U. Vt., 1955; M.S., SUNY-Syracuse, 1960. Intern SUNY Med. Ctr.-Syracuse, 1955-56, resident, 1957-60; assoc. prof. physiology UCLA, 1964-66; prof. physiology, chmn. dept. U. Okla., Oklahoma City, 1966-71, U. Tex.-Houston, 1971-77; assoc. dean Coll. Medicine, U. Cin., 1977-83, vice dean, 1983-85; dean Sch. Medicine, U. Kans., Kansas City, 1985—; cons. Upjohn Co., Kalamazoo, 1969—, USPHS, Bethesda, Md., 1968-72; chmn. Nat. Commn. on Digestive Diseases, U.S. Congress, Washington, 1977-79; mem. nat. digestive diseases adv. bd. NIH, Bethesda, 1985—. Contbr. articles to profl. jours., chpts. to books. Mem. editorial bd. several jours. Served to maj. U.S. Army, 1956-64. Recipient Disting. Alumnus award Coll. Medicine, U. Vt., 1980. Mem. Am. Gastroent. Assn. (gov. bd. 1976-79, disting. service award 1980), Am. Physiol. Soc. (com. on coms. 1975-77), Am. Soc. Clin. Investigation, Am. Heart Assn. (del. 1975). Avocations: rose growing, travel. Office: Sch Medicine U Kans Med Ctr Kansas City KS 66103

JACOBSON, GLORIA NADINE, coll. adminstr.; b. Jewell, Iowa, July 12, 1930; d. Christian Frederick and Amanda M. (Englebart) Larson; B.B.A., U. Iowa, 1974; m. Richard T. Jacobson, July 22, 1951; children—Richard Thomas, Douglas L., William Andrew. Mem. adminstrn. staff U. Iowa, Iowa City, 1950—, asst. to the dean Coll. of Pharmacy, 1981—. Mem. Phi Gamma Nu, Kappa Epsilon. Republican. Lutheran. Home: 415 Ridgeview Iowa City IA 52240 Office: U of Iowa Coll of Pharmacy Iowa City IA 52242

JACOBSON, JOAN, speech pathologist, audiologist, educator; b. Hull, Iowa, Apr. 26, 1924; d. Fred and Mary (Hoogechagen) Elsinga; m. John Jacobson, June 1, 1945 (div. 1952). B.A., Morningside Coll., 1944; M.A., Syracuse U., 1948, Ph.D., 1958. Cert. of clin. competence in speech pathology and audiology. Speech clinician Brookline Pub. Schs., Mass. Gen. Hosp., 1951-57; research assoc. Syracuse U., N.Y., 1957-58; asst. prof. speech pathology and audiology Eastern Ill. U., Charleston, 1958-62; faculty St. Cloud State U., Minn., 1962—, now prof. Mem. Am. Acad. Rehabilitive Audiology, Am. Cleft Palate Assn., Minn. Speech Lang. and Hearing Assn. (recipient honors 1984), Am. Auditory Soc. Presbyterian. Avocation: tournament bridge. Home: 412 1/2 7th Ave S Saint Cloud MN 56301 Office: St Cloud State U Speech Clinic Saint Cloud MN 56301

JACOBSON, MICHAEL HAROLD, educational administrator; b. Lajunta, Colo., Feb. 16, 1945; s. Irving Ralph and Bernice Marie (Rubin) J. B.S., Loyola U., Chgo., 1967; LL.B., LaSalle U., 1971; M.A., Northeastern Ill. U., 1970; Ph.D., Sussex Coll. (Eng.), 1973; L.H.D. honoris causa, London Inst., 1974, D.M., 1976; M.B.A., Keller Grad. Sch. Mgmt. Tchr., Chgo. Bd. Edn., 1967-71, counselor, 1971-76; pres. Chgo. Counseling Assocs., 1971-74; regional coordinator Chgo. Region, Effectiveness Tng. Assocs., 1972-73; Ill. state rep. Universal Life Ch., 1975—; prof. psychology Foster G. McGaw Grad. Sch., Nat. Coll. Edn., Chgo., 1975-80; dir. guidance services Orr High Sch., Chgo., 1976-78; assoc. prin. Dunbar Vocat. High Sch., 1978-79, Phillips High Sch., 1979-80; prin. Abbott Elem. Sch., Chgo., 1980—. Dist. commr. Boy Scouts Am., Chgo., 1975-82, asst. dist. commr., 1973-75, mem. sea exploring com., 1980—; staff officer public edn. USCG Aux., 1979-81, div. staff officer pub. affairs, 1981-82, asst. dist. staff officer communications, 1982-83, vice comdr., 1984, flotilla comdr., 1984, div. staff officer, 1983—. Served to capt. USNR; Vietnam. Decorated Meritorious Service medal (USN), Naval Commendation medal, Naval Achievement medal, Res. Commendation medal; Vietnamese Cross of Gallantry. recipient Dist. award of Merit Boy Scouts Am., 1976, Wood badge, 1977, named explorer advisor of the year, 1974; decorated Knight Sovereign Order of Lichstenstine; Knight commdr. Order Sursum Corda; Knight Order of Constantine. Mem. U.S. Naval Inst., Am. Assn. Sex Educators Counselors and Therapists (cert. sex educator and sex therapist), Assn. for Supervision and Curriculum Devel., Chgo. Prins. Assn., U.S. Naval League, Spl. Elite Forces Soc., Mensa, Am. Legion, Psi Chi, Phi Delta Kappa, Phi Delta Epsilon, Alpha Phi Omega (nat. exec. alumni com. 1974—). Contbr. articles to profl. jours., also books. Home: 5547 W Higgins Rd Chicago IL 60630 Office: 3630 S Wells St Chicago IL

JACOBSON, NORMAN LEONARD, university administrator, researcher; b. Eau Claire, Wis., Sept. 11, 1918; s. Frank R. and Elma (Baker) J.; m. Gertrude A. Neff, Aug. 24, 1943; children—Gary, Judy. B.S., U. Wis.-Madison, 1940; M.S., Iowa State U., Ames, 1941, Ph.D., 1947. Asst. prof. dept. animal sci. Iowa State U., Ames, 1947-49, assoc. prof., 1949-53, prof., 1953—, disting. prof. agr., 1963—, assoc. dean Grad. Coll., 1973—, assoc. v.p. research, 1979—. Contbr. numerous articles to profl. jours., chpts. to books. Served with USNR, 1942-46. Fellow AAAS; mem. Am. Dairy Sci. Assn. (past pres.), Am. Feed Mfrs. Assn. (assn. award 1955, Borden award 1960), Am. Soc. Animal Sci. (Morrison award 1970), Am. Inst. Nutrition. Republican. Presbyterian. Home: 339 Hickory Dr Ames IA 50010 Office: Iowa State U 201 Beardshear Hall Ames IA 50011

JACOBSON, PHILLIP GORDON, optometrist; b. Milw., Jan. 27, 1918; s. Morris D. and Edith M. (Stein) J.; children—Eric M., Gary J., Steven L. B.A., U. Wis., Madison, 1936; O.D., Ill. Coll. Optometry, Chgo., 1942. Gen. practice optometry, Milw., 1946—; pres. Wis. State Bd. Examiners in Optometry, 1960-67; specialist in vision for partially sighted, Milw., 1966—, specialist in orthokeratology, Milw., 1984—. Pres. Vliet St. Assn., Milw., 1950-58; mem. mayor's adv. council City Milw., 1950; active Boy Scouts Am. Served with USAF, 1943-46. Recipient Disting. Citizen award State of Wis., 1956-68. Fellow Royal Soc. Health, Am. Sch. Health Assn., Orthokeratology-Nat. Edn. Research Found.; mem. Wis. Optometric Assn., Am. Optometric Assn. (legis. keyman 1970—), Milw. County Optometric Soc. (pres. 1952-53, 62, 72, 73). Lodges: Elks, Masons, Kiwanis (pres. 1979-84). Avocation: entertaining at children's hospitals. Home: 2330 W Dickinson Ct 102 N Mequon WI 53092 Office: 8500 W Capitol Dr Milwaukee WI 53222

JACOBSON, RONALD LEE, hospital executive; b. Webster, S.D., Jan. 11, 1948; s. Milton John and Gertrude Olive (Conklin) J.; m. Carol Louise Fisher, Nov. 2, 1968; children—Brent Ronald, Sara Lynn, Keith Lawrence, Mark Fisher. B.S. in Nursing, S.D. State U., 1970; CAS in Hosp./Health Care Adminstrn., U. Minn., 1978, M.Hosp. Adminstrn., 1981. Dir. nursing Community Meml. Hosp., Elbow Lake, Minn., 1971; dir. nursing services St. Mary's Hosp., Detroit Lakes, Minn., 1971-74; adminstr. Day County Hosp., Webster, S.D., 1974-78, Stevens County Meml. Hosp., Morris, Minn., 1978—. Hosp. rep., bd. dirs. Blue Cross Blue Shield Minn. Kellogg Found. grantee, 1980. Mem. Am. Hosp. Assn., Am. Coll. Hosp. Adminstrs., Minn. Hosp. Assn. (trustee 1981—), Morris Area C. of C. (v.p 1980-81). Republican. Lutheran. Clubs: Shriners, Kiwanis (pres. 1981-82); Coteau Lodge (Webster, S.D.). Home: 13 Westwood Acres Morris MN 56267 Office: 400 E 1st St Morris MN 56267

JACOBY, HENRY ALBERT, police chief, law enforcement educator; b. Wauseon, Ohio, Dec. 13, 1915; s. Carl and Katherina Elizabeth (Eichorn) J.; m. Lauretta Bullock, Nov. 11, 1939 (div. 1956); children—Barbara, Kathleen; m. Catherine G. Herzog, Nov. 8, 1958; 1 child, Alan. Cert. FBI seminar Sandusky Police Dept., 1947, Ohio Bur. Criminal Investigation, 1957. Patrolman Sandusky Police Dept., Ohio, 1942-49, detective, 1949-56, detective sgt., 1956-62, chief detectives, 1962-65; chief of police Port Clinton Police Dept., Ohio, 1966—; staff member Nat. Rifle Assn. Police Firearms workshop, Camp Perry, Ohio, 1967—, Sandusky Police Acad., 1976—; sch. comdr. advanced police scis. Terra Tech. Coll., Fremont, Ohio, 1976; dir. Northstar Regional Enforcement, six county area, 1972-75. Author: Criminal Investigation, 1960. Mem. North Central Ohio Crime Clinic (pres. 1970-72), U.S. Olympic Com. for Ottawa County (chmn. 1982—), Project Info (dir. 1972—), Internat. Assn. Chiefs Police, Ohio Chiefs of Police Assn., Fraternal Order of Police Assn. Lodge: Elks (chmn. Drug Awareness Program). Avocation: collecting police memorabilia. Office: Port Clinton Police Dept Adams & Second St Port Clinton OH 43452

JACOX, JOHN WILLIAM, engineering and consulting company executive; b. Pitts., Dec. 12, 1938; s. John Sherman and Grace Edna (Herbster) J.; B.S. in M.E., B.S. in Indsl. Mgmt., Carnegie Mellon U., 1962; 1 son, Brian Erik. Mfg. engr., Nuclear Fuel div. Westinghouse Elec. Co., Pitts., 1962-65; data processing salesman IBM, Pitts., 1965-66; mktg. mgr. nuclear products MSA Internat., Pitts., 1966-72; v.p. Nuclear Consulting Services, Inc., Columbus, Ohio, 1973-84; v.p. NUCON Internat., 1981-84; dir. NUCON Europe Ltd., London; pres. Jacox Assocs.; cons., lectr. Nat. Center for Research in Vocat. Edn., 1978—; presenter, session chmn. nuclear air cleaning confs., 1974—; adv. bd., exec. com., co-chmn. program subcom. Tech. Alliance Central Ohio, 1984—. Coop. edn. adv. com. Otterbein Coll., 1978-82. Mem. ASME (code com. nuclear air and gas treatment, exec. com., legis. services commn., chmn. subcom. testing), Am. Nuclear Soc. (pub. info. com.), N.Y. Acad. Scis., Ohio Acad. Sci., Inst. Environ. Scis., Electric Overstress-Electrostatic Discharge Assn. Columbus Area C. of C. (tech. roundtable 1983), Mensa, Nat. Rifle Rifle Assn. (life), Sun Bunch (pres. 1980-81). Home: 5874 Northern Pine Pl Columbus OH 43229 Office: 1445 Summit St Columbus OH 43201

JACQUEZ, JOHN ALFRED, physiologist, biomathematician; b. Pfastatt, France, June 26, 1922; came to U.S., 1929, naturalized, 1937; s. Francois Albert and Victorine (Oestermann) J.; m. Marianne Rose Reibel, Mar. 20, 1948; children—Albert R., Nicholas P., Geoffrey M., Phillip F. Student Cornell U., 1940-43, M.D., 1947. From research fellow to asst. Sloan Kettering Inst., N.Y.C., 1947-53; intern Kings County Hosp., Bklyn., 1955-56; from assoc. to assoc. mem. Sloan Kettering Inst., 1956-62; assoc. prof. physiology and biostatistics U. Mich., Ann Arbor, 1962-69, prof., 1969—; cons. RAND Corp., Santa Monica, Calif., 1959-64. Author: A First Course in Computing and Numerical Methods, 1970; Compartmental Analysis in Biology and Medicine, 1972, 2 edit., 1985; Respiratory Physiology, 1979. Editor: The Diagnostic Process, 1964; Computer Diagnosis and Diagnostic Methods, 1972. Editor Math. Bioscis., 1975—. Served to capt. U.S. Army, 1953-55. Nat. Cancer Inst. Research fellow, 1948-50; scholar in residence Fogarty Internat. Ctr., 1983-84. Mem. AAAS, Am. Physiol. Soc., Biophys. Soc., Soc. Indsl. and Applied Math., Soc. Math. Biology (pres. 1985-86). Home: 490 Huntington Dr Ann Arbor MI 48104 Office: 7712 Med Scis II U Mich Ann Arbor MI 48109

JAEKEL, BARBARA DOROTHY, public relations company executive; b. San Mateo, Calif., Apr. 9, 1958; d. Ralph Carl and Dorothy Willene J. B.S., Syracuse U., 1978; M.S., U. Tenn., 1983. News anchor, dir. pub. affairs Sta. WOLF, Syracuse, N.Y., 1977-78; news dir., investigative reporter Sta. WSKG, Endicott, N.Y., 1978-81, news dir., Knoxville, Tenn., 1981-82; freelance pub. relations cons., Knoxville, 1982-83; pub. relations mgr. Campbell & Co., Detroit, 1983—; account exec. Ford-Lyn St. James Program, 1983—, Lincoln-Mercury Cellular Communications Program, 1982—. Mem. Nat. Assn. Broadcast Engrs. and Technicians, Soc. Profl. Journalists, Am. Bus. Women's Assn. Avocations: running; hiking; gardening; writing poetry. Home: 13236 Joslin Lake Rd Gregory MI 48137 Office: Campbell & Co PO Drawer 490 Dearborn MI 48121

JAENIKE, VAUGHN, college dean, music educator; b. David City, Nebr., Sept. 30, 1930; s. Carl Albert and Lula (Egly) J.; m. Ruth Louise Lemke, June 27, 1953; children—Fritz, Kurt, Kristen, Katherine, Gretchen. B.Mus. in Edn., U. Nebr., 1952, M.Mus., 1955, Ed.D., 1967. Music tchr. pub. schs., Newman Grove, Nebr., 1952-56; jr. high music tchr. Englewood Pub. Schs., Colo., 1956-65; asst. prof. secondary edn. and music edn. U. Nebr., Lincoln, 1967-70, assoc. prof., 1970-72; spl. asst. to pres. U. Nebr. System, Lincoln, 1972-74; dean Coll. Fine Arts, Eastern Ill. U., Charleston, 1974—. Mem. Ill. Humanities Council Bd., 1976-80, exec. com. 1979-80. Grantee Nat. Endowment for the Arts, 1975, 78, Ill. Arts Council, 1974—. Mem. Internat. Council Fine Arts Deans (exec. com. 1979-82), Central Ill. Arts Consortium (pres. 1976-78). Ill. Arts. Alliance (sec. 1982-84), Charleston Area C. of C. (bd. dirs. 1984). Lutheran. Lodge: Rotary. Avocations: railroading, photography, cartography. Home: 1001 Colony Ln Charleston IL 61920 Office: Dean of Fine Arts Eastern Ill Univ Charleston IL 61920

JAFFE, DONALD NOLAN, lawyer; b. East Cleveland, Ohio, Feb. 20, 1938; s. David Baer and Vivian (Kramer) J.; m. Sandra Lois Katz, Aug. 11, 1963; children—Deborah Susan, Charles Edward. A.B., Case Western Res. U., 1959, J.D., 1961. Bar: Ohio. Law clk. U.S. Ct. Appeals (6th cir.), Cleve., 1962-64; asst. law dir. City of Cleveland Heights, Ohio, 1964-66; trust officer Union Commerce Bank, Cleve., 1966-69; asst. U.S. atty. Dept. Justice, Cleve., 1969-72; sole practice law, Cleve., 1972-82; of counsel Persky, Marken, Konigsberg & Shapiro Co., L.P.A., Cleve., 1982—; acting judge Cleveland Heights, Mcpl. Ct., 1972-75, Shaker Heights Mcpl. Ct., Ohio, 1982—; arbitrator Am. Arbitration Assn., Ohio State Employment Relations Bd., Cuyahoga County Common Pleas Ct. Author article in field. Councilman City of Cleveland Heights, 1976; mem. Gallon Club, ARC, Cleve., 1978; pres. No. Ohio council Am. Jewish Congress, 1972. Mem. Ohio State Bar Assn. (council of dels. 1984—), Bar Assn. Greater Cleve., Tau Epsilon Rho (supreme recorder 1979, pres. Cleve. grad. chpt. 1971), Delta Sigma Rho, Pi Sigma Alpha, Kappa Kappa Psi. Clubs: Ripon, Hawthorne Valley Country. Avocations: tennis; swimming; jogging; chess. Home: 32449 Chestnut Ln Pepper Pike OH 44124 Office: Persky Marken Konigsberg & Shapiro Co LPA 900 One Pub Sq Cleveland OH 44113

JAFFE, EUGENE J., oral surgeon, educator; b. Chgo., Mar. 6, 1924; s. Harry J. and Dora (Katz) J.; student Wilson City Coll., 1942-43; D.D.S., Loyola U., 1946; m. Adelyne Marshak, Oct. 20, 1946; children—Sally, Patti, Francine. Oral surgery resident Cook County Hosp., 1950-51; pvt. practice oral surgery, Chgo., 1952-69, Oak Lawn, Ill., 1969—. Asst. prof. oral surgery Loyola U. Sch. Dentistry, 1959-67; asst. prof. oral surgery U. Ill., 1967—; clin. asst. prof. surgery Lincoln Sch. Medicine, 1967—; mem. attending staff Cook County Hosp., Michael Reese Hosp. and Med. Center. Served with USAF, 1946-48. Fellow Internat. Assn. Oral and Maxillofacial Surgeons, Am. Coll. Oral and Maxillofacial Surgeons, Internat. Coll. Dentists, Am. Assn. Oral and Maxillofacial Surgeons, Am. Dental Soc. of Anesthesiology, Am. Coll. Dentists; mem. Am., Ill., Chgo. (pres. 1964-65) socs. oral and maxillofacial surgeons, Englewood Dental Soc. (pres. 1968-69). Office: 4435 W 95th St Oak Lawn IL 60453 also 7625 W 159th St Tinley Park IL 60477

JAFFE, MARTIN ELLIOT, career counselor, journalist; b. Cleve., Apr. 3, 1951; s. Ben and Elsie (Kaplan) J. B.A., Cleve. State U., 1973; M.A., Ohio U., 1974; M.S.L.S., Case Western Res. U., 1976. Adult services librarian Lorain Pub. Library, Ohio, 1976-82, dir. project Adult Career Planning Ctr., ACTION, 1982—; feature writer, book reviewer Cleve. Jewish News, 1982—; workshop leader. Author articles and book revs. Recipient Jesse Hauk Shera award Sch. Library Sci., Case Western Res. U., 1976; Ohio State Library grantee, 1983—. Mem. Am. Assn. Counseling and Devel. Democrat. Jewish. Home: 1102 E Erie St Apt 5 Lorain OH 44052 Office: Lorain Pub Library 351 6th St Lorain OH 44052

JAFFE, THERESA ANN, health agency administrator; b. Dover, N.J., Oct. 4, 1948; d. Edward Paul and Sophia Olga (Durda) Sheplak; m. Kent Edward Jaffe, Apr. 22, 1972. B.A., Kean Coll., 1970; M.S., Hunter Coll., 1971; Ed.S., U. Iowa, 1979. Asst. dir. Title I Project, Chgo., 1975-78; program coordinator Ill. Deaf-Blind Ctr., Chgo., 1978-79; mgmt. cons. T. Jaffe & Assocs., Chgo., 1978—; exec. dir. Easter Seal Soc., Chgo., 1980—; grad. instr. Nat. Coll., Chgo., 1976-77. Mem. adv. bd. Council for Exceptional Children, chmn. Exceptional Children's Week, Chgo., 1978, 79; founder Avondale Community Orgn., Chgo., 1980; mem. exec. bd. Scouting for Handicapped, Chgo., 1975—, Am. Chamber Symphony, Chgo., 1981-83; bd. dirs. Legal Clinic for Disabled, Chgo., 1985. Rotary scholar, 1966; Hunter Coll. fellow, 1971. Mem. Am. Mgmt. Assn., Nat. Soc. of Fundraising Execs.

JAHN, HELMUT, architect; b. Nurnberg, Germany, Jan. 4, 1940; came to U.S., 1966; s. Wilhelm Anton and Karolina (Wirth) J.; m. Deborah Ann

Lampe, Dec. 31, 1970; 1 child, Evan. Dipl. Ing.-Architect, Technische Hochschule, Munich, Fed. Republic Germany, 1965; postgrad. Ill. Inst. Tech., 1966-67; D.F.A. (hon.), St. Mary's Coll., Notre Dame, Ind., 1980. With P.C. von Seidlein, Munich, 1965-66; with C.F. Murphy Assocs., Chgo., 1967-81, asst. to Gene Summers, 1967-73, exec. v.p., dir. planning and design, 1973-81; prin. Murphy/Jahn, Chgo., 1981-82, pres., 1982—, chief exec. officer, 1983—; design studio faculty U. Ill.-Chgo., 1981; Elliot Noyes prof. archtl. design Harvard U., Cambridge, Mass., 1981; Davenport vis. prof. archtl. design Yale U., New Haven, 1983. Prin. works include Kemper Arena, Kansas City, Mo., 1974 (Nat. AIA honor award, Bartelt award, Am. Inst. Steel Constrn. award), Auraria Library, Denver, 1975, Fourth Dist. Cts. Bldg., Maywood, Ill., 1976, John Marshall Cts. Bldg., Richmond, Va., 1976, H. Roe Bartle Exhbn. Hall, Kansas City, Mo., 1976, Michigan City Library, Ind., 1977 (AIA Ill. Council honor award, AIA-ALA First honor award, Am. Inst. Steel Constrn. award), St. Mary's Athletic Facility, 1977 (AIA Ill. Council honor award, Am. Inst. Steel Constrn. award, AIA Nat. honor award), Monroe Garage, Chgo., 1977, Springfield Garage, Ill., 1977, Glenbrook Profl. Bldg., Northbrook, Ill., 1978, La Lumiere Gymnasium, La Porte, Ind., 1978, Rust-Oleum Corp. Hdqrs., Vernon Hills, Ill., 1978 (Am. Inst. Steel Constrn. award), Prairie Capital Convention Ctr.-Parking Garage, Springfield, Ill., 1979, W.W. Grainger Corp. Hdqrs., Skokie, Ill., 1979, Xerox Centre, Chgo., 1980, De La Garza Career Ctr., East Chicago, Ind., 1981 (ASHRAE Energy award), Oak Brook Post Office, Ill., 1981, Commonwealth Edison Dist. Hdqrs., Downers Grove, Ill., 1981 (ASHRAE Energy award), Area 2 Police Hdqrs., Chgo., 1981, Argonne Program Support Facility, Ill., 1982 (Owens-Corning Fiberglas Energy Conservation award), First Source Ctr., South Bend, Ind., 1982, One South Wacker Office Bldg., Chgo., 1982, Addition to Chgo. Bd. of Trade, 1982 (Reliance Devel. Group Inc. award for Disting. Arch., Am. Inst. Steel Constrn. award, Structural Engring. Assn. Ill. award), Mercy Hosp. Addition, Chgo., 1983, 11 Diagonal St., Johannesburg, Republic of South Africa, 1983, U. Ill. Agrl. Engring. Sci. Bldg., Champaign, 1984, Learning Resources Ctr., Coll. of Du Page, Glen Ellyn, Ill., 1984, Plaza East, Milw., 1984 (Disting. Architect award Milw. Art Commn.), Shand Morahan Corp. Hdqrs., Evanston, Ill., 1984, 701 Fourth Ave. S., Mpls., 1984, O'Hare Rapid Transit Sta., Chgo., 1984, State of Ill. Ctr., Chgo., 1985 (Structural Engring. Assn. Ill. award). Contbr. to numerous group and solo exhbns. of archtl. drawings and design. Recipient Arnold W. Brunner Meml. Prize in Arch., 1982, Progressive Arch. Design citation, 1977, 78, Progressive Arch. award for Chgo. Central Area Plan, 1985. Mem. AIA (numerous Chgo. chpt. awards 1975—). Roman Catholic. Clubs: Arts, Chgo. Athletic. Office: Murphy/Jahn 35 E Wacker Dr Chicago IL 60601

JAHNKE, FRED JOHN, electrical company executive; b. Milw., May 12, 1951; s. Fred Walter and Frieda (Hruz) J.; m. Mary Koch, July 13, 1974; children—Eric James, Mark Andrew. B.S. in Elec. Engring., Marquette U., 1973. Registered profl. engr., Minn., Fla. Draftsman, estimator Premier Electric, Aurora, Ill., 1973-74, project mgr., 1974-78, gen. mgr., Mpls., 1978-84, v.p., 1984—; sec., treas. Profl. Engr. in Constrn., Mpls., 1983—. Mem. Nat. Soc. Profl. Engrs., IEEE, Eta Kappa Nu. Roman Catholic. Lodges: K.C., Rotary. Advocations: water skiing; snow skiing; basketball; racquetball. Home: 5940 Kirkwood Circle Plymouth MN 55427 Office: Premier Electric Constrn 2221 Edgewood Ave S St Louis Park MN 55426

JAHNS, ARTHUR WILLIAM, educational administrator; b. Milw., Jan. 23, 1929; s. Arthur Victor and Vera (Kranz) J. B.S. in Secondary Edn., U. Wis.-Milw., 1953; M.Ed. in Guidance and Adminstrn., Marquette U., 1964. Tchr., counselor Milw. Pub. Schs., 1959-66, guidance dir., curriculum coordinator, 1967; asst. prin. Burrough Jr. High Sch., Milw., 1967-79; prin. Daniel Webster Middle Sch., Milw., 1980-83, Riverside U. High Sch., 1983—; cons. edn. ptnr. Met. Milw. C. of C., 1984—; ptnr. prin. Milw. Pub. Schs. Corp. Partnership Program, 1983—; cons. secondary edn. U. Wis.-Milw., 1984—. Coordinator, prin. acad. program devel. Riverside U. University Preparatory Program, 1984; ptnr., developer Profl. Partnership program, 1985; participant University-Bus. Cooperative Effort, 1982; co-author, developer Data Processing Programs Middle School Programming, 1979. Evaluator North Central Assn. for Accreditation, Madison, 1985—; mem. Harvard Grad. Sch. Edn., 1983—; adv. Milw. Inter-High Council, 1965-66; mem. steering com. U. Wis. Milw./Riverside U. High Sch. Partnership in Excellence Program, 1983—. Served to capt. USN, 1953-76. Named Outstanding Educator Marquette U., 1981; recipient Most Outstanding Support and Service award United Negro Coll. Fund, 1984. Mem. Naval Res. Assn. (life) (local pres. 1973-76, Outstanding service award 1976), Res. Officer Assn. (life), Assn. Sch. Curriculum Devel., Wis. Assn. Student Councils (adv.), Milw. Adminstrs. and Suprs. Council (various positions 1974—), U. Wis.-Milw. Alumni Assn. (life), Wis. Farm Bur., Milw. High Sch. Prins. Assn. Republican. Lutheran. Avocations: gardening; business; farming; collecting; music. Home: 3223 North Lake Dr Milwaukee WI 53211 Office: Riverside University High Sch 1615 East Locust St Milwaukee WI 53211

JAIN, JAY L., business administration educator; b. Haryana, India, Jan. 10, 1942; came to U.S., 1968; s. Phool Chand and Chanda Jain; m. Shubbi Jain, Feb. 26, 1967; children—Ashu, Manu. B.S., Punjab U., Chandigarh, India, 1965; M.S., U. Minn., 1970, Ph.D., 1972. Sub-div. officer Beas Project, Talward, India, 1965-68; computer programmer Compace Corp., Mpls., 1969-70; research fellow U. Minn., Mpls., 1969-72; systems engr. Engrs. India Ltd., New Delhi, 1972-73; indsl. engr. Dispatch Oven Co., Mpls., 1973—; asst. prof. bus. adminstrn. Detroit Inst. Tech., 1973-76, chmn., assoc. prof. dept. mgmt., 1976-78, dean, assoc. prof. Coll. Bus. Orgnl. Sci., 1978-80; prof., head dept. bus. adminstrn. St. Francis Coll., Fort Wayne, Ind., 1980—; pres. Lakshmi Investment Group, West Bloomfield, Mich., 1984; cons. in field. Contbr. articles to profl. publs. Recipient Outstanding Faculty award Detroit Inst. Tech., 1976. Mem. Fin. Exec. Inst. (treas. Fort Wayne chpt.), Midwest Bus. Adminstrn. Assn., Am. Prodn. and Inventory Control Soc. Home: 4815 Pasture Gate Fort Wayne IN 46804

JAKIEL, JAN J., chamber of commerce executive; b. Buffalo, Jan. 26, 1934; s. Stanley B. and Alvira Z. (Woyski) J.; m. Edith Marie McDonald, June 27, 1969. B.A., SUNY-Buffalo, 1956, M.B.A., 1966. Gen. mgr. Automotive Sales Dealership, Buffalo, 1958-62, Western Electric Co., Buffalo, 1962-69; bus., membership mgr. Buffalo Area C. of C., 1969-73, v.p. ops., 1973-82, v.p. econ. devel., 1982-83; pres. South Bend/Mishawaka Area C. of C., Ind., 1983—; dir., pres., treas. Consumer Credit Counseling, Buffalo, 1976-84; treas., dir. Buffalo Urban League, 1978-84; exec. v.p. ENIDC, Buffalo, 1982-84. Sec., Buffalo Chamber Found., 1978-84; treas. W. N.Y. Polit. Action Com., Buffalo, 1980-84. Served with U.S. Army, 1956-58. Mem. Am. C. of C. Execs., U.S. C. of C., Ind. C. of C. Execs. Assn. (bd. dirs. 1985-86). Clubs: South Bend Country, Morris Park Country (South Bend). Avocations: skiing; golfing; boating. Office: South Bend/Mishawaka Area C of C 401 E Colfax Ave PO Box 1677 South Bend IN 46634

JAKOBSEN, JANE ROBINETTE, statistician; b. Springfield, Mo., Aug. 19, 1930; s. John Thomas and Mary Catharine (Cook) Robinette; m. James Fredrik Jakobsen, Aug. 11, 1951; children—Thomas James, Janet Ruth. B.S., B.S. in Edn., Southwest Mo. State U., 1951; M.A., U. Mo.-Columbia, 1959. Statistician, Sheller-Globe, Inc., Iowa City, Iowa, 1968-72; research asst. Conduit, Iowa City, 1974-79; statistician Coll. Dentistry, U. Iowa, Iowa City, 1979—. Contbr. articles on dental research to profl. jours. Commr. Planning and Zoning Commn., Iowa City, 1975-85, chmn. 1980-82; chmn. County Lung Assn., Iowa City, 1973; stated clk. St. Andrew Presbyterian Ch., Iowa City, 1970; rep. Synod of Lakes and Praires, Mpls., 1981-85; pres. Longfellow PTA, Iowa City, 1966. Mem. Am. Pub. Health Assn., Internat. Assn. Dental Research, Am. Statis. Assn. Office: U Iowa N337 DSB Iowa City IA 52242

JAKUBAS, RICHARD GEORGE, software computer systems company manager; b. Beaconsfield, Eng., July 10, 1949; came to U.S., 1951, naturalized, 1956; s. Bronislaw and Maria (Kwiatkowska) J. Student U. Ill.-Urbana, 1967-69, U. Ill.-Chgo., 1969-71; B.S. in Math., U. Houston, 1974-76. Application engr. Baker Automation System Co., Houston, 1972-76; mgr., application engr. Kobe Systems-BASIC, Houston, 1976-78; corp. devel. mgr. BWT-BASIC, Inc., Houston, 1978-81; v.p. BWT-Data Processors Co., Houston, 1981-82; dir. MIS, Powell Industries, Inc., Houston, 1982-83; regional support mgr. ASK Computer Systems, Inc., Hinsdale, Ill., 1983—. Inventor software system. Vol. tchr. sch., Prairie du Chien, Wis., 1967. Mem. ASK South Central Regional Users Group (pres. 1982-83). Republican. Avocations: piano; computers; skiing; woodworking; photography. Home: 1905 Stanford Dr Naperville IL 60565 Office: ASK Computer Systems Inc 907 N Elm St Hinsdale IL 60521

JAMES, CHARLES FRANKLIN, JR., college dean, engineering educator, consultant; b. Des Arc, Mo., July 16, 1931; s. Charles Franklin and Beulah Frances (Kyte) J.; m. Mollie Keeler, May 18, 1974; children—Thomas Elisha, Matthew Jeremiah. B.S. in Mech. Engring., Purdue U., 1958, M.S. in Indsl. Engring., 1960, Ph.D., 1963. Prodn. engring. trainee Shampaine Co., St. Louis, 1949-51; asst. dir. class schedules and acad. space Purdue U., 1960-61, dir. counseling, 1955-63, instr., 1959-63; sr. engr. McDonnell-Douglas Co., 1963; asst. prof. engring. U. R.I., 1963-66, prof., chmn. dept. indsl. engring., 1967-83; assoc. prof. U. Mass., 1966-67; C. Paul Stocker Disting. vis. prof. engring. Ohio U., 1982-83; dean Coll. Engring. and Applied Sci., U. Wis. Milw., 1983—; cons. in field; vis. faculty Massey U., Palmerston North, N.Z., 1979; labor mgmt. arbitrator. Contbr. articles to profl. jours. Served as staff sgt. USAF, 1951-55. Mem. Am. Inst. Indsl. Engrs. (chpt. bd. dirs. 1974-77, pres. 1972-74, editor newsletter 1982-83); ASME, Soc. Mfg. Engrs., Am. Foundrymen's Soc., Am. Soc. Engring. Edn., AAUP, Am. Arbitration Assn., Soc. Profls. in Dispute Resolution, Engrs. and Scientists of Milw., Sigma Xi, Alpha Pi Mu, Pi Tau Sigma, Tau Beta Pi (Eminent Engr. award 1978). Republican. Club: University (Milw.). Home: 9100 W Hawthorne Rd Mequon WI 53092 Office: U Wis PO Box 784 Coll Engring and Applied Sci Milwaukee WI 53201

JAMES, CHARLES RAYMOND, mechanical contracting company executive; b. Mason City, Iowa, Feb. 14, 1934; s. John Wesley and Dora Mary (O'Donnel) J.; m. Arlene Jean Fonte, Aug. 3, 1963; 1 son, Michael Charles. M.E., Missouri Sch. Mines, 1956. Vice pres. Climatemp, Inc., Chgo., 1958-66; v.p. R. Irsay Co., Skokie, Ill., 1966-78, exec. v.p., 1978—. Served to cpl., U.S. Army, 1956-58. Mem. ASME. Roman Catholic.

JAMES, DENNIS WAYNE, medical supply company executive; b. Buffalo, Aug. 30, 1947; s. Rex Willard and Donna Kay (Langhaus) J.; m. Stephanie Kay Judkins, Sept. 7, 1968; children—Brian, Heather, Holly. Student U. Nebr.-Omaha, 1974-77. Staff respiratory therapist Bryan Hosp., Lincoln, Nebr., 1970-72; staff respiratory therapist Clarkson Hosp., Omaha, 1972-73, supr. respiratory therapy, 1974-78; dir. respiratory therapy Behlen Community Hosp., Columbus, Nebr., 1974; staff respiratory therapist St. Elizabeth Hosp., Lincoln, 1974; pres. Pulmonary Service Co., Inc., Omaha, 1978—. Mem. Am. Assn. for Respiratory Therapy, Nebr. Soc. for Respiratory Therapy (del. 1973, dir. 1977-78). Democrat. Methodist. Home: 6729 S 139th Avenue Circle Omaha NE 68137 Office: Pulmonary Service Co Inc 10135 J St Omaha NE 68127

JAMES, ERNEST WILBUR, lawyer; b. N.Y.C., July 21, 1931; s. Ernest Leaman and Lola Marguerita (Clancy) J.; B.S., U.S. Naval Acad., 1956; M.S.A.E., U.S. Naval Postgrad. Sch., 1964; J.D., St. Louis U., 1979; m. Jane Gallagher; children—Ernest Jude, Sean Patrick, Patrick Logan, Sharon Ann; 1 stepdau., Susan Bartsch. Title examiner Queens County Registrar's Office, N.Y.C., 1949-51; commd. ensign U.S. Navy, 1956, advanced through grades to comdr., 1971; designated naval aviator, 1958; aviation maintenance mgmt., 1956-69; maintenance mgmt. engr. planning, 1969-76; ret., 1976; admitted to Mo. bar, 1979; atty., dir. risk mgmt. Bi-State Devel. Agy., St. Louis, 1979-85; mem. Haley Fredrickson & Walsh, St. Louis, 1985—; adj. prof. safety Central Mo. State U. Active Maryville Homecoming Assn.; vol. fire insp. Maryville Fire Dept. Decorated D.F.C., Air medal (3), Navy Commendation medal. UMTA grantee, 1978. Mem. ABA, Mo. Bar Assn., Met. St. Louis Bar Assn., Met. St. Louis Safety Council, Naval Acad. Alumni Assn., U.S. Naval Inst., Am. Def. Preparedness Assn., Met. St. Louis Lawyers Club, VFW. Home: 7416 Foley Dr Belleville IL 62223

JAMES, FRANCIS EDWARD, JR., investment counselor; b. Woodville, Miss., Jan. 5, 1931; s. Francis Edwin and Ruth (Phillips) J.; m. Iris Rae Senn, Nov. 3, 1952; children—Francis III, Barry, David. B.S., La. State U., Baton Rouge, 1951; M.S., Rensselaer Poly. Inst., Troy, N.Y., 1966, Ph.D., 1967. Commd. 2d lt. U.S. Air Force, 1951; advanced through grades to col., 1972; prof. mgmt. and statistics Wright Patterson AFB, Fairborn, Ohio, 1967-74, chmn. quantitative studies, 1967-71, dir. grad. mgmt. programs, 1972-74; ret., 1974; pres. James Investment Research Inc., Alpha, Ohio, 1973—; chmn. bd. PAK Software Systems, Inc., Alpha, 1984—. Author: A Matrix Solution to the General Linear Regression Model, 1974. Contbr. articles to profl. jours. Decorated Legion of Merit, D.F.C.; recipient Eckles award Soc. Logistics Engr., 1980; NSF grantee, 1970. Mem. Am. Statis. Assn., Am. Fin. Assn., Investment Council Assn. Am., Market Technicians Assn., Sigma Iota Epsilon. Republican. Avocations: swimming, fishing, karate. Home: 2604 Lantz Rd Xenia OH 45385 Office: James Investment Research Inc PO Box 8 Alpha OH 45301

JAMES, JEFFERSON ANN, artistic director, dancer, choreographer, educator; b. Washington, July 12, 1943; d. Robert Mitchell and Dorothea Jefferson (Lewis) Miller; m. Martin Edward James, June 16, 1964; 1 child, Rachel Eleanor. Student Juilliard Sch. Music, N.Y.C., 1961-63, Columbia U., 1963-64; B.F.A., Coll. Conservatory Music, U. Cin., 1970. Vis. prof. Western Coll., Oxford, Ohio, 1970-74; artistic dir. Dance '70, Cin., 1970-71, Contemporary Dance, Theater, Cin., 1972—; bd. dirs. Cin. Commn. on Arts. 1981—, Ohio Dance, Assn. Ohio Dance Cos., Cleve., 1984—. Choreographer: Corbett Awards Finalist, 1975; dir. Corbett Awards (Arts Orgn. 1982); NEA fellow, 1978; Individual Artist Fellow, 1978-79; Contemporary Dance Theater chosen to present dance Nat. Performance Spaces NEA; recognition OAC, NEA, Cin. Fine Arts Fund. Mem. Cin. Bicentennial Comn., Dance Cin. (mem. adv. bd. 1983—). Avocations: tennis, gardening, sewing, knitting and travel. Office: Contemporary Dance Theater Inc PO Box 19220 Cincinnati OH 45219

JAMES, MARION RAY, editor; b. Bellmont, Ill., Dec. 6, 1940; s. Francis Miller and Alma Lorraine (Wylie) J.; B.S., Oakland City Coll., 1964; postgrad. U. Evansville, 1966; M.S., St. Francis Coll., 1978; m. Janet Sue Tennis, June 16, 1960; children—Jeffrey Glenn, David Ray, Daniel Scott, Cheryl Lynne. Sports and city editor Daily Clarion, Princeton, Ind., 1963-65; English tchr. Jac-Cen-Del High Sch., Osgood, Ind., 1965-66; indsl. editor Whirlpool Corp., Evansville and LaPorte, Ind., 1966-68; indsl. editor Magnavox Govt. and Indsl. Electronics Co., Fort Wayne, Ind., 1968-79; pres., editor, pub. Bowhunter mag. Blue-J Pub. Co., Fort Wayne, 1971—; instr. Ind.-Purdue U., Ft. Wayne, 1980—. Recipient Best Editorial award United Community Services Publs., 1970-72; named Oakland City Coll. Alumnus of Yr., 1982; named to Mt. Carmel High Sch. Hall of Fame (Ill.), 1983. Mem. Outdoor Writers Assn. Am., Fort Wayne Assn. Bus. Editors (Fort Wayne Bus. Editor of Year 1969, pres. 1975-76), Alpha Phi Gamma, Alpha Psi Omega, Mu Tau Kappa. Club: Toastmasters (Able Toastmaster award). Author: Bowhunting for Whitetail and Mule Deer, 1975; Successful Bowhunting, 1985; editor: Pope and Young Book World Records, 1975; Bowhunting Adventures, 1977. Home: 6142 W Hamilton Rd Fort Wayne IN 46804 Office: 3150 Mallard Cove Ln Fort Wayne IN 46804

JAMES, MICHAEL EDWARD, management services corporation executive; b. Atlanta, Oct. 10, 1951; s. Walter Simeon and Anne (Pappenheimer) J.; m. Anne Marie Dahlstrom, Aug. 5, 1978; 1 son, Ian Michael. B.A., U. Ga., 1974; postgrad. U. Cin., 1983—. News producer, reporter Sta. WTVC-TV, Chattanooga, 1975-79; news producer Sta. WKRC-TV, Cin., 1979-80; dir. Batesville Mgmt. Services div. Hillenbrand Industries, Ind., 1980—; lectr. in field. Area fund raiser Am. Cancer Soc., 1983—. Mem. Sigma Delta Chi. Republican. Episcopalian. Author: (brochure) Estate Planning (Silver Screen award 1982), 1982; author, copywriter various brochures, audio-visual programs for profl. use. Office: Batesville Mgmt Services PO Drawer 90 Batesville IN 47006

JAMES, SYDNEY VINCENT, history educator; b. Chgo., Mar. 9, 1929; s. Sydney Vincent and Caroline Beatrice (Topping) J.; m. Jean Wooster Middleton, July 8, 1950; children—Samuel W., Catherine Lyon. A.B. cum laude, Harvard U., 1950, A.M., 1951, Ph.D., 1958. Instr. history Kent (Ohio) State U., 1956-58; asst. prof. history Brown U., Providence, 1959-62; asst. prof. history U. Oreg., Eugene, 1962-65; assoc. prof. history U. Iowa, Iowa City, 1965-67, prof., 1967—, chmn. dept. history, 1970-74. Am. Council Learned Socs. research grantee, 1964-65; NEH research grantee, 1972-74; Charles Warren Ctr. for Studies in Am. History, Harvard U. research grantee, 1979-80. Fellow R.I. Hist. Soc.; mem. Am. Hist. Assn., Orgn. Am. Historians, Colonial Soc. Mass., Internat. Commn. for History of Rep. and Parliamentary Insts., Am. Soc. Legal History. Democrat. Club: Cliff Dwellers (Chgo.). Author: A People Among Peoples: Quaker Benevelence in Eighteenth Century America, 1963; Colonial Rhode Island-A History, 1975; editor books; contbr. articles to profl. jours. Home: 1101 Kirkwood Ave Iowa City IA 52240 Office: Dept History U Iowa Iowa City IA 52242

JAMES, WALTER, retired computer information specialist, state official; b. Mpls., June 8, 1915; s. James Edward and Mollie (Gress) Smoleroff; B.Ch.E., U. Minn., 1938, postgrad, 1945-60; m. Jessie Ann Pickens, Dec. 27, 1948; 1 son, Joel Pickens. Process designer Monsanto Chem. Co., St. Louis, 1940-45; instr. math U. Minn., Mpls., 1945-60, extension div., 1950—; researcher computer based applied math. 3M Co., St. Paul, 1960-68; info. systems planner State of Minn., St. Paul, 1968-85; ret., 1985. Mem. Am. Math. Assn., AAAS, Sigma Xi. Contbr. articles to profl. jours. Home: 6228 Brooklyn Dr Brooklyn Center MN 55430

JAMES, WILLIAM MEREDITH, scientific company executive; b. Madelia, Minn., Nov. 3, 1931; s. Howard Meredith and Gertrude Virginia (Pinney) J.; m. Almarie Helen Fell, Sept. 18, 1954; children—Scott G., Mark D., Bradley M., W. Craig, Jeffrey F. B.A., Macalester Coll., 1953; M.B.A., Temple U., 1957. Br. mgr. Scherr-Tumico N.Y., Inc., N.Y.C., 1958-62; v.p. sales, v.p. mfg. Scherr-Tumico Inc., St. James, Minn., 1962-68, pres., 1968-72; mgr. indsl. sales and mfg. Gaertner Sci. Corp., Chgo., 1973-75, exec. v.p., 1975-76, pres., chmn. bd., 1977—. Mem. Am. Soc. for Quality Control (rep. Z-1 com. 1977-83). Republican. Presbyterian. Lodges: Masons, Shriners. Avocations: sailing, golf. Office: Gaertner Sci Corp 1201 Wrightwood Ave Chicago IL 60614

JAMES, WILLIAM THOMAS, computer systems architect, consultant; b. Pine Bluff, Ark., Mar. 21, 1934; s. Russell Robertson and Florence (Arseneau) J.; m. Sue Hampton, Apr. 6, 1958; children—Russell, Neenah, Karen. B.S.M.E., U. Ark., 1955; M.B.A., U. Pitts., 1964. Registered profl. engr., Pa. Systems mgr. Harris Systems Inc., Melbourne, Fla., 1966-68; resource mgr. Martin Marietta Co., Orlando, Fla., 1969-74; v.p. SPM Corp., Orlando, 1974-76, Watkins Assoc. Industries, Lakeland, Fla., 1976-77; systems architect Blue Cross & Blue Shield, Indpls., 1977—; chmn. IDEAS, Inc., Atlanta, 1983-84. Chmn., Pub. Edn. Com., Rockledge, Fla., 1974-75. Recipient Westinghouse Advanced Design award Westinghouse Electric Corp., 1959, Indpls. Key to City by City of Indpls., 1984. Mem. Am. Soc. Engrs., Ins. Developers Efficient Acctg. Systems (past chmn.). Methodist. Avocations: old sports cars; skiing; golf. Office: Blue Cross & Blue Shield Co 120 W Market St Indianapolis IN 46204

JAMES, WILLIAM W., banker; b. Springfield, Mo., Oct. 12, 1931; s. Will and Clyde (Cowdrey) J.; A.B., Harvard U., 1953; m. Carol Ann Muenter, June 17, 1967; children—Sarah Elizabeth, David William. Asst. to dir. overseas div. Becton Dickinson & Co., Rutherford, N.J., 1956-59; stockbroker Merrill Lynch, Pierce, Fenner & Smith, Inc., St. Louis, 1959-62; with trust div. Boatmen's Nat. Bank St. Louis, 1962—, v.p. in charge estate planning, 1972—, sr. v.p., 1984—; dir. Heer-Andres Investment Co., Springfield. Mem. gift and bequest council Barnes Hosp., St. Louis, 1963-67, St. Louis U., 1972-78. Served with U.S. Army, 1953-55. Mem. Estate Planning Council St. Louis, Mo. Bankers Assn., Bank Mktg. Assn., Am. Inst. Banking. Republican. Clubs: Harvard (pres. 1972-73), Mo. Athletic, Noonday (St. Louis). Office: Boatmen's Nat Bank PO Box 7365 Saint Louis MO 63166

JAMES, WILLIAM WESLEY, JR., utility executive; b. Gulfport, Miss., Feb. 24, 1936; s. William Wesley and Mamie (Swanner) J.; m. Beverly Elaine Banderet, Oct. 28, 1952; children—William Wesley, Cheryl Elaine, Carl Byron, Troy Lee. B.E.E., Miss. State U., 1958. Registered profl. engr., Fla. With Fla. Power & Light Co., Miami, 1957-77, systems ops. mgr., 1969-72, supr. distbn., 1972-73, mgr. apprentice tng., 1973-77; vice gen. mgr. Big Rivers Electric Corp., Henderson, Ky., 1977-80; dir. ops. Seminole Electric Coop., Inc., Tampa, Fla., 1981-82; dir. engring. and ops. Wabash Valley Power Assn., Indpls., 1982—; mem. faculty Manatee Jr. Coll., Bradenton, Fla., 1959-69, U. Miami, 1970-77. Coach basketball and football Boys' Club, Brandenton, 1958-64; football coach Pop Warner League, Miami, 1970-77; youth basketball coach Suniland, Miami, 1974-77; mem. gen. adv. bd. tech. edn. Manatee Jr. Coll., 1959-69, Manatee Profl. Guidance Bd., Pub. Schs., Bradenton, 1961-68, council Manatee County PTA, 1964-67; mem. adv. com. Henderson (Ky.) Community Coll., 1978-81, U. Evansville (Ind.) Ctr. Mgmt. Edn., 1979-81; mem. ofcl. bd. 1st Meth. Ch., Bradenton, 1959-69. Named Ky. col., 1980. Mem. Ind. Soc. Profl. Engrs., Nat. Soc. Profl. Engrs., IEEE, Ind. Engring. Soc., Gt. Lakes Electric Consumer Assn. (transmission task force 1982—, bd. dirs. 1983—). Office: 722 N High Sch Rd PO Box 24700 Indianapolis IN 46224

JAMIESON, NORMAN CLARK, research and development executive; b. Edinburgh, Scotland, Nov. 21, 1935; came to U.S., 1966; s. Thomas D. and Jane E. M. (Peattie) J.; m. Wilma D. Cuddihy, Aug. 14, 1964; 1 dau., Anne K. B.Sc. with honors in Chemistry, U. Edinburgh, Scotland, 1958; M.Sc., U. Atla., Can., 1961; Ph.D., U. Adelaide, Australia, 1966. Postdoctoral assoc. Rensselaer Poly. Inst., 1966-67; research chemist Merck & Co., Rahway, N.J., 1967-70; research assoc. Mallinckrodt, Inc., St. Louis, 1970-80, dir. research and devel., 1980—. Contbr. articles to tech. jours. Patentee in field. Mem. Am. Chem. Soc., Royal Inst. Chemistry. Club: Toastmasters. Avocation: running. Home: 14 Webster Acres Webster Groves MO 63119 Office: Mallinckrodt Inc PO Box 5840 Saint Louis MO 63134

JAMIESON, SCOTT ALLAN, orthodontist; b. Detroit, Oct. 27, 1947; s. Douglas James and Allana Maria (Minifie) J.; m. Claudia Jane Grzemski, July 29, 1972; children—Jeffrey Allan, Jody Ann, Jayme Allana, Jillian Amanda. D.D.S., Northwestern U., 1972, M.S., 1974; B.A., Aquinas Coll., 1982. Staff orthodontist Northwestern U., Chgo., 1976-77; orthodontics assoc. H.T. Perry, Jr., Elgin, Ill., 1976-77; pvt. practice orthodontist, Marquette, Mich., 1977—; lectr. Northwestern U., 1982—. Eucharist minister St. Peters Cathedral, Marquette, 1980—; active Marquette Sch. Bd., 1983—, Rotary Internat., 1984—. Served to lt. comdr. USNR, 1972-74. Decorated Commendation of Achievement medal U.S. Army, 1976. Mem. ADA, Mich. Dental Assn., Superior Dist. Dental Soc. (pres. 1983-84), Am. Assn. Orthodontists, Gt. Lakes Soc. Orthodontists, Mich. Soc. Orthodontists (pres.-elect 1984-85), Acad. Dental Materials, Mich. Cleft Lip and Palate Assn. Republican. Roman Catholic. Avocations: cross-country skiing; fishing; hunting; woodworking.

JAMISON, CHRIS MARK, electrical engineer; b. Ft. Lauderdale, Fla., Jan. 13, 1953. B.S. with honors in Elec. Engring., Valparaiso U., 1975; M.S. in Elec. Engring., Purdue U., 1980. Registered profl. engr., Ind. Engring. intern, Sargent & Lundy, Chgo., 1974; electronics engr. Naval Avionics Ctr., Indpls., 1975-81; sr. devel. engr. Ransburg Corp., Indpls., 1981—; pres. Electronic Assocs., Inc., Hybrid Computer Users Group, N.Am. chpt., 1980 Mem. IEEE (sr., chmn. 1985-86), Soc. Mfg. Engrs. (sr.), Indpls. Sci. and Engring. Found., IEEE Computer Soc. Office: PO Box 88512 Indianapolis IN 46208

JAMISON, ROGER W., pianist, piano educator; b. Marion, Ohio, June 18, 1937; s. Harold Theodore and Martha Louise (Haas) J.; m. Caroline R. Hansley, Jan. 26, 1957; children—Lisa Renee, Eric Karl. B.S., Ohio State U., 1959, M.A. (scholar), 1961; postgrad. Oberlin Conservatory, Oakland U.; student George Haddad, Columbus, Ohio, Mischa Kottler, Detroit. Piano faculty mem. Detroit Conservatory of Music, 1964-68, Cranbrook Schs., Bloomfield Hills, Mich., 1981-84; performer in one-man musical presentation Spirits of Great Composers, 1979—; dir. music Birmingham Temple, Farmington Hills, Mich., 1984—; soloist Brunch with Bach series Detroit Inst. Arts., Detroit Symphony Orch.'s Internat. Brahms Festival; cons. Royal Oak Arts Council; adjudicator Am. Coll. Musicians. Mem. Nat. Guild of Piano Tchrs. (pres. Oakland-Macomb chpt.) Address: 2300 Bedford Rd Bloomfield Hills MI 48013

JANECEK, LENORE ELAINE, chamber of commerce executive; b. Chgo., May 2, 1944; d. Morris and Florence (Bear) Picker; M.A.J. in Speech Communications (talent scholar), Northeastern Ill. U., 1972; postgrad. (Ill. Assn. C. of C. Execs. scholar) Inst. for Organizational Mgmt., U. Notre Dame, 1979-80; M.B.A., Columbia Pacific U., 1982; cert. in C. of C. mgmt. U. Colo., 1982; m. John Janecek, Sept. 12, 1964; children—Frank, Michael. Adminstrv. asst., exec. dir. Ill. Mcpl. Retirement Fund, Chgo., 1963-65; personnel mgr. Profile Personnel, Chgo., 1965-68; personnel rep. Marsh Instrument Co., Skokie, Ill., 1971-73; restaurant mgt. Gold Mine Restaurant and What's Cooking Restaurant, Chgo., 1974-76; pres., owner Secretarial Office Services, Chgo., 1976-78; founder, pres. Lincolnwood (Ill.) C. of C. and Industry, 1978—; rep. 10th dist. U.S. C. of C., 1978—. Mem. mktg. bd. Niles Twp. Sheltered Workshop; pres. Lincolnwood Sch. Dist. 74 Sch. Bd. Caucus; bd. mem., officer, founder Ill. Fraternal Order Police Ladies Aux.; bd. dirs., officer Lincolnwood Girl's Softball League, PTA; bd. dirs. United Way, 1982-83; mem. sch. curriculum com. Lincolnwood Bd. Edn. Mem. Am. C. of C. Execs., Ill. Assn. C. of C. Execs., Women in Mgmt., Nat. Assn. Female Execs., Am. Notary Soc., Ill. Nat. Council Jewish Women, Hadassah. Jewish. Home: 6707 N Monticello St Lincolnwood IL 60645 Office: 4433 W Touhy Suite 264 Lincolnwood IL 60646

JANECKE, RONALD BRIAN, editor; b. Rock Island, Ill., June 6, 1939; s. Duval Ronald and Berneice (Borell) Janecke. A.B. in History, Augustana Coll., 1961. Asst. sports editor Moline Dispatch (Ill.), 1963-64, asst. mng. editor,

1964-66; asst. news editor St. Louis Globe-Democrat, 1967-79, sports editor, 1979-83, assoc. editor, 1984—. Democrat. Home: 50 Plaza Sq Apt 401 Saint Louis MO 63103 Office: St Louis Globe Democrat 710 N Tucker Blvd Saint Louis MO 63101

JANES, DENNIS WAYNE, medical supply company executive; b. Buffalo, Aug. 30, 1947; s. Rex Willard and Donna Kay (Langhaus) J.; m. Stephanie Kay Judkins, Sept. 7, 1968; children—Brian, Heather, Holly. Student U. Nebr.-Omaha, 1974-77. Staff respiratory therapist Bryan Hosp., Lincoln, Nebr., 1970-72, Clarkson Hosp., Omaha, 1972-73, shift supr. respiratory therapy, 1974-78; dir. respiratory therapy Behlen Community Hosp., Columbus, Nebr., 1973-74; staff respiratory therapist St. Elizabeth Hosp., Lincoln, 1974; pres. Pulmonary Service Co., Inc., Omaha, 1978—; del. Nebr. Soc. Respiratory Therapy, 1973, dir., 1977, 78. Mem. Am. Assn. Respiratory Therapy. Democrat. Methodist. Home: 6729 S 139 Ave Circle Omaha NE 68137 Office: Pulmonary Service Co Inc 10135 J Omaha NE 68127

JANESS, ROBERT JAMES, health and beauty aid manufacturing executive; b. Chgo., July 18, 1942; s. Chester O. and Genevieve Bernice (Mossman) J.; Janet Lucille Arch, Aug. 15, 1964; children—Brian Patrick, Christine Marie, Scott Andrew. B.A., Marquette U., 1964. Sales rep. Owens-Ill., Los Angeles, Chgo., 1964-70; sales rep. Boise Cascade Corp., Los Angeles, 1970-73, sales mgr., Chgo., 1973-76; regional mgr. Blistex, Inc., Chgo., 1976-79, dir. sales, 1979-83, v.p. sales, 1983—. Pres. sch. bd. Western Springs, Ill., 1982-83; mem. exec. senate Marquette U., Milw., 1984. Mem. Gen. Mdse. Distbr. Council (adv. bd. 1984—), Nat. Assn. Service Merchandisers, Nat. Assn. Tobacco Distbrs. (exec. council), Great Lakes Travelers Assn. Republican. Roman Catholic. Avocations: golf; tennis; snowmobiling; boating; hunting. Office: Blistex Inc 1800 Swift Dr Oakbrook IL 60521

JANEWAY, CORNELL, engineering company executive; b. Dayton, Ohio, Mar. 9, 1923; s. Robert N. and Grace (Muffson) J.; m. Barbara Brenner, Nov. 24, 1949 (wid. Apr. 1978); children—Karen, David; m. Betty Jo Levine, Dec. 2, 1979; children—Peter, Marne. B.S.M.E., U. Mich., 1943. Test engr. Ethyl Corp., Detroit, 1946-49; devel. engr. Reo Motors, Lansing, Mich., 1949-53; design engr. Taub Engring., Washington, 1953-56; head research, devel., Am. Brake Shoe, Rochester, N.Y., 1956-59; ptnr., owner Janeway Engring., Troy, Mich., 1959—. Inventor muffler, throttle control, 1953, filters 1984. Served to lt. USN, 1943-46, PTO. Recipient award Mich. Edn. Dept. Vocational Service, 1978-84. Mem. Am. Soc. Testing Materials (com. chmn. 1966-84; Daniel Green award 1984), Soc. Automotive Engrs. (com. chmn. 1959-64). Clubs: Great Lakes Cruising (Chgo.), Hunters Run Golf & Tennis (Boynton Beach, Fla.). Avocations: sail cruising Great Lakes; tennis; golf. Home: 18210 Wildemere Detroit MI 48221 Office: Janeway Engineering Co 326 Park Troy MI 48084

JANIAK, THOMAS ANTHONY, educator; b. Oak Park, Ill., July 16, 1949. A.S. in Media, Coll. DuPage, Glen Ellyn, Ill., 1971; B.A. in Communications, Sangamon State U., Springfield, Ill., 1973, M.S. in Ednl. Adminstrn., Nat. Coll. Edn., Evanston, Ill., 1979. Media technician Sch. Dist. 201, Cicero Ill., 1969-71; dir. media, activities, supr. performing arts Argo High Sch. Dist. 217, Summit Ill., 1973-83; gen. mgr. Cable channel Cablevision of Chgo., 1975—; project dir. Resource Devel. and Mgmt. Inst. of Chgo., 1980-82, dir. activities, 1984—; ind. cons. on cable TV, 1980—; prof. mass communications Moraine Valley Community Coll., 1984—. Asst. dist. commr. Boy Scouts Am., 1970-72, post advisor, 1972—, chmn., 1979-80, council mem.-at-large, 1985—; commr. cable, Summit, Ill., 1981—; mem. adv. cable commn., Bridgeview, Ill., 1983—; bd. dirs. Hull House Desplaines Valley Community Center, 1975-76. Mem. ALA, Ill. Library Assn., Am. Assn. Supervision and Curriculum Devel., Assn. Ednl. Communication and Tech., Nat. Assn. Broadcasters, Nat. Assn. Ednl. Broadcasters, Assn. Secondary Sch. Prins., Owassippi Staff Assn. (bd. dirs.). Home: 8937 S Roberts Rd Hickory Hills IL 60457 Office: 7329 W 63rd St Summit IL 60501

JANIK, BOREK, science company executive; b. Brno, Czechoslovakia, Oct. 29, 1933; came to U.S., 1968, naturalized, 1975; s. Borivoj and Helena (Macku) J.; m. Alice M. Bednarova; children—Dasha, Peter. Ph.D. in Chemistry and Biophysics, Inst. Biophysics, Brno, 1964; D. Life Scis., U. J.E. Purkyne, Brno, 1966; Research assoc. Inst. Biophysics, Brno, 1960-66; post doctoral fellow U. Mich., Ann Arbor, 1966-67, research assoc., 1968-69; various positions in research products and Ames divs., also mgr. research and devel. Miles Labs., Elkhart, Ind., 1969-79; dir. lab. product devel. Gelman Sci, Inc., Ann Arbor, 1979—. Author: Physicochemical Characteristics of Polynucleotides, 1971; Electrophoresis, 1985. Contbr. articles to sci. publs. Recipient Outstanding Tech. Communication award Soc. Tech. Communication, 1981. Mem. Am. Assn. Clin. Chemists, Electrophoresis Soc., Assn. Clin. Sci., Internat. Soc. Clin. Enzymology, Mich. Tech. Council (chmn. biomed. com.), Nat. Com. Clin. Lab. Standards. Avocations: skiing, canoeing, windsurfing, backpacking, gardening. Home: 13805 Waterloo St Chelsea MI 48118 Office: Gelman Scis 600 S Wagner St Ann Arbor MI 48106

JANIS, AARON MARK, optometrist; b. Chgo., Nov. 16, 1955; s. Lawrence N. and Ann I. J. B.A., Northwestern U., 1977; B.S.V.S., Ill. Coll. Optometry, 1979, O.D., 1981. Gen. practice optometry, Chgo., 1981—. Contbr. articles to profl. jours. Fellow Internat. Orthokeratology Soc. Mem. Nat. Eye Research Found., Am. Optometric Assn., Ill. Optometric Assn., Internat. Orthokeratology Soc., Gold Key Internat. Optometric Honor Soc. (pres. 1980-81). Avocations: computer systems analysis, skiing, golf. Office: 4256 W 63rd St Chicago IL 60629

JANIS, LARRY WILLIARD, educator; b. St. Louis, Dec. 17, 1937; s. Jesse Williard and Mary Helen (McClanahan) J.; m. Patsy Jeanne Rucker, Apr. 29, 1966; 1 dau., Susan Annalee. Student U. Md., 1961-64, Mo. Bapt. Coll., 1965, Forest Park Community Coll., 1966-68; B.S. in Elem. Edn., U. Mo.-St. Louis, 1972; postgrad. U. Alaska-Anchorage, 1972-79; M.Ednl. Adminstrn., U. So. Miss., 1981. Lifetime cert. elem. edn., jr. high sci., high sch. biology, Mo. Dictaphone repairman Dictaphone Corp., 1964-65; customer engr. IBM, 1965-69; custodian Tower Grove Bapt. Ch., 1969-72; tchr. sci., math., art Wasilla Jr. High Sch. (Alaska), 1972-80; tchr. math. and sci. Tower Grove Christian Sch., St. Louis, 1980—; black-light chalk artist for ch./sch. programs. Mem. Wasilla Bicentennial Commn., 1975-76; mem. dist. com. in support presdl. candidate Ronald Reagan, Republican Party, Wasilla, 1976. Served with U.S. Army, 1955-58, USAF, 1960-64. U.S. Govt. edn. grantee, 1974-75, 75-76. Mem. Mo. Assn. Creation. Baptist. Led students to design and build 50-foot hist. totem pole, Wasilla, 1976. Home: 3647 Virginia Saint Louis MO 63118

JANIS, WALTER GERALD, dentist; b. Chgo., Feb. 19, 1945; s. Walter James and Eleanore Irene Janis; married Aug. 1, 1970; (div. Aug. 1982); 1 child, Matthew Neal. B.S., Elmhurst Coll., 1967; B.S. in Dentistry, U. Ill.-Chgo., 1969, D.D.S., 1971. Gen. practice dentistry, Villa Park, Ill., 1971—. Mem. Chgo. Dental Soc., Suburban Dental Soc., ADA. Republican. Roman Catholic. Lodge: Rotary (sgt.-at-arms 1981-83). Avocations: fishing; sailing; hunting; photography. Home: 915 N York Rd Apt 301 Elmhurst IL 60126 Office: 1634 S Ardmore Ave Villa Park IL 60181

JANKE, KENNETH, association executive; b. Ft. William, Ont., Can., May 13, 1934; s. Adolf Earthman and Julianna (Dika) J.; m. Sally Mildred Roach, June 29, 1957; children—Kenneth Stuart, Laura Lynn, Julie Ann. Student Mich. State U., 1952-56. Asst. mgr. Household Fin. Co., Detroit, 1958-60; gen. mgr. Nat. Assn. Investors, Royal Oak, Mich., 1960-76, pres., 1976—; bd. dirs. Investment Edn. Inst., Royal Oak, 1965—, World Fedn. Investment Clubs, Brussels, 1976—. Author: Ask Mr. Naic, 1982. Columnist mag. Better Investing. Contbg. editor FACT. Chmn. Mich. Golf Hall of Fame, Lake Orion; pres. Am. Cancer Soc.-Oakland Country, Southfield, Mich., 1974-75. Served with U.S. Army, 1956-58, ETO. Recipient Disting. Service award Investment Edn. Inst., 1972, Founder award Am. Cancer Soc., 1970. Fellow Fin. Analysts Soc. of Detroit (pres. 1984—), Fin. Analysts Fedn.; mem. Nat. Investor Relations Inst. (v.p. Detroit 1984—). Republican. Episcopalian. Clubs: Indianwood Golf and Country (Lake Orion); Renaissance (Detroit); Nat. Football League Alumni (Fort Lauderdale, Fla.). Lodge: Mason. Avocations: golf; golf collecting. Home: 4305 W Maple Birmingham MI 48010 Office: Nat Assn Investors 1515 E Eleven Mile Royal Oak MI 48067

JANKE, RONALD ROBERT, lawyer; b. Milw., Mar. 2, 1947; s. Robert Erwin and Elaine Patricia (Wilken) J.; m. Mary Ann Burg, July 3, 1971; children—Jennifer, William, Emily. B.A. cum laude, Wittenberg U., 1969; J.D. with distinction, Duke U., 1974. Bar: Ohio 1974. Assoc. Jones, Day, Reavis & Pogue, Cleve., 1974-83, ptnr., 1983—. Served with U.S. Army, 1970-71, Vietnam. Mem. ABA (chmn. environ. control com. 1980-83), Ohio Bar Assn., Greater Cleve. Bar Assn. Office: Jones Day Reavis & Pogue 1700 Huntington Bldg Cleveland OH 44115

JANKLOW, WILLIAM JOHN, governor of South Dakota; b. Chgo., Sept. 13, 1939; B.S., J.D., U. S.D.; m. Mary Dean; children—Russell, Pamela, Shawna. Staff atty., later directing atty. and chief officer S.D. Legal Services System, 1967-73; chief prosecutor Office Atty. Gen. of S.D., 1973-74, atty. gen., 1975-78; gov. of S.D., 1979—; practice law, Pierre, S.D., 1972-73. Served with USMC, 1956-59; Vietnam. Mem. Am., S.D. trial lawyers assns., Nat. Govs. Assn. (exec. com.), Am. Judicature Soc., ABA, S.D. Bar Assn. Recipient Nat. award for Legal Excellence and Skill, Office of Equal Opportunity Legal Services. Office: Office of Gov State Capitol Pierre SD 57501*

JANKOWSKI, EDWARD JULIAN, computer company executive; b. Heilbronn, W.Ger., Sept. 10, 1948; came to U.S., 1953; s. Bleslaw Olgierd and Marianna (Kolodziej) J.; m. Rita Louise Hoolahan, Mar. 8, 1975; 1 child, Kelly Marie. A.S., Electronics Inst., Pitts., 1967; postgrad. U. Pitts., 1970-76. Engring. specialist Gen. Electric Co., Utica, N.Y., 1967-70; systems analyst U. Pitts., 1970-76; quality control mgr. On-Line Systems, Pitts., 1976-79; fin. mgr. United Telecom. Computer Group, Pitts., 1979-81, mgr. mgmt. info. systems, 1981-84; mgr. software support UIS Co., Kansas City, Kans., 1984—. Mem. Am. Mgmt. Assn. Republican. Roman Catholic. Home: 10312 Haskins St Lenexa KS 66215 Office: UIS Co Fin Div 9300 Metcalf St 7th Floor Room 721 Overland Park KS 66212

JANKOWSKI, FRANK DAVID, mechanical engineer; b. Cleve., Nov. 26, 1946; s. Frank Chester and Janet Agnes (Jakubowski) J.; m. Linda Elizabeth Pristas, Aug. 31, 1974. B.S. in Mech. Engring., Ohio U., 1969; M.S. in Mech. Engring., Cleve. State U., 1980. Registered profl. engr., Ohio, Mech. engr. Babcock & Wilcox, Akron, Ohio, 1969-71, Stone & Webster, Boston, 1971-74, 75; planner Toledo Edison, Ohio, 1974-75; engr. H.K. Ferguson, Cleve., 1975-77; sr. planner Cleve. Electric Illuminating, 1977—; co. rep. generation res. panel East Central Area Reliability Council. Co-author tech. paper. Mem. ASME. Republican. Roman Catholic. Avocations: Cross country skiing, golf. Home: 7942 Gallowae Ct Mentor OH 44060 Office: Cleve Electric Illuminating Co PO Box 5000 Cleveland OH 44101

JANOV, BARRY ALLAN, dentist; b. Chgo., Oct. 21, 1935; s. Michael Morris and Idelle Elaine (Cutler) J.; m. Sandra Lee Wolf., Sept. 17, 1964; children—Jill Andrea, Robert Steven. B.S., U. Ill., 1957, D.D.S., 1959. Gen. practice dentistry, Chgo., 1961-75, Des Plaines, Ill., 1975—. Served to capt. U.S. Army, 1959-61. Mem. ADA, Ill. State Dental Soc., Chgo. Dental Soc., Am. Analgesia Soc., Acad. Gen. Dentistry, Acad. History of Dentistry, Antique Radio Club of Ill. (co-founder, v.p. 1980—), Antique Radio Club of Am., Antique Wireless Assn., Ind. Hist. Radio Soc., Sigma Alpha Mu. Avocations: collecting antique dental and antique radio memorabilia. Home: 1304 Cariann Ln Glenview IL 60025 Office: 2434 Dempster St Des Plaines IL 60016

JANOVER, ROBERT H., lawyer; b. N.Y.C., Aug. 17, 1930; s. Cyrus J. and Lillian D. (Horwitz) J.; B.A., Princeton U., 1952; J.D., Harvard U., 1957; m. Mary Elizabeth McMahon, Oct. 23, 1966; 1 dau., Laura Lockwood. Admitted to N.Y. State bar, 1957, U.S. Supreme Ct. bar, 1961, D.C. bar, 1966, Mich. bar, 1973; practice law, N.Y.C., 1957-65; cons. Office of Edn. HEW, 1965, legis. atty. Office of Gen. Counsel, HEW, 1965-66; asst. gen. atty. Mgmt. Assistance Inc., N.Y.C., 1966-71; atty. Ford Motor Credit Co., Dearborn, Mich., 1971-74; mem. firm Freud, Markus, Slavin, Toohey & Galgan, Troy, Mich., 1974-79; sole practice law, Detroit, 1979—. Bd. dirs. Oakland Citizens League, 1976—, v.p., 1976-79, pres., 1979—; bd. dirs. Civic Searchlight, 1979—. Served to 1st lt. U.S. Army, 1952-54. Mem. Mich. State Bar, Am., N.Y. State, Detroit bar assns., Bar Assn. D.C., Assn. Bar of City of N.Y. Clubs: Univ., Players (Detroit), City (Bloomfield Hills), Harvard (N.Y.C.). Home: 685 Ardmoor Dr Birmingham MI 48010 Office: 21 E Long Lake Rd Suite 202 Bloomfield Hills MI 48013

JANSEN, MARGERY HUNTER, pharmacist, miniature horse breeder; b. Lima, Ohio, Apr. 10, 1938; d. Charles Milton and Edna (Barr) Hunter; m. Anthony Albert Jansen, Dec. 26, 1963; children—Julia Elizabeth, Tony Charles. B.S., Purdue U., 1960. Registered pharmacist, Ohio, Wis. Pharmacist Hunter's Drugstore, Lima, Ohio, 1960-63, Organon Drug Co., Oss, Holland, 1963; hosp. pharmacist Waukesha Hosp., Wis., 1963-65; relief pharmacist Milw. area, 1965-81; pharmacist Germantown Pharmacy, Wis., 1981-84, Mallach Pharmacy, Watertown, Wis., 1984-85, New Berlin Pharmacy, Wis., 1985—; advanced 1st aid instr. instr. Milw. unit ARC, 1984—. Ski patroller Nat. Ski Patrol, Little Switzerland, 1984—; 4-H leader, Waukesha. Mem. Purdue Alumni Assn. Republican. Episcopalian. Clubs: Waukesha Clown, U.S. Pony, Heart of Am. Miniature Equine. Avocations: dressage, downhill skiing, swimming, clowning, driving miniature horses. Home: N 67 W 27019 Silver Spring Sussex WI 53089

JANSEN, WILLIAM ALLEN, civil engineer; b. Louisville, Oct. 6, 1939; s. John William and Anna Mae (Langley) J.; m. Anna Kraft, June 10, 1961; 1 child, Laura Ann. B.S., USCG Acad., 1961; B.S. in Civil Engring., U. Ill., 1967. Registered profl. engr., Ill., N.C. Mgr., Safety Guide Products, Scottsburg, Ind., 1970-71; asst. chief div. boating N.C. Wildlife Commn., Raleigh, 1971-80; chief engr. Ill. Dept. Conservation, Springfield, 1980—. Served to lt. cmmdr. USCG, 1961-70. Mem. Assn. Conservation Engrs. (pres. 1977-78), Am. Soc. Civil Engrs., Ill. Soc. Prof. Engrs. (chmn. com. 1984-85), Nat. Soc. Profl. Engrs. Republican. Home: 3509 Bluff Rd Springfield IL 62707 Office: Dept Conservation 524 S 2d St Springfield IL 62706

JANSSEN, ROBERT BRUDER, manufacturing company executive; b. Kansas City, Mo., Aug. 10, 1932; s. Victor Ernst and Clara Helen (Bruder) J.; m. Suzanne Roberts, Mar. 20, 1954; children—Michael George, Carolyn Louise. A.A., U. Minn., 1952, B.A., 1954. Sales rep. Can. Life Assurance Co., Mpls., 1957-58; asst. to sales mgr. Quality Park Products, St. Paul, 1958-62, customer service mgr., 1962-63, exec. asst., 1963-66, asst. plant supt., 1966-73, plant supt., dir. nat. sales, 1974—. Author: Minnesota Birds, 1975; Birds in Minnesota, 1985. Editor The Loon, 1959—. Served to 1st lt. U.S. Army, 1955-57. Recipient T. S. Roberts award, Minn. Ornithologists Union, Mpls., 1976. Mem. Am. Ornithologists Union, Minn. Ornithologists Union (editor 1958—). Democrat. Methodist. Home: 10521 S Cedar Lake Rd #212 Minnetonka MN 55343 Office: Quality Park Products 2520 Como Ave St Paul MN 55108

JANTZE, MARGARET LORRAINE, business educator, university administrator; b. Mpls., Feb. 5, 1925; d. Clarence A. and Laura I. (Pegel) Pederson; m. R. Dale Jantze, June 5, 1962. B.S., Union Coll., 1947; M.Ed., U. Nebr., 1959, Ed.D., 1965. Instr. Sunnydale Acad., Centralia, Mo., 1947-48, Air Capital Bus. Coll., Wichita, Kans., 1962-65; instr. Union Coll., Lincoln, Nebr., 1948-49, 1951-55, asst. prof., 1955-60, assoc. prof., 1960-61; part-time instr. U. Nebr., Lincoln, 1962; instr. Wichita State U., Kans., 1965-66, asst. prof., 1966-68, assoc. prof., chairperson dept. bus. edn., 1968—. Mem. exec. bd. Am. Bus. Ctr., Inc., Wichita, 1974—. Mem. Nat. Bus. Edn. Assn. (membership dir. Kansas, 1974-77, reg. dir. membership for Mountain-Plains Region 1973-76, 1982—), Nat. Assn. for Bus. Tchr. Edn. (Wichita State U. rep. 1968—), Mountain-Plains Edn. Assn. (mem. exec. bd. 1973-79, 1982—, various com. and rep. positions), Kans. Bus. Edn. Assn. (reporter Kansas Bus. Tchr. 1970-72, treas. 1971-73, pres. elect 1973-74, pres. 1974-75), Wichita State Univ. Council of Univ. Women (v.p. 1970-71, pres. 1971-72, chairperson program com. 1975, chairperson scholarship com. 1977-78), Adminstrv. Mgmt. Soc. (mem. program com. 1970-71), Nat. Assn. Tchr. Edn. for Bus. Edn., Seventh-day Adventist Bus. Edn. Assn., Assn. of Information Systems Profls., Pi Omega Pi (Epsilon Mu chpt. sponsor 1980—), Delta Pi Epsilon, Pi Lambda Theta, Phi Kappa Phi. Avocations: music; travel. Home: 2301 Westport Wichita KS 67203 Office: Wichita State U 1845 Fairmount St Wichita KS 67208

JANUARY, LEWIS EDWARD, physician, educator; b. Haswell; Colo., Nov. 14, 1910; s. Frank Puleng and Estella (Miller) J.; m. Virginia Eloise Taylor, Sept. 13, 1941; children—Alan Frank, Craig Taylor. B.A., Colo. Coll., 1933, D.Sc. (hon.), 1966; M.D., U. Colo., 1937. Diplomate Am. Bd. Internal Medicine. Intern, resident in internal medicine, then asst. physician U. Iowa Hosps., Iowa City, 1937-42, dir. cardiovascular tng. program, mem. staff, dir. heart sta., 1946-79; faculty Coll. Medicine, U. Iowa, Iowa City, 1946—, prof. medicine, 1953-81, emeritus, 1981—, assoc. chmn. clin. programs dept. medicine, 1973-81, spl. asst. to chmn., 1981—; mem. staff VA Hosp., Iowa City; mem. Inter-Soc. Commn. Heart Disease Resources, 1968-71; vis. prof. Ein Shams U., Cairo, 1972; mem. cardiovascular tng. com. Nat. Heart and Lung Inst., 1972-74; mem. heart adv. com. Joint Commn. Accreditation Hosps., 1974. Contr. articles to profl. jours. Mem. editorial bd. Circulation, 1969-74, Am. Heart Jour., 1974-80. Bd. dirs. Community Health, 1966-67, Found. for Joffrey Ballet, 1979—. Served to lt. col. M.C., AUS, 1942-46. Recipient Honors Achievement award Angiology Research Found., 1965, Silver and Gold award U. Colo. Sch. Medicine, 1971, Helen B. Taussig award, 1972, Whitaker Teaching award Iowa Med. Soc., 1977, spl. citation for disting. service to internat. cardiology, 1978, Tchr. of Yr. award U. Iowa, 1981, Disting. Alumni award U. Iowa, 1983. Master ACP; fellow Am. Coll. Cardiology, Council Clin. Cardiology (chmn. 1961-63); mem. AMA, Am. Clin. and Climatol. Assn. (council 1973-77), Am. Fedn. Clin. Research, Am. Heart Assn. (bd. dirs. 1955-71), pres. 1966-67, internat. program com. 1968-78, Gold Heart award 1969, International Achievement award 1977), Iowa Heart Assn. (bd. dirs. 1948-52, heart fund chmn. 1963, pres. 1952-53), Assn. U. Cardiologists (council 1973-76), Am. Soc. Internal Medicine, AAUP, Central Soc. Clin. Research (council 1951-54), Central Clin. Research Club (pres. 1954), Iowa Clin. Med. Soc., Pan Am. Med. Soc. (life), Inter Am. Soc. Cardiology (bd. dirs. 1968-76), Internat. Cardiology Fedn. (v.p. 1970-78), Internat. Soc. and Fedn. Cardiology (exec. bd. 1976-78), Sigma Xi, Phi Delta Theta, Nu Sigma Nu, Alpha Omega Alpha. Club: Univ. Athletic (Iowa City) (pres. 1961-64). Avocation: gardening. Home: 3324 Hanover Ct Iowa City IA 52240 Office: U Ia Hosps Iowa City IA 52242

JANUSZEWSKI, JOHN ANTHONY, bank executive; b. Chgo., Mar. 25, 1945; s. John Joseph and Ann Bernice (Dybas) J.; m. Diane Marie, Jan. 13, 1968; children—John Joseph, James Anthony. B.S.B.A., Northwestern U., 1967. Asst. cashier Central Nat. Bank, Chgo., 1967-72; asst. v.p. Lake View Trust & Savs., Chgo., 1972-76; v.p. Libertyville Nat. Bank (Ill.), 1976-78; v.p., sr. lending officer Bank of Lincolnwood (Ill.), 1978—. Ill. State scholar, 1963-67; Jewel Food Cos. scholar, 1963-67. Mem. Robert Morris Assocs., No. Ill. Indsl. Assn., Assn. Equipment Lessors. Republican. Roman Catholic. Office: Bank of Lincolnwood 4433 W Touhy Ave Lincolnwood IL 60646

JANUSZEWSKI, RICHARD, pharmacist; b. St. Cloud, Minn., Jan. 19, 1951; s. Vincent and Agnes (Sopkowiak) J.; 1 child, Cynthia. B.S., U. Minn., 1976, M.S., 1983. Pharmacist Erickson Value Drug, St. Peter, Minn., 1977-78, K-Mark Pharmacy, Burnsville, Minn., 1978-79, Mount Sinai Hosp., Mpls., 1980-81, Home Health Cons., Mpls., 1981-84, Pharmacy Corp. of Am., Mpls., 1984—. Recipient Outstanding Young Men of Am. award Jaycees, 1984. Fellow Am. Soc. Cons. Pharmacists; mem. Am. Pub. Health Assn., Am. Pharm. Assn., Minn. State Pharm. Assn. (chmn. 1980-83, bd. dirs. 1983—), Rho Chi. Avocations: camping, skiing, traveling. Home: 9425 Cedar Lake Rd Saint Louis Park MN 55426 Office: Pharmacy Corp of Am 155 26th Ave SE Minneapolis MN 55414

JANZEN, ERNST KRIJGERS, orthodontist; b. The Netherlands, Sept. 22, 1932; s. Willem Krijgers and Geria (Noteboom) J.; D.D.S., Utrecht State U., The Netherlands, 1957; Ph.D., U. Zurich, Switzerland, 1962; D.D.S., Northwestern U., 1965, M.S., 1965; m. Agnes Pot, Jan. 24, 1959; children—Marita, Annette, Nicolette. Came to U.S., 1962, naturalized, 1967. Pvt. practice dentistry, specializing in orthodontics, Northbrook, Ill., 1966—; guest lectr. orthodontics Northwestern U. Served to capt., M.C., Royal Dutch Army, 1957-59. Recipient 1st prize Ann Research Contest, Am. Assn. Orthodontists, 1966, Milo Hellman Research award, 1966. Mem. Am. European, Ill. (exec. bd.) assns. orthodontists, Am. Dental Assn., Dutch Dental Soc. Republican. Presbyn. (trustee). Rotarian. Contbr. articles profl. jours. Home: 2240 Chestnut St Northbrook IL 60062 Office: 1220 Meadow Rd Northbrook IL 60062

JANZEN, NORINE MADELYN QUINLAN, medical technologist; b. Fond du Lac, Wis., Feb. 9, 1943; d. Joseph Wesley and Norma Edith (Gustin) Quinlan; B.S., Marian Coll., 1965; med. technologist St. Agnes Sch. Med. Tech., Fond du Lac, 1966; M.A., Central Mich. U., 1980; m. Douglas Mac Arthur Janzen, July 18, 1970; 1 son, Justin James. Med. technologist Mayfair Med. Lab., Wauwatosa, Wis., 1966-69; supr. med. technologist Dr.'s Mason, Chamberlain, Franke, Klink & Kamper, Milw., 1969-76, Hartford-Parkview Clinic, Ltd., 1976—. Substitute poll worker Fond du Lac Democratic Com., 1964-65; mem. Dem. Nat. Com., 1973—. Mem. Nat. (awards com. 1984-87), Wis. (chmn. awards com. 1976-77, 84-85, treas. 1977-81, pres.-elect 1981-82, pres. 1982-83, dir. 1977-84, 85-87, Mem. of Yr. 1982, numerous service awards), Milw. (pres. 1971-72; dir. 1972-73) socs. med. technologists, Communications of Wis. (originator, chmn. 1977-79), Southeastern Suprs. Group (co-chmn. 1976-77), LWV, Alpha Delta Theta (nat. dist. chmn. 1967-69; nat. alumnae dir. 1969-71), Methodist. Home: N 98 W 17298 Dotty Way Germantown WI 53022 Office: 1004 E Sumner St Hartford WI 53027

JARBOE, EVERETT ESTEL, retired teacher educator; b. Henryville, Ind., Aug. 16, 1918; s. William Andrew and Edith Hazel (Gabbert) J.; m. Betty M. McCoy, July 22, 1944; 1 child, John Andrew (dec.). B.S., Evansville Coll., 1940; M.S., Ind. U., 1948, Ed.D., 1949. Asst. prof. edn. North Tex. State U., Denton, 1949-52, assoc. prof., 1952-55; prof. edn. D.C. Tchrs. Coll., Washington, 1956-65; prof. edn. Ind. U., Bloomington, 1965-84, emeritus prof. edn., 1984—; lic. commr. Ind. State Dept. Edn., 1971-79; dir. div. of edn. Ind. U.-Purdue, Indpls., 1969-76. Served with M.C., U.S. Army, 1942-46, ETO. Mem. Ind. State Bd. Edn. Methodist. Lodges: Masons. Shriners. Home: 2711 N Dunn Bloomington IN 47104 Office: Sch Edn Ind U Bloomington IN 47406

JARED, PATSY MCCLURE, civic worker; b. Macomb, Ill., Apr. 8, 1934; d. George Darwin and Ruth Lenora (Hackett) McClure; m. Alva H. Jared, July 23, 1955; children—Jennifer Lynne Anderson, Elizabeth Joan. B.S., U. Wis.-Platteville, 1974. Substitute tchr. Platteville Sch. System, Wis., 1974-78. Troop leader Green Hills council Girl Scouts U.S.A., 1969-79, town chmn., 1979-84, dist. nominating com., 1975-84, council trainer dist. 3, 1975-83, council nominating com., 1981—, bd. dirs., 1981—, sec. bd. dirs., 1981-85, property devel. com., 1976-81; mem. edn. bd. United Meth. Ch., 1977-79, alter com., 1980-82; mem. nominating com. United Meth. Women, 1982-85; bd. dirs. Surgeons Quarters, Portage, Wis., 1985-88. Named Outstanding Leader, Wis. Jaycettes, Platteville, Wis., 1970, Town Chmn. of Yr., Green Hills council Girl Scouts U.S.A., Freeport, Ill., 1981. Mem. DAR (chpt. regent 1985), Univ. Women Club., Platteville. Club: 20 Year (Platteville). Avocations: genealogy; plants; knitting; sewing; birds. Home: 945 St James Circle Platteville WI 53818

JAROS, KEVIN LARSON, food co. exec.; b. Virginia, Minn., Aug. 29, 1951; s. Floyd D. and Joyce Marilyn (Larson) J.; A.B. (N.W. Paper Found. scholar 1969-73), Brown U., 1973; M.B.A. (fellow, 1974-76), Harvard U., 1976; m. Margaret Helen Bernhard, Nov. 3, 1979. Asst. to controller NW Paper div. Potlatch Corp., Cloquet, Minn., 1973-74; mktg. asst. Flour div. Gen. Mills, Mpls., 1976-77, asst. product mgr., Cereal div., 1977-78, product mgr. New Cereals Group, Big "G„ div., Mpls., 1979-81, product mgr. Nature Valley snacks, 1981-83, dir. mktg. new cereals, 1983—; tutor Harvard Bus. Sch., Cambridge, Mass., 1975-76. Mem. Delta Phi Omega. Home: 14027 Orchard Rd Minnetonka MN 55343 Office: Gen Mills Big G 9200 Wayzata Blvd Minneapolis MN 55440

JAROSZCZYK, TADEUSZ, research engineer; b. Grezow, Poland, Dec. 10, 1938; came to U.S., 1981; s. Alesander and Zofia (Trojanek) J.; m. Dorota-Barbara Pieczara, Sept. 15, 1960; children—Malgorzata, Thomasz-Michal. Prodn. technician, Technicum of Mech. Engring.-Poland, 1956; Mech. Technician, Mil. Officers Sch. in Engring.-Poland, 1960; M.Sc. in Mech. Engring., Mil. Acad. Tech.-Warsaw, 1970; Ph.D., Mil. Acad. Tech., 1975. Process technician Warsaw Tool Assn., Poland, 1956-57; chief repair shop Mil. Service, Poland, 1960-65; mgr. filtration lab. Mil. Acad. Tech., Warsaw, 1970-77; mgr. filtration lab. Radom Inst. Tech., Poland, 1977-79; mgr. filtration and ventilation lab. Central Inst. Occupational Safety & Health, Warsaw, 1979-81; research engr. Nelson Industries, Inc., Stoughton, Wis., 1982—; air and oil filtration expert Polish Central Engrs. Assn., 1975-81. Co-author: Oil, Fuel and Air Filtration for Piston Engines, 1977. Contbr. articles to profl. jours. Inventor in field. Served to lt. col. Polish Army, 1957-77. Recipient 2d Degree Individual award Minister Sci., Higher Edn. and Tech., Warsaw, 1979; 3d Degree award, Minister Nat. Def., Warsaw, 1975. Mem. Soc. Automotive Engrs., Air Pollution Control Assn. Avocations: travelling; history. Home: 1526 Kenilworth Ct Apt 5 Stoughton WI 53589 Office: Nelson Industries Inc Hwy 51 W Box 428 Stoughton WI 53589

JARRELL, ROBERT HOMER, management consultant, accounting educator; b. Harrisburg, Ill., July 16, 1923; s. John L. and Catherine (Grace) J.; B.S., U. Ill., 1946; M.S., Ill. Inst. Tech., 1961; m. Elizabeth Jane Beidelman, Feb. 26, 1949; children—Katherine, Michael, Steven, Peter. Accountant, Ill. Farm Supply Co., 1947-50; asst. comptroller Ill. Inst. Tech., 1950-54, comptroller, 1954-62, bus. mgr., 1962-83, lectr. in acctg., 1961-82; treas. Argonne U. Assocs., 1979-83; owner, prin. Robert H. Jarrell & Assocs., mgmt. cons., Naperville, Ill., 1983—. Chmn. edn. div. Ill. Cancer Crusade, Am. Cancer Soc., 1960-63, 65, 66; mem. adv. bd. Salvation Army Settlement, Chgo., chmn., 1975-77; mem. pub. edn. com. Chgo. unit Am. Cancer Soc., vice chmn., 1974-79, chmn., 1979-81; mem. adv. com. Sch. Dist. 203, 1967, 71-72; town clk. Lisle Twp., 1973—; jury commr. 18th Jud. Dist. Ill., 1975—, chmn., 1979—; chmn. Lisle Twp. Republican Orgn., 1976-78; mem. exec. com. Du Page County Central Rep. Com., 1976-78. Mem. Fin. Execs. Inst. (sec. 1964-65), Nat. Assn. Ednl. Buyers (sec.-treas. Ill.-Wis. sect. 1969, chmn. 1971), Nat., Central assns. coll. and univ. bus. officers, Alpha Kappa Psi, Delta Sigma Rho. Republican. Congregationalist. Club: Rotary. Home: 1204 Cardinal Ln Naperville IL 60540

JARRETT, JERRY THOMAS, lawyer; b. Ripley, Tenn., Oct. 26, 1954; s. Lawrence Volly and Rosie B. (Harston) J.; m. Theresa Burnett, Dec. 15, 1984. B.A. in History, Langston U., 1977; J.D., Valparaiso. U., 1981. Bar: Ind. 1981, U.S. Dist. Ct. (no. and so. dists.) Ind. 1981. Law clk. Lake County Prosecutor's Office, Ind., 1979-81, dep. pros. atty., 1981-83; sole practice, Hammond, Ind., 1981—; asst. city atty. City of Hammond, 1984—; atty. Hammond Housing Authority, 1984—; atty. Ind. State Black Expo, Hammond, 1981—; participating atty. pro-bono project Cook County Bar Assn., Chgo., 1981—; bd. dirs. legal rev. com. Greater Hammond Community, 1984—. Bd. dirs. Bethany Day Care Ctr., Hammond, 1982—, Mt. Zion Housing Authority, Inc., Hammond, 1983—. Recipient Recognition award Ind. Black Expo, Inc., 1982, Recognition award N.W. Ind. Open Housing Ctr., Gary, 1983. Mem. Black Am. Law Students' Assn. (pres. 1979-80, Service award 1980), Ind. State Bar Assn., Hammond Bar Assn., ABA, Assn. Trial Lawyers Am., Thurgood Marshall Law Assn., NAACP, Kappa Alpha Psi. Democrat. Baptist. Home: 927 Ames St Hammond IN 46320 Office: 5917 State Line Ave Hammond IN 46320

JARRETT, JERRY VERNON, banker; b. Abilene, Tex., Oct. 31, 1931; s. Walter Elwood and Myrtle Elizabeth (Allen) J.; B.B.A., U. Okla., 1957; M.B.A., Harvard U., 1963; m. Martha Ann McCabe, June 13, 1953; children—Cynthia Ann, Charles Elwood, Christopher Allen, John Carlton. Gen. sales mgr. Tex. Coca-Cola Bottling Co., Abilene, 1957-61; exec. v.p. Marine Midland Bank, N.Y.C., 1963-73; exec. v.p. Cleve. Trust Co., 1973-76, vice-chmn., 1976-78, pres., from 1978; pres. Cleve. Corp.; chmn., chief exec. officer AmeriTrust Corp., 1983—. Served with USAAF, 1950-54. Mem. Phi Gamma Delta. Co-author: Creative Collective Bargaining, 1964. Office: AmeriTrust 900 Euclid Ave Cleveland OH 44101*

JARVIS, DAVID JAMES, banker; b. New Bremen, Ohio, Aug. 8, 1958; s. James Arthur and Irene (Berg) J.; m. KaBeth Ann Gilbert, Oct. 20, 1984. Student, Ohio State U., 1976-78; degree in bus. Wright State U., 1984. Teller 1st Nat. Bank, New Bremen, 1978-79, data processing mgr., 1979-84, v.p., 1985—; dir. Home Benefit Co. Mem. Am. Bankers Assn., Ohio Bankers Assn. Republican. Clubs: Porsche Am. (Toledo, Ohio); Sports Car Am. (Dayton, Ohio). Avocations: auto crossing; car collecting; travelling; off road running.

JARVIS, GILBERT ANDREW, humanities educator, writer; b. Chelsea, Mass., Feb. 13, 1941; s. Vernon Owen and Angeline M. (Burkard) J.; m. Carol Jean Ganter, Jan. 26, 1963; children—Vicki Lynn, Mark Christopher. B.A., St. Norbert Coll., De Pere, Wis., 1963; M.A., Purdue U., 1965, Ph.D., 1970. Prof. Ohio State U., Columbus, 1970—, chmn. humanities edn., 1980—, assoc. chmn. dept. theory and practice, 1983—; cons. Internat. Edn. Program, U.S. Dept. Edn., Washington, 1977—. Author: Et Vous?, 1983; Invitation, 2d edit., 1984; Y tu?, 1985. Editor: The Challenge for Excellence, 1984. Mem. editorial bd. Modern Lang. Jour., 1979—; adv. bd. Can. Modern Lang. Review, 1982—. Mem. Am. Ednl. Research Assn., Am. Council Teaching Fgn. Langs., Phi Delta Kappa. Avocations: Running, marine aquariums, travel, sports. Home: 8337 Evangeline Dr Worthington OH 43085 Office: Ednl Theory and Practice Ohio State U 1945 N High St Columbus OH 43210

JARVIS, MICHAEL RICHARD, osteopathic physician; b. Detroit, Aug. 30, 1949; m. Colleen Curran; children—Amy, J. Michael. B.S., Western Mich. U., 1971; D.O., Des Moines Coll. Osteo. Medicine and Surgery, 1976. Diplomate Am. Bd. Surgery. Intern, Detroit Osteo. Hosp., 1976-77; resident in gen. surgery Grand Rapids Osteo. Hosp., Mich., 1977-81; practice medicine specializing in gen. surgery, Grand Rapids, 1981—; chmn. nutritional support com. Met. Hosp., Grand Rapids, 1984—, sec. dept. surgery, 1983—, chmn. trauma com., 1984—. Mem. Am. Coll. Osteo. Surgeons, Am. Osteo. Assn., Mich. Assn. Osteo. Physicians and Surgeons, Am. Coll. Emergency Physicians, Kent County Assn. Osteo. Physicians and Surgeons. Republican. Roman Catholic. Avocations: golf, skiing. Office: Michael R Jarvis DO 2424 Barton St SE Grand Rapids MI 49506

JASPER, BARRY LEWIS, dentist; b. St. Louis, Nov. 14, 1939; s. Milton Harvey and Dorothy (Polinsky) J.; m. Bett Ragin, Dec. 24, 1961; children—Stacey Gwenn, Daniel Ragin. Student Johns Hopkins U., 1957-59; A.B., Washington U., St. Louis, 1961, D.D.S. cum laude, 1964; M.S. in Dentistry, Boston U., 1966. Prin. Milton & Barry Jasper D.D.S., Clayton, Mo., 1966-70; v.p., sec. M.H. & B.L. Jasper D.D.S., Inc., Clayton, 1970-84, pres., 1984—; asst. prof. Washington U. Sch. Dental Medicine, 1966-76. Pres. bd. dirs. Central Agy. for Jewish Edn., St. Louis, 1976-78; bd. dirs. Jewish Fedn. of St. Louis, 1973-79, Jewish Community Ctr. Assn., St. Louis, 1979-81, Jewish Ctr. for Aged, St. Louis, 1974-83, United Hebrew Congregation, St. Louis, 1976-82. Recipient award of Merit Jewish Ctr. for Aged, 1983, David Grosberg Leadership award Jewish Fedn. St. Louis, 1974. Mem. Pierre Fauchard Acad. Greater St. Louis Dental Assn., Mo. Dental Assn., ADA, Alpha Omega (pres. local chpt. 1970), Omicron Kappa Upsilon (pres. local chpt. 1971). Home: 2450 Hermitage Hill Ln Frontenac MO 63131 Office: 8000 Bonhomme Clayton MO 63105

JASPER, ELBERT BAKER, veterinarian; b. Berea, Ohio, May 11, 1923; s. Jay Elbert and Marion Bethia (Baker) J.; student Baldwin Wallace Coll., 1941-42; D.V.M., Ohio State U., 1949; m. Carolyn Agatha Beach, Oct. 27, 1951. Area veterinarian U.S. Dept. Agr., Ohio, 1949-54, Kans., 1955-56, asst. veterinarian in charge State of N.J., 1956-59, asst. veterinarian in charge State of Tenn., 1959-61, mem. program appraisal staff, Washington, 1961-63, veterinarian in charge State of Md., 1963-65, mem. import export staff, Hyattsville, Md., 1965-71; gen. practice veterinary medicine specializing in small animals, Berea, 1973-83. Served with Veterinary Corps, U.S. Army, 1944-46; CBI. Mem. Am., Ohio veterinary med. assns., Cleve. Acad. Veterinary Medicine, U.S. Power Squadron (advanced pilot). Methodist. Club: Masons. Home: 84 West St Berea OH 44017

JASPER, MICHAEL LEE, investment brokerage firm executive; b. Mankato, Minn., Jan. 14, 1956; s. Leonard A. and Janet Kay (Krause) J. B.S. in Acctg., Murray State U., 1978. C.P.A., Ind., Ky. Acct. Ernst & Whinney, Louisville, Ky., 1978-81, Brinkerhoff, Franklin & Co., Indpls., 1982; account exec. Thomson McKinnon Securities Inc., Indpls., 1983—. Vol. Richard Lugar Re-election Campaign, Indpls., 1982, Crossroads of Am. council Boy Scouts Am., 1983. Named hon. Ky. col., 1982; recipient Thomas Arkle Clark award Zeta Lambda chpt. Alpha Tau Omega, 1978. Mem. Am. Inst. C.P.A.s, Ind. Soc. C.P.A.s, Indpls. C. of C., Indpls. Jaycees. Republican. Roman Catholic. Club: Indpls. Athletic. Home: 1130 N Tecumseh Apt 3 Indianapolis IN 46201 Office: Thomson-McKinnon Securities Inc 200 Circle Tower Bldg Indianapolis IN 46204

JASPER, ROBERT GORDON, JR., county official, consultant; b. Winthrop Harbor, Ill., Jan. 25, 1917; s. Robert Gordon and Martha Ellen (Durham) J.; m. M. Jean Cannon, Jan. 2, 1942; children—Sandra Jasper Drew, Leslie Jasper Heberlein, Robin Jasper Sprague, James R. Student Coll. of Lake County, 1960-61. Cert. rev. appraiser, Ill., assessment officer, Ill. Indsl. engr. Marshall Field and Co., Zion, Ill., 1935-52; machinist Johnson Motors, Waukegan, Ill., 1952-58; supr. assessments Lake County, Waukegan, Ill., 1958—; cons. Former trustee Village of Winthrop Harbor (Ill.); active Lake County Republican Fedn. Served with U.S. Army 1942-45. Mem. Internat. Assn. Assessing Officers, Nat. Assn. Rev. Appraisers (past regional gov.), County Assessment Officers Assn. (pres. 1960-61), Lake-McHenry Assessors Assn., Am. Legion. Clubs: Lions (Winthrop Harbor); Moose (Zion). Home: 530 Kirkwood Winthrop Harbor IL 60096 Office: 18 N County St Room 603 Waukegan IL 60085

JAY, STEPHEN JORDAN, physician, researcher, educator; b. Indpls., June 2, 1941; s. Arthur Nottingham and Hilda (Jordan) J.; m. Anne Marie Beegan, July 12, 1969; children—Stephen, Audrey, Matthew, Alan. Student Wabash Coll., 1959-62; M.D., Ind. U.-Indpls., 1966. Diplomate Am. Bd. Internal Medicine. Intern, Parkland Hosp., Dallas, 1966-67; resident in medicine, 1969-71, fellow in pulmonary medicine, 1971-73; asst. prof. medicine U. Tex. Health Sci. Ctr., Dallas, 1973-74, U. Ky. Med. Ctr., Lexington, 1974-76; assoc. prof., chief pulmonary sect. Wishard Hosp., Ind. U. Sch. Medicine, 1976-80, prof., asst. dean, 1980—; v.p. acad. affairs Methodist Hosp. Ind., Indpls., 1980—. Pres.-elect Am. Lung Assn. Ind. Served to lt. USN, 1967-69. Recipient award in recognition excellence of sci. paper Am. Assn. for Med. Systems and Informatics, 1983. Fellow Am. Coll. Chest Physicians, ACP; mem. AAAS, Am. Fedn. for Clin. Research, Royal Soc. Medicine, AMA, Ind. Thoracic Soc. (pres.), Marion County Med. Soc. (dir. 1982—), Sigma Xi, Alpha Omega Alpha. Methodist. Contbr. chpts. to books, articles to profl. jours. Office: Methodist Hosp Ind Inc 1604 N Capital Ave Indianapolis IN 46202

JAYDOS, ROBERT ANTHONY, architect; b. Chgo., Feb. 5, 1938; s. Anthony Walter and Angeline Rita J.; B.Arch., U. Ill., 1968; children by previous marriage—Robert Anthony, Christine Marie, Shari Anne. Designer, Perkins & Will, Chgo., 1968-69; designer, asst. job capt. Loebl, Schlossman, Bennett & Dart, Chgo., 1969-71; draftsman Graham, Anderson, Probst & White, Chgo., 1971-72; job capt. Marshall Lieb & Assos., Chgo., 1972-73; pres., design cons. Smith & Jaydos Inc., Elk Grove Village, Ill., owner, operator Jaydos & Assocs., Architects Ltd., Elk Grove Village, 1973-80, pres., 1980—. Served with USAF, 1955-59. Mem. Easter Seals Com., 1983. Registered architect, Ill., Nebr., Iowa, Ohio; lic. comml. pilot. Mem. AIA, Nat. Council Archtl. Registration Bds., U. Ill. Alumni Assn. (life), Art Inst. Chgo. Club: Rotary. Office: Jaydos & Assocs Architects Ltd 311 W Superior St Chicago IL 60610

JAYE, DAVID ROBERT, hospital administrator; b. Chgo., Aug. 15, 1930; s. David R. and Gertrude (Gibfried) J.; m. Mary Ann Scanlan, June 6, 1953; children—David, Jeffrey, Kathleen. B.S., Loyola U., Chgo., 1952; M.S.H.A., Northwestern U., 1954. Adminstrv. asst. Chgo. Wesley Meml. Hosp., 1952-54; asst. adminstr. Sharon Gen. Hosp., Pa., 1957-60; assoc. adminstr. St. Joseph Hosp., Joliet, Ill., 1960-65; adminstr. Sacred Heart Hosp., Allentown, Pa., 1965-69; pres. St. Joseph's Hosp., Marshfield, Wis., 1969—. Served to 1st lt. USAF, 1954-57. Fellow Am. Coll. Hosp. Adminstrs. (bd. regents 1978-81); mem. Am. Hosp. Assn. (del.), Wis. Hosp. Assn. (trustee 1973-79), Cath. Health Assn. (trustee 1975-79). Roman Catholic. Lodges: Rotary, Elks. Home: 1125 Ridge Rd Marshfield WI 54449 Office: St Joseph Hosp 611 St Joseph Ave Marshfield WI 54449

JAYNE, THEODORE DOUGLAS, technical research and development company executive; b. Painesville, Ohio, Dec. 3, 1929; s. Earl Douglas and Mary Griffin (Erskine) J.; m. Penelope Sanders, Mar. 7, 1959 (div. Sept. 1980); children—Douglas T., Virginia M., Jillanne M. B.A., U. Chgo., 1950; postgrad. Case Inst. Tech., 1950-54. Head materials, instr. labs. Rand Devel. Corp., Cleve., 1950-64; dir. labs. Gen. Tech. Services, Upper Darby, Pa., 1964-69; tech. dir., prin. T. Jayne Co., Painesville, 1969—. Patentee in field. Office: T Jayne Co 10234 Johnnycake Painesville OH 44077

JEBE, EMIL HENRY, statistician, educator, local government officer; b. Clutier, Iowa, Feb. 26, 1909; s. Jurgen Friedrich and Theresa (Arp) J.; m. Noma Lureen Rupprich, June 16, 1941. B.S. in Economics, Iowa State Coll., 1938, M.S. in Agrl. Economics, 1941; Ph.D. in Stats., N.C. State U., 1950. Worker family farm Benton County, Iowa, 1925-34; state supr. U.S. Dept. Agriculture and WPA, Iowa, 1940-41; assoc. prof. Iowa State U., Ames, 1949-59; research mathematician U. Mich., Ann Arbor, 1959-73; statistician emeritus Environ. Research Inst. Mich., Ann Arbor, 1974—. Author (with others); Statistical Design of Fatigue Experiments, 1975, An Alternative View of Estimation in Linear Models, 1984. Chmn. Scio Twp. Planning Commn., Washtenaw County, Mich., 1967-74, Scio Twp. Zoning Bd. Appeals, 1976—. Served to maj. U.S. Army, 1938-46, Korea; lt. col. USAR Ret., 1962—. Recipient commendation citation Washtenaw County Bd. Commrs., Ann Arbor, 1972, Scio Twp., 1974. Fellow ASTM (award of merit 1985), Am. Statis. Assn. (com. chmn., 1983—; Youden award); mem. Internat. Biometric Soc., Bernoullie Soc., Internat. Assn. Survey Statisticians. Lutheran. Avocations: family genealogy; photography; brick collecting; sailing. Home: 2650 Laurentide Dr Ann Arbor MI 48103 Office: ERIM 3300 Plymouth Rd Box 8618 Ann Arbor MI 48107

JEBSEN, HARRY ALFRED ARTHUR, JR., college dean; b. Chgo., Apr. 8, 1943; s. Harry Alfred Arthur Jebsen; m. Elaine Claire Melchert, Sept. 5, 1964; children—Timothy Paul, Christopher Warren. B.A., Wartburg Coll., 1965; M.A., U. Cin., 1966, Ph.D., 1971. Prof. history Texas Tech U., Lubbock, 1969-81, dir. urban studies, 1972-81, assoc. dean arts and scis., 1980-81; dean Coll. of Arts and Scis., Capital U., Columbus, Ohio, 1981—. Author: History of Dallas, Texas Park System, 1971. Contbr. articles to profl. jours. Bd. dirs. Luth. Council for Community Action, Lubbock, 1970-78, U. Ministries of Lubbock, 1971-81, Luth. Social Services of Central Ohio, Columbus, 1984—. Recipient Fish and Loaves award Luth. Council for Community Action, Lubbock, 1977; NDEA fellow, Cin., 1966-69. Mem. Am. Assn. Higher Edn., Am. Assn. Colls., N. Am. Soc. Sport Histories. Democrat. Avocations: golf, reading. Home: 2406 N Havenwood Dr Bexley OH 43209 Office: Capital U 2199 E Main St Columbus OH 43209

JECKLIN, LOIS U., art corporation executive, consultant; b. Manning, Iowa, Oct. 5, 1934; d. J.R. and Ruth O. (Austin) Underwood; m. Dirk C. Jecklin, June 24, 1955; children—Jennifer Anne, Ivan Peter. Student State U. Iowa, 1953-55, 60-61, 74-75. Residency coordinator Quad City Arts Council, Rock Island, Ill., 1973-78; field rep. Affiliate Artists, Inc., N.Y.C., 1975-77; mgr., artist in residence Deere & Co., Moline, Ill., 1977-80; dir. Vis. Artist Series, Davenport, Iowa, 1978-81; pres. Vis. Artists, Inc., Davenport, 1981—; cons. writer's program St. Ambrose Coll., Davenport, 1981, 83, 85; mem. com. Iowa Arts Council, Des Moines, 1983-84; panelist Chamber Music Am., N.Y.C., 1984, Pub. Art Conf., Cedar Rapids, Iowa, 1984; panelist, mem. com. Lt. Gov.'s Conf. on Iowa's Future, Des Moines, 1984. Trustee Davenport Art Gallery; mem. steering com. Iowa Citizens for Arts, Des Moines, 1970-71; bd. dirs. Tri-City Symphony Orchestra Assn., Davenport, 1968-83; founding mem. Urban Design Council, HOME, City of Davenport Beautification Com., all Davenport, 1970-72. Recipient numerous awards Izaak Walton League, Davenport Art Gallery, Assn. for Retarded Citizens, Am. Heart Assn., Ill. Bur. Corrections, many others; LaVernes Noyes scholar, 1953-55. Mem. Am. Council for Arts, Ptnrs. for Livable Places, Ann. Coll. Univ. Community Arts Adminstrs., Iowa Assembly Local Arts Agys. (state exec. com.), Nat. Assembly Local Arts Agys., Am. Assn. Mus., Crow Valley Golf Club, Lindsay Yacht Club. Republican. Episcopalian. Club: Outing. Home: 2717 Nichols Ln Davenport IA 52803 Office: Vis Artists Inc 106 E 3rd St Suite 220 Davenport IA 52801

JECMEN, JOHN JOSEPH, manufacturing company executive; b. Chgo., Jan. 16, 1916; s. James and Marie (Steker) J.; student DePaul U., 1933-37, Ill. Inst. Tech., 1942; m. Betty R. Malek, June 18, 1938. Chmn. bd. Harris Preble Co. mfg. elevator doors, Cicero, Ill., 1933—. Mem. adv. council Coll. Commerce, DePaul U. Mem. NAM, Dist. Export Council, Nat. Assn. Elevator Contractors, Ill. Mfrs. Assn., Internat. Bus. Council, Execs. Club Chgo., Chgo. Assn. Commerce and Industry, Briarwood Lakes Community Assn., French-Am., Finnish-Am., German-Am., Mid-Am. Arab chambers commerce, C. of C. U.S., U.S., Western golf assns. Moose. Club: Butterfield Country (Oak Brook, Ill.). Patentee in field. Home: 210 Briarwood Pass Oak Brook IL 60521 Office: 4608 W 20th St Chicago IL 60650

JEDLICKA, DIANE SCHWEDE, nursing educator; b. Cleve., June 20, 1946; d. Harold Edward and Elsie Margaret (Hatala) Schwede; m. Ronald Louis Jedlicka, May 10, 1975; children—Peter Louis, Dana Marie, Michael Louis. R.N., St. Vincent Charity Hosp., 1967; B.S. in Nursing, Ohio State U., 1972, M.S., 1976. Clinic nurse Ohio State U. Hosp., Columbus, 1969, ICU nurse, 1970-72; staff nurse, supr. Appalachian Regional Hosp., McDowell, Ky., 1969-70; instr. Grant Hosp. Sch. Nursing, Columbus, Ohio, 1972-80, staff devel. instr., 1980-81; asst. prof. Otterbein Coll., Westerville, Ohio, 1981—; flight nurse Grant Hosp., 1985—. Critical care cons. ANCER, 1983—; lectr., cons. Continuing Profl. Edn., 1980—; lectr. Profl. Med. Edn., Grove City, Ohio, 1979—. Mem. Am. Assn. Critical Care Nurses, Nat. Flight Nurses Assn., Sigma Theta Tau. Home: 475 S Main St Pataskala OH 43062 Office: Otterbein Coll Dept Nursing Westerville OH 43081

JEDLICKA, RONALD LOUIS, real estate broker; b. Cleve., Feb. 23, 1944; s. Louis Joseph and Mary (Maline) J.; m. Diane Schwede, May 10, 1975; children—Peter, Dana, Michael. B.A., Ohio State U., 1972; A.B.A., Cuyahoga Community Coll., 1966. Project asst. North Excavating, Cleve., 1962-69; real estate broker Brashear Realty Co., Augusta, Ga., 1969-72; real estate cons. Borden, Inc., Columbus, Ohio, 1972-73; with real estate/spl. projects dept. Ohio Dept. Transp., Columbus, 1973-75; facilities planner Bur. of Real Estate, Columbus, 1975—; real estate broker Meridian Realty Co., Pataskala, Ohio, 1975—. Founder, Newark, Heath & Buckeye Lake Scenic Ry., non-profit community r.r. Author: Lancaster Street Railway, 1983. Served with U.S. Army, 1967-69. Mem. Soc. Indsl. Realtors, N. Am. Railway Hist. Assn. (pres. 1980—). Lodge: Lions. Home: 475 S Main St Pataskala OH 43062

JEFFERIES, MARK GERARD, financial analyst, petroleum geologist; b. Elmwood Park, Ill., Nov. 4, 1959; s. Albert Glen and Louis Ann (Fitzsimmons) J. B.A. in Geology, St. Louis, 1981. Wellsite geologist Core Labs., Midland, Tex., 1981-82; geol. research asst. St. Louis U., 1982—; matching analyst Fed. Res. Bank of St. Louis, 1983—; cons. geologist Wagner Oil Corp., Alton, Ill., 1982—. Contbr. articles on geol. research to jours. Mem. Rankin Neighborhood Redevel. Assn., 1983—. Mem. Am. Assn. Petroleum Geologists. Republican. Roman Catholic. Avocations: photography, biking, woodworking. Home: 4420 Arco St Saint Louis MO 63110

JEFFERIS, ROBERT ALLEN, information and computer engineer; b. Cleve., Oct. 12, 1957; s. Richard Hall and Bernice Martha (Knautz) J. B.A. cum laude, Ohio Wesleyan U., 1979; M.S., Ohio State U., 1980; postgrad. Case Western Res. U., 1982—. Grad. teaching assoc. Ohio State U. Coll. Engring., Columbus, 1979-80; programmer Cole Nat. Corp., 1981, application analyst, 1982-83, info. ctr. cons., 1983-84; systems engr. Database and Info. Ctr., Cullinet Software, Inc., 1984—. Synthesized new organic compound, 1978. Mem. Cleveland Heights Democratic Caucus. Mem. assn. for Computing Machinery, Audubon Soc., Sierra Club, Nat. Eagle Scout Assn., Cleve. Natural History Mus., Phi Mu Epsilon, Chi Gamma Nu. Methodist.

JEFFERS, MARK THOMAS, lawyer; b. Kansas City, Mo., July 2, 1953; s. Robert Grant and Lurlene Lucille (Caruthers) J.; m. Claudia Marie Brownfield, Jan. 21, 1978; children—Brian Alan, Nicole Marie. B.S., Pittsburg State U., 1975; J.D., Washburn U., 1979. Bar: Kans., 1979, U.S. Dist. Ct. Kans. 1979, U.S. Ct. Appeals (10th cir.) Kans. 1979. Sole practice, Overland Park, Kans., 1979—; staff atty. Legal Services for Prisoners, Inc., Lansing, Kans., 1981-82. Mem. Kans. Bar Assn., Kans. Trial Lawyers Assn., Assn. Trial Lawyers Am. Johnson County Bar Assn., Kansas City Bar Assn. Home: 7645 Marty St Overland Park KS 66204 Office: 8000 Foster St Overland Park KS 66204

JEFFERSON, ARTHUR, superintendent schools; b. Dec. 1, 1938; married; 2 children. B.S., Wayne State U., 1960, M.A. in Polit. Sci., 1963, Ed.D., 1973. Cert. secondary tchr., Mich. Tchr. Detroit Pub. Schs., 1960-66; coordinator Tri-Area Integration Project, Detroit Pub. Schs., 1966-68; instr. Inst. on Desegregation, U. Detroit, 1967-68; polit. sci. instr., supr. Wayne County Community Coll., Mich., 1969-71; adminstrv. asst. Office of Exec. Dep. Supt., Detroit Pub. Schs., 1968-69; staff devel. adminstr. tchr. edn. dept. Office Adult and Continuing Edn., Detroit, 1969-70; asst. region supt. Region Three, Detroit Pub. Schs., 1970-71, region supt., 1971-75, interim gen. supt., 1975, gen. supt., 1975—; staff cons. Citizens Action Com. on Fin., Detroit Pub. Schs., 1968-69; mem. Council for Basic Edn., nat. rev. panel Study of Sch. Desegregation, Duke U., Met. Task Force Youth Employment-United Community Services. Active Wayne State Fund, ACLU, NAACP; corp. mem. Boys and Girls Clubs Met. Detroit, mem. Nat. PTA Urban Adv. Task Force; mem. exec. bd. Detroit Area Council Boy Scouts Am.; bd. dirs. Coll. Bd., Detroit Ednl. TV Found., Detroit Symphony, Detroit Tchrs. Credit Union, Jr. Achievement Southeastern Mich., Magnet Schs. Am., Inc., Music Hall Ctr., United Found., YMCA Met. Detroit; adv. bd. Ctr. for Peace Conflict Studies, Close Up, Detroit Pre-Employment Tng. Ctr., Instr. Mag., Met. Detroit chpt. March of Dimes, Nat. Reading Olympics; trustee Bus.-Edn. Alliance, Detroit Econ. Growth Corp., Franklin-Wright Settlement, Inc., Joint Council Econ. Edn., Met. Affairs Corp., New Detroit, Inc., Traffic Safety Assn. Detroit; pres. Council Great City Schs., 1983-84; v.p. Univ. Cultural Ctr. Assn. Mem. Wayne State U. Edn. Alumni Assn. (bd. govs. 1968-71, 79-82), Wayne State U. Alumni Assn. (trustee 1968-71), Nat. Acad. Edn. (panel mem.), Nat. Inst. Edn. (law and govt. study group), Nat. Council Social Studies, Mich. Council Social Studies, Assn. Supervision and Curriculum Devel., Mich. Assn. Supervision Curriculum Devel., Am. Assn. Sch. Adminstrs., Mich. Assn. Sch. Adminstrs., Met. Detroit Soc. Black Ednl. Adminstrs., Nat. Alliance Black Sch. Educators, Inst. Devel. Ednl. Activities, Inc. (adv. bd.), Univ. Council Ednl. Adminstrn. (cons. bd. jour.), Phi Delta Kappa, Pi Sigma Alpha. Home: 19445 Gloucester Detroit MI 48203 Office: Gen Supt Detroit Pub Schs 5057 Woodward Ave Detroit MI 48202

JEFFERSON, BETTY, educational administrator; b. Lake Providence, La., Nov. 28, 1938; d. Mose and Angeline (Harris) J.; divorced; 1 dau., Angela Coleman. B.S. in Foods and Nutrition, So. U., Baton Rouge, 1961; M.A. in Adminstrn., Roosevelt U., 1978; Ed.D. in Ednl. Adminstrn., Vanderbilt U., 1981. Food supr. Michael Reese Hosp., Chgo., 1961-62; dietitian Mercy Hosp., Chgo., 1962-63; social worker, unit supr., trainer spl. programs Cook County Dept. Pub. Aid, Chgo., 1963-65; tchr., reading coordinator, supr. instructional programs sci. Chgo. Bd. Edn., 1965—. Community organizer 29th Ward. Mem. Assn. Black Sci. Educators, Nat. Assn. Black Sch. Educators, Assn. Supervision and Curriculum Devel., Internat. Reading Assn., Nat. Assn. Tchr. Edn., Phi Delta Kappa. Democrat. Baptist. Home: 1440 N Massasoit Chicago IL 60651

JEFFERSON, JOHN LARRY, See *Who's Who in America,* 43rd edition.

JEFFERSON, MELVIN DORSEY, fire commissioner of Detroit; b. Phila., July 5, 1922; s. Charles and Leona J.; student Temple U.; m. Helen Cuzzens, July 5, 1947; children—Joyce, Melvin. Pres., Superior Beauty and Barber Supply Co., Inc., Detroit; mem. Detroit Bd. Fire Commrs., 1969-74, fire commr., 1974—, exec. commr. Detroit Fire Dept.; mem. Detroit Bd. Suprs.; dir. Johnson Products. Bd. dirs. Econ. Devel. Corp., Coop. Assistance, Boy Scouts Am., North Detroit Gen. Hosp., United Found.; past mem. Detroit Airport Commn.; past bd. dirs., treas. Detroit Urban League. Served to lt. USAF. Mem. NAACP (life), Detroit C. of C. Club: One Hundred. Episcopalian. Office: 250 W Larned St Detroit MI 48226*

JEFFERSON, NAOMI JEAN, city official; b. Madisonville, Ky., Jan. 18, 1935; d. William H. and Helena (Render) Pritchett; m. Melvin J. Jefferson, Aug. 13, 1981; 1 child, Leslie Cumby. Student U. Ill., 1951, Ill. Sch. Nursing, 1952-55, Ind. U., 1977. Loan officer, adminstr. Housing Conservation Program, City of Gary (Ind.), 1972-77, adminstrv. asst. Mayor's Office of Housing Conservation, 1977-80, asst. dir. planning Dept. Planning and Devel., 1983—, interim dir. Mayor's Office of Conservation, City of Gary, 1984—, rehab. loan officer, counselor, neighborhood organizational coordinator; bd. dirs., v.p. Housing and Neighborhood Devel. Services, Ft. Wayne, Ind., 1980-82. Mem. Mayor's Task Force, 1985; active Rebeccas of St. Timothy Ch., Gary. Recipient Ambridge Mann Social Services merit award, 1978; Employee of Month award, City of Gary, 1979; Summer Youth Program Counselor award City of Gary, 1980. Mem. Nat. Assn. Female Execs., Nat. Assn. Housing and Redevel. Ofcls. (steering com., past sec. Fedn. Neighborhood Block Orgn.). Democrat. Club: Progress (Gary). Office: 824 Broadway 2d Floor Gary IN 46402

JEFFERSON, WAYNE, broadcasting executive; b. Norwalk, Conn., June 12, 1948; s. David and Josephine (Williams) J.; m. Patricia Ann McAllister, Feb. 24, 1979; children—Brandie Michelle, Brian Jordan. B.S., NYU, 1971; A.A.S., Bronx Community Coll., 1968. Sr. auditor Price Waterhouse, N.Y.C., 1971-75, CBS, Inc., N.Y.C., 1975-76, mgr. internat. audit, N.Y.C., 1976-79, dir. internal audit, N.Y.C., 1979-82; dir. fin. and adminstrn. CBS/WBBM Radio, Chgo., 1982—. Home: 2506 Grant St Evanston IL 60201 Office: WBBM Radio 630 N McClurg Ct Chicago IL 60611

JEFFREY, HARRY PALMER, lawyer; b. Dayton, Ohio, Dec. 26, 1901; s. Samuel E. and Grace Sims (Wilson) J.; m. Susan Virginia Gummer, Sept. 11, 1935; B.A., Ohio State U., 1924, J.D., 1926; LL.D. (hon.), Wright State U.,

1980. Bar: Ohio 1926, U.S. Supreme Ct. 1943. Assoc. Vorys, Sater, Seymour & Pease, Columbus, Ohio, 1926-27; assoc. D.W. and A.S. Iddings, Dayton, Ohio, 1930-34; ptnr. Iddings, Jeffrey & Weisman and successor firms (presently Jeffrey, Snell, Rogers & Greenberg), Dayton, 1934—; asst. atty. gen. Ohio, 1932-36; sec. and gen. csl. Foremanship Found., Dayton, 1945-71. Mem. 78th Congress, 3rd Dist. Ohio, 1943-44; trustee Wright State U., 1966-76. Served to 2d lt. USAR, 1927-30. Mem. ABA, Ohio Bar Assn., Dayton Bar Assn. (pres. 1955-56), Am. Coll. Trial Lawyers, Judicature Soc., Acad. Polit. Sci., Order of Coif, Phi Beta Kappa. Republican. Presbyterian. Clubs: Dayton Country, Dayton Bicycle. Home: 2230 S Patterson Blvd Dayton OH 45409 Office: Jeffrey Snell Rogers & Greenberg 2160 Kettering Tower Dayton OH 45423

JEFFRIES, CHARLES DEAN, scientist, educator; b. Rome, Ga., Apr. 9, 1929; s. Andrew Jones and Rachel Lucinda (Ringer) J.; B.S., N. Ga. Coll., 1950; M.S., U. Tenn., 1955, Ph.D., 1958; postgrad. Purdue U., 1955-56; m. Virginia Mae Alford, Sept. 6, 1953. Technician, Ga. Pub. Health Dept., Rome, 1950-51; instr. microbiology Wayne State U., Detroit, 1958-60, asst. prof., 1960-65, assoc. prof., 1965-70, prof., 1970—, acting chmn. dept., 1972-73, assoc. dermatology, 1968—, asst. dean for curriculum affairs, dir. grad. programs Sch. Medicine, 1975-80; guest researcher Center for Disease Control, USPHS, Dept. Health and Human Services, Atlanta, 1980-81. Fulbright-Hays lectr., Cairo, Egypt, 1965-66; examiner bacteriology Bd. Basic Scis. State Mich., 1967-72, v.p., 1970-72; councilor Am. Assn. Basic Sci. Bds., 1970-72; mem. sci. adv. bd. Mich. Cancer Found., 1970-79; mem. Am. Inst. Biol. Scis.-EPA, Adv. Panel, 1979-80. Served with AUS, 1951-53. NIH grantee, 1958-70; NSF grantee, 1959-69. Fellow Am. Acad. Microbiology; mem. Am. Soc. for Microbiology (councilor 1976-78, chmn. med. mycology div. 1977-78), Nat. Registry Microbiologists, Soc. Gen. Microbiology, Soc. Exptl. Biology and Medicine, Internat. Soc. Human and Animal Mycology, Sigma Xi. Contbr. articles to profl. jours. Home: 22513 Raymond Ave St Clair Shores MI 48082 Office: Dept Immunology and Microbiology Sch Medicine Wayne State U 540 E Canfield Detroit MI 48201

JEFFRIES, DOROTHY M., sales and marketing executive consultant; b. Pitts., Jan. 9, 1951; d. Murrell Moore and Frances Elizabeth (Moore) J. B.A. in Classics, Western Res./U., 1973. Counselor, Innisfree, Maple City, Mich., 1973-75; store mgr. Nature Co., Berkeley, Calif., 1975-78; dir. mus. store Mus. Sci. and Industry, Chgo., 1979-83; dir. sales and mktg. Here's Chicago!, 1983-85; ptnr., mktg. dir. City Garden, Chgo., 1985—; cons. Discovery Place, Charlotte, N.C., 1982, Field Mus. Natural History, Chgo., 1984—. Bd. dirs. Passage Theater, Chgo., 1984—. Mem. Women's Advt. Club, Chgo. Assn. Direct Mktg. Presbyterian. Avocations: sewing, cooking, tennis, skating, reading. Home: 807 N Wabash Ave Apt 2F Chicago IL 60611 Office: City Garden 312 S Dearborn St Chicago IL 60604

JEFFRIES, ROBERT WAYNE, clinical psychologist; b. Indpls., Aug. 4, 1949; s. Kenneth Robert and Isabelle Joyce (Stafford) J. Ph.D., Purdue U., 1980. Lic. in psychology, Ind. Behavioral clinician Ind. Boys Sch., Plainfield, 1975-78; clin. psychology intern VA Med. Ctr., Danville, Ill., 1978-80; clin. psychologist Ctr. for Mental Health, Anderson, Ind., 1980—; pvt. practice psychology, Indpls., 1981—. Mem. Am. Psychol. Assn., Ind. Psychol. Assn., Internat. Neuropsychol. Soc., Sigma Chi. Office: 1950 W 86th St Suite 205 Indianapolis IN 46260

JEGHERS, HAROLD JOSEPH, physician, educator; b. Jersey City, Sept. 26, 1904; s. Albert and Matilda (Gerckens) J.; m. Isabel Jean Wile, June 21, 1935; children—Harold Joseph, Dee, Sanderson, Theodore. B.S. in Biology, Rensselaer Poly. Inst., 1928; M.D., Western Res. U., 1932; D.Sc. (hon.), Georgetown U., 1975, Coll. Medicine and Dentistry of N.J., 1976. Med. intern Boston City Hosp., 1932-34; resident in medicine 5th Boston U. Med. Service, 1935-37, vis. physician, 1937-41, physician-in-chief, 1941-46, cons. in medicine, 1946-66; dir. Tufts U. Med. Service, 1969-71; research fellow Evans Meml. Inst. Med. Research, Mass. Meml. Hosp., Boston, 1934-35; asst. prof., then. assoc. prof. medicine Boston U., 1937-46; prof., dir. dept. medicine Georgetown U., Washington, 1946-56, Seton Hall Coll. Medicine (name changed to N.J. Coll. Medicine and Dentistry 1965), Jersey City, 1956-66; prof. medicine Tufts U., Boston, 1966-74; med. dir. St. Vincent Hosp., Worcester, Mass., 1966-78, emeritus and cons. in med. edn., 1978—; prof. med. edn. Northeastern Ohio U. Coll. Medicine, Rootstown, 1977-85, prof. emeritus, 1985—; cons. physician Jersey City Med. Ctr., 1956-58, dir. med. service, 1958-66; cons. in med. edn. St. Elizabeth Hosp. Med. Ctr., Youngstown, Ohio, 1977—, Cleve. Health Scis. Library, Case-Western Res. U. 1979—, Cleve. Med. Library Assn., 1979—. Contbr. numerous articles to profl. jours., chpts. to med. textbooks. Creator Jeghers Med. Index System. Recipient Laetare award Guild of St. Luke, Boston, 1958, Disting. Alumni award Case-Western Res. U., 1974, Centennial Celebration award and citation for disting. achievement in medicine Boston City Hosp., 1964. Fellow ACP (rep. NRC 1950-53); mem. So. Soc. Clin. Research (v.p. 1948-49), Am. Soc. Clin. Research, AMA, Assn. Am. Physicians, Assn. Profs. Medicine, Am. Soc. Clin. Investigation. Roman Catholic. Home: PO Box 1063 Marshfield MA 02050 Office: St Elizabeth Hosp Med Ctr 1044 Belmont Ave Youngstown OH 44501

JELEPIS, LEONARD T(HOMAS), marketing executive; b. Cleve., Sept. 7, 1927; s. Thomas and Mary Katherine (Mavrikis) J.; m. Joanne Stecker, Aug. 21, 1954; children—Thomas, James. B.A. in Mktg., Case Western Res U., 1955. With Monumental Life Ins., Baltimore, 1953-56, Mutual of Omaha Ins., Cleve., 1956-60; ins. broker Chapel Hill Assocs., Cleve., 1960-70; owner Inland Sales, Cleve., 1970—; cons. Water Purification Systems, Cleve., 1980-83; cons. Ohio Paralegal Inst., Cleve., 1970-77. Mem. Kidney Found., Cleve., 1978. Served with USAAF, 1945-47. Republican. Presbyterian. Club: Ripon. Lodges: Masons, Ashlar (Newburgh Heights, Ohio). Address: PO Box 41136 Brecksville OH 44141

JELKS, EDWARD BAKER, archeologist, educator; b. Macon, Ga., Sept. 10, 1922; s. Oliver Robinson and Lucille (Jarrett) J.; B.A., U. Tex., 1948, M.A., 1951, Ph.D., 1965; m. Juliet Elizabeth Christian, Aug. 12, 1944; 1 child, Edward Christian. Archeologist, Smithsonian Instn., 1950-53; research scientist U. Tex., Austin, 1958-65; assoc. prof. anthropology So. Meth. U., Dallas, 1965-68; prof. anthropology Ill. State U., Normal, 1968-84, dir. Midwestern Archeol. Research Center, 1981-84, prof. emeritus, 1984—; mem. Hist. Commn., Pan Am. Inst. Geography and History, 1981—; active archeol. field research Tex., La., Ill., Va., N.Y., Mo., Nfld., Micronesia; mem. Ill. Adv. Council on Hist. Preservation, 1977-78, 82-84. Served with USN, 1942-44. Recipient Ann. award for Oustanding Contbns. to Field of Preservation, Assn. Preservation of Va. Antiquities, 1982; Clarence Webb award for outstanding contbns. to Caddoan archeology; cert. of Merit for Significant Contbn. to Hist. Preservation in Ill., 1980; Smithsonian Instn. research fellow, 1968. Fellow AAAS, Am. Anthropol. Assn.; mem. Soc. Profl. Archeologists (pres., 1976-77, dir. 1979-81), Soc. Hist. Archaeology (pres., 1968-69), Am. Soc. for Conservation Archaeology, Soc. for Am. Archaeology, McLean County Hist. Soc. (pres. 1983-85), Assn. Field Archaeology, Archaeol. Inst. Am., Delta Chi. Co-author: Handbook of Texas Archeology, 1954; Trick Taking Potential, 1974; The Joachim De Brum House, Likiep, Marshall Islands, 1978; author: Archaeological Explorations at Signal Hill, Newfoundland, 1973; co-author: Jonas Short and Coral Snake Mounds, 1980. Home: 605 N School St Normal IL 61761 Office: 105 Edwards Hall Ill State U Normal IL 61761

JELLISON, JAMES LOGAN, II, marketing executive; b. Chgo., June 3, 1922; s. James Logan and Ethel (Reynolds) J.; Ph.B., DePaul U., Chgo., 1943; B.M.E., Northwestern U., 1948; M.B.A., U. Louisville, 1959; m. Charlotte Jean Scott, Oct. 20, 1951; children—James Logan, Jeanene Lynn, Jennifer Lee. Mgr. mktg. research Gen. Electric Co., Holland, Mich., 1961—. State and County Conv. del. Republican Party; bd. dirs. Ottawa County ARC; chmn. bd. govs. Fountain St. Ch., Grand Rapids, Mich. Served to 1st lt. AUS, 1943-46, ETO. Decorated Bronze Star, Purple Heart; registered profl. engr. Mem. Am. Mktg. Assn., Am. Legion, Elfun Soc., Kappa Sigma. Republican. Home: 729 Lugers Rd Holland MI 49423 Office: 570 E 16th St Holland MI 49423

JELLISON, RICHARD MARION, history educator; b. Muncie, Ind., Dec. 26, 1924; s. Carl R. and Leora Melvina (Folkner) J.; B.S., Ball State U., 1948; A.M., Ind. U., 1949, Ph.D., 1953; m. Kathleen Elizabeth Frick, May 5, 1945; children—Richard G., Stephanie L., Leslie N. Instr. history Ind. U., 1952-56; instr. Mich. State U., 1956-58; asso. prof. Eastern Ill. U., 1958-62; prof. Miami U., Oxford, Ohio, 1962—, chmn. dept. history, 1971—; lectr. U. Berlin, 1966, U. Siena, Italy, 1968, Budapest, Hungary, 1974. Served with U.S. Navy, 1942-44. Colonial Williamsburg summer research fellow, 1958-62. Mem. Am. Hist. Assn., Inst. Early Am. Culture, Am. Assn. History Medicine, Orgn. Am. Historians, Internat. Soc. History Medicine, Ohio, Ind., S.C. hist. socs., AAUP (pres. Miami U. chpt. 1967). Author: Society, Freedom & Conscience: The American Revolution in Virginia, Massachusetts and New York, 1976. Contbr. articles to profl. jours. Home: 6 Chestnut Hill Oxford OH 45056 Office: History Department Miami University Oxford OH 45056

JEN, PHILIP HUNG SUN, science educator, researcher; b. Hung, Hunan, China, Jan. 11, 1944; came to U.S., 1969, naturalized, 1980; m. Betty Yu, Feb. 20, 1971. M.A., Washington U., St. Louis, 1971, Ph.D., 1974. Asst. prof. U. Mo., Columbia, 1975-80, assoc. prof., 1980-83, prof., 1984—; vis. prof. Frankfurt U., W. Ger., 1979. Grantee NSF, 1978-84, NIH, 1980-84. Mem. Soc. Neuroscis., Acoustic Soc. Am., Am. Soc. Zoologists, Internat. Soc. Neuroethology, Northwest Acad. Scis. Avocation: fishing. Office: U Mo 208 Lefevre Hall Columbia MO 65122

JENEFSKY, JACK, wholesale executive; b. Dayton, Ohio, Oct. 27, 1919; s. David and Anna (Saeks) J.; B.S. in Bus. Adminstrn., Ohio State U., 1941; postgrad. Harvard Bus. Sch., 1943; M.A. in Econs., U. Dayton, 1948; m. Beverly J. Mueller, Feb. 23, 1962; 1 dau., Anna Elizabeth; 1 stepdau., Cathryn Jean Mueller. Surplus broker, Dayton, 1946-48; sales rep. Remington Rand-Univac, Dayton, 1949-56, mgr. AF account, 1957-59, br. mgr. Dayton, 1960-61, regional mktg. cons. Midwest region, Dayton, 1962-63; pres. Bowman Supply Co., Dayton, 1963—. Selection adv. bd. Air Force Acad., 3d congl. dist., chmn., 1974-82; chmn. 3d. dist. screening bds. Mil. Acad., 1976-82; coordinator Great Lakes region, res. assistance program CAP, 1970-73. Served from pvt. to capt. USAAF, 1942-46; CBI; maj. USAF, 1951-53; col Res. Mem. Air Force Assn. (comdr. Ohio wing 1957-58, 58-59), Res. Officers Assn. (pres. Ohio dept. 1956-57, nat. council 1957-58, chmn. research and devel. com. 1961-62), Dayton Area C. of C. (chmn. spl. events com. 1970-72, chmn. research com. on mil. affairs 1983—), Miami Valley Mil. Affairs Assn. (trustee 1985—), Ohio State U. Alumni Assn. (pres. Montgomery County, Ohio, 1959-60), Nat. Sojourners (pres. Dayton 1961-62). Jewish. Club: Harvard Bus. Sch. Dayton (pres. 1961-62). Lodge: Lions. Home: 136 Briar Heath Circle Dayton OH 45415 Office: c/o Bowman Supply Co PO Box 1404 Dayton OH 45401

JENISON, EDWARD HALSEY (NED), newspaper publisher, editor; b. Paris, Ill., Jan. 6, 1932; s. Edward Halsey and Barbara (Weinbrugh) J.; m. Margaret Danner, June 18, 1954; children—Kevin, James, Stephen. B.A. in Journalism, U. Ill., 1954. Farm editor Champaign-Urbana Courier, Urbana, Ill., 1956-58; editorial staff Paris Beacon-News, Ill., 1958—, assoc. pub., gen. mgr., 1980—. Trustee Paris Community Hosp., 1981—; mem. United Way, Paris Community YMCA, Edgar County Children's Home, 1960—. Served with U.S. Army, 1954-56. Mem. Inland Daily Press Assn., Sigma Delta Chi, Paris C. of C., Mental Health Assn. (bd. dirs., pres. 1968-1977). Republican. Methodist. Avocations: sailing, camping. Office: Paris Beacon Publishing Co 218 N Main St Paris IL 61944

JENKINS, GEORGE HENRY, photographer, educator; b. Shanghai, China, Oct. 24, 1929 (parents Am. citizens); s. Clarence O. and Efransinia M. (Pomorenkoff) J.; grad. N.Y. Inst. Photography, 1952; student Purdue U., 1952-55; student Ind. U., 1955-58, B.B.A., Ind. No. U., 1972; M.Ed., Wayne State U., 1976, postgrad., 1976—; Ph.D., Columbia Pacific U., 1984; m. Madge Marie Vickroy, Aug. 19, 1967. Photographer, Ft. Wayne (Ind.) Jour.-Gazette, 1952-55; computer programer Gen. Electric Co., Ft. Wayne, 1955-61; data processing mgr. Columbia Record Club subs. CBS, Terre Haute, Ind., 1961-63; adminstrv. coordinator Capitol Record Club, Scranton, Pa. and Toronto, Ont., Can., 1963-64; mktg. systems analyst Xerox Corp., Detroit, 1964-66; dir. systems and data processing Nicholson File Co., Anderson, Ind., 1966-69; hosp. adminstr. Wayne County Gen. Hosp., Eloise, Mich., 1969-78; asst. prof. bus. Western Washington U., Bellingham, 1978-80; asst. prof. Lima (Ohio) Tech. Coll., 1980-83; assoc. prof. Findlay (Ohio) Coll., 1983—; freelance photographer, 1969—, writer/producer, 1984—. Chmn. supervisory bd. Eloise Credit Union, 1972-76. Served with USAF, 1948-52. Cert. data processor, data educator, systems profl. Mem. Photog. Soc. Gt. Britian, Photog. Soc. Am., Assn. System Mgmt., Am. Prodn. and Inventory Control Soc., Human Factors Soc., Am. Inst. Indsl. Engrs., Data Processing Mgmt. Assn. of Lima (pres.). Presbyterian. Clubs: 8-16 Cine, Detroit Yacht Lodge: Elks. (Van Wert, Ohio). Home: 710 W Main St Cairo OH 45820 Office: Findlay Coll Findlay OH 45840

JENKINS, GEORGE L., lawyer, fast food company exectuve; b. Wheeling, W.Va., Jan. 30, 1940; s. George Addison and Mildred Irene (Liggett) J. A.B. magna cum laude, Kent State U., 1963; J.D. with honors, U. Mich., 1966. Bar: Ohio 1966. Assoc., Vorys, Sater, Seymour & Pease, Columbus, Ohio, 1966-71, ptnr., 1975—; first asst. atty. gen. State of Ohio, Columbus, 1971-75; dir. Fleagane Enterprises, Inc., Columbus, 1977—, C'est Cheese, Inc., 1980, Jet Sales, Inc., 1984—. Bd. dirs. Columbus Urban Environ. Workshop, 1968-70. Mem. ABA, Ohio State Bar Assn., Columbus Bar Assn. (chmn. various coms. 1966—). Democrat. Methodist. Club: Columbus Athletic. Avocations: racquetball; tennis; jogging; travel; reading; Office: Vorys Sater Seymour & Pease 52 E Gay St Columbus OH 43215

JENKINS, JOHN ANTHONY, lawyer; b. Cin., Apr. 11, 1926; s. John A. and Norma S. (Snyder) J.; m. Patricia Stone, Dec. 20, 1952; children—Julie Anne, John A. B.E.E., Ohio State U., 1951; LL.D., 1953. Bar: Ohio 1954. Assoc. Knepper, White, Richards & Miller, Columbus, 1954-58, ptnr., 1958—; mem. mgmt. com. Arter & Hadden, Cleve., 1984—; dir. Gen. Exploration Co., Dallas, 1972-80; pres. Mummy Mountain Devel. Co., Phoenix, 1978—; gen. ptnr. Columbus Lasher P/S, Ohio, 1976—; gen. ptnr. Indian Bend Ltd. P/S, Phoenix, 1978—. Contbr. articles to profl. jours. Trustee Citizens Research, Inc., Columbus, 1960-72. Served with U.S. Army, 1944-46. Fellow ABA (chmn. various coms. 1960—); mem. Ohio State Bar Assn. (chmn. various coms.), Columbus Bar Assn. (chmn. various coms.), Beta Theta Pi (pres. bldg. assn. Columbus 1972-76). Republican. Clubs: Athletic, Muirfield Country, Scioto Country, The Golf. Lodges: Masons, Shriners. Home: 2303 Yorkshire Rd Columbus 43221

JENKINS, ROYAL GREGORY, manufacturing executive; b. Springville, Utah, Dec. 11, 1936; s. Chester W. and Sarah E. (Finch) J.; m. Donna Jeanne Jones, Aug. 3, 1957; children—Brad, Kent. B.S. in Engring., San Jose State U., 1959; M.B.A., U. Santa Clara, 1968. Registered profl. engr., Calif. Indsl. engr. Lockheed Corp., Sunnyvale, Calif., 1959-64; controller ICORE Industries, Sunnyvale, 1964-68; div. v.p. fin. Dart Industries, Los Angeles, 1968-74; dir. planning, div. v.p. Avery Label Group, Avery Internat., Los Angeles, 1974-81, group v.p. Materials Group, Painesville, Ohio, 1981—. Republican. Avocations: golf, racquetball. Office: Avery Internat 250 Chester St Painesville OH 44077

JENKINS, WALTER KIMBALL, oil company executive; b. Council Bluffs, Iowa, July 25, 1929; s. Walter Lot and Ruth Elizabeth (Kimball) J.; B.S. in Chem. Engring., Iowa State U., 1951; M.B.A., State U. N.Y. at Buffalo, 1960; m. Mary Elizabeth Erler, July 25, 1953; children—Donald, Cindy, Nancy, Pat. Ops. supt. U.S. Indsl. Chem. Co., Tuscola, Ill., 1958-64; acting plant mgr. Apple River Chem. Co., East Dubuque, Ill., 1964-67; ops. mgr. Atlantic Richfield Co., Fort Madison, Iowa, 1967-69; project mgr. Procon Inc., gen. contractor petroleum refineries, Des Plaines, Ill., 1970-72; supervising engr. Union Oil Co., Lemont, Ill., 1972—. Co-chmn. steering com. Douglas County Hosp., 1964; active Boy Scouts Am. Bd. dirs. S.E. Iowa Community Coll.; pres Naperville Council of Chs., 1978. Served as 1st lt. Signal Corps., AUS, 1951-53. Registered profl. engr., Ill. Mem. Tuscola C. of C. (pres. 1963), Am. Inst. Chem. Engrs. (chmn. Joliet sect. 1976). Presbyn. (dir. ch.) Rotarian. Home: 1156 Elizabeth Ave Naperville IL 60540 Office: Union Oil Refinery Lemont IL 60439

JENKINS, WILLIAM ATWELL, educational administrator, educator; b. Scranton, Pa., Nov. 18, 1922; s. William Arthur and Thelma Marie (Atwell) J.; m. Gloria Hyam, Mar. 12, 1944 (div. 1974); m. Alice Wyne Carney, Nov. 1, 1974. B.S., NYU, 1948; M.S., U. Ill., 1949, Ph.D., 1954. Mem. faculty U. Wis.-Milw., 1953-70, assoc. dean, dir. tchr. edn. and grad. studies, 1963-70; dean sch. edn. Portland State U., Oreg., 1970-74; acad. v.p. Fla. Internat. U., Miami, 1974-78; acad. vice chancellor U. Colo., Denver, 1978-80; chancellor U. Mich.-Dearborn, 1980—. Author numerous textbooks in reading and lang. Editor: Elementary English, 1963-70. Contbr. articles to profl. jours. Mem. Portland Devel. Commn., 1972-73, chmn., 1973-74. Served to 1st lt. U.S. Army, 1943-46, ETO, PTO. Mem. Nat. Council Tchrs. English (pres. 1968-69, Disting. Service award 1976), Wis. Council Tchrs. English (pres. 1966-67, Chisolm award 1970), Kappa Delta Pi, Phi Kappa Phi, Phi Delta Kappa, Pi Lambda Theta. Avocations: reading, writing, tennis, model railroads. Home: 551 Golfcrest Dr Dearborn MI 48124 Office: U Mich 4901 Evergreen Rd Dearborn MI 48129

JENKINS, WILLIAM WESLEY, retired pharmaceutical company executive; b. Chgo., Oct. 22, 1917; s. Carl Huber and Hermine Lucy (Schaub) J.; m. Elizabeth Ann Tucker, Mar. 8, 1952; children—Elizabeth, John, Douglas. A.B., DePauw U., 1939; M.S., Loyola U., Chgo., 1942; Ph.D., Northwestern U., 1950. With G.D. Searle & Co., Skokie, Ill., 1954-83, dir. devel., 1969-73, dir. product affairs, 1973-79, dir. preclin. ops., 1979-83, ret. 1983; cons. in field. Patentee in field. Author tech. papers. Served to lt. USNR, 1943-46. Standard Oil Co. of Ind. fellow 1949. Mem. Am. Chem. Soc. (emeritus, medicinal sect., Chgo. sect.), Am. Pharm. Soc., Acad. Pharm. Sci., Sigma Xi, Phi Lambda Upsilon, Sigma Chi. Episcopalian. Club: Wilmette Golf (Ill.). Avocations: golf, fishing, travel, woodworking. Home: 623 Washington Ave Wilmette IL 60091

JENKS, DOWNING BLAND, railroad executive; b. Portland, Oreg., Aug. 16, 1915; s. Charles O. and Della (Downing) J.; B.S., Yale U., 1937; m. Helen Pelton, Feb. 2, 1985; children—Downing B., Nancy Randolph. Chainman Spokane Portland & Seattle Ry., Portland, 1934-35; asst., engr. corps Pa. R.R., N.Y. div., 1937-38; successively roadmaster, div. engr., trainmaster various divs. G.N. Ry., 1938-47, div. supt., Spokane, Wash., 1947-48; gen. mgr. C. & E.I. R.R., 1949-50; asst. v.p. ops. Rock Island Lines, Chgo., 1950-51, v.p. ops., 1951-53, exec. v.p., dir., 1953-55, pres., 1956-61; pres. M.P.R.R., 1961-71, chmn., 1972-83, also dir.; chmn., chief exec. officer, dir. Mo. Pacific Corp., 1971-83; dir. Bankers Life Co., Centerre Bancorp., Union Pacific Corp. Life trustee Northwestern U.; nat. pres. Boy Scouts Am., 1977-80. Served from 1st lt. to lt. col. 704th Ry. Grand Div., AUS, 1942-45; ETO, MTO. Mem. Tau Beta Pi. Home: 4 Greenbriar Saint Louis MO 63124 Office: 9900 Clayton Rd Saint Louis MO 63124

JENKS, JEFFREY, state official; b. Detroit, Mar. 21, 1939; s. Bernard H. Jenks and Dorothy J. (Weitzman) Koploy; m. Natividad Lim, Jan. 10, 1971. Student U. Mich., 1957-60; B.A., Eastern Mich. U., 1962; postgrad. Ateneo de Manila, 1963, Wayne State U., 1966-69. Asst. to dean edn. Wayne State U., Detroit, 1966-67, asst. dir. research and adminstrn., 1967-69; coordinator program devel. Mich. Dept. Civil Rights, Detroit, 1969-72, dir. research, 1972—; cons. on aging; travel cons. Travel Counselors, Bloomfield Hills, Mich., 1981—. Mng. editor Jour. of Intergroup Relations, 1983—. Mem. exec. com. Mich. unit Am. Jewish Com., 1981—; v.p. Interfaith Ctrs. for Racial Justice, Detroit, 1979—; mem. housing com. New Detroit, Inc., 1979—. Asian Soc. grantee, 1968. Mem. Am. Soc. Pub. Adminstrn. (bd. dirs. 1978-83), Nat. Assn. Human Rights (bd. dirs. 1984—), Urban and Regional Info. Systems, Mich. Library Consortium (trustee 1982—), Mich. Assn. Human Rights Workers (v.p. 1983-85). Democrat. Avocation: travelling. Home: 13361 Ludlow St Huntington Woods MI 48070 Office: Mich Dept Civil Rights 1200 6th St Detroit MI 48070

JENNER, ALBERT ERNEST, JR., lawyer; b. Chgo., June 20, 1907; s. Albert Ernest and Elizabeth (Owens) J.; m. Nadine Newbill, Mar. 19, 1932; 1 dau., Cynthia Lee; J.D., U. Ill., 1930; LL.D., John Marshall Law Sch., 1952, Northwestern U., 1975, Columbia Coll., 1974, U. Notre Dame, 1975, William B. Mitchell Sch. Law, 1976, U. Mich., 1976; Bar: Ill. 1930. Mem. firm Jenner & Block, Chgo., 1933—; prof. law Northwestern U., 1952-53; dir., mem. exec. com. Gen. Dynamics Corp.; spl. asst. to atty. gen. Ill., 1956-68 83—; chmn. U.S. Supreme Ct. Adv. Com. on Fed. Rules of Evidence, 1965-75; chmn. Ill. Commn. on Uniform State Laws, 1951-81; mem. Nat. Conf. Commn. on Uniform State Laws in U.S., pres., 1969-71; mem. U.S. Supreme Ct. Adv. Com. Fed. Civil Rules, 1960-70; mem. Nat. Conf. Bar Assn. Pres. U.S., pres., 1952-53; mem. U.S. Presdl. Loyalty Rev. Bd., 1952-53; mem. council U. Ill. Law Forum, 1948-51; sr. counsel Presdl. Commn. to Investigate the Assassination Pres. Kennedy (Warren Commn.), 1964; law mem. Ill. Bd. Examiners Accountancy, 1948-51; mem. Pres.'s Nat. Commn. on Causes and Prevention of Violence in U.S. (Eisenhower Commn.), 1968-69; chief spl. counsel to minority Ho. of Reps. Judiciary Com. Conducting Impeachment Inquiry Pres. Nixon, 1974. Bd. dirs. Center for Study Democratic Instns., from 1975; trustee Fund for Republic, recipient Robert Maynard Hutchins Disting. Service award, 1976; sec. U.S. Navy Found., from 1977; bd. dirs. or trustee Evanston Glenbrook Hosp., Columbus Coll., Ill. Arthritis Found., Cerebral Palsy Found., Northwestern U. Library Found. Recipient Disting. Service award for outstanding public service Chgo. and Ill. Jr. chambers commerce, 1939, U. Ill. Disting. Alumnus award, 1962, Disting. Civic Achievement award Am. Jewish Com., 1973, Disting. Citizens award N.Y. U., 1975; named Chicagoan of Yr., Chgo. Press Club, 1975, laureate Lincoln Acad. of Ill. Fellow Am. Coll. Trial Lawyers (bd. regents, pres. 1958), Internat. Acad. Trial Lawyers; mem. Ill. Soc. Trial Lawyers, Nat. Assn. Def. Lawyers in Criminal Cases, ABA (Ill. state del. ho. of dels. 1948-75, state del. 1975-78, chmn. standing com. on fed. judiciary 1965-68, chmn. sect. on individual rights and responsibilities 1973-74, mem. council, sect. on legal edn. 1967-75, bd. govs. 1977-80), Ill. Bar Assn. (pres. 1949-50), Chgo. Bar Assn. (sec. 1947-49), Am. Judicature Soc. (pres. 1958, recipient Herbert Harley award 1981), Am. Inst. Jud. Adminstrn., Bar Assn. U.S. Ct. Appeals (gov.), Am. Law Inst., ACLU (dir. 1976), Order of Coif, Alpha Chi Rho, Phi Delta Phi. Clubs: Skokie Country, Law, Legal, Chgo. Press, Tavern, Chicago. Author, co-author: Ill. Civil Practice, Annotated; Smith-Hurd Ill., Annotated Statutes, 1934-80, 8 vols. on Pleading and Practice Procedure. Mem. permanent editorial bd. Uniform Commercial Code. Contbr. articles to law revs., legal publs. Office: One IBM Plaza Chicago IL 60611

JENNER, WILLIAM ALEXANDER, meteorologist; b. Indianola, Iowa, Nov. 10, 1915; s. Edwin Alexander and Elizabeth May (Brown) J.; A.B., Central Meth. Coll., Mo., 1938; certificate meteorology U. Chgo., 1943; M.Ed., U. Mo., 1947; postgrad. Am. U., 1951-58; m. Jean Norden, Sept. 1, 1946; children—Carol Beth, Paul William, Susan Lynn. Instr. U. Mo., 1946-47; research meteorologist U.S. Weather Bur., Chgo., 1947-49; staff Hdqrs. Air Weather Service, Andrews AFB, Md., 1949-58, Scott AFB, Ill., 1958-84, dir. tng., 1960-84. Mem. O'Fallon (Ill.) Twp. High Sch. Bd. Edn., 1962—, sec., 1964-71, pres., 1971-83; mem. O'Fallon Planning Commn., 1973-84, sec., 1979-81, sub-div. chmn., 1978-84; alderman City of O'Fallon, 1984—. Served with AUS, 1942-46. Recipient Disting. Service award O'Fallon PTA, 1968; Exceptional Civilian Service award Dept. Air Force, 1984; Jenmer Award established by Air Weather Service, 1984. Mem. Am. Psychol. Assn., Wilson Ornithological Soc., Am. Philatelic Soc., Am. Philatelic Congress, Am. Meteorol. Soc., AAAS, Nat. Soc. Study Edn., Am. Legion, Phi Delta Kappa, Psi Chi. Clubs: Masons, Shriners, O'Fallon Sportsmen's, Toastmasters Internat. Home: 307 Alma St O'Fallon IL 62269

JENNINGS, EDWARD HARRINGTON, university president; b. Mpls., Feb. 18, 1937; s. Edward G. and Ruth (Harrington) J.; B.S., U. N.C., 1959; M.B.A., Western Res. U., 1963; Ph.D. (NDEA Title IV fellow), U. Mich., 1969; m. Mary Eleanor Winget, Nov. 4, 1958; children—William Francis, Steven Winget. With Deering Milliken Service Corp., 1959-61, Merck & Co., 1963-65; acad. positions at various instns., 1969-74; prof. fin. U. Iowa, 1974-75, asst. dean faculties, dir. summer sessions, 1975-76, prof. fin., 1976-79, v.p. for fin. and univ. services, 1976-79; pres. U. Wyo., Laramie, 1979-81; pres. Ohio State U., Columbus, 1981—; dir., Ohio Bell, BancOne, Inc.; bd. dirs. Columbus C. of C. Club: Rotary (Columbus). Author: (with R.A. Stevenson) Fundamentals of Investments, 1976. Office: Office of Pres Ohio State U Columbus OH 43210

JENNINGS, JAMES BLANDFORD, history educator; b. Ironwood, Mich., Jan. 23, 1922; s. Blandford and Anne (Heise) J.; B.E., Ill. State U., 1947, M.Ed., 1948; postgrad. U. Wis., 1950-51, Washington U., 1956, Ripon Coll., 1961, Northwestern U., 1965, Southern Ill. U., Edwardsville, 1970, 71. Instr. polit. sci. and econs. Mc Kendree Coll., Lebanon, Ill., 1948-49; tchr. social studies high sch., Pleasant Hope, Mo., 1950; tchr. history Howe (Ind.) Mil. Sch., 1951-52; tchr. social studies Center Twp. Sch., LaPorte, Ind., 1952-54; tchr. history East High Sch., Aurora, Ill., 1954-67, Maine Twp. High Sch. West, Des Plaines, Ill., 1967-69; instr. history State Community Coll. East St. Louis, 1969—, chmn. humanities, 1972-75; mem. faculty adv. com. Ill. Bd. Higher Edn., 1980-83. Co-chmn. Search for the Am. Dream in East St. Louis, 1976. Served with AUS, 1943-45. Decorated Bronze Star, Purple Heart with 2 oak leaf clusters. Mem. Nat. Forensic League (dist. chmn. 1962-65), Aurora Edn. Assn. (pres. 1961-62), NEA, Ill. Community Coll. Faculty Assn. (editor newsletter 1981-84, treas. 1984—), Am. Hist. Assn., Ill. Hist. Assn., Abraham Lincoln Assn., AAUP, Pi Kappa Delta, Pi Gamma Mu. Home: 7746 Rannells Maplewood MO 63143 Office: 601 James R Thompson Blvd East St Louis IL 62201

JENNINGS, JOE, building trades educator; b. Rosharon, Tex., Sept. 27, 1928; s. Henry and Violet Catherine J.; m. Vernetta Marie Battle, Dec. 14, 1956 (div.); 1 dau., Joetta Renae. Student Tex. So. U., 1946-48, Prairie View A&M U., 1948-50, Pittsburg (Kans.) State U., 1971-73. Carpenter, cabinet maker, Houston, 1950-60; tchr. Jackson High Sch., Corsicana, Tex., 1960-65; bldg. trades tchr. Gary Job Corp, San Marcos, Tex., 1968-70; instr. bldg. trades Sumner High Sch., Kansas City, Kans., 1970-73; bldg. trades instr. Area Vocat. Tech. Sch., Kansas City, 1973—. Served with U.S. Army, 1950-52. Recipient Outstanding Tchr. award Gary Job Corp, 1969; Frontiers Internat. award, 1983. Mem. NEA, Am. Vocat. Assn., Kans. Indsl. Edn. Assn., Vocat. Indsl. Clubs Am. Methodist. Clubs: Jayhawk Frontiers (Kansas City, Kans.). Home: 616 Stewart St PO Box 1131 Kansas City KS 66101 Office: 2220 N 59th St Kansas City KS 66106

JENNINGS, LEE W., accounting firm executive; m. Kosciusko, Miss., Dec. 12, 1928; s. Samuel T. and Cora E. (Bell) J.; m. Billye Lee; 1 son, Darrell Lee. Student, Tex. Christian U., 1957; B.S. in Acctg., U. Houston, 1957-59, M.B.A., 1962. C.P.A. Cons., Peat, Marwick, Mitchell & Co., Dallas, 1963-65, Houston, 1965-67, partner-in-charge mgmt. cons., Houston/Southwest region, 1967-71, Chgo., 1971-77, mng. partner, 1977—, mem. operating com., security clearance com. Sustaining fellow Art Inst. Chgo.; bd. dirs., mem. exec. com. Lyric Opera Chgo.; bd. dirs. Protestant Found. Greater Chgo.; trustee, mem. fin. com. Michael Reese Hosp. and Med. Center; trustee Chgo. Symphony Orch.; assoc. bd. dirs. United Charities, Chgo.; mem. exec. com. Ill. br. U.S. Olympic Com.; mem. bd. assocs. Chgo. Theol. Sem.; chief crusader Chgo. com. Crusade of Mercy; mem. communications com., comml. arbitration com. Chgo. Econ. Devel. Commn.; sec.-treas. Center Performing Arts, Chgo.; mem. Chgo. Crime Commn. Served with USAF, 1951-55. Recipient Disting. Leadership award Pace Inst., Chgo., 1983; awards Crusade of Mercy, 1977-83. Mem. Am. Inst. C.P.A.s, Ill. Soc. C.P.A.s, Chgo. Assn. Commerce and Industry (dir.), Chgo. Council on Fgn. Relations. Clubs: Econ., Comml., Chicago, Tavern, Racquet (Chgo.); Hundred of Cook County; Assocs. Northwestern U.; Bull Valley Hunt (Woodstock, Ill.); Glenview (Golf, Ill.); Old Elm (Ft. Sheridan, Ill.); Country of Fla. (Golf). Home: 1110 N Lake Shore Dr Chicago IL 60611 Office: Peat Marwick Mitchell & Co 303 E Wacker Dr Chicago IL 60601

JENNINGS, MARK ALLAN, safety professional; b. Lawrenceville, Ill., Sept. 7, 1956; s. Veris Earl and Helen Ruth (Barnett) J.; B.A. in Biology, Eastern Ill. U., 1979; M.S. in Edn., Southern Ill. U., 1984. Comml. underwriter Golden Rule Ins. Co., Lawrenceville, 1982-85; safety and workmans compensation Snap-On Tools Corp., Mt. Carmel, Ill., 1985—. Author: Industrial Health Underwriting of Oil Refinery Employees, 1984. Vol. Am. Nat. Red. Cross, Vincennes, Ind., Mem. Am. Soc. Safety Engrs., Phi Kappa Phi. Lodge: Elks. Home: RR 1 Box 356 Lawrenceville IL 62439 Office: Snap-On Tools Corp 1200 W 7th Ave Mount Carmel IL 62863

JENNINGS, MYRA FERN, savings and loan executive; b. Alton, Ill., Mar. 15, 1941; d. Henry Martin and A. Mae (Nixon) J. A.Acctg., So. Ill. U., 1975, B.S. in Bus. Adminstrn.-Acctg., 1978; grad. diploma Inst. Fin. Edn., 1972 C.P.A., Ill. Teller Citizens Savs. and Loan Assn., East Alton, Ill., 1959-70, treas., 1970—, head acctg. dept., 1969—, dir., 1977—; instr. Lewis and Clark Coll., Godfrey Inst. Fin. Edn. Organist 1st United Meth. Ch., East Alton, 1976—. Mem. Fin. Mgrs. Soc., Women in Savs. Assn. State of Ill., Am. Inst. C.P.A.s, Ill. Soc. C.P.A.s, Fin. Inst. Edn. (pres. chpt. 1981-84). Republican. Home: 620 Valley Dr East Alton IL 62024 Office: 700 Berkshire Blvd East Alton IL 62024

JENNINGS, VIVIEN LEE, bookstore management and licensing organization executive; b. Little Rock, Ark., Mar. 7, 1945; d. Loron and Mildred Louise (Wright) Bolen; m. Richard Walker Jennings, Sept. 1, 1967; children—Geoffrey, Alison. B.A., Rhodes Coll., Memphis, 1967. Women's fiction cons. Ballantine Books, Inc., N.Y., 1981-82, Berkeley Pub. Group, N.Y., 1982-83; pres. Rainy Day Books, Inc., Fairway, Kans., 1975—. Editor: nat. weekly bus. letter Boy Meets Girl. Exec. editor serialized women's fiction project Day Dreams, 1984. Author: The Romance Wars. Contbr. articles to profl. publs. Featured on nat. pub. radio and nat. tv programs. Mem. Greater Kansas City Booksellers Assn., Romance Writers Am., Inc. (bd. dirs.). Episcopalian. Club: Carriage (Kansas City). Home: 5413 Norwood Rd Fairway KS 66205 Office: Rainy Day Books Inc 2812 W 53d St Fairway KS 66205

JENNINGS, WILLIAM GEORGE, dentist; b. Detroit, Aug. 17, 1946; s. George Leo and Geraldine Mary (Tholl) J. D.D.S., U. Mich., 1971. Lic. dentist, Mich., Va. Gen. practice dentistry, Grosse Pointe, Mich., 1973-76; pres. Jennings Dental Assocs., P.C., Grosse Pointe, 1976—; adv. bd. Blue-Cross/Blue Shield, Detroit, 1984—; mem. staff Cottage Hosp., Grosse Pointe Farms, 1983—. Adviser Grosse Pointe Schs.-Vocat. Edn., 1976—; mem. Grosse Pointe Community Health Council, 1980-82. Served to lt. USN, 1971-73. Recipient Vol. award Grosse Pointe Schs., 1983. Mem. Am. Acad. of Dental Practice Adminstrn., ADA, Am. Soc. Dentistry for Children, Mich. Dental Assn. (trustee 1985—), Detroit Dist. Dental Soc. (pres. 1985, bd. dirs. 1976—), Eastern Dental Soc. (pres. 1979, bd. mem. 1976-80), Detroit Clinic Club, Francis B. Vedder Crown and Bridge Soc., Pierre Fauchard Acad., Delta Sigma Delta. Republican. Roman Catholic. Club: Grosse Pointe Yacht (bd. mem. 1982-83). Avocations: sailing; scuba diving; hockey. Home: 561 Hollywood Grosse Pointe Woods MI 48236 Office: Jennings Dental Assocs PC 383 Fisher Rd Grosse Pointe MI 48230

JENS, ARTHUR MARX, JR., insurance company executive; b. Winfield, Ill., June 26, 1912; s. Arthur M. and Jeanette Elizabeth (Vinton) J.; m. Elizabeth Lee Shafer, Aug. 14, 1937; children—Timothy Vinton, Christopher Edward, Jeffrey Arthur. B.S., Northwestern U., 1934; J.D., Kent Coll. Law, Ill. Inst. Tech., 1939. Bar: Ill. 1939. Ins. underwriter, claim mgr. Continental Casualty Co. and Royal Globe Group, Chgo., 1934-39; sec., asst. treas. TWA, Kansas City, Mo., 1939-47; v.p., pres., chmn. bd. Fred S. James & Co. Inc., Chgo., 1947-76, hon. chmn. bd.; dir. Airline Service Corp. and all TWA subs., Comml. Resources Corp.; founder, dir. 6 First Security Banks of DuPage County; chmn. Jenson Corp. Life gov. Central DuPage Hosp.; mem. Ill. Gov.'s Panel on Racing. Mem. Ill. State Bar Assn., ABA, Nat. Assn. Ins. Agts. and Brokers (dir.). Republican. Presbyterian. Clubs: Chgo. Golf (past pres.), Mid-Day (trustee), Chgo. Club Room 19; Thunderbird Country (Palm Springs, Calif.). Contbr. articles to air transp. and ins. journs. Home: 22 W 210 Stanton Rd Glen Ellyn IL 60137 Office: 230 W Monroe St Chicago IL 60606

JENS, ELIZABETH LEE SHAFER (MRS. ARTHUR M. JENS, JR.), civic worker; b. Monroe, Mich., Jan. 25, 1915; d. Frank Lee and Mary (Bogard) Shafer; student Kalamazoo Coll., 1932-34, U. Wis., summer 1935; B.S., Northwestern U., 1936; postgrad. Wheaton Coll., summer 1965; L.P.N., Triton Coll., 1969; m. Arthur M. Jens, Jr., Aug. 14, 1937; children—Timothy V., Christopher E., Jeffrey A. Gray Lady, Hines, (Ill.) Hosp., 1948-49, 51-53; vol. Elgin (Ill.) State Hosp., 1958-72; writer Newsletter Vol. Planning Council, 1960-62; mem. Family Service Assn. Du Page County; vol. coordinator, chmn. bd. dirs., treas. Thursday Evening Club; social club for recovering mental patients Du Page County, 1966—; vol. FISH orgn., 1973-84. Bd. dirs. Du Page County Mental Health Soc., 1962-68, sec., 1963-64, 65-68, chmn. forgotten patient com., 1963-68, chmn. new projects, 1965-68; co-chmn. Glen Ellyn unit Central Du Page Hosp. Assn. Women's Aux., 1959-60; bd. dirs. chmn. com. on pesticides, Ill. Audubon Soc., 1963-73; mem. Ill. Pesticide Control Com., 1963-73, Citizens Com. Dutch Elm Disease, Glen Ellyn, 1960; bd. dirs. Natural Resources Council Ill., 1961-67, sec., 1961-64; bd. dirs. Du Page Art League, 1958-68, chmn. bd., 1961-63, chmn. new bldg. com., 1968-75; bd. dirs. mem. planning com., publicity chmn. Du Page Fine Arts Assn., 1965-67; bd. dirs. Friends Library Glen Ellyn, 1967-68, Rachel Carson Trust for Living Environment 1971-74; bd. dirs. Du Page Mental Health Assn., 1973—, sec., 1973-75, pres., 1980-81, chmn. community liaison, 1981—, mem. action group, 1976—; mem. Du Page Subarea adv. council Suburban Cook County-Du Page County Health Systems Agy., 1977-83; chmn. bd. dirs. Du Page County Comprehensive Health Planning Agy., 1976; citizens adv. bd. to mental health div. Du Page Bd. Health, 1977—; mem. com. on midlife and older women Ill. Commn. on Status of Women, 1978-85; bd. dirs., publicity chmn., DuPage County Council Vol. Coordinators, 1977-78; bd. dirs., membership chmn. Homemakers Equal Rights Assn. in DuPage County, 1979-84; publicity chmn. Homemakers Coalition for Equal Rights, 1984—; mem. DuPage County Health Planning Council; now chmn. Grass Roots Com. to Pass Ill. Marital Property Act. Hon. mention in Nat. Sonnet contest, 1967; Vol. of Year, Ill. Mental Health Assn., 1975; Service award Ill. Rehab. Assn., 1980; named DuPage County Outstanding Woman Leader in Arts and Culture, W. Suburban YWCA, 1984. Mem. Wilderness Soc., W. Suburban Humane Soc., Du Page County Hist. Soc., Glen Ellyn Hist. Soc., Nat., Du Page Audubon socs., Nat. Writers Club (monthly meeting chmn. Midwest chpt. 1973-74, 4th award Ann. Mag. Con. test 1978), Defenders of Wildlife, Theosophical Soc. Am., Nature Conservancy Ill. (hon.), NAACP, Chgo. Art Inst. (life), Ill. Assn. Mental Health (dir. 1966-68), Pi Beta Phi. Writer column Mental Health and You for Press Publs., 1969—, Life Newspapers, 1982—, Pioneer Newspapers, 1984—. Home: 22 W 210 Stanton Rd Glen Ellyn IL 60137

JENSEN, ANNETTE MARIE FERANDO, cable company training coordinator; b. Sioux City, Iowa, Feb. 11, 1948; d. Thomas V. and Angeline R. (Bucchino) Ferando; m. Thomas R. Jensen, Dec. 17, 1981. B.S. in Child Devel., Iowa State U., 1970; M.S. in Edn., U. Nebr.-Omaha, 1975, postgrad. in bus. adminstrn., 1980—. Tchr. Omaha Pub. Schs., 1970; dir. devel. ctrs. Eastern Nebr. Human Services Agy., 1971-75; edn. dir. Head Start Child Devel. Corp., 1975-82; tng. coordinator Cox Cable, Omaha, 1982—. Women's Ednl. Equity Act grantee HEW, 1978. Mem. Women in Cable, Am. Soc. Tng. and Devel., Nat. Assn. Female Execs., Gamma Phi Beta. Author: Resource Handbook for Single Mothers, 1982. Office: 5011 Capitol St Omaha NE 68154

JENSEN, DALE IVER, electric fan and motor manufacturing company executive; b. Bismarck, N.D., July 30, 1956; s. Donald E. and Irene C. (Sperle) J.; m. Renee D. Kluksdahl, May 27, 1977; children—David M., Kevin D. B.S. in Mech. Engring., U. N.D., 1978. Sales engr. Universal Electric Co., Owosso, Mich., 1978-80, account exec., 1980-82; mgr. engring. services and mech. design Howard Industries div. MSL Industries, Milford, Ill., 1982, purchasing mgr., 1982-85, product mktg. mgr., Carmel, Ind., 1985—. Mem. ASME (assoc.). Lodge: K.C. Avocations: golf; bowling; camping; wood refinishing. Office: Howard Industries div MSL Industries 11555 N Meridian Carmel IN 46032

JENSEN, ERIK HUGO, pharmaceutical company executive; b. Fredericia, Denmark, June 27, 1924; came to U.S. 1950, naturalized 1962; s. Alfred Marinus and Clara Krista (Sorensen) J.; m. Alice Emy Olesen, Oct. 8, 1949; children—Ian Peter, Lisa Joan, Linda Ann. B.S., Royal Danish Sch. Pharmacy, Copenhagen, 1945, M.S., 1948, Ph.D., 1954. Head product development AB Ferrosan, Malmo, Sweden, 1955-57; research scientist Upjohn Co., Kalamazoo, Mich., 1957-62, head quality control, 1962-63, mgr. quality control, 1963-66, asst. dir. quality control, 1966-81, dir. quality control, 1981—. Author: A Study on Sodium Borohydride, 1954; also articles. Patentee in field. Bd. dirs. Kalamazoo Inst. Arts, 1971-73, treas., 1973-74, pres., 1974-75. Recipient W.E. Upjohn Co., 1962. Mem. Pharm. Mfr.'s Assn. (quality control sect. recorder 1971-78, vice chmn. 1978-80, chmn. 1980-83), Acad. Pharm. Scis. (vice chmn. 1968-69, chmn. 1971-72) Lodge: Kiwanis (treas. 1962-65). Avocations: painting, sculpting, photography. Office: Upjohn Co 7171 Portage Rd Kalamazoo MI 49001

JENSEN, ERIK MICHAEL, law educator; b. Washington, D.C., Aug. 26, 1945; s. Wayne Ivan and Anna Elizabeth (Nelson) J.; m. Helen Burgin, May 4, 1981. S.B., MIT, 1967; M.A., U Chgo., 1972; J.D., Cornell U., 1979. Bars: N.Y. 1980, U.S. Tax Ct. 1981, U.S. Dist. Ct. (so. dist.) N.Y. 1983, U.S. Ct. Appeals 1983. Law clk. to Judge Monroe G. McKay, Salt Lake City, 1979-80; assoc. Sullivan & Cromwell, N.Y.C., 1980-83; asst. prof. law Case Western Reserve U., Cleve., 1983—. Author: (with others) book supplement Federal Income Taxation of Oil and Gas Investments, 1984. Mem. adv. council Musical Arts Assn. of Cleve. Orchestra, 1984-85. Served to specialist 4th class U.S. Army, 1968-70. Mem. ABA, Am. Polit. Sci. Assn. Home: 3215 Warrington Rd Shaker Heights OH 44120 Office: Case Western Res U Sch Law 11075 East Blvd Cleveland OH 44106

JENSEN, ERLING N., retired college president; b. Des Moines, Sept. 3, 1908; s. Jens Lars and Efra (Nielsen) J.; m. Ruth McElhinney, Aug. 9, 1936; children—Richard Erling, Carl Harold, Edward Erik, David Paul. A.B., Drake U., 1932; LL.D. (hon.), 1969; A.M., Columbia U., 1933; Ph.D., Iowa State U., 1947; Litt.D. (hon.), Lafayette Coll., 1962; LL.D. (hon.), Muhlenberg Coll., 1969, Lehigh U., 1969. Prof. physics, sr. physicist Inst. Atomic Research, Iowa State U., Ames, 1943-61, prof. physics, 1969-73, prof. emeritus, 1973—; pres. Muhlenberg Coll., Allentown, Pa., 1961-69, emeritus, 1969—. Contbr. articles on nuclear physics to profl. jours. Active campus, local, state, nat. and internat. activities Lutheran Ch. in Am. mem. Allentown Charter Study Commn., 1966; mem. exec. com. Commn. Ind. Colls. and Univs. in Pa., 1965-68, Citizens Com. for Progress Lehigh County, Pa., 1966-69; adviser Pa. Council Higher Edn., 1967-69; chmn. bd. dirs. Grand View Coll., Grand View Sem., 1951-62; bd. dirs. Indsl. Devel. Corp. Lehigh County, 1964-69, Muhlenberg Med. Ctr., 1962-69, United Fund Lehigh County, 1964-69, Super Sr. Tennis, 1977—. Recipient Disting. Service award Allentown-Lehigh County C. of C., 1969, Disting. Service award Drake U., 1965, Double D award Drake U., 1968; named to Iowa Tennis Hall of Fame, 1974. Fellow Am. Phys. Soc., Iowa Acad. Sci.; mem. Am. Assn. Physics Tchrs., Am. Fedn. Scientists, Phi Beta Kappa, Sigma Xi, Phi Kappa Phi, Kappa Phi Kappa, Pi Mu Epsilon. Address: 2522 Pierce Ave Ames IA 50010

JENSEN, ETHEL ROXANNE, hotelier; b. Minot, N.D., Oct. 5, 1938; d. Lyle James Thompson and Hazella Marion (Jones) Blake; m. J. Walter Richard Peters, Nov. 14, 1959 (div. 1975); 1 son, Jay Chandler; m. Ivan Raymond Jensen, June 1, 1978. Cert. secondary tchr., N.D. Adminstrv. officer U. N.D. Grad. Sch., Grand Forks, 1974-78; owner, mgr. Ambassador Motel, Grand Forks, 1978—. Author weekly newspaper column Valley View, 1980-82. Bd. dirs. Greater Grand Forks Symphony, 1979-80; founding mem., treas. Greater Grand Forks Arts and Humanities Council, 1980-81; charter v.p. Greater Grand Forks Conv. Bur., 1981-82, pres., 1982-83, 83-84. Mem. Am. Hotel/Motel Assn., Greater Grand Forks Hotel/Motel Assn. (pres. 1979-81), Phi Beta Kappa. Unitarian. Club: Quota (treas. 1982-83). Lodge: Lioness (charter pres. 1982-83). Avocations: art, music, lit. Home: 3707 Belmont Rd Grand Forks ND 58201 Office: Ambassador Motel 2021 S Washington St Grand Forks ND 58201

JENSEN, GREG FREDERICK, optometrist; b. Sheboygan, Wis., Sept. 13, 1951; s. Walter Voss Jensen and Georgia Harriet Hartwig; m. Doreen Elizabeth Ruppel, Aug. 20, 1977. O.D., Ill. Coll. Optometry, Chgo., 1975. Lic. optometrist, Wis., Ill. Optometrist, Associated Optometrists of Oshkosh, Inc., Wis., 1975-83; pvt. practice optometry, Oshkosh, 1983—. Mem. Wis. Optometric Assn., Am. Optometric Assn., Beta Sigma Kappa, Phi Theta Upsilon. Lutheran. Avocations: cross country skiing; boating. Home: 2075 Allerton Oshkosh WI 54911 Office: 422 N Main Oshkosh WI 54911

JENSEN, JOHN WARNER, music educator, concert pianist; b. Lynn, Mass., Dec. 27, 1944; s. Knute Werner and Myrtle Christine (Munson) J. B.A., Occidental Coll., 1966; Mus.M., U. So. Calif., 1968. Instr. piano Cerritos Jr. Coll., Norwalk, Calif., 1970-72; lectr. music history Glendale Jr. Coll., Calif., 1972-73; staff accompanist Calif. State U., Fullerton, 1973-75; artist-in-residence Grinnell Coll., Iowa, 1975—; mem. MT3, Inc., A Profl. Piano Trio, Grinnell and Los Angeles, 1973—. Democrat. Avocations: cooking, reading, race car driving. Home: 1421 Broad St Grinnell IA 50112 Office: Grinnell Coll Park St Grinnell IA 50112

JENSEN, KAREN SUE, feminist bookseller, catalog editor; b. Mpls., Dec. 8, 1950; d. Richard W. and Jeanne-Marie (Empey) Jensen. Student Inst. for Am. Univs., 1970-71; B.A. in Internat. Studies, Miami U., Oxford, Ohio, 1972. Research assoc. Archlab Cons., Columbus, Ohio, 1973-74; asst. mgr. Little Prof. Bookstore, Columbus, 1975-76; researcher project on community action strategies to stop rape Women Against Rape, Columbus, 1976-80; treas., co-founder Fan the Flames Feminist Bookstore, Columbus, 1974—; library asst., catalog editor State Library of Ohio, Columbus, 1980—. Author: (with others) Freeing our Lives: A Feminist Analysis of Rape Prevention, 1978; coordinator Her Soul Lives On multi-media presentation on violence against women, Columbus, 1975-80. Trustee Women's Action Collective, Columbus, 1976-84; co-founder Rape Crisis Ctr., Columbus, 1973-76; participant Internat. Women's Studies Inst., Greece, 1984. Mem. Communication Workers of Am. (council pub. workers). Office: Fan the Flames Feminist Bookstore 65 S 4th St Columbus OH 43215

JENSEN, KATHRYN LENORA, pharmacist; b. Ft. Wayne, Ind., Mar. 1, 1959; d. Harold Richard and Madeleine Marie (Meunier) J. B.S. in Pharmacy, Butler U., 1982. Registered pharmacist, Ind. Staff pharmacist Wishard Meml. Hosp., Indpls., 1982—, emergency drug box coordinator, 1982—. Mem. Am. Soc. Hosp. Pharmacists, Ind. Soc. Hosp. Pharmacists, Ind. Soc. Hosp. Pharmacists Region I. Republican. Roman Catholic. Avocations: reading; music; jogging. Home: 5043 Boulevard Pl Indianapolis IN 46208 Office: Wishard Meml Hosp 1001 W 10th St Indianapolis IN 46204

JENSEN, LYNN EDWARD, medical association executive, economist; b. Rock Springs, Wyo., May 27, 1945; s. Glen and Helen (Anderson) J.; m. Carol Jean Lombard, June 10, 1967; children—Chelsea, Kara. B.A., Idaho State U., 1967; Ph.D., U. Utah, 1979. Research assoc. U.S. Dept. Commerce, Washington, 1967, U. Utah, 1971-74, Utah State Planning Office, 1971-74; economist AMA Research Ctr., Chgo., 1974-75, div. dir., 1975—; mem. Robert Wood Johnson Found. Adv. Com., Princeton, N.J., 1983-84. Editor-in-chief Intermountain Economic Review, 1972-73; assoc. editor Jour. Bus. and Econ. Stats., 1981—; contbr. articles to profl. jours. Served with U.S. Army, 1968-70, West Germany. Mem. Assn. Am. Med. Soc. Execs., Am. Econ. Assn., Western Econ. Assn., Am. Pub. Health Assn., Nat. Assn. Bus. Economists, Methodist. Avocations: jogging; swimming; photography. Home: 4 E Brookwood Ct Arlington Heights IL 60004 Office: AMA 535 N Dearborn St Chicago IL 60610

JENSEN, MICHAEL EUGENE, lumber company executive; b. Council Bluffs, Iowa, June 15, 1951; s. Clarence Morton and Louise Ruth (Parr) J.; m. Linda Kay Thomas, Nov. 26, 1971; children—Breck Lynn, Eric Michael. Student Iowa State U., 1969-70, U. Nebr.-Omaha, 1970. Carpenter various cos., Iowa, 1964-69; asst. mgr. Fullerton Lumber Co., Sioux City, Ia., 1970-71; mem. inside sales staff Jordan Millwork Co., Omaha, 1971-72, mem. territory sales staff, 1972-81; sales mgr. Morgan Distbn., Lenexa, Kans., 1981—. County chmn. Re-election of Gov. Ray, Montgomery County, Iowa, 1978. Mem. Mid Am. Lumberman's Assn., Mo.-Kans. Lumber Dealers Assn. (bd. dirs. 1985), Kansas City Home Builders Assn. Republican. Episcopalian. Home: 10434 Hauser St Lenexa KS 66215 Office: Morgan Distbn Box 14490 Lenexa KS 66215

JENTES, WALTER KENNETH, manufacturing company executive; b. Western Port, Md., May 18, 1941; s. Walter and Lydia (Walthert) J.; m. Shirley Dianne Richardson, Nov. 9, 1966; children—Jennifer Lynn, Kenneth Jason. M.S., Cin. U., 1963; B.S. in Acctg., U. Cin., 1973; M.B.A., Xavier U., 1973. Gen. mgr. Whitbeck-Wheeler, Belvidere, Ill., 1965-68; asst. to controller Vulcan Mfg.-Zurn Industries, Cin., 1968-72; plant controller Hillenbrand Industries, Batesville, Ind., 1972-76; v.p. fin. Cin. Time-Gen. Signal, Cin., 1976-86; v.p. ops., plant engring. PME, Cin., 1986—; dir. Richardson Realty, Cin., Old Town Investments, Cin. Editor: Direct Costing, 1980. Mem. Nat. Assn. Accts., Am. Prodn. and Inventory Control Soc. Lodge: Masons.

JEPSEN, ROGER WILLIAM, U.S. senator; b. Cedar Falls, Iowa, Dec. 23, 1928; s. Ernest and Esther (Sorensen) J.; B.S., Ariz. State U., 1950, M.A., 1953; m. Dee Ann Delaney, Sept. 26, 1958; children—Jeffrey, Ann, Craig, Linda, Deborah, Coy. Br. mgr. Conn. Gen. Life Ins. Co., Davenport, Iowa, 1956-72; exec. v.p. Agridustrial Electronics Co., Bettendorf, Iowa, 1973-76; pres. H.E.P. Mktg. Co., Davenport, 1976-78; mem. Iowa Senate, 1967-69; lt. gov. State of Iowa, 1969-73; mem. U.S. Senate from Iowa, 1979-85; chmn. Nat. Orgn. Lt. Govs., 1971-72; instr. mktg. U. No. Iowa, 1955. Supr., Scott County (Iowa), 1962-66. Served to capt. U.S. Army, 1946-47. Mem. Nat. Assn. Life Underwriters, Gen. Agts. and Mgrs. Assn., Assn. Mentally Retarded, Davenport YMCA (dir.), Res. Officers Assn. Republican. Lutheran. Clubs: Shriners, Moose, Jesters. Office: 736 Jackson Pl NW Washington DC 20503

JEPSON, ROBERT SCOTT, JR., international investment banking specialist; b. Richmond, Va., July 20, 1942; s. Robert Scott and Inda (Hodges) J.; B.S., U. Richmond, 1964, M.Commerce, 1975; m. Alice Finch Andrews, Dec. 28, 1964; children—Robert Scott, John Steven. With Va. Commonwealth Bankshares, Richmond, 1966-68; v.p. corp. fin. Birr Wilson & Co., Inc., San Francisco, 1968-69; with Calif. Capital Mgmt. Corp., Irvine, 1970-73; pres. Calcap Securities Corp., Los Angeles, 1970-73; v.p., dir. corp. fin. Cantor Fitzgerald & Co., Beverly Hills, Calif., 1973-75; dir. corp. planning and devel. Campbell Industries, San Diego, 1975-77; v.p., mgr. merger and acquisition div. Continental Ill. Bank, Chgo., 1977-82; sr. v.p., group head U.S. Capital Markets Group, 1st Nat. Bank Chgo., 1982-83; chmn. bd. Jepson Corp., Chgo., Signet Optical Co., San Diego, Armorlite, Inc., San Marcos, Calif., Emerson Quiet Kool Corp., Woodbridge, N.J., Air-Maze Corp., Cleve., Hedstrom Corp., Bedford, Pa., Gerry Sportswear Corp., Denver; vice chmn. bd. Hill Refrigeration, Trenton, N.J.; asst. prof. fin. Nat. U., 1976. Trustee, Gonzaga U., Spokane, Wash., 1982—. Served to 1st lt. M.P., Corps, AUS, 1964-66. Mem. Omicron Delta Kappa, Alpha Kappa Psi. Republican. Clubs: Mid-Am., Chgo. Home: 65 Hills and Dales Rd Barrington Hills IL 60010 Office: 340 W Butterfield Rd Elmhurst IL 60126

JERELE, JOSEPH JAMES, JR., radiologist; b. Cleve., Mar. 1, 1945; s. Joseph James and Margaret Louise (Meares) J.; m. Linda Sue Wells, June 29, 1973; children—Jordan, Joe, Jacob. B.A., Taylor U., 1968; D.O., Kirksville Coll. Osteo. Medicine, 1972. Intern Doctor's Hosp., Columbus, Ohio, 1972-73; emergency room physician Orlando Gen. Hosp., Fla., 1973-74; radiology and nuclear medicine resident Doctor's Hosp., Columbus, 1974-77, sr. attending staff radiologist, 1977—, treas., 1980-81; asst. clin. prof. radiology Ohio U. Athens, 1980—. Contbg. author: X-ray Technology Textbook, 1980. Contbr. book revs. to profl. jours. Recipient Mead Johnson award, 1976. Mem. Am. Osteo. Coll. Radiology (treas. 1982—, bd. dirs. 1982—, cert. radiologist), Am. Osteo. Assn., Ohio Osteo. Assn., Central Ohio Radiol. Assn., Am. Inst. Ultrasound in Medicine, Radiol. Soc. N.Am., Am. Osteo. Coll. Nuclear Medicine (cert. nuclear medicine). Republican. Mem. Grace Brethren Ch. Avocations: triathlons; distance running; soccer; racquetball. Home: 697 Gatehouse Ln Worthington OH 43085 Office: Doctors Hosp 1087 Dennison Ave Columbus OH 43201

JEREN, JOHN ANTHONY, JR., lawyer; b. Youngstown, Ohio, Feb. 23, 1946; s. John A. and Irene E. (Struharik) J.; m. Marjorie C. Barbarie, July 11, 1973; children—Lisa Ann, Christine Alicia, Suzanne Beth, John A. III. B.S. in Bus., Ohio State U., 1968; J.D., Ohio No. U., 1973. Bar: Ohio 1973, U.S. Dist. Ct. (no. dist.) Ohio 1974. Ptnr. Wellman & Jeren Co., L.P.A., Youngstown, 1973—. Served to 1st lt. U.S. Army, 1968-70. Recipient Willis Soc. award Ohio No. U., 1974; named Protestant Man of Yr. Orgn. Protestant Men, 1984. Mem. ABA, Assn. Trial Lawyers Am., Ohio Trial Lawyers Assn., Nat. Orgn. Social Security Claiment's Reps. Democrat. Baptist. Home: 8199 Burgess Lake Dr Poland OH 44514 Office: Wellman & Jeren Co 67 Westchester Dr Youngstown OH 44515

JERSE, DOROTHY WEINZ, health association administrator; b. Chgo., Dec. 15, 1926; d. Louis Arthur and Ruby (Reckner) W.; m. Frank William Jerse, Aug. 9, 1947; children—Thomas, Mary, Ann, James. B.A., St. Mary-of-the-Woods Coll., 1975. Teen, youth dir. YWCA, Terre Haute, Ind., 1970-74, exec. dir., 1983—; curator, Vigo County Hist. Soc., Terre Haute, 1974-82. Co-author: On the Banks of the Wabash; A Photograph Album of Greater Terre Haute, 1900-50, 1983. Contbr. articles to prof. jours. Mem. bd. Covered Bridge council Girl Scouts of Am., Terre Haute, 1968-71, United Way of Wabash Valley, Terre Haute, 1975-78, Goodwill Industries, Terre Haute, 1984—; com. mem. Max Ehrmann Centennial, Terre Haute, 1972. Recipient Book of Golden Deeds award Exchange Club, 1975, Woman of Yr. award Girls Club, 1977, Outstanding Contbr. award Wabash Valley Council Internat. Reading Assn., 1980; named Banks of the Wabash Festival Belle, Festival Assn., 1981. Mem. Terre Bus. and Profl. Women (Woman of Community 1979, Woman of Yr. 1982), P.E.O., Delta Kappa Gamma (hon.). Democrat. Unitarian. Clubs: Altrusa of Terre Haute, Wabash Valley Press. Home: 1001 Royce Ave Terre Haute IN 47802 Office: YWCA 951 Dresser Dr Terre Haute IN 47807

JESKA, EDWARD LAWRENCE, veterinary pathology educator; b. Erie, Pa., Aug. 6, 1923; s. Francis Alexander and Martha Irene (Nowak) J.; children—Judith, Theodore, Cheryl, Meribeth. B.A., Gannon U., 1951; M.S., Marquette U., 1954; Ph.D., U. Pa., 1966. Asst. prof. U. Pa., Phila., 1966-67; assoc. prof. Iowa State U., Ames, 1968-75, prof. vet. pathology, 1975—; collaborator Nat. Animal Disease Ctr., U.S. Dept. Agr., Ames, 1975—; research expert panel Spl. Grants Div., Washington, 1980-85; ednl. cons. Fed. U. Rio de Janeiro, Brazil, 1984-85. Office: Vet Medicine Research Inst Iowa State Univ Vet Coll S Beach St Ames IA 50011

JESS, JOHN MICHAEL, state water resources administrator; b. Fremont, Nebr., Feb. 4, 1944; s. H. Albert Jess and Georgia R. (Hansen) Jess Broihier; m. Carol J. Henderson, May 23, 1969; children—Kelly, Scott, Adam. B.S., U. Nebr., 1968. M.S., 1969. Registered profl. engr., Ill., Nebr. Hydrologist cons.

and survey div. U. Nebr., Lincoln, 1968-70; Ill. Water Survey, Champaign, 1972-75; dir. Nebr. Dept. Water Resources, Lincoln, 1975—. Contbr. articles to profl. jours. Chmn. summer water resources tours U. Nebr.-Lincoln. Served to 1st lt. U.S. Army, 1970-72. Mem. ASCE (pres. local chpt. 1980-81). Episcopalian. Lodge: Rotary. Avocations: cabinet making; gardening; hunting. Home: 2535 Stockwell St Lincoln NE 68502 Office: Nebr Dept Water Resources PO Box 94676 Lincoln NE 68509

JESSUP, FLORENCE REDDING, Spanish educator, department administrator; b. Indpls., Apr. 8, 1934; d. Gerald Raymond and Dorothy Ellen (Moore) Redding; m. Robert Lowell Jessup, Oct. 18, 1958; children—Elizabeth Redding, Benjamin Lowell, Jonathan R. B.A., Wellesley Coll., 1956; M.A., Ind. U., 1958; Ph.D., 1975. From instr. to assoc. prof. Spanish Butler U., Indpls., 1962-85, prof., 1985—, acting head dept., 1982-84, head dept. modern fgn. langs., 1984—. Contbr. articles to profl. jours. Mem. Am. Assn. Tchrs. Spanish and Portuguese, AAUP, Am. Council Tchrs. Fgn. Langs., MLA, Midwest MLA, Phi Kappa Phi, Sigma Delta Pi, Phi Sigma Iota, Delta Kappa Gamma. Democrat. Office: Butler U 4600 Sunset Indianapolis IN 46208

JESTER, GUY E., construction executive. B.S. in Engring., U.S. Mil. Acad, 1951; M.S. in Civil Engring., U. Ill., 1958; postgrad. Columbia U., 1963-65, U.S. Army War Coll.; Ph.D., U. Ill., 1969; postgrad. U. Pitts., 1973. Registered profl. engr., Tex. Dep. dir. and acting dir. Corps of Engrs., Waterways Expt. Sta., 1965-67; div. engr. U.S. Army, 9th Inf. Div., 1968-69; office chief research and devel. U.S. Army Asst. to chief Research & Devel. and chief info. system, 1968-71; dist. engr. U.S. Army Corps of Engrs., St. Louis, 1971-73; v.p. spl. projects J.S. Alberici Constrn. Co., Inc., St. Louis, 1973—. Vice chmn. bd. transp. St. Louis Regional Commerce and Growth Assn.; v.p., dir. Internat. Waste Energy Systems; chmn. bd. and pres. Assn. for Improvement of Miss. River; bd. dirs. Thermal Resources of St. Louis; mem. vestry and sr. warden St. Timothy's Episcopal Ch.; former vice chmn. council Diocese of Mo., Episcopal Ch.; vice chmn. Profl. Code Com. of St. Louis. Recipient Award of Appreciation, Soc. Am. Mil. Engrs., 1983; Presdl. citation, ASCE, 1979; Cert. of Appreciation, U.S. Army, C.E., 1974; Award of Merit, Engrs. Club of St. Louis, 1981; Spl. Service award, Fed. Exec. Bd., 1972, 73; named St. Louis Constrn. Man of Yr., 1980. Fellow Soc. Am. Mil. Engrs. (past pres., past regional v.p., dir.); mem. ASCE (past pres. St. Louis sect.), Am. Gen. Contractors, Engrs. Club of St. Louis, U. Ill. Civil Engr. Alumni Assn., West Point Soc. St. Louis, Sigma Xi, Phi Kappa Phi. Address: 2150 Kienlen Ave Saint Louis MO 63121

JESTER, LINDA R., state government official; b. Indpls., June 30, 1944; d. Edwin A. and Lula M. (Richardson) J. B.A. in Biology, Ind. Central U., 1966. Dir. div. tourism Ind. Dept. Commerce, Indpls., 1972-76; dir. pub. relations Airport Assocs., Indpls., 1976-77; dir. econ. devel. Ind. Dept. Commerce, Indpls., 1977-81; exec. dir. Ind. Office Occupational Devel., Indpls., 1981—. Bd. dirs. Indpls. Shakespeare Festival Inc., 1984, 85. Republican. Methodist. Home: 4273 Woodsage Trace Indianapolis IN 46237 Office: Ind Office Occupational Devel 150 W Market Indianapolis IN 46204

JETT, MILDRED SUNDAY, nurse, administrator; b. Bessmer, Ala., July 1, 1947; d. Jimmie and Inez (Norwood) Sunday; B.S.N. magna cum laude, U. Mich., 1975; L.P.N. diploma No. Mich. U., 1967; m. Arthur Robert Jett, Aug. 15, 1970; children—Nataki Elissar, Kanye Kamau. Lic. practical nurse Providence Hosp., Southfield, Mich., 1968-70; nurse St. Luke's Hosp., Marquette, Mich., 1970-72; lic. practical nurse Univ. Hosp., Ann Arbor, Mich., 1972-74, staff nurse, 1976-77; inservice instr. Kirwood Gen. Hosp., Detroit, 1976-77, dept. head, ednl. dir. hosp. staff devel., 1977—; tchr. CPR to sr. citizens. Capt., Nurses Corps, USAR. Mem. Detroit Black Nurses Assn. (2d v.p. 1978-80, 80-82), Am. Nurses Assn., Nat. Black Nurses Assn., Met. Detroit Health Edn. Council, Met. Detroit Coalition for Blood Pressure Control, Mich. Soc. Instructional Tech., Cable Health Coalition, Delta Sigma Theta, Sigma Theta Tau (membership com. 1975-76). Mem. Christian Ch. Office: 4059 W Davison Detroit MI 48238

JETTKE, HARRY JEROME, government official; b. Detroit, Jan. 2, 1925; s. Harry H. and Eugenia M. (Dziatkiewicz) J.; B.A., Wayne State U., 1961; m. Josefina Suarez-Garcia, Oct. 22, 1948; 1 dau., Joan Lillian Jettke Sorger. Owner, operator Farmacia Virreyes/Farmacia Regina, Toluca, Mex., 1948-55; intern pharmacist Cunningham Drug Stores, Detroit, 1955-63; drug specialist, product safety specialist FDA, Detroit, 1963-73; acting dir. Cleve., U.S. Consumer Product Safety Commn., 1973-75, compliance officer, 1975-78, supr., investigations, 1978-82, regional compliance officer, 1982-83, sr. resident, 1983—. Served with Fin. Dept., U.S. Army, 1942-43. Drug specialist FDA. Mem. Am. Soc. for Quality Control (sr., chmn. Cleve. sect. 1977-78, cert. quality technician, cert. quality engr.), Asociación Nacional Mexicana de Estadistica y Control de Calidad, policy com. Cleve. Fed. Exec. Bd., 1985. Roman Catholic. Home: 25715 Yoeman Dr Westlake OH 44145 Office: US Consumer Product Safety Commn One Playhouse Sq 1375 Euclid Ave Cleveland OH 44114

JEWELL, E. HARVEY, musician, educator, conductor; b. Cuba, N.Y., Oct. 24, 1942; s. Clarence Wade and Erma (Sears) Marriott J.; m. Mary Elizabeth Johnson, Dec. 28, 1968; children—Melody Elaine, Eric Harmony. B.Mus. in Music Edn. and Performance, Houghton Coll., 1964; D.Mus. Arts in Orchestral and Opera Conducting, U. Wash., 1976; additional studies Eastman Sch. Music, 1964-65, SUNY-Geneseo, 1964-65, Instituto Nacional de Msica, Panama City, 1966-67, Canal Zone Coll., Balboa, 1966-67, Oberlin Coll., 1968—, Minn. Opera Inst., Am. Symphony Orch. League Conducting Inst., The Grantsmanship Ctr. Tng. Program, Instrumental music dir. Houghton Acad., N.Y., 1963-64; tchr. instrumental music Bd. Cooperative Ednl. Services, Leicester, N.Y., 1964-65; lectr. music Union Coll., Schenectady, 1967-68; dir. strings and orchestral programs East Greenbush Central Sch. Dist., N.Y., 1967-68; prin. oboist Omaha Symphony Orch., 1968-69; Rockefeller fellow to Contemporary Group, U. Wash., Seattle, prin. oboist U. Symphony, Festival Opera Orch., Contemporary Group Woodwind Quintet, Sinfonietta, 1969-72; asst. prof. music, condr. Symphony Orch., Wind Ensemble, Coll. Choir and Opera Theatre, Cornell Coll., Mount Vernon, Iowa, 1972-74; instr. music Coll. Great Falls, Mont., 1974-78; music dir., condr. and prin. adminstr. Symphony Orch., Chamber Orch., Symphonic Choir, Great Falls Symphony Assn., Inc., 1974-79; instr. music Brookhaven Coll., Farmers Branch, Tex., 1979-80; asst. prof. music, dir. instrumental music U. Tex. at Dallas, Richardson, 1978-80; assoc. prof. music, music/drama dept. chmn., music dir./conductor Music. Theatre and String Orch., dir./player Collegium Musicum and Wind Octet, U. Sci. and Arts Okla., Chickasha, 1980-84; dean, oboist Woodwind Quintet, violist Chamber Orch., instr. string methods Am. Conservatory Music, Chgo., 1984—; dir. Dansville Community Chorus, N.Y., 1964-65; prin. oboist Geneseo Symphony and Woodwind Quintet, 1964-65; oboist Albany Symphony, Vt. State Symphony, 1967-68; oboist Seattle Opera Orch., 1971-72; founder, dir., player Auloi Double Reed Ensemble, 1972-74; prin. oboist Cedar Rapids Symphony Orch., 1972-74; music dir./condr. Greater Dallas Community Chamber Orch., 1978-80; dir./player Woodwind Quintet, Jazz Ensemble, Recorder Consort, 1978-80; violinist Lawton Philharmonic Orch., Okla., 1983-84; guest condr. Oakland Ballet Co., Ron Guidi, Artistic Dir., N.W. Jazz Sextet, Helena Symphony, Mont., Waterloo-Cedar Falls Symphony, Iowa, Cedar Rapids Youth Symphony, Iowa. Served with U.S. Army, 1965-67. Mem. Am. Fedn. Musicians, Coll. Music Soc. (life), Nat. Assn. Schs. Music. Home: 1006 N Humphrey Oak Park IL 60302 Office: Am Conservatory Music 116 S Michigan Ave Chicago IL 60603

JEWELL, RICHARD BARKLEY, agricultural equipment manufacturing executive; b. Decatur, Ill., Nov. 28, 1945; s. Albert W. and M. Helen (Taggart) J.; m. Cynthea Jensen, Apr. 17, 1970; children—Jennifer Christine, Catherine Elizabeth. B.S. in Acctg., No. Ill. U., 1970; M.B.A., Ill. State U., 1976. Cert. ins. broker. Staff auditor Price Waterhouse & Co., Chgo., 1970-71; acctg. mgr. Am. Hosp. Supply Co., McGaw Park, Ill., 1971-72; spl. project analyst Honeggar & Co., Inc., Fairbury, Ill.; corp. sec. Wheels Leasing, Inc., Fairbury, Ill., 1972-74, JLW Holding Co., Paxton, Ill., 1972-74, Agrl. Comml. Inc., Paxton, 1974-83; controller, corp. sec. Big Wheels Internat. Co., Paxton, 1974—; v.p. mktg. Rhino Robots Inc., Champaign, Ill., 1983 exec. v.p., 1983-84; treas. Big Wheels, Inc., 1984—; del. Gov.'s First Small Bus. Conf., Ill. Social events chmn. local Am. Cancer Soc. Mem. Am. Prodn. and Inventory Control Soc. (dir.). Methodist. Club: Lakeview Country (Loda). Contbr. articles on robots to publs. Home: POB 305 Loda IL 60948 Office: PO Box 113 Paxton IL 60957

JEWELL, RICHARD DANIEL, dentist; b. Reedsburg, Wis., Feb. 12, 1936; s. Ernest L. and Adele Dorthea (Gall) J.; m. Jeanette Marie Brown, Apr. 15, 1962; children—Todd E., Lisa M. B.A., Luth. Coll., 1958; D.D.S., Marquette Dental Coll., 1962. Practice dentistry, Madison, Wis., 1964—. Served to capt. USAF, 1962-64. Mem. ADA, Dane County Dental Soc., Wis. Dental Assn. Lodges: Masons, Elks. Avocations: soap stone carving; stamp collecting; stained glass. Office: 5011 Monona Dr Madison WI 53716

JEWSON, RUTH HATHAWAY, retired association administrator, consultant; b. Ellendale, N.D., Mar. 3; d. Floyd Cecil and Mabel (Hay) Hathaway; m. W. Vance Jewson, Mar. 19, 1938; children—Douglas, Meredith, Roberta, Dwight. Ph.D., U. Minn.-St. Paul, 1978. Tchr. Avon-Growe Consol. High Sch., Avondale, Pa., 1935-37, Hudson Pub. High Sch., Wis., 1937-38, U. Minn. High Sch., Mpls., 1939-40, adult edn. Mpls. Pub. Schs., 1951-69; research asst. U. Minn., Mpls., 1938-39; exec. officer Nat. Council on Family Relations, St. Paul, 1956-84; cons. Minn. State Dept. Edn., St. Paul, Mpls. Pub. Schs. Consumer Homemaking adv. com.; mem. Minn. Gov.'s Adv. Com. on Families, 1981, steering com. Minn. Gov.'s Commn. on Stress and the Family, 1981, Minn. Gov.'s Commn. on Work and the Family, 1981, Nat. Task Force White House Conf. on Families, 1981, Nat. Task Force White House Conf. on Aging; bd. dirs. Groves Conf. on Marriage and the Family, 1981-85; Christian Children's Fund, Richmond, Va., 1970-84. Recipient Disting. Service to Families award Nat. Council on Family Relations, 1974, Ruth Hathaway Jewson Disting. Service award Minn. Council on Family Relations, 1982, Bldg. Family Strengths award Nat. Symposium on Bldg. Family Strengths, 1984. Mem. Nat. Council on Family Relations (sect. chair 1985—), Am. Home Econs. Assn., Minn. Home Econs. Assn., Minn. Council on Family Relations (pres. 1983-84), Mortar Bd., Phi Upsilon Omicron, Omicron Nu. Methodist. Avocations: travel, volunteer work, reading. Home: 5515 E Oberlin Circle Minneapolis MN 55432

JEZOWSKI, MARIANNE MIKA, computer science and mathematics educator; b. Oklahoma City, June 3, 1943; d. Walter Francis and Ann (Labosh) Mika; m. John Joseph Jezowski, Aug. 14, 1965; 1 child, Michele. B.A., Clarke Coll., 1965; M.Ed., Loyola U.-Chgo., 1977. Math. tchr. Community Consol. Sch. Dist. #15, Palatine, Ill., 1965-69, River Trails Sch. Dist. #26, Mount Prospect, Ill., 1972—. Math. tchr. Coll. of DuPage, Glen Ellyn, Ill., 1984—. Mem. Nat. Council Tchrs. Math., Ill. Edn. Assn., NEA, River Trails Edn. Assn. Roman Catholic. Office: River Trails Jr High Sch 1000 N Wolf Rd Mount Prospect IL 60056

JILANI, ATIQ AHMED, electronic company executive; b. Amroha, India, Feb. 1, 1948; s. Siddiq Ahmed and Nasima (Khatoon) J.; B.E., N.E.D. Engring. Coll., Karachi U., 1969; M.S., Tuskegee Inst., Ala., 1971; cert. in mgmt., Purdue U., 1978, Northwestern U., 1980, Wharton Sch. Mgmt., U. Pa., 1982; m. Khalida Bano Naqvi, Dec. 25, 1975; children—Hussain, Ibrahim. Script writer Karachi (Pakistan) TV, 1967-70; mem. research staff AEC, Tuskegee, Ala., 1970-71; design engr. Lummus Industries, Columbus, Ga., 1971-73; product engr. Borg-Warner Corp., Chgo., 1974-78, mem. cost and productivity com., 1976, mgr. engring. Chgo. Marine Containers div. Sea Containers, Broadview, Ill., 1978-80; v.p., chief operating officer, gen. mgr. Borg-Erickson Corp., Chgo., 1980-85; pres., chief exec. officer Circuit Systems Inc., 1985—, dir., 1985—; cons. in industry and agr. UN, including work in South Asia, 1981. Registered profl. engr., Ill.; cert. mfg. engr.; cert. plant engr. Mem. Nat., Ill. socs. profl. engrs., Am. Soc. Agrl. Engrs., ASME, Assn. Energy Engrs. (charter), Thinkers Forum (pres. 1967-70). Muslim. Contbr. articles to profl. jours. Patentee (U.S. and internat.) in field agrl. equipment. Home: PO Box 3212 Oak Brook IL 60521

JILG, MICHAEL FLORIAN, artist, art educator; b. Great Bend, Kans., June 28, 1947; s. Paul Florian and Mildred Amelia (Mausolf) J.; m. Joyce Seeman. B.A., Fort Hays State U., 1969, M.A., 1970; M.F.A., Wichita State U., 1972; postgrad., Kent State U., 1972, Studio Camnitzer (Italy), 1984. Secondary edn. instr. High Sch., Dodge City, Kans., 1968; grad. tchr. Fort Hays State U., Kans., 1969-70, asst. prof. art, 1981—; grad. tchr., Wichita State U., Kans., 1970-72. Exhibited in numerous group shows, Kans., Mo., Colo. N.D., Italy. One-man shows include Kans. Cultural Arts Commn., Fredonia, 1972, Butler County Community Coll., El Dorado, Kans., 1972, Barton County Community Coll., Great Bend, Kans., 1972, Burger Sandzen Meml. Gallery, Lindsborg, Kans., 1974, Davis Gallery, Hays, 1974, Cummins Meml. Gallery, Larned, Kans., 1975, Hutchinson Library, Kans., 1976, Co-op Gallery, Hays, 1976, Wichita State U., Kans., 1976, Marymount Coll., Salina, Kans., 1976, Ark Gallery, Brookville, Kans., 1976, Bette Moses Gallery, Great Bend, 1979, Hays Art Council Gallery, 1979, Cloud County Coll., Concordia, Kans., 1983, Pratt Community Coll., Kans., 1984, Stone Gallery, Hays, 1984. Represented in permanent collections Joslyn Art Mus., Wichita Art Mus., Kans. Arts Commn., Wichita State U., Kent State U., St. Anns Catholic Ch., Fort Hays Kans. State U., Ellis Bd. Edn., McCracken Library; numerous pvt. collections. Past bd. dirs. Hays Arts Council. Grantee Fort Hays State U. 1983, 1984, 1985, Stauffer Research grant 1984. Mem. Kans. Watercolor Soc., Boston Printmakers, Phila. Print Club. Lodge: KC. Avocations: reading; sailing. Home: 317 W 20th Hays KS 67601 Office: Visual Arts Ctr 600 Park St Hays KS 67601-4099

JILKA, ROBERT LAURENCE, biomedical researcher; b. Salina, Kans., Nov. 26, 1948. B.S., Kans. State U., 1970, M.S., 1972; Ph.D., St. Louis U., 1975. Postdoctoral fellow Roche Inst. Molecular Biology, Nutley, N.J., 1975-78; staff scientist VA Med. Ctr., Kansas City, Mo., 1978—; research asst. prof. U. Kans. Med. Ctr., Kansas City, 1979—. Contbr. articles to profl. jours. NIH grantee, 1983—. Mem. Am. Soc. Biol. Chemists, Am. Soc. Bone and Mineral Research. Office: VA Med Ctr 4801 Linwood Blvd Kansas City MO 64128

JOB, REUBEN P., clergyman. Bishop Iowa conf. United Methodist Ch. Office: 1019 Chestnut St Des Moines IA 50309*

JOBE, RONALD LEE, laundry machinery company executive; b. Birmingham, Ala., Jan. 19, 1948; s. Robert Lee and Eloise Dean (Glass) J.; m. Beverly W. Whitehead, Sept. 14, 1968; 1 son, Jason Robert. B.S. in Indsl. Engring., U. Ala., 1970. Methods engr. Butler Mfg. Co., Birmingham, 1973-76; v.p. House of Metals, Inc., Birmingham, 1976-78; v.p. sales and mktg. Arrowhead Grating and Metalworks, Kansas City, Mo., 1978-81; v.p., gen. mgr. Columbia Laundry Machinery Co., Kansas City, 1981—. George C. K. Johnson scholar, 1970. Mem. Am. Inst. Indsl. Engrs. (pres. 1970-71), Ala. Bass Fisherman's Assn. (pres. Tuscaloosa 1971-72), Kansas City C. of C., Alpha Pi Mu (pres. 1969-70). Home: 7919 Hallet Lenexa KS 66215 Office: Columbia Laundry Machinery Co 2210 Campbell Kansas City MO 64108

JOBST, CAROLINE BRIGGS, mfg. co. exec.; b. Asheville, N.C., May 7, 1919; d. Horace Gladstone and Erma Parham Briggs; student Cecil's Coll., 1937-38; m. Conrad Jobst, June 16, 1941 (dec.). Pres., chief exec. officer Jobst Inst., Inc., Toledo, Ohio, 1957—; dir. Toledo Trust Co. Bd. dirs. Community Chest; mem. Pres.'s Council, Toledo Mus. Art; Golden Baton assoc., bd. dirs. Toledo Symphony Orch.; mem. vestry Trinity Episc. Ch. Mem. Am. Mgmt. Assn., Aerospace Med. Assn., Nat. Mgmt. Assn. (mem. adv. bd., Silver Knight award 1980), Nat. Assn. Hosiery Mfrs., Employers Assn. Toledo, Toledo Area C. of C. (bd. dirs.). Episcopalian. Club: Toledo. Home: 418 Riverside Dr Rossford OH 43460 Office: 653 Miami St Toledo OH 43605

JOCKE, RALPH EDWARD, lawyer; b. Berea, Ohio, Apr. 7, 1953; s. Ralph F. and Joan M. (Kaskey) J.; m. Patricia A. Walker, Oct. 8, 1982. B.M.E., Cleve. State U., 1976; J.D., Cleve. Marshall Coll. Law, 1981. Bar: Ohio 1981, U.S. dist. ct. (no. dist.) Ohio 1981, U.S. ct. appeals (6th cir.) 1982, U.S. Patent Bar 1983, U.S. Supreme Ct. 1985. Registered profl. engr., Ohio Engr., Union Carbide Corp., Cleve., 1973-77; product equipment designer Ford Motor Co., Cleve., 1977-79; mgr. mfg. engring. Donn Corp., Westlake, Ohio, 1979-81; litigation assoc. Squire Sanders & Dempsey, Cleve., 1981-83; legal counsel. Diebold Inc., North Canton, Ohio, 1983—. Recipient Am. Jurisprudence award, Coll. Law, 1979, Pres.' award Cleve. State U., 1976, G. Brooks Earnest award Fenn Coll. Engring., 1976. Mem. Soc. Automotive Engrs. (outstanding sr. award 1976), ABA, Ohio Bar Assn., Cuyahoga County Bar Assn., Bar Assn. Greater Cleve., Fed. Bar Assn. Office: Diebold Inc 5995 Mayfair Rd North Canton OH 44720

JODELKA, EDWARD STEFAN, manufacturing company executive; b. Emsdetten, Germany, Sept. 26, 1949; came to U.S., 1951, naturalized, 1966; s. Stefan and Maria (Budnik) J.; B.S. indsl. Edn., Chgo. State U., 1971, postgrad., 1971, 72-73; m. Deborah Lee Boykovsky, July 3, 1971; children—Melissa Lynn, Thomas Edward, David Edward. With Radiant Products Co., Inc., Chgo., 1965-83, v.p. 1978-83; with Binks Mfg. Co., Franklin Park, Ill., 1983—; vocat. guidance counselor, sch. programmer, tchr. Cregier Vocat. High Sch., Chgo., 1972-74. Mem. Internat. Entrepreneurs Assn., Am. Entrepreneurs Assn., Am. Mgmt. Assn. Republican. Office: Binks Mfg Co Inc 9201 W Belmont Ave Franklin Park IL 60131

JOERN, CHARLES EDWARD, JR., lawyer; b. Oak Park, Ill., Apr. 27, 1951; s. Charles Edward and Eleanor (Lambert) J.; m. Christine Mary Lake, July 28, 1973; children—Jessica, William, Marisa, Angela. B.A., Knox Coll., 1973; M. Urban Affairs, U. Colo., 1976; J.D., De Paul U., 1980. Bar: Ill. 1980, U.S. Dist. Ct. (no. dist.) Ill. 1980, U.S. Ct. Appeals (7th cir.) 1981. Asst. to planning cons. J. R. Crowley and Assocs., 1973-74; systems analyst U. Colo. sponsored systems analysis of the Aravada, Colo. Bldg. Inspection Div., 1974-75; student intern div. comprehensive health planning Colo. Dept. Health, 1976; law clk. Cook County Legal Assistance Found., Ill., 1978, consumer fraud div. Office Ill. Atty. Gen., 1979-80; assoc. Pope, Ballard, Shepard & Fowle, Ltd., Chgo., 1980—; staff mem. Family in Crisis Conf., Galesburg, Ill., 1973; panel atty. Chgo. Vol. Legal Services Found. Bd. advisers N.C. Outward Bound Sch., Morganton, 1983—; bd. dirs. Richport YMCA, LaGrange, Ill., 1984—. Fellow in pub. affairs U. Colo., 1976. Mem. Ill. State Bar Assn., ABA (litigation sect.), Chgo. Bart Assn. (child abuse and neglect com.), Pi Alpha Alpha. Republican. Roman Catholic. Office: Pope Ballard Shepard & Fowle Ltd 69 W Washington St Chicago IL 60602

JOFFE, WILLIAM IRVING, priest, educator; b. Oak Park, Ill., Mar. 24, 1931; s. Irving B. and Minna (Coia) J. A.B., Loras Coll., 1953; M.A., Mt. St. Bernard Sem., 1957; M.A. in Journalism, Marquette U., 1959; D.Ministry, St. Mary U., Balt., 1983. Ordained priest Roman Catholic Ch., 1957; tchr. high sch. Aurora, Sterling and Woodstock, Ill., 1960-82; asst. editor diocesan newspaper The Observer, Rockford, Ill., 1959-62; dir. vocations Diocese of Rockford, 1959-61; pastor St. Joseph Ch., Harvard, Ill., 1983; chmn. bd. Cath. edn. McHenry County; owner, mgr. horse farm. Mem. Nat. Psychology Assn., Nat. Priests Senate, Am. Quarter Horse Assn. Author: The Triple Way, 1956; contbr. articles to profl. jours. Office: St Joseph Ch 206 E Front St Harvard IL 60033

JOHANNES, JOHN ROLAND, political science educator; b. Milw., Dec. 15, 1943; s. Jerome Fridolin and Theresa (Stoiber) J.; m. Frances Virginia Slater, Aug. 5, 1967; children—Teresa, Michael, James. B.S., Marquette U., 1966; A.M., Harvard U., 1968, Ph.D., 1970. Asst. prof. polit. sci. Marquette U., Milw., 1970-75, assoc. prof., 1975-84, prof., 1984—. Author: Policy Innovation in Congress (monograph), 1972; To Serve the People, 1984. Contbr. articles to profl. jours. Am. Philos. Soc. grantee, 1978; Everett Dirksen Ctr. grantee, 1981, 82. Mem. Am. Polit. Sci. Assn., Midwest Polit. Sci. Assn., So. Polit. Sci. Assn., Western Polit. Sci. Assn. Home: 1218 E Courtland Place Whitefish Bay WI 53211 Office: Marquette U Dept Polit Sci Milwaukee WI 53233

JOHANNSEN, KENNETH M., surgeon; b. Denison, Iowa, Oct. 17, 1930; s. Wilbert Johannsen and Irene Krohnke; m. Audrey J. Leidholdt, Apr. 17, 1953; children—Mark, Jess, Seth. B.A., U. Iowa, 1953; M.D., U. Nebr. 1965. Diplomate Am. Bd. Surgery. Intern, Bryan Meml. Hosp., Lincoln, 1965-66; resident VA Hosp., Des Moines, 1973-77; practice medicine specializing in gen. surgery, Spencer, Iowa, 1966-73; gen. surgeon Buena Vista Clinic, Storm Lake, Iowa, 1977—. Served to 1st lt. USMC, 1953-55. Fellow Am. Coll. Surgeons; mem. Iowa Med Soc., AMA. Republican. Lutheran. Home: 1605 Shoreway Rd Storm Lake IA 50588 Office: Buena Vista Clinic 620 Northwestern Dr Storm Lake IA 50588

JOHANSEN, DONALD ANTHONY, state education official, consultant; b. Wishek, N.D., June 11, 1929; s. Torolf and Anna Margretha (Stevens) J.; m. Jean Adell Sandberg, June 28, 1953; children—Mark Steven, Philip Bruce, Michael Donald, Pamela Jean, Peter Leslie. B.S., Bemidji State U., 1951; M.Ed., U. of N.D., 1958; Ph.D., U. of Minn., 1982. Tchr., prin. Deer Creek High Sch., Minn., 1953-57; prin. Wadena High Sch., Minn., 1957-69; asst., head prin., Robbinsdale Schs., Minn., 1969-78, dir. careers project, 1971-74; supr. secondary edn. Minn. Dept. of Edn., St. Paul, 1978—; liaison Commn. on Excellence, Minn., 1984, Task Force on Ednl. Adminstrn., Minn., 1984—; cons. Legis. Coop. Sch. Study, Minn., 1984—. Author: Looking Forward to a Career, 1973. Contbr. articles to ednl. jours. Mem. Community Action Council, Ottertail, Wadena Counties, 1965-69; chmn. Minn. Concentrated Employment Program 13, Central Minn. Counties, 1967-69; mem. New Hope Environ. Commn., Minn., 1972-74. Served to 2nd lt. USAF, 1951-53. Recipient Appreciation award Minn. State Distributive Club Am., 1968; Service award Community Action Council, 1975, Southwest Ednl. Coop. Service Unit, Marshall, Minn., 1983. Mem. NEA (life, Minn. del. assembly 1960), Nat. Minn. Assn. Secondary Sch. Prins. (bd. dirs. 1969, 78-82, Disting. Service award 1985), Nat. Assn. Supts. and Dirs. of Secondary Edn. (nat. sec. 1979), Minn. Assn. Alternative Edn. (organizer 1983, dir. 1983—), Minn. Assn. Supervision and Curriculum Devel, Phi Delta Kappa. Lodge: Rotary Internat. (Wadena, Minn.) (pres. 1968-69). Avocations: singing; automobile repair; building a cabin. Lutheran. Home: 4801 Decatur Ave N New Hope MN 55428 Office: Minn Dept of Edn 550 Cedar St St Paul MN 55101

JOHANSEN, GREGORY JAMES, pharmacist; b. Belmond, Iowa, Oct. 5, 1954; s. Raymond Louie and Billie Virginia (Whitten) J.; m. Kathleen Renee Porter, Sept. 20, 1975; children—Erika Lynn and Jennifer Erin (twins). B.S. in Pharmacy, Drake U., 1976; student U. Iowa, 1975. Registered pharmacist Iowa. Staff pharmacist McLean Drug, Indianola, Iowa, 1976-83; owner-mgr. Medicap Pharmacy, Indianola, 1983—. Chmn. Winifred Law Care Rev. Com., Indianola, 1984; fin. chmn. Planned Parenthood of Central Iowa, 1984; chmn. Warren County Democrats, 1984. Mem. Iowa Pharm. Assn., Polk County Pharm. Assn. Indianola C. of C. (legis. chmn. 1984). Lutheran. Avocations: furniture refinishing; old house restoration; antiques; politics. Home: 412 West Iowa Indianola IA 50125 Office: Medicap Pharmacy 208 E Euclid Indianola IA 50125

JOHN, DEBORAH ROEDDER, educator; b. St. Louis, Aug. 24, 1952; d. Charles George and Ruth Helen (Buchanan) R.; B.S.B.A. summa cum laude, St. Louis U., 1974; M.B.A., Kent State U., 1976; Ph.D., Northwestern U., 1980. Teaching fellow Kent (Ohio) State U., 1975-76; instr. Northwestern U., Evanston, Ill., 1979-80; asst. prof. Grad. Sch. Mgmt. UCLA, 1980-82, asst. prof. Grad. Sch. Bus., U. Wis., Madison, 1982—; cons. in field. Recipient doctoral dissertation award, Am. Psychol. Assn., 1981; Am. Mktg. Assn. doctoral dissertation grantee, 1978; Kent State U. grad. fellow, 1974-75; Northwestern U. grad. fellow, 1976-79. Mem. Am. Mktg. Assn., Am. Psychol. Assn., Assn. for Consumer Research, Alpha Sigma Nu, Beta Gamma Sigma. Contbr. articles to profl. jours. Home: 3516 Valley Ridge Rd Middleton WI 53562 Office: 1155 Observatory Dr Madison WI 53706

JOHN, GERALD WARREN, hospital pharmacist; b. Salem, Ohio, Feb. 16, 1947; s. Harold Elba and Ruth Springer (Pike) J.; m. Jean Ann Marie Orris, Nov. 5, 1977; children—Patrick Warren, Jeanette Lynn. B.S.Ph., Ohio No. U., 1970; M.S., U. Md., 1974. Registered pharmacist, Ohio, Md. Staff pharmacist North Columbiana County Community Hosp., Salem, 1970-72; asst. resident in hosp. pharmacy U. Md. Hosp., Balt., 1972-73, sr. resident, 1973-74, chmn. patient care pharmacies, 1974-76; dir. pharmacy Ohio Valley Hosp., Steubenville, Ohio, 1976—; preceptor profl. externship program Ohio No. U. Sch. Pharmacy, 1977—; adj. clin. instr. practical experience program Duquesne U. Sch. Pharmacy, 1976—. Named Hosp. Pharmacist of Yr., Md. Soc. Hosp. Phamacists, 1976, Outstanding Young Man of Am., U.S. Jaycees, 1977. Mem. Am. Soc. Hosp. Pharmacists, Ohio Soc. Hosp. Pharmacists, Am. Pharm. Assn., Jefferson County Acad. Pharmacy, Ohio Pharm. Assn., Southeastern Ohio Soc. Hosp. Pharmacists, Rho Chi. Methodist. Mem. adv. bd. Contemporary Pharmacy Practice, 1977-83.

JOHN, MERTIS, JR., record company executive; b. Detroit, May 22, 1932; s. Mertis and Lillie G. (Robinson) J.; m. Essie M. Wincher, June 16, 1957; 1 son, Darryl E.; m. Olivia M. Fuller, Aug. 6, 1978. A.A., Wayne Coll., 1978. Songwriter for King Records, Cin. and N.Y.C., 1955-67; founder Mertis Music Co., Detroit, 1962—; founder, pres. Meda Record Co., 1981—; co-producer Inside Music, 1977; also musician, songwriter. Served with U.S. Army, 1952-54. Mem. Broadcast Music Assn., Detroit Soc. Musicians and Entertainers (chmn. bd. dirs. 1984—), Am. Fedn. Musicians, Broadcast Music Inc. (corr.). Baptist. Lodge: Masons. Composer over 300 songs; author (poem) Christmas Morn, 1982. Office: 8130 Northlawn Detroit MI 48204

JOHNEY, GLENN ERIC, aerospace engineer; b. Kansas City, Mo., July 15, 1956; s. Eugene Albert and Czerna Bye (Cruce) J. B.S. in Aerospace Engring., U. Mo.-Rolla, 1978. Specialist engr. Boeing Mil. Aircraft Co., Wichita, Kans., 1978—; freelance computer programmer Glenn Johney Enterprises, Wichita, Kans., 1984—. Mem. bd. edn. Grace Luth. Ch., Wichita, 1979-80; v.p. Aid Assn. for Lutherans Br., Wichita, 1985. Mem. AIAA (newsletter editor 1980-81). Avocations: photography; computers; swimming; skiing; travel. Home: 1911 Marion Rd Wichita KS 67216 Office: Boeing Mil Airplane Co 3801 S Oliver St Wichita KS 67210

JOHNS, ANTIONETTE FRANCIS, educational administrator; b. Detroit, July 22, 1944; d. Francin James and Annottillie (Turley) Kolvoord; m. William Max Johns, June 19, 1964; children—Cori Lyne, Heather. Student Kellog Community Coll., 1964, U. Mich., 1965; B.A. in Elem. Edn. and Spl. Edn., Western Mich. U., 1969, M.A., 1973; cert. sch. psychologist, Western Mich. U., 1974; Ed.D., U. No. Colo., 1977; postgrad. in ednl. adminstrn. U. Minn., 1981. Tchr. mentally retarded Galesburg (Mich.) High Sch., 1968-69, Comstock (Mich.) Elem. Sch., 1969-73; cons. Sci. Research Assocs., Chgo., 1973-75; instr. Western Mich. U., Kalamazoo, 1973-75; coordinator Eastern Service Area, Kalamazoo Intermediate Sch. Dist., Comstock, Mich., 1972-75; instr. U. No. Colo., Greeley, 1975-77; dir. spl. edn. 916 Spl. Intermediate Dist., White Bear Lake, Minn., 1977—; chmn. East Met. Spl. Edn. Consortium, 1982-83; cons. McKnight Found., 1983, JWK Corp., Washington; chmn. Ramsey County Mental Retardation Adv. Com. Human Services Com.; mem. St. Paul Assn. Retarded Children, Council Exceptional Children. Bush fellow, 1982-83. Mem. Am. Vocat. Assn., Am. Assn. Edn. Severely and Profoundly Handicapped, Minn. Assn. Sch. Adminstrs. (chmn. statewide edn. policy com. 1982-83), Minn. Adminstrs. Spl. Edn., Am. Soc. Tng. and Devel., Kappa Eta Sigma, Phi Delta Kappa, Kappa Delta Pi. Lutheran. Author: Classification Tasks with Mentally Retarded and their Predictor Variables for Success., 1977; co-author research papers. Home: 6 White Oaks Ln Saint Paul MN 55110 Office: 3300 Century Ave N White Bear Lake MN 55110

JOHNS, JERRY WAYNE, county sheriff; b. Monon, Ind., Nov. 21, 1940; s. Harry Edward and Valeria Goldie (Bulington) J.; m. Nancy Lee Burns, Dec. 2, 1961 (div. 1979); children—Lori Ann, Tracy Lyn, Michelle Elaine; m. Mary Margaret Hackl, June 17, 1984; children—Bryan Paul Hietpas, Jodi Marie Hietpas. Grad. Law Enforcement Acad., 1973. Produce mgr. Annis I.G.A., Monon, Ind., 1955-60; safety and security officer R.C.A. Corp., Monticello, Ind., 1960-73; dep. sheriff White County Sheriff Dept., Monticello, 1973-82, sheriff, 1982—. Mem. Fraternal Order Police (pres. 1980-81). Republican. Avocations: Spectator sports-football, basketball, boating and summer sports. Home: RR 3 Box 200 Monticello IN 47960 Office: White County Sheriffs Dept 315 N Illinois St Monticello IN 47960

JOHNS, MICHAEL RICHARD, regional planner; b. Chgo., Aug. 23, 1952; s. Carl Richard and Josephine Elizabeth (Jacobs) J.; m. Carol Beth Quigley, Aug. 2, 1979; children—Geoffrey Andrew, Rebecca Renee. B.A., U. Minn., 1975; M.A., Mankato State U., 1978; postgrad. U. Okla., 1982. Cert. planner. Program asst. spl. projects and program devel. Arrowhead Regional Devel. Commn., Duluth, Minn., 1976-78; state land use planner Iowa Office for Planning and Programming, Des Moines, 1978-79; exec. dir. Green Hills Regional Planning Commn., Trenton, Mo., 1979—; program mgr. Green Hills Rural Devel. Inc., Trenton, 1981—; Recipient Outstanding Young Am. award Jaycees, 1981, 82, Creative Writing award Masonic Lodge, Minn., 1970. Mem. Amer. Inst. Cert. Planners, Amer. Planning Assn. (dir. Mo. chpt. 1981-83), Mo. Assn. Councils Govt. Dirs. Com., Amer. Econ., Devel. Council, Nat. Assn. Housing Rehab. Officers, Mo. C. of C. Dirs. Assn. Roman Catholic. Clubs: Trenton Rotary. Contbr. articles to profl. publs. Office: 815 Main St Trenton MO 64683

JOHNSEN, DONALD EDWARD, pharmacist; b. Hammond, Ind., June 29, 1952; s. Donald Edward and Louise Agnes (Farni) J.; m. Linda Beth Elliott, June 10, 1972; children—Amy, Sara, Donald. B.S. in Pharmacy. Staff pharmacist Community Hosp., Munster, Ind., 1975-78, dir. pharmacy, 1978-81, Our Lady of Mercy Hosp., Dyer, Ind., 1981—; externship preceptor Purdue U., West Lafayette, Ind., 1978—. Mem. Am. Soc. Hosp. Pharmacists, Ind. Soc. Hosp. Pharmacists, Am. Soc. Cons. Pharmacists, Jaycees (pres. 1978-79). Avocations: marathon running, basketball referee. Home: 2661 Lakewood Dr Dyer IN 46311 Office: Our Lady of Mercy Hosp US Hwy 30 Dyer IN 46311-1799

JOHNSGARD, PAUL AUSTIN, biological science educator, author; b. Fargo, N.D., June 28, 1931; s. Alfred Bernard and Yvonne Marguerite (Morgan) J.; m. Lois Miriam Lampe, June 25, 1956; children—Jay Erik, Scott Kenneth, Ann Yvonne, Karin Luisa. B.S., N.D. State U., 1953; M.S., Wash. State U., 1956; Ph.D., Cornell U., 1959; postgrad. Bristol U., 1959-61. Postdoctoral fellow Bristol U., Eng., 1959-61; instr. U. Nebr., Lincoln, 1961-62, asst. prof., 1962-63, assoc. prof., 1965-68, prof. biol. sci., 1968-80, found. prof. biol. sci., 1980—. Author: Handbook of Waterfowl Behavior, 1965; Animal Behavior, 1967; Waterfowl: Their Biology and Natural History, 1968; Grouse and Quails of North America, 1973; Song of the North Wind: A Story of the Snow Goose, 1974; American Game Birds of Upland and Shoreline, 1975; Waterfowl of North America, 1975; Ducks, Geese and Swans of the World, 1978; Birds of the Great Plains; Breeding Species and Their Distribution, 1979; A Guide to North American Waterfowl, 1979; Sandpipers and Snipes of the World, 1981; Those of the Gray Wind: The Sandhill Cranes, 1981; Teton Wildlife: Observations by a Naturalist, 1982; (with K. Johnsgard) Dragons and Unicorns: A Natural History, 1982; Hummingbirds of North America, 1983; Cranes of the World, 1983; Grouse of the World, 1983; The Platte: Channels in Time, 1984; Pheasants of the World, 1985; Birds of the Rocky Mountains, 1985; Loons, Grebes and Auks of North America, 1985; Prairie Children, Mountain Dreams, 1985. Contbr. articles to profl. jours. Editor: The Bird Decoy: An American Art Form, 1976. Recipient Disting. Teaching award U. Nebr., Lincoln, 1968, Research and Creative Activity award U. Nebr., Lincoln, 1984, Mari Sandoz Lit. award Nebr. Library Assn., 1984; J.S. Guggenheim fellow, 1970. Fellow Am. Ornithol. Union; mem. Cooper Ornithol. Soc., Wilson Ornithol. Soc., Nebr. Ornithologists Union (hon. life). Unitarian. Avocations: drawing; photography; sculpture. Home: 7341 Holdrege St Lincoln NE 68505 Office: Sch Biol Scis U Nebr Lincoln NE 68588

JOHNSON, ALAN EDWARD, lawyer; b. Hibbing, Minn., Sept. 3, 1946; s. Robert Eugene and Georgia Viola (Webb) J.; married June 10, 1973 (div. Sept. 15, 1981); 1 son, Robert Edward. B.A., U. Chgo., 1968, M.A., 1971; J.D., Cleve. State U., 1979. Bar: Ohio 1979, U.S. Dist. Ct. (no. dist.) Ohio 1979, U.S. Ct. Appeals (6th cir.) 1981. Research assoc. Ednl. Research Council Am., Cleve., 1972-78; founder, pres. Johnson Legal Research, Cleve., 1978-81; sole practice, Cleve., 1979-81; assoc. editor Lawyers Co-op. Pub. Co., Rochester, N.Y., 1981-83; assoc. Hendershott, Huffman & Peckinpaugh Co., L.P.A., Cleve., 1983—. Co-author series: Concepts and Inquiry, 1972-78; Federal Procedures, Lawyers Edition, 1983. Office: Hendershott Huffman & Peckinpaugh Co LPA 600 Citizens Fed Tower Cleveland OH 44111

JOHNSON, ALBERT EDDIE, publisher; b. Chgo., Dec. 10, 1932; s. Albert Elwood and Evelyn Margret Jessie (Morgan) J.; student Loop Jr. Coll., Chgo., 1962-63, U. Chgo., 1963, Inst. Contemporary Latin Am. Studies, 1968; m. Annette Dial, Nov. 15, 1955; children—Martin, Charles, Michael, Albert, Aquanette, Andray, Toni. With Ill. Bell Telephone Co., Chgo., 1957-70, community relations mgr., 1968-70; pres. Al Johnson & Assos., Inc., Chgo., 1970—; chmn. bd. Act V Prodns., Inc., 1965; pub.-editor Chgo. Shoreland News, weekly, 1975—; dir. Ebony Talent Assos., Inc.; cons. Mem. Coalition Community Action, Black Strategy Center; bd. dirs. Sears YMCA, Midwest Community Council. Served with AUS, 1950-53. Decorated Purple Heart; recipient Nat. Lane Bryant award, Joint Action Dirs. award, Vision Found. for Blind Youth award, Maury Hoffberg Meml. Found. award, Nat. Eye Research Found. award, Philander Smith Coll. award, Jobs for Youth Service award, BMI Pubs. award, Black Media Reps. award, Sears YMCA Service award, Chgo. I Will award. Mem. Nat. Black Media Inc., Nat. Newspaper Pubs. Assn. Creator, author: Time's Running Out, 1969; Where Do I Go From Here?, 1967; The Easter Story, 1966; The Easter Story Record, 1966; The Johnson's View. Office: 1020 S Wabash Ave Chicago IL 60605*

JOHNSON, ARTHUR SUNE, veterinarian; b. Mpls., Aug. 13, 1927; s. Richard E. and Marie (Johanson) J.; B.S., U. Minn., 1953, D.V.M., 1955; m. Carol Lou Stedman, July 21, 1951; children—Ann Marie, Arthur Mark. Veterinarian, small animal practice All Pets Hosp., Mpls., 1958—; pres. Arthur S. Johnson Corp., investments, 1965—, chmn. bd., 1965—; ordained to ministry Pentecostal Ch., 1969; radio evangelist Selby Gospel Broadcasting, Inc., St. Paul, 1970—; evangelist Harvest Field Mission, Mpls., 1967—, Northside Outreach Worker Program, Mpls., 1971. Precinct chmn. Rep. party, 1966-69; bd. dirs. Kings Acad., Young Am. Encounter. Served with USMCR, 1945-46. Mem. AVMA, Minn. Veterinary Med. Assn., Am., Met. animal hosp. assns., Am. Pub. Health Assn., Nat. Assn. Professions, Full Gospel Businessmen Fellowship Internat., Am. Legion, Gideons Internat. (Bible sec. 1968-71). Clubs: Kiwanis; Forest Hills Golf (Forest Lake, Minn.). Home: 907 51st Ave NE Minneapolis MN 55421 Office: 5100 Central Ave NE Minneapolis MN 54421

JOHNSON, BARBARA JANE, sales representative; b. Chgo., Aug. 19, 1946; d. Sidney and Norma Mona Shaffer; B.A. in Sociology and Psychology, U. Ill., 1968; postgrad. M.B.A. program, Roosevelt U., 1971-72; m. Gary Johnson, Aug. 25, 1968; 1 child, Eric Michael. Asst. personnel dir. Associated Mills, Chgo., 1967-69, Scholl Mfg. Co. Inc., Chgo., 1969-71; nurse recruiter Cook County Hosp. Governing Com., Chgo., 1971-73; recruiter Mt. Sinai Hosp., Chgo., 1973-76; sales rep. Stryker Corp., Kalamazoo, 1976-81, area trainer; sales rep. Physio Control, Schaumberg, Ill., 1981—; with Sensormedics Corp., Anaheim, Calif.; founder Chgo. Area Nurse Recruiters; cons. positions as nurse recruiter. Vice pres. Budlong Community Action Group, 1979—; advisor Jr. Achievement, 1969-72; auction com. Ednl. TV; trustee Mt. Sinai/Schwab Rehab. Ctr., 1983—. Recipient Lee Stryker sales award, 1979. Mem. Assn. of Operating Room Nurses (sponsor). Recipient first place Recruitment Brochure for Chgo. Area Bus. Communicators, 1975; salesman of year, 1979; first woman to achieve nat. award, 1979.

JOHNSON, BARRY LEE, safety and health association executive; b. Sanders, Ky., Oct. 24, 1938; s. Otto Lee and Sarah Josephine (Deatherage) J.; m. Billie Reed, Aug. 19, 1960; children—Lee, Clay, Scott, Reed, Sarah. B.S., U. Ky., 1960; M.S., Iowa State U., 1962, Ph.D., 1967. Bioengr. U.S. EPA, Cin., 1962-71, Nat. Inst. for Occupational Safety & Health, 1971—. Editor: Neurotoxicology; Archives Environ. Health, Toxicology Indsl. Health. Commendation medals USPHS, 1978, 84. Mem. Am. Pub. Health Assn., Permanent Commn. Occupational Health, Am. Conf. Govt. Indsl. Hygienists, Sigma Xi. Home: 8393 Summitridge Cincinnati OH 45230

JOHNSON, BETTY JEAN, state educational administrator; b. Indpls., July 16, 1944; d. Hezekiah and Easter Gertrude (Lewis) Hill; m. William George Ryder, July 17, 1965 (div. Mar. 1974); 1 son, Mark Oliver; m. Steven Maurice Johnson, Nov. 2, 1977. B.Ed., Butler U., 1965, M.Ed., 1969. Tchr., Indpls. pub. schs., 1965-69, reading tchr., 1969-71, elem. cons., 1972-73; reading cons. Ind. Pub. Instrn. Dept., Indpls., 1973-77; assoc. prof. edn. Ind. U.-Purdue U.-Indpls., 1974-76; asst. dir. div. reading effectiveness Ind. Dept. Pub. Instrn., Indpls., 1977-78, dir. div. reading effectiveness, 1978—. Bd. dirs. Operation PUSH, 1977-82, 500 Festival Assocs.; state vice-chmn. Am. Cancer Soc., 1976-77; state vice-chmn. Black Republicans, 1975-77. Mem. Internat. Reading Assn., Nat. Tchrs. Council English, Nat. Alliance Black Educators, Nat. Assn. State English and Reading Specialists, NAACP (edn. chmn. 1980), Alpha Kappa Alpha. Republican. Club: Jack and Jill of Am.

JOHNSON, BRUCE ROSS, educator; b. La Porte, Ind., May 18, 1949; s. Egbert Johannes Daniel and Ruth Elvera (Johnson) J. B.S., Ball State U., Muncie, Ind., 1971; M.Edn., Valparaiso U., 1975; postgrad. Nat. Coll. Edn., Evanston, Ill., 1974. Cert. elem. sch. tchr., Ind. Vol. tchr. Peace Corps, St. Vincent, W.I., 1971-72; tchr. South Central Sch., Union Mills, Ind., 1972-76, 77—; missionary tchr. Luth. Ch., Liberia, West Africa, 1976-77; vis. educator U. London, 1974, U. Moscow, 1974, U. Paris, 1974. Contbr. articles to newspapers. Pres. People to People Internat., La Porte, Ind., 1981-83, trustee, Kansas City, Mo., 1983—; mem. ch. council Bethany Luth. Ch., La Porte, 1983—; v.p. Friends of La Porte County Library, 1984; trustee La Porte County Hist. Soc., 1985—; v.p. Ind. Geneal. Soc., 1981-82; pres. Community Concert Assn., La Porte, 1984. State finalist NASA Tchr.-in-Space project, 1985. Mem. NEA (life), Ind. State Tchrs. Assn., Phi Delta Kappa. Clubs: Amateur Music (pres. 1982-83) (La Porte), Little Theater (bd. dirs. 1980-83), Lions (bd. dirs. 1983—). Avocations: Performing in musical theater, collecting foreign coins, traveling, gardening. Home: 2012 S Village Rd La Porte IN 46350 Office: South Central Community Schs 9808 S 600 W Union Mills IN 46382

JOHNSON, C. E., diversified manufacturing company executive. Pres., chief operating officer, dir. Borg-Warner Corp., Chgo. Office: Borg-Warner Corp 200 S Michigan Ave Chicago IL 60604*

JOHNSON, CALVIN KEITH, research executive, chemist; b. Litchfield, Minn., Dec. 15, 1937; s. Delphin J. and Iva Mae (Watkins) J.; m. Constance S. Hoffman, June 18, 1960; children—Eric O., Judd. F., Malinda K. B.A., Olivet Nazarene Coll., Ill., 1959; Ph.D. in Chemistry, Mich. State U., 1963. Postdoctoral fellow Columbia U., N.Y.C., 1963-64; research chemist 3M Co., St. Paul, 1964-67; group leader CPC Internat., Summit, Ill., 1967-69; mgr. research and devel. Acme Resin Corp. unit CPC Internat., Forest Park, Ill., 1969-71, tech. dir., 1971-76, v.p., tech. dir., 1977—. Patentee in field (10). Contbr. articles to tech. jours. Mem. ch. bd. 1st Ch. of Nazarene, Lemont, Ill., 1969—, Sunday Sch. supt., 1977-83; chmn. bd. Olivet Research Assocs., Kankakee, Ill., 1982—; mem., fundraiser Chickasaw Homeowners Assn., Lockport, Ill., 1979—. NSF fellow, 1961; NIH fellow, 1963. Mem. Am. Chem. Soc., Am. Foundrymen's Soc. (chmn. com.), Soc. Petroleum Engrs., AAAS, Research Dirs. Assn. Chgo., Sigma Xi. Republican. Avocations: gardening; fishing. Home: 13725 Potawatomi Lockport IL 60441 Office: Acme Resin Corp 1372 Circle Ave Forest Park IL 60130

JOHNSON, CHARLES PHILIP, business executive; b. Darien, Wis., May 9, 1922; B.A., U. Wis., 1947, L.L.B., 1949; m. Frances V. Huber, June 17, 1944; children—Philip C., Jennifer S., Kristi L., Jay L., Craig R. Admitted to Wis. bar, 1949; partner-operator Johnson Farms, Darien, 1950-69, Jon-Dyke, Inc., Agri-Bus., Darien, 1969-75, Johnson & Danielson, Inc., Ins. and Real Estate, Darien, 1954-74, Darien Hardware Co., 1961-73; prin. C. Phil Johnson, Agcons., Darien, 1976-82; now with Starview Capital Co., Inc., Williams Bay, Wis. Pres. Village of Darien, 1951-52; treas. Darien Consol. Schs., 1960-64, pres., 1965-69; treas. Walworth County March of Dimes, 1950-58; mem. exec. com Walworth County Farm Bur., 1955-59; dir. Wis. div. Nat. Farmers Orgn., 1965-69; area rep. Tri County State Line council Boy Scouts Am., 1954-66; bd. dirs. Family Motor Coach Assn., 1972-80, v.p., 1972-73, pres., 1974-77; bd. dirs. Wis. Vocat. and Tech. Adult Edn., 1972-78, pres., 1976-78; bd. dirs. Wis. Higher Edn. Aids, 1973-80, Wis. Regents, 1976-78, Coop. Edn. Service Agy., 1967-71; pres. Wis. Found. Vocat., Tech. and Adult Edn., 1977-83. Home: 237 E Jackson St Darien WI 53114 Office: Starview Capital Co Inc 154 Elkhorn Rd Williams Bay WI 53191

JOHNSON, CHERYL STEWART, educator, school administrator; b. Dayton, Ohio, Oct. 26, 1944; d. William Edward and Dorothy Mae (Ware) S.; m. Victor Jerome Johnson, Mar. 12, 1966; 1 child, Derrick Scott. B.S. in Edn., Central State U., 1966, M.S. in Edn. Adminstrn., 1970; M.Ed., Wright State U., 1978. Personnel test adminstr. Nat. Cash Register Co., Dayton, 1965-66; tchr. Dayton Pub. Schs., 1966-69, media specialist, 1969-71, asst. prin., 1971-79, elem. prin., 1979-82, prin. jr. high. sch., 1982—; cons. Dayton Citizens Community Edn. Council, Adelphi U. Nat. Tng. Inst., Dayton City Schs. Curriculum Task Force. Bd. dirs. YMCA, YWCA, Dayton Sch. Mgmt. Assn., Bethel Bapt. Ch. Fed. Credit Union. Recipient Outstanding Adminstr. award Dayton Edn. Assn., 1984. Mem. NAACP, Dayton Adminstrs. Assn. (sec. 1979-81), Ohio Assn. Secondary Sch. Prins., Nat. Assn. Secondary Sch. Prins., Delta Sigma Theta, Phi Delta Kappa. Democrat. Baptist. Club: Twentig, Jack & Jill. Avocations: bolwing; music; photography; interior design. Home: 4200 Brookhill Ln Dayton OH 45405

JOHNSON, CLEO VERNON, hospital administrator; b. Lowell, Kans., Oct. 28, 1936; s. Raymond Lester and Bernice Adelia (Brock) J.; m. Shirley Mae Frick, June 8, 1958; children—Randal Linn, LaVonne Rene Johnson Dye. B.S. in Bus. Adminstrn., Union Coll., 1958; M.B.A., Andrews U., 1971. Bookkeeper, accountant, chief accountant Boulder Meml. Hosp., Colo., 1958-64; bus. mgr. Benghazi Adventist Hosp., Libya, North Africa, 1965-69, Bandung, Java, Indonesia, 1971-73, Seoul Adventist Hosp., Korea, 1974-76; asst., assoc. exec. dir. Shawnee Mission Med. Center, Kans., 1977-82, pres., 1982—; dir. Moberly Regional Med. Center, Mo., Osborne Meml. Hosp., Kans.; regional v.p. Adventist Health System/Eastern & Middle Am., Shawnee Mission, 1982—. Mem. Am. Coll. Hosp. Adminstrs., Merriam C. of C. (v.p. 1980-81), Overland Park C. of C. Seventh-day Adventist. Lodge: Rotary. Avocation: art work. Home: 7123 Halsey Shawnee KS 66216 Office: Shawnee Mission Med Center 74th & Grandview Shawnee Mission KS 66201

JOHNSON, CURTIS MILTON, educator, ednl. adminstr.; b. St. Paul, Feb. 29, 1928; s. Vivian W. and Emma (Bethke) J.; B.S., St. Cloud State U., 1952; M.A., St. Thomas Coll., 1965; A.B.D., Ohio U., 1974; m. Jewel M. Troyer, July 22, 1949; children—Wendy, Cheryl, Brant, Jay, Dana, Todd. Indsl. arts tchr. Clarkfield (Minn.) Schs., 1952-56; indsl. arts tchr., chmn. dept. Sibley Sr. High Sch., West Saint Paul, Minn., 1956-66; adminstrn. fellowship Ohio U., 1966-67, dir. continuing edn., 1967-69, dir. Ext. Div., 1969-80, dir. internat. edn., 1980—, asst. prof. engring. graphics, 1976—. Pres., South St. Paul (Minn.) Public Schs. Bd. Edn., 1964-66; chmn. Dakota County (Minn.) Jr. Coll. Com., 1965-66; chmn. Athens Twp. Zoning Commn., 1973-74; dir., pres. Athens County Regional Planning Commn., 1975—. Served with USCGR, 1946-47. Recipient Nat. Ford Indsl. Arts award, Bush Found. Leadership fellow. Mem. Nat. Univ. Continuing Edn. Assn., Ohio Coll. Assn., Ohio Adult Edn. Assn., Ohio Council on Higher Continuing Edn., Phi Delta Kappa. Rotarian. Home: Route 1 Box 48F Athens OH 45701 Office: 302 Tupper Hall Ohio Univ Athens OH 45701

JOHNSON, DANA ERNEST, pediatrician, neonatologist, researcher; b. Worcester, Mass., Dec. 28, 1948; s. Ernest Albin and Virginia Edith (Peterson) J.; m. Maureen Ellen Crowley, Mar. 24, 1973; children—Rachael Virginia, Elizabeth Marie. B.A., North Park Coll., 1970; M.D., U. Minn., 1975, Ph.D., 1982. Diplomate Am. Bd. Pediatrics, Am. Bd. Neonatal Medicine. Intern, resident fellow U. Minn. Hosps.; instr. in pediatrics U. Minn., Mpls., 1979-80, asst. prof. pediatrics, 1980-84, assoc. prof. pediatrics, 1984—; co-ordinator Twin Cities Com. for Neonatal Life Support Policy, 1982—; neonatal cons. Internat. Mission of Hope, Calcutta, India, 1984—. Contbr. numerous articles to sci. jours. Fellow Am. Acad. Pediatrics. Mem. Evangel. Covenant Ch. Avocations: gardening; cooking; travel. Office: Box 211 University Hosps U Minn 420 Delaware SE Minneapolis MN 55455

JOHNSON, DAVID CHESTER, dean, sociology educator; b. Jan. 21, 1933; s. Chester Laven and Olga Henriett (Resnick) J.; m. Jean Ann Lunnis, Sept. 10, 1955; children—Stephen, Andrew, Jennifer. B.A., Gustavus Adolphus Coll., 1954; M.A., U. Iowa, 1956, Ph.D., 1959. Instr. to prof. sociology Luther Coll., Decorah, Iowa, 1957-69; dean arts and scis. East Stroudsburg State Coll., Pa., 1969-76; v.p. acad. affairs St. Cloud State U., Minn., 1976-83; dean Gustavus Adolphus Coll., St. Peter, Minn., 1983—. Vice chmn. curriculum adv. com. Minn. Higher Edn. Coordinating Bd., St. Paul, 1984—. NSF sci. faculty fellow Inst. Social Research, Oslo, 1965-66; Adminstrv. fellow Am. Council Edn., Luther Coll., 1968-69, Summer Leadership fellow Bush Found., Inst. Edn. Mgmt., Harvard U., 1981; grantee Kennedy Swedish Fund, Sweden, 1976. Mem. Am. Scandinavian Found., Am. Council Acad. Deans, Am. Assn. Higher Edn., St. Peter C. of C. Democrat. Lutheran. Lodge: Rotary. Home: 821 S 4th St Saint Peter MN 56802 Office: Gustavus Adolphus Coll Saint Peter MN 56082

JOHNSON, DAVID LEWIS, research director, materials researcher; b. Indpls., Mar. 29, 1946; s. William Lewis and Lula (Zoitos) J.; m. Kathleen Faye Bradley, Sept. 2, 1967; children—Bill, Brad, Brian. B.S. in Metall. Engring., Purdue U., 1968, Ph.D. in Material Sci., 1973. Metallurgist, Argonne Nat. Lab., Ill., 1973-79; dir. materials research InterNorth, Inc., Omaha, 1979—. Contbr. articles to profl. jours. Inventor Prestressed Impact Testing Device, 1984. Mem. Am. Soc. Metals, Am. Welding Soc., Welding Inst. Canada. Presbyterian. Avocations: softball; coaching youth sports; furniture refinishing; auto restoration. Office: Inter North Inc 4840 F St Omaha NE 68117

JOHNSON, DAVID WARREN, audiologist; b. Duluth, Minn., Feb. 13, 1944; s. Gustaf Adolph and Anna Margurite (Sjogren) J.; m. Cynthia Stephanie Brecke, Nov. 9, 1973; children—Michael, Matthew. B.A., U. Minn.-Duluth, 1966; M.A., U. Oreg., 1969; M.S., Portland State U., 1971. Tchr. Atlanta Community Sch. (Mich., 1967-68, Mt. Hood Community Coll., Gresham, Oreg., 1968-71, Portland Community Coll. (Oreg.), 1969-71; audiologist; dept. otolaryngology Hennepin County Med. Ctr., Mpls., 1972—; clin. instr. dept. otolaryngology U. Minn. Med. Sch., 1973—. Contbr. papers to profl. publs. Pres., chmn. bd. Minn. Found. for Acoustical Edn. and Research, Richfield, 1981—; Minn. Hearing Inst., Mpls., 1984—; mem. Mpls. Med. Research Found., 1982—; assoc. mem. Am. Acad. Otolaryngology-Head and Neck Surgery Found., 1984—; vice chmn. Richfield Adv. Bd. Health, 1980-84. Mem. Acoustical Soc. Am. (pres. Upper Midwest chpt. 1976-77), Am. Speech-Lang.-Hearing Assn. Council for Accreditation in Occupational Hearing Conservation (course coordinator 1977—), Minn. Speech-Lang.-Hearing Assn. (v.p. for govtl. affairs 1980-82), Linguistic Soc. Am., Pi Gamma Mu. Lutheran. Office: Audiology 824 Dept of Otolaryngology Hennepin County Med Ctr 701 Park Ave Minneapolis MN 55415

JOHNSON, DENNIS WILLIAM, printing company executive; b. Rockford, Ill., Mar. 10, 1938; s. Harry C. and Alice E. (Greenberg) J.; student Bethel Coll., 1956-58, Rockford Coll., 1958-59; m. Evelyn Jo Stahl, Aug. 12, 1961; children—Tonya, Cary, Rynn. Sec., treas. H.C. Johnson Press, Inc., Rockford, 1958—; pres. Versatile Ventures, Inc., Rockford, 1966—; sec.-treas. Johnson Graphics, Inc., Dubuque, Ill., Sundberg Printers, Inc., Rockford, Ill., Johnson Printing Corp., DeKalb, Ill., Lawrence Travel Internat., Phoenix, Clinic Profl. Weight Control, Rockford; dir. Camelot World Travel, Inc., Rockford, Guaranty Nat. Bank, Rockford. Mem. Bd. Suprs. Winnebago County, Rockford, 1965-68; alderman City of Rockford, 1968-83; mem. No. Ill. Law Enforcement Commn., Rockford, 1969-76; bd. dirs. No. Ill. Multiple Sclerosis Bd., 1971-73; co-chmn. Winnebago County Bicentennial Commn., 1976-77; chmn. Police and Fire Commn., Rockford, 1983; trustee Judson Coll., Elgin, Ill.; bd. dirs. Inst. for Holyland Studies, Jerusalem, Bibles for India, Grand Rapids, Mich., Johnson Found., Rockford. Named Outstanding Young Legislator, Rockford Jr. C. of C., 1969. Mem. Printing Industry of Ill., Christian Businessmen's Com., C. of C., Gideons Republican. Mem. Free Ch. Home: 3134 Talbot Trail Rockford IL 61111 Office: 2801 Eastrock Dr Rockford IL 61125

JOHNSON, DIANE MARIE, hospital administrative official; b. Superior, Wis., Aug. 9, 1957; d. Gordon Charles and Dorothy Elaine (Jacobson) Johnson. B.A. in Health Info. Adminstrn., Coll. of St. Scholastica, Duluth, Minn., 1979. Chief med. info. sect. VA Med. Center Saginaw, Mich., 1979-83, adminstrv. specialist to dir., 1983-84, adminstrv. asst. to chief of staff, 1984—. Mem. Am. Med. Record Assn., Mich. Med. Record Assn., East Central Mich. Med. Record Assn., Coll. Young Hosp. Adminstrs., Mich. Assn. Quality Assurance Profls. Office: 1500 Weiss St Saginaw MI 48602

JOHNSON, DONALD LOREN, hospital administrator; b. Madelia, Minn., Aug. 3, 1936; s. Loren Edward and Marian Grace (Harris) J.; m. Annette Mae Kriens, Dec. 1, 1957; children—Monica Lauren, Sonya Ann. B.A., Metropolitan U., 1977. Registered x-ray technologist. Lab. and x-ray technician Windom Hosp., Minn., 1955-56, Spencer Municipal Hosp., Iowa, 1966-67; hosp. adminstr. Watonwan Meml. Hosp., St. James, Minn., 1967—; chmn. bd. vol. Hosps. Am., Inc. InterCare, Redwood Falls, Minn., 1982—; dir. North Star Mut. Assurance Ltd., Hamilton, Bermuda, InterHome Care, Redwood Falls, Minn., 1983—. Mem. Minn. EMS Task Force, Mpls., 1980, Am. Registry of Radiol. Technologists, Mpls., St. James Housing Redevel. Authority, Minn., 1980. Mem. Minn. Hosp. Assn. Methodist. Lodge: Eagles. Avocations: travel; reading; gardening. Office: Watonwan Meml Hosp 1207 6th Ave S Saint James MN 56081

JOHNSON, DONALD OTTO, geologist; b. Chgo., July 9, 1941; s. Ronald Raymond Johnson and Irene Louise (Beckmann) Vinyard; m. Michele Dougherty, Aug. 19, 1967. B.S., No. Ill. U., 1965, M.S., 1966; Ph.D., U. Ill., 1972. Geologist, Ill. State Geol. Survey, Champaign, 1965-72; coal geologist Ohio Geol. Survey, Columbus, 1972-74; dep. dir. phys. scis. research, land reclamation program Energy and Environ. Systems Div., Argonne Nat. Lab., Ill., 1974-79; asst. dir. environ. research Gas Research Inst., Chgo., 1977-85; pres. Donald O. Johnson & Assoc., Inc., Naperville, Ill., 1985—; cons. geologist, Columbus, 1972-74. Contbr. articles to profl. publs. Mem. Naperville Heritage Soc., 1975—; treas. East Central Homeowners Orgn., Naperville, 1976-78; bd. trustees Alliance Française, DuPage County, Ill., 1977-79. Mem. Air Pollution Control Assn., Am. Assn. Petroleum Geologists (jr. mem.). Avocations: travel, classical music, wine. Home: 127 S Wright Naperville IL 60540

JOHNSON, DONALD RICHARD, immunology researcher, educator; b. Duluth, Minn., June 11, 1947; s. Theodore Richard and Eleanor Ann (Carlson) J. B.A., U. Minn., 1970; Ph.D., U. Ill., 1977. Research assoc. Karolinska Inst., Stockholm, Sweden, 1977-81; asst. prof. U. Nebr. Med. Ctr., Omaha, 1981—. Contbr. articles to profl. jours. John C. Dawn Found. scholar, 1965-69; fellow Am. Cancer Soc., 1977-79, Cancer Research Inst., 1979-81; NIH grantee, 1982—. Mem. Am. Assn. Immunologists. Home: 1516 N 51st St Omaha NE 68104 Office: Dept Pathology and Lab Medicine U Neb Med Ctr 42d and Dewey Ave Omaha NE 68105

JOHNSON, DOROTHY PHYLLIS, counselor, art therapist; b. Kansas City, Mo., Sept. 13, 1925; d. Chris C. and Mabel T. (Gillum) Green; B.A. in Art, Ft. Hays. State U., 1975, M.S. in Guidance and Counseling, 1976, M.A. in Art, 1979; m. Herbert E. Johnson, May 11, 1945; children—Michael E., Gregory K. Art therapist High Plains Comprehensive Mental Health Assn., Hays, Kans., 1975-76; art therapist, mental health counselor Sunflower Mental Health Assn., Concordia, Kans., 1976—, co-dir. Project Togetherness, 1976-77, coordinator partial hospitalization, 1978—, out-patient therapist, 1982—; dir. Swedish Am. State Bank, Courtland, Kans., 1960—, sec., 1973-77. Mem. Kans., Am. art therapy assns., Am. Mental Health Counselors Assn., Am. Personnel and Guidance Assn., Assn. Specialists in Group Work, Phi Delta Kappa, Phi Kappa Phi. Contbr. articles to profl. jours. Home: Box 183 Courtland KS 66939 Office: 520 B Washington St Concordia KS 66901

JOHNSON, DOUGLAS, small business consultant; b. Norfolk, Va., Aug. 31, 1952; s. Henry and Nancy Jean (Kurfess) Kowalchick; m. Janis Marie Johnson, Aug. 23, 1980. B.A. in Philosophy (citation), Dartmouth Coll., 1974. Dir. prodn. WQSR Radio, Sarasota, Fla., 1975-78; announcer, personality Embrescia Communications, Cleve., 1978-81; pres. HW Enterprises, Cleve., 1979-83, Concepts, Inc., Lodi, Ohio, 1983—. Author: (plays) Lingua Canis, 1973; The Chalice, 1976; Festival, 1977. Speaker, Citizen's Choice, Cleve., 1982-83. Mem. Christian Ch. Address: 7860 Prouty Rd Lodi OH 44254

JOHNSON, DOUGLAS ALLAN, plastic manufacturing company executive; b. St. Paul, Jan. 18, 1942; s. Edgar L. and Luella Johanna (Rahn) J.; m. Carol Francis Semlak, Mar. 3, 1962; children—Theresa, Julie, Darren. Student U. Minn., 1961-65. Acct., Armour & Co., South St. Paul, Minn., 1963-68; plant mgr. Plastics Products, Lindstrom, Minn., 1968-79; owner Grantsburg Molded Products (Wis.), 1979-82; v.p., gen. mgr. Hartzell Mfg., St. Croix Falls, Wis., 1982—. Mem. Soc. Plastics Engrs. Republican. Lutheran. Club: Rotary. Home: 33160 Nueman Ct Lindstrom MN 55045 Office: 911 Pine St Saint Croix Falls WI 54024

JOHNSON, DOUGLAS BLAIKIE, engineer, corporate planning counsel; b. Chgo., Sept. 13, 1952; s. Marvin Melrose and Anne Stuart (Campbell) J.; m. Pamela Jane Tomlinson, Aug. 1, 1975; children—Richard Aaron, Lauren Stuart, Diana Blaikie, Scott Nathaniel. B.S.M.E., U. Nebr., 1974; J.D., Seton Hall U., 1980. Bar: Nebr. 1980, U.S. Dist. Ct. Nebr. 1980; registered profl. engr., Nebr. Project engr. Dupont, Cleve., 1974-75; project engr. Exxon Chems., Linden, N.J., 1975-78, cost engr., 1978-80; sr. engr. InterNorth, Inc., Omaha, 1980-82, market planner, 1982-84, corp. planner, 1984-85, bus. mgr., 1985—. Loaned exec. United Way of Midlands, Omaha, 1982, Midland council Boy Scouts Am., 1984, Jr. Achievement, Cleve., 1974. Mem. ABA, Fed. Energy Bar Assn., Assn. Trial Lawyers Am., Nebr. Bar Assn., Omaha Bar Assn., Sigma Tau, Pi Tau Sigma, Triangle. Republican. Presbyterian. Home: 14705 U Plaza Omaha NE 68137 Office: InterNorth Inc 2223 Dodge St Omaha NE 68102

JOHNSON, DOUGLAS LEE (EDDIE FINGERS), broadcasting executive, copywriter, producer, performer; b. Dayton, Ohio, Feb. 17, 1957; s. Clyde Harold and Genivee (Rock) J. B.A., U. Dayton, 1979. Announcer Sta. WVUD-FM, Dayton, 1977-79, Sta. WQMF-FM, Louisville, 1981-82, Sta. WWWM-FM, Cleve., 1982; prodn. dir. Sta. WSAI-FM, Cin., 1979-80; creative dir. O'Connell & Assocs. Advt., Cin., 1980-81; asst. program dir. Sta. WSKS-FM, Cin., 1982—; on-call talent Radio Theatre Group, Cin., 1984—. Mem. Alpha Epsilon Rho. Democrat. Avocations: poetry; wine collecting; basketball; baseball. Home: 73 Fawn Dr #10 Fairfield OH 45014 Office: WSKS-FM 3 East 4th St Cincinnati OH 45202

JOHNSON, DOUGLAS NEIL, educational administrator; b. Chgo., June 25, 1950; s. Roland Raymond and Bernice Evelyn (Stowowy) J.; m. Karen Elaine Jacobson, Oct. 14, 1972. B.A., St. Olaf Coll., Northfield, Minn., 1972; M.A., U. Minn.-Mpls., 1980. Cert. secondary edn. tchr., Minn. Buyer, Donaldsons Dept. Store, Mpls., 1972-76; coordinator community edn. Anoka-Hennepin Pub. Sch., Coon Rapids, Minn., 1976-79; dir. community edn. Columbia Heights Pub. Schs., Minn., 1979-80; exec. dir. Project Concern-Minn., Mpls., 1980-81; dir. community ctrs. Edina Pub. Schs., Minn., 1981—. Co.-chmn. Edina Expo '85; mem. Edina Community Orgns. Coop; mem. Performing Arts Ctr., Edina. Mem. Minn. Community Edn. Assn., Edina C. of C. Lutheran. Home: 5119 Valley View Rd Edina MN 55436 Office: Edina Community Ctr 5701 Normandale Rd Edina MN

JOHNSON, EARLE BERTRAND, insurance company executive; b. Otter Lake, Mich., May 3, 1914; s. Bertrand M. and Blanche (Sherman) J.; B.S., U. Fla., 1937, J.D., 1940; m. Peggy Minch Rust, Apr. 30, 1972; children by previous marriage—Earle Bertrand, Victoria, Julia, Sheryl. With State Farm Ins. Cos., Bloomington, Ill., 1940—, regional agy. dir., 1958-60, regional v.p., 1960-65, v.p., sec. State Farm Mut. Automobile Ins. Co., 1965-80, dir., 1967—, also mem. exec. com., chmn. bd. State Farm Life Ins. Co., 1970—, also mem. exec. com.; dir. State Farm Fire & Casualty Co., State Farm Internat. Services, Inc., 1967—; dir. State Farm Gen. Ins. Co. First v.p., dir. S.W. Ins. Information Service, 1963-65; mem. U. Tex. Ins. Advt. Bd., 1964; trustee Life Underwriter Tng. Council. Mem. Agy. Officers Round Table (exec. coms.), Am., Fla. bar assns., Phi Alpha Delta, Phi Kappa Tau. Office: State Farm Life Ins Co One State Farm Plaza Bloomington IL 61701*

JOHNSON, EDWARD SANDS, civil engineer; b. Walkerville, Ont., Can., Nov. 30, 1931; came to U.S., 1931; s. Charles Edward and Alice (Sands) J.; m. Donna Jean Treiber, May 18, 1957; children—Peter, Susan, David, Michael. B.S. in Civil Engring., Wayne State U., Detroit. Registered profl. engr., Mich. Design engr. Civil Engrs., Inc., Detroit, 1955-59, Mcpl. Cons. Service, Hazel Park, Mich., 1959-61; sr. asst. civil engr. Detroit Water and Sewerage Dept., 1961-65, assoc. civil engr., 1965-68, sr. assoc. civil engr., 1968-72, engr. water systems, 1972-79, head water systems engr., 1979—. Served with U.S. Army, 1956-57. Mem. Am. Water Works Assn., Water Pollution Control Fedn. Episcopalian. Lodge: Elks.

JOHNSON, EDWIN BARNER, mining company executive; b. Ishpeming, Mich., Oct. 21, 1923; s. Edwin William and Blanche (Carlson) J.; m. Lois Millman, Apr. 28, 1944; children—Scott, Vicki Johnson Caneff, Marsha Johnson Nardi. B.S. in Metallurgy, Mich. Tech. U., 1947. Chief metallurgist Cleveland-Cliffs Iron Co., Ishpeming, 1963-64, asst. mgr., 1964-66, mgr. Mich. Mines, 1966-71, gen. mgr. mines, Cleve., 1971-73, v.p. ops., 1973-75, sr. v.p., 1975-83, pres., 1983—, also dir.; dir. Society Corp., Cleve., Society Nat. Bank, Cleve., Mich. Mfg. Assn., Lansing. Bd. dirs. Fairview Found., Cleve., 1982; trustee Mich. Tech. U. Fund, Houghton, 1981; mem. Baldwin Wallace Bus. Adv. Council, Berea, Ohio, 1977. Served with AUS, 1942-45; ETO. Mem. Am. Iron and Steel Inst., Am. Iron Ore Assn., AIME. Republican. Presbyterian. Clubs: Union, Westwood Country (Cleve.); Lodge: Elks. Office: Cleveland-Cliff Iron Co 14th Floor Huntington Bldg Cleveland OH 44115

JOHNSON, EMORY EMANUEL, civil engineering educator, consultant; b. Ceresco, Nebr., May 3, 1914; s. Arthur E. and Emmy Josephine (Wedberg) J.; m. Margaret Joanne Heimberger, Sept. 30, 1939; children—Carolyn Anne, Stanley Allen. B.S. in C.E., U. Nebr., 1936; M.S., U. Mich., 1941. Registered profl. engr., S.D.; registered land surveyor. Clk., draftsman Nebr. Dept. Rds., Lincoln, 1936-37; instr. math. Mo. Sch. Mines, Rolla, 1937-41; asst. prof. civil engring. S.D. State Coll., Brookings, 1941-43, U. Kans., Lawrence, 1943-46; assoc. prof. civil engring. Colo. State Coll., Ft. Collins, 1946; prof. civil engring., head dept. S.D. State U., Brookings, 1947-79, prof. emeritus, 1979—; forensic engr. attys. and ins. cos., S.D., Minn., 1950—; land surveyor, S.D., 1947—; faculty cons. Boeing Airplane Co., Seattle. Chmn. Planning Commn., Brookings, S.D., 1961-64. Fellow ASCE (dir. 1967-71); mem. Am. Concrete Inst. (life), Nat. Soc. Profl. Engrs., S.D. Engring. Soc. (exec. sec. 1977-82, outstanding engr. 1982), Chi Epsilon (pres. supreme council 1978-80), Tau Beta Pi (dist. dir. 1977-80). Lodge: Kiwanis (lt. gov. 1971-72). Avocations: photography; travel; profl. meetings. Home: 515 13th Ave Brookings SD 57006 Office: SD State U Civil Engring Dept Brookings SD 57006

JOHNSON, ERNEST MCCABE, human resources executive, consultant; b. Evanston, Ill., May 7, 1944; s. Ernest A. and Ruth Alice (McCabe) J.; m. Linda Sue Millett, Jan. 22, 1966; children—Timothy Ernest, Darin Edward, Elizabeth Linda. B.A., U. Ill., 1970, M.A., 1971. Instr. psychology Parkland Coll., Champaign, Ill., 1970-73; regional psychologist U.S. Office Personnel Mgmt., Phila., 1973-75; personnel psychologist City of Milw., 1975-79; personnel dir. City of Green Bay (Wis.), 1979-83; v.p. human resources Firemans Fund Employers Ins. Co., 1983—; cons. personnel, Green Bay, 1974—; corp. mem. Curative Workshop, Green Bay, 1981-82. Served to sgt. USAF, 1965-69. Mem. Am. Psychol. Assn., Am. Mgmt. Assn. Home: 1013 Redwood Dr Green Bay WI 54304 Office: Firemans Fund Employers Ins Co PO Box 1100 Green Bay WI 54344

JOHNSON, FRANCIS WILLARD, clergyman; b. Haxtun, Colo., Mar. 13, 1920; s. Aaron William and Lettie Victoria (Lindgren) J.; m. Ruth Marian Palm, Sept. 11, 1945; children—Christine Louise Johnson Sleight, Roland Wayne. B.A., Augustana Coll., 1943; B.D., Augustana Theol. Sem., 1946; M.Div., Luth. Sch. Theology, 1971; D.Min. summa cum laude, 1977. Ordained to ministry Lutheran Ch. Am., 1946. Pastor Bethany Luth. Ch., Laurens, Iowa, 1946-50, Mamrelund Luth. Ch., Stanton, Iowa, 1950-69; sr. pastor St. Mark's Luth. Ch., Washington, Ill., 1969—; sec. Iowa Conf. Stewardship Com., Des Moines, 1951-59, stewardship dir., 1953-58, chmn. commn. on social action, 1956-62; dir. Luth. World Action, Des Moines, 1955-59; dist. supr. Christian Rural Overseas Program, Stanton, Iowa, 1958; exec. bd. Iowa Synod Luth. Ch. Am., Des Moines, 1962-68. Chmn. library bd. Pub. Library, Laurens, Iowa, 1948-50; chmn. bd. trustees Pub. Hosp., Laurens, 1949-50; mem. Montgomery County Farm Bur., Red Oak, Iowa, 1951-69; bd. dirs. Luth. Social Services, Chgo., 1973-76, Luth. Home for Aged, Peoria, Ill., 1978-83, 85—, Sr. Center, Washington, 1982—. Mem. Washington Ministerial Assn. (pres. 1974, 76, 77, 82), Ill. Synod Ministerium (Service award 1981), Ministerium of Luth. Ch. Am., Peoria Dist. Ministerium (dean 1973-83). Republican. Home: 606 Yorkshire Dr Washington IL 61571 Office: St Mark's Luth Ch 101 Burton St Washington IL 61571

JOHNSON, FRANK EDWARD, surgeon, educator; b. Evanston, Ill., Oct. 28, 1943; s. Frank E. and Beryl Madeline (Johnson) J. m. Tamiko Asato, Jan. 24, 1976; children—Mariko, Michael, Eric, David. B.A., U. Minn., 1964, M.D., 1967. Diplomate Am. Bd. Surgery. Intern, UCLA affiliated hosps., 1967-78; resident in surgery U. Wash., Seattle, 1972-74, U. Colo., 1974-77; research fellow U. Calif.-San Francisco, 1975-76; fellow in surg. oncology Meml. Sloan-Kettering Cancer Ctr., N.Y.C., 1977-79; clin. instr. surgery Cornell U., N.Y.C., 1977-79; asst. prof. surgery St. Louis U. Med. Ctr., 1979-84, assoc. prof. surgery, 1984—. Contbr. articles to profl. jours. Author 2 med. films. Co-founder Children's Heart Fund, Mpls., 1969. Served to lt. commander USN, 1969-71, Vietnam. Decorated Bronze Star; grantee, NIH, Am. Cancer Soc. Mem. Soc. Surg. Oncology, Am. Gastroent. Assn. AMA, Am. Fedn. Clin. Research, Am. Soc. Clin. Oncology, Am. Assn. Cancer Edn., Am. Assn. Cancer Research, ACS, Am. Pancreatic Assn., Am. Radium Soc., Am. Soc. Preventive Oncology, Southwestern Surg. Congress.

JOHNSON, FRANKLIN AGRIPPA, police chief; b. Bloomfield, Iowa, Apr. 2, 1936; s. Frederic F. and Gwendolyn F. (Westbrook) J.; m. Sandra Zoe Silka, Dec. 27, 1959; children—Scott B., Suzanne, Wendy R. A.A., Kirkwood Community Coll., 1971; B.A., Mt. Mercy Coll., 1979; grad. FBI Nat. Acad., 1975. Communications officer Iowa City Police Dept., 1965, patrolman, 1965-71, detective, 1971-77, sr. patrol officer, 1977-81; chief of police Fairfield Police Dept., Iowa, 1981—. Ambassador, Fairfield C. of C., 1983-84; treas. Crisis Line Jefferson County, 1984. Served with USN, 1959, Army N.G., 1982. Mem. Iowa Assn. Chiefs of Police and Peace Officers (2d v.p. 1985—), Johnson County Peace officers Assn. (past pres. and treas.), Iowa State Policemen's Assn., Iowa Police Exec. Forum, Internat. Assn. Chiefs of Police. Democrat. Baptist. Avocation: genealogy. Home: 1226 Glenview Circle Fairfield IA 52556 Office: 200 W Briggs St Fairfield IA 52556

JOHNSON, GARY DEAN, dental company sales executive; b. Madison, Wis., Mar. 8, 1947; s. Oscar William and Lavina Amelia (Marks) J.; m. Judith Lynn Bernhardt, May 6, 1972; children—Amanda Lynn, Brett Andrew. Vice pres. Wright's Inc., Milw., 1970-81; br. mgr. Patterson Dental Co., Milw., 1981—. Served with U.S. Army, 1966-69; Vietnam. Republican. Lutheran. Home: 3013 Mesa Verde Dr Waukesha WI 53186 Office: Patterson Dental Co 2063 S 116th St West Allis WI 53227

JOHNSON, GEORGE EMIL, real estate appraiser, broker, contractor; b. Mpls., Jan. 21, 1921; s. Frank Emil and Gertrude (Aase) J.; m. Veronica Susan Bagger, Aug. 11, 1918; children—Marie Susan, Paul Steven. Student U. Minn., 1941, 1945. Welding engr. Internat. Harvester Co., St. Paul, 1945-50; foreman Fabricform Metal Products, Calif., 1950-53; owner, pres. Appraisal Valuation Analysts, George E. Johnson Realtors, Johnson Enterprises, Mpls., 1953—; appraisal instr. various orgns.; cons. in field. Chmn. Mpls. Truth in Housing Examining Bd. Served with USNR, 1942-45. Mem. Nat. Assn. Realtors, Nat. Assn. Ind. Fee Appraisers (nat. pres. 1968; Man of Yr. 1974), Nat. Assn. Rev. Appraisers, Am. Arbitration Assn. (arbitrator), Internat. Inst. Valuers. Democrat. Roman Catholic. Clubs: Sons of Norway, Masons, Shriners. Contbr. articles to profl. jours. Home: 2832 Stinson Blvd NE Minneapolis MN 55418 Office: 2841 Johnson St NE Minneapolis MN 55418

JOHNSON, GEORGE TAYLOR, aircraft company official; b. Kansas City, Mo., Jan. 12, 1930; s. George Dewey and Geneva (Van Leu) J.; B.A., Columbia Coll., 1977; m. Pamela Kay Cole, Aug. 30, 1981; children—Van L., Victoria Johnson-Beineke, Wendell O., Marcella Johnson-Bruce. Enlisted in U.S. Army, 1947, served to 1967; chief instr. rotary wing sect. U.S. Army Transp. Sch., Ft. Eustis, Va., 1965-67; ret., 1967; group leader aerospace publs. Beech Aircraft Corp., Wichita, Kans., 1968-79, adminstr. aerospace logistics programs, 1979—. Mem. Community Action Agy., Wichita, 1973-75; founder U.S. Army Black Pilots Reunions, U.S. Army Black Aviators Assn. Served with U.S. Army, 1947-67. Decorated D.F.C., Air medal with V and four oak leaf clusters. Mem. Negro Airmen Internat. (state dir.), Nat. Bus. League, NAACP, Army Aviation Assn. Am., Assn. U.S. Army, Soc. Logistics Engrs., VFW, 9th and 10th Cav. Assn. Baptist. Club: Optimist. Home: 202 Miles Ave Valley Center KS 67147 Office: 9709 E Central Wichita KS 67201

JOHNSON, GLENDORA SHANNON, printing company executive; b. McFarland, Kans., Aug. 17, 1919; d. Arthur and Julia Mary (Mooney) Shannon; m. Clyde W. Talley, Jan. 11, 1937 (div. 1955); m. William Johnson, Nov. 13, 1959. Diploma, Strickler's Bus. Coll., 1937. Gen. adminstrv. mgr. Lago & Whitehead Advt. Agy., Wichita, Kans., 1950-61; adminstrv. asst. to pres. Lawrence Photo Supply, 1961-65; v.p., gen. mgr. Wichita Automotive & Tech. Sch., 1965-69; dir. prodn. services, McCormick-Armstrong Advt. Agy., 1969-84; co-owner-sales mgr. Johnson Printing, 1984—; pres. Adminstrv. Mgmt. Soc., Wichita, 1967-68, Advt. Club of Wichita, 1978-79. Pres. Wichita Women's Polit. Caucus. Named Wichita Ad Woman of Yr., 1984. Mem. Bus., Profl. Women, Nat. Assn. Women Bus. Owners. Democrat. Catholic. Club: Zonta (pres. 1970-73). Avocations: bowling; walking; reading; teaching. Home: 423 Topaz Wichita KS 67209

JOHNSON, GLENN EDWARD, air force officer, hospital administrator; b. Andalusia, Ala., Sept. 25, 1930; s. Dezzie and Lois Leslie (Carter) J.; m. Janet Elaine Johnson, Dec. 13, 1952; children—Julia Farris, Judith, Jann. Ahacupce, Columbia, 1962; student, N.M. State U., 1958-60. Pvt. Armed Forces Staff Coll., 1972, advanced through grades to lt. col., 1973; comdr. U.S. Air Force Clinic, Syracuse, N.Y., 1973-75; hosp. adminstr. U.S. Air Force, Albuquerque, 1975-76, chief med. adv. team, Tehran, Iran, 1976-78, regional health facilities officer, Atlanta, 1978-80, project health facilities officer, Wright-Paterson AFB, Ohio, 1980—; v.p. Southwest Health Resources, Albuquerque, 1978—. Republican. Methodist. Lodge: Masons. Avocations: classic automobiles. Home: 627 Q St Area B Wright-Patterson AFB OH 45433 Office: DET WPAT/PHFO Bldg T-B31A Wright-Patterson AFB OH 45433-5000

JOHNSON, GLENN RUSSELL, dentist; b. Elyria, Ohio, June 7, 1938; s. Russell Wise and Myrtle (Wildman) J.; m. Anne Louise Carpenter, June 15, 1963 (div. Oct. 1982); one child, Wendy Sue Johnson. B.S., Western Res. U., 1962, D.D.S., 1964. Lic. dentist, Ohio. Intern, Chattahoochee State Mental Hosp., Fla., 1964-65, gen. practice dentistry, Elyria, 1965—. Chmn. artificial reef com. Sea. grant, Ohio State U., 1981—. Mem. North Coast Planning Assn., Am. Walleye Assn., Polish Fishermans Club, Lorain County Dental Soc., Ohio Dental Soc., ADA, Elyria Meml. Hosp. Staff (pres. 1975), Central Basin Charter Boat Assn. Lodge: Elks. Avocations: fitness, fishing. Office: Glenn R Johnson DDS 124 Middle Ave Suite 602 Elyria OH 44035

JOHNSON, HAROLD ROBERT, social work educator, dean; b. Windsor, Ont., Can., Jan. 9, 1926; came to U.S., 1963; s. Lee and Catherine Anne (Brown) J.; m. Marion Cowie, June 13, 1953; children—Robert Harold, Karen Elizabeth, Alan Douglas. B.A., U. We. Ont.-Assumption Coll., 1950; M.S.W., Wayne State U., 1957; Ph.D. (hon.), Yeungnam U., Daegu, Korea, 1984. Internat. rep. Brewery & Distillery Workers Am., Can., 1951-57; exec. dir. Labour Com. for Human Rights, Windsor, Ont., Can., 1951-57; planning cons. United Community Services, Detroit, 1957-61; assoc. dir. Neighborhood Services Orgn., Detroit, 1961-69; prof. social work U. Mich.-Ann Arbor, 1969—, dir. Inst. Gerontology, 1975-81, dean Sch. Social Work, 1981—. Contbr. articles to sci., profl. jours. Chmn., White Ho. Conf. on Aging, Com. on Edn., Washington, 1980-81; vice-chmn. Mich. Commn. on Criminal Justice, Lansing, 1968-75. Served with Can. Army, 1944-46. Fellow Gerontol Soc. Am., Acad. Cert. Social Workers; mem. Nat. Assn. Social Workers, Nat. Assn. Black Social Workers, Assn. Gerontology in Higher Edn. (past pres.), Council on Social Work Edn. Democrat. Home: 2739 Appleway Ann Arbor MI 48104 Office: Sch Social Work U Mich Ann Arbor MI 48109

JOHNSON, HENDERSON ANDREW, III, dentist, management consultant, management consulting firm executive; b. Nashville, Dec. 19, 1929; s. Henderson Andrew Johnson and Minerva Azalea (Hatcher) Johnson Hawkins; m. Gwendolyn Cassie Gregory, June 14, 1952; children—Gregory Paul, Andrea Lynn, Henderson Andrew IV. B.S., Fisk U., 1950; M.S., Springfield Coll., Mass., 1951; R.P.T., Med. Coll. Va., 1952; D.D.S., Western Res. U., 1959. Practice dentistry, Shaker Heights, Ohio, 1959—; v.p., treas. Mgmt. Office Design, Shaker Heights, 1982—; clin. instr. Dental Sch., Western Res. U., Cleve., 1963-69; chief dental dept. Cuyahoga Hills Boys' Sch., Warrensville, Ohio, 1969-71; trustee Cleve. Pub. Radio, 1982—; v.p., bd. dirs. Ctr. for Human Relations, Cleve., 1984—. Pres. Shaker Heights Pub. Library, 1978-84. Served to 1st lt. USAF, 1952-54. Fellow Pierre Fauchard Acad.; mem. Cleve. Dental Soc., Ohio Dental Soc., ADA. Democrat. Congregationalist. Avocations: creative writing; sports. Home: 16506 Fernway Rd Shaker Heights OH 44120 Office: Mgmt Office Design Inc 16611 Chagrin Blvd Shaker Heights OH 44120

JOHNSON, HERBERT LAVERN, audiovisual educator; b. Princeville, Ill., July 11, 1936; s. Harold Elgin and Lorene Florence (Kramer) J.; m. Helen Joan Ford, Aug. 25, 1957; children—Helen Rachel, Harold Lane, Hope Elizabeth. B.A., McPherson Coll. (Kans.), 1958; M.S. in Edn., So. Ill. U., 1971. Tchr., Thayer High Sch. (Nebr.), 1958-60, Elk Horn High Sch. (Iowa), 1960-70; dir. learning resources McPherson Coll., 1970—; mem. standing com. on techs. for resource sharing Kans. Library Network, 1984—; cons. Kansas Green Thumb, McPherson, 1984—. Producer, dir. Kans. Union Catalog, 1984. Precinct chmn., county del., state del. Republican Party, Elk Horn, 1968. Named Profl. Tchr. Yr. Shelby County Tchrs. Assn., 1963. Mem. Kans. Assn. Ednl. and Tech., Assn. Ednl. Communication and Tech., NEA (life mem.). Mem. Ch. of the Brethren. Avocations: History, Mississippian Indian study, hunting, fishing. Home: 407 S Grand McPherson KS 67460 Office: McPherson Coll Media Ctr McPherson KS 67460

JOHNSON, HOWARD ARTHUR, JR., operations research analyst; b. Indpls., July 25, 1952; s. Howard Arthur Sr. and Joy (Nelson) J.; m. Teresa Thirsk, Aug. 11, 1979. B.A. in Polit. Sci. and Ops. Research Analysis, U. Kans., 1974; M.A. in Internat. Studies and Mgmt., U. Wyo., 1984. Ops. research analyst Armament Systems, Inc., Ft. Walton Beach, Fla., 1980-81, EG&G InterTech, Inc., Arlington, Va., 1981-84, dep. to U.S. dir. plans and budgets, Royal Saudi Navy, Saudi Arabian Ministry Def. and Aviation, Riyadh, Saudi Arabia, 1981-82; ops. research analyst FMC Corp., Mpls., 1984—; cons. U.S. Navy, Coronado, 1977-78. Sustaining mem. Republican Nat. Com., Washington, 1984—. Served to lt. USN, 1974-78. U.S. Navy scholar, 1970-74; grad. acad. scholar U. Wyo., 1983-84. Mem. AAAS, Ops. Research Soc. Am., Acad. Internat. Bus., Inst. Mgmt. Scis., Fgn. Policy Research Inst., Tau Kappa Epsilon. Home: 3376 Brunswick Ave S Saint Louis Park MN 55416 Office: FMC Corp 4800 E River Rd Minneapolis MN 55421

JOHNSON, HOWARD PAUL, agricultural engineering educator; b. Odebolt, Iowa, Jan. 27, 1923; s. Gustaf Johan and Ruth Helen (Hanson) J.; m. Patricia Jean Larsen, June 15, 1952; children—Cynthia, Lynette, Malcolm. B.S., Iowa State U., 1949, M.S. in Agrl. Engring., 1950; M.S. in Hydraulic Engring., U. Iowa, 1954; Ph.D., Iowa State U., 1959. Registered profl. engr., Iowa. Engr., Soil Conservation Service, Sioux City, Iowa, 1949; instr. Iowa State U., Ames, 1950-53, 54-59, asst. prof., 1959-60, assoc. prof., 1960-62, prof. agrl. engring., 1962—, head dept., 1980-85; cons., 1960-80. Contbr. numerous articles, papers to profl. lit. Co-editor Hydrologic Modeling, 1981. Patentee flow meter. Pres., Sawyer Sch. PTA, Ames, 1965; precinct rep. Republican party, Ames, 1980. Served with AUS, 1943-46, ETO. Recipient Iowa State U. Gamma Sigma Delta Merit award, 1983; EPA grantee, 1975-80. Fellow Am. Soc. Agrl. Engrs. (div. chmn. 1969-70, tech. council 1974-76; Engr. of Yr. Iowa sect. 1981, Mid-Central sect. 1982). Baptist. Lodge: Rotary. Avocations: reading; photography; fishing. Office: Dept Agrl Engring 100 Davidson Hall Iowa State U Ames IA 50011

JOHNSON, IRENE HARRIS, educational administrator; b. Miami, Fla.; d. Benjamin Franklin and Ollie Lee (Jennings) H.; children—Gordon, Eric, Reginald. B.S., Hampton Inst., 1960; M.S., Purdue U., 1980, Ph.D. candidate, 1985—. Med. technician Kecoughton VA Hosp., 1960-61; tchr. sci. Dade County Pub. Schs., Miami, Fla., 1961-64; chmn. dept. sci. Richmond (Va.) Pub. Schs., 1964-65; cons. sci. D.C. Pub. Schs., 1965-72; tchr. biology Fairfax County Pub. Schs., Vienna, Va., 1972-77; coordinator minorities sci. program Purdue U., 1977—, dir. tutorial program, Sch. Sci., 1978-80, dir. Summer Outreach Program, 1979-81; cons. coll. relations IBM, Rochester, Minn., 1984—. Chmn. edn. com. NAACP, 1983-84; chmn. Purdue Black Caucus of Faculty and Staff, 1983—. NSF grantee, 1962, 69, 74. Mem. Nat. Assn. Negro Women (1st v.p. 1975), Ind. Coalition of Blacks in Higher Edn., Assn. Counseling and Devel., AAAS, Assn. for Non-White Concerns in Personnel and Guidance, Nat. Assn. Student Personnel Adminstrs., Nat. Acad. Adv. Assn. Baptist. Avocations: Gardening, reading, swimming, matchbooks and recipes collecting. Office: Purdue U Sch Sci Math Bldg 250 West Lafayette IN 47907

JOHNSON, IZONA VAUGHN, educator; b. E. St. Louis, Ill., June 9, 1933; d. Major and Izona Veola (Hawkins) Vaughn; m. LaSalle Hernando Johnson, Dec. 20, 1931; children—Keith Lamont, Vince Lydell. B.S., Central States U., 1957; M.S., U. Ill., 1965. Tchr. phys. edn. East St. Louis Sr. High Sch., 1960—, chmn. phys. edn. dept., 1969-74, head volleyball coach, 1974-77, supr. secondary phys. edn. Dist. 189, 1978—; coordinator fitness workshop Lewis & Clark Coll., 1983; condr. workshops. Active PTA, East St. Louis, 1981—. Mem. Ill. Assn. Health, Phys. Edn. and Recreation (dist. chmn., pres. 1982-83, mem. govtl. affairs com. exec. bd. 1983-84), AAHPER, Nat. Council Negro Women, Phi Delta Kappa. Baptist. Contbr. articles to profl. jours. Address: 8921 Woestboul Dr Loisel Hills East Saint Louis IL 62203

JOHNSON, JAMES ALAN, resort executive; b. Denver, Apr. 16, 1953; s. Otto Rexford and Faith Lucy (Meppen) J.; m. Michele Ann McNally, June 25, 1977; children—Hillary Hope, Eric Alan. B.S., U. S.D., 1975. Cert. tchr. S.D., cert. park operator. English tchr. Washington High Sch., Sioux Falls, S.D., 1975-77; gen. mgr. Palmer Gulch Resort, Hill City, S.D., 1977—. Pres. Heart of Hills Action Group, Hill City, 1981. Named Pres. Class Kampgrounds of Am. Mgmt. Class, 1979. Mem. Kampgrounds of S.D. (pres. 1983—, sec. 1981-82), S.D. Campground Owners Assn. (v.p. 1984—, treas. 1982-83), Black Hills Badlands & Lakes Assn. (dir. 1982-84). Republican. Presbyterian. Avocations: basketball, basketball officiating. Home and Office: Mt Rushmore KOA Box 295 Hill City SD 57745

JOHNSON, JAMES DUKE, mfg. co. exec.; b. St. Louis, Jan. 21, 1941; s. James Monroe and Frances Miriam (Duke) J.; m. Cathy Lynn. B.A., Washington U., St. Louis, 1959-63; children—James Michael, James Duke. With Duke Mfg. Co., St. Louis, 1961—, v.p. mktg., 1968-71, pres., chief exec. officer, 1971—. Active Jr. Achievement, St. Louis, 1970—; fund raiser Boy Scouts Am., St. Louis, 1975—; bd. dirs. Independence Ctr. Mem. Nat. Assn. Food Equipment Mfrs., Food Equipment Distbrs. Assn., Young Presidents Orgn. Episcopalian. Clubs: Glen Echo Country, St. Louis, Mo. Athletic,

Confederate Air Force. Patentee in field. Office: 2305 N Broadway Saint Louis MO 63102

JOHNSON, JAMES FREEMAN, office furniture manufacturing company executive; b. Cedar Rapids, Iowa, Oct. 30, 1932; s. Freeman and Marie Rose Johnson; B.A., Knox Coll., 1954. Salesman, Am. Chicle Co., Minn., 1954-57; advt. mgr., Toronto, Ont., Can., 1962-65; regional sales mgr. Warner Lambert, Chgo., 1969-71; dir. sales, mgr. Europe, Am. Optical Co., South Bridge, Mass., 1971-75; dir. nat. sales Am. Chicle div. Warner Lambert, Morris Plains, N.J., 1976-79; v.p. sales and mktg. The HON Co., Muscatine, Iowa, 1979—. Served with U.S. Army, 1954-56. Home: Route 3 Box 42 Muscatine IA 52761 Office: The HON Co 200 Oak St Muscatine IA 52761

JOHNSON, JAMES ROBERT, executive scientist, educator, consultant; b. Cin., Jan. 2, 1923; s. Charles William and Della Romona (Schubert) J.; m. Virginia May Bowen, Apr. 3, 1945; children—Cathy Johnson Whitman, Barbara Johnson Kallusky, Randy, John, Jamie Johnson Myers, Brian. B. Ceramic Engring., Ohio State U., 1947, M.S., 1948, Ph.D., 1950. Asst. prof. U. Tex., Austin, 1950-51; tech. adv. Oak Ridge Nat. Lab., 1951-56; research dir., exec. scientist 3M Co., St. Paul, 1956-79, ret. 1979; adj. prof. U. Wis., Stout, Menomonie, 1979—; spl. asst. to dean Grad. Sch., U. Minn., Mpls., 1979—; mem. vis. com. U. Wash., Seattle, 1982—, MIT, Boston, 1978-84. Bd. dirs. Sci. World, Madison, Wis., 1983—. Served to 1st lt. U.S. Army, 1943-46, ETO. Recipient Disting. Alumnus award Ohio State U., 1970; Engr's. Achievement award Am. Soc. Metals, 1981; James R. Johnson award U. Wis.-Stout, 1983. Fellow Wis. Acad. Sci.; mem. Internat. Tech. Edn. Assn. (bd. advs. 1981—), Am. Ceramic Soc. (disting. life mem.) (pres. 1973-74), Nat. Inst. Ceramic Engrs. (Greaves-Walker award 1985), Research Soc. Am., Nat. Acad. Engring., Minn. Acad. Sci. (bd. dirs., past pres.), Minn. High Tech. Council (bd. dirs.), Sigma Xi. Avocations: making fine porcelain; fishing; gardening. Home: Rt 1 Box 231 B River Falls WI 54022 Office: U Minn Grad Sch 417 Johnston Hall Minneapolis MN 55456

JOHNSON, JAMES WILLIAM, hospital administrator; b. Gallipolis, Ohio, Dec. 24, 1935; s. James Austin and Marguerite Elizabeth (Harrington) J.; m. Nancy Sue Rawlings, July 13, 1959; children—Kimberly Sue Johnson Shipp, Jeffrey Allen. B.A., Capital U., 1979; cert. health services adminstrs. program U. Ala., 1970. Ins. agt. Barnes-Simpson Ins. Agy., Middleport, Ohio, 1961-65; bus. mgr. Meigs Gen. Hosp., Pomeroy, Ohio, 1965-67; bus. mgr. Meml. Hosp. of Union County, Marysville, Ohio, 1967-70, asst. adminstr., 1970-76, assoc. adminstr., 1976-78, adminstr., 1978—; dir. M.I.S., Inc.-Hosp. Shared Engring. Services, Grosse Pointe, Mich., 1979-83, Central Ohio Psychiat. Hosp., Columbus, 1977-83. Served with U.S. Army, 1957-59. Mem. Am. Acad. Health Adminstrs., Central Ohio Health Adminstrs. Assn., C. of C., Am. Hosp. Assn., Ohio Hosp. Assn. Presbyterian. Club: Racquet of Columbus. Home: 300 Grove St Marysville OH 43040 Office: Meml Hosp of Union County 500 London Ave Marysville OH 43040

JOHNSON, JAMES WINSTON, chemical engineering educator; b. Quinton, Okla., May 25, 1930; s. Fred M. and Lois Amelia (Sands) J.; m. Vera Mae Hamman, Oct. 10, 1954; children—Christopher James, Victor Andrew. A.S., Eastern Okla. A&M, 1951; B.S. in Edn., Southeastern Okla. State, 1953; B.S. in Chem. Engring, Mo. Sch. Mines, 1957, M.S. in Chem. Engring, 1958; Ph.D. in Chem. Engring., U. Mo.-Columbia, 1961. Research assoc. U. Pa., Phila., 1962-63; from instr. to asst. prof. chem. engring. Mo. Sch. Mines, Rolla, 1958-64; assoc. prof. U. Mo., Rolla, 1964-67, prof., 1967—, chmn. dept., 1979—. Contbr. articles to profl. jours. Served to sgt. U.S. Army, 1953-54. Fellow Atomic Energy Commn., 1957-58, NSF, 1960-61. Mem. Electrochem. Soc., Am. Inst. Chem. Engrs., Nat. Assn. Corrosion Engrs., Am. Soc. Engring. Educators, Tau Beta Pi, Phi Kappa Phi. Republican. Lodge: Rotary. Avocations: antiques, raising cattle. Home: PO Box 486 Rolla MO 65401 Office: U Mo Chem Engring Dept Rolla MO 65401

JOHNSON, JAY BRESTEL, insurance company executive; b. Columbus, Ohio, Oct. 13, 1946; s. Stewart Pearl and Luetta (Brestel) J.; m. Joanne Hollander, Aug. 30, 1969; children—Blair Geoffrion, Kyle Stewart. B.S., Mich. State U., 1969. Claims adjustor Mich. Millers Mut. Ins. Co., Lansing, 1969-71; v.p. Insurco, Inc., Tampa, Fla., 1971-75; pres., owner Blair Corp., Tampa, 1975-77; mktg. rep. Delta Dental Plan of Mich., Okemos, Mich., 1978-81; v.p. mktg. Delta Dental Plan of Ohio, Columbus, 1981—. Instr., Project Bus., Jr. Achievement, Lansing, 1981, 80; treas. George Sheldon Campaign for Fla. Ho. of Reps., Tampa, 1972, 74; vice chmn. Great Issues, Associated Students of Mich. State U. Student Govt., East Lansing, 1968. Home: 5140 Parkmoor Dr Westerville OH 43081 Office: Delta Dental Plan of Ohio Inc 1880 E Dublin Granville Rd Columbus OH 43229

JOHNSON, JEFFREY TAYLOR, osteopathic physician, educator; b. Los Angeles Sept. 16, 1945; s. William Taylor and Reba Eunice (Harper) J.; m. Ruth Elaine Lageschulte, 1968; 3 children. B.S., Wheaton Coll., 1967; student Central Mich. U., 1967-68; D.O., Chgo. Coll. Osteo. Medicine, 1973. Cert. Am. Bd. of Family Practice. Intern Grandview Hosp., Dayton, Ohio 1973-74; practice medicine specializing in osteo medicine, Winfield, Ill. 1974—; chmn. dept. of family practice, Central Dupage Hosp., Winfield, Ill. 1984—; instr. Chgo. Coll. Osteo. Medicine, 1976—; preceptor Chgo. Med. Sch., North Chgo., 1983—; Rush Med. Coll., Chgo., 1982—, Ill. Benedictine Coll., Lisle, Ill. 1983-84; emergency room physician Central Dupage Hosp., Winfield, Ill. 1974—; med. dir. Alcoholism Treatment Center of Central DuPage Hosp., Winfield, Ill., 1982—; Dir. Health Chgo. Health Maintenance Orgn., Oak Brook, Ill. Contbr. articles to newspapers on alcoholism. Bd. dirs. United Way Winfield/Warrenville. Mem. AMA, Ill. State Med. Soc., Dupage County Med. Soc., Am. Osteo. Assn. Ill. Assn. Osteo. Physicians and Surgeons; Am. Heart Assn., Winfried C. of C. Club: Wheaton Community Radio Amateurs. Avocations: amateur radio; fishing; music; family outings. Office 150 Winfield Rd Winfield IL 60190

JOHNSON, JERRY MARVIN, retail firm executive; b. Barron, Wis., Oct. 21, 1944; s. John Anthony and Lorraine Ethylm (Johnson) J.; m. Patricia Leona Berg, Oct. 2, 1965; children—Laura Rae, Jarrod Micah, Melody Lynn. Assoc., U. Minn., 1971. Shipping and receiving clk. Pioneer Hydraulics, Mpls., 1965-66; auto mechanic various firms, Minn., 1966-69; service mgr. Firestone, St. Paul, 1969-70; owner, pres. Carrousel House, Columbia Heights, Minn., 1971-76; supr. 10,000 Auto Parts, Mpls., 1972-73; v.p. Big Wheel/Rossi Auto Stores, Mendota Heights, Minn., 1973—. Mem. Planning and Zoning Commn., City of Andover, Minn., 1981-82; mem. council Faith Lutheran Ch., Coon Rapids, Minn., 1983—; sec. Crooked Lake Civic Assn., Andover, 1984—; del. county, dist. and state convs. Democratic Farm Labor Party Minn., to 1980. Avocations: fishing, reading, tennis, spectator sports. Home: 13522 Gladiola St NW Andover MN 55304 Office Big Wheel/Rossi Auto Stores 1335 Mendota Heights Rd Mendota Heights MN 55120

JOHNSON, JOHN ARTHUR, technology executive; b. Oak Park, Ill., Oct. 10, 1943; s. Russell Arthur and Loretta Jean (Schneider) J.; m. Carol Ann Maddock, Aug. 31, 1963; children—John Michael, Stephen Russell. B.S. in Engring. Physics with honors, U. Ill., 1964. M.S. in Physics, 1965; postgrad., Cambridge U., 1966; J.D., U. Chgo., 1969. Bar: Ill. 1969. Adminstrv. assoc. U.S. Steel Corp., Pitts., 1969-72, project coordinator internat., 1972-75; asst. to gen. supt., Gary, Ind., 1975-76, asst. supt. coke plant, 1976-77; gen. mgr. Ind. Gen. Co., Valparaiso, Ind., 1977-80, v.p., gen. mgr., 1980-83; owner, pres. I G Technologies, Inc., Valparaiso, 1983—. Gen. campaign mgr. United Way of Porter County, Ind., 1982. Recipient Lisle Abbot Rose award Coll. Engring. U. Ill., Urbana, 1964; Churchill Found. scholar Cambridge U., Eng., 1964; U.S. Steel indsl. fellow, Pitts., 1967-69.

JOHNSON, JOHN HAROLD, magazine publisher; b. Arkansas City, Ark., Jan. 19, 1918; s. LeRoy and Gertrude (Jenkins) J.; student U. Chgo., Northwestern U.; LL.D., Shaw U., Benedict Coll., Carnegie-Mellon Inst., Central State Coll., Eastern Mich. U., Hamilton Coll., Lincoln U., Malcolm X Coll., Morehouse Coll., N.C. Coll., N.C. A. and T. State U., Upper Iowa Coll., Wayne State U., Pratt Inst.; m. Eunice Rivers Walker, June 21, 1951; children—John Harold, Linda Eunice. Pres., pub. Johnson Pub. Co., pubs. Ebony, Jet, Black Stars Ebony Jr.!, mags., Chgo., 1942—; pres. Sta. WJPC, Chgo.; dir. Marina Bank, Greyhound Corp., Twentieth-Century-Fox Film Corp., Zenith Radio Corp. Bd. dirs. Harvard Grad. Sch. Bus., United Negro Coll. Fund, NCCJ, Chgo., United Negro Coll. Fund; trustee Art Inst. Chgo. Named 1 of 10 outstanding young men of yr. U.S. Jaycees, 1951; recipient Henry Johnson Fisher award Mag. Pubs. Assn., 1972; Communicator of Year award U. Chgo. Alumni Assn., 1974; Columbia Journalism award, 1974; Horatio Alger award, 1966. Fellow Sigma Delta Chi; mem. Mag. Pubs. Assn., Opportunities Industrialization Centers. Office: 820 S Michigan Ave Chicago IL 60616*

JOHNSON, JOHN PRESCOTT, philosophy educator; b. Tumalo, Oreg., Apr. 24, 1921; s. John Edward and Caroline Prescott (Eaton) J.; m. Mable Alice Dougherty, June 9, 1943; children—Grace Beth, John Paul, Carol Ruth. A.B., Pitts State U., 1947, M.S., 1958; Ph.D., Northwestern U., 1959. Asst. prof. philosophy Bethany Nazarene Coll., Okla., 1949-57, U. Okla., Norman, 1957-62; prof. Monmouth Coll., Ill., 1962—; cons. U.S. Office Edn., 1967. Contbr. articles to profl. jours. Mem. Ill. Philos. Assn., (pres. 1971-73), Am. Philos. Assn. Democrat. Office: Monmouth Coll 700 E Broadway Monmouth IL 61462

JOHNSON, JORENE KATHRYN, community organization director; b. Rockville Centre, N.Y., Jan. 6, 1931; d. Adam and Kathryn Lillian (Schoen) Freitag; B.F.A., Pratt Inst., 1952; M.P.A., U. Cin., 1975; student Mt. St. Joseph Coll., 1977-78; m. Roland E. Johnson, Oct. 10, 1954; children—Lorin, Melissa. Furniture designer Jacques Bodart, Inc., N.Y.C., 1952-54; interior decorator Albert Parvin Co., Los Angeles, 1955-57, Maria Bergson Assocs., N.Y.C., 1957-61; office mgr., research asst. The Cin. Inst., 1973-74, research mgr., 1974-75; exec. dir. Friends of Cin. Parks Inc., 1975-77; community coordinator College Hill Forum, Cin., 1977-84; sec., insp. Green Twp. Zoning Bd., 1982-84; dir. The Program for Cin., 1984—. Mem. Cin. Mayor's Energy Policy Com., 1982-83; chmn. com. Mayor's Budget Task Force, 1984; vice-chmn. Monfort Heights Civic Assn., 1977, chmn., 1978; mem. Leadership Cin. Class III, 1979-80; mem. planning com. Community Chest, 1982—; mem. planning com. Program for Cin., 1982-83; mem. steering com. Congress of Neighborhood Groups, 1983-85; bd. dirs. Hamilton County Assn. Retarded Citizens, 1983—. Mem. Met. Exchange of Cin., Internat. Platform Assn., Cincinnatus Assn., Mensa. Home: 5200 Race Rd Cincinnati OH 45247 Office: 230 E 9th St Cincinnati OH 45202

JOHNSON, JOSEPH ALAN, physiologist, educator; b. West Palm Beach, Fla., Feb. 1, 1933; s. Eli Allen Johnson and Emily Kate (Percy) Wilcher; m. Janice Louise Van de Water, July 21, 1956; children—Robert Alan, Gary Francis. B.A. in Zoology, Butler U., 1963; Ph.D. in Physiology, Ind. U. Med. Ctr., 1968. Postdoctoral fellow U. Mo., Columbia, 1968-71, asst. prof., 1971-78, assoc. prof. physiology, 1978—; research physiologist Truman Meml. VA Hosp., Columbia, 1974—. Co-editor: Comparative Endocrinology of Prolactin, 1977; The Renin-Angiotensin System, 1980. Contbr. articles to profl. pubis. Fellow Am. Heart Assn. (council for high blood pressure research); mem. Am. Physiol. Soc., Endocrine Soc., Am. Soc. Nephrology. Avocations: canoeing, hiking. Home: 3100 Timberhill Trail Columbia MO 65201 Office: Truman Meml VA Hosp Research 151 Columbia MO 65201

JOHNSON, JOYCE MARIE BETTS, stockbroker, columnist, radio personality; b. East Chicago, Ind., Jan. 18, 1938; d. Hobart and Mattie (Upshaw) Betts; B.S. magna cum laude, U. Md., 1976; m. Emmitt Johnson, July 6, 1959; children—Roderick, Terence. Tchr. shorthand Univ. Lang. Center, Taipei, Taiwan, 1963; adminstrv. asst. exec. sec. U.S. Army Intelligence, Munich, Germany, 1969-73; tchr. McArthur Jr. High Sch., Ft. Meade, Md., 1974-75; bus. mgr. The Reading Center, Gary, Ind., 1976-77; stockbroker A.G. Edwards Co., Merrillville, Ind., 1977—; columnist Info Newspaper, Gary, Dollars & Sense mag., 1978-81, Post Tribune, Gary, Chgo. Defender, Chgo., The Capital City Argus, Austin, Tex., The Herald, Savannah, Ga.; host Money Talks, radio sta. WLTH, Gary; participant profl. confs. Bd. dirs. Northwest Ind. Symphony Soc., Friends Lake County Library, 1978, Internat. Women's Econ. Devel. Corp.; mem. adv. bd. Businesswomen's Ednl. Programs; mem. Delta Econ. Adv. Council; pres. chpt. Jack and Jill. Recipient Black Achievement award HELP, Inc., Appreciation award Delta Sigma Pi, Bus., Community Service and Journalism award Phi Beta Sigma. Mem. Nat. Council Negro Women, PUSH Internat. Bur. Trade, Am. Bus. Women's Assn., AMEX Club, Nat. Assn. Securities Profls. (founder), AAUW (dir. Gary-Merrillville br. 1977—), Am. Soc. Women Accts., Nat. Soc. Registered Reps., NAACP, League Black Women, Chgo. Urban League, Phi Kappa Phi, Alpha Sigma Lambda, Delta Sigma Theta. Club: Civitan. Co-author: The Money Workbook, 1983. Office: 222 S Riverside Plaza Suite 720 Chicago IL 60606

JOHNSON, JUDITH ANNE, English educator; b. Fargo, N.D., Aug. 31, 1934; d. Raymond Orlando and Floy Blanche (Beatty) Gregerson; m. Neil B. Johnson, Aug. 14, 1956 (div. May 1974); children—Catherine Elisabeth, Wendy Gillian; m. Alfred L. Freeland, Mar. 26, 1977. B.A., Carleton Coll., 1956; M.A. N.D. State U., 1965; Ph.D., U. Mich., 1969. Teaching asst. N.D. State U., Fargo, 1963-65; lectr. Moorhead State Coll., Minn., 1965-66; teaching fellow, lectr. U. Mich., Ann Arbor, 1966-70; instr., prof. Eastern Mich. U., Ypsilanti, 1970-81, head dept. English, 1981—. Author: Writing Strategies for ESL Students, 1983, A Transformational Analysis of the Syntax of Africa's Lives of Saints, 1975. Fellow Coll. English Assn.; mem. Assn. Depts. English, MLA, Phi Beta Kappa. Avocations: raising Paso Fino horses, golden retrievers. Office: Dept English Eastern Mich U Ypsilanti MI 48197

JOHNSON, JUDITH LYNNE, medicinal chemist; b. Casper, Wyo., Jan. 25, 1942; d. Morgan Parke and Amelia (Kupke) Huntington; m. Dale Raymond Johnson, June 17, 1967; children—Heidi Elizabeth, Karsten Dale. B.A., Lindenwood Coll., 1964; M.S., Iowa State U., 1967. Research assoc. nutrition dept. Iowa State U., Ames, 1966-67; assoc. chemist Parke Davis Co., Ann Arbor, Mich., 1967-77; sr. assoc. chemist Warner Lambert-Parke Davis Co., 1977—. Woodrow Wilson fellow, 1964; NIH fellow, 1967. Mem. Am. Chem. Soc. Democrat. Lutheran. Avocations: running; gardening; swimming; tennis. Home: 2779 Ellis Rd Ypsilanti MI 48197 Office: Warner Lambert-Parke Davis Co 2800 Plymouth Rd Ann Arbor MI 48106

JOHNSON, KATHRYN MARY, sociology educator, researcher, consultant; b. Moline, Ill., July 18, 1952; d. Arthur Gordon and Eleanor C. (Lange) J.; m. Steven Charles Kuemmerle, Oct. 4, 1980; B.S., U. No. Colo., 1975, M.A., 1978; Ph.D., Western Mich. U., 1981. Instr., U. No. Colo., 1976-78, Chapman Coll., 1977-78, Western Mich. U., Kalamazoo, 1979-81; researcher, cons. Ctr. for Social Research, Kalamazoo, 1980-81, Grand Rapids (Mich.) pub. schs., 1979—; asst. prof. sociology Ind. U. N.W., Gary, 1981—. Author: If Your Are Raped: What Every Woman Needs to Know, 1984. Contbr. articles to profl. jours. Bd. dirs. Chgo. Abused Women Coalition. Recipient Founder's Day Teaching award Ind. U. N.W., 1983; Ind. U. N.W. Faculty fellow, 1983, 85. Mem. Am. Sociol. Assn., Am. Ednl. Research Assn., North Central Sociol. Assn., NOW, Sociologists for Women in Society. Democrat. Episcopalian. Home: 4059 N Greenview Apt 3N Chicago IL 60613 Office: Ind U NW Dept Sociology Gary IN 46408

JOHNSON, KAY MARIE, hospital medical records administrator; b. Independence, Mo., Oct. 16, 1936; d. Clarence Joseph and Naoma Muriel (Upham) Price; m. William Francis Burgess, Oct. 1, 1954; children—Deborah Kay Burgess Tinker, William Edward, Phillip Eugene; m. 2d, Travis Oscar Johnson, Nov. 16, 1964; 1 son, Steven Travis; m. 3d, Alfred H. Yale, Aug. 19, 1983. B.A. in Health Care Mgmt., Park Coll., 1978. Accredited records technician. Med. records technician St. Luke's Hosp., Kansas City, Mo., 1973-76; asst. dir. Kansas City Coll. Osteopathic Medicine, 1976-78; med. records dir. Toledo Hosp., 1978-83; dir. med. records Service Med. Ctr. of Beaver County, Beaver, Pa., 1983—; cons., lectr. in field. Assoc. counselor to dir. of Personal and Family Services, Independence, Mo., 1976-78. Mem. Am. Med. Records Assn., Ohio Med. Record Assn., N.W. Ohio Med. Record Assn.

JOHNSON, KEITH DONALD, lawyer; b. Mpls., July 18, 1954; s. Dennis Axel and Dorraine Jeannette (Hennen) J. B.A., Marquette U., 1976; J.D., U. Minn., 1979. Bar: Minn. 1979, U.S. Dist. Ct. Minn. 1980. Assoc. Theodore R. Mellby & Assocs., P.A., Montgomery, Minn., 1979-84; ptnr. Wold, Jacobs, & Johnson, Mpls., 1984—. Mem. Assn. Trial Lawyers Am., Minn. Trial Layers Assn., Minn. State Bar Assn., Hennepin County Bar Assn., Phi Beta Kappa. Roman Catholic. Office: Wold Jacobs & Johnson 247 Third Ave S Minneapolis MN 55415

JOHNSON, KEVIN BLAINE, lawyer, educator; b. Wichita, Kans., Aug. 28, 1956; s. Howard Blaine and Ruth Signe (Hornlund) J.; m. Suzanne Kay Wright, Aug. 29, 1981. B.A., Wichita State U., 1978; J.D., Washburn U., 1981. Bar: Kans. 1982, U.S. Dist. Ct. Kans. 1982. Sole practice, Overland Park, Kans., 1981-82; asst. dist. atty. Wyandotte, County, Kans., 1982-84; assoc. Law Office of A. B. Fletcher, Wichita, Kans., 1984—; prof. law Kans. Newman Coll., Wichita, 1984—. Author: The 11th Kansas Volunteer Cavalry, 1986. Mem. Wichita Citizen Participation Orgn. Council, 1985—. Contbr. articles to profl. jours. Drum instr. Sky Ryders Drum and Bugle Corps, Hutchinson, Kans., 1978-81. Mem. Assn. Trial Lawyers Am., Wichita Bar Assn. Republican. Lutheran. Home: 8406 Castle Dr Wichita KS 67207 Office: Law Office of Andrew B Fletcher 2409 E Pawnee Wichita KS 67211

JOHNSON, LARRY G., computer leasing executive; b. Granite City, Ill., Sept. 9, 1947; s. Russell F. and Olga R. (Kozak) J.; m. Marilyn R. Westenberg, May 17, 1984; children—Cris, Aaron, David, Marcus, Isaac. B.S. in Engring. Mgmt., U. Mo.-Rolla, 1970. Mktg. rep. Data Processing div. RCA, St. Louis, 1970-71; sr. mktg. rep. Honeywell Info. Systems, Lansing, Mich., 1972-73; mktg. mgr. Docutel Corp., Southfield, Mich., 1973-75; nat. account mgr. Storage Technology Corp., Southfield, 1975-77, br. mgr., 1977-78; pres. N.Am. Computer Equipment, Inc., Bloomfield Hills, Mich., 1978—. Recipient national and regional sales and mktg. awards. Office: 1145 W Long Lake Rd Bloomfield Hills MI 48013

JOHNSON, LEONARD MARTIN, chemical company executive; b. Mpls., May 7, 1936; s. Leonard J. and Martha A. (Jacobson) J.; B.S., Yale U., 1959; m. Charlotte G. Seymour, Nov. 28, 1959; children—Laurie, Leonard Martin, Kimberly, Michael, Kristina, Katherine. Sales engr. Elec. Products div. 3M Co., 1959-63, tech. service engr., 1963-65, analyst mktg. research elec. group, 1965-67, mgr. internat. devel., 1967-70, mgr. market planning Sumitomo-3M, Tokyo, 1970-72, mgr. bus. planning tape group, 1972-77, mgr. global planning and internat. mktg.-Packaging Systems div., St. Paul, 1975-77, mgr. bus. devel. tape group, 1977-78; dir. corp. planning Allied Corp., Morristown, N.J., 1978-79, mem. corp. acquisition task force, 1979; v.p. planning and devel. Allied Chem. Co., Morristown, N.J., 1979-83; v.p. planning and acquisitions Hartzell Corp., St. Paul, 1983—. Bd. dirs., mem. exec. com. Goodwill Agy., Mpls., 1978; vice chmn. Morris Area Planning and Adv. Com., 1989-81; chmn. adv. com. United Way First Call for Help, 1981-83; bd. dirs. Breck Sch., Mpls., 1984, Source Tech. Biols., Mpls., 1984, Natures Moods, Long Valley, N.J., 1984. Mem. Comml. Devel. Assn., N.Am. Soc. Corp. Planners, Chem. Mktg. Research Assn. Home: 195 S Brown Rd Long Lake MN 55356 Office: 2515 Wabash St Saint Paul MN 55114

JOHNSON, LINDA OLSON, educator, consultant; b. Beloit, Wis., July 25, 1946; d. Russell Raymond and Iris (Smout), Olson; m. Philip Charles Johnson, June 29, 1968; children—Melissa Anne, Russell Charles. B.A. in Spanish, Northwestern U., 1968; M.A. in Spanish and Edn., U. Wis.-Madison, 1979; postgrad. U. Wis.-Whitewater. Cert. Spanish tchr., Wis. Tchr. Spanish, Delavan-Darien High Sch., Darien, Wis., 1968—; pres. Johnson & Danielson, Inc.; cons. ins., income tax preparation, and fin. Trustee, chmn. fin. com. United Ch. of Christ. Mem. Am. Council on Teaching Fgn. Langs., Wis. Assn. Fgn. Lang. Tchrs., Am. Assn. Tchrs. Spanish and Portuguese. Home: 514 McDowell St Delavan WI 53115 Office: Johnson & Danielson Inc 10 Wisconsin St Darien WI 53114

JOHNSON, LONNELL EDWARD, pharmacist, educator; b. Gary, Ind., June 17, 1942; s. Lonnie and Jessie Marie (Garrett) J.; m. Brenda Joyce Warren, Aug. 31, 1973; children—Melissa Dawn, Angela Renee. B.S., Purdue U., 1965; B.Th., Way Coll. Bibl. Research, Rome City, Ind., 1975; M.A., Emporia State U. (Kans.), 1978; Ph.D., Ind. U., 1985. Registered pharmacist, Ind. Info. analyst Pharm. Mfrs. Assn., Washington, 1969-71; assoc. editor The Way Internat., New Knoxville, Ohio, 1975-77; dir. publ. relations, 1979-81; news writer Emporia State U. (Kans.), 1977-78; staff pharmacist Bloomington Hosp. (Ind.), 1981-85; assoc. instr. Emporia State U., 1977-78, Ind. U., Bloomington, 1983-85; asst. prof. English, Fayetteville U., N.C., 1985—, adj. faculty Way Coll. Emporia, 1976-81. Author: (poems) Ears Near to the Lips of God, 1984. Contbr. articles to profl. pubis. Served with U.S. Army, 1967-69. Recipient Orrison Challenge award The Way Internat., 1970; consortium in Instn. Cooperative fellow, 1981. Mem. Soc. Bibl. Lit., Alpha Phi Alpha. Avocations: Jogging, gourmet cooking, poetry, handicrafts, gardening. Office: Ind U Ballantine Hall 447 Bloomington IN 47401

JOHNSON, LORETTA RENEE, manufacturing company executive; b. Concord, N.C., Nov. 7, 1950; d. Paul and Elmira (Epps) Giles; m. John David Johnson (dec. July 11, 1975); 1 child, Corwin Dwayne. Student Bowling Green U., Findlay Coll., Tiffin U. Adminstrv. asst. Atlas Crankshaft Corp., Fostoria, Ohio, 1980-83, orgnl. devel. specialist, 1983-85, mfg. supr. comml. products, 1985—. Sec., Fostoria YMCA, 1982; 2d v.p. Fostoria United Way, 1983, 1st v.p., 1984, 85. Mem. Altrusa Club, Bus. and Profl. Women. Avocations: writing; music; computer; racquetball; autocross racing. Home: 234 Watson Ave Fostoria OH 44830 Office: Atlas Crankshaft Corp US Route 23 South Fostoria OH 44830

JOHNSON, LOWELL C., state legislator; b. Dodge County, Nebr., June 12, 1920; B.S. in Mech. Engring., U. Nebr., 1942; m. Ruth Marion Sloss, June 21, 1943; children—Mark C., Kent R., James S., Nancy L. Farm and property mgmt. exec.; pres. Johnson-Sloss Land Co., North Bend, Nebr.; mem. Nebr. Legislature, 1980—. Mem. USDA Nat. Adv. Council on Rural Devel.; former trustee Meml. Hosp. Dodge County; former mem. adv. council Nebr. Dept. Labor; former mem. citizens adv. com. Immanuel Hosp., Omaha; former mem. County Sch. Reorgn. Com.; former field rep. Congressman Charles Thone; pres. bd. dirs. North Bend Sr. Citizens Home. Mem. Am. Legion, Fremont and North Bend C. of C. Clubs: Masons, Shriners, Rotary. Address: RFD 2 North Bend NE 68649

JOHNSON, LOWELL THOMAS, dentist, educator, consultant; b. Muskegon, Mich., July 25, 1930; s. Philip Oliver and Dona Marie (Michaud) J.; m. Catherine Doris von Glahn, June 26, 1954; children—Thomas Andrew, Ann Elizabeth, Margaret Carol. A.B., U. Mich., 1953; D.D.S., Marquette U., 1961. Diplomate Am. Bd. Forensic Odontology. Clin. prof. Marquette U., Milw., 1961—; gen. practice dentistry, Glendale, Wis., 1961—; cons. County Med. Examiners Office, Milw., 1963—, Wis. Dept. of Justice, Madison, 1978—. Served with USAF, 1953-57. Fellow Am. Acad. of Forensic Sci., Internat. Coll. Dentists; mem. Internat. Orgn. Forensic Odontostomatology, AMA (spl. affiliate), Omicron Kappa Upsilon. Lodge: Kiwanis Internat. (Brown Deer, Wis.) (sr. mem. 1962) Home: 6040 N Kent Ave Whitefish Bay WI 53217 Office: 5900 N Port Washington Rd Glendale WI 53217

JOHNSON, LUCIE JENKINS, social worker, educator; b. Elizabethtown, Ky., Feb. 10, 1927; d. Alex Heady and Mary Lee (Igleheart) Jenkins; B.A. magna cum laude, Wake Forest U., 1949; M.S.W., Tulane U., 1953; postgrad. Va. Poly. Inst. and State U., 1974-80; m. Glenn E. Johnson, Oct. 24, 1952; children—Alexander, Rebecca, Catherine, Elizabeth. Psychiat. social worker with families in public/pvt. service, 1952-67; chief psychiat. social worker Youth Services, Va. Dept. Welfare and Instns., Richmond, 1967-69; asst. prof. Va. Commonwealth U., 1969-74; asst. prof., coordinator continuing edn. in social work Wayne State U., Detroit, 1977-81; supr. oncology social work Harper Hosp./Wayne State U., Detroit, 1981-84. Mem. Nat. Assn. Social Workers, Acad. Cert. Social Workers, Mich. Soc. Clin. Social Work, Mich. Oncology Social Work Assn. (chmn.), AAUP. Democrat. Presbyterian (elder). Home: 79 Kenwood Rd Grosse Pointe Farms MI 48236

JOHNSON, SISTER MARIE INEZ, librarian; b. Mitchell, S.D., June 2, 1909; d. Charles and Inez L. (Williams) Johnson; B.A. in English, Coll. St. Catherine, 1929, B.S. in L.S., 1939; M.S., in L.S., Columbia, 1940; postgrad. U. Denver, 1951-52, U. So. Calif., 1953-54. Joined Sisters St. Joseph Carondolet, 1926; tchr. elementary schs. St. Paul, 1930-38; librarian Coll. St. Catherine, St. Paul, 1940-42, head librarian, 1942-73. Mem. steering com. U. Minn. Workshop for Librarians, 1956; library cons. survey Mt. Mercy Coll., Cedar Rapids, Iowa, 1963-64; bldg. cons. Fontbonne Coll., St. Louis, 1964—. Mem. Conf. Am. Folklore for Youth, St. Paul Speakers Bur., com. standard catalog for high sch. Cath. Support, Children's Lit. TV Series; trustee James J. Hill Library, 1970—. Butler Fgn. Study fellow Coll. St. Catherine, 1958. Named Minn. Librarian of Year, 1967. Mem. Am. (various coms.), Cath. (various coms.) library assns. Editor column Cath. Library World, 1954—. Contbr. articles to profl. jours. Address: Coll St Catherine St Paul MN 55105

JOHNSON, MARLENE, lieutenant governor of Minnesota; b. Braham, Minn., Jan. 11, 1946; d. Beauford Johnson and Helen Johnson. B.A., Macalester Coll., 1968. Founder, pres. Split Infinitive, Inc., 1970-82; pres. bd. Face to Face Health and Counseling Clinic, 1977-78, Working Opportunities for Women, 1977; lt. gov. State of Minn., St. Paul, 1983—. Chmn. Minn. Women's Polit. Caucus, 1973-76; membership dir. Nat. Women's Polit. Caucus, 1975-77; chmn. Democrat-Farmer-Labor Small Bus. Task Force,

1978; vice chmn. Minn. Small Bus. Task Force, 1978; co-chmn. Minn. Del. to White House Conf. on Small Bus., 1980; co-founder Minn. Women's Campaign Fund, 1982; Recipient Disting. Service award St. Paul Jr. C. of C., 1980; Outstanding Achievement award St. Paul YWCA, 1980; named Outstanding Young Minnesotan, Minn. Jr. C. of C., 1980; Disting. Citizen citation Macalester Coll., 1982. Mem. Nat. Assn. Women Bus. Owners (pres. 1981-82). Address: 122 State Capitol Saint Paul MN 55155*

JOHNSON, MARSHALL BOYD, product designer; b. Mineola, N.Y., Dec. 5, 1938; s. Loyal Robert and Madeline Margaret (Ramsauer) J.; m. Katherine Jean Wright, Aug. 1, 1964; children—Margaret Jean, Patricia Lyn. B.F.A., R.I. Sch. Design, 1960; student Harford Community Coll., 1962-63. Package engr. Black & Decker, Towson, Md., 1960-61, indsl. designer, 1961-67; sr. indsl. designer Aluminum Co. of Am., Pitts., 1967-71; product design coordinator Wear-Ever Aluminum, Chillicothe, Ohio, 1971-82; corp. product designer Wear-Ever/Proctor-Silex, Chillicothe, 1982—; cons. in field. Patentee in field. Mem. Civic Band Organizing Com., Bel Air, Md., 1962; v.p. South Central Ohio Speech & Hearing Ctr., Chillicothe, 1971-74, Citizens Ednl. Adv. Com., 1971-74, Bd. Deacons, 1st Presbyterian Ch., 1971-74, Peoples Reps. on Mass Pub. Transit, Pitts., 1970; instr. Project Bus. of Central Ohio, 1972—. Recipient Alcoa Tech. award, 1980, 81, Appreciation award Goodwill Industries, 1983. Mem. Indsl. Designers Soc. Am. (chmn. Ohio Valley chpt. 1972-76), Color Mktg. Group, Human Factors Soc., Ross County Hist. Soc. Libertarian, Jaycees (pres. 1963-65). Clubs: Chillicothe Art League (pres. 1982). Avocations: trombone; Dixieland jazz; photography; restoration of vehicles; cartoons. Home: 120 Eastview Ave Chillicothe OH 45601 Office: Wear-Ever/Proctor Silex 1089 Eastern Ave Chillicothe OH 45601

JOHNSON, MARSHALL DUANE, theology educator, editor; b. Middle River, Minn., Nov. 15, 1935; s. Ingvald and Bertha Sylvia (Maijala) J.; m. Alice Joy Peterson, May 31, 1959; children—Nathan Erick, Catherine Florence, Jennifer Beth. B.A., Augsburg Coll., 1957, B.Th., 1961; Th.D., Union Theol. Sem., 1966. Vis. prof. Lutheran Sem., Phila., 1965-66; prof. religion Wartburg Coll., Waverly, Iowa, 1966-85; acad. editor Augsburg Pub House, Mpls., 1984—. Author: The Purpose of Biblical Genealogies, 1969; The Life of Adam and Eve, 1985. Contbr. articles to profl. jours. Fulbright lecturer, researcher U. Bergen, Norway, 1976; mem. NEH summer seminar, 1980. Mem. Soc. Bibl. Lit. Avocations: Music, swimming, traveling. Home: 5413 Morgan Ave S Minneapolis MN 55419 Office: Augsburg Pub House Box 1209 Minneapolis MN 55440

JOHNSON, MARTHA CELESTIA, civic organization executive; b. Odessa Twp., Mich., Nov. 17, 1903; d. Charles Jefferson and Charlotte (Musgrove) Koutz; m. Harley D. Johnson, June 8, 1934; children—Alicia Marjorie Johnson Walker, Phyllis Charlene Johnson Carter. Grad. Lansing Bus. U., 1925. Order clk. Lansing Co., Mich., 1926-28; bookkeeper Pingry Tractor and Equipment Co., Grand Rapids, Mich., 1928-33; typist, clk. Dept. Mil. Affairs, State of Mich., Lansing, 1955-56, driver improvement clk., 1957-66; exec. sec. Michigan Pure Water Council, Lansing, 1971—. Pianist Wesleyan Methodist Ch., East Odessa, Mich., 1946-51, Sunday Sch. sec., 1946-51; mem. Heritage Found., Washington, 1975, Republican Presdl. Task Force, 1982-85, Rep. Nat. Com., 1980, Citizens Clearing House for Hazardous Waste, 1983, Project CURE, 1984; mem. Friends of Mich. Schs., 1963—. Recipient Liberty award Congress of Freedom, 1972-73; cert. of achievement Central Ch. of the Nazarene, Lansing, 1975; cert. recognition Hale Found., 1984; spl. tribute State of Mich., 1984. Mem. WCTU, Fedn. of Homemakers, Nat. Health Fedn. (life), Clubs: Safe Water (bd. dirs. 1979-85), Organic Garden (Lansing).

JOHNSON, MARVIN FREDERICK, insurance executive; b. Balt., July 19, 1925; s. John Frederick and Jessie (Gadd) J.; m. Grace Verna Rose, Sept. 26, 1946 (dec.); 1 child, Carol Lynn Johnson Rush; m. Dorothea Lee Myers, Aug. 25, 1972; stepchildren—Joy Lee Mitchell, Randall Eric Mitchell, Dennis Alan Mitchell. A.A., U. Balt., 1948, LL.B., 1951. Supt. life and health claims Zurich Ins. Co., Chgo., 1950-58, corp. planning officer, 1970-74; life mktg. dir., life and health claim dir. Allstate Ins. Co., Northbrook, Ill., 1958-69, v.p. internat. ops., 1974-81; ins. mgmt. cons., Chgo., 1969-70, 81—. Author: Life and Health Claim Reference Guide, 1958-59. Contbr. articles to profl. jours. Chmn. stock casualty ins. div. Am. Cancer Soc., Chgo., 1956; div. capt. Northwest Community Hosp. Bldg. Fund, Arlington Heights, Ill., 1956; pres. Balt. Young Men's Democratic Club, 1954. Served with USNR, 1943-46, PTO. Recipient award of Merit Am. Cancer Soc., 1956. Mem. Internat. Claim Assn. (mem. uniform forms com. 1959), Chgo. Claim Assn., C. of C. of U.S. (mem. life ins. com., internat. ins. adv. com.). Republican. Lutheran. Home: 2531 Honeysuckle Ln Rolling Meadows IL 60008

JOHNSON, MARVIN MELROSE, industrial engineer, educator; b. Neligh, Nebr., Apr. 21, 1925; s. Harold Nighram and Melissa (Bare) J.; B.S., Purdue U., 1949; postgrad. Ill. Inst. Tech., 1953; M.S. in Indsl. Engring., U. Iowa, 1966, Ph.D., 1968; m. Anne Stuart Campbell, Nov. 10, 1951; children—Douglas Blake, Harold James, Phyllis Anne, Nighram Marvin, Melissa Joan. Quality control supr., indsl. engr. Houdaille Hershey, Chgo., 1949-52; sr. indsl. engr. Bell & Howell, Chgo., 1952-54; with Bendix Aviation Corp., Davenport, Iowa, 1954-64, successively chief indsl. engr., staff asst., supr. procedures and systems, 1954-63, reliability engr. Pioneer Central Div., 1963-64, cons., 1964—; lectr. indsl. engr. State U. Iowa, 1963-64; instr. indsl. engring. U. Iowa, 1965-66; assoc. prof. U. Nebr., 1968-73, prof., 1973—; U.S. AID adviser mgmt. engring. and food processing Kabul (Afghanistan) U., 1975-76; vis. prof. U. P.R., Mayaguez, 1982-83. NSF trainee U. Iowa, 1964-67. Served with AUS, 1943-46, ETO. Registered profl. engr., Iowa, Mo., Nebr. Fellow Am. Inst. Indsl. Engrs.; mem. Am. Soc. Engring. Educators, Am. Statis. Assn., ASME, Ops. Research Soc. Am., Inst. Mgmt. Sci., Sigma Xi, Tau Beta Pi, Pi Tau Sigma, Alpha Pi Mu. Presbyterian. Home: 2507 Ammon Ave Lincoln NE 68507 Office: 175 Nebraska Hall U Nebr Lincoln NE 68588

JOHNSON, MARY JANE JACQUELIN, Realtor; b. Mpls., Aug. 12, 1929; d. Belmont LeRoy and Lauretta Frances (Cunningham) Oddson; m. Franklin Keith Johnson, May 21, 1948; children—Deborah, Randolph, Scott, Timothy, Eric. Ed. in St. Paul. Saleswoman, Fedders AC Heating Co., Mpls., 1972-75; owner, mgr. Off-Sale Liquor Co., Crosslake, Minn., 1975-80; Realtor, Century 21-Goedker Co., Crosslake, 1981-85; broker/owner Realty World-Shores & More, Crosslake, 1985—. Dir., writer, producer local theatre; sec.-treas. Crosslake Parks, Recreation, Crosslake, 1977-83. Recipient sales awards. Mem. Brainerd Bd. Realtors (communication com.), Crosslake C. of C. (treas. 1976-77). Roman Catholic. Club: Pine Cone Players (pres. 1982). Home: Star Rte 1 Pequot Lakes MN 56472 Office: Box 345 Crosslake MN 56442

JOHNSON, MARYL RAE, cardiologist; b. Fort Dodge, Iowa, Apr. 15, 1951; d. Marvin George and Beryl Evelyn (White) J. B.S., Iowa State U., 1973; M.D., U. Iowa, 1977. Diplomate Am. Bd. Internal Medicine. Intern, U. Iowa Hosps., Iowa City, 1977-78, resident, 1978-81; assoc. in cardiology U. Iowa Hosps. and Clinics, Iowa City, 1982—. Mem. Nat. Heart Lung and Blood Adv. Council, Bethesda, Md., 1979-83. Barry Freeman scholar, 1974; recipient Jane Leinfelder Meml. award U. Iowa Coll. Medicine, 1977, Clin. Investigator award NIH, 1981. Mem. AMA, Am. Heart Assn., Johnson County Med. Soc., Iowa Med. Soc., Am. Fedn. Clin. Research, AAAS, Am. Coll. Cardiology, ACP, Order of the Rose, Alpha Lambda Delta, Phi Kappa Phi, Iota Sigma Pi, Alpha Omega Alpha. Office: U Iowa Hosps and Clinics Dept Internal Medicine Iowa City IA 52242

JOHNSON, MICHAEL ALBERT, SR., distributing company executive; b. Joliet, Ill., Oct. 20, 1957; s. Donald Laverne and Teresa (Grenchik) J.; m. Frances Ann Carlino, May 28, 1977; children—Donald Joseph, Michael Albert, Robert Mattew. Student Lewis U., Romeoville, Ill., 1977-81. Lic. real estate broker. Acct. Royal Crest Homes, Joliet, Ill., 1976-80; controller Avionics Assocs., Inc., Joliet, 1980-83; exec. v.p., 1983—, also dir. dir. Communication Assocs., Inc., Joliet. Mem. Gen. Aviation Credit Group, Ill. State C. of C. Republican. Roman Catholic. Club: Die-Hard Cub Fan (Chgo.). Avocations: coin collecting; softball. Home: 2504 Caddy Ln Joliet IL 60435 Office: Avionics Assocs Inc 305 Republic Ave Joliet IL 60435

JOHNSON, NELS JOEL, JR., arborist; b. Chgo., Mar. 30, 1942; s. Nels Joel and Ruth V. (Gustafson) J.; m. Margaret Louise Vikner, 1965; children—Matthew, Erik, John, Lisa. Grad. Augustana Coll., 1965. Lic. tree expert, Ill. Flight instr., pilot Air Wis., 1967-69; v.p. Nels J. Johnson Tree Experts Inc., Evanston, Ill., 1969—. Mem. tree expert examiners com. Ill. Dept. Registration and Edn. Mem. Nat. Arborist Assn., Internat. Soc. Arboriculture, Ill. Comml. Arborists. Republican. Lutheran. Club: Waukegan Yacht. Office: 912 Pitner Evanston IL 60202

JOHNSON, NOEL MCKINLEY, psychiatrist; b. San Antonio, Mar. 2, 1936; s. Charles Nelson and Florence (McKinley) J.; m. Anita DeArmond, Nov. 28, 1964; children—Michael E., Wendy S. B.A., U. Kans., 1958, Exchange Scholar U. of Exeter, England, 1958-59; M.D. (Regional Scholar), Washington U., St. Louis, 1963. Diplomate Am. Bd. Psychiatry and Neurology. Intern, Ind. U. Med. Center, Indpls., 1963-64; resident in psychiatry Washington U. Med. Sch. Hosp., St. Louis, 1966-69; asst. chief dept. neuro-psychiatry U.S. Army Hosp., Stuttgart, Germany, 1964-66; pvt. practice gen. psychiatry, Springfield, Mo., 1969-72; chief Mental Health Clinic, Student Health Center, U. S.C., Columbia, 1973-76; staff psychiatrist McKinley Student Health Center, U. Ill., Urbana, 1977-79; chief psychiatry service VA Med. Center, Danville, Ill., 1979—; assoc. clin. prof. U. Ill. Coll. Medicine, Champaign-Urbana. Served to capt. U.S. Army, 1964-66. Mem. Am. Psychiat. Assn., Royal Coll. of Psychiatry (Engl.) Corr. Affiliate, Phi Beta Kappa. Office: VA Med Center 1900 E Main St Danville IL 61832

JOHNSON, NORMA JEANETTE, specialty wool grower; b. Dover, Ohio, Aug. 30, 1925; d. Jasper Crile and Mildred Catherine (Russell) J.; student Heidelberg Coll., 1943; cert. drafting techniques Case Sch. Applied Sci., 1944; student Western Res. U., 1945-47, Ohio State U., 1951, Muskingum Coll., 1965; A.A., Kent State U., 1979, Buckeye Joint Vocat. Sch., 1979-84; m. Robert Blake Covey, Oct. 7, 1951 (div. 1960); 1 dau., Susan Kay. Instr. arts and crafts Univ. Settlement House, Cleve., 1944; mech. drafstwoman Nat. Assn. Civil Aeros., Cleve., 1944-46; mfrs. rep. Nat. Spice House, 1947-49; tchr. econs., home econs., English, math, history, high sch., Tuscarawas County Sch. System, New Philadelphia, Ohio, 1962-69; owner, mgr. Sunny Slopes Farm, producer of specialty wools, Dover, Ohio, 1969—. Tchr., Meth. Sunday Sch., 1956-61; chaplain Winfield PTA, 1960; program dir. Brandywine Grange, 1960-62; troop leader Girl Scouts, U.S.A., 1961-70; mem. Tuscarawas County Jail Com., 1981. Recipient cert. of merit Tuscarawas County Schs., 1965, Ohio Wildlife Conservation award Tuscarawas County, 1972, 1st and 3d premiums for handspinning fleece, Ohio State Fair, 1984. Mem. Mid States Wool Growers, Am. Angus Assn., Club: Nat. Grange. Designer, constructor interior facilities for a Scheuer-Haus. Home and Office: Route 1 Box 398 Dover OH 44622

JOHNSON, NORMAN J., health and physical education educator; b. Cape Girardeau, Mo., Sept. 8, 1919; s. Louis Henry and Anna Lou (Cravens) J.; m. Helen Louise Watkins, June 12, 1954; 1 child, Michael O. A.B., Ky. State U., 1941; M.A., U. Mich., 1948 Ed.D., 1960. Prof., dept. dir. Xavier U., New Orleans, 1948-49; prof. dept. chmn. Bluefield State Coll., W.Va., 1951-56; prof.-in-charge Prairie View A&M U., Tex., 1956-63; prof. dept. chmn. Lincoln U., Jefferson City, Mo., 1963—, also Curators disting. prof. Bd. dirs. Nat. Found. March of Dimes, Am. Nat. Red Cross; commr. Boy Scouts Am. Served to 1st lt. horse calvary U.S. Army, 1942-46. Mem. AAHPERO, Am. Assn. Health and Phys. Edn. (v.p. 1970-71), Mo. Assn. Health and Phys. Edn. (pres. 1971-72), Am. Sch and Community Safety Assn. Roman Catholic. Lodges: Kiwanis, K.C. Avocation: back packing. Home: 807 Jackson St Jefferson City MO 65101 Office: Lincoln U Jefferson City MO 65101

JOHNSON, ORA J., clergyman; b. Oakland City, Ind., Aug. 31, 1932; s. Ora F. and Thelma Pauline (Julian) J.; B.S., Oakland City Coll., 1971; m. Wanda Mae Lockamy, Aug. 11, 1952; children—David Russell, Kent Alan, Vicki Jeanne. Ordained to ministry Baptist Ch., 1966; sales rep., staff sales mgr. Western & So. Ins. Co., Evansville, Ind., 1956-70, also pastor Corydon (Ky.) Gen. Bapt. Ch., 1965-68, Wadesville (Ind.) Gen. Bapt. Ch., 1968-70, North Haven Gen. Bapt. Ch., Evansville, 1970-75; nat. dir. evangelism and ch. growth Gen. Bapt. Hdqrs., Poplar Bluff, Mo., 1976-82; pastor 1st Gen. Bapt. Ch., Malden, Mo., 1982—; producer, dir. weekly TV program Moments of Worship, 1973-74; pres. Greater Evansville Sunday Sch. Assn., 1975; pres. Gen. Bapt. Home Mission Bd., 1972-73, Gen. Bd. Gen. Bapts., 1972-73; pres. Evansville Clergy Assn., 1975-76. Named Outstanding Theolog of 1971, Gen. Bapt. Brotherhood; recipient Good Shepherd award Boy Scouts Am., 1980. Mem. Christian Resource Assos., Evangelization Forum, Nat. Assn. Evangelicals, Malden Ministerial Alliance (pres. 1983), Malden C. of C. (pres. 1985-86). Club: Malden Optimist. Lodge: Kiwanis (dir. Evansville 1975, dir. Poplar Bluff 1981-83). Home: 611 Barrett Dr Malden MO 63863 Office: 1st Gen Bapt Ch Bldg 601 Barrett Dr Malden MO 63863

JOHNSON, OWEN VERNE, history educator; b. Madison, Wis., Feb. 22, 1946; s. Verner L. and Marianne V. (Halvorson) J.; m. Marta Kucerova, July 17, 1969; children—Eva, Hana. B.A. in History with distinction, Wash. State U., 1968; M.A. in History, U. Mich., 1970, Ph.D. in History, 1978; cert. Russian and East European studies, 1978. Reporter Pullman (Wash.) Herald, 1961-67; reporter, announcer Sta. KWSU Radio/TV, Pullman, 1965-68; producer, editor, reporter Sta. WUOM, Ann Arbor, Mich., 1969-77; adminstrv. asst. U. Mich. Russian and European Inst., 1978-79; asst. prof. So. Ill. U., Carbondale, 1979-80, Ind. U., Bloomington, 1980—; lectr. U. Mich., 1978-79, teaching fellow, undergrad. adviser, 1975; Danforth teaching fellow dept. history U. Mich., 1970; mem. rev. com. Polish Studies Ctr., 1983-84; mem. scholarship selection com. Ind. U. High Sch. Journalism Inst., 1983-85; mem. exec. com. Russian and East European Inst. Ind. U., 1981—, mem. fin. aid com., 1982—; mem. Studia Academica Slovaca, Comenius Univ. Czechoslovakia, 1973, Modern Sweden Seminar, 1967; frequent lectr. Author: Slovakia 1918-1938: Education and the Making of a Nation, 1985. Mem. editorial bd. Slovakia, 1978—; cons. Slavic Rev., 1985—. Book reviewer. Contbr. numerous articles to profl. jours. Served to capt. USAR, 1971-79. Judge Ind. State Women's Press Club, 1982. Recipient Rackham prize U. Mich. Grad. Sch., 1971-72, Sigma Delta Chi Excellence in Journalism award State of Wash., 1966; Ernest O. Holland Study Abroad scholar Wash. State U., 1967, Internat. Research and Exchanges Bd. scholar, 1973-74, 82; Mellon summer research fellow, 1984; grantee Am. Council of Learned Societies/Social Sci. Research Council Joint Com. on Eastern Europe Conf., Russian and Eastern European Inst. Ind. U., fall 1983; Am. Philos. Soc. grantee, 1979; James and Helen Hovorka Found. grantee, 1978, Fulbright-Hays doctoral dissertation fellow, 1973-74. Mem. Am. Hist. Assn., Am. Assn. for Advancement of Slavic Studies, Assn. Edn. in Journalism and Mass Communication (editor newsletter, sec. history div., 1983-84, head history div. 1985-86), Czechoslovak History Conf. (editor newsletter 1980-84), Immigration History Soc., Internat. Assn. for Mass Communication Research, Orgn. Am. Historians, Slovak Studies Assn. (mem. exec. com. 1980-82), Swedish Am. Hist. Soc., Sigma Delta Chi (nat. conv. del. 1967), Alpha Epsilon Rho. Democrat. Presbyterian. Office: Sch of Journalism Ind U Bloomington IN 47405

JOHNSON, PATRICK VINCENT, lawyer; b. Mpls., May 20, 1953; s. Vincent Eugene and Ruby Helen (Johnson) J.; m. Mary Carol Cordell, June 13, 1981; children—Eva Marie, Emily Christine. B.A., U. Minn., 1975; J.D., Hamline U., 1978. Bar: Minn. 1978, U.S. Dist. Ct. Minn. 1978. Atty., ptnr. Speeter, Johnson, Hautman & Olson, Mpls., 1977—; chief exec. officer TOJ Prodns., Inc., Mpls., 1982—. Author screenplay: It Came From Somewhere Else, 1981, dir. motion picture, 1984. Mem. Uptown Community Clinic Adv. Com., Mpls., 1982-84; mem. Basilica of St. Mary, Mpls., 1980-84. Recipient Am. Jurisprudence award Lawyer's Coop. Pub. Co., 1976. Mem. Minn. Trial Lawyers Assn., Hennepin County Bar Assn., Hennepin County Referral. Democratic Farm Labor. Roman Catholic. Club: Rosehill Golf Assn. (Mpls.). Home: 2620 Colfax Ave S Minneapolis MN 55408 Office: Speeter Johnson Hautman & Olson 2100 First Bank Pl W Minneapolis MN 55402

JOHNSON, PAUL EDWARD, financial consultant, accountant; b. Toledo, May 19, 1952; s. William Arthur and Edith (Dooley) J.; m. Denise Anne Connelly, Dec. 27, 1975; children—Ellen, Stephen. B.A., Villanova U., 1974; M.B.A., Syracuse U., 1976. C.P.A., Ohio. Mem. audit staff, cons. Arthur Young & Co., Toledo, 1977-82, mgr. entrepreneurial services group, 1982—. Bd. dirs. Catholic Social Services, Toledo, 1983—; loan exec., firm chmn. United Way, Toledo, 1983—. Mem. Ohio Soc. C.P.A.s, Am. Inst. C.P.A.s, Nat. Cash Mgmt. Assn., Govt. Fin. Officers Assn., Soc. Advancement Mgmt., Alliance Francaise (treas. Toledo 1980-82), Toledo Orgn. for Mgmt. Democrat. Roman Catholic. Club: Toledo. Home: 2665 Meadowwood Dr Toledo OH 43606 Office: Arthur Young & Co 3130 Executive Pkwy Toledo OH 43606

JOHNSON, PAUL JAMES, consultant; b. Bay City, Mich., Nov. 6, 1946; s. William and Helen Harriet (Stevens) J.; m. Valorie Jean Huff, Aug. 28, 1976; children—Christopher, Stephen, Derek, Dustin. B.S.E., U. Mich., 1968, M.A., 1976, M.S.W., 1976. Admissions counselor U. Mich., Ann Arbor, 1968-69; tchr. Girmingham Sch. System (Mich.), 1969-70; program analyst Exec. Office State Mich., Lansing, 1970-73; profl. devel. cons. Mich. Edn. Assn., East Lansing, Mich., 1973—. Author: Native American Curriculum Handbook, 1981. Mem. state bd. dirs. Mich. YMCA, Torch Lake, Mich., 1983—. Mem. ASTD, Assn. Suprs. Curriculum Devel., Am. Mgmt. Assn., NEA. Club: U. Mich. M. Avocations: athletic activities. Home: 1187 Buckingham Rd Haslett MI 48840 Office: Mich Edn Assn 1216 Kendale Blvd East Lansing MI 48823

JOHNSON, PAUL STEVEN, real estate appraiser, consultant; b. Mpls., Feb. 17, 1950; s. George Emil and Veronica Susan (Bagger) J. B.A. in Sociology, Ethics, St. Norbet Coll., 1972. Cert. review appraiser. Agt., appraiser George E. Johnson Realtors, Mpls., 1968-74; appraiser, cons. Appraisal Valuation Analysts, Mpls., 1974-78, v.p., 1978-81, 82—, pres., 1981-82; instr. real estate valuation. Named Nat. Man of Yr., Nat. Assn. Ind. Fee Appraisers, 1978, recipient Nat. Recognition award, 1979, Appreciation award, 1982. Mem. Nat. Assn. Ind. Fee Appraisers (past nat. dir.), Nat. Assn. Rev. Appraisers, Nat. Assn. Realtors. Club: Aircraft Owners and Pilot's Assn. Contbr. articles in field to profl. jours. Home: 3235 Pierce St NE Minneapolis MN 55418 Office: 2841 Johnson St NE Minneapolis MN 55418

JOHNSON, PHYLLIS AUDREY, auditor; b. Darwin, Minn., July 25, 1923; d. John Emmanuel and Emma Elizabeth (Scheidegger) Nelson; B.A., Met. State U., St. Paul, 1973; B.Applied Sci., U. Minn., 1974; diploma U. Wis. Grad. Sch. Banking, 1973; cert. Am. Inst. Banking, 1975; cert. tchr.; lic. real estate sales; m. Ellsworth Orr Johnson, Apr. 6, 1943; children—Elwood Oren (dec.), Christine Marie Johnson Wilbur, Elizabeth Ann Johnson Milne, Eric Christian. Asst. cashier Farmers State Bank, Darwin, 1941-42; asst. cashier State Bank Anoka (Minn.), 1944; cost accountant Red Wing Boat Works (Minn.), 1956-57; banking generalist First Bank Southdale, Edina, Minn., 1960-70; asst. v.p. ops., personnel and purchasing S.W. Fidelity State Bank, Edina, 1970-71; auditor First Nat. Bank Glenwood City (Wis.), 1973—, Hiawatha Nat. Bank, Hagen City, Wis., 1973—; employment mgr., personnel officer Bank Shares, Inc., Mpls., 1973-77; mortgage loan officer St. Anthony Park State Bank, St. Paul, 1978-79; pres. DAAV Banking Services, 1984—; instr. bus. mgmt. Mpls. Tech. Inst., 1979—, mem. adv. com. bus. mgmt. and banking, 1975—; adv. com. banking program Suburban Hennepin Tech. Inst., White Bear Lake, Minn., 1972-77; speaker in field, 1974—. Precinct chmn. Edina Ind. Republicans, 1970-74; chmn. service unit, mem. coms., leader Edina and Red Wing councils Girl Scouts, 1958-68; sec. Edina United Fund, 1963-64; pres. St. Paul's Lutheran Ch., Mankato, Minn., 1965-67, St. Paul's Luth. Ch., Red Wing, 1950-58, Bethlehem Luth. Ch., Mpls., 1959—. Mem. Am. Mgmt. Assn., Am. Banking Assn., Nat. Assn. Women Bus. Owners, Am. Bus. Women's Assn., Nat. Bus. Edn. Assn., Am. Vocat. Assn., Minn. Bus. Edn. Assn., Minn. Vocat. Assn. Clubs: Normandale Tennis, Winterset and Marti Grau Dance, Interlachen Country. Home: 5301 Ayrshire Blvd Edina MN 55436 Office: 1415 Hennepin Ave S Minneapolis MN 55403

JOHNSON, PHYLLIS ELAINE, chemist; b. Grafton, N.D., Feb. 19, 1949; d. Donald Gordon and Evelyn Lorraine (Svaren) Lanes; m. Robert S.T. Johnson, Sept. 12, 1969; children—Erik, Sara. B.S., U.N.D., 1971, Ph.D., 1976. Instr. chemistry Mary Coll., Bismarck, N.D., 1971-72; postdoctoral research fellow U.N.D., Grand Forks, 1975-79, chemist, 1977-79; research chemist U.S. Dept. Agr. Human Nutrition Research Ctr., 1979—. Editor: Stable Isotopes in Nutrition, 1984. Contbr. articles to profl. jours. Chmn. Parents of Gifted and Talented, 1984—. Mem. Am. Chem. Soc., Am. Soc. Mass Spectrometry, Am. Inst. Nutrition, Minn. Chromatography Forum, Soc. Exptl. Biology and Medicine, Phi Beta Kappa, Sigma Xi. Lutheran. Lodge: Sons of Norway (dist. v.p. 1984—). Avocations: cooking; skiing; needlework; camping. Home: 4809 4th Ave N Grand Forks ND 58201 Office: US Dept Agr Human Nutrition Research Ctr PO Box 7166 University Sta Grand Forks ND 58202

JOHNSON, RALPH STERLING, JR., metallurgical engineer; b. Shickshinny, Pa., Apr. 2, 1926; s. Ralph Sterling and Hilda Flo (Camp) J.; m. Margaret Louise Master, Dec. 1, 1951; 1 child, Ralph Sterling III. B.S. in Physics, U. Akron, 1957, M.S. in Physics, 1960; Ph.D. in Metall. Engring., Materials Sci., U. Mich., 1970. Registered profl. engr., Calif. Sr. devel. engr. Goodyear Aerospace, Akron, Ohio, 1949-61; staff engr., supr. Bendix Aerospace, Ann Arbor, Mich., 1962-72; engring. supr. Bechtel Corp., San Francisco, 1973-79; staff metallurgist, supr. Aramco, Dhahran, Saudi Arabia, 1979-81; sr. cons. Sohio Petroleum Co., Cleve., 1981—. Commr. Sci. Adv. Commn. for Alaska Found., Anchorage, 1984—; scoutmaster Ann Arbor council Boy Scouts Am., 1968-69. Served with USAF, 1944-45. Recipient Apollo Achievement award NASA, 1969. Mem. Nat. Soc. Corrosion Engrs. (chpt. chmn. 1982-84), AIME, Nat. Soc. Profl. Engrs., Am. Soc. Metals, N.Y. Acad. Sci., Sigma Xi. Republican. Lodge: Masons (32 degree). Home: 9009 Crow Dr Macedonia OH 44056 Office: Sohio Petroleum Co Tech Ctr 1 Lincoln Ctr 5400 LBJ Freeway Dallas TX 75240

JOHNSON, RICHARD ARNOLD, statistics educator; b. St. Paul, July 10, 1937; s. Arnold Verner and Florence Dorothy Johnson; m. Roberta Ann Weinard, Mar. 21, 1964; children—Erik Richard, Thomas Robert. B.A. in Elec. Engring., U. Minn., 1960, M.S. in Math., 1963, Ph.D. in Stats., 1966. Asst. prof. stats. U. Wis., Madison, 1966-70, assoc. prof., 1970-74, prof., 1974—, chmn. dept. stats., 1981-84; cons. Dept. Agr., 1978—, Dept. Energy, 1983—. Co-author: Statistical Concepts and Methods, 1977; Applied Multivariate Statistical Analysis, 1982; Statistics-Principles and Methods, 1985. Editor jour. Statistics and Parability Letters, 1982—. Contbr. articles to profl. publs. NATO fellow, 1972; grantee NSF, Office Naval Research U.S. Air Force, NASA. Fellow Inst. Math. Statistics (program sec. 1980—, mem. council 1980—), Am. Statis. Assn. (council 1980-82), Royal Statis. Soc.; mem. Internat. Statis. Inst. Lutheran. Office: U Wis Dept Statistics 1210 W Dayton Madison WI 53706

JOHNSON, RICHARD KEITH, petroleum/transportation/computer software company executive; b. Hutchinson, Kans., Feb. 24, 1939; s. Glenford Carl and Marjory Eloise (Jackson) J.; m. Shanon Athy, June 27, 1964; children—Reed Athy, Deborah Diane. B.S., Kans. U., 1964. With credit and sales dept. Am. Can Co., Neenah, Wis., 1964-67; prodn. supr. Kay Electronics, Kansas City, Mo., 1967-68; exec. v.p. Robo-Wash, Inc., Kansas City, Mo., 1968-70; leasing mgr. United Telecom, Shawnee Mission, Kans., 1970-72; cons. Lawrence-Leiter, Kansas City, 1972-74; pres. Pronto Systems, Shawnee Mission, 1972—, Trans-Oil, Ltd., Kansas City, 1979—, Computer Programs, Ltd., Kansas City, 1983—. Pres. Johnson County Soccer League, 1982-83, treas., 1979-82. Mem. Am. Petroleum Inst. Lodges: Optimist. Home: 5208 Mansfield Ln Shawnee KS 66203 Office: Trans-Oil Ltd 4303 Speaker Rd Kansas City KS 66106

JOHNSON, RICHARD MATHIAS, dentist; b. Duluth, Minn., Jan. 21, 1946; s. Theodore Mathias and Nahhah Indred (Peterson) J.; m. Patricia Lea Perkins, Sept. 6, 1969; children—Jennifer Lea, Tiffany Dawn, Scott Mathias. B.S., U. Minn.-Mpls., 1968; D.D.S., 1970. Pvt. Practice dentistry, Superior, Wis. 1971—. Mem. Am. Dental Assn. (pres. 1977-79), Acad. Gen. Dentistry (pres. 1976-77). Republican. Presbyterian. Avocations: Fishing, hunting, skiing. Home: 130 Billings Dr Superior WI 54880 Office: 1507 Tower Ave Room 427 Superior WI 54880

JOHNSON, RICHARD WALTER, lawyer; b. Mpls., Oct. 10, 1951; s. Richard Walter Johnson and Dolores Elaine (Diggles) Hancock; m. Julie Harris, Jan. 22, 1983. B.A. summa cum laude, U. Minn., 1975, J.D., 1978. Bar: Minn. 1979, U.S. Dist. Ct. Minn. 1979, U.S. Ct. Appeals (8th cir.) 1979, Nebr. 1982. Assoc. Babcock, Locher, Neilson & Mannella, Anoka, Minn., 1978-81; v.p., gen. counsel Modern Equipment Co., Inc., Omaha, 1981—; dir. Western Securities Co. Del., Omaha. Mem. Nebr. Bar Assn., Omaha Bar Assn., Phi Beta Kappa. Episcopalian. Home: 9394 Cady Ct Omaha NE 68134 Office: Modern Equipment Co Inc 2011 Cuming St Omaha NE 68102

JOHNSON, ROBERT HUGH, financial planner; b. Cleve., Dec. 22, 1934; s. Robert Hugh and Kathleen (McElroy) J.; m. Louise Marie Schulte, July 16, 1960; children—Anne Marie, Jane Ellen, Robert Hugh III, Mary Margaret. B.S., Yale U., 1959; M.B.A., Harvard U. 1961; M.S., Am. Coll., 1983. C.L.U.; chartered fin. cons. Mgr. Container Corp., Chgo., 1961-65; sr. assoc. Hinsdale Assocs., 1966—. Author: Microwave Communications, 1961. Pres. Seton Montessori Sch., Clarendon Hills, Ill., 1965-70; v.p. Am. Montessori Soc., N.Y.C., 1969-70. Named Man of Yr., No. Ill. Gen. Agts., 1968. Mem. Nat. Assn. Life Underwriters, Am. Soc. C.L.U.s, Million Dollar Round Table (chmn. program arrangements 1980), Ill. Life Underwriters (sec.-treas. 1982-84, pres. 1984-85). Roman Catholic. Club: Salt Creek. Avocations: skiing;

running; bread baking. Office: The Hinsdale Assocs 119 E Ogden Ave Hinsdale IL 60521

JOHNSON, ROBERT OLIVER, JR., educational administrator; b. Galesburg, Ill., Mar. 10, 1940; s. Robert Oliver and Veda Margaret J.; B.S., Western Ill. U., 1963, M.S., 1968, Ed.S., 1972; Ed.D., Western Colo. U., 1975; m. Patricia Ann O'Field, Apr. 7, 1979; children—Ray, Greg, William. Tchr., adminstr. Ill. schs., 1963—; prin. Knoxville (Ill.) Jr. High Sch., 1973—, curriculum coordinator, 1970—, asst. supt., 1983—; alderman Knoxville City Council. Bd. dirs. Carl Sandburg Jr. Coll. Found. Mem. Ill. Jr. High Sch. Assn. (pres.), Assn. Ill. Middle Schs., Phi Delta Kappa (pres.-elect Galesburg chpt.). Club: Masons. Home: 208 W North St Knoxville IL 61448 Office: 700 E Mill St Knoxville IL 61448

JOHNSON, ROBERT PAUL, broadcast engineer; b. Bluefield, W.Va., Aug. 18, 1929; s. William W. and Minnie M. (Lewis) J.; m. Pauline Dora Johnson, Mar. 14, 1953; children—Jessica Jean, Christopher Howard. Student Capitol Radio Engring. Inst. 1951; Cert. sr. broadcast engr. Lab. technician Raytheon Mfg. Co., Waltham, Mass., 1954-55, Spl. Techniques Lab. Electronics Corp. of Am., Cambridge, Mass, 1955-58; field engr. Sprague Electric Co., North Adams, Mass., 1958-60; chief engr. Sta. WBEC, Pittsfield, Mass., 1960-66, Sta. WISN/WLPX, Milw., 1966—. Served to staff sgt USAF, 1951-54. Mem. Soc. Broadcast Engrs. Home: 1043 Saratoga Ct Oconomowoc WI 53066 Office: 759 N 19th St Sta WISN Milwaukee WI 53233

JOHNSON, ROBERT SWIFT, accounting educator, consultant; b. Greenwood, Miss., July 22, 1942; s. Lewis Dilliard and Dorothy Sue (Swift) J.; m. Judy Lynn Foster, Aug. 20, 1964 (div. Jan. 1974); m. Andrea Joyce Kraus, Oct. 16, 1981. C.P.A., Mo. Gen. mgr. Office Machine & Equipment Co., Clarksville, Tenn., 1963-75; instr. acctg. Middle Tenn. State U., Murfreesboro, 1975-76; prof. acctg. Jefferson Coll., Hillsboro, Mo., 1976—, chmn. dept., 1979—. Cons. in field. Author: Public School Accounting, 1979. Served in Air N.G., 1963-69. Mem. Am. Inst. C.P.A.s, Mo. Soc. C.P.A.s, Am. Acctg. Assn. Clubs: Kiwanis (Disting. Pres., Disting. Gov. Mo.-Ark.), Elks. Home: 6713 Moss Hollow Rd Barnhart MO 63012 Office: Jefferson Coll Arts and Sci Hillsboro MO 63050

JOHNSON, ROBERT WILLIAM, photography educator; b. San Diego, Aug. 21, 1923; s. John and Marie Pauline (Eastin) J.; m. Patricia L. Pedler, June 22, 1947; children—Judith A. Johnson Root, Carol J. Johnson Aylesworth, Robert S. A.B. in History, U. So. Calif., 1947, M.A. in Cinematography, 1953; Ed.D. Nova U., 1977. Enlisted U.S. Navy, 1942, advanced through grades to lt. condr., 1969; asst. photog. officer Naval Forces, Far East, 1952-54; producer, dir. Navy Tng. Films, 1957-59; officer-in-charge Photo Triangulation Group, 1959-61; photog. officer, Point Arguello, Calif., 1963-65; dir. tng. Navy Schs. Photography, Pensacola, Fla., 1965-69. Prof. Coll. of DuPage, Glen Ellyn, Ill., 1970—; edn. cons. Profl. Photographers of Am., Des Plaines, Ill., 1975-81. Recipient Navy Medal of Merit, 1969. Mem. Ret. Officers Assn. Republican. Episcopalian. Avocations: numismatics; oil painting; photography. Office: Coll of DuPage 22nd St and Lambert Rd Glen Ellyn IL 60137

JOHNSON, RON J., wildlife biologist, educator; b. Dayton, Ohio, Sept. 26, 1946; s. Chester E. and Lizzie E. (Thacker) J.; m. Mary McLean Beck, June 18, 1983; 1 child, Lindsay McLean. B.S. with distinction, Ohio State U., 1968, M.S., 1973; Ph.D., Cornell U., 1979. Instr. Ohio State U., Columbus, 1974-75; asst. prof. wildlife sci. U. Nebr., Lincoln, 1979-85, assoc. prof., 1985—; cons. Airport Planning Group Central N.Y., 1978, Gt. Lakes Fisheries, Bayfield, Wis., 1983, Conservation-Tillage Info. Ctr., Washington, 1983—. Contbr. articles to profl. publs., chpts. to books. Served to 1st. lt. U.S. Army, 1968-71, Vietnam. Recipient Excellence in Programming award U. Nebr., 1983; grantee Research Council, U. Nebr., 1983. Mem. Wildlife Soc., Wilson Soc., Nebr. Acad. Scis., Sigma Xi, Gamma Sigma Delta. Avocations: running; photography; guitar playing. Office: 202 Natural Resources Hall U Nebr Lincoln NE 68583-0819

JOHNSON, RONALD HARRY, business educator; b. Moline, Ill., May 17, 1931; s. Harry Carl and Jane Agatha (Young) J.; B.A. in Bus. Adminstrn., St. Ambrose Coll., 1954; M.A. in Bus. Edn., U. Iowa, 1964; postgrad. U. Santa Clara, 1975, Western Ill. U., 1976, 80; m. Ruth Beverly Ashton, June 10, 1955; children—Michael James, Andrew Ashton, Daniel Ronald. In shipping and receiving positions Sears Roebuck & Co., Moline, 1946-52, salesman, 1952-54; mgr. sporting goods dept., Davenport, Iowa, 1954-57, mgr. automotive dept., Moline, 1957-62, mgr. automotive service, 1962-63; tchr. bus. Central High Sch., Davenport Community Sch. Dist., 1964—. Instr., ARC, 1961—; active Boy Scouts Am., 1965-76, scout master troop 4 Illowa council, 1971-76; swim ofcl. Iowa AAU, 1962—; head scorer 1st Iowa Girls Swim Meet, Iowa Girls High Sch. Athletic Union, 1967; chmn. fin. Sacred Heart Roman Catholic Parish Council, Davenport, 1980-82, v.p. council, 1981-82. Served to cpl. arty. U.S. Army, 1951-52. Mem. Davenport Edn. Assn. (pres. 1968-69, exec. bd. 1969-78), Iowa Edn. Assn. (exec. bd. 1974-78), NEA (rep. del. assembly 1976-78), Gt. River Uniserve Unit (exec. bd. 1982-84), Adminstrv. Mgmt. Soc. (edn. chmn. Quad-Cities chpt. 1970-71, exec. bd. 1970-71, 79-80), Iowa Bus. Edn. Assn. (S.E. Dist. Outstanding Bus. Tchr. award 1969, treas. and mem. exec. bd. 1974-75), Pi Kappa Alpha, Delta Pi Epsilon. Clubs: Sky Cats Flying (treas., exec. bd.), K.C. Home: 2627 Middle Rd Davenport IA 52803 Office: 1020 Main St Davenport IA 52803

JOHNSON, ROY RAGNAR, fusion company executive, researcher; b. Chgo., Jan. 23, 1932; s. Ragnar Anders and Ann Viktoria (Lundquist) J.; m. Martha Ann Mattson, June 21, 1963; children—Linnea Marit, Kaisa Ann. B.S.E.E., U. Minn., 1954, M.E.E., 1956, Ph.D., 1959. Research fellow U. Minn., Mpls., 1957-59; research scientist Boeing Sci. Research Labs., Seattle, 1959-72; prin. scientist KMS Fusion, Inc., Ann Arbor, Mich., 1972-74, dir. fusion experiments, 1974-78, tech. dir., 1978-85, head dept. fusion and plasmas, 1985—; bd. indsl. advs. Rose-Hulman Inst. Tech., Terre Haute, Ind., 1982—. Mem. editorial bd. Proceedings on Plasma Science, N.Y.C., 1972-76. Author: Non-Linear Effects in Plasmas, 1969, Plasma Physics, 1977. Patentee computer element, 1963, repetitive laser fusion, 1975. Decorated comdr. Torpar Riddar Orden (Sweden); knight Order St. George; comdr. Order Holy Cross (Jerusalem). Fellow Am. Phys. Soc.; mem. IEEE (mem. exec. com. plasma sci. 1972-75), N.Y. Acad. Sci., AAAS, Swedish Am. Hist. Soc., Am. Swedish Inst., Swedish Council Am. Lutheran. Clubs: Swedish, Corinthian Yacht (Seattle); Scandinavian (Ann Arbor). Lodge: Vasa. Avocations: skiing; sailing; ice hockey; windsurfing. Home: 671 Adrienne Ln Ann Arbor MI 48103 Office: KMS Fusion Inc 3621 South State Rd Ann Arbor MI 48104

JOHNSON, RUSSELL CLARENCE, microbiologist educator, researcher; b. Wausau, Wis., Aug. 3, 1930; s. Clarence Nels and Esther Mae (Bachman) J.; m. Patricia Ann Struck, June 25, 1955; children—Linda, Kimberly, Kristine. B.S., U. Wis., Madison, 1957, M.S., 1958, Ph.D., 1960. Research council mem. Nat. Acad. Sci., Fort Derrick, Frederick, Md., 1960-61; research microbiologist, 1961-62; instr. and asst. prof. U. Minn., Mpls., 1962-69, assoc. prof., 1969-74, prof. microbiology, 1974—; cons. Office of Surgeon General, U.S. Army, 1970-72; mem. subcom. Taxonomy of Leptospira and Spirochaetales, 1969, comn. viral infections, Armed Forces Epidemiological Bd., 1970-73. Editor: Biology of the Parasite Spirochetes, 1976. Served to cpl. U.S. Army, 1952-54. USPHS fellow, 1963-65. Research grantee NIH, 1966. Fellow Am. Acad. Microbiology; mem. AAAS, Am. Soc. Microbiology (mem. ed. bd. 1979, 1982—, sect. ed. 1979, 85), Soc. Exptl. Biology Medicine (mem. ed. bd. 1975), Am. Leptospirosis Research Conf. (hon. life), Sigma Xi. Home: 1030 W County Rd D St Paul MN 55126 Office: U Minn Med Sch Dept Microbiology 420 Delaware St SE Minneapolis MN 55455

JOHNSON, RUTH BEVERLY ASHTON, physical education educator; b. Clinton, Iowa, Sept. 20, 1933; d. Ned Lowell and Gladys Mae (Brooker) Ashton; m. Ronald Harry Johnson, June 10, 1955; children—Michael James, Andrew Ashton, Daniel Ronald. B.A., U. Iowa, 1955; M.A., Northeast Mo. State U., 1977. Dir. swimming program Davenport Parks (Iowa), 1955-68; tchr. Frank L. Smart Jr. High Sch., Davenport, 1955-56; active Lend-A-Hand Swim Program, Davenport, 1956-57; tchr. St. Katherine's Sch., Davenport, 1957-68, Davenport West High Sch., 1968—; coach water polo, competitive swimming and diving, field hockey, synchronized swimming, girls' gymnastics, soccer; nat. synchronized swimming judge, Synchronized Swimming Clinic, 1970, 77; organizer, meet referee Iowa State High Sch. Swimming Meets, 1967; bd. dirs. Iowa Girls High Sch. Athletic Union, 1969-78; mem. Iowa High Sch. Swimming Adv. Com., 1969—; swimming coach, 1956—. Contbr. writings to publs. in field. Water safety instr., trainer ARC, 1961—, mem. nat. resolutions com., 1965, water safety chmn. Scott County, 1956-71, bd. dirs. Quad City chpt., 1971-77. Mem. NEA, Iowa Edn. Assn. Davenport Edn. Assn., AAHPERD, Iowa Assn. Health, Phys. Edn., Recreation and Dance (treas. 1980-83, pres. 1985), Am. Swimming Coaches Assn., Iowa High Sch. Swimming Coaches Assn., Synchronized Swimming Coaches Acad., U.S. Synchronized Swimming and Gymnastics Coaches Acad., U.S. Gymnastics Safety Assn., Field Hockey Coaches Acad., U.S. Field Hockey Assn., AAU (nat. bd. govs. 1961-73, women's water polo chmn. 1966-70, synchronized swimming chmn. Iowa chpt. 1970-74, Iowa devel. chmn. 1979-81, Iowa ofcls. chmn. 1982—, Iowa women's swimming chmn., age group swimming chmn. or gen. swimming chmn. 1956-68), DAR, Phi Beta Kappa, Pi Lambda Theta, Chi Omega. Home: 2627 Middle Rd Davenport IA 52803 Office: West High Sch 3505 W Locust Davenport IA 52804

JOHNSON, RUTH MARIE, national collection agency and computer service company executive; b. St. Paul, Jan. 24, 1917; d. Louis H. and Sylvia Marie (Bricko) Berke; divorced; 1 child, John A. Erickson. Pres., I. C. System, Inc., St. Paul, 1961-84, chmn. bd. dirs., chief exec. officer, 1984—; dir. Am. Nat. Bank, St. Paul, 1978-80. Mem. exec. com. Minn. Leadership Council, St. Paul, 1984; mem. St. Paul Exec. Postal Council, 1979—. Mem. Am. Collectors Assn., Minn. Assn. Commerce and Industry (recipient Hall of Fame award 1983), U.S. SBA, C. of C. Republican. Clubs: North Oaks Country (Minn.), John's Island (Vero Beach, Fla.). Office: I C System Inc 444 E Hwy 96 St Paul MN 55164

JOHNSON, SAM MAYES, III, banker; b. Vernon, Tex., June 12, 1945; s. Sam Mayes and Mary Frances (Kayser) J.; m. Angela Catherine Christakos, Aug. 21, 1965 (div.); 1 dau.; Renee Catherine; m. 2d, Emojean Kay Hesse, Nov. 27, 1974; children—Jacqueline Ann, Heather Leigh, Sonya Marie. Student Parks Coll., 1963-65, Providence Coll., 1964. Asst. v.p. Bank of Cahokia (Ill.), 1965-69; asst. v.p. Deland State Bank (Fla.), 1969-70; exec. v.p. Commerce Bank of Florissant (Mo.), 1970-80; chmn., pres. Commerce Bank-No. County Spanish Lake (Mo.), 1980—; cons., Florissant, Mo., 1971—; broker real estate, Florissant, Mo., 1974—. Bd. dirs. Am. Cancer Soc., Florissant, 1978—; v.p., bd. dirs. Chapel of Cross, Florissant, 1983—. Named Bus. Person of Yr. Am. Bus. Women's Assn., St. Louis, Mo., 1983. Mem. Am. Inst. Banking (dir. 1974-77), Robert Morris Assocs., Bank Adminstrn. Inst., Real Estate Bd. of Metro. St. Louis, Florissant C. of C. (dir. 1981—, pres. 1983). Republican. Lutheran. Clubs: Rotary (charity chmn. 1983-84), Kiwanis (treas. 1970-74). Home: 360 Afshari Dr Florissant MO 63034 Office: Commerce Bank No County 1626 Pattern Dr St Louis MO 63138

JOHNSON, STANLEY R., economist, educator; b. Burlington, Iowa, Aug. 26, 1938; married; 2 children. B.A. in Agrl. Econs., Western Ill. U., 1961; M.S., Tex. Tech. U., 1962; Ph.D., Tex. A&M U., 1966. Asst. prof. dept. econs. U. Mo., Columbia, 1964-66, assoc. prof. depts. econs. and agrl. econs., 1967-70, prof., 1970-85, chmn. dept. econs., 1972-74; assoc. prof. dept. agrl. econs. U. Conn., Storrs, 1966-67; prof., dir. Ctr. for Agrl. and Rural Devel., dept. econs. Iowa State U., Ames, 1985—; vis. assoc. prof. agrl. econs. U. Calif.-Davis, 1970, Purdue U., 1971-72; economist Agr. Can., Ottawa, 1975; vis. prof. econs. U. Ga., 1975-76, U. Calif.-Berkeley, 1981; cons. and lectr. in field. Author: Advanced Econometric Methods, 1984; Demand Systems Estimation, 1984. Assoc. editor Am. Jour. Agrl. Econs. Contbr. chpts. to books, articles to profl. jours. Recipient Chancellor's award for outstanding research, 1980; numerous grants in econs. Mem. Mo. Valley Econ. Assn. (bd. dirs. 1977-82, pres.-elect 1979-81). Office: Dept Econs Iowa State U Ames IA 50011

JOHNSON, STEPHEN CARL, educator, consultant; b. Joliet, Ill., Mar. 17, 1940; s. Harold Carl and Virginia Lee (Berst) J.; m. Sharon Kay Thomas, June 13, 1965; children—Shelley Marie, Kimberly Ann. B.S. in Edn., Ill. State U., 1962, M.S. in Edn., 1966; Ed.D., Ind. U., 1971. Dir. summer camp Joliet YMCA, Joliet, 1959-62; tchr. librarian Bloomington, Ill. Pub. Schs., 1962-66; faculty Audiovisual Ctr., Sch. Edn., Ind. U., Bloomington, 1967-76, dir. field services, asst. prof. of edn., 1971-76; asst. prof. info. scis. Ill. State U., Normal, 1976-80, assoc. prof. library media Ala. A&M U., Normal, 1977; pres. Behavioral Images, Inc., Bloomington, 1976—; dir. mktg., pub. relations U. Ill. Film Ctr., Champaign, 1980—; cons. for major producers and distributors of ednl. media in the U.S. and Can., 1976—. Bd. mem. The Wesley Found., Normal, Ill., 1976—; sec. Union of Profl. Employees at U. of Ill., Urbana-Champaign, 1984—. Mem. Ednl. Film Library Assn. (pres. 1974-76), Am. Soc. of Indexers, Phi Delta Kappa. Democrat. Methodist. Avocations: physical fitness; jogging; bicycle touring. Home: 302 Leland St Bloomington IL 61701 Office: U of Ill Film Ctr 1325 S Oak St Champaign IL 61820

JOHNSON, TERESA MARIE, nurse, educator; b. Miami Beach, Fla., July 28, 1953; d. Robert Roy and Evelyh Ophelia (Mullins) Mandrell; m. Barry James Johnson, Aug. 18, 1975; children—Lisa Ann, Scott Anthony. A.A., Mo. Bapt. Coll., 1977; B.S. in Nursing, St. Louis U., 1985. Cert. critical care nurse. Staff nurse St. Elizabeth Hosp., Granite City, Ill., 1974-75, Wood River Twp. Hosp. (Ill.), 1975-78, head nurse intensive care, 1978-79, staff nurse, 1979-80; cardiopulmonary rehab. nurse St. Elizabeth Med. Center, Granite City, 1980-83, pulmonary staff devel. asst., 1983-84, pulmonary clinician, 1984—; mem. Midwestern Nursing Diagnosis Conf. Group, 1984, Patient Edn. Research Interest Group, So. Ill. U., 1985; lectr. in field. Mem. Assn. Rehab. Nurses, Am. Assn. Critical Care Nurses. Baptist. Home: 1844 Bremen Ave Granite City IL 62040 Office: Four Doctors Unit St Elizabeth Med Center 2100 Madison Ave Granite City IL 62040

JOHNSON, TIMOTHY PETER, state senator, lawyer; b. Canton, S.D., Dec. 28, 1946; s. Vandal C. and Ruth J. Johnson; m. Barbara Brooks, June 6, 1969; children—Brooks Dwight, Brendan Vandal, Kelsey Marie. B.A., U.S.D., 1969, M.A., 1970, J.D., 1975; postgrad. Mich. State U., 1970. Bar: S.D. 1975. Fiscal analyst appropriations com. Mich. State Senate, Lansing, 1971, 72; sole practice, Vermillion, S.D., 1975—; mem. S.D. Ho. of Reps., 1978-82; mem. S.D. Senate, Vermillion, 1982—; adj. instr. law and social work U. S.D., Vermillion, 1974-83. Mem. S.D. Bar Assn., Clay County Bar Assn., Phi Beta Kappa, Omicron Delta Kappa, Pi Sigma Alpha. Democrat. Lutheran. Lodge: Rotary. Office: 119 E Main St Vermillion SD 57069

JOHNSON, TODD ARTHUR, clinical pharmacist; b. St. Paul, Minn., Sept. 25, 1951; s. Arthur L. and Doreen B. (Borgstrom) J.; B.S., U. Minn.-Mpls., 1974, D.Pharm., 1976. Lic. pharmacist, Minn. Asst. prof. pharmacy U. Minn.-Mpls., 1976—; clin. pharmacist Lake Region Hosp., Fergus Falls State Hosp., Fergus Falls, Minn., 1976—; adj. prof. Moorhead State U., 1980—; cons. pharmacist, 1976—. Contbr. articles to sci. jours. Mem. Am. Soc. Cons. Pharmacists, Am. Soc. Hosp. Pharmacists, Minn. State Pharm. Assn. Lutheran. Avocations: Sports. Home: 521 W Cavour Ave Fergus Falls MN 56537 Office: Lake Region Hosp 712 S Cascade St Fergus Falls MN 56537

JOHNSON, VIRGINIA MAE, educator, job coordinator; b. New Ulm, Minn., June 28, 1927; d. Edward and Rosalia (Mieske) Frahm; m. Roger LeRoy Johnson, Sept. 25, 1949 (div.); 1 dau., Bonnie Mae (dec.); m. 2d, Lallof Shellum, Dec. 29, 1983. B.S. in Vocat. Home Edn., Mankato State U., 1960, M.S. in Service Occupations, 1970. Exptl. home economist Green Giant Co., LeSueur, Minn., 1960-63; sr. high sch. econs. tchr. Madelia, Minn., 1963-70; secondary home econs. tchr. New Ulm, Minn., 1970-74; secondary food service instr. Viking Vocat. Ctr., Hanska, Minn., 1974—; tchr. adult in-service Mankato Tech. Inst., Minn., 1982—; adv. bd. Home Econs.; youth group adviser. Chmn. Nicollet County chpt. Am. Cancer Soc., 1980-82. Mem. NEA, Minn. Edn. Assn., Am. Vocat. Assn., Minn. Vocat. Assn., Am. Home Econs. Assn., Minn. Home Econs. Educators, Delta Kappa Gamma. Republican. Lutheran. Clubs: P.O.L.K.A. Am. Polka Dancers. Home: 811 6th St Box 255 Nicollet MN 56074

JOHNSON, VIVIAN MARIE, nursing adminstrator; b. Chgo., Jan. 20, 1940; d. Edward T. and Vesta C. (Landingham) Crowley; m. Merrill Johnson, Feb. 15, 1958; children—Jeffrey, Jill, Gregg. B.S.N., No. Ill. U.; M.A., Roosevelt U. Cert. emergency nurse, trauma nurse specialist. Supr. McHenry Hosp. (Ill.), 1971-76; instr. trauma nursing St. Joseph Hosp., Elgin, 1976-79, asst. dir. nursing critical care, 1982—; regional nursing coordinator Ill. Dept. Pub. Health Emergency Med. Service, Springfield, 1979-82; program coordinator trauma/spl. care symposia; mem. speakers bur. Co-author: Curriculum for Trauma Nurse Specialist, 1980. Mem. Am. Assn. Critical Care, Emergency Dept. Nurses Assn. (founder Greater N.W. chpt.), Soc. Tchrs. Emergency Medicine (pres. 1980), Sigma Theta Tau, Phi Kappa Theta, Phi Kappa Phi. Roman Catholic. Home: 2404 Timber Trail Crystal Lake IL 60014 Office: St Joseph Hospital 77 N Airlite Elgin IL 60120

JOHNSON, WALLACE, army officer; b. Oklahoma City, Aug. 8, 1939; s. Carroll Wallace and Pauletta (Bibbs) J.; B.S., U. Okla., 1961; M.B.A., Ala. A&M U., 1973; m. Lela Mae Johnson, Dec. 25, 1959; children—Wallace, Steven, Valerie Lynne, Sharon Denise. Commd. 2d lt. U.S. Army, 1961, advanced through grades to lt. col., 1978; spl. forces detachment comdr., Vietnam, 1966-67; exec. officer 101st Ordnance Bn., Heilbronn, W. Ger., 1976-78; surety insp. Office of Insp. Gen., Heidelberg, W. Ger., 1978-79; logistics instr. Command and Gen. Staff Coll., Ft. Leavenworth, Kans., 1979—; instr. U.S. Army service schs. Mem. U.S. Congressional Adv. Bd. Decorated Combat Inf. Badge, Bronze Star, Army Commendation medal, Meritorious Service medal. Mem. Assn. U.S. Army, Am. Def. Preparedness Assn., Internat. Platform Assn. Democrat. Baptist. Clubs: Jaywalkers of Ft. Leavenworth (v.p. 1980-82), Sertoma (pres. 1981-84). Home: 2 Buckner Dr Fort Leavenworth KS 66027 Office: Dept Combat Support US Army Command and Gen Staff Coll Fort Leavenworth KS 66027

JOHNSON, WARREN EDWIN, electrical supply company executive; b. East Lansing, Mich., May 31, 1929; s. Edwin Peter and Mildred Frances (Wilcox) J.; m. Gloria Love, June 10, 1952; children—Virginia Louise, Katherine Anne, Rose Marie. B.S., Va. Poly. Inst., 1951. Field rep. Sylvania Electric Products Inc., St. Louis, 1955-56; regional sales mgr. GTE Sylvania, Melrose Park, Ill., 1966-68; pres. Stitzell Electric Supply Co. Inc., Des Moines, 1968—. Bd. dirs. Better Bus. Bur., Des Moines, 1983-84. Paul Harris fellow Rotary Internat., 1979. Served as 1st lt. U.S. Army, 1951-55, Korea. Mem. Nat. Assn. Elec. Distbrs. (lamp com. 1979—, area chmn. 1980-82), Illuminating Engring. Soc. (assoc., dir. 1959-75). Republican. Clubs: Des Moines, Wakonda (Des Moines). Office: Stitzell Electric Supply Co Inc 101-107 12th St Des Moines IA 50308

JOHNSON, WAYNE RICHARD, utility environmental engineer; b. Kansas City, Kans., Sept. 3, 1921; s. Willis Richard and Pearl May (White) J.; m. Marguerite Elinor Hunzicker, Aug. 14, 1943; children—Steven Wayne, Jerry Wayne. B.S., U. Kans., 1948. Registered profl. engr., Mo. Engr., Kans. City Power & Light Co., Kansas City, 1948-57, project engr., 1957-59, supt. stores, 1959-60, mgr. internal services, 1960-61, engr., 1961-64, maintenance supr., 1964-67, staff engr., 1967-70, supt. Hawthorn Sta., 1970-71, mgr. prodn., 1971-78, asst. to pres., chief environmental engr., 1978—. Served to lt., USNR, 1942-45. Mem. ASME, Air Pollution Control Assn. Republican. Lodge: Mason (Shriner). Club: Kansas City. Home: 6316 Woodson Dr Mission KS 66202 Office: Kansas City Power & Light Co 1330 Baltimore Ave Kansas City MO 64105

JOHNSON, WILLIAM BENJAMIN, transportation executive; b. Salisbury, Md., Dec. 28, 1918; s. Benjamin A. and Ethel (Holloway) J.; A.B. maxima cum laude, Washington Coll., 1940, LL.B. (hon.), 1975; LL.B. cum laude, U. Pa., 1943; m. Mary Barb, Dec. 19, 1942; children—Benjamin H., Kirk B., John P., Kathleen M. Admitted to Md. bar, 1943, Pa. bar, 1947; atty. U.S. Tax Ct., 1945-47; asst. solicitor Pa. R.R., 1947-48, asst. gen. solicitor, 1948-51, asst. to gen. counsel, 1951-52, asst. gen. counsel, 1952-59; pres., dir. REA Express (formerly Ry. Express Agy., Inc.), N.Y.C., 1959-66, chmn. bd., 1966; pres., chief exec. officer, dir. Ill. Central Industries and I.C. R.R., 1966-68; chmn., pres., chief exec. officer Ill. Central Industries, 1968-72, chmn., chief exec. officer, 1972—; chmn., chief exec. Officer I.C. R.R., 1969-72, chmn. exec. com., 1972-76; dir. Hussmann Corp., Bridgeton, Mo., Pneumo Corp., Boston, Abex Corp., N.Y.C., Ill. Central Gulf R.R., Midas-Internat., Chgo., Pet Inc., St. Louis, Pepsi-Cola Gen. Bottlers, Inc., Chgo. Bd. dirs. Chgo. Central Area Com., Am. Productivity Ctr.; trustee Com. for Econ. Devel.; life trustee, mem. citizen's bd. U. Chgo.; bd. overseers U. Pa.; mem. Northwestern U. Assocs. Served as spl. agt., Security Intelligence Corps, AUS, 1943-45. Mem. Am., Phila. bar assns., ICC Practitioners Assn., Juristic Soc., Conf. Bd., Newcomen Soc. N.Am., Transp. Assn. Am. (hon. life), Nat. Def. Transp. Assn. (life; past chmn. bd.), Md. Soc. Pa., S.A.R., Order of Coif, Kappa Alpha, Omicron Delta Kappa. Clubs: Sky, Economic, Links (N.Y.C.); Commercial, Economic, Chicago, Executives, Metropolitan, Mid-America (Chgo.); Onwentsia (Lake Forest); Old Elm (Highland Park). Editor-in-chief U. Pa. Law Rev. Office: Room 2700 111 E Wacker Dr Chicago IL 60601

JOHNSON, WILLIAM CUMMING, JR., civic worker, former educator; b. Memphis, June 26, 1904; s. William Cumming and Evangeline (Harvey) J.; B.S., Princeton U., 1925; E.E., Rensselaer Poly. Inst., 1927; postgrad. in engring. Gen. Electric Co., 1927-30; m. Mayo Crew, Feb. 5, 1926; children—Kenn Harvey, Carel Crew, EveAnne. With Gen. Electric Co., Schenectady, 1927-33; asst. prof. Rensselaer Poly. Inst., 1933-39; asso. prof. Va. Poly. Inst., 1939-43; research and devel. Goodyear Aerospace Corp., Akron, Ohio, 1943-65; asst. prof. Kent State U., 1965-74; vol. Western Res. Hist. Soc., Cleve., 1970-81, trustee, 1982—; registrar Ohio soc. Order Founders and Patriots Am., 1977-81. Mem. AIAA, Ohio Geneal. Soc. (v.p. 1974-80), Phi Beta Kappa, Sigma Xi. Quaker. Developed method for calculation stresses in helicopter rotor blades; patentee airship-enclosed radar. Home: 11687 Vaughn Rd Hiram OH 44234

JOHNSON, WILLIAM DUNCAN, hospital administrator, consultant; b., Kansas City, Kans., June 30, 1932; s. George William and Iva May (Browning) J.; m. Patricia JoAnn Stewart, May 6, 1955; children—Michael Dean, Douglas William. B.A., Kansas City U., 1956. Treas. Midstates Cons., Denver, 1963-65; sr. acct. Lee J. Cooper, C.P.A., Mission, Kans., 1965-70; owner, chief exec. officer Johnson & Assocs., Westwood, Kans., 1970-79, cons., Lenexa, Kans., 1984—; v.p. Mgmt. Concepts Corp., 1984—; adminstr. McDonagh Med. Ctr., Gladstone, Mo., 1979-84. Contbr. articles to trade jours. Pres. Midwest Cardiac Rehab. Ctr., Gladstone, 1979-84; dir. agt. Orange Program for Vietnam Vets., Lenexa, 1981-84; scoutmaster Kaw council Boy Scouts Am., 1969-74; mem. Exec. Forum Jackson County, Kansas City, Mo., 1983-84. Recipient Boss of Yr. award Am. Bus. Women's Assn., Kansas City, 1982, Humanitarian award Vietnam Vets. Am., 1984. Fellow Am. Acad. Homeopathic Medicine; mem. Am. Acad. Preventive Medicine, Nat. Assn. Atomic Vets., Midwest Acad. Preventive Medicine (founder, exec. dir. 1980-84), Kansas City C. of C. (fin. com. 1982-83), North Kansas City C. of C. (ways and means com. 1982). Republican. Lutheran. Club: Brookridge Country (Overland Park, Kans.). Lodge: Order of De Molay. Avocations: hunting; backpacking; golf; black powder gun building; bowling. Home: 13329 W 77th Terr Lenexa KS 66216

JOHNSON, WILLIAM E., JR., hospital executive; b. Mpls., Oct. 11, 1933; s. William E. and Dorothy A. (Peterson) J.; m. Julia Anderson, May 14, 1960; children—Jill, Karen, Steve. B.S., U. Minn., 1955, M.H.A., 1958. Administrv. resident Swedish Hosp., Mpls., 1957-58; asst. adminstr. Madison Gen. Hosp., Wis., 1958-64; adminstr. Methodist Hosp., Madison, 1964-74, pres., 1974-82; pres. Meth. Health Services, Inc., Madison, 1982—. Contbr. articles to profl. jours. Served to 2d lt. U.S. Army, 1956-57. Recipient Merit award Tri-State Hosp. Assembly, 1977. Fellow Am. Coll. Hosp. Adminstrs. (chmn.-elect 1984); mem. Wis. Hosp. Assn. (Harold M. Coon award 1977, cert. in hosp. mgmt.). Lutheran. Lodges: Masons (33 deg.), Shriners (mem. divan). Avocations: golf; skiing; spectator sports. Home: 6405 Keelson Dr Madison WI 53705 Office: Methodist Hosp 309 W Washington Ave Madison WI 53703

JOHNSON, WILLIAM GEORGE, communications system consultant; b. Cleve., May 12, 1950; s. William Yancey and Reather (Swindler) J. Photographer, Ohio Bell, Cleve., 1968-70, central office repair, 1970-75, market adminstr., 1975-79, communications system rep., 1979-82, market adminstr., 1982-83, communications system cons. ATT Communications, Cleve., 1983—. Mem. Council on Black Am. Affairs, Cleve., 1983; trustee Black Profl. Assn., Cleve., 1983. Recipient Outstanding Sales Performance award Ohio Bell, 1978. Fellow Black Profl. Assn. (greatest contbg. mem. 1982). Democrat. Methodist. Home: 3213 E 119th St Cleveland OH 44120

JOHNSON, WILLIAM H., JR., sales executive; b. Chgo., Jan. 24, 1943; s. William H. and Lois C. (Banks) J.; m. Joan C. Cervantes, Dec. 22, 1972 (div. Jan. 1985); children—Kevin L., Marvin E. B.S., Bradley U., 1965. Tchr. pub. schs., Evanston, Ill., 1965; design engr. Conveyor Systems, Inc., Morton Grove, Ill., 1965-67; with IBM Corp., 1967—, dist. sales mgr., Rolling Meadows, Ill., 1984—; dir. edn. tech. div. Nexus, Chgo., 1985—; com. mem. CC&Q, Atlanta, 1985; cons. computer game America Us, 1985. Mem. com. United Negro Coll. Fund, N.Y.C. Recipient Black Achiever award YMCA, Boston, 1979. Mem. Cell Found. Democrat. Methodist. Avocation: tennis. Office: IBM Corp 1701 Golf Rd Rolling Meadows IL 60008

JOHNSON, WILLIAM HERBERT, emergency medicine physician, aerospace physician, air national guard officer; b. Elkhart, Ind., Dec. 12, 1928; s. Herbert John and Lorene Wilhemena (Johnson) J.; m. Ann Marie Bacon, Oct.

17, 1964; children—Ernest Michael, Jennifer Lynn. A.B., Augustana Coll., 1951; M.D., Ind. U., 1958. Intern, Indpls. Gen. Hosp., 1958-59; resident in internal medicine Ind. U. Med. Ctr., Indpls., 1960-61; practice medicine specializing in gen. medicine, East Gary, Ind., 1959-60; asst. surgeon U.S. Steel Co., Gary Works (Ind.), 1959-60; ptnr. Gary Clinic (now Ross Clinic), 1962-69; staff physician student health services Western Mich. U., 1969-74; staff physician Trauma and Emergency Ctr., Bronson Methodist Hosp., Kalamazoo, Mich., 1969—, chmn., 1972-74; asst. clin. prof. medicine Mich. State U. Coll. Human Medicine, East Lansing, 1976—; mem. staffs Borgess Med. Ctr., Community Hosp. Assn., Leila Y. Post Montgomery Hosp., Three Rivers Hosp.; med. dir. emergency dept., mem. exec. bd. Elkhart (Ind.) Gen. Hosp., Goshen (Ind.) Gen. Hosp.; med. dir. Emergency Med. System, Elkhart County, Ind.; pres. Elkhart Emergency Physicians, Inc. Pres. Corey Lake Improvement Assn., 1978-80. Served with USAF, 1951-53, 61-62; brig. gen. Air N.G. Decorated Air N.G. Meritorious Service award; nominee Malcolm C. Grove award USAF Flight Surgeon of Yr., 1971; Mem. Kalamazoo Acad. Medicine, Mich. Med. Soc., AMA Physician's Recognition award 1983), Am. Coll. Emergency Physicians (pres. Mich. chpt. 1976-78, dir.), Calhoun County Med. Soc., Univ. Assn. for Emergency Medicine, Aerospace Med. Assn., Soc. USAF Flight Surgeons (constn., by-laws com.), Alliance of Air N.G. Flight Surgeons (dir., mem. membership com., chmn. nominating com., past pres.), Assn. Mil. Surgeons U.S., Mich. Assn. of Professions, Res. Officers Assn., Air Force Assn. Lutheran. Lodge: Elks. Contbg. editor to books, articles to profl. jours.; contbg. editor, mem. editorial bd. Annals of Emergency Medicine, 1972—; mem. editorial bd. Aviation, Space and Environ. Medicine, 1981—, editor book rev. sect., 1984—. Home and Office: 11451 Coon Hollow Rd Three Rivers MI 49093

JOHNSON, WILLIAM JOSEPH, physician; b. Valrea, Venezuela, Nov. 17, 1924; came to U.S., 1937; s. Charles George and Hannah (Fex) J.; m. Jean Catherine Boone; children—Carol, Linda, Kevin, Charles. B.S. summa cum laude, Wheaton Coll. (Ill.), 1948; M.D., Yale U., 1952; M.S., U. Minn., 1957. Diplomate Am. Bd. Internat. Medicine. Intern Mary Fletcher Hosp., U. Vt., Burlington, 1952-53; resident Mayo Clinic, Rochester, Minn., 1954-57; cons. Grisinger Med. Ctr., Danville, Pa., 1957-63; cons. Mayo Clinic, 1962—, dir. artificial kidney ctr., 1973-83; chmn. Renal Network Coordinating council of Upper Midwest, Inc., Mpls., 1975-82. Contbr. articles to profl. publs., chpts. to books. Served to staff sgt. U.S. Army, 1944-46. Grantee USPHS, 1966-77, Wyeth, Merrill Cipa, 1974—. Fellow ACP; mem. Am. Soc. Nephrology, Internat. Soc. Nephrology, Minn. State Med. Assn. (chmn. com. 1965-75), AMA. Republican. Mem. Covenant Ch. Avocation: Tree farmer. Office: Mayo Clinic 200 1st St SW Rochester MN 55905

JOHNSON, WILLIAM LOUIS, heating and air conditioning educator, consultant; b. Chgo., Dec. 29, 1955; s. William Carroll and Mary Alice (Wallace) J.; m. Bernadette Marie Simpson, Mar. 15, 1980; children—William, Joseph. Student, Green Tech. Inst., 1975, Moraine Valley Coll., 1978. Service mgr. heating and air conditioning G.R.S. Corp., Hickory Hills, Ill., 1977-79; instr. Moraine Valley Coll., Palos Hills, Ill., 1980—; owner, mgr. Energy Systems, 1979—. Served to sgt. USMC, 1975-77. Mem. Am. Solar Energy Soc., ASHRAE, Cook County Roundtable. Home: 13767 S Lavergne St Crestwood IL 60445 Office: Moraine Valley Community College 10900 S 88th Ave Palos Hills IL 60465

JOHNSON, WILLIAM THOMAS, endodontics educator, endodontist; b. Des Moines, Apr. 11, 1949; s. Gaillard Xenton and Alvah (Monson) J.; m. Georgia Kay Tonn, Aug. 25, 1974. B.A., Drake U., 1971; D.D.S., U. Iowa, 1975, cert. endodontics, 1981, M.S., 1981. Diplomate Am. Bd. Endodontics. Resident U. Iowa, Iowa City, 1979-81, asst. prof., 1981-82; pvt. practice endodontics, Des Moines, 1982-83; asst. prof. endodontics U. Nebr., Lincoln, 1983—; pvt. practice dentistry, Cedar Rapids, Iowa, 1977-79. Contbr. articles to profl. jours. Served to capt. U.S. Army, 1975-77; to maj. Iowa N.G., 1977—. Mem. Am. Assn. Endodontists, ADA, Am. Assn. Dental Schs., Delta Sigma Delta. Lutheran. Avocation: photography. Home: 2831 S 74th St Lincoln NE 68506 Office: U Nebr Med Ctr Coll Dentistry 40th and Holdrege St Lincoln NE 68583

JOHNSON, WILLIE, JR., educational administrator; b. Tyler, Tex., Oct. 21, 1940; s. Willie and Mattie Ardalia (Chadwick) J.; m. Lorraine Antoinette Griffin, Nov. 26, 1983; 1 child, Brandon Grant. B.S. in Edn., Kans. State Tchrs. Coll., 1967; M.A., U. Colo., 1970. Cert. tchr., adminstr., Kans. Tchr. Mathewson Jr. High Sch., Wichita, Kans., 1967-70; asst. prin. Heights High Sch., Wichita, 1970-73, Southeast High Sch., Wichita, 1973-81; asst. dir. upward-bound Wichita State U., 1970-75; prin. Marshall Jr. High Sch., Wichita, 1981-84, Coleman Jr. High Sch., Wichita, 1984—; cons. employment City of Wichita, 1984; cons. tchr. edn. Wichita State U., 1984. Painting exhibited in one-man shows, Colo., Tex., Kans., 1969. Co-founder sports devel. Loff/John, Wichita, 1975; chmn. bd. dirs. Youth Devel. Services, Wichita, 1983. Names to Outstanding Young of Am., Jaycees, 1979. Fellow Inst. Devel. Ednl. Activity; mem. Wichita Ednl. Mgmt. Assn., Nat. Assn. Secondary Sch. Prins., Emporia State U. Alumni Assn. (bd. dirs.), Kappa Alpha Psi. Democrat. Baptist. Clubs: Excelsiors (Wichita) (sec. 1982-83), McAdams Golf. Avocations: golf, junior golf programs, reading, cross country driving, painting, drawing. Office: Coleman Jr High Sch 1544 N Governeour Wichita KS 67206

JOHNSON, WYATT, consulting engineer, land surveyor; b. Indpls., June 12, 1947; s. Wylie LeFlore and Gertrude Mae (Daupert) J.; m. Nancy Lee Pore, Jan. 2, 1971; children—Carrie Lee, Seth Adam. B.S., Purdue, 1970. Registered profl. engr., Ind. Engr., land surveyor, road design Ind. State Hwy. Dept., Indpls., 1970-73, constrn. engr., 1973-75; engr. Tipton County, Ind., 1975-78; owner, mgr. Wyatt Johnson P.E., L.S., Tipton, 1978—. Mem. Ind. Soc. Profl. Land Surveyous, Am. Congress Surveying and Mapping. Republican. Home and Office: 215 N West St Tipton IN 46072

JOHNS-REMBLE, MERRY ELIZABETH, dentist, educator; b. Argos, Ind., Mar. 8, 1949; d. Nicholas and Doris Ann (Douglas) J.; m. John Richard Remble, Dec. 22, 1977. A.B. in zoology, Ind. U., 1971; D.D.S., Ind. U., Indpls., 1975. Lic. dentist, Ind., Ariz. Resident dentist, VA Hosp., Washington, 1975-76, practice dentistry, Phoenix, 1977-82; dir. dental clinic Teledyne Job Corp., Phoenix, 1982-84; gen. practice dentistry, Phoenix, 1982-84, Carmel, Ind., 1984—; asst. prof. Ind. U., Indpls., 1984—; pub. relations cons. Ind. Dental Assn., Indpls., 1984—. Editor: Newsletter Conner Prairie Hist. Mus. Vol. Alliance, 1984—. Fellow Acad. Gen. Dentistry, 1982; mem. ADA, Ind. Dental Assn., Jr. League of Indpls. Avocations: sailing, antique restoration, decorating.

JOHNSTON, DENNIS HARRY, farm manager; b. Saskatoon, Sask., Can., June 22, 1946; came to U.S., 1972; s. James T. and Mary (Weibe) J.; m. Connie L. Isaacs, Nov. 10, 1973; children—Shane, Richelle. Student U. Sask., 1965-66. Beef cattle herdsman Glenkirk Farm, Maysville, Mo., 1968-73; gen. mgr. Paul Deer Farm, Springfield, Ohio, 1974-82, Northcote Farm, Forest, Va., 1984—. Mem. Springfield C. of C. (agr. relations com. 1981-84), Ohio Polled Hereford Assn. (bd. dirs. 1979-83), Ohio Simmental Assn. (bd. dirs. 1976-79), Chianina Assn. Ohio (bd. dirs. 1975-78). Republican. Methodist. Avocation: golf.

JOHNSTON, JOHN WAYNE, educational administrator; b. McAlester, Okla., Oct. 8, 1943; s. Cecil Wayne and Hazel Elena (Robinson) J.; m. Lynda Faith Gee, Feb. 4, 1971 (div.); 1 son, Ian Sean. Student Graceland Coll., 1961-62, William Jewell Coll., 1962-63; B.S. in Journalism, Kans. U., 1964; M.A. in Edn. and Sociology, U. Mo.-Kansas City, 1966; M.A. in Polit. Sci. and Econs., Goddard Coll., 1972; Ph.D. (hon.), Calif. Western U., 1975; Ph.D. in Social Psychology, Internat. U., 1975. Personnel mgmt. specialist VA Hosp., Kansas City, Mo., 1968-69; instr. Central Mo. State U., Independence, 1969-72; founder, chancellor The Internat. U., Independence, 1973—; freelance writer and researcher, 1968-73. Bd. dirs. Good Govt. League, Independence, Com. for County Progress, Jackson County, Mo. Republican. Mem. Reorganized Church of Jesus Christ of Latter Day Saints (ordained minister). Lodge: Lions (Independence). Author: Divided for Plunder; Turmoil in the North.

JOHNSTON, LANNY RAY, vocational administrator; b. Escanaba, Mich., June 17, 1941; s. Charles Arthur and Helen (Smith) J.; m. Sharon Anne Thompson, July 1, 1961 (div.); children—Lanny Ray, Locki Lynn, Erika Jean Johnston Steinbrecher; m. 2d, Barbara Ann Edwards, June 10, 1978. B.S., Ferris State Coll., 1971; M.A., Western Mich. U., 1976; cert. U. Mich. Vocat. Leadership Devel. Program, 1975. Vocat. job placement coordinator high sch., Battle Creek, Mich., 1983—; owner print shop; competency based edn. trainer Mich. Dept. Edn.; vocat. printing tchr., 1971-80. Mem. Mich. Assn. Sch. Placement Personnel (exec. bd.), Am. Vocat. Assn., Mich. Occupational Edn. Assn., Mich. Assn. Area Sch. Adminstrs., Marshall C. of C. (chmn. edn. com.), Albion C. of C. (chmn. edn. com.). Democrat. Lutheran.

JOHNSTON, MARILYN FRANCES-MEYERS, physician, medical educator; b. Buffalo, Mar. 30, 1937; B.S., Dameon Coll., 1966; Ph.D., St. Louis U., 1970, M.D., 1975. Diplomate Am. Bd. Pathology, Diplomate Nat. Bd. Med. Examiners. Fellow in immunology Washington U., St. Louis, 1970-72; resident in pathology Washington U. Hosp., St. Louis, 1975-77, St. John's Mercy Med. Ctr., St. Louis, 1977-79; research fellow hematology St. Louis U. Sch. Medicine, 1979-80; instr. biochemistry St. Louis U., 1972-75, asst. prof. pathology, dir. transfusion service, 1980—; med. dir. Mo./Ill. Regional Red Cross, 1983—; area chmn. for inspection and accreditation Am. Assn. Blood Banks, Arlington, Va., 1984. Author: Transfusion Therapy, 1985. Recipient Transfusion Medicine Acad. award Nat. Heart, Blood and Lung Inst., 1984; Goldberger fellow AMA, 1979. Mem. Am. Assn. Blood Banks, Am. Assn. Immunologists, Sigma Xi. Office: St Louis U Hosps 1325 S Grand Blvd St Louis MO 63104

JOHNSTON, ROBERT KENT, seminary dean; b. Pasadena, Calif., June 9, 1945; s. Roy G. and Naomi (Harmon) J.; m. Anne R., Dec. 14, 1968; children—Elizabeth, Margaret. A.B., Stanford U., 1967; B.D., Fuller Theol. Sem., 1970; Ph.D., Duke U., 1974. Ordained to ministry Evang. Covenant Ch., 1975. Asst. prof. Western Ken. U., Bowling Green, 1974-78, assoc. prof., 1978-82; vis. prof. New Coll., Berkeley, Calif., 1980-81; dean, assoc. prof. theology North Park Sem., Chgo., 1982—. Author: Evangelicals at an Impasse, 1979, Psalms for God's People, 1982, The Christian at Play, 1983. Editor: The Use of the Bible in Theology: Evangelical Options, 1985. Mem. Am. Acad. Religion, Phi Beta Kappa. Democrat. Avocations: contemporary fiction, handball. Home: 613 Central Ave Wilmette IL 60091 Office: North Park Theol Sem 5125 N Spaulding Ave Chicago IL 60625

JOHNSTON, ROBERT LEE, banker; b. Logansport, Ind., Dec. 18, 1950; s. Cecil E. and Anna M. (Pfisterer) J.; m. Susan M. Kozusko, Mar. 26, 1972; children—Stefanie Rae, Lindsay Brie. B.S., Ind. State U., 1972. Math. tchr. Kankakee Valley Sch. Corp., Wheatfield, Ind., 1972-73; sales and service rep. Met. Life Ins. Co., Lafayette, Ind., 1973-74; personnel mgr. Wagner Industries, Inc., Plymouth, Ind., 1974-78; human resourses mgr. Universal Cooperatives, Inc., Goshen, Ind., 1978-84; personnel mgr. Am. Nat. Bank, Vincennes, Ind., 1984—; instr. Vincennes U., 1984—. Mem. Emergency Med. System, Goshen, 1983, 84, 85; mem. Vincennes U. Indsl. Adv. Com., 1984—. Mem. Goshen C. of C., Vincennes C. of C., Am. Soc. Personnel Adminstrs., Vincennes Personnel Assn., Valley Mgmt. Assn. Lodge: Elks. Avocations: reading, bicycling, camping, swimming. Home: 522 N 3rd St Vincennes IN 47591 Office: Am Nat Bank Vincennes 302 Main St Vincennes IN 47591

JOHNSTON, WILLIAM KEITH, county sheriff; b. Ashtabula, Ohio, Jan. 16, 1942; s. Albert Henry and Sylvia Marie (Hietikko) J.; m. Judy Kaye Foust, Dec. 22, 1960; children—Shelly, Tammy, William. Student Ashtabula, Ohio pub. schs. Dep. sheriff Ashtabula County Sheriff's Dept., Jefferson, Ohio, 1968-75, sheriff, 1977—; mem. Community Crisis Adv. Com., Council of Govt., Served to staff sgt. USMC, 1960-67. Named Ashtabula County Law Enforcement Officer Yr., Congressman Eckart, 1983; recipient Disting. Service medal Ashtabula County Fireman's Assn., 1983. Mem. Nat. Assn. Jail Mgrs., Nat. Assn. Chiefs of Police, Buckeye State Sheriff's Assn. (redistricting com. 1977-84), Nat. Sheriff's Assn. (detentions and corrections bd. 1977-84), Am. Correctional Assn., Ohio State Assn. Township Trustees and Clerks, Ohio Crime Prevention Assn., Fraternal Order of Police, VFW. Lodges: Elks, Moose. Office: Ashtabula County Sheriff's Dept 25 W Jefferson St Jefferson OH 44047

JOHNSTON, WILLIAM LESLIE, osteopathic physician, educator; b. Sault Ste. Marie, Ont., Can., Feb. 17, 1921; s. Roy Leslie and Eva Pearl (Osborn) J.; m. Margaret MacFarlane, Jan. 1945; children—Merilyn, Gail; m. Anne McCabe, Mar. 18, 1979. D.O., Chgo. Coll. Osteo. Medicine, 1943. Intern, Mass. Osteo. Hosp., Boston, 1944; pvt. practice medicine, Manchester, N.H., 1945-73; mem. faculty Mich. State U. Coll. Osteo. Medicine, East Lansing, 1973—, prof. biomechanics, 1973-81, prof. dept. family medicine, 1981—; cons. staff Lansing Gen. Hosp.; courtesy staff dept. family practice Ingham Med. Hosp. Contbr. numerous articles to profl. publs. Mem. Am. Acad. Osteopathy (cert.; chmn. Conclave of Fellows 1972-74, 1983-84), Am. Osteo. Assn., Mich. Assn. Osteo. Physicians and Surgeons, N.H. Osteo. Assn. (pres.). Home: 830 N Harrison Rd East Lansing MI 48823 Office: Coll Osteopathic Medicine Mich State Univ B216 West Fee East Lansing MI 48824

JOHNSTONE, LEA MAE, fashion merchandising educator; b. Little Falls, Minn., Feb. 12, 1947; d. Ole J. and Marian M. (Scott) Erickson; m. Thomas J. Johnstone, Aug. 22, 1981. Student Moorhead State U., 1965-69; B.A., N.D. State U. 1968, B.S. in Home Econs. Edn., 1970; postgrad. U. Minn., 1972—. With Waterman's, Moorhead, Minn., 1966-67, S & L, Fargo, N.D., 1967-68, Jackson Graves, Mpls., 1969; dept. mgr., asst. mgr. Buttrey's, Southdale, Minn., 1969-72; with 3M Co., Mpls., 1974; sr. instr. fashion sales and merchandising program Dist. 916 Vo-Tech., White Bear Lake, Minn., 1972—; lectr. in field. Mem. Minn. Vocat. Assn., Am. Vocat. Assn., Nat. Assn. Distributive Edn. Tchrs., Distributive Edn. Clubs Am., Nat. Retail Mchts. Assn., Minn. Assn. Distributive Educators, Fashion Group, Kappa Alpha Theta. Lutheran. Club: Midland Hills Country. Home: 600 Gosiwin Ct Mahtomedi MN 55115 Office: 3300 Century Ave N White Bear MN 55110

JOHNSTONE, ROBERT HARLOW, hospital administrator; b. Bloomington, Ill., Aug. 13, 1920; s. Andrew J. and Helen (Amsbary) J.; m. Anne McGorrisk, May 8, 1943; children—Robert H., Michael S., Julianne Weiss, Jill Astorino. B.S., U. Ill., 1942; M.B.A., Xavier U., 1963. Super. Gen. Electric, Schenectady, 1946-59; specialist AVCO, Cin., 1960; asst. adminstr., controller William Booth Hosp., Covington, Ky., 1961-63; asst. adminstr. Drake Hosp., Cin., 1964-65; asst. dir. grad. sch. hosp. adminstr. Xavier U., Cin., 1966-67; asst. adminstr. Drake U., 1968-69; pres. Good Samaritan Hosp., Sandusky, Ohio, 1970-83; pres. Sandusky Area Health Services, 1984—. Bd. dirs. Sandusky Goodwill, Sandusky Youth Group, LPN Sch., Sandusky Congl. Ch. Served to capt. USAF, 1946. Fellow Am. Coll. Hosp. Adminstrs., Hosp. Fin. Mgmt. Assn. Club: Plum Brook Country. Lodge: Rotary. Avocations: Philatelist, travel, models. Address: SAHS Sandusky OH 44870

JOHNSTONE, ROBERT MORTON, JR., political science educator; b. Nashville, Dec. 20, 1939; s. Robert M. and Georgia (Byrum) J.; m. Marjorie A. White, May 10, 1980; 1 child, Gwyneth, 1 stepson, Eric. B.A., Vanderbilt U., 1962; M.A., Cornell U., 1970, Ph.D., 1972. Lectr. politics Cornell U., Ithaca, N.Y., 1970-72; asst. prof. Wilson Coll., Chambersburg, Pa., 1972-75; asst. prof. Earlham Coll., Richmond, Ind., 1975-79, assoc. prof., 1979-82, prof., 1982—. Author: Jefferson and the Presidency, 1978; also chpt. to book. Bd. dirs. Whitewater Opera Co., Richmond, 1977-80, Richmond Symphony Orch., 1984—. Served to lt. USN, 1962-67. Recipient Disting. Teaching award Wilson Coll., 1973. Mem. Am. Polit. Sci. Assn., Ind. Polit. Sci. Assn. Democrat. Methodist. Avocations: singing; acting; music. Home: 1117 Abington Pike Richmond IN 47374 Office: Dept Polit Sci Earlham Coll Richmond IN 47374

JOINER, CHARLES WYCLIFFE, judge; b. Maquoketa, Iowa, Feb. 14, 1916; s. Melvin William and Mary (von Schrader) J.; B.A., U. Iowa, 1937, J.D., 1939; m. Ann Martin, Sept. 29, 1939; children—Charles Wycliffe, Nancy Caroline, Richard Martin. Admitted to Iowa bar, 1939, Mich. bar, 1947; with firm Miller, Huebner & Miller, Des Moines, 1939-47; part-time lectr. Des Moines Coll. Law, 1940-41; faculty U. Mich. Law, 1947-68, assoc. dean, 1960-65, acting dean, 1964-65, dean Wayne State U. Law Sch., Detroit, 1968-72; U.S. dist. judge, Detroit, 1972—, sr. judge, 1984—; assoc. dir. Preparatory Commn. Mich. Constl. Conv., 1961, co-dir. research and drafting com., 1961-62; civil rules adv. com. U.S. Jud. Conf. Com. Rules Practice and Procedure, 1959-70, evidence rules adv. com., 1965-70; rep. Mich., Atty. Gens. Com. Ct. Congestion, 1959-60. Mem. charter rev. com. Ann Arbor Citizens Council, 1959-61; mem. Mich. Commn. on Uniform State Laws, 1963—. Mem. Ann Arbor City Council, 1955-59. Served to 1st lt. USAAF, 1942-45. Fellow Am. Bar Found. (chmn. 1977-78); mem. ABA (chmn. com. specialization 1952-56, spl. com. uniform evidence rules fed. cts. 1959-64; adv. bd. jour. 1961-67, spl. com. on specialization, 1966-69, ethics com. 1961-70, council mem. sect. individual rights and responsibilities 1967-77, chairperson 1976-77), State Bar Mich. (pres. 1970-71; chmn. joint com. Mich. procedural revision 1956-62, commr. 1964—), Am. Judicature Soc. (chmn. publs. com. 1959-62), Am. Law Student Assn. (bd. govs.), Am. Law Inst., Am. Bar Found., Scribes (pres. 1963-64). Author: Civil Justice and the Jury, 1962; Trials and Appeals, 1957; Trial and Appellate Practice, 1968. Co-author: Introduction to Civil Procedures, 1949; Jurisdiction and Judgments, 1953; (with Delmar Karten) Trials and Appeals, 1971. Office: 200 E Liberty Suite 400 Box 7880 Ann Arbor MI 48107

JOINER, GAYLE ANN, nurse; b. Warren, Ohio; d. James Allen Lipscomb and Delores Pauline (Vauple) Swindler; m. Philip Douglas Joiner, Aug. 2, 1980. B.S.N., Kent State U., 1980, M.S.N., 1985. Staff nurse Robinson Meml. Hosp., Ravenna, Ohio, 1980-84, charge nurse spl. care unit, 1983—, now asst. head nurse ICU. Mem. Am. Assn. Critical Care Nurses, Nat. League Nursing, Sigma Theta Tau. Republican.

JOIST, JOHANN HEINRICH, hematologist, medical researcher, educator; b. Bergisch, Gladbach, West Germany, Jan. 9, 1935; came to U.S., 1972; s. Heinrich and Katharina (Hasbach) J.; m. Nancy Lee Maxeiner, July 25, 1966; children—Bettina Lynn, Catherine Anne, Heidi Elaine. M.D., U. Cologne, West Germany, 1962; Ph.D., McMaster U., Hamilton, Ont., Can., 1977. Lic. physician and surgeon, Mo. Sr. research fellow McMaster U., 1970-72; asst. prof. medicine Washington U., St. Louis, 1972-78; assoc. prof. medicine/pathology St. Louis U., 1978-82, prof. medicine, pathology, 1982—; dir. hemostasis lab. Barnes Hosp., St. Louis, 1972-78; dir. div. hematology-oncology St. Louis U. Med. Ctr., 1978—. Editor: Venous and Arterial Thrombosis, 1979. Mem. hemophilia adv. com. Mo. Div. Health; chmn. med. adv. com. Mo./Ill. region ARC, Mo./Ill. region ARC Blood Services, 1981-84; assembly del. Am. Heart Assn. Council Thrombosis, Dallas, 1982; chmn. Mo. affiliate Am. Heart Assn., mem. research and research peer rev. com., 1984-85. NIH research fellow, 1964-65; Ont. Heart Assn. research fellow, 1970-72; NIH grantee, 1982. Fellow ACP; mem. Am. Heart Assn., Am. Soc. Hematology, Central Soc. Clin. Research, Am. Assn. Pathologists, St. Louis Soc. Internal Medicine. Home: 716 S Central Ave Clayton MO 63105 Office: Div Hematology-Oncology St Louis U Med Ctr 1402 Grand Blvd St Louis MO 63104

JOLIET, LEO JOSEPH, lawyer, real estate title specialist; b. Cleve., June 24, 1925; s. Louis C. and Margaret Mary (Kennedy) J. A.B., John Carroll U., 1946; LL.B., Western Res. U., 1948. Escrow, title officer Lawyers Title Ins. Corp., Cleve., 1947-84; sr. v.p., chief title officer Midland Title Security, Inc., Cleve., 1984—; lectr. on real estate titles throughout Ohio. Author: (with others) Principles of Ohio Real Estate Titles, 1984. Contbr. articles to legal jours. Recipient various awards Ohio Legal Ctr., Ohio Land Title Assn. Mem. ABA, Ohio State Bar Assn., Cleve. Bar Assn. (various awards), Democrat. Roman Catholic. Club: Mid Day (Cleve.). Avocations: classical music; modern languages, stamp and coin collecting. Home: 1545 Parkwood Rd Lakewood OH 44107 Office: 1404 E 9th St Cleveland OH 44114

JONAS, JAN HANZEL, college administrator; b. Barberton, Ohio, Oct. 6, 1942; d. George Frank and Grace Naomi (Carillon) H.; m. Stephen Jonas, June 19, 1966. B.A., Ohio State U., 1964; M.S., Ind. U., 1966, Ed.D., 1974. Assoc. dir. U. Wis., Madison, 1966-69; head counselor Ind. U., Bloomington, 1969-71; asst. to exec. vice chancellor Cuyahoga Community Coll., Cleve., 1976-79, dir. program devel., 1979-81, dean of instrn., Parma, 1981-84, provost/v.p., Warrensville Twp., Ohio, 1984—; cons., evaluator North Central Assn., Chgo., 1982—. Mem. Am. Assn. Higher Edn., Am. Assn. Women in Community and Jr. Colls., Phi Beta Kappa. Jewish. Avocations: sailing; reading; travel. Office: Cuyahoga Community Coll 4250 Richmond Rd Warrensville Township OH 44122

JONES, A. CLIFFORD, state senator; b. St. Louis, Feb. 13, 1921; s. Wilbur B. and Irene (Clifford) J.; A.B., Princeton U., 1942; J.D., Washington U., St. Louis, 1948; children—A. Clifford, Irene, Wesley, Janet; m. 2d, Nan Thornton, Nov. 1974. City clk. Ladue (Mo.), 1948-50; mem. Mo. Ho. of Reps., Jefferson City, 1950-58, minority floor leader, 1956-58; mem. Mo. Senate, Jefferson City, 1964—, minority floor leader, 1968-76; pres. Mo. Polaris Corp., Aluminum Truck Bodies, Inc.; sec.-treas. Hewitt-Lucas Body Co., Inc. Pres. Mo. Assn. for Social Welfare, 1953-54; trustee St. Louis Country Day Sch., 1948-50. Served with USNR, 1942-46; ETO, PTO. Recipient award Jaycees of St. Louis, 1952, Globe Democrat award for pub. service, 1958, 65, 69, 76. Mem. Mo., St. Louis (Bicentennial award) bar assns., Am. Legion, John Marshall Club. Republican. Congregationalist. Lodge: Masons (32 deg.). Home: 7 Willow Hill Ladue MO 63124 Office: State Capitol Bldg Jefferson City MO 65101

JONES, ADRIENNE EILEEN, sch. prin.; b. Hamtramck, Mich., Dec. 7, 1946; d. Sidney Minrose and Rosa Eileen (McKinney) J.; B.A., U. Mich., 1969, M.A., 1973; m. John William Crockett, June 27, 1981. Tchr., Bloomfield Hills (Mich.) Schs., 1969-77, adminstrv. intern, 1977-78, prin., 1978—. Vice pres. Bloomfield Hills Adminstrv. Council, 1980-81. Organist, St. Peters African Meth. Episcopal Zion Ch., 1974-79; fin. sec., treas. Brazeal Dennard Chorale, 1973—; dir. Christian edn. bd., St. Peters, 1980—. Recipient Opportunity grant U. Mich., 1965-69. Mem. Internat. Reading Assn., Nat. Assn. Elem. Sch. Prins., Mich. Elem. and Middle Sch. Prins Assn., U. Mich. Alumni Club, One Hundred Club U. Mich. Home: 22950 Mapleridge St Southfield MI 48075 Office: 1101 Westview St Eastover Sch Bloomfield Hills MI 48013

JONES, AGNES MARIE ANDERSEN, home economics administrator, educator, librarian, academic and career services counselor; b. Withee, Wis., Dec. 23, 1915; d. Sam K. Andersen and Kathrine (Jacobsen) A.; m. James Lawrence Jones, June 5, 1943 (div.); 1 son, James Lee. B.S. in Home Econs. Edn., U. Wis., 1937, M.S. in Home Econs., 1943; Ph.D. in Tchr. Edn. and Supervision, 1954. Tchr. home econs., 1937-41, Wis., 1941-43; coop. tchr. home econs. student tchrs. U. Wis., Madison, 1941-43, librarian, home econs. tchr. educator and supr. off-campus student tchrs., 1943-54; head home econs. No. Ill. State U., DeKalb, 1954-55; instr. foods and supr. off-campus student tchrs. U. Wis., Madison, 1955-56, head home econs. and assoc. dean Coll. Profl. Studies, Stevens Point, 1956-81, acad. and career services counselor, 1981—; cons. in field. Grantee Head Start, Allied Health, Dept. Pub. Instrn. Home Econs. Mem. Am. Home Econs. Assn., Wis. Home Econs. Assn., Nat. Ret. Tchrs. Assn., Portage County Home Econs. Orgn., Wis. Assn. Adult and Continuing Edn., Phi Upsilon Omicron, Pi Lambda Theta. Lutheran. Clubs: Stevens Point Country, Central Wis. Rose Soc. Home: 603 Soo Marie Ave Stevens Point WI 54481 Office: Student Assistance Ctr and Career Services Office U Wis Stevens Point WI 54481

JONES, ALAN HEDRICK, editor, publishing company executive; b. Ann Arbor, Mich., Apr. 18, 1937; s. Volney Hurt and Joyce (Hedrick) J.; m. Susan Holtzer, June 2, 1960; 1 son, Mason Todd. B.A. in Social Sci., U. Mich., 1959, M.A. in Comparative Edn., 1961, Ph.D. in Social Founds. of Edn., 1971. Cert. tchr., Mich. Teaching fellow Sch. Edn., U. Mich., 1959-62, instr., 1965-68; tchr. Ann Arbor (Mich.) Pub. Schs., 1962-65; asst. prof. Coll. Edn., Eastern Mich. U., 1968-72; chmn. dept. edn. Sacred Heart U., Bridgeport, Conn., 1972-73; dir. research, long range planning com. U. Mich., 1973-74; coordinator External Assessment Pilot Project Commn. for Tchr. Preparation and Licensing, State of Calif., 1974-76, chief Office of Planning and Govtl. Relations, 1978-81; exec. sec. Mich. Conf. AAUP, 1976-78; mng. editor Edn. Digest, Ann Arbor, 1981—, also mng. editor Sch. Shop; exec. editor Prakken Publs. Inc.; sec.-treas. EDCON Assocs., Inc., Ann Arbor. Mem. Am. Ednl. Studies Assn., Ednl. Press Assn. Am., Michigamua. Democrat. Author: Philanthropic Foundations and the University of Michigan, 1922-1965, 1972; The CASA Handbook, 1984. Editor: Civic Learning for Teachers, 1985. Contbr. numerous articles to profl. jours. Home: 1205 Olivia Ann Arbor MI 48104 Office: 416 Longshore Dr PO Box 8723 Ann Arbor MI 48107

JONES, ALICE HANSON, economist; b. Seattle, Nov. 7, 1904; d. Olof and Agatha Marie (Tiegel) Hanson; A.B., U. Wash., Seattle, 1925, M.A., 1928; Ph.D., U. Chgo., 1968; m. Homer Jones, Apr. 21, 1930; children—Robert Hanson, Richard John, Douglas Coulthurst. Teaching fellow U. Wash., 1927-28; fellow, research asst. econs. U. Chgo., 1928-29, 32-34; asst. editor Ency. Social Scis., N.Y.C., 1930; researcher, writer Pres.'s Com. Social Trends, N.Y.C., 1931; economist, asst. chief Cost of Living div. Bur. Labor Stats., Washington, 1934-44; economist div. statis. standards Bur. Budget, Washington, 1945-48; sec. com. nat. accounts Nat. Bur. Econ. Research, Washington, 1957; supervising economist, cons. Dept. Agr., Washington, 1958-61; lectr. econs. Washington U., St. Louis, 1963-68, asst. prof., 1968-71, asso. prof., 1971-73, adj. prof., 1973-77, prof. emeritus, 1977—; prin. investigator Social Sci. Inst., 1969—; adj. prof. econs. Claremont Men's Coll., 1973-74; econ.

adviser Bank of Korea, AID, 1967-68. Named Woman of Achievement, St. Louis Globe-Dem., 1980; NSF research grantee, 1969-75; Nat. Endowment Humanities research grantee, 1970-76. Mem. Am. Econ. Assn., Econ. History Assn. (v.p. 1976-77, pres.-elect 1981-82, pres. 1982-83, trustee 1983-84), Orgn. Am. Historians. Internat. Assn. Research in Income and Wealth, Social Sci. History Assn., Soc. Profs. Emeriti Washington U. (pres.-elect, sec. 1982), Mortar Bd., Phi Beta Kappa, Beta Phi Alpha (nat. pres. 1932-34), Delta Zeta (Nat. Woman of Yr. 1981), Omicron Delta Epsilon. Congregationalist. Author: American Colonial Wealth: Documents and Methods, 3 vols., rev. edit., 1978; Wealth of a Nation to Be: The American Colonies on the Eve of the Revolution, 1980. Home: 404 Yorkshire Pl Webster Groves MO 63119 Office: Dept Economics Washington U Saint Louis MO 63130

JONES, ANABEL RATCLIFF, anesthesiologist; b. Lafayette, Ind., Sept. 6, 1933; d. Frank William and Mary Rovene (Holt) Ratcliff; A.B., Ind. U., 1955, M.D., 1959; m. Wiley A. Jones, Oct. 4, 1975; 1 son by previous marriage, Warren Lee. Intern, Meth. Hosp., Indpls., 1959-60; resident anesthesiology Ind. U. Med. Center, Indpls., 1960-62; staff anesthesiologist VA Hosp., Indpls., 1962-63; practice medicine, specializing in anesthesiology, Lafayette, 1963—; mem. staff St. Elizabeth Hosp., Home Hosp., Purdue U. Hosp.; instr. Ind. U. Med. Center, Indpls., 1962—. Piano accompanist civic chorus, also combined civic vocal groups; mem. governing bd. Lafayette Symphony Orch., 1971—. Diplomate Am. Bd. Anesthesiology. Mem. Am. Soc. Anesthesiologists, Internat. Anesthesia Research Soc., Ind. Med. Assn., Ind. Soc. Anesthesiologists, AMA, DAR (gen. Lafayette chpt.), Kappa Kappa Kappa, Delta Delta Delta. Methodist. Home: 3301 Cedar Ln Lafayette IN 47905 Office: Life Bldg Lafayette IN 47901

JONES, B. J., lawyer; b. Iowa City, Iowa, Sept. 28, 1920; s. M.P. and M.E. Jones; B.S. in Bus. Adminstrn., State U. Iowa, 1942; M.A., U. Miami, 1946; Ph.D., UCLA, 1948, J.D., 1952; m. Estelle Perry, June 3, 1950 (dec. 1960). Founder, pres., chmn. bd. Exec. Consultants Inc., Miami Beach, Fla., 1953-78; dir. indsl. relations and labor law, v.p. Internat. Harvester, 1946-53; founder, developer, pres., chmn. bd. Paradise Haven Villa, La Jolla, Calif., 1978-84, also Aloha Paradise Haven, Honolulu; founder KCID-TV/AM-FM, Iowa City; personnel dir., asst. city mgr., exec. dir. City of Berkeley (Calif.), 1945-48. Served to maj. USAF, 1942-45. Decorated Purple Heart with 6 clusters, Silver Star, Congressional Medal of Honor with 3 clusters. Mem. Personnel and Indsl. Relations Execs. Assn. (past pres.), Indsl. Relations and Labor Law Execs. Club (Los Angeles, past pres.), Phi Beta Kappa, Phi Delta Theta (past pres.). Clubs: Rotary (past pres.), Kiwanis (past pres.), U. Iowa Athletic, K.C. (4th deg., grand knight), Lions. Author numerous books in field. Home: 715 N Van Buren St Iowa City IA 52240 also S Torrey Pines Rd La Jolla CA 92123

JONES, BERNARD IRVIN, architectural company executive; b. Estherville, Iowa, Mar. 19, 1933; s. Lawrence Laverne and Beatrice Rebecca (French) J.; m. Jane Ellen Hutchinson, Jan. 19, 1958; children—Tamera Jane, Leslie Anne. A.A., Estherville Jr. Coll., 1953; B.S., Iowa State U., 1957. Registered architect, NCARB cert. Constrn. engr. W.A. Klinger, Inc., Sioux City, Iowa, 1957-58, 60-64; architect, structural engr. James M. Duffy, Sioux City, 1964-68; v.p. DeWild Grant Reckert, Sioux City, 1968-75; pres. FEH Assocs. Inc., Sioux City, 1975-84; owner, prin. Garrison-Jones Architects Inc., Carbondale, Ill., 1984—. Mem., pres. Iowa State Bd. Archtl. Examiners, 1979-84 (GSA Value Engring. Cert.). Served to 1st lt. C.E., U.S. Army, 1958-60. Mem. AIA, Constrn. Specifications Inst., Profl. Services Mgmt. Assn. Club: Jackson Country. Avocations: golf; tennis; woodworking. Home: Heritage Hill #43 Carbondale IL 62901 Office: Garrison Jones Architects Inc 1118 W Main St Carbondale IL 62901

JONES, BERNARD WALTER, II, corporate executive, former state official; b. Oak Park, Ill., July 5, 1930; s. Harry Bernard and Ann C. Jones; m. Irma L. Gardner, Sept. 18, 1954; 1 dau., Jane E. Jones Hurst. B.S., Culver-Stockton Coll., 1954; M.A., Sangamon State U., 1981. Credit mgr. Gen. Electric Co., Chgo., 1954-59; gen. credit mgr. Ill. Tool Works, Inc., Chgo., 1959-65; factoring credit mgr. Walter E. Heller & Co., Chgo., 1965-67; loan officer SBA, Springfield, Ill., 1967-73; pres., fin. cons. B.W.J. Fin. Services, Inc., Springfield, 1973—; acctg. exec. Ill. State Govt., 1977—. Republican. Roman Catholic. Home and office: 8 Oakdale Dr Springfield IL 62707

JONES, BILLY DIOWADE, pharmacist; b. Gideon, Mo., Feb. 17, 1927; s. Marion Earl and Nellie Mae (Barnes) J.; m. Joy Lee Mculloch, Dec. 15, 1946 (dec. Dec. 10, 1980); children—Bradley Wade, Stanley Earl; m. Margie York, Nov. 24, 1982. Grad. Gideon High Sch. Registered pharmacist, Mo., Nev. Pharmacist, Hayden Drug Store, Caruthersville, Mo., 1947-55; owner, pharmacist Jones Family Pharmacy, Lilbourn, Mo., 1955—. Mem. Lilbourn City Council, 1960-66. Served with USN, 1945-46. Named Lilbourn Man of Yr., Citizens of Lilbourn, 1977; recipient Scouters Key, 1968, Order of Merit, 1969, Order of Arrow, 1971, Silver Beaver award, 1972, Boy Scouts Am. Mem. Semo Mo. Pharm. Assn. (pres. 1981-82), Mo. Pharm. Assn. Democrat. Baptist. Lodges: Kiwanis (pres. 1970, Legion of Honor 1981), Gideons, Masons. Home and Office: 101 N Third Lilbourn MO 63862

JONES, BRUCE EDWARD, Realtor; b. Anderson, Ind., Nov. 21, 1947; s. George Lewis and Hazel Marie (Crull) J.; B.S., Ball State U., 1970, M.A., 1974; m. Laura Dana Harrell. Tchr., Pendleton (Ind.) Community Schs., 1970-74; tchr. Ball State U.-Burris Lab. Sch., 1974-75; res. dep. sheriff, Madison County, Ind., 1972-74; pres. Bernard Realty Co., Anderson, 1974—; pres. BEJ Cattle Ranch; mgmt. broker VA. Precinct election insp., judge, poll taker, Anderson. Served as comdr. USCG Aux., 1977-78. Named Tchr. of Yr., Current Events Club, 1974. Lic. prin., Ind.; cert. hunter instr., boating instr. Mem. AAUP, Nat. Rifle Assn., Chief Ind. Tng. Officers, Nat. Assn. Realtors, Anderson Bd. Realtors, Am. Assn. Cert. Appraisers (lic. appraiser), Nat. Assn. Realtors, Phi Delta Kappa. Republican. Baptist. Clubs: Fall Creek Valley Conservation (chmn. bd. trustees), B.A.S.S., Lincoln, Moose Lodge, Young Republicans (officer 1968-70). Home: 4231 W Cross St Anderson IN 46011 Office: 424 Citizens Bank Bldg Anderson IN 46016

JONES, C. W., banker; b. Murdock, Kans., Oct. 20, 1921; s. Claude C. and Ina (Silvius) J.; student Kansas City Jr. Coll., 1942-43, Park Coll., 1943-44; m. Helen Johnson, Sept. 15, 1946; children—Marcia A. (Mrs. James R. Steele III), Mark A., Jeffrey L. With Jones Investment Corp., Independence, Mo., 1955—; with Jomaco, Inc., Independence, Mo., 1958—; pres. Chrisman-Sawyer Bank, Independence, Mo., 1962—; real estate development builder, 1953—. Life mem. hon. bd. Baptist Hosp., Kansas City. Mem. Am. Bankers Assn., Home Builders Assn., Independent Bankers Assn., Mo. Bankers Assn. Baptist. Office: 201 W Lexington St Independence MO 64051

JONES, CARL HUGH, museum curator, steamboat historian; b. Huron, N.Y., July 10, 1936; s. Elihu Roe and Helga (Petersen) J.; m. Gloria Reese, Sept. 18, 1959; children—Bruce Reese, Kent Reese, Carla, Michael Reese, Sandra Reese. B.S. in Archaeology, Brigham Young U., 1959, M.S. in Archaeology, 1961; postgrad. Utah State U., 1964-65. Teaching asst. Brigham Young U., Provo, Utah, 1956-61; archaeology field asst. Smithsonian Inst., Lincoln, Nebr., summers 1956-58; archeology crew foreman Nat. Park Service, Mesa Virde, Colo., summer 1959; curator, librarian Utah State U., Logan, 1963-65; curator Neb. State Historical Soc., Lincoln, 1968-81, Missouri River History Museum, Brownville, Nebr., 1981—; first co-ordinator Utah Museums Conf., Salt Lake City, 1964. Co-author (with John Q. Magie): A History and Historic Sites Survey of Johnson, Nemaha, Pawnee, and Richardson Counties in Southeastern Nebraska, 1969, (with Persiijs Kolberg) A Survey of Historic, Architectural and Archaeological Sites of the Eleven County Eastern Nebraska Urban Region, 1971. Book reviewer. Contbr. numerous articles to profl. jours. Missouri River corr. for Waterways Jour. Mem. Am. Assn. Mus., Mountain-Plains Mus. Conf. State Rep., Soc. for Early Historic Archaeology, Nebr. State Hist. Soc. Republican. Mormon. Home: 2240 S 46th Lincoln NE 68506 Office: Mus of Missouri River History PO Box 124 Brownville NE 68321

JONES, CHRISTOPHER ALLEN, financial executive; b. Flint, Mich., Nov. 29, 1954; s. Robert E. and Joanne J. (Jakeway) J.; m. Wendy J. Wendrick, Nov. 1, 1973; children—Jason A., Katie E. A.A., Schoolcraft Coll. 1977, B.B.A., Eastern Mich. U., 1982. Cost analyst Massey Ferguson, Detroit, 1974-82, Cyclops Corp., Detroit, 1982-83; div. controller A A R Brooks Perkins Co., Livonia, Mich., 1983-84; div. controller Robotron div. Midland Ross Corp., Southfield, Mich., 1984—. Mem. Nat. Assn. Accts., Inst. Mgmt. Accts. Avocations: camping; fishing; golf. Home: 400 2d St South Lyon MI 48178 Office: Robotron Div Midland Ross Corp 21300 W 8 Mile Rd Southfield MI 48046

JONES, CLARA DELL, telephone company administrator; b. Bunkie, La., Sept. 2, 1941; d. Alfred and Neola Ray Joe; m. Leyton C. Jones, Aug. 29, 1969; children—Paula D., Kenneth A., Nichon R. B.S. in Social Work, Tex. Women's U., 1974; M.A. in Urban Affairs, St. Louis U., 1979. With Southwestern Bell, 1966—; personnel staff specialist Centralized Services, St. Louis, 1982—. Vice pres. Carver House bd., 1980-82; mem. bd. Consol. Neighborhood Services Inc.; vol. First Bapt. Ch. Alcohol Youth Preventive Program. Mem. NAACP, Alpha Kappa Delta, Delta Sigma Theta. Office: 1010 Pine Room 635 St Louis MO 63101

JONES, CLAUDELLA ARCHAMBEAULT, medical institute administrator, educational administrator, consultant, researcher; b. Holgate, Ohio, Sept. 25, 1938; d. Claude Edmund and Marjorie Elizabeth (Warren) Archambeault; m. Christopher Mark Jones; children—Christopher Mark, Daniel Sullivan, Anne Elizabeth. R.N. diploma Mercy Sch. Nursing, Toledo, 1959; N.C.F.D., U. Mich., 1972. Lic. nurse, Mich.; R.N., Ohio. Mem. staff surg. ward St. Charles Hosp., Toledo, 1959; asst. to staff physician for Casa Marina Hotel and USCG, Key West, Fla., 1959-60; charge nurse labor and delivery Monroe County Gen. Hosp., Key West, 1959-60; charge nurse emergency room Jackson Meml. Hosp., Miami, Fla., 1960; mem. staff operating room Good Samaritan Hosp., Los Angeles, 1961; charge nurse, medicine, surgery, pediatrics Defiance (Ohio) Hosp., 1961-62; staff nurse, rehab. Tampa Gen. Hosp., 1961-62; float and pvt. duty nurse U. Mich., 1962-64, mem. staff in neurosurgery, otology, ophthalmology U. Mich. Med. Ctr., Ann Arbor, 1964-66, head nurse burn unit, 1966-68; mem. project staff Evaluation and Demonstration of a Model Burn Unit, Ann Arbor, 1968-71; dir. burn care technician program U. Mich. Burn Ctr., St. Joseph Mercy Hosp., 1969-71; editor publs. dept. Nat. Inst. for Burn Medicine, Ann Arbor, 1971—, ednl. coordinator, 1971-75, dir. edn., 1975—, adminstr. inst., 1982—; project mgr. Nat. Burn Info. Exchange, 1972—, W.K. Kellogg Found. Gt. Lakes Regional Burn Care Demonstration Project, 1975-77; mgr. Burn Info. Triage System, 1976-78; co-chmn. Rehab. of Burned Patient Seminars, 1975—; guest speaker, faculty mem., moderator, panelist and participant burn nursing and intensive care nursing seminars and ednl. programs at local, state, nat. and internat. levesl, 1967—. Mem. Am. Burn Assn. (Disting. Service award 1978), Assn. Critical Care Nurses, Mich. Nurses Assn., Am. Nurses Assn. Roman Catholic. Author books, including: (with I. Feller) Nursing the Burned Patient, 1973, Procedures for Nursing the Burned Patient, 1975, Teaching Basic Burn Care, 1975; (with Feller and K.E. Richards) Emergent Care of the Burn Victim, 1977; contbr. articles, editorials to profl. publs.; editor: A Decade of Progress in Burn Medicine: NIBM, 1980; Reconstruction and Rehabilitation of the Burned Patient (I. Feller, W.C. Grabb), 1980; editor Am. Burn Assn. newsletter, 1970, NBIE Newsletter, 1980; mem. editorial bd. Dimensions of Critical Care Jour., 1981-82, Burns, Jour. of Burn Care and Rehab., 1982. Office: 909 E Ann St Ann Arbor MI 48104

JONES, CLIFF CLOON, JR., mutual funds executive; b. Kansas City, Mo., May 11, 1919; s. Cliff Cloon and Elizabeth (Smith) J.; m. Patricia Maude Busler, Sept. 13, 1947; children—Elizabeth Schellhorn, Leigh Jones-Bamman, Cliff C. A.B., Princeton U., 1941. Chmn., R.B. Jones Corp., Kansas City, Mo., 1960-75; chmn., founder Jones & Babson Inc., Kansas City, Mo., 1960—; dir. Bus. Men's Assurance Corp., Kansas City, 1968—, Tower Properties Inc., Kansas City, 1983—; pres. Market Area Devel. Corp. Author: Winning Through Integrity, 1985. Chmn. bd. dirs. Old Town Redevel. Corp., Kansas City, 1983—; adv. council U. Kans. Med. Ctr.; trustee Kansas City Assn. Trusts and Founds.; bd. govs. William Rockhill Nelson Gallery of Art; adv. dir. Kansas City Regional Council for Higher Edn.; mem. Civic Council of Greater Kansas City; active Country Club Christian Ch.; formerly chmn. adv. bd. Salvation Army, Kansas City. Served to lt. USNR, 1942-45. Mem. Nat. Assn. Casualty and Surety Agts. (past pres.), Greater Kansas City C. of C. (past pres.). Republican. Clubs: Kansas City Country (bd. dirs. 1983-85), The River (Kansas City). Avocations: tennis, hiking. Home: 6408 Aberdeen Rd Shawnee Mission KS 66208

JONES, CLOYZELLE KARRELLE DELEJQON, educator, consultant. B.S. in Mental Retardation, Wayne State U., 1968, M.Ed. in Supervision of Spl. Edn., 1969, Ed.D. in Curriculum Devel., 1970. Dir. programming Boys Clubs Am., Detroit, 1962-66; tchr. spl. edn. Detroit Pub. Schs., 1966-69; prof. intern Wayne State U., Detroit, 1969-70; asst. prof. div. edn. U. Mich.-Dearborn, 1970-74, assoc. prof., 1974-79, prof., 1979—, acad. coordinator program acad. support, 1976-79, dir. urban and regional studies, 1979-81; prof. cons. in edn., locally and nationally, 1969—; research assoc. community edn. div. U. Wis.-Milw., edn. clinic U. No. Iowa, Coll. Edn., Wayne State U. Bd. govs. Wayne State U. Coll. Edn., also mem. President's Commn. on Excellence, 1983—; mem. Mich. Gov.'s Task Force for Talented and Gifted; mem. exec. bd. Better Edn. through Spelling; mem. edn. com. New Detroit Inc.; mem. adv. council Mich. Council for Arts; mem. sub coms. on rape and govtl. service Detroit City Council, 1984—; bd. dirs. street Law Jud. Commn., Detroit, 1984—; mem. blue-ribbon adv. commn. to oversee Wayne County Community Coll., Mich. Dept. Pub. Instrn., 1984—. Recipient Disting. Ednl. Leadership award OME Ednl. Testing Service, 1981; commendation for teaching excellence Detroit City Council, 1982; ofcl. commendation for teaching excellence Office of Mich. Gov., 1982; Disting. Faculty Teaching award U. Mich.-Dearborn, 1983; Crutchfield Community Leadership award Wayne State U., 1983; commendation Mich. Legislature, 1983 Mem. Mich. Assn. Children with Learning Disabilities, Assn. for Study Afro-Am. Life and History (dir.), Assn. Urban Educators (dir. 1977-78), Nat. Urban Edn. Assn. (pres. 1978—, editor publ. proc. 1980-82, coordinator nat. conf. on computer edn. 1983), Detroit Assn. Black Orgns. (trustee), Phi Delta Kappa (Educator of Yr. award Wayne State U. chpt. 1980). Editorial reviewer Educating Exceptional Children, 1979-80; editor Renaissance, Nat. Urban Edn. Assn. jour., 1983; cons. editor Urban Rev., 1980-81. Home: 18110 Birchcrest Rd Detroit MI 48221 Office: 4901 Evergreen Rd Dearborn MI 48128

JONES, DONALD WEIL, superintendent schools; b. Cin., Mar. 20, 1922; s. Harry Herbert and Lauretta Frances (Weil) J.; m. Betty Louise Beyer, Nov. 1, 1947; 1 dau., Judith Lynn Lackey. B.S. in Edn., U. Cin., 1947, Ed.M., 1957; Cert. supt., Ohio. Sr. corr. in pub. relations Wright Aero. Corp., Cin., 1944; exec. YMCA, Cin. and Flint, Mich., 1946-50; owner ins. agy., Hamilton, Ohio, 1951-60; pub. sch. tchr., prin. S.W. Ohio, 1955-68; supt. schs. Guernsey County, Ohio, 1969—; mem. Ohio Supts. Exec. Com. vice pres. Concert Bd.; chmn. bd. Community Theater, 1972; pres. Jr. Achievement, 1972-73; div. chmn. County 175th Anniversary, 1973; pres. Citizen's Scholarship Found., 1976-78. Served with USMCR, 1942-44. Mem. East Central Ohio Schoolmasters (pres. 1971-72), Northeastern Ohio County Sch. Supts. (pres. 1975-76), Am. Assn. Sch. Adminstrs., Buckeye Assn. Sch. Adminstrs., Phi Delta Kappa. Republican. Methodist (lay leader, chairperson bd. adminstrn.). Clubs: Cambridge Rotary (bd. dirs.), U. Cin. Alumni —C—. Contbr. music revs. to newspapers, ednl. articles to gen. mags. Home: Barton Manor Cambridge OH 43725 Office: County Administration Bldg Cambridge OH 43725

JONES, DONNA RUTH, librarian; b. Denver, June 23, 1948; d. Don and Ruth Virginia (Hampton) Lusk; m. Thomas W. Jones, June 7, 1969; 1 child, Matthew Trevor. A.A., Colby Community Coll., Kans., 1967; B.A., Frot Hays Kans. State U., 1969; M.L.S., Emporia Kans. State U., 1972. Librarian, instr. Colby Community Coll., 1969-76; dir. library services Pioneer Meml. Library, Colby, 1976-85; dir. Ark. Valley Regional Library Service System, Pueblo, Colo., 1985—; adj. prof. library sci. Fort Hays State U., 1972-73, 78-80; cons. Northwest Kans. Library System, 1970-71, 74, humanities cons., 1979—. Researcher: (movie and brochure) Country School Legacy: Humanities on the Frontier, 1980-82. Mem., chmn. Kans. Com. for Humanities, Topeka, 1979-85; pres. Thomas County Day Care, Colby, 1983-85. Recipient Jr. Mems. Round Table award 3-M, 1975, Young Alumni award Fort Hays State U., 1979; named Sister of Yr., Beta Sigma Phi. Mem. Mountain Plains Library Assn. (pres. 1984-85), ALA, State Steering Com. for Humanities in Pub. Libraries (chmn. 1980-85), Beta Sigma Phi. Democrat. Methodist. Lodge: Order of Eastern Star.

JONES, E(BEN) BRADLEY, former steel company executive; b. Cleve., Nov. 8, 1927; s. Eben Hoyt and Alfreda Sarah (Bradley) J.; B.A., Yale U., 1950; m. Ann Louise Jones, July 24, 1954; children—Susan Robb, Elizabeth Hoyt, Bradley Hoyt, Ann Campbell. With Republic Steel Corp., Cleve., 1954-84, v.p. mktg., Cleve., 1971-74, v.p. comml., 1974-76, exec. v.p., 1976-79, pres., 1979-80, pres., chief operating officer, 1980-82, chmn., chief exec. officer, 1982-84. officer and/or dir. subs. and affiliates; chmn., chief exec. Office LTV Steel Co., 1984; dir. Nat. City Bank Cleve., Nat. City Corp., TRW Inc. Trustee, v.p., mem. exec. com. Cleve. Clinic Found.; trustee, exec. com. Univ. Sch., Cleve.; trustee Cleve. Mus. Art. Served with U.S. Army, 1950-53. Mem. Delta Kappa Epsilon.

JONES, EDWARD, physician, pathologist; b. Willington, Kans., Mar. 21, 1935; s. Thomas S. and Grace M. (Sydebotham) Imel; m. Barbara A. Blount, Aug. 30, 1956; children—Kimberly Riegel, Sheila, Matt, Tom. A.B. in Chemistry, U. Kans., 1957, M.D., 1961. Diplomate Am. Bd. Anatomic Clin. Pathology. Intern St. Francis Hosp., Wichita, Kans., 1951-62; sr. asst. USPHS, Yuma, Ariz., 1962-64; gen. practice, medicine Lawrence Meml. Hosp., Kans., 1964-65; resident in pathology St. Luke's Hosp., Kansas City, Mo., 1965-69; pathologist Central Kans. Med. Ctr., Great Bend, 1969—; physician cons. Hoisington Luth. Hosp., Kans., 1969—, St. Joseph's Meml. Hosp., Larned, Kans., 1969—, Edwards County Hosp., Kinsley, Kans., 1969—; dir. Central Kans. Med. Center, Great Bend, 1974-76, pres., 1976-78. Bd. dirs. Cedar Park Place, Great Bend, 1980—. Fellow Coll. Am. Pathologists (del., foreman 1978—), Am. Soc. Clin. Pathologists; mem. Kans. Soc. Pathologists (pres. 1980-81). Republican. Congregationalist. Club: Great Bend Community Theater. Avocations: theater, musical theater. Home: 3208 Broadway Great Bend KS 67530 Office: Central Kans Med Center 3515 Broadway Great Bend KS 67530

JONES, EDWARD WITKER, See *Who's Who in America,* 43rd edition.

JONES, ENDSLEY TERRENCE, university dean, political consultant; b. Kansas City, Mo., Aug. 25, 1941; s. Endsley and Mary Teresa (Donovan) J.; m. Ruth Helene Schuessler, Feb. 12, 1966 (div. Sept. 1976); 1 son, Mark Penfield. B.S. in Econs., St. Louis U., 1963; Ph.D. in Polit. Sci., Georgetown U., 1967. Asst. prof. polit. sci. Kans. State U., Manhattan, 1966-69; from asst. prof. to prof. U. Mo.-St. Louis, 1969—, dir. pub. policy program, 1976-83, dean Coll. Arts and Scis., 1983—; pres. Community Cons., Inc., St. Louis, 1975—. Author: Conducting Political Research, 2d edit. 1983; contbr. articles to profl. publs. Bd. dirs. Confluence St. Louis, 1984—; polit. analyst Sta. KMOX, St. Louis, 1979—. Served to staff sgt. USAR, 1966-72. Fellow NSF, 1965-66, Am. Council on Edn., 1981-82; named Outstanding Tchr., AMOCO, 1974-75. Mem. Am. Polit. Sci. Assn., Am. Soc. Pub. Adminstrn. Home: 8570 Colonial Ln Saint Louis MO 63124 Office: U Mo-St Louis 8001 Natural Bridge Rd Saint Louis MO 63121

JONES, GARY EDMOND, school principal; b. Youngstown, Ohio, Nov. 27, 1938; s. Alvey Edmond and Gladys Louise (Probert) J.; m. Marilyn June Merritt, Nov. 21, 1970; children—Elizabeth Victoria, Merritt Edmond. B.S., Youngstown State U., 1962; M.S., Ind. U., 1967; Ed.D., 1972; postgrad. Valparaiso U., Kent State U. Adminstrv. asst. to supt. schs. Geneva (Ohio) Area City Schs., 1962, tchr., 1964-66; tchr. Calumet Jr. High Sch., Gary, Ind., 1966-68; research analyst, coordinator dropout study Lake Ridge Schs., Gary, 1968, dir. Title I ESEA, 1968-71; prin. Stanbery Freshman Sch., Lancaster, Ohio, 1972-76; prin. Donald E. Gavit Jr. Sr. High Sch., Hammond, Ind., 1976—. Bd. dirs. Lake Area Blood Service div.; chmn. Lake County chpt. ARC, Ind.; bd. dirs. Hammond Edn. Found; bd. mgrs. Ind. Congress Parents and Tchrs., mem. council Christ Luth. Ch., Hammond, 1980-82. Served with AUS, 1962-64. Recipient Outstanding Prin. award Ind. Congress Parents and Tchrs., 1985. Mem. Ind. Secondary Sch. Adminstrs. (outstanding secondary sch. adminstr. award 1982), fed. relations coordinator Ind., exec. com.), Nat. Assn. Secondary Sch. Prins., Assn. Supervision and Curriculum Devel., Nat. Soc. Study Edn., Nat. Council Social Studies, Ind. U. Alumni Assn., Am. Legion, Sigma Phi. Clubs: Masons, K.T.

JONES, GLORIA ELLEN, corporate design firm executive; b. Beaver Dam, Wis., Aug. 30, 1948; s. Henry P. and Theresa Sylvia (Alsum) Westra; m. Jerald W. Kuiper, June 21, 1965 (div. Jan. 1975); children—Bill, Bob, Heather; m. Robert W. Jones, Jr., July 16, 1977. Student U. Wis.-Oshkosh, 1970-73, Harvard Sch. Design, 1985. Sales dir. The Star, Oshkosh, 1975-76; account exec. The Post Corp., Appleton, Wis., 1976-78; prin. Rehab. Specialists, Appleton, 1978-82, Jones Appraisal Service, Appleton, 1978-82, Interior Design Firm, Appleton, 1980-82; v.p. Bischoff/Lincoln, Chgo., 1982—. Bd. sec. A Better Chance, Oshkosh, 1974. Named Mrs. Wisconsin, Wis. chpt. of Mrs. Am., 1980. Mem. Internat. Assn. Bus. Communicators, Young Execs. (v.p. communications 1984-85), Women in Mgmt. (v.p. mktg. 1984, 2d v.p. 1985). Democrat. Presbyterian. Avocations: writing; reading; golf. Home: 1927 Sherman Ave Apt 1S Evanston IL 60201 Office: Bischoff/Lincoln 55 W Monroe St Suite 3690 Chicago IL 60603

JONES, HENRY VINTON, insurance company executive; b. McKeesport, Pa., July 10, 1938; s. Robert Evan and Norma Winnifred (Vinton) J.; m. Carol Anne Stelter, July 23, 1966; children—Bruce Vinton, Stephanie Ruth. A.S., Tampa Coll., 1977; B.S. magna cum laude, Jones Coll., 1979; student Ashland Coll., 1982—. Casualty underwriter Nat. Union Ins. Co., Pitts., 1960-62; spl. agt. CNA, Erie, Pa., 1962-65; multi-line underwriter Ohio Casualty Co., St. Petersburg, Fla., 1965-75; mgr. Aetna Ins. Co., Columbia, S.C., 1975-81; asst. v.p., dir. casualty underwriting Lumbermen's Mut. Ins. Co., Mansfield, Ohio, 1981—. Mem. expansion fund com. Mansfield Gen. Hosp., 1982. Served with AUS, 1956-60. Mem. Soc. Ins. Research. Republican. Lutheran. Home: 44 Norfolk Dr Lexington OH 44904 Office: 900 Springmill St Mansfield OH 44907

JONES, IRMA JEWEL, social worker; b. Alton, Ill., Apr. 6, 1934; d. Damon and Willie Ann Jones; student So. Ill. U., Carbondale, 1952-54, San Francisco-Columbia Sch. Broadcasting, St. Louis, 1969-72. With Madison County (Ill.) Dept. Public Aid, 1956-72, 76—, social worker, caseworker, 1976—; adminstrv. sec., clk. III, So. Ill. U., Edwardsville, 1973-76; religious music radio announcer, producer, coordinator Sta. WOKZ, Alton, 1974—; pub. speaker; ch. sch. Writer. Lic. missionary, lay reader African Meth. Epis. Ch.; lic. radiotelephone operator. Mem. Nat. Assn. Colored Women's Clubs (past 2d and 3d v.p.), Fedn. Methodist Women, Nat. Gospel Announcers Guild, Alton Tri Del Federated Club Women, Ill. Assn. Club Women and Girls, Ill. Welfare Assn., Internat. Platform Assn., Smithsonian Assocs., Alton Area Bus. and Profl. Women's Club, Alton Ch. Women United (Southwest area), African Meth. Epis. Missionary Soc., Alton Area Alliance Religious Leaders, Alton Women's History Week Coalition, Jones Sisters Ensemble Kompany, Central Assn. Colored Women's Clubs, Nat. Assn. Female Execs., Gospel Music Workshop Am. Mem. A.M.E. Ch. Club: Alton Suburbia Toastmistress Author: Irma's Kreative Book of Religious and Kontemporary Works of Art, 1975—. Office: PO Box 985 Alton IL 62002

JONES, JAMES EDWARD, osteopath; b. Poplar Bluff, Mo., Apr. 17, 1939; s. Arthur Lee and Juanita M. (Huffman) J.; m. June Westaver, Apr. 2, 1966; children—James E., Julie Ann. Student N.E. Mo. State U., 1957-61; Western Ill. U., summer 1961; D.O., Kirksville Coll. Osteo. Medicine, 1966. Intern, Normandy Osteo. Hosp., St. Louis, 1966-67; practice osteo. medicine, St. Peters, Mo., 1967—; chief of staff St. Peters Community Hosp., 1982, now mem. bd. trustees. Mem. AMA, Mo. State Med. Assn., Am. Coll. Gen. Practice, Lincoln/St. Charles County Med. Assn. Republican. Lutheran. Home: PO Box 10 Saint Peters MO 63376 Office: 418 S Church St Saint Peters MO 63376

JONES, JAMES ERNEST, social work administrator; b. Woodstock, Ill., July 26, 1946; s. Jack E. and Gladys L. (Scudder) J.; m. Jan. 26, 1968 (div. Nov. 1981); children—Shannon, Shane. B.A., Adrian Coll., 1968; M.S.W., U. Mich., 1972. Probation officer Juvenile Ct., Adrian, Mich., 1968-71; enforcement officer Friend of the Ct., Ann Arbor, Mich., 1971-72; social work cons. Adrian Intermediate Sch. Dist., 1972-73; mem. faculty Adrian Coll., 1978-80; exec. dir. Call Someone Concerned, Inc., Adrian, 1970—; field instr. U. Mich., 1973-74. Pres. Catholic Social Services, Adrian, 1973-76, Social Forum Lenawee County, 1972. Club: Civitan (pres. 1980-81; Disting. Pres. award 1981; Honor Club 1981; Service award 1984). Avocation: handball. Home: 7330 Walnut Hill-Devils Lake Manitou Beach MI 49253 Office: Call Someone Concerned Inc 227 N Winter St Suite 21 Adrian MI 49221

JONES, JANET LEE, insurance company executive; b. Saginaw, Mich., Sept. 16, 1942; d. Max Loren and Joyce Eleanor (Burlingame) Bowyer; m. Larry Jack Jones, Sept. 8, 1962; children—Melissa J., Audra L., Sarah J. Lic. Ins. Counselor. Claim clk. Frankenmuth Mut., Frankenmuth, Mich., 1965-70; asst. Judd Ins. Agy., Birch Run, Mich., 1970-78; asst. mgr. mktg. Penn Gen. Agy., Saginaw, Mich., 1978-80; mgr. mktg. Ferguson Ins. Agy., Saginaw, Mich., 1980-82; account exec., agt. Universal Underwriters, Birmingham, Mich., 1982—. Coach, mgr. Albee Athletic Assn., Burt, Mich., 1979-81; v.p. Little Six Athletic Assn., 1979-81. Fellow Ins. Women Saginaw County, Soc. Cert. Ins.

Counselors. Independent. Episcopalian. Home: 12620 Lincoln Rd Burt MI 48417

JONES, JOHN BAILEY, federal judge; b. Mitchell, S.D., Mar. 30, 1927; s. John B. and Grace M. (Bailey) J.; m. Rosemary Jones; children—John, William, Mary Louise, David, Judith, Robert. B.S., U. S.D., 1951, LL.B., 1953. Bar: S.D. 1953. Sole practice, Presho, S.D., 1953-67; circuit judge S.D., Kennebec, 1967-81; judge U.S. Dist. Court, Sioux Falls, S.D., 1981—. Mem. S.D. Ho. of Reps., 1956-60. Served with USN, 1945-47. Office: US Dist Court 400 S Phillips Sioux Falls SD 57102

JONES, JOHN ROBERT, university administrator; b. Seaboard, N.C., May 1, 1943; m. Aretha Hopson, Dec. 7, 1967; children—Jeffrey, Jason. B.A., Shaw U., 1966; M.S., Tenn. State U., 1968; Ed.D., U. Mo., 1978. Asst. dir. Tenn. State U., Nashville, 1968-71; dir. Trio Programs Lincoln U., Jefferson City, Mo., 1971-78; exec. dir. Com. Programs, U. Pacific, Stockton, Calif., 1978-83; dir. Office of Acad. Assistance U. Mo., Columbia, 1983—; cons. U.S. Dept. Edn., Kansas City, Mo., 1973-74; presenter papers profl. confs. Mem. Area Com. Human Devel. Corp., Columbia, 1978; co-chmn. United Way Funding Com., Stockton, 1981; v.p. bd. Opportunities Industrialization Ctr., San Joaquin Community Action Council, Stockton, 1982. Recipient commendation Bd. Suprs., Stockton, 1983, Ho. of Reps. Calif., Sacramento, 1981, Calif. Senate, Sacramento, 1983, City Council Stockton, 1983. Mem. Phi Beta Sigma. Lodge: Capitol City (warden 1975-78). Avocations: fishing; tennis; model cars and airplanes. Home: 3415 Bray Ave Columbia MO 65201 Office: Office of Acad Assistance 207 Jesse Hall U MO Columbia MO 65211

JONES, JOHNNIE LOIS, student program administrator, counselor: b. Cleve., May 19, 1957; d. Paul Jesse and Mary Modean (Treadwell) J. B.A., Kent State U., 1980; M.A. in Student Personnel, Bowling Green State U., 1985. Residence staff advisor Kent State U., Ohio, 1976-78, registration aide, 1978-79, ednl. dir. Black-Greek Council, 1979-80; tchr. Cleve. Bd. Edn., 1980-83; acad. counselor, advisor student devel. program Bowling Green State U., Ohio, 1983—. Named one of Outstanding Young Women of Am., 1982; recipient Community Service award Kent State U. Black United Students, 1980. Mem. Mid-Am. Assn. for Ednl. Opportunity Program Personnel, Am. Coll. Personnel Assn., Am. Assn. Counseling and Devel., Assn. for Non-White Concerns in Personnel and Guidance, The Third World Grad. Assn. (v.p. Bowling Green State U. sect. 1984—), Blue Key, Kent State U. Alumni Assn., Sigma Gamma Rho (Ohio undergrad. coordinator 1981-83, campus advisor Cleve. State U. 1982-83, campus advisor Bowling Green State U. 1983—, Cleve. grad. chpt. scholar 1984, Outstanding Mem. of Yr. 1980, officer local chpts. 1978—). Democrat. Baptist. Avocations: bowling; basketball; video games; table tennis; tennis. Home: 426 S Enterprise St #D Bowling Green OH 43402 Office: Student Devel Program Bowling Green State U 424 Student Services Bldg Bowling Green OH 43403

JONES, KAREN BAGLEY, educator; b. Detroit, Sept. 18, 1951; d. James and Joyce (Ramsey) Bagley. B.A., U. Ill., 1974, M.Ed., 1977. Tchr. English, A.B.I., Chgo., 1984—; tchr. English, City Colls., Chgo., 1984, U. Chgo., Office Spl. Programs, 1985—; corp. sec. Harper Sq. Housing Corp., Chgo., 1982-84; communications chmn. U. Ill. Black Alumni Assn., Chgo., 1982—. Vice chmn. 4th Ward Citizens Com., Chgo., 1983—; area coordinator Washington for Mayor, Chgo., 1983-84. Mem. Nat. Assn. Univ. Women, Alpha Kappa Alpha. Democrat. Avocations: travel; gourmet dining.

JONES, KATHERINE ANN, health educator; b. Jackson, Mich., Mar. 22, 1953; d. Harry Irvin and Norma Joanne (Long) J. B.S., Central Mich. U., 1979, M.A., 1984. Grad. intern St. Lawrence Hosp., Lansing, Mich., 1979; health edn. mgr. St. Lawrence Hosp., Lansing, 1979—. Recipient Diabetes Edn. award Mich. Dept. Pub. Health, 1983. Mem. AAHPER and Dance, Soc. Pub. Health Edn. (pres. Great Lakes chpt. 1984-85), Nat. Soc. Pub. Health Edn., Am. Pub. Health Assn., Eta Sigma Gamma. Office: St Lawrence Hosp 1210 W Saginaw St Lansing MI 48915

JONES, KENSINGER, advertising educator, advertising consultant; b. St. Louis, Oct. 18, 1919; s. Walter Clare and Anna Lee (Kensinger) J.; m. Alice May Guseman, Oct. 7, 1944; children—Jeffrey K., Janice A. Student Washington U., St. Louis, 1939-40. Writer Land We Live In, KMOX-KSD, St. Louis, 1945-52; TV copywriter Leo Burnett Co., Chgo., 1952-57; TV creative dir. Campbell-Ewald Co., Detroit, 1957-59, exec. v.p., creative div., 1959-68; sr. v.p., exec. creative dir. Leo Burnett Co., Detroit, Chgo., Sydney, Australia, Singapore, 1968-76; creative cons. Wilding Advt., Southfield, Mich., 1977-79; creative supr. Biggs/Gilmore Advt., Kalamazoo, Mich., 1980-82; dir. Cello-Foil Co., Battle Creek, Mich.; lectr. advt. Mich. State U., East Lansing, 1982—. Author: (with others) Rebellious Colonel Speaks, 1965; Enter Singapore, 1975; Cable-New Ways to New Selling, 1984; writer film: The Horse and the Fiddle, 1959; producer film; Importance of Being Interesting, 1963; writer, producer film: Child of his Own, 1975. Bd. dirs. World Med. Relief, Detroit, 1965—; mem. Nat. Exec. Res., Detroit, Chgo., 1965—; mem. Mich. Planning Bd., Lansing, 1963-65; mem. Mich. Cultural Commn., Lansing, 1966-67; chmn. Pub. Service Communications Com., Chgo., 1972-73; chmn. Planning and Zoning, Parks and Recreation Commns., Barry County, Mich., 1980-83; mem. nat. communications com. Boy Scouts Am., 1966—. Served with U.S. Army, 1941-45, PTO. Recipient Clio awards Am. TV Comml. Festival, N.Y.C., 1958, 59, 60, 61, 1st place awards Cannes and Venice Film Festivals, 1962, 63, 64, Silver Beaver award Boy Scouts Am., 1966, Silver Salute, Mich. State U., 1981; Freedoms Found. award, 1985. Mem. Adcraft Club Detroit, Alpha Delta Sigma. Presbyterian. Clubs: Circumnavigators (Detroit); Am. Tree Farmers, Am. Angus Assn., Vet. Car Club Am. Avocations: farming; fishing; hunting; antique cars. Home: Aurohn Lake 425 Pritchardville Rd Hastings MI 49058 Office: 312 Communications Arts Bldg Mich State U East Lansing MI 48824

JONES, KENT, state agricultural administrator; b. Webster, N.D., Apr. 26, 1926; s. John D. and Katherine (Jones) J.; m. Helen L. Johnson, Sept. 10, 1947; children—Deborah, Jeff, Sara, Rebecca. B.S. in Agr., N.D. State U. Farmer, Ramsey County, N.D.; commr. N.D. Dept. Agr., Bismarck, 1981—. Mem. N.D. Ho. of Reps., 1967-69, N.D. State Senate, 1971-79. Served with U.S. Army, 1946-47. Republican. Episcopalian. Lodges: Elks, Masons. Avocations: walking; reading. Office: ND Dept Agr 601 State Capitol Bismarck ND 58505

JONES, LAWRENCE WILLIAM, physics educator; b. Evanston, Ill., Nov. 16, 1925; s. Charles Herbert and Fern (Storm) J.; m. Ruth R. Drummond, June 24, 1950; children—Douglas W., Carol Jones Dwyer, Ellen Jones Dillman. B.S., Northwestern U., 1948, M.S., 1949; Ph.D., U. Calif.-Berkeley, 1952. Research asst. Radiation Lab., Berkeley, 1950-57; physicist Midwestern U. Research Assoc., Madison, Wis., 1956-57; fellow CERN, Geneva, 1961-62; prof. physics U. Mich., Ann Arbor, 1952—, chmn. dept. physics, 1982—; vis. scientist Fermi Nat. Accel. Lab., Batavia, Ill., 1972—, Brookhaven Nat. Lab., Upton, N.Y., 1962-79. Contbr. articles (over 150) to profl. jours. Bd. dirs. Ecology Ctr., Ann Arbor, 1973-76; trustee U. Research Assn., Washington, 1981—; chmn. organ com. 1st Congl. Ch., Ann Arbor, 1981-84. Gugenheim fellow, Geneva, 1965, Sci. Research Council fellow, London, 1977; vis. prof. Tata Inst., Bombay, India, 1979. Fellow Am. Phys. Soc.; mem. AAAS. Avocations: amateur radio; sailing; skiing. Home: 2666 Park Ridge Dr Ann Arbor MI 48103 Office: Dept Physics Univ Michigan Ann Arbor MI 48109-1120

JONES, LEANDER CORBIN, educator, media specialist; b. Vincent, Ark., July 16, 1934; s. Lander Corbin and Una Bell (Lewis) J.; A.B., U. Ark., Pine Bluff, 1956; M.S., U. Ill., 1968; Ph.D., Union Grad. Sch., 1973; m. Lethonee Angela Hendricks, June 30, 1962; children—Angela Lynne, Leander Corbin. Tchr. English pub. high schs., Chgo. Bd. Edn., 1956-68; vol. English-as-fgn. lang. tchr. Peace Corps, Mogadiscio, Somalia, 1964-66; TV producer City Colls. of Chgo., 1968-73; communications media specialist Meharry Med. Coll., 1973-75; assoc. prof. Black Americana studies Western Mich., U., 1975—, chmn. African studies program, 1980-81, co-chmn. Black caucus, 1983, corr. sec., 1984—; dir. 7 art workshop Am. Negro Emancipation Centennial Authority, Chgo., 1960-63. Mem. Mich. Commn. on Crime and Delinquency, 1981-83; mem. exec. com. DuSable Mus. African Am. History, 1970—; mem. Prisoners Progress Assn., 1977-82, South African Solidarity Orgn., 1978—, Dennis Brutus Def. Com., 1980-83; chmn. Kalamazoo Community Relations Bd., 1977-79; bd. dirs. Kalamazoo Civic Players, 1981-83. Served with U.S. Army, 1956-58. Mem. Assn. Study African-Am. History (exec. com. 1978-82), NAACP, Prisoners Progress Assn., Theatre Arts and Broadcasting Skills Ctr. Studies, Nat. Council Black Studies, Popular Culture Assn., 100 Men's Club, Am. Muslim Dawah Com. Dir. for South Side Center of Performing Arts, Chgo., 1968-69, Progressive Theatre Unltd., Nashville, 1974-75; writer, producer, dir. TV drama: Roof Over my Head, Sta. WDCN, Nashville 1975; designer program in theatre and TV for hard-to-educate; developer edn. programs in Ill. State Penitentiary, Pontiac, and Cook County Jail, Chgo., 1971-73. Writer, dir. 10 Score!, 1976, Super Summer, 1978; dir. Trouble in Mind, Black Theatre of Kalamazoo Civic Players, 1979, chmn. Black Theatre com., 1980-82, also bd. dirs.; chmn. Kalamazoo Community Relations Bd., 1978, mem. bd., 1979-80; featured in Great White Hope, Civic Auditorium, Kalamazoo, 1979, in Moon on a Rainbow Shawl, Kalamazoo Carver Arena, 1980; Africa Is for Reel, 1983. Home: 2226 S Westnedge Ave Kalamazoo MI 49008 Office: Black Americana Studies Western Mich U Kalamazoo MI 49001

JONES, LELAND EVERETTE, retired executive; b. Barneveld, Wis., Mar. 5, 1915; s. Everette Roland and Pearl (Liddle) J.; children from former marriage: Louise Marie, Judith Ann, Kathleen Mary, Rita Carol, Thomas Everette, Gerald Cecil. Ed., Commerce Coll., Whitewater, Wis. Mem. Internat. Lions, Whitewater, 1962—, sec., 1983-84; charter mem., active VFW, Whitewater, 1946—. Served as sgt. U.S. Army, 1940-45, ETO. Mem. Am. Legion. Roman Catholic. Lodges: Masons. Avocations: all sports; coin collecting; civic work. Address: 1061 W Blackhawk Dr Whitewater WI 53190

JONES, MARVIN ENNIS, judge; b. Bernie, Mo., June 8, 1921; s. James Tribble and Ora Blanch (Walker) J.; m. Vivian Pauline Norman, Nov. 10, 1943; children—Marcia Lynn Jones Norman, Susan Carole Jones Pudlowski, Emily Ann. J.D., U. Mo.-Columbia, 1950. Bar: Mo. Claims atty. MFA Mut. Ins. Cos., Dexter, Mo., 1951-58; ptnr. Powell, Jones & Ringer, Dexter, 1958-67; vice chmn. Mo. Pub. Service Commn., Jefferson City, 1967-71, chmn., 1971-73; adminstrv. law judge U.S. EPA, Kansas City, Mo., 1973—. Contbr. articles to profl. jours. Pres. United Fund, Dexter, 1960; deacon First Baptist Ch., Dexter, 1961-67, Wornall Rd. Baptist Ch., Kansas City, 1977—. Served to 1st lt. USAF, 1942-45, ETO. Decorated Purple Heart, Air Medal. Mem. Fed. Adminstrv. Law Judges Conf., Mo. Bar Assn. Democrat. Lodges: Kiwanis (pres. 1965), Masons. Home: 608 West 50th St Kansas City MO 64112

JONES, MELVIN, publisher, lawyer; b. Hayti, Mo., Jan. 4, 1954; s. Ernest Eugene and Musetta (Simpson) J.; m. Sharon Butcher, July 5, 1975; children—Caleb Martin, Joshua Eugene. B.S., Lincoln U., 1975; J.D., Cornell U., 1979. Bar: Mo. 1979. Jr. ptnr. Bryan, Cave, McPheeters & McRoberts, St. Louis, 1979-81; gen. mgr. St. Louis Am. Newspaper, 1981-82; pres. Community Communications, St. Louis, 1982—. Bd. dirs. Childhaven, St. Louis, 1985, St. Louis Opportunities Industrialization Ctr., 1982—. Served to 1st lt. USMC, 1977-79. Mem. Mo. Bar Assn. Democrat. Presbyterian. Club: 100 Black Men. Home: 5816 Waterman Saint Louis MO 63112 Office: Community Communications Corp 306 N Grand Saint Louis MO 63103

JONES, MICHAEL HOUSTON, insurance company executive; b. Sikeston, Mo., Sept. 5, 1942; s. Venson Bruce and Vanita Elizabeth (Fenimore) J.; m. Kathryn Fay Reed, June 10, 1977; children—Richard, Michael, Christy, Allison. B.A., Central Meth. Coll., 1964. Real estate broker, owner Sportsman, Inc., Sikeston, Mo., 1964-68; sales rep. Mut. of Omaha, Sikeston, 1968-73, dist. mgr., Cape Girardeau, Mo., 1973-80, regional sales dir. midwest, Omaha, 1980-81, gen. mgr., Mansfield, Ohio, 1981—. Mem. Nat. Assn. Life Underwriters (polit. action com. 1983). Republican. Methodist. Home: 12 Sussex Ct W Lexington OH 44904 Office: Mut of Omaha 2282 Village Mall Dr Mansfield OH 44906

JONES, NATHANIEL P., federal judge. Judge U.S. Ct. Appeals Sixth Cir. Office: US Ct Appeals 541 US Post Office Bldg and Courthouse Cincinnati OH 45202*

JONES, NELSON, marketing consultant; b. Chgo., May 21, 1947; s. George and Rosa Mae (Grant) J.; B.S. in B.A., Roosevelt U., 1969; M.B.A. (Mgmt fellow), U. Chgo., 1974; m. Valerie Ann Hughes, June 21, 1966 (div. 1973); children—Selene Tess, Nelson, Manuel. Sales trainee/sales trainee mgr. Gen. Foods Corp., Chgo., 1968-70; computer marketing rep. IBM, Chgo., 1971-73; program marketing analyst Xerox Corp., Rochester, N.Y., 1973-75; industry account exec. 3M Co., Chgo., 1975-76; asso. dir. mktg. Nat. Minority Purchasing Council, Chgo., 1976-78; mktg. exec. NCR Corp., 1978-80; Midwest regional sales mgr. Blackfeet Indian Writing Co., 1981—; mktg. cons. computer systems/word processing and computerized display systems. Mem., supporter WTTW/Channel 11, Chgo. Pub. TV, 1977—, Easter Seal Soc., Chgo., 1977—, Masca-Sickle Cell Anemia, 1977—. Boost fellow, Roosevelt U., 1965-69. Mem. Am. Mktg. Assn., Assn. of MBA Execs., Nat. Splty. Merchandisers Assn., Air Force Mus. Found., Grant Park Concerts Assn., Mus. Sci. and Industry, Internat. Platform Assn. Contbr. articles in field to profl. jours. Home and Office: 333 E Ontario St Chicago IL 60611

JONES, NORMA LOUISE, educator; b. Poplar, Wis.; d. George Elmer and Hilma June (Wiberg) Jones; B.E., U. Wis.; M.A., U. Minn., 1952; postgrad. U. Ill., 1957; Ph.D., U. Mich., 1965. Librarian, Grand Rapids (Mich.) pub. schs., 1947-62; Grand Rapids (Mich.) Pub. Library, 1948-49; instr. Central Mich. U., Mt. Pleasant, 1954, 55; librarian Benton Harbor (Mich.) pub. schs., 1962-63; lectr. U. Mich., Ann Arbor, 1954, 55, 61, 63-65, asst. prof., 1966-68; asst. prof. dept. library sci. U. Wis.-Oshkosh, 1968-70, asso. prof., 1970-75, prof., 1975—, chmn. dept. library sci., 1980—; mem. com. on certification of sch. librarians State of Wis., 1972—. Recipient Disting. Teaching award U. Wis., 1977, Mem. ALA (chmn. reference conf. 1975), Wis. Library Assn., Am. Assn. Sch. Librarians, Spl. Libraries Assn., Assn. Am. Library Schs., Soc. Am. Archivists, Phi Beta Kappa, Phi Kappa Phi, Pi Lambda Theta, Beta Phi Mu, Sigma Pi Epsilon. Home: 1220 Maricopa Dr Oshkosh WI 54901

JONES, NORMAN HARRY, human resource and development consulting firm executive, education counselor; b. Battle Creek, Mich., June 4, 1936; s. Harry Charles and Ernestine (Smith) J.; m. Patricia Claire Walsh, June 18, 1960; children—Denise, Diane, Deborah. B.A., Ball State U., 1959, M.A., 1963; Ed.D. in Counseling and Ednl. Psychology, U. Miss., 1977. Tchr., coach North Vernon (Ind.) High Sch., 1959-61; counselor, tchr., coach Salem (Ind.) High Sch., 1961-66; pupil personnel counselor Palatine (Ill.) High Sch., 1966—; pres. Communications Unltd., Inc., Palatine, 1979—; lectr. on communication skills, motivation, encouragement and mgmt. techniques. Bd. dirs. Community Child Care Ctr., Palatine, 1982-83. Recipient Kiwanis Achievement award, 1954. Mem. No. Ill. Ednl. Research and Edn. Devel., Ill. Personnel and Guidance Assn. (pres. N. Suburban chpt. 1980), Am. Personnel and Guidance Assn. Author: Keep In Touch, 1981. Office: 1111 Rohlwing Rd Palatine IL 60067

JONES, NORMAN M., savings and loan association executive. Chmn., chief operating officer, dir. Met. Fed. Bank FSB, Fargo, N.D. Office: Metropolitan Federal Bank FSB 215 N Fifth St Fargo ND 58102*

JONES, PAUL WILLIS, former editor, historian, importer; b. Washington Court House, Ohio, Oct. 28, 1913; s. Walter W. and Ida (Junk) J.; m. Maurine Hasseltine Wilson, Dec. 28, 1940; 1 child, Ann Ferrell Jones Austin. B.A., Ohio Wesleyan U., 1936; M.A., Bowling Green State U., 1961. Editor, Bowling Green Daily Sentinel-Tribune, Ohio, 1936-41; state editor Columbus Citizen, Ohio, 1936-41; dir. news bur., mem. journalism faculty Bowling Green State U., 1941-53, asst. prof., 1949-53; dir. N.W. Buckeye Council, nat. Assn. Investors Corp., 1980—, chmn., 1981-84. Author: Presbyterians in Bowling Green, Ohio, 1855-1980, 1980; also articles. Mem. editorial staff: Bowling Green, Ohio: A Sesquicentennial History, 1985. Bd. dirs., past treas. Friends of Wood County Pub. Library. Served with USNR, 1943-46. Recipient Disting. Service award Kiwanis Club, Bowling Green, 1980; 1st place editorial award UPI Assn. Ohio, 1962. Mem. Expo Collectors and Historians Orgn., Maumee River Scenic and Historic Hwy. Assn. (v.p.), Maumee Valley Hist. Soc., Ohio Assn. Hist. Socs. and Mus., Sigma Delta Chi (chpt. pres. 1958), Ohio Geneal. Soc. (chpt. historian), Wood County Hist. Soc., Ohio Hist. Soc., Blue Pencil Club Ohio (past pres.), UPI Editors Assn. Ohio (past pres.), Alpha Phi Omega, Delta Sigma Rho, Phi Gamma Delta (bd. chpt. advisors), Pi Delta Epsilon, Kappa Tau Alpha. Elder, deacon, historian Presbyterian Ch. Republican. Club: Junto (pres. 1960-61, 72-73) (Bowling Green). Lodge: Kiwanis (pres. 1951) (Bowling Green). Avocations: local history; postcard collecting.

JONES, PHILLIP ERKSINE, university dean; b. Chgo., Oct. 26, 1940; m. Jo Lavera Kennedy, Jan. 18, 1964; children—Phyllis Lavera, Joel Erskine. B.S., U. Ill., 1963; M.A., U. Iowa, 1967, Ph.D., 1975. Group work counselor Chgo. Youth Ctrs., 1963-64; tchr. phys. edn., psychology Flint Community Schs., Mich., 1967-68; coordinator ednl. opportunity programs U. Iowa, Iowa City, 1968-70, dir. spl. support services, 1970-75, asst. v.p., dir. affirmative action, asst. prof. counselor edn., 1975-78, assoc. dean student services, asst. prof., 1978-83, dean student services, 1983—. Contbr. articles to profl. jours. Mem. Am. Assn. Higher Edn., Nat. Assn. Student Personnel Adminstrs. Avocations: phys. fitness; jazz. Office: U Iowa 105 Jessup Hall Iowa City IA 52242

JONES, RAYMOND BOLIN, ceramic engineering consultant; b. Vicksburg, Miss., May 4, 1920; s. Alva Lewis and Flora Belle (Bolin) J.; m. Roberta Ownby, June 22, 1947; children—Raymond B. Jr., Karin Sue, Robert L., Elizabeth Ann. B.S. in Ceramic Engring., Mo. Sch. Mines, 1946. Vice pres., treas. Ceramo Co., Jackson, Mo., 1946-52; v.p. mfg. Nat. Tile Co., Anderson, Ind., 1952-62; ops. mgr. color div. Ferro Corp., Cleve., 1962-72, mgr. electronic materials, 1972-80, bus. devel. mgr. color div., 1980-82; cons. ceramic engring., Bay Village, Ohio, 1982—; cons. Glass Beads Co., Latrobe, Pa., 1982—. Contbr. articles to profl. jours. Patentee in field. Fellow Am. Ceramic Soc. Republican. Methodist. Home and Office: 26907 Lake Rd Bay Village OH 44140

JONES, RICHARD CYRUS, lawyer; b. Oak Park, Ill., Oct. 20, 1928; s. Ethler E. and Margaret S. (Stoner) J.; Ph.B., DePaul U., 1960, J.D., 1963; children—Richard C., Carrie, William. Bar: Ill. 1963. Dept. mgr. Chgo. Title & Trust Co., 1947-64; mem. firm Sachnoff, Schrager, Jones, Weaver & Rubenstein Ltd. and predecessor firms, Chgo., 1964-81; of counsel Sachnoff, Weaver & Rubenstein, 1981—; instr. Real Estate Inst., Chgo., 1970—. Served with U.S. Army, 1951-52. Decorated Bronze Star, Combat Inf. badge. Mem. ABA, Ill. Bar Assn., Chgo. Bar Assn. (com. chmn. real property law 1970-72, 76—), Chgo. Council Lawyers, Delta Theta Phi. Kiwanian. Home: 1044 Forest Ave River Forest IL 60305 Office: 30 S Wacker Dr 29th Floor Chicago IL 60606

JONES, RICHARD JEFFERY, physician, educator; b. Cleve., Apr. 6, 1918; s. Edward Safford and Frances Christine (Jeffery) J.; m. Helen Hart, Oct. 5, 1946; children—Christopher, Ruth, Jeffery, Catherine. A.B., Oberlin Coll., 1938; M.A., U. Buffalo, 1942, M.D., 1943. Diplomate Am. Bd. Internal Medicine. Intern, U. Chgo. Hosps., 1944; resident, 1947-49; assoc. prof. medicine U. Chgo., 1958-76; assoc. prof. clin. medicine Northwestern U., Chgo., 1976—. Author: Chemistry and Therapy of Chronic Cardiovascular Disease, 1961. Editorial bd. Nutrition Revs., 1964-72. Served to lt. USNR, 1944-46, PTO. Recipient Presl. Letter Commendation, Pres. Truman, 1946, vis. assoc. prof. Rockefeller U., 1985. Fellow Am. Heart Assn.; mem. AMA (dir. scientific activites 1976-83, council sec. 1976-83), Central Soc. Clin. Research, Soc. Experimental Biol. and Med. (editorial bd. 1964-74). Unitarian. Home: 4820 S Kenwood Ave Chicago IL 60615 Office: Northwestern Meml Hosp 251 E Chicago Ave Chicago IL 60611

JONES, ROBERT BROOKE, microbiologist and immunologist educator; b. Knoxville, Tenn., Sept 14, 1942; s. Robert Melvin and Evaleen (Brooke) J.; m. Barbara Burgess McLawhorn, Sept. 7, 1963; children—Julia Ashley, Jonathan Davis, Quinnette Brooke. A.B. in Chemistry, U. N.C., 1964, M.D., 1970, Ph.D. in Biochemistry, 1970. Diplomate Am. Bd. Internal Medicine. Intern U. Wash., Seattle, 1970-71; resident U. Wash., Seattle, 1974-76; fellow in infectious diseases, 1976-78; asst. prof. Ind. U. Sch. Medicine, Indpls., 1978-83, assoc. prof. medicine, microbiology and immunology, 1983—; dir. Ind. Sexually Transmitted Diseases Research Ctr., Indpls., 1983—. Contbr. sci. articles to profl. jours. Served to lt. comdr. U.S. Navy, 1971-74. NIH grantee, 1983. Fellow ACP; mem. Am. Venereal Disease Assn. (bd. dirs. 1983—), Am. Soc. Microbiology, Infectious Disease Soc. Am., Am. Fedn. Clin. Research, Order Golden Fleece, Sigma Xi, Alpha Omega Alpha. Republican. Mem. Society of Friends. Office: Ind U Dept Medicine Emerson 302 Indianapolis IN 46223

JONES, ROBERT C., orchestra executive. Exec. dir. Indpls. Symphony Orch. Office: Indpls Symphony Orch Circle Theatre 45 Monument Circle Indianapolis IN 46204*

JONES, ROBERT E., company executive; m. Mary Jane Jones; 1 child, Tom. Student Washington U. With The Jones Co., St. Louis, 1953—, pres., 1961—, chmn. bd.; dir. St. John's Bank and Trust Co. Chmn. labor com. Home Builders Assn. Greater St. Louis; tech. advt. com. St. Louis County Planning Commn.; chmn. bd. Met. St. Louis Sewer Dist. Mem. Nat. Assn. Home Builders (life dir.). Address: 13100 Manchester Rd Suite G55 Saint Louis MO 63131

JONES, ROBERT GILBERT, dentist, fast food francise owner; b. Kansas City, Mo., Aug. 13, 1945; s. Clarence C. and Kathrine Jones; m. Virginea Elizabeth Merrinan, May 9, 1975; children—Lisa, Zach. B.S. in Biology, Baker U., 1971; D.D.S., U. Mo.-Kansas City, 1976. Gen. practice dentistry, Hannibal, Mo., 1976—; v.p., owner, Wendy's, Hannibal, 1984—; staff dentist Bethaven Nursing Home, Hannibal, 1976—; staff mem. St. Elizabeth Hosp., Hannibal, 1980—, Levering Hosp., Hannibal, 1980—. Fin. chmn. St. Johns Luth. Sch., Hannibal, 1982; bd. dirs. United Way, Hannibal, 1983, Salvation Army, Hannibal, 1984; sr. warden Trinity Episc. Ch., Hannibal, 1984. Served as E-5 U.S. Army, 1966-68, Vietnam. Recipient Outstanding Trainee award, U.S. Army, 1966, Army Commendation medal, 1968, Combat Medic Medal, 1968. Mem. ADA, Mo. Dental Soc., Am. Straight Wire Orthodontic Soc., Grant River Dental Soc., Am. Prosthetic Soc., Hannibal C. of C. Republican. Episcopalian. Club: Hannibal Country. Lodge: Rotary. Home: 4105 W Ely Hannibal MO 63401 Office: 2319 Broadway Hannibal MO 63401

JONES, SANDRA YVONNE, lawyer; b. Chgo., July 13, 1952; d. Fred Alexander and Luenettie (Joiner) J. B.S., U. Ill., 1975; J.D., Valparaiso U., 1977; diploma Nat. Jud. Coll., 1981. Bar: Ill. 1978, U.S. Dist. Ct. (no. dist.) Ill., U.S. Supreme Ct. 1983. Legal asst. Porter County Prosecutor's Office, Valparaiso, Ind., 1977; legal counsel Cook County Legal Asst.'s Office, Maywood, Ill., 1978-81; adminstrv. law judge Human Rights Commn., Chgo., 1981-85; asst. regional civil rights counsel Office Civil Rights, U.S. Dept. Edn., Chgo., 1985—. Author: Tenant's Guide to Self-Help, 1981. Mem. ABA, Ill. Assn. Adminstrv. Law Judges (v.p. 1984—), Ill. Assn. Trial Lawyers, Chgo. Bar Assn., Ill. Bar Assn. Home: 3316 S Calumet Chicago IL 60616 Office: Human Rights Commn 32 W Randolph Chicago IL 60601

JONES, STANLEY ARDEN, aerial applicator; b. Phillipsburg, Kan., May 20, 1947; s. Vinton and Mildred Evelyn (Yancy) J.; m. Phyllis Jean Jones, June 1, 1966; children—Shawn David, Stacy Daree. A.A. in Bus., McCook Jr. Coll., 1967. Air traffic controller FAA, Cedar Rapids, Iowa, 1970-74; v.p. Top Hat Aerial, Benkelman, Nebr., 1974-80, pres., 1980—; pres. Top Crop Fertilizer, Benkelman, Nebr., 1979—, Top Hat Flying Service, Benkelman, 1983; sec. Nat. Agrl. Research & Edn. Found., Washington, 1983—. Pres., Dundy County Agrl. Soc., 1982-84; bd. dirs. City Council, Terrytown, Nebr., 1969-70. Recipient Outstanding Service award Nat. Agrl. Aviation Assn., 1983; Allied Industry award, 1983; Falcon Club award, 1983. Mem. Nebr. Aviation Trades Assn. (dir. 1976-83, pres. 1984), Nat. Agrl. Aviation Assn. (dir. 1978-84, treas. 1985). Republican. Methodist. Lodge: Shriners. Address: Top Hat Aerial Applicators Inc Jones Airport Benkelman NE 69021

JONES, STANLEY WILLIAM, JR., wholesale distributing company executive; b. Kalamazoo, Sept. 5, 1935; s. Stanley William and Eddi Fern (Bullock) J.; m. Mary Louise Hamilton, Sept. 20, 1954; children—Karen, Mark, Sharen, Kevin. Cert. in pulp and paper making Internat. Corr. Sch. Trainee, Bond Supply, Kalamazoo, 1957-61; salesman Bard Tool & Equipment, 1961-63; estimator, salesman Miller Steel & Supply Co., Elkhart, Ind., 1963-64; br. mgr. Morley Bros., Flint, Mich., 1964-67; v.p. sales Keppels, Inc., Holland, Mich., 1967-71; pres. Oshtemo Hill, Inc., Kalamazoo, Lansing and Grand Rapids, Mich., 1972—; dir. Assoc. Builders and Contractors, Grand Rapids, Mich. Served with USMC, 1950-51. Republican. Club: Pennisular. Avocations: flying; boating. Home: 1918 Lake St Holland MI 49423 Office: Oshtemo Hill Inc 2050 Turner NW Grand Rapids MI 49504

JONES, STEPHAN LOWRY, financial executive; b. Sac City, Iowa, Nov. 4, 1935; s. Zardus and Opal Baxter (Lowry) J.; m. Linda Ann Vernon, June 30, 1962; children—Carrie Elizabeth, Stephan Vernon. B.A., Grinnell Coll., 1957; postgrad. Grad. Sch. Banking, Madison, 1971-73. With Francis I. duPont & Co., Storm Lake, Iowa, 1964-71; corr. bank officer Central Nat. Bank, Des

Moines, 1971-73; v.p. Hawkeye Bankcorp., Des Moines, 1973-82, sr. v.p., 1982—; dir. Hawkeye Investment Mgmt., Inc. Mem. Bank Mktg. Assn., Nat. Investor Relations Inst., Bank Investor Relations Assn. (dir. 1981), Fin. Analysts Fedn., Des Moines C. of C. Republican/Presbyterian. Clubs: Des Moines, Des Moines Country. Address: Hawkeye Bankcorporation 600 Stephens Bldg Des Moines IA 50307

JONES, TERRENCE DALE, university dean, arts administrator; b. Kansas City, Mo., Jan. 11, 1948; s. Bobby J. and Ida Lorene (Overstreet) J.; m. Marla Jean Carr, Sept. 23, 1972; 1 child, Eryn. B.S., U. Kans., 1970, M.A., 1972; M.F.A., U. Ga., 1971. Mgr., dir. Bradford Repertory Theatre, Vt., 1970-71; designer, instr. Miami-Dade Community Coll., Fla., 1972-74; designer, asst. prof. Grinnell Coll., Iowa, 1974-76; mng. dir., asst. prof. Kirkland Fine Arts Ctr., Millikin U., Decatur, Ill., 1976-81; gen. mgr., asst. dean Clowes Meml. Hall/Jordan Coll. Fine Arts, Butler U., Indpls., 1981—. Recipient Service award Univ. Theatre, U. Kans., Lawrence, 1969-70; study grantee Assn. Coll., Univ. and Community Arts Adminstrs./NEA, 1978, 81, 85, Ford Found./-Grinnell Coll., 1975, 76. Mem. Internat. Assn. Auditorium Mgrs., Internat. Soc. Performing Arts Adminstrs., Assn. Coll., Univ. and Community Arts Adminstrs., Ind. Presenter's Network. Methodist. Lodge: Rotary. Office: Clowes Meml Hall 4600 Sunset Ave Indianapolis IN 46208

JONES, THEODORE, hospital dietetic services executive; b. Gould, Ark., June 22, 1940; s. James and Erma Mae (Weston) J.; m. Freddie Faye Frierson, Mar. 8, 1961; children—Sharon, Theodore, Pamela. Student U. Ark., Pine Bluff, 1958-62. Waiter, Franke Restaurant, Little Rock, 1961-74; asst. dir. dietetic services Doctors Hosp., Little Rock, 1974-77; dir. dietetic services Am. Internat. Hosp., 1977—. Mem. Nat. Restaurant Assn., Am. Soc. Food Service Adminstrs. (speaker on nutrition 1977—). Baptist. Contbr. articles to Hosp. Nutritional News. Office: 2500 Emmans Ave Zion IL 60099

JONES, TREVOR OWEN, automobile company executive; b. Maidstone, Kent, Eng., Nov. 3, 1930; s. Richard Owen and Rudy Edith (Martin) J.; came to U.S., 1957, naturalized, 1971; Higher Nat. Certificate in Elec. Engring., Aston Tech. Coll., Birmingham, Eng., 1952; Ordinary Nat. Certificate in Mech. Engring., Liverpool (Eng.) Tech. Coll., 1957; m. Jennie Lou Singleton, Sept. 12, 1959; children—Pembroke Robinson, Bronwyn Elizabeth. Student engr., elec. machine design engr. Brit. Gen. Electric Co., 1950-57; project engr., project mgr. Nuclear Ship Savannah, Allis-Chalmers Mfg. Co., 1957-59; with Gen. Motors Corp., 1959-78, staff engr. in charge Apollo computers, 1967, dir. electronic control systems, 1970-72, dir. advanced product engring., 1972-74, dir. Gen. Motors Proving Grounds, 1974-78; v.p. engring., automotive worldwide TRW Inc., 1978-80, v.p., gen. mgr. transp. electronics group, 1980—; vice chmn. Motor Vehicle Safety Adv. Council, 1971; chmn. Nat. Hwy. Safety Adv. Com., 1976. Trustee Lawrence Inst. Tech., 1973-76; mem. exec. bd. Clinton Valley council Boy Scouts Am., 1975; gov. Cranbrook Inst. Sci., 1977. Served as officer Brit. Army, 1955-57. Recipient Safety award for engring. excellence U.S. Dept. Transp., 1978. Registered profl. engr., Wis.; chartered engr., U.K. Fellow Brit. Instn. Elec. Engrs. (Hooper Meml. prize 1950), IEEE (exec. com. vehicle tech. soc. 1977—, Edison medal Cleve. sect. 1983), Soc. Automotive Engrs., Soc. Automotive Engrs. (Arch T. Colwell paper award 1974, 75, Vincent Bendix Automotive Electronics award 1976); mem. Nat. Acad. Engring., Engring. Soc. Detroit and Cleve. Republican. Episcopalian. Clubs: Birmingham (Mich.) Athletic; Capitol Hill (Washington); Kirtland Country. Author, patentee automotive safety and electronics. Home: 18400 Shelburne Rd Shaker Heights OH 44118 Office: TRW Inc 30000 Aurora Rd Solon OH 44139

JONES, WILLIAM AUGUSTUS, JR., bishop; b. Memphis, Jan. 24, 1927; s. William Augustus and Martha (Wharton) J.; B.A., Southwestern at Memphis, 1948; B.D., Yale U., 1951; m. Margaret Loaring-Clark, Aug. 26, 1949; 4 children. Ordained priest Episcopal Ch., 1952; priest in charge Messiah Ch., Pulaski, Tenn., 1952-57; curate Christ Ch., Nashville, 1957-58; rector St. Mark Ch., LaGrange, Ga., 1958-65; assoc. rector St. Luke Ch., Mountainbrook, Ala., 1965-66; dir. research So. region Assn. Christian Tng. and Service, Memphis, 1966-67, exec. dir., 1968; rector St. John's, Johnson City, Tenn., 1972-75; bishop of Mo., St. Louis, 1975—. Office: 1210 Locust St Saint Louis MO 63103

JONES, WILLIAM MCKENDREY, English educator; b. Dothan, Ala., Sept. 19, 1927; s. William McKendrey and Margaret (Farmer) J.; m. Ruth Ann Roberts, Aug. 14, 1952; children—Margaret, Elizabeth, Bronwen. B.A., U. Ala., Tuscaloosa, 1949, M.A., 1950; Ph.D., Northwestern U., Evanston, Ill., 1953. Asst. prof. Wis. State U., Eau Claire, Wis., 1953-55; asst. prof. U. Mich., Ann Arbor, 1955-59; asst. prof. U. Mo., Columbia, 1959-61, assoc. prof., 1961-64, prof., 1964—. Communications cons. Nat. Inst. of Health, NASA, Washington, 1964-74; writer USIA, Washington, 1974—. Author: Living in Love, 1975; Two Careers— One Marriage, 1979; Survival, 1979; Protestant Romance, 1980. Served to sgt. U.S. Army, 1946-47. Presbyterian. Home: 209 Russell Blvd Columbia MO 65203 Office: Dept English U Mo Columbia MO 65211

JONES, ZENOBIA, educational counselor; b. Okmulgee, Okla., July 22, 1923; d. John and Leatchie (Brigham) White; m. Otha Jones, June 19, 1945. B.S., Eastern Mich. U., 1957, M.A., 1960, Ed.S., 1969; Ed.D., Wayne State U., 1982. Elem., spl. edn. and secondary cert., Mich. Elem. tchr. Woodson Elem. Sch., Inkster, Mich., 1957-62; remedial reading tchr. Fellrath Middle Sch. and Inkster High Sch., 1962-67; curriculum coordinator Inkster Pub. Schs., 1967-76; tutorial asst. Madonna Coll., Livonia, Mich., 1980-81; cons. Okmulgee (Okla.) Pub. Schs.; asst. mgr. Zeco's Party Store, Romulus, 1968—. IDEA fellow, summer 1975. Mem. AAUW, Assn. Supervision and Curriculum Devel., Phi Delta Kappa, Alpha Kappa Alpha. Home: 11060 Gabriel St Romulus MI 48174

JONTE, JOHN HAWORTH, chemistry educator; b. Moscow, Idaho, Oct. 21, 1918; s. John Herbert and Bada Sophia (Johnson) J.; m. Eloise Nyra, June 15, 1942; children—Barbara Ellen Jonte Boswell, Sharon Louise Jonte Page, J. Michael, Dorothy Ann. A.B., U. of Pacific, 1940; M.S., Washington State U., 1942; student Iowa State U., 1946-51; Ph.D., U. Arks., 1956. Chemist U.S. Bur. Mines, Reno, 1942-44, Shell Devel. Co., Emeryville, Calif., 1944-46; instr. Iowa State Univ.; Am Ames, 1946-51; research asst. Univ. Arks., Fayetteville, 1951-55; research chemist Texaco Inc., Bellaire, Tex., 1955-66; prof., dept. chmn. S.D. Sch. Mines & Tech., Rapid City, 1966-85. Mem. Am. Chem. Soc., AAAS, Am. Inst. Chemists. Geochemical Soc., N.Y. Acad. Sci., Alpha Chi Sigma (v.p. 1966-70, pres. 1970-72). Republican. Methodist. Lodge: Elks. Avocations: photography, backpacking. Home: 2126 Cedar Dr Rapid City SD 57702

JORDAN, CHARLES EDWIN, agricultural, pharmaceutical products company executive; b. South Charleston, Ohio, Jan. 2, 1927; s. Author Wesley and Daisy Lenor (Schreck) J.; m. Joyce Fox, Jan. 17, 1954; children—David, Pamela, Jennifer. B.S., Ohio State U., 1951; M.S., Purdue U., 1955, Ph.D., 1958. Registered profl. animal scientist. Asst. prof. Purdue U., West Lafayette, Ind., 1958-59; sr. animal scientist Eli Lilly & Co., Greenfield, Ind., 1959-65, head animal nutrition, 1965-70, dir. agr. research Lilly Research Ctr., Windlesham, Surrey, Eng., 1970-74, dir. Animal Sci. Field Research, Research Labs., Greenfield, 1975-81, exec. dir., 1981—; dir. product coordination Elanco Products Co., Indpls., 1974-75; mem. Antibiotics in Feeds Task Force Animal Health Inst., Washington, 1970-71. Patentee Cephalosporin C, Diethylstilbestrol+ testosterone. Past pres. Greenfield Planning Commn., The Bridge (community drug abuse orgn.); past chmn. Hancock County Cancer Fund Crusade, Greenfield; bd. dirs. Greenfield Revitalization, Inc. Named to Ohio State U. Dept. Animal Sci. Hall of Fame, 1975. Fellow Am. Soc. Animal Sci.; mem. AAAS, Am. Inst. Biol. Scis., Animal Nutrition Research Council. Republican. Methodist. Home: RR 1 Box 425 Greenfield IN 46140 Office: Lilly Research Labs PO Box 708 Greenfield IN 46140

JORDAN, CHARLES NATHANIEL, education consultant; b. N.Y.C., Mar. 10, 1912; s. Walter Henry and Myrtle (Muntz) J.; m. Jewel Corine, Dec. 22, 1945; 1 son, Charles N. Student Ill. State U., 1931-33; A.B., W.Va. State Coll., 1938; M.A., Western Res. U., 1950, Ed.D., 1961. Cert. supt., elem. prin., ednl. researcher. Prin. Cadiz Pub. Schs. (Ohio), 1945-47; tchr. Cleve. Pub. Schs., 1947-57, asst. prin., 1957-61, asst. chief bur. ednl. research, 1961-66, dir. major work and honors program, 1966-78; mng. ptnr. Jordan Jones Jordan, Lakewood, Ohio, 1979—; asst. prof. edn. Kent State U., 1966-69, instr., part-time 1973; vis. lectr. Cleve. State U., 1969, John Carroll U., 1970, 72, 75, 76, Case-Western Res. U., 1970, Notre Dame Coll., 1977; cons. State of Ohio, 1967, Baldwin-Wallace Coll., 1969, U.S. Office Edn., Washington, 1972-80, Ohio Dept. Edn., 1966-78, Ohio Assn. for Gifted, 1960-80, Council for Exceptional Children, Reston, Va., 1972-80; mem. project staff on sch. orgn. Ohio Bd. Edn.; chmn. adv. council Ohio Dept. Edn. ESEA Title IV; speaker and presenter various ednl. confs. Author monographs in field. Contbr. to book Gifted Case Studies, 1972. Contbr. report to Congress on education of gifted, 1972. Bd. mgrs. Cleve. YMCA, 1960-64; bd. dirs. Forest City Hosp., Cleve., 1960-65, Karamu House, Council Human Relations, Cleve. Hearing and Speech Ctr., Health and Rehab. Rev. and Allocation Com., Welfare Fedn. of Cleve., Seattle Country Day Sch. pres. Friends of Cleve. Pub. Library, 1983-85; trustee Ohio Conf. United Ch. of Christ. Served to lt. col. Q.M.C., U.S. Army, 1942-45, ETO. Recipient Alumnus of Yr. award W.Va. State Coll. Alumni Assn., 1973. Mem. Ohio Assn. Gifted Children (pres. 1969, Disting. Educator Hall of Fame award 1972), Assn. Supervision and Curriculum Devel., Am. Ednl. Research Assn., Nat. Council Measurement in Edn., Phi Delta Kappa (past pres. Greater Cleve. Univ. chpt., Disting. Service award 1978). Home: 12900 Lake Ave Suite 609 Lakewood OH 44107

JORDAN, DAVID CHARLES, statistician; b. Batesville, In., June 3, 1950; s. Elmer Fred and Melba Regina (Steuver) J.; m. Mary Anna Kaiser, June 5, 1971; children—Barbara, Julie, Jennifer. B.S. in Math., Rose-Hulman Inst. Tech., Terre Haute, In., 1971; M.S. in Statistics, U. Ky., 1974, Ph.D. in Stats., 1977. Sci. programmer Mead Johnson, Evansville, Ind., 1971-73, statistician, 1977-80, mgr. clin. stats. and data services 1981-82; sect. head clin. stats. Abbott Labs., North Chicago, Ill., 1983—. Contbr. articles to profl. publs. Fellow U. Ky. Grad. Sch., 1973-76. Mem. Am. Statis. Assn., Biometric Soc., Soc. Clin. Trials, Sigma Xi. Club: Triangle (nat. council 1981-83, nat. v.p. 1984—). Home: 916 Fairlawn Libertyville IL 60048 Office: Abbott Labs Dept 432/AP9A-2 North Chicago IL 60064

JORDAN, DENVER CHRISTIAN, lawyer; b. Indpls., Oct. 14, 1953; s. Denver Cecil Rhodes and Emily Christine (Sorhage) J.; m. Marsha Ann Shaffer, Oct. 29, 1983. B.S. in Bus., Purdue U., 1976, B.A. in Am. History, 1976, M.S.I.A., Krannert Sch., 1977; J.D., Ind. U., 1980. Bar: Ind. 1980, U.S. Dist. Ct. (no. and so. dists.) Ind. 1980, U.S. Ct. Appeals (7th cir.) 1983. Adminstrv. asst. Ind. U., Bloomington, 1978-80; assoc. Raver & Assocs., Fort Wayne, Ind., 1980-84; ptnr. Raver, Jordan & Assocs., Fort Wayne, 1985—; TV show host; lectr. in field. Pres. Directors, Fort Wayne, 1980-84. Mem. ABA, Assn. Trial Lawyers Am., Allen County Bar Assn. (dir. Speaker's Bur.). Club: U.S. Power Squadron. Lodges: Lions (sec. 1982-84), Masons. Home: 2734 Westmore Dr Fort Wayne IN 46825 Office: Raver Jordan & Assocs 520 S Calhoun St Fort Wayne IN 46802

JORDAN, DIANA, education educator; b. Altadena, Calif., Feb. 24, 1940; d. Roy R. and Nola (LaVern) J. B.A., Cornell Coll., 1961; M.S. in Math Edn., Syracuse U., 1962; PhD. in Tchr. Edn. and Ednl. Psychology, Wayne State U., 1969; postgrad. Cleve. State U., 1978-79, cert. in indsl. relations. Instr. math. and sci. edn. Iowa State U., Ames, 1966-67; instr. tchr. edn. Wayne State U., Detroit, 1967-69; asst. prof. tchr. edn. U. Mo.-St. Louis, 1969-70; asst. prof. tchr. edn., dir. Research and Demonstration Ctr., SUNY-Potsdam, 1974-76; asst. prof. math. edn. Cleve. State U., 1970-71, assoc. prof., 1976—, chmn. dept. specialized instrnl. programs, 1976-81, chmn. dept. infant and early childhood edn., 1970-71; prin. East Lansing (Mich.) Pub. Schs., 1971-74. Mem AAUW (corp. rep.), Nat. Council Accreditation Tchr. Edn. (asst. chmn.), Assn. Supervision and Curriculum Devel., Assn. Tchrs. Edn., Nat. Council Tchrs. Math., Nat. Soc. Study Edn., Ohio Assn. Tchr. Educators (life). Contbr. articles to profl. jours. Office: Rhodes Tower 1336 Cleveland State U Cleveland OH 44115

JORDAN, FRANK ROBERT, army officer; b. Warren, Pa., July 15, 1949; s. Glenn Ray and Dorothy Rachel (Graziano) J.; m. Denise Marie Yezzi, Sept. 4, 1976; 1 child, Christopher Lawrence. B.S., Gannon U., 1972; M.A., Webster U., 1985; postgrad. Armed Forces Staff Coll., Norfolk, Va., 1985—. Commd. 2d lt. U.S. Army, 1972, advanced through grades to maj., 1984; instr. U.S. Army Field Artillery Sch., Fort Sill, Okla., 1979-82; chem. br. adviser U.S. Army Readiness Group, St. Louis, 1982-85. Decorated 2 Army Commendation medals, 2 Meritorious Service medals. Mem. Assn. Chem. Officers. Roman Catholic. Avocations: amateur ornithology and philately.

JORDAN, JAMES FRANCIS, nutritional supplement merchant; b. Lima, Ohio, Nov. 5, 1917; s. William Edward and Cora Marie (Griggs) J.; m. Norma Marie Glick, Dec. 26, 1942; 1 son, James Lan. Owner, mgr. Jordan's, Lima, Ohio, 1958—. Mem., St. Rita's Hosp. Mercy Club. Served with AUS, 1942-46. Mem. Lima Better Bus. Bur., Lima C. of C., Greater Downtown Assocs. Republican. Roman Catholic. Home: 552 W O'Connor Ave Lima OH 45801

JORDAN, JESSIE MAE, educator; b. Leadwood, Mo., May 25, 1921; d. Thomas and Dora J.; B.S. in Elem. Edn., U. Mo., Columbia, 1948, M.Ed. in Spl. Edn. and Reading, 1956; postgrad. in learning disabilities Fontbonne Coll., St. Louis. Tchr. grade 3 Leadwood (Mo.) Sch. R-IV, 1944-52; tchr. spl. edn. Leadwood Sch., 1952-71; reading specialist West County RIV Public Schs., 1971—; speaker in field. Active, East Side Ch. of God. Mem. St. Francois County, Mo. State tchrs. assn., Council Exceptional Children (nat., local-mem. chmn.), Internat. Reading Assn. (past pres. Mineral area chpt., mem. research com., treas. 1981-82, 83-84). Specialist in spl. edn., educable mentally retarded, home-bound cerebral palsy, emotionally disturbed, reading specialist. Home: 205 E 9th St Leadwood MO 63653 Office: West County RIV Public Schs 1124 Main St Leadwood MO 63653

JORDAN, JIM, association executive; b. Muskogee, Okla., Aug. 29, 1926; s. Tom M. and Ruby M. (Stapleton) J.; m. Betty Lloyd, Nov. 22, 1946; 1 child, James D. Cert. chamber exec., indsl. developer, Mich. Mgr. Agrl.-Area Devel., Muskogee, 1956-62; gen. mgr. C. of C., Muskogee, Okla., 1962-67; v.p. econ. devel. Buffalo Area C. of C., 1967-79; proprietor Jordan Transport Service, Buffalo, 1979-81; exec. v.p. Lansing Regional C. of C., Mich., 1981—. Served with USNR, 1944-46, 1950-52. Mem. Am. C. of C. Execs. Assn., Am. Econ. Devel. Council. Home: 980 Touraine Ave East Lansing MI 48823 Office: 510 W Washtenaw PO Box 14030 Lansing MI 48901

JORDAN, JOHN R., JR., accountant; b. Houston, Jan. 7, 1939; m. Anne Jordan; children—John Jennifer, Stephanie, Anne-Marie, Suzanne. B.A. with highest honors, U. Tex.-Austin, 1961; M.B.A. with high distinction, Harvard Bus. Sch., 1963. With Price Waterhouse, St. Louis, mng. ptnr., mem. policy bd. and ptnr. admissions com. Contbr. articles to profl. jours. Trustee Barnes Hosp., St. Louis; bd. dirs. Washington U. Med. Ctr., Cath. Charities, Archdiocese of St. Louis; vice chmn. bd. dirs. Jr. Achievement of Miss. Valley, YMCA of Met. St. Louis; mem. acctg. adv. council U. Tex.-Austin; exec. bd. St. Louis Area council Boy Scouts Am.; fin. com. St. Joseph's Acad.; bd. dirs., treas. Arts and Edn. Council. Mem. Mo. Soc. C.P.A.s, Am. Inst. C.P.A.s, Phi Beta Kappa, Beta Gamma Sigma. Clubs: Bogey, Noonday, Old Warson Country, St. Louis, Harvard Bus. Sch. Avocations: golf; tennis; jogging; photography; reading. Address: Price Waterhouse One Centerre Plaza Saint Louis MO 63101

JORDAN, JOSEPH PATRICK, JR., box company executive, lawyer; b. Buffalo, June 21, 1937; s. Joseph Patrick, Sr. and Helen (Mahoney) J.; m. Sheila Mary O'Loughlin, Aug. 19, 1961; children—Jennifer, Julie, Jodi, Melissa, Michelle. B.S., Xavier U., 1959; J.D., Marquette U., 1962. Bar: Ohio, Wis., U.S. Dist. Ct. (no. dist.) Ohio, U.S. Dist. (ea. dist.) Wis., U.S. Ct. Appeals (6th cir.). Asst. law dir. City of Toledo, Ohio, 1965-81; assoc. Jordan, Warrick & Disalle, Toledo, 1972-82; pres. Gen. Box Co., Toledo, 1982—. Thomas Moore scholar Marquette U., 1959-62. Mem. ABA, Ohio Bar Assn., Toledo Bar Assn., Lucas County Bar Assn. Republican. Roman Catholic. Clubs: Sylvania Country (Ohio) (v.p.), Toledo. Avocation: athletics. Home: 5235 Carlingfort Dr Toledo OH 43623 Office: Gen Box Co 5656 Opportunity Toledo OH 43623

JORDAN, LLOYD JEROME, lawyer; b. Chgo., July 25, 1955; s. Arthur Livingston and Dorothy (Morton) J. B.S. in Computer Engring. and Applied Math., Washington U., St. Louis, 1977; J.D., St. Louis U., 1981. Bar: Mo. 1981, U.S. Dist. Ct. Mo. 1981, U.S. Ct. Appeals (8th cir.) 1981, Ill. 1982, U.S. Supreme Ct. 1984. Ptnr., Bussey and Jordan, St. Louis, 1981—; Bd. dirs. St. Louis Vocat. Counseling and Rehab., St. Louis, Wesley House, St. Louis. Mem. ABA, St. Louis Bar Assn., Mound City Bar Assn., Assn. Trial Lawyers Am., Omega Psi Phi (bd. dirs. 1976-82, Outstanding Service award 1984, Man of Yr. award 1977). Office: Bussey and Jordan 721 Olive Suite 515 Saint Louis MO 63101

JORDAN, PHILIP HARDING, JR., college president; b. N.Y.C., June 2, 1931; B.A. in Philosophy summa cum laude, Princeton U., 1954; M.A. in History (Univ. fellow), Yale U., 1956, Ph.D. in History (Conn. Soc. Colonial Dames fellow), 1962; m. Sheila Anne Gray; children—Philip Harding, III, John, II. Asst. in instrn. Yale U., 1956-57, 58-59; instr. in history Conn. Coll., 1959-63, asst. prof. history, 1963-67, asso. prof., 1967-73, prof., 1973-75, asso. dean acad. affairs, 1968-69, dean of faculty, 1969-74; pres. Kenyon Coll., 1975—; mem. governing bd. Conn. Faculty Talent Search for recruitment of black faculty into Conn. colls. and univs., 1970-75; mem. regional adv. council Mohegan Community Coll., 1974-75; mem. faculty cons. examiners, com. on asso. degree Conn. Bd. State Acad. Awards, 1974-75; mem. Ohio Com. Public Programs in Humanities, 1977-79; dir. First-Knox Nat. Bank, Mt. Vernon, Ohio. Trustee Williams Sch., New London, Conn., 1971-75, Pine Point Sch., Stonington, Conn., 1973-75, Rutherford B. Hayes and Lucy Webb Hayes Found., 1977—, Lawrenceville Sch., 1979—; bd. dirs. Am. Council Edn., 1982—1984-85, chmn., 1985-86. Recipient Class of 1869 prize in ethics Princeton U., 1954, Salgo-Noren prize Conn. Coll., 1965. Mem. AAUP (ad hoc com. to investigate acad. freedom and tenure at Tufts U. 1964-65), Assn. Ind. Colls. and Univs. Ohio (vice chmn. 1977-79, dir. 1975—, chmn. 1980-82), Ohio Coll. Assn. (exec. com.), Phi Beta Kappa. Author: Student Guide to Accompany John A. Garraty's The American Nation, 1966; (with Patrick J. Abbazia) Instructor's Manual to Accompany John A. Garraty's The American Nation, 1966. Office: Office of Pres Kenyon Coll Gambier OH 43022

JORDAN, ROBERT MANSCAU, animal science educator; b. Mpls., Feb. 13, 1920; s. Philip S. and Imadee M. (Fraiken) J.; m. Harriet Frances Granger, Dec. 31, 1942 (div. 1974); children—Barbara Dee, Robert M. Jr., Susan Scobel Davies; m. Ann Whitfield Summers, June 8, 1974. B.S., U. Minn., 1942; M.S., S.D. State U., 1949; Ph.D., Kans. State U., 1953. Instr., U. Minn., Grand Rapids, 1942-44; salesman Lyon Chem. Co., St. Paul, 1944-47; asst. prof. S.D. State U., Brookings, 1947-54; prof. animal sci. dept. U. Minn., St. Paul, 1954—. Author: Nutrient Requirements of Horses, 1978; Nutrient Requirements of Sheep, 1985; also bulls., book chpts., sci. and popular articles on sheep and horse prodn. and nutrition. Named Hon. State Farmer, Minn. Future Farmers Am., 1965; recipient Pipestone award Pipestone Sheep Project, Minn., 1975, Silver Bell award Minn. Sheep and Lamb Producing Assn., 1983; R.E. Jacobs award U. Minn., St. Paul, 1983. Fellow Am. Soc. Animal Sci (Animal Mgmt. award 1983); mem. Ramsey County Hist. Soc. (pres. 1963), Sigma Xi. Avocations: fishing; gardening. Home: 7143 Manning Ave N Stillwater MN 55108 Office: Univ Minn Dept Animal Sci 120 Peters Hall 1404 Gortner Ave Saint Paul MN 55108

JORDAN, SHARON ANN, clinical social worker, child and family psychotherapist; b. Detroit, July 22, 1953; d. Benneal and Myrtice Marie J., A.B. in Journalism, U. Mich., 1975, M.Urban Planning, 1977, M.S.W., 1979. Intern, research asst. City of Ann Arbor (Mich.), 1976-77; caseworker asst. Ann Arbor Community Center, 1977-78; caseworker aide ARC, 1978-79; parent orientation coordinator U. Mich., 1978, resident dir. housing, 1975-79; adminstrv. intern City of Ann Arbor, 1979; social worker, counselor, staff devel. coordinator U. Mich. opportunity program, 1979-84; clin. social worker U. Mich. Children's Psychiat. Hosp., 1984—. U. Mich. fellow, 1976-77. Mem. Nat. Assn. Social Workers (sec. Huron Valley chpt.), Acad. Cert. Social Workers, Phi Beta Kappa. Home: 300 N Ingalls Box 50 Ann Arbor MI 48109 Office: 300 N Ingalls St Box 50 Ann Arbor MI 48109

JORDAN, THURMAN, manufacturing company executive; b. Harrisburg, Ill., Dec. 2, 1936; s. Joseph and Lutishia (Threadgill) J.; m. Teiko Ann Ijichi, Jan. 26, 1963; children—Eric Ichiro, Neal Kiyohiko, Philip Takashi. B.S.B.A., Roosevelt U., Chgo., 1966; M.B.A., U. Chgo., 1982. C.P.A., Ill. Audit mgr. Arthur Andersen & Co., Chgo., 1966-77; corp. controller Signode Corp., Glenview, Ill., 1977-82; v.p., corp. controller Signode Industries, Inc., Glenview, 1982—. Bd. dirs. Evanston United Way, 1978-84, United Way of Suburban Chgo., 1982—, Evanston Art Ctr.; trustee Earn and Learn. Served with Army N.G., 1961-62. Recipient Black Achiever award YMCA, 1977. Mem. United Ch. of Christ. Club: Executive (Chgo.). Office: 3600 W Lake Ave Glenview IL 60025

JORDAN, WILLIAM LEE, college administrator; b. Iroquois, S.D., Sept. 20, 1931; s. William Laverne and Imogene Alpha (Stoner) J.; m. Barbara Averill Boettcher, Oct. 24, 1954; children—Kirk, Kelly, Craig. B.S., No. State Coll., Aberdeen, S.D., 1954, M.S., 1958; Ph.D., U. Minn., 1965. chmn. div. phys. edn. Black Hills State Coll., Spearfish, S.D., 1967—; 2d v.p. Nat. Assn. Intercollegiate Athletics, Kansas City, Mo., 1984—. Served to 1st lt. USMC, 1954-56. Named to Hall of Fame, No. State U., 1980, S.D. Intercollegiate Conf., 1982. Mem. AAHPERD. Avocations: golf; golf club repair. Home: 711 10th Spearfish SD 57783 Office: Black Hills State Coll 1200 University Spearfish SD 57783

JORDAN, ZEMA LOUISE, educational administrator; b. Huntsville, Ala.; d. Willie Davey and Hattie (Jobe) Jordan; B.A., Tenn. A&I State U., 1953; M.Ed., Wayne State U., 1963, now doctoral candidate. Instr. English, Liberty (Miss.) High Sch., 1953-54; instr. English, part-time guidance counselor Wilson Jr. High Sch., Florence, S.C., 1954-64; instr. English, Hutchins Jr. High and Southwestern High Sch., Detroit, 1964-68; head English dept. Farwell Jr. High Sch., Detroit, 1968-75; instr. English, Wayne County Community Coll., Detroit, part-time, 1969—; adminstrv. unit head Richard Middle Sch., Detroit, 1976-77, Von Steuben Middle Sch., Detroit, 1977—; curriculum cons. Profl. Growth Center, Detroit Pub. Schs., Wayne State Univ., 1980—. Mem. Adult Great Books Discussion Group, Detroit, 1965-81, vol. leader Jr. Great Books Discussion Group, 1983—. Mem. Orgn. Sch. Adminstrs. and Suprs., Met. Detroit Alliance Black Sch. Educators, Nat. Alliance Black Sch. Educators, TESOL, Nat. Council Tchrs. English, Mich. Council Tchrs. English, Met. Detroit Reading Council, NAACP, Internat. Platform Assn., Delta Sigma Theta, Pi Lambda Theta. Methodist. Contbr. articles to profl. jours. Office: Von Steuben Middle Sch 12300 Linnhurst St Detroit MI 48205

JORGENS, THOMAS PHILLIP, regional planner; b. Bertha, Minn., July 14, 1947; s. Joseph Anthony and Anna Marie (Fjeld) J.; B.A., U. Minn., 1969, M.A., 1971; m. Michal Kulenkamp, June 13, 1970; children—Gwendolyn Anna, Amber Blythe. Instr. econs. and history U. Minn., Mpls., 1970-73, researcher, 1974-75; planning dir. Upper Minn. Valley Regional Devel. Commn., Appleton, 1975-79; exec. dir. N.W. Regional Devel. Commn., Crookston, Minn., 1979—; exec. vice chmn. Minn. Assn. Regional Commns., 1982-83; mem. Intergovtl. Info. Systems Adv. Council, 1980-83. Bd. dirs. Appleton Cultural Affairs Com., 1976-79; chair policy com. Internat. Coalition, 1984-85. McMillan fellow, 1972-73. Mem. Am. Planning Assn., Minn. Planning Assn., Soil Conservation Soc. Am., Minn. Waterfowl Assn., Phi Alpha Theta. Clubs: Lions, Ducks Unltd. (chpt. dir. 1980-84, chair 1985). Author: The Fiscal Impact of Federal and State Waterfowl Production Areas on Local Units of Government in West Central Minnesota, 1979. Home: 309 Leonard Ave Crookston MN 56716 Office: 425 Woodland Ave Crookston MN 56716

JORGENSEN, GERALD THOMAS, psychologist, educator; b. Mason City, Iowa, Jan. 15, 1947; s. Harry Grover and Mary Jo (Kollasch) J.; m. Mary Ann Reiter, Aug. 30, 1969; children—Amy Lynn, Sarah Kay, Jill Kathryn. B.A., Loras Coll., Dubuque, 1969; M.S., Colo. State U., Ft. Collins, 1970, Ph.D., 1973. Lic. psychologist, Iowa. Psychology intern Counseling Ctr., Colo. State U., Ft. Collins, 1971-72, VA Hosp., Palo Alto, Calif., 1927-73; psychologist Loras Coll., 1973-76, Clarke Coll., Dubuque, 1973-76; asst. prof. psychology, Loras Coll., 1976-80, assoc. prof., 1981—, dir. Ctr. for Counseling and Student Devel., 1977—; cons. and supervising psychologist Dubuque/Jackson County Med. Health Ctr., 1975—; chairperson Iowa Bd. Psychology Examiners, Des Moines, 1984—, continuing edn. coordinator, 1981. Contbr. articles to profl. jours. Treas. Dubuque County Assn. Mental Health Inc., Dubuque, 1975-82. NDEA fellow, 1969. Mem. Am. Coll. Personnel Assn. (chmn. com. VII 1980-82), Am. Assn. Counseling Devel., Am. Psychol. Assn., Iowa Psychol. Assn. (mem. exec. council), Iowa Student Personnel Assn., Delta Epsilon Sigma, Phi Kappa Phi, Sigma Tau Phi. Democrat. Roman Catholic. Home: 2183 Saint Celia St Dubuque IA 52001 Office: Loras Coll 1450 Alta Vista St Dubuque IA 52004-0178

JORGENSEN, RONALD ALAN, banker; b. Sioux City, Iowa, May 17, 1957; s. Kenneth Warren and Ruth (Mjoen) J.; m. Kathryn Ann Ricke, May 9, 1981. B.S. in Bus. Adminstrn., Morningside Coll., Sioux City, 1979. Staff acct. First Nat. Bank, Sioux City, 1979-82, acctg. officer, 1982-84, auditor, 1984-85, controller, 1985—. Treas., bd. dirs. March of Dimes, Sioux City, 1981-83.

Mem. Nat. Assn. Accts. (chpt. v.p. 1983-84), Am. Inst. Banking (chpt. pres. 1984—), Jaycees. Republican. Lutheran. Avocations: reading, golf. Home: 3000 S Cypress St Sioux City IA 51106 Office: First Nat Bank 501 Pierce St Sioux City IA 51101

JORGENSON, DALE ALFRED, music educator, arts administrator, minister; b. Litchfield, Nebr., Mar. 20, 1926; s. Alfred E. and Laura Irene (Thickett) J.; m. Mary Lee Strawn, May 29, 1947; children—Dale A. Jr., Rebecca Lee, Mark Steven, Janet Irene, Eric Leon. B.A. in Music, Harding Coll., 1948; M.A. in Music, Geo. Peabody Coll., 1950; Ph.D., Ind. U., 1957; cert. arts adminstrn., Harvard, 1972. Instr. Southeastern Christian Coll., Winchester, Ky., 1950-54, 1956-58; asst. prof. music Tex. Women's Univ., Denton, 1958-59; head dept. music Bethany Coll., W. Va., 1959-62; dir. fine arts Milligan Coll., Tenn., 1962-63; head div. fine arts N.E. Mo. State U., Kirksville, Mo., 1963—; summer tchr. Dartington Sch. Arts, Devonshire, Eng., 1976, Opera Workshop, Oglebay Park, Wheeling, W. Va., 1962, 63. Author: Christianity & Humanism, 1983. Contbr. articles to profl. jours. Served to sgt. USAAF, 1944-46, PTO. Mem. Music Educators Nat. Conf., Internat. Council Fine Arts Deans, Nat. Assn. Schs. Music (bd. dirs. 1978-81), Am. Musicol. Soc. (chmn. Allegheny chpt. 1961-62). Republican. Mem. Christian Ch. Home: 1512 S Cottage Grove Kirksville MO 63501 Office: Northeast Mo State U Head Div Fine Arts Kirksville MO 63501

JORND, RONALD WAYNE, police chief; b. Chgo., Dec. 7, 1942; s. Russell M. and Francis (Pincin) J.; m. Rita Mae Moore, Feb. 8, 1964; 1 child, Tammy Rae. B.S. in Bus. Adminstrn., Franklin U., 1972; M.Edn., Ohio State U., 1980. Patrolman, U. Ohio State U. Police, Columbus, 1966-76; asst. chief U. Houston Police, 1976-78; instr. mgmt. Ohio Peace Officer Acad., London, 1978-83; chief Minerva Police Dept., Ohio, 1983—; mem. council Ohio Peace Officer Tng., London, 1983—, chmn., 1984—; dir. Stark County Crime Prevention, Canton, Ohio, 1984—. Contbr. articles to profl. jours. Served with USAF, 1962-66, Korea. Recipient Stark County Highway Safety award Ohio Highway Safety, Canton, 1983. Mem. Internat. Assn. Chiefs Police, Ohio Assn. Chiefs Police, Stark County Police Chiefs Assn. Lodge: Mason (degree staff 1975). Office: Minerva Div Police 209 N Market St Minerva OH 44657

JOSCELYN, KENT BUCKLEY, research scientist, lawyer; b. Binghamton, N.Y., Dec. 18, 1936; s. Raymond Miles and Gwen Buckley (Smith) J.; B.S., Union Coll., 1957; J.D., Albany Law Sch., 1960; m. Mary A. Komoroske, Nov. 20, 1965; children—Kathryn Anne, Jennifer Sheldon. Bar: N.Y. 1961, U.S. Ct. Mil. Appeals 1962, D.C. 1967, Mich. 1979. Atty., adviser Hdqrs. USAF, Washington, 1965-67; asso. prof. forensic studies Coll. Arts and Scis., Ind. U., Bloomington, 1967-76, dir. Inst. Research in Pub. Safety, 1970-75; head policy analysis div. Hwy. Safety Research Inst., U. Mich., 1976-81, dir. transp. planning and policy, Urban Tech., Environ. Planning Program, 1981-84; partner firm Joscelyn & Treat, P.C., 1981—; cons. Law Enforcement Assistance Adminstrn., U.S. Dept. Justice, 1969-72; Gov.'s appointee as regional dir. Ind. Criminal Justice Planning Agy., also vice chmn. Ind. Organized Crime Prevention Council, 1969-72; commr. pub. safety City of Bloomington, 1974-76. Served to capt., USAF, 1961-64. Mem. Transp. Research Bd. (chmn. motor vehicle and traffic law com. 1979-82), Nat. Acad. Sci., NRC, Am. Soc. Criminology, AAAS, Soc. Automotive Engrs., Am. Soc. Pub. Adminstrn., Acad. Criminal Justice Scis., ABA, D.C., Mich., N.Y. State bar assns., Internat. Assn. Chiefs Police (asso.), Nat. Safety Council, Sigma Xi. Editor Internat. Jour. Criminal Justice. Office: 325 E Eisenhower Pkwy Ann Arbor MI 48104

JOSE, PHYLLIS ANN, librarian; b. Detroit, Mar. 15, 1949; d. William Henry and Isobel Eleanor (Mundle) J.; B.A., Mich. State U., 1971, M.A., 1972; M.A. in Library Sci., U. Mich., 1975. Library aide audio-visual div. Dearborn (Mich.) Dept. Libraries, 1973-76, librarian gen. info. div., 1976-77; reference library dir. Oakland County (Mich.) Library, 1977—. Officer Southfield Economic Devel. Corp., 1980—; mem. Southfield Tax Increment Fin. Authority, 1981—; bd. dirs. Southfield Arts Council, 1983—, Poetry Resource Ctr. Mich., 1983—; coordinator Southfield Arts Festival, 1984, 85. Mem. ALA, Mich. Library Assn., Spl. Library Assn., LWV Southfield, Lathrup Village and Oak Park. Presbyterian. Office: 1200 N Telegraph Rd Pontiac MI 48053

JOSEPH, EARL CLARK, futurist; b. St. Paul, Nov. 1, 1926; s. Clark Herbert and Ida Bertha (Schultz) J.; A.A., U. Minn., 1947, B.A., 1951; m. Alma Caroline Bennett, Nov. 19, 1955; children—Alma (Mrs. Richard Chadner), Earl, Vincent, René. Mathematician/programmer Remington Rand Univac, Arlington, Va., 1951-55, supr., St. Paul, 1955-60, systems mgr. Sperry Univac, St. Paul, 1960-63, staff scientist-futurist, 1963-82; pres. Anticipatory Scis., Inc., 1981—; scholar Scholar Leadership Enrichment Program, Okla. U., 1984; vis. lectr. U. Minn., Mpls., 1971—; mem. Sci. and Mgmt. Adv. Com., U.S. Army, 1972-74. Futurist-in-residence Sci. Mus. of Minn., 1973-82; chmn. bd. Future Systems, 1979-81. Chmn., Met. Young Adult Ministry, 1967-69; mem. Gov.'s Planning Commn. for City Center Learning, 1968. Served with USNR, 1944-46. Disting. lectr. IEEE Computer Soc., 1971-72, 76-82, Assn. Computer Machinery. Mem. IEEE (sr.), Minn. Futurists (founder, dir., past pres.), World Future Soc., Soc. for Gen. Systems Research, Assn. Computer Machinery (gen. chmn. 1975, pres. chpt. 1976-77), AAAS, Data Processing Mgmt. Assn., Beta Phi Beta. Patents, publs. in field; co-author 50 books; founding editor jour. Futurics; editor Future Trends Newsletter, System Trends Newsletter; adv. editor Jour. Cultural and Ednl. Futures. Home: 365 Summit Ave St Paul MN 55102 Office: ASI/Wesley Bldg Suite 702 123 E Grant St Minneapolis MN 55403

JOSEPH, LESTER MARK, lawyer; b. Chgo., May 8, 1950; s. Paul Arthur and Irene (Tichauer) J.; m. Sarah Ann Rockwell, May 23, 1980. B.A., U. Mich., 1971; J.D., John Marshall Law Sch., 1980. Bar: Ill. 1980. Asst. state's atty. Cook County State's Atty.'s Office, Chgo., 1981-84; trial atty. U.S. Dept. Justice, Washington, 1984—. Mem. ABA.

JOSEPH, MONICA ANNA BILCHECK, music educator; b. Orient, Pa., Sept. 3, 1926; d. John and Mary Elizabeth (Blachak) B.; m. Jamele E. Joseph, Aug. 18, 1973. B.Music, Marywood Coll., Scranton, Pa., 1966; M.Music, DePaul U., Chgo., 1970. Tchr. pvt. schs., Trenton, N.J., 1948-50, 56-58, Scranton, Pa., 1950-53, Gary, Ind., 1953-55; adminstr. St. Mary's Sch., Freeland, Pa., 1960-63, Holy Ghost Sch., Jessup, Pa., 1963-66, St. Michael's Sch., Gary, Ind., 1958-60, 66-69; music supr. parochial schs. Diocese Gary, 1969-72; tchr. pub. schs. Waterford and Westwood Heights, Mich., 1972-75; asst. prof. class piano C.S. Mott Community Coll., Flint, Mich., 1975—; pvt. piano tchr. Flint. Monterrey (Mex.) Inst. Tech. Fulbright-Hays grantee, 1970. Mem. Nat. Music Tchrs. Assn., Mich. Music Tchrs. Assn., Flint Music Tchrs. Assn. (pres. 1978-80, Tchr. of Yr. 1981-82), Nat. Fedn. Music, NEA. Roman Catholic. Clubs: St. Cecilia Soc., Altrusa (pres. 1981-85). Home: 6989 Wedgewood Dr Grand Blanc MI 48539 Office: 1025 E Kearsley St Flint MI 48502

JOSEPH-FELDMAN, DIANE, appraiser; b. Chgo., May 21, 1933; d. Wilfried Elmer and Rose (Kopca) Davis; ed. Am. Acad. Art, Art Inst. Chgo., Stone-Camryn Sch. Ballet; m. Z. Albert Joseph, 1957 (div. 1969); m. Hy Feldman, Feb. 14, 1979; children—Diana Jill Joseph, John Alan Joseph. Soloist, tchr. ballet Interlochen (Mich.) Nat. Music Camp, 1954-55; soloist in Brigadoon, N.Y.C. Center, 1956, My Fair Lady, other musicals; dancer WGN-TV and Lyric Opera Ballet, Chgo., 1955-58; founder, pres. Heritage Appraisal Service, Inc., Wilmette, Ill., 1971-82. Vol., Hospice of North Shore, Cancer Care Ctr. of Evanston Hosp., Y-Me Breast Cancer Support Group, Planned Parenthood. Mem. Simon Wiesenthal Center, Democratic Nat. Orgn. Mem. Internat. Soc. Appraisers (rec. and corr. sec. Chgo. chpt.), New Eng. Appraisers Assn., ACLU, NOW, Audubon Soc. Address: 2201 Crestview Ln Wilmette IL 60091

JOSEPHS, SHELDON B., hospital administrator; b. Buffalo, Apr. 10, 1957; s. Edward and Edith (Scharf) J.; m. Diane Joan Josephs, May 30, 1982. B.S. in Mgmt. Sci., SUNY-Binghamton, 1978; M.Health Services Adminstrn., Ariz. State U., 1981. Coordinator info. systems Nassau County Med. Ctr., E. Meadow, N.Y., 1981-82; adminstrv. asst. Mt. Sinai Med. Ctr., Cleve., 1982-84, asst. v.p., 1985—. Mem. Am. Coll. Hosp. Adminstrs., Am. Hosp. Assn., Health Care Adminstrs. Assn. N.E. Ohio. Office: Mt Sinai Med Ctr University Circle Cleveland OH 44106

JOSEPHSON, KENNETH, photographer; b. Detroit, July 1, 1932; m. Carol Compeau, 1954 (dec. 1958); m. Sherrill Petro, 1960 (div. 1972); m. Sally Garen, 1973 (div. 1978); children—Matthew (dec. 1980), Bradley, Anissa. B.F.A., Rochester Inst. Tech., 1957; M.S., Inst. Design, Ill. Inst. Tech., 1960. Photographer, Chrysler Corp., Detroit, 1957-58; free-lance photographer, Chgo., 1958—; one-man shows: Konstfackskolan, Stockholm, 1966, Visual Studies Workshop, Rochester, N.Y., 1971, Art. Inst. Chgo., 1971, 291 Gallery, Milan, 1974, U. Iowa, Iowa City, 1974, Cameraworks Gallery, Los Angeles, 1976, Galerie die Brucke, Vienna, 1976, Barat Coll., Lake Forest, Ill., 1977, So. Ill. U., Carbondale, Fotoforum der Gesamthoschschule, Kassel, W.Ger., P.P.S. Gallery, Hamburg, W.Ger., Photographer's Gallery, London, Open Eye Gallery, Liverpool, Eng., 1979, Young Hoffman Gallery, Chgo., 1981, Delpire Galerie, Paris, 1981, Orange Coast Coll., Costa Mesa, Calif., 1982, Baker Gallery, Kansas City, Kans., 1984, Vision Gallery, Boston, 1983, The Friends of Photography, Carmel, Calif., 1984; retrospective exhbn. Mus. Contemporary Art, Chgo., 1983; numerous group shows include: The Photographer's Eye, Mus. Modern Art, N.Y.C., 1964, 78, Nat. Gallery Can., Ottawa, Ont., 1967, Parcheggio Villa Borghese, Rome, 1973, Mus. Contemporary Art, Chgo., 1977, Kunsthaus, Zurich, Switzerland, 1977, R.I. Sch. Design, Providence, Moderna Museet, Stockholm, Art Inst. Chgo., 1979, Light Gallery, N.Y.C., 1980; represented in permament collections: Mus. Modern Art, Joseph E. Seagram and Sons, N.Y.C., Internat. Mus. Photography, George Eastman House, Rochester, N.Y., Mus. Fine Arts, Boston, R.I. Sch. Design, Art Inst. Chgo., Mus. Fine Arts Houston, U. N.Mex., Albuquerque, Ctr. Creative Photography, U. Ariz., Tucson, UCLA, Bibliothèque Nationale, Paris; books include: The Bread Book, 1973; Portfolio: Kenneth Josephson (with introduction by Alex Sweetman), 1975; Underware, 1976; Kenneth Josephson, postcard portfolio Fotofolio, N.Y., 1980, Mus. of Contemporary Art, Chgo, 1983; prof. Sch. Art Inst. Chgo., 1961—; exchange tchr. Konstfackskolan, Stockholm, 1966-67; asso. prof. U. Hawaii, Honolulu, 1967-68; vis. prof. Inst. Design, Ill. Inst. Tech., 1969, R.I. Sch. Design, 1973, U. Minn., Mpls., 1974, Tyler Sch. Art, Temple U., Phila., 1975. Served with U.S. Army, 1953-55. Guggenheim fellow, 1972; Nat. Endowment Arts grantee, 1975, 79; Ruttenberg Arts Found. grantee, 1983. Office: Sch Art Inst Chicago Columbus Dr and Jackson Blvd Chicago IL 60603

JOURDIAN, GEORGE WILLIAM, biological chemistry educator; b. Northampton, Mass., Apr. 21, 1929; s. Charles Loomis and Florence (Brooks) J.; m. Joan Kettell, June 12, 1953; children—Susan, Robert. B.A., Amherst Coll., 1946, M.S., 1950; Ph.D., Purdue U., 1958. Instr. biol. chemistry U. Mich., Ann Arbor, 1961-63, asst. prof., 1963-65, research assoc., 1965-74, assoc., prof., 1965-74, prof., 1974—. Contbr. articles to profl. jours. Mem. editorial bd. Jour. Biol. Chemistry, 1984—. Mem. med. and sci. com. Mich. chpt. Arthritis Found., 1974-81, 84—; mem. research com. Nat. Arthritis Found., 1984—. NIH grantee, 1965—; Arthritis Found. grantee, 1965—. Mem. Am. Soc. Biol. Chemists, Am. Chem. Soc., Soc. Complex Carbohydrates. Avocations: hiking; fishing; hunting. Home: 4455 Kuebler Ct Ann Arbor MI 48103 Office: U Mich Rackham Arthritis Research Unit Box 018 Ann Arbor MI 48109

JOY, MARLENE FAYE SEVERIN, coach; b. Lincoln, Nebr., Nov. 13, 1939; d. Marvin Milton and Viola Lena (Horstman) Severin; children—Cristy Kay, Tracey Dawn. B.S., U. Nebr., 1962; M.S. in Edn., Northwest Mo. State U., 1969. Cert. tchr., Mo. Instr., Eagle River High Sch. (Wis.), 1962-63, Doane Coll., Crete, Nebr., 1963-69; athletic dir. and coach Peru State Coll. (Nebr.), 1975-78; instr. and coach Mo. Valley Coll., Marshall, 1978—; women's program dir. YMCA, Wichita, Kans., 1973-75. Project leader 4-H, Marshall, 1982—; mem. Wal-Mart Scholarship Found. Selection Com., Marshall, 1983. Mem. Nat. Assn. Intercollegiate Athletics Dist. 16 (exec. com. 1980-85, basketball com. 1980-83, softball com. 1980-82), Heart of Am. Athletic Conf. (basketball com. 1978—, volleyball com. 1979-82), Nebr. Assn. Intercollegiate Athletics for Women (treas. 1977-78). Republican. Mem. Christian Ch. Club: Valley Dames (Marshall, treas. 1979-80). Office: Mo Valley Coll 500 E College Marshall MO 65349

JOY, RICHARD HENRY, association executive, communications consultant, writer; b. Detroit, Oct. 2, 1932; s. William Raymond and Helen Elizabeth (Jamieson) J.; divorced; children—Kenneth R., Karen L., R. Scott. B.A. in Speech, U. Mich., 1954. Dir. liaison, sales, prodn. The Jam Handy Orgn., Detroit, 1956-61; mgr. corp. audio-visual and photographic services Burroughs Corp., 1961-76; cons., writer, dir., 1976—; exec. dir. Audio-Visual Mgmt. Assn., Royal Oak, 1979—. Served to 1st lt. AUS, 1954-56. Recipient —The Bennie— award Printing Industries of Am., 1973; Disting. Achievement award Ind. Audio-Visual Assn., 1974; CINE Golden Eagle, 1984. Mem. Detroit Producers Assn. Presbyterian. Clubs: U. Mich. of Detroit, High Noon Old Pro League. Editor/producer Village Vision for Presbyterian Village, Inc. Writer/-dir. numerous sales and ednl. motion pictures, slide presentations, speeches, articles, brochures, and videotape presentations. Home and Office: 3633 Crooks Rd #4 Royal Oak MI 48073

JOYCE, BLAINE RICHARD, chemical engineer; b. Jeannette, Pa., Nov. 13, 1925. B.S. in Chem. Engring., U. Pitts., 1949; M.S. in Indsl. Engring., U. Toledo, 1965. Research assoc. Mellon Inst. Research, Pitts., 1949-51; devel. engr. Union Carbide Corp., Fostoria, Ohio, 1953-60, mgr. activated carbon devel., 1960-81; tech. dir. Witco Chem. Corp., Berea, Ohio, 1981—. Patentee in field. Contbr. articles to profl. jours. Served with U.S. Army, 1951-53. Mem. Am. Chem. Soc., Am. Inst. Chem. Engrs., ASTM (chmn. 1984 chmn. subcom. on activated carbon 1984-85).

JOYCE, DAVID LEE, health care company executive; b. Logansport, Ind., Apr. 25, 1944; s. Lloyd Wayne and Catherine (Kiesling) J.; m. Donna Maria Castelli, June 27, 1970; children—Jeffrey David, Colleen Elizabeth, Shannon Christine. B.A., DePauw U., 1966; postgrad. U. Ill., 1967. Lic. real estate broker, Mo. Adminstrv. asst. St. Louis Football Cardinals, 1967-70, bus. mgr., 1970-73; co-founder Spectrum Emergency Care, St. Louis, 1973-83; founder StaffMark Corp., St. Louis, 1983—; owner, pres. Ind. Lumber Corp., Greencastle, 1985—; vis. lectr. St. Louis U. M.B.A. program, 1981—; dir. Mark Twain Nat. Bank, St. Louis, 1981—. 1967-73. Mem. Am. Acad. Med. Adminstrs., Emergency Medicine Mgmt. Assn., Am. Mgmt. Assn. Republican. Club: Hon. Order of Ky. Cols. (Louisville). Office: 555 N New Ballas Rd Suite 150 Saint Louis MO 63141

JOYCE, GREGORY PAUL, optometrist; b. El Dorado, Kans., Oct. 24, 1954; s. Jean Dallas and Dorothy Lou (Harper) J.; m. Helen Annette Prather, Aug. 2, 1975; children—Jaime Anne, Katie Ellen. B.S. in Optometry, U. Houston, 1977, D.Optometry, 1977. Ptnr. Drs. Joyce and Joyce, El Dorado, Kans., 1981—. Fin. dir. El Dorado Thunderboat Regatta, 1980; scouting coordinator Sea Scout Ship 200 Boy Scouts Am., El Dorado, 1982, 85. Mem. Am. Optometric Assn., Kans. Optometric Assn. (pub. info. chmn. 1981-83, standards and cert. co-chmn. 1984, edn. chmn. 1985), Heart of Am. Contact Lens Soc., El Dorado C. of C. (treas. 1980, 81, 1st v.p. 1982), Gold Key. Republican. Methodist. Lodge: Kiwanis (pres. 1983-84). Avocations: sailing; tennis. Home: 1005 Rimrock St El Dorado KS 67042 Office: Drs Joyce and Joyce 120 S Gordy El Dorado KS 67042

JOYCE, THOMAS JOSEPH, antiquarian bookseller, book appraiser; b. Hessville, Ind., Sept. 16, 1949; s. Thomas Joseph and Sarah Johanna (Flaherty) J.; m. Kathleen Keenan, Aug. 19, 1972 (div. Jan. 1980). A.B., Loyola U., 1972, M.A., 1973. Mgr., J&S Graphics, Chgo., 1973-75; pres., owner Scholar Gypsy, Ltd., Geneva, Ill., 1975-83, Thomas J. Joyce and Co., Chgo., 1983—; lectr. New Trier Extension, Wilmette, Ill., 1979—. Author: (with others) Geneva, Illinois: A History, 1976. Recipient Horace Harker award Hugo's Companions, 1981. Mem. Antiquarian Booksellers Assn. Am. (chmn. midwest chpt. 1982—), The Midwest Bookhunters (pres. 1981, 82). Roman Catholic. Clubs: Hugo's Companions (Chgo.) (sec. 1979-82, pres. 1982-84), Caxton (Chgo.). Home: PO Box A3566 Chicago IL 60690 Office: Thomas J Joyce & Co 431 S Dearborn St Chicago IL 60605

JOYNER, PAUL JAY, optometrist; b. Dayton, Ohio, Nov. 3, 1954; s. Ralph Delmer and Marjorie Jean (Hake) J.; m. Sally Sue Smith, July 12, 1981. B.S., Ind. U., 1977, O.D., 1978. Diplomate Nat. Bd. Optometry, state cert., Ind., Ill., Mo. Pvt. practice optometry, Fort Wayne, Ind., 1978-79, with Dr. White, Kendallville, Ind., 1978-79, with Dr. David Tavel, Indpls., 1979-82; optometrist Pearle Vision Ctr., Indpls., 1982-83, Evansville, Ind., 1982-83, Merrillville, Ind., 1983—. Recipient Roy E. Denny Meml. award Ind. Acad. Optometry, 1978. Democrat. Unitarian-Universalist. Avocation: bicycling. Office: Pearle Vision Ctr 7756 Broadway Merrillville IN 47410

JOYNER, WILLIAM LYMAN, physiology educator; b. Farmville, N.C., June 10, 1939; s. William L. Joyner and Hazel (Riley) Sandlin; m. Delorise Fowler, Sept. 12, 1964 (div. 1980); m. Christine Ann Eccleston, Dec. 23, 1982; children—William Jeffrey, Candace Darlene, Andrew William. B.S. in Biology, Davidson Coll., 1965; M.S. in Parasitology, U. N.C., 1967, Ph.D. in Physiology, 1971. Postdoctoral fellow Duke U. Med. Ctr., Durham, N.C., 1971-73; asst. prof. U. Nebr. Med. Ctr., Omaha, 1973-77, assoc. prof., 1977-83, prof. physiology and biophysics, 1983—; vis. prof. numerous univs., 1969-83; lectr. in field; chmn. research com. Am. Heart Assn., Nebr. affiliate, 1982; dir. Am. Heart Assn. Nebr. affiliate, 1981-84; editorial bd. jour. Microvascular Research, 1981—; ad hoc reviewer numerous sci. jours.; NIH study sect., 1981-84. Contbr. numerous articles to profl. jours. Served with U.S. Army, 1960-63, Korea. Recipient Pharmacia Travel award Microcirculatory Soc., 1975, Merit award U. Nebr. Coll. Medicine, 1983; NSF fellow; fellow Council on Circulation Am. Heart Assn.; vice chmn. Regional research rev. and adv. com. Am. Heart Assn., 1982, chmn. 1984; Mid Am. honor lectr. U. Nebr. Med. Ctr. Mem. Am. Physiol. Soc., Circulation Group, AAAS, Internat. Soc. Lymphology (North Am. chpt.), Microcirculatory Soc. (program com., 1976, fin. com., 1977, fin. com. chmn., 1978-79, awards com., 1980-83, exec. council, 1980-82, ad hoc com. soc. affiliations, 1983-84). Democrat. Methodist. Avocations: hunting; fishing; wood working. Home: 5009 Chicago Ave Omaha NE 68123 Office: U Nebr Coll Medicine Dept Physiology and Biophysics 42nd and Dewey Ave Omaha NE 68105

JUDD, DOROTHY HEIPLE, educator; b. Oakwood, Ill., May 27, 1922; d. Eldridge Winfield and Mary Luciel (Oliphant) Heiple; B.A., Ind. U., 1944; M.Ed., U. Toledo, 1971; Ed.S., Troy State U., 1976; Ed.D., No. Ill. U., 1981; m. Robert Carpenter Judd, Sept. 19, 1964; children by previous marriage—Patricia Ann Konkoly, Catherine Rafferty, Deborah Brown, Nancy Lee Arrington; stepchildren—Dianna Kay Judd Carlisi, Nancy Carol Judd Wilber, Linda Judd Marinaccio Pucci. Head lang. arts dept. Eisenhower Jr. High Sch., Darien, Ill., 1961-70; instr. devel. edn. Owens Tech. Coll., Perrysburg, Ohio, 1971-73; instr. edn. Troy State U., Montgomery, Ala., also right-to-read coordinator State of Ala., 1975-76; core dept. chair Community Consol. Sch., Dist. 15, Palatine, Ill., 1977-79; asst. prof. curriculum and instrn. No. Ill. U., 1979-83; asst. prof. edn. Southeastern La. U., Hammond, 1984—; pres. R.C. Judd & Assos., Bloomingdale, Ill., 1980—. Mem. Assn. Ednl. Data Systems, Assn. Supervision and Curriculum Devel., Assn. Tchr. Edn., Internat. Council Computers in Edn., Internat. Reading Assn., Nat. Council Social Studies, Nat. Council Tchrs. of English, Pi Lambda Theta. Author: Mastering the Micro, 1984. Contbg. editor Ednl. Computer mag., 1981-84, Electronic Edn., 1984—; mem. editorial bd. Computers, Reading and Language Arts; contbr. articles to profl. jours. Home: 1990 Flagstaff Ct Glendale Heights IL 60139

JUDD, JAMES JUSTICE, physical education educator; b. North Baltimore, Ohio, Dec. 29, 1937; s. Kenneth Wilbur and Elsia (Nigh) J.; m. Bea Mae Carpenter, June 11, 1961; children—James C., J. Todd. B.S., Findlay Coll., 1962; M.Ed., Bowling Green State U., 1965. Tchr. Otsego (Ohio) Local Schs., 1962-64, Ottawa-Glandorf (Ohio) Pub. Schs., 1964-65, Spencerville (Ohio) High Sch., 1965-68; instr. phys. edn., wrestling coach, golf coach Southwestern Mich. Coll., Dowagiac, 1968—; head coach Mich. Hawks, semi-profl. football team, 1971-72; mem. Region XII wrestling com. Nat. Jr. Coll. Athletic Assn. Mem. Econ. Devel. Corp. Dowagiac, 1976—; councilman, City of Dowagiac, 1982—, mayor protem, 1984. Served with paratroopers U.S. Army, 1956-58. Coached winning wrestling team Nat. Acad. All-Am. Team Championship, 1973. Mem. Mich. Mcpl. League, Ohio Edn. Assn., U.S. Team Handball Fedn., Am. Tae Kwan Do Assn., Nat. Jr. Coll. Athletic Assn. Wrestling Coachs' Assn., Mich. Mcpl. League (fin. and taxation com. 1983-85), Jr. C. of C. Lodges: Elks, K.P. Home: 318 E Division St Dowagiac MI 49041 Office: Cherry Grove Rd Southwestern Mich College Dowagiac MI 49041

JUDD, JOHN HARVEY, educational administrator; b. Oconto Falls, Wis., Apr. 14, 1934; s. Harvey John and Marie (Housner) J.; m. Patricia Eggert, June 26, 1955 (dec. 1984); children—Debra, Susan, Jerome. B.S. in Edn., U. Wis.-Stevens Point, 1956; M.S., U. Mich., 1964; Ph.D., U. Wis.-Madison, 1969. Asst. dean U. Wis.-Milw., 1968-69; research assoc. State Univ. Coll., Oswego, N.Y., 1969-71; assoc. dir. Sea Grant Int., N.Y., 1971-78, U. Mich., 1978-84; assoc. program dir. Mich. State U., East Lansing, 1984—; cons. in field. Chmn. Environ. Conservation Commn., East Greenbush, N.Y., 1976-78; chmn. adv. com. Internat. Joint Commn., 1977; budget com. Council Sea Grant Dirs., 1979-80. Recipient Recognition award N.Y. Sea Grant Inst., 1978, Cert. of Appreciation, Internat. Joint Commn., 1983, Cert. of Recognition, U.S. Office Personnel Mgmt., 1983. Mem. Am. Soc. Limnology and Oceanography, Internat. Assn. Great Lakes Research, N.Am. Benthol. Soc., Societas Internationalis Limnologia, Sea Grant Assn. (treas. 1976-81). Avocations: Antique restoration; ship model construction. Home: 1803 Oneida Dr Okemos MI 48864 Office: Mich State U 334 Natural Resources East Lansing MI 48824

JUDGE, CHARLES JOSEPH, dentist, consultant, researcher; b. Cin., Oct. 31, 1940; s. Robert Thomas and Marie (Barlow) J. m. Kathleen Cain, May 5, 1973; children—Charles, Marc. Grad. Xavier U., 1961; D.D.S., Loyola U., Chgo., 1965. Dental surgeon Meth. Home, Cin., 1969-78; pvt. practice dentistry, Cin., 1965—. Mem. Clifton Town Meeting, Cin., 1965—, Clifton Bus. Assn., 1965—. Recipient Am. Coll. Surgery award of merit, 1965; R.C.A. Corp. award of merit, 1958; J.D. Squire award, 1973; Ky. Col., 1983. Mem. Greater Cin. Dental Study Club (sec. 1975-78, pres. 1980), Cin. Dental Soc. (chmn. access councilmen 1983-85), Ohio Dental Soc. (councilman 1983-85), Am. Dental Soc. (advisor, councilman 1983-85), Pub. Dental Service Soc. (pres. 1980-82, clinician and advisor 1965-79, trustee 1979—), Cin. C. of C., Xavier U. Alumni Assn., Loyola U. Alumni Assn. Republican. Roman Catholic. Clubs: Kiwanis, Camera (pres.), One Hundred of Cin. Avocations: photography; electronics; computers; travel; hunting; fishing. Office: 3349 Whitfield Ave Cincinnati OH 45220

JUDGE, EDWARD RICHARD, farmer; b. Boone, Iowa, Apr. 21, 1945; s. William Henry and Dorothy Marie (Healy) J.; m. Mary Beth Peterson, Apr. 22, 1967; children—David R., Richard P. B.S. in Agronomy, Iowa State U., 1968. Ptnr. Judge Bros. Inc., Ames, Iowa, 1968—. Mem. United Community Sch. Bd. Boone, Iowa, 1980—, pres., 1984—. Chmn. Boone County Extension Council, 1977-79, 80; mem. West Story Vol. Fire Agy., Kelly, Iowa, 1974—. Democrat. Roman Catholic. Home: Route 3 Ames IA 50010 Office: United Community Sch Dist Rural Route 1 Boone IA 50036

JUDGE, GEORGE GARRETT, economics educator; b. Carlisle, Ky., May 2, 1925; s. William Everitt and Etna (Perkins) J.; m. Sue Dunkle, Mar. 17, 1950; children—Lisa C., Laura S.; m. Margaret C. Copeland, Oct. 8, 1976. B.S., U. Ky., 1948; M.S., Iowa State U., 1949, Ph.D., 1952; Asst. prof. U. Conn., Storrs, 1951-55; prof. U. Okla., Stillwater, 1955-58; vis. prof. Yale U., New Haven, 1958-59; prof. econs. U. Ill., Urbana, 1959—; vis. disting. prof. U. Ga., 1977-79; cons. Internat. Wool Secretariat, London, 1976-77. Author: Theory and Practice of Econometrics, 1980, 85; Pre-Test and Stein Rule Estimates, 1978; Spatial Equilibrium, 1972; Markov Processes, 1970. Served with USAAF, 1943-45; PTO. Fellow Social Sci. Research Council, 1958-59, NSF, 1965-66; NSF grantee, 1976—. Mem. Econometric Soc., Am. Statis. Assn., Am. Econ. Assn. Club: Dial. Avocations: golf, tennis. Home: 4004 Farhills Dr Champaign IL 61821 Office: Dept Econs U Ill Champaign IL 61820

JUDGE, JOHN EMMET, marketing consultant; b. Grafton, N.D., May 5, 1912; s. Charles C. and Lillian (Johnson) J.; B.S., U. N.D., m. Clarita Garcia, Apr. 18, 1940; children—Carolyn (Mrs. Samuel Stanley), J. Emmet Jr., Maureen (Mrs. William Barron), Eileen, Susan (Mrs. Ralph Lloyd). Asst. to adminstr. Fed. Works Agy., Washington, 1939-42; staff mem. Wallace Clark & Co., mgmt. cons., 1942-46; v.p. Morgan Furniture Co., Asheville, N.C., 1946-48; mgr. financial analysis Lincoln Mercury div., Ford Motor Co., 1949-53, asst. gen. purchasing agt., 1953-55, merchandising mgr., 1955-58, mgr. Mercury mktg., 1958-60, mgr. product planning office, 1960-62; v.p. mktg. services Westinghouse Electric Corp., Pitts., 1963-67; v.p. marketing Indian Head Inc., 1967-68; mktg. cons., Birmingham, Mich., 1968—. Dir. Intertek Industries Inc., Cambridge Instruments, Kratos Inc. Mem. nat. adv. com. mktg. to sec. commerce. Chmn. library study com., Birmingham, Mich.,

1957; dir. Boysville of Mich., 1957. Mem. Am. Def. Preparedness Assn., Soc. Advancement Mgmt., Engring. Soc. Detroit, Am. Soc. M.E., Nat. Assn. Accountants, Soc. Automotive Engrs., U.S. C. of C. (consumer com.), N.A.M. (mktg. com.), Newcomen Soc. N.Am., Sigma Tau, Alpha Tau Omega. Roman Catholic. Clubs: Detroit Athletic, Economic (Detroit); Orchard Lake County (dir.). Address: Shore Dr Harbor Springs MI 49740

JUDILLA, LAURA JANE, nurse anesthesist, resort executive; b. Erie, Pa., May 25, 1946; d. Laurence Henry and Patricia Elizabeth (Elis) Sydow; m. Francisco Gerona Judilla, Jr., Oct. 27, 1973; children—Marea, Francis III. Diploma Sch. Practical Nursing, 1965; student Pa. State U.-Behrend, 1970-73; B.S.N. cum laude, Wichita State U., 1981; B.S.N.A., St. Francis Sch. of Nurse Anesthesia, Kans. Newman Coll., 1984. Cert. nurse anesthesist; R.N. L.P.N., St. Vincent's Regional Med. Ctr., Erie, Pa., 1965-73, Beth Israel Med. Ctr., Newark, N.J., 1973-76; R.N., Med. Personnel Pool, Wichita, 1979-80; Wesley Med. Ctr., Wichita, 1981-82, R.N.A. med. anesthesia services, 1985—; dir. nursing Christ Villa Nursing Ctr., Wichita, 1980-81; inservice edn. coordinator, acting nursing dir. Cherry Creek Village, Wichita, 1981. Active mem. St. Francis Aux. Ronald McDonald House, Wichita, 1985; educator ARC, Wichita, 1978—; hypertension screener, caseworker, blood mobile vol. health fair, Wichita, 1985—; good neighbor Meals on Wheels, Wichita, 1985—; internat. health caseworker Sedgwick Med. Aux., Wichita, 1979—. Mem. U. Assn. Women, Am. Assn. Nurse Anesthesists, Am. Assn. Critical Care Nurses, Branson C. of C., Sigma Theta Tau (hon.). Republican. Lutheran. Avocations: antiques; flower gardening; fishing; children and gerontology advocate; ikebana. Home: 16 Douglas Ave Wichita KS 67206 Office: Med Anesthesia Service 2322 E Central Wichita KS 67214

JUDSON, JOHN PAUL, cardiovascular and thoracic surgeon; b. Washington, July 14, 1939; s. John H. and Joyce Mary (Duffield) J.; m. Ann Marie Ull, June 20, 1964; children—Ruth, Andrea, Sarah, Christopher, Therese. B.S. in Chemistry, Villanova U., 1961; M.D., Georgetown U., 1965. Diplomate Nat. Bd. Med. Examiners, Am. Bd. Surgery, Am. Bd. Thoracic Surgery. Resident in surgery Yale-New Haven Hosp., 1965-71, instr. surgery Yale U., 1970-71; surgeon, pres. Surgical Assocs. of Blacksburg, Va., 1971-77; resident in cardiac surgery U. Utah, Salt Lake City, 1977-79; fellow in cardiac surgery Mayo Clinic, Rochester, Minn., 1979-80; chief cardiovascular surgery Tex. Tec. U., Lubbock, 1980-82; surgeon, pres. Berrien Cardiovascular Surgery, Benton Harbor, Mich., 1982—; research asst. VA Hosp., Washington, 1963; chief dept. surgery Montgomery County Hosp., Blacksburg, 1971-75, chief of staff-elect, 1976-77; mng. ptnr. Profl. Assocs., 1973-77; mem. profl. adv. com. Beverly Home Health Care of St. Joseph, Mich., 1984; mem. med. adv. com. Hospice at Home, Inc., 1984; pres. Berrien County Heart Unit, Benton Harbor, Mich., 1984—; mem. staff Southwest Mich. Health Care Assn.; Meml. Hosp., St. Joseph; Watervilet Community Hosp., Mich.; Burgess Med. Ctr., Kalamazoo. Contbr. articles to profl. jours.; lectr., speaker, presenter profl. assns., socs. Fellow Am. Coll. Surgeons, Med. Soc. Va., Med. Soc. Am. Coll. Surgeons, Am. Soc. Abdominal Surgery, Southeastern Surg. Congress, So. Med. Soc., Flying Physicians Assn., Am. Coll. Chest Physicians, Soc. Thoracic Surgeons. Roman Catholic. Avocations: aviation. Office: 777-D Riverview Dr Suite 115 Benton Harbor MI 49022

JUDSON, LYMAN SPICER VINCENT, speech pathologist, educator; b. Plymouth, Mich., Mar. 27, 1903; s. Ernest W. and Fannie Louise (Spicer) J.; A.B. in Biol. Scis., Albion Coll., 1925; M.S. in Med. Scis., U. Mich., 1929; Ph.D., U. Wis., 1933; postgrad. S.E. Mich. U., 1926, U. Iowa, 1929-30, U. So. Calif., 1927, Harvard U., 1942, U. San Francisco, Palma, Mallorca, Spain, 1967; m. E. Ellen MacKechnie, 1933 (dec. 1964); m. 2d, S. Adele H. Christensen, 1968. Chmn. dept. sci. Las Vegas (Nev.) High Sch., 1925-27; instr. speech, studio dir. Sta. KUSD, U. S.D., 1927-28; instr. speech U. Mich., 1928-29; research assoc. speech pathology U. Iowa, 1929-30; assoc. prof. Kans. State Tchrs. Coll., summers 1929, 30; chmn. dept. speech Ala. Poly. Inst., Auburn, 1930-31; asst. prof. speech U. Ill., 1933-35; prof. speech Kalamazoo Coll., 1936-42; chief motion picture and visual edn. divs. Pan Am. Union, OAS, 1946-50; served to comdr. USNR, 1942-65; mem. joint bd. control USN tng. films, 1944-46; chmn. dept. speech, dir. public relations Babson Coll. Bus. Adminstrn., 1950-55; vis. prof. Latin Am. affairs Assn. Am. Colls., 1952; speech writer Hon. Christian A. Herter, 1954-57; asst. to pres. Alfred U., 1955-57; dir. devel. Ripon Coll., 1957-63; lectr. U. Wis., 1963-64; prof. speech Minn. State U., Winona, 1964-71; staff Supreme Allied Comdr. Atlantic, liaison officer staff Supreme Allied Comdr. Europe and European Hdqrs., dir. gen. NATO, 1953-54; spl. mission Vietnam and 7th Fleet, 1966; TV cons. Johnson Found., 1963-64; devel. and long-range planning cons., 1965—; Mem. Explorers Scout bd., cabinet mem., bd. mem., exec. com. mem., treas. Twin Lakes council Boy Scouts Am., 1972-73. Fellow Am. Geog. Soc.; mem. AAAS, Inter-Am. Soc. Anthropology and Geography, Soc. Am. Archeology, Am. Soc. Agrl. Scis., Am. Acad. Polit. and Social Scis., Public Relations Soc. Am., Wis. Arts Council, Boston Athenaeum (propr.), Explorers Club (N.Y.C.), Archeol. Inst. Am. (pres. Winona-Hiawatha Valley chpt.), Service Corps Ret. Execs., Navy League, Sigma Xi, Alpha Phi Omega, Delta Sigma Rho (nat. sec., nat. editor), Tau Kappa Alpha, Pi Kappa Delta, Sigma Delta Chi, Sigma Chi. Episcopalian. Clubs: Rotary; Cosmos (Washington). Author: Preliminary Study of the Offerings of Speech-Content Courses in the Technical Colleges of the United States, 1932; The Vegetative Versus the Speech Use of Biological Systems, 1932; Basic Speech and Voice Science, 1933; The Fundamentals of the Speaker-Audience Relationship, 1934; Modern Group Discussion, 1935; Manual of Group Discussion, 1936; Public Speaking for Future Farmers, 1936; After-Dinner Speaking, 1937; Winning Future Farmers Speeches, 1939; The Student Congress Movement, 1940; The Monroe Doctrine and the Growth of Western Hemisphere Solidarity, 1941; Voice Science, 1942, rev. edit., 1965; The Judson Guides to Latin America, including: Let's Go to Colombia, 1949, Let's Go to Guatemala, 1950, Let's Go to Peru, 1951, Your Holiday in Cuba, 1952; Report of Command Information Bureau 47 on Operation Inland Seas, 1959; The Interview, 1966; The Business Conference, 1969; Vincent Judson: The Island Series, 1973; Solution: PNC and PNCLAND, 1973; The AQUA Declaration, 1976; Happy 60th Birthday, 1982; The Shadow(s), 1983. Address: PO Box 277 Rochester MN 55903-0277

JUENEMANN, SISTER JEAN, hospital administrator, nun; b. St. Cloud, Minn., Nov. 19, 1936; d. Leo A. and Teresa M. (Oster) Juenemann. Diploma St. Cloud (Minn.) Sch. Nursing, 1957; student Coll. St. Benedict, 1957-59; B.S. cum laude in Nursing, Seattle U., 1967; M.H.A., U. Minn., 1977. Joined Order of St. Benedict, Roman Catholic Ch., 1959; asst. head nurse orthopedics St. Cloud Hosp., 1960-62; dir. nursing service St. Michael's Hosp., Richfield, Utah, 1962-63; dir. nursing service Queen of Peace Hosp., New Prague, Minn., 1963-65, 67-77, asst. adminstr., 1967-77, chief exec. officer, 1977—; speaker at confs. Chmn. Community Com. for Prevention Chem. Abuse, New Prague, 1975-80; bd. dirs. St. Cloud (Minn.) Hosp., 1979—. Named participant Itasca Seminar on Leadership, Mpls. Found., 1979; Bush Found. summer fellow Cornell U., U. Calif., Berkeley, 1982. Mem. Am. Hosp. Assn., Cath. Hosp. Assn., Am. Coll. Hosp. Adminstrs., AAUW (past pres. New Prague chpt.), Eleven Fifteen Club-Women in Health Care Leadership, Sigma Theta Tau.

JUERGENSMEYER, JOHN ELI, lawyer; b. Stewardson, Ill., May 14, 1934; s. Irvin Karl and Clara Augusta (Johannaber) J.; m. Elizabeth Ann Bogart, Sept. 10, 1963; children—Margaret Ann, Frances Elizabeth. B.A., U. Ill., 1955, J.D., 1963; M.A., Princeton U., 1957, Ph.D., 1960. Bar: Ill. 1963. Mem. faculty extension div. U. Ill., 1961-63, U. Hawaii, 1958-60; mem. firm Kirkland, Brady, McQueen, Martin & Schnell, Elgin, Ill., 1963-64; founder, sr. ptnr. Juergensmeyer, Zimmerman, Smith & Leady, Elgin, 1964-81, Juergensmeyer & Assocs., 1981—; mgr., owner Tollview Office Complex, 1976—; asst. pub. defender Kane County, 1964-67, asst. states atty., 1976-78; spl. asst. atty. gen. State of Ill., 1978—; hearing officer Ill. Pollution Control Bd., 1971-74; commr. U.S. Nat. Commn. on Libraries and Info. Scis., 1982—; lectr. Inst. for Continuing Legal Edn., Ill Bar Assn., 1971-73; trustee ALA Endowment Fund, 1979-84; assoc. prof. Judson Coll., Elgin, 1963—. Chmn. Hiawatha Dist. Boy Scouts Am.; v.p. Elgin Family Service Assn., 1967-71; sec. Lloyd Morey Scholarship Fund, 1967-73; commr. Elgin Econ. Devel. Commn., 1971-75; chmn. Elgin Twp. Republican Central Com., 1978-80; adv. bd. Ill. Youth Commn., 1964-68; bd. dirs. Wesley Found. of U. Ill., 1971-75; pres. adv. bd. Elgin Salvation Army, 1973-75. Served to capt. Intelligence Service, USAF, 1958-60. Recipient Anti-Pollution Echo award Defenders of the Fox River, Inc., 1971, Cert. Merit, Heart Fund, 1971, Outstanding Young Man award Jr. C. of C., Elgin, 1967; Princeton U. fellow, 1955-56, Merrill Found. fellow, 1956-58. Mem. Assn. Trial Lawyers Am., ABA, Ill. Bar Assn. (chmn. local govt. com. 1974-75, editor local govt. law newsletter 1973-74), Chgo. Bar Assn. (chmn. local govt. com. 1975-76), Kane County Bar Assn., Am. Arbitration Assn. (arbitrator), Am. Polit. Sci. Assn., Izaak Walton League, Fed. Bar Assn., Phi Beta Kappa, Phi Alpha Delta, Alpha Kappa Lambda. Author: President, Foundations, and the People-to-People Program, 1965. Contbr. to publs. in field. Methodist. Club: Union League (Chgo.). Lodges: Masons, Shriners, Elks, Rotary (pres. 1977-78). Office: 707 A Davis Rd Elgin IL 60120

JUETTNER, PAUL GERARD, lawyer; b. Evanston, Ill., Nov. 16, 1954; s. Thomas Richard and Vivian Dorthy (Bajork) J.; m. Mary Rose Angeleri, Nov. 13, 1982; 1 child, Thomas Joseph. B.S.C.E., U. Ill., 1977; J.D. with high honors, Chgo. Kent. Coll. Law, 1981. Bars: Ill. 1981, U.S. Dist. Ct. (no. dist.) Ill. 1981, U.S. Ct. Appeals (7th cir.) 1981, U.S. Patent Office (agent 1981) 1982. Civil engr. Harza Engring. Co., Chgo., 1974-79; assoc. Gary, Juettner & Pyle, Chgo., 1979—. Tchr., Chgo. Coalition for Law Related Edn., 1984. Mem. ABA, Chgo. Bar Assn., Patent Law Assn. Chgo. Roman Catholic. Home: 5872 Leonard St Chicago IL 60646 Office: Gary Juettner & Pyle 33 N Dearborn St Chicago IL 60602

JUILLERAT, ERNEST EMANUEL, JR., safety professional; b. Portland, Ind., Dec. 2, 1921; s. Ernest Emanuel and Anna Liza Etta (Stanley) J.; m. Mary Frances Knakal, Nov. 18, 1945; children—Mary Anne Juillerat Koepfler, Martha Grace. B.B.A., Capitol City Coll., 1951; postgrad. W.Va. State Coll., 1959-61. With Union Carbide Corp., Institute, W.Va., 1947-61; mgr. fire analysis dept. Nat. Fire Protection Assn., Boston, 1961-70; asst. exec. dir. Nat. Sch. Bds. Assn., 1971-73; asst. dir. safety and fire protection dept. pub. safety Northwestern U., Evanston, Ill., 1973—; cons. in field; lectr. in field. Bd. dirs. Bel Canto Found., 1979—, Northwestern Library Council, 1972—. Served with USCG, 1942-46; PTO. Decorated Silver Star. Mem. Am. Soc. Safety Engrs., Nat. Fire Protection Assn., Nat. Safety Council, Campus Safety Assn., U.S. Naval Inst., Am. Legion. Republican. Presbyterian. Clubs: Masons, Shriners. Author: Campus Fire Safety, 1978; contbr. articles to profl. jours. Home: 628 Colfax St Evanston IL 60201 Office: 1819 Hinman Ave Evanston IL 60201

JULIAR, MARVIN DALE, banker; b. Mankato, Minn., Jan. 12, 1934; s. Milton O. and Alma (Knutson) J.; m. Barbara Boberg, Nov. 29, 1957; children—Jane Juliar Crabtree, Kristin, Mark. B.A., U. Minn., 1956, M.B.A., 1958. Vice-pres. First Nat. Bank Chgo., 1958-73; pres. Air Fin. Internat., Elk Grove Village, Ill., 1973-75; v.p. LaSalle Nat. Bank, Chgo., 1975-80, Algemene Bank Nederland, Chgo., 1980—. Alderman City of Evanston, Ill., 1982—. Served with U.S. Army, 1956-63. Club: Union League. Home: 1225 Sheridan Rd Evanston IL 60202 Office: Algemene Bank Nederland NV 135 S LaSalle St Chicago IL 60603

JULIUS, RONALD LYNN, quality assurance engineer; b. Kokomo, Ind., June 6, 1950; s. William Howard and Mary Lou (Hudson) J.; m. Judith Ann Bell, Sept. 19, 1970; children—Michael Lynn, Tamara Michelle. Tech. cert. United Electronics, Louisville, 1970. Dial technician Delco Electronics Corp., Kokomo, 1975, service technician, 1975-77, service trainer, 1977-78, service lab. supr., 1978-80, regional service mgr., Los Angeles, 1980-84, sr. engr., Kokomo, 1984—. Served with AUS, 1970-72. Avocations: computers; fishing. Home: 136 Maplewood Dr Noblesville IN 46060

JUMP, DONALD BRADLEY, biochemist, educator; b. Dover, Del., Oct. 6, 1949; s. Josiah Temple and Evelyn (Bradley) T., Jr.; m. Claudia Lorene Moritz, Mar. 19, 1977; children—Marc Lindsy, Megan Louise. B.S., Del. State U., 1971; M.S., Rutgers U., 1973; Ph.D., Georgetown U., 1979. Research asst. Inst. Med. Research, Camden, N.J., 1972-73, Oreg. State U., Corvallis, 1973-76; pre-doctoral fellow Georgetown U., Washington, 1977-79; postdoctoral fellow in endocrinology U. Minn., Mpls., 1979-81, asst. prof. medicine, 1981-83, asst. prof. medicine and cell biology, 1983—. Contbr. articles to profl. publs. Recipient Nat. Research Service award NIH-USPHS, 1979, 81. Mem. N.Y. Acad. Scis., AAAS, Endocrine Soc., Sigma Xi. Republican. Lutheran. Club: Flying Scot Sailing Assn.

JUN, CHOLL KYU, materials scientist; b. Taegu, Korea, Jan. 19, 1939; came to U.S., 1962; s. Ryong A. and Hae (Kim) J.; m. Young Arlene Kwon, June 25, 1966; children—Susie, Steve, Helen. B.S. in Metall. Engring., Chosum U., Korea, 1961; M.S. in Metall. Engring., U. Cin., 1964, Ph.D. in Materials Sci., 1967. Postdoctoral research materials sci., U. Cin., 1967-69; sr. research assoc. Carborundum Co., Niagara Falls, N.Y., 1969-73; mgr. research projects Kennametal, Inc., Greensburg, 1973-80; dir. carbide tool div. Korea Tungsten Mining Co., 1980-81, dir. central research and devel. div. 1981-83; adj. prof. Korea Advanced Inst. Sci. and Tech., 1982-83; project mgr. Gen. Electric Carboloy Systems Dept., Detroit, 1983—. Recipient Indsl. Research 100 award, 1973. Mem. Am. Ceramic Soc., Am. Soc. Metals, Am. Powder Metallurgy Inst. Office: Gen Electric CSBD Box 237 GPO Detroit MI 48232

JUNE, BRIAN GREGORY, real estate executive, consultant; b. Flint, Mich., July 18, 1954; s. Raymond Carl and Bethany Joan (Aldred) J.; m. Valerie Lynne McLucas, June 28, 1975. Assoc. Aviation Tech. with high distinction, Mott Community Coll., 1975, Assoc. Bus. Adminstrn. with high distinction, 1975; B.B.A. with distinction, U. Mich., 1976. Vice-pres. Skybolt Aviation, Inc., Flint, 1977-78; treas. Allen June Allen, Inc., Flint, 1978-79; pres. Data Gen. Realty Group, Inc., Flint, 1981-84; chmn. The Morgan Cos., 1984—; guest lectr. real estate investment devel. and syndication U. Mich., 1981. Mem. Nat. Assn. Realtors, Realtors Nat. Mktg. Inst., Real Estate Securities and Syndication Inst. (chmn. state regulatory, legislation and taxation com. Mich. chpt. 1, specialist in real estate securities 1984), Mich. Assn. Realtors, Mich. Assn. Real Estate Exchangors, C. of C. Republican. Lutheran. Contbr. articles on real estate to Flint Jour. Office: 2707 E Court St Flint MI 48503

JUNG, JAMES, state education official. Exec. sec., State Higher Ednl. Aids Bd., Madison, Wis. Office: State Higher Ednl Aids Bd 137 E Wilson St Madison WI 53702*

JUNG, ROBERT JOHN, broadcast executive; b. Manitowoc, Wis., May 2, 1949; s. John Earnest and Berniece Irene (Dawes) J.; m. Barbara Rich, June 16, 1973; children—Jonathan, Andrew. Grad., Wis. State U., Oshkosh, 1971; degree in radio and TV broadcasting Brown Inst. Broadcasting, 1973. Sports dir., announcer, ops. dir. Sta. WTIQ, Manistique, Mich., 1973-74; sports dir., announcer Sta. WOMT, Manitowoc, 1974-78, program dir., 1978-80; sta. mgr. WQTC-FM, Two Rivers, Wis., 1980-81; ops. mgr. Seehafer Broadcasting Corp., Manitowoc, 1981—. Chmn. services north Manitowoc United Way Campaign, 1982; bd. dirs. Lakeshore All-Sports Hall of Fame. Mem. Bowling Writers Assn. Am. Methodist. Lodge: Rotary. Home: 1405 Lee Circle Manitoqoc WI 54220 Office: 3730 Mangin St Manitowoc WI 54220

JUNGEBERG, THOMAS DONALD, lawyer; b. Berea, Ohio, June 12, 1950; s. Wilbert Donald and Carolyn Francis (Gaube) J.; m. Kathleen Ann Killmer, Oct. 5, 1973; children—Kimberlee Ann, Allison Lynn, Zebulun Thomas, Nathan Aaron. B.A., Kent State U., 1972; J.D., Cleve. State U., 1976. Bar: Ohio 1976, U.S. Dist. Ct. (no. dist.) Ohio 1977, U.S. Tax Ct. 1980, U.S. Supreme Ct. 1980. Tchr., Berea City Schs., Ohio, 1972-75; staff atty. Palmquist & Palmquist, Medina, Ohio, 1977-80, Gibbs & Craze, Parma Heights, Ohio, 1980-81; sole practice, Medina, 1981—. Tchr., First Baptist Christian Sch., Medina, 1981-84; bd. dirs. Tech. Leaders, Inc., Cleve., 1984—; elder, sec. First Bapt. Ch. of Medina, 1979—, chmn. First Bapt. Christian Sch., Medina, 1984. Mem. Ohio State Bar Assn., Medina County Bar Assn. Republican. Avocations: piano; golf; archery. Home: 911 Lancaster Dr Medina OH 44256 Office: Thomas D Jungeberg Atty Law 331 N Broadway St Medina OH 44256

JUNKINS, JOANN, dental group executive; b. Oskaloosa, Iowa, Aug. 14, 1936; d. Lawrence Nicholas and Helen Maxine (Dusenberry) Vander Linden; m. Larry James Junkins, Dec. 18, 1955 (div. Aug. 1971); children—Dennis L., Debra Suzanne. Diploma Lacey Consol., New Sharon, Iowa, 1954. Typist, Meredith Pub., Des Moines, 1954-55; sec. Messer, Hamilton, Cahill, Iowa City, 1955-58, Univ. Iowa, Iowa City, 1958-62, Dan Neviaser, Madison, Wis., 1969-76, Wm. Krell, Madison, 1977; exec. dir. Am. Acad. Dental Group Practice, Madison, 1985—; real estate broker J.J. Realty, Madison, 1973—. Avocations: traveling, reading, softball, bowling. Home and Office: Am Acad Dental Group Practice 2425 Ashdale Dr #35 Austin TX 78758 also #2 Lakewood Gardens Ln Madison WI 53704

JURCISIN, DALE ALAN, lawyer; b. Cleve., July 2, 1949; s. Andrew and Irene Marie (Kmecik) J.; m. Barbara K. Newth, Aug. 31; children—Andrew, Michael, Marc. B.A., U. Mich., 1971; J.D., Wayne State U., 1974. Bar: Mich. 1974, U.S. Dist. Ct. Mich. 1974. Assoc. Bokos, Jones & Plakas, Westland, Mich., 1975-82; asst. city atty. City of Westland, 1974-83; dept. exec. to sheriff of Wayne County, Detroit, 1983—. Del., Democratic Nat. Conv., 1976-84; mem. Livonia Cable Commn., Mich., 1982-83, Livonia Civil Service Commn., 1984—. Mem. ABA, Assn. Trial Lawyers Am. Mich. Trial Lawyers Assn., Internat. Personnel Mgmt. Assn. Mem. exec. bd. Democratic 15th Congl. Dist., 1983—, Democrat 2d Congl. Dist., 1980-83. Home: 14743 Yale St Livonia MI 48154 Office: 1231 St Antoine Detroit MI 48226

JURGENSEN, LYLE RODNEY, antique service company executive; b. Andrew, Iowa, Dec. 4, 1937; s. Herman and Adela (Schroeder) J.; m. Verla Lee Seehase, July 13, 1957; children—Rodney, Sherry, Gail, Carla. Bookkeeper Green Bay Lumber Co., Sumner, Iowa, 1961-62; route salesman Sumner Bakery, 1962-67; owner, mgr. Antique Service Ctr., Inc., sumner, 1967—. Chmn. Bd. Adjustments, Sumner, 1979—. Served with U.S. Army, 1955-61. Decorated Letter of Commendation, 1960, 61, Good Conduct medal, 1961; Republican. Lutheran. Avocations: hunting; fishing; bowling. Home: 813 W 3rd St Sumner IA 50674 Office: Antique Service Ctr Inc 109 E 1st St Sumner IA 50674

JUSTAK, SUSAN, nurse; b. Hammond, Ind., Nov. 3, 1953; d. John Stephen and Helen Marie (Mihalov) Markovich; m. Jeffrey Eugene Justak, Apr. 29, 1972; children—Jeffrey Jerome, Christine Marie. R.N., St. Margaret Hosp., 1979; A.A.S., Purdue U., 1980, student, 1985—. Staff nurse St. Margaret Hosp., Hammond, 1979—. Mem. Emergency Dept. Nurses Assn. (cert.). Democrat. Roman Catholic. Home: 1625 Central Ave Whiting IN 46394 Office: St Margaret Hosp 5454 Hohman Ave Hammond IN 46320

JUSTEN, FRANK A., lawyer; b. Toledo, June 17, 1940; s. Frank C. and Virginia B. (Janicki) J.; m. Betty Jane Jones, Sept. 7, 1963; children—Scott, Jeffery, Amy, Andy. B.B.A., U. Toledo, 1963, J.D., 1969. Bar: Ohio 1970, Mich. 1970. Asst. U.S. atty. U.S. Dept. Justice, Toledo, 1971-74; sole practice, Toledo, 1975—; dir. Gen. Aluminum and Chem., Toledo. Pres. adv. bd. Vols. of Am., Toledo, 1972—, bd. dirs., New Orleans, 1984. Mem. ABA, Toledo Bar Assn. Republican. Roman Catholic. Avocations: golf; racquetball; bridge. Home: 5627 Bonniebrook Sylvania OH 43560 Office: 4930 Holland-Sylvania Sylvania OH 43560

JUSTICE, GLORIA JANE SMITH, public relations executive; b. Detroit, Mar. 14, 1951; d. H. James and Irene Margaret (Lulenski) Smith; m. Bruce Lloyd Justice, June 11, 1982. B.A. in Journalism, U. Mich., 1973. Mem. info. task force, Charter Revision, Commn., City of Detroit, 1972; editor Commn. on Profl. and Hosp. Activities, Ann Arbor, Mich., 1973-77; pub. relations dir. Port Huron Hosp. (Mich.), 1977—. Bd. mem. Vis. Nurse Assn. of St. Clair County, 1982; mem. regional council Lung Assn. Mich., 1978-79. Mem. Am. Soc. Hosp. Pub. Relations (cert.), Mich. Assn. Hosp. Pub. Relations (dir. 1981—), Southeastern Mich. Hosp. Pub. Relations Assn. (dir. 1982-83), Women in Communications. Editor: Your Magazine, 1975. Home: 1115 Rawlins St Port Huron MI 48060 Office: Port Huron Hosp 1001 Kearney St Port Huron MI 48061

JUSTICE, JAY DAVID, savings association executive; b. Kansas City, Kans., Dec. 29, 1952; s. John Edward and Jacqueline Louise (Wiant) J.; m. Mary Alice Eschbacher, Aug. 9, 1975; children—Sarah Marie, Patrick David, Anne Catherine. B.A., Rockhurst Coll., 1974; J.D., Washburn U., 1976. Bar: Kans. 1977. Asst. city atty., chief labor counsel City of Kansas City (Kans.), 1977-79; atty. Alder, Zemites, Nelson & McKenna, Overland Park, Kans., 1979-80; v.p., dir. human resources Farm & Home Savs. Assn., Nevada, Mo., 1980—. Bd. dirs. United Community Fund, 1983—; vice chmn. Mo. Pvt. Industry Council, 1983—. Mem. Am. Soc. Personnel Adminstrs., Kans. Bar Assn. Roman Catholic. Home: 620 S Adams St Nevada MO 64772 Office: 221 W Cherry St Nevada MO 64772

JYUNG, WOON HENG, biology educator; b. Sanchung, Korea, Mar. 12, 1934; came to U.S. 1958, naturalized 1974; s. Hack Yang and Yun Soo (Oh) J.; m. Kap See Sung, Dec. 25, 1961; children—Earl, Robert. B.S., Seoul Nat. U., 1957; M.S., Mich. State U., 1959, Ph.D., 1963. Grad. research asst. Mich. State U., East Lansing, 1960-63, research assoc., 1963-64; asst. prof. biology U. Toledo, Ohio, 1964-69, assoc. prof., 1969-74, prof., 1974—, chmn., 1976—. Contbr. articles to profl. jours. Served with Korean Army, 1957-58. Grantee NSF 1965, 66, 70, Univ. Toledo 1969, 74-76, 83-84. Mem. Am. Soc. Plant Physiologists, Scandinavian Soc. Plant Physiology, Am. Soc. Agronomy, Crop Sci. Soc. Am., Soil Sci. Soc. Am. Office: Biology Dept U Toledo Toledo OH 43606

KABARA, JON J., medical educator; b. Chgo., Nov. 26, 1926; m. Virginia Christie, 1948 (dec.); 4 children; m. Annette Sproull, 1971; 2 children. B.S., St. Mary's Coll., Minn., 1948; M.S. in Organic Chemistry, U. Miami, 1950; Ph.D. in Pharmacology and Biochemistry, U. Chgo., 1957. Research asst. U. Ill., 1948, U. Miami, 1949-53, U. Chgo., 1953-57; asst. prof. dept. chemistry U. Detroit, 1957-60, dir. chemistry research, 1957, assoc. prof., 1960-65, prof., 1965-69; prof. pharmacology, assoc. dean Mich. Coll. Osteo. Medicine, East Lansing, 1968-70; prof. pharmacology, assoc. dean Mich. State U. Coll. Osteo. Medicine, East Lansing, 1970-71, prof. dept. biomechanics, 1971—; curriculum coordinator Joe Berg Found. High Sch. Program, Detroit, 1958-60; dir. NSF Summer Inst. High Sch. Students, 1959; cons. clin. chemistry Bon Secours Hosp., Grosse Pointe, Mich., 1959-61; dir. biochemistry research Mt. Carmel Mercy Hosp., Detroit, 1960-62; cons. Detroit Dept. Medicine, 1962; dir. life scis. Council United Research in Devel. and Aging, 1965; dir. Osteo. Regional Med. Program, Mich., 1968-69. Contbr. numerous articles to profl. jours. Patentee in field (7). Recipient citation of merit Nat. Multiple Sclerosis Soc., 1961, Mich. Acad. Sci., Arts and Letters, 1966; Bishop Heffron award St. Mary's Coll., 1970; Sigma Pi Founders award, 1964; Educator of Yr. award Alpha Epsilon Delta, 1964; grantee Am. Osteo. Assn., Ashland Oil Co., Ciba Pharms., U. Detroit, Med-Chem Labs., Mich. Cancer Found., Mich. Heart Assn., Mich. Lung Assn., Mich. Osteo. Coll. Found., Muscular Dystrophy Assn., NIH, Nat. Multiple Sclerosis Soc., NSF, Reichhold Found., Dept. Army, also others; Damon Runyon fellow, 1949-50; Mt. Sinai fellow, 1949-51; U. Chgo. scholar, 1953-54, 56-57). Fellow Am. Inst. Chemists; mem. Am. Chem. Soc., N.Y. Acad. Scis., Assn. Analytical Chemists, Brit. Biochem. Soc., Mich. Nucleonic Soc., AAAS, Am. Soc. Clin. Pathologists, Albertus Magnus Guild, Am. Assn. Clin. Chemists, Am. Oil Chemists Soc., Soc. Exptl. Biology and Medicine, Fedn. European Biochem. Socs., Sigma Xi, Alpha Epsilon Delta, Sigma Pi. Office: Mich State U Coll Osteo Medicine East Lansing MI 48824

KABAT, KEVIN THOMAS, human resources executive, educator; b. Huntington, N.Y., Feb. 15, 1957; s. Harry and Gena (Lorenzetti) K.; m. Patricia Lorraine Bullis, Aug. 18, 1979; children—Matthew Kevin, Jennifer Patricia. B.A., Johns Hopkins U., 1979; M.S., Purdue U., 1981. Cons. orgnl. devel. Mchts. Nat. Bank, Indpls., 1980-82; officer personnel Old Kent Bank, Grand Rapids, Mich., 1982-83, asst. v.p., 1984—; adj. prof. Purdue U., Indpls., 1980-82, Grand Valley State Coll., Allendale, Mich., 1982, Davenport Coll., Grand Rapids, 1983—. Mem. Am. Soc. Personnel Profls. Office: Old Kent Bank and Trust 1 Vandenberg Ctr Grand Rapids MI 49503

KABLER, MICHAEL LEE, school psychologist, educator, consultant; b. Ripley, Ohio, Sept. 24, 1943; s. Howard L. and Mary Helen (Schuman) K.; m. Diane Ellen Wells, Aug. 17, 1968; children—Heather Lee, Heidi Anne. B.S., Ohio State U., 1966, M.A., Ohio State U., 1968, Ph.D., 1976. Lic. psychologist, Ohio, profl. sch. psychologist, Ohio. Tchr., Westerville (Ohio) Pub. Schs., 1966-69, dir pupil services, 1984— psychologist Franklin County (Ohio) Pub. Schs., 1970-72; chief sch. psychologist Franklin County (Ohio) Pub. Schs., 1972-74; ednl. cons. Ohio Dept. Edn., Columbus, 1976-77, coordinator program rev. 1977-79, cons. sch. psychol. services, 1982-84; asst. prof. Ohio State U., Columbus, 1980-82, adj. asst. prof. 1982—; adminstr. multihandicapped unit Ohio State Sch. for Blind, Columbus, 1984-85; mem. Ohio Sch. Psychology Exam. Com.; assoc. editor The Directive Teacher mag., Spl. Services in the Schs. jour. Grantee Ohio Dept. Edn. 1980, Spencer Found., 1981. Mem. Am. Psychol. Assn., Council Exceptional Children, Ohio Sch. Psychologists Assn., Nat. Assn. Pupil Personnel Adminstrs., Nat. Assn. Sch. Psychologists, Assn. Pupil Personnel Adminstrs., Ohio Assn. Pupil Personnel Adminstrs., Phi Delta Kappa. Author: (with Dardig and Heward) Leaders Manual—Sign Here, 1977; (with Crisci, Garwood and Wendt) The Ohio School

Psychologists Association Handbook on Law, 1978; contbr. articles to profl. jours. Office: 336 S Otterbein Ave Westerville OH 43081

KACHEL, CHARLES ALBERT, hospital administrator; b. South Bend, Ind., Nov. 23, 1939; s. Albert Philip and Helen Louise (Peterson) K.; m. Susan Rebecca Bouvy, June 23, 1962; children—Ann, Alan, Chris, Andy. B.A., Ind. U., 1962, postgrad., 1962; postgrad. Butler U., 1963. Registered central service technician. Ins. adjuster Aetna Life Ins., Indpls., 1963-66; pharm. salesman Ciba-Geigy Corp., South Bend, Ind., Flint, Mich., 1966-73; lab. supr., central service supr. Flint Osteo. Hosp., 1973—. Chmn. fund drive United Way, Flint Osteo. Hosp., 1977. Mem. Internat. Assn. Hosp. Central Service, Mich. Soc. Hosp. Central Service, Mid-Mich. Central Service Assn. Roman Catholic. Avocations: cooking; classical music; opera. Home: 1010 Southlawn Flint MI 48507 Office: Flint Osteopathic Hosp 3921 Beecher Rd Flint MI 48502

KADERLAN, NORMAN STANLEY, performing arts administrator, management consultant; b. Bklyn., Aug. 26, 1943; s. Sidney Arthur and Tauba (Knight) K.; m. Alice Youngerman, Dec. 28, 1969 (div. Jan. 1985); 1 child, Joshua. B.S. in Biology, MIT, 1965; M.S. in History of Sci., U. Wis., 1966, Ph.D. in Arts Adminstrn., 1970. Performing arts supr. Arlington County, Va., 1970-75; dir. cultural programs Nat. Pub. Radio, Washington, 1975-79; cons. mgmt., Akron, Ohio, 1979—; gen. dir. Opera/Omaha, 1980-81; gen. mgr. Ohio Ballet, Akron, 1983-85; pres. Kaderlan Group, Akron, 1985—; bd. dirs. Ohio Dance, Cleve., 1984-85; mem. program panel Nebr. Arts Council, Omaha, 1982; chmn. Parks, Arts and Leisure Project, Washington, 1972-75. Author: (monograph) The Role of the Arts Administrator, 1972. Bd. dirs. Akron Regional Devel. Bd., 1984-85; participant Leadership Akron, 1984-85; fin. dir. Fellman for Congress, Omaha, 1982; mem. CATV Adv. Com., Arlington, Va., 1973-74. Recipient Karl T. Compton prize Mit, 1965. Office: Kaderlan Group 89 Edgerton Rd Akron OH 44303

KADISH, STEPHEN LEONARD, lawyer; b. N.Y.C., Oct. 3, 1938. B.A., Williams Coll., 1960; LL.B., Columbia U., 1963; LL.M. in Taxation, Georgetown U., 1966. Bar: N.Y. 1965, Ohio 1965, U.S. Tax Ct. 1965. Ptnr., Burke, Haber & Berick, Cleve., 1965-71; v.p. Metzenbaum, Gaines & Stern Co., L.P.A., Cleve., 1971-75; pres. Kadish & Krantz Co., L.P.A., Cleve., 1975-84, Kadish & Bender, Cleve., 1984—. Contbr. articles to profl. jours. Mem. Greater Cleve. Bar Assn. (chmn. gen. tax com. 1975-77), Cuyahoga County Bar Assn. (chmn. tax com. 1975-77, 80), Ohio State Bar Assn., Fed. Bar Assn., ABA, Tax Club of Cleve. (pres., dir. 1983—). Office: 1717 E 9th St #1212 Cleveland OH 44114

KADIYALA, KOTESWARA RAO, econometrics educator; b. Mustabada, India, Apr. 20, 1933; came to U.S. 1962, naturalized 1981; s. Venkayya and Anna Poorna (Korivi) K.; m. June 15, 1957; children—Ravindra Kumar, Rajendra Kumar, Rajeswarrao, Suseela Anna. B.Sc. with honors, Andhra U., 1957; M.S. in Stats., Indian Statis. Inst., 1959; Ph.D., Minn. U., 1966. Asst. prof. Wayne State U., Detroit, 1966-67; asst. prof. U. Western Ont., London, Can., 1967-69, assoc. prof., 1969-70, prof., 1970-71; prof. Purdue U., West Lafayette, Ind., 1971—. Mem. Am. Statis. Assn. Home: 484 Littleton St West Lafayette IN 47906 Office: Purdue U Krannert Bldg West Lafayette IN 47906

KADLEC, ROBERT HENRY, engineering educator, consultant; b. Racine, Wis., June 11, 1938; s. Henry and Alice Blanche (Chernohorsky) K.; m. Kathleen Grace Benson, Apr. 20, 1957 (div. 1978); children—Debra, Christopher, Jonathan; m. D. Kay Ferris, Sept. 28, 1979; children—Sheldon McCracken, Laura McCracken. B.S., U. Wis.-Madison, 1958; M.S., U. Mich., 1959, Ph.D., 1961. Registered profl. engr., Mich. Prof. engineering U. Mich., Ann Arbor, 1961—. Editor Am. Inst. Chem. Engring. Jour., 1977—. Contbr. articles to profl. jours. Recipient Outstanding Teaching and Leadership award Phi Lambda Upsilon, 1971-72, Am. and Mich. Cons. Engrs. Council award, 1976. Mem. Am. Inst. Chem. Engrs. (Chem. Engr. of Yr. Detroit chpt. 1985), Am. Soc. Engring. Edn., Soc. Wetland Scis., Internat. Peat Soc., Internat. Soc. Ecologial Modeling, Nat. Soc. Profl. Engrs., Mich. Soc. Profl. Engrs. Avocations: Wilderness canoeing; tennis. Office: 3094 Dow Bldg Ann Arbor MI 28109-2136

KADLUBOWSKI, MICHAEL GEORGE, business executive; b. Reno, Feb. 17, 1945; s. Stanley Laurance and Constance Sadie (Colby) K.; B.A. in Accounting with honors, North Eastern Ill. U., Chgo., 1978; children—Michelle Leigh, Jeffrey Kurtis. Chief accountant Pyle Nat. Corp., Chgo., 1969-72; corp. controller Doncor, Inc., Chgo., 1972-73; controller Emconite div., Chgo., 1973-77; corp. controller, chief fin. officer, v.p. Bearcat Tire Co., 1977-81; v.p. fin. Rescar Inc., Chgo., 1982—. Served with USN, 1965-69. Mem. Am. Acctg. Assn., Am. Mgmt. Assn., Shellback Fraternity, Good Samaritan Hosp. Aux., Beta Alpha Psi. Home: 107 Regency Dr Lombard IL 60148 Office: 1101 31st St Suite 110 Downers Grove IL 60515

KAEHR, ROBERT EUGENE, librarian, educator; b. Bluffton, Ind., July 2, 1942; s. William Edward and Vendetta Edna (Hupp) K.; m. Winnifred Helen Bertha Suski, Aug. 14, 1965; children—Renee Helen, Thomas Ryan. B.S., Huntington Coll., 1964; M.S., No. Ariz. U., 1972; M.L.S., George Peabody Coll. for Tchrs., Nashville, 1976. Tchr. Edon Sch. Dist. (Ohio), 1964-65, Huntington Sch. Corp. (Ind.), 1965-68, Window Rock Sch. Dist. (Ariz.), 1968-76; librarian, asst. prof. library sci. and dir. library services Huntington Coll., 1976—; chmn. planning small coll. com. Office Mgmt. Studies. Mem. Ind. Library Assn. (coll. and Univ. library div., exec. bd. mem. at large), Assn. Christian Librarians, Tri-Area Library Services Authority (exec. bd., mem. planning and evaluation com.), Beta Phi Mu. Mem. United Brethren Ch. Book reviewer Christian Librarian, Fortress Press. Office: 2303 College Ave Huntington IN 46750

KAGAN, ANDREW AARON, engineering company executive, author; b. St. Louis, Sept. 22, 1947; s. William and Rose (Gerber) K. A.B., Wash. U., 1969; M.A., Harvard U., 1971, Ph.D., 1977. Critic-in-residence Bennington Coll., Vt., 1973; critic art, music, architecture St. Louis Globe-Democrat, 1977-80; contbg. editor, assoc. editor Arts Mag., N.Y.C., 1975—; pres., chief exec. officer Aalco Engring. Corp., St. Louis, 1978—; vis. prof. art history Wash. U., 1980-81; fine arts cons., St. Louis, 1977—. Author: Paul Klee Art and Music, 1983; Mark Rothko, 1985. Contbr. numerous articles to profl. jours. Nominator awards in The Visual Arts, Atlanta, 1982; advisor, cons. NASA Art in Space Program, Washington, 1983; mem. adv. panel Mo. Arts Council, Jefferson City, 1985—. Ford Found grantee, 1968-69; Kingsbury fellow, 1970-73, Harvard traveling fellow, 1973-77. Mem. Phi Beta Kappa. Avocations: golf; bridge; chess; sky diving. Home: 3434 Shenandoah St St Louis MO 63104

KAGAN, ANDREW BESDIN, lawyer; b. Pittsfield, Mass., Apr. 26, 1949; s. David Bernard and Irene Sylvia (Besdin) K. B.A. in Psychology, Syracuse U., 1971; M.A. in Psychiat. Social Work, U. Chgo., 1975; J.D. with honors, Rutgers U., 1980. Bar: Ill. 1980, U.S. Dist. Ct. (no. dist.) Ill. 1980, U.S. Ct. Appeals (7th cir.) 1980. Psychiat. social worker Austen Riggs Ctr., Stockbridge, Mass., 1971-73, Michael Reese Hosp., Chgo., 1975-77; assoc. Mandel, Lipton & Stevenson, Ltd., Chgo., 1980-82; sole practice, Chgo., 1982—; arbitrator, comml. panel Am. Arbitration Assn., Chgo., 1984, Better Bus. Bur., Chgo., 1984; instr. Northeastern Ill. U., Chgo., 1984. Recipient Am. Jurisprudence award Lawyer's Coop. Pub. Co., Rochester, N.Y., 1980. Mem. Ill. Bar Assn., Chgo. Bar Assn. (mem. lawyer referral service 1984). Home: 1121 Washington Blvd Oak Park IL 60302 Office: 69 W Washington St Suite 1154 Chicago IL 60602

KAGAN, DAVID DENNIS, priest, communications administrator; b. Spring-Grove, Ill., Nov. 9, 1949; s. Louis Leigh and Catherine Ruth (Hoffman) K. B.A. summa cum laude, Loras Coll., 1971; St.B. magna cum laude, Pontifical Gregorian U., Rome, 1975, J.C.L. magna cum laude, 1979. Ordained priest Roman Catholic Ch., 1975; assoc. pastor St. Patrick Parish, Dixon, Ill., 1975-77; instr. Newman Cath. High Sch., Sterling, Ill., also campus minister Sauk Valley Coll., 1975-77; advocate, judge and vice officialist Diocesan Tribunal, Rockford, Ill., 1976-78, 79—, diocesan dir. office communications, 1982—; instr. Boylan Central Cath. High Sch. Mem. Canon Law Sc. Am., Cath. Theol. Soc. Am. (assoc. mem.). Office: 850 N Church Suite 300-301 Rockford IL 61103

KAGAN, GEORGE IRWIN, dentist; b Brookline, Mass., Aug. 8, 1939; s. Abraham and Sylvia (Coleman) K. S.B., U. Chgo., 1961, B.S. in Dentistry, 1963; D.D.S., U. Ill., 1965. Nursing technician Cook County Sch. Nursing, Chgo., 1964-65; intern U. Chgo., 1965-66; staff dentist Chgo. Bd. Health, 1966-68; Stickney Twp. Pub. Health Dist., Burbank, Ill., 1969; dental health care provider State of Ill., 1969-79; gen. practice dentistry, Chgo., 1968—; table clinician Chgo. Dental Soc., 1980—, Ariz. State Dental Soc., Phoenix, 1983-85. Served to capt. USAR, 1965-67. Fellow Acad. Gen. Dentistry, Royal Soc. Health; mem. Chgo. Dental Soc., Royal Coll. Dental Surgeons Ont. (licentiate), Ill. State Dental Soc., ADA. Republican. Club: Ill. Railway Museum (Union). Avocations: railroading, restoration of classic autos, motorsports, touring. Office: 1525 E 53d St #516 Chicago IL 60615

KAGLER, WILLIAM G., retail company executive. Pres., dir. The Kroger Co., Cin. Office: The Kroger Co 1014 Vine St Cincinnati OH 45201*

KAHLE, CATHY BENNING, librarian; b. Huntingburg, Ind., June 21, 1956; d. Leonard Henry and Anna Mae (Johnson) B.; m. Wayne Kahle, June 29, 1985. B.S., Elmhurst Coll. (Ill.), 1979; M.L.S., Ind. U., 1981. Instructional media asst. A.C. Buehler Library Elmhurst Coll., 1976-79; readers asst. Lilly Library Ind. U., Bloomington, 1980; asst. librarian Jasper Pub. Library-Dubois County Contractual Library, Jasper, Ind., 1981-84, dir., 1984—; bd. dirs. Ind. Coop. Library Services Authority, Indpls., 1981—. Bd. dirs. St. Paul United Ch. of Christ, Holland, Ind., 1983—. Mem. ALA, Ind. Library Assn. (chairperson Dist. VII 1982-83). Office: Jasper Pub Library-Dubois County Contractual Library 1116 Main St Jasper IN 47546

KAHLENBECK, HOWARD, JR., lawyer; b. Fort Wayne, Ind., Dec. 7, 1929; s. Howard and Clara Elizabeth (Wegman) K.; B.S. with distinction, Ind. U., 1952; LL.B., U. Mich., 1957; m. Sally A. Horrell, Aug. 14, 1954; children—Kathryn Sue, Douglas H. Admitted to Ind. bar, 1957; partner Krieg, DeVault, Alexander & Capehart, Indpls., 1957—; sec., dir. Maul Tech. Corp. (formerly Buehler Corp.), indsl. equipment mfg., Indpls., 1971-81, Am. Monitor Corp., med. equipment mfg., Indpls., 1971—, Am. Interstate Ins. Corp. Wis., Milw., 1973-84, Am. Interstate Ins. Co. Ga., 1973—, Am. Underwriters Group, Inc., ins. holding corp., Indpls., 1973—. Served with USAF, 1952-54. Mem. Am., Ind., Indpls. bar assns., Alpha Kappa Psi, Delta Theta Phi, Beta Gamma Sigma, Delta Upsilon Internat. (sec., dir. 1971-83, chmn., dir. 1983—). Lutheran. Home: 6320 Old Orchard Rd Indianapolis IN 46226 Office: 2800 Indiana National Bank Tower Indianapolis IN 46204

KAHN, CHARLES FREDERICK, JR., lawyer; b. Milw., Apr. 19, 1949; s. Charles Frederick and Louise Ann (Hartmann) K.; m. Elizabeth Martha Brauer, Dec. 28, 1975. B.A., George Washington U., 1971; J.D., U. Wis., 1974. Bar: Wis. 1975, U.S. Dist. Ct. (ea. and we. dists.) Wis. 1975, U.S. Supreme Ct. 1983. Staff atty. Wis. Indian Legal Services, Keshena, 1975-76; trial atty. misdemeanor and felony divs. Legal Aid Soc. Milw., 1976-78, chief staff atty. juvenile div., 1978; ptnr. Kahn & Levine, 1979-83; sr. atty. Charles Kahn & Assocs., Milw., 1983—; spl. prosecutor pro tem Milw. County, 1981-82; counsel for Bd. of Attys. Profl. Responsibility, 1981—; cir. ct. commr., part-time 1983—; mng. v.p. Colby-Abbot Bldg. Co., 1980—; vis. lectr. dept. criminal justice U. Wis.-Milw., 1982-85; moderator, speaker, panelist profl. seminars and convs.; testimonial witness Wis. Senate and Assembly, 1981, 83. Contbr. writings to profl. publs. Bd. dirs. Parents Anonymous of Greater Milw., 1980-84; vice chmn. Milw. County North Shore Unit, Democratic Party of Wis., 1982-84; mem. Gov.'s Exec. Trade Delegation to Israel, 1985. Recipient Pro Bono award Posner Found., 1983; named Outstanding Young Lawyer 1980, Milw. Jaycees. Mem. ABA, Milw. Bar Assn., Wis. Acad. Trial Lawyers, Bar Assn. 7th Fed. Cir., ACLU, Am. Jewish Com., Bldg. Owners and Mgrs. Assn. (bd. dirs. polit. action com. 1983-84), Milw. Young Lawyers Assn. (chmn. criminal justice com. 1980-81), Met. Milw. Assn. Commerce, Nat. Audubon Soc., Wis. Environ. Decade. Club: Photo Club of Schlitz Audubon Ctr. Home: 2105 E Newton Ave Milwaukee WI 53211 Office: 759 N Milwaukee St Suite 500 Milwaukee WI 53202

KAHN, DAVID, dermatologist, dermatology educator; b. Bay City, Mich., Sept. 21, 1912; s. Alexander and Augusta (Dreyer) K.; m. Carrol Mae Green, Apr. 6, 1941; children—Wendy, Susan. A.B., U. Mich., 1934, M.D., 1938; M.S. in Dermatology, U. Chgo., 1942. Diplomate Am. Bd. Dermatology. Intern Harper Hosp., Detroit, 1938-39; resident U. Chgo. Clinics, 1939-41, resident instr. dermatology, 1941-42; practice medicine specializing in dermatology, Lansing, Mich., 1946—; prof. dermatology Mich. State U., East Lansing, 1973—. Contbr. articles to profl. jours. Bd. dirs. Community Services Council, Lansing, 1952-58, Community Chest, Lansing, 1955-61. Served to maj. U.S. Army, 1942-46, ETO. Co-author landmark article republished in centennial issue Archives Dermatology, 1982. Fellow Am. Acad. Dermatology; mem. Central States Dermatol. Soc., Internat. Soc. Tropical Dermatology, Mich. Dermatol. Soc. (pres. 1964), Ingham County Med. Soc. (pres. 1961). Jewish. Office: Lansing Dermatology PC 2909 East Grand River St Lansing MI 48912

KAHN, JAN EDWARD, manufacturing company executive; b. Dayton, Ohio, Aug. 29, 1948; s. Sigmond Lawrence and Betty Jane K.; B.S. in Metall. Engring., U. Cin., 1971; m. Deborah Ann Deckinga, Nov. 28, 1975; children—Jason Edward, Justin Allen. Mgmt. trainee U.S. Steel Corp., Gary, Ind., 1971-72; plant metallurgist Regal Tube Co., Chgo., 1972-74, gen. foreman, 1974-76, supt., 1976-77, mgr. tech. service, 1978-80, materials mgr., 1980-81; mgr. quality control Standard Tube Co., Detroit, 1977-78; dir. ops. Boye Needle Co., Chgo., 1981-82, v.p. ops., 1982-83, v.p., gen. mgr., 1984-85, pres., 1985—. Mem. Am. Soc. Metals, AIME, ASTM, Ravenswood Indsl. Council (bd. dirs. 1983-84, pres. 1985—). Republican. Christian Reformed Ch. Club: Triangle. Home: 9135 S Mulligan Oak Lawn IL 60453 Office: 4343 N Ravenswood Chicago IL 60613

KAHN, MARK LEO, arbitrator, educator; b. N.Y.C., Dec. 16, 1921; s. Augustus and Manya (Fertig) K.; B.A., Columbia U., 1942; M.A., Harvard U., 1948, Ph.D. in Econs., 1950; m. Ruth Elizabeth Wecker, Dec. 21, 1947 (div. Jan. 1972); children—Ann Mariam, Peter David, James Allan, Jean Sarah. Asst. economist U.S. OSS, Washington, 1942-43; teaching fellow Harvard U., 1947-49; dir. case analysis U.S. WSB, Region 6-B Mich., 1952-53; mem. faculty Wayne State U., Detroit, 1949-85, prof. econs., 1960-85, prof. emeritus, 1985—, dept. chmn., 1961-68, dir. indsl. relations M.A. Program, 1978-85; arbitrator union-mgmt. disputes, specializing in airline industry. Bd. govs. Jewish Welfare Fedn. Detroit, 1976-82; trustee Mich. Quality of Work Life Council, 1978—; bd. dirs. Jewish Home for Aged, Detroit, 1978—. Served to capt. AUS, 1943-46. Decorated Bronze Star. Mem. Indsl. Relations Research Assn. (pres. Detroit chpt. 1956, exec. sec. 1979—; exec. bd. 1986—), Am. Econ. Assn., AAUP (past chpt. pres.), Nat. Acad. Arbitrators (bd. govs. 1960-62, v.p. 1976-78, chmn. membership com. 1979-82, pres. 1983-84). Co-author: Collective Bargaining and Technological Change in American Transportation, 1971; contbr. articles to profl. jours. Home and Office: 4140 2d Ave Detroit MI 48201

KAHN, SANDRA S., psychotherapist; b. Chgo., June 24, 1942; d. Chester and Ruth (Goldblatt) Sutker; m. Jack Murry Kahn, June 1, 1965; children—Erick, Jennifer. B.A., U. Miami, 1964; M.A., Roosevelt U., 1976. Tchr. Chgo. Pub. Schs., 1965-67; pvt. practice psychotherapy, Northbrook, Ill., 1976—; host Shared Feelings, Sta. WEEF, Highland Park, Ill., 1983—. Author: The Kahn Report on Sexual Preferences, 1981. Mem. Ill. Psychol. Assn., Chgo. Psychol. Assn. Jewish. Office: 2970 Maria Ave Northbrook IL 60062

KAHNWEILER, WILLIAM MARK, management consultant, trainer; b. Chgo., May 4, 1950; s. Louis S. and Ruth M. (Markus) K.; m. Jennifer Boretz, June 17, 1973; children—Lindsey Meg, Jessie Beth. B.A., Washington U., St. Louis, 1972, M.Ed., 1973; Ph.D., Fla. State U., 1979. Program adminstr. Adolescent Counseling Ctr., Amherst (Mass.) High Sch., 1973-76; instr., cons., researcher, therapist Fla. State U., Fla. Correctional Inst., Tallahassee, 1976-79; asst. prof. Miami U., Oxford, Ohio, 1979-80; mgmt. trainer, cons. Gen. Electric Co., Cin., 1980-83; mgmt. cons. Hay Mgmt. Cons., Cin., 1983—; cons. indsl., fin., service and health care orgns.; cons. to sch. systems, 1976-79; adj. prof. U. Cin., Miami U., 1980—. Mem. Am. Psychol. Assn. (div. indsl. and organizational psychology), Am. Soc. Tng. and Devel., Phi Beta Kappa. Club: Athletic (Cin.). Contbr. articles to profl. jours. Office: First Nat Bank Ctr 425 Walnut St Cincinnati OH 45202

KAIGHIN, BARBARA ANN, police officer; b. St. Louis, Dec. 29, 1946; d. William Wesley and Kathleen Majorie (Vadner) Fisher; m. Donald Charles Kaighin, Nov. 4, 1975; (dec. Jan. 1982); children—Charles Jay, Angela Kay. Grad. Greater St. Louis Police Acad., 1973; B.S. in Criminal Justice, Northeast Mo. State Univ., 1978; M.A. in Mgmt., Webster Univ., 1983; postgrad. St. Louis U. Police officer St. Louis County Police, St. Louis, 1973-80; security police officer McDonnel Douglas Security, St. Charles, Mo., 1980-81; police officer City of Ballwin, Mo., 1982—; trainee/advisor Police Reserves/Scouts, Ballwin, 1982—. Named Disting. Expert (Firearms) St. Louis Police Acad., 1973; Am. Business Women's Assn. scholar, 1983. Mem. Internat. Order Women Police, Mo. Assn. Women Police, Am. Soc. Tng. and Devel., Am. Assn. Counseling and Devel. Republican. Roman Catholic. Avocations: coach teen girls softball team; travel. Home: 4 Kilkenny Hills Pacific MO 63069 Office: Ballwin Police Dept 300 City Hall Dr Ballwin MO 63011

KAISER, MARK STEVEN, biometrician, government official; b. St. Louis, July 7, 1958; s. Eldor Carl and Delores Ruth (Garberding) K. B.S. magna cum laude, in Wildlife, Univ. Mo., Columbia, 1980, M.S. in Wildlife, 1982, M.A. in Stats., 1984. Research assoc. Dept. Agr., Columbia, 1982-84; biometrician U.S. Fish and Wildlife Service, Columbia, 1984—; cons. in field. Contbr. articles to Col. Waterbirds, Jour. Wildlife Mgmt., Wilson Bull. Lobyist Alaska Coalition, Washington, 1978. Curators scholar U. Mo., 1976, Univ. scholar, 1977-79; Love Conservation Found. fellow, 1981-82. Mem. Am. Statis. Assn., Biometric Soc., Am. Ornithologist's Union, Wildlife Soc., Sierra Club (past officer 1978-79). Lutheran. Avocations: Waterfowl decoy carving. Home: 1506 Fir Pl Columbia MO 65201 Office: Columbia Nat Fisheries Research Lab Route #1 Columbia MO 65201

KAISER, PAUL JACOB, consulting engineer, retired county official; b. Calumet, Mich., Dec. 5, 1925; s. William Lewis and Elizabeth Theresa (Marston) K.; m. Bette Ruth Hore, July 28, 1951; children—William G., Catherine M. Kaiser Bolton, Susan E. B.S. in Civil Engring., Mich. Tech. U., 1953. Registered profl. engr., Mich. Project engr. Houghton County Road Commn., Hancock, Mich., 1946-50; county hwy. engr. Baraga County Road Commn., L'Anse, Mich., 1950-51; engr., supt. C.G. Bridges Constrn. Co., Escanaba, Mich., 1951-52; county hwy. engr. mgr. Van Buren County Road Commn., Lawrence, Mich., 1953-85, ret., 1985; now cons. engr. Mem. regional exec. bd. Boy Scouts Am., 1980—. Served with C.E., U.S. Army, 1943-46. Mem. Nat. Assn. County Engrs., Am. Road and Transp. Builders Assn., Mich. Engring. Soc., County Road Assn. Mich., Am. Legion. Republican. Presbyterian. Contbr. articles to profl. jours. Home: 51693 351/2th St Paw Paw MI 49079

KAISER, RAYMOND LEROY, business office procedures educator; b. Strasburg, Ohio, Dec. 23, 1929; s. George Edward and Anna Marie (Shear) K.; m. Anna Mae Gerber, July 17, 1952; children—James Robert, Patricia Ann, Terry Lee. B.S. in Edn. cum laude, Kent State U., 1955, M.E. in Edn., 1960. Cert. tchr., Ohio. Acct., Arthur G. McKee Co., 1950-52; tchr. bus. edn. Baltic (Ohio) High Sch., 1954-60; tchr. acctg. typing, shorthand, bus. English, bus. math. and vocat. acctg. Washington High Sch., Massillon, Ohio, 1960—. Mem. Ohio Edn. Assn., Ohio Vocat. Educators Assn., Kappa Delta Pi. Republican. Mem. Nazarene Ch. Clubs: Ashland Pioneer Coin and Investment Guild, Masons, Grange.

KAKAR, SATYA NARAIN, geneticist; b. Multan, Panjab, India (now Pakistan), Oct. 2, 1933; came to U.S., 1980; s. Krishan Narain and Leela Wati (Gandhi) K.; m. Sushem Trehan, Oct. 14, 1966; children—Rajat, Bharat. B.Sc. with honors in Botany, Delhi U. (India), 1953, M.Sc. in Botany, 1955; Ph.D. in Genetics, U. Wash., 1961. Prof., sr. prof., chmn. dept. Haryana Agrl. U., Hissar, India, 1967-72, dean basic scis., 1972—; vis. prof. Mich. State U., East Lansing, 1980-81, 82-84; vis. scientist U. Wash., Seattle, 1981-82; scientist Corn Products Corp., Summit-Argo, Ill., 1985—; cons. Cold Spring Harbor Lab. (N.Y.), 1984, RECOMTEX, East Lansing, 1984; mem. Internat. Com. on Yeasts; mem. ad hoc com. of rev. for Internat. Union Biol. Scis., com. on data coding and processing World Fedn. Culture Collection; former mem. Univ. Grants Commn. India, panel for biol. sci. and dean's com. for basic sci. Indian Council for Agrl. Research. Mem. Genetics Soc. Am., Sigma Xi. Avocations: badminton; bridge; camping; music; reading. Office: Moffett Tech Ctr Corn Products Corp Box 345 Summit-Argo IL 60501

KALB, MARTY JOEL, art educator, artist; b. Bklyn., Apr. 13, 1941; s. Herman A. Kalb and Rosalyn (Hersh) Goldway; m. Joan Bernhard, June 22, 1963; children—Peter, Rachel. B.A., Mich. State U., 1963; B.F.A., Yale U., 1964; M.A., U. Calif.-Berkeley, 1966. Instr., U. Ky., Lexington, 1966-67; faculty Ohio Wesleyan U., Delaware, 1967—, prof. art, 1981—. Exhibited one-man shows: Allan Stone Gallery, N.Y.C., 1980, Canton Art Inst., Ohio, 1981, Wright State U., Dayton, 1982, Denison U., Granville, Ohio, 1982; works represented in pub., pvt., corp. art collections. Ohio Arts Council fellow, 1979. Home: 165 Griswold St Delaware OH 43015 Office: Dept Fine Arts Ohio Wesleyan U 60 E Sandusky St Delaware OH 43015

KALBFLEISCH, GIRARD EDWARD, district court judge; b. Piqua, Ohio, Aug. 3, 1899; s. Oscar Conrad and Magdalena Margueret (Gerstmeyer) K.; m. Chattie Lenore Spohn, May 1, 1929. LL.B., Ohio No. U., 1923, LL.D. (hon.), 1960. Bar: Ohio 1924. Pros. atty. Richland County, Ohio, Mansfield, 1928-33; judge Mansfield Mcpl. Ct., 1936-42, Richland County Common Pleas Ct., 1943-59, U.S. Dist. Ct., Cleve., 1959—. Served with U.S. Army, 1918. Fellow Ohio State Bar Found.; mem. ABA, Ohio State Bar Assn., Fed. Bar Assn., Richland County Bar Assn., Ct. Nisi Prius, Soc. Benchers, Common Pleas Judges Assn. Ohio (pres. 1952). Lodges: Masons, Elks. Home: 545 Stewart Ln Mansfield OH 44907

KALDOR, NANCY ELIZABETH, educational administrator; b. Rochester, Minn., Feb. 10, 1942; d. Robert Benjamin and Helen Laura (Priebe) Kuhle; m. Richard H. Kaldor, June 15, 1963; children—Katheryn Rae, Kristin Rosalie, Kori Lynn. B.S., Mayville State Coll., 1963; cert. reading specialist, U. Minn., 1967; M.S., Kans. State U., 1979, Ph.D., 1983. Tchr. chemistry, English, Fisher High Sch., Minn., 1963-64; tchr. reading, English Cleveland Jr. High, St. Paul, Minn., 1966-68; Dist. 475, Junction City, Kans., 1973-80; prin. Dist. 481, White City, Kans., 1983—. Mem. United Sch. Adminstrn., Nat. Assn. Secondary Sch. Prins., Am. Assn. Curriculum Devel., AAUW, Kans. Assn. Secondary Prins., Am. Ednl. Research Assn., Kans. State Univ. Alumni, Harvard Dames, Internat. Reading Assn., Phi Delta Kappa, Phi Kappa Phi. Lutheran. Avocations: snow skiing, swimming, playing piano, crewel, walking. Home: 1013 K Kingsbury Dr Junction City KS 66441 Office: USD # 481 White City KS 66872

KALET, SYDNE JO, communications company sales executive; b. Buffalo, Mar. 24, 1946; d. Sidney Ralph and Caryl Jane (Cohen) K. B.S. in Speech, NYU, 1967. Profl. actress, N.Y.C., 1967-69; office adminstr. Nat. Hockey League, N.Y.C., 1969-76; owner, designer SK Designs, Ortonville, Mich., 1976-81; salesperson So. Pacific Communications, Birmingham, Mich., 1981-82; dist. sales mgr. GTE Sprint, Southfield, Mich., 1983—. Mem., past rec. sec. Lakeland Players, Waterford, Mich., 1979—; patron Detroit Inst. Arts. Mem. Internat. Orgn. of Wo/Men in Telecommunications, (past treas.), Armed Forces Communications and Electronics Assn., Nat. Assn. Female Execs., Profl. Women in Sales. Jewish. Avocations: community theatre; singing; reading; physical fitness. Home: 7043 Hillside Dr Clarkston MI 48016 Office: GTE Sprint Communications 3000 Town Center #300 Southfield MI 48075

KALISCH, BEATRICE JEAN, nursing educator, administrator; b. Tellahoma, Tenn., Oct. 15, 1943; d. Peter and Margaret Peterson; m. Philip A. Kalisch, Apr. 18, 1964; children—Philip Peter, Melanie Jean. B.S. in Nursing, U. Nebr., 1965; M.S., U. Md., 1967, Ed.D., 1970; postgrad. Case Western Res. U., 1977. Pediatric staff nurse Centre County Hosp., Bellefonte, Pa., 1965-66; instr. nursing Philipsburg State Gen. Hosp. Sch. Nursing, Pa., 1966; pediatric staff nurse Greater Balt. Med. Ctr., Towson, Md., 1967; asst. prof. maternal-child nursing Am. U., Washington, 1967-68; clin. nurse specialist N.W. Tex. Hosp., Amarillo, 1970; assoc. prof. maternal-child nursing, curriculum coordinator nursing Amarillo Coll., 1970-71; assoc. prof. nursing, dir. undergrad. program U. So. Miss., Hattiesburg, 1971-74; prof. nursing, chmn. dept. parent-child nursing, dir. grad. program in parent-child nursing, project dir., pediatric nurse practitioner program U. Mich. Sch. Nursing, Ann Arbor, 1974-77, Shirley C. Titus Disting. prof. nursing, chairperson dept. parent-child nursing, dir. grad. program parent-child nursing, 1977—; vis. disting. prof. U. Ala. Sch. Nursing, Birmingham, 1979, U. Tex.-San Antonio Sch. Nursing, summer 1981, Tex. Christian U., Harris Coll. Nursing, Ft. Worth, summer 1983. Mem. editorial adv. bd. Nursing Research, 1978—, Nursing Forum, 1981—, Nursing Outlook, 1982—. Mem. editorial bd. Springer Pub. Co., 1982—, Nursing Success Today, 1983—. Co-author: The Advance of American Nursing, 1978; Nursing Involvement in Health Planning, 1978; Child Abuse and Neglect, 1978; Politics of Nursing, 1982; Images of Nurses on Television, 1983. Editor monographs: Patient Teaching by Registered Nurses, 1982; Nurses and Physicians in Transition, 1982; others; contbr. numerous articles to profl. jours. Co-prin. investigator U.S. Cadet Nurse Corps, 1943-48, USPHS Div. Nursing, 1977-83; U.S. Steel Co. grantee, 1982, 83-84; Mich. Dept. Pub. Health Tng. grantee, 1974-77; USPHS grantee, 1976-81, 82-86. Mem. Am. Nurses' Assn., Mich. Nurses' Assn., Nat. League for Nursing, Mich. League for Nursing, Am. Pub. Health Assn., Internat. Soc. History of Nursing, Am. Heart Assn., AAAS, Am. Acad. Polit. and Social Sci., Am. Polit. Sci. Assn., Nurses' Coalition for Action in Politics, Am. Rural Health Assn. Home: 5663 Glen Oak Ct Saline MI 48176 Office: U Mich 400 N Ingalls Bldg Room 1166 Ann Arbor MI 48109

KALLESTAD, JAMES STUART, laboratory executive; b. Mpls., Jan. 21, 1941; s. Hursel O. and Helen (Dela) K. A.A. in Psychology, U. Minn., 1965, Assoc. Liberal Arts in Chemistry, 1967, cert., 1971; cert. Advanced Mgmt. Research, Inc., 1969, 72, 73, Am. Mgmt. Assn., 1970. Co-founder, part owner Kallestad Labs., Inc., Mpls., 1978—, ops. controller, 1968-69, treas., 1969-70, mktg. mgr., 1970-72, dir. mktg., 1972-73, v.p. mktg., 1973-74, tech. salesman, 1975-82, cons., 1983—; pres. Kallestad Properties, Inc., Miami, Fla., Kallestad Charters, Inc., Miami. Served with USMC, 1959-63. Mem. Am. Mktg. Assn., AAAS, Am. Mgmt. Assn., Natl Contract Mgmt. Assn., U.S. Yacht Racing Union, Biscayne Bay Yacht Racing Assn., Performance Handicap Racing Fleet, Internat. Offshore Racing Assn., Fla. Ocean Racing Assn., So. Ocean Racing Conf. (award). Clubs: Coconut Grove Sailing; St. George Sports and Yacht (Bermuda); BellAire Yacht, Lake Minnetonka. Home: 55 Holly Ln Wayzata MN 55447 Office: 1000 Lake Hazeltine Dr Chaska MN 55318

KALMON, BEN, physicist, educator; b. N.Y.C., July 9, 1913; s. Samuel and Sarah Ethel (Davidson) K.; m. Muriel Weinberg, Jan. 4, 1942; children—Judith Williamson, Sharon Weed. B.S., U. Akron, 1936, M.S., 1938. Physicist, NASA, Cleve., 1941-53, Goodyear Atomic Corp., Piketon, Ohio, 1953-75; instr. physics Shawnee State Community Coll., Portsmouth, Ohio, 1963-72, 75—. Inventor in field. Jewish. Lodges: Elks, Masons, B'nai B'rith (pres. 1975—).

KALSBEEK, DAVID HOWARD, university administrator, educational consultant, researcher; b. Cin., Jan. 16, 1956; s. Theodore William and Lewise (Wickersham) K.; m. Mary Katherine Poniatowski, Aug. 23, 1980; 1 dau. Sarah Lewise. B.A., Muskingum Coll., 1978; M.A., Ohio State Univ., 1980; postgrad. St. Louis U., 1984—. Research asst. Ohio State Univ., Columbus, 1978-80; residence edn. coordinator Mercer U., Macon, Ga., 1980-82; dir. student life studies St. Louis U., 1982—, asst. v.p. for student devel., 1985—; sr. cons. Myers-Briggs Workshops, St. Louis, 1984, 85. Mem. Am. Coll. Personnel Assn. (outstanding research award 1981, Annuit Coeptis award 1983, chmn. retention com., chmn. research and evaluation com.), Assn. Instl. Research, Nat. Assn. Student Personnel Adminstrs., Phi Sigma Tau (New Concord chpt. pres. Ohio 1977-78). Avocations: photography; computers. Office: St Louis U Student Life Studies 221 N Grand St St Louis MO 63103

KALVER, GAIL ELLEN, dance company manager; musician; b. Chgo., Nov. 25, 1948; d. Nathan Eli and Alice Martha. (Jaffe) K.; B.S. in Music Edn., U. Ill., 1970; M. in Clarinet, Chgo. Musical Coll., Roosevelt U., 1974. Profl. musician, Chgo., 1970-77; assoc. mgr. Ravinia Festival, Highland Park, Ill., 1977-83; gen. mgr. Hubbard Street Dance Co., Chgo., 1984—; bd. dirs., sec. Chicago Dance Art Coalition, 1984—; dir. Sheffield Winds, Chgo., 1982—, Ill. Arts Alliance, 1985—; mem. dance panel Ill. Arts Council, Chgo., 1983—; mem. grants panel Chgo. Office Fine Arts, 1985; cons. music Nat. Radio Theatre, Chgo., 1983. Editor: Music Explorer (for music edn.), 1983—. Office: Hubbard Street Dance Co 218 S Wabash Ave Chicago IL 60604

KALYAWONGSA, WORALAK, anesthesiologist; b. Bangkok, Thailand, Jan. 1, 1947; came to U.S., 1972; s. Nguan and Lian (Kuan) Liang. B.S., Mahidol U., 1969, M.D., 1971. Diplomate Am. Bd. Anesthesiology. Intern, Miriam Hosp., Brown U., Providence, R.I., 1972-73; resident in anesthesiology Northwestern U., Chgo., 1973-76; chief, anesthesia dept. St. Joseph Hosp., Mishawaka, Ind., 1977-81; v.p. med. staff St. Joseph Hosp., 1982, assoc. anesthesiologist, 1983—, chief anesthesia dept., 1984—; pres. Kaly Med. Corp., 1977—. Mem. AMA, Am. Soc. Anesthesiologists, Ind. Soc. Anesthesiologists. Office: PO Box 125 215 W Fourth St Mishawaka IN 46544

KAMIKOW, NORMAN B., publishing company executive; b. Chgo., Dec. 25, 1943; s. Howard M. and Ethel (Morris) K.; B.A. in Journalism, Drake U., 1967 (div.); children—Jeffrey R., David A. Account exec. Chgo. Tribune, 1967-69; account exec., dir. sales devel. Branham Newspapers, Chgo., 1969-72; asso. Chgo. mgr. Seventeen mag., 1972-76; Midwest advt. dir. Penthouse Internat., Chgo., 1976-82; pres. Kamikow & Co., Pubs.' Reps., 1982—, Decks, Inc., 1984—; dir. D.E.K. Properties, Power Advt.; guest lectr. U. Ill. Mem. Chgo. Advt. Club, Nat. Assn. Pubs. Reps. Clubs: Plaza, East Bank, Agate of Chgo.; Variety of Ill. Office: 1309 Rand Rd Arlington Heights IL 60004

KAMIN, KAY HODES, lawyer, educational historian; b. Chgo., July 3, 1940; d. Barnet and Eleanor (Cramer) Hodes; m. Malcolm S. Kamin, June 12, 1963; children—Kim Alison, Kyle Barret. B.A., Vassar Coll., 1961, M.A., U. Chgo., 1962, Ph.D., 1970; J.D. cum laude, Northwestern U., 1981. Bars: Ill. 1981, U.S. Dist. Ct. (no. dist.) Ill. 1981. Cert. tchr., Ill. History tchr. Lincoln Park High Sch., Chgo., 1963-67; social studies coordinator U. Chgo., 1968-69; assoc. prof. edn. Rosary Coll., River Forest, Ill., 1970-76; jud. law clk. Ill. Appellate Ct., Chgo., 1981-83; assoc. Mayer, Brown & Platt, Chgo., 1983—. Co-author: Contract Law, 1983. Contbr. articles to profl. jours. Pres., Chgo. Council for Social Studies, 1967-69, Soc. Contemporary Art (pres.), Chgo. Art Inst., 1974-76; governing life mem. Chgo. Art Inst., 1974—. Grad. fellow U. Chgo., 1967-70. Mem. Chgo. Bar Assn., Ill. Bar Assn., ABA, Chgo. Council Lawyers. Club: Arts. Office: Mayer Brown & Platt 231 S LaSalle St Chicago IL 60604

KAMINSKI, ROBERT STANLEY, fastner company executive; b. Youngstown, Ohio, Feb. 3, 1936; s. Stanley and Agnes (Javorsky) K.; m. Mary Ann Bell, Feb. 9, 1957; children—Robert M., Janice M., David M. B.E. in Chem. Engring., Youngstown U., 1961. Dept. mgr. Brush Wellman, Elmore, Ohio, 1971-73, div. mgr., 1973-75; v.p. ops. S.K. Wellman, Bedford, Ohio, 1975-81, Janesville Products, Norwalk, Ohio, 1981-83; pres. Continental/Midland, Park Forest, Ill., 1983—. Mem. Am. Inst. Chem. Engrs., Jaycees. Lodge: KC. Avocations: golf; Little League coaching; Sunday School teaching. Home: 3500 Parthenon Way Olympia Fields IL 60461 Office: Continental/Midland 25000 S Western Ave Park Forest IL 60466

KAMINSKY, ALBERT ABRAHAM, jeweler, watchmaker; b. Toronto, Ont., Can., Jan. 18, 1921; came to U.S., 1922-23; s. Morris Isaac and Anna Altah (Eichenthal) K.; m. Alice Patricia Harris, Apr. 15, 1952; children—Gary Earl, Deborah Ann, Steven Mark. Cert. master watchmaker. Ptnr. Kaminsky Jewelers, Fostoria, Ohio, 1945—; Findlay, Ohio, 1964-83, owner, pres., 1983—. Mem. Bd. Health, Fostoria, 1960. Served as staff sgt. USAF, 1942-45, ETO. Mem. Horological Inst. Am., Am. Watchmakrs Inst. Democrat. Jewish. Lodges: Masons, Shriners. Avocations: literature; music; swimming; restoration of antique watches. Home: 1804 Hilton Ave Findlay OH 45840 Office: Kaminsky Jewelers 414 S Main St PO Box 964 Findlay OH 45839

KAMINSKY, LON ARDEN, chiropractic physician; b. Oshkosh, Wis., June 12, 1944; s. Harold William and Ethel Vivian (Pultz) K.; m. Terry Wright, June 14, 1978; children—Cara Dawn, Michael Arden, Katherine Darice. B.A., Andrews U., Berrien Springs, Mich., 1968; D.Chiropractic, Northwestern Coll., St. Paul, 1978; M.D., Kepler U., Zurich, Switzerland, 1980. Diplomate Am. Bd. Chiropractic Examiners; cert. homeopathic physician. Mktg. mgr. Standard Oil Co., Eau Claire, Wis., 1965-73; intern Stewartville (Minn.) Clinic, 1976-77; resident in family practice, Lafayette, Ind., 1977-78; pvt. practice chiropractic medicine, West Lafayette, Ind., 1978—; lectr. in preventive medicine. Mem. Internat. Acad. Preventive Medicine, Am. Chiropractic Physicians Assn., Am. Nutritional Cons., N.Y. Acad. Scis. Republican. Seventh-Day Adventist. Home: 6425 State Rd 25 N Lafayette IN 47905 Office: 6027 State Rd 43 N West Lafayette IN 47906

KAMRATH, RANDY PAUL, state senator, farmer; b. Canby, Minn., May 23, 1954; s. Paul Elmer and Verna Marie (Haugen) K. Student pub. schs., Canby. Farmer, Canby, 1973—; mem. Minn. Senate, St. Paul, 1981—. Home: Route 2 Box 214 Canby MN 56220 Office: Minn State Senate 133 State Office Bldg Saint Paul MN 55155

KANABROCKI, EUGENE LADISLAUS, chemist; b. Chgo., Apr. 18, 1922; s. Paul and Jeanette (Tyrala) K.; m. Rose Marie Spata, Nov. 5, 1950; children—Joseph, Paul. B.S. in Chemistry, DePaul U., 1948; M.S. in Chemistry, Loyola U., Chgo., 1969; Dr.Sci. in Chronobiochemistry, Jagiellonian U., Krakow, Poland, 1983. Registered chemist Nat. Registry in Clin. Chemistry. Clin. chemist VA Hosp., Hines, Ill., 1946-71, Bethesda Hosp., Chgo., 1971-73; chemist regional lab. U.S. Customs Service, Chgo., 1973-83; research chemist VA Hosp., Hines, 1984—; dir. Cardiovascular Lab., Evergreen Park, Ill., 1977-78; cons. chemist Edward Hosp., Naperville, Ill., 1981-85. Contbr. articles to profl. jours. Served with U.S. Army, 1943-46, ETO, col. USAR. Decorated Meritorious Service medal. WHO grantee, 1970. Mem. Am. Chem. Soc., Health Physics Soc., Sigma Xi. Roman Catholic. Home: 151 Braddock Dr Melrose Park IL 60160 Office: VA Hosp Nuclear Medicine Service Hines IL 60141

KANDAH, WALID FUAD, osteopathic physician; b. Ramallah, Jordan, July 18, 1952; came to U.S., 1957; naturalized, 1957; s. Fuad Saliba and Helen Fuad (Kazaleh) K.; m. Randa Zanayed, July 17, 1983. B.S., U. Mich., 1974; D.O., Kansas City Coll., 1980. Diplomate Am. Bd. Family Practice, Nat. Bd. Examiners in Osteo. Medicine. Intern, Mt. Clemens (Mich.) Gen. Hosp., 1980-81; resident in family practice St. Joseph Hosp., Flint, Mich., 1981-83; emergency dept. physician Ionia County (Mich.) Meml. Hosp., 1982-83, Hills and Dales Gen. Hosp., Cass City, Mich., 1981-83, Sinai Hosp. of Detroit, 1983-84, Garden City Hosp., 1984—; clin. instr. family practice Mich. State U., East Lansing, 1981-83. Mem. Am. Acad. Family Physicians, Am. Osteo. Assn., Mich. Acad. Family Physicians, Mich. Assn. Osteo. Physicians and Surgeons, Psi Sigma Alpha. Democrat. Home: 9136 Henry Ruff Rd Livonia MI 48150

KANE, DAVID SHERIDAN, insurance company executive; b. Deadwood, S.D., July 12, 1940; s. Arthur Sheridan and Grace Marie K.; m. Oline. Ph.B., U. N.D., 1964. Agt., Fidelity Union Life Ins. Co., Grand Forks, N.D., 1963-65, gen. agt., 1965; pres., founder D.S. Kane & Assocs., Inc., Fargo, N.D., 1968—; pres., founder, dir. Midwest Internat. Life Ins. Co., Fargo, 1976—; nat. dir. sales ITT Life, 1980-81; dir. Target Energies. Mem. Nat. Assn. Life Underwriters, Fargo-Moorhead Life Underwriters Assn. (pres. 1980), Am. Soc. C.L.U., Sigma Nu (pres. ednl. found.). Lutheran. Office: D S Kane & Associates Inc PO Box 5676 University Station Fargo ND 58105

KANE, MARY GLORIA, gastroenterologist; b. Chgo., Apr. 11, 1953; d. James Michael and Gloria (D'Ambrosio) Kane; m. Vern Hiram Kerchberger, Sept. 10, 1983. B.A., Middlebury Coll., Vt., 1974; M.D., Johns Hopkins U., 1978. Diplomate Bd. Internal Medicine. Intern in internal medicine Parkland Meml. Hosp., Dallas, 1978-79, resident in internal medicine, 1979-80, chief resident in internal medicine, 1980-81, fellow gastroenterology, 1981-83; research fellow Washington U. Sch. Medicine, St. Louis, 1983-84; practice medicine specializing in gastroenterology, 1984—. Contbr. articles to med. publs. Mem. ACP, Am. Gastroent. Assn., AMA, Phi Beta Kappa. Roman Catholic. Office: 33 W Higgins Rd Suite 5000 South Barrington IL 60010

KANE, WILLIAM MATTHEW, obstetrician, gynecologist; b. Bridgeport, Conn., Oct. 5, 1927; s. William Matthew and Mary (Fekete) K.; m. Shirley Rita Steeves, Aug. 26, 1950; children—William, Claire, Daniel, Mary Kathleen, Susan, John. A.B., Holy Cross Coll., 1950; M.D., George Washington U., 1954. Diplomate Am. Bd. Ob-Gyn. Rotating intern St. Vincents Hosp., Bridgeport, Conn., 1954-55, resident in ob-gyn, 1955-57; resident in ob-gyn St. Francis Hosp., Bridgeport, 1957-59; practice medicine specializing in ob-gyn, Trumbull, Conn., 1959-61, The Eddy Clinic, Hays, Kans., 1961-78, Canterbury Women's Clinic, Hays, 1978—. Bd. dirs. United Fund, Hays, 1968-70; dist. chmn. Coronado Council Wheatland Dist. Boy Scouts Am., Hays; chmn. fund drive Hays Pub. Library. Served with U.S. Army, 1946-47. Mem. AMA, Kans. Med. Soc., Kans. Ob-Gyn Soc. (pres.1972-73), Am. Fertility Soc., Am. Coll. Ob/Gyn. Club: Smoky Hill Country (Hays) (bd. dirs.). Avocations: fishing; sailing; magic; photography. Office: 2503 Canterbury Rd Hays KS 67601

KANG, TAI KYUN, psychiatrist; b. Kwangju, Korea, Oct. 15, 1933; s. Pan Suck and Ae Bock (Yoon) K.; came to U.S., 1964, naturalized, 1968; M.D., Chunnam U., 1959; m. Won-Sook Hong, Dec. 17, 1971; children—Sora, Sumi, Daniel. Intern, Worcester (Mass.) Meml. Hosp., 1964-65; resident in psychiatry Conn. Valley Hosp., Middleton, Conn., 1965-68; dir. psychiat. unit Mt. View Hosp., Lockport, N.Y., 1968-69; program dir. Genesee County Community Mental Health Services, Flint, Mich., 1969-72; dir. methodone program Genesee County Regional Drug Abuse Commn., City of Flint, also chief methadone investigator HEW, Flint, 1970-72; practice medicine specializing in psychiatry, Flint, 1972—; asst. clin. prof. Mich. State U., East Lansing, 1972-82, clin. assoc. prof., 1982—; chmn. dept. psychiatry McLaren Gen. Hosp., Flint, 1980—; mem. mental health com. G.L.S. Health Systems, Inc., 1980—; critical care cons. Region V Council, Mich. Emergency Med. Service, 1980. Chmn. treatment and rehab. sub-com. Citizens Narcotic Action Com., Flint, 1969-70. Served to capt. Korean Army, 1959-64. Research grantee Sandoz Pharm. Co., 1971, Lederle Labs., 1975. Diplomate Am. Bd. Psychiatry and Neurology. Mem. Korean Am. Assn. Flint (pres. 1979—), Chunnam U. Med. Sch. Alumni Assn. Am. (pres. Mid-eastern chpt. 1979—, pres. assn. 1980—), AMA, Genesee County Med. Assn., Mich. Med. Assn., Mich. Psychiat. Assn., Am. Psychiat. Assn., Am. Acad. Psychosomatic Medicine. Clubs: Rotary, Lions, Flint Swimming and Racquet, Shussmeister Ski, Warwick Hills Country. Contbr. articles to profl. jours. Home: 9395 Burning Tree Grand Blanc MI 48439 Office: 2765 Flushing St Flint MI 48504

KANGER, DAVID WAYNE, petroleum retailing company executive; b. Springfield, Ill., Jan. 30, 1946; s. John James Kanger and Mary Anne (Mesich) Neitzelt; m. Deborah Anne Freeman, Jan. 24, 1970; children—James Scott, David Andrew. Student Danville Jr. Coll., 1964-67; B.A. in Biology, Elmhurst Coll., 1969. Mgr. Bill's Shell Service, Lisle, Ill., 1967-72; ptnr. Oak Hill Shell, Lisle, 1979-84, Maple Grove Automotive, Downers Grove, Ill., 1980-83; owner, operator Dave's Shell Auto Care, Lisle, 1972-84; pres. K-Kar Service Ctrs., Lisle, 1984—; pres., chmn. bd. dirs. D & D Kwik Marts, Inc., Lisle, 1984—. Scoutmaster West Suburban council Boy Scouts Am., 1979-84, leadership tng. com., 1982-84, 1st asst. scoutmaster, 1985. Served with U.S. Army, 1969-71, Vietnam. Recipient Top Performance award Shell Oil Co., 1972-83, Dealer of Yr. award Shell Oil, 1980. Mem. Lisle C. of C., Nat. Rifle Assn. Republican. Lodge: Lions (v.p. 1975-79). Avocations: big game and upland hunting; backpacking; canoeing; reloading. Home: 5639 Elinor Ave Downers Grove IL 60516 Office: K-Kar Service Ctrs Inc 1117 Maple Ave Lisle IL 60532

KANNADY, DONALD RAY, counselor, former army officer; b. Collinsville, Okla., Aug. 18, 1936; s. Francis William and Alpha May (Hilderbrand) K.; m. Gisela Muuss Oct. 10, 1964 (div. Nov. 1978); children—Alan Ray, Arian Solveigh. B.S., Okla. State U., 1958; M.Ed., U. Mo.-St. Louis, 1984. Cert. Nat. Bd. Cert. Counselors. Commd. 2d lt. U.S. Army, 1958, advanced through grades to lt. col., 1972; co. comdr. Second Armored Div., Ft. Hood, Tex., 1960-62; advisor 22d ARVN Div., RVN, 1966; assoc. PMS, U. Ark. 1967-69; personnel staff officer Hdqrs. U.S. Army, Europe, 1975-78; ret., 1981; counselor, St. Louis, 1984—; co-leader therapy group Mo. State Bd. Probation and Parole, 1982-84. Decorated Bronze Star, others. Mem. Am. Assn. Counseling and Devel. Republican. Baptist. Avocation: jogging. Home: 114 Francis Ct St Charles MO 63303 Office: 3466 Bridgeland Bridgeton MO 63044

KANNE, MICHAEL STEPHEN, federal judge; b. Rensselaer, Ind., Dec. 21, 1938; s. Allen Raymond and Jane (Robinson) K.; m. Judith Ann Stevens, June 22, 1963; children—Anne, Katherine. Student St. Josephs Coll., Rensselaer, Ind., 1957-58; B.S., Ind. U., 1962, J.D., 1968; postgrad. Boston U., 1963, U. Birmingham (Eng.), 1975. Bar: Ind. 1968, U.S. Dist. Ct. (no. dist.) Ind. 1968. Assoc., Nesbitt & Fisher, Rensselaer, 1968-71; sole practice, Rensselaer, 1971-72; atty. city of Rensselaer, 1972; judge 30th Jud. Circuit of Ind., Rensselaer, 1972-82; judge U.S. Dist. Ct. No. Dist. Ind., Hammond, 1982—; lectr. in field. Bd. dirs. Sagamore council Boy Scouts Am., 1979—; trustee St. Joseph's Coll., 1984—. Served to 1st lt. USAF, 1962-65. Recipient Disting. Alumni Service award St. Josephs Coll., 1973. Mem. ABA, Fed. Bar Assn., Ind. State Bar Assn. (recipient Presidential citation 1979), Am. Judicature Soc., Jasper County Bar Assn. Roman Catholic. Club: Nat. Lawyers (Washington). Office: 205 Federal Bldg Hammond IN 46320

KANTER, MORTON JAY, editor; b. Chgo., Apr. 7, 1942; s. Isadore and Esther Barbara (Holtzman) K.; B.S. with honors, U. Ill., 1963, Ph.D. (NIH fellow 1963-66), 1966; m. Linde L. Anderson, Nov. 22, 1966; 1 dau., Traci. Research scientist Texaco Research Co., Beacon, N.Y., 1966-68; sr. editor Chem. Abstracts Service, Columbus, Ohio, 1968—; dir. Nat. Center for Pet Info. Jewish. Club: B'nai B'rith. Home: 103 S Dawson Rd Columbus OH 43209 Office: PO Box 3012 Columbus OH 43210

KANTOFF, JOYCE, court probation officer; b. Chgo., Apr. 13, 1945; d. Morton H. and Selma (Shapiro) K.; m. Apr. 3, 1973 (div. Jan. 1977). B.S., Loyola U., 1968. Field worker Juvenile Ct. Cook County, Chgo., 1968-79; complaint screener probation officer, 1981—. Mem. Wilderness Soc., Defenders of Wildlife, Greenpeace, Ctr. for Environment Edn., Nature Conservatory, Animal Protection Fund, Whale Protection Fund, World Wildlife Fund., Lincoln Park Zoo, Seal Rescue Fund. Democrat. Jewish. Office: 1100 S Hamilton St Chicago IL 60612

KANTOFF, SHELDON LEE, real estate development executive, lawyer; b. Chgo., Aug. 12, 1936; s. Nathan S. and Rosamond (Cohan) K.; m. Barbara Sue Pomeranz, Dec. 17, 1961; children—Stuart Alan, Howard David. B.S.C.E., Ill. Inst. Tech., 1957; J.D., Loyola U., 1964. Bar: Ill. 1964, U.S. Ct. Appeals (7th cir.) 1964; real estate broker, Ill. Vice pres. Urban Investment & Devel. Co., Chgo., 1969-72, Draper & Kramer, Inc., Chgo., 1978-84, Leisure Care, div., Leisure & Tech., Inc., Northbrook, Ill., 1984—; exec. v.p. Hollywood Builders, Chgo., 1972-74, prin. Interbuild, Inc., Chgo., 1974-78, v.p., gen. mgr. Dearborn Park Corp., Chgo., 1978-84; treas., dir. South Loop Planning Bd., Chgo., 1979-84; mem. housing task force Chgo. Central Area Com., 1983—. Pres. Dearborn Park Community Assn., Chgo., 1983-84. Served to capt. USAF, 1957-59. Recipient Humanitarian award St. Matthews AMFE Ch., Chgo., 1980. Mem. ABA, Ill. State Bar, Urban Land Inst. (assoc.), Ill. Assn. Home Builders, Nat. Assn. Home Builders, Multifamily Housing Assn. Ill. (bd. dirs. 1983-84). Club: Monroe (Chgo.). Home: Wilmette IL Office: Leisure & Tech Leisure Care Div 666 Dundee Rd #1903 Northbrook IL 60062

KANTON, KURT GOTTFRIED, pharmacist; b. St. Louis, Oct. 21, 1958; s. Erich and Herta (Rauskolb) K. B.S., St. Louis Coll. Pharmacy, 1982. Registered pharmacist, Mo. Purchasing and inventory control Lindenwood Drug, 1983-84, Watson Profl. Pharmacy, 1984—. Mem. Am. Pharm. Assn. Roman Catholic. Avocations: philately, model rocketing. Home: 4254 Carrollton Dr Bridgeton MO 63044-1921

KANTOR, NEIL MICHAEL, osteopathic physician; b. N.Y.C., July 4, 1940; m. Felice M. Zimmerman, June 20, 1965; children—Robert Joseph, Sheryl Beth, Michelle Jayne, Adam Scott. B.A., NYU, 1961; D.O., Phila. Coll. Osteo. Medicine, 1965. Diplomate Am. Bd. Pediatrics, Am. Bd. Neonatal-Perinatal Medicine, Am. Bd. Neonatology, Am. Bd. Osteo. Pediatricians. Intern, Doctor's Hosp., Columbus, Ohio, 1965-66; resident in pediatrics Grandview Hosp., Dayton, Ohio, 1966-68; practice osteo. medicine specializing in pediatric critical care and neonatology, Dayton, 1968-75, 83—, Jacksonville, Fla., 1975-81, Omaha, 1981-83; chmn. dept. pediatrics Grandview Hosp., Dayton, 1971-75; chmn. dept. pediatrics Jacksonville Gen. Hosp., 1975-78, fellow in neonatal-perinatal medicine Univ. Hosp., Jacksonville, 1975-78, assoc. dir. regional neonatal intensive care ctr., 1979-81; med. dir. neonatal intensive care nursery Jacksonville Children's Hosp., 1979-81; dir. pediatric critical care medicine div. St. Joseph Hosp., Omaha, 1981-83; dir. nurseries regional perinatal ctr. Miami Valley Hosp., Dayton, 1983—; clin. instr. dept. pediatrics Wright State Sch. Medicine, Dayton, 1974-75; asst. prof. U. Fla., Jacksonville, 1978-81; assoc. prof. Creighton U., Omaha, 1981-83; adj. clin. prof. Univ. Osteo. Med. and Health Scis., Des Moines, 1982—; assoc. clin. prof. Wright State U. Sch. Medicine, Dayton, 1983—; clin. prof. Ohio U. Coll. Osteo. Medicine, 1983—; med. cons. pediatrics State of Ohio Aid Dependent Children, 1971-75; med. cons. neonatalogy State of Fla. Children's Med. Services, Health and Rehab. Services, 1976-81; med. cons. United Cerebral Palsy Duval County, Jacksonville, 1979-81; med. cons. Nebr. Dept. Child and Maternal Welfare, 1981—; cons. Am. Bd. Neonatology, Am. Bd. Osteo. Pediatricians. Bd. dirs. Speech and Hearing Council Met. Dayton, 1971-75; mem. med. adv. com. Am. Diabetes Assn., Montgomery County, Dayton, 1973-75; mem. com. Prevention Lead Poisoning, State of Ohio, 1975-76; mem. med. adv. bd. Tay-Sach's Screening Program, Jacksonville, 1976-77; mem. Fla. Infant Screening Adv. Council, 1978, Genetic Adv. Council, 1978; mem. med. adv. com. March of Dimes, 1981-83; bd. dirs. Hillel Acad., Dayton, 1972-73, Beth Israel Synagogue, Omaha, 1982-83. Recipient Resident Tchr. award Grandview Hosp., 1972; award Recognition Am. Reyes Syndrome Assn., 1982; numerous research grants. Fellow Am. Acad. Pediatrics; mem. Am. Osteo. Assn., Ohio Osteo. Assn., Am. Coll. Osteo. Pediatricians (sr. mem., dir., pres. 1985-86), Greater Plains Orgn. Perinatal Care. Author: (with R.D. Garrison) neonatal Transport Handbook, 1979; (with T. Chiu, R.D. Garrison) Houseofficers Manual for Intensive Care Unit, 1978, 1983; editor (with A. Tolaymat, S. Deering) Training Modules in Pediatrics, 1980; editorial cons. Jour. Am. Osteo. Assn., 1976—; contbr. articles to profl. jours.

KAPACINSKAS, JOSEPH, engineer, author; b. Mazuciai, Lithuania, Oct. 20, 1907; came to U.S., 1949, naturalized, 1956; s. George and Teofile (Baskeviciute) K.; Civil Engr., Tech. Coll., Ausburg, Germany, 1948; student Ill. Inst. Tech., 1950-51; B. Indsl. Engring., Allied Inst. Tech., Chgo., 1960; m. Marie Kulikauskas, Dec. 27, 1952; 1 son, Joseph-Vytautas. Employee, City of Kaunas Municipal Govt., Lithauania, 1929-39, Nat. R.R., Lithuania, 1940-44, Nat. R.R., Treuchtlingen, Germany, 1944-45; instr., chief electrician UNRRA, Weissenburg, Germany, 1946-47; electrician Burlington No. R.R., Inc., Chgo., 1951-72; editor Sandara, weekly Lithuanian League newspaper, Chgo., 1973-76. Mem. Am. Lithuanian Engrs. and Architects Assn., Lithuanian Journalists Assn., Am. Tool and Mfg. Engrs., AAAS, Internat. Platform Assn., Intercontinental Biog. Assn., Lithuanian Alliance of Am. Author: Siaubingos Dienos-Horrifying Days, 1965; Iseivio Dalia-Emigrant's Fate, 1974; Spaudos Baruose-Within the Press, 1979. Contbr. articles on Lithuanian culture and social life to newspapers. Home: 6811 S Maplewood Ave Chicago IL 60629

KAPER, HANS GERARD, mathematician, researcher; b. Alkmaar, Netherlands, June 10, 1936; came to U.S., 1969; s. Gerrit and Trijntje (Reine) K.; m. Hillegonde J. van Biezen, July 17, 1962; children—Tasso, Bertrand. Ph.D., Rijksuniversiteit, Groningen, Netherlands, 1965. Sr. mathematician Argonne Nat. Lab., Ill., 1969—; vis. prof. Northwestern U., 1984-85; adj. prof. No. Ill. U., DeKalb, 1982—. Author: Mathematical Theory of Transport Processes in Gases, 1972; Spectral Methods in Linear Transport Theory, 1982; contbr. research articles to profl. jours. Pres. Downers Grove Concert Assn., 1978—, trustee, 1972—. NATO sci. fellow, 1966-67. Mem. Am. Math. Soc., Soc. Indsl. and Applied Math., Wiskundig Genootschap Amsterdam. Avocation: music. Home: 731 59th St Downers Grove IL 60516 Office: Argonne Nat Lab 9700 S Cass Ave Argonne IL 60439

KAPILA, VED PARKASH, engineer, surveyor, builder; b. Lopon, India, Dec. 27, 1932; s. Baboo Ram and Amravati (Vasishta) K.; came to U.S., 1963; naturalized, 1977; student Punjab U., India, 1949-51; diploma in civil engring Civil Engring. Sch., Lucknow, Ind., 1951-53; B.S. in Civil Engring., U. Mich., 1964, M.S. in Civil Engring., 1965; M.B.A., Wayne State U., 1970, value engring. orientation, 1970; m. Pushpa Pipat, Nov. 18, 1952; children—Shashi, Rajnish, Rita, Renu. Engring. sect. officer Punjab State Public Works Dept., India, 1953-63; design, engr. Ayres, Lewis, Norris & May, Ann Arbor, Mich., 1964-65; Obenchain Corp., Dearborn, Mich., 1965-66; v.p., chief civil and structural engr. O. Germany, Inc., Warren, Mich., 1966-76; dir. project services and chief planning and scheduling, chief quality assurance, chief client purchasing Hoad Engrs., Inc., Ypsilanti, Mich., 1976-78; pres. Kapila Constrn. Co., Inc., Kapila Contracting Co., Inc., Kapila & Assocs., 1968—. Registered profl. engr. Mich., Ga., Va., Punjab State (India); registered land surveyor, Mich.; licensed builder, Mich.; certified Nat. Council Engring. Examiners. Mem. ASCE, Am. Congress Surveying and Mapping, Am. Concrete Inst., Am. Inst. Steel Constrn., Mich. Soc. Registered Land Surveyors, Am. Soc. Quality Control, Soc. Am. Value Engrs., Nat. Soc. Profl. Engrs. Home: 1878 Canterbury Ct Bloomfield Hills MI 48013 Office: 31333 Thirteen Mile Rd Farmington Hills MI 48018

KAPLAN, ALAN MICHAEL, lawyer; b. Chgo., May 2, 1951; s. Milton and Evelyn (Davis) K. B.S.E., Northwestern U., 1973, M.A., 1975; J.D., DePaul U., 1980. Bar: Ill. 1980, U.S. Dist. Ct. (no. dist.) Ill. 1984. Research and devel. specialist U.S. League Savs. Assns., Chgo., 1976-78; atty., appeals officer Freedom of Info. Act, NLRB, Washington, 1980-82, field atty. NLRB, Chgo., 1982—. Contbr. articles to profl. jours. Mem. ABA, Chgo. Bar Assn. Home: 233 E Wacker Dr Apt 2201 Chicago IL 60601

KAPLAN, ARTHUR LEWIS, nuclear engineer; b. Boston, Mar. 13, 1933; s. Herbert and Stella (Trieger) K.; m. Edith J. Berger, June 30, 1957; children—Harrison, Judith. B.S. in Physics, MIT, 1954, MS. in Nuclear Engring., 1955. Physicist, Tech. Ops., Inc. Burlington, Mass., 1957-60; engr. Gen. Electric Co, Syracuse, N.Y., 1960-64; physicist Tech. Ops., Inc., 1964-72; engr. Gen. Electric Co., Wilmington, N.C., 1972-81, engring. mgr., 1981—. Mem.

Framingham Town Meeting, Mass., 1966-72, Framingham Democratic Town Com., 1968-72. Served to capt. USAF, 1955-57. Mem. Am. Phys. Soc., Am. Nuclear Soc., Health Physics Soc., Illuminating Engring. Soc., Air Force Assn. (life). Democrat. Jewish. Lodge: B'nai B'rith (pres. 1978-81). Avocations: tennis; chess; golf. Home: 25422 Bryden Rd Beachwood OH 44122 Office: Gen Electric Co Nela Park East Cleveland OH 44112

KAPLAN, ETHAN ZADOK, urban planner-analyst; b. Pontiac, Mich., May 9, 1935; s. Morris J. and Certie (Bock) K.; B.A., U. Chgo., 1955, M.A., 1958; postgrad. Washington U. at St. Louis, 1960-62; m. Jane B. Breese, Dec. 23, 1958; children—Mark, Alan. Sr. planner St. Louis County Planning Com., 1962-66, prin. planner, 1967-69; chief advanced planning City Alexandria, Va., 1966-67; research planner Health and Welfare Council St. Louis, 1969-75; pvt. cons., 1975-78; exec. dir. Southeast Kans. Regional Planning Commn., 1978—. Served with AUS, 1958-60. Mem. Am. Inst. Cert. Planners, Nat. Con. Social Welfare, Am. Planning Assn., Am. Sociol. Assn. Home: 630 S Evergreen St Chanute KS 66720

KAPLAN, HOWARD GORDON, lawyer; b. Chgo., June 1, 1941; s. David I. and Beverly Kaplan. B.S., U. Ill., 1962; J.D., John Marshall Law Sch., Chgo., 1967. Bar: Ill. 1967, D.C. 1980, N.Y. 1982, Wis. 1983, U.S. Supreme Ct. 1971, Acct., Chgo., 1962-67; practiced, Chgo., 1967—; ptnr. Angell, Kaplan & Zaidman, 1975—; asst. prof. Chgo. City Colls., 1967-78. C.P.A., Ill. Mem. ABA, Ill. Bar Assn., Chgo. Bar Assn., Bar Assn. 7th Circuit, Decalogue Soc., Am. Inst. C.P.A.s, Ill. Soc. C.P.A.s. Clubs: Chgo. Athletic Assn., Standard, Covenant, Bryn Mawr Country (Chgo.); B'nai B'rith; Friars (Los Angeles). Author papers in field. Office: 180 N LaSalle St Chicago IL 60601

KAPLAN, LAURA KAY, marketing executive; b. Chippewa Falls, Wis., Apr. 12, 1958; d. Robert Raymond and Frances Darlene (Schnabel) K. B.F.A., Drake U., 1980. Mktg. rep. Mademoiselle Mag., N.Y.C., 1977-80; asst. to pres. Hutson Advts., La Crosse, Wis., 1979; acct. exec., creative dir. Gerdes Advt., Des Moines, 1979-80; acct. exec., sr. writer Colle & McVoy Advt., Mpls., 1981-82; mktg. mgr. Jostens, Inc., Mpls., 1982—; cons., lecturer, author. Mem. Walker Art Ctr., Mpls., Inst. Arts, Redheads Club Internat.; loaned exec. United Way of Mpls., 1985. Named Outstanding Mem. AD/2 Twin Cities, 1982; Drake Art scholar, 1976-80. Mem. Am. Advt. Fedn., Art Dirs., Copywriter's Club, Jewelers of Am., Am. Mgmt. Assn., Women in Communications, Mpls. C. of C. (mem. tourism com. 1980-82), Drake Alumni Assn., Chi Omega Alumni Assn. Republican. Congregationalist. Author: They Never Said It Would be Like This, 1984; contbr. articles to profl. mags. Office: 5501 Norman Ctr Dr Minneapolis MN 55437

KAPLAN, MICHAEL DAVID, health management consultant; b. N.Y.C., Nov. 4, 1940; s. Harry J. and Rose K. Kaplan; B.A., Syracuse U., 1962, postgrad., 1963; postgrad. N.Y.U., 1964; m. Barbara Oberstein, Aug. 30, 1964; children—Jeremy Scott, Abigail Sarah. Polit. reporter AP, N.Y.C., 1965-69; v.p. mktg. First Healthcare Corp., Chgo., 1969-74; pres. Resource Dynamics, Inc., Chgo., 1974-79, also dir.; pres. Randmark Corp., Louisville, 1979—, also dir.; pres., chmn. bd. Rand Mgmt. Corp., Peoria, 1981—, Pavilion Healthcare Centers, 1981—, Pavilion Healthcare Ctrs. of Louisville, Inc., Richwoods Terrace of Peoria, Inc., Pavilion Oaks of Peoria, Inc., Pavilion Healthcare West, Inc., Pavilion Healthcare South, Inc., Central Dietary Systems, Inc., Pavilion Healthcare North, Inc.; lectr. Acad. Gerontol. Edn. and Devel. Bd. dirs. Louisville Jewish Community Fedn., Kenesth Israel Synagogue, Louisville, Bur. Jewish Edn., Louisville. Author: Comprehensive Guide to Health Care Marketing, 1974; contbr. articles to profl. jours.; contbg. editor Nursing Homes mag., 1978—. Office: 222 S 1st St Louisville KY 40202

KAPLAN, ROBERT, steel co. exec.; b. Chgo., Jan. 20, 1907; s. Max S. and Jennie K.; Ph.B., U. Chgo., 1929; m. Virginia M. George, July 1, 1943; children—Miriam Kaplan Schwartz, Donna L. Kaplan Rautbord, Patricia K. Mem. Midwest Stock Exchange, 1929-37; pres. Filshie Lead Head Nail Co., Chgo., 1935-39; v.p. Paumar Engring. Co., Gary, Ind., 1939-43; pres. Sun Steel Co., Chicago Heights, Ill., 1943—; dir. M.S. Kaplan Co. Bd. dirs., v.p. Nat. Found. for Progressive Relaxation. Mem. Am. Assn. for Advancement Tension Control (dir.). Clubs: Presidents (U. Chgo.), Standard. Patentee lead head nails, vinyl coating sheet steel, reclamation of steel from slag. Home: 1040 Lake Shore Dr Chicago IL 60611 Office: 2500 Euclid Ave Chicago Heights IL 60411

KAPLAN, SAMUEL, microbiologist, researcher, educator; b. Yonkers, N.Y., Feb. 13, 1934; s. Harry Benjamin and Pauline (Kaplan) K.; m. Deanna Faith Palmer, Dec. 19, 1961; children—Idanna, Ilania. B.S., Cornell U., 1959; M.S., Yale U., 1961; Ph.D., U. Calif.-San Diego, 1963. Postdoctoral fellow Molecular Biology Labs., Cambridge, Eng., 1964-66; asst. prof. Western Res. U., Cleve., 1966-67; asst. prof. U. Ill.-Urbana, 1967-70, assoc. prof., 1971-73, prof., 1974—, head dept. microbiology, 1983-84, dir. sch. life scis., 1984—; cons. Eli Lilly, Indpls., 1982—, Amoco, Naperville, Ill., 1984—. Contbr. articles to profl. jours. Recipient NIH fellow, 1959, 64; Research Scholar award Am. Cancer Soc., Eng., 1974; Pasteur award Ill. Soc. Microbiology, 1980. Mem. Am. Soc. Microbiology, Genetics Soc. Am., AAAS, Am. Inst. Biol. Scis., Am. Soc. Biol. Chemists. Jewish. Office: U Ill 407 S Goodwin Ave Urbana IL 61801

KAPLAN, WILFRED, mathematics educator; b. Boston, Nov. 28, 1915; s. Jacob Joseph and Anne Sabin (Levinson) K.; m. Ida Roettinger, Aug. 16, 1938; children—Roland, Muriel. A.B., Harvard U., 1935, A.M., 1936, Ph.D., 1939. Instr. Coll. William and Mary, Williamsburg, Va., 1939-40; prof. U. Mich., Ann Arbor, 1940—. Author: Advanced Calculus, 1952; Ordinary Differential Equations, 1958; Advanced Mathematics for Engineers, 1981. Pres. Washtenaw Council for Arts, Ann Arbor, 1980-84. Recipient Guggenheim fellow, 1949-50; Amoco Teaching award, 1984. Fellow AAAS; mem. Am. Math. Soc., Am. Phys. Soc., Can. Math. Soc. (dir. 1981-84), French Math. Soc. Democrat. Unitarian. Avocation: music. Office: U Mich Math Dept 347 W Engring Bldg Ann Arbor MI 48109

KAPLER, JOSEPH EDWARD, biology educator; b. Mar. 13, 1924; s. Albert Frank and Mary (Drilling) K.; m. Helen Therese Bamrick, Aug. 22, 1959; children—David J., Mark A., Mary B., Joseph Edward II. B.S., Loras Coll., 1948; M.S., Marquette U., 1953; Ph.D., U. Wis.-Madison, 1958. Instr. biology Loras Coll., Dubuque, Iowa, 1948-51, 54-55, from asst. to assoc. prof. biology, 1957-69, prof., 1969—; instr. zoology Marquette U., Milw., 1953-54. Contbr. articles to profl. jours., 1956-84. Recipient Forest Conservation award Iowa Wildlife Fedn., 1966. Fellow Iowa Acad. Sci.; mem. Entomol. Soc. Am., Am. Registry Profl. Entomologists, Dubuque County Conservation Soc., Assn. Midwestern Coll. Biology Tchrs. (hon. life). Home: 5135 Asbury Rd Dubuque IA 52001 Office: Loras Coll Dept Biology 1450 Alta Vista St Dubuque IA 52001

KAPP, ROBERT GEORGE, farmer; b. Curtice, Ohio, Feb. 22, 1932; s. Erwin William and Florence (Meyer) K.; m. Carolyn Belle Guy, Nov. 7, 1953; children—Lucinda, Brenda, Roert E., Gary, Steven, Lisa. Grad. high sch., Millbury, Ohio. Sr. mem. and principle owner of family farm operation, 1953—; dir. Farmers Savings Bank, Northwood, Ohio. Mem. Ohio Sch. Bds. Assn., 1970—, trustee, 1980, 83, 84, exec. com., 1983-84; mem. Lake Local Bd. Edn., Millbury, Ohio, 1970—, pres. bd., 1972—; mem., treas. Vol. Fire Dept., Millbury, 1962-78. Served to cpl. inf. U.S. Army, 1951-53. Mem. Future Farmers of Am. (state sec. 1950-51), Ohio Farm Bur. Republican. Mem. United Ch. of Christ. Home: 5113 Walbridge Rd Northwood OH 43619

KAPPY, WILLIAM FRED, educator, consultant; b. Cleve., Oct. 26, 1919; s. William Ernest and Lena Maria (Scherler) K.; children—William John, Amy Lyn Douglass. Grad. Kent State U., 1969. Pipe welder Standard Oil Co., 1939-65; tchr. welding Thomas Edison High Sch., 1965-70, Martin Luther King High Sch., 1970-79; vocat. welding instr. East Tech. Sch., Cleve., 1980—; tchr. adult edn. Manpower Tng. Ctr., 1967-75, Cuahoga Valley Joint Vocat. Sch., 1981-83; cons. welding, 1965-80. Served with USAF, 1942-47; PTO. Mem. Am. Welding Soc., Am. Vocat. Assn., Iota Lambda Sigma. Office: East Tech Sch 55th and Scovill Sts Cleveland OH 44104

KAPSALIS, THOMAS HARRY, art educator, artist; b. Chgo., May 31, 1925; s. Harry Thomas and Adamentia (Tzitziafianou) K.; m. Stella Manos, May 13, 1956; children—Adamandia Eugenia, Harry Thomas. B.A.E., Sch. Art Inst. Chgo., 1949, M.A.E., 1957. Assoc. prof. drawing and painting Sch. Art Inst. Chgo., 1954—; lectr. painting Northwestern U., Chgo., Evanston, Ill., 1968-71. Two-person exhibits include: Art Inst. Chgo., 1979; exhibited in group shows: Pa. Acad. Fine Arts, Phila., 1946, Art Inst. Chgo., 1950, 52, 53, 55, 56, 60, 63, 67, 68, 69, 71, 76, 81, Barone Gallery, N.Y.C., 1956, Corcoran Gallery Art, Washington, 1961, Ill. Arts Council Traveling exhbn., 1971, Hyde Park Group Exhibit, Chgo., 1976, Hyde Park Art Ctr., Chgo., 1983. Served with U.S. Army, 1944-45, ETO. Recipient Pauline Palmer prize Art Inst. Chgo., 1960, Julie F. Brower prize Art Inst. Chgo., 1969; Fulbright grantee, Stuttgart, Fed. Republic Germany, 1953-54, Huntington Hartford Found grantee, 1956, 59. Eastern Orthodox. Office: Sch Art Inst Chgo Columbus at Jackson Sts Chicago IL 60603

KAPTUR, MARCY C., congresswoman; b. Toledo, June 17, 1946; d. Stephen Jacob Kaptur and Anastasia Delores (Rogowski) K. B.S., U. Wis., 1968; M.S., U. Mich., 1974; postgrad. MIT, 1982—. Mem. Lucas County Democratic Exec. Com., Ohio, 1969-83; asst. dir. urban affairs White House Domestic Policy Staff, Washington, 1977-79; mem. 98th-99th Congresses from 9th Dist. Ohio, 1983—. Mem. Am. Planning Assn. Democrat. Roman Catholic. Address: 1228 Longworth House Office Bldg Washington DC 20515

KAPUR, KAILASH CHANDER, industrial engineering educator; b. Rawalpindi, Pakistan Aug. 17, 1941; s. Gobind Ram and Vidya Vanti (Khanna) K.; m. Geraldine Palmer, May 15, 1969; children—Anjali Joy, Jay Palmer. B.S., Delhi U., 1963; M.Tech., Indian Inst. Tech., Kharagpur, 1965; M.S., U. Calif.-Berkeley, 1968, Ph.D., 1969. Registered profl. engr., Mich. Sr. research engr. Gen. Motors Research Labs., Mich., 1969-70; sr. reliability engr. TACOM, U.S. Army, Mich., 1978-79; mem. faculty Wayne State U., Detroit, 1970—, assoc. prof. indsl. engring. and ops., 1973-79, prof., 1979—; vis. prof. U. Waterloo (Can.), 1977-78; vis. scholar Ford Motor Co., Mich., summer 1973. Author: Reliability in Engineering Design, 1977; contbr. articles to profl. jours. Gen. Motors grantee, 1974-77; U.S. Army grantee, 1978-79; U.S. Dept. Transp. grantee, 1980-82. Mem. IEEE (sr.), Ops. Research Soc. Am. (sr.), Inst. Indsl. Engrs. (assoc. editor 1980—). Assoc. editor Jour. Reliability and Safety, 1982—. Home: 17291 Jeanette St Southfield MI 48075 Office: Dept Indsl Engring Wayne State U Detroit MI 48202

KAPUSTA, MILA LYNN, patient ombudsman; b. Cleve., Dec. 30, 1956; d. Milan John and Janet (Sadlowski) Kapp. B.A., Macon Woman's Coll., 1978; postgrad. Detroit Coll. Law, 1981-85. Legis. page Ohio Ho. of Reps., Columbus, 1976-77; intern Legal Aid Soc. Greater Lynchburg (Va.), 1977-78; lobbyist State of Ohio (ORTA), Columbus, 1978-80; pub. relations rep. Allstate Ins. Co., Southfield, Mich., 1981; patient ombudsman Harper-Grace Hosp. Corp., Detroit, 1981—; mem. career mktg. bd. Madmoiselle mag. Mem. Am. Hosp. Assn. Soc. of Patient Reps., Mich. Hosp. Assn. Soc. Patient Reps., ABA (student div.), Mich. Bar Assn. (student div.), 1st Soc. of Detroit, Sigma Nu Phi. Republican. Home: 2923 Moon Lake Dr West Bloomfield MI 48033

KARABATSOS, GERASIMOS JOHN, chemistry educator; b. Chomatada, Greece, May 17, 1932; came to U.S., 1950, naturalized, 1963; s. John P. and Athena (Papadopoulou) K.; m. Marianna Marris, Dec. 16, 1956; children—Lelena, Yanna, Jason, Byron. A.B., Adelphi Coll., 1954; M.A., Harvard U., 1956, Ph.D., 1959. Asst. prof. chemistry Mich. State U., East Lansing, 1959-63, assoc. prof., 1963-66, prof., 1966—, dept. chmn., 1975—. Mem. Am. Chem. Soc., Chem. Soc. London, Sigma Xi. Home: 1623 Old Mill Rd East Lansing MI 48823 Office: Mich State U Dept Chemistry 320 Chemistry Bldg East Lansing MI 48824

KARANT, DANIEL GRANT, pharmacist; b. Long Beach, Calif., Apr. 11, 1954; s. Thomas Karant and Genevieve Rochelle (Sanscrainte) Karant Lauer; m. Tamara Sue Zunk, July 30, 1977; children—Alyssa Renee, Amy Catherine. B.S. in Pharmacy, Ohio No. U., 1977. Registered pharmacist, Ohio. Pharmacy mgr. Clark's Pharmacy, Ravenna, Ohio, 1979-80, K-Mart Pharmacy #3142, Tallmadge, Ohio, 1981-83; staff pharmacist Northfield Drug, Ohio, 1980-81; staff pharmacist Youngfellow Drug #86, Akron, Ohio, 1983-84, pharmacy mgr. #71, 1984—. Faculty speaker Summit Portage Area Health Edn. Network, Akron, 1984. Mem. Ohio State Pharm. Assn. (conv. del. 1981-84, conv. chmn. 1983-84, mem. pharmacy econ. com. 1982—), Summit County Pharm. Assn. (mem. speaker's bur. 1981—, council 1982—), Kappa Psi (chaplain 1973-74, vice regent 1974-75, province V historian 1974-75, inter-fraternity rep. 1975-76). Avocations: philately; tennis; racquetball; billiards; bowling. Home: 1788 Tonawanda Ave Akron OH 44305 Office: Youngfellow Drug #71 25 W Miller Ave Akron OH 44305

KARARA, HOUSSAM MAHMOUD, civil engineering educator; b. Cairo, Egypt, Sept. 5, 1928; came to U.S., 1957; s. Mahmoud M. and Amna (El-Kashef) K.; m. Albertina G. Panchetti, May 14, 1956; children—Anna Maria, Mervet. B.Sc. with honors, Cairo U., 1949; Dr.Sc.Techn., Swiss Fed. Inst. Tech. (ETH), Zurich, 1956. Registered profl. engr., Ill. Surveying engr. Ministry of Pub. Works, Cairo, Egypt, 1949-51; sci. collaborator Inst. Photogrammetry, Zurich, 1956-57, Wild-Heerbrugg Co., Switzerland, 1957; asst. prof. U. Ill., Urbana, 1957-60, assoc. prof., 1961-66, prof. civil engring., 1966—; cons. photogrammetry Fairfax County Water Authority, Annandale, Va., 1972-74, Wild-Heerbrugg Instrument, Inc., 1974-76. Editor-in-chief: Handbook of Non-Topographic Photogrammetry, 1979. Recipient Research prize, ASCE, 1963. Mem. Am. Soc. Photogrammetry (cert., bd. dirs. 1969-72, 76-78, Fairchild Photogrammetric award, 1974, Talbert Abrams award, 1959, 61, Presdl. Meritorious award, 1966, 71, 72, 76, 78, 79), Am. Congress on Surveying and Mapping, Can. Inst. Surveying, Belgian Soc. Photogrammetry, Brit. Soc. Photogrammetry, French Soc. Photogrammetry, German Soc. Photogrammetry. Avocations: photography; hiking; swimming. Home: 1809 Coventry Dr Champaign IL 61821 Office: Newmark Civil Engring Lab 208 N Romine St Urbana IL 61801

KARATHANOS, DEMETRIUS, statistics educator; b. Argos Orestikon, Greece, Dec. 28, 1941; came to U.S., 1960, naturalized, 1972; s. Nikolas and Anthi (Papadimitriou) K.; m. Patricia Ruth Hager, June 9, 1969; children—Nikolas, Byron, Katya. B.S. in Engring., So. Ill. U., 1964, M.S. in Engring., 1969; Ph.D. in Applied Stats., U. No. Colo., 1975. Instr. Math. Murray State U., Ky., 1966-68; research and devel. engr. H.K. Porter Co., Chgo., 1969-73; dir. instnl. research Imperial Valley Coll., Calif., 1975-79; assoc. prof. mgmt. sci. Southeast Mo. State U., Cape Girardeau, 1979—. Pres. Cape Area Youth Soccer Assn., Cape Girardeau, 1981-82. Mem. Am. Statis. Assn., Am. Inst. Decision Scis. Avocations: tennis, soccer. Home: 1824 Lawanda Cape Girardeau MO 63701 Office: Southeast Mo State U Cape Girardeau MO 63701

KARIM, M. REZA-UL, microbiologist, educator; b. Noakhali, Bangladesh, India, Nov. 1, 1941; came to U.S., 1963, naturalized, 1974; student Ahsannauallah Engring. Coll., Pakistan, 1956-58; B.Sc. with honors in Microbiology (gold medalist), U. Karachi (Pakistan), 1962; M.S., U. Minn., 1966; Ph.D., U. Mont., 1974; m. Agnes A. Mullenbach, Feb. 4, 1967; children—Lisa Mona, Sarah Ranee. Teaching asst. dental microbiology U. Minn., 1963-64; instr. Bengali lang. Peace Corps Tng. Program, 1963-64; instr. biology U. Wis., Eau Claire, 1966-67; asst. prof. gen. biology, physiology and microbiology No. State Coll., Aberdeen, S.D., 1968-70, research and teaching asst. virology U. Mont., Missoula, 1970-71; asso. prof. organic chemistry, gen. biology dept. natural scis. No. State Coll., Aberdeen, S.D., 1972-75, prof., 1975—, also chief health professions advisor, 1976—, coordinator health scis. program and health scis. research, 1981—, chmn. dept. math., natural scis. and health profession, 1982—; dir. DeVries project on quality control of milk, 1969; dir. various workshops on sanitation and public health, 1973-75. Mem. Am. Acad. Microbiology, Am. Soc. Microbiology, Pakistan Soc. Microbiology, NEA, S.D. Edn. Assn., S.D. Assn. for Health Educators and Practitioners, S.D. Acad. of Sci., Central Assn. Advisors for Health Professions, S.D. Cancer Soc., Gerontology Assn. of S.D., N.Y. Acad. Sci., Minn. Alumni Assn., Sigma Xi, Phi Sigma. Clubs: Elks, Cosmopolitan. Contbr. articles to sci. jours. Home: 1714 S 8th St Aberdeen SD 57401 Office: Northern State College Aberdeen SD 57401

KARKUT, ANN LOUISE, editor; b. Bellwood, Ill., June 30, 1924; d. Walter and Anna (Jacobs) Knippenberg; student LaSalle U.; m. Edward Karkut, Mar. 20, 1943; children—Patricia, Edward, Stanley, Susan, Christopher. Asst. editor, Lockport (Ill.) Herald, 1960-63, editor, 1963-69; asst. editor Naperville (Ill.) Sun, 1969-70; editor Joliet (Ill.) Circle, 1970; editor Pointer Publs., Riverdale, Ill., 1970-72; asst. editor Lisle (Ill.) Sun, 1972-74; asst. editor Big Farmer mag., Frankfort, Ill., 1974-81. Sec., Homer Fire Dept. Aux., 1962, Dist. 92 Band Parents, 1967; mem. Homer Republican Precinct Com., 1976—; Homer Twp. clk., 1981—; bd. dirs. Will County Hist. Soc. Mem. Lockport Bus. and Profl. Women's Club (charter mem., past pres., named Woman of Yr. 1979), Ill. Bus. and Profl. Women's Club (bull. editor 1983-84), Ill. Fedn. Bus. and Profl. Women's Clubs Found. (dir. Dist. 5), Ill. Press Women's Assn. Roman Catholic. Club: Waa-Shee Riders (pres.). Home: Rt 2 Box 26 Gougar Lockport IL 60441 Office: 143d St Lockport IL 60441

KARLAN, MARC SIMEON, surgeon educator, consultant; b. N.Y.C., Sept. 10, 1942; s. Henry Milton and Alexandria (Stambler) K.; m. Lynn Hoggatt, May 29, 1983; children—Laura, Dean. B.A. magna cum laude, Tufts Coll., 1964; M.D., U. Pa., 1968; postdoctoral (Physicians and Surgeons fellow) Columbia U., 1970-73. Diplomate Am. Bd. Otolaryngology. Intern, Montefiore Hosp. and Med. Center, Bronx, N.Y., 1968-69; resident in otolaryngology Presbyn. Hosp., N.Y.C., 1970-73; vis. lectr. Med. Coll. Va., 1973-75; asst. prof., then assoc. prof. dept. surgery, dept. communicative disorders Grad. Sch. Arts and Scis., Coll. Engring. U. Fla. Sch. Medicine, Gainesville, 1975-79; vis. fellow U. Zurich (Switzerland), 1979-80; assoc. prof. surgery Northwestern U. Med. Sch., Chgo., 1980—; bd. dirs. Northwestern Med. Faculty Found., 1982-83; cons. FDA Bur. Med. Devices, NIH, Ill. Med. Legal Affairs; dir. research Milton Med. Co. Contbr. articles to profl. jours. Served to maj. U.S. Army, 1973-75. Recipient Tchr. Investigator award NIH, 1976-80. Mem. AMA, Ill. State Med. Soc., Am. Acad. Facial Plastic Surgery (chmn. research com., mem. awards and edn. coms., recipient Ira Tresley award for outstanding research 1977), Am. Acad. Otolaryngology, Assn. Research in Otolaryngology, Soc. of Univ. Otolaryngologists, Sigma Chi. Jewish. Office: 150 E Huron St Suite 902 Chicago IL 60611

KARLINS, MARTIN WILLIAM, composer, educator; b. N.Y.C., Feb. 25, 1932; s. Theodore and Gertrude Bertha (Leifer) K.; m. Mickey Cutler, Apr. 6, 1952; children—Wayne, Laura. Mus. B., Manhattan Sch. Music, 1961, Mus.M., 1961; Ph.D. in Composition, U. Iowa, Iowa City, 1965; studied with Frederick Piket, Vittorio Giannini, Stefan Wolpe, Philip Bezanson, Richard Hervig. Composer: Concert Music 1 through 5, Lamentations-In Memoriam, Reflux (concerto for double bass), Symphony No. 1, Concerto Grosso I and II, Woodwind Quintet I and II, Saxophone Quartet I and II, 3 Piano Sonatas, Outgrowths-Variations for Piano, Catena I, II and III, Chameleon for solo harpsichord, Birthday Music I and II, Variations on Obiter Dictum, Music for Cello Alone I and II, Infinity, Quintet for alto saxophone and string quartet, numerous others; recordings include: Music for Tenor Saxophone and Piano, Variations on Obiter Dictum, Solo Piece with Passacaglia for clarinet; quintet for alto saxophone and string quartet; asst. prof. music Western Ill. U., 1965-67; assoc. prof. theory and composition Northwestern U., 1967-73, prof., 1973—, dir. Contemporary Music Ensemble, 1967-81; coordinator Composer's Workshops 1976 Internat. World Congress of Saxophones, London; lectr., composer-in-residence and panelist World Saxophone Congress, Bordeaux, France, 1974. Grantee MacDowell Colony, Nat. Endowment for the Arts, 1979, 85, Meet the Composer, 1980, 84, 85, Ill. Arts Council, 1985. Mem. Am. Composers Alliance, Am. Soc. Univ. Composers, Chgo. Soc. Composers, Am. Music Center, Pi Kappa Lambda. Office: Northwestern U Sch of Music Evanston IL 60201

KARLSON, BEN EMIL, kitchen design company executive; b. Hedemora, Sweden, Aug. 27, 1934; came to U.S., 1954, naturalized, 1960; s. Emil W.J. and Ester Linnea (Hellman) Karlsson; student bus. mktg. Alexander Hamilton Inst., N.Y.C., 1967, Am. Inst. Kitchen Designers, 1972; grad. Dale Carnegie Inst., 1972; m. Susan Jo Kaupert, Feb. 7, 1958; children—David, Kristine, Thomas. Salesman, Edward Hines Lumber Co., Chgo., 1954-63; v.p., gen. mgr. Lake Forest Lumber Co. (Ill.), 1963-67; pres. Karlson Home Center, Inc., Evanston, Ill., 1967—, Poggenpohl-Midwest/USA, Inc., Evanston, Atag USA Corp., Evanston; dir. tng. U.S. Poggenpohl, Herford, W. Ger., 1981—; pres. Bank Lane Investors, Lake Forest, 1971-72; founder chmn. Evanston Home Show, 1973, 74; judge, Nat. Design Contest, 1974; showroom design cons., Ill., Poggenpohl Kitchens Germany; speaker in field; lectr. on kitchen bus. and design at univs. and convs. Mem. steering com. Covenant Meth. Ch., Evanston, 1968-69; bd. dirs. Evanston Family Counseling Service, 1973-75, Evanston United Community Services, 1974-75, mid-Am. chpt. No. region ARC, 1974; chmn. bus. div. Evanston United Fund, 1974, gen. campaign chmn., 1975. Recipient awards for community service. Cert. kitchen designer. Mem. Am. Inst. Kitchen Designers (pres. 1975-76), Evanston C. of C. (dir. 1973-74, v.p. 1975, pres. 1976), Westmoreland C. of C., Nat. Fed. Ind. Bus., Mid-Am. Swedish Trade Assn. Club: Evanston Rotary (pres. 1984-85). Contbr. kitchen designs to nat. mags. Home: 2311 Central Park Ave Evanston IL 60201 Office: 1815 Central St Evanston IL 60201

KARNEMAAT, JOHN NATHANIEL, analytical chemist, product researcher; b. Fremont, Mich., Oct. 19, 1926; s. Koos and Etta (Wile) K.; m. Mildred Arlene Thomas, Sept. 13, 1952; children—Janet, Richard, Paul, Julia. B.A., Western Mich. U., 1948. Dir. Bioclin. Lab., Kalamazoo, Mich., 1956-77; v.p. KAR Labs., Inc., Kalamazoo, 1960—; pres. Interfibe Research Corp., Portage, Mich., 1983—; bd. dirs. Vanco Mfg. Co., Portage, 1983—, Country Queen Inc., Grand Rapids, Mich., 1977 –. Author: Methods of Biochemical Analysis; patentee in field. Mem. Am. Assn. Ofcl. Agrl. Chemists. Avocations: music; travel. Home: 7350 E ML Ave Kalamazoo MI 49001 Office: Interfibe Research Corp 1615 Vanderbilt Rd Portage MI 49002

KARNES, EVAN BURTON, II, lawyer; b. Chgo.; s. Evan Burton and Mary Alice (Brosnahan) K.; m. Bridget Anne Clerkin, Oct. 9, 1976; children—Kathlen Anne, Evan Burton III, Molly Aileen. A.B., Loyola U., Chgo., 1975; J.D., DePaul U., 1978. Bar: Ill. 1978, U.S. Dist. Ct. (no. dist.) Ill. 1978, U.S. Ct. Appeals (7th cir.) 1978, U.S. Supreme Ct. 1983. Trial atty. Chgo. Milw. St. Paul & Pacific R.R., Chgo., 1978-81; litigation dept. Baker & McKenzie, Chgo., 1981—. Mem. Chgo. Bar Assn., Def. Research Inst., Nat. Assn. R.R. Trial Counsel, Blue Key (sec. Loyola U. chpt. 1974-75), Pi Sigma Alpha, Phi Alpha Delta. Club: Union League (Chgo.). Office: Baker & McKenzie 130 E Randolph St Suite 2700 Chicago IL 60601

KARNS, ANTHONY WESLEY WARREN, geol. cons.; b. Kansas City, Mo., Dec. 15, 1936; s. Anthony Wesley and Madge Pearl (Hill) K.; A.A., Coffeyville (Kans.) Coll., 1956; B.S. in Geology, Colo. State U., 1960; M.S. in Geology, Okla. U., 1961; children by previous marriage—Anthony Wesley, Shawn Michelle. With Mobil Oil Co., U.S., North Africa and Can., 1961-68, Magellan Petroleum, Australia, North Africa, N.Z., Tonga, Fiji, 1968-71; pres., founder Earth Scientists, Ltd., Australia, N.Z., Can., U.S. and New Hebrides, 1971—. Mem. Am. Assn. Petroleum Geologists, Geol. Soc. Am., Am. Assn. Scientists, N.Z. Geol. Soc., Four Corners Geol. Soc., Sigma Xi, Sigma Gamma Epsilon. Republican. Contbr. chpt. in book. Home: Route 1 Box 15AA Coffeyville KS 67337 Office: 806 Hickman St Coffeyville KS 67337

KARPICKE, JOHN ARTHUR, systems engineer, experimental psychologist; b. Saginaw, Mich., Nov. 26, 1945; s. Herbert August and Eleanor Louise (Stafford) K.; m. Susan Gail Denyes, Aug. 5, 1972; children—Jeffrey Denyes, Jennifer Denyes. B.S., Mich. State U., 1972; Ph.D., Ind. U., 1976. NIH postdoctoral fellow in psychobiology Fla. State U., Tallahassee, 1976-77; asst. prof. psychology Valparaiso (Ind.) U., 1977-81, research fellow, 1978, 79, 80; mem. tech. staff human factors group Bell Telephone Labs., Indpls., 1981-82; mem. tech. staff system architecture group AT&T Consumer Products Labs., Indpls., 1983-84; mem. tech. staff functional systems design and software group AT&T Consumer Products Labs, Indpls., 1984-85, mem. tech. staff advanced cellular technologies design group, 1985—. Served with USNR, 1969-71; Vietnam. NIMH research grantee, 1979-80. Mem. AAAS, N.Y. Acad. Scis. Contbr. numerous articles to psychology jours. Office: 6612 East 75th St PO Box 1008 Indianapolis IN 46206

KARR, GERALD LEE, agrl. economist, state senator; b. Emporia, Kans., Oct. 15, 1936; s. Orren L. and Kathleen M. (Keller) K.; B.S., Kans. State U., 1959; M.S. in Agrl. Econs., So. Ill. U., 1962, Ph.D. in Econs., 1966; m. Sharon Kay Studer, Oct. 18, 1959; children—Kevin Lee, Kelly Jolleen. Livestock mgr. Eckert Orchards Inc., Belleville, Ill., 1959-64; grad. asst. So. Ill. U., Carbondale, 1960-64; asst. prof. econs. Central Mo. State U., Warrensburg, 1964-67; asst. prof. agrl. econs., head dept. Njala U., Sierra Leone, West Africa, 1967-70; asst. prof. agrl. econs. U. Ill., Urbana, 1970-72; asso. prof. agrl. econs., chmn. dept., mgr. coll. farms Wilmington (Ohio) Coll., 1972-76; farmer, Emporia, Kans., 1976—; mem. Kans. Senate, 1981—; research advisor Bank of Sierra Leone, Freetown, summer 1967; agrl. sector cons. Econ. Mission to Sierra Leone, IBRD, 1973. Mem. Am. Agrl. Econs. Assn., Lyon County Farmer Union, Lyon County Farm Bur., Lyon County Livestock Assn., Omicron Delta Epsilon, Farm House. Contbr. articles to profl. jours. Democrat. Methodist. Club: Kiwanis.

KARR, JOHN F., See *Who's Who in America,* 43rd edition.

KARR, WILLIAM LEE, land surveyor; b. Alexandria, Va., June 24, 1951; s. Raymond A. and Margaret E. (Richards) K.; m. Patricia A. Brotherton, Nov. 14, 1970; children—William R., Matthew T. B.S., Mich. Tech. U., 1975. Lic. land surveyor, lic. forester. Survey mgr. Estes park Surveyors, Colo., 1977-79, Granger Engring., Sault Ste. Marie, Mich., 1979-81; prin., pres. Northwoods Land Surveying, Inc., Sault Ste. Marie 1981—; dir. Easter Upper Peninsula Regional Planning com., 1981—; mem. Mich. Bd. Registration for Land Surveyors, Profl. Engrs.; Chippewa County Surveyor, Mich., 1983—. Mem. Soc. Am. Mil. Engrs. (pres. 1983-84), Mich. Soc. Registered Land Surveyors (Upper Peninsula chpt. rep. to state bd. 1980-83), Am. Congress Surveying and Mapping, Nat. Soc. Profl. Surveyors. Democrat. Baptist/Methodist. Lodge: Kiwanis (local pres. 1982-83, Disting. past pres. award 1983). Avocations: hunting; canoeing; gardening. Home: 806 Court St Sault Ste Marie MI 49783 Office: Northwoods Land Surveying Inc 125 Arlington St Suite 1 Sault Ste Marie MI 49783

KARRAKER, LOUIS RENDLEMAN, manufacturing company executive; b. Jonesboro, Ill., Aug. 2, 1927; s. Ira Oliver and Helen Elsie (Rendleman) K.; B.A., So. Ill. U., 1949, M.A., 1952; postgrad. U. Wis., 1951-52, Washington U., 1954-56; m. Patricia Grace Stahlheber, June 20, 1952; children—Alan Louis, Sharon Elaine. Asst. prof. Augustana Coll., 1956-60, acting chmn. div. social scis., 1960-61, asst. to pres., 1962-64; personnel mgr. Parker Pen Co., Janesville, Wis., 1964-67, personnel mgr., asst. to chmn., 1967-68, gen. asst. to chmn., 1968-69; v.p. personnel Am. Appraisal Assos., Inc., Milw., 1969-73, v.p. adminstrn., 1973-74, group v.p., dir., 1974-77, exec. v.p., dir., 1977-79, pres., dir., 1979-82; mgmt. cons., 1982-85; exec. v.p. Columbia ParCar Corp., Deerfield, Wis., 1985—. Served with USNR, 1952-53. Republican. Lutheran. Home: 3035 Applewood Ct Brookfield WI 53005 Office: Columbia ParCar Corp Deerfield WI

KARSON, ALLEN RONALD, aerospace company executive; b. Chgo., June 18, 1947; s. Bruno Stanley and Rose Jean (Nowakowski) Kasprzyk; m. Bonnie Jean Pazdziora, Sept. 1, 1968. B.S. in Acctg., Bradley U., 1970; postgrad. DePaul U., 1972. C.P.A., Ill. Corp. controller Time Industries, Inc., Chgo., 1973-77; controller U.S. ops. Indal, Inc., Toronto, Ont., Can., 1977; v.p. fin. affairs Rentco Internat., Inc., subs. Fruehauf Corp., The Hague, The Netherlands, 1977-83; pres., chief exec. officer Ideal Aerosmith, Inc., Cheyenne, Wyo., 1983-84, East Grand Forks, Minn., 1984—. Apptd. hon. consul of The Hague, 1985; chmn. bus. devel. bd. East Grand Forks, Minn. Mem. Am. Inst. C.P.A.s, Ill. Soc. C.P.A.s, Minn. Soc. C.P.A.s, Planning Execs. Inst., Nat. Assn. Accts. (bd. dirs. Netherlands chpt. 1981-83). Roman Catholic. Lodge: Rotary Internat. Office: Ideal Aerosmith Inc Hwy 2 East Grand Forks MN 56721

KARTHIKEYAN, GOPALASRINIVASA, physician; b. Tirapattur, India, Jan. 15, 1948; s. Gopalasrivivasa Verkataraman and Sundari (Krishnasawamy) Gpalasrinivasa; m. Uma Siva, May 23, 1973; children—Tharun, Hrishikesh, Omkar. Student St. Joseph's Coll., Bangalore, India, 1964; B.S., Madras Med. Coll., India, 1971, M.B., 1971. Diplomate Am. Bd. Internal Medicine, Am. Bd. Rheumatology. Asst. physician E.S.T. Hosp., Coimbatore, India, 1971-72, Chingleput Med. Coll., India, 1972-73; intern Jewish Hosp., Bklyn. N.Y., 1973-74; resident Med. Ctr. of Bklyn., 1974-76, fellow rheumatology, 1976-78; staff physician VA Med. Center, Iron Mountain, Mich., 1978—. Mem. Am. Rheumatism Assn. Hindu. Office: VA Med Center H St Iron Mountain MI 49801

KASDORF, JOHN COLIN, investment company executive; b. Milw., Mar. 12, 1943; s. Clifford Carl and Jane E. (Henderson) K.; m. Cheryl Nicks, June 15, 1969; children—Kurt P., David J., Michael C. B.S. in Fin., Northwestern U., 1965; M.B.A., U. Wis.-Madison, 1970. Investment advisor Newton & Co., Milw., 1971-75; cons. Hewitt Assocs., Milw., 1975-79; pres. Kaztex Fin., Inc., Brookfield, Wis., 1979—. Mem. fund raising com. United Performing Arts Fund, Milw., 1982. Served to lt. comdr. USN, 1965-69. Fellow Fin. Analysts Fedn.; mem. Milw. Fin. Analyst Soc. Republican. Lutheran. Avocations: sporting activities. Home: 1080 Madera Circle Elm Grove WI 53122

KASHYAP, MOTI LAL, physician, medical educator, researcher; b. Singapore, Feb. 19, 1939; came to U.S., 1970, naturalized, 1975; s. Ram Nath and Vidya Vati (Bedi) K.; m. Suman Prakash, Dec. 8, 1970; children—Gauri Tillotma, Vikram Aditya, Ishaan Pururava. M.B., B.S., U. Singapore, 1964; M.S., McGill U., 1967. Intern U. Singapore Teaching Hosps., 1964-65; resident, fellow McGill U., Montreal, Que., Can., 1965-70, U. Calif.-San Francisco, 1970-71; sr. lectr., head dept. physiology U. Singapore, 1971-74; asst. prof., then assoc. prof. U. Cin., 1974-81, prof. medicine, 1981—, prof. medicine and pathology, 1981—; dir. Apolipoprotein Lab., Cin., 1974—, assoc. dir. Lipid Research Div., 1974—; cons. physician Univ. and Holmes Hosps., Cin., 1974—. Contbr. articles to profl. jours. U. Singapore scholar, 1960. Am. Heart Assn. fellow, 1971; grantee NIH, Am. Heart Assn., 1974—. Fellow ACP, Arteriosclerosis Council Am. Heart Assn., Royal Coll. Physicians Can.; mem. Central Soc. Clin. Investigation, Can. Soc. Endocrinology, Am. Fedn. Clin. Research. Home: 3033 Burning Tree Ln Cincinnati OH 45237 Office: U Cin Med Ctr K Pavilion 231 Bethesda Ave Cincinnati OH 45267

KASICH, JOHN R., congressman; b. McKee's Rocks, Pa., May 13, 1952. B.A. in Politics and Govt., Ohio State U. Admin. asst. to State Senator Donald Luken's, 1975-77; mem. Ohio Senate, 1978-82; mem. 98th-99th Congresses from 12th Dist. Ohio; legis. dir. Desautels & Assocs. Recipient Outstanding Young Men in Am. award, 1976; Watchdog of the Treasury award, 1979; Watchdog of the Treasury's "Golden Bulldog" award, 1983-84; Leadership award Am. Security Council, 1983-84. Office: 1133 Longworth House Office Bldg Washington DC 20515*

KASKEY, BAYLEN, communications corporation executive; b. Phila., Apr. 1, 1929; s. Sydney S. and Selma (Silver) K.; m. Marjorie Ann Updegrove, June 27, 1954; children—Jeffrey Allen, Cynthia Louise, Michael Andrew. B.S. in Mech. Engring., U. Pa., 1950; cert. communications and electronics, Bell Labs. Community Devel., N.Y.C., 1953. Faculty, Kans. State Coll., Manhattan, 1950-51; mem. tech. staff Bell Labs., Whippany, N.J., 1951-58, supr., 1958-62, dept. head Bellcomm, Inc., Washington, 1962-67, Columbus, Ohio, 1967-80, dir. Bell Labs., Naperville, Ill., 1980—. Author: (with others) Telecommunications, An Interdisciplinary Survey, 1979; Innovations in Telecommunications, 1982. Contbr. articles to profl. jours. Chmn., PTA, Worthington, Ohio, 1974, council rep., 1977; founder, v.p. Citizens for Union Sta. Architecture, Columbus, 1977-80; founder, bd. dirs. Columbus Landmark Found., 1978-80; mem. Friends of Danata Forest Preserve, Wheaton, Ill., 1983—. Served with AUS, 1954-56. Mem. AIAA, ASME, Am. Mgmt. Assn., Tau Beta Pi, Sigma Tau. Avocations: orchid culture; historic preservation. Office: AT&T Bell Labs Naperville-Wheaton Rds Naperville IL 60566

KASPERS, LAMBERT MANN, manufacturing executive; b. Evanston, Ill., Sept. 19, 1919; s. Lambert and Florence A. (Mann) K.; m. June Motter, June 4, 1944; children—Karen Kaspers Jackson, William Freeman, Richard Lambert, Robert Lawrence, John Newton. A.B., U. Rochester, 1940; postgrad. Harvard Grad. Sch. Bus. Adminstrn., 1944. Gen. mgr., dir. Towne-Robinson Fastener, Dearborn, Mich., 1968-79; chmn. bd., chief exec. officer, v.p., Fastener Group, dir. Key Internat. Mfg. Inc., Southfield, Mich., 1969—. Active, Birchwood Farms Property Owners Assn., Nat. Republican Party. Served to lt. USNR, 1942-45. Mem. Indsl. Fasteners Inst. (bd. govs.). Presbyterian. Clubs: Orchard Lake Country, Innisbrook Golf and Country (Tarpon Springs, Fla.); Birchwood Farms Golf and Country (Harbor Springs, Mich.). Home: 651 Orchard Ridge Rd Bloomfield Hills MI 48013 Office: 24175 Northwestern Hwy Southfield MI 48075

KASPRISIN, ARLENE THERESA, audiology and speech pathologist; b. Braddock, Pa., July 4, 1945; d. John A. and Margaret R. (Ulakey) Kasprisin; m. Dana Michael Astry, Sept. 30, 1982. B.A., Indiana U. of Pa., 1967; M.A., Northwestern U., 1969; Ph.D., U. Pitts., 1976. Adj. clin. instr. U. Pitts., 1972-74; chief audio/speech pathology service VA Med. Ctr., Butler, Pa., 1972-74; asst. prof. speech pathology Northwestern U., Evanston, Ill., 1978—; asst. prof. psychology U. Health Scis./Chgo. Med. Sch., 1978—, asst. prof. neurology, 1978—; chief audio/speech pathology VA Med. Ctr., North Chicago, Ill., 1974—; cons. VA Med. Ctr., Erie, Pa., 1973-74; research asst. stuttering project U. Pitts. Bd. dirs. Am. Cancer Soc., 1977—, also state del.; profl. mem. Lake County Lost Chord Club; mem. employee of yr. com. Chgo. Fed. Exec. Bd., 1980—; bd. dirs. Easter Seal Soc., Heart Assn. and Cardiac Charities of Lake County, Ill., 1977-79. Recipient cert. of appreciation Heart Assn. of Lake County, 1976, Am. Cancer Soc. of Lake County, 1980, Chgo. Fed. Exec. Bd., 1981; merit award Nat. Am. Cancer Soc., 1981; named profl. fed. employee of yr., Chgo., 1979. Mem. Am. Speech-Lang.-Hearing Assn., Am. Mgmt. Assn., Internat. Assn. Logopedics and Phoniatrics. Contbr. articles on speech and hearing disorders to profl. jours. Office: Audio/Speech Pathology Service (126) VA Med Center North Chicago IL 60064

KASS, DAVID RICHARD, pension actuary; b. Bklyn., Nov. 16, 1931; s. Harry M. and Vivian S. Kass; m. Carole J. Black, June 4, 1956; children—Ruth, Michael, Sara. A.B. magna Cum Laude, Princeton U., 1952; With Mut. of N.Y., N.Y.C., 1954-69, assoc. group actuary, 1965-68, asst. v.p., 1969; v.p. E. M. Klein & Assocs., Cleve., 1969-70; founder, pres. Kass, Germain & Co., Shaker Heights, Ohio, 1970-83, v.p. Kass, Germain div. Johnson & Higgins Co. of Ohio, 1983—. Served with U.S. Army, 1952-54. Fellow Soc. Actuaries; mem. Am. Acad. Actuaries (charter), Midwest Pension Conf., Am. Pension Conf. Office: 2600 National City Ctr Cleveland OH 44114

KASSEBAUM, NANCY LANDON, U.S. senator; b. July 29, 1932; d. Alfred M. and Theo Landon; B.A. in Polit. Sci., U. Kans., 1952; M.Diplomatic History, U. Mich., 1956; m. Philip Kassebaum, 1955 (div. 1979); children—John Philip, Linda Josephine, Richard Landon, William Alfred. Mem. Kans. Govtl. Ethics Commn., Kans. Com. for Humanities, Maize (Kans.) Sch. Bd.; mem. Washington staff Sen. James B. Pearson of Kans., 1975-76; v.p. KFH-KLZS-FM stas.; mem. U.S. Senate from Kans., 1979—, mem. Fgn. Relations Com., Commerce, Sci. and Transp. Com., Budget Com., Select Com. on Ethics. Recipient Matrix award Women in Communications. Republican. Episcopalian. Office: 304 Senate Russell Office Bldg Washington DC 20510

KASTELLE, RUSSELL ERVIN, surveyor, educator; b. Fergus Falls, Minn., Jan. 28, 1933; s. George A. and Edna L. (Baumgarten) K.; m. Darlene A. Greenquist Walstad, June 8, 1963; children—Gregg L. Greenquist, Eric L. Greenquist. Diploma in Architecture N.D. State Sch. Sci., 1958, A.S. in Civil Engring. Tech., 1970, A.S. in Computer Tech., 1974; B.S. in Tech. Edn. Moorhead State U., 1975. Mil. surveyor U.S. Army, 1953-55; cons. engr. K.B.M. Inc., Grand Forks, N.D., 1958-61; city engr., Breckenridge, Minn., 1961-65; instr. N.D. State Sch. Sci., Wahpeton, 1965—; owner, prin. Kastelle Land Surveying, Breckenridge, 1971—. Contbr. articles to profl. jours. Creator Trigstar, nat. trigonometry skills award. Past chmn. Intra State Airport Commn., Wahpeton; vol. Breckenridge Fire Dept.; organizer S.D. Soc. Profl. Land Surveyors. Mem. Am. Congress on Surveying and Mapping, Nat Soc. Profl. Surveyors (bd. govs. 1981—), Am. Tech. Edn. Assn., N.D. Soc. Profl. Land Surveyors. Lutheran. Club: Head of the Red Trap (dir. 1961—), Head of the Red Shooting Grounds (founder). Avocations: Trapshooting, genealogist. Office: Kastelle Land Surveying 518 Minnesota Ave Breckenridge MN 56520

KASTEN, LLOYD AUGUST WILLIAM, emeritus medieval Spanish studies educator, researcher; b. Watertown, Wis., Apr. 14, 1905; s. William Frederick and Emilie Friedericke (Kluetzmann) K. B.A., U. Wis., Madison, 1926, M.A., 1927, Ph.D., 1931; Litt.D., U. of South, 1981. Instr. U. Fla., Gainesville, 1927-28; instr. U. Wis., Madison, 1929-37, asst. prof., 1937-42, assoc. prof., 1942-47, prof. medieval Spanish studies, 1947-75, prof. emeritus, 1975—; pres. Hispanic Sem. Medieval Studies, 1972—. Editor: Luso-Brazilian Rev., 1965-75; co-editor: Alfonso X General Estoria, 1957-61. Co-author, co-editor dictionaries. Mem. Medieval Acad. Am., Linguistic Soc. Am., Am. Oriental Soc., MLA, Dictionary Soc. N.Am., Academia Norteamericana de la Lengua Española (academician), Royal Spanish Acad. (corr. mem.), Hispanic Soc. Am., Phi Beta Kappa, Phi Lambda Beta (hon. nat. pres.). Republican. United Methodist. Avocations: photography; music; gardening. Home: 3734 Ross St Madison WI 53705 Office: U Wisconsin 1130 Van Hise Hall Madison WI 53706

KASTEN, ROBERT W., JR., U.S. Senator; b. Milw., June 19, 1942; s. Robert W. and Mary (Ogden) K.; B.A., U. Ariz., 1964; M.B.A., Columbia U., 1966. With Genesco, Inc., Nashville, 1966-68; dir., v.p. Gilbert Shoe Co., Thiensville, Wis., 1968-75; mem. Wis. Senate, 1972-75, mem. joint fin. com., 1973-75, chmn. joint survey com. on tax exemptions, after 1973; designee Eagleton Inst. Politics, 1973; mem. 94th-95th Congresses from 9th Wis. Dist.; mem. U.S. Senate from Wis., 1980—. Alt. del. Republican Nat. Conv., 1972, del., 1976. Mem. Milw. Council Alcoholism, Milw. Soc. Prevention of Blindness; regional dir. Milw. Coalition for Clean Water; hon. assoc. Harvard U. Inst. of Politics. Served to 1st lt. USAF, 1967-72. Named Jaycee of Year, 1972, Legis. Conservationist of Year, 1973. Mem. Nat. Audubon Soc., Sigma Nu, Alpha Kappa Psi. Office: 110 Hart Senate Office Building Washington DC 20510*

KASTEN, ROGER NEIL, JR., petroleum geologist, consultant; b. St. Georges Parish, Bermuda, U.K., Mar. 15, 1959; came to U.S., 1961, naturalized, 1959; s. Roger Neil and CoNette Lee (Nofzinger) K.; m. Leah Ann Peterson, Aug. 21, 1982. B.S. in Geology, Wichita State U., 1982. Apprentice baker Ketteman's Bakery, Wichita, Kans., 1973-75; mechanic Hillcrest Co., Wichita, 1975-77; salesman Kellogg-Buck Furniture Co., Wichita, 1977-79; lighting technician Am. Electric Co., Wichita, 1979-80; asst., geologist Goodin Trust Petroleum Co., Wichita, 1980-81; staff petroleum geologist D.R. Lauck Oil Co., Inc., Wichita, 1981—. Ricks scholar, 1982. Mem. Am. Assn. Petroleum Geologists (energy and minerals divs.), Kans. Geol. Soc., Wichita Area C. of C. (state legis. com. 1984—, water resources com. 1984—), Jaycees (bd. dirs. 1983-84, v.p. 1984-85), Sigma Gamma Epsilon (pres. 1981-82). Republican. Mem. Christian Ch. (Disciples of Christ). Avocations: kayaking; real estate "high end" audiophile equipment. Home: 928 N Dellrose St Wichita KS 67208 Office: D R Lauck Oil Co Inc 221 S Broadway Suite 400 Wichita KS 67202

KASTENMEIER, ROBERT WILLIAM, congressman; b. Beaver Dam, Wis., Jan. 24, 1924; s. Leo H. and Lucille (Powers) K.; LL.B., U. Wis., 1952; m. Dorothy Chambers, June 27, 1952; children—William, Andrew, Edward. Branch office dir. Claims Service, War Dept., Philippines, 1946-48; admitted to Wis. bar, 1952; practiced Watertown, Wis., 1952-58. Mem. 86th-99th Congresses from 2d Dist. Wis.; mem. house jud. com.; chmn. judiciary subcom. on cts., civil liberties and adminstrn. of justice. Served to 1st lt. Inf., AUS, 1943-46. Philippines. Office: 2328 Rayburn House Office Bldg Washington DC 20515

KASUM, JAMES KENNETH, computer science educator; b. Milw., Sept. 2, 1943; s. Anton and Katherine Susan (Boden) K.; m. Mary Margaret Pahler, May 30, 1970; children—Kelly, Kathleen, Christine. B.S. in Math., U. Wis.-Milw., 1966, M.S. in Math., 1968, Ph.D. in Math., 1974, M.S. in Engring., 1985. Asst. prof. Cardinal Stritch Coll., Milw., 1971-82, assoc. prof., 1984—, dir. grad. program ednl. computing, dir. computer services, 1984—; asst. prof. U. Wis.-Milw., 1982-84; cons. Owensboro Pub. Schs., Ky., 1976, Computrek Bus. Systems, Milw., 1978, Oster Mfg. Co., Milw., 1982. Vol. computer curriculum cons. St. Monica Sch., 1983—, St. Eugene Sch., 1984—. Wis. Alumni Research Found. grantee, 1972. Mem. Math. Assn. Am., Nat. Council Tchrs. Math., Wis. Math. Council (exec. council 1980-82), Assn. Computing Machinery, Milw. Ednl. Computing Assn. (pres. elect 1985-86), Phi Kappa Phi, Delta Chi Sigma, Delta Epsilon Sigma. Roman Catholic. Avocations: cycling; swimming; music. Home: 416 E Fox Dale Ct Fox Point WI 53217 Office: Cardinal Stritch Coll 6801 N Yates Rd Milwaukee WI 53217

KATE, CHRISTINE JANE, educator; b. Massillon, Ohio, Nov. 12, 1955; d. Paul H. and Esther J. (Waltz) K. B.S. in Edn., Kent State U., 1977; M.S. in Edn., U. Akron, 1981. Supr. cert., Ohio; vocat. cert., Ohio; high sch. cert., Ohio. Tchr. home econs. McKinley Sr. High Sch., Canton, Ohio, 1977, Hartford Jr. High Sch., Canton, 1977—. Mem. Assn. for Supervision and Curriculum Devel., Ohio Assn. Supervision and Curriculum Devel., Internat. Home Econs. Assn. (chmn. for Ohio), Am. Home Econs. Assn. Ohio Home Econs. Assn. (nominating com., program and conv. planning com., chmn. internat. sect.), Am. Vocat. Assn., Ohio Vocat. Assn. (chmn. membership com.), Am. Home Econs. Educators Assn., Nat. Assn. Vocat. Tech. Edn. Tchrs., Stark County Home Econs. Assn., Kappa Omicron Phi, Kappa Delta Pi. Home: Route 1 Strasburg OH 44680 Office: Hartford Jr High Sch 1824 3d St SE Canton OH 44707

KATES, SAMUEL SIMON, lawyer, labor arbitrator; b. Cleve., Nov. 10, 1901; s. Harry and Sarah (Rosenberg) K.; m. Dorothy Davis, July 16, 1929; children—Robert D., Alix Kates Shulman. L.L.B., Cleve. Law Sch. Baldwin Wallace U., 1925. Bar: Ohio 1925. Sole practice, Cleve., 1925-51; ptnr. Hertz & Kates, 1951-74, Hertz, Kates, Friedman & Kammer, Cleve., 1974-85; sole practice labor arbitration, 1985—. Contbr. articles on aspects of arbitration to profl. jours. Mem. Cleve. adv. bd. SSS, 1942-45. Mem. Nat. Acad. Arbitrators, ABA (hon.), Ohio State Bar Assn. (hon.), Greater Cleve. Bar Assn. (hon., exec. com. 1936-39), Cuyahoga County Bar Assn. (hon.). Office: Hertz Kates Friedman & Kammer 1020 Leader Bldg Cleveland OH 44114

KATHMAN, MICHAEL DENNIS, university executive; b. Quincy, Ill., Dec. 12, 1943; s. William J. and Beatrice (Costigan) K.; m. Jane McGurn, Nov. 26, 1971; children—Kevin, Cara. B.A., St. Procopius Coll., 1966; A.M.L.S., U. Mich., 1967, A.M. in Am. Studies, 1969; postgrad., St. Cloud State U., 1973-74. Reference, periodicals librarian Monroe County Community Coll., Monroe, Mich., 1968-70; asst. dir. learning resources Wayne County Community Coll., Detroit, 1970-72; dir. pub. services Alcuin Library, St. John's U., Collegeville, Minn., 1972-73, library dir., 1973-80, colloquium instr., 1974-76, 1977-80, dir. libraries and media services Coll. St. Benedict, St. John's U., 1980—; cons. Assn. Coll. and Research Libraries, 1982-84, Adv. Com. on Acad. Computer Services, 1983—; chmn. search com. Minn. Interlibrary Telecommunications Exchange, 1983-84, Contbr. articles and book revs. to profl. jours. Editor (with Virgil F. Massman) Assn. Coll. and Research Libraries Nat. Conf., 1981. Presenter talks on managing student workers to numerous groups. Mem. Diocesan Commn. on Baptism, 1975-76; instr. Pre-Cana Conf., 1975-76, St. Boniface Parish Baptism Program, 1975-76; mem. Cold Spring Planning Commn., 1977-80, Cold Spring City Council, 1978—; negotiator City of Spring, Minn., 1980-81. Mem. ALA (mem. Assn. Coll. & Research Libraries, Resources and Tech. Services, Reference and Adult Services), Minn. Library Assn. (vice chmn., chmn.-elect acad. div. 1976, bd. dirs. 1982—, v.p. 1982-83, pres. 1983-84). Roman Catholic. Office: St Johns University Collegeville MN 56301

KATSCHKE, RICHARD NORMAN, university administrator; b. Chgo., June 23, 1949; s. Norman George and Lucille Victoria (Watson) K.; m. Vickie Lee Wagaman, Sept. 13, 1980; 1 child, Richard Norman. B.S., No. Ill. U., 1972; M.A., Northeastern Ill. U., 1983. Asst. dir. devel. and pub. relations Resurrection Hosp., Chgo., 1971-72; dir. pub. relations St. Anthony Hosp., Rockford, Ill., 1972-76; pub. relations specialist U. Chgo., 1976-79; dir. univ. relations Northeastern Ill. U., Chgo., 1979—. Mem. jury Chgo. Internat. Film Festival. Mem. Pub. Relations Soc. Am. (accredited), Sigma Delta Chi, Phi Kappa Sigma. Lutheran. Home: 1134 Cernan Ct Elk Grove Village IL 60007 Office: Northeastern Ill U 5500 N St Louis Ave Chicago IL 60625

KATZ, FRANK M., manufacturing executive; b. Cin., Jan. 26, 1927; s. Julien E. and Edith (Shott) K.; m. Susan Stix, June 12, 1951 (dec. Dec. 1977); children—Nancy, David, William; m. Carol Joy Paseley, Sept. 9, 1979; stepchildren—James Klein, Steven Klein. M.E., U. Cin., 1951. Pres., Shott Mfg. Co., Cin., 1943—. Rear comdr. U.S. Power Squadrons, 1981-84; pres. Maketewah Neighborhood Assn., Cin., 1983-84. Served with USN, 1945-46. Mem. Ohio Home Furnishings Assn., Cin. Wholesale Home Furnishing Club (pres. 1959), Cin. Propeller Club (pres. 1970-71). Jewish. Club: Ohio River Launch (Cin.). Avocation: boating. Home: 1015 Towanda Terr Cincinnati OH 45216 Office: 3168 Beekman St Cincinnati OH 45223

KATZ, JONATHAN ISAAC, astrophysicist, educator; b. N.Y.C., Jan. 5, 1951; s. Shlomo and Rebecca Leah (Samuels) K.; m. Lilly Margaret Canel, Mar. 15, 1982; 1 child, Shlomo. A.B., Cornell U., 1970, A.M., 1971, Ph.D., 1973. Mem. Inst. Advanced Study, Princeton, N.J., 1973-76; assoc. prof. astrophysics UCLA, 1976-81, Washington U., St. Louis, Mo., 1981—; cons. various corps. and sci. labs., 1973—; mem. NASA Adv. Council, Washington, 1983—, NAS-NRC Com. Atmospheric Effects Nuclear War, Washington, 1983-84. Contbr. articles to profl. jours. Alfred P. Sloan Found. fellow, 1977-81. Mem. Am. Phys. Soc., Am. Astron. Soc. Jewish. Home: 3 Tuscany Park Clayton MO 63105 Office: Washington U Saint Louis MO 63130

KATZ, LAWRENCE S., banker, lawyer; b. Milw., Feb. 22, 1912; s. Samuel and Rose (Grossman) K.; m. Florence Cohen, June 12, 1938; children—Alan James, Steven Alexander. J.D., Marquette U., 1934. Bar: Wis. 1934. Examiner Wis. Indsl. Commn., Milw., 1936-46; pres. Met. Constrn. Co., Milw., 1946-61; dir. FHA, Wis., 1961-71; sr. v.p. First Bank, Milw., 1971—; cons. Sec. HUD, 1972. Co-chmn. NCCJ, 1978—; chmn. Anti-Defamation League, Wis., 1982—, Milw. County Cultural Council, 1984—. Mem. Wis. Mortgage Bankers Assn. (pres. 1980-82). Democrat. Jewish. Lodge: B'Nai Brith. Office: First Bank 201 W Wisconsin Ave Milwaukee WI 53259

KATZ, MYER, industrial metals company executive, educator, biologist, historian; b. Winona, Minn.; s. William Udell and Anna Sara (Schochett) K.; B.E. in Biol. Sci. and History, U. Wis.; M.A. in Biol. Scis., George Washington U.; postgrad. U. Wis., U. Minn., U. Chgo., Am. U., Western Wis. Tech. Inst. Sec.-treas., Katz Indsl. Metals, Inc., La Crosse, Wis., 1959—; exec. v.p. Gateway Plastics Corp., La Crosse, 1965-69; instr. bus. mgmt. Western Wis. Tech. Inst., La Crosse, 1969-71; instr. Am. history and gen. scis. Central High Sch., La Crosse; research biologist and writer U.S. Dept. Agr., Washington, U.S. Dept. Interior, Washington; office mgr. Wis. Dept. Hwys., Madison; guest lectr. U. Wis. Library Sch., 1972-73; lectr. local, state and Jewish history to various sch., civic and ch. groups in Wis., 1970-85; editorial writer La Crosse Tribune, 1977-85, spl. features writer, 1980-85. Pres., La Crosse Public Library Friends, 1969-71; mem. Mayor's Bicentennial Commn., La Crosse, 1975-76, chmn. heritage div., 1975-76; mem. U. Wis. Bicentennial Commn.; mem. La Crosse City and County Historic Sites Commn., 1973-78, chmn., 1973-78; bd. curators Swarthout Hist. Mus., 1975—; bd. dirs. Congregation Sons of Abraham, La Crosse, 1974-76, La Crosse Public Library, 1968-72; bd. dirs. Mississippi River Sci. and Industry Center, La Crosse, 1979—, hist. adv., 1979—; bd. dirs. Wis. Libraries Friends, 1969-72; del. Wis. Gov.'s Conf. on Libraries, 1978; bd. advisers Riverside U.S.A., 1982—. Served with U.S. Army Mil. Welfare, field dir. ARC. Recipient Bronze Plaque award La Crosse County Hist. Soc., 1976; award of Recognition Luther Rice Soc., George Washington U., 1972; Blue Ribbon for meritorious contbns. to Am. Bicentennial Year, 1976; nat. award of Commendation, Am. Assn. State and Local History, 1977; award of Merit, State Hist. Soc. Wis., 1974; 1st citizen award City of La Crosse, 1980, disting. service award Phi Delta Kappa, 1981, achievement award Hist. Preservation Soc. Am., 1980, recognition award George Washington U., 1972. Mem. Am. Bibl. Archeol. Soc., Wis. Archeol. Soc., Coalition for Regional Environ. Studies, Washington Biol. Soc., AAAS, Wis. Soc. Jewish Learning, Wis. Acad. Scis., Arts and Letters, Am. Ornithologists Union, Nat. Audubon Soc., Smithsonian Instn., Costeau Soc., Hist. Preservation Alliance of La Crosse, La Crosse Writers Club, U. Wis. Alumni Assn., George Washington U. Alumni Assn., La Crosse County Hist. Soc. (dir. publs. 1973-77, pres. 1975-76, museum dir. 1973-75), Wis. State Hist. Soc. (spl. commendation 1976), John Quincy Adams Assocs., George Washington Univ., Tau Alpha Omega. Lodge: B'nai B'rith. Author: History of Jews and Judaism in La Crosse Area (State award), 1974; Pictorial History of Mayors of La Crosse, 1974; History of Rabbinate of La Crosse, 1979; History of Onalaska, Wis., 1974; The Caves of Barre Mills, Wis., 1975; History of Hebrew Chirography, The Hirshheimer Saga, 1976, Echoes of Our Past, 1985; contbr. articles on local and state history to scholarly publs. Home: 1525 State St La Crosse WI 54601 Office: 2535 E Ave South La Crosse WI 54601

KATZEL, JEANINE ALMA, journalist; b. Chgo., Feb. 20, 1948, d. LeRoy Paul and Lia Mary (Arcuri) Katzel; B.A. in Journalism, U. Wis., 1970; M.S. in Journalism, Northwestern U., 1974. Publs. editor U. Wis. Sea Grant Program, Madison, 1969-72; editor research div. agrl. sch. U. Wis., Madison, 1972; research editor Prism mag. AMA, Chgo., 1972-73; free lance writer, 1974-75; lit. editor Plant Engring. mag. Tech. Pub. Co., Barrington, Ill., 1975-76, news editor, 1976-77, asso. editor, 1977-79, sr. editor, 1979—. Judge assoc. ann. competition Engring. Coll. Mag., 1978-83, 85—. Recipient Elsie Bullard Morrison prize in Journalism, U. Wis., 1969; Peter Lisagor award in bus. journalism, 1983. Mem. Women in Communications, Am. Soc. Bus. Press Editors (pres. Chgo. chpt. 1977-78), Soc. Profl. Journalists, Soc. Fire Protection Engrs., Am. Inst. Chem. Engrs., Am. Chem. Soc., Nat. Audubon Soc., Nat. Fire Protection Assn. (tech. com. on fire pumps), Am. Soc. Safety Engrs., Internat. Soc. Fire Service Instrs., Chgo. Computer Club, AAUW, Phi Kappa Phi. Home: 16 Boxwood Ln Cary IL 60013 Office: 1301 S Grove Ave Barrington IL 60010

KATZEN, RAPHAEL, consulting chemical engineer; b. Balt., July 28, 1915; s. Isidor and Esther (Stein) K.; m. Selma M. Siegel, June 19, 1938; 1 child, Nancy. B.Chem. Engring. cum laude, Poly. Inst. N.Y., 1936, M.Chem. Engring., 1938, D.Chem. Engring., 1942. Tech. dir. Northwood Chem. Co., Phelps, Wis., 1938-42; project mgr. Diamond Alkali Co., Painesville, Ohio, 1942-44; mgr. engring. div. Vulcan Cin., 1944-53; mng. ptnr. Raphael Katzen Assocs., Cin., 1953-80; pres., owner Raphael Katzen Assocs. Internat., Inc., Cin., 1956—; cons. ITT Rayonier, Stamford, Conn., 1953—, Union Carbide

Corp., Danbury, Conn., 1966-83; mem. Air Pollution Adv. Bd. City of Cin., 1972-75; panel mem. Am. Arbitration Assn., Cin., 1975; dir. Biol. Energy Corp., Valley Forge, Pa.; pres. C.P. Assocs., Ltd., Montreal, Que., Can., 1974—. Contbr. articles on process tech. to profl. jours. Patentee in field. Recipient Disting. Alumnus award Poly. Inst. N.Y., 1970, Disting. Cons. award Ohio Assn. Cons. Engrs., 1978, Profl. Accomplishment award Tech. and Sci. Soc. Council, 1978, Disting. Engr. award Tech. and Sci. Soc. Council, 1979. Fellow Poly. Inst. N.Y., Am. Inst. Chem. Engrs., Am. Inst. Chemists; mem. TAPPI, Can. Pulp and Paper Assn., Am. Chem. Soc. Republican. Jewish. Clubs: Chemists (N.Y.C.); Univ. (Cin.); Am. (Miami). Avocations: photography; shooting; swimming.

KATZMAN, ELLEN JO, community center administrator; b. Indpls., June 16, 1957; d. Abraham and Riva L. (Tuch) K. B.S. in Criminal Justice, Ind. U., 1980, M.S.W., 1982. Youth and young adult dir. Jewish Community Ctr., Indpls., 1982-85, program dir., 1985—; Dor L' Dor Israel seminar participant, 1984. Jewish Welfare Fedn. Scholar, 1981-82. Mem. Nat. Assn. Social Workers (bd. dirs. 1980—), Nat. Council of Jewish Women, Orgn. for Rehab. Through Tng. (v.p. 1983-84), Assn. Jewish Ctr. Workers. Office: Jewish Community Ctr 6701 Hoover Rd Indianapolis IN 46260

KAUFFMAN, ANDRENE, artist, educator; b. Chgo., Apr. 19, 1905; d. George Francis and Charlotte Camille (Henriksen) K.; B.F.A., Art Inst. Chgo., 1939, M.F.A., 1941. Prof. painting, sculpture, ceramics and history art Rockford Coll., Ill., 1942-58; faculty Sch. Art Inst. Chgo., 1927-67, chmn. Div. Fine Arts, 1963-66; prof. emeritus, 1967—. Exhibited continuously Art Inst. Chgo.; one-man shows include San Diego Fine Arts Mus., Mt. Mary Coll., Vanderpoel Gallery, Burpee Gallery, Univ. Club Chgo., Rosary Coll., Loyola U. Chgo., represented in permanent collections Art Inst. Chgo., Elmhurst Art Mus., Beverly Art Ctr., Sears Tower, Hull House. Fellow John Quincy Adams; numerous awards. Mem. The Arts Club of Chgo., Nat. Soc. Mural Painters, Chgo. Soc. Artists, AAUP, Coll. Art Assn. Home and Office: 411 N West Ave Elmhurst IL 60126

KAUFFMAN, DONNA MAY, nursing educator; b. Rochester, Ind., July 6, 1947; s. Charles Edward and Donnabelle (Newell) K. Diploma Marion County Gen. Hosp. Sch. Nursing, Indpls., 1968; B.S.N., Ind. U., Indpls., 1974; M.S., Ball State U., 1979. Head nurse CICU, Meml. Hosp., Logansport, Ind., 1968-73; staff nurse Howard Community Hosp., Kokomo, Ind., 1973-74; staff nurse Gen. Hosp., Ft. Walton Beach, Fla., 1974-75; vis. lectr. nursing Ind. U., Kokomo, 1976-79; asst. prof. nursing Purdue U., West Lafayette, Ind., 1979—, asst. head student affairs, 1982—; dir. IndiMed Cons., Inc. Judge, Regional Sci. Fair, Lafayette, 1983, 84, counselor Area IV Council Aging, 1982; bd. dirs. Tippecanoe County Heart Assn., 1979-81. Mem. Ind. Nurses Assn. (dist. 8 bd. dirs. 1982-83), Sigma Theta Tau. Methodist. Office: Purdue U Sch Nursing Northwestern Ave West Lafayette IN 47907

KAUFFMAN, EWING MARION, pharm. co. exec., baseball exec.; b. 1916; s. John S. and Effie May (Winders) K.; Asso. Sci., Kansas City Jr. Coll.; D.Sci., Union Coll.; m. Muriel Irene McBrien, Feb. 28, 1962; children—Larry, Sue, Julia Moore. Founder, chmn. bd. Marion Labs., Inc., Kansas City, Mo., 1950—; majority owner, chmn. Kansas City Royals Baseball Club, 1969—. Mem. Civic Council Kansas City, Kansas City Sports Commn., Mayor's Corps of Progress; pres. Ewing M. Kauffman Found. Served with USN. Recipient Horatio Alger award Am. Schs. and Colls. Assn.; Disting. Eagle, Boy Scouts Am.; Disting. Service award Fellowship Christian Athletes; named to Mo. Sports Hall of Fame. Clubs: Indian Hills Country, Kansas City, Eldorado Country. Office: Marion Labs Inc 9221 Ward Pkwy Kansas City MO 64114

KAUFFMAN, JOSEPH FRANK, educator, university administrator; b. Providence, Dec. 2, 1921; s. Frank J. and Lena (Andelman) K.; m. Gladys Davidson, June 20, 1943; children—Marcia Lee, Glenn Frank. A.B., U. Denver, 1948; M.A., Northwestern U., 1951; Ed.D., Boston U., 1958. Dr. Pedagogy (hon.), U. R.I., 1973, R. I. Coll., 1977. Asst. to pres. Brandeis U., Waltham, Mass., 1952-56, dean students, 1956-60; exec. v.p. Jewish. Theol. Sem. of Am., N.Y.C., 1960-61; dir. tng. U.S. Peace Corps, Washington, 1961-63; staff assoc. Am. Council on Edn., Washington and dir. higher edn. services Am. Personnel and Guidance Assn., Washington, 1963-65; dean student affairs U. Wis., Madison, 1965-68; pres. R.I. Coll., Providence, 1968-73; exec. v.p. U. Wis. Systems, Madison, 1980-83; prof. dept. ednl. adminstrn. U.Wis.-Madison, 1973—; commr. North Central Assn. Colls. and Schs., Chgo., 1982—; mem. Commn. on Leadership Devel., Am. Council on Edn., Washington, 1985—. Author: Education, 1968; The Selection of College Presidents, 1974; At the Pleasure of the Board, 1980; co-editor: The College and the Student, 1965. Trustee St. Norbert Coll., De Pere, Wis., 1976—. Served with U.S. Army, 1942-45; ETO. Mem. Am. Assn. for higher Edn. (chmn.-elect 1985—), Assn. for Study of Higher Edn. (pres. 1981-82). Democrat. Jewish. Home: 1426 Annen Ln Madison WI 53711 Office: U Wis 1025 W Johnson St Madison WI 53706

KAUFFMAN, RICHARD VANCE, economist; b. Louisville, July 22, 1946; s. Robert Earl and Josephine Jane (Flower) K.; m. Suzanne L. King, Dec. 31, 1966 (div. 1974); children—Kelley Louise, Mark Richard; m. Deborah Ann Absey, Dec. 22, 1975; 1 child, Stacy Leigh. B.A., U. No. Colo., 1967, M.A., 1968; Ph.D., Colo. State U., 1975. Asst. prof., dir. Ctr. Econ. Edn., U. N.D., Grand Forks, 1974-78, assoc. prof., chmn. dept. econs., 1978-85. Editor: Statistical Abstract of North Dakota, 1979. Contbr. articles to profl. jours. Bush Found. fellow, 1984. Mem. Western Social Sci. Assn., Midwest Econs. Assn., N.D. Council Econ. Edn. (exec. dir. 1980-83, trustee 1983—). Avocation: classical guitar playing. Home: 3551 11th Ave N Grand Forks ND 58201 Office: Dept Econs U ND Gamble Hall Grand Forks ND 58202

KAUFFMAN, STEPHEN BLAIR, law librarian; b. St. Louis, Sept. 25, 1948; s. William Porter and Patricia Mary (Cain) Kauffman Supernois; m. Susan Heffernan, Jan. 24, 1971 (dec. Aug. 1972); children—Ashley, Stephanie, Cameron; m. Mary Ann Royle, Aug. 24, 1979. B.S., U. Mo., St. Louis, 1971; J.D., U. Mo., Kansas City, 1975, LL.M., 1976; M.L.L., U. Wash. 1977. Law librarian Reiderer, Eisberg, Kansas City, Mo., 1973-75; law library asst. U. Wash., Seattle, 1976-77; law librarian Nat. Jud. Coll., Reno, 1977-81; law library dir. No. Ill. U., DeKalb, 1981—. Bd. dirs. Ill. Bar Automated Research, Chgo., 1982—; mem. adv. bd. Washoe County Law Library, Reno, 1978-81. Contbr. articles to profl. jours. Mem. Am. Assn. Law Libraries, Chgo. Assn. Law Libraries, Mid Am. Assn. Law Libraries, Spl. Libraries Assn., Mo. Bar Assn. Democrat. 630 Grove St DeKalb IL 60115 Office: Coll Law Library No Ill U DeKalb IL 60115

KAUFMAN, ALBERT NICK, manufacturing executive; b. Warsaw, Ind., May 16, 1924; s. Emanuel Kaufman; student Ind. U., 1948; m. Gwendolyn Ione, May 1, 1943; children—Victoria Joyce, Timothy N. With Arnolt Corp., Indpls., 1942-62, advancing through various positions and serving as v.p. mfg., dir., 1953-62; pres. K-T Corp., 1962—; pres., chmn. bd. Kaufman Enterprises, Inc., 1977—; sec.-treas. Kaufman Energy Devel. Corp.; v.p. Splty. Products Group, ALCO Standard Corp.; pres. ALCO Aerospace Co., 1981—; dir. Accudyne Corp., 1983—. Vice pres. bd. pensions Ch. of God Anderson, Ind. Served with USNR, World War II. clubs: Masons, Shriners. Home: 6220 N Chester Ave Indianapolis IN 46220 Office: 8445 Keystone Crossing Suite 230 Indianapolis IN 46240

KAUFMAN, CHARLES EDWARD, university administrator; b. Kendallville, Ind., Jan. 22, 1926; s. Edward Ernest and Marguerite Albert (Smith) K.; m. Joyce Elaine Friar, Aug. 6, 1950; children—Kim Edward, Gregory Lawrence, Richard Charles. B.S., Ball State U., 1950, M.S., 1954; postgrad. St. Francis Coll., 1962-63, Ind. U., 1964-65. Cert. guidance counselor, prin., Ind. Tchr., coach Bluffton Community Schs. (Ind.), 1950-56; counselor, tchr. Culver Mil. Acad. (Ind.), 1956-60; dir. guidance Huntington Community Schs. (Ind.), 1960-66; dir. pre-admission services Ball State U., Muncie, Ind., 1966—; cons. in field. Dist. adminstr. Circle K, 1977-80; sec. Ind. Kiwanis Found., 1980. Served with USN, 1944-46; PTO. Recipient WASSON achievement award Kiwanis Internat., 1979. Mem. Ind. Assn. Coll. Admissions Counselors, Nat. Assn. Coll. Admissions Counselors, Ind. Assn. Registrars and Admissions Officers, Nat. Assn. Registrars and Admissions Officers, Ind. Sch. Adminstrs. Assn., Ind. State Tchrs. Assn., Phi Delta Kappa. Republican. Methodist. Lodge: Kiwanis (lt. gov. 1983-84). Author: Academic Planning for High School & College and How to Pay the Bills, 1983. Home: 3510 Brook Dr Muncie IN 47304 Office: 2000 University Ave Ball State U Muncie IN 47306

KAUFMAN, GERRY LEE, dentist; b. Huntington, Ind., May 10, 1937; s. Glenn Wilbur Kaufman and Mary Jane (Cretsinger) Didier; m. Linda Hendry Cross, June 30, 1962; children—Karen Elizabeth, Cynthia Ann. B.A., Hanover Coll., 1959; D.D.S., Ind. U., 1967. Practice dentistry Gerry L. Kaufman, DDS, Ft. Wayne, Ind., 1967—. Class rep. Hanover Coll. Alumni Fund (Ind.), 1971; dir. New Glenwood Civic Assn., Ft. Wayne, 1976-78. Fellow Acad. of General Dentistry; mem. Acad. of Operative Dentistry, Pierre Fauchard Acad., Isaac Knapp Dist. Dental Soc. (sec. 1975-77, pres. 1979-80, bd. dirs. 1972—), Ind. Dental Assn., (trustee 1982—, chmn. council on dental edn. 1974-82), Am. Dental Assn. (del. 1979—), Phi Delta Theta (warden 1957, pres. 1959). Republican. Unitarian. Club: Wildwood Summit City Court (Ft. Wayne). Lodge: Rotary. Avocations: sailing; tennis; jogging; cross country skiing; reading. Home: 5421 Chantilly Dr Fort Wayne IN 46815 Office: Gerry L Kaufman DDS PC 4606-BE State Blvd Fort Wayne IN 46815

KAUFMAN, KENTON RICHARD, agricultural engineer; b. Mitchell, S.D., Feb. 19, 1952; s. Richard and Leona Wilma (Herbst) K.; m. Nancy Ann Brockel, June 3, 1978. B.S., S.D. State U., 1974, M.S., 1976, Registered profl. engr., N.D. With Caterpillar Tractor Co., Peoria, Ill., summer 1974; grad. research asst. S.D. State U., Brookings, 1975-76; asst. prof. N.D. State U., Fargo, 1976—; cons. UN Indsl. Devel. Orgn., Vienna, Austria, summer 1983. F.O. Butler scholar, 1971; 3M Co. scholar, 1972; Ralston Purina scholar, 1973; grantee Internat. Harvester Co., Allis Chalmers Co., U.S. Dept. Agr. Mem. Am. Soc. Agrl. Engrs., Nat. Strength and Conditioning Assn., Sigma Xi, Alpha Epsilon, Tau Beta Pi, Phi Kappa Phi, Gamma Sigma Delta, Lutheran. Contbr. articles to profl. jours. Home: 3213 Maple St Fargo ND 58102 Office: Agrl Engring Dept ND State U Fargo ND 58105

KAUFMAN, LAWRENCE CLARK, city administrator; b. Oklahoma City, Mar. 21, 1950; s. Clark Ernest and Barbara Jo (Landsberger) K.; m. Deborah Anne Deckard, Sept. 26, 1972. B.S. in Pub. Adminstrn., Southwest Mo. State U., 1972. Adminstrv. asst. City of Independence (Mo.), 1972-76, community devel. dir., 1976-78, asst. to city mgr., 1978—. Mem. Internat. City Mgmt. Assn. (assoc.), Mo. City Mgmt. Assn., Am. Pub. Works Assn., Am. Soc. for Pub. Adminstrn., Nat. Corvette Owners Assn. (charter), Nat. Corvette Restorers Soc. Contbr. articles to profl. jours. Office: 111 E Maple St Independence MO 64050

KAUFMAN, MILDRED KANTOR, sociologist; b. Bronx, N.Y., Jan. 28, 1930; d. David E. and Henrietta May (Friedlander) Kantor; m. Robert L. Kaufman, May 19, 1968; children—David Jay. Student U. Rochester, 1951; M.A., U. N.C.-Chapel Hill, 1954, Ph.D., 1956. Project dir. mental health research St. Louis County Health Dept., Clayton, Mo., 1955-61, dir. vital stats., 1961-73; dir. Health Data Ctr., St. Louis County Dept. Community Health and Med. Care, St. Louis, 1973—; assoc. program dir. tng. program for social sci. research in community mental health Social Sci. Inst., Washington U., St. Louis, 1958-67, co-dir., 1968-69; asst. clin. prof. community medicine St. Louis U. Sch. Medicine, 1969-78, assoc. clin. prof., 1979—; key census person St. Louis Met. area U.S. Bur. Census, 1966—; mem. adv. com. Nat. Ctr. Health Stats., HEW, 1969-72. Editor: Mobility and Mental Health, 1965. Contbr. articles to profl. jours. Rochester City scholar, 1947-51; co-recipient Ernest W. Burgess award, 1958. Milbank Meml. Fund grantee, 1959-61; USPHS grantee, 1969-71. Fellow Am. Pub. Health Assn., Am. Sociol. Assn.; mem. Am. Assn. Vital Records and Pub. Health Stats., Am. Statis. Assn., Internat. Union Sci. Study of Population, Midwest Sociol. Soc., Mo. Assn. Social Welfare, Mo. Sociol. Soc., Population Assn. Am., Phi Beta Kappa. Club: Woman's of Washington University (St. Louis). Home: 7249 Greenway University City MO 63130 Office: St Louis County Dept Community Health 801 S Brentwood Blvd Saint Louis MO 63105

KAUFMAN, ROBERT J., plant sciences director; b. St. Louis, Nov. 28, 1947; s. Oliver W. and Margaret J. (Williams) K.; m. Janice M. Schmidt, Aug. 29, 1970; children—Emily, Angela. B.S. in Chemistry, U. Mo., 1970; Ph.D. in Chemistry, MIT, 1974. Sr. research chemist Monsanto, St. Louis, 1974-77, group leader, 1977-78, research mgr., 1978-81, research dir. plant scis., 1981-83, dir. plant scis., 1983—. Author profl. writings in field. Avocations: hiking; hockey; guitar; handball. Office: Monsanto 700 Chesterfield Village Pkwy Saint Louis MO 63198

KAUFMAN, ROBERT WILLIAM, political science educator; b. Fond du Lac, Wis., Dec. 23, 1923; s. Andrew Carl and Helen (Ohring) K.; m. Ellen Frasier Anders, Sept. 19, 1953; children—Marianne, Julie, Carol. B.S., U. Wis., 1948; M.A., Am. U., 1953, Ph.D., 1961. Researcher, writer Congl. Quar., Washington, 1954-59; asst. prof. Western Mich. U., Kalamazoo, 1959-64, assoc. prof., 1964-71, prof. polit. sci., 1971—, dir. Univ. Ctr. for Environ. Affairs, Sci. for Citizens Ctr., 1979-84, S.W. Mich. Ground Water Survey and Monitoring Program, 1983-84; acting exec. dir. S. Central Mich. Planning Council, Kalamazoo, 1973-74. Author: (with others) Coping with Energy Limitation in Transportation - Proposals for Michigan, 1979; also articles. Cons. Calif. State Assembly, Sacramento, 1967-68; mem. Mich. Transp. Research Adv. Com., 1976-82; chmn. citizens adv. com. Kalamazoo Area Transp. Study, 1976-78; pres. Hackett High Sch. Bd. Edn., Kalamazoo, 1980-81; v.p., bd. dirs. Lake Mich. Fedn., Chgo., 1981-82. Served to lt. comdr. USNR, 1943-46, PTO. Establish a Sci. for Citizens Ctr. grantee NSF, 1980, Establish S.W. Mich. Ground Water Survey and Monitoring Program grantee W.K. Kellogg Found., 1984; Nat. Ctr. for Edn. in Politics fellow, 1967. Mem. Mich. Assn. Environ. Profls. (pres. 1980-81), Mich. Conf. Polit. Scientists (pres. 1970-71), Internat. Studies Assn. (exec. com. 1970-71), Pi Sigma Alpha. Democrat. Avocations: tennis; skiing; swimming; hiking. Home: 1000 Carolee Ln Kalamazoo MI 49008 Office: Dept Polit Sci Western Michigan U Kalamazoo MI 49007

KAUFMAN, ROLF M., information services manager; b. Frankfurt, Ger., Nov. 25, 1935; came to U.S., 1940; s. Dolf and Lore W. (Kornsand) K.; m. Elinor Weisbaum, Apr. 4, 1959; children—Janine, Michael F. B.E.E., CCNY, 1958. Programmer/project leader Western Electric Co., N.Y.C., 1958-69; mgr. fin. systems Borden, Inc., Columbus, Ohio, 1969-72; mgr. systems and programming Amerace Corp., Columbus, 1972-75; mgr. data ctr. Ranco Inc., Columbus, 1975-79; dir. mgmt. info. services White Castle, Columbus, 1979-82; mgr. mgmt. info. services Midland-Ross Corp., Columbus, 1982—. Officer civic assn., 1973—. Served to 2d lt. U.S. Army, 1958-60. Mem. Am. Mgmt. Assns., Assn. Systems Mgmt. Jewish. Avocations: philately; long distance walking; sports; reading. Office: Midland Ross Corp 4200 Surface Rd Columbus OH 43228

KAUFMAN, SUZANNE DRYER, art educator, artist; b. Indpls., Oct. 10, 1927; d. Gerald and Iola (Callier) Mahalowitz; m. Joseph G. Dryer, Oct. 18, 1948 (div. 1964); children—Janet Dryer Ross, Jeffrey (dec.), Joel. Student, Purdue U., 1944-46; B.A., Rockford Coll., 1965; M.A., No. Ill. U., 1968. Cert. tchr., Ill. Asst. editor William H. Block & Co., —Block's Booster—, Indpls., 1946-49; tchr. art Rockford (Ill.) Sch. Dist., 1965-70; instr., asst. prof., assoc. prof., prof. art Rock Valley Coll., Rockford, Ill., 1970—; lectr. Rockford Coll.; art critic New Art Examiner, Rockford Register Star, WREX-TV; cons. A.C.T.S. Inc., Glencoe, Ill.; judge for juried art competitions; lectr. in field; over 400 art works in pub. and pvt. collections, 14 one man shows, 49 group and invitational exhibits, 31 juried exhibits. Initiator gift fund and presentation Lindisfarne Gospels from Rockford Coll. to Holy Island, Eng., 1970; mem. visual arts panel Ill. Arts Council, 1975; mem. Mayor's Urban Design Rev. Com., Rockford, 1974-76, sculpture com. for Rockford Symbol, 1974-77; co-founder Rockford Gifted Child Assn.; v.p., sec. Rockford Art Assn. bd., 1972-82; mem. Rockford Hosp. Vols. bd., 1959-64; bd. dirs., v.p., sec. chmn. center mgmt. com. Jewish Community Center, 1960-65; vol. Highland Park Hosp., 1955-59; mem. Ind. Jewish Community Relations bd., 1948-52; chmn. Indpls. Jewish Community Center adult activities, 1950-52. Recipient Outstanding Vol. of Yr. award Sinnissippi Lung Assn., 1983, 84; 10 Yr. Service award Rockford Art Assn., 1982; numerous service awards from Rockford Meml. Hosp., Highland Park Hosp., Temple Beth El Sisterhood; 15 Yr. Service award Rock Valley Coll.; named Disting. Alumnus of Yr., No. Ill. U., 1985, also award for outstanding profl. achievement Dept. Art Alumni, 1985. Mem. Coll. Art Assn., Community Coll. Humanities Assn., Community Coll. Faculty Assn. Club: Figure Skating of Rockford. Home: 240 Lovesee Rd Roscoe IL 61073 Office: 3301 N Mulford Rd Rockford IL 61101 Studio: Stone Hollow Studio 3318 N Main St Rockford IL 61103

KAUFMAN-CODJOE, KAREN, physician; b. Memphis, Sept. 23, 1952; d. Ellis and Mildred Kaufman; m. Bernard A. Codjoe, Oct. 11, 1975; children—Ellis, John, Anna. B.A., Macalester Coll., St. Paul, 1973; M.D., U. Tenn., 1978. Intern, Breckenridge Hosp., Austin, Tex., 1979-80, resident, 1980-82; instr. pediatrics Central Tex. Med. Found., Austin, 1982-83; dir. ambulatory pediatrics St. Elizabeth Hosp., Youngstown, Ohio, 1983—, asst. dir. dept. pediatrics, 1984—. Fellow Am. Acad. Pediatrics (jr.). Home: 514 Tod Ln Youngstown OH 44504 Office: 1044 Belmont Ave Youngstown OH 44501

KAUNLEY, RUTH HOWARD, guidance counselor; b. Kansas City, Mo., June 24, 1951; d. Gail and Maxine (Hunter) Howard; m. Samuel Maurice Kaunley, Dec. 1, 1973; 1 child, Nathanael. B.S. in Edn., Evangel Coll., 1973; M.A. in Guidance and Counseling, S.W. Mo. State U., 1979. Asst. research analyst Gospel Pub. House, Springfield, Mo., 1974-75; sec. Mo. Bd. Probation and Parole, Branson, 1977-80; guidance counselor Central Bible Coll., Springfield, 1980—. Mem. Am. Assn. Counseling Devel., Mo. Coll. Personnel Assn. Mem. Assembly of God Ch. Home: 3965 N Bannister St Springfield MO 65803 Office: 3000 N Grant St Springfield MO 65803

KAUTZ, RICHARD CARL, chemical and feeds company executive; b. Mucatine, Iowa, Aug. 1, 1916; s. Carl and Leah (Amlong) K.; student U. Ariz., 1936-37; B.S. with high distinction, U. Iowa, 1939; D.H.L., George Williams Coll., 1973; m. Mary Elda Stein, Dec. 24, 1939; children—Linda, Judith (Mrs. J. David Curb), John Terry, Thomas R., Susan E. (Mrs. Donald C. Teeple), Sarah J. (Mrs. Harold Aavang), Mary Catherine (Mrs. Jay S. Huff), Jennifer W. (Mrs. Donald W. Kreger). Supr. in fin. dept. Gen. Electric Co., 1939-43; with Grain Processing Corp. and Kent Feeds, Inc., Muscatine, 1943—, chmn. bd., dir., mem. exec. com., 1966—. Mem. citizens com. Rock Island dist. U.S. Army Engrs.; chmn. bd. trustees mem. exec. com. Herbert Hoover Presdl. Library Assn., 1976—; chmn. bd. Nat. Council YMCA, 1970-73, now mem., mem. exec. com. and bd.; N.Am. regional v.p. World Alliance YMCA's, 1973—, mem. pres.'s com., exec. com.; bd. dirs. U. Iowa Found.; mem. Bd. Trustees YMCA's; trustee Center for Study of Presidency, 1977—; mem. Bus.-Industry Polit. Action Com., 1977—; mem. adv. com. Export-Import Bank U.S., 1984. Mem. NAM (dir., chmn. exec. com. 1977, chmn. fin. com. 1978, vice chmn. 1975, chmn. 1976), Iowa Mfrs. Assn. (dir.), Muscatine C. of C., DeMolay Legion of Honor, Beta Gamma Sigma (dirs. table), Sigma Chi (named Significant Sig.). Presbyterian. Clubs: Union League (Chgo.); Met., Capitol Hill (Washington); Marco Polo, Met., Canadian (N.Y.C.); University Athletic, U. Iowa Presidents (Iowa City); Des Moines, Lincoln (Des Moines). Lodges: Masons, Shriners, Elks, Rotary. Home: Rural Route 4 Box 201 Muscatine IA 52761 Office: 1600 Oregon St Muscatine IA 52761

KAVAN, JOSEPH ORIN, lawyer, tax consultant; b. Omaha, Feb. 17, 1957; s. Orin Joseph and Jane Ann Beckel, July 18, 1980; children—Brooke Ann, Molly Elizabeth. B.A., Creighton U., 1979, J.D., 1982. Bars: Nebr. 1982, U.S. Tax. Ct. 1982, U.S. Dist. Ct. Nebr. 1982. Tax. cons. Touche Ross and Co., Omaha, 1980-82; mng. ptnr. Kavan, Smart and Davis, Omaha, 1982—. Contbr. monthly article to Western Livestock Jour., 1982-84. Mem. ABA (blockbuster wills com. 1982—), Assn. Trial Lawyers Am., Nebr. Assn. Trial Attys., Nebr. State Bar Assn., Omaha Bar Assn. (exec. planning com. 1984—). Home: 5412 S 107th St Omaha NE 68127 Office: Kavan Smart & Davis 3929 Harney St Omaha NE 68131

KAVANAUGH, CHARLES EDWARD, orthodontist, bank owner; b. Hamilton, Mo., Sept. 25, 1937; s. Edward C. and Audentia (Miller) K.; m. Gladene Sherard, Aug. 20, 1958; children—Kurt Edward, Kirby Lee, Kelly Kirk. B.S. in Secondary Edn., Northwest Mo. U., 1960; D.D.S., U. Mo.-Kansas City, 1964, Grad. orthodontic degree, 1966. Practice orthodontics, Kansas City, Mo., 1966—, Sedalia, Mo., 1966-69, Marshall, Mo., 1969-73, Chillicothe, Mo., 1973-74, Excelsior Springs, Mo., 1974-77, Cameron, Mo., 1977-82, Warsaw, Mo., 1982-83, Albany, Mo., 1983, Platte City, Mo., 1983; mem. staff Children's Mercy Hosp., Kansas City; pres. Kirby Devel. Co., Kansas City; assoc. clin. prof. U. Mo. Sch. Dentistry, Kansas City; pres. Kavanaugh Bancshares, Kansas City. Mem. Kansas City Crime Commn., 1978; pres. Kansas City Bd. Police Commrs., 1979; trustee Mo. Valley College, Marshall, 1984. Mem. Am. Assn. Orthodontists, Clay Platte Dental Soc. (pres. 1969-70), Greater Kansas City Dental Soc. (pres. 1973-74), ADA, Mo. Dental Assn. (past bd. govs.), Xi Psi Phi. Club: Pierre Fauchard Acad. Home: 2600 NE 76th Box 10744 Kansas City MO 64118 Office: 4420 Chouteau Trafficway Kansas City MO 64117

KAWITT, ALAN, lawyer; b. Chgo., 1937. J.D., Chgo.-Kent Coll. Law, 1965; postgrad. Lawyers Inst. John Marshall Law Sch., 1966-68. Bar: Ill. 1966, U.S. Dist. Ct. (no. dist.) Ill. 1967, U.S. Ct. Appeals (7th cir.) 1971, U.S. Supreme Ct., 1971. Owner Law Offices of Alan Kawitt, Chgo., 1970—. Mem. Am. Arbitration Assn. (arbitrator), Trial Lawyers Assn., Ill. Bar Assn., Ill. Trial Lawyers Assn., Chgo. Bar Assn., Decalogue Assn. Lawyers (coms. bankruptcy and reorgn., tort law, admiralty and maritime law, civil practice, communications law). Office: Law Offices of Alan Kawitt 30 W Washington St Chicago IL 60602

KAY, H. DAVID, medical educator, research immunologist, cancer research consultant; b. Glendale, Ohio, Sept. 6, 1943; s. Herbert Ralph and Adrienne Wilhelmina (Spruit) K.; m. Judith Jean Willeke, July 12, 1968; children—Carrie Sue, Emily Jennifer. B.S., Rensselaer Poly. Inst., 1966; M.S. in Cell Biology, Iowa State U., 1969, Ph.D. in Immunology, 1972. Postdoctoral tng. U. Tex. M.D. Anderson Hosp., Houston, 1972-73, staff scientist, 1973-75; vis. scientist Nat. Cancer Inst., Bethesda, Md., 1975-78; asst. prof., then assoc. prof. U. Va. Sch. Medicine, Charlottesville, 1978-82, dir. rheumatology research, 1980-82, cell sorter lab. 1980-82; assoc. prof. medicine U. Nebr. Med. Ctr., Omaha, 1983—, dir. Exptl. Immunology Lab., 1983—, chmn. Immunology Council, 1984—. Contbr. articles to profl. jours. Inventor of blood defibrinator. Soloist, adult tchr. First Covenant Ch., Omaha, 1983—; mem. Omaha Youth Symphony Assn., 1984. NIH fellow; grantee NIH, Nat. Cancer Inst., Am. Cancer Soc. Mem. Am. Assn. Immunologists, Am. Rheumatism Assn., Internat. League Against Rheumatism, Am. Assn. Cancer Research, Am. Fedn. Clin. Research, Am. Sci. Affiliation (publicity chmn. Houston chpt. 1974-75, v.p. Washington chpt. 1977-78), Nat. Audubon Soc., Nat. Arbor Day Found. Democrat. Avocations: photography; amateur astronomy; tennis; skiing; singing. Home: 10309 Z St Omaha NE 68127 Office: Dept Internal Medicine Sect Rheumatology and Immunology U Nebr Med Ctr Omaha NE 68105

KAY, THOMAS OBED, history educator, university administrator; b. Geneva, Ill., Dec. 20, 1932; s. Obed S. and Margaret A. (Brown) K.; m. Janice Cave, Apr. 25, 1959; children—Catherine, Robert, John. A.B., Wheaton Coll., 1953; M.A., U. Chgo., 1954, Ph.D., 1974. Instr. Wheaton Coll., Ill., 1955, summer 1957, 1959-61, asst. prof., 1961-75, assoc. prof., 1975—, chmn. dept. history, 1980—, chmn. Lutherfest, 1983; instr. Wartburg Coll., Waverly, Iowa, 1957-59. Contbr. articles to United Evangelical Action, New Oxford Rev. Author: The Christian Answer to Communism, 1961. Chair Ch. Centennial Program, Wheaton, 1977-78, City Council Nominating Assembly, Wheaton, 1974-78, Scout Troop Com., 1983—; precinct committeeman 1976—; del. to state conv., 1980, 82. Mem. Am. Hist. Assn., Conf. on Faith and History (bd. dirs. 1984—), Ill. Assn. Advancement of History (pres. 1984-85), Assn. of Ancient Historians, Ill. State Hist. Soc. Republican. Home: 1319 Irving Wheaton IL 60187 Office: Wheaton Coll Wheaton IL 60187

KAY, WEBSTER BICE, chemical engineer, chemistry educator; b. Hammond, Ind., Dec. 8, 1900; s. Howard Lincoln and Bessie (Bice) K.; m. Ruth St John, June 4, 1939; children—Bonnie J., Bruce W. B. Chem. E., Ohio State U., 1922; Ph.D., U. Chgo., 1926. Registered profl. engr., Ohio. Research engr. Standard Oil Co. (Ind.), Whitting, 1926-47; prof. chemical engring. Ohio State U., Columbus, from 1947, now prof. emeritus. Author: Solvent Fractionation, 1937; Isomerizing Paraffinic Napthas, 1944; Manufacturing of Pour Point Depressors, 1938, also research papers pub. Ch. com. activities North Broadway Methodist Ch., Columbus, 1947—; active alumnus U. Chgo., 1947—. Mem. Am. Chem. Soc., Am. Inst. Chem. Engrs., Inst. Am. Chemists, Sigma Xi. Democrat. Club: Ohio State U. Faculty. Avocations: travel, music, glassblowing, gardening. Home: 139 Fenway Rd Columbus OH 43214 Office: Ohio State U 140 W 19th Ave Columbus OH 43210

KAYAFAS, NICHOLAS, transportation company executive, author; b. New Kensington, Pa., May 6, 1931; s. Steve and Mary K.; B.B.A., U. Pitts., 1954, M.B.A., 1960; m. Helen Herouvis, July 8, 1956; 1 dau., Stephanie Ann (Mrs. Charles O. Bryant). Indsl. engr. Crucible Steel Co. Am., Pitts., 1956-60; programmer and systems analyst Nat. Steel Corp., Portage Ind., 1960-63; chief indsl. engr., GATX Corp., Chgo., 1963-68, terminal engr., 1968-72, plant safety dir., 1972-78, mgr. indsl. hygiene and safety, 1978—; chmn. Orgn. Resources Counselors Task Force on OSHA Marine Terminal Regulations, Washington.

Author: Employee Health and Industrial Hygiene, 1984; Why Not Write a Little Poetry, 1985. Served with AUS, 1954-56. Cert. hazard control mgr. Mem. Am. Soc. Safety Engrs., Am. Welding Soc., Am. Indsl. Hygiene Assn., Nat. Fire Protection Assn., Robotics Internat., Air Pollution Control Assn. Greek Orthodox. Home: 612 E Wilson Rd Lombard IL 60148 Office: 120 S Riverside Plaza Chicago IL 60606

KAYE, MICHAEL PETER, physician, educator; b. Chgo., Feb. 10, 1935; s. Theodore J. and Florence C. (OBraitis) K.; m. Mary E. Livingston, Nov. 5, 1960; children—Michael, Robert, Christopher, Mary Dorinda, Eric. Student, St. Louis U., 1952-55; M.S., Loyola U., Chgo., 1959, M.D., 1959. Diplomate Am. Bd. Surgery, Am. Bd. Thoracic Surgery. Asst. prof. surgery and physiology Loyola U., Chgo., 1967-70, assoc. prof., 1970-71; sci. dir. Ill. Inst. Tech. Research Inst., Chgo., 1971-73; assoc. prof. surgery Mayo Med. Sch., Rochester, Minn., 1974-79, prof., 1979—; dir. cardiovascular surgery research Mayo Clinic and Found., Rochester, 1974—. Assoc. editor Jour. Thoracic and Cardiovascular Surgery, 1978—. Contbr. articles to profl. publs. Served to capt. U.S. Army, 1964-66. Fellow Am. Coll. Caridology, ACS; mem. Am. Assn. Thoracic Surgery, Am. Heart Assn., Internat. Soc. Heart Transplantation (sec.-treas. 1982—). Home: Route 3 Box 128 Stewartville MN 55976 Office: Mayo Clinic Rochester MN 55905

KAYLOE, JUDITH CAROLYN, psychotherapist; b. Bronx, N.Y., Aug. 9, 1941; d. Isadore C and Myra (Simon) Rubin; m. Alvin Kayloe, June 15, 1967; children—Lili, Jordan, Rachel. B.A. in Psychology, Wittenberg U., 1969; M.A. in Clin. Psychology, U. Dayton, 1976; postgrad. Kent State U. Care agy. counselor, psychotherapist, 1977—. Mem., exec. com. citizens council Fedn. Community Planning, 1980—; instr. local community colls., community edn. Recipient Richter Fund award, Jewish Found. Edn. Girls, 1974-75. Mem. Am. Psychol. Assn., Ohio Assn. Counseling Devel. Cleve. Psychol. Assn., Internat. Assn. Psycho-Social Rehab. Democrat. Jewish. Founder FIND program for after-care of psychiat. patients. Home: 19482 Albion Rd Strongville OH 44136 Office: Far West Center 29133 Health Campus Dr Westlake OH 44145

KAYLOR, JOHN WILLIAM, educational administrator; b. Sidney, Ohio, Nov. 18, 1949; s. Robert Milton and Dorothy Jane (Ullery) K.; m. LuAnn Wise, June 7, 1980; children—Amy Nicole, Joshua Edwin. B.S., Bowling Green State U., 1972; M.S., U. Dayton, 1977. Cert. tchr., prin., supt., Ohio. Tchr., coach Findlay Schs., Ohio, 1972-79; assoc. prin. Rossford Schs., Ohio, 1979-84; prin. Montpelier Schs., Ohio, 1984—. Mem. Ohio Assn. Secondary Sch. Adminstrs., Phi Delta Kappa. Republican. Methodist. Office: Montpelier High Sch 309 E Main Montpelier OH 43543

KAYNE, JON BARRY, industrial psychologist; b. Sioux City, Iowa, Oct. 20, 1943; s. Harry Aaron and Barbara Valentine (Daniel) K.; B.A., U. Colo., 1973; M.S.W., U. Denver, 1975; Ph.D., U. No. Colo., 1978; m. Bunee Ellen Price, July 25, 1965; children—Nika Jenine, Abraham; m. Sandra Kay Fossbender, Jan. 5, 1985. With spl. services Weld County Sch. Dist. 6, Greeley, Colo., 1975-77; forensic diagnostician Jefferson County (Colo.) Diagnostic Unit, 1977-78; assoc., dir. mktg. 1 Dow Center, assoc. prof. psychology Hillsdale (Mich.) Coll., 1978—; pres. Jon B. Kayne, P.C., Hillsdale, 1980—; pres., chief exec. officer Am. Internat. Mgmt. Assocs., Ltd., Denver, 1984—. chmn. bd. dirs. Domestic Harmony, 1979-82; dir. religious sch., Greeley, 1975-77; candidate for sheriff of Boulder County, 1974. Served with USAR, 1962. Mem. Am. Psychol. Assn., Am. Soc. Clin. Hypnosis, Am. Statis. Assn., Internat. Neuropsychol. Soc., Mich. Soc. Investigative and Forensic Hypnosis (chmn. bd., pres. 1982), N.Y. Acad. Scis., Phi Delta Kappa, Psi Chi, Alpha Gamma Sigma. Home: 205 Chestnut St Reading MI 49274 Office: Dow Center Hillsdale College Hillsdale MI 49242

KAZERSKI, KENNETH CARL, international trade consultant; b. Detroit; s. Michael and Theresa (Wisniewski) K.; m. Susan Caroline Gilbert, Oct. 10, 1962; children—Kenneth Carl, Jr., Linda Susan. B.S. in Acctg., Wayne State U., 1964; postgrad. U. Wis., 1972. Vice pres. Bank of Commonwealth, Detroit, 1960-72; sr. v.p. Liberty State Bank, Detroit, 1972-82; exec. v.p. Sims, Inc., Detroit, 1982-84; pres. Metier Service Corp., Detroit and Hong Kong, 1984—; chmn., pres. Detroit Central Hosp., 1980-84. Mem. Soc. Mfg. Engrs. Lutheran. Clubs: Grosse Pointe Yacht (Grosse Pointe Shores, Mich.) (bd. dirs. 1982—); Grosse Pointe Sail (Mich.). Office: Metier Service Corp 7/F Cosmos Bldg 8-11 Lan Kwai Fong Hong Kong

KEAIRNS, RAYMOND EARL, dentist; b. nr. Jackson, Ohio, July 27, 1912; s. Gus Earl and Ethel Jane (McClure) K.; student Rio Grande Coll., 1931-33, Ohio State U., summers, 1934-37, 39; D.D.S., Ohio State U., 1943; m. Alice Genevieve Poston, Aug. 21, 1946. Tchr. elem. schs., Jackson County, Ohio, 1933-39; pvt. practice dentistry, Logan, Ohio, 1946—; pres. Keairns, Inc., Lancaster, Ohio, U-Do-It Laundromat, Logan, Speed Queen Coin-Op Laundry, McArthur, Ohio, Served with USN, 1943-46. Mem. Nat. Automatic Laundry and Cleaning Council, Am. (life mem.), Ohio, Logan dental assns., Logan Area C. of C., U.S. C. of C. (bus. mem.) Presbyn. Kiwanian (dir. 1955-57, 62-64). Home: 36660 Hocking Dr Logan OH 43138 Office: 9 E 2d St Logan OH 43138

KEARL, BRYANT EASTHAM, university administrator; b. Paris, Idaho, Sept. 21, 1921; s. Chase and Hazel Loveless K.; m. Ruth Warr, Sept. 5, 1941; children—Susan DeJongh-Kearl, Richard B., Katheryn Dammon, Robert. Student, U. Idaho, 1936-37; B.S., Utah State U., 1941; M.S., U. Wis., 1942; Ph.D., U. Minn., 1951. Instr. U. Wis., 1944-46, asst. prof., 1947-49, assoc. prof., 1950-51, prof. agrl. journalism, 1952—, assoc. dean, 1963-67, vice chancellor, 1967-70, acting chancellor, 1968, vice chancellor acad. affairs, 1978—; vice prof. Friedrich Wilhelms U., Bonn, 1961-62; sr. planning officer U. East Africa, 1964-65; exec. dir. Asia Office Agrl. Devel. Council, 1970-74; mem. com. on weather info. systems NRC, 1979-80; cons. FAO World Conf. on Agrarian Reform and Rural Devel., 1979; mem. study team for CGIAR Rev. of Internat. Agrl. Research Ctrs., 1980-81. Mem. Midwest U. Consortium Bd., 1965-70, 74—, vice chmn., 1967—; trustee U. Wis. Hosps., 1977—; mem. council Elvehjem Art Mus., 1978—. Served with USN, 1944-46. Decorated Bronze Star. Mem. Assn. Edn. Journalism, Am. Agrl. Coll. Editors (past pres.), AAUP, AAAS, Alpha Zeta, Epsilon Sigma Phi. Mormon. Home: 2807 Ridge Rd Madison WI 53705 Office: 150 Bascom Hall U Wis Madison WI 53706

KEARNEY, ALBERT JOHN, retail executive; b. Phila., Feb. 5, 1941; s. Eugene Albert and Anna Marie (Cunnane) K.; m. Theresa Hirschinger, Sept. 22, 1973; children—Thomas Albert, Theresa Anne, Joseph Albert. B.S., Loyola U., Chgo., 1965. Vice pres. human resources retail stores div. Hartmarx Corp. (formerly Hart, Schaffner & Marx), Chgo., 1968—. Mem. Human Resources Mgmt. Assn. Chgo. (dir.). Home: 635 Garden Ct Glenview IL 60025 Office: Hartmarx Corp 101 N Wacker Dr Chicago IL 60606

KEARNEY, WILLIAM MICHAEL, metals company safety executive; b. Orange, Tex., July 8, 1943; s. William Harold and Totsy (Rogers) K.; m. Charlene Patten, Aug. 28, 1965; children—Mary Deirdre, Kevin Charles, Brendon Michael. B.S. in Physics, Va. Mil. Inst., 1965; cert. in meteorology, Tex. A&M U., 1967. Salesman, Home Life Ins. Co., Newport News, Va., 1972-73; indsl. hygiene engr. Newport News Shipbuilding, 1973-74; environ. control engr. Kennecott Copper Co., Hayden, Ariz., 1974-77; environ. engr. Amax Lead Co., Boss, Mo., 1977-81, dir. safety health and environ., 1981—. Contbr. articles to publs. Packmaster Cub Scouts Am., Kearny, Ariz., 1976. Served to capt. USAF, 1966-70. Decorated Bronze Star. Mem. Air Pollution Control Assn. Roman Catholic. Lodge: Kiwanis. Avocation: woodworking. Home: 121-1 Bixby Star Route Salem MO 65560 Office: Amax Lead Co Boss MO 65440

KEARNS, MARY LOU, coroner, nurse; b. Chgo., May 5, 1944; d. Joseph Michael and Mary (Comiskey) Kearns; 1 son, Joseph Michael. R.N., St. Anne's Hosp., 1965; B.S., No. Ill. U., 1976; M.P.H., U. Ill.-Chgo., 1981. R.N. Staff nurse med. and trauma units, Cook County Hosp., Chgo., 1965-66; coronary and intensive care nurse Delnor Hosp., St. Charles, Ill., 1966-67; trauma nurse specialist, head nurse and inservice instr. Cook County Hosp., 1967-72; hosp. care program coordinator Chgo. Med. Found., State of Ill., 1972-73; emergency room nurse St. Joseph Hosp., Elgin, Ill., 1974-75; nursing supr. Community Hosp., Geneva, Ill., 1976; elected coroner of Kane County, Geneva, 1976-80, re-elected coroner, 1980—; lectr. in field. Contbr. articles to med. and nursing jours. Named Ill. Outstanding Women of Yr., 1978; recipient Resolution of Commendation Ill. Nurses Assn., 1977. Fellow Am. Acad. Forensic Sci.; pres. Kane County Chiefs Assn. (pres. 1983), Ill. Coroners Assn. (v.p. 1983, pres. elect 1984), Internat. Coroners and Med. Examiners, Nat. Women's Polit. Caucus. Democrat. Roman Catholic. Club: Zonta. Home: 603 S 13th Ave Saint Charles IL 60174 Office: Kane County Govt 719 Batavia Ave Geneva IL 60134

KEASTER, ARMON JOSEPH, entomology educator; b. Lilbourn, Mo., Mar. 12, 1933; s. John Powell and Nora E. (Cato) K.; m. Mona Lee Scott, June 3, 1956; children—Scott, Aaron. Student Southeast Mo. State U., Cape Girardeau, 1955-57; B.S. in Agr., U. Mo.-Columbia, 1959, M.S. in Entomology, 1961, Ph.D. in Entomology, 1965. Assoc. prof. entomology U. Mo., Columbia, 1970-76, prof., 1977—; technologist in entomology S.E. Mo. Research Sta., U. Mo.-Sikeston, 1959-61; instr. U. Mo. Delta Ctr., Portageville, 1962-65, asst. prof., 1965-70. Chmn. editorial bd. Insecticide Acaricide News, 1984—. Contbr. articles to profl. jours. Served with U.S. Army, 1953-55, Korea. Mem. Entomol. Soc. Am. (chmn. auditing com. N. Central br. 1969-70, mem. nominating com. 1979-80, membership com. 1979-80, J.E. Bussart Meml. award 1984), N.E. Br. Entomol. Soc. Am., Kans. Entomol. Soc., Sigma Xi, Alpha Zeta, Gamma Sigma Delta. Methodist. Club: Old Wheels Car (Columbia) (treas. 1983—). Avocations: restoring antique cars, jogging. Home: 606 E Rockcreek Dr Columbia MO 65203 Office: U Mo Dept Entomology 1-87 Agr Bldg Columbia MO 65211

KEATING, MICHAEL JOSEPH, lawyer; b. St. Louis, June 8, 1954; s. John David and Patricia Ann (Sullivan) K.; m. Maureen Ann Moder, Aug. 28, 1981; 1 dau., Sarah Kathleen. A.B., Washington U., St. Louis, 1976; J.D., St. Louis U., 1979. Bar: Mo. 1979, Ill. 1980. Law clk. Mo. Ct. Appeals, St. Louis, 1979-80, U.S. Dist. Ct. (ea. dist.) Mo., St. Louis, 1980-81; assoc. Bryan, Cave, McPheeters & McRoberts, St. Louis, 1981-83; sr. atty. Emerson Electric Co., St. Louis, 1983—. Mem. St. Louis U. Law Jour., 1977-79, mng. editor, 1978-79. Mem. ABA (chmn. subcom. on product liability compliance program litigation sect. 1984—), Sigma Alpha Epsilon, Phi Delta Phi, Pi Sigma Alpha. Roman Catholic. Club: Mo. Athletic (St. Louis). Home: 891 Totem Woods Ct Saint Louis MO 63011 Office: Emerson Electric Co PO Box 4100 8000 W Florissant Saint Louis MO 63136

KEATING, WILLIAM JOHN, newspaper executive, former congressman; b. Cin., Mar. 30, 1927; s. Charles H. and Adele (Kipp) K.; B.B.A., U. Cin., 1950, J.D., 1950, LL.D., 1975; m. Nancy Nenninger, Sept. 22, 1951; children—Nancy C. (Mrs. Dale E. Hoe), William J., Michael K., Daniel N., Susan (Mrs. John C. Lame), Thomas J., John S. Bar: Ohio 1950. Asst. atty. gen. Ohio, 1957-58; judge Cin. Municipal Ct., 1958-65, presiding judge, 1962-63; judge Ct. Common Pleas, Hamilton County, Ohio, 1965-67; mem. Cin. City Council, 1967-70, majority leader, chmn. finance com.; mem. 92d-93d Congresses from 1st Dist. Ohio, 1970-74; pres. Cin. Enquirer, Inc., 1973-79, pres. and pub., 1979—; pres. Gannett Central Newspaper Group, 1979—; dir. Fifth Third Bank. Co-chmn. Cin. Bus. Com., 1983-85. Bd. dirs. AP, Kenton County Airport, Served with USNR, World War II. Mem. Ohio Newspaper Assn., West Shell, Inc. Am. Newspaper Pubs. Assn., Am. Soc. Newspaper Editors, Former Mems. Congress, Am. Legion, Sigma Chi. Office: 617 Vine St Cincinnati OH 45201

KEATS, GLENN ARTHUR, manufacturing company executive; b. Chgo., July 1, 1920; s. Herbert J. and Agnes H. (Streich) K.; m. Olga Maria Loor Hurtado, Feb. 13, 1946; children—Maria Susana Keats Eggemeyer, Allwyn Dolores Keats Gustafson. B.S. in Commerce, Northwestern U., 1941. Sales exec. Keats-Lorenz Spring Co., Chgo., 1947-56; controller, auditor Plantaciones Ecuatorianas, S.A., Guayaquil, Ecuador, 1956-58; co-founder, sec.-treas. Keats Mfg. Co., Evanston, Ill., 1958—. Sec. Hispanic Soc. Chgo., 1965—. Served to lt. comdr. USN, 1941-47. Mem. Spring Mfrs. Inst., Northwestern U. Alumni Assn., Sigma Nu. Republican. Lutheran. Club: Evanston Golf. Home: 368 Woodland Rd Highland Park IL 60035 Office: 1227 Dodge Ave Evanston IL 60202

KEATS, ROGER ALAN, state senator, business executive; b. Cleve., Aug. 12, 1948; s. Robert L. and Margaret Anne (Achelpohl) K.; B.A., U. Mich.; M.A., U. Ill. Mem. Ill. Ho. of Reps., 1976-79; mem. Ill. Senate, 1979—. Served with armor br. U.S. Army, 1972-74. Republican. Evangelical. Office: State Capitol Springfield IL 62706

KECK, C(HARLES) DON, educational administrator; b. Lone Jack, Mo., Jan. 12, 1938; s. William Earl and Vera Nancy (Alley) K.; m. Delorris Ruth Reed, Nov. 11, 1960; children—Michael Don, Steven Charles. B.S. in Edn., Central Mo. State U., 1960, Edn. Specialist, 1968; M.Edn., U. Mo., 1966; Ed.D., Okla. State U., 1971. Cert. tchr., Mo., Okla., cert. sch. adminstr., Mo., Okla. Asst. supt. schs. Duncan Pub. Schs., Okla., 1970-72; supt. schs. Richmond Pub. Schs., Mo., 1972-73; asst. prof. edn. Chadron State Coll., Nebr., 1973-74; dir. continuing edn. Wayne State Coll., Nebr., 1974-76, edn. and psychol. div. head, 1976-79; ednl. adminstrn. dept. head Southwest Mo. State U., Springfield, 1979—. Contbr. articles to profl. publs. Chmn. exec. com. Wayne council Boy Scouts Am., 1976-79; chmn. Strafford Planning and Zoning Commn., Mo., 1981—. Recipient Disting. Service award Jaycees, 1971; HEW grantee, 1981, 82. Mem. SW Mo. Adminstrs. Assn. (sec.-treas. 1980—), Mo. Assn. Sch. Adminstrs. (mem. exec. com. 1982—), Mo. Assn. Elem. Sch. Prins. (advisor 1981—), Am. Assn. Sch. Adminstrs., Council Adminstrs. Spl. Edn., Council Exceptional Children, Profs. Ednl. Adminstrn. Methodist. Lodge: Elks. Avocations: hunting, fishing, reading, team sports, handball. Office: Southwest Mo State U 901 S National Springfield MO 65804

KECK, ROBERT CLIFTON, lawyer; b. Sioux City, Iowa, May 20, 1914; s. Herbert A. and Harriet (McCutchen) K.; A.B., Ind. U., 1936; J.D., U. Mich., 1939; L.H.D., Nat. Coll. Edn., 1973; m. Ruth P. Edwards, Nov. 2, 1940; children—Robert Clifton, Laura E. Simpson, Gloria E. Sauser. Bar: Ill. 1939. Practiced in Chgo., 1939—, mem. firm Keck, Mahin & Cate, 1939—, partner, 1946—; dir. Union Spl. Corp., Schwinn Bicycle Co., Methode Electronics, Inc. Chmn. bd. trustees Nat. Coll. Edn.; bd. dirs. Sears Roebuck Found., 1977-79. Served with USNR, 1943-45. Mem. ABA, Fed., Ill., Chgo. bar assns., Bar Assn. 7th Fed. Circuit (past pres.), Am. Coll. Trial Lawyers, Phi Gamma Delta. Republican. Clubs: Westmoreland Country (Wilmette, Ill.); Chicago, Metropolitan, Law, Legal, Economic, Executives (Chgo.); Biltmore Forest Country (Asheville); Glen View (Golf, Ill.). Lodge: Masons. Home: 1043 Seneca Rd Wilmette IL 60091 Office: 233 Wacker Dr Chicago IL 60606

KECKLER, MARK PURDUM, pharmacist; b. Warren, Ohio, Oct. 27, 1954; s. Norman F. and Jane E. (Purdum) K.; m. Susan L. Alm, June 18, 1977; children—Kelly M., Kyle J. Student Kent State U., 1972-73; B.S. in Pharmacy, Ohio State U., 1977. Registered pharmacist, Ohio. Audio-visual aide Kent State U., Canton, Ohio, 1972-73; pharmacy intern Barberton Citizens Hosp., Ohio, 1974-75, Riverside Hosp., Columbus, 1975-77; staff pharmacist Aultman Hosp., Canton, 1977-82, pharmacist supr., 1982—; part-time pharmacist Finney's Drugs, Canton, 1980—. Recipient Outstanding Achievement in Clin. Pharmacy award Smith, Kline, French Co., 1977. Mem. Akron Area Soc. Hosp. Pharmacists, North Canton Jaycees. Republican. Lutheran. Avocations: basketball; swimming; softball. Home: 6294 Bayside St NW Canton OH 44718 Office: Aultman Hospital Pharmacy 2600 Sixth St SW Canton OH 44710

KEDDLE, DAVID GLEN, library administrator; b. Howell, Mich., Jan. 27, 1951; s. Glen Joseph and Burla Alfreda (Doherty) K.; m. Cynthia Louise Conley, Jan. 12, 1980; children—Jenny Sue, Michael David. A.A. in Bus. and Library, Lansing Community Coll. (Mich.), 1972. Dir., John W. Chi Meml. Med. Library, Ingham Med. Ctr., Lansing, 1973—. Sec., Livingston County Republican Com., 1974-78. Mem. Lansing Area Library Assn. (pres. 1979-80), Mich. Health Scis. Library Assn. (bd. dirs. 1977-80), Med. Library Assn., Capital Area Library Network (bd dirs. 1981—), Mich. Health Scis. Libraries Assn. (state council bd. 1984-86), Spl. Library Assn., ALA, Mich. Library Assn., Mid-Mich. Health Scis. Library Assn. (chmn. 1974-79; ad hoc com. electronic mail 1985), Jaycees (Holt chpt., newsletter editor 1984-85, individual devel. v.p. 1985-86), Methodist. Office: Ingham Med Ctr Med Library 401 W Greenlawn Ave Lansing MI 48909

KEEGAN, DANIEL PATRICK, management consultant; b. Cleve., May 23, 1939; s. Daniel Francis and Genevieve (Stanton) K.; m. Barbara Boyle, Sept. 5, 1963; children—Daniel, Michel, David. B.S., John Carroll U., 1962; M.B.A., U. Pitts., 1963. Cert. mgmt. cons. Engr., Exxon, Morristown, N.J., 1963-64; staff cons. Price Waterhouse, Cleve., 1966-67, mgr., Columbus, Ohio, 1967-74, prin., Columbus, Cleve., 1974—. Bd. dirs. Combined Health Appeal, Columbus, 1983—. Served to 1st lt. AUS, 1962-64. Mem. Inst. Mgmt. Cons., Columbus Area C. of C. (chmn. 1983). Club: Muirfield Golf; Columbus Athletic. Roman Catholic. Home: 440 Mediatation Ln Worthington OH 43085 Office: Price Waterhouse 180 E Broad St Columbus OH 43085

KEEHN, SILAS, banker; b. New Rochelle, N.Y., June 30, 1930; s. Grant and Marjorie (Burchard) K.; m. Marcia June Lindquist, Mar. 26, 1955; children—Elisabeth, Britta, Peter. A.B. in Econs., Hamilton Coll., 1952; M.B.A. in Fin., Harvard U., 1957. With Mellon Bank N.A., Pitts., 1957-80, v.p., then sr. v.p., 1967-78, exec. v.p., 1978-79, vice chmn., 1980; v.p. Mellon Nat. Corp., 1979-80, vice chmn., 1980; chmn. bd. Pullman, Inc., Chgo., 1980; pres. Fed. Res. Bank Chgo., 1981—. Charter trustee Hamilton Coll.; trustee Rush-Presbyn.-St. Luke's Med. Ctr., Chgo.; bd. dirs. Chgo. Council on Fgn. Relations, United Way of Chgo. Served with USNR, 1953-56. Clubs: Fox Chapel Golf, University (Chgo.); Links (N.Y.C.); Rolling Rock (Ligonier, Pa.); Chicago, Economic, Commercial (Chgo.). Office: 230 S LaSalle St Chicago IL 60690*

KEEL, LAURA LEE, nurse; b. Geneva, Ohio, June 14, 1952; d. Richard Wright and Emily Ruth (Curtiss) Warner; m. C.E. Keel, Dec. 23, 1972; children—Lewis R., Amanda L. A.A.S., Kent State U., Ashtabula, Ohio, 1981; student B.S.N. program Pa. State U.-Shenango Valley. R.N., Ohio. Nurse in pediatrics Warren Gen. Hosp., Ohio, 1981-82, nurse in med.-surgery, 1982—. Methodist. Home: 5983 Hoagland-Blackstub Rd Cortland OH 44410

KEELINE, THOMAS JOHN, accountant; b. Putnam, Conn., Feb. 21, 1950; s. William S. and Loraine (Kitson) K.; Marilyn McCarthy, June 17, 1983; 1 child, Thomas J. B.S. in Econs., U. Pa., 1972, J.D., 1975. Bar: Mo. 1975; C.P.A., Mo. Acct., Touche Ross & Co., St. Louis, 1975—. Author: NLRB and Judicial Control of Union Discipline, 1976. Mem. ABA, Mo. Bar Assn., Am. Inst. C.P.A.s, Mo. Soc. C.P.A.s, Bar Assn. Met. St. Louis. Roman Catholic. Club: Mo. Athletic. Lodge: Rotary. Home: 6236 Alamo Saint Louis MO 63105 Office: Touche Ross & Co 2100 Railway Exchange Bldg Saint Louis MO 63101

KEELING, JOSEPH TIMOTHY, systems designer; b. Caracas, Venezuela, Nov. 27, 1952; s. Joe Alfred and Mary Jon (Brasel) K.; m. Roberta Ann Pautler, June 7, 1980; children—Elizabeth Ann, Stephanie Katherine. B.B.A., Pan Am. U. Sr. systems analyst Blue Cross/Blue Shield, Rochester, N.Y., 1981-84; systems designer Marion Labs., Kansas City, Mo., 1984—. Served to capt. USMC, 1978-81. Mem. Assn. Systems Mgmt. Presbyterian. Avocations: running, triathlons. Home: 1016 NE Cedar St Lee's Summit MO 64063 Office: Marion Labs 10236 Bunker Ridge Rd Kansas City MO 64137

KEEN, ROBERT CLEVELAND, management consultant, agricultural economist; b. Clanton, Ala., Mar. 22, 1948; s. Lonnie Warren and Zelma (Wilkins) K.; m. Margaret Ellen Dunlap, Sept. 29, 1973; 1 child, Ashley Margaret. B.S., Auburn U., Ala., 1970, M.S., 1972; Ph.D., Purdue U., 1985. Research asst. Auburn U., 1970-72, asst. to dean, 1972-74; instr. Purdue U., West Lafayette, Ind., 1974-78, dir. assoc. degree programs, 1978-80; dir. program devel. Agri Bus. Assocs., Indpls., 1980—. Author, editor tng. programs. Contbr. articles to profl. pubs. Served to maj. USAR. Mem. Am. Agrl. Econ. Assn., Nat. Agrl. Mktg. Assn., Am. Soc. Tng. and Devel. (dirs. elect 1984—), Gamma Sigma Delta, Alpha Zeta, Omicron Delta Epsilon. Baptist. Clubs: Farm House Social Fraternity (Saint Joseph, Mo.); Spades. Avocation: golf. Home: 435 W 65th St Indianapolis IN 46260 Office: Argi Bus Assocs 8777 Purdue Rd Suite 220 Indianapolis IN 46268

KEENE, BARRY RICHARD, systems specialist; b. Norfolk, Va., Aug. 31, 1946; s. Richard R. and Mary E. (Malone) K.; m. Nellie Louise McLawhorn, Feb. 18, 1966; children—Tracy Jane, Corey Lynn. A.A., Leoiir Community Coll., N.C., 1971; B.A. with honors, U. N.C.-Chapel Hill, 1973. Cert. systems profl. Systems supr. Nationwide Ins. Co., Columbus, Ohio, 1973-77; mgr. systems and programming Motorists Ins. Co., Columbus, 1977—. Active Jr. Achievement, 1978-81. Served with USAF, 1966-70. Mem. Assn. Systems Mgmt. Democrat. Roman Catholic. Avocations: running; softball; home computers; photography; paleontology. Home: 1828 Arlington Ave Upper Arlington OH 43212 Office: Motorists Ins Cos 471 E Broad St Columbus OH 43215

KEENER, C(HARLES) RICHARD, food company information systems executive; b. Durant, Okla., Sept. 8, 1939; s. Otis R. and Annie Idell (Hay) K.; m. Linda Kay Vaughan, Jan. 22, 1959; children—Kerri Kaye, C. Kevin. B.S. in Bus., Southeastern Okla. State U., 1961; M.B.A., Exec. Program, U. Chgo., 1976; grad. advanced mgmt. program Harvard U., 1982. With Kraft Foods, Garland, Tex., 1961-67, sr. programmer, Chgo., 1967-69, systems mgr., 1969-71; with Kraft, Inc., Glenview, Ill., 1971—, dir. systems mgmt. ops. group, 1977—, v.p., dir. systems services, 1978—; bd. dirs. Transp. Data Coordinating Com., Washington; mem. steering com. Uniform-Communications Standards for Grocery Industry; chmn. Dart & Kraft Info. Systems Council. Advisor Computer Ctr., Chgo. Urban League, Served to sgt. U.S.N.G., 1956-64. Recipient Beautiful People award Chgo. Urban League, 1979. Mem. Soc. Info. Systems (Disting. Service award 1979), Grocery Mfrs. Am. (dir. adminstrv. systems com.). Methodist. Home: 1203 S Fernandez Arlington Heights IL 60005

KEEPPER, JOHN HERRIN, investment specialist; b. Waukegan, Ill., Oct. 17, 1938; s. Lester H. and Martha (Herrin) K.; m. Elizabeth Ouida Bamford, July 10, 1965; children—David, Peter, Kathryn, Andrew. B.A., Lake Forest Coll., 1961. Cert. investment agt., Ill. Salesman, Ayars & Assocs., Northbrook, Ill., 1965-68; pres. Keepper Nagel, Lake Forest, Ill., 1969-76, Keepper & Co., Lake Bluff, Ill., 1977-81; investment specialist Coldwell Banker Comml. Real Estate Service, Chgo., 1982—; founder, pres. Reimcon, Waukegan, Ill., 1971-81. Served to lt. USNR, 1961-65, Vietnam. Mem. Central Assn. Real Estate Exchangers (Exchange of Yr. award 1980, founder, dir., pres. 1975-81), Soc. Exchange Counselors, Grad. Realtors Inst. Republican. Episcopalian. Club: Lake Bluff Yacht (fleet capt.). Lodge: Kiwanis (dir. 1966). Office: Coldwell Banker Comml Real Estate Service 200 E Randolph Dr 6509 Chicago IL 60601

KEGARISE, SCOTT MARTIN, petroleum laboratory executive; b. Cleve., Oct. 3, 1950; s. Donald Arthur and Kaye Darlene (La Pira) K.; m. Charlotte Ann Seaton, May 28, 1971; children—Scott Martin, Kevin Michael, Charles Arthur Allan. Grad. high sch. Hollidaysburg, Pa. Salesman, serviceman Euclid Inc., Cleve., 1968; div. mgr. Watchdog Inc., Spokane, Wash., 1975-78; area mgr. Analysts Inc., Linden, N.J., 1978-79, Hoffman Estates, Ill., 1979—. Vice pres. Citizens Adv. Council Sch. Dist. 54, Schaumburg, Ill., 1983. Served to staff sgt. USAF, 1968-75. Mem. Truck Maintenance Council Am. (sec. oil analysis task force 1982—). Republican. Methodist. Clubs: Schaumburg Athletic (1st v.p. 1983), Schaumburg Soccer Assn. (head commr. 1984), Jaycees (bd. dirs. 1983-84). Avocations: soccer, golf, bowling, sport fishing. Home: 18 Essex Ct Schaumburg IL 60194 Office: Analysts Maintenance Labs Inc 2450 Hassell Hoffman Estates IL 60195

KEGEL, PAUL LINKEN, college dean, educator; b. Milw., July 28, 1935; s. Paul William and Voga Louise (Linken) K.; m. Ann Catherine McGarry, June 12, 1965 (div. 1984); m. Patricia Underkofler, Aug. 19, 1984; children—Patrick, Brian, Thomas, Lynn Ann. B.A. cum laude, Ripon Coll., 1957; M.S. in Guidance, U. Wis.-Madison, 1958, M.S. in English, 1963, Ph.D. in English, 1976. Cert. post-secondary tchr., Iowa. English tchr. Evergreen Park High Sch. (Ill.), 1964-65; English instr., student activities dir. U. Wis., Marshfield, 1965-68; dir. student affairs U. Wis.-Washington, West Bend, 1968-69; dean of students Worthington Community Coll. (Minn.), 1970-77; dean, pres. Marshalltown Community Coll. (Iowa), 1977—; cons., evaluator No. Central Assn., Chgo., 1980—; adj. English instr. Buena Vista Coll., Marshalltown, 1983—. Contbr. articles to profl. jours. Founder, Worthington Montessori Sch., 1971; mem. com. Vietnamese Resettlement So. Asian Refugee, Worthington, 1975—; mem. gov.'s task force Pub. Radio State of Minn., 1976; bd. dirs. Ripon Coll. Alumni Assn., 1979-82; del. Iowa Democratic Conv., 1980, 84. Served with U.S. Army, 1959-60, USNG, 1960-65. Mem. Nat. Council Community Relations. Episcopalian. Lodge: Rotary. Avocations: writing; reading; fine arts; fishing; skiing. Home: 807 Henry Dr Marshalltown IA 50158 Office: Marshalltown Community Coll 3700 S Center St Marshalltown IA 50158

KEHLER, CLAIR DOUGLAS, marketing administrator, auto sales executive; b. Warsaw, Ind., Jan. 26, 1939; s. Clair Hatfield and Catherine Lucille (Kennedy) K.; m. Virginia Diane Heckrotte, July 1, 1961 (div.); children—Christopher, Shawn, Mitch. Student Grace Coll., Winona Lake, Ind., 1961, Ind. U.-Fort Wayne, 1964. Sales promotion supr., staff asst. L.M. Berry & Co., Warsaw, 1956-73; asst. supr. resdl. products, services, supr. advt., promotion United Telephone Co., Warsaw, 1979—; propr. automobile dealership; grad. asst. Dale Carnegie courses, Warsaw, 1962; guest speaker advt. class Grace Coll., Winona, Ind., 1982. Publicity chmn. United Way campaign, 1974; advt.

chmn. Com. to Elect The Mayor, Warsaw, 1983. Recipient 1st place Mktg. award Ind. Telephone Assn., 1980; 1st place award World's Greatest Promotion contest, Incentive Travel Mgr. mag., 1983. Republican. Club: Toastmaster's (Warsaw) Lodge: Elks (3 terms exalted ruler). Home: PO Box 123 Warsaw IN 46580 Office: PO Box 391 Warsaw IN 46580

KEHLER, PAUL, physicist; b. Mariampole, Lithuania, Mar. 5, 1931; s. Otto and Wanda (Haak) Kehler; M.S., U. Freiburg (Germany), 1955; m. Luise M. Hofflin, June 4, 1960; children—Elvira, Victoria. Came to U.S., 1956, naturalized, 1962. With Dresser Industries, Dallas, 1956-59, Phillips Petroleum Co., Bartlesville, Okla., 1960-62; with Bell Aerosystems Co., Buffalo, 1963-71; owner, gen. mgr. Frontier Technologies Co., Niagara Falls, N.Y., 1971; pres. Applied Inventions Corp. (Del.), Mishawaka, Ind., 1972—. Mem. Am. Phys. Soc., Am. Nuclear Soc., I.E.E.E. Soc. Profl. Well Log Analysts, Internat. Platform Assn. Contbr. articles to profl. jours. Patentee in field. Home: 17305 Fergus Dr South Bend IN 46635 Office: Box 826 Mishawaka IN 46544

KEIDERLING, TIMOTHY ALLEN, chemistry educator, researcher; b. Waterloo, Iowa, June 22, 1947; s. Glenn Allen and Ethel V. (Kalainoff) K.; m. Candace Ruth Crawford, Sept. 4, 1976; 1 son, Michael Crawford. B.S., Loras Coll., 1969; M.A., Princeton U., 1971, Ph.D., 1974. NSF fellow Princeton U., 1969-72; research assoc. U. So. Calif., Los Angeles, 1973-76; asst. prof. U. Ill., Chgo., 1976-81, assoc. prof. chemistry, 1981-85, prof., 1985—. Contbr. articles to profl. jours. Fellow NSF 1969-72, Fulbright Found. 1984; grantee NSF, NIH, Petroleum Research Found., 1976—. Mem. Am. Chem. Soc., Am. Phys. Soc. Office: U Ill Dept Chemistry Box 4348 Chicago IL 60680

KEIFER, MARY CARTER, law educator; b. Charlottsville, Va., Sept. 21, 1946; d. Carter Lewis and Anne Harrison (Crathorne) Loth; m. John Louis Keifer, Aug. 29, 1970; children—Marcy, Lisa, Kate, Kristin. A.B. in Math., Converse Coll., 1968; J.D., U. Va., 1971. Bar: Ohio 1971, U.S. Dist. Ct. 1974. Staff atty. Toledo Legal Aid Soc., 1971-74; asst. prof. bus. law Ohio U., Athens, 1974—. Contbr. papers to legal procs. Mem. Athens City Recreation Bd., 1978-83, pres., 1980; mem. Athens City Bd. Edn., 1978—, pres., 1984; officer Athens Coop. Nursery Bd., 1975-77; bd. dirs. Athens Swim Club. Mem. Ohio State Bar Assn., Athens City Bar Assn. Presbyterian. Club: Athens Jr. Women's. Avocations: reading; lap swimming. Home: 201 Longview Heights Athens OH 45701 Office: Ohio U 216 Copeland Hall Athens OH 45701

KEIM, MARYBELLE CHASE ROCKEY, educator; b. Odebolt, Iowa, July 28, 1933; d. Kermit M. and Ardythe J. (Putnam) Chase; m. Harry C. Rockey; children—Don, Dale, Douglas, David, Daryl; m. William A. Keim, June 15, 1979. B.A., U. No. Iowa, 1955; M.A., U. No. Colo., 1958; Ph.D., Mich. State U., 1972. Counselor, instr. Fla. State U., Tallahassee, 1959-62; asst. dean student State U. Coll., Oswego, N.Y., 1962-66; dean of women, assoc. dean students Central Wash. U., Ellensburg, 1966-71; asst. prof. Va. Poly. Inst. and State U., Blacksburg, 1972-79; vis. prof. U. Mo., Kansas City, 1979-81; counselor, researcher Kansas City Regional Council for Higher Edn., Mo., 1981-84; vis. prof. So. Ill. U., Carbondale, 1985-86. Editor: (monograph) Directory of Graduate Programs in College Student Personnel, 1973, 77, 80, 84; Marketing the Program, 1981. Mem. Am. Coll. Personnel Assn. (exec. council 1974-77), AAUW (corp. del. 1966-71), Am. Assn. Counseling and Devel., Am. Assn. for Higher Edn., Assn. for Study Higher Edn., DAR, Phi Delta Kappa. Recipient Leadership, Service and Accomplishment award Am. Coll. Personnel Assn., 1984, 85; Excellence in Teaching award Va. Poly. Inst. and State U., 1974, 75. Avocations: genealogy; travel; music. Home: 9904 Taylor Dr Overland Park KS 66212 Office: Coll Edn Southern Illinois Univ Carbondale IL 62901

KEISER, JEFFREY EARL, chemistry educator, researcher; b. Kalamazoo, Mich., Feb. 25, 1941; s. Earl Dale and Donia Beryl (Blakeslee) K.; divorced; children—Grant, Sarah. A.B., Kalamazoo Coll., 1962; Ph.D., Wayne State U., Detroit, 1966. Asst. prof. chemistry Coe Coll., Cedar Rapids, Iowa, 1966-72, assoc. prof., 1972-81, prof., 1981—, chmn. chemistry dept., 1976—; research cons. U. Iowa, Iowa City, 1978-83. Contbr. articles to profl. jours. Grantee Johnson's Wax Fund, 1980, 81, 82, NSF, 1972. Mem. Am. Chem. Soc., Central Advisers Health Professions (bd. dirs.), AAAS, Cedar Rapids Lit. Club. Democrat. Avocations: tennis, microcomputers.

KEITH, BRIAN DUNCAN, petroleum geologist, consultant; b. El Paso, Tex., Nov. 29, 1943; s. Stanton Baker and Elizabeth (Abernathy) K.; m. Jean Elizabeth Scott, Dec. 17, 1966; children—Colin McLean, Ian Andrew, Arlyn Elizabeth, Logan Charles. B.A., Amherst Coll., 1965; M.S., Syracuse U., 1971; Ph.D., Rensselaer Poly. Inst., 1974. Cert. prof. geologist, Ind. Exploration geologist Chevron Oil Co., Oklahoma City, 1969-71; research scientist Amoco Prodn. Co., Tulsa, 1974-78; geologist Ind. Geol. Survey, Bloomington, 1978—; cons. Amoco Exploration Tng., Tulsa, 1981—; asst. prof. Ind. U., Bloomington, 1982—; assoc. instr. Gerry Exploration, Inc., Troy, N.Y., 1984—. Editor: Trenton of Eastern North America, 1985. Contbr. articles to profl. jours., maps and State of Ind. publs. NSF trainee, 1967; research grantee Sigma Xi, 1972, Am. Assn. Petroleum Geologists, 1972, Pub. Service of Ind., 1978. Mem. Soc. Econ. Paleontologists and Mineralogists, Ind.-Ky. Geol. Soc., Am. Assn. Petroleum Geologists, Ind. Acad. Sci. Democrat. Avocations: science fiction. Office: Ind Geol Survey 611 N Walnut Grove Ave Bloomington IN 47405

KEITH, DAMON J., federal judge. U.S. cir. judge U.S. Ct. Appeals Sixth Cir., Mich. Office: US Ct Appeals Rm 240 231 West Lafayette St Detroit MI 48226*

KEITH, DAVID LEE, entomologist; b. Mankato, Minn., Dec. 7, 1940; s. Wendell Gregory and Verdeen Marcella (Wohlrabe) K.; m. Brenda Jane Pick, June 4, 1961; children—Becky E., Jennifer L., Melissa J., Rachele M. B.Sc., Gustavus Adolphus Coll., 1962; M.Sc., U. Minn., 1965; Ph.D., U. Nebr., 1971. Research asst. U. Minn., St. Paul, 1962-65; teaching asst. U. Nebr., Lincoln, 1965-66, research asst., 1966-67, extension-survey entomologist, 1967-81, extension entomologist, 1981—. Recipient award merit Nebr. Honey Producers Assn., 1983. Mem. Nebr. Coop. Extension Assn. (sec. 1982-83, pres. specialists sect. 1983-84, recipient Disting. Service award 1984), Entomol. Soc. Am., Am. Registry Profl. Entomologists, Sigma Xi, Gamma Sigma Delta, Epsilon Sigma Phi. Democrat. Lutheran. Club: Ptnrs of Ams. (sec.-treas. 1980-82, citation 1983). Avocation: gardening, beekeeping, fishing, hunting. Home: 3247 S 40th St Lincoln NE 68506 Office: U Nebr Dept Entomology IANR/UNL Pl209 Lincoln NE 68583

KEITH, GEORGE FRANCIS, educational adminstrator, communications consultant; b. Detroit, July 18, 1942; s. Fred Marion and Mary (Cimbalik) K.; m. Cecilia Elena Colasanti, Aug. 20, 1966; A.B., U. Detroit, 1964, M.M.A., 1966; postgrad. Wayne State U. 1966. Dept. chmn. Oakland Community Coll., Bloomfield Hills, Mich., 1968-84, academic dean, 1984—; pvt. practice communications cons., West Bloomfield, 1982—; regular book reviewer West Bloomfield Libraries, 1974—. Mem. Soc. Tech. Communications, Nat. Council Tchrs. English, Midwest Regional Conf. English in the Two-Yr. Coll. Democrat. Roman Catholic. Avocations: book collecting, skiing, racquetball. Home: 5963 Barnstable Ct West Bloomfield MI 48033 Office: Southeast Campus Oakland Community Coll 739 S Washington Royal Oak MI 48067

KEITH, ROBERT LEWIS, college counselor; b. Louisville, Nov. 8, 1954; s. Cecil Morton and Frances (Meadors) K. B.S., Eastern Ky. U., 1978, M.A., 1981. Chpt. cons. Sigma Pi, Vincennes, Ind., 1978-79, dir. chpt. services, 1979; asst. dir. student activities Eastern Ky. U., Richmond, 1980-81; coordinator Greek affairs Ohio Wesleyan U., Delaware, Ohio, 1981-84; counselor DeVry Inst. Tech., Columbus, Ohio, 1984—. Vol. emergency services North Central Mental Health Services, Columbus, 1984, Democratic campaign Mondale-Ferraro, 1984. Recipient Outstanding Campus Interfrat. Service award Eastern Ky. U., 1980; Outstanding Young Men in Am., 1981. Mem. Am. Assn. Counseling and Devel., Am. Coll. Profl. Assn., Nat. Assn. Gay Alcoholism Profls., Nat. Orgn. Changing Men, Assn. Fraternity Advs. (mid Am. rep 1983-84). Roman Catholic. Avocations: cooking, weightlifting, music, breeding cockatiels. Office: DeVry Inst Tech 1350 Alum Creek Dr Columbus OH 43209

KEITH, THEO GORDON, JR., mechanical engineering educator; b. Cleve., July 2, 1939; s. Theo Gordon and Dorothy (Meech) K.; m. Sandra Jean Finzel, Aug. 20, 1960; children—Robin Lynne, Nicole Heather. B.Mech. Engring., Fenn Coll., 1964; M.S., U. Md., 1968, Ph.D., 1971. Mech. engr. Naval Ship Research and Devel. Ctr., Annapolis, Md., 1964-71; faculty U. Toledo, 1971—, prof., chmn. mech. engring., 1977—; prin. investigator, wind turbine modeling grantee NASA Lewis Research Ctr., Cleve., 1979—, prin. investigator, combustor modeling grantee, 1982—. Recipient Outstanding Teaching award U. Toledo, 1977; Phi Kappa Phi scholar, 1968. Mem. ASME, AIAA, Soc. Automotive Engrs. (Ralph Teetor award 1978), Am. Soc. Engring. Edn., Sigma Xi, Pi Tau Sigma. Home: 3866 LaPlante Rd Monclova OH 43542 Office: Dept Mech Engring Univ Toledo 2801 W Bancroft St Toledo OH 43606

KEITHLEY, RICHARD ERNEST, lawyer; b. Kansas City, Kans., Mar. 12, 1948; s. Marion C. and Elsie V. (Hatch) K.; A.A., Donnelly Coll., 1968; B.A., Kans. U., 1970, J.D., 1974; children—Shannon Eileen, Heather Dawn; m. Angela Michelle, Mar. 28, 1985. Admitted to Kans. bar, 1974, Fed. bar, 1974, U.S. Supreme Ct. bar, 1977, U.S. Ct. of Appeals bar for 10th Circuit, 1977; clk. to Dist. Judge Kenneth Harmon, Leavenworth, Kans, 1973; individual practice law, Kansas City, 1974-75, Olathe, Kans., 1985—. asst. city atty. City of Kansas City, 1975-77; dep. county counselor Johnson County (Kans.), 1983-85; lectr. in field. Democratic nominee Kans. Ho. of Reps., 1972. Mem. Kansas City Jaycees, Phi Alpha Delta, Delta Sigma Phi. Democrat. Episcopalian. Home: 1960 Sheridan Bridge Ln Olathe KS 66062 Office: Johnson County Courthouse Olathe KS 66061

KELCH, ROBERT PAUL, hospital administrator, physician; b. Detroit, Dec. 3, 1942; m. Jeri Anne Parker; children—Randall Paul, Julie Marie. Ph.B., Monteith Coll., 1963; M.D., U. Mich., 1967. Diplomate Am. Bd. Pediatrics. Intern U. Mich., Ann Arbor, 1967-68, resident in pediatrics, 1968-70; research fellow U. Calif.-San Francisco, 1969-70, NIH trainee, 1970-72; asst. prof. U. Mich., 1972-75, assoc. prof., 1975-77, prof. pediatrics, 1977—, chmn. dept. pediatrics, 1981—; physician-in-chief C.S. Mott Children's Hosp., Ann Arbor, 1983—; pediatric cons. Westland Med. Ctr., Mich., 1973—, St. Joseph Mercy Hosp., Pontiac, Mich., 1983—, Ctr. Disease Control, Humachao, P.R., 1984—. Author: (with Bacon and Spencer) A Practical Approach to Pediatric Endocrinology, 1975; (with Bacon, Spencer and Hopwood) A Practical Approach to Pediatric Endocrinology, 1982. Served to lt. comdr. USNR, 1966-77. Fellow Am. Acad. Pediatrics; mem. Midwest Soc. Pediatric Research (pres. 1983—), Am. Pediatric Soc., AMA. Home: 3525 Charter Pl Ann Arbor MI 48105 Office: U Mich Dept Pediatrics D1109 MPB Box 45 Ann Arbor MI 48109

KELEHER, BRENDAN, lawyer; b. Chgo., Aug. 23, 1954; s. John T. and Dorothy (Catalano) K.; m. Mary E. Rose, Sept. 2, 1984. B.A. cum laude in Polit. Sci., Loyola U., Chgo., 1976, J.D., 1980. Bars: Ill. 1980, U.S. Dist. Ct. (no. dist.) Ill. 1980. Law clk. to presiding justice Circuit Ct. Cook County, Chgo., 1980; assoc. William D. Maddux & Assocs., Chgo., 1980—. Ill. State scholar, 1972-76; Chgo. Motor Club scholar, 1972. Mem. ABA, Ill. Trial Lawyers Assn. (profl. negligence com. 1982-85), Assn. Trial Lawyers Am., Chgo. Bar Assn., Ill. Bar Assn., Am. Judicature Soc., Alpha Sigma Nu. Democrat. Roman Catholic. Office: William D Maddux & Assocs 1 N La Salle St Suite 3800 Chicago IL 60602

KELEHER, JAMES, clergyman. Bishop, Diocese of Belleville (Ill.), Roman Catholic Ch. Office: Chancery Office 220 Lincoln St Belleville IL 62221*

KELL, LEONE BOWER, retired home economics educator, researcher; b. Dighton, Kans., Nov. 27, 1898; d. Carroll and Nettie Maxon (Cheever) Bower; m. William Edgar Kell, June 23, 1924 (dec. 1955); stepchildren—George (dec.), Ruth Kell Noble, Eugene R. (dec.). B.S., Kans. State U., 1923, M.S., 1928; postgrad. Cornell U., 1937-38, Stanford U., 1946. Tchr. elem. schs., Lane County, Kans., 1917-19; tchr. Manhattan High Sch. (Kans.), 1923-24; grad. asst. child devel. Kans. State U., Manhattan, 1927-28, instr., 1929-37, asst. prof., 1938-40, assoc. prof. family and child devel., 1940-46, prof., 1947-65, family economist, 1953-65, prof. emeritus, 1965—; prof. home econs. Kobe Coll., Nishinomiya, Japan, 1967-70. Missionary, United Ch. Bd. for World Ministries, United Ch. of Christ, Japan, 1967-70; dir. nursery sch. Kans. State U. Mem. Am. Home Econs. Assn., Nat. Council on Family Relations, Soc. for Research in Child Devel., LWV, Phi Kappa Phi, Omicron Nu, Delta Kappa Gamma. Democrat. Congregationalist. Contbr. articles to profl. jours. Home: Brewster Pl 1205 W 29th St Apt 525 Topeka KS 66611

KELLER, DENNIS JAMES, management educator, business executive; b. Chgo., July 6, 1941; s. Ralph and Dorothy (Barckman) K.; m. Constance Bassett Templeton, May 28, 1966; children—Jeffrey Breckenridge, David McDaniel, John Templeton. A.B., Princeton U., 1963; M.B.A., U. Chgo., 1968. Account exec. Motorola Communications, Chgo., 1964-67; v.p. fin. Bell & Howell Communications, Waltham, Mass., 1968-70; v.p. mktg. Bell & Howell Schs., Chgo., 1970-73; pres. Keller Grad. Sch. Mgmt., Chgo., 1973-81, chmn., chief exec. officer, 1981—; cons., evaluator North Central Assn., Chgo., 1979—; chmn. bd. Precision Plastics, Inc., Columbia City, Ind., 1981—; chmn. exec. com. Templeton Kenly & Co., Bensenville, Ill., 1975—; dir. Admiral Steel Co., Alsip, Ill. Trustee Glenwood Sch. for Boys, Ill., 1980—, Chgo. Zool. Soc., Brookfield, Ill., 1979—, Lake Forest Acad.-Ferry Hall, Ill., 1980—; chmn. Community House, Hinsdale, Ill., 1985. Nat. Merit scholar, 1959-63; U. Chgo. Grad. Sch. Bus. fellow, 1967-68. Commr. North Central Assn.-Commn. on Instns. of Higher Edn., 1985—. Republican. Mem. United Ch. of Christ. Clubs: Hinsdale Golf (bd. dirs.); Chgo. Avocations: skiing; windsurfing; scuba diving; mountain climbing. Home: 324 E 7th St Hinsdale IL 60521 Office: Keller Grad Sch Mgmt 10 S Riverside Plaza Chicago IL 60606

KELLER, ELIOT AARON, broadcasting executive, consultant; b. Davenport, Iowa, June 11, 1947; s. Norman Edward and Millie (Morris) K.; m. Sandra Kay McGrew, July 3, 1970; 1 child, Nicole. B.A., U. Iowa, 1970; M.S., San Diego State U., 1976. Correspondent, newsman, photographer for various radio and tv stations, newspapers, 1969-77; dir., pres. KRNA, Inc., Iowa City, 1971—, gen. mgr. KRNA-FM, 1974—; adjunct instr. in communication studies U. Iowa, Iowa City, 1983, 84. Mem. Radio TV News Dirs. Assn., Broadcast Financial Mgmt. Assn. Jewish. Home: 609 Keokuk Ct Iowa City IA 52240-4659 Office: KRNA Inc 2105 ACT Circle Iowa City IA 52240-9560

KELLER, HAROLD WILLIAM, chemical company executive; b. Grand Forks, N.D., Aug. 24, 1922; s. Charles Earl and Margaret Ann (Carlson) K.; student U. N.D., 1940-42, 46-48; m. S. Betty Larsen, Oct. 31, 1947; children—Charles William, Kenneth Earl. Asst. dir. research Ill. Water Treatment Co., Rockford, 1952-68, service mgr., 1968-69, mgr. market devel., 1969-72; v.p. Techni-Chem, Inc., Cherry Valley, Ill., 1972-77, pres., 1977—, also owner, corp. exec., dir. Served with USAAF, 1942-46. Mem. Am. Chem. Soc., Am. Oil Chemists Soc., Am. Inst. Chem. Engrs., Am. Soc. Sugar Beet Tech., Lambda Chi Alpha. Home: 7633 Lucky Ln Rockford IL 61108 Office: 6853 Indy Dr Belvidere IL 61008

KELLER, HARRY STEVENS, graphic designer; b. Chgo., Mar. 21, 1943; s. Harry Ralph and Cynthia Francis (Stevens) K.; m. Margaret Carol, June 11, 1966; children—Laura Jean, Thomas Burton, Nancy Jane. B.S., Ill. Inst. Tech., 1967, postgrad., 1969-70. Design asst. Container Corp. Am., Chgo., 1966-68; designer Ctr. for Advanced Research in Design, 1969-72; design dir. C.F. Murphy Assoc., 1972-79; ptnr. Keller, Lane & Waln, Inc., 1979—. Dir., producer Bumeln (film), 1970. Fulbright scholar, Fed. Republic Germany, 1968-69. Mem. Soc. Environ. Graphic Designers, Chgo. 27 Designers. Republican. Avocations: mountaineering; canoeing, skiing; sailing. Home: 515 Scranton Ave Lake Bluff IL 60044 Office: Keller Lane & Waln Inc 8 S Michigan Ave Chicago IL 60603

KELLER, JEANNE ALLIE, social worker; b. Chgo., Nov. 1, 1948; d. Chester and Emma Evelyn (Todd) K.; 1 son, Kenyon Todd. Student So. Ill. U., 1966-67, DePaul U., 1968; B.A., Roosevelt U., 1971; M.A., Gov. State U., 1975. Registered social worker, Ill. Social worker Chgo. Assn. Retarded Children, 1972; program coordinator Clair-Christian Ctr., Chgo., 1972-73; social worker Westside Parents Exceptional Children, Chgo., 1973-76; dist. coordinator Chgo. Police Dept., 1977—; notary pub., Ill., Chmn. criminal justice com. Lawndale Peoples Planning and Action Conf., Chgo.; mem. Lawndale adv. council Chgo. Dept. Human Services; bd. dirs. Westside Assn. Community Action, Brotherhood Against Slavery Addiction; mem. Lawndale Conservation Community Council, Chgo. Dept. Housing; mem. Little Village Community Council. Mem. Sigma Gamma Rho (1st anti-basileus 1973-75). United Methodist. Home: PO Box 867 Chicago IL 60690 Office: 10th Dist Beat Representative Program 2434 S Pulaski Rd Chicago IL 60623

KELLER, JO ELLEN, speech communication educator, consultant; b. Huntington, Ind., Mar. 4, 1948; d. John Frederick and Miriam Lucile (Kindy) Young; children—Sarah Kate, John Christian. B.A., Manchester Coll., 1969; M.A., U. Kans., 1977, Ph.D., 1980. English tchr. Crestwood Schs., Dearborn Heights, Mich., 1969-70; English tchr. Fenton High Sch., Bensenville, Ill., 1970-73; asst. instr. U. Kans., Lawrence, 1977-79; asst. prof. Ind. U.-Purdue, Ft. Wayne, Ind., 1979-82; assoc. prof. Manchester Coll., North Manchester, Ind., 1982—. Recipient E. C. Buehler award U. Kans., 1978; grantee NEH, 1983. Mem. Ind. Speech Assn., Central States Speech Assn. (Outstanding Young Educator award, 1982), Speech Communication Assn. Home: 1206 N Wayne St North Manchester IN 46962 Office: Manchester Coll Box 122 North Manchester IN 46962

KELLER, JOHN MAHLON, biological chemistry educator; b. Sussex, N.J., Mar. 10, 1939. A.B., Princeton U., 1961; Ph.D., MIT, 1966. Nat. Cancer Inst. fellow U. Calif.-Berkeley, 1966-68; Leukemia Soc. Am. fellow U. Chgo., 1968-70; asst. prof. U. Wash., Seattle, 1970-76; assoc. prof. biol. chemistry Chgo. Med. Sch.-Univ. Health Sci., North Chicago, 1977-81, prof., 1981—; vis. scientist Max Planck Inst. Biochemistry, Martinsried, Fed. Republic Germany, 1983-84. Am. Heart Assn. investigator, 1971-76; Am. Cancer Soc. scholar, 1983-84. Mem. Am. Soc. Biol. Chemists, Am. Soc. Cell Biology, Am. Soc. Microbiology, Am. Chem. Soc. Office: Chgo Med Sch Dept Biol Chemistry 3333 Green Bay Rd North Chicago IL 60064

KELLER, JOHN MILTON, gynecologist/obstetrician, educator; b. Phila., Jan. 12, 1922; s. Frederick E. and Ruth (Lock) K.; m. Ruth C. Stranford, Apr. 28, 1929; children—John Frederick, Brian Keith. B.A., W. Va. U., 1943; M.D., Jefferson Med. Coll., 1946. Diplomate Am. Bd. Ob-Gyn. Resident in ob-gyn St. John's Hosp., Bklyn., 1951-54; clin. fellow Am. Cancer Soc., SUNY, Bklyn., 1954-55; attending obstetrician/gynecologist Williston, N.D., 1955-62, Geisinger Med. Ctr., Danville, Pa., 1962-69; assoc. prof. Abraham Lincoln Sch. Med., U. Ill., Chgo., 1969-70, U. Health Scis., Chgo. Med. Sch., 1971-74; prof. univ. health scis. Chgo. Med. Sch., 1974-80; assoc. clin prof. Peoria Sch. Medicine, U. Ill., 1982—; attending chief ob-gyn Fairbury (Ill.) Hosp., 1980-84; sr. attending Colposcopy Clinic, St. Francis Hosp., Peoria, 1981-84; attending ob-gyn St. Elizabeth Hosp., Bryan Meml. Hosp., Lincoln Gen. Hosp., Nebr., 1984—; obstetrician-gynecologist Health Am., Lincoln, 1984—. Served with M.C., U.S. Army, 1947-49. Geisinger Med. Ctr. grantee, 1968; U. Ill. grantee, 1971-72. Mem. ACS, Am. Coll. Ob-Gyn, Am. Soc. Colposcopy, Am. Inst. Ultrasound in Medicine, Chgo. Gynecol. Soc., AMA, Nebr. Med. Soc., Lancaster County Med. Soc. Republican. Lutheran. Club: Masons (32 deg.), Shriner. Contbr. articles to profl. jours. Office: 17th & N Sts Lincoln NE 68508

KELLER, JOHN PAUL, industrial company executive; b. Cleve., July 26, 1939; s. Paul And Jane (Beeson) K.; m. Judith Klein, Aug. 6, 1960; children—Lizabeth, Susan, Jack. B.S., Yale U., 1961; M.B.A., Harvard U., 1963. Product planner Ford Motor Co., Dearborn, Mich., 1963-64; asst. to publisher Time, N.Y.C., 1964-66, bus. mgr., 1966-70; pres. Pioneer Press Limited, Inc., Wilmette, Ill., 1970-71, Keller Steel Co., Northfield, Ill., 1972—; dir. AM Castle, Chgo., 1980—, UniBanc Trust Co., Chgo., 1984—. Mem. Young Pres's. Orgn. (dir. 1983—). Clubs: Cypress Point (Carmel, Calif.), Glen View (Ill.). Home: 1095 Pine St Winnetka IL 60093 Office: Keller Steel Co One Northfield Plaza Northfield IL 60093

KELLER, KENNETH CHRISTEN, advertising executive; b. Toledo, Feb. 17, 1939; s. Theodore G. and Edna L. (Christen) K.; m. Mary Carolyn Folsom, Sept. 10, 1960; children—Kathryn Elizabeth Keller Oulevey, David Folsom. Student Ohio State U., 1957-59. Part-time staff announcer Sta. WMNI, Columbus, Ohio, 1958-59, Sta. WTVN, Columbus, 1959, Sta. WBNS-TV, Columbus, 1959; staff announcer Sta. WRFD, Worthington, Ohio, 1959-61; staff announcer, news supr., program dir. Sta. WOSU, Columbus, 1961-65; on-air talent Sta. WBNS, Columbus, 1962-65; copywriter Joe Hill & Assocs., Columbus, 1965-66; creative dir. Myers, Ault & Assocs., Columbus, 1966-70; co-owner, account exec. Angeletti, Wise & Keller, Columbus, 1970-72; co-owner TRIAD, Columbus, 1972—, v.p., dir. creative services, 1972-85, pres., 1985—; owner Radio City Music Hole. Bd. dirs. Friends of WOSU, 1981—, sec. bd., 1982-83, v.p and pres.-elect, 1983-85, pres., 1985—. Lyricist, co-composer Best Radio Comml. award Internat. Assn. Fairs and Expns., Ohio State Fair, 1978, 81; Champion Papers award, 1976. Mem. AFTRA (pres. chpt. 1978). Home: 270 Park Blvd Worthington OH 43085 Office: TRIAD 6525 Busch Blvd Columbus OH 43229

KELLER, PAUL ALAN, lawyer; b. Bucyrus, Ohio, Aug. 12, 1954; s. Darl Emerson and Maxine Delores (Beamer) K.; m. Jacquelyn Sue Walter, Nov. 20, 1976; 1 child, Katie Alanna. B.S. magna cum laude, U. Cin., 1977; J.D. cum laude, U. Mich., 1980. Bar: Mich. 1980, U.S. Dist. Ct. (ea. dist.) Mich. 1980, U.S. Ct. Appeals (6th cir.) 1981. Carpenter Bob Nigh Builder, Bucyrus, 1972; coop. engr. Gen. Telephone Co., Marion, Ohio, 1973, Dugan & Myers Constrn. Co., Blue Ash, Ohio, 1974, EPA, Cin., 1975-77; research asst. U. Mich. Law Sch., Ann Arbor, 1979-80; assoc. Harness, Dickey & Pierce, Birmingham, Mich., 1980-84, ptnr., 1984—. Vice-pres. Beverly-Golfhurst Homeowners Assn., Birmingham, 1982-83; chmn. adminstrv. bd. Beverly Hills United Meth. Ch., Birmingham, 1985—. Recipient All-State Basketball award Ohio High Sch. Athletic Assn., 1972; Timken scholarship, 1972-77; Charles B. Herfurth scholarship U. Cin. Coll. Engring., 1976-77; Book award U. Mich. Law Sch., 1980. Mem. Oakland County Bar Assn., State Bar Mich., ABA, Am. Intellectual Property Law Assn., Mich. Patent Law Assn., Assn. Trial Lawyers Am., Chi Epsilon, Tau Beta Pi. Club: Am. Youth Hostels. Home: 19519 Riverside Birmingham MI 48009 Office: Harness Dickey & Pierce 1500 N Woodward Ave Birmingham MI 48011

KELLER, THOMAS KENNETH, JR., association administrator; b. Cin., Oct. 20, 1947; s. Thomas Kenneth and Frances I. (Green) K.; m. Sally S.; 1 child, Evan L. B.A. with honors in English, U. Cin., 1972; cert. mil. journalism Def. Info. Sch., 1968. Pub. relations copywriter EPA, Cin., 1970-73; advt. copywriter NCR Corp., Dayton, Ohio, 1973-76; nat. dir. communications DAV, Cin., 1976—. Bd. dirs. Tng. in Ind. Living, 1978-80; mem. nat. adv. com. on scouting for the handicapped Boy Scouts Am., 1983-84. Served in USAF, 1968-70. Recipient Philipson Found. award 1972. Mem. Pub. Relations Soc. Am. (dir. Cin. chpt. 1981-82), Greater Cin. C. of C., No. Ky. C. of C., DAV, VFW, Nat. Order Trench Rats. Episcopalian. Office: 807 Maine Ave SW Washington DC 20024

KELLER, WALTER DAVID, geology educator; b. North Kansas City, Mo., Mar. 13, 1900; s. Theodore and Marie (Schulz) K.; widowed; children—David, Dwight. A.B., U. Mo., 1925, Ph.D., 1933; B.S. in Ceramic Engring., U. Mo.-Rolla, 1930; M.A., Harvard U., 1932. From asst. prof. geology to prof. geology U. Mo., Columbia, 1932-70; ceramic technologist A.P. Green Refractories Co., Mexico, Mo., 1929-31; cons. intermittent basis U.S. Geol. Survey. Author: Principles of Chemical Weathering, 1954; Principles of Geology, 1957; Chemistry in Introductory Geology, 1952; Common Rocks and Minerals of Missouri, 1945. Served with AUS, 1918. Recipient Twenhofel award Soc. of Econ. Paleontologists and Mineralogists, 1981; Neil A. Miner award Nat. Assn. Geology Tchrs., 1967; Hardinge award Am. Inst. Mining and Metall. Engrs., 1979; named Disting. Faculty Mem., U. Mo. Fellow Geol. Soc. Am., Mineral. Soc. Am., AAAS; disting. mem. Clay Minerals Soc., Soc. Mining Engrs. Lodge: Masons. Avocations: photography. Office: Dept Geology U Mo Columbia MO 65211

KELLER-MARESH, JOAN MAE, nursing educator; b. Chgo., July 29, 1938; d. Joseph F. and Marie L. (Nelson) Keller; m. Richard Joseph Maresh, June 20, 1970; children—Karin Ann, Daniel Joseph. B.S., Marymount Coll., 1963; M.S.N., St. Louis U., 1967. Registered nurse, Wis. Supr., surg. nurse St. John's Hosp., Saline, Kans., 1962-64, 67-70; spl. care unit nurse Orange County Med. Ctr., Orange, Calif., 1970-71; instr. Boulder County Practical Nurse Program, Boulder, Colo., 1971-73; childbirth educator, 1974-80; asst. prof. nursing Viterbo Coll., LaCrosse, Wis., 1980—. Pregnancy counselor/cons. for schs. on women's issues. Mem. Citizens Advocacy Wis., 1982, LaCrosse Ministry Program, 1981-83. Mem. Am. Nurses Assn., Leleche League, Am. Soc. Psychoprophylaxis in Obstetrics, LaCrosse Dist. Nurses Assn., Friends of the Earth. Democrat. Roman Catholic. Home: 213 3d Ave Holmen WI 54636 Office: Viterbo Coll Dept Nursing 815 S 9th St LaCrosse WI 54601

KELLEY, BARBARA CARTIER, information specialist, artist; b. Ludington, Mich., May 15, 1928; d. Warren Raphael Cartier and Mary Josephine (Hendry) C.; m. Roger F. Kelley, Apr. 22, 1950 (div.); children—Brian, Stephen, Susan, Peter. Student, St. Mary-of-the-Woods Coll., 1945-47; B.S., Mich. State U., 1950; M.L.S., U. Mich., 1978. Info. specialist Market Opinion Research, Detroit, 1978—. Patron Birmingham/Bloomfield Art Assn., Surface Design Assn., Founders Soc., Detroit Inst. Arts, Am. Craft Council; Friends of Detroit

Pub. Library, Bloomfield Twp. Library; mem. allocations com. United Way of Mich.; mem. adv. bd. Women United Found. Mem. Spl. Library Assn. Roman Catholic. Home: 1040 Stratford Ln Bloomfield Hills MI 48013 Office: Market Opinion Research 550 Washington Blvd Detroit MI 48226

KELLEY, EDGAR ALAN, teacher educator; b. Bath, Mich., Aug. 1, 1940; s. Clarence E. and Cora (Bollinger) K.; B.A., Mich. State U., 1961, M.A., 1965, Ph.D., 1970; m. Marie Elaine Foerch, Aug. 10, 1963; 1 son, Wesley Lynn. Tchr., Ovid Elsie (Mich.) Area Schs., 1961-67; sch. adminstr. Colon (Mich.) Community Schs., 1967-69; asst. prof. ednl. adminstrn. and secondary edn. Tchrs. Coll., U. Nebr., Lincoln, 1970-74, assoc. prof. ednl. adminstrn., curriculum and instrn., 1974-79, prof., 1979-84; prof., chmn. dept. ednl. leadership Western Mich. U., Kalamazoo, 1984—. Recipient Disting. Teaching award U. Nebr., 1979. Mem. Assn. Supervision and Curriculum Devel. (exec. bd. 1978-83), Nat. Assn. Secondary Sch. Prins. (Disting. Service award), Nebr. Assn. Supervision and Curriculum Devel. (Disting. Service award 1979, 83), Nat. Soc. Study Edn., Nebr. Council Sch. Adminstrs. (Disting. Service award 1983), Phi Delta Kappa (Outstanding Young Leaders in Edn. award 1981). Editor: Catalyst, 1977-82; co-editor UCEA monograph series 1983—; contbr. articles to profl. jours. Home: 6875 Glen Creek SE Caledonia MI 49316 Office: 3312 Sangren Hall Western Mich U Kalamazoo MI 49008

KELLEY, FRANK JOSEPH, attorney general of Michigan; b. Detroit, Dec. 31, 1924; s. Frank Edward and Grace Margaret (Spears) K.; pre-law cert. U. Detroit, 1948, J.D., 1951; m. Josephine Palmisano, June 30, 1945; children—Karen Ann, Frank Edward, Jane Francis. Admitted to Mich. bar, 1952; practice law, Detroit, 1952-54, Alpena, Mich., 1954-61; public adminstr. Alpena County, Mich., 1956; atty., Alpena, 1958-61; atty. gen. Mich., 1962—; instr. econs. Alpena Community Coll., 1955-56; instr. real estate law U. Mich. extension, 1957-61. Mem. Alpena County Bd. Suprs., 1958-61; founding dir., 1st sec. Alpena United Fund, 1955; founding dir., 1st pres. Northeastern Mich. Child Guidance Clinic, 1958; pres., dir. Northeastern Mich. Cath. Family Sers. Council, 1956. Mem. Am., 26th Jud. Circuit (pres. 1956) bar assns., State Bar Mich., Internat. Movement Atlantic Union, Nat. Assn. Attys. Gen., Alpha Kappa Psi. Lodge: K.C. (4 deg.). Office: Law Bldg 525 W Ottawa Lansing MI 48913*

KELLEY, GLENN E., state supreme court justice; b. St. Edward, Nebr., Apr. 25, 1921; s. Glenn O. and Sigrid O. Kelley; m. Margaret A. Kelley, July 25, 1946; children—Glenn A., David P., Anne L. B.S., No. State Coll., 1943; LL.B., U. Mich., 1948. Bar: Minn. Judge Minn. 3d Jud. Dist. Ct., 1969-81; assoc. justice Minn. Supreme Ct., 1981—. Served with USAAF, 1942-45. Office: Minn Supreme Court 230 State Capitol Saint Paul MN 55155

KELLEY, GORDON EDWARD, health educator, dentist; b. Fairland, Ind., Aug. 5, 1934; m. Gail Ruth Gallinger, Aug. 2, 1958; children—Elizabeth, Pamela and Priscilla (twins), Marcella. B.S., Ind. U., 1957, D.D.S., 1964; M.S.D., Ind. Sch. Dentistry, 1967. Med. lab. tech. Meml. Hosp., Mattoon, Ill., 1958-59; dir. Ind. fluride programs Ind. Univ. Sch. of Dentistry, Indpl., 1965-71, asst. prof., 1967-71, dir. allied health programs Ind. State Univ., Evansville, 1971-78, chmn. div. of allied health 1978—; Head Start cons. Dept. Health and Human Services, Chgo., 1976—. Contbr. articles to profl. jours. Actioneer Pub. T.V., Evansville, 1976—; vice chmn. Met. Emergency Services Council, Evansville, 1980-84; adv. com. Ind. Vocat.-Tech. Coll., Evansville, 1982—. Served to 2nd lt. U.S. Army, 1957-58. Mem. ADA, Ind. Dental Assn., Am. Assn. Dental Schs., Am. Soc. Allied Health Professions, Ind. Soc. for Hosp. Edn. and Tng. (pres. 1976-77). Avocations: pilot; old radios and programs; photography; old coins; computer programming. Home: 620 Drexel Dr Evansville IN 47712 Office: U So Ind Evansville 8600 University Blvd Evansville IN 47712

KELLEY, PAMELA LACKO, choreographer, artistic director; b. East Chicago, Ind., June 29, 1948; d. Anthony Valentine and Anne Cathrine (Yelinich) Lacko; m. Robert Jerome Kelley, June 17, 1972; children—Robert Jerome III., Jonathan Anthony. B.S., St. Joseph's Calumet Coll., 1971. Choreographer East Chicago Jr. Tamburitzans, 1969-72; tchr. Clark Grade Sch., Hammond, Ind., 1971-72; artistic dir., choreographer Zivili Kolo Ensemble, Columbus, Ohio, 1971—; guest choreographer East Chicago Jr. Tamburitzans, 1976, Cleve. Jr. Tamburitzans, 1982-83, Vela Luka Ensemble, Anacortes, Wash., 1980, Mandala Ensemble, Boston, 1984. Choreographer of ethnic dances, 1969-84. Choreography fellow Ohio Arts Council, 1978, 80-81, 83, 85. Mem. Ohio Dance. Lodge: Croatian Fraternal Union. Avocations: singing, playing the tamburitza. Home: 336 Guernsey Ave Columbus OH 43204 Office: Zivili Kolo Ensemble 12 Clover Ct Granville OH 43023

KELLEY, ROBERT J., labor leader; b. St. Louis; m. Barbara Kelley; children—Colleen, Amy, Melissa, Erin, Michael, Meghan. Student pub. schs., St. Louis. With United Food and Comml. Workers, Local #665, AFL-CIO, St. Louis, dir. organizing; sec.-treas. Greater St. Louis Labor Council, 1975-78, pres., 1978—. Vice chmn. United Way of Greater St. Louis, bd. dirs., exec. com. and fin. com.; bd. dirs. St. Louis Area council Boy Scouts Am., Cath. Charities, St. Patrick's Ctr., St. Louis Arts and Edn. Council; bd. dirs. Backstoppers, St. Louis; exec. bd. Mo. State Labor Council, AFL-CIO; mem. Nat. AFL-CIO adv. com. Address: 1401 Hampton Ave Saint Louis MO 63139

KELLEY, RONALD WILLIAM, physician, microbiologist; b. Flint, Mich., Feb. 25, 1945; s. William Martin and Beulah Mae (Vieu) K.; m. Mary Jane Hillier, Aug. 1, 1970; children—Molly, Cyndy, William. Supr. chief microbiology and urology lab. Flint Osteo. Hosp. (Mich.), 1969-73, intern, 1975-76; practice medicine specializing in family medicine, Gaylord, Mich., 1976—; chief of staff Otsego Meml. Hosp., Gaylord, 1981—; med. examiner Otsego County (Mich.). Recipient student assistantships Mich. State U., 1969, 73. Mem. Am. Osteo. Assn., Mich. Assn. Osteo. Physicians and Surgeons, Osteo. Gen. Practitioners of Mich., Northeastern Mich. Osteo. Assn. Office: 850 N Otsego St Gaylord MI 49735

KELLEY, TIMOTHY MICHAEL, environmental engineer, consultant; b. Batesville, Ind., Apr. 21, 1952; s. Robert Leo and Bernice Elizabeth (Gonder) K.; m. Darcy Kay Pierce, Aug. 2, 1975; children—Jessica, Courtney. B.S. in Environ. Sci., Ind. State U., 1974. Health insp. City of Madison, Wis., 1973; sanitarian NIH, USPHS, Bethesda, Md., 1974; sanitarian hazardous waste sect. Ind. State Bd. Health, Indpls., 1977-81; environ. engr. Roll Coater, Inc., Greenfield, Ind., 1981—. Mem. South Deanery Indpls. Bd. Cath. Edn., 1984, St. Roch Cath. Sch. Bd. Edn., Indpls., 1985. Mem. Nat. Coil Coaters Assn. (environ. chmn. 1982—, asst. tech. sec. 1984—), Air Pollution Control Assn., Ind. Water Pollution Control Assn. Roman Catholic. Avocations: scuba diving; hunting; fishing.

KELLEY, WENDELL J., utilities exec.; b. Champaign, Ill., May 2, 1926; s. Victor W. and Erma (Dalrymple) K.; B.S. in Elec. Engring., U. Ill., 1949; m. Evelyn Kimpel, June 12, 1947; children—Jeffrey, David, Alan, Stephen, John. With Ill. Power Co., Decatur, 1949—, mgr. personnel, 1959-61, v.p., 1961-66, pres., 1966-76, chmn. and pres., 1976—, also dir.; dir. Millikin Nat. Bank, Decatur, Electric Energy, Inc., Millikin Mortgage Co., Franklin Ins. Co., Springfield. Former chmn. Mid-Am. Interpool Network, 1969-71, vice chmn., 1975-77, former mem. exec. com.; bd. dirs. Edison Electric Inst., Washington, 1974-77, 80-83; former trustee Nat. Electric Reliability Council, vice chmn., 1975-77, chmn., 1978-80; past mem. Ill. Council on Econ. Edn.; mem. citizens com. U. Ill.; past mem. U. Ill. Found.; past mem. adv. council St. Mary's Hosp., Decatur, pres., 1972-73; past bd. dirs. Shults-Lewis Children's Home, Valparaiso, Ind. Served with USAAF, 1944-45. Recipient Alumni Honor award Coll. Engring., U. Ill., 1974, Alex Van Praag, Jr. disting. engring. award, 1983. Registered profl. engr., Ill. Fellow IEEE (past chmn. central Ill. sect.); mem. Elec. Engring. Alumni Assn. U. Ill. (past pres., Disting. Alumnus award 1973), Ill. State C. of C. (chmn. 1973-74, past. dir.), U. Ill. Alumni Assn. (past dir.), Nat., Ill. socs. profl. engrs., Eta Kappa Nu. Mem. Ch. of Christ (elder). Home: 65 Dellwood Dr Decatur IL 62521 Office: 500 S 27th St Decatur IL 62525

KELLOGG, CHARLES PEZAVIA, SR., religious organization executive; b. Steubenville, Ohio, Jan. 3, 1927; s. William Pitt and Fannie Laura (Gassaway) K.; m. Nora Lee Spotts, Aug. 23, 1948; children—Brenda C. Kellogg Jones, Saundra A. Kellogg Green, Charles Pezavia. B.S., Wittenberg U., 1949; M.A., Kent State U., 1950; LL.B., Blackstone Sch. Law, 1952; LL.D. (hon.), Bethune Cookman Coll., 1968; postgrad. John Carroll U., 1951-52, United Theol. Coll., 1970-71, U. West Indies. Instr. polit. sci. Elizabeth City (N.C.) State Coll., 1949-52; tchr. Turtle Mountain Indian Sch., Belcourt, N.D., 1952-54; instr. Glenville High Sch., Cleve., 1955-64; mem. exec. staff Gen. Bd. of Laity, United Methodist Ch., Evanston, Ill., 1964-72, Gen. Bd. Discipleship, Nashville, 1972-74; exec. dir. health and welfare div. Bd. Global Ministries, United Meth. Ch., Evanston, Ill. and N.Y.C., 1974—. Served with USAAF, 1945-46. Mem. NEA. Home: 1708 Keeney St Evanston IL 60202 Office: Bd Global Ministries United Methodist Church 1200 Davis St Evanston IL 60202 also 475 Riverside Dr New York NY 10115

KELLOGG, RICHARD CARLTON, engineer; b. Sioux City, Iowa, May 11, 1951; s. Jack Alvin and Shirley Lilian (Annable) K.; m. Deborah Kay Wortman, Nov. 3, 1984. B.S. in Mech. Engring., U. Nebr., 1974. Engr., Omaha Pub. Power Dist., 1974-77, sr. engr., 1977-81, supr., 1981—. Mem. Am. Soc. Metals, ASME (exec. com. Nebr. sect. 1984—), Exptl. Aircraft Assn. Avocations: aviation, camping, photography. Home: 5853 Elm St Omaha NE 68106 Office: Omaha Pub Power Dist 1623 Harney St Omaha NE 68102

KELLY, DENNIS MICHAEL, lawyer; b. Cleve., May 6, 1943; s. Thomas Francis and Margaret (Murphy) K.; m. Marilyn Ann Divoky, Dec. 28, 1967; children—Alison, Meredith. B.A., John Carroll U., 1961-65; J.D., U. Notre Dame, 1968. Bar: Ohio 19—. Law clk. U.S. Ct. Appeals (8th cir.), Cleve., 1968-69; assoc. Jones, Day, Reavis & Pogue, Cleve., 1969-75, ptnr., 1975—; chmn. environ. law sect. Jones, Day, Reavis & Pogue, Cleve., 1975—. Trustee Diabetes Assn. Greater Cleve., 1982—. Mem. ABA, Ohio Bar Assn., Bar Assn. Greater Cleve. Office: Jones Day Reavis & Pogue 1700 Huntington Bldg Cleveland OH 44115

KELLY, DONALD PHILIP, investment company executive; b. Chgo., Feb. 24, 1922; s. Thomas Nicholas and Ethel M. (Healy) K.; student Loyola U., Chgo., 1953-54, De Paul U., 1954-55, Harvard U., 1965. Mgr. tabulating United Ins. Co. Am., 1946-51; mgr. data processing A.B. Wrisley Co., 1951-53; mgr. data processing Swift & Co., 1953-65, asst. controller, 1965-67, controller, 1967-68, v.p. corp. devel., controller, 1968-70, fin. v.p., dir., 1970-73; fin. v.p., dir. Esmark, Inc., Chgo., 1973, pres., chief operating officer, 1973-77, pres. chief exec. officer, 1977-82, chmn., pres., chief exec. officer, 1982-84, also dir.; pres. Kelly Briggs & Assocs., Inc., Chgo., 1984—; dir. Gen. Dynamics Corp., Inland Steel Co. Trustee Michael Reese Hosp. and Med. Center, Chgo., Com. for Econ. Devel., Washington, Mus. Sci. and Industry, Chgo. Served in USNR, 1942-46. Mem. Fin. Execs. Inst. Clubs: Chgo., Comml., Econ. (Chgo.). Office: 55 E Monroe St Suite 3822 Chicago IL 60603

KELLY, EARL PATRICK, social services agency administrator; b. Newton, Iowa, Feb. 17, 1940; s. Earl Patrick and Ismene Beatrice (Bianchi) K.; B.A., U. Iowa, 1962; M.S.W., St. Louis U., 1966; Ed.D., Drake U., 1978; m. Madleine Carol Vivone, Aug. 11, 1962; children—Anne, Kathleen, Michael. Tchr. public schs., Sheboygan, Wis., 1962-63; staff social worker Cath. Social Services, Des Moines, 1963-69; with Orchard Place, Des Moines, 1969—, exec. dir., 1975—; instr. Drake U., 1971—. NIMH grantee, 1965-66. Mem. Iowa Coalition Family and Children's Services (pres. 1981-82), Child Welfare League (exec. adv. com. 1982). Home: 1335 SW Thornton Ave Des Moines IA 50315 Office: 925 SW Porter Ave Des Moines IA 50315

KELLY, EUGENE KEVIN, lawyer; b. Sioux City, Iowa, Jan. 22, 1943; s. John C. and Dorothy F. (Hagan) K.; m. Judith Ann Gurney, Sept. 3, 1966 (div. Apr. 1978); children—Timory Lynn, Tracy Ann; m. Carole Jean Eichhorn, Dec. 2, 1978. B.A., Gonzaga U., 1965; J.D., U. S.D., 1968. Bar: Iowa 1968. Asst. county atty. Woodbury County, Sioux City, 1968-71; mem. Iowa Ho. of Reps., 1970-73; chief exec. trust dept. Northwestern Nat. Bank, Sioux City, 1973-76; mem. Iowa State Senate, 1973-78; prin. Kelly Law Firm, Des Moines, 1976—; legis. counsel Iowa Def. Council, 1979—; sec.-treas. Iowa Travel Council, 1980—; exec. dir. Iowa Recreational Vehicle Assn., 1978—. State sec. Nature Conservancy; nat. treas. U.S. Masters Swimming. Recipient Vol. award Gov. Iowa, 1976, 77. Mem. ABA, Iowa Bar Assn. (com.), Polk County Bar Assn., Iowa Soc. Assn. Execs., Def. Research Inst., Des Moines C. of C. (com.), Ducks Unltd. (chmn. region 1985-86; Nat. Conservation Service award 1972; nat. trustee 1973-77), Des Moines Com. Fgn. Relations. Avocations: swimming; skiing; hunting; biking. Office: 1400 Dean Ave Des Moines IA 50316

KELLY, JERRY BOB, social services administrator; b. Chgo., Feb. 6, 1942; s. Robert Lee and Mildred Florence (Griffin) K.; B.S. in Acctg., Roosevelt U., 1968; m. Diane Joyce Wilburn, Nov. 29, 1969; children—Jerold Robert, Joycelyn Renée. Lic. real estate salesman and life ins. producer, Ill. Br. mgr. Chgo. Econ. Devel. Corp., 1970-77; acct. Weather Bloc Mfg. Co., Chgo., 1967-68; programmer Morton Salt Co., Chgo., 1968-69; ptnr. Smith Distbrs., 1977-79; mgr. fin. and adminstrn. Suburban Cook County Area Agy. on Aging, Chgo., 1979-85; exec. dir. Lawndale Bus. and Local Devel. Corp., Chgo., 1985—. Treas. Day Care Crisis Council Met. Chgo., 1973-76, appreciation award; 1st v.p. West Side Health Planning Orgn., 1974-76, appreciation award; treas. Met. Chgo. chpt. Nat. Caucus and Ctr. on Black Aged. Served with AUS, 1964-67. Recipient appreciation award Chgo. Black Caucus, Am. Fedn. Tchrs., Chgo. Bd. Election Commrs., Comprehensive Health Planning Orgn. Chgo. Mem. Assoc. Photographers Internat. Baptist. Club: Elks (2d v.p. Ill.-Wis., past grand exalted ruler). Research on redevel. plans for East Garfield. Home: 1415 N Mayfield Ave Chicago IL 60651 Office: 1111 S Homan Ave Chicago IL 60624

KELLY, JOHN GEORGE LEE, veterans organization executive; b. Takoma Park, Md., Aug. 12, 1932; s. Fred Colburn and Patrice Louise (Boswell) K.; m. Glenda Merle Karns, June 20, 1959 (div. June 22, 1963); children—David Thomas Colburn, Catherine Marie Kelly Houk. A.A. in Bus. Mgmt., Columbus Tech. Inst., 1982. Notary public, Tex., Ohio. Truck driver Ohio State U., Columbus, 1962-63; taxicab driver, Columbus, 1963-68; factory laborer Westinghouse, Columbus, 1963-64; letter carrier, mail handler U.S. Postal Service, Columbus, 1964-75; exec. sec. 12th Dist. Council Am. Legion, Columbus, 1976—; organizer Veterans Day Parade, 1976-83. Author, editor monthly bulletin Am. Legion, 1976—. Election Day Com. worker, Ward 8C Columbus, 1984; 12th Dist. Chaplain Am. Legion Ohio, 1981—; asst. chaplain Franklin County Jail, Franklin County Workhouse, 1983—. Served with USAF, 1958-62. Recipient Vigil Honor, 1973, Order of Arrow, Boy Scouts Am. Mem. Am. Law Enforcement Officers Assn., Nat. Lodge Fraternal Order of Police. Republican. Mem. DAV (life), AMVETS. Roman Catholic. Lodges: Rosicrucian Order, Moose, K.C. Home: PO Box 93 Columbus OH 43216-0093 Office: 12th Dist Council Dept Ohio Am Legion 250 W Broad St Room 21 Columbus OH 43215

KELLY, MARGARET TERESA, pharmacist; b. Waterloo, Iowa, Oct. 14, 1950; d. Eugene Francis and Elizabeth Marie (Hayes) K. A.A., Iowa Central Community Coll., 1970; B.S., S.D. State U., 1973; M.S., U. Minn., 1984. Registered pharmacist Ill., Iowa, Minn., S.D. Pharmacist, Walgreen Drug Co., Sioux City, Iowa, 1973-76; pharmacist St. John's Hosp., Springfield, Ill., 1977, pharmacy supr., 1977-82; pharmacy resident Univ. Minn. Hosp., Mpls., 1982-84; pharmacist, doctoral candidate Univ. Minn., Mpls., 1984—. Den leader Abraham Lincoln council Boy Scouts of Am., Springfield, 1977-82. Mem. Am. Soc. Hosp. Pharmacists, Am. Pharm. Assn., Minn. Soc. Hosp. Pharmacists, Ill. Council Hosp. Pharmacists, Phi Kappa Phi, Rho Chi. Roman Catholic. Clubs: Am. Youth Hostel (Mpls.), League of Am. Wheelmen (Balt.). Avocations: bicycling; walking; cooking; needlework. Home: 3446 Garfield Ave S Minneapolis MN 55408 Office: Univ of Minn Coll of Pharmacy HSUF 7-152 308 Harvard St SE Minneapolis MN 55408

KELLY, NELSON ALLEN, research scientist; b. Lakewood, Ohio, Aug. 6, 1951; s. John Louis and Laura Katherine (Nelson) K.; m. Suzanne May Gerou, Sept. 4, 1982; 1 child, Benjamin. B.S., Miami U., Oxford, Ohio, 1973; Ph.D., Pa. State U., 1977. Sr. research scientist Gen. Motors, Warren, Mich., 1977-82, staff research scientist, 1982—. Contbr. articles to profl. jours. Sci. reader Recording for the Blind, Inc., 1982—. Harvey Clayton Brill scholar Miami U., 1972. Mem. Air Pollution Control Assn. (chem. com. 1982—), Am. Chem. Soc., Inter-Am. Photochem. Soc., Sigma Xi. Avocations: golf; bowling; billiards; barbershop harmony; bridge. Home: 11722 Fairview Sterling Heights MI 48077 Office: Gen Motors Research Labs Environ Sci Dept Warren MI 48090

KELLY, PATRICK F., federal judge; b. Wichita, Kans., June 25, 1929; s. Arthur J. and Reed (Skinner) K.; B.A., Wichita U., 1951; LL.B., Washburn Law Sch., 1953; m. Joan Y. Cain, Jan. 3, 1953; children—Deanna Kelly Riepe, Patrick F. Admitted to Kans. bar; individual practice law, Dunn & Hamilton, 1955; from asso. to partner firm Kahrs & Nelson, 1955-59; partner firm Frank & Kelly, 1959-68, Render, Kamas & Kelly, 1968-76; individual practice law, Patrick F. Kelly, P.A., Wichita, 1976-80; judge U.S. Dist. Ct., Dist. of Kans., Wichita, 1980—. Trustee, Wichita State U., 1969-74, chmn., 1972-74; chmn. Midway chpt. ARC, 1967. Served with JAGC, USAF, 1953-55. Fellow Am. Coll. Trial Lawyers; mem. Am. Bar Assn., Kans. Bar Assn., Kans. Trial Lawyers Assn., Am. Arbitration Assn. (arbiter), Internat. Soc. Barristers, Am. Bd. Trial Advocates. Office: 232 Federal Bldg Wichita KS 67202*

KELLY, RAYMOND JOHN, III, brokerage firm executive; b. Norfolk, Va., Feb. 1, 1943; s. Raymond John and Katherine Elizabeth (Levasseur) K.; m. Kathleen Elizabeth Brennan, Oct. 25, 1969; children—Raymond John IV, Deirdre Elizabeth, Laura Clare, Timothy Spencer, David Patrick. B.A., U. Notre Dame, 1963; B.A., Oxford (Eng.) U., 1965, M.A., 1969. Restaurant and hotel tester Egon Ronay Guides, London, 1965; broker William C. Roney & Co., Flint, Mich., 1969—, br. mgr., 1974—, ptnr., 1978—; mem. faculty Baker Bus. Coll., Flint, 1972-74; dir. Kelly-Younger Interiors, Ceallaigh Corp. Pres. edn. com. St. Robert's Parish Council, Flushing, Mich., 1979-82, pres. council, 1981—; trustee Flint Inst. Music, 1983—. Served to 1st lt. Intelligence, U.S. Army, 1965-69; Vietnam. Decorated Bronze Star, Air medal. Republican. Roman Catholic. Clubs: Univ. (Flint); Flushing Golf. Lodge: Kiwanis. Home: 1020 E Main St Flushing MI 48433 Office: G-4444 W Bristol Rd Flint MI 48507

KELLY, SANDRA ROSEMARY, special education educator; b. Columbia, Miss., Feb. 9, 1956; s. Cephus Moore and Ethel Doretha (Kelly) Brundidge. B.S., Ill. State U., 1977; M.S., Chgo. State U., 1983. Cert. tchr. spl. edn. K-12. Waitress, cashier Faber Enterprises, Chgo., 1971-73; cafeteria worker Walker Hall, Ill. State U., Normal, 1974-75, audio-visual tester, distbr. Univ. Union, 1975-76; pvt. tchr. English and math., Chgo., 1976; mag. phone solicitor Dial Am. Mktg., Chgo., 1977-78; tchr. Chgo. Pub. Schs., 1977—; pvt. tutor, Chgo., 1982; dance choreographer, Chgo., 1982-83; counselor intern psychology dept. Chgo. State U., 1983. Voter registration trainer Panhellenic Community Action Council, Chgo., 1982, chmn., 1983—; organizer Roland Burris campaign, Chgo., 1983. Recipient Civic cert., Near Northwest Civic Community, 1979; Dedicated Service plaque, Hal Jackson Talented Teen Contestants, 1983. Mem. Am. Personnel and Guidance Assn., Nat. Assn. Female Execs., Nat. Employment Counselors Assn., Friends of DuSable Mus. Afro-Am. History (v.p. membership), Sigma Gamma Rho (telethon worker Easter Seal Chgo. 1982). Democrat. Baptist. Home: 7930 S Wabash Apt 1A Chicago IL 60619 Office: Panhellenic Community Action Council Alpha Phi Alpha Fraternity Hdqrs Chicago IL 60653

KELLY, TIMOTHY MICHAEL, computer company executive; b. Rochester, N.Y., Sept. 26, 1953; s. Edward F. and Mary Ellen (Coughlin) K.; m. Sharon Lynn Villa, July 17, 1976. B.S. in Econs., Boston Coll., 1975. Ter. mgr. Burroughs Corp., Rochester, 1975-77; regional mgr. Infortext, Chgo., 1977-79, nat. accounts mgr., 1979-80, nat. sales mgr., 1980-81, exec. v.p., 1981—. Bd. dirs. Youth Football League, Arlington Heights, Ill., 1982. Mem. Am. Mgmt. Assn. Avocations: skiing; youth football. Home: 1110 W Maude Ave Arlington Heights IL 60004 Office: Infortext 1067 E State Pkwy Schaumburg IL 60195

KELLY, TIMOTHY WILLIAM, lawyer; b. Chgo., Apr. 27, 1953; s. George Raymond and Mary Therese (Kelly) K.; m. Mary Teresa Harms, May 24, 1980; 1 child, Ryan Timothy. B.S. in Bus. Adminstrn., U. Dayton, 1975, J.D., 1978. Bar: Ill. 1978, U.S. Dist. Ct. (so. dist.) Ill. 1979. Staff counsel Praire State Legal Aid, Bloomington, Ill., 1978-81; felony asst. McLean County Pub. Defenders, Bloomington, 1981-83; assoc. Jerome Mirza & Assocs., Bloomington, 1983—; asst. prof. polit. sci. Ill. State U., Normal, 1980-83. Bd. dirs. Bloomington/Normal Day Care Assn., 1982-83. Mem. Ill. State Bar Assn., Ill. Trial Lawyers Assn., Assn. Trial Lawyers Assn., Chgo. Bar Assn., McLean County Bar Assn. (sec. 1984-85). Democrat. Roman Catholic. Office: Jerome Mirza & Assocs 705 E Washington St Bloomington IL 61701

KELLY, WILLIAM CODY, lawyer; b. Cin., Mar. 1, 1922; s. Garrard Elliott and Lucy Orr (Gayle) K.; m. Karen Lucile Brown, Dec. 21, 1970; children—Patrick, Shannon, Michael, William Cody; 1 stepson, Marshall Garrison. B.A., Yale U., 1943; LL.B., U. Cin., 1949. Bar: Ohio 1949. Mem. Brooks, Kelly & Barron, Cin., 1954—; pres. Kelly Broadcasting Co., Carson City, Nev., 1970—, Barbuda Devel. Co., Ltd., Antigua, W.I., 1960—, Uppaway Devel. Co., Glenbrook, Nev., 1977—. Councilman City of Cin., 1953-59, vice mayor, 1957-59; chief asst. to chmn. Republican Nat. Com., 1965; chmn. Yale Alumni Fund Class of 1944, 1969-74; mem. Yale Devel. Bd., 1972—. Named Outstanding Young Man of Yr., U.S. Jr. C. of C., 1954. Home: PO Box 135 Glenbrook NV 89143 Office: 1410 Central Trust Tower Cincinnati OH 45202

KELLY, WILLIAM EDWARD, engineering educator; b. June 25, 1942; s. William Adrian and Mary (Barrett) K.; m. Carolyn Young, Sept. 9, 1967; 1 child, Susanna. B.S., U. Notre Dame, 1965, M.S., 1969, Ph.D., 1972. Registered profl. engr., R.I., Nebr. Faculty dept. architecture U. Notre Dame, Rome, 1971; faculty dept. civil engring. U. R.I., Kingston, 1972-76, prof., chmn. dept. civil engring., 1976-82, dir. Water Center, 1980-82; prof. chmn. dept. civil engring. U. Nebr., Lincoln, 1982—; cons. industry and govt., 1974—. Contbr. articles to profl. jours. Mem. Zoning Bd. Review, S. Kingston, R.I., 1978-82. Served to lt. USMC, 1965-67; Viet Nam. Grantee NSF, 1974-78. Mem. ASCE, Am. Geophys. Union. Roman Catholic. Avocations: gardening, tennis. Home: 1490 Plum Ridge Rd Lincoln NE 68257 Office: Dept Civil Engring W 348N NH Lincoln NE 68588

KELLY, WILLIAM EDWARD, lawyer; b. Chgo., Sept. 9, 1938; s. William H. and Edna Mae (Brunner) K.; m. Sarah Ann Mulrey, Apr. 20, 1963; children—William P., John F., Michael A., Brian D. B.B.A. in Accounting, U. Notre Dame, 1961, J.D., 1962. Bar: Ill. 1962, Ind. 1962, U.S. Dist. Ct. (no. dist.) Ind. 1962, U.S. Dist. Ct. (no. dist.) Ill. 1964, U.S. Ct. Appeals (7th cir.) 1963, U.S. Supreme Ct. 1978. Law clk. to chief judge U.S. Dist. Ct., Ind., 1962-64; assoc. Pope, Ballard, Kennedy, Shepard & Fowle, Chgo., 1964-69; ptnr. Pope, Ballard, Shepard & Fowle, Ltd., Chgo., 1970—; special asst. corp. counsel, City of Chgo., 1980; lectr. various law insts. Contbr. articles to profl. jours. Dir. Wilmette United Way, Ill., 1976-78; exec. chmn. Eighth Annual Conv. of Nat. Conf. of Law Reviews, 1962; founding mem. Free Far North Legal Clinic, Chgo. Mem. ABA, Ill. Bar Assn., Chgo. Bar Assn., Seventh Fed. Circuit Bar Assn., Ill. Trial Lawyers Assn., Loyola Acad. Hockey Club, Inc. (dir. 1981—), Wilmette Hockey Assn. (dir. 1976-77). Roman Catholic. Club: University (Chgo.). Office: Pope Ballard Shepard & Fowle Ltd 69 W Washington St Chicago IL 60602

KELMAN, STEPHEN JAY, chiropractor; b. Louisville, Feb. 11, 1944; s. Ben and Billie Ethel (Hark) K.; A.A., U. Louisville, 1968; D.Chiropractic magna cum laude, Palmer Coll. Chiropractic, 1971; m. Delores Sue Callaway, Feb. 11, 1968; children—Jason David, Rachel Leah. Dir., Chiropractic Arts Center, Fort Wayne, Ind., 1971-72; owner, Three Rivers Chiropractic Center, Ft. Wayne, Ind., 1972—Bd. dirs. Allen County chpt. Am. Cancer Soc., 1976-79. Rep., Ft. Wayne Jewish Fedn., 1975-79, 80-81; bd. dirs. N.E. Subarea adv. council No. Ind. Health Systems Agy., 1977-82; bd. dirs. B'nai Jacob Synagogue, 1973-76, 78-79, 80-82, pres. Men's Club, 1978-79; advisor B'nai B'rith Youth Orgn., 1972-79. Served with U.S. Army, 1964-66. Recipient Service awards Ind. State Chiropractic Assn., 1974, 75, 81; Service award B'nai Jacob Synagogue, 1980; Merit award B'nai B'rith Youth Orgn., 1981; Ky. Col. Mem. Am. Chiropractic Assn. (alt. state del. 1977-83), Ky. Assn. Chiropractors, Ky. Chiropractic Soc., Ind. Chiropractic Assn., Inc. (dir. 1973-81, 2d v.p. 1977-78, 1st v.p. 1978-79, pres. 1979-80, sec. 1982-83, chmn. council on ins. 1981-84, peer rev. chmn. 1981—, chiropractor of Yr. award 1982), Allen County Chiropractic Soc. (pres. 1973-75), Palmer Coll. Alumni Assn. Ind. (pres. 1984—), Delta Delta Pi, Pi Tau Delta. Jewish. Lodge: B'nai B'rith. Home: 7408 Kingsway Dr Fort Wayne IN 46809 Office: 3310 E State Blvd Fort Wayne IN 46805

KELPE, SUSAN LOUISE, educator; b. St. Louis, Jan. 12, 1954; d. Robert Fredrick and Doris Jean (Wood) Kelpe. B.S. in Edn., U. Kans., 1976, postgrad., 1981—. Cert. water safety instr. Phys. educator, volleyball coach Old Mission Jr. High Sch., Shawnee Mission, Kans., 1976-79; aquatic specialist, swimming coach Johnson County Park and Recreation, Shawnee Mission, 1979-80; tchr. math., volleyball and basketball coach Shawnee Mission West High Sch., 1980-83, math. tchr., swimming coach, 1980—; pool mgr., swimming program mgr. City of Leawood, Kans., summers, 1976, 77, 78, 79, pool mgr., swimming coach, summer, 1983; asst. coach Kans. City Blazers, Shawnee Mission, 1979—; sponsor Fellowship of Christian Athletes, Kansas City, 1979—. Recipient swimming awards. Mem. Am. Swim Coaches Assn., Nat. Interscholastic Swim Coaches Assn., Nat. Council Math. Tchrs., Kans. Edn. Assn., NEA. Republican. Clubs: K-Club, Spike (Lawrence, Kans.).

KELSO, HAROLD GLEN, physician; b. Newport, Ky., Apr. 1, 1929; s. Harold Glen and Alvina Marie (Hehl) K.; B.S., U. Dayton 1951; M.D., St. Louis U., 1955; m. Janet Rae Cooper, Aug. 12, 1950; children—Harold Glen III, Susan Annette. Intern St. Elizabeth Hosp., Dayton, Ohio, 1955-56; practice medicine specializing in family practice, Centerville, Ohio, 1956—; mem. teaching staff St. Elizabeth Hosp., Dayton, mem. staff Kettering (Ohio) Meml. Hosp., chief staff, 1975-76, now chief dept. family practice; chief staff Sycamore Med. Center, 1978-79; clin. prof. family practice Wright State U.; mem. faculty Kettering Coll. Med. Arts; med. dir. Kettering Convalescent Center. Pres., vice mayor, Centerville, 1960-62; pres. Bd. Edn., Centerville city schs., 1969-72; trustee Western Ohio Found. Med. Care, Kettering Med. Center, Sycamore Med. Center, Engring. and Sci. Hall of Fame, Miami Valley Coalition on Health Care. Served to capt. U.S. Army, 1957-59. Named Ky. Col. Diplomate Am. Bd. Family Practice. Fellow Am. Acad. Family Practice; mem. AMA (del. hosp. med. staff sect.), Ohio (del.), Montgomery County (sec. 1970, pres. 1984) med. assns., Phi Chi. Clubs: Rotary (pres. local club 1974-75, Paul Harris fellow 1979), Dayton Racquet. Home: 2212 E Alex-Bellbrook Rd Centerville OH 45459 Office: 330 N Main St Centerville OH 45459

KELSO, J. RICHARD, utility company executive; b. Student Geneva Coll., U. Pitts. Dir. Ameritrust Co., Ameritrust Corp., Cleve. until 1948; with Peoples Natural Gas Co., 1948-56; gen. sales mgr. Hope Natural Gas Co., 1956-67; asst. v.p. mktg. Consol. Gas Supply Corp., 1967-74; pres. mktg. The Rivers Gas Co., 1974-78; v.p. mktg. East Ohio Gas Co. subs. Consol. Natural Gas Service Co., Cleve., 1978-80, pres.; dir., 1980—. Office: East Ohio Gas Co 1717 E 9th St Cleveland OH 44114*

KELTY, PAUL DAVID, physician; b. Louisville, Oct. 2, 1947; s. William Theadore and Mary Frances (Hinton) K.; m. Connie Darlene Wilkerson, Apr. 16, 1983. B.E.E., U. Louisville, 1970; M.S., Ohio State U., 1971; M.D., U. Louisville, 1978. Mem. tech. staff Bell Labs., Whippany, N.J., 1970-72; design engr. Gen. Electric Co., Louisville, 1972-74; intern St. Mary's Med. Center, Evansville, Ind., 1978-79, resident in ob-gyn, 1979-82; practice medicine, specializing in ob-gyn, Corydon, Ind., 1982—. Mem. AMA, N.Y. Acad. Scis., Sigma Xi, Phi Kappa Phi, Tau Beta Pi, Sigma Tau, Sigma Pi Sigma, Eta Kappa Nu, Gamma Beta Phi, Omicron Delta Kappa. Roman Catholic. Home: 1355 Park Ave NW Corydon IN 47112 Office: 245 Hospital Dr Corydon IN 47112

KELZ, ARNOLD, psychiatrist, hospital administrator; b. N.Y.C., Apr. 15, 1933; s. Benjamin and Florence (Rubin) K.; m. JoAnne Harlow, Dec. 21, 1971; m. 2d Anne Judith Klarman, Apr. 8, 1979. B.S., L.I. U., 1954; D.O., Chgo. Coll. Osteo. Medicine, 1959; M.D., Wash. Coll. Physicians and Surgeons, 1964. Intern Pontiac (Mich.) Osteo. Hosp., 1959-60; resident Northville (Mich.) State Hosp., 1973-75, Lafayette Clinic, Detroit, 1975-76; physician, surgeon Wixom (Mich.) Med. Clinic, 1960-73; med. dir. Bloomfield Psychol. Services, Bloomfield Hills, Mich., 1976-78, Suburban West Community Ctr., Detroit, 1978-80; chief psychiatry Southfield (Mich.) Rehab. Ctr., 1980-82; clin. dir. dept. psychiatry KSB Hosp., Dixon, Ill., 1982—; cons. in field; clin. instr. psychiatry Mich. State U., 1976-78. Fellow Am. Nat. Bd. Psychiatry (life); mem. Am. Osteo. Assn., Am. Psychiat. Assn., Nat. Psychiat. Assn., Ill. Psychiat. Soc., Ill. Med. Soc., AMA, Lee County Med. Soc. Home: 323 Boyd Dixon IL 61021 Office: 403 E First St Dixon IL 61021

KEMP, DANIEL WARREN, lawyer; b. Ironton, Ohio, Oct. 7, 1945; s. Warren Daniel and Evelyn Mary (Ball) K.; m. Judith Elizabeth Renz, Aug. 28, 1965; children—Brian Daniel, Nicole Elizabeth. B.A., Ohio U., 1967; J.D., U. Cin., 1970. Bar: Ohio 1970. Counsel Cin. Gas & Electric Co., 1970-81; asst. counsel Armco Inc., Middletown, Ohio, 1981-84, assoc. counsel, 1985—, Contbr. articles to profl. jours. Mem. ABA, Ohio Bar Assn., Cin. Bar Assn. (com. chmn. 1976-78), Butler County Bar Assn. Republican. Presbyterian. Lodge: Masons. Avocations: outdoor sports. Home: 7879 Ironwood Way West Chester OH 45069 Office: Armco Inc 703 Curtis St Middletown OH 45043

KEMP, HILDA THIGPEN, educator; b. Henderson, N.C., Oct. 16, 1927; d. Zeno E. and Carrie B. (Wilkins) Thigpen; m. Jerahn T. Kemp, June 7, 1952 (div.); children—Jerahn T. III, Jeannette, Jon. B.S., St. Paul's Coll., 1950; M.S., Ind. U., 1970. Tchr., N.C. Pub. Schs., 1951-52, Palmer Inst., Sedalia, N.C., 1952-53, Warrenton, Ga., 1953-55; tchr. Monroe County Community Schs., Bloomington, Ind., 1969—. Mem. NEA, Ind. Tchrs. Assn., Monroe County Edn. Assn., Delta Sigma Theta. Episcopalian. Club: Order Eastern Star. Home: PO Box 1184 Bloomington IN 47402

KEMP, JOHN DANIEL, biotechnology company executive, plant pathology educator; b. Mpls., Jan. 20, 1940; s. Dean Dudley and Catherine Georgia (Treleven) K.; m. Marilyn Irene Mather, Aug. 12, 1961 (div. June 1974); children—Todd A., Christine C., Laura K. B.A., UCLA, 1962, Ph.D., 1965. Chemist Dept. Agr., Madison, Wis., 1968-81; from asst. to assoc. prof. plant pathology U. Wis., Madison, 1968-77, prof., 1977—; head microbiology Agrigenetics, Corp., Madison, 1981-84, dir., 1984—. Contbr. chpts., numerous research articles on plant genetic engring. to profl. publs. Patentee in field. NIH postdoctoral fellow, 1965-67; grantee Dept. Agr., 1968-80, NSF, 1968-80. Mem. Sigma Xi. Club: Mt. Horeb Flying (treas. 1972-75, pres. 1976) (Wis.). Avocations: flying glider, single engine land; commercial balloon flying. Office: Agrigenetics Corp 5649 E Buckeye Rd Madison WI 53716

KEMPE, LLOYD LUTE, chemical engineering and microbiology educator, consultant; b. Pueblo, Colo., Nov. 26, 1911; s. Henry Edwin and Ida Augusta (Pittelkow) K.; m. Barbara Jean Bell, June 27, 1938; 1 child, Marion Louise Kempe Palmer. B.S. in Chem. Engring., U. Minn., 1932, M.S., 1938, Ph.D., 1948. Registered profl. engr., Minn., Mich. Research asst. dept. soils U. Minn., St. Paul, 1934-35, research assoc., 1940-41, teaching asst. chem. engring. dept., Mpls., 1946-48; asst. sanitary engr. Minn. Dept. Health, Mpls., 1935-40; instr. bacteriology U. Mich. Med. Sch., Ann Arbor, 1948-49, asst. prof. bacteriology, 1949-50, asst. prof. chem. engring. and bacteriology, 1952-55, assoc. prof., 1955-58, prof., 1958-60, prof. chem. engring. and sanitary engring., 1960-64, prof. chem. engring., 1964-67, prof. chem. engring., microbiology and immunology, 1967-81, prof. emeritus chem. engring., microbiology and immunology, 1981—; asst. prof. food technology U. Ill.-Urbana, 1950-52; cons. biochem. engring. Upjohn Co., Kalamazoo, 1952-82, Gen. Mills Inc., Mpls., 1955-75, Nat. Sanitation Found., Ann Arbor, 1984. Author books in field, also numerous articles. Served to col. AUS, 1940-46. Decorated Bronze Star. Fellow Am. Inst. Chem. Engrs.; mem. Am. Acad. Environ. Engrs., Water Pollution Control Fedn., Soc. Indsl. Microbiologists, Am. Soc. Microbiology, Inst. Food Technologists, Sigma Xi, Tau Beta Pi, Phi Lambda Upsilon, Alpha Chi Sigma. Republican. Presbyterian. Lodges: Masons, Kiwanis. Home: 3020 Exmoor Ann Arbor MI 48104 Office: Dept Chem Engring U Mich Dow Bldg Ann Arbor MI 48109

KEMPER, DAVID WOODS, II, See *Who's Who in America,* 43rd edition.

KEMPER, JAMES MADISON, JR., See *Who's Who in America,* 43rd edition.

KEMPER, WALKER WARDER, JR., dentist, educator; b. Indpls., Aug. 26, 1924; s. Walker Warder Sr. and Margaret Louise (Mast) K.; m. Janet Morene Cottingham, June 10, 1950 (div. Oct. 1973); children—Walker Warder III, Todd Geller; m. Stephanie Ann Brean, June 24, 1978; stepchildren—Jeffrey L., Michael L., Scott L. B.S., Butler U., 1949; D.D.S., Ind. U., 1953, M.Sci. Dentistry, 1965. Clin. instr. Ind. U., Indpls., 1953-65; practice dentistry specializing in prosthodontics, Indpls., 1953—; dentistry prof., Ind. U., 1979—; chief dental sect. St. Vincent Hosp. and Health Care Ctr., 1976—, exec. com., 1976—; mem. Ind. State Bd. Dental Examiners, 1971-77; dental dir. Marquette Manor Retirement Home, Indpls., 1975—. Active in Ind. U. Century Club, Indpls., 1968—, Butler U. Pres.'s Club, 1966—; bd. dirs. Little Read Door Cancer Soc., 1970-74. Served to staff sgt. USAF, 1943-46. Mem. East African Hunters Assn. (hon.), ADA, John F. Johnston Soc. (pres. 1982, exec. com. 1977—), Ind. State Dental Assn., Indpls. Dist. Dental Assn. (pres. 1970-71), Am. Assn. Dental Examiners, Am. Coll. Dentists, Am. Acad. Crown and Bridge, Am. Acad. Dental Medicine, Safari Club Internat. (pres. 1982-83 Ind. chapt.), Adult Firecrafter, Phi Delta Theta, Omicron Kappa Upsilon, Psi Omega. Republican. Methodist. Clubs: Meridian Hills Country, Columbia (Indpls.). Avocations: big game hunting; fishing; scuba diving; swimming; skiing; golf. Home: 7574 N Morningside Dr Indianapolis IN 46240 Office: 8402 N Harcourt Rd Suite 404 Indianapolis IN 46260

KEMPSON, STEPHEN ALLAN, physiology educator; b. Walsall, Staffordshire, Eng., July 2, 1948. Ph.D., U. London, 1975. Asst. prof. physiology Ind. U. Med. Sch., Indpls., 1982—. Mem. Am. Physiol. Soc., Am. Soc. Nephrology, Am. Soc. Renal Biochemistry and Metabolism. Office: Ind U Med Sch Dept Physiology 635 Barnhill Dr Indianapolis IN 46223

KEMPTHORNE, OSCAR, statistics educator; b. Jan. 31, 1919; s. James T. and Emily F. (Cobeldick) K.; m. Valda M. Scales, June 10, 1949; children—Jill, Joan, Peter. B.A., Cambridge U., Eng., 1940, M.A., 1943, Sc.D., 1960. Statistician Rothamsted Expt. Sta., Eng., 1941-46; assoc. prof. Iowa State U., Ames, 1947-51, prof. stats., 1951—, disting. prof., 1964—. Author: Design and Analysis of Experiments, 1952; Introduction to Genetic Statistics, 1957; Probability, Statistics, and Data Analysis, 1971. Editor: Proceedings of the International Conference on Quantitative Genetics, 1977. Recipient Alumni Assn. Faculty Citation, Iowa State U., Ames, 1977. Fellow Am. Statis. Assn., Inst. Math. Stats. (pres. 1984-85), Am. Statis. Assn. for Advancement Sci., Royal Statis. Soc.; mem. Internat. Statis. Inst. Home: 2020 Ashmore Dr Ames IA 50010 Office: Dept Stats Iowa State U 111A Snedecor Hall Ames IA 50011

KEMPTON, ALAN GEORGE, microbiologist; b. Toronto, Aug. 21, 1932; s. Albert Edward and Velma Pearl (Williams) K.; m. Suzanne Philp, Aug. 13, 1955; children—Alan Scott, Kathryn Suzanne. B.S.A., U. Toronto, 1954, M.S.A., 1956; Ph.D., Mich. State U., 1958. Research officer Agr. Can., Swift Current, Sask., 1958-60; chemist U.S. Army, Natick, Mass., 1960-64; chief bacteriologist Can. Packers Ltd., Toronto, 1964-66; prof. biology U. Waterloo (Ont.), 1966—; cons. food industry. Fellow AAAS; mem. N.Y. Acad. Scis., Soc. Indsl. Microbiology, Can. Soc. Microbiologists, Can. Coll. Microbiologists. Bioadsorption patentee; contbr. articles to profl. jours. Home: 117 Moccasin Dr Waterloo ON N2L 4C2 Canada Office: U Waterloo University Ave Waterloo ON N2L 3G1 Canada

KENDALL, CYNTHIA ELLEN, immunologist, researcher; b. Evansville, Ind., Sept. 14, 1950; d. James William and Jeanette (LaGrange) K.; m. John Allen Wareham, Dec. 11, 1978; 1 child, Scott Douglas. Student Hanover Coll., 1968-70; B.S., Purdue U., 1972; Ph.D., U. Tex.-Austin, 1977. Postdoctoral fellow U. Tex. System Cancer Ctr., Smithville, 1978-80; research assoc. Baylor Coll. Medicine, Houston, 1980-82; research asst. prof. U. Mo., Columbia, 1982—. Patentee Immunoassay employing monoclonal antibody and biotin-avidin detection system, 1982; contbr. articles to profl. jours. U. Mo. Faculty grantee, 1983, COR grantee, 1983-84, 84-85. Mem. Am. Assn. Lab. Animal Sci., Alpha Omicron Pi. Avocations: outdoor activities; hiking; tennis; photography. Home: 4416 Georgetown Dr Columbia MO 65203 Office: U Mo Vet Med Diagnostic Lab Columbia MO 65211

KENDALL, GEORGE PRESTON, SR., retired insurance company executive; b. Seattle, Aug. 11, 1909; s. George R. and Edna (Woods) K.; B.S., U. Ill., 1931; m. Helen A. Hilliard, Sept. 30, 1933; children—George Preston, Thomas C., Helen R. With Washington Nat. Ins. Co., Evanston, Ill., 1931-76, sec., 1950-76, exec. v.p., 1956-62, pres., 1962-67, chmn. bd., 1968-76, also chief exec. officer, dir.; chmn. bd., chief exec. officer, dir. Washington Nat. Corp., 1969-82, dir., hon. chmn., 1982—; dir. State Nat. Bank, Evanston. Served from 2d lt. to 1st lt., inf. AUS, 1942-45. Decorated Purple Heart. Mem. Northwestern U., Assos., Nat. Coll. Edn. Assos., Kendall Fellows of Kendall Coll., Theta Chi. Mason (K.T. Shriner). Clubs: Univ. (Evanston); Westmoreland Country (Wilmette, Ill.); Bankers (Chgo.).

KENDALL, JAMES WILLIAM, manufacturing company executive; b. Ashland, Ky., June 9, 1932; s. J. William and Mary Lee (Wright) K.; m. Mary Ann Smith, June 26, 1955; children—Susan Lupton, Thomas Fairchild, James William, Sally Ann. B.A., DePauw U., Greencastle, Ind., 1954. Bus. mgr. Rev. Pub. Co., Indpls., 1960-62; sales mgr. Elec. Metals Corp., Indpls., 1962-63; asst. advt. mgr. Am. United Life Ins. Co., Indpls., 1963-66; spl. accounts mgr. Arvinyl Div., Arvin Industries, Columbus, Ind., 1966-74, v.p. market devel., 1974-77, v.p., personnel, Metals, 1977—. Bd. dirs. Arvin Found., Columbus, 1978—; vice chmn. S. Central Pvt. Industry Council, 1984-85; pres., bd. dirs. Columbus Visiting. Visitors Series, Columbus, 1978-79, Bartholomew Consol. Sch. Found., Columbus, 1978-79, United Way Bartholomew County, Columbus, 1979-80. Served to 1st lt. USAF, 1955-57. Mem. Adminstrv. Mgmt. Soc., Am. Metal Stamping Assn., Am. Soc. Personnel Adminstrn., Ind. Personnel Assn. Republican. Methodist. Avocations: tennis, sailing, civic activities, reading. Home: 4566 Carya Sq Columbus IN 47201 Office: Arvin Industries Inc 1531 13th St Columbus IN 47201

KENDALL, KENNETH EDWARD, business educator; b. Buffalo, June 12, 1948; s. Edward J. and Julia A. (Bebenek) K.; m. Julie Ellen Tukua, June 11, 1976. B.S., Canisius Coll., 1969; M.B.A., SUNY-Buffalo, 1970, Ph.D., 1974. Research assoc. SUNY-Buffalo, 1972-74; asst. prof. U. Minn., Mpls., 1974-76; U. Wis.-Milw., 1976-78; assoc. prof. mgmt. info. systems U. Nebr., Lincoln, 1978—; cons. ARC, 1969-74, 79—, Milw. Blood Ctr., 1977. Contbr. chpts. to books, articles to profl. jours. Patron, Lincoln Community Playhouse; mem. Sheldon Art Soc., Lincoln; critic U. Nebr. Theatre. Grantee U. Minn., 1975, U. Wis., 1977, U. Nebr., 1981, 83. Mem. Inst. Mgmt. Scis., Ops. Research Soc. Am., Am. Inst. Decision Scis. (publs. com. 1980-82), Soc. Info. and Mgmt., Am. Assn. Blood Banks. Avocations: microcomputers; photography; theatre; flying. Office: U Nebr 255 CBA Lincoln NE 68588

KENDALL, ROBERT LLEWELLYN, contractor; b. Mishawaka, Ind., May 3, 1923; s. Harold E. and Jessie (Pettengill) K.; student pub. schs., Cadillac, Mich.; m. Betty Louise Powers, July 23, 1943; children—Stephen, Jane, Kay, Holly, David, Roberta. Owner, Kendall Constrn. Co., Cadillac, 1945-63, Cadillac Lumber Co.; pres. Robert Kendall, Inc.; v.p. Hungerford Constrn. Co., Jackson, Mich. Mayor, Cadillac, 1953-55; mem. Wexford County Bd. Suprs., County Social Welfare Bd., County and City Planning Bds.; chmn. Bd. Edn., 1948-50; pres. Mich. Extended Care Bldg. Corp.; dir. phys. plant services, mem. adminstrv. staff Chelsea Community Hosp. Served from pvt. to capt. USAAF, 1942-45; ETO. Mem. C. of C. (pres. 1958-60), Am. Soc. Hosp. Engring., Am. Soc. Profl. Cons. Am. Legion. Presbyterian (deacon). Club: Elks. Home: 340 Edward St Jackson MI 49201 Office: Chelsea Community Hosp 775 S Main St Chelsea MI 48110

KENDZIOR, ROBERT JOSEPH, fast food chain marketing executive; b. Chgo., Mar. 24, 1952; s. Joseph W. and Josephine R. Kendzior; B.Arch., Ill. Inst. Tech., 1975. Account supr. Burger King Corp., Rogers Merchandising, Inc., Chgo., 1975-77; account exec. Walgreen Corp., Eisaman, Johns & Laws Advt., Inc., Chgo., 1977-78; dir. mktg. Midwest region, Dunkin' Donuts Am., Inc., Park Ridge, Ill., 1978—. Recipient Most Valuable Promotion award PepsiCo, 1984. Mem. Triangle Fraternity, Chgo. Advt. Club. Home: Glencoe IL 60022 Office: 1550 Northwest Hwy Park Ridge IL 60068

KENNEDY, CHARLES ALLEN, lawyer; b. Maysville, Ky., Dec. 11, 1940; s. Elmer Earl and Mary Frances Kennedy; m. Patricia Ann Louderback, Dec. 9, 1961; 1 child, Mimi Mignon. A.B., Morehead State Coll., 1965, M.A. in Edn., 1968; J.D., U. Akron, 1969; L.L.M., George Washington U., 1974. Bar: Ohio 1969. Asst. cashier Citizens Bank, Felicity, Ohio, 1961-63; tchr. Triway Local Sch. Dist., Wooster, Ohio, 1965-67; with office of gen. counsel Fgn. Agr. and Spl. Programs Div., U.S. Dept. Agr., Washington, 1969-71; ptnr. Kauffman, Eberhart, Cicconetti & Kennedy Co., Wooster, 1972—. Mem. ABA, Fed. Bar Assn., Assn. Trial Lawyers Am., Ohio State Bar Assn., Ohio Acad. Trial Lawyers, Wayne County Bar Assn., Phi Alpha Delta, Phi Delta Kappa. Republican. Club: Exchange (Wooster). Lodges: Lions, Elks. Home: 1770 Burbank Rd Wooster OH 44691 Office: Kauffman Eberhart Cicconetti & Kennedy 517 N Market St Wooster OH 44691

KENNEDY, CHARLES FERGUSON, III, lawyer; b. Van Wert, Ohio, Jan. 31, 1948; s. Edward S. and LuVerne (Jones) K.; m. Jane Louise Elder, July 29, 1967; children—Jill Ann, Michael E., Tyson A. B.A., Bowling Green State U., 1970; M.P.A., U. Okla., 1975; J.D., Ohio No. U., 1979. Bar: Ohio 1979, U.S. Dist. Ct. (no. dist.) Ohio 1980. Assoc. Runser & Hatcher, Van Wert, 1979-82; sole practice, Van Wert, 1982—. Editor Ohio No. Law Rev., 1979. Mem. Regional Planning Commn., Van Wert County, Ohio, 1984—; bd. dirs. Camp Fire, Inc., Van Wert, 1984—. Served to capt. U.S. Army, 1970-76; Vietnam. Mem. Van Wert County Bar Assn., N.W. Ohio Bar Assn., ABA, Ohio Acad. Trial Lawyers, Assn. Trial Lawyers Am., Am. Legion, VFW. Lodges: Kiwanis (bd. dirs. local club), Elks, Moose. Home: Rural Route 4 Box 168 Van Wert OH 45891 Office: C F Kennedy III Co LPA 101 E Main St Van Wert OH 45891

KENNEDY, COLLEEN MARGARET, machine tool company marketing executive; b. Detroit, Oct. 28, 1957; d. John James and Margaret Mary (Healy) K.; m. James Francis Giovanni, July 2, 1983. A. Applied Sci., Schoolcraft Coll., 1977; B.B.A., Wayne State U., 1980; postgrad. Sinclair Coll., 1980-82. Application engr. A&M div. Bendix, Dayton, Ohio, 1980-81, market analyst, 1981-82; product mgr. M&M div. Acme Cleve., West Carrollton, Ohio, 1982—. Vol. Big Bros. and Big Sisters Program, Dayton, 1980-84. Avocations: sports, horticulture, interior design. Home: 1360-30 Black Forest West Carrollton OH 45449 Office: M&M Precision Systems 300 Progress Rd West Carrollton OH 45449

KENNEDY, CORNELIA G., federal judge. U.S. cir. judge U.S. Ct. Appeals Sixth Cir., Mich. Office: US Ct Appeals 744 Federal Bldg Detroit MI 48226*

KENNEDY, DAVID BURL, physician; b. Indpls., Jan. 26, 1950; s. Robert Dean and Esther Evelyn (Stephani) K.; m. Barbara Anne Ehrgott, Jan. 6, 1973; children—Elizabeth Anne, Jeffrey Townsend. B.S., Ind. U., 1972, M.D., 1975. Diplomate Am. Bd. Psychiatry and Neurology. Intern, resident Ind. U. Med. Ctr., Indpls., 1975-78; consulting psychiatrist Psychiat. Clinics of Ind., Anderson, 1977, Four County Mental Health Ctr., Logansport, Ind., 1980—; staff psychiatrist Regional Mental Health Ctr., Kokomo, Ind., 1978-80; pres. David B. Kennedy, M.D., Inc. and Kennedy Clinics, Indpls. and Kokomo, 1980—; asst. clin. prof. psychiatry Ind. U. Sch. Medicine, Indpls., 1978—; mem. adv. bd. Profl. Communications, Inc., Teaneck, N.J., 1984. Mem. AMA, Ind. State Med. Assn., Marion County Med. Soc., Am. Psychiat. Assn., Ind. Psychiat. Soc., Phi Beta Kappa. Club: Columbia (Indpls.). Avocations: boating; computers. Office: 4954 E 56th St Indianapolis IN 46220

KENNEDY, DAVID DEE, conservation executive; b. Metropolis, Ill., Sept. 5, 1938; s. David Deskin and Hazel (Yost) K.; m. Susan Knupp, Aug. 12, 1961; children—Jodie, John David. Assoc. Tech., So. Ill. U., 1959, B.A., 1962, M.S., 1972. Area mgr. Ind. Dept. Natural Resources, Howe, 1963-65; refuge supr. and staff biologist Ill. Dept. Conservation, Anna, 1965-75, dir. bur. natural resources, 1975-76; regional dir. and supr. Ducks Unlimited, Inc., Long Grove, Ill., 1976-83, field ops. supr., 1983—. Author: A Waterfowl Hunters Guide to Illinois, 1973; In Search of the Canada Goose, 1974. Served with U.S. Army, 1962-63. Mem. Wildlife Soc. Avocations: running; hunting. Home: Route 2 Box 401 Anna IL 62906 Office: Ducks Unlimited Inc 1 Waterfowl Way Long Grove IL 60047

KENNEDY, GENE V, lobbyist; b. Merrill, Iowa, Oct. 28, 1927; s. Eugene Michael and Lillian Irene (Banks) K.; m. Dorothy Evelyn Sell, May 21, 1952; children—Candace, Michael, Mary, Theresa, Patrick, Diana, Maurreen, Edward. B.A., Loras Coll., 1948. Hwy. patrolman, Iowa, 1950-54; ind. ins. adjustor, Crocker Claims Service, Omaha, 1954-70; state rep. Dubuque, Iowa, 1968-70; state senator, Iowa, 1970-74; lobbyist Des Moines, 1974—. Asst. floor leader Senate, Des Moines, 1972-74; chmn. Schaben for Gov., Des Moines, 1974; Iowa campaign mgr. Shriver for Pres., 1976. Democrat. Roman Catholic. Avocations: golf, fishing. Home and Office: 912 11th St West Des Moines IA 50265

KENNEDY, GEORGE DANNER, natural resource company executive; b. Pitts., May 30, 1926; s. Thomas Reed and Lois (Smith) K.; student Williams Coll., 1947; m. Valerie Putis; children—Charles Reed, George Danner, Jamey Kathleen, Susan Patton, Timothy Christian. With Scott Paper Co., 1947-52, Champion Paper Co., 1952-65; exec. v.p. Brown Co., 1965-71, also dir.; exec. v.p. Internat. Minerals & Chem. Corp., Northbrook, Ill., 1971-78, pres., 1978—, chief exec. officer, 1983—, also dir.; dir. Brunswick Corp., Kemper Corp. Chmn. bd. dirs. Children's Meml. Hosp., Chgo.; trustee Orch. Soc. of Chgo. Symphony; mem. Chgo. Com.; mem. bus. adv. council Grad. Sch. Indsl. Adminstrn., Carnegie-Mellon U., Pitts.; bd. dirs. Chgo. Council Fgn. Relations, Northeast Ill. council Boy Scouts Am. Served with U.S. Navy. Mem. Econs. Club Chgo., Chgo. Assn. Commerce and Industry (bd. dirs.). Clubs: N.Y. Athletic, Bd. Room (N.Y.C.); Sle.py Hollow Country (Scarborough N.Y.); Larchmont (N.Y.) Yacht; Skokie Country (Glencoe, Ill.); Commercial of Chgo. Office: 2315 Sanders Rd Northbrook IL 60062

KENNEDY, GEORGE EDWARD, marketing executive; physical therapist; b. Scottsbluff, Nebr., Nov. 10, 1951; s. George Elmer and Patricia Jean (Carpenter) K.; m. Mary Lou Kinsinger, June 7, 1975; 1 child, Sarah Marie. A.S., Nebr. Western Coll., 1972; B.S., Chadron State Coll., 1974; cert. in phys. therapy U. Iowa, 1975. Cert. profl. phys. therapist, Ind., Iowa, Ky., Mich., Oreg. staff phys. therapist Restorative Services, Inc., Hobart, Ind., 1975-76, chief phys. therapist, 1976-79, dir. ops., 1979-83, v.p. and chief mktg. exec., 1984—. Mem. adv. bd. Upjohn Home Health Agency, Hammond, Ind., 1984—. Mem. Am. Phys. Therapy Assn. (bd. dirs. Ind. chpt. 1984—, jus. com. chmn. 1984). Republican. Lutheran. Clubs: Jr. Investment (Merrillville, Ind.) (pres. 1981-82), Gary Country (Ind.). Home: 6334 Hayes St Merrillville IN 46410

KENNEDY, JOHN A., company executive; b. Chgo., Apr. 22, 1918; s. James A. and Mary Agnes (Casey) K.; married; children—Patrick M., Mary Agnes, Kathleen, James M. A.S. SUNY-Albany, 1980; B.S. in Engring., Calif. Coast U., 1983, M.S. in Engring., 1984. Cert. and explosion investigator. Prin. John A. Kennedy & Assocs., Chgo., 1955—; pres. Investigation Inst., Chgo., 1960—; instr., cons. in field; condr. fire tng. schs. and seminars for city, state and fed. govtl. agys. at numerous univs., cities and fire depts. throughout the U.S., also conducted seminars and tng. for fire dept. Caracas, Venezuela; expert photographer on fires and explosions; expert ct. hearings witness in field of fire and explosion investigations; determination of their cause and origin; established and popularized system for tracing fire to its source; conducted numerous experiments in field. Author: Fire Investigating, 1955, Fire and Arson Investigation, 1962, Fire, Arson and Explosion Investigation, 1977; Determination of Cause and Origin of Fires and Explosions, 1985. Contbr. articles to profl. jours. Served to comdr. USNR, 1941-78, ret. Fellow Am. Assn. Forensic Scitists.; mem. Am. Assn. Criminology (hon. life, chmn. fire com.), Nat. Assn. Fire Investigators (charter mem., pres. 19—), Nat. Fire Protection Assn., Spl. Agts. Assn. (pres. 1962, bd. dirs.). Roman Catholic. Avocation: photography. Office: 53 W Jackson Blvd Chgo IL 60604

KENNEDY, MARGARET ANN, music store executive; educator; b. Terre Haute, Ind., Oct. 31, 1946; d. Billy Carter and Virginia Belle (Zerweck) Riley; m. John Leslie Kennedy; children—Kathleen, Rebecca. B.S., Ind. State U., 1969, M.S., 1973. Cert. tchr., Ind. English tchr. Mooresville Consol. Sch. Corp., Ind., 1969-75; substitute tchr. Brownsburg Community Sch. Corp., Ind., 1976, 82-83; writer, editor, co-owner Community Mag., Brownsburg, 1984; bus. mgr., co-owner Edn. Arts Ctr., Brownsburg, 1983-85, Main St. Music Store, Brownsburg, 1984—; bus. mgr., tchr. After Sch. Program, Brownsburg, 1984—. Precinct committeeman Democratic Party, Lincoln Twp., Hendricks County, 1975-82, state conv. del., 1978, 80; bd. dirs. Youth Variety Festival, Brownsburg, 1979-81; pub. relations dir. Brownsburg Halloween House, 1979—, Indpls. Zoo Guild, 1980-83; bus. mgr. Brownsburg Players, 1982-83. Recipient Best Marching Unit award Brownsburg Lion's Club, 1979, Outstanding Performance award Pittsboro July 4 Com., 1980, Best Performance award Plainfield Merchant's Assn., 1980. Mem. Brownsburg C. of C., AAUW. Lutheran. Avocations: piano; violin; mandolin; theatre; needlecraft. Home: 27 Southridge Dr Brownsburg IN 46112 Office: Main St Music Store 24 W Main St Brownsburg IN 46112

KENNEDY, MARY ELLEN, librarian, educator; b. Pitts., Feb. 28, 1939; d. Joseph Michael and Stella Marie (Kane) K.; B.A., Villa Maria Coll., 1961; M.L.S., U. Pitts., 1970, Ph.D., 1980. Tchr., Pitts. Catholic Schs., 1962-65; tchr., Anne Arundel County Schs., Annapolis, 1965-67; legal sec., firm Joseph M. Kennedy, Pitts., 1967-70; cataloger Newport News (Va.) Library System, 1970-71; reference librarian Glenville (W.Va.) State Coll., 1971-80; asst. prof. library sci. Ball State U., Muncie, Ind., 1980-83; reference librarian, asst. prof. Purdue U., West Lafayette, Ind., 1983—. Sec. women Glenville Presbyn. Ch., 1973-74, pres., 1974-76, bd. deacons, 1979-80; chmn. library com. Presbyn. Ch. Muncie, 1981—; mem. belle com. W.Va. Folk Festival, 1973-80. Recipient Title III advanced study grant, 1977-78. Mem. ALA (reference books rev. com. 1979-82), Ind. Library Assn., Spl. Libraries Assn., Assn. Coll. and Research Libraries, Assn. Ind. Media Educators, Assn. Am. Library Schs., AAUW (corr. sec. 1981-82), Delta Kappa Gamma, Sigma Sigma Sigma. Democrat. Home: 203 Montefiore Dr Apt 218 Lafayette IN 47905 Office: HSSE Library Purdue Univ West Lafayette IN 47907

KENNETT, KEVIN LEE, corporate controller; b. Midland, Mich., Aug. 16, 1956; s. Wilbur W. and Bonnie H. (Horman) K.; m. Ilisapesi Maafu, July 15, 1982; B.B.A., U. Mich., 1978. Sales assoc. Calcomp, Chgo., 1978-80; bus. advisor Peace Corps, Kingdom of Tonga, 1980-82; acctg. tchr. Mailefihi High Sch., Varau, Tonga, 1982, U. of S. Pacific, 1981; corp. controller Pendell Printing, Inc., Midland, Mich., 1983—. Republican campaign vol., Midland, 1983-84. Presbyterian. Club: Varau Tennis. Avocations: duplicate bridge; tennis; personal robots. Home: 2311 Alta Ct Midland MI 48604 Office: Pendell Printing Inc 1700 James Savage Rd Midland MI 48604

KENNEY, CHARLES SAMUEL, lawyer; b. Bay City, Mich., July 26, 1917; s. Samuel Charles and Kathern C. (McClellan) K.; B.C.S., Cleary Coll., 1937; B.S., Eastern Mich. U., 1940; J.D., Wayne State U., 1951; m. Ellen G. Hilbert, Oct. 8, 1944; children—Barbara (Mrs. William M. Silvis), Peter C., William S., Scott S. Admitted to Mich. bar, 1952; tchr. Woodland (Mich.) High Sch., 1940-42; auditor Mich. State Accident Fund, 1945-52; partner firm Archer, Kenney, & Wilson, Dearborn, Mich., 1952—. Pres., Western Wayne Homeowners Assn., 1966, Woodland Tchrs. Assn., 1941. Served with U.S. Army, 1942-45. Mem. Dearborn (pres. 1965), Mich., Am. bar assns., Am. Coll. Probate Counsel, Delta Theta Phi. Presbyn. (deacon 1972—). Home: 8909 Beck Rd Plymouth MI 48170 Office: 20390 W Outer Dr Dearborn MI 48124

KENNEY, ESTELLE KOVAL, artist; b. Chgo., Feb. 15, 1928; d. Hyman English and Florence (Browman) Koval; B.F.A., Art Inst. Chgo., 1976, M.F.A., 1978; postgrad. Yale U., 1980; m. Herbert Kenney, Feb. 6, 1948; children—Carla, Robert. Art therapist Grove Sch., Lake Forest, Ill., 1973-78, New Trier High Sch. and Central High Sch., Winnetka, Ill., 1978-79, Mosely Sch., Chgo., 1979, Cove Sch., Evanston, Ill., 1979-82; dir. art therapy concentration, instr. painting and drawing Loyola U., Chgo., 1981—; v.p., art dir. Nuts on Clark Inc., Chgo.; one woman shows: Evanston (Ill.) Library, 1971, Zaks Gallery, Chgo., 1977, 79, 82, Renaissance Soc.-Bergman Gallery, U. Chgo., 1980; group shows include: Ill. State Mus., 1975, Women Artists, Here and Now, 1976, Chgo. Connections travelling exhbn., 1976-77, Nat. Women's Caucus for Art, 1977, Nancy Lurie Gallery, 1978, Marycrest Coll. Gallery, Davenport, Iowa, 1982, Chgo. Internat. Art Expo, 1981, 82, 83, Notre Dame U. Gallery, South Bend, Ind., 1982; represented in permanent collections: Ill. State Mus., Springfield, Union League Club of Chgo. Mem. Am. Art Therapy Assn., Ill. Art Therapy Assn. (pres. 1979—), Coll. Art Assn. Home: 3830 N Clark St Chicago IL 60613 Office: Loyola University of Chicago Dept Fine Arts 6525 N Sheridan Rd Chicago IL 60626

KENT, HOMER AUSTIN, JR., seminary and college president, clergyman; b. Washington, Aug. 13, 1926; s. Homer Austin and Alice Ethel (Wogaman) K.; m. Beverly Jane Page, Aug. 1, 1953; children—Rebecca, Katherine, Daniel. B.A. cum laude, Bob Jones U., 1947; B.D. summa cum laude, Grace Theol Sem., 1950, Th. M., 1952, Th. D., 1956. Ordained to ministry Fellowship of Grace Brethren Ch., 1951. Prof. Grace Theol. Seminary, Winona Lake, Ind., 1951—, dean, 1962-76, pres. Grace Theol Seminary and Grace Coll., 1976—; cons. New Internat. Version com. on Bible translation, 1967-73; moderator Fellowship of Grace Brethren Chs., 1983; dir. Lake City Bank, Warsaw, Ind. Author: A Heart Opened Wide: Studies in II Corinthians, 1982; Treasures in Wisdom: Studies in Colossians and Philemon., 1978; The Freedom of God's Sons: Studies in Galatians, 1976; Light in the Darkness; Studies in the Gospel of John, 1974; Jerusalem to Rome: Studies in the Book of Acts, 1972; The Pastoral Epistles, 1958. Mem. Evang. Theol. Soc. (chmn. Midwestern sect. 1970), Near East Archeol. Soc., Chamber of Commerce Warsaw. Lodge: Kiwanis. Avocations: philately, photography. Home: 305 6th St Winona Lake IN 46590 Office: Grace Theol Seminary and Coll 200 Seminary Dr Winona Lake IN 46590

KENT, ROLLIN MICHAEL, newspaper editor; b. Lebanon, Ind., May 8, 1945; s. Stanley Roy and Frances Anne (English) K.; m. Janet K. Prather, Sept. 15, 1972 (div. 1975); 1 child, Keri; m. Mary Ellen Lawler, Jan. 21, 1979; children—Robert, Christopher, Lisa. B.S., Butler U.; postgrad., Ind. U. Asst. mng. editor The Collegian, Butler U., Indpls., 1965-67; copy editor Post-Tribune, Gary, Ind., 1967, news editor. Editor: The American Middle-Sized City, 1978. Bd. dirs., treas. Valparaiso (Ind.) Jaycees, 1974-77. Indpls. News scholar, 1964. Mem. Sigma Delta Chi. Office: The Post Tribune 1065 Broadway St Gary IN 46383

KENT DONAHUE, LAURA, state senator; b. Quincy, Ill., Apr. 22, 1949; d. Laurence S. and Mary Lou (McFarland) Kent; m. Michael A. Donahue, July 16, 1983. B.A. in Phys. Edn., Stephens Coll., 1971. Mem. Ill. Senate, 1981—minority spokesman pub. health, welfare, corrections com., mem. agr., conservation and energy com. Mem. Ill. Fedn. Republican Women, Am. Legis. Exchange Council, P.E.O. Club: Lincoln of Adams County (Ill.); Altrusa (Quincy). Methodist. Office: State Senate Dist Office 400 Maine St Quincy IL 62301

KENYON, CHARLES KYLE, JR., lawyer; b. Tomah, Wis., June 24, 1953; s. Charles Kyle and Xena Burnette (Cade) K.; m. Debra B. Schroeder, Dec. 30, 1977. B.A., U. Wis.-Madison, 1975, J.D., 1978, postgrad. in bus., 1977-80. Bar: Wis. 1979, U.S. Dist. Ct. (we. dist.) Wis. 1979. Ptnr. Winslow & Kenyon, Madison, 1980-81; assoc. Kenyon Law Offices, Tomah, 1981—; instr. in bus. law Western Wis. Tech. Inst., Tomah, 1982—. Mem. ABA, Assn. Trial Lawyers Am., Wis. Acad. Trial Lawyers, Monroe County Bar Assn. (sec.-treas. 1984-85), Tomah Jaycees (v.p. 1983-85), Phi Alpha Delta (justice 1979-80), Beta Alpha Psi. Home: PO Box 263 Tomah WI 54660

KEPKA, DOUGLAS JOSEPH, advertising executive; b. Ellsworth, Kans., Jan. 26, 1948; s. Leo Joseph and Betty Jean (Andreasen) K.; m. Honor Louise Fiddler, June 9, 1973; children—Beth Anne, Thomas Christopher. B.S., Ft. Hays State U., 1970. Tchr. art St. John (Kans.) High Sch., 1972-73; drill press operator, fluid power div. Cessna, Inc., Hutchinson, Kans., 1973-74; gen. assignment reporter Ellsworth (Kans.) Reporter, 1974-75; pub. Chase (Kans.) Index, 1975-77; advt. rep. Great Bend (Kans.) Tribune, 1978-81; advt. dir. G.E. Stockton, Inc., Gt. Bend, 1981-84; advt. mgr. Broken Arrow Scout, Tulsa, 1984—; tchr. advt. Barton County Community Coll., 1984—. Mayor, City of Chase, 1977-79; precinct committeeman Lincoln Twp.; Rice County coordinator John Carlin for Gov., 1979; Barton County co-coordinator for Gov. Carlin, 1982. Democrat. Roman Catholic. Home: 1813 S 7th St Broken Arrow OK 74012 Office: 8545 E 41st St Tulsa OK 74145

KEPLEY, BENJAMIN FRANKLIN, oral and maxillofacial surgeon, educator; b. Detroit, June 20, 1937; s. Benjamin Franklin and Martha Mae (Crawford) K.; m. Sandra Lee Basch, Sept. 11, 1961; children—Franklin Kyle, Damon Kirk. D.M.D., U. Louisville, 1962. Diplomate Am. Bd. Oral and Maxillofacial Surgery. Asst. dir. oral and maxillofacial surgery residency program Naval Hosp., Oakland, Calif., 1976-79, chief of dental service, Pensacola, Fla., 1979-82; clinic dir. Naval Dental Clinic, San Diego, 1982-84; dir. oral and maxillofacial surgery residency program Naval Hosp., Great Lakes, Ill., 1984—; cons. Loyola U., Chgo., 1984—, VA Hosp., North Chicago, 1984—. Recipient Humanitarian medal U.S. Navy, 1976, Fellow Am. Assn. Oral and Maxillofacial Surgeons, Internat. Coll. Dentists; mem. Am. Dental Soc. of Anesthesiology, ADA, Ky. Dental Assn. Avocations: phys. fitness; golf. Home: 1213 Green Tree Ct Libertyville IL 60048 Office: Oral Surgery Dept Naval Hosp Great Lakes IL 60088

KEPNER, JAMES LEE, mathematics educator, researcher, consultant; b. Chgo., May 10, 1943; s. Robert Franklin and Mary E. (Durbin) K.; m. Barbara Ellen Johnson, Aug. 21, 1965; children—Diane Lynn, Jennifer Lynn. B.S. in Math., Ill. State U., 1965, M.S. in Math., 1968; M.S. in Math. Stats., U. Iowa, 1976, Ph.D., in Math. Stats., 1979. Instr. math. Ill. Central Coll., East Peoria. Ill., 1968-69, Kirkwood Community Coll., Cedar Rapids, Iowa, 1969-75; grad. asst. U. Iowa, Iowa City, 1975-79; asst. prof. stats. U. Fla., Gainesville, 1979-83; assoc. prof. math. St. Cloud State U., Minn., 1983—; cons. Nat. Assn. Coll. Admissions Officers, 1983-85, City of Albany, Minn., 1983-85, City of Little Falls, Minn., 1984-85; mem. Joint Com. on Curriculum in Stats. and Probability, Am. Statis. Assn. and Nat. Council Tchrs. Math., 1985-87. Contbr. articles to profl. jours. Mem. ch. council Univ. Luth. Ch., Gainesville, Fla., 1981-83, treas. 1982-83; treas. Salem Luth. Ch., St. Cloud, Minn., 1984—; treas. Butternut Condominium Assn., Balsam Lake, Wis., 1984—. Mem. Am. Statis. Assn., Inst. Math. Stats., Nat. Council Tchrs. Math. Avocations: studying stats.; boating; swimming; fishing; ice skating. Home: Route 2 Saint Cloud MN 56301 Office: Dept Math and Computer Sci St Cloud State U Saint Cloud MN 56301

KEPPLER, JAMES GEORGE, nuclear regulation administrator; b. Syracuse, N.Y., Mar. 19, 1934; s. Harold George and Genevieve Velma (Parrott) K.; m. Marietta Estelle Farrell, Oct. 6, 1956; children—James R., Timothy J., Melinda J. B.S. in Physics, LeMoyne Coll., 1956. Reactor physicist Gen. Electric Co., Cin., 1956-61, San Jose, Calif., 1961-65; reactor insp. AEC, Chgo., 1965-67, br. chief, Bethesda, Md., 1967-73; regional dir. U.S. Nuclear Regulation Commn., Chgo., 1973-81, regional adminstr., 1981—. Recipient Presdl. Meritorious award, Washington, 1982. Roman Catholic. Avocation: golf. Office: US Nuclear Regulatory Commission 799 Roosevelt Rd Glen Ellyn IL 60137

KER, (ALICE) ANN STEELE, music educator, composer, organist, choir director; b. Warsaw, Ind., Nov. 10, 1937; d. George Arthur and Winifred Pauline (Foster) Steele; m. Charles Arthur Ker, Sept. 8, 1957 (div.); children—Kelly Lynne, Karen Elizabeth, Kristin Ann. Student DePauw U., 1955-57, Butler U., 1957-58; B.M.E., Ind. U., 1974; postgrad. Notre Dame U. Organist, 1st Presbyn. Ch., Warsaw, 1969-79; dir. music Central Christian Ch., Huntington, Ind., 1980; mem. faculty Huntington Coll., 1975—; dir. music Redeemer Lutheran Ch., Warsaw, 1980—; festival condr. Luth. Circuit Festival Chorus; co-founder, bd. mem. No. Ind. Opera Assn.; mem. Lakeland Community Concert Assn., concert critic, bd. mem., 1976-80. Active Kosciusko Community Hosp. Aux., 1975—. Winner 1st place composition competition St. Francis Coll., 1974. Mem. Internat. League Women Composers, Am. Guild Organists (dir. 1978-81), Am. Choral Dirs. Assn., Nat. Guild Piano Tchrs., Am. Musicol. Soc., Music Tchrs. Nat. Assn., Women in Music. Republican. Lutheran. Compositions include: Hear This!, 1973; Triptych, 1980; Three Men on Camelback, 1982; One Glorious God, 1982; For Me, O Lord, 1983; Softly, 1983; Ways to Praise, 1983; The House of the Lord, 1984. Home: 1607 N Springhill Rd Warsaw IN 46580 Office: Music Dept Huntington Coll Huntington IN 46750

KERAN, DOUGLAS CHARLES, natural resources consultant, educator; b. Mpls., Nov. 12, 1943; s. Philip Leroy and Charlotte Virginia (Hoaglund) K.; m. Julie Doris Godtland, May 12, 1979; children—Douglas, Kevin, Shane, Brianna. B.S., U. Minn., 1965; M.A., St. Cloud U., 1976. Researcher, U. Minn. Cedar Creek Natural History Area, 1964-65; dir. Crow Wing Natural History Area, Brainerd, Minn., 1969-73; instr. fisheries and wildlife Brainerd Area Vocat. Tech. Inst., 1973—; pres. Kerdolian, Inc., Brainerd, 1981—, wildlife cons., 1980—; night sch. instr. Brainerd Vocat. Tech. Inst., 1973—. Served with USCG, 1965-69. Named Outstanding Reservist in Minn., Res. Forces Component, 1972; Profl. Environ. Quality award, 1984; Minn. Nongame Wildlife Program grantee, 1982—. Mem. Nat. Wildlife Soc., Raptor Research Found., N. Central Wildlife Soc., Minn. Wildlife Soc., Kestrel Karetakers, Am. Fisheries Soc., Minn. Ornithological Union, Minn. Wildlife Assistance Coop. Lutheran. Club: Bee Nay She Council (Brainerd). Contbr. articles to profl. jours. Home: Route 7 Box 14 Brainerd MN 56401 Office: 300 Quince St Brainerd MN 56401

KERBER, CHARLES, farm supply company executive. Pres. Ind. Farm Bur. Coop. Assn. Inc., Indpls., also dir. Office: Ind Farm Bur Coop Assn Inc 120 E Market St Indianapolis IN 46204*

KEREK, KATHY ZABKAR, technical writer; b. Berea, Ohio, July 9, 1957; d. Edward A. and Elizabeth (Gazdik) Zabkar; m. Wayne Lewis Kerek, Aug. 30, 1980; 1 dau., Amber Elizabeth. Student Bowling Green State U., 1975-77; B.A., Baldwin-Wallace Coll., 1979. C.P.A., Ohio. Acctg. intern AmeriTrust, Cleve., 1978; acctg. systems coordinator Parker-Hannifin Corp., Cleve., 1979-80; systems sr. tech. writer Ernst & Whinney, Cleve., 1980—. Mem. Ohio Soc. C.P.A.s (assoc.). Avocations: swimming; aerobics; cooking; piano; ballet. Office: Ernst & Whinney 2000 National City Ctr Cleveland OH 44114

KERES, KAREN LYNNE, English educator; b. Evanston, Ill., Oct. 22, 1945; d. Frank and Bette (Pascoe) K.; B.A., St. Mary's Coll., 1967; student U. Notre Dame, 1967-68; M.A., U. Iowa, 1969. Asst. to editor U. Chgo. Press, 1968; assoc. prof. English lit., composition William Rainey Harper Coll., Palatine, Ill., 1969—; cons. bus. communications. Mem. MLA, Ill. Assn. Tchrs. English, Am. Fedn. Tchrs., Nature Conservancy. Home: 222 Fairfield Dr Island Lake IL 60042 Office: Dept Liberal Arts William Rainey Harper Coll Palatine IL 60067

KERICH, JAMES PATRICK, manufacturing company executive; b. Wichita, Kans., May 25, 1938; s. Bernard William and Helen Marie (Hendrickson) K.; m. Julia Jean Grosjean, June 28, 1958; children—Marie Suzanne, Julie Ann, Wendy Kathryn. Student Kans. U. Dir. ops. Skyline Corp., Elkhart, Ind., 1974-79, v.p., officer, 1982—; pres. ON TV, Detroit, 1979-81; sports negotiator, cons., investor Pay TV, Chgo., Detroit and Dallas, 1981-82; cons. Buford TV, Chgo., 1981, Golden West Broadcasting, Los Angeles, 1981. Republican. Roman Catholic. Clubs: South Bend Country; Sugar Mill Country (New Smyrna Beach, Fla.). Lodge: Elks. Home: 1525 Greenleaf Blvd Elkhart IN 46514 Office: Skyline Corp 2520 By Pass Rd Elkhart IN 46514

KERLAGON, RAYMOND LEE, telephone company executive; b. St. Louis, Dec. 15, 1945; s. Lawrence Raymond and Lola Louise (Isgrig) K.; A. Sci.-and Commerce in Econs., St. Louis U., 1971, M.B.A., 1976; B.S. in Bus. Adminstrn., Washington U., 1974; m. Jane Arlene Schnurer, Nov. 6, 1965; children—Sherri Lynn, Michael James. Spl. rep. Southwestern Bell Telephone Co., St. Louis, 1965-69, communications cons., 1977, phone power specialist, 1977, account exec., 1977-79, staff specialist promotions and motivation, 1979-80, industry mgr., 1980-81, staff mgr. competitive tactics, 1981, staff mgr. sales devel., 1981—; field sales rep. Xerox Corp., 1969-72; sr. customer service rep. Monsanto, 1972-74, voice communications analyst, 1974-76; zone mgr. Ford Motor Co., 1976-77; adj. prof. Meramec Community Coll.; faculty investments and fin. mgmt. Webster U. Troop capt. Greater St. Louis council Girl Scouts U.S.A., 1974; mem. curriculum adv. com. St. Louis Community Coll., 1983—; asst. mgr. Ballwin Baseball, 1980-82. Recipient Dist. Profl. award Southwestern Bell, 1979. Mem. Nat. Assn. Securities Dealers. Baptist. Contbr. to profl. jours. and booklets. Home: 15494 Strollways Dr Chesterfield MO 63017 Office: 1625 Des Peres Suite 404 Saint Louis MO 63131

KERLEY, RICHARD ALLEN, radiology technologist, administrator; b. Dixon, Ill., Dec. 13, 1947; s. Thoy D. and Phyllis I. (Gallentine) K.; m. Rita Louise McDonnell, Mar. 20, 1976; children—Kathryn Lynn, Richard Allen, Sean Edward. A.A.S., Sauk Valley Coll., 1970; postgrad. Triton Coll., Western Mich. U., 1980—, DePaul U., 1969-70. Cert. Am. Registry Radiologic Tech. Staff technician Rockford (Ill.) Meml. Hosp., 1970; staff technician Community Gen. Hosp., Sterling, Ill., 1973-78, adminstrv. dir. radiology, 1978—; clin. dir. and cons. Sauk Valley Coll. Bd. dirs. Ch. of Brethern, 1982—. Served to lt. (j.g.) USN, 1971. Mem. Am. Soc. Radiologic Technologists, Ill. State Soc. Radiologic Technologists, Am. Hosp. Radiology Adminstrs., Am. Fedn. Musicians. Club: Optomists. Office: Community Gen Hosp 1601 1st Ave Sterling IL 61081

KERN, LILLIAN MURPHY, judge; b. N.Y.C., Sept. 9, 1931; d. Martin and Elizabeth Murphy; m. Thomas W. Kern. A.B. cum laude, U. Miami, Fla., 1951; J.D., U. Cin., 1964. Bar: Ohio, U.S. Dist. Ct. (so. dist.) Ohio, U.S. Ct. Appeals (6th cir.), U.S. Supreme Ct. 1971. Sole practice, Dayton, Ohio, 1964-76; asst. pros. atty. Montgomery County, Ohio, 1966-76; chief to Civil Div. Office of Pros. Atty., Ohio, 1971-76; judge Div. Domestic Relations, Common Pleas Ct., Dayton, 1977—. Trustee, Buckeye Trails council Girl Scouts U.S.A.; mem. Kidney Found. of Miami Valley. Served to lt. USN, 1954-57. Recipient 304 award Big Brothers and Big Sisters; Ten Top Women Contest Judges award, 1978; Superior Service award Supreme Ct. Ohio, 1981, 82. Mem. ABA, Ohio Bar Assn., Dayton Bar Assn., Nat. Assn. Women Judges, Nat. Council Juvenile Ct. Judges, Assn. Women Execs. Republican. Roman Catholic. Club: Altrusa. Office: Montgomery County Common Pleas Ct Div Domestic Relations 303 W 2nd St Dayton OH 45422

KERN, THOMAS LEE, manufacturing company executive; consultant; b. Cleve., July 23, 1946; s. Elroy J. and Carol L. (Scheuerman) K.; m. Dorothy Weitzel, Jan. 27, 1967; children—Michelle, Lynette, Bryan, Christine. B.S.B.A., Bowling Gren State U., 1968. Machinist, Hartland Machine, Norwalk, Ohio, 1962-66; machinist-assembler Printainer Corp., Norwalk, 1966-68; gen. foreman Clevite Corp., Milan, Ohio, 1968-69, indsl. engr., 1969-70; v.p., gen. mgr. Poly-Foam Internat., Fremont, Ohio, 1970-72, pres., chief exec. officer, 1972—; ptnr. Hartland Auto Stores, Clyde, Ohio, 1973—; pres. Top Distbrs., Clyde, 1978—; dir. PFI Transport, Fremont. Recipient W. C. Coleman award Coleman Co., Wichita, Kans., 1983. Mem. Warehouse Distbrs. Assn. Republican. Presbyterian. Home: 179 Saint Thomas Dr Fremont OH 43420 Office: Poly Foam Internat Inc 600 Hagerty Dr Fremont OH 43420

KERN, TIMOTHY LYNN, lawyer; b. Valparaiso, Ind., Sept. 21, 1956; s. Harold Isaac and Dorothy (Gerken) K. B.A., Valparaiso U., 1978, J.D., 1981. Bar: Ind. 1981. Dep. pros. atty. Tippecanoe County Prosecutor's Office, Ind., 1981—. Exec. editor Valparaiso U. Law Rev., 1980-81. Ind. Bar Found. scholar Valparaiso U. Sch. Law, 1980. Mem. Ind. State Bar Assn., ABA, Assn. Trial Lawyers Am. Democrat. Lutheran. Home: 1999 State St Lafayette IN 47905 Office: Tippecanoe County Prosecutor's Office Courthouse Room 14 Lafayette IN 47901

KERN, TIMOTHY SCOTT, experimental pathologist, researcher; b. Spring Valley, Ill., Apr. 19, 1951; s. Atherton C. and Jean Ruth (Ingram) K.; m. Carol Ann Lewandowski, Sept. 7, 1974; 1 child, Collen Ann. B.S. in Biochemistry and Zoology, U. Wis., 1973, Ph.D. in Pathology, 1980. Research specialist U. Wis., Madison, 1973-76, postdoctoral fellow in opthalmology, 1980-82, asst. scientist, 1982—. Contbr. articles to profl. jours., chpt. to book. Mem. AAAS, Am. Diabetes Assn. (Research and Devel. award 1984—), Assn. Research in Vision and Ophthalmology (Young Investigator award 1983). Home: 5217 Odana Rd Madison WI 53711 Office: Dept Ophthalmology U Wis 1300 University Ave Madison WI 53706

KERNAN, EDWARD JAMES, legal administrator; b. Two Harbors, Minn., Mar. 22, 1926; s. Edward James and Edith A. (Scott) K.; B.S., U. Minn., 1948; M.Ed., U. Wis., Superior, 1962; m. Barbara Louise Iverson, Sept. 28, 1948; children—Edward James, Barbara Lee, James E. Coach and athletic dir. Robbinsdale (Minn.) High Sch., 1948-53, Northland Coll., Ashland, Wis., 1954-64; placement dir. U. Minn., Duluth, 1965; adminstrv. and personnel mgr. Price Waterhouse, Cleve., 1966-73; adminstrv. dir. Sidley & Austin, Chgo., 1974—. Pres. Ashland Little League, 1959-64, Badger-Gopher Conf., 1964-65; chmn. Citizen's Com. for Sch. Bond Issue, Rocky River, Ohio, 1973. Served with USAAF, 1944-45. Mem. Law Office Mgrs. Assn. (dir. 1976-79), Assn. Legal Adminstrs. (dir. 1977-80, v.p. 1982, pres. 1983, regional v.p. 1985-86), Cocker Spaniel Club Midwest. Roman Catholic. Clubs: Glenflora Country, Pickwick Golf. Coached three Badger-Gopher Coll. Conf. basketball championships. Home: 1205 Candlewood Hill Northbrook IL 60062 Office: One First National Plaza Chicago IL 60603

KERNEN, WILL, lawyer; b. Boston, July 4, 1951; s. Judson and Olive (Bardsley) K.; m. Cindy M. Krueger, June 21, 1970; children—Kerry, Kurt, Kyle. B.A., Bridgewater State Coll., 1974; J.D., Ohio State U., 1976. Bar: Ohio, U.S. Dist. Ct. (so. dist.) Ohio. Mem. Lappen, Lilley, Kernen & Co., L.P.A., Logan, Ohio, 1977—; law dir. City of Logan, 1978-79; law librarian Hocking County Law Library, 1980-83; acting judge Hocking County Mcpl. Ct., Logan, 1983—. Bd. mem. Logan-Hocking City Sch. Dist., 1979-83; counsel Hocking County Republican Party, 1979—. Served with U.S. Army, 1968-71, Germany. Mem. ABA, Ohio Bar Assn., Hocking County Bar Assn. (v.p. 1978-79), Jaycees (pres. Logan 1983-84, dist. dir. Ohio 1984-85). Home: 481 Henrietta Ave Logan OH 43138 Office: Lappen Lilley Kernen & Co LPA PO Box 588 Logan OH 43138-0588

KERNIS, MARTEN MURRAY, medical school administrator; b. Chgo., Sept. 21, 1941; s. Alvin and Esther (Katz) K.; m. Janet Tockman, Nov. 25, 1982; 1 child: Ariel Fern. B.S., Roosevelt U., Chgo., 1963; Ph.D., U. Fla., 1968. Asst. prof. anatomy U. Ill. Coll. Medicine, Chgo., 1968-70, asst. prof. anatomy, ob-gyn., 1970-73, assoc. prof., 1973-76, asst. dean Coll. Medicine, 1972-74, assoc. dean, 1974-76, assoc. prof. anatomy, 1978—, dep. exec. dean, 1978-83, acting exec. dean, 1982-83, exec. assoc. dean, 1983—; assoc. prof. anatomy Jefferson Med. Coll., Thomas Jefferson U., Phila., 1976-78, dean Coll. Allied Health Scis., 1976-78. Contbr. articles to profl. jours. Population Council research grantee, N.Y.C., Mem. Teratology Soc., Assn. Am. Med. Colls., Liason Com. of Med. Edn. (asst. sec.), Ill. Council on Continuing Med. Edn. (bd. dirs. 1979—). Home: 2205 Beechwood Ave Wilmette IL 60091 Office: U Ill 1853 W Polk St Chicago IL 60612

KERNS, GERTRUDE YVONNE, psychologist; b. Flint, Mich., July 25, 1931; d. Lloyd D. and Mildred C. (Ter Achter) B.; B.A., Olivet Coll., 1953; M.A., Wayne State U., 1958; Ph.D., U. Mich., 1979. Sch. psychologist Roseville (Mich.) Pub. Schs., 1958-68, Grosse Pointe (Mich.) Pub. Schs., 1968—; pvt. practice psychology, 1980—; instr. psychology Macomb Community Coll., 1959-63. Mem. Mich., Am. psychol. assns., Mich., Nat. socs. sch. psychologists, NEA, Psi Chi. Home: 28820 Grant St St Clair Shores MI 48081 Office: 63 Kercheval Suite 205 Grosse Pointe MI 48236

KERNS, MICHAEL DENNIS, county official; b. Council Bluffs, Iowa, Feb. 17, 1947; s. Francis Albert and Juanita Jean (Heady) K.; m. Linda Elizabeth Powell, May 11, 1968 (div. 1976); children—Kristine Lynn, Michael Charles; m. Nina Marie Espersen, Apr. 9, 1977; 1 child, Amanda Marie. A.A., Iowa Western, 1972; B.A., Buena Vista Coll., 1978. Investigator Pottawattamie County atty., Council Bluffs, 1970-73; road dep. Pottawattamie County sheriff, Council Bluffs, 1973-76, investigator, 1976-80, sgt., 1980-81, lt., 1981-83, sheriff, 1983—. Served with USN, 1966-69. Mem. Iowa State Sheriffs and Deps. Assn. Republican. Presbyterian. Lodge: Optimists. Avocations: antique cars; hunting; reading; camping. Office: Pottawattamie County Sheriff 227 S 6th St Council Bluffs IA 51501

KERR, DOUGLAS STUART, pediatrics and biochemistry educator; b. Beirut, Lebanon, Oct. 29, 1936; s. Stanley E. and Elsa L. (Reckman) K.; m. Mary Ann DuMond, June 12, 1965; children—Laura Diane, Daniel Ross. B.A., Haverford Coll., 1958; M.D., Western Res. U., 1965, Ph.D. in Biochemistry, 1965. Diplomate Am. Bd. Pediatrics. Intern Johns Hopkins Hosp., Baltimore, 1965-66, resident, 1968-70; Helen Hay Whitney fellow U. W.I., Kingston, Jamaica, 1970-73; asst. prof. Case Western Res. U., Cleve., 1973-82, assoc. prof. in pediatrics, biochemistry, 1982—; grant reviewer NIH, Bethesda, Md., 1977-78, 85; com. mem. Nat. Acad. Scis., Washington, 1984—. Contbr. articles in field of metabolism and nutrition to profl. jours., chpts. in books. Bd. dirs., sec. Diabetes Assn. Greater Cleve., 1974—. Research grantee NIH. Mem. Am. Diabetes Assn., No. Ohio Pediatric Soc., Soc. Inherited Metabolic Disorders. Democrat. Avocation: backpacking. Home: 2930 Coleridge Rd Cleveland Heights OH 44118 Office: Case Western Res U Rainbow Babies and Children's Hosp Cleveland OH 44106

KERR, ELIZABETH MARGARET, educator, author; b. Sault Ste Marie, Mich., Jan. 25, 1905; d. John Arthur and Katherine Dorothy (Hirth) Kerr; B.A., U. Minn., 1926, M.A., 1927, Ph.D., 1941. Instr. English, Tabor Coll., Hillsboro, Kans., 1929-30, U. Minn., Mpls., 1930-37, 38-43, Coll. of St. Catherine, St. Paul, 1937-38; asst. prof. Rockford (Ill.) Coll., 1943-45; instr. Milw. State Coll., 1945-55; asso. prof. U. Wis., Milw., 1956-59, prof., 1959-70, prof. emeritus English, 1970—. MLA research grantee, 1942; Summer Salary Support grantee U. Wis., Milw., 1959, 1961. Mem. MLA, Dickens Studies, Soc. for Study So. Lit. Democrat. Congregationalist. Author: Bibliography of the Sequence Novel, 1950; Yoknapatawpha: Faulkner's Little Postage Stamp of Native Soil, 1969; William Faulkner's Gothic Domain, 1979; William Faulkner's Yoknapatawpha: —A Kind of Keystone in the Universe,— 1984. Home: 4259 N Sercombe Rd Milwaukee WI 53216

KERR, NANCY KAROLYN, pastor, mental health consultant; b. Ottumwa, Iowa, July 10, 1934; d. Owen W. and Iris Irene (Israel) Kerr; student Boston U., 1953; A.A., U. Bridgeport, 1966; B.A., Hofstra U., 1967; postgrad. in clin. psychology Adelphi U. Inst. Advanced Psychol. Studies, 1968-73; m. Richard Clayton Williams, June 28, 1953 (div.); children—Richard Charles, Donna Louise. Pastoral counselor Nat. Council Chs., Jackson, Miss., 1964; dir. teen program Waterbury (Conn.) YWCA, 1966-67; intern in psychology N.Y. Med. Coll., 1971-72; research cons., 1972-73; coordinator home services, psychologist City and County of Denver, 1972-75; cons. Mennonite Mental Health Services, Denver, 1975-78; asst. prof. psychology Messiah Coll., 1978-79; mental health cons., 1979-81; called to ministry Mennonite Ch., 1981, pastor Cin. Mennonite Fellowship, 1981-83, adv. ch. curriculum, 1981, coordinator campus peace evangelism, 1981-83, mem. central dist. peace and justice com., 1983—, mem. Gen. Conf. Peace and Justice Reference Council, 1983—; instr. Associated Mennonite Bibl. Sems.; teaching elder Assembly Mennonite Ch., 1985—; mem. Tri-County Counseling Clinic, Memphis, Mo., 1980-81; spl. ch. curriculum Nat. Council Chs., 1981; mem. Central Dist. Conf. Peace and Justice Com., 1981—. Mem. Waterbury Planned Parenthood, 1964-67; mem. MW Children's Home Bd., 1974-75; mem. Boulder (Colo.) ARC, 1977-78. Mem. Am. Psychol. Assn., Am. Assn. Mental Deficiency, Soc. Psychologists for Study of Social Issues, Am. Acad. Polit. and Social Scientists. Office: Associated Mennonite Biblical Seminaries 3003 Benham Ave Elkhart IN 46517

KERR, WILLIAM ANDREW, lawyer, educator; b. Harding, W.Va., Nov. 17, 1934; s. William James and Tocie Nyle (Morris) K.; m. Elizabeth Ann McMillin, Aug. 3, 1968. A.B., W.Va. U., 1955, J.D., 1957; LL.M., Harvard U., 1958; B.D., Duke U., 1968. Bar: W.Va. 1957, Pa. 1962, Ind. 1980. Assoc. McClintic, James, Wise and Robinson, Charleston, W.Va., 1958, Schnader, Harrison, Segal and Lewis, Phila., 1961-64; asst. prof. law Cleve. State U., Coll. Law, 1966-67, assoc. prof., 1967-68; assoc. prof. Ind. U. sch. Law, Indpls., 1968-69, 72-74, prof., 1974—; asst. U.S. atty. So. Dist. Ind., Indpls., 1969-72; exec. dir. Ind. Jud. Ctr., 1974—; dir. research Ind. Pros. Attys. Council, 1972-74; mem. Ind. Criminal Law Study Commn., 1973—, sec., 1973-83; reporter speedy trial com. U.S. Dist. Ct. (so. dist.) Ind., 1975-84; trustee Ind. Criminal Justice Inst., 1983—; dir. Indpls. Lawyers Commn., 1975-77, Ind. Lawyers Commn., 1980-83; mem. Ind. Supreme Ct. Records Mgmt. Com., 1983—. Bd. dirs. Ch. Fedn. Greater Indpls., 1979—. Served to capt. JAGC, USAF, 1958-61. Decorated Air Force Commendation medal; Ford Found. fellow Harvard Law Sch., 1957-58; recipient Outstanding Prof. award Students of Ind. U. Sch. Law, 1974; Outstanding Service award Indpls. chpt. Fed. Bar Assn., 1975; Disting. Service award Ind. Council Juvenile Ct. Judges, 1979; Outstanding Jud. Edn. Program award Nat. Council Juvenile and Family Ct. Judges, 1985. Mem. Ind. State Bar Assn., Indpls. Bar Assn., Phila. Bar Assn., W.Va. Bar Assn., Am. Judicature Soc., Fed. Bar Assn., Nat. Assn. State Jud. Educators, Order of Coif, Phi Beta Kappa. Office: 735 W New York St Indianapolis IN 46202

KERREY, ROBERT, governor of Nebraska; b. Lincoln, Nebr., Aug. 27, 1943; s. James and Elinor K.; children—Benjamin, Lindsey. B.S. in Pharmacy, U. Nebr., 1965. Ptnr., Grandmother's Skillet Restaurant, Omaha, from 1972, Sun Valley Bowl, then Wall-Bankers Racquetball Club and Fitness Ctr., Lincoln; gov. State of Nebr., 1982—. Served with USNR, 1966-69. Decorated Congl. medal of Honor, Bronze Star medal, Purple Heart. Mem. Am. Legion, VFW, DAV, Lincoln C. of C. (mem. coms.). Congregationalist. Lodges: Sertoma, Lions. Office: Office of Governor 2d floor State Capitol Bldg Lincoln NE 68509*

KERSHASKY, MICHAEL JOSEPH, retired pulp and paper company executive; b. Nekoosa, Wis., July 3, 1913; s. Joseph and Anna (Stambor) K.; m. Elizabeth Lutz, Apr. 20, 1938; children—James, Joseph, John, Jerome, Jennifer, Jeanne. Student Stevens Point U., 1932-33, U. Wis.-Madison, 1933-34. Paper tester Nekoosa Edwards Paper Co., Port Edwards, Wis., 1934-40; paper maker U.S. Dept. Agr. and Forest Service, Madison, Wis., 1940-46; paper tester, boiler water and feed clk. Nekoosa Papers, Port Edwards, 1946-78. Recipient Yrs. of Dedicated Service award Central Labor Council, Wisconsin Rapids, 1984, service award State of Wis. Legislature, Madison, 1984. Mem. Wisconsin Rapids Area Sr. Citizens Assn. (pres. 1984-85), Wood County Sr. Citizens Civic Club (pres. 1978-84). Roman Catholic. Avocation: politics. Home: 631 11th Ave S Wisconsin Rapids WI 54494

KERSHAW, STEWART, conductor, music director; b. Oxford, Eng., Apr. 11, 1941; s. Harvey and Molly (Brownlow) K. Student, Royal Acad. Music, London, 1957-62, Conservatoire de Paris, 1962-64. With Royal Ballet, 1966-69, Opera De Lyon (France, 1970-71, Munich Opera House, 1971-74, Stuttgart Opera House (W. Ger.), 1974-80, Paris Opera, 1977-80, Kyoto Symphony (Japan), 1978-80; condr., music dir. Evansville Philharmonic (Ind.), 1980—. Office: 14 1/2 SE 2d St Evansville IN 47708

KERSHNER, CARL JOHN, chemist; b. Lima, Ohio, Dec. 15, 1934; s. Fred William and Florence Elizabeth (Kundert) K.; m. Doris Elizabeth Grieve, Aug. 23, 1958; children—Jeffrey John, Jean Elizabeth. Student, Ohio No. U., Ada, 1952-54; B.S., Capital U., Columbus, Ohio, 1956; Ph.D., Ohio U., Athens, 1961. Sr. research chemist Monsanto Research Corp., Miamisburg, Ohio, 1961-63, group leader, 1963-66, sect. mgr., 1966-68, sr. research specialist, 1968-70, fellow, 1970-79, sr. fellow, 1979—; adj. prof. Ohio State U., Columbus, 1980-81. Contbr. articles to sci. jours. Patentee in field. Mem. Am. Chem. Soc., Am. Phys. Soc., Royal Soc. Chemistry, Sigma Xi. Avocations: Tennis, skiing, flying. Office: Monsanto Research Corp Box 32 Miamisburg OH 45342

KERTZ, ALOIS FRANCIS, agricultural researcher, b. Bloomsdale, Mo., Sept. 15, 1945; s. Andrew Nicholas and Hilda Frances (Fallert) K.; m. Molly Ann Corcoran, July 25, 1969; children—Julia, Emily, Nicholas, Mary. B.S. in Agr., U. Mo., 1967, M.S. in Dairy Nutrition, 1968; Ph.D. in Animal Nutrition, Cornell U., 1973. Grad. research asst. U. Mo., Columbia, 1967-68, Cornell U., Ithaca, N.Y., 1970-73; research nutritionist Ralston Purina Co., St. Louis, 1973-75, mgr. dairy research, 1975—. Contbr. articles to profl. jours. Served to 1st lt. U.S. Army, 1968-70. Fellow Ralston Purina, 1967-68; Liberty Hyde Bailey fellow, 1970-73. Mem. AAAS, Am. Dairy Sci. Assn., Am. Soc. Animal Sci., Nutrition Today Soc., Am. Inst. Nutrition, U. Mo.-Columbia Agrl. Alumni Assn. (sec.-treas. 1983—). Roman Catholic. Office: Ralston Purina Co Checkerboard Square St Louis MO 63164

KESSEL, BARRY LEE, advertising and marketing executive; b. Chgo., June 5, 1949; s. Charles and Molly (Wool) K.; m. Maria Cristina Cardenas, Aug. 12, 1972; children—Leah C., Eliot Benjamin. B.A., Kent State U., 1971; postgrad Am. U., 1972. Sr. producer, Communitape, Inc., Washington, 1972-73; mktg. mgr. Numa Ltd., Akron, Ohio, 1973-74; advt. mgr. Williams & Wilkins, Balt., 1975-76; v.p. mktg. Volair Ltd., Kent, Ohio, 1977-80; creative dir. World Book Ency., Chgo., 1980-83; sr. v.p. Stone & Adler, Inc., Chgo., 1983—. Editor: The Complete Audubon, 10 vols., 1977; editor/designer: History of the Indian Tribes of North America (named Best Book Overall, Binding Inst. Am. 1979), 1978. Mem. Homewood-Flossmoor High Sch. Found., Ill., 1984. Recipient 3 awards Chgo. Assn. Dir. Mktg., 1984. Mem. Direct Mktg. Assn. (Echo awards 1984, 84). Jewish. Avocations: bridge, chess, basketball, poetry. Home: 2310 MacDonald Ln Flossmoor IL 60422 Office: Stone & Adler Inc 1 S Wacker Dr Chicago IL 60606

KESSEN, DONALD JOSEPH, hospital administrator; b. Spearville, Kans., Mar. 2, 1942; s. Paul B. and Helen A. (Fitzgerald) K.; m. Julia Marie Knoeber, May 11, 1963; children—Christine, Gregory, Marsha. Student Dodge City Jr. Coll., 1960; student U.S. Naval Sch. Radiologic Technology, 1962-63. Dir. x-ray sch. Asbury Hosp., Salina, Kans., 1965-66; dir./instr. sch. Trinity Hosp., Dodge City, Kans., 1966-71; owner/mgr. Jerry Lewis Cinema, Dodge City, 1971-75; mgr. Honda, Dodge City, 1975-79; x-ray technologist Spearville Dist. Hosp., Kans., 1979; adminstr. Spearville Hosp. Complex, 1979—. First-aid tchr. Spearville council Boy Scouts Am., 1977. Served with USN, 1960-65. Mem. Am. Registry Radiologic Technologists, S.W. Kans. Soc. X-ray Technologists (pres. 1968-69), Kans. Assn. Health Care Execs. (bd. dirs. 1983—), Kans. Hosp. Assn. (vice chmn. conv. com. 1983-84). Roman Catholic. Lodge: K.C. (grand knight 1981-82). Avocations: boating; hunting; motorcycle riding; sports. Home: Box 6 Route 2 Spearville KS 67876 Office: Spearville Dist Hosp PO Box 156 Spearville KS 67876

KESSLER, ANN ELIZABETH, social sciences educator; b. Aberdeen, S.D., Jan. 28, 1928; d. George and Elizabeth (Sahli) K. B.A., Mt. Marty Coll., 1953; M.A., Creighton U., 1957; Ph.D., U. Notre Dame, 1963. Instr. Sacred Heart Sch., Yankton, S.D., 1947-49, Mt. Marty High Sch., Yankton, 1952-56, St. Otto Grade Sch., Webster, S.D., 1957-58; prof. Mt. Marty Coll., Yankton, 1962—; vis. prof. Marquette U., Milw., 1969-70. Contbr. articles to profl. jours. Cand. state Democratic Party, S.D., 1972, 74, 76; party chairperson Yankton County Dem. Party, 1974-75; publs. com. S.D. Centennial Commn., Sioux Falls, 1984. Mem. Am. Polit. Sci. Assn., S.D. Social Sci. Assn. Roman Catholic. Home: 1005 W 8th St Yankton SD 57078 Office: Mt Marty Coll Yankton SD 57078

KESSLER, DORIS HENRIETTA, army officer; b. New Kensington, Pa., Sept. 19, 1935; d. Francis Arthur and Dora Mary Molinari; B.S., Pa. State U., 1957; m. Otto F. Kessler, June 1958 (div.). Tchr., Duquesne (Pa.) High Sch., 1958-68; commd. 1st lt. U.S. Army, 1968, advanced through grades to lt. col. Adj. Gen.'s Corps, 1984; instr. Ft. McClellan, Ala., 1968-69; recruiting officer, N.Y.C., 1970-72; chief tng. mgmt. div. Ft. Belvoir, Va., 1972-73; co. comdr., Ft. Jackson, S.C., 1973-75; bn. exec. officer, Ft. Jackson, 1975; ADP officer Computer Systems Command, Ft. Belvoir, 1975-79; project officer Women in the Army Study, Dept. Army, 1977-78; chief staff support sect., software, command, control and communications, Command in Chief Pacific Staff, Camp Smith, Hawaii, 1980-83, chief adminstrv. team U.S. Army Readiness Group, Ft. Sheridan, Ill., 1983-84; automation mgmt. officer 4th Army Planning Group, Ft. Sheridan, 1983-84; dir. adminstrv. and logistical support U.S. Army Res. Components Personnel and Adminstrv. Ctr., St. Louis, 1984—. Committeewoman, Allgheny County, Pitts., 1963-67. Decorated Meritorious Service medal, Army Commendation medal (2). Mem. Nat. Assn. Female Execs., Assn. U.S. Army, Internat. Platform Assn., Met. Opera Guild, Met. Mus. Art, St. Louis Symphony Assn., Lafayette Sq. Restoration Com. Club: Mil. Dist. Washington Officers. Office: US Army Res Components Personnel and Adminstrv Ctr 9700 Page Blvd Saint Louis MO 63132

KESSLER, DUANE KEITH, college administrator; b. Robinson, Ill., June 23, 1935; s. Oscar Clyde and Susan Pauline (Osborn) K.; m. Mary Jo Keen, Sept. 7, 1957; children—Kristen, Duane K., Robert. B.S., U. Ill., 1958, M.A., 1959. Mktg. analyst Shell Oil Co., St. Louis, 1960-61; bus. adminstr. Centralia High Sch., Ill., 1961-67; dean adminstrv. services Kaskaskia Coll., 1967—, instr. econs., 1967—; dir. Home Fed. Savs. & Loan. Bd. dirs. Marion County Bd., 1984—. Served to 1st lt. U.S. Army, 1959-60. Mem. Ill. Assn. Sch. Bus. Ofcls., Ill. Community Coll. Bus. Adminstrs., Assn. Sch. Bus. Ofcls. of U.S. and Can., Centralia C. of C. Republican. Methodist. Lodges: Rotary, Elks. Avocation: golf. Home: 14 Orchard Dr E Centralia IL 62801 Office: Kaskaskia Coll Shattuc Rd Centralia IL 62801

KESSLER, JOHN W, college president; b. Gunn City, Mo., July 2, 1919; s. James Ruben and Nannie Bell (Cox) K.; m. Bernice Hubick, June 18, 1947; children—John W., David. B.S., S.E. Mo. State Coll., 1940; M.S., George Williams Coll., 1949; D. Humanics (hon.), Springfield Coll., 1985. Gen. exec. Oak Park YMCA, Ill., 1962-68; pres. Met. Mpls. YMCA, 1969-84, chmn. exec. com., 1984; pres. George Williams Coll., Downers Grove, Ill., 1984—. Contbr. articles to profl. jours. Active local sch. bds., Mass., 1954-62. Served to sgt. USAF, 1943-45, NATOUSA. Mem. Assn. for Profl. Devel.-YMCA, Nat. Assn. of Social Workers, YMCA Urban Group (chmn. 1974-78). Republican. Clubs: Minneapolis; Bell Aire Yacht. Avocations: boating, music, reading. Office: George Williams Coll 555 31st St Downers Grove IL 60515

KESSLER, JOHN WEBSTER, judge, lawyer; b. Dayton, Ohio, Oct. 27, 1942; s. Raymond W. and Ruth (mager) K.; m. Mary Sue Hanson, June 19, 1965: children—Christine, Daniel. B.A., Miami U., Oxford, Ohio, 1965; J.D., U. Toledo, 1968. Bar: Ohio 1968, U.S. Dist. Ct. 1969. Asst. pros. atty. Montgomery County, Dayton, 1968-71, chief pub. def., 1971-78; mng. ptnr. Hunt, Dodge & Kessler, LPA, Dayton, 1978-81; common pleas judge Montgomery County, 1981—. Mem. ABA, Dayton Bar Assn., Ohio State Bar Assn., Am. Judges Assn., Am. Judicature Soc. Democrat. Home: 215 Dellwood Ave Dayton OH 45419 Office: Montgomery County Common Pleas Ct 41 N Perry St Dayton OH 45402

KESSLER, NATHAN, manufacturing company executive; b. St. Louis, Aug. 19, 1923; s. Isadore Harry and Esther (Becker) K.; m. Sara Ellen Potashnick, June 21, 1947; children—Joy Sandra, Gail Sue, Margie Ann. B.S. in Chem. Engring., Washington U., St. Louis, 1944, M.S. in Chem. Engring., 1944. Registered profl. engr., Ill. Chief chem. engr. A.E. Staley Mfg. Co., Decatur, Ill., 1944-63, plant supt., 1962-63, gen. supt., 1963-67, v.p. mfg., 1967-70, v.p. tech., 1970—, also dir.; pres. Staley Techventures Co., 1984—; dir. Source Tech. Biologicals, Mpls., Bio-Tech. Resources, Manitowoc, Wis. Pres., United Way, Decatur, 1976; v.p. Progress Resources, Decatur, 1978-80; adv. bd. Community Health Improvement Clinic, Decatur, 1981—; bd. dirs. Macon County Mental Health Bd., 1985—; pres. Ill. Bd. JETS, Champaign, 1983-85. Fellow White-Rodgess, 1944. Mem. Am. Inst. Chem. Engrs., Am. Oil Chemists Soc., Am. Chem. Soc., Univ. Ill. Inds. Research Assn. (adv. bd.), Tech. Transfer Soc. (bd. dirs., pres.-elect 1985—). Republican. Jewish. Lodge: B'nai Brith (pres. 1968-69). Avocation: gardening. Home: 49 Allen Bend Dr Decatur IL 52521 Office: A E Staley Mfg Co P O Box 151 Decatur IL 52525

KESSLER, WAYNE VINCENT, health sciences educator, researcher, consultant; b. Milo, Iowa, Jan. 10, 1933; s. Joseph Edward and Genevieve (Frueh) K.; m. Olive Beatrice Buremaster, Sept., 10, 1953; children—Katherine Marie, Karl Matthew. B.S., N.D. State U., 1955, M.S., 1956; Ph.D., Purdue U., 1959. Asst. prof. pharm. chemistry N.D. State U., Fargo, 1959-60; asst. prof. health physics Purdue U., W. Lafayette, Ind., 1960-64, assoc. prof., 1964-68, prof. bionucleonics, 1968-79, prof. health scis., 1979—; cons. Mead Johnson Inc., Evansville, Ind., 1968-69, Miles Labs., Elkart, Ind., 1970. Author: Cadmium Toxicity, 1974. Purdue Research Found. fellow, 1957. Fellow AAAS, Acad. Pharm. Scis., Phi Kappa Phi; mem. Health Physics Soc. Presbyterian. Avocations: woodworking; traveling. Home: 2825 Forest Ln Lafayette IN 47904 Office: Purdue U Sch Health Scis West Lafayette IN 47907

KESTEN, JACK LEONARD, architect; b. N.Y.C., Nov. 4, 1935; s. Herman and Bessie (Peckerman) K.; m. Elaine Adele Lapofsky, May 18, 1976. Cert. in Architecture, Cooper Union for Advancement of Sci. and Art, 1955; B.Arch., MIT, 1958. Registered architect, N.Y., N.J., Mo. Staff architect William B. Tabler, F.A.I.A., N.Y.C., 1958-66; job capt. William Lescaze, F.A.I.A., N.Y.C., 1966-67; project mgr. Pomerance and Breines, Architects, N.Y.C., 1968-69; prin. architect Vollmer Assocs., N.Y.C., 1969-70; project architect Morris Lapidus Assocs., N.Y.C., 1970-71; project mgr., job capt., rep. field The Gruzen Partnership, N.Y.C., 1971-78; project architect, design architect HBE Corp., St. Louis, 1978—. Prin. works include residence for Hon. V.P. Nelson A. Rockefeller, Pocantico Hills, N.Y., Yorkville Subway Sta., N.Y.C., renovation of Commodore Hotel to Grand Hyatt Hotel, N.Y.C., U.S. Atty. Office Bldg. Met. Correctional Ctr., N.Y.C., cell block revisions Attica Correctional Facility, N.Y., York Coll. Lab. Facilities, Jamaica, N.Y., South Park Hosp., Shreveport, La., new and remodeled hosps. in Ariz., Bermuda, Colo., Ga., Maine, Mass., N.J., N.Y., S.C., S.D., Tex., W.Va., HBE Corp. Hdqrs., St. Louis, Adam's Mark Hotel, St. Louis, Retirement Community, Sun City, Ariz. Emil Schweinburg postgrad. scholar, 1955, Nat. Bd. Fire Underwriters scholar, 1957. Mem. AIA (St. Louis chpt.), Mo. Council Architects, MIT Club. Avocatons: sailing; photography; ice hockey fan; ice skating; bicycling. Home: 1771 Canyon View Ct Chesterfield MO 63017

KETTINGER, BURTON EDWARD, JR., clergyman, musician; b. Zanesville, Ohio, Nov. 19, 1944; s. Burton Edward and Mary Jane (Probst) K.; m. Sharon Rose Meads, June 22, 1968; 1 child, Shauna Rae. B.A., Spring Arbor Coll., Mich., 1967; M.A., Am. Conservatory Music, Chgo., 1978. Ordained to ministry Free Methodist Ch. N.Am., 1975. Tchr. Turner Jr. High Sch., Warren, Ohio, 1967-69, Wheaton Christian High Sch., West Chicago, Ill., 1972-74; minister youth and music Free Methodist Ch., Indpls., 1969-71, Winona Lake, Ind., 1971-72; free lance musician, minister, Wheaton, Ill., 1974—; vocal soloist Moody Bible Inst., Chgo., 1974—; dir., cons. Free Spirit Music Ministry, Winona Lake, 1971-76; bd. dirs. Timberlee Christian Ctr., East Troy, Wis.; chaplain-minister Fellowship of Christian Peace Officers, Chgo., 1977—. Named Young Leader of Yr., Spring Arbor Coll., 1976. Mem. Free Ch. Ministerial Assn., West Suburban Ministerial Fellowship. Republican. Avocation: golfing. Home: 1523 Gainesboro Dr Wheaton IL 60187 Office: PO Box 1098 Wheaton IL 60189

KETTLER, THOMAS DALE, realtor; b. Cuba City, Wis., Aug. 29, 1944; s. Dale Orville and Julia Mary Patricia (Boyle) K.; m. Susanne Margot Klingler, July 13, 1968; children—John Thomas, Christine Susanne. B.A., Marquette U., 1972. Real estate sales assoc. Rite Realty Corp. Milw., 1974-77, sales mgr., 1977-78; v.p., gen. mgr., 1978-80; owner, pres. Ketco Corp., Rite Realty, Milw., 1980—. Served with USN, 1966-72. Mem. Milw. Bd. Realtors, Wis. Realtors Assn., Nat. Assn. Realtors. Roman Catholic. Avocations: Traveling; reading; golfing; gardening. Office: Rite Realty 5910 W Forest Home Ave Milwaukee WI 53220

KEY, HELEN ELAINE, accounting, consulting company executive; b. Cleve., Jan. 16, 1946; d. Maud and Helen (Key) Vance. B.S., W.Va. State Coll., 1968; M.Ed., Cleve. State U., 1977. Tchr. Cleve. Bd. Edn., 1968—; instr. Cuyahoga Community Coll., Cleve., part-time, 1969-78, Dyke Coll., Cleve., part-time, 1979—; pres. H.E. Key & Assos., Cleve., 1983—; treas. BK4W Inc., Cleve., 1981. Mem. Am. Assn. Notary Pubs., Women Bus. Owners Assn., AAUW, NAACP, Cleve. Area Bus. Tchrs., NEA, Pi Lambda Theta, Alpha Kappa Alpha. Democrat. Baptist. Club: Toastmistress (sec. 1978) (Cleve.). Home: 23951 Lakeshore Blvd Apt 608B Euclid OH 44123

KEYES, JAMES ALAN, police chief; b. Hillsdale, Mich., Nov. 14, 1934; s. George W. and Clara (Kemp) K.; m. Nancy Sue Westin, Mar. 20, 1954; children—Alan George, Kevin Kraig, James Alan, Jr. B.S., Mich. State U., 1973, M.S., 1973. Police officer Albion Police Dept., Mich., 1961-63; dep. sheriff Calhoun County Sheriff Dept., Marshall, Mich., 1963-69, chief dep., 1969-73; mgmt. cons. Northwestern U., Evanston, Ill., 1973-76, chmn. traffic option, 1976-79; dep. chief Woodridge Police Dept., Ill., 1979-81, chief of police, 1981—; mem. exec. bd. DuPage Co. Chiefs of Police, Ill. Author: Driving Under the Influence, 1973. Bd. dirs. DuPage-McHenry Counties Lung Assn., Wheaton, Ill., Salvation Army, Woodridge, 1981—; asst. dist. commr. DuPage Area council Boy Scouts Am., 1980—. Served to staff sgt. USAF, 1955-61. Recipient Cert. of Appreciation, VFW, 1983. Mem. DuPage County Chief's of Police, Ill. Assn. Chief's of Police, Internat. Assn. Chief's of Police. Avocations: running; weight lifting. Office: Woodridge Police Dept 2900 W 83rd St Woodridge IL 60517

KEYES, PAUL LANDIS, phyisology educator; b. Thomasville, N.C., July 7, 1938; s. Paul Spring and Helen Cecilia (Presgrave) K.; m. Sharon Joann Shull, June 19, 1966; children—Jeffrey Landis, Christopher Allan. Student, Randolph-Macon Coll., Ashland, Va., 1955-58; B.S., N.C. State U., 1960, M.S., 1962; Ph.D., U. Ill., 1966. Postdoctoral fellow Harvard Med. Sch., Boston, 1966-68; research asst. prof. physiology Albany Med. Coll., N.Y., 1968-72; asst. prof. U. Mich., Ann Arbor, 1972-75, assoc. prof., 1975-84, prof., 1984—; mem. ad hoc clin. fellowship com. NIH, 1979-81. Editor: Endocrinology, 1979-82. Contbr. articles to profl. jours., chpt. to books. NIH grantee, 1972—; NIH sr. fellow 1983-84. Mem. Soc. Study Reproduction, Endocrine Soc., Am. Physiol. Soc., Soc. Study Fertility, Phi Kappa Phi. Methodist. Home: 609 Sunset Rd Ann Arbor MI 48103

KHACHATURIAN, HENRY, anatomist, neuroendocrinologist; b. Tehran, Iran, Oct. 19, 1951; s. Shahen and Emma (Babayan) K.; m. Ellen Catherine Quinn, June 24, 1983. B.S., SUNY-Brockport, 1974, M.S., 1976; Ph.D., U. Rochester, 1981. Postdoctoral scholar Mental Health Research Inst., U. Mich., Ann Arbor, 1981-83, research investigator, 1983—; instr. human gross anatomy U. Rochester Med. Sch., 1978-79. Contbr. articles to profl. jours. Recipient John R. Bartlett prize in neurosci. Center for Brain Research, U. Rochester, 1979; Outstanding Research award Sch. Medicine, U. Rochester, 1980; Best Tchr. award U. Rochester, 1980. Mem. Soc. for Neurosci. Office: Mental Health Research Inst Dept Psychiatry Univ Mich Ann Arbor MI 48109

KHAN, BASHIR AHMAD, statistics educator; b. Jampur Punjab, Pakistan; June 10, 1951; came to U.S., 1982; s. Ghulam Qadir and Amna K.; m. Shaista Bashir, Apr. 14, 1977; children—Rabia, Usman. B.Sc., Punjab U., Lahore, 1970, M.Sc., 1972; postgrad. U. Mo.-Columbia, 1985—. Lectr. Gomal U., D.I. Khan, Pakistan, 1974-81, chmn. stats. dept., 1978-81. Mem. Am. Statis. Assn. Islam. Avocation: reading. Home: Al-Qadir Farid Abad Colony D G Khan Punjab Pakistan Office: Stats Dept U Mo Columbia MO 65211

KHAN, KALIM ULLAH, project engineer, consultant; b. Kanpur, India, Feb. 9, 1937; naturalized Am. citizen; s. Abdul Hai and Salamat (Begam) K.; m. Florence Dedes, Sept. 5, 1954 (dec.). Diploma engring. Aligarh Muslim U., (India), 1959; M.E., Goethe Inst. (W.Ger.), 1963; cert. Vickers Hydraulic Inst., 1971. Engr., M-A-N, A.G., Mainz-Gustavsburg, W.Ger., 1961-63; designer U.S. Industries, Inc., Chgo., 1964-65; project engr. Grotnes Metalforming Systems, Inc., Chgo., 1965-83; cons. engr. Wm. Wrigley Jr. Co., Chgo., 1983—; owner, cons. Khan Hydraulics, Inc., Evanston, Ill. Vol., FISH, Evanston, 1976—; mem. Citizen's Com. to Control Cable TV, Evanston, 1981—. Mem. ASME, Soc. Automotive Engrs., Fluid Power Soc. Republican. Moslem. Clubs: Rotary, Engineering. Home: 850 Mark Ln Suite 221 Wheeling IL 60090

KHAN, M. ALI, municipal air quality control administrator; b. India, Apr. 28, 1940; came to U.S., 1968, naturalized, 1971; m. Zarina Ansari, July 4, 1968; 1 child. B.Engring., India, 1965; M.S. in Engring., U. Miss., 1970. Registered profl. engr., Ill., Ind. Research asst. U. Miss., Oxford, 1968-70; engr. Air Quality Control, East Chicago, Ind., 1971-72, asst. dir., 1972—. Mem. Air Pollution Control Assn., IEEE, Am. Planning Assn. Avocations: tennis; hiking. Office: Dept Air Quality Control City of East Chicago 4525 Indianapolis Blvd East Chicago IN 46312

KHAN, MOHAMMED ABDUL QUDDUS, biology educator; b. Kaimgunj, India, Mar. 15, 1939; s. Mohammed Hanif and Maryam (Khan) K.; m. Anwarun Nisa, Apr. 18, 1957; children—Sarah, Samreen, Yaseen. B.S., Karachi U., Pakistan, 1957, M.S., 1959; Ph.D., U. Western Ont., London, 1964; M.D., Universidad Autonoma de Ciudad Juarez, Mexico, 1984. Postdoctoral fellow N.C. State U., Raleigh, 1965-67, Oreg. State U., Corvallis, 1967-68, Rutgers U., New Brunswick, N.J., 1968-69; mem. faculty U. Ill., Chgo., 1969—, assoc. prof., 1969-74, prof. biology, 1974—; vis. scientist NIH, Research Triangle Park, N.C., 1975-76; vis. chemist EPA, Corvallis, Oreg., 1980. Editor: Pesticides in Aquatic Environments, 1977. Co-editor: Survival in Toxic Environments, 1976; Pesticide and Xenobiotics in Aquatic Organisms, 1979; Toxicology of Halogenated Hydrocarbons, 1980. Editor in chief Jour. Biochem. Toxicology, 1985—. Research grantee USPHS, NIH, 1972, 1977. Mem. Am. Chem. Soc., AAAS, Entomol. Soc. Am., Sigma Xi. Democrat. Islam. Avocations: Urdu poetry, prose composing. Home: 5931 Clarendon Ct Hanover Park IL 60103 Office: Biol Scis U Ill PO Box 4348 Chicago IL 60680

KHAN, MOHAMMED VAHID HUSAIN, physician; b. Hyderabad, India, Oct. 31, 1927; came to U.S., 1958, naturalized, 1972; s. Mohammed Ameen and Amina (Begum) K.; m. Georgia Kelley, Sept. 2, 1960; children—Talat M., Sarwat A., Irshad H., Farhat A., Nurul A. F.Sc., Osmania U., 1945; M.B., B.S., Dow Med. Coll., Karachi, Pakistan, 1955; D.T.M. and H., London Sch. Hygiene and Tropical Medicine, 1962. House physician Civil Hosp., Karachi, 1955-56; med. officer Govt. of Bahrain, 1957-58; rotating intern Cook County Hosp., Chgo., 1959; resident internal medicine Mo. Pacific Hosp., St. Louis, 1960; edn. council Fgn. Med. Grads., 1964; gen. practice medicine Nat. Health Service, London, 1962-63; med. officer Preston Hall Chest Hosp., Maidstone, Kent, Eng., 1964-65; resident internal medicine Wyckoff Heights Hosp., Bklyn., 1965-68; practice medicine specializing in internal medicine, Lake Grove, N.Y., 1968-78, Smithtown, N.Y., 1968-78; assoc. attending physician Smithtown Gen. Hosp., 1968-78; civilian med. officer internal medicine U.S. Gen. Leonard Wood Army Hosp., Fort Leonard Wood, Mo., 1978-79; staff physician VA Med. Ctr., St. Louis, 1979-82; mem. attending staff internal medicine St. Charles Hosp., Port Jefferson, N.Y., 1968-78; staff assoc. attending internal medicine Mather Hosp., Port Jefferson, 1968-78; assoc. attending internal medicine St. John's Smithtown (N.Y.) Hosp., cons. Pilgrim State Hosp., Brentwood, N.Y., 1969; cons. examiner State of N.Y., Bur. Disability Determinations, 1974. Mem. Republican Presdl. Task Force, 1985. Suffolk Acad. Medicine fellow, 1969-78; N.Y. Cardiol. Soc. assoc. fellow, 1973. Fellow Royal Soc. Tropical Medicine; mem. Brit. Med. Assn., AMA, Am. Soc. Internal Medicine, Am. Soc. Tropical Medicine, Islamic Med. Assn. U.S.A. and Can., N.Y. State Soc. Internal Medicine, Mo. State Soc. Internal Medicine. Islam. Home: 9939 Affton Pl St Louis MO 63123

KHAN, SHAHID NISAR, physician; b. Nowshera, Pakistan, Dec. 3, 1949; came to U.S., 1973; s. Nisar Ahmed Khan and Mustafai Nisar; m. Farzana Zahour, Mar. 14, 1976; children—Faiza, Sophia. F.Sc., Forman Christian Coll., Lahore, Pakistan, 1967; M.B.B.S., King Edward Med. Coll., Lahore, 1973. Diplomate Am. Bd. Pediatrics. Intern, St. Francis Hosp., Trenton, N.J., 1973-74; resident Bklyn.-Cumberland Med. Ctr., 1974-76; neonatologist William Beaumont Hosp., Royal Oak, Mich., 1978-79, 80—; practice medicine specializing in neonatology Corning Pediatric Assocs., Corning, N.Y., 1979-80; neonatologist William Beaumont Hosp., Royal Oak, Mich.; cons. Children Hosp., Detroit, 1981—. Contbr. articles to profl. jours. Fellow Am. Acad. Pediatrics; mem. Perinatal-Neonatal Assn., Assn. Pakistani Physicians, Perinatal Assn. Mich. Moslem. Avocations: skiing, photography. Office: William Beaumont Hosp 3601 W 13 Mile Rd Royal Oak MI 48072

KHO, EUSEBIO, surgeon; b. Philippines, Dec. 16, 1933; s. Joaquin and Francisca (Chua) K.: came to U.S., 1964; A.A., Silliman U., Philippines, 1955; M.D., State U. Philippines, 1960; fellow in surgery, Johns Hopkins, 1965-67; m. Grace C. Lim, May 24, 1964: children—Michelle Mae, April Tiffany, Bradley Jude, Jaclyn Ashley, Matthew Ryan. Intern in surgery Balt. City Hosp., 1964-65, resident in gen. surgery, 1965-67; research asso. pediatric surgery U. Chgo. Hosps., 1967-68; resident in gen. surgery, then chief resident U. Tex. Hosp., San Antonio, 1968-70; hosp. surgeon St. Anthony Hosp., Louisville, 1970-72; practice medicine specializing in surgery, Scottsburg, Ind., 1972—; chmn. dept. surgery Scott County Meml. Hosp., 1973—; cons. surgeon Washington County Meml. Hosp., Salem, Ind., also Clark County Meml. Hosp., Jeffersonville, Ind., 1973—; courtesy surgeon Suburban Hosp., Louisville, 1973—; gen. surgeon U.S. Army Hosp., Louisville, 1980—. Served to lt. col. M.C., USAR, 1980—. Diplomate Am. Bd. Surgery. Fellow A.C.S., Am.

Soc. Abdominal Surgeons; mem. Am. Coll. Internat. Physicians (founding mem., trustee 1974—), AMA (Physician's Recognition award 1969, 72), Ind., Ky., Philippine med. assns., Internat. Coll. Surgeons, Soc. Philippine Surgeons in Am. (life), Assn. Philippine Practicing Physicians in Am. (life), Assn. Mil. Surgeons of U.S., Res. Officers Assn. of U.S., Mark Ravitch Surg. Assn., Bradley Aust Surg. Soc., N.Y. Acad. Scis. Presbyterian. Clubs: Optimists, Masons. Home: 14 Carla Ln Scottsburg IN 47170 Office: 137 E McClain Ave Scottsburg IN 47170

KHOO, CHENG HOR, systems analyst; b. Bukit Mertajam, Penang, Malaysia, Jan. 21, 1955; came to U.S., 1976; s. Cheow Hock and Gaik Choo (Ch'ng) K.; m. Lee Khuen Yau, Aug. 28, 1984. B.S. in Math., U. Wis.-Stevens Point, 1980; M.S. in Ops. Research, Case Western Res. U., 1982. Research analyst Lorain County Community Coll., Elyria, Ohio, 1980-83, systems analyst, 1983—. Mem. Ops. Research Soc. Am., Assn. Systems Mgmt., Data Processing Mgmt. Assn., Assn. Computing Machinery, Omega Rho. Avocation: photography. Home: 1439 Jalan Tan Sai Gin Bukit Mertajam Penang Malaysia Office: Lorain County Community Coll 1005 N Abbe Rd Elyria OH 44035

KHOURY, GEORGE GILBERT, printer, baseball association executive; b. St. Louis, July 30, 1923; s. George Michael and Dorothy (Smith) K.; m. Colleen E. Khoury Czerny, Apr. 3, 1948; children—Colleen Ann, George Gilbert. Grad. St. Louis U., 1946. Vice pres. Khoury Bros. Printing, St. Louis, 1946—; exec. dir. George Khoury Assn. Baseball Leagues, Inc., St. Louis, 1967—. Served with U.S. Army, 1943-45, NATOUSA, MTO. Decorated Purple Heart with oak leaf cluster. Roman Catholic. Office: George Khoury Assn Baseball Leagues Inc 226 Lemay Ferry Rd Saint Louis MO 63125

KIDDLE, LAWRENCE BAYARD, emeritus Spanish language educator; b. Cleve., Aug. 20, 1907; s. Bayard Taylor and Emma Melvina (Volmar) K.; B.A. magna cum laude, Oberlin (Ohio) Coll., 1929; M.A., U. Wis. at Madison, 1930, Ph.D., 1935; m. Allene Cornelia Houglan, June 29, 1932; children—Sue (Mrs. Loche Van Atta), Mary Ellen. Teaching asst. Spanish and French, U. Wis., 1929-35; instr. U. N.Mex., Albuquerque, 1935-37, asst. prof., 1937-38; instr. Spanish, Princeton, 1938-40; asst. prof. Romance langs. Tulane U., New Orleans, 1940-41, assoc. prof., 1941-43; asst. prof. Spanish, Romance linguistics U. Mich., Ann Arbor, 1947-48, assoc. prof., 1948-54, prof., 1954-78, prof. emeritus, 1978—. Fulbright prof. linguistics Instituto Caro y Cuervo, Bogotá, Colombia, 1963-64. Served to lt. comdr. USNR, 1943-47. Decorated comandante Orden Militar de Ayacucho (Peru). Mem. Hispanic Soc. Am. (corr.), MLA, Am. Assn. Tchrs. Spanish and Portuguese (pres.), Linguistic Soc. Am. Democrat. Editor: (with J.E. Englekirk) Los de Abajo (Mariano Azuela), 1939; Veinte Cuentos Hispanoamericanos del Siglo Veinte, 1956; El Libro de Las Cruzes (Alfonso El Sabio), 1961; Cuentos Americanos y Algunas Poesías, 1970; La Barraca (Blasco Ibáñez), 1961. Home: 2654 Englave Dr Ann Arbor MI 48103

KIDDY, CHARLES AUGUSTUS, agricultural researcher, administrator; b. Boston, Apr. 14, 1931; s. Charles Stanley and Mary Agnes (O'Neil) K.; m. Beverly Elaine Fournier, Dec. 22, 1951; children—Kenneth Charles, Kathleen Mary, Christopher Jay (dec.), Thomas Lee, Michael Paul. B.S., U. Mass., 1951; M.S., U. Wis., 1955, Ph.D., U. Wis., 1958. With Agrl. Research Service, Dept. Agr., Beltsville, Md., 1958-84, nat. program leader, 1979-84, dir. U.S. Dairy Forage Research Ctr., Madison, Wis., 1984—. Contbr. articles to profl. jours. Pres. parish conf. St. Vincent de Paul Soc., 1975-84. Served to capt. USAFR, 1951-62. Recipient Outstanding Performance award Dept. Agr.; 1963, 81, Sustained Outstanding Performance award, 1965. Mem. Am. Dairy Sci., Assn., Am. Soc. Animal Sci., AAAS. Avocations: breeding Am. quarter horses and simmental cattle. Home: 5594 Alpine Rd Brooklyn WI 53521 Office: US Dairy Forage Research Ctr 1925 Linden Dr W Univ Wis Madison WI 53706

KIEFER, KAREN HOPE, psychiatrist, hypnoanalyst; b. New Britian, Conn., May 31, 1947; d. Lester Fuog and Esther Edna (Bohn), Spencer; m. Richard Curtis Kiefer, Aug. 25, 1973 (dec. May, 1981); 1 child, Kristian Jacob. B.A., SUNY Oneonta, 1970; M.S., SUNY-Buffalo, 1976; D.O., Chgo. Coll. Osteo. Medicine, 1976. Diplomate Am. Bd. Psychistry and Neurology, cert. in adult and child psychiatry Am. Osteo. Bd. Pediatric Neurology and Psychiatry, cert. in adult and pediatric psychiatry. Oncological fellow Nat. Cancer Inst., Bethesda, Md., 1971-72; rotating intern Lansing Gen. Hosp., Mich., 1976-77; resident in psychistry Mich. State U., Grand Rapids, Mich., 1977-79; Case Western Res. U. Hosp., 1981-82; staff psychiatrist Ohio Dept. Mental Health, Cleve., 1981—; cons. Bellefaire Residential Treatment Ctr., Cleve., 1984—; asst. clin. prof. Case Western Res. U., 1982—. Mem. Am. Coll. Neuropsychiatrists, Am. Osteo. Assn.; Am. Psychiat. Assn., Am. Soc. Clin. Hypnosis, Ohio Psychiat. Assn., Soc. Med. Hypnoanalysts. Office: PO Box 20789 Cleveland OH 44120

KIEFER, WILLIAM LEE, computer marketing executive; b. St. Louis, Aug. 19, 1946; s. A.A., St. Louis Community Coll., 1971; B.S., U. Mo., St. Louis, 1975; m. Joyce Ann Cwiklowski, Aug. 15, 1970; children—Jason Lee, William Andrew. Ins. agt. Liberty Mut. Ins. Co., St. Louis, 1973-75; Democratic dir. elections City of St. Louis, 1975; mktg. specialist GAF Corp., Lincolnwood, Ill., 1976-79; with Microdata Corp., St. Louis, 1979-83, Honeywell, Inc., St. Louis, 1983-85, Harris Computer Systems Div 7980 Clayton Rd Ward committeeman Dem. party City of St. Louis, 1976-79, mem. ward steering com., 1974-79, campaign mgr., 1974-76. Served with USMC, 1965-69. Mem. Am. Inst. Design and Drafting, Soc. Mfg. Engrs., Assn. Integrated Mfg., Internat. Computer Consultants Assn., Engring. Reprographics Soc., Data Processing Mgmt. Assn., St. Louis Jaycees, North Park Neighborhood Assn. (chmn.), Assn. Computer Users, VFW, Am. Legion, U. Mo.-St. Louis Alumni Assn. (v.p.), Alumni Alliance U. Mo. System, U. Mo.-St. Louis Bus. Alumni Assn. (pres. 1980-81). Democrat. Roman Catholic. Club: St. Louis Engrs. Home: 1656 Grape St Saint Louis MO 63147 Office: Saint Louis MO 63117

KIEGERL, SIEGFRIED MATHIAS, rehabilitation management company executive; b. Mannheim, Ger., Apr. 8, 1939; s. Heinrich and Erna Maria (Duczek) K.; m. Marguerite Evelyn French, Nov. 2, 1963; children—Erna, Mathias, Christine. B.A., Park Coll., 1976; M.A., Am. Grad. Sch. Internat. Mgmt., Glendale, Ariz., 1977. Profl. rehab. counselor; cert. rehab. counselor. Cons., SMK, Inc., Kansas City, Mo., 1970-75; pres. Profl. Rehab. Mgmt. Inc., Olathe, Kans., 1977—; adj. prof. St. Mary's Coll., Kansas City, Kans., 1978-81. Contbr. articles to profl. jours. Mem. Nat. Assn. Rehab. Profls. in Pvt. Sector, Nat. Rehab. Counseling Assn., Nat. Rehab. Assn. Republican. Roman Catholic. Home: Rt 3 Ward Cliff Rd Olathe KS Office: Profl Rehab Mgmt Inc 201 E Santa Fe St Olathe KS 66061

KIEL, FREDERICK ORIN, lawyer; b. Columbus, Feb. 22, 1942; s. Fred Otto and Helen Louise (Baird) K.; m. Vivian Lee Naff, June 2, 1963; 1 child, Aileen Vivian. A.B. magna cum laude, Wilmington Coll., 1963; J.D., Harvard U., 1966. Bar: Ohio 1966, U.S. Supreme Ct. 1972. Assoc. firm Peck, Shaffer & Williams, Cin., 1966-71, ptnr., 1971-80; ptnr. firm Taft, Stettinius & Hollister, Cin., 1980—; lectr. Contbr. articles on mcpl. bond fin. to profl. jours. Mem. Wilmington Coll. Alumni Council, 1984—. Recipient Bond Atty.'s Workshop Founder's award, 1982. Mem. Nat. Assn. Bond Lawyers (dir. 1979-84, pres. 1982-83, hon. dir. 1984—, editor Quarterly Newsletter 1982—; mem. Bond Attys. Workshop steering com. 1976, 83, 85), Ohio State Bar Assn., Cin. Bar Assn. Republican. Clubs: Queen City, Terrace Park Country, Queen City Mcpl. Bond. Office: Taft Stettinius & Hollister 1800 First Nat Bank Ctr 425 Walnut St Cincinnati OH 45202

KIELHOFER, JOHN DALE, sales executive, pilot; b. Chgo., Dec. 17, 1955; s. Gene Dale and Janice Elizabeth (Buslee) K.; m. Barbara Sue Bernhardt, July 2, 1981; children—Carrie Leigh Clark, Kenneth Andrew Clark, Barbara Janice. Assoc. in Mktg. Mgmt., Oakton Community Coll., Morton Grove, Ill., 1977. Part owner, apprentice Neumann-Buslee & Wolfe, Des Plaines, Ill., 1971-79, sales exec., 1977-79; sales exec. Ingredient Tech., Des Plaines, 1979-84; pres. Another Era, Ltd., Bloomingdale, Ill., 1984—, Bloomin T's Ltd., Bloomingdale, Ill. Com. mem. Cub Scouts Am., 1983; bd. dirs. Notre Dame High Sch. Alumni Assn.; v.p. Old Town Bloomingdale Mchts. Assn., 1984-85, pres., 1985—. Recipient award for meritorious service Notre Dame High Sch. Fathers Club, Niles, Ill., 1972, 73, 74. Mem. Am. Assn. Cereal Chemists, Chgo. Perfumery Soap and Extract Assn., Bloomingdale C. of C. (assoc. dir. 1985, bd. dirs. 1985—), Aircraft Owners and Pilots Assn., Exptl. Aircraft Assn. Republican. Roman Catholic. Club: Oakton Flying of Morton Grove (founding pres. 1975-76). Home: 570 Northport Dr Elk Grove Village IL 60007 Office: 108 S 3d St Bloomingdale IL 60108

KIELINEN, CYNTHIA ELIZABETH, nursing educator; b. Gloucester, Mass., Feb. 19, 1944; d. John N. and Sylvia W. (Jacobson) K. B.S., Boston U., 1967, M.S., 1972; Ed.D., Columbia U. Tchrs. Coll., 1979. R.N. Staff nurse Salem Hosp., Mass., 1964-67, faculty/coordinator Sch. Nursing, 1965-71; instr. Salem State Coll., 1972-76, assoc. project dir., 1978-81; assoc. prof., chair dept. nursing baccalaureat Calvin Coll./Hope Coll., Holland, Mich., 1981—. Mem. N.E. Mass. Heart Assn., Mich. Nurses Assn., Nat. League Nurses, Am. Assn. Colls. Nursing, Sigma Theta Tau. Episcopalian. Avocations: music; sewing; knitting. Home: 968 Acorn Dr Holland MI 49423 Office: Hope College Holland MI 49423

KIELMAN, RICHARD CHARLES, hospital administrator, management educator; b. Sioux Falls, S.D., Mar. 15, 1946; s. Herman and Viola Frances Geneva (Oihus) K.; m. Cheryl Rae Prins, Jan. 25, 1969 (div. Sept. 1983); children—Christopher Charles, Tamra Lynn. B.S., U. S.D., 1968, M.B.A., 1971. Instr., Benedictine Coll., Atchison, Kans., 1972-75, chmn., asst. prof., 1975-77; dir. edn. Meml. Hosp., Fremont, Nebr., 1977-78, dir. support service, 1978-80, v.p., 1980—; mgmt. instr. Met. Community Coll., Omaha, 1979—. Bd. dirs. Health Planning Council of the Midlands, Omaha, 1980-81. Served to 1st lt. U.S. Army, 1968-70. Mem. Am. Soc. Hosp. Planning, Am. Mgmt. Assn., Am. Acad. Med. Adminstrs., Am. Coll. Hosp. Adminstrs., Nebr. Hosp. Assn. Republican. Club: Sertoma (Fremont, Nebr.).

KIELY, DENNIS LEE, physician; b. Grayling, Mich., June 3, 1950; s. Robert Burton and Betty Mae (Bloom) K.; m. Chelo Mae Merritt, Nov. 13, 1982; 1 child, Timothy Allen. A.S., Delta Coll., 1970; B.S., Mich. State U., 1974, D.O., 1977. Registered histologist Am. Soc. Clin. Pathologists. Intern, Bay Osteo. Hosp., Bay City, Mich., 1977-78; resident in pediatrics Chgo., 1978-79; gen. practice osteo. medicine Pub. Health Dept., Mt. Pleasant, Mich., 1982-83, The Community Clinic, Weidman, Mich., 1984—; gen. practice osteo. medicine, Midland, Mich., 1983-84; med. dir. Branch County Clinic, Coldwater, Mich., 1984; med. cons. Tri-County Center, Midland, 1983-84, 1016 House (drug rehab.), Midland, 1983-84. Com. mem. Lake Huron Area Council Boy Scouts Am., Weidman, 1985; scout master, asst. scout master Paul Bunyan Council Boy Scouts Am., 1961-68 (recipient Eagle, God, Country awards). Mem. Am. Osteo. Assn., Osteo. Gen. Practioners of Mich., Am. Coll. Osteo. Pediatricians (assoc.). Presbyterian. Avocations: hunting, camping, fishing, horseback riding. Home and Office: 3180 First St PO Box 215 Weidman MI 48893

KIES, CONSTANCE VIRGINIA, nutrition educator, scientist; b. Blue River, Wis., Dec. 13, 1934; d. Guerdon Francis and Gertrude Caroline (Pitts) K. B.S., U. Wis.-Platteville, 1955, M.S., U. Wis.-Madison, 1960, Ph.D., 1963. Lic. dietitian, Tex.; lic. tchr., Wis. English tchr. Rothschild-Schofield area schs., Wis., 1955-56; tchr., librarian Pontage High Sch., Wis., 1956-58; research asst. U. Wis., Madison, 1960-63; dietition instr. Madison Gen. Hosp., Wis., 1960-63; asst. prof. U. Nebr., Lincoln, 1963-65, assoc. prof., 1965-68, prof. human nutrition, 1968—. Editor: Bioavailability of Iron, 1983; Bioavailability of Calcium, 1985. Assoc. editor Nutrition Reports Internat. Contbr. articles to profl. jours. Recipient Disting. Alumni award U. Wis., Platteville, 1974. Grantee Ross-Abbott Labs., 1982. Mem. Am. Chem. Soc., Inst. Nutrition, Soc. for Clin. Nutrition, Am. Assn. Cereal Chemists, Am. Dietetics Assn. (registered dietitian), Am. Oil Chemists Assn., Soc. Enteral and Parenteral Nutrition, Am. Home Econs. Assn. (Borden award 1973). Congregationalist. Home: 3341 Holdredge Apt 9 Lincoln NE 68503

KIESOW, LINDA F., data processing executive; b. Rock Island, Ill., July 5, 1953; d. Oscar R. and Helen F. (Junk) McElroy; m. James Thomas Kiesow, May 26, 1973. B.Bus. in Acctg., Western Ill. U., 1979; M.B.A., U. Iowa, 1985. Cert. data processor. Produce mgr. Carthage Super Valu, Ill., 1974-75; aggregate sample analyst Valley Quarry, St. Augustine, Ill., 1975-76; data processing mgr. Moline Consumers Co., Ill., 1979—. Fulbright scholar Western Ill. U., Macomb, 1977; Coll. Bus. Scholar, Western Ill. U., 1978; Acctg. Dept. scholar Western Ill. U., 1978. Mem. Acctg. Soc. (mem. banquet com. chmn., v.p. 1977-78), Nat. Assn. Female Execs., Data Processing Mgmt. Assn., Assn. of Inst. for Cert. of Computer Profls., Alpha Lambda Delta, Phi Kappa Phi. Republican. Baptist. Avocations: reading; sports. Home: 4907 48th Ave Moline IL 61265 Office: Moline Consumers Co 313 16th St Moline IL 61265

KIFFEL, WILLIAM GILBERT, research scientist; b. Kenosha, Wis., Apr. 5, 1932; s. Herman and Hertha (Heimsoth) K.; m. Gloria Mae Vite, June 23, 1956; children—Kevin William, Kurtis Anthony, Karon Monica. B.S. in Chemistry, U. Wis.-Milw., 1959; cosmetic sci. diploma, Roosevelt U., 1972. Chemist Am. Motors Corp., Kenosha, 1959-62; chemist to research assoc. Internat. Personal Care Div., S.C. Johnson & Son Inc., Racine, Wis., 1962—. Patentee in field. Bd. dirs. Troop 491, Gateway council Boy Scouts Am., Kenosha, 1967-77. Served to sgt. U.S. Army, 1952-54. Mem. Soc. Cosmetic Chemists (com. chmn. 1972), Am. Chem. Soc. Lodge: Moose. Home: 2015 22nd St Kenosha WI 53140 Office: SC Johnson & Son Inc 1525 Howe St Racine WI 53140

KIFFMEYER, JAMES GEORGE, priest, pharmacist, educator; b. Cin., Mar. 2, 1957; s. James Costello and Patricia Mary (Fessler). B.S., U. Cin., 1980; M.A., Athenaeum of Ohio, 1985, M. Div., 1985. Registered pharmacist, Ohio; cert. secondary tchr. Ohio. Ordained priest Roman Catholic Ch., 1985. Pharmacist, St. George Hosp., Cin., 1980-81, Moore's Pharmacy, Cin., 1981-84; tchr. McNicholas High Sch., Cin., 1983-84; Roman Catholic deacon Archdiocese of Cin., 1984-85; chaplain Carroll High Sch., Dayton, Ohio, 1984-85. Mem. Hamilton County Pharm. Assn., Ohio State Pharm. Assn., Catholic Pharmacist Guild. Avocations: photography, racketball. Home: 462 Considine Ave Cincinnati OH 45205 Office: St Mary Ch 3917 Central Ave Middletown OH 45044

KIHNE, JOHN FRANKLIN, educator; b. Grafton, N.D., Dec. 5, 1950; s. Joseph R. and Holmfridur (Asmundson) K.; m. Susan Amelia Hoffman, Aug. 14, 1971; children—Jason Alexander, Nancy Jo. B.S. in Edn. U. N.D., 1973. Tchr. indsl. arts Turtle Mountain Community Sch., Belcourt, N.D., 1973-77; tchr. indsl. arts Mandan (N.D.) High Sch., 1977—, asst. coach in cross country, track, 1980—. Served to 1st lt. USAR, 1973-81. Mem. N.D. Indsl. Arts Assn. (Tchr. of Yr. award 1982), Am. Indsl. Arts Assn., N.D. Vocat. Assn., Am. Vocat. Assn., N.D. Edn. Assn., NEA, Am. Legion. Democrat. Roman Catholic. Lodges: K.C., Elks. Home: 1202 3rd St NE Mandan ND 58554 Office: 905 8th Ave NW Mandan ND 58554

KIKUCHI, CHIHIRO, physics educator; b. Seattle, Sept. 26, 1914; s. Naoki and Mitsuye (Ichinomiya) K.; m. Grace Keiko Fujii; children—Naomi, Carl, Gary. B.S. in Physics, U. Wash., 1939, Ph.D. in Physics, 1944; M.A. in Math., U. Cin., 1943. Instr. Haverford Coll., Pa., 1943-44, Mich. State U., East Lansing 1944-53; research physicist U.S. Naval Research Lab., Washington, 1953-55; prof. physics U. Mich., Ann Arbor, 1955—; vis. research physicist Brookhaven Nat. Lab., Upton, N.Y., 1951-52; tech. specialist IAEA, Taiwan, 1964; internat. collaborator Atomic Energy Instn., Brazil, 1976-77. Author: Nuclear Power, 1979. Fellow Am. Physical Soc., Am. Nuclear Soc. Democrat. Congregationalist. Home: 1050 Wall St Apt 5D Ann Arbor MI 48105 Office: Dept Nuclear Engring U Mich Ann Arbor MI 48109

KILBANE, THOMAS JAMES, lawyer; b. Cleve., Aug. 19, 1937; s. Thomas Bryan and Nora (Coyle) K.; m. Lucy Clay Ryan, July 31, 1965; children—Nora, Sarah, Thomas, Clare, Brendan, Terrence, Grace, Egan. B.A., Holy Cross Coll., 1959; M.S., Western Res. U., 1960; J.D., Capital U., 1967. Bar: Ohio 1968, U.S. Dist. Ct. (so. dist.) Ohio 1978. Dist. mgr. Williams & Co., Inc., Charleston, W.Va., 1960-69; gen. referee Franklin County Probate Ct., Columbus, Ohio, 1970-73; assoc. Bessey & Kilbane, Columbus, 1973-75; sole practice, Columbus, 1975—; mem. faculty Ohio Legal Ctr. Inst.; lectr. Capital U. Continuing Edn. Faculty. Mem. adv. bd. Salvation Army, Columbus, 1981—; trustee Birthright of Columbus, 1974-77. Mem. Ohio State Bar Assn., Columbus Bar Assn. (fee arbitration panel, chmn. probate law com.), Columbus Lawyers Club (pres.). Address: 2715 Wexford Rd Columbus OH 43221

KILBANE, THOMAS STANTON, lawyer; b. Cleve., Mar. 7, 1941; s. Thomas Joseph and Helen (Stanton) K.; m. Sally Conway, June 4, 1966; children—Sarah, Thomas, Eamon, James, Carlin. B.A., magna cum laude, John Carroll U., 1963; J.D., Northwestern U., 1966. Bar: Ohio 1966, U.S. Ct. Claims 1981, U.S. Ct. Appeals (6th cir.) 1982, U.S. Supreme Ct. 1975. Assoc. Squire, Sanders & Dempsey, Cleve., 1966-76, ptnr., 1976—. Democratic precinct committeeman, Rocky River, Ohio, 1974-76. Served to capt. USAR, 1967-69, Vietnam. Decorated Bronze Star. Mem. ABA, Ohio Bar Assn., Greater Cleve. Bar Assn. Republican. Roman Catholic. Clubs: Union (Cleve.), Athletic (Cleve.), Mid-Day (Cleve.). Home: 22800 Lake Rd Rocky River OH 44116 Office: 1800 Huntington Bldg Cleveland OH 44115

KILBO, MELVIN HERMAN, police chief; b. Sebeka, Minn., Dec. 23, 1928; s. Gustu Herman and Esther Laura (Pantsari) K.; m. Mary Ellen Quady, Jan. 20, 1951; children—Erik, Brian. A.S., North Hennepin Jr. Coll., 1972; B.A., Minn. Met. State U., 1976. Lic. police officer, Minn. Patrolman, Golden Valley Police Dept., Minn., 1958-64, uniform sgt., 1964-72, detective sgt., 1972-73, watch comdr., 1973-75; chief of police City of Orono, Crystal Bay, Minn., 1975—. Served with U.S. Army, 1950-51. Mem. Minn. Chiefs of Police Assn. (pres. 1983-84, bd. dirs. 1979), Hennepin County Police Chiefs Assn. (pres. 1981), Suburban Law Enforcement Assn. (life), Minn. Police and Police Officers Assn., Internat. Assn. Chiefs of Police, Am. Soc. Indsl. Security. Roman Catholic. Avocations: bowhunting; fishing; travel. Office: Orono Police Dept 1330 Brown Rd Crystal Bay MN 55323

KILBY, JAN ELIZABETH, university administrator; b. New Haven, Jan. 4, 1949; d. Robert H. and Rosalie R. (Costello) Kilby. B.A., St. Mary's U., San Antonio, 1970; M.A., Southwest Tex. State U., 1972; Ph.D., U. Tex., 1978; postdoctoral fellow U. Ill., 1981-83. Instr. English, St. Mary's U., San Antonio, 1972-78; asst. dir. United Colls. of San Antonio Consortium, 1974-75; instr. Austin Community Coll., Tex., 1975-77; instr. div. edn. U. Tex., San Antonio, 1978; dir. project on career and English, Nat. Council Tchrs. English, Urbana, Ill., 1978-79; dir. edn. placement U. Ill., Urbana, 1979-83; asst. dean student affairs U. Minn., Mpls., 1983—. Author: Career Education and English, K-12, 1980. Editor: Job Search Handbook for Educators, 1980-81. Contbr. articles to profl. jours. Editorial reviewer Jour. Tchr. Edn., 1984—. Mem. Nat. Council Tchrs. English, Nat. Career Development Assn., Am. Assn. for Counseling and Devel., Am. Coll. Personnel Assn., Am. Assn. for Higher Edn., Assn. Tchr. Educators. Office: U Minn Coll Edn 1425 University Ave SE Minneapolis MN 55414

KILDEE, DALE E., congressman; b. Flint, Mich., Sept. 16, 1929; s. Timothy Leo and Norma Alicia (Ullmer) K.; B.A., Sacred Heart Sem., 1952; tchr.'s certificate U. Detroit, 1954; M.A., U. Mich., 1961; postgrad. (Rotary Found. fellow) U. Peshawar (Pakistan), 1958-59; m. Gayle Heyn, Feb. 27, 1965; children—David, Laura, Paul. Tchr., U. Detroit High Sch., 1954-56, Flint Central High Sch., 1956-64; mem. Mich. Ho. of Reps. from 81st Dist., 1964-74; mem. Mich. Senate from 29th dist., 1975-77; mem. 95th-99th Congresses from 7th Mich. dist., 1977—. Mem. Am. Fedn. Tchrs., Urban League, Phi Delta Kappa. Clubs: K.C., Optimists. Office: 2432 Rayburn House Office Bldg Washington DC 20515 also 400 N Saginaw St Flint MI 48502

KILGORE, JOE MOFFATT, editor; b. Clifton, Tex., Sept. 9, 1916; s. Walter Louis and Mary Alice (Gallagher) K.; B.J. magna cum laude, Temple U., 1950; M.S.J., UCLA, 1951; m. Cathryn McCormick, Feb. 4, 1965; 1 dau., Linda Kilgore Brandon. Mng. editor Three Sons Publ. Co., Niles, Ill., 1961—; realtors assoc. ERA Gudgeon & Assocs., Inc., Lake Zurich, Ill. Mem. Constl. Amendment Conv., 1977. Served with USN, 1939-46. Mem. Nat. Assn. Realtors, Lake County Bd. Realtors. Home: 134 Eastwood Ln Route 4 Barrington IL 60010 Office: 6311 Grosse Pointe Rd Niles IL 60068

KILLIAN, WILLIAM FRANCIS, periodontist, air force officer; b. Balt., Sept. 8, 1943; s. William Frank and Elizabeth Mary (Schmidt) K.; m. Melanie Cecelia Reese, June 8, 1968; children—William F., Brian D., Ashley E. B.A., Loyola Coll., Balt., 1965; D.D.S., U. Md.-Balt., 1969; M.S., U. Tex.-Houston, 1976. Commd. 2d lt. U.S. Air Force, 1966, advanced through grades to col., 1984; chief gen. dentistry USAF Hosp., Fairchild AFB, Wash., 1971-73; resident in periodontics Wilford Hall Med. Ctr, San Antonio, 1973-76; chief periodontics USAF Clinic, Charleston AFB, S.C., 1976-79, Hickam AFB, Hawaii, 1979-83, USAF Med. Ctr., Scott AFB, Ill., 1983—; cons., 1983—. Mem. Am. Acad. Periodontology, ADA, Omicron Kappa Upsilon, Beta Beta Beta, Gorgas Dental Honor Soc. Republican. Roman Catholic. Avocation: woodworking. Home: 807 Meadowlark Dr O'Fallon IL 62269 Office: USAF Med Ctr Scott AFB IL 62225

KILLIN, ARTHUR MARION, consulting engineer, business consultant; b. Dayton, Ky., June 3, 1907; s. Ralph Waldo and Marjorie Eloise (Davidson) K.; m. Miriam Helen Van Dusen, June 25, 1936. B.S. in Elec. Engring., Purdue U., 1930, profl. degree in Elec. Engring., 1934. Registered profl. engr., N.Y. With Union Carbide Corp., Sault Ste. Marie, Mich., 1930-48, Niagara Falls, N.Y., 1949-60, N.Y.C., 1961-63, plant mgr., Ashtabula, Ohio, 1963-67; cons. U.S. Small Bus. Adminstrn., Cleve., 1969-85. Served as col. C.E., U.S. Army, 1930-62. Life mem. IEEE (pres. 1971), Air Pollution Control Assn. Republican. Clubs: Niagara; Rotary. Home: 3916 Edgewater Dr Ashtabula OH 44004

KILLINGBECK, JANICE LYNELLE (MRS. VICTOR LEE KILLINGBECK), journalist; b. Flint, Mich., Nov. 11, 1948; d. Leonard Paul and Ina Marie (Harris) Johnson; B.A., Mich. State U., 1970; postgrad. Delta Coll., 1971-72; m. Victor Lee Killingbeck, Sept. 26, 1970; children—Deeanna Dawn, Victor Scott. Tourist counselor Mich. Dept. State Hwys., Clare, 1969; copy editor Mich. State News, East Lansing, 1969-70; gen. reporter Midland (Mich.) Daily News, 1970; tchr. Saginaw (Mich.) Public Schs., 1971; public relations teller 1st State Bank of Saginaw, 1971-75; crew leader spl. census in Buena Vista Twp., Detroit Regional Office, U.S. Bur. Census, 1976, interviewer ann. housing survey-standard met. statis. areas, 1977-78, interviewer on-going health surveys, 1979—, Nat. Crime Survey, 1985—; editor AMEN newsletter United Meth. Women, Saginaw, 1984-85. Mem. Women in Communications, Sigma Delta Chi. Methodist. Home and Office: 4946 Hess Rd Saginaw MI 48601

KILLOY, WILLIAM JOHNI, periodontics dentist; b. Butte, Mont., July 29, 1936; s. John B. and Marie (Bursken) K.; m. Patricia Ann Jones; children—Diane, John, Richard, Kristine. Student, Carroll Coll., 1953-55; D.D.S., Creighton U., 1959; M.S., U. Tex., 1968. Diplomate Am. Bd. Periodontology. Dental officer U.S. Air Force, 1958-79, ret. col., 1979; chmn. dept. periodontics Wilford Hall U.S. Air Force Med. Ctr., Lackland AFB, Tex., 1976-79; dir. grad. periodontics U. Mo., 1979-84, chmn., 1984—; cons. periodontics VA, Kansas City, Mo., 1979—, Leavenworth, Kans., 1979—. Contbg. author: The Periodontics Syllabus, 1985. Contbr. articles to profl. jours. Mem. ADA, Am. Acad. Periodontology, Midwestern Soc. Periodontology, Mo. Dental Assn., Omicron Kappa Upsilon. Roman Catholic. Avocations: fishing; skiing. Home: 8931 Twilight St Lenexa KS 66219 Office: U Mo 650 E 25th St Kansas MO 64108

KILLPACK, JAMES ROBERT, banker; b. Persia, Iowa, Aug. 11, 1922; s. James Marion and Dorothy (Divelbess) K.; B.S., Miami U., Oxford, Ohio, 1946; m. Norma Hewett, June 11, 1949; children—James, John, Steven. With Peat, Marwick, Mitchell & Co., Cleve., 1946-58; treas. Ferro Corp., Cleve., 1958-66; fin. v.p. Island Creek Coal Co., Cleve., 1966-68; dir. corp. planning Eaton Corp. (formerly Eaton Yale & Towne Inc.), Cleve., 1968-69, v.p. corp. planning, 1969, v.p. adminstrn., 1970, v.p. fin., 1970-78, exec. v.p. fin. and adminstrn., 1978; pres. Nat. City Bank, Cleve., 1979-84, dir., 1979—; pres., dir. Nat. City Corp., 1981—; dir. Sherwin-Williams Co., 1979, Weatherchem, 1981. Served with AUS, 1942-45. C.P.A., Ohio. Mem. Fin. Execs. Inst. (dir. Cleve. chpt., pres. 1970-71), Am. Inst. C.P.A.s. Mem. Christian Ch. Clubs: Tavern, Union (Cleve.); Shaker Country (Shaker Heights, Ohio); Pepper Pike, The Country (Pepper Pike); Rolling Rock (Pa). Home: 13901 Shaker Blvd Cleveland OH 44120 Office: 1900 E 9 St 35th Floor Cleveland OH 44114

KIM, DAVID YOUNG, psychiatrist; b. Seoul, Korea, Apr. 23, 1945; came to U.S., 1974, naturalized 1980; s. Hyun-oo and Janran (Jung) K.; m. Jennifer Park, Mar. 17, 1971; children—Emily, Park. B.S., U. Korea, Seoul, 1967, M.D., 1971. Diplomate Am. Bd. Psychiatry and Neurology. Resident in psychiatry Nassau County Med. Ctr., East Meadow, NY., 1974-77; asst. clin. prof. Med. Coll. Wis., 1980; practice medicine specializing in psychiatry, Racine, Wis., 1980—; assoc. clin. dir. Mental Health Mgmt., Racine, 1984—; chmn. dept. psychiatry St. Lukes Hosp., Racine, 1984—. Bd. dirs. Bell City Learning Ctr., Racine, 1982. Recipient Excellence in Clin. Practice award, State of Wis., 1978. Mem. Am. Psychiat. Assn., Wis. Med. Soc. Republican.

KIM, KWAN S(UK), economist, educator, consultant; b. Pusan, Korea, Oct. 8, 1936; came to U.S., 1959, naturalized, 1970; s. Joon W. and Bok Hee (Yoo) K.; m. Gloria Jean Letourneau, Mar. 19, 1966; children—Kevin Christopher, Malaika Nicole. B.A., Seoul (Korea) Nat. U., 1959; M.A. in Polit. Sci., U.

Minn., 1961, Ph.D. in Econs., 1967. Research economist North Star Research and Devel. Inst., Mpls., 1964; econometrician Pillsbury Co., Mpls., 1964-66; instr. U. Minn., Mpls., 1966-67; asst. prof. econs. U. Notre Dame (Ind.), 1967-75, assoc. prof., 1975—; vis. lectr. U. Nairobi (Kenya), 1971-73; vis. prof. U. Dar es Salaam (Tanzania), 1975-77; econ. policy adviser AID, Washington, 1979-81; vis. prof. Universidad Autonoma de Nuevo Leon (Mexico), 1982; econ. adviser Nacional Financiera, Mexico, 1984; vis. prof. Delft Inst. Mgmt. Sci., The Netherlands, 1984; cons. AID, 1983. Recipient Merit award AID, 1980; Asian Research Inst. fellow Pan-Asia Inst., Washington, 1970-71; Rockefeller Found. grantee, 1971-73, 75-77. Mem. Am. Econ. Assn., Econometric Soc. N.AAm. Econ. and Fin. Assn. Roman Catholic. Club: Atari Computer (South Bend, Ind.). Co-author: Papers on the Political Economy of Tanzania, 1979; Korean Agricultural Research, 1982; Debt and Development in Latin America, 1985; contbr. numerous articles to profl. jours. Home: 414 Napoleon Blvd South Bend IN 46617 Office: Decio 110 U Notre Dame Notre Dame IN 46556

KIM, MICHAEL WOOKUN, physician; b. Pusan, Korea, Mar. 15, 1940; came to U.S., 1970, naturalized, 1976; s. Pora and Bogryun (Park) K.; m. Catherine Soyoung Park, June 14, 1969; 1 child, David Paul. M.D., Seoul Nat. U. (Korea), 1964. Diplomate Am. Bd. Internal Medicine, Am. Bd. Hematology. Attending physician Bay State Med. Ctr., Springfield, Mass., 1977-80; instr. Tuft U., Boston, 1978-80, asst. prof., 1980; clin. asst. prof. Med. Coll. Ohio, Toledo, 1981—; practice medicine specializing in hematology and oncology, Lima, Ohio, 1981—. Served to capt. Army Republic of Korea, 1965-69. Mem. Am. Coll. Physicians, Am. Soc. Hematology. Office: 718 W Market St Lima OH 45801

KIM, SUNG KYU, physics educator; b. Soonchun, Korea, Jan. 12, 1939; came to U.S., 1954, naturalized, 1970; m. Sherry J. Erickson, Aug. 24, 1968; children—Robert, Jennifer, Alicia, Alexander. B.S., Davidson Coll., 1960; A.M., Duke U., 1964, Ph.D., 1965. Asst. prof. physics Macalester Coll., St. Paul, 1965-70, assoc. prof., 1972-75, prof., 1975—; asst. prof. U. Calif., Irvine, 1970-71; prof. Bethel Coll., St. Paul, 1978-79; vis. scholar U. Chgo., 1980-81. Author: Physics: The Fabric of Reality, 1975; (with E.N. Strait) Modern Physics for Scientists and Engineers, 1978. Mem. Am. Phys. Soc., Am. Assn. Physics Tchrs., History of Sci. Soc. Presbyterian. Home: 3134 N Victoria St St Paul MN 55112 Office: Macalester Coll 1600 Grand Ave St Paul MN 55105

KIM, SUN-KEE, biologist, researcher, educator; b. Seoul, Korea, Dec. 11, 1937; came to U.S., 1961, naturalized, 1967; m. Sandra Lee, June 7, 1963; children—Karen Lee, Steven Michael. B.S., Yon-Sei U., Korea, 1960; M.S., U. Rochester, 1964, Ph.D., 1970. Predoct. trainee U. Rochester, N.Y., 1965-68; research biologist VA Med. Ctr., Ann Arbor, 1968—; research assoc. U. Mich. Med. Sch., Ann Arbor, 1971-74, asst. prof., 1974-81, assoc. prof., 1981—. Contbr. articles to profl. jours. Mem. Am. Soc. Cell Biology, Am. Assn. Anatomists, Internat. Assn. Dental Research, Gerontol. Soc. Methodist. Home: 2802 Torrey Ave Ann Arbor MI 48104 Office: Research Service VA Med Ctr 2215 Fuller Rd Ann Arbor MI 48105

KIM, YEONG ELL, physics educator, researcher, consultant; b. Cheju, Korea, Aug. 12, 1933; s. Chi Joon Kim and Sook Yang Koh; m. Kyung Sook Lim, 1960; children—Julia Mihyung, Anne Syl. B.S., Lincoln Meml. U., 1959; Ph.D., U. Calif.-Berkeley, 1963. Mem. tech. staff Bell Telephone Lab., Murray Hill, N.J., 1963-65; post-doctoral fellow Oak Ridge Nat. Lab., Tenn., 1965-67; prof. physics Purdue U., West Lafayette, Ind., 1967—; cons. Los Alamos Nat. Lab., 1973—; dir. Nuclear Theory Group, Purdue U., 1971—. Contbr. numerous research articles to profl. jours. Recipient Sr. Scientist award Humboldt Found., W. Ger., 1977. Fellow Am. Physical Soc., Korean Physical Soc. Home: 1834 Sheridan Rd West Lafeyette IN 47906 Office: Dept of Physics Purdue U West Lafayette IN 47907

KIM, YUNG DAI, research scientist; b. Seoul, Korea, Mar. 24, 1936; came to U.S., 1957, naturalized, 1971; s. Ik S. and Jung H. (Juhn) K.; m. Young S. Chyung, June 17, 1967; children—Jean Ok, Sue Ok. Ph.D., U. Minn., 1968. Vis. scientist Kettering Research Lab., Yellow Springs, Ohio, 1968-69; NIH fellow Northwestern U., Evanston, Ill., 1969-71; NIH research fellow U. Pa., Phila., 1971-73; immunochemist Worthington Biochem. Co., Freehold, N.J., 1973-74; sr. scientist Abbott Labs., North Chicago, Ill., 1974—. Mem. Am. Assn. Immunologists, Am. Chem. Soc., Sigma Xi, Phi Lambda Upsilon. Contbr. articles to profl. jours.; patentee in field. Home: 75 N Rolling Ridge Lindenhurst IL 60046 Office: Cancer Research Lab D90C Abbott Labs North Chicago IL 60064

KIMBALL, OLIVE CORNISH, educational administrator; b. Laurium, Mich., Aug. 19, 1930; d. William Verran and Jennie (Oliver) Cornish; children—Karen Lee, Paul Gordon. B.S. with honors in Gen. Sci., Mich. Technol. U., 1952; M.S. in Secondary Edn., No. Ill. U., 1969, Ed.D. in Ednl. Psychology, 1973; postgrad. Inst. Ednl. Mgmt., Harvard U., 1980. Research technologist Argonne Nat. Lab., Ill., 1952-53; ednl. diagnostician, DeKalb, Ill., 1970-73; asst. prof. No. Ill. U., DeKalb, 1973-79, dir., chmn. dept. allied health, 1974—, asst. dean profl. studies, 1975, assoc. dean, 1980-81, dir. univ./industry research, 1984—; accreditation survey evaluator for allied health AMA, Chgo., 1976—; corp. rep. AAUW, 1983—; project dir. several fed. and state funded research and demonstration projects. Contbr. articles in field to profl. publs. Recipient Bd. Control Silver Medal, Mich. Technol. U., 1984; Profl. Recognition award Ill. Med. Tech. Assn., 1984. Mem. Am. Pub. Health Assn., Am. Soc. for Allied Health Professions, Am. Assn. for Higher Edn., Am. Ednl. Research Assn., Am. Soc. Med. Tech., Am. Soc. Clin. Pathologists (assoc.), Alpha Eta. Home: 202 Knollwood Dr DeKalb IL 60115 Office: No Ill U DeKalb IL 60115

KIMBALL, PAUL CLARK, molecular biology researcher; b. New London, Conn., Jan. 26, 1946; s. Burton Clark and Carol (Williams) K.; B.S., MIT, 1968; Ph.D., U. Calif.-Berkeley, 1972. Instr. dept. microbiology U. Ill. Med. Ctr., Chgo., 1972; sr. scientist Meloy Labs., Springfield, Va., 1973-75; research assoc., asst. prof. Ohio State U., Columbus, 1975-81; prin. research scientist Battelle, Columbus, 1982-83, sr. research scientist, 1983-84, research leader, 1984—. Author: Virology, 1982. Contbr. articles to profl. jours. Grantee Nat. Cancer Inst. 1981-85, NSF 1980-85. Mem. AAAS, Am. Soc. Microbiology. Avocations: Tae Kwon Do; Amateur Radio; sailing. Home: 122 Forest Ridge Pl Worthington OH 43085 Office: Battelle 505 King Ave Columbus OH 43201

KIMBLE, JAMES A., management consultant, accountant; b. Owosso, Mich., June 6, 1937; s. Gaylord Browning and Iva I. (Ansted) K.; m. Virginia Ruth Humphreys, June 20, 1959 (div. 1970); children—Kim, Katherine, Kerri, Charles; m. Anne Park, June 13, 1970; 1 child, Jeffrey. B.B.A., U. Toledo, 1959. Treas. The PM Group-Toledo, Inc., 1961—; mgmt. cons., Toledo, 1978—. Pres. Citizens for Metroparks, Toledo, 1976-77; v.p., commr. Met. Park Dist., 1977—. Recipient Treasury Card IRS, 1976. Mem. Soc. Profl. Bus. Cons. (bd. dirs. 1977-80, cert.), Inst. Cert. Profl. Bus. Cons., Black & Skaggs Assocs. Republican. Avocation: fishing; travel; photography. Office: The PM Group Toledo Inc 3150 Republican N Toledo OH 43615

KIMBROUGH, WILLIAM WALTER, III, psychiatrist; b. Cleve., Sept. 26, 1928; s. William Walter and Minerva Grace (Champion) K.; student Cornell U., 1945-46; B.S., U. Mich., 1948, M.D., 1952; m. Jo Ann Greiner, July 6, 1953; children—Elizabeth, Douglas. Intern, Ohio State U. Health Center, Columbus, 1952-53; resident U. Chgo. Clinics, 1955-56, Ypsilanti (Mich.) State Hosp., 1956-59; asso. psychiatrist U. Mich. Health Service, Ann Arbor, 1959-61; practice medicine specializing in psychoanalytic psychiatry, Ann Arbor, 1961—; cons. atty. gen. U.S., 1958—, Center for Forensic Psychiatry, 1974—, Brighton Found. for Alcoholism, 1961—, Washtenaw County (Mich.) Community Mental Health Services, 1978—, Mich. Dept. Social Services, 1978—; clin. dir. Livingston County (Mich.) Community Mental Health Services, 1983—, Mich. Dept. Corrections, 1985—. Served to col. USPHS(R), 1953-81. Recipient Physicians Recognition awards AMA, 1972-84. Fellow Am. Acad. Psychiatry and Law, Am. Soc. Psychoanalytic Physicians; mem. Am. Acad. Psychotherapists, Am. Psychiat. Assn., Ann Arbor Psychiatric Assn., Mich. Psychiat. Assn., N.Y. Acad. Sci., AAAS, Hon. Order Ky. Cols., Sigma Alpha Epsilon, Phi Rho Sigma. Clubs: Ann Arbor Town, Ann Arbor Racquet, Univ., Travis Pointe Country (Ann Arbor); Little Harbor (Harbor Springs, Mich.). Home: 520 Hillspur Rd Barton Hills Village MI 48105 Office: 400 Maynard St Ann Arbor MI 48104

KIME, HARRIET RUTH, nurse; b. Sandusky, Ohio, June 13, 1955; d. Homer Lee and Maxine Mary (Null) K. B.S. in Nursing, U. Akron, Ohio, 1982. R.N., Ohio. Staff nurse St. Thomas Hosp. Med. Ctr., Akron, 1982—. Democrat. Mem. Ch. of the Nazarene. Office: St Thomas Hosp Med Ctr 444 N Main St Akron OH 44310

KIMEL, WILLIAM ROBERT, college dean; b. Cunningham, Kans., May 2, 1922; s. Chester LeRoy and Klonda Florence (Harte) K.; m. Mila Brown, Aug. 14, 1952. B.S. in Mech. Engring., Kans. State U., 1944, M.S. in Mech. Engring., 1949; Ph.D. in Mechanics, U. Wis., 1956. Registered profl. engr., Mo., Kans. Devel. engr. Goodyear Tire and Rubber Co., Akron, Ohio, 1944-46; instr. Kans. State U., 1946-48, asst. prof., 1948-54; engr. Boeing Airplane Co., Wichita, Kans., summer 1953, Westinghouse Electric Co., Kansas City, Mo., summer 1954; assoc. prof. Kans. State U., 1954-58, prof., head dept. nuclear engring., 1958-68; fellow U. Wis., 1955-56; engr. U.S. Forest Products lab., Madison, Wis., 1955-56; resident research assoc. Argonne Nat. Lab., 1957-58; dean U. Mo.-Columbia Coll. Engring., 1968—, dir. Engring. Expt. Sta., 1968-70, prof. nuclear engring. 1968—; cons. G.P.U. Parsippany, N.J., 1979-80, 84—, Inst. Nuclear Power Operation, Atlanta, 1980—, N.Y. Regents, Albany, 1983—; mem. nuclear engring. educ. com. Argonne U. Assn., Chgo., 1959—. Contbr. numerous articles to profl. jours. Chmn. Columbia Area Indl. Devel. com., 1970-76. Recipient Disting. Service in Engring. award Kansas State U., 1972, Faculty, Alumni award U. Mo.-Columbia, 1979, Bliss award Am. Soc. Mil. Engrs., 1982, Disting. Service citation U. Wis., 1982, award of merit Engring. Club St. Louis, 1983. Fellow Am. Nuclear Soc. (bd. dirs. pres. 1978-79), ASME; mem. Nat. Soc. Profl. Engrs. (exec. bd., bd. govs. 1984—), Mo. Soc. Profl. Engrs. (bd. dirs., pres. 1983-84), JETS (pres. 1980-81). Lodge: Rotary (pres. 1981-82). Home: 900 Yale St Columbia MO 65211 Office: Univ Mo-Columbia Coll Engring Columbia MO 65211

KIMES, ROBERT HILLMER, interior designer; b. Freeport, Ill., June 4, 1927; s. Thomas Albert and Marion E. (Hillmer) K.; m. Fawn Gray, Dec. 28, 1950; children—Bradford, E., Tracy M., Grant T. B.S., Knox Coll., 1950. Mgr. Bldg. & Design Ctr., Freeport, 1953-60; owner, mgr. Robert Kimes Designs, Freeport, 1956—. Pres. Greater Downtown Freeport, 1968-69; bd. dirs. YMCA, Freeport, 1983—. Served with USN, 1945-46. Recipient Liberty Bell award ABA, 1968. Mem. Am. Soc. Interior Designers (bd. dirs. 1973-74, v.p. 1977). Republican. Methodist. Lodge: Rotary (Freeport) (v.p. 1984-85, pres. 1985—). Home: Hickory Hill Freeport IL 61032 Office: Robert Kimes Designs 9 N Chicago Ave Freeport IL 61032

KIMM, JAMES WILSON, cons. engr.; b. Huron, S.D., Sept. 26, 1925; s. Arthur A. and Mary (Fry) K.; B.S., U. Iowa, 1950; m. Dorothy A. Madsen, Aug. 16, 1952; children—Mary L., Jill A., Tobias J. Pub. health engr. Iowa State Dept. Health, Des Moines, 1950-55; head san. engring. report sect. Stanley Engring. Co., Muscatine, Iowa, 1955-61; pres. Veenstra & Kimm, Inc., Engrs. and Planners, West Des Moines, Iowa, 1961—, West Des Moines Devel. Corp. Served with AUS, 1943-45. Named Engr. Distinction, Engrs. Joint Council. Mem. Iowa Water Pollution Control Assn. (past pres.), Iowa Engring Soc., Nat. Soc. Profl. Engrs., C. of C., Cons. Engrs. Council Iowa, Water Pollution Control Fedn. (dir.), Tau Beta Pi, Chi Epsilon. Presbyterian (elder). Contbr. articles and papers to profl. jours. Home: 3932 Ashworth Rd West Des Moines IA 50265 Office: 300 West Bank Bldg 1601 22 St West Des Moines IA 50265

KIMMEL, JOE ROBERT, physician, hospital administrator, biochemistry educator; b. DuQuoin, Ill., May 3, 1922; s. Maurice Edward and Sara Roberta (Pyatt) K.; m. Merolyn Jean Howell, Apr. 3, 1947; children—Phillip H., Lynn, Ellen, Bruce E. A.B., DePauw U., 1943; M.D. Johns Hopkins U., 1947; Ph.D., U. Utah, 1954. Intern, Salt Lake Gen. Hosp., 1947-49; resident in internal medicine U.S. Naval Hosp., Oakland, Calif., 1950-52; from instr. to assoc. prof. biochemistry U. Utah Med. Sch., Salt Lake City, 1954-64; prof. U. Kans. Med. Sch., Kansas City, 1964—, assoc. dean, 1970-76; assoc. chief staff/research VA Hosp., Kansas City, Mo., 1983—. Contbr. articles to profl. jours. Pres. Kaw Valley div. Am. Heart Assn.; mem., pres. Kansas City Youth Symphony Bd. Recipient Career Devel. award USPHS, 1960. Mem. Am. Soc. Biol. Chemistry, Endocrine Soc., AAAS, Sigma Xi. Democrat. Presbyterian. Avocations: sailing, railroads. Home: 11416 Marty Overland Park KS 66210 Office: VA Med Ctr Med Research Service 4801 Linwood Blvd Kansas City MO 64128

KIMMLE, BARBARA LOUISE, real estate broker; b. Belleville, Ill., Mar. 1, 1939; d. William Henry and Regina Marie (Hemmer) Koch; m. Albert Alfred Kimmle, Mar. 16, 1957; 1 child, Chrystia Jane. Student Belleville Area Coll., 1981-82. Legal sec. Jones, Ottesen & Fleming, Belleville, Ill., 1956-57, 1961-63; exec. v.p., dir. First Nat. Holding Corp., O'Fallon, Ill., 1963-82; v.p. Fulford Realty, Inc., O'Fallon, 1982—. Mem. O'Fallon C. of C. (sec. 1968-69; dir. 1973-76), Belleville Bd. Realtors, Multiple Listing Service (vice chmn. 1983), Ill. Assn. Realtors, Nat. Assn. Realtors, Women's Council Realtors (chpt. pres. 1974, 79), Wives of Ill. Assn. Hwy. Engrs. Roman Catholic. Club: St. Clare Altar Sodality (O'Fallon). Home: 402 E Jefferson St O'Fallon IL 62269 Office: 312 S Lincoln Ave O'Fallon IL 62269

KIMURA, JAMES HIROSHI, biochemistry educator; b. Kona, Hawaii, Oct. 29, 1944; s. Robert Takenori and Adelaide Yoshi K.; m. Pamela Sue Simmons, Apr. 26, 1975; children—Melissa Hanako, Daniel Takenori. B.S., U. Hawaii, Honolulu, 1971; Ph.D., Case Western Res. U., 1976. Postdoctoral fellow Case Western Res. U., Cleve., 1976. Nat. Inst. Child Health and Human Devel., Bethesda, Md., 1976-78; NIH staff fellow Nat. Inst. Dental Research, Bethesda, 1978-80, NIH sr. staff fellow, 1980-81; asst. prof. dept. orthpedic surgery and biochemistry Rush Med. Coll., Chgo., 1981-84, assoc. prof. biochemistry, 1984—. Mem. editorial bd. Jour. Biol. Chemistry, 1984—. Mem. Am. Soc. Biol. Chemists, AAAS, Orthopaedic Research Soc. Home: 632 S Clarence Oak Park IL 60304 Office: Rush Med Coll Dept Biochemistry 1753 W Congress Pkwy Chicago IL 60612

KINCAID, ARTHUR ROY, lawyer; b. Gardner, Kans., Apr. 24, 1911; s. Roy Porter and Sadie (Arnold) K.; m. Marion King, May 23, 1942; 1 dau., Carol Ann. A.B., William Jewell Coll., 1932; LL.B., U. Kansas City, 1941. Bar: Mo. 1941. Ptnr. firm Hale, Kincaid, Waters, and Allen, P.C., Liberty, Mo., 1944—, sr. mem., 1976—, pres., 1979—; mem. Mo. Ho. of Reps., 1937-42; city atty., Liberty, 1944-50. Chmn. bd. Liberty Pub. Works, 1960-70. Served to pvt. U.S. Army, 1943. Mem. ABA, Mo. Bar Assn., Clay County Bar Assn. Democrat. Mem. Christian Ch. Club: Rotary (Liberty). Home: 726 W Mississippi St Liberty MO 64068 Office: Hale Kincaid Waters Allen 17 W Kansas St Liberty MO 64068

KINCAID, DAVID MICHAEL, optometrist; b. Columbus, Nebr., Dec. 5, 1951; s. Milo Charles and Arlene E. (Johnson) K.; m. Diana Lynn Taschner, June 22, 1974; children—Samuel D., Daniel J. Assoc. Sci., Platte Coll., 1972; B.S. in Visual Sci., Ill. Coll. Optometry, 1977, O.D., 1977. Pvt. practice optometry, South Sioux City, Nebr., 1978—. Mem. Am. Optometric Assn., Nebr. Optometric Assn. Republican. Baptist. Lodge: Rotary (pres. 1984-85). Avocations: raise, breed, train Paso Fino horses; field trial Brittany bird dogs. Home: 508 Timber Line Dr South Sioux City NE 68776 Office: 114 S Ridge Plaza South Sioux City NE 68776

KINCANNON, L. E., petroleum refining company executive. Chmn., dir. Rock Island Refining Corp., Indpls. Office: Rock Island Refining Corp PO Box 68007 Indianapolis IN 46268*

KINDERS, ROBERT JAMES, biologist, researcher; b. Chgo., Feb. 12, 1948; s. Robert Peter and Clara Victoria (Marek) K.; m. Patricia M. Fogli, Mar. 10, 1980. Student Northwestern U., 1976-77; B.S., Loyola U., 1970, M.S., 1975; Ph.D., Kans. State U., 1980. Post-doctoral scientist Kans. State U., Manhattan, 1980-82; lab. head Ctr. Basic Cancer research, 1982-83; staff scientist Abbott Labs., North Chgo., 1983—. Contbr. articles to profl. jours. Served to SP5 U.S. Army, 1970-73, Vietnam. State of Ill scholar 1966; fellow Northwestern U. 1976, USPHS, NIH, Nat. Cancer Inst. 1977; USPHS NIH, Nat. Cancer Inst. grantee 1982. Mem. Am. Soc. Cell Biology, Cell Cycle Soc., Sigma Xi (assoc.). Avocations: music; athletics; computers. Office: Abbott Labs Bldg R1A North Chicago IL 60064

KINDNESS, THOMAS NORMAN, congressman; b. Knoxville, Tenn., Aug. 26, 1929; s. Norman G. and Christine (Gunn) K.; A.B. in Polit. Sci., U. Md., 1951; LL.B., George Washington U., 1953; m. Averil J. Stoneback, Jan. 7, 1984; children by previous marriage—Sharon L., David T., Glen J., Adam B. Admitted to D.C. bar, 1954; practiced in Washington, 1954-57; asst. counsel Champion Internat. Corp., Hamilton, O., 1957-73; mem. 94th-99th Congresses from 8th Dist. Ohio, 1975—, mem. judiciary, govt. operations coms. Mem. Hamilton City Council, 1964-69, mayor, 1964-67; mem. Ohio Ho. of Reps., 1971-74. Republican. Home: 646 High St Hamilton OH 45011 Office: Room 2417 Rayburn House Office Bldg Washington DC 20515

KINDRICK, ROBERT LEROY, educator; b. Kansas City, Mo., Aug. 17, 1942; s. Robert William and Waneta LeVeta (Lobdell) K.; B.A., Park Coll., 1964; M.A., U. Mo., 1967; Ph.D., U. Tex., 1971; m. Carolyn Jean Reed, Aug. 20, 1965. Instr., Central Mo. State U., Warrenburg, 1967-69, asst. prof., 1969-73, asso. prof., 1973-78, prof. English, 1978-84, head dept. English, 1975-80; dean Coll. Arts and Scis., also prof. English, Western Ill. U., Macomb, 1980-84; v.p. acad. affairs, prof. English, Emporia State U., Kans., 1984—. Chmn. bd. dirs. Mo. Com. for Humanities, 1979-80. U. Tex. fellow, 1965-66; Am. Council Learned Socs. travel grantee, 1975; Nat. Endowment for Humanities summer fellow, 1977; Mediaeval Acad. Am. grantee, 1976; Mo. Com. Humanities grantee, 1975-76; Assn. Scottish Lit. Studies grantee, 1979. Mem. Mo. Assn. Depts. English (pres. 1978-80), Mo. Philological Assn. (founding pres. 1975-77), Medieval Assn. Midwest (councillor 1977—), Ill. Medieval Assn. (founding exec. sec. 1984—), Mid-Am. Medieval Assn., Rocky Mountain MLA, Assn. Scottish Lt. Studies, Mo. Assn. Depts. English, Early English Text Soc., Société Rencesvals, Medieval Acad. N.Am. (exec. sec. com. on ctrs. and regional assns.), Internat. Arthurian Soc., Sigma Tau Delta, Phi Kappa Phi. Club: Rotary. Author: Robert Henryson, 1979; A New Classical Rhetoric, 1980; editor: Teaching the Middle Ages; contbr. articles to profl. jours. Home: 1005 State St Emporia KS 66801

KINDS, HERBERT E(UGENE), educator; b. Cleve., Feb. 25, 1933; s. Levander and Esther (Johnson) K. B.S. (Tyng scholar), Williams Coll., 1951-55; postgrad. Harvard U., 1955-58, Case Western Res. U., 1972, 80-81. Instr. Natchez (Miss.) Jr. Coll., 1958-68, registar, 1967, dean, 1968; tchr. Cleve. Pub. Schs., 1968—; owner Kinds Tutorial Service, 1972—; tutor Cuyahoga Community Coll., 1975-81, instr. chemistry. Deacon, Mt. Herodon Bapt. Ch. Mem. Math. Assn. Am., Am. Chem. Soc., Internat. Platform Assn., Phi Beta Kappa. Baptist. Baptist. Clubs: Williams of N.Y., Williams of Northeastern Ohio. Home: 9023 Columbia Ave Cleveland OH 44108

KINDSCHI, PAUL DOUGLAS, educational administrator, mathematics educator; b. Mitchell, S.D., Feb. 15, 1941; s. Paul Lorenz and Alberta L. (Klatt) K.; m. Barbara Jean Pechuman, Aug. 17, 1962; children—Elizabeth, Paul Aaron, Jennifer, Nicole. B.A., Houghton Coll., 1962; student U. Chgo., 1962-64; M.A., U. Wis.-Madison, 1967, Ph.D., 1972. Asst. prof. mathematics Sangamon State U., Springfield, Ill., 1970-76, dean ednl. services, 1973-76; dean Kirkhof Coll. Grand Valley State U., Allendale, Mich., 1976-83, prof. mathematics, 1982—, dean sci., mathematics, 1982—; cons. U. Chgo., 1980-81; regional cons. Am. Coll., Bryn Mawr, Pa., 1980—; project dir. Oakes Coll. U. Calif., Santa Cruz, 1978-80. Contbr. articles to profl. jours. Mem. exec. com. West Mich. Tourist Assn., Grand Rapids, 1981; bd. dirs. West Mich. Telecommunication Found., Grand Rapids, 1981. Kent fellow Danforth Found.; NSF fellow; Woodrow Wilson fellow. Fellow Soc. for Values in Higher Edn.; mem. Sigma Xi (pres. chpt. 1984-85), Phi Kappa Phi. Presbyterian. Home: 6761 Shady Oak Ln Hudsonville MI 49426 Office: Grand Valley State Coll 330 Loutit Allendale MI 49401

KINER, CAROL ANN, home economist; b. Chgo., July 22, 1954; s. Daniel Charles and Doris Elaine (Balling) K.; m. David Allen Howerton, Oct. 2, 1982. B.S. with honors, U. Ill., 1976, M.Ed. with highest honors, 1979. Tchr. home econs. Fenton High Sch., Bensenville, Ill., 1976-81; cons. home econs. Ill. Bd. Edn., Springfield, 1981-82; nat. mktg. services mgr. Forecast for Home Econs. mag., Scholastic, Inc., Chgo., 1982—. Bd. dirs. Greenwing Camp Mem. Am. Home Econs. Assn. (nat. resolutions com.), Chgo. Home Economists in Bus. (chmn. elect), Am. Vocat. Assn., Nat. Assn. Vocat. Home Econs. Tchrs., Ill. Home Econs. Assn., Ill. Vocat. Assn., Ill. Vocat. Home Econs. Tchrs. Assn. (Outstanding mem. 1985), Home Econs. Edn. Assn., Ill. Found. Future Homemakers Am. (bd. dirs. 1984—), U. Ill. Home Econs. Alumni Assn., Phi Upsilon Omicron, Kappa Delta Pi. Lutheran.

KING, ALBERT SIDNEY, management educator, administrator; b. Pampa, Tex., Nov. 16, 1939; s. John Thomas and Bonnie (Merle-Lambstein) K.; m. Sondra L. Heinze, Sept. 1, 1961 (div. 1983); children—Kim, Lynn, Karisa Leigh. Instr. mgmt. Tex. Tech. U., 1966-69; asst. prof. mgmt. Kans. State U.-Manhattan, 1969-72, assoc. prof., 1972-75, Troy State U., 1975; assoc. prof. No. Ill. U., 1975-79, prof., chmn. dept., 1979—, mem. senate Coll. Bus., 1984-85. Contbr. articles to bus. jours. Mem. DeKalb Environ. Research Com., 1984-85, mem. technol. transport com., 1984-85, mem. comml. Airtransport com., 1984-85. Mem. Acad. Mgmt., Assn. Bus. Simulation and Exptl. Learning, Midwest Bus. Adminstrn. Assn., Midwest Am. Inst. Decision Scis., Inst. Mgmt. Scis., Alpha Kappa Psi, Sigma Iota Epsilon. Office: Dept Mgmt No Ill U Wirtz Hall Room 122 DeKalb IL 60115

KING, BRUCE DEXTER, chemical company executive, researcher; b. Vidalia, Ga., Dec. 29, 1950; s. Tholan Frederick and Carolyn Ethyl (Fountain) K.; m. Teresa Ann Herndon, Oct. 23, 1982. B.S., Armstrong State Coll., 1973; M.S., U. Ga., 1976, Ph.D., 1979. Faculty U. Mo., Columbia, 1979-81; tech. services coordinator Syntex, Springfield, Mo., 1981-84, group product mgr., 1984—. Contbr. articles to profl. jours. Active Syntex Christmas Com., 1982-84; contbr. John Ashcroft for Gov., Springfield, 1984. Mem. Am. Soc. Animal Sci., Am. Dairy Sch. Assn., Poultry Sci. Assn., Am. Assn. Bakery Engrs., Soc. Environ. Geochemistry and Health, Am. Feed Mfrs. Assn. (vice chmn. com. 1984-86). Avocations: jogging; sailing; football; skiing; tennis. Home: 3447 S Rogers Springfield MO 65804 Office: Syntex Agribus Inc PO Box 1246 SSS Springfield MO 65805

KING, CHARLES ROSS, physician; b. Nevada, Iowa, Aug. 22, 1925; s. Carl Russell and Dorothy Sarah (Mills) K.; student Butler U., 1943; B.S. in Bus., Ind. U., 1948, M.D., 1964; m. Frances Pamela Carter, Jan. 8, 1949; children—Deborah Diane, Carter Ross, Charles Conrad, Corbin Kent. Dep. dir. Ind. Pub. Works and Supply, 1949-52; salesman Knox Coal Corp., 1952-59; rotating intern Marion County Gen. Hosp., Indpls., 1964-65; family practice medicine, Anderson, Ind., 1965—; sec.-treas. staff Community Hosp., 1969-72, pres. elect, dir., chief medicine, 1973—, also bd. dirs., 1973-75; sec.-treas. St. John's Hosp., 1968-69, chief medicine, 1972-73, chief pediatrics, 1977—; dir. Rolling Hills Convalescent Center, 1968-73; pres. Profl. Center Lab., 1965—. Vice-chmn. Madison County Bd. Health, 1966-69; dir. First Nat. Bank Madison County, Anderson. Bd. dirs. Family Service Madison County, 1968-69, Madison County Assn. Mentally Retarded, 1972-76; chmn., bd. dirs. Anderson Downtown Devel. Corp., 1980—. Served with AUS, 1944-46. Diplomate Am. Bd. Family Practice. Recipient Physician's Recognition award AMA, 1969, 72, 75, 78. Fellow Royal Soc. Health, Am. Acad. Family Practice (charter); mem. AMA, Ind., Pan Am. med. assns., Am. Acad. Gen. Practice, Madison County (pres. 1970), 8th Dist. (sec.-treas. 1968) med. socs., Anderson C. of C. (dir. 1979—), Indpls. Mus. Art (corp. mem.). Phi Delta Theta Alumni Assn. (pres. 1952), Phi Delta Theta, Phi Chi. Methodist. Club: Anderson Country (dir. 1976-79). Home: 920 N Madison Ave Anderson IN 46011 Office: 1933 Chase St Anderson IN 46014

KING, CHRISTOPHER MIDDLETON, ophthalmologist; b. Cleve., May 11, 1934; s. Douglass Stone and Kathryn Middleton K.; m. Marilyn Jackson, Sept. 5, 1959; children—Richard Douglass, Christopher Jackson, Lisa Kathryn. Cert. Mercersburg Acad., 1953; B.S., Mt. Union Coll., 1957; M.D., Ohio State U., 1960. Intern Miami Valley Hosp., Dayton, Ohio; resident Univ. Hosp., Ohio State U., Columbus; practice medicine specializing in ophthalmology, Alliance Eye & Ear Clinic, Ohio, 1968—; moderator Pub. TV med. talk show Feedback, 1981—; pres. med. staff Alliance City Hosp., 1974. Pres., Carnation City Players, 1978. Served as capt. MC, AUS, 1966-68. Fellow Am. Acad. Ophthalmology, ACS. Mem. United Ch. of Christ. Lodge: Rotary (bd. dirs. 1971-73). Avocations: acting; scuba diving; flying; photography; cross-country skiing. Home: 11181 McCallum Ave Alliance OH 44601 Office: Alliance Eye & Ear Clinic 985 S Sawbury Ave Alliance OH 44601

KING, DAVID MERVIN, investment management company executive; b. nr. Ottawa, Kans., July 3, 1927; s. Alvin Jesse and Gertrude Beatrice (Jones) K.; B.S., Emporia (Kans.) State U., 1950; m. Bernice Arlene Owen, June 11, 1950; 1 dau., Elizabeth A. Salesman, Mut. Life of New York, Wichita, Kans., 1950; mgr. Colby (Kans.) C. of C., 1952-54; self employed, 1954-56; dist. mgr. King Merritt & Co. Investments, Colby, 1956-60; v.p., regional mgr. Westam. Securities, Inc., Hays, Kans., 1960-78; v.p. Investment Mgmt. and Research Co., 1978—; pres. David M. King and Assos., Ltd., King Fin. Services Corp.;

partner Berdeak Assos.; chmn. bd. trustees Coll. Fin. Planning. Served with USMCR, 1945-46, 50-52. Mem. Internat. Assn. Fin. Planners, Inst. Cert. Fin. Planners (pres. 1978), Hays C. of C. Republican. Presbyn. Mason (Shriner), Rotarian. Home: 3007 Tam O'Shanter St Hays KS 67601 Office: Box 707 Hays KS 67601

KING, EDWARD ALVIN, city official; b. Pratt City, Ala., Sept. 4, 1919; s. Fred Elijah and Phyllis Ann (Robertson) K.; A.B., Del. State Coll., 1943; M.S.W., Atlanta U., 1947; m. Beatrice Pitts, Nov. 14, 1980; children by previous marriage—Linda Ann, Antone J. Scrivens, Daniel Scrivens. Dir. group work, community relations Grand Rapids (Mich.) Urban League, 1947-53; community relations specialist Boston Urban League, 1953-57; supr. Pitts. Human Relations Commn., 1957-63; exec. dir. Dayton (Ohio) Human Relations Council, 1963—; instr. U. Dayton, 1968-71. Bd. dirs. Johnson C. Smith Sch. Theology, 1975—; sr. elder Trinity United Presbyn. Ch., 1973—. Served with AUS, 1943-46. Recipient Public Service awards Rotary Club, 1973, Kiwanis Club, 1979, U. Dayton, 1979, Optimist Club, 1974, Dayton Bd. Edn., 1980. Mem. Internat. Assn. Ofcl. Human Rights Agys., Nat. Assn. Human Rights Workers, NAACP, Alpha Phi Alpha. Club: Kiwanis (dir. 1976-80). Home: 1828 Ruskin Dr Dayton OH 45406 Office: Dayton Human Relations Council Suite 721 40 S Main St Dayton OH 45402

KING, EVERETT CLINTON, copper product company executive; b. Kansas City, Kans., Dec. 9, 1955; s. Everett Meryl and Lillian Ester (Mercer) K.; m. Connie Marie Lowry, Dec. 17, 1977. B.B.A., U. Mo.-Kansas City, 1977. Inventory control clk. Swift Premium Co., Kansas City, 1978; office mgr. Lanter Distbg. Co., Kansas City, 1978; controller Fair Mercantile Furniture, St. Louis, 1978-79; cost acct. Consol. Aluminum, Madison, Ill., 1979-81; cost analyst Courion Industries, St. Louis, 1981; office mgr. Cerro Copper Products Co., Shelbina, Mo., 1981-85, mgr. acctg., Sauget, Ill., 1985—. Treas. Nazarene World Mission Soc., mem. ch. bd. Southwest Ch. of Nazarene. Recipient cert. achievement in bus. mgmt. Marmon Group, 1984. Republican. Nazarene. Avocation: woodworking. Home: 4978 Tyrolean Saint Louis MO 63109 Office: Cerro Copper Products Co Hwy 3 Alton and Southern Tracks Sauget IL 62201

KING, FRED LEE, radiologist, author; b. Queen City, Mo., Aug. 9, 1931; s. Fred and Lillian D. (Campbell) K.; m. Anita Marie White, Aug. 12, 1956; children—Vincent, Christopher, Phyllis. B.S., N.E. Mo. State U., 1959; D.O., Kirksville Coll. Osteo. and Surgery; LL.B., LaSalle Extension U., Chgo., 1967. Cert. Roentgenology Am. Osteo Coll. Radiology. Practice gen. medicine and radiology Laughlin Hosp., Kirksville, Mo., 1961-83, Samaritan Meml. Hosp., Macon, Mo., 1983—. Author: weekly newspaper column "Nostalgia", 1983—; contbr. articles to med. jours. Served with USN, 1951-55; Mem. Am. Osteo. Assn., Mo. Osteo. Assn., Am. Osteo. Coll. Radiology, Northeast Mo. Osteo. Assn., Republican. Lodge: Masons. Avocations: writing; antique collecting; history; old radio tapes. Home: 508 Sunset Dr Macon MO 63552 Office: Samaritan Meml Hosp N Jackson St Macon MO 63552

KING, GARY HAMILTON, college administrator, educator; b. Columbus, Kans., July 2, 1940; s. Gurney Deward and Roxie (Hamilton) K.; m. Judith Gail Holman, Dec. 18, 1971; children—David, Jim. B.B.A., Southwestern Coll., 1963. Cost acct. Gen. Motors, Santa Barbara, Calif., 1963-68; divisional controller Applied Magnetics, Santa Barbara, 1968-72; systems analyst County of Orange, Santa Ana, Calif., 1972-77; asst. prof. computer sci., dir. info. services Southwestern Coll., Winfield, Kans., 1977—. Mem. Data Processing Mgmt. Assn., Pi Gamma Mu. Home: 0707 College St #8 Winfield KS 67156 Office: Southwestern Coll 100 College St Winfield KS 67156

KING, GEORGE RALEIGH, manufacturing company executive; b. Benton Harbor, Mich., May 13, 1931; s. Maurice Peter and Opal Ruth (Hart) King; m. Phyllis Stratton, Apr. 10, 1950; children—Paula King Zang, Angela King Moleski, Philip. Student Adrian Coll., 1950-51. Cert. purchasing profl. exec. status. With Kirsch Co., Sturgis, Mich., 1951—, data processing trainee, 1951-53, data processing mgr., 1953-59, asst. purchasing agt., 1959-62, purchasing agt., 1962-68, asst. dir. purchasing, 1968-71, dir. purchasing, 1971—. Author: Rods & Rings, 1972. Elder, 1st Presbyterian Ch., Sturgis, 1970; pres. Sturgis Civic Players, 1972. Recipient citation Boy Scouts Am., 1966, Jr. Achievement, 1967; nominated candidate for adminstr. Fed. Procurement Policy, Reagan Adminstrn., Washington, 1980. Mem. Am. Purchasing Soc. (pres. 1979-81), Nat. Assn. Purchasing Mgmt., Southwestern Purchasing Assn. Clubs: Klinger Lake Country, Exchange (pres. Sturgis 1959, dist. gov. dist and nat. clubs 1961). Masons, Elks. Home: 906 S Lakeview Sturgis MI 49091 Office: Kirsch Co 309 N Prospect St Sturgis MI 49091

KING, (JACK) WELDON, photographer; b. Springfield, Mo., Jan. 19, 1911; s. Clyde Nelson and Mary Blanche (Murphy) K.; B.A., Drury Coll., 1934, Mus.B., 1934. Chief still photographer African expdns. including Gatti-Hallicrafters Expdn., 1947-48, 12th Gatti Expdn., 1952, Wyman Carroll Congo Expdn., 1955, 13th Gatti Expdn., 1956, 14th Gatti Expdn., 1957; also free-lance photog. expdns., Africa, 1960, 66, 76-77; trips for GAF Corp. to S.Am., 1962, 63, 77-78, Australia and N.Z., 1972-73; Alaska, 1982, Europe, 1983, also numerous assignments throughout contiguous states U.S. Served as photographer with Coast Arty. Corps, U.S. Army, 1941-42; PTO; Japanese prisoner of war, 1942-45. Decorated numerous service ribbons and battle stars. Mem. Space Pioneers, Am. Theatre Organ Soc., Humane Soc. U.S., Friends Animals, Nat. Parks and Conservation Assn., Animal Protection Inst. Am., African Wildlife Leadership Found., Internat. Platform Assn., World Wildlife Fund, Am. Defenders of Bataan and Corregidor, Am. Ex-Prisoners War, Lambda Chi Alpha. Democrat. Roman Catholic. Contbr. to numerous art books including Africa is Adventure, 1959, also French and German edits.; Primitive Peoples Today, 1956; Africa: A Natural History, 1965; South American and Central America, 1967; Animal Worlds, 1963; Living Plants of the World, 1963; The Earth Beneath Us, 1964; Living Trees of the World; The Life of the Jungle, 1970; Living Mammals of the World. Contbr. photographs to mags., encys., textbooks. Address: 1234 E Grand Ave Springfield MO 65804

KING, JAMES ROLAND, tobacco company executive; b. Springfield, Mo., Dec. 28, 1946; s. Joseph Franklin and Viola (Potter) K.; m. Karen Sue Wilson, Apr. 28, 1967; children—Jennifer, Julie, Jill. B.S. in Bus. Adminstrn. and Mktg., Southwest Mo. State U., 1969. With R.J. Reynolds Tobacco Co., 1969—, sales rep., St. Louis, 1969-71, asst. div. mgr., Toledo, 1971-79, div. mgr. North Chicago and Arlington Heights, Ill., 1979-80, West Chicago and Carol Stream, Ill., 1980-82, regional tng. and devel. mgr., Lombard, Ill., 1982—. Served to capt. USMC, 1969-70. Mem. Tobacco Action Network. Democrat. Presbyterian. Home: 130 Aspen Dr Schaumburg IL 60194

KING, JANE LESLIE, research lawyer, paralegal educator; b. Lower Weedon, Northamptonshire, Eng., June 29, 1949; came to U.S., 1961, naturalized, 1972; d. Ronald George King and Olive Grace (Hutchins) King Betts. B.A. with high distinction in English, with high honors in L.A.S., U. Ill., 1974, J.D., 1981. Bars: Ill. 1982, Colo. 1982, U.S. Dist. Ct. Colo. 1982. Asst. editor Matthew Bender & Co., San Francisco, 1976-77; research asst. Community Research, Champaign, Ill., 1978-81; editor/researcher Office of Legal Counsel, Springfield, Ill., 1980; legal editor Shepard's/McGraw-Hill Co., Colorado Springs, Colo., 1981-82; dir. legal research Champaign County Circuit Ct., Urbana, Ill., 1982—; instr. Am. Inst. Paralegal Studies, Chgo., 1984—. Author: Comparative Analysis of Juvenile Codes, 1980. Assoc. editor Jour. Legal Medicine, 1981—. Contbr. articles to profl. jours. Mem. Humane Soc., Champaign, 1982-84, Grassroots Group Second Class Citizens, Champaign, 1983-84; treas. Citizens Party, Champaign, 1984. Mem. Ill. Bar Assn. Home: 612 1/2 W Union Champaign IL 61820 Office: Circuit Ct Champaign County 101 E Main Urbana IL 61801

KING, JENNIFER LAINE, college administrator, psychology educator; b. Pitts., Sept. 6, 1950; d. Donald Frederick and Nancy Elaine (Clark) K. B.A., Allegheny Coll., 1972; M.A., Bowling Green State U., 1973. Residence hall dir. Bowling Green State U. (Ohio), 1973-77; asst. dir. student life Wilmington Coll. (Ohio), 1977-78; dir. residence life Allegheny Coll., Meadville, Pa., 1978-82; grad. asst. U. Pitts., 1982-83; asst. to dean for student services U. Cin., Clermont Coll., Batavia, Ohio, 1983—. Adviser Dan Beard council Boy Scouts Am., 1984—; mem. choir Our Lady of Grace Ch., Pitts., 1982-83, St. Veronica's Ch., Cin., 1983-84. Mem. Am. Coll. Personnel Assn., Ohio Coll. Personnel Assn. Avocations: Computer programming, reading, canoeing, hiking, camping, sewing, latchhooking. Office: Clermont Gen and Tech Coll Coll Dr Batavia OH 45103

KING, JOHN B., trailer company executive; b. Ardmore, Okla., Sept. 10, 1916; s. Felix Jennings and Rachel Caroline (Boyd) K.; m. Anna Belle Fuson, Aug. 10, 1941; children—Anna Marie, Louis John. Assoc. Engring., Murray State Coll., 1936; B.S. in Engring., Okla. A&M U., 1941. Registered profl. engr., Okla. Sr. project engr. Remington Arms, Independence, Mo., 1941-44; chief engr. Hutchens Metal, Springfield, Mo., 1945-47; v.p. Wilco, Kenton, Ohio, 1948-50; v.p., plant mgr. Hwy. Trailer, Edgerton, Wis. and Cin., 1952-54; dir. tank engring. Heil Co., Milw., 1954-57; v.p. mfg. engring. Trailer div. Clark Equipment, Michigan City, Ind., Spokane, Wash. and Reading, Pa., 1968-72; v.p. sales and engring. Hutchens Industries, Springfield, Mo., 1972-81, v.p. new products, 1981—. Served with U.S.N.G., 1934-37. Mem. Soc. Profl. Engrs., ASME. Roman Catholic. Author text book on tank trailer design; numerous patents on suspension designs for trailers. Home: 2155 Valley Rd Springfield MO 65804 Office: 215 N Patterson Springfield MO 65805

KING, JOHN EDWIN, internist, gastroenterologist, consultant; b. Charleston, W.Va., Nov. 10, 1939; s. Edward Peter and Frances Ewing (Smith) K.; m. Judith Louise Wharton, July 21, 1962; children—Randall Wharton, Catherine Louise. A.B., Northwestern U., 1961, M.D., 1965. Diplomate Am. Bd. Internal Medicine. Intern, Passavant Meml. Hosp., Chgo., 1965-66; resident in internal medicine and gastroenterology Mayo Grad. Sch. Medicine, Rochester, Minn., 1966-70; practice medicine specializing in internal medicine and gastroenterology, Rochester, 1972—. Cons., physician Mayo Clinic, Rochester, 1972—; asst. prof. medicine Mayo Med. Sch., chmn. 2d-yr. medicine curriculum. Served to maj. USAF, 1970-72. Fellow ACP; mem. N.Y. Acad. Scis., Am. Soc. Gastrointestinal Endoscopy, Am. Gastroent. Assn., Sigma Xi. Republican. Methodist. Contbr. articles to profl. jours. Office: Mayo Clinic W 19-A 200 First St Rochester MN 55901

KING, JOSEPH CLEMENT, physician; b. Colorado Springs, Colo., Aug. 20, 1922; s. Charles Clement and Gladys (Ascher) K.; B.S., Tulane U., 1944, M.D., 1946; m. Margie Freudenthal Lepold, Apr. 2, 1947; children—Leopold Ascher, Jocelyn King Tobias. Instr. zoology Tulane U., 1941-42; rotating intern Michael Reese Hosp., Chgo., 1946-47, resident in internal medicine, 1947-50; assoc. with Dr. Sidney Portis, Chgo., 1950-51; practice medicine specializing in internal medicine, Chgo., 1953-77, Palm Springs, Calif., 1977-79; attending staff Louis A. Weiss Hosp., Chgo., 1953-77, hon. staff, 1979—; attending staff Desert Hosp., 1977-79; med. dir. Life Extension Inst., Chgo., 1979-80; dir. employee health services Continental Ill. Nat. Bank, Chgo., 1980—; asst. to asso. clin. prof. internal medicine Northwestern U. Med. Sch., Chgo., 1954-67; clin. asst. prof. medicine Abraham Lincoln Sch. Medicine U. Ill., 1973-77; clin. asst. prof. preventive medicine and community health Northwestern U. Med. Sch., 1980—. Served to capt. M.C., AUS, 1944-46, 1951-53. Diplomate Am. Bd. Internal Medicine. Fellow ACP; mem. Chgo. Soc. Internal Medicine, Chgo. Med. Soc., Am., Ill. med. assns., Am. Heart Assn., Chgo. Heart Assn. (bd. govs.), Am. Rheumatism Assn., Med. Dirs. Club Chgo. (pres.), Bank Med. Dirs. Club, Am. Acad. Occupational Medicine, Central States Occupational Med. Assn. (bd. govs.), Am. Occupational Med. Assn., Tulane Med. Alumni Assn. (past dir.), Phi Beta Kappa, Beta Mu, Alpha Omega Alpha. Contbr. numerous articles in field to med. jours. Home: 1100 Lake Shore Dr Chicago IL 60611 Office: 231 S LaSalle St Room 2048 Chicago IL 60697

KING, KENNETH EDWARD, library executive; b. Bklyn., July 9, 1925; s. Joseph and Mary (Fereira) K.; m. Ruth Boulter, Dec. 27, 1951 (dec.); children—Karen, Kenneth. B.A., Brown U., 1950; M.S.L.S., Simmons Coll., 1951. Cert. Librarian. Assoc. dir. br. services Detroit Pub. Library, 1963-73; dir. Mount Clemens Pub. Library, Mich., 1973—. Co-editor: Centennial History of Mount Clemens, Michigan, 1879-1979, 1980. Pres. Mount Clemens Regional Arts Council, 1977—; chmn. Bright Future Mount Clemens Com., 1977—. Served with U.S. Army, 1943-46, ETO. Recipient Outstanding Community Service award Mount Clemens C. of C. 1976; named Mich. Librarian of Yr., 1976; recipient award of merit Macomb County Hist. Soc., 1985. Mem. AIA (adult services div. v.p. 1956-66). Clubs: Torch of Detroit (pres. 1985—), Econ. of Detroit. Lodge: Rotary. Office: Mount Clemens Pub Library 150 Cass Mount Clemens MI 48043

KING, LARRY L., electronics information scientist; b. Lawton, Okla., Aug. 1, 1958. B.B.A., U. Wis.-Eau Claire, 1981; postgrad. DePaul U., Chgo., 1984—. Cert. in data processing. Applications systems support supr. GTE Communications Systems, Northlake, Ill., 1981-84; system analyst AT&T Techs., Warrenville, Ill., 1984—; cons. in field. Mem. Am. Prodn. and Inventory Control Soc., Data Processing Mgmt. Assn. Avocations: studying architecture and architectural design. Home: 30W229 Briar Ln Naperville IL 60540 Office: AT&T Techs 28W 615 Ferry Rd PO Box 450 Warrenville IL 60555

KING, LYNDEL IRENE, art museum administrator, art historian; b. Enid, Okla., June 10, 1943; d. Leslie Jay and Jennie Irene (Duggan) Saunders; m. Blaine Larman King, June 12, 1965. B.A., U. Kans., 1965; M.A., U. Minn., 1971, Ph.D., 1982. Dir., Univ. Art Mus., U. Minn., Mpls., 1979—; dir. exhbns. and mus. programs Control Data Corp., Mpls., 1979, 80-81; exhbn. coordinator Nat. Gallery of Art, Washington, 1980. Recipient Honor award Minn. Soc. Architects, 1979, Cultural Contbn. of Yr. Mpls. C. of C., 1978. Mem. Assn. Art Mus. Dirs. (assoc.), Internat. Council Mus., Am. Assn. Mus., Assn. Coll. and Univ. Mus. and Galleries, Art Mus. Assn. (v.p. 1984—), Upper Midwest Conservation Assn. (sec. 1980—), Minn. Assn. Mus. (steering com. 1982—). Home: 326 W 50th St Minneapolis MN 55419 Office: Univ Art Mus U Minn 110 Northrop Meml Auditorium Minneapolis MN 55455

KING, PAUL MAX, college administrator; b. Logan County, Ohio, Apr. 17, 1929; s. Alva Jay and Lulu Marie (Keenen) K.; m. Lois Irene Marquart, Oct. 11, 1952; children—Bruce Marquart, Timothy Paul, John Eric. B.S., Bluffton Coll., 1957; C.L.U., Am. Coll., 1977. With sales dept. Nationwide Ins. Co., Bluffton, Ohio, 1957-60, with sales mgmt., Bowling Green, Ohio, 1960-75; investment estate planning Bluffton Coll., Ohio, 1975-78, dir. devel., 1978—; ins. cons. M.M.A.S., Bluffton, 1977—; dir. Goodville Mut. Casualty Co., New Holland, Pa., 1977—; pres. Bluffton Slaw Cutter, 1983—. Writer, editor estate planning mag. Spirit, 1981—. Served with USAF, 1951-55. Mem. Estate Planning Council, Bluffton C. of C. Republican. Mennonite. Lodge: Optimist. Avocations: flying; skiing; woodwork. Home: 9220 Bixel Rd Bluffton OH 45817 Office: Bluffton Coll College Ave Bluffton OH 45817

KING, PEGGY SUE, banker; b. Marengo, Iowa, Dec. 25, 1950; d. Marvin Clark and Eunice Mildred (Jordan) Morse; B.A. magna cum laude in History, Trinity Coll., Deerfield, Ill., 1973; M.A. in European History, U. Iowa, Iowa City, 1974; M.B.A., Drake U. 1983; m. Merrill Jack King, June 26, 1976. Asst. head teller Iowa-Des Moines Nat. Bank, 1975-77; head teller Bankers Trust Co., Des Moines, 1979, consumer banker, 1980, asst. mng. officer, 1981-82, mng. officer, 1982-83; comml. loan officer United Fed. Savs. Bank, Des Moines, 1983—; treas., stockholder Piccadilly Spoke & Tread Ltd., Des Moines. Mem. Nat. Assn. Bank Women (vice chair central Iowa group 1984-85), Nat. Assn. Profl. Saleswomen, Women's C. of C. Greater Des Moines, Beta Gamma Sigma. Home: 1070 35th St Des Moines IA 50311 Office: Locust at 4th Des Moines IA 50309

KING, RALEIGH WAYNE, beauty school executive; b. Camden, N.J., Oct. 18, 1945; s. Travis Greer and Eva Virginia K.; student U. Md., 1969-71, Belleville Area Coll., 1972-74. Instr., Coiffure Sch. Beauty Culture, Belleville, Ill., 1978-79, dir., 1979—; educator Revlon-Realistic, 1981—; stylist Roux Inc., 1983; co-chmn. Sch. Continuing Cosmetology Edn., So. Ill. U., 1983. Bd. dirs. Ill. Assn. Cosmetology Schs., 1981; permanent mem. Ill. Hair Fashion Com.; chmn. cosmetology adv. council Belleville Area Coll. Served with USAF, 1965-76. Mem. Nat. Hairdressers and Cosmetologists Assn. (pres. affiliate 40 1979-80), Ill. Hairdressers and Cosmetologists Assn. (2d v.p. 1981-82, 5th v.p. 1982-83). Home: Ash Creek Manor Rural Route 1 Box 711 Belleville IL 62221 Office: Coiffure Sch Beauty Culture 402 E Main St Belleville IL 62220

KING, ROBERT HOWARD, publisher; b. Excelsior Springs, Mo., June 28, 1921; s. Howard and Nancy (Henry) K.; student Kenyon Coll., Gambier, Ohio, 1940-42; m. Marjorie Kerr, Mar. 14, 1975; children—John McFeeley, Mary Nan King Murphy, Sarah Ann. Vice pres. sales Ency. Brit., Inc., 1946-61; pres., Spencer Internat. Press, Inc., 1961-66; v.p. Dill-Clitherow & Co., 1966-68; pres. Time-Life Libraries, Inc., 1968-79; chief exec. officer, chmn. bd. World Book-Childcraft Internat., Inc., Chgo., 1979-83, vice chmn., 1983—; chmn. bd. World Book Enterprises, Inc., World Book Life Ins. Co.; pres. Consumer Mktg. Services, Inc., 1983—, Beachbuilders of Am., 1983—; dir. World Book Fin. Co., Field Enterprises Internat., Inc., Inroads Chgo., Inc. Pres. Howard V. Phalin Found. Grad. Study. Served to capt. AUS, 1942-46. Mem. World Fedn. Direct Selling Assns. (chmn. 1978-81), Direct Selling Edn. Found. (past chmn.), Direct Selling Assn. (past chmn. bd.), Sales and Mktg. Execs. Internat., Internat. Trade Club. Clubs: Chicago, Chgo. Yacht, Lighthouse Point Yacht, Ocean Reef, Racquet. Office: 3440 Hollywood Blvd Hollywood FL 33021

KING, RUDOLPH HENRY, office products company executive; b. Evanston, Ill., Oct. 26, 1934; s. Arthur Charles King and Marian (Keitel) King Bishop; m. Nancy Jo Flanagan, June 29, 1956; children—Cynthia Lynn King Dell, Sharon King Wencel, Jennifer. B.A., Brown U., 1956. Sales trainee Ryerson Steel Co., Chgo., 1956-58; salesman Mead Papers, Chgo., 1958-65; v.p., gen. mgr. Boise Cascade, Chgo., 1965-69; sales mgmt. staff Mead Papers, 1969-71; pres. Wis. Office Supply Co., Madison, 1971—; dir., sec.-treas. Wis. Graphic Forms, Madison, 1971—; dir., v.p. Bus. Graphics, Madison, 1971—, AD Madison, 1982—; dir. M&I Bank of Jamestown, Madison, 1978—. Bd. dirs. Chgo. Boys Club, 1969-71, Orchard Ridge Community Assn., Madison, 1976-78. Served with U.S. Army, 1956-57, 60-61. Mem. Sales and Mktg. Execs. Assn. (pres. 1979-80, Best Club Internat. award 1980), Pi Sigma Epsilon. Republican. Presbyterian. Avocations: athletics; reading; gardening; cooking. Home: 42 Oak Creek Trail Madison WI 53717 Office: Wis Office Supply Co 3120 Syene Rd Madison WI 53713

KING, TERRY LEE, statistician, mathematician; b. Akron, Iowa, Feb. 24, 1945; s. Stanley W. and Hazel M. (Peck) K.; m. Carol Elizabeth Glass, June 12, 1971; children—Kevin, Shawn, Heather. B.A. cum laude, Westmar Coll., 1967; M.S., U. Iowa, 1969; Ph.D., Pa. State U., 1980. Instr., Thiel Coll., Greenville, Pa., 1969-71; statistician Desmatics, Inc., State College, Pa., 1975-79; instr. Frostburg State Coll., Md., 1979-81; assoc. prof. math./stats. N.W. Mo. State U., Maryville, 1981—. Editorial collaborator Current Index to Statistics, 1980—. Mem. Am. Statis. Assn. (membership com. 1982-84), Math. Assn. Am., Biometric Soc., Phi Kappa Phi, Kappa Mu Epsilon, Pi Mu Epsilon. Office: NW Mo State U Maryville MO 64468

KING, WILLIAM ROBERT, II, lawyer; b. Kansas City, Kans., July 23, 1954; s. William Robert and Dorothy Mae (Skelly) K.; m. Mary Kathleen Taylor, June 9, 1978; 1 child, Kathleen Suzanne. A.A., Donnelly Coll., 1974; B.A. in Acctg. and Bus. Adminstrn., U. Kans., 1976; J.D., Washburn U., 1979. Bar: Mo. 1979, U.S. Dist. Ct. (we. dist.) Mo. 1979, U.S. Ct. Appeals (8th cir.) 1980, U.S. Tax Ct. 1983. Law clerk legal div. Kans. State Ins. Co., Topeka, 1977-79; ptnr. Morris, Larson, King, Stamper & Bold, Kansas City, Mo., 1979—, shareholder, dir., v.p., 1984—. Mem. Mo. Bar Assn., ABA, Kansas City Bar Assn., Lawyers Assn. Kansas City, Trial Lawyers Assn. Am. Clubs: Hillcrest Country, Victory Hills Country (Kansas City). Home: 9204 Cherokee Ln Leawood KS 66206

KINGDON, JOHN WELLS, political science educator; b. Wisconsin Rapids, Wis., Oct. 28, 1940; s. Robert Wells and Catherine (McCune) K.; m. Kirsten Ingrid Berg, Aug. 18, 1941; children—James, Tor. B.A., Oberlin Coll., 1962; M.A., U. Wis., 1963, Ph.D., 1965. Asst. prof. dept. polit. sci. U. Mich., Ann Arbor, 1965-70, assoc. prof., 1970-75, prof., 1975—, dept. chmn., 1982— guest scholar Brookings Inst., 1969, 76-77. Social Sci. Research Council grantee, 1969-70; NSF grantee, 1978-82; Guggenheim fellow, 1979-80. Mem. Am. Polit. Sci. Assn., Midwest Polit. Sci. Assn. Author: Candidates for Office, 1968; Congressmen's Voting Decisions, 1973, 2d edit., 1981; Agendas, Alternatives, and Public Policies, 1984. Office: Dept Polit Sci U Mich Ann Arbor MI 48109

KINGDON, ROBERT MCCUNE, historian; b. Chgo., Dec. 29, 1927; s. Robert W. and Anna Catherine (McCune) K. A.B., Oberlin Coll., 1949; M.A., Columbia U., 1950, Ph.D., 1955; postgrad. U. Geneva, 1951-52. Instr., asst. prof. history U. Mass., Amherst, 1952-57; asst. prof. State U. Iowa, Iowa City, 1957-59, assoc. prof., 1959-61, prof., 1961-65; prof. history U. Wis., Madison, 1965—, mem. Inst. Research Humanities, 1974—, dir., 1975—. Bd. dirs. Ctr. Reformation Research, St. Louis, 1963—, pres., 1967—. Mem. Am. Soc. Ch. History (pres. 1980), Am. Soc. Reformation Research (pres. 1971), Central Renaissance Conf., Renaissance Soc. Am. (exec. bd. 1972—), Internat. Fedn. Socs. and Insts. for Study Renaissance (sec.-treas. 1967—). Author: Geneva and the Coming of the Wars of Religion in France, 1555-1563, 1956; Geneva and the Consolidation of the French Protestant Movement, 1564-1572, 1967; The Political Thought of Peter Martyr Vermigli, 1980; editor: 16th Century Jour., 1973—; contbr. articles on history to profl. jours. Home: 4 Rosewood Circle Madison WI 53711 Office: University of Wisconsin Madison WI 53706

KINGSBURY, ARTHUR ADAMS, college dean; b. Joplin, Mo., Aug. 20, 1939; s. Charles Hardwick and Bea (Rich) K. A.A., Daytona Beach Community Coll., 1964; B.S., Fla. State U., 1966; M.S., Mich. State U., 1968; Ph.D., Wayne State U., 1976. With Volkswagen of Am., Sterling Heights, 1981-82; asst. dir. crim. justice dept. U. Wis.-Platteville, 1968-69; assoc. dean bus. and pub. service dept. Macomb Community Coll., Mt. Clemens, Mich., 1969—; cons. in field. Author: (text) Introduction to Security and Crime Prevention Surveys, 1973, Security Administration: An Introduction, 4th edit., 1985, others. Contbr. articles to profl. jours. Mem. Am. Soc. Indsl. Security (bd. dirs., officer, pres. profl. certification bd.). Office: Macomb Community Coll 44575 Garfield Mount Clemens MI 48044

KINGSLEY, JAMES GORDON, college president; b. Houston, Nov. 22, 1933; s. James G. and Blanche (Payne) Peak; m. Elizabeth Sasser, Aug. 26, 1956; children—Gordon Alan, Craig Emerson. B.A., Miss. Coll., 1955; M.A., U. Mo.-Columbia, 1956; B.D., New Orleans Bapt. Sem., 1960, Th.D., 1965. Instr. Miss. Coll., Clinton, 1956-58, Tulane U., New Orleans, 1958-60; from asst. prof. to prof. William Jewell Coll., 1960-1976, dean, 1976-80, pres., 1980—. Author: A Time For Openness, 1973; Frontiers, 1983. Pres. English Speaking Union, Kansas City, Mo., 1980-81. LaRue fellow Kansas City Regional Council, 1976. Baptist. Clubs: Kansas City, University. Lodge: Rotary (pres. 1979). Avocations: theatre, marathons. Home: 510 E Mississippi St Liberty MO 64068 Office: William Jewell Coll Jewell St Liberty MO 64067

KINGSRITER, DAYTON ALBERT, college dean; b. Mankato, Minn., Sept. 5, 1943; s. Harland A. and Dorris V. (Williams) K.; m. Marilyn G. Jones, Dec. 16, 1965; children—H. Bradford, Roslynn. B.S.Ed., Evangel Coll., Springfield, Mo., 1965; M.Ed., U. Mo., 1973, Ed.S., 1974, Ed.D., 1981. Cert. elem. sch. tchr., sch. supt., Mo.; ordained to ministry Assemblies of God Ch., 1976. Tchr. Springfield R-12 Sch., 1965-68; supt. Hi-Way R-III Sch., Mexico, Mo., 1974-76; minister of music and Christian edn. Pawnee Assembly, Ill., 1976-78; dir. Christian edn. The Stone Ch., Palos Heights, Ill., 1978-80; ch. adminstr. Oak Brook Christian Ctr., Ill., 1980-82; acad. dean Trinity Bible Coll., Ellendale, N.D., 1982—. Vice pres. Ellendale Civic Assn., 1984—; mem. Ellendale Pub. Sch. Bd., 1984—. Served with USAF, 1968-72. Mem. Pi Mu Alpha Sinfonia, Phi Delta Kappa, Kappa Delta Pi. Republican. Avocations: golf; tennis; biking. Home: 79 3d St N Ellendale ND 58436 Office: Trinity Bible Coll 50 6th Ave S Ellendale ND 58436

KINGTON, LOUIS BRENT, art educator, artist, sculptor; b. Topeka, July 26, 1934; s. Louis William and Isabele Evoria (Baley) K.; m. Diana Sue Daaton, June 5, 1959; children—Tod Lindsay, Brooke. B.F.A., U. Kans., 1957; M.F.A., Cranbrook Acad. Art, 1961. Lectr. So. Ill. U., Carbondale, 1961-62, from asst. prof. to assoc. prof. art, 1962-72, prof., 1972—. Prin. works include sculpture Cranbrook Mus., Mich., Nat. Ornamental Metal Mus., Tenn., State Mus., Ill., Swope Art Gallery, Ind. (award for Excellence 1982). Served with USAR, 1957-63. Craftsman fellow Nat. Endowment Arts, 1974, 1981. Fellow Am. Crafts Council (trustee 1976-80), Artist-Blacksmith Assn. N.Am. (dir. 1975-79, disting. service award 1983), Soc. N.Am. Goldsmiths (pres. 1970-74). Home: Route 2 Box 254 Makanda IL 62958 Office: So Ill U Sch Art Carbondale IL 62901

KINKOPF, EDWARD JOHN, physician; b. Alliance, Ohio, Oct. 8, 1952; s. Edward John and Marjorie Pauline (Stalzer) K.; m. Marion Gaye Russell, July 12, 1980; children—Laura, Brett. B.S., Mt. Union Coll., 1974; D.O., Chgo. Coll. Osteo. Medicine, 1979. Diplomate Am. Bd. Family Practice. Intern, Grandview Hosp., Dayton, Ohio, 1979-80, resident, 1980-81; pres./owner Centerville Family Practice, Inc., Ohio, 1981—; ptnr. West Carrollton Med. Ctr., Ohio, 1983—; med. dir. Crawford Convalescent Ctr., Dayton, 1982—; med. adv. Ohio Coll. Bus. and Tech., Middletown, 1984—. Trustee, Grandview Hosp., Dayton, 1984—. Mem. Dayton Acad. Osteo. Medicine, Ohio Osteo. Assn., Am. Osteo. Assn., Sigma Sigma Phi, Phi Sigma. Republican. Roman Catholic. Avocations: skiing; water skiing; racquetball; antiques. Office: 1147 D Lyons Rd Centerville OH 45459

KINNEAR, CHERYL JEAN, computer programmer; b. Girard, Kans., Aug. 29, 1951; d. Clarence A. and Harriett J. (Black) Kern; m. Connie Kinnear, Jan. 26, 1973; children—Cynthia Annette, Cassie Jeanette. A.A., Ft. Scott Community Coll., Kans., 1972; B.S.B.A., Pittsburg State U., Kans., 1974. Programmer, McNally Mfg. Co., Pittsburg, 1974-77; supr. data processing ops. Mt. Carmel Med. Ctr., Pittsburg, 1978-80; programmer Red River Credit Union, Texarkana, Tex., 1981-82; dir. info. systems Talbot Industries, Neosho, Mo., 1984-85. Pittsburg State U. sr. scholar, 1974. Mem. Phi Kappa Phi, Delta Mu Delta. Republican. Methodist. Avocations: Bicycling; horseback riding; skiing; swimming; sewing. Home: 1709 Ankney Pl Neosho MO 64850

KINNEARY, JOSEPH PETER, U.S. judge; b. Cin., Sept. 19, 1905; s. Joseph and Anne (Mulvihill) K.; B.A., U. Notre Dame, 1928; LL.B., U. Cin., 1935; m. Byrnece Camille Rogers, June 26, 1950. Bar: Ohio 1935; U.S. Supreme Ct., 1960; pvt. practice in Cin. and Columbus, 1935-61; asst. atty. gen. Ohio, 1937-39, 1st asst. atty. gen., 1949-51, spl. counsel to atty. gen., 1959-61; U.S. atty. So. Dist. Ohio, 1961-66; judge U.S. Dist. Ct., So. Dist. Ohio, 1966—, chief judge, 1973-75; lectr. law trusts Coll. Law, U. Cin., 1948. Delegate Democratic Nat. Conv., 1952. Served to capt. AUS, World War II. Decorated Army Commendation ribbon. Mem. Phi Delta Phi. Roman Catholic. Office: 319 US Courthouse 85 Marconi Blvd Columbus OH 43215

KINNEY, EARL ROBERT, See *Who's Who in America*, 43rd edition.

KINNEY, JOHN JAMES, mathematics and statistics educator; b. Dansville, N.Y., Aug. 2, 1932; s. RayStephen and Evelyn (White) K.; m. Cherry Carter, July 7, 1962; 1 child, Kaylyn. B.S., St. Lawrence U., 1954; A.M.T., Harvard U., 1955; M.S., U. Mich., 1960; Ph.D., Iowa State U., 1971. Instr., asst. prof. St. Lawrence U., Canton, N.Y., 1955-64; assoc. prof. SUNY-Oneonta, 1964-68; asst. prof. U. Nebr., Lincoln, 1971-74; assoc. prof. Rose 1-1 Hulman Inst., Terre Haute, Ind., 1974-77, prof. math. 1977—. Pres., Dixie Bee PTA, 1979; v.p. Covered Bridge council Girl Scouts, 1982—. NSF fellow, 1968. Mem. Am. Statis. Assn., Assn. Computing Machinery, Sigma Xi, Phi Beta Kappa. Lodge: Rotary (pres. 1980-81). Home: 221 Highland Rd Terre Haute IN 47802 Office: Rose 1-1 Hulman Inst Tech 5500 Wabash Ave Terre Haute IN 47803

KINSEL, MICHAEL LESLIE, museum director; b. Council Bluffs, Iowa, May 5, 1947; s. Leslie Henry, Jr. and Stella Julia Sophia (Pedersen) K. B.A., Augustana Coll., 1969; postgrad. Luth. Sch. Theology, Chgo., 1969-73. Asst. to dir. devel. Luth. Sch. Theology, Chgo., 1970-73; dir. devel. Suomi Coll., Hancock, Mich., 1973; account exec. Knaphurst Co., Chgo., 1973-74; dir. Western Heritage Mus., Omaha, 1974—, tchr. edn. dept., 1982—. Part-time instr. Lifelong Learning Ctr., Creighton U., Omaha; fund-raising cons. Mem. Am. Assn. Mus., Am. Assn. State and Local History, Nat. Soc. Fund-Raising Execs., Lewis and Clark Found., Mus. Council Greater Omaha, Western History Assn., Nat. Trust Hist. Preservation, Mountain-Plains Mus. Conf., Omaha Com. Fgn. Relations, Omaha Westerners, Omaha Bacchanialian Soc. Republican. Lutheran. Clubs: Omaha Press, Kiwanis (Omaha).

KINSEY, WALTER JAMES, JR., sales consultant; b. St. Joseph, Mich., Jan. 5, 1948; s. Walter James Kinsey, Sr. and Della Edith Mae (Davidson) Bassett; m. Elizabeth Jean Koets, June 8, 1974; children—Walter James III, Kathleen Beth, Heather Ann, Sarah Jane. Retail salesman Norman Camera Co., Battle Creek, Mich., 1970-72; printer G.M. Litho, Sturgis, Mich., 1972-73; salesman Donaldson Supply Inc., Sturgis, 1973-76; sales cons. WCMR/WFRN Radio, Elkhart, Ind., 1976-80, A.L. Williams, Inc., Atlanta, 1984—, WTRC Radio, Elkhart, 1980—; cons. Pro-Life Activity Group, Goshen, Ind., 1984—. Republican. Club: f-8 Camera (Sturgis) (treas. 1977—). Avocations: Photography, model railroading, reading. Home: 430 E Congress St Sturgis MI 49091 Office: WTRC Radio PO Box 699 Elkhart IN 46515

KINSMAN, ROBERT DONALD, ART mus. adminstr.; b. Bridgeport, Conn., Sept. 13, 1929; s. Cummings Sanborn and Sarah Elizabeth (Barton) K.; B.S., Columbia U., 1958, M.A. in Art History, 1966, A.B.D. in Art History; m. Patricia Ann Mulreed, Oct. 3, 1953. Asst. curator Nat. Gallery Art, Washington, 1961-62; instr. art history Mary Washington Coll., U. Va., Fredericksburg, 1962-63; curator contemporary art Detroit Inst. Arts, 1963-65; asst. prof. art history and dir. duPont Art Galleries, Mary Washington Coll., 1966-68; asst. prof. art history SUNY, Albany, 1968-77; dir. Sheldon Swope Art Gallery, Terre Haute, Ind., 1978—. Bd. dirs. Arts Illiana, Inc., 1981—. Served with U.S. Army, 1951-53. Mem. Am. Assn. Museums, AAUP, Coll. Art Assn. Am. Contbr. articles to profl. jours. Home: 4591 Dixie Bee Rd Terre Haute IN 47802 Office: 25 S 7th St Terre Haute IN 47807

KINTNER, ROBERT ROY, chemistry educator; b. Weeping Water, Nebr., Apr. 3, 1928; s. Elmer Hayes and Rae Imogene (Swartwout) K.; m. Helen Ruth Remmers, Aug. 31, 1952; children—Timothy Roy, Melinda Rae Kintner Hooper, SueLynn Reneé. B.S. in Chem. Tech., Iowa State U., 1953; Ph.D. in Organic Chemistry, U. Wash., Seattle, 1957. Prof. chemistry Augustana Coll., Sioux Falls, S.D., 1957—; vis. prof. chemistry, U. Wash., Seattle, summer 1959; U. Nebr., Lincoln, 1980-81, U. Md., Munich, Fed. Republic Germany 1985; cons., co-principle investigator Augustana Research Inst., Sioux Falls, 1978-80. Author: (with others) Chemistry of the Carbonyl Group, 1966. Contbr. articles to profl. jours. Served to cpl. USMC, 1946-49. Petroleum Research Fund faculty fellow U. Wash., Seattle, 1964-65; NSF faculty fellow U. Calif.-Santa Cruz, 1971-72. Mem. ASTM (faculty fellow), Midwestern Assn. Chem. Tchrs. in Liberal Arts Colls., Am. Chem. Soc. (pres. Sioux Valley sect. 1965-66), S.D. Acad. Sci. (pres. 1970), Sigma Xi, Phi Lambda Upsilon. Lutheran. Avocations: hiking; camping; biking; nutrition; youth ministries. Office: Univ Md Munich Campus APO New York NY 09407

KINTZ, JOHN FRANK, civil engineer, structural engineer; b. Richland Center, Wis., Sept. 8, 1941; s. Milford Clark and Mildred (Eaton) K.; m. Penny Proctor, June 15, 1980; children by previous marriage—Kirk, John, Craig. B.S. in Civil Engring., Wis. State U.-Platteville, 1965. Registered profl. engr. Iowa, Wis., N.D., Ill., Tenn., Pa. Engr. Peterson and Appell, Des Moines, 1965-68, Vawter and Walter, Des Moines, 1968-71, Brooks, Borg and Skiles, Des Moines, 1971-74, Brown Engring. Co., Des Moines, 1974—. Tchr. Jr. Achievement Project Bus., Des Moines, 1981-82; pres. bd. dirs. Des Moines Community Playhouse, 1975. Mem. Iowa Engring. Soc. Nat. Soc. Profl. Engrs. (chmn. continuing edn. 1983-84, chmn. scholarship 1984—, Outstanding Pub. Service award 1982). Republican. Methodist. Avocations: golf; tennis; singing; income tax preparation. Home: 1598 NW 91st Des Moines IA 50322 Office: Brown Engring Co 1001 Office Park Rd West Des Moines IA 50265

KIP, HERBERT WEBSTER, village manager; b. N.Y.C., Oct. 27, 1915; s. Charles Jay and Lillian Annie (Webb) K.; m. Alice Marie Kreher, June 15, 1942; children—Sandra Diane Murphy, Linda Carol Hatt; m. Gloria Mary Unico, Feb. 3, 1967. Student Rutgers U., 1934-36. With Standard Oil Co. N.J. (now Exxon Corp.), N.Y.C., 1934-51, bus. history researcher, 1947-51; v.p. Floyd L. Carlisle Co., N.Y.C., 1951-57; city coordinator, city mgr., dir. parks and recreation City of West Palm Beach (Fla.), 1957-66; town mgr. Springfield (Vt.), 1967-70; bus. adminstr. City of Bridgeton (N.J.), 1970-73; city mgr. Garfield (N.J.), 1973-74, Northlake (Ill.), 1974-75; village mgr. Vernon Hills (Ill.), 1976—. Served with USAF, 1942-45. Mem. Internat. City Mgmt. Assn., Am. Pub. Works Assn., Ill. City Mgmt. Assn., Metro Mgrs. Assn. (dir.). Home: 10 Crestview Ln Apt 3 Vernon Hills IL 60061 Office: 290 Evergreen Dr Vernon Hills IL 60061

KIRBY, KENNETH W., company executive; b. Mankato, Minn., July 1, 1923; s. William F. and Irene (Moeri) K.; m. Bernice Hallman, July 26, 1947; children—Carol, Robert. B.A., Gustavus Adolphus Coll., 1945; M.S., Purdue U., 1956, Ph.D., 1958. Research chemist Green Giant Co., LeSueur, Minn., 1945-53, Penick & Ford, Ltd, Cedar Rapids, Iowa, 1958-65, 1967-77, 1982—, R.J. Reynolds Tobacco Co., Winston-Salem, N.C., 1965-67; control chemist Purdue U., Lafayette, Ind., 1953-56; project dir. U. Iowa, Oakdale, 1977-82; v.p., gen. mgr. ops. Penick & Ford, Ltd., Cedar Rapids, 1984—; cons. Iowa Electric L & P, Cedar Rapids, 1980-82. Pres., Community Concert Assn., Cedar Rapids, 1965, Fine Arts Council, Cedar Rapids, 1976. Mem. Am. Chem. Soc. (chmn. 1983), TAPPI, Inst. Food Tech., Cereal Chemists, Textile Colorists and Chemists. Presbyterian. Club: Cedar Rapids Country; Cedar Rapids Literary (chmn. 1982). Home: 2800 Indian Hill Rd SE Cedar Rapids IA 52403 Office: Penick & Ford Ltd 1001 1st St SW Cedar Rapids IA 52406

KIRBY, MICHAEL CLEMENS, railroad executive; b. Chgo., May 10, 1937; s. Ernest James and Lorraine (Lubinski) K.; m. Elizabeth C. Cosgrove, June 27, 1959; children—Elizabeth Anne Kirby Potter, Michael Edward. B.S. in Bus. Adminstrn., Marquette U., 1959; M.Ed., DePaul U., 1965. Cert. adminstr., tchr., Ill. Tchr., coach high schs., Chgo., 1959-66; various positions C.W.P. & S. R.R. Co., Chgo., 1963-73; pres. Mfrs. Junction Ry. Co., Cicero, Ill., 1973—; exec. com. Mid-West Adv. Bd., Mt. Prospect, Ill., 1980—; chmn. Asst. Mgrs. Conf., Chgo., 1984-85; com. chmn. oral presentation Boxcar Deregulation, 1984. Pres. South Side Crippled Childrens Aid, Chgo., 1977-81. Recipient Community Service award Mayor of Chgo., 1979. Mem. Am. Assn. R.R. Supts. (treas. 1980-84), Chgo. Car Assn., Roadmasters and Maintenance of Way Assn., Chgo. Freight Agts., Chgo. R.R. Supts. Assn. (pres. 1979), Am. St. Line R.R. Assn. (regional v.p. 1979—). Roman Catholic. Clubs: Kiwanis (pres. S.W. Club Chgo. 1976, lt. gov. Ill. E. Iowa, 1980, chmn. Council Chgo. 1981-83, Outstanding Pres. award 1976), Hawthorne (pres. Chgo. 1984). Avocations: Electronic kit building; fishing; camping. Home: 2255 W 108th Pl Chicago IL 60643 Office: Mfrs Junction Ry Co 2335 S Cicero Cicero IL 60650

KIRCH, WILLIAM, chemical engineer; b. Cin., May 20, 1927; s. Nicholas John and Barbara Lena (Junger) K.; m. Leonore Ida Neumann, May 19, 1956; children—Barbara, Nicholas. Ch.E., U. Cin., 1952. Sr. project engr. Am. Synthetic Rubber Corp., Louisville, 1952-57; mgr. U.S. Indsl. Chems., Cin., 1957-68; dir. tech. devel. Chemplex Co. (name now Norchem div. HNG/Internorth), 1968—. Patentee in field. Served with U.S. Army, 1945-46. Mem. Am. Inst. Chem. Engrs. Office: Norchem PO Box 819 Clinton IA 52732

KIRCHER, DUDLEY PAUL, forest products company executive; b. Dayton, Ohio, Nov. 12, 1934; s. Ralf Charles and Mary Virginia (Paul) K.; m. Carole A. Jacobs; children—Christopher, Stacy, Ralf Edward. B.A., Ohio U., 1957; M.B.A., Harvard U., 1960. Cons. Logistics Mgmt. Inst., Washington, 1963-65; cons., assoc. Booz, Allen & Hamilton Assocs., Washington, 1965-69; v.p. Kircher, Helton & Collett Inc., Dayton, Ohio, 1969-72; v.p., dir. Dayton Devel. Council, 1972-79; v.p. Mead Corp., Dayton, 1979—; dir. Gem Savs. Assn., Dayton, Van Dyne Crotty, Dayton, Greater Dayton Pub. TV. Dir. Dayton Mus. Natural History, 1971—, U.S. Aviation Hall of Fame, Dayton, 1978—; Republican candidate for U.S. Congress, 3rd Dist. Ohio, 1978. Named Mktg. Man of Yr., Am. Mktg. Assn., 1975, Man of Yr., Air Force Assn., Dayton, 1976, Outstanding Pub. Servant, Sta. WKEF-TV, Dayton, 1976. Mem. Dayton Area C. of C. (pres. 1974-78). Episcopalian. Clubs: Moraine Country (bd. dirs. 1970-85), Dayton Racquet (bd. dirs. 1976—). Home: 235 W Thruston Blvd Dayton OH 45419 Office: Mead Corp Courthouse Plaza NE Dayton OH 45463

KIRCHNER, RICHARD JAY, educator; b. Schenectady, Feb. 17, 1930; s. Richard Jacob and Leah (Williams) K.; B.S., U. Wis., 1952, M.S., 1955, postgrad., 1956; Ed.D., Mich. State U, 1962; m. Barbara Ann Crane, Feb. 2, 1952; children—Richard Alec, Barbara Jayne, Carolyn Diane, Robert Jay, Kathleen Kay. Instr. wrestling and track coach St. Cloud (Minn.) Tchrs. Coll., 1955-56; asst. prof., coaching staff Central Mich. U., Mt. Pleasant, 1956-62, prof. recreation, chmn. dept., 1962—, chmn. pres.'s adv. com.; camp program dir., camp dir. Elkton-Pigeon-Bayport Sch. Camp, Caseville, Mich., 1962; municipal recreation dir. Petoskey (Mich.), 1963, cons., 1964-74; vice chmn. citizens adv. com. Recreation Services div. Mich. Dept. Conservation, 1966-67. Pres. Mt. Pleasant Intermediate Sch. PTA, 1968-69; chmn. tech. planning com. Mt. Pleasant Recreation Commn. Served to capt. USMCR, 1952-54. Mem. AAHPER (v.p. Mich. 1966-67, v.p. Midwest dist. 1973-74), Nat Recreation and Parks Assn., Am. Assn. Leisure and Recreation (nat. pres. 1976-77, nat. accreditation council 1978-83, vice chmn. 1979-81, chmn. 1981-83), Am. Camp Assn., Mich. Soc. Arts, Sci. and Letters, Mich. Soc. Gerontology, Outdoor Edn. and Camping Council (charter), Mich. Recreation and Parks Assn. (v.p. 1968-70), Phi Eta Sigma, Phi Epsilon Kappa, Phi Delta Kappa. Home: 6953 Riverside Dr Mount Pleasant MI 48858

KIRCHSTEIN, JAMES EDWARD, electronics engineer, consultant; b. Madison, Wis., Mar. 28, 1931; s. Frank Henry and Helen Elenor (Callaway) K.; m. Nancy Jeanne Mathews, June 26, 1976; children—Betty Lou, Vicki Lynn, Helen Susan, James Esteban, Lydia Ann, Mathew James, Daniel Warren, Eva Marie. B.S.E.E., U. Wis., 1958. Lic. comml. pilot. Exec. dir. Sauk Prairie Radio, Sauk City, Wis., 1964-67; pres. Am. Music Corp., Sauk City, 1967, Seven Sounds Pub., Sauk City, 1970; dir. elec. media U. Wis., Madison, 1968-82; elec. engr. dept. adminstrn. Bur. Engring., State of Wis., Madison, Madison, 1982—. Explorer advisor, 1968-70. Served with USN, 1950-54; Korea. Mem. Audio Engring. Soc., Soc. Motion Picture Engrs., Aircraft Owners and Pilots Assn. Mem. United Ch. of Christ. Clubs: August Derleth Soc. (dir.); Sauk Prairie Optimist (pres. 1969). Developer spl. accoustical ceiling for sound rec.; created largest catalog of ethnic music in world, 1961-72. Home: 3830 Sth 78 Mount Horeb WI 53572

KIRK, MILDRED THOMAS, educator; b. St. Louis, Apr. 1, 1927; d. Robert and Annie Laura (Poole) Thomas; B.S., U. Mo., 1975; m. Isaac Wilson Kirk, Apr. 10, 1948; 1 son, Isaac Douglas. Acctg. clk. Southwestern Bell Telephone Co., St. Louis, 1950-75; tchr. Buder Sch., St. Louis, 1976-83; tchr. Shenandoah Valley Sch., Chesterfield, Mo., 1983-84, Barretts Sch., Des Peres, Mo., 1984-85. Mem. Assn. Supervision and Curriculum Devel., NEA, U. Mo. Alumni Assn., Nat. Writers Club. Lutheran. Author: A Different Kind of Birthday, 1980. Home: 5919 Evergreen St Saint Louis MO 63134

KIRKENDALL, RONALD WAYNE, author, police dispatcher; b. Barada, Nebr., Oct. 13, 1939; s. Roy Ervin and Merna Nedra (Vice) K.; m. Barbara Ann Campbell, Oct. 29, 1961 (div. 1969); children—Todd Wayne, Michelle Rene; m. Janyce Maxine Schuler, Dec. 23, 1972; Asst. office mgr. Mo. Beef Packers, Rockport, 1973-75; office mgr. Flying L, Inc., Falls City, Nebr., 1976-82; dispatcher Falls City Police Dept., 1984—; advt. copywriter Mktg. Support Service, St. Joseph, Mo., 1984—; corr. St. Joseph Gazette, 1984—. Author poetry: Quill and Palette, 1981; Plainsong, 1980; song: Cotton Row Recording, 1984; also greeting cards. Active Falls City Jaycees, 1963-64; v.p. Falls City Vol. Ambulance Squad, 1980, pres., 1981, chmn. bd., 1982. Republican. Lodge: Elks. Avocations: music; creative writing; water sports. Home: Box 143 717 E 21st St Falls City NE 68355

KIRKHAM, JAMES ALVIN, business executive; b. Sumner County, Tenn., June 18, 1935; s. Shirley Barnes and Ouida Redempta (Bursby) K.; m. Shirley Ann Clouse, Sept. 3, 1954; children—Denise Anne, James Alvin II, Hughe Allan. Welder, Ind. Wire Co., 1952-54; truck driver Arthur Lowe Cigar & Candy Co., 1954-56; time study Insley Mfg. Co., 1957; salesman Am. Chicle Co., 1958-59; mgr. Ace Battery, Inc., Indpls., 1960-67, pres., 1967—; v.p. L P Industries, Inc., Indpls., 1977—; ptnr. TKT Leasing, Indpls., 1978—, LDJ Leasing, Indpls., 1979—. Bd. dirs. English Ave. Boys Club, State 4-H Horse and Pony Orgn.; pres. PTO, Clark Twp. Sch. Dist.; v.p. Johnson County 4-H Fairboard; active Boy Scouts Am. Recipient Golden Boy award Indpls. Boys Club Alumni Assn., 1970; named Outstanding Show Mgr., Ind. State Fair, 1971. Mem. U.S. C. of C., Ind. Motor Truck Assn., Indpls. Motor Truck Assn., Indpls. C. of C. Clubs: Ind. Pony Exhibitors, Ind. Pony of Am., Ind. Shetland Pony Breeders, Ind. Saddle Horse Assn., Am. Hackney, Am. Horse Show Assn., Masons, Shriners, Moose. Home: Rural Route 1 Box 35 Greenwood IN 46142 Office: 2166 Bluff Rd Indianapolis IN 46225

KIRKPATRICK, ELWOOD, milk association executive. Pres., dir. Mich. Milk Producers Assn., Detroit. Office: Michigan Milk Producers Assn 26300 Northwestern Southfield MI 48219*

KIRKWOOD, JAMES JOHN, sales manager; b. Newark, Dec. 27, 1945; s. James McComiskey and Dorothy F. (Theile) K.; m. Mary Barnes Meeler, Feb. 2, 1967; children—Jessica Ann, James John. B.A., Rutgers U., 1969; M.B.A., No. Ill. U., 1986. Salesman, Parke-Davis Co., Teterboro, N.J., 1969-73, Travenol Labs., Deerfield, Ill., 1973-78; sales mgr. Pilling Co., Inc., Ft. Washington, Pa., 1978—. Republican. Presbyterian. Avocations: travel; reading; racquetball; acting. Home: 912 Oxford Ct Palatine IL 60067 Office: Pilling Co 420 Delaware Dr Fort Washington PA 19034

KIRSCHENBAUM, STUART EDWARD, podiatrist; b. Bklyn., Jan. 23, 1945; s. Albert Barry and Eleanor K.; B.S., Mich. State U., 1965; D.P.M., N.Y. Coll. Podiatric Medicine, 1970; m. Janice Beardslee, July 27, 1967; children—Jennifer Robin, Storm Tyler. Resident in foot surgery Grand Community Hosp., Detroit, 1970-71; gen. practice podiatry, Detroit, 1970—; founder, pres. Foot Surgeons of Detroit, P.C., 1970—; chief podiatry services, trustee Monsignor Clement Kern Hosp. for Spl. Surgery, 1979-81; nat. lectr. in foot surgery; bd. dirs. Mich. Foot Health Found.; bd. dirs. Detroit Jr. Action Youth Services; mem. adv. bd. Am. Assn. Improvement of Boxing; Profl. and amateur boxing judge Mich. Athletic Commn.; judge World Boxing Assn.; judge U.S. Amateur Boxing Fedn., World Boxing Council, World Athletic Assn., U.S. Boxing Assn., N. Am. Boxing Fed., Internat. Boxing Fedn.; chairperson Mich. Athletic Bd. Control, 1982—; mem. World Congress of Ring Ofcls. Diplomate Am. Bd. Podiatric Surgery, Nat. Bd. Podiatry Examiners. Fellow Royal Soc. Health, Am. Coll. Foot Surgeons, Am. Soc. Podiatric Dermatology, Am. Soc. Hosp. Podiatrists, Am. Soc. Podiatric Medicine; mem. Am. Podiatric Med. Assn., Mich. Podiatric Med. Assn. (ethics com.), Mich. Pub. Health Assn., Am. Pub. Health Assn. (chmn. substance abuse: categorical podiatric health concerns com.), Am. Med. Writers Assn., Am. Coll. Sports Medicine (chmn. boxing com.), Acad. Podiatric Medicine, World Med. Assn., Am. Soc. Podiatric Sports Medicine, Am. Acad. Podiatric Acupuncture, World Boxing Historians Assn., U.S. Amateur Boxers and Coaches Assn., Am. Running and Fitness Assn., Internat. Platform Assn., Internat. Vet. Boxers Assn. (podiatry cons.). Author publs. on foot surgery and sports medicine. Home: 27080 Wellington Rd Franklin MI 48025 Office: 8300 Mack Ave Detroit MI 48214 also 8319 Grand River Detroit MI 48204

KIRSCHNER, BARBARA STARRELS, pediatric gastroenterologist; b. Phila., Mar. 23, 1941; m. Robert H. Kirschner. M.D., Woman's Med. Coll. of Pa., 1967. Diplomate Am. Acad. Pediatrics. Intern, U. Chgo., 1967-68, resident, 1968-80; co-dir. sect. pediatric gastroenterology Wyler Children's Hosp., U. Chgo., 1984—, assoc. prof. pediatrics, 1984—. Contbr. articles to profl. jours. Mem. Am. Gastroenterologic Assn., N.Am. Soc. Pediatric Gastroenterology, Soc. Pediatric Research. Office: U Chgo 5825 S Maryland St Chicago IL 60637

KIRSHBAUM, RONALD MICHAEL, business executive; b. Chgo., Apr. 20, 1938; s. Charles C. and Frances (Walker) K.; m. Adrienne C. Kaufman, Aug. 22, 1965; children—Benjamin, Jonathan, Sarah, Daniel. B.A. cum laude, Northwestern U., 1960; M.S. in Indsl. Mgmt., MIT, 1962. Mktg. research analyst Swift & Co., Chgo., 1962-64; asst. product mgr. Alberto Culver Co., Melrose Park, Ill., 1964-65, product mgr., 1965-67, group product mgr., 1967-69, dir. mktg., 1969-73, gen. mgr. Household/Grocery div., 1973-77, v.p., gen. mgr. Food Service div., 1977-84, v.p., gen. mgr. Food Service and Splty. Products dir., 1984—; bus. cons. Served with U.S. Army, 1962-68. Jewish. Home: 154 Green Bay Rd Highland Park IL 60035 Office: Alberto Culver Co 2525 Armitage Ave Melrose Park IL 60160

KIRSNER, JOSEPH BARNETT, medical educator; b. Boston, Sept. 21, 1909; s. Harris and Ida (Waizer) K.; m. Minnie Shneider, Jan. 6, 1934; 1 child, Robert S. M.D., Tufts U., 1933; Ph.D., U. Chgo., 1942. Asst. in medicine U. Chgo., 1935-39, from instr. to assoc. prof., 1939-1951, prof., 1951—, chief of staff, dep. dean, 1971-76; med. cons. Gastro-Intestinal Research Found., 1962—, Cancer Research Found., 1978—; exec. council Nat. Found. Ileitis Colitis, N.Y., 1976—. Author: Crohn's Desease of the Gastrointestinal Tract, 1980. Editor: Inflammatory Bowel Disease, 1975, 1980. Contbr. articles to profl. jours. Adv. com. med. exhibits Mus. Sci. and Industry, 1981—; mem. Horatio Alger Assn., 1979—, Crusade of Mercy com., Chgo., 1982—. Served to maj. U.S. Army, 1943-46, Europe, Pacific. Recipient Friedenwald medal Am. Gastroenterological Assn., 1975, John Phillips Meml. award ACP, 1984, Geo. Howell Coleman medal Inst. Medicine Chgo., 1984, Rudolph Schindler award Am. Soc. Gastrointestinal Endoscopy, 1984, Louis Block Disting. Service Prof. of Medicine, U. Chgo., 1974. Mem. Am. Gastroenterological Assn. (sr., treas., v.p., pres. elect, pres.), ACP, AMA, Am. Assn. Physicians, Am. Soc. Clin. Investigation. Jewish. Club: Quadrangle (Chgo.). Office: U Chgo Med Ctr 5841 S Maryland Ave Chicago IL 60637

KIRWAN, JAMES ROBERT, management consulting company executive; b. N.Y.C., Oct. 14, 1931; s. James Christopher and Catherine Verona (Flynn) K.; m. Ann Harkin, Aug. 7, 1951; children—James, Katherine, Ann, Eileen, Patti, Jerry, Jack, Peggy, Kelly. B.B.A., Pace U., 1961. Mgr. Touche, Ross, N.Y.C., 1961-65; sr. v.p. Diners Club, N.Y.C., 1965-69; pres. Banc Systems, Cleve., 1969-71, —Fore— Assocs., Cleve., 1971-76, Mgmt. Horizons, Columbus, 1976-78, J. R. Kirwan and Co., Columbus, 1978—. Office: 6469 Masefield St Worthington OH 43085

KISER, BONNIE BEA, educator; b. Fort Wayne, Ind., Feb. 3, 1945; d. Andrew U. and Marian M. (Carr) Smith; m. John T. Kiser, Oct. 5, 1968; 1 son, J. Christopher. B.S., Findlay Coll. (Ohio), 1963; M.S. Ind. U.-Fort Wayne, 1983. Cert. tchr. Calif., Ind. Sci. tchr. Carey Schs. (Ohio), 1967-68; math./sci. tchr. Oklahoma City Schs., 1968-69, Corona-Norco Unified Schs., Corona, Calif., 1969-78; math. tchr. Windsor Schs. (Mo.), 1971-72; math./sci. tchr. East Allen County Schs., Fort Wayne, Ind., 1978—; lectr. in field. Sponsor, Civic Theatre, Fort Wayne. Mem. NEA, Nat. Council Tchrs. Math., Ind. State Tchrs. Assn., East Allen Edn. Assn. (treas.), Phi Delta Kappa. Methodist.

KISER, JOHN L., surgeon; b. Wichita, Kans., Apr. 10, 1937; s. Willard J. and Alice M (Walker) K.; children—Julie Diane, John Loren Jr.; m. Sharon Lyn Hartzell, Oct. 21, 1972; 1 child, Jason Kier. B.S., So. Meth. U., 1958; M.D., Washington U., 1962. Diplomate Am. Bd. Surgery. Resident in surgery Barnes Hosp., St. Louis, 1962-67; practice medicine specializing in surgery, Wichita, Kans., 1967—; attending surgeon Wesley Med. Ctr., 1967—; clin. faculty Kans. U. Med. Sch., 1975—. Contbr. articles to profl. jours. Fellow ACS. Congregationalist. Home: 7765 Killarney Wichita KS 67206 Office: 3243 E Murdock Wichita KS 67208

KISHPAUGH, ALLAN RICHARD, mechanical engineer; b. Dover, N.J., Aug. 31, 1937; B.S. in Mech. Engring., N.J. Inst. Tech., 1967; m. Maryann M. Bizub, July 31, 1965. Engring. technician Stapling Machines Co., Rockaway, N.J., 1956-65; design engr. Airoyal Engring. Co., Livingston, N.J., 1965-66; project engr. Simautics Co., Fairfield, N.J., 1966-67; design engr. Pyrofilm Resistor Mfg. Co., Cedar Knolls, N.J., 1967-68; sr. engr., project mgr. Packaging Systems div. Standard Packaging Corp., Clifton, N.J., 1968-77; sr. machine design engr. Travenol Labs., Round Lake, Ill., 1977-79; dir. engring. TEC, Inc., Alsip, Ill., 1979-80; mgmt. cons., machine developer, Palos Heights, Ill., 1980—; owner Ark Internat., 1981—. Councilman, Borough of Victory Gardens (N.J.), 1969-71, council pres., 1971, police commnr., 1970-70, chmn. fin. com., 1970; pres. Pompton River Assn., Wayne, N.J., 1976-77; mem. Wayne Flood Control Commn., 1976-77; past deacon, elder, Sunday sch. tchr. and supt. local Presbyn. chs. Served with Air N.G., 1960-61, 62-65, with USAF, 1961-62. Registered profl. engr., N.J., Ill. Mem. ASME (vice chmn. N.J. sect. 1973-74, numerous other regional offices, food, drug and beverage com. 1983—), Nat. Soc. Profl. Engrs., Ill. Soc. Profl. Engrs. (chpt. officer 1984—), Chgo. Assn. Commerce and Industry. Patentee mechanism for feeding binding wire, wirebound box-making machine, method packaging granular materials, others in field. Address: 6118 W 123d St Palos Heights IL 60463

KISKER, C. THOMAS, physician, medical educator; B.A., Johns Hopkins U., 1958; M.D., U. Cin. Coll. Medicine, 1962. Diplomate Am. Bd. Pediatrics, AM. Bd. Pediatric Hematology-Oncology. Licensed physician Ohio, Iowa. Intern, U. Oreg. Coll. Medicine, 1962-63; sr. asst. surgeon NIH, 1963-65; jr. resident pediatrics Children's Hosp., Cin., 1965-66, sr. resident pediatrics, 1966-67; fellow pediatric hematology, 1967-69; asst. attending pediatrician, 1968-69, attending pediatrician, 1969-73; dir. hemophilia project, 1971-73, dir. clin. hematology lab., 1972-73; asst. prof. pediatrics U. Cin., 1969-72, assoc. profl pediatrics, 1972-73; assoc. prof. pediatrics U. Iowa, Iowa City, 1973-79, dir. div. pediatric hematology-oncology, 1973—, prof. pediatrics, 1979—; med. lectr. various student and profl. groups; active mem. Pediatric Hematology-Oncology Group, Cin., Children's Cancer Study Group, Los Angeles; councilor Midwest Blood Club; mem. editorial bd. Pediatrics Today; mem. adv. council Nat. Hemophilia Ctrs., 1979—. Contbr. numerous sci. papers to profl. jours. and chpts. to books. Mem. Iowa Found. Fund Raising Com. Lederle Med. Student Research fellow, 1959; recipient state and fed. grants. Mem. Am. Soc. Hematology, Mid-west Soc. for Pediatric Research, Am. Fedn. for Clin. Research, Am. Heart Assn., Internat. Soc. Thrombosis and Haemostasis (sub-com. on neonatal hemostasis), Central Soc. for Pediatric Research, Soc. for Pediatric Research, Johnson County Med. Soc., Prairie Region Affiliated Blood Services, Am. Pediatric Soc. Office: Univ of Iowa Hosps 2520 JCP Iowa City IA 52242

KISPERT, DONALD EUGENE, engineering executive; b. Clinton, Ind., Sept. 1, 1928; s. Ortie Curtis and Euphemia (Broatch) K.; B.S. in Civil Engring., Ind. Inst. Tech., 1951; m. Nancy Marie Berghoff, Aug. 27, 1950; children—Robert Calvin, Donna Jean, Linda Sue. Field project engr. E.I. DuPont Co., Ind., Ga., N.J., 1951-54, 55-56; constrn. supr. Socony Mobil Oil Co., New Goshen, Ind., 1954-55; field supt. Fruin-Colnon Constrn. Co., Indpls., 1956-59; design engr. Clyde Williams & Assoc., Indpls., 1956-59, E.R. Hamilton & Assos., 1959-60;

bldg. and maintenance mgr. R.R. Donnelley & Sons Co., Warsaw, Ind., 1960-70, group mgr. engring., 1970-78, 84—, quality and services group mgr., 1978-82, materials group mgr., 1982-84. Bd. dirs. Warsaw YMCA, 1965-72. Served with U.S. Army, 1946-48. Licensed profl. engr., Ind. Mem. Nat., Ind. socs. profl. engrs. Republican. Presbyterian. Clubs: Optimists, Masons. Home: 1933 E Clark St Warsaw IN 46580 Office: RTE 30 W Warsaw IN 46580

KISS, JANOS, music educator, composer, condr.; b. Hungary, Mar. 21, 1920; s. Andras and Maria (Laszlo) K.; came to U.S., 1956, naturalized, 1973; teaching diploma Bela Bartok Conservatory of Music, Budapest, 1954; conducting diploma People's Ednl. Inst., Budapest, 1956; Franz Liszt Acad. Music, Budapest, 1954-56; student music edn. sci. Western Res. U., 1960-64; m. Josephine Anna Recse, July 27, 1963. Tchr. brasses Cleve. Music Sch. Settlement, 1964-79; chmn. music dept. St. Luke Sch., Lakewood, Ohio, 1966-70; dir. orch., composer in residence, tchr. instruments Western Res. Acad., Hudson, Ohio, 1967-72; tchr., composer in residence St. Edward High Sch., Lakewood, Ohio, 1968-74; composer in residence Luth. High Sch., Rocky River, Ohio, 1973-76; chmn. music dept. Holy Family Sch., Parma, Ohio, 1974-82, St. Ann's Sch., Cleveland Heights, 1974-75; co-founder, condr., music dir. West Suburban Philharmonic Orch., 1969—; hon. mem. Zoltan Kodaly Acad. and Inst., Chgo. Mem. Am. Soc. Univ. Composers, Nat. Assn. Composers U.S.A., Music Tchrs. Nat. Assn., Ohio Music Tchrs. Assn., Cleve. Fedn. Musicians, Am. Music Center, ASCAP. Composer: Black Rose of the Alamo, 1964; Spring-At-Las, 1970; String Bass Concerto, 1970; Flute Concerto, 1970; Concerto for Trombone, 1971; On the Wing, for flute and guitar, 1972; Josepha, quintet for alto recorder with violin, viola, cello and harp, 1973; Concerto for B-Flat Clarinet, with orch., 1974; Celebration and Challenge, for wind ensemble with electronics, 1974; Western Legend, rhapsody for harp and orch., 1975; Twilight Mist, for string quartet and organ, 1975; Impression, for trumpet and piano, 1975; Adagio for Viola, with two violins, cello and harp, 1975; Silent Presence, tone poem for clarinet, viola and organ, 1975; winter's Sonnet, flute-harp-organ, 1975; Ballet for Harps, 1975; Concerto for violoncello and orch., 1976; Lexington '76, Bicentennial Rhapsody for Orch., 1976; Divertimento, solo violin, solo viola, solo string bass, harp and chamber ensemble, 1977; Episode for oboe, french horn, bassoon and harp, 1977; In Homage for harp ensemble, 1977; Suite in Stilo Antico for orch. with harpsichord, 1977; Salute-in Retrospect, cimbalo solo with orch., 1977; Chorale Prelude, organ, 1977; Via Lactea (The Galaxy), symphonic fantasy, 1978; Rhapsody for Cimbalom and Orch., 1978; Dance of Colors on the Black Hills of South Dakota, for harp ensemble, 1978; Sinfonia Atlantis, for orch., 1979; Canzone da Sacra for string quartet, 1979; Let Me Be Near for voice and orch., 1980; Las Vegas (The Meadows), cimbalom solo with orch., 1980; Ave Maria for voice and organ, 1980; Benedictus Dominus for orch. and mixed voices, 1981; Mount of Atlantis clarinet solo with synthesizer and orch., 1981; Agnus Dei for orch. and mixed voices and organ, 1981; trumpet solo, 1984.

KIST, GERALDINE F., manufacturer's representative; b. Chgo., July 13, 1942; s. Frank S. and Gertrude (Manuszak) Tutlewski; m. Charles J. Kist, Jan. 31, 1962 (dec. 1974); children—Steven, Sondra, Douglas. R.N., St. Mary of Nazareth Coll., Chgo.; B.S.N., DePaul U. Staff nurse St. Mary of Nazareth, Chgo., 1958-59, Resurrection Hosp., Chgo., 1959-68, Holy Family Hosp., Des Plaines, 1968-69; pres. Kist Assocs. Ltd., Northbrook, Ill., 1969—; nat. sales mgr. Glenn Electric Inc., Orland Park, Ill., 1979—; nat. field rep. mgr. Systems Material Handling, Overland Park, Kansas, 1983—. Mem. Republican Nat. Com., 1983; charter mem. Republican Presdl. Task Force, 1983. Mem. Mfrs. Agt. Nat. Assn., Material Handling Equipment Dealers Assn., Internat. Material Mgmt. Soc., Am. Material Mgmt. Soc. Roman Catholic. Club: U.S. Senatorial. Home: 3029 Rennes Ct Northbrook IL 60062

KIST, NICOLAAS CHRISTIAAN, consulting engineer; b. S.I., N.Y., Aug. 8, 1928; s. Herman Jacob and Ernestine Clara (Nickenig) K.; m. Nancy Prichard Jones, Apr. 24, 1954; children—Cornelia Helena, Johanna Claire, Susanna Maria. M.S. in Civil Engring., Technische Hogeschool, Delft, Netherlands, 1953. Registered profl. engr., Ill. Jr. and field engr. Chgo. Bridge and Iron, Chgo., 1957-59, project mgr., Italy, 1959-60, constrn./sales/engring. service mgr., Netherlands, 1960-67, internat. engr. standards coordinator, Oak Brook, Ill., 1967-68, asst. dir. corp. nuclear quality assurance, 1968-72; pres. N.C. Kist & Assocs., Inc., Naperville, Ill., 1972—; speaker, cons. in quality assurance. Served to lt. (j.g.) USN, 1953-57. Mem. Am. Soc. Quality Control (regional councilor 1981—), Am. Arbitration Soc. (arbitrator 1979), ASME, ASCE, Royal Soc. Engrs. (Netherlands). Republican. Methodist. Avocations: backpacking; art history; travel; observing nature. Home: 900 E Porter Ave Naperville IL 60540 Office: N C Kist & Assocs Inc 127-A S Washington Naperville IL 60540

KIST, ROBERT THOMAS, real estate consultant; b. Eagle Grove, Iowa, Mar. 8, 1920; s. Joseph J. Kist and Verna E. Klaas; m. Bernadine Williams, May 9, 1942 (dec. Feb. 1984); children—Cheryl Lynn, Scott. Cert. in real estate Washington U., St. Louis, 1949. Salesman, Keeney-Toelle, St. Louis, 1945-50; ptnr. Marr-Kist-Bell, St. Louis, 1950-53; regional v.p. Equitable Ins. Co., N.Y.C., 1953-82; cons. Solon Gershman, Inc. and Edward J. Jones, St. Louis, 1982—; dir. Clayton Merc. Bank, St. Louis. Bd. dirs. Boy Scouts Am., 1970—, Jr. Achievement, St. Louis, 1971, St. Luke's Hosp., St. Louis, 1979, Clayton Employee Pension Fund, 1982; trustee Goodwill Industries. Served with USAF, 1940-45. Recipient Silver Beaver award Boy Scouts Am., 1979. Mem. Am. Inst. Real Estate Appraisers, Omega Tau Rho, Lambda Alpha. Republican. Presbyterian. Clubs: Sunset Country, Missouri Athletic (St. Louis) (sec. 1979-80). Avocations: golfing; antique golf club collecting. Home: 8041 Daytona Dr Saint Louis MO 63105 Office: Gershman Investment Co 7 N Bemiston St Saint Louis MO 63105

KISTNER, RICHARD ALLEN, city official; b. Greensburg, Pa., May 1, 1948; s. Paul Richard and Margaret Melinda (Haney) K.; m. Karen Jane Remy, Aug. 31, 1974; children—Richard Allen, Rachel Ann, Ryan Alexander. B.A. in Urban Studies, Wright State U., 1975; M. Pub. Adminstrn., U. Dayton, 1981. Police officer City of Fairborn, Ohio, 1970-77; dir. pub. safety City of New Lebanon, Ohio, 1977-81; Chief of Police, City of Liberal, Kans., 1981—; instr. Seward County Community Coll., Liberal, Kans., 1982—, St. Mary of the Plains, Dodge City, Kans., 1983—. Contbr. articles to profl. jours. Bd. dirs. Community Concerts, Inc., Liberal, 1984; bd. dirs. Rainbow Players Community Theatre, Liberal, 1984; adv. bd. Sta. KANZ Pub. Radio, Pierceville, Kans., 1984. Served to sgt. USAF, 1966-70. Recipient Extraordinary Service award Office Spl. Investigations, Washington, 1976, Blue Coat award Ohio K.C., 1976, Govs. Traffic Safety award Ohio Traffic Safety Commn., Columbus, 1980, Recognition award Miami Valley Civil Def., Dayton, Ohio, 1981. Mem. Internat. Assn. Chiefs of Police, Kans. Peace Officers Assn., Kans. Assn. Chiefs of Police (bd. dirs. 1983—), Liberal C. of C. (bd. dirs. 1984—). Roman Catholic. Club: Sertoma (Fairborn) (v.p. 1975-77). Lodge: Fraternal Order of Police. Avocation: piano. Home: 1309 Fairview Ave Liberal KS 67901 Office: PO Box 830 Liberal KS 67901

KITHIER, KAREL, physician, pathology educator; b. Prague, Czechoslovakia, Dec. 6, 1930; came to U.S. 1968, naturalized, 1978; s. Karel and Marie (Bohackova) K.; m. Viktorie Svecova, May 6, 1961; 1 child, Karel. M.D., Charles U., Prague, 1962, Ph.D., 1967. Research scientist Research Inst. for Child Devel., Prague, 1967-68, Child Research Ctr. of Mich., Detroit, 1968-71, Mich. Cancer Found., Detroit, 1972-74; asst. prof. pathology Wayne State U Sch. Medicine, Detroit, 1974-78, assoc. prof. pathology, 1978—; chief, clin. immunology Detroit Receiving Hosp., Detroit, 1978—, assoc. head clin. chemistry, 1978—; staff pathologist VA Med. Ctr., Allen Park, Mich., 1976—. Contbr. articles to profl. jours. Fellow Nat. Acad. Clin. Biochemistry; mem. Am. Assn. Cancer Research, Am. Assn. Immunologists, Am. Assn. Clin. Chemists, Internat. Soc. Oncodevelopmental Biology and Medicine. Avocation: fishing. Office: Wayne State U Sch Medicine 540 E Canfield St Detroit MI 48201

KITOS, PAUL ALAN, biochemistry educator; b. Saskatoon, Saskatchewan, Can., May 31, 1927; s. Richard Joseph and Ellen (McGinn) K.; m. Gwenyth Theresa Heffernan, May 24, 1952; children—Theresa, Peter, John, Anne Marie, Richard, Emily. B.S.A., U.B.C., Can., 1950, M.S.A., 1952; Ph.D., Oreg. State U., 1956. Research chemist E.I. duPont, Newark, 1956-59; asst. prof. U. Kans., Lawrence, 1959-64, assoc. prof., 1964-69, prof. biochemistry, 1969—; vis. prof. Harvard Med. Sch., Boston, 1971-72; vis. scientist L'Institut d'Embryologie, Nogent-sur-Marne, France, 1983. Recipient Amoco award U. Kans., 1974. Mem. Am. Chem. Soc., Am. Soc. Biol. Chemists, AAAS, Tissue Culture Assn., Sigma Xi. Home: 2136 Terrace Rd Lawrence KS 66044 Office: Dept Biochemistry Univ Kans Lawrence KS 66045

KITSIS, ARLEN THOMAS, confectionary company executive; b. Mankato, Minn., Jan. 16, 1935; s. Louis and Florence (Marcus) K.; m. Tybelle Scherling, June 17, 1956; children—Steven, Mindy, Edward. A.A., U. Minn., 1956. Vice pres. sales Shari Candies, Inc., Mankato, 1956-66, exec. v.p., 1966-76, owner/pres., 1984—; pres. confectionary div. CFS Continental, Chgo., 1976-84. Bus. chair chpt. Am. Cancer Soc., 1975-78; mem. exec. com. City of Hope, 1980-85. Recipient Golter award City of Hope, 1976. Mem. Mankato C. of C. (Minn. Viking Chair 1965-80), Nat. Candy Wholesalers Assn. Trustee, B'nai Emet Synagogue, 1981-83. Republican. Jewish. Club: Golden Valley Country (Mpls.). Lodges: B'nai B'rith (pres. 1958-80), Shriners. Avocations: golf; music; sports; travel. Home: 6601 Parkwood Rd Edina MN 55436 Office: Shari Candies 5780 Lincoln Dr Edina MN 55436

KITTELL, THEODORE HARMON, hospital executive; b. Bloomfield, N.Mex., Jan. 19, 1934; s. Arthur Callen and Virginia Anne (Harmon) K.; B.B.A., U. N.Mex., 1955; M.H.A., U. Minn., 1963; Ph.D., Walden U., 1975; m. Martha H. Kittell, Nov. 30, 1958; 1 dau., Mary. Commd. 2d lt. U.S. Air Force, 1957; advanced through grades to capt., 1963; bus. mgr. Malcolm Grow U.S. Air Force Hosp., Elmendorf, Alaska; adminstrv. resident Wilford Hall Air Force Hosp., San Antonio; adminstrv. officer, Eglin AFB, Fla.; ret., 1967; pres. Pulaski Meml. Hosp., Winamac, Ind., 1967-80, Apple River Valley Meml. Hosp., Amery, Wis., 1980—; mem. Ind. Health Careers Bd., 1973-76. Internat. Farm Youth Exchange fellow, 1956. Mem. Am. Coll. Hosp. Adminstrs., Am. Public Health Planning Assn., Am. Hosp. Assn. Methodist. Lodges: Lions, Mason, Shriners. Home: 705 Harriman St S Amery WI 54001 Office: 221 Scholl St Amery WI 54001

KITTELSON, JOHN EDWARDS, insurance field underwriter; b. Beresford, S.D. July 19, 1936; s. Helmey and Ella (Grunning) K.; m. Marcia Lea Gunderson, June 28, 1959; children—John Olaf, Susan Marie. B.S. in Math., Augustana Coll., 1961; postgrad. Northwest Mo. State U., 1973; grad. U.S. Air Force Command and Staff Coll., 1969. Registered health underwriter. System simulation designer System Devel. Corp., Santa Monica, Calif., 1961-63; engring. mgr. Raven Industries, Inc., Sioux Falls, S.D., 1963-68, mgr. mktg. and sales, 1969-72; field underwriter N.Y. Life Ins. Co., Sioux Falls, 1973—; admission liaison officer U.S. Air Force Acad., Colorado Springs, 1975-81, liaison officer comdr. for S.D., 1981—; fighter pilot, dir. pub. affairs U.S. Air Force, Calif. Air N.G., S.D. Air N.G., 1955-84; col. USAFR, 1984—. Pres., Nordland Fest Assn., Inc., Sioux Falls, 1983; bd. dirs. Nordland Heritage Found., Sioux Falls, 1982—, Nordland Fest Assn., Inc., Sioux Falls, 1983—, S.D. Children's Home Soc., Sioux Falls, 1981—; mem. council First Lutheran Ch., Sioux Falls, 1978-81, dir. parish edn., 1978-81; mem. S.D. Com. on Employers Support of Guard and Res., Sioux Falls, 1982-85; chmn. U.S. Sen. Pressler's Selection Com. for Mil. Acad. Nominations, Sioux Falls, 1978-82; mem. center com., Bergland Sr. Citizens Ctr., Sioux Falls, 1977—. Serves as col. with USAFR. Decorated Meritorious Service medal, Commendation medal (USAF); Humanitarian Service medal, 1977. Fellow Augustana Coll.; mem. Air Force Assn. (v.p. S.D. 1983-84, pres. 1984—), Res. Officer Assn. (pres. S.D. 1979-80, Reservist of Yr. 1981, nat. councilman 1984—), N.G. Assn. (exec. com. S.D. 1980-82), Estate Planning Council (bd. dirs. 1980-82), Sioux Falls Life Underwriters (treas. 1982-83, sec. 1983-84, v.p. 1984-85, pres. elect 1985-86), Sioux Falls Area C. of C. (bd. dirs. 1980-83, chmn. aviation com. 1978-80, chmn. mil. and vets. affairs com. 1983—). Lodges: Rotary Internat., Optimists Internat. (Disting. lt. gov. 1968; pres. Sioux Falls 1966-67; lt. gov. Dakota-Man.-Minn. 1967-68), Elks. Home: 2012 S Holly Sioux Falls SD 57105 Office: 141 N Main Suite 308 Sioux Falls SD 57102

KIVETT, MARVIN F., anthropologist; b. Nebr., Mar. 10, 1917; s. Thomas and Murl (Mark) K.; A.B., U. Nebr., 1942, M.A., 1951; m. Caroline Ritchey, Sept. 12, 1941; 1 son, Ronald Lee. Archeologist, Smithsonian Instn., 1946-49; mus. dir. Nebr. Hist. Soc., Lincoln, 1949-63, adminstrv. dir., 1963-85; dir. Nebr. Hist. Soc. Found., 1985—. Served with AUS, 1942-46. Editor: Nebraska History, 1963—. Contbr. articles to profl. jours. Home: 5425 Franklin Lincoln NE 68501 Office: 1500 R Box 82554 Lincoln NE 68501

KIZER, BERT L., management consultant; b. Montpelier, Ohio, Oct. 27, 1930; s. Weldon William and Nina Dell (Oberlander) K.; m. Patricia Jean Minard, Apr. 10, 1971; 1 son, Geoffrey Minard. B.S. in Bus. Adminstrn., Miami U., Ohio, 1952. With sales and mktg. depts. Mead Corp., Dayton, Ohio, 1956-65; mgr. paperboard ops. Scholle Container Corp., Northlake, Ill., 1965-66; owner, pres. Bert L. Kizer & Assocs., Inc., Hinsdale, Ill., 1966—. Mem. Hinsdale Village Caucus, 1977-80. Served to lt. (j.g.), U.S. Navy, 1952-55. Mem. TAPPI. Republican. Presbyterian. Club: Edgewood Valley Country (LaGrange, Ill.). Home: 1148 Laurie Ln Burr Ridge IL 60521 Office: 930 York Rd Suite 202 Hinsdale IL 60521

KIZER, LEONARD LEROY, data processing executive; b. Flint, Mich., Apr. 11, 1941; s. Leonard Leroy and Helen Evelyn (Rugg) K.; m. Ruth Ellen Hansen, Mar. 12, 1965; children—Thomas, Matthew, Laura. A.A., Ferris State Coll., 1963; cert. in computer programming Brockton Inst., 1965; cert. in TV and radio repair DeVry Inst. Tech., 1971; B.S., Aquinas Coll., 1974. Cert. systems profl. Inst. for Cert. Computer Profls. Surveyor, Mich. Dept. Transp., 1960-65; computer operator Rapistan, Inc., Grand Rapids, Mich., 1965-66, programmer, analyst, 1966-74, supr. programming, 1974-78; mgr. systems and programming Lear Siegler, Inc., Grand Rapids, 1978-81; dir. info. services Rospatch Corp., Grand Rapids, 1981—. Mem. Assn. Systems Mgmt. Avocations: reading; hunting; fishing; photography; music. Home: 8139 Belmont Ave NE Belmont MI 49306 Office: Rospatch Corp PO Box 2738 Grand Rapids MI 49501

KIZZIER, DONNA LORRAINE, educator; b. Beatrice, Nebr., Jan. 16, 1951; d. Willard Henry and Emma (Johnson) McAlister; m. Roy James Kizzier, Dec. 19, 1971; children—Nicole, Ryan. B.S., U. Nebr., 1972, M.E., 1978, Ed.D., 1985. Bus. instr. Hildreth (Nebr.) Pub. Schs., 1973-75; bus. tchr., vocat. coordinator Lexington (Nebr.) Sr. High Sch., 1973-75; instr. bus. Kearney (Nebr.) State Coll., 1975-81, prof. bus., 1982—, exec. v.p. acad. affairs, 1985—; adminstrv. intern Lincoln (Nebr.) Pub. Schs. and Nebr. Dept. Edn., summer 1981; cons. Bd. dirs. Kearney Campfire Assn., 1982—; tchr. Sunday sch. Methodist Ch., 1976-78. Recipient Dean's Council Research award Kearney State Coll., 1983. Mem. Women in Mgmt. Assn. Central Nebr. (pres. 1980), Nat. Bus. Edn. Assn., Nebr. Bus. Edn. Assn. (conf. dir. 1983), Am. Vocat. Assn., Nebr. Vocat. Assn., Soc. Data Educators, Nat. Assn. Tchr. Educators, Delta Pi Epsilon (state pres. 1982, nat. council rep. 1983-85, nat. research council rep. 1984), Phi Delta Kappa. Club: Shrine Aux. Home: 2010 W 35th St Kearney NE 68847 Office: Kearney State Coll Bus Dept Office Bldg Kearney NE 68849

KJELLSTRAND, CARL MAGNUS, medical educator; b. Svenljunga, Sweden, Feb. 19, 1936; came to U.S., 1962, naturalized, 1978; s. Torsten Fritiof and Aja M. (Breimer) K.; m. Kerstin Clifford, Aug. 27, 1958; children—Torsten, Cecilia. Medic Kand., U. Lund, 1956, M.D., 1962. Intern medicine U. Minn., Mpls., 1968, asst. prof. medicine and surgery, 1969-71, assoc. prof., 1971-74, prof., 1974—. Contbr. 300 articles to profl. jours. Served to capt. Swedish Army, 1954-67. Fellow ACP; mem. Am. Soc. Artificial Internal Organs (pres. 1982), Internat. Soc. Artificial Organs (v.p. 1982—), Central Soc. Clin. Research, European Dialysis Transplant Assn., Peruvian Soc. Pediatrics (hon.), Peruvian Soc. Nephrology (hon.), Venezuelan Soc. Nephrology (hon.). Avocations: reading; writing; skiing; canoeing. Home: 1367 Shryer Ave W St Paul MN 55113 Office: U Minn Hennepin County Med Ctr Dept Medicine Minneapolis MN 55415

KLAMERUS, KAREN JEAN, pharmacist, educator; b. Chgo., Aug. 10, 1957; d. Robert Edward and Jane Mary (Nawoj) K.; m. Frederick P. Zeller. B.S. in Pharmacy, U. Ill., 1980; Pharm. D., U. Ky., 1981. Registered pharmacist Ky., Ill. Staff pharmacist Haggin Meml. Hosp., Harrodsburg, Ky., 1980-81, Regional Med. Ctr., Madisonville, Ky., 1982; critical care liasion, 1982; clin. pharmacist resident U. Nebr., Omaha, 1983; clin. pharmacist cardiothoracic surgery U. Ill., Chgo., 1983—, clin. asst. prof. dept. pharmacy practice, 1983—; cons. Dimensional Mktg. Inst., Chgo., 1983—, Channing, Weinbergs' Co., Inc., N.Y.C., 1983—. Mem. rev. bd. Am. Jour. Hosp. Pharmacy, Clin. Pharmacy, Drug Intelligence and Clin. Pharmacy. Mem. Am. Assn. Colls. Pharmacy, Am. Coll. Clin. Pharmacy, Am. Heart Assn., Am. Soc. Hosp. Pharmacists, No. Ill. Soc. Hosp. Pharmacists, Rho Chi. Avocations: computers, sports, gardening, sewing. Office: U Ill Chgo 833 S Wood St Room 244 Chicago IL 60612

KLARNER, DANIEL WILLIAM, engineer; b. Kaukauna, Wis., Feb. 1, 1957; s. Norman Joseph and Elizabeth Ann (Zahn) K.; m. Patricia Liala Anderson, Dec. 27, 1980. B.S. in Mech. Engring., U. Wis.-Platteville, 1979. Registered profl. engr., Wis., Minn. Material handler Pierce Mfg., Appleton, Wis., 1976-79; engr. Lakehead Pipe Line Co., Superior, Wis., 1979—. Club: LPL Activity (pres. 1984—) (Superior). Lodge: Moose. Avocations: woodworking; stained glass; bowling; swimming; volleyball. Home: 1707 Susquehanna Ave Superior WI 54880 Office: Lakehead Pipe Line Co Inc 3025 Tower Ave Superior WI 54880

KLATT, LOIS ANN, educator; b. Phila., July 18, 1938; d. Alferd John and Marion (Simpson) Klatt. B.S., West Chester State U., 1960; M.S., U. Wis., 1965; P.E.D. (grad. asst.), Ind. U., 1977. Instr., Milw. Luth. High Sch., 1960-63; assoc. prof. anatomy, physiology and biomechanics Concordia Coll., River Forest, Ill., 1963—, dir., 1980—; cons. Midwest Sports Medicine, Chgo., 1981—; researcher U.S. Olympic Com., 1982—; clinician Ill. High Sch. Assn., 1975—. Contbr. articles on sports medicine to profl. jours. Mem. ch. council Lutheran Ch.-Mo. Synod, Elmwood Park, Ill., 1978-82; active Luth. World Relief, 1978—; trainer, instr. ARC Ill.-Ind., 1963—; instr. CPR, Am. Heart Assn., Chgo., 1981—. Recipient award Ill. Bd. Ofcls., 1981, Ill. High Sch. Assn., 1978, 81, 83. Fellow Internat. Soc. Biomechanics; mem. AAHPER, Am. Coll. Sports Medicine, U.S. Field Hockey Assn. (hon.; adminstrv. v.p. 1978-81), Luth. Edn. Assn., Milw. Field Hockey Assn. (hon.), Sports Medicine Ofcls. Club Chgo. (leader 1980—, chmn. 1976-80). Republican. Office: Concordia College Human Performance Lab 7400 Augusta St River Forest IL 60305

KLAUS, ANDREW PETER, cardiologist; b. Columbus, Ohio, Nov. 7, 1941; s. Emmett John and Mary Louise (Wochos) K.; m. Jean Ann Poling, June 19, 1965; children—David, Jennifer, Kevin. B.S., Northwestern U., 1963, M.D., 1966. Diplomate Am. Bd. Internal Medicine, subsplty. bd. cardiology. Intern, resident Ward Med. Service, Barnes Hosp., St. Louis, 1966-68; fellow in cardiology Johns Hopkins Hosp., Balt., 1970-72; physician, chief of cardiology, dir. cardiac catheterization lab., dir. CCU, Frederick C. Smith Clinic and Community Meml. Hosp., Marion, Ohio, 1972-75; founding ptnr. Cardiology, Inc., Columbus, Ohio, 1975—; clin. instr. in cardiology Ohio State U. Coll. Medicine, Columbus, 1972-81, clin. asst. prof. medicine, 1981—; dir. cardiac noninvasive lab. Mount Carmel Med. Ctr., 1980—; chmn. clin. research rev. com. Mt. Carmel Hosp., 1978—; chief cardiology, dir. CCU, Mount Carmel East Hosp., 1979—. Contbr. articles to profl. jours. Served as surgeon USPHS, 1968-70. Fellow Am. Coll. Cardiology, Am. Heart Assn. (Council on Clin. Cardiology, pres., bd. dirs. Central Ohio chpt.); mem. Alpha Omega Alpha, Phi Beta Kappa. Republican. Avocations: golf; boating. Home: 4839 Stonehaven Dr Columbus OH 43220 Office: 777 W State St Columbus OH 43222

KLECZKA, GERALD D., congressman; b. Milw., Nov. 26, 1943; ed. U. Wis., Milw; married Bonnie Scott, 1978. Mem. Wis. Assembly, 1968-72, Wis. Senate, 1974-84. Mem. 98th-99th U.S. Congresses from 5th District, Wisconsin. Del., Democratic Nat. Conv. Served with Wis. Air NG, 1963-69. Mem. Polish Nat. Alliance, Wilson Park Advancement Assn., Polish Assn. Am., South Side Businessmen's Club, Milw. Soc. Democrat. Address: 226 Cannon House Office Bldg Washington DC 20515*

KLEIMAN, BERNARD, lawyer; b. Chgo., Jan. 26, 1928; s. Isadore and Pearl (Wikoff) K.; B.S., Purdue U., 1951; J.D., Northwestern U., 1954; m. Lenore Silver, Apr. 27, 1959; children—Leslie, David. Bar: Ill. 1954. Practice law in assn. with Abraham W. Brussell, 1957-60; dist. counsel United Steel Workers Am., 1960-65, gen. counsel, 1965—; ptnr. Kleiman, Cornfield & Feldman, Chgo., 1960-75, B. Kleiman, P.C., 1976-77, Kleiman & Whitney, P.C., Chgo., 1978—; mem. top industry-wide joint collective bargaining coms. in steel, aluminum, can mfg. and other industries; lectr. in field. Bd. dirs. Breast Cancer Support Program. Served with AUS, 1946-48. Mem. Am., Ill., Chgo., Allegheny County bar assns., Ill. Labor History Soc., Phi Alpha Delta. Contbr. articles to legal jours. Office: 1 E Wacker Dr Chicago IL 60601

KLEIMAN, DAVID HAROLD, lawyer; b. Kendallville, Ind., Apr. 2, 1934; s. Isador and Pearl (Wikoff) K.; m. Meta Dene Freeman, July 6, 1958; children—Gary, Andrew, Scott, Matthew. B.S., Purdue U., 1956; J.D., Northwestern U., 1959. Bar: Ind. 1959. Assoc. Bamberger & Feibleman, Indpls., 1959-61; ptnr. Bagal, Talesnick & Kleiman, Indpls., 1961-73; ptnr. Dann, Pecar, Newman, Talesnick & Kleiman, Indpls., 1973—; dep. pros. atty. 1961-62; counsel Met. Devel. Commn., 1965-75, Ind. Heartland Coordinating Commn., 1975—. Chmn., Young Leadership Council, 1967; v.p. Indpls. Hebrew Congregation, 1973; pres. Jewish Community Ctr. Assn., 1972-75; v.p. Jewish Welfare Fedn., 1975—; bd. govs. United Way of Greater Indpls., 1979—; bd. dirs. New Hope Found., 1981-83. Recipient Young Leadership award, 1968. Mem. ABA, Ind. Bar Assn., Indpls. Bar Assn., Comml. Law League Am. Club: B'nai B'rith. Editor: Jour. of Air, Law and Commerce, 1958-59. Office: 1600 Market Square Center Indianapolis IN 46204

KLEIMAN, MORTON, chemist consulant; b. Kansas City, Mo., Mar. 8, 1916; s. Saul and Esther (Schiller) K.; 2 children. B.S. in Chemistry, U. Mich., 1937, M.S., 1983; Ph.D., U. Chgo., 1942. Dir. research Velsicol Corp., Chgo., 1948-53; pres., dir. research Chemley Products Co., Skokie, Ill., 1953-82; dir., chem. cons. M. Kleiman & Assocs., Skokie, 1982—. Patentee in field. Mem. Am. Chem. Soc., Sigma Xi. Address: 8033 Ridgeway Ave Skokie IL 60076

KLEIN, CHARLES HENLE, lithographing co. exec.; b. Cin., Oct. 5, 1908; s. Benjamin Franklin and Flora (Henle) K.; student Purdue U., 1926-27, U. Cin., 1927-28; m. Ruth Becker, Sept. 23, 1938; children—Betsy (Mrs. Marvin H. Schwartz), Charles H., Carla (Mrs. George Fee III). Pres., Progress Lithographing Co., Cin., 1934-59, Novelart Mfg. Co., Cin., 1960—; dir. R.A. Taylor Corp. Founding mem. Chief Execs. Forum. Clubs: Losantiville Country, Queen City, Bankers (Cin.). Home: 6754 Fairoaks Dr Amberley Village Cincinnati OH 45237 Office: 2121 Section Rd Amberley Village Cincinnati OH 45237

KLEIN, DALE H., SR., financial executive; b. Manitowoc, Wis., Mar. 6, 1946; S. Arthur J. and Josephine K.; m. Karen A. Weina, June 19, 1965; children—Dale H. Jr., Tina M. Student Lake Shore Tech. Inst., 1969-71. Supr. acctg. Kargard Co., Marinette, Wis., 1971-72; div. controller toy div. Connor Forest Industries, Wausau, Wis., 1972-75; acctg. mgr. Universal Foundry, Oshkosh, Wis., 1975-79; acctg. mgr., controller, treas. Mill-Craft Bldg. Systems, Inc., Waupaca, Wis., 1979-85; controller Davis Indus., Nappanee, Ind., 1985—. Office: Davis Industries DBA Heckaman Homes PO Box 229 Nappanee IN

KLEIN, DAVID MARK, mechanical engineer, executive; b. Appleton, Wis., Nov. 16, 1944; s. Mark Michael and Marie Catherine (Sheleski) K.; m. Kathleen A. Skovera, Oct. 4, 1974; children—Kelly L., Kerri L., Matthew D., Amanda E. B.S., U. Wis.-Madison, 1970; M.B.A., U. Wis.-Oshkosh, 1976. Registered profl. engr., Wis. Chief engr. TEC Systems Inc., DePere, Wis., 1969-74; sr. engr. C. A. Lawton, DePere, 1974-75; engring. mgr. Am. Can Co., Green Bay, Wis., 1976-79; dir. engring. TEC Systems, W.R. Grace, DePere, 1979-82, gen. mgr., v.p., 1982—. Patentee in field. Mem. Tech. Assn. Pulp and Paper Industry. Republican. Lodge: Kiwanis (bd. dirs. 1982-84). Avocations: fishing; hunting; snowmobiling. Home: 134 Lorrie Way DePere WI 54115 Office: TEC Systems W R Grace & Co 830 Prosper Rd DePere WI 54115

KLEIN, EILEEN LASHELLE, account coordinator; b. Independence, Mo., Mar. 26, 1955; d. Virgil Lee and Virginia Lee (DeBerry), K. B.S. Southwest Mo. State U., 1977. Data input operator Syntex Agribusiness Inc., Springfield, Mo., 1977-78; mktg. sec., 1978-79, account coordinator, 1979—. Mem. Young Democrats, Springfield, 1975-77, v.p., 1977, big sister Big Brothers-Big Sisters of Ozarks, Springfield, 1984—. Mem. Quality of Work Life Circle, 1982-84, Steering Com Policies and Procedures, 1984—. Lodge: Order Eastern Star. Home: 419 N Oak Grove Springfield MO 65802 Office: Syntex Nutrition and Chemical Div 1915 W Sunshine Springfield MO 65805

KLEIN, GEORGE DEVRIES, geologist; b. Den Haag, Netherlands, Jan. 21, 1933; came to U.S., 1947, naturalized, 1955; s. Alfred and Doris (deVries) K.; B.A. in Geology, Wesleyan U., 1954; M.A. in Geology, U. Kans., 1957; Ph.D. in Geology, Yale U., 1960; m. Chung Sook Kim, May 23, 1982; children—Richard L., Roger N. Research sedimentologist Sinclair Research, Inc., 1960-61; asst. prof. geology U. Pitts., 1961-63; asst. prof. to assoc. prof. U. Pa., 1963-69; prof. geology U. Ill., Urbana, 1970—; vis. fellow Wolfson Coll., Oxford U., 1969; vis. prof. geology U. Calif., Berkeley, 1970; vis. prof. oceanography Oreg. State U., 1974; CIC vis. exchange prof. geophys. sci. U.

Chgo., 1979-80; chief scientist Deep Sea Drilling Project Leg 58, 1977-78; continuing edn. lectr.; assoc. Ctr. Advanced Study, U. Ill., 1974, 83; vis. prof. oceanography Seoul Nat. U., 1980; vis. research prof. Ocean Research Inst., U. Tokyo, 1983. Recipient Outstanding Paper award Jour. Sedimentary Petrology, 1970, Erasmus Haworth award in geology U. Kans., various NSF grants; Japan Soc. Promotion of Sci. sr. research fellow, 1983. Fellow AAAS, Geol. Soc. Am. (chmn. div. on sedimentary geology), Geol. Assn. Can.; mem. Am. Geophys. Union, Am. Inst. Profl. Geologists, Soc. Econ. Paleontologists and Mineralogists, Internat. Assn. Sedimentologists, Am. Assn. Petroleum Geologists, Netherlands Geol. and Mining Soc., Sigma Xi. Author: Sandstone Depositional Models for Exploration for Fossil Fuels, 1975, 2d edit., 1980, 3d edit., 1985; Clastic Tidal Facies, 1977; Holocene Tidal Sedimentation, 1975; assoc. editor Geol. Soc. Am. Bull., 1975-81; chief cons. adv. editor CEPCO div. Burgess Pub. Co., 1979-82; series editor Geol. Sci. monographs IHRDC, 1982—; mem. adv. editorial bd. Sedimentary Geology. Office: Dept of Geology U Ill 254 Natural History Bldg 1301 W Green St Urbana IL 61801-2999

KLEIN, JAMES WALTER, paper mill executive; b. Appleton, Wis., Apr. 30, 1940; s. George R. and Josephine Ann (Fetterer) K.; m. Mary Frances Vandercook, Aug. 11, 1962; children—Kathleen, Jennifer, Jeffrey. Student, St. Norbert Coll., 1958-59; B.S., U. Minn., 1962, M.S., 1969. Mgmt. trainee Container Corp. Am., Chgo., 1969-70, mill mgr., 1970-74; mill mgr. Clevepak Corp., Dallas, 1974-75, asst. pres. mill div., 1975-76; v.p., gen. mgr. Wis. Paperboard Corp., Milw., 1976—. Served to capt., C.E., U.S. Army, 1962-68. Homolite Forestry scholar, 1962. Mem. Soc. Am. Foresters, TAPPI, Am. Mgmt. Assn., Paper Industry Mgmt. Assn., Nat. Rifle Assn., Xi Sigma Pi. Club: YMCA. Home: 9914 Huntington Dr Mequon WI 53092 Office: 1514 E Thomas Ave Milwaukee WI 53211

KLEIN, JERRY EMANUEL, insurance and financial planning; b. Cin., Apr. 4, 1933; s. Milton H. and Ida S. (Dunsker) K.; m. Arlene Ruth Rosen, July 3, 1957 (dec. Nov. 1974); children—Marjorie, Bradley, Amy; m. Nancy Cohen Hahn, Aug. 7, 1982. B.Mech. Engring., Cornell U., 1956; M.B.A., Ohio State U., 1959. C.L.U.; chartered fin. cons., 1984. Fin. engring. Avco Electronics, Cin., 1959-61; spl. agt. Northwestern Mut. Life of Milw., Cin., 1961—. Vice chmn. Am. Jewish Com., 1978; pres. Social Health Assn., 1964-66, Jewish Vocat. Service, 1978-80, Cancer Family Care, 1981-83; chmn. fin. com. Jewish Fedn., 1981-83, treas., mem. exec. com., 1981-84; bd. dirs. Children Psychiat. Ctr., Jewish Family Service, Jewish Vocat. Service, Cinti Jewish Fedn.; chmn. HILB Scholarship Com. Served to 1st lt. USAF, 1956-58. Recipient Kate S. Mack award Jewish Fedn., 1975. Mem. Million Dollar Round Table, Nat. Assn. Life Underwriters, Assn. C.L.U.s. Jewish. Office: Northwestern Mut Life of Milw 635 W 7th St Suite 202 Cincinnati OH 45203

KLEIN, JOHN RICHARD, auto manufacturing company executive; b. Cleve., Nov. 21, 1938; s. John A. and Sophie Theresa (Marko) K.; m. Patricia Ann Holtschult, July 11, 1964; children—John Thomas, Karen E., Debra L., Kathleen M. B.S.S., John Carroll U., 1960; M.A., Kent State U., 1965. With Ford Motor Co., various locations, 1964—, policy planning mgr. Ford Parts and Service div., Dearborn, Mich, 1971-80, market research coordinator, 1980—. Mem. Auto Market Research Council. Roman Catholic. Avocations: photography; golf; stamp collecting; jogging. Home: 5627 Hobnail Circle West Bloomfield MI 48033 Office: Ford Parts and Service Div 3000 Schaefer Rd Bus Planning and Strategy Dept Dearborn MI 48033

KLEIN, MAX, physicist; b. New Bedford, Mass., Feb. 5, 1925; s. Morris and Jennie (Liss) K.; m. Ruhama Demiel, June 14, 1954 (dec. 1976); children—Nehemiah, David, Sara; m.2d Suzette Alden, Mar. 10, 1985. B.S. cum laude, U. Mass., 1948; Ph.D., U. Md., 1962. Physicist, Nat. Bur. Standards, Washington, 1950-63, Weizmann Inst., Rehovoth, Israel, 1963-65; supervisory physicist Nat. Bur. Standards, Gaithersburg, Md., 1965-81; sr. scientist Gas Research Inst., Chgo., 1981—; program mgr. NSF, Washington, 1980-81. Editor spl. publs. Contbr. articles to profl. jours. Served with USN, 1944-46. Recipient Dept. Silver medal U.S. Dept. Commerce, 1978. Mem. Am. Physical Soc., AAAS, Am. Inst. Chem. Engrs. (vice chmn. research com. 1981—), Am. Chem. Soc., N.Y. Acad. Scis., Sigma Xi. Jewish. Avocations: Photography, investments, religious study. Home: 6308 N Richmond St Chicago IL 60659 Office: Gas Research Inst 8600 W Bryn Mawr Chicago IL 60631

KLEIN, MICHAEL DAVID, pediatric surgeon; b. Cleve., Jan. 17, 1944; s. Barney and Lillian (Deitch) K.; m. Margaret G. Sharpe, April 20, 1979; children—Alisa, Andrew, Elizabeth. A.B. U. Chgo., 1965; postgrad. Princeton U., 1965-66; M.D. Case Western U., 1971. Cert. Nat. Bd. Med. Examiners; diplomate Am. Bd. Surgery. Intern, U. Wash. Hosps., Seattle, 1971-72; asst. resident Harvard Surg. Service, Deaconess Hosp., Boston, 1972-74, chief resident, 1976-77; sr. asst. resident, research assoc. Children's Hosp. Med. Ctr., Boston, 1974-76; instr. surgery Harvard Med. Sch., 1976-77; assoc. chief resident, chief resident Children's Hosp. of Mich., Detroit, 1977-79, dir. surg. edn., 1983-84, assoc. chief pediatric gen. surgery, 1984—; asst. prof. surgery and pediatrics U. N.Mex., 1979-80; asst. prof. surgery U. Mich. Med. Sch., 1980-83; assoc. prof. surgery Wayne State U., Detroit, 1983—. Fellow ACS, Am. Acad. Pediatrics; mem. Assn. Acad. Surgery, Am. Pediatric Surg. Assn., Mich. Pediatric Surg. Soc. (pres. 1980—), AAAS. Home: 1049 Kensington Grosse Pointe Park MI 48230 Office: Children's Hosp of Mich 3901 Beaubien Detroit MI 48201

KLEIN, MILES VINCENT, physics educator; b. Cleve., Mar. 9, 1933; s. Max Ralph and Isabelle (Benjamin) K.; m. Barbara Judith Pincus, Sept. 2, 1956; children—Cynthia Klein Banay, Gail. B.S., Northwestern U., 1954; Ph.D., Cornell U., 1961. NSF postdoctoral fellow Max Planck Inst., Stuttgart, Germany, 1961; prof. U. Ill. Urbana, 1962—. Author: Optics, 1970. Contbr. articles to profl. jours. A.P. Sloan Found. fellow, 1963. Fellow Am. Phys. Soc. (chmn. Condensed Matter div. 1985—); mem. IEEE (sr.), Optical Soc. Am., AAAS. Office: Loomis Lab U Ill 1110 W Green St Urbana IL 61801

KLEIN, PAULA SCHWARTZ, hospital development officer; b. Chgo., Oct. 16, 1941; d. Arthur A. and Rosalyn (Davidson) Schwartz; student Mich. State U., 1959-60; B.A., Governors State U., 1974, M.A., 1975; m. Sanford David Klein, Dec. 18, 1960 (div. 1981); children—Gregory Scott, Julie Ann. Mem. editorial staff Okinawa Morning Star, Machinato, 1960-63; exec. dir. Bloom Twp. Com. on Youth, Chicago Heights, Ill., 1975-81; dir. fund devel. and public relations South Chgo. Community Hosp., 1981-84; v.p. South Chgo. Health Care Found., 1982-84; dir. devel. and public relations Chgo. Crime Comm., 1985—. Mem. Calumet Area Indsl. Commn. Mem. Nat. Soc. Fund Raising Profls., Nat. Assn. Prevention Profls., So. Suburban Youth Service Alliance, Criminal Def. Consortium, Nat. Assn. Hosp. Devel., Twp. Ofcls. Ill., Youth Network Council, Sierra Club. Jewish. Home: 2100 Lincoln Park West Chicago IL 60614 Office: Chgo Crime Commission 79 W Monroe St Chicago IL 60603

KLEIN, RICHARD EARL, mechanical engineering educator, consultant; b. Stratford, Conn., Feb. 11, 1939; s. Albert Wilhelm and Ellen Moeller (Kristensen) K.; m. Marjorie Ann Maxwell, Sept. 1, 1963; children—Victoria Ellen, Timothy Maxwell. B.S. in Mech. Engring., Pa. State U., 1964, M.S. in Mech. Engring., 1965; Ph.D. in Mech. Engring., Purdue U., 1968. Asst. prof. mech. engring. U. Ill., Urbana, 1968-71, assoc. prof., 1971—; cons. dynamic systems, automatic control systems to firms. Served with USAR, 1956-63. Mem. ASME, IEEE, AAAS, Nat. Rifle Assn. (life), Sigma Xi. Presbyterian. Patentee electro hydraulic steering device, assigned to Caterpillar Tractor Co., 1972. Author: (with L.D. Metz), Man and the Technological Society, 1973. Contbr. articles to engring. jours. Home: Rural Route 1 Box 182 Dewey IL 61840 Office: 1206 W Green St Room 354 Urbana IL 61801

KLEIN, ROBERT EDWARD, publishing company executive; b. Cin., Dec. 27, 1926; s. Albert and Elisabeth (Muschnau) K.; A.B., Kenyon Coll., 1950; M.B.A., Cornell U., 1952; A.M., U. Chgo., 1969, Ph.D., 1983; m. Nancy Minter, May 25, 1958; children—Robert Schuyler, Elisabeth Susan. With McGraw Hill Co., Chgo., 1969—, dist. mgr. Housing mag., 1980, now dist. mgr. Modern Plastics mag., Modern Plastics Internat. mag., Chem. Week mag. cons. to Time/Life Books, 1980; lectr. in history Mallinckrodt Coll., 1983-85. Served with U.S. Army, 1944-46. Grolier scholar, 1952. Mem. Am. Legion, Am. Hist. Assn., Beta Theta Pi. Republican. Clubs: Westmoreland Country, Cornell. Home: 633 Park Dr Kenilworth IL 60043 Office: McGraw Hill Co 645 N Michigan Ave Chicago IL 60611

KLEIN, SHAWNEE GEETING, data systems executive; b. Hollywood, Calif., Sept. 27, 1943; d. Lloyd Elsworth and Cherie Emmert (Shoun) Geeting; m. Richard H. Klein, Dec. 26, 1970 (div. Aug. 1980); children—Shawna Cherie, Larke Nicole, Ariel Lara. B.A. in English, Otterbein Coll., 1965; postgrad. Miami U., Oxford, Ohio and Wright State U., 1972—; E.M.T., Grandview Hosp., 1978; Dale Carnegie courses, 1979, 81. Tchr. English high schs., West Alexandria, Ohio and Richmond, Ind., 1965-72; coll. recruiter Miami Jacobs, Dayton, Ohio, 1978-79; account exec. Applied Communications, Dayton, 1979-81; sales rep. Standard Register Co., Dayton, 1981-85; communications cons. to fed. govt., 1985—. Vol., Ohio Assn. for Retarded Children, Dayton, 1980—, Aim for Handicapped Children, Dayton, 1980—, Residential Home for Mentally Retarded, Cin., 1980-81, Kettering Devel. Ctr. for Handicapped, Dayton, 1977-78. Mem. Internat. Assn. Bus. Communicators, Tau Epsilon Mu (alumni sec. Westerville, Ohio 1965-66). Club: Advertising (Dayton). Home: 1388 Elmdale Dr Kettering OH 45409 Office: Standard Register Sales Office 3411 Office Park Dr Dayton OH 45439

KLEIN, SHEFFIELD, symphony orchestra manager; b. New Brunswick, N.J., Feb. 22, 1918; s. Julius and Ida (Schneider) K.; m. Gisela H. Stetter, Jan. 12, 1964; children—Michael, Susanna, Randi. Student CCNY, 1936-41; B.S., Columbia U., 1946, M.A., 1947, Ed.D., 1956. Dir. instrumental music Battle Creek (Mich.) Schs., 1950-54; dir. sch. sales World Book Ency., Chgo., 1958-77; gen. mgr. Sioux City Symphony (Iowa), 1979—; music instr., Atlantic City, 1947-50, Tchrs. Coll. Columbia U., 1954-56. Served as fighter pilot USAAF, 1941-46; maj. USAFR ret. Decorated Air medal. Mem. Am. Symphony Orch. League, Met. Orch. Mgrs. Assn., Phi Mu Alpha. Lodge: Rotary. Author: Community Music, 1957. Home: 3048 Cheyenne Blvd Sioux City IA 51104 Office: 370 Orpheum Bldg Sioux City IA 51101

KLEINGARTNER, LARRY, agricultural association executive; b. Kulm, N.D., Mar. 14, 1945; s. William Fred and Elsie (Riebhagen) K.; m. Nancy Lee Brand, Sept. 2, 1978; children—Jessie Lee, Britta Paula. A.A., Bismarck Jr. Coll., 1965; B.A., Jamestown Coll., 1967; M.A., U. Hawaii, 1974. Vol., U.S. Peace Corps, Maharastra, India, 1968-71; dir. mktg. N.D. Dept. of Agr., Bismarck, N.D., 1975-79; exec. dir. Nat. Sunflower Assn., Bismarck, 1980—. Contbr. articles on agr. to profl. jours. Vice pres. New Horizons Foreign Adoption Services, Bismarck, 1983—; bd. dirs. Bismarck Mandan Civic Chorus, 1980; Sunday sch. tchr. Lord of Life Lutheran Ch., Bismarck, 1978—, council mem. 1984—. Nat. Def. Lang. fellow, 1972-74. Avocations: cross-country skiing; horseback riding; music. Home: 2876 Woodland Pl Bismarck ND 58501 Office: Nat Sunflower Assn Box 2533 Bismarck ND 58502

KLEINMAN, JACK G., medical educator, biomedical researcher; b. N.Y.C., Feb. 8, 1944; s. Martin and Dorothy (Friedman) K.; m. Lynne Holland, June 12, 1966; children—Gabrielle, Jason. B.A., Columbia U., 1964; M.D., NYU, 1968. Diplomate Am. Bd. Internal Medicine. Research staff Walter Reed Army Inst. Research, Washington, 1973-75; intern, resident Univ. Hosps. of Cleve., 1968-71; fellow in nephrology Northwestern U. Med. Sch., 1971-72, Walter Reed Army Med. Ctr., 1972-73; staff physician VA Med. Ctr., Wood, Wis., 1975—; asst. prof. medicine, assoc. prof. Med. Coll. of Wis., Milw., 1975—; chmn. profl. edn. com. Nat. Kidney Found. of Wis., 1982-84; mem. research com. Wis. Affiliate, Am. Heart Assn. 1984—. Served to maj. U.S. Army, 1972-75. Grantee VA, 1976—, Nat. Kidney Found. Mem. Central Soc. Clin. Investigation, Am. Soc. Nephrology, Am. Fedn. Clin. Research, Am. Heart Assn., Nat. Kidney Found., Am. Physiol. Soc. Avocations: playing violin; running; tennis. Office: Renal Sect VA Med Ctr 5000 W National Milwaukee WI 53193

KLEINMAN, KENNETH MARTIN, psychology educator; b. Bklyn., Aug. 10, 1941; s. Paul and Belle (Sieven) K.; m. Linda Rochelle Senat (div.); children—Seth Michael, Scott Elliott; m. Sheila LaVon O'Brien, Aug. 14, 1982. B.A., Grinell Coll., 1962; M.A., Washington U., St. Louis, 1964, Ph.D. with honors, 1967. Instr. dept. psychiatry U. Mo. Sch. Medicine, 1967-69; asst. prof. dept. psychology So. Ill. U., 1969-73, assoc. prof., 1973-78, prof., 1978—, chmn. dept., 1979—; research cons. St. Louis VA Hosp. Med. Research Service of VA grantee, 1975-77. Mem. Am. Psychol. Assn., Soc. Psychophysiol. Research, Sigma Xi, Psi Chi. Cons. editor profl. jours.; contbr. articles to profl. jours. Home: 930 Thunderhead Ct Saint Louis MO 63138 Office: Dept Psychology So Ill Univ Edwardsville IL 62026

KLEINSORGE, CLINTON ARTHUR, management consulting company executive; b. St. Louis, May 12, 1947; s. Clarence Jerome and Laura Virginia (Fuchs) K.; m. Kathleen Muldowny, Feb. 1, 1975. Student Forest Park Community Coll., 1968-70. Computer operator Wagner Electric Co., St. Louis, 1965-67, programmer/analyst Internat. Shoe Co., St. Louis, 1967-69; project mgr. ITT Hamilton Life Ins. Co., St. Louis, 1969-71; sr. programmer/analyst Market Devel. Corp., St. Louis, 1971-75; mgr. new devel. Comml. State Life Ins. Co., St. Louis, 1975-77; br. mgr. Analysts Internat. Corp., St. Louis, 1977-83, mktg. dir. 1983-84; br. mgr. Applied Info. Devel., St. Louis, 1984—; dir. Fed. Systems. Recipient Pres.' Quar. Efficiency award Analysts Internat. Corp., 1981 (2), 1982, 83. Mem. Am. Prodn. and Inventory Control Soc., Nat. Assn. Accts., Data Processing Mgmt. Assn., Assn. for Systems Mgmt., St. Louis Regional Commerce and Growth Assn. Lodge: Rotary. Home: 1456 Gettysburg Landing Saint Charles MO 63301

KLEMAN, JEROME ARTHUR, hospital laboratory manager; b. Delphos, Ohio, Jan. 27, 1948; s. Charles L. and Ruth V. (Dunlap) K.; m. Wilma Jean Hunt, June 21, 1969; children—Christina M., Tiffany R., Tammy L., Kevin L. Diploma, Cleve. Jr. Coll., 1967. Registered med. technologist; cert. clin. technologist. Lab. mgr. Union City Meml. Hosp., Ind., 1967—. Officer, Randolph County Vols. in Probation, Winchester, Ind., 1969-81; chmn. Union City Republican Com., 1983. Mem. Am. Assn. Med. Technologists, Ind. Soc. Med. Technologists (bd. dirs. 1972-78), Ind. Assn. Blood Banks, Union City Jaycees. Roman Catholic. Lodges: K.C. (4th degree, dist. dep. 1979-81, state health service chmn. 1981-82). Avocations: gardening; golf, tennis. Home: 1239 Beverly St Union City IN 47390 Office: 900 N Columbia St Union City IN 47390

KLEMER, ROBERT WADSWORTH, textile company executive; b. Faribault, Minn., Aug. 21, 1910; s. Frank Henry and Eleanor Myrtle Klemer; m. Anna Margaret Danielson, July 15, 1936; children—Susan, Anne, Mary. Student, U. Minn., 1928-30; B.S., Phila. Coll. Textiles and Sci., 1932. Supt. Faribault Woolen Mill Co., Faribault 1940-49, pres., 1949-77, chmn., 1977—. Bd. dirs. emeritus Faribault YMCA; mem. Faribault Bd. Edn., 1948-53. Served to capt. U.S. Army, 1942-46. Recipient Service To Mankind award Sertoma Club. Mem. Nat. Wool Mfrs. Assn. (dir., v.p.), Am. Textile Mfrs. Inst. (dir. wool div.), Minn. Assn. Commerce and Industry (dir.), C. of C. of Faribault, Phi Psi. Republican. Congregationalist. Clubs: Lions, Faribault Country.

KLEMKE, JUDITH ANN, mortgage banking executive; b. Berwyn, Ill., July 22, 1950; d. John Stanley and Mildred Lucille (Baldwin) K.; m. Keith Michael Kurzeja, Nov. 6, 1976. B.S., U. Ill., 1972. With Ben Franklin Savs., Oak Brook, Ill., 1973-74, asst. v.p., Skokie, Ill., 1975; asst. v.p. 1st Fin. Savs. & Loan Assn., Downers Grove, Ill., 1975-76, v.p., 1977-80, sr. v.p., 1981-82; v.p. First Family Mortgage Corp., Lisle, Ill., 1980—. Mem. Am. Mortgage Bankers Assn., Ill. Mortgage Bankers Assn., Nat. Assn. Female Execs., Am. Soc. Profl. and Exec. Women, AAUW, Bus. and Profl. Women, U. Ill. Alumni Assn. (life), Alpha Gamma Delta. Home: 18 W 206 Lathrop Villa Park IL 60181 Office: 2900 Ogden Ave Lisle IL 60532

KLEMM, JAMES LOUIS, systems analyst; b. South Bend, Ind., Oct. 30, 1939; s. Paul Otto and (Margaret) Grace (Taylor) K.; m. Barbara Elaine Whitten, June 3, 1965 (div. 1976); children—Paul Andrew, Sarah Ruth; m. 2d, Martha Ruth Ritchie, Aug. 1, 1981. B.S., U. Chgo., 1961; M.S., Purdue U., 1963; Ph.D., Mich. State U., 1970. Grad. asst. in math. Purdue U., 1961-65; asst. prof. math. Indiana U. of Pa., 1965-67; grad. asst. Mich. State U., 1967-70; asst. prof. engring. analysis U. Cin., 1970-77; sr. publs. specialist NCR Corp., Dayton, Ohio, 1977-80, systems analyst, 1980-81, sr. prin. systems analyst, 1981-83, cons. analyst, 1983—. NSF grantee, 1971-72. Methodist. Mem. Sigma Xi. Office: NCR Corp Dayton OH 45479

KLEMS, GEORGE JIRI, metallurgist; b. Brno, Moravia, Czechoslovakia, May 4, 1936; s. Oldrich and Ludmila (Pokorny) K.; m. Judith Louise Kyle, Oct. 19, 1968; children—Kyle, Ryan. A.B., Harvard Coll., 1958; M.S., Ill. Inst. Tech., 1961; Ph.D., Case Western Res. U., 1971. Instr. dept. metall. engring. Ill. Inst. Tech., Chgo., 1961-64; research metallurgist Republic Steel Research Ctr., Independence, Ohio, 1964-72, project leader, 1972-73; mktg. and application metallurgist Molycorp Inc., Pitts., 1973-76; product metallurgist Republic Steel, Cleve., 1976-84; div. metallurgist LTV Steel Co., Whiting, Ind., 1984—. Editor: Microalloying '75, 1975. Patentee in field. Chmn. administrv. bd. Brunswick United Meth. Ch., Ohio, 1982-84; trustee Medina County Dist. Library, Ohio, 1984. Mem. Am. Soc. Metals (mem. exec. com. Calumet chpt. 1984—, mem. editorial com. Metal Progress 1982—), AIME (mem. ferrous metallurgy com. 1974-77), Soc. Automotive Engrs., Sigma Xi, Tau Beta Pi. Avocations: photography; music; reading; computer programming; traveling; cooking. Home: 300 Michele Ave Crown Point IN 46307-4923 Office: LTV Steel Co Flat Rolled Div 2500 New York Ave Whiting IN 46394

KLEPERIS, JOHN VICTOR, aerospace executive, former air force officer; b. Jaunrauna, Latvia, June 19, 1935; came to U.S., 1950, naturalized, 1955; s. Otto and Elza Otilija (Zarins) K.; m. Margaret Dean, Dec. 28, 1957; children—John V., Jr., Richard W. B.A. in Math., U. Conn., 1957; M.S. in Materials Engring., Air Force Inst. Tech., 1964. Registered profl. engr., Ohio. Commd. 2d lt. U.S. Air Force, 1957, advanced through grades to col., 1977; dir. program mgmt. Andrews Air Force Base, Md., 1976-77; dir. simulator SPO, Aeronautical Div., Wright Patterson Air Force Base, Ohio, 1977-79, dir. SPO cadres, 1979-80, dir. F-15 projects, 1980-82, dir. tactical planning, 1982-84; retired, 1984; dir. advanced projects SAIC, Dayton, Ohio, 1984—. Decorated Legion of Merit, D.F.C., Air medal (8). Mem. Air Force Assn., Am. Def. Preparedness Assn., Soc. Old Crows, Sigma Phi Epsilon, Tau Beta Pi. Republican. Avocations: Gourmet cooking; sports cars. Home: 2399 Meadowgreen Dr Beavercreek OH 45431 Office: Sci Applications Internat Corp 1010 Woodman Dr Dayton OH 45432

KLERKX, MARTIN ALAN, information management executive; b. Detroit, Dec. 1, 1942; s. Walter Martin and Sylvia Imogene (Greene) K.; B.S., Mich. State U., 1964; m. Ruth Ann Bouchard, Dec. 27, 1982; children by previous marriage—Gregory William, David Walter. Staff systems analyst Mich. Consol. Gas Co., Detroit, 1968-69; systems cons. Univ. Computing Co., Detroit, 1969-72; mgmt. cons. Ernst & Whinney, 1972-73; info. systems dir. Mich. Judicial Data Center, 1973-81; mgmt. cons. Peat Marwick Mitchell & Co., 1981-82; gen. mgr. Info. Systems div. TIC Internat., Indpls., 1982-83; dir. info. services agy. City of Indpls. and Marion County, 1984—. Served with USN, 1964-68. Mem. Am. Mgmt. Assn., Soc. Mgmt. Info. Systems, Naval Inst. Methodist. Home: 3522 Hyannis Port Dr Indianapolis IN 46224 Office: 1960 City County Bldg Indianapolis IN 46204

KLIEWER, HENRY B., educator, farmer, lay minister; b. Henderson, Nebr., Sept. 1, 1904; s. Peter J. and Susanna (Buller) K.; A.B., York Coll., Nebr., 1931; A.M., U. Nebr., 1939; postgrad. Kans. State U., Emporia, 1953-67; m. Eva Peters, Aug. 18, 1927; children—Marion Waller, Lowell Joyce, Herald James, Ruth Elaine. Tchr. rural schs., Nebr., 1923-29; tchr. Henderson High Sch., 1931-35, prin., 1935-39; supt. Henderson Public Schs., 1939-48; prin. Hillsboro (Kans.) High Sch., 1948-55; supt. Unified Sch. Dist. 410, Hillsboro, 1955-69, Corn (Okla.) Bible Sch., 1969-72; instr. Bible, Tabor Coll., Hillsboro, 1972-75; ordained minister Mennonite Brethren Ch., 1943, pastor, Henderson, also Corn, 1969-72; sec. Mennonite Aid Plan, Dist. 25, Hillsboro, 1978—, chmn. Mennonite Brethren Bd. Publs., 1954-57; mem. Parkside Homes, Inc.; coordinator Parkside Fund Drive. Mem. Hillsboro C. of C., Nebr. Tchrs. Assn., Kans. Tchrs. Assn., Am. Assn. Sch. Adminstrs., NEA. Club: Kiwanis (pres. Hillsboro 1976-77, lt. gov. Div. V, Kans. dist. 1979-80). Home and office: 110 N Adams St Hillsboro KS 67063

KLIEWER, KENNETH LEE, research and development administrator; b. Mt. Lake, Minn., Dec. 31, 1935; s. Henry G. and Susan (Epp) K.; m. Kathleen Kay Zimmermann, Aug. 30, 1959; children—Steven, Lisa, Christopher. B.S. in Elec. Engring., U. Minn., 1957, M.S.E.E., 1959; Ph.D., in Physics, U. Ill., 1964. Asst. prof., assoc. prof., prof. dept. physics Iowa State U., Ames, 1963-81; assoc. physicist, physicist, sr. physicist Ames Lab., Dept. Energy, 1963-81; program dir. solid state physics, 1974-78, assoc. dir. sci. and tech., 1978-81; assoc. lab. dir. phys. research Argonne Nat. Lab., Ill., 1981—; temporary program officer U.S. Dept. Energy, Washington, 1979-80; guest prof. Fritz-Haber Inst., Berlin, 1974, 75; guest prof. U. Hamburg and Deutsches Electronen Synchroton, Hamburg, W.Ger., 1972-73. Editor: (with others) Non-Traditional Approaches to the Study of the Solid-Electrolyte Interface, 1980. Illini fellow U. Ill., 1959, U.S. Steel Found. fellow U. Ill., 1961. Fellow Am. Phys. Soc.; mem. AAAS, Sigma Xi, Eta Kappa Nu, Tau Beta Pi. Home: 714 S Charles St Naperville IL 60540 Office: Argonne Nat Lab 9700 S Cass Ave Argonne IL 60439

KLIMEK, EDWARD MARK, pediatrician, educator; b. Warren, Ohio, May 17, 1950; s. Joseph and Ruth Marie (Blystone) K.; m. Nancy Rae Kearbey, June 12, 1976; children—Joseph Eugene, Stephanie Lynn. B.S. in Biology, Youngstown State U., 1972; postgrad., 1972-73; D.O., Coll. Osteo. Medicine and Surgery, Des Moines, 1976. Diplomate Nat. Bd. Examiners Osteo. Physicians and Surgeons, Am. Osteo. Bd. Pediatrics. Rotating intern Grandview Hosp., Dayton, Ohio, 1976-77; resident in pediatrics Chgo. Osteo. Hosp., 1977-79, chief pediatric resident, 1978-79, asst. prof. pediatrics, 1979-85, assoc. prof. pediatrics, 1985—, assoc. chmn. dept. pediatrics, 1984—, resident trainer, program dir. dept. pediatrics, 1984—; sec., treas. staff Chgo. Osteo. Hosp., Olympia Fields Osteo. Med. Ctr., 1981-82, vice chief of staff, 1982-83; acting chmn. dept. pediatrics Chgo. Coll. Osteo. Medicine, 1984—; mem. staff, 1979—; mem. staff Olympia Field Osteo. Med. Ctr., 1979—; mem. exec. staff Chgo. Coll. Osteo. Medicine, 1981—. Contbr. articles to profl. jours. Named Resident of Yr. Chgo. Coll. Osteo. Medicine, 1979, Outstanding Educator, 1984; recipient 1st place writing award Am. Coll. Osteo. Pediatrics, 1979. Mem. Student Osteo. Med. Assn., Am. Osteo. Assn., Ill. Assn. Osteo. Physicians and Surgeons, Am. Coll. Osteo. Pediatricians (sr.), AMA, Chgo. Med. Soc., Ill. State Med. Soc. Baptist. Avocations: photography, stamp collecting. Office: Olympia Fields Osteo Med Ctr 20201 S Crawford Ave Olympia Fields IL 60461

KLIMON, ELLEN LOUISE, lawyer, educator, consultant; b. Harrisburg, Pa., Jan. 17, 1946; d. George Michael and Irene Catherine (Gregor) Schmeltzer; m. William Wayne Dolph (div.); m. Craig Bernard Klimon, Jan. 4, 1974; children—William Michael, Ian Christopher. A.B. in Psychology, Rosemont Coll., 1972; J.D., U. Cin., 1978. Bar: Ohio 1978, U.S. Dist. Ct. (so. dist.) Ohio 1979. C.P.C.U. Occupational analyst Commonwealth of Pa., Harrisburg, 1972-74; ins. adjuster Lloyd Deist, Inc., Cin., 1977-78; asst. editor FC&S Bulls., Nat. Underwriter Co., Cin., 1978-81; assoc. dir. risk mgmt. U. Cin., 1981-84, dir. risk mgmt., 1984—; ptnr. Fischer, Klimon, Salman & Harpster, Cin., 1984—; cons. Don Malecki & Assocs., Fort Thomas, Ky., 1983—; asst. atty. gen. State of Ohio, Columbus, 1983—; asst. prof. family medicine U. Cin., 1984—; legal adviser Children's Internat. Summer Villages, Cin., 1984—. Editor: Insuring the Lease Exposure, Part II, 1981. Mem. Our Lady of Rosary Sch. Bd., Greenhills, Ohio, 1974-81; v.p. Covered Bridge Civic Assn., Cin., 1979-81, area rep., 1979-82; pres. Nat. Underwriter Co. Fed. Credit Union, Cin., 1980-81. Pa. Higher Edn. Assistance Agy. scholar Rosemont Coll., Phila., 1971-72. Mem. ABA, Ohio Bar Assn., Cin. Bar Assn., Soc. C.P.C.U.s, Am. Soc. Law and Medicine, Am. Soc. Hosp. Risk Mgrs., Univ. Risk Mgmt. and Ins. Assn. Republican. Roman Catholic. Office: U Cin 234 Goodman St Cincinnati OH 45267

KLINCK, BRUCE DEE, operations director; b. Toledo, Ohio, Nov. 24, 1940; s. Norman Earl and Minnie Mary K.; student U. Toledo, 1958-59, Owens Tech. Coll., 1975-78; m. Carole Faye Henson, Oct. 7, 1961; children—Bruce Allen, Lisa Michelle. Sample maker, photo specialist Owens Ill. Glass Co., Toledo, 1959-63; with Toledo Police, 1963-84, with selective enforcement units, 1967-73, with planning and research unit, 1974-84; cons./specialist crowd control, pre-planning mass crowd events, indsl. and retail security, 1979—, on constrn. and remodelling of police facilities. Recipient 1st place award Internat. Chiefs of Police Facilities Workshop, 1978. Mem. Ohio Police Planners Assn., Nat. Assn. Police Planners (charter mem.). Democrat. Lutheran. Office: Five Seagate 408 N Summit St Toledo OH 43604

KLINE, GEORGE HOWARD, insurance company executive; b. Leonia, N.J., Sept. 15, 1916; s. Hibberd Van Buren and Helen (Howard) K.; m. Marjorie Beach, June 1, 1940; children—Patricia Kline Hoffman, Janet Kline McGee. A.B., Syracuse U., 1938; M. Pub. Adminstrn., Maxwell Sch. Pub. Adminstrn., 1940; J.D., Syracuse Coll. Law, 1947. Bar: N.Y. 1947, Ill. 1954. Dep. supt. N.Y. Ins. Dept., N.Y.C., 1947-54; v.p., sec., gen. counsel Allstate Ins. Co., Northbrook, Ill., 1954-74; chmn. bd. First Wis. Mortgage Trust, Chgo., 1974-80, Novus Property Co., Chgo., 1980-83, United Equitable Ins. Group, Lincolnwood, Ill., 1983—. Served to 1st lt. U.S. Marine Corps, 1942-46. Mem. ABA, N.Y. Bar Assn., Ill. Bar Assn., Am. Soc. Pub. Adminstrn., Assn. Life

Ins. Counsel, Justinian Soc., Phi Beta Kappa. Home: 643 Spring Rd Glenview IL 60025 Office: 7373 N Cicero Ave Lincolnwood IL 60646

KLINE, JAMES EDWARD, lawyer, manufacturing company executive; b. Fremont, Ohio, Aug. 3, 1941; s. Walter J. and Sophia Cecelia K.; m. Mary Ann Bruening, Aug. 29, 1964; children—Laura Anne, Matthew Thomas, Jennifer Sue. B.S. in Social Sci., John Carroll U., 1963; J.D., Ohio State U., 1966. Bar: Ohio 1966. Assoc., Eastman, Stichter, Smith & Bergman (now Eastman & Smith), Toldeo, 1966-70, ptnr., 1970-84; ptnr. Shumaker, Loop & Kendrick, 1984—; corp. sec. Sheller-Globe Corp., Toledo, 1977-84. Trustee, Kidney Found. of Northwestern Ohio, 1972-81, pres., 1979-80; mem. bd. dirs. Crosby Gardens, Toledo, 1974-80, pres. 1977-79; trustee Toledo Symphony Orch., 1981—, Home Away From Home, Inc. (Ronald McDonald House of N.W. Ohio), 1983—; bd. dirs. Toledo Zool. Soc., 1983—, Toledo Area Regional Transit Authority, 1984—; mem. Securities Adv. Com., Ohio Div. of Securities, 1979—. Fellow Ohio State Bar Found., mem. ABA, Ohio State Bar Assn. (mem. corp. law com.; sec. 1973-76, v. chmn. 1977-82, chmn., 1983—), Toledo Bar Assn., Am. Soc. of Corp. Secs., Toledo Area C. of C. Roman Catholic. Clubs: Inverness, Toledo. Lodge: Rotary. Home: 5958 Swan Creek Dr Toledo OH 43614 Office: 1000 Jackson Blvd Toledo OH 43624

KLINE, JOHN ALFRED, osteopathic physician; b. Carson, Iowa; Aug. 25, 1906; s. Daniel Morse and Luella Elizabeth (Wolfe) K; m. Helen Rebecca Gilbert, Sept. 16, 1934; children—Carolyn Joan Henderson, Diane Elayne Schroeder. Student, Iowa State Coll., 1923-24, Peru State Teachers Coll., 1925; D.O., Kirksville Coll. Osteo Medicine, 1930. Pvt. practice gen. osteo. medicine, Malvern, Iowa, 1930-85; cons., referral privileges area hosps. Past city health physician City of Malvern; 30 yr. mem. Malvern Vol. Fire Dept.; formerly active Cemetery Bd., Comml. Club, Jaycees. Recipient Community award for outstanding service Malvern Betterment Assn., 1977. Mem. Am. Osteo. Assn. (life), Iowa Osteo Med. Assn., Iowa Soc. Osteo Physicians Surgeons, Sigma Sigma Phi. Republican. Baptist (treas. 10 yrs.). Club: Fairview Country. Lodge: Masons (50 yr. 1986), Order Eastern Star. Home: 710 Marion Ave Malvern IA 51551

KLINE, JOHN ANDREW, osteopathic physician, pathologist; b. Lancaster, Pa., Jan. 2, 1930; s. Ellis Preston and Lola Imogene (Welchans) K.; m. Gloria Charollotte Ziliak, June 13, 1955; children—Kevin A., Stephan M., Gayle T.; m. 2d. Jane Ann Moore, July 27, 1974. B.S., Franklin and Marshall Coll., 1951; D.O., Phila. Coll. Osteopathy, 1955. Gen. practice, Cumberland (Maine) Ctr., 1956-60; resident in pathology Osteo. Hosp. Maine, Portland, 1960-62, Flint (Mich.) Osteo. Hosp., 1962-63; assoc. pathologist Chgo. Coll. Osteopathy, 1963-64; chmn. dept. pathology Waterville (Maine) Osteo. Hosp., 1964-67; chmn. dept. pathology Grand Rapids (Mich.) Osteo. Hosp., 1967-74; assoc. pathologist Kirksville (Mo.) Coll. Osteo. Medicine, 1974-78, prof., dept. chmn., 1978-80; pathologist Grim Smith Hosp., Kirksville, Mo., 1980—; dir. Regional Clin. and Pathology Reference Labs. N.E. Mo., Inc. Chmn. Coalition for Mandatory Spl. Edn., Mich., 1970-72; mem. Mo. Mental Health Commn., 1982—, sec., 1983-84, chmn., 1984-85. Named Citizen of Yr., Mich. Council for Exceptional Children, 1972; Citizen of Yr., Kent County (Mich.) Assn. for Mentally Handicapped, 1972. Mem. Am. Osteo. Assn. Am. Coll. Osteo. Pathologists (past pres.), Mo. Assn. Osteo. Physicians and Surgeons, N.E. Mo. Assn. Osteo. Physicians and Surgeons, Am. Registry Pathology (Armed Forces Inst. Pathology). Republican. Methodist. Lodge: Masons. Contbr. articles to profl. jours. Home: 3 Woodland Ln Kirksville MO 63501 Office: Grim Smith Hosp 1211 S Franklin St PO Box 917 Kirksville MO 63501

KLINE, MABLE CORNELIA PAGE, educator; b. Memphis, Aug. 20, 1928; d. George M. and Lillie (Davidson) Brown; 1 dau., Gail Angela Page. Student LeMoyne Coll.; B.S.Ed., Wayne State U., 1948, postgrad. Tchr., Flint, Mich., 1950-51, Pontiac, Mich., 1953-62; tchr. 12th grade English, Cass Tech High Sch., Detroit, 1962—, coordinator Summer Sch. High Sch. Proficiency Program. Life mem. YWCA, NAACP. Mem. NEA (life), Assn. Supervision and Curriculum Devl., Am. Fedn. Tchrs., Nat. Council Tchrs. English, Internat. Platform Assn., Wayne State U. Alumni Assn., Delta Sigma Theta. Episcopalian. Home: 1101 Lafayette Towers W Detroit MI 48207 Office: 2421 2d Ave Detroit MI 48207

KLINE, ROBIN SANDERS, rehabilitation executive; b. Norfolk, Va., Apr. 16, 1953; d. George Harding and Sylvia Emma (Wudel) Sanders; m. Ted Arnold Kline, May 25, 1974; 1 child, Jay Arnold. B.S., U. Wis., 1974; M.S., DePaul U., 1979. Dir. rehab. Goodwill Industries, Des Moines, 1974-79; exec. dir. Boone County Developmental Disabilities Council, Boone, Iowa, 1979-80; ctr. dir. Assn. Retarded Citizens of Polk County, Des Moines, 1980-82; extended employment coordinator, program evaluator Opportunity Workshop, Minnetonka, Minn., 1982—. Surveyor, Commn. on Accreditation Rehab. Facilities, Tucson, 1978—. Mem. Nat. Rehab. Assn., Iowa Rehab. Assn., Vocat. Evaluation and Work Adjustment Assn., Minn. Rehab. Assn. Avocations: camping; canoeing; computers. Office: Opportunity Workshop Inc 5500 Opportunity Ct Minnetonka MN 55343

KLINENBERG, EDWARD LEE, communications company executive; b. Chgo., Mar. 21, 1942; s. Jerome Jacob and Muriel (Abrams) K.; B.A. in English, U. Mich., 1963; postgrad. U. Paris, 1964-65; children—Eric Martin, Danielle Elyse. Public info. dir. Chgo. unit Am. Cancer Soc., 1966-67; account exec. Stral Advt. Co., Chgo., 1967-69; pres. Precise Communications, Inc., Chgo., 1969—; leader seminars, speaker in field. Bd. dirs., v.p. public relations Hull House Assn., Chgo., 1977—; bd. dirs. Internat. Visitors Center Chgo., 1975-77; pres. Old Town Triangle Assn., 1975-77. Served with AUS, 1965-66. Mem. Chgo. Council Fgn. Relations (dir. 1969-76), Com. on Fgn. and Domestic Affairs (exec. com. 1978—). Club: Columbia Yacht (Chgo.). Office: 233 E Erie St Chicago IL 60611

KLING, S. LEE, banker; b. St. Louis, Dec. 22, 1928; m. Rosalyn Hauss; 4 children. B.S.B.A., Washington U. Chmn. bd., chief exec. officer Landmark Bancshares Corp., St. Louis, 1974—; asst. spl. counselor on inflation White House, Washington, 1978-79; adv. vice chmn. bd. U.S. div. Reed Stenhouse, Inc.; dir. various corps., including E. Systems, Inc., Dallas, Horn & Hardart Co., N.Y.C., Flaacon Products, Inc., St. Louis, Reed Stenhouse, Inc., Landmark Bancshares Corp., Bright Star Holding, Inc., Tampa, Fla., Medicare-Glaser Corp., St. Louis. Bd. trustees Congl. award; bd. dirs. Civic Entrepreneurs Orgn. St. Louis, Jewish Hosp. St. Louis, YMCA, St. Louis, Lindenwood Coll., St. Charles, Mo., Washington Internat. Horse Show, Pres.'s Council, St. Louis U., Exec. Com., NCCJ, St. Louis, Caribbean Central Am. Action; fin. chmn. Dem. Nat. Com., 1974-77; treas. Dem. Nat. Conv., 1976; chmn. 1977 Nat. Dem. House and Senate Dinner and founder, chmn. Dem. House and Senate Council; nat. treas. Carter-Mondale Re-election com.; co-chmn. Citizens Com. for Ratification of Panama Canal Treaties; U.S. econ. advisor representing pvt. sector during peace negotiations between Isreal and Egypt, 1979; co-chmn. Coalition for enactment of Caribbean Basin Initiative Legislation, 1982-83. Mem. Am. Bus. Conf., Sr. Exec. Orgn. Clubs: 1925 "F" St., Univ., Georgetown (Washington); Standard (Chgo.); Westwood Country, St. Louis (St. Louis). Address: Landmark Bancshares Corp 10 S Brentwood Blvd Saint Louis MO 63105

KLINGLER, EUGENE ALBERT, JR., surgeon, b. Kansas City, Kans., Mar. 26, 1935; s. Eugene Albert and Louise Elizabeth (Roth) K.; m. Norma Sue Walling, June 28, 1959; children—Rebecca, Leah, Heidi, Doug. A.B., Doane Coll., 1957; M.D., U. Kans., 1962. Diplomate Am. Bd. Surgery. Intern Menorah Med. Ctr. Kansas City, Mo., 1962-63; resident in surgery, U. Kans. Med. Ctr., Kansas City, Kans., 1963-67, resident, pediatric surgery, 1967-68; practice medicine specializing in surgery, Surgical Assocs. P.A., Manhattan, Kans., 1968—; attending staff, St. Mary and Meml. Hosp., Manhattan, 1968—; cons. Irwin Army Hosp., Ft. Riley, Kans., 1970—; preceptor, U. Kans. Sch. Medicine, 1973—. City commr., City of Manhattan, 1979—, mayor, 1981-82; trustee Doane Coll., Crete, Nebr., 1976—. Recipient Builder award Doane Coll., 1982. Fellow A.C.S., Southwestern Surg. Congress; mem. Kans. Med. Soc., Riley County Med. Soc. (pres. 1973), Manhattan C. of C. (v.p., dir. 1974-79). Republican. Presbyterian. Lodge: Optimists (dir.) (Manhattan). Avocations: skiing; fishing; swimming. Office: 1 Surg Assocs PA 1133 College Ave Manhattan KS 66502

KLINT, THEODORE CHARLES, toy manufacturing company executive; b. Rockford, Ill., Mar. 19, 1945; s. Bernard Carl and Grace Hulda (Frisk) K.; m. Patricia Eleanor, Nov. 22, 1975; children—Sarah Eleanor. B.A., Drake U., 1968. Mgmt. trainee Nylint Corp., Rockford, Ill., 1968-70, credit mgr., 1970-76, advt. mgr., 1971-79, v.p. ops., 1979-81, pres., chief operating officer, 1982—; dir. Colonial Nat. Bank, Rockford, Dongkook Nylint Ltd., Seoul, Korea. Patentee 4 wheel drive toy vehicles. Served with USAR, 1967-73. Mem. Toy Mfg. Assn. Am. (chmn. Midwest credit 1973-74, bd. dirs.).

KLODZINSKI, JOSEPH ANTHONY, data communications executive, consultant; b. Chgo., Aug. 19, 1942; s. Joseph Fabian and Haline Ann (Bieganski) K.; m. Mary Margaret Osten, Nov. 19, 1966; children—Joseph II, Catherine Ann, Patricia Ann. B.B.A., Loyola U., Chgo., 1964; M.Ed., Boston U., 1968; M.B.A., Northwestern U., 1971. Packaging engr. Westvaco, Chgo., 1969-72; regional mgr. MacMillan, Chgo., 1972-74; fin. applications cons. IC Systems Corp., Schaumburg, Ill., 1974-77; mgmt. info. systems salesman Honeywell, Chgo., 1977-80; mgmt. info. systems and communications cons. Intertel, Chgo., 1980-82; Midwest dist. mgr. UDS/Motorola, Chgo., 1982—. Contbr. articles to profl. jours. Mem. parish council Ch. of Holy Spirit, Schaumburg, 1980-85. Served to capt. U.S. Army, 1965-69; Vietnam. Decorated Bronze Star; named Pacesetter, Honeywell Mktg. Mgmt., 1978, Top Sales Mgr., IC Systems Corp., 1975-76, MacMillan, 1974; fellow Lions Clubs Internat. Found., 1984. Life mem. Am. Numismatic Assn. Roman Catholic. Lodges: K.C., Elks, Lions (pres. Schaumburg 1980-82, DG cabinet No. Ill., DG awards 1983, 84, 85; fellow Internat. Found. 1984—). Home: 1419 Chalfont Dr Schaumburg IL 60194 Office: UDS/Motorola 3801 W Lake Ave Glenview IL 60025

KLOESEL, CHRISTIAN JOHANNES WILHELM, English educator, editor, researcher; b. Breslau, Silesia, Fed. Republic Germany; came to U.S., 1965, naturalized 1984; s. Josef H. F. and Felicitas H. M. (Glusa) K.; m. Cheryl Knapp, Sept. 4, 1966 (div. Oct. 1977); 1 child, Alicia; m. Lynn Franken, Jan. 6, 1979. B.A. U. of Bonn, Fed. Republic Germany, 1965; Certificat Superieur U. de Caen, France, 1964; M.A., U. Kans., 1967, M. in Philosophy, 1970; Ph.D. in English, 1973. Asst. prof. English, Tex. Tech U., Lubbock, 1971-76; asst. prof. English, assoc. editor Ind. U.-Indianapolis, 1976-79, assoc. prof., assoc. editor, 1979-83, assoc. prof., sr. assoc. editor, 1983-84, assoc. prof., editor, dir. Peirce Edition Project, 1984—. Editor, translator: English Novel Explication, 2 vols., 1976, 1981; Writings of Charles S. Peirce, 3 vols, 1982, 84, 85. Contbr. articles on Peirce, Semiotics, Medieval Lang. and Lit. to profl. jours. Recipient Teaching Excellence award Tex. Tech U., 1972; Recent Ph.D. Recipients fellow Am. Council of Learned Socs., 1976; short-term research grant Texas Tech U., 1974, Indiana U., 1981, Am. Council Learned Socs. travel grants, 1979, 1984. Mem. Medieval Acad. of Am., Modern Lang. Assn., Semiotic Soc. of Am. (program com. 1981-84), Charles S. Peirce Soc. (pres. 1983-84), Am. Philos. Assn. Democrat. Avocations: Tennis; physical fitness. Office: Peirce Edit Project Ind Univ 425 Agnes St Indianapolis IN 46202

KLOHN, FRANKLIN JAMES, JR., psychologist, educator; b. Galion, Ohio, Aug. 8, 1951; s. Franklin J. and Ruth (Dorchester) K.; m. Suzanne M. Clark, Dec. 28, 1981; 1 child, Katherine Susanne. B.S., U. Dubuque, 1974; M.S., Central Mo. State U., Warrensburg, 1978; Ph.D., Calif. Sch. Profl. Psychology, Fresno, 1984. Counselor, Mercy Med. Ctr., Dubuque, 1973-76; dir. conf. ctr. Central Mo. State U., 1976-77; psychologist IV, coordinator psychol. services Galesburg Mental Health Ctr., Ill., 1977-85; instr. Carl Sandburg Coll., Galesburg, 1978-85; crisis counselor Valley Med. Ctr., Fresno, Calif., 1983-84; neuropsychology behavioral medicine intern Fresno Community Hosp. and Med. Ctr., 1982-84; cons. in field. Cons. North East Iowa council Boy Scouts Am., Dubuque, 1971-76; group leader Family Action Support Team Fresno Community Med. Ctr., 1982-84. Mem. Am. Psychol. Assn., Assn. Advancement of Behavior Therapy, Assn. Advancement Psychology, Assn. Behavior Analysis, Ill. Psychol. Assn., Midwest Psychol. Assn., Psi Chi. Episcopalian. Home: 1115 N Academy St Galesburg IL 61401 Office: Galesburg Mental Health Ctr 1801 N Seminary St Galesburg IL 61401

KLOOSTER, DALE H., publishing company executive; b. Ellsworth, Minn., July 12, 1944; s. John J. and Anna B. (Buus) K.; m. Judith Lynn Williams, Sept. 28, 1973; children—Nathan, Matthew. A.A., U. Minn., 1966; B.S., Mankato State U., 1969, M.S., 1975; Ed.D., U. No. Colo., 1978. Cert. data educator. Systems programmer Red Owl Stores, Inc., Mpls., 1966-68, ComputoService, Inc., Mankato, Minn., 1968-69; chmn. data processing Mankato Area Voc-Tech. Inst., 1969-82; v.p., dir. electronic pub. South-Western Pub. Co., Cin., 1982—; v.p. computer sci. and info. systems. Recipient certs. of Appreciation and Service, Minn. State Dept. Edn., 1982. Mem. NEA, Am. Vocat. Assn., Assn. Ednl. Data Systems, So. Minn. Data Processing Assn. (past pres.). Author: Automated Accounting for the Macrocomputer, 1982; Integrated Accounting on Microcomputers, 1983; Automated Accounting Practice Sets, 1983. Home: 952 Creek Knoll Dr Milford OH 45150 Office: 5101 Madison Rd Cincinnati OH 45227

KLOPFER, ERIC LESLIE, data processing executive; b. Dayton, Ohio, Oct. 9, 1947; s. Leslie Edward and Loretta Florence (Wendling) K.; m. Claudia Gail Karns, Mar. 6, 1976; children—marriage: Eric Neil, Samantha Erin. 1 child by previous marriage: Christopher Leslie. A.A. in Libral Arts, Sinclair Community Coll., 1978; B.S. in Data Porcessing, Rockwell U., 1982. Cert. data processor, systems profl. Analyst/programmer Reynolds & Reynolds, Dayton, Ohio, 1969-77; systems analyst NCR Corp., Dayton, 1977; programmer-/analyst Allied Tech., Dayton, 1977-78; mgr. data processing Ledex, Inc., Dayton, 1978—. Mem. Data Processing Mgmt. Assn., Assn. for Cert. of Computer Profls. Address: 968 Rayberta Dr Vandalia OH 45377

KLOPMAN, GILLES, chemistry educator; b. Brussels, Belgium, Feb. 24, 1933; came to U.S., 1965; s. Alge and Brana (Brendel) Klopman; m. Malvina Pantiel, Sept. 5, 1957. B.A., Athenee d'Ixelles (Belgium), 1952; lic. chemistry, U. Brussels, 1956; D.Chemistry, 1960. Research scientist Cyanamid European Research Inst., Geneva, Switzerland, 1960-67; postdoctoral fellow U. Tex., 1964-65; assoc. prof. Case Western Res. U., Cleve., 1967-69, prof. chemistry, 1969—, chmn. dept., 1981—. Recipient Kahlbaum prize Swiss Chem. Soc., 1971; grantee NSF, NIH, EPA, PRF. Mem. Am. Chem. Soc., Brit. Chem. Soc. Belgium Chem. Soc. (Stas Spring medal 1960), Swiss Chem. Soc., AAUP, Sigma Xi. Author: All Valence Electrons SCF Calculations, 1970; Chemical Reactivity and Reaction Paths, 1974; contbr. articles to profl. jours. Home: 2153 Lee Blvd E Cleveland OH 44112 Office: 2074 Adelbert Rd Case Western Reserve U Cleveland OH 44106

KLOSKA, RONALD FRANK, corporate executive; b. Grand Rapids, Mich., Oct. 24, 1933; s. Frank B. and Catherine (Hilaski) K.; student St. Joseph Sem., Grand Rapids, Mich., 1947-53; Ph.B., U. Montreal, Que., Can., 1955; M.B.A., U. Mich., 1957; m. Mary F. Minick, Sept. 7, 1957; children—Kathleen Ann, Elizabeth Marie, Ronald Francis, Mary Josephine, Carolyn Louise. Staff accountant Lybrand Ross Bros. & Montgomery, Niles, Mich., 1957, staff to sr. accountant, 1960-63; treas., v.p. Skyline Corp., Elkhart, Ind., 1963-67, exec. v.p. finance, treas., 1967-74, pres., 1974—, also dir.; dir. Midwest Commerce Banking Co., Elkhart. Mem. adv. bd. Salvation Army, Elkhart; bd. dirs. Stanley Clark Sch., South Bend, Ind. Served to 1st lt. AUS, 1957-60. Mem. Am. Inst. C.P.A.s, Mich., Ind. assns. C.P.A.s. Roman Catholic. Club: South Bend Country. Home: 1329 E Woodside St South Bend IN 46614 Office: 2520 By Pass Rd Elkhart IN 46514

KLOSTERMAN, MARK VENANTIUS, judge; b. Celina, Ohio, May 11, 1930; s. Aloys H. Klosterman and Agnes Gillig; m. Diane M. Weber, June 19, 1965; children—Kara, Kevin, Kip, Kory. B.C.E., U. Detroit, 1953; LL.B., U. Mich., 1960. Bar: Ohio. Sole practice law, Celina, 1960-80, 81-85; mcpl. judge Celina Mcpl. Ct., 1980-81; probate judge Mercer County, Ohio, Celina, 1985—; dir. Mercer Savs. Bank, Celina, 1981—; dir. various small corps. Served to lt. (j.g.) USN, 1953-57, Philippines. Mem. Am. Judges Assn., Ohio State Bar Assn., Mercer County Bar Assn. Republican. Roman Catholic. Club: Sertoma (pres. Celina 1970). Lodge: KC. Avocations: Flying; sailing; travel; windsurfing; snowmobiling. Home: 609 Harbor Point Dr Celina OH 45822 Office: Mercer County Courthouse Celina OH 45822

KLOTE, LUANNA MAE, accountant; b. Carrollton, Mo., Feb. 1, 1951; d. Earl Edwin and Ethel Louise (Lungren) Bell; m. Paul Joseph Klote, Feb. 27, 1982. B.S., Central Mo. State U., 1973; M.B.A., U. Mo.-Kansas City, 1978; postgrad Johnson County Community Coll., 1983—. C.P.A., Mo., Kans.; cert. mgmt. acct. Jr. acct. Panhandle Eastern Pipe Line Co., Kansas City, Mo., 1973-75, acct., 1975-77, sr. acct., 1977—. Mem. Friends of the Zoo. Mem. Nat. Assn. Accts. (assoc. dir. 1979-82, assoc. dir. spl. activities 1983-84, dir. IMA programs 1984-85, assoc. dir. tech. programs 1984-85), Central Mo. State U. Alumni Assn., U. Mo.-Kansas City Alumni Assn., Inst. Mgmt. Acctg., Mo. Soc. C.P.A.s, Acctg. Assn., Acctg. Club, Beta Alpha Psi, Alpha Phi Delta. Home: 6852 Mastin Dr Merriam KS 66203 Office: Panhandle Eastern Pipe Line Co 3444 Broadway Kansas City MO 64111

KLOTZ, CHARLES ROBERT, diversified industry executive; b. Wheeling, W.Va., Oct. 10, 1938; s. Helen (Kerringer) K. B.M.E., Fenn Coll., 1962; M.S. in Mech. Engring., Calif. Inst. Tech., 1963; postgrad. Case Western Res. U., 1966-67, Cleve. State U., 1982-83. Propulsion engr. N.Am. Aviation, Downey, Calif., 1962; research engr. Calif. Inst. Tech., Pasadena, 1963; staff engr. Chrysler Space Corp., New Orleans, 1964; prin. research engr. Boeing Co., New Orleans, 1964; pres., prin. scientist C.R. Klotz & Co., Washington, 1965; staff engr. Lear-Siegler, Inc., Cleve., 1965-66; chmn. bd., chief exec. officer Midwest Controls Corp., Cleve., 1967-76; pres. Klotz Aerospace, Klotz Bank, Klotz Consol., Klotz Controls, Klotz Internat., Klotz Law Orgn., 1976—; cons. to various corps.; adv. to Govt. France, French Navy. ASHRAE scholar, 1961; Earle C. Anthony scholar, 1962-63; U.S. Steel Found. fellow, 1963-64; Charles W. Bingham fellow, 1966-67. Mem. ASME, Air Force Assn., Am. Security Council, U.S. Naval Inst., Sigma Xi, Tau Beta Pi, Pi Mu Epsilon. Office: 4241 W 50th St Cleveland OH 44144

KLUG, JENNINGS BENJAMIN, engineer; b. Alliance Twp., Minn., Feb. 4, 1923; s. Ewald Henry and Dorothea (Kuehl) K.; m. Olivia Norma Gilbertson, Aug. 21, 1946; children—JoAnne (dec.), Rodney, Dorothy, Bonnie, William, Randee. B.S. in Archtl. Engring., N.D. State U., 1950. Sales engr. Smith, Inc., Fargo, N.D., 1950-55, Fargo Foundry, 1955-62, Structural Products, Inc., Fargo, 1962-63, Rusco Window, Inc., Moorhead, Minn., 1963-64; architect 91 Civil Engring. Minot AFB, N.D., 1964-83, protective coatings engr., 1965-83, sonic boom investigator, 1965-83; civil engr. Hdqrs. U.S. Air Force Europe Planning and Programming Dept., Ramstein AB, Fed. Republic Germany, 1983—. Co-founder North Hill Improvment Corp., Minot, N.D., 1966, Served with USN, 1943-46, PTO. Named Citizen of Yr., North Hill Improvement Corp., 1979. Mem. Soc. Am. Mil. Engrs. (past pres. local chpt.), Am. Security Council, Am. Legion, V.F.W. Clubs: Toastmasters Internat. (various positions; gov. Dist. 20, 1979-80; Disting. Toastmaster 1979, Select Disting. Dist., 1979), TM (Ramstein AB, Germany); K-Towners Square Dancers (Kiaserslautern, Germany). Avocations: writing. Home: 1916 3d St NW Minot ND also Baumschulstr 12 6751 Rodenbach Federal Republic Germany Office: HQU-SAFE/DEPPD Box 9966 Ramstein AB APO New York NY 09012 Federal Republic Germany

KLUNZINGER, THOMAS EDWARD, writer, accountant, reapportionment specialist; b. Ann Arbor, Mich., Sept. 11, 1944; s. Willard Reuben and Katherine Eileen (McCurdy) K.; B.A. cum laude in Advt., Mich. State U., 1966. Copywriter, Campbell-Ewald Advt. Co., Detroit, 1966-70; travel cons. Moorman's Travel Service, Detroit, 1973-74; media dir. Taylor for Congress campaign, East Lansing, Mich., 1974; communications specialist House Republican Staff, Lansing, 1975-80; trustee Meridian Twp., Ingham County, Mich., 1980-84; vice chmn. Econ. Devel. Corp., 1982-84; mktg. dir. The Eyde Co., Lansing, 1985—. Mem. Ingham County Republican Com., 1976—, Mich. Rep. State Com., 1981-85. Mem. Dramatists Guild, Am. Numismatic Assn., Mich. Numismatic Soc., Zero Population Growth, Mensa, Internat. Platform Assn. Author: Chester!, 1981; Heavy Lady, 1983; Double Standards, 1985; A Villa in Unadilla, 1985. Address: PO Box 16231 Lansing MI 48901

KLUTE, ALLAN ALOYS, physicist, economist, consultant; b. St. Louis, July 19, 1916; s. Aloys J. Henry and Noelie Constance (Jeep) K. A.B., Washington U., St. Louis, 1949, postgrad., 1949-50. Supr. technics office Aero. Chart and Info. Center, St. Louis, 1951-72; pvt. practice as economist and investor, Imperial, Mo., 1972—; investment cons. Active St. Louis Council on World Affairs, UN Assn., Conservation Fedn. Mo. Served to 2d lt. USAAF, 1942-45; prisoner-of-war, Germany, 1944-45. Decorated Air medal, Purple Heart; recipient organizational excellence award USAF, 1970. Mem. Am. Assn. Individual Investors, Mil. Order World Wars, Air Force Assn. Co-developer system of mapping surface of moon.

KLUVER, HERMAN CHRISTOF, ophthalmologist; b. Audubon, Iowa, Feb. 25, 1902; s. Christian F. and Pauline A. (Hahn) K.; B.S. with honors, U. Chgo., 1924, M.D., 1927; m. Lois Heward Cobb, Dec. 25, 1935 (dec. 1969); 1 son, Charles Ross Hansen; m. 2d, Ruth Schroeder Carlson, 1970. Intern, Charity Hosp., New Orleans, 1928-29; asst. otolaryngologist Univ. Hosps., U. Iowa, 1929-31, asst. ophthalmologist, 1931-36; practice medicine specializing in ophthalmology and otolaryngology, Fort Dodge, Iowa, 1936—; asso. Martin, Kluver, Coughlan, 1940-50, Kluver, Coughlan & Allen, 1959-68; pres. Melville Farms, Inc., 1959-68, Kluver Land and Cattle Co., 1968-75; cons. Trinity Regional Hosp., Fort Dodge; mem. med. adv. bd. Selective Service, 1941-42. Served to comdr. USNR, 1942-46. Diplomate Am. Bd. Ophthalmology. Fellow A.C.S., Am. Acad. Ophthalmology and Otolaryngology; mem. AMA, Pan Am. Ophthalmology, Am. Soc. Ophthalmology and Otolaryngology Allergy, Iowa Med. Soc., Am.-Internat. Charolois Assn., Iowa Beef Improvement Assn., Am. Rifle Assn., V.F.W., Am. Legion. Mason (Shriner), Elk. Author: Cluverii Chronica, 1958, Cluver'sche Familien Archiv, 1961. Contbr. to profl. publs. in field. Home: 331 Wraywood Manor Fort Dodge IA 50501

KLUZNIK, JOHN COOKE, psychiatrist; b. Hibbing, Minn., June 24, 1941; s. John Cooke and Ruth Elizabeth (Sandberg) K.; B.A., U. Minn., 1967, M.D., 1971; 1 dau., Katherine Elizabeth. Intern, resident U. Minn. Hosps., Mpls., 1971-74; asst. prof. U. Minn., Mpls., 1974-75, 80—; staff psychiatrist St. Paul-Ramsey County Hosp., 1974-75; instr. psychiatry Harvard Med. Sch., Boston, 1975-76; asst. psychiatrist McLean Hosp., Belmont, Mass., 1975-76; dep. med. dir. Mass. Correctional Inst., Bridgewater, practice medicine specializing in psychiatry, Mpls.-St. Paul, 1977—; staff psychiatrist VA Hosp., Mpls., 1979—; cons. St. Paul-Ramsey County Med. Center, Forensic Psychiatry Service, 1978-81. Mem. Minn. Supreme Ct. Commn. on Mentally Disabled and The Cts., 1977-79. Served with USN, 1959-63. Diplomate Am. Bd. Psychiatry and Neurology. Mem. AMA, Am. Psychiat. Assn., Minn. Med. Soc., St. Paul Soc. Psychiatry and Neurology, Ramsey County Med. Soc., Minn. Psychiat. Soc., Minn. Orch. Assn., Mpls. Soc. Fine Arts, Common Cause, Union of Concerned Scientists. Democrat. Lutheran. Office: 527 Medical Arts Bldg Minneapolis MN 55402

KMENTA, JAN, economics educator; b. Prague, Czechoslovakia, Jan. 3, 1928; came to U.S., 1963; m. Joan Helen Gaffney, Aug. 9, 1959; children—David, Steven. B.Econs. with 1st class honors, Sydney U., 1955; M.A., Stanford U., 1959, Ph.D., 1964. Lectr., U. N.S.W., Sydney, 1957-61; sr. lectr. Sydney U., 1961-63; asst. prof. U. Wis.-Madison, 1963-65; prof. Mich. State U., East Lansing, 1965-73; prof. U. Mich., Ann Arbor, 1973—; vis. prof. U. Bonn, Germany, 1971-72, 1979-80, U. Saarland, Saarbrucken, Germany, 1984. Author: Elements of Econometrics, 1971. Editor: (with others) Evaluation of Econometric Models, 1980, Large-Scale Macro-Econometric Models, 1981. Contbr. articles to profl. jours. Recipient U.S. Sr. Scientist Prize, Humboldt Found., Bonn, 1979; Fulbright scholar, 1957-59. Fellow Am. Statis. Assn., Econometric Soc.; mem. Am. Econ. Assn., Czechoslovak Soc. Arts and Scis. in Am. Home: 2511 Londonderry St Ann Arbor MI 48104 Office: Dept Econs U Mich Ann Arbor MI 48109

KNABE, ARTHUR TOMPKINS, lawyer; b. Cin., Feb. 17, 1929; s. Arthur J. and Ida J. (Tompkins) K.; m. Peggy Lou Wullenweber, May 21, 1955; children—Janny Lou Knabe Gebhardt, Arthur T. Jr., Sally Ann Knabe Bender, Bruce David. B.B.A., U. Cin., 1951; J.D., No Ky. U., 1957. Supr. prodn. planning and inventory control Kroger Co., Cin., 1953-59; assoc. McIntosh & McIntosh, Cin., 1959-69; ptnr. McIntosh, McIntosh & Knabe, Cin., 1969—. Mem. Hamilton County Rural Zoning Commn., Cin., 1971—. Served with U.S. Army, 1951-53. Mem. Cin. Bar Assn., Cin. Lawyers' Club, Ohio State Bar Assn., ABA, Delta Tau Delta Alumni. Republican. Lutheran. Club: Western Hills Optimist (pres. 1969-70). Office: McIntosh McIntosh & Knabe 3312 Caren Tower Cincinnati OH 45202

KNACKSTEDT, CAMERON DEL, osteopathic physician, educator; b. Wichita, Kans., Sept. 5, 1948; s. Delmer R. and Glennys J. (Carlson) K.; m. Barbara A. Becker, June 3, 1966; children—Nathaniel Clay, Jason Ryan. B.S., Emporia State U., 1970; D.O., Kansas City Coll. Osteo. Medicine, 1975. Grad. instr. Emporia (Kans.) State U., 1970-71; intern U. Health Scis., Kansas City, Mo., 1975-76; family practice in osteo. medicine Phillips County Med. Clinic, Phillipsburg, Kans., 1976—; dep. dist. coroner Phillips County; instr. med. U. Health Scis.; mem. Kans. Bd. Healing Arts. Mem. Am. Coll. Gen. Practioner Osteo. Medicine and Surgery, Am. Osteo. Assn., Kans. Assn. Osteo. Medicine, Nat. Bd. Med. Examiners, Kans. Osteo. Assn. (pres.-elect). Club: Elks. Office: Box 547 Phillipsburg KS 67661

KNAPP, DONALD ROY, musician, educator; b. Mpls., Dec. 26, 1919; s. Roy Cecil and Nellie Anette (Johnson) K.; m. Loretto C. Downes, June 5, 1960 (dec. 1975); m. Kimberly J. Carr, May 9, 1977 (div. 1980); 1 child, Deidre. Student Met. Sch. Music, Voss Bus. Coll. Percussionist Sauter-Finegan Band, N.Y.C., 1962-64, Shubert Theater, Chgo., 1970-75, Arie Crown Theater, Chgo., 1975-77, mus. show Annie, N.Y.C., 1978-82, Lyric Opera of Chgo., 1955-57; prof. percussion Met. Sch. Music, Chgo., 1945-48; instr. percussion Roy C. Knapp Sch. Percussion, Chgo., 1948-52; played in Broadway musicals including original prodns. of West Side Story, Hello Dolly, Guys and Dolls, Gypsy, Kismet, Cabaret, Can Can, Fiddler on the Roof. Served with USN, 1941-45, PTO. Mem. Chgo. Fedn. Musicians (bd. dirs. 1983-84), Musicians Union of Greater N.Y.C., Musicians Union of Los Angeles. Republican. Lodges: Masons, K.T., Shriners (band). Home: 2828 Pine Grove Chicago IL 60657

KNAPP, MILDRED FLORENCE, social worker; b. Detroit, Apr. 15, 1932; d. Edwin Frederick and Florence Josephine (Antaya) K.; B.B.A., U. Mich., 1954, M.A. in Community and Adult Edn. (Mott Found. fellow 1964), 1964, M.S.W. (HEW grantee 1966), 1967. Dist. dir. Girl Scouts Met. Detroit, 1954-63; planning asst. Council Social Agencies Flint and Genessee County, 1965; sch. social worker Detroit public schs., 1967—; field instr. grad. social workers. Mem. alumnae bd. govs. U. Mich., 1972-75, scholarship chmn., 1969-70, 76-80, chmn. spl. com. women's athletics, 1972-75, class agt. fund raising Sch. Bus. Adminstrn., 1978-79; mem. Founders Soc. Detroit Inst. Art, 1969—, Friends Children's Museum Detroit, 1978—, Women's Assn. Detroit Symphony Orch., 1982—; trustee Children's Mus. Recipient various certs. appreciation. Mem. Nat. Assn. Social Workers, Acad. Cert. Social Workers, Nat. Community Edn. Assn. (charter), Outdoor Edn. and Camping Council (charter), Mich. Sch. Social Workers Assn. (pres. 1980-81), Detroit Sch. Social Workers Assn. (past pres.), Detroit Assn. U. Mich. Women (pres. 1980-82), Detroit Fedn. Tchrs. Methodist. Clubs: Detroit Boat, Detroit Women's City. Home: 702 Lakepointe Grosse Pointe Park MI 48230 Office: 4300 Marseilles Detroit MI 48224

KNAPP, WILLIAM BERNARD, cardiologist; b. Paterson, N.J., Oct. 26, 1921; s. Joseph and Mary (Cannon) K.; m. Jeannette C. Zarnowiecki, Jan. 31, 1948; children—William, Thomas, Bernadette, Richard, Suzanne. Attending physician Cook County Hosp., Chgo.; asst. prof. medicine Loyola U., Chgo.; chmn. medicine Little Co. of Mary Hosp., 1960-80; chmn. Holy Cross Hosp., Suburban Hosp., Hinsdale, Ill., 1976-81; practice medicine specializing in cardiology; chmn. S.W. Hosp. Planning, Chgo. Bd. dirs. Retirement Village, Civic Assn., Geneva Lake, Wis., 1970—; dir. water safety patrol, Geneva Lake, 1970—. Served with U.S. Army, 1943-46. Recipient Research award Ill. Inst. Medicine. Fellow Am. Coll. Cardiology; mem. N.Am. Soc. Pediatric Physiology, AMA, ACP, Ill. Med. Soc., Chgo. Med. Soc., Inst. Medicine Chgo. Roman Catholic. Clubs: Butterfield Country (Oak Brook, Ill.); Big Foot Country; Beverly Country (Chgo.); Tracer; Whitehall. Office: 3900 W 95th St Evergreen Park IL 60642

KNAUF, KONRAD STEVE, Christmas light company executive; b. Sheboygan, Wis., Aug. 20, 1944; s. Edmund Reiss and Mary E. (Testwuide) K.; m. Mary Joann Day, Feb. 25, 1968; children—Majo, Heidi. B.B.A. in Acctg., Notre Dame U., 1966; M.S. in Computer Sci., U. Wis., 1972. With sales dept. Phillips Petroleum Co., Chgo., 1966; cons. Arthur Young & Co., Milw., 1972-80; v.p., treas. NOMA WorldWide, Forest Park, Ill., 1980—. Served to maj. U.S. Army, 1966-71; ETO; Vietnam. Home: 202 W Highview Dr Mequon WI 53092

KNAUSS, DALTON L., electronics company executive. Chmn., chief exec. officer, dir. Square D Co., Palatine, Ill. Office: Square D Co 1415 S Roselle Palatine IL 60067*

KNEELAND, MUNROE HAZEN, osteopathic physician; b. St. Albans, Vt., Jan. 23, 1919; s. Guy Franklin and Althea Diantha (Reynolds) K.; m. Dorothy Violet Robinson, June 28, 1942; 1 dau., Betty Guyleen Galvan. Student N.E. Mo. State U., 1937; D.O., Kirksville Coll. Osteo Medicine, 1941. Physician, Liberal Community Clinic, Mo., 1944-85; cons. physician Barton County Hosp., Lamar, Mo., Oak Hill Hosp., Joplin, Mo. Bd. dirs. Water and Light Dept., Liberal, Mo., 1955-78, city physician water analysis, 1955-85; bd. dirs. Farmers State Bank, Liberal, 1970-85. 25 Yr. Sch. Physician Service award, Liberal, Mo. PTA, 1976. Mem. Am. Osteo. Assn., Am. Acad. Osteopathy, Am. Acad. Family Physicians, Civil Aviation Med. Assn., Am. Coll. Gen Practictioners Osteo. Med and Surgery, Mo. Pilots Assn., Republican. Congregationalist, Methodist. Club: South West Mo. Pilots. Lodges: Lions, Masons. Avocations: aviation; forestry; wildlife conservationist. Home: 215 Denton St Liberal MO 64762 Office: Liberal Community Clinic 125 Main St Liberal MO 64762

KNEEN, JAMES RUSSELL, health care administrator; b. Kalamazoo, Dec. 16, 1955; s. Russell Packard and Joyce Elaine (Knapper) K.; m. Peggy Jo Howard, Aug. 4, 1979; 1 son, Benjamin Russell. B.A., Alma Coll., 1978; M.H.A., U. Mo., 1982. Systems analyst Bronson Meth. Hosp., Kalamazoo, 1976-79; adminstrv. resident Meth. Hosp. Ind., Indpls., 1981-82; div. dir. psychiat. care services Parkview Meml. Hosp., Ft. Wayne, Ind., 1982—. Bd. dirs. Washington House Alcoholism Treatment Ctr. Mem. Allen County Mental Health Assn., Am. Coll. Hosp. Adminstrs., Am. Hosp. Assn. Office: 2200 Randallia Dr Fort Wayne IN 46805

KNELL, KENNETH WARREN, educator; b. Dewey, Ill., June 21, 1921; s. Charles W. and Maude Artilla (Miller) K.; m. Dorothy Lucile Denne, Aug. 29, 1942; children—Philip Denne, Charles Denne, Suzanne. B.S. in Agr., U. Ill., 1948, M.Ed., 1954, Advanced Cert. in Edn., 1969. Vocat. agr. instr. Mahomet (Ill.) Sch. Dist. 3, 1947-67; regional dir. adult edn. Region 4, State of Ill., Springfield, 1967-68; instr., researcher vocat. and tech. edn. dept. U. Ill., Urbana, 1968-69; regional vocat. adminstr. Region 4, Ill. Bd. Edn., Dept. Adult, Vocat. and Tech. Edn., Springfield, 1969—; instr. Am. Meat Inst., Washington, 1970—. Served to 1st lt. U.S. Army, 1943-46; ETO. Decorated Bronze Star. Mem. Am. Vocat. Assn., Ill. Vocat. Assn., Ill. Council Local Adminstrs., Ill. Guidance and Vocat. Services Assn., Farm Bur., Am. Legion, Phi Delta Kappa. Republican. Methodist. Clubs: Lions, Moose. Home: 307 W Main St Mahomet IL 61853 Office: 100 N 1st St Springfield IL 62777

KNEPPER, EUGENE ARTHUR, realtor; b. Sioux Falls, S.D., Oct. 8, 1926; s. Arlie John and May (Crone) K.; B.S.C. in Acctg., Drake U., Des Moines, 1951; m. LaNel Strong, May 7, 1948; children—Kenton Todd, Kristin Rene. Acct., G.L. Yager, pub. acct., Estherville, Iowa, 1951-52; auditor R.L. Meriwether, C.P.A., Des Moines, 1952-53; acct. govt. renegotiation dept. Collins Radio Co., Cedar Rapids, Iowa, 1953-54; head acctg. dept. Hawkeye Rubber Mfg. Co., Cedar Rapids, 1954-56; asst. controller United Fire & Casualty Ins. Co., Cedar Rapids, 1956-58; sales assoc. Equitable Life Assurance Soc. U.S., Cedar Rapids, 1958-59; controller Gaddis Enterprises, Inc., Cedar Rapids, 1959-61; owner Estherville Laundry Co., 1959-64; sales assoc., comml. investment div. mgr. Tommy Tucker Realty Co., Cedar Rapids, 1961-74; owner Real Estate Investment Planning Assocs., Cedar Rapids, 1974—; controlling ptnr. numerous real estate syndicates; cons. in field, fin. speaker; guest lectr. Kirkwood Community Coll., Cedar Rapids, Mt. Mercy Coll., Cedar Rapids, Cornell Coll., Mt. Vernon; creative financing instr. Iowa Real Estate Commn.-Iowa Assn. Realtors. Patron Cedar Rapids Symphony, 1983—, treas., mem. exec. com., bd. dirs.; bd. dirs. Oak Hill-Jackson Outreach Fund, 1970-83, pres., 1973-74; bd. dirs. Consumer Credit Counseling Service Cedar Rapids-Marion Area, 1974-80, pres., 1974-80. Served with USNR, 1945-46. Recipient Storm Manuscript award, 1976. Mem. Nat. Assn. Realtors (state mcpl. legis. com., subcom. on multi-family housing), Iowa Assn. Realtors (pres. comml. investment div. 1973, 80; state legis. com., savs. and loan formation feasibility com., mcpl. and county legis. com.), Nat. Assn. Accountants, Nat. Inst. Real Estate Brokers (membership chmn. Iowa 1972-73, regional v.p.), Real Estate Securities and Syndication Inst. (small group investment council, steering com. 1985, vice chmn. regional officers and state officers devel. com.; gov. Iowa div.), Cedar Rapids Bd. Realtors, Internat. Platform Assn., Internat. Inst. Valuers. Methodist. Clubs: Cedar Rapids Optimist (past chmn. boys work com.); Eastern Iowa Execs. (dir., pres. 1981-82). Contbr. articles to profl. jours. Home: 283 Tomahawk Trail SE Cedar Rapids IA 52403 Office: 1808 IE Tower Cedar Rapids IA 52401

KNIGHT, CHARLES F., electric equipment manufacturing executive; b. Lake Forest, Ill., 1936. B.M.E., Cornell U., M.B.A. Pres., Lester B. Knight Internat. Corp., 1961-63; pres., chief exec. officer Lester B. Knight & Assocs., 1963-72; vice chmn. bd., chief exec. officer, Emerson Electric Co., St. Louis, 1973, chmn., chief exec. officer, dir., 1974—; dir. Southwestern Bell Telephone Co., Cox Broadcasting Corp., Standard Oil Co. of Ohio, Centerre Bancorp., Baxter Travenol Labs., Inc., McDonnell Douglas Corp. Office: Emerson Electric Co Inc 8100 Florissant Ave Saint Louis MO 63136*

KNIGHT, CHRISTOPHER JOHN, lawyer; b. Fostoria, Ohio, Feb. 13, 1952; s. Howard Allen and Joyce E. (Reinhart) K.; m. Mary Francis Hoffman, Sept. 23, 1978; children—Sarah Elizabeth, Aaron Christopher. B.S., Heidelbert Coll., 1974; J.D., U. Toledo, 1978. Bars: Ohio 1978, U.S. Dist. Ct. (no. dist.) Ohio 1978. Ptnr. Bennett & Knight, Clyde, Ohio, 1978—. County commr. Sandusky County, Fremont, Ohio, 1979-81. Mem. Assn. Trial Lawyers Am., Ohio Trial Lawyers Assn., Ohio Bar Assn., Sandusky County Bar Assn. Republican. Home: 1653 Swiss Rd Fremont OH 43420 Office: Bennett & Knight 107 W Buckeye St Clyde OH 43410

KNIGHT, CLARENCE LAWRENCE, U.S. postal service executive; b. Thompson, Ga., Aug. 18, 1943; s. James and Minnie (Ivory) K.; m. Jacqueline Coleman, Jan. 10, 1964 (div. Jan. 1984); children—Sheldon G.; Erik C. Grad. high sch., Detroit; student Lawrence Inst., 1969-70; cert. Rets Electronic Sch., Detroit, 1970; Student Wayne Community Coll., 1972-74. Mail flow controller U.S. Postal Service, Allen Park, Mich., 1975-77, mail processing supr., 1977-79, master instr., Oak Brook, Ill., 1980, regional postal ops. analyst, Chgo., 1980-82, regional maintenance officer, 1983—, acting mgr. plant maintenance, St. Louis, 1982-83, acting dir. mail processing dept., Allen Park, 1985; chmn. affirmative action program, U.S. Postal Service, Chgo., 1984—. Adminstrv. asst. Boy Scouts Am., Downers Grove, Ill., 1980; assoc. Smithsonian Inst., Washington, 1984; pres. Mendota Block Club, Detroit, 1967. Mem. Am. Mgmt. Assn., Nat. Assn. Postal Suprs. (pres. 1977-78, corr. sec. Mich. br. 1978-79, Cert. of Recognition 1981, Letter of Appreciation 1981, Cert. of Achievement 1982, Cert. of Appreciation 1984). Lutheran. Lodges: Wolverine (degree team 1978), Masons (32 degree). Avocations: fishing; painting; bowling; boating. Home: 1646 Barnsdale Rd Apt 305 LaGrange IL 60525

KNIGHT, JOHN LORD, tool manufacturing company executive; b. Chgo., Mar. 16, 1936; s. William Windus and Elsie (Stranahan) K.; m. Sharon Dempsey, Sept. 24, 1958 (div. Aug. 1962); children—Katherine, Deborah; m. Darlene Bock, May 9, 1963 (div. Sept. 1983); children—John Lord, Angela, Robert; m. Beverly Larson, June 16, 1984. B.A., Colo. Coll., 1958; M.B.A., Harvard U., 1962. With devel. dept., tech. div. Libbey Owens Ford Glass Co., Toledo, 1958-60; various mgmt. positions Dana Corp., Ind. and Mich., 1962-70; pres., chief exec. officer Viking Drill & Tool, Inc., St. Paul, 1970—. Charter trustee Colo. Coll., Colorado Springs. Mem. Soc. Mfg. Engrs., Metal Cutting Tool Inst. (dir.), Cutting Tool Mfrs. Am. (dir.). Republican. Mem. Evangelical Free Ch. Home: 13 Evergreen Rd North Oaks MN 55110 Office: Viking Drill & Tool Inc PO Box 3278 Saint Paul MN 55165

KNIGHT, LESTER BENJAMIN, JR., consulting engineer; b. Albany, N.Y., June 29, 1907; s. Lester B. and Louise (Vaast) K.; M.E., Cornell U., 1929; student Chgo. Kent Coll. Law, 1932-34; m. Elizabeth Anne Field, Mar. 5, 1935 (dec. 1978); children—Charles Field, Leslie Knight; m. Frances T. Edens, Mar. 22, 1980. Vice pres. Nat. Engring. Co., Chgo., 1930-43; chmn., chief exec. officer Lester B. Knight & Assos., Inc., mgmt. and cons. engrs., Chgo., 1945—; chmn. Lester B. Knight Internat. Corp., Chgo., 1952—; A.B. Knight, Karlstad, Sweden, 1962—; dir. Knight Wendling, Zurich, Switzerland, Knight Wendling Ltd., London; spl. research foundry mgmt., operation, design, automation and mechanization. Pres., adminstrv. dir. Travelers Aid Soc. Chgo., 1958-60, pres. sponsoring bd., exec. com., 1960—; mem. pres.'s council Cornell U., U. Ill. Served to lt. comdr. USNR, 1943-45. Mem. Am. Foundrymen's Soc., ASME, Am. Mgmt. Assn., Assn. Cons. Mgmt. Engrs., Chgo. C. of C. (dir., v.p. indsl. devel. and policy com.), Ill. Engr. Council (1st v.p., dir., exec. com.), Alpha Tau Omega. Clubs: University, Mid-America, Chicago, Econ. (dir.) (Chgo.); Glenview (Ill.) Golf; Army-Navy (Washington); Country of Fla. (Golf); Quail Ridge Golf and Country (Boynton Beach, Fla.). Home: 1616 Sheridan Rd Wilmette IL 60091 Office: 549 W Randolph St Chicago IL 60606

KNIGHT, ROBERT EDWARD, banker; b. Alliance, Nebr., Nov. 27, 1941; s. Edward McKean and Ruth (McDuffee) K.; B.A., Yale U., 1963; M.A., Harvard U., 1965, Ph.D., 1968; m. Eva Sophia Youngstrom, Aug. 12, 1966; Asst. prof. U.S. Naval Acad., Annapolis, Md., 1966-68; lectr. U. Md., 1967-68; fin. economist Fed. Res. Bank of Kansas City (Mo.), 1968-70, research officer, economist, 1971-76, asst. v.p., sec., 1977, v.p., sec., 1978-79; pres. Alliance (Nebr.) Nat. Bank, 1979—, now also chmn.; pres. Robert Knight Assocs., banking and econ. cons., Alliance, 1979—; mem. faculty Stonier Grad. Sch. Banking, 1972—, Colo. Grad. Sch. Banking, 1975-82, Am. Inst. Banking, U. Mo., Kansas City, 1971-79, Prochnow Grad. Sch. Banking, U. Wis. Trustee, Knox Presbyn. Ch., Overland Park, Kans., 1965-69; bd. regents Nat. Comml. Lending Sch., 1980—; chmn. Downtown Improvement Com., Alliance, 1981—; trustee U. Nebr. Found.; bd. dirs. Stonier Grad. Sch. Banking; mem. fin. com. United Meth. Ch., Alliance, 1982—; ambassador Nebr. Diplomats. Woodrow Wilson fellow, 1963-64. Mem. Am. Econ. Assn., Am. Fin. Assn., So. Econ. Assn., Nebr. Bankers Assn. (com. state legis. 1980—, com. comml. loans and investments), Am. Inst. Banking (state com. for Nebr. 1980—), Am. Bankers Assn. (econ. adv. com. 1980-83, community bank leadership council), Western Econ. Assn., Econometric Soc. Clubs: Rotary, Masons. Contbr. articles to profl. jours. Home: Drawer E Alliance NE 69301 Office: Alliance Nat Bank Alliance NE 69301

KNIGHT, ROBERT G., mayor; b. Wichita, Kans.; m. Jane; 3 children. B.A., Wichita State U., 1970. Elected Wichita Bd. City Commrs., 1979-83, 83—; served as mayor Wichita, 1980-81, 84—; v.p. Ranson & Co., Wichita; adv. bd. Kans. Foodbank, Inc.; mem. Nat. League Cities Steering Com. Adv. bd. Salvation Army; trustee Southwestern Coll. Bd.; adv. bd. United Meth. Urban Ministeries; active First United Meth. Ch. Mem. Wichita Area C. of C. Address: 455 N Main St Wichita KS 67202

KNIGHT, ROBERT MONTGOMERY, basketball coach; b. Massilon, Ohio, Oct. 25, 1940; s. Carroll and Hazel (Henthorne) K.; B.S., Ohio State U., 1962; m. Nancy Lou Knight, Apr. 17, 1963; children—Timothy Scott, Patrick Clair. Asst. coach Cuyahoga Falls (Ohio) High Sch., 1962-63; freshman coach U.S. Mil. Acad., West Point, N.Y., 1963-65, head basketball coach, 1965-71; head basketball coach Ind. U., Bloomington, 1971—. Recipient Coach of Year award Big Ten, 1973, 75, 76, 80; named Coach of Year, AP and Basketball Weekly, 1976. Mem. Nat. Assn. Basketball Coaches (dir.). Office: Indiana Univ Basketball Office Assembly Hall Bloomington IN 47405*

KNIGHT, ROBERT PERKINS, sales executive; b. Evanston, Ill., Oct. 10, 1924; s. Francis M. and Helen (Perkins) K.; m. Andrea Saladine, Mar. 12, 1949; children—Robert P. Jr., Susan, Margaret. Student Hotchkiss Sch., 1942; A.B. in Econs., Yale U., 1948. C.P.C.U. 1954. Asst. v.p. Marsh & McLennan Inc., Chgo., 1956-62, v.p., 1962-70, sr. v.p., 1970—; sr. v.p. prodn., past pres. Evanston Charitable Assn., Chgo. Trustee Northland Coll., Ashland, Wis. Winnetka Congl. Ch.; bd. dirs. Children's Meml. Hosp., Duncan YMCA; former dir. United Charities, Mental Health Soc. Chgo., Inroads. Served to sgt. USAF, 1942-45. Mem. Nat. Assn. Ins. Brokers (former dir.), Ill. Assn. Ins. Brokers, Soc. C.P.C.U. Republican. Congregational. Clubs: Economic, University, Chicago Yacht, Metropolitan, Commonwealth (Chgo.); Indian Hill (Winnetka). Office: 222 S Riverside Plaza Chicago IL 60606

KNIGHT, SUSAN SINGER, advertsing executive; b. Chgo., Oct. 17, 1952; d. Joseph and Florence (Goldman) Singer; m. Robert Alan Knight, June 4, 1972 (div. Dec. 1979); 1 son, Benjamin Sierra. Student U. Ariz., 1970-72, Weber State U., 1972-76; B.A., Calif. State U.-Sacramento, 1979. Freelance artist, 1972-78; Alpha Baking Co., Rosen's Rye Bread, Century 21/Mitchell Bros., 1979-80; advt. dir. Reiter's Inc., Chgo., 1980-83; asst. advt. sales promotion dir. Beltone Electronic Corp., Chgo., 1983—. Mem. Council Fgn. Relations, Sierra Club, Human Soc., Field Mus., Lincoln Park Zool. Soc. Club: East Bank (Chgo.). Office: 4201 W Victoria Ave Chicago IL 60046

KNIGHTON, HARRY SEVILLE, electronics technician, association executive; b. Columbus, Ohio, July 23, 1915; s. Ervin William and Elsie Alice (Dixon) K.; m. Elsie Louise Webb, July 2, 1937. Electrician, Wheeling Steel Corp., Portsmouth, Ohio, 1934-43; electronic technician Empire Detroit Steel, Portsmouth, 1945-80. Editor: The Mycophile, 1963—. Dist. commr. Scioto Area council Boy Scouts Am., 1953-55; mem. Salvation Army Adv. Bd., Portsmouth, 1983-84. Served as staff sgt. U.S. Army, 1943-45; PTO. Recipient Ohio State Conservation Achievement award Dept. Natural Resources, 1983. Mem. North Am. Mycological Assn. (exec. dir. Portsmouth chpt. 1967—, nat. chmn. Forays 1963-84, Contbns. to Amateur Mycology award 1965). Methodist. Avocations: naturalist; stamp collector. Home: 4345 Redinger Rd Portsmouth OH 45662

KNILANS, MICHAEL JEROME, See *Who's Who in America,* 43rd edition.

KNIPP, RICHARD HENRY, building contractor; b. Tipton, Mo., Nov. 14, 1914; s. Carl Henry and Rosa Elizabeth (Hartmen) K. Owner Knipp Constrn. Co., Columbia, Mo., 1940—; v.p. Central Mo. Abstact and Title Co.; v.p. Glenview Drug Co., Columbia, 1965; trustee Mo-Kan Teamsters Pension Trust Fund, 1971—. Mem. Columbia City Council, 1963-73, 79-81, Columbia Planning and Zoning Commn., 1981—; mem. Our Lady of Lourdes Ch. Mem. Kansas City Builders Assn., Assoc. Gen. Contractors Am. Roman Catholic. Club: Country of Mo., Columbia Country. Lodges: Lions, Elks, K.C. Home: 210 W Forest Ave Columbia MO 65203 Office: Richard Knipp Assoc 1204 Pannell St Columbia MO 65201

KNITTEL, ROBERT EDWARD, social and health programs consultant; b. St. Louis, July 22, 1923; s. George Ernest and Paula Marie (Fischer) K.; student St. Louis U., 1941-42, 45-46; B.J., U. Mo., 1948; Ph.D. in Anthropology, So. Ill. U., 1967; m. Elizabeth Rita Geers, June 5, 1948; children—George Randall, David Allen, Rita Marie. Asst. mgr. Doubleday Book Shop, St. Louis, 1948-50, mgr., New Orleans, 1950-52, Clayton, Mo., 1952-54; community relations cons. Housing Rehab. project City of St. Louis, 1954-56; community cons. Community Devel. Services So. Ill. U., 1956-57, asst. dir., 1957-59, dir., 1959-65, asst. dir. research, 1965-67, community cons. area services studies, 1967-68, research asso., 1969-74; coordinator Gulfstream Area Agy. on Aging, Palm Beach, Fla., 1974-75; asso. prof. dept. regional and community affairs U. Mo., 1975-79; pvt. practice social and health programs consulting, St. Louis, 1979—; owner, mgr. Grass-Hooper Press. Active Boy Scouts Am., Murphysboro, Ill., 1963-71; chmn. bd. St. Andrews Parochial Sch., Murphysboro, 1968. Served with U.S. Navy, 1943-46. Fellow Am. Anthrop. Assn., Soc. Applied Anthropology; mem. AAAS, Am. Public Health Assn., Community Devel. Soc. Am., Soc. Med. Anthropology, So. States Anthropl. Assn., Mo. Playwrights Assn. (pres. 1981). Author: Walking in Tower Grove Park, 1978, rev. edit., 1983. Author play: Prometheus (recipient Mo. Council for the Arts Playwrighting contest award), 1978. Editor: A Missouri Playwrights Anthology, 1981. Home and Office: 4030 Connecticut St Saint Louis MO 63116

KNOCHE, HERMAN WILLIAM, biochemist, researcher, educator; b. Stafford, Kans., Nov. 15, 1934; s. Herman William and Ollie Emeline (Keller) K.; m. Darlene K. Bowman, Feb. 5, 1955; children—Kimberly K., Christopher Lynn. B.S., Kans. State U., 1959, Ph.D., 1963. Instr. biochemistry U. Nebr., Lincoln, 1962-63, asst. prof., 1963-68, assoc. prof., 1968-73, prof., 1973—, head dept. agrl. biochemistry, 1974—; research assoc. Harvard U., Cambridge, Mass., 1971-72; cons. Norden Labs., Lincoln, Nebr., 1973—, Vets. Hosp., Lincoln, 1975—, Dorsey Labs, 1980—. Author: Essentials of Organic Chemistry, 1985. Contbr. articles to profl. jours. Served with U.S. Army, 1954-56. Grantee NSF, 1968-81 U.S. Dept. Agr., 1985—. Mem. Am. Soc. Biol. Chemists, Am. Chem. Soc., Am. Legion, Sigma Xi. Republican. Methodist. Home: Route 2 Box 36A Ceresco NE 68017 Office: Univ Nebr Dept Agrl Biochemistry Lincoln NE 68583

KNOCK, GARY HOWARD, university official, educational psychologist; b. Eau Claire, Wis., July 18, 1936; s. Fred John and Agnes (Bjorklund) K.; m. Barbara Marie Kjustad, June 21, 1958; children—Cynthia, Elizabeth. B.S., U. Wis.-Eau Claire, 1958; M.S., U. Wis.-Madison 1961; Ed.D., Ind. U., 1965. Lic. psychologist, Ohio. Tchr. Beloit Pub. Schs., Wis., 1958-61; counselor Mankato State U., Minn., 1961-63; asst. prof., dept. counselor edn. U. Mo., Kansas City, 1965-66; from asst. prof. to prof. dept personnel and guidance Miami U., Oxford, Ohio, 1966-78, chmn. dept. personnel and guidance, 1978-79, assoc. dean Grad. Sch., 1979—. Contbg. author; Establishing Effective Student Service Programs, 1985. Editor Perspectives on the Preparation of Student Affairs Professionals, 1977. Mem. Am. Psychol. Assn., Assn. Counseling and Devel., Am. Coll. Personnel Assn., Midwest Assn. Grad. Schs. (chmn. membership com. 1984-85). Lutheran. Club: 1809 (Oxford) (treas. 1981-82).

KNODELL, ROBERT JAMES, mfg. co. exec.; b. Chgo., May 28, 1932; s. Homer Edward and Mildred Jenette (Miller) K.; student Morton Jr. Coll., 1962-65; m. Jean Marie Klean, Jan. 29, 1955; children—James, Sandra, Richard. Lab. tech. Indsl. Bio-Test Labs., Northbrook, Ill., 1962-70; service sta. dealer Standard Oil of Ind., Brookfield, Ill., 1971-77; service tech. Hobart Corp., Broadview, Ill., 1977—; also freelance writer. Bd. dirs. Library Bd., Brookfield, 1977-81; Dem. precinct capt., 1965—. Mem. Chgo. Council on Fgn. Relations, Am. Enterprise Inst. for Pub. Policy Research. Democrat. Presbyterian. Club: Kiwanis. Home: 9317 Jackson Ave Brookfield IL 60513 Office: 2747 S 25 Ave Broadview IL 60153

KNOEBEL, SUZANNE BUCKNER, medical educator; b. Ft. Wayne, Ind., Dec. 13, 1926; d. Doster and Marie (Lewis) Buckner. A.B. Internat. Relations, Goucher Coll., Balt., 1948; M.D., Ind. U.-Indpls., 1960. Diplomate Am. Bd. Internal Medicine. Intern, Ind. U. Med. Ctr., 1960-61, resident in medicine, 1962-65; asst. prof. medicine Ind. U.-Indpls., 1966-69, assoc. prof., 1969-72, prof., 1972-77, Krannert prof., 1977—, asst. dean research, 1975—; asst. chief cardiology sect. Richard L. Roudebush VA Med. Ctr., Indpls., 1982—. Recipient Matrix award Indpls. chpt. Women in Communications, 1983. Mem. Am. Fedn. Clin. Research, Assn. Univ. Cardiologists, Am. Coll. Cardiology (pres. 1982-83). Contbr. articles sci. jours. Office: Ind U Sch Medicine 1100 W Michigan St Indianapolis IN 46223

KNOEDLER, THOMAS BERNARD, computer analyst and programmer; b. Springfield, Ill., Jan. 20, 1952; s. Joseph Bernard and Rose Louise (Geier) K.; B.A. in Math. Systems, Sangamon State U., 1974, M.A. in Math. Systems/Computer Sci., 1981. Mgmt. analyst, programmer II, Sangamon State U., Springfield, 1977—. Mem. Assn. Computer Programmers and Analysts, L5 Soc., Planetary Soc., U.S. Chess Fedn. (life). Roman Catholic. Club: Springfield Chess (v.p.). Office: PAC 595 Shepherd Rd Springfield IL 62708

KNOERLE, JEANNE, nun, college chancellor; b. Cleve., Feb. 24, 1928. B.A. in Journalism, St. Mary of the Woods Coll., 1949; M.A. in Journalism, Ind. U., 1961, Ph.D. in Comparative Lit., 1966, LL.D. (hon.), 1975; LL.D. (hon.), Ind. State U., 1972, St. Mary's Coll.-Notre Dame, Ind., 1981; Litt. D. (hon.), Rose-Hulman Inst. Tech., 1971; D.D. (hon.), Ind. Central U., 1978. Joined Sisters of Providence, Roman Cath. Ch., 1949. Tchr. Cath. schs., Chgo., Ind., and Washington, D.C., 1952-54; chmn. dept. journalism St. Mary of the Woods Coll., Ind., 1954-63; vis. prof. Providence Coll., Taichung, Taiwan, 1966-67; asst. to pres., assoc. prof. Asian Studies St. Mary of the Woods Coll., 1967-68, pres., 1968-84, chancellor, dir. endowment program, 1984—. Author: The Dream of the Red Chamber, A Critical Study, 1972. Contbr. articles to profl. jours. Pres. Ind. Conf. on Higher Edn., 1973-74, Alliance for Growth and Progress, Econ. Devel. Group, Terre Haute, Ind., 1983—; bd. dirs. Fed. Home Loan Bank of Ind., 1973, Union Hosp. of Terre Haute, 1973, Commn. on Women in Higher Edn., 1976-79, Am. Council on Edn., 1979-80, Aquinas Coll., 1978-80, Ind. Acad. in the Pub. Service, 1980-82, Council of Ind. Colls., 1980-83, Fund for the Improvement of Post Secondary Edn., 1982—; sec., treas. Ind. Colls. and Univs. of Ind., 1979-80. Recipient Advisor of Yr. award Cath. Sch. Press Assn., 1960; Mother Theodore Guerin medal St. Mary of the Woods Coll., 1975; Fulbright fellow, 1966. Mem. Assn. Cath. Colls. and Univs. (chmn. 1978-80), Assn. Am. Colls., Nat. Cath. Edn. Assn., Terre Haute Med. Edn. Found., Internat. Assn. Univ. Pres., Mental Health Assn. Vigo County, NIH, Assn. Colls. Ind. (pres. 1982-84). Home and Office: St Mary of the Woods Coll Saint Mary of the Woods IN 47876

KNOPF, HARRY LOUIS, ophthalmologist; b. Trenton, N.J., Apr. 17, 1941; m. Karen Sue Lipschultz, June 12, 1964; children—Joelyn, Aaron. B.A. in Biology cum laude, Harvard U., 1963, M.D., 1967. Dilomate Am. Bd. Ophthalmology. Intern Duke U. Med. Ctr, Durham, N.C., 1967-68; staff assoc. NIH, Bethesda, Md., 1968-70, sr. fellow ocular infectious disease, 1970-71; resident dept. ophthalmology Washington U., 1971-74; clin. instr., 1974-78, asst. clin. prof., 1978—; mem. staff Barnes Hosp., Jewish Hosp., Children's Hosp., St. Louis County Hosp., St. Luke's Hosp. Contbr. articles to profl. jours. Fellow Am. Acad. Ophthalmology; mem. AMA, Mo. State Med. Assn., Mo. Ophthal. Soc. (pres. 1983-84), St. Louis Met. Med. Soc., St. Louis Ophthal. Soc. (treas. 1979-80, sec. 1980-81, v.p. 1981-82, pres. 1982-83). Avocations: gardening, singing, cooking. Office: 211 N Meramec Clayton MO 63105

KNORR, FRANK LAWRENCE, college administrator; b. Phila., July 25, 1937; s. Frank Russell and Eleanor Magdalene (Lawrence) K.; m. Jean Ann Warren, June 22, 1963; children—Eric Arthur, Elisabeth Ann. B.A., Coll. Wooster, 1959; M.A., U. Rochester, 1966, postgrad., 1966-70. Cert. Sch. Dist. Administr. N.Y. Dir. radio broadcasting Haverford Schs., Phila., 1959-61; instr. Am. history, Econs. Webster Schs., Rochester, 1961-66, T.V. coordinator, 1966-68; asst. supt. schs. Brighton Schs, Rochester, 1968-74; dir. alumni relations Coll. Wooster, Ohio, 1974-82, dir. devel., 1982—, asst. prof. edn., 1974—; tenure hearing officer Commr. Edn., Albany, N.Y., 1972-74; assoc. tchr. edn. Ford Found. Project, Rochester, 1962-64. Co-founder, producer Ohio Light Opera, Wooster, 1978-83; gen. chmn. YMCA Rochester & Monroe County-Camps, 1972-74, fin. chmn. 1966-72; bd. dirs. Rochester Oratorio Soc., 1973-74; ruling elder Third Presbyn. Ch., Rochester, 1973-74, Westminster Presbyn. Ch., Wooster, 1976-79. Recipient Opera Co. of Year award No. Ohio Live Mag. 1983. Mem. Ind. Coll. Advancement Assn. (pres. 1978-79), Council Advancement and Support of Edn. (conf. speaker 1979, 80, 81, 82). Republican. Club: Sodus Bay Heights Country (Rochester). Avocations: golf, classical music, gardening, travel. Home: 5 Smith Ln Wooster OH 44691 Office: Dir Devel Coll Wooster Alumni House Wooster OH 44691

KNORR, JOHN CHRISTIAN, music and entertainment executive, band leader, show producer; b. Crissey, Ohio, May 24, 1921; s. Reinhold Alfred and Mary (Rieth) K.; m. Jane Lucy Hammer, Aug. 10, 1922; children—Gerald William, Janice Grace Knorr Wilcox. Student Ohio No. U., 1940-41. Violin soloist with Helen O'Connell, 1934-35; reed sideman Jimmy Dorsey, Les Brown and Sonny Dunham orchs., 1939-48; mem. theater pit orchs. and club shows, Ohio, 1949-57; leader Johnny Knorr Orch, Toledo, 1958—; mgr. Centennial Terr.; owner Johnny Knorr Entertainment Agy.; band leader, show producer. Bd. trustees Presbyterian Ch. Served to cpl. AUS, 1944-45. Recipient outstanding dance band citations, Chgo., 1966, Des Moines, 1968, Las Vegas, 1969, Nat. Ballroom Operators Assn., Omaha, 1970, Entertainment Operators Assn., 1973; named Grand Duke of Toledo, King of the Hoboes, 1975. Mem. Am. Fedn. Musicians, Am. Legion. Clubs: Exchange, Circus Fans Am., Masons, Shriners, Ind. Order Foresters. Recordings: Live at Franklin Park Mall, 1973; Let's Go Dancing, 1979; Encore, 1984; TV spl. An Era of Swing, 1973. Home and Office: 1751 Fallbrook Rd Toledo OH 43614

KNOTT, CAROL REDE, interior designer; b. Weston, W.Va., Mar. 18, 1930; d. Marion Wyllys and Mary Warren Rede; student Rollins Coll., 1948-49; B.A., Northwestern U., 1966; m. Richard F. Knott, Nov. 26, 1949; children—Diana Despard, Richard F., Thomas Read, Sally Oliver. Designer, Betty Lotz Interiors, Winnetka, Ill., 1966-73; owner Carol R. Knott Interior Design, Kenilworth, Ill., 1973—; tchr. Wilmette Park Dist. Mem. Am. Soc. Interior Designers (dir.), Chgo. Designers Club, Colonial Dames, Desc. Signers Declaration of Independence. Republican. Episcopalian. Clubs: Farmington Country (Charlottesville, Va.); Mchts. and Mfrs. (Chgo.). Office: 430 Green Bay Rd Kenilworth IL 60043

KNOTT, JOHN R., JR., English language educator; b. Memphis, Tenn., July 9, 1937; s. John Ray and Wilma (Henshaw) K.; m. Anne Percy; children—Catherine, Ellen, Walker, Anne. B.A., Yale U., 1959; Ph.D., Harvard U., 1965. Instr. English, Harvard U., 1965-67; asst. prof. to prof. English, U. Mich., Ann Arbor, 1967—, assoc. dean Coll. Lit. Scis. and Arts, 1977-80, acting dean, 1980-81, chmn. dept. English, 1981—. Author: Milton's Pastoral Vision, 1971; The Sword of the Spirit, 1980. Editor: The Triumph of Style, 1969, Mirrors: An Introduction to Literature, 1972, 75. Carnegie fellow Yale U., 1959, NEH fellow, 1973. Mem. Modern Lang. Assn., Milton Soc., Renaissance Soc. Am. Home: 1945 Cambridge Rd Ann Arbor MI 48104 Office: Dept English Univ Mich Ann Arbor MI 48109

KNOTT, WILEY EUGENE, electronics engineer; b. Muncie, Ind., Mar. 18, 1938; s. Joseph Wiley and Mildred Viola (Haxton) K.; B.S. in Elec. Engring., Tri-State U., 1963; postgrad. Union Coll., 1970-73; children—Brian Evan. Asso. aircraft engr. Lockheed-Ga. Co., Marietta, 1963-65; tech. publs. engr. Gen. Electric Co., Pittsfield, Mass., 1965-77,sr. publs. engr., 1977-79, group leader, 1967-79; specialist engr. Boeing Mil. Airplane Co., Wichita, Kans., 1979-81, sr. specialist engr., 1981—; part-time bus. cons., 1972—. Active Am. Security Council, 1975—, Nat. Republican Senatorial Com., 1979—, Nat. Rep. Congressional Com., 1979—, Rep. Nat. Com., 1979—, Rep. Presdl. Task Force, 1981—; state advisor U.S. Congl. Adv. Aboard, 1981—. Served with AUS, 1956-59. Mem. Am. Def. Preparedness Assn. (life), U.S. Golf Assn., M.B.A. Assn. Methodist. Home: 2006 S Dellrose Wichita KS 67218 Office: Boeing Mil Airplane Co 3801 S Oliver St Wichita KS 67210

KNOUSE, CHARLES ALLISON, osteopathic physician, pathology educator; b. Plattsburg, Mo., Mar. 14, 1921. S. Charles Albert and Alice Susan May (Trout) K.; m. Iris Christine Ehrenreich, May 21, 1944; children—Thea Christine Knouse Price, Charles Allison, Karen Elizabeth Knouse Brungardt, John Arthur. Grad. Emmettsburg (Iowa) Jr. Coll., 1941; student U. Chgo., 1941-42; D.O., Kansas City Coll. Osteopathy and Surgery, 1949. Diplomate Nat. Bd. Examiners Osteo. Physicians. Gen. practice medicine, Howard City, Mich., 1950-55; asst. to editor. Am. Osteo. Assn., Chgo., 1955; gen. practice, Seattle, 1956; resident Hosps. Kansas City Coll. Osteopathy and Surgery, 1958-61; mem. faculty Kirksville (Mo.) Coll. Osteopathy and Surgery, 1961-65; mem. staff Kirksville Osteo. Hosp., 1961-65; prof. pathology, chmn. dept. Univ. Health Scis., Kansas City (Mo.), 1965-68; chmn. dept. pathology Meml. Osteo. Hosp., York, Pa., 1968-78; prof. pathology Ohio U. Coll. Osteo. Medicine, 1978—, also dir. lab. services; gen. clinician Ohio U. Osteo. Med. Ctr.; adj. prof. pathology W.Va. Sch. Osteo. Medicine; mem. vis. faculty U. New Eng. Coll. Osteo. Medicine; cons. pathology Nat. Bd. Examiners for Osteo. Physicians and Surgeons. Elder 1st Christian Ch., Athens, Ohio. Served with U.S. Mcht. Marine, 1942-44, U.S. Army, 1944-46; ETO. U. Chgo. scholar, 1941. Fellow Am. Osteo. Coll. Pathlogists; mem. Am. Osteo. Assn. (del. to Am. Blood Commn. 1975—), Ohio Osteo. Assn., Am. Acad. Osteopathy, AAUP, Am. Assn. Automotive Medicine, Am. Med. Writers Assn., Psi Sigma Alpha. Mem. Disciples of Christ Ch. Contbr. articles to osteo. jours. Home: 85 S May Ave Athens OH 45701 Office: Grosvenor Hall Ohio U Coll Osteo Medicine Athens OH 45701

KNOWLES, MARYELLEN SHANK, public school administrator; b. Saginaw, Mich., Aug. 25, 1940; d. Arlo Van and Orpha Mae (Knowles) Shank; m. Richard Adolph Fluck, June 2, 1962 (div.); 1 son, Ronald Edwin. B.A. in Edn., Greenville Coll., 1962; M.S., No. Ill. U., 1976, Cert. Advanced Study, 1977, Ed.D., 1979. Cert. tchr. adminstr. Ill., Iowa. Tchr. Waterford (Mich.) Pub. Schs., 1962-63, Wyanet (Ill.) Pub. Schs., 1963-65; tchr. Woodridge (Ill.) Pub. Schs., 1967-71, dir. Learning Ctr., 1971-76; tchr. Fenton (Ill.) Pub. Schs., 1977-78; curriculum cons. Clinton (Iowa) Pub. Schs., 1979-81, spl. edn. dir., prin. sch. for handicapped, 1981—. Bd. dirs Clinton YWCA, Women's Resource Ctr.; bd. dirs., newsletter editor Eagle Point Nature Soc. active Divorce Support Groups. Mem. Iowa Assn. Supervision and Curriculum Devel. (state pres.), Am. Assn. Supervision and Curriculum Devel., Shepherd's Flock Curriculum Orgn. Iowa (exec. sec.) Mem. United Ch. of Christ. Contbr. articles to profl. jours. Home: 1045 8th Ave N Clinton IA 52732 Office: Clinton Community Schools 600 S 4th St Clinton IA 52732

KNOWLTON, AUSTIN E. (DUTCH KNOWLTON), See *Who's Who in America,* 43rd edition.

KNOWLTON, RICHARD L., food products company executive; b. 1932; B.A., U. Colo., 1954; married. With Geo. A. Hormel & Co., Austin, Minn., 1948—, salesman, 1953-59, mgr. Minn. route car div., 1959-61, central mgr. Minn. and Wis. sales div., 1961-63, mgr. route car sales, 1963-67, mgr. meat products div. and route car sales, 1967-69, asst. mgr. Austin plant, then gen. mgr. Austin plant, 1969-74, group v.p. ops., 1974-79, pres., 1979—, chief exec. officer, 1981—, chmn., 1984—, also dir.; dir. 1st Nat. Bank Mpls., 1st Nat. Bank Austin, 1st Bank Mpls., Can. Packers, Inc., Nat. Live Stock and Meat Bd. Trustee U. Minn. Found.; bd. dirs. Hormel Found. Served to 1st lt. USAF, 1954-56. Mem. Am. Meat Inst. (dir.). Office: Geo A Hormel & Co 501 16th Ave NE Austin MN 55912

KNOX, ARTHUR LLOYD, investment banker; b. Perkins, Okla., May 12, 1932; s. Myrl Frank and Margaret (Grant) K.; B.S., Okla. State U., 1955; m. Earlene Lois Luff, Feb. 19, 1955; children—Arthur Earl, Angela Marie. With Lincoln (Nebr.) Steel Corp., 1957-84, exec. v.p., chief operating officer, 1979-81, pres., 1981-84; sr. v.p. Commerce Capital Inc., 1984—; ptnr. Reinox Devel., 1984—; partner 2LK Horse & Cattle Co., K&L Leasing Co., Knox Rentals; dir. Cornhusker Bank, Lincoln; adv. bd. Nebr. Dept. Econ. Devel., 1979-83; del. White House Conf. Small Bus., 1974—. Chmn., Lancaster County Young Republicans, 1966-67, Nebr. Fedn. Young Reps., 1967-68, Lancaster County Rep. Com., 1972-76; asst. chmn. Nebr. Rep. Party, 1979-80; mem. Rep. Nat. Com., 1980-84; bd. dirs. Lower Platte S. Natural Resources Dist., 1974—; presdl. elector for Nebr., 1976—. Served with AUS, 1955-57. Recipient various Rep., Jaycee awards. Mem. Am. Welding Soc., Nebr. Assn. Commerce and Industry, Associated Industries Lincoln, Lincoln C. of C. (dir. 1981—), Farmhouse. Republican. Presbyterian. Clubs: Rotary (bd. dirs.), Elephant. Home: 920 Pine Tree Ln Lincoln NE 68521 Office: 646 NBC Ctr Lincoln NE 68508

KNOX, CHERYL ANNE, biologist; b. Fayetteville, Ark., Sept. 17, 1948; d. Harold Frank and Bonnie Mae (Fife) Prescott; m. Hugh David Knox, Aug. 3, 1968; 1 child, Ahern Prescott. B.A., U. Tex.-Austin, 1970; M.A., U. Tex-Arlington, 1975; Ph.D., Tex. A&M U., 1980. Plant tissue culturist Tex. A&M U., College Station, 1976-80; researcher molecular biology U. Tex.-Dallas, Richardson, 1980-83; plant molecular biologist Kans. State U., Manhattan, 1983—. Contbr. articles to profl. jours. Mem. Am. Soc. Plant Physiologists, Internat. Soc. Plant Molecular Biology. Office: Kans State U Dept Biochemistry Willard Hall Manhattan KS 66506

KNOX, JAMES MARSHALL, lawyer; b. Chgo., Jan. 12, 1944; s. Edwin John and Shirley Lucille (Collett) K.; m. Janine Lenar, July 18, 1964; children—Erik M., Christian S. B.A., U. Ill., 1968; M.A. in L.S., Rosary Coll., 1973; J.D., DePaul Coll. of Law, 1979. Bar: Ill. 1979, U.S. Dist. Ct. (no. dist.) Ill. 1979, U.S. Ct. Appeals (7th cir.) 1980. Assoc., Fishman & Fishman, Ltd., Chgo., 1979—. Vestryman St. Mark's Episc. Ch., Evanston, Ill., 1980-83. Mem. ABA, Ill. State Bar Assn., Chgo. Bar Assn. (civil practice com. 1984—, indsl. commn. com. 1984—). Republican. Home: 806 Hamlin St Evanston IL 60201 Office: Fishman & Fishman Ltd 134 N LaSalle Suite 1016 Chicago IL 60602

KNOX, JANICE ANN, data processing executive; b. Chgo., Mar. 18, 1948; d. James W. and Lucy Olivia (Williams) Knox; B.A. in Math., Northeastern Ill. U., 1971; postgrad. Northwestern U. With First Nat. Bank Chgo., 1971—, programming instr., 1973-76, systems mgr., 1976—, systems officer, 1979-82, application devel. and support mgr., 1982—; programming instr. Malcolm X Coll., Chgo., 1974; tng. specialist urban skills City Colls. Chgo., 1978—. Bd. dirs., trustee Beacon Neighborhood House, 1983—; bd. dirs., chmn. state coordinating com. NAACP, 1983—, mem. exec. bd. Chgo. Southside br., 1983—, 1st v.p. women's aux., 1981-83. Grantee NSF, 1964-65. Mem. Assn. Computing Machinery, Pansophic Users Learning and Sharing Exchange. Office: 1 First Nat Plaza Suite 0272 Chicago IL 60670

KNUDSON, CURTIS LEE, chemist; b. Grand Forks, N.D., Jan. 2, 1944; s. Clarence Edward and Ina Elvira (Quammen) K.; m. Karol-lyn Mercia Howe, Aug. 16, 1969; children—Carl, Brant. Student St. Olaf Coll., 1962-64; B.A., Augsburg Coll., 1969; M.S., U. N.D., 1972, Ph.D., 1975. Project mgr. Grand Forks Energy Tech. Ctr. (N.D.), 1974-82; chemist, research cons. Research Computer Services, Grand Forks, 1982-83; sr. research assoc. U. N.D. Energy Research Ctr., 1984—; cons. Alta. Research Council, Edmonton, Northwest Research Co., Grand Forks. Served with U.S. Army, 1964-67. Mem. Am. Chem. Soc., Sigma Xi. Contbr. articles to profl. jours.; patentee process for conversion of coal. Address: 711 N 25th St Grand Forks ND 58201

KNUDSON, MARK BRADLEY, medical corporation executive; b. Libby, Mont., Sept. 24, 1948; s. Melvin R. and Melba Irene (Joice) K.; m. Susan Jean Voorhees, Sept. 12, 1970; children—Kirstin Sue, Amy Lynn. B.S., Pacific Luth. U., 1970; Ph.D., Wash. State U., 1974. Asst. prof. U. Wash., Seattle, 1977-79; physiologist Cardiac Pacemakers, Inc., St. Paul, 1979-80, mgr. research, 1980-82, dir. applied research, 1983; pres., chmn. bd. SenTech Med. Corp., St. Paul, 1983—; lectr. in field. NIH fellow, 1975-76. Mem. AAAS, Am. Heart Assn. Republican. Lutheran. Contbr. articles to profl. jours.; patentee in field. Office: 3771 Lexington Ave North Arden Hills MN 55126

KNUDSON, ROBERT LELAND, communications specialist; b. Newman Grove, Nebr., Aug. 8, 1951; s. Leland H. and Arlene (Grace) K.; m. Christine Marie Petrini, Sept. 23, 1978; children—Cassandra Jane, Melissa Lynn. B.A. in Journalism, U. Nebr., 1973. Editor, Sun Newspapers of Omaha, 1971-74; staff writer InterNorth, Inc., Omaha, 1978; mktg. dir. Priesman Graphics, Omaha, 1979; spl. events coordinator Omaha World-Herald, 1979—. Contbr. articles to mags. Mem. Pub. Relations Soc. Am., Internat. Assn. Bus. Communicators Internat. News Promotion Assn., Omaha Fedn. Advt., Omaha Jaycees, Nebr. Jaycees, Omicron Delta Kappa, Lambda Chi Alpha. Democrat. Methodist. Club: Omaha Press. Home: 13517 Frances St Omaha NE 68144 Office: Omaha World-Herald World-Herald Sq Omaha NE 68102

KNUDSON, THOMAS JEFFERY, journalist; b. Manning, Iowa, July 6, 1953; s. Melvin Jake and Coreen Rose (Nickum) K. B.A. in Journalism, Iowa State U., 1980. Reporter/intern Wall Street Jour., Chgo., summer 1979; staff writer Des Moines Register, 1980—. Author: (series) A Harvest of Harm: The Farm Health Crisis, 1984 (Pulitzer prize 1985). Recipient James W. Schwartz award Iowa State U., 1985. Office: Des Moines Register PO Box 957 Des Moines IA 50304

KNULL, HARVEY ROBERT, biochemist; b. Thorsby, Alta., Can., Sept. 15, 1941; s. Herman B. and Molly Louise (Connolly) K.; m. Diane Roberta Zessin, July 3 1965; children—Tania, Tami. B.S., U. Alta., 1963; M.S., U. Nebr., 1965; Ph.D., Pa. State U., 1970. Postdoctoral fellow Pa. State U., 1970, Mich. State U., East Lansing, 1970-73; asst. prof. U. Man., Winnipeg, Can., 1973-80; assoc. prof. U. N.D., Grand Forks, 1980—. Contbr. articles to profl. jours. Mem. Am. Soc. Biol. Chemists, Am. Soc. Neurochemistry, Can. Soc. Biochemistry, Internat. Soc. Neurochemistry. Home: 1316 Noble Cove Grand Forks ND 58201 Office: Dept Biochemistry U ND Grand Forks ND 58202

KNUTSON, HOWARD ARTHUR, state senator, lawyer; b. Grand Forks, N.D., May 16, 1929; s. Arthur K. and Ella M. (Kamplin) K.; m. Jerroldine M. Sundby, Oct. 5, 1958; children—David, Douglas, Eric, Annette, Amy. Student Wabash Coll., 1947-49; A.B., Luther Coll., 1951; J.D., William Mitchell Coll. Law, 1959. Bar: Minn. 1959, U.S. Dist. Ct. Minn. 1959. Claims mgr. Federated Ins., 1953-60; ptnr. Bergman, Knutson, Street & Ulmen, Mpls., 1959-79; mem. Minn. Ho. of Reps., 1967-72; mem. Minn. Senate, 1972—; prin. Knutson Law Office, Burnsville, Minn., 1979—. Bd. dirs. Fairview Community Hosp., Fairview-Southdale Hosp., Ebenezer Soc. Served with U.S. Army, 1951-53. Recipient Disting. Service award Minn. Social Services Assn., 1974; Pub. Service award Met. State U. Alumni Assn., 1984. Mem. Hennepin County Bar Assn., Dakota County Bar Assn., Minn. Bar Assn., ABA, Nat. Conf. State Legislators. Republican. Lutheran. Home: 1907 Woods Ln Burnsville MN 55337 Office: 14500 Burnhaven Dr Burnsville MN 55337

KNUTSON, MARK STEVEN, lawyer; b. El Paso, Tex., June 13, 1953; s. Eugene B. and Jacqueline (Hall) K.; m. Patricia B., Aug. 16, 1975; children—Kristin Lynn, Kathrine Elizabeth. B.A., St. Mary's Coll., Winona, Minn., 1975; J.D., Loyola U., Chgo., 1978. Bar: Wis. 1978. Mem. Bissonnette & Knutson, S.C., Beaver Dam, Wis., 1981—. Mem. Wis. Bar Assn., ABA, Dodge County Bar Assn., Wis. Trial Lawyers Assn. Lodge: Optimists (pres. 1983-84). Office: Bissonnette & Knutson SC 105 Front St Beaver Dam WI 53916

KOBAK, ALFRED JULIAN, JR., obstetrician-gynecologist; b. Chgo., Feb. 10, 1935; s. Alfred J., and Rose B. (Baron) K.; m. Sue B. Stein, May 3, 1959; children—William, Steven, Jane, Deborah. B.S., U. Ill., 1957, M.D., 1959. Diplomate Am. Bd. Ob-Gyn. Intern Michael Reese Hosp., Chgo., 1959-60; resident Cook County Hosp., 1960-62, 64-65; practice medicine specializing in ob-gyn., Valparaiso, Ind., 1965—; mem. med. staff Parker Meml. Hosp., Valparaiso, 1965—, pres., 1981-82; asst. clin. prof. ob-gyn Ind. U.; clin. instr. ob-gyn Rush Med. Sch., Chgo.; pres. Ob-Gyn Assocs., Valparaiso, 1970—. Bd. dirs. Northwest Ind. Jewish Fedn. Served to capt. USAF, 1962-64. Fellow ACS, Internat. Coll. Surgeons, Am. Coll. Ob-Gyn.; mem. AMA, Am. Fertility Soc., Ind. Med. Assn., Central Assn. Obstetricians and Gynecologists, Porter County Med. Soc. (pres. 1979). Republican. Clubs: Valparaiso Country. Contbr. articles to med. jours. Office: 1101 E Glendale Valparaiso IN 46383

KOBER, ARLETTA REFSHAUGE (MRS. KAY L. KOBER), ednl. adminstr.; b. Cedar Falls, Iowa, Oct. 31, 1919; d. Edward and Mary (Jensen) Refshauge; B.A., State Coll. Iowa, 1940; M.A., U. No. Iowa; m. Kay Leonard Kober, Feb. 14, 1944; children—Kay Mary, Karilyn Eve. Tchr. high schs., Soldier, Iowa, 1940-41, Montezuma, Iowa, 1941-43, Waterloo, Iowa, 1943-50, 65-67, co-ordinator Office Edn. Waterloo Community Schs., Waterloo, Iowa, 1967—; head dept. co-op. career edn. West High Sch., Waterloo, 1974—. Mem. Waterloo Sch. Health Council; nominating com. YWCA, Waterloo; Black Hawk County chmn. Tb Christmas Seals; ward chmn. ARC, Waterloo; co-chmn. Citizen's Com. for Sch. Bond Issue; pres. Waterloo PTA Council, Waterloo Vis. Nursing Assn., 1956-57, Kingsley Sch. PTA, 1959-60; v.p. Waterloo Women's Club, 1962-63, pres., 1963-64, trustee bd. clubhouse dirs., 1957—; mem. Gen. Fedn. Women's Clubs, Nat. Congress Parents and Tchrs.; Presbyterial world service chmn. Presbyn. Women's Assn.; bd. dirs. Black Hawk County Republican Women, 1952-53, United Services of Black Hawk County, Broadway Theatre League, St. Francis Hosp. Found. Mem. AAUW (v.p. Cedar Falls 1946-47), NEA, LWV (dir. Waterloo 1951-52), Black Hawk County Hist. Soc. (charter), Delta Pi Epsilon (v.p. 1966-67), Delta Kappa Gamma. Club: Town (dir.) (Waterloo). Home: 1046 Prospect Blvd Waterloo IA 50701 Office: West High Sch Waterloo IA 50702

KOBLENZER, MARGARET ETHRIDGE, clinical social worker; b. Huntington, N.Y., June 27, 1954; d. Mark Foster and Margaret Burns (Furbee) Ethridge; m. Warren Dale Koblenzer, Aug. 11, 1979. B.A., Ohio Wesleyan U., 1977; M.S. in Social Adminstrn., Case Western Res. U., 1980. Clin. social worker Catholic Service League, Akron, Ohio, 1980-81; psychiat. social worker Akron Child Guidance Ctr., 1981-84; clin. social worker Psychotherapy Assocs., Akron, 1983—. Mem. vestry Ch. of Our Savior, Akron; active United Way Summit County. Mem. Nat. Assn. Social Workers, Acad. Cert. Social Workers, Jr. League of Akron, Kappa Kappa Gamma. Democrat. Episcopalian. Club: Portage Country (Akron). Office: 3200 W Market St Akron OH 44313

KOBS, ANN ELIZABETH JANE, nursing administrator, consultant; b. Clinton, Iowa, Feb. 13, 1944; d. Francis Hubert and Leora Elizabeth (Sodeman) Boeker; m. Dennis Raymond Kobs, Oct. 15, 1966; children—Michael, Peter, Amy. Diploma, Mercy Hosp. Sch. Nursing, 1965; B.S. in Nursing, Marycrest Coll., 1978; M.S. in Nursing Adminstrn., No. Ill. U., 1981. Staff charge nurse Mercy Hosp., Davenport, Iowa, 1965-66; clin. instr. Marycrest Coll., Davenport, 1967; cons. to physicians in pvt. practice, Rock Island, Ill., 1973-75; pre-reviewer for continuing edn. and career counselor in residence Ill. Nurses Assn., Chgo., 1978-80; career devel. cons. Ill. Hosp. Assn., Oak Brook, 1980-81, staff specialist nursing, 1981-83, dir. nursing, Naperville, 1983-84; dir. nursing surg./maternal-child health Alexian Bros. Med. Ctr., Elk Grove Village, Ill., 1984—; lectr. No. Ill. U., 1981-83. Mem. City Beautification Commn. Rock Island, 1972-76, also sec., vice-chmn. Mem. Am. Soc. Nursing Services Adminstrs., Ill. Soc. Nurse Adminstrs. (mem. exec. com., chmn. Task Force on Sunset Ill. Nursing Act 1984—), Nat. League Nursing, Ill. League Nursing, Women's Health Exec. Network, Nat. Forum Adminstrs. of Nursing Services, Nat. Assn. Female Execs., Sigma Theta Tau. Roman Catholic. Editor: Ill. Nurses Assn. Directory of Baccalaureate Degree Completion Programs for RNs in Ill., 1979; writer, producer, dir.: Nursing: Opportunities Unlimited, 1980.

KOCH, ALBERT ACHESON, acctg. co. exec.; b. Atlanta, May 16, 1942; s. Albert H. and Harriet M. (Acheson) K.; B.S. cum laude, Elizabethtown Coll., 1964; m. Bonnie Royce, June 6, 1964; children—Bradford Allen, David Albert, Robert Acheson, Donald Leonard. With Ernst & Whinney, 1964—, nat. dir. client services nat. office, Cleve., 1977-81, mng. partner Detroit office, 1981—; mem. adv. com. on replacement cost implementation SEC, 1976. Bd. dirs. Harper-Grace Hosps., 1982—, HGH Health System, 1983—, Radius Health Services, 1984—, New Detroit, 1985—, Elizabethtown Coll., 1981—, Met. Detroit YMCA, 1982—, Mich. Colls. Found., 1981—, Detroit Symphony Orch., 1983—. Served to 1st lt. Fin. Corps, USAR, 1966-72. Recipient Elijah Watt Sells Gold Medal award Am. Inst. C.P.A.s, 1965, Educate for Service award Elizabethtown Coll., 1966. Fellow Life Mgmt. Inst.; mem. Am. Inst. C.P.A.s, Mich. Assn. C.P.A.s. Clubs: Bloomfield Hills Country, Orchard Lake Country, Detroit, Detroit Athletic, Renaissance, Econ. Detroit (dir. 1981—). Co-author: SEC Replacement Cost Requirements and Implementation Manual, 1976. Office: 200 Renaissance Center Suite 2300 Detroit MI 48243

KOCH, CHARLES G., petroleum company executive. Chmn., dir. Koch Industries, Inc., Wichita, Kans. Office: Koch Industries In PO Box 2256 Wichita KS 67201*

KOCH, DOUGLAS CHARLES, newspaper manager; b. Two Rivers, Wis., July 10, 1938; s. Charles E. and Faith H. Koch; m. Adele M. Mrozinski, Feb. 7, 1959; children—Kevin Douglas, Student pub. schs. Vice pres. Brown County Pub. Co., Denmark, Wis., 1976—. Contbr. articles to various mags. Bd. dirs. Manitowoc Maritime Mus., Manitowoc, Wis., 1978—, pres., 1980-82. Mem. Wis. Advt. Pubs. Assn. (pres. 1985). Clubs: Rotary, Optimists. Home: 4823 Morgan Dr Manitowoc WI 54220 Office: Lakeshore Chronicle 2115 Washington St Two Rivers WI 54241

KOCH, GARY EDWARD, legislative accounting administrator; b. Jacksonville, Ill., Sept. 24, 1950; s. Byron Edward and Paula Elizabeth (Scoggins) K.; m. Valerie Jean Ludden, Dec. 8, 1979. B.A., Ill. Coll., Jacksonville, 1972; M.A., Sangamon State U., 1973, postgrad., 1980-85. Reporter, State Jour.-Register, Springfield, Ill., 1973; legis. aide Ill. Ho. Reps., 1973-74; pub. info. officer Ill. Dept. Local Govt. Affairs, Springfield, 1974-79, Ill. Dept. Commerce and Community Affairs, Springfield, 1979-82; exec. dir. Legis. Local Acctg. Task Force, Springfield, 1982-84; adminstrv. asst. Office of State Comptroller, Springfield, 1984—; mem. State Comptroller's Local Govt. Adv. Bd., 1984—; spokesman Gov.'s Adv. Commn. on Taxes, 1978-79, mem. Gov.'s Task Force on Reorgn. State Govt., 1978-79. Mem. Ill. Press Assn., Pub. Relations Soc. Am., Internat. Assn. Bus. Communicators, Scott County Hist. Soc., Springfield Jaycees, Sangamon State Alumni Assn. Democrat. Lutheran. Co-editor: Simplified Financial Management Manual for Illinois Park Districts, 1976. Home: 2206 Makemie St Springfield IL 62704 Office: 325 W Adams 4th Floor Springfield IL 62706

KOCH, ROBERT MARTIN, industrial executive; b. Chgo., Oct. 21, 1930; s. Martin and Pearl (Unison) K.; m. Anita Ernst, Dec. 6, 1952; children—Susan Ellen, Cathy Lynn, Robert Ernst (dec.), Jeffrey John. Student U. Ill.-Chgo., 1948-50; B.A. cum laude, Augustana Coll., 1952. Engr., sales engr., asst. mgr. Sears Roebuck & Co., Moline and Chgo., Ill., 1952-55; engr., gen. foreman, prodn. mgr. Advance Transformer Co., Chgo., 1955-62; ops. and plant mgr. Grand Sheet Metal Products Co. Melrose Park, Ill., 1962-65; v.p., exec. v.p., gen. mgr., pres. Standard Transformer Co., Warren, Ohio, 1965-72; dir. and v.p. ops. Bastian Blessing and Rego divs. Golconda Corp., Grand Haven, Mich. and Chgo., 1972-83; v.p. mfg. Fort Lock Corp., River Grove, Ill., 1983—. Home: 2805 Weller Ln Northbrook IL 60062

KOCH, ROBERT MILTON, research geneticist; b. Sioux City, Iowa, May 15, 1924; s. William F. and Geneva E. (Skinner) K.; m. Virginia Lee Terrett, July 12, 1946; children—William Terrett, James Robert, Richard Lee. B.S., Mont. State U., 1948; M.S., Iowa State U., 1950, Ph.D., 1953. Asst. prof. Animal sci. U. Nebr., Lincoln, 1950-55, assoc. prof., 1955-59, prof., 1959—; chmn. animal sci. dept., 1959-66. Editor: Breeding and Genetics Sect. Jour. Animal Sci., 1985—. Contbr. articles to profl. jours. Served to 1st lt.; U.S. Army, 1943-46, ETO. Elected to Nebr. Hall Agrl. Achievement, 1965; recipient Livestock Service award U. Nebr., 1978, Pioneer Service award Beef Improvement Fedn., 1979. Fellow AAAS, Am. Soc. Animal Sci. (Animal Breeding and Genetics award 1976); mem. Sigma Xi, Alpha Zeta, Gamma Sigma Delta, Phi Kappa Phi. Office US Meat Animal Research Ctr PO Box 166 Clay Center NE 68933

KOCH, ROBERT WARREN, foods manufacturing executive; b. Chgo., Jan. 5, 1927; s. Otto C. and Florence G. (Brown) K.; m. Florence Mary Rooney, 1949 (dec. 1961); children—Robert Warren, Jr., Kathleen P.; m. Anne M. Donnelly, 1963; children—Mark Uhler, Amy D. B.S. in Bus. Adminstrn., Northwestern U., 1949, postgrad., 1950-57. Acct., Busby & Oury, C.P.A.s, Chgo., 1949-50; with Food Materials Corp., Chgo., 1950—, v.p., 1955-56, exec. v.p., 1956-58, pres., 1958-72, 85—, chmn., 1972-84. Vice-pres., Culver Legion Culver Mil. Acad. Served with AC, U.S. Army, 1946-47. Mem. Flavor & Extract Mfrs. Assn. (past pres.), Sigma Nu Alumni Assn. (v.p., sec.-treas. 1975-85). Club: Chgo. Yacht. Home: 2137 N Cleveland Ave Chicago IL 60614 Office: 2711 W Irving Park Rd Chicago IL 60618

KOCH, WILLIAM JOSEPH, advertising and public relations agency executive; b. Celina, Ohio, June 6, 1949; s. George Albert and Helen Marie (McKovich) K.; B.A., U. Akron, 1974; m. Susan Margaret Griffith, June 14,

1969; children—Brian William, Dana Marie. Draftsman, Summit County Engr.'s Office, Akron, Ohio, 1968-72; public info. officer Ohio Dept. Transp., Ravenna, 1972-75; asst. dir. mktg. and public relations Metro Regional Transit Authority, Akron, 1975-78; sr. account exec. Meeker-Mayer Agy., Akron, 1978-83; v.p. Meeker-Mayer Pub. Relations, 1983—; exec. v.p. David A. Meeker & Assocs., Inc./Pub. Relations, 1984—. Trustee All-Am. Soap Box Derby, Inc., 1978—; trustee Weathervane Community Playhouse; trustee Tourette Syndrome Assn. Ohio; trustee Metro Regional Transit Authority. Mem. Public Relations Soc. Am., Advt. Club Akron, Akron Press Club. Democrat. Roman Catholic. Clubs: Jaycees (senator, Disting. Service award 1983). Home: 1369 Hilton Dr Akron OH 44313 Office: One Cascade Plaza 19th Floor Akron OH 44308

KOCHANCZYK, BRONISLAW JOZEF, safety engineer; b. Skole, Poland, Dec. 15, 1918; came to U.S., 1951, naturalized, 1956; s. Michal J. and Barbara M. (Bielak) K.; m. Yvonne Marie Valentin, Aug. 16, 1950; children—Elizabeth, Barbara. Ed. tech. pre-coll., Polish Mil. Acad. Officers Sch., 1936-39. Formerly with Willis Overland Tool & Die, Toledo, Dura Corp. Leader-Tool & Die, Toledo, exptl. engr. fishing div. Sheakspear Sports, Kalamazoo; safety engr. Parker-Hannifin Co., Otsego, Mich., 1972—. Active Allegan County (Mich.) Civil Def., ARC, Am. Heart Assn., Sheriff's Dept.; trustee Pipp Hosp. Served to lt. Polish army in exile, World War II. Decorated Krzyz Zaslugi (2), Krzyz Walecznych (2) Mem. Am. Soc. Safety Engrs., Nat. Safety Mgmt. Soc., Kalamazoo Area Safety Engrs. Assn., Western Mich. Indsl. Hygienists Assn., Kalamazoo Area Safety Council, Occupational Hearing Technician, Roman Catholic. Clubs: Lions, Polish Am. Congress, Elks. Office: Parker Hannifin Co 300 Parker Dr Otsego MI 49078

KOCHAR, MAHENDR SINGH, physician, educator, administrator, researcher, writer; b. Jabalpur, India, Nov. 30, 1943; came to U.S., 1967, naturalized, 1978; s. Harnam Singh and Chanan Kaur (Khaturia) K.; M.B., B.S., All India Inst. Med. Scis., New Delhi, 1965; M.Sc., Med. Coll. Wis., 1972; m. Arvind Kaur, 1968; children—Baltej, Ajay. Intern, All India Inst. Med. Scis. Hosp., New Delhi, 1966, Passaic (N.J.) Gen. Hosp., 1967-68; resident in medicine Allegheny Gen. Hosp., Pitts., 1968-70; fellow in clin. pharmacology Milw. VA Med. Center, 1970-71, attending physician, 1973; fellow in nephrology and hypertension Milwaukee County Gen. Hosp., 1971-73, attending physician, 1973—; attending physician St. Mary's Hosp., 1973-76; attending physician St. Michael Hosp., Milw., 1974—, dir. hemodialysis unit, 1975-80; clin. asst. prof. medicine and pharmacology and toxicology Med. Coll. Wis., Milw., 1973-75, asst. prof., 1975-78, assoc. prof., 1978-84, prof. 1984—; attending physician St. Joseph's Hosp., Milw., 1975—; cons. nephrology Elmbrook Meml. Hosp., Brookfield, Wis., 1976—; chmn. medicine Northpoint Med. Group, Milw., 1974-75; chief Hypertension Clinic, St. Mary's Hosp., Milw., 1974-75; dir. Milw. Blood Pressure Program, 1975-78; dir. Hypertension Clinic, Milwaukee County Downtown Med. and Health Services, 1975-79; chief hypertension sect. VA Med. Center, Milw., 1978—, asso. chief staff for edn., 1979—. Diplomate Am. Bd. Internal Medicine and Nephrology, Am. Bd. Family Practice. Fellow A.C.P. Cardiology, Am. Acad. Family Physicians, Royal Coll. Physicians Can., Am. Coll. Clin. Pharmacology; mem. Am. Acad. Med. Dirs., AMA, Royal Coll. Physicians (London), Internat. Soc. Nephrology, AAAS, Am. Fedn. Clin. Research, Am. Heart Assn., Am. Soc. Nephrology, Am. Soc. Internal Medicine, Am. Med. Writers Assn., Am. Diabetic Assn., council Biology Editors, Milw. Acad. Medicine, Mensa. Author: Hypertension Control, 1978, 2nd rev. edit., 1985. Editor: Textbook of General Medicine, 1983. Home: 18630 LeChateau Dr Brookfield WI 53005 Office: Clement Zablocki VA Medical Center 5000 W National Ave (14-A) Milwaukee WI 53193

KOCHELL, RICHARD LEE, obstetrician and gynecologist; b. Williamaport Ind., Sept. 27, 1937; s. Glen Cletus and Wilma Jean (Hare) K.; m. Carol Marsue Starkey, Aug. 16, 1959 (div. Sept. 1981); children—Krista Carol, Melissa Carol, Jay Richard-Bryan. Student Purdue U., 1955-58; M.D., Ind. U., 1962. Diplomate Am. Bd. Ob-Gyn. Intern, then resident Ind. U., Bloomington, 1962-66; obstetrician Arnet Clinic, Lafayette, Ind., 1966-67, Janesville Woman's Clinic, Wis., 1967-75, Janesville Med. Ctr. Ltd., 1975—. Contbr. articles to profl. jours. Sec., treas. Mercy Hosp. Med. Staff, Janesville, 1968-69; pres. Rock County Surg. Soc., Janesville Wis., 1978—. Served to capt. USAR, 1965-67. Fellow Am. Coll. Ob-Gyn; mem. AMA, Am. Soc. Fertility and Sterility. Republican. Methodist. Office: Janesville Med Ctr Ltd 2020 E Milwaukee St Janesville WI 53545

KOCHER, RICHARD B., pharmaceutical company executive. Pres., dir. Miles Labs, Inc., Elkhart, Ind. Office: Miles Labs Inc 1127 Myrtle St Elkhart IN 46515*

KOCHMAN, THOMAS, communications educator, consultant; b. Berlin, Germany, May 19, 1936; came to U.S., 1937, naturalized, 1944; s. Max and Ellen (Samson) K.; children—Adrienne, Svitlana. B.A., CCNY, 1958; M.A., NYU, 1962, Ph.D., 1966. English tchr. Wagner Jr. High Sch., N.Y.C., 1961-66; asst. prof. linguistics Northeastern Ill. U., Chgo., 1966-70; assoc. prof. communication U. Ill., Chgo., 1970-74, prof. communication, 1974—. Author: Black and White Styles in Conflict, 1981. Editor: Rappin and Stylin Out; Communication in Urban Black America, 1972. Fellow Am. Anthrop. Assn., Soc. for Applied Anthropology; mem. MLA. Avocations: chess, tennis. Home: 5453 N Virginia Chicago IL 60625 Office: Dept Communication Box 4348 Chicago IL 60680

KOCORAS, CHARLES PETROS, Federal judge; b. Chgo., Mar. 12, 1938; s. Petros K. and Constantina (Cordonis) K.; student Wilson Jr. Coll., 1956-58; B.S., Coll. of Commerce, DePaul U., 1961, J.D., Coll. Law, 1969; m. Grace L. Finlay, Sept. 22, 1968; children—Peter, John, Paul. Admitted to Ill. bar, 1969; asst. atty. office U.S. Atty., U.S. Dept. Justice, No. Dist. Ill., 1971-77, U.S. dist. judge, U.S. Dist. Ct., Chgo., 1980—; chmn. Ill. Commerce Commn., Chgo., 1977-79; partner firm Stone, McGuire, Benjamin and Kocoras, Chgo., 1979-80; instr. trial practice, evening div. John Marshall Law Sch., 1975—. Served with Army N.G., 1961-67. Mem. Fed. Criminal Jury Instruction Com. Seventh Circuit. Greek Orthodox. Office: US Dist Court 219 S Dearborn St Chicago IL 60604

KODNER, LESLEY, flooring contracting company executive; b. Chgo., Oct. 20, 1917; s. Louis and Ollie Kodner; m. Denise Friedman, June 17, 1945; children—David, Peter. Student Northwestern U., 1943-45. Lic. judge Am. Kennel Club. Reporter, Chgo. Herald Am., Chgo., 1940-43, Chgo. Sun Times, 1943-45; from salesman to pres. Morton Floors, Inc., Lincolnwood, Ill., 1946-75, chmn. 1982—. Served to sgt. U.S. Army, 1941-43. Mem. Profl. Flooring Installers (past pres.), Chgo. Chpt. of Am. Subcontractors Assn. (past v.p.). Clubs: Metropolitan (Chgo.), Mchts. and Mfrs. Lodges: Masons, Shriners. Office: Morton Floors Inc 6525 N Proesel St Lincolnwood IL 60645

KODOSKY, THOMAS MICHAEL, financial executive; b. Lilly, Pa., May 20, 1942; s. Michael and Rose (Sopchak) Drengacz; m. Catherine Marie Reizer, May 30, 1964; children—David, Stephen, Cynthia, Christopher. B.B.A., Loyola U., 1966; M.B.A., U. Chgo., 1975. C.P.A., Ill. Mem. audit staff Arthur Young & Co., Chgo., 1964-71; asst. v.p. F.H. Prince & Co., Inc., Chgo., 1971-82; corp. controller Elkay Mfg. Co., Oakbrook, Ill., 1982—. Mem. Am. Inst. C.P.A.s, Ill. Soc. C.P.A.s. Roman Catholic. Office: Elkay Mfg Co 2222 Camden Ct Oakbrook IL 60521

KOEHLER, KENNETH JOSEPH, statistics educator, consultant; b. Waukesha, Wis., July 25, 1950; s. Francis I. and Alice C. (Bishel) K.; m. Susan Overend, June 10, 1978; children—Kristine, John. B.S., U. Wis.-Parkside, Kenosha, 1972; Ph.D., U. Minn. 1977. Asst. prof. stats. Iowa State U., Ames, 1977—; statis. cons. govt. and industry, Ames, 1977—. Contbr. articles to profl. jours. Mem. Am. Statis. Assn. (gov. 1983-85), Royal Statis. Soc., Biometric Soc., AAAS, Inst. Math. Stats. Roman Catholic. Office: Iowa State U 121 Snedecor Hall Ames IA 50011

KOENE, WAYNE GEORGE, agricultural educator, radio broadcasting executive; b. Kiel, Wis., Sept. 22, 1937; s. George Henry and Norma Louise (Laux) K.; m. Mary Ann Hanseter, July 17, 1965 (div. June 1982); children—Noreen, M., David J.; m. Helen May Kratz Bloch, Oct. 19, 1984. B.S., U. Wis.-Madison, 1960, M.S., 1963. Cert. agrl. edn., vocat. edn., ednl. adminstrn., cheese-making, Wis. Vocat. agr. instr. Glenwood City High Sch., 1961-66; farm editor Sta. WBAY-TV, Green Bay, Wis., 1966-67, food sci. instr. Moraine Park Tech. Inst., Fond du Lac, Wis., 1967-69, div. chmn., 1969—; farm dir. Sta. KFIZ, Fond du Lac, 1978—; adj. faculty U. Wis.-Stout, Menomonie, 1973-79; adv. bd. AVI Pub. Co., Westport, Conn., 1967-74. Contbr. articles on agr. to profl. jours. Pres. Fond du Lac County Agrl. agencies, pres. Kiel Future Farmers Alumni Assn., 1978-79; bd. dirs. Fond du Lac Area Agribus. Council, 1980-84. Served to maj. USAR, 1960-81. Recipient Tchr. of Tchrs. bronze and silver awards Nat. Vocat. Agr. Instrs. Assn., 1970, 75, State Winner Sound Off for Agr. award Nat. Vocat. Agr. Instrs. Assn., 1978, 79. Mem. Wis. Assn. of Vocat. Agr. Instrs. (pub. relations chmn. 1961-76, 30-Minute Club award 1963, 64, 69, 71, 74), Am. Vocat. Assn., Wis. Vocat. Assn., Wis. Agr. Coordinators Assn. (pres. 1977-78), Nat. Assn. Farm Broadcasters, Nat. Environ. Tng. Assn., U. Wis. Alumni Assn. Lodges: Kiwanis (pres. 1977-78, Disting. Service award). Avocations: reading non-fiction books; photography; travel; collecting records and books. Home: 40 S Pioneer Pkwy Fond du Lac WI 54935 Office: Moraine Park Tech Inst 235 N Nat Ave Fond du Lac WI 54935

KOENIG, ERNEST JOSEPH, sales executive; b. Cleve., Apr. 23, 1924; s. Anthony and Anna (Kraker) Hutter K.; m. Rita Mary Louis Silvester, Oct. 6, 1956; children—Ronald, MaryLou, Robert. Student Fenn Coll., 1945-48. Salesman Holden Engring. Co., Cleve., 1954-58; salesman W.G. Hayden Co., Cleve., 1958-61; asst. sales mgr. Hydyn Inc., Cleve., 1961-63; sales mgr. Stratton Equip. Co., Solon, Ohio, 1963-65; sales rep., Walker Butler Co., Brecksville, Ohio, 1965-82; owner, sales rep. Co-Flo Systems, Inc., Wickliffe, Ohio, 1982—. Organizer, pres. Wickliffe Civic Ctr., 1980—; candidate chmn. Wickliffe Council Pres., 1979—; organizer, chmn. Wickliffe Town Meeting, 1975; bd. dirs. pres. Lake Geauga Catholic Youth Orgn., Mentor, Ohio, 1977-83; bd. dirs. Catholic Charities of Cleve., 1983—; mem. Wickliffe United Way Services, 1983—. Served with U.S. Army, 1943. Named Man of Yr. Holy Name Soc., Wickliffe, 1971; Man of Yr., Wickliffe Jaycees, 1981. Mem. Mfrs. Agts. Nat. Assn., Instrument Soc. Am., Wickliffe C. of C. (v.p.). Republican. Roman Catholic. Clubs: Denim Dancers (Cleve. pres. 1951-59), Cayomaw (Cleve. chmn. 1945-48). Lodge: First Austrian Mut. Aid Soc. (v.p. 1968-72). Office: CO-FLO Systems Inc PO Box 341 Wickliffe OH 44092

KOENIG, KARL WILLIAM, computer services executive; b. Milw., Sept. 1, 1954; s. William C. and Irene (Marten) K.; m. Roberta Ruth Schwartz, Jan. 4, 1980. B.A., U. Wis., Madison, 1979. Sales rep., account exec. Constrn. Computer Control Corp., Madison, 1976-79, account exec. vendor contracts, 1979-81, v.p. systems and programming, 1981-82, v.p. client services, systems and programming, 1982-83, exec. v.p., 1983—. Mem. Assn. Gen. Contractors (mem. computer task force 1981-83, computer com. 1985—), Assn. Data Processing Service Orgns. (sales seminar leader 1980), Council of Ind. Mgrs., Ind. Bus. Mgrs. Assn. of Wis. Clubs: Milw. Athletic, Milw. Yacht. Avocations: sailboat racing; skiing. Office: System 5/Construction Computer Control Corp 615 E Michigan St Milwaukee WI 53202

KOENINGS, CHARLES PETER, social worker; b. West Bend, Wis., Oct. 16, 1953; s. Christ Peter and Elizabeth Agatha (Bahr) K.; m. Judith Griesbach, Sept. 8, 1984. B.S., U. Wis., Milw., 1975, M.S.W., 1977. Cert. sch. social worker. Day camp counselor Neighborhood House Milw., summer 1975; sch. social worker Coop. Ednl. Service Agy. 9, Green Bay, Wis., 1977-82; social worker Big Bros./Big Sisters Met. Milw., Inc., 1982-85, Oconomowoc Devel. Tng. Ctr., 1985—; coach basketball and soccer teams. Home: W 169 N 8757 Sheridan Dr Menomonee Falls WI 53051 Office: 36100 Genesee Lake Rd Oconomowoc WI 53066

KOEPKE, DONALD HERBERT, packaging company executive; b. Milw., Sept. 19, 1923; s. Herbert Hugo and Lillie (Kirchen) K.; B.A. in Bus., Valparaiso U., 1949; B.S. in Mech. Engring., Purdue U., 1951; m. Mary Ruth Brudi, June 16, 1951; children—Debora, Andrew, Thomas. Vice pres. dealer relations Valeer Industries, Inc., Mundelein, Ill., 1974-76; dir. engring. Respiratory Care, Inc., Arlington Heights, Ill., 1976-80; pres. Sorbets, Inc., Hampshire, Ill., 1980-83; pres. Liquorland Enterprises, Inc., Elgin, Ill., 1962-84, also dir.; chief engr. Rinn, Inc., Elgin, 1984—. Served with U.S. Army, 1943-46. Cert. mfg. engr. Mem. Soc. Automotive Engrs., Soc. Mfg. Engrs., Soc. Am. Value Engrs. Republican. Lutheran. Clubs: Elgin Country, Anvil, Lions. Contbr. articles to profl. jours.; patentee in field. Home: 532 N Melrose Ave Elgin IL 60120 Office: 1212 Abbott Dr Elgin IL 60120

KOETTING, ROBERT A., optometrist; b. St. Louis, Nov. 1, 1925. Student St. Louis U., 1943; O.D., So. Coll. Optometry, 1947. Sole practice optometry, practice limited to contact lenses, St. Louis, 1962—; asst. adj. prof. Ill. Coll. Optometry, 1983—, U. Mo., St. Louis, 1985—; assoc. prof., adj. clin. faculty So. Coll. Optometry, 1981-82; lectr. in field. Contbr. articles to profl. jours. Patentee in field. Mem. editorial staff Contact Lens Forum, Contacto, Optometric Mgmt. Adv. Bd., St. Louis Area Council on Aging, 1982-84. Named Optometrist of Yr., Mo. Optometric Assn., 1978; recipient Grand Honors, Nat. Eye Research Found., 1980, Boys Town of Mo. Service award, 1983. Fellow Southwest Contact Lens Soc.; mem. Am. Acad. Optometry, Am. Optometric Assn. (pres.-elect), Am. Soc. Contact Lens Specialists (sec.), Better Vision Inst. (bd. dirs.), Heart of Am. Contact Lens. Soc. (pres. 1967-68, Optometrist of Yr. 1967), Internat. Soc. Contact Lens Research (council), Nat. Eye Research Found. (bd. dirs.), St. Louis Optometric Soc. (pres. 1983-84), Sociedad Americana Ofthalmologia y Optometria, Internat. Soc. Contact Lens Specialists, Nat. Acad. Practice, Beta Sigma Kappa. Lodges: Rotary, Toastmasters. Home: 1034 S Brentwood Saint Louis MO 63117

KOGAN, BERNARD ROBERT, English language educator, author; b. Chgo., May 16, 1920; s. Isaac and Ida (Perlman) K.; m. Irene Wishnewsky, Aug. 19, 1962; children—Henry, Sophia, Naomi, Sara. B.A., U. Chgo., 1941, M.A., 1946, Ph.D., 1953. Instr. English, Ind. U., Bloomington, 1946-48; instr. humanities U. Chgo., 1949-51; from asst. prof. to prof. English, U. Ill.-Chgo., 1952—. Author: The Chicago Haymarket Riot: Anarchy on Trial, 1959; Darwin and His Critics, 1960. Contbr. articles to prof. jours. Served with USNR, 1941-45. Mem. AAUP (pres. local chpt. 1984—), MLA, Phi Beta Kappa (pres. U. Ill.-Chgo. chpt. 1977-79, Chgo. area pres. 1984—). Democrat. Jewish. Avocations: amateur letter-press printing; recorder playing; tennis; bicycling. Home: 612 Lake Ave Wilmette IL 60091 Office: Dept English U Ill-Chgo Box 4348 Chicago IL 60680

KOGLIN, NORMAN ALFRED, architect; b. Chgo., May 5, 1928; s. Alfred Ernst and Elizabeth Maria (Faselt) K.; m. Bernice E. Morrell, May 22, 1982; children—Eric Norman, Andrew Mc Clean, Lisa, Susan Jane. B.S. in Architecture, U. Ill., 1951. Architect Skidmore, Owings & Merrill, architects, Chgo., 1957-61; partner Tigerman & Koglin, architects, Chgo., 1961-64; asso. partner C.F. Murphy & Assos., architects, Chgo., 1965-67; pres. Norman A. Koglin Assos., Ltd., Chgo., 1967—; Served with C.E. U.S. Army, 1951-53. Mem. AIA. Clubs: Economic, Monroe, Mid-Day, Sports Car of Am. (Chgo.). Office: 111 W Monroe St Chicago IL 60603

KOHLAN, WILLIAM GEORGE, lawyer; b. Mpls., Feb. 13, 1910; s. George and Anastasia (Leschisin) K.; LL.B., Mpls. Coll. Law (William Mitchell Coll. Law), 1932; m. Helen Marie Peterson, Nov. 25, 1947. Admitted to Minn. bar, 1932; practice in Mpls., counsel and dir. misc. groups. Mem. Hennepin County Central com. Democratic Farmer Labor party, 1948-67; ward chmn. and ward vice chmn., 1954-59, del. Dem. Farmer Labor convs., 1948-78. Served in USAF, World War II. Recipient medal of Merit, Air Force Assn., 1957; Distinguished Service award Minn. State Bar Assn., 1959, City of Mpls., 1975. Mem. Minn., Hennepin County bar assns., Air Force Assn. (charter life mem.; past nat. v.p.), Air Force Hist. Found., DAV (past judge adv. Minn. dept., past vice comdr. Mpls. chpt.), Mpls. Joint Vets. Council (past pres.). Home: 1610 5th St NE Minneapolis MN 55413 Office: Gorham Bldg Minneapolis MN 55402

KOHLENBERG, EILEEN MIERAS, nurse educator, administrator; b. Sioux City, Iowa, Apr. 10, 1954; d. Howard Charles and Esther Rosella (Van Roekel) Mieras; m. Randy Bryan Kohlenberg, Mar. 17, 1979. B.S. in Psychology, B.S. in Nursing, Morningside Coll., 1977; M.S. in Nursing, U. Tex., Austin, 1982; postgrad., 1984—. Registered nurse, Iowa, Nebr. Registered nurse Marian Health Ctr., Sioux City, 1977-79; instr. nursing Morningside Coll., Sioux City, 1979-83, chmn. nursing edn., 1983—, dir. workshops in microcomputers, testing and phys. assessment of geron., 1984-85, coordinator Sci. and Tech. Forum, 1983. Organist, pianist Sioux City Symphony, 1983—. Mem. Iowa Nurses' Assn. (sec., dir. 1980—), Iowa League Nursing (mem. com. 1983—), AAUW (treas., by-laws chmn. local chpt.), Briar Cliff Honor Soc. (community nurse leader 1984—). Episcopalian. Clubs: Morningside (pres. 1983-84), Women's. Avocations: Organist, seamstress. Home: 2536 S Paxton St Sioux City IA 51106 Office: Morningside College Dept of Nursing Edn Sioux City IA 51106

KOHN, FRANK SOLIS, pharmaceutical company executive, microbiologist, consultant; b. Bristol, Pa., June 21, 1942; s. Frank S. and Julia (Hutchinson) K.; m. Marge Mussig, Sept. 26, 1984; children—Frank A., David G. Diploma in med. tech. cum laude, Franklin Sch. Sci., 1961; Assoc. Sci., Trenton Jr. Coll., 1963; B.A., N.J. State Coll., 1969; M.S., Drexel U., 1972; P.D., U. Wis.-Madison, 1978. Pres., Bristol San. Corp., Pa., 1960-63; research scientist N.J. Dept. Health, Trenton, 1963-69; dir. ops. Schering-Plough-Inc., Madison, Wis., 1969-78; dir. malts mgmt. Schering-Plough Inc., Union, N.J., 1978-80; dir. mfg. Revon Corp., Kankakee, Ill., 1980-82, Am. Home Products, Fort Dodge, Iowa, 1982—; instr. mgmt. Iowa Central Commn. Coll., Fort Dodge, 1983—; cons. Media Tape Corp., Phila., 1975-80. Bd. dirs. Ft. Dodge Mus. Recipient H. Burrows award in clin. chemistry. Mem. Am. Soc. Microbiology, Am. Soc. Indsl. Engrs., Parenteral Drug Assn., Supr. and Mgmt. Program (adv. 1983—), Nat. Registry Microbiologists (specialist microbiologist), Am. Soc. Med. Tech. (registered med. tech.) Clubs: Sertoma Noon (Ft. Dodge, Iowa) (v.p., pres. 1984—) Elks. Avocations: stained glass; running; antique toys. Home: N 332 Twin Lakes St RR1 Manson IA 50563 Office: Am Home Products PO Box 508 Fort Dodge IA 50501

KOHN, JULIEANNE, travel agent; b. Detroit, Apr. 15, 1946; d. Ralph Merwin and Jane Tacke (Meyers) K.; B.A., Heidelberg Coll., Tiffin, Ohio, 1968; postgrad. Eastern Mich. U., 1969-70; diploma Inst. Cert. Travel Agts., 1979. Travel agt. Am. Express Co., Detroit, 1970-73, Thomas Cook Inc., Detroit, 1973-75; mgr. Island Traveller, Grosse Ile, Mich., 1975-76; pres., owner Flying Suitcase, Inc., Grosse Ile, 1976—; ptnr. Tri-Kohn Investments, Grosse Ile, Mich., 1983—. Mem. Am. Soc. Travel Agts., Episcopalian. Club: Grosse Ile Golf and Country. Home: 27081 E River Rd Grosse Ile MI 48138 Office: 8117 Macomb St Grosse Ile MI 48138

KOHN, MARY LOUISE BEATRICE, nurse; b. Yellow Springs, Ohio, Jan. 13, 1920; d. Theophilus John and Mary Katharine (Schmitkons) Gaehr; A.B., Coll. Wooster, 1940; M.Nursing, Case Western Res. U., 1943; m. Howard D. Kohn, 1944; 1 dau., Marcia R. Nurse, Univ. Hosps., Cleve., 1943-44, Atlantic City Hosp., 1944, Thomas M. England Gen. Hosp., U.S. Army, Atlantic City, 1945-46, Peter Bent Brigham Hosp., Boston, 1947, Univ. Hosps., Cleve., 1946-48; mem. faculty Frances Payne Bolton Sch. Nursing Case Western Res. U., 1948-52; vol. nurse Blood Service, ARC, 1952-55; office nurse, Cleve., part time 1955—; free-lance writer. Bd. dirs. Aux. Acad. Medicine Cleve., 1970-72, officer, 1976—; mem. Cleve. Health Mus. Aux.; mem. women's com. Cleve. Orch., 1970; women's council WVIZ-TV. Mem. Am., Ohio nurses assns., alumni assns. Wooster Coll., Frances P. Bolton Sch. Nursing (pres. 1974-75), Assn. Operating Rm. Nurses, Antique Automobile Assn. Am., Western Res. Hist. Soc., Am. Heart Assn., Cleve. Playhouse Aux., U.S. Humane Soc., Friends of Cleve. Ballet, Smithsonian Instn., Council World Affairs, Orange Community Arts Council. Clubs: Cleve. Racquet, Women's City, Women's of Case-Western Res. U. Sch. Medicine. Author: (with Atkinson) Berry and Kohn's Introduction to Operating Room Technique, 5th edit., 1978, 6th edit., 1986. Asst. editor Cleve. Physician, Acad. Medicine Cleve., 1966-71. Home: 28099 Belcourt Rd Cleveland OH 44124

KOHN, NORMAN VITA, neurologist; b. Cleve., Sept. 26, 1951; s. Howard M. and Orietta (Vita) K.; m. Lisa Salkovitz, Mar. 11, 1979; children—Isaac V., Russell J. S.B., MIT, 1972; M.D., Yale U., 1976. Diplomate Am. Bd. Psychiatry and Neurology. Resident in medicine Case Western Res. U., Cleve., 1976-77; resident in neurology U. Chgo., 1977-80, neuroimmunology fellow, 1980-82; practice medicine specializing in neurology, Chgo., 1982—; mem. staff Mt. Sinai Hosp., 1980—; chmn. neurology dept., 1984—. Mem. Am. Acad. Neurology, Am. Assn. Electromyography and Electrodiagnosis. Office: Mt Sinai Hosp California Ave at Ogden Chicago IL 60608

KOHOUTEK, FRANK LEO, JR., educator, athletic coach; b. LaMoure, N.D., May 31, 1931; s. Frank Leo and Margaret Mabel (Sandeen) K.; m. Joan Peggy Case, Aug. 9, 1953; children—Linda, Frank Leo, Kathleen, Karen. B.S., Jamestown Coll. (N.D.), 1954; M.Ed., U. N.D., 1964. Cert. tchr., N.D., Minn.; cert. coach, Minn. Tchr., coach Drayton High Sch. (N.D.), 1956-60, Newfolden High Sch. (Minn.), 1960-65, Sebeka High Sch. (Minn.), 1965-70, Wadena High Sch. (Minn.), 1970—. Mem. Minn. State Softball Adv. Council, 1980-83; Coach Minn. State Champion Softball Team, 1979, Minn. State Tournament Softball Team, 1980, 81. Served with U.S. Army, 1954-56. Mem. U.S.-China Peoples Friendship Assn., NEA, Minn. Edn. Assn., Minn. State Softball Coaches (pres. 1982), Minn. State High Sch. Coaches, Assn. for Girls Sports, Inc., Nat. Wood Carvers Assn. Methodist. Lodge: Masons, Lions (pres. 1965). Home: 121 Colfax Ave SW Wadena MN 56482

KOKORON, NICKOLAS STEVEN, accountant; b. Chgo., Apr. 4, 1947; s. Nickolas Vincent and Eva (Bleizeffer) K.; m. Barbara Darlene Zadny, July 14, 1978; children—Heather, Nickolas J., Bradley J. B.S., Ill. Inst. Tech., 1970. Auditor, Price Waterhouse & Co., Chgo., 1970-72; controller Pansophic Systems Inc., Oak Brook, Ill., 1972-74; ptnr. Kokorn, Monco & Co., Arlington Heights, Ill., 1974—; dir. Finenco Inc., Arlington Heights, Vogel Tool & Die Co., Stone Park, Ill. Commr. River Trails Park Dist. Mem. Am. Inst. C.P.A.s, Ill. Soc. C.P.A.s. Club: Rolling Meadows Social (officer 1979-84). Lodge: Masons. Home: 1112 Dogwood Ln Mount Prospect IL 60056 Office: Kokoron Monco & Co 1845 E Rand Rd Arlington Heights IL 60004

KOLA, ARTHUR ANTHONY, lawyer; b. New Brunswick, N.J., Feb. 16, 1939; s. Arthur Aloyisius and Blanche (Raym) K.; m. Jacquelin Lou Draper, Sept. 3, 1960 (div. 1976); 1 child, Jill Ann; m. Anna Molnar, Apr. 15, 1977; children—Jean Rebecca, Jennifer Anna. A.B., Dartmouth Coll., 1961; LL.B., Duke U., 1964. Bar: Ohio 1964. Assoc. Squire, Sanders & Dempsey, Cleve., 1964-65, 68-74; asst. prof. law Ind. U., Bloomington, 1967-68; ptnr. Squire, Sanders & Dempsey, Cleve., 1974—; bd. visitors Duke U. Sch. Law; mem. nat. council Duke Law Sch. Fund, 1981—. Served to capt. U.S. Army, 1965-66. Mem. ABA, Ohio Bar Assn., Greater Cleve. Bar Assn., Phi Beta Kappa. Club: Cleve. Athletic. Avocations: bicycling; skiing. Office: 1800 Huntington Bldg Cleveland OH 44115

KOLAR, JIRI FRANTISEK, aeronautical engineer; b. Prague, Czechoslovakia, Jan. 29, 1940; came to U.S., 1970, naturalized, 1977; s. Roman and Zdena (Kunstova) K.; m. Jaroslava Sladkova, 1962 (div. 1969); 1 dau., Michaela; m. Marie Stoupova, June 19, 1977; 1 son, Jan Jiri. Masters degree, M.E., Mil. Tech. U., 1969. Project engr. Williams Internat., Walled Lake, Mich., 1978—. Republican. Roman Catholic.

KOLB, JOHN CARL, family therapist, clergyman; b. Bay City, Mich., Apr. 6, 1943; s. Carl Henry Edwin and Renate Marie (Krieger) K.; m. Malinda Marie Hartman, June 5, 1966; children—Rebecca Marie, Debra Renee, Charles Walter. B.A., Concordia Sr. Coll., 1964; M.Div., Concordia Sem., St. Louis, 1968; M.S.T., Christian Theol. Sem., Indpls., 1972; student McCormick Theol. Sem., 1975-76. Ordained to ministry, Lutheran Ch., 1968; pastor Emanuel Luth. Ch., Arcadia, Ind., 1968-72; pres. Hamilton County (Ind.) Mental Health Assn., 1971-72; pastoral resident Luth. Gen. Hosp., Park Ridge, Ill., 1972-73; mental health therapist Northwestern Meml. Hosp. and Northwestern Inst. Psychiatry, Chgo., 1973-76; pastoral care fellow, chaplain Evanston (Ill.) Hosp., 1974-75, social worker, group therapist, asst. team leader Refocus Program, 1976-78; family therapist Luth. Child and Family Services, Indpls., 1978—; pastor Hosanna Luth. Ch., Oaklandon, Ind., 1980—; vis. prof. Concordia Theol. Sem., Ft. Wayne, 1984—; counselor Indpls. Area Luth. Laymen's League; mem. chaplaincy com. Fedn. Indpls. Luth. Chs. Pres., Trinity Luth. Parent Tchr. League, 1982-84; mem. spl. services com. Fedn. Indpls. Luth. Chs., 1982-84. Garret Theol. Sem. fellow, 1974-75. Mem. Am. Assn. Pastoral Counselors (pastoral affiliate). Contbr. articles to religious publs. Home: 2613 Sheffield Dr Indianapolis IN 46229 Office: 1525 N Ritter St Indianapolis IN 46219

KOLB, MARY LORRAINE, banker; b. La Crosse, Wis., Jan. 26, 1947; d. Thomas and Lorriane Marie (Schaffer) Sagear; m. Jerry Robert Kolb, May 29, 1971; children—James Thomas, Kelly Robert. Grad. high sch., Holmen, Wis. Loan and compliance officer Bank of Holmen, 1968—. Leader, Long Coulee 4-H Club, Holmen, 1983—; mem. ARC Disaster Action, La Crosse, 1983—. Mem. Nat. Assn. Bank Women, Bus. and Profl. Women. Avocations: family camping; raising quarter horses. Home: N7795 Amsterdam Prairie Rd Holmen WI 54636 Office: Bank of Holmen 1248 Main St Holmen WI 54636

KOLB, ROBERT ALLAN, religious educator; b. Fort Dodge, Iowa, June 17, 1941; s. Ralph Orrin and Eva Ann (Holm) K.; m. Pauline Joanne Ansorge, Aug. 14, 1965. B.A., Concordia Coll., 1963; M. Divinity, Concordia Sem., 1967; S.T.M., 1968; Ph.D., U. Wis., Madison, 1973. Ordained to ministry Lutheran Ch., 1972. Exec. dir. Ctr. for Reformation Research, St. Louis, Mo., 1972-77; mem. faculty Concordia Coll., St. Paul, Minn., 1977—, assoc. prof., 1981—, chmn. Div. Religion, 1982—. Mem. Commn. Theology and Ch. Relations, Luth. Ch.-Mo. Synod, 1984—. Author: Andreae and the Formula of Concord, 1977; Nikolaus von Amsdorf, 1978; Speaking the Gospel Today, 1984. Assoc. editor: The Sixteenth Century Jour., 1977—. Contbr. numerous articles to various periodicals. Mem. bd. Lexington-Hamline Community Council, St. Paul, 1980—. Mem. 16th Century Studies Conf. (pres. 1980-81), Am. Soc. Ch. History (mem. council 1978-81; mem. membership com. 1984—), Am. Soc. Reformation, Republican. Home: 1292 Marshall Ave St Paul MN 55104 Office: Concordia Coll Hamline and Marshall Ave St Paul MN 55104

KOLDA, THOMAS JOSEPH, college executive; b. Chgo., Dec. 1, 1939; s. Amos Joseph and Cecilia Marie (Baxa) K.; B.A., Coe Coll., 1961; postgrad. U. Iowa, Iowa City, 1961; m. Gail Judith Kettler, June 30, 1962; children—Brian Joseph, Jeffrey Thomas. Dir devel./pub. relations Mt. Mercy Coll., Cedar Rapids, Iowa, 1965-69; v.p. devel. St. Mary's Coll., Orchard Lake, Mich., 1969-71; dir. devel. Roman Catholic Diocese, Tucson, 1971-74; dir. devel.-/community relations St. Mary's Hosp., Milw., 1974-75; dir. devel./pub. relations The Pontifical Coll. Josephinum, Columbus, Ohio, 1975-77; dir. trusts and estates Ohio State U. Devel. Fund, Columbus, 1977-85; v.p. devel. Coe Coll., Cedar Rapids, Iowa, 1985—. Commr., Perry Twp. (Ohio) Zoning Bd. Cert. fund raising exec. Mem. Nat. Soc. Fund Raising Execs. (past pres. Central Ohio chpt.), Council Advancement and Support Edn., Lambda Chi Alpha. Roman Catholic. Club: Kiwanis (bd. dirs., pres. Worthington-Linworth, Ohio). Home: 2111 Sandalwood Dr NE Cedar Rapids IA 52402 Office: 1220 1st Ave NE Cedar Rapids IA 52402

KOLENBRANDER, HAROLD MARK, college administrator, consultant; b. Sibley, Iowa, Oct. 7, 1938; s. Dirk J. and Nellie (Van Heukelom) K.; m. Laurie L. Bouma, Aug. 28, 1958; children—Kimberly, Kirk, Kerri. B.A., Central Coll., 1960; Ph.D., U. Iowa, 1964. From asst. prof. to prof. chemistry Central Coll., Pella, Iowa, 1964-71, chmn. chemistry dept., 1967-71, provost, dean coll., 1975—; dean acad. planning Grand Valley State Coll., Allendale, Mich., 1971-75; cons. Council Ind. Colls., Washington, 1979—; cons. evaluator N. Central Assn. Colls., Chgo., 1980—, commr.-at-large, 1982—. Contbr. articles to profl. jours. NIH fellow, 1961-64, 69-70. Mem. Am. Assn. Higher Edn., Royal Soc. Chemistry, Biochem. Soc. Club: Rotary (pres. 1980). Avocation: personal computing. Home: 1204 1/2 Franklin Pella IA 50219 Office: Central Coll 812 University Pella IA 50219

KOLESON, DONALD RALPH, college dean, educator; b. Eldon, Mo., June 30, 1935; s. Ralph A. and Fern M. (Beanland) K.; children—Anne, David, Janet. B.S. in Edn., Central Mo. State U., 1959; M.Ed., So. Ill. U., 1973. Mem. faculty So. Ill. U., Carbondale, 1968-73; dean tech. edn. Belleville (Ill.) Area Coll., 1982—. Mem. Am. Vocat. Edn. Assn., Am. Welding Assn., Nat. Assn. Two-Year Schs. of Constrn. (pres. 1984-85). Clubs: Masons; Shriners, Jesters.

KOLF, JAMES, home health care service manager; b. Detroit, July 22, 1948; s. John A. and Mary M. (Whalen) K.; m. Marie Anne Mace, Nov. 25, 1970; children—Heather Anne, Rebecca Lynn, Kelly Marie. B.S., Wayne State U., 1970, postgrad., 1972-73. Cert. tchr., Mich. Tchr. St. Raymond Sch., Detroit, 1970-73; pharm. sales Eaton Labs., Norwich, N.Y., 1973-74; ter. mgr. Baxter Travenol Labs., Deerfield, Ill., 1974-75, field tng., 1976-81; med. edn. coordinator Mt. Carmel Hosp., Detroit, 1975-76; area mgr./antibiotic/TPN specialist Home Health Care Am., Newport Beach, Calif., 1981—. PTO grantee, 1971. Mem. Assn. Hosp. Med. Edn., Sigma Pi (sec. 1967-68). Republican. Roman Catholic.

KOLICK, DANIEL JOSEPH, lawyer; b. Lakewood, Ohio, May 12, 1950; s. Joseph Frank and Agnes Helen (Lusnak) K. B.A., Holy Cross Coll., 1972; J.D., Case Western Res. U., 1975. Bar: Ohio 1975. Sole practice, North Olmsted, Ohio, 1976-85; ptnr. Kolick & Kondzer, Westlake, Ohio, 1985—; asst. law dir. City of Strongsville, Ohio, 1976—; dir. law Village of Lindale, Cleve., 1975-76. Chmn. North Olmsted Charter Rev. Commn., 1981, 83; mem. council St. Richard's Parish Council, North Olmsted, 1980-82, tchr. Sch. Religion, 1979-81. Mem. Cuyahoga County Law Dirs. Assn., Cuyahoga County Bar Assn., Ohio Sch. Bd. Assn., Ohio State Bar Assn., ABA. Roman Catholic. Club: North Olmsted Exchange (trustee, treas. 1977-78). Avocations: softball; racquetball; tennis. Home: 20686 Wildwood Lane Strongsville OH 44136 Office: Kolick & Kondzer 24500 Center Ridge #175 Westlake OH 44145

KOLINEK, ROBERT BRETT, marketing executive; b. Chgo., Sept. 20, 1954; s. Jerry W. and Renee C. K.; B.S. in History, U. Wis., 1975; postgrad. in econ. studies U. Chgo., 1976. With Helen Brett Enterprises, Inc. and R.B.K. Enterprises, Ltd., Chgo., 1976—, exec. v.p., 1980—; pres. Petro-Tech Expos., Ltd., trade show mgmt. co. oil and gas industry, Chgo., 1981—. Mem. Nat. Assn. Exhbn. Mgrs. (chmn. new memberships, treas. 1982, sec. 1983), Internat. Technol. Exchange (bd. dirs.). Winner NAIA Vault Championship, horizontal bar Championship. Ill. champion, 1973. Office: Helen Brett Enterprises Inc 1 Quincy Ct Chicago IL 60304

KOLKS, KIM ELAINE, practical nurse; b. Leesville, La., Dec. 30, 1957; d. Merlin Eloy and Jocelyn Germaine (Leibach) Kreftmeyer; m. David Lee Kolks, Oct. 11, 1980; 1 dau., Erin Leigh. Grad. Washington Sch. Practical Nursing. Lic. practical nurse, Mo. Practical nurse Hermann Area Hosp. (Mo.), 1978—. Candystriper, Candystripers of Hermann Hosp., 1972-76. Recipient cert. of recognition State of Mo., 1976. R. Bozzo scholar, 1978. Mem. Mo. Assn. Lic. Practical Nurses. Republican. Mem. United Ch. of Christ. Home: 335 W 10th St Hermann MO 65041 Office: Hermann Area Hosp W 18th St Hermann MO 65041

KOLL, RICHARD LEROY, chemical company executive; b. Muscatine, Iowa, Mar. 16, 1925; s. Charles C. and Emma (Schafer) K.; m. Patricia Ann Grunder, Jan. 2, 1955; children—Craig, Christine, Cary. B.S. in Mech. Engring., U. Iowa, 1951. Mgr. plant Grain Processing Corp., Muscatine, Iowa, 1971-72, v.p., 1972-77, sr. v.p., 1977—. Served with USMCR, 1944-46. Republican. Lutheran. Club: University Athletic. Lodge: Elks. Home: 1317 Oakland Dr Muscatine IA 52761 Office: 1600 Oregon St Muscatine IA 52761

KOLLAR, JOHN ANTON, III, commodity trader; b. Harvey, Ill., Nov. 7, 1947; s. John Anton and Joan T. (Donnellan) K.; m. Catherine Nellson, May 6, 1972; children—John, Timothy. B.A., U. Denver, 1970. Account exec. Blyth Eastman Dillon, Chgo., 1971-74; asst. mgr. Beef Baron/Skokie Hilton, Skokie, Ill., 1974-75; gen. mgr. Beer & Brat Restaurants, Mount Prospect, Ill., 1975-77; pres., chmn. bd. OOM-PA-PA Restaurants, Inc., Northbrook, Ill., 1977-79; assoc. mem. Chgo. Bd. Trade, 1979—. Served with U.S. Army, 1970-71. Recipient Man of Yr. award Phi Kappa Sigma, 1970. Mem. Chgo. Bd. Trade (vice-chmn. floor conduct com., assoc. members com., mem. pit com. 1983-84). Republican. Roman Catholic. Club: Yacht (Chgo.). Home: 620 Earl Dr Northfield IL 60093 Office: CC&J Inc Suite 2640 141 W Jackson St Chicago IL 60604

KOLLER, DIANE SNYDER, educational administrator, nursing educator; b. Freeport, Ill., May 17, 1936; d. Harold Texas and Violet (Sundstrom) Snyder; m. Robert Walter Koller, Aug. 23, 1959 (div. 1984); children—Lisa Ann, Craig William, Michelle Lynn. B.A. magna cum laude in Psychology, St. Norbert Coll., West De Pere, Wis., 1972; M.S. in Curriculum and Instrn., U. Wis.-Madison, 1976, Ph.D. in Ednl. Adminstrn., 1983. Obstetric nurse Madison Gen. Hosp., 1965; psychiat. nurse St. Vincent Hosp., Green Bay, Wis., 1966; home health nurse Walworth County Pub. Health Dept., Elkhorn, Wis., 1967-68; instr. Bellin Coll. Nursing, Green Bay, 1968-77, dean, dir., 1977—; ad hoc faculty mem. U. Wis.-Green Bay, 1981-82; sec. Wis. League Nursing, 1976-78; ednl. cons. St. Joseph Hosp., Marshfield, Wis., 1984—. Vol. Aging Americans Program, Green Bay, 1968; mem. plan coordinating com. NEW Health Systems Agy., Green Bay, 1975-79; mem. allocations com. United Way, Green Bay, 1981-84. Mem. Am. Hosp. Assn. (hosp. sch. planning com. 1983—, gov. council 1983—), Wis. Assn. Diploma Schs. (chmn. 1983-84), Green Bay Dist. Nurses Assn. (bd. dirs. 1976-77, state del. 1975-77), Am. Nursing Assn. (nat. del. 1980), Phi Delta Kappa. Avocations: sailing; swimming; yoga; flying. Home: 300 Little Rd Green Bay WI 54301 Office: Bellin Coll Nursing Box 1700 Green Bay WI 54301

KOLLER, MARVIN ROBERT, sociology educator, writer; b. Cleve., Feb. 24, 1919; s. Julius George and Margaret Cecilia (Spitz) K.; m. Pauline Esther Steinfeld, Jan. 27, 1945; 1 son, Robert Lee. B.S. in Edn., Kent State U., 1940; M.A. in Sociology, Ohio State U., 1947, Ph.D., 1950. Tchr., Westlake (Ohio) High Sch., 1945-46; asst. instr., sociology, Ohio State U., 1946-49; instr. sociology Kent (Ohio) State U., 1949-50, asst. prof., 1950-58, assoc. prof. 1958-61, prof., 1961—. Served with U.S. Army, 1941-45; PTO. Nat. Faculty fellow in social gerontology, 1959; NSF award in anthropology, 1962, Nat. Endowment for Humanities award, 1980. Mem. Gerontol. Assn., AAUP, Am. Sociol. Assn., North Central Sociol. Assn., Nat. Council Family Relations. Author: Sociology of Childhood, 1964, 2d edit. 1978; Modern Sociology, 1965, 3d edit., 1974; Social Gerontology, 1968; Families, A Multigenerational Approach, 1974; co-Author: (with David King) Foundations of Sociology, 1975. Office: Sociology/Anthropology Kent State U Kent OH 44242

KOLLINS, MICHAEL JEROME, automotive engineer, historian; b. St. Clairsville, Ohio, Mar. 20, 1912; s. Michael Arthur and Mary Ann (Peck) K.; student Coll. City Detroit, 1928-32; m. Julia Dolores Advent, Jan. 16, 1934; children—Michael Lewis, Richard, Laura. Chief sect. service engring. and tech. data Studebaker-Packard Corp., Detroit, 1945-55; mgr. tech. services Chrysler Corp., Detroit, 1955-64, mgr. warranty adminstrn., 1964-68, mgr. Highland Park Service center, 1968-75; pres. Kollins Design & Engring., Detroit, 1975—. Pres., Oakland (Mich.) U. Chorus, 1969-71, Home Owners Assn. of Eastover Farms No. 1, 1981—; trustee Nat. Automotive Hist. Collection, 1982—; bd. dirs. Capuchin Charity Guild, 1983—; active Birmingham (Mich.) Chorale, Meadowbrook (Mich.) Festival Chorus; mem. adv. bd. Am. Security Council, 1972—. Served with USN, 1942-45. Mem. U.S. Auto Club (vice-chmn. tech. com. 1971-82, dir. cert. com. 1983—), Am. Automobile Assn. (contest bd.), Soc. Automotive Engrs., Soc. Automotive Historians, Engring. Soc. Detroit (industry ambassador 1972—). Contbr. articles to profl. publs. Designer racing cars, 1932-39, sports cars, spl. luxury vehicles, 1951—, automotive performance and safety devices, 1946—. Home: 821 Highwood Dr Bloomfield Hills MI 48013 Office: Kollins Design & Engring PO Box 214 Bloomfield Hills MI 48013

KOLLY, DOUGLAS PAUL, lawyer; b. Detroit, Feb. 13, 1951; s. Leonard Edward and Monica Marie (Stephens) K.; m. Carolyn Lisa Louie, June 21, 1974; 1 child, Andrew Lee. B.S., Western Mich. U., 1973; J.D., Detroit Coll. Law, 1978. Bar: Mich. 1978, U.S. Dist. Ct. (ea. dist.) Mich. 1978. Tchr., cons., dept. head Bloomfield Pub. Schs., Bloomfield Hills, Mich., 1974-78; assoc. James O. Flynn, P.C., Pontiac, Mich., 1978-84; sole practice, Birmingham, Mich., 1984—. Mem. Council Exceptional Children (pres. 1972-73), ABA, Mich. Bar Assn., Mich. Trial Lawyers Assn., Assn. Trial Lawyers Am., Delta Kappa Pi. Democrat. Office: 400 W Maple St Suite 300 Birmingham MI 48011

KOLMER, LEE ROY, college dean, educator; b. Waterloo, Ill., Jan. 4, 1928; s. Arthur and Carmelita (Vogt) K.; m. Wilma Jean O'Brien, Apr. 19, 1952; children—Diane, James, John. B.S., So. Ill. U., 1952; M.S., Iowa State U.-Ames, 1952, Ph.D., 1954; student U. Ill.-Urbana, 1945-46. Extension economist Iowa State U.-Ames, 1953, 1956-65, state leader agrl. and econs., 1965, asst. dean, dir. coop. extension, 1967-70, dean, dir. Coll. Agr. and Home Econs. Expt. Sta., 1973—; asst. prof. So. Ill. U., 1954-55; assoc. dean, dir. cooperative extension service Coll. Agr., Oreg. State U.-Corvallis, 1971-73; dir. United Central Bancshares, Des Moines, Midamerica Internat. Agrl. Consortium, Columbia, Mo.; trustee Farm Found., Oak Brook, Ill. Served with AUS, 1946-48. Mem. Am. Agrl. Econs. Assn., AAAS, Gamma Sigma Delta, Phi Kappa Phi, Alpha Zeta. Independent. Roman Catholic. Avocation: Woodworking. Home: 4118 Phoenix St Ames IA 50010 Office: Iowa State U 124 Curtiss Hall Ames IA 50011

KOLODZIEJ, JOAN HELEN, public affairs specialist; b. Detroit, July 29, 1938; d. Joseph and Valeria (Bujak) K.; B.A., Mich. State U., 1960. Women's editor Ford Motor Co., 1964-65; promotion writer Sta. WWJ-TV, Detroit, 1961-68; public service mgr. Detroit Free Press, 1968-71; public info. dir. Mich. Cancer Found., 1971-73; exec. dir. Project HOPE, 1973-74; asst. v.p. Bank of the Commonwealth, Detroit, 1974-77; public affairs specialist Southeastern Mich. Transp. Authority, Detroit, 1977-82; mgr. media relations and customer communications Mich. Wis. Pipe Line Co., 1982—. Mem. public relations adv. com. ARC, Detroit, 1978—. Mem. Internat. Assn. Bus. Communicators, Public Relations Soc. Am., Detroit Press Club, Econ. Club Detroit, Women's Advt. Club Detroit, Detroit Zool. Soc. Roman Catholic. Home: 27602 Parkview Blvd #104 Warren MI 48092 Office: 660 Woodward Detroit MI 48226

KOMINSKY, CYNTHIA CECELIA, optometrist; b. Dearborn, Mich., Sept. 1, 1957; d. Andrew and Angeline (Laorno) K. Student Oakland U., Rochester, Mich., 1976-77; O.D. magna cum laude, Ferris Coll. Optometry, 1981. Lic. optometrist, Mich. Intern, Optometric Inst. and Clinic of Detroit, 1980, Ferris State Coll., Big Rapids, Mich., 1980, Jackson Prison (Mich.), 1981; assoc. in pvt. practice, Warren, Mich., 1981-82; optometrist Pearle Vision Ctr., Sterling Heights, Mich., 1982-85, K Mart Optical Ctr., Sterling Heights, 1982—; provided eye care to nursing homes, Mt. Clemens, Mich. Inventer binocular low vision aid device. Avocations: music; sports, bicycling. Home: 42123 MacRae Dr Sterling Heights MI 48078 Office: K Mart Optical Ctr 2051 18 Mile Rd Sterling Heights MI 48078

KOMMEDAHL, THOR, plant pathology educator; b. Mpls., Apr. 1, 1920; s. Thorbjorn and Martha (Blegen) K.; m. Faye Lillian Jensen, June 4, 1924; children—Kris Alan, Siri Lynn, Lori Anne. B.S., U. Minn., 1945, M.S., 1947, Ph.D., 1951. Instr., U. Minn., St. Paul, 1946-51, asst. prof. plant pathology, 1953-57, assoc. prof., 1957-63, prof., 1963—; asst. prof. Ohio Agrl. Research and Devel. Center, Wooster and Ohio State U., Columbus, 1951-53; cons. botanist and taxonomist Minn. Dept. Agr., 1954-60. Guggenheim fellow, 1961; Fulbright scholar, 1968. Fellow AAAS, Am. Phytopathol. Soc. (councilor 1958-60, pres. 1971, publs. coordinator 1978-84, Disting. Service award); mem. Am. Inst. Biol. Scis., Bot. Soc. Am., Council Biology Editors, Internat. Soc. Plant Pathology (councilor 1971-78, sec.-gen. and treas. 1983-88), Mycol. Soc. Am., Minn. Acad. Sci., N.Y. Acad. Scis., Soc. Scholarly Publs., Weed Sci. Soc. Am. (award of excellence 1968). Baptist. Contbr. articles to profl. jours.; cons. editor McGraw-Hill Ency. Sci. and Tech., 1972-78; editor-in-chief Phytopathology, 1964-67; editor Procs. IX Internat. Congress Plant Protection, 2 vols., 1981; sr. editor: Challenging Problems in Plant Health, 1983. Home: 1840 W Roselawn Ave Falcon Heights MN 55113 Office: 495 Borlang Hall Univ Minn 1991 Buford Circle Saint Paul MN 55108

KOMP, BARBARA ANN, technical writer; b. La Porte, Ind., Nov. 3, 1954; d. Gerald Lee and Betty Mae (Schelin) K. B.A. in Elem. Edn., Ball State U., 1977; student Mech. Engring. Tech., Purdue U., 1984—, Elec. Engring. Tech., 1984—. Quality control insp. Foreman Mfg. Co., Rolling Prairie, Ind., 1978-80; quality control insp. Weil-McLain Co., Michigan City, Ind., 1980-81, jr. quality control engr., 1981-84, tech. writer, 1984—. Adviser Jr. Achievement, Michigan City, 1982-83. Mem. Am. Soc. Quality Control (cert., membership chmn. 1981-83, treas. 1984—). Office: Weil-McLain-A Marley Co Blaine St Michigan City IN 46360

KOMULA, SANFRID EDWIN, airport planner; b. San Diego, May 10, 1949; s. Sanfrid E. and Faye (Ivie) K. B.S., UCLA, 1971, M.S., U. Calif.-Berkeley, 1972. Engr. Bechtel, San Francisco, 1972-77, 82; planner, Kansas City, Mo., 1977-82; planner dept. aviation Kansas City Internat. Airport, 1982—. Vol. Big Bros., Kansas City, Children's Hosp., Kansas City. U. Calif.-Berkeley fellow, 1972. Mem. AIAA, Am. Assn. Airport Execs. Lodge: Rotary (bd. dirs. 1982—). Avocations: volleyball, basketball, coaching. Home 7308 NW 78th St Kansas City MO 64152 Office: Aviation Dept Kansas City Internat Airport 1 Internat Sq PO Box 20047 Kansas City MO 64195

KONDELIK, JOHN PREMYSL, librarian; b. Chgo., Jan. 28, 1942; s. John P. and M. Kathleen (Vaught) K.; m. Marlene R. Rosenthal, May 14, 1967; 1 dau., Vicki Jane. B.A., U. Fla., 1964; M.L.S., Fla. State U., 1966; postgrad. U. Mich., 1980—. Acquisition librarian Fla. Presbyterian Coll., St. Petersburg, 1966-68, cataloger, 1968-71; cataloger Eckerd Coll., St. Petersburg, 1968-71; acting librarian, 1971, asst. librarian, 1972-74; dean libraries Olivet Coll., Mich., 1974-83; dir. Irwin library system Butler U., Indpls., 1984—; chmn. resource sharing com. Central Ind. Area Library Services Authority, Indpls., 1984—. Mem. ALA, Ind. Library Assn., Assn. Coll. and Research Libraries. Home: 1521 Lancashire Ct Indianapolis IN 46260 Office: Irwin Library Butler U 4600 Sunset Ave Indianapolis IN 46208

KONLE, MARY CAROLINE, educator; b. Morgantown, W.Va., Nov. 28, 1923; d. John Malcolm and Mary Barriere (Tomlinson) Orth; m. Robert Louis Konle, June 30, 1945; children—Dale Reed Konle, Kathleen Konle Schneider. Student Morris Harvey Coll., 1940-42; B.A., W.Va. U., 1944; M.S. in Guidance, U. Wis.-Milw., 1961, postgrad., 1961-82; Ed.D., Marquette U., 1976; postgrad. Inst. Norte Americano, San Luis Potosi, Mex., summer 1981. Tchr. cert., Wis. Tchr. schs., Harpers Ferry, W.Va., 1944-45, Trenton, N.D., 1945-46; tchr. phys. edn. Bradenton (Fla.) High Sch., 1946-47; elem. tchr. New Berlin (Wis.) Pub. Schs., 1956-69; tchr. New Berlin High Sch., 1969-77; reading specialist Glen Park Middle Sch., New Berlin, 1978—; a founder, dir. Friendship Center Reading Camp, Dodgeville, Wis., 1970—. Contbg. mem. Am. Friends Service Com., 1947-82; mem. dirs. Am. Youth Hostels, Milw., 1978-81; adv. Am. Field Service, 1970-74. Recipient service award Am. Youth Hostels, 1953. Mem. Internat. Reading Assn., Wis. Reading Assn., Assn. Supervision and Curriculum Devel., NEA, Wis. Edn. Assn., New Berlin Edn. Assn., Common Cause, World Federalist Assn., Servas, Audubon Soc., Kappa Delta Pi. Quaker. Home: 12418 W Rosemary St New Berlin WI 53151 Office: 3500 S Glen Park Rd New Berlin WI 53151

KONOPINSKI, VIRGIL JAMES, industrial hygienist; b. Toledo, Ohio, July 11, 1935; s. Mack and Mary Veronica (Jankowski) K.; m. Joan Mary Wielinski, June 27, 1964; children—Ann Marie, Carol Sue, Peter James. B.S. in Chem. Engring., U. Toledo, 1956; M.S. in Chem. Engring., Pratt Inst., Bklyn., 1960; M.B.A., Bowling Green State U., 1971. Registered profl. engr., Ohio, Ind., Calif.; cert. indsl. hygienist; cert. safety profl. Assoc. engr. Owens Illinois, Toledo, 1956, 60; real estate developer, Grand Rapids, Ohio, 1961; chem. engr. USPHS, Cin., 1961-64; sr. environ. engr. Vistron Corp., Lima, Ohio, 1964-67; environ. specialist, asst. to dir. environ. control Owens Corning Fiberglas, Toledo, 1967-72; gen. mgr. Midwest Environ. Mgmt., Maumee, Ohio, 1972-73; staff specialist, indsl. hygienist Williams Bros. Waste Control., Tulsa, Okla., 1973-75; dir. div. indsl. hygiene and radiol. health Ind. State Bd. Health, Indpls., 1975—, dir. IOSHA indsl. hygiene, 1975-83; cons., lectr. Served with USNR, 1956-59. Mem. Am. Indsl. Hygiene Assn., Am. Conf. Govtl. Indsl. Hygienists, Am. Soc. Safety Engrs., U.S. Naval Inst., Toledo Zool. Soc. Republican. Roman Catholic. Contbr. articles to profl. jours. Home: 60 Irongate Dr Zionsville IN 46077 Office: 1330 W Michigan Indianapolis IN 46206

KONOPKA, MARY ANN STEPHANY, container mfg. co. exec.; b. Chgo., Jan. 30, 1933; d. Thomas Stephen and Mary Irene (Plucinski) Poltorak; student public schs., Chgo.; m. Louis Steven Konopka, Nov. 22, 1964 (dec. 1976); stepchildren—Linda Marie Konopka Orseno, Lorraine Louise Konopka Capra. With Continental Group, Inc., West Chicago, Ill., 1952—, project control supr., 1978—. Mem. Am. Inventory and Prodn. Soc., Nat. Assn. Female Execs., Am. Soc. Profl. and Exec. Women, U.S. CB Radio Assn. Democrat. Roman Catholic. Club: Northwest Internat. Trade. Home: 526 E Pomeroy St West Chicago IL 60185 Office: Continental Group Inc 1700 Harvester Rd West Chicago IL 60185

KONOWALOW, STEPHEN, counselor, educator, behaviorist, stress management specialist; b. Bklyn., Oct. 26, 1941; s. Julius Lewis and Terry (Stolzenberg) K.; divorced; children—Rhonda Leigh, Erika Reuben; m. Kathy Jo Eschtruth, Oct. 24, 1981; children—Robert Isaac, Terry Anne. B.A., SUNY-Buffalo, 1963; M.A., Central Mich. U., 1968, Ed.S., 1973; Ed.M., Duke U., 1975; Ph.D., Wayne State U., 1980. Cert. counselor, social worker. Coordinator student activities Broome Community Coll., Binghamton, N.Y., 1965-66; dir. student activities Delta Coll., University Ctr., Mich., 1966-69, counselor, 1970-72, 73—, sociology instr., 1972-73; counselor, research asst. Duke U., Durham, N.C., 1969-70; pres. Success Seminars, Bay City, Mich., 1983—; owner, operator Cassettes for Success, Bay City, 1983—; exec. dir. Brahman Enterprises, Bay City, 1975—. Author: Rekindling the Fires, 1985; Journal, 1985; Up Up and Away, 1985; Stress Break, 1985; articles, texts, workbooks, lectures, seminars and cassettes on stress and behavioral management. Adv. bd. dirs. Delta Family Clinic, P.C., Bay City, 1982-84; bd. dirs. Mich. Human Services Inc., Ann Arbor, Mich., 1978-82. Recipient 10 Yr. Gold cert. for volunteerism Sta. WUCM-TV, 1982, Recognition cert. Mich. Human Services, 1980. Mem. Am. Asn. Counsel Devel., Am. Assn. Higher Edn., AAUP, Mich. Assn. Specialists in Group Work, Mich. Personnel Guidance Assn., Kappa Delta Pi. Democrat. Jewish. Avocations: writing; lecturing; traveling. Office: Delta Coll Counseling Ctr University Center MI 48706

KONZELMANN, DAVID PAUL, educational administrator; b. Greensburg, Ind., Jan. 12, 1936; s. Paul William and Miriam Frances (Jones) K.; m. Karen Louise Wortley, June 8, 1958; children—Jeffrey Allen, Scott David. B.S., Butler U., 1960; M.S., Purdue U., 1964. Cert. tchr., Ind. Tchr., counselor LaPorte Schs. (Ind.), 1960-63; dir. guidance Bremen Community Schs. (Ind.), 1963-66; admissions, registration, fin. aid officer Purdue North Central, Westville, Ind., 1966-79; assoc. dir. admissions and fin. aid Purdue Calumet, Hammond, Ind., 1979-81; assoc. dir. admissions Purdue U., West Lafayette, Ind., 1981—. Gen. Electric fellow, 1965. Mem. Nat. Assn. Collegiate Registrars and Admissions Officers (state reporting officer 1982—), Ind. Assn. Collegiate Registrars and Admissions Officers (com. mem. 1976-79), Ind. Assn. Coll. Admissions Counselors (exec. com., chmn. membership com. 1982—). Democrat. Office: Purdue U Office Admission Hovde Hall West Lafayette IN 47907

KONZELMANN, HENRY JOSEPH, pediatrician; b. Elizabeth, N.J., Aug. 11, 1935; s. Henry Joseph and Marianne Jahn K.; B.S. in Biology, Holy Cross Coll., 1956; M.D., Georgetown U., 1960; married; children—Suzanne, Kathleen, Henry, Robert, Daniel, Agnes, John. Intern, Harrisburg (Pa.) Hosp., 1960-61; resident in pediatrics U. Md., Balt., 1963-66; practice medicine specializing in pediatrics, Springfield, Ill., 1966—; chmn. pediatrics dept. St. John's Hosp.; assoc. clin. prof. pediatrics So. Ill. U. Med. Sch. Bd. dirs. Med. Found. Central Ill. Served with USPHS, 1961-63. Diplomate Am. Bd. Pediatrics. Mem. AMA, Am. Acad. Pediatrics, Ill. Med. Soc., Sangamon County Med. Soc. Conservative Republican. Roman Catholic. Home: 1520 W Lake Dr Springfield IL 62707 Office: 2657 W Lawrence Ave Springfield IL 62704

KONZEN, JON LEO, physician; b. Toledo, July 23, 1934. M.D., U. Ottawa, Ont., 1960; M.P.H., U. Mich., 1965. Diplomate Am. Bd. Preventive Medicine. Physician in charge Ford Motor Co., Trenton, Mich., 1967-78; med. dir. Owens-Corning Fiberglas Corp., Toledo, 1968—. Contbr. chpt. to Occupational Medicine: Principles and Practical Applications, 1975, Occupational and Industrial Dermatology, 1982. Fellow Am. Coll. Preventive Medicine, Am. Occupational Med. Assn., Am. Acad. Occupational Medicine. Office: Owens-Corning Fiberglas Corp Fiberglas Tower Toledo OH 43659

KOO, CHARLES MINGYAN, sociologist, photographer, media consultant; b. Guangdon, China, Feb. 22, 1950; came to U.S., 1977; s. Albert and Yukyu (Yu) K. Diploma in communications Hong Kong Baptist Coll., 1975; M.S. in Edn., U. So. Calif., 1978; M.A. in Journalism, U. Wis.-Madison, 1980, Ph.D., 1984. Asst. info. officer Family Planning Assn., Hong Kong, 1975; publicity officer Rank Xerox (Far East) Ltd., Hong Kong, 1975-76; head edn. media ctr. Delia Meml. Sch., Kung Tong, Kowloon, Hong Kong, 1976-77; media cons. Environ. Awareness Ctr., U. Wis.-Madison, 1982—; cons., tchr. Summer traveling grantee Inst. Internat. Edn., 1980; summer fellow Freedom Found., 1982. Mem. Assn. Edn. in Journalism and Mass Communications, Am. Sociology Assn., Communication Assn. Pacific, Internat. Communication Assn., Internat. Assn. Mass Communication Research, Midwest Social. Soc., Soc. Studies Social Problems, Assoc. Photographers Internat., U. So. Calif. Gen. Alumni Assn. (life). Contbg. author to profl. publs. Home: 548 W Johnson St Apt 608 Madison WI 53703 Office: 3473 Dept Sociology U Wis Madison WI 53706

KOO, PETER HUNG-KWAN, immuno-biochemist, educator; b. Shanghai, China; came to U.S., 1959, naturalized, 1975; s. Yung-Foo and Shun-Wa (Ko) K.; B.A., U. Wash., 1964; Ph.D., U. Md., 1970; m. S. Alice Hotapichayawivat, Dec. 23, 1967; children—David G., Christopher G. Research asso. Johns Hopkins U., 1970-74, asst. prof. oncology and radiology, 1975-77; staff fellow NIH, Bethesda, Md., 1974-75; asst. prof., assoc. prof. microbiology/immunology Northeastern Ohio Univs. Coll. Medicine, Rootstown, 1977—; adj. assoc. prof., depts. chemistry and biology Kent (Ohio) State U.; chmn. profl. edn. com. Am. Cancer Soc. Deacon, 1st Christian Ch. of Kent, 1978—, mem. fin. com., 1982—; bd. dirs. Portage County (Ohio) chpt. Am. Cancer Soc. Recipient Cystic Fibrosis Care Fund award 1979, 82; NIH grantee, 1978-82; Am. Cancer Soc. grantee, 1979, 82; United Way Health Found. grantee, 1982; MEFCOM Found. grantee, 1983—; NAF grantee, 1984—. Mem. N.Y. Acad. Scis., Am.

Assn. Immunologists, Johns Hopkins Med. Surg. Assn., AAAS, Am. Chem. Soc., Am. Soc. for Microbiology, Ohio Acad. Sci., Sigma Xi. Research, publs. in field. Office: Northeastern Ohio Univs Coll Medicine Rootstown OH 44272

KOON, CARL DANIEL, information systems executive; b. Watseka, Ill., Sept. 11, 1942; s. Carl Dwight and Helen Madge (Arbuckle) K.; m. Patricia Brannon, Apr. 29, 1966 (div. Dec. 1980); children—Kathleen Gayle, Mary Patricia, Erin Colleen; m. 2d, Mary Carolyn Hiner DeMyer, Jan. 24, 1981; stepchildren—Catherine Jane Wright, Karen Margaret Wright. Student computer sci., Purdue U., 1966-69. Mgr. info. systems Ind. Bell Telephone Co., Indpls., 1967-83; dir. mktg. info. systems Ameritech Communications Inc., Chgo., 1983—. Sports host Nat. Sports Festival, Indpls., 1982; pres. Westlane Little League, Indpls., 1981-82; awards chmn. Nat. Rowing Championships, Indpls., 1983; coach Catholic Youth Orgn., Indpls., 1970-75. Served with USAF, 1962-66. Democrat. Roman Catholic. Home: 1070 Whirlaway St Naperville IL 60540 Office: Ameritech Communications Inc 300 S Riverside Suite 1218 Chicago IL 60606

KOONSVITSKY, BURTON PHILLIP, biochemist; b. Pitts., July 13, 1943; s. Aaron Albert and Sarah (Mervis) K.; m. Bonnie Lois Newman, Dec. 26, 1965; children—Mara Susan, Brian Alan. B.S. Carnegie Mellon U., 1965; Ph.D. U. So. Ill., 1965-70; postdoctoral U. Cin., 1971-73. Cert. chemist, organic chemist, Ohio. Sect. head Procter & Gamble Co., Cincinnati, 1973—. Bd. dirs. Jewish Community Relations Council, Cin., 1976-80, Cin. Community Hebrew Schs., 1982—. Fellow research So. Ill. U., 1965-70, postdoctoral U. Cin. Med. Sch., 1971-73. Recipient Best Paper of Yr. Soc. Cosmetic Chemists, 1980. Mem. Am. Chem. Soc., Ohio Valley Sect. Soc. Exptl. Biology and Medicine, Am. Acad. Dermatology. Avocations: photography; canoeing; hiking. Home: 4302 Berryhill Ln Cincinnati OH 45242

KOONTZ, RAYMOND, See *Who's Who in America,* 43rd edition.

KOPAC, MILAN JAMES, microsurgery cons., cell biologist; b. Ravenna, Nebr., Mar. 12, 1905; s. James and Mary B. (Skala) K.; B.S., U. Nebr., 1927, M.S., 1929, D.Sc. (hon.), 1962; Ph.D., U. Calif., Berkeley, 1934. Research asso. biology N.Y. U., 1934-38; vis. asst. prof., 1938-43, asst. prof., 1944-46, asso. prof., 1947-49, prof. biology, 1949-73, prof. emeritus, 1973—, head all-univ. dept. biology, 1963-70, dir. Robert Chambers Lab. Microsurgery, 1968-77; specialist in microsurgery; vis. instr. U. Nebr., 1934, vis. prof. biology, 1962; mem. physiology fellowships panel NIH, 1962-66; chmn. Gordon Research Conf. Cancer, 1964. Sci. adv. com. Damon Runyon Mel. Fund Cancer Research, 1950-73, chmn., 1966-69, sci. dir., 1967-69; adv. com. instnl. grants Am. Cancer Soc., 1963-66. Served to 2d lt., inf., USAR, 1927-37. Fellow N.Y. Acad. Scis. (councilor, v.p. 1958, pres. 1960, trustee 1960-62, Gold medal award 1969); mem. Am. Soc. Cytology (founder), Harvey Soc. (life), Am. Assn. Cancer Research, Sigma Xi. Cons. editor: Mechanisms of Cell Division, 1951; Cancer Cytology and Cytochemistry, 1956; contbr. articles to tech. and sci. jours. Home: 521 Brookside Dr Lincoln NE 68528

KOPERSKI, ROSEANN ELIZABETH, insurance agency executive; b. Toledo, Ohio, Mar. 8, 1947; d. Anthony John and Stella Elizabeth (Guziolek) Rogowski; m. Kenneth James Koperski, Aug. 20, 1966; children—Karleen Marie, Kristin Marie, Kelly Ann. Client service rep. W.F. Roemer Ins., Inc., Toledo, 1965-83, asst. v.p. comml. lines underwriting, 1983—. Mem. Profl. Ins. Agts. Assn., Ins. Women Toledo (welfare chmn. 1973-74). Democrat. Roman Catholic. Home: 3863 Almeda Dr Toledo OH 43612 Office: WF Roemer Ins Inc 3912 Sunforest Ct Toledo OH 43623

KOPF, GEORGE MICHAEL, physician, b. Chilton, Wis., Oct. 20, 1935; s. George and Mary (Schmid) K.; m. Sandra Mary Nolte, Dec. 29, 1962; children—Karen, Jennifer, Nancy. B.S., U. Wis.-Madison, 1958, M.D., 1961. Diplomate Am. Bd. Ophthalmology. Intern Luther Hosp., Eau Claire, Wis., 1961-62; resident in surgery Milw. County Hosp., 1962-63; resident in ophthalmology Detroit Gen. Hosp., 1965-68; practice medicine specializing in ophthalmology, Zanesville, Ohio, 1968—; mem. med. staff Bethesda Hosp., Zanesville; mem. med. staff Good Samaritan Med. Ctr., Zanesville, pres., 1978, also dir. Served to capt. USAF, 1963-65. Fellow Am. Acad. Ophthalmology, ACS; mem. Ohio Ophthal. Soc. (pres. 1976-77), Muskingum County Acad. Medicine (pres. 1983), AMA. Republican. Roman Catholic. Lodges: Elks, Rotary. Avocations: Tennis; swimming; sailing; reading; traveling. Home: 2950 Ash Meadows St Zanesville OH 43701 Office: Ophthalmologists Inc 2315 Maple Ave Zanesville OH 43701

KOPP, CARL ROBERT, advertising agency executive; b. Detroit, Apr. 8, 1921; s. Andrew Russell and Bertha (Hecke) K.; student Ill. Inst. Tech.; grad. Advanced Mgmt. Program, Harvard U.; m. Jenna Lou Sandburg, Apr. 15, 1978; children—Suzie Sandburg Simon, Deborah Kopp Poulin, Sally Sandburg, Jeffrey. Salesman, sales mgr., advt. mgr. Marathon Corp., Menasha, Wis., 1947-53; account exec. Needham, Louis & Brorby, Chgo., 1953-55; account exec. Leo Burnett Co., Inc., Chgo., from 1955, now chmn. audit com., chmn. bd., chief exec. officer. Mem. Chgo. Crime Commn., The Chgo. Com. Served with U.S. Army; World War II; Korea. Decorated Bronze Star, Combat Inf. badge, Purple Heart. Clubs: Bob O'Link Golf, Glen View; Tavern, Mid-Am., Chgo. (Chgo.); Lost Tree Village; Jupiter Hills; N.Y. Athletic. Office: Leo Burnett Co Prudential Plaza Chicago IL 60601

KOPP, DAVID JEROME, data processing systems engineer; b. St. Louis, Dec. 31, 1937; s. Jules H. and Frances (Levy) K.; m. Anita Louise Soffer, June 12, 1960 (dec. 1983); children—Gary Alan, Susan Lynn. B.S. in Elec. Engring., Purdue U., 1960; M.B.A., Washington U., 1962. Sr. systems engr. IBM, St. Louis, 1962—. Bd. dirs. Ladue Sch. Bd., Mo., 1980-85. Served as 1st lt. U.S. Army, 1961. Home: 10910 Brooktrail Ct Creve Coeur MO 63141 Office: 500 Maryville College Dr Creve Coeur MO 63141

KOPPERUD, ROY MILTON, farmer; b. Lake Preston, S.D., Apr. 18, 1914; s. Arthur and Nellie (Knutson) K.; grad. high sch. Engaged in farming, Lake Preston, 1933—; dir. Farmers Union Oil Co., Lake Preston, 1958-85, ret., pres., 1960—; asst. sec., treas., dir. CENEX, wholesale farm supplies, South St. Paul, 1974-85, ret.; partner Kopperud Bros. Farms. Served with AUS, 1941-45. Democrat. Lutheran. Address: RFD 1 Lake Preston SD 57249

KOPRIVICA, DOROTHY MARY, management consultant, real estate and insurance broker; b. St. Louis, May 27, 1921; d. Mitar and Fema (Guzina) K. B.S., Washington U., St. Louis, 1962; cert. in def. inventory mgmt. Dept. Def., 1968. Mgmt. analyst Transp. Supply and Maintenance Command, St. Louis, 1954-57, Dept. Army Transp. Materiel Command, St. Louis, 1957-62; program analyst Dept. Army Aviation System Command, St. Louis, 1962-74, spl. asst. to comdr., 1974-78; ins. broker D. Koprivica, Ins., St. Louis, 1978—; real estate broker Century 21 KARE Realty, St. Louis, 1978—, also dir.; dir. KARE Constrn., St. Louis. Mem. Bus. and Profl. Women (pres. 1974-75). Eastern Orthodox. Lodge: Order Eastern Star.

KOPSAFTIS, PETER, florist; b. Karyae, Greece, Jan. 24, 1948; s. Peter G. and Stella (Karagiannis) K.; m. Frances Tomaras; children—Peter, Ted, Esther. Student Wright Coll., 1967-70, Midwest Stock Exchange, 1972. Salesman, Cutler & Yantis, Chgo., 1970-71, Dun & Bradstreet, Chgo., 1972-73, Acme Freight, Chgo., 1971-72; sales mgr. Nicherson & Collins, Des Plaines, Ill., 1973-78; pres. Jeromes Flowers, Chgo., 1978—, Jeromes Lake Point, 1982—, Jeromes Plants, 1982—. Mem. Republican Nat. Com., 1983. Served with AUS, 1967-73. Mem. Am. Florists Assn., Florafax, Am. Mgmt. Assn. Greek Orthodox. Club: Nat. U.S. Citizen (Washington). Home: 8218 Enger Ln River Grove IL 60610 Office: Jeromes Lake Point 505 N Lake Shore Dr Chicago IL 60610

KOPSTAIN, CLEMENT CRAIG, university executive; b. Berwyn, Ill., Nov. 28, 1938; s. Clement Joseph and Priscilla Ann (Parsons) K.; m. Judith Anna Stoneberg, Jan. 12, 1963; children—Lori Kristine, Eric Craig. B.S. in Bus. Adminstrn., Roosevelt U., 1969; Cert. in Advanced Mgmt., U. Chgo., 1970; M.A., Northwestern U., 1978. Corp. trust adminstr. Continental Ill. Nat. Bank, Chgo., 1962-64; asst. personnel dir. Vapor Corp., Niles, Ill., 1964-72; mgr. compensation and staffing Honeywell Corp., Arlington Heights, Ill., 1972-74; assoc. dir. Northwestern U., Evanston, Ill., 1974-78; mgr. Deloitte Haskins & Sells, Chgo., 1978-85; dir. engring. placement Northwestern U., 1985—; vice chmn. Task Force on Correctional Industries, State of Ill., 1972-74; cons. USN, 1978. Author: Basic Intelligence Tng. and Evaluation, 1982. Pres. Wheeling High Sch. Career Adv. Council, Ill., 1972-75; bd. dirs., corp. sec. Pace Inst., Chgo., 1973-75. Served to cmdr. USNR. Recipient John Howard award John Howard Assn., 1970. Mem. Naval Res. Assn., Res. Officers Assn., Phi Delta Kappa, Beta Gamma Sigma. Lutheran. Lodge: Elks (treas. 1959-60). Home: 623 N Elmhurst Ave Mount Prospect IL 60056

KOPTIK, TRACY IRENE, accountant; b. Chgo., Nov. 22, 1943; d. Charles and Grace Elizabeth (Zimmerman) Koptik. B.S. in Acctg., U. Ill., 1967. C.P.A., Ill. Staff acct. Coopers & Lybrand, Chgo., 1967-71; dir. fin. City of Naperville, Ill., 1971-72; asst. dir. fin. City of Elmhurst, Ill., 1972—. Mem. Am. Inst. C.P.A.s, Ill. Soc. C.P.A.s. Home: PO Box 936 Addison IL 60101 Office: City of Elmhurst 119 Schiller St Elmhurst IL 60126

KORBITZ, BERNARD CARL, oncologist-hematologist, medical educator, medical-legal consultant; b. Lewistown, Mont., Feb. 18, 1935; s. Fredrick William and Rose Eleanore (Ackmann) K.; m. Constance Kay Bolz, June 22, 1957; children—Paul Bernard, Guy Karl. B.S. in Med. Sci., U. Wis.-Madison, 1957, M.D., 1960, M.S. in Oncology, 1962; LL.B., LaSalle U., 1972. Asst. prof. medicine and clin. oncology, U. Wis. Med. Sch., Madison, 1967-71; dir. medicine Presbyn. Med. Ctr., Denver, 1971-73; practice medicine specializing in oncology, hematology, Madison, 1973-76; med. oncologist, hematologist Radiologic Ctr. Meth. Hosp., Omaha, 1976-82; practice medicine specializing in oncology, hematology, Omaha, 1982—; sci. advisor Citizen's Environ. Com., Denver, 1972-73; mem. Cancer Com. Bergan Mercy Hosp., Omaha, 1982—; Meth. Hosp., Omaha, 1977—; dir. Bernard C. Korbitz, P.C., Omaha, 1983—. Contbr. articles to profl. jours. Webelos leader Denver area Council, Mid. Am. Council of Nebr. Boy Scouts Am.; bd. elders King of Kings Luth. Ch., Omaha, 1979-80; mem. U.S. Senatorial Club, 1984, Republican Presdl. Task Force, 1984. Served to capt. USAF, 1962-64. Fellow ACP, Royal Soc. Health; mem. Am. Soc. Clin. Oncology, Am. Coll. Legal-Medicine, Am. Soc. Internal Medicine, AMA, Nebr. Med. Assn., Omaha Med. Society, Omaha Clin. Soc., Phi Eta Sigma, Phi Beta Kappa, Phi Kappa Phi, Alpha Omega Alpha. Avocations: photography fishing, travel. Home: 9024 Leavenworth St Omaha NE 68114 Office: 8300 Dodge St Suite 226 Omaha NE 68114

KORCZAK, EDWARD STANLEY, association executive; b. Chgo., July 12, 1945; s. Stanley and Helen (Dzik) K.; m. Linda Marie Venzon, May 30, 1969; children—Jori, Dana; m. Jacqueline Mandy Utt, Oct. 16, 1977; children—Grant, Dirk. B.A., Northeastern Ill. U., 1973; postgrad. Harper Coll., 1973-76; Assn. Mgmt. Degree, U. Notre Dame/U.S. C. of C., 1977. With Charles Pfizer Co., Chgo., 1963-67; sales mgr. Kaynar Mfg. Co., Chgo., 1967-69; asst. exec. dir. Profl. Photographers Am., Des Plaines, Ill., 1969-78; exec. dir. Retail Floorcovering Inst., Inc., Chgo., 1978—. Bd. dirs. Floor Covering Industry Edn. Found.; pres. Nat. Council for Small Bus. Devel., Chgo., 1974-75; council mem., com. chmn. Resurrection Luth. Ch., 1981-84. Served with U.S. Army, 1965-67. Mem. Am. Soc. Assn. Execs., Chgo. Soc. Assn. Execs., U.S. C. of C. Republican. Lutheran. Office: 1890 Merchandise Mart Chicago IL 60654

KORDING, SIRI KAREN, purchasing agent; b. Vallejo, Calif., Oct. 25, 1942; d. Edward Wallingford and Doris Lucille (Cook) Price; m. Glenn Condo Kording, Aug. 7, 1964; children—Wendy, Jason. A.A., Solano Coll., 1962. With Stanley Cons., Muscatine, Iowa, 1974—, contract adminstr., purchasing agt., 1980—. Treas., Grant pack Cub Scouts Am., 1983, Grant PTO, Muscatine, 1983; sec. Great River P.R.I.D.E., 1984; bd. dirs. Muscatine United Way, 1985—. Republican. Lutheran. Avocations: reading; cooking. Home: 805 Robin Rd Muscatine IA 52761 Office: Stanley Cons Stanley Bldg Muscatine IA 52761

KORF, KILEY KAY, insurance agent; b. Red Cloud, Nebr., May 12, 1948; d. Robert Barta and Shirley (Stewart) Barta; m. Sherwood Joseph Korf, Aug. 8, 1970; children—Jennifer, Jami Jodi. B.A. in Edn., Kearney State Coll., 1970. Tchr. English, McCook, Nebr., 1970-73; sec. Hal D. Mason, McCook, 1979-81, agt. 1981—. Mem. adv. bd. Order Rainbow for Girls. Mem. Bus. and Profl. Women, Beta Sigma Phi (pres. 1983-84, Girl of Yr. 1983-84). Republican Methodist. Avocations: reading; college business courses; crocheting. Home: HC30 Box 161 McCook NE 69001 Office: Hal D Mason Ins 110 East C McCook NE 69001

KORGESKI, GREGORY PAUL, clinical psychologist; b. Scranton, Pa., May 15, 1954; s. Frank Alexander and Shirley Josephine (Fitch) K.; m. Elaine Jeanne Madigan, July 15, 1978; 1 stepson, Michael L. Madigan. B.S., U. Scranton, 1976; Ph.D., U. Minn., 1981. Lic. cons. psychologist, Minn. Supr., Walk-In Counseling Ctr., Mpls., 1979—; psychologist Washington County Human Services, Oakdale, Minn., 1981—; dir. counseling ctr. Hamline U., St. Paul, 1983—; Cons. Kiel Mgmt. Counsellors, 1985—. Recipient Richard Elliott award U. Minn., 1982. Mem. Am. Psychol. Assn., Minn. Psychol. Assn. Contbr. articles to profl. jours. Office: Hamline U Counseling Ctr Saint Paul MN 55104

KORMAN, KEITH EDWIN, hospital, nursing home administrator; b. Bottineau, N.D., Oct. 11, 1941; s. Edwin R. and Mabel (Patterson) K.; m. Sharon Anne Simek, Aug. 29, 1960; children—Kimberly, Kerri, Michael, Kristi, Nicole. Student N.D. State U., 1959-60. Office mgr. Gamble Robenson, Williston, N.D., 1960-63, T & K Rambler, Bottineau, 1963-64; credit mgr., asst. adminstr. St. Andrews Hosp., Bottineau, 1964-70, adminstr., 1970-82, St. Andrews Hosp., Rolla Hosp., 1982—; alt. del. Am. Hosp. Assn., Chgo., 1981—. Mem. N.D. Hosp. Fin. Assn., N.D. Hosp. Assn. (chmn. bd. 1982), Blue Cross of N.D. (bd. dirs. 1973-83). Republican. Presbyterian. Club: N.D. Wildlife. Lodge: Eagles. Avocations: hunting; fishing; camping; golf. Home: 310 W 13th Bottineau ND 58318 Office: St Andrew's Hosp 316 Ohmer St Bottineau ND 58318

KORNFEIN, WILLIAM, lawyer, real estate agent; b. Zurich, Switzerland, Mar. 9, 1947; came to U.S., 1954; s. Max and Amalie (Mermelstein) K.; m. Peggy Ellen Goalstone, June 6, 1971; 1 child, Kimberly Clare. B.S. in Edn., U. Kans., 1969; J.D., U. Mo., 1972. Bar: Mo. Asst. city counselor City of St. Louis, 1972-75; atty.-advisor Office of Hearings and Appeals, Brentwood, Mo., 1975—; instr. Acad. Real Estate, Creve Coeur, Mo., 1985—. Recipient Spl. Achievement awards Office Hearings and Appeals, Arlington, Va., 1982, 84. Mem. ABA, Mo. Bar Assn., Met. Real Estate Bd. St. Louis. Jewish. Avocations: photography; stamps; softball. Home: 835 Weatherwood Dr Manchester MO 63011 Office: Office Hearings and Appeals 8706 Manchester Rd Brentwood MO 63144

KORNHABER, BERNARD R(AYMOND), diversified manufacturing company executive; b. N.Y.C., 1924; s. A. and R. (Rothman) K.; A.B. cum laude with honors in Econs., Bklyn. Coll., 1949; A.M. in Econs., U. Pa., 1950; m. Susan W., children—Marda J., Peter O. Trainee. Internat. Playtex Corp., Dover, Del., 1950-55, mgr. sales stats., 1953-54, sr. economist, 1954-55; mgr. sales devel. internat. div. Allied Chem. Corp., N.Y.C., 1956-61; with Brunswick Corp., Skokie, Ill., 1962—, mktg. mgr., 1964-66, v.p. mktg., dir. corp. planning, 1975—; speaker in field; bd. dirs. Strategic Planning Inst. Served with Security Agy., U.S. Army, 1944-46. Mem. Assn. Corp. Growth (pres. Chgo. chpt. 1980, dir. chpt. 1981—), Planning Execs. Inst., Midwest Planning Soc., Am. Mktg. Assn. Clubs: Chgo. Yacht, Rotary; Skyline Country (Tucson). Home: 100 17th St Wilmette IL 60091 Office: One Brunswick Plaza Skokie IL 60077

KORSAK, MICHAEL THOMAS, educator; b. Chgo., Nov. 24, 1952; s. Norbert Thomas and Adeline (Muslak) K. B.S.Ed., Chgo. State U., 1973, M.S.Ed., 1976; postgrad. St. Xavier Coll., 1976-81, U. Chgo., 1978, Nat. Coll. Edn., 1982. Indsl. edn. instr. Carl Sandburg High Sch., Orland Park, Ill., 1974-81; lectr. Chgo. State U., 1981; dept. chmn. Victor J. Andrew High Sch., Tinley Park, Ill., 1981—; part-time instr. Moraine Valley Coll., 1981—; cons. Tech. Edn. Research Corp., 1974. Pres. Hurley Homeowners Civic Assn., Chgo., 1976. Recipient Award of Merit Am. Vocat. Assn., 1982. Mem. Nat. Assn. Secondary Sch. Prins., Phi Delta Kappa, Epsilon Phi Tau. Roman Catholic. Home: 3726 W 68th Pl Chicago IL 60629 Office: 171st and 90th Aves Tinley Park IL 60477

KORTE, RALPH, construction company executive. B.S. in Bus. Adminstrn., So. Ill. U. Founder Ralph Korte Constrn. Co., St. Louis, 1958, now chmn. bd.; dir. Mark Twain St. Louis Bank. Pres. So. Ill. U. Found., Edwardsville, 1982-83; pres. Cahokia Mound council, Boy Scouts Am., 1980-81, N. Central Regional bd. dirs.; exec. bd. St. Louis Regional Commerce and Growth Assn.; adv. bd. Belleville Area Coll., Granite City Ctr.; bd. dirs. New Age Coll. for Living, Webster Groves, Mo. Recipient Alumnus of Yr. award So. Ill. U., 1978; Silver Beaver award, 1984. Mem. Assoc. Gen. Contractors Am. (nat. bd. dirs.), So. Ill. Builders Assn. (past pres.), Young Pres.'s Orgn., Highland C. of C. (past pres.). Club: Rotary. Address: Ralph Korte Constrn Co Inc 8860 Ladue Rd Saint Louis MO 63124

KORTE, R(EINHARDT) FREDERICK, lawyer, real estate developer; b. Decatur, Ill., Feb. 19, 1945; s. Reinhard Albert and Ruby Arnold (Arnold) K.; m. Barbara Ann Simlek, Apr. 26, 1980; children—Kathrine Ann, Sara Lynn. B.S., So. Ill. U., 1970; J.D., Thomas M. Cooley Law Sch., 1981. Bar: Ill. 1981, U.S. Dist. Ct. (cen. dist.) Ill. 1981, Tex. 1985. Ptnr., Bennett-Korte & Assocs., Decatur, 1981—; corp. counsel Lake Ozark Acres, Inc., Laurie, Mo., 1984—; pres. Shoreline Enterprises, 1984—. Contbr. weekly article to newspaper, 1984. Bd. dirs. Lake Ozarks Real Estate Devel. Com., Lake of the Ozarks, 1984. Served capt. U.S. Army, 1968-70. Mem. Ill. Bar Assn., Ill. Trial Lawyers Assn., Christian Lawyers Assn., ABA. Independent. Home: 1 Kenwood Ct Decatur IL 62521 Office: Suite 529 Millikin Ct Decatur IL 62523

KORTH, OTTO KARL, pilot; b. Chgo., Sept. 17, 1930; s. Otto Karl and Erma Bethel (Oothoudt) K.; m. Patricia Sirena Bahcman, Dec. 21, 1974; children—Jeffrey, Dawn, Gregory. B.A., Manchester Coll., 1956; postgrad. U. Minn., 1958-59. Internat. jet capt. 3M Co., St. Paul, 1959—; asst. adj. gen. Minn. Air Guard, St. Paul, 1983—; dir. Minn. Air Guard Hist. Found., St. Paul, 1983—. Served to brig. gen. USAF, from 1948. Mem. N.G. Assn. U.S., N.G. Assn. Minn., Air Force Assn., Minn. Bus. Aircraft Assn., Nat. Bus. Aircraft Assn., Aircraft Owners and Pilots Assn. Avocations: hunting, fishing, golf, tennis, skiing. Home: 540 Varner Circle Golden Valley MN 55427 Office: Aviation Dept 3M Co St Paul Downtown Airport Saint Paul MN 55107

KOSA, SAMUEL JOHN, rubber manufacturing company executive, consulting engineer; b. Youngstown, Ohio, June 4, 1947; s. Victor and Anna Marie (Blotor) K.; m. Barbara Ann Popa, Sept. 4, 1971; children—Katherine Marie, Laura Ann. B.Engring. in Civil Engring., Youngstown State U., 1971, postgrad., 1973, 75. Registered profl. engr., Ohio, Pa., N.Y., Iowa. Engr., J.N. Cernica & Assocs., Youngstown, 1965-72; v.p., ptnr. Concrete Testing Services, Inc., Youngstown, 1969-74; chief engr. Inter-Lock Steel Co., Sharon, Pa., 1972; underground support engr. Comml. Shearing, Inc., Youngstown, 1972-74; project engr. Hale & Kullgren, Inc., Akron, Ohio, 1974; cons. engr. Samuel J. Kosa & Assocs., Canton, Ohio, 1974—; chief civil/structural engr. C.F. Simmers div. Pollock Research & Design, Inc., Canfield, Ohio, 1974-76; instr. Youngstown State U., 1976-77; project engr. Firestone Tire & Rubber Co., Akron, 1977—. Mem. Nat. Soc. Profl. Engrs., Ohio Soc. Profl. Engrs., ASCE (pres. Youngstown br. 1975-76), Mahoning Valley Tech. Socs. Council (vice-chmn. 1976-77). Republican. Byzantine Catholic. Home: 6517 Lake O'Springs NW Canton OH 44718 Office: Firestone Tire & Rubber Co 1200 Firestone Pkwy Akron OH 44317

KOSCIERZYNSKI, RONALD JOHN, educator; b. Detroit, July 18, 1947; s. William Joseph and Jean Mary (Sloncz) K.; m. Barbara Renata, Aug. 19, 1972; children—Anne Marie, John Joseph. A.T., Macomb County (Mich.) Community Coll., 1968; B.S.Ed., Wayne State U., 1970, M.Ed., 1973, Ed.D., 1979. Tchr. electronics Utica (Mich.) Community High Sch., 1972—, chmn. indsl. arts dept., 1981—, chmn. system-wide indsl. edn., 1975-79; instr. Macomb County Community Coll., 1977-81; tchr. electronics Hazel Park (Mich.) Adult Edn., 1972-77. Served with AUS, 1970-72. Fin. dir. Our Lady Queen of Apostles Parish, 1978-80. Recipient Paul M. Shilling Disting. Service award Mich. Indsl. Edn. Soc., 1981. Mem. AMVETS (AMVET of yr. Mich., 1982, cmdr. dist. 1 Mich. 1982-83, fin. officer 1984-85), Mich. Indsl. Edn. Soc. (membership dir. 1981-84, treas., 1977-80), Am. Indsl. Arts Assn., Am. Polish Engring. Assn., Am. Vocat. Assn., Electricity Electronics Tchrs. Mich., Mich. Occupational Edn. Assn., Mich. Trade and Tech. Educators, Nat. Assn. Indsl. and Tech. Tchrs. Educators, Vocat. Indsl. Clubs Am., Phi Delta Kappa. Club: K.C. Contbr. articles to profl. jours. Office: 47255 Shelby Rd Utica MI 48087

KOSHAL, MANJULIKA, production management educator, researcher; b. Eastern India, Aug. 21, 1938; came to U.S., 1968, naturalized, 1980; d. Indrajit and Saytyawati (Puri) Badhwar; m. Rajindar Kumar Koshal, Aug. 12, 1966; children—Vinita, Vipin. Higher Secondary, Calcutta U., India, 1953; Intermediate in Arts, Bihar U., India, 1955; B.A. with honors, Patna U., India, 1957, M.A., 1959, Ph.D., 1964. Lectr. Patna U., India, 1965-67; counsellor to women students Ohio U., Athens, summer 1968; part-time instr., 1969, 77, asst. prof., 1979-82, assoc. prof., 1983—; vis. research assoc. SRI RAM Inst Indsl. Relations, New Delhi, India, 1973-74. Author: (with others) Management by Japenese Systems, 1982. Contbr. articles to profl. jours. Grantee AAAU, 1974-75, Ohio U., 1981-82. Mem. Inst. Mgmt. Scis., Acad. Mgmt., Am. Econs. Assn., AAAU (corp. del. 1984—), Am. Inst. Decision Scis. Avocations: reading, travel. Home: 7 Canterbury Dr Athens OH 45701 Address: Ohio U 406C Copeland Hall Athens OH 45701

KOSHICK, JOHN CHARLES, theatrical management firm executive; b. Milw., Aug. 13, 1955; s. John Stanley and Charlotte Cecilia (Herro) K.; m. Heidi Rae Tennant, Dec. 22, 1979 (div. Apr. 1983). Student, U. Wis.-Milw. Lic. booking agt. Pres., Utopia Prodns., Milw., 1973-76, Internat. Talent Assn., N.Y.C., 1976-78; co. mgr. Broadway nat. tour Passion of Dracula, N.Y.C., 1978; gen. mgr. Gordon Crowe Prodns., N.Y.C., 1978-79; pres. Jack Koshick Mgmt., Milw., 1980—; personal mgr. Badfinger Rock Act, Liverpool, Eng., 1980—; tour mgr. Searchers Rock Act, London, 1983; talent coordinator Festa Italiana, Milw., 1985. Democrat. Melkite. Avocations: karate; jogging; song writing. Office: Jack Koschick Mgmt PO Box 54 Hales Corners WI 53130

KOSHY, GEORGE PYNUMMOOTTIL, reliability engineer; b. Trivandrum, Kerala, India, Jan. 15, 1941; came to U.S., 1966; s. Pynummoottil T. and Annamma (Mathai) K.; m. Alice G. Abraham, Aug. 18, 1966; children—Ann, Abraham. B.S., Kerala U., India, 1961; M.S., Agra U., Uther Pradesh, India, 1964; Ph.D., Sussex Coll. Tech., 1981. Cert. quality engr. Lectr. Kerala U., India, 1964-66; statistician IBM, Phila., 1967-69; mgr. quality assurance/quality control Inst. Sci. Info., Phila., 1972-78; quality control engr. Conrail, Phila., 1978-84; sr. reliability engr., founder statis. quality control and reliability system Gen. Electric - Power Supply Operation, Ft. Wayne, Ind., 1984—; founder statis. quality control system Inst. Sci. Info., Phila., 1972-78; founder component quality measurement system Conrail, Phila., 1978-84. Mem. Am. Soc. Quality Control, Am. Statis. Assn. Republican. Avocations: reading; research. Home: 3030 Padago Ct Fort Wayne IN 46815 Office: Gen Electric Power Supply Operation 1701 College St 26-4 Fort Wayne IN 46801

KOSIAK, MICHAEL J., leisure and recreation company executive; b. Chgo., Dec. 11, 1943; s. Michael and Emma (Gedmin) K.; m. Carol M. Weis, Sept. 5, 1979. B.B.A., Loyola U., Chgo., 1965; M.B.A., U. Chgo., 1978. Dir. group acctg. Maremont Corp., Chgo., 1969-72, regional controller, 1972-75; asst. to controller Canteen Corp., Chgo., 1975-76, dir. acquisitions, 1976-81, staff v.p., 1981—, dir. ops. concessions div., 1982—; sr. v.p. TWA Services, Chgo., 1981—; dir. First Penn Pacific Life Ins. Co., Oakbrook, Ill., 1980-82. Mem. Nat. Restaurant Assn., U. Chgo. Club Met. Chgo., U. Chgo. Exec. Club, West Highland White Terrier Club No. Ill., West Highland White Terrier Club Am., Delta Theta Phi, Alpha Kappa Psi. Republican. Roman Catholic. Office: Canteen Corp Merchandise Mart Chicago IL 60054

KOSKINEN, DONALD S(TEWARD), printing company executive; b. Hamilton, Ohio, Oct. 18, 1928; s. Einar T. and Rachael (Steward) K.; m. Jean Alexander, Aug. 28, 1954; children—Walter, Anne, David, John. B.S., Lawrence U., 1950. Pres., Banta Co., Inc., Menasha, Wis., 1972—; dir. George Banta Co., Inc., Murray Machinery, Inc., Wausau, Wis., Twin City Savs. & Loan. Trustee, Lawrence U., 1965—, chmn. bd. trustees, 1981-83; trustee Theda Clark Regional Med. Ctr., Neenah, Wis., 1982—; bd. dirs. Neenah chpt. Am. Cancer Soc., 1978—, pres. bd. dirs., 1978-80; trustee Wayland Acad., Beaver Dam, Wis., 1978-81. Served to 1st lt. U.S. Army, 1951-53. Mem. Book Mfrs. Inst. (pres. 1984—), Wis. Paper Group (pres. 1973, treas. 1974—), Fox Cities C. of C. (bd. dirs., exec. com.). Republican. Presbyterian. Clubs: North Shore Golf (Menasha); Rainbo Lodge (Land O'Lakes, Wis.); Wausau; Plum Lake Golf (Sayner, Wis.). Lodge: Elks. Home: 315 Lake Rd Menasha WI 54952 Office: Banta Co Curtis Reed Plaza Menasha WI 54952

KOSLOSKY, PIERCE ANDREW, JR., metal company executive; b. Newark, June 18, 1950; s. Pierce Andrew and Helen May (Benton) K.; m. Judith Ellen Riddle, July 22, 1971 (div. 1983); m. Candice M. Cuttler, Apr. 27, 1985. B.A. in Psychology, Duke U., 1972. Psychol. asst. N.C. Dept. Corrections, Raleigh, 1972-74; v.p. sales Magnolia Metal Corp., Omaha, 1975—. Recipient 3rd place Poetry for Nebr., Am. Acad. Poets, 1979. Mem. Am. Foundrymen's Soc. Republican. Mem. Assembly of God Ch. Avocations: writing; film; travel.

Home: 2512 N 53d St Omaha NE 68104 Office: Magnolia Metal Corp 6161 Abbott Dr Omaha NE 68110

KOSS, GREGORY ALAN, architect; b. Tallahassee, Fla., Dec. 19, 1952; s. John Peter and Jacquelyn Elizabeth (Moore) K.; m. Mary Beth Botzum, Aug. 4, 1973; children—Jennifer, Jonathan. B.A. in Architecture, U. Mich., 1975, M.Arch. with distinction, 1976. Cert. AIA, Nat. Council Archtl. Registration Bds. Plan examiner City of Dayton (Ohio), 1976; project architect Kleski & Assocs., Dayton 1977-78; project mgr. The Austin Co., Cleve., 1979-83, project planner, 1983—. Mem. AIA, Architects Soc. Ohio. Roman Catholic. Home: 3630 Northcliffe Rd University Heights OH 44118 Office: Austin Co 3700 Mayfield Rd Cleveland Heights OH 44121

KOSTEL, MARY LOU, librarian; b. Tabor, S.D., Mar. 18, 1949; d. Lawrence William and Tillie Georgina (Novotny) Herman; m. Roger Dale Kostel, Aug. 22, 1970. Student So. State Coll., Springfield, S.D., 1967, 68, 69, 70, 71. Tchr., Scotland Sch. Dist. (S.D.), 1968-69, St. Wenceslaus, Tabor, S.D., 1969-71; med. librarian S.D. Human Services Ctr., Yankton, 1971—. Med. library resource improvement grantee Nat. Library of Medicine, S.D. Human Services Ctr. Med. Library, 1980. Mem. S.D. Hosp. Library Assn., S.D. Council Health Scis. Libraries, Greater Midwest Regional Med. Library Network. Democrat. Roman Catholic. Home: 1015 E 15th St Yankton SD 57078 Office: SD Human Services Ctr Med Library Yankton SD 57078

KOSTYRA, EUGENE MICHAEL, province official; b. Winnipeg, Man., Can., June 19, 1947; s. Albert and Jean (Swetz) K.; m. Jeri McKee, Feb. 1, 1985. Electrician, Man. Hydro Co., Winnipeg, Can., union rep. Can. Union Pub. Employees; minister of industry, trade and tech. Province of Man., Winnipeg, 1983—, minister of the crown Govt. of Man., Winnipeg, 1981—. Mem. New Democratic Party. Office: Govt of Manitoba Room 358 Legis Bldg 450 Broadway Ave Winnipeg MB R3C 0V8 Canada

KOTCH, ALEX, chemistry educator, university administrator; b. Edwardsville, Pa., Aug. 18, 1926; s. Alex and Irene (Hazilla) K.; m. Anny Marie Brinkman, Mar. 5, 1952; children—Marianne (Mrs. Gerald L. Cassell), Axel, Robert, Jennifer. Student, Bucknell Jr. Coll., 1943-44; B.S., Pa. State U., 1946, M.S., 1947; Ph.D., U. Ill., 1950. Arthur D. Little postdoctoral fellow Mass. Inst. Tech., 1951-52; research chemist central research dept. E.I. duPont de Nemours & Co., Wilmington, Del., 1952-54, chemist organic chems. dept. Deepwater Point, N.J., 1954-59; assoc. program dir. for chemistry NSF, Washington, 1959-63, program dir. for organic chemistry, 1963-65; chief biosciences div. Office of Saline Water, Dept. Interior, Washington, 1965-66; staff assoc. univ. sci. devel. sect. NSF, Washington, 1966-67; prof. chemistry, assoc. chmn. U. Wis., Madison, 1967-77; asst. dir. info. edn. and internat. programs Solar Energy Research Inst., 1977-78, spl. asst. to dir., 1978-79, mgr. univ. programs office, 1979-82; prof. chemistry, dir. Office of Research and Program Devel. U. N.D., 1982—; cons.-examiner North Central Assn. Colls. and Schs., commr.-at-large, 1984—; bd. dirs. Associated Western Univs., 1982—. Evan Pugh scholar Pa. State U., 1946; fellow Monsanto Chem. Co., 1949-50, Fulbright fellow Tech. U. Delft, Netherlands, 1950-51. Mem. Am. Chem. Soc., AAAS, Nat. Council Univ. Research Adminstrs., Soc. Research Adminstrs., Sigma Xi, Alpha Chi Sigma, Phi Kappa Phi, Phi Lambda Upsilon, Pi Mu Epsilon. Home: 3502 Belmont Rd Grand Forks ND 58201 Office: Univ ND Office Research & Program Devel Box 8138 University Station Grand Forks ND 58202

KOTICK, ROBERT ANDREW, computer software company executive; b. N.Y.C., Mar. 1, 1963; s. Charles M. and Judith Elizabeth (Fremer) K. Student U. Mich., 1981—. Chmn. Arktronics Corp., Ann Arbor, Mich., 1983—. Office: Arktronics Corp 520 E Liberty St Ann Arbor MI 48104

KOTTMAN, ROY MILTON, agriculture research administrator, consultant; b. Thornton, Iowa, Dec. 22, 1916; s. William D. and Millie J. (Christensen) K.; m. Wanda L. Moorman, Dec. 31, 1941; children—Gary R., Robert W., Wayne D., Janet K. B.S. in Agr., Iowa State U., 1941, Ph.D. in Animal Breeding, 1952; M.S. in Genetics, U. Wis., 1948; LL.D. (hon.), Coll. Wooster, 1972. Asst. dean Coll. Agr., Iowa State U., Ames, 1951-54, assoc. dean, 1954-58; dean, dir. Coll. Agr. and Home Econs. W.Va. U., Morgantown, 1958-60; dean, dir. Coll. Agr. and Home Econs., Ohio State U., Columbus, 1960-82, v.p. for agrl. adminstrn., 1982, acting assoc. dir. Nev. Agrl. Expt. Sta., 1982-83; coordinator estate gifts, Ohio State U., 1983-84; cons. to chancellor U. Puerto Rico, Mayaguez, 1984-85; mem. adv. bd. Cancer Research Ctr., Coll. Medicine, Ohio State U., 1972-82, mem. adv. com. Ctr. for Lake Erie, Area Research, Ohio State U., 1972-82; mem. exec. com. sci. adv. bd. DNA Plant Tech. Corp., Cinnaminson, N.J., 1982—; Speaker various orgns. Recipient Disting. Service award Ohio Farm Bur. Fedn., 1981, Golden Rose award Ohio Outdoor Hist. Assn., 1982, Disting. Service award Am. Agr. Editors Assn., 1983; commencement speaker Ohio State U., 1982; named to Ohio Agr. Hall Fame, 1983. Fellow Am. Soc. Animal Sci; mem. Soil Conservation Soc. Am. (honor award 1975), Agr. Research Inst. (hon. life, v.p. 1980-81), Farm Fedn. (trustee 1978—), People-to-People Internat. Republican. Presbyterian. Home: 1375 Kirkley Rd Columbus OH 43221 Office: Coll Agr 2120 Fyffe Rd Columbus OH 43210

KOTTMEIER, JAMES ALAN, communication and meeting consultant, executive; b. Cedar Rapids, Iowa, Sept. 9, 1944; s. William Henry and Hildegarde Caroline (Rabus) K.; m. Cheryl Chase, Aug. 28, 1984; 1 son, James Blair. B.S. in Bus. Adminstrn., U. Minn., 1971. Design draftsman Collins Radio Corp., Cedar Rapids, 1962-63; sr. designer Strom Engring. Corp., Hopkins, Minn., 1963-66; asst. plant mgr. GAF Corp., Mpls., 1968-71; mktg. bus. mgr. Control Data Corp., Mpls., 1971-80, meeting mgr., 1980-84, tng. cons., 1977-81; now pres. Twin Cities Unltd., Travel and Meeting Services. Contbr. articles to profl. jours. Musician-drummer RUMC Players, Richfield, Minn., 1978-84. Served with U.S. Army, 1966-68. Methodist. Home: 2000 W 86th St Bloomington MN 55431 Office: Twin Cities Unltd 5748 Nicollet Ave S Minneapolis MN 55419

KOUBA, LISA MARCO, lawyer; b. Chgo., July 1, 1957; d. Edward Samuel and Phyllis Lavergne (Pincus) Marco; m. Kenneth Edward Kouba, Sept. 24, 1983. B.A. with honors, U. Ill., 1978; J.D. cum laude, Loyola U., Chgo., 1981. Bar: Ill. 1981, U.S. Dist. Ct. (no. dist.) Ill. 1981, U.S. Ct. Appeals (6th, 7th, 8th and 10th cirs.) 1982. Assoc. Clausen, Miller, Gorman, Caffrey & Witous, P.C., Chgo., 1981—. Editor Loyola Law Jour., 1981. Mem. Chgo. Bar Assn. (chmn. young lawyers sect. on appellate law 1982-83), Ill. Bar Assn., Appellate Lawyers Assn., Chgo. Council on Foreign Relations. Office: Clausen Miller Gorman Caffrey & Witous PC 5400 Sears Tower Chicago IL 60606

KOUMOULIDES, JOHN THOMAS ANASTASIOS, history educator; b. Greece, Aug. 23, 1938; s. Anastasios Lazaros and Sophia (Theodosiadou) K.; came to U.S., 1956, naturalized, 1969; A.B., Montclair (N.J.) State Coll., 1960, A.M., 1961; Ph.D., U. Md., 1968; student Fitzwilliam Coll., Cambridge (Eng.) U., 1965-67, vis. fellow, 1971-72. Grad. asst. U. Md., 1961-63; asst. prof. history Austin Peay State U., Clarksville, Tenn., 1963-65, Vanderbilt U., summer 1968; vis. tutor Campion Hall, Oxford (Eng.) U.; mem. faculty Ball State U., Muncie, Ind., 1968—, prof. history, 1975—. Named Archon Chartophylax of Ecumenical Patriarchate of Constantinople, 1979. Research grantee Ball State U., 1969, 70, 74, 79, Am. Philos. Soc., 1973, 80; Am. Council Learned Socs. grantee, 1969, 71, 74; Fulbright-Hays research awardee, Greece, 1977-78; guest scholar Woodrow Wilson Internat. Ctr. for Scholars, 1982; Dumbarton Oaks research grantee, 1982, 83-86; recipient Outstanding Research award Ball State U., 1983; vis. fellow Wolfson Coll., Oxford U., 1983-84. Mem. Am., Brit., Cambridge U. hist. assns., Archaeol. Inst. Am., AAUP, Modern Greek Studies Assn., Soc. Promotion Hellenic Studies, Cambridge U. Philol. Assn., Phi Alpha Theta, Alpha Tau Omega. Author: Cyprus and the Greek War of Independence, 1821-1829, 2d edit., 1974; Byzantine and Post-Byzantine Monuments at Aghia in Thessaly, Greece: The Art and Architecture of the Monastery of Saint Panteleimon, 1975; (with others) Churches of Aghia in Larissa, 1985; also monographs, articles; editor: Greece in Transition: Essays in the History of Modern Greece 1821-1974, 1977; Greece: Past and Present, 1979; Hellenic Perspectives: Essays in the History of Greece, 1980; Greece and Cyprus in History, 1984; co-editor: Perspectives in Byzantine History and Culture 1984.

KOUTROULIS, ARIS GEORGE, artist, educator; b. Athens, Greece, May 14, 1938; came to U.S., 1953; s. George Aris and Julia (Eftimiades) K.; m. Mary Ann Schmid, 1964 (div. 1973); m. Jill Warren, July 4, 1982; 1 dau., Georgina. B.F.A., La. State U., 1961; Master Printer, Tamarind Lithography Workshop, Los Angeles, 1964; M.F.A., Cranbrook Acad. Art, Bloomfield Hills, Mich., 1966. Chmn. bd. Willis Gallery, Detroit, 1970-71; pres. Common Ground of the Arts, Detroit, 1969-72; guest artist Ox-Bow Summer Sch. Art, Saugatuck, Mich., 1973, co-dir., 1975; assoc. prof. art Wayne State U., 1966-75; head painting dept. Ctr. Creative Studies, Detroit, 1975-81, chmn. Fine Arts Dept., 1981—; exhibited one-man shows, Hanamura Gallery, Detroit, 1966, Montgomery Mus. Fine Arts, Ala., 1966, Va. Poly. Inst., 1968, Baton Rouge Gallery, 1968, Wayne State U., 1969, Mich. Council for Arts, 1969, Gertrude Kasle Gallery, Detroit, 1970, Detroit Artists Market, 1973, Klein-Vogel Gallery, Detroit, 1974, Detroit Inst. Arts, 1976, Gloria Cortella Gallery, N.Y.C., 1977, Gallery Renaissance, Detroit, 1980, Haber-Theodore Gallery, N.Y.C., 1980; OK Harris Gallery, N.Y.C., 1980, 81, 82, 83, 85, Mich. Traveling Exhbn., 1981, Cantor/Emberg Gallery, Birmingham, Mich., 1982, Dubins Gallery, Los Angeles, 1984; exhibited group shows Decorative Arts Ctr., N.Y.C., 1973, Detroit Inst. Arts, 1974, Bykert Gallery, N.Y.C., 1974, Bklyn. Mus., 1977, Brooks Meml. Art Gallery, Memphis, 1977, La. State U. Gallery, 1978, Tyler Sch. Art, Temple U., 1978, Mus. Fine Arts, Springfield, Mass., 1978, Van Doren Gallery, San Francisco, 1978, Consulate Gen. Greece, N.Y.C., 1978, Landmark Gallery, N.Y.C., 1978, Cranbrook Mus. Art, Bloomfield Hills, Mich., 1979, Detroit Inst. Arts, 1980; represented in pub. collections including Mus. Modern Art, Nat. Gallery Art, Detroit Inst. Arts, Los Angeles County Mus. Art, Cranbrook Mus. Art, Detroit Engring. Soc., Detroit Pub. Library, U. Mich. Art Mus., Anglo-Am. Mus., Amon Carter Mus. Western Art, Ft. Worth, UCLA Grunwald Graphic Arts Found., Ball State U. Art Mus.; represented in corp. collections; commd. Standard Oil Corp., San Ramon, Calif., Arbor Drugs, Inc., Focus Gallery, Bracewell/Patterson, Washington, Mich. Found. for Arts, Detroit Engring. Soc., Art for Detroit, City of Detroit, WDIV-TV4, Detroit. Address: Center for Creative Studies Dept Fine Arts 245 E Kirby St Detroit MI 48202

KOVACH, ILDIKO MARIA, pharmaceutical chemist, researcher; b. Nagykanizsa, Hungary, June 22, 1939; came to U.S., 1966, naturalized, 1972; d. Istvan O. and Maria M. (Kratky) Lugos; m. Gyula F. Kovach, Sept. 20, 1958; children—Adam, Adrienne. Diploma in Pharmacy with honors, Med. U. Budapest, 1964; M.S. in Pharm. Chemistry, U. Kans., 1972, Ph.D., 1974. Lic. pharmacist, Hungary. Research assoc. dept. chemistry U. Kans., 1974-78, ind. research, 1978-80; asst. scientist Ctr. for Biomed. Research, U. Kans., 1980-85, assoc. scientist, 1985—. Reviewer Jour. Am. Chem. Soc., 1983—, Jour. Organic Chemistry, 1980—. Contbr. articles to profl. jours. Mem. Am. Chem. Soc., Acad. Pharm. Assocs. Roman Catholic. Avocations: fine arts, music, swimming, water-skiing. Office: CBR Univ Kans 2099 Constant Ave Lawrence KS 66045

KOVACIK, VICTOR PAUL, industrial control systems manufacturing company executive; b. St. Louis, Aug. 2, 1927; s. Paul and Anna (Matusovic) K.; m. Winifred Ann Hartzell, July 9, 1955; 1 child, Ellissa. B.S. in Mech. Engring., Washington U., St. Louis, 1948; M.S. in Aero. Engring., Purdue U., 1949; M.B.A., Harvard U., 1957; diploma Oak Ridge Sch. Reactor Tech., 1951. Project engr. Wright Air Devel. Ctr., Dayton, Ohio, 1949-55; engr. supr. Pratt & Whitney Div. United Tech., Boston, 1956-57; mgr. elec. products dept. TRW, Inc., Cleve., 1957-69; dir. new tech. ventures Studebaker Worthington Corp., N.Y.C., 1969-70; founder Cyberex, 1968, dir., 1968-80; pres., dir. Frolic Friends, Mentor, Ohio, 1971—; pres. Orttech, Inc., Willoughby, Ohio, 1980—; dir., chmn. bd. Cyberex, Inc., Mentor, 1968-81; pres. Mead Dijit Inc., subs. Mead Corp., Dayton, 1973-75; dir. Mitech Inc., Willoughby, 1983—. Author: Impact of High Temperature Technology, 1947. Patentee torpedo propulsion system; developer ink jet printing system. Served with USN, 1945-46, to 1st lt. USAF, 1953-55. Recipient IR-100 award Mead Corp., 1973. Mem. IEEE, Soc. Mfg. Engrs., Greater Cleve. Growth Assn., Council Small Bus. Enterprises. Home: 522 Saddleback Ln Gates Mills OH 44040 Office: Orttech Inc 4760 Beidler Rd Willoughby OH 44094

KOVACS, GAIL LOUISE PATEK, hospital administrator, nurse, biologist; b. Cleve., Feb. 17, 1949; d. Louis Cornelius and Veronica Rose (Skerl) Patek; m. John Joseph Kovacs, June 24, 1972 (div.); 1 son, Jeffrey Joseph. B.A. in Biology cum laude, Ursuline Coll., 1971; R.N., Cleve. Met. Sch. Nursing, 1975; M.B.A. magna cum laude, Cleve. State U., 1982. Med. technologist Cleve. Clinic Found., 1971-72; immunology research asst. Case Western Res. U., Cleve., 1972-73; staff nurse Mt. Sinai Hosp., Cleve., 1975-76; staff nurse Cleve. Met. Gen. Hosp., 1976, infectious disease nurse, 1976-78; assoc. dir. supply services Univ. Hosps of Cleve., 1978-79, asst. dir. material mgmt., 1979, administrv. assoc., 1979-80, assoc. dir. material mgmt., 1980-84, asst. gen. mgr. adminstrn., 1984—; lectr. epidemiology, material mgmt. Cleve. Found. grantee, 1980, 81; recipient Paul Widman Meml. award Ctr. Health Affairs/Greater Cleve. Hosp. Assn., 1985. Mem. Health Care Fin. Mgmt. Soc., Health Care Material Mgmt. Soc. (v.p.; presdl. citation 1985), Internat. Material Mgmt. Soc., Soc. for Hosp. Purchasing and Material Mgmt., N.E. Ohio Soc. for Health Care Material Mgmt., Beta Gamma Sigma. Roman Catholic. Home: 1450 Blossom Park Ave Lakewood OH 44107 Office: Univ Hosps of Cleveland 2074 Abington Rd Cleveland OH 44106

KOVACS, JOHN JOSEPH, lawyer; b. Elyria, Ohio, Nov. 5, 1947; s. John Joseph and Elizabeth (Fusa) K.; 1 child, Jeffrey Joseph. B.A., Borromeo Coll. Ohio, 1969; J.D. cum laude, Cleve. State U., 1977. Bar: Ohio. Probation officer Ohio Adult Parole Authority, Elyria, 1969-72, dist. supr., Cleve., 1972-79; asst. prosecutor Lorain County, Elyria, 1980-83; sole practice, Elyria, 1979—; arbitrator Lorain County Common Pleas Court, Elyria, 1979—. Mem. ABA, Ohio State Bar Assn., Lorain County Bar Assn., Jaycees (bd. dirs., legal counsel, 1981-82). Roman Catholic. Avocations: hiking; tennis; swimming; horseback riding. Home: 1416 Lewis Dr Apt 102 Lakewood OH 44107 Office: Lessing Schnitkey & Kovacs 422 EST Bldg Elyria OH 44035

KOVACS, SANDOR JANOS, JR., scientist, physician; b. Budapest, Hungary, Aug 17, 1947; s. Sandor and Julianna (Weisz) K.; m. Diane Frances Merritt, Apr. 16, 1983; 1 child, Sándor Ádám. B.S., Cornell U., 1969; M.S., Calif. Inst. Tech., 1972, Ph.D. in Theoretical Physics, 1977; M.D., U. Miami, Fla., 1979. Diplomate Am. Bd. Internal Medicine. Intern, Barnes Hosp., St. Louis, 1979-80, resident 1980-82; mem. house staff internal medicine Washington U. Med. Ctr., Barnes Hosp., St. Louis, 1979-82, fellow in cardiology, 1982-85, instr. in medicine, 1985-86. Contbr. articles to various publs. Mem. ACP, Am. Coll. Cardiology, Internat. Soc. Gen. Relativity and Gravitation, N.Y. Acad. Sci., AAAS, Sigma Xi, Tau Beta Pi.

KOVELESKI, KATHRYN DELANE, educator; b. Detroit, Aug. 12, 1925; d. Edward Albert Vogt and Delane (Bender) Vogt; B.A., Olivet (Mich.) Coll., 1947; M.A., Wayne State U., Detroit, 1955; m. Casper Koveleski, July 18, 1952; children—Martha, Ann. Tchr. schs. in Mich., 1947—; tchr. Garden City Schs., 1955-56, 59—, resource and learning disabilities tchr., 1970—. Mem. NEA, Mich. Edn. Assn., Garden City Edn. Assn., Bus. and Profl. Women (pres. Garden City 1982-83, Woman of Yr. 1983-84). Congregationalist. Clubs: Wayne Lit. (past pres.), Sch. Masters Bowling League (v.p. 1984-86), Odd Couples Bowling League (pres. 82-83). Office: 33411 Marquette St Garden City MI 48135

KOVITZ, ARTHUR A., mechanical engineering educator; b. Detroit, Aug. 6, 1928; s. Hyman and Rose (Zuzel) K.; m. Valerie Silverman, June 30, 1957; children—Claudia Rose, Jordan Aaron. B.S., U. Mich., 1950, M.S., 1951; Ph.D. in Aero. Engring., Princeton U., 1957. Asst. prof. mech. engring. Northwestern U., Evanston, Ill., 1958-61, assoc. prof., 1961-69, prof., 1969—. Mem. Am. Phys. Soc. Office: Northwestern U Dept Mech Engring 2145 Sheridan Rd Evanston IL 60201

KOWALCZEWSKI, DOREEN MARY THURLOW, communications company executive; b. London, May 5, 1926; came to U.S., 1957, naturalized, 1974; d. George Henry and Jessie Alice (Gray) Thurlow; B.A., Clarke Coll., 1947; postgrad. Wayne State U., 1959-62, Roosevelt U., 1968; m. Witold Dionizy Kowalczewski, July 26, 1946; children—Christina Julianna, Janet Alice, Stephen Robin. Agy. supr. MONY, N.Y.C., 1963-67; office mgr. J.B. Carroll Co., Chgo., 1967-68; mng. editor Sawyer Coll. Bus., Evanston, Ill., 1968-71; mgr. policyholder service CNA, Chgo., 1971-73; EDP coordinator Canteen Corp., Chgo., 1973-75; mgr. documentation and standards LRSP, Chgo., 1975-77; data network mgr. Computerized Agy. Mgmt. Info. Services, Chgo., 1977—; founder, chmn. Tekman Assos., 1982—. Pres., Univ. Park Assn., 1980-84. Mem. Nat. Assn. Female Execs., Women in Info. Processing, Chgo. Orgn. Data Processing Educators, Women in Mgmt., Mensa. Home: 3712 Madison St Brookfield IL 60513

KOWALSKI, CASIMIR J., college dean; b. Poland, Apr. 9, 1942, came to U.S., 1951; m. Johanna Kowalski; children—Joseph, Matthew, Peter, Robert. B.S. in Edn., SUNY-Oswego, 1965; M.A. in Guidance and Counseling, Western Ky. U., 1972; Ed.S. in State Personnel Services, 1973; Ed.D. in Administrn., Ind. U., 1974. Tchr. elem. edn. Syracuse Bd. Edn., N.Y., 1965-68; tchr., phys. edn. dir. N.Am. Sch. U.S. Steel Corp., Puerto Ordaz, Venezuela, 1968-71; counselor, instr. Western Ky. U., Bowling Green, 1971-72, research and adminstrv. asst., 1972-73; counselor, instr. Ind. U., Bloomington, 1973-74; asst. dir. U. Ky. Henderson Community Coll., 1975-77; v.p. acad. affairs SUNY-Morrisville, 1977-80; dean instructional services Marion Tech. Coll., Ohio, 1980—; cons. numerous insts. and orgns. Contbr. articles to profl. jours. Mng. editor Psychology, 1978—. Mem. Nat. Assn. Gifted Children (nat. bd. dirs. 1972-73). Office: Marion Tech Coll Marion OH 43302

KOWALSKI, RAYMOND ALOIS, design executive; b. Erie, Pa., June 21, 1933; s. John and Anna (Wisniewski) K. B.F.A., Cleve. Inst. Art, 1957. Exec. dir. design Am. Greetings, Cleve.; lectr. in field. Numerous exhibits and one man shows in water color, acrylic and collage. Program dir. Shaker Heights Hist. Mus., Ohio; jurist various art competitions, Cleve. Served with U.S. Army, 1957-59. Mem. Design Mgmt. Inst., Soc. Illustrators. Avocations: collector, researcher Am. Shaker furniture. Home: 2780 Berkshire Rd Cleveland Heights OH 44106

KOWALSKI, ROBERT JAMES, lawyer; b. Evanston, Ill., June 11, 1947; s. Walter J. and Sue L. (Poleski) K.; m. Carol J. Holt, Sept. 27, 1969 (div. Jan. 1981); children—Lauren Sue, Melissa Kay, Deanna Lynn. B.S. in Bus. Adminstrn., U. Tex.-Corpus Christi, 1969; J.D., Ill. Inst. Tech. Chgo. Kent Sch. Law, 1973. Bar: Ill. 1973, U.S. Dist. Ct. (no. dist.) Ill. 1973, U.S. Supreme Ct., 1980, U.S. Ct. Appeals (7th cir.) 1981, U.S. Tax Ct. 1985; lic. real estate broker, Ill.; cert. instr. polygraph interns, Ill. Real estate broker, Chgo., 1967-73; traffic safety educator Cook County, Chgo., 1969-73; instr. Aerospace Inst., Chgo., 1971-73; asst. states atty. Cook County, 1974-81; sole practice, Chgo., 1981—. Legal adviser Photog. Arts and Sci. Found., Des Plaines, Ill., 1981—, chpt. 3438 Am. Assn. Ret. Persons, Des Plaines, 1982—, Copernicus Found., Chgo., 1982—. Mem. Chgo. Bar Assn., Am. Judicature Soc., ABA, Ill. State Bar Assn., Northwest Suburban Bar Assn., Advs. Soc., Am. Arbitration Assn. (arbitrator), Delta Theta Phi. Roman Catholic. Office: Law Offices R J Kowalski PC 134 N LaSalle Chicago IL 60602

KOZAR, JENNIFER LEA, osteopathic physician; b. Mexia, Tex., Mar. 10, 1948; d. James Marlin and Betty Jo (Long) Wrenn; m. Raymond Davis Brendle, Nov. 8, 1968 (div. 1980); m. Bradley Kenneth Kozar, June 19, 1982. B.A., Austin Coll., 1975; D.O., Kirksville Coll. Osteo. Medicine, Mo., 1980. Intern Okla. Osteo. Hosp., Tulsa, 1980-81; gen. practice osteo. medicine, Westside Clinic, Mount Pleasant, Mich., 1981—; chmn. family practice dept., chief staff, trustee Central Mich. Community Hosp. Bd. dirs. Sexual Assault Task Force, Mount Pleasant, 1983-85; physician advisor Hospice Central Mich., Mount Pleasant, 1984-85. Mem. Am. Osteo. Assn., Mich. Assn. Osteo. Physicians and Surgeons, Mich. State Med. Soc., Mount Pleasant C. of C., Delta Omega. Republican. Episcopalian. Lodge: Zonta. Avocations: travel; swimming. Home: 1333 E Bennett Mount Pleasant MI 48858 Office: Westside Clinic PC 709 S Adams Mount Pleasant MI 48858

KOZBERG, STEVEN FREED, psychologist; b. Mpls., Apr. 30, 1953; s. Martin L. and Lois (Bix) K. B.A., Macalester Coll., 1975; M.A., U. Minn.-Duluth, 1978; Ph.D., U. Wis.-Madison, 1981. Lic. cons. psychologist, Minn. Research asst. dept. counseling and guidance U. Wis.-Madison, 1978-79, teaching asst., 1980-81, research asst. Guidance Inst. for Talented Students, 1979-80; counseling psychologist, asst. prof. psychology Carleton Coll., Northfield, Minn., 1981—. Mem. Am. Psychol. Assn., Am. Assn. Counseling and Devel., Sigma Xi, Phi Kappa Phi, Pi Lambda Theta. Home: 6400 Barrie Rd Apt 606 Edina MN 55435 Office: Carleton Coll Northfield MN 55057

KOZELKA, EDWARD WILLIAM, seed and feed company executive; b. Monona, Iowa, July 19, 1912; s. William Frank and Elizabeth (Tayek) K.; student Loras Coll., 1929-31; m. Beulah Annette Gunderson, Feb. 24, 1941; 1 dau., Gail Kathleen. Gen. mgr. Hall Roberts' Son, Postville, Iowa, 1932-46, v.p., gen. mgr., 1946-75, treas., 1975—; salesman Dean Real Estate, Postville, 1975—; dir. Postville State Bank, Postville Telephone Co. Mem. Postville City Council, 1960-61; pres. Postville Hist. Soc., 1975-78; treas. Upper Explorerland Resource, Conservation and Devel. Com., 1969—; chmn. Upper Explorerland Regional Planning Commn., 1971-80; chmn. N.E. Iowa River Basin Com., 1976-79; mem. Iowa Policy Adv. Council on Water Quality, 1976-82; mem. citizens adv. council Dept. Transp., 1977—; mem. planning and fin. com. Postville Hosp., 1959-60; chmn. bldg. com. Postville Hosp., 1960-61; co-chmn. fund raising com. Postville Good Samaritan Center, 1968; bd. dirs. Big 4 Fair, 1946-74; mem. adv. council Area Aging Com., 1983—. Recipient Disting. Service award Jaycees, 1966; hon. future farmer FFA. Mem. Iowa Seed Dealers Assn. (pres. 1972), Iowa Grain and Feed Assn., Western Seed Dealers Assn. Republican. Roman Catholic. Clubs: Kiwanis, Postville Comml. Home: 205 Williams St W Postville IA 52162 Office: PO Box 396 Postville IA 52162

KOZLOFF, GEORGE ARTHUR, JR., insurance company official; b. Detroit, Sept. 24, 1952; s. George Arthur and Jacquiline M. (Thebo) K.; m. Janice LaFleur, June 16, 1979; children—Kristine, Katherine. A.A., Oakland Community Coll., 1973; postgrad., U. Mich., 1973-74; B.B.A., Eastern Mich. U., 1977. Adminstrv. intern Hurley Med. Ctr., Flint, Mich., 1977-80; systems-procedures analyst Kelly Services, Troy, Mich., 1981-82; methods analyst Citizens Ins. Co., Howell, Mich., 1983—. Loan exec. Genesee County United Way, Flint, 1977-78; vol. Genesee-Flint Internat. Inst., Flint, 1980. Mem. Assn. Systems Mgmt. (profl. mem.), Sigma Chi (chpt. advisor). Avocations: photography; gardening; travel; sports. Home: 1202 W Hamilton Ave Flint MI 48504

KOZMA, PAUL DENNIS, pharmacist, funeral director; b. Syracuse, N.Y., Mar. 25, 1952; s. Joseph and Hilda Nellie (Blanchard) K.; m. Carmella Antoinette Ellwein, Feb. 14, 1982. Student So. State Coll., 1970-71; A.A.S., Onondaga Community Coll., 1975; student in mortuary sci., Simmons Coll., 1974-75; B.S. in Pharmacy, N.D. State U., 1982. Lic. funeral dir., N.Y.; pharmacist, N.D., Iowa. Funeral dir. intern McGrath Funeral Home, Bronxville, N.Y., 1975-76; Sutton Funeral Home, Clintondale, N.Y., 1976; funeral dir. Parsky Funeral Home, Rochester, N.Y., 1977; pharmacist intern St. John's Hosp., Fargo, N.D., 1982-83; pharmacist K-Mart Corp., Clinton, Iowa, 1983—. Recipient Outstanding Athlete award Morris Machine Works, 1970; Most Individual award N.D. State Coll. Pharmacy, 1982. Mem. Iowa Pharmacy Assn. Republican. Methodist. Avocations: volleyball and softball coach; running; record album collecting. Home: 1215 7th Ave Apt 303 Camanche IA 52730

KRAATZ, ROLAND LEE, utility company executive; b. Evanston, Ill., May 18, 1943; s. Arthur William Kraatz and Dorothy Loraine (Strauss) Keyes; m. Gloria Jean Hohisel, Sept. 4, 1965. B.S. in Elec. Engring., Bradley U., 1965; M.B.A., U. Chgo., 1971. Registered profl. engr., Ill. Engr., Commonwealth Edison Co., Maywood, Ill., 1965-68, Joliet, Ill., 1969-71, Chgo., 1971-82, dir. econ. research, 1982-85, dir. rates, 1985—. Mem. IEEE (sr.), Western Soc. Engrs. Home: 1857 Mission Hills Ln Northbrook IL 60062

KRABACH, RICHARD, state education official. Chmn., Bd. Regents (higher edn.) State of Ohio, Columbus. Office: Bd Regents Higher Edn 30 E Rd St Columbus OH 43215*

KRAEMER, ELIZABETH EMERSON, clinical psychologist, educator; b. Lynchburg, Va., Mar. 1, 1936; d. Cameron and Leona (Greene) King; children—Mark Karl, Kristina Marie, Katherine Ann, Teresa Kelle. A.B., U. Mo., 1970, M.A., 1971, Ph.D., 1978. Asst. dir. Psychol. Clinic, U. Mo., Columbia, 1974-75; clin. psychologist Mark Twain Mental Health Ctr., Kirksville, Mo., 1975-78; dir., pvt. practice clin. psychology Profl. Counseling Services, Kirksville, 1978—; mem. faculty Northeast Mo. State U., 1978—. Bd. dirs. ARC, 1979-82, Kirksville Crisis Line, 1978-83, Transisition Care Ctr., 1980-82. Mem. Am. Psychol. Assn., Phi Beta Kappa. Democrat. Roman Catholic. Office: 404 S Franklin St Suite 3 Kirksville MO 63501

KRAESZIG-MULCAHY, KARLA MARIA, optometrist; b. Indpls., Oct. 29, 1951; d. Harry E. and Lillian (Lieland) K.; m. James George Mulcahy, Oct. 11, 1980; 1 child, James Lionel. B.S., Ind. U., 1973, O.D., 1975. Optometrist, Arner & Kraeszig, Rockford, Ill., 1976-82, Kraeszig-Mulcahy, Byron, Ill., 1982—. Mem. Vol. Optometric Services to Humanity, 1980—. Mem. World Wildlife

Fund, Audubon Soc., Smithsonian Instn., Byron C. of C., Am. Optometric Assn. (contact lens sect.), No. Ill. Optometric Soc. (past pres.), Ill. Optometric Assn., Phi Beta Kappa, Omega Epsilon Phi. Club: Womanspace (past pres.). Avocations: growing orchids, growing grapes, making fine wines. Office: 137 N Walnut St Byron IL 61010

KRAFT, SUMNER CHARLES, physician, educator; b. Lynn, Mass., Aug. 21, 1928; m. Patricia F. Pink; children—Gary Andrew, Jennifer Rose, Steven Russell. B.S., Tufts U., 1948; A.M., Boston U., 1949; M.D., U. Chgo., 1955. Diplomate Am. Bd. Internal Medicine. Intern Boston City Hosp., 1955-56; jr. asst. resident U. Chgo. Hosp., 1956-57, sr. asst. resident, 1957-58, resident, 1958-59, physician student health service, 1958-59, instr. medicine, 1959-61, USPHS spl. fellow, 1961-66, research fellow immunology Scripps Clinic & Research Found., 1964-66, assoc. prof. medicine, 1967-73, USPHS Research Career Devel. fellow, Nat. Inst. Allergy and Infectious Diseases, 1967-72, prof. medicine, 1974—; staff mem. U. Chgo. Med. Ctr. Ad hoc cons. food allergy and gastrointestinal immunology; faculty lectr. Cook County Grad. Sch. Medicine, Chgo., 1969—; vis. prof. of medicine, then affiliated prof. medicine Uniformed Services U. of Health Scis., Bethesda, Md., 1979—. Chmn. editorial bd. Jour. Medicine on the Midway. Contbr. articles to med. jours. Merit badge counselor Calumet council Boy Scouts Am., former scoutmaster, troop com. chmn., 1966—; judge Chgo. Non-Pub. Sch. Sci. Exposition, 1981-82. Served to col. with USAR, 1957—. Recipient William Beaumont award for clin. research, 1977. Fellow Am. Coll. of Physicians; mem. AAAS, Am. Assn. Immunologists, Am. Fedn. Clin. Research, Am. Gastroent. Assn. (editorial bd. 1976-81), Am. Soc. Gastrointestinal Endoscopy, Assn. Mil. Surgeons of U.S., Central Soc. Clin. Research, Chgo. Assn. Immunologists, Chgo. Soc. Gastroenterology (organizing com. 1967-68, exec. com. 1968-71, pres. 1969-70), Chgo. Soc. Gastrointestingal Endoscopy, Chgo. Soc. Internal Medicine, Midwest Gut Club (steering com. 1969-72), N.Y. Acad. of Scis., Res. Officers Assn. (life), Soc. for Exptl. Biology and Medicine, U.S. Army War Coll. Alumni Assn., Sigma Xi. Office: U Chgo 5841 S Maryland Ave Chicago IL 60637

KRAFVE, ALLEN HORTON, management consultant; b. Superior, Wis., Jan. 26, 1937; s. Richard Ernest and Frances Virginia (Horton) K.; m. Lois Anne Reed, Aug. 15, 1959; children—Bruce Allen, Anne Marie, Carol Elizabeth. B.S. in Mech. Engring., U. Mich., 1958, M.B.A., 1960, M.S. in Mech. Engring., 1961. Asst. prof. mech. engring. San Jose State U. (Calif.), 1961-65; various positions including quality control mgr. Ford Motor Co., Dearborn, Mich., 1965-77; engring. mgr. Kysor/Cadillac, Cadillac, Mich., 1977-82; mgmt. cons., Lake City, Mich., 1982—. Co-author: Reliability Considerations in Design, 1962, internat. conf. paper, 1961. Bd. dirs. Crooked Tree council Girl Scouts U.S.A., Traverse City, Mich., 1983. Mem. ASME, Soc. Automotive Engrs., Am. Soc. Quality Control, Am. Soc. Engring. Edn. Republican. Methodist. Home: 145 Duck Point Dr Lake City MI 49651 Office: Allen H Krafve Cons 457 Pearl St Cadillac MI 49601

KRAGER, LUANN LESLIE, educational administrator; b. Holstein, Iowa, Nov. 9, 1954; d. Eldon Lester and Lorraine Ann (Wunschel) K. B.A., Midland Luth. Coll., 1976; M.A. in Psychol. Counseling, U. Nebr., 1977; postgrad., 1984—. Asst. dir. residential life Morningside Coll., Sioux City, Iowa, 1977-79, dir. life learning ctr., 1979-81; asst. instr. U. Nebr., Lincoln, 1981-84, asst. to dean of students, 1984—. Contbr. chpt. to book, article to jour. Bd. dirs. Ctr. for Women, Sioux City, 1980-81; mem. planning com. Community Career Planning Info. Service, 1980; mem. singers group Sioux City Community Theatre, 1981; entertainer USO, Orient, 1974. Recipient Cert. Recognition for Teaching U. Nebr.-Lincoln, 1983; named Greek Faculty Mem. of Yr. Morningside Coll. Greek Letters Socs., 1980. Mem. Am. Assn. Counseling and Devel., Am. Coll. Personnel Assn. (Annuit Coeptis award 1983). Democrat. Lutheran. Avocations: racquetball; jogging; singing; playing guitar. Office: III Tchrs Coll U Nebr Lincoln NE 68588

KRAINIK, ARDIS, opera company executive; b. Manitowoc, Wis., Mar. 8, 1929; d. Arthur Stephen and Clara (Bracken) K.; B.S., Northwestern U., 1951; postgrad. in music, 1953-54. Tchr. drama, public speaking Horlick High Sch., Racine, Wis., 1951-53; mezzo soprano appearing with Chgo. Lyric Opera, 1955-59, Ft. Wayne (Ind.) Philharm. Orch., Tri-City Symphony, Davenport, Iowa, Cameo Opera Co., Chgo., North Shore Symphony, Winnetka, Ill., Lake Forest (Ill.) Symphony, 1954—; appeared in oratorio performances throughout Mid-West on Artists Showcase, NBC-TV, in recitals throughout area; soloist 17th Ch. Christ Scientist, Chgo., 1969-77; exec. sec., office mgr. Lyric Opera of Chgo., 1954-59, asst. mgr., 1960-76, artistic adminstr., 1976-81, gen. mgr., 1981—. Bd. dirs. Chgo. br. English Speaking Union, from 1963; charter mem. Chgo. Council Fine Arts, from 1976, Northwestern U. Women's Bd., from 1978. Mem. Mortar Bd., Pi Alpha Lambda, Phi Beta, Chi Omega. Christian Scientist. Office: Office of Ardis Krainik Lyric Opera of Chgo 20 N Wacker Dr Chicago IL 60606

KRAJEWSKI, LEE JEROME, management educator, consultant; b. Milw., Apr. 26, 1942; s. Jerome John and Virginia Pearl (Kozlowski) K.; m. Judith Ann Tower, Aug. 31, 1963; children—Gary, Jeffrey, Daniel, Jonathan. B.S., U. Wis., 1964, M.S., 1966, Ph.D., 1969. Faculty, Ohio State U., Columbus, 1969—, prof. mgmt., 1976—, chmn. dept., 1983—; cons. to various orgns., Columbus, 1972—; acad. dir. IBM Materials Mgmt. Seminars, Columbus, 1983—. Author: Management Science, 1980. Contbr. articles to profl. jours. Recipient Disting. Teaching award Ohio State U. Alumni, 1976; research grantee U.S. Postal Service, 1972, Westinghouse Corp., Pitts., 1980. Mem. Inst. Mgmt. Scis., Am. Inst. Decision Scis., Ops. Mgmt. Assn. (v.p. 1980-82), Am. Prodn. and Inventory Control Soc. (acad. liaison local chpt. 1979—, editor jour. 1980-83, Pres.'s award 1983). Roman Catholic. Avocation: photography. Home: 682 Mohican Way Westerville OH 43081 Office: Dept Mgmt Ohio State Univ 1775 S College Rd Columbus OH 43210

KRAKORA, JAMES V., association executive; b. Cleve., Oct. 1, 1909; s. Frank Vincent and Marie Theresa (Rericha) K.; m. Rose Emma Cerveny, July 20, 1935; children—Richard James. Student pub. schs., Coeve. Asst. to the sec. CSA Fraternal Life (formerly Czechoslovak Soc. Am.), Cleve., 1928-32, asst. to the pres., Cicero, Ill., 1933-42, sec., Berwyn, Ill., 1943-82, pres., chief exec. officer, 1982—; treas. Czechoslovak Nat. Council Am., Cicero, 1966—; pres. Svobodna Obec, Cicero, 1980—; trustee Bohemian Nat. Cemetery Assn., Chgo., 1980—. Author: (hist. record) 100 years of Bohemian Nat. Cemetery Assn., 1977. Bd. dirs. Morton Coll. Endowment Fund, Cicero, 1977-78. Served with UNRRA, 1945-56. Recipient DeMolay Legion of Honor award Grand chpt. Order of DeMolay for Boys, Cleve., 1931. Mem. Ill. Fraternal Congress (pres. 1952-53), Nat. Fraternal Congress Am. (dir. 1954-55, past pres. secs. and state congresses sect.), Captive Nations Com. Chgo. Lodges: Masons, Odd Fellows, Am. Sokol Orgn., Western Fraternal Life Assn., Slavonic Benevolent Order of State of Tex.; others. Office: CSA Fraternal Life 2701 S Harlem Ave Berwyn IL 60402

KRAKOWSKI, RICHARD JOHN, lawyer, public relations executive; b. Meppen, W.Ger., Apr. 3, 1946; came to U.S., 1951, naturalized, 1962; s. Feliks and Maria (Chilinski) K. M.B.A., DePaul U., 1979; J.D., John Marshall Law Sch., 1983. Bar: Ill. 1984. Personnel dir. Andy Frain, Inc., Chgo., 1973-78; pub. relations dir. Chgo. Health Systems Agy., 1978-84; assoc. firm Mangum, Smietank & Johnson, Chgo., 1984—; lectr. in field. Fundraising and pub. relations dir. Cabrini-Green Sandlot Tennis program, Chgo., 1979-83; sustaining mem. Republican Nat. Com., 1981—. Served to capt. U.S. Army, 1969-72. Mem. ABA, Ill. Bar Assn., Chgo. Bar Assn., Chgo. Council Fgn. Relations, Advocates Soc., Lyric Opera Guild. Roman Catholic. Club: Publicity (Chgo.). Co-author: Health Care Financing and Policy Making in Chicago and Illinois, 1982. Home: 65 E Scott St Apt 12C Chicago IL 60610 Office: 35 E Wacker Dr #2130 Chicago IL 60601

KRALOVEC, J. MARTIN, retired insurance agency executive and savings and loan executive; b. Cary, Ill., July 2, 1919; s. George W. and Anna M. Z. K.; m. Mikeline H. Sutkus, Apr. 20, 1946 (dec. 1963); children—Alice C. Kralovec Nye, Claudia A.; m. 2d Harriette M. McNellis, Mar. 24, 1966. B.A. in Psychology, Beloit Coll., 1942. Researcher, MIT, 1943-46; v.p., sec. J.M. Kralovec & Son, Inc., Cicero, Ill., 1946—; acting chmn. bd. Hawthorne Savs. & Loan Assn., Naperville, Ill., 1983—, also dir.; mem. agts. council Continental Ins. Co.; sec. agt. council Northwestern Nat. Ins. Co., 1972-74. Bd. dirs. Oak Park (Ill.) Art League, Cicero Community Fund. Served to capt. Signal Corps, U.S. Army, World War II. Mem. Ret. Officers Assn., Sigma Chi. Roman Catholic. Clubs: Riverside Golf (pres. 1980-82, bd. dirs. 1977-82) (North Riverside, Ill.); Eastern Srs. Golf Assn., Par, Caribbean Sailing Yachts (skipper), Country of Blue Water Bay. Lodge: Elks (Cicero). Address: 223 Dominica Circle Niceville FL 32578

KRAMER, JONATHAN DONALD, composer, educator; b. Hartford, Conn., Dec. 7, 1942; s. Maxwell and Pauline (Klein) K.; m. Norma Berson, Aug. 28, 1966; children—Zachary, Stephanie. A.B. magna cum laude, Harvard U., 1965; M.A., U. Calif.-Berkeley, 1967, Ph.D., 1969; postgrad. U. Calif.-Irvine, 1976. Lectr. music theory and composition U. Calif., Berkeley, 1969-70; prof. conservatory music Oberlin (Ohio) Coll., 1970-71; prof. dept. music Yale U., New Haven, 1971-78, dir. undergrad. composition, 1972-78; prof., dir. electronic music Coll. Conservatory Music, U. Cin., 1978—; hon. research assoc. U. London, 1985-86; program annotator San Francisco Symphony, 1967-70; program annotator Cin. Symphony, 1980—, new music advisor, 1984—; weekly radio program host Sta. WGUC, Cin., 1982—; lectr. in field. Cons., Ohio Arts Council, Meet the Composer. U. Calif.-Irvine fellow, 1976; Nat. Endowment Arts grantee, 1976, 85; NEH grantee, 1976, 85; Meet the Composer grantee, 1982, 84; Martha Baird Rockefeller Fund grantee, 1978; Morse fellow, 1975; Ohio Arts Council grantee, 1982, 84. Mem. Cin. Composers Guild (chmn. adv. bd.), Nat. Assn. Composers (nat. council), Soc. Music Theory (publs. com.), Am. Soc. Univ. Composers (dir. nat. festival), AAUP, Coll. Music Soc., Internat. Soc. for Study of Time, Am. Music Ctr. Compositions performed at Lincoln Ctr., Aspen Music Festival, Carnegie Hall, World Music Days, Composers, Forum, Peru, Brazil, Denmark, Israel, Argentina, Norway, France, Can., Germany, Belgium, Austria, Holland; composer: music for orch., chorus, piano, clarinet, band, dance, theater, electronics, chamber ensembles, percussion.; compositions rec. by Grenadilla, Opus One, Orion Records, pub. by G. Schirmer; contbr. articles to profl. jours. Office: Coll Conservatory Music U Cincinnati Cincinnati OH 45221

KRAMER, LOIS BETH, clinical dietetics manager, consultant; b. Orange City, Iowa, Feb. 27, 1944; d. Lawrence and Johanna (Punt) VandeBerg; m. Gary Eugene Kramer, Aug. 17, 1963 (div. Mar. 1984); 1 child, Brent Alan. Student Central Coll., 1961-63; B.S., Mundelein Coll., 1965. Clin. dietitian Hines VA Hosp., Ill., 1966-67, research dietitian, 1968-73; clin. dietitian St. Vincent Hosp., Sioux City, Iowa, 1974-77; mgr. clin. dietetics Marian Health Center, Sioux City, 1977—; cons. research dietitian Hines VA Hosp, 1973—; mem. speakers bur. Mead Johnson Nutrition Div., Evansville, Ind., 1978—. Contbr. articles to profl. jours. Mem. Am. Soc. Clin. Nutrition, Am. Inst. Nutrition, Am. Dietetic Assn., Iowa Dietetic Assn. (treas. 1983—). Republican. Avocations: reading; playing piano. Home: 2300 Indian Hills Dr # 302 Sioux City IA 51104 Office: Marian Health Center 801 5th St Sioux City IA 51101

KRAMER, PAMELA KOSTENKO, librarian; b. Chgo., Mar. 5, 1944; d. Barry Michael and Helene (Ullrich) Kostenko; m. Claude Richard Kramer, Aug. 17, 1966. A.B., U. Ill., 1966; M.A.L.S., Rosary Coll., 1973. Tchr. English United Twp. High Sch., E. Moline, Ill., 1966-70, audiovisual librarian, 1970-76; instr. Marycrest Coll., Davenport, Iowa, 1973-75; librarian United Twp. High Sch., E. Moline, 1976-81, librarian, audio visual dept. head, 1981—. Author audiovisual software revs. for Previews mag. Sch. Library Jour., 1973—. Edmund J. James scholar, 1962-66. Mem. ALA, Women in Edn. Adminstrn., Ill. Library Assn., Ill. Assn. Ednl. Communications and Tech., NEA, Ill. Edn. Assn., Classroom Tchrs. Assn., Ill. Assn. Tchrs. English, Ill. Assn. Media in Edn., Am. Assn. Sch. Librarians, Assn. Supervision and Curriculum Devel., Delta Kappa Gamma, Beta Phi Mu. Home: 3441 60th St Apt 5C Moline IL 61265 Office: United Twp High Sch Archer Dr and 42d Ave East Moline IL 61244

KRAMER, TIMOTHY EUGENE, lawyer; b. Cleve., Mar. 21, 1943; s. Theodore Eugene and Margaret Agnes (Vargo) K.; m. Jacqueline Marie Rini, May 30, 1969; children—Thomas, Kathleen, Anne. B.A., John Carroll U., 1965; J.D., Case Western Res. U., 1968. Bar: Ohio 1969. Law clk. Cuyahoga County Common Pleas Ct., 1970-73; asst. counsel Jacobs, Visconsi & Jacobs Co., Cleve., 1973-78; corp. counsel Revco D.S. Inc., Twinsburg, Ohio, 1978—; lectr. in field. Served with U.S. Army, 1968-70. Mem. Ohio State Bar Assn. Roman Catholic. Home: 31710 Birch Circle Solon OH 44139 Office: Revco D S Inc 1925 Enterprise Pkwy Twinsburg OH 44087

KRAMER, YALE, business appraiser, broker; b. St. Louis, Oct. 21, 1944; s. Paul and Evelyn (Reiss) K.; m. Mary Helene Miller, Feb. 17, 1968; children—Christopher, Paul, Jonathon. B.A., Drake U., 1967, J.D., 1969, M.B.A., 1971; student law Washington U., St. Louis, 1966-68. C.P.A., Iowa. Sr. tax specialist Peat Marwick Mitchell, Des Moines, 1970-72; v.p. R.G. Dickinson Co., Des Moines, 1972-78; pres. Iowa Capital Corp., Des Moines, 1978-80; pres. Reiss Corp., Des Moines, 1980—, V R Bus. Brokers, Des Moines, 1982—. Fellow Des Moines Soc. Fin. Analysts; mem. Am. Soc. Appraisers (sr. mem.; mem. bus. valuation com. 1981—), Am. Inst. C.P.A.s (mem. bus. law com. 1983—), Iowa Soc. C.P.A.s (bd. dirs. 1980-83). Home: 2004 80th St Des Moines IA 50322 Office: Reiss Corp 8033 University St Des Moines IA 50311

KRAMPITZ, SYDNEY DIANE, nurse educator, consultant; b. Conneaut, Ohio, Jan. 29, 1935; m. David R. Krampitz; children—Rebecca, Kathleen, Cynthia. B.S. in Nursing, SUNY-Buffalo, 1966; M.S. in Nursing, St. Xavier Coll., Chgo., 1969; Ph.D., U. Chgo., 1978. Mem. faculty Cooperative Edn. Services, Buffalo, 1963-65; supervising nurse State of Ill., Chgo., 1967-70; dir. Sch. Nursing, Evang. Hosp. Assn., Oak Lawn, Ill., 1969-71; dir. Ctr. Nursing Edn., Elmhurst Coll., 1971-79; assoc. chief nursing service Hines (Ill.) VA Hosp., 1979-81; assoc. dean, dir. grad. programs U. Kansas, Kansas City, 1981—; cons. U.S. Air Force Surgeon Gen.'s Office, Washington, 1979—, VA Med. Ctr., Kansas City, 1982—; dir. Kansas City Health Care. Author: Psychiatric Nursing, 1977. Editor: Readings in Nursing Research, 1981. Dir. crisis com. ARC, 1984—. Maj. USAFR, 1972—. Fellow Inst. Medicine Chgo.; assoc. fellow Aerospace Med. Assn.; mem. Johnson County Mental Health Assn. (dir., mem. governing bd.), Internat. History of Nursing Soc. (past pres.), Am. Nurses Assn., Ill. Nurses Assn., Kans. Nurses Assn., Council Nursing Researchers. Avocations: Sports; flying. Home: 12727 W 100th St Lenexa KS 66215

KRANTZ, BEATRICE V., ednl. adminstr.; b. Chgo.; d. Andrew S. and Beatrice K.; B.A., Lake Forest Coll.; M.A. in Public Law, Columbia U.; postgrad. Northwestern U., 1944-60, U. Ill., 1960-62, No. Ill. U., 1964, Ill. Inst. Tech., 1969. Formerly adminstrv. asst. to lawyer, Chgo.; tchr. social studies Deerfield (Ill.) Shields High Sch.; tchr. govt., econs. and history High Sch. Dist. 218, Blue Island, Ill., 1936-47; asst. county supt. schs., dir. tchr. personnel and placement Cook County Schs., Chgo., 1947-51, asst. supt. secondary edn., scholarships, guidance, 1967-70, asst. supt. in charge West area Ednl. Service Region, Cook County, 1970—; adminstrv. asst. to supt. Dist. 88, Du Page County, 1951-59, dean of girls, Elmhurst, Ill., 1960-66; ednl. cons., 1974—. Past mem. exec. com. Heart Assn. W. Cook Regions for County. Recipient Distinguished Alumni award Lake Forest Coll., 1976. Mem. NEA, Am. Assn. Sch. Adminstrs., No. Ill. Supts. Round Table, Pan Hellenic Assn., Delta Kappa Gamma, Alpha Xi Delta. Research in field. Office: 1032 Washington Blvd Oak Park IL 60302

KRASNAPOLSKY, YURI, conductor. Ed. Tanglewood, Juilliard Sch. Music; pvt. study, Vienna. Asst. condr. N.Y. Philharmonic, condr. orchs. Wolf Trap, Vancouver Internat. Festival, also orchs. of Tulsa, Okla. Miami, Fla., Omaha, Bklyn. Philarm.; now music dir., condr. Des Moines Symphony; numerous tours Europe and U.S. Ford Found. fellow. Recs. EMI Records. Address: Shops Bldg Des Moines IA 50309*

KRATT, PETER GEORGE, lawyer; b. Lorain, Ohio, Mar. 7, 1940; s. Arthur Leroy and Edith Ida (Dietz) K.; m. Sharon Amy Maruska, June 15, 1968; children—Kevin, Jennifer. B.A., Miami U., Oxford, Ohio, 1962; J.D., Case Western Res. U., 1966. Bar: Ohio 1966. Atty. Cleve. Trust Co., 1966-72; assoc. counsel AmeriTrust Co., 1974-84, sec., assoc. counsel, 1984—. Mem. Am. Soc. Corp. Secs., Ohio Bar Assn. Methodist. Lodge: Lions. Office: Ameritrust Co E 9th and Euclid Sts Cleveland OH 44101

KRATZ, MILDRED SANDS, artist; b. Pottstown, Pa.; d. M. Stanley Q. and Ann (Hohl) Sands; m. Lowell F. Kratz (div.); children—Melissa and Melinda (twins); m. Richard Keith Johnson, Sr. Grad. high sch., Pottstown. One-woman shows include: Gallery Madison 90, N.Y.C., Piccolo Mondo, Palm Beach, Fla., Little Gallery, Phila; exhibited in group shows, U.S. and Can.; represented in permanent collections: Reading Mus., General Mills. Recipient Senatorial Citation, Pa. Senate, 1976. Recipient 100 awards, 6 gold medals in nat. competition. Mem. Pottstown Area Artists (co-founder, pres. 1963), Am. Watercolor Soc., Ohio Watercolor Soc., Am. Artist Prof. League, Allied Artists, Nat. Arts Club, Phila. Watercolor Club. Avocations: skiing; tennis. Home and Office: 2988 Silverview Dr Silver Lake OH 44224

KRAUSE, JAMES WILLIAM, management consultant; b. Fergus Falls, Minn., May 21, 1930; s. William Otto and Esmere (Tomhave) K.; m. Roselyn Soniette Olson, Aug. 15, 1959; children—Paul Frederick, Alan James, John William. B.A., Concordia Coll., 1951; J.D., U. Minn., 1954; postgrad. U. Harvard Grad. Sch. Bus. Adminstrn., 1966-67. Bar: Minn. 1954, N.D., 1954; C.L.U. Trust officer, 1st Bank N.D., Fargo, 1954-58; head bus. and econs. dept., assoc. prof. Concordia Coll., Moorhead, Minn., 1958-61; practice law, Fargo and Moorhead, 1958-61; legal counsel Lutheran Brotherhoods Ins., Mpls., 1961-66, sr. v.p. adminstrn. and investments, 1967-77; pres. Luth. Brotherhood Securities Corp., 1970-77; prin. Saks, Inc., Mpls., 1975—; dir., exec. com. Luth. Brotherhood Ins. Co., 1967—, chmn. audit com., 1983 —. Pres. Minn. Higher Edn. Coordinating Bd., 1980-82, bd. dirs., 1978-82. Recipient Bush Leadership award Bush Found., 1966. Mem. North Central Mgmt. Assn. (pres. 1978—), Minn. Bar Assn., Minn. Bd. Continuing Legal Edn., Soc. Advancement Mgmt., Am. Mgmt. Assn., World Futurist Soc. Clubs: Minnesota; Harvard Bus. Sch. Minn. Office: 5300 Glenwood Ave Minneapolis MN 55422

KRAUSE, JOHN L., optometrist; b. Portland, Oreg., Oct. 26, 1917; m. Nancy D., Sept. 30, 1942; children—Diana L., Karen L., Ronald L. O.D., Ill. Coll. Optometry, 1947. Practice optometry, Niles, Ill., 1947—; USAF Med. Service liaison officer, Northwestern U. Med. Sch., Chgo., 1964—. Author: Sight Check Your Child, 1961. Patentee card holder, 1967. Served with U.S. Army, 1941-45, to lt. col. USAF. Decorated Bronze Star with cluster. Mem. Am. Optometry Assn., Ill. Optometric Assn., Am. Optometric Found., Nat. Eye Research Found., Am. Interprofl. Assn., Armed Forces Optometric Soc. Avocations: golf; stamp collecting; bowling. Home: PO Box 122 Glenview IL 60025 Office: 9475 N Milwaukee Ave Niles IL 60648

KRAUSE, MAUREEN THERESE, educator; b. Evanston, Ill., June 17, 1947; d. Walter William and Eileen Ann (Gill) K.; m. David Lawrence Francoeur, July 28, 1978. B.A., Northwestern U., 1969; student Inst. Advanced Studies, Stanford U., 1969; M.A. (univ. fellow), Ohio State U., 1970, Ph.D., 1980. Teaching assoc. German, Ohio State U., Columbus, 1970-74, 77-78, 79-80, instr., 1980-81; sr. transl. aide Battelle Columbus Labs., 1974-77; asst. prof. German, Rose-Hulman Inst. Tech., Terre Haute, Ind., 1981-85, assoc. prof., 1985—; mem. editorial staff New German Critique, 1981; bibliographer Soc. German-Am. Studies, 1979-82. Vol., Am. Cancer Soc., 1982—; instl. del. Arts Illiana, 1983; active Vigo County Hist. Soc., 1981-84, Audubon Soc., 1983-84. Fulbright grantee, 1983; recipient Deptl. Disting. Teaching award Ohio State U., 1971. Mem. Am. Assn. Tchrs. of German, Am. Council Teaching of Fgn. Langs., Hoffmann-Gesellschaft (Ger.), N.W. MLA, MLA, Soc. German-Am. Studies, Western Assn. German Studies. Office: Rose Hulman Inst Tech Terre Haute IN 47803

KRAUSE, WILLIAM RICHARD, industrial arts educator; b. Chgo., May 7, 1949; s. Richard Joseph and Mary (Reczek) K.; m. Roberta Ann Schmidt, July 8, 1972; children—Thomas Joseph, Amanda Elizabeth. B.S., Western Ill. U., 1971; M.Ed., U. Ill., 1976, Advanced Cert. Edn., 1980. Cert. tchr., adminstr., Ill. Tchr., Proviso Twp. (Ill.) High Schs., 1971—; instr. Triton Jr. Coll., 1974-75; prin. Olde Tyme Toys Co., 1976-78. Mem. Oak Brook (Ill.) Civic Assn., 1978—, Oak Brook Library Assn., 1978—, Oak Brook Community Caucus, 1980—, Ben Fuller Assn., Oak Brook, 1981—; treas. Brook Forest Community Assn., 1982—; trustee York Twp. Youth Commn., 1984—. Mem. Am. Vocat. Assn., Ill. Vocat. Assn., Am. Indsl. Arts Assn., Ill. Indsl. Edn. Assn., Chgo. Area Roundtable. Club: Oak Brook Racquet. Contbr. articles to indsl. arts jours. Home: 9 Lambeth Ct Oak Brook IL 60521 Office: Wolf and Harrison Sts Hillside IL 60162

KRAUSEN, ANTHONY SHARNIK, surgeon; b. Phila., Feb. 22, 1944; s. B.M. and Kay S. (Sharnik) K.; m. Susan Elizabeth Park, Sept. 6, 1970; children—Nicole, Allison. Student Germantown Acad., 1949-61; B.A., Princeton U., 1965; M.D., U. Mich., 1969. Intern, Presbyn. Med. Center, Denver, 1969-70; resident St. Joseph Hosp., Denver, 1970-71, Barnes Hosp., St. Louis, 1972-76; with Milw. Med. Clinic, 1976—, head dept. facial plastic surgery, 1984—; mem. staffs Columbia, St. Michael, Children's hosps., Milw.; instr. Med. Coll. Wis., Milw., 1976-84. Pres., Contemporary Art Soc., Milw. Art Mus., 1983, bd. dirs. Friends of Art. Served with U.S. Army Nat. Guard, 1970-76. Fellow Am. Acad. Facial Plastic and Reconstructive Surgery, Am. Acad. Otolaryngology, Soc. Univ. Otolaryngologists, A.C.S.; mem. Wis. Otolaryngological Soc. Clubs: Ivy (Princeton, N.J.); Ausblick Ski (Milw.). Office: 3003 W Good Hope Rd Milwaukee WI 53209

KRAUSS, ALAN ROBERT, physicist, consultant; b. Chgo., Oct. 3, 1943; s. Paul and Shirley (Shapiro) K.; m. Julie Emelie Rosado, Aug. 28, 1965; 1 child, Susan. B.S. in Physics, U. Chgo., 1965; M.S. in Physics, Purdue U., 1968, Ph.D. in Physics, 1972. Research assoc. U. Chgo., Ill., 1971-74; physicist Argonne Nat. Lab., Ill., 1974—; publicity chmn., editor, mem. adv. com. Fusion Tech. div. Am. Vacuum Soc., N.Y.C., 1981—; cons. Microdyne Assocs., Plainfield, Ill., 1982—. Contbr. articles to profl. jours. Inventor self-sustaining coatings. Recipient Research award Dept. of Energy, 1984. Mem. Am. Phys. Soc., Am. Vacuum Soc. (exec. com. Ill. chpt. 1985—), Sigma Xi, Sigma Pi Sigma. Club: Downers Grove Camera (treas. 1979-83). Avocations: photography; computers; electronics. Office: Argonne Nat Lab Materials Sci & Tech Div Argonne IL 60439

KRAUSS, WILLIAM EDWARD, engineer; b. Cleve., May 12, 1928; s. Jacob and Helen (Fuchs) K.; m. Barbara Allen Marlin, Aug. 3, 1957; children—Vicki, Ellen, Lori Anne. B.M.E., Ohio State U., 1950, M.S., 1953; Ph.D., U. Fla., 1970. Profl. engr., Fla., Ohio, Tex. Engring. mgr. Martin Marietta Corp., Orlando, Fla., 1959-74; chief engr. Mechtron Internat. Corp., Orlando, 1974-77; sr. staff mem. Brunswick Corp., Deland, Fla., 1976-77; mgr. product devel. Midland Ross, Toledo, 1977-79; v.p. engring. Cleaver Brooks, Milw., 1979-82; dir. Gas Research Inst., Chgo., 1982—. Contbr. articles to profl. publs. Mem. ASME, Nat. Soc. Profl. Engrs. (sr. mem.), Am. Soc. Engring. Edn., Sigma Xi, Phi Beta Phi, Tau Beta Pi. Avocations: gardening, home renovation. Home: 2030 Creekside Ave Wheaton IL 60187 Office: Gas Research Inst 8600 W Bryn Mawr Chicago IL 60631

KRAVIS, DAVID SCOTT, food company executive; b. Bklyn., Jan. 9, 1951; s. Samuel Joseph and Beryl (Gittelman) K.; m. Lynn Barbara Ferszt, May 26, 1979. B.S., Va. Poly. Inst., 1973; postgrad. Bus. Sch., U. Cin., 1975-78. Staff engr. Procter & Gamble, Cin., 1973-77, group leader, 1977-78; group leader ITT Continental, Rye, N.Y., 1978-80, mktg. mgr., 1980-81, mgr. research and devel., 1981-82; dir. research and devel. Bunge Edible Oil Corp., Kankakee, Ill., 1982—. Mem. Ill. Public Action Council, 1983—. N.Y. Regents scholar, 1969. Mem. Inst. Shortening and Edible Oils, Inst. Food Technologists (exec. com. food engring. div. 1984—), Am. Inst. Chem. Engrs., Am. Oil Chemists Soc. (found. action bd. dirs. 1984—), Am. Assn. Cereal Chemists, Am. Inst. Baking (sci. adv. council 1984—), Research and Devel. Assocs., Am. Mgmt. Assn., Alpha Chi Sigma. Republican. Patentee meaty flavored deep-fat frying compositions; contbr. articles to profl. jours. Home: 2748 2d Private Rd Flossmoor IL 60422 Office: PO Box 192 Kankakee IL 60901

KRAVITZ, MARSHALL CRAIG, sales and marketing executive; b. Chgo., Aug. 20, 1954; s. Ben and Francine (Rosenberg) K.; m. Rhonda Korey, June 2, 1985. B.A. in History, U. Ill.-Chgo., 1976, M.A. in History, 1977; M.S. in Mktg. and Advt., Roosevelt U., 1979. Direct mail cons. Bosler Co., Chgo., 1980-81; pres., prin. Marsh & Assocs., Chgo., Cons., 1980—; collateral communications cons. Johns-Byrne Co. Chgo., 1981-84, Chgo. Press Corp., 1984-85, Kentex Corp., 1985—. Adminstrv. asst., legis. aide Chgo. City Council, 1975-79; bd. dirs. Hollywood-North Park Improvement Assn., 1979-80; mem. young leadership div. Jewish United Fund, Chgo. Mem. Printing Industries Ill., Zionist Orgn. Chgo. Democrat. Lodges: B'nai B'rith, Maccabi Assn. (exec. v.p. Chgo. region 1981-84). Author: The Mayors of Chicago—1837-Present, 1976. Home and Office: 514 Hill St Highland Park IL 60035 Office: 1201 W 37th St Chicago IL 60609

KRCHNIAK, NANCY SPICER, educational administrator; b. Waterville, Maine, Jan. 11, 1934; d. George William and Blanche Rosalie (Grondin) Spicer; m. Stefan Paul Krchniak, July 15, 1961; children—Catherine, Steven. B.S., SUNY-New Paltz, 1955; M.A., Columbia U., 1961; Ed.S., So. Ill. U., 1972.

Tchr. art K-12, N.Y. State Pub. Schs., 1955-57; tchr., Plainview, L.I., 1958-66; instr. sch. edn. So. Ill. U., Edwardsville, 1969-74; cons. Ill. Bd. Edn. in Arts-in-Edn., 1976—; adminstr. Office of Regional Supt. Schs., Madison County, Edwardsville, Ill., 1980—; comml. artist, editor various local orgnl. pubs. Exec. dir. Madison County Arts Council, 1981—; chmn. Madison County Curriculum Council, 1980—; pres. PTA, 1976-77; bd. dirs. Ill. Women Adminstrs. and Prevention Resource Ctr., Springfield, Ill., 1982—. Alcohol Drug Abuse Prevention Edn. program grantee, 1981—. Mem. Assn. Supervision and Curriculum Devel., Ill. Women Adminstrs., Nat. Assn. Gifted Children, Delta Kappa Gamma, Phi Delta Kappa. Democrat. Club: Sunset Hills Country. Editor Madison County Schs. Newsletter, 1980—; curriculum devel. project dir.: Drugs: A Guide Towards Prevention of Abuse, K-6, 1981. Home: 1514 Weber Dr Edwardsville IL 62025 Office: 201 Hillsboro Ave Edwardsville IL 62025

KRCO, CHRISTOPHER JOSEPH, immunologist; b. Chgo., July 17, 1950; s. Christopher Joseph and Catherine Pearl (Miloslavich) K.; m. Deborah Carol Newman, June 10, 1979; 1 child, David Jonathan. B.S. with honors and distinction, U. Ill.-Chgo., 1972; Ph.D., U. N.Mex., 1977. Postdoctoral fellow Mayo Clinic, Rochester, Minn., 1977-83, assoc. cons., 1983—. Contbr. articles to profl. jours. Nat. Merit scholar, 1968-72; U. N.Mex. fellow, Albuquerque, 1974-76; grantee NIH, Am. Cancer Soc. Mem. AAAS, Am. Assn. Immunologists. Avocations: reading, swimming, bicycling. Office: Dept Immunology Mayo Clinic Rochester MN 55905

KREAGER, EILEEN DAVIS, bursar; b. Caldwell, Ohio, Mar. 2, 1924; d. Fred Raymond and Esther (Farson) Davis. B.B.A., Ohio State U., 1945. With accounts receivable dept. M & R Dietetic, Columbus, Ohio, 1945-50; complete charge bookkeeper Magic Seal Paper Products, Columbus, 1950-53, A. Walt Runglin Co., Los Angeles, 1953-54; office mgr. Roy C. Haddox and Son, Columbus, 1954-60; bursar Meth. Theol. Sch. Ohio, Delaware, 1961—; ptnr. Coll. Administrv. Sci., Ohio State U., 1975-80; seminar participant Paperwork Systems and Computer Sci., 1965, Computer Systems, 1964, Griffith Found. Seminar Working Women, 1975; pres. Altrusa Club of Delaware, Ohio, 1972-73. Del. Altrusa Internat., Montreal, 1972, Altrusa Regional, Greenbrier, 1973. Assoc. Am. Inst. Mgmt. (exec. council of Inst., 1979); mem. Am. Soc. Profl. Cons., Internat. Platform Assn., Ohio State U. Alumna Assn., AAUW, Kappa Delta. Methodist. Clubs: Ohio State U. Faculty, Delaware Country. Home: PO Box 214 Worthington OH 43085

KREBS, WILLIAM PAUL, management consultant; b. Sioux City, July 19, 1928; s. Claude Gottlieb and Edna Louise K.; B.S.C., U. Iowa, 1952; m. Corinne Ann Brockmeier, Dec. 20, 1958; children—Leslie, Alison, Thomas. Home office rep., Group and Pension div. Aetna Life & Casualty Co., various locations, 1952-67; mgr. Life and Group Dept., Youngberg-Carlson Co., Chgo., 1967-68; cons. employee benefit plans, Chgo., 1968-70; sr. cons. Johnson & Higgins, 1970-72; mng. partner Krebs & Sisler, mgmt. cons.'s, Chgo., 1972—. Served with USN, 1946-48, USAFR, 1952-57. Mem. Planning Execs. Inst., Am. Soc. Quality Control, Am. Statis. Assn., Midwest Planning Assn. Home: 315 Poplar St Winnetka IL 60093 Office: Krebs & Sisler 209 S LaSalle St Chicago IL 60604

KREGEL, ANNA MAY, piano tchr.; b. Nebraska City, Nebr., Apr. 11, 1916; d. Robert W. and Ann (Kerrick) Kregel. B.A. cum laude, Mo. Valley Coll., 1938, Mus.B., 1939; M. Music Edn., U. Mo., Kansas City, 1976. Tchr. high sch., DeWitt, Mo., 1938-39, Kidder, Mo., 1940-42; with Kansas City Star, 1942-44; secretarial position Trans World Airlines, 1945, Thompson Hayward Chem., 1946, Johnson Sales, 1948; exec. sec. Line Material Co., 1949-51, Kansas City Philharmonic, 1951-52, City Plan Dept., Kansas City, Mo., 1952-60; tchr. Woods Studio, 1963-65, Pauline Wright Studio, 1966-70; ch. organist First Ch. Christ Scientist, Merriam, Kans., 1954-59, 73-79; ch. organist, asst. to ch. clk. First Ch. of Christ Scientist, Kansas City, Mo., 1985—; pvt. tchr. piano, organ and harmony, Kansas City, Mo., 1961—; real estate salesperson, Mo., 1980—; piano and organ judge Mid Am. Festival, 1966-68; free-lance organist, 1979—. Judge Spl. Olympics Music and Art Festival, 1976, 77, 78, 79, 80, 81, 82, organizer 1st state-wide competition, 1979. Mem. Music Tchrs. Nat. Assn., Mo., Kansas City music tchrs. assn., Federated Tchrs. of Music and Fine Arts Greater Kansas City, Nat. Secs. Assn. (editor Rainbow chapt. 1948-50), Cert. Profl. Secs. Christian Scientist. Home: PO Box 4853 Kansas City MO 64109

KREIDER, GARY P., lawyer; b. Newark, Ohio, June 7, 1938; s. Kenneth Kirby and Josephine (Stare) K.; m. Barbara B. Brown, Aug. 25, 1962; children—Kenneth, Katherine, Krista, Karen, Kimberly. B.A., U. Cin., 1960, M.A. in History, 1961, J.D., 1964. Bar: Ohio 1964, U.S. Dist. Ct. (so. dist.) Ohio 1964, U.S. Supreme Ct. 1971. Ptnr. Keating, Muething & Klekamp, Cin., 1963—; adj. prof. law securities regulation U. Cin., 1977-84; lectr. in field. Contbr. articles to profl. jours. Pres. New Richmond Exempted Village Bd. Edn. Mem. Ohio State Bar Assn. (mem. corp. law com.), ABA (mem. corp. counsel sect., chmn. securities subcom. real estate syndications and condominiums 1977-79), Cin. Bar Assn. (mem. corp. counsel sect., chmn. corp. and banking com. 1972-75, del.-at-large 1969-71), Nat. Assn. Securities Dealers, Inc. (arbitrator). Republican. Roman Catholic. Club: Bankers. Avocations: fox hunting; farming. Office: Keating Muething & Klekamp 1 E 4th St Cincinnati OH 45202

KREIDER, JAMES NICHOLAS, electronic equipment manufacturing company executive; b. Celina, Ohio, Dec. 29, 1945; s. Perry Eldon and Dorotha Ruth (Brown) K.; m. Vickie Lynn Hank, Jan. 7, 1977; children—Jason, Rachael, Alexander, Jessee. B.A., Ohio State U., 1968, M.B.A., 1975. Budget analyst Nuclear Regulatory Commn., Washington, 1975-76; assoc. Booz Allen & Hamilton, Bethesda, Md., 1976-80; mgr. cost control Fairchild Industries, Germantown, Md., 1980-82; dir. fin. planning NWL Control Systems, Kalamazoo, 1982—. Author: Cost of Ships, 1978. Served to lt. USNR, 1968-72. Mem. DAV. Avocations: harness racing; furniture refinishing. Home: 4079 N 8th St Kalamazoo MI 49009 Office: NWL Control Systems 2220 Palmer Ave Kalamazoo MI 49002

KREIDLER, HARRY MARTIN, pharmacist, executive; b. La Porte, Ind., May 19, 1927; s. Harry John and Florence (Kampf) K.; m. Juanita Jean Northam, Sept. 4, 1949; children—Jeffrey, Gregory, Kimberly. B.S., Purdue U., 1950. Pharmacist Theatre Pharmacy, La Porte, Ind., 1950-51; pharmacist, asst. mgr. Tams Drug Co., Huntington, Ind., 1951-52; pharmacist Hilbish Drug Co., La Porte, 1952; owner, pharmacist Northside Pharmacy, La Porte, 1953-84; pharmacist, pres. La Porte Northside Pharmacy Inc., 1957—; dir. 1st Nat. Bank, La Porte, 1972—; mem. drug div. La Porte County Sherriffs Dept., 1984—. Pres. Jaycees, La Porte, 1962; leader United Ch. of Christ Youth Fellowship, La Porte; asst. scoutmaster Boy Scouts Am., La Porte, 1957; pres. La Porte C. of C., 1965; v.p. La Porte Indsl. Devel. Corp., 1965; mem. expansion com. La Porte High Sch., 1976; bd. dirs. Vis. Nurses Assn., La Porte, 1966-67. Recipient Keyman award Jaycees, 1961, Disting. Service award, 1962, named Senator, 1964. Mem. La Porte County Pharm. Assn. (pres. 1963-64), Nat. Assn. Retail Druggists, Am. Legion, Purdue Alumni Assn., Purdue North Central Alumni Assn., Jaycees (pres. 1963-64), Kappa Psi, Rho Chi. Republican. Lodges: Rotary (pres. 1976-77), Mason, Demolay, Elks (past exalted ruler 1973, chaplin 1974-75). Avocations: skiing; fishing; golf; tennis; coins. Home: 206 Canterbury Dr La Porte IN 46350 Office: La Porte Northside Pharmacy 121 Pinelake Ave La Porte IN 46350

KREININ, MORDECHAI ELIAHU, economist, educator; b. Tel Aviv, Israel, Jan. 20, 1930; came to U.S., 1951, naturalized, 1960; B.A., U. Tel Aviv, 1951; M.A., U. Mich., 1952, Ph.D., 1954; m. Marlene Miller, Aug. 29, 1956; children—Tamar, Elana, Miriam. Office mgr. Efroni Advt., Israel, 1950-51; research asst. dept. econs. U. Mich., Ann Arbor, 1952-53, asst. study dir. Survey Research Center, 1954-55, study dir., 1955-56, lectr. econs., U. Mich., 1956-57; asst. prof. econs. Mich. State U., East Lansing, 1957-59, assoc. prof., 1959-61, prof., 1961—, mem. sterring com. acad. council, 1981—, chmn. steering com., 1984—; vis. prof. econs. UCLA, summer 1969, UN, Geneva, 1971-73, U. So. Calif., Los Angeles, summer, 1974, N.Y. U., summer, 1975, U. Hawaii, Honolulu, summer, 1977, U. Toronto (Ont., Can.), summer, 1978; vis. scholar Inst. for Internat. Econ. Studies, U. Stockholm (Sweden), 1978-80, U. B.C., summer 1983; world lectr. tours on behalf USIA, 1974-82; cons. to U.S. Dept. Commerce, 1964-66, U.S. Dept. State, 1972-74, UN, Council on Fgn. Relations, N.Y., 1965-67, Brookings Inst., 1972-75, Central Am. Common Market, 1972-75, IMF, 1976, various bus. corps, 1960-80, NSF, 1982-84. Recipient Disting. Faculty award Mich. State U., 1968; State of Mich. Collegiate award, 1984, NSF fellow, 1964-73, Ford Found. fellow, 1960-61. Mem. Am. Econ. Assn., Midwest Econ. Assn., Western Econ. Assn., AAUP, Royal Econ. Soc. Jewish. Author: Israel and Africa: A Study in Technical Cooperation, 1964; Alternative Commercial Policies—Their Effects on the American Economy, 1967; International Economics-A Policy Approach, 4th edit., 1983; Trade Relations of the EEC-An Empirical Investigation, 1974; (with L. Officer) The Monetary Approach to the Balance of Payments: A Survey, 1978; Economics, 1983; contbr. articles to profl. jours. Home: 1431 Sherwood St East Lansing MI 48823 Office: Econ Dept Mich State Univ East Lansing MI 48824

KREISER, FRANK DAVID, real estate exec.; b. Mpls., Sept. 20, 1930; s. Harry D. and Olive W. (Quist) K.; student U. Minn., 1950-51; m. Patricia Williams, Aug. 23, 1973; children—Sally, Frank David, Susan, Paul, Mark, Patti, Richard. Founder, owner Frank Kreiser Real Estate, Inc., Mpls., 1966—, pres., 1979—; partner, founder B & K Properties Co., Mpls., 1976—; chmn. bd., founder Transfer Location Corp., Atlanta, 1979—. Served with U.S. Army, 1948-50, Korea. Certified resdl. specialist and resdl. broker. Mem. Nat. Assn. Realtors, Mpls. Bd. Realtors (dir. 1972), St. Paul Bd. Realtors, Dakota County Bd. Realtors, Minn. Assn. Realtors, Realtors Nat. Mktg. Inst., Employers Relocation Council. Lutheran. Club: Decathlon Athletic. Address: 5036 France Ave S Minneapolis MN 55410

KREISMAN, JEROLD JAY, psychiatrist; b. St. Louis, Dec. 28, 1947; s. Erwin and Frieda Marion (Pokres) K.; m. Judith Irene (Korn), Aug. 9, 1970; children—Jennifer Laine, Brett Joshua. B.S., B.A., Washington U., 1969; M.D., Cornell U., 1973. Diplomate Am. Bd. Psychiatry and Neurology. Intern, Denver Gen. Hosp., 1973-74; resident St. Elizabeth's Hosp./NIMH, Washington, 1974-76, St. Louis U., 1976-77; practice medicine specializing in psychiatry; mem. staff St. John's Mercy Med. Ctr.; asst. clin. prof. St. Louis U., 1982—. Served with USPHS, 1974-76. Mem. AMA, Am. Psychiat. Assn., Am. Group Psychotherapy Assn., Internat. Psychogeriatric Assn., Am. Soc. Adolescent Psychiatry, Assn. Acad. Psychiatry, Eastern Mo. Psychiat. Soc. (pres. 1985-86), Phi Beta Kappa. Jewish. Office: 621 S New Ballas St Suite 4018 Saint Louis MO 63141

KREJCSI, CYNTHIA ANN, textbook editor; b. Chgo., Dec. 28, 1948; d. Charles and Dorothea Bertha (Hahn) K. B.A., North Park Coll., 1970; student Nat. Coll. Edn. Evanston, Ill., 1983—. Prodn. editor Ency., Brit. Chgo., 1970-71, style editor, 1971—; asst. editor Scott, Foresman & Co., Glenview, Ill., 1972-77, assoc. editor, 1977, editor, 1978-84, sr. editor, 1984—; sr. editor Benefic Press, Westchester, Ill., 1977-78. Mem. Nat. Assn. Female Execs., Chgo. Council on Fgn. Relations, Field Mus. Natural History, Chgo. Women in Pub., Internat. Reading Assn. Democrat. Lutheran. Office: Scott Foresman & Co 1900 E Lake Ave Glenview IL 60025

KREMER, EUGENE R., architecture educator; b. N.Y.C., Jan. 4, 1938; s. John and Ida (Applegreen) K.; m. Sara Lillian Kimmel, June 30, 1960; children—Michael, Ian. B.Arch., Rensselaer Poly. Inst., 1960; postgrad. U. Pa., 1960-61; M.Arch., U. Calif., 1967. Registered architect, N.Y., Kans. Architect, Ulrich Franzen assoc., N.Y.C., 1963-66; asst. prof. Washington U., St. Louis, 1967-70; lectr. Portsmouth Poly. Inst., Eng., 1970-71, Poly. Central London, 1971-72; dir. Inst. Environ Design, Washington, 1972-73; prof., head dept. architecture Kans. State U., Manhattan, 1973-85, dir. programs and devel. Coll. Architecture and Design, 1985—; mem. editorial bd. Jour. Arch. and Planning Research, Arlington, Tex., 1983—; mem. State Bldg. Adv. Bd., Topeka, Kans., 1984—. Author: Careers in Architecture, 1967; Leadership Meetings in Environmental Design, 1973. Author/editor newsletter Architecture Update, 1983—. Contbr. articles to profl. publs. Chmn. Adv. Bd. Gifted, Talented, Creative, Manhattan, 1974-75, Convocations Com., Manhattan, 1984—; mem. Truman Scholarship Com., Manhattan, 1980-84; v.p. Friends of Farrell Library, Manhattan, 1985-86. Recipient Spl. Service award Kans. Soc. Architects, 1984. Fellow AIA; mem. Environ. Design Research Assn., Assn. Collegiate Schs. Arch. (treas. 1976-80, pres. 1981-82, Service award 1983), Tau Sigma Delta, Tau Beta Pi, Tau Epsilon Phi (pres. 1959-60). Avocations: Reading, photography. Office: Kans State U Dept Architecture 211 Seaton Hall Manhattan KS 66506

KREMSNER, FRANK FRED, real estate executive; b. Chgo., Nov. 7, 1917; s. Richard and Anna (Blaskovits) K.; grad. high sch. Warehouse foreman Campbell Soup Co., Chgo., 1945-52, Wright Sales, 1952-54; with Goldblatt Bros. Dept. Store, Chgo., 1954-80, v.p., dir. ops., 1968-80; owner, pres. Rensmerk Co., 1981—; broker Century 21, Beacon Realty, 1982—. Served with AUS, 1942-45. Mem. Nat. Guild Profl. and Bus. Graphologists (pres. 1973-77), Internat. Material Mgmt. Soc., Field Mus. Natural History, First Burgenlaender Soc., Soc. of the Little Flower, Am. Legion. Home and Office: 7749 S Kenneth Ave Chicago IL 60652

KRENTZIN, EARL, sculptor, silversmith; b. Detroit, Dec. 28, 1929; s. Harry and Anna (Kievski) K.; m. Lorraine Joan Wolstein, Aug. 15, 1954; 1 child, Alexander. B.F.A., Wayne State U., 1952; M.F.A., Cranbrook Acad., 1954; student Royal Coll. Art, London, 1957-58. Instr. art dept. U. Wis., Madison, 1956-60; freelance sculptor, silversmith, Detroit area, 1960—; vis. prof. Kans. U., Lawrence, 1965-66; vis. lectr. Fla. State U., Talahassee, 1969. Metal work and sculpture exhibited in many regional, nat. and internat. exhibitions, 1954—. Recipient L. C. Tiffany award, 1966, awards and prizes for works in numerous pvt. and pub. collections; Fulbright grantee, 1957-58. Mem. Am. Crafts Council. Avocation: collection art and antiques. Home and Office: 412 Hillcrest Grosse Pointe Farms MI 48236

KRENZLER, ALVIN IRVING, See *Who's Who in America*, 43rd edition.

KRETSCHMAR, WILLIAM EDWARD, lawyer, state legislator; b. St. Paul, Aug. 21, 1933; s. William Emanuel and Frances Jane (Peterson) K. B.S., Coll. St. Thomas, 1954; LL.B., U. Minn., 1961. Bar: N.D. 1961. Ptnr. Kretschmar & Kretschmar, Ashley, N.D., 1962—; mem. N.D. Ho. of Reps., Bismarck, 1972—. dir. N.W. G.F. Mut. Ins. Co., Eureka, S.D., Central Dakota Bank, Lehr, N.D., N.W. G.F. Investment Co., Eureka. Del. N.D. Constl. Conv., Bismarck, 1971-72. Mem. State Bar Assn. N.D., ABA. Republican. Roman Catholic. Lodges: Lions (pres. local club 1972-73), Jaycees (pres. local club 1967-68), Elks. Avocations: hunting; swimming; hiking; bicycling; skiing. Home: 22 East Ln Venturia ND 58489 Office: Kretschmar & Kretschmar 211 W Main Ashley ND 58413

KRETSINGER, TOM BARK, JR., lawyer; b. Kansas City, Mo., Dec. 12, 1955; s. Tom Bark and Carolyn (Trimble) K.; m. Jo Annis Hetherington, May 22, 1982; 1 child, Mary Jo. B.A., William Jewell Coll., 1978; J.D., U. Mo., 1981. Bars: Mo. 1981, U.S. Dist. Ct. (we. dist.) Mo. 1981, U.S. Ct. Appeals (8th cir.) 1983. Ptnr., v.p. Kretsinger & Kretsinger, P.C., Liberty, Mo., assoc. prof. bus. law William Jewell Coll., Liberty, 1984-85. Campaign Coordinator Missourians for Roy Blunt, Clay County, 1984. Mem. ABA, Mo. Bar Assn., Kansas City Bar Assn., Clay County Bar Assn. (sec./treas. 1983), Assn. Trial Lawyers Am., Transp. Lawyers Assn. Republican. Espicopalian. Home: 139 N Water St Liberty MO 64068 Office: Kretsinger & Kretsinger PC 20 E Franklin Liberty MO 64068

KRETZSCHMAR, WILLIAM ADDISON, JR., English language and literature educator, editor; b. Ann Arbor, Mich., Sept. 13, 1953; s. William Addison and Audrey June (Krauss) K.; m. Claudia Suzanne Miller. A.B., U Mich., 1975; M.A. in Medieval Studies, Yale U., 1976; Ph.D. English, U. Chgo., 1980. English instr. Mundelein Coll., Chgo., 1977-82, summer sch. dir., 1979-81; asst. prof. English, U. Wis., Whitewater, Wisc., 1982—; editor, Linguistic Atlas Middle and South Atlantic States, Chgo., Linguistic Atlas North-Central States, 1984—. Editor: Dialects in Culture (R.I. McDavid, Jr.), 1979. Editor, Jour. English Linguistics, 1983—. Contbr. articles to profl. jours. Mem. MLA (regional del. 1983—), Am. Dialect Soc., Linguistic Soc. Am., Medieval Acad. Am., Conf. Editors of Learned Jours. Home: 5914 Anthony Pl Monona WI 53716 Office: English Dept U Wis Whitewater WI 53190

KREUTZER, PAUL, JR., interior designer; b. Sharon, Pa., Jan. 22, 1954; s. Paul and Maria (Schuster) K. A. in Specialized Tech., Art Inst. Pitts., 1973. With Hume's Carriage House, Youngstown, Ohio, 1974-84, buyer, 1978-79, sr. staff designer, 1979-84; propr. Paul Kreutzer Interiors, 1984—. Mem. Am. Soc. Interior Designers (assoc.). Lutheran. Clubs: Alliance Transylvanian Saxons (U.S. group leader 8th internat. youth rally 1984) (Cleve.); Youngstown Saxon (asst. fin. sec. 1984, 85), Youngstown Saxon Culture Group (v.p. 1977, 84, pres. 1985, trustee 1976, youth advisor 1970-71, news corr. 1974, 80, 81, 82). Home: 198 Wychwood Ln Youngstown OH 44512 Office: 198 Wychwood Ln Youngstown OH 44512

KREUTZKAMPF, JUNE ELIZABETH, social studies and home economics educator; b. Estherville, Iowa, June 13, 1940; d. Albert Olaf Theodore and Pearl Pauline (Wede) K. B.S., Iowa State U., 1962, M.S., 1970; Ph.D., U. Minn., 1978. Tchr. pub. schs. Hawarden, Maquoketa and Jefferson, Iowa, 1962-69; asst. prof. SUNY-Buffalo, 1971-74; vis. asst. prof. Brigham Young U., Provo, Utah, 1975-76; asst. prof. Peru State Coll., Nebr., 1979-80; asst. prof., chmn. dept. home econs. and instructional sci. U. Minn.-Duluth, 1980-84, coordinator social studies program, 1984—. Bd. dirs. Spirit Mountain Recreational Area Authority, Duluth, 1983—. Mem NEA, Am. Edn. Research Assn., Am. Home Econs. Assn., AAUW, Assn. Tchr. Educators, Assn. for Supervision and Curriculum Devel., Phi Delta Kappa, Omicron Nu, Kappa Omicron Phi, Alpha Delta Kappa, Beta Sigma Phi. Democrat. Methodist. Advocations: traveling; reading; sewing; photography. Home: 312 Hawkins St Duluth MN 55811 Office: U Minn 221 Bohannon Hall Duluth MN 55812

KREWSON, JAMES WILLARD, architect; b. St. Louis, Aug. 21, 1929; s. Oscar and Thelma Leola (Eleam) K.; B.S. in Archtl. Engring., Washington U., St. Louis, 1951; M.Arch., Columbia Pacific U., 1979, Ph.D. in Arch., 1980; m. Marlene Orf, Oct. 19, 1985. Architect, Bell System, St. Louis, N.Y.C. and Los Angeles, 1951-70; architect, Indio, Calif., 1971-73, Chgo., 1973-74, St. Louis, 1964-65; prin. firm Jim Krewson AIA Architect, Hannibal, Mo., 1975—. Dist. chmn., mem. exec. bd. Gt. Rivers council Boy Scouts Am., 1975—; adv. St. Louis Jr. Achievement, 1953-54; coach and adv. Hannibal YMCA, 1975-76; mem. Citizens Adv. Bd., Hannibal Bd. Edn., 1979—; adv. Hannibal Vocat. Tech. Sch., 1976-79, Hist. Hannibal, 1976-78; bd. dirs. Hannibal Arts Council; mem. Mark Twain Historic Dist. Bd. Rev. Recipient Bausch & Lomb Hon. Sci. award, 1951; Danforth Found. award, 1951, 5 nat. design awards in architecture, 1956. Mem. Internat. Platform Assn., AIA, Nat. Com. Architects for Commerce and Industry, St. Louis Engrs. Club, Nat. Council Archtl. Registration Bds. Republican. Clubs: Kiwanis, St. Louis Met. Toastmasters, Hannibal Country. Home: 838 Country Club Dr Hannibal MO 63401 Office: 2333 Palmyra Rd Hannibal MO 63401

KRIEG, DENNIS GEORGE, psychology educator; b. St. Louis, Oct. 12, 1952; s. George Valentine and Irma Marie (Seper) K. Adj. prof. Parks Coll., St. Louis, 1984—. Mem. Am. Psychol. Assn.

KRIEGER, GEORGE KENNETH, educator, musician; b. Cape Girardeau, Mo., Mar. 21, 1939; s. Clarence William Martin and Eula Mae (Hanners) K.; m. Arliss Sigrid Niemann, July 21, 1967; children—Katherine Elizabeth, Rachel Esther, Nathan George. Student St. Paul's Coll., Concordia, Mo., 1952-58; B.S. in Edn., Concordia Coll., River Forest, Ill., 1960; postgrad. Eastman Sch. Music, 1962-63; Orff-Schulwerk tchrs. cert. Royal Conservatory of Music, Toronto, Can., 1971; postgrad. Canisius Coll., Buffalo, 1974-75; M.S. in Edn., Kans. State U., 1978; postgrad. Salzburg Coll. (Austria), summer 1980, U. Iowa, 1982—. Cert. tchr., Iowa. Organist, choir dir. Holy Cross Luth. Ch., Chgo., 1958-60; with J. Neils Lumber Co., summer 1959; tchr. Topeka Luth. Sch., 1961-64; dir. music St. John's Luth. Ch., Topeka, 1961-64; tchr., dir. music St. Mark's Evang. Luth. Ch., North Tonawanda, N.Y., 1964-76; tchr., dir. music St. Paul's Evang. Luth. Ch., Ft. Dodge, Iowa, 1976—; mem. worship com. Iowa dist. W. Luth. Ch. Mo. Synod. Mem. Am. Orff-Schulwerk Assn. (pres. Iowa 1st chpt.), Music Educators Nat. Conf., Internat. Reading Assn., Assn. Supervision and Curriculum Devel., Choristers Guild, Royal Sch. Ch. Music, Fedn. Internationale des Choeurs d'Enfants, Ft. Dodge YMCA. Democrat. Lutheran. Research on music curriculum for early childhood music. Home: 1312 6th Ave S Fort Dodge IA 50501 Office: 1217 4th Ave S Fort Dodge IA 50501

KRIEGER, MICHAEL PARIS, neurologist; b. Bay City, Mich., Sept. 13, 1942; s. Maurice Harold and Elinor L. (Kuttner) K.; m. Sherry A. Saunders, Feb. 14, 1983; children—William Harvey, Elizabeth Maurine. A.B., Dartmouth Coll., 1964; M.D., N.Y. Med. Coll., 1968. Diplomate Am. Bd. Psychiatry and Neurology. Resident in internal medicine Meadowbrook Hosp., Long Island, N.Y., 1969-70; resident in neurology Walter Reed Army Med. Ctr., Washington, 1970-73; chief neurology sect. Walson Army Hosp., Ft. Dix, N.J., 1973-75; clin. neurologist, mng. ptnr. Neurol. Assocs. N. Central Ohio Inc., Mansfield, 1975-83; pres., practice medicine specializing in neurology Neurol. Services Inc., Mansfield, 1983—; cons. neurology, epilepsy Rehab. Ctr. N. Central Ohio, Mansfield, 1976—. Bd. dirs. Multiple Sclerosis Soc., Mansfield, 1976-78. Served to maj. U.S. Army, 1970-75. Mem. AMA, Am. Acad. Neurology, Am. Soc. Internal Medicine, Ohio State Med. Assn., Richland County Med. Soc., Am. Legion. Club: Mens Garden (Mansfield). Avocations: gardening; skiing. Office: Neurol Services Inc 233 Marion Ave Mansfield OH 44903

KRIER, CURTIS GENE, acctg. and fin. cons.; b. Mpls., Aug. 11, 1948; s. Curtis George and Jeanne Dale K.; B.A., U. Minn., 1970, B.S.B., 1978; M.B.A., Mankato State U., 1978; m. Nancy D. Carlson, Sept. 1980. Asst. to bank ops. officer 3d. Northwestern Nat. Bank, Mpls., 1972-75; staff acct. Robert G. Engelhart & Co., Burnsville, Minn., 1978-79, House & Nezerka, C.P.A.s, 1979-80; controller Calc-Type, Inc., Mpls., 1980-81; pres. Curtis G. Krier & Co., acctg. and fin. cons., Edina, Minn., 1981—. Cert., Am. Inst. Banking. Mem. Nat. Assn. Accts. (dir., sec. chpt. 1982-84). Home and Office: 5817 Grove St Edina MN 55436

KRIESHOK, THOMAS STEPHEN, psychology educator, consultant; b. Granite City, Ill., Mar. 10, 1952; s. Peter G. and Ruth M. (Hagnauer) K.; m. Susan Mary Isbell, Jan. 5, 1974; children—Benjamin, Aaron, Gabriel. B.S. in Psychology, U. Ill., 1974; M.A. in Counseling, Bradley U., 1979; Ph.D. in Counseling Psychology, U. Mo., 1982. Cert. psychologist, Kans. Adminstrv. asst. U. Mo. Career Planning and Placement Ctr., Columbia, 1979-80; psychology intern U. Mo. Counseling Services, 1980-82; asst. dir. Univ. Counseling Ctr., U. Kans., Lawrence, 1984—, asst. prof. counseling psychology, 1982—; psychologist, 1982—. Contbr. articles to profl. jours. James scholar, 1970, Merle Kaufman scholar, 1979, Carol and Adolph Frank scholar, 1980. Mem. Am. Psychol. Assn., Am. Assn. Counseling and Devel., Am. Coll. Personnel Assn. Office: Univ Counseling Ctr U Kans 116 Bailey Hall Lawrence KS 66045

KRIKORIAN, ROBERT V., manufacturing company executive; b. New Haven, 1919; B.S., Yale U., 1950. With Rexnord Inc., Milw., 1950—, v.p. constrn., 1962-63, exec. v.p., 1963-67, pres., 1967-78, vice chmn., chief exec. officer, 1978-80, chmn. bd., 1980—, chief exec. officer, 1980-85, also dir.; dir. Parker Pen Co., Mueller Co., Black & Decker Mfg. Co., Beloit Corp. Chmn. bd. Ethics Resource Center. Mem. Machinery and Allied Products Inst. (exec. com.). Office: Rexnord Inc 350 N Sunny Slope Rd Brookfield WI 53005*

KRISCH, ALAN DAVID, physics educator; b. Phila., Apr. 19, 1939; s. Kube and Jeanne (Freiberg) K.; m. Jean Peck, Aug. 27, 1961; 1 child, Kathleen Susan. A.B., U. Pa., 1960; Ph.D., Cornell U., 1964. Instr. Cornell U., 1964; mem. faculty U. Mich., Ann Arbor, 1964—, assoc. prof. high energy physics, 1966-68, prof., 1968—; vis. prof. Niels Bohr Inst., Copenhagen, 1975-76. Trustee Argonne Nat. Lab., 1972-73, 80-82, chmn. zero gradient syncrotron users group, 1973-75, 78-79; chmn. internat. com. for high energy spin physics symposia, 1978-88. Guggenheim fellow, 1971-72. Fellow Am. Phys. Soc.; mem. AAAS. Discovered heaviest elem. particle, also structure within the proton, 1966, scaling in inclusive reactions, 1971, spinning core within proton, 1977; inventor inclusive reactions; developed high energy polarized proton beam, 1973. Office: Randall Lab U Mich Ann Arbor MI 48109

KRISHNAN, E. RADHA, consulting chemical engineer; b. Calcutta, India, Feb. 21, 1952; came to U.S., 1974; s. S.E. and Swarna (Rajagopal) Raman; m. Sara Clem, Dec. 1, 1979 (div. Oct. 1982). B.S. in Chem. Engring., Jadavpur U., Calcutta, 1974; M.S. in Chem. Engring., U. Cin., 1976. Registered profl. engr., Ohio. Research chem. engr. Battelle Meml. Inst., Columbus, Ohio, 1977-78; tech. info. specialist Nat. Inst. Occupational Safety and Health, Cin., 1979; project mgr. PEI Assocs., Inc., Cin., 1980—; lectr. chem. engring. U. Cin., 1981—. Contbr. articles to tech. jours. Univ. grad. scholar U. Cin., 1974. Mem. Am. Inst. Chem. Engrs., Phi Lambda Upsilon. Avocations: square dancing; racquetball; music. Home: 599 Beaufort Ct Cincinnati OH 45240 Office: PEI Assocs Inc 11499 Chester Rd Cincinnati OH 45246

KRIST, DONALD EUGENE, insurance association executive; b. Topeka, June 26, 1926; s. George M. and Florence (McInerny) K.; B.A., Drake U., 1951; m. Marilyn McClurkin, May 29, 1948; children—Lisa Ann, James Eric. Public relations dir. U.S. Jr. C. of C., 1953-55, Meredith Co., 1955-60; exec. v.p. Iowa Consumer Fin. Assn., 1960-66, Profl. Ins. Agts. Iowa, West Des Moines, 1973—; owner, mgr. Donald Krist & Assos., Inc., public relations consultants, Des Moines, 1966-73; instr., lectr. public relations Drake U., Des Moines, 1957-70. Served with USN, 1943-46. Cert. assn. exec. Recipient Outstanding Achievement award Iowa 1752 Club, 1980. Mem. Am. Soc. Assn. Execs. (Mgmt. Achievement award 1976), Iowa Soc. Assn. Execs., Smithsonian Instn. Assos. Clubs: Des Moines, Des Moines Press (pres. 1959). Editor Iowa Ins. Interpreter mag., 1973—. Home: 800 52d Ct West Des Moines IA 50265 Office: Westgate Plaza Suite 12 1000 73d St Des Moines IA 50311

KRITSAS, ZOE PANAS, nurse; b. Mazatlan, Sinaloa, Mex., Sept. 5, 1933; came to U.S., 1957; d. John D. and Helen (Kutrumpusi) Panas. B.A., U. So. Calif., 1951; B.S., U. Guadalajara, 1953; R.N., Triton Coll., Maywood, Ill., 1979. Cert. obstet. nurse; disaster nurse ARC. Sec.-treas. Am. consulate, Guadalajara, 1952-55; coordinator State Fair, Govt. of Jalisco (Mex.), 1950-51; mem. staff Hosp. Service League, Chgo., 1968—; nurse Resurrection Hosp., Chgo. Author children's stories. Active ARC; interpretor Cook County Ct. Systems, 1981-82; chmn. Community Health Services No. Cook County Republican. Greek Orthodox. Office: Resurrection Hosp Chicago IL

KRIVOSHA, NORMAN MARVIN, chief justice Nebraska Supreme Court; b. Detroit, Aug. 3, 1934; s. David B. and Molly Krivosha; B.S. in Law, U. Nebr., 1956, J.D., 1958; m. Helene Miriam Sherman, July 31, 1955; children—Terri Lynn, Rhonda Ann. Bar: Nebr. Ptnr., Ginsburg, Rosenberg, Ginsburg & Krivosha, Lincoln, Nebr., 1958-78; chief justice Nebr. Supreme Ct., Lincoln, 1978—; city atty. City of Lincoln, 1969-70; gen. counsel Lincoln Electric System, 1969-78, Lincoln Gen. Hosp., 1969-78; mem. Uniform Law Commn., from 1973. Pres. Lincoln council Camp Fire Girls, Congregation Tifereth Israel, Lincoln, bd. dirs., nat. v.p. United Synagogue of Am.; bd. govs. Nebr. Wesleyan U., Lincoln; bd. dirs. YMCA, Lincoln; Nebr. chmn. Israel Bonds; chmn. fund drive Lincoln Jewish Welfare Fedn.; mem. Lincoln Charter Revision Commn.; bd. dirs. Ramah Commn., Camp Ramah, Wis. Recipient Outstanding Jewish Leader award State of Israel Bonds, 1978. Mem. ABA (sect. exec. council 1983—), Nebr. Bar Assn. (chmn. com. procedure), Lincoln Bar Assn., Nebr. Assn. Trial Attys. (sec. 1961-64, v.p. 1964-65), Am. Trial Lawyers Assn., Am. Soc. Hosp. Attys., Nat. Conf. Chief Judges (chmn. coordinating council an lawyer competence 1982—), Am. Public Power Assn. (chmn. legal sect.), Lincoln C. of C. (bd. dirs.), Sigma Alpha Mu (nat. pres. 1981-84). Office: State Capitol Suite 2214 Lincoln NE 68509

KROCH, CARL ADOLPH, retail book business executive; b. Chgo., June 21, 1914; s. Adolph Alfred and Gertrude Marie (Horn) K.; B.A., Cornell U., 1935; m. Jeanette Kennelly, Aug. 12, 1939. With Kroch's Bookstore, Inc., Chgo., 1935-54, pres., 1950-54, also dir.; pres., chief exec. officer Kroch's & Brentano's, Inc., Chgo., 1954—, also dir.; pres., chief exec. officer Booksellers Catalog Service, Inc., Chgo., 1954—; ptnr. Cin. Reds Baseball Club; dir. Nat. Blvd. Bank Chgo. Bd. dirs. Northwestern Meml. Hosp., Chgo., Better Bus. Assn. Chgo., Ill. Humane Soc., USO, Chgo., Center for Book, Library of Congress, Washington; life presdl. councillor Cornell U. Served to lt. USNR, 1942-45. Mem. Ill. Retail Mchts. Assn. (dir.), Am. Booksellers Assn. Clubs: Tavern, Univ. Chgo., Chgo. Yacht, Mid-Am., North Shore Country, Pauma Valley Country; Queen City (Cin.). Author: So Red The Nose, 1935; American Booksellers and Publishers: A Personal Perspective, 1981. Office: 29 S Wabash Ave Chicago IL 60603

KROETCH, PATRICIA ANN ROBINSON, educational diagnostician, educator; b. Tucson, Feb. 16, 1935; d. Lloyd Madison and Edith Beatrice (Kellogg) Robinson; m. George Duane Kroetch, July 3, 1955; children—Gregory, Sheron, Erika. Student San Jose State Coll., 1952-55; B.S. in Elem. Edn., Dominican Coll., Racine, Wis., 1956; M.Ed., S.D. State U., 1968. Elem. tchr. cert., Wis., S.D.; elem. adminstrn. cert., S.D. Tchr., Horicon (Wis.) pub. schs., 1956-57, Elk Mound Consol. Sch., Elk Mound, Wis., 1958-59; elem. tchr. Douglas Sch. System, Ellsworth AFB, S.D., 1964-80, Title I diagnostician, 1980-83, prin. elem. sch., 1983—; instr. S.D. State U., Brookings, 1979. Bd. dirs. Black Hills Waldorf Sch., 1981. AAUW scholar, 1965. Mem. Nat. Council Tchrs. Math., Internat. Reading Assn., Assn. Supervision and Curriculum Devel., Collegial Assn. for Devel. and Renewal of Educators, Delta Kappa Gamma, Alpha Delta Kappa. Republican. Episcopalian. Home: 1011 Franklin St Rapid City SD 57701 Office: Douglas School System Ellsworth Air Force Base SD 57706

KROGH, LESTER CHRISTENSEN, research and development executive; b. Ruskin, Nebr., Aug. 22, 1925; s. Jens Clarence and Clara Elizabeth (Christensen) K.; m. Rosa Christina Knickrehm, Dec. 23, 1946; children—Christine Krogh Brown, Charles John Krogh. B.S. in Ch.E., U. Nebr.-Lincoln, 1945, M.S. in Organic Chemistry, 1948; Ph.D., U. Minn.-Mpls., 1952. Sr. research chemist 3M Co., St. Paul, Minn., 1952-54, supr., mgr., asst. tech. dir., tech. dir., 1954-64, dir. corp. tech. planning and coordination, 1964-69, gen. mgr. new bus. ventures dir., 1969-70, exec. dir. Cen. Research Lab., 1970-73, div. v.p., 1973-81, v.p. research and devel. indsl. and consumer sector, 1981-82, v.p. research and devel., 1982—. Patentee in field. Served with USNR, 1944-46. Mem. Am. Chem. Soc., AAAS, Am. Inst. Chem. Engrs., Minn. Acad. Sci., Chem. Mfrs. Assn., Sigma Xi, Sigma Tau, Phi Lambda Upsilon. Republican. Methodist. Avocations: photography; golfing, handball; gardening. Office: 3M Co 3M Center 220-14W Saint Paul MN 55144-1000

KROGSTAD, JAMES GREGORY, insurance executive; b. Plum City, Wis., Mar. 18, 1950; s. Roland J. and Irma (Beatrice) K.; m. Jill Vanessa Pinzer, May 21, 1983. B.A., U. Wis.-Madison, 1973, postgrad., 1974-76. Loan officer trainee Thorp Fin., Portage and Platteville, Wis., 1976-77; v.p. Mortenson-Matzells & Assocs., Inc., Madison, 1977—. Fundraiser Arthritis Found., 1984, Am. Cancer Soc., 1982; sustaining mem. Boy Scouts Am. Recipient Disting. and Exceptional Service award Phi Gamma Delta, 1984. Mem. Nat. Assn. Life Underwriters, Madison Assn. Life Underwriters, So. Wis. Ofcls. Assn. (v.p. 1985), Nat. Assn. Sports Ofcls., Phi Gamma Delta (sec. 1970-71, treas. 1982—), Tri Bucks Investment Club (pres. 1983—), RMK Investment Club (v.p. 1984—). Methodist. Avocations: sports officiating; golf; softball; coin collecting; jogging. Home: 4329 Windflower Way Madison WI 53711 Office: 2009 W Beltlin- Hwy Madison WI 53713

KROGSTAD, WILBUR DONALD, JR., electrical engineer, land surveyor; b. Lebanon, Mo., July 8, 1944; s. Wilbur Donald and Caroline Eleanor (Bowman) K.; m. Freida Mae Sanning, Dec. 20, 1969; children—Cynthia Jean, Judith Ann. B.S.E.E., U. Mo.-Rolla, 1967. Registered profl. engr., land surveyor, Mo. San. engr. Clean Water Commn., Jefferson City, Mo., 1967-69; design engr. Lake of the Ozark Regional Planning Commn., Camdenton, Mo., 1971-72; cons. engr. Mo. Engring. Corp., 1972-74; design engr. Div. Design and Constrn., Mo. Office of Adminstrs., Jefferson City, 1974-77, chief design engr., 1977—. Active Holts Summit Civic Assn. Served with U.S. Army, 1969-71. Mem. Nat. Soc. Profl. Engrs., Mo. Soc. Profl. Engrs. (bd. dirs.), Mo. Assn. Registered Land Surveyors. Republican. Methodist. Office: Mo Office of Adminstrn Box 809 Jefferson City MO 65102

KROL, KENNETH HENRY, lawyer, educator; b. Cleve., Jan. 11, 1955; s. Henry C. and Helen M. (Kwiatkowski) K.; m. Maureen Ann Freas, Oct. 14, 1978; 1 child, Lauren Mary. B.A. in Social Studies, Cleve. State U., 1977; J.D., Cleveland Marshall Law Sch., 1981. Bar: Ohio 1981. Tchr. Magnificat High Sch., Rocky River, Ohio, 1977-81; atty., dist. hearing officer Indsl. Commn. Ohio, Cleve., 1981—; presenter Ohio Social Studies Conf. Moderator consumer rights Magnificat Consumer Protection Agy., 1981. Roman Catholic. Home: 5525 Delora Ave Cleveland OH 44144 Office: 615 Superior Ave NW Cleveland OH 44113

KROMER, SUSAN LEIGH, aerospace engineer; b. Cin., Dec. 3, 1958; d. Jack Karl and Betty Jane (Gillespie) K. B.S. in Aerospace Engring., U. Cin., 1981. Engr., Gen. Electric Co., Cin., 1981—. Mem. AIAA. Club: Cin Bridge Assn. Lodges: Eastern Star, Ladies Oriental Shrine. Avocations: softball; soccer; bowling. Office: Gen Electric Co 1 Neumann Way Evendale OH 45215

KRONENBERG, JACOB ARTHUR HERBERT, lawyer, educator; b. Cleve., July 7, 1951; s. Louis David and Shirley Evelyn (Weiskopf) K. A.B., Kenyon Coll., 1971; J.D., George Washington U., 1974. Bar: D.C. 1974, Ohio 1976, U.S. Dist. Ct. (no. dist.) Ohio 1976, U.S. Ct. Appeals (6th cir.) 1980. Sole practice, Cleve., 1976-79; ptnr. Kronenberg & Kronenberg, Cleve., 1979—; instr. legal research and writing Cleve. Marshall Coll. Law, 1982—. Mem. Greater Cleve. Bar Assn., Cuyahoga County Bar Assn. (grievance com. 1977—), Ohio State Bar Assn., D.C. Bar Assn., Assn. Trial Lawyers Am. Democrat. Office: Kronenberg & Kronenberg 857 Leader Bldg Cleveland OH 44114

KRONICK, PETER ALAN, physician; b. North Adams, Mass., Aug. 17, 1935; s. Jack B. Kronick; m. Maxine Rosenholtz, Aug. 9, 1958 (div. 1984); children—Brian, Scott, Dana, Erin. B.S., U. Detroit, 1957; D.O., Kirksville Coll. Osteopathy, 1961. Intern Flint Osteo. Hosp., Mich., 1962; gen. practice medicine, Flint, Mich., 1962—; mem. depts. ob-gyn, family practice, mem. Flint Osteo. Hosp.; mem. courtesy staff; Genesee Meml. Hosp.; assoc. prof. Mich. State U.; instr. Kirksville Coll.; chief staff Flint Osteo. Hosp., 1971, trustee, 1972; chmn. dept. family practice, 1969, chmn. various coms. Bd. dirs. Am. Cancer Soc. Genesee County Div., chmn. profl. relations com. Bruin Club Mott Community Coll. Scholarship Div., 1977; chmn. dept. ethics and credentials Genesee County Osteo. Assn., pres., 1973-74, 1979-80; v.p. Regional Comprehensive PSRO, Lapeer and Shiawasee counties; state del. Nat. Am. Osteo. Assn.; del. Mich. Assn. Osteo. Physicians and Surgeons. Mem. Genesee Med. Corp., Ind. Physicians Assn. Avocations: golfing; bowling; coin collecting; collecting limited edition items. Home: 1200 River Valley P-11 Flint MI 48504 Office: Peter A Kronick DO PC 3169 Beecher Rd Flint MI 48504

KROSSNER, WILLIAM JOHN, JR., psychologist; b. Newark, Oct. 19, 1939; s. William J. and Dora (Bruder) K.; B.Chem. Engring., Cornell U., 1961; Ph.D. (NIMH fellow), Harvard U., 1965; m. Rhonda A. Parrella, Sept. 4, 1977. Asst. prof. Vassar Coll., Fordham U., N.Y.C., 1966-74; assoc. prof. psychology and medicine U. Minn., Duluth, 1974-78; pres. PsyMinn Corp., Duluth, 1975—, Med. Psychometrics Inc., Duluth, 1980—; head dept. psychology St. Luke's Hosp., Duluth, 1978-84. Bd. dirs. St. Louis Center for Alcohol and Drug Problems, 1978-82. Center for Urban and Regional Affairs grantee, 1974-75. Mem. Am. Psychol. Assn., Minn. Psychol. Assn., Am. Statis. Assn., Minn. Biofeedback Soc. Club: Harvard. Home: 1045 Brainerd Ave Duluth MN 55811 Office: PsyMinn Corp 915 E 1st St Duluth MN 55805

KRUCKS, WILLIAM, electronics manufacturing company executive; b. Chgo., Dec. 26, 1918; s. William and Florence (Olson) K.; B.S., Northwestern U., 1940; postgrad. Loyola U., Chgo., 1941-42; m. Lorraine C. Rauland, Oct. 23, 1947; children—William Norman, Kenneth Rauland. Auditor, Benefit Trust Life Ins. Co., Chgo., 1940-42; chief tax acct., asst. to comptroller C.M., St.P.&P. R.R., Chgo., 1942-56; asst. comptroller, dir. taxation, asst. treas. C. & N.W. Ry., Chgo., 1956-58, treas., 1968-75; asst. treas. N.W. Industries, Inc., 1968-72; chmn. bd., chief exec. officer, pres. Rauland-Borg Corp.; pres., dir. Rauland-Borg (Can.) Inc., Mississauga, Ont.; dir. ATR Mfg. Ltd., Kowloon, Hong Kong. Bd. dirs. Civic Fedn. Chgo. Mem. Nat. Tax Assn., Tax Execs. Inst., Assn. Am. Railroads, Internat. Bus. Council Mid-Am., Ill. C. of C. Republican. Methodist. Clubs: Tower; Execs., Union League. Home: 21 Indian Hill Rd Winnetka IL 60093 Office: 3535 W Addison St Chicago IL 60618

KRUEGER, BONNIE LEE, editor, writer; b. Chgo., Feb. 3, 1950; d. Harry Bernard and Lillian (Soyak) Krueger; m. James Lawrence Spurlock, Mar. 8, 1972. Student Morraine Valley Coll., 1970. Adminstrv. asst. Carson Pirie Scott & Co., Chgo., 1969-72; traffic coordinator Tatham Laird & Kudner, Chgo., 1973-74; traffic coordinator J. Walter Thompson, Chgo., 1974-76; prodn. coordinator, 1976-78; editor-in-chief Assoc. Pubs., Chgo., 1978—; editor-in-chief Sophisticate's Hairstyle Guide, 1978—, Sophisticates Beauty Guide, 1978—, Complete Woman, 1981—; pub., editorial services dir. Sophisticate's Black Hair Guide, 1983—. Mem. Statue of Liberty Restoration Com., N.Y.C., 1983; campaign worker Cook County State's Atty., Chgo., 1982; poll watcher Cook County Dem. Orgn., 1983. Mem. Soc. Profl. Journalists, Nat. Assn. Female Execs., Sigma Delta Chi. Lutheran. Clubs: Sierra, Cousteau Soc. Office: Associated Publications Inc 1165 N Clark St Chicago IL 60610

KRUEGER, DANIEL CARL, county government official; b. Muskegon, Mich., May 4, 1946; s. John Albert Carl and Dorothy Jane (Vos) K.; m. Nancy Anne Dornbos, May 25, 1966; children—Heather Daniele, Daniele Denise. B.A., Hope Coll., Holland, Mich., 1968; M.A., Mich. State U., 1979. Cert. tchr., Mich. Tchr., West Ottawa Pub. Schs., Holland, Mich., 1968-77; asst. prin., 1977-78; county clk. Ottawa County, Grand Haven, Mich., 1978—. Mem. exec. com., del. Ottawa County Republican Party, Holland, 1974—, chmn., 1980-82; candidate state rep. Mich. Republican Party, Lansing, 1976, 82, conv. del.; bd. dirs., chmn. Hollard Community Hosp., 1977—; bd. dirs. Ottawa County Sch. Employees Credit Union, Grand Haven, 1978-79. Mem. Mich. Assn. County Clks., Internat. Assn. Clks., Recorders, Election Ofcls. and Treas. Mem. Reformed Ch. Am. Avocations: golf; baseball; woodworking; photography, gardening. Home: 14117 Brooklane Holland MI 49423

KRUEGER, DARRELL WILLIAM, college dean; b. Salt Lake City, Utah, Feb. 9, 1943; s. William T. and E. Marie (Nelson) K.; m. Verlene Terry, July 1, 1965 (dec. Jan. 1969); 1 child, William; Nancy Leane Jones, Sept. 2, 1969; children—Tonya, Amy, Susan. B.A. So. Utah State Coll., 1967; M.A. U. Ariz., 1969, Ph.D., 1971. Asst. prof. N.E. Mo. State U., Kirksville, 1971-73, dean instrn., 1973—. Author: (with others) Using Outcome Assessment: A Case Study in Institutional Change. Bd. dirs. Gt. Rivers council Boy Scouts Am., 1971—, SSS, 1982—. Mem. Am. Assn. State Colls. and Univs., Acad. Affairs Resource Ctr., Phi Beta Kappa. Republican. Mem. Ch. of Jesus Christ of Latterday Saints. Avocation: running. Home: 10 Catalina Dr Kirksville MO 63501 Office: Northeast Missouri State University Kirksville MO 63501

KRUEGER, DAVID ALBERT, JR., pharmacist; b. Hibbing, Minn., July 15, 1955; s. David Albert and Doris Mae (Anderson) K., Sr. A.A., Hibbing Community Coll., 1975. Assoc. Sci., 1975; B.S. in Pharmacy, N.D. State U., 1978. Registered pharmacist, Minn., N.D. Pharmacist, Pamida Pharmacy, Hibbing, 1978-80; pharm. rep. E.R. Squibb & Sons, Princeton, N.J., 1980—. Mem. U.S. Republican. Senatorial Com., Washington, 1984. Bristol scholar, 1978. Mem. Am. Pharm. Assn., Minn. State Pharm. Assn. (dist. rep. 1980-83, mem. state welfare task force com. 1984), Am. Legion (award 1973), Rho Chi, Phi Kappa Phi. Avocations: fishing, hunting, photography, skiing, backpacking, camping, American history. Home: Star Route 3 Hibbing MN 55746

KRUEGER, LESTER EUGENE, psychology educator; b. Chgo., Nov. 6, 1939; s. Carl and Helen (Milanowski) K.; Ph.D., Harvard U., 1969. Asst. prof. CCNY, 1969-72, assoc. prof., 1973-74; asst. prof. psychology Ohio State U., Columbus, 1974-76, assoc. prof., 1976-80. prof., 1980—. Served with U.S. Army, 1957. NIH grantee, 1970-76; NIMH grantee, 1979-80. Fellow Am. Psychol. Assn.; mem. Psychonomic Soc., Midwestern Psychol. Assn., AAUP, Sigma Xi. Cons. editor Memory and Cognition, Perception and Psychophysics; contbr. articles to profl. jours. Home: 2036-D Northwest Blvd Columbus OH 43212 Office: 404B W 17th Ave Columbus OH 43210

KRUEGER, NORMAN LELAND, physician; b. Bagley, Iowa, Dec. 5, 1915; s. Charles William and Helen Young (McLellan) K.; B.A., McPherson Coll., 1941; M.D., U. Iowa, 1950; m. Alma McLamb, June 26, 1948; children—Jean, Charles. Intern, St. Francis Hosp., Wichita, Kans., 1950-51, resident in pathology, 1954-55; resident in internal medicine, VA Hosp., Wood, Wis., 1955-57; practice medicine, Casey, Iowa, 1957—; clin. instr. Marquette U., 1955-57. Served with USN, 1942-45. Mem. Iowa Med. Soc., AMA, AAAS, Am. Coll. Angiology, Am. Assn. Physicians and Surgeons, Alpha Kappa Kappa. Republican. Mem. Church of the Brethren. Office: Hayes Bldg Casey IA 50048

KRUG, JOHN CARLETON (TONY), college administrator, library consultant; b. Evansville, Ind., Nov. 27, 1951; s. John Elmer and Mary Ellen (Moore) K.; m. Anna Marie Waters, July 3, 1983. B.A., Ind. State U., 1972, M.L.S., 1973; Ph.D., So. Ill. U.-Carbondale, 1985. Lic. minister Baptist Ch. Exec. dir. Olney (Ill.) Carnegie Pub. Library, 1973-74; assoc. dean Wabash Valley Coll., Mt. Carmel, Ill., 1974-84; mem. Com. for U.S. Depository State Plan, Springfield, Ill., 1982-84; dir. libraries Maryville Coll., St. Louis, 1984—; sec. pro-tem Ill. Basin Coal Mining Manpower Council, Mt. Carmel, 1974-79. Author computer programs. Vice pres. bd. dirs. Wabash Area Vocat. Enterprises, Mt. Carmel, 1979-81; mem. pres. bd. edn. Wabash Community Unit, Mt. Carmel, 1980-83; mem. exec. com. Community Edn. and Arts Assn., Carbondale, 1983-84; mem. visual arts adv. com. Ill. Arts Council, Chgo., 1982-84; pastor Hopewell United Meth. Ch., Bridgeport, Ill., 1976-77; lic. minister Terre Haute 1st Bapt. Ch. (Ind.), 1972—. Conf. speaker Kans. State U., 1982. Mem. ALA, Mo. Library Assn., Nat. Assn. for Preservation and Perpetuation of Storytelling, So. Ill. Learning Resources Consortium (del.), St. Louis Regional Library Network (del. 1985—), St. Louis Med. Librarians Assn. Mem. Christian Ch. Home: 121 Solley Dr Winchester MO 63021 Office: Maryville College 13550 Conway Rd Saint Louis MO 63141

KRUGER, WILLIAM ARNOLD, consulting civil engineer; b. St. Louis, June 13, 1937; s. Reynold and Olinda (Siefker) K.; B.C.E., U. Mo.-Rolla, 1959; M.S., U. Ill., 1968; m. Carole Ann Hofer, Oct. 17, 1959. Civil engr. City of St. Louis, 1959; with Clark, Dietz & Assocs., and predecessors, Urbana, Ill., 1961-79, sr. design engr., 1963-67, dir. transp. div., 1968-79; civil engr. div. hwys. Ill. Dept. Transp., Paris, 1979-83; part-owner ESCA Cons., Inc., Urbana, 1983—; instr. Parkland Coll., Champaign, 1972; mem. Ill. Profl. Engrs. Examining Com., 1982—. Served with C.E., AUS, 1959-61. Registered profl. engr., Ill., Mo., Fla., Miss., N.Y., Iowa, Del., Ohio, Ind. Mem. Nat. Ill. (chpt. pres. 1974, state chmn. registration laws com. 1973, 78) socs. profl. engrs., Ill. Assn. Hwy. Engrs., ASCE (br. pres. 1982-83), Am. Pub. Works Assn. (sect. dir. 1974-77, 80), Inst. Transp. Engrs., Ill. Registered Land Surveyors Assn., Soc. Am. Mil. Engrs., Nat. Council Engring. Examiners, ASTM, Urbana C. of C., U. Mo.-Rolla Alumni Assn., Theta Tau, Tau Beta Pi, Chi Epsilon, Pi Kappa Alpha. Clubs: Urbana Sportsmans, Champaign Ski. Home: 1811 Coventry Dr Champaign IL 61821 Office: 1606 Willow View Rd Urbana IL 61801

KRUGLIK, MEYER, psychiatrist; b. N.Y.C., Nov. 3, 1914; s. Max and Sarah (Fratkin) K.; m. Gertrude Barbara Ginsburg, Feb. 6, 1938; children—Michael, Gerald, Sally Kruglik Bauer, Martin. B.S., U. Ill., 1936, M.D., 1939. Intern, Univ. Hosp., Cook County Hosp., 1938-41; resident VA, 1942-47; practice medicine specializing in psychiatry, Chgo., 1947—; mem. faculty Chgo. Med. Sch., 1948-58; cons. Ill. Dept. Corrections, 1947—. Served to capt. U.S. Army, 1942-46. Mem. Am. Psychiat. Assn. (life), Ill. Psychiat. Soc. (life), Chgo. Med. Soc. (emeritus), Ill. Med. Soc., AMA. Office: 6 N Michigan Ave Chicago IL 60602

KRUH, ROBERT F(RANK), university foundation executive, chemist, university dean; b. St. Louis, June 15, 1925; s. Frank O. and Nelle (Dee) K.; B.A., Washington U., St. Louis, 1948, Ph. D., 1951; m. Janet Jackson, Dec. 19, 1948; children—Lindsay J., Nancy D. Asst. prof. chemistry DePauw U., 1951-52; asst. prof. U. Ark., 1952-55, asso. prof., 1956-60, prof., 1961-67; dean Coll. Arts and Scis., 1964-67; dean Grad. Sch., prof. chemistry Kans. State U., 1967—; vis. prof. Washington U., 1960-61; trustee Argonne (Ill.) Univs. Assn., Argonne Nat. Lab., 1970-76; pres. Kans. State U. Research Found., 1971—; mem. Grad. Record Exams. Bd., 1978-83, vice chmn., 1980-81, chmn., 1981-82; chmn. policy council, Test of English as Fgn. Lang., Ednl. Testing Service, Princeton, N.J., 1978-80; mem. Commn. on Instns. of Higher Edn., North Central Assn., 1983—. Served with U.S. Army, 1943-46; ETO. Mem. Council Grad. Schs. in U.S. (bd. dirs. 1977-80, chmn. 1978-79), Midwestern Assn. Grad. Schs. (pres. 1975-76, exec. sec. 1976—), Blue Key, Phi Beta Kappa, Sigma Xi, Omicron Delta Kappa. Lutheran. Research, publs. on determination of structure of crystals and liquids by means of x-ray diffraction. Office: Grad Office Kans State U Manhattan KS 66506*

KRULL, EDWARD ALEXANDER, dermatologist; b. Oakville, Conn., Oct. 25, 1929; s. Alexander and Marian (Ruppert) K.; m. Joan Marie Adams, Sept. 7, 1955; children—Alisa M., Lael Adams, Edward A., Jr. Student Yale U., 1948-51, M.D., 1955. Diplomate Am. Bd. Dermatology (bd. dirs. 1984—). Intern San Francisco City-County Hosp., 1955-56; resident Henry Ford Hosp., Detroit, 1960-63, staff physician dept. dermatology, 1965-76, chmn. 1976—; practice medicine specializing in dermatology, Grand Rapids, Mich., 1963-65; bd. dirs. Skin Cancer Found., 1977—, Found. Internat. Dermatologic Edn., 1980—; mem. residency rev. com. in dermatology, 1984—. Editorial bd. Jour. Dermatol. Surg. and Oncology, 1976—. Served to capt. M.C., U.S. Army, 1957-60, Iran. Fellow Am. Dermatol Assn., Am. Coll. Chemosurgery, Am. Acad. Dermatology (editorial bd. 1979—, chmn. task force on surgery 1978-84, presdl. blue ribbon com. 1984—, exec. com. adv. bd. 1974-76, chmn. task force surgery Council and Lab. Services, 1978—, bd. dirs. 1982—, exec. com. bd. dirs. 1984—, Bronze award exhibit, 1969), Mich. Dermatol. Soc. (chmn. liaison Blue Cross Blue Shield 1971-72, sec. treas. 1973-75, pres. 1976-77), AMA, Mich. State Med. Soc. (sec. dermatology sect. 1972-73, pres. 1973-74), Wayne County Med. Soc., Am. Soc. Dermatologic Surg. (pres. elect. 1980-81, pres. 1982, bd. dirs., 1973-76, 79—, chmn. resident com., scholarship com., 1976-81, cons. bd. dirs. 1976-79, chmn. educ. coordinating com., 1978—). Episcopalian. Avocations: tennis, trout fishing, golf. Home: 422 Univsity St Grosse Pointe MI 48230 Office: Henry Ford Hosp Dept Dermatology 2799 W Grand Blvd Detroit MI 48202

KRUMM, CAROL RHODEBACK, librarian; b. Pataskala, Ohio, June 17, 1923; d. Donald F. and Ethel Irene (Stevenson) Rhodeback; m. Delbert Russell Krumm, July 28, 1946 (div. Aug. 1981); 1 child, Carolyn Dee Krumm Heffner. B.A. cum laude, Capital U., 1945; B.S. in L.S., Case Western Res. U., 1946. Asst. librarian Otterbein Coll., Westerville, Ohio, 1946-51; cataloger Ohio State U., Columbus, 1952-53, 59-65, 82—, catalog maintenance librarian, head bibliog. records div., 1965-71, 71-76, head serial holdings conversion div., 1976-80, librarian tech. service, 1980-82; serial cataloger Cleve. Pub. Library, 1957-58. Indexer: Ohio State U. Monthly, 1953-57. Tchr., leader Methodist Chs., Columbus, 1958-81, librarian, 1968—. Mem. ALA, Ohio Library Assn., Ohio Valley Group of Tech. Service Librarians, Acad. Library Assn. Ohio (editor newsletter 1976-78). Republican. Clubs: Kiwanikwee (Columbus); New Century (Westerville). Home: 5768-B Pine Tree St N Columbus OH 43229 Office: Ohio State U Libraries 1858 Neil Ave Mall Columbus OH 43210

KRUMM, DANIEL JOHN, home appliance manufacturing company executive; b. Sioux City, Iowa, Oct. 15, 1926; s. Walter A. and Anna K. (Helmke) K.; B.A. in Commerce, U. Iowa, 1950; postgrad. U. Mich., 1955; D.B.A. (hon.), Westmar Coll., Le Mars, Iowa, 1981, Luther Coll., Decorah, La., 1983; m. Ann L. Klingner, Feb. 28, 1953; children—David Jonathan, Timothy John. With Globe Office Furniture Co., Mpls., 1950-52; with Maytag Co., Newton, Iowa, 1952—, mgr. European ops., Belgium and W. Ger., 1962-67, adminstr. asst. to pres., 1967-70, v.p., 1970-71, exec. v.p., 1971-72, pres., treas., 1972—, chief exec. officer, 1974—, also dir.; pres. Maytag Co. Ltd., Toronto, 1970—; dir. Centel Corp., Chgo., Bankers Life, Des Moines, Snap-on-Tools Corp., Kenosha, Wis. Mem. Newton Community Theater; pres. Maytag Co. Found., Inc.; bd. dirs. Iowa Natural Heritage Found.; chmn. bd. dirs. Grand View Coll., Des Moines; past pres. Des Moines Symphony Assn.; chmn. Newton Community Drive, 1976; bd. govs. Iowa Coll. Found.; past mem. Iowa Gov.'s Task Force on Ethics in State Govt., Iowa Gov.'s Dist. Jud. Nominating Commn.; chmn. Iowa Gov.'s Venture Capital Fund; former del. to nat. conv. Luth. Ch. Am. Served with USNR, 1944-46. Recipient Gold Knight of Mgmt. award Nat. Mgmt. Assn., 1978, Oscar C. Schmidt Iowa Bus. Leadership award, 1983; Disting. Achievement award U. Iowa Alumni Assn., named outstanding chief exec. of yr. in appliance industry Fin. World mag., 1979, 81, 84. Mem. Am. Mktg. Assn. (past pres. Iowa), NAM (bd dirs.), Newton C. of C. (past dir., Community Service award 1980), Maytag Mgmt. Club. Republican. Lutheran (council). Club: Newton Country. Office: Dependability Sq Newton IA 50208

KRUMSKE, WILLIAM FREDERICK, JR., marketing and research consultant; b. Chgo., Dec. 17, 1952; s. William Frederick and Harriet Marie (Piwowarczyk) K.; B.S., Ill. Inst. Tech., 1974; M.S. in Bus. Adminstrn., No. Ill. U., 1978; postgrad. in mktg., U. Ill.-Urbana-Champaign, 1983—. Salesman, warehouse mgr. Lus-Ter-Oil Beauty Products, Palos Heights, Ill., 1972-74; pub. relations dir. Crouching Lion Inn, Alsip, Ill., 1974; mgr. food and beverage Inn Devel. & Mgmt., Chicago Heights, Ill., 1974-75; v.p., dir. mktg. DeKalb (Ill.) Savs. and Loan Assn., 1975-81; sr. v.p. mktg. Regency Fed. Savs. and Loan Assn., Naperville, Ill., 1981-83; mktg. and research cons., Champaign, Ill., 1983—; dir. Rock Valley Network, Inc., Rockford, Ill., 1981-82; instr. Coll. Bus., No. Ill. U., 1978-83; mktg. mgr. Jordan Gallagher for State's Atty. campaign, 1976. Recipient William J. Hendrickson award No. Ill. U. Alumnus, 1980. Mem. Am. Mktg. Assn., Ill. Savs. and Loan League (mktg. com. 1977-81, chmn. 1979-80), Quill and Scroll, Beta Gamma Sigma. Lutheran. Contbr. articles to profl. jours. Home: 1903 Nancy Ct 5 Champaign IL 61821 Office: 339 Commerce W U Ill Champaign IL 61820

KRUPANSKY, ROBERT B., federal judge. U.S. cir. judge U.S. Ct. Appeals Sixth Cir., Ohio. Office: US Ct Appeals 250 US Courthouse Cleveland OH 44114*

KRUSE, AUDREY ANN, nursing administrator, registered nurse; b. Denver, Oct. 4, 1935; d. Clarence Chester and Marjorie Mona (Jones) Johnson; m. Eugene Kruse, Aug. 17, 1958; children—Elizabeth Kruse Borgman, Katharine, Marjorie, Mark, John. B.S.N., Augustana, Coll., Sioux Falls, S.D., 1957. R.N., Mo., S.D., Tex., Ohio, Ill., Colo. Various supervisory positions, 1961-68; instr. Area Vocat. Sch. Practical Nursing, Springfield, Ill., 1968-69, coordinator, 1970-71; office nurse, Parkston, S.D., 1972-75; staff nurse, night supr. Community Hosp., Sweet Springs, Mo., 1976-80, dir. nursing, 1980—, dir. in-service edn., project dir. Swingbed grant project. Campaign worker Republican Party, 1976—; active Lutheran Women's Missionary League Internat., Luth. Ch.-Mo. Synod. Served to lt. Nurse Corps, U.S. Army, 1957-58.

KRUTH, LAWRENCE FRANCIS, steel fabricating company executive; b. Sharpsburg, Pa., Nov. 13, 1953; s. Lawrence Herman and Emma (Bennardo) K.; m. Linda Kay Ankeny, Sept. 10, 1977; children—James Andrew, Adam David. B.S. in Civil Engring. Tech., U. Pitts.-Johnstown, 1976. Registered profl. engr., Pa., Mich. Engr., Franklin Assocs., Inc., Somerset, Pa., 1976-80; staff engr. Master Engrs. Corp., Pitts., 1980-81; sr. engr. Raymond Kaiser Engrs., Pitts., 1981-84; contracts mgr. H&G Steel Fabricating, Inc., Grand Ledge, Mich., 1984; project mgr. Douglas Steel Fabricating, Inc., Lansing, Mich., 1984—. Mem. ASCE. Republican. Lutheran. Club: Internat. Apple Core (Santa Clara, Calif.). Avocations: computer programming; computer graphics; computer aided drafting; design and engring. Home: 614 Belknap St Grand Ledge MI 48837 Office: Douglas Steel Fabricating Inc 1312 S Waverly Rd Lansing MI 48909

KRYN, RANDALL LEE, public relations exec.; b. Chgo., Oct. 12, 1949; s. Chester N. and Beatrice K. Kryn; A.A., Morton Coll., 1970; B.S. in Journalism, No. Ill. U., 1973. Writer and researcher William M. Young & Assocs., Oak Park, Ill., 1977; asst. public relations dir. Oak Park Festival, 1978; founder Oak Park Ctr. of Creativity, 1978, pres., 1978—, public relations dir., 1978—; founder, dir. Reality Communication, Oak Park, 1976—; dir. publicity campaigns for communication related orgns., 1976—. Legis. aide to rep. 21st dist. Ill. Gen. Assembly, 1980-83; Republican candidate for Ill. State Senate, 1982. Recipient Golden Trumpet award Publicity Club of Chgo., 1979; named One of 48 Outstanding Young Men of Am. from Ill., Ill. Jaycees, 1980; ambassador for Canberra, Australia, 1982. Mem. Public Relations Soc. Am., Seward Gunderson Soc. (co-founder 1978), Mensa. Columnist, Village Economist newspaper, 1977-78, Oak Leaves newspaper, 1978-79. Home and Office: 1030 Wenonah St Oak Park IL 60304

KRYSL, SHANNON SUE, lawyer, educator, administrative law judge; b. Phillipsburg, Kans., Aug. 21, 1955; d. Stanley and Betty Jo (Henry) K.; m. Dwight A. Corrin, June 5, 1982. Student Washburn U., 1973-75, J.D., 1980; B.S., U. Kans., 1977. Bars: Kans. 1980, U.S. Dist. Ct. Kans. 1980, U.S. Ct. Appeals (10th cir.) 1982. Staff atty. North Central Kans. Legal Services, Salina, 1980-81, Wichita Legal Aid Soc., Kans., 1981-82; sole practice, Wichita, 1982-84; adj. prof. law Wichita State U., 1982—; adminstrv. law judge State of Kans., Wichita, 1982—; ptnr. Corrin & Krysl, Chartered, Wichita, 1984—. Co-v.p. Mid Town Citizens Assn., Wichita, 1981; bd. dirs. Community Food Bank, Wichita, 1982, Child Care Assn., Wichita, 1982—; vol. Young Lawyers-Patterning Program, Wichita, 1983—. Mem. ABA, Kans. Bar Assn., Assn. Trial Lawyers Am., Kans. Trial Lawyers Assn., Wichita Bar Assn., Wichita Young Lawyers Assn., Order of Barristers. Home: 1919 Park Pl Wichita KS 67203 Office: Corrin & Krysl Chartered PO Box 2075 Wichita KS 67201

KRZYCH, JAMES, songwriter, publisher; b. Milw., Oct. 3, 1950; s. James Edward and Arvella Mary (Grier) K.; m. MaryJane Rondeau, Aug. 6, 1971 (div.); children—Joshua James, Samuel Dan, Simon Thomas. Student pub. schs., Wis. Guitarist and vocalist with groups Rubberband, 1968-70, Grain, 1970-71, Rio, 1976-78, Arroyo, 1978-82; owner Chenequa Music, Milw., 1980—. Composer/publisher: Can't Shake the Feeling, 1980; Run Out of Time, 1980; Gotta Have You, 1980; On Our Own, 1979; co-writer/publisher: Stronger Than Before, 1980; Little Miss Twister, 1980; Just Take a Hold of It (with Derrick Procell), 1980; producer/artist album Arroyo. (Album of Yr. and Best Prodn., Southeastern Wis. Music Awards), 1981. Address: 2404 S Howell Ave Milwaukee WI 53207

KRZYS, ROBERT MICHAEL, pharmacist; b. Youngstown, Ohio, Feb. 6, 1945; s. Fred and Joan (Kumiga) K.; m. Patricia M. Klinger, Aug. 28, 1971; children—Anne Michele, Wendy Dawn. B.S. in Pharmacy, Ohio No. U., 1973. Registered pharmacist, Ohio, 1974. Pharmacist, Norton Pharmacy, Ohio, 1973; pharmacist, asst. mgr. Super X Drugs, Youngstown, Ohio, 1974-77, Wittenauer Pharmacy, Poland, Ohio, 1977-79; pharmacist, mgr. Thrift Drug, Canfield, Ohio, 1979—. Served as sgt. USMC, 1966-70, Vietnam. Mem. Ohio State Pharmacy Assn., Eastern Ohio Pharmacy Assn. Roman Catholic. Avocation: racquetball. Home: 844 Indianola Rd Boardman OH 44512 Office: Thrift Drug 431 E Main St Canfield OH 44406

KU, HAN SAN, physiologist, biochemist, researcher; b. Hsin-chu, Taiwan, Nov. 20, 1935; s. Hsin-Nan and Tou-Mei (Liu) K.; m. Lily S. H. Lim., June 27, 1965; children—David, Timothy. B.S., Nat. Taiwan U., 1958; M.S., Osaka Pref. U., 1960, Sc.D., 1964; Ph.D., U. Calif.-Davis, 1968. Research assoc. U. Calif.-Davis, 1967-68, Purdue U., 1968; group leader Allied Chem. Co., Morristown, N.J., 1968-70; plant biochemist Mich. State U., 1970-73; sr. research assoc. Diamond Shamrock, Painesville, Ohio, 1973—, sr. research assoc. S.D.S. Biotech., 1983—, mgr., 1985—; cons. chem. cos., 1970-73. Contbr. articles to sci. jours. Patentee in field. Grant reviewer NSF, 1980—. Served to lt. U.S. Army, 1958-60. Mem. Am. Chem. Soc., Am. Weed Scientists, Am. Plant Physiologists, Am. Plant Growth Regulator, Japanese Plant Physiologist. Christian. Office: S D S Biotech Corp PO Box 348 Painesville OH 44077

KUBE, FRANK CARL, dentist, consultant; b. Arcadia, Wis., May 29, 1949; s. Frank Carl and Joyce (Severson) K.; m. Heidi Marie Harrison, July 22, 1972; children—Erik, Erin, Elissa. B.A. with honors, Luther Coll., 1971; D.D.S., Marquette U., 1975. Practice gen. dentistry, Reedsburg, Wis., dental cons. Reedsburg Meml. Hosp., 1975—, Synder Nursing Home, Reedsburg, 1975—, Sauk County Health Care Ctr., Reedsburg, 1976—; chief dentist Mobile Dentistry to Homebound, Reedsburg, 1983—. Contbr. articles to profl. jours. Bd. dirs. Sauk County Humane Soc., 1983—. Fellow Acad. Forensic Odontology; mem. ADA (Continuing Edn. award 1976-78, 1979-81), Sauk Juneau Dental Soc. (sec.-treas. 1978-79), Wis. Dental Assn., Acad. Gen. Dentistry, Acad. Soc. Geriatric Dentistry, Acad. Sports Denistry (founding). Lodge: Lions (pres. 1979-80). Lutheran. Avocations cross country skiing; swimming music. Home: Route 2 Reedsburg WI 53959 Office: 118 S Walnut St Reedsburg WI 53959

KUBE, MICHAEL ROBERT, lawyer; b. Cleve., Aug. 29, 1941; s. Mike and Herta Kube; m. Mary Junp, June 29, 1963; children—Scott, Julie. B.A., Baldwin-Wallace Coll., 1963; J.D., Case Western Res. U., 1967. Bar: Ohio 1967. Ptnr. Kube & Weinberger, Cleve., 1984—. Mem. Ohio Acad. Trial Attys. (treas. 1984-85, sec. 1985-86), Cleve. Acad. Trial Attys. (pres. 1980). Address: 118 St Claire NE Suite 103 Cleveland OH 44114

KUBINEC, JOSEPH THOMAS, accountant, financial consultant; b. Cleve., July 2, 1947; s. Joseph and Anne Louise (Silak) K.; m. Marjorie Jean Kubinec, Nov. 18, 1983; 1 dau., Suzanne. B.B.A., Cleve. State U., 1969. C.P.A., Ohio. Tax specialist McCarthy, Crystal et al, Cleve., 1967-70; tax ptnr. Lewandowski, Veres & Co., Cleve., 1970-72; mng. ptnr. Kubinec & Burg, Cleve., 1972—; dir. fin. Royal Petroleum, Cleve., 1980—; tax cons. Pavonia S.A., Panama City, Panama, 1977—; projects dir. Royal Belize (C. Am.), 1983; dir. Fin. Ninera Natalgua, Santiago, Chile. Fund raiser Republican Party, Cleve., 1981-83; mem. fin. com. Cuyahoga County Rep. Com. Mem. Ohio Soc. Pub. Accts., Nat. Soc. C.P.A.s. Clubs: Cleve. Athletic, University, Ionosphere, Admirals, Red Carpet, Clipper, Executives, Delta Crown. Home: 12203 Bluffside Ct Strongsville OH 44136 Office: Kubinec & Burg 1248 Standard Bldg Cleveland OH 44113

KUBISTAL, PATRICIA BERNICE, elementary school principal; b. Chgo., Jan. 19, 1938; d. Edward John and Bernice Mildred (Lenz) Kubistal; A.B. cum laude, Loyola U. of Chgo., 1959, A.M., 1964, A.M., 1965, Ph.D., 1968; postgrad. Chgo. State Coll., 1962, Ill. Inst. Tech., 1963, State U. Iowa, 1963, Nat. Coll. Edn., 1974-75. With Chgo. Bd. Edn., 1959—, tchr., 1959-63, counselor, 1963-65, adminstrv. intern, 1965-66, asst. to dist. supt., 1968-69, prin. spl. edn. sch., 1969-75, prin. Simpson Sch., 1975-76, Brentano Sch., 1975—, supr. Lake View Evening Sch., 1982—; lectr. Loyola U. Sch. Edn., Nat. Coll. Edn. Grad. Sch., Mundelein Coll.; coordinator Upper Bound Program of U. Ill. Circle Campus, 1966-68. Active Crusade of Mercy; mem. com. Ill. Constnl. Conv., 1967-69; mem. Citizens Sch. Com., 1969-71; mem. edn. com. Field Mus., 1971; ednl. advisor North Side Chgo. PTA Region, 1975; gov. Loyola U., 1961—. NDEA grantee, 1963, NSF grantee, 1965, HEW Region 5 grantee for drug edn., 1974; U. Chgo. adminstrv. fellow, 1984; Chgo. Bd. Edn. Prins.' grantee for study robotics in elem. schs.; recipient Outstanding Intern award Nat. Assn. Secondary Sch. Prins., 1966; named Outstanding History Tchr., Chgo. Pub. Schs., 1963, Outstanding Ill. Educator, 1970, Outstanding Women of Ill., 1970; St. Luke's-Logan Sq. Community Person of Yr., 1977. Mem. Ill. Personnel and Guidance Assn., NEA, Ill., Chgo. edn. assns., Am. Acad. Polit. and Social Sci., Chgo. Prins. Club (pres. aux.), Nat. Council Adminstrv. Women, Chgo. Council Exceptional Children, Chgo. Council Fgn. Relations, Chgo. Urban League, Loyal Christian Benevolent Assn., Kappa Gamma Pi, Pi Gamma Mu, Phi Delta Kappa, Delta Kappa Gamma, (parlimentarian 1979-80, Lambda state editor 1982—), Delta Sigma Rho, Phi Sigma Tau. Book review editor of Chgo. Prins. Jour., 1970-76, gen. editor, 1982—. Home: 5111 N Oakley Ave Chicago IL 60625 Office: 2723 N Fairfield St Chicago IL 60647

KUBLY, A(LVIN) RAY, seed company executive, agronomist; b. Watertown, Wis., May 22, 1924; s. Rudolf and Anna (Richard) K.; m. Ruth Audrey Wegwart, Sept. 4, 1948; children—Roger Ray, Joan Kristine, Carol Ann, Mary Lee. B.S. in Agr., U. Wis., 1952. Cert. profl. agronomist. Dist. sales mgr. Cargill, Inc., Mpls., 1952-59, Teweles Seed Co., Milw., 1959-61; v.p., gen. sales mgr. Dairyland Seed Co., West Bend, Wis., 1961—. Chmn. bd. dirs. Immanuel Lutheran Ch., Watertown, Wis., 1967-69; pres. Watertown Unified Sch. Dist., 1966-81, Coop. Service Ednl. Agy., Waupun, Wis., 1971-76. Served to 2d lt. USAF, 1944-45, prisoner of war, 1944; ETO; lt. col. Res. ret. Decorated Purple Heart, Air medal. Mem. Agronomy Soc., Wis. Soybean Assn. (bd. dirs. 1971-76), Res. Officer's Assn. (life), VFW, Am. Legion, DAV (life), Air Force Assn. (life), U. Wis. Alumni Assn. Lutheran. Lodge: Elks. Home: 1204 Amber Ln Watertown WI 53094 Office: Office: Dairyland Seed Co Inc PO Box 958 West Bend WI 53095

KUBO, GARY MICHAEL, advertising agency executive; b. Chgo., Aug. 15, 1952; s. Robert S. and Hideko K.; B.S., Ill. State U., 1974; m. Harriet Davenport, June 14, 1975. Research project dir. Foote, Cone & Belding Communicatins, Chgo., 1974-76, account research supr., 1976-79, research mgr., 1979-80; assoc. research dir. Young & Rubicam, Chgo., 1980-83; group research dir. Tatham, Laird & Kudner Advt., Chgo., 1983—. Mem. Advt. Research Found., Am. Mktg. Assn. Home: 2587 Oakton Ct Lisle IL 60532 Office: 980 N Michigan Ave Chicago IL 60611

KUCERA, MARY ANN, school board president; b. Iowa City, Iowa, July 18, 1936; d. James Leland and Mary Louise (Hickok) Turnbull; m. Howard Leo Kucera, Sept. 7, 1957; children—Charles, Elizabeth. B.A., Coe Coll., 1958. Cert. secondary tchr., Iowa. Tchr. Cedar Rapids Community Sch. Dist., Iowa, 1964-74, mem. sch. bd., 1974—, pres., 1983—. Pres. Children's Theatre, 1973; treas. Jr. League of Cedar Rapids, 1971; sec. Cedar Rapids Community Theatre, 1967-73; bd. dirs. Cedar Rapids YWCA. Recipient Community Service to the Arts award Cedar Rapids/Marion Fine Arts Council, 1978. Mem. Iowa Sch. Bd. Assn., Am. Assn. of Sch. Adminstrs. Avocations: reading, travel. Home: 2160 Larry Dr NE Cedar Rapids IA 52402

KUCHAR, WILLIAM RUDOLPH, mechanical designer, architectural design consultant; b. Grand Forks, N.D., May 30, 1955; s. Rudolph Joseph and Donna Mae (Yeager) K.; m. Kimberley Ann Monson, June 4, 1977; children—Michael, William, David, Joseph. Student U. N.D., 1974-75, State Sch. Sci., Wahpeton, N.D., 1976-78, N.D. State U., 1979-80. Surveyor, K.B.M. Consultants, Grand Forks, 1972-73; mech. designer Mobility Inc., Mpls., 1980-84, Food Engring. Co., Mpls., 1984-85, Simer Pump Co., Mpls., 1985—; cons. Merrill Lynch, Mpls., 1984—. Mem. Wahpeton Jaycees. Roman Catholic. Lodge: Elks. Home: 11215 51st Ave N Plymouth MN 55442 Office: Simer Pump Co 5960 Main St NE Minneapolis MN 55432

KUCHARO, DONALD DENNIS, JR., manufacter's representative; b. Des Moines, Mar. 25, 1946; s. Donald Dennis and Billie Wenonah (Stanford) K.; m. Carole Lee Toran, Sept. 11, 1971; children—Brian Neal, Bradley Alan. B.S.E.E., U. Iowa, 1969. Sales rep. Montgomery Elevator Co., Moline, Ill., 1970-73; v.p. Donald D. Kucharo Co., Davenport, Iowa, 1973-82, pres., 1982—; safety cons., leader product seminars. Mem. Soc. Mfg. Engrs. Republican. Unitarian. Club: Lindsay Park Yacht. Home: 2753 Nichols Ln Davenport IA 52803 Office: PO Box 727 Bettendorf IA 52722

KUCHTA, JOHN ALBERT, chemical company executive; b. Chgo., June 3, 1955; s. John and Janet Mary (Ivancak) K.; B.S. in Math., Northwestern U., 1982. Work coordinator Continental Ill. Nat. Bank & Trust Co., Chgo., 1974-78; lab. technician Kasar Labs., Chgo., 1975-76, supr. quality control, 1976-77; supr. weights and measures Bell Chem. Co., Chgo., 1977-78, quality control chemist, 1978-82, asst. ops. mgr., 1982—. Active Best Off Broadway Theatre, Music On Stage Theatre, Des Plaines Theatre Guild; music arranger community theatre. Mem. Am. Soc. Quality Control, Am. Prodn. and Inventory Control Soc., N.Y. Acad. Scis., Alpha Sigma Lambda. Roman Catholic. Home: 8023 N Wisner St Niles IL 60648 Office: 411 N Wolcott Ave Chicago IL 60622

KUCZYNSKI, JOHN RAYMOND, lawyer, banker; b. New Britain, Conn., July 3, 1953; s. Raymond John and Lucy (Giuliani) K.; m. Barbara Bowman, July 31, 1976; 1 child, John Robert. B.A. with honors, U. Notre Dame, 1975; J.D., St. Louis U., 1978. Bar: Ill. 1979. With law office R.H. Shultz, Walnut, Ill., 1978-80; v.p., asst. sec. Central of Ill., Inc., Sterling, 1980—; v.p., counsel Central Nat. Bank of Sterling, 1980—, Illini Life Ins. Co., Phoenix. Treas., bd. dirs. Ill. div., Whiteside unit Am. Cancer Soc., 1981—; mem. Indsl. Devel. Commn., City of Sterling. Mem. ABA, Ill. Bar Assn., Whiteside County Bar Assn. Republican. Roman Catholic. Club: Notre Dame of Rock River Valley (pres. 1980—). Lodge: Rotary (com. chmn. 1980—). Office: Central Nat Bank of Sterling 302 1st Ave PO Box A Sterling IL 61081

KUDRYK, OLEG, librarian; b. Rohatyn, Ukraine, Dec. 14, 1912; s. Theodosius and Olga (Spolitakevich) K.; diploma Conservatory Music, Lviv, 1934; LL.M., U. Lviv, 1937, M.A. in Econ. Sci., 1938; postgrad., U. Vienna, 1945-46; M.A. in Library Sci., U. Mich., 1960; Ph.D. in Polit. Sci., Ukrainian Free U., Munich, 1975; m. Sophie H. Dydynski, Feb. 5, 1944. Came to U.S., 1949, naturalized, 1954. Mgr., legal advisor Coop. Agrl. Soc., Chodoriv, Ukraine, 1938-39; mgr. Import Export Corp., Cracow, Poland, 1940-44; tchr. Comml. Sch., Ulm, Germany, 1946; adminstr. UNRRA, and Internat. Refugee Orgn., Stuttgart, Germany, 1947-49; asst. treas., mgr. Self-Reliance Fed. Credit Union, Detroit, 1953-60; rep., cons. Prudential Ins., Detroit, 1955-60; catalog librarian Ind. Univ., Bloomington, 1960-63, head order librarian, 1963-70, head acquisitions librarian, 1971-81, librarian for spl. projects and asst. to assoc. dean, 1982—; lectr. Ukrainian Free U., 1975—; guest lectr. Indiana Univ. Sch. Library and Info. Sci., 1965—. Recipient grant to survey West European book trade, Indiana Univ. Office Research and Advanced Studies Internat. Programs, 1972. Mem. Ukrainian Library Assn. Am. (v.p. 1972-75; exec. bd. mem. 1975—), AAUP (chpt. treas., mem. exec. bd. 1976—), Am. Library Assn., Assn. Coll. Research Libraries, Am. Econ. Assn., Am. Acad. Polit. and Social Scis., Shevchenko Sci. Soc. Contbr. articles to various publs. Home: 409 Clover Lane Bloomington IN 47401 Office: Indiana Univ Library Bloomington IN 47405

KUEHL, HAL C., See *Who's Who in America,* 43rd edition.

KUEHL, RICHARD JOHN, chemical company executive; b. Chgo., July 30, 1930; s. John Christen Fredrick and Josephine Louise (Schmidt) K.; m. Ina Lea Judy, Dec. 20, 1951; children—Diane Louise, Dale Richard, Kathryn Lee. B.E.E., Rose Poly. Inst., 1950. Sales engr. Allis Chalmers, St. Louis, 1950-57; project engr. Dow Chem. U.S.A., Baton Rouge, 1957-67, plant supt., 1967-70, prodn. mgr., Sarnia, Ont., Can., 1970-74, purchasing mgr., Midland, Mich., 1974-82, project mgr., Bay City, Mich., 1983—; cons. Pres. Reagan's Pvt. Sector Survey on Cost Control (Grace Commn.), 1982, Nat. Inst. Bldg. Scis., Washington, 1982-83. Served as 1st lt. C.E., U.S. Army, 1951-53. Clubs: Men of Music (pres. 1976-79). Home: 600 Harper Ln Midland MI 48640 Office: Dow Chem USA 4675 E Wilder Rd Bay City MI 48707

KUEHNI, NORMAN ARNOLD, private investigator, researcher; b. New Glarus, Wis., July 17, 1928; s. Arnold Samuel and Amelia (Mani) K.; m. Joanne Beth Voeck, Sept. 4, 1948; children—Kathleen Ann Porta, Barbara Dawn Rector, Pamela Jo Zulzer. Student U. Wis., 1946-49. With Dane County Traffic Dept., Madison, Wis., 1954-63; criminal investigator Bur. Alcohol, Tobacco and Firearms, U.S. Treasury Dept., Chgo., 1963-66, area supr., 1966-70, coordinator organized crime drive, 1970-72, spl. agt. in charge Washington Field Office, 1972-73, regional insp., Washington, 1973-75, dep. asst. dir. inspection, Washington, 1975-79, spl. agt. in charge, St. Paul, 1979-83; pvt. investigator, owner Eagle Eye Detective Agy., Hudson, Wis., 1983—. Served with U.S. Army, 1947-48. Recipient cert. of merit State of Minn., 1983, Badge of Royal Can. Mounted Police, 1983, Albert Gallatin award U.S. Treasury Dept., 1983, Spl. Agt. Retirement award U.S. Dept. of Treasury, 1983, cert. of appreciation Fed. Drug Enforcement Agy., 1983. Mem. Mensa, Fraternal Order Police, Wis. Private Investigators, Wis. Law Enforcement Assn. Lutheran. Club: Westwood Country (Vienna, Va.). Lodges: Masons, Order Eastern Star. Avocations: travel. Home and Office: 906 Sommer St N Hudson WI 54016

KUEKER, VIOLET LOUISE, educator; b. East St. Louis, Ill., June 27, 1929; d. Marcellus C. and Mildred M. (Meyer) Hartman; student MacMurray Coll., 1947-49; B.S. in Edn., So. Ill. U., Carbondale, 1951; M.Ed., U. Ill., 1957; m. Edmund E. Kueker, Mar. 31, 1951. Home econs. tchr. Zeigler (Ill.) High Sch., 1951-52, Waterloo (Ill.) Public High Schs., 1952—. Past mem. North Central Evaluation Team; mem. Ill. Vocat. Evaluation Team, 1981—. Recipient Outstanding Tchr. award Waterloo High Sch., 1982. Mem. NEA (life), Am. Home Econs. Assn., Nat. Assn. Vocat. Home Econs. Tchrs., Am. Vocat. Assn., Am. Council Consumer Interests, Ill. Coop. Vocat. Edn. Coordinators Assn., Ill. Consumer Edn. Assn., Ill. Edn. Assn., Ill. Home Econs. Assn., (pres. dist. V 1981-82), Ill. Vocat. Home Econs. Tchrs. Assn. (chair region V, 1983-85), Ill. Vocational Assn., Monroe County Homemakers Extension Assn., Monroe County Fair Assn., Monroe County Hist. Soc., Waterloo Classroom Tchrs. Assn., Delta Kappa Gamma. Mem. United Ch. of Christ. Clubs: Evening Women's Guild; Peterstown Heritage Soc. Waterloo IL 62298 Office: Bellefontaine Dr Waterloo IL 62298

KUENZEL, NANCY VARDE, photographic products company executive; b. Evanston, Ill., Mar. 31, 1925; d. Christ Michael and Ruth A. (Forester) Varde; m. Aug. 31, 1946 (div. Sept. 1975); children—Robert, Thomas, Chrisanne, Kimberly. B.S., Northwestern U., 1947; postgrad. paralegal studies Mallinckrodt Coll., Wilmette, Ill., 1976. Account exec. Bell & Howell subs. Columbia Pictures, Northbrook, Ill., 1976—. Mem. Women in Cable (rec. sec. Chgo. chpt. 1983, nat. bd. dirs. 1984—), Nat. Cable TV Assn. Republican. Presbyterian. Club: Evanston Jr. League. Office: Bell & Howell/Columbia Pictures 720 Landwehr Rd Northbrook IL 60062

KUETTNER, KLAUS EDUARD, biochemistry educator; b. Bunzlau, Germany, June 25, 1933; came to U.S., 1962, naturalized, 1969; s. Gerhard Paul and Elfriede (Oelze) Küttner; m. Yolanda Adler, Aug. 25, 1975. B.S., Minden, Fed. Republic Germany, 1956; M.S., U. Freiburg, Fed. Republic Germany, 1958; Ph.D., U. Berne, Switzerland, 1961. Research assoc. Presbyterian St. Luke's Hosp., Chgo., 1964-66; instr. biol. chemistry U. Ill. Coll. Medicine, Chgo., 1964-65; asst. prof. dept. biochemistry Rush Med. Coll., Rush Presbyn.-St. Luke's Med. Ctr., Chgo., 1971-72, assoc. prof. dept. orthopedic surgery and biochemistry, 1972-77, prof. biochemistry and orthopedics, 1980—, chmn. dept. biochemistry, 1980; chmn. chemistry, physiology and structure of bones and teeth Gordon Research Conf., 1978; chmn. Proteoglycon Gordon Research Conf., 1984; co-chmn. fellowship subcom. Nat. Arthritis Found., 1981-82. CIBA fellow, Basel, Switzerland, 1961-62; AEC fellow, 1962-64. Mem. Am. Soc. Biol. Chemists, Am. Soc. Cell Biology, Am. Chem. Soc., Orthopedic Research Soc. Internat. Assn. Dental Research. Office: Rush Presbyterian St Luke's Med Ctr Dept Biochemistry 1753 W Congress Pkwy Chicago IL 60612

KUFELDT, GEORGE, biblical educator; b. Chgo., Nov. 4, 1923; s. Henry and Lydia (Dorn) K.; m. Kathryn Rider, July 24, 1943 (dec. July 1956); children—Anita Kay Kufeldt Shelton, Kristina Sue Kufeldt Schmidt; m. 2d, Claudena Eller, June 21, 1957 (dec. Sept. 1978); m. 3d, Lydia Borgardt, Aug. 12, 1980. A.B., Anderson Coll., Ind., 1945, Th.B., 1946, M.Div., 1953; Ph.D., Dropsie U., 1974. Ordained to ministry Ch. of God, 1949; pastor Ch. of God, Homestead, Fla., 1948-50, Ch. of God, Cassopolis, Mich., 1954-57, Ch. of God, Lansdale, Pa., 1957-61; prof. O.T. and Hebrew, Anderson Coll., 1961—. Dropsie U. fellow, 1961, 63; Land of the Bible Workshop grantee N.Y.U., 1966. Mem. Soc. Bibl. Lit., Nat. Assn. Profs. of Hebrew, AAUP. Lodge: AHEPA (rec. sec.). Contbr. to Wesleyan Bible Commentary, Vol. II, 1968, Nelson's Expository Dictionary of the Old Testament, 1980. Home: 907 N Nursery Rd Anderson IN 46012 Office: School of Theology Anderson College Anderson IN 46012

KUGLER, IDA CAROLYN, museum director; b. Bancroft, Nebr., Dec. 22, 1905; d. Herman and Petrine (Pedersen) Grunke; cert. Montevideo (Minn.) Tchr. Tng. Dept., 1925; A.A. with honors, St. Cloud (Minn.) State U., 1931; B.S. with distinction, U. Minn., 1941, M.A., 1956; Ph.D., Walden U., Naples, Fla., 1972; m. William John Kugler, Nov. 8, 1940. Tchr., Chippewa County, Minn., 1925-30, Rushford, Minn., 1930-31, Lakefield, Minn., 1931-35, St. Paul Public Schs., 1935-61; pioneering prin. Aiyepe High Sch., Ogun State, Nigeria, 1961-65; tchr. St. Paul Public Schs., 1965-74; v.p. Kugler Musical Instrument Mus., St. Paul, 1974—, also edn. dir., registrar. Chmn. Chippewa County Field Day, 1929; tchr. English to Chinese immigrants from Hong Kong, 1965—; nat. adv. bd. Am. Security Council; mem. Republican Nat. Com., U.S. Senatorial Club. Mem. St. Paul Ret. Tchrs. Assn., Nat. Ret. Tchrs. Assn., Am. Assn. Museums, OAS, Cath. Golden Age. Roman Catholic. Office: 1124 Dionne Ave Saint Paul MN 55113

KUH, GEORGE DENNIS, educator, educational administrator; b. Chgo., Mar. 26, 1946; s. Rudolph George and Anne (Sulovsky) K.; m. Kristi M. Buckneberg, July 7, 1968 (dec. 1976); m. Martha May McCarthy, Dec. 17, 1977; children—Kari Ann, Kristian R. B.A., Luther Coll., 1968; M.S., St. Cloud State Coll., 1971; Ph.D., U. Iowa, 1975. Admissions officer Luther Coll., Decorah, Iowa, 1968-72; asst. prof. U. Iowa, Iowa City, 1975-76; assoc. prof. Ind. U., Bloomington, 1977-83, prof., 1984—, assoc. dean acad. affairs, 1985—. Author publs., monographs. Contbr. articles to prof. jours. Mem. Am. Coll. Personnel Assn., Nat. Assn. Student Personnel Administrs., Am. Ednl. Research Assn., Assn. Study of High Edn. Avocations: running, alpine skiing, tennis. Office: Wright Edn Bldg 227 Bloomington IN 47405

KUHAR, JUNE CAROLYNN, retired fiberglass manufacturing company executive; b. Chgo., Sept. 20, 1935; d. Kurt Ludwig and Dorothy Julia (Lewand) Stier; student William Rainey Harper Coll., Chgo.; m. G. James Kuhar, Feb. 5, 1953; children—Kathleen Lee, Debra Suzanne. Engaged in fiberglass mfg., 1970—; sec.-treas. Q-R Fiber Glass Industries Inc., Elgin, 1970—. Mem. Multiple Sclerosis Soc., Nat. Fedn. Ileitis and Colitis, Mt. Prospect Bus. and Profl. Woman's Club (pres. 1984—). Home: 9723 Arthur Dr Algonquin IL 60102 Office: 701 N State St Elgin IL 60120

KUHLMAN-HARRISON, JUDY RAE, university research and grants administrator; b. Sedalia, Mo., Dec. 9, 1946; d. Delbert and Alyce Lou (Judd) Bearce; m. Gary Paul Kuhlman, June 12, 1969 (div. Aug. 1974); 1 son, Erik Paul; m. 2d, Lindell Lee Harrison, Aug. 11, 1979. B.A., Central Mo. State U., 1968, M.S., 1977; Ph.D., U. Mo.-Columbia, 1981. Cert. tchr. Mo., 1973. Traffic coordinator Sta. KMBC-TV, Kansas City, Mo., 1968-69; tchr. English, Smithton (Mo.) High Sch., 1969-74; dir. career edn. programs State Fair Community Coll., Sedalia, Mo., 1974-80; dir. research and grants Central Mo. State U., 1980—; cons. U.S. Office Edn., Ohio State U., Phoenix (Ariz.) Sch. Dist. EPDA fellow, 1974; named Outstanding Educator, Pettis County, Mo., 1971. Mem. Nat. Council Research Administrs., Soc. Research Administrs., Nat. Experience-Based Career Edn. Assn., Am. Vocat. Assn., Mo. Vocat. Assn., LWV, Nat. Fedn. Bus. and Profl. Women's Clubs (pres. Sedalia chpt. 1982-83), Phi Delta Kappa. Meth. Home: RR 3 Walnut Hills Box 307R Sedalia MO 65301 Office: Central Mo State U Adminstrn 314 Warrensburg MO 64093

KUHLMANN, FRED L., brewery consultant; b. St. Louis, Apr. 24, 1916; s. Fred A. and Meta (Borrenpohl) K.; A.B., J.D., Washington U., St. Louis, 1938; LL.M., Columbia U., 1942; m. Mildred E. Southworth, July 11, 1941; children—Marilyn (Mrs. John W. Brickler), Fred M. Admitted to Mo. bar, 1938; partner Stolar, Kuhlmann, Heitzmann & Eder, St. Louis, 1956-67; gen. counsel Anheuser-Busch, Inc., St. Louis, 1967-70, v.p., gen. counsel, 1971-74, sr. v.p. adminstrn. and services, dir., 1974-77, exec. v.p., 1977-84, vice chmn. bd., 1979—; exec. v.p., chief operating officer St. Louis Nat. Baseball Cardinals, Inc., 1984—; dir. Anheuser-Busch Cos., Inc., Mercantile Bancorp., Mercantile Trust Co., St. Louis Nat. Baseball Club. Mfrs. Ry. Co., Concordia Pub. House, St. Louis, Aid Assn. for Luths., Appleton, Wis. Bd. dirs. Civic Center Corp. Mem. Am., St. Louis bar assns., Mo. Bar, Order of Coif, Phi Beta Kappa. Clubs: St. Louis, Bellerive Country. Contbr. articles to legal publs. Home: 6 Coach N Four Frontenac MO 63131 Office: 250 Stadium Plaza Saint Louis MO 63102

KUHN, DAVID ALAN, lawyer; b. Cleve., Ohio, May 7, 1929; s. Irwin Albert and Margaret (Janke) K.; m. Jacqueline McColloch, July 2, 1955; children—David McColloch, Douglas Alan. A.B., Kenyon Coll., 1951; J.D., Case Western Res. U., 1954. Bar: Ohio 1954. Asst. to sec. Warner & Swasey Co., Cleve., 1956-59; staff atty. Oglebay Norton Co., Cleve., 1959-70, asst. sec., 1970-80, sec., counsel, 1980—. Trustee Kenyon Coll., 1983—. Mem. Cleve. Bar Assn., Ohio State Bar Assn., Am. Soc. Corp. Secs., Kenyon Coll. Alumni Assn. (pres. 1974; named Outstanding Alumni 1976-77), Delta Tau Delta. Served to capt. USAF, 1954-56. Clubs: Cleve. Yachting (sec. 1983—), Cleve. Athletic. Republican. Home: 337 Morewood Pkwy Rocky River OH 44116 Office: Oglebay Norton Co 1100 Superior Ave Cleveland OH 44114

KUHN, GLORIA JEAN, physician; b. Detroit, Oct. 25, 1943; d. Edward and Dorothy (Schweig) Houseman; m. John Robert Kuhn, Sept. 5, 1964; children—David, Deena, Michael. D.O., Chgo. Coll. Osteo. Medicine, 1970. Staff emergency physician Riverside Osteo. Hosp., Trenton, Mich., 1971-72, Martin Pl. Hosp., Madison Heights, Mich., 1973-77, Detroit Gen. Hosp., 1977-79, Mt. Carmel Mercy Hosp., Detroit, 1979—, St. Joseph Mercy Hosp., Pontiac, Mich., 1984—; dir. resident edn. dept. emergency medicine Mt. Carmel Mercy Hosp., Detroit, 1982—. Contbr. articles to profl. jours. Fellow Am. Coll. Emergency Physicians; mem. Emergency Med. Residency Assn., Am. Coll. Osteo. Emergency Physicians, Soc. Tchrs. Emergency Medicine, U. Assn. Emergency Medicine. Democrat. Jewish. Avocations: reading, needlework. Office: Mount Carmel Mercy Hosp 6071 W Outer Dr Detroit MI 48235

KUHN, JOHN FERDINAND, English educator; b. Hamtramck, Mich., Mar. 26, 1940; s. John F. and Lillian (Dudzinski) K.; m. Sara Lynn Goldhammer, Nov. 12, 1966; children—Deborah, David. A.B., Loyola U., Chgo., 1963, M.A., 1967; Ph.D., U. Notre Dame, 1973. Instr., No. Mich. U., Marquette, 1966-69, asst. prof., 1973-76, assoc. prof., 1976-79, prof. English, 1979—, head dept., 1977—, dir. freshman writing, 1972-77; grad. asst. U. Notre Dame, Ind., 1969-71; dir. Upper Peninsula Writing Project, Marquette, 1979-82. Contbr. sect. to book; also articles. Chmn. adminstrn. commn. St. Michael's Roman Catholic Parish, Marquette, 1982—; v.p. Upper Peninsula chpt. March of Dimes, 1983—. U. Notre Dame fellow, 1970-72; NEH grantee, 1976, 77. Mem. MLA, Mich. Acad. Arts, Sci. and Letters, Mich. Assn. Depts. English. Democrat. Avocations: cross-country skiing, swimming, walking, reading, computers, attending sporting events. Home: 1609 Gray St Marquette MI 49855 Office: Dept English No Mich U Marquette MI 49855

KUHN, PAUL ANTON, engineer; b. Chgo., Mar. 21, 1931; s. Anthony Joseph and Paula Theresa (Carstensen) K.; m. Sharon Lee Dreymiller, Sept. 10, 1955; children—Mark Anton, Cinda Lee, Sarah Lynne. Student in Civil Engring., Northwestern Tech. Inst., Evanston, Ill., 1948-51; B.S. in San. Engring., U. Ill., 1954; M.S. in Civil Engring., U. Wis.-Madison, 1956. Registered profl. engr., Ill., Iowa, Mo., Minn., Miss., Calif., Va., Wis., Ind., Ky., Nebr., Colo., Ohio, Mich., S.D. Engr., Pacific Flush Tank Co., Chgo., 1954-55; research asst. U. Wis. Madison, 1955-56; engr., head san. design sect. Stanley Engring. Co., Muscatine, Iowa, 1956-61; engr., project mgr. Greeley and Hansen, Chgo., 1961-68, assoc., 1969-71, ptnr., 1971—. Treas. Northbrook Caucus Com., Ill., 1967-68, holdover mem., 1968-69. Served with U.S. Army, 1951-53. Walter Murphy scholar, 1949-51, N.O. Nelson scholar, 1954; recipient Ira O. Baker prize civil engring. dept. U. Ill., 1954. Fellow ASCE v.p. Tri-City sect. 1961, (pres. Ill. sect. 1970-71, nat. v.p. 1981-83); mem. Water Pollution Control Fedn. (bd. dirs. 1978-81, Arthur Sidney Bedell award 1978), Central States Water Pollution Control Assn. (pres. 1975-76), Am. Water Works Assn. (Harry E. Jordan scholar 1955), Am. Pub. Works Assn., Nat. Soc. Profl. Engrs., Ill. Soc. Profl. Engrs., Am. Cons. Engrs. Council (chmn. environ. com. 1976-79), Cons. Engrs. Council Ill., Am. Underground Space Assn., Constrn. Specifications Inst., Tau Beta Pi, Chi Epsilon, Sigma Tau, Phi Kappa Phi. Republican. Methodist. Club: Union League (Chgo.) (chmn. camera group). Avocations: photography, gardening, fishing. Office: Greeley and Hansen 222 S Riverside Plaza Chicago IL 60606

KUHN, PAUL HUBERT, JR., investment counsel; b. Chattanooga, Sept. 7, 1943; s. P. Hubert and Pauline Anna (Byrnes) K.; m. Jeanne Bartlett Elmore, June 7, 1966; children—Katherine, Christopher. B.A., Vanderbilt U., 1965; M.B.A., Ind. U., 1971. Chartered investment counselor. Investment counsel Stein Roe & Farnham, Chgo., 1971—; v.p. Stein Roe Spl. Fund, Chgo., 1983—. Mid-West coordinator Nat. Orgn. for Reform Marijuana Laws, Chgo., 1973-77; bd. dirs. Augustana Hosp., Chgo., 1980-83, USO of Chgo.; pres. Lincoln Park Renewal Corp., Chgo. Served to lt. USN, 1965-69. Mem. Investment Analysis Soc., Phi Beta Kappa, Omicron Delta Kappa. Republican. Roman Catholic. Clubs: Tavern (Chgo.); Long Beach Country (Ind.). Home: 1716 Crilly Ct Chicago IL 60614 Office: Stein Roe & Farnham One S Wacker Dr Chicago IL 60606

KUHN, RICHARD R., lawyer; b. Pitts., Oct. 10, 1951; s. Thomas A. and Mary Sue (Austin) K.; m. Patricia S. Skelley, June 30, 1973; children—Matthew, Lindsay. B.A., Coll. of Wooster, 1973; J.D., U. Akron, 1980. Bar: Ohio 1980, U.S. Dist. Ct. Ohio, 1980. Staff atty. Stark County Pub. Defender's Office, Canton, Ohio, 1980-83; sole practice, Canton, 1983—. Home: 1713 Frazer Ave NW Canton OH 44703 Office: 335 McKinley Ave NW Canton OH 44702

KUHNERT, BETTY ROSE, analytical pharmacologist; b. N.Y.C., Dec. 16, 1944; d. Walter and Esther (Wallach) Goldstein; m. Paul M. Kuhnert, Sept. 12, 1969; children—Kathleen Lesley, Natalie Laura. B.S., Kent State U., 1966, M.S., 1968, Ph.D., 1972. Instr., then asst. prof. Cuyahoga Community Coll., Cleve., 1971-74; instr. Case Western Res. U., Cleve., 1974-75, asst. prof., 1975-84, assoc. prof., 1984; dir. labs. Perinatal Clin. Research Ctr., Cleve., 1984—. Contbr. articles to profl. jours. Mem. Am. Soc. Pharmacology and Exptl. Therapeutics, Am. Soc. Clin. Pharmacology and Therapeutics, Perinatal Research Soc., Soc. Obstetric Anesthesia and Perinatology, N.Y. Acad. Scis. Office: Perinatal Clin Research Ctr CMGH 3395 Scranton Rd Cleveland OH 44109

KUIPERS, JACK, mathematician, educator, consultant; b. Grand Rapids, Mich., Mar. 27, 1921; s. Bernard Jacob and Grace (Werkema) K.; m. Lois Belle Holtrop, Mar. 25, 1948; children—Benjamin Jack, Emily Louise, Joel Corneal, Alison Jane, Lynne Marie. A.B., Calvin Coll., 1942; B.S.E.E., U. Mich., 1943, M.S.E., 1958, Info. and Control Engr.'s degree, 1966; postgrad. U. Calif.-Santa Barbara, 1967-70. Asst. to dir. research Electric Sorting Machine Co., Grand Rapids, 1946-50; project engr. Flight Reference and Autopilot Systems, Lear, Inc., Grand Rapids, 1950-53, sr. project engr., analytical design, 1954-59; chief engr. instrument div. R.C. Allen Bus. Machines, In., Grand Rapids, 1953-54; sr. physicist Instrumentation and Control Div. Cleve. Pneumatic Industries, Grand Rapids, 1959-62; lectr. Horace B. Rackman Sch. of Grad. Studies, U. Mich., Ann Arbor, 1962-67, research engr. NASA Apollo Applications Inst. of Sci. and Tech., 1962-67; prof. math. Calvin Coll., Grand Rapids, 1967—; cons. in aerospace tech., math. models. Served with U.S. Army, 1942-46. Mem. Math. Assn. of Am., IEEE, Sigma Xi. Mem. Christian Reformed Ch. Patentee: SPASYN, electromagnetic tracking device and other devels. in field; frequent guest lectr.; contbr. articles to profl. jours. Home: 3085 Baker Park Dr SE Grand Rapids MI 49508 Office: Dept of Math Calvin Coll Grand Rapids MI 49506

KUKLA, KENNETH JAMES, veterans organization official; b. Bay City, Mich., Sept. 13, 1953; s. Richard Charles Kukla and Joan Lorraine (Zelno) Kukla Williams; m. Marlene Marie Trudell, Apr. 15, 1975; children—Michael Paul Coron, Brian James, Kevin Richard. Student No. Mich. U., 1977-79. Sales mgr. Meldisco Shoe Co., Bay City, Mich., 1974-76; laborer Forsyth Twp., Gwinn, Mich., 1977-78; disabled vets. outreach worker Mich. Employment Security Commn., Marquette, 1978-79; field service officer AMVETS, Marquette, 1979—; adviser Six County Tng. Consortium, Escanaba, Mich., 1980-82. Served with U.S. Army, 1973-74. Recipient Comdrs. Disting. Service award AMVETS, 1980, 81, 82, Cert. Appreciation Mich. Vets. Trust Fund, 1981. Roman Catholic. Avocations: hunting, fishing, reading, World War II buff. Office: AMVETS 2833 US 41 W Marquette MI 49855

KULECK, WALTER JULIUS, psychologist, consultant; b. Phila., Aug. 25, 1945; s. Walter J. and Alma Kuleck; m. Carol S. Edmonson, June 15, 1968 (div.); 1 son, Julian James; m. 2d Catharine C. Knight, Jan. 2, 1983. B.S. in Aero. Engring., MIT, 1967, M.S. in Aero. Engring., 1968; M.A. in Psychology, U. Mich., 1974, Ph.D. (Ctr. for Creative Leadership fellow), 1976. Lic. psychologist, Ohio. Engr., Vertol div. Boeing, Phila., 1966-71; parts and accessories mgr. West Chester Honda (Pa.), 1971-72; NIMH trainee, asst. research dir. Inst. for Social Research, U. Mich., Ann Arbor, 1972-76; postdoctoral fellow Ctr. for Creative Leadership, Greensboro, N.C., 1976-77; staff psychologist William, Lynde & Williams, Inc., Painesville, Ohio, 1977-83; pres. Cognitive Processes, Inc., Cleveland Heights, Ohio, 1983—; founding prin. ProTrane, Detroit, 1984—; cons. psychologist The Creative Thinking Ctr., Hudson, Ohio, 1983-85; dir. Innovative Health Systems, Inc., 1984—; mgmt. psychologist; creativity cons. Mem. Am. Psychol. Assn., Cleve. Venture Club (founder), Ruger Collectors' Assn. Republican. Lutheran. Club: Solon Sportsman's (Ohio). Contbr. articles to profl. jours. Office: 3631 Fairmount Blvd Cleveland Heights OH 44118

KULI, AMIEL MICHAEL, airline executive; b. Akron, Ohio, Aug. 5, 1942; s. Amiel Michael and Margaret Emma (Brady) K.; m. Carolyn Elizabeth Phinney, Sept. 26, 1964; children—Michelle Marie. Student AG Aviation Acad., Reno, Nev., 1967-68, Akron U., 1969-70, Kent State U., 1971-72. Airline transport pilot, jet capt. Airborne Express, Wilmington, Ohio, 1976-78, chief pilot, dir. flight ops., 1978-79, dir. ops., 1979, v.p. air contract ops., 1979-80, v.p. ops., 1980-83, v.p. govt. affairs, 1983—; pres. Escort Air, Inc., Akron, Ohio, 1973-76; chief pilot Forest City Enterprises, Cleve., 1970-73. Served with USN, 1960-64, Cuba. Mem. Quiet Birdmen, Nat. Street Rod Assn., Am. Legion, VFW (nat. com. 1976). Methodist. Avocations: automobiles; motorcycles; water skiing. Office: Airborne Express Inc 145 Hunter Dr Wilmington OH 45177

KULICH, BETTY ALICE, home economics educator; b. Columbus, Ohio, Jan. 15, 1952; d. Russell and Virginia Lee (Jaynes) Rodgers; m. Richard Alexander Kulich, Jan. 20, 1973; 1 dau., Carrie Ann. B.S. in Home Econs., Ohio State U., 1974, M.S. in Early Childhood Edn., 1980. Cert. home economist, Ohio. Home econs. tchr. and job tng. child care services and multi-area instr. Columbus (Ohio) Pub. Schs., 1974—; pub. relations spokesman Ohio Vocat. Legis. Network, 1978-80. Active Future Home Makers Am., Home Econs. Related Occupations, 1974—. Author curriculum guide. Recipient Outstanding Service award Redeemer's Ch., Columbus, Ohio, 1978. Mem. NEA, Ohio Edn. Assn., Columbus Edn. Assn. (union bldg. rep. 1981—), Central Ohio Tchrs. Assn., Nat. Vocat. Assn., Ohio Vocat. Assn., Columbus Home Econs. Assn. (pres. 1979-80). Office: 546 Jack Gibbs Columbus OH 43215

KULTGEN, JOHN MARVIN, investment executive; b. Chgo., July 27, 1950; s. John Henry and Phyllis Hoyt (Biggs) K.; m. Jill Anne Weiss, Oct. 7, 1979; 1 child, Sarah Elizabeth. B.A., U. Mo., 1972, M.B.A., 1977. Mgr. Shakespeare's Pizza Corp., Manhattan, Kans., 1973-75; research analyst U. Mo., Columbia, 1978-79, Pub. Service Commn., State of Mo., 1978-79; v.p. Stern Bros. & Co., Kansas City, Mo., 1979—. Mem. Kansas City Soc. Fin. Analysts, Kansas City Council Bus. Economists, Kansas City Securities Assn. Roman Catholic. Avocation: physical fitness. Home: 12806 Pembroke Circle Leawood KS 66209 Office: Stern Bros & Co Suite 2200 City Center Sq 1100 Main St PO Box 13486 Kansas City MO 64199

KUMAR, KRISHNA, physics educator; b. Meerut, India, July 14, 1936; came to U.S., 1956, naturalized, 1966; s. Rangi and Susheila (Devi) Lal; m. Katharine Johnson, May 1, 1960; children—Jai Robert, Raj David. B.Sc. in Physics, Chemistry and Math., Agra U., 1953, M.Sc. in Physics, 1955; M.S. in Physics, Carnegie Mellon U., 1959, Ph.D. in Physics, 1964. Research assoc. Mich. State U., 1963-66, MIT, 1966-67; research fellow Niels Bohr Inst., Copenhagen, 1967-69; physicist Oak Ridge Nat. Lab., 1969-71; assoc. prof. Vanderbilt U., Nashville, 1971-77; fgn. collaborator AEC of France, Paris, 1977-79; Nordita prof. U. Bergen, Norway, 1979-80; prof. physics Tenn. Tech. U., Cookeville, 1980-82, Univ. prof. physics, 1983—; lectr. in field. cons. various research labs. Sec. India Assn. Pitts., 1958-59. Recipient Gold medal Agra U., 1955; NSF research grantee, 1972-75. Mem. AAAS, Am. Phys. Soc., N.Y. Acad. Scis., Planetary Soc., Sigma Pi Sigma, Sigma Xi. Republican. Hindu. Lodge: Cookeville Rotary. Author: Nuclear Models and the Search for Unity in Nuclear Physics, 1984. Contbr. articles profl. jours., chpts. in books.

KUMAR, ROMESH, chemical engineer, researcher, consultant; b. Rajpura, Punjab, India, Oct. 18, 1944; s. Kundan Lal and Prakash (Wati) Agarwal; m. Kumkum Khanna, Feb. 22, 1976; children—Rahul, Ritu. B.S., Panjab U., Chandigarh, India, 1965; M.S., U. Calif.-Berkeley, 1968, Ph.D., 1972. Postdoctoral Fellow Argonne Nat. Lab., Ill., 1972-73, asst. chem. engr., 1973-76, chem. engr., 1976—; free lance cons., 1984—; tchr. Tex text formatting Argonne Nat. Lab., 1982—. Author: (with J.M. Prausnitz) Weisburger's Techniques in Chemistry, 1973. Contbr. articles to profl. jours. Patentee in field. Recipient Silver medal Panjab U., 1965. Mem. Am. Inst. Chem. Engrs., AAAS. Home: 1028 Emerald Dr Naperville IL 60540 Office: Argonne Nat Lab 9700 S Cass Ave Argonne IL 60439

KUMAR, SUDHIR, biochemistry and neurology educator, researcher; b. Anjhi, India, Sept. 16, 1942; came to U.S., 1965, naturalized, 1982; s. Sita Ram and Sarla (Agarwal) K.; m. Nilima Jain, Jan. 5, 1969; children—Avanti, Anjali. B.S. in Biology, U. Rajasthan, Jaipur, India, 1959, M.S. in Biochemistry, 1961; Ph.D. in Biochemistry and Neurochemistry, U. Lucknow, India, 1966; postdoctoral Baylor Med. Sch., 1965-67. Sr. research scientist N.Y. State Res. Inst. of Neurochemistry, Wards Island, 1967-69; chief biochemist Methodist Host., Bklyn., 1969-73; research biochemist V.A. Hosp., Bklyn., 1973-75; dir. perinatal lab Christ Hosp., Oak Lawn, Ill., 1975-82; asst. prof. biochemistry and neurology Rush Med. Coll., Chgo., 1976-79, assoc. prof. 1979-83; dir., pres. clinical diagnostics Hazel Crest, Ill., 1982—; prof. Rush Med. Coll. Chgo., 1983—; cons. scientist V.A. Med. Center, Hines, Ill., 1977-80; dir. Avanti Enterprises, Inc., Hazel Crest, 1982—, Edn. Services, Inc., Flossmoor, Ill., 1982—. Editor: Biochemistry of Brain, 1980, Perinatal Medicine Vol. 1, 2, and 3, 1979-82, Advances in Brain Biochemistry, 1984. Patentee in field. Contbr. articles to profl. jours. Pres. Lucknow U. Alumni Assn., 1976-78, 83—; nat. v.p. Assn. Indians in Am., 1982, 83—, pres. Ill. chpt., 1983—; bd. dirs. Festival of India, Ill., 1984—. Recipient Outstanding New Citizen award Citizenship Council of Chgo., 1983; Research fellow C.S.I.R. 1962-65, UNESCO & INSERM, 1971-73, Dreyfus Found., 1971-73; Travel grant Am. Inst. of Nutrition, 1981. Fellow N.Y. Acad. Scis., Nat. Acad. Clin. Biochemists, Royal Inst. Chemistry; mem. Am. Soc. Biol. Chemists, Am. Soc. Clin. Nutrition, Am. Soc. Neurochemistry, Soc. Pediatric Research, Am. Soc. Microbiology, Nat. Acad. Clin. Biochemists, Sigma Xi. Jain-Hindu. Club: Flossmoor Country. Lodge: Rotary. Avocations: stamp and coin collecting; tennis; travel. Home: 18901 Springfield Flossmoor IL 60422 Office: Clinical Diagnostics 3611 W 183rd St Hazel Crest IL 60429

KUMARAN, ALAPATI KRISHNA, biology educator, researcher; b. Govada, India, July, 17, 1932; came to U.S., 1968, naturalized, 1975; s. Venkatakrishnaiah and Seethamma (Saranu) A.; m. Jyoti Thummala, May 4, 1956; 1 child, Nanda Krishna. B.Sc., Madras U., India, 1950, M.Sc., 1955, Ph.D., 1959. Lectr. S.V. U., Tirupati, India, 1957-62; vis. asst. prof. Western Res. U., Cleve., 1965; reader Osmania U., Hyderabad, India, 1965-68; assoc. prof. biology Marquette U., Milw., 1969-73, prof., 1973—; vis. scholar Harvard U., Cambridge, Mass., 1983; research assoc. Case Western Res. Cleve., 1968-69; exchange prof. Czechoslovak Acad., Prague, 1978. Co-author: Biology, 1985. Editor: Biology for 9th Grade in Telugu, 1968. Founder, mem. India Religious Ctr., Milw., 1973. Fellow AAAS (cell biology, devel. biology, zoology, entomology sects.). Avocations: history, philosophy. Home: 1843 Jeffery Ln Waukesha WI 53186 Office: Biology Dept Marquette U 530 N 15th St Milwaukee WI 53233

KUMP, LARRY D., public employee labor leader; b. Chambersburg, Pa., Jan. 27, 1948; s. Willis Theodore and Betty Ann (Steinbach) K.; m. Carolyn Anne Daniels, Dec. 3, 1976 (div. Sept. 1979); children—David Christopher, Sarah Elizabeth. Student Hagerstown Jr. Coll., 1965-68; B.S., Frostburg State Coll., 1970; postgrad. U. Md., 1974, Ind. U., 1980. Arbitrator Am. Arbitration Assn. Chief exec. asst. to senate minority leader Pa. Senate, 1972; labor relations rep. Md. Classified Employees Assn., 1972-78; exec. dir. Ind. State Employees Assn., Indpls., 1978—; guest lectr. labor relations Ind. U., 1981—. Republican candidate for Md. Ho. of Dels., 1974; vice precinct committeeman Rep. party, Indpls., 1981; mem. Marion County exec. com. Libertarian party, 1982-83; vol. arbitrator Better Bus. Bur., 1982-83; elder Ch. Jesus Christ of Latter-day Saints. Named hon. Ky. col., 1984. Mem. Assembly Govtl. Employees (pres. central region, nat. bd.). Home: 1517 E Ruth Dr Ravenswood IN 46240 Office: 17 W Market St Suite 328 Indianapolis IN 46204-2972

KUNDERT, ALICE E., state ofcl.; b. Java, S.D., July 23, 1920; d. Otto J. and Maria (Rieger) Kundert; ed. North State Tchrs. Coll. Tchr. pub. schs., Campbell County, S.D., 1939-43, 49-54; from clk to mgr., buyer, dept. store and dress shop, Calif., 1943-48; dep. supt. schs. Campbell County, 1954; county clk of cts., 1955-60; county register of deeds, 1961-68; sec.-treas. Campbell County Republican party, 1962-64, finance chmn., 1962-68, vice chmn., 1964-68; presdl. elector Rep. Party of S.D., 1964; town treas., Mound City, S.D., 1965-68; state auditor S.D., 1969-79, sec. state, 1979—. Leader, project leader, 4-H; acting chmn., vice chmn. Black Hills Leaders Lab., exec. sec. citizen's responsibility com. Internat. Leaders Tng. Lab., Ireland, 1963; mem. S.D. Local Study Commn., 1967—; mem. state and local adv. coms. Office Equal Opportunity. Named Outstanding Teen Age Republican adviser, 1971-72, 76; recipient Alumni award No. State Coll. Congregationalist. Author: History of the County of Campbell, 1960. Office: State Capitol Bldg Pierre SD 57501

KUNIN, MYRON, hair care company executive. Chmn., pres. Regis Corp., Edina, Minn., also dir. Office: Regis Corp 5000 Normandale Rd Edina MN 55436*

KUNKLER, ARNOLD WILLIAM, surgeon; b. St. Anthony, Ind., Nov. 18, 1921; s. Edward J. and Selma (Hasenour) K.; A.B., Ind. U., 1943, M.D., 1949; m. Muriel Helen Burns, May 22, 1954; children—Lisa, Arnold William, Carolyn, Christine, Phillip, Kevin. Intern Ind. U. Med. Center, Indpls., 1949-50, asst. resident in surgery, also fellow vascular surg. research, 1950-54, resident in surgery, 1954-55; faculty, 1955—, clin. prof. surgery, 1976—; practice medicine, specializing in gen. surgery, Terre Haute, Ind., 1955—; dir. med. edn. Terre Haute Regional Hosp., 1970-78, now mem. staff, chmn. bd., 1981-83; staff Terre Haute Center Med. Edn.; pres. Terre Haute Med. Edn. Found., 1972-73, 78-80, bd. dirs. 1967—; pres. community adv. council Terre Haute Center Med. Edn., 1976-78; treas. Wabash Valley Community Blood Program, 1974-76. Served with U.S. Army, 1943-46; ETO. Diplomate Am. Bd. Surgery. Fellow ACS (dir. Ind. chpt. 1973-81, pres. 1981-82); mem. Terre Haute C. of C., Vigo County Cancer Soc., Vigo County Med. Soc., Ind., Am., Pan Am. med. assns., Pan Pacific Surg. Assn., Aesculapian Soc. Wabash Valley, Soc. Abdominal Surgeons, Midwest Surg. Soc., Ind. Soc. Chgo. Democrat. Roman Catholic. Club: Country of Terre Haute. Contbr. articles to profl. publs. Home: 3515 Ohio Blvd Terre Haute IN 47803 Office: 4333 S 7th St Terre Haute IN 47802

KUNTZ, JOHN KENNETH, religion educator; b. St. Louis, Jan. 20, 1934; s. John Frederick and Zula Belle (Reed) K.; m. Ruth Marie Stanley, July 7, 1962; children—David Kenneth, Nancy Ruth. B.A., Grinnell Coll., 1956; B.D., Yale U., 1959; Ph.D., Union Theol. Sem., 1963. Ordained to ministry, 1961. Tutor in O.T., Union Theol. Sem., N.Y.C., 1961-63; instr. Bibl. history Wellesley (Mass.) Coll., 1963-65, asst. prof., 1965-67; asst. prof. religion U. Iowa, Iowa City, 1967-70, assoc. prof., 1970-76, prof., 1976—, chmn. grad. studies Sch. Religion, 1980-83, chmn. lectures com., 1983—. Minister South Bethel United Methodist Ch., Tipton, Iowa, 1974-79. Recipient Huber faculty research award Wellesley Coll., 1966; Old Gold faculty research award U. Iowa, 1970, 79; Nat. Endowment Humanities grantee, 1971, 84; Dozentenstipendium Germany fellow, 1971-72, 73, 79. Mem. Iowa Meth. Conf. Bd. Ministry. Am. Acad. Religion, Soc. Bibl. Lit., Am. Schs. Oriental Research, Cath. Bibl. Assn., Council Grad. Studies in Religion (sec.-treas.), Phi Beta Kappa. Democrat. Author: The Self-Revelation of God, 1967; The People of Ancient Israel; An Introduction to Old Testament Literature, History and Thought, 1974; contbr. articles to profl. jours. Home: 321 Koser Ave Iowa City IA 52240 Office: 313 Gilmore Hall U Iowa Iowa City IA 52242

KUNZ, CHRISTINA LYNN, legal educator, writer; b. Indpls., Sept. 10, 1952; d. Halbert William and Ruth Louise (Gottschall) K. B.S., U. Wis.-Madison, 1975; J.D., Ind. U.-Indpls., 1978. Bar: Ind. 1979, U.S. Dist. Ct. (so. dist.) Ind. 1979. Professorial lectr. Ind. U., Indpls., 1978-80; asst. prof. William Mitchell Coll. Law, St. Paul, 1980-82, assoc. prof., 1982-84, prof. law, 1984—, legal writing dir., 1981-83, legal writing coordinator, 1984—. Author: (with others) Appellate Advocacy Videotape Manual, 1981, The Process of Legal Research, 1986. Contbr. articles to profl. jours. Contbr. chpt. to The Indiana Water Resource, 1980. Mem. Assn. Am. Law Schs., Ind. State Bar Assn., Minn. State Bar Assn., Sierra Club. Mem. Democratic Farm Labor Party. Methodist. Office: William Mitchell Coll Law 875 Summit Ave Saint Paul MN 55105

KUNZE, MARY HELEN MONSEN, hospital administrator; b. Milw., Mar. 17, 1938; d. Maynard Adolph and Milda Frances (Seidl) Monsen; m. Peter Kurt Kunze, Jan. 21, 1961; children—Christopher Peter, Joseph Maynard, Elizabeth Irmgard, Anne Ludmilla. M.B.A., J.L. Kellogg Grad. Sch. Mgmt., Northwestern U., 1984. Adminstr. pediatrics dept. Med. Coll. Wis., Milw., 1976-80; dir. pediatric adminstrn. Milw. Children's Hosp., 1976-80, v.p. ambulatory services, 1980—; dir. Guadalupe Clinic, Milw., 1978—, Coalition Community Health Ctrs., Milw., 1980—. Bd. dirs. Health Care for the Homeless, 1984—, Robert Wood Johnson Found., 1984—. Mem. Ambulatory Assn. Roman Catholic. Clubs: Elm Grove Women's, Zonta, Tempo. Home: 1065 Lower Ridgeway Elm Grove WI 53122 Office: 1700 W Wisconsin St Milwaukee WI 53233

KUNZE, WALTER EDWARD, JR., civil engineer; b. St Paul, Jan. 3, 1924; s. Walter Edward and Carolina Frieda (Brenning) K.; m. Frances Anne Halverson, June 20, 1947; children—Anne Catherine, Jean Marie, Elizabeth Joan. B.S. in Civil Engring., The Citadel, 1949; S.M. in Civil Engring., MIT, 1950. Registered profl. engr., S.C. Structural engr. Metcalf & Eddy, Boston, 1950-52, Toltz, King & Day, St. Paul, 1952; structural engr. Portland Cement Assn., Skokie, Ill., 1952-65, regional mgr., 1965-70, v.p. regional ops., 1970-71; group v.p. research and devel. Constrn. Tech. Labs., Skokie, Ill., 1971—. Served to 1st lt. inf. AUS, 1943-46. Decorated Bronze Star, Purple Heart, Silver Star. Fellow ASCE, Am. Concrete Inst. (v.p.); mem. Prestressed Concrete Inst., ASTM. Republican. Avocation: photography. Home: 530 S Newbury Pl Arlington Heights IL 60005 Office: Constrn Tech Labs 5420 Old Orchard Rd Skokie IL 60077

KUPERMAN, JESSE PAUL, physician; b. Jersey City, N.J., Mar. 20, 1918; s. Benjamin and Sophie (Bercowitz) K.; m. Lois Hauptman, 1951 (div. 1972); children—Kathy, Donald Bruce, Douglas Alan, Peggy; m. Rita Gwendolyn Cooper, Dec. 18, 1977. B.A., Duke U., 1938; M.D., Johns Hopkins Med. Sch., 1942. Diplomate Am. Bd. Internal Medicine. Asst. clin. prof. of medicine Ohio State U., Columbus, 1950-64; practice medicine specializing in internal medicine and neurology, Dayton, 1949—; cons. in neurology VA Hosp., Dayton, Ohio, 1950-63; mem. cons. staff Good Samaritan Hosp., Dayton, 1970—. Pres. Montgomery County unit Am. Cancer Soc., 1961-62. Served to maj. M.C., AUS, 1943-46, ETO. Mem. ACP, Am. Acad. Neurology, AMA, Ohio State Med. Assn., Montgomery County Med. Assn., Am. Geriatric Soc. Avocations: golf, reading, watercolors. Home: 2810 Dennis Ct Beavercreek OH 45385 Office: 2716 W Hillcrest Ave Dayton OH 45406

KUPLEN, ALBERT CLIFTON, lawyer, former insurance company executive, consultant; b. Crawford County, Kans., May 4, 1915; s. Albert and Goldie (Markey) K.; m. Ruth Caroline Laney, Feb. 13, 1937; children—Albert Clifton, Gregory Edward. Student Kans. State Coll., Pittsburg, 1933-35; J.D., U. Mo.-Kansas City, 1939. Bar: Mo. 1939, U.S. Supreme Ct. 1939. Assoc., Heckle Bros., Kansas City, Mo., 1939; sole practice, Kansas City, Mo., 1940-43, Lees Summit, Mo., 1946-47; claims atty. Western Ins. Cos., Fort Scott, Kans., 1947-67, asst. sec., 1967-72, asst. v.p., 1972-73, v.p. claims, claims atty., 1973-81; cons. in field; dir. Western Casualty & Surety Co., Western Firm Ins. Co.; mem. Kans. Gov.'s Adv. Com. on Workers Compensation, 1963-69.

Served with JAGC, U.S. Army, 1943-46, Res., 1946-53. Mem. Mo. Bar Assn., Central Claims Execs. Assn. Episcopalian. Club: Ft. Scott Country. Home and Office: 1394 Marblecrest Dr Fort Scott KS 66701

KUPPLER, KARL JOHN, hospital administrator; b. Painesville, Ohio, June 22, 1955; s. Herman Gustav and Audrey Jean (Dumbeck) K.; m. Susan Marie Kompes, Aug. 18, 1979; 1 child, Jason Karl. B.S. in Econs. and Bus., Allegheny Coll., 1977; M.S. in Hosp. and Health Services Adminstrn., Ohio State U., 1979. Grad. adminstrv. assoc. Ohio State U. Hosps., 1978-79; adminstrv. asst. Trumbull Meml. Hosp., Warren, Ohio, 1979, asst. exec. dir., 1979—. Loaned exec. United Way of Trumbull County, 1983—. USPHS grantee, 1979. Mem. Am. Coll. Hosp. Adminstrs., Forum Health Service Adminstrn. (chmn. program com. 1982-83, pres. 1984-85), Jacyees of Warren. Lutheran. Lodge: Lions (treas. 1982-83, sec. 1983-85, pres. 1985-86). Home: 281 Corriedale Dr Cortland OH 44410 Office: 1350 E Market St Warren OH 44482

KUPSCHE, DANIEL WILLIAM, vending service executive; b. Chgo., Oct. 19, 1923; s. William and Freida (Ruesch) K.; divorced; children—Steven, Randall, Marilyn, Bradley. Founder, operator Dan's Vending Service, Fox Lake, Ill., 1951—; bd. govs. Ill. Automatic Merchandising Council, 1979-82. Mem. Republican Presdl. Task Force, 1980—, Nat. Fedn. for Decency, 1972—, Ams. Against Union Control of Govt., 1969—; Nat. Congl. Club, 1971—, Conservative Caucus, Inc., 1978—, Nat. Taxpayer's Union, 1974—, Rep. Nat. Com., 1980—; U.S. Senatorial Club, 1979—, Nat. Right to Work Com., 1967—. Served with U.S. Army, 1943-45. Decorated Purple Heart, Bronze Star, Silver Star. Mem. Nat. Automatic Merchandising Assn., Ill. Automatic Merchandising Council, Better Vendors Assn., Ill. C. of C., Zion C. of C. Office: 64 Sayton Rd Fox Lake IL 60020

KURATKO, DONALD F., business educator, consultant, funeral director; b. Chgo., Aug. 27, 1952; s. Donald W. and Margaret M. (Browne) K.; m. Deborah Ann Doyle, Dec. 28, 1979; 1 child, Christina Diane. B.A. in Econs., John Carroll U., 1974; M.S. in Mortuary Sci. and Adminstrn., Worsham Coll., 1975; M.B.A. in Mktg.-Mgmt., Ill. Benedictine Coll., 1979; D.B.A. in Small Bus. Mgmt., Nova U., 1984. Lic. funeral dir., Ill. Tchr., chmn. bus. dept. Immaculate Conception High Sch., Elmhurst, Ill., 1975-78; prof. bus. Ill. Benedictine Coll., Lisle, 1979-83; prof., coordinator small bus.-mgmt. and entrepreneurship Ball State U., Muncie, Ind., 1983—; funeral dir. Kuratko Funeral Home, North Riverside, Ill., part-time, 1975—; cons. Kendon Assocs., Riverside, 1983—; dir. Ind. Cert. Devel. Corp., Indpls.; cons. Small Bus. Devel. Ctr., Muncie C. of C., 1985. Author: Management, 1984; Effective Small Business Management, 1985. Mem. editorial bd. Mid-Am. Bus. Jour., 1985—. Contbr. articles in field to profl. jours. Mem. Small Bus. Council, Muncie, 1984—. Named Tchr. of Yr., Immaculate Conception High Sch., Elmhurst, 1977, Prof. of Yr., Ill. Benedictine Coll., 1981, 83, Prof. of Yr., Ball State U., Muncie, 1984, 85, Outstanding Young Hoosier, Ind. Jaycees, 1985. Mem. Nat. Acad. Mgmt., Internat. Council for Small Bus., Midwest Bus. Adminstrn. Assn., Midwest Case Writers Assn. Roman Catholic. Avocations: weightlifting; jogging. Home: 3500 S Robinwood Dr Muncie IN 47304 Office: Ball State U Coll Bus Muncie IN 47306

KURIT, NEIL, lawyer; b. Cleve., Aug. 31, 1940; s. Jay and Rose (Rainin) K.; m. Doris Tannenbaum, Aug. 9, 1964. B.S., Miami U., 1961; J.D., Case Western Res. U., 1964. Bar: Ohio 1964. Prin. Kahn, Kleinman, Yanowitz & Arnson Co., L.P.A., Cleve., 1964—. Co-author Handbook for Attorneys and Accountants, Jewish Community Fedn. Endowment Fund. Trustee, v.p. Montefiore Home, 1983—; trustee Jewish Community Fedn. Cleve., 1983—. Mem. ABA, Ohio State Bar Assn. Home: 2774 Meldon Blvd Beachwood OH 44122 Office: Kahn Kleinman Yanowitz & Arnson Co LPA 1300 Bond Ct Bldg Cleveland OH 44114

KURTICH, JOHN WILLIAM, architect, film-maker, educator; b. Salinas, Calif., Oct. 18, 1935; s. John Joseph and Elizabeth (Lyons) K.; B.A. in Theatre and Cinematography, UCLA, 1957; B.Arch., U. Calif.-Berkeley, 1966; M.S. in Architecture and Urban Design (William Kinne fellow, Fgn. Travelling fellow), Columbia U., 1968. Film-maker SMP, Architects, San Francisco, 1960-61; film-maker, archtl. draftsman McCue & Assocs., San Francisco, 1962-66; freelance film-maker, designer Friedberg, N.Y., 1968; instr. Sch. of Art Inst. Chgo., 1968-70, asst. prof., 1970-74, assoc. prof., 1974-82, prof., 1982—, chmn. dept. design and communication, 1977—, area head interior architecture; staff architect Am. Excavations, Samothrace, Greece, 1970—; archtl. cons. Fed. Res. Bank Chgo., 1978. Served with USNR, 1957-60. Recipient Architecture medal Alpha Rho Chi, 1966; grantee NEA, 1972, Woman's Bd. Art Inst. Chgo., 1973, Union Independent Colls. Art, 1974, Fulbright-Hays (Eng.), 1976, Fulbright-Hays (Jordan), 1981. Fellow Royal Soc. Arts (London); mem. AIA (corp. mem.), Soc. Archtl. Historians, Archaeol. Inst. Am. (asso. mem.), Oriental Inst. Multi-media productions include: Hellas, Columbia U., N.Y.C., 1968, Art Inst. Chgo., 1971, 79; Muncie: Microcosm of America (NEA grant), Muncie, Ind., 1972; Legend of the Minotaur, Art Inst. Chgo., 1973; The Seasons, Shapes, Contrasts, Art Inst. Chgo., 1977, 1983, 84. Home: 2054 N Humboldt Blvd Chicago IL 60647 Office: Dept Design and Communication Sch of Art Inst Chgo Columbus Dr and Jackson Blvd Chicago IL 60603

KURTIDES, EFSTRATIOS STEPHEN, physician; b. Kilkis, Greece, July 4, 1930; came to U.S. 1955, naturalized 1963; s. Theodore and Agapy (Papadopoulos) K.; m. Elli Hamali, Aug. 8, 1958; children—Pauline, Theodore, Carl, John. Diploma Gymnasium, Kilkis, Greece; M.D., Aristotle U. Thessaloniki, Greece, 1954. Diplomate Am. Bd. Internal Medicine. Instr., research fellow Northwestern U. Med. Sch., Chgo., 1961-63; assoc. in medicine, attending physician Northwestern and Evanston Hosps., Chgo. and Evanston, 1963-66, asst. prof. and sr. attending physician, 1966-76; assoc. prof., chmn. St. Joseph Hosp., Chgo., 1977-79; prof., chmn. Evanston Hosp., Ill., 1979—; bd. dirs. Evanston Hosp., 1980—, Northwestern Infirmary, Student Health Service, 1979—. Contbr. articles to med. jours. Mem. Sch. Bd. Caucus Dist. 65, Evanston, 1963-68. Named Physician of Yr., Evanston Hosp., 1966, 72, 73, 80; recipient Silver Plaque, Evanston Hosp. Medical Staff, 1977. Fellow ACP; mem. AMA, Am. Soc. Hematology, AAAS, Am. Soc. Internal Medicine, Am. Hosp. Assn., N.Y. Acad. Scis., Alpha Omega Alpha. Greek Orthodox. Club: Mich. Shores (Wilmette, Ill.). Avocations: reading; debate; backgammon; biking. Office: Dept Medicine Evanston Hosp 2650 Ridge Ave Evanston IL 60201

KURTZ, CHARLES JEWETT, III, lawyer; b. Columbus, Ohio, May 13, 1940; s. Charles Jewett, Jr. and Elizabeth Virginia (Gill) K.; m. Linda Rhoads, Mar. 18, 1983. B.A., Williams Coll., 1962; J.D., Ohio State U., 1965. Bar: Ohio 1965. Law clk. Ohio Supreme Ct., Columbus, 1965-67; assoc. Porter, Wright, Morris & Arthur, Columbus, 1967-71, ptnr., 1972—. Mem. ABA, Columbus Bar Assn., Def. Research Inst., Columbus Def. Assn. (pres. 1976), Ohio Civil Trial Attys. Assn. Clubs: University, City (Columbus). Office: 37 W Broad St Columbus OH 43215

KURTZ, HAROLD PAUL, hospital administrator; b. Milw., May 21, 1936; s. Henry John and Minnie Christina (Olson) K.; m. Grace Jahn Kurtz, June 16, 1963; children—Steven, David. B.A., Wartburg Coll., 1958; M.S., U. Wis., 1961. Journalist, Post-Crescent, Appleton, Wis., 1961-63; dir. pub. relations Lutheran Gen. Hosp., Park Ridge, Ill., 1963-73, Med. Coll. Wis., Milw., 1973-77, Children's Hosp., St. Paul, 1977—. Author: Public Relations for Hospitals, 1969; Public Relations and Fund Raising for Hospitals, 1981; (with M. Burrows) Effective Use of Volunteers, 1971. Editor: Toward a Creative Chaplaincy, 1973. Bd. dirs. Bd. Edn., Dist. 621, Mounds View, 1985—, United Hosp. Edn. and Research Inst., St. Paul, 1978-84, Minn. Internat. Health Vols., 1984—. Recipient Community Service citation Wartburg Coll., 1970; named Boss of Yr., Internat. Assn. Bus. Communications. Mem. Chgo. Hosp. Pub. Relations Soc. (pres. 1971-72), Wartburg Coll. Alumni Assn. (bd. dirs. 1962-66). Lutheran. Home: 1465 17th Ave NW New Brighton MN 55112 Office: Children's Hosp 345 N Smith Ave Saint Paul MN 55102

KURTZ, JAMES FRANCIS, training director; b. Chgo., Feb. 17, 1953; s. Stanley Joseph and Loretta Eileen (Cook) K. Student Mayfair Jr. Coll., 1971-73; B.A., Loyola U., Chgo., 1978. Safety and security supr. Schwinn Bicycle, Chgo., 1973-80; tng. dir. Leaf Confectionery, Inc., Chgo., 1980—. Mem. Am. Soc. Safety Engrs., VFW.

KURTZ, ORVILLE IRVIN, architect; b. Arlington Heights, Ill., May 10, 1924; s. Orville Thorsen and Laura A. (Garms) K.; m. Jessie P. Stacy, Mar. 16, 1946; children—Stacie, Janice, Karen; m. 2d, Lucille Marie Monicke Nehmzow, June 5, 1982. Student Bradley U., 1946-48; B.S. in Archtl. Engring., U. Ill., 1950. Registered architect, Ill., Ind., Mich., Minn., Wis. Project planner Pub. Housing Adminstrn., Chgo., 1950-53; job capt. Sumner Sollit Co., Chgo., 1953-55; staff architect Cities Service Oil Co., Chgo., 1955-59; architect/owner Orville I. Kurtz & Assoc., Ltd., Des Plaines, Ill., 1959—; tchr. blueprint reading. Pres. and dir. Rotary Club Des Plaines; chmn. Archtl. Commn. Des Plaines. Served with USAF, 1942-46. Recipient Archtl. Achievement award Des Plaines C. of C., 1975, 83. Mem. AIA, Am. Registered Architects, Nat. Council Architects Registration Bds. Lodge: Elks. Home: 628 Thistle Ln Rob Roy Country Club Village Prospect Heights IL 60070 Office: 1401 Oakton St Des Plaines IL 60018

KURTZ, TERRENCE STEVEN, utility executive, mechanical engineer; b. Chgo., Feb. 16, 1948; s. Bernard Laurence and Rosaleen (Kaminski) K.; m. Linda Dianne Keeney, Apr. 27, 1974; children—Amy, Brian. B.S. in Mech. Engring., Bradley U., 1970, M.B.A., 1979. Start-up engr. Gen. Electric Co., Schnectady, 1970-75; staff mech. engr. Central Ill. Light Co., Peoria, 1975-79, supr. of maintenance, 1979-81, plant mgr., 1981-84, controller, 1984—. Assoc. mem. ASME. Republican. Methodist. Lodge: Sertoma (pres. 1984—). Avocations: ice skating, golf, home improvements. Home: 11 Burning Tree Ln Pekin IL 61554 Office: Central Ill Light Co 300 Liberty St Peoria IL 61602

KURTZ, WINIFRED MARY, club woman; b. Washington, Iowa, Aug. 28; d. Charles Sanford and Gertrude Josephine (Swift) Ragan; student Washington Jr. Coll., 1949-50, St. Ambrose Coll., Davenport, Iowa, 1950; m. Robert Kurtz, Sept. 12, 1951; 1 son, Michael R. Hostess, waitress Grand Lake Lodge, Colo., 1946; desk clk. Cosmopolitan Hotel, Denver, 1946; cashier Sears Roebuck & Co., Kansas City, Mo., 1947; tchr. Pleasant Hill Sch., Washington County, Iowa, 1950-51, Riverside Sch., Brighton, Iowa, 1952-53. Pres. dist. 11, Diocesan Council Cath. Women, 1972-74, 76-78, parish rep., 1970—, mem. nominating com., 1983; mem. legis. commn. Davenport Diocesan Council, 1983-84; Sunday sch. tchr. St. Joseph's Ch. East Pleasant Plain, Iowa, 1960-70, v.p. Altar and Rosary Soc., 1980-81; sec. Writers Round Table, 1966-80; asso. Citizens for Decency through Law, 1974—; pres. Pleasant Plain (Iowa) Sch. PTA, 1966-68; state historian Daus. Am. Colonists, 1966-68, state corr. sec., 1968-70, state 1st vice regent, 1972-74, state regent, 1974-76, 81-83, chmn. nat. def., 1976-78, vice-chmn. flag U.S.A., 1976—, chmn. state nominating com. 1982, mem. state nominating com., 1983-84, del. state assembly, 1983; state chmn. flag of U.S.A., DAR, 1976-78, nat. vice chmn. flag U.S.A., 1976-80, chpt. regent, 1971-73, 80-83, del. state conv., 1983; mem. Iowa Button Club. Republican. Home: Route 2 Brighton IA 52540

KURZ, JERRY BRUCE, lawyer; b. Chgo., June 21, 1949; s. Jack and Delores Estelle (Koss) K. B.S., U. Okla., 1971; J.D., No. Ill. U., 1979. Bar: Ill. 1980, U.S. Dist. Ct. (no. dist.) Ill. 1980, U.S. Ct. Appeals (7th cir.) 1980, U.S. Dist. Ct. (cen. dist.) Ill. 1983, U.S. Supreme Ct. 1984. Tchr., pub. schs., Chgo., 1972-79; ptnr. Hall & Kurz, Chgo., 1980—; dir. Met. Football League, Chgo., 1983—, Free Agt. Scouting Combine, Chgo., 1983—, Minor Profl. Football Assn., 1980—. Served to capt. U.S. Army, 1968-69, Vietnam. Mem. Nat. Assn. Criminal Def. Lawyers, Chgo. Bar Assn., ABA, Assn. Trial Lawyers Am., Phi Alpha Delta. Democrat. Jewish. Home: 233 E Wacker Dr Apt 3503 Chicago IL 60601 Office: Hall & Kurz 127 N Dearborn Suite 1011 Chicago IL 60602

KUSEY, JULIUS, educator; b. Omer, Mich., July 1, 1931; s. Toney F. and Rose A. (Tellish) K.; B.S., Central Mich. U., 1957; M.S. in Art Edn., U. Wis., Madison, 1964. Tchr. art Rochester (Mich.) Community Sch. Dist., 1957—, kindergarten-through 12th grades art coordinator, 1975-81, art cons., 1957—; bd. dirs. Rochester Arts Commn., 1979-80. Sch. chmn. United Found., Rochester, 1959—; mem. Oakland County (Mich.) Cultural Councl, 1980—. Served with M.C., U.S. Army, 1952-55. Recipient Silver C Club award Central Mich. U., 1982, 25 Yrs. Continuous Teaching award Rochester Community Schs., 1982. Mem. Mich. Art Edn. Assn. (Elem. Art Tchr. of Yr. award 1971, Mich. Art Educator of Yr. 1983, pres. 1980-82, 82-84), Mich. Edn. Assn., Nat. Art Edn. Assn. (State Art Educator award Western region 1984), Am. Crafts Council, Internat. Soc. Edn. Through Art, Am. Hort. Soc., Am. Primrose Soc. Democrat. Roman Catholic. Office: 522 W Fourth St Rochester MI 48063

KUSHNER, GARY B., employee benefits consultant; b. N.Y.C., Apr. 18, 1955; s. Alvin L. and Ruth (Kaiser) K.; m. Lila Pride, Aug. 6, 1978; children—Kelly Michelle, Jeffrey Alan. B.A., Franklin and Marshall Coll., 1977; M.A., Western Mich. U., 1980. Personnel dir. Bur. Med. Assistance, Lansing, Mich., 1977-78, Calhoun County, Mich., 1978-79; human resources dir. Walker Parking Cons., Kalamazoo, 1979-82; pres. Kushner & Co., Inc., Kalamazoo, 1982—. Mem. editorial adv. bd. Personnel Adminstr., 1983—. Bd. dirs. H.O.M.E., Inc., Marshall, 1984—. Mem. Employers Council on Flexible Compensation, Kalamazoo Personnel Assn. (sec. 1984—), Am. Soc. Personnel Adminstrn. (region program chair 1984), Am. Mgmt. Assns. Jaycees. Avocation: sports officiating. Office: 2121 Hudson Ave Suite 101 Kalamazoo MI 49008

KUSHNER, IRVING, medical educator; b. N.Y.C., Jan. 16, 1929; s. Boris and Rose (Klausner) K.; m. Enid Pearl Lupeson, Jan. 2, 1955; children—Ellen Ruth, Philip Seth, David Micah. B.A., Columbia U., 1950; M.D., Washington U., St. Louis, 1954. Diplomate Am. Bd. Internal Medicine, Am. Bd. Rheumatology. Intern in medicine Grace-New Haven Community Hosp., 1954-55; resident in medicine Harvard med. services Boston City Hosp., 1957-58; asst. prof. medicine Case Western Res. U., Cleve., 1964-69, assoc. prof. medicine, 1969-73, prof. medicine, 1974—; prof. medicine West Va. U., Morgantown, 1973-74; med. dir. Highland View Rehab. Hosp., Cleve., 1985—. Editor: C-reactive Protein and the Plasma Protein Response to Tissue Injury, 1982; Understanding Arthritis, 1984. Contbr. articles to profl. jours. and chpts. to books. Trustee Arthritis Found., Cleve., 1974—. Recipient Nat. Vol. award Arthritis Found., 1982. Fellow ACP; mem. Am. Rheumatism Assn. (pres. central region 1980), N.Y. Acad. Sci., Am. Assn. Immunologists, Phi Beta Kappa, Alpha Omega Alpha. Jewish. Avocations: travel, photography, books, print collecting. Home: 22149 Rye Rd Shaker Heights OH 44122 Office: Cleve Met Gen Hosp/Highland View 3995 Scranton Rd Cleveland OH 44109

KUSLER, JAMES O'DELL, farmer, state senator; b. Bismarck, N.D., Dec. 10, 1947; s. John and Alma (Buechler) K.; m. Barbara Carmen Braun, Nov. 16, 1952. Ph.B., U. N.D., 1972, M.A. in Communications, 1979; M. in Internat. Mgmt., Am. Grad. Sch. Internat. Mgmt., Glendale, Ariz., 1976. Media coordinator Link-Sanstead Campaign, Bismarck, N.D., 1976; market research analyst Meyer Broadcasting Co., Bismarck, 1977-78; research and info. asst. Gov. N.D., Bismarck, 1978-81; asst. to state tax commr. N.D. Tax Dept., Bismarck, 1981-82; wheat and cattle farmer, Beulah, N.D., 1982—; mem. N.D. Senate, 1983—. Democrat. Congregationalist. Home and Office: Rural Route 1 Box 160-C Beulah ND 58523

KUSPAN, JOSEPH FRANCIS, JR., sales executive; b. Struthers, Ohio, June 13, 1925; s. Joseph Francis and Cecilia Agnes Kuspan; m. Shirley Ruth Black, Jan. 3, 1950; 1 child, Joseph F. Grad. high sch., Struthers. Sales service mgr. Harvell Mfg. Corp., Hubbard, Ohio, 1954-59, R.D. Werner Co., Inc., Greenville, Pa., 1959-67; sales mgr., nat. accounts R.D. Werner Co., Inc., 1968-78, gen. sales mgr., 1978—. Bd. dirs. Struthers Community Chest, 1951. Served with USAAF, 1943-46, PTO. Democrat. Roman Catholic. Mem. VFW (comdr. 1950-51). Avocations: gardening; fishing. Home: 270 Overlook Blvd Struthers OH 44471 Office: R D Werner Co Inc Werner Rd PO Box 580 Greenville PA 16125

KUSSEL, RICHARD JOHN, mechanical engineer; b. Chgo., June 3, 1931; s. Ferdinand Mario and Julia Ann (Drapalik) K.; married; children—Richard, Fred, Julie Ann. B.S. in Mech. Engring., U. Ill., 1958; postgrad. Ill. Inst. Tech., 1958-60. Lic. real estate agt., Ill. Chief engr. Greenlee Foundry Co., Cicero, Ill., 1956-65; pres., entrepreneur Casting Masters, Elk Grove, Ill., 1965-77; dir. engring. projects Alliance Steel, Franklin Park, Ill., 1978-80; sr. project mgr. R.B.C., Inc., Villa Park, Ill., 1980-83; chief engr., mgr. Helmold Co., Inc., Elk Grove Village, Ill., 1983—; cons. engr. Datum Engring. Co., Itasca, Ill., 1978—; entrepreneur Goodlife Co., Itasca, 1982—. Served with USN, 1951-55. Mem. ASM, Nat. Assn. Die Designers, Soc. Die Casting Engrs., ASME. Club: Elmhurst Ski (v.p. 1960-62). Avocations: horse breeding and riding; skiing; boating. Home: 5N560 Rholwing Rd Itasca IL 60143

KUTSCHER, GORDON RALPH, educator; b. Jackson, Mo., Jan. 3, 1934; s. Richard Henry and Emilie (Kasten) K.; B.S., S.E. Mo. State Coll., 1957; M.Ed., U. Mo., 1961; student Mo. Sch. Mines, summer 1958; m. Louanna Mae Dickerson, Aug. 15, 1954; children—Richard Gordon, Randy Keith, Robert Clark. Instr. math. Sch. Dist. R-4, Benton, Mo., 1955-57, Rolla (Mo.) Sr. High Sch., 1957-59, head dept. math., 1959-61; sch. psychol. examiner, counselor, dir. guidance Rolla Jr. High Sch., 1962-67; dir. guidance Rolla Pub. Schs., 1967, supr. guidance services Mo. Dept. Edn., 1967-70, asst. dir. Research Coordinating Unit, 1970-71; exec. sec., dir. Mo. Adv. Council Vocat. Edn., 1971—; mem. State Employment and Tng. Council; co-chmn. Nat. Bicentennial Conf. on Vocat. Edn.; del. Mo. Gov.'s Conf. on Edn.; sr. research asst., Freshman orientation counselor U. Mo. at Rolla, summer 1966. Mem. Rolla Community Betterment Program, 1964; past pres. Trinity Lutheran Ch., past chmn. bd. stewardship; committeeman explorer post and scout troop Boy Scouts Am.; past bd. dirs. Cole County Conservation Commn. Mem. NEA (life), Mo. State Tchrs. Assn., Rolla Community Tchrs. Assn. (past pres.), Phelps County Mental Health Assn. (past pres.), Mo. (past pres.; editor emeritus quar. jour.), South Central (past pres.) guidance assns., Am. Personnel and Guidance Assn., Am. Sch. Counselor Assn., Nat. Vocat. Guidance Assn., Assn. Measurement and Evaluation in Guidance, Am. (life), Mo. vocat. assns., Nat. Assn. Exec. Dirs. State Vocat. Adv. Councils (past v.p.), Phi Delta Kappa (life), Council Vocat. Educators. Optimist (past pres. Jefferson City, lt. gov. Mo. dist. 1970-71, dist. boys work chmn. 1971-72, dist. community service chmn. 1972-73, dist. oratorical chmn. 1974-75, dist. sec./treas. 1975-76, 79-82, dist. gov. 1977-78, dist. candidate qualifications chmn. 1978-79, mem. internat. achievement and awards com. 1979-80, dist. fin. chmn. 1980-83). Author: 1965 Graduates Responses and Data Survey, 1968; Structure, Function and Use of Local Advisory Committees in Vocational Education, 1974; co-author: Handbook for Local Vocational Advisory Committees, 1977; The Impact of Local Vocational Advisory Committees in Missouri, 1982; Analysis of a Formula for the Distribution of Federal Funds, 1982; contbr. articles to profl. jours. Home: 1815 Swift's Hwy Jefferson City MO 65101

KUTSKO, HARLENE MARY, trucking company executive; b. Massillon, Ohio, Aug. 9, 1943; d. Harlan Harold and Helen Margurite (Holzbach) Hicks; m. Mark Lee Kutsko, Feb. 24, 1968. B.A. in English, U. Akron, 1965, postgrad., 1965-67. Pres., Kutsko Trucking, North Canton, Ohio, 1980-81, v.p., 1981—. Mem. Phi Sigma Alpha. Office: Kutsko Trucking 6967 Promway NW North Canton OH 44720

KUTTEN, L.J., lawyer, high technology writer, consultant; b. St. Louis, May 10, 1953; s. Joseph and Carolyn Jane (Yalem) K.; m. Linda Gail Ishibashi, Oct. 20, 1979; 1 child, Carolyn. B.A., Claremont McKenna Coll., 1974; J.D., Washington U., St. Louis, 1977. Bar: Mo. 1977, Ill. 1978. Assoc., Mann & Poger, Clayton Mo., 1977-78; ptnr. Chartrand, Harvey, Kutten, St. Louis, 1978-81. Author: Computer Buyer's Protection Guide: How to Protect Your Rights in the Micro-computer Marketplace, 1984. Contbr. articles to mags. including: Bus. Computing, Computer Shopper, Computer World, EDN, Infoworld, Mini-Micro, Today, Videotex/Computer Mag. Office: PO Box 16185 Clayton MO 63105

KUTTEN, MICHAEL JAY, dentist; b. St. Louis, Nov. 3, 1950; s. Eli Aaron and Sally (Schnitzer) K.; m. Elizabeth Fink, June 6, 1981. B.S., Tulane U., 1972; D.M.D., Washington U., 1976. Pvt. practice dentistry, St. Louis, 1976—. Mem. ADA, Pierre Fauchard Acad., Mo. Dental Assn., St. Louis Dental Soc. Clubs: Westwood Country, Frontenac Raquet (St. Louis). Home: 41 Willow Hill Rd Saint Louis MO 63124 Office: 225 S Meramec Suite 311 Saint Louis MO 63105

KUZNIAR, JOSEPH ALPHONSE, interior designer, lighting consultant; b. Chgo., Aug. 7, 1946; s. Stanley and Meta (Jedresak) K. Student Acad. of Lighting Arts, Chgo., 1965-66, Chgo. Acad. Fine Arts, 1965-68. Cert. residential lighting cons. Dir. store planning Homemakers Furniture, Schaumburg, Ill., 1973-76, Nelson Bros. Furniture, Ill. and Wis., 1977-78, Darvin Furniture, Orland Park, Ill., and Chgo., 1979-82; interior designer Kuzniar's Elegant Interiors, Chgo., 1978—; interior design cons. Darvin Furniture and Nelson Bros. Furniture. Mem. Am. Soc. Interior Designers (assoc.), Interior Design Soc. Ill., Inst. of Bus. Designers. Roman Catholic. Avocations: church organist. Home: 523 S Lincoln Ave Addison IL 60101 Office: 711 N Leavitt Chicago IL 60101

KVIZ, FREDERICK JAMES, epidemiology-biometry educator; b. Berwyn, Ill., Oct. 3, 1946. B.A. in Sociology, U. Ill.-Chgo., 1971, M.A., 1972, Ph.D., 1975. Asst. prof. Coll. Nursing U. Ill-Chgo., 1975-79, asst. prof. Sch. Pub. Health, 1979-81, assoc. prof., 1981—; research assoc. prof. Survey Research Lab., Chgo., 1981—; cons. Ill. Cancer Council, Chgo., 1980—. Author: Statistics for Nurses, 1981 (Book of Yr. award 1981). Assoc. editor Jour. Health and Social Behavior, 1984—. Contbr. articles to profl. jours. Recipient Outstanding Service award Chgo. Lung Assn., 1981. Mem. Am. Assn. Pub. Opinion Research, Am. Pub. Health Assn., Am. Sociol. Assn. Home: 2484 Lakeside Dr Aurora IL 60505 Office: Sch Pub Health Epidemiology-Biometry Program Box 6998 U Ill Chicago IL 60680

KWART, WILLIAM ROBERT, newspaper executive; b. Detroit, July 7, 1903; s. Joseph and Frances (Kozniacki) K.; children—Patricia, Laureen. Student Detroit pub. schs. Advt. mgr. Sears, Ft. Wayne; with advt. dept. Detroit Times, 1943-48, Detroit Free Press, 1948-81; mgr. auction advt. sales dept. Conquest Newspaper, Detroit, 1981—. Roman Catholic. Clubs: Ad Craft, English Speaking Union. Lodges: Lions, K.C. Home: 8900 E Jefferson St Detroit MI 48214 Office: Conquest Newspaper 9149 E Jefferson Detroit MI 48214

KWASNIEWSKI, BRENDA JOAN, secondary school administrator, business educator; b. Faulkton, S.D., April 6, 1950; d. Frank Xavier and Rhea Joyce (Jansen) Barondeau; m. Duane Raymond Kwasniewski, Jan. 15, 1972; children—Devon Andre, Amber Linea. B.A. in Bus. Edn., No. State Coll., S.D., 1972, M.A. in Secondary Adminstrn., 1977. Cert. tchr. and adminstr., S.D. Bus. tchr. Bridgewater High Sch., S.D., 1971—, secondary prin., 1977—. Mem. Southeast Area Secondary Prins. (sec.), Pi Omega Pi, Sigma Delta Epsilon. Democrat. Roman Catholic. Avocations: reading, latchhook, embroidery, word puzzles. Home: Box 251 Bridgewater SD 57319 Office: Bridgewater High Sch Box 251 Bridgewater SD

KWASNIEWSKI, HELEN THERESA, principal; b. New Philadelphia, Pa., July 31, 1937; d. William Joseph and Catherine Blanche (Bender) Butvich; m. Leonard Daniel Kwasniewski, July 16, 1972; stepchildren—Kenneth, Richard, William. B.A., Marywood Coll., 1962; Licentiate in Theology, Providence Coll., 1965; M.Ed., Nat. Coll. Edn., Evanston, Ill., 1982. Tchr. elem. grades, Mass., Fla., Chgo., 1957-70; tchr. St. Domitilla Sch., Hillside, Ill., 1970-73, Immaculate Conception Sch., Elmhurst, Ill., 1973-75; adminstr. St. Piux X Sch., Stickney, Ill., 1968-70, Notre Dame Sch., Clarendon Hills, Ill., 1975-78, St. Alexis Sch., Bensenville, Ill., 1978-81; prin. Immaculate Conception Grade Sch., Elmhurst, 1981—; Savs. counselor St Paul Fed. Savs. & Loan, part time 1971-73; mem. Joliet Diocesan Schs. Evaluation Team, 1978, 79. Mem. Nat. Council Tchrs. English, Assn. Supervision and Curriculum Devel., Nat. Cath. Edn. Assn. Democrat. Office: 132 Arthur St Elmhurst IL 60126

KWEDER, ANTHONY KARL, automotive cooling systems repair service executive; b. Chgo., Apr. 4, 1946; s. Anthony and Agnes (Waclawski) K.; m. Kathryn Jean Schickling, Apr. 1, 1967; children—Steven Anthony, Kenneth Eugene. Machinist, Electro-Motive div. Gen. Motors, McCook, Ill., 1967; salesman Prudential Ins. Co., Blue Island, Ill., 1967-69; ptnr. Tony's Radiator/Battery Service, Oak Forest, Ill., 1969-72; owner, operator Tony's Radiator Service Inc., Oak Forest, 1972-79, pres., 1979—. Pres. Oak Forest C. of C., 1980-83, bd. dirs. Roman Catholic. Office: Tonys Radiator Service Inc 5141 W 159th St Oak Forest IL 60452

KWON, O KEY, mechanical engineer, researcher; b. Euisung, Korea, May 5, 1950; came to U.S., 1977; s. Young-Sook and Wee-Sook (Lee) K.; m. Young-Mee Kim, Aug. 24, 1978; children—Eunice, Eugene. B.E., Hanyang U., Seoul, Korea, 1971; student Carleton U., Ottawa, Can., 1976-77; M.S., Iowa State U., 1978, Ph.D., 1981. Teaching asst. Carleton U., 1976-77; research asst. Korea Atomic Energy Research Inst., Seoul, 1974-76, Iowa State U., Ames, 1977-81; research engr. Belcan Corp., Indpls., 1981-82; sr. project engr. Allison Gas Turbine div. Gen. Motors Corp., Indpls., 1982—. Contbr. tech. papers to sci. jours. Served to lt. Korean Navy, 1971-74. Mem. AIAA, ASME, Phi Kappa Phi, Sigma Xi. Home: 1212 W 78th St Indianapolis IN 46260 Office: Allison Gas Turbine Div GMC PO Box 420 T-9 Indianapolis IN 46206

KYES, HELEN G. (MRS. ROGERS M. KYES), civic leader; b. Marion, Ohio; d. Benjamin and Bess (Gilmore) Jacoby; B.A., Oberlin Coll., 1926; Ph.D. (hon.), Oakland U., 1980; m. Roger M. Kyes, June 5, 1931; children—Carolyn Kyes Eggert, Frances (dec.), Katharine Kyes Leab, Anne Kyes Smith. Sec., pres. Federated Women's Club, Marion, Ohio, 1927-31; bd. dirs. Cleve. Coll. Club, 1936-41, Cleve. YWCA, 1938-41; mem. bd. Woman's Nat. Farm and Garden, 1943-56, 60—, sec., 1943-45, 54-55; dir. Children's Aid and Home Friendless, 1949—, v.p., 1961—; bd. dirs. Brookside Sch., Cranbrook, 1952-58, sec., 1957-58; bd. dirs. Kingswood Sch., Cranbrook, 1968—; charter mem. bd. trustees Oakland U. Found., 1958, v.p. exec. bd., 1960—; trustee Oakland U., 1970—; mem. Woman's Assn. Detroit Symphony; com. 100 Detroit Met. Opera; capt. spl. gifts Detroit United Fund, 1959-61; mem. Detroit Mus. Art Founders Soc.; mem. com. Detroit Foster Home Edn. and Recruitment Program, 1960—. Mem. DAR, AAUW (past treas., v.p. Marion). Presbyterian (vice moderator deacons). Clubs: Bloomfield Hills Country, Detroit, Village Woman's; Ocean (Delray Beach, Fla.); Gulfstream Bath and Tennis. Home: 945 Cranbrook Rd Bloomfield Hills MI 48013 also 6861 N Ocean Blvd Ocean Ridge FL 33435

KYLE, GENE MAGERL, merchandise presentation artist; b. Phila., Oct. 11, 1919; d. Elmer Langham and Muriel Helen (Magerl) K.; student Center for Creative Studies, Detroit, 1938-45. Mdse. presentation artist D. J. Healy Shops, Detroit, 1946-50, Saks Fifth Ave., Detroit, 1950-58, J.L. Hudson Co., Detroit, 1958-84; tchr. workshop classes; exhibited in shows at Mich. Water Color Soc., 1944, 53, 74, Mich. Artists Exhbn., 1962, 64, Scarab Club, 1948, 49, 52, Detroit Artists Market, 1946—. Recipient various art awards. Mem. Detroit Inst. Arts Founders Soc., Mich. Water Color Soc., Windsor Art Gallery.

KYLE, GEORGE WILLIAM, nuclear controls and instrumentation systems engineer, consultant; b. Westerly, R.I., Aug. 9, 1945; s. Albert Groves and Dorothy Ella (Hill) K.; m. Miriam Angela Dupree, Feb. 1970. A.A. in Personnel Mgmt., A.S. in Data Processing, Southwestern Coll., 1976; B.G.S. in Computer Sci., Roosevelt U., 1982. Data systems tech., chief petty officer U.S. Navy, various locations, 1963-83; supr. plant computers Clinton Power Station, Ill. Power Co., Clinton, 1983, supr. nuclear info. systems, 1983-85, nuclear controls and instrumentation systems engr., 1985—; owner, cons. Kyle Enterprises, Clinton, 1983—. Recipient 2nd Place Business award Bank of Am., 1976; Disting. Service award Arthritis Found., 1981; Appreciation award Mid-Pacific Roadrunners Club, 1982. Mem. Alpha Gamma Sigma (pres. 1975). Club: Mid-Pacific Roadrunners. Lodge: Masons. Avocations: running, leather-work, scuba diving. Home: 1 Nancy Ln RR 2 Box 156 Clinton IL 61727 Office: Clinton Power Station Route 54 Clinton IL 61727

KYLE, MARTIN LAWRENCE, research and development executive, chemical engineer; b. Akron, Ohio, Jan. 2, 1935; s. John C. and Miriam (Martin) K.; m. Evelyn Mae Sveda, May 25, 1957. B.S. in Chem. Engring., Notre Dame U., 1956; M.S. in Chem. Engring., Purdue U., 1959; M.B.A., U. Chgo., 1971. Mgr. materials and services Argonne Nat. Lab., Ill., 1960—. Mem. Wheaton Environ. Commn., Ill., 1975. Served to 1st lt., U.S. Army, 1956-59. Mem. Am. Chem. Soc. Home: 1105 Delles Rd Wheaton IL 60187 Office: Argonne Nat Lab 9700 S Cass Ave Argonne IL 60439

KYLE, ROBERT CAMPBELL, publishing executive; b. Cleve., Jan. 6, 1935; s. C. Donald and Mary Alice (King) K.; m. Barbara Ann Battey, June 8, 1957; children—Peter F., Christopher C., Scott G. B.S., U. Colo., 1956; M.A., Case Western Res. U., 1958; M.B.A., Harvard U., 1962, D.B.A., 1966. Ptnr. McLagan & Co., Chgo., 1966-67; founder, pres. Devel. Systems Corp. (now subs. Longman Group USA), 1967-82, pres. Longman Group USA, Chgo., 1982—; dir. Grubb & Ellis Co., San Francisco, 1976—. Author: Property Mamangement, 1979; co-author: Modern Real Estate Practice, 1967. Mem. Real Estate Educators Assn. (pres. 1981), Info. Industry Assn., Internat. Assn. Fin. Planning. Clubs: Harvard (N.Y.C.), Economic (Chgo.), Chgo. Yacht. Avocations: Competitive yacht racing; tennis. Home: 935 Private Rd Winnetka IL 60093 Office: Longman Group USA Inc 500 N Dearborn St Chicago IL 60610

KYLES, CALVIN EUGENE, manufacturing company marketing executive; b. Lake Charles, La., Oct. 26, 1937; s. William and Hattie (Hagger) K.; student McNeese State Coll., 1957; B.B.A., Tex. Southern U., 1977; m. Girtha Lee Little John, Jan. 5, 1965; 1 dau., Yolanda Yvette. With Riverside Gen. Hosp., Houston, 1964-77, asst. adminstr., 1974-76, project dir. met. health founds. health maintenance orgn. feasibility study, 1974-76; system engr. Automated Health Services div. McDonnell Douglas Co., St. Louis, from 1977, now mktg. specialist. Pres., young adults NAACP, Lake Charles, 1959-61; scoutmaster Boy Scouts Am., 1959-61; pres. PTA Elementary Sch., Houston, 1974-77; mem. citizens participating com. City of Florissant (Mo.). Served with AUS, 1961-63. Recipient Parent Year award Fairchild Elementary sch., 1977; named Teammate of Distinction, McDonnell Douglas Co. Pres. sr. choir St. John Bapt. Ch., Houston. Home: 2085 Teakwood Manor Dr Florissant MO 63031 Office: 5775 Campus Pkwy Hazelwood MO 63042

KYNER, JOSEPH LATSHAW, medical educator; b. Wilson, Kans., Aug. 3, 1934; s. Joseph L. and Jane (Smith) K. B.A., U. Kans., 1956, M.D., 1960. Diplomate Am. Bd. Internal Medicine. Intern U. Kans. Med. Ctr., Kansas City, 1960-61, resident, 1961-62, 64-66, fellow, 1966-70; Fellow Joslin Diabetes Found., 1966-70; asst. prof. U. Kans. Sch. Medicine, Kansas City, 1970-75, assoc. prof., 1975-81, prof. medicine, 1981—; clin. dir. Cray Med. Research Found., Kansas City. Contbr. articles to med. jours. Served to capt. U.S. Army, 1962-64. Recipient Mosby Scholarship award, 1957, Intern of Yr. award, 1960-61. Fellow ACP; mem. Am. Diabetes Assn., Am. Fedn. Clin. Research, Am. Diabetes Assn. (bd. dirs. Johnson County Chpt. 1982—), U. Kans. Internal Medicine Found. (bd. dirs. 1981-82), Greater Kansas City Soc. Internists, Sigma Xi, Alpha Omega Alpha. Avocations; tennis, Kansas history. Home: 7233 Eby Merriam KS 66204 Office: U Kans Med Ctr 39th Rainbow Kansas City KS 66103

LAAKSO, LIISA LYDIA JOHANNA, osteopathic physician; b. Boston, May 20, 1951; d. Perttu Vihtori and Toini Viola (Hartikainen) Laakso; m. Ronald Lennox Walsh, May 21, 1977. B.S. in Biology, U. Ill., 1973; D.O., Chgo. Coll. Osteo. Medicine, 1977. Diplomate Am. Bd. Radiology. Staff radiologist, asst. prof. radiology, now assoc. prof. radiology Chgo. Coll. Osteo. Medicine at Olympia Fields (Ill.) Osteo. Med. Ctr., 1981—; tchr.; lectr. Mem. Radiol. Soc. N.Am., Am. Osteo. Assn., Am. Osteo. Coll. Radiology, Dartmouth Road Soc. Office: Olympia Fields Osteo Med Ctr 20201 S Crawford Olympia Fields IL 60461

LABABIDI, ZUHDI A., pediatric cardiologist, pediatrics educator; b. Yafa, Palestine, July 20, 1939; came to U.S., 1967, naturalized, 1970; s. Ali S. and Jamila (Umari) L.; m. Cynthia J. Landis, June 14, 1969; children—Dina, Sami. B.Sc., Am. U., Lebanon, 1962, M.D., 1966. Diplomate Am. Bd. Pediatrics. Resident in pediatrics U. Iowa, 1967-70; Instr. U. Mo., Columbia, 1970-71, asst. prof., 1971-76, assoc. prof., 1976-82, prof. pediatrics, 1982—, dir. pediatric cardiology, 1970—. Contbr. articles to profl. jours. Served to col. USAR, 1973—. Fellow Am. Acad. Pediatrics, Am. Coll. Cardiology, Am. Heart Assn.; mem. Mid-West Pediatric Cardiology Soc., Mo. Med. Assn. Avocations: jogging; tennis. Home: Route 4 Box 323 Columbia MO 65201 Office: Univ Hosp 1 Hospital Dr Columbia MO 65212

LABARBERA, ANDREW RICHARD, physiology educator; b. Teaneck, N.J., Oct. 6, 1948; s. Mario Richard and Georgine (Mart) L. B.S. cum laude, Iona Coll., 1970; M.Phil., Columbia U. Coll. Physicians and Surgeons, 1974, M.A., 1974, Ph.D., 1975. Instr. dept. biology Iona Coll., 1970; NIH predoctoral trainee, 1971-75; staff assoc. Ctr. Reproductive Scis., Columbia U., N.Y.C., 1975-77; research fellow Mayo Grad. Sch. Medicine, Rochester, Minn., 1977-80; asst. prof. physiology Northwestern U. Med. Sch., Chgo., 1980—; dir. R.I.A. labs. Ctr. for Endocrinology, Metabolism and Nutrition, 1980-85, asst. prof. obstetrics and gynecology, 1985—; also dir. in vitro fertilization labs Prentice Women's Hosp. and Maternity Ctr. Contbr. articles to profl. jours. Bd. dirs. West Wellington Condominium Assn., 1984-85. Recipient New Investigator award Am. Diabetes Assn., 1982; grantee Population Council, 1972-75, Northwestern U., 1980-81, USPHS-NIH, 1982—. Mem. AAAS, Am. Inst. Biol. Sci., Am. Physiol. Soc., Am. Soc. Zoologists, Chgo. Assn. Reproductive Endocrinologists, Endocrine Soc., Soc. Expl. Biology and Medicine, Soc. Study of Reproduction (chmn. info. mgmt. com. 1983—), Tissue Culture Assn., Lyric Opera Guild, Chgo. Symphony Soc., Art Inst. Chgo., Field Mus. Natural History, Sigma Xi, Beta Beta Beta. Avocation: music. Home: 913 W Van Buren 4D Chicago IL 60607 Office: Prentice Women's Hosp and Maternity Ctr 333 E Superior St Chicago IL 60611

LABATE, DAVID FREDERICK, financial analyst; b. Akron, Nov. 12, 1953; s. Frederick and Lenora (Long) LaB.; m. Frances Ann Paridon, June 4, 1976 (div. Dec. 1979); 1 son, Christopher Michael. B.S., U. Akron, 1975; M.B.A., 1979. Claims investigator Hartford Ins. Co., Akron, 1976-78; pricing analyst TLT Babcock Inc., Fairlawn, Ohio, 1978-79, fin. analyst, 1979-80; supr. gen. acctg. Lawson Co., Cuyahoga Falls, Ohio, 1980, fleet adminstr./fin. analyst, 1980-82, mgr. fin. analysis and fleet adminstrn., 1983—. Roman Catholic. Home: 461 Loomis Ave Cuyahoga Falls OH 44221 Office: The Lawson Co 210 Broadway E Cuyahoga Falls OH 44222

LABATH, OCTAVE AARON, mechanical engineer; b. Milw., Sept. 22, 1941; s. Octave Adrain and Bertha Jane (Johnson) LaB.; m. Carole Marion Clay, Jan. 23, 1965; children—Melissa, Michelle, Mark. B.S. in Mech. Engring., U. Cin., 1964, M.S., 1969. Registered profl. engr., Ohio. Chief indsl. engr. Cin. Gear Co., 1972—. Contbr. articles to profl. jours. Mem. Am. Gear Mfg. Assn. (vice chmn. com. gear rating 1984), ASME, Assn. Iron and Steel Engrs. Methodist. Club: Cin. Day Users Group. Home: 5105 Kenridge Dr Cincinnati OH 45242 Office: Cin Gear Co 5657 Wooster Pike Cincinnati OH 45227

LABORDE, RONALD GARRETT, mathematics educator; b. Fond du Lac, Wis., Aug. 23, 1955; s. Garrett Sheldon and Janet Victoria (Thorpe) LaB.; m. Tina Maria Ponzer, May 8, 1981. B.S., U. Wis.-Oshkosh, 1979, M.S., 1981. Lectr. math. U. Wis., Oshkosh, 1980-84; asst. prof. math. Marian Coll., Fond du Lac, Wis., 1984—. Mem. Math. Assn. Am., Nat. Council Tchrs. Math., Wis. Math. Council, Kappa Delta Pi. Methodist. Home: 4227 A Omro Rd Oshkosh WI 54901 Office: Marian Coll 45 S National Ave Fond du Lac WI 54935

LABSVIRS, JANIS, economist, emeritus educator; b. Bilska, Latvia, Mar. 13, 1907; s. Karlis and Kristina L.; Mag.Oec., Latvian State U., 1930; M.S., Butler U., 1956; Ph.D., Ind. U., 1959. Tchr., Latvia, 1930-36; dir. dept. edn. Fedn. Latvian Trade Unions, 1936-37; v.p. Kr. Baron's U., Extension, Riga, Latvia, 1938-40, also exec. v.p. Filma, Inc., 1939-40; with UNRRA and Internat. Refugee Orgn., Esslingen, Germany, 1945-50; asst. prof. econs. Ind. State U., Terre Haute, 1959-62, assoc. prof., 1963-68, prof., 1969-73, prof. emeritus, 1973—; head dept. public and social affairs Latvian Ministry for Social Affairs, 1938-40; dir. Sch. of Commerce and Gymnasium, Tukums, Latvia, 1941-44. Danforth grantee, 1961; Ind. State U. research grantee, 1966. Mem. Am. Latvian Assn., Am. Assn. Advancement Slavic Studies, Assn. Advancement Baltic Studies, Am. Econ. Assn., Royal Econ. Soc. Lutheran. Author: Local Government's Accounting and Management Practices, 1947; A Case Study in the Sovietization of the Baltic States: Collectivization of Latvian Agriculture 1944-1956, 1959; Atminas un Pardomas, 1984; contbr. articles profl. jours. Home: 3313 Hovey St Indianapolis IN 46218

LACAMPAGNE, CAROLE BAKER, mathematician educator; b. San Francisco, Sept. 12, 1933; d. Ruel and Charlotte (Alde?) Baker; children—Richard, Suzanne, Loren, John. Student U. Calif.-Berkeley, 1951-53; B.A., U. Pacific, 1959; M.A., Tchrs. Coll., Columbia U., 1972, Ed.D., 1979. Assoc. prof. math. Bergen Community Coll., Paramus, N.J., 1972-82; clin. asst. Tchrs. Coll., Columbia U., N.Y.C., 1977-79; assoc. prof. math. U. Mich., Flint, 1982—; lectr. in field.. Contbr. articles to profl. jours. Mem. Am. Math. Soc. (chmn. com. status women in math. scis. 1979—), Math. Assn. Am., Assn. Women in Math., Women and Math. (nat. dir. 1979—), Women and Math. Edn., Nat. Council Tchrs. Math. Avocation: piano. Office: U Mich Dept Math Flint MI 48503

LACEY, CHARLOTTE LORA, nurse educator; b. Birmingham, Ala., Oct. 29, 1953; d. James Carl and Charlotte Rachel (Bailey) Lacey; children—Kathereen Rachel, Tara Michelle. B.S. in Nursing, U. Ala., 1977, M.S., 1981; postgrad. U. Mo.-Kansas City, 1983—. Staff nurse Children's Hosp., Birmingham, 1977; pediatric nurse practitioner newborn intensive care unit U. Ala., Birmingham, 1977-81, instr. nursing, 1980-81; asst. prof. nursing U. Mo., Kansas City, 1981—. Mem. Am. Nurses Assn., Nurses Assn. of Am. Coll. Obstetricians and Gynecologists, Sigma Theta Tau. Democrat. Methodist. Office: Univ Mo 2220 Holmes Kansas City MO 64108

LACEY, HOWARD RAYMOND, food technologist; b. Fitchburg, Mass., Mar. 18, 1919; s. Clarence Frederick and Sarah Lovisa (Hancock) L.; m. Dorothy Louise Daulton, Aug. 23, 1947; children—Howard R., Janet H. Lacey Wanink. B.S. in Chemistry, U. Mass., 1942. Processed foods inspector USDA, various locations, 1942-46; tech dir. P.J. Ritter Co. (now Curtice-Burns, Inc.), Bridgeton, N.J., 1946-67; gen. mgr., v.p. mfg. Brooks Foods (now Curtice-Burns, Inc.), Mt. Summit, Ind., 1967-74, tech. dir., 1974-85; pres. Lacey Assocs., Inc., 1985—; cons. Cape May Canners, N.J., Party Tyme Corp., N.Y.C.; instr. Better Process Control Sch., Purdue U., West Lafayette, Ind., 1981—. Inventor 100% corn sweetner added to catsup, improved method for firming diced red peppers, Stannous chloride added to asparagus. Asst. mgr. Little League Baseball, Bridgeton, N.J., 1958-61; merit badge counselor Boy Scouts Am., 1957-67; contbg. mem. U.S. Senatorial Club (Republican), Washington, 1978—, Rep. Nat. Com., 1982—. Recipient New Foods award Canner/Packer Mag., Bridgeton, 1957-67. Mem. Inst. Food Tech. (nat., Hoosier chpt., quality assurance sect.), Phi Tau Sigma. Club: Toastmasters (Bridgeton). Lodges: Masons, Elks. Avocations: tennis; reading; bicycling.

LACEY, JEROME, college dean; b. Grenada, Miss., July 21, 1940; m. Ella M. Phillips, Mar. 18, 1962. B.S., So. Ill. U., 1963, M.S., 1968, Ph.D., 1975. Elem. tchr. Dist. 95 Schs., Carbondale, Ill., 1963-65; field rep. Ill. Office Econ. Opportunity, Carbondale, 1965-67; exec. dir. Jackson/Williamson Community Action Agy., Carbondale, 1967-69; coordinator U. services So. Ill. U., Carbondale, 1969-73, asst. to pres. affirmative action office, 1970-73, spl. asst. to v.p. devel. and services office, 1973-75, spl. asst. to v.p. univ. relations office, 1975-79, assoc. v.p., 1979-81, asst. v.p. acad. affairs and research office, 1981-83, assoc. dean student services office, 1983—; adj. instr. Rehab. Inst. So. Ill. U., Carbondale, 1967-70, asst. prof. human resources, 1977-84, asst. prof. dept. curriculum, instrn. and media, Coll. Edn., 1984—. Adv. com. Elem. Sch. Dist. Title VI, Carbondale, 1979-82; mem. state writing com. Ill. Vocat. Edn. Bd., Carbondale, 1970; sec. bd. Carbondale Elem. Sch. Dist. Bd. Edn., 1967-73; chmn. bd. govs. Attucks Multi-Purpose Community Ctr., Carbondale, 1969-72; chmn. Fair Housing Bd., Carbondale, 1968-72; chmn. com. housing Carbondale Human Relations Commn., Carbondale, 1966-71; council mem., vice chmn. Ill. Title XX Citizens Adv. Council, Springfield, 1979-83, chmn. State Task Force on Tng., 1979-80, chmn. 1979-80; vice chmn. central region minority assembly Assn. Community Coll. Trustees, Carterville, Ill., 1984, chmn. central region nominating com., 1983; vice chmn. Southeastern Regional Trustees Assn., Carbondale, 1982-83, chmn., 1983—; various positions Ill. Community Coll. Trustees Assn., Springfield, 1980—. Recipient Pres. Cert. of Merit, Coll. and U. Personnel Assn., 1972, Merit award Ill. Assn. Sch. Bds. 1973, Black Excellence award Black Alumni Assn. So. Ill. U. 1981, Cert. award Outstanding Leadership Black Affairs Council So. Ill. U. Mem. Nat. Assn. Affirmative Action Officers (charter), Ill. Affirmative Action Officers Assn. (charter), Ill. Econ. Opportunity Adv. Com., Am. Assn. Higher Edn., Nat. Assn. Student Personnel Adminstrs., Am. Assn. Counseling and Devel., Soc. Ethnic and Spl. Studies, Am. Coll. Personnel Assn., Nat. Alliance Black Sch. Educators (commn. on higher edn.), Post-doctoral Acad. Higher Edn. (charter), Phi Delta Kappa (past v.p., pres. Gamma Lambda chapt.). Democrat. African Methodist Episcopal. Avocations: flying, golf; photography, coaching jr. sports basketball, little league baseball coach. Home: Rural Route 7 Box 181C Carbondale IL 62901

LACEY, JOHN WILLIAM, data processing and finance company executive; b. London, May 1, 1930; s. William J. and Florence (Farbus) L.; m. Edna Winifred Burns, July 28, 1951; children—Jonathan Charles, Erika Jane. B.A. with honors in Physics, Oxford, U., Eng., 1952, M.A., 1956. Sr. sci. officer Govt. of U.S., 1952-60; U.S. liaison officer Brit. Embassy, Washington, 1956-60; mgr. research and devel., spl. systems Control Data Corp., Bloomington, Minn., 1960-63, dir. ops., 1963, pres. Control Corp. subs., 1964-65, gen. mgr. Devel. and Standard Systems div., 1965, v.p. computer equipment group, 1966-67, v.p. corp. devel., 1967-71, v.p., sr. staff officer corp. plans and controls, 1971-73, sr. v.p. corp. plans and controls, chmn. mgmt. com., 1973-77; pres. Control Data Edn. Co., 1977-79, Control Data Info. and Edn. Systems Co., 1979-81; exec. v.p. Control Data, 1982—; dir. Graco, Inc., Semicondr. Research Corp., 1982—, Microelectronics and Computer Tech. Corp., 1983—; chmn. bd. Control Corp., Adcomp Corp., 1963-65. Bd. dirs. Jr. Achievement Greater Mpls., 1966-77, Mpls. Acquatennial, 1975-82, Mpls. C. of C., 1974-78, Guthrie Theatre, Mpls., 1983—. Home: 7141 Gleason Rd Edina MN 55435

LACH, ALMA ELIZABETH, food and cooking writer, consultant; b. Petersburg, Ill.; d. John H. and Clara E. (Boeker) Satorius; diplome de Cordon Bleu, Paris, 1956; m. Donald F. Lach, Mar. 18, 1939; 1 dau., Sandra Judith. Feature writer Children's Activities mag., 1954-55; creator, performer TV show Let's Cook, children's cooking show, 1955; performer TV show Over Easy, PBS, 1977-78; food editor Chgo. Daily Sun-Times, 1957-65; pres. Alma Lach Kitchens Inc., Chgo., 1966—; dir. Alma Lach Cooking Sch., Chgo.; lectr. U. Chgo. Downtown Coll., Gourmet Inst., U. Md., 1963, Modesto (Calif.) Coll., 1978, U. Chgo., 1981; resident master Shoreland Hall, U. Chgo., 1978-81; food cons. Food Bus. Mag., 1964-66, Chgo.'s New Pump Room, Lettuce Entertain You, Bitter End Resort, Brit. V.I., Midway Airlines, Flying Food Fare, Inc., Berghoff Restaurant; columnist Modern Packaging, 1967-68, Travel & Camera, 1969, Venture, 1970, Chicago mag., 1978, Bon Appetit, 1980, Tribune Syndicate, 1982. Recipient Pillsbury award, 1958; Grocery Mfrs. Am. Trophy award, 1959, certificate of Honor, 1961; Chevalier du Tastevin, 1962; Commanderie de l'Ordre des Anysetiers du Roy, 1963; Confrerie de la Chaine des Rotisseurs, 1964; Les Dames D'Escoffier, 1982. Mem. U. Chgo. Settlement League, Am. Assn. Food Editors (chmn. 1959), Internat. Platform Assn. Clubs: Tavern, Quadrangle (Chgo.). Author: A Child's First Cookbook, 1950; The Campbell Kids Have a Party, 1953; The Campbell Kids at Home, 1953; Let's Cook, 1956; Candlelight Cookbook, 1959; Weekly TV food show CBS, 1962-66; Cooking a la Cordon Bleu, 1970; Alma's Almanac, 1972; Hows and Whys of French Cooking, 1974. Contbr. to World Book Yearbook, 1961-75, Grolier Soc. Yearbook, 1962. Home and Office: 5750 Kenwood Ave Chicago IL 60637

LACK, RICHARD FREDERICK, painter, educator; b. Mpls., Mar. 26, 1928; s. Frederick August and Mildred Carolyn (Petersen) L.; m. Katherine Elizabeth Vietorisz, Sept. 12, 1955; children—Susanna, Peter, Michael. Student, Mpls. Sch. Art, 1947-49, R.H. Gammell Studio, Boston, 1950-57. Dir. Atelier Lack, Mpls., 1968—. Author: On the Training of Painters, 1973. Commd. portraits of Joseph P. Kennedy, Jr., 1960, Sen. Wendell Anderson, 1981, Gov. Albert Quie, 1984. Served as cpl. U.S. Army, 1951-53. Recipient Gold medal Am. artist Profl. League, 1967, 68, 69 Copley Soc., 1960. Mem. Twin City Guild Painters and Sculptors, New Am. Acad. Art. Avocation: violin. Home and Studio: 5827 Louis Ave Minnetonka MN 55345 Office: Atelier Lack 2908 Hennepin Ave S Minneapolis MN 55408

LACKNER, THOMAS EDWARD, pharmaceutical educator; b. St. Paul, Oct. 22, 1954; s. Edward Andrew and Ruth Florence (Beckman) L.; m. Laura Therese Rogowski, Mar. 18, 1978; children—Jeffrey, Stephen. B.S., U. Minn., 1979, Pharm.D., 1980. Asst. prof. clin. pharmacy St. Louis Coll. Pharmacy, 1980—. Contbr. articles to profl. jours. Samuel W. Melendy Meml. scholar, 1977-78. Mem. Am. Assn. Colls. Pharmacy, Am. Soc. Hosp. Pharmacists, Drug Info. Assn., Minn. Soc. Hosp. Pharmacists, Rho Chi Soc. (v.p. student chpt. 1978-79, award 1976-77). Roman Catholic. Avocations: tennis; golf; lapidary. Home: 815 Palm Bay Dr Saint Louis MO 63011

LACOUR, BLAIR PAUL, paint company executive; b. Phila., Jan. 28, 1947; s. Richard Dean and Hedwig Katherine (Kordwitz) L.; m. Linda Ellen Kenney, June 13, 1970; children—Blair Ashley, Danielle Marie, Richard Kenney. B.B.A. in Mktg., U. Notre Dame, 1969; M.B.A. in Mktg. Mgmt., Calif. State U., Fresno, 1973. Sales rep. 3M Co., Fresno and Valencia, Calif., 1970-77, mktg. mgr., St. Paul, 1977-80, regional sales mgr., Cleve., 1980-81; v.p., dir. sales Sherwin Williams Co., Cleve., 1981-82, v.p. sales, mktg., 1982—. Mem. Paint Body and Equipment Assn., Motor Equipment Mgmt. Assn., Automotive Service Industry Assn., Truck Body and Equipment Assn., Distbrs. Inst. Avocations: golf; tennis. Home: 17704 Fairfax Ln Strongsville OH 44136 Office: Sherwin Williams Co 101 Prospect Ave Cleveland OH 44101

LACY, ALAN JASPER, food company executive; b. Cleveland, Tenn., Oct. 19, 1953; s. William J. and Mary (Leigh) L.; m. Caron Ann Cap, May 16, 1981; 1 child, Daniel Alan. B.S.I.M., Ga. Inst. Tech., 1975; M.B.A., Emory U., 1977. Chartered fin. analyst. Fin. analyst Holiday Inns, Inc., Memphis, 1977-79; mgr. investor relations Tiger Internat., Los Angeles, 1979-80, Dart Industries, Los Angeles, 1980-81; dir. corp. fin. Dart & Kraft, Northbrook, Ill., 1981-82, asst. treas., 1982-83, treas., v.p., 1984—. Mem. Fin. Analysts Fedn., Fin. Execs. Inst., Investment Analysts Soc. Chgo., Inst. Chartered Fin. Analysts. Clubs: University, Economic (Chgo.); Exmoor Country (Highland Park, Ill.). Office: Dart & Kraft 2211 Sanders Rd Northbrook IL 60062

LACY, HERMAN EDGAR, management consultant; b. Chgo., June 21, 1935; s. Herman E. and Florence L.; children—Frederick H., Carlton E., Douglas H., Jennifer S., Victoria J., Rebecca M. B.S. in Indsl. Engring., Bradley U., 1957; M.B.A., U. Chgo., 1966. Plant mgr., indsl. engring. supr. Hammond Organ Co., Chgo., 1961-66; mgr. corp. indsl. engring. Consol. Packaging Corp., Chgo., 1966-68; mgr. mgmt. cons. Peat, Marwick, Mitchell & Co., Chgo., 1968-70; dir. ops. Wilton Enterprises, Inc., Chgo., 1970-77; v.p., gen. mgr. Intercraft Industries Corp., Chgo., 1978-79; pres. Helmco Cons., Inc., Glenview, Ill., 1979—; instr. Roosevelt U., Oakton Coll., Harper Coll. Served to capt. USAF, 1957-61; Germany. Mem. Inst. Indsl. Engrs. (past pres., founder North suburban Ill. chpt.), Am. Mgmt. Assn., Internat. Material Mgmt. Soc., Soc. Mfg. Engrs., Inst. Mgmt. Cons. Home: 930 Huber Ln Glenview IL 60025 Office: 1920 Waukegan Rd Glenview IL 60025

LACY, MARGRIET BRUYN, French language educator, university dean; b. Amsterdam, Netherlands, Apr. 4, 1943; came to U.S., 1969; d. Pieter and Greet (Holtrop) Bruyn; m. Gregg Lacy, Aug. 28, 1970 (div. 1982). Kandidaats in French, U. Amsterdam, 1966, Doctoraal, 1969; M. Phil., U. Kans., 1971, Ph.D., 1972. Asst. prof. French, N.D. State U., Fargo, 1974-78, assoc. prof., 1978-83, prof., 1983—, assoc. dean, 1984-85, dean, 1985—. Contbr. articles to profl. jours. Mem. Am. Assn. for Netherlandic Studies (mem. exec. bd. 1984—), MLA. Home: 117 NE 35th Ave Fargo ND 58102 Office: ND State U Deans Office Fargo ND 58105

LADAGE, WANDA LEE MAXSON, nursing educator; b. Elm Grove Twp., Kans., Dec. 5, 1929; d. Irvin Ray and Geneva Irene (Duncan) M.; m. Jack C. Goodwin, Aug. 14, 1947; children—Penny Bennett, Paula Van Nice, Kim McMunn, Mona Garrett; m. 2d, Dwayne Curtis Ladage, May 19, 1979. A.D.Nursing, Labette Community Coll., 1972; B.S.N., Kans. State Coll., Pittsburg, 1976; M.S., Pittsburg State U., 1979, Ed.S., 1980; Ph.D., Kans. State U., 1985. Staff nurse Coffeyville (Kans.) Meml. Hosp., 1972-74, house supr., 1974-76; dir. edn. Parsons (Kans.) State Hosp. & Tng. Ctr., 1976-77; nursing instr. Labette Community Coll., Parsons, Kans., 1977-81, dir. nursing edn., 1981—. Mem. adv. bd. and pharmacy bd. Elm Haven Nursing Home; active Am. Heart Assn., Am. Diabetes Assn., others. Named Student Nurse of Yr., Labette Community Coll., 1972; Employee of Yr., Coffeyville Meml. Hosp., 1975. Mem. Am. Nurses Assn., Nat. League Nursing, Am. Vocat. Assn., Kans. State Nurses Assn., NEA, Kans. Edn. Assn. Adult and Occupational Edn. Club, Labette County Farm Bur., Women's Bowling Assn., Katy Golf Assn., Sigma Theta Tau. Democrat. Mem., Ch. of the Brethren. Clubs: Order Eastern Star, Swing 'n Twirl Square Dance.

LADD, JAMES CHARLES, lawyer; b. Miami, Fla., Nov. 10, 1951; s. Joseph Montgomery and Mildred Pauline (Pogozelski) L.; m. Sandra Jean Hedgepeth, June 18, 1977; 1 child, Megan Rae. B.S., Western Ky. U., 1977; J.D., No. Ky. U., 1980. Bar: Ky. 1980, U.S. Dist. Ct. (we. dist.) Ky. 1981, U.S. Dist. Ct. (so. dist.) La. 1983, U.S. Dist. Ct. (so. dist.) Tex. 1984. Trial commr. Hart Dist. Ct., Munfordville, Ky., 1981-82; asst. Commonwealth atty., Hart County, Ky., 1984—. Served with U.S. Army, 1971-74, Vietnam. Mem. Ky. Bar Assn., Ky. Acad. Trial Attys., ABA, Hart County Bar Assn., Munfordville Battlefield Assn. (chmn. 1983-84). Democrat. Home: Route 1 Box 127 Canmer KY 42722 Office: Baird & Ladd 10 Main St Munfordville KY 42765

LADD, KAREN LOUISE, psychologist; b. Niles, Mich., Feb. 26, 1948; d. Gemroe and Amy Jean (Thomas) Fletcher; B.Sacred Lit. (essay contest scholar, 1966), Gt. Lakes Bible Coll., 1970; M.Ednl. Psychology, Andrews U., 1974, postgrad.; m. S. Lee Ladd, June 29, 1969; children—Christopher Lee, Matthew Lee. Therapist, Christian Counseling Services, Indpls., 1973-83; therapist Agape Counseling Services, Greenwood, Ind., 1983—; asst. prof. psychology and sociology, Ind. Christian U., 1978-79; chmn. psychology div. textbooks adoptions com. State of Ind., 1979. Mem. Am. Assn. Christian Counselors, Am. Personnel and Guidance Assn., Am. Businesswomen's Assn., Nat. Speakers Assn., Christian Assn. for Psychol. Studies. Mem. Christian Ch. (non-denominational). Composer song: Why, Lord?, 1973; author booklet: Meeting the Needs of the Inmate, 1976; contbr. articles to publs. in field. Home: 2233 Darlene Ct Greenwood IN 46142 Office: 537 Turtle Creek S Dr Suite 14D Indianapolis IN 46227

LADD, KENNETH PAUL, clergyman, counselor; b. Delphos, Ohio, Aug. 3, 1938; s. Lawrence Andrew and Velma (May) L.; m. Kay Elaine Saunders, July 15, 1961; children—Kristine Lynn (dec.), Kevin Lee, Kim Leann, Karin Lynette. B.A., Huntington Coll., 1962; M.Div., United Thwol. Seminary, 1966; Ph.D., U. Beverly Hills, 1983. Cert. tchr., Ohio. Ordained to ministry United Methodist Ch., 1966; pastor Antioch Christian Ch., Ottoville, Ohio, 1958-59, Goblesville Cir. Evangel. United Brethren Ch., Huntington, Ind., 1960-62, Salem Evangel. United Brethren Ch., Bettsville, Ohio, 1962-65, First Evangel. United Brethren Ch., Wauseon, Ohio, 1965-67, St. Paul's United Meth. Ch., Bloomville, Ohio, 1967-68; chaplain Maumee Youth Camp, Liberty Center, Ohio, 1968-80; dir. Counseling Center, Wauseon, 1980—; pastor Taylor United Meth. Ch., Delta, Ohio, 1980, Beulah United Meth. Ch., Winameg, Ohio, 1981—. Bd. dirs. Valley Oak Council Camp Fire Youth, 2d v.p.; chmn. Ohio Youth Commn. Chaplains. Mem. Ohio State Chaplains Assn. (1st v.p.), Wauseon Ministerial Assn. (past pres.), Am. Assn. Counseling and Devel., Ohio Mental Health Counselors Assn., Ohio Assn. Counseling and Devel., Am. Assn. Profl. Hypnotherapists, Am. Personnel and Guidance Assn., Am. Mental Health Counselors Assn., Am. Assn. Profl. Hypnotherapists, Ohio Mental Health Counselors Assn., Ohio Assn. Counseling and Devel., Hope (dir.), Fellowship Christian Magicians, Internat. Brotherhood of Magicians, Soc. Am. Magicians. Contbr. chpts. to books; author courses of study for use with alienated youth; developer workshops under fed. grant. Home: 234 E Superior St Wauseon OH 43567 Office: 120 W Chestnut St Wauseon OH 43567

LADENBERGER, DONALD ALLAN, engineering administrator; b. Rockford, Ill., Feb. 25, 1945; s. Philip F. Edna (Mueller) L.; m. Diane M. Bomback, Sept. 17, 1981; children—Erin, Amy, Kent, Andrew. B.S. in Mech. Engring., Ill. Inst. Tech., 1969. Registered profl. engr., Ill. Mgr. engring. Nagle Pumps Inc., Chicago Heights, Ill., 1982; design engring. mgr. Aurora Pump Co., Aurora, Ill., 1975-82; design engr. Chgo. Bridge & Iron Co., Oakbrook, Ill., 1969-75. Mem. ASME. Roman Catholic. Home: 230 Acorn Ridge Frankfort IL 60423 Office: 1249 Center Ave Chicago Heights IL 60411

LADENSON, JACK HERMAN, clinical chemist, researcher, pathology educator; b. Phila., Apr. 8, 1942; s. Paul J. and Lillian B. (Vinokur) L.; m. Ruth E. Carroll, June 23, 1968; children—Michele, Jeff. B.S., Pa. State U., 1964; Ph.D., U. Md., College Park, 1971. Asst. dir. clin. chemistry Barnes Hosp., St. Louis, Mo., 1972-76, co-dir. clin. chemistry, 1976-79, dir. clin. chemistry, 1980—; asst. prof. pathology Washington U., St. Louis, 1972-79, assoc. prof., 1979-84, prof., 1984—; dir. Am. Bd. Clin. Chemistry, N.J., 1979—; v.p. Commn. on Accreditation in Clin. Chemistry, Chgo., 1981—; mem. Nat. Com. Clin. Lab. Standards. Contbr. articles to profl. jours. Mem. Am. Assn. Clin. Chemistry (pres. 1985, dir. 1981-83), Acad. Clin. Lab. Physicians and Scientists, Endocrine Soc., Am. Fedn. Clin. Research, Am. Assn. Pathologists, Am. Chem. Soc. Office: Washington U Sch Medicine Div Lab Medicine Box 8118 Saint Louis MO 63110

LADISCH, MICHAEL R., biochemical engineering educator; b. Upper Darby, Pa., Jan. 15, 1950; s. Rolf Karl and Brigitte M. (Gareis) L.; m. Christine Schmitz, July 25, 1975; children—Sarah, Mark. B.S. in Chem. Engring., Drexel U., Phila., 1973; M.S. in Chem. Engring., Purdue U., 1974, Ph.D. in Chem. Engring., 1977. Research engr. Lab. Renewable Resources Engring. and dept. chem. engring. Purdue U., West Lafayette, Ind., 1977-78, asst. prof. food and agrl. engring., asst. prof. chem. engring., 1978-81, assoc. prof., 1981-85, prof., 1985—. Contbr. articles to profl. publs. Patentee in field. Recipient U.S. Presdl. Young Investigator award NSF, 1984. Mem. Am. Chem. Soc. (librarian 1982-84, chmn.-elect., 1985—, program chmn. 1985—, W.H. Peterson award microbial div. 1977), Am. Inst. Chem. Engring., Am. Soc. Agrl. Engrs., N.Y. Acad. Sci. Home: 1228 Ravinia Rd West Lafayette IN 47906 Office: Purdue U LORRE West Lafayette IN 47907

LADO, ROBERT ANTHONY, chiropractor; b. Rome, N.Y., Mar. 23, 1944; s. Anthony Louis and Wanda Lucille (Linke) L.; m. Sandy Krider, Oct. 16, 1982; children—Kristin, Derek. B.S., Palmer Coll. Chiropractors, 1969, D. Chiropractic Medicine, 1969. Pres., dir. Lado & Lado Clinic, P.C., Grand Rapids, Mich., 1982—; cons. Clinic Masters Inc., Kansas City, Mo., 1982—. Contbr. articles to profl. jours. Instr. ARC, 1970-81. Recipient Eagle Scout award Boy Scouts Am., Rome, N.Y., 1958, Badge of Honor award Clinic Masters, 1976, Boss of Yr. award La Grande Vitesse, 1979. Mem. Internat. Chiropractic Assn., Mich. State Chiropractic Assn. (Dist. Pres. Yr. award 1978). Republican. Lodges: Moose (jr. gov. 1970-71), Rotary (pres. 1978-79). Avocations: travel, learning, helping others. Home: Kissing Rock Lowell MI Office: 5344 Plainfield NE Grand Rapids MI 49505 and Riverview Plaza Jenison MI 40428

LA DU, BERT NICHOLS, JR., educator; b. Lansing, Mich., Nov. 13, 1920; s. Bert Nichols and Natalie Jessie (Kerr) La D.; B.S., Mich. State Coll., 1943; M.D., U. Mich., 1945; Ph.D., U. Calif. at Berkeley, 1950; m. Catherine Shilson, June 14, 1947; children—Elizabeth, Mary, Anne, Jane. Intern, Rochester (N.Y.) Gen. Hosp., 1945-46; research asso. N.Y. U. Research Service, Goldwater Meml. Hosp., N.Y.C., 1950-53; sr. asst. surgeon USPHS, Nat. Heart Inst., 1954-57; surgeon, sr. surgeon, med. dir. Nat. Inst. Arthritis and Metabolic Diseases, 1957-63; prof., chmn. dept. pharmacology N.Y. U. Med. Sch., N.Y.C., 1963-74; prof., chmn. dept. pharmacology U. Mich. Med. Sch., Ann Arbor, 1974-80, prof., 1980—. Mem. adv. com. Roche Inst. Molecular Biology, 1972-74; mem. toxicology adv. com. FDA, 1975-77; mem. nat. adv. com. NIH study sects., 1964-70, Nat. Inst. Arthritis and Metabolic Diseases Council, 1975-78. Served with AUS, 1943-45. Mem. AAAS, Am. Chem. Soc., Am. Soc. Biol. Chemists, Am. Soc. Pharmacology and Therapeutics, Am. Soc. Human Genetics, Biochem. Soc. (Gt. Britain), N.Y. Acad. Scis. Editor: (with others) Fundamentals of Drug Metabolism and Drug Disposition; contbr. articles to profl. jours. Home: 817 Berkshire Rd Ann Arbor MI 48104 Office: 6322 Med Sci Bldg I U Mich Med Sch Ann Arbor MI 48109

LAFF, CHARLES RUDER, health care executive, financial consultant; b. Chgo., Mar. 17, 1942; s. Milton M. and Bertha (Ruder) L.; m. Judith Ann Kramer, Nov. 20, 1965; children—Michael, Joshua. B.S. in Accountancy, U. Ill., 1963. C.P.A., Ill. Treas. Budget Rent-a-Car, Chgo., 1965-71, v.p., fin. treas., 1971-73; v.p. InterContinental Service, Chgo., 1973-75; pres. In Home Health Care, Morton Grove, Ill., 1975—; fin. cons. Charles R. Laff, Northbrook, Ill., 1976—, Pub. Funding Corp., Morton Grove, 1982—. Contbr. article to publ. Mem. Am. Inst. C.P.A.s, Nat. Assn. for Home Care (membership com.), Ill. Soc. Home Health Agys. Republican. Jewish. Home: 2668 Lisa Ct Northbrook IL 60062

LA FOLLETTE, BRONSON CUTTING, atty. gen. Wis.; b. Washington, Feb. 2, 1936; s. Robert Marion, Jr. and Rachel Wilson (Young) LaF.; children—Robert M., Deborah C.; B.A., U. Wis., 1958, J.D., 1960. Bar: Wis. 1960, U.S. Supreme Ct. 1966. Individual practice law, Madison, Wis., 1960-62; asst. U.S. atty. Western Dist. Wis., 1962-64; atty. gen. Wis., Madison, 1964-68, 74—; Democratic nominee for Gov. Wis., 1968; lectr. Am. Specialist Abroad Program U.S. Dept. State, India, Sri Lanka, 1965. Mem. Pres.'s Consumer Adv. Council, 1966-69, chmn., 1968-69; bd. dirs. Consumers Union, Inc., 1968-76; mem. adv. bd. Sister Cities Internat., Inc.; pres. Dane County Exchange Project to Prevent Child Abuse, 1982—. Mem. Wis., Dane County bar assns., Nat. Assn. Atty. Gen. (exec. com.). Office: Justice Dept PO Box 7857 Madison WI 53707*

LA FOLLETTE, DOUGLAS J., state official; b. Des Moines, June 6, 1940; s. Joseph Henry and Francis (VanderWilt) LaF. B.S., Marietta Coll., 1963; M.S., Stanford U., 1964; Ph.D., Columbia U., 1967. Asst. prof. chemistry, ecology U. Wis.-Parkside, 1969-72; mem. Wis. Senate, 1972-74; sec. of state State of Wis., Madison, 1974-78, 83—; asst. dir. Mid-Am. Solar Energy Ctr., Mpls., 1979-80; dir. tng. and devel. Energy Mktg. Group, Ind., Petoskey, Mich., 1981-82. Recipient Wis. Jaycees Outstanding Man of the Yr. award, 1971; EPA Environ. Quality award, 1976; U. Freiberg Internat. Research fellow, 1967-68. Mem. Fedn. Am. Scientists, Wis. Environ. Decade, Council Econ. Priorities, Audubon Soc., Friends of the Earth. Democrat. Author: Wisconsin Survival Handbook, 1971. Home: 715 S Few St Madison WI 53705 Office: State Capitol Madison WI 53702

LAFOLLETTE, WILLIAM ROBERT, business educator, former air force officer; b. Elwood, Ind., Dec. 25, 1935; s. Walter F. and Kathryn E. (Arnott) LaF.; m. Mary Elizabeth Chapman, Sept. 26, 1958; children—Elizabeth Anne, Mary Katherine. B.A., Butler U., 1957; M.B.A., U. Mo., 1968; D.B.A., Ind. U., 1973. Commd. 2d lt. U.S. Air Force, 1957, advanced through grades to lt. col., 1981; asst. prof. Ball State U., Muncie, Ind., 1973-77, assoc. prof., 1977-81, prof. mgmt., 1981—, chmn. dept., 1977-85, coordinator TV instrn. Coll. Bus., 1985—. Contbr. articles to bus. and psychol. jours. Decorated D.F.C., Air medal with six oak leaf clusters, Air Force Commendation medal, also others. Mem. Acad. Mgmt., Am. Inst. Decision Scis., Ind. Acad. Social Scis., Muncie C. of C. (small bus. council 1980—), Internat. Council Small Bus., Beta Gamma Sigma (pres. 1984-85), Sigma Iota Epsilon (faculty adviser 1980—). Republican. Roman Catholic. Lodge: Masons. Avocations: gardening, reading. Home: Rural Route 6 Box 202 Muncie IN 47302 Office: Ball State U Muncie IN 47306

LAGOS, JAMES HARRY, lawyer, small business advocate; b. Springfield, Ohio, Mar. 14, 1951; s. Harry Thomas and Eugenia (Papas) L.; m. Nike Daphne Pavlatos, July 3, 1976. B.A. cum laude, Wittenberg U., 1969; J.D., Ohio State U., 1972. Bar: U.S. Supreme Ct. 1976, U.S. Ct. Appeals (6th cir.) 1979, U.S. Dist. Ct. (so. dist.) Ohio 1973, U.S. Tax Ct. 1975, Ohio Supreme Ct. 1973. Asst. pros. atty. Clark County, Ohio, 1972-75; ptnr. Lagos & Lagos, Springfield, 1975— mem. Springfield Small Bus. Council, past chmn., 1977—; del. Ohio Small Bus. Coalition, 1980—, past chmn., now vice chmn. fed. action; del. Ohio, Small Bus. United, v.p. issues, 1982—; del. Small Bus. Nat. Issues Conf., 1984, Ohio Gov.'s Conf. Small Bus., 1984, resource person regulatory and licensing reform com., 1984. Bd. dirs., pres. Greek Orthodox Ch., 1974—; past chmn. Clark County Child Protection Team, 1974-82; mem. Clark County Young Republican Club, past pres., sec., treas., 1968-76. Served to staff sgt. with Ohio Air Nat. Guard, 1970-76. Recipient Dr. Melvin Emanuel award West Central Ohio Hearing and Speech Assn., 1983; Outstanding Young Man of Am., 1978; Disting. Service award Springfield-Clark County, 1977. Mem. Am. Hellenic Inst. (pub. affairs com.), Am. Hellenic Ednl. Progressive Assn. (past treas), C. of C. (past bd. dirs.), Ohio C. of C. (small bus. com. 1983—), Jaycees (past chmn. several coms. 1977—, Spoke award 1974), ABA, Ohio State Bar Assn., Springfield Bar and Law Library Assn. (past sec., exec. com. 1973—), West Central Ohio Hearing and Speech Assn. (bd. dirs., pres., v.p. 1973-84), Alpha Alpha Kappa, Phi Eta Sigma, Tau Pi Phi, Pi Sigma Alpha. Home: 2023 Audubon Park Dr Springfield OH 45504 Office: Lagos & Lagos 31 E High St Suite 500 Springfield OH 45502

LAHEY, PAUL DAVID, legal investigator; b. Green Springs, Ohio, Aug. 7, 1923; s. William Edward and Grace Ann (Eckel) L.; m. Eleanor Alice McGuire, July 2, 1947; children—Janet, Steven, Denise. Student parochial schs., Pontiac, Mich. Officer Ohio State Patrol, 1953-75, sgt., 1964-75; investigator Pros. Atty.'s Office, Wauseon, Ohio, 1975—, dir. deferred prosecution program, 1975—; bd. dirs. 5 County Alcohol Program, Defiance, Ohio, 1976—, Ohio Investigator's Office, 1976—. Served to cpl. U.S. Army, 1943-46; PTO. Fellow Nat. Dist. Atty's Assn.; mem. Ohio Prosecutor's Investigators (sec. 1984). Republican. Roman Catholic. Lodge: K.C. Home: 1-6714-3 Swanton OH 43558 Office: Pros Atty's Office 114 W Chestnut St Wauseon OH 43567

LAHR, JOHN WILLIAM, optometrist; b. Lafayette, Ind., June 11, 1950; s. Willard Keith and Verly Marion (Westfall) L.; m. Mary Jo Geffert, Sept. 11, 1976; children—Brian, Jennifer, Suzanne. B.S., Ind. U., 1972, O.D., 1974. Assoc., Dr. Earl Doelle, Grand Rapids, Minn., 1974-75; assoc. Dr. G. T. Gibbons, Cambridge, Minn., 1975-77; pres. Cambridge (Minn.) Eye Clinic, 1977—. Cons., Grand Rapids Vocat. Tech. Inst., 1974-75, Cambridge State Hosp., St. Cloud Vocat. Tech. Inst., 1979—, Sandstone Fed. Corr. Inst., 1982—; dir. mktg. America's Doctors of Optometry, Tracy, Minn., 1982—. Fellow Am. Acad. Optometry; mem. Am. Optometric Assn., Minn. Optometric Assn., Met. Dist. Optometric Soc., Cambridge C. of C. Republican. Methodist. Club: Rum River Pilots. Home: 514 Winnetka Pl Cambridge MN 55008 Office: 120 E 1st Ave Cambridge MN 55008

LAHTI, LESLIE ERWIN, engineering educator, consultant; b. Floodwood, Minn., July 27, 1932; s. Frank Leon and Esther (Baaso) L.; m. Alma L. Kelley, May 19, 1956; children—David L., Mark S., Paul A. B.S. in Chem. Engring., Tri-State U., Angola, Ind., 1954; M.S. in Chem. Engring., Mich. State U., 1958; Ph.D., Carnegie Tech. U., 1964. Registered profl. engr., Ohio. Glass technologist Corning Glass, Albion, Mich., 1955-57; process engr. Ron Plastics, Lansing, Mich., 1957-58; assoc. prof. Tri-State U., Angola, Ind., 1958-60; asst. prof. Purdue U., Lafayette, Ind., 1963-67; mem. faculty U. Toledo, 1967—, assoc. prof., 1967-72, prof. engring., 1972—, dean, 1980—; cons. Great Lakes Chem., Lafayette, Ind., 1965-68, Inland Chems., Toledo, 1968-70, Stubbs-Overbeck, Inc., Houston, 1978-81. Contbr. articles to various publs. Vice chmn. Area Council Tech., 1984—. Ford Found. fellow, 1960-63; recipient Shreve Prize, Purdue U., 1967; Herb Thorber award Toledo sect. Am. Inst. Chem. Engring., 1978; named Ohio Engring. Educator, Ohio Soc. Profl. Engrs., 1978. Mem. Toledo Soc. Profl. Engrs. (bd. trustees 1981—, vice chmn. 1985—), Am. Inst. Chem. Engrs. (bd. dirs. 1975-80), Am. Chem. Soc., Am. Soc. Engring. Edn. Lutheran. Home: 2460 Valleybrook Toledo OH 43615 Office: U Toledo 2801 W Bancroft Toledo OH 43606

LAHTI, ROBERT ALLAN, biochemist; b. Iron Mountain, Mich., Dec. 29, 1933; s. Henry E. and Ellen (Stephens) L. B.S. in Secondary Edn., Western Mich. U., 1960; Ph.D. in Biochemistry, U. N.C., 1968. Sr. Scientist Upjohn Co., Kalamazoo, Mich., 1967—. Contbr. articles to profl. jours. Mem. Bd. Edn., Galesburg, Mich., 1980—, pres., 1983—. Served with USMC, 1953-56, Korea. Recipient Am. Cancer Soc. award, 1960; Sabbatical award, Upjohn Co., 1978-79. Mem. Am. Soc. Pharmacology and Exptl. Therapeutics, Internat. Narcotic Research Conf. Avocations tennis; skiing; music. Office: CNS Disease Research Upjohn Co Henrietta St Kalamazoo MI 49001

LAIER, PHILIP MARTIN, engineering company executive; b. Flint, Mich., June 19, 1938; s. Alois and Pauline (Karr) L.; m. Mary Anne McGinty, May 30, 1960; children—Caroline, Louise, Christine, Patty. B.M.E., Gen. Motors Inst. Engring. Mgmt., 1962. Process engr. Chevrolet, Ft. Washington, Pa., 1962-67; sr. engr. Honeywell, Ft. Washington, 1967-70, engring. supr., 1970-72, vertical line mgr., 1972-77, product line mgr., 1977-79, program mgr., 1979-80, factory ops. mgr., 1980-82; exec. v.p. Ardac, Inc., Eastlake, Ohio, 1982-83, pres., 1983—; cons. Honeywell Med. Instruments, N.Y.C., 1981-82, AutoTank, Eastlake, 1983. Coach Warrington Athletic Assn. (Pa.), 1971-74. Served with U.S. Army, 1956-57. Named Chmn. Yr., Suburban Bucks Jaycees, Warminster, Pa., 1970. Republican. Roman Catholic. Author: Reduction in Cost of Manufacturing Quality Connecting Rods, 1962. Home: 8785 Arborhurst Ln Kirtland OH 44094 Office: Ardac Inc 34000 Vokes Dr Eastlake OH 44094

LAIKIN, GEORGE JOSEPH, lawyer; b. Milw., June 21, 1910; s. Isadore and Bella (Schoene) L.; m. Sylvia Goldberg, Jan. 20, 1935; children—Michael B., Barbara Laikin Funkenstein. B.A., LL.B., U. Wis., 1933. Bar: Wis. 1933, D.C. 1944, Ill. 1945, Calif. 1972, N.Y. 1980; cert. taxation specialist, Calif. Pvt. practice law, Milw., 1933-42; spl. asst. to U.S. atty. gen., tax div. Dept. Justice, Washington, 1942-45; pvt. practice law, Wis., 1945, Milw. and Washington, 1945—; pres. Laikin & Laikin, S.C., Milw., 1980—; gen. counsel, Milw. Assn. Life Underwriters, 1953-85, Wis. Assn. Life Underwriters, 1955-85; gen. counsel, dir. Schwerman Trucking Co., Milw., 1955-84, Continental Bank and Trust Co., Milw., 1963-70, Empire Gen. Life Ins. Co., Los Angeles, 1973-77, U.S. Life Ins. Co., Hinsdale, Ill., 1971-76; counsel, dir. Mirish Motion Pictures, Hollywood, Calif., 1960—; chmn. bd., gen. counsel Univ. Nat. Bank, Milw., 1971-76; gen. counsel Liberty Savs. and Loan Assn., Milw., 1979—; spl. atty. M & I Marshall & Ilsley Bank, Milw., 1973—; writer, lectr. in field. Contbr. articles to profl. publs. Chmn. spl. gifts and bequests com. Marquette U., 1967-70; pres. Wis. Soc. Jewish Learning, 1967-71. Mem. ABA, Wis. Bar Assn., Ill. Bar Assn., Calif. Bar Assn., Bar Assn. D.C., Milw. Estate Planning Council, Assn. Trial Lawyers of Am., Nat. Assn. Criminal Def. Lawyers. Clubs: Milw. Athletic, Milw. Yacht; Standard (Chgo.); Carmel Yacht (Haifa, Israel). Home: 1610 N Prospect Ave Milwaukee WI 53202 Office: 825 N Jefferson St Milwaukee WI 53202

LAINSON, HARRY ACKLEY, JR., manufacturing company executive; b. Fairbury, Nebr., Aug. 7, 1912; s. Harry Ackley and Celia W. (Jennings) L.; m. Gretchen Helen Hollman, Jan. 2, 1938; children—Margaret Helen Lainson Hermes, Mary Catherine Lainson Olsen. A.B., Hastings Coll., 1934, LL.D. 1982; LL.B., Whitworth Coll., 1965. Warehouseman, Dutton-Lainson Co., Hastings, Nebr., 1932-34, advt. mgr., 1934, warehouse mgr., 1935, sec., 1936, traffic mgr., personnel mgr., 1937-48, v.p., gen. mgr., 1948-50, pres., 1950-74, chmn., 1960—, chmn., chief exec. officer, 1974—; pres. Midland Corp., Jaden Mfg. Co.; dir. City Nat. Bank, Lincoln Telephone and Telegraph Co., Lincoln TeleCom, Alarm Systems Nebr. Mem. Civil Service Commn., Hastings; mem. Gov.'s Task Force, 1981; trustee Hastings Mus.; bd. dirs. Hastings Carnegie Library; mem. shell com. Dept. War; past pres. bd. trustees Hastings Coll.; nat. bd. dirs. SBA; founder, incorporator Nebr. Ind. Coll. Found. Mem. NAM, Assoc. Industries Nebr. (bd. dirs.), Am. Ordnance Assn. (life), Navy League U.S. (dir., state pres.). Republican. Presbyterian. Club: Lochland Country (Hastings). Lodge: Masons. Home: 229 University Blvd Hastings NE 68901 Office: 2d and St Joseph Ave Hastings NE 68901

LAINSON, PHILLIP A., dental educator; b. Council Bluffs, Iowa, Feb. 11, 1936; s. Donald Wesley and Olive Ione (Stageman) L.; m. Mary Margaret Tangney, June 18, 1960; children—David, Michael, Elizabeth. B.A., U. Iowa, 1960, D.D.S., 1962, M.S., 1968; Dental Intern Cert., USAF Malcom Crow Hosp., 1963. Diplomate Am. Bd. Peridontology. Instr. dept. periodontics U. Iowa, Iowa City, 1965-69, asst. prof., 1969-71, assoc. prof., 1971-75, prof., 1975—, head dept. periodontics, 1976—; cons. in periodontics VA Hosp., Knoxville, Iowa, 1967—, Iowa City, 1976—, Central Regional Dental Testing Service, Topeka, Kans., 1977-81, Commn. on Dental Accreditation, Chgo., 1984-86. Contbr. articles to profl. jours. Editor newsletter Midwest Soc. Periodontology, 1982-85. Assoc. editor Iowa Dental Jour., 1974-76. Chmn., Bd. in Control of Athletics U. Iowa, 1984-86. Served to capt. USAF, 1962-65, Iowa Army N.G., 1973—. Am. Coll. Dentists fellow, 1976. Mem. Iowa Soc. Periodontology (pres. 1976-78), U. Dist. Iowa Dental Assn. (pres. 1979-80), Midwest Soc. Periodontology (v.p. 1985-86), Am. Acad. Periodontology, Internat. Assn. Dental Research, Am. Dental Assn., Am. Assn. Dental Schs., Sigma Xi, Omicron Kappa Upsilon. Republican. Roman Catholic. Lodge: Rotary. Avocations: sailing; fishing; biking; tennis. Home: 16 Ridgewood Ln Iowa City IA 52240 Office: Coll Dentistry Univ Iowa Iowa City IA 52242

LAITY, RONALD LEONARD, consulting engineer; b. Hancock, Mich., July 16, 1927; s. Leonard Benjamin and Ida Sophia (Baakko) L.; B.S. in Elec. Engring., Mich. Technol. U., 1953; m. Leola Gladys Upton, Nov. 26, 1948; children—Kathryn, Teresa, Matthew. With Commonwealth Assos. Inc., Jackson, Mich., 1953-83, sr. staff engr. power and indsl. systems div., asst. treas., 1972-83; coordinator of projects Wolf Wineman Engrs., Inc., Southfield, Mich., 1984—, v.p., 1985—. Served with USAF, 1945-47. Mem. Nat. Soc. Profl. Engrs., Mich. Soc. Profl. Engrs., IEEE, Engring. Soc. Detroit, Tau Beta Pi, Eta Kappa Nu. Presbyterian. Home: 3239 McCain Rd Jackson MI 49203 Office: Wolf Wineman Engrs 17570 W Twelve Mile Rd Southfield MI 48076

LAIVINIEKS, GEORGE JURIS, lawyer; b. Riga Latvia, Oct. 21, 1937; came to U.S., 1951, naturalized, 1959; s. Arvids and Herta Laivinieks; m. Margaret Schuetz (div. 1974); children—Monika, Anita; m. 2d Inese Skujins, Mar. 7, 1975; 1 dau., Sonja. B.A. in Polit. Sci., U. Ill., 1962, J.D., 1965. Trust officer Continental Bank, Chgo., 1965; sole practice, Chgo., 1966—. Served with U.S. Army, 1956-59. Mem. ABA, Ill. State Bar Assn., Baltic League Lawyers (pres.), Jurists, Phi Delta Phi. Lutheran. Office: 7 S Dearborn St Suite 1440 Chicago IL 60603

LAJOIE, WILLIAM R., professional baseball executive. Vice-pres., gen. mgr. Detroit Tigers. Office: Detroit Tigers Tiger Stadium Detroit MI 48216*

LAKIN, DUANE EDWARD, industrial psychologist; b. St. Joseph, Mo., Feb. 22, 1948; s. Edward Daniel and Margaret Evelyn (Gregory) L.; m. Melanie Catherine Gimbut, Mar. 16, 1969; 1 child, Jennifer Elizabeth. B.A. in Psychology, U. Minn., 1970, Ph.D. in Psychology in Schs. Tng. Program, 1978. Evaluation dir. Lake Minnetonka Mental Health Ctr., Minn., 1974-78; cons. psychologist, v.p. Mgmt. Psychologists, Inc., Chgo., 1978-80; pres. Lakin Assocs., Chgo., 1980—. Composer: (song book) Get It Together, 1970; author book chpt., articles. Mem. adv. bd. Sisters of St. Joseph, LaGrange, Ind., 1984—. Mem. Am. Psychol. Assn., Am. Prodn. and Inventory Control Soc. Home: 2105 Willow Run Wheaton IL 60187 Office: Lakin Assocs 20 N Wacker Dr Suite 1828 Chicago IL 60606

LAKSHMINARAYANAN, KRISHNAIYER, microbiologist, corporate executive; b. Bikshandarkoil, Madras, India, July 5, 1924; came to U.S., 1967; s. Valadi and Muthulakshmi (Ammal) K.; m. Kamakshi Ramaiya, May 2, 1960; children—Gayathri, Venkatesh. M.Sc., U. Madras, 1950, Ph.D., 1956. Project leader John Labatt Ltd., London, Ont., Can., 1961-67; dir. research and devel. Dawe's Lab. Inc., Harbor Beach, Mich., 1967-71; mgr. process devel. Searle Biochemics, Arlington Heights, Ill., 1971-76; pres. Bio-Tech. Inc., Bensenville, Ill., 1976—; hon. lectr. U. West Ont., London, 1963-67. Patentee indsl. fermentations. Fellow Nat. Inst. Scis. India, 1955-56, Nat. Research Council Can., 1956-58. Fellow Royal Inst. Chemistry, Chem. Inst. Can. Home: 1310 N Belmont Ave Arlington Heights IL 60004 Office: Bio-Tech Inc 692 Industrial Dr Bensenville IL 60106

LAMB, GAIL APPIANI, counseling service administrator, educator, psychotherapist; b. Medford, Mass., Jan. 5, 1943; d. Leo Armando and Alice Harriet (Tarr) Appiani; m. Douglas Hart Lamb, Aug. 20, 1966; children—David Scott Rogers, Deborah Tarr. B.S., Bridgewater State Coll., 1964; M.A., Ohio U., 1966. Dir. residence Osceola Hall, Fla. State U., Tallahassee, 1966-67; counselor residence Woman's Coll. Duke U., Durham, N.C., 1967-68; dir. counseling services Mennonite Hosp. Sch. Nursing, Bloomington, Ill., 1978-83, Mennonite Coll. Nursing, Bloomington, 1983—, asst. prof., 1983—; pvt. practice psychotherapy, Bloomington, 1983—. Developed 8 courses on personal growth for nursing schools, 1978-80. Mem. McClean County Mental Health Assn., Am. Assn. Counseling and Devel., Ill. Assn. Counseling and Devel. (editorial bd. 1983—, chmn. govt. relations 1984—), Am. Coll. Personnel Assn., Ill. Coll. Personnel Assn. Avocations: home remodeling, jogging, yoga. Office: Mennonite Coll Nursing 804 N East St Bloomington IL 61701

LAMBDIN, WILLIAM CHARLES, electrical company executive, consultant; b. Elkhart, Ind., June 18, 1943; s. Cecil Curtis and Dorothy May (Markel) L.; m. Ann Kathleen Miller, Aug. 25, 1944; children—Laura Ann, Thad Philip, Amanda Ruth. B.S.I.M., Purdue U., 1968. Sales engr. Gen. Electric Co., York, Pa., 1969-72, mgr. strategy devel., Ft. Wayne, Ind., 1972-76, nat. acctg. exec., Grand Rapids, Mich., 1976-78, mgr. sales and internat., Holland, Mich., 1978-83, mgr. programs, Tyler, Tex., 1983—, adviser GATT negotiations, N.Y.C., 1972-74. Recipient Pub. Service award Am. Radio Relay League, West Hartford, Conn., 1966; Recognition award Purdue U., 1968; Best. Bus. Planner award Gen. Electric Co., 1972, Holt Mktg. award, 1977, Quest award, 1984. Mem. Elfun Soc. Republican. Baptist. Home: 7206 Pinetree Pl Tyler TX 75703 Office: Gen Electric Co 5620 Old Bullard St Suite 121 Tyler TX 75703

LAMBERT, CARL FREDERICK (NICK), risk management executive; b. Kansas City, Mo., Sept. 29, 1932; s. Carl Frederick and Genevieve Elizabeth (Corbin) L.; m. Mary Jo Lee, Dec. 2, 1961 (div. Feb. 1977); children—Corbin F., Bryan J. Student U. Va., 1950-53. Participant internat. yacht racing, Fla., Cuba, 1954; life ins. salesman and mgr., regional dist. mgr. Equitable Life Assurance Soc., Lakeland, Fla., 1968-72; v.p. Consol. Investors Life Assurance Co., Coral Gables, Fla., 1972-76; mgr. safety and compliance Hannah Marine Corp., Lemont, Ill., 1977-82; mgr. loss control/loss prevention Canonie, Inc., Muskegon, Mich., 1982—. Served to maj. SAC, USAF, 1955-68. Mem. Am. Soc. Marine Artists, Midwest Watercolor Soc. Club: Propeller of U.S. (1st v.p. Port of Chicago 1982-83). Home: 575 Lake Forest Ln Apt L-10 Muskegon MI 49441 Office: 559 E Western Ave Muskegon MI 49443

LAMBERT, JONATHAN ROY, engineering technology educator, industrial consultant; b. Quincy, Ill., Oct. 11, 1951; s. Lavern F. and Patricia J. Lambert; m. Deborah A. Doehler. A.A.S. in Engring. Tech., Black Hawk Coll., 1971; B.S. in Engring. Tech., Bradley U., 1973. Quality control engr. Motorola Inc., 1974-75; chief engr. Sta. WQPT-TV, 1975-77; instr. engring. tech. dept. Black Hawk Coll., Moline, Ill., 1977-80, lead instr., 1980—; instrument and control system cons. to local industries. Mem. Am. Soc. Engring. Educators, Instrument Soc. Am. (sr.). Home: 2221 Barnard Ct Moline IL 61265 Office: Black Hawk Coll 6600 34th Ave Moline IL 61265

LAMBERT, JOSEPH BUCKLEY, chemistry educator; b. Ft. Sheridan, Ill., July 4, 1940; s. Joseph Idus and Elizabeth Dorothy (Kirwan) L.; m. Mary Wakefield Pulliam, June 27, 1967; children—Laura Kirwan, Alice Pulliam, Joseph Cannon. B.S., Yale U., 1962; Ph.D., Calif. Inst. Tech., 1965. Asst. prof. Northwestern U., Evanston, Ill., 1965-69, assoc. prof., 1969-74, prof., 1974—; dir. integrated sci. program, 1982-85 vis. assoc. British Museum, 1973; Nat. Acad. Scis. exchange fellow to Poland, 1985. Polish Acad. Sci. vis. scholar, 1981; recipient Nat. Fresenius award, 1976; Guggenheim fellow, 1973; Alfred P. Sloan fellow, 1968-70. Fellow AAAS, Brit. Interplanetary Soc., Japan Soc. Promotion Sci.; mem. Ill. Acad. Sci., Internat. Soc. Magnetic Resonance, Soc. of Archaeol. Scis., Am. Chem. Soc., Royal Soc. Chemistry, Phi Beta Kappa,

Sigma Xi. Author: Organic Structural Analysis, 1976; Physical Organic Chemistry Through Solved Problems, 1978; The Heteronuclear Approach to NMR Spectroscopy, 1983; Archaeological Chemistry III, 1984; others; contbr. articles to profl. jours. Home: 1956 Linneman St Glenview IL 60025 Office: Dept Chemistry Northwestern Univ Evanston IL 60201

LAMBERT, LECLAIR GRIER, arts administrator, writer, lecturer; b. Miami, Fla., s. George F. and Maggie (Grier) L.; B.S., Hampton Inst., 1959; postgrad. Harvard U., 1959, U. Munich (Germany), 1965-66. Researcher, copy reader Time-Life Books, 1961-64; tchr. biology and Eng. lit., secondary level U.S. Dependent's Schs. Overseas, Tripoli, Libya, 1964-65; biology editor of high sch. textbooks Holt, Rinehart & Winston, N.Y.C., 1966-69; biology editor and writer Ency. Britannica, N.Y.C., 1969; copy editor Russian sci. monographs The Faraday Press, N.Y.C., 1970-71; writer Med. World News, N.Y.C., 1971; pub. relations writer Nat. Found./March of Dimes, White Plains, N.Y., 1972; lectr. community and human relations, Black cultural heritage at local schs. and colls., 1977—; radio commentator Sta. KEEY, 1975—; reporter Twin Cities Courier, Mpls., 1976—; free lance writer and designer of brochures and pamphlets, 1974—; dir. communications St. Paul Urban League, 1972-80, asst. to exec. dir., 1977-80; exec. dir. African Am. Mus. Art and History, 1980—; info. officer Mpls. Urban League, 1978-79. Founder, bd. dirs. Summit-University Free Press, 1974—; bd. dirs. H.E.A.R.T., 1978—; adv. bd. Concordia Coll. Minority Program, 1979—, U. Minn. Black Learning Resource Center, 1980-83; mem. Twin Cities Cable Arts Consortium, Roy Wilkins Meml. Com., St. Paul; mem. state meml. com. Martin Luther King; mem. Ethiopian Famine Relief Com.; mem. rev. com. Twin Cities Mayors' Public Art Awards, 1981. Served to 1st lt., Chem. Corps., U.S. Army, 1959-61. Recipient Community Martin Luther King Communications award, 1978; spl. recognition award Mpls. St. Acad., 1983; spl. achievement award Roosevelt High Sch., 1985. Mem. Pub. Relations Soc. Am., Twin Cities Black Journalists Assn., African-Am. Mus. Assn. (nat. legis. edn. com. 1983, exec. council, Midwest region rep. 1984-87). Club: Minn. Press. Author: Reflections of Life-Poems, Prose and Essays, 1981; editor, writer: Minnesota's Black Community, 1977. Office: 2429 S 8th St Minneapolis MN 55454

LAMBERT, SUSAN SHEA, book-search service manager; b. Corona, Calif., Apr. 22, 1954; d. E. Roy Wilson and Virginia Merrill (Mitchell) Mongno; m. Stephen Knowlton Lambert, Feb. 15, 1975; children—Jennifer Ann, Stephen K., II. Lic. realtor. Sec. Hobart Corp., Greenville, Ohio, 1976-77; salesman Beavercreek Realty, Dayton, Ohio, 1980-82, Ann Burns Real Estate, Greenville, 1981—; exercise instr. Greenville YMCA, 1985—; owner, mgr. Dormant Inventory Clearing House, Greenville, 1983-84, A Book Search by Susan, Greenville, 1983—. Author promotional articles and newsletter. Vice pres. PTA, Gettysburg, Ohio, 1984-85. Avocations: piano; needlepoint; snow skiing; tennis; racquetball. Office: A Book Search by Susan 8050 US Route 127 N Greenville OH 45331

LAMBETH, DAVID ODUS, biochemistry educator; b. Carthage, Mo., June 16, 1941; s. James O. and Jewell (Rosebrough) L.; m. Sharon Oldham, Dec. 1, 1962; children—Gregory Scott, Judith Christine. B.S., U. Mo., 1962; M.S., Purdue U., 1967; Ph.D., U. Wis., 1971. Chemistry tchr. Hickman High Sch., Columbia, Mo., 1962-67; NIH fellow U. Mich., Ann Arbor, 1971-73; asst. prof. biochemistry U. South Fla., Tampa, 1973-77; prof. U. N.D., Grand Forks, 1977—. Contbr. articles to profl. jours. Mem. Am. Soc. Biol. Chemists, Am. Chem. Soc., Sigma Xi, Pi Lambda Upsilon, Pi Mu Epsilon. Avocations: birds, photography, travel. Home: 1909 20th Ave S Grand Forks ND 58201 Office: U ND Dept Biochemistry Grand Forks ND 58202

LAMBO, MICHELE DIANE, interior designer; b. Jackson, Mich., June 13, 1951; d. Angelo Marko and Florence (Petroff) L. Student Jackson Community Coll., 1970-71; B.A. in Interior Design, Mich. State U., 1975; postgrad. Bowling Green State U., 1978—. With Jacobson's Furniture Galleria, Ann Arbor, Mich., 1976, interior designer, salesperson, Toledo, 1976-77; tchr., coordinator Rogers High Sch., Toledo, 1977-78; interior designer, salesperson Johnson's Fine Furniture, Toledo, 1978-79; interior designer, draftsperson Crown Store Equipment Co., Holland, Ohio, 1980—; cons. interior design Weight Watchers, Inc., Lansing, Mich., 1984-85, others; lectr. in field. Dancer, Lansing Ballet Co., Mich., 1972-75, Kitka Dance Ensemble, Toledo, 1977-82, Toledo Sch. Ballet, 1980—; vol. Am. Cancer Soc., Toledo, 1985, Epilepsy Ctr. Northwest Ohio, 1985; blood donor ARC, 1971—. Jackson County Rosequeen Pageant scholar, 1971, 72; Toledo Sch. Ballet scholar, 1983. Mem. Am. Soc. Interior Designers, Inst. Bus. Designers. Club: Ladies Guild (pres. 1983-85). Avocations: dancing; sewing; singing; running; skiing; swimming. Address: 319 Dulton Dr Toledo OH 43615-5106

LAMBOWITZ, ALAN MARC, biochemistry educator; b. Bklyn., Dec. 24, 1947; s. Michael Peter and Eva (Feldman) L.; m. Sheila Helene Mintz, Dec. 24, 1968. B.S., Bklyn. Coll., 1968; M. Philosophy, Yale U., 1970, Ph.D., 1972. Postdoctoral fellow U. Pa., Phila., 1972-73; research assoc. Rockefeller U., N.Y.C., 1973-75; sr. staff fellow NIH, Bethesda, Md., 1975-76; asst., then assoc. prof. St. Louis U., 1976-82, prof. biochemistry, 1982—; with molecular biology study sect. NIH, 1982—; with policy com. Neurospora, 1982—; cons. and sci. adv. bd. Panlabs Internat., Seattle, 1983—. Contbr. articles to profl. jours. Patentee in field. Grantee NIH, NSF, March of Dimes, Mem. Am. Soc. Microbiology, Am. Soc. Cell Biology, Sigma Xi, Phi Beta Kappa. Office: St Louis Med Sch 1402 S Grand Blvd St Louis MO 63104

LAMBRECHT, MARGE ANN, public relations administrator; b. Rock Island, Ill., July 15, 1949; d. Jack L. and Darlene (Langford) Simpson. B.A. cum laude, Augustana Coll., 1974. Staff writer The Daily Dispatch, Moline, Ill., 1974-77; dir. communications United Way of Rock Island, Ill., 1980—. Producer-dir.: (films) Winners, 1982; Reach Out, 1983; Better Tomorrow, 1984; Through Rain, 1985; coordinator: (multi-media) It's An Uphill Climb, 1984; Fitness: Feel it!, 1985 Dir. pub. relations Quad City Music Guild, 1984—; bd. dirs. Quad City Arts Council, 1984—; promotions coordinator Fit Fest, Davenport, Iowa, 1984-85. Recipient first place, Feature Stories, Ill. Press Assn., Dorothy Dawe award Chgo. Mart, 1975, 76, Pub. Relations award for merit and art, 1983; best of show-best of pub. relations award, Quad City Advt. Club, 1982. Mem. Pub. Relations Soc. Am. (N.P. Quad Cities chpt. 1983, bd. dirs.). Avocations: Piano, arts activities, travel. Office: United Way of the Quad Cities Area 1705 2d Ave Rock Island IL

LAMBROS, THOMAS DEMETRIOS, U.S. judge; b. Ashtabula, Ohio, Feb. 4, 1930; s. Demetrios P. and Panagoula (Bellios) L.; student Fairmount (W.Va.) State Coll., 1948-49; LL.B., Cleveland-Marshall Law Sch., 1952; m. Shirley R. Kresin, June 20, 1953; children—Lesley P., Todd T. Admitted to Ohio bar, 1952; partner firm Lambros and Lambros, Ashtabula. 1952-60: judge Ct. Common Pleas, Jefferson, Ohio, 1960-67; judge U.S. Dist. Ct., No. Dist. Ohio, Cleve., 1967—; mem. faculty Fed. Jud. Center. Mem. exec. bd. N.E. Ohio council Boy Scouts Am.; pres. Ashtabula county chpt. National Found. Served with U.S. Army, 1954-56. Recipient Disting. Service award Ashtabula Jr. C. of C., 1962; Outstanding Young Man of Ohio award Ohio Jaycees, 1963 Man of Yr. award Delta Theta Phi, 1969; Outstanding Alumnus award Cleveland Marshall Coll. of Law, 1974. Fellow Internat. Acad. Law and Sci.; mem. Am., Ohio, Ashtabula County (past pres.) bar assns., Atty. Gen. Advocacy Inst. Contbr. articles legal publs.; innovator of summary jury trial. Office: US Dist Ct 106 US Courthouse Cleveland OH 44114*

LAMELAS, GUSTAVE FELIX, accountant; b. Havana, Cuba, Feb. 21, 1930; came to U.S., 1965, naturalized, 1970; s. Francisco Jose and Blanca Maria (Blanco) L.; m. Martha A. Fernandez, July 12, 1964; children—Gustavo, Peter. M.B.A., Havana U., Cuba; postgrad. Mich. U., Dominican Coll., U. Wis.-Milw. C.P.A., Cuba. Gen. ptnr. C.P.A. firm, Havana, 1951-61; pres. Laboratorios Rea, SA, Havana, 1954-64; corporate acct. J. E. Case, Racine, Wis., 1965-67; asst. controller Aqua-Chem., Inc., Milw., 1968-71; controller Arco Wheel, Inc., West Allis, Wis., 1971-75; acctg. mgr. Milw. County, 1975—. Gen. chairperson Hispanics Internat. Inst. Milw. Holiday Folk Fair, 1980-84. Mem. Nat. Assn. Accts. Republican. Roman Catholic. Clubs: Spanish (Milw.) (bd. dirs. 1983-84), Village (Greendale, Wis.,). Avocations: reading, walking, swimming. Home: 2314 W Manchester Ave Milwaukee WI 53221 Office: Dept Social Services Milwaukee County 1220 W Vliet St Milwaukee WI 53205

LAMKA, PHILIP CHARLES, broadcasting company executive; b. El Reno, Okla., Feb. 10, 1947; s. Charles Edwin and Ardelle (Johns) L.; m. Sharman Stewart, Nov. 14, 1981; children by previous marriage—Michael Charles, Philip Glenn. Sales rep. William H. Rorer Pharms., Houston, 1970-73; acct. exec. Sta. KYOK, Houston, 1973-76, local sales mgr., 1977-80; acct. exec. Sta. KLYX, Houston, 1976-77; gen. mgr. Sta. WBOK, New Orleans, 1980-81; gen. mgr. Sta. WWWW, Detroit, 1981—. Mem. Nat. Radio Broadcasters Assn., Nat. Assn. Broadcasters, Mich. Assn. Broadcasters, Detroit Radio Broadcasting Group. Club: Detroit Yacht. Office: 2930 E Jefferson St Detroit MI 48207

LAMMERS, JOSEPH EDWIN, hospital executive; b. Archie, Mo., July 28, 1935; s. Melvin Edwin and Emma Victoria L.; m. Dorothy L. Howe, Sept. 14, 1957; children—Sean, Elizabeth, Kristen. B.S., Central Mo. State U., 1957. Office mgr. Firestone Tire and Rubber Co., Independence, Mo., 1957-60; area mktg. mgr. Phillips Petroleum Co., San Francisco, 1960-70; asst. adminstr. Independence (Mo.) Sanitarium and Hosp., 1970-79, exec. dir., 1979—; dir. Blue Cross, Profl. Standards Rev. Orgn. Bd. dirs. YMCA, 1982; pres. Am. Cancer Soc., 1979. Served with U.S. Army, 1958. Mem. Am. Hosp. Assn., Kansas City Hosp. Assn. (treas., chmn. bd. dirs. 1985—), Am. Coll. Hosp. Adminstrs., Mo. Hosp. Assn. (bd. dirs.), Am. Protestant Hosp. Assn., Independence C. of C. (bd. dirs. 1979—, div. v.p. 1980-82; chmn.-elect 1985—). Mem. Reorganized Ch. of Jesus Christ of Latter-day Saints (ordained minister). Lodge: Kiwanis (pres. 1977) (Independence). Home: 3324 Phelps Rd Independence MO 64055 Office: 1509 W Truman Rd Independence MO 64050

LAMMERS, NICK JAY, sales executive; b. Loup City, Nebr., Aug. 13, 1953; s. Donald Ray and Erma Louise (Luce) L.; m. Patricia Lee Bernet, May 28, 1972; children—Deena, Kylee, Chelsie. B.S. in Agr. with distinction, U. Nebr., 1975, M.S., 1977. Tchr. vocat. agr. Sutton Pub. Schs., Nebr., 1975-77, Wood River Rural High Sch., Nebr., 1977-80; dist. sales mgr. Stauffer Seeds, Inc., Phillips, Nebr., 1980-81, regional sales mgr., 1981—. Vice pres. Wood River Elem. Sch. Bd., 1983, pres., 1984. Named Outstanding Young Educator, Nebr. Vocat. Agr. Tchrs. Assn., 1979. Mem. Nat. Agrl. Mktg. Assn. Lutheran. Lodge: Lions. Avocations: computers; hunting; fishing; camping. Home: 1411 Lilley St Wood River NE 68883 Office: Stauffer Seeds Phillips NE 68865

LAMMERS, THOMAS DEAN, lawyer; b. Celina, Ohio, Oct. 19, 1951; s. Calvin Dean and Dorothy (Gilmore) L.; m. Kimberly Sue Stubbs, Mar. 18, 1980. Village solicitor Villages of Fort Recovery and Montezuma, Ohio, 1978—; ptnr. Purdy, Hogan & Lammers, Celina, 1980—; adj. prof. bus. law Wright State U., Dayton, Ohio, 1982—. Chmn. Sesqicentennial Com. Celina, 1984; bd. dirs. Tri-County Mental Health Bd., Celina, 1977-83, Mercer County Hospice, Inc. Mem. Mercer County Bar Assn. (treas. 1983-85, v.p. 1985—), Ohio Bar Assn. (del. 1984-85), Phi Delta Phi. Democrat. Lutheran. Lodge: Rotary (pres. Celina 1984-85). Home: 1009 Lilac St Celina OH 45822 Office: Purdy Hogan & Lammers 113 E Market PO Box 404 Celina OH 45822

LAMMERT, LELAND VAL, system consultant; b. Portland, Oreg., Jan. 6, 1955; s. Valentine Frank and Louise Marie (Gerfe) L.; B.S.E.E., U. Mo., 1976; M.S.E.E., So. Meth. U., 1979; Ph.D., Calif. Western U., 1982; m. Nancy Jane Wright, May 6, 1978. Design engr. Tex. Instruments, Sherman, Tex., 1977-79; sr. systems engr. Emerson Electric, St. Louis, 1979-82; pres. Omnitec Corp., St. Louis, 1980—, System Research Assocs., St. Louis, 1982-84, Omnitec Ventures Corp., 1983—; propr. Orion Systems, Creve Coeur, Mo., 1981-83; v.p. MLD Computer Services, St. Louis, 1982—; exec. dir. Triad Found., 1985—. Mem. Ind. Computer Cons. Assn., IEEE, ACM, Am. Entrepreneurs Assn., Nat. Soc. Profl. Engrs., Mo. Soc. Profl. Engrs., Sigma Xi. Contbr. articles to profl. jours. Address: PO Box 12747 Saint Louis MO 63141

LAMONICA, JOHN ANTHONY, financial analyst; b. Chgo., May 21, 1951; s. John A. and Dorothy (Marth) LaM.; m. Mary F. Dibelka, June 21, 1975; children—Drake Edward, Trent Peter. B.S., Ohio State U., 1973; M.B.A., DePaul U., 1982. Retail store mgr. Goodyear Tire and Rubber Co., 1974-77; sales adminstr. SCM/Durkee Foods, 1977-81, budget analyst, 1981-83; fin. analyst Am. Hosp. Assn., Chgo., 1983-85, sr. fin. analyst, 1985—. Home: 434 Provident Ave Winnetka IL 60093 Office: Am Hosp Assn 840 N Lake Shore Dr Chicago IL 60611

LA MOTHE, WILLIAM E., food manufacturing company executive; b. Bklyn., 1926; B.S., Fordham U. With Kellogg Co., Inc., Battle Creek, Mich., 1950—, v.p. and asst. to pres., 1962-65, v.p. corp. devel., 1965-70, sr. v.p. corp. devel., 1970-72, exec. v.p. ops., 1972-73, pres., chief operating officer, 1972-81, chief exec. officer, 1980—, chmn. bd., 1981—, also dir. Office: Kellogg Co Inc 235 Porter St PO Box 3423 Battle Creek MI 49016*

LAMOUREUX, GERARD WILLIAM, container manufacturing company executive; b. Chgo., July 27, 1946; s. Donald Benjamin and Anna Rita (Williamson) L.; B.S. in Mech. Engring. Tech., Purdue U., 1970; m. Gloria Jean Kempa, Feb. 13, 1971; children—Gerard Joseph, Jennifer Ann, Brian Gerard. Design draftsman Whiting Corp., Harvey, Ill., 1967-69; plant engr. DeSoto, Inc., Chicago Heights, Ill., 1970-74; maintenance mgr. Panduit Corp., Tinley Park, Ill., 1974-75; plant engr., plant supt. Container Corp. Am., Dolton, Ill., 1975-79, plant engr., Anderson, Ind., 1979-84, sr. staff engr., Carol Stream, Ill., 1984—. Mem. mech. adv. bd. Thornton Community Coll., South Holland, Ill., 1975-79. Mem. South Holland United Fund-Crusade of Mercy Com., 1976-78; bd. dirs. Madison County Jr. Achievement, 1980-83. Mem. Am. Inst. Plant Engrs., Madison County Mgmt. Club (v.p. 1984), TAPPI, Anderson Jaycees, Anderson YMCA, Christian Fellowship Businessmen, Full Gospel Businessmen's Fellowship Internat., Purdue U. Alumni Assn., South Holland Jaycees (pres. 1978-79, state dir. 1976-77). Roman Catholic. Home: 505 Longmeadow Circle Saint Charles IL 60174 Office: 500 E North Ave Carol Stream IL 60188

LAMP, WILLIAM OWEN, entomologist; b. Omaha, June 19, 1951; s. Donald George and Marjorie (Knpp) L.; m. Josephine Ann Smith, May 19, 1973; children—Thomas Smith, Kathryn Ann. B.S., U. Nebr., 1973; Ph.D., 1980; M.S., Ohio State U., 1976. Teaching asst. Ohio State U., Columbus, 1974-76; research asst. U. Nebr., Lincoln, 1977-80; asst. profl. scientist Ill. Natural History Survey, Champaign, 1980—. Contbr. articles to profl. jours. Mem. Entomol. Soc. Am., Weed Sci. Soc. Am., Central States Entomol. Soc., North Central Entomol. Soc. (Grad. Student award 1980). Home: 1107 W Charles Champaign IL 61821 Office: Illinois Natural History Survey 607 E Peabody Champaign IL 61820

LAMPING, WILLIAM JAY, lawyer; b. Detroit, Aug. 27, 1954; s. William Jay and Marilyn Alice (Welsand) L.; m. Kathryn Szczepanik, July 18, 1981; children—Elizabeth, Jacqueline. B.S., U. Mich., 1976; J.D., Wayne State U., 1979. Bar: Mich. 1979, U.S. Dist. Ct. (ea. dist.) Mich. 1979, U.S. Ct. Appeals (6th cir.) 1981. Research asst. Law Sch., Wayne State U., Detroit, 1978-79; clk. Wayne County Cir. Ct., Detroit, 1979-80; assoc. Kiefer, Allen, Cavanagh & Toohey, Detroit, 1980-82; ptnr. Fieger, Fieger & Lamping, Southfield, Mich., 1982-84, William J. Lamping, P.C., Birmingham, Mich., 1984—; ptnr. Woodward Fin. Services Group, Birmingham, 1984—; arbitrator Better Bus. Bur., Detroit, 1981. Mem. steering com. Ann Arbor Tenants Union, Mich., 1976. Nat. Merit scholar U. Mich., Ann Arbor, 1972. Mem. ABA, State Bar Mich. (unauthorized practice of law com.), Assn. Trial Lawyers Am., Mich. Trial Lawyers Assn., Detroit Bar Assn. Democrat. Roman Catholic. Club: Detroit Yacht. Lodge: Optimists. Home: 34209 Banbury Farmington Hills MI 48018 Office: William J Lamping PC 401 S Woodward Suite 430 Birmingham MI 48011

LAMPKY, JAMES ROBERT, bacteriology and mycology educator; b. Battle Creek, Mich., June 19, 1927; s. Howell Clayton and Viva Fay (McNally) L.; m. Shirley Ann Kellett, Dec. 28, 1971; children—Dawne, Diane, Judi, Lynda, Richard, Mark. B.S., Eastern Mich. U., 1955-59; M.A., U. Mo., 1961, Ph.D., 1966. Asst. prof. U. Wis.-Whitewater, 1962-66; from asst. prof. to prof. bacteriology and mycology Central Mich. U., Mt. Pleasant, 1966—. Contbr. articles to profl. jours. Fungal identification person Western Mich. Poison Control Ctr., Grand Rapids, 1978—. Served with U.S. Army, 1945-46. Mem. Am. Soc. Microbiology, Mich. Acad., Mycol. Soc., Soc. Indsl. Microbiology. Avocations: golfing, hunting, fishing, fine furniture making. Home: 1016 E Preston Rd Mount Pleasant MI 48858 Office: Central Michigan Univ Biology Dept Mount Pleasant MI 48859

LAMPORT, DEREK THOMAS ANTHONY, plant biochemist; b. Brighton, Eng., Dec. 1, 1933; came to U.S., 1961, naturalized; s. Henry Thomas and Laura Anna (Tune) L.; m. Inez JoAnn Daly, June 1, 1963; children—Laura, Derek, Victoria, Christopher, Joseph. B.A., U. Cambridge, Eng., 1958, Ph.D., 1963. Staff scientist Research Inst. for Advanced Studies, Balt., 1961-64; from asst. prof. to prof. Mich State U. Plant Research Lab., East Lansing, 1964—. Contbr. articles to profl. jours. Guggenheim fellow, 1976. Mem. Am. Soc. Biol. Chemists, Am. Soc. Plant Physiologists, Am. Chem. Soc. Avocations: gardening, running, opera, chess. Home: 762 W Columbia Rd Mason MI 48854 Office: Mich State U Plant Research Lab East Lansing MI 48824

LAMSON, GEORGE HERBERT, economics educator, researcher; b. Hartford, Conn., Feb. 21, 1940; s. Arroll and Marguerite (Brechbuhler) L.; m. Susan Kathryn Lippert, Sept. 7, 1968; children—Scott, Brandon. A.B., Princeton U., 1963; M.A., Northwestern U., 1966, Ph.D., 1971. Research asst. Northwestern U. Econ. Survey of Liberia, Monrovia, 1962-63; instr. dept. econs. Loyola U., Chgo., 1967-68, U. Conn., Storrs, 1968-69; asst. prof. dept. econ. Carleton Coll., Northfield, Minn., 1969-76, assoc. prof. 1976-80, prof., chmn., Williams prof. econs., 1980—; cons. Minn. High Edn. Coordinating Bd., St. Paul, 1971-72; textbook reviewer John Wiley & Son, N.Y.C., 1979-82. Author: (with others) Africa: From Political to Economic Independence, 1973, Income-Contingent Loans, 1972. Recipient Faculty Devel. award NSF, 1979; Internat. Studies fellow, Northwestern U., 1966-67. Mem. Am. Econ. Assn., Minn. Econ. Assn. (pres. 1983-84). Republican. Home: 614 E 5th St Northfield MN 55057 Office: Dept Econs Carleton Coll Northfield MN 55057

LAN, CHUAN-TAU EDWARD, aerospace engineering educator; b. Kangshan, China, Apr. 21, 1935; came to U.S., 1961, naturalized, 1972; s. Tu-sen and Tsai-mei Lan; m. Sumy Chen, Feb. 12, 1961; children—Susan, Justin, Austin. B.S., Nat. Taiwan U., 1958; M.S., U. Minn., 1963; Ph.D., NYU, 1968. Asst. engr. N.Y.C. Bd. Water Supply, 1963-65; asst. prof. dept. aerospace engring. U. Kans., Lawrence, 1968-74, assoc. prof., 1974-78, prof., 1978—; prin. investigator Ctr. for Research, Inc., Lawrence, 1972—. Author: Airplane Aerodynamics and Performance, 1981. Contbr. articles to profl. jours. NASA grantee, 1972—. Fellow AIAA (assoc.); mem. Sigma Gamma Tau, Tau Beta Pi. Avocation: classical music. Home: 3328 W 8th St Lawrence KS 66044 Office: U Kans Dept Aerospace Engring Lawrence KS 66045

LANCASTER, NORMAN THOMAS, design draftsman; b. Winfield, Kans., Aug. 8, 1940; s. Charles Freeman and Ida Bernice (Beloit) L.; m. Carla Slaton Payne, Aug. 16, 1974; 1 child, Georgia Lynn. Cert. computer aid design operator. Adminstrv. tech. Kans. Army N.G., Winfield, Kans., 1972-73; foreman Tweco Products, Wichita, Kans., 1973-75; draftsman Uniflo Conveyor, Wichita, 1977-78; elec. draftsman, Cessna, Wichita, 1978-80; design draftsman Boeing, Wichita, 1980—; advisor Wichita Vocat. Tech. Sch., 1980—. Mem. Nat. Republican Senatorial Com., Washington, 1983. Served with U.S. Army, 1972-75. Mem. AIAA. Baptist. Avocations: computers; reading; hunting; fishing; shooting. Home: 5100 S Kansas Wichita KS 67216

LANDAZURI, COLLEEN ANN, public health nurse; b. Fond du Lac, Wis., Sept. 8, 1950; d. James Edward and Elizabeth Ann (Masloff) Flood; m. Gabriel Landazuri, Oct. 26, 1974; children—Dario James, Patrick Xavier, Alexander Gabriel. B.S. in Nursing, Marquette U., 1972, postgrad., 1976-77. Staff nurse Nursing Bur., Milw. Health Dept., 1972-75, Lady Pitts program nurse, 1975-76, dist. supr., 1976-80, dir. prenatal edn. and assessment program, 1980—; fed. nurse trainee, 1976-77, coordinator interdisciplinary dental and nursing student program Marquette U. Sch. Dentistry, 1976-77. Mem. Greater Milw. Com. for Unmarried Parent's Services, 1980—, vice co-chmn., 1985; mem. critical health problems curriculum adv. com. Milw. Pub. Schs., 1980—, chmn., 1982-84; mem. adv. com., sch. aged parents program Lady Pitts Ctr., 1980—; mem. adv. com. Family Hosp. Teen Pregnancy Service, 1984—, nurse adv. com. March of Dimes, 1985—. Mem. Life Options Coalition, Orgn. Twin-Blessed Mothers (sec. 1984), Sigma Theta Tau. Roman Catholic. Home: 3368 N 44th St Milwaukee WI 53216 Office: 841 N Broadway Suite 228 Milwaukee WI 53202

LANDERS, CRAIG CLARK, medical administrator; b. Omaha, Aug. 29, 1957; s. Allan Campbell and Deneen Diane (Clark) L.; m. Julie Des Enfants, Dec. 29, 1979. B.A., Hastings Coll., 1979; M.S. in Pub. Health Adminstrn., U. Mo.-Columbia, 1982. Adminstrv. resident U. Mo. Med. Ctr., Columbia, 1980, fiscal analyst, 1980-81; asst. adminstr. Kneibert Clinic, Poplar Bluff, Mo., 1981—. Active U.S. Jaycees, Poplar Bluff, 1981—; com. mem. Am. Cancer Soc., Poplar Bluff, 1982—, bd. dirs. Am. Heart Assn., Poplar Bluff. Mem. Mo. Med. Group Mgmt. Assn.; assoc. mem. Med. Group Mgmt. Assn. Republican. Methodist. Avocations: racquetball; golf; biking; skiing; camping. Home: 744 Vine St Poplar Bluff MO 63901 Office: Kneibert Clinic 686 Lester Poplar Bluff MO 63901

LANDERS, RAY DANIEL, musician, author, composer, lecturer, educator; b. Kissimmee, Fla., Nov. 17, 1942; s. John Silvey and Jewel Oline (Fain) L.; Mus.B., Sherwood Conservatory of Music, 1964; Mus.M., Northwestern U., 1966; Mus.D., Ind. U., 1974. Assoc. instr. Sch. Music, Ind. U., 1966-71; instr. dept. music Chgo. State U., 1971-75, asst. prof., 1975-79, assoc. prof., 1979-80; founder, dir. Suzuki Music Acad. of Chgo., 1975—, Chicagoland Suzuki Music Festival, 1981—, Chgo. Summer Suzuki Inst., 1982—; mem. faculty Am. Suzuki Inst., U. Wis., 1976—; pianist, clinician, U.S., Can., Europe, Australia; participant Tchaikovsky Internat. Competition, Moscow, 1970, Vianna da Motta Competition, Lisbon, 1971, Rockefeller Competition for Excellence in Am. Music, Chgo., 1978; performed concertos with Sherwood Symphony Orch., Chgo. Chamber Orch., Ind. U. and Gold Coast orchs. Mem. Music Educators Nat. Conf., Music Tchrs. Nat. Assn., Ill. State Music Tchrs. Assn., Suzuki Assn. Americas (chmn. publ. com.). Composer numerous mus. compositions. Author: The Talent Education School of Shihichi Suzuki - An Analysis; Second Piano Accompaniments for Teachers and Students; Is Suzuki Education Working in America?; also articles. Home: 1560 N Sandburg Terr Apt 3504 Chicago IL 60610 Office: Suzuki Music Acad Chgo Fine Arts Bldg Suite 401 410 S Michigan Ave Chicago IL 60605

LANDFIELD, BARBARA JENSWOLD, editor, bookseller; b. Duluth, Minn., July 27, 1921; d. John Darrah and Marion M. (Townsend) Jenswold; m. Sidney Landfield, Feb. 27, 1945 (dec. Apr. 1977); children—Bruce, Susan, Scott, Robert. Student Mills Coll., 1939-40; B.A., U. Mich., 1943. Reporter, City News Bur., Chgo., 1943-44; asst. editor World Book Ency., Chgo., 1945-47; assoc. editor Am. Educator Ency., Lake Bluff, Ill., 1960-66; owner The Book Post, Duluth, Minn., 1971—; an editor Lake Superior Port Cities mag., Duluth, 1983—. Co-author: The Other Side of the Sheet, 1965. Mem. Kappa Kappa Gamma. Home: 2234 Woodland Ave Duluth MN 55803 Office: 325 Lake Ave S Duluth MN 55802

LANDHOLM, KATHY JO, pharmacist; b. Kansas City, Mo., Dec. 30, 1957; d. Joseph Enrod and Sonya Merline (Brink) L. D.Pharm., U. Nebr., 1981. Registered pharmacist, Nebr., Iowa. Pharmacy resident Univ. Heights Hosp., Albuquerque, 1981-82; clin./unit dose pharmacist U. Iowa Hosps. and Clinics, Iowa City, 1982—; cons. pharmacist Free Med. Clinic, Iowa City, 1982—; lectr. in field. Mem. Am. Soc. Hosp. Pharmacists, Iowa Soc. Hosp. Pharmacists, Nebr. Alumni Assn. Democrat. Presbyterian. Club: P.E.O. (Lexington, Nebr.). Avocations: skiing; weight lifting; swimming; expressive drawing; literature. Home: 80 Broadmeadows Blvd #5422 Columbus OH 43214 Office: U Iowa Hosps and Clinics Dept Pharmacy Newton Rd Iowa City IA 52242

LANDHUIS, LEO RAY, ophthalmologist, educator; b. Marshalltown, Iowa, Apr. 21, 1935; s. Cornelius and Dorothy Lois (Rolston) L.; m. Mary Alice Smith, June 29, 1957 (div. 1981); children—Louis Wayne, Mark David, Laura Ann, Mary Jane; m. Charlotte Kolb, Apr. 10, 1982. A.A., Northwestern Coll., Orange City, Iowa, 1954; B.S., McPherson Coll., 1969; M.D., State U. Iowa, 1959. Diplomate Am. Bd. Ophthalmology. Intern, Broadlawns Polk County Hosp., Des Moines, 1959-60; resident U. Mo. Sch. Medicine, Columbia, 1964-67; exec. com. Kersten Clinic, Fort Dodge, Iowa, 1963-64; med. examiner Webster County, Fort Dodge, 1963-64; head Lions Eye Tissue Bank, U. Mo., Columbia, 1966-74; v.p. Drs. Cheek and Landhuis Eye Cons., Columbia, 1970-80; med. dir. Lions Eye Bank, Eye Research Found. Mo., Columbia, 1973—; pres. Landhuis Ophthalmic Care, Ltd., Columbia Eye Cons., Columbia, 1980—; mem. staff Boone County Hosp., Columbia, 1969—, Columbia Regional Hosp., Columbia, 1974—; bd. govs. Eye Research Found. Mo., Ind., Columbia, 1973—; clin. prof. ophthalmology U. Mo., Sch. Medicine, Columbia, 1980—. Recipient Disting. Service award Northwestern Coll., 1983,; named Alumnus of Yr. Northwestern Coll., 1984. Fellow Am. Acad. Ophthalmology; mem. Mo. Ophthal. Soc., Eye Bank Assn. Am. (pres. 1979-80), Am. Intracoular Implant Soc., Midwest Corneal Assn., Castroviejo Soc., Boone County Med. Soc., Mo. State Med. Assn. Home: 3400 Woodrail Terr Columbia MO 65203 Office: Eye Research Found Mo 404 Portland St Columbia MO 65201

LANDINI, RICHARD GEORGE, university president; b. Pitts., June 4, 1929; s. George R. and Alice (Hoy) L.; A.B., U. Miami, 1954, M.A., 1956, LL.D.

(hon.), 1981; Ph.D., U. Fla., 1959; m. Phyllis Lesnick, Nov. 26, 1952; children—Richard, Gregory, Matthew, Cynthia, Vincent. Asst. prof. to prof. Ariz. State U., 1959-70, asst. dean grad. coll., 1965-67, dean Litchfield Coll., 1967-70, asst. to pres., 1968-70; prof. English U. Mont., 1970-75, acad. v.p., 1970-75; pres. Ind. State U., 1975—; pres. Ind. Partners of Americas, 1976-79; bd. dirs. Ind. Corp. Sci. and Tech. Served with U.S. Army, 1948-51. Mem. Am. Assn. Higher Edn., MLA, Nat. Council Tchrs. English, Am. Council on Edn. (com. on athletics), Ind. Conf. Higher Edn., Phi Beta Kappa, Phi Kappa Phi, Phi Alpha Theta, Sigma Tau Delta, Phi Delta Kappa, Beta Gamma Sigma. Roman Catholic. Contbr. in field. Office: President's Office Ind State Univ Terre Haute IN 47809

LANDIS, BRUCE RICHARD, optometrist; b. Monticello, Iowa, Dec. 28, 1954; s. Royal Richard and Verona Margaret (Kromminga) L.; m. Betty Ardis Roepke, Oct. 17, 1984; children—Adam Aric Larson, Bridget Ann Larson. B.S., U. Iowa, 1976; O.D., Ind. U., 1980. Lic. optometrist, Iowa. Gen. practice optometry, Elkader, Iowa, 1982—. Mem. Am. Optometric Assn., Iowa Optometric Assn., Upper Iowa Optometric Assn. (chmn. 1982—), Vol. Optometric Service to Humanity, Jaycees. Republican. Mem. United Ch. Christ. Lodge: Lions (sec. 1983—). Home: 409 2d St NW Elkader IA 52043 Office: PO Box 100 Elkader IA 52043

LANDIS, DAVID MORRISON, state legislator; b. Lincoln, Nebr., June 10, 1948; B.A., U. Nebr., Lincoln, 1970, J.D., 1971; m. Melodee Ann McPherson, June 6, 1969; children—Matthew, Melissa. Admitted to Nebr. bar, 1972; practice law, Lincoln, 1972-74; mem. Nebr. Legislature, 1978—; adj. faculty mem. dept. pub. adminstrn. U. Nebr., Omaha, 1984; adj. mem. bus. faculty Doane Coll., 1985—. Bd. dirs. Lower Platte S. Natural Resources Dist., 1977-78; officer PTA, 1979-80; adminstrv. law judge Dept. Labor, 1977-78. Home: Lincoln NE

LANDIS, GEORGE HARVEY, psychotherapist; b. Newton, Kans., Dec. 12, 1918; s. Melvin D. and Erie Emma (Byler) L.; student Baker U., 1937-38; B.A., John Fletcher Coll., 1941; M.S.W., U. Nebr., 1948; m. Lois I. Donaldson, Sept. 26, 1943; children—Judy Carol Landis Forsman, Richard G. Caseworker, Family Service of Omaha, 1948-50; psychotherapist Midwest Clinic, Omaha, 1950—. Served with U.S. Army, 1941-46. Mem. Acad. Cert. Social Workers, Registry Clin. Social Workers. Home: 4628 Hascall St Omaha NE 68106 Office: 105 S 49th St Omaha NE 68132

LANDIS, JAMES RAYMOND, data processing administrator; b. Rochelle, Ill., Nov. 9, 1955; s. Raymond James and Irene Modina (Woolbright) L.; m. Nancy Mary Lamermayer, Oct. 6, 1984; 1 child, Christina. Student Ill. State U., 1973-76, Troy State U., 1977-79; B.S., Northwestern Coll., Tulsa, 1981; postgrad. in bus. adminstrn. St. Ambrose Coll., 1984—; Cert. data processor. Programmer analyst 1st Nat. Bank, Louisville, 1979-80; sr. programmer analyst Nat. Bank & Trust Co., Sycamore, Ill., 1980-81; project mgr. Caron Internat., Rochelle, Ill., 1981-82; asst. dir. data processing Swiss Valley Farms Co., Mt. Joy, Iowa, 1982-83; data processing mgr. Davenport Community Sch Dist., Iowa, 1983—; ptnr., cons. Mgmt. Decision Systems, Davenport, 1984—. Trustee, Kishwaukee Community Coll., Malta, Ill., 1981-82. Served with USAF, 1976-79. Mem. Assn. Systems Mgmt. Republican. Roman Catholic. Club: Cornbelt Running. Avocations: long-distance running, golf. Home: 507 W 61st St Davenport IA 52806 Office: Davenport Community Sch Dist 1001 Harrison St Davenport IA 52803

LANDO, HARRY ALAN, psychology educator; b. New Haven, Conn., Sept. 6, 1946; s. Harry and Anne Lindsey (Wolf) L.; m. Lois Irene Hamilton, June 1, 1978; children—Elizabeth Anne, Ruth Ellen. B.A., George Washington U., 1968; Ph.D., Stanford U., 1973. Asst. prof. Iowa State U., Ames, 1972-77, assoc. prof., 1977-81, prof. psychology, 1981—; cons. Nat. Heart, Lung, Blood Inst., Bethesda, Md., 1979—, Nat. Inst. on Drug Abuse, Rockville, Md., 1982—. Contbr. chpts. to profl. jours. Co-campaign chmn. Hamilton for County Supr., Story County, Iowa, 1982; mem. Substance Abuse Adv. Bd., Ames, 1981-83; mem. smoking com. Lung Assn., Des Moines, 1981—, Heart Assn. Risk Factors Subcom., Des Moines, 1982—. Recipient Psi Chi psychology hon. award George Washington U., 1967; Stanford U. fellow, 1968, 71. Fellow Am. Psychol. Assn.; mem. Nat. Cancer Inst. (grant review com. 1983-87, cons. 1979—), AAAS, Sigma Xi (sci. hon.). Democrat. Home: 1303 Jefferson Ames IA 50010 Office: Iowa State U Dept Psychology Ames IA 50011

LANDON, ROGER J., utility company professional; b. Lansing, Mich., Aug. 25, 1949; s. John T. and Margaret Ella (Scott) L.; m. Deborah Elaine Staples, Dec. 11, 1971; children—Matthew R., Kevin R., Andrew R. B.S., Mich. State U., 1977, M.S., 1977. Cons. Snell Environ. Group, Lansing, Mich., 1974; assoc. planner, staff biologist Tri County Regional Planning Commn., Lansing, 1975-77; licensing engr. Gilbert Commonwealth, Jackson, Mich., 1977-79; sr. licensing specialist Morrison Knudson Co., Boise, Idaho, 1981-83; sr. nuclear licensing analyst Consumers Power Co., Jackson, Mich., 1979-81, 83—. Mem. Air Pollution Control Assn., Beta Beta Beta. Republican. Avocations: HO model railroads, motorcycling, bicycling, camping, sailing. Home: 2121 Mark Ave Lansing MI 48912 Office: Consumers Power Co 1945 W Parnall Rd Jackson MI 49201

LANDREMAN, URBAN EDWARD, data processing systems administrator, data analyst; b. DePere, Wis., Feb. 22, 1951; s. Edward Joseph and Leona Rita (Greatens) L.; m. Mary Ann Boley, Aug. 5, 1978; 1 Child, Matthew. B.S. in Math., Coll. St. Thomas, 1973; M.S. in Ops. Research, Case Western Res. U., 1974. Acad. computing coordinator Coll. St. Thomas, St. Paul, 1974-81; dir. program devel. Minn. Dept. Human Services, St. Paul, 1981—; cons. Guthrie Theater, Mpls., 1979—. Recipient Outstanding Contbn. to State Govt., Gov. Albert Quie, 1982. Mem. Assn. Computing Machinery, Am. Statistics Assn. Club: Sierra. Avocations: outdoors; photography. Home: 1184 Portland Ave Saint Paul MN 55104 Office: Minn Dept Human Services 444 Lafayette Rd Saint Paul MN 55101

LANDRUM, BAYLOR, III, theatre administrator, arts management consultant; b. Louisville, June 17, 1949; s. Baylor and Mary Wallis (Evans) L. Student U. Ky., 1968-70; cert. Middle Mgmt. Program, New London, Conn., 1978, Comml. Theatre Inst., N.Y.C., 1984. Subscription asst. N.Y.C. Ballet & Opera, 1970-72; box office mgr. McCarter Theatre, Princeton, N.J., 1972-74; gen. mgr. Acad. Festival Theatre, Lake Forest, Ill., 1974-78; adminstrv. dir. Va. Mus. Theatre, Richmond, 1978-81; mng. dir. Cin. Playhouse in the Park, 1981—; prin. cons. FEDAPT, N.Y.C., 1982—, co-dir. middle mgmt. program-fin. mgmt., 1983. Mem. Cin. Citizens Cable Bd., 1984—. U. Ky. summer fellow, 1969. Mem. Cin. Commn. on Arts, Ohio Theatre Alliance, A.R.T. New York. Democrat. Avocations: fishing; travel. Home: 453 Milton St Cincinnati OH 45210 Office: Cin Playhouse in the Park PO Box 6537 Cincinnati OH 45206

LANDSKE, DOROTHY SUZANNE, state senator; b. Evanston, Ill., Sept. 3, 1937; d. William Gerald and Dorothy Marie (Drewes) Martin; m. William Steve Landske, June 1, 1957; children—Catherine Suzanne Hudson, Jacqueline Marie Stoops, Pamela Florence, Cheryl Lynn, Eric Thomas. Student St. Joseph's Coll., Ind. U., U. Chgo. Receptionist Cedar Lake Med. Clinic (Ind.) 1959-62; owner, operator Sues Bridal House, 1967-75; dep. clk.-treas., Cedar Lake, 1975; chief dep. twp. assessor Center Twp., Crown Point, Ind., 1976-78, twp. assessor, 1979-84, mem. Ind. Senate, 1984—. Vice chmn. Lake County Republican Central Com., 1978—; Lake County rep. to 5th Congl. Dist.; mem. Women's Week panel Purdue U.-Calumet. Mem. Council State Govts., Nat. Order Women Legislators. Roman Catholic.

LANDSKRONER, LAWRENCE, lawyer; b. N.Y.C., June 9, 1927; s. Jack and Jean (Hershofsky) L.; m. Florence Alberta Blawes, July 2, 1957; children—Leigh, Lynn, Kathy, Jack. Student Dennison U., 1945, Union Coll., 1945, Miami U., Oxford, Ohio, 1946; LL.B., Vanderbilt U., 1950, J.D., 1979. Diplomate Nat. Bd. Trial Advocacy; bar: Ohio 1950. Sole practice, Cleve., 1950-52; gen. counsel Region 2 UAW, W. Pa., No. Ohio, 1970-81; sr. ptnr. Landskroner & Phillips, Cleve., 1952—; spl. counsel to atty. gen. State of Ohio, Cleve., 1970—; acting judge Arbitration Common Pleas Ct., Am. Arbitration Assn.; part-time lectr. law Case Western Res. U. Law Sch., Cleve. State U. Law Sch.; moot ct. judge Case Western Res. Law Sch.; gen. counsel Fraternal Order of Police of Ohio, 1975—; lectr. Contbr. articles to legal jours. Bd. dirs. Legal Aid Soc., Cleve., 1978—; bd. dirs. Cleve. Met. Gen. Hosp., 1974—, No. Ohio March of Dimes, Cleve., 1977—, Kolff Found., Cleve., 1979-80. Served with USNR, 1945-46. Mem. Assn. Trial Lawyers Am. (lectr. 1960—), Ohio Bar Assn., Cuyahoga County Bar Assn., Cleve. Bar Assn., Ohio Trial Lawyers Assn., Vanderbilt Alumni Assn. (pres. No. Ohio 1975-81, Inner Circle Advocates 1985). Club: Lakeside Yacht (Cleve.) (vice commodore 1965, trustee).

LANDSMAN, SANDRA GILBERT, psychologist, transactional analyst; b. Detroit, Jan. 5, 1933; d. Arthur Bernard and Ida Myra (Finkelstone) G.; B.S., Wayne State U., 1966, M.A., 1970, Ph.D., 1984; m. Rodney Glenn Landsman, Apr. 3, 1955; children—Victoria Louise Landsman Peterson, Jonathan Gilbert, Faith Susan, Jill Barbara. Cons., counselor Continuum Center for Women, Oakland U., Rochester, Mich., 1970-77; pvt. practice transactional analysis, Farmington Hills, Mich., 1971—; clin. cons., U.S., Can., Europe; transactional analyst, clin. supr. North Metro & Dearborn Downriver Growth Centers, Rochester and Allen Park, Mich., 1975-78; mem. faculty Macomb County (Mich.) Community Coll., 1976-79; dir. clin. and edn. services Landsman/-Foner & Assocs., West Bloomfield, Mich., 1977-82; disting. lectr. Sch. Social Work, Mich. State U., 1975-78; cons. in field. Cert. social worker, Mich. Fellow Inst. Gerontology; mem. Internat. Transactional Analysis Assn. (cert. tchr., mem. editorial bd.), Nat. Assn. Social Workers, Am. Assn. for Counseling and Devel., Am. Coll. Personnel Assn., Assn. Specialists in Group Work, Mich. Assn. for Counseling and Devel., Mich. Coll. Personnel Assn., Mich. Assn. Specialist Group Work (past pres.), Mich. Assn. Women Deans, Adminstrs. and Counselors, New Directions in Edn. and Psychotherapy (charter, trustee). Author: Affective Disorders: The Assessment, Development, and Treatment Strategies of Manic-Depressive Structure. Contbr. articles to profl. publs. Home: 34316 Thornbrook Dr Farmington Hills MI 48018 Office: 34316 Thornbrook Dr Farmington Hills MI 48018

LANDWEHR, WILLIAM CHARLES, museum director; b. Milw., Sept. 19, 1941; s. Frank Albert and LaVerna Gertrude (Schumacher) L.; B.S., U. Wis., Stevens Point, 1964; M.A., U. N.D., 1968; 1 dau., Leslie Lynne. Dir. S.D. Meml. Art Center, Brookings, 1969-71, Quincy (Ill.) Art Center, 1971-73; curator exhbns. Mint Mus. Art, Charlotte, 1973-76; dir. Springfield (Mo.) Art Mus., 1976—. Mem. Am. Assn. Mus., Mo. Mus. Assocs., Art Mus. Assn. (trustee 1978-80). Author exhbn. catalogs, including The Lithographs and Etchings of Philip Pearlstein, 1978; editor: Selections from the Permanent Collection of the Springfield Art Museum, 1980. Office: 1111 E Brookside Dr Springfield MO 65807

LANE, CONSTANCE CARMICHAEL RENICK, ednl. adminstr.; b. Rockford, Ill., Nov. 9, 1921; d. James Alexander and Nozella (Oda) Carmichael; B.S. in Edn. magna cum laude, W.Va. State Coll., 1943; M.A., Northwestern U., 1962; m. Andrew J. Lane, June 20, 1964; children—Betty Anne Renick (Mrs. Flynn Jefferson), James Renick. Tchr., Rockford Pub. Schs., 1954-62, helping tchr. elementary math., 1962-63; prin. Henrietta Primary and Intermediate Schs., Rockford, 1963-66; prin. W. Ray McIntosh Sch., Rockford, 1966—; Area IV coordinator Rockford Pub. Schs., after 1971, asst. supt. elem. edn., 1979—; part-time instr. Rockford Coll., evenings 1964-79. Mem. Taus, Inc. (pres. 1960-63, 74-78, treas. 1972-74), Ill., Rockford edn. assns., NEA, AAUW, Nat. Council Tchrs. Math., Assn. Supervision and Curriculum Devel., Rockford Prins. Assn., Nat. Elementary Prins. Assn., Delta Kappa Gamma, Phi Delta Kappa. Episcopalian. Contbr. articles to profl. jours. Home: 2224 Clover Ave Rockford IL 61102 Office: Rockford Bd Edn 201 S Madison St Rockford IL 61101

LANE, EUGENE NUMA, classics educator; b. Washington, Aug. 13, 1936; s. George Sherman and Colette (Resweber) L.; m. Carol Downes Gault, Aug. 22, 1964; children—Michael Franklin, Helen Taylor. A.B., Princeton U., 1958; M.A., Yale U., 1960, Ph.D., 1962. Asst. prof. classics U. Va., 1962-66; assoc. prof. classical studies U. Mo., Columbia, 1966-76, prof. classics, 1976—, chmn. dept., 1981-84. Fulbright grantee, 1960-61; Am. Council Learned Socs. grantee, 1972-73; others. Mem. Am. Philol. Assn., Archaeol. Inst. Am., Classical Assn. Middle West and South. Episcopalian. Author: Corpus Monumentorum Religionis Dei Menis, 4 vols., 1971-78; Corpus Cultus Iovis Sabazii, II, 1985; contbr. articles to profl. jours. Home: 813 Maupin Rd Columbia MO 65201 Office: 420D General Classroom Bldg Univ MO Columbia MO 65211

LANE, WILLIAM IRWIN, service technologies company executive; b. N.Y.C., Sept. 14, 1936; s. Jacob and Miriam (Steinberg) L.; m. Jill Fruchtman, Nov. 6, 1976; children—Elizabeth, Jennifer; children by previous marriage—Samuel, Howard. B.S., in Chemistry, Toledo U., 1959, B.S. in Pharmacy, 1962. Registered pharmacist, Ohio. Owner, Southbriar Pharmacies, Sylvania, Ohio, 1962-74; dir. planning Donovan Wire & Iron Co., Toledo, 1976-81; adminstrv. v.p. Central Steel Tube Co., Clinton, Iowa, 1981-82; dir. corp. devel. DST Industries, Clinton, Mich., 1982-83; pres., chief operating officer Diversified Service Techs., Clinton, 1984—. Mem. Am. Mgmt. Assn., Bus. and Profl. Advisory Assn. Republican. Jewish. Avocations: Reading; tennis. Home: 4635 Woodland Ln Sylvania OH 43560 Office: Diversified Service Techs 303 W Michigan Ave Clinton MI 49236

LANG, CHARLES EBERHARDT, college administrator, priest, chemist; b. Chgo., Feb. 10, 1933; s. Charles Eberhardt and Genevieve (O'Connor) L. B.S., Loyola U., 1955, M.S., 1956; Ph.D., Iowa State U., 1960; postgrad. Mt. St. Bernard Sem., 1961-65; M.A., Aquinas Inst., 1962; postdoctoral student in clin. psychology Loyola U., 1971-72. Prof. chemistry Loras Coll, Dubuque, Iowa, 1965-71, assoc. dean of students, 1971-72, dean of students, 1972-77, v.p. student affairs, 1977-85, v.p. coll. advancement, 1985—; lectr. on theology, psychology, and sci. Author: Student Affairs Research, Student Development, 1981; Chemical Research Chemical Effects of Nuclear Reactions, 1963. Treas. Dubuque Symphony Orch., 1981. Fellow Am. Inst. Chemists (cert. 1971), Iowa Student Personnel Assn. (pres. 1982, sec.-treas. 1980, adv. bd. 1979-83), Iowa Assn. Cons. and Devel., Am. Assn. Cons. and Devel., Am. Coll. Personnel Assn., Assn. Religious and Value Issues in Cons., Sigma Xi, Phi Lamda Upsilon. Lodge: Rotary. Avocations: swimming, reading, music. Home: 1450 Alta Vista St Dubuque IA 52001 Office: Loras Coll 1450 Alta Vista St Dubuque IA 52001

LANG, DOUGLAS RICHARD, pharmacist, hospital administrator; b. St. Louis, Aug. 14, 1956; s. Richard Thomas and Marilyn Ruth (Maurer) Lang Vitale; m. JoAnn Embry, Mar. 9, 1979; children—Joshua Ryan, Erin Dyan. A.A. in Life Scis., St. Louis Community Coll., 1977; B.S. in Pharmacy, St. Louis Coll. Pharmacy, 1981. Registered pharmacist, Mo. Staff pharmacist satellite coordinator St. Louis U. Hosp., 1981-84, asst. dir. pharmacy, 1984—; clin. instr. health careers St. Louis Coll., 1984—. Mem. Am. Soc. Hosp. Pharmacists, Mo. Soc. Hosp. Pharmacists, St. Louis Soc. Hosp. Pharmacists (treas. 1983-84, pres. elect, 1984-85, pres. 1985-86), Kappa Psi (Outstanding Sr. award St. Louis chpt. 1981, Man of Yr. award 1984, pres. grad. chpt. 1983—). Office: St Louis Univ Hosp 1325 S Grand Blvd St Louis MO 63104

LANGBEIN, JOHN HARRISS, law educator; b. Washington, Nov. 17, 1941. S. I.L. and M.V. (Harriss) L.; m. Kirsti Hiekka, June 24, 1973; children—Christopher, Julia, Anne. A.B. in Econs., Columbia U., 1964; LL.B. magna cum laude, Harvard U., 1968; LL.B. with 1st class honours, Cambridge U. (Eng.), 1969, Ph.D., 1971. Bar: D.C. 1969, Inner Temple 1969, Fla. 1971. Asst. prof. U. Chgo. Law Sch., 1971-73, prof., 1973-80, Max Pam prof. and fgn. law, 1980—. Vis. fellow Max Planck Inst. Criminal Law, Freiburg, Ger., 1973, Max Planck Inst. European Legal History, Frankfurt, 1969-70, 77, All Souls Coll., Oxford, 1977. Mem. ABA, Am. Law Inst., Am. Hist. Assn., Am. Soc. Legal History, Selden Soc., Gesellschaft für Rechtsvergleichung. Author: Prosecuting Crime in the Renaissance (Yorke prize Cambridge U.), 1974; Torture and the Law of Proof: Europe and England in the Ancien Régime, 1977; Comparative Criminal Procedure: Germany, 1977; also numerous articles. Office: U Chgo Law Sch 1111 E 60th St Chicago IL 60637

LANGE, CRYSTAL MARIE, nursing educator; b. Snover, Mich., Aug. 22, 1927; d. Bazil H. and Crystal S. (Hilborn) Morse; m. Elmer William Lange, June 10, 1961; children—Gregory, Frederick, Helen, Charles, G. Benson, Robert, Larry. B.S. in Nursing, U.Mich., 1949; M.S. in Nursing, Wayne State U., 1961; Ph.D., Mich. State U., 1972. Pvt. duty nurse, Richmond, Ind., 1949-50; asst. dir. nursing, nursing supr., instr. St. Mary's Hosp., Tucson, Ariz., 1950-58; night supr. Pima County Hosp., Tucson, 1958-59; asst. dir. Sch. Nursing, Saginaw Gen. Hosp., Mich., 1959-60; instr. to prof., chmn. div. Delta Coll., University Center, Mich., 1962-76; dean Sch. Nursing and Allied Health Scis., asst. to v.p. acad. affairs Saginaw Valley State Coll., University Center, 1976—; mem. vis. com. Med. Ctr., U. Mich., 1978-81. Author: Leadership for Quality, 1966; Instructor's Guide - Nursing Skills and Techniques, 1969; The Use of the Auto-tutorial Laboratory and the Mobile Tutorial Unit in Teaching, 1969; Instructor's Guide - Nursing Skills and Techniques - Films 76-126, 1972; Instructor's Guide - Nursing Skills and Techniques - Films 127-151, 1971; Auto-Tutorial Techniques in Nursing Education, 1971; Future Education: Diagnosis Prescriptions Evaluation, 1971. Contbr. articles to profl. jours. Bd. dirs. Saginaw chpt. ARC, 1982—, Saginaw Vis. Nurse Assn., 1980—. Recipient award Mich. Acad. Sci., Arts and Letters, 1970, Monsour Found. Lectureship award Health Edn. Media Assn., 1977; NEH fellow, 1983. Fellow Am. Acad. Nursing; mem. Am. Acad. Arts and Scis., Am. Acad. Nursing (governing council, sec. 1978-80), AAUP (chpt. v.p. 1976, award citation 1970), Am. Ednl. Scis., Am. Nurses Assn., Mich. Nurses Assn., Saginaw Dist. Nurses Assn. (bd. dirs. 1976—), U. Mich. Alumnae Assn., Wayne State U. Alumnae Assn., Phi Kappa Phi, Sigma Theta Tau. Home: 4135 Kochville Rd Saginaw MI 48604 Office: Saginaw Valley State Coll University Center MI 48710

LANGE, FREDERICK EMIL, lawyer; b. Washington, May 24, 1908; s. Emil F. and Jane (Austin) L.; A.B., U. Nebr., 1928; J.D., M.P.L., Washington Coll. Law, 1932; m. Leila M. Benedict, Sept. 11, 1930; children—Frederick Emil, David W., James A. Admitted to D.C. bar, 1932, Minn. bar, 1943; examiner U.S. Patent Office, 1929-35; patent lawyer Honeywell, Inc., 1935-63, mgr. Mpls. patent dept., 1954-63; partner firm Dorsey, Marquart, Windhorst, West & Halladay, Mpls., 1965-73; individual practice law, Mpls., 1973-78; with Kinney & Lange, P.A., Mpls., 1978—; spl. lectr. patent law U. Minn., 1949-51, Minn. Continuing Legal Edn., 1976. Bd. trustees 1st Unitarian Soc., 1970-71; chmn. Minn. br. World Federalists, 1958-60, nat. exec. com., 1958-64; bd. dirs. Group Health Plan, Inc., 1967-84, 1st v.p., 1975-78; bd. dirs. St. Paul Civic Symphony Assn., 1976-81, Environ. Learning Center, 1977-79, Minn. Funeral and Meml. Soc. Recipient Distinguished Service award U. Nebr., 1968. Mem. Am., Minn., D.C., Hennepin County bar assns., Am., Minn. (pres. 1954-55) patent law assns., Am. Judicature Soc., Sigma Nu Phi (lord high chancellor 1984—). Holder U.S. patents. Home: 1235 Yale Pl Apt 210 Minneapolis MN 55403 Office: 625 4th Ave Suite 1500 Minneapolis MN 55415

LANGE, THOMAS LLOYD, shoe company executive; b. Belleville, Ill., May 23, 1942; s. Leslie Rudolph and Bessie (Lloyd) L. B.S. in Bus Adminstrn., McKendree Coll., 1964. Visual coordinator Stix, Baer & Fuller, St. Louis, 1964-65; spl. events display Famous-Barr Co., St. Louis, 1965-69; display dir. Macy's, Kansas City, Mo., 1969-71; self-employed design cons., St. Louis, 1971-73; dir. visual presentation Wohl Shoe Co., St. Louis, 1973—. Creative designer Connie and Fanfare Shops, 1976. Recipient ann. Display award Nat. Assn. Display Industries, 1974; Best Supporting Role award Wohl Shoe Co., 1976, 83. Mem. Internat. Profl. Display Assn., Nat. Retail Mchts. Assn. Home: 5630 Pershing Ave Apt 11 St Louis MO 63112 Office: Wohl Shoe Co 811 Hanley Indsl Park St Louis MO 63144

LANGELER, GEORGE HARRIS, college dean; b. Elmhurst, Ill., Dec. 2, 1927; s. George A. and Mary E. (Santee) L. B.S. in Biology, Elmhurst Coll., 1949; M.S., U. Ill., 1950, postgrad., 1951; Ph.D. in Higher Edn., U. Mich., 1959. Instr. biology Elmhurst Coll., 1950-54, asst. prof., 1954-55, head resident, 1951-55; acting assoc. dean arts and scis. Oberlin Coll., Ohio, 1959, registrar, 1959-62, dir. fin. aid, 1962-64, assoc. dean arts and scis., 1964-66, dean of students, 1966—, lectr. biology, 1961—, lectr. human devel., 1975—; examiner, cons. N. Central Assn. Colls. and Schs., 1961—, mem. com. undergrad. edn., 1973-76; mem. faculty Workshop Inst. for Living Learning, N.Y.C., 1979—. Contbr. articles to profl. jours. Trustee, Elmhurst Coll., 1974—, mem. exec. com., 1978—; mem. citizens com. Lorain County Community Coll. Dist., 1962-64; bd. dirs. Oberlin chpt. ACLU, 1971-74, 79-81. Named Alumnus of Yr., Elmhurst Coll., 1968. Mem. Am. Assn. Higher Edn., Nat. Assn. Student Personnel Adminstrs., Am. Assn. Counseling and Devel., AAAS, AAUP, Am. Coll. Personnel Assn., Phi Kappa Phi, Phi Delta Kappa. Home: 173 Hollywood St Oberlin OH 44074 Office: 109 Peters Hall Oberlin College Oberlin OH 44074

LANGEMO, KATHY DIANE, financial administrator; b. Rochester, Minn., Aug. 21, 1950; d. Albert Robert and Elaine Ramona (Schacht) L.; m. Darrell Lee Dugdale, May 23, 1982. B.A., Augsburg Coll., 1972; M.B.A., Coll. of St. Thomas, 1979. Acctg. clk. Hansord Pontiac, Mpls., 1972-74; payroll adminstr. Mpls. Electric Steel Castings Co., Mpls., 1974-77, staff acct., 1977-78; fin. analyst Fairview Hosp., Mpls., 1980-81; regional control mgr. Datapoint Corp., Mpls., 1981-82; asst. v.p. fin. Coll. St. Scholastica, Duluth, Minn., 1982—; mem. planning com. Am. Council Edn., Mpls., 1984—. Mem. citizen budget panel United Way of Duluth, 1984. Mem. Adminstrv. Mgmt. Soc. (bd. dirs. 1984—), Duluth Women's Network (treas. 1983), Minn. Women's Network, Nat. Assn. Coll. and Univ. Bus. Officers. Avocations: reading, cross country skiing, piano. Home: 13712 W Hwy 23 Superior WI 54880 Office: Coll St Scholastica 1200 Kenwood Ave Duluth MN 55811

LANGENBAHN, JAY RICHARD, lawyer; b. Covington, Ky., Apr. 25, 1950; s. John William and Ruth Marion (Grefer) L.; m. Sally Ann Strother, Aug. 17, 1973; children—Jeffrey R., Alison Taaffe. B.S. in Acctg., U. Ky., 1972; J.D., Samuel P. Chase Coll. Law, Covington, Ky., 1976. Bar: Ohio 1976, Ky. 1983. Assoc. McIntosh, McIntosh & Knabe, Cin., 1977-78, Lindhorst & Dreidame, Cin., 1978—. Mem. Cin. Bar Assn., Ohio Bar Assn., Ky. Bar Assn., ABA. Home: 773 Maidstone Ct Cincinnati OH 45230 Office: 1700 Central Trust Ctr Cincinnati OH 45202

LANGENBERG, DONALD NEWTON, physicist, educational administrator; b. Devils Lake, N.D., Mar. 17, 1932; s. Ernest George and Fern (Newton) L.; m. Patricia Ann Warrington, June 20, 1953; children—Karen Kaye, Julia Ann, John Newton, Amy Paris. B.S., Iowa State U., 1953; M.S., UCLA, 1955; Ph.D. (NSF fellow), U. Calif.-Berkeley, 1959. Electronics engr. Hughes Research Labs., Culver City, Calif., 1953-55; acting instr. U. Calif.-Berkeley, 1958-59; mem. faculty U. Pa., Phila., 1960-83, prof., 1967-83; dir. Lab. for Research on Structure of Matter, 1972-74; vice-provost for grad. studies and research, 1974-79; chancellor U. Ill.-Chgo., 1983—; maitre de conference associe Ecole Normale Superieure, Paris, France, 1966-67; vis. prof. Calif. Inst. Tech., Pasadena, 1971; guest researcher Zentralinstitut fur Tieftemperaturforschung der Bayerische Akademie der Wissenschaften and Technische Universitat Munchen, 1974; dep. dir. NSF, 1980-82. Recipient John Price Wetherill medal Franklin Inst., 1975; NSF Postdoctoral fellow, 1959-60; Alfred P. Sloan Found. fellow, 1962-65; Guggenheim fellow, 1966-67. Fellow Am. Phys. Soc., AAAS, Sigma Xi. Home: 3750 N Lake Shore Dr Chicago IL 60613 Office: U Ill-Chgo Box 4348 Chicago IL 60680

LANGENBERG, FREDERICK CHARLES, steel company executive; b. N.Y.C., July 1, 1927; s. Frederick C. and Margaret (McLaughlin) L.; B.S., Lehigh U., 1950, M.S., 1951; Ph.D., Pa. State U., 1955; postgrad. execs. program Carnegie-Mellon U., 1962; m. Jane Anderson Bartholomew, May 16, 1953; children—Frederick C., Susan Jane. With U.S. Steel Corp., 1951-53; vis. fellow MIT, 1955-56; with Crucible Steel Corp., Pitts., 1956-68, v.p. research and engring., 1966-68; pres. Trent Tube div. Colt Industries, Milw., 1968-70; exec. v.p. Jessop Steel Co., Washington, Pa., 1970, pres., 1970-75, also dir.; pres., dir. Am. Iron and Steel Inst., Washington, 1975-78; pres., dir. Interlake, Inc., Oak Brook, Ill., 1979-81; pres., chief exec. officer, dir. Interlake OakBrook, 1982-83, chmn., chief exec. officer, 1983—; dir. People's Energy, Cartech Corp., Chgo. & Northwestern Transp. Corp. Trustee Ill. Inst. Tech. Served with USNR, 1944-45. Alumni fellow Pa. State U., 1977. Fellow Am. Soc. Metals (Disting. life mem.; trustee, David Ford McFarland award Penn State chpt. 1973, Pittsburgh Nite lectr. 1970, Andrew Carnegie lectr. 1976); mem. ASME, Am. Iron and Steel Inst., Assn. Iron and Steel Engrs., Am. Ordnance Assn., Northwestern Univ. Assocs., Phi Beta Kappa, Sigma Xi, Tau Beta Pi. Clubs: Duquesne, St. Clair Country, Laurel Valley Golf Rolling Rock (Pitts.); University, Congressional, Burning Tree, Carlton (Washington); Butler Nat. Golf, Chgo. Golf, Chicago (Chgo.). Contbr. articles to tech. jours. Patentee in field. Home: 22 Bradford Ln Oak Brook IL 60521 Office: Commerce Plaza 2015 Spring Rd Oak Brook IL 60521

LANGENBERG, PATRICIA WARRINGTON, biostatistics educator, consultant; b. Des Moines, Sept. 10, 1931; d. Harold Paris and Rose Marie (Thompson) Warrington; m. Donald Newton Langenberg, June 20, 1953; children—Karen, Julia, John, Amy. B.S. in Math. Stats., Iowa State U., 1953; M.A. in Math., Temple U., 1975, Ph.D. in Math., 1978. Asst. prof. LaSalle Coll., Phila., 1977-80, Temple U., Phila., 1980-83; asst. prof. biostats. U. Ill., Chgo., 1983—; treas. Com. of Pres of Stats. Socs., 1981— Contbr. articles to biometric jours. Mem. Am. Statis. Assn., Biometric Soc., Assn. Women in Math., Caucus for Women in Stats. Democrat. Home: 3750 N Lake Shore Dr Apt 9A Chicago IL 60613 Office: Sch Pub Health U Ill 557 SPH-West Box 6998 Chicago IL 60680

LANGENDORF, RICHARD, cardiologist; b. Prague, Czechoslovakia, July 11, 1908; came to U.S. 1939, naturalized 1944; s. Gustav Langendorf and Olga Lederer; m. Raya Burakoff, 1944; children—Frederick, Trudi, Stephen. M.D., German U. Prague, 1932. Diplomate Am. Bd. Internal Medicine, 1948, Am. Bd. Cardiovascular Disease, 1951. Intern, then resident I. Medizinlsche Universitatsklinik, Prague, 1933-38; research assoc. Cardiovascular Inst., Michael Reese Hosp., Chgo., 1939—, mem. staff dept. medicine, 1955—; emeritus clin. prof. medicine U. Chgo., 1965—. Author: (with A. Pick) Interpretation of Complex Arrhythmias, 1979. Contbr. articles to profl. jours. Fellow ACP, Am. Coll. Cardiology (gifted tchr. award 1975); mem. Med. Alumni Assn. U. Chgo. (disting. Service award 1974). Jewish. Avocation: music. Home: 1765 E 55th St Chicago IL 60615 Office: 111 N Wabash Ave Chicago IL 60602

LANGENHEIM, RALPH LOUIS, JR., geology educator; b. Cin., May 26, 1922; s. Ralph Louis and Myrtle Rosalia (Helmers) L.; m. Jean Cloteal Harmon, 1946 (div. 1962); m. Virginia Amelia Knobloch, June 5, 1962 (div. 1970) children—Victoria Elizabeth, Ralph Louis III; m. Shirley Louise Blair, Jan. 5, 1970. B.S. in Geol. Engring, U. Tulsa, 1943; M.S. in Geology, U. Colo., 1947; Ph.D. in Geology, U. Minn., 1951. Teaching asst. U. Colo., Boulder, 1946-47; teaching asst., fellow U. Minn., Mpls., 1947-50; asst. prof. geology Coe Coll., Cedar Rapids, Iowa, 1950-52; asst. prof. paleontology U. Calif.-Berkeley, 1952-59; asst. prof. geology dept. U. Ill., Urbana, 1959-61, assoc. prof., 1962-66, prof., 1967—; ptnr. Lanman Assoc., Urbana, 1975—; cons. Central Geol. Survey, Republic of China, Taipei, 1982, Geol. Survey of Iran, Tehran, 1974, Inst. Geol. Nat., Colombia, Bogota, 1953; tech. officer Geol Survey Can., Ottawa, 1967. Author: (with others) Correlation of Great Basin Stratigraphic Units, 1973; Cenozoic Reef Biofacies etc., 1974; coordinator Handbook Paleontological Techniques, 1965. Served to lt. (j.g.) USN, 1943-46, lt. comdr. Res. Grantee Arctic Inst. N.Am., 1956, NSF, 1962-64, AEC, 1973-76. Fellow Geol. Soc. Am., AAAS; mem. Am. Assn. Petroleum Geologists, Paleontol. Soc. (sec. 1963-71), Geol. Soc. London, Swiss Geol. Soc., Soc. Econ. Paleontologists and Mineralogists, Explorers Club. Democrat. Presbyterian. Lodge: Rotary. Home: 401 W Vermont St Urbana IL 61801 Office: Dept Geology U Ill 245 NHB 1301 W Green St Urbana IL 61801

LANGER, EDWARD GREGORY, lawyer; b. Watertown, Wis., Jan. 4, 1954; s. Francis James and Gertrude (Hofmann) L. B.A., Lawrence U., 1976; J.D., U. Wis.-Madison, 1979, postgrad. Bus. Sch., 1979. Bar: Wis. 1979, U.S. Tax Ct. 1980, U.S. Ct. Appeals (7th cir.) 1983; C.P.A., Wis. Atty. Dist. Counsel's Office, IRS, Milw., 1980—. Recipient Elijah Watts Sells cert. Bd. Examiners of Am. Inst. C.P.A.s, 1980. Mem. Wis. Inst. C.P.A.s, Milw. Bar Assn., Wis. Bar. Roman Catholic. Club: Milw. Liederkranz (treas. 1981-85). Office: IRS Dist Counsel 310 W Wisconsin Ave Milwaukee WI 53203

LANGEWISCH, WILLIAM HENRY, physician, university official; b. Evanston, Ill., July 1, 1922; s. William Henry and Edith Anne (Nelson) L.; m. Dorothy May Bagley, Sept. 27, 1946; children—Judith, William. M.D., Northwestern U., 1948. Diplomate Am. Bd. Pediatrics. Intern, Evanston Hosp., 1948-49; resident in pediatrics Children's Meml. Hosp., Chgo., 1949-51; practice medicine specializing in pediatrics, Rockford, Ill., 1953-85; assoc. dean U. Ill. Coll. Medicine, Rockford, 1977—. Contbr. articles to profl. publs. Served to capt. USAF, 1951-53. Fellow Am. Acad. Pediatrics. Home: 407 N Gardiner Ave Rockford IL 61107 Office: U Ill Coll Medicine 1601 Parkview Ave Rockford IL 61107

LANGFORD, TRAVIS ALLEN, telecommunications company executive; b. Baytown, Tex., Nov. 9, 1940; s. Travis Culberson and Emma Myrtle (Delawder) L.; m. Marilyn Joyce Manville, May 14, 1966; children—Audra Elizabeth, Ashley Joyce. B.E.E., Tex. Tech U., 1963. Dist. mgr. AT&T Overland Park, Kans. Councilman Town of Cortlandt, N.Y., 1973-76. Served to capt. USAR, 1963-65. Republican. Methodist. Lodge: Lions (v.p. 1982-83). Avocations: pilot; hunting; fishing. Home: 7620 Haskins St Lenexa KS 66216 Office: AT&T 10881 Lowell St Overland Park KS 66210

LANGLAND, HAROLD REED, sculptor, educator; b. Mpls., Oct. 6, 1939; s. Carl and Helen (Kimmey) L.; m. Janice Clemens, Aug. 25, 1962; children—Susan Elizabeth, Victoria Ann. B.A. in Art, U. Minn., 1961, M.F.A. in Sculpture, 1964. Asst. lectr. Carlisle Coll. Art, Eng., 1964-65, Sheffield Coll. Art, Eng., 1965-67; asst. prof. Murray State U., Ky., 1967-71; assoc. prof. Ind. U. at South Bend, 1971-77, prof., 1978—; vis. prof. N. Staffordshire Poly., Stoke-on-Trent, Eng., 1977-78; collections include: Midwest Mus. Am. Art, Elkhart, Ind., Calhoun St. Pedestrian Mall, Ft. Wayne, Ind., Beatrice Foods, Chgo., Morris Civic Auditorium, South Bend, Stanley Iron Works, Mpls., U. Minn., Mpls., Ind. U. at South Bend, Notre Dame U., South Bend; regional exhbns. include: Art Ctr., Inc., South Bend, 1982, Midwest Mus. Am. Art, 1981, No. Ind. Artists, Munster, 1983 (Best in Show award), 1984, Hoosier Salon Show, Indpls., 1980, 82, 84 (Outstanding Work in Sculpture awards), J.B. Speed Mus., Louisville, 1983; nat. exhbns. include: Dogwood Internat., Atlanta, 1982, 83, N.Am. Sculpture Exhbn., Foothills Art Ctr., Golden, Colo., 1981, 82, 83, 84, NAD, N.Y.C., 1982, 83, Salmagundi Club, N.Y.C., 1982, 83, Terrence Gallery Show (Honorable Mention award), Palenville, N.Y., 1982, Shelby Art League, N.C., 1983, 84, Audubon Artists, N.Y.C., 1984; international exhbns. include: Royal Festival Hall, London, 1980, Ind. State Mus., Indpls., 1981, Indpls. Art League, 1982, Midwest Mus. Am. Art, Elkhart, Ind., 1982, St. Paul Acad. and Summit Sch., 1983, Mpls. Inst. Art, 1983, Goshen Coll., Art Gallery, Ind., 1984. Recipient grants Ind. Arts Commn., 1980, U.S. Ednl. Found. India, 1982. Mem. Am. Portrait Soc., Artnet (dir. 1984—). Avocations: choral singing; swimming. Home: 12632 Anderson Rd Granger IN 46530

LANGLEY, ELIZABETH MARIE, college dean; b. Roanoke, Va., Jan. 29, 1923; d. Ernest Stanley and Anna (Grzesiakowski) Hickok; m. Paul Bates Langley (dec.), July 1, 1944; children—Michael Paul, Robert Thomas, Joanne Margaret. B.A., Whittier Coll., 1952; M.A., Loyola U., 1963, Ph.D., 1968. Cert. elem. tchr., high sch. tchr., Ill. Tchr. Santa Ana City Schs., Calif., 1952-60; lectr. Loyola U., Chgo., 1964-67; prof. Northeastern Ill. U., Chgo., 1966—, chmn. counselors edn., 1970-75, assoc. dean grad. coll., 1976—. Contbr. articles to profl. jours. Served with USMC, 1943-44. Mem. Nat. Vocat. Guidance Assn., Am. Sch. Counselors Assn., Am. Assn. Counseling and Devel., AAUW, AAUP, Catholic War Veterans (Ill. trustee 1984—), Catholic War Veterans Post 198 (comdr. 1984-85). Avocation: travel. Home: 3831 N Nora Ave Chicago IL 60634 Office: Northeastern Ill U 5500 N St Louis Ave Chicago IL 60625

LANGLEY, JOHN ARTHUR, engineer; b. Monroe County, Ind., Oct. 31, 1923; s. John P. and Laura E. (Polley) L.; m. Mary Ward, Aug. 14, 1949; children—Stephen W., John P., Dennis D. B.S., Purdue U., 1949; cert. in mgmt. Lake Forest Coll., 1968. Engr.-in-tng. Lauson div. Harte-Carter, New Holstein, Wis., 1950-51; planning engr., project engr. Nat. Presto Industries, Eau Claire, Wis., 1951-54; project engr. research Continental Motors, Detroit, 1954-57; head research, chief engr. Oliver Outboards, Battle Creek, Mich., 1957-60; project engr. Outboard Marine Corp., Waukegan, Ill., 1960-62, engring., mgr., 1962—; cons. in marine accident investigations and litigation; Patentee in field; contbr. articles to profl. jours. Cubmaster Boy Scouts Am., 1961-75; first aid instr. ARC, Waukegan, 1964-71. Served with U.S. Army, 1942-45. Mem. Internat. Standards Orgn., Am. Boat and Yacht Council, Nat. Fire Protection Assn., Am. Power Boat Assn. (chmn. safety and regatta mgmt. commn. 1969—), Soc. Automotive Engrs. (chmn. power unit subcom. 1977—), Marine Engine Mfrs. Assn., Lake County Radio Control Club (pres. 1982). Club: Zion Benton Athletic Booster. Home: 11184 W Wadsworth Rd Zion IL 60099 Office: Outboard Marine Corp 300 Sea Horse Dr Waukegan IL 60089

LANGLOIS, DONALD HAROLD, clergyman; b. Rochester, N.Y., Nov. 25, 1940; s. Harold Lionel and Eleanor Emma (Stout) L.; m. Ullrike Frances Baudisch, Aug. 28, 1965; children—Stephen, Eric. A.B., Kenyon Coll., 1962; M.Div., Gen. Theol. Sem., 1966; M.L.S., Queens Coll., 1973. Ordained priest Episcopal Ch., 1967. Asst. Christ Episcopal Ch., Hornell, N.Y., 1966-67; vicar Ch. of Redeemer, Addison, N.Y., 1967-72; librarian Martin Luther High Sch., Maspeth, N.Y., 1973-76; asst. St. George's Ch., Flushing, N.Y., 1973-76; dean Star Prairie Deanery, Rice Lake, Wis., 1981-84; rector Grace Episcopal Ch., Rice Lake, 1976-85; rector Holy Trinity Episc. Ch., Danville, Ill., 1985—; chmn. Diocesan Communications Dept., 1980—; clerical del. Province V Synod, 1983-85. Editor The Herald, 1980-85. Contbr. articles to profl. jours. Bd. dirs. No. Pines Unified Services Ctr., Cumberland, Wis., 1980-85, Rice Lake Pub. Library, 1982-85; bd. dirs. Friends of Rice Lake Pub. Library, 1984-85, pres., 1979; gen. leader Knapp Street Hustlers 4-H, Rice Lake, 1982-85. Mem. Soc. of King Charles the Martyr, Sisterhood of Holy Nativity (priest assoc.), Beta Phi Mu. Avocations: camping; photography; sightseeing; reading; stamp collecting. Home: 1226 N Vermilion St Danville IL 61832 Office: Holy Trinity Ch PO Box 822 Danville IL 61832

LANGOWSKI, LAWRENCE LEONARD, computer system administrator, consultant; b. Chgo., July 13, 1948; s. Leonard Peter and Victoria Ann (Slimkowski) L.; m. Maria Guadalupe Mendoza, Dec. 11, 1982. M.A. in Econs. with honors, Roosevelt U., 1981; student Moody Bible Inst., 1981-82; M.B.A. in Finance with honors, DePaul U., 1985. Telephone repairman Ill. Bell, Chgo., 1969-84; computer system adminstr., 1984—; pvt. practice real estate consulting, developing, Chgo., 1974—. Vol. Grant Hosp., Chgo., 1982—. Served as sp/4 U.S. Army, 1966-69, Vietnam. Mem. Nat. Vietnam Vets. Network, Wycliff Assocs., Delta Mu Delta. Democrat. Mem. Evang. Ch. Club: 11 Armored Calvary Assn. (Ft. Knox, Ky.). Avocation: stock and option trading. Home: 1931 W Evergreen St Chicago IL 60622 Office: Ill Bell Telephone Co 225 W Randolph St Chicago IL 60604

LANGSLEY, DONALD GENE, psychiatrist, educator, administrator; b. Topeka, Oct. 5, 1925; s. Morris J. and Ruth (Pressman) L.; m. Pauline Royal, Sept. 9, 1955; children—Karen Jean, Dorothy Ruth, Susan Louise. B.A., SUNY-Albany, 1949; M.D. U. Rochester, 1953. Diplomate Am. Bd. Psychiatry and Neurology (dir. 1976-80). Intern, USPHS Hosp., San Francisco, 1953-54; resident in psychiatry U. Calif.-San Francisco, 1954-59, mem. faculty, 1959-61; assoc. prof. psychiatry U. Colo. Sch. Medicine, Denver, 1961-68; prof. and chmn. dept. psychiatry U. Calif.-Davis Sch. Medicine, 1968-76, U. Cin. Sch. Medicine, 1976-80; exec. v.p. Am. Bd. Med. Spltys., Evanston, Ill., 1981—; prof. psychiatry and behavioral scis. Northwestern U. Sch. Medicine, Chgo., 1981—; clin. practice psychiatry. Served with U.S. Army, 1943-46; with USPHS, 1953-54. Recipient Colo. Assn. Mental Health Spl. award, 1968; Harold Miles award, 1977; Sacramento Mental Health Assn. spl. award, 1973. Fellow Am. Coll. Psychiatrists; mem. Am. Psychiat. Assn. (pres. 1980-81, v.p. 1978-80, chmn. council med. edn. 1981-84; Hofheimer prize 1971), Hong Kong Psychiat. Soc. (hon.), Am. Psychoanalytic Assn., Chgo. Med. Soc., Ill. Med. Assn., AMA, Soc. Med. Adminstrs. Author: The Treatment of Families in Crisis, 1968; Mental Health Education in the New Medical Schools, 1973; A Manual of Psychiatric Peer Review, 1976; Handbook of Community Mental Health; Legal Aspects of Certification and Accreditation, 1981; contbr. numerous articles, revs. and abstracts to profl. jours. Home: 9445 Monticello Ave Evanston IL 60203 Office: One American Plaza Suite 805 Evanston IL 60201

LANGSTON, ROSEMARY FLORENCE, college dean, nursing educator; b. Rochester, N.Y., June 6, 1938; d. Michael and Rose (Maniscalco) Andaloro; m. John A. Langston, Nov. 20, 1965; 1 child, Michael. BSS., SUNY-Buffalo, 1960; M.S., Tex. Woman's U., Houston, 1973; Ph.D., U. Minn., 1981. R.N., Minn. Adminstrv. asst. div. disease control Alameda County Health Dept., Oakland, Calif., 1961-64; pub. health nurse III, chronic disease coordinator Houston City Health Dept., 1965-66; aftercare coordinator St. Joseph Community Mental Health Ctr., Houston, 1966-68; from instr. to asst. prof. community health nursing U. Tex., Galveston, 1973-74, Tex. Woman's U., Houston, 1974-76, Coll. St. Theresa, Rochester, Minn., 1977-78; asst. prof. community nursing Winona State U., Minn., 1978-81, dean nursing, 1981-85, dean nursing and health services, 1985—. mem. nursing adv. com. Rochester Community Coll., Minn., 1984—; Mem. scholarship com. Watkins Home, Winona, 1983—; group leader I Can Cope community program for cancer patients, Rochester, Minn., 1984; del. to polit. conv., Minn., 1982; Mem. Midwest Alliance in Nursing (program com. 1982—), Minn. League for Nursing (bd. dirs., vice chmn. edn. council 1985—, service award 1984), Am. Pub. Health Assn., Minn. Assn. Colls. Nursing, Soc. Research in Nursing Edn., Minn. Intersystem Nursing Forum, Nat. League for Nursing (accreditation site visitor council baccalaureate and higher degree programs 1985), Sigma Theta Tau, Phi Kappa Phi. Avocations: music, golf. Home: 2502 4th Ave NW Rochester MN 55901 Office: Winona State Univ Winona MN 55987

LANIGAN, ROBERT J., container manufacturing company executive. Chief exec. officer, dir. Owens-Ill., Inc., Toledo. Office: Owens-Illinois Inc One Seagate Toledo OH 43666*

LANING, EVERETT LAIDLEY, sociology educator, clergyman; b. Chgo., Jan. 31, 1931; s. Harry Burnham and Helen Irene (Laidley) L.; m. Ruth Woolson, Sept. 4, 1954; children—Yvonne Marie, Brent Woolson, Jolene Kay. A.A., Kendall Coll., Evanston, Ill., 1951; B.A., Simpson Coll., Indianola, Iowa, 1953; B.D., Garrett-Evangelical Theol. Sch., Evanston, 1957; M.A., Northwestern U., 1959; Ph.D., Iowa State U., 1965. Ordained to ministry United Meth. Ch., 1959. Pastor United Meth. Ch., Milo and Green Plain, Iowa, 1957-60, Luther and Napier, Iowa, 1960-63; grad. asst. Iowa State U., Ames, 1960-64; from asst. prof. to prof. Simpson Coll., 1964—; vis. lectr. Drake U., Des Moines, 1967, 70; vis. prof. Rust Coll., Holly Springs, Miss., 1970-71; cons. Better Homes and Gardens, Des Moines, 1971. Designer logo Town & Country Commn., 1963. Author multimedia event Iowa's Rainbow People, 1982. Pres. Y's Mens Club, Indianola, 1974, Red Rock Area Community Action Program, Iowa, 1980-82. Mem. Am. Sociol. Assn., Midwest Sociol. Soc., Iowa Sociol. Assn. (pres. 1967-68, sec.-treas. 1983—), Iowa Consortium for Social Work Educators, Iowa Assn. Criminal Justice Educators (treas. 1983—). Democrat. Lodge: Rotary (pres. 1984). Avocations: photography, carpentry, cabinet-making, auto mechanics. Home: 612 W 1st Ave Indianola IA 50125 Office: Simpson Coll Dept Sociology and Applied Social Sci Indianola IA 50125

LANKSTON, ROBERT JASON, mechanical engineer; b. Bridgeport, Ill., Mar. 19, 1927; s. Jason Franklin and Elva Grace (Foss) L.; m. Evelyn Bailey, July 1, 1950; children—Kathy, Jeffrey, Nancy, Richard. B.S. in Mech. Engring., U. Ill., 1950. Registered profl. engr., Ill., Kans. Sales engr. Chgo. Pneumatic Tool Co., 1950-52; project engr. Taylor Forge Inc., Chgo., 1952-64, chief engr., Paola, Kans., 1964-67; mgr. engring. Taylor Forge Engring. div. Gulf & Western, Paola, 1967-84, Taylor Forge Engineered Systems, Inc., Paola, 1984—; mem. pressure vessel research com. Welding Research Council, N.Y.C., 1970—. Patentee in field. Contbr. articles to profl. jours. Served with USN, 1945-46. Mem. ASME, Am. Welding Soc., Am. Soc. Metals. Lodge: Lions (treas. 1962-64). Avocation: ham radio. Home: 4876 Black Swan Dr Shawnee KS 66216 Office: Taylor Forge Engineered Systems 1st and Iron Sts Paola KS 66071

LANO, CHARLES JACK, mfg. co. exec.; b. Port Clinton, Ohio, Apr. 17, 1922; s. Charles Herbin and Antoinette (Schmitt) L.; B.S. in Bus. Adminstrn. summa cum laude, Ohio State U., 1949; m. Beatrice Irene Spees, June 16, 1946; children—Douglas Cloyd, Charles Lewis. With U.S. Gypsum Co., 1941-46, Ottawa Paper Stock Co., 1946-47; accountant Arthur Young & Co., C.P.A.'s, Tulsa, 1949-51; controller Lima div. Ex-Cell-O Corp., 1951-59, electronics div. AVCO Corp., 1959-61, Servomation Corp., 1961; asst. comptroller Scovill Mfg. Co., Waterbury, Conn., 1961-62, comptroller, 1962-67; controller CF&I Steel Corp., Denver, 1967-69, v.p., controller, 1969-70; controller Pacific Lighting Corp., 1970-76; exec. v.p. Arts-Way Mfg. Co., Armstrong, Iowa, 1976—, dir., 1981—. Served with USMCR, 1942-45. C.P.A., Okla. Mem. Am. Inst. C.P.A.'s, Calif. Soc. C.P.A.'s, Iowa Soc. C.P.A.'s, Financial Execs. Inst., Nat. Assn. Accountants. Home: PO Box 198 Armstrong IA 50514 Office: Arts-Way Mfg Co Armstrong IA 50514

LANPHIER, EDWARD HOWELL, physiologist, clergyman; b. Madison, Wis., May 29, 1922; s. Ira Burton and Beatrice (Howell) L.; m. Karron Ruth Baird, Apr. 9, 1978. B.S., U. Wis.-Madison, 1946; M.S. in Pharmacology, U. Ill. Coll. of Medicine, Chgo., 1949, M.D., 1949; M.Div., Nashotah Sem., Wis., 1976. Ordained priest Episcopal Ch., 1975. Intern Hosp. of U. Pa., Phila., 1949-50; Assoc. prof. physiology SUNY-Buffalo, 1959-73; sr. scientist dept. preventive medicine U. Wis., Madison, 1976—, asst. dir. for research U. Wis. Biotron. Contbg. editor: The New Science of Skin and Scuba Diving, 1957; U.S. Navy Diving Manual, 1959; Fundamentals of Hyperbaric Medicine, 1966. Contbr. articles to profl. jours. and chpts. to books. Vicar St. Andrew's Episcopal Ch., Monroe, Wis., 1979—. Served from lt. (j.g.) to lt. comdr. M.C., USN, 1951-59. Recipient Borden research award, 1949, 1st Place award Phi Beta Pi essay competition, 1949. Mem. Am. Physiol. Soc., Aerospace Med. Assn., Am. Coll. Sports Medicine, Undersea Med. Soc. (exec. com. 1972-73, Behnke award 1977), Am. Thoracic Soc. Republican. Avocations: multimedia photography, woodworking, camping, language. Home: 208 Highland Ave Madison WI 53705 Office: U Wis Biotron 2115 Observatory Dr Madison WI 53706

LANTRY, JAMES JOHN, coast guard officer; b. Jersey City, Jan. 1, 1942; s. Walter James and Bertha May (Henkel) L.; m. Charlene Linda Ogden, Jan. 28, 1964; children—Dawn Christina, Michael James. B.S., U.S. Coast Guard Acad., 1963; M.B.A., George Washington U., 1970. Commd. ensign U.S. Coast Guard, 1963, advanced through grades to capt., 1984; exec. officer U.S. Coast Guard Cutter Conifer, Portsmouth, Va., 1969-70, contracting officer U.S. Coast Guard Hdqrs., Washington, 1970-73; comdg. officer U.S. Coast Guard Cutter Clover, Sitka, Alaska, 1973-75; comptroller Coast Guard Tng. Ctr., Alameda, Calif., 1975-79, 9th Coast Guard Dist., Cleve., 1979-85. Mem. Am. Soc. Mil. Comptrollers. Democrat. Roman Catholic. Clubs: Bay Soccer (Bay Village, Ohio) (commr. 1983-84); Sunday Stumblers Soccer League (Cleve.) (founder, pres. 1979-85). Advocations: soccer, running, racketball. Home: 30328 Provincetown Ln Bay Village OH 44140 Office: 9th Coast Guard Dist (F) 1240 E 9th St Cleveland OH 44199

LANTZ, GEORGE BENJAMIN, JR., corporation executive; b. Buckhannon, W.Va., Feb. 6, 1936; s. George Benjamin and Georgia Myrtle (Bodkin) L.; m. Mary Sue Powell, Feb. 25, 1957; children—Mary Lynne, Marsha, Kimberly, Rebecca, Todd. A.B. with honors, W.Va. Wesleyan Coll., 1960; S.T.B. with honors, Boston U. Sch. Theology, 1964, Ph.D., 1971. Ordained elder United Methodist Ch. Prof. W.Va. Wesleyan Coll., Buckhannon, 1967-73, chmn. div. Humanities, prof. humanities and religion, 1974-75; asst. to pres., Am. Council on Edn. fellow in acad. adminstrn. Ohio Wesleyan U., Delaware, 1973-74; dean Mount Union Coll., Alliance, Ohio, 1975-80, pres., 1980-85; v.p. acquisitions and adminstrn. Nesco, Inc., Cleve., 1985—; cons. HEW, Washington, 1968-69; commr. North Central Assn. Colls. and Schs., Chgo., 1978—; cons. Council of Ind. Colls., Washington, 1982—. Contbr. articles to profl. jours. Vice pres. Upshur County Bd. Edn., Buckhannon, 1972-78; mem. Mayor's Commn. on Sr. Citizens, Alliance, 1978—; bd. dirs. Alliance unit ARC, 1980—; trustee Canton Symphony Orch., Ohio, 1983—. Served with U.S. Army 1954-56, Korea. Lucinda Bidwell Beebe fellow; Roswell Robinson fellow; W.Va. Wesleyan Key scholar, Walker scholar; recipient Francis Asbury award, Cokesbury Grad. award, Alliance Sr. Citizens Ann. Citizenship award, 1980. Mem. Am. Assn. Higher Edn., AAUP, Soc. Bibl. Lit., Alliance C. of C. (bd. dirs. 1981—), Omicron Delta Kappa, Psi Kappa Omega. Republican. Clubs: University (N.Y.C.), Wranglers. Avocations: golf, hunting, fishing, horseback riding. Home: 7800 Salem Dr Hudson OH 44236 Office: 19201 Villaview Dr Cleveland OH 44119

LANTZ, RICHARD DALE, building materials company official; b. Berne, Ind., Oct. 29, 1951; s. Dale Bernell and Ruby Maxiene L.; m. Debra Sue Spichiger, July 29, 1972; children—Krista, Jessica, Gregory. B.S., Ind. U., 1974. Sales rep. Owens Corning Fiberglas, Oklahoma City, 1974-76, sr. sales rep., Tulsa, 1976-77, supply mgr., Oklahoma City, 1977-78, Cin., 1978-81, br. mgr., Chgo., 1981-84, mktg. mgr., Toledo, 1984—. Mennonite. Home: 2548 Wealdstone Toledo OH 43615

LANTZSCH, HANS EDWIN, school superintendent; b. Krogis, Germany, Aug. 7, 1923; s. Rheinhold Edwin and Louise (Ettmeier) L.; came to U.S., 1927, naturalized, 1934; B.A., Central Mich. U., 1948; M.A., U. Mich., 1950; postgrad. Wayne State U., 1952-63; m. Dora Jablinskey, June 19, 1948; children—James Edwin, Susan Elizabeth, Thomas Paul. Asst. and acting supt. Ecorse (Mich.) Pub. Schs., 1948-67; supt. Trenton (Mich.) Pub. Schs., 1967-71, Gerrish Higgins Sch., Roscommon, Mich., 1971—. Dir. Community Resources Workshop, Mich. State U., 1955-72; asst. dir. NSF Chemistry Inst., Mont. State Coll., 1958. Chmn. sch. liaison Met. Detroit Sci. Fair, 1957-68; mem. com. Wayne County Intermediate Sch. Dist. Occupational Edn., 1969-71; mem. Com. for Educating New Supts. in Mich., 1973-83. Trustee, Mich. Council for Econ. Edn., 1965-68; mem. exec. bd. Down River Learning Disability Ctr., Wyandotte, Mich., 1966-71. Served with AUS, 1943-46. Decorated Bronze Star. Mem. Am. Assn. Sch. Adminstrs. (life, del. assembly 1981, 82, 83), Mich. Edn. Assn. (life), No. Mich. Supts. Assn. (pres. 1977-78), Internat. Platform Assn., Phi Delta Kappa (life). Office: Gerrish Higgins Bd Edn Roscommon MI 48653

LANZL, LAWRENCE HERMAN, medical physics educator; b. Chgo., Apr. 8, 1921; s. Hans and Elsa (Seitz) L.; m. Elisabeth Farber, Sept. 18, 1947; children—Eric Lawrence, Barbara Jane. B.S., Northwestern U., 1943; M.S., U. Ill., 1947, Ph.D., 1951. Diplomate Am. Bd. Radiology. Asst. prof. U. Chgo., 1956-57, assoc. prof., 1959-68; 1st officer Internat. AEC, Vienna, Austria, 1967-68; prof. med. physics U. Chgo., 1968-80, prof. emeritus dept. radiology, 1980—; prof., dir. med. physics Rush U., Chgo., 1980—. Editor: Med. Physics World, 1982. Chmn., Radiation Protection Adv. Council, Springfield, Ill., 1971. Fellow Am. Coll. Radiology; Health Physics Soc.; mem. Am. Assn. Physicists in Medicine (Farrington Daniels award 1984), Internat. Orgn. Med. Physics (v.p. 1982-85, pres. 1985—). Club: Quadrangle. Home: 5750 S Kenwood Ave Chicago IL 60637 Office: Sect Med Physics Rush Presbyn St Luke's Med Ctr 1750 W Congress Pkwy Chicago IL 60612

LAPENSKY, M. JOSEPH, airline executive; b. Mpls., Nov. 27, 1918; s. Frank J. and Mary (Mulkern) L.; B.A., Coll. St. Thomas, St. Paul, 1940; m. Joan M. LaCroix, Nov. 14, 1942; children—John, Stephen, Rosemary, Julianne, Michael, Joseph. With Northwest Air Lines, Inc., 1945—, comptroller, 1960-66, v.p. econ. planning, 1966-73, v.p. fin., 1973-76, pres., chief operating officer, 1976-83, chief exec. officer, 1979-85, chmn., 1983—, also dir. Bd. dirs. St. Mary's Jr. Coll., Mpls.; chmn. bd. trustees Acad. Holy Angels; trustee St. Thomas Coll.; mem. Am. adv. bd. Sogang U., Seoul, chief Mem. Mpls. C. of C. Clubs: Decathlon, Mpls., Minikahda (Mpls.); Minn. (St. Paul). Office: Northwest Air Lines Inc Mpls-St Paul Internat Airport Saint Paul MN 55111*

LAPIN, ANDREW WILLIAM, lawyer; b. Chgo., Feb. 2, 1953; s. Robert Allan and Elaine (Muhlrad) L.; m. Debra Nan Goldberg, July 7, 1979; 1 child, Lauren Elise. B.A., Ind. U., 1975; J.D., John Marshall Law Sch., 1978. Bar: Ill. 1978, U.S. Dist. Ct. (no. dist.) Ill. 1978. Sole practice, Chgo., 1978-79, 81—; assoc. Tash & Slavitt, Ltd., Chgo., 1979-81. Mem. ABA, Chgo. Bar Assn., Ill. State Bar Assn. Office: 35 E Wacker Dr 34th Fl Chicago IL 60601

LAPLACA, LAURA LYN, lawyer; b. Newark, May 8, 1956; d. Peter John and JoAnne Ruth (Olson) LaP.; m. Craig R. Culbertson, Sept. 17, 1983. B.A., Ill. Wesleyan U., 1978; J.D., Loyola U., Chgo., 1981. Bar: Ill. 1981, U.S. Dist. Ct. (no. dist.) Ill. 1982. Assoc. Jenner & Block, Chgo., 1981—. Vol. advisor Anti-Cruelty Soc., Chgo., 1982—. Republican. Lutheran. Office: Jenner & Block 1 IBM Plaza Chicago IL 60611

LAPLANTE-SOSNOWSKY, FRANCES, educational administrator; b. Lawrence, Mass., June 4, 1941; d. Francis and Genevieve (Rogoz) LaPlante; m. William P. Sosnowsky; 2 children. A.A.S., Immaculata Coll., Hamburg, N.Y., 1961; B.S., Marywood Coll., Scranton, Pa., 1965; M.Ed., Marygrove Coll., Detroit, 1970; Ed.D., Wayne State U., 1975. Mem. Order Franciscan Sisters of St. Joseph, Roman Catholic Ch., 1954-69; tchr. St. Hedwig Sch., Detroit, 1961-69, Corpus Christi Sch., Buffalo, 1960-61; cons. programs for speech and lang., impaired dept. spl. Edn. Archdiocese Detroit, 1968-71; dir. Macomb/St. Clair Diagnostic-Assessment Ctr., Dept. Spl. Edn., Ednl. Service Center, Macomb Intermediate Sch. Dist., Macomb County Mt. Clemens, Mich., 1973—, pres. Cranford Terrances, Inc., 1976-80; mem. adv. council Bur. Rehab. Mich. Grantee Mich. Dept. Edn., 1972, U.S. Office Edn., 1973; U.S. Office Edn. fellow, 1968-69. Mem. Wayne State U. Edn. Alumni Assn. (gov.), Am. Assn. Sch. Adminstrs., Council Exceptional Children, Council Adminstrs. Spl. Edn., Nat. Orgn. Legal Problems in Edn., Mich. Assn. Adminstrs. Spl. Edn., Mich. Council Exceptional Children, Macomb County Assn. Adminstrs. Spl. Edn., Phi Delta Kappa, Pi Lambda Theta. Office: 44001 Garfield Rd Mt Clemens MI 48044

LAPOSKY, BEN FRANCIS, comml. artist; b. Cherokee, Iowa, Sept. 30, 1914; s. Peter Paul and Leona Anastasia (Gabriel) L. Free-lance comml. artist, oscillographic designer, 1938; creator electronic abstractions, Oscillons, 1952; one-man shows include: USIA, France, 1956; group shows include: Cybernetic Serendipity, London, 1968; Computer Art, N.Y.C., 1976; Computer Art Internat., Lawrence Hall of Sci., U. Calif., Berkeley, 1979; others; contbr. articles to art jours. Recipient Gold Medal award N.Y. Art Dirs. Club, 1957. Subject of article Arts Mag., June 1980. Home and office: 301 S 6th St Cherokee IA 51012

LAPP, CHARLES JOSEPH, physician; b. Detroit, Jan. 10, 1927; s. Willard Ross and Hattie Louise (Kay) L.; m. June Vera Labatt, June 11, 1951; children—Cynthia, Christopher, Linda, Pamela, Charles, Jr. B.S., Wayne State U., 1949, M.D., 1952. Diplomate Am. Bd. Family Practice. Intern, Detroit

Meml. Hosp.; ptnr. family practice, Glendale, Ariz., 1953-54; gen. practice medicine Luna Pier, Mich., 1954-55, Utica, Mich., 1957—; anesthesiologist Weiss, Palaus, Atler, Lapp, Toledo, Ohio, 1955-57; asst. clinical prof. Dept. Family Practice Wayne State Coll. Medicine; coroner, Macomb County. Served to seaman lc USNR, 1944-46. Mem. AMA, Mich. State Med. Soc., Macomb County Med. Soc., Acad. Family Practice. Republican. Lutheran. Avocations: photography; electronic experimenting; auto repair. Home: 8830 Suncrest Sterling Heights MI 48078 Office: Charles J Lapp MD PC 7817 McClellan Utica MI 48087

LAPP, JOHN ALLEN, history educator, college administrator; b. Lansdale, Pa., Mar. 15, 1933; s. John E. and Edith (Nyce) L.; m. Alice Weber, Aug. 20, 1955; children—John F., Jennifer, Jessica. B.A., Eastern Mennonite Coll., 1954; M.A., Case Western Res. U., 1958; Ph.D., U. Pa., 1968. From asst. prof. to prof. Eastern Mennoite Coll., Harrisonburg, Va., 1960-69; prof. history, dean Goshen Coll., Ind., 1972-82, prof. history, provost, 1982-84; exec. sec. Mennonite Central Com., Akron, Pa., 1985—; campus visitor North Central Assn. Schs. and Colls., 1975—. Author: The Mennonite Church in India, 1972, The View From East Jerusalem, 1980. Contbr. articles to profl. jours. Chmn. commn. Mennonite Central Peace Sect., Akron, 1973-78; bd. dirs. Mennonite Central Com., Akron, 1980-84. Mem. Conf. Faith and History.

LAPRE, KATHRYN MARY, computer scientist; b. Manchester, N.H., May 3, 1939; d. Clayton Gerald and Margaret May (Flood) Hobbs; B.A. magna cum laude, Providence Coll., 1972, M.B.A., 1976, C.D.P., 1977; m. Robert Henry Lapre, Sept. 30, 1959 (div.); children—Donna Marie, Robert James, Michael Jon. With Raytheon Co., 1961-69; programmer analyst Kay Windsor, New Bedford, Mass., 1969-70; programmer analyst Providence Pile Fabric, Fall River, Mass., 1970-72; systems analyst Citizens Bank, Providence, 1972-74; project leader, lead analyst R.I. Hosp. Trust Nat. Bank, Providence, 1974-77; instr. bus. and computer sci. Providence Coll., 1977-81; research and devel. systems coordinator U. Fla. Gainesville, 1981-82, now adj. instr.; mgr computer services GMI Engring. and Mgmt. Inst., Flint, Mich., 1982-84; dir. computer ctr. Denison U., Granville, Ohio, 1984—; Bd. dirs. Camp Fire Girls, 1972-73; active Explorer Scouts, 1982-84, chmn. Post 407, 1983-84. Author: Getting Started in BASIC, 1980. Served with USAF, 1957-58. Mem. Assn. Systems Mgmt. (sec. 1979-80), Assn. Women in Computing. Home: 102 Chapin Pl Granville OH 43023 Office: Computer Ctr Fellows Hall Denison U Granville OH 43023

LARDY, HENRY ARNOLD, biological science educator; b. Roslyn, S.D., Aug. 19, 1917; s. Nicholas and Elizabeth (Gebetsreiter) L.; m. Annrita Dresselhuys, Jan. 21, 1943; children—Nicholas, Diana, Jeffrey, Michael. B.S., S.D. State U., 1939; M.S., U. Wis.-Madison, 1941, Ph.D., 1943; D. Sc. (hon.) S.D. State U., 1978. Asst. prof. U. Wis.-Madison, 1945-47, assoc. prof. 1947-50, prof. biochemistry, 1950—, chmn. sect. II Inst. Enzyme Research, 1950—, Vilas prof. biol. scis., 1966—. Editor: Respiratory Enzymes, 1948, The Enzymes, 1959-63 (eight books); contbr. articles to profl. jours.; patentee in field. Pres. Citizens vs. McCarthy, Wis., 1950. Recipient Wolf Prize in Agr., Wolf Found., Israel, 1981. Mem. Am. Soc. Biol. Chemists (pres. 1964), Am. Chem. Soc., Soc. for Study of Reproduction (Carl Hartman award), Biochem. Soc. (U.K.), Am. Philos. Soc., Am. Acad. Arts and Sci. (Armory prize 1984). Democratic. Avocations: riding; hunting; tennis. Home: 1829 Thorstrand Rd Madison WI 53705 Office: Enzyme Inst 1710 Univ Ave Madison WI 53705

LARGENT, ALFRED JOSEPH, power company official; b. Cadillac, Mich., June 19, 1930; s. Alfred Clay and Cecilia M. (Long) L.; ed. Traverse City (Mich.) public and parochial schs., DeForrest Radio and Electronics Sch., Internat. Corr. Schs.; m. Caroline C. Weber, June 17, 1950; children—Edward, Robert, Linda, Sherri. With Traverse City Light & Power Co., 1948—, beginning as meter reader, successively polyphase meter reader, line crew, journeyman lineman, 1948-68, supt. transmission and distbn., 1968—; mem. Grand Traverse County Bd. Commrs., 1968-82. Active Boy Scouts Am., Community Chest, Walking Blood Bank. Mem. Mich. Assn. Commrs., Mich. Elec. Assn. Democrat. Roman Catholic. Club: K.C. Home: 857 Kinross St Traverse City MI 49684 Office: 400 Boardman Ave Traverse City MI 49684

LARIMORE, HAROLD CORDELL, optometrist; b. Hull, Ill., Sept. 12, 1915; s. Albert Roy and Angeline (Oitker) L.; m. Ruth M. Ross, Aug. 13, 1937; children—Albert Leslie, Cynthia Ann, David Ross O.D., Ill. Coll. Optometry, Chgo., 1959. Gen. practice optometry, Springfield, Mo., 1940-68; optometrist, sec., treas. Larimore, Baker, Brown & Assocs., Inc., Springfield, 1968—. Active Springfield Boys Club, pres. 1956-58. Recipient Legion of Honor award De Molay, 1959. Mem. Am. Optometric Found. (life), Am. Optometric Assn., Mo. Optometric Assn. (trustee 1953-59), Illuminating Soc. of Am., Greater Ozarks Optometric Soc. (pres. 1947-58, sec., treas. 1959-64). Republican. Episcopalian. Lodges: Sertoma (Springfield) (pres. 1953-56), Sertoma Internat. (life), Elks, Masons (32 degree), Shriners. Avocations: fishing, painting, charity work. Office: Larimore Baker Brown & Assocs Inc 601 South Ave Springfield MO 65806

LARKIN, JEAN ARIEL, book and antique shop owner, operator, book restorer; b. Topeka, Kans., May 5, 1928; d. Robert Gault and (Clara) Elizabeth (McClelland) Gross; m. Storey Judson Larkin, Jan. 3, 1948; children—Barbara Voorhees, Josephine Susan Larkin Smith, Midge E. Larkin Sheahan. Grad. South High Sch., Denver, 1946; student Kiswaukee Jr. Coll. Office worker Texaco, Denver, 1947-48; antique shop owner, operator Storeybook Antiques, De Kalb County, Ill., 1972-81, antique and book shop, Sycamore, Ill., 1981—. Pres. Glen Ellyn, Ill., PTA, 1960; Sunday sch. tchr. St. Marks Episcopal Ch., Glen Ellyn, 1960s; librarian St. Peter's Episcopal Ch., Sycamore, 1979—; leader DuPage County Council Girl Scouts U.S., 1960s; vol. rare book preservationist Morton Arboretum Library, Lisle, Ill., 1980—. Mem. Altrusan Internat., Midwest Book Hunters, No. Ill. Antique Dealers Assn. (sec. 1970s). Republican. Clubs: Columbian Literary (Sycamore) (sec.), Wheaton-Glen Ellyn Book. Avocations: reading, cooking, walking, travel, dress design. Home: Rural Route 1 Box 151 Sycamore IL 60178 Office: Storeybook Antiques & Books 11325 E State Sycamore IL 60178

LARRABEE, GENE ROSS, health care executive; b. Hammond, Ind., Nov. 30, 1947; s. James F. and Kathryn J. (Eggers) L.; B.A., U. Iowa and Winona (Minn.) State U., 1970; postgrad. U. Toledo, 1970-71; M.H.A., Governors State U., Park Forest South, Ill., 1972; children—Brent E.J., Kirk F.J., Aaron A.R. Unit adminstr. Elisabeth Ludeman Mental Retardation Center, Park Forest, Ill., 1972-73; adminstr. RN Convalescent Home, Berwyn, Ill., 1973-74; adminstr. Niles Manor Nursing Center, Niles, Ill., 1974; adminstr. Park Rehab. Center, Euclid, Ohio, 1974-82, chmn. bd., 1982—; pres. Primus Inter Pares Health Cons., Inc., 1982—; pres. Medi-Pro Employment Services, Inc., 1981—; pres. Consultronics Corp., Euclid, 1975—; v.p. Euclid Park Nursing Center Pharmacy, Euclid, 1975—, Hermetic Chem. Labs., Inc., Euclid, 1976—; mem. seminar faculty Ohio U.; treas. St. Anthony's Continuing Care Center, Rock Island, Ill., 1978-79; mem. Gov.'s Commn. on Ohio Health Care Costs, 1983. Mem. Ohio Acad. Nursing Homes (bd. dirs. 1980-85, chmn. legal com., mem. legis. com. 1980-81, treas. 1980-81, pres. 1981-83, mem. geriatric polit. action com., pres. 1981-83), Am. Coll. Nursing Home Adminstrs., Am. Health Care Assn., Ohio Health Care Assn., N.E. Ohio Nursing Home Assn., Am. Assn. Rehab. Facilities. Home: 5191 B Liberty Ln Willoughby OH 44094 Office: 20611 Euclid Ave Euclid OH 44117

LARSEN, LINDA ELYSE, information official; b. Chgo., Aug. 1, 1946; d. Martin M. and Reah R. (Goldstein) Brin; m. Laird L. Larsen, June 22, 1968. B.A., U. Ill.-Chgo., 1971; postgrad. No. Ill. U., 1977-79. Officer admissions Columbia Coll., Chgo., 1971-74; bus. Librarian Blue Cross Blue Shield Assns., Chgo., 1975-81; mgr. info. ctr. A.T. Kearney, Inc., Chgo., 1981—. Mem. Spl. Libraries Assn. Office: AT Kearney Inc 222 S Riverside Plaza Chicago IL 60606

LARSEN, MARK LEIF, construction executive, accounting and management executive; b. Elgin, Ill., Sept. 20, 1956; s. Donald Ernst and Corinna (Gessa) L. B.S. in Bus. Adminstrn., U. Ill., 1978. Field engr. Thorleif Larsen & Son, Inc., Itasca, Ill., 1978-79, project mgr., estimator, 1979-81, v.p. adminstrn., 1981—; pres. GM Acctg./Mgmt. Services, Inc., Itasca, 1983. Republican. Clubs: Medinah (Ill.) Country; Chgo. Athletic Assn. Home: 1030 N State St Suite 52H Chicago IL 60610 Office: Thorleif Larsen & Son Inc 801 W Thorndale Ave Itasca IL 60143

LARSON, ANDREW ROBERT, lawyer; b. Pine County, Minn., Feb. 25, 1930; s. Gustaf Adolf and Mary (Mach) L.; B.A., U. Minn., 1953, B.S. Law, St. Paul Coll. Law, 1956; LL.B., William Mitchell Coll. Law, 1958; m. Evelyn Joan Johnson, Sept. 12, 1953 (div. 1980); children—Linda Suzanne, Mark Andrew. Bar: Minn. 1958. With Armour & Co., 1953-56, Minn. Dept. Taxation, 1956-58; individual practice law, Duluth, Minn., 1958—; municipal judge Village of Proctor, part-time 1961-74; dir., sec. various bus., real estate corps.; pres. Larson, Huseby and Brodin, Ltd.; v.p., sec. Sea Jay Corp. Arbitrator Minn. Bur. Mediation Services. chmn. Duluth Fair Employment and Housing Commn., 1965-76; vice chmn. Mayor's Arena Auditorium Com., Duluth, 1964-65; active United Way; mem. State Bd. Human Rights, 1967-73; Midwest regional rep. nat. standing com. on legislation United Cerebral Palsy, 1967-71, bd. dirs. nat. assn., 1971-72; bd. dirs. United Day Activity Center, 1969-76, Am. Cancer Soc., 1973-75, Light House for Blind, 1975-79, 80—, Environ. Learning Center, 1978-81; mem. Greater Downtown Council. Recipient awards including Humanitarian Service award United Cerebral Palsy, 1965, Republican party I Care award for work in civil rights, aid to handicapped, 1964, Jr. C. of C. Disting. Service award, 1965. Mem. Minn. Bar Assn., Minn. Jud. Council, Am. Arbitration Assn., Nat. Fedn. Ind. Businessmen, Nat. Assn. Accts., Fresh Water Soc., Minn. League Municipalities, Hist. Soc., NAACP, ACLU, C. of C., U.S. C. of C., Minn. Arrowhead Assn., Western Lake Superior Recreation Assn., Boat Owners Assn. U.S., Nat. Wildlife Fedn., Minn. Pub. Radio, Beta Phi Kappa. Republican. Unitarian-Universalist. Clubs: 242 Yacht, Duluth Keel. Lodge: Kiwanis. Home: 3002 E Superior St Duluth MN 55812 Office: 333 W Superior St Duluth MN 55802

LARSON, BRUCE LINDER, biochemistry educator; b. Mpls., June 24, 1927; s. Leif Raeder and Olive Hazel Rosetta (Linder) L.; m. Marjorie Helen Hersleth, Sept. 24, 1954; children—Eric Martin, David Bruce, Brian Linder. B.S., U. Minn., 1948, Ph.D., 1951. Instr. biochemistry U. Ill., Urbana, 1951-53, asst. prof., 1953-59, assoc. prof., 1959-66, prof., 1966—. Author, editor: Lactation: A Comprehensive Treatise, 4 vols., 1974, 78; Lactation, 1985. Contbr. articles to profl. jours. Commr. Urbana Park Dist., 1967—, pres., 1970—. Grantee NSF, 1959-74, 79-82 NIH, 1972-75, Nat. Dairy Council, 1976-79. Mem. Am. Chem. Soc., Am. Soc. Biol. Chemists, AAAS, Am. Dairy Sci. Assn. Lutheran. Club: Exchange. Avocations: wilderness canoe, camping. Home: 506 E Pennsylvania Ave Urbana IL 61801 Office: Dept Animal Sci U Ill 1207 W Gregory Dr Urbana IL 61801

LARSON, CLIFFORD EMIL, marketing educator, corporate consultant; b. Rice Lake, Wis., May 31, 1928; s. Casper Paul and Augusta Louise (Kinn) L.; m. Winifred Esther Wentorf, June 19, 1954; children—Karl C., David R., Ann L., Jane E. B.B.A., U. Wis., 1950, M.B.A., 1951, Ph.D., 1957. Bd. dirs. TIME Ins. Corp., Milw., 1973-78, TEKRA Corp., New Berlin, Wis., 1983—, H.C. Prange Co., Sheboygan, Wis., 1983—; dean coll. bus. admin. U. Wis.-Oshkosh, 1969-84, prof. mktg., 1969—; pres. Bethel Home, Oshkosh, 1984—, bd. dirs., 1980—. Bd. dirs. Oshkosh Symphony, 1980—, pres. 1980-82; mem. Milw. Symphony State Adv. Bd., 1980-82, Adv. Bd., Oshkosh, 1979—; bd. dirs. Work Adjustment Services, Inc., Wis. Citizens for Arts, Inc., 1985—. Mem. Am. Assembly Collegiate Sch. Bus. (accreditation chmn., various chairs 1973-84), Am. Mktg. Assn., Fin. Execs. Inst. Midwest Mktg. Assn., Beta Gamma Sigma (bd. govs. 1976-80). Republican. Congregationalist. Avocations: model railroading; railroad history; sailing; cross-country skiing. Home: 940 Windward Ct Oshkosh WI 54901 Office: Coll Bus Admin U Wis Oshkosh WI 54901

LARSON, DALE ALAN, solid fuel safety technician; b. Eau Claire, Wis., Sept. 19, 1953; s. Lawrence Christian and Mary Elaine (Anderson) L.; m. Bonita Louise Buttenhoff, Feb. 14, 1978; children—Dustin Levi, Dalton Jon. Grad. North High Sch., Eau Claire, 1971. Optical lab. technician Benson Optical Co., Eau Claire, 1976-81; prin. Mr. Sweep Inc., Lake Hallie, Wis., 1978—; agent Buttenhoff Ins. Co., Eau Claire, 1982—; cons. solid fuel safety to consumers. Served with U.S. Army, 1971-74; Germany. Mem. Nat. Chimney Sweep Guild (cert., Wis. state rep. 1983—), Wis. Guild Chimney Sweeps, Wood Heating Alliance, Energy Alternatives Inst. (cert.), Wood Heat Edn. Research Found. (cert.), Ind. Safety Commn. (cert.). Home: 5707 Lakeshore Dr Chippewa Falls WI 54729

LARSON, DAVID CHRISTOPHER, lawyer, judge; b. Spencer, Iowa, Sept. 4, 1955; s. Leonard and Margaret Roxanne (Proctor) L.; m. Carol Ann Kuntz, Sept. 17, 1983. B.S. in Constrn. Engring., Iowa State U., 1978; J.D., Creighton U., 1981. Bar: Iowa 1981, U.S. Patent Office 1981, U.S. Dist. Ct. (no. dist.) Iowa 1981, U.S. Ct. Appeals (8th cir.) 1981. Law clk. Henderson & Sturm, Omaha, 1981; ptnr. Stoller & Larson, Spirit Lake, Iowa, 1981-84; sole practice, 1984—; alt. dist. assoc. judge Iowa Jud. Dist. 3A, 1983—. Mem. Iowa State Bar Assn. (com. on patents, trademarks and copyrights 1982—), Dist. 3A Bar Assn. (pres. 1983-84), Dickinson County Bar Assn. (chmn. Am. citizen com. 1982-83, pres. 1983-84), ABA, Iowa Patent Law Assn., Iowa Great Lakes C. of C. (ambassador 1982—). Republican. Methodist. Club: Okoboji Yacht (trophy chmn. 1984—). Lodge: Kiwanis (fin. com. chmn. 1983, bd. dirs. 1984). Home: Rural Route 5520 Spirit Lake IA 51360 Office: PO Box 246 Spirit Lake IA 51360

LARSON, DAVID ELI, lawyer; b. Dayton, Ohio, Feb. 9, 1945; s. Eli Christian and Myrtle Lorene (Heeren) L.; m. Beverly Jean Farlow, June 17, 1967 (div.); m. Roberta Elizabeth Longfellow, Aug. 25, 1979; 1 child, Jessica Deane Longfellow. B.A., Wittenberg U., 1967; M.P.A., U. N.C., 1974; J.D., Ohio State U., 1979. Bar: Ohio 1979, U.S. Dist. Ct. (so. dist.) Ohio 1980. Vol. Peace Corps, Turkey, 1968; community devel. rep. HUD, Columbus, Ohio, 1970-73, multifamily housing rep., 1975-76; community devel. dir. City of Miamisburg, Ohio, 1973-75; assoc. Law Clinic of D.W. Bench, Dayton, 1980-83; ptnr. Certo and Larson, Kettering, Ohio, 1983—. Lyricist: Rain and Gray Eyes, 1981. Co-chmn. and mem. commn. on ch. and soc. Grace United Methodist Ch., Dayton, 1981; bd. dirs. Dayton Area Heart Assn., 1982. Recipient cert. of commendation Montgomery County Mental Health Assn., Ohio, 1983; Wittenberg Alumni scholar Wittenberg U., 1963; study fellow for internat. devel. U. N.C., Chapel Hill, 1969. Mem. Dayton Bar Assn. Democrat. Home: 836 Belmonte Park N Dayton OH 45405 Office: Certo and Larson 2278 S Smithville Rd Kettering OH 45420

LARSON, DAVID JAMES, plant maintenance engineer; b. Mpls., Dec. 30, 1946; s. James Howard and Virginia Doyle (Smart) L.; m. Nancy Patricia Aber, Oct. 9, 1970; children—Chad Christian, Scott David, Stephanie Brita. Student U. Minn., 1966, U.S. Navy Nuclear Power Sch., 1968. Mem. maintenance staff St. Mary's Hosp., Mpls., 1972-76; maintenance foreman Wolkerstorfer Plating, Mpls., 1976-77; electrician John Morrell Mends, St. Paul, 1977-79; maintenance mgr. M.A. Gedney Co., Chaska, Minn., 1979-81; plant maintenance engr. Swiss Miss div. Beatrice Co., Menomonie, Wis., 1981—. Fund raiser Menomonie United Way, 1984—. Served with U.S. Navy, 1966-72. Mem. Toastmasters, Soc. for Advancement of Mgmt. (sec. 1984—), Am. Inst. Plant Engrs., Am. Mgmt. Assn. Republican. Mem. Missionary Alliance. Avocations: jogging, golf, fishing. Home: 208 Sunset Dr Menomonie WI 54751 Office: Swiss Miss div Beatrice Co 104 River Rd Menomonie WI 54751

LARSON, DONALD NORMAN, linguist, educator, consultant; b. Chgo., Nov. 1, 1925; s. Norman and Ferne Eleanor (Sellstrom) L.; m. Llewellyn Marie Johnson, July 14, 1949; children—Jeffrey, Rebecca, Brett. B.A., Wheaton Coll., 1949; M.A., U. Chgo., 1957, Ph.D., 1965. Research dir. Toronto Inst. Linguistics, Ont., Can., 1957—; prof. linguistics and anthropology Bethel Coll., St. Paul, 1966—; exec. dir. Communication Mgmt. Services, St. Paul, 1982—; cons. Fgn. Mission Bd. So. Bapt. Conv., Richmond, Va., 1972—, Link-Care, Fresno, Calif., 1979—. Author: Structural Approach to Greek, 1958; Becoming Bilingual, 1972; Guidelines for Barefoot Language Learning, 1984; also articles. Bd. dirs. Minn. Internat. Health Vols., Mpls., 1981—. Served with USNR, 1944-46. Tuition scholar U. Chgo., 1952-65. Fellow Am. Anthrop. Assn.; mem. Linguistic Soc. Am., Am. Soc. Missiology. Avocations: fishing; boating; photography. Home: 3570 Rice St Saint Paul MN 55112 Office: Dept Linguistics Bethel Coll 3900 Bethel Dr Saint Paul MN 55112

LARSON, DOUGLAS CARL, municipal executive; b. Big Rapids, Mich., Feb. 13, 1950; s. Carl E. and Ellen M. (Adolphson) L.; m. JoAnne Roemisch, Mar. 18, 1972; children—Stacy Joan, Jillian Suzanne. Real Estate cert. Ferris State Coll., 1976, A.A.S., 1976, B.S. in Bus. Adminstrn., 1978; postgrad. Central Mich. U., 1977—. Cert. level III assessor, personal property examiner, Mich., 1977. Student mgr. Ferris State Coll., Big Rapids, Mich., 1973-75, legal asst. to v.p., 1976; asst. assessor City of Big Rapids, 1976-78, assessor, 1978-80, mgr. data processing, assessment, 1980-81; adminstrv. asst., 1981-83; city mgr., Algonac, Mich., 1983—; instr. Ferris State Coll., 1979-81. Mem. Mecosta County Assessors Assn., Mich. Assessors Assn. (legis. com. mem.), Indsl. Devel. Corp (bd. dirs.), Internat. Assessors Assn., Internat. City Mgrs. Assn. Methodist. Club: Rotary (v.p., 1983) Home: 1828 St Clair Blvd Algonac MI 48001 Office: City of Algonac 805 St Clair River Dr Algonac MI 48001

LARSON, EMILIE G., retired educator; b. Northfield, Minn., Apr. 28, 1919; d. Melvin Cornelius and Frieda (Christiansen) L.; A.B., St. Olaf Coll., 1940; M.A., Radcliffe Coll., 1946; student U. Chgo., 1951-52. Tchr. Hanska (Minn.) High Sch., 1940-42, Two Harbors (Minn.) High Sch., 1942-43; tchr. J.W. Weeks Jr. High Sch., Newton, Mass., 1946-56, guidance counselor, 1956-81; counselor Warren Jr. High Sch., Newton, 1979-81. Deacon, Univ. Luth. Ch., 1979. Mem. AAUW (state v.p. for program devel., topic chmn. Mass. div. 1975-76; corp. rep., area rep. for internat. relations Minn. div. 1984-86), Mass., Newton tchrs. assns., St. Olaf Coll. Alumni Assn. (dir. 1982-85), PEO, Virginia Gildersleeve Internat. Fund for Univ. Women Inc. (membership com.), Pi Lambda Theta. Lutheran. Club: Women's City (Boston). Contbr. articles to profl. jours. Address: 1110 W 1st St Northfield MN 55057

LARSON, ERIC ALFRED, college dean; b. Syracuse, N.Y., May 22, 1945; s. Kenneth George and Kathryn Elouise (Keiper) L.; m. Susan Wright, July 1, 1967 (div. 1981); children—Shannon, Christopher, David; m. Sharon Anne Burian Fisher, Oct. 16, 1981. B.A., Franklin Pierce Coll., 1967; M.B.A., Syracuse U., 1969. Tchr. Onondaga County Bd. Coop. Ednl. Services, Syracuse, 1967-69; instr. Onondaga Community Coll., 1969-78; dean Elgin Community Coll., Ill., 1978—; cons., owner Fisher-Larson & Larson, Elgin, 1984—. Mem. Greater Elgin City Commn., 1984—. Mem. Nat. Assn. Mgmt. Educators (chmn. bd. 1983-85), Ill. Vocat. Assn., Am. Vocat. Assn., Ill. Bus. Edn. Assn., Chgo. Area Bus. Edn. Assn. Republican. Lodge: Masons. Avocation: golf. Office: Elgin Community Coll 1700 Spartan Dr Elgin IL 60120

LARSON, INGEMAR WALLACE, biology educator; b. Clarissa, Minn., Dec. 4, 1928; s. David and Gertrud Larson; m. Katherine Ekstrom, Aug. 18, 1963. B.A., Concordia Coll., 1951; M.S., Kans. State U., 1957; Ph.D., 1964. Research assoc. Oreg. State U., 1963-66; asst. prof. biology Augustana Coll., Rock Island, Ill., 1966-69, assoc. prof., 1969-77, prof., 1977—, chmn. dept., 1977-83. Served with U.S. Army, 1952-54. Mem. Am. Soc. Parasitologists, Am. Micros. Soc., Ill. Acad. Sci., Sigma Xi. Democrat. Lutheran. Office: Dept Biology Augustana Coll Rock Island IL 61201

LARSON, JACQUELINE FAY, media specialist; b. S. Gate, Calif., Nov. 6, 1940; d. Joseph F. and Neta Elizabeth (Hill) McPherron; m. Donald Lee Larson, Feb. 23, 1963; children—Gregory Paul, Kimberly Ann, Jill Marie. B.S., N.W. Mo. State U., 1965; M.S. in Edn., Ft. Hays State U. (Kans.), 1982. Library asst. Clarinda Pub. Library, Iowa, 1964-65; bookmobile librarian Mpls. Pub. Library, 1966-67; librarian Unified Sch. Dist. 273, Beloit, Kan., 1968—; com. mem. North Central Eval. Team, Belleville and Oberlin, Kans., 1982, 83; speaker in field. Contbr. articles to profl. jours. Vol., Multiple Sclerosis, Am. Cancer Soc., ARC. Mem. Kans. Assn. Sch. Librarians (sec. 1978-80), ALA, Am. Assn. Sch. Librarians, Young Adult Services, Kans. Assn. Ednl. Communications Tech., Phi Delta Kappa. Lutheran. Lodge: Eagles. Home: 213 N Campbell St Beloit KS 67420 Office: Beloit Jr-Sr High Sch 1711 N Walnut St Beloit KS 67420

LARSON, JAMES GORDON, farmer, agriculture company executive; b. Sioux Rapids, Iowa, Jan. 13, 1947; s. E. Fordan and Edna Marie (Olsen) L.; m. Marcia Arlene Morse, May 26, 1968; children—Karl, Susan, Benjamin. B.S., Iowa State U. Sales rep. Am. Breeders Service, Defores, Wis., 1977—. Central com. Clay County Republicans, 1973—; pres. Rembrandt Ch., Iowa, Clay County Farm Bur., Spencer, 1979, 80; trustee Douglas Twp.; dir. Clay County Cattleman, 1984—. Served to 1st lt. USNG, 1967-73. Lutheran. Avocation: farming. Home: Rural Route 2 Box 62 Sioux Rapids IA 50585

LARSON, JANE BALE, interior designer; b. Dickinson, N.D., Sept. 30, 1946; d. Stanley Walter and Hazel Eleanor (Bartow) Bale; m. James W. Emison III, Feb. 14, 1983. B.S., N.D. State U., 1968. Home fashion coordinator Montgomery Wards, Mpls., 1968-69; staff interior designer McClain, Hedman & Schultz, St. Paul, 1969-72; sales, design mgr. Dayton's Contract Interiors, Mpls., 1972-73; v.p., contract mgr. Contemporary Designs, Inc., Mpls., 1973-79; pres., owner J.B. Larson Assocs., Inc., 1979-83; cons. interior design Jane Larson-Emison Designs, Mpls., 1983—. Mem. adv. bd. design dept. U. Minn. Coll. Home Econs., 1982-84. Recipient Merit award Minn. Soc. AIA, 1979, Architecture Minn. Pubs. Design award, 1980, Architecture Minn. Advt. award excellence, 1981, Honor award Minn. AIA, 1983. Mem. Mpls. C. of C. (cultural activities com. 1980). Clubs: Wayzata Country (Minn.); Minikahda (Mpls.). Home: 19255 Cedarhurst St Deephaven MN 55391 Office: Jane Larson-Emison Designs 19255 Cedarhurst Deephaven MN 55391

LARSON, JERRY L., state supreme court justice; b. Harlan, Iowa, May 17, 1936; s. Gerald L. and Mary Eleanor (Patterson) L.; B.A., State U. Iowa, 1958, J.D., 1960; m. Linda R. Logan; children—Rebecca, Jeffrey, Susan, David. Bar: Iowa. Partner firm Larson & Larson, 1961-75; dist. judge 4th Jud. Dist. Ct. Iowa, 1975-78; justice Iowa Supreme Ct., 1978—; county atty. Shelby County (Iowa), 1965-69. Mem. Iowa State Bar Assn., Iowa Judges Assn. Office: State House Des Moines IA 50319

LARSON, JOSEPH, wholesale agricultural company executive. Chmn., dir. Farmers Union Central Exchange, Inc., Inver Grove Heights, Minn. Office: Farmers Union Central Exchange Inc 5500 Cenex Dr Inver Grove Heights MN 55075*

LARSON, LARRY G., optical company executive; b. New Effington, S.D., Aug. 26, 1931. B.S. in Elec. Engring., U. Minn., 1959; postgrad. in fin., U. Calif. Research engr. Econs. Lab., Inc., St. Paul, 1957-59; sr. devel. engr. Philco Western Devel. Lab., 1959-60; supr. Lockheed Missiles and Space Co.; group mgr. Honeywell, to 1968; dir. programs Textron, Inc., Dalmo Victor Co., Belmont, Calif., 1968-69; pres., chief exec. officer EOCOM Corp., Irvine, Calif., 1969-79; exec. Electro-Optics div. Honeywell, Inc., 1979-84; pres., chief exec. officer RECON/Optical, Inc., Barrington, Ill., 1984—. Contbr. articles to profl. jours. Contbg. editor Am. Prodn. News. Served with USAF, 1950-54. Recipient citations U.S. Air Force, B'nai Brith, U. Minn.; appointed Pres. Carter to serve UN Day Chmn., 1977. Mem. Am. Electronics Assn., Am. Def. Preparadness Assn., Am. Security Council, IEEE; Optical Soc. Am., Am. Inst. Physics, AAAS, and others. Address: Recon/Optical Inc 550 W Northwest Hwy Barrington IL 60010

LARSON, MARIAN GERTRUDE, catalog sales company executive; b. Madison, Wis., Aug. 22, 1927; s. Guy Henry and Gertrude Francis (Everett) L. B.A., U. Wis., 1948; M.B.A., U. Chgo., 1982. Mgr. continuity, Sta. WISC, Madison, 1948-53; copy chief Spiegel, Inc., Chgo., 1953-58, editor-in-chief women's, 1958-62, catalog mgr., domestics and shoes, 1962-76, group catalog mgr. hardlines, 1976-79, v.p. advt., Oak Brook, Ill., 1979—; pres. Spiegel Pub. Co., Oak Brook, 1979—. Bd. dirs. Hinsdale United Way; alumni bd. U. Chgo. Grad. Sch. Bus. Mem. Chgo. Advt. Club, Nat. Assn. Women Bus. Owners, Direct Mktg. Assn. Office: Regency Towers Oak Brook IL 60521

LARSON, OBERT LEROY, former banker; b. Worth County, Iowa, Apr. 9, 1916; s. Lauritz Nicholi and Anna Otillie (Storre) L.; student Waldorf Jr. Coll., Forest City, Iowa, 1936; B.A., Luther Coll., Decorah, Iowa, 1939; cert. banking U. Wis., 1967; m. Mary Lou McGrath, June 4, 1944; children—Mary Lynne, John Lauritz. Bookkeeper, Peterson Oil Co., Ft. Dodge, Iowa, 1939-40; retail dealer petroleum products, Eagle Grove, Iowa, 1940-41, 46-48; partner Chevrolet/Pontiac retail dealership, Eagle Grove, 1948-54, owner, 1954-56; with Security Savs. Bank, Eagle Grove, 1956-66; exec. v.p. Farmers Trust and Savs. Bank, Williamsburg, Iowa, 1966-67, pres., 1967-81, chmn. bd., 1972-81; chmn. Iowa Bankers and Ins. Services Inc., 1972-75, dir., 1971-81. Treas., corr. Rotary Ann Home sr. citizens, 1962-66; treas. Eagle Grove Community Sch. Bd., 1958-66; v.p. Wright County (Iowa) Fair Bd., 1951-66; chmn. Iowa County Cancer Crusade, 1975-76, Iowa County Am. Heart Assn., 1977, River City SCORE, 1984-85; mem. Iowa County Airport Commn., 1974—, Iowa County Quality Water Study Com., 1977—. Served with USNR, 1941-45. Decorated D.F.C., Air medal with cluster. Mem. Iowa Ind. (dir. 1974-76), Iowa, Am. Ind., Am. bankers assns., Am. Inst. Banking (charter), Eagle Grove C. of C. (pres. 1950, 58), Williamsburg C. of C. (dir. 1967-69). Republican. Lutheran. Club: Sport Hill Golf and Country. Lodges: Rotary (pres. Eagle Grove 1960), Kiwanis. Home: 24 Oak Dr Mason City IA 50401

LARSON, SANDRA MAE, nursing educator; b. Chgo., Apr. 21, 1944; d. Richard Milward and Eldred Gertrude (Piehl) Blackburn; m. Eric Richard Larson, Nov. 25, 1967; children—Sarah, Keith. B.S., No. Ill. U., 1966, M.S., 1978. R.N., Ill. Nursing educator Lutheran Hosp., Moline, Ill., 1968-70; charge nurse ICU, Peninsula Hosp., Burlingame, Calif., 1970-72; staff nurse Illini Hosp., Silvis, Ill., 1972-76; nursing educator Black Hawk Coll., Moline, 1976—, chmn. assoc. degree program, 1983—; mem. audit com. Rock Island County Health Dept., Ill., 1983—; mem. long-term care tech. adv. com. Western Ill. Area Agy. on Aging, Rock Island, 1984—; presenter radio program on stress Sta. KIIK, Moline, 1980; interviewer Am. Cancer Soc., Moline, 1982, 84. Mem. Am. Nurses Assn., Ill. Nurses Assn. (bd. dirs. 5th dist. 1979-82, treas., 1982-84, pres. 1984—), Sigma Theta Tau. Democrat. Congregationalist. Avocations: camping; reading. Home: 1812 24th Ave Moline IL 61265 Office: Black Hawk Coll 6600 34th Ave Moline IL 61265

LARSON, SIDNEY, art educator, artist, painting conservator; b. Sterling, Colo., June 16, 1923; s. Harry and Ann (Levin) L.; m. George Ann Madden, Aug. 30, 1947; children—Sara Catherine, Nancy Louise. B.A., U. Mo., 1949, M.A. in Art, 1950. Prof. art Columbia Coll., Mo., 1951—; art curator State Hist. Soc. Mo., 1962—; painting conservator, Columbia, 1960—. Exhibited paintings and drawings in group shows in Midwest and N.Y.; executed mural Daily News, Rolla, Mo., Shelter Ins., Columbia, Mo., Mcpl. Bldg., Jefferson City, Mo., Centerre Bank, Columbia, Mo., chs. in Okla. and Ark. Adv. Mo. State Council on Arts, 1960. Served with USN, 1943-46, PTO. Recipient Commendation award Senate of State of Mo., 1977; fellow Huntington Hartford Found., 1972. Mem. Am. Inst. Conservation of Hist. and Artistic Works (assoc. mem.), Internat. Inst. Conservation of Hist. and Artistic Works (assoc. mem.), Nat. Assn. Mural Painters. Avocations: world travel, reading. Home: 2025 Crestridge Dr Columbia MO 65201 Office: Columbia Coll Art Dept 10th & Rogers St Columbia MO 65216

LARSON, THOMAS DANA, dental educator, dentist; b. St. Paul, Dec. 5, 1944; s. Harold Floyd and Marie Harriet (Tufts) L.; m. Maureen Naomi Cady, Sept. 2, 1967; children—Dawn Marie, Matthew Thomas, Heather Anne. B.A., St. Mary's Coll.-Winona, 1966; B.S., D.D.S., U. Minn., 1970, M.S.D., 1976. Gen. practice dentistry, Bloomington, Minn., 1970-71; gen. practice part-time dentistry, St. Cloud Reformatory for Men, 1971-72, Mendota, Minn, 1971-72, U. Minn., 1972—; clin. instr. dept. operative dentistry U. Minn. Sch. Denistry, 1971-72, instr., 1972-76, asst. prof., 1976-82, assoc. prof. 1982—; clin. staff U. Minn. Hosps. Dental Clinic, 1976—, Chubb Group Ins. Cos., 1980—, 3M Co. 1983—. Contbr. articles to profl. jours. Recipient Cert. Appreciation Minn. Dental Assn., 1973, 76, 77, 81, Acad. Operative Dentistry, 1979, ADA, 1980. Mem. Minn. Dist. Dental Soc., Minn. Dental Assn., ADA, Acad. Operative Dentistry, G.V. Black Study Club (pres. 1979-85), Am. Acad. Gold Foil Operators (edn. com. 1982—), Beta Beta Beta, Omicron Kappa Upsilon. Office: Univ Minn Sch Dentistry 515 Delaware St SE Minneapolis MN 55455

LARSON, WILLIAM JOHN, safety engineer; b. Benton, Ill., Mar. 8, 1923; s. Thure Alfred and Ruth Esther (Anderson) L.; student U. Nebr., 1943-44; E.E., U. Mich. and Mich. State U., 1945; B.S.M.E., Ill. Inst. Tech., 1948; m. Ruth Virginia Cannon, Mar. 17, 1945; children—Barbara Lee Larson Biskie, John Philip. Coop. student to safety engr. Hartford Accident & Indemnity Co., 1941-43, 46-57; safety engr. Argonne (Ill.) Nat. Lab., 1957-71, safety engrng. supr., 1971—, supr. fire protection and safety engr., 1972—; compliance officer Dept. of Labor, 1971; safety cons. and instr. Republican precinct committeeman, 1965-71; vol. Joliet Area Community Hospice, 1983—. Served with Signal Corps, AUS, 1943-46. Cert. safety profl.; registered profl. engr. Calif. Mem. Ill. Engring. Council, Am. Soc. Safety Engrs., Indsl. Conf., Nat. Safety Council (exec. com. research and devel. sect., chmn. research and devel. sect. 1984-85 4 Cameron awards). Mem. Evangelical Covenant Ch. Adv. bd. Am. Soc. Safety Engrs. Jour., 1967-75, chmn., 1972-75; contbr. numerous articles to safety jours. Home: 2212 Mayfield Ave Joliet IL 60435 Office: Argonne National Laboratory 9700 S Cass Ave Argonne IL 60439

LARTER, RAIMA MARZEE, chemistry educator; b. Kingsville, Tex., May 1, 1955; d. Gary Duane and Edith Marie (Carpenter) L.; m. Kenneth Barry Lipkowitz, June 12, 1977; children—Nathaniel Larter, Benjamin Larter. B.S. in Chemistry, Mont. State U., 1976; Ph.D. in Phys. Chemistry, Ind. U., 1980. Research assoc. Princeton U., N.J., 1980-81; vis. prof. chemistry Ind.-Purdue U.-Indpls., 1981-83, asst. prof., 1983—. Contbr. articles to profl. jours. Research Corp. research grantee, 1984; Ind. U. summer faculty fellow, 1984. Mem. Assn. Women in Sci. (nat. exec. bd. 1982—; pres. Ind. chpt. 1982—), Am. Chem. Soc., Am. Phys. Soc., Internat. Soc. Bioelectricity, Am. Inst. Chem. Engrs., Ind. Acad. Scis., Hoosier Assn. Sci. Tchrs. Home: 4506 Dickson Rd Indianapolis IN 46226 Office: Chemistry Dept Ind U-Purdue U 1125 E 38th St Indianapolis IN 46223

LARUE, RICHARD ALLEN, computer systems analyst; b. Bedford, Ohio, Nov. 20, 1947; s. Wesley Ernest and Bertha Elizabeth (Bott) LaR.; s. Sharon Ann Rabold, Oct. 20, 1973; 1 son, Brian Richard. B.A. in Math., Hiram Coll., 1969; M.A. in Math., U. Cin., 1971. Computer programmer trainee Navy Fin. Ctr., Cleve., 1972-73, programmer, 1973-75, sr. programmer, 1975-80, systems analyst, 1980-83, sr. systems analyst, 1983—; former instr. math. Cuyahoga Community Coll. Methodist. Home: 8680 Royalview Dr Parma OH 44129 Office: Navy Fin Ctr 1240 E 9th St Code 5121 Cleveland OH 44129

LA RUSSA, ANTHONY (TONY), professional baseball manager, lawyer; b. Tampa, Fla., Oct. 4, 1944; s. Tony and Oliva (Cuervo) La R.; B.A., U. South Fla., 1969; J.D. with honors, Fla. State U., 1978; m. Elaine Coker, Dec. 31, 1973; children—Bianca Tai, Devon Kai. Profl. baseball player with Oakland A's, Atlanta Braves, Chgo. Cubs, Pitts. Pirates, St. Louis Cardinals, Chgo. White Sox, 1962-77; field mgr. White Sox AA minor league team, Knoxville, Tenn., 1978, AAA minor league team, Des Moines, 1979; 1st base coach Chgo. White Sox, 1978, mgr., 1979—; admitted to Fla. bar, 1980; assoc. Thorp, Reed and Armstrong, Sarasota, Fla., from 1981. Democrat. Roman Catholic. Office: Comiskey Park Dan Ryan Expressway at 35th St Chicago IL 60616

LASATER, DONALD, See *Who's Who in America,* 43rd edition.

LASEMI, YAGHOOB, petroleum geologist; b. Kilan, Iran, June 24, 1949; came to U.S., 1973; s. Ali and Sedigheh (Jamsheedi) L. B.S., Teheran Tchrs. Coll., 1972; M.S., Mich. State U., 1975; Ph.D., U. Ill., 1980. Tchr. natural sci. Farvardin High Sch., Kilan, Damavand, Iran, 1972-73; research asst. Ill. State Geol. Survey, Urbana, 1977-79; exploration geologist Great Southwest Oil & Gas Corp., Lawrenceville, Ill., 1981-83; cons. petroleum geologist, Lawrenceville, Ill., 1983—. Iranian Ministry of Sci. scholar, 1973-79. Mem. Am. Assn. Petroleum Geologists, Soc. Petroleum Engrs., Ill. Geol. Soc. Office: Lawrenceville Nat Bank Bldg Suite 2 1124 Jefferson St Lawrenceville IL 62439

LASH, FREDERICK FRANKLIN, stockbroker; b. Lash, Pa., June 13, 1916; s. Jesse and Mary Ellen (Brocker) L.; m. Kathryn Witt, Aug. 10, 1946; children—Frederick F., Jr., Herbert, Leslie, JoAnne. B.S., U. Md., 1955; postgrad. Indsl. Coll. Armed Forces, 1959-60. Commd. 2d lt. U.S. Army, 1941, advanced through grades to col., 1964, ret. 1971; stockbroker Harris Upham, Kansas City, Mo., 1971-74, Blyth Eastman, Kansas City, 1975-79; v.p. Paine Webber, Kansas City, 1980—; nat. def. exec. reservist Fed. Emergency Mgmt. Agy., Washington, 1976—. Decorated Legion of Merit, Silver Star, Bronze Star, Purple Heart, Pacificador, Govt. of Brazil. Mem. Assn. U.S. Army, Mil. Order of World Wars, Nat. Assn. Security Dealers. Clubs: Optimist (v.p. 1974-75); Cosmopolitan (Overland Park, Kans.) (v.p. 1974-75). Lodge: Masons. Home: 9926 Roe Ave Overland Park KS 66207 Office: Paine Webber One Ward Pkwy Kansas City MO 64212

LASLEY, JOHN FOSTER, retired animal scientist, genetics consultant; b. Liberal, Mo., Jan. 26, 1913; s. Foster Dunn and Emma Mae (Williams) L.; m. Gladys Marie Lamont, Mar. 22, 1940; children—Joan Carol Ann, Donna Marie. B.S., U. Mo., 1939, A.M., 1940, Ph.D., 1943. Agr. extension agt. U.S. Dept. Interior, San Carlos, Ariz., 1943-49; assoc. prof. animal sci. U. Mo., Columbia, 1949-52, prof., 1952-79, ret., 1979. Author: Genetics of Livestock Improvement, 1963; Genetic Principles of Horse Breeding, 1976; (with Foley and Osweiler) Abnormalities of Companion Animals, 1979; Beef Cattle Production, 1981; the Science of Animals that Serve Humanity, 3d edit., 1985. Contbr. articles to profl. jours. Chmn. March of Dimes, Columbia, Mo., 1974; mem. Mo. Gov.'s Sci. Adv. Com., 1962-64. Fellow AAAS, Am. Soc. Animal Sci. (pres. midwestern sect. 1971, disting. tchr. award 1978); mem. Am. Genetic Assn. Republican. Mem. Ch. of Christ. Avocations: photography, writing, gardening. Home: 2207 Bushnell Dr Columbia MO 65201

LASLEY, THOMAS J., educator; b. Delaware, Ohio, July 23, 1947; s. Thomas J. and Anna F. (Cooper) L.; m. Janet O. Olney, Apr. 21, 1973; children—Julie Marie, Elizabeth Ann. B.S., Ohio State U., 1969, M.A., 1972, Ph.D., 1978. Cert. tchr. and administr., Ohio. Tchr., Upper Arlington, Ohio, 1969-75; research assoc. Ohio State U., 1975-77; cons. Ohio Dept. Edn., 1977-80, asst. dir. tchr. edn. and cert., 1980-83; assoc. prof. U. Dayton (Ohio), 1983—; cons. on sch. research and disruptive student behavior. Mem. Am. Ednl. Research Assn., Assn. Supervision Curriculum Devel., Phi Delta Kappa. Co-author: Biting the Apple, 1980; Handbook of Schools with Good Discipline, 1982; editor Jour. Tchr. Edn.; numerous articles. Office: Chaminade Hall U Dayton Dayton OH 45469

LASSILA, KENNETH EINO, physicist, educator; b. Hancock, Mich., Apr. 27, 1934; s. Eino Isaac and Anja Helmi (Heikkinen) L.; m. Jean Hannah Day, Mar. 17, 1957 (div. Nov. 9, 1982); children—Kathrin, Erik, Kirsten. B.S., U. Wyo., 1956; M.S., Yale U., 1959, Ph.D., 1962. Postdoctoral assoc. Case Western Res. U., Cleve., 1961-63, Stanford (Calif.) U., 1966; asst. prof. Iowa State U., Ames, 1963-64, 66-67, assoc. prof., 1967-69, prof. physics, 1969—, spokesman high energy theory Ames Lab., 1978-84; sr. research assoc. U. Helsinki (Finland), 1964-66. Contbr. articles to profl. jours. Fulbright research scholar U. Helsinki, 1965, Fulbright lectr. U. Oulu (Finland), 1972; NORDITA prof. Finland, 1973. Fellow Am. Phys. Soc.; mem. Finnish Phys. Soc. Lutheran. Office: Iowa State University Dept Physics Ames IA 50011

LASSMAN-EUL, MARK F., educator, university official; b. Milw., Sept. 18, 1957; s. Donald Matthew and Carol Ann (Wieczorek) Eul; m. Karen Elaine Lassman, July 3, 1982. B.A. in History and Geography, Carroll Coll., Waukesha, Wis., 1979; M.S. in Edn., U. Wis.-Milw., 1982. Cartographer, S.E. Wis. Planning Commn., Waukesha, 1978; housing coordinator Carroll Coll., Waukesha, 1979-83, freshman advisor, instr. Miami U., Oxford, Ohio, 1983—, mem. speaker's bur., 1984; presentor to confs. Author poetry. Bd. dirs. Waukesha Mental Health Assn., 1982; usher, Sunday sch. tchr. Methodist Ch., Oxford, 1983-84. Mem. Assn. Coll. and Univ. Housing Officers (com. on profl. devel. 1980-82), Am. Coll. Personnel Assn., Ohio Coll. Personnel Assn. (new profls. task force 1983-84), Am. Assn. for Counseling and Devel. Avocation: running; sports; poetry; jazz music; history. Office: Miami U 111 Warfield Hall Oxford OH 45056

LASSUS, JON FRANCIS, oil company executive; b. Fort Wayne, Ind., May 21, 1937; s. Elmer F. and Madeline (Boedeker) L.; m. Kathleen McCoy, Aug. 22, 1959; children—Jon R., Michelle, Todd, Gregory. B.A., Xavier Coll., Cin., 1960. Exec. v.p. Lassus Bros. Oil, Inc., Fort Wayne, 1965-72, pres., chief exec. officer, 1972—; pres. Lasco Leasing Co., Inc., 1974—, Handy Dandy Food Stores, Inc., 1982—, Anthony Wayne Vending Co., Inc., 1980—; v.p. Century Dynamics, 1975—; dir. Summit Bank, Wayne Pipe & Supply Co. Bd. dirs. Jr. Achievement Fort Wayne, St. Francis Coll., YMCA, Better Bus. Bur., ARC, Catholic Social Service, Public TV Fort Wayne; past pres. Covington Lake Assn.; mem. council parish St. Patrick's Catholic Ch., also past pres. Mem. Fort Wayne C. of C., Ind. Oil Marketers, N.E. Ind. Oil Men's Club, Bus. Forum, Young Pres. Orgn., St. Joseph Hosp. Health Found. Clubs: Fort Wayne Country (past dir.), Mad Anthonys. Lodge: Rotary (past dir.). Home: 3216 LaBalme Trail Fort Wayne IN 46804 Office: Lassus Bros Oil Inc 4600 W Jefferson Blvd Fort Wayne IN 46804

LASTER, HOWARD JOSEPH, physics educator; b. Jersey City, N.J., Mar. 13, 1930; s. Harry Lionel and Yetta (Adelman) L.; m. Miriam Edna Sargeant, Apr. 26, 1952; children—Elizabeth, Jonathan, Jane, Sarah. A.B. summa cum laude, Harvard U., 1951; Ph.D., Cornell U., 1957. Mem. Faculty U. Md., College Park, 1956-77, chmn. physics and astronomy, 1965-75; prof. physics U. Iowa, 1977—, dean liberal arts, 1977-84; vis. fellow Clare Hall, Cambridge U., Eng., 1970-71, 84; vis. program assoc. NSF, Washington, 1975-76; dir. Atlantic Research Corp., Alexandria, Va., 1972—. Mem. Md. Gov.'s Sci. Adv. Council, Annapolis, 1965-77, chmn., 1973-75; mem. Iowa Gov.'s Sci. Adv. Council, Des Moines, 1981-83; bd. dirs. Council Colls. Arts and Scis., Manhattan, Kans., 1981-84; vice chmn. Md. Panel on Pub. Policy on Nuclear Energy for Electricity, College. Park, 1975-76. Fellow Am. Phys. Soc., Royal Astron. Soc.; mem. AAAS, Am. Assn. Physics Tchrs., Soc. Internat. Devel. Democrat. Avocations: reading; music; tennis. Home: 891 Park Pl Iowa City IA 52240 Office: U Iowa Dept Physics and Astronomy Iowa City IA 52242

LATCHAW, MARTIN LEON, accountant; b. Marion, Ind., Dec. 23, 1948; s. B. Dale and Margaret L. (Pattison) L.; m. Sue Ellen Copenhaver, Oct. 30, 1971; children—Casey, Mindi, Corey. B.A. in Acctg., Mich. State U., 1980. C.P.A., Mich. Staff acct. D. D. Criss, C.P.A., Charlotte, Mich., 1980-84; ptnr. Criss, Latchaw & Co., C.P.A.s, Charlotte, 1984—. Treas. First Congl. Ch., Charlotte, 1982-84; mem. Charlotte Fire Dept., 1978-84; sub-com. chmn. Citizen Adv. Com., Charlotte, 1984—. Served with U.S. Army, 1970-72, Vietnam. Decorated Bronze Star; named Outstanding Young Man, Charlotte Jaycees, 1983. Mem. Am. Inst. C.P.A.s, Mich. Assn. C.P.A.s (small practioners com.). Lodge: Rotary (treas. 1983-84). Avocations: swimming instruction, skiing, computers. Home: 930 Forest St Charlotte MI 48813 Office: Criss Latchaw & Co CPAs 115 S Cochran St Charlotte MI 48813

LATESSA, EDWARD JAMES, criminal justice educator; b. Youngstown, Ohio, July 13, 1954; s. Edward James and Amelia (Stephens) L.; m. Sally Mae Wakefield, Aug. 4, 1979; 1 dau., Amy. B.S., Ohio State U., 1976, M.A., 1977, Ph.D., 1979. Asst. dir. program study of crime and delinquency Ohio State U., Columbus, 1978-79; asst. prof. criminal justice U. Ala., Birmingham, 1979-80; assoc. prof. U. Cin., 1980—; cons. Lucas County Adult Probation Dept., Toledo, 1978—. Author: (with others) Probation and Parole in America, 1985; contbr. articles to profl. jours. Mem. Am. Soc. Criminology, Acad. Criminal Justice Scis. (trustee), Midwest Criminal Justice Assn., Tau Kappa Epsilon. Democrat. Roman Catholic. Home: 3945 Mantell Ave Cincinnati OH 45236 Office: U Cin Criminal Justice Dept 108 Cincinnati OH 45221

LATIMER, GEORGE, mayor; b. Poughkeepsie, N.Y., June 20, 1935; s. William Wilbur and Dorothy L.; B.S. cum laude, St. Michael's Coll., 1958; LL.B., Columbia U., 1963; m. Nancy Moore Latimer, June 20, 1959; children—Faith, George, Phillip, Kate, Tom. Practice law, St. Paul, 1963-76; mayor, St. Paul, 1976—. Pres. League of Minn. Cities, 1979-80; chmn. Dist. Heating Devel. Co., 1979-84, community devel., housing and econ. devel. standing com. U.S. Conf. of Mayors, 1980-81, Minn. Tax Commn., 1983-84; chmn. com. on energy, environmental quality and natural resources Nat. League of Cities, 1980, bd. dirs., 1980-84, pres., 1983-83; mem. St. Paul Sch. Bd., from 1970; regent U. Minn., 1975-76. Democrat. Roman Catholic. Office: 347 City Hall Saint Paul MN 55102*

LATRONICO, KENNETH ALBERT, lawyer, educator; b. Chgo., Oct. 25, 1948; s. Albert and Sophie Latronico; m. Susan Katherine Shumaker, Aug. 20, 1976; children—Thomas Barker, Mark. B.A. in English Literature, Loyola U., Chgo., 1970, J.D., 1981; M.Ed. in Ednl. Adminstrn., U. Ill., 1975. Bars: Ill. 1981, U.S. Dist. Ct. (no. dist.) Ill. 1981, U.S. Ct. Appeals (7th cir.) 1981. Tchr. Chgo. Bd. Edn., 1970-71; assoc. Lawrence L. Kotin, Ltd., Chgo., 1981-82, Garretson & Santora, Chgo., 1983; staff atty. Law Offices of Thomas J. Keevers, Chgo., 1984—. Mem. ABA (citizenship edn. com. 1981-83), Ill. Bar Assn., Chgo. Bar Assn. (jud. evaluation com. 1981—). Office: Law Offices of Thomas J Keevers 230 W Monroe St Chicago IL 60606

LATTA, DELBERT L., congressman; b. Weston, Ohio, Mar. 5, 1920; A.B., LL.B., Ohio No. U.; m. Rose Mary Kiene; children—Rose Ellen, Robert Edward. Admitted to Ohio bar, 1944; state senator, Ohio, 3 terms; mem. 86th to 99th Congresses, 5th Ohio Dist. Republican. Lodge: Mason (33d degree). Office: 2309 Rayburn House Office Bldg Washington DC 20515*

LATTA, JEAN CAROLYN, financial analyst; b. Chgo., Oct. 11, 1943; d. John Oscar and Katherine Helen (Schnitzer) Latta. B.S. in Chemistry, U. Ill., 1966; M.S. in Chemistry, Ill. Inst. Tech., 1970; M.B.A., U. Chgo., 1976. Asst. research chemist Gillette Co., Chgo., 1969-73; product designer Bunker-Ramo Corp., Chgo., 1973-75; staff exec. George S. May Internat. Co., Park Ridge, Ill., 1977; controller, ind. cons. Bayou City Service Co., Houston, 1978; staff acct., Chemtrust Industries, Franklin Park, Ill., 1979; fin. analyst U. Chgo., 1979—. Patentee in field. Mem. U. Chgo. Women's Bus. Group. Republican. Roman Catholic. Office: U Chgo 1225 E 60th St Chicago IL 60637

LATTANZI, THERESA MARZIO, educational administrator; b. Youngstown, Ohio, Oct. 22, 1951; d. Victor Leonard and Julia Marie (Liberato) Marzio; m. Roger Lawrence Lattanzi, Dec. 13, 1975; 1 dau., Lisa Anne. A.A.B. in Secretarial Studies, Youngstown State U., 1973, B.S. in Edn., 1976; M.S. in Vocat. Edn. Adminstrn., Kent State U., 1982. Cert. supr., Ohio. Instr. dictation and transcription Youngstown (Ohio) Coll. of Bus., 1976; tchr. bus. Union Area High Sch., New Castle, Pa., 1976-77; clk. typist tchr. Ashtabula County Joint Vocat. Sch., Jefferson, Ohio, 1977, job placement and trade indsl. supr., 1978—, intern supr., 1978-79; advanced secretarial instr. Choffin Career Ctr., Youngstown city schs., 1977-78; cons. bus. and office edn. services Ohio Dept. Edn., 1983; lectr. in field. Bd. dirs. YMCA-YWCA membership campaign, Big Bros./Big Sisters Mahoning Valley, ARC. Named Big Sister of Yr., 1982. Mem. Catholic Collegiate Assn., Ohio Assn. for Secondary Sch. Adminstrs., Am. Soc. Personnel Adminstrn., Nat. Assn. Industry-Edn. Coop., Am. Vocat. Assn., Ohio Vocat. Assn., Ohio Bus. Tchrs. Assn., Ashtabula County Indsl. Devel. Assn., Nat. Bus. Edn. Assn. Home: 5370 Old Oxford Ln Youngstown OH 44512 Office: 1565 State Route 167 Jefferson OH 44047

LATTANZIO, RICK JAMES, data processing company official; b. Chgo., May 12, 1953; s. Glenn and Maryann (Crivello) L.; m. Christine Marie Migala, June 12, 1976. B.S., Wright Coll., 1975. Field sales mgr. Pitney Bowes, Arlington Heights, Ill., 1975-78; dir. mktg. Vaxar, Inc., Des Plaines, Ill., 1978-80; regional mgr. Computer Sharing, Chgo., 1980—. Mem. Chgo. Commerce and Industry.

LATZ, WILLIAM MICHAEL, accountant; b. Logansport, Ind., Oct. 14, 1944; s. John William and Mary Katherine (Broderick) L.; m. Diane Marie Wolfangle, May 16, 1970; 1 son, Kenneth Michael. B.S. in Bus., Ind. U., 1972. C.P.A., Ind.; lic. pilot. Staff acct. Michael C. Latz & Assocs., Indpls., 1968-72; ptnr. Nyikos & Latz, CPAs, Indpls., 1972-81, Ashby, Brown, Latz, Maudlin & Co., Indpls. and Anderson, Ind., 1981-83; pres., chief exec. officer, tax ptnr. Latz & Maudlin, Inc. CPAs, Indpls., 1983—; dir. KML Enterprises, Inc., Plainfield, Ind. Served with U.S. Army, 1966-68; Viet Nam. Mem. Am. Inst. C.P.A.s, Ind. C.P.A. Soc., Aircraft Owners and Pilots Assn. Republican. Roman Catholic. Office: 8750 Purdue Rd Indianapolis IN 46268

LAUBER, JACK MOORE, history educator; b. Archbold, Ohio, Oct. 8, 1934; s. William Burke and Velma Mae (Moore) L.; m. Margaret Jean Carlson, Aug. 7, 1964; children—Chad William, Megan Margaret. B.S., Bowling Green State U., Ohio, 1959, M.A., 1960; Ph.D., U. Iowa, 1967. Instr. Ohio State U., Columbus, 1964-67; asst. prof. history U. Wis.-Eau Claire, 1967-69, assoc. prof., 1969-77, prof., 1977—, dept. chmn., 1982—. Contbr. articles to profl. jours. Served with USN, 1953-57. Mem. Am. Hist. Assn., Am. Assn. for Advancement Slavic Studies, Phi Alpha Theta. Avocations: reading; chess. Office: Dept History U Wis Eau Claire WI 54701

LAUDE, RAYMOND JOSEPH, securities corp. exec.; b. Anchorville, Mich., Nov. 1, 1903; s. Edward T. and Mary (Neibeur) L.; student U. Detroit, 1920-22; m. Carol J. Henderson, July 2, 1968. Securities broker 1st of Mich. Corp., Troy, 1973—. Trustee, Alma Coll., 1955-73, emeritus, 1973—; treas. Ferndale-Pleasant Ridge Sch. Dist., 1952. Mem. Nat. Assn. Investors Brokers (past pres.), Security Traders. Republican. Presbyterian. Clubs: Bond of Detroit, Detroit Athletic, Masons; Fort Hill of Boston. Home: 5911 Orchard Bend Birmingham MI 48010 Office: 1st Mich Corp 2401 W Big Beaver St Troy MI 48084

LAUDICK, BONNIE BROUWER, therapeutic recreation specialist, consultant; b. Ft. Wayne, Ind.; d. Lester Jay Brouwer and Geraldine (Smith) Webber; children—William, Robert. B.S., Ind. U., 1965. Dir. recreation therapy and phys. edn. Ill. Children's Hosp. Sch., Chgo., 1965-68; day supr., activity therapy Henry Horner Children's Ctr., Chgo. Read Mental Health Ctr., Chgo., 1975-76; dir. recreational therapy and spl. services Orangegrove Rehab. Hosp., Garden Grove, Calif., 1976-78; cons. activity therapy Hosp. Affiliates Internat., Inc., Nashville, 1980-81, Hosp. Corp. Am., Nashville, 1982—; dir. activity therapy Riveredge Hosp., Forest Park, Ill., 1978—; speaker local, state and nat. confs. therapeutic recreation assns. Mem. Forest Park Community Edn. Adv. Council, 1981-82. Recipient Outstanding Service award Nat. Cystic Fibrosis Found., 1973, 74, 75, Top Fundraiser award, 1971, 72, 73; Outstanding Achievement in Activity Therapy award Hosp. Affiliates Internat., Inc., 1979, Outstanding Dept. award, 1980. Mem. Nat. Recreation and Parks Assn., Nat. Therapeutic Recreation Soc. (joint commn. on accreditation hosps. com. 1981, 82, co-chmn., 1983—, mem. mental health com. 1982), Ill. Parks and Recreation Assn. (mem. awards com. 1981-82), Ill. Therapeutic Recreation Sect. (bd. dirs. 1981—, sec.-treas. 1983—, Outstanding Program award 1980), West Suburban Juvenile Officers Assn. Contbr. to profl. publs. Office: 8311 W Roosevelt Rd Forest Park IL 60130

LAUER, ROBERT LEE, consumer products company executive; b. Crook, Colo., Oct. 25, 1933; s. Martin F. and Mary A. (Hofsetz) L.; m. Mary Redman, Aug. 25, 1956; children—Anne, Lisa, John. B.S., Bowling Green State U., 1956. Mgr., Procter & Gamble Co., Cin., 1962-69; accounts supr. Harshe-Rotman & Druck, Los Angeles, 1969-70; mgr. corporate relations Clorox Co., Oakland, Calif., 1970-77; dir. pub. affairs S.C. Johnson & Son, Inc., Racine, Wis., 1977-81; v.p. corporate affairs Sara Lee Corp., Chgo., 1981—; dir. Second Harvest Nat. Food Bank Network. Served with U.S. Army, 1956-58. Mem. Pub. Relations Soc. Am., Econ. Club Chgo. Clubs: Univ. (Chgo.), Commonwealth (San Francisco). Office: Sara Lee Corp 3 1st Nat Plaza Chicago IL 60602

LAUER, RONALD MARTIN, pediatric cardiologist, researcher; b. Winnipeg, Man., Can., Feb. 18, 1930; m. Eileen Pearson, Jan. 12, 1959; children—Geoffrey, Judith Lauer. B.S., U. Man., 1953, M.D., 1954. Diplomate Am. Bd. Pediatrics. Asst. prof. pediatrics U. Pitts., 1960-61; asst. prof. pediatrics U. Kans., 1961-67, assoc. prof. pediatrics, 1967-68; prof. pediatrics, dir. pediatrics cardiology U. Iowa, 1968—, vice chmn. pediatrics, 1974-82, prof. pediatrics and preventive medicine 1980—. Home: RD 6 Steward Rd Iowa City IA 52240 Office: U Iowa Hosps Clin Dept Pediatrics Div Pediatric Cardiology Iowa City IA 52240

LAUGHLIN, JOAN, textiles educator; b. Council Bluffs, Iowa, Sept. 11, 1940; d. Matthew John and Helen Frances (Roscoe) L. B.S., Coll. of St. Mary, 1962; M.S., Iowa State U., 1965; Ph.D., Pa. State U., 1974. Tchr. home econs., Lake City and Carson, Iowa, 1962-65; chmn. home econs. Mt. St. Clare Jr. Coll., Clinton, Iowa, 1965-69; asst. prof. U. No. Iowa, Cedar Falls, 1969-72; grad. research asst. Pa. State U., University Park, 1972-74; prof., chmn. dept. clothing, textiles and design, U. Nebr., Lincoln, 1974—; cons. Am. Linen and Laundry Coll., Richmond, Ky., 1976-85; cons. Consumer Product Safety Com., Washington, 1978-80. Contbr. articles to profl. jours. Recipient Excellence in Research award Man-Made Fibers Assn., 1984; named Disting. Prof., U. Nebr., Lincoln, 1982. Mem. Am. Home Econs. Assn. (bd. dirs. 1979-81), Assn. Coll. Profs. Textiles and Clothing (pres. 1979-80, nat. exec. bd. 1985—), Am. Assn. Textile Chemists and Colorists (second place tech. paper competition 1983), ASTM (faculty fellow), Omicron Nu. Roman Catholic. Avocations: genealogy; swimming. Office: 234 Home Econs Bldg U Nebr Lincoln NE 68583

LAUGHLIN, MARK HAMILTON, osteopathic physician; b. Kirksville, Mo., Oct. 2, 1943; s. Earl Herbert and Margaret Hardman (Biggerstaff) L.; B.A., Pomona Coll. 1965; D.O., Kirksville Coll. Osteo. and Surgery, 1969. Intern Lansing Gen. Hosp., Mich., 1969-70; practice medicine specializing in osteo. medicine, Kirksville, 1970—. Bd. dirs. Adair County Family YMCA, 1982—; curator Adair County Hist. Soc. Mus., 1984. Mem. Am. Osteo. Assn., N.E. Mo. Osteo. Assn., Mo. Osteo. Assn. Home: PO Box 846 Kirksville MO 63501 Office: 902 E La Harpe St Kirksville MO 63501

LAUGHLIN, TERRY XAVIER, management consultant; b. Oskaloosa, Iowa, Dec. 7, 1936; s. John Dwight and Beryle Beatrice (Bible) L.; m. Marilyn Jean Bendig, May 14, 1966. B.B.A., U. Notre Dame, 1960; LL.B., Blackstone Sch. Law, 1967; Ps.D., Coll. Metaphysics, 1971. Real estate broker, Ill., 1965-66; div. mgr. Britannica Schs., Chgo., 1966-68; pres. Laughlin Assocs., Inc., Roselle, Ill., 1968—. Mem. Am. Soc. Profl. Cons., N.W. Suburban Assn. Commerce and Industry. Republican. Roman Catholic. Clubs: Ventura 21 (Roselle, Ill.); KC; Toastmasters (v.p.). Home: 56 N Salt Creek Rd Roselle IL 60172 Office: 100 E Irving Park Rd Roselle IL 60172

LAUNHARDT, GREG ARNOLD, tax lawyer, accountant, consultant; b. Chgo., Nov. 16, 1953; s. Arnold John and Evelyn (Milas) L.; m. Theresa Michele Boulicault, May 18, 1984. B.S. in Fin., U. Ill., 1975; M.B.A., So. Ill.

U., 1979, J.D., 1979. Bars: Ill. 1980, U.S. Tax Ct. 1980, Mo. 1984; C.P.A., Ill., Mo. Tax acct. Touche Ross & Co., St. Louis, 1979-84; tax atty. Ralston Purina Co., St. Louis, 1984-85; tax supr. Coopers & Lybrand, St. Louis, 1985—. Ill. State scholar, 1971. Mem. ABA, Am. Inst. C.P.A.s, Alpha Sigma Phi, Phi Alpha Delta. Republican. Lutheran. Home: 3654-A Arsenal Saint Louis MO 63116 Office: Coopers & Lybrand One Merc Ctr Saint Louis MO 63101

LAUNSTEIN, HOWARD CLEVELAND, educator; b. Flushing, Mich., Oct. 15, 1922; s. John Henry and Jennie Grace (Cleveland) L.; student Central Mich. U., 1941-43; B.A., Mich. State U., 1947, M.A., 1948; Ph.D., Ohio State U., 1956; m. Elizabeth June Snyder, May 22, 1943; children—Robert John, Howard Elmer. Grad. asst. Mich. State U., 1947-48, instr. acctg., 1948-56; asst. prof. State U. Iowa, Iowa City, 1956-58; asso. prof. Marquette U., Milw., 1958-64, prof. fin., 1964—, chmn. dept., 1959-67; ins. agt. Guarantee Mut. Life Ins. Co., Lansing, Mich., 1948-51; instr. C.P.C.U. program, 1954-55, C.L.U. programs, 1959-81; ins. cons. Marquette U., 1958—; mem. ednl. adv. com. Wis. Real Estate Examining Bd., 1976-78; mem. adv. com. Wis. Ins. Examining Bd., 1977-78; dir., auditor Red Cedar Coop. Assn., East Lansing, 1949-52. Asst. cub master, treas. Greendale (Wis.) cub pack Boy Scouts Am., 1960-66, committeeman Boy Scouts, 1963-66; mem. citizens com. bonding issues Greendale Sch., 1959-61. Bd. govs., dir. Nat. Inst. Consumer Credit Mgmt., 1965—; mem. bd. electors Ins. Hall of Fame, 1982—. Served with USAAF, 1942-45. Decorated Air medal. Mem. Internat. Ins. Seminars (bd. govs. 1965—, moderator 1965-71, research directorate 1979—), Am. Fin. Assn., Midwest Econ. Assn., Am. Acctg. Assn., Am. Fin. Mgmt. Assn., Am. Risk and Ins. Assn., Beta Alpha Psi, Delta Sigma Pi, Sigma Epsilon, Beta Gamma. Methodist. Contbr. chpts. to books, articles to profl. jours. Chmn. awards com. Nat. Assn. Ind. Insurers Jour. Ins., 1962-63, 68-69, 72-74. Home: 5854 Glen Flora Greendale WI 53129 Office: Marquette U Milwaukee WI 53233

LAURENCE, MICHAEL MARSHALL, magazine publisher, writer; b. N.Y.C., May 22, 1940; s. Frank Marshall and Edna Ann (Roeder) L.; m. Patricia Ann McDonald, Mar. 1, 1969; children—Elizabeth Sarah, John Marshall. A.B. cum laude, Harvard U., 1963. Sr. editor Playboy mag., Chgo., 1967-69, contbg. editor, 1969-72, asst. pub., 1977-82; mng. editor Oui mag., Chgo., 1973-77; editor/pub. Linn's Stamp News, Sidney, Ohio, 1982—, also columnist Editor's Choice; co-founder, dir. U.S. 1869 Pictorial Research Assocs., 1975-82. Author: Playboy's Investment Guide, 1971; also articles. Editor: U.S. Mail and Post Office Assistant, 1975. Recipient G.M. Loeb award for disting. mag. writing U. Conn., 1968. Mem. Internat. Soc. Philatelic Journalists, Am. Stamp Dealers Assn., U.S. Philatelic Classics Soc. (Elliott Perry award 1975; bd. dirs. 1975-81). Clubs: Harvard (N.Y.C.); Collectors (bd. dirs. 1978-82) (Chgo.). Avocations: stamp collecting; gardening. Office: PO Box 29 Sidney OH 45365

LAURENT, STEPHAN (FAESI), choreographer, artistic director, ballet teacher; b. Lausanne, Vaud, Switzerland, June 24, 1948; came to U.S., 1973; s. Hugo Max and Annette Eva Faesi; m. Martha Anne Denton, Nov. 10, 1973; children—Christopher Michael, Daniel Monroe. Baccalaureat es Lettres, Gymnase du Belvedere, Lausanne, 1964; B.F.A., So. Meth. U., 1974, M.F.A. summa cum laude, 1979. Dancer, Ballet Royal de Wallonie, Charleroi, Belgium, 1974-75, Scapino Ballet, Amsterdam, the Netherlands, 1975-77; guest artist, various ballet cos. in Europe and U.S., 1972-82; ballet master Ballet Del Monte Sol, Santa Fe, 1978, Repertory Dance Co., Dallas, 1978-79; asst. prof. dance U. Wis.-Milw., 1979-82; artistic dir. Des Moines Ballet Co., 1982—; dance critic Feuille d'Avis de Lausanne, Switzerland, 1968-72; cons. Wis. Arts Bd., 1980-84, Iowa Arts Council, 1982—, Affiliated Arts Agys., Mpls., 1982—; coach Swiss team Internat. Ballet Competition, Varna, Bulgaria, 1976. Choreographer: Journey Into Elsewhere, 1980; The Nutcracker, 1982, Coppelia, 1984; 1-act ballet The Hunchback of Notre-Dame, 1984 (commn. Iowa Arts Council 1984), others. Canton of Zurich Scholar, 1973-77; Steo Found. grantee, Zurich, 1977. Office: Des Moines Ballet Co 4333 Park Ave Des Moines IA 50321

LAURILA, MELVIN JAMES, coal preparation engineer, consultant; b. Ishpeming, Mich., June 3, 1957; s. Felix Theodore and Edna Miriam (Mannikko) L.; m. Anna Marie Schoonover, Aug. 20, 1977; 1 child, Elizabeth Ann. B.S., Mich. Tech. U., 1979, M.S., 1980. Metallurgical engr. Cleve. Cliffs Iron, Ishpeming, 1978; coal preparation engr. Paul Weir Co., Chgo., 1980-82; mgr. mining Arthur D. Little, Inc., Cambridge, Mass., 1982-84; sr. coal preparation engr. Norton, Hambleton, Inc., Ann Arbor, Mich., 1984-85; gen. mgr. NH Tech., Inc., Ann Arbor, Mich., 1985—; cons. Arthur D. Little, Inc., Cambridge, 1984; lectr. Argonne Nat. Lab., 1983, Mich. Tech. U., 1983, 84, U.S. Geol. Survey, 1985. Contbr. articles to profl. jours. Mem. Am. Inst. Mining Engrs., Can. Inst. Mining Engrs., ASTM. Methodist. Home: 5561 Grayfield Circle Ypsilanti MI 48197 Office: Norton Hambleton Inc 3135 Professional Dr Ann Arbor MI 48104

LAURING, RICHARD STANLEY, pharmacist; b. Coleraine, Minn., Feb. 9, 1940; s. Stanley W. and Muriel (Efnor) L.; m. Marjorie Huls, July 16, 1966; children—Heidi, Holly, Heather. B.S. in Pharmacy, U. Minn., 1963. Pharmacist Truman Drug, Minn., 1968—. Served with USAF, 1963-68. Mem. Minn. State Pharmacist Assn., Rho Chi. Lutheran. Avocations: flying; antique cars; genealogy. Home: Truman MN 56088

LAURMANN, JOHN ALFRED, fluid dynamicist; b. Cambridge, Eng., Aug. 8, 1926; s. Emil and Elizabeth (Laurmann; m. Giselle Vanessa Bardenleben, July 5, 1957; children—Lawrence Oliver, Sylvia Irene. B.A., Cambridge U., 1947, M.A., 1951; M.S., Cranfield Inst. Tech., Eng., 1951; Ph.D. U. Calif.-Berkeley, 1958. Mem. tech. staff Gen. Research Corp., Santa Barbara, Calif., 1963-69, Inst. Def. Analysis, Washington, 1969-70; exec. sec. Nat. Acad. Sci./Nat. Acad. Engring., Washington, 1970-74; dir. climate research Ocean Data Systems Monterey, Calif., 1974-75; sr. research assoc. Stanford U., Calif., 1976-82; exec. scientist Gas Research Inst., Chgo., 1982—; cons. Rand Corp., NOAA, EPA, Occidental Research Corp., SRI Internat., also others. Author: Wing Theory, 1955. Editor: Rarefied Gas Dynamics, 1963. Contbr. articles to profl. jours. Grantee U.S. Air Force, 1975-76, NASA, 1977-80, Occidental Research Corp., 1979-81. Mem. N.Y. Acad. Scis., AAAS, Am. Geophys. Union, Am. Meteorol. Soc., Am. Phys. Soc. Home: 3372 Martin Rd Carmel CA 93923 Office: Gas Research Inst 8600 W Bryn Mawr Ave Chicago IL 60631

LAUTERBACH, WESLEY VERN, educational administrator; b. Wichita, Kans., Jan. 9, 1929; s. John George and Anna Lee (Loosley) L.; m. Shirley Anne Coffey, July 10, 1953; children—Douglas Wesley, Kathy Lynn, Anne Renee. B.A., Friends U., Wichita, 1951; M.A., Wichita State U., 1954; Ed.D., U. No. Colo., 1961. Cert. adminstr., Kans. Social studies tchr. North High Sch., Wichita, 1952-55, asst. prin. student activities, 1955-57, vice prin., 1957-64; prin., Southeast High Sch., Lincoln, Nebr., 1964—; summer instr. U. Nebr., Lincoln, 1965—. Contbr. articles to profl. publs. Mem. Nebr. State Centennial Com., Lincoln, 1966-67; bd. elders Ch. of Christ, Lincoln, 1968—; bd. dirs. Catholic Social Service Bur., Lincoln, 1970-73. Mem. Nebr. State Edn. Assn. (local pres. 1964-75), Nebr. Sch. Activities Assn. (local pres. 1964), Nat. Assn. Secondary Sch. Prins. (Nebr. coordinator 1955—, nat. com. on ednl. tech. 1971-73, chmn. nat. council nat. honor soc. 1982), NEA (nat. convention del. 1951—), Nebr. Council Sch. Adminstrs. (exec. bd. 1970-82, Disting. Service award 1983). Club: Nebr. Schoolmasters (Lincoln). Lodge: Kiwanis (bd. dirs. 1967-70). Avocations: genealogy; gardening; woodcarving; philately. Home: 4111 South Gate Blvd Lincoln NE 68506 Office: Lincoln Southeast High Sch 2930 S 37th St Lincoln NE 68506

LAUTH, LOUIS FREDERICK, JR., publishing executive; b. Chgo., Nov. 17, 1923; s. Louis Frederick and May H. (Stanek) L.; m. Bonnie K. Fisher, Feb. 27, 1945; children—Constance, Patrick, Kathleen, Irene, Michael, John, Mark, Amy. B.Naval Sci., U. Notre Dame, 1945, B.S. in Commerce in Bus. Adminstrn., 1947. Vice pres. ops. M.P. Brown, Inc., also editor-in-chief Working Press of Nation, Burlington, Iowa, 1963-73; mktg. dir. Nat. Catholic Rep. Pub. Co., Kansas City, Mo., 1973-77; direct mail mgr. Andrews & McMeel, Mission, Kans., 1977-80; book projects mgr. Modern Handicraft Inc., Kansas City, Mo., 1980—. Editor: Workbench Treasuries series, 1982—, Aunt Ellen's Handbooks series, 1982—, Who's Who in Public Relations, 1972—. Served with USN, 1943-46, PTO. Mem. Kansas City Mail Mktg. Assn. Democrat. Roman Catholic. Avocations: fishing, camping, woodworking, writing, gardening. Home: 5235 Howe Dr Roeland Park KS 66205 Office: Modern Handcraft Inc 4251 Pennsylvania Ave Kansas City MO 64111

LAUVER, EDITH MARIE GEDEON, educator; b. Lakewood, Ohio, Mar. 28, 1926; d. George Joseph and Martha Louise Emma (Blankenburg) G.; m. Milton R. Lauver, July 17, 1948; children—Patricia E., Janet M., James M., Susan E. B.A., Western Res. U., 1948; M.Ed., Kent State U., 1968. Cert. tchr., Ohio. Substitute tchr. pub. schs., N.J., 1948-49; substitute tchr. North Olmsted (Ohio) Pub. Schs., 1960-61, tchr., 1962—, tchr. Spruce Sch., 1967—. Tchr. Sunday sch. Bethal Bible class Ascension Lutheran Ch., Mo. Synod. Named Master Tchr., Supt. Schs. North Olmsted, 1969-70. Mem. North Olmsted Edn. Assn. (pres. 1963-64), Ohio Edn. Assn. (life), NEA, Internat. Reading Assn. Home: 28385 Holly Dr North Olmsted OH 44070 Office: Spruce Sch 28590 Windsor St North Olmsted OH 44070

LAVELLE, GEORGE CARTWRIGHT, scientist, educator; b. Mpls., Dec. 1, 1937; s. John Joseph and Agnes Evelyn (Cartwright) L.; m. Rosalie Kathryn Freiling, Aug. 13, 1966; children—Georgianne, Daniel, Nathaniel, Christopher. B.A. in Natural Sci., St. John's U., Collegeville, Minn., 1959; Ph.D. in Microbiology, U. Notre Dame, 1967. Research assoc. Johns Hopkins U., Balt., 1967-69; staff fellow USPHS, Hamilton, Mont., 1969-71, Bethesda, Md., 1971-73; prin. investigator Oak Ridge Nat. Lab., 1973-79; dir. genetic toxicology Hill Top Research, Inc., Cin., 1980—; mem. research faculty U. Tenn.-Oak Ridge, 1974-79; assoc. prof. Bemidji State U., Minn., 1979-80. Contbr. articles to profl. jours., chpts. to books. Grantee Nat. Cancer Inst., 1976, Oak Ridge Nat. Lab., 1976, U.S. Dept. Energy, 1979. Mem. Environ. Mutagen Soc., Genetic Toxicology Assn., ASTM. Home: 9079 Shadetree Dr Cincinnati OH 45242 Office: Hill Top Research Inc PO Box 42501 Cincinnati OH 45242

LAVIN, JEFFREY NATHAN, educator; b. Columbus, Ohio, June 13, 1953; s. Lloyd M. and Mary R. (Feldman) L.; m. Debra Lynn Berlas, Mar. 26, 1977. Student, Miami U., Oxford, Ohio, 1971-75; B.S., Kent State U., 1976; M.Ed., John Carroll U., 1980. Tchr., Fairfax Elem. Sch., Cleveland Heights-University Heights Bd. Edn., 1977-82, remedial reading and remedial math. tchr. Wiley Jr. High Sch., 1982—, boys' baseball coach, 1983—, girls' tennis coach, 1983—; union steward AFL-CIO, Local 795, 1979-83. Mem. Assn. Supervision and Curriculum Devel., Ohio Assn. Elem. Sch. Adminstrs. Democrat. Jewish. Club: South Euclid Boosters. Author: The Buck Starts Here, 1978; Mass O'Matics, 1978; Social Studies Curriculum Guide, 1979; Elementary School Science Program, 1981. Home: 4126 Stilmore Rd Cleveland OH 44121 Office: 2181 Miramar Blvd Cleveland OH 44118

LAW, FREDERICK WING-KAI, college administrator, consultant; b. Hong Kong, May 6, 1951; came to U.S., 1971; s. Tin Tak and Tak Chong (Lai) L.; m. Edwina Yuen-Wa Chiu, Apr. 30, 1976; children—Janice Chung-See, Jonathan Ho-Yin. Student York Coll., 1971-72; B.S., U. Wis.-Madison, 1974; M.S., W.Va. U., 1976; postgrad. Ohio U., 1983—. Med. technologist W.Va. U. Hosp., Morgantown, 1974-76; sr. instr. Shawnee State Coll., Portsmouth, Ohio, 1976-79, asst. prof. med. lab. scis., 1979-82, program dir. med. tech., 1982—; cons. Vallege Diagnostic Lab., Gallipolis, Ohio, 1981-82. Author Shawnee State lab manuals, 1979; contbg. author: NCA Review for Clinical Laboratory Sciences, 1985. Mem. speakers bur. Shawnee State Community Coll., 1982—. Mem. Nat. Cert. Agy. for Clin. Lab. Personnel (cert., exam. council 1981-83), Clin. Lab. Mgmt. Assn., Am. Soc. Clin. Pathologists (cert.), Am. Soc. Med. Tech. Office: Shawnee State Community Coll 940 Second St Portsmouth OH 45662

LAWHORN, MICHAEL RAY, police administrator, security consultant; b. Cin., Oct. 14, 1945; s. John William and Harriet (Baker) L.; m. Kathleen E. Renner, May 1968 (div. Jan. 1984); 1 child, Lisa; m. Carol Wells, Jan. 19, 1985. Student Middletown Bus. Coll., 1975, Clark Tech. Coll., 1975, Ohio State Patrol Acad., 1976. Chief of police Monroe Div. of Police, Ohio, 1977—; pres., security cons. Lawhorn & Assocs., Middletown, Ohio, 1984—. Served with USMC, 1965-67, Vietnam. Decorated Meritoris Mast. Mem. Miami Valley Police Assn. (pres. 1972), Internat. Assn. Police Chiefs, Nat. Chiefs of Police Assn., Butler County Chiefs Assn., Am. Soc. Indsl. Security. Avocations: music, racquetball. Home: 7310 Michael Rd Middletown OH 45042 Office: Div Police 201 S Main St Monroe OH 45050

LAWLER, DENNIS ALBERT, environmental program manager; b. Marshalltown, Iowa, July 17, 1945; s. Albert Daniel and Gwendolyn (Cahill) L.; m. Marilyn Jo Budde, May 24, 1969; children—Christopher Michael, Rebecca Jo. B.S. in Physics cum laude, Loras Coll., 1967; M.S. in Meteorology, U. Wis., 1974. Cert. cons. meteorologist. Specialist Ill. Environ. Protection Agy., Springfield, 1975-77, supr. air quality unit, 1978-83, mgr. air quality planning sect., 1984—; instr. enrichment program Sch. Dist. 186, Springfield, 1981, 84. Contbr. articles to profl. jours. Pres. Westwood Forum Neighborhood Assn., Springfield, 1981-82, Sandburg Sch. Parent Orgn., Springfield, 1982. Served with USAF, 1969-73. Mem. Am. Meteorol. Soc., Air Pollution Control Assn. Roman Catholic. Avocations: coaching youth baseball and soccer. Home: 2616 Bennington Dr Springfield IL 62704 Office: Ill Environ Protection Agy 2200 Churchill Rd Springfield IL 62706

LAWLER, JAMES WILLIAM, hosp. exec.; b. Cudahy, Wis., Mar. 13, 1921; s. Edward F. and Ida M. (Martin) L.; Ph.B., Marquette U., 1942; M.Social Adminstrn., Loyola U., Chgo., 1948; m. Rita Cecelia Tabat, Dec. 27, 1947; children—Kathleen, Mark, Margaret, Maureen, Patrick, Michael. Account supr. Blue Cross Plan for Hosp. Care, Chgo., 1948-49; personal mgr. Wallace Supplies Mfg. Co., Chgo., 1949-50; order supt. Norge div. Borg-Warner Corp., Chgo., 1950-53; asst. personnel dir. Kleinschmidt Labs., Deerfield, Ill., 1953-55; personnel mgr. George S. May Co., Chgo., 1956-60; personnel mgr. Airway Products Corp., Schiller Park, Ill., 1960-62; dir. personnel and public relations Holy Cross Hosp., Salt Lake City, 1962-65; dir. personnel and public relations Holy Cross Hosp., Jacksonville, Ill., 1965-68; v.p. devel. and human resources Holy Family Hosp., Des Plaines, Ill., 1968-81; dir. personnel Walther Meml. Hosp., Chgo., 1981—. Served with U.S. Army, 1942-45. Decorated Bronze Star. Mem. Am. Soc. for Hosp. Personnel Dirs., Am. Mgmt. Assn., Am. Hosp. Assn., Inst. Public Relations Mgmt., Chgo. Assn. Commerce and Industry. Club: Lions. Contbr. articles to profl. publs. Home: 5101 Carriage Way Dr Rolling Meadows IL 60008 Office: 1116 N Kedzie Ave Chicago IL 60651

LAWN, JACK, JR., printing company sales executive; b. Youngstown, Ohio, May 11, 1946; s. Jack and Charlotte May (Daniels) L.; m. Judith Ann Pflughaupt, May 31, 1975; children—Pamela Ann, Jill Ann. Sales rep. Friden div. Singer Co., Youngstown, 1969-71; sales rep. John Henry Co., Lansing, Mich., 1971-75, regional sales mgr., Fremont, Calif., 1975-78, nat. sales mgr., Lansing, 1978—; com. mem. Florists Transworld Delivery Trade Fair, Detroit, 1982-85; chmn. Wholesale Florists and Florist Suppliers of Am. Trade Fair, Atlanta, 1983-86. Pres. Verndale Condominium Assn., Lansing, 1983. Served to sgt. U.S. Army, 1966-68. Republican. Methodist. Home: 930-D Montevideo Dr Lansing MI 48917 Office: John Henry Co PO Box 17099 Lansing MI 48901

LAWRENCE, DAVID WILSON, foundation executive; b. Worcester, Mass., June 3, 1942; s. Linwood Reed and Emilie (Wilson) L.; m. Susan Gardner Dogherty, June 26, 1965; children—Peter David, Christopher David. A.B., Miami U., Oxford, Ohio, 1964; M.A. in Edn., George Washington U., 1970. Dir. devel. Miami U., 1970-80, assoc. v.p. univ. affairs, 1980-82; vice chmn. bd. devel. Mayo Clinic/Found., Rochester, Minn., 1982—; pres. Rochester Airport Co., 1985—; cons. Phi Kappa Tau, Oxford, 1980-83. Mem. exec. com. Rochester Civic Music, 1983-85; bd. dirs. Oxford C. of C., 1979-82. Served to lt. USN, 1964-70; to capt. Res. Decorated Navy Commendation medal; recipient Admiral Sidney W. Souers award Miami U., 1983. Mem. Council for Advancement and Support of Edn. Republican. Presbyterian. Lodge: Rotary. Home: 1607 20th Ave NE Rochester MN 55904 Office: Section Devel Mayo Clinic/Found Rochester MN 55905

LAWRENCE, JAMES LESTER, college dean and official; b. N.Y.C., Oct. 22, 1941; s. Ernice B. and Telete Zorayda (Lester) L.; B.A., Tex. Christian U., 1963, M.A., 1965; Ph.D., U. Maine, 1968. Asst. prof. biology Hartwick Coll., Oneonta, N.Y., 1968-70, asst. dean faculty, 1970-71, asst. v.p., assoc. dean of coll., 1971-74, v.p. ednl. affairs, dean coll., 1974-75; dean of coll. Huron Coll., S.D., 1979-81; sr. v.p., dean of coll. Marycrest Coll., Davenport, Iowa, 1981—; mem. student life council Colls. Mid-Am., Sioux Falls, S.D., 1979-81, mem. deans' council, Sioux Falls, 1979-81, chmn., 1981; mem. adv. bd. Huron Coll./Huron Regional Med. Ctr. Sch. Nursing, 1979-81, mem. com. accreditation, 1980-81; mem. Council Ind. Colls. Nat. Cons. Network, Washington, 1980—; mem. program rev. panel Quad-Cities Grad. Study Ctr., Rock Island, Ill., 1981—; presenter workshops and seminars. Contbr. articles and poetry to profl. publs. Fulbright fellow, 1972-73; Helene Wurlitzer Found. grantee, 1975. Bd. dirs. Community Chorale, Oneonta, N.Y., 1974-78, Huron Symphony, 1979-81, Community Theatre, Huron, 1980-81, Glimmerglass Opera Theatre, Cooperstown, N.Y., 1976-78, Davenport Med. Ctr., Iowa, 1985—; vestryman Grace Ch., Huron, 1980-81, chmn. religious edn. com., 1980-81; mem. Friends of Art, Davenport Art Mus., 1984—. Mem. Davenport C. of C. (edn. com. 1981-83), Huron C. of C. (edn. com. 1980-81), Am. Assn. Higher Edn., Am. Assn. Acad. Deans, Council Advancement Exptl. Learning, Nat. Assn. Advisers for Health Professions. Democrat. Episcopalian. Avocations: writing, cooking, singing. Home: 112 Slavens Manor Bettendorf IA 52722 Office: Marycrest Coll 1607 W 12th St Davenport IA 52804

LAWRENCE, JOHN KIDDER, lawyer; b. Detroit, Nov. 18, 1949; s. Luther Ernest and Mary Anna (Kidder) L.; m. Jeanine Ann DeLay, June 20, 1981. A.B., U. Mich., 1971; J.D., Harvard U., 1974. Bar: Mich. 1974, D.C. 1978, U.S. Supreme Ct. 1977. Assoc., Dickinson, Wright, McKean & Cudlip, Detroit, 1973-74; staff atty. Office of Judge Adv. Gen., Washington, 1975-78; assoc. Dickinson, Wright, McKean, Cudlip & Moon, Detroit, 1978-81; ptnr. Dickinson, Wright, Moon, VanDusen & Freeman, Detroit, 1981—. Patron, Founders Soc. Detroit Inst. Arts, 1979—; mem. founds. com. Detroit Symphony Orch., 1983—. Served with U.S. Navy, 1975-78. Mem. ABA, State Bar Mich., D.C. Bar Assn., Am. Judicature Soc., Internat. Bar Assn., Detroit Com. on Fgn. Relations, Am. Hist. Assn., Phi Eta Sigma, Phi Beta Kappa. Democrat. Episcopalian. Club: Detroit. Office: Dickinson Wright Moon VanDusen & Freeman 800 First Nat Bldg Detroit MI 48226

LAWRENCE, JOHN WARREN, business and broadcasting executive; b. Kalamazoo, Mar. 25, 1928; s. William Joseph and Borgia Marie (Wheeler) L.; m. Joanne Myrtle McDonald, Oct. 27, 1956; children—Joni Lawrence Knapper, Jane Ellen, John Warren, Jeffrey Michael. B.S., Western Mich. U., 1949; M.B.A., U. Mich., 1950. Gen. mgr. Ill. Envelope, Inc., Kalamazoo, 1958-66, pres., 1958-80, chmn. bd., 1980-85; sec.-treas. Superior Pine Products Co., Fargo, Ga., 1967—; pres. Channel 41, Inc., Battle Creek, Mich., 1972—; chmn. MCE, Inc., Kalamazoo, 1980—; founder, chmn. bd. Lawrence Prodns., Inc., Kalamazoo, 1985—; dir. Am. Nat. of Mich., Kalamazoo, 1966—, Am. Nat. Holding Co., Kalamazoo, 1972—. Trustee Starr Commonwealth Schs., Albion, Mich., 1969-83; vice chmn., trustee Borgess Med. Ctr., Kalamazoo, 1982—; trustee Gull Lake Sch. Found., Richland, Mich., 1983—; bd. dirs. United Way of Mich., 1976-80; chmn. bd. trustees Nazareth Coll., Kalamazoo, 1979—. Served to lt. (j.g.) USNR, 1952-55. Recipient Mich. Citizen's award Greater Mich. Found., 1963. Roman Catholic. Clubs: Park (Kalamazoo); Gull Lake Country (Richland, Mich.); Carlton (Chgo.). Office: 157 S Kalamazoo Mall Suite 250 Kalamazoo MI 49007

LAWRENCE, MARY MARGARET, hospital volunteer administrator, freelance writer; b. Cleve., Jan. 23, 1953; d. Raymond Anthony and Mary Arleen (McCarthy) Moenich; m. Edward Lawrence, Jr., June 13, 1976; children—Justin Bruce, M. Olivia, Ben Mathias. Cert. program in vol. mgmt Barat Coll., 1980; cert. advanced mgmt. vol. programs, U. Colo., 1980. Asst. dir. vol. services Decatur (Ill.) Meml. Hosp., 1976-77; coordinator vol. services Miami Valley Hosp., Dayton, Ohio, 1978-79; dir. vol. services Condell Meml. Hosp., Libertyville, Ill., 1979-82, St. Joseph Hosp., Chgo., 1982—; cons. in field. Bd. dirs. Family Service Agy. North Lake County, Ill., Ill. Hosp. Assn. Council on Vols. Mem. Am. Hosp. Assn., Am. Soc. Dirs. Vol. Services, Ill. Soc. Dirs. Vol. Services, Chgo. Council Dir. Hosp. Vols. Developed, designed and wrote brochures, newsletters and other publs. in field. Office: St Joseph Hosp 2900 N Lake Shore Dr Chicago IL 60657

LAWRENCE, THOMAS HOEL, management consultant; b. New Orleans, July 21, 1913; s. Thomas Hoel and Rebecca (Marks) L.; m. Bettie Byrd Rogers, Oct. 17, 1936; children—Thomas Hoel III, Kathryn Byrd Lawrence Harsh. B.A., Yale U., 1935. Certified mgmt. cons. Dir. tng. Procter & Gamble, Cin., 1935-48, Hallmark, Inc., Kansas City, Mo., 1948-49; asst. to pres. Great Lakes Pipeline, Kansas City, 1949-50; founder, pres., chmn. emeritus Lawrence-Leiter & Co., Kansas City, 1950—. Contbr. articles to profl. jours. Recipient citation USAF, 1970. Mem. Inst. Mgmt. Cons. (sr. assoc., pres. 1978-81), Assn. Mgmt. Cons. Firms (pres. 1969-70), Kansas City C. of C. (com. chmn. 1961). Republican. Episcopalian. Clubs: Kansas City Country, Mercury (Kansas City, Mo.). Avocation: golf.

LAWRENCE, WILLARD EARL, statistics educator, consultant; b. Chassell, Mich., Apr. 8, 1917; s. William and Ruth Marie (messner) L.; m. Lorayne Adalayde Williams, June 12, 1943; children—Victoria Lawrence Barton, Barbara Lawrence Columbia, Joan Lawrence Wilger, Willard, Mark. Student Ripon Coll., 1947-49; B.S., Marquette U., 1951, M.S., 1953; postgrad. U. Wyo., 1959, Iowa State U., 1961; M.S., U. Wis., 1962, Ph.D., 1964. Mem. faculty Marquette U., Milw., 1953—, chmn. dept. math. and stats. 1973-79, prof. math. and stats., 1979—; cons. Statpower, Milw., 1970—, AID, India, 1966-68. Author: Introduction to the Theory of Probability, 1967; Probability: A First Course, 1970; also articles. Served to capt. U.S. Army, 1941-46. Decorated Bronze Star medal; NSF fellow, 1961. Mem. Math. Assn. Am., Am. Statis. Assn., Wis. Geol. Soc. (v.p. 1983-84). Republican. Roman Catholic. Avocations: golf; choir; rockhounding. Home: 6823 Kinsman St Wauwatosa WI 53213 Office: Dept Math Statistics and Computer Sci Marquette U Milwaukee WI 53233

LAWS, LEONARD STEWART, mathematics educator, management consultant; b. Pocasset, Okla., Dec. 29, 1917; s. Samuel M. and Ruth W. L.; m. Janet Owen, Aug. 29, 1943; children—Gregory, Kenneth, David, Rebecca. A.B., Willamette U., 1939; A.M., Stanford U., 1941; postgrad. U. Minn., 1941-43; Ed.D., Mich. State U., 1953; postgrad. Stanford U., 1961-62, 74. Teaching asst. in math. Stanford U., Palo Alto, Calif., 1939-41; teaching asst. in math. and mechanics U. Minn., Mpls., 1941-43, instr., 1943-48, asst. prof., 1948-52; prof. math. scis. Southwestern Coll., Winfield, Kans., 1953—; assoc. McElrath & Assocs., Inc., Mpls., 1964-70, 80—. NSF faculty fellow, 1961. Mem. Am. Soc. Quality Control, Am. Statis. Assn., NEA (life). Methodist. Avocation: sculptor. Office: Southwestern Coll 100 College St Winfield KS 67156

LAWSON, DAVID JERALD, bishop; b. Princeton, Ind., Mar. 26, 1930; s. David Jonathon and Bonnetta A. (White) L.; m. Martha Ellen Pegram, July 16, 1950; children—John Mark, Karen Sue Lawson Strang. A.B., U. Evansville, 1955; M.Div., Garrett Theol. Sem., 1959; D.D., U. Evansville, 1977. Ordained to ministry United Methodist Ch. Pastor, Tell City United Meth. Ch., Ind., 1956-67, Beach Grove United Meth. Ch., Indpls., 1967-72; dist. supt. So. Ind. Conf., 1972-76, conf. council dir., 1976-82; pastor Carmel United Meth. Ch., Ind., 1982-84; bishop United Meth. Ch., Sun Prairie, Wis., 1984—; trustee North Central Coll., Naperville, Ill., 1984—, Meth. Health Service, 1984—, Cedar Crest Home, Janesville, Wis., 1984—, Christian Community Home, Hudson, Wis., 1984—. Author monograph: Administrative Spirituality. Contbr. articles to profl. jours. Mem. Wis. Coordinating Com., Nicaraqua, 1984, Community Dept. of Instnl. Chaplains of State, City Traffic Commn., Ind., Marion County Bd. Zoning Appeals, Ind. Democrat. Lodge: Lions (membership sec. Indpls. 1967-72). Home: 5113 Comanche Way Madison WI 53704 Office: United Meth Episcopal 750 Windsor St Suite 303 Sun Prairie WI 53590

LAWSON, E. THOMAS, religion educator; b. Capetown, Republic of South Africa, Nov. 27, 1931; s. Robert Edward and Emily Gertrude (Swart) L.; m. Ruth Ann Jones, July 30, 1966; children—Sonya, Jennifer. B.D., U. Chgo., 1958, M.A., 1961, Ph.D., 1963. Instr. religion Western Mich. U., Kalamazoo, 1961-63, asst., 1963-65, assoc., 1965-67, prof., 1967—. Author: Religions of Africa: Traditions in Transformation, 1984. Contbr. articles to profl. jours. Postdoctoral fellow Soc. for Values in Higher Edn., Council for Philos. Studies. Mem. Am. Acad. Religion, Soc. for Philosophy and Psychology, Philosophy of Sci. Assn. Democrat. Avocations: painting; piano; computing. Home: 121 Monroe St Kalamazoo MI 49001 Office: Dept Religion Western Mich U Kalamazoo MI 49001

LAWSON, JAMES GREGORY, hospital administrator; b. Superior, Wis., Jan. 13, 1943; s. John Stuart and Barbara Levina (Rauchenstein) L.; m. Michaela Lee Yilk, Apr. 1, 1968; children—Deborah Paige, Terry Katherine, Michael James. B.S., U.S. Air Force Acad., 1965; M.B.A., U. Minn., 1975. instr. dept. family practice, Mpls., 1971-80; project dir. St. Joseph-Cold Spring Hosp., Minn., 1977-79; asst. adminstr. Willmar Med. Ctr., Minn., 1979-80; adminstr. Tri-County Hosp., Wadena, Minn., 1980—. Author: Starting and Managing Your Practice, 1983. Del. Ind. Republican State Conv., 1984. Served to capt. USAF, 1965-70. Mem. Minn. Hosp. Assn. (fin. com. 1984—, chmn. dist. D 1985), Central Minn. Health Systems Agy. Task Force. Roman

Catholic. Lodge: Rotary. Avocations: jogging; reading; gardening. Office: Tri-County Hosp 418 N Jefferson St Wadena MN

LAWSON, KENNETH RICHARD, state trooper, association executive; b. Greenfield, Mass., June 9, 1950; s. John Edmund and Ruby Harriet (Hutchinson) L.; m. Barbara Ann Webb; children—Michael K., Jennifer K., Jason K., Kimberly R. B.A. in Theology, Union Coll., 1976. Minister Seventh-day Adventist Ch., Wis., Mo., 1976-80; state trooper III, Wis. State Patrol, Madison, 1980—. Founder, pres. Friends of Missing Children, Madison, 1982—. Served with U.S. Army, 1970-72. Recipient Wis. State Patrol Outstanding Service award Ind. Ins. Agts. Wis., 1981. Avocations: amateur radio, outdoor sports. Home: 1401 Jasper Circle Sun Prairie WI 53590 Office: Friends of Missing Children PO Box 8848 Madison WI 53708

LAWSON, MATTHEW S., electronics industry executive; b. New Fairfield, Conn., Aug. 8, 1946; m. Mary Coryn, Jan. 2, 1978. A.B., Hamilton Coll., 1968; M.B.A. with honors, U. Chgo., 1985. Account exec. Foote, Cone & Belding Advt., Inc., Los Angeles, 1969-71, account dir., 1971-72; corp. pub. affairs mgr. Mazda Motors Am., Inc., Los Angeles, 1972-74; v.p. Eisaman, Johns and Laws Advt. Inc., Los Angeles, 1974-76; dep. news sec. to Gov. Ronald Reagan Presdl. Campaign, 1976, 80; dir. corp. communications Computer Scis. Corp., El Segundo, Calif., 1977-82; dir. investor relations Gould Industries, Rolling Meadows, Ill., 1982—. Mem. Calif. Republican Central Com., 1969-71; dir. Calif. Rep. Assembly, 1969-73; communications dir. for Lt. Gov. John Harmer, 1974. Mem. IEEE, N.Y. Soc. Security Analysts, Nat. Investor Relations Inst., Soc. Automotive Engrs. Club: Meadow. Home: 1505 E Central Rd Arlington Heights IL 60005 Office: 10 Gould Center Rolling Meadows IL 60008

LAWSON, ROBERT DAVIS, theoretical nuclear physicist; b. Sydney, Australia, July 14, 1926; s. Carl Herman and Angeline Elizabeth (Davis) L.; came to U.S., 1949; m. Mary Grace Lunn, Dec. 16, 1950 (div. 1976); children—Dorothy, Katherine, Victoria; m. 2d, Sarah Virginia Roney, Mar. 13, 1976. B.S., U. B.C., 1948, M.S., 1949; Ph.D., Stanford U., 1953. Research assoc. U. Calif.-Berkeley, 1953-57, Fermi Inst. U. Chgo., 1957-59; assoc. physicist Argonne Nat. Lab. (Ill.), 1959-65, sr. physicist, 1965—; vis. scientist U.K. Atomic Energy Authority, Harwell, Eng., 1962-63; vis. prof. SUNY-Stony Brook, 1972-73; vis. fellow Australian Nat. U., Canberra, 1982; vis. prof. U. Groningen, 1973, U. Utrecht, 1974, Technische Hochschule, Darmstadt, 1975, 78, Free U., Amsterdam, 1976, 81, others. Author: Theory of the Nuclear Shell Model, 1980; contbr. articles to sci. jours. Weizmann Inst. Sci. (Israel) fellow, 1967-68; Niels Bohr Inst. (Copenhagen) Nordita fellow, 1976-77. Fellow Am. Phys. Soc. Home: 1590 Raven Hill Dr Wheaton IL 60187 Office: Bldg 316 Argonne Nat Lab Argonne IL 60439

LAWTON, DAVID L., linguistics educator; b. N.Y.C., Mar. 20, 1924; s. Charles E. and Gladys E. (Cooke) L.; m. Jean Margaret Hahn, 1949; children—Robin, Martin. B.A., Hiram Coll., 1949; M.A., Western Res. U., 1950; Ph.D., Mich. State U., 1963. Instr. Alpena Community Coll., Mich., 1954-57; chmn. Lansing Community Coll., Mich., 1957-64; assoc. prof. Inter Am. U., San German, P.R., 1964-65, prof., dean faculty, Hato Rey, P.R., 1965-68; prof. linguistics Central Mich. U., Mount Pleasant, 1968—; Smith-Mundt prof. U. Guadalajara, Mex., 1960-62; Fulbright prof. U. Quito, Ecuador, 1971. Precinct del. Mount Prospect Democratic Com., 1980. Recipient Premier Performance award Central Mich. U., 1971, 75, 76; NSF fellow, 1977, Am. Council Learned Socs. fellow, 1977. Mem. Mich. Linguistic Soc. (sec.-treas. 1971—, editor, 1973-76), Linguistic Soc. Am., Internat. Soc. Caribbean Linguists, Am. Dialect Soc. Democrat. Episcopalian. Avocations: sailing, camping. Home: 1314 E Bennett St Mount Pleasant MI 48858 Office: Anspach 230 Central Mich Univ Mount Pleasant MI 48859

LAWYER, VERNE, lawyer; b. Indianola, Iowa, May 9, 1923; s. Merrill Guy and Zella (Mills) L.; LL.B., Drake U., 1949; m. Sally Hay, Oct. 5, 1946; 1 dau., Suzanne; m. 2d, Vivian Jury, Oct. 25, 1959; children—Michael, Steven. Admitted Iowa bar, 1949, also U.S. Supreme Ct. bar; practice law, Des Moines, 1949—; mem. firm Law Offices of Verne Lawyer. Mem. Iowa Aeros. Commn., 1973-75. Trustee ATL Roscoe Pound Found., 1965-71, fellow, 1973—; trustee Melvin M. Belli Soc. Recipient Outstanding Law Alumni award Phi Alpha Delta, 1964. Fellow Internat. Acad. Trial Lawyers, Am. Coll. Trial Lawyers, Am. Bd. Trial Advs., Internat. Soc. Barristers, Am. Bar Found.; mem. ABA (state chmn. membership com. of ins., negligence and compensation law 1970—, com. trial techniques 1969-70, com. on aviation litigation 1983-84), Iowa (spl. comn. on fed. practice 1971-78, spl. automobile reparations com. 1972—), Polk County bar assns., Assn. Trial Lawyers Am. (v.p. Iowa chpt. 1956-57, nat. sec. 1963-64, 67-68, bd. govs. 1962-63, chmn. for Iowa 1972-74, mem. internat. aviation com. 1973—, trial advs. scholarship soc. com. 1973—), Iowa Acad. Trial Lawyers (sec.-treas. 1962—, editor Newsbull. 1962—, editor Weekly Verdict Summary 1970—, editor Acad. Alert 1979—, editor Court Says 1978—), N.Y. State Trial Lawyers Assn., Calif. Trial Lawyers Assn., Okla. Trial Lawyers Assn., Tex. Trial Lawyers Assn., Assn. Trial Lawyers Iowa, Law Sci. Acad. Am., Lawyer-Pilots Bar Assn., Am. Judicature Soc., World Assn. Lawyers (founding), World Peace Through Law Center, Trial Lawyers Assn. Des Moines, Phi Alpha Delta, Sigma Alpha Epsilon. Author: Trial by Notebook, 1964; author: Art of Persuasion in Litigation, 1966, How to Defend a Criminal Case from Arrest to Verdict, 1967; The Complete Personal Injury Practice Manual, 1983. Contbr. articles law jours. Home: 5831 N Waterbury Rd Des Moines IA 50312 Office: Fleming Bldg Des Moines IA 50309

LAWYER, VIVIAN JURY, lawyer; b. Farmington, Iowa, Jan. 7, 1932; d. Jewell Everett Jury and Ruby Mae (Schumaker) Brewer; m. Verne Lawyer, Oct. 25, 1959; children—Michael Jury, Steven Verne. Tchr.'s cert. U. No. Iowa, 1951; B.S. with honors, Iowa State U., 1953; J.D. with honors, Drake U., 1968. Bar: Iowa 1968. Home econs. tchr. Waukee High Sch. (Iowa), 1953-55; home econs. tchr. jr. high sch. and high sch., Des Moines Pub. Schs., 1955-61; sole practice law, Des Moines, 1972—; dir. Micah Corp.; chmn. juvenile code tng. sessions Iowa Crime Commn., Des Moines, 1978-79, coordinator workshops, 1980; assoc. Law Offices of Verne Lawyer, Des Moines, 1981—; co-founder, bd. dirs. Youth Law Center, Des Moines, 1977—; mem. com. rules of juvenile procedure Supreme Ct. Iowa, 1981—; trustee Polk County Legal Aid Services, Des Moines, 1980-82; mem. Iowa Dept. Human Services and Supreme Ct. Juvenile Justice County Base Joint Study Com., 1984—; mem. Iowa Task Force permanent families project Nat. Council Juvenile and Family Ct. Judges, 1984—; mem. substance abuse com. Commn. Children, Youth and Families, 1985—. Editor: Iowa Juvenile Code Manual, 1979, Iowa Juvenile Code Workshop Manual, 1980; author booklet in field, 1981. Mem. Polk County Citizens Commn. on Corrections, 1977. Iowa Dept. Social Services grantee, 1980. Mem. ABA, Iowa Bar Assn., Polk County Bar Assn., Polk County Women Attys. Assn., Assn. Trial Lawyers Am., Assn. Family Counseling in Juvenile and Family Cts., Purple Arrow, Phi Kappa Phi, Omicron Nu. Republican. Home: 5831 N Waterbury Rd Des Moines IA 50312 Office: 427 Fleming Bldg Des Moines IA 50309

LAXPATI, SHARAD RANJITLAL, educator; b. Bombay, India, July 16, 1938; came to U.S., 1960; s. Ranjitlal P. and Arvinda R. (Zaveri) L.; m. Maureen A. Burns, Nov. 26, 1983. B.E., Gujarat U., India, 1957; M.S., U. Ill., 1961, Ph.D., 1965. Jr. sci. officer Atomic Energy Establishment, Bombay, 1958-60; asst. prof. Pa. State U., University Park, 1965-69; assoc. prof. dept. info. engring. U. Ill.-Chgo., 1969—; cons. Naval Research Lab., Washington, 1979—, Locus Inc., Alexandria, Va., 1984—, Motorola Inc., Schaumburg, Ill., 1976-77. Contbr. articles to profl. jours. Mem. IEEE, Instn. Elec. Engrs. (London), Internat. Radio Sci. Union. Home: 6067 N Whipple St Chicago IL 60659 Office: M/C 154 Dept EECS Univ Ill at Chicago PO Box 4348 Chicago IL 60680

LAY, DONALD POMEROY, U.S. judge; b. Princeton, Ill., Aug. 24, 1926; s. Hardy W. and Ruth (Cushing) L.; student U.S. Naval Acad., 1945-46; B.A., U. Iowa, 1948, J.D., 1951; L.L.D. (hon.) Wm. Mitchell Coll. Law, 1985; m. Miriam Elaine Gustafson, Aug. 6, 1949; children—Stephen Pomeroy (dec.), Catherine Sue, Cynthia Lynn, Elizabeth Ann, Deborah Jean, Susan Elaine. Admitted to Nebr. bar, 1951, Iowa bar, 1951, Wis. bar, 1953; with firm Kennedy, Holland, DeLacy & Svoboda, Omaha, 1951-53, Quarles, Spence & Quarles, Milw., 1953-54, Eisenstatt, Lay, Higgins & Miller, 1954-66; U.S. circuit judge 8th Circuit U.S. Ct. Appeals, 1966—, chief judge, 1980—; faculty mem. on evidence Nat. Coll. Trial Judges, 1964-65. Pres., Douglas County (Nebr.) Dystrophy Assn., 1964; bd. dirs. Hattie B. Monroe Home, Omaha, 1961-67. Served with USNR, 1944-46. Recipient Hancher-Finkbine medal U. Iowa, 1980. Fellow Internat. Acad. Trial Lawyers; mem. ABA, Nebr., Iowa bar assns., Am. Judicature Soc. (dir. 1976-82, exec. bd. 1979-82), Jud. Conf. U.S., Law Sci. Acad. (v.p. 1960), Am. Trial Lawyers Assn. (bd. govs. 1963-65), U. Iowa Alumni Assn. (pres. Omaha-Council Bluffs chpt. 1958), Order of Coif, Delta Sigma Rho, Phi Delta Phi. Methodist (ofcl. bd. 1965-68). Mem. editorial bd. Iowa Law Rev., 1950-51. Contbr. articles to legal jours. Home: 17 Eagle Ridge Rd Saint Paul MN 55110 Office: PO Box 75908 Saint Paul MN 55175

LAYBOURN, HALE, insurance company executive; b. Cedar Rapids, Iowa, July 20, 1923; s. Harold Hale and Reba S. (Strudevant) L.; B.S.B.A., U. Wyo., 1949; m. Barbara G., Dec. 21, 1947; children—Lillian Louise Laybourn Casares, Constance Grace Laybourn Harb, Deborah Hayle Laybourn Davis, Paul James, Richard Tod, Dorothy M. Asst. bus. mgr. Cheyenne (Wyo.) Newspapers, Inc., 1949-50; fiscal and personnel officer, dir. hosp. facilities Wyo. Dept. Health, 1950-60; dir. internal ops. Blue Cross and Blue Shield, Cheyenne, Wyo., 1960-65; pres. Blue Cross N.D., Fargo, 1965—; pres., chief exec. officer Dental Service Corp., Vision Service, Inc., 1976—; Coordinated Ins. Service, 1982—; chmn. bd. No. Plains Life Ins. Co., 1983—; v.p. Care Plan HMO; bd. dirs. Nat. Blue Cross Assn., 1973-77; chmn. Dist. X Plan Pres's., 1970-73; dir. West Fargo State Bank. Pres., Fargo-Moorhead Civic Opera Co., 1968-81, chmn. bd., 1981—; chmn. United Fund, Fargo, 1972. Served with inf. U.S. Army, 1942-45. Mem. Fargo C. of C. (pres. 1977). Republican. Episcopalian. Clubs: Elks, Kiwanis. Office: 4510 13th Ave SW Fargo ND 58121

LAYMAN, ROBERT CARL, optometrist, educator; b. Toledo, Ohio, Oct. 15, 1955; s. Carl Wesley and Elaine Edna (Rothacker) L. B.A. in Pre-Med., Univ. Toledo, 1973-78; B.S. in Physiol. Optics, Ohio State Univ., Columbus, 1980, O.D., 1982. Pvt. practice optometry Toledo, 1982—, Lambertville, Mich., 1985—; mem. faculty (part-time) Owens Tech. Coll., Toledo, 1983—. Mem. Am. Optometric Assn., Ohio Optometric Assn. (Outstanding Sr. Student 1982), Am. Pub. Health Assn. (vision care sect.), Toledo Jaycees (pres. 1984-85), Epsilon Psi Epsilon (dir. 1982-84). Republican. Lutheran. Lodge: Kiwanis (dir. 1983-85). Avocations: skiing; running; racket sports; tinkering with cars. Home: 1910 Fairfax St Toledo OH 43613 also 8050 Summerfield Rd Lambertville MI 48144

LAYNE, DONALD JAY, educational administrator; b. Chgo., Sept. 14, 1929; s. Duff B. and Elsie C. (Hemme) L.; m. Sylvia J. Lemanski, June 16, 1956; children—Mark, Robert, Leslie. Student U. Ill., 1947-49; B.S. in Edn., Ill. State U., 1952, M.S. in Edn., 1953; postgrad. Ill. State U., Bradley U., U. of Ill., 1954-73, U. Ill., Loyola U., Western Ill. U., 1974—. Tchr. Rochelle Twp. High Sch., Ill., 1955-57, York Community High Sch., Elmhurst, Ill., 1957-66; driver edn. supr. Addison Trail High Sch., Ill., 1966-76, dean of boys, 1967-68, athletic dir., 1971-72, asst. prin., 1976-83, prin., 1983—. Chmn. Village of Addison Liquor Commn., 1968—; coordinator, chmn. Village of Addison Substance Commn., 1975—; active Village of Addison Intergovtl. Agy., Addison Trail Parent Adv. Council, Addison Park Dist. Citizens Adv. Council, Village of Addison Police Fire Merit Rev. Bd., 1981—; mem. services bd. Lutherbrook Children's Ctr. Served with U.S. Army, 1953-55. Mem. Ill. Assn. Secondary Sch. Adminstrs., Ill. Prins. Assn. (region VIII program chmn.), Suburban Prins. Assn., Prins. Share, Assn. for Supervision and Curriculum Devel. Republican. Lodges: Kiwanis (pres. 1977, sec. 1975-76), Friars Cove (sec., treas. 1969-82). Avocations: sports; golf; hunting; fishing. Home: 262 Haddon Pl Addison IL 60101 Office: Addison Trail High Sch 213 N Lombard Rd Addison IL 60101-1999

LAYTON, MICHAEL LEROY, defense security assistance educator; b. Spokane, Wash., Oct. 17, 1935; s. Albert and Mae (Leata) L.; m. Victoria Layton, Jan. 11, 1964; children—Lisa, Brian. B.S. in Agronomy, Mont. State U., 1957; M.A. in Internat. Relations, Boston U., 1972; M.A. in Pub. Adminstrn., Central Mich. U., 1979; D. Pub. Adminstrn., Nova U., 1985. Research coordinator Infantry Sch., Fort Benning, Ga., 1967-69; chief Civil Mil. Ops. Community Comdrs. Office, Heidelberg, Fed. Republic Germany, 1970-74; ops. and tng. advisor U.S. Mil. Group, LaPaz, Bolivia, 1974-76; mem. Dept. Army Study Group, Washington, 1977; assoc. prof. Def. Inst. Security Assistance Mgmt., Wright Patterson AFB, Ohio, 1978—; staff officer Fgn. Mil. Tng. U.S. Army Tng. Command, Fort Monroe, Va., 1976-77; mem. DISAM Mobil Tng. Team, Australia, 1982, Kenya, 1984. Author: (with others) Security Assistance Training Management, 1984, Foreign Training Officers Guide, 1984; (contbr.) The Management of Security Assistance, 1984. Trustee Forest Ridge Assn., Mad River, Ohio, 1979—; dist. commr. Chattahoochee council Boy Scouts Am., 1967-69, scoutmaster, LaPaz, Bolivia, 1974-76, asst. scoutmaster, Dayton, Ohio, 1979-83. Decorated Army Commendation medals, Meritorious Service medal, Bronze Star, Air medal, Joint Service Commendation medal. Mem. Am. Def. Preparedness Assn. (chpt. treas. 1982—), Am. Soc. Pub. Adminstrn., Ctr. for Study of Presidency, Acad. Polit. Sci., Sigma Iota Epsilon, Alpha Gamma Rho. Republican. Roman Catholic. Lodges: Lions (Chile); La Sertoma (Ga.); Nat. Sojourners (pres. 1972-73), Masons, Shriners. Avocations: soccer referee; skiing; hunting; fishing. Home: 5530 Honeyleaf Way Dayton OH 45424

LAZAR, HAROLD PAUL, physician, consultant; b. Ellenville, N.Y., Nov. 19, 1928; s. Ephraim Baruch and Fannie (Springfield) L.; m. Molly Kailen Beck, June 20, 1953; children—Richard, Flora, Emily. A.B., Harvard U., 1948; M.D., N.Y. Med. Coll., 1952. Diplomate Am. Bd. Internal Medicine, Am. Bd. Gastroenterology. Intern U. Chgo. Clinics, 1952-53; resident in labs. Mt. Sinai Hosp., N.Y.C., 1953-54; asst. resident Montefiore Hosp., N.Y.C., 1954, Michael Reese Hosp., Chgo., 1956-58, V.A. Research Hosp., Chgo., 1958-59; research asst. in gastroenterology Mt. Sinai Hosp., 1959-71; asst. prof. medicine Northwestern U. Med. Sch., Chgo., 1971-80, assoc. prof. clin. medicine, 1980—; cons. gastroenterology V.A. Lakeside Hosp., Chgo., 1971—. Author: (with Leo Vander Reis) The Human Digestive System, 1972. Contbr. articles to profl. jours. Served to capt. USAF, 1954-56. Fellow Am. Coll. Physicians; mem. Am. Gastroent. Assn., Am. Soc. Gastroent. Endoscopy, Am. Coll. Gastroenterology. Democrat. Jewish. Clubs: Harvard (Mid Hudson Valley, Chgo., N.Y.C.)(pres. Mid Hudson Valley 1960-71, program chmn. Chgo., 1972-77). Avocations: jazz; squash. Home: 340 Sheridan Rd Winnetka IL 60093 Office: 676 N St Clair St Chicago IL 60611

LAZAR, LEE ALAN, transportation company executive; b. Pitts., Dec. 29, 1951; s. Bernard and Ethel L.; m. Karen Laine, Sept. 3, 1978; children—Stephen, Wendy. B.A., George Washington U., 1973; J.D., Washington U. St. Louis, 1976. Bar: Pa. 1976. Assoc. Kuhn, Engle & Stein, Pitts., 1976-79; labor counsel Leaseway Transp. Corp., Cleve., 1979-80, gen. mgr. personnel leasing div., 1980—. Pres. Temple Emanuel Young Peoples Congregation. Mem. Driver Leasing Council Am. (treas.). Contbr. articles to profl. jours. Home: 1811 Edenhall Dr Lyndhurst OH 44124 Office: 3700 Park East Dr Cleveland OH 44122

LAZAR, LINDA FRANCINE, physician; b. N.Y.C., Nov. 24, 1951; d. Solomon and Dorothy (Flakowitz) Zishuk; m. Rande Harris Lazar, Aug. 11, 1974. B.S., Bklyn. Coll., 1973; M.D., U. Autonoma de Guadalajara, Mex./N.Y. Med. Coll., 1979. Intern in pediatrics L.I. Jewish Hosp., New Hyde Park, N.Y., 1979-80; resident in pediatrics Rainbow Babies and Children's Hosp., Cleve., 1980-82, fellow in pediatric gastroenterology, 1982-84; instr. gastroenterology U. Tenn., 1984—; adj. instr. Cuyahoga Community Coll., Parma, Ohio, 1983-84. Mem. Am. Med. Women's Assn., AMA, Am. Soc. Parenteral and Enteral Nutrition.

LAZERE, MONICA BRIDGET, social work educator, therapist; b. Berlin, July 29, 1938; came to U.S., June 28, 1949, naturalized, 1957; d. Frederick O. and Maria Hart; m. Sydney H. Lazere, Nov. 9, 1958; children—Michael, Robert, Steven, Edward. B.S.W., Briarcliff Coll., Sioux City, Iowa, 1976; M.S.W., U. Iowa, 1979. Counselor, Planned Parenthood, Sioux City, 1974-79, exec. dir., 1979-81; prof. social work Morningside Coll., Sioux City, 1981-85, chmn. dept., 1982-85; sex therapist, Sioux City, 1981-85; leader workshops in field. Mem. CSC, Sioux City, 1979-85; chmn. allocations United Way, Sioux City, 1983-84; mem. fin. com. Woodbury County Democratic Com., 1983-84. Mem. Nat. Assn. Social Workers, Acad. Cert. Social Workers, Am. Assn. Sex Educators, Counselors and Therapists, Assn. Sci. Study of Sex, Interprofl. Inst. (v.p. 1980-81). Democrat. Jewish. Avocations: travel, people, Vietnam veterans rap group, reading. Home: 1026 La Crosse St Onalaska WI 54650

LAZZARA, DENNIS JOSEPH, dentist, orthodontist; b. Chgo., Mar. 14, 1948; s. Joseph James and Jacqueline Joan (Antonini) L.; m. Nancy Ann Pirhofer, Dec. 18, 1971; children—Kristin Lynn, Bryan Matthew, Matthew Dennis, Kathryn Marie. B.S., U. Dayton, 1970; D.D.S., Loyola U., 1974. M.S. in Oral Biology, 1976, cert. orthodontics, 1976. Practice dentistry specializing in orthodontics, Geneva, Ill., 1976—; sec. dental staff Community Hosp., Geneva Hosp., 1978-80, v.p., 1980-82, pres., 1982-84, exec. com., 1982-84. Recipient Award of Merit, Am. Coll. of Dentists, 1974, Harry Sicher honorable mention Council on Research, Am. Assn. Orthodontists, 1977. Mem. Am. Assn. Orthodontists, Midwestern Soc. of Orthodontists, Ill. Soc. Orthodontists, ADA, Fox River Valley Dental Soc. (bd. dirs. 1983—), Blue Key Nat. Honor Soc. Roman Catholic. Avocations: sailing, golf, tennis. Office: 1725 South St Box 575 Geneva IL 60134

LAZZARO, S. ROBERT E., lawyer, restaurant executive; b. Cleve., Mar. 25, 1953; s. Robert A. and Jan N. Lazzaro. B.A., Miami U., Oxford, Ohio, 1975; J.D., Dayton U., 1978. Bar: Ohio 1978, U.S. Dist. Ct. Ohio 1984. Ptnr. Costanzo & Lazzaro, Lakewood, Ohio, 1978—, Madison Avenue Land Co., Lakewood, 1983—; v.p. Glaw Bird, Inc., Cleve., 1983—. Served with USN, 1971-73. Mem. Cuyahoga Bar Assn., Greater Cleve. Bar Assn. Democrat. Roman Catholic. Clubs: Party Time II (pres.) (Middleburg Heights, Ohio); Parma Town Shell Softball (Parma Heights, Ohio). Office: Costanzo & Lazzaro 13317 Madison Ave Lakewood OH 44107

LEA, ALBERT ROBERT, manufacturing executive; b. Melrose, Mass., May 27, 1921; s. Robert Wentworth and Lillian (Ryan) L.; A.B., Amherst Coll., 1943; student Harvard Grad. Sch. Bus. Adminstrn., 1943; m. Joyce Winona Padgett, May 17, 1943 (div.); children—Patricia, Jennifer, Anne, Melissa Lea; m. 2d, Helen Clay Jones, May 12, 1961; children—Albert Robert, Robert Wentworth II. Exec. v.p. Ashcraft Inc., Kansas City, 1957-67, 83—, pres., 1967-83, also dir. Trustee Westminster Coll., Fulton, Mo., 1983—. Served as lt. Supply Corps, USNR, 1943-46. Mem. Phi Gamma Delta (trustee). Clubs: Mission Hills Country: University, Kansas City (Kansas City); Met. (N.Y.C.). Home: 625 W Meyer Blvd Kansas City MO 64113 Office: 816 Locust St Kansas City MO 64106

LEACH, DONALD PAUL, institute executive; b. Mount Vernon, N.Y., Mar. 17, 1945; s. Alfred Grahame and Anne Marie (Hantz) L.; B.S., Cedarville Coll., 1968; M.B.A., U. Dayton, 1974; m. Nancy Lynne Davis, Jan. 30, 1967; children—Donald Paul, Brian, Deborah. Accountant, mem. corp. staff Top Value Enterprises, Dayton, Ohio, 1969-72; tax analyst, corp. staff Philips Industries, Inc., Dayton, 1972-73; tax mgr. Danis Industries Corp., Dayton, 1973-76, asst. v.p., 1976-78, v.p., treas. constrn. products group, 1978-82; v.p., treas. Moody Bible Inst., Chgo., 1982—; instr. acctg. Sinclair Community Coll., Dayton, 1974-82. Mem. fin. com. Dayton Christian Schs., 1981-82; trustee Washington Hts. Bapt. Ch., Dayton, 1981-82, supt., 1977-80; deacon Faith Bapt. Ch., Winfield, Ill., 1984-86; treas. Alumni Council of Cedarville (Ohio) Coll., 1981-83, chmn., 1983-87; pres. Dayton Tax Club, 1977-78. Served with U.S. Army, 1967. Mem. Nat. Assn. Accountants, Inst. Internal Auditors. Home: 1481 Fanchon St Wheaton IL 60187 Office: Moody Bible Inst 820 N La Salle St Chicago IL 60610

LEACH, JIM, congressman; b. Davenport, Iowa, Oct. 15, 1942; s. James Albert and Lois (Hill) L.; m. Elisabeth Foxley, Dec. 6, 1975; 1 son, Gallagher Hill. B.A., Princeton U., 1964; M.A., Johns Hopkins U., 1966. Mem. staff Congressman Donald Rumsfeld, 1965-66; U.S. fgn. service officer, 1968-73; adminstrv. asst. to dir. OEO, 1969-70; mem. U.S. Delegation Geneva Disarmament Conf., 1971-72; mem. U.S. Delegation UN Gen. Assembly, 1972; pres. Flamegas Cos.; 1973-76; dir. Fed. Home Loan Bank, Des Moines, 1976; mem. 95th-99th Congresses from 1st Iowa Dist. mem. com. on banking, fin. and urban affairs, com. on fgn. affairs, chmn. Arms Control and Fgn. Policy Caucus of U.S. Congress. Mem. Nat. Fedn. Ind. Bus., Ripon Soc. (chmn.), C. of C., Rotary Club, Elks, Moose. Home: 20 Forest Rd Davenport IA 52803 Office: 1514 Longworth House Office Bldg Washington DC 20515*

LEACH, RONALD GEORGE, librarian; b. Monroe, Mich., Feb. 22, 1938; s. Garnet W. and Erma (Leach) L.; m. Joy A. Moore, Dec. 21, 1956; children—Ronald George, Debra, Catherine, Shane. B.S., Central Mich. U., 1966; M.L.S., U. Mich., 1969; Ph.D., Mich. State U., 1980. Head librarian Ohio State U., Mansfield, 1969-70; asst. library dir. Lake Superior State Coll., Sault Ste. Marie, Mich., 1970-75, acctg. library dir., 1975-76; assoc. library dir. Central Mich. U., Mt. Pleasant, 1976-80; dean of libraries Ind. State U., Terre Haute, 1980—. Evaluator, North Central Assn. Accreditation, Chgo., 1982—. Contbr. articles to profl. jours. Mem. ALA, Ind. Coop. Library Services Authority (dir. 1980—), Assn. Coll. and Research Libraries, Am. Soc. Info. Sci., Library Adminstrv. and Mgmt. Assn. (pres. 1985-86). Home: Rural Route 32 Box 199 Terre Haute IN 47803 Office: Ind State U Libraries 6 1/2 and Sycamore Sts Terre Haute IN 47809

LEACOCK, ROBERT ARTHUR, physicist, educator; b. Detroit, Oct. 3, 1935; s. Robert Cowles and Kathleen Francis (Maguire) L.; m. Jean Mackenzie Searles, Dec. 2, 1961; children—Nina Kathleen, Nicole Irene, Alexis Catherine. B.S., U. Mich., 1957, M.S., 1960, Ph.D., 1963. Instr. U. Mich., Ann Arbor, 1963-64; vis. fellow CERN, Geneva, 1964-65; postdoctoral assoc. Ames Lab., U.S. Dept. Energy, Iowa, 1965-67, assoc. physicist, 1967-71, physicist, 1971—; asst. prof. Iowa State U., Ames, 1967-71, assoc. prof. 1971—. Contbr. articles to profl. publs. Fellow Corning Glass Works, 1962-63, Am.-Swiss Found., 1964-65. Mem. Am. Phys. Soc., Sigma Xi. Home: 2323 Donald St Ames IA 50010 Office: Iowa State U Dept Physics Ames IA 50011

LEACOX, WILLIAM BRAMMER (LEE WILLIAMS), stockbroker; b. Coon Rapids, Iowa, Mar. 9, 1918; s. Glen F. and Neta (Brammer) L.; m. Winifred Duncan, Mar., 1935; children—Paul, Suzanne; m. 2d, Laura Beth Mahorney, Aug. 28, 1953; children—Paula Beth, Brent, Scott. Student Northwestern Mo. U., 1935-36, U. No. Iowa, 1938-39. Band leader, 1937-52; entertainment rep., 1952-59; with Harold Helme Investment Co., Omaha, 1960-65; v.p. Robert E. Schweser Co., Omaha, 1965-67; sr. v.p. Piper, Jaffray & Hopwood, Omaha, 1968—. Vol. Mid-Am. council Boy Scouts Am. Served to sgt. U.S. Army 1944-46. Mem. Omaha-Lincoln Fin. Analysts. Republican. Clubs: Omaha Press, West Omaha Cosmopolitan (past pres.), Oak Hills Country, Masons, Scottish Rite, Downtown Kiwanis, Shriners (Omaha); Elks (Shenandoah). Home: 6249 Oak Hills Plaza Omaha NE 68137 Office: 910 N 96th St Suite 200 W Omaha NE 68114

LEAHY, JAMES MICHAEL, real estate broker; b. Milw., Mar. 20, 1943; s. Robert Eugene and Virginia Estelle (Drolshagen) L.; student Mich. State U., 1965; 1 dau., Kelly. Vice pres. Leahy Builders, Inc., Birmingham, Mich., 1965-67; salesman Weir, Manuel, Snyder & Ranke, Inc., Realtors, Birmingham, 1967-72, mgr., Troy, Mich., 1973-79; part owner, mgr. Re/Max of Troy Realtors, 1979—; owner, pres. Re/Max of West Bloomfield, 1979—; part-owner Re/Max of Royal Oak Realtors, 1979—, Remax Assocs., Birmingham. Mem. bd. mgmt. YMCA, 1969-73, mem. bd. pub. relations com., 1970-71, chmn. phys. com. and mems., 1971-72. Served with Air NG, 1965-66. Mem. Birmingham Jr. C. of C. (chmn. youth devel. 1969), Mich. Assn. Realtors (dir. 1979—), Birmingham-Bloomfield Bd. Realtors (chmn. profl. standards com. 1977-78, pres. 1979, bd. dirs.), Sigma Alpha Epsilon. Roman Catholic. Home: 5397 Breeze Hill Pl Troy MI 48098 Office: 725 S Adams Birmingham MI 48011

LEAVENWORTH, RICHARD ORMOND, ophthalmologist; b. Mpls., Nov. 24, 1923; s. Richard Ormond and Geneva May (Hilton) L.; m. Ann Athens, June 21, 1951; children—Nancy, Suzanne, Georgia. B.S. in Medicine, U. Minn., 1948, M.D., 1950, M.D., 1951. Diplomate Am. Bd. Ophthalmology. Practice medicine specializing in ophthalmology, St. Paul, 1954-55, St. Louis Park Med. Ctr. (named changed to Park Nicollet Med. Ctr.), Mpls., 1955—; Contbr. articles to profl. jours. Precinct and area chmn. Republican Party, Excelsior, Minn. Served as ensign USNR, 1944-46. Fellow Am. Acad. Ophthalmology, Minn. Acad. Opthalmology and Otolaryngology (sec. 1958-59); mem. AMA, Minn. Med. Assn., Minn. Assn. Ophthalmology (bd. dirs., pres., treas. 1965—). Mem. United Church of Christ. Avocations: sailing, tennis, duck hunting. Home: 28070 Woodside Rd Shorewood MN 55331 Office: Park Nicollet Med Ctr 17821 Hwy 7 Minnetonka MN 55345

LEAVITT, GUY ORRIN, educational adminstrator; b. LaCrosse, Wis., Mar. 18, 1955; s. Orrin Miles and Esther Gladys (Stensven) L.; m. Rita Ann Reincke, June 14, 1980; children—Adam Michael, Amber Marie, Alec Miles. B.S. in Teaching, Winona State U., 1978, M.S. in Secondary Sch. Adminstrn., 1984. Tchr. Kiel Middle Sch., Wis., 1979-80, Mauston High Sch., Wis., 1980-84; jr.-sr. high sch. prin. Athens High Sch., Wis., 1984—; extension adv. bd. N.

Central Tech. Inst., Wausau, Wis., 1984—. Mem. Trempealeau Vol. Fire Dept., Wis., 1977-79. Mem. Nat. Assn. Secondary Sch. Prins., Assn. Wis. Sch. Adminstrs., Mauston Edn. Assn. (pres. 1983-84). Club: Jaycees (Tempealeau, Wis.). Lodge: Masons. Avocations: woodworking; biking; reading; automobiles. Home: 702 Damon St Athens WI 54411 Office: Sch Dist Athens 601 W Limits Rd Athens WI 54411

LEAVITT, LEWIS A., pediatrician, medical educator; b. N.Y.C., Nov. 7, 1941; s. Isidore and Sarah (Fishkowitz) L.; m. Judith E. Walzer, July 2, 1966; children—Sarah Abigail, David Isaac. B.S., U. Chgo., 1961, M.D., 1965. Diplomate Am. Bd. Pediatrics. Intern, resident Albert Einstein Coll. Medicine, Jacobi Hosp., Bronx, N.Y., 1965-68; prof. pediatrics U. Wis., Madison, 1984—, head infant devel. lab. Waisman Ctr. Mental Retardation and Human Devel., 1973—. Contbr. articles to profl. jours. Served to lt. comdr. USN, 1968-70. Mem. Soc. Research in Child Devel., Am. Acad. Pediatrics. Office: U Wis 1500 Highland Ave Madison WI 53706

LEAVY, THOMAS GREGORY, lawyer; b. Oakland, Calif., May 11, 1946; s. Patrick Drury and Natalie F. (Malida) L.; m. Mary Lou Hugh, 1969; children—John, Shannon, Heather, Elizabeth, Meaghan. A.A., Wright City Coll., 1972; B.A. with honors, Roosevelt U., 1975; J.D., John Marshall Law Sch., 1978. Bar: Ill. 1978, U.S. Dist. Ct. (no. dist.) Ill. 1978, Trial Bar U.S. Dist. Ct. (no. dist.) Ill. 1983. Assoc., Judge, Drew, Cipolla & Kurnik, Ltd., Park Ridge, Ill., 1978-82, Judge & Knight, Ltd., Park Ridge, 1982-84, ptnr., 1983—; judge John Marshall Moot Ct. Program, 1984; lectr., cons. in field. Contbr. sections to profl. publs. Solicitor, Crusade of Mercy, 1978. Served to cpl. USMC, 1964-68; Vietnam. Chgo. Bar Assn. scholar, 1976-77; named to Gavel Soc., John Marshall Law Sch., 1975; recipient Dean's Letter of Commendation, 1977. Fellow Nat. Assn. Criminal Def. Lawyers; mem. Ill. Bar Assn., ABA, John Marshall Alumni Assn. (trustee 1977—, Cert. of Appreciation 1983), Delta Theta Phi (master of rolls 1976-77), Forum Legal Frat. Group. Roman Catholic. Home: 5712 N West Circle Ave Chicago IL 60631 Office: Judge & Knight Ltd 422 N Northwest Hwy Park Ridge IL 60068

LEBAMOFF, IVAN ARGIRE, lawyer; b. Ft. Wayne, Ind., July 20, 1932; s. Argire V. and Helen A. (Kachandonov) L.; m. Katherine S. Lebamoff, June 9, 1963; children—Damian I., Jordan I., Justin A. A.B. in History, Ind. U., 1954, J.D., 1957. Bar: Ind. 1957, U.S. Ct. Dist. Ct. for no. and so. dists Ind. 1958, U.S. Supreme Ct. 1963. Sole practice law, Ft. Wayne, 1957-68; ptnr. firm Lebamoff, Ver Wiebe & Snow, Ft. Wayne, 1968-71; mayor City of Ft. Wayne, 1972-75; sole practice Lebamoff Law Offices, Ft. Wayne, 1975—; U.S. commr. No. Dist. Ind., 1957-62; fgn. service officer USIA, Dept. Commerce, Bulgaria, 1963; vis. prof. dept. urban affairs Ind. U.-Purdue U., Ft. Wayne, 1976-77. Chmn. Allen County Democratic Com., 1968-75; pres. Ft. Wayne Bd. Park Commrs., Ft. Wayne Dept. Parks and Recreation. Served with USAF, 1958-64. Mem. Allen County Bar Assn., Ind. Bar Assn., Am. Trial Lawyers Assn., Ind. Trial Lawyers Assn. Eastern Orthodox. Clubs: Kiwanis (Ft. Wayne); Masons. Home: 205 E Packard Ave Fort Wayne IN 46806 Office: 918 S Calhoun St Fort Wayne IN 46802

LEBANO, EDOARDO ANTONIO, French and Italian educator; b. Palmanova, Italy, Jan. 17, 1934; s. Nicola and Flora (Puccioni) L.; came to U.S., 1957, naturalized, 1961; m. Mary Vangeli, 1957; children—Tito Nicola, Mario Antonio. Student Biennio, U. Florence, 1955; M.A., Catholic U. Am., 1961, Ph.D., 1966. Tchr. high sch., Florence, Italy, 1955-57; Italian lang. specialist Bur. Programs and Standards, CSC, Washington, 1958; lang. instr. Sch. Langs., Fgn. Services Inst., Dept. State, Washington, 1959-61; lectr. Italian, U. Va., Charlottesville, 1961-66; asst. prof. Italian, U. Wis.-Milw., 1966-69; assoc. prof., assoc. chmn. dept. French and Italian, 1969-71; assoc. prof. dept. French and Italian, Ind. U., Bloomington, 1971-83, prof., 1983—. Author: A Look at Italy, 1976; Buon giorno a tutti, 1983; L'Insegnamento dell'italiano nei colleges e nelle universita del nordamerica, 1983. Contbr. articles to profl. jours. Recipient Uhrig award Faculty U. Wis., 1968. Mem. MLA, AAUP, Am. Assn. Tchrs. Italian (sec. treas. 1980-84, pres. 1984—), Dante Soc. Am., Renaissance Soc. Am., Boccaccio Soc. Am., Nat. Italian Am. Found., Am. Italian Hist. Assn., Am. Assn. Italian Studies, Midwest MLA. Home: 715 Plymouth Rd Bloomington IN 47401 Office: Ctr for Italian Studies Ind U Bloomington IN 47405

LEBEDA, KAY ELLEN, college official; b. Cedar Falls, Iowa, Nov. 15, 1945; d. Robert Earl and Katharine Madeline (Gallagher) Lamb; m. James William Lebeda, Jan. 11, 1969; children—Michael James, Sara Katherine. B.S. cum laude, Marywood Coll., 1967. Tchr. bus. Sidney Community Schs., N.Y., 1967-68; bookkeeper Standard Mfg. Co., Cedar Falls, 1968-69; sec., bookkeeper Real Estate Inc., Ames, Iowa, 1970-71, Mgmt. Recruiters, Des Moines, 1971-73; asst. to alumni dir. Simpson Coll., Indianola, Iowa, 1975-79, asst. dir. devel., 1979-80, alumni dir., 1980—. Contbg. author and editor Alumnus Mag., 1980—. Republican. Roman Catholic. Club: Simpson Guild (Indianola). Avocations: snow skiing, boating, home decorating, ch. and community choir. Home: 807 N 8th St Indianola IA 50125 Office: 701 North C St Indianola IA 50125

LEBIECKI, LAWRENCE LOUIS, business administrator; b. Gilman, Wis., Aug. 6, 1939; s. Joseph and Louise Cecelia (Zaborowski) L.; m. Avis Arlene Bremer, Aug. 26, 1961; 1 child, Robyn Lee. B.S. in Edn., U. Wis.-LaCrosse, 1962; M.S. in Edn., Northern Ill. U., 1968. Tchr. English Aurora E. Pub. Sch., Ill., 1962-65; asst. bus. mgr. Sch. Dist. 15, Palatine, Ill., 1965-67; asst. dean bus. Waubonsee Community Coll., Aurora, 1967-68; bus. adminstr. U. Wis., LaCrosse, 1968—; research interviewer LaCrosse C. of C., 1983-84; mgmt. audit team U. Wis. System, Whitewater, 1977. Contbr. articles to profl. jours. Photography pub. in various nat. mags. Bd. dirs. LaCrosse Area Day Care Center, Inc., 1973-76; bd. dirs., sec. LaCrosse Area Crime Stoppers, Inc., 1984—. Mem. Nat. Assn. Coll. and Univ. Bus. Officers, Central Assn. Coll. and Univ. Bus. Officers. Club: LaCrosse Quarterback (sec. 1984—). Avocations: photography, sports, cross country skiing. Home: W5190 Kiel Coulee Rd LaCrosse WI 54601 Office: U Wis LaCrosse 1725 State St LaCrosse WI 54601

LEBLANC, RALPH LOUIS, JR., marketing executive, international relations educator; b. Winthrop, Mass., Feb. 17, 1947; s. Ralph Louis and Rita Ellen (Downs) LeB.; m. Eileen C. Ralls, Mar. 6, 1982; divorced; children—Renee, Juliet. B.A., Boston Coll., 1976, M.A., 1980. Mem. tech. staff Mitre Corp., Bedford, Mass., 1971-84; dir. mktg. Integral Systems, Inc., Omaha, 1984—; prof. internat. relations U. Nebr., Omaha, 1982—. Contbr. articles to profl. jours. Chmn. Wakefield Republican Town Com., Mass., 1978; treas. Wakefield Housing Authority, 1979. Served with USAF, 1967-71. Mem. Armed Forces Communications and Electronics Assn. Air Force Assn., Republican. Wakefield Jaycees (v.p. 1977). Avocations: reading; golf. Home: 4321 Amos Gates Dr Omaha NE 68123 Office: Integral Systems Inc 9701 Philadelphia Ct Lanham MD 20706

LEBRETON, PIERRE ROBERT, chemistry educator; b. Chgo., Sept. 17, 1942; s. Robert Pierre and Irene Josephine (Mozzi) LeB.; m. Laura Hartwell Wessman, Oct. 25, 1969; children—Paul, David. B.S., U. Chgo., 1964; M.A., Harvard U., 1966, Ph.D., 1970. Postdoctoral fellow Physikalisches Inst., U. Freiburg, Fed. Republic Germany, 1971-72, Calif. Inst. Tech. and Jet Propulsion Lab., Pasadena, 1972-73; asst. prof. chemistry U. Ill.-Chgo., 1973-78, assoc. prof., 1978—. Contbr. articles to profl. jours., chpts. to books. Mem. Network 44, Chgo., 1985. CNRS fellow U. Louis Pasteur, 1980. Mem. Am. Chem. Soc., Internat. Soc. Quantum Biology. Avocations: hiking, camping, diving, skiing, travelling. Office: Dept Chemistry U Ill Chicago IL 60680

LEDDICK, GEORGE RUSSELL, counseling and educational psychologist; b. Newman, Calif., April 6, 1948; s. Kenneth L. and Margaret R (McIntosh) L.; B.A., DePauw, U., 1970; M.A., Fisk U., 1977; Ph.D., Purdue U., 1980. Cert. clin. mental health counselor. Instr. Purdue U., West Lafayette, Ind., 1979-80; asst. prof. edn., coordinator counseling Ind.-Purdue U., Ft. Wayne, 1980—; pres. Ind. Specialists in Group Work. Fellow, Internat. Council Sex Edn. and Parenthood; mem. Am. Assn. Marriage and Family Therapy (clin.), Am. Psychol. Assn., Am. Assn. for Counseling and Devel. (pres.-elect), Ind. Assn. Counseling and Devel. (pres.), Ind. Counselor Edn. and Supervision, Ind. Specialists in Group Work (past pres.), Assn. Counselor Edn. and Supervision (chmn. supervision com.), Am. Mental Health Counselors Assn., Phi Delta Kappa. Mem. editorial bd. Jour. Specialists in Group Work, Clin. Supr.; contbr. articles to profl. jours., other publs.

LEDERMAN, LEON MAX, physicist, educator; b. N.Y.C., 1922; m. Ellen Carr; children—Rena, Jesse, Heidi. B.A., CCNY, 1943; M.A., Columbia U., 1948, Ph.D., 1951; D.Sc., U. Chgo., 1983, No. Ill. U., 1983. Faculty Columbia U., N.Y.C., now Eugene Higgins Prof., dir. Nevis Labs., Irvington, 1962-79; dir. Fermi Nat. Accelerator Lab., Batavia, Ill., 1979—; collaborator in research Nevis Lab. program Brookhaven Nat. Lab., European Center for Nuclear Research, Geneva, Fermilab and SUNY-Stony Brook. U.S. rep. to Internat. Com. for Future Accelerators; mem. AEC Adv. Panel of High Energy Physics. Ford Found. fellow, 1958-59; John Simon Guggenheim fellow, 1958-59; European Center for Nuclear Research fellow, 1958-59; Ernest Kempton Adams fellow, 1961; NSF fellow, 1967; recipient Nat. Medal of Sci. by Pres. Lyndon Johnson, 1965, Townsend Harris medal City of N.Y., 1973, Elliot Cresson medal Franklyn Inst., 1976, Wolf prize in physics, 1982. Fellow Am. Phys. Soc., Am. Acad. Arts and Scis., AAAS; mem. Nat. Acad. Sci. Co-discoverer two kinds of neutrinos, 1961, parity violations in the decay of mu mesons, 1957, long-lived neutral K-meson, 1956, second neutrino associated with muon, 1961, existence of large transverse momentum pions, 1972, Upsilon particles, 1977; co-researcher muon decay, 1957. Office: Fermi Nat Accelerator Lab PO Box 500 Batavia IL 60510*

LEDVINA, LEE CARL, sheriff; b. Green Bay, Wis., Aug. 8, 1952; s. Leonard Ernest and Gloria Victoria (Novitski) L.; m. Joanne Ledvina, Feb. 8, 1975; children—Jason Lee, Jonathan Ardeal, Justin Leonard. A.A., N.W. Tech. Inst., 1974. Vice pres. L&M Security, Green Bay, 1975-78; spl. investigator Kewaunee County Sheriff, Wis., 1979-81, under sheriff, 1979-81, radio operator, 1981-82, sheriff, 1982—; sec., recorder Badger Sheriffs, Wisconsin Rapids, Wis., 1984—. Chorer, lectr. St. Joseph's Parish, Pilsen, Wis., 1985. Served to staff sgt. USAF, 1970-74. Mem. Gov.'s Council on Hwy. Safety. Lodge: K.C. Home and Office: 620 Juneau St Kewaunee WI 54216

LEDWIDGE, PATRICK JOSEPH, lawyer; b. Detroit, Mar. 17, 1928; s. Patrick Liam and Mary Josephine (Hooley) L.; m. Rosemary Lahey Mervenne, Aug. 3, 1974; stepchildren—Anne Marie, Mary Clare, John, David, Sara Mervenne. A.B., Coll. Holy Cross, 1949; J.D., U. Mich., 1952. Bar: Mich., 1952. Assoc. Dickinson, Wright, Moon, Van Dusen & Freeman, Detroit, 1956-63, ptnr. 1964—. Served to lt. (j.g.) USN, 1952-55. Mem. ABA, Mich. Btate Bar, Am. Law Inst. Roman Catholic. Clubs: Detroit, Athletic, Golf (Detroit). Home: 777 N Williamsbury Birmingham MI 48010 Office: 800 First National Bldg Detroit MI 48226

LEE, ALBERTA MAXINE, county official, realtor; b. Lima, Ohio, May 17, 1933; d. Ralph Virgil and Mary Kathryn (Wellbaum) Vermillion; m. Richard Franklin Lee, Sept. 11, 1950; 1 child, Brett Alan. Realtor, prin. Alberta Lee Realty, Lima, 1956—; recorder Allen County, Lima, 1981—. Pres. Lima City Bd. Edn., 9 yrs. Mem. Lima Bd. Realtors (pres. 1971, 78; Realtor of Yr. 1969), Ohio Assn. Sch. Bds. (named to All Ohio Sch. Bd. 1980), Lima PTA Council (life), Ohio Recorders Assn. (v.p. 1985), Lima Area C. of C. (bd. dirs. 1978), Fed. Relations Network Nat. Sch. Bds. Lima Bus. and Profl. Women (past pres.). Republican. Mem. Ch. Brethren. Lodges: Soroptimists (past pres., Soroptimist of Yr. 1971). Home: 700 Maplewood Dr Lima OH 45805 Office: Allen County Recorder 301 N Main St Lima OH 45801

LEE, AMY HSUAN, mechanical engineer; b. Swatow, Kwangtung, China, Oct. 27, 1952; d. Paul Sewtuk and Sally (Sharping) L. B.S. in Mech. Engring., Ill. Inst. Tech., 1979, M.S.M.E. with honors, 1982. Sr. engr., mfg. devel. engring. Travenol Labs., Round Lake, Ill., 1982-83, prin. engr. Fenwal product devel., 1983—. Mem. ASME, Soc. Women Engrs., Sigma Xi, Tau Beta Pi, Pi Tau Sigma. Home: B40 W Irving Park Rd Suite 227 Chicago IL 60613 Office: Baxter Travenol Labs Route 120 and Wilson Rd Round Lake IL 60073

LEE, ANTHONY L., chemical engineer; b. Qingdao, China, Nov. 16, 1934; came to U.S., 1953, naturalized, 1962. B.S., U. Calif.-Berkeley, 1957; M.S., Mo. Sch. Mines, 1961. Registered profl. engr., Ill., Ont., Can. Researcher Calif. Inst. Tech., Pasadena, 1957-59; instr. Mo. Sch. Mines, Rolla, 1959-61; engr. Stepan Chem. Co., Chgo., 1960-61; sr. chem. engr. Inst. Gas Tech., Chgo., 1961—. Author: Viscosity of Hydrocarbons, 1965; Viscosity of Natural Gases, 1970. Contbr. articles on catalysis, Kinetics and phys. properties to profl. jours. Patentee raw gas conversion processes, preparation of pipeline gas from synthesis gas. Mem. Am. Inst. Chem. Engrs., Am. Chem. Soc., Am. Soc. Petroleum Engrs. Office: Inst Gas Tech 3424 S State St Chicago IL 60616

LEE, CHENG-FEW, finance educator; b. Tao-Yuen, Taiwan, Jan. 29, 1939; s. Wan-Chen and Chi-Mei (Chang) L.; m. Schwinne Chwen Tzen, Oct. 20, 1966; children—John C., Alice C. B.S. in Econs., Nat. Taiwan U., 1962; M.S. in Stats., W.Va. U., 1970; Ph.D. in Econs., SUNY-Buffalo, 1973. Mem. staff Bank of China, Taipei, Taiwan, 1963-68; asst. prof. U. Ga.-Athens, 1973-76; assoc. prof. fin. U. Ill.-Champaign, 1976-78, prof., 1978-82, Ill. Bus. Edn. prof., 1982—; research advisor Fed. Res. Bank of Chgo., 1984—. Editor, Advances in Financial Planning and Forecasting, 1983—; assoc. editor Jour. Financial and Quantitative Analysis, 1977-83; editor: Readings in Investments, 1980, Readings in Financial Analysis and Planning, 1983; author: Financial Analysis and Planning, 1985. Wharton Sch. Ins. Research Inst. grantee, 1978, Chgo. Merc. Exchange grantee, 1980. Mem. Am. Econs. Assn., Am. Fin. Assn., Am. Statis. Assn., Western Fin. Assn. Home: 601 Shurts St Urbana IL 61801 Office: Dept Finance U Ill 1206 S 6th St Champaign IL 61820

LEE, DANIEL ANDREW, osteopathic physician, optometrist; b. Bklyn., Aug. 20, 1951; s. Jack W. and Lily (Ho) L.; m. Janet Lynne Eng, June 14, 1975; children—Jason Matthew, Brian Christopher. B.S. in Psychobiology, SUNY-Stony Brook, 1973; B.S. in Biology, Westminster Coll., 1973; cert. in emergency medicine tech. Mohawk Valley Community Coll., 1978; O.D., Pa. Coll. Optometry, 1977; D.O., Ohio U., 1984. Lic. optometrist, N.J., N.Y., Pa., Ohio; cert. in low vision proficiency N.Y. State Optometric Assn. Teaching asst. Westminster Coll., New Wilmington, Pa., 1971-72; teaching and research asst. Pa. Coll. Optometry, Phila., 1975-77; instr. Mohawk Valley Community Coll., Rome, N.Y., 1978-80; pvt. practice optometry, Utica, N.Y., 1978-80, Chauncey, Ohio, 1981-84, Dayton, Ohio, 1984—; teaching asst. Ohio U. Coll. Osteo. Medicine, Athens, 1983-84; intern Grandview Hosp., Dayton, 1984, mem. staff, 1984-85, ophthalmology resident, 1985—; cons. Rome Sch. Dist., Central Assn. for Blind, Utica, Kernan Sch. for Multiple Handicapped, Utica; speaker various profl. orgns. and confs.; mem. curriculum adv. com. Deer Creek Curriculum Rev. Conf., 1982. Contbr. articles to profl. jours. Mem. adv. bd. ARC, Rome, 1977-80; mem. Mohawk Valley Chinese Cultural Assn., Rome, 1977-80; nominated People to People Optometry Delegation to People's Republic of China, 1985. Served with USAF, 1977-80, to lt. USNR, 1981—. Fellow Am. Acad. Optometry; mem. Am. Osteo. Assn. (student rep. nat. com. on colls. 1984), Ohio Osteo. Assn., Ohio Optometric Assn., Dayton Area Chinese Assn., Gold Key, Beta Beta Beta. Episcopalian. Avocations: hunting; fishing; target shooting; guitar; mandolin. Home: Apt 17 D 434 Grand Ave Dayton OH 45405 Office: Grandview Hosp 405 Grand Ave Dayton OH 45405

LEE, DAVID RAY, immunogeneticist, researcher; b. Jackson, Miss., Feb. 16, 1953; s. Jack Ray Lee and Judith (McCoy) Lee Brown; m. Melissa Ann Johnson, Aug. 1, 1976; 1 child, Forrest Mathew. B.A., U. Calif.-Santa Barbara, 1975; Ph.D., U. Va., 1980. Postdoctoral fellow Washington U., St. Louis, 1980-83, research assoc., 1983—. Contbr. (with others) articles to profl. jours. and chpt. to Ann. Rev. Genetics, vol. 18, 1984. Grantee NIH, Leukemia Soc. Am. Democrat. Office: Washington Univ Sch Medicine Dept Genetics 660 S Euclid Ave St Louis MO 63110

LEE, DOYLE WAYNE, instrument company executive; b. Cogar, Okla., May 28, 1937; s. Walter S. and Mattie (Beavor) L.; m. Betty Sue Risner, Dec. 28, 1958; children—Doyle S., Julia R., Steven W. B.S., Ind. U., 1960; M.B.A., Baldwin Wallace Coll., 1983. Dir. employee relations N-L Industries, various locations 1960-73, N.Y.C., 1969-73; dir. indsl. relations Chase Brass, Wickliffe, Ohio, 1973-75; dir. customer and employee services Bailey Controls Co., Beachwood, 1975—. Leader Boy Scouts Am., 1979. Mem. Assn. Field Service Mgrs., Am. Assn. Personnel Adminstrs. Avocations: golf; bowling. Home: 7613 Huntington Dr Hudson OH 44236

LEE, ELL LOUIS, oral surgeon; b. Marshfield, Wis., May 21, 1940; s. Ell Louis and Mary Charlotte (Gile) L.; m. Donna Lee Kissling, Dec. 26, 1960 (div. June 1978); Annette Mary Schmitz, July 9, 1980; children—Patrick Ell, Julie Ann. D.D.S., Marquette U., 1964. Diplomate Am. Bd. Oral and Maxillofacial Surgery. Practice medicine specializing in oral and maxillofacial surgery, Green Bay, Wis., 1969—; cons. Green Bay Correctional Inst., 1969—, Dept. Vocat. Rehab., Green Bay, 1969—, Brown County Coroner's Office, Green Bay, 1982—. Served to capt. U.S. Army, 1965-72. Fellow Am. Assn. Oral and Maxillofacial Surgeons (trustee 1982), Am. Dental Soc. Anesthesia; mem. ADA. Republican. Lutheran. Avocations: motorcycles, shooting, golf. Home: 723 Brookridge St Green Bay WI 54301 Office: Oral Surgery Assocs Green Bay 704 S Webster Green Bay WI 54301

LEE, EUGENE, bank official; b. Flint, Mich., July 16, 1950; s. Colonel and Eliza L. Student Am. Inst. Banking; B.S., Gramblin U., 1972; postgrad. Central Mich. U., 1982—; m. Cathis Thompson, June 6, 1976; children—Laquan Thompson, Derrick. Bank teller Citizens Bank, Flint, Mich., 1972-76, mktg. rep., 1976-79, corp. rep., 1979-81, EEO specialist, 1981—; sales and mktg. dir. Vines Mag., 1979-80; instr. Jordan Coll., 1980-82. Bd. dirs. Jr. Achievement Greater Genesee Valley, Inc., 1980-82; chmn. fanfare com. United Way of Genesee and Shiawasee Counties, 1979, 80, 81; vol. salesman Flint C. of C., 1978. Recipient Disting. Salesman's award Citizen Bank, 1980. Home: 4010 Donnelly St Flint MI 48504 Office: 1 Citizens Banking Center S Saginaw St Flint MI 48502

LEE, JACK K., marketing executive; b. Chgo., June 23, 1953; s. Joe D. and Jane (Yung) Lee; m. Diana Dong, Dec. 22, 1979. B.S., U. Ill., 1976; postgrad. Nanzan U., Nagoya, Japan, 1976, Loyola U., 1984—, Columbia Pacific U., 1985. Lic. real estate and life ins. sales rep. Ill. Div. sales mgr. Sears, Roebuck & Co., Ann Arbor, Mich., 1976-77; asst. mktg. mgr. Chgo. Fed. Savs. Assn., 1977-81; account exec. CNA Fin. Assn., Chgo., 1982-84; div. mgr. advt. service The Jewel Co., Chgo., 1984—; tchr. English, tutor Nagoya Internat. Tng. Ctr., 1975-76. Youth advisor Jr. Achievement, Cin., 1977; coordinator Combined Appeal, Cin., 1977, promotion supporter, Chgo., 1982-83. Fgn. exchange student Ill. State U., Japan, 1975. Mem. Am. Mktg. Assn. (promotion services com. 1984). Republican. Avocations: reading mktg. topics, tennis, photography. Home: 1033 Ontario St Oak Park IL 60301 Office: White Hen Pantry Div Jewel Co 666 Industrial Dr Elmhurst IL 60126

LEE, JERRY WAYNE, lawyer; b. Columbus, Ohio, Nov. 3, 1944; m. Judith Ann Skulski, Nov. 27, 1965; children—Bryan D., Kirsten N. B.S. in Edn., Bowling Green State U., 1966, M.A., 1968; J.D., U. Toledo, 1978. Bar: Ohio 1978, U.S. Dist. Ct. (no. dist.) Ohio 1979, U.S. Supreme Ct. 1982. Tchr. Otsego Local Schs., Tontogany, Ohio, 1966-67; teaching asst. Bowling Green State U., Ohio, 1967-68; instr. speech Ohio No. U., Ada, 1968-74; jud. clk. Wood County Ct. Common Pleas, Bowling Green, 1978-79; assoc. Reddin, Reddin & Lee, Bowling Green, 1979-81, ptnr., 1981—; v.p. Research and Devel. Co., Toledo, 1974-75. Bus. editor U. Toledo Law Rev., 1977-78. Contbr. articles to profl. jours. Asst. den leader Toledo Area Cub Scouts Am., 1973-74, asst. troop leader Boy Scouts Am., 1976-81; past pres., trustee Autistic Community of N. W. Ohio, Whitehouse, 1976—, Bowling Green PeeWee League, Inc., 1978-82; mem. Wood County Democratic Exec. Com., Bowling Green, 1979—; trustee Indsl. and Devel. Corp. Bowling Green, 1985—; vice-chmn. Bowling Green Housing Commn., 1981-82; chmn. Bowling Green Cable Vision Com., 1982-83; mem. city council, Bowling Green, 1983, mem. cablevision com., 1984—; trustee Wood county chpt. Am. Diabetes Assn., Bowling Green, 1984—, v.p., trustee Ohio affiliate; bd. dirs. Wood County unit Am. Cancer Soc., 1984—; trustee Wood County Mental Health Ctr., Inc., 1985—. Recipient Resolution for Community Service Univ. Circle, Bowling Green State U. Alumni Assn., 1984. Mem. Ohio State Bar Assn., Ohio Trial Lawyers Assn., ABA, Assn. Trial Lawyers Am., Wood County Bar Assn., Bowling Green C. of C. (chmn. econ. devel. com.), Jaycees (bd. dirs. 1979-80, Phi Alpha Delta. Democrat. Clubs: Falcon, Bowling Green Country. Lodges: Elks, Kiwanis (bd. dirs. 1985—), Optimists (bd. dirs. 1979). Home: 226 Sandridge Rd Bowling Green OH 43402 Office: Reddin Reddin & Lee 136 N Main St Bowling Green OH 43402

LEE, KYO RAK, radiologist; b. Seoul, Korea, Aug. 3, 1933; s. Ke Chang and Ok Hi (Um) L.; came to U.S., 1964, naturalized, 1976; M.D., Seoul Nat. U., 1959; m. Ke Sook Oh, July 22, 1964; children—Andrew, John. Intern, Franklin Sq. Hosp., Balt., 1964-65; resident U. Mo. Med. Center, Columbia, Mo., 1965-68; instr. dept. radiology U. Mo., Columbia, 1968-69, asst. prof., 1969-71; asst. prof. dept. radiology U. Kans., Kansas City, 1971-76, assoc. prof., 1976-81, prof., 1981—. Served with Republic of Korea Army, 1950-52. Diplomate Am. Bd. Radiology. Recipient Richard H. Marshak award Am. Coll. Gastroenterology, 1975. Fellow Am. Coll. Radiology; mem. Radiol. Soc. N.Am., Am. Roentgen Ray Soc., Assn. Univ. Radiologists, Kans. Radiol. Soc., Greater Kansas City Radiol. Soc., Wyandotte County Med. Soc. Presbyterian. Contbr. articles to med. jours. Home: 9800 Glenwood St Overland Park KS 66212 Office: U Kans 39th St and Rainbow Blvd Kansas City KS 66103

LEE, MARGARET BURKE, college administrator, consultant, educator; b. San Diego, Dec. 28, 1943; d. Peter John and Margaret Mary (Brown) Burke; m. Donald Harry Lee, June 30, 1973; children—Katherine Louise, Kristopher Donald. B.A. summa cum laude, Regis Coll., 1966; M.A. with honors, U. Chgo., 1970, Ph.D., 1978. Asst. to humanities MIT, Cambridge, 1969; instr. Dover-Sherborn High Sch., Dover, 1973-75; instr. Alpena Community Coll., Mich., 1975-80, dean liberal arts, 1980-82; dean instrn. Kalamazoo Valley Community Coll., 1982-85; v.p. Oakton Community Coll., Des Plaines, Ill., 1985—; cons. evaluator North Central Assn., Chgo., 1982—; cons., field faculty Vt. Coll., Montpelier, 1982—. Mem. Career Edn. Planning Dist., Kalamazoo, 1982, Kalamazoo Forum/Kalamazoo Network, 1982, Needs Assessment Task Force, 1984. Ford Found. fellow, 1969-73; Woodrow Wilson Found. fellow, 1975; fed. grantee, 1978-84. Mem. Am. Assn. Community and Jr. Colls., Mich. Assn. Community Coll. Instrnl. Adminstrs. (pres. 1983-85), Mich. Occupational Deans Adminstrs. Council (exec. bd. 1983-85), Mich. Women's Studies Assn. (honors selection com. 1984), Kalamazoo Consortium Higher Edn. (pres.'s council coordinating com. 1982-85), Kalamazoo C. of C. (vocat. edn. subcom. indsl. council 1982). Democrat. Lutheran. Avocations: quilt collecting; reading; listening to classical music; sports spectating; theatre-going. Home: 875 Tree Ln 201 Prospect Heights IL 60070 Office: Oakton Community Coll 1600 E Golf Rd Des Plaines IL 60016

LEE, MARGARET NORMA, artist; b. Kansas City, Mo., July 7, 1928; d. James W. and Margaret W. (Farin) Lee; Ph.B., U. Chgo., 1948; M.A., Art Inst. Chgo., 1952. Lectr., U. Kansas City, 1957-61; cons. Kansas City Bd. Edn., Kansas City, Mo., 1968—guest lectr. U.Mo.-Columbia, 1983; one-woman shows Univ. Women's Club, Kansas City, 1966, Friends of Art, Kansas City, 1969, Fine Arts Gallery U. Mo. at Columbia, 1972, All Souls Unitarian Ch. Kansas City, Mo., 1978; two-Woman show Rockhurst Coll., Kansas City, Mo., 1981 exhibited in group shows U. Kans., Lawrence, 1958, Chgo. Art Inst., 1963, Nelson Art Gallery, Kansas City, Mo., 1968, 74, Mo. Art Show, 1976, Fine Arts Gallery, Davenport, Iowa, 1977; represented in permanent collections Amarillo (Tex.) Art Center, Kansas City (Mo.) Pub. Library, Park Coll., Parkville, Mo. Mem. Coll. Art Assn. Roman Catholic. Contbr. art to profl. jours.; author booklet. Home and studio: 4109 Holmes St Kansas City MO 64110

LEE, MORDECAI, state legislator, political scientist; b. Milw., Aug. 27, 1948; s. Jack Harold and Bernice (Kamesar) L.; m. Storm Garrison, Apr. 15, 1984; stepchildren—Benjamin, Alyssa, Alexandra. B.A., U. Wis., 1970, M.P.A., Syracuse U., 1972, Ph.D., 1975. Guest scholar Brookings Instn., Washington, 1972-74; legis. asst. to Congressman Henry Reuss, Washington, 1975; asst. prof. polit. sci. U. Wis.-Whitewater and Parkside, 1976; mem. Wis. Ho. Reps., 1977-82; mem. Wis. Senate, 1982—; adj. prof. govt. U. Wis.-Milw. Democrat. Jewish.

LEE, NORMAN KEITH, mathematics educator; b. Frankfort, Ind., Feb. 3, 1934; s. Harvey George and Adeline Mae (Robison) L.; m. Barbara Jean Robison, June 11, 1956; children—Michael D., Bruce K. A.B., Hanover Coll., 1956; M.A., Vanderbilt U., 1958; postgrad. Washington U., St. Louis, 1962-65; Ph.D., Purdue U., 1969. Asst. prof. math. Ball State U., Muncie, Ind., 1958-66, assoc. prof., 1969—; sr. instr. Somerset City Coll., Ky., 1968-69. Mem. AAMS. Republican. Presbyterian. Avocations: reading; hunting. Home: 401 W Main St Ridgeville IN 47380 Office: Ball State U Math Dept Muncie IN 47306

LEE, PAUL WARREN, lawyer; b. St. Petersburg, Fla., Jan. 14, 1948; s. Paul William and Lilly Evelyn (Smith) L. B.S., Ohio State U., 1970; J.D., Capital U., Columbus, Ohio, 1978. Bar: Ohio 1978, Fla. 1978. Asst. prosecutor Franklin County Pros. Atty.'s Office, Columbus, 1979—. Home: 1320 Bryden Rd Columbus OH 43205

LEE, RICHARD FRANK, general and home building contracting company executive; b. Richland Center, Wis., Nov. 19, 1941; s. Clarence Arlington and Vivian Clare (Postel) L.; m. Judith Ann Jordan, July 9, 1966; children—Jeffrey

Alan, Jennifer Ann. B.S., Wis. State U., 1964. Lic. fire instr. 1, Wis. Mgr., Janeff Credit Corp., Madison, Wis., 1965-66; with A.B.C. Builders, Madison, 1966—, owner, pres., 1976—. Mem. Fitchburg (Wis.) Vol. Fire Dept., 1970-83. Served with Wis. Air N.G., 1964-70. Mem. Builders Assn. Lutheran. Lodges: Optimists, Masons, Scottish Rite, Shriners. Home: 2762 Marledge St Madison WI 53711 Office: 6213 Monona Dr Madison WI 53716

LEE, ROBERT EUGENE, medicinal chemistry educator; b. West Salem, Ohio, Nov. 19, 1941; s. Clarence William Lee and Irene (Frary) Tanner; m. Jane Alice Wasson, Nov. 1968; children—Heather Ann, Jaclyn Elise, James Edward Bryan. B.S. in Pharmacy, Ohio No. U., 1963; Ph.D. in Med. Chemistry, Purdue U., 1968. Postdoctorate U. Mich., Ann Arbor, Mich., 1968-70; asst. prof. medicinal chemistry U. Cin., 1970-76, assoc. prof., 1976-83, prof., 1983—, asst. dean, 1978—. Contbr. articles to profl. jours. Bd. trustees United Methodist Ch., Monfort Heights, Ohio, 1978-83, chmn. fin. com., 1983-84, pastor parish relations com., 1984—; bd. dirs., treas. Taylor's Creek Youth Orgn., Miamitown, Ohio, 1984—. Mem. Am. Assn. Colls. Pharmacy, Am. Chem. Soc., Am. Pharm. Assn., Ohio State Pharm. Assn., Acad. Pharm. Scis. Republican. Avocations: outdoor sports, coaching youth soccer. Home: 8630 Strimple Rd Cleves OH 45002 Office: U Cin Med Ctr Coll Pharmacy ML-4 Cincinnati OH 45267

LEE, ROBERTO, chemical engineer; b. Shanghai, China, Jan. 10, 1937; came to U.S., 1954; s. Kin Wood and Yueh Chiu (Liu) L.; m. Alice Ong, Jan. 26, 1963; children—Vivienne, Denise. B.S., U. Ill., 1958; M.S., Purdue U., 1960, Ph.D., 1964. Registered profl. engr., Mo. Chem. engr. Corning Glass Works, N.Y., 1960; research engr. DuPont Co., Wilmington, Del., 1961; engring. group cons. Monsanto Co., St. Louis, 1963—. Patentee in field. Mem. Am. Chem. Soc., Am. Inst. Chem. Engrs. (nat. bd. dirs. 1985-87), Sigma Xi. Avocations: tennis; jogging; table tennis. Home: Saint Louis MO 63141 Office: Monsanto Co 800 N Lindbergh Blvd Saint Louis MO 63167

LEE, SANG MOON, management educator, consultant; b. Choongju, Korea, Apr. 1, 1939; came to U.S., 1961; s. Chang Woo and Duck Soon (Bahng) L.; m. Laura M. Moncrief, Apr. 20, 1968; children—Tosca M., Amy L. B.A., Seoul Nat. U., 1961; M.B.A., Miami U., Oxford, Ohio, 1963; Ph.D., U. Ga., 1968. Instr. U. Ga., Athens, 1966-68; mem. faculty Va. Poly. Inst., Blcksburg, 1968-76; disting. prof., chmn. dept. mgmt. U. Nebr., Lincoln, 1976—; cons. to industry. Author: Japanese Management, 1982; Management by Multiple Objectives, 1982; Introduction to Management Science, 1983; also 17 others. Mem. Nebr. Gov.'s Commn. on Trade, 1984-85. Recipient Outstanding Research award U. Nebr., 1981, Disting. Teaching award, 1983. Fellow Am. Inst. Decision Scis. (pres. 1984-85, Disting. Service award 1981); mem. Acad. Mgmt., Inst. Mgmt. Sci., Ops. Research Soc. Am. Democrat. Lodge: Elks. Avocations: racquetball; painting. Home: 7245 N Hampton Rd Lincoln NE 68506 Office: U Nebr 210 CBA Lincoln NE 68588

LEE, SHIU TAO, statistician; b. Taichung, Taiwan, Mar. 19, 1940; came to U.S. 1967, naturalized 1975; d. Su and Yei Nu (Liu) Hung; m. Chun-Cheng Lee, Jan. 8, 1967; children—Eming R., Cincy H. B.A., Taiwan Normal U., 1965; M.Stats., N.C. State U.-Raleigh, 1970, postgrad. 1971-72. Statis. analyst N.C. State Govt., Raleigh, 1973-74; programmer/analyst Power & Light Co., Raleigh, 1974-75; scientist N.C. Power & Light Co., Raleigh, 1975-76; statistician NIOSH, Cin., 1976—; cons. in field. Contbr. articles to profl. jours. Home: 10285 Gentlewind Dr Cincinnati OH 45242 Office: Nat Inst Occupational Safety and Health 4676 Columbia Pkwy Cincinnati OH 45226

LEE, SHUISHIH SAGE, pathologist; b. Soo-chow, Kiang Su, China, Jan. 5, 1948; came to U.S., 1972, naturalized, 1979; d. Wei-ping Wilson and Min-chen (Sun) Chang; m. Chung Seng Lee; children—Yvonne Claire; Michael Chung. M.D. Nat. Taiwan U., 1972; Ph.D., U. Rochester, 1976. Resident in pathology Strong Meml. Hosp., Rochester, N.Y., 1976-78, Northwestern Meml. Hosp., Chgo., 1978-79; dir. cytology and electron microscopy Parkview Meml. Hosp., Ft. Wayne, Ind., 1979—. Contbr. articles to profl. jours. Fellow Coll. Am. Pathologists, Am. Soc. Clin. Pathologists; mem. AMA, Ind. Med. Assn., N.E. Ind. Pathologists Assn. (sec. 1984), Ind. Assn. Pathologists, N.Y. Acad. Scis., Am. Assn. Pathologists, Am. Soc. Cytology, Internat. Acad. Pathology, Buckeye Soc. Cytology, Electron Microscopy Soc. Am. Home: 5728 Poophet Pass Fort Wayne IN 46825 Office: Parkview Meml Hosp 2200 Randalia Dr Fort Wayne IN 46825

LEE, SOO K., pediatrician; b. Korea, Mar. 1, 1940; s. Kun D. and Kae S. (Kim) L.; M.D., Kyungpook Nat. U., 1965; m. Seung Ja Seo, June 9, 1966; children—Greg, Young, Janet. Intern, resident in pediatrics Michael Reese Hosp., Chgo., 1969-72; fellow in pediatric nephrology LaRabida Hosp.- U. Chgo., 1972-74; attending pediatric physician Cook County Hosp., Chgo., 1974-76; practice medicine, specializing in pediatrics, Joliet, Ill., 1976—; instr. pediatrics U. Ill., 1974-76. Med. cons. Parent Power, 1976-80. Served to capt. M.C., Korean Army, 1966-69. Mem. Am. Acad. Pediatrics, AMA. Roman Catholic. Office: 210 N Hammes Ave Joliet IL 60435

LEE, TERRANCE RILEY, educator; b. Jamestown, N.D., June 16, 1940; s. Riley Ever and Ina Lois (Didier) L. B.A., St. Cloud State U., 1966; M.A.T. in Chemistry, U. Wis., 1973. Tchr. Cromwell Wright Pub. Sch., Cromwell, Wis., 1967-68, Owen Pub. Schs., Wis., 1968-69, Winter Pub. Schs., Wis., 1969—. Democrat. Lodges: Masons, Shriners. Avocations: folk music; stamps. Home: Rural Route 1 Box 44 Winter WI 54896

LEE, TIMOTHY EBY, automobile manufacturing company executive; b. Lorain, Ohio, Feb. 5, 1951; s. Robert Alfred and Jean (Thomas) L.; m. Deborah Katherine Sulpizio, Dec. 18, 1971; children—Matthew David, Elizabeth Anne, Allison Anne. B.A., Gen. Motors Inst., 1973; M.A., Purdue U., 1974. Labor relations specialist Fisher Body div. Gen. Motors Co., Hamilton, Ohio, 1974-76, labor relations supr., Trenton, Ohio, 1977-79, adminstr. personnel, 1979-81, personnel dir., Hamilton 1982-85; prodn. mgr. Chevrolet-Pontiac-GM of Can. Car Group, Hamilton-Fairfield, 1985—. Trustee Mercy Hosps. of Hamilton and Fairfield, 1982—; mem. Butler County Pvt. Industry Council, 1985—; mem. pub. relations com. United Way of Hamilton-Fairfield, 1985—. Republican. Roman Catholic. Home: 5691 Green Oak Ct Fairfield OH 45014 Office: 4400 Dixie Hwy Hamilton OH 45014

LEE, WAYNE CYRIL, author; b. Lamar, Nebr., July 2, 1917; s. David Elmer and Rosa Belle (Deselms) L.; m. Pearl May Sheldon, Mar. 17, 1948; children—Wayne Sheldon, Charles Lester. Rural mail carrier, Lamar, 1951-77; instr. Writer's Digest Sch., 1976—; author non-fiction: Scotty Philip, the Man Who Saved the Buffalo, 1975; Trails of the Smoky Hill, 1980; author fiction: Shadow of the Gun, 1981; Guns at Genesis, 1981; Putnam's Ranch War, 1982; The Violent Trail, 1984; War at Nugget Creek, 1985; Massacre Creek, 1985; many others. Served with Signal Corps, U.S. Army, 1945. Named Historian of Year, High Plains Preservation of History Commn., 1981. Mem. Western Writers Am. (pres. 1970-71), Nebr. Writers Guild (pres. 1974-76), Nebr. State Hist. Soc. Found. (dir. 1975—). Republican. Mem. Christian Ch. Club: Toastmasters (pres. 1964-65, 72-73) (Imperial, Nebr.). Home and Office: Lamar NE 69035

LEE, WILLIAM CHARLES, federal judge; b. Fort Wayne, Ind., Feb. 2, 1938; s. Russell and Catherine (Zwick) L.; m. Judith Anne Bash, Sept. 19, 1959; children—Catherine L., Mark R., Richard R. A.B., Yale U., 1959; J.D., U. Chgo., 1962. Bar: Ind. 1962. Ptnr., Parry, Krueckeberg & Lee, Fort Wayne, 1964-70; dep. pros. atty. Allen County, Fort Wayne, 1963-69, chief dep., 1967-69; U.S. atty. No. Dist. Ind., Fort Wayne, 1970-73; ptnr. Hunt, Suedhoff, Borror, Eilbacher & Lee, Fort Wayne, 1973-81; U.S. Dist. judge No. Dist. Ind., Fort Wayne, 1981—; instr. Nat. Inst. Trial Advocacy. Co-chmn. Fort Wayne Fine Arts Operating Fund Drive, 1978; past bd. dirs., v.p. Fort Wayne Philharm. Orch., Fort Wayne Fine Arts Found., Hospice of Fort Wayne, Inc.; past bd. dirs. Fort Wayne Civic Theatre, Neighbors; past bd. dirs., pres. Legal Aid of Fort Wayne, Inc.; past mem. Trinity English Lutheran Ch. Council; trustee Fort Wayne Community Schs., 1978-81, pres., 1980-81; trustee Fort Wayne Mus. Art, 1984—. Griffin scholar, 1955-59; Weymouth Kirkland scholar, 1959-62. Fellow Am. Coll. Trial Lawyers, Ind. Bar Found.; mem. ABA, Allen County Bar Assn., Ind. State Bar Assn., Fed. Bar Assn., Seventh Cir. Bar Assn. Republican. Lutheran. Office: US Dist Court 243 Federal Bldg Fort Wayne IN 46802

LEE, WILLIAM JOHNSON, lawyer; b. Oneida, Tenn., Jan. 13, 1924; s. William J. and Ara (Anderson) L.; student Akron U., 1941-43, Denison U., 1943-44, Harvard U., 1944-45; J.D., Ohio State U., 1948. Bar: Ohio 1948, Fla. 1962. Research asst. Ohio State U. Law Sch., 1948-49; asst. dir. Ohio Dept. Liquor Control, chief purchases, 1956-57, atty. examiner, 1951-53, asst. state permit chief, 1953-55, state permit chief, 1955-56; asst. counsel, staff Hupp Corp., 1957-58; spl. counsel City Attys. Office Ft. Lauderdale (Fla.), 1963-65; asst. atty. gen. Office Atty. Gen., State of Ohio, 1966-70; adminstr. State Med. Bd. Ohio, Columbus, 1970-85, also mem. Federated State Bd.'s Nat. Commn. for Evaluation of Fgn. Med. Schs., 1981-83; Mem. Flex 1/Flex 2 Transitional Task Force, 1983-84; pvt. practice law, Ft. Lauderdale, 1965-66; acting municipal judge, Ravenna, Ohio, 1960; instr. Coll. Bus. Adminstrn., Kent State U., 1961-62. Mem. pastoral relations com. Epworth United Meth. Ch., 1976; chmn. legal aid com. Portage County, Ohio, 1960; troop awards chmn. Boy Scouts Am., 1965; mem. ch. bd. Melrose Park (Fla.) Meth. Ch., 1966. Mem. Am. Legion, Fla., Columbus, Akron, Broward County (Fla.) bar assns., Delta Theta Phi, Phi Kappa Tau, Pi Kappa Delta. Served with USAAF, 1942-46. Editorial bd. Ohio State Law Jour., 1947-48; also articles. Home: 4893 Brittany Ct W Columbus OH 43229

LEECH, CHARLES RONALD, educator; b. Itawamba County, Miss., Aug. 29, 1932; s. Mary Cestus Leech; m. Elinor Ann Stoltz, Dec. 27, 1959; children—Paul, Mark. B.S.Ed., Ill. State U., 1959; M.A., Northwestern U., 1964. Asst. mgr. A&P, various locations, 1953-59; English tchr. Waukegan Pub. Schs., Ill., 1959—; owner Bonnie Brook Computing, Waukegan, 1980—. Mem. Thoreau Soc., Mark Twain Soc., Am. Fedn. Tchrs., Ill. Assn. Tchrs. of English. Presbyterian. Avocations: amateur radio; computing; reading. Home: 2935 W Bonnie Brook Waukegan IL 60087 Office: Waukegan East High Sch 1011 Washington St Waukegan IL 60085

LEECH, PHYLLIS MILLER, college official; b. Wheeling, W.Va., Sept. 18, 1944; d. Bernard Joseph and Thelma Louise (Hopkins) Miller; m. Harry William Leech, July 16, 1966; 1 son, Albert Benjamin. Student West Liberty (W.Va.) State Coll., 1962-65; B.S., U. Md., 1975; postgrad. U. New Haven, 1978; M.B.A., Ohio U., 1985. Acct., asst. supr. Gladstone Assocs., Washington, 1975-76; cost analyst treas. office Yale U., New Haven, 1977-78; asst. bus. mgr. Jefferson Tech. Coll., Steubenville, Ohio, 1979-80, treas., bus. mgr., 1980—, treas. to bd. trustees, 1980—. Mem. Ohio Assn. Coll. and Univ. Bus. Officers, Central Assn. Coll. and Univ. Bus. Officers, Am. Assn. Women in Community and Jr. Colls., Ohio Tech. and Community Coll. Assn. Fiscal Officers (chmn. 1983—). Republican. Office: 4000 Sunset Blvd Steubenville OH 43952

LEEPER, ROSS ALLEN, music educator; b. Madison County, Iowa, Nov. 27, 1933; s. Merle Jasper and Ruth Estella (DeVault) L.; m. Shirley Ann Paasch, Sept. 28, 1956; children—Jeffrey Allen, Kristen Lynn. Student Simpson Coll., 1951-53; B.M.E., Drake U., 1955, M.M.E., 1960. Cert. tchr., Iowa. Dir. bands Exira (Iowa) Pub. Schs., 1955-56, Eagle Grove (Iowa) Community Schs., 1958—; musical dir., condr. Ft. Dodge (Iowa) Area Symphony Orch., 1978—; guest condr. at clinics and honor band festivals. Served with US Army, 1955-56. Named One of 10 Most Outstanding Music Educators in U.S. and Can., Sch. Musician mag., 1977; recipient MAC award as outstanding band dir. in Iowa, First Chair of Am., 1978. Mem. Am. Sch. Band Dirs. Assn. (past pres.), Iowa Bandmasters Assn. (pres.), Am. Fedn. Musicians. Methodist. Office: NW 2nd and Fort Sts Eagle Grove IA 50533

LEESON, JANET CAROLINE TOLLEFSON, cake specialties company executive; b. L'Anse, Mich., May 23, 1933; d. Harold Arnold and Sylvia Aino (Makikangas) Tollefson; student Prairie State Coll., 1970-76; master decorator degree Wilton Sch. Cake Decorating, 1974; grad. Cosmopolitan Sch. Bus., 1980; m. Raymond Harry Leeson, May 20, 1961; 1 son, Barry Raymond; children by previous marriage—Warren Scott, Debra Delores. Mgr., Peak Service Cleaners, Chgo., 1959; co-owner Ra-Ja-Lee TV, Harvey, Ill., 1961-66; founder and head fgn. trade dept. Wilton Enterprises, Inc., Chgo., 1969-75; tchr. cake decorating J.C. Penney Co., Matteson, Ill., 1975; office mgr. Pat Carpenter Assocs., Highland, Ind., 1975; pres. Leeson's Party Cakes, Inc., cake supplies and cake sculpture, Tinley Park, Ill., 1975—; lectr. and demonstrator cake sculpture and decorating; lectr. small bus. and govt. Sec., Luth. Ch. Women; active worker Boy Scouts Am. and Girl Scouts U.S.A., 1957-63; bd. dirs. Whittier PTA, 1962-70; active Bremen Twp. Republican party. Recipient numerous awards for cake sculpture and decorating, 1970—. Mem. Internat. Cake Exploration Soc. (charter, Outstanding Mem. Ill. 1984), Retail Bakers Am., Chgo. Area Retail Bakers Assn. (1st pl. in regional midwest wedding cake competition 1978, 80, 1st pl. nat. 1982, others), Am. Bus. Women's Assn. (chpt. publicity chmn., hospitality chmn. 1982-83), Ingalls Meml. Hosp. Aux, Lupus Found. Am. Lutheran. Home: 6713 W 163d Pl Tinley Park IL 60477 Office: Leeson's Party Cakes Inc 6713 W 163d Pl Tinley Park IL 60477

LEET, RICHARD HALE, oil company executive; b. Maryville, Mo., Oct. 11, 1926; s. Theron Hale and Helen Eloise (Rutledge) L.; B.S. in Chemistry, N.W. Mo. State Coll., 1948; Ph.D. in Phys. Chemistry, Ohio State U., 1952; m. Phyllis Jean Combs, June 14, 1949; children—Richard Hale II, Alan Combs, Dana Ellen. Research chemist Standard Oil Co. (Ind.), Whiting, 1953-64; dir. long-range and capital planning, mktg. dept. Am. Oil Co., Chgo., 1964-68, mgr. ops. planning, mfg. dept., 1968-70, regional v.p., Atlanta, 1970-71, v.p. supply, Chgo., 1971-74; v.p. planning and adminstr. Amoco Chems. Corp., Chgo., 1974-75, v.p. mktg., 1975-77, exec. v.p., 1977-78, pres., 1978-83; exec. v.p., dir. Standard Oil Co. (Ind.), 1983—. Vice chmn. bd. mgrs. Met. YMCA, Chgo.; regional pres. Boy Scouts Am.; trustee Crusade of Mercy, Ill. Cancer Council. Served with USNR, 1944-46. Mem. Am. Chem. Soc., Soc. Chem. Industry (exec. com.), Am. Petroleum Inst., Société Industrielle de Chemie, Phi Sigma Epsilon, Gamma Alpha. Office: 200 E Randolph St Chicago IL 60601

LEEVER, DONALD FRANK, industrial sales executive; b. Kansas City, Kans., Oct. 6, 1943; s. Donald Ray and Lorraine Francis (Gunner) L.; m. Mildred Jean Dieu, Sept. 5, 1965; children—David J., John D., Rebecca J. B.B.A., Kans. State Coll., 1965. Acct. Trans World Airlines, Kansas City, Mo., 1966-69; systems analyst Thompson-Hayward Chem. Co., Kansas City, Kans., 1969-74; owner, operator Kansas City Washers, Mo., 1974-78; dist. mgr. Certanium Alloys, Kansas City, 1978-82; nat. accounts mgr. Electro Dynamics, Mission, Kans., 1982—. Methodist. Avocations: snow skiing; collecting razors. Home: 13906 W 47th Terr Shawnee KS 66216 Office: Electro Dynamics 5625 Foxridge Dr Mission KS 66202

LEFEBVRE, EUGENE ALLEN, ecology educator, researcher; b. St. Paul, Oct. 18, 1929; s. Clarence Joseph and Lucille (Carolina) LeF.; m. Mary Ellen Schultz Aug. 26, 1966; children—Ann-Marie, Charles Allen. B.S., U. Minn.-St. Paul, 1952; M.S., U. Minn.-Mpls. 1958, Ph.D., 1962. Research fellow Univ. Minn., Mpls., 1960-61, research assoc., 1961-65; asst. prof. ecology Southern Ill. Univ., Carbondale, 1966-71, assoc. prof. ecology, 1972—. Contbr. articles to profl. jours. Bd. dirs. So. Ill. Bird Observatory, Carbondale, 1976-78, chmn., 1978-82; bd. dirs. Minn. Chpt. Nature Conservancy, Mpls. Served with the U.S. Army, 1954-56. Recipient Avian Ecology Investigator award Ill. Dept. Conservation, 1981-82; NIH grantee, 1960-66, NSF grantee, 1968-83. Mem. Am. Ornithol. Union, British Ornithol. Union, Cooper Ornithology Soc., Ecol. Soc. Am., Sigma Xi. Avocations: camping; photography. Home: Box 112 Route 1 Carterville IL 62918 Office: Dept Zoology SIU-C Southern Ill Univ Carbondale IL 62901

LEFEVER, MAXINE LANE, educator, consultant; b. Elmhurst, Ill., May 30, 1931; d. Thomas Clinton Lane and Georgia Marie (Hampton) L.; m. Orville Joseph Lefever, Aug. 18, 1951 (div.). Student Ill. Wesleyan U., 1949-51; B.A., Western State Coll., 1958; M.S., Purdue U., 1964, postgrad., 1965. Elem. sch. tchr. Leaf River (Ill.) Pub. Schs., 1953-54, Mancos (Colo.) Pub. Schs., 1954-56; elem./jr. high sch. tchr. Cortez (Colo.) Pub. Schs., 1956-60; grad. teaching asst. band dept. Purdue U., Lafayette, 1962-65, edn. dept., 1964-65, instr. bands, 1965-79, asst. prof., 1980—; cons. numerous festivals and contests; pres. music/edn1. travel corp., 14 years. Hon. mem. U.S. Navy Band; recipient citation of excellence Nat. Band Assn.; Star of Order of Merit, J.P. Sousa Found. Mem. Ind. Music Educators Assn., Music Educators Nat. Conf., Nat. Band Assn. (v.p., exec. sec.), Coll. Band Dirs. Nat. Assn., Percussion Arts Soc., John Philip Sousa Found. (exec. sec.), Big Ten Band Dirs. Assn., Alpha Lambda Delta, Delta Omicron, Tau Beta Sigma, Kappa Kappa Psi (hon.), Phi Sigma Kappa (hon.). Contbr. articles to profl. jour.; composer percussion ensembles. Home: PO Box 2454 2924 Wilshire St West Lafayette IN 47906 Office: Purdue Univ Bands West Lafayette IN 47907

LEFEVRE, HARVARD STANLEY, engineering company executive; b. Stephenson, Mich., Oct. 3, 1920; s. Louis and Delia (Gardner) L.; m. Mary Lee Moore, Apr. 10, 1943; children—Linda, Terese, Stephen. Student U.S. Army Air Force Tech. Sch., 1943, San Angelo Army Air Field Bombardier Sch., 1943, Sch. Bus. Adminstrn., U. Mich., 1952; exec. tng. Alexander Hamilton Inst., 1955. With King Engring. Corp., Ann Arbor, Mich., 1941—, exec. v.p., 1956-67, pres., 1967—, acting chmn. bd., 1970-76, chmn. bd., 1976—, treas., 1970—, also dir. Served with USAAF, 1942-46. Mem. Engring. Soc. Detroit, Soc. Mfg. Engrs., Am. Mgmt. Assn., Ann Arbor Mfrs. Assn., Ann Arbor C. of C. (dir. 1976—), Ann Arbor Personnel Assn. Roman Catholic. Patentee gas dispersoid separator. Home: 801 Mount Pleasant St Ann Arbor MI 48103 Office: King Engring Corp 3201 S State St Ann Arbor MI 48106

LEFEVRE, JAMES JOSEPH, printer; b. Appleton, Wis., Nov. 19, 1949; s. John Earl and Monica Ann (Reince) Le F. Printer J&J Printing, Appleton, 1966—. Lodge: Optimists (sec. 1975-80, 83—, v.p. 1981-83). Home: 725 E Brewster St Appleton WI 54911 Office: J&J Printing 1410 N Meade St Appleton WI 54911

LEFF, ALAN RICHARD, medical educator, researcher; b. Pitts., May 23, 1945; s. Maurice D. and Grace Ruth (Schwatz) L.; m. Donna Rae Rosene, Feb. 14, 1975; children—Marni, Karen, Alison. A.B. cum laude, Oberlin Coll., 1967; M.D., U. Rochester, 1971. Diplomate Am. Bd. Internal Medicine, Am. Bd. Pulmonary Disease. Intern U. Mich. Hosp., Ann Arbor, 1971-72, resident, 1974-76; fellow U. Calif.-San Francisco, 1976-77, postdoctoral fellow, 1977-79; asst. prof. medicine U. Chgo., 1979-84, assoc. prof., 1985—, dir. pulmonary medicine service, 1984—, Pulmonary Function Lab., 1979—; advisor San Francisco Dept. Pub. Health, 1977-79, Chgo. Dept. Health, 1979—; bd. dirs. Chgo. Lung Assn., 1984—. Contbr. articles to profl. jours. Served with USPHS, 1972-74. Recipient Citation of merit Chgo. Lung Assn., 1974; Leopold Schepp Found. fellow, 1967-69. Fellow Am. Coll. Chest Physicians; mem. Am. Fedn. Clin. Research (councilor 1983—), Am. Soc. Clin. Investigation. Avocation: music. Home: 5730 S Kimbark Ave Chicago IL 60637 Office: Box 98 Dept Medicine Sect Pulmonary/Critical Care Medicine 5841 S Maryland Ave Chicago IL 60637

LEFTWICH, SAMUEL GILMER, retail company executive; b. Homer, Nebr., Dec. 10, 1926; s. Samuel Abel and Norma Emma (Ritchison) L.; B.S. in Bus. Adminstrn., U. Nebr., Omaha, 1949; m. Doris Mae Krupa, Oct. 1, 1950; children—James, Scott, Sharon, Thomas, Robert, William. With K Mart Corp. (formerly S.S. Kresge Co.), 1949—, dir. food ops. K mart Internat. Hdqrs., Troy, Mich., 1974-75, v.p. personnel and employee relations, Troy, 1976-79, sr. v.p. personnel and mgmt. devel., 1979-81, pres., chief operating officer, dir., 1981-85, vice chmn., 1985—. Served with AC, USN, 1944-46; PTO. Office: KMart Corp 3100 W Big Beaver Troy MI 48084*

LEGACY, JAMES WILLIAM, agricultural educator; b. Malone N.Y., Sept. 12, 1945; s. Bert James and Marcella May (Enos) L.; m. Betty Sue Rankin, Apr. 23, 1966; children—Peter, Lisa. B.S., Cornell U., 1968, M.S., 1971, Ph.D., 1976. Tchr. agrl. Hammond High Sch., N.Y., 1971-74; lectr. Cornell U., Ithaca, N.Y., 1974-75, research asst., 1975-76; asst. prof. Purdue, U., West Lafayette Ind., 1976-77; prof., chmn. Southern Ill. U., Carbondale, Ill., 1977—; program asst. U.S. AID State Dept., Apia Western Samoa, 1982—; program devel. U. Hawaii, Hilo, 1984. Author: Program Development in Agriculture Extension, 1981; Research Methods in Vocational Education, 1982; Agriculture & Society, 1982; Microcomputing in Agriculture, 1984. Adv. bd. Jackson County 4-H Clubs, Murphysboro, Ill., 1977-82, Kaskaskia Coll., Centralia, Ill., 1980—; bd. dirs. Jackson County YMCA, Carbondale, 1978-83. Served to sgt. E-5 U.S. Army, 1966-68. Recipient Tchr. of Yr. award Coll. Agriculture, 1981; various grants. Mem. Am. Assn. Tchrs. Agr., Am. Vocat. Assn., Nat. Assn. Tchrs. of Agr., Ill. Vocat. Assn., Ill. Vocat. Agr. Tchrs. Assn. Avocations: coin and stamp collecting. Home: Route 2 Box 294-D Murphysboro IL 62966 Office: AGEM Dept Southern ILL U Carbondale IL 62901

LEGGITT, DOROTHY, educator; b. Oblong, Ill., Feb. 19, 1903; d. Clarence C. and Louise Frances (Muchmore) L.; diploma Eastern Ill. State U., 1923, L.H.D. (hon.), 1977; Ph.B., U. Chgo., 1930, M.A., 1933, postgrad., intermittently, 1937-62. Tchr. rural schs., Jasper & Crawford Counties, Ill., 1920-22; tchr. high sch., Glen Ellyn, Ill., 1923-35; lectr., prof. No. Ill. State U., DeKalb, 1936-37; tchr. social studies, counselor Clayton (Mo.) pub. schs., 1937-52; tchr. Decatur (Ill.) pub. schs., 1952-54, Park Ridge (Ill.) pub. schs., 1954-61; reading specialist Joliet (Ill.) Jr. Coll., 1961-62, Niles West High Sch., Skokie, Ill., 1962-63; reading cons. Kenosha High Schs., Kenosha, Wis., 1963-65; head study skills dept. Palm Beach (Fla.) Jr. Coll., 1965-73, prof. emeritus, 1973—; summer lectr. various colls. and univs. Field rep. grad. edn. and social sci. depts. U. Chgo.; mem. found. bd. Eastern Ill. U. Recipient Walgreen Found. award in social, econ. and polit. instns., 1948, scholarship award Pi Lambda Theta, 1948, Distinguished Alumni award Eastern Ill. U., 1974. Mem. Newberry Library Assn. (assoc.), Ill. Edn. Assn., AAUW, Internat. Platform Assn. Author: Basic Study Skills and Workbook, 1942. Contbr. articles to profl. jours. Home: Grand Ohio Venture 211 E Ohio St Chicago IL 60611 Mailing Address: PO Box 1432 Chicago IL 60690

LEGGON, HERMAN WESLEY, chem. co. exec.; b. Cleve., Sept. 20, 1930; s. Charles W. and Ombra Novella (Reese) L.; B.S., Case Inst. Tech., 1953; M.S., John Carroll U., 1966; m. Zara M. Kerr, Aug. 14, 1976. Head organic lab. Crobaugh Labs., Cleve., 1955-59; analytical chemist Union Carbide Corp., Cleve., 1959-67, systems analyst Parma Tech. Center, 1967—; guest lectr. Atlanta U., 1973—; instr. Dyke Coll., 1979—. Service dir. Oakwood Village, 1969-70, councilman, 1970-71, councilman-at-large, 1971-73, pres. council, 1973-75. Recipient commendation Oakwood Village, 1962. Mem. ASTM (chmn. subcom. on nomenclature), Alpha Phi Alpha. Home: 3470 Belvoir St Beachwood OH 44122 Office: PO Box 6116 Cleveland OH 44101

LEGLER, LARRY EDWARD, physician; b. Kansas City, Kans., Dec. 20, 1950; s. Gilbert Lawrence and Madera Anna (DeAngeli) L.; m. Beth Jeanine Pounds, June 12, 1976; 1 child, Kristina Renee. B.S. in Chemistry, U. Mo., 1972; M.D., Baylor Coll. Medicine, 1975. Diplomate Am. Bd. Family Practice. Resident in family practice U. Ill.-Peoria, 1975-78; practice medicine specializing in family medicine, Independence, Mo., 1978—; staff Independence Sanitarium and Hosp., 1978—, Med. Ctr. of Independence, 1978—. Fellow Am. Acad. Family Physicians; mem. Kansas City S.W. Clin. Soc., Jackson County Med. Soc., Mo. Med. Assn. Office: 17611 E 24 Hwy Independence MO 64056

LEGLER, PAUL KEVIN, lawyer; b. Lisbon, N.D., Oct. 2, 1955; s. Victor Wilbert and Marlys B. (Timm) L.; m. Julie M. Wild, Sept. 12, 1979; 1 child, Alison. B.A., U. N.D., 1976; J.D., U. Minn., 1979. Bar: Minn. 1979, N.D. 1981, U.S. Dist. Ct. Minn. 1980, U.S. Dist. Ct. N.D. 1981, U.S. Ct. Appeals (8th cir.) 1982. Staff atty. Western Minn. Legal Services, Willmar, 1979-81; sole practice, Fargo, N.D., 1981—; instr. Moorhead State U., Minn., 1983—; contract atty. Legal Aid of N.D., Bismarck, 1984—. Mem. Assn. Trial Lawyers Am., Minn. State Bar Assn., N.D. State Bar Assn., Cass County Bar Assn., Clay County Bar Assn., Phi Beta Kappa. Democrat. Presbyterian. Home: 1542 S 8th St Fargo ND 58103 Office: 2501 13th Ave S Fargo ND 58103

LEGUEY-FEILLEUX, JEAN-ROBERT, political scientist, educator; b. Marseilles, France, Mar. 28, 1928; came to U.S., Aug. 1949; s. E. Feilleux and Jeanne (Leguey) Feilleux Levassort; m. Virginia Louise Hartwell, Sept. 19, 1953; children—Michele, Monique, Suzanne, Christiane. M.A., Ecole Superieure de Commerce, France, 1949; Diplome Superieur d'Etudes Coloniales, U. d'Aix-Marseille, France, 1949; M.A., U. Fla., 1951; Ph.D., Georgetown U., 1965. Lectr. Sch. Foreign Service Georgetown U., Washington, 1957-66; dir. research Inst. World Policy Georgetown U., 1960-66; asst. prof. St. Louis U., 1966-70, assoc. prof., 1970—, chmn. polit. sci. dept., 1983—; vis. scholar Harvard Law Sch., Cambridge, Mass., 1974-75; chmn. Fulbright Commn. for France Inst. Internat. Edn., N.Y.C., 1974-76; vis. researcher UN, N.Y.C., 1981. Author (with others): Law of Limited International Conflict, 1965. Contbr. chpt. to Implications of Disarmament, 1977. Contbr. articles to profl. jours. Author testimony Pres.'s Commn. on 25th Anniversary of UN, 1970. Recipient Medaille d'Or Institut Comml., France, 1949, Fulbright award U.S. State Dept., 1950, Cert. Disting. Service Inst. Internat. Edn., 1976; named Outstanding Educator Nutshell Mag., 1982. Mem. UN Assn. (mem. nat. council chpt. and div. pres. 1972-73, steering com. 1973-75), Internat. Human Rights Task Force (chmn. 1975-81), Character Research Assn. (pres. 1980-83), Phi Alpha Theta, Pi Sigma Alpha, Delta Phi Epsilon, Pi Delta Phi. Roman Catholic. Home: 6139 Kingsbury Ave Saint Louis MO 63112 Office: Political Science Dept Saint Louis Univ 221 N Grand Blvd Saint Louis MO 63103

LEHMAN, DAVID HAYES, marketing communications company executive; b. Columbus, Ohio, Apr. 26, 1949; s. Robert Hayes and Teresa (Keller) L.; m. Deborah Lee Phillips, June 19, 1971; children—Sarah Phillips, Matthew Keller. B.A., Miami U., Oxford, Ohio, 1971; M.S. in Journalism, Ohio U., 1972. Lic. real estate broker, Ind. Staff writer Ohio U. Office Pub. Info., Athens, 1971-72; advt. exec. Concepts Unltd., Inc., Ft. Wayne, Ind., 1972-75; pres. Lehman Co., Ft. Wayne, 1976—. Active United Way of Allen County (Ind.), 1974—; media adviser/advt. dir. U.S. Congressman Dan Quayle, 1978; media adviser, advt. dir. U.S. Congressman Daniel R. Coats, 1980, campaign mgr., 1982. Recipient First Place Addy awards Northeastern Ind. chpt. Ft. Wayne Advt. Club, 1974. Mem. Am. Mktg. Assn. (v.p. bd. dirs. Northeast Ind. chpt. 1979-82), Ft. Wayne C. of C., Miami U. Alumni Assn., Beta Theta Pi, Phi Kappa Phi. Methodist. Lodges: Rotary, Masons (Ft. Wayne). Author sales tng. booklets.

LEHMAN, DENNIS DALE, chemistry educator; b. Youngstown, Ohio, July 15, 1945; s. Dale Vern and Coryn Eleanor (Neff) L.; m. Maureen Victoria Tierney, July 19, 1969 (div. Mar. 1981); children—Chris, Hillary; m. Kathleen Kim, Kuchta, May 15, 1983. B.S., Ohio State U. 1967; M.S., Northwestern U., 1968, Ph.D., 1972. Prof. chemistry Chgo. City Colls., 1968—, Northwestern U., Evanston, Ill., 1974—; lectr. biochemistry Northwestern U. Med. Sch., Chgo., 1979—; cons. Chgo. Bd. Edn. Bd. dirs. First Congregational Ch. of Wilmette (Ill.). Mem. Am. Chem. Soc., AAAS, Royal Chem. Soc., Sigma Xi. Club: Lake Forest Swim. Author: Chemistry for the Health Sciences, 1981; Laboratory Chemistry for the Health Sciences, 1981. Home: 3940 Elm Ln Waukegan IL 60087 Office: Dept Chemistry Northwestern U Evanston IL 60201

LEHMAN, JOHN FREDERICK, advertising agency executive; b. Chgo., June 8, 1941; s. Edward Henry and Grace (Solway) L.; m. Patricia Whyte, Oct. 13, 1967; children—John Karl, Pamela Christine. B.A., Notre Dame U., 1963; M.A., U. Mich., 1972. Tchr. Whitehall Dist. Sch., Mich., 1972-79; owner, mgr. Gate of Horn Art Gallery, Whitehall, 1973-76; pres. Storyboard, Inc., Madison, Wis., 1980—; advt. dir. INSUL-CRETE Co., Inc., McFarland, Wis., 1983-85. Author: (poems) Quick Blue Gathering, 1977. Founder Muskegon Area Tchrs. of English, Mich., 1978. Served to capt. Med. Service Corps, U.S. Army, 1963-69. Decorated Bronze Star. Mem. Madison Advt. Fedn., Sales and Mktg. Execs. Madison. Home: 315 N Ingersoll Madison WI 53703 Office: Storyboard Inc 615 E Washington Ave Madison WI 53703

LEHNEN, ROBERT GEORGE, public affairs educator, consultant; b. Danville, Ill., June 22, 1942; s. Fred John and Valeria Joan (DalMolin) L.; m. Sandra Baird Buck, Oct. 10, 1969; children—Laura Catherine, John Frederick. B.A., DePauw U., 1964; M.A., U. Iowa, 1966, Ph.D., 1968. Asst. prof. U. N.C., Chapel Hill, 1968-72; assoc. prof. U. Houston, 1972-76, prof. Ind. U., Indpls., 1978—; cons. U.S. Dept. Justice, Washington, 1976-78; guest lecturer U. Colonge, W. Ger., 1981. Author: American Institutions, Political Opinion, & Public Policy, 1976; (with others) Public Program Analysis, 1981. Scoutmaster Crossroads of Am. council Boy Scouts Am., 1984-85; adult leader Nat. Jamboree Boy Scouts Am., 1985. Nat. Def. Edn. Act fellow U. Iowa, 1964-68. Mem. Am. Statis. Assn. (v.p. Central Ind. chpt. 1982-83, pres. 1983-84), Am. Sociol. Assn., Am. Soc. Pub. Adminstrn. Democrat. Club: Nat. R.R. Hist. Soc. (Danville Junction Chpt. Ill.) Avocation: model railroading. Office: Pub and Environ Affairs Ind U Indianapolis IN 46223

LEHNHOFF, HENRY JOHN, JR., physician; b. Lincoln, Nebr., Sept. 13, 1911; s. Henry John and Rae (Challis) L.; m. JoAnn Milliken, Sept. 16, 1939; children—Henry John III, James Wood. B.A., U. Nebr., 1933; M.D., Northwestern U., 1938. Diplomate Am. Bd. Internal Medicine, Am. Bd. Med. Examiners. Intern Kings County Hosp., Bklyn., 1937-39; resident in internal medicine Mayo Found., Rochester, Minn., 1939-42; practice medicine specializing in internal medicine, Omaha, 1946—; sr. staff Bishop Clarkson Meml. Hosp., Nebr. Meth. Hosp.; med. dir. Northwestern Bell Telephone Co., Omaha, Woodmen of World Life Ins. Soc., Omaha; prof. internal medicine U. Nebr. Med. Ctr., Omaha, endowed professorship, 1984—. Contbr. articles to profl. jours. Served to lt. col. AUS, 1942-46. Recipient Disting. Service to Medicine award U. Nebr. Med. Ctr., 1980. Fellow ACP; mem. AMA, Nebr. Med. Assn., Am. Soc. Internat. Medicine, AM. Heart Assn., Royal Soc. Medicine (London), Am. Coll. Occupational Medicine, Am. Rheumatism Assn., Am. Fedn. Clin. Research. Republican. Unitarian. Clubs: Omaha, Omaha Country. Office: Internal Medicine Assocs PC 650 Doctors Bldg North Tower 4242 Farnam Omaha NE 68131

LEHODEY, JOHN FRANCOIS, hotel company executive; b. Paris, July 27, 1933; came to U.S., 1960; s. Jacques and Gabrielle (Godard) L.; 1 child, Jacques. B.S. in Hotel Adminstrn. Hotel Sch., Thonon, France, 1953. Purser S.S. Liberté, S.S. Ile de. France, French Line, Le Havre-N.Y., 1955-60; mgr. rooms div. Waldorf Astoria Hotel, N.Y.C., 1963-71; mgr. Novotel, Paris, 1972-78; gen. mgr., v.p. Sofitel div. Accor N.Am., Mpls., 1979—. Served with French Navy, 1953-55. Mem. French-Am. C. of C., Chaine des Rotisseurs. Home: 5601 W 78th St Minneapolis MN 55435 Office: Accor NAm 2 Overhill Dr Scarsdale NY 10583

LEHR, GLENN CARLTON, dentist; b. Grand Rapids, Mich., Apr. 16, 1934; s. Glenn Cecil and Nella (Van Ian Waarden) L.; m. Maria Rhodes, Jan. 25, 1959; children—Glenn Christopher, Michael David, Victoria Alice. B.A., U. Nebr.-Omaha, 1962; D.D.S., U. Mich., 1968. Gen. practice dentistry, Manchester, Mich., 1968-83; pres. Am. Dental Health, Ypsilanti, Mich., 1982—, Retail Dentistry, Inc., Ypsilanti, 1983—; dir. Mason Dental Ceramics, Livonia, Mich. Pres. Assn. Performing Arts; Athletic Boosters; bd. dirs. Emmanual Ch.; chmn. United Way, 1981-82; mem. exec. bd. Wolverine council Boy Scouts Am. Served to capt. USAF, 1955-64. Mem. Am. Dental Soc., Mich. Dental Soc., Chgo. Dental Soc., Detroit Dental Soc., Vedder Crown and Bridge Soc., Bunting Periodontal Study Club, Am. Acad. Group Practice, Manchester C. of C. (pres. 1974), Am. Soc. Preventive Dentistry (bd. dirs.). Republican. Lodge: Optimists. Home: 19220 Sanborn Manchester MI 48158 Office: Am Dental Health 3825 Carpenter Ypislanti MI 48197

LEHR, LEWIS WYLIE, manufacturing company executive; b. Elgin, Nebr., Feb. 21, 1921; s. Lewis H. and Nancy (Wylie) L.; B.S. in Chem. Engring., U. Nebr., D.S. (hon.), 1977; m. Doris Stauder, Oct. 13, 1944; children—Mary Lehr Makin, William L., Donald D., John M. With 3M Co., 1947—, v.p. tape & allied products group, 1974-75, pres. U.S. ops., 1975-79, vice chmn., chief exec. officer, 1979-80, chmn., chief exec. officer, 1980—; dir. Gen. Mills, Inc., Mpls., Shell Oil Co., Houston, United Telecommunications, Inc., Pacific Southwest Airlines, San Diego. Trustee Hamline U., St. Paul, Fairview Community Hosps., Mpls. Served with U.S. Army, 1943-46. Mem. U. Nebr. Alumni Assn. (recipient Alumni Achievement award), Am. Chem. Soc. Clubs: N. Oaks Golf, St. Paul Athletic, White Bear Yacht, Minn. Office: 3M Co 3M Center Saint Paul MN 55144*

LEHTINEN, JOHN L., physician; b. Hancock, Mich., Dec. 10, 1946; s. Lauri E. and Ann M. (oikarinen) L.; m. Linda D. Erickson, Aug. 1, 1970; children—John, Robert. B.S., Mich. Technol. U., 1970; M.D., Wayne State U., 1974. Diplomate Am. Bd. Family Practice. Resident in family practice St. John's Hosp., Detroit, 1974-77, dir. family practice, 1977-80; dir. family practice Upper Penninsula Health Edn. Corp., Marquette, Mich., 1980-84, Marquette Gen. Hosp., 1984—; clin. instr. Wayne State U., Detroit, 1977—; assoc prof. family practice Mich. State U., East Lansing, 1980—. Bd. dirs. Marquette Jr. Hockey, 1984—. Mem. Am. Acad. Family Physicians (Mead Johnson award 1977), Mich. Med. Soc., Marquette-Alger Med. Soc., Mich. Acad. Family Physicians (sec., treas. 1980). Avocations: coaching hockey, baseball, soccer. Office: 1414 W Fair Marquette MI 49855

LEIBENSPERGER, WILLIAM PAUL, financial company manager; b. Columbus, Ohio, Sept. 12, 1923; s. Paul Jesse and Geneva Jo (Westlake) L.; m. Ruth Wylie, July 1, 1944; children—Edward Paul, Susan Kay Wylie, William W., Beth Ann Leibensperger Harroff. Student Am. Coll., 1968. Staff mgmt. and sales Prudential Co., Columbus, 1951-56, agy. mgr., 1956-59; agy. mgr. Acacia Mut. Co., Columbus, 1959-62, The Bankers Life Co., 1962—. Trustee Nat. Ch. Residences, Inc., Columbus, 1969-82. Served to lt. USAF, 1943-46, ETO. Melvin Jones fellow, 1982. Mem. C.L.U. Assn., Nat. Assn. Life Underwriters, Gen. Agts. and Mgrs. Assn. (pres. Columbus chpt. 1968-69, Mgmt. Achievement 1975, 76, 77), Internat. Assn. Lions Clubs (bd. dirs. 1977-79, Ambassador of Good Will, 1979). Republican. Presbyterian. Avocation: golf. Home: 4217 Edgehill Dr Columbus OH 43220 Office: Bankers Life Co PO Box 14404 3620 N High St Columbus OH 43214

LEIBIG, EDWARD CHARLES, JR., electronics company executive; b. Corning, N.Y., Sept. 13, 1933; s. Edward Charles and Anne L.; m. Mary Lou Davia, June 25, 1955; children—Lori, Lindi, Luci, Edward. B.S.M.E., U. Rochester, 1955. With Honeywell, Freeport, Ill., 1960-74, program mgr., 1974-79, dir. mktg., 1979-80; pres. ITT Datanetics, Fountain Valley, Calif., 1980-82; pres. ITT Shadow, Eden Prairie, Minn., 1982—. Served to lt. USN, 1955-58. Mem. Am. Electronics Assn. Office: ITT Shadow 8081 Wallace Rd Eden Prairie MN 55344

LEIBMAN, JORDAN HARVEY, law educator, researcher; b. Chgo., June 5, 1930; s. Harry and Rose (Bodanis) L.; m. Joan Zabronsky, Oct. 26, 1952; children—Theodore, Rachel, Sara, Dena, Maya. B.A., U. Chgo., 1950, M.B.A., 1955; J.D., Ind. U., 1979. Bars: Ind. 1979, U.S. Dist. Ct. (so. dist.) Ind. 1979. Prodn. control mgr. Star Products, Chgo., 1953-56; indsl. engr. Hamilton Industries, Chgo., 1956-57; v.p., plant gen. mgr. Imperial Packaging Co., Indpls., 1957-76; asst. prof. bus. law Ind. U. Sch. Bus., Indpls., 1979-82, assoc. prof., 1982—. Note and devel. editor Ind. Law Rev., 1978-79. Contbr. articles to profl. jours. Pres., Met. Arts Council Indpls., 1970-71, Contemporary Art Soc., Indpls., 1978-80; mem. nat. alumni cabinet U. Chgo., 1970-73, 82-84; vice chmn. bd. Ind. Repertory Theatre, Indpls., 1972-76. Mem. Am. Bus. Law Assn. (staff editor jour. 1983-86), Ind. Bar Assn. (publ. com. 1982-85), ABA, Phi Delta Phi, Beta Gamma Sigma. Democrat. Jewish. Home: 6808 N Sherman Dr Indianapolis IN 46220 Office: Ind Univ Sch Bus Box 647 801 W Michigan St Indianapolis IN 46223

LEIBOVICH, SAMUEL JOSEPH, biochemist, researcher; b. Southport, Eng., June 21, 1948; s. Mendel and Ruth (Riseman) L.; m. Susan Deborah Scheiner, July 11, 1976; children—Esther, Dahlia. B.Sc. with honors, U. Manchester (Eng.), 1968, Ph.D., 1971. Postdoctoral fellow U. Wash., Seattle, 1972-74; sr. scientist The Weizmann Inst. Sci., Rehovot, Israel, 1974-80; assoc. prof. dept. oral biology Northwestern U., Chgo., 1980—. Served to cpl. Israeli Army, 1980. Mem. AAAS, N.Y. Acad. Sci., Sigma Xi. Jewish. Contbr. articles to profl. jours. Home: 9101 Pottawattami Dr Skokie IL 60076 Office: Dept Oral Biology Northwestern U 311 E Chicago Ave Chicago IL 60611

LEIBOVIT, MARK ALBERT, stock market technical analyst; b. Miami, Fla., July 21, 1948; s. Meyer and Geraldine (Selzer) L.; m. Alice Wintz, Sept. 7, 1969; 1 son, Jeremy. B.S. in Broadcast Journalism, U. Fla., 1972, M.Edn., 1974. Registered investment advisor SEC. Market maker, specialist Chgo. Bd. Options Exchange, 1976-78, Midwest Options Exchange, Chgo., 1978-79; dir. research, chief market strategist Freehling & Co., Chgo., 1979—; commentator, moderator TV Channel 26, Chgo., 1980—; guest analyst Nightly Bus. Report, Miami, 1981—; guest commentator Fin. News Network, Santa Monica, Calif., 1983—; editor, pub. The Volume Reversal Surrey. Mem. Market Technicians Assn. Jewish. Contbr. articles to profl. jours. Office: Freehling & Co 120 S LaSalle St Suite 910 Chicago IL 60603

LEIBOVITZ, ROBERT DEANE, fire chief; b. Monmouth, Ill., Jan. 22, 1933; s. Michael and Mabel Grace (Fernald) L.; m. Shirlee JoAnne Simmons, Oct. 1, 1954; children—David, Daren, Dana. Student Augustana Coll., Rock Island, Ill., Blackhawk Coll. Owner, mgr. Am. Plumbing, Silvis, Ill., 1955-76; lt. Silvis Fire Dept., 1968-72, asst. chief, 1972-78, chief, 1978—. Alderman City of Silvis, 1964-72; chmn. Silvis Country Music Fest, 1980—. Mem. Internat. Assn. Fire Chiefs, Ill. Fire Chiefs Assn., Ill. Fire Fighters Assn., Bi-State Fire Chiefs (pres. 1979), Miss. Valley Fire Assn. (bd. dirs.). Democrat. Jewish. Club: Silvis Optimists (pres. 1965, 73). Home: 318 5th St Ct Silvis IL 61282 Office: Silvis Fire Dept 1040 1st Ave Silvis IL 61282

LEIGH, GARY DEAN, lawyer; b. Danville, Ill., Jan. 14, 1955; s. Donald Dean and Myra Elizabeth (Stipp) L. B.A., U. Miami, 1978; J.D., John Marshall Law Sch., 1981. Bar: Ill. 1981, Calif. 1981, U.S. Dist. Ct. (no. dist.) Ill. 1981, U.S. Dist. Ct. (no. dist.) Calif. 1982, U.S. Dist. Ct. (so. dist.) Calif. 1982, U.S. Ct. Appeals (7th cir.) 1981, U.S. Ct. Appeals (9th cir.) 1982. Assoc. Leonard M. Ring & Assocs., Chgo., 1981-83, Susan E. Loggans & Assocs., Chgo., 1983-84; ptnr. Fisher, Leigh & Assocs., Chgo., 1984—. Contbr. articles to profl. jours. Mem. Assn. Trial Lawyers Am. (advanced trial advocacy cert. 1983), Ill. Trial Lawyers Assn. (products liability com. 1981—), Calif. Trial Lawyers Assn., Chgo. Bar Assn. (trial techniques sect. 1981—), Ill. State Bar Assn., ABA (tort and ins. practice sect. 1981—). Home: 1247 N State Pkwy Chicago IL 60610 Office: Fisher Leigh & Assocs 180 N LaSalle St Suite 1818 Chicago IL 60601

LEIGH, WILLIAM ERNEST, computer science educator; b. Memphis, Sept. 9, 1948; s. William Ernest and Evelyn (Evans) L.; m. Alice Newsom, Oct. 5, 1958 (div. 1975); children—Alyson, William; m. Noemi Myriam Paz, June 4, 1982; children—Clara, Rachel. B.S. Millsaps Coll., 1968; M.S., Rensselaer Poly. Inst., 1974; M.B.A., U. Cin., 1975, Ph.D., 1984. Systems engr. IBM Corp., Cin., 1969-73; dir. info. systems Ambulatory Patient Care, Inc., Cin., 1974-75; cons. Data Methods Corp., Con., 1975-78; asst. prof. No. Ky. U., Cin., 1979-83; Purdue Sch. Sci., Ind. U., Indpls., 1984—. Author: Programming Business Systems with Basic, 1984. Mem. Assn. Computing Machinery. Office: Ind U Purdue Sch Sci Dept Computer and Info Sci 1125 E 38th St PO Box 647 Indianapolis IN 46223

LEIGHTON, GEORGE NEVES, judge; b. New Bedford, Mass., Oct. 22, 1912; s. Antonio N. and Anna Sylvia (Garcia) Leitao; A.B., Howard U., 1940; LL.B., Harvard, 1946; LL.D., Elmhurst Coll., 1964, John Marshall Law Sch., Southeastern Mass. U., 1975, New Eng. U., 1978; m. Virginia Berry Quivers, June 21, 1942; children—Virginia Anne, Barbara Elaine. Admitted to Mass. bar, 1946, Ill. bar, 1947, U.S. Supreme Ct. bar, 1958; partner Moore, Ming & Leighton, Chgo., 1951-59, McCoy, Ming & Leighton, Chgo., 1959-64; judge Circuit Ct. Cook County, Ill., 1964-69, Appellate Ct., 1st Dist., 1969-76, U.S. Dist. Ct., 1976—. Commr., as mem. character and fitness comm. for 1st Appellate Dist., Supreme Ct. Ill., 1955-63, chmn. character and fitness comm., 1961-62; mem. joint com. for revision jud. article Ill. and Chgo. bar assns., 1959-62, joint com. for revision Ill. Criminal Code, 1959-63; chmn. Ill. adv. com. U.S. Commn. on Civil Rights, 1964; mem. pub. rev. bd. UAW, AFL-CIO, 1961-69. Asst. atty. gen. State of Ill., 1950-51; pres. 3d Ward Regular Democratic Orgn., Cook County. Ill., 1951-53, v.p. 21st Ward, 1964. Bd. dirs. United Ch. Bd. for Homeland Ministries, United Ch. of Christ, Grant Hosp., Chgo.; trustee Notre Dame U., 1979-83, trustee emeritus, 1983—; bd. overseers Harvard U., 1983—. Served to capt., inf. AUS, 1942-45. Decorated Bronze Star; recipient Civil Liberties award Ill. div. ACLU, 1961; named Chicagoan of Year in Law and Judiciary, Jr. Assn. Commerce and Industry, 1964. Fellow Am. Bar Found.; mem. Howard U. Chgo. Alumni Club (chmn. bd. dirs.), John Howard Assn. (dir.), Chgo., Ill. bar assns., NAACP (chmn. legal redress com. Chgo. br.), Nat. Harvard Law Sch. Assn. (mem. Council), Phi Beta Kappa (hon.), Gamma of D.C. Contbr. articles to legal jours. Office: Dirksen Fed Bldg Chicago IL 60604

LEIGHTON, JACQUELINE ELEANOR, immunobiologist, researcher; b. Glasgow, Scotland, Oct. 3, 1952; came to U.S., 1978; d. Rudolph Francis and Ellen Cary (Oppler) L.; m. Phillip John Grieves, Oct. 7, 1971 (div. 1982). HNC, Paisley Tech. Inst., Glasgow, 1976; ONC, David Dale Coll., Glasgow, 1974. Research technician Sch. Vet. Medicine, U. Glasgow, 1970, dept. devel. biology, 1972-74, dept. genetics and virology, 1974-76, dept. biochemistry, 1976-78; research technician Imperial Coll. Sci. and Tech., London, 1970-71; project supr. dept. zoology research U. Wis., Madison, 1979-82; research assoc. Agrigenetics Corp., Madison, 1982—. Contbr. research articles to immunological publs. Mem. South Wis. Am. Assn. Lab. Animal Sci. Avocations: horseback riding, running, body-building, swimming, bicycle riding. Office: Agrigenetics Corp Advanced Research Labs 5649 E Buckeye Rd Madison WI 53716

LEIKER, SHEILA M., dairy farmer; b. Hays, Kans., Oct. 9, 1942; d. Edmund and Martina (Gottschalk) Roth; m. Adrian Leiker, Oct. 22, 1960 (dec. May 1979); children—Linette, Brenda, Keith. Grad. high sch. Dairy herd improvement supr. Kans. Dairy Herd Improvement Assn., 1974—, sec., 1982—. Chair sch. bd. Sch. Dist. 432, Victoria, Kans., 1984; treas. Ellis County Soil Conservation, 1984, Kans. Assn. Conservation Dists., 1984. Named Supr. of Yr., Kans. Dairy Herd Improvement Assn., 1980. Democrat. Roman Catholic. Avocations: music; reading. Home: Route 1 Box 68 Victoria KS 67671

LEIMKUHLER, FERDINAND FRANCIS, industrial engineering educator, university official, consultant, researcher; b. Balt., Dec. 31, 1928; s. Ferdinand Frank and Louise Theresa (Kimmel) L.; m. Natalie Theresa Morin, July 4, 1956; children—Kristin, Margaret, Jean, Benedict, Thomas, Ernest. B.S., Loyola Coll., Balt., 1950; B.Engring. Sci., Johns Hopkins U., 1952, Dr. Engring., 1962. Engr. Dupont Co., Wilmington, Del., 1952-57; research asst. Johns Hopkins U., Balt., 1957-61; assoc. prof. indsl. engring. Purdue U., West Lafayette, Ind., 1961-67, prof., 1967—, head Sch. Indsl. Engring., 1969-74, 81—; vis. prof. U. Calif.-Berkeley, 1968; disting. lectr. Am. Assn. Info. Sci., 1971. Author: Transportation of Nuclear Waste, 1962; also research papers, chpts. Served with U.S. Army, 1952-54. Fulbright fellow, Yugoslavia, 1974. Mem. Inst. Indsl. Engrs. (sr.), Ops. Research Soc. Am. (sr.), Inst. Mgmt. Sci. (sr.), Tau Beta Pi, Alpha Pi Mu. Democrat. Roman Catholic. Avocations: hiking; woodwork. Home: 101 E Stadium Ave West Lafayette IN 47906 Office: Purdue U Sch Indsl Engring West Lafayette IN 47907

LEINIEKS, VALDIS, classics educator; b. Liepaja, Latvia, Apr. 15, 1932; came to U.S., 1949, naturalized, 1954; s. Arvid Ansis and Valia Leontine (Brunaus) L.; B.A., Cornell U., 1955, M.A., 1956; Ph.D., Princeton U., 1962. Instr. classics Cornell Coll., Mount Vernon, Iowa, 1959-62, asst. prof. classics, 1962-64; assoc. prof. classics, Ohio State U., 1964-66; assoc. prof. classics U. Nebr., Lincoln, 1966-71, prof. classics, 1971—, chmn. dept. classics, 1967—, chmn. program comparative lit., 1970—, interim chmn. dept. modern langs., 1982-83. Mem. AAUP, Am. Philol. Assn., Archaeol. Inst. Am. Republican. Author: Morphosyntax of the Homeric Greek Verb, 1964; The Structure of Latin, 1975; Index Nepotianus, 1976; The Plays of Sophokles, 1982; contbr. articles to profl. jours. Home: 2505 A St Lincoln NE 68502 Office: Dept Classics U Nebr Lincoln NE 68588

LEININGER, ELMER, emeritus chemistry educator; b. Milw., Apr. 19, 1900; s. Philip Henry and Louise (Hardtke) L.; B.S., Carroll Coll., 1923; postgrad. U. Wis., 1923-24; M.S., Mich. State U., 1931; Ph.D., U. Mich., 1941; m. Hazel Ann MacNamara, Dec. 30, 1924 (dec. June 1961); 1 dau., Mary Louise (Mrs. Robert Reed); m. 2d, Byrnice L. Dickinson, 1964. Instr. chem. Mich. State U., 1924-30, prof. chemistry, head analytical chemistry sect. 1930-65, prof. emeritus, 1965—; chem. cons., 1965—. Sec., dir. Geneva Lake Civic Assn., 1968-76, 79—; bd. dirs., moderator Pilgrim Ch. Mem. Am. Chem. Soc. (chmn., councilor Mich. sect.), Am. Philatelic Soc., Sigma Xi, Alpha Chi Sigma, Phi Lambda Upsilon. Republican. Clubs: Lake Geneva Country; Green Valley (Ariz.) Country. Editorial adv. bd. Analytical Chemistry. Contbr. articles to profl. jours. Address: S Lake Shore Dr Rural Route 1 Box 70 Lake Geneva WI 53147

LEININGER, GARY GEORGE, oil company executive; b. Buffalo, Dec. 7, 1942; s. George J. and Gladys M. (Radke) L.; m. Ellen C. Velie, Dec. 26, 1964; children—Brian, Michael, Kristen. B.E.E., SUNY-Buffalo, 1965, M.E.E., 1968, Ph.D. in Elec. Engring., 1970. Prof. elec. engring. U. Toledo, 1970-78; prof. mech. engring. Purdue U., West Lafayette, Ind., 1978-83; research supr. Standard Oil Co., Cleve., 1983—. Editor: CAD of Control Systems, 1979. Contbr. articles to profl. publs. Mem. IEEE, Internat. Fedn. Automatic Control. Home: 5466 Clarendon Dr Solon OH 44139 Office: Sohio Research and Devel 4440 Warrensville Center Rd Cleveland OH 44128

LEININGER, RICHARD KEITH, geochemist; b. Whitefish, Mont., Sept. 6, 1921; s. Albert Guy and Emma Eva (Dickerson) L.; m. Elaine Seeger, Mar. 8, 1945; children—Mari Lane, Mark Edward, Matthew John, Marshall Eliot. A.B., Miami U., Oxford, Ohio, 1943; M.A., Ind. U., 1957. Spectrographer, Armco Steel Co., Middleton, Ohio, 1946-48, Ind. Geol. Survey, Bloomington, 1948-52, geochemist, head geochemistry sect., 1952—. Contbr. papers to profl. publs. Mem. Owen County Sch. Bd., Ind., 1979-84. Served to lt. (j.g.) USNR, 1943-46, PTO. Mem. Geochem. Soc., Am. Chem. Soc., Clay Minerals Soc., Soc. Applied Spectroscopy, Mineral. Assn. Can., Phi Eta Sigma. Avocations: travel, art glass, glass tumblers. Home: Route 1 Box 374 Spencer IN 47460 Office: Ind Geol Survey 611 N Walnut Grove Ave Bloomington IN 47405

LEIS, JONATHAN PETER, biochemistry educator, researcher; b. Bklyn., Aug. 17, 1944; s. Morris and Beatrice (Sperber) L.; m. Susan Lyndia Schoenfeld, Dec. 20, 1970; children—Benjamin, Betsy. B.A. in Chemistry, Hofstra U., 1965; Ph.D. in Biochemistry, Cornell U., 1970. Postdoctoral fellow Albert Einstein Coll. Medicine, Bronx, N.Y., 1970-73; asst. prof. Duke U. Med. Ctr., Durham, N.C., 1974-79; assoc. prof. biochemistry Case Western Res. U. Sch. Medicine, Cleve., 1979—. Contbr. articles and abstracts to profl. jours. Cubmaster Boy Scouts Am., Shaker Heights, Ohio, 1982-84. Recipient Career Devel. award NIH, 1974-79; Hofstra U. scholar, 1962-65, Leukemia Soc. scholar, 1974; NIH trainee, 1965-70; grantee Damon Runyon Research, 1974, Am. Cancer Soc., 1974-75, 79, 81, 82, 83-84, 84, Nat. Cancer Inst., 1979-82, 84—, NSF, 1977-78, 79-80, 80-85. Mem. Am. Soc. Microbiology, Am. Soc. Biol. Chemists, Am. Cancer Soc. (grant rev. study sect. Ohio div. 1981—). Avocations: stamps; tennis. Home: 3628 Palmerston Rd Shaker Heights OH 44122 Office: Dept Biochemistry Case Western Res U Sch Medicine 2119 Abington Rd Cleveland OH 44106

LEISE, FRED, music company administrator; b. Washington, Sept. 15, 1949; s. David and Phyllis Rhea (Fleitman) L. B.S. in math., U. Md.-College Park, 1974. Asst. to gen. mgr. Buffalo Philharm., 1976-77; mgr. Albany Symphony, N.Y., 1977-80; gen. mgr. Waverly Consort, N.Y.C., 1981-82; bus. mgr. Music of the Baroque, Chgo., 1982-84, dir. fin., 1984—; dir. Ill. Arts Alliance Chgo., 1984—, Ill. Arts Action Coalition, Chgo., 1984—. Dir. N.Y.C. Gay Men's Chorus, 1981-82; mem. Windy City Gay Chorus, Chgo., 1983—, dir., 1983. Mem. Am. Symphony Orch. League. Avocations: choral singing; rare book collecting. Home: 900 W Ainslie St Chicago IL 60640 Office: Music of the Baroque 343 S Dearborn Chicago IL 60604

LEISNER, ANTHONY BAKER, publishing company executive; b. Evanston, Ill., Sept. 13, 1941; s. A. Paul and Ruth (Solms) L.; B.S., Northwestern U., 1964, M.B.A., 1983; children—Justina, William. Salesman, Pitney Bowes Co., 1976-77; with Quality Books Inc., Northbrook, Ill., 1968—, v.p., 1972—, gen. mgr., 1979—; adj. faculty Lake Forest (Ill.) Sch. Mgmt., 1983—. Pres. bd. dirs. Lake Villa (Ill.) Public Library, 1972-78; bd. dirs. No. Ill. Library Systems, 1973-78; chmn. Libertarian Party Lake County (Ill.), 1980-81; probation officer Lake County CAP, 1981. Mem. ALA, Ill. Library Assn. (Gerald L. Campbell award 1980), Am. Booksellers Assn., Acad. Mgmt., Internat. Platform Assn., World Future Soc., World Isshin Ryu Karate Assn. Methodist. Author: Official Guide to Country Dance Steps, 1980; also articles. Home: 898 Elm St Winnetka IL 60093 Office: 400 Anthony Trail Northbrook IL 60062

LEISTICO, MILDRED FAE, bank executive; b. Hobart, Okla., July 4, 1947; d. Walter D. and Ethel Marie (Koehn) Goossen; student Wichita Bus. Coll., 1965-66; m. Melvin Allen Leistico, May 17, 1975; 1 son, Sean Duane. Sec., Farmers Ins. Group, Wichita, Kans., 1965-66; asst. cashier Nat. Life & Accident Ins., Enid, Okla., 1966; typist Dow Chem. Co., Freeport, Tex., 1967; supply clk. Kans. U. Med. Ctr., Kansas City, 1968; statis. sec. Centerre Bank of Kansas City (Mo.) (Formerly Columbia Union Nat. Bank), 1969-70, 73-79, analyst, 1979-80, info. processing mgr., 1980—; sec. First Nat. Bank, Lake Jackson, Tex., 1970-71; statis. typist Arthur Andersen & Co., Kansas City, Mo., 1972. Mem. adv. bd. Fort Osage Vo-Tech., 1983-85. Mem. Assn. Info. Systems Profls. formerly Internat. Word Processing Assn. (bd. dirs. 1982-83, 84-85, v.p. membership 1983-84), Internat. Platform Assn. Asst. editor Christ For Me, Inc., 1980—. Office: Centerre Bank of Kansas City 900 Walnut St Kansas City MO 64106

LEISTNER, MARY EDNA, educator; b. Evanston, Ill., Apr. 13, 1929; d. Joseph W. and Edna C. (Moe) Cox; m. Delbert L. Leistner, Sept. 30, 1950; children—David, Martha, Joseph. B.S. in Chemistry, Purdue U., 1950; M.Ed., Miami U., 1964. Tchr. sci. and math. Central Jr. High Sch., Sidney, Ohio, 1962-66; tchr. chemistry, biology, advanced chemistry Sidney High Sch., 1966—; mem. high sch. chemistry test com. Nat. Sci. Tchrs. Assn. Am. Chem. Soc., 1983-85. Mem. exec. com. Ohio Dist. Luth. Women's Missionary League, Columbus, 1978-82, pres. Miami Valley zone, 1985-87; pres. Redeemer Ladies Soc., Sidney, Ohio, 1980—. Mem. Nat. Sci. Tchrs. Assn. (Cadre 100 award), Western Ohio Sci. Tchrs. Assn. (pres. 1972-73), Sci. Edn. Council Ohio (dist. rep. exec. bd. 1984-86), Sidney Edn. Assn. (treas. 1980-82, 85-86). Republican. Lutheran. Office: Sidney High Sch 1215 Campbell Rd Sidney OH 45365

LEITNER, B. DEAN, city official; b. McDonald, Kans., June 7, 1933; s. Henry D. and Annabel N. (Rowland) L.; B.A., U. Nebr., 1974; grad. Traffic Inst., Northwestern U.; m. Rose Termine, Sept. 4, 1956; children—Gregory Dean, Debora LuAnn. With Lincoln (Nebr.) Police Dept., 1957—, sgt., 1960-68, lt., 1968-74, capt., 1974-77, asst. chief, 1977-79, chief police, 1979—; mem. Nebr. State Crime Commn., 1979—. Bd. dirs. Salvation Army, Lincoln. Served with U.S. Army, 1953-55. Mem. Internat. Assn. Chiefs Police, VFW, Police Officers Assn. Nebr., Northwestern U. Alumni Assn., U. Nebr., Alumni Assn.

Republican. Lutheran. Lodges: Masons, Shriners, Rotary. Office: 233 S 10th St Lincoln NE 68508

LELLO, ANTHONY PAUL, JR., lawyer; b. Evergreen Park, Ill., Dec. 3, 1953; s. Anthony P. and Anne Marie (Seman) L.; m. Susan Anne Laidley, Nov. 21, 1981. B.A., St. Mary's Coll. Winona, Minn., 1976; J.D., John Marshall Law Sch., 1980. Bar: Ill. 1980, U.S. Dist. Ct. (no. dist.) Ill. 1981, U.S. Tax Ct., 1984. Assoc., Zukowski, Poper, Rogers & Flood, Crystal Lake, Ill., 1981-82; title counsel N. Am. Title Co., Crystal Lake, 1982-83; also dir.; pres. First Comml. Title & Escrow Inc., Mt. Prospect, Ill., 1983-84; ptnr. Lello & Wittmeyer, Mount Prospect, 1984—. Mem. task force Project L.E.A.P., Chgo., 1977-80; com. mem. Task Force on Illegal Election Practices, Chgo., 1977-80, election judge, 1977-80. John Marshall Law Sch. Scholar, 1978, pres. Gavel Soc., 1979. Mem. Ill. Bar Assn., N.W. Suburban Bar Assn. (vice chmn. com. on law practice econs.), Mount Prospect Jaycees, Phi Delta Phi (conv., del. 1979, historian, cert. of merit 1980). Roman Catholic. Lodges: K.C., Lions. Office: Lello & Wittmeyer 209 S Main St Mount Prospect IL 60056

LEMANSKI, DENNIS RICHARD, osteopathic physician and surgeon; b. Detroit, June 21, 1949; s. Richard S. and Stella (Krystyniak) L.; m. Barbara Ann Tarwacki, Nov. 28, 1975; 1 child; Michelle. B.S., Wayne State U., 1971; D.O., Chgo. Coll. Osteo. Medicine, 1976. Diplomate Nat. Bd. Osteo. Med. Examiners, Am. Coll. Osteo. Gen. Practice. Rotating intern Riverside Osteo. Hosp., Trenton, Mich., 1976-77; asst. clin. prof. medicine Mich. State U. Coll. Osteo. Medicine, East Lansing, 1979—; dir. med. edn. Detroit Osteo. Hosp. Corp., 1984—; chmn. dept. gen. practice Riverside Osteo. Hosp., Trenton, 1983-84, sec. med. staff, 1983-84, dir. med. edn., 1984—; corp. mem. Horizon Health Systems, Oak Park, Mich., 1980-84; chmn. nutrition com. Seaway Hosp., Mich., 1983-84. Active Mich. Assn. Adoptive Parents MA-PA, Inc. Mem. Am. Osteo. Assn., Mich. Assn. Osteo. Physicians and Surgeons, Mich. Assn. Osteo. Dirs. Med. Edn., Nat. Assn. Osteo. Dir. Med. Edn., Wayne County Osteo. Assn., Chgo. Coll. Osteo. Medicine Alumni Assn. Roman Catholic. Club: Grosse Ile Golf and Country (Mich.). Avocations: golf, hockey. Home: 20627 Churchill Ave Trenton MI 48183 Office: Riverside Osteo Hosp Medical Edn 150 Truax Trenton MI 48183

LEMBERGER, AUGUST PAUL, pharmacy educator, university dean; b. Milw., Jan. 25, 1926; s. Max N. and Celia T. (Gehl) L.; m. Charlyne A. Young, June 30, 1947; children—Michael, Mary, Thomas, Terrence, Ann, Kathryn, Peter. B.S. in Pharmacy, U. Wis., 1948, Ph.D. in Pharmacy, 1952. Sr. chemist Merck & Co. Inc., Rahway, N.J., 1952-53; from asst. prof. to prof. U. Wis., Madison, 1953-69, dean Sch. Pharmacy, 1980—; dean Coll. Pharmacy, U. Ill., Chgo., 1969-80. Contbr. articles to profl. jours. Served to 1st lt. U.S. Army, 1944-46. Recipient Kiekhofer Meml. Teaching award U. Wis., 1957, citation of merit, 1977; Disting. Service award Wis. Pharm. Assn., 1969. Fellow Acad. Pharm. Scis. (pres. 1983-84), AAAS; mem. Am. Pharm. Assn. (trustee 1985-88), Am. Assn. Colls. Pharmacy, Rho Chi (pres. 1982-84). Roman Catholic. Office: U Wis Sch Pharmacy 425 N Charter St Madison WI 53706

LEMBERGER, LOUIS, pharmacologist, physician; b. Monticello, N.Y., May 8, 1937; s. Max and Ida (Seigel) L.; B.S. magna cum laude, Bklyn. Coll. Pharmacy, L.I. U., 1960; Ph.D. in Pharmacology, Albert Einstein Coll. Medicine, 1964, M.D., 1968; m. Myrna Sue Diamond, 1959; children—Harriet Felice, Margo Beth. Pharmacy intern VA Regional Office, Newark, summer 1960; postdoctoral fellow Albert Einstein Coll. Medicine, 1964-68; intern medicine Met. Hosp. Center, N.Y. Med. Coll., N.Y.C., 1968-69; research asso. NIH, Bethesda, Md., 1969-71; practice medicine specializing in clin. pharmacology, Bethesda, 1969-71, Indpls., 1971—; clin. pharmacologist Lilly Lab. Clin. Research, Eli Lilly & Co., Indpls., 1971-75, chief clin. pharmacology, 1975-78, dir. clin. pharmacology, 1978—, clin. research cons., 1982—; asst. prof. pharmacology Ind. U., 1972-73, asst. prof. medicine, 1972-73, asso. prof. pharmacology, 1973-77, asso. prof. medicine, 1973-77, prof. pharmacology, medicine and psychiatry, 1977—, mem. grad. faculty, 1975—; adj. prof. clin. pharmacology Ohio State U., 1975—; physician Wishard Meml. Hosp., 1976—; cons. U.S. Nat. Commn. on Marihuana and Drug Abuse, 1971-73, Can. Commn. of Inquiry into Non-Med. Use of Drugs, 1971-73; guest lectr. various univs., 1968—. Post adviser Crossroads of Am. council Boy Scouts Am., 1972-77. Served with USPHS, 1969-71. Fellow ACP, N.Y. Acad. Scis., Am. Coll. Neuropschopharmacology, Am. Coll. Clin. Pharmacology, AAAS; mem. Am. Soc. Pharmacology and Exptl. Therapeutics (com. div. clin. pharmacology 1972-78, chmn. 1978-82, councillor 1980-83, chmn. 2d World Conf. Clin. Pharmacology), Am. Soc. Clin. Pharmacology and Therapeutics (chmn. neuropsychopharmacology sect. 1973-80, dir. 1975-81, chmn. fin. com. 1976-82, pres. 1983-84), Am. Soc. Clin. Investigation, Collegium Internat. Neuro-Psychopharmacologicum, Am. Fedn. Clin. Research, Central Soc. Clin. Research, Soc. Neuroscis., AMA, Sigma Xi, Alpha Omega Alpha, Rho Chi. Jewish. Author: (with A. Rubin) Physiologic Disposition of Drugs of Abuse, 1976; contbr. numerous articles on biochemistry and pharmacology to sci. jours.; editorial bd. Excerpta Medica, 1972—, Clin. Pharmacology and Therapeutics, 1976—, Psychopharmacology, 1975-81, Pharmacology, Internat. Jour. Exptl. and Clin. ; Trends in Pharm./Scis., 1980—, Ann. Rev. of Pharmacology, 1983—. Office: Lilly Lab Clin Research Wishard Memorial Hosp Indianapolis IN 46202

LEMIRE, JEROME ALBERT, oil company executive, lawyer, geologist; b. Cleve., June 4, 1947; s. George A. and Matilda (Simon) L.; m. Sandra Marsick, Oct. 1, 1976; children—Laura, Lesley, Thomas. B.S. in Geology, Ohio State U., 1969, M.S. in Geology, 1973, J.D., 1976. Bar: Ohio 1976. Geologist United Petroleum Co., Columbus, Ohio, 1976-77; assoc. Brownfield, Bowen & Bally, Columbus, 1977-79; land mgr. POI Energy Inc., Cleve., 1979-81; cons., Jefferson, Ohio, 1981-83; v.p. Carey Resources Inc., Jefferson, 1984—. Vice chmn. Tech. Adv. Council, Columbus, 1984—. Served to 1st lt. U.S. Army, 1970-72. Mem. ABA, Ohio Bar Assn., Am. Assn. Petroleum Geologists, Am. Assn. Petroleum Landman, Internat. Assn. Fin. Planning. Democrat. Roman Catholic. Home: 838 State Route 46 N Jefferson OH 44047 Office: Carey Resources Inc 12 W Jefferson St Suite 202 Jefferson OH 44047

LEMKE, CARL RICHARD, paper company executive; b. Neenah, Wis., Aug. 4, 1943; s. Carl John and Alma Caroline (Berge) L.; m. Jennifer Jane Johnson, Oct. 2, 1976; children—Nicole, Paul, David, Sarah, Joel. B.B.A., U. Wis., 1965. Group leader Bendix Corp., Teterboro, N.J., 1965-67; asst. sec. Consol. Papers, Inc., Wisconsin Rapids, Wis., 1967—; dir. South Wood County Econ. Devel. Corp., Wisconsin Rapids, 1977—. Avocations: travel; sports; boating. Home: 420 Witter St Wisconsin Rapids WI 54494

LEMKE, CORRINE LARUE, university official; b. Sabin, Minn., May 25, 1934; d. Oswald Edward and Ida M. (Krabbenhoft) L. B.A. in Philosophy, Moorhead State U., 1972. Notary pub., Minn. With WDAY radio and TV sta., Fargo, N.D., 1953-67; fin. aid grant coordinator Moorhead State U., 1967—, mem. task force study of changing student mix, 1983-84. Vol. Comstock Hist. House, Moorhead. Recipient cert. Gov. Minn., 1976, 10 yr. service award Moorhead State U., 1980, letter of commendation U.S. Dept. Edn., 1983. Mem. Minn. Hist. Soc., State Hist. Soc. Wis., Concordia Hist. Inst. of St. Louis, Phoenix Soc. of Moorhead, Concordia Coll. Alumni Assn., Moorhead State U. Alumni Assn. Lutheran. Author pvt. family history publs. Home: 128 Pierce Trailer Ct Moorhead MN 56560 Office: Moorhead State U Moorhead MN 56560

LEMKE, LEROY WALTER, lawyer, state senator; b. Chgo., Sept. 24, 1935; s. Otto Mark and Myrtle Theresa L.; B.S.B.A., Drake U., 1959; J.D., John Marshall Law Sch., 1964; children—Lee Alan, Ronda Lee Lemke Alvarado, Kevin Keith. Bar: Ill. Individual practice law, Chgo., 1973; rep. Ill. Legislature, 1973-75; mem. Ill. State Senate, 1975—. Founder, chmn. Ill. Ethnic Heritage Commn. Named Outstanding Senator, Ill. Fedn. Pvt. Univs. and Colls.; Outstanding Legislator, Ill. Pro Life Coalition, Polish Community Council. Mem. ABA, Ill. Bar Assn., Chgo. Bar Assn., Bohemian Bar Assn., Casimir Pulaski Civic League, Archer Heights Civic League, West Elsdon Civic League. Democrat. Club: Little Village Lions. Office: 5838 S Archer Ave Chicago IL 60638

LEMKIN, JOYCE ALDA, radiologist; b. Boston, June 18, 1947; d. Harold Jacob and Sally (Berkowitz) L. B.S., U. Mass., 1969; Ph.D., U. Rochester, N.Y., 1976, M.D., 1976. Diplomate Am. Bd. Radiology. Intern, U. Va. Hosp., Charlottesville, 1976-77; resident Rochester Gen. Hosp., N.Y., 1977-80, fellow in interventional and neuroradiology, 1980-82; radiologist, mem. staff Sinai Hosp. Detroit, 1982—; mem. program tng. for clin. investigation Nat. Inst. Arthritis, Metabolism and Digestive Diseases, 1973-76. Contbr. articles to sci. publs. Recipient Sci. Achievment award Chem. Rubber Corp., 1966; NIH grantee, 1969-76. Mem. AMA, Mich. State Med. Soc., Wayne County Med. Soc., Am. Coll. Radiology, Radiol. Soc. N. Am., Am. Heart Assn. (mem. council on cardiovascular radiology). Office: Sinai Hosp Detroit Dept Radiology 6767 W Outer Dr Detroit MI 48235

LEMMON, WILLIAM ARTHUR, communications engineer; b. Orlando, Fla., Oct. 4, 1939; s. John Wilson and Suzanne Isabelle (Black) L.; m. Betty Elaine Franklin, Dec. 21, 1963 (div. 1970); m. Mary Joyce Gillihan, Aug. 31, 1973; stepchildren—Stuart Belcher, Jr., Melanie Roy, James Belcher; 1 foster dau., Michelle. Student U. Orlando, 1967-68, Orlando Jr. Coll., 1958-61. Clk., Orlando Daily News, 1956-62; printer Quick Service Printing, Orlando, 1962-63; asst. engr. Phys. Standards Lab., Cape Kennedy, Fla., 1966-72; chief engr. Quality Broadcasting, Daytona, Fla., 1973-78; tech. dir. Pathfinder Communications Corp., Fort Wayne, Ind., 1978—; broadcasting cons. Served with U.S. Army, 1963-66. Mem. Soc. Broadcast Engrs. Republican. Baptist. Office: 2916 Maples Rd Fort Wayne IN 46896

LEMMONS, JAMES CURTIS, manufacturing company executive; b. Jonesboro, Ark., July 8, 1948; s. Charles Norman Lemmons and Betty Jo (Knotts) Albertina; m. Dianne Louise Feller, Apr. 24, 1983. B.S. in Indsl. Engring., U. Ill., 1972; M.B.A., DePaul U., 1976. Mfg. engr. Elkay Mfg. Co., Broadview, Ill., 1972-78; plant mgr. Dayton-Ogden Corp., Ogden, Utah, 1978-83; dir. mfg. engr. Elkay Mfg. Co., 1983; v.p. mfg. Fed. Signal Corp., University Park, Ill., 1983—. Clubs: Fedn. Fly Fisherman (West Yellowstone, Mont.); Amateur Trap-Shooting Assn. (Vandalia, Ohio). Avocations: trap shooting; fly fishing; alpine skiing. Home: 1131 Spring Garden Circle Naperville IL 60540 Office: Fed Signal Corp 2645 Federal Signal Dr University Park IL 60466

LEMMONS, MIRIAM ELISE, nurse, social worker, rehabilitation counselor; b. New Orleans, Jan. 3, 1932; d. Walter Simpson and Ola Adele (Carruth) Weathersby; Asso. Nursing, Iowa Lakes Community Coll., 1977; B.A., Buena Vista Coll., 1978; M.S., Mankato State U., 1981; m. Ronald Lemmons, June 22, 1962; children—Robert, Linda, Mark, Kevin, Robin. R.N., Holy Family Hosp., Estherville, Iowa, 1977-82, dir. med. social services, 1981—, dir. home health dept., hospice, med. social services, 1981—; dir. Hospice, 1982—. Bd. dirs. Good Samaritan Nursing Home; mem. Estherville City Council, 1985—. Mem. Nat. Hospice Assn., Am. Nurses Assn., Nat. League Nursing, Assn. Rehab. Nurses, Nat. Rehab. Assn., NOW, Social Workers in Health Facilities, Am. Soc. Profl. and Exec. Women, Nat. Assn. Rehab. Profls., Am. Pub. Health Assn., Iowa Hospice Orgn. (bd. dirs., mem. exec. com.), AAUW, LWV, Am. Nurses Found., Iowa Med. Soc. Aux., ACS Aux., Internat. Coll. Surgeons Aux. Democrat. Methodist. Club: Century Home: 33 Manor Circle Estherville IA 51334 Office: 826 N 8th St Estherville IA 51334

LEMON, CHESTER EARL (CHET), professional baseball player. Outfielder Detroit Tigers. Office: Detroit Tigers Tiger Stadium Detroit MI 48216*

LEMON, GARY L., heat transfer manufacturing executive; b. Washington, Ind., Oct. 2, 1942; s. William A. and Joan (Jones) Henson L.; m. Rita I. Martin; children—Andrea, Heather, Adam, Brad. Student Vincennes U., 1969. Inventory planner heat transfer div. McCord, Washington, Ind., 1967-75, purchasing mgr., Canton, S.D., 1975-78, materials mgr., 1978-81, mfg. mgr., 1981-82, plant mgr., 1982-85, v.p. ops., 1985—. Contbr. articles to profl. publs. Mem. Ex-Cell-O Polit. Action Com., S.D. Mem. Canton C. of C. Republican. Lodge: Rotary. Avocations: sports; fishing; antiques. Home: 506 E 2d St Canton SD 57013

LEMOND, JUDITH ELLEN, insurance broker; b. Lafayette, Ind., July 25, 1947; d. William Henry and Frances Elizabeth (Thoennes) L. Student Eureka Coll. (Ill.), 1965-67, 68-69. Clk., United Fedn. Tchrs., N.Y.C., 1967-68; sr. casualty underwriter Ins. Co. N. Am., St. Louis, 1969-77, mktg. mgr., 1978-79; mktg. v.p. Assoc. Underwriters, St. Louis, 1977-78; unit mktg. mgr. Reed Stenhouse, St. Louis, 1979-81; mktg. mgr. Corroon & Black, St. Louis, 1981—. Office: Corroon & Black of St Louis Inc 8850 Ladue Rd Saint Louis MO 63124

LENARD, MICHAEL JOHN, postal clerk, philatelist; b. Wausau, Wis., July 5, 1943; s. Alexander T. and Genevieve M. (Stoltz) L.; m. Tangie Jean Rusch, Nov. 2, 1974; children—Andrew James, April Jan. Student Marathon County U. Wis., 1963-65. With Wausau Homes, Inc., 1965-66; postal clk., machine operator U.S. Postal Service, Wausau, 1966—. Served with USMC, 1967. Recipient First Place and Grand awards stamp shows, 1973—. Mem. Am. Philatelic Soc., Croatian Philatelic Soc. Democrat. Mem. Ch. Jesus Christ of Latter-day Saints. Expert on Yugoslavian stamps. Home: 1514 N 3d Ave Wausau WI 54401

LENERTZ, THOMAS CLARENCE, hospital administrator; b. Mankato, Minn., Sept. 5, 1936; s. Clarence Robert and Nona Cathryn (Dorn) L.; m. Patricia Ann Muellerleile, July 16, 1960; children—Laura Marie, Bradley Thomas. B.A. in Bus. Adminstrn., Mankato State U., 1960. Auditor Arthur Andersen & Co., Mpls., 1960-65; asst. controller Am. Rehab. Found., Mpls., 1965-68; asst. adminstr. Mt. Sinai Hosp., Mpls., 1968-73; exec. v.p. Riverview Hosp. Assn., Crookston, Minn., 1973—; treas., dir. North Star Hosp. Mut., Bermuda, 1977—; dir. Agassiz Health Systems Agy., Grand Forks, N.D., 1983—, Polk County Group Homes, 1985—. Bd. dirs. United Way of Crookston, Minn., 1981—; mem. adv. com. Agassiz Valley Vocat. Tech. Inst. Served with U.S. Army, 1956-58, PTO. Recipient William G. Follmer award Hosp. Fin. Mgmt., 1969, Robert H. Reeves award, 1973. Mem. Am. Colls. Hosp. Adminstrs. Roman Catholic. Lodges: Lions, Eagles, K.C. Avocations: fishing; winemaking; gardening. Home: 511 Euclid Ave S Crookston MN 56716 Office: Riverview Hosp Assn 323 S Minnesota St Crookston MN 56716

LENGEMANN, ROBERT ALLEN, chemical engineer, marketing executive; b. Winnett, Mont., June 25, 1934; s. Henry G. and Eva O. (Doman) L.; m. Mary Jane Spangler, Sept. 9, 1961; children—Susan, James. B.S., Mont. State U., 1956, M.S., 1957. With exptl. devel. dept. UOP Process div. UOP Inc., Des Plaines, Ill., 1957-69, European mktg. mgr., London, 1969-76, v.p. engring. research and devel., Des Plaines, 1976-79; v.p. sci. and tech. parent co. World Hdqrs., Des Plaines, 1979-84, v.p. mktg. UOP Process div., 1984—. Office: UOP Inc Algonquin and Mt Prospect Rds Box 5017 Des Plaines IL 60017

LENHART, GARY MICHAEL, court official; b. Defiance, Ohio, Jan. 10, 1956; s. John J. and Pauline (Liska) L. B.S., B.E., Findlay Coll., 1978. Cert. tchr. learning disability-behavioral disability (K-12), elem. edn. (grades 1-8). Treatment specialist Starr Commonwealth, Van Wert, Ohio, 1978-80; juvenile programs coordinator Defiance County Juvenile Ct., Ohio, 1981-84; restitution coordinator Lucas County Juvenile Ct., Toledo, 1984—; exec. sec. Ohio Restitution Del Inc., 1981-84. Author: (with others) Juvenile Restitution Manual, 1983. Scoutmaster Shawnee council Boy Scouts Am., 1978-80, dist. roundtable chmn. Bluejacket dist., 1983-84. Mem. Nat. Criminal Justice Assn., Defiance County Law Assistance Assn., Theta Chi. Democrat. Roman Catholic. Avocations: stamp and coin collecting, sports, camping, travel. Home: 302 Plymouth St Toledo OH 43605 Office: Family Ct 429 Michigan St Toledo OH 43624

LENNES, GREGORY, finance company executive; b. Chgo., Aug. 5, 1947; s. Lawrence D. and Genevieve (Karoll) L.; m. Maryann Meskers, July 27, 1968; children—Robert, Sandra, Ryan. B.A., U. Ill., 1969, M.A., 1971, postgrad., 1971-73. Archivist, Internat. Harvester Co., Chgo., 1973-80, asst. sec., 1980—, corp. sec., Internat. Harvester Credit Corp., 1980—. Mem. Am. Soc. Corp. Secs., Am. Assn. for State and Local History, Soc. Am. Archivists, Assn. Records Mgrs. and Adminstrs. Home: 14637 Atlantic Ave Dolton IL 60419 Office: Internat Harvester Co 401 N Michigan Ave Chicago IL 60611

LENNICK, THEOPHILE VERNON, engineer; b. Hebron, N.D., Nov. 6, 1931; s. Jacob and Lydia (Imhoff) L.; m. Julie Eslick, Sept. 26, 1953; children—Bruce, Steven, Susan. B.S.E.E., U. N.D., 1957. Registered profl. engr., Minn., High voltage test engr. Line Material Industries, Milw., 1957-59; chief engr. Central Power, Minot, N.D., 1959-63; chief engr. Coop Power Assn., Mpls., 1963-74, gen. mgr., 1974—; dir., v.p. Elec. Info. Council, Grand Forks, N.D., 1982—; dir. Nat. Food and Energy, Columbus, Mo., Norwest Bank, Bloomington, Minn. Served to 1st lt. U.S. Army, 1951-53. Mem. Mid-Continent Area Power Pool Assn. (mgmt. com. 1974—, exec. com. 1985—). Republican. Presbyterian. Avocations: photography, skiing. Office: Coop Power Assn 14615 Lone Oak Rd Eden Prairie MN 55344

LENNING, JAMES ERIC, banker; b. Dayton, Ohio, Sept. 1, 1947; s. George H. and Annabel Jane (Romig) L.; m. Mary Lynn Thompson, Dec. 19, 1970; children—Bradford, Blaire. B.B.A., U. Cin., 1970, M.B.A., 1973. Mgr. nat./regional corp. banking group Central Trust Co., Cin., 1977—, v.p., 1977-83, sr. v.p., 1983—. Trustee, Wyoming Civic Ctr., Ohio, 1983—; participant Leadership Cin., 1980. Mem. Beta Gamma Sigma. Republican. Avocations: golf; tennis; reading; travel. Home: 905 Springfield Park Wyoming OH 45215 Office: Central Trust Co Central Trust Ctr Cincinnati OH 45202

LENNON, JERRY WINDSOR, graphic arts communication executive, consultant; b. Chgo., June 18, 1947; s. Samuel Charles and Alice Kathleen (Range) L.; m. Karen Skubish, Oct. 22, 1971 (div. June 1975); m. Martha Elizabeth Rennison, Feb. 14, 1981; 1 child, Kimberley. Student phys. sci. U. Calif.-Berkeley, 1964-66, Radio Inst., Washington, 1967; student cinematography Columbia Coll., Chgo., 1967-69; A.Holography, Lake Forest Coll., Ill., 1978. Press photographer AP, Chgo., 1969-75; mgr. art and photography Unique Color, Chgo., 1974-79; sales mgr. TDS Color, Chgo., 1979-81; regional mgr. E/S Color Lab., Chgo., 1981-84; lectr. in field; cons. on electronic info. systems. Photographer: Atlas Project, 1974. Fellow Tech. Assn. Graphic Arts. Democrat. Clubs: East Bank, M & M (Chgo.). Home: 3422 N Harding St Chicago IL 60618

LENNOX, DONALD D(UANE), truck and engine manufacturing company executive; b. Pitts., Dec. 3, 1918; s. Edward George and Sarah B. (Knight) L.; m. Jane Armstrong, June 11, 1949; children—Donald D., J. Gordon. B.S. with honors, U. Pitts., 1947. C.P.A., Pa. With Ford Motor Co., 1950-69; corp. v.p., sr. v.p. info. tech. group, Xerox Corp., Rochester, N.Y., 1969-73, sr. v.p., sr. staff officer, Stamford, Conn., 1973-74, group v.p., pres. info. tech. group, Rochester, 1973-75, group v.p., pres. info. systems group, 1975-80, also dir.; sr. v.p. ops. staff Internat. Harvester Corp., 1980-81, exec. v.p., 1981-82, pres., chief operating officer, 1981-82; pres., chief exec. officer, 1982-83, chmn., chief exec. officer, 1983—; dir. Sybron Corp., Schlegel Corp. Vice chmn. bd. trustees St. John Fisher Coll. Served with AC, USN, 1942-45. Decorated D.F.C. with 2 gold stars, Air medal with 4 gold stars. Mem. Rochester Area C. of C. (pres. 1979), Soc. Automotive Engrs., Soc. Mfg. Engrs., Order of Artus, Beta Gamma Sigma. Republican. Clubs: Country of Rochester, Genesee Valley; Saddle and Cycle, Econ., Mid-Am., Chgo. (Chgo.).

LENNY, MARY RUTH, college administrator, nursing educator; b. Potosi, Mo., Nov. 24, 1922; d. Joseph Lynn and Katherine (Kelsey) Thurman; m. Norman K. Lenny, Sept. 4, 1949; children—David, Douglas, Deborah, Noel, Alan, Catherine, Cynthia. Diploma, St. John's Hosp. Sch. Nursing, St. Louis, 1943, B.S. in Nursing, Washington U., St. Louis, 1949; M.S. in Psychiat. Nursing, 1963; Ph.D. in Higher Edn. Adminstrn., St. Louis U., 1980. Instr., course coordinator Mo. Baptist Hosp., St. Louis, 1958-62, 1965-67, Belleville Area Coll., Ill., 1967-80; div. chmn. McKendree Coll., Lebanon, Ill., 1980-81, MacMurray Coll., Jacksonville, Ill., 1981—; cons. St. Elizabeth Hosp., Granite City, Ill., 1973—, St. Mary's Hosp., East St. Louis, Ill., 1975-80, Belleville Meml. Hosp., 1968-70. Contbr. articles to profl. jours. Served to lt. (j.g.) USN, 1944-46. Recipient Alumnae Book award Washington U., 1963; Dr. Scholl grantee, 1982-84. Mem. Ill. Nurses Assn. (10th dist. pres., 9th dist. pres.-elect 1983-85), AAUP (pres. 1973-75, bd. dirs. 1968-73), Internat. Toastmistresses, Delta Kappa Gamma. Roman Catholic. Avocations: Swimming; bicycling; dancing; doll collecting. Home: 1058 W College Ave Jacksonville IL 62650 also 2435 England Town Rd Saint Louis MO 63129 Office: MacMurray Coll Jacksonville IL 62650

LENO, MELVIN JOHN, social science educator; b. Tuttle, N.D., Nov. 20, 1944; s. William and Katherine Leno; m. Barbara Carol Sorenson, July 3, 1967, children—Teresa, Laree, Terra Lynn. B., U. N.D., 1967; M.S., N.D. State U.-Fargo, 1972. Tchr. Kindred Pub. Schs., N.D., 1967-69; grad. asst. N.D. State U., Fargo, 1969-72, instr. N.D. State U., Bottineau, 1972—; vice chmn. N.D. Humanities Council, 1983—; chmn. N.D. Consortium on Gerontology, 1982; mem. N.D. Hist. Preservation Review Bd., 1984-85. Grantee NEH, Washington, 1976, Bush Found., 1983. Mem. Am. Hist. Assn., N.D. Hist. Soc., Bottineau County Hist. Soc., Ducks Unltd. Democrat. Lutheran. Lodge: Eagles. Avocations: photography, hunting, woodworking. Home: 719 E 5th St Bottineau ND 58318 Office: North Dakota State U Bottineau 1st and Simrall Sts Bottineau ND 58318

LENON, RICHARD ALLEN, minerals and chem. co. exec.; b. Lansing, Mich., Aug. 4, 1920; s. Theodore and Elizabeth (Amon) L.; B.A., Western Mich. Coll., 1941; postgrad Northwestern U., 1941-42; m. Helen Johnson, Sept. 13, 1941; children—Richard Allen, Pamela A., Lisa A. Mgr. fin. div. Montgomery Ward & Co., Chgo., 1947-56; v.p. fin. Westinghouse Air Brake Co., Pitts., 1963-67, treas., 1965-67; v.p., treas. Internat. Minerals & Chem. Corp., Northbrook, Ill., 1956-63, group v.p. fin. and adminstrn., 1967-68, exec. v.p., 1968-70, pres., 1970-78, chief exec. officer, 1971-83, chmn. bd., 1977—, also dir.; dir. Am. Standard Inc., Allis-Chalmers Corp., Bankers Trust Co., Fed. Paper Bd. Co., The Signal Cos. Served with USNR, 1942-47. Clubs: Univ. (Chgo.); Glen View (Golf, Ill.); Bankers (N.Y.C.). Office: 2315 Sanders Rd Northbrook IL 60062

LENT, ROBERT WILLIAM, counseling psychologist; b. Bklyn. Apr. 1, 1953; s. Jack Harvey and Gladys (Unger) L. B.A., SUNY-Albany, 1975; M.A., Ohio State U., 1977, Ph.D., 1979. Lic. cons. psychologist. Teaching assoc. Ohio State U., Columbus, 1976-77; psychology intern Mpls. VA Hosp., 1977-78; psychology intern Ohio State U., 1978-79; asst. prof. student counseling bur., U. Minn., 1979-84, assoc. prof., 1984-85; asst. prof. counseling psychology Mich. State U., East Lansing, 1985—. Vol. counselor Walk-in Counseling Ctr., Mpls., 1977-78. Mem. Am. Psychol. Assn., Minn. Psychol. Assn., Am. Assn. Counseling and Devel., Phi Beta Kappa. Co-author profl. publs., tng. films; co-editor Handbook of Counseling Psychology. Office: Counseling Psychology Mich State U 513 Erickson St East Lansing MI 48824

LENTZ, GORDON FRANKLIN, muffler franchise company executive; b. Milan, Mich., Apr. 16, 1936; s. Leonard Leo and Clarice Hubba (Albright) L.; m. Gloria Jean Plummer, Oct. 4, 1958; children—Brad, Jeff, Greg. B.A., Wayne State U. Sales rep. Bankers Life & Casualty Co., Southfield, Mich., 1961-65; gen. agt. Wayne Nat. Life Ins. Co., Detroit, 1965-66; sales engr. Dexion Inc., Warren, Mich., 1966-72; franchisee Tuffy Muffler, Kalamazoo, Mich., 1972-83; pres., chief exec. officer Lentz U.S.A. Mufflers, Kalamazoo, 1983—. Served with AUS, 1959-61. Mem. Ind. Muffler Dealers Assn. (v.p. 1978-85). Congregationalist (moderator 1978).

LENZ, ROBERT THOMAS, business educator; b. New Albany, Ind., May 12, 1947; s. Robert Lee and Ruth Day (Kist) L.; m. Marla Kay Clark, Aug. 21, 1977; 1 child, Abigail Clark. B.S. with high distinction, Ind. U., 1969, D.B.A., 1978; M.B.A., U. Louisville, 1972. Process control engr. Gen. Electric Co., Bloomington, Ind., 1971-73, mgr. quality control, 1973-74; asst. prof. bus. Ind. U.-Indpls., 1978-81, assoc. prof. bus. adminstrn., 1982—, chmn. exec. M.B.A. program, 1985—; resident dir. Tilburg Program, John F. Kennedy Inst., U. Tilburg (Netherlands), 1984; dir. Guarantee Auto Stores, Inc. Recipient Teaching Excellence award M.B.A. Career in Progress Student Adv. Com., 1978, 79, 80, 82, 83; Amoco Found. Teaching Excellence award; grantee Strategy Research Ctr., 1983. Mem. Acad. Mgmt. (exec. com., bus. policy and planning div. 1985—), Planning Execs. Inst., Beta Gamma Sigma, Sigma Iota Epsilon. Methodist. Club: Economics (Indpls.). Mem. editorial rev. bd., contbr. articles to Strategic Mgmt. Jour. and Acad. of Mgmt. Rev. Contbr. articles to profl. jours. Office: 801 W Michigan St Suite 4012 Indianapolis IN 46223

LENZ, WILLIAM C., clergyman; b. Appleton, Wis., 1958; s. David and Jan (Verhagen) L.; m. Janet Gregg; children—Benji, Nathanael. Grad. David Wilkeson Inst. Christian Tng., Lindale, Tex., 1980. Ordained to ministry Christian Ch., 1981; exec. dir. Solid Rock Ministries, Appleton, 1980—, counselor to drug addicts-abusers, alcholics, suicidals, 1980—; pastor New Cornithian Chapel, Appleton, 1983—; speaker numerous youth and civic groups, 1980—. Served with USCG, 1976-80. Recipient Speaking award Appleton Kiwanis Club, 1983, Services award Appleton Salvation Army, 1983. Mem. World Challenge, United Evangel. Churches. Avocations: hunting, fishing, backpacking, swimming, skiing. Home: 927 Wilson St Little Chuts WI 54140

LEON, ARTHUR SOL, research cardiologist, exercise physiologist; b. Bklyn., Apr. 26, 1931; s. Alex and Anne (Schrek) L.; B.S. with high honors in Chemistry, U. Fla., Gainsville, 1952; M.S. in Biochemistry, U. Wis., Madison, 1954, M.D., 1957; m. Gloria Rakita, Dec. 23, 1956; children—Denise, Harmon,

Michelle. Intern, Henry Ford Hosp., Detroit, 1957-58; fellow internal medicine Lahey Clinic, Boston, 1958-60; fellow cardiology U. Miami (Fla.) Sch. Medicine, Jackson Meml. Hosp., Miami, 1960-61; chief gen. medicine, cardiology, dir. intern edn. 34th Gen. U.S. Army Hosp., Orleans, France, 1961-64; research cardiologist Walter Reed Army Inst. Research, Washington, 1964-67; dir. Hoffmann-La Roche Clin. Pharmacology Research Unit, Newark Beth Israel Med. Center, 1969-73; instr. dept. medicine Coll. Medicine and Dentistry N.J., Newark, 1967-69, asst. prof., 1969-72, asso. prof., 1972-73; asso. prof. medicine, physiol. hygiene, nutrition and physiology Med. Sch. and Sch. Pub. Health, U. Minn., Mpls., 1973-79, prof., 1979—; dir. grad. studies, 1974-83, applied physiology and nutrition sects. Lab. Physiol. Hygiene U. Minn., 1973—, also chief cardiologist Lipid Research Clinic; col., chief cardiology 5501 U.S. Army Hosp., Ft. Snelling, Minn., 1973—, chief profl. services, 1983—; mem. Med. Evaluation Team Gemini and Apollo Projects, Washington, 1964-67. Bd. dirs. Vinland Nat. Sports Health Center, 1978—. Served with M.C., U.S. Army, 1961-67. Decorated Army Commendation medal; Am. Heart Assn. fellow, 1960-61; recipient William G. Anderson award AAHPER, 1981. Fellow Am. Coll. Cardiology, Am. Coll. Chest Physicians, Am. Coll. Clin. Pharm., N.Y. Acad. Sci., Am. Coll. Sports Medicine (trustee 1976-78, 81-83, v.p. 1977-79, pres. Northland chpt. 1976); mem. Am. Physiol. Soc., Soc. Clin. Pharm. and Therapeutics, Am. Inst. Research, Am. Heart Assn. (v.p. Hennepin div. 1980, pres. 1982-83), Am. Coll. Nutrition, Am. Fedn. Clin. Research, Am. Soc. Biol. and Exptl. Therapeutics, Phi Beta Kappa, Phi Kappa Phi. Jewish. Contbr. articles in exercise physiology, exercise in prevention, treatment of coronary heart disease, cardiology, biochemistry, clin. pharmacology to med. jours., books. Participant White House Conf. Health and Physical Activity, 1976, 81. Home: 9701 Oak Ridge Trail Minnetonka MN 55343 Office: Div Epidemiology Sch Pub Health U Minn Stadium Gate 27 Minneapolis MN 55455

LEONARD, CHARLES ALEXANDER, political science educator; b. Phila., Aug. 7, 1929; s. Charles Hawkins and Rose Teresa (Murray) L.; m. Emily Louise Velde, June 6, 1970. A.B., Catholic U. Am., 1952; Litt.M., U. Pitts., 1957; M.A., U. Notre Dame, 1962, Ph.D., 1967. Tchr. La Salle High Sch., Phila., 1953-61; asst. prof. La Salle U., Phila., 1964-68; assoc. prof., prof. dept. polit. sci. Western Ill. U., Macomb, 1968—. Author: A Search for a Judicial Philosophy, 1972. Contbr. articles to profl jour. NEH summer grantee, 1977. Mem. Am. Polit. Sci. Assn., Midwest Polit. Sci. Assn., Acad. Polit. Sci., Am. Judicature Soc., Supreme Ct. Hist. Soc. Democrat. Roman Catholic. Home: 130 Carriage Hill Macomb IL 61455 Office: Polit Sci Dept Western Ill U Macomb IL 61455

LEONARD, EUGENE A., banker; b. St. Louis. Ph.D. in Econs., U. Mo., 1962; Grad. Stonier Grad. Sch. Banking, Rutgers U. Economist, Fed. Res. Bank, St. Louis, 1961-67; v.p. Fed. Res. Bank, Memphis, 1967-70, 1st v.p., 1971-77; sr. v.p. Mercantile Bancorp. Inc. and Mercantile Trust Co., St. Louis, 1977—, head banking div., chmn. funds mgmt. com. Chmn. bd. dirs. Logos Sch., Repertory Theatre, St. Louis. Mem. Conf. State Bank Supervisors (state rep.), Mo. Bankers Assn. (pres.-elect), U. Mo.-Columbia Alumni Assn. (past pres., bd. dirs. devel. fund). Office: Mercantile Bancorp Inc Mercantile Tower Box 524 St Louis MO 63166

LEONARD, HARRY ELVIN, industrial relations consultant; b. Ottowa, Ill., Mar. 5, 1899; s. Andrew and Hannah (Weberg) L.; student U. Minn., 1920-21; m. Louise Anne Olson, May 13, 1940; children—Terri Lou (Mrs. Gordon Buhrer), Jacqueline Lee (Mrs. Robert Posner). With No. States Power Co., Mpls., 1923-40; asst. bus. mgr. Local 160 Internat. Brotherhood Elec. Workers, Mpls., 1940-41, union organizer, 1942-43, bus. mgr., 1944-64; maintenance supr. East Side Neighborhood Services, Mpls., 1966-67; indsl. relations cons. Minn. Nurses Assn., St. Paul, 1968-81; arbitrator for public and pvt. employees in State of Minn., 1973-81; dir., Service Savs. and Loan Assn., St. Paul, 1956-66; instr. labor relations U. Minn. Evening Sch., 1950-51, mem. adv. council Indsl. Relations Center, 1950—. Mem. exec. com. Citizens League Greater Mpls., 1953-54; mem. staff Coummunity Chest, Mpls. 1944; commr. Mpls. Charter Commn., 1958-70, chmn., 1963-64. Chmn. 3d Ward Democratic Farmer Labor Club, 1941-46; del. Dem. Nat. Conv., 1948. Bd. dirs. Hennepin County Cancer Soc., 1959-71, hon. life mem., 1971—, 2d v.p., 1963-66. Served with U.S. Army, 1918. Named Labor Man of Year Mpls. Jr. C. of C., 1958. Mem. Amicus, Assn. for Non-Smokers Rights. Unitarian. Clubs: Masons, Shriners, Eagles (life). Home: 2939 Grand St NE Minneapolis MN 55418

LEONARD, PAUL ROGER, mayor of Dayton, lawyer; b. Dayton, Ohio, July 3, 1943; s. Paul Roger and Ida H. (Miller) L. B.S. with honors in Journalism, Ohio U., 1965; J.D., Salmon P. Chase Coll. Law, Cin., 1969. Bar: Ohio. Labor relations rep. Gen. Motors Corp., 1966-69; asst. pros. atty., Montgomery County, Ohio, 1969-72; mem. Ohio Ho. of Reps., vice chmn. judiciary com., 1972-80; mayor City of Dayton (Ohio), 1981—; dir. Abington Steel Corp.; ptnr. firm Hunt, Skilken, Leonard & Wehner, Dayton, 1981—; mem. urban econ. com. U.S. Conf. Mayors; mem. fin., adminstrn. and intergovtl. relations policy com. Nat. League of Cities. Bd. dirs. Dayton Urban League; mem. Miami Valley Cancer Consortium. Recipient Outstanding Grad. award Dayton Pub. Schs., 1983, Medal of Merit, mem. Alumni Hall of Fame, Ohio U., 1983. Mem. Nat. Conf. Democratic Mayors. Roman Catholic. Democratic. Lodge: K.C. Office: 101 W 3d St Dayton OH 45402*

LEONARD, PETER, conductor; b. Boston, July 18, 1952; s. John Francis and Ethel (Walker) L.; m. Paula Jeanne Leavy, Aug. 7, 1976; 1 son, Alexander Robert. B.Mus., Juilliard Sch., 1972, M.Mus., 1974; postgrad. Aspen Music Sch., 1972, Salzburg Mozarteum, 1973. Assoc. condr. Greenwich Philharmonia (Conn.), 1972-76; assoc. then prin. guest condr. L.I. Symphony, 1978-82; music dir. Bergen Philharm. (N.J.), 1979—; condr. in residence Louisville Orch., 1978-81; conductor N.Y. Lyric Opera, 1978-80; music dir. Youngstown Symphony Orch. (Ohio), 1981—, Shreveport Symphony, 1984—; numerous guest appearances. Recipient ASCAP award for orchestral programming, 1979-80; Nat. Arts Assoc. award Sigma Alpha Iota, 1983; Fromm fellow, Tanglewood, 1970; grantee in field. Office: 260 Federal Plaza W Youngstown OH 44503 or Shaw Concerts 1995 Broadway New York NY 10023

LEONARD, WILLIAM JOHN, pharmacist; b. San Diego, Aug. 4, 1953; s. Milton John and Agnes Maureen (Moreland) L.; m. Jill Marie Brown, Dec. 27, 1973; children—Tracy, John, Mary. B.S. in Pharmacy, U. Ill. Chgo., 1978. Registered pharmacist, Ill., Ind. Pharmacist Cavett Drug Store, Chicago Heights, Ill., 1978-80; pharmacist, asst. mgr. Hoosier Drug Store, Whiting, Ind., 1980-84; pharmacist, mgr. Olympia Fields Profl. Pharmacy, Ill., 1984—. Elder Tinley Park Ch. of Christ, Ill., 1982—. Avocations: sports, reading. Home: 17056 Forestview Dr Tinley Park IL 60477 Office: Olympia Fields Profl Pharmacy 20303 S Crawford Olympia Fields IL 60461

LEONIDA, DOMINGO DOMINIC JOSEPH, physician; b. Honolulu, July 3, 1927; s. Fernando Gabriel and Fortunata (Ragas) L.; B.S., Marquette U., 1951; M.S., U. Cin., 1953, M.D., 1959; M.P.H., U. Mich., 1962; postgrad. (fellow) Computer Sci., U. Ill., 1978-80; m. Madelaine Ching Hua Kao, Aug. 7, 1954; children—Mark Huaming Patrick, Clara HuaCin Catherine. Intern, Mercy Hosp., Toledo, 1959-60; resident U. Mich. Hosp., Ann Arbor, 1961-62; research biochemist U.S. Indsl. Chem.-Nat. Distillers Corp., Cin., 1955-56; epidemiologist Ohio Dept. Health, Columbus, 1962-64, chief chronic diseases, 1964-65; fellow Physicians Alcohol Studies Inst., Rutgers U., New Brunswick, N.J., 1964; med. dir. immunol. activities and grants, epidemiologist N.Y. Dept. Health, Albany, 1965-67; med. dir. Skokie (Ill.) Health Dept., 1967-69, Kenosha (Wis.) Health Dept., 1969-71; family practice, indsl. practice medicine, Lincoln, Ill., 1971—; instr. Coll. Medicine, Ohio State U., 1963-64, spl. edn. Ill. State U., 1973-74, Coll. Medicine, U. Ill., Peoria, 1971-77; clin. asst. prof. occupational medicine Coll. Medicine, U. Ill., Chgo., 1980—; mem. staff Meth. Hosp., Peoria, Pekin (Ill.) Hosp., Warner Hosp., Clinton, Ill. Chmn. camping health and safety coms. Kenosha council Boy Scouts Am., 1970-71. Served with inf. U.S. Army, 1946-48; lt. M.C., USN, 1960-61; lt. col. M.C., Army Res. N.G., 1978—; comdr. USNR, 1984—. Mental health profl., Hamilton, Ohio. Fellow Am. Coll. Preventive Medicine, Am. Acad. Family Practice; mem. AAAS, Ecol. Soc. Am., AMA, Ill. State, Logan County Med. Socs., Am. Heart Assn. (Chgo. br.), N.Y. Public Health Assn. Roman Catholic. Contbr. articles to med. jours. Home and Office: 42 Northbrook St Lincoln IL 62656 Office: OWCP 230 S Dearborn St Chicago IL 60604

LEOPOLD, JERRY LEE, optometrist; b. Colby, Kans., Dec. 29, 1952; s. Dale Melville and Linnie Irene (Gilbert) L.; m. Deanna Rose Allmon, May 18, 1980. Student B.S., U. Houston, 1974, O.D., 1976. Optometrist, Drs. Aplin & Leopold, P.A., McPherson, Kans., 1976—. Chmn. Cobb for Treas. Campaign, McPherson, 1984; chmn. bd. dirs. McPherson County Diversified Services, 1978, 79, 84, 85, treas., 1981-83. Mem. Kans. Optometric Assn. (zone pres. 1982-85, chmn. polit. action com. 1982-85, mem. assistance to grads. and undergrads. com. 1982-85, chmn. ins. com. 1985), Am. Otometric Assn. (coordinator State polit. action com. 1985—). Republican. Methodist. Lodges: Optimists (McPherson) (project chmn. 1977-85); Elks (dist. dep. grand exalted ruler 1984-85, Elk of Yr. 1985, bd. dirs. tng. ctr. for handicapped). Home: 1009 Heatherwood Pl McPherson KS 67460 Office: 1233 Main St PO Box 306 McPherson KS 67460

LEOPOLD, ROBERT BRUCE, lawyer; b. Toledo, Ohio, June 25, 1949; s. James A. and Florence B. (Barnett) L.; m. Cathryn Lucy Hagler, Nov. 2, 1978. A.B., in Polit. Sci., Ind. U., 1971; J.D., Valparaiso U., 1974. Bar: Ill., Ind. 1975. Dep. prosecutor Lake County, Ind., 1975-76; assoc. Cohen, Cohen & Bullard, East Chicago, Ind., 1977-78; sole practice law, Munster, Ind., 1978—. Pres., Westlake Unit of Northwest Ind. div. Am. Heart Assn., 1982-85. Mem. ABA, Ind. Bar Assn., Ill. Bar Assn., Assn. Trial Layers of Am., Delta Theta Phi. Address: 9335 Calumet Ave Suite D Munster IN 46321

LEPKOWSKI, JAMES MICHAEL, biostatistician, research scientist; b. Dearborn, Mich., July 18, 1948; s. Eugene Walter and Ellen Josephine (Courtney) L.; m. Alicia Ann Thayer, Feb. 1, 1975; children—Matthew James, Alexander John, Michael Andrew. B.S., Ill. State U., 1970; M.P.H., U. Mich., 1976, Ph.D., 1980. Vol. U.S. Peace Corps, Addis Ababa, Ethiopia, 1970-72; cons. WHO, Juba, Sudan, 1972-73; research asst. U. Mich., Ann Arbor, 1977-79; staff fellow Ctrs. for Disease Control, Kathmandu, Nepal, 1980; research investigator U. Mich., Ann Arbor, 1980-82, study dir., 1982—. Contbr. articles to profl. jours. Mem. Am. Statis. Assn., Soc. Epidemiologic Research, Internat. Assn. Survey Statisticians. Baptist. Home: 406 Manor Dr Ann Arbor MI 48105 Office: Inst Social Research U Mich 426 Thompson Ann Arbor MI 48104

LERSTEN, NELS RONALD, botany educator; b. Chgo., Aug. 6, 1932; s. Einar Anders and Elvira Maria (Bloom) L.; m. Patricia Anne Brady, June 13, 1958; children—Samuel, Andrew, Julie. B.S., U. Chgo., 1958, M.S., 1960; Ph.D., U. Calif.-Berkeley, 1963. Asst. prof. botany Iowa State U., Ames, 1963-67, assoc. prof., 1967-70, prof., 1970—. Contbr. articles to profl. publs., chpts. to books. Served with USCG, 1952-55. Fellow Iowa Acad. Sci. (editor Proc. 1977-82); mem. Am. Soc. Plant Taxonomists, Bot. Soc. Am. (treas. 1981—), Internat. Soc. Plant Taxonomists, Sigma Xi. Office: Dept Botany Iowa State U Ames IA 50011

LESH-LAURIE, GEORGIA ELIZABETH, university administrator, biology educator, researcher; b. Cleve., July 28, 1938; d. Howard Frees and Josephine Elizabeth (Taylor) Lesh; m. William Francis Laurie, Aug. 16, 1969. B.S., Marietta Coll., 1960; M.S., U. Wis., 1961; Ph.D., Case Western Reserve U., 1966. Asst. prof. SUNY, Albany, 1966-69; asst., then assoc. prof. Case Western Reserve U., 1969-77, asst. dean, 1973-76; interim dir. Cleve. State U., Ohio, 1980, prof., chairperson, 1977-81, dean grad. studies, 1981—; cons. in field; reviewer numerous granting agencies, profl. jours., 1968—; advanced placement exam. Edn. Testing Service, Princeton, N.J., 1982-83. Contbr. sci. articles to profl. pubs. Trustee Marietta Coll., Ohio, 1980-84, 85—; mem. city/univ. interchange com., Cleve., 1983—. Fellow NSF, NIH; grantee NIH, Am. Cancer Soc., Am. Heart Assn., Research Corp., 1968—; Recipient Wright fellowship Bermuda Biol. Station. Mem. Am. Soc. Zoologists, Soc. Devel. Biology, Am. Soc. Cell Biology, AAAS, Phi Beta Kappa. Office: Coll of Grad Studies Cleveland State Univ Cleveland OH 44115

LESKE, LARRY OMER, pharmacist; b. Stewartville, Minn., Apr. 18, 1951; s. Omer A. and Mildred G. (Wilson) L.; m. Lonnie M. Lange, May 23, 1973; 1 child, Steven A. Student S.W. State Coll., Marshall, Minn., 1969-71; B.S. in Pharmacy, S.D. State U., 1974. Registered pharmacist, Minn. Intern pharmacist Dan's Rexall Drug, Springfield, Minn., 1974-75; pharmacist Brix Drug, Redwood Falls, Minn., 1975—; drug information lectr. Redwood County, Minn., 1982—; participant Burroughs-Welcome County Pharmacy Edn. Program. Commr. Redwood Falls Police Dept., chmn. Police Commn., 1982—. Mem. Am. Pharm. Assn., Minn. Pharm. Assn., Nat. Rifle Assn. Republican. Methodist. Avocations: hunting; motorcycle riding; reading. Home: 108 Cypresswood Ln Redwood Falls MN 56283 Office: Brix Drug 216 S Washington Redwood Falls MN 56283

LESKOVYANSKY, JOHN JOSEPH, judge; b. Senecaville, Ohio, Mar. 28, 1925; s. Stephen and Susan (Younger) L.; m. Ethel Virginia Drew, 1948; children—John Joseph, Paul James, Mark Jeffrey, Susan Jennifer. Student Youngstown State U., 1947-49, Ohio No. U., 1949-50; J.D., Youngstown State U., 1953, Bar: Ohio. First asst. prosecutor City of Youngstown, Ohio, 1954-59, 1st asst. law dir., 1959-61; judge Youngstown Mcpl. Ct., 1961-73; judge domestic relations div. Ct. Common Pleas, Youngstown, 1973—; seminar lectr., 1973-84; lectr. Ohio Acad. Trial Lawyers, Ohio Jud. Coll.; dir. child support enforcement project Nat. Council Juvenile and Family Ct. Judges, 1982. Author chpt. in book. Pres. conv. 1st Catholic Slovak Union, Ohio, 1973-76, pres., Cleve., 1983—; chmn. Am. Slovak Bicentennial, Youngstown, 1976; com. mem. Mahoning County and Youngstown Bicentennial Com. Ohio, 1976; 2d v.p. Ohio Family Support Assn., 1978; pres. Ohio Burs. Support Assn., 1980; bd. dirs. Mahoning Valley council Boy Scouts Am., 1970—; appt. chmn. child support enforcement and family law task force State of Ohio. Served with USN, 1943-46, PTO. Recipient St. George award Mahoning Valley council Boy Scouts Am., 1970, Silver Beaver award, 1976; Superior Jud. Service award Ohio Supreme Ct., 1981; named Man of Yr., Slovak Am. Soc., Youngstown, 1982. Mem. Ohio Bar Assn. (family com. com.); Ohio Jud. Conf. (2d v.p. 1985), Woodrow Wilson Alumni Assn. (pres.). Democrat. Roman Catholic. Lodge: K.C. Home: 2714 Shirley Rd Youngstown OH 44502 Office: Mahoning County Courthouse 4th Floor 120 Market St Youngstown OH 44503

LESLIE, ROBERT WENDELL, manufacturing company executive; b. Lincoln, Nebr., June 28, 1933; s. Oliver Wendell and Hazel R. (Barnett) L.; m. Janet C. Deckinger, June 5, 1957; children—Steven, David, Mark B.A., Nebr. Wesleyan U., 1957; M.A., U. Nebr., 1960. Tchr./coach schs. in Nebr. and Calif., 1957-66; from salesman to v.p. sales Jostens, Inc., Bloomington, Minn., 1966-71, v.p. scholastic div., 1971-74, exec. v.p. ops., 1974-77, pres., chief operating officer, 1977—; past dir. Jewelers Vigilance Com. Bd. dirs., pres. Jr. Achievement Twin Cities; bd. dirs. United Way Mpls., chmn., 1984-85; trustee Nebr. Wesleyan U. Mem. Bloomington C. of C. (chmn. pres.'s adv. council 1980-81). Office: Jostens Inc 5501 Norman Center Dr Minneapolis MN 55437

LESSER, FRANCES SHAIMAN, lawyer; b. Wilkes-Barre, Pa., Aug. 5, 1954; d. Jerome and Doris Lee (Kaufman) Shaiman; m. Steven David Lesser, Jan. 1, 1978; children—Bethany, Natalie. B.A., U. Pitts., 1976; J.D., Capital U., 1979. Bar: Ohio 1979, U.S. Dist. Ct. (so. dist.) Ohio 1979. Legal intern Legal Aid Soc., Columbus, Ohio, 1977-78; research asst. Capital U. Law Sch., Columbus, 1978-79; mediator for city prosecutor, Columbus, 1978-79; legal counsel to treas. State of Ohio, Columbus, 1979—. Treas. Women's Am. Orgn. for Rehab. through Tng., Columbus, 1979-81, 83—, v.p., 1982; bd. mem. Centennial Com. YWCA, Columbus, 1981—. Legal Aid Soc. scholar, 1977. Mem. Columbus Bar Assn. (fin. instns. com., pub. funds com.), Women Lawyers of Franklin County. Democrat. Jewish. Office: Treas of State's Office 30 E Broad St 9th Floor Columbus OH 43215

LESSING, ROBERT ERNEST, JR., lawyer; b. Akron, Ohio, Jan. 30, 1944; s. Robert E. and Jean E. (Garrett) L.; m. Bonnie L. Havel, June 29, 1968; children—David R., Scott A. B.A., Capital U., 1966; J.D., Valparaiso U., 1969. Bar: Ohio 1969. Atty. Nat. City Bank, Cleve., 1969-73, West, West & Sherman, Elyria, Ohio, 1973-76; sole practice, Elyria, 1976-83; mng. ptnr. Lessing, Schnitkey & Kovacs, Elyria, 1983—; mem. charter bd. Lorain County Estate Planning Council, Elyria, 1975—, pres. 1976-77. Author: Law Office Staff Manual, 1983. Chmn. Elyria Citizens for Edn., 1974, Elyria Town Meeting, 1976, Elyria Bd. Bldg. Appeals, 1978-79, Taxpayer's Com. Eaton Twp., 1982-83; mem. Zoning Commn. Eaton Twp., 1985—; Republican precinct committeeman City of Elyria, 1976-79; trustee United Health Found., 1978-84, pres., 1981-83; trustee Family Services Assn. Lorain County., 1983—, pres., 1985-87 Recipient Honor medal Chgo. Tribune, 1964. Mem. Ohio State Bar Assn., Lorain County Bar Assn. (chmn. community relations com. 1982-84), Jaycees (pres. 1975-76). Republican. Lutheran. Lodge: Kiwanis. Avocations: skiing; travel; gardening; baseball, jogging. Home: 118 Country Pl Grafton OH 44044 Office: Lessing Schnitkey & Kovacs Attys at Law 422 E S T Bldg Elyria OH 44035

LESTER, BRUCE PAUL, computer science educator; b. Phila., Sept. 12, 1947. B.S., MIT, 1971, M.S., 1971, Ph.D., 1974; M.S.C.I., Maharishi European Research U., Seelisberg, Switzerland, 1977. Lectr. Princeton U., 1973-75; prof. dept. computer sci. Maharishi Internat. U., Fairfield, Iowa, 1979—, chmn. dept. computer sci., 1982—. Mem. Assn. Computing Machinery, IEEE Computer Soc. Office: Maharishi Internat U Dept Computer Sci Fairfield IA 52556

LESTER, SANDRA KAY, social worker; b. Kalamazoo, Sept. 18, 1944; d. LeRoy Clifford and Maxine Blenn (Stafford) Butcher; m. Edward Bernard Lester, Sept. 1, 1978; children—Kevin Craig, Julie Kathleen, Nicholas, Edward. B.S., Western Mich. U., 1970, postgrad., 1979—. Case mgr. Mich. Dept. Social Services, Kalamazoo, 1971, interagency foster care liaison, 1973-77, recruiter, trainer for foster care, 1977-80, purchase of service contract specialist, 1980-83, employment and tng. counselor, 1983—, contract mgr., 1984—; instr. Kalamazoo Valley Community Coll., 1976-77. Bd. dirs. Continuing Edn. for Young Families, 1981; pres., bd. dirs. Regional Interagency Council for Developmentally Disabled, 1973-76. Mem. Network, Internat. Platform Assn., Internat. Personnel Mgmt. Assn. Democrat. Lutheran. Home: 3822 Mt Olivet St Kalamazoo MI 49004 Office: 322 Stockbridge St Kalamazoo MI 49001

LETO, GLENN KEITH, educator; b. Chgo., Sept. 8, 1946; s. Samuel and Ann (Dulek) L. B.S., No. Ill. U., 1968, M.S., 1972. Educator, Dist. 220, Barrington, Ill., 1970—; cons. Mus. Sci. and Industry, Chgo., 1985, Tech. Pub. Co., Barrington, 1984-85, State of Ill. Dept. Edn., Springfield, 1979. Author: (with others) Biology, 1985; co-author tng. manual Force & Motion, 1986. Am. Assn. Physics Tchrs. grantee, 1982, State of Ill. grantee, 1983; Kellogg Found. fellow, 1983, 84. Mem. Nat. Sci. Tchrs. Assn., Nat. Assn. Biology Tchrs., Mus. Sci. and Industry, Common Cause, Sigma Xi. Avocations: photography; computer applications; hiking. Home: 10013 Hillshire Dr W Richmond IL 60071 Office: Barrington High Sch 616 W Main St Barrington IL 60013

LETO, JOHN ANTHONY, trucking firm executive; b. Des Moines, Sept. 19, 1962; s. Paul Joseph and Elsa Mae (Domres) L. Student Grand View Coll., 1981-83, Drake U., 1983—. Treas. City Wide Cartage Inc., Des Moines, 1975-84, pres., 1984—. Republican. Roman Catholic. Avocations: photography; golf; bowling. Home: 10617 Greenbelt Dr Des Moines IA 50322 Office: City Wide Cartage Inc 1617 NE 51st Ave Des Moines IA 50313

LETSON, ALAN DOUGLAS, ophthalmologist, vitreo-retinal surgeon, educator; b. C.Z., Apr. 6, 1951; s. Holton Charles and Betty Jean (Mellinger) L.; m. Susan Reade, Aug. 2, 1975; children—Robert Alan, Charles Venning. B.A., Miami U., 1973; M.D., Case Western Res. U., 1977. Diplomate Am. Bd. Ophthalmology. Intern, St. Luke's Hosp., Cleve., 1977-78; resident Ohio State U., Columbus, 1978-81, fellow in vitreo-retinal surgery, 1981-82; practice medicine specializing in vitre-retinal surgery, Columbus, Ohio, 1982—; clin. instr. Ohio State U., 1978-82, clin. asst. prof., 1982—, clin. research, 1978—; cons. Dayton VA Hosp., 1982-84. Contbr. articles to sci.-ophthalmic jours. Mem. med. adv. com. Nat. Soc. to Prevent Blindness, 1982—. Recipient AMA Physicians' Recognition award, 1981, 83. Fellow Am. Acad. Ophthalmology; mem. AMA, Ohio Ophthal. Soc., Ohio State Med. Assn., Columbus Ophthal. and Otolaryn. Soc. Avocations: long distance running, computers, backpacking, reading, photography, painting, music. Home: 1810 Waltham Rd Upper Arlington OH 43221 Office: 393 E Town St Suite 228 Columbus OH 43215

LETSON, WILLIAM NORMAND, lawyer; b. N.Y.C., Mar. 24, 1930; s. Benjamin Hugle and Ellen (Skon) L.; m. Barbara C. Briggs, Jan. 22, 1956 (div. May 1980); children—Benjamin B., Katherine L., William C.; m. Brenda Powell, Oct. 10, 1981. A.B. cum laude, Harvard U., 1952, J.D. magna cum laude, 1955. Bar: Ohio 1955, N.Y. 1956, D.C. 1973, Pa. 1975. Assoc. Shearman & Sterling, N.Y.C., 1955-62; ptnr. Letson, Letson & Kightlinger, Warren, Ohio, 1962-71; gen. counsel U.S. Dept. Commerce, Washington, 1971-73; v.p., gen. counsel, sec. Westinghouse Electric, Pitts., 1973-76; ptnr. Schiff, Hardin & Waite, Washington, 1977-79, Letson, Griffith, Woodall & Lavelle, Warren, Ohio, 1979—; dir. HON Industries, Muscatine, Iowa, 1977—, Therm-o-Link, Inc., Garrettsville, Ohio, 1979—. Mem. Pres. Commn. on Personnel Interchange, Washington, 1976-80; mem. U.S.-USSR Sci. and Tech. Commn., Washington, 1972-73; mem. State Com. to Elect Clarence Brown Gov., 1982; mem. law sch. adv. com. U. Akron, 1981—. Mem. ABA, Ohio State Bar Assn., Warren Area C. of C. (dir. 1984-85). Republican. Episcopalian. Clubs: Duquesne, Fox Chapel (Pitts.); Metropolitan (Washington); Trumbull Country, Buckeye (Warren). Avocations: skiing; sailing; fly fishing; tennis. Home: 930 Fairway Dr Warren OH 44483 Office: Letson Griffith Woodall & Lavelle PO Box 151 155 S Park Ave Warren OH 44482

LEUENBERGER, JAMES MONROE, advertising/public relations executive; b. Decorah, Iowa, Oct. 23, 1946; s. Clinton Monroe and Mary (Silhacek) L.; m. Glenda Gay Fike, Feb. 28, 1970; children—Jeffrey, Jennifer, Jeremy. B.S., Iowa State U., 1968, M.S., 1970. 4-H youth agt., Winneshiek County, Iowa, 1968; dir. info. Nat. Holstein Assn., Brattleboro, Vt., 1970-75; dir. advt./pub. relations 21st Century Genetics Coop., Shawano, Wis., 1975—. Served with Vt. N.G., 1968-74. Named Disting. Pres., Shawano Optimist Club, 1980, Editor of Outstanding A.I. Newsletter, Nat. Assn. Animal Breeders, 1979. Mem. Coop. Editorial Assn., Internat. Assn. Bus. Communicators, Nat. Dairy Shrine (dir., sec.), Nat. Post-Sec. Agr. Student Orgn. (dir.). Democrat. Roman Catholic. Club: Optimist. Home: 305 Prospect Circle Shawano WI 54166 Office: RFD 2 Shawano WI 54166

LEUKART, RICHARD HENRY, II, lawyer; b. Detroit, Mar. 15, 1942; s. Richard Henry and Marjorie Ruth (Smith) L.; m. Barbara Joan Gottfried, Oct. 7, 1977; children—Elisabeth, Jennifer, Kathleen, Richard Henry III, Brian. A.B., Dartmouth Coll., 1964; A.B., Amos Tuck Sch. Bus., 1964; J.D., U. Mich., 1967. Bar: Ohio 1967. Ptnr. Baker & Hostetler, Cleve., 1967—. Bd. trustees Hudson Heritage Assn., 1984—. Alfred P. Sloan Found. scholar, 1960-62; Daniel Webster scholar, 1963-64. Mem. ABA, Ohio Bar Assn., Cleve. Bar Assn. Republican. Presbyterian. Home: 7255 Valley View Rd Hudson OH 44236 Office: Baker & Hostetler 3200 National City Ctr Cleveland OH 44114

LEUNG, BENJAMIN SHUET-KIN, biochemist, educator, researcher; b. Hong Kong, June 30, 1938; came to U.S., 1961, naturalized, 1970; s. Frank Yun-Pui and Ken-Yau (Lee) L.; m. Helen T. Hsu, Oct. 19, 1964; children—Kay, Titus, Steven. Student in chemistry and zoology, Hong Kong Baptist Coll., 1960-61; B.S. cum laude in Chemistry and Zoology, Seattle Pacific U., 1963; Ph.D. in Biochemistry, Colo. State U., 1969. Postdoctoral fellow Vanderbilt U., Nashville, 1969-71; dir. Clin. Research Ctr. Lab., Portland, Oreg., 1971-76; from asst. prof. to assoc. prof. dept. surgery Dept. Oreg. Health Service, Portland, 1971-76; sr. research scientist Sinai Med. Ctr., Los Angeles, 1976-78; assoc. prof. ob-gyn U. Minn., Mpls., 1978-84, prof. ob-gyn, 1984—, research dir. Endocrine Fellowship, 1978—, head div. cell biology and reprodn., 1984—; ad hoc cons. NIH, NCI, NSF, 1972—. Editor: Hormonal Regulation of Mammary Tumors, Vols. I and II, 1982; contbr. articles to profl. jours. Chmn. Dad's Club Bridlemile Sch., Portland, 1975-76; resource person Community Resource Pool of Edina (Minn.), 1980—. Fellow NIH, Ford Found., 1966-71; grantee NIH, NCI, and others, 1971—. Mem. Am. Soc. Biol. Chemists, Endocrine Soc., Am. Assn. Cancer Research, Soc. Gynecol. Investigation, Minn. Chromatography Forum (chmn. program com. 1983-84). Republican. Home: 6076 Olinger Blvd Edina MN 55436 Office: U Minn Dept Obstetrics and Gynecology 420 Delaware St SE PO Box 395 Mayo Minneapolis MN 55455

LEURGANS, SUE ELLEN, statistics educator; b. Denver, Jan. 9, 1952; s. Paul J. and E. Lois (Cook) L. A.B., Princeton U., 1974; Ph.D., Stanford U., 1978. Asst. prof. stats. U. Wis., Madison, 1978-84; vis. asst. prof. U. Wash., Seattle, 1983-84; assoc. prof. stats. Ohio State U., Columbus, 1984—. Mem. Am. Statis. Assn. (assoc. editor 1983—), Inst. Math. Stats., Royal Statis. Soc., AAAS, Sigma Xi. Home: 4847 Hollingbourne Ct Columbus OH 43214 Office: Stats Dept Ohio State U 1958 Neil Ave Columbus OH 43210-1247

LEUTHER, MICHAEL DOYLE, research biochemist; b. St. Louis, Feb. 15, 1948; s. Elmer Carl and Doyle Price (Bennett) L.; m. Regalia Jean Simons, Mar. 29, 1969 (div.); 1 dau., Danielle Renea; m. 2d, Kathlee Mae Schnabel, Sept. 20, 1981. B.A. in Biology, U. Mo.-St. Louis, 1970; Ph.D. in Biochemistry, St. Louis U., 1983. Product mgr. monoclonal hepatitis diagnostics A.D.D. Abbott Labs., Abbott Park, North Chgo., 1981—. Served to capt. USAF, 1971-75. Decorated Unit Merit Citation. Named Citizen of Month, St. Louis Bd. Police Commrs., Dec. 1968; recipient Presdl. award of achievement, Abbott Labs., 1983. Mem.

Sci. Research Soc., AAAS, Sigma Xi. Republican. Presbyterian. Contbr. articles to profl. publs. Home: 17574 W Winnebago Dr Wildwood IL 60030 Office: Abbott Labs 9ZR - AP1O Abbott Park North Chicago IL 60064

LEV, MAURICE, pathologist; b. St. Joseph, Mo., Nov. 13, 1908; m. Lesley Beswick, Sept. 7, 1947; children—Benita Lev Lyons, Peter. B.S., NYU, 1930; M.D., Creighton U., 1934; M.A., Northwestern U., 1966. Diplomate Am. Bd. Pathology. Intern, resident, resident in pathology Michael Reese Hosp., Chgo., 1935-40; instr. pathology U. Ill.-Chgo., 1939-46, asst. prof., 1947-48, assoc. prof., 1948-51; asst. prof. Creighton U., Omaha, 1946-47; assoc. prof. U. Miami, Coral Gables, Fla., 1951-56, prof., 1956-57; prof. Northwestern U., Chgo., 1957-77; dir. clin. lab. Deborah Heart & Lung Ctr., Browns Mills, N.J., 1982—; clin. prof. pathology Temple U., Phila., 1983—, Milton S. Hershey Med. Ctr., Pa. State U., Hershey, 1983—. Served to lt. col. U.S. Army, 1942-46; ETO. Fellow AMA, Am. Coll. Cardiology, Am. Soc. Clin. Pathologists, Am. Coll. Chest Physicians, Coll. Am. Pathologists, Am. Heart Assn., N.Y. Acad. Scis., Inst. Medicine Chgo.; mem. Am. Soc. Pathologists and Bacteriologists, Am. Assn. Anatomists, Gerontol. Soc., Midwest Soc. Electron Microscopists, Histochem. Soc., Phi Delta Epsilon, Sigma Xi, Alpha Omega Alpha. Contbr. numerous articles to profl. jours.

LEVAK, BARBARA ANN, educator; b. Lorain, Ohio, June 29, 1949; d. Martin Michael and Olga (Mihalsky) L. B.S. cum laude, Bowling Green State U., 1971; M.Ed., Ohio State U., 1983; tng. Adelphi U. Nat. Tng. Inst., 1981. Cert. tchr., Ohio. Tchr., Fremont (Ohio) City Schs., 1971-73; tchr. Reynoldsburg (Ohio) City Schs., 1973—, bldg. coordinator English dept., 1978—, curriculum coordinator, 1984— mem. Sch. and Dist. Think Tank, 1981—; mem. Prin.'s Adv. Com., 1979-81; mem. Supt.'s Adv. Com., 1980-81. Mem. Reynoldsburg Com. for Prevention of Substance Abuse, 1981; mem. resource bd. Spl. Wish Found. Grantee Tchr. Center of Franklin County, 1982. Mem. Reynoldsburg Edn. Assn. (exec. com.), Ohio Edn. Assn., NEA, Assn. Supervision and Curriculum Devel., Central Ohio Assn. Curriculum Devel. and Supervision, Bowling Green State U. Alumni Assn., Phi Delta Kappa. Eastern Orthodox. Home: 5880 Parliament Dr Columbus OH 43213 Office: 2300 Baldwin Dr Reynoldsburg OH 43068

LEVANDOWSKI, BARBARA SUE, educational administrator; b. Chgo., Mar. 16, 1948; d. Earl F. and Ann (Klee) L.; B.A., North Park Coll., 1970; M.S., No. Ill. U., 1975, Ed.D., 1979; Tchr., Round Lake (Ill.) Sch. Dist., 1970-75; tchr., asst. prin. Schaumburg (Ill.) Sch. Dist., 1975—; curriculum cons. Spring Grove (Ill.) Sch. Dist., 1980—; presenter various confs. Contbr. articles to profl. jours. Mem. staff Round Lake Park Dist., 1973—. Recipient numerous awards for excellence in teaching. Mem. Ill. Assn. Women Adminstrs., Ill. Assn. for Supervision and Curriculum Devel. (chmn. research com.), Assn. Supervision and Curriculum Devel., Ill. Prins. Assn., Phi Delta Kappa. Mem. editorial bd. Ill. Sch. Research and Devel. Jour., 1981—. Home: 508 Garfield St Ingleside IL 60041 Office: 1100 Laurie Ln Hanover Park IL 60103

LEVANDOWSKI, DONALD WILLIAM, geosciences educator, administrator; b. Stockett, Mont., Dec. 20, 1927; s. Anthony and Ann (Hudak) L.; m. Martha Mary Midlik, June 4, 1955; children—Mari Ann, Laura Joan. B.S., Mont. Coll. Mining, Sci. and Tech., 1950; M.S., U. Mich., 1952, Ph.D., 1956. Cert. profl. geol. scientist. Adminstrv. asst. Chevron Oil Field Research Co., La Habra, Calif., 1963-65; prof. Purdue U., West Lafayette, Ind., 1967—, assoc. head dept. geosciences, 1970-78, head dept. geosciences, 1978—; research geologist Chevron Oil Field Research Co., La Habra, 1955-65; research geophysicist Standard Oil Co. of Calif., La Habra, 1965-67. Fellow Geol. Assn. Can., Geol. Soc. Am., Explorers Club; mem. Am. Assn. Petroleum Geologists, Am. Soc. Photogrammetry, Am. Inst. Profl. Geologists. Republican. Roman Catholic. Home: 3711 Capilano Dr West Lafayette IN 47906 Office: Purdue Univ Dept of Geosciences West Lafayette IN 47907

LEVEY, DON, advertising filmmaker and photographer; b. Chgo., July 30, 1947; s. Nathan and Grace (Bloom) L.; m. Rebecca Maria LaMake, Apr. 23, 1983. Producer Don Levey Studio, Chgo., 1970—. Mem. Assn. Ind. Comml. Producers. Avocations: martial arts; weightlifting; antique autos. Office: Don Levey Studio Inc 15 W Delaware Pl Chicago IL 60610

LEVICH, CALMAN, physicist, radiation and reactor physics consultant; b. Iowa City, Iowa; s. Jacob and Edith (Subotnik) L.; m. Eva B. Lindas, Sept. 22, 1946; children—Judith, David, Rebecca, Miriam. B.S., Morningside Coll., 1949; Ph.D., Catholic U. of Am., 1966. Research projects dir. Armed Forces Radiobiology Research Inst., Bethesda, Md., 1961-68; chmn. physics dept. Seton Hall U., S. Orange, N.J., 1968-70; prof., chmn. physics dept. Central Mich. U., Mount Pleasant, 1970-83; v.p. Caleb Assocs., Pentwater, Mich., 1983—; mem. Mich. State Radiation Adv. Bd., Lansing, 1982—; mem. Mich. State Task Force on High Level Waste, Lansing, 1983—. Contbr. articles to profl. jours. Served to comdr. USN, 1941-67. Mem. Radiation Research Soc., Biophysical Soc., Am. Assn. Physics Tchrs., AAUP, AAAS, Sigma Xi. Office: Caleb Assocs 55 E Lowell St Pentwater MI 49449

LEVIN, CARL, U.S. senator; b. Detroit, June 28, 1934; s. Saul R. and Bess L. (Levinson) L.; B.A., Swarthmore Coll., 1956; LL.B., Harvard U., 1959; m. Barbara Halpern, Aug. 31, 1961; children—Kate, Laura, Erica. Admitted to Mich. bar, 1959, practice in Detroit, 1959-64; asst. atty. gen., gen. counsel Mich. Civil Rights Commn., Detroit, 1964-67; chief dep. defender Detroit Defender's Office, 1968-69; mem. Detroit City Council, 1970-77, pres., 1974-77; U.S. Senator from Mich., 1979—. Instr. Wayne U. Law Sch., Detroit, 1970, U. Detroit, 1966, 68. Mem. Am., Mich., Detroit bar assns. Democrat. Office: 459 Russell Senate Office Bldg Washington DC 20510

LEVIN, CHARLES L., state supreme court justice, lawyer; b. Detroit, Apr. 28, 1926; s. Theodore and Rhoda (Katzin) L.; m. Patricia Joyce Oppenheim, Feb. 21, 1956; children—Arthur, Amy, Fredrick. B.A., U. Mich., 1946, LL.B., 1947; LL.D., Detroit Coll. Law. Bar: Mich. ptnr. firm Levin, Levin, Garvett & Dill, 1951-66; judge Mich. Ct. Appeals, 1966-72; justice Mich. Supreme Ct., Southfield, 1973—. Fellow ABA; mem. Am. Law Inst., Am. Judicature Soc., State Bar Mich., Assn. Bar City of N.Y. Jewish. Office: 26555 Evergreen Rd 1008 Travelers Tower Southfield MI 48076*

LEVIN, DEBBE ANN, lawyer; b. Cin., Mar. 11, 1954; d. Abram Asher and Selma Ruth (Herlands) L. B.A., Washington U., St. Louis, 1976; J.D., U. Cin., 1979; LL.M., NYU, 1983. Bar: Ohio. Staff atty. U.S. Ct. Appeals 6th Circuit, Cin., 1979-82; assoc. Schwartz, Manes & Ruby Co., L.P.A., Cin., 1983—. Recipient Judge Alfred Mack prize U. Cin., 1979. Mem. ABA, Cin. Bar Assn., Ohio Bar Assn., Order of Coif. Office: Schwartz Manes & Ruby Co LPA 36 E 4th St Cincinnati OH 45202

LEVIN, JON, bookstore executive; b. Lindsborg, Kans., Dec. 16, 1935; s. Joseph A. and Amy E. (Nelson) L.; m. Lila J. Orme, Aug. 19, 1956; children—Jeffrey, Steve, Susan. B.S. in Bus. Adminstrn., Kans. State U., 1957. Book mgr. Varney's Bookstore, Inc., Manhattan, Kans., 1957-74, gen. mgr., 1974—; dir. Citizens Bank, Manhattan. Pres. United Way, Manhattan, 1969-70; bd. dirs. Red Cross, Manhattan, 1978; trustee Leadership Kans., Topeka, 1984—. Served to 2d lt. U.S. Army, 1960-62. Recipient Outstanding Service award United Cerebral Palsy of Kans., 1969, 70. Mem. Nat. Assn. Coll. Stores, Kans. Retail Council (bd. dirs. 1982—); Manhattan C. of C. (bd. dirs.). Republican. Presbyterian. Club: Rotary (bd. dirs. 1970-71). Avocation: golf. Office: Varney's Bookstore Inc 623 N Manhattan Ave Manhattan KS 66502

LEVIN, MYRON JAME, physician, educator, consultant; b. Los Angeles, Mar. 6, 1912; s. Ben S. and Elsie (Jame) L.; m. Anita Dresner, July 7, 1940; children—Harold D., Marilyn Jean. B.S., U. Ill., 1935, M.S. in Bacteriology, 1937, M.D., 1937. Diplomate Am. Bd. Anesthesiology. Intern, Woodlawn Hosp., Chgo., 1937-38; resident in anesthesiology Hines VA Hosp. (Ill.), 1949-51, asst. chief anesthesiology, 1951-72, cons., 1951—; dir. anesthesiology Am. Hosp., Chgo., 1956-70; chmn. anesthesiology Gottlieb Meml. Hosp., Melrose Park, Ill., 1961-78, cons., 1978—; sr. attending anesthesiology, chmn. dept. Pain Mgmt. Clinic, Cook County Hosp., Chgo., 1981—; clin. assoc. prof. anesthesiology U. Ill. Coll. Medicine, Chgo., 1951-75; clin. prof. anesthesiology Chgo. Med. Sch., 1975—, acting chmn. anesthesiology, 1980-81; cons. VA Hosp., North Chicago, Ill., 1979—; field rep. Joint Commn. on Accreditation of Hosps., 1976-78. Contbr. articles to profl. jours., chpts. to books. Served to capt. M.C., AUS, 1942-46. Fellow Am. Coll. Anesthesiologists, Internat. Coll. Surgeons; mem. AMA, Chgo. Med. Soc., Ill. State Med. Soc., Am. Soc. Anesthesiologists, Ill. Soc. Anesthesiologists, Chgo. Soc. Anesthesiologists (pres. 1956-57). Lodges: Masons, Shriners. Home: 1280 Rudolph Rd #3H Northbrook IL 60062 Office: Cook County Hosp Dept Anesthesiology 1835 W Harrison St Chicago IL 60612

LEVIN, PATRICIA OPPENHEIM, educator; b. Detroit, Apr. 5, 1932; d. Royal A. and Elsa (Freeman) Oppenheim; A.B. in History, U. Mich., 1954, Ph.D., 1981; M.Ed., Marygrove Coll., 1973; m. Charles L. Levin, Feb. 21, 1956; children—Arthur David, Amy Suzanne, Fredrick Stuart. Substitute tchr. Oak Park (Mich.) Schs., 1955-67; substitute tchr. Detroit Pub. Schs., 1960-67, reading and learning disabled tchr., cons., 1967-76; guest lectr. Marygrove Coll., 1974-76, coordinator spl. edn., 1976—; lectr., conf. presenter. Mem. Mich. regional bd. ORT, 1965-68; v.p. women's aux. Children's Hosp. Mich.; bd. dirs. women's com. United Community Services, 1968-73; women's com. Detroit Grand Opera Assn., 1970-75; mem. coms. Detroit Symphony Orch., Detroit Inst. Arts; torch drive area chmn. United Found., 1967-70. Mem. Friends of Detroit Pub. Library, NAACP (life), Internat. Reading Assn., Nat. Council Tchrs. of English, Assn. Supervision and Curriculum Devel., Nat. Assn. Edn. of Young Children, Assn. Children and Adults with Learning Disabilities, Mich. Assn. Children with Learning Disabilities (edn. v.p., exec. bd.), Council Exceptional Children, Assn. Gifted and Talented Children Mich., Mich. Assn. Emotionally Disturbed Children, Orton Soc., Phi Delta Kappa, Pi Lambda Theta. Home: 30840 Running Stream #1 Farmington Hills MI 48018 Office: 8425 W McNichols St Detroit MI 48221

LEVIN, PETER FREDERIC, financial executive; b. Flushing, N.Y., Apr. 22, 1936; s. Leo C. and Ruth (Feitelberg) L.; m. Mary Wolf, Aug. 27, 1960; children—Kate, Jean, Anne. B.A. in History, Williams Coll., 1958; J.D., U. Mich., 1961. Chartered fin. analyst. Trader rep. David J. Joseph Co., N.Y.C., 1962-68; stockbroker Gradison & Co., Cin., 1968-70; sales mgr. Bartlett & Co., Cin., 1970—. Bd. dirs. Jewish Fedn., Cin., 1980-84, Am. Jewish Com., Cin., 1984—, Cin. Psycoarpeytic Found., 1981-84; singer May Festival Chorus, Cin., 1984—. Mem. Fin. Analysts Soc., Ohio Bar Assn. Jewish. Avocations: skiing, horseback riding, piano, singing. Home: 1 Linden Ln Cincinnati OH 45215 Office: Bartlett & Co 120 E 4th St Cincinnati OH 45202

LEVIN, SANDER MARTIN, congressman; b. Detroit, Sept. 6, 1931; s. Saul Levin and Bess (Levinson) L.; m. Victoria Schlafer, 1957. B.A., U. Chgo., 1952; M.A., Columbia U. 1954; LL.B., Harvard U. 1957. Supr. Oakland County Bd. Suprs., 1961-64; mem. Mich. Senate, 1965-70; fellow Kennedy Sch. Govt., Inst. Politics, Harvard U., 1975; asst. adminstr. AID, Washington, 1977-81; assoc., ptnr. firm Schwartz, O'Hare & Levin, 1957-64, Jaffe, Snider, Raitt, Garrett & Heuer, 1971-74, Beer & Boltz, 1975-77; adj. prof. law, Wayne State U., Detroit, 1971-74; mem. 98th-99th Congresses from 17th dist. Mich. Chmn. Mich. Democratic Com., 1968-69. Address: 17117 W 9 Mile Rd Southfield MI 48075

LEVINE, BARUCH, social worker, consultant; b. Windsor, Ont., Can., Sept. 10, 1933; came to U.S., 1948; naturalized, 1950; s. Maurice and Shifrah Levine; m. Virginia Gallogle, Oct. 20, 1974; children—Shauna, David, Richard. B.S., U. Ill., 1954; M.S.W., U. Ill.-Chgo., 1956; Ph.D., U. Chgo., 1968. Asst. prof. U. Chgo., 1964-71; assoc. prof. U. Ill.-Chgo., 1971—; pvt. practice social work, Chgo., 1969—; local, state, nat. and internat. mental health and social welfare service delivery systems cons., 1963—. Author: Fundamentals of Group Treatment, 1967, Group Psychotherapy Practice and Development, 1979. Mem. Nat. Assn. Social Workers (past nat. chmn. group work). Home: 1440 N Dearborn Chicago IL 60610

LEVINE, FREDERICK HUGH, cardiovascular surgeon; b. N.Y.C., May 9, 1943; s. Alexander Benjamin and Thelma (Marcus) L.; m. Patricia Beverly Zimmerman, July 3, 1965; children—Shira, Hallie. A.B., Columbia U., 1964; M.D., Harvard U., 1968. Diplomate Am. Bd. Surgery, Am. Bd. Thoracic Surgery. Intern and resident in surgery Mass. Gen. Hosp., Boston, 1968-75, resident in cardiovascular and thoracic surgery, 1976; instr., asst. prof. surgery Mass. Gen. Hosp., Harvard Med. Sch., Boston, 1977-81; chmn. dept. cardiovascular and thoracic surgery Sinai Hosp. of Detroit, 1981—; assoc. clin. prof. surgery Wayne State U., Detroit, 1981—. Contbr. articles to med. jours. Served to lt. comdr. USPHS, 1970-72. NIH grantee, 1977-81. Mem. Assn. for Acad. Surgery, AMA, N.Y. Acad. Scis., Am. Heart Assn., Am. Coll. Cardiology, ACS, Soc. Thoracic Surgeons, Soc. Univ. Surgeons, Am. Assn. for Thoracic Surgery, Internat. Cardiovascular Soc. Jewish. Office: Sinai Hosp of Detroit 6767 W Outer Dr Detroit MI 48235

LEVINE, JEFFREY LURIE, real estate executive, lawyer; b. Springfield, Ohio, June 1, 1951; s. Martin A. and Harriett (Lurie) L.; m. Ellen Martha Kepnes, June 2, 1974; children—Jeffrey Kyle, Peter Kepnes. B.S., Miami U., Ohio, 1973; J.D., Capital U., 1976. Bar: Ohio 1976. Vice-pres., counsel Levine Realty Co., Springfield, 1976-83, pres., 1983—; prin. Convest Mgmt. Corp., Columbus, Ohio; mng. ptnr. Main Assocs., Springfield, Southwest Realty Assocs., Springfield; officer, dir. Assoc. Real Estate Investors, Inc., Springfield, Levine Investment Co., Springfield; pres. Real Estate Ctr. Assocs., Inc., Springfield; exec. v.p. Feesavers, Inc., Springfield; ptnr. Second Equity Co., Springfield; dir. Huntington Nat. Bank, Springfield, Fin. Land Corp., Springfield. Bd. dirs. Core Renewal Corp., Springfield; mem. fin. adv. com. Mercy Med. Ctr.; trustee Friends of Mercy, United Way Clark County, 1980; mem. exec. com. Springfield Arts Ctr., also chmn. devel. com.; mem. exec. bd. Clark County chpt. ARC, also chmn. personnel com. Mem. ABA, Ohio Bar Assn., Springfield Bar and Law Library Assn., Springfield Real Estate Bd., Ohio Assn. Realtors, Internat. Council Shopping Ctrs., Nat. Assn. Realtors. Republican. Jewish. Clubs: Springfield Country, University (Springfield). Lodge: Rotary (Springfield). Avocations: tennis; skiing. Office: 501 W High St PO Box 1848 Springfield OH 45501

LEVINE, MYRON, genetics educator, researcher, consultant; b. Bklyn., July 28, 1926; s. Irving and Sarah (Perr) L.; m. Barbara Ruth Kohn, Feb. 4, 1950; children—Peter Arthur, Sura. B.A., Bklyn. Coll., 1947; Ph.D., Ind. U., 1952. Research assoc. U. Ill.-Urbana, 1954-56; from asst. to assoc. Brookhaven Nat. Lab., Upton, N.Y., 1956-61; vis. assoc. prof. UCLA, 1960; assoc. prof. human genetics U. Mich., Ann Arbor, 1961-67, prof. human genetics, 1967—; Commonwealth Fund fellow Inst. Molecular Biology, U. Geneva, 1966-67; vis. scientist Imperial Cancer Research Fund, London, 1973-74, Cambridge U., Eng., 1982. Contbr. articles to profl. jours. Recipient Disting. Faculty Achievement award U. Mich., 1980. Mem. Genetics Soc. Am., Am. Soc. Microbiology, Am. Soc. Virology, AAUP, Sigma Xi. Home: 356 Hilldale Dr Ann Arbor MI 48105 Office: U Mich Dept Human Genetics 1137 E Catherine Ann Arbor MI 48109

LEVINE, NATHALIE CHRISTIAN, performing arts adminstr., choreographer, ballerina; b. Las Animas, Colo., July 21, 1929; d. Fleming V. and Juanita J. (Jobe) Christian; B.A. in Polit. Sci., UCLA, 1958; student Royal Ballet Sch., London, 1959-60; student Michel Panaieff, Los Angeles, 1945-48, Mia Slavenska, Los Angeles, 1948-53, Rozelle Frey, Los Angeles, and others; m. Victor Theodore LeVine, July 19, 1958; children—Theodore Vincent, Nicole Jeanette. Tchr., Wilcoxon Sch. of Dance, Los Angeles, 1946-48, Sutro-Seyler Studio, Los Angeles, 1949-51; mem. faculty Brown Gables Conservatory of the Arts, Los Angeles, 1952-61, Ecole de Danse, Cameroun, W. Africa, 1961-62; pvt. tchr. ballet and dance, St. Louis, 1963-67; tchr. dance Dawn Quist Sch. of Dance, Accra, Ghana, W. Africa, 1969-70; mem. faculty dance div. Washington U., St. Louis, 1967-69, 70-71; prin. tchr. Le Vine Acad. of Ballet, St. Louis, 1964—; co-artistic dir. St. Louis Dance Theater, 1966-72, also choreographer, 1966-72; founder Metropolitan Ballet of St. Louis, 1974, artistic dir., 1974—; participant planning dance performances, St. Louis, 1964—; cons. to Phelps County Dance Assn., 1978-79, Rolla (Mo.) Bd. of Parks and Recreation, 1978-79; guest tchr. various dance schs. and theaters, 1964—; soloist Ballet de Los Angeles, 1948-49; soloist Radio City Music Hall, N.Y.C., 1952-53; appeared in various TV and stage prodns., Los Angeles, 1946-48, Santa Monica, Calif., 1945-50, Laguna Beach, Calif., 1946-51; appeared in Greatest Show on Earth, other motion pictures, 1950-52. Mem. Nat. Soc. Arts and Letters, Phi Beta Kappa. Office: 11607 Olive Blvd St Louis MO 63141

LEVINE, NEIL MARSHAL, obstetrician, gynecologist, medical educator; b. N.Y.C., Nov. 9, 1947; s. Victor and Beatrice (Sclar) L.; m. Judith Klein, June 21, 1975; children—Rachel Beth, Ari Daniel. B.S., Tulane U., 1968; D.O., Chgo. Coll. Osteo. Medicine, 1974; student Cleve. Marshall Coll. Law. Diplomate Nat. Bd. Examiners Osteo. Physicians and Surgeons. Intern, Chgo. Osteo. Hosp., 1974-75; resident in obstetrics and gynecology Normandy Hosps., St. Louis, 1976-79; asst. prof. obstetrics and gynecology Tex. Coll. Osteo. Medicine, Fort Worth, 1979-81; practice osteo. medicine specializing in obstetrics and gynecology, Lakewood, Ohio, 1981—; tchr. med. students dept. obstetrics and gynecology Fairview Hosp., Cleve. Recipient Obstetrics and Gynecology award Chgo. Coll. Osteo. Medicine, 1974; Research award Mead Johnson Co., 1977, 78. Mem. Am. Osteo. Assn., Ohio Osteo. Assn., Am. Fertility Soc., Am. Assn. Gynecologic Laparoscopists. Jewish. Contbr. articles to profl. jours. Office: 1392 Warren Rd Suite 2 Lakewood OH 44107

LEVINE, NORMAN DION, parasitologist, protozoologist, educator; b. Boston, Nov. 30, 1912; s. Max and Adele (Daen) L.; m. Helen Marie Saxon, Mar. 2, 1935. B.S., Iowa State Coll., 1933; Ph.D., U. Calif.-Berkeley, 1937. With Coll. Vet. Medicine, U. Ill., Urbana, 1937—, now prof. emeritus, Author: Protozoan Parasites of Domestic Animals and Man, 1961, 2d edit. 1973; Nematode Parasites of Domestic Animals and of Man, 1968, 2d edit., 1980; Textbook of Veterinary Parasitology, 1978; Veterinary Protozoology, 1985. Author and editor: Malaria in the Interior Valley of North America, 1964; Human Ecology, 1975. Editor: Pavlovsky's Natural Nidality of Transmissible Diseases, 1966; The Ecology of Animals, 1972. Contbr. numerous sci. papers to profl. publs. Served to maj. U.S. Army, 1942-46; PTO. Decorated Bronze Star, Philippine Liberation medal. Mem. Soc. Protozoologists (pres. 1959-60), Am. Microscopical Soc. (pres. 1968-69), Ill. Acad. Sci. (pres. 1966-67), World Assn. Advancement Vet. Parasitology, Am. Soc. Parasitologists (pres. 1980), Phi Sigma. Home: 702 LaSell Dr Champaign IL 61820 Office: Coll Vet Medicine U Ill Urbana IL 61801

LEVINE, RANDALL STEWART, lawyer; b. Ann Arbor, Mich., Apr. 27, 1954; s. Alvin and Blanche (Cutler) L.; m. Sharan Lee. B.A., Mich. State U., 1976; J.D., Cooley Law Sch., Lansing, 1979. Bar: Mich. 1979, U.S. Dist. Ct. (we. dist.) Mich. 1981. Asst. prosecutor Barry County, Hastings, Mich., 1980-82; assoc. Vlachos, Jerkins & Hurley, Kalamazoo, 1983—. Mem. Nat. Assn. Criminal Def. Lawyers, Assn. Trial Lawyers Am., ABA, Kalamazoo County Trial Lawyers Assn. Jewish. Office: Vlachos Jerkins & Hurley 729 Academy St Kalamazoo MI 49007

LEVING, JEFFERY MARK, matrimonial lawyer; b. Chgo., July 2, 1951; s. Al and Rebecca Leving; B.S., So. Ill. U., 1974; J.D., Chgo.-Kent Coll. Law, 1979. Bar: Ill. 1979, U.S. Dist. Ct. (no. dist.) Ill. 1979, U.S. Ct. Appeals (7th cir.) 1980. Fed. tax law editor Commerce Clearing House, Chgo., 1979-80; staff atty. Chgo. Vol. Legal Services, 1980-81; sole practice, Chgo., 1981—; guest speaker various radio and TV programs. Mem. Chgo. Bar Assn. (matrimonial law com.), Ill. Bar Assn. (commendation and recognition 1983), Fathering Support Services, Decalogue Soc. Democrat. Jewish. Office: 123 W Madison Suite 606 Chicago IL 60603

LEVINS, MICHAEL, clinical psychologist; b. Chgo., Sept. 14, 1949; s. Milton and Mildred (Greenberg) L.; divorced. Ph.D., Calif. Sch. Profl. Psychology, 1980. Cert. clin. psychologist, Ill., Wis. Intern, Calif. Men's Colony Prison, San Luis Obispo, 1976-77, Fresno (Calif.) VA Hosp., 1977-78, Visalia (Calif.) Community Mental Health Clinic, 1978-79; cons. Midwest Actors' Equity Assn., Chgo., 1980, Faith Ch. Crisis Ctr., Chgo., 1980, Transition Midwest Gender Identity Agy., Evanston, Ill., 1980-81; staff psychologist Du Page County (Ill.) Dept. Health, 1982; pvt. practice clin. psychologist, Chgo., 1979—; chief psychologist Ill. Youth Ctr., St. Charles, 1983—; staff therapist Edgewater-Uptown Community Mental Health Ctr., Chgo., 1982-83. Mem. Am. Psychol. Assn., Ill. Psychol. Assn., Nat. Register Health Service Providers in Psychology. Office: 333 N Michigan Ave Suite 2121 Chicago IL 60601

LEVINSKAS, GEORGE JOSEPH, toxicologist; b. Tarriffville, Conn., July 9, 1924; s. Joseph John and Frances Julia (Eurkunas) L.; Sr.; m. Ruth Irene Hublitz, Dec. 28, 1946; children—Robert John, Nancy Jane Levinskas Armstrong, Edward Joseph. A.B., Wesleyan U., Middletown, Conn., 1949; Ph.D., U. Rochester. 1953. Diplomate Am. Bd. Toxicology, Acad. Toxicological Scis. Research assoc. atomic energy project U. Rochester (N.Y.), 1952-53; research assoc., lectr., then asst. prof. Grad. Sch. Pub. Health, U. Pitts., 1953-58; chief indsl. toxicologist, dir. environ. health lab., central med. dept. Am. Cyanamid Co., Stamford, Conn. and Princeton, N.J., 1958-71; mgr., then dir. environ. assessment and toxicology, dept. medicine and environ. health Monsanto Co., St. Louis, 1971—. Served to 2d lt. U.S. Army, 1943-46, ETO. AEC fellow, 1949-52. Fellow AAAS; mem. Soc. Toxicology (charter mem.), Am. Chem. Soc., Am. Indsl. Hygiene Assn., Environ. Mutagen Soc., Am. Assn. Pharmacology and Exptl. Therapeutics, N.Y. Acad. Scis., Phi Beta Kappa, Sigma Xi. Avocations: Woodworking, gardening. Office: Monsanto Co G2WE Dept Medicine and Environ Health 800 N Lindbergh Blvd Saint Louis MO 63167

LEVINTHAL, MARK, biology educator, research scientist; b. Bklyn., Mar. 3, 1941; s. Louis and Bertha (Nissenbaum) L.; m. Maxine Kassiola, Dec. 23, 1963; children—Peter Steven, Sarita. B.A., Bklyn. Coll., 1962; Ph.D., Brandeis U., 1966. Postdoctoral fellow Johns Hopkins U., Balt., 1966-68; staff fellow NIH, Bethesda, Md., 1968-72; assoc. prof. biology Purdue U., West Lafayette, Ind., 1973—. Contbr. articles to profl. jours. Coordinator New Mobilization to End War, Washington, 1971; chmn. Moratorium Com. NIH/NIMH, Bethesda, 1969. NIH grantee 1973-76, fellow, 1965-66. Mem. N.Y. Acad. Scis., Genetics Soc. Am., Am. Soc. Microbiology Socita Italiano Biologia Moleculare, Sigma Xi. Buddist. Club: Bklyn. (Lafayette). Avocations: bicycling; baseball. Home: 909 Sarasota Dr Lafayette IN 47905 Office: Purdue U Dept Biol Scis West Lafayette IN 47907

LEVITAN, THOMAS, college official; b. New Orleans, Mar. 29, 1951; s. Samuel Theodore and Gertrude Rachel (Koniarski) L. B.A., La. State U., 1973; M.Ed., U. Houston, 1978. Activities advisor U. Houston, 1973-76; program dir. Northwestern U., Evanston, Ill., 1976-77; asst. dean students, union dir. Macalester Coll., St. Paul, 1977—; cons. on leadership and group tng. to various other univs. Contbr. articles to profl. jours. Mem. zoning task force St. Paul Planning Commn., 1982; bd. dirs. St. Paul United Jewish Fund and Council, 1984—, chmn. campus services com., 1982—. Mem. Assn. Coll. Unions Internat. (internat. conf. program com. 1978, 80, regional conf. program com. 1982, 83), Assn. Coll. Personnel Adminstrs. Avocations: reading fiction and travel essays; attending concerts. Home: 1314 Grand Ave Saint Paul MN 55105 Office: Macalester Coll 1600 Grand Ave Saint Paul MN 55105

LEVITAN-GERSON, DEBORAH ANNE, obstetrician-gynecologist; b. N.Y.C., July 18, 1952; d. James Abraham and Ruth Terry (White) Levitan; m. Stanton Lawrence Gerson, June 18, 1976; children—Ruth Sarah, James Nathan. B.A., Yale U., 1973; M.D., Harvard U., 1977. Intern, Hosp. U. of Pa., Phila., 1977-78, resident in ob-gyn, 1977-81; clin. instr. ob-gyn dept. Hahneman Med. Sch., Phila., 1981-83; practice medicine specializing in ob-gyn, Ohio, 1983—. Fellow Am. Coll. Ob-Gyn. Home: 2463 Snowberry Ln Pepper Pike OH 44124 Office: 3619 Park East Beachwood OH 44122 also 34055 Solon Rd Solon OH 44139

LEVITAS, JOHN ROBERT, orthopedic surgeon; b. Green Bay, Wis., Dec. 18, 1924; s. Isaac Edward and Gloria Faye (Zucker) L.; m. Marcia Corinne Siegel, June 19, 1951; children—Cynthia, Paul, Lori, Edward. Student U. Wis., 1942-44; B.S., Northwestern U., 1948, M.D. 1949. Diplomate Am. Bd. Orthopedic Surgery. Intern, Cook County Hosp., Chgo., 1948-50; resident Cin. Jewish Hosp.-1950-52, U. Cin., 1954-57; practice medicine, specializing in orthopedic surgery, Louisville, 1957-59, Cin., 1959—; mem. staffs Cin. Jewish Hosp., Cin. Children's Hosp., Holmes Hosp., Univ. Hosp., Providence Hosp.; asst. clin. prof. orthopedic surgery U. Cin. Served with M.C., USAF, 1952-54. Fellow ACS, Am. Acad. Orthopedic Surgeons. Home: 6745 E Beechlands St Cincinnati OH 45237 Office: 400 Melish Ave Cincinnati OH 45229

LEVITETZ, CARLETON SAMUELS, food company executive; b. Chgo., Dec. 9, 1931; s. Charles L. and Fae (Samuels) L.; m. Judith Goldman, Jan. 22, 1977; children—Jeffrey Allen, Debra Lynn; 1 stepchild, Deborah Figeura. B.B.A., U. Mich., 1953. Gen. sales mgr. Hinckley & Schmitt, Chgo., 1957-60; regional sales mgr. Swanee Paper Co., N.Y.C., 1960-62; pres. Purity Bottling Co., Schaumburg, Ill., 1962—. Founder Falcon Hockey Assn., Deerfield, Ill., 1964; dist. adminstrv. asst. U.S. Coast Guard Aux., Chgo., 1977-84. Served with U.S. Army, 1953-55. Mem. Grocery Mfrs. Sales Execs., Internat. Bottled Water Assn., Am. Legion. Republican. Jewish. Clubs: Waukegan Yacht, U. Mich. (Chgo.). Avocation: boating. Home: 2397 Riverwoods Rd Riverwoods IL 60015 Office: Purity Bottling Co Inc 1220 Remington Road Schaumburg IL 60195

LEVITT, LEROY PAUL, psychiatrist; b. Plymouth, Pa., Jan. 8, 1918; s. Samuel and Paula (Goldstein) L.; B.S., Pa. State U., 1939; M.B., Chgo. Med. Sch., 1943, M.D., 1944; m. Jane Glaim, Apr. 7, 1971; children—Steven, Susan, Jeremy, Sara. Intern, Beth David Hosp., N.Y.C., 1943-44; resident Elgin (Ill.) State Hosp., Ill. Neuropsychiat. Inst., Inst. for Juvenile Research, vet. Rehab. Center, 1947-49; practice medicine specializing in psychiatry, Chgo., 1949—; dir. psychiat. edn. Chgo. Med. Sch., 1964-66, dean, 1966-73, prof., 1966-73; dir. dept. mental health and devel. disabilities State of Ill., 1973-76; prof. psychiatry Rush Med. Coll., Chgo., 1976—, chmn., 1982—; v.p. med. affairs Mt. Sinai Hosp. Med. Center, Chgo., 1976-82, chmn. dept. psychiatry, 1982—; pres. Chgo. Bd. Health, 1979-83. Served to capt. M.C., U.S. Army, 1944-46. Recipient Disting. Alumnus award Chgo. Med. Sch., 1970; named Prof. of Yr., Chgo. Med. Sch., 1964; Tchr. of the Year, Ill. State Psychiat. Inst., 1966; Gold Medal Sci. award Phi Lambda Kappa, 1974; WHO fellow in geriatrics, 1970; diplomate Am. Bd. Psychiatry and Neurology. Mem. Am. Psychiat. Assn., Am. Coll. Psychoanalysts (pres. 1983), Ill. Psychiat. Soc., Internat. Psychoanalytic Assn., Am. Psychoanalytic Assn., Am. Coll. Psychiatrists, Midwest Profs. Psychiatry, Nat. Assn. State Mental Health Dirs., Inst. Medicine Chgo., AMA, Chgo. Psychoanalytic Soc., Council Med. Deans. Jewish. Contbr. articles and book revs. to profl. jours. Home: 1626 St Michael's Ct Chicago IL 60614 Office: Mt Sinai Hosp Med Center California Ave at 15th St Chicago IL 60608

LEVITT, MORTON HILL, physician, hospital administrator; b. N.Y.C., May 28, 1946; s. Benjamin and Lillian (Bernard) L.; married; children—Lisa Michelle, Nicole Valerie, Tamara Lynn. B.S. in Engring., Princeton U., 1968; M.D., Duke U., 1972; M.Health Adminstrn., 1981. Intern, Duke U. Hosp., Durham, N.C., 1972-73, resident in pathology, 1973-74; practice medicine specializing in pathology, 1972—; assoc. div. of cancer cause and prevention Nat. Cancer Inst., Bethesda, Md., 1974-80, acting dir. gastrointestinal tract prostate cancer program, 1977-79; spl. asst. to chmn. dept. health adminstrn. Duke U., Durham, N.C., 1982; asst v.p. Methodist Hosps. of Memphis, 1982-84; v.p. clin. services Research Med. Ctr., Kansas City, Mo., 1984-85; v.p. med. affairs Jewish Hosp., Louisville, Ky., 1985—. Served to lt. commdr. USPHS, 1974-80. Recipient C.V. Mosby award Duke U. Sch. Medicine, 1972; Physician's Recognition award AMA 1976, 1979. Fellow Coll. Am. Pathology; mem. Am. Coll. Hosp. Adminstrs., Am. Hosp. Assn., Tenn. Hosp. Assn., Assn. Mil. Surgeons U.S. Club: Pinceton of N.Y.

LEVITT, WILLIAM MARK, real estate executive; b. Detroit, Mar. 9, 1933; s. Edward Joseph and Minna (Jacobson) L.; m. Barbara Salzman, Oct. 23, 1962; 1 child, Judith Ellen. B.A., Wayne State U., 1954; J.D., U. Detroit, 1957. Bar: Mich. 1957, N.Y. 1958, Fla. 1958. Pres. Realty Services Inc., Southfield, Mich., 1984—. Mem. Mich. Bar Assn., Fla. Bar Assn., N.Y. State Bar Assn., Mich. Assn. Realtors (pres. 1972-73, Realtor of Yr. 1972), Nat. Assn. Realtors, others. Republican. Jewish. Clubs: Knollwood Country (West Bloomfield, Mich.); Standard City (Southfield). Avocations: golf; bridge. Office: Realty Services Inc 16500 North Park Dr Suite 110 Southfield MI 48075

LEVY, ARNOLD S(TUART), real estate company executive; b. Chgo., Mar. 15, 1941; s. Roy and Esther (Scheff) L.; m. Eva Cichosz, Aug. 8, 1976; children—Adam, Rachel. B.S., U. Wis., 1963; M.P.A., Roosevelt U., 1970. Dir. Neighborhood Youth Corps, Chgo., 1966-68; v.p. Social Planning Assn., Chgo., 1968-70; planning dir. Office of Mayor Chgo., 1970-74; dep. dir. Mayor's Office Manpower, Chgo., 1974-75; sr. v.p. Urban Investment & Devel. Co., Chgo., 1975—; pres. Ritz-Carlton of Chgo., 1984—; lectr. at univs. Pres. Ark, Chgo., 1970-72, Parental Stress Services, Chgo., 1978-79; del. Mid-Term Democratic Nat. Conf., Memphis, 1978; v.p. Inst. Urban Life, Chgo., 1983—. Home: 5445 N Sheridan Rd Chicago IL 60640 Office: Urban Investment & Devel Co 333 N Wacker Dr Chicago IL 60606

LEVY, JERRE, psychobiology educator; b. Birmingham, Ala., Apr. 7, 1938; s. Jerome Milton and Marie (Ullman) L.; m. Thomas Andrew Nagylaki, Jan. 30, 1969; children—Marie Basch, Todd Basch. B.A., U. Miami, 1962, M.S., 1966; Ph.D., Calif. Inst. Tech., 1970. Postdoctoral fellow U. Colo., Boulder, 1970-71, Oreg. State U., 1971-72; asst. to assoc. prof. U. Pa., Phila., 1972-77; assoc. prof. to prof. U. Chgo., 1977—. Cons. editor Jour. Exptl. Psychology: Human Perception and Peformance, 1972-84; assoc. editor Brain and Cognition, 1982—; editorial bd. Human Neurobiology, 1985—; contbr. articles to profl. jours. and books. Grantee Spencer Found. 1979—, NIMH, 1979—. Mem. Internat. Neuropsychol. Symposium, Behavior Genetics Assn. Avocations: reading, traveling. Office: Univ Chgo 5848 S University Ave Chicago IL 60637

LEVY, MARTIN BERYL, physical therapist, rehabilitation consultant, educator; b. N.Y.C., June 17, 1927; s. William Harold and Ethel Marie (Ament) L.; m. Helen E. Lipkin, June 6, 1954; children—Elizabeth, Patricia. B.S. NYU, 1951, M.A., 1956. Lic. phys. therapist, Ohio. Staff therapist Inst. Phys. Medicine and Rehab., N.Y.C., 1955, for pvt. physician, Cedarhurst, L.I., N.Y., 1956; coordinator rehab. Drake Meml. Hosp., Cin., 1957-83; dir. rehab. Community Multi-care Ctr., Fairfield, Ohio, 1983—; phys. therapy cons., mem. adv. com. home health services Cin. Health Dept. Served to 2d lt. USAF, 1952-53. Mem. Am. Phys. Therapy Assn. Jewish. Home: 840 Yorkhaven Rd Cincinnati OH 45240 Office: Community Multi-care Ctr 908 Symmes Rd Fairfield OH 45014

LEVY, MATTHEW NATHAN, physiology educator, biomedical engineering researcher; b. N.Y.C., Dec. 2, 1922; s. David Leonard and Rose (Flomenhaft) L.; m. Ruth Selma Joseph, Mar. 20, 1946; children—Donald, Garry, James. B.S., Western Reserve U., Cleve., 1943, M.D., 1945. Dept. physiology Western Reserve U., Cleve., 1949-52, Albany Med. Coll., N.Y., 1953-57; dir. research div. St. Vincent Charity Hosp., Cleve., 1957-67; chief, investigative medicine Mt. Sinai Hosp., Cleve., 1967—; prof. physiology, bio-medical engring., Case Western Res. U., Cleve., 1968—. Author: (with others) Cardiovascular Physiology, 1981, Excitation and Neural Control of the Heart, 1982, Physiology, 1983. Consulting editor: Circulation Research. Served with U.S. Army, 1943-48. Recipient Julius E. Goodman Memorial award Mt. Sinai Med. Ctr., 1974, Disting. Physiologist award Southwestern Med. Sch., 1978; Shanes Memorial lectr. Cardiac Muscle Group, 1972. Mem. Am. Physiol. Soc. (Wiggers award, 1983), Am. Heart Assn. (pres. Northeastern Ohio affiliate 1981-83). Democrat. Jewish. Avocations: tennis, photography. Home: 2439 Elmdale Rd University Heights OH 44118 Office: The Mt Sinai Medical Ctr University Circle Cleveland OH 44106

LEVY, NELSON LOUIS, physician, scientist; b. Somerville, N.J., June 19, 1941; s. Myron L. and Sylvia (Cohen) L.; m. Joanne Barnett, Dec. 21, 1963 (div. 1972); children—Scott, Erik, Jonathan; m. Louisa Douglass Stiles, Dec. 21, 1974; children—Michael, Andrew, David. B.A./B.S., Yale U., 1963; M.D., Columbia U., 1967; Ph.D., Duke U., 1972. Diplomate Am. Bd. Allergy and Immunology. Intern, U. Colo. Med. Ctr., Denver, 1967-68; resident Duke U. Med Ctr., Durham, N.C., 1970-73; research assoc. NIH, Bethesda, Md., 1968-70; asst. prof. immunology Duke U. Med. Ctr., 1972-75, assoc. prof. immunology and neurology, 1975-80, prof., 1980-81; dir. biol. research Abbott Labs., Abbott Park, Ill., 1981, v.p. research, 1981-84; pres. Nelson L. Levy Assocs., Inc., 1984—; cons. Upjohn Co., Inc., Kalamazoo, 1976-77, G.D. Searle Inc., Skokie, Ill., 1984—, Erbamont Inc., Stamford, Conn., 1984—. Editor several books. Contbr. articles to profl. publs., chpts. to books. Served with USPHS, 1968-70. Grantee Am. Cancer Soc., 1970-75, NIH, 1971-81, Nat. Multiple Sclerosis Soc., 1974-81. Mem. Am. Assn. Immunologists, Am. Assn. Cancer Research, Phi Beta Kappa, Alpha Omega Alpha, Phi Gamma Delta. Republican. Jewish. Avocations: Tennis, running, philately, car mechanics, history of art. Home and office: 1391 Concord Dr Lake Forest IL 60045

LEVY, STANLEY ROY, educational administrator; b. Bklyn., July 19, 1934; s. Abraham and Rose (Weinberger) L.; m. Joan Weinberg, June 15, 1963; children—Scott, Marcia. B.A., U. Mich., 1955, M.A., 1959, Ph.D., 1964. Assoc. dean students U. Ill., Urbana, 1968-73, asst. vice chancellor, 1973-76, assoc. vice chancellor, 1976-78, acting vice chancellor, 1978-79, vice chancellor, 1979—. Bd. dirs. Arrowhead Council Boy Scouts Am., 1983, United Way of Champaign County, 1976—. Served to 1st lt. U.S. Army, 1955-57, Germany. Mem. Am. Assn. Higher Educ., Nat. Assn. Student Personnel Adminstrs. (v.p. 1976-78). Jewish. Lodge: B'nai Brith. Home: 3006 Meadowbrook Ct Champaign IL 61821 Office: 601 E John St Champaign IL 61820

LEWERENZ, DAVID CHARLES, optometrist; b. Herington, Kans., Nov. 1, 1952; s. Victor Edward Theodore and Elsie Mary (Riffel) L.; m. Patrice Murphy, Mar. 5, 1971; children—Heather Maureen, Daniel David, Andrea Elizabeth. Student Kans. State U., 1971-73; B.S., U. Ala., 1975, O.D., 1977. Gen. practice optometry, Salina, Kans., 1977-84. Contbr. articles to profl. jours. Fellow Am. Acad. Optometry; mem. Kans. Optometric Assn., Am. Optometric Assn. United Ch. of Christ. Lodge: Lions. Home: 2307 Melrose Salina KS 67401 Office: 903 Elmhurst Salina KS 67401

LEWIN, CAROLINE TOEPFER, clinical psychologist; b. Newark, Feb. 17, 1944; d. Chester Leon Throckmorton and Caroline Amanda Lange; B.A. in Psychology (Cleve. Found. scholar), Kent State U., 1965, M.A., 1967, Ph.D. (NIMH fellow), 1969; m. William Lewin II, Sept. 10, 1979; 1 son, Neil Norval. Social worker Fallsview Mental Health Center, 1965, Sagamore Hills Children's Psychiat. Hosp., 1966; psychologist Portage County Welfare Dept., 1966-68; intern Univ. Hosps., Case Western Res. U., 1968; asst. prof., dir. student interns Slippery Rock State Coll., 1969-75; pvt. practice clin. psychology Youngstown, Ohio, 1974-80, Columbus, Ohio, 1980—; cons. Bur. Disability Determination, Bur. Vocat. Rehab., St. Vincent's Children's Center; speaker, guest lectr.; condr. workshops; ptnr. Legal Ease, Columbus. Mem. Selective Service Bd. 41. Lic. clin. psychologist, Ohio. Mem. Am. Psychol. Assn., Ohio Psychol. Assn., Psi Chi. Editor: Supplementary Readings in Applied Psychology and Human Behavior, 1970; (with Bicknell, Fox, Kirk and Sayre) Environmental Psychology, 1972. Home: 6473 Borr Ave Reynoldsburg OH 43068 Office: PO Box 2485 Columbus OH 43216

LEWIS, ASLE KINGSLEY, physician, surgeon; b. Hettinge, N.D., July 26, 1920; s. Carl William and Grace Josephine (Gronna) L.; m. Mada Hubbard Eppler, Sept. 21, 1942; children—Barry, Jon, Scott. B.A., U. N.D., 1942, B.S. in Medicine, 1943; M.D., U. Ill.-Chgo., 1944. Diplomate Am. Bd. Family Practice. Intern Los Angeles County Hosp., 1944-45; resident in ob-gyn St. Mary's Hosp., Mpls., 1946-47; preceptor ob-gyn Dakota Clinic, Fargo, N.D., 1947-50; gen. practice medicine, Lisbon, N.D., 1950—. Bd. dirs. Lisbon Pub. Schs. Served to lt. (j.g.) with USN, 1942-45. Served to lt. col. Army N.G. 1980-84. Fellow Am. Acad. Family Practice (charter); mem. Sigma Xi, Alpha Omega Alpha. Republican. Lutheran. Club: Toastmasters (Lisbon) (pres.). Lodge: Kiwanis (pres.). Avocations: hunting; golfing; commercial pilot. Office: Lisbon Clinic 819 Main St Lisbon ND 58054

LEWIS, BERNARD, dentist, consultant; b. Detroit, Jan. 5, 1938; s. Phillip and Ida Sarah (Litvack) L.; m. Sherrill Lois Marblestone, Dec. 24, 1961; children—Alicia Lynne, Randall Michael, Kenneth Evan. Student U. Mich., 1955-57, Wayne State U., 1957-58; D.D.S., U. Detroit, 1962. Gen. practice dentistry, Oak Park, Mich., 1964-65; dentist, hematologist, cons., tchr. Children's Hosp. Mich., Detroit, 1968—; dentist for pvt. corp., Warren, Mich., 1965—; lectr. on dentistry for hemophiliacs at profl. meetings, 1970—; mem. med. adv. com. Hemophilia of Mich., Ann Arbor, 1975—. Served to capt. USAF, 1962-64. Fellow Acad. Gen. Dentistry, ADA, Macomb Dental Soc., Mich. Dental Assn. Jewish. Avocations: tennis, photography, contesting, numistmatics. Home: 4330 Ramsgate Ln Bloomfield Hills MI 48013 Office: Lewis Schreibman & Rochlen PC 30825 Ryan St Warren MI 48092

LEWIS, BRINSLEY BOSWELL, sales and marketing executive; b. June 17, 1954; came to U.S., 1973; s. Alfonso Thomas and Ermine (Bacchus) L.; m. Betty Dasilva, Apr. 29, 1979. B.S., Andrews U., 1977; grad. respiratory therapy U. Chgo., 1979. Registered respiratory therapist; cert. respiratory therapy technician. Staff respiratory therapist Mercy Hosp., Benton Harbor, Mich., 1977-79; supr. respiratory therapy Suburban Hosp., Hinsdale, Ill., 1979-81; respiratory staff therapist Vita-Medics, Lombard, Ill., 1981-82, dir. patient services, 1982-83, dir. sales and mktg., 1983—. Mem. Am. Assn. Respiratory Therapy, Am. Soc. Clin. Pathologists. Seventh-day Adventist. Avocations: piano; organ. Office: Vita-Medics Ltd 651 E Butterfield St Lombard IL 60148

LEWIS, CHRISTOPHER MATTHEW, electronic company executive; b. Chgo., Sept. 19, 1952; s. John F. and Helen L. (Goss) L.; m. Janice L. Zimmerman, Sept. 5, 1981. B.S. in Computer Sci. and Math., U. Ill.-Chgo., 1976; M.B.A., DePaul U., 1982. Programmer, analyst Arthur Andersen Co., Chgo., 1976-78, Baxter Travenol Labs., Deerfield, Ill., 1978-79; systems analyst Motorola Inc., Schaumburg, Ill., 1979-82, project leader, 1982-84, project mgr., 1984—. Office: Motorola Inc 1301 Algonquin Rd Schaumburg IL 60196

LEWIS, CRAIG JAY, medical laboratory science educator; clin. lab. scientist; b. Iowa City, Sept. 7, 1951; s. Robert James and Emily Doris (Lorack) L.; B.S. in Med. Tech., Moorhead State U., 1973; M.S. in Edn., U. N.D., 1982. Cert. clin. lab. scientist. Asst. lab. supr. St. Francis Hosp., Breckenridge, Minn., 1973-74; staff technologist St. John's Hosp., Fargo, N.D., 1974-76; health occupations div. chmn., med. lab. sci. program dir. East Grand Forks (Minn.) Area Vocat. Tech. Inst., 1976—; hematologist, med. technologist, lab. safety officer United Hosp., Grand Forks, 1977-84; pvt. mgmt. and ednl. cons. in health care C.J. Lewis & Assocs., Fargo, N.D., 1984—. Asst. dist. commr. No. Lights council Boy Scouts Am., also past asst. council commr. tng. Mem. Am. Soc. Clin. Pathologists, Am. Soc. Med. Tech., N.D. Soc. Med. Tech. (edn. chmn.), NEA, Am. Vocat. Assn., Assn. M.B.A. Execs. Home: 2402 S 17th St #206 Grand Forks ND 58103 Office: CJ Lewis & Assocs Box 7304 Fargo ND 58103

LEWIS, DALE ARTHUR, insurance company executive; b. Detroit, Jan. 29, 1947; s. Robert Dale and Vernetta (Dibler) Steinmetz L.; m. Cynthia Anne Kopczyk, Apr. 21, 1971; children—Andrew D., Lisa A., Brian A. C.L.U. Agt., Aid Assn. for Lutherans, Appleton, Wis., 1971-73, bus. ins. adminstr., 1977-80; supr. Conn. Mut. Life, Detroit, 1973-75; 2d v.p. Fed. Home Life Ins. Co., Battle Creek, Mich., 1980—; pres. Decorating Systems-Great Lakes; sec.-treas. Decorating Den of Battle Creek (Mich.); mem. Calhoun County Estate Planning Council, 1980-84. Sustaining mem. Republican Nat. Com. Served with U.S. Army, 1966-68. Mem. Am. Soc. C.L.U.s (Gold Key Soc.) (pres. S. Mich. chpt.), Battle Creek C. of C., Nat. Assn. Life Underwriters, DAV (life), Midwest Tng. Dirs. Assn. (pres. 1984-85). Lutheran. Home: 149 Birch Ln Battle Creek MI 49015 Office: Fed Home Life Ins Co 78 W Michigan Mall Battle Creek MI 49017

LEWIS, DAVID RICHARD, physician, surgeon; b. Rushville, Ill., July 9, 1929; s. Dana Mendel and Gladys Elizabeth (Hersman) L.; m. Katherine Rose Governale, June 25, 1955 (dec. Apr. 1962); children—David, Lizette; Cheri Lee Kruse, Nov. 27, 1965; children—Cara, Derek. B.S., U. Ill., 1950, M.D., 1954; Diplomate Am. Bd. Surgery, Am. Bd. Thoracic Surgery. Pres. Sherman Hosp. Staff, Elgin, Ill., 1984—. Mem. AMA, Kane County Med. Soc., Chgo. Med. Soc., Ill. Med. Soc., Midwest Surg. Soc., Ill. Thoracic Surg. Soc., Am. Coll. Chest Physicians, Priestley Surg. Soc., Am. Clin. Alumni Assn., Mayo Clinic Alumni Assn. Republican. Presbyterian. Avocation: farming. Office: 860 Summit Elgin IL 60120

LEWIS, DAVID SLOAN, JR., aircraft company executive; b. North Augusta, S.C., July 6, 1917; s. David S. and Reuben (Walton) L.; student U. S.C., 1934-37; B.S. in Aero. Engring., Ga. Inst. Tech., 1939; m. Dorothy Sharpe, Dec. 20, 1941; children—Susan, David Sloan III, Robert, Andrew. Aerodynamicist, Glenn L. Martin Co., Balt., 1939-46; chief aerodynamics McDonnell Aircraft Corp., St. Louis, 1946-52, chief preliminary design, 1952-55, mgr. sales, 1955-56, mgr. projects, 1956-57, v.p. project mgmt., 1957-59, sr. v.p. ops., 1960-61, exec. v.p., 1961-62, pres., 1962-67; pres. McDonnell-Douglas Co., also chmn. Douglas Aircraft Co. div., 1967-70; chmn., chief exec. officer Gen. Dynamics Corp., 1970—; dir. Ralston Purina Co., Mead Corp., St. Louis, BankAm. Corp., San Francisco, Cessna Aircraft Co. Alderman, Ferguson, Mo., 1951-54; trustee Washington U., St. Louis. Fellow AIAA. Episcopalian. Office: Pierre Laclede Center Saint Louis MO 63105

LEWIS, DOUGLAS EDWARD, clinical toxicologist, consultant; b. Elmhurst, Ill., May 31, 1949; s. David O. and Margery Ellen (Fletcher) L.; m. Veronica Armenouhi Nichols, Aug. 7, 1982. B.A. in Chemistry, Grinnell Coll., 1972; postgrad. U. Ill. Med. Ctr., 1972-77; Ph.D., U. S.Africa, 1980. Postdoctoral fellow Ill. Masonic Med. Ctr., Chgo., 1980-82; head sect. toxicology Children's Meml. Hosp., Chgo., 1982—; asst. prof. clin. pathology Northwestern U. Med. Sch., Chgo., 1983—; clin. asst. prof. U. Ill. Med. Ctr., Chgo., 1984; v.p. tech. services Bio-Analytical Technologies, Chgo., 1985—. Contbr. articles to prof. jours. USPHS fellow, 1972. Mem. Am. Assn. Clin. Chemistry. Home: 1131 W Oakdale Ave Chicago IL 60657 Office: Children's Meml Hosp 2300 Children's Plaza Chicago IL 60614

LEWIS, EVELYN, communications and public relations executive; b. Goslar, Germany, Sept. 19, 1946; came to U.S. 1952, naturalized 1957; d. Gerson Emanuel and Sala (Mendlowicz) L. B.A., U. Ill.-Chgo., 1968; M.A., Ball State U., 1973, Ph.D., 1976. Research analyst Comptroller, State Ill., Chgo., 1977-78; lectr. polit. sci. dept. Loyola U., Chgo., 1977; asst. to commr. Dept. Human Services, Chgo., 1978-81; group mgr. communications Arthur Anderson & Co., Chgo., 1981-84; dir. communications and pub. relations Heidrick & Struggles, Inc., Chgo., 1984—. Mem. Children of the Holocaust, Chgo., 1982. Mem. Internat. Assn. Bus. Communicators, Publicity Club Chgo., Nat. Assn. Female Execs. Jewish. Club: Metropolitan (Chgo.). Avocations: writing, poetry, biking, hiking. Office: Heidrick & Struggles Inc 125 S Wacker Dr Chicago IL 60606

LEWIS, GARRY LINUEL, lawyer, real estate developer; b. Lilbourn, Mo., Dec. 4, 1946; s. William Merlin and E. Ivadell (Crawley) L.; m. Brenda Gayle Harper, June 3, 1967; children—Carrie, Drake, Benjamin, Joshua. B.A., U. Mo., 1968; J.D., 1979. Bars: Mo. 1979, U.S. Dist. Ct. (we. dist.) Mo. 1979, La. 1980, U.S. Dist. Ct. (ea. dist.) Mo. 1980, U.S. Ct. Appeals (5th cir.) 1982, U.S. Dist. Ct. (we. dist.) La. 1984. Sole practice, Columbia, Mo., 1979—; pres. Earth Resources Engring., Inc., Columbia, 1983—. Served from ensign to lt. USN, 1968-76; comdr. Res. Mem. ABA, Mo. Bar Assn., La. Bar Assn. Democrat. Mem. Pentecostal Ch. Home: 3008 Westcreek Circle Columbia MO 65201 Office: 108 Green Meadows Columbia MO 65201

LEWIS, GERALD DAVID, music educator; b. Elkhart, Ind., Dec. 14, 1922; s. Russell Kinkaid and Ruth Elnora (Horein) L.; m. Marjorie Louise Lewis, June 17, 1951; children—Julia, Scott, Jacqueline. B.S., Juilliard Sch. Music, N.Y.C., 1950; M.M., U. So. Calif., 1954. Violinist, St. Louis Symphony and Sinfoniette, 1950-53, Los Angeles Philharm., 1953-57; tchr. South Bend (Ind.) Community Schs., 1960-70; concertmaster South Bend Symphony, 1960-70; assoc. prof. violin and theory Gustavus Adolphus Coll., St. Peter, Minn., 1970—, also dir. orch.; tchr. New Eng. Music Camp, Oakland, Maine, summers 1978—; past sec. Minn. String Task Force. Served with U.S. Army, 1943-46. Decorated Bronze Star. Mem. Am. Fedn. Musicians, Music Educators Nat. Conf., Am. String Tchrs. Assn. (Gold Merit award Ind. chpt. 1964). Home: 418 N 3d St Saint Peter MN 56082 Office: Gustavus Adolphus Coll Saint Peter MN 56082

LEWIS, JAMES MICHAEL, electronics engineer; b. Ft. Wayne, Ind., Sept. 6, 1947; s. James Trueman and Ruth Margaret (Luyben) L.; m. Sandra Kay Rediger, Mar. 1, 1969; children—Shane, Mindelle. B.S. in Elec. Engring. Tech., Purdue U., Ft. Wayne, Ind., 1979. Inventory control supr. Stanscrew Dist. Ctr., Garrett, Ind., 1971-74; estimator Mid. Am. Electronics, Auburn, Ind., 1974-76; with Dana Corp., Auburn, 1976—, plant engr., 1982—. Sound technician Bible Baptist Ch., Auburn, Ind., 1982—; basketball coach Faith Christian Acad., Auburn, 1982-83. Republican. Home: 0811-CR28 Corunna IN 46730 Office: Dana Corp 5th and Brandon Sts Auburn IN 46706

LEWIS, JOHN BALLARD, agricultural products company executive; b. St. Louis, Mar. 31, 1937; s. C. Carter and Elizabeth (Ballard) L.; m. Florence Bradford Johnson, Oct. 24, 1964; children—Alice Carter, Harriet Bradford, Florence Elizabeth. A.B., Washington U., St. Louis, 1958, LL.B., 1961, M.B.A., 1962. Mgr. fin. Monsanto Agrl. Products Co., St. Louis, 1969-72, mgr. planning, 1972-74, 1977-78, projects mgr., 1974-77, 1978-81, projects dir., 1981—. Elder Covenant Presbyterian Ch., St. Louis, 1972-85; scoutmaster St. Louis council Boy Scouts Am., 1965-69; trustee Covenant Theol. Seminary, St. Louis, 1975-85. Mem. Am. Mgmt. Assn. Republican. Home: 810 S Warson Rd Saint Louis MO 63124 Office: 800 N Lindbergh C3NA Saint Louis MO 63167

LEWIS, JOSEPH DAVID, physician, surgeon, educator; b. Orange, N.J., Oct. 7, 1937; s. Joseph and Ada Elizabeth (Jones) L.; m. Judith Irene Stanier, June 25, 1960; children—Jean Evelyn, Joan Elizabeth, Joseph David II, Janet Elaine. A.B., Oberlin Coll., 1959; M.D., U. Tenn. 1962. Diplomate Am. Bd. Surgery. Intern Buffalo Gen. Hosp., 1963; resident Marquette U. Affiliated Hosps., Milw., 1966-70; from instr. to assoc. prof. surgery Med. Coll. Wis., Milw., 1970-78; assoc. clin. prof., 1978—; surgeon Gen. Clinic of West Bend, Wis., 1978—; area med. dir. Wisc. div. Am. Cancer Soc., Madison, 1979—. Contbr. articles to profl. jours. Served to surgeon USPHS, 1964-66. Fellow ACS (chpt. pres. 1981-82); Wis. Surg. Soc. (bd. dirs. 1981-84), Milw. Acad. Surgery, Wis. Med. Soc., Central Surg. Assn. Avocations: skiing, golf. Home: 668 Highland View Dr West Bend WI 53095 Office: Gen Clinic of West Bend 279 S 17th Ave West Bend WI 53095

LEWIS, LARRY LYNN, college official, minister; b. Mexico, Mo., Jan. 27, 1935; s. Artie Francis and Mary Lue (Whiteside) L.; m. Betty Jo Cockerell, Feb. 28, 1964; children—Janet Lynn, Christy Ann, Mark Ray. A.A., Hannibal-LaGrange Coll., 1954; B.A., U. Mo., 1956; B.D., Southwestern Bapt. Sem., 1960, M.R.E., 1960; D.Ministry, Luther Rice Sem., 1978. Ordained to ministry Southern Bapt. Conv., 1954; pastor Parsons Bapt. Ch., Columbus, Ohio, 1961-66, Delaware Valley Bapt. Ch., Willingboro, N.J., 1966-71; dir. religious edn. Bapt. Conv. Pa./South Jersey, Harrisburg, Pa., 1971-74; pastor Tower Grove Bapt. Ch., St. Louis, 1974-81; pres. Hannibal-LaGrange Coll., Hannibal, Mo., 1981—; minister edn., youth Tri-Village Bapt. Ch., Columbus, 1961-62; pub. sch. tchr. Columbus Pub. Sch., 1962-63; ch. growth cons. Bapt. Sunday Sch. Bd., Nashville, 1971-74; pres. Tower Grove Christian Sch., 1978-81; pres. Mo. Bapt. Pastors Conf., 1979; v.p. Southern Bapt. Pastors Conf., Southern Bapt. Conv., 1980. Bd. dirs. Hannibal YMCA. Author: The Bus Ministry, 1971; (with others) Outreach with Church Buses, 1973; Organize to Evangelize, 1980. Editor: Walking with God, 1972. Contbr. articles to various ch. mags. Mem. Mo. Edn. Assn., Hist. Hannibal Assn., Hannibal C. of C. (pres. 1985). Lodge: Hannibal Rotary. Avocation: farming. Home: 3035 Muir St Hannibal MO 63401 Office: Office of President Hannibal-LaGrange College 2800 Palmyra Rd Hannibal MO 63401-1999

LEWIS, LENA ARMSTRONG, physiologist, chemist, educator; b. Lancaster, Pa.; d. John Wythe and Lena (Armstrong) L.; A.B., Lindenwood Coll., 1931, LL.D., 1952; Med. Technologist, Lancaster Gen. Hosp., 1934; M.A., Ohio State U., 1938, Ph.D., 1940. Research asst. Ohio State U., Columbus, 1936-40, research assoc., 1940-41; research fellow in endocrinology, Cleve. Clinic Found., 1941-43, staff mem., 1943-75, emeritus, 1975—; clin. prof. chemistry Cleve. State U., 1962—. Author: Electrophoresis in Physiology, 1950, 2d edit., 1960. Editor: Handbook of Electrophoresis (4 vols.), 1980-83. Contbr. numerous articles to sci. publs. Mem. Quota Club. Fellow N.Y. Acad. Sci., Nat. Acad. Clin. Biochemistry; mem. Am. Assn. Clin. Chemistry (Behringer-Mannheim award 1974, Reiner award 1984), Endocrine Soc., Physiol. Soc., AAAS, Sigma Xi. Avocations: travel, hand crafts. Home: 386 S Belvoir Blvd South Euclid OH 44121 Office: Cleve Clinic Found 9500 Euclid Ave Cleveland OH 44106

LEWIS, LYNN L., automotive company research executive; b. Terra Alta, W.Va., Mar. 2, 1929; s. Asa Ray Lewis and Edna May Cuppett; m. Ruth Elizabeth Carter, June 12, 1954; children—Deborah, Jennifer, Cynthia, Stuart. B.S., W.Va. Wesleyan Coll., 1950; M.S., Marshall U., 1952; Ph.D., U. Tenn., 1955. Research scientist U.S. Steel Corp., Monroeville, Pa., 1955-64; sr. research scientist IBM, Yorktown Heights, N.Y., 1964-66; asst. dept. head Gen. Motors Research Labs., Warren, Mich., 1966-76, dept. head, 1976—; mem. sci. evaluation panel Nat. Bur. Standards, 1978-81; mem. sci. adv. com. Oak Ridge Nat. Lab., 1979-82. Co-editor: Determination of Gaseous Elements in Metals, 1974. Contbr. articles to profl. jours. Mem. Am. Chem. Soc. (reagent chems. com. 1980—, adv. com. analytical chemistry 1976-78, div. program chair 1978, chair 1979), ASTM, Soc. Applied Spectroscopy, Electron Microscopy Soc. Am., Sigma Xi. Home: 454 Fairfax Birmingham MI 48009 Office: Gen Motors Research Labs 12 Mile and Mound Rds Warren MI 48090

LEWIS, MICHAEL EDWARD, hospital administrator; b. Pawtucket, R.I., Apr. 23, 1950; s. Robert Henry and Ethel Irene (Nolte) L.; m. Charlotte Arleen Jackson, Aug. 10, 1974; children—Eric Jason, Michael Edward, Jennifer Elizabeth. B.A., U. R.I., 1972; M.A., U. Nev., 1978. Ednl. aide Children's Ctr. Sch., Providence, 1972-73; psychology intern Eastern State Hosp., Williamsburg, Va., 1973-74; psychology asst. Bronx VA Hosp. (N.Y.), 1974; psychology researcher Nev. State Hosp., Reno, 1974-78; instr. Ind. U.-Purdue U., Columbus, 1980—; adminstr. Muscatatuck State Hosp., Butlerville, Ind., 1978—. NIMH fellow, 1974-78. Mem. Am. Philatelic Soc. Office: Muscatatuck State Hosp PO Box 77 Butlerville IN 47223

LEWIS, R. DENNIS, physical education educator; b. Chgo., Feb. 19, 1943; m. Sharon Joyce Macejak, Sept. 4, 1965; 1 child, Shaun Lewis. B.S., North Central Coll., Ill., 1965; M.S., No. Ill. U., 1966; postgrad., 1967—. Dir.

athletics Newman Central High Sch., Sterling, Ill., 1966-68; assoc. prof., dir. athletics Wilbur Wright Coll., Chgo., 1968-77, prof., athletic dir., 1977—. Author intramural handbooks. Pres., La Grange Park Park Dist., Ill., 1981-85, park commr., 1971—; bd. dirs. La Grange Park Little League, 1975-80; mgr. Babe Ruth and Tee Ball, 1975—. Served to 1st lt. USMC, 1961-65. Named Skyway Conb. Basketball Coach of Yr., 1983, 85. Mem. Nat. Jr. Coll. Athletic Assn., AAHPER, Nat. Athletic Dirs. Assn., Ill. Real Estate Assn., Ill. Park Dist. Assn. Home: 530 Barnsdale La Grange Park IL 60525 Office: Wilbur Wright College 3400 N Austin Ave Chicago IL 60634

LEWIS, RICHARD STANLEY, pharmacist; b. Windom, Minn., Jan. 7, 1926; s. Clifford Henry and Hellen Hayden (Brubacher) L.; m. Lucille Bonevieve Pierson, June 2, 1956; children—Steven Richard, Jane Helen. A.A., Worthington Community Coll., 1948; B.S. in Pharmacy, S.D. State U., 1953, B.S. in Edn., 1961. Registered pharmacist; cert. tchr. Instr. Freeman Jr. Coll. and Acad., S.D., 1962-65; tchr. Sanborn Pub. Schs., Minn., 1965-68; pharmacist Windom Drug Inc., 1965-84; inservice pharm. instr. Windom Hosp., 1976-77; resource instr. macroecons. Worthington Community Coll., Minn., 1979, 84. Mem. Distributive Edn. Clubs. Am. adv. bd. Windom Pub. Schs., 1975-77. Served with USN, 1944-46, PTO, NSF grantee, U. S.D., 1964-65. Mem. Nat. Pharm. Assn., Minn. Pharm. Assn., S.D. Pharm. Assn. Republican. Lutheran. Lodges: Kiwanis, Sons of Norway. Avocation: reading. Home: 1048 Prospect Ave Windom MN 56101

LEWIS, ROBERT ALAN, musician; b. Oshkosh, Wis., Jan. 23, 1936; s. Barton Evan and Dorothy Marie (Sprister) L.; m. Myrna Kay Mayette, Jan. 6, 1962 (div.); 1 dau., Laura Marie. Mus.B., U. Wis., 1957, Mus. M., 1958. Profl. musician trumpet and flugel horn, Chgo., 1961—; recorded over 6000 commercials, records, films; co-leader Ears-Jazz of All Eras; leader Forefront Trumpet Ensemble; soloist Chgo. Symphony Orch.; music dir. Miss Peggy Lee. Served with U.S. Army, 1959-60. Nat. Endowment Arts grantee, 1974, 75. Mem. ASCAP, Nat. Assn. Rec. Artists, Nat. Trumpet Guild, Nat. Jazz Educators, Jazz Inst. Chgo. Composer for trumpet (15 etudes), others.

LEWIS, ROBERT DAVID, ophthalmologist, educator; b. Thomasville, Ga., Aug. 27, 1948; s. Ralph N. and E. Margaret (Klaus) L.; m. Frances Elizabeth Golys, Aug. 29, 1970. B.S., St. Louis Coll. Pharmacy, 1971; M.D., St. Louis U., 1975. Diplomate Am. Bd. Ophthalmology; registered pharmacist. Intern, Cardinal Glennon Hosp. Children, St. Louis, 1975-76; resident St. Louis U., 1976-79; practice medicine specializing in ophthalmology, St. Louis, 1979—; dir. pediatric ophthalmology St. Louis U., 1980—, asst. prof., 1980—; dir. pediatric ophthalmology Cardinal Glennon Hosp. for Children, St. Louis, 1980—; mem. adv. bd. Delta Gamma Found. for Visually Handicapped Children. Recipient St. Louis U. Award for Teaching, 1982. Fellow ACS, Am. Coll. Emergency Physicians; mem. AMA, Mo. Med. Assn., St. Louis Med. Soc., Am. Acad. Ophthalmology, Assn. for Research in Vision and Ophthalmology, Contact Lens Assn. Ophthalmology, Internat. Assn. Ocular Surgeons, Am. Intraocular Implant Soc. Office: 1034 S Brentwood Blvd Saint Louis MO 63117 also 1361 Manchester Rd Manchester MO 63011

LEWIS, ROBERT IAN, osteopathic urologic surgeon, educator; b. N.Y.C., Apr. 28, 1951; s. Sy and Florence (Miller) L.; m. Jean Keefer, Feb. 18, 1978; children—Rachel, David. B.A., La Salle Coll., 1973; D.O., Phila. Coll. Osteo. Medicine, 1977. Diplomate Nat. Bd. Osteo. Medicine, Am. Osteo. Bd. Surgery, Am. Bd. Urology. Intern, Southeastern Med. Ctr., North Miami Beach, Fla., 1977-78; resident in surgery Allentown (Pa.) Osteo. Hosp., 1978-79; resident in urologic surgery U. Miami Med. Ctr. Hosps., 1979-82; assoc. Surgery and Gynecology, Inc., Columbus Ohio, 1982—; mem. staff Doctor's Hosp., Columbus, 1982—, Childrens Hosp., Columbus, 1982—, St. Ann's Hosp., Columbus, 1983—; clin. asst. prof. Sch. Osteo. Medicine, Ohio State U.; lectr. in field. Recipient Achievement award Class of 1977, Phila. Coll. Osteo. Medicine. Mem. Am. Osteo. Assn., Ohio Osteo. Assn., Pa. Osteo. Med. Assn., Fla. Osteo Med. Assn., Columbus Acad. Osteo. Medicine, Am. Coll. Osteo. Surgeons (Merck, Sharpe and Dohme Resident's award 1982), Central Ohio Urology Soc., Am. Fedn. Physicians, Uro Dynamics Soc., Med. Amateur Radio Council, Columbus Amateur Radio Assn., Central Ohio Amateur Radio Emergency Services, Am. Radio Relay League, Lamda Omicron Gamma. Clubs: Capital City Rotary, Capital City Repeater Assn. Contbr. articles to profl. pubs. Office: Surgery and Gynecology Inc 50 Old Village Rd Columbus OH 43228

LEWIS, RONALD STEPHEN, pharmacist; b. Ripley, W.Va., Mar. 3, 1958; s. Clifford Royal and Janet Lorene (Monday) L.; B.S. in Pharmacy, Ohio No. U., 1981; postgrad. Kent State U. Registered pharmacist. Pharmacist Finney's Drug Stores, Canton, Ohio, 1981-82; staff pharmacist Timken Mercy Med. Ctr., Canton, 1982—. Mem. Ohio Pharm. Assn. (hosp. spl. interest group, young pharmacist spl. interest group, 1984), Stark County Acad. Pharmacy. Democrat. Baptist. Avocations: skiing, guitar, bicycling, softball, golf. Home: 1279 Kingwood Dr Bolivar OH 44612 Office: Timken Mercy Med Ctr Pharmacy 1320 Timen Mercy Dr Canton OH 44718

LEWIS, SALLY BUTZEL (MRS. LEONARD THEODORE LEWIS), civic worker; b. Detroit, June 29, 1912; d. Leo Martin and Caroline (Heavenrich) Butzel; B.A., Vassar Coll., 1934; m. Leonard Theodore Lewis, Apr. 4, 1935; 1 son, Leonard Theodore. Mem. Women's City Club of Detroit, 1932-67, dir., 1935-38; dir., chmn. community services com. Village Woman's Club of Birmingham-Bloomfield dir. Franklin-Wright Settlement, Inc., Detroit, 1939—, pres. 1959-60; trustee Oakland County Children's Aid Soc., 1950-64, Oakland U. Found., 1973-82; mem. exec. com. Detroit Fedn. Settlements, 1961; mem. steering com., women's orgn. United Fund, 1960-61; mem. Oakland planning div. United Community Services, Met. Detroit, 1959-70; membership chmn. Bloomfield Art Assn., Birmingham, Mich.; mem. scholarship com. Meadow Brook Sch. Music, Meadow Brook Festival, Rochester, Mich.; treas. Cranbrook Music Guild, Inc., 1959, dir., 1958-63, sec., 1960-61; mem. women's com. Cranbrook Art Acad. and Mus., Bloomfield Hills; exec. com. Meadow Brook Festival, Rochester, Md., 1969-76. Mem. Nat. Council Jewish Women, Am. Jewish Com., Women's Assn. Detroit Symphony, Friends Detroit Symphony. Clubs: Women's Nat. Farm and Garden, Village, Ibex. Home: 1763 Alexander Dr Bloomfield Hills MI 48013

LEWIS, STEPHEN BLAINE, lawyer; b. Indpls., July 16, 1952; s. Ted B. and Phyllis J. (Keyser) L.; m. Kathryn L. Ruff, May 10, 1980. B.A., DePauw U., 1974; J.D., Ind. U., 1977. Bar: Ind. 1978, U.S. Dist. Ct. (no. dist.) Ind. 1978, Ill. 1980, U.S. Dist. Ct. (no. dist.) Ill. 1980. Law clk. Ind. Nat. Bank, Indpls., 1975-78, counsel, 1978-80; counsel Continental Bank, Chgo., 1980-82, Borg-Warner Corp., Chgo., 1982—. Bd. dirs., 2d v.p. Aux. bd. North Ave. Day Nursery, Chgo., 1983—; dir. aux. bd. Henrotin Hosp., Chgo., 1983—; bd. dirs., treas. Legal Clinic for Disabled, Chgo., 1984—; mem. exec. bd. Chgo. Area council Boy Scouts Am., 1984—. Mem. ABA (chmn. internat. lawyers young lawyers div. 1984—), Chgo. Bar Assn. (dir. young lawyers sect. 1985-86, mem. exec. council 1984—, chmn. law explorers com. 1984-85), Ill. State Bar Assn., Ind. State Bar Assn. Club: Union League of Chgo. Lodge: Masons. Home: 875 N LaSalle St #2-S Chicago IL 60610 Office: Borg-Warner Corp Fin Services 225 N Michigan Ave Chicago IL 60601

LEYDA, JAMES PERKINS, pharmaceutical company executive; b. Youngstown, Ohio, Oct. 2, 1935; s. Walter Cletus and Dorothy Eleanor (Perkins) L.; m. Barbara Marie Dykstra, Sept. 9, 1967; children—Jason Walter, Jeffrey Albert, Justin Michael. B.S. in Pharmacy, Ohio No. U., 1957; M.Sc. in Pharmacy, Ohio State U., 1959, Ph.D., 1962. Registered pharmacist, Ohio. Devel. chemist Lederle Labs., Pearl River, N.Y., 1962-66; mgr. new product devel. Cyanamid Internat., Pearl River, 1966-69; dir. new product devel. Merrell Internat., N.Y.C. also Westport, Conn., 1969-81, dir. pharmacy research Merrell Dow Pharm., Cin., 1981-83, dir. comml. devel., 1983—. Contbg. author: Pharmaceutical Chemistry, 1964; contbr. articles to profl. jours. Recipient Ohio No. U./Bristol Labs. Bristol award, 1957; Richardson Merrell Inc. Lunsford Richardson award, 1960; NIH Predoctoral Fellowship award, 1960. Mem. Am. Pharm. Assn., Acad. Pharm. Scis., N.Y. Acad. Scis., AAAS, Sigma Xi. Avocations: Tennis, golf. Home: 10597 Tanager Hills Dr Cincinnati OH 45249 Office: Merrell Dow Pharmaceuticals Inc 12345 Alliance Dr Cincinnati OH 45242

L'HEUREUX, JACQUES JEAN, astrophysicist; b. Three Rivers, Que., Can., Dec. 20, 1939; came to U.S., 1961; s. Sammy and Simone (Baril) L'H.; m. Linda L. Roark, Aug. 4, 1984; children—Elizabeth, Ingrid, Valerie; stepchildren—Michael, Daniel, Michelle. B.Sc., U. Montreal, 1961, M.Sc., 1962; Ph.D., U. Chgo., 1966. Research assoc. U. Chgo., 1966-69, asst. prof., 1969-73, sr. research assoc. 1977—; research asst. prof. U. Ariz., Tucson, 1973-77. Fellow Am. Phys. Soc. Home: 805 Exmoor Rd Olympia Fields IL 60461 Office: U Chgo 933 E 56th St Chicago IL 60637

LI, NORMAN L., state ofcl.; b. Hong Kong, Mar. 11, 1947; came to U.S., 1971; s. Po On and Lena (Lam) L.; 1 son, David T. B.A., Nat. Taiwan U., 1971; M.A., Central Mo. State U., 1974; m. Judy Cheng, May 8, 1976. Internat. mktg. dir. Tataicheong Co. Ltd., Hong Kong, 1970-72; mgr. New Moon of Merrillville Inc. (Ind.), 1974-79; trade specialist Ill. Dept. Commerce and Community Affairs, Chgo., 1979-82; mng. dir. Ill. Far East Bur., Hong Kong, 1982—; leader state trade missions to China, Hong Kong, Korea, Singapore, Taiwan; developer trade promotion agreement between Ill. and Taiwan, 1979, between Ill. and Liaoning, China, 1983. Mem. Am. C. of C. in Hong Kong. Home: 4974 W 87th Pl Crown Point IN 46307 Office: 310 S Michigan Ave Suite 1000 Chicago IL 60604

LI, STEPHEN KU-CHING, architect; b. Taipei, Taiwan, Republic of China, Sept. 10, 1948; came to U.S., 1974, naturalized, 1982; s. Jun-te and Yue-hsia (Chou) L.; m. Annie Ho, Dec. 6, 1975. B.Arch, Chung Yuan Coll., 1972; M.Arch, Ill. Inst. Tech., 1976. Registered architect, Calif., Ill., Wis. Designer, Martin Oil Service Co., Alsip, Ill., 1975-77; draftsman Schiller & Frank, Wheeling, Ill., 1977; designer Perkins & Will, Chgo., 1977-79; job capt. L.B. Knight & Assocs., Chgo., 1979-81; mgr. J.A. Iacopi & Assocs., Northbrook, Ill., 1981-83; owner, mgr. K.C. Li & Assocs., Roselle, Ill., 1983—. Mem. AIA. Avocations: tennis; soccer.

LI, THOMAS MING-TING, chemist; b. Hong Kong, Oct. 8, 1946; came to U.S., 1968, naturalized, 1981; s. Yiu-Hoi and Yuk-Chun (Cheng) L.; B.S. with honors and highest distinction in Chemistry, U. Ill., 1972, M.S., 1974, Ph.D., 1976; m. Janey O. Loh, Sept. 19, 1973; children—Diane K., Stephen Michael. Postdoctoral fellow NIH, Inst. for Cancer Research, Phila., 1976-78; research scientist Miles Labs., Inc., Elkhart, Ind., 1978-79, sr. research scientist, 1980-81; supr. Ames Immunochemistry Lab., 1981-83, dir. diagnostics research Axonics, Inc., Mountain View, Calif., 1983-84; research group leader Syntex Med. Diagnostics, Palo Alto, Calif., 1984—. Edmund J. James scholar, 1969-72; Haas Found. fellow, 1972-73; USPHS fellow, 1976-78; recipient Benjamin Freund award in chemistry, 1971; Am. Inst. Chemists Outstanding award, 1972. Mem. N.Y. Acad. Sci., Am. Assn. Clin. Chemistry, Am. Chem. Soc., Biophys. Soc., Sigma Xi, Phi Kappa Phi. Contbr. articles to profl. jours.; patentee in field; contbr. to: Immunoassays Clinical Laboratory Techniques for the 1980's, 1980; Clinical Immunochemistry: Principles of Methods and Applications, 1984; prin. developer of Optimate, clin. fluorometer/photometer. Office: 3300 Hillview Ave Palo Alto CA 94304

LI, TIEN-YI, educator; b. Juyang, Honan, China, Mar. 14, 1915; s. Kuei-hsin and Hsin Li; m. Julia Liu, Sept. 14, 1963; children—Pin-wen, Norman. B.A., Nankai U. (China), 1937; M.A., Yale U., 1946, Ph.D., 1950. Asst. prof. Chinese lang. and lit. Yale U., New Haven, 1950-59, assoc. prof. Chinese lang. and lit., 1959-62, prof. Chinese lit. and culture, 1962-69; Mershon prof. Chinese lit. and history, Ohio State U., Columbus, 1969-85, prof. emeritus, 1985—; chmn. dept. East Asian langs. and lits., 1971-75; chmn. dept. history Chinese U. Hongkong, 1975-77, dir. Inst. Chinese Studies, 1975-77. Mem. Chinese Lang. Tchrs. Assn., Chinese Am. Assn. Chinese Studies (pres. 1981-83), Am. Hist. Assn., Am. Oriental Soc. Author: Woodrow Wilson's China Policy, 1913-17, 1952; P'ai-an ching-ch'i, 1967; Chinese Fiction: A Bibliography of Books and Articles in Chinese and English, 1968; Chinese Historical Literature, 1977; Erh-k'o p'ai-an ching-ch'i, 1980. Office: 390 Cunz Hall 1841 Millikin Rd Columbus OH 43210

LIANOS, ELIAS A., physician, educator; b. Athens, Greece, Sept. 14, 1949; came to U.S., 1973; s. Apostolole and Euphemia (Frangoulis) L. M.D., U. Athens, 1973. Clin. nephrology fellow SUNY-Buffalo, 1977-80, research fellow, 1980-83; clin. fellow in nephrology Case Western Res. U., Cleve., 1980-83; asst. prof. medicine Med. Coll. Wis., Milw., 1983—. Mem. Am. Soc. Nephrology. Office: Med Coll Wis 9200 W Wisconsin Ave Milwaukee WI 53226

LIBBY, JUDITH LYNN, lawyer; b. Elgin, Ill., Oct. 20, 1948; d. Jules Leon and Virginia Marie (Marshall) L.; B.A. in English Lit., Roosevelt U., 1970; J.D. with highest distinction (Scholar), John Marshall Law Sch., 1977; m. Richard J. Coffee, II; 1 son, David Patrick. Tchr. humanities Craigmore High Sch., Smithfield, South Australia, Australia, 1971-73; admitted to Ill. bar, 1977; assoc. firm Taussig, Wexler & Shaw, Ltd., Chgo., 1977-78; chief counsel Ill. Dept. Ins., Springfield, 1978-80; ptnr. Libby & Coffee Law Office, Springfield, 1981-84; implementation dir. Ill. Coalition Against Sexual Assault, 1984-85. Mem. ABA, Ill. State Bar Assn., Central Ill. Women's Bar Assn. (pres. 1984-85), Sangamon County Bar Assn., Chgo. Bar Assn.

LIBMAN, GARY N., pharmaceutical company executive, quality assurance consultant; b. Chgo., May 4, 1943; s. Ben and Frieda (Sax) L.; m. Norma Esther Granat, June 27, 1965; children—Daniel, Amy, Marc. B.S. in Biology, U. Ill.-Chgo., 1966; M.S. in Microbiology, Roosevelt U., 1970; M.B.A. in Indsl. Mgmt., DePaul U., 1977. Cert. quality engr. Microbiologist, Kendall Co., Barrington, Ill., 1967-75; mgr. sterilization and microbiology Abbott Labs., North Chicago, Ill., 1975-77, mgr. solutions and devices, 1977-80, div. mgr. quality assurance Latin Am. and Can., 1980—; cons., instr. Oakton Community Coll., Des Plaines, Ill., 1973-78. Contbr. articles to sci. jours., papers to profl. confs. Patentee devices for bacteriuria. Cubmaster N.W. Ill. council Boy Scouts Am., Des Plaines, 1976-78. Mem. Am. Soc. Microbiology (workshop coordinator 1981), Am. Soc. Quality Control, Art Inst. Chgo., Delta Mu Delta. Avocations: computer applications in quality; photography. Office: Abbott Internat Ltd Abbott Park North Chicago IL 60064

LICHT, CHARLES ALBERT, mechanical engineer, consultant; b. N.Y.C., Oct. 15, 1924; s. Benjamin H. and Frances Licht; m. Phyllis Aaron, Nov. 25, 1951 (dec. July 1970); children—Heidi, Jonathan Marc, Alisa Sue; m. Dolores Jean Lewin, Feb. 13, 1971; step-children—Richard, Alan, Lori. B.S.M.E., MIT, 1948, B.S. in Bus. and Engring. Adminstrn., 1949. Registered profl. engr., Ill., Calif., N.Y., N.J. Constrn. engr. Am. Steel Foundry, East Chicago, Ind., 1948-50; plant mgr. Specialloy Inc., Chgo., 1950-53; research engr. Apex Smelting, Cleve., 1953-54; v.p., engr. U.S. Reduction Co., East Chicago, 1954-68; pres. Charles Licht Engring. Assocs., Inc., Olympia Fields, Ill., 1968—. Mem. Olympia Field Park Bd., 1960-65, Olympia Fields Zoning Bd. Appeals, 1969-75. Served to lt. (j.g.) USNR, 1943-46, PTO. Mem. Am. Acad. Environ. Engrs. (diplomate), ASME, Am. Soc. Metals, AIME, Ill. Soc. Profl. Engrs., Nat. Soc. Profl. Engrs., Air Pollution Control Assn., Am. Inst. Plant Engrs. Soc. Die Casting Engrs., Nat. Assn. Recycling Industries (affiliate), Am. Foundrymen's Soc., Water Pollution Control Fedn., Ill. Water Pollution Control Assn., Ill. Soc. Environ. Profls., ASHRAE, Internat. Precious Metals Inst. Jewish. Club: Ravisloe Ctr. (Homewood, Ill.). Office: Charles Licht Engring Assocs Inc PO Box 315 Olympia Fields IL 60461

LICHTENBERG, DON BERNETT, physics educator; b. Passaic, N.J., July 2, 1928; s. Milton and Ida (Krulewitz) L.; m. Rita Kalter, Jan. 10, 1954; children—Naomi, Rebecca. B.A., NYU, 1950; M.S., U. Ill., 1951, Ph.D., 1955; Research assoc. Ind. U., Bloomington, 1955-57, assoc. prof., 1963-66, prof. physics, 1966—; asst. prof. Mich. State U., 1958-61, assoc. prof., 1961-63; physicist Stanford Linear Accelerator Ctr., 1962-63; vis. prof. U. Hamburg, Germany, 1957-58, Tel-Aviv U., 1967-68, Imperial Coll., London, 1971; vis. sr. fellow Oxford U., 1979-80. Author: Meson and Baryon Spectroscopy, 1965; (with K. Johnson, J. Schwinger, S. Weinberg) Particles and Field Theory, 1965, Unitary Symetry and Elementary Particles, 1970, 2d edit., 1978. Contbr. articles to profl. jours. Fellow Am. Phys. Soc., Phi Beta Kappa, Sigma Xi. Home: 715 S Fess Ave Bloomington IN 47401 Office: Physics Dept Ind U Bloomington IN 47405

LICHTENFELD, MELVIN ALLEN, pharmacist; b. Gary, Ind., June 13, 1927; s. Albert Isidore and Sidell (Korenthal) L.; m. Elaine Kaplan, Apr. 6, 1952; children—Dean Howard, Jan Rae, Michelle Ann, Bruce Harvey. B.S. in Pharmacy, Purdue U., 1951. Staff pharmacist Walgreen Drug Co., Gary, 1951-52; pharmacist, mgr. Hobart Drugs, Hobart, Ind., 1952-60; owner, pharmacist Mel's Pharmacy, Gary, 1960-70; chief pharmacist, dir. pharmacy Ross Med. Pharmacy, Merrillville, Ind., 1970—; corp. sec. Merrillville Health Ctr. Pharmacy, 1970—; regional dir. Bank of Indiana, Merrillville, 1984—. Author: Man Power in Pharmacy, 1976. Recipient Bowl of Hygeia A.H. Robins Co., 1980. Mem. Nat. Assn. Retail Druggists (Leadership award 1980), Am. Pharm. Assn., Ind. Pharmacist Assn. (pres. 1978-79), Lake County Pharmacist Assn. (pres. 1961-62), Merrillville C. of C. Club: Lofs Golf Assn. (Crown Point Ind.). Lodges: Masons, Lions, B'nai B'rith. Avocations: golf, racquetball, photography, travel. Home: 3037 Sunrise Dr Lofs Crown Point IN 46307

LICHTENSTEIN, IRVIN YALE, mortgage banking company executive; b. Columbus, Ohio, Dec. 21, 1924; s. Samuel and Bessie Lichtenstein; m. Mitzi Lee Shaucet, Aug. 31, 1947; children—Hindi Lee, Jeffrey Alan. Student Ohio State U., 1942-43, 46-47. With Yerke Mortgage Co., Columbus, Ohio, 1954—, v.p., 1960-73, exec. v.p., 1973—; instr. post licensing courses Columbus Bd. Realtors; speaker numerous seminars conducted by local newspapers; expert commentator local TV stas. on residential mortgage financing; speaker on specialty, FHA and VA govt. insured mortgages. Served to sgt. AC, U.S. Army, 1943-45. Decorated Air medal with 2 oak leaf clusters. Mem. Columbus Bd. Realtors, Mortgage Bankers Assn. (pres. 1963). Republican. Jewish. Club: Winding Hollow Country (Columbus). Lodge: B'nai B'rith. Office: 145 E Rich St Columbus OH 43215

LICHTY, WARREN DEWEY, JR., lawyer; b. Colorado Springs, Colo., Dec. 17, 1930; s. Warren D. and Margaret (White) L.; m. Margaret Louise Grupy, Dec. 8, 1962. Student Chadron State Coll., 1948-50; B.S. in Law, U. Nebr., 1952, J.D., 1954. Bar: Nebr. 1954, U.S. Dist. Ct. Nebr., 1954, U.S. Ct. Appeals (8th cir.) 1973, U.S. Supreme Ct. 1979. Spl. agt. CIC, 1955-58; county judge Dawes County, Nebr., 1958-61; spl. asst. atty. gen. Nebr. Dept. Justice, Lincoln, Nebr., 1961-69; asst. atty. gen., chief counsel Nebr. Dept. Roads, Lincoln, 1969—; lectr. law Chadron State Coll., 1959-60; mem. com. on eminent domain and land use, transp. research bd. Nat. Acad. Sci.-NRC. Bd. dirs. Scottish Rite Found. Nebr., 1981—, DeMolay Found. Nebr., 1980—, Nebr. Masonic Home Corp., 1979—. Served with U.S. Army, 1954-58. Mem. Nebr. Bar Assn., Lincoln Bar Assn., Am. Assn. State Hwy. and Transp. Ofcls. (subcom. on legal affairs), Am. Legion. Republican. Episcopalian. Clubs: Hiram (past pres.), Nebraska (Lincoln). Lodges: Masons (33 deg., grantmaster Nebr. 1979; vice chmn. conf. Grand Masters of N.Am., 1980), Shriners, Royal Order of Scotland, Philalithes Soc., Elks. Home: PO Box 2559 Lincoln NE 68502 Office: PO Box 94759 Lincoln NE 68509

LIDDELL, LEON MORRIS, educator, librarian; b. Gainesville, Tex., July 21, 1914; s. Thomas L. and Minnie Mae (Morris) L.; B.A., U. Tex., 1937, J.D., 1937; B.L.S., U. Chgo., 1946; grad. study Internat. Law, Faculty of Polit. Sci., Columbia. Admitted to Tex. bar, 1937; claims dept. Hartford Accident and Indemnity Co., Houston, 1937-38; pvt. practice Gainesville, 1938-39; claim dept. Pacific Mutual Life Ins. Co., Kansas City, Mo., 1939-41; asst. prof. law and law librarian U. Conn., 1946-47; asst. prof. law U. Minn., 1949-50, asso. prof. law and law librarian, 1950-54, prof., 1954-60; prof. of law, law librarian U. Chgo., 1960-74, emeritus, 1974—; librarian, prof. law Northwestern U., Chgo., 1974-80. Served from 2d lt. to maj. AUS, 1941-46. Mem. Tex. State Bar, Am. Assn. Law Libraries, Spl. Libraries Assn. Home: 880 Lake Shore Dr Chicago IL 60611 Office: 357 E Chicago Ave Chicago IL 60611

LIDGE, RALPH THEODORE, orthopaedic surgeon; b. Tacoma Park, Md., Mar. 19, 1921; s. Ernest F. and Renee (Engel) L.; m. Jacquelyn Ann Johnson, June 1, 1946; children—Ralph Theodore, Patricia Ann, Christpher Dale. B.S., Northwestern U., 1942, M.D., M.B., 1945. Diplomate Am. Bd. Orthopaedic Surgery. Resident, Ill. Research and Ednl. Hosps., Chgo., 1945-46, resident in orthopaedics, 1948-51; practice medicine specializing in orthopaedic surgery, Chgo., 1951—; attending staff N.W. Community Hosp., Arlington Heights, Ill., 1959—; clin. assoc. prof. orthopaedic surgery Abraham Lincoln Sch. Medicine, U. Ill. Med. Ctr., Chgo. Mem. Am. Acad. Orthopaedic Surgeons, ACS, AMA, Am. Geriatrics Soc., Am. Orthopaedic Assn., Am. Orthopaedic Soc. for Sports Medicine, Am. Rheumatism Assn., Am. Trauma Soc., Chgo. Orthopaedic Soc., Chgo. Med. Soc., Clin. Orthopaedic Soc., Ill. Med. Soc., Ill. Orthopaedic Soc. (founding mem.), Internat. Arthroscopy Assn. (founding mem., dir.), Internat. Soc. of the Knee, Internat. Soc. Orthopaedic Research and Traumatology (founding mem.), Internat. Soc. Orthopaedic Surgery and Traumatology, Inst. Medicine of Chgo., Lamplighters Orthopaedic Soc., Mid-Am. Orthopaedic Assn. (charter mem.), Orthopaedic Research and Edn. Found. (nat. chmn. fund raising and devel. com. 1973-77). Contbr. articles to profl. jours. Address: 1300 E Central Rd Arlington Heights IL 60005

LIDMAN, J(OHN) KIRBY, transportation planner; b. Dickens, Iowa, July 12, 1930; s. John Harold and Marie (Sorenson) L.; B.S., Iowa State U., 1961. Mem. Iowa Hwy. Commn., 1958-60, 61-62; wind-tunnel design engr. airframe and rotorcraft div. B & C Splty., Inc., Ames, Iowa, 1963-69; project engr. Iowa Hwy. Commn., 1969-75; transp. planner Iowa Dept. Transp., 1975—. Registered profl. engr., Iowa. Fellow Brit. Interplanetary Soc.; mem. AIAA, Aircraft Owners and Pilots Assn., Air Force Assn., Civil Air Patrol, Soaring Soc. Am., ASCE, Exptl. Aircraft Assn., Nat. Aeros. Assn., Nat. Soc. Profl. Engrs., Am. Soc. Pub. Adminstrn. Home: 607 Carroll Av Ames IA 50010 Office: Iowa Dept Transp Ames IA 50010

LIEBENOW, ROLAND RUDOLPH, insurance company medical director; b. Jefferson County, Wis., Sept. 17, 1922; s. Rudolph F. and Elma L. (Loper) L.; B.S., U. Wis., Madison, 1944, M.D., 1948; m. Martha E. Anderson, May 5, 1950; children—Linda S., Ronald M., Kurt S. Intern, Colo. Gen. Hosp., Denver, 1948-49; gen. practice medicine, Stevens Point, Wis., 1949-50; practice medicine specializing in medicine and surgery, Lake Mills, Wis., 1950-67; asso. med. dir. Northwestern Mut. Life Ins. Co., Milw., 1967-82; v.p., med. dir. CUNA Mut. Ins. Group, 1982—. teaching asst. in anatomy Med. Sch., U. Wis., 1944, research asst. in pharmacology, 1946-47; mem. med. staffs Deaconess Hosp., Milw., Watertown Meml., Ft. Atkinson Meml. hosps.; pres. exec. com. Marquardt Manor Nursing Home, Watertown, Wis., 1972-74; pres. med. staff St. Mary's Hosp., Watertown, 1959; vice chief of staff Ft. Atkinson (Wis.) Meml. Hosp., 1967; clin. asst. prof. Med. Coll. Wis., 1976-84. Chmn. troop com. Sinnissippi council Boy Scouts Am., 1965-76; vice chmn. bd. elders Lake Mills Moravian Ch., 1972-75; appointed to Wis. State Task Force on Alzheimer's Disease, 1984. Served to capt. M.C., U.S. Army, 1953-55. Named Alumnus of Year, Lake Mills Alumni Assn., 1972. Diplomate Am. Bd. Family Practice; cert. Bd. Life Ins. Medicine. Fellow Am. Acad. Family Practice; mem. Jefferson County Med. Assn. (pres. 1959-60), Wis. State Med. Soc. (mem. ho. of dels. from Jefferson County 1980-81, mem. Fed. legislation com. 1981, mem. com. aging 1982— chmn. extended care facilities 1983—), AMA, Wis. Acad. Arts and Scis., Assn. Life Ins. Med. Dirs., Am. Council Life Ins. (legis. com., med. sect.), Aerospace Med. Assn., U. Wis. Med. Alumni Assn. (bd. dirs. 1985—), Soc. for Prospective Medicine, Am. Legion, Phi Kappa Phi. Republican. Clubs: Northwestern Mut. Stamp (pres. 1972-76), Philatelic Classics Soc., Masons, Rotary. Co-author monograph on chloroform, 1951. Home: 309 Lakeview Ave Lake Mills WI 53551 Office: 5910 Mineral Point Rd Madison WI 53705

LIEBERMAN, DAVID JOSEPH, physician, county health administrator; b. Phila., Feb. 2, 1928; s. Wolf Meyer and Anne (Elman) L.; student Temple U., 1946; M.D., Jefferson Med. Coll., Phila., 1950; postgrad. U. Pa., 1952-53, 66; M.P.H., Harvard U., 1966. Rotating intern Phila. Gen. Hosp., 1950-52; camp physician Camp Pinecrest, Dingman's Ferry, Pa., 1951; ship surgeon Grace Line, N.Y.C., 1952-53; resident gen. surgery Albert Einstein Med. Center, Phila., 1953-56; tour physician Harlem Globetrotters Basketball Exhbn. World Tour, 1956; practice medicine specializing in gen. surgery Albert Einstein Med. Center, Phila., 1956-59; instr. surgery Albert Einstein Med. Center, No. Div., 1956-59, Albert Einstein Med. Center Sch. Nursing, 1956-59, Temple U. Sch. Medicine, 1956-59; asso. surgeon Rush Hosp. for Diseases of Chest, 1956-59; surgeon Home for the Jewish Aged, 1956-59; mem. courtesy surg. staff Germantown Hosp., Rolling Hill Hosp., 1956-59; ship surgeon U.S. Lines, N.Y.C., 1960; chief surg. services Warren (Pa.) State Hosp., 1960-64; physician I, Pa. Dept. Health, Bur. Field Services, 1964-65; asst. dist. health dir. Phila. Dept. Pub. Health, Bur. Dist. Health Services, 1966-67; dir. Bur. Med. Policies and Standards, Office Med. Services and Facilities, Pa. Dept. Pub. Welfare, Harrisburg, 1968-69, med. assistance adminstr. Bur. Med. Assistance, Office Family Services, 1967-68; exec. med. dir. med. assistance program N.Y.C. Dept. Health, 1969-71; dir. Dept. Ambulatory Care Services and Community Medicine, French and Polyclinic Med. Sch. and Health Center, N.Y.C., 1971-74; dir. Monroe County Health Dept., Monroe County Med. Examiner, Monroe, Mich., 1975—; mem. med. staff Mercy-Meml. Hosp., Monroe, 1975—; non-resident lectr. dept. health planning and adminstrn. U. Mich. Sch. Public Health, 1976-83; mem. tech. adv. council Mich. Cancer Found. Community Outreach Detection and Care Project, 1975-77; mem. Monroe County Substance Abuse Adv. Council, 1975-81; lectr. emergency med. technicians course Monroe County Community Coll., 1977—; bd. dirs., pres. elect Monroe Boys Club, 1976-78; bd. dirs. Monroe chpt. Mich. Soc. Mental Health, 1977-78; mem. exec. com. Monroe County Health Planning Council,

1975—, chmn., 1977-78; mem. exec. com. Monroe County Emergency Med. Services Council, 1975—, chmn., 1977-78, mem. med. control bd., 1982—; health services coordinator Monroe County Office Civil Preparedness, 1975—; mem. Monroe County Commn. Aging, 1975—; bd. dirs. Monroe County Opportunity Program, 1975-81; mem. environ. health adv. com. Mich. Dept. Public Health, 1976—; gen. mem. Comprehensive Health Planning Council Southeastern Mich., 1975—; bd. dirs. Southeastern Mich. Council on Emergency Med. Services, 1977-81, Monway Citizens Health Council, 1978—; trustee Monroe County unit Mich. Cancer Found., 1978-81; mem. profl. edn. com. Monroe unit Am. Cancer Soc., 1978-79; chmn. physicians subcom. United Way Monroe County, 1975, chmn. profl. div., 1976; div. co-chmn. Monroe County Health Day, Mich. Week, 1979; mem. adv. council Area Agy. on Aging, 1985—; chmn. Monroe County Employees Assistance Program Com., 1984—; bd. dirs. South Monroe County Citizens Health Council, 1979—; bd. dirs. Southeastern Mich. Substance Abuse Services, 1982—. Recipient Dr. Francis W. Shain prize, Gold medal in surgery Jefferson Med. Coll., 1950, Best Resident prize Albert Einstein Med. Center Phila., 1956; USPHS traineeship grantee, 1965-66. Fellow Am. Public Health Assn. (governing council 1978), Royal Soc. Health; mem. Am. Coll. Preventive Medicine, Southeastern Mich. Health Assn. (dir. 1975—, pres. 1983-84), 1981-82, 1st v.p. 1982-83, pres. 1983—), Mich. Public Health Assn. (dir. 1978-80, 84—, chmn. awards com. 1984— chmn. adminstrv. div. 1978-79), Alcohol and Drug Problems Assn. N.Am., Mich. Health Officers Assn. (dir. 1977-80, 83—, sec. 1983-84, pres.-elect 1985—, chmn. environ. and occupational health com. 1977-80, 81-82, , com. on med. examiner system 1978-80, 81-83), Mich. Alcohol and Addiction Assn. (dir. 1979-80), Nat. Assn. County Health Officers, Nat. Assn. Med. Examiners, Am. Med. Soc. on Alcoholism, Am. Assn. Public Health Physicians, Met. Opera Guild, Detroit Grand Opera Assn., Am. Hort. Soc., Warren (Pa.) Jaycees (pres. 1963-64). Jewish. Club: Harvard of Eastern Mich. Home: 3861 N Custer Rd Monroe MI 48161 Office: 650 Stewart Rd Monroe MI 48161

LIEBERMAN, PEARL NAOMI, philatelist; b. Chgo., Aug. 24, 1918; d. Harry and Katherine (DeKoven) Feldman; m. Eugene Lieberman, Aug. 3, 1947; children—Mark Joel, Robert Frederic, Steven Terry. B.A., U. Ill., 1940. Tchr. bus. edn. Chgo. Pub. Schs., 1946-83, Roberto Clemente High Sch., 1975-83; philatelist, 1945—. Served with AUS, 1943-45: CBI, PTO. Recipient Silver medal Internat. Philatelic Exhbn., Taipei, 1981; Gold medal Compex Vatican Exhbn., 1978; Silver medal Can. Nat. Philatelic Exhbn., 1981; Silver medal Internat. Philatelic Exhbn., Korea, 1984, Australia, 1984. Mem. Chgo. Bus. Tchrs. Assn. Club: Ill. Athletic (Chgo.). Home: 801 LeClaire Ave Wilmette IL 60091

LIEBERTHAL, MILTON M., medical consultant, gastroenterologist; b. Jewett City, Conn., Oct. 30, 1911; s. Robert Henry and Erna (Bloomfield) L.; m. Naomi Ruth Burd, June 9, 1935; children—David Henry, Kenneth Guy, Gary Burd. A.B., Dartmouth Coll., 1932; M.D., NYU, 1935. Diplomate Am. Bd. Internal Medicine. Intern, Phila. Gen. Hosp., 1935-37, resident in internal medicine and gastroenterology, 1937-39; practice medicine, Phila., 1939-41; practice medicine specializing in gastroenterology, Bridgeport, Conn., 1946-71; dir. investigative gastroenterology Merrell-Nat. Labs., 1972-76; med. cons. Merrell Dow Pharms., Cin., 1977—; clin. prof. medicine U. Cin. Served to maj. M.C., AUS, 1942-45. Fellow ACP; mem. Am. Gastroent. Assn., Am. Soc. Gastrointestinal Endoscopy, Alpha Omega Alpha. Club: Kenwood Country (Cin.). Author: (with H.O. Conn) The Hepatic Coma Syndromes and Lactulose, 1979; The Lighter Side of Life, 1973; contbr. articles to profl. books and jours.

LIEBHART, MARK MICHAEL, information management executive; b. N.Y.C., Aug. 26, 1949; s. Edward Patrick and Bette Elizabeth (Zwall) L.; m. Jeanne Lou Audsley, Aug. 1, 1969; children—Juliet, Steven, Melisa, Andrea, Joshua, Michal. B.S. in Edn., Central Mo. State U., 1972. Asst. to mktg. mgr. Harmon Industries, Warrensburg, Mo, 1973-73; salesman, sales mgr. David Kahn, Inc., Kansas City, Mo. and St. Louis, 1973-80; salesman Bankers Box, St. Louis, 1980-84; area sales mgr. Fellowes Mfg. Co., St. Louis, 1984—. Central Mo. State U. scholar, 1967; Nat. Student Def. grantee, 1967-71. Mem. Midwest Travelers Club (v.p. St. Louis 1982-83, exec. v.p. 1983-84, pres. 1984-85), Nat. Office Products Assn., St. Louis Office Products Assn., Assn. Records Mgrs. and Adminstrs. Avocations: sports; camping; fishing. Home: 140 Wild Oak Ct Ballwin MO 63011

LIEBMAN, SHELDON WAYNE, book editor, literary critic; b. Pitts., Nov. 17, 1940; s. Abe and Sadie Saundra (Sakolsky) L.; m. Gale Steinfeld, June 13, 1965; children—Sarah, Rebecca. B.S. in Econs., U. Pa., 1962; M.A., in English, U. Pitts., 1964; Ph.D. in English, U. Pa., 1972. Tchr., Allegheny County Pub. Schs., Pitts., 1962-64; asst. prof. Glassboro State Coll. (N.J.), 1964-66; instr., then asst. prof. Lafayette Coll., Easton, Pa., 1966-73; asst. prof. U. Ill.-Chgo., 1974-80; editor Crain Communications, Inc., Chgo., 1980-81; asst. dir. Office for Intellectual Freedom, ALA, Chgo., 1981-82; editor Crain Books, Chgo., 1982-84, PCM Newsletter, 1984—; lectr. Northwestern U., 1983—, Roosevelt U., 1985—; editorial cons. CMD Corp., 1983—. Chmn. Oak Park (Ill.) Literary Map Com. NEH summer fellow, 1976; Lafayette Coll. summer fellow, 1968; U. Ill.-Chgo. summer fellow, 1974. Democrat. Jewish. Co-editor Newsletter on Intellectual Freedom, 1981-82; contbr. articles profl. jours. Home: 409 N Taylor Ave Oak Park IL 60302 Office: 6445 W North Ave Oak Park IL 60302

LIEDER, MARY ANDREA, sales and marketing consulting company executive; b. Mpls., Sept. 6, 1938; d. William H. and Anne J. (Gamradt) Berney; m. James Edward Lieder; children—Timothy, Jon, William, Kristin. A. Liberal Arts, U. Minn., 1958; B.A., Met. State U., 1976. Lic. real estate broker, Minn. Property mgr. Sage Co., Madsen Constrn. Co., Mpls., 1967-69; cons. Coult Mortgage Co., St. Paul, 1969-77; social worker Courage Ctr., Mpls., 1977-78; dir. sales and mktg. Swanson Abbott Devel. Co., Mpls., 1978-81; dir. condominium and townhouse div. Edina Realty, Mpls., 1981-83; pres., owner Lieder Corp., Mpls., 1983—; mem. examining bd. Truth in Housing, City of Mpls., 1984—; bd. dirs. Project for Pride in Living, Mpls. Mem. Minn. Multi-Housing Assn. Republican. Roman Catholic. Avocation: painting in oils and mixed media. Home: 2501 Kyle Ave N Minneapolis MN 55422 Office: Lieder Corp 3100 W Lake St Minneapolis MN 55416

LIEDTKE, CAROLE MARGARET, biochemistry educator, researcher; b. Lakewood, Ohio, Jan. 8, 1944; d. Kenneth Harold and Angela Mary (Wagner) L.; m. William Patrick Liedtke, June 8, 1973; 1 child, Christine Marie. B.A. magna cum laude, Miami U., 1966; Ph.D., Case Western Res. U., 1980. Jr. research asst. Case Western Res. U., Cleve., 1966-68, sr. research asst., 1968-74, Nat. Research Service predoctoral fellow 1977-79, Nat. Research Service postdoctoral pulmonary fellow, 1980-81, instr. pediatrics, 1981-83, asst. prof., 1983—; moderator SPACE program, 1983; recorder Cystic Fibrosis Found., Bethesda, 1984. Recipient Herbert S. Steuer Meml. award Case Western U., 1980; Gen. Motors scholar Miami U., 1962-66; Kappa Kappa Gamma scholar Miami U., 1966; grantee NSF Ohio State U., 1965, Case Western Res. U., 1974-77. Res. Mem. Biophys. Soc. (co-chmn. meeting session 1985), Am. Physiol. Soc. (research award 1983), Soc. Gen. Physiologists, AAAS, Phi Beta Kappa. Avocations: reading, sewing. Office: Case Western Reserve Univ 2101 Adelbert Rd Cleveland OH 44106

LIEU, JOHN, physician; b. Hankow, China, Aug. 15, 1904; s. Fan Hou and Sing Ten (Chen) L.; M.D., St. John's U., Shanghai, China, 1926; D.T.M., Liverpool (Eng.) U., 1939; m. Dorothy A. Irwin, Aug. 31, 1974; children—John, Gladys. Came to U.S., 1959, naturalized, 1964. Supt. Works & Mine Hosp., Tayeh, Hupeh, China, 1928; asst. med. officer, Shanghai Mcpl. Council, 1929-36; doctor-in-charge Mcpl. Hosp., Shanghai, 1936-45; chief surgeon Soochow (China) Hosp., 1945-46; pvt. practice, Soochow, 1946-49, Columbus, Ohio, 1962—; chief surg. dept. Mcpl. Sixth Hosp., Shanghai, 1949-57; asst. port health officer, Hongkong; dir. Emerick Hosp., Columbus State Inst., 1961-65; mem. staff Grant Hosp., Columbus. Rockerfeller scholar, 1940. Fellow Royal Soc. Health, Eng.; mem. Am., Ohio med. assns., Acad. Medicine, AAAS, Ohio Acad. Sci. Presbyn. (deacon 1968). Home: 645 Neil Ave Columbus OH 43215 Office: 370 E Town St Columbus OH 43215

LIFSON, HUGH ANTHONY, artist, art educator; b. N.Y.C., Nov. 7, 1937; s. David Lifson and Dorothy (Heilbrunner) Janney; m. Delores Sue Jannes, Dec. 23, 1961; children—Jeffrey Aaron, Amy Rebecca. B.A., Wesleyan U., 1959; M.F.A., Pratt Inst., 1962. Instr. Newark Sch. Art, 1961-62; assoc. prof. LeMoyne Coll., Memphis, 1962-63; prof. dept. art Cornell Coll., Mt. Vernon, Iowa, 1963—, chmn. dept., 1971-74, 79—; vis. lectr. Drake U., 1970, Bristol Poly. Inst., Eng., 1980. One-man shows include Davison Art Ctr., Middletown, Conn., 1957-59, Whittingham Gallery, Boston, 1958, Pratt Inst., Bklyn., 1961, Cornell Coll., 1963-69, 71, 73, 75, 76, 79, 81, 83, East End Gallery, Provincetown, Mass., 1964, Coe Coll., 1967, 70, 72, DeMena Gallery, N.Y.C., 1968, Ohio State U., 1972, Clinton Art Assn., 1973, Extension 4 Gallery, Dubuque, Iowa, 1978, 80, Jail Gallery, Dubuque, 1981, Century Ctr., South Bend, Ind., 1982, Stone City Gallery, 1982; exhibited in group shows at Whittingham Gallery, Provincetown, Mass., 1958, Greenwood Gallery, Hartford, Conn., 1958-59, Tirza Karlis Gallery, Provincetown, 1959, East End Gallery, Provincetown, 1960-61, Mus. Modern Art, 1962, Waverly Gallery, N.Y.C., 1962, Martin Gallery, Mpls., 1970-71, Son Raed Gallery, N.Y.C., 1971, Morton Boyd Gallery, Columbus, Billy Son Gallery, Corallville, Iowa, 1973-74, Am. Gothic Galleries, Cedar Rapids, Iowa, 1975, The Corner Gallery, Cedar Rapids, 1976, The Cothran Gallery, Cedar Rapids, 1976, Ward Nasse Gallery, N.Y.C., 1977-79, Frank Marino Gallery, N.Y.C., 1978, G&G Gallery, Vinton, Iowa, 1983—; represented in permanent collections U. Wis., Wesleyan U., Davenport Art Mus., Chiam Gross, Irving Marantz, Arthur Collins, Collins Radio, Leonard Bocour, SUNY-Potsdam, Carl Shorske, Cedar Rapids Art Ctr., Coe Coll., Richard Kostelanetz. Art editor, contbr. Cardinal; art critic Wesleyan Argus, 1958. Grantee N.Y. State Dept. Edn., 1966, Cornell Coll./Ford Found., 1969, HEW, 1976, 84, Cornell travel grantee, Turkey and Iran, 1973, NIH fellow, Chgo., 1984. Mem. AAUP, Phi Eta Sigma. Home: 219 6th Ave N Mount Vernon IA 52314 Office: Cornell Coll Mount Vernon IA 52314

LIFTON, HERMAN MANUEL, dentist, nutritionist; b. Detroit, Apr. 3, 1919; s. Isadore and Esther (Zieve) L.; m. Pola Winokur, Sept. 17, 1944; children—Estralee, Cathy, James. D.D.S., U. Detroit; D.Nutripathy, Am. Coll. Nutripathy, 1981; 1983; M.Herbology, Emerson Coll. Herbology, 1981. Practice preventive gen. dentistry, 1943—; practice nutrition, analysis and counseling, 1970—; mem. staff diagnostic sect. Sinai Hosp. Dental Clinic, Detroit; lectr. various colls. and univs. Contbr. articles on nutritional subjects to profl. jours. Served to 1st lt. U.S. Army, 1943-46. Fellow Acad. Gen. Dentistry, Internat. Acad. Applied Nutrition, Internat. Acad. Med. Preventics; mem. ADA (life), Mich. State Dental Assn. (life), Detroit Dist. Dental Soc. (life), Southwestern Dental Soc. (life), Am. Assn. Nutritional and Dietary Consultants, Am. Acad. Oral Medicine (pres. Mich. sect. 1964-65, chmn. ann. internat. meeting 1965), Internat. Coll. Applied Nutrition, Internat. Acad. Med. Preventives, Price-Pottenger Nutritional Found., Detroit Dist. Clinic Club-Periodontal sect., Russell Bunting Periodontal Study Club, N.Y. Acad. Scis., Nutrition Today Soc., Acad. Gen. Dentistry, Alpha Omega. Office: 2930 Oakwood Blvd Melvindale MI 48122

LIGGETT, TWILA MARIE CHRISTENSEN, instructional TV co. exec.; b. Pipestone, Minn., Mar. 25, 1944; d. Donald L. and Irene E. (Zweigle) Christensen; B.S., Union Coll., Lincoln, Nebr., 1966; M.A., U. Nebr., 1971, Ph.D., 1977; m. Kenneth R. Liggett, June 2, 1966. Dir. vocal and instrumental music Sprague (Nebr.)-Martell Public Sch., 1966-67; tchr. vocal music public schs., Syracuse, Nebr., 1967-69; tchr. Norris Public Sch., Firth, Nebr., 1969-71; cons. fed. reading project public schs., Lincoln, 1971-72; curriculum coordinator Westside Community Schs., Omaha, 1972-74; dir. State program Right-to-Read, Nebr. Dept. Edn., 1974-76; asst. dir. Nebr. Commn. on Status of Women, 1976-80; asst. dir. devel. and acquisitions Great Plains Nat. Instructional TV Library, U. Nebr., Lincoln, 1980—; exec. producer Reading Rainbow, Pub. Broadcasting System nat. children's series; cons. U.S. Dept. Edn., 1981; Far West Regional Lab., San Francisco, 1978-79. Bd. dirs. Planned Parenthood, Lincoln, 1979-81. Mem. Assn. Supervision and Curriculum Devel., Phi Delta Kappa. Presbyterian. Home: 3001 Kipling St Lincoln NE 68516 Office: PO Box 80669 Lincoln NE 68501

LIGGETT, WILLIAM N., retired banker; b. Ripley, Ohio, Apr. 29, 1917; s. N. and Ida (Montgomery) L.; B.S., Miami U., Oxford, Ohio, 1939, LL.D., 1974—; grad. U. Wis. Sch. Banking, 1950; m. Marjorie Lloyd, May 15, 1940; children—William Reese, Lloyd N., Ann, Jane. Asst. cashier Citizens Nat. Bank, Ripley, 1940; past field sec. Ohio Bankers Assn.; with 1st Nat. Bank Cin., 1948-84, v.p., 1949-64, exec. v.p., 1964-68. pres., chief exec. officer, 1968-72, chmn. bd., chief exec. officer, 1972-81, also dir.; chmn., chief exec. officer 1st Nat. Cin. Corp., 1974-83; examiner FDIC, 1942-48; dir. Ancast Indsl. Corp., Cin. Gas & Electric Co., Midland Co., Morris Bean & Co., Hennegan Co., Schauer Mfg. Co. Served to lt. (j.g.) USNR, 1944-46. Mem. Am. (v.p. Ohio 1955), Ohio (treas. 1958-59, v.p. 1979-80, pres. 1980-81) bankers assns., Newcomen Soc. N. Am. Office: Nat'l Bank PO Box 1038 Cincinnati OH 45201

LIGHT, ALBERT, biochemistry educator, researcher; b. Bklyn., June 19, 1927; s. David and Sarah (Edinoff) L.; m. Tobia L. Lipsher, May 18, 1952; children—Pamela S., Audrey L. B.S. in Chemistry, CCNY, 1948; Ph.D. in Biochemistry, Yale U., 1955; postdoctoral in biochemistry, Cornell Med. Sch., 1955-57. Research instr. U. Utah, Salt Lake City, 1957-59, asst. research instr., 1959-63; assoc. prof. biochemistry UCLA, 1963-65; assoc. prof. chemistry Purdue U., West Lafayette, Ind., 1965-77, head. div. biochemistry, 1978-82, prof. biochemistry, 1977—; vis. scientist NIH, 1972; cons. DuPont Co., 1983, Eli Lilly Co., 1983-84; mem. editorial bd. Jour. Biol. Chemistry, 1982—, Analytical Biochemistry, 1984—. Author: Proteins-Structure and Function, 1974. Contbr. articles to sci. jours. Bd. dirs. Ind. Civil Liberties Union, 1981-82. Served with USN, 1944-45. Grantee NSF, NIH. Mem. Am. Chem. Soc., Am. Soc. Biol. Scis., AAAS. Club: Lafayette Sailing (bd. govs. 1984—). Avocations: photography, sailing, skiing, travel. Home: 2307 Carmel Dr West Lafayette IN 47906 Office: Purdue U Chemistry Bldg West Lafayette IN 47907

LIGHT, CHRISTOPHER UPJOHN, writer, computer musician; b. Kalamazoo, Jan. 4, 1937; s. Richard and Rachel Mary (Upjohn) L.; A.B., Carleton Coll., 1958; M.S., Columbia U., 1962; M.B.A., Western Mich. U., 1967; Ph.D., Washington U., 1971; m. Lilykate Victoria Wenner, June 22, 1963; children—Victoria Mary, Christopher Upjohn. Editor, pub. The Kalamazoo Mag., 1963-66; pres. Mich. Outdoor Pub. Co., Kalamazoo, 1965-68; chmn. fin. dept. Roosevelt U., Chgo., 1975-78; free-lance writer, computer musician, Chgo. Trustee Harold and Grace Upjohn Found., 1967-84. Recipient Mich. Welfare League ann. press award, 1967. Mem. Am. Econs. Assn., Fin. Mgmt. Assn., Soc. Profl. Journalists. Contbr. articles to profl. and microcomputer jours. Record albums: Apple Compote, 1983; One-Man Band, 1985. Office: 400 N Michigan Ave Suite 2002 Chicago IL 60611

LIGHT, JOHN RICHARD, investment consultant; b. Kalamazoo, Oct. 11, 1940; s. Richard Light and Rachel Mary (Upjohn) L.; B.A., Yale U., 1962; m. Frances Mary Hesser, June 21, 1969; 1 dau., Aimee Upjohn. Asst. advt. mgr. Verson Allsteel Press Co., Chgo., 1967-68; pub. relations copywriter Barton Brands, Chgo., 1970; investment cons., Chgo., 1972—. Bd. dirs. Juvenile Protective Assn., Chgo., 1975—, Kalamazoo Child Guidance Clinic, 1969—, Lakeside Boys and Girls Home, 1979—. Recipient Distinguished Service award Publicity Club Chgo., 1972. Roman Catholic. Clubs: Gull Lake Country (Richland, Mich.); Publicity (Chgo.) (dir. 1975-77, mgr. club publs. 1972-73, chmn. seminar com. 1976-77). Lodge: Kiwanis (Kalamazoo and Chgo.). Editor: Impact Machining, 1968. Home: 4866 E Gull Lake Dr Hickory Corners MI 49060 Office: 720 Comerica Bldg 151 S Rose St Kalamazoo MI 49007

LIGHTFOOT, JIM, U.S. Congressman; b. Fremont County, Iowa; m. Nancy L.; children—Terri, Jamie, Allison, James. Mem. U.S. Ho. of Reps., 5th Iowa Dist., mem. coms. Pub. Works and Transp., Govt. Ops., Select Com. on Aging, House Republican Agr. Task Force, Task Force on Rural Elderly, Mil. Reform Caucus. Farm editor Sta. KMA, Shenandoah, Iowa. Participant numerous world confs. to promote agr. Vol. safety counselor FAA. Served with U.S. Army. Recipient Outstanding Service award FAA. Mem. Farm Bur., U.S. Feed Grains Council, Soybean Assn., Nat. Agr. Mktg. Assn. (Ag spokesman of Yr. award), Iowa Park Producers Assn., Iowa Cattleman's Assn. (Broadcasting award). Address: 1609 Longworth Bldg Washington DC 20515

LIKAVEC, MATT JOHN, neurosurgeon, physician; b. Cleve., Aug. 15, 1948; s. Methodius Joseph and Catherine (Popovich) L.; m. Laura Wolfson, Feb. 9, 1974; children—Adam, Aaron, Sarah. B.A. magna cum laude, Coll. Holy Cross, 1970; M.D., Harvard U., 1974. Diplomate Am. Bd. Neurol. Surgery. Intern, Case Western Res. U. Cleve., 1974-75, resident in surgery, 1975-76, resident in neurosurgery, 1976-80; staff neurosurgeon Cin. VA Hosp., 1980-82, dir. neurosurgery, 1982; staff neurosurgeon Cleve. Met. Gen. Hosp., 1982—. Instr. Advanced Trauma Life Support/Ohio State Med. Soc., 1983. Fellow ACS; mem. AMA, Congress Neurol. Surgeons, Am. Assn. Neurol. Surgeons. Roman Catholic. Avocations: Swimming, running, collecting stamps. Office: Cleve Met Gen Hosp Div Neurosurgery 3395 Scranton Blvd Cleveland OH 44109

LILEY, ARTHUR, company executive; b. London, Ont., Can.; m. Betty Liley; children—Brian, Katherine. B. Indsl. Mgmt. U. Toronto; A.M.P., Harvard Bus. Sch. Vice pres., gen. mgr. Parker-Hannifin Can. Ltd., Westinghouse Air Brake Co., Fluid Power Div., Lexington, Ky.; v.p., chief operating officer Bellows Internat., Akron, Ohio; v.p., gen. mgr. Weatherhead Co., Cleve.; now group mgr., v.p. Dana Corp., Ft. Wayne and pres. Spicer Axel Div.; chmn. bd. START, Inc. Mem. Greater Ft. Wayne C. of C. (dir.). Address: Dana Corp Spicer Axel Div PO Box 750 Fort Wayne IN 46801

LILJEGREN, FRANK SIGFRID, artist, art educator; b. N.Y.C., Feb. 23, 1930; s. Josef Sigfrid and Ester (Davidsson) L.; m. Donna Kathryn Hallam, Oct. 12, 1957. Student Art Students League, N.Y.C., 1950-55. Fine art tchr. Westchester County Ctr. Art Workshop, White Plains, N.Y., 1965-77, Art Students League, N.Y.C., 1975-76, Wassenberg Art Ctr., Van Wert, Ohio, 1977-80, White Studios, Decatur, Ind., 1981-83, Wright State U., br. campus, Celina, Ohio, 1982-83, Liljegren Studios, Van Wert, 1980—. Active Van Wert County Hist. Soc., 1978—. Served with U.S. Army, 1951. Recipient Gold medal of Honor for oil painting Hudson Valley Art Assn., 1967; First prize oil painting Council Am. Artists Socs., 1964; Frank V. Dumond award oil painting Salmagundi Club, 1968; Lucien Schimpf award oil painting Acad. Artists Assn., 1970. Mem. Allied Artists Am. (pres. 1970-72, bd. dirs. 1973-75; recipient 42 awards), Artists Fellowship Inc., Art Students League. Home and Studio: 203 S Cherry St Van Wert OH 45891

LILLIE, RICHARD HORACE, investor, real estate developer, retired surgeon; b. Milw., Feb. 3, 1918; s. Osville Richard and Sylvia Grace (Faber) L.; B.S., Haverford Coll., 1939; M.D., Harvard U., 1943; M.S. in Surgery, U. Mich., 1950; m. Jane Louise Zwicky, Sept. 24, 1949; children—Richard Horace, Diane Louise. Intern, U. Mich. Hosp., Ann Arbor, 1943-44, resident, 1946-50; chief of surgery, Milw. Hosp., 1968-80; practice medicine specializing in surgery, Milw., 1951-81; clin. prof. emeritus Med. Coll. Wis.; pres. Lillie 18-94 Corp.; trustee Northwestern Mut. Life Ins. Co., The Bradley Trusts; dir. Djinnii Industries, Inc.; investor, real estate developer, 1981—. Bd. dirs. Goodwill Industries. Served with M.C. AUS, 1944-46. Mem. Am. Bd. Surgery, A.C.S., Central Surg. Assn., AMA, Wis. Surg. Soc. Episcopalian. Clubs: Univ. of Milw., Milw. Yacht, Town. Contbr. articles to surg. jours. Home: 6500 N Lake Dr Milwaukee WI 53217 Office: 811 E Wisconsin Ave Milwaukee WI 53202

LILLY, ALFRED FORREST, JR., insurance company computer executive; b. Aruba, Netherlands Antilles, Dec. 4, 1938; s. Alfred Forrest and Bertha May (Walsh) L. (parents Am. citizens); A.A., Johnson County (Kan.) Community Coll., 1974; B.A., Rockhurst Coll., 1978; m. Loree Adele Plattner, Jan. 27, 1972; children—Diana Laurene, Jennifer Ann, Robert Kyle. Asst. mgr. computer programming Kansas City (Mo.) Life Ins. Co., 1965-67; supr. computer services, 1967-73, dir. computer ops., 1973-75, dir. computer planning, 1975-83, asst. v.p. computer planning, 1984—; owner, founder Flower Software Co. Mem. Citizens Assn., Kansas City, Mo., 1962. Served with Signal Corps, AUS, 1956-59; Korea, 1958-59. Mem. Univac Users Assn., Univac Sci. Exchange (sec. Kansas City chpt. 1976-77, vice chmn. 1977-78), Kansas City Jr. C. of C. Methodist. Home: 7701 Westgate Dr Lenexa KS 66216 Office: PO Box 139 Kansas City MO 64141

LIM, RAMON (KHE-SIONG), neuroscience educator; b. Cebu City, Philippines, Feb. 5, 1933; came to U.S., 1959; s. Eng-Lian and Su (Yu) L.; m. Victoria K. Sy, June 21, 1961; children—Jennifer, Wendell, Caroline. A.B., U. Santo Tomas, Manila, 1953, M.D. cum laude, 1958; Ph.D. in Biochemistry, U. Pa., 1966. Research neurochemist U. Mich., Ann Arbor, 1966-69; asst. prof. biochemistry U. Chgo., 1969-76, assoc. prof. Brain Research Inst., 1976-81; prof. dept. neurology U. Iowa, Iowa City, 1981—, dir. div. neurochemistry and neurobiology, 1981—. Mem. editorial bd. Internat. Jour. Devel. Neurosci., 1984—. Contbr. articles to sci. jours. Discovered Glia Maturation Factor, 1972. Grantee NIH, 1971—, NSF, 1979—, VA, 1983—. Mem. Am. Soc. Biol. Chemists, Internat. Soc. Neurochemistry, Am. Soc. Neurochemistry, Soc. Neurosci., Am. Soc. Cell Biology. Avocations: Calligraphy; painting; writing; music. Home: 118 Richards St Iowa City IA 52240 Office: U Iowa Iowa City IA 52242

LIM, SOON-SIK, chemical engineering educator; b. Kaesung, Korea, Mar. 2, 1944; came to U.S., 1973, permanent resident, 1982; s. Bo-Young and Young-Ae (Lee) L.; m. Jae-Yeon Yoo, Apr. 21, 1973; children—Steve, Anna. B.S., Yonsei U., Seoul, Korea, 1971; M.S., Wayne State U., 1975; Ph.D., 1981. Registered profl. engr., Ohio. Research engr. Pacific Chem. Co., Seoul, Korea, 1971-73; grad. research asst. Wayne State U., 1976-81; assoc. prof. chem. and metall. engring. dept. Youngstown State U., 1981—. Contbr. articles to profl. jours. Wayne State U. scholar, 1974, grad. fellow, 1977. Mem. Am. Inst. Chem. Engrs., Am. Chem. Soc., Am. Soc. Engring. Edn., Sigma Xi, Phi Lambda Upsilon. Home: 3890 Ayrshire Dr Youngstown OH 44511 Office: Chem and Metall Engring Dept Youngstown OH 44555

LIM, TOH-HOAI, internist; b. Xiamen, Fukien, China; Dec. 9, 1939; s. Si-Sin and Po-Sio (Kwa) L.; m. Pein-Kwan Chwa, Mar. 9, 1968; children—Katherine, Joseph, Christine. M.D., U. Rangoon, Burma, 1963. Diplomate Am. Bd. Internal Medicine, Am. Bd. Allergy and Immunology, Am. Bd. Family Practice. Intern Def. Services Hosp., Mingaladon, Burma, 1963-64; resident Shan States, Burma, 1964-66; clin. instr. Med. Sch., Rangoon, 1966-68; intern Cook County Hosp., Chgo., 1968-69, resident in internal medicine, 1969-72; attending physician Swedish Covenant Hosp., Chgo., 1972—; practice medicine specializing in internal medicine, Chgo., 1972—; clin. instr. Rush Med. Sch., Chgo., 1974—. Recipient Tchr. of Yr. award Swedish Covenant Hosp., Chgo., 1974. Fellow ACP, Am. Assn. Cert. Allergists; mem. AMA, Am. Soc. Internal Medicine. Avocations: piano, violin, table tennis, swimming. Office: 5131 N Lincoln Ave Chicago IL 60625

LIMANNI, MARK ANTHONY, lawyer; b. Paulsboro, N.J., Apr. 2, 1956; s. John Timothy and Mary (DiStefano) L. B.A., Temple U., 1978; J.D., DePaul U., 1982. Bar: Ill. 1982, U.S. Dist. Ct. (no. dist.) Ill. 1982, U.S. Ct. Appeals (4th cir.) 1983. Law clk., assoc. Hoellen, Lukes & Halper, Chgo., 1980-82; pros. atty. City of Chgo., 1982—. Organizer 47th ward Republican Com., Chgo. Recipient Outstanding Prosecutor award S.E. Chgo. Commn.-U. Chgo., 1984. Roman Catholic. Home: 2233 W Eastwood St Chicago IL 60640 Office: Office of Corp Counsel City Hall Room 511 121 N LaSalle St Chicago IL 60602

LIN, ANDY CHIUN TSU, aerospace engineer; b. Pingtung, Republic of China, Sept. 24, 1944; came to U.S., 1971; s. Ma-Chuan and Yu (Wu) L.; m. Susan T.K. Su, Dec. 27, 1970; children—Robert, Cindy. B.S., Nat. Cheng-Kung U., Taiwan, 1967; M.S., Northwestern U., 1973, Ph.D., 1975. Registered profl. engr., N.Y.; registered archtl. engr. Taiwan. Sr. engr. Bechtel Power Corp., Gaithersburg, Md., 1976-77; supr. Combustion Engring., Inc., Wellsville, N.Y., 1977-79; sr. specialist engr. The Boeing Co., Wichita, Kans., 1980—. Mem. Am. Acad. Mechanics, AIAA. Avocation: sports. Home: 8210 E Mt Vernon St Wichita KS 67207 Office: Boeing Mil Airplane Co 3801 S Oliver St Wichita KS 67210

LIN, FU-SHAN, physician; b. Taiwan, China, Oct. 15, 1941; s. Chow-Lian and Pen (Ding) L.; came to U.S., 1971, naturalized, 1977; B.M., Taipei Med. Coll., 1967; m. Chung Chiou-Jin, Nov. 17, 1968; children—Ki-Hon, Wan-In, James Anthony, Robert John. Intern, Taipei City Hosp., Taiwan, 1966-67; resident in pediatric MacKay Meml. Hosp., Taiwan, 1968-71; rotating intern Barberton (Ohio) Citizen Hosp., 1971-72; resident in pediatrics Trumbull Meml. Hosp., Warren, Ohio, 1972-73, Akron (Ohio) Children's Hosp., 1973-74; physician The Windham (Ohio) Clinic, Inc., 1974-80, Robinson Meml. Hosp., Ravenna, Ohio, 1974—; practice medicine specializing in pediatrics and family practice, Ravenna, 1980—; instr. pediatrics Northeastern Ohio Univs. Coll. Medicine, 1980—. Served with China Air Force, 1967-68. Diplomate Am. Bd. Pediatrics, Am. Bd. Family Practice. Mem. AMA, Am. Acad. Pediatrics, Am. Acad. Family Physicians, Ohio Med. Assn., Portage County Med. Soc. Office: 6693 N Chestnut St Ravenna OH 44266

LIN, HSIU-SAN, radiology educator, cell biologist; b. Nagoya, Japan, Mar. 15, 1935; came to U.S., 1962, naturalized, 1976; s. Mao-Sung and Tao (Chuang) L.; m. Su-Chiung Chen, Sept. 22, 1962; children—Kenneth, Bertha, Michael. M.D., Nat. Taiwan U., 1960; Ph.D. in Microbiology, U. Chgo., 1968. Diplomate Am. Bd. Therapeutic Radiology. Intern, Cook County Hosp., Chgo., 1962-63; resident in radiation oncology Washington U. Hosps., St. Louis, 1979-81; asst. prof. Washington U., St. Louis, 1971-76, assoc. prof., 1976-84, prof. radiology, 1984—; vis. scientist U. Oxford, Eng., 1977-78. Bd.

dirs. Orgn. Chinese Ams., St. Louis, 1983-85; pres. Taiwanese Assn., St. Louis, 1984. Recipient Research Career Devel. award Nat. Cancer Inst., 1974-79; grantee Nat. Heart, Lung Inst., 1976-88, Nat. Inst. Allergy Infectious Diseases, 1980-88. Mem. Am. Soc. Therapeutic Radiology and Oncology, Am. Assn. Cancer Research, Am. Soc. for Microbiology. Home: 10651 Speed View Ct Saint Louis MO 63141 Office: Washington U 510 S Kings Highway Saint Louis MO 63110

LIN, JAMES C., electrical and biomedical engineer, educator; b. Seoul, Korea, Dec. 29, 1942; m. Mei Fei, Mar. 21, 1970; children—; Janet, Theodore, Erik. B.S., U. Wash., 1966, M.S., 1968, Ph.D., 1971. Asst. prof. U. Wash., Seattle, 1971-74; from assoc. prof. to prof. Wayne State U., Detroit, 1974-80; prof. U. Ill.-Chgo., 1980—, prof., head dept. bioengring., 1980—, dir. robotics and automation lab., 1982—; cons. Battelle Meml. Inst., Columbus, Ohio, 1973-75, SRI Internat., Palo Alto, Calif., 1978-79, Arthur D. Little, Inc., Cambridge, Mass., 1980-83, Ga. Tech. Research Inst., 1984—. Author: Microwave Auditory Effects and Applications, 1978; also numerous papers. Panelist NSF Presdl. Young Investigator award com., Washington, 1984, mem. diagnostic radiology spl. study sect., 1981-85. Recipient IEEE Transaction Best Paper award, 1975; Nat. Research Services award, 1982. Sr. mem. Biomed. Engring. Soc., Robotics Internat.; IEEE (robotics automation council); mem. Bioelectromagnetics Soc. Office: U Ill Chgo Dept Bioengring Box 4348 Chicago IL 60680

LIN, YA-TAI, civil engineer; b. Taipei, Republic of China, Jan. 24, 1932; came to U.S., 1959, naturalized, 1970; s. Y.L. and F.N. (Kao) L.; m. Shelley S. Lee, Dec. 23, 1957; children—Annie, Eugene, Elise, Francis. B.S.C.E., Nat. Taiwan U., 1955; M.S. in Hydraulics, State U. Iowa, 1960; Ph.D. in Environ. Engring., Ill. Inst. Tech., 1970. Registered profl. engr., Ill., Ohio; registered structural engr., Ill. Engr., Allied Engring. Service, Taipei, 1956-58, Am.-Chinese Joint Commn. Rural Constrn., Taipei, 1958-59; engr. Alvord, Burdick & Howson, Chgo., 1960-80, ptnr., 1980—. Mem. Am. Acad. Environ. Engrs. (diplomate), ASCE, Am. Water Works Assn., Water Pollution Control Fedn., Western Soc. Engrs. Home: 535 Exmoor Rd Kenilworth IL 60043 Office: Alvord Burdick & Howson 20 N Wacker Dr Room 1401 Chicago IL 60606

LIN, YEONG-JER, atmospheric sciences educator; b. Taipei, Taiwan, Nov. 11, 1936; came to U.S., 1962; m. Chiung Chen Wang, June 8, 1966; children—Kathleen, Diana. B.S., Nat. Taiwan U., 1959; M.S., U. Wis., 1964; Ph.D., NYU, 1969. Asst. prof. atmospheric scis. St. Louis U., 1969-72, assoc. prof., 1972-76, prof., 1976—. NSF grantee, 1971—. Mem. Am. Meteorol. Soc., Am. Geophys. Union. Office: Dept Earth and Atmospheric Scis St Louis U Saint Louis MO 63103

LIND, MARILYN MARLENE, artist, writer, genealogist; b. New Ulm, Minn., Aug. 15, 1934; d. Fred S. and Emma L. (Steinke) Thiem; student pub. schs., Aitkin, Minn.; m. Charles R. Lind, Aug. 22, 1952; children—Michael, Bonnie, Vickie. Photographic asst., Aitkin, 1951-52; bookkeeper, office mgr. Rural Electric Assn., Aitkin, 1953-54; office mgr. N.E. Minn. Edn. Assn., Cloquet, 1970-77; pres. The Linden Tree, Cloquet, 1981-85; exhibited in one-woman shows: Lake Superior Art Center, Duluth, 1972, Old Towne Gallery, Duluth, 1983; group shows include: Lutheran Brotherhood Ctr. Gallery, Mpls., 1977, Centre Internationale d'Art Contemporain de Paris, 1983. Precinct chmn. Ind. Republicans Minn., 1976-77, co-chmn. Carlton County/Senate Dist. 14, 1977-80, vice-chmn. Carlton County, 1984-85, 8th Congl. Dist. Com., 1977-80, mem. Minn. state central com., 1977-82, county, dist. and state conv. del., 1076-85. Recipient Gallery awards, Duluth, 1972, Mpls., 1977. Mem. Geneal. Soc. Carlton County (founding mem., bd. dirs. 1977-86, v.p. 1980-81, sec. 1982-84). Lutheran. Author: Christoph and August, A Dream and a Promise, 1981; various publs. in field of genealogy research, including: Beginning Genealogy, 1983; Using Maps and Aerial Photography in your Genealogical Research, 1984; Immigration, Migration and Settlement in the United States, 1985. Home and Office: 1204 W Prospect St Cloquet MN 55720

LIND, STEPHEN MICHAEL, lawyer; b. Danville, Ill., Oct. 27, 1951; s. Richard Dean and Joan (Rewerts) L.; m. Carolyn Eva Peck, May 25, 1974 (div. Mar. 1978); m. Rita Ann West, Mar. 12, 1983. B.S., U. Wis., 1973; J.D., Washburn U., 1979; postgrad. U. So. Calif. 1980. Bar: Kans. 1979, U.S. Dist. Ct. Kans. 1979. Gen. mgr. Security Systems, Inc., Topeka, 1976-77; claims examiner Assoc. Aviation Underwriters, Detroit, 1979-81, claims atty., 1981-83; claims mgr., asst. v.p., Chgo., 1983—; ops. officer CAP, USAF, Wausau, Wis., Topeka, 1967-69, 76-79. Mem. Republican Presdl. Task Force, Washington, 1984. Served to 1st lt. U.S. Army, 1973-75. Recipient Am. Vet. award VFW, Stevens Point, Wis., 1973, Am. Jurisprudence award West Pub. Co., Topeka, 1978, Bronze medal of valor CAP/Red Cross, Topeka, 1979. Mem. Lawyers Pilots Bar Assn., Orgn. Flying Adjusters (assoc.), Aviation Ins. Assn. (cons. 1983—), DAV, Soc. of the Big Red One. Republican. Lutheran. Clubs: Radio Control Flyers (Manhatten, Kans.); The Man Will Never Fly Meml. Soc., Inc. (Kill Devil Hills, N.C.). Home: 23 W 134 Sherbrooke St Glen Ellyn IL 60137 Office: Assoc Aviation Underwriters 20 N Wacker Dr Suite 1475 Chicago IL 60606

LINDAMAN, LINDA JANE, computer science educator; b. Milw., Nov. 24, 1949; d. Kenneth Earl and Rita Jane (Lindow) Mickelson; m. David William Lindaman, Nov. 28, 1970; children—Brian, Benjamin. B.S., Iowa State U., 1971; M.S. Ed., No. Ill. U., 1973. Assoc. prof. Black Hawk Coll., Moline, Ill., 1971—. Mem. Clarence-Lowden Bd. Edn., Iowa, pres., 1983—. Mem. Ill. Adult Continuing Educators Assn., Phi Delta Kappa. Lutheran. Club: P.E.O. (Charles City, Iowa). Avocations: needlework, sewing, home computing. Home and Office: Rural Route Box 175 Lowden IA 52255

LINDBERG, CHARLES DAVID, lawyer; b. Moline, Ill., Sept. 11, 1928; s. Victor S. and Alice Christine (Johnson) L.; A.B., Augustana Coll., 1950; LL.B., Yale U., 1953; m. Marian J. Wagner, June 14, 1953; children—Christine, Breta, John, Eric. Admitted to Ohio bar, 1954—; assoc. firm Taft, Stettinius and Hollister, Cin., 1953-61, partner firm, 1961—; dir. Arga Co., Bellefontaine, Ohio, 1975—, Cup Vending Co. of Ohio, Cin., 1976-82, Coca-Cola Bottling Corp. of Cin., 1976-82, Taft Broadcasting Co., Cin., 1979—, Cin. Reds, Inc., 1969-80, Cin. Bengals Profl. Football Team, 1980—, Citation-Walther Corp., 1980—; corp. sec. Taft Broadcasting Co., Cin., 1973—, Hanna-Barbera Prodns., Inc., Good Samaritan Hosp., Cin., 1975—. Chmn. law firm div. Cin. United Appeal, 1976; chmn. policy com. Hamilton County Republican Party, 1981—; pres. City of Cin. Bd. Edn., 1971, 74; pres. Zion Luth. Ch. of Mt. Washington, Cin., 1966-69; mem. Cin. Recreation Commn., 1972-73; chmn. local govt. com. Cin. C. of C., 1977; bd. dirs. Augustana Coll., Rock Island, Ill., 1978—, chmn. bd., 1983—; trustee Greater Cin. Center for Econ. Edn., 1976—, Pub. Library of Cin. and Hamilton County (Ohio), 1982—. Mem. Am. Bar Assn., Ohio Bar Assn., Cin. Bar Assn. Republican. Lutheran. Clubs: Queen City, Commonwealth, Queen City Optimists, Cin. Country. Editorial bd. Nat. Law Jour., 1978—. Home: 1559 Moon Valley Ln Cincinnati OH 45230 Office: 1800 First National Bank Center Cincinnati OH 45202

LINDBERG, DAVID CHARLES, history of science educator; b. Mpls., Nov. 15, 1935; s. Milton Benjamin and Elizabeth Amy (MacKinney) L.; m. Greta Johnson, June 20, 1959; children—Christin Lisa, Erik David. B.S., Wheaton Coll., 1957; M.S., Northwestern U., 1959; Ph.D., Ind. U., 1965. Asst. prof. history U. Mich., Ann Arbor, 1965-67; asst. prof. history of sci. U. Wis., Madison, 1967-69, assoc. prof., 1969-72, prof., 1972-82, Evjue-Bascom prof. history of sci., 1982—; mem. Sch. Hist. Studies, Inst. for Advanced Study, Princeton U., 1970-71; Guggenheim fellow, 1977-78; NSF grantee; Nat. Endowment for Humanities grantee. Mem. History of Sci. Soc. (council 1970-72, 81-83), Mediaeval Acad. Am., Renaissance Soc. Am., Brit. Soc. for History of Sci. Author: John Pecham and the Science of Optics, 1970; Theories of Vision from al-Kindi to Kepler, 1976; Roger Bacon's Philosophy of Nature, 1983; editor: Sci. in the Middle Ages, 1978; assoc. editor Ency. Americana; adv. editor Isis, 1975-80. Home: 5038 Marathon Dr Madison WI 53705 Office: Dept History Sci 4143 H C White Hall U Wis Madison WI 53706

LINDBERG, ELAYNE VERNA, art gallery administrator; b. Browerville, Minn., Apr. 27, 1926; d. Leslie and Velma (Breighhaupt) Averill; ed. U. Minn.; m. Russell H. Lindberg, July 26, 1941; children—Gary, Bonnie Lindberg Carlson. Cert. appraiser fine art. With Dayton's Dept. Store, Mpls., 1965-71; owner, chief exec. officer Elayne Galleries, Inc., Mpls., 1970—; appraiser and restorer paintings. Mem. Am. Soc. Appraisers (cert.), World Assn. Document Examiners (charter), Internat. Soc. Appraisers, New Eng. Appraisers Assn., Cert. Antique and Art Appraisers, Fine Art Trade Guild (London), West Suburban C. of C., Francis Hook Scholarship Fund. Clubs: Calhoun Beach, Soroptomists (Mpls.). Co-author, composer verse, sacred music, choir arrangements, including A Broken Heart I Gave, There Are Times. Pioneer in handwriting analysis of questioned documents. Home: 2950 Dean Blvd Minneapolis MN 55416 Office: 6111 Excelsior Blvd St Louis Park MN 55416

LINDBERG, WILLIAM HENRY, lawyer, publishing company executive; b. Elmhurst, Ill., July 15, 1948; s. Lloyd Magnus and Helen Camille (Nelson) L.; m. Susan Irene Schieber, Aug. 26, 1972; children—Daniel, Peder, Anna. B.A., St. Olaf Coll., 1970; J.D., U. Minn., 1973. Bar: Minn. 1974. Assoc. Murphy, Lano & Kalar, Grand Rapids, Minn., 1977-78; staff atty., adminstr. Westlaw, West Pub. Co., St. Paul, 1978—. Home: 4732 10th Ave S Minneapolis MN 55407 Office: West Pub Co 50 W Kellogg Blvd St Paul MN 55102

LINDBLOM, LANCE EDMUND, foundation executive, lawyer; b. Chgo., June 17, 1948; s. Edmund John and Barbara Jean (Sahlberg) L.; m. Marjorie Press, June 13, 1971; children—Derek Press, Ian Press. B.A. magna cum laude in Govt., Harvard U., 1970; M.Pub. Affairs, Woodrow Wilson Sch. Princeton U., 1972; J.D., U. Chgo., 1978. Bar: Ill. 1978, U.S. Dist. Ct. (no. dist.) Ill. 1979, U.S. Ct. Appeals (7th cir.) 1980. Econ. and program analyst Ill. Econ. and Fiscal Commn., Ill. Gen. Assembly, 1972-73; sr. program analyst, budget examiner Ill. Bur. Budget, Exec. Office of Gov., Springfield, 1973-75, chief spl. projects unit, 1973-75; assoc, Jenner & Block, Chgo, 1978-79, 79-80; dep. dir. Mayor's Office of Budget and Mgmt., City of Chgo., 1979-80; exec. dir. J. Rocerick McArthur Found., Niles, Ill., 1980-84, pres., 1984—; sec. adv. bd. J. Roderick MacArthur Enterprises, Niles, 1981-84; dir. Donors Forum, Chgo., 1985—. Named Young Leader, Atlantik-Brucke and Am. Council on Germany, 1982. Mem. Acad. Polit. Sci., ABA (vice chmn. com. on internat. human rights of individual rights and responsibility sect.), Chgo. Council on Fgn. Relations. Avocations: reading; films; travel. Office: J Roderick Mac Arthur Found 9333 N Milwaukee Ave Niles IL 60648

LINDE, RONALD KEITH, conglomerate executive; b. Los Angeles, Jan. 31, 1940; s. Morris and Sonia Doreen (Hayman) L.; m. Maxine Helen Stern, June 12, 1960. B.S., UCLA, 1961; M.S., Calif. Inst. Tech., 1962, Ph.D., 1964. Engr., cons. scientist, dept. head Litton Industries, Inc., Beverly Hills, Calif., 1961-63; lab. chief exec., dir. phys. scis., Stanford Research Inst., Menlo Park, Calif., 1964-71; chmn., pres. Envirodyne Industries, Inc., Chgo., 1970—. Tech. reviewer sci. jours., 1967-72. Contbr. articles to jours., books and mags. Patentee in field. Mem. Founding Friends of Harvey Mudd Coll., Claremont, Calif., 1974—, Northwestern U. Assocs., Evanston, Ill., 1978—; mem. regional adv. council Calif. Inst. Tech., Pasadena, 1979—. Calif. Inst. Tech. scholar, 1961-62; Rutherford scholar, 1962-63. Mem. Sigma Xi, Tau Beta Pi, Phi Eta Sigma. Office: Envirodyne Industries Inc 222 W Adams St Suite 1200 Chicago IL 60606

LINDEBORG, RICHARD ANDREW, editor; b. Lansing Mich., Dec. 24, 1946; s. Robert Gustav and Margaret Eloise (Isley) L.; m. Susan McCreight, Mar. 30, 1970. B.A., N.Mex. Highlands U., 1968; M.S., Syracuse U., 1973; student Dartmouth Coll., 1964-65. Acting chmn. dept. communication Baker U., Baldwin, Kans., asst. prof. journalism, 1974-76; adminstrv. technician U.S. Dept. Agr. Forest Service, Sante Fe Nat. Forest, Pecos, N.Mex., 1976-78, sci. editor Rocky Mountain Forest and Range Expt. Sta., Fort Collins, Colo., 1979-82; chief sci. editor, head publs. U.S. Forest Products Lab., Madison, Wis., 1982—; instr. journalism Colo. State U., 1980, cons. speech research to pres., 1981-82. Bd. dirs. Larimer Choral Soc.; vice cmn. Community Devel. Block Grant program Ft. Collins, 1981; bd. dirs. Sante Fe County Red Cross, 1977-78. Served with U.S. Army, 1968-71. Decorated Bronze Star, Army Commendation medal; recipient Forest Service Achievement award, 1978, 81, 83, 84; John Ben Snow research asst., 1971-74. Mem. Sigma Delta Chi. Democrat. Deacon, Presbyterian Ch. Contbr. articles to profl. jours. Office: Gifford Pinchot Dr Madison WI 53705

LINDELL, ANDREA REGINA, college dean, registered nurse; b. Warren, Pa., Aug., 21, 1943; d. Andrew D. and Irene M. (Fabry) Lefik; m. Warner E. Lindell, May 7, 1966; children—Jennifer I., Jason M. B.S., Villa Maria Coll., 1970; M.S.N. Catholic U., 1975, D.N.Sc., 1975; diploma R.N., St. Vincent's Hosp., Erie, Pa. Instr. St. Vincent Hosp. Sch. Nursing, 1964-66; dir. Rouse Hosp., Youngsville, Pa., 1966-69; supr. Vis. Nurses Assn., Warren, Pa., 1969-70; dir. grad. program Cath. U., Washington, 1975-77; chmn., assoc. dean U. N.H., Durham, 1977-81; dean, prof. Oakland U., Rochester, Mich., 1981—; cons. Moorehead U., Ky., 1983. Editor; Jour. Profl. Nursing, 1985; contbr. articles to profl. jours. Mem. sch. bd. Strafford Sch. Dist., N.H., 1977-80; Gov.'s Blue Ribbon Commn. Direct Health Policies, Concord, N.H., 1979-81; vice chmn. New England Commn. Higher Edn. in Nursing, 1977-81; mem. Mich. Assn. Colls. Nursing, 1981—. Named Outstanding Young Woman Am., 1980. Mem. Nat. League Nursing, Am. Assn. Colls. Nursing, Sigma Theta Tau. Democrat. Roman Catholic. Avocations: water skiing; roller skating; reading; fishing; camping; Office: Oakland U 428 O Dowd Hall Rochester MI 48063

LINDELOW, DANIEL MARTIN, insurance company executive; b. Pottstown, Pa., Apr. 26, 1951; s. Daniel L. Beury and Jeanne (Fogarty) Beury Lindelow; m. Mary L. Kociban, May 11, 1974. B.A., U. Pitts., 1972. Systems analyst Nationwide Ins. Cos., Columbus, Ohio, 1975-78, methods engring. sr. analyst, 1978-80, methods engring. supr., 1980-82, data quality mgr., 1982-85, ops. controls mgr.-west, 1985—. Mem. jr. arts council Columbus Mus. Art, 1984-85. Mem. Adminstrv. Mgmt. Soc. (bd. dirs. 1983-85). Republican. Roman Catholic. Club: Toastmasters. Avocations: building antique furniture reproductions; bonsai; bicycling; reading. Home: 6646 Merry Ln Columbus OH 43229 Office: Nationwide Ins Cos One Nationwide Plaza 31-T Columbus OH 43229

LINDEMAN, LENORE HELEN, jewelry company executive; b. Evanston, Ill., Oct. 4, 1949; d. Walter E. and Gladys H. (Sykora) L. B.S. in Communications, U. Ill., 1971. Copywriter Marshall Field & Co., Chgo., 1971-73, Hart Schaffner & Marx, Chgo., 1973-75; asst. to dir. corp. communications Apeco Corp., Evanston, 1975-76; buyer Beeline Fashions Inc.-Act II Jewelry, Bensenville, Ill., 1976-81; merchandise mgr. Act II Jewelry, Bensenville, 1981-84, v.p., 1984—. Mem. Direct Selling Assn., Direct Mktg. Assn. Lutheran. Office: Act II Jewelry Inc 101 Leland Ct Bensenville IL 60106

LINDEMEYER, MICHAEL ROBERT, optometrist, church musician; b. Balt., Apr. 29, 1957; s. Robert William and Alice Elizabeth (Moose) L.; m. Marilyn Ann Lueth, Aug. 25, 1984; 1 stepson, Matthew Todd. Student U. Md., 1975-78; B.S., So. Coll. Optometry, 1980, O.D., 1982. Lic. optometrist, Wis., N.Y., Mo. Optometrist, Pearle Vision Ctr., Milw., 1982—. Organist, Beautiful Savior Luth. Ch., Memphis, 1980-82, Pentecost Luth. Ch., Milw., 1982—. Republican. Avocation: jogging; swimming; bowling; reading; music. Home: 10543 Beacon Hill Ct E Franklin WI 53132 Office: Pearle Vision Ctr 2812 S 108th St West Allis WI 53227

LINDER, FRANK WALTER, utility company executive; b. Washington, Ill., Mar. 23, 1918; s. Walter Henry and Louise (Lowell Miller) L.; m. Kathleen Almira Reese, Sept. 10, 1947; children—Jean, Mark, Kay, Greg. B.E.E., U. Ill., 1940. Elec. engr. Rural Electrification Adminstrn., 1940-47; chief elec. engr. Dairyland Power Coop., 1947-73, asst. gen. mgr., 1973-78, gen. mgr., 1978—; dir. Norwest Bank La Crosse, N.A., Inst. Nuclear Power Ops., Chippewa Flambeau Improvement Co. Chmn. Bd. Elec. Examiners, City of La Crosse. Recipient Nikola Tesla award Westinghouse Electric Corp., 1984. Mem. IEEE, Power Engring. Soc. Methodist. Lodge: Kiwanis. Home: 2416 Hoeschler Dr La Crosse WI 54601 Office: 2615 East Ave S La Crosse WI 54601

LINDGREN, WILLIAM DALE, librarian; b. Peoria, Ill., Mar. 8, 1936; s. Hugh Gottfried and Olive Kathryn (Myer) L. B.A., Bradley U., 1958, M.A., 1959; M.S. in L.S., U. Ill., 1967. Tchr., Limestone High Sch., Bartonville, Ill., 1960-68; asst. dir. Learning Resources Center, Ill. Central Coll., East Peoria, 1968-73, dir., 1973—. Chmn. East Peoria Oral History Com., 1983-84. Mem. ALA, Ill. Library Assn., Assn. Ednl. Media Tech., Assn. Ednl. Media and Tech. Ill., Council Library Technology. Club: Creve Coeur (Peoria). Office: Ill Central Coll East Peoria IL 61635

LINDHOLM, CARL EDWARD, auto manufacturing company executive; b. N.Y.C.; s. Carl Edward and Elsie (Krone) L.; m. Louise MacDonald, June 14, 1952; children—Jeffrey, Julia, Claire. B.S., Webb Inst., 1950; M.S. in Indsl. Engring., NYU, 1952, M.B.A., 1954. With Motorola Corp., Schaumburg, Ill., 1967—, sr. v.p., gen. mgr. Auto div., 1975-78, sr. v.p., gen. mgr., auto and indsl. electronics group, 1978-84, exec. v.p., gen. mgr., 1984—. Office: Motorola Inc Auto and Indsl Electronics Group 1299 E Algonquin Rd Schaumburg IL 60196

LINDNER, CARL HENRY, financial holding company executive. Chmn., chief exec. officer United Brands Co., N.Y.C., Am. Fin. Corp., Cin. Office: Am Fin Corp One E 4th St Cincinnati OH 45202*

LINDSETH, VIRGINIA MACDONALD, educational psychologist; b. Ithaca, N.Y., Apr. 17, 1935; d. John Winchester and Mary Elizabeth (Browne) MacDonald; m. Jon Andrew Lindseth; children—Andrew, Steven, Karen, Peter. B.A., Cornell U., 1956; M.A., John Carroll U., 1975; Ph.D., Case Western Res. U., 1980. Cert. sch. counselor, Ohio. Dean of students Hathaway Brown Sch., Shaker Heights, Ohio, 1970-75, head Upper Sch., 1974-75; dir. studies Univ. Sch. Upper Sch., Hunting Valley, Ohio, 1975-79; asst. dir., dir. studies Lower Sch., Shaker Heights, 1979—. Mem. Am. Psychol. Assn. Republican. Roman Catholic.

LINDSEY, BEVERLY SUE, educator; b. Muncie, Ind., June 14, 1930; d. Rollin William and Merkel May (Ruckman) L.; diploma Meth. Hosp. Sch. Nursing, Indpls., 1952; B.S. in Nursing, U. Mo., 1962; M.S. in Nursing, U. Colo., 1972; postgrad. U. Kans., 1979-80, U. Mo., 1980—. Gen. duty nurse U. Kans. Med. Center, 1952-53; staff nurse med.-surg. intensive care unit VA Hosp., Kansas City, Mo., 1953-55, head nurse, 1957-60; instr. med.-surg. nursing U. Mo., Columbia, 1962-64; sch. nurse tchr. Kansas City (Mo.) Bd. Edn., 1964; med.-surg. coordinator Research Hosp. and Med. Center, Kansas City, Mo., 1964-65; instr. practical nurse program Kansas City Bd. Edn., 1965-66; nurse instr. cardiology Kansas City (Mo.) Gen. Hosp. and Med. Center, 1966-68, edn. coordinator programmed cardiovascular care project, 1968-71; asst. prof., U. Mo. Med. Sch., Kansas City, 1967-71; asst. prof. nursing Avila Coll., Kansas City, Mo., 1972-75, asso. prof., 1975—, acting chmn. dept. nursing, 1978-79, 80-82, asso. chmn., 1979-80, asso. chmn., curriculum coordinator, 1982—; reviewer grant projects HEW, 1974-75; lectr. in field. Served to brig. gen. Nurse Corp USAFR, 1960—. Decorated Air Force Commendation medal, Air Force Meritorious Service medal. Mem. Am. Nurses Assn., Mo. Nurses Assn., Res. Officers Assn., Nat. League Nursing, Sigma Theta Tau. Club: Order Eastern Star. Contbr. articles to profl. jours. Home: 107 W Bannister Rd Kansas City MO 64114 Office: 11901 Wornall Rd Kansas City MO 64145

LINDSLEY, HERBERT PIPER, life insurance agent; b. Wichita, Kans., Dec. 16, 1913; s. Herbert Kitchel and Jessie McMahon (Piper) L.; A.B., U. Wichita, 1935; M.B.A., U. Pa., 1937; m. Barbara Irene Benzinger, Dec. 31, 1938; childen—Herbert Benzinger, Barbara Kitchel, Thomas Roland. Agt., Northwestern Mut. Ins. Co., N.Y.C., 1937-38; v.p., ednl. dir. Farmers & Bankers Life, Wichita, 1939-48; gen. agt. Occidental Life Calif., Wichita, 1948—; dir. Electric Furnace Co., Salem, Ohio; chmn. bd. Motel Devel. Corp., Wichita. Mem. Wichita Bd. Edn., 1951-59, pres., 1955; mem. Wichita City Commn., 1959-63, mayor, 1961-62. Republican. Congregationalist. Home: 230 N Terrace Dr Wichita KS 67208 Office: 200 E 1st Suite 407 Wichita KS 67202

LINEBERRY, ROBERT LEON, university dean; b. Oklahoma City, May 4, 1942; s. John and Julia (Flemming) L.; m. Nita Ann Ray, Sept. 5, 1964; children—Mary Nicole, Robert Keith. B.A., U. Okla., 1964; Ph.D., U. N.C., 1968. From asst. prof. to assoc. prof. polit. sci. U. Tex.-Austin, 1967-74; prof. polit. sci. Northwestern U., Evanston, Ill., 1974-81; dean Coll. Liberal Arts and Scis., U. Kans.-Lawrence, 1981—. Author: Equality and Urban Policy, 1977, Government in America, 2d edit., 1983; co-author: Urban Politics and Public Policy, 3d edit., 1978. NSF grantee, 1972, Law Enforcement Assistance Adminstrn. grantee, 1978. Mem. Am. Polit. Sci. Assn., Policy Studies Orgn. (past pres.), Council Colls. Arts and Scis. (dir. 1983-84). Democrat. Avocation: Skiing. Home: 321 Settlers Dr Lawrence KS 66044 Office: Coll Liberal Arts and Scis Univ Kans Lawrence KS 66045

LINEHAN, STEPHEN DAVID, health care insurance company executive; b. Moorhead, Minn., Apr. 14, 1950; s. John David and Florence Lorraine (Volkmann) L.; B.S.B.A., U. N.D., 1973; M.B.A., Lindenwood Coll., 1980; m. Christy Fay Zilson, June 8, 1974; 1 dau., Lisa. Med. rep. Arnar Stone Labs., 1973-74; with Aladdin Synergetics, 1975-81, dist. mgr., 1976-78, regional mgr., St. Louis, 1978-80, corp. sales mgr., 1981; dir. mktg. Concordia Pub. Co., St. Louis, 1981-85; dir. mktg. and devel. Met Life Health Care Mgmt. Corp., St. Louis, 1985—. Mem. Bd. of Aldermen, City of Lake St. Louis (Mo.), 1980—, pres., 1982-83, mayor, 1983—, mem. Planning and Zoning Commn., 1983—; v.p. St. Charles County Mcpl. League. Mem. Mo. Mcpl. League, Sales and Mktg. Execs., Am. Assn. Indsl. Mgmt., Lake St. Louis Community Assn. Lutheran. Home: 9 Rouen Ct Lake Saint Louis MO 63367 Office: 14500 S 40th Outer Rd Suite 110 Saint Louis MO 63017

LING, ALEXANDER, neurological surgeon; b. Tientsin, Hopei, China, June 24, 1922; came to U.S., 1941; s. Ping and Clara (Soo-Hoo) L.; m. Flora Lee Silver, Apr. 1, 1946; children—Alexander, Cynthia Ling Cheng. B.S., St. John's U., Shanghai, China, 1941; M.D., Washington U., St. Louis, 1944. Diplomate Am. Bd. Neurol. Surgery. Intern, Union Meml. Hosp., Balt., 1944-45; fellow Columbia U. Med. Ctr., N.Y.C., 1947-48; resident Cleve. Clinic, 1949-52; practice medicine, specializing in neurol. surgery, Cleve., 1952—. Served to capt. M.C., U.S. Army, 1945-47; Korea. Mem. Am. Assn. Neurol. Surgeons, Congress Neurol. Surgeons, AMA, ACS. Republican. Presbyterian. Lodge: Rotary. Avocations: skiing; scuba diving. Office: Neurosurgical Assocs NE Ohio 822 Keith Bldg Cleveland OH 44115

LING, SUMY H.C., design engineer; b. Tainan, Taiwan, Jan. 24, 1938; d. Yuan H. Wu and Jean Y. Lee; m. Cheng C. Ling, Sept. 27, 1963; children—Katherine A., Enid A. B.S., Cheng-Kung U., Taiwan, 1960; M.S., U. Cin., 1965. Design engr. Hazelet & Erdal, Cin., 1965-73; design engr. Stacey Mfg. Co., Cin., 1973-74, mgr. design engring., 1974-77, chief engr., 1977—. Mem. Archtl. Engring. Soc. Taiwan. Buddhist. Patentee in field. Home: 7831 Shadowhill Wy Cincinnati OH 45242 Office: 259 Township Ave Cincinnati OH 45216

LINN, DIANNE, media specialist; b. Decatur, Ind., Aug. 12, 1933; d. Lawrence Edward and Veronica F. (Anker) Linn. Student Hanover Coll., 1951-53; B.A., St. Francis Coll., 1963; M.L.S., Ind. U., 1966. Clerk stenographer Gen. Electric Co., Ft. Wayne, 1953-60; asst. librarian Decatur Pub. Library, 1960-62; English tchr., media specialist North Adams Community Schs., Decatur, 1963—; dir., past officer Area Library Services Authority. Sec. Decatur City Plan Commn., 1971—; past sec. Decatur Community Fund Bd.; mem. Adams County Bicentennial Com.; past officer Young Democrats; del. Democratic State Conv.; treas., librarian First Presbyn. Ch., Decatur; past pres. local United Presbyn. Women. Mem. North Adams Tchrs. Assn., Ind. State Tchrs. Assn., Ind. Hist. Soc., Adams County Hist. Soc., NEA, Assn. Ind. Media Educators, Ind. U. Alumni Assn., Ch. Women United (pres.), Alpha Delta Pi, Kappa Kappa Kappa. Home: 355 Mercer Ave Decatur IN 46733 Office: North Adams Community Schools 901 Everhart Dr Decatur IN 46733

LINN, ROBERT DALTON, financial executive; b. Ft. Dodge, Iowa, Mar. 29, 1941; s. Willis Leroy Linn and Alta Bernice (Lumsden) Fuhrman; m. Marie Leanna Long, Sept. 3, 1961; children—Luann Marie, Robert Dalton. B.S.B.A., Simpson Coll., 1963; M.B.A., U. Wis., 1973; cert. accomplishment Fox Valley Tect. Inst., 1975, Minn. Mgmt. Inst. Grad. Sch., 1981. Mgmt. trainee S.S. Kresge Co., Des Moines, 1963; assoc. mgr. Avco Fin. Co., Des Moines, 1964-67; mgr. credit, accounts receivable Koehring Farm Equipment, Appleton, Wis., 1967-76; corp. credit mgr. E.F. Johnson Co., Waseca, Minn., 1976—; v.p., gen. mgr. Johnson Credit Corp., Waseca, 1981—. Author instl. and ops. workbook The Choice Program, 1983. Treas. United Methodist Ch., Waseca, 1979-82. Mem. Nat. Assn. Credit Mgmt. (charter mem.), Am. Assn. Equipment Lessors, Land Mobile Group, Nat. Assn. Credit Mgmt. Clubs: Waseca Sno-Secas (bd. dirs. 1980-83); Business Club (Indianola, Iowa) (sec. 1961-63). Avocations: golf, fishing, camping, touring. Home: 408 4th Circle NW Waseca MN 56093 Office: E F Johnson Co 299 Johnson Ave Waseca MN 56093

LINNE, ROBERT STEVEN, lawyer; b. Indpls., Nov. 15, 1943; s. Robert Joseph and Edithe Blanch (Davison) L.; m. Beverly Christine Alexander, Apr. 26, 1969; children—R. Scott, Benjamin J. B.S. in Metall. Engring., Purdue U., 1968; J.D., Woodrow Wilson U., 1980; LL.M., Atlanta Law Sch., 1982. Bar: Ga. 1980, U.S. Patent Office 1976, U.S. Ct. Appeals (5th cir.) 1981. Research engr. Caterpillar Tractor Co., Peoria, Ill., 1968-71; patent atty. Southwire Co., Carrollton, Ga., 1971-84, Cabot Corp., Kokomo, Ind., 1984—. Patentee (5).

Mem. ABA, Ga. Bar Assn. Home: 11917 Birdie Ct Kokomo IN 46901 Office: Cabot Corp 1020 W Park Ave Kokomo IN 46901

LINNEMAN, CALVIN CUMMINS, JR., physician, researcher, educator; b. Durham, N.C., June 29, 1940; s. Calvin Cummins and Adelia (Park) L.; m. Patricia Gross, June 17, 1966; children—Timothy, Catherine, Mark. B.A., Duke U., 1961, M.D., 1965. Diplomate Am. Bd. Internal Medicine, Am. Bd. Infectious Diseases. Intern, U. Wash., Seattle, 1965-66; resident Emory U., Atlanta, 1968-70; asst. prof. medicine U. Cin., 1972-76, assoc. prof., 1976-82, prof., 1982—, dir. clin. virology lab., 1978—, dir. infection control dept. Med. Ctr., 1972—. Contbr. articles to profl. jours. Fellow ACP, Infectious Diseases Soc. Am., Am. Coll. Epidemiology. Home: 5885 Graves Lake Dr Cincinnati OH 45243 Office: U Cin Coll Medicine Div Infectious Diseases Dept Medicine Mail Location 560 Cincinnati OH 45267

LINSENMANN, WILLIAM MICHAEL, insurance company executive, lawyer; b. Cleve., Mar. 25, 1919; s. Gust C. and Genevieve L.; m. Darla G. Carlson, June 11, 1942; children—Karen Kay Linsenmann Okamoto, Darla Robin Linsenmann Brown. A.B., Kent State U., 1941; J.D. magna cum laude, Cleve. Marshall Law Sch., 1950. Bar: Ohio, 1950. Adjuster, Liberty Mut. Ins. Co., 1940-41; with Gen. Accident Ins. Co., 1945-50; adjuster Ohio Casualty Ins. Co., Cleve., 1950-52, supr., 1952-53, claim mgr., Warren, Ohio, 1953-68, Cin., 1968-69, asst. v.p., 1969-71, v.p., 1971-80, sr. v.p., 1980—. Trustee, Mercy Hosp. Served to 1st lt. U.S. Army, 1941-45. Mem. Ohio Bar Assn., Internat. Assn. Ins. Counsel, Ohio Def. Assn., Ohio Trial Lawyers Assn., Def. Research Assn. Lodge: Elks (Hamilton, Ohio). Home: 628 Sanders Dr Hamilton OH 45013

LINSON, WILLIAM EDGAR, JR., hospital public relations executive; b. Hammond, Ind., Nov. 11, 1939; s. William E. and Dora Myrlie (Hutson) L.; children—Thaddeus Michael, Lori Melissa; m. Sue Howard Lencke, Oct. 24, 1981. B.S., Ind. State U., 1965. Sports editor Robinson (Ill.) Daily News, 1965-66; sports info. dir. Ind. State U., Terre Haute, 1966-71; asst. sports info. dir. Purdue U., West Lafayette, Ind., 1971-73; asst. commr. Mid.-Am. Athletic Conf., Columbus, Ohio, 1973-79; pub. relations dir. Grant Hosp., Columbus, 1979—; pub. info. dir. Cox Med. Ctr., Springfield, Mo., 1983—; pub. relations cons. Health Mgmt. Services, Inc., 1980-83. Mem. Am. Soc. Hosp. Pub. Relations, Mo. Soc. Hosp. Pub. Relations, Pub. Relations Soc. Am. (2d v.p.). Lutheran. Office: 1423 N Jefferson St Springfield MO 65802

LINTNER, BARBARA JEAN, librarian; b. Decatur, Ill., June 1, 1942; d. Kenneth Robert and Margaret Rose (Westervelt) Bauman; m. Michael Alan Lintner, Apr. 17, 1966 (dec. 1973); children—Jeffrey Clements, Natalie Elaine. B.A., Millikin U., 1964; M.L.S., U. Ill., 1965. Extramural librarian U. Ill., Urbana, 1965-66; ref. librarian Wilmington Inst. Free Pub. Library, Del., 1966-67; children's librarian Allerton Pub. Library, Monticello, Ill., 1976-83, dir., 1984—. Pres., Piatt County Unit Am. Cancer Soc., 1976-77; leader Girl Scouts U.S.A., 1979—; troop com. mem. Boy Scouts Am., Monticello, 1980-83. Mem. ALA, Ill. Library Assn. (Davis Cup award 1981), Lincoln Trails Librarians Assn. (pres. 1981-82). Republican. Presbyterian. Club: Homemakers Extension. Home: 814 Robert Webb Monticello IL 61856 Office: Allerton Pub Library 201 N State St Monticello IL 61856

LINTON, IRMA ALBERTA, librarian; b. Indpls., Sept. 13, 1914; d. Charles Henry and Ella Theresa (Griffin) Frazier; m. Charles Edward Linton, June 11, 1949; 1 son, Thomas Edward; 1 dau., Lois Ellen Stevens. B.S., Butler U., 1936, library cert., 1969; A.M., Ind. U., 1946. Elem. tchr. Indpls. Pub. Schs., 1937-51, 61-69, library services, 1961—, media profl. Montessori Sch. #55, #58, 1984—. Mem. Delta Kappa Gamma. Republican. Roman Catholic. Home: 936 N Rochester Ave Indianapolis IN 46222

LINVILLE, JUDITH ANN, writer; b. Tulsa, Jan. 21, 1943; d. James A. and Frances E. (McElyea) Burch; m. Norman D. Linville, Aug. 24, 1968. B.A., U. Ark., 1965, M.A., 1966. Cert. secondary tchr. English, Ark. Instr. Pittsburg State U. (Kans.), 1966-70; library asst. Pub. Library Denver, 1971-73; freelance writer, St. Louis, 1973-75; features editor Jour. Newspapers, St. Louis, 1975-80; asst. editor Decor mag., St. Louis, 1980-82; sr. info. specialist U. Mo.-St. Louis, 1982—, vis. lectr., 1983; Author: We Have New Life To Share, 1979; contbr. feature articles to newspapers, 1974—, articles to mags., 1980—. Mem. Women in Communications, Phi Beta Kappa. Mem. Christian Ch. (Disciples of Christ). Office: U Mo 421 Woods Hall 8001 Natural Bridge Saint Louis MO 63121

LINZ, ANTHONY JAMES, osteopathic physician, consultant; b. Sandusky, Ohio, June 16, 1948; s. Anthony Joseph and Margaret Jane (Ballah) Linz; m. Kathleen Ann Kovach, Aug. 18, 1973; children—Anthony Scott, Sara Elizabeth. B.S., Bowling Green State U., 1971; D.O., Des Moines Coll. Osteo. Medicine and Surgery, 1974. Diplomate Nat. Bd. Osteo. Examiners; bd. cert., diplomate Am. Osteo. Bd. Internal Medicine, Internal Medicine and Med. Diseases of Chest. Intern, Brentwood Hosp., Cleve., 1974-75, resident in internal medicine, 1975-78; subsplty. fellow in pulmonary diseases Riverside Meth. Hosp., Columbus, Ohio, 1978-80; med. dir. pulmonary services Sandusky Meml. Hosp., 1980—, also cons. pulmonary diseases and internal medicine, active staff sect. internal medicine, chmn. dept. medicine, head div. pulmonary medicine; cons. staff dept. medicine Good Samaritan Hosp., also sect. internal medicine specializing pulmonary diseases; cons. pulmonary and internal medicine Providence Hosp., Sandusky, Willard Area Hosp.; clin. assoc. prof. internal medicine Ohio U. Coll. Osteo. Medicine; mem. respiratory therapy adv. bd. Firelands Campus, Bowling Green State U., 1983—;39 Contbr. article on early detection lung cancer to profl. jour. Water safety instr. ARC; med. dir. Camp Superkid Asthma Camp. Recipient Sr. award in pharmacology Coll. Osteo. Medicine and Surgery, 1974. Fellow Am. Coll. Chest Physicians; mem. Am. Osteo. Assn., Ohio Osteo. Assn. (sec.-treas. 5th dist. acad.), Am. Coll. Osteo. Internists, Am. Heart Assn., Am. Thoracic Soc., Ohio Thoracic Soc., Am. Lung Assn. (med. adv. bd. chmn., exec. bd. dirs., bd. dirs. Ohio's So. Shore sect.), Nat. Assn. Med. Dirs. Respiratory Care, Ohio Soc. Respiratory Therapy (med. adviser/dir.), Alpha Epsilon Delta, Beta Beta Beta, Atlas, Pi Kappa Alpha, Atlas Med. Fraternity. Roman Catholic.

LIPETZ, LEO ELIJAH, biophysics educator, researcher; b. Lincoln, Nebr., Aug. 10, 1921; s. Elijah Y. and Ruth D. (Leavitt) L.; m. Dorothea Ogulnick, July 4, 1947; children—Philip David, Timothy Joseph, Robert Eugene. B.E.E., Cornell U., 1942; Ph.D., U. Calif.-Berkeley, 1953. Jr. engr. U.S. Signal Corps, Balt., also Phila., 1942-43; mem. tech. staff Bell Telephone Labs., N.Y.C., 1943-46; instr. Ohio State U., 1954-55, asst. prof., 1955-60, assoc. prof., 1960-65, prof. biophysics dept., 1965-81, prof. zoology dept., 1981—, chmn. dept. biophysics, 1965-76; U.S. del. UN Sci. Com. on Effects of Atomic Radiation, 1960; mem. NRC Com. on Vision, 1962-69. Contbr. articles to sci. jours. Postdoctoral fellow Nat. Found. Infantile Paralysis, 1953-54; sr. fellow NIH, Paris, France, 1962-63, Japan Soc. Promotion of Sci., 1981. Mem. Biophys. Soc. (founder), Soc. Neurosci., (pres. central Ohio chpt. 1975-76), Assn. Research in Vision and Ophthalmology. Home: 2395 Sheringham Rd Columbus OH 43220 Office: Ohio State Univ 1314 Kinnear Rd Columbus OH 43212

LIPIN, S. BARRY, business executive, investor; b. Chgo., Oct. 7, 1920; s. Bernard and Mary (Schrier) L.; m. Priscilla Richter, Oct. 7, 1952; m. 2d, Rachel Kucheck, Nov. 21, 1976. Student Ill. Inst. Tech., 1939-41, DePaul U. Commerce, 1943-44, DePaul Coll. Law, 1944-45. Founder/owner new and used automobile sales co., Chgo., 1945—, U.S. Auto Leasing Co., Chgo., 1954; chmn., chief exec. officer Lipin Enterprises Inc. (U.S. Auto Leasing Co., Lipin Rent-A-Car, Automobile Corp. N.Am., Rifco Auto Leasing Co., Modern Cars Inc.), Chgo., 1982—; pres., chief exec. officer Paul-Sey Investment Corp. Bd. dirs. Am. Hearing Research Found., Lipin Found. Recipient State of Israel Bonds award, 1980; Automotive Industry-Leasing Div. Man of Yr. award; Spirit of Life award City of Hope, 1983. Mem. Am. Automotive Leasing Assn., Chgo. Assn. Commerce and Industry, Ill. C. of C., Phi Kappa Tau. Clubs: Variety; Canyon Country (Palm Springs, Calif.); Covenant, Mid-America, Executive. Office: 1800 N Ashland Ave Chicago IL 60622

LIPINSKI, WILLIAM OLIVER, United States congressman; b. Chgo., Dec. 22, 1937; s. Oliver and Madeline (Collins) L.; m. Rose Marie Lapinski; children—Laura, Dan. Student pub. schs. Alderman Ward 23, Chgo., 1975-83; commr. Ward 23, Democratic Com., Chgo., 1975—; del. Ill. State Platform Conv., 1974, Dem. Nat. Com. Mini Conv., Kansas City, 1974, Dem. Nat. Conv., San Francisco, 1984; mem. 98th Congress from 5th Dist., Ill., 1983—; mem. staff Chgo. Park and Recreation Dept., 1958-75. Recipient Businessman and Mchts. award 43d Ward, 1977; Archer Heights Civic Assn. award, 1979; named Man of Yr., Chgo. Park Dist., 1983. Mem. Chgo. Hist. Soc. Roman Catholic. Address: 1032 Longworth House Office Bldg Washington DC 20515

LIPMAN, DAVID, editor; b. Springfield, Mo., Feb. 13, 1931; s. Benjamin and Rose (Mack) L.; B.J., U. Mo., 1953; m. Marilyn Lee Vittert, Dec. 10, 1961; children—Gay Ilene, Benjamin Alan. Sports editor Jefferson City (Mo.) Post-Tribune, 1953, Springfield Daily News, 1953-54; gen. assignment reporter Springfield Leader and Press, 1956-57; reporter, copy editor Kansas City (Mo.) Star, 1957-60; sports reporter St. Louis Post-Dispatch, 1960-66, asst. sports editor, 1966-68, news editor, 1968-71, asst. mng. editor, 1971-78, mng. editor, 1979—; v.p., dir. Pulitzer Prodns. Inc., 1981—; guest lectr. Am. Press Inst., Columbia Journalism Sch., 1967-70; mem. alumni publs. bd. U. Mo. Bd. dirs. Mid-Am. Press Inst., 1973—, chmn., 1975-77; bd. dirs. Mid-Am. Newspaper Conf., 1973-75; trustee United Hebrew Congregation, 1975-77. Served to 1st lt. USAF, 1954-56. Mem. Football Writers Assn. Am. (bd. dirs. 1968), U. Mo. Sch. Journalism Nat. Alumni Assn. (nat. chmn. 1980-82), Sigma Delta Chi (pres. St. Louis chpt. 1976-77), Kappa Tau Alpha, Omicron Delta Kappa. Jewish. Author: Maybe I'll Pitch Forever, 1962; Mr. Baseball, The Story of Branch Rickey, 1966; Ken Boyer, 1967; Joe Namath, 1968; co-author: The Speed King, The Story of Bob Hayes, 1971, Bob Gibson Pitching Ace, 1975, Jim Hart Underrated Quarterback, 1977. Office: 900 N Tucker Blvd Saint Louis MO 63101

LIPNICK, STANLEY MELVIN, lawyer; b. Washington, Nov. 14, 1934; s. Max and Cecilia (Hollins) L.; m. Judith Sara Berman, Nov. 19, 1961; children—Stuart, Laura Gail. B.A., Columbia Coll., N.Y.C., 1956; J.D. with honors, George Washington U., 1960. Bar: D.C. 1960, Colo. 1967, Ill. 1968, Fla. 1983. Law clk. U.S. Ct. Appeals, Washington, 1960-61; trial atty. FTC, Washington, 1961-66; assoc. Ireland, Stapleton, Pryor & Holmes, Denver, 1966-68; ptnr. Arnstein, Gluck, Lehr, Barron & Milligan, Chgo. and West Palm Beach, 1968—. Mem. ABA, Bar Assn. D.C., Chgo. Bar Assn. Office: Arnstein Gluck Lehr Barron & Milligan 7500 Sears Tower Chicago IL 60606

LIPNIK, MORRIS JACOB, physician; b. Detroit, Aug. 27, 1922; s. Louis and Lillian (Portney) L.; m. Lois Russine Wertheimer, Dec. 8, 1946; children—Susan, Carol. B.A., Wayne State U., 1943, M.D., 1946. Diplomate Am. Bd. Dermatology. Intern, Detroit Receiving Hosp., 1946-47; resident Johns Hopkins Hosp., Balt., 1947-48, Hosp. of U. Pa., 1949-51; practice medicine specializing in dermatology, Southfield, Mich., 1953—; mem. staff Sinai Hosp., Detroit, 1954-60, Cottage Hosp., Grosse Pointe, Mich., 1957-60, St. John Hosp. Detroit, 1954-60, Mt. Carmel Hosp., Detroit, 1966—; spl. lectr. U. Detroit Dental Sch., 1958-63; adj. clin. prof. dermatology Marygrove Coll., Detroit, 1979—. Contbr. articles to med. jours. Mem. Founders' Soc. Detroit Inst. Arts, 1962; pres. Center Theatre, Detroit, 1963; patron Detroit Symphony Orch., 1978, Mich. Opera Theatre, Detroit, 1980, Detroit Community Music Sch., 1981, 82, 83. Served to capt. AUS, 1947-49. Mem. Mich. Dermatol. Soc., AMA, Am. Acad. Dermatology, Phi Delta Epsilon. Clubs: Renaissance (Detroit); Standard (North Southfield). Office: M J Lipnik PC 17000 W 8 Mile Rd Suite 226 Southfield MI 48075 also 29829 Telegraph Rd Southfield MI 48034

LIPSCHULTZ, M. RICHARD, accountant; b. Chgo., July 5, 1913; s. Morris David and Minnie (Moskowitz) L.; student Northwestern U., 1930-35; J.D., De Paul U., 1948; m. Evelyn Smolin, May 16, 1945 (dec. 1963); m. Phyllis Siegel, July 11, 1965; children—Howard Elliott, Carl Alvin, Saul Martin. Admitted to Ill. bar, 1948; auditor State of Ill., Chgo., 1938-41; conferee IRS, Chgo., 1941-49; tax acct. A.I. Grade & Co., C.P.A.s, Chgo., 1949-50; sr. ptnr. Lipschultz Bros., Levin and Gray and predecessor firms, C.P.A.s, Chgo., 1950-82; fin. v.p., dir. Miller Asso. Industries, Inc., Skokie, 1973-74; dir. Miller Builders, Inc.; dir., chmn. exec. com. Portable Electric Tools, Inc., Geneva, Ill., 1963-67; mem. exec. com. Midland Screw Corp., Chgo., 1958-66; faculty John Marshall Law Sch., 1951-64. Bd. dirs., sec., treas. Phil Pekow Family Found.; pres. bd. dirs. Lipschultz Bros. Family Found. Served with USAAF, 1943-46. C.P.A., Ill. Mem. Ill. Soc. C.P.A.s, Am. Inst. C.P.A.s, ABA, Fed., Chgo., Ill. bar assns., Decalogue Soc. Lawyers, Am. Legion, Nu Beta-Epsilon. Mem. B'nai B'rith. Clubs: Standard (Chgo.); Ravinia Green Country (Deerfield, Ill.). Contbr. articles to profl. jours. Home: 1671 E Mission Hills Rd Northbrook IL 60062

LIPSCHULTZ, MAURICE ALLEN, machinery co. exec.; b. Chgo., Aug. 5, 1912; s. Isadore M. and Minnie (Tuchow) L.; student Crane Jr. Coll., 1928-29, U. Chgo., 1929-30; m. Sarah Goldsher, Aug. 29, 1934; children—Nathan M., Arthur H., Martin P. Pres. Malco Machinery Co., Chgo., 1939—; sec.-treas. Continental Drill Corp., Chgo., 1951-65; chmn. Viking Drill and Tool Co., St. Paul, 1965—; chmn. Reltool Corp., St. Paul, 1965—; chmn. Namco Devel. Corp., Eye Corp.; partner Namco Mgmt. Co., Namco Devel. Co.; treas. Conwell Bldg. Corp., 1960—; dir. AIM Cos., Detroit, 1969—. Mem. art vis. com. U. Chgo.; mem. art adv. bd. Spertus Mus.; bd. dirs. Gottlieb Meml. Hosp., Museum Contemporary Art, Chgo., Evanston (Ill.) Art Center, D'Arcy Galleries, Loyola U., Chgo., Ukrainian Mus. Modern Art, Boca Raton Ctr. for Arts. Jewish (dir. temple). Mason. Club: Covenant (Chgo.). Home: 1342 Jackson Ave River Forest IL 60305 Office: 214 S Clinton St Chicago IL 60606

LIPSCOMB, JACK EUGENE, advertising executive; b. Springfield, Mo., Aug. 30, 1927; s. Forest W. and Elizabeth (Cotner) L.; m. Cathryn Cox, June 25, 1949; children—Cynthia Lipscomb Daniel, Lawrence W. B.A. in Bus., U. Mo., 1951. Pres. Overland Outdoor Advt., Poplar Bluff, Mo., 1960—, Pioneer Advt. Co., Springfield, 1970—, Superior Outdoor Advt., Springfield, 1970—, Modern Neon and Plastics, Springfield, 1970—, Lipscomb Bros. Co., Springfield, 1980—; v.p. Lipscomb Grain and Seed Co., Springfield, 1980—; dir. Boatmen's Nat. Bank, Springfield. Bd. dirs. Springfield Airport, 1959-66. Served to maj. USAFR, 1951-60. Mem. Nat. Outdoor Advt. Assn. Am. (vice chmn., Bd. dirs. 1958-66), Sigma Nu. Presbyterian. Club: Hickory Hills Country (Springfield). Lodges: Masons, Shriners (potentate Abou Ben Adhem 1972-73). Avocations: travel; golf. Home: 2909 Southern Hills Springfield MO 65804 Office: Pioneer Advt Co 3121 E Elm St Springfield MO 65803

LIPTON, MICHEL JOHN, consulting engineering executive; b. Paris, France, Apr. 10, 1928; s. Gerald D. and Germaine (Chaison) L.; m. Elizabeth Mary Wittlin, Feb. 2, 1951; 1 child, James B. B.S., MIT, 1947. Registered profl. engr., N.Y. From asst. v.p. to sr. v.p. PRC Harris, Madrid (Spain) and N.Y., 1962-78; from v.p. to sr. v.p. PRC Engring., N.Y.C., 1978-83, div. pres., Chgo., 1983—. Mem. ASCE. Home: 666 N Lake Shore Dr Chicago IL 60611 Office: PRC Engineering 303 E Wacker Dr Chicago IL 60601

LIS, LAWRENCE FRANCIS, facsimile company executive; b. Blue Island, Ill., Jan. 27, 1941; s. Anthony C. and Ann Marion (Galazin) L.; student DeVry Inst. Tech., 1958-59; m. Barbara Jean Lisak, Oct. 19, 1963; children—Christ and Connie (twins), David S. With Telautograph Corp., Chgo., 1959-64; regional mgr. Datalog div. Litton Industries, Chgo., 1964-74; regional mgr. Rapicom Inc., Chgo., 1974-78, nat. dir. field service ops., Hillside, Ill., 1978-79, v.p. customer service div., 1979—, v.p. customer service div. Ricoh Corp. and Rapifax of Can. Ltd. subs. Ricoh Ltd., 1980—. Lt. col. CAP, 1957—, dep. research and devel., 1972-75, dir. communications Ill. wing, group comdr., 1983-84, dep. wing comdr., 1984—; dir. Emergency Services and Disaster Agy., Village of Chicago Ridge, 1977-82; mem. Ill. CD Council. Mem. Assn. Field Service Mgrs. (pres. Chgo. chpt. 1984-85), Armed Forces Communications and Electronics Assn., Suburban Amateur Radio Assn., Mendel High Sch Alumni Assn. Home: 10401 Leslie Ln Chicago Ridge IL 60415 Office: 4415 W Harrison St Hillside IL 60162

LISEC, W(ARREN) MICHAEL, architect; b. Chgo., Mar. 26, 1938; s. Otto and Irene Ann (Minarik) L.; m. Katherine Ann Miller, Dec. 19, 1959; children. B.Arch., U. Ill., 1961. Designer, project architect Harry Weese & Assocs., Chgo., 1961-76, pres., 1976-77; founder, pres. Lisec & Biederman Ltd., Architects and Planners, Chgo., 1977—. Bd. dirs. Unity Temple Restoration Found., Oak Park, Ill., chmn. archtl. adv. com.; v.p. Friends of Downtown (Chgo.). Mem. AIA, Landmark Preservation Council Ill., Nat. Trust Hist. Preservation. Contbr. articles to profl. jours. Home: 718 Bonnie Brae River Forest IL 60305 Office: 407 S Dearborn St Suite 505 Chicago IL 60605

LISHER, JAMES RICHARD, lawyer; b. Aug. 28, 1947; s. Leonard B. and Mary Jane (Rafferty) L.; m. Martha Gettelfinger, June 16, 1973; children—Jennifer, James Richard II. A.B., Ind. U., 1969, J.D., 1975. Bar: Ind. 1975, U.S. Dist. Ct. (so. dist.) Ind. 1975. Assoc. Rafferty & Wood, Shelbyville, Ind., 1976, Rafferty & Lisher, Shelbyville, 1976-77; dep. prosecutor Shelby County Prosecutor's Office, Shelbyville, 1976-78; ptnr. Yeager & Lisher, Shelbyville, 1977—; pros. atty. Shelby County, Shelbyville, 1983—. Editor: (seminar manual) Traffic Case Defenses, 1982. Bd. dirs. Girls Club of Shelbyville, 1979-84, Bears of Blue River Festival, Shelbyville, 1982—. Recipient Citation of Merit, Young Lawyers Assn. Mem. State Bar Assn. (bd. dirs.), Ind. State Bar Assn. (bd. dirs. young lawyer sect 1979—), Shelby County Bar Assn., Ind. Pros. Attys. Assn. (bd. dirs. 1985—). Democrat. Lodges: Masons, Elks, Lions. Home: 48 W Mechanic St Shelbyville IN 46176 Office: Yeager & Lisher Law Firm 406 S Harrison St Shelbyville IN 46176

LISHER, JOHN LEONARD, lawyer; b. Indpls., Sept. 19, 1950; s. Leonard Boyd and Mary Jane (Rafferty) L.; m. Mary Katherine Sturmon, Aug. 17, 1974. B.A. with honors in History, Ind. U., 1975, J.D., 1975. Bar: Ind. 1975. Dep. atty. gen. State of Ind., Indpls., 1975-78; asst. corp. counsel City of Indpls., 1978-81; assoc. Osborn & Hiner, Indpls., 1981—. Vol. Mayflower Clasic, Indpls., 1981—; asst. vol. coordinator Marion County Republican Com., Indpls., 1979-80; vol. com. to re-elect Theodore Sendak, Indpls., 1976—, Don Bogard for Atty. Gen., Indpls., 1980, Steve Goldsmith for Prosecutor, Indpls., 1979, 83, Sheila Suess for Congress, Indpls., 1980. Recipient Outstanding Young Man of Am. award Jaycees, 1979, Indpls. Jaycees, 1980. Mem. ABA, Ind. State Bar Assn., Indpls. Bar Assn. (membership com.), Assn. Trial Lawyers Am., Ind. U., Alumni Assn., Hoosier Alumni Assn. (charter, founder, pres.), Ind. U. Coll. Arts and Scis. (bd. dirs. 1983—), Wabash Valley Alumni Assn. (charter), Founders Club, Presidents Club, Phi Beta Kappa, Eta Sigma Phi, Phi Eta Sigma, Delta Xi Alumni Assn. (charter, v.p., sec., Delta Xi chpt. Outstanding Alumnus award 1975, 76, 79, 83), Delta Xi Housing Corp. (pres.), Pi Kappa Alpha (midwest regional pres. 1977—, parliamentarian nat. convention 1982, del. convs. 1978-80, 82, 84). Presbyterian. Avocations: reading; golf; jogging; Roman coin collecting. Home: 7919 Buckskin Dr Indianapolis IN 46250 Office: Osborn & Hiner 2511 E 46th St Bldg U Indianapolis IN 46205

LISMAN, MICHAEL RAY, government administrator, clergyman; b. Richlands, Va., Feb. 3, 1952; s. Daniel and Rosevet W. Lisman. m. Diedre Lynn Payne, Sept. 15, 1972; children—Mich'El, Alexandria. B.A. in Communications, Kent State U., 1977; M.R.E., Berean Bible Coll., 1980. Ordained to ministry Apostolic Faith, 1980. Acad. dean Berean Bible Coll., Akron, Ohio, 1981-83; adj. faculty Youngstown State U., Ohio, 1982-84; retng. mgr. Alt. EEO Office and SYEP Coordinator Pvt. Ind. Council, Akron, 1982—; youth motivator Youth Motivational Task Force, Akron, 1983—; chmn. bus devel. com. 4th Ward Council, Akron, 1984—; owner, mgr. Alexandria's Books & Christian Supply, Akron, 1983—. Founding minister Maranatha Apostolic Ministries. Mem. Christian Booksellers Assn. Office: Pvt Industry Council 480 W Tuscarawas Barberton OH 44203

LISOWSKI-GLAD, SUZANNE JANET, consulting forensic psychologist; b. Chgo., Aug. 7, 1952; s. Edward A. and Rose (Plonka) L.; m. Wayne R. Glad, Sept. 11, 1982. B.A., St. Mary-of-the-Woods Coll., 1973; M.S., Ind. State U., 1975; Ph.D., U. Wis.-Milw., 1981. Community mental health worker Hamilton Mental Health Ctr., Terre Haute, Ind. 1973-75; psychometric asst. Behavioral Services Ltd. Milw., 1977-81; clin. psychology intern Chgo.-Read Mental Health Ctr., 1978-79; staff psychologist Maine Ctr. for Mental Health, Park Ridge, Ill., 1978-81; cons. psychologist Behavioral Services Ltd., Milw., 1981-82, North Shore Psychol. Services, Libertyville, Ill., 1982—; cons. forensic psychologist, Milw., 1982—; mentor Alverno Coll. Mem. Am. Psychol. Assn., Wis. Psychol. Assn. (chmn. pub. relations), Milw. Area Psychol. Assn., Soc. Clin. and Cons. Psychologists, Nat. Register Health Service Providers in Psychology, NOW. Home: 2525 South Shore Dr Milwaukee WI 53207 Office: 4022 W Burleigh St Milwaukee WI 53210

LIST, ARTHUR DAVID, lawyer; b. Newark, Ohio, Aug. 24, 1935; s. Arthur David and Goldie Mae (Imhoff) L.; m. Mary Jo Williams, Jan. 11, 1964; children—David Andrew, Barbara Lynn, Sarah Mary. B.A., Ohio State U., 1956; J.D., 1958. Bar: Ohio 1958. Ptnr., Jones, Norpell, List, Miller & Howarth, Newark, 1959—; solicitor City of Newark, 1962-67. Mem. Licking County Bar Assn. ABA, Order of Coif. Republican. Methodist. Club: Moundbuilders Country. Lodge: Rotary. Home: 724 Snowdon Dr Newark OH 43055 Office: 2 N 1st St PO Box 4010 Newark OH 43055

LIST, CHARLES EDWARD, management and organization development consultant; b. Chgo., May 9, 1941; s. Kermit Paul and Johanna Emma (Staat) L.; B.A., Valparaiso U., 1963; M.A., St. Marys Coll., Winona, Minn., 1980; Ph.D. in Orgn. Devel., Union Coll., Cin., 1984; m. Susan Mary Nelson, July 20, 1968; children—Andrea Sarang, Darcy Young. Mem. personnel staff Control Data Corp., Mpls., 1965-72; mgr. human resource center Supervalu Stores, Mpls., 1973-74; dir. personnel Internat. Dairy Queen, Mpls., 1974-77; mgr. mgmt. and orgn. devel. Cardiac Pacemakers Inc., St. Paul, 1977-82; adj. faculty instr. U. Minn., Normandale Community Coll.; instr. Met. State U., St. Paul, 1972—. Served with USMC, 1963-64. Recipient Instr. Recognition award Met. State U., 1975, 80. Mem. Am. Soc. Personnel Adminstrn., Am. Soc. Tng. and Devel. Episcopalian. Contbr. articles to profl. jours. Home: 4940 Wintersét Dr Minnetonka MN 55343

LIST, GLORIA TAMARA, dental educator, dentist; b. Madison, Wis., Aug. 22, 1938; d. August Heinrich and Teresa Ethel (Hoffer) L. B.S., Mount Mary Coll., Milw., 1962; D.D.S., Marquette U., 1964, M.A., 1981. Joined Sch. Sisters Notre Dame, 1958. Dentist, Sch. Sisters Notre Dame, Mequon, Wis., 1964—; tchr. high sch. sci. Caroline Acad., Mequon, 1966-69; mem. faculty Marquette U., Milw., 1970—; dental missionary Archdiocese Milw., Asunción, Paraguay, summer 1968. Bd. dirs. Mount Mary Coll., Milw., 1983—. Mem. Am. Dental Assn., Am. Assn. Dental Schs., Wis. Dental Assn., Greater Milw. Dental Assn. Roman Catholic. Avocation: needlework. Home: 5522 W Bluemound Rd Milwaukee WI 53208 Office: Marquette U Sch Dentistry 604 N 16th St Milwaukee WI 53233

LISTER, CHARLES FREDERICK, county official; b. Champaign, Ill., Mar. 6, 1949; s. Clifford George Lister and Nellie Busey (Sturts) Lister Garret; m. Kathryn L. Lusader, June 1, 1974; 1 child, Caitlin Louise. A.A., Parkland Jr. Coll., 1973; B.A., Eastern Ill. U., 1975. Laborer, U. Ill., Champaign, 1967-68; personnel analyst Ill. Dept. Personnel, Springfield, 1975-76; asst. dir. Coles County Assn. for Retarded, Charleston, Ill., 1976-78; sheriff Coles County Sheriff's Dept., 1978—; cons. Nat. Inst. Corrections, Boulder, Colo., 1979-80, Ill. Dept. Corrections, Springfield, 1979—. Charter mem. Coles County Coalition of Domestic Violence, Charleston, 1981. Served as sgt. U.S. Army, 1968-71, Vietnam. Named Employer of Yr., Am. Bus. Women's Assn., 1981. Mem. Ill. Sheriffs Assn. (mem. exec. bd. 1980—), Nat. Sheriffs Assn., Internat. Chiefs of Police Assn., Am. Correctional Assn., Chi Psi. Democrat. Club: Coles County Corvette (Charleston). Avocations: weight lifting; restoration of old cars, motorcycles. Home: Box 270 Rural Route 3 Mattoon IL 61938

LITCHFIELD, JOHN HYLAND, microbiologist; b. Scituate, Mass., Feb. 13, 1929; s. Frank Albert and Alma (Hyland) L.; m. Dianne Chappell, Apr. 15, 1966; 1 child, Robert Chappell. S.B., MIT, 1950; M.S., U. Ill., 1954, Ph.D., 1956. Chemist, Searle Food Corp., Hollywood, Fla., 1950-51; research food technologist Swift & Co., Chgo., 1956-57; asst. prof. Ill. Inst. Tech., Chgo., 1957-60; research leader Battelle Meml. Inst., Columbus, Ohio, 1960—; cons. to food industry, Chgo., 1951-60; adj. assoc. prof. Ohio State U., Columbus, 1977-79. Co-author: Food Plant Sanitation, 1962. Contbr. articles to sci. jours. Patentee in field. Served to 1st lt. U.S. Army, 1951-53. Fellow Am. Acad. Microbiology, AAAS, Am. Inst. Chemists, Am. Pub. Health Assn., Inst. Food Technologists (Disting. service award Ohio Valley sect. 1980), Royal Soc. Health; mem. Soc. Indsl. Microbiology (pres. 1970-71); Charles Porter award 1977). Home: 255 Bryant Ave Worthington OH 43085 Office: Battelle Meml Inst 505 King Ave Columbus OH 43201

LITES, DAYLE EMORY, city official; b. Many, La., Sept. 4, 1932; s. Joseph G. and Myrtle (Bryant) L.; m. Leona LaFleur, May 7, 1955 (dec. 1969); children—Lynn M., Daniel B.; m. Rene Hand, Mar. 4, 1972; 1 child, Christopher D.; m. Joan E. Johnson, July 23, 1983. B.A., Northeastern Ill. U., 1978; grad. FBI Nat. Acad., 1973. Patrolman, Glenview Police Dept., Ill., 1958-66, sgt., 1966-69, lt., 1969-79, comdr. patrol, 1974-78, comdr. criminal investigations, 1968-73; chief of police, chief adminstr. Roselle Police Dept., Ill., 1979—. Served as sgt. USAF, 1951-55. Mem. Internat. Assn. Chiefs Police, FBI Nat. Acad. Assn., Ill. Police Assn. Avocation: golf. Home: 862 Springfield Dr Roselle IL 60172 Office: Roselle Police Dept 103 S Prospect Roselle IL 60172

LITTLE, EUGENE ROLAND, architect; b. Canton, Ohio, Jan. 30, 1928; s. George C. and Iva L. (Boron) L.; m. Marilyn Alice Aman, June 13, 1953;

children—Eugene Roland, Kimberly Dewitt, G. Bradley, Jonathan, W. Garth. B.Arch. U. Notre Dame. Registered architect, Ohio. Architect John L. Kline, Springfield, Ohio, 1953-63; ptnr. Screiber, Little & Assocs., Springfield, 1963—. Served with U.S. Army, 1946-48. Mem. AIA, Springfield C. of C., U.S. Power Squadrons, Dayton Power Squadron (lt. col.) Order of Foresters. Roman Catholic. Home: 3473 Rocky Point Rd Springfield OH 45502 Office: 352 E High St Springfield OH 45505

LITTLE, RICHARD ALLEN, mathematics and computer science educator; b. Coshocton, Ohio, Jan. 12, 1939; s. Charles M. and Elsie Leanna (Smith) L.; m. Gail Louann Koons, June 12, 1960; children—Eric, J. Alice, Stephanie. B.S. in Math. cum laude, Wittenberg U., 1960; M.A. in Edn., Johns Hopkins U., 1961; Ed.M. in Math., Harvard U., 1965; Ph.D. in Math. Edn., Kent State U., 1971. Tchr. Culver Acad., Ind., 1961-65; instr., curriculum cons. Harvard U., Cambridge, Mass. and Aiyetoro, Nigeria, 1965-67; from instr. to assoc. prof. Kent State U., Canton, Ohio, 1967-75; from assoc. prof. to prof. Baldwin-Wallace Coll., Berea, Ohio, 1975—; cons. in field; lectr. various colls. and univs. Contbr. articles to profl. jours. Catechism tchr. St. Paul Luth. Ch., Berea, 1976-84, lector, 1980—; bd. deacons Holy Cross Luth. Ch., Canton, 1968-74, chmn., 1971-74; bd. dirs. Canton Symphony Orch., 1973-75. Mem. Ohio Council Tchrs. Math. (pres. 1974-76, v.p. 1970-73, sec. 1982-84), Greater Cleve. Council Tchrs. Math. (bd. dirs. 1979-82), Greater Canton Council Tchrs. Math. (pres. 1969-70), Math. Assn. Am. (pres. Ohio sect. 1983-84, editor 1978-83). Avocations: jogging, tennis, handball. Home: 243 Kraft St Berea OH 44017 Office: Baldwin-Wallace Coll Math and Computer Sci Dept Berea OH 44017

LITTLE, ROGER WILLIAM, sociology educator; b. Moose Lake, Minn., Feb. 3, 1922; s. Emmet Joseph and Frances Cecelia (Spencer) L.; m. Irmgard Elizabeth Schmidtmann, Sept. 11, 1948; children—Thomas, Anne, Mary, Erika. A.B., Harvard U., 1948; M.A., U. Chgo., 1949; Ph.D., Mich. State U., 1955. Commd. 2d lt. U.S. Army, 1940, advanced through grades to lt. col., 1966, instr. U.S. Mil. Acad., West Point, N.Y., 1962-66; prof. U. Ill.-Chgo., 1966—; cons. U.S. Army C.E., Champaign, Ill., 1974—, Argonne Nat. Lab., Ill., 1978-82. Editor: Handbook of Military Institutions, 1971; Selective Service and American Society, 1969 Mem. Am. Sociol. Assn., Midwest Sociol. Assn. Democrat. Roman Catholic. Avocations: photography; woodwork; bicycling. Home: 226 10th St Wilmette IL 60091 Office: U Ill at Chgo PO Box 4348 Chicago IL

LITTLEFIELD, VIVIAN M., nursing educator, administrator; b. Princeton, Ky., Jan. 24, 1938; d. Willard Anson and Hester V. (Haydon) Moore; children—Darrell, Virginia. B.S. magna cum laude, Tex. Christian U., 1960; M.S., U. Colo., 1964; Ph.D., U. Denver, 1979. Staff nurse USPHS Hosp., Ft. Worth, Tex., 1960-61; instr. nursing Tex. Christian U., Ft. Worth, 1961-62; nursing supr. Colo. Gen. Hosp., Denver, 1964-65, pvt. patient practitioner, 1974-78; asst. prof. nursing U. Colo., Denver, 1965-69, asst. prof., clin. instr., 1971-74, asst. prof., 1974-76, acting asst. dean, assoc. prof. continuing edn., regional perinatal project, 1976-78; assoc. prof., chair dept. women's health care nursing U. Rochester Sch. Nursing, N.Y., 1979-84; clin. chief ob-gyn., nursing U. Rochester Strong Meml. Hosp., N.Y., 1979-84; prof., dean U. Wis. Sch. Nursing, Madison, 1984—; cons. and lectr. in field. Author: Maternity Nursing Today, 1973, 76; Education for Women in Health and Illness; Process and Content, 1985. Contbr. articles to profl. jours. Bur. Health Professions Fed. trainee, 1963-64; Nat. Sci. Service award, 1976-79. Mem. Am. Nurses Assn., Health Care for Women Internat. (editorial bd. 1984—), Midwest Nursing Research Soc., Sigma Theta Tau (v.p.). Avocations: golf; tennis. Office: U Wis Madison Sch Nursing 600 Highland Ave H6/150 Madison WI 53792

LITTLER, JOHN DOUGLAS, die casting company executive; b. Portland, Ind., Feb. 1, 1951; s. Frank Perry and Julia Agnes (Younce) L.; m. Katherine Wells Countryman, July 21, 1973; children—Douglas Robert, Kathryn Ann, Mark Daniel. B.S. in Bus., Ind. U., 1972. With Littler Diecast Corp., Albany, Ind., 1972—, treas., chmn. bd., 1977—; ptnr. Priority Components, Albany, 1982—; dir. 1st State Bank Dunkirk. Mem. Albany Town Bd., 1976-79, Albany Planning Com., 1976-82; co-founder Albany Concerned Citizens Assn., 1982; chmn. Albany Republican Town Com., 1982; cubmaster Albany Cub Scout Pack 37, 1984—. Named Outstanding Young Man Am., Albany Jaycees, 1978. Mem. Soc. Die Castings Engrs. (pres.'s adv. com., area dir., nat. dir., tech. council, nat. sec. exec. com.), Methodist. Club: Ind. U. Varsity. Lodges: Elks, Lions. Home: 116 Gillcrest Dr Albany IN 47320 Office: Littler Diecast Corp 500 W Walnut St Albany IN 47320

LITTLEWOOD, THOMAS BENJAMIN, journalism educator; b. Flint, Mich., Nov. 30, 1928; s. Thomas N. and Louise E. (Grebenkemper) L.; m. Barbara Elaine Badger, June 9, 1951; children—Linda Littlewood Johnson, Lisa Littlewood Ratchford, Thomas S., Leah. Student DePauw U., 1948-51; B.S., Northwestern U., 1952, M.S., 1953. Reporter, Chgo. Sun-Times, 1953-77; staff asst. to U.S. Senator Robert Dole, Washington, 1977; prof., head dept. journalism U. Ill.-Urbana, 1977—. Author: Horner of Illinois, 1969; The Politics of Population Control, 1977. Fellow John F. Kennedy Inst. Politics, Harvard U., 1975; recipient Disting. Reporting award Am. Polit. Sci. Assn., 1957. Mem. N.Am. Soc. Sport History, Ill. State Hist. Soc., Sigma Delta Chi. Home: 1303 Brighton Dr Urbana IL 61801 Office: U Ill 119 Gregory Hall Urbana IL 61801

LITTRELL, DONALD WATTS, community development educator; b. Moberly, Mo., May 21, 1936; s. Waldo Watts and Mildred Katherine (Forrest) L.; m. Doris Sue Painter, Jan. 31, 1958; children—Charles Watts, William Painter. B.S., U. Mo.-Columbia, 1959, M.S., 1964. Mem. faculty U. Mo., Columbia, 1967—, chmn. community devel. dept., extension project leader, 1983—; cons. U.S. Dept. Agr., 1975-76, univs. and state govts. Ark., Minn., N.D., Ga., Nebr. and Mo., 1972—; dir. nat. staff devel. project FHA, Washington, 1978-81; bd. dirs., cons. TVA, Knoxville, 1982-83. Author: Theory and Practice of Community Development, 1972; also chpts. in books. Mem. Boone County Democratic Com., 1984—; mem. adv. bd. Mo. 4-H Club, 1977-80. Recipient 3 certs. of appreciation U.S. Dept. Agr., 1976-78, cert. appreciation U.S. Community Services Adminstrn., Washington, 1978; Extension fellow U. Mo., Columbia, 1984-85; scholar Farm Found., Chgo., 1984. Mem. Community Devel. Soc. (a founder, bd. dirs. 1977-78), Am. Soc. Tng. and Devel. Baptist. Avocations: fishing, hunting, reading. Home: 1309 Dawn Ridge Columbia MO 65202 Office: Univ Mo-Columbia 723 Clark Hall Columbia MO 65211

LITTS, BONNIE JEANE, computer systems adminstrator; b. Battle Creek, Mich., Feb. 2, 1947; d. Mason E. and Jeane E. (Dickerson) L. Assoc. Gen. Study, Kellogg Community Coll., 1968; student Grand Rapids Jr. Coll., 1979-80, Davenport Coll., Grand Rapids, 1981, Aquinas Coll., 1982. Bank teller Mich. Nat. Bank, Battle Creek, 1967-69; acctg. clk. Battle Creek San. Hosp., 1969-73; computer operator Shawnee Mission Med. Ctr., Merriam, Kans., 1973-78; computer operator Zondervan Corp., Grand Rapids, Mich., 1978-82, computer programmer/analyst, 1982-83, OIS/DVX adminstr., 1983—. Mem. Assn. Info. Systems Profls., Internat. Soc. Wang Users, Assn. Systems Mgrs. Avocations: reading, travel, photography. Office: Zondervan Corp 1415 Lake Dr SE Grand Rapids MI 49506

LITVIN, MARTIN JAY, author, lecturer; b. Galesburg, Ill., Mar. 31, 1928; s. Ben and Sylvia (Gillis) L. B.S. in Social Studies, U. So. Calif., 1949. Author: Sergeant Allen and Private Renick, 1971; Voices of the Prairie Land, 2 Vols., 1972; Black Angel, 1973; Hiram Revels in Illinois, 1974; Chase the Prairie Wind, 1975; The Young Mary, 1976; The Journey, 1981; A Rocking Horse Family, 1982; A Daring Young Man, 1983; Black Earth, 1984; lectr. in field. Served with U.S. Army, 1950-52. Mem. Dramatists Guild (assoc.), Alumnus of Tau Epsilon Phi. Office: care Frank A Ward PO Box 1205 Galesburg IL 61402

LITZ, NORMAN GERALD, engineering company executive, consultant; b. Bronx, N.Y., Oct. 23, 1930; s. Benjamin and Sophie (Madrick) L.; m. Helen Clare Berger, Feb. 4, 1951 (dec. Feb. 1977); m. 2d, Patricia Bridget Scott, Jan. 7, 1979; children—Michael H., Thomas A., R nee Kohn. A.B., Washington U., St. Louis. Textile salesman, 1950-51; with Bennat Corp., 1953-55; founder, pres. Hillsboro Garment Co. (Ill.), 1955-69, Benld Garment Co. (Ill.), 1957-69, Loopex Co., Litchfield, Ill., 1957-69, Eldorado Garment Co., Decatur, Ill., 1962-69, Mt. Carmel Garment Co. (Ill.), 1964-68, Whirlwind Products Co., St. Louis, 1979—, PB Scott & Co (doing business as Tech. Sales & Services Co.), St. Louis, 1979—; v.p. Plastic Bottle Corp., St. Louis, 1960-69, pres., 1969-77; chmn. N.G.L. Enterprises, Litchfield, 1964-69; pres. Plasco div. Nixdorff-Krein Industries, St. Louis, 1977-79; v.p. acquisitions MKI, St. Louis, 1977-79; pres. Tara Products Corp., Leominster, Mass., 1978-79; mgmt. cons. Mem. Mo. Bd. Mediation. Served with AUS, 1951-53. Mem. Soc. Plastics Engrs., Soc. of Plastics Industry. Jewish. Clubs: Meadowbrook Country, Engineers (St. Louis). Patentee Loopex belt loop machine. Home: 57 Meadowbrook Country Club Ballwin MO 63011 Office: Technical Sales and Services Co 4607 McRee Ave Saint Louis MO 63110

LIU, CHEN-YA, scientist; b. Shanghsien, China, Sept. 21, 1924; came to U.S., 1954, naturalized, 1959; s. Hsiang-Po and Hsiu-Chen (Wee) L.; m. Siuha Anita Go, Oct. 20, 1956; children—Leo, Isabel, Ursula. B.S., Central U., Nanking, China, 1948; M.M.E., NYU, 1955; D.Eng., 1959. Registered profl. engr. N.Y., Ohio. Instr. NYU, 1955-59; asst. prof. Carnegie Inst. Tech., Pitts., 1959-61; sr. research engr. B.F. Goodrich Co., Brecksville, Ohio, 1961-65; assoc. fellow Battelle Meml. Inst., Columbus, Ohio, 1965-68, fellow, 1968-72, sr. scientist, 1972—. Recipient Founders Day award NYU, 1959, TECH award NASA, 1972. Fellow AIAA; mem. Sigma Xi. Home: 3007 Avalon Rd Upper Arlington Ohio 43221 Office: Battelle Meml Inst 505 King Ave Columbus OH 43201

LIU, KHANG-LEE, dentist, educator; b. China, Aug. 5, 1939; came to U.S., 1972, naturalized, 1982; s. T.P. and K.H. (Lu) L.; m. Nancy S.Y. Lee (div.); children—Christine, Helen. B.D.S., Nat. Def. Med. Ctr., Faculty of Dentistry, Taipei, 1964; M.A., U. Chgo., 1974. Asst., Nat. Def. Med. Ctr., Taipei, Taiwan, 1964-67; instr. Med. Ctr., Republic of China, 1968-72; asst. prof. U. Chgo., 1972-76; assoc. prof. Nat. Def. Med. Ctr., 1976-77; from asst. prof. to assoc. prof. dentistry Northwestern U., Chgo., 1977—; dir. McCormick Boys and Girls Dental Clin. Mem. ADA, Chgo. Dental Soc., Am. Soc. Dentistry for Children, Internat. Assn. Dental Research, Am. Acad. Pediatric Dentistry. Office: 2929 N Central St Chicago IL 60634

LIU, LEE, JR., utility company executive. Chmn., pres., chief exec. officer, dir. Iowa Electric Light and Power Co., Cedar Rapids. Office: Iowa Electric Light and Power Co PO Box 351 Cedar Rapids IA 52406*

LIU, PING YUAN, chemist, researcher; b. Hwai-an, China, May 12, 1931; came to U.S., 1959, naturalized, 1973; s. Soo-noon and Chee (Hang) L.; m. Lily Tehyu Chen; children—Henry Heng, Ingrid Ying. B.S., Nat. Taiwan U., 1955; M.S., Case Western Res. U., 1962, Ph.D., 1966. Research chemist Monsanto, Bloomfield, Conn., 1972-74, Amoco Chem. Corp., Naperville, Ill., 1974-77; advanced devel. chemist Gen. Electric Co., Mt. Vernon, Ind., 1977—. Translator: Chemical Plant Design with Fiber Reinforced Plastics, 1970. Patentee in field. Fellow Soc. Plastics Engrs.; mem. Am. Chem. Soc., Soc. Rheology. Avocation: bridge. Office: Gen Electric Co Hwy 69 South Mount Vernon IN 47620

LIVENTALS, HARRY HAROLD, osteopathic physician; b. Madona, Latvia, Apr. 6, 1938; s. Janis and Milda (Kaminskis) L.; m. Patsy Jean Sup, Sept. 7, 1970; children—Chad, Summer. B.S., U. Iowa, 1966, postgrad., 1967-68; D.O., Coll. Osteo. Medicine, Des Moines, 1967-75; practice osteo. medicine, Indianola, Iowa, 1976—; pres. Liventals Investment Corp., 1981—; mem. staff Mercy Med. Ctr., Des Moines Gen. Hosp. Served with USMC, 1957-59. Mem. Iowa Soc. Osteo. Physicians, Am. Osteo. Assn., Latvian Vets. Assn., Latvian Soc. Iowa. Republican. Office: 124 W Ashland St Indianola IA 50125

LIVESEY, ROBERT SHAW, architect; b. Montclair, N.J., Jan. 25, 1947; s. Robert Ellis and Maureen (Shaw) L.; m. Diana Maragret Josephine Rose, Apr. 30, 1977; children—Jessica, Cecilia. A.B., Princeton U., 1969; M.Arch., Havard U., 1972. Designer, I.M. Pei & Ptnrs., N.Y.C., 1976-78; ptnr. Livesey Rosenstein Assocs., N.Y.C., 1978-81; assoc. Stirling/Wilford Assocs., N.Y.C., 1978-81; dir. design CUH2A, Princeton, N.J., 1981-83; prof. architecture, chmn. dept. Ohio State U.-Columbus, 1983—; vis. critic U. Pa., Phila., 1978-80, Yale U., 1976-83. Recipient Sheldon Traveling Fellowship award Harvard U., 1972; Rome prize, 1973-75; Yale U. Sch. Architecture Judith M. Capen award, 1980. Fellow Am. Acad. Rome; mem. AIA, Architects Soc. Ohio (bd. dirs. 1984-85). Home: 2481 Sherwood Rd Columbus OH 43209 Office: Dept Architecture Ohio State Univ 190 W 17th Ave Columbus OH 43210

LIVINGSTON, HOWARD MITCHELL, manufacturing company executive; b. Leatherwood, Ky., Jan. 3, 1951; s. Howard Francis and Catherine Marie (Anderson) L.; m. Rita Rene McMillan, June 21, 1969. A. Engring., Allied Inst. Tech., Chgo., 1972. Machinist, F.J. Littell Co., Chgo., 1969-71; mech. engr. Machine Products Co., Skokie, Ill., 1971-73, dir. engring., 1973-75, v.p., 1975-82; pres. Helio Precision Products, Inc., Deerfield, Ill., 1982—. Sec., Riverwoods Residents Assn., 1980, 2d v.p., 1981, 1st v.p., 1982. Indsl. Arts Commn. scholar, 1969. Mem. Soc. Auto. Engrs (assoc.), Am. Soc. Quality Control, Soc. Mfg. Engrs., Ill. Mfrs. Assn., Aircraft Owners and Pilots Assn. Republican. Lodge: Optimists. Home: 475 White Oak Ln Riverwoods IL 60015 Office: Helio Precision Products Inc 725 County Line Rd Deerfield IL 60015

LIVINGSTON, JAMES MICHAEL, air force officer, entomologist, toxicologist; b. Philadelphia, Miss., June 26, 1944; s. Arthur L. and Carmen J. L.; m. Venita Ann Upton, June 6, 1965; children—James Robert, Suzanne Michelle. B.S., Miss. State U., 1969; M.S., U. Ark., 1971, Ph.D., 1978; Research asst. U. Ark., Fayetteville, 1971-73; commd. 1st lt. U.S. Air Force, 1973, advanced through grades to lt. col. 1979; cons. entomologist USAF Environ. Health Lab., Kelly AFB, Tex., 1973-75; environ. entomologist USAF Occupational and Environ. Health Lab., Brooks AFB, Tex., 1978-80; chief environ. quality br. Air Force Aerospace Med. Research Lab., Wright Patterson AFB, Ohio, 1980-82, staff biomed. scientist for programs, 1982-83; biotech. rep., dep. for devel. planning Aero. Systems Div., Wright Patterson AFB, 1983—; adj. prof. biology Wright State U., Dayton, Ohio; cons. toxicologist USAF Surgeon Gen., 1983. Scoutmaster Tecumseh council Boy Scouts Am. Decorated Air Force Commendation medal with oak leaf cluster. Mem. Entomol. Soc. Am., Soc. Environ. Toxicology and Chemistry, Sigma Xi, Alpha Zeta, Gamma Sigma Delta. Presbyterian. Contbr. articles on insect virology, ecol. and pub. health aspects of pesticides, insect population dynamics, ecol. impact of hydrocarbon fuels to profl. jours. Home: 3133 Suburban Dr Beavercreek OH 45432 Office: Devel Objectives Office Dep for Devel Planning Aero Systems Div Wright Patterson AFB OH 45433

LIVINGSTON-DUNN, CONNIE LYNN, art therapist; b. Mt. Morris, Ill., Oct. 16, 1940; d. Samuel Herman and Opal Zelinda (Kretsinger) Frey; m. David William Livingston, Feb. 10, 1959 (div. 1975); children—Penni, David William, Polli; m. 2d, Mervin Keith Dunn, Mar. 3, 1978 (div. 1980). A.A., Sauk Valley Coll., 1970; B.A., No. Ill. U., 1978, M.A., 1982. Registered art therapist. Activity therapist Dixon Developmental Ctr. (Ill.), 1966—; dir. art therapy clin. program Mt. Mary Coll., Milw., 1984-85, inst. instr., 1985—; group shows include: Rockford (Ill.) ann. juried show, Nat. Art Edn. Assn., Marriott Hotel, Chgo., 1981, Merseyside County Mus., Liverpool, Eng., 1981-83, Beloit (Wis.) ann. exhbn., 1983, Daley Civic Ctr., Chgo., 1983, Firebird Gallery, Alexandria, Va., 1984, Ill. Art Edn. Assn., 1984-85; represented in permanent collection: Sauk Valley Coll., Dixon, Ill. Mem. Nat. Art Edn. Assn., Am. Art Therapy Assn., Ill. Art Therapy Assn. Contbr. papers to profl. confs. and publs. Home: 107 E Oregon St Polo IL 61064 Office: 2600 N Brinton Ave Dixon IL 61064

LIVINGSTONE, FRED JOSEPH, lawyer; b. Cleve., Feb. 20, 1926; s. Charles Leonard and Libbie (Warshawsky) L.; m. Pearl Schwartz, Aug. 21, 1955; children—David, Ruth, Daniel. LL.B., Harvard U., 1950. Bar: Ohio 1950, U.S. Dist. Ct. Ohio 1953, U.S. Supreme Ct. 1973. Assoc., Charles L. Livingstone, Cleve., 1950-52, Rocker, Zaller & Kleinman, Cleve., 1952-61; gen. counsel Community Devel., Inc., Cleve., 1961-63; sole practice, Cleve., 1963-64; ptnr. Kelley, McCann & Livingstone, Cleve., 1964—. Mem., chmn. Brecksville Civil Service Commn., Ohio, 1961-81; bd. govs., treas. Cleve. Coll. Jewish Studies, Beechwood, Ohio, 1975-82, 84—. Served to cpl. USAF, 1944-45. Mem. ABA (urban affairs com. 1969-73). Democrat. Jewish. Avocations: Judaic studies; swimming; hiking. Home: 12916 Parkview Rd Brecksville OH 44141 Office: 300 National City-E 6th Bldg 1953 E 6th St Cleveland OH 44114

LIVSEY, ROBERTA, product/business planning analyst; b. Dayton, Ohio, Dec. 9, 1955; d. L.C. and Alberta (Steele) L. B.S.B.A., Ohio State U., 1977, M.B.A., 1978. Fin. analyst Parts and Service div. Ford Motor Co., Dearborn, Mich., 1978-81, Anaconda Industries, Rolling Meadows, Ill., 1981-82; sr. acctg. analyst Oldsmobile div. Gen. Motors Corp., Lansing, Mich., 1982-84; product/bus. planning analyst, bus. planning staff, Buick-Oldsmobile-Cadillac group, 1985—. Gen. Motors scholar, 1973. Mem. Planning Execs. Inst. Home: 2190 Regency Dr East Lansing MI 48823 Office: BOC Group Gen Motors Corp 920 Townsend St Lansing MI 48921

LIZAK, JOHN BERNARD, energy company executive, consultant; b. Northhampton, Pa., Apr. 26, 1953; s. John Bernard and Mary (Groller) L.; m. M. Frances D'Amico, May 6, 1978. B.S. in Engring. Geology, Lehigh U., 1975; M.S. in Geology, Purdue U., 1977; B.S. in Mining Engring., U. So. Ind., 1983. Registered profl. geologist, Ind. Exploration geologist Exxon Co. (Carter Oil), Houston, 1977-78; devel. geologist Exxon Coal Resources, Houston, 1978-80; geol. project mgr. Standard Oil Ohio, Evansville, 1980-84; pres. Diversified Mineral & Land and Lizak Geology & Engring., 1984—. Mem. Am. Assn. Profl. Geologists, AIME, Am. Assn. Petroleum Geologists (del. 1976—), Ind. and Ky. Geol. Soc. (treas. 1985). Lodge: Kiwanis. Avocations: swimming, backpacking, gardening. Home: 6600 Whispering Hills Evansville IN 47712 Office: Diversified Mineral & Land 1006 Diamond Ave Evansville IN 47711

LJUNG, DONOVAN ALLEN, physicist; b. Alexandria, Minn., July 16, 1943; s. Allen Latimer and Irene Margaret (Hanson) L.; m. Ellen Jo Szabad, Sept. 5, 1968; children—Michael Allen, David Jeffrey. Grad. Phillips Exeter Acad., 1961; B.A. in Physics, Carleton Coll., 1965; M.A., U. Wis., 1966, Ph.D., 1972. Research assoc. Fermi Nat. Accelerator Lab., Batavia, Ill., 1972-74, physicist, 1979-81; instr. physics Yale U., New Haven, 1974-75, asst. prof., 1975-79; mem. tech. staff AT&T Bell Labs., Naperville, Ill., 1981—, supr., 1985—. Contbr. articles to profl. jours. Bd. dirs., sec. Temple B'nai Israel, Aurora, Ill., 1981—; pres., founder Blackberry Homeowners Assn., Geneva, Ill., 1980-81, pres., 1985. Mem. Am. Phys. Soc., IEEE. Avocations: skiing, gardening; bicycling. Home: 2257 Clover Ln Geneva IL 60134 Office: AT&T Bell Labs Indian Hill Room 2B 268 Naperville Wheaton Rd IL 60566

LLOYD, LEONA LORETTA, lawyer; b. Detroit, Aug. 6, 1949; d. Leon Thomas and Naomi Mattie (Chisolm) L. B.S., Wayne State U., 1971, J.D., 1979. Bar: Mich. Speech, English tchr. Detroit Bd. Edn., 1971-75; instr. criminal justice Wayne State U., Detroit, 1981; sr. ptnr. Lloyd and Lloyd, Detroit, 1982—. Wayne State U. scholar, 1970, 75; recipient Kizzy Image award, 1985; named to Black Women Hall of Fame, Fred Hampton Image award, 1984. Mem. ABA, Wolverine Bar Assn., Mary McLeod Bethune Assn. Office: Lloyd and Lloyd Law Firm 600 Renaissance Ctr Suite 1400 Detroit MI 48243

LLOYD, MICHAEL STUART, newspaper editor; b. Dickinson, N.D., Aug. 11, 1945; s. James William and Mary Marie (Ripley) L.; m. Judith Ann Baxter, May 24, 1966; children—Matthew James, Kristen Ann. B.Jour., U. Mo., 1967. Reporter Grand Rapids (Mich.) Press, 1967-70, copy editor, 1970-72, asst. city editor, 1972-74, city editor, 1975-77, editor-in-chief, 1978—. Bd. dirs. Youth Commonwealth, Grand Valley State Coll. Found.; chmn. Celebration on Grand Com.; treas., trustee Citizens Bee. Mem. Am. Soc. Newspaper Editors. Office: 155 Michigan St Grand Rapids MI 49503

LLOYD, PHILIP ARMOUR, lawyer; b. Youngstown, Ohio, Feb. 13, 1947; s. Robert Brill and Blanche (Butler) L.; m. Margaret McDowell, Aug. 9, 1969; children—Kimberly, Beatrice. B.A., Ohio Wesleyan U., 1969; J.D., U. Akron, 1972. Bar: Ohio 1972. Mem. firm Brouse & McDowell, Akron, 1972—, ptnr., 1977—. Trustee U. Akron Sch. Law Alumni Assn., Bd. Mental Retardation, Summit County, Ohio, Akron City Hosp. Found., Summit County Defenders Assn., Fairlawn West United Ch.; past trustee Old Trail Sch., Perkiomen Sch., Akron City Club, United Cerebral Palsy and Services for Handicapped; pres. United Cerebral Palsy and Services for Handicapped, 1982-83. Mem. Akron Bar Assn., Ohio Bar Assn., ABA. Republican. Mem. United Ch. of Christ. Avocations: skiing; flying. Office: 500 First National Tower Akron OH 44308

LO, SUNNY JOAN, chemist, corporate executive; b. N.Y.C.; d. Samuel and Marilyn Ruth Belchis; m. Peter Yin Kwai Lo, July 16, 1978. B.A., Lake Forest Coll., 1975; M.S., U. Mich.-Ann Arbor, 1977, Ph.D., 1981. Project chemist Dow Corning Corp., Midland, Mich., 1981-83, research specialist, 1983-84, mgr. tech. planning, 1984—. Contbr. articles to tech. jours. Vol., John Anderson Election Campaign, 1980. Mem. Am. Chem. Soc., Sigma Xi. Avocations: Ice skating, jazzercize.

LOBANOV-ROSTOVSKY, OLEG, orchestra executive; b. San Francisco, July 12, 1934; s. Andrei and Grace S. (Pope) Lobanov-Rostovsky; m. Berkeley Blashfield, 1959 (div. 1977); children—Christopher, Nicholas; m. 2d, Susan Waters, Sept. 8, 1979; 1 dau., Alexandra. Community concert rep. Columbia Artists Mgmt. Inc., 1958-59; mng. dir. Columbus Symphony Orch. (Ohio), 1959-62, Hartford Symphony Orch. (Conn.), 1962-65, Balt. Symphony, 1965-69; program office div. humanities and arts Ford Found., 1969-75; exec. dir. Denver Symphony Orch., 1975-77; mng. dir. Nat. Symphony Orch., Washington, 1977-80; cons. Fed. Council on Arts, 1980-81; exec. dir. Del. Ctr. for Performing Arts, 1981-82; exec. v.p., mng. dir. Detroit Symphony Orch., 1982-83, pres., 1983—. Mem. Am. Symphony Orch. League (past dir.). Clubs: Renaissance, Grosse Pointe Hunt. Home: 871 Grand Marais St Grosse Pointe Park MI 48230 Office: Ford Auditorium Detroit MI 48226

LOBENHOFER, LOUIS FRED, legal educator; b. Denver, Mar. 24, 1950; s. Frederick C. and Betty Lobenhofer; m. Carol E. Clarkson, June 16, 1973; children—Kristina M., Lauren E. A.B., Coll. William and Mary, 1972; J.D., U. Colo., 1975; LL.M., U. Denver, 1979. Bar: Colo. 1975, Tax Ct. 1982. Assoc. law firm Charles H. Booth, Denver, 1975-78; asst. prof. law Ohio No. U., 1979-82, assoc. prof., 1982-85, prof., 1985—. Denver Tax Inst. scholar, 1979. Mem. ABA, Soc. Am. Law Tchrs., Phi Beta Kappa, Omicron Delta Kappa, Delta Theta Phi. Republican. Roman Catholic. Office: Pettit Coll Law Ohio No U Ada OH 45810

LOBER, PAUL HALLAM, medical educator; b. Mpls., Sept. 25, 1919; s. Harold A. and Minnie (Toraason) L. B.S., U. Minn., 1942, M.D., 1944, Ph.D in Pathology, 1951. Diplomate Am. Bd. Pathology. Intern, Gen. Hosp. Mpls., 1944, resident, 1944-46; surg. pathologist U. Minn. Hosp., Mpls., 1951-74; pathologist Abbott-Northwestern Hosp., Mpls., 1974—; prof. U. Minn. Med. Sch., Mpls., 1963—. Served to capt. U.S. Army, 1946-48; PTO. Fellow Coll. Am. Pathologists; mem. Am. Soc. Clin. Pathologists, Internat. Acad. Pathology, Am. Soc. Cytologists, AMA, N.Y. Acad. Sci. Home: 5800 View Ln Edina MN 55436 Office: 800 E 28th St Minneapolis MN 55407

LOBER, TERENCE ALLEN, lawyer; b. Panama, C.Z., Jan. 31, 1954; came to U.S., 1956; d. William J. and Marjorie E. (Donahue) L. B.S., Kans. State U., 1976; J.D. with honors, Washburn Law Sch., 1979. Bar: Kans. 1979, U.S. Dist. Ct. Kans. 1979, U.S. Ct. Appeals (10th cir.) 1984. Ptnr. Crow & Lober, Leavenworth, Kans., 1983—; assoc. prof. law Orange County Community Coll., Calif., New Hampshire Coll., 1981-83. Served to lt. JAGC, USN, 1979-83. Mem. ABA. Republican. Home: Box 142 Rural Route 2 Leavenworth KS 66048

LOBERG, THOMAS JOHN, accountant; b. St. Paul, Mar. 14, 1955; s. Robert John and Rose Kathryn (Ginnaty) L.; m. Carolyn Ann Woodruff, June 30, 1979; B.S. in Acctg., U. Minn., 1976. C.P.A., Minn. Sr. auditor Arthur Andersen Co., St. Paul, 1977-79; mgr. audit Borowicz, Holmgren, Burnsville, Minn., 1980-81, audit ptnr. Borowicz, Holmgren, Loberg Co., 1981-83; ptnr., audit practice dir. Bergren, Borowic, Holmgren, Johnson, Loberg & Co., 1983—; dir. Metrinch Tool Co., Twin City Computure User Newspaper. Treas. Penny Route Charity, 1983; adviser Jr. Achievement of St. Paul, 1977-81. Named Jr. Achievement Outstanding Achiever, 1973; recipient Reader's Digest Seminar award, fall 1974. Mem. Am. Inst. C.P.A.s, Minn. Soc. C.P.A.s, Alpha Kappa Psi (alumni chpt. v.p., 1983-84), Jr. C. of C., Travelers Protective Assn. Am. Republican. Roman Catholic. Clubs: Bracketts Crossing Country (Mpls.), Mendakota Country (West St. Paul). Lodges: Elks.

LOBOSCHEFSKI, GARETH CHARLES, pharmicist; b. Toledo, Dec. 24, 1946; s. Edward John and LaVaughn (Friedley) L.; m. Shannon Marie Nelson, Nov. 12, 1983; children—Brandon Scott, Donald Allen Dotson, Amber Lynn. B.A., Denison U., 1969; B.S., U. Toledo, 1975. Lic. pharmacist, Ohio. Pharmacist St. Luke's Hosp., Maumee, Ohio, 1971-78, owner Whitehouse Apothecary, Ohio, 1978-83; mgr., pharmacist Medicine Shoppe, Fremont, Ohio, 1983—; Served with U.S. Army. Mem. Toledo Hosp. Pharmacists Assn. (pres. 1976-78). Home: 1009 Hayes Ave Fremont OH 43420 Office: Medicine Shoppe 824 W State St Fremont OH 43420

LOCASCIO, JOSEPH JASPER, research methodologist, statistician, educator, consultant; b. Chgo., Mar. 15, 1950; s. Dominic and Angela (Lipari) L. B.S., Loyola U., 1972; M.A., U. Kans., 1974; Ph.D., Northwestern U., 1982. Statistician Mental Health div. Chgo. Dept. Health, Chgo., 1975-76, coordinator research and evaluation, 1976-79; tchr. Northwestern U., Evanston, Ill., 1982; research assoc., asst. prof. U. Chgo., 1983—; dir. data analysis, Mental Health Clin. Research Ctr. Ill. State Psychiatric Inst., Chgo., 1983—. Contbr. articles to profl. jours. Northwestern U. scholar; postgrad. fellow U. Ill., 1983. Mem. Am. Psychol. Assn., Am. Statis. Assn. Roman Catholic. Avocations: graphic art; music; fiction writing. Home: 2909 W 65th St 2d Floor Chicago IL 60629 Office: Mental Health Clin Research Ctr Ill State Psychiat Inst 1601 W Taylor St Chicago IL 60612

LOCH, JOHN ROBERT, educational administrator; b. Sharon, Pa., Aug. 25, 1940; s. Robert Addison and Mary Virginia (Beck) L.; student Waynesburg Coll., 1958; A.B., Grove City Coll., 1962; postgrad Pitts. Theol. Sem., 1962; M.Ed., U. Pitts., 1966, Ph.D., 1972; cert. Harvard U. Inst. for Mgmt. of Lifelong Edn., 1984; m. Nov. 26, 1969 (div. 1979). Asst. to dean men U. Pitts., 1963-64, dir. student union, 1964-70, dir. student affairs research, 1970-71, dir. suburban ednl. services Sch. Gen. Studies, 1971-75; dir. continuing edn. and pub. service Youngstown (Ohio) State U., 1975-82, dir. continuing edn./edn. outreach, 1982—, assoc. mem. grad. faculty, 1980—; research assoc. Pres's Commn. on Campus Unrest, 1970. Trustee, Mahoning Shenango Health Edn. Network, 1976—, Career Devel. Center for Women, 1978-80; trustee Youngstown Area Arts Council, 1980-85, pres., 1981-83; bd. dirs. Protestant Family Services, 1981-83; trustee Mahoning County RSVP, 1983—, chmn. evaluation com., 1983-84, chmn. personnel com., 1984-85; coordinator fund raising Nat. Unity Campagn, Mahoning County, 1980; state chmn. Young Republican Coll. council Pa., 1960. Mem. Adult Edn. Assn. U.S.A., Am. Assn. Higher Edn., Nat. U. Continuing Edn. Assn., Ohio Council Higher Continuing Edn. (pres. 1979-80), Ohio Continuing Higher Edn. Assn. (co-chmn. constn. com. 1982, v.p. state univs. 1984-85), Druids, Omicron Delta Kappa, Kappa Kappa Psi, Phi Kappa Phi (pres. 1980-81), Alpha Phi Omega, Alpha Sigma Lambda. Presbyterian. Clubs: Kiwanis (dir. 1981-82), Youngstown Traffic (hon. life). Home: 242 Upland Ave Youngstown OH 44504 Office: Youngstown State U Youngstown OH 44555

LOCHER, RALPH S., justice Ohio Supreme Ct.; b. Moreni, Romania, July 24, 1915; s. Ephraim and Natalie (Voigt) L.; B.A. with honors, Bluffton Coll., 1936; LL.B., Case Western Res. U., 1939; m. Eleanor Worthington, June 18, 1939; 1 dau., Virginia Lynn. Admitted to Ohio bar, 1939; former sec. to Gov. Ohio; former law dir. City of Cleve.; former mayor Cleve.; judge Ohio Ct. Common Pleas Cuyahoga County, 1969-72, Cuyahoga County Ct. Probate Div., 1973-77; justice Supreme Ct. Ohio, 1977—. Mem. ABA, Bar Assn. Greater Cleve., Cuyahoga County Bar Assn. Democrat. Office: State Office Tower 30 E Broad St Columbus OH 43215*

LOCHER, RICHARD EARL, editorial cartoonist; b. Dubuque, Iowa, June 4, 1929; s. Joseph John and Lucille (Jungk) L.; student Loras Coll., 1948, Chgo. Acad. Fine Arts, 1949-51; B.F.A., Art Center, Los Angeles, 1954, postgrad., 1955-56; m. Mary Therese Cosgrove, June 15, 1957; children—Stephen Robert, John Joseph, Jana Lynne. Asst. writer, artist Buck Rogers Comic Strip, 1954-57, Dick Tracy Comic Strip, 1957-61, Martin Aerospace Co., Denver, 1962-63; art dir. Hansen Co., Chgo., N.Y.C., 1963-68; founder, pres. Novamark Corp., Chgo., 1968-72; editorial cartoonist Chgo. Tribune, 1972—; cons. McDonalds Corp., Oakbrook, Ill.; tchr. art at local high schs. and colls. Served with USAF, 1951-53. Recipient Dragonslayer award U.S. Indsl. Council, 1976, 77, 78; Overseas Press Club award, 1982, 82; recipient Sigma Delta Chi Journalism award, 1983; Pulitzer prize, 1983. Mem. Assn. Am. Editorial Cartoonists. Author: Dick Locher Draws Fire, 1980; Send in the Clowns, Flying Can Be Fun. Patentee, Poker Face device to play poker without cards. Office: Chgo Tribune 435 N Michigan Ave Chicago IL 60611

LOCHIANO, STEPHEN ANTHONY, controller; b. Liberal, Kans., Mar. 2, 1949; s. Rocco LoChiano and Margie Louise (Pitts) LoChiano Wooden; m. Ellen Jane Walker, Aug. 28, 1971; children—Anthony Paul, Ryan Michael, Eric Stephen. B.S. in Bus. Adminstrn., U. Nebr., Lincoln, 1975; postgrad. U. Nebr., Omaha, 1980—. Office mgr. trainee Roberts Dairy, Omaha, 1976-78; controller Security Internat., Omaha, 1978, Jubilee Mfg. Co., Omaha, 1978-80, Omaha Box Co., 1983—; plant acct. Weyerhaeuser Co., Omaha, 1980-83. Served as sgt. U.S. Army, 1973-75. Mem. Nat. Assn. Accts. (controllers council 1984—), Nat. Assn. Credit Mgrs., Internat. Soc. Wang Users, Toastmasters (dist. treas. 1980-81). Republican. Lutheran. Club: Park Ave. Health (Omaha). Avocations: camping, computer programming. Home: 10205 R St Omaha NE 68127 Office: Omaha Box Co PO Box 1172 Omaha NE 68101

LOCHOWITZ, RICHARD THOMAS, dentist; b. Milw., Oct. 18, 1949; s. Norbert James and Rosemary Elizabeth (Waltz) L.; m. Mary Bambic, May 27, 1972; children—Michael Richard, Kathryn Marie. B.S., Marquette U., 1971, M.S., 1973, D.D.S., 1977. Gen. practice dentistry, Milw., 1977-83; staff dentist Midwest Dental Care, Sheboygan, Wis., 1983-84; chief dentist Family Dental Ctr. at Shopko, Green Bay, Wis., 1984—. Mem. ADA, Am. Soc. of Forensic Odontology, Wis. Dental Assn., Brown-Door-Kewaunee Dental Soc. Club: Med. Amateur Radio Council Ltd. Avocations: reading; amateur radio; photography; archery. Home: 1171 Cormier Rd Green Bay WI 54304 Office: Family Dental Ctr at Shopko 2401 S Oneida St Green Bay WI 54304

LOCK, JOE M(ICHAEL), trucking company executive; b. Carrollton, Mo., Oct. 11, 1940; s. Albert Paul and Clara (Tonnar) L.; m. Patricia Ann Slezak, June 23, 1961; children—Kimberly Ann, Sally Ann. B.A., Rockhurst Coll., Kansas City, Mo., 1961. Vice pres. Leonard Bros. Transport Co. Inc., Kansas City, Mo., 1961—. Contbr. articles to profl. jours. Mem. Utility Conservation Commn., Prairie Village, Kans., 1980-84, All Sports Booster Club, Shawnee Mission East High Sch., Prairie Village, 1980-84. Mem. Regional and Distbn. Carriers Conf. (dir. 1974-83), Kans. Motor Carriers Assn. (dir. 1978-81), Distbrs. and Consolidators Am. (dir. 1978-81, sec. 1980-82, pres. 1982-84). Republican. Roman Catholic. Office: Leonard Bros Transport Co 1528 W 9th Kansas City MO 64101

LOCKE, CARL EUGENE, educator; b. Beach Grove, Tenn., Oct. 22, 1933; s. Carl B. and Laura Ann (Wilson) L.; m. Minnie Helen Cotner, July 4, 1954; 1 dau., Ravine Locke Ferguson. B.S., Knoxville Coll., 1954; M.S. Case Western Res. U., 1970, Ph.D., 1977; M.S., John Carroll U., 1972. Prin., tchr., Lake City, Tenn., 1954-56; sci. tchr., coach State Vocat. Tng. Sch., Pikeville, Tenn., 1956-60, Nelson Merry High Sch., Jefferson City, Tenn., 1960-65; tchr., chmn. dept. sci. John Marshall High Sch., Cleve., 1965—. Martha Holden Jennings Found. scholar, 1969-70, 78-79; fellow Case Western Res. U., 1974-75; named an Outstanding Coll. Alumnus United Negro Coll. Fund, 1979; named 1 of 6 Outstanding Educators in Cleve. Pub. Schs., 1982; named Outstanding Sci. Educator in Northeastern Ohio, IEEE, Inc., 1984-85. Mem. Am. Chem. Soc., Nat. Sci. Tchrs. Assn., Regional Council Sci. Tchrs., Assn. Supervision and Curriculum Devel. Democrat. Baptist. Clubs: Knoxville Coll. Alumni, Cleve. Council Black Coll. Alumni. Contbr. articles to profl. jours. Home: 12701 Firsby Ave Cleveland OH 44135 Office: John Marshall High School 3952 West 140th St Cleveland OH 44111

LOCKE, CHARLES STANLEY, manufacturing company executive; b. Laurel, Miss., Mar. 5, 1929; s. Richard C. and Florence (Parker) L.; B.B.A., U. Miss., 1952, M.S., 1955; m. Nora Fulkerson, Mar. 15, 1952; children—Cathy, Stanley, Lauren, Pamela. With Corvey Engring. Co., Inc., Washington, 1952, Price Waterhouse & Co., C.P.A.'s, New Orleans, 1955-58, Westvaco, Inc., 1958-64; controller A.E. Staley Mfg. Co., 1964-69; v.p. Brown Co., Pasadena, Calif., 1969-73, also dir., mem. exec. com.; sr. v.p. Allen Group Inc., Melville, N.Y., 1973-75; v.p. fin. Morton-Norwich Products, Inc. (now Morton Thiokol Inc.), Chgo., 1975-80, treas., dir., 1975-76, pres., 1980-81, 83-84, chief exec. officer, 1980—, chmn. bd., 1980—; dir. Avon Products, Inc., NICOR, First Chgo. Corp. Served with AUS, 1952-54. Mem. Nat. Assn. Accts., Mid-Am. Com., Beta Alpha Psi. Methodist. Clubs: Economic, Mid-America, Tower, Metropolitan, Sunset Ridge Country, Sky. Office: Morton Thiokol Inc 110 N Wacker Dr Chicago IL 60606*

LOCKOWITZ, PAMELA ANN, medical malpractice claims consultant; b. Chgo., Sept. 17, 1954; d. Paul Joseph and Josephine Lucille (Dicosola) Romito; m. Thomas Gerald Lockowitz, June 12, 1976; 1 son, Matthew Vincent. B.S., U. Ill., 1976; M.S., No. Ill. U., 1981. R.N., Ill. Nurse clinician Luth. Gen. Hosp., Park Ridge, Ill., 1976-77, head nurse, 1977-79, dir. risk mgmt., 1979-83; claims cons. Hosp. Shared Services Inc., 1983—; mem. seminar faculty for hosp. shared services, ednl. program Luth. Sch. Nursing. Mem. Am. Soc. Hosp. Risk Mgmt., Hosp. Risk Mgmt. Soc. Met. Chgo., Alpha Lambda Delta. Office: Hosp Shared Services Inc 2275 Half Day Rd Bannockburn IL 60015

LOCKRIDGE, KAREN SUE, marketing executive; b. Goshen, Ind., Nov. 23, 1948; d. Leslie Eugene and Rhea Jean (Reed) L.; B.A., Purdue U., 1971. With Allen & O'Hara, Inc., mgrs. Holiday Inns, 1967-82, sales dir., asst. gen. mgr. Holiday Inn, Tampa, Fla., 1975-82; corp. dir. sales Midway Motor Lodges, Brookfield, Wis., 1982-84; v.p. sales and mktg. Midway Mgmt. Group, Inc., 1984-85; owner, operator Apricot Annie's Cafe & Bar, 1985—. Bd. dirs. Milw. Conv. and Visitors Bur. Recipient Human Relations award City of Tampa, 1980. Mem. Am. Soc. Assn. Execs., Religious Conv. Mgrs. Assn., Nat. Tour Brokers Assn., Am. Bus. Assn., Milw. Conv. and Visitors Bur., Meeting Planners Internat., Sales and Mktg. Execs. of Milw., Wis. Soc. Assn. Execs. Episcopalian. Home: 2025 E Greenwich St Milwaukee WI 53211 Office: 275 W Wisconsin Ave Milwaukee WI 53203

LODWICK, KATHLEEN LORRAINE, historian, educator; b. St. Louis, Feb. 7, 1944; d. Algha Claire and Kathryn Elizabeth (Worthington) L.; B.S. with honors, Ohio U., 1964, M.A., 1965; Ph.D., U. Ariz., 1976; postgrad. U. Hawaii, 1966-67, Nat. Taiwan Normal U., 1967-68. Asst. prof. history U. No. Colo., 1976-77; asst. prof. history Ind. State U., 1977-78; research asso. John King Fairbank Center for East Asian Research, Harvard U., 1978-79; asst. prof. history S.W. Mo. State U., Springfield, 1979-82, assoc. prof., 1982—; dir. index/biog. guide to Chinese Recorder and Missionary Jour. project, 1977—. Mem. AAUW, Am. Hist. Assn., Assn. Asian Studies, Nat. Assn. Fgn. Student Affairs, UN Assn., Phi Alpha Theta. Democrat. Mem. Soc. of Friends. Home: 2934 E Southeast Circle Springfield MO 65802 Office: History Dept SW Mo State U Springfield MO 65802

LOEFFLER, LOWELL FREDERICK, life insurance agent; b. Grand Island, Nebr., Nov. 7, 1913; s. Frederick Frank and Eva S. (Stearns) L.; m. Wilma Aria Smith, June 16, 1940; children—Mark, Alan, Kent, Bruce. A.B., Doane Coll., 1937; M.B.A., U. Mich., 1942; C.L.U. Spl. agent Bankers Life Nebr., Lincoln, 1949-58, gen. agent, 1958-65; gen. agent Midland Nat. Life, Sioux Falls, S.D., 1965—. Chmn. State bd. dirs. Child Evangelism Fellowship of Nebr., Hampton, chmn. 1981—; nat. trustee Child Evangelism Fellowship, Inc., Warrentown, Mo., 1970—. Mem. Omaha Assn. Baptist Men (pres. 1983—). Served as lt. (j.g.) USN, 1943-46, PTO. Republican. Baptist. Club: Golden K Kiwanis (Fremont) (pres. 1983-84). Avocations: golfing; fishing; Bible teaching; working with youth. Home: 1443 W Linden St Fremont NE 68025

LOEFFLER, VERNON DENNIS, pharmacist; b. Shreveport, La., Mar. 30, 1952; s. Ralph Anthony Loeffler and Agnes Marie (Eisenbath) Hoffman; m. Janet Elayne Hollinsworth, Dec. 29, 1973; children—Jennifer Dawn, Jason Michael. B.S., St. Louis Coll. Pharmacy, 1975. Registered pharmacist, Mo., Ill. Pharmacy intern Katz Drug, St. Charles, Mo., 1970-72; admissions office clk. St. Louis Pharmacy, 1971-74; pharmacy intern St. Charles Rexall, Mo., 1972-75; staff pharmacist Walgreen Drug Store, Quincy, Ill., 1975—, St. Mary Hosp., Quincy, 1984—. Bd. dirs. Am. Cancer Soc. Adams County, Quincy, 1983—. Mem. Adams County Pharmacists Assn. (sec. 1978-79, pres. 1979-82; Service award 1982), Ill. Pharmacists Assn. (regional dir. 1979-84; Service award 1984), Phi Delta Chi (pres. 1973-74). Avocations: hunting, fishing, camping, archery, tropical fish. Home: 1225 Daniel Ct Quincy IL 62301 Office: Walgreen Drug Store #821 600 Maine St Quincy IL 62301

LOESCH, KATHARINE TAYLOR (MRS. JOHN GEORGE LOESCH), educator; b. Berkeley, Calif., Apr. 13, 1922; d. Paul Schuster and Katharine (Whiteside) Taylor; student Swarthmore Coll., 1939-41, U. Wash., 1942; B.A., Columbia U., 1944, M.A., 1949; grad. Neighborhood Playhouse Sch. of Theatre, 1946; postgrad. Ind. U., 1953; Ph.D., Northwestern U., 1961; m. John George Loesch, Aug. 28, 1948; 1 son, William Ross. Instr. speech Wellesley (Mass.) Coll., 1949-52, Loyola U., Chgo., 1956; asst. prof. English and speech Roosevelt U., Chgo., 1957, 62-65; assoc. prof. communication and theatre U. Ill. at Chgo., 1968—. Active ERA, Ill., 1975-76. Recipient Golden Anniversary Prize award Speech Assn. Am., 1969. Am. Philos. Soc. grantee, 1970; U. Ill., Chgo., grantee, 1970. Mem. Am. Soc. Aesthetics, Linguistics Soc. Am., Speech Communication Assn. (Golden Anniversary prize award 1969, chmn. interpretation div. 1979-80), MLA, Honorable Soc. Cymmrodorion, Pi Beta Phi. Episcopalian. Contbr. writings to profl. publs. Office: Dept Communication and Theatre Box 4348 U Ill Chicago IL 60680

LOEWEN, LORAINE ATWOOD, school administrator; b. Cuyahoga Falls, Ohio, July 31, 1955; d. Howard Wright and Isabelle (Parseghian) A.; m. Gregory M. Loewen, Mar. 17, 1982; 1 child, Jennifer Lee. Student, U. Akron, 1973-75; B.S., Auburn U., 1977, M.B.A., 1978. Acctg. supr. Park Hill Sch. Dist., Kansas City, Mo., 1978-81; internal auditor Falls Savs. & Loan, Cuyahoga Falls, 1981-82; bus. mgr. Hathaway Brown Sch., Cleve., 1982—; mem. evaluation team Ind. Sch. Assn. Central States. 1984—. Mem. Nat. Assn. Ind. Schs., Midwest Assn. Ind. Schs. Bus. Mgrs., Ohio Assn. Ind. Schs., Cleve. Council Ind. Schs. (div. pres. 1985-86). Republican. Congregationalist. Home: 3252 E Fairfax Rd Cleveland Heights OH 44118 Office: 19600 N Park Blvd Cleveland OH 44122

LOEWENTHAL, LAWRENCE MICHAEL, ophthalmologist; b. Detroit, Apr. 14, 1943; s. Erry S. and Renee T. (Gamsu) L.; m. Shirley Faye Rosenberg, June 27, 1965; children—Robert, Jeffrey, Lisa. B.S., Wayne State U., 1964, M.D., 1968. Diplomate Am. Bd. Ophthalmology. Pres. Vision Inst. Mich., Sterling Heights, 1974—. Contbr. articles on glaucoma and cataracts to Am. Intraocular Implant Soc. Jour., Glaucoma, Jour. Ophthalmology. Pres. Detroit Friends of Shaarey Zedeh Hosp., 1983—; chmn. bd. dirs. Young Israel of Southfield, 1983—, Alkiva Hebrew Day Sch., Southfield, 1984—; bd. dirs. Hebrew Free Loan, Southfield, 1980—. Served to lt. USPHS, 1969-71. Fellow Am. Acad. Ophthalmology; mem. Keratorefractive Soc. Avocations: skiing; sailing. Office: Vision Inst Michigan 44750 Delco Blvd Sterling Hts MI 48078

LOFGREN, JOHN ZAMÉO, museum director, curator; b. Sweden, Apr. 3, 1944; s. Birger Zaméo and Mary Margaret (Carl) L.; m. Inger Kristina Edemalm, Aug. 6, 1965; children—Kersti My, Carl Zaméo, Erik Zaméo. B.A., U. Oreg., 1969, M.A., 1972, Ph.D., 1976. Exec. sec. Coop. Sci. Mus., Eugene, Oreg., 1975-76; exec. dir., curator Am. Swedish Inst., Mpls., 1982—. Mem. adv. bd. Met. Med. Ctr. U. Calif. scholar, 1970; Soc. for Advancement Scandinavian Studies scholar, 1974-75; Samuel H. Kress Found. fellow, 1973-74. Mem. Am. Assn. Museums, Coll. Arts Assn., Swedish Council Am. (dir.). Author: The American Swedish Institute Collections and Swan J. Turnblad Mansion, 1979; contbr. articles to profl. jours. Office: 2600 Park Ave Minneapolis MN 55407

LOFTON, JAMES DAVID, See *Who's Who in America,* 43rd edition.

LOFTUS, DANIEL GEORGE, lawyer; b. Chgo., June 27, 1952; s. George Edward and Dorothy Elizabeth (Chapek) L. B.A., No. Ill. U., 1974; paralegal cert. Roosevelt U., 1974; J.D., John Marshall Law Sch., Chgo., 1980. Bar: Ill. 1980, U.S. Dist. Ct. (no. dist.) Ill. 1980. Paralegal, Karlin & Fleischer, Chgo., 1975-76, Rooks, Pitts, Fullager & Poust, Chgo., 1976-79, Kaplan, Gold & Gallagher, Ltd., Chgo., 1979-80; assoc. Hayt, Hayt & Landau, Evanston, Ill., 1980-83; sole practice, Chgo., 1983—. Mem. Chgo. Bar Assn., Northwest Suburban Bar Assn. Democrat. Roman Catholic. Clubs: Appalachian Mountain, Green Mountain. Office: PO Box 39053 Chicago IL 60639

LOGAN, GEORGE EDWARD, television station administrator; b. Boonville, Mo., Feb. 6, 1936; s. George H. and Bessie E. (Rush) Loesing; m. Sarah Overstreet, June 11, 1956 (div. 1978); 1 child, Janet Marie; m. Jessie M. Hughes, May 17, 1979. B.S., U. Mo.-Columbia, 1957. Info. specialist USDA, Washington, 1957-60; farm dir. Sta. WLW-TV/Radio, Cin., 1960-65, Sta. WIBW-TV/Radio, Topeka, 1965-74; nat. sales mgr. Sta. WIBW, Topeka, 1974-75; gen. mgr. Sta. KGNC, Amarillo, Tex., 1975-77, Sta. WIBW-TV, Topeka, 1977—. Chmn. Citizens Adv. Com. Topeka State Hosp., 1981, CrimeStoppers of Topeka, 1982-83. Recipient Oscars in Agr. award, 1973; Town Crier award, 1972; Outstanding Farm Broadcaster award, 1965. Mem. Kans. Assn. Broadcasters (bd. dirs., pres. 1983-84), Nat. Assn. Farm Broadcasters (exec. sec., pres., 1972-73). Republican. Club: Rotary of Topeka. Avocations: flying; motorcycling; music. Home: 4822 W Hills Dr Topeka KS 66606 Office: WIBW-TV Box 119 Topeka KS 66601

LOGAN, JAMES KENNETH, judge; b. Quenemo, Kans., Aug. 21, 1929; s. John Lysle and Esther Maurine (Price) L.; A.B., U. Kans., 1952; LL.B. magna cum laude, Harvard, 1955; m. Beverly Jo Jennings, June 8, 1952; children—Daniel Jennings, Amy Katherine, Sarah Jane, Samuel Price. Admitted to Kans. bar, 1955, Calif. bar, 1956; law clk. U.S. Circuit Judge Huxman, 1955-56; with firm Gibson, Dunn & Crutcher, Los Angeles, 1956-57; asst. prof. law U. Kans., 1957-61, prof., dean Law Sch., 1961-68; partner Payne and Jones, Olathe, Kans., 1968-77; judge U.S. Circuit Ct., 10th Circuit, 1977—; Ezra Ripley Thayer teaching fellow Harvard Law Sch., 1961-62; vis. prof. U. Tex. Law Sch., 1964, Stanford, 1969, U. Mich., 1976; commr. U.S. Dist. Ct., 1964-67. Candidate for U.S. Senate, 1968. Served with AUS, 1947-48. Rhodes scholar, 1952. Mem. Am., Kans. bar assns., Phi Beta Kappa, Order of Coif, Beta Gamma Sigma, Omicron Delta Kappa, Pi Sigma Alpha, Alpha Kappa Psi, Phi Delta Phi. Democrat. Presbyterian. Author: (with W.B. Leach) Future Interests and Estate Planning, 1961; Kansas Estate Administration, 4th edit., 1980; (with A.R. Martin) Kansas Corporate Law and Practice, 2d edit., 1979; also articles. Office: Box 790 1 Patrons Plaza Olathe KS 66061*

LOGAN, SERGE EDWARD, editor, wax company executive; b. Chgo., Feb. 7, 1926; s. Carl and Alexandra (Honcharik) L.; student Superior (Wis.) State U., 1946-48; B.A. magna cum laude, U. Minn., 1950. Reporter, asst. city editor, Sunday editor Racine (Wis.) Jour.-Times, 1950-60; publs. mgr. S. C. Johnson & Son, Inc., Racine, 1960-65, community affairs mgr., editor, 1965-68, communications mgr., 1968-71, communications dir., 1971-81, asst. to vice chmn., 1981-82, dir. corporate social responsibility, 1982—, editor Johnson Mag., 1960-79. Active as scoutmaster, explorer adviser, commnr., mem. exec. bd. S.E. Wis. council Boy Scouts Am., 1951—, pres., 1966-68; sec. Johnson Wax Fund, Inc., 1965-68, trustee, 1978-81, 85—, v.p., 1982-85; public relations chmn. United Fund, 1967, 70, 72, 73. Served with USNR, 1944-46; PTO. Named Outstanding Young Man of Year, Racine Jr. C. of C., 1961; recipient Silver Beaver award Boy Scouts Am., 1963, Silver Antelope, 1973. Am. Polit. Sci. Assn. Congl. fellow on Senate staff Hubert H. Humphrey, Ho. of reps. staff James Wright, 1956-57. Mem. C. of C. (publs. com. 1967—), Meeting Planners Internat. (officer, dir. Wis. chpt.), Phi Beta Kappa. Methodist (steward). Home: 1737 Wisconsin Ave Racine WI 53403 Office: 1525 Howe St Racine WI 53403

LOGEMANN, JERILYN ANN, speech pathologist, communicative disorders educator; b. Berwyn, Ill., May 21, 1942; d. Warren F. and Natalie M. (Killmer) L. B.S., Northwestern U., 1963, M.A., 1964, Ph.D., 1968. Instr. Mundelein Coll., Chgo., 1967-71; research asst. Northwestern U., Evanston, Ill., 1970-74, asst. prof. communicative disorders, 1974-78, assoc. prof., 1978-83, prof., 1983—, chmn. dept. communicative disorders, 1982—; assoc. staff mem. Northwestern Meml. Hosp., Chgo., 1972—; cons to hosps., Chgo., 1983—. Author: Evaluation and Treatment of Swallowing Disorders, 1983. Grantee Nat. Cancer Inst., 1977, 83-85, Am. Cancer Soc., 1982. Mem. AAUP, Am. Speech-Lang.-Hearing Assn. (cert.), Ill. Speech and Hearing Assn., Am. Cleft Palate Assn., Speech Communication Assn. Home: 1002 Greenleaf Wilmette IL 60091 Office: Northwestern U 303 E Chicago Ave Chicago IL 60611

LOGIUDICE, ROSEMARY JOANNE, veterinarian; b. Albany, N.Y., Feb. 5, 1955; d. Frank Joseph and Mafalda Rosalie (DeVirgilio) LoG. B.S. with honors in Agr., U. Ill., 1977, B.S. in Vet. Medicine, 1979, D.V.M., 1981. Lic. veterinarian. Student vet. asst. Oak Knoll Animal Hosp., Ltd., Moline, Ill., 1974-81; vet. Plato Computer programmer Coll. Vet. Medicine, U. Ill., Urbana, 1978-81; student vet. asst. Quad City Downs and Friendship Farms, East Moline, Ill., 1974-79; staff veterinarian Ingmire Large Animal Clinic, Joliet, Ill., 1981-83, staff veterinarian, corp. ptnr., 1983—; Dept. Agr. meat inspector Illini Beef Packers, Inc., Geneseo, and Wilson Foods, Monmouth, Ill., 1979. Editor U. Ill. Coll. Vet. Medicine Yearbook, 1980. Choir dir. St. John's Cath. Chapel, Champaign, Ill., 1974-79; mem. Peoria Cath. Diocese Liturgical Music Commn., 1975-77; coach nat. champion team Ill. Arabian Horse Assn. Youth Horse Judging Team, 1978, also mem. nat. res. champion team, 1972; mem. U. Ill. Women's Glee Club, 1973-79, pres., 1975-76, tour mgr., 1973-74; mem. U. Ill. Horse Judging Team, 1975-77; coach youth horse judging team Will County 4-H Clubs, Joliet, Ill., 1981-82; alto soloist Joliet Community Chorale, 1982—. Recipient U. Ill. Mother's Assn. award, 1973. Mem. Am. Assn. Equine Practitioners, Ill. State Vet. Med. Assn. (equine practitioners com. 1981—, pub relations com. 1985—), Kankakee Valley Vet. Med. Assn. (pres. 1984-85, program chmn. 1983-84), AVMA (Outstanding Service award U. Ill. Student chpt.), Mortar Bd. (pres. 1977), Omega Tau Sigma (pres. 1980, Outstanding Sr. award 1981), Gamma Sigma Delta, Alpha Zeta, Atius, Alpha Lambda Delta. Roman Catholic. Club: Upper Midwest Competitive and Endurance Ride Assn. (ride veterinarian 1981—). Office: Ingmire Large Animal Clinic Ltd 1410 Mills Rd Joliet IL 60433

LOGUE, MARSHALL W., chemistry educator; b. Danville, Ky., June 4, 1942; s. William A. and Elva Ray (Woford) L.; m. Joan Karen Newell, Nov. 28, 1980; 1 child, Timothy Gale. B.A., Centre Coll., 1964; Ph.D., Ohio State U., 1969. Postdoctoral research asst. U. Ill., Urbana, 1969-71; asst. prof. U. Md. Baltimore County, Catonsville, 1971-77, N.D. State U., Fargo, 1977-81; assoc. prof. chemistry Mich. Technol. U., Houghton, 1981—. Contbr. articles to profl. jours. Grantee Petroleum Research Fund, 1972, Am. Cancer Soc., 1975, 76, 77, Nat. Cancer Inst., 1984. Mem. Am. Chem. Soc. (exam. com. 1980—), Royal Soc. Chemistry, AAAS, N.Y. Acad. Scis. Methodist. Avocations: bicycling, amateur astronomy. Office: Dept Chemistry Mich Technol U Houghton MI 49931

LOHR, KENNETH RAYBORNE, pharmacist, drug analyst; b. Quincy, Ill., Dec. 19, 1922; s. Rayborne Peter and Sarah Elizabeth (Houdyshell) L.; m. Eleanor Lucille Hetzler, July 23, 1943; children—Denise, Debra. B.S. in Pharmacy, U. Ill., 1950. Ptnr., mgr. Owl Drug Store, Quincy, 1951-58, Lohr's Prescription Shop, Quincy, 1958—; dir. St. Drug Analysis Service, Quincy. Served with U.S. Army, 1943-45. Recipient A.H. Robbins Bowl of Hygeia award, 1974. Fellow Am. Coll. Apothecaries; mem. Am. Inst. History of Pharmacy, Am. Pharm. Assn., Ill. Pharmacists Assn., Nat. Assn. Retail Druggists, Quincy C. of C. (dir. 1956-59). Republican. Lutheran. Contbr. articles in field to profl. jours. Home: 905 Payson Ave Quincy IL 62301 Office: 1301 Broadway St Quincy IL 62301

LOK, SILMOND RAY, pharmacist, pharmaceutical salesman; b. Columbus, Ohio, Dec. 14, 1948; s. Fee and Oilene (Yee) L.; m. Thresa Carlene Dale, Aug. 27, 1978. B.S. in Pharmacy, Ohio State U., 1973; M.B.A., Capital U., 1982. Registered pharmacist. Pharmacist, Federated Stores, Columbus, Ohio, 1975-82; pharm. salesman Ives Labs., Columbus, 1982, Squibb, Columbus, 1982-85; dir. pharmacy services Wendt-Bristol Co., 1985—. Mem. Grove City Civic Assn. Served to 1st lt. USAF, 1973-75. Mem. Central Ohio Acad. Pharmacy, Sigma Phi Epsilon, Kappa Psi (grand regent grad. chpt. 1973-75). Avocation: Kenpo karate (brown belt, 2d degree). Home: 2591 McDonald Ct Grove City OH 43123

LOKEN, BARBARA JEAN, marketing educator, social psychologist; b. Owatonna, Minn., Aug. 22, 1951; d. Gordon Keith and June Rosaline (Iverson) Anderson; m. Ronald Leland Hinkle, Feb. 11, 1982. B.A. in Psychology magna cum laude, U. Minn., 1973; M.A., NYU, 1976; Ph.D. in Social Psychology, U. Ill., 1981. Research and statis. asst. Nat. Soc. Prevention Blindness, N.Y.C., 1974-76; research asst. dept. psychology U. Ill., 1976, 78-80, instr., 1977-78; cons. Champaign County Mental Health Bd., 1977-78; NIMH trainee in measurement, 1979-80, asst. prof. dept. mktg. U. Minn., 1980—, co-dir. edn. evaluation Minn. heart health project Sch. Pub. Health, 1982—. Research grantee Sch. Mgmt., U. Minn., 1981-84. Mem. Am. Psychol. Assn., Am. Mktg. Assn., Assn. Consumer Research. Contbr. articles to profl. jours. Home: 3615 15th Avenue S Minneapolis MN 55407 Office: Management and Econ Bldg U Minn Minneapolis MN 55455

LOLLAR, ROBERT MILLER, indsl. mgmt. exec.; b. Lebanon, Ohio, May 17, 1915; s. Harry David and Ruby (Miller) L.; Chem.E., U. Cin., 1937, M.S., 1938, Ph.D., 1940; m. Dorothy Marie Williams, Jan. 1, 1941; children—Janet Ruth (Mrs. David Schwarz), Katherine Louise (Mrs. James Punteney, Jr.). Cereal analyst Kroger Food Found., Cin., 1935-37; devel. chemist Rit Product div. Corn Products, Indpls., 1937-39, 40-41; asso. prof. U. Cin., 1941-59; tech. dir. Armour & Co., Chgo., 1959-73; mgmt. and tech. cons., pres. Lollar and Assos., 1973—; tech. dir. Tanners Council Am., Cin., 1975—. Dir. OSRD, 1942-45. Recipient Alsop award Am. Leather Chemists Assn., 1954. Mem. Am. Leather Chemists Assn. (pres., editor-in-chief), Inst. Food Technologists, Am. Chem. Soc. (nat. councillor), Am. Soc. Quality Control, World Mariculture Soc., Sigma Xi, Tau Beta Pi, Alpha Chi Sigma. Address: 5960 Donjoy Dr Cincinnati OH 45242

LOLLI, RICHARD JOHN, lawyer; b. Alliance, Ohio, Feb. 11, 1951; s. Robert and Carmela J. (Corbisella) L.; m. Sheila Marie Mann, Sept. 21, 1980; children—Alyson Christina, Hilary Catherine. B.S. in Fgn. Service, Georgetown U., 1973; J.D., Case-Western Res. U., 1976. Bar: Ohio 1976, U.S. Dist. Ct. (no. dist.) Ohio 1977. Practice law, Alliance, Ohio, 1976—; pres. Colonial Title Co., 1985—; asst. law dir. City of Alliance, 1984—; ct. arbitrator Stark County Ct. Common Pleas, Canton, 1977—. Big Bro. Cath. Big Bros., Cleve., 1974-76; mgr., chmn. Thomas Walsh's Campaign for Ohio Senate, Canton, 1978; bd. dirs., chmn. com. Am. Lung Assn. Stark-Wayne, Canton, 1981—; bd. dirs. Am. Lung Assn. of Ohio. Mem. Alliance Jaycees, Ohio State Bar Assn., Stark County Bar Assn. Home: 1060 Oakwood Dr Alliance OH 44601 Office: 2045 Cherry Ave Alliance OH 44601

LOMAX, RICHARD EARL, land surveyor, state government official; b. Gratiot County, Mich., Jan. 25, 1936; s. Earl Bell and Lola Pearl (Sabin) L.; m. Linnie S. Sharp, Sept. 1957 (div.); children—Richard L., Rhonda L., Brian A., Robert E., John R.; m. Doye Juanita Rogers Pullano, Aug. 25, 1973. Student Chgo. Tech. Coll., 1954-55, Mich. State U., 1955-59, Lansing Community Coll., 1979-80. Registered land surveyor, Mich. Draftsman Dept. of Hwys., State of Mich., Lansing, 1954-61, plat examiner Dept. Auditor Gen., 1961-66, supr. plat sect. Dept. Treasury, 1966-70, mgr. subdiv. control Dept. Treasury, 1970-81, adminstr. subdiv. control and county zoning Dept. Commerce, 1981—; prin. Richard Lomax, Surveyor, Charlotte, Mich., 1973-76; mem. Ingham County Remonumentation and Survey Bd., Mich., 1977-81. Co-editor: Mich. Surveyor mag., 1983-85. Chmn. Charlotte City Planning Commn., 1976-85; sec. Tri- County Regional Planning Commn., Lansing, 1979-85. Fellow Mich. Soc. Registered Land Surveyors (dir. 1976—, pres. 1985), Am. Congress on Survey and Mapping (chmn. Gt. Lakes council of affiliates 1982-84); mem. Nat. Soc. Profl. Surveyors. Republican. Home: 243 S Sheldon St Charlotte MI 48813

LOMBARDO, (GUY) GAETANO, factory automation manufacturing company executive; b. Salemi, Italy, Feb. 4, 1940; came to U.S., 1947; s. Salvatore and Anna Maria L.; Sc.B. with honors, Brown U., 1962; Ph.D. in Physics, Cornell U., 1971; m. Nancy B. Emerson, Sept. 2, 1967; children—Nicholas Emerson, Maryanne Chilton. Sr. staff Arthur D. Little Inc., Cambridge, Mass., 1967-77; v.p. logistics Morton Salt Co., Chgo., 1977-78; dir. logistics and distbn. Gould Inc., Chgo., 1978-80; corp. dir. Bendix Corp., Southfield, Mich., 1980-82; group v.p. worldwide bus. devel. Bendix Indsl. Group, 1982-84; pres. Comau Productivity Systems, Troy, Mich., 1984—; vis. prof. ops. mgmt. Boston U., 1973. Contbr. articles on physics and bus. mgmt. to profl. jours. Home: 900 Timberlake Dr Bloomfield Hills MI 48013 Office: Comau Productivity Systems 750 Stephenson Hwy Troy MI 48084

LOMBARDY, ROSS DAVID, food co. exec.; b. Cleve., Mar. 20, 1920; s. David Ross and Minnie (Roberto) L.; student pub. schs.; m. Louise Adelaide McMahon, Oct. 28, 1940; children—Louise, Ross David, David J., Kathleen L., Mary A., Thomas J. Pres. David Lombardy Co., Cleve., 1942-57; v.p., sec. Seaway Foods, Inc., Bedford Heights, Ohio, 1957-79, exec. v.p., 1979—. Recipient Grocery Man of Year award, 1973. Mem. Internat. Order Alhambra (Grand Comdr.). Roman Cathloic (pres. Holy Name Soc. 1955). K.C. (4 deg.). Club: K-C (trustee South Euclid, Ohio). Home: 4991 Countryside Ln Lyndhurst OH 44124 Office: 22801 Aurora Rd Bedford Heights OH 44146

LONDON, ANNE ODEAN, pharmacist, author; b. Hamilton, Ind., Mar. 7, 1934; d. Harry C. and Frances E. (Kepler) Fee; m. Russell Henry Meyer, June 5, 1955 (div. Mar. 1959); 1 child, Kenton H. (dec.); m. Norman Homner Lanza, June 16, 1961 (div. Oct. 1975); 1 child, Kimberlee Anne Lanza Lee. B.S. Purdue U., 1956. Cert. real estate counselor; registered pharmacist, Ill., Mich., Ind., Ohio. Pharmacist, Brookhaven Drugs, Darien, Ill., 1968-72; broker McNeil Realtors, Downers Grove, Ill., 1972, Circle Real Estate, Downers Grove, 1973-78; broker/mgr. Bankman & Best, Downers Grove, 1979; realtor/broker, mgr. Dixon Gallery of Homes, Bolingbrook, Ill., 1979-85; guest speaker Eye on Classics, Cable-TV, 1985. Author (pen name A. Lee Hamilton): Prose by a Dead Poet, 1985. Mem. Realtors PAC, Notaries Assn. Ill., Will County Bd. Realtors, DuPage County Bd. Realtors. Republican. Clubs: Bridging the Arts (Downers Grove) (pres. 1984); Choralers, WRX and WCCR Radio (Purdue U.). Avocations: art; music; bridge. Office: Dixon Gallery of Homes 4954 Main St Downers Grove IL 60515

LONE, HARRY EDWIN, waterproofing company executive, vehicle leasing company executive; b. Council Bluffs, Iowa, Oct. 20, 1923; s. Harry Edwin and Lula (Wakefield) L.; m. Wanda Lu Selindh, Mar. 16, 1946; children—Stanley Craig, Allen Eugene, Gregory Lynn, Janet Elaine Lone Davis. Student Princeton U., 1945, DePauw Coll., Greencastle, Ind., 1945-46, Purdue U., Lafayette, Ind., 1946. Motor machinist apprentice Rock Island R.R., Des Moines, 1946-47; bakery sales Continental Bakery, Des Moines, 1947-49; dairy route sales A&E Dairy, Des Moines, 1949-52; route supr. Hilan Dairy, Ames, Iowa, 1953-60; route sales mgr. Borden Co., Marshalltown, Iowa, 1960-63; ter. mgr. Gen. Foods Corp., White Plains, N.Y., 1963-78; pres., chief exec. officer Central States Waterproofing, St. Louis, 1978—; pres. Gold Key Enterprises, Maryland Heights, Mo., 1982—, Lone Advt., Maryland Heights, 1982—. Mem. nat. and state elections com. Mo. Republican Com., 1983; mem. Rep. Nat. Com., Washington, 1983; mem. Rep. Senatorial Com., Washington, 1983. Recipient Pres.' Medal of Merit, Republican Presdl. Task Force, 1982. Mem. Nat. Assn. for Remodeling Industry, Nat. Fedn. Ind. Bus., Nat. Assn. Waterproofing, Homebuilders Assn. Kansas City. Club: U.S. Senatorial. Lodges: Eagles, Toastmasters. Home: 14864 Grassmere Ct Chesterfield MO 63017 Office: Central States Waterproofing of MO Inc 13738 Rider Trail N Earth City MO 63045

LONG, CHARLES ALAN, biology educator, museum curator; b. Pittsburg, Kans., Jan. 19, 1936; s. Dorsey Arnold and Mary Bell (Seelig) L.; m. Claudine Fern Lowder, Aug. 28, 1960; children—Charles Alan, John Edward. B.S., Pittsburg State U., Kans., 1957, M.S., 1958; postgrad. U. Wash., summer 1960; Ph.D., U. Kans., 1963. Grad. fellow Pittsburg State U., 1957-58; teaching asst. U. Kans., Lawrence, 1959-61, research asst., 1961-63; instr. U. Ill.-Urbana, 1963-65, asst. prof., 1965-66; asst. prof. biology U. Wis.-Stevens Point, 1966-68, assoc. prof., 1968-70, prof., 1970—, curator of mammals Mus. Natural History, 1967—, founder, dir. mus., 1968-83; prof. Rocky Mountain Research Lab., Gunnison, Colo., summer 1966; cons. Argonne Nat. Lab., Ill., 1973-75, Lake Superior Ojibway Tribe, Lac du Flambeau, Wis., 1981-84. Author: The Mammals of Wyoming, 1965; The Mammals of the Lake Michigan Drainage Basin, 1974; co-author: The Badgers of the World, 1983; contbr. numerous articles to profl. jours., chpts. to books. Bd. dirs., co-founder Portage County Humane Soc., Stevens Point, 1967-68, mem. steering com. Greek Revival Architecture Ch. Mus., Plover, Wis., 1979-81; bd. dirs. Portage County Hist. Soc., 1979-81; co-founder Lac du Flambeau Indian Mus., 1983—. Served to capt. USAR, 1957-68. Fulbright schoar, 1976; Named Outstanding Scholar, U. Wis., 1983-84. Grantee NSF, Am. Inst. Museums, Dept. Interior, others. Mem. Am. Soc. Museums, Am. Assn. Sci. Mus. Dirs., Internat. Council Museums, Am. Naturalists, Am. Soc. Mammalogists, Southwestern Naturalists, Kappa Mu Epsilon, Phi Sigma, Sigma Xi. Lutheran. Avocations: art nouveau; kids basketball coach; canoeing; poetry; traveling. Home: 3531 Yvonne Dr on McDill Pond Stevens Point WI 54481 Office: Dept Biology U Wis Stevens Point WI 54481

LONG, CHARLES HENRY, JR., clergyman, publisher; b. Phila., Feb. 13, 1923; s. Charles Henry and Evelyn Agnes (Boyd) L.; m. Nancy Ingham, Feb. 14, 1946; children—Christine, Charles H. III, Robert, Jeremy. B.A. Yale U., 1944; D.Min., Va. Sem., 1946, D.Div., 1976; S.T.M., Phila. Luth. Sem., 1966; S.T.D. Episcopal Sem. Ky., 1983; L.H.D. Episcopal Sem. Southwest, 1984. Ordained priest Episcopal Ch., 1945. Missionary, Episcopal Ch., Nanking, China, 1946-49; far east rep. Yale-China Assn., Hong Kong, 1954-58; study sec. World Student Christian Fedn., Geneva, Switzerland, 1958-60; rector St. Peter's Ch., Glenside, Pa., 1960-73; exec. dir. World Council of Chs., N.Y.C., 1974-78; pub., editor Forward Movement Publs., Cin., 1978—. Author: Vancouver Voices, 1983. Editor: The Compulsion of the Spirit, 1983; various religious guides; asst. editor: Anglican Theol. Rev. Vice-pres. Greater Phila. Council of Chs., 1963-66. Fellow Coll. of Preachers; mem. Evang. Edn. Soc. (bd. mgrs. 1963—, v.p. 1969-78), Soc. Promotion Christian Knowledge (trustee 1984—), Yale-China Assn. (trustee 1961-73). Clubs: University (Cin.), Literary. Avocations: music, golf. Office: Forward Movement Pubs 412 Sycamore St Cincinnati OH 45202

LONG, DWIGHT EDWARD, audio-visual company executive; b. Cin., Sept. 23, 1936; s. Richard C. and Charlene (O'Kelly) L; m. Ethel Burroughs (div. Mar. 1981); m. Nancy Elizabeth Morris, Apr. 17, 1982; children—Connie, Lee, Cheryl, Darrell, Beth, Amy. Grad. high sch. Mgr. photo/graphics dept. Procter & Gamble Co., Cin., 1957-78; pres. Cin. Audio Visual Design, 1978-82; pres. audio/visual design div. David Douglas Corp., Cin., 1982—. Pres. Mt. Washington Pee Wee Football Assn. Mem. Assn. Multi-Image, Profl. Photographers Am., Internat. Communications Industries Assn. Avocations: photography; music; woodworking; hunting. Home: 3664 Hopper Ridge Rd Cincinnati OH 45230 Office: The David Douglas Corp 700 Walnut St Cincinnati OH 45202

LONG, ERNESTINE MARTHA JOULLIAN, educational consultant; b. Ladue, Mo., Nov. 14, 1906; d. Ernest Cameron and Alice (Joullian) Long; A.B., U. Wis., 1927; M.S., U. Chgo., 1932; Ph.D., St. Louis U., 1975; postgrad. (NSF fellow), So. Ill. U., 1969-70. Tchr. scis. Normandy High Sch., St. Louis, 1927-64; with City St. Louis Health Dept. and U.S. Maternal Child Health Div., Children's Bur., Washington, 1964; chmn. sci. dept. Red Bud (Ill.) High Sch., 1965-70, St. Louis pub. schs., 1971-75; assoc. coordinator continuing edn. U. Mo.-St. Louis, 1976-79; ednl. cons. Docent, St. Louis Symphony Orch. Recipient Community Service award St. Louis Newspaper Guild, 1978; NSF fellow, 1967-68. Mem. Am. Assn. Counseling Devel. (treas. St. Louis br. 1954), Am. Chem. Soc. (com. for revision high sch. chemistry, women's nat. service com.), Central Assn. Sch. Sci. and Math. Tchrs., AAAS, Am. Physics Tchrs. Assn., Assn. for Supervision and Curriculum Devel., Am. Assn. for Microbiology, Nat. Sci. Tchrs. Assn., Am. Guild Organists, NEA. Author: Living Chemistry. Author numerous sci. edn. articles. Composer: Organ preludes, 1945; Hymns, 1967-69; research on edn.

LONG, EVERETT LEE, history educator; b. Hindsville, Ark., Jan. 8, 1938; s. Oakley Charles and Anna Ruth (Enyart) L.; m. Ellen Joyce Baker, June 10, 1961; children—Paula, Laura, Douglas. B.A., Ouachita Bapt. U., 1958; M.A., U. Ark., 1961; Ph.D., U. Mo., 1966. Asst. prof. history U. Wis.-Whitewater, 1965-67, assoc. prof., 1967-75, prof., 1975—. Mem. Orgn. Am. Historians, Soc. Historians of the Early Republic. Home: 1259 Satinwood Lane Whitewater WI 53190 Office: U Wis History Dept 800 W Main St Whitewater WI 53190

LONG, GEORGE STEPHEN, lawyer; b. Memphis, Mar. 22, 1952; s. George Gilmore and Betty Lou (McKee) L.; m. Mary Margaret Johannes, Sept. 2, 1972; 1 dau., Alysia Christine. B.A. with honors, Harvard U., 1974; J.D. with honors, U. Wis., 1977. Bar: Mo. 1978, U.S. Dist. Ct. (we. dist.) Mo. 1979, U.S. Ct. Appeals (8th cir.) 1981. Law clk. to chief judge U.S. Dist. Ct. (we. dist.) Mo., Kansas City, 1977-79; assoc. Shughart, Thomson & Kilroy, P.C., Kansas City, Mo., 1979-83, ptnr., 1983—; city atty. and prosecutor City of Parkville, Mo., 1981-83. Contbr. Communication as Identification, 1975. Precinct chmn. Johnson County Democratic Com., Kans., 1984. Named to Outstanding Young Men Am., U.S. Jaycees, 1983. Mem. Kansas City Bar Assn., Young Lawyers Assn. of Kansas City, Mo. Bar, ABA, Kansas City C. of C. (congl. affairs com. 1984). Presbyterian. Clubs: Harvard Varsity (Cambridge, Mass.); Harvard of Kansas City. Office: Shughart Thomson & Kilroy PC 922 Walnut St Kansas City MO 64106

LONG, JOHN VERNON, clergyman; b. Texhoma, Okla., May 13, 1946; s. Floyd Alva and Verna Blanche (Gaddy) L.; m. Diana Lee Burton, June 7, 1969; children—Anne Melinda, Nathaniel Lawrence, Jennifer Lee. Student Panhandle State Coll., 1964-65; B.Sacred Lit., Th.B., Ozark Bible Coll., 1971. Ordained to ministry Christian Ch., 1969. Pastor, Alba (Mo.) Christian Ch., 1970-73, Humboldt (Kans.) Christian Ch., 1973; asst. pastor Shelbina (Mo.) Christian Ch., 1974-76; minister Youth Brownsburg (Ind.) Christian Ch., 1976-78; pastor Brook (Ind.) Christian Ch., 1978-80, First Christian Ch., Villa Grove, Ill., 1980—; bd. advs. Milligan Coll., 1978-80, Christian Campus House, U. Ill., 1981-82. Mem. physician selection com., Newton City, Ind., 1979-80; pres. George Ade Hosp. Chaplain Assn., 1979-80; asst. mgr. Villa Grove Little League, 1980. Named Outstanding Young Religious Leader, Villa Grove Jaycees, 1982; recipient Cert. of Appreciation, S. Newton High Sch., 1979. Mem. Nat. Assn. Nouthetic Counselors, Villa Grove Ministerial Alliance (pres.), Newton City Assn. Chs. (pres.), Villa Grove C. of C., Alumni Assn. Ozark Bible Coll. Club: Rotary (pres.) (Villa Grove). Home: Rural Route 1 Box 2 McCoy Addition Villa Grove IL 61956 Office: Route 130 N Box 42 Villa Grove IL 61956

LONG, PATRICK DAVID, lawyer; b. Middletown, Ohio, Jan. 4, 1951; s. John Clarence and Marilyn (Greenfield) L.; m. Jennifer Rapp, Aug. 16, 1975; children—James, Erin. B.A. in Speech and English, Western Ky. U., 1973; postgrad. U. Ky., 1974-75; J.D., U. Dayton, 1977. Bar: Ohio 1977. Assoc. Tracy & Tracy, Franklin, Ohio, 1977-82; ptnr. Tracy & Long, Franklin, 1982—; contact atty. Pub. Children Services Assn., 1983—. Mem. Warren County Democratic Central Com., 1976-82; pres. Franklin Area Community Services, 1983—; Editor Jour. Honors Bull., 1973. Mem. ACLU (cooperating atty. 1980—), ABA, Warren County Bar Assn., Ohio Bar Assn., Cin. Bar Assn., Assn. Trial Lawyers Am., Ohio Acad. Trial Lawyers. Lodges: Lions, Rotary. Avocation: amateur radio. Office: Tracy & Long 8 E 5th St Franklin OH 45005

LONG, ROBERT BASIL, typographer, publisher; b. Keokuk, Iowa, Sept. 16, 1945; s. John Carl and Grace Marie (Gilbert) L.; m. Mercedes Ann Peitzmeier, Dec. 28, 1965 (dec. Mar. 1984); children—Robert B. II, Christine J., Nathan E. B.A., St. Ambrose Coll., 1967; M.S., Western Ill. U., 1969. Tchr., instr. Western Ill. U., Macomb, 1968-69; mathematician Rodman Lab., Rock Island, Ill., 1967-77; pres. Thinker's Press, Davenport, Iowa, 1967—, Chessco, Davenport, 1971—, typefaces, inc., Davenport, 1980—. Editor Lasker & His Contemporaries, 1978— The Sorcerer's Eyes, 1979, The Chess Atlas, 1978-82. Recipient Yr. Chess Profl. award U.S. Chess Fedn., 1984. Mem. U.S. Chess Fedn., Typographers Internat. Assn. Roman Catholic Club: Illowa Chess (Rock Island, Ill.) (all offices 1967-84) Avocations: computers; Sherlock Holmes; stamps; mathematics; bridge. Home: 1026 Arlington Ct Davenport IA 52803 Office: typefaces inc 331 Union Arcade Bldg Davenport IA 52801

LONG, ROBERT JEFFREY, lawyer; b. Waukegan, Ill., July 25, 1954; s. John George and Virginia Marguerite (Kierland) L.; m. Marcia Ann Korducki, Aug. 16, 1980. B.A., U. Ill., 1976; J.D., DePaul U., 1981. Bar: Ill. 1981, U.S. Dist. Ct. (no. dist.) Ill. 1981, U.S. Dist. Ct. (ea. and we. dists.) Wis. 1984. Assoc. Law Offices A. Denison Weaver Ltd., Chgo., 1981-84, Law Offices Howard M. Lang, Libertyville, Ill., 1984—; classical guitarist. Recipient Am. Jurisprudence award in Torts, Lawyers Coop. Pub., 1978. Mem. Assn. Trial Lawyers Am., Ill. Trial Lawyers Assn., Cook County Bar Assn., Lake County Bar Assn. Presbyterian. Office: 800 S Milwaukee Ave Libertyville IL 60048

LONG, ROLAND JOHN, secondary school principal; b. Chgo., Nov. 15, 1921; s. John and Lillian Catherine (Sigmund) L.; B.S., Ill. State Normal U., 1949; M.A., Northwestern U., 1951; Ed.D., Ill. State U., 1972; m. Valerie Ann Zawila, Nov. 13, 1954; children—Ronald J., Thomas E. Instr. of social sci. Ball State U., Muncie, Ind., 1951; comdt. Morgan Park Mil. Acad., Chgo., 1952-54; tchr. history Hyde Park and Amundsen high schs., Chgo., 1955-62; prin. Hubbard Elementary Sch., Chgo., 1962; founder, prin. Hubbard High Sch., Chgo., 1963—; mem. doctoral advisory com. of Ill. State U., 1973-75; panelist Gen. Assembly State of Ill. Sponsored Conf. Ednl. Reform. Mem. Chgo. Police Dist. 8 steering com., 1974-77; bd. dirs. West Communities YMCA, Chgo., Greater Lawn Mental Health Center, Chgo. Served to 1st lt., inf., U.S. Army; ETO. Decorated Silver Star, Purple Heart, Bronze Star; Ford Found. fellow, 1973; recipient Sch. Mgmt. citation Ill. Gen. Assembly, 1972; mem. Accademia Italia, 1983. Fellow (hon.) Harry S. Truman Library Inst.; mem. Ill. Assn. for Supervision and Curriculum Devel., Nat. Assn. of Secondary Sch. Prins., Am. Legion, Phi Delta Kappa (Educator of Yr. award 1980), Pi Gamma Mu, Kappa Delta Pi. Club: Elks. Author: Dr. Long's Old-Fashioned Basic Report Card and Parent Helper, 1977. Home: 6701 N Ionia Ave Chicago IL 60646 Office: 6200 S Hamlin Ave Chicago IL 60629

LONG, SANDRA JEAN, lawyer; b. Anderson, Ind., Feb. 18, 1955; d. Donald Allen and Jean Frances (Loudenback) L. B.A. summa cum laude, Butler U., 1977; J.D. summa cum laude, Ind. U., 1980. Bar: Ind. 1980, U.S. Dist Ct. (so. dist.) Ind. 1980, U.S. Ct. Appeals (7th cir.) 1984. Assoc., Barnes & Thornburg and predecessor firm Barnes, Hickam, Pantzer & Boyd, Indpls., 1980—. Chmn. attys. div. United Way Greater Indpls., 1984—; leader troop Girl Scouts Am., 1982-83. Mem. ABA, Ind Bar Assn., Indpls. Bar Assn., 7th Cir. Bar Assn., Assn. Trial Lawyers Am. Home: 5426 Graceland Ave Indianapolis IN 46208 Office: Barnes & Thornburg 1313 Mchts Bank Bldg Indianapolis IN 46204

LONG, WRITESMAN, business educator; b. Hume, Ill., Sept. 16, 1934; s. H. Montelle and Mary Louvene (Writesman) L. B.S., Eastern Ill. U., 1956; M.S., U. Ill., 1959, advanced cert. in edn., 1965; D.Edn., No. Ill. U., 1977. Instr. bus. Blue Mound (Ill.) High Sch., 1956-64; chmn. dept. bus. edn. Kankakee (Ill.) Sr. High Sch., 1964-66; supr. bus. edn. Kankakee Eastridge and Westview High Schs., 1966-68; vis. lectr. U. Ill., Urbana, 1966, 67, 68; chmn. bus. div. Kankakee Community Coll., 1968-73, dir. instrn. and personnel, 1973-77, v.p. bus. affairs and personnel, 1977-81, instr. bus., 1981—. Mem. Am. Vocat. Assn., Nat. Bus. Edn. Assn., North Central Bus. Edn. Assn., Ill. Vocat. Assn., Ill. Bus. Edn. Assn. (disting. service award 1977), Chgo. Area Bus. Educators Assn., Delta Pi Epsilon, Phi Delta Kappa. Home: 720 Riverside Ct Kankakee IL 60901 Office: Box 888 Kankakee IL 60901

LONGHOFER, PAUL DAVID, educational administrator; b. Junction City, Kans., July 22, 1938; s. Fred Godfrey and Emily Pearl (Mott) L.; m. Janet Lenore Davis, Aug. 14, 1960; children—Kirk David, Stanley David. B.S., Kans. State U., 1960; M.Ed., U. Mo., 1963; Ed.D., U. Kans., 1967. Cert. school adminstr. Dir. spl. projects Topeka Pub. Sch., 1965-69; dir. employment relations Wichita Pub. Sch. Kans., 1969-74; prin. Truesdell Jr. High Sch., Wichita, 1974-77, North High Sch., Wichita, 1977-84, East High Sch., Wichita, 1984—; profl. negotiator Bd. Edn., Kans. Okla., Colo., 1969-84; guest faculty, Emporia State U., Wichita State U., 1972-79; guest lectr. various univs., 1971-79. Contbr. articles to profl. jours. Adv. bd., Booths Childrens Home, Wichita, 1981—; bd. dirs. Boys Club Topeka, 1967. Fellow NDEA, Mem. Assn. Edn. Negotiators (pres. 1972-73), Nat. Assn. Secondary Sch. Prins., Kans. Assn. Secondary Sch. Prins., Wichita Edn. Mgmt. Assn. (exec. bd. 1984), Phi Delta Kappa. Methodist. Lodge: Rotary. Avocations: skiing; reading. Home: 319 N Dellrose Wichita KS 67208

LONGLEY, WILLIAM WARREN, physicist, computer science educator; b. Hanover, N.H., Aug. 30, 1937; s. William Warren and Anita Grace (Sallans) L.; m. Patricia Ann Sweetman, July 3, 1960; children—Elizabeth Ann, Harold William. B.A., U. Colo., 1958, M.A., 1959, Ph.D., 1963. Engr. aerospace div. Martin-Marietta Corp., Denver, 1959-63; postdoctoral fellow U. Alta., Edmonton, 1963-64; assoc. physicist Midwest Research Inst., Kansas City, Mo., 1964-68; assoc. prof. physics, computer ctr. dir. Upper Iowa U., Fayette, Iowa, 1968-81; assoc. prof. computer sci. St. Cloud State U. (Minn.), 1981-83; assoc. prof. computer sci. Peru State Coll. (Nebr.), 1983—; cons. data processing. Mem. AAAS, Am. Phys. Soc., Am. Econ. Assn., Sigma Xi. Office: Peru State Coll Peru NE 68421

LONGMEYER, JUDITH A. SHULMISTRAS, marketing executive; b. Chgo., Aug. 30, 1943; d. John A. and Ann (Jakaitis) Shulmistras; m. Joseph F. Longmeyer, Apr. 28, 1962 (div. May 1978). A.A., Chgo. City Coll., 1962; B.A., Roosevelt U., 1970; M.B.A., Northwestern U., 1975. Mem. pub. relations mktg. staff Skil Corp., Chgo., 1964-72; asst. mgr. pub. relations McGraw Edison Co., Elgin, Ill., 1973-74; ptnr. Advocates Agy., McHenry, Ill., 1975-76; mgr. mktg. services Switchgear div., Allis Chalmers, West Allis, Wis., 1976-80; mgr. mktg. communications Micro Design div. Bell & Howell Co., Hartford, Wis., 1980—. Instr., Milw. Area Tech. Coll., West Allis, 1979-80; owner Intercom, Milw., 1980—. Mem. Bus. Profl. Advt. Assn., Iota Sigma Epsilon. Home: 9215 W Adler St Milwaukee WI 53214 Office: Micro Design Div Bell & Howell Co 857 W State St Hartford WI 53027

LONGMIRE, WILBERT THOMAS, musician; b. Mobile, Ala., Dec. 2, 1943; s. William T. and Mildred (Stallworth) L.; m. Ollie V. Alexander, Nov. 7, 1959; children—Sharon, Carmen, Wilbert Thomas, Mark, Linda, Cherilynne; m. Esther Marie Brabson, Mar. 11, 1977; children—Chris, Lisa. Grad. Moler Barber Coll.; Cert. profl. musician. Performer from age of 13 as violinist, guitarist, pianist, bass; rec. artist United Artist Records, 1968, Columbia Records, 1978; pres. Cintown Records, 1971—; performer at schs., prisons, nursing homes, also concerts, radio and TV performances U.S. and abroad, 1965—. Mem. Am. Fedn. Musicians, Cin. Musicians Assn., AFTRA, Broadcast Music, Methodist. Ind. producer sound records.

LONGMORE, WILLIAM JOSEPH, biochemist, researcher, educator; b. LaJolla, Calif., Oct. 7, 1931; s. Joseph Henry and Sophie Mary (Smith) L.; m. Martha Baxter, Oct. 2, 1953; children—David, Brian, Timothy, Christopher. Student San Diego State Coll., 1949-51; A.B. in Biochemistry, U. Calif.-Berkeley, 1957; Ph.D. in Biochemistry, U. Kans., 1961. Postdoctoral fellow Scripps Clinic and Research Found., LaJolla, 1961-63, assoc., 1963-66; asst. prof. St. Louis U., 1966-69, assoc. prof., 1969-73, prof., 1973—, interim chmn. biochemistry, 1982-84; vis. prof. State U., Utrecht, Netherlands, 1977-78. Contbr. chpts. to books, articles to profl. jours. Served with USAF, 1951-55. USPHS fellow, 1961-63; Research Career Devel. awardee USPHS, 1966-76, fellow, 1977-78. Mem. Am. Soc. Biol. Chemists, Am. Physiol. Soc., Am. Thoracic Soc., Am. Chem. Soc., Perinatal Research Soc., AAAS, Sigma Xi. Democrat. Presbyterian. Avocations: woodworking; antique autos. Home: 517 Beaucaire Dr Warson Woods MO 63122 Office: St Louis U Dept Biochemistry 1402 S Grand Blvd Saint Louis MO 63104

LONGSTRETH, FRANK HOOVER, educator, tour director, camp director; b. Haverford, Pa., Oct. 30, 1921; s. William Collins and Nella (Thacher) L.; m. Martha C. Bush, Nov. 27, 1943 (div.); children—Frank Jr., Helen T. Kimber, Lucy B.; m. 2d, Cynthia Sykes Shepherd, Dec. 20, 1968; stepchildren—Eliz, Sam, Victoria Anne. A.B., Princeton U., 1944; M.A., U. Pa., 1947; postgrad. Am. Acad., Rome, 1960, Vergilian Soc. Sch. at Cumae, 1960. Tchr., Haverford Sch., 1945-48; tchr. Latin, coach track, swimming and tennis, Western Res. Acad., Hudson, Ohio, 1948—; asst. dir. Camp Choconut, Friendsville, Pa., 1944-52; dir. Camp Conestoga, Minerva, Ohio, 1953, Camp Arrowhead, Jackson, Ohio, 1961-64, dir. Western Res. Acad. Day Camp; tour dir. to France, Germany, Gr. Britain, Italy, Greece. Active March of Dimes Bike-athon, 1975—, chmn., 1979; pres., bd. dirs. Hudson Players. Served with USMCR, 1942-45. Track facility named in his honor. Mem. Classical Assn. of Midwest and South (holder Independence Found. Chair, recipient Outstanding Tchr. award), Vergilian Soc., Am. Acad. in Rome, Ohio Classical Assn., Nat. Coaches Assn. Quaker. Address: Western Res Acad Hudson OH 44236

LONGSWORTH, ROBERT MORROW, college dean; b. Canton, Ohio, Feb. 15, 1937; s. Robert H. and Margaret Elizabeth (Morrow) L.; m. Carol Herndon, Aug. 16, 1958; children—Eric D., Margaret W., Ann E. A.B., Duke U., 1958; M.A., Harvard U., 1960, Ph.D., 1965. Asst. prof. Oberlin Coll., 1964-70, assoc. prof., 1970-75, prof. English, 1975—, dean Coll. Arts and Scis., 1974-84. Author: The Cornish Ordinalia, 1967, The Design of Drama, 1972. Contbr. articles to profl. jours. Danforth Found. fellow. Fellow Am. Council Learned Socs., Nat. Humanities Ctr.; mem. MLA, Medieval Acad. Am., Cornwall Archaeol. Soc., Phi Beta Kappa.

LONNING, ROGER DEAN, school media supervisor; b. Iowa City, Iowa, Feb. 12, 1927; s. Lennie B. and Leona Beatrice (Hanson) L.; m. Marjorie Ann Moe, Aug. 16, 1953; children—Stuart Eric, Kathy Linnea, Steven Roger. B.A., Iowa State Tchr's. Coll., 1954, M.A. in Edn., 1957; M.A.L.S., U. Minn., 1971. Librarian pub. schs., Clarion, Iowa, 1954-56; tchr. 6th grade Hawthorne Sch., Albert Lea, Minn., 1957-61; librarian Lea Coll., Albert Lea, Minn., summers 1968, 69; instr. Mankato State U. (Minn.), summers 1976, 82; media supr. High Sch. Albert Lea, 1961—; mem. adv. bd. Albert Lea Pub. Library, 1968-71. Trustee Freeborn County Hist. Soc., Albert Lea, 1966—, pres., 1971, 72, treas., 1981—; mem. Planning Zoning Commn., Albert Lea, 1979-83, Southeast Minn. Arts Council, 1984—. Served with USN, 1945-52; Atlantic, Pacific, Japan. Mem. ALA, NEA, Minn. Edn. Assn., Albert Lea Edn. Assn., Minn. Assn. Sch. Librarians (pres. 1969-70), Minn. Edn. Media Orgn. (sec. 1976-77), Phi Delta Kappa. Republican. Office: Sr High Sch 504 W Clark Albert Lea MN 56007

LOOK, DAVID CHARLES, research physicist, consultant; b. St. Paul, Dec. 19, 1938; s. Oliver Ardell and Hyacinth Harriet (Hanson) L.; m. Rita Marie Beatty, Oct. 19, 1968; children—James Wesley, Christine Marie. B.Physics, U. Minn., 1960, M.S., 1962; Ph.D., U. Pitts., 1966; M.S., U. Dayton, 1978. Research physicist U. Dayton, Ohio, 1969-71, sr. research physicist, 1971-80; sr. research physicist Wright State U., Dayton, 1980—; pres. DCL Semiconductor Co., Dayton, 1984—; dir. Systems for Sci., Cleve., 1983—; cons. Keithley, Inc., Cleve., 1981—, Morgan Semiconductor, Inc., Dallas, 1985—. Author: Semi-Insulating III-V Materials, 1984; contbr. articles to jours.; patentee Toneburst NMR Relaxation. Leader Spinning Rd. Baptist Ch., Dayton, 1972—. Served to capt. USAF, 1966-69. Andrew W. Mellon fellow, 1962; NSF fellow, 1963. Fellow Am. Phys. Soc.; mem. Am. Sci. Affiliation. Avocations:

tennis; volleyball. Home: 1851 Stonewood Dr Dayton OH 45432 Office: Wright State Univ University Research Center Dayton OH 45435

LOONEY, MARY LOU, equipment company executive; b. Carroll, Iowa, July 30, 1948; d. Vincent Patrick and Edna Margaret (Schultz) Rowan; m. W. J. Pick, Jan. 7, 1967 (div.); children—Rebecca Ann, Brenda Louise; m. 2d, Ralph Bernard Looney, Oct. 1, 1977. Student U. S.D., 1972, Met. Tech. Community Coll., 1980. Sec., Wall Lake Community Sch. (Iowa), 1966-67; adminstrv. asst. U. S.D., Vermillion, 1969-73; mgr., buyer The Rocking Horse, Vermillion, S.D., 1973-75; bookkeeper Nebr. Builder's Product, Omaha, 1975-76; office mgr. Restaurant Mgmt., Omaha, 1976-80; controller LaGrange Equipment Co., Omaha, 1976-80, pres., 1982—. Mem. PTA, Omaha, 1975—; mem. Keystone Little League Assn., Omaha, 1977—. Mem. Nat. Assn. Female Execs., Profl. Woman's Assn., Greater Resources for Omaha Women. Home: 11412 Queens Dr Omaha NE 68164 Office: LaGrange Equipment Co 8714 Washington St Omaha NE 68127

LOPEZ, ANN M., utility company regulatory executive; b. Coldwater, Mich., Oct. 28, 1952; d. Robert J. and Margaret M. (Earley) Lopez. B.A. in Econs., U. Mich., 1973. With Mich. Bell Telephone Co., 1974—, assoc. dist. mgr. revenues, Detroit, 1978-80, dist. mgr. mktg. staff, 1980-83, br. mgr. mktg. Farmington Hills, Mich., 1983-84, regulatory, 1984—, mem. women's adv. panel, 1978-81. Pack master Cub Scout Pack 1688, North Trails council Boy Scouts Am., 1979-81. Mem. Women's Econ. Club, Women In Mgmt., Beacon Sq. Civic Assn., U. Mich. Alumni Assn. Republican. Jewish. Lodge: B'nai B'rith (Southfield, Mich.). Office: Mich Bell Telephone Co Room 1540 444 Michigan Ave Detroit MI 48226

LOPEZ, FRANCISCO VICARIO, radiologist; b. Los Angeles, Aug. 9, 1934; s. Frank Rangel and Amparo (Congreras) L.; m. Gayle Barnikow, Oct. 7, 1981; children—Alejandro, Ruy, Eric. B.A. in Zoology, UCLA, 1958; M.D., Nat. Autonomous U. Mexico, 1967. Rotating intern Gen. Hosp. S.S.A., Mexico City, 1964; intern Cedars-Sinai Med. Ctr., Los Angeles, 1969-70; gen. practice medicine Artesian Med. Ctr., Artesia, Calif., 1970-71; resident in radiology U. Ill.-Chgo., 1971-73, Cook County Hosp., Chgo., 1973-74; staff radiologist Westside VA, Chgo., 1974-81, dir. diagnostic radiology, nuclear medicine and ultrasound, 1975-82; dir. radiology Chgo.-Read Mental Health Ctr., Chgo., 1975-82; assoc. radiologist North Suburban Clinic, Skokie, Ill., 1975-82; dir. emergency radiology Holy Cross Hosp., Chgo., 1975-82 dir. radiology Bellevue Hosp. (Ohio), 1982—. Founder Internat. Youth Soccer, Norwalk, Ohio, 1983. Mem. AMA, Am. Thoracic Soc. Home: 80 W Elm St Norwalk OH 44857 Office: Bellevue Hosp 811 Northwest St Bellevue OH 44811

LOPEZ, OSVALDO INOCENTE, ophthalmology educator; b. Havana, Cuba, Dec. 28, 1941; came to U.S., 1962, naturalized, 1963; s. Marcos O. and Noemi J. (Sierra) L.; m. Maria J. Garcia, June 24, 1962; children—Marie A., Tania I., Noemi K., Marcos O. B.S., Northwestern U., 1967, M.D., 1970. Diplomate Am. Bd. Opthalmology. Intern, Passavant Meml. Hosp., Chgo., 1970-71; resident Michael Reese Hosp., Chgo., 1971-74, chief resident, 1973-74, sr. attending, 1974—; clin. asst. prof. ophthalmology U. Ill.-Chgo., 1983—; chmn. dept. ophthalmology Ill. Masonic Hosp., Chgo., 1985—, Grant Hosp., Chgo., 1980-85; lectr. throughout world. Editor Medico jour., 1982—. Inventor in field. Named Citizen of Yr., Lions of Am., 1980; recipient Humanitarian award Am. Lebanese Women's Soc., 1984. Fellow Am. Acad. Opthalmology, Interam. Coll. Physicians and Surgeons, Internat. Coll. Surgeons; mem. Barraquer Inst. Ophthalmolgoy (hon.), Am. Implant Soc. Republican. Roman Catholic. Office: Chgo Eye Inst 111 N Wabash Chicago IL 60602

LOPINA, LAWRENCE THOMAS, mfg. co. exec.; b. Chgo., Nov. 9, 1930; s. Thomas F. and Augustine A. (Schwantes) L.; Ph.B., U. Notre Dame, 1952; M.B.A., DePaul U., 1953; M.B.A., U. Chgo., 1963; m. Marion T. Toomey, Nov. 5, 1955; children—Joseph D., Lawrence M., Mary E., Celeste N., James P. Jr. acct. Haskins & Sells, C.P.A.s, Chgo., 1952-53; acctg. positions with Motorola, Inc., Chgo., 1953-63; div. controller then v.p. fin. fluid power group Applied Power, Inc., Milw., 1963-74; v.p. fin. Broan Mfg. Co., Inc., Hartford, Wis., 1974—, former dir. Served with AUS, 1953-55. C.P.A., Wis. Mem. Nat. Assn. Accts., Fin. Execs. Inst., Wis. Inst. C.P.A.s, Beta Gamma Sigma. Club: KC. Office: 926 W State St Hartford WI 53027

LORD, DAWN DIEZMAN, psychologist; b. Ravenna, Ohio, June 8, 1952; d. Paul Edward and Betty Jane (Harter) Diezman; m. Robert George Lord, Dec. 19, 1977. B.A. cum laude, Kent (Ohio) State U., 1975; M.A. in Clin. and Counseling Psychology, U. Akron, 1977, Ph.D., 1981. Cert. psychologist, Ohio. Asst. instr. U. Akron, 1977-80, research psychologist, 1978-82; research cons. Bd. Edn. Akron Sch. Dist., 1978-82; postdoctoral psychology trainee Fallsview Psychiat. Hosp., 1980-81; staff psychologist Akron Child Guidance Ctr., 1981-83, supervising psychologist, 1984—; supervising psychologist Northeast Summit Family Services, 1983—; pvt. practice, 1984—. Mem. Am. Psychol. Assn., Ohio Psychol. Assn., Am. Personnel and Guidance Assn., Ohio Acad. Sci. Contbr. articles to profl. jours. Office: 2975 W Market St Suite 204 Akron OH 44313

LORD, JAMES GREGORY, marketing and fundraising consultant; b. Cleve., Aug. 23, 1947; s. James Nelson and Esther L.; student U. Md., Far East Campus, 1966-68, Cleve. State U., 1968-72; m. Wendy Franklin, July 10, 1977. TV news producer Far East Network, Tokyo, 1965-68; wire editor News-Herald, Willoughby, Ohio, 1968-69; pub. relations assoc. United Way, Cleve., 1969-70; free-lance pub. relations person, Cleve., 1970-72; dir. pub. relations Ketchum, Inc., Pitts., 1972-77; cons. mktg., devel. philanthropic instns., Cleve., 1977—; lectr. Served with USN, 1964-68; Japan. Author: Philanthropy and Marketing, 7th edit., 1981; The Raising of Money, 1983; Communicating with Donors, 1984; Building Your Case, 1984; The Campaign Manuals, 1985; The Development Consultant, 1985; contbr. numerous articles on philanthropy, mktg. and quality of life in Am. cities to various publs.; developed one-man photography exhbns., 15 worldwide sites, 1968-72. Home: 28050 S Woodland Rd Pepper Pike OH 44124 Office: care Third Sector Press 2000 Euclid Ave PO Box 18044 Cleveland OH 44118

LORD, MILES WELTON, federal judge; b. Pine Knoll, Minn., Nov. 6, 1919; s. Frank Kendall and Rachel Ann (Terry) L.; B.S.L., U. Minn., 1946, LL.B., 1948; m. Maxine Fay Zontelli, Aug. 26, 1940; children—Priscilla Ann, Miles Welton, James Frank, Virginia. Admitted to Minn. bar, 1948; practiced law, Mpls., 1948-51; asst. U.S. dist. atty. Dist. Minn., 1951-52; atty. gen. State Minn., 1955-60; U.S. atty., St. Paul, 1961-66; U.S. dist. judge Dist. Minn., 1966—, now chief judge. Candidate Minn. Legislature, 1950. Mem. Nat. Assn. Attys. Gen. (chmn. Midwestern conf. 1957), Fed. (Minn. pres. 1962), Am., Minn., Hennepin County bar assns., Citizens League Greater Mpls., Minn. Hist. Soc. Lutheran. Mason. Office: 684 US Court House 110 S 4th St Minneapolis MN 55401*

LORENSEN, LAWRENCE WILLIAM, political science educator; b. Rock Island, Ill., Nov. 29, 1937; s. Lawrence E. and Patricia Ann (McLeod) L.; m. Mary Katherine Fleischman, Aug. 26, 1961; children—Jean, Jane, Julie. B.A. in Polit. Sci., St. Ambrose Coll., 1959; M.A. in Govt., George Washington U., 1964. Social sci. instr. Alleman High Sch., Rock Island, Ill., 1964-66; prof. govt. Black Hawk Coll., Moline, Ill., 1966—; nat. govt. affairs cons. Ill. Quad-Cities C. of C., 1984—; mayor City of Moline, 1977-81. Alderman, City of Moline, 1966-77; vice chmn. Bi-State Met. Planning Commn., Rock Island, 1979-81. Mem. Ill. Polit. Sci. Assn., Midwest Polit. Sci. Assn. Democrat. Roman Catholic. Avocations: reading; golf; model railroading. Home: 2608 Second St Moline IL 61265 Office: Black Hawk Coll 6600 34 Ave Moline IL 61265

LORENZ, KEVIN J., lawyer; b. St. Louis, Feb. 28, 1955; s. Alois Joseph and Dorothy Cecilia (O'Connor) L.; m. Margaret Mary Risch, Oct. 2, 1981; 1 dau., Coleen Elizabeth. B.A., St. Louis U., 1977, J.D., 1981. Bar: Mo. 1982, U.S. Dist. Ct. (ea. dist.) Mo. 1982, U.S. Ct. Appeals (8th cir.) 1982, Ill. 1983. Assoc. Sale, Evans, Phelps, Coffin, Adreatta & Lorenz, P.C., Clayton, Mo., 1981-84, ptnr., 1984—. West County coordinator McGovern for Pres., 1972. Mem. Assn. Trial Lawyers Am., Mo. Assn. Trial Lawyers, Lawyers Assn. Democrat. Roman Catholic. Club: Forest Hills Country. Home: 7216 Clayton Rd Saint Louis MO 63117 Office: Phelps Coffin Andreatta & Lorenz PC 230 S Bemiston Suite 1000 Clayton MO 63105

LORGE, GERALD DAVID, lawyer, former state senator; b. Bear Creek, Wis., July 9, 1922; s. Joseph J. and Anna M. (Peterson) L.; J.D., Marquette U., 1952; m. Christina C. Ziegler, Apr. 15, 1958; children—Robert G., William D., Anna Marie, Julie Agnes, Christina Marie. Admitted to Wis. bar, 1952; gen. practice, Bear Creek, 1952—; mem. Wis. Gen. Assembly, 1951-54, Wis. Senate, 1954-85, past chmn. com. on committees, past chmn. com. on judiciary and ins., past mem. com. on legis. procedure, past mem. judiciary and consumer affairs coms. Former mem. Wis. Legis. Council, Interstate Coop.; former past chmn. Justice and Law Enforcement Study com. Midwestern Council Govts., also past mem. jud. council; mem. ins. laws rev. com. Served with USMCR, 1942-45. Mem. Wis., Outagamie bar assns., Nat. Conf. Ins. Legislators (dir. 1971-85, pres. 1973-74, exec. com.), Am. Legion, DAV (life). Republican. K.C. Home: PO Box 47 Bear Creek WI 54922 Office: 204 Railroad Ave Bear Creek WI 54922

LORIA, LANCE SAVERIO, accountant, hospital and health care consultant; b. Long Island, N.Y., July 24, 1950; s. Saverio and Viola (DeCostanza) L.; m. Claire New Woody, Apr. 4, 1981; 1 dau., Melissa Claire. B.B.A. in Acctg., Stetson U., 1972. C.P.A., Fla., Ill. With Coopers & Lybrand, 1972—, mgr. Health Care Services Group, Miami, Fla., 1977-79, asst. to nat. dir. Health Care Services Group, Chgo., 1979-80, dir. Midwest Health Care Services Dept., Chgo., 1980—. Served to capt. USAR, 1972-81. Mem. Am. Inst. C.P.A.s, Ill. C.P.A. Soc., Hosp. Fin. Mgmt. Assn., Am. Hosp. Assn., Contbr. articles to profl. jours. Home: 1064 W North Shore Ave Apt 1-W Chicago IL 60626 Office: Coopers and Lybrand 222 S Riverside Plaza Suite 1700 Chicago IL 60606

LORMAN, BARBARA KAILIN, state senator, corp. exec.; b. Madison, Wis., July 31, 1932; d. Clarence and Edith (Choffnes) Kailin; student U. Wis., 1950-53, Whitewater, 1978-79; m. Milton Lorman, Feb. 1, 1953; children—Carol R. Lorman Weinstein, William Joseph, David B. Pres., Lorman Iron & Metal Co., Inc., Ft. Atkinson, Wis., 1979—; mem. Wis. State Senate, 1980—, minority caucus sec., 1983, mem. edn., govt. ops., agr., health and human services, aging, taxation, banking and comml. credit coms. Mem. exec. council Sinnissippi council Boy Scouts Am.; bd. dirs. Wis. Soc. Jewish Learning, Fort Atkinson Hosp. Bd.; past chmn. Fort Atkinson Assn. Milw. Symphony; past pres. Fort Atkinson Devel. Council. Mem. Fort Atkinson Hist. Soc., Nature Conservancy, Wis. Women's Council, Forward Wis. Republican. Jewish. Office: 140 S State Capitol Madison WI 53538

LOSIN, EDWARD THOMAS, research scientist; b. Racine, Wis., July 9, 1923; s. John and Sophia (Jamroz) L.; m. Laura Joy Soderstrom, June 10, 1950; children—Peter, Eric, Martha. B.S., U. Ill., 1948; M.A., Columbia U., 1950, Ph.D., 1955. Supr. high pressure lab. Columbia U., N.Y.C., 1950-54; postdoctoral fellow U. Mich., Ann Arbor, 1954-57; research chemist Union Carbide Corp., Tarrytown, N.Y., 1957-61; mgr. chemist dept. Isomet Corp., Palisades Park, N.J., 1961-63; sr. research scientist Allis-Chalmers Corp., Milw., 1963—. Served with USN, 1943-46; ETO. Esso postdoctoral fellow, 1954-57. Mem. Am. Chem. Soc., AAAS, N.Y. Acad. Sci., Combustion Inst., Sigma Xi, Phi Lambda Upsilon. Congregationalist. Contbr. articles to profl. jours. Home: 10000 N Sheridan Dr Mequon WI 53092 Office: PO Box 512 Milwaukee WI 53201

LOSONCI, GEORGE BERNARD (GYORGY LEFKOVITS), pharmacist; b. Satoralyaujhel, Zemplen, Hungary, Feb. 7, 1947; came to U.S. 1959, naturalized, 1965; s. Leslie and Magdolna (Landsberger) L.; m. Karin Roberts, Aug. 4, 1974 (div. Feb. 19, 1981); 1 child, Leslie Aaron; m. Michele Nickin, Nov. 6, 1983; 1 child, Sara Gita. B.A. in Polit. Sci., Western Mich. U., 1969; B.S. in Pharmacy, Wayne State U., 1975. Pharmacist G & W Drugstore, Livonia, Mich., 1975—. Mem. Md. Pharmacist Assn., Step Family Assn., Mich. Assn. Children and Adults with Learning Disabilities, Jewish Hist. Soc., Jewish. Avocation: geneologist. Home: 18240 Onyx Dr Southfield MI 48075

LOTITO, MICHAEL JAMES, chiropractic physician; b. Chgo., Nov. 2, 1945; s. Angelo Joseph and Nadine (Mendell) L.; D. Chiropractic, B.S., Palmer Coll. Chiropractic, 1976; B.A., Northeastern U., 1970, Postgrad., 1970-73; m. Karen Aleta Diggle, Dec. 28, 1973; children—Elizabeth Ann, David Michael. Tchr., Bellwood Bd. Edn., Ill., 1970-73; instr. psychology Blackhawk Coll., Moline, Ill., 1974-75; staff psychologist, asst. to dir. physiology dept., supr. x-ray dept. Palmer Coll. Chiropractic, Davenport, Iowa, 1973-76; gen. practice chiropractic, Oak Park, Ill., 1976-79; chief examining doctor Kellenburger Clinic, Elgin, Ill., 1979-80; gen. practice chiropractic, Forest Park, Ill., 1980—; clinic supr. Fullerton Clinic, Chgo., 1980-81; mem. staff patient research ctr. Nat. Coll. Chiropractic, Lombard, Ill. 1983—. Mem. Am. Chiropractic Assn., Ill. Chiropractic Assn., Internat. Found. Preventive Medicine, Am. Holistic Med. Inst., Sports, Safety and Health Care Soc., Psi Chi. Office: 7318 W Madison St Forest Park IL 60130

LOTT, DONALD CHARLES, graphic arts company executive; b. Phila., Nov. 12, 1937; s. Raymond Allen and Lois Marie (Pounding) L.; m. Joyce Elizabeth Block, Jan. 11, 1964 (div. May 1983); children—Kelly Elizabeth, Paul Timothy; m. 2d, Sallie Lou Rhoads, Oct. 2, 1983. A.B. in Bus. Adminstrn., Rutgers U., 1959. Asst. v.p. Fidelity Mut. Life Co., Phila., 1964-73; mgr. service engring. Am. Motors Co., Southfield, Mich., 1973-80; owner Genesus I, Inc., Southfield, 1980—. Served to lt. (j.g.) USNR, 1960-63. Mem. Mensa. Republican. Home: 1058 Wakefield Birmingham MI 48009 Office: Genesus I Inc 29600 Northwestern Hwy Southfield MI 48034

LOTTES, J. OTTO, orthopedic surgeon; b. Altenberg, Mo., Oct. 15, 1906; s. Andreas and Birdie (Dockins) L.; 1 son, George Andreas. Ph.B., St. Louis Coll. Pharmacy, 1926, Ph.G., 1928; A.B., U. Mo.-Columbia, 1934, B.S., 1935; M.D., U. Louisville, 1937. Diplomate Am. Bd. Orthopedic Surgery. Intern, St. Louis City Hosp., 1937-38, resident, 1946-48; resident in orthopedic surgery Barnes Hosp., St. Louis, 1948-51; asst. prof. clin. orthopedic surgery Washington U., St. Louis, 1958—; sect. chief orthopedic surgery St. Louis City Hosp., 1951-65; sect. chief orthopedic surgery Lutheran Med. Ctr., St. Louis, 1951-70, pres., 1976-77; sect. chief orthopedic surgery St. Anthony's Med. Ctr., St. Louis, 1951-66, pres., 1965. Served to col. M.C., U.S. Army, 1946; ETO; PTO. Recipient Meritorius award U. Mo.-Columbia Med. Sch., Lutheran Med. Ctr., St. Anthonys Med. Ctr. Fellow ACS; mem. AMA, So. Med. Assn., Clin. Orthopedic Soc., Mid Central States Orthopedic Soc., Mid-Am. Orthopedic Assn., Am. Acad. Orthopedic Surgeons, Mo. State Orthopedic Assn., St. Louis Orthopedic Soc. (past pres.), Mo. State Med. Assn., St. Louis Med. Soc. (past pres., meritorious award). Republican. Clubs: Jefferson (U. Mo.-Columbia); antique auto clubs. Address: 2646 Michigan Saint Louis MO 63118

LOTUACO, LUISA GO, physician; b. Gapan, Nueva Ecija, Philippines, Jan. 29, 1938; came to U.S., 1972; d. Galicano Yuzon and Alicia (Go) L.; m. George Garrett Shepherd, Aug. 7, 1976; 1 child, Lara. A.A., U. Santo Tomas, Manila, Philippines, 1951-53, D.M., 1960. Diplomate Am. Bd. Coll. Am. Pathology Pathologist, Manila Sanitarium and Hosp., Manila, Philippines, 1969-72; instr. pathology Kansas U., Kansas City, 1972, asst. prof., 1974—; pathologist St. Catherine Hosp., East Chgo., Ind., 1973-74, VA Med. Ctr., Kansas City, Mo., 1974—. Fellow Coll. Am. Pathology, Am. Assn. of Clin. Pathologists; mem. Philippe Med. Soc. of Kansas City (pres. 1981-83), Am. Med. Women's Assn., Philippine Med. Soc. Avocations: stamps; ceramics; antiques. Home: 1215 W 66th Terr Kansas City MO 64113 Office: VA Med Ctr 4801 Linwood Blvd Kansas City MO 64128

LOTZER, WILLIAM JOHN, aviation company executive; b. Fond du Lac, Wis., Feb. 20, 1917; s. Jake and Margaret (Feldner) L.; student Ripon Coll., 1935-36, Marquette U., 1936-40; m. Irene B. Fleager; children by previous marriage—Margaret Reinders, John, Michael. Pres., chmn. Gran Aire, Inc., Milw., 1946—; former pilot examiner FAA. Bd. dirs. Youth in Aviation. Served with A.C., U.S. Navy, 1944-45. Mem. Wis. Aviation Trades Assn. (pres. 1950-53, dir. 1979-83), Wis. Hockey Hall Fame (pres. 1976-79), Nat. Aviation Trades Assn. (pres. 1958-59), Nat. Air Transp. Assn. (steering com.), Exptl. Aircraft Assn. (charter). Republican. Roman Catholic. Club: Blue Line (Fond du Lac, Wis.). Mailing Address: 8741 N 72d St #3 Milwaukee WI 53223 Office: Gran Aire Inc 9305 W Appleton Ave Milwaukee WI 53225

LOUCKS, VERNON REECE, JR., hospital supply company executive; b. Kenilworth, Ill., Oct. 24, 1934; s. Vernon Reece and Sue (Burton) L.; B.A. in History, Yale U., 1957; M.B.A., Harvard U., 1963; m. Linda Kay Olson, May 12, 1972; children—Charles, Greg, Suzy, David, Kristi, Eric. Sr. mgmt. cons. George Fry & Assocs., Chgo., 1963-65; with Baxter Travenol Labs., Inc., Deerfield, Ill., 1966—, exec. v.p., 1973-76, dir., 1975—, pres., chief operating officer, 1976-80, pres., chief exec. officer, 1980—; dir. Dun & Bradstreet Corp., Emerson Electric Co., Quaker Oats Co.; mem. adv. com. to dir. NIH. Bd. dirs. Lake Forest Hosp.; chmn. suburban campaign Met. Crusade of Mercy, 1977; bd. dirs. John L. and Helen Kellogg Found., Protestant Found., Econ. Club of Chgo.; trustee Rush-Presbyn.-St. Luke's Med. Center; assoc. Northwestern U.; former alumni trustee Yale Corp. Served to 1st lt. USMC, 1957-60. Mem. Health Industry Mfrs. Assn. (chmn. 1983). Episcopalian. Clubs: Chgo. Commonwealth, Comml. Office: One Baxter Pkwy Deerfield IL 60015

LOUGEAY, J. ALAN, health care administrator; b. St. Louis, Aug. 16, 1948; s. Milford E. Lougeay and Betty Lou (Weiss) Young; m. Lynn Ellen Kerr, Dec. 21, 1974; children—Ryan, Christopher, Jessica, Jacob. B.S. in Recreational Adminstrn., U. No. Colo., Greeley, 1971; M.A. in Health Adminstrn., Lincolnwood Coll., St. Charles, Mo., 1982—. Asst. dir. Sherwood Forest Camp, St. Louis, 1971-72, exec. dir., 1972-81; adminstr. Fin. Mgmt., St. Louis, 1981, St. Louis Med. Clin, 1982—. Mem. Am. Camping Assn. (pres. St. Louis sect. 1979-80), Am. Coll. Med. Group Adminstrs., Med. Group Mgmt. Lutheran. Avocations: biking, hiking, racquetball. Home: 12745 Big Bend Rd Kirkwood MO 63122 Office: St Louis Med Clinic Inc 3009 N Ballas Suite 100 Saint Louis MO 63131

LOUGHEED, THOMAS ROBERT, solar energy construction company executive; b. Detroit, July 8, 1941; s. Aloysius V. and Ruth S. (Stait) L.; m. Nancy E. Godt, Mar. 28, 1970; children—Thomas S., Patrick R. Student Wayne State U., 1961, postgrad., 1969-74; student Welch Sch. Acctg., Detroit, 1962; B.S., Central Mich. U., 1964, M.B.A., 1966, M.A., 1967; postgrad., MIT, 1968. Cost auditor Fisher Body div. Gen. Motors Co., Flint, Mich., 1964; staff acct. Jim Robbins Co., Troy, Mich., 1964-66; owner Dyn-A-Systems, Flint, 1966-83; treas., sec., ptnr. Talo Enterprises, Ltd., Fenton, Mich., 1976-77; v.p., treas. Dyn Am. Land, Inc., Swartz Creek, Mich., 1972-76, pres., 1976—; officer Creative Ekistic Systems and Solar Unique Networks, Ltd., Swartz Creek, 1980—; instr. statis/research design Eastern Mich. U., Flint, 1970-71; prof. Mott Community Coll., Flint, 1966-85; instr. Mich. Dept. Treasury, Mich. State U., Flint, 1972-77. Councilman City of Swartz Creek, 1976-80, mem. Planning Commn., 1976-80. Mem. Nat. Home Builders Genesee County, Am. Solar Soc., Mich. Soc. Planning Ofcls., Assn. Govtl. Accts., Pi Sigma Alpha, Alpha Kappa Psi. Democrat. Lutheran. Avocations: music, water sports. Home: 6449 Bristol Rd Swartz Creek MI 48473

LOUIS, DAVID JOHN, college dean; b. Pontiac, Ill., Dec. 21, 1945; s. John Leo and Mary Kathryn (Verdun) L.; m. Mary Anne Ferrari, Aug. 30, 1969; children—Brian and Kevin. B.A., St. Ambrose Coll., 1968; M.A., No. Ill. U., 1973, Ed.D., 1978. Jr. high tchr. St. Joseph Grade Sch., Rock Island, Ill., 1968-69; dir. guidance, football, basketball Newman High Sch., Sterling, Ill., 1971-73; counselor, dir. fin. aid Kishwaukee Coll., Malta, Ill., 1973-77, adminstrv. dean, 1977—. Chmn. edn. commn. St. Patrick's Parish, Rochelle, Ill., 1979-82; chmn. Ogle City Commn. Mental Health Bd., Oregon, Ill., 1981—. Recipient Ill. Mental Health Vol. award, 1983. Club: Sports Booster (Rochelle) (v.p. 1982-84). Lodge: Rotary (pres. 1984-85). Advocations: volunteer baseball coach; camping. Home: 323 N Knoll Dr Rochelle IL 61068 Office: Office Adminstrv Dean Route 38 & Malta Rd Malta IL 60150

LOUIS, WILLIAM JOSEPH, theatre educator, actor, director; b. Castorland, N.Y., Mar. 5, 1928; s. Loren A. and Laura Ruth (Hirschey) L. B.A., Boston Coll., 1957, M.A., 1959; Ph.D., Stanford U., 1969; postdoctoral U. Nice, France, 1967-68, 69, Lee Strasberg Acting Inst., Hollywood, Calif., summer 1976. Instr., LeMoyne Coll., Syracuse, N.Y., 1958-60; asst. prof. theatre U. B.C., Vancouver, Can., 1968-70; chmn. drama dept. Western N.Mex. U., Silver City, 1971-73; chmn. performing and visual arts dept. Avila Coll., Kansas City, Mo., 1973—; actor. Mem. screening com. Mo. Arts Council, 1975. Served with U.S. Army, 1943-47. Named Hon. Citizen of Silver City, 1971. Mem. Actors Equity, Am. Coll. Theatre Assn., Speech and Theatre Assn. Mo., Mo. Citizens for the Arts, Kansas City Arts Council, VFW, Alpha Sigma Nu. Democrat. Roman Catholic. Avocations: painting; poetry; skating; dancing; weight-lifting. Home: 109 Glen Arbor Rd Kansas City MO 64114 Office: 11901 Wornall Rd Kansas City MO 64145

LOURENCO, RUY VALENTIM, physician, educator; b. Lisbon, Portugal, Mar. 25, 1929; came to U.S., 1959, naturalized, 1966; s. Raul Valentim and Maria Amalia (Gomes-Rosa) L.; M.D., U. Lisbon, 1951; m. Susan Jane Loewenthal, Jan. 18, 1960; children—Peter Edward, Margaret Philippa. Intern, Lisbon City Hosp., 1951-53, resident in internal medicine, 1953-55; instr. U. Lisbon, 1955-59; fellow dept. medicine Columbia U.-Presbyn. Med. Center, N.Y.C., 1959-63, asst. prof. medicine N.J. Coll. Medicine, Jersey City, 1963-66, asso. prof., 1966-67; practice medicine specializing in pulmonary medicine, 1967—; attending physician, dir. respiratory physiology lab. Jersey City Med. Center, 1963-67; asso. prof. medicine and physiology U. Ill., Chgo., 1967-69, prof., 1969—, chmn. dept. medicine, 1977—, Foley prof. medicine, 1978—; dir. respiratory research lab. Hektoen Inst., Chgo., 1967-71; dir. pulmonary medicine Cook County Hosp., Chgo., 1969-70; attending physician U. Ill. Med. Center, Chgo., 1967—, dir. pulmonary sect. and labs 1970-77, physician-in-chief, 1977—, pres. med. staff, 1980-81; cons. task force on research in respiratory diseases NIH, 1972, mem. pathology study sect., 1972-76; mem. rev. bd. for Spl. Centers of Research program, 1974; cons. career devel. program VA, 1972—; mem. nat. com. Rev. Sci. Basis of Respiratory Therapy, 1973-74. Bd. dirs., mem. exec. com. Chgo. Lung Assn., 1974-82; bd. dirs. Hektoen Inst. for Med. Research, 1977—. Fellow AAAS, ACP, Am. Coll. Chest Physicians (pres. Ill. chpt. 1974-75, vice chmn. com. on environ. health 1981-82); mem. Am. Fedn. Clin. Research, Am. Heart Assn., Am. Physiol. Soc., Am. Soc. Clin. Investigation, Am. Thoracic Soc. (chmn. sci. assembly 1974-75), Am. Lung Assn. (com. on smoking and health 1981-83), Internat. Acad. Chest Physicians and Surgeons of Am. Coll. Chest Physicians (chmn. nominating com. 1984—), Assn. Am. Physicians, Assn. Profs. Medicine, Central Soc. Clin Research (councillor 1973-77), Soc. Exptl. Biology and Medicine, Central Research Club, Sigma XI, Alpha Omega Alpha (faculty), Phi Kappa Phi. Editorial bd. Jour. Lab. and Clin. Medicine, 1973-77, 85—, Am. Rev. of Respiratory Diseases, 1985—. Contbr. numerous articles on pulmonary diseases, respiratory physiology and biochemistry to med. jours. Home: 1000 N Lake Shore Dr Chicago IL 60611 Office: 840 S Wood St Chicago IL 60612

LOUSBERG, PETER HERMAN, lawyer; b. Des Moines, Aug. 19, 1931; s. Peter J. and Ottilia M. (Vogel) L.; A.B., Yale U., 1953; J.D. cum laude, U. Notre Dame, 1956; m. JoAnn Beimer, Jan. 20, 1962; children—Macara Lynn, Mark, Stephen. Bar: Ill. 1956, Fla. 1972. Clk. Ill. Appellate Ct., 1956-57; asst. states atty. Rock Island County, Ill., 1959-60; partner firm Lousberg, McClean, Snyder & Schwarz and predecessors, Rock Island, Ill., 1960—; opinion commentator Sta. WHBF, 1973-74; lectr. Ill. Inst. Continuing Edn., chmn., 1981-82; lectr. Ill. Trial Lawyers seminars. Chmn. crime and juvenile delinquency Rock Island Model Cities Task Force, 1969; chmn. Rock Island Youth Guidance Council, 1964-69; adv. bd. Ill. Dept. Corrections Juvenile Div., 1976—; Ill. commr. Nat. Conf. Commrs. Uniform State Laws, 1976-78; treas. Greater Quad City Close-up Program, 1976-80. Bd. dirs. Rock Island Indsl.-Comml. Devel. Corp., 1977-80; bd. govs. Rock Island Community Found., 1977-82. Served to 1st lt. USMC, 1957-59. Fellow Am. Bar Found., Ill. Bar Found.; mem. Am., Ill. (past gov. 1969-74, chmn. spl. survey com. 1974-75, chmn. com. on mentally disabled 1979-80), Rock Island bar assns., Fla. Bar Assn. (chmn. out-of-state practitioners com. 1985-86), Rock Island C. of C. (treas. 1975, pres. 1978), Am., Ill. (bd. mgrs. 1974-78) trial lawyers assns., Am. Judicature Soc., Nat. Legal Aid and Defenders Assn. (chmn. membership campaigns for Ill. 1969-71, for Midwest dist. 2 1974-75), Quad Cities Council of Chambers Commerce (1st chmn. 1979-80), Ill. Inst. Continuing Legal Edn. (bd. dirs. 1980-83, chmn. 1981-82), Lawyers Trust Fund Ill. (dir.), Ill. Quad. Cities Rotary (v.p. 1985—). Roman Catholic. Clubs: Notre Dame, Quad Cities (Rock Island). Lodge: Rotary (dir. Quad Cities). Contbr. articles to profl. jours. Home: 2704 27th St Rock Island IL 61201 Office: PO Box 1088 Rock Island IL 61201

LOVE, DAVID BRUCE, lawyer; b. Royal Oak, Mich., Oct. 23, 1956; s. Bruce Webster and Ruth Anne (Cooper) L. B.A., Northwestern U., 1977; J.D., U. Mich., 1980. Bar: Ill. 1980, U.S. Dist. Ct. (no. dist.) Ill. 1980, U.S. Ct. Appeals (7th cir.) 1983. Assoc. Winston & Strawn, Chgo., 1980—. Home: 1503 Oak St Apt 408 Evanston IL 60201 Office: Winston & Strawn One First Nat Plaza Suite 5000 Chicago IL 60603

LOVE, EVELYN MCMICHAEL, counselor, human development educator; b. Cleve., July 5, 1945; d. Marion Joseph and Lilly Bell (Cobbs) McMichael; m. Bernard Love, Mar. 18, 1978; children—Kevin, Randy. A.A., Cuyahoga Community Coll., 1968; B.A., Kent State U., 1970, M.Ed., 1971. Nat. cert. counselor. Youth program dir. YWCA, Cleve., 1971-72; tchr., counselor Cleve. State U., 1973-77; counselor, asst. prof. Cuyahoga Community Coll., Cleve.,

1977—, counselor, workshop facilitator Career Devel. Inst., 1982-83. Recipient Teaching Excellence award, 1985. Mem. Edn. Network, Cleve., 1971-72; chmn. scholarship com. Beth-el A.M.E. Zion Ch., Cleve., 1980—. Mem. Am. Assn. Counseling and Devel., Am. Coll. Personnel Assn., Ohio Coll. Personnel Assn., Assn. for Humanistic Edn. Devel., Alpha Kappa Alpha. Democrat. Avocations: reading; singing. Office: Cuyahoga Community Coll 2900 Community Coll Ave Cleveland OH 44115

LOVE, KENYON D., lawyer; b. Canton, Ohio, July 1, 1922; s. William Love and Nellie Braunstein; m. Lenore Clair Wolman. LL.B., William McKinley Sch. Law, 1951. Bar: Ohio 1952. From v.p. to pres. Colonial Foundry Co., Louisville, Ohio, 1942-73; sole practice law, Canton, 1962—; instr. acctg. Canton Coll., 1964-66; spl. counsel Ohio Atty. Gen., 1962-66; pres. U.S. Trading and Service Corp., 1954-80; pres. Love Properties, Inc., 1979—. Candidate judge Canton Mcpl. Ct., 1977; mem. Ohio State Bd. Edn., 1966-67. Mem. Ohio State Bar Assn. (mem. uniform state laws com.), Stark County Bar Assn. (mem. legal aid com.). Republican. Club: Toastmasters. Avocations: paper furniture design, cerplastic formulations, personal computer systems, writing. Home: 4110 Logan Ave NW Canton OH 44702 Office: 740 Renkert Bldg Canton OH 44702

LOVE, MILDRED LOIS (JAN), public relations executive; b. Iowa City, July 9, 1928; d. Joseph R. and Gladys M. (Parsons) Casey; B.S. in Bus. Adminstrn., U. Iowa, 1951; m. Gerald Dean Love, Apr. 4, 1952; children—Laura Anne Love Parris, Cynthia Love-Hazel, Gregory Alan, Linda Jayne, Geoffrey Dare. Vocal soloist Sta. KXEL, Waterloo, Iowa, 1944-46; sec. to lawyer, La Porte City, Iowa, 1944-46; administrv. aide Office of Supt., La Porte City High Sch., 1947-48; office mgr. Minn. Valley Canning Co., Iowa div. offices, LaPorte City, 1947-48; sec. dept. mktg. U. Iowa, 1948-51; asst. dept. public relations Chgo. Bd. Trade, 1949-51; exec. sec. patent dept. Collins Radio Co., Cedar Rapids, 1951-52; vol. VA Hosp., Albany, N.Y., 1965-73; adminstrv. dir. Tri-Village Nursery Sch., Delmar, N.Y., 1960-61; participant Internat. Lang. Teaching Exchange, Cambodia, 1961; vol. hosps. in Concord, N.H., 1963-64; vol. Chgo. Maternity Center, 1973-74; mgr. Wolf Trap Assos. Gift Shop, Vienna, Va., 1975-80; gen. mgr. Travelhost of Washington, 1980-81; cons. mgmt., 1980—; chair Nat. Cherry Blossom Festival, Washington. Participant community pageants on local and dist. levels, Iowa, 1950-51; Sunday sch. tchr. Meth. Ch., 1941-61; mem. Flossmoor (Ill.) Planning and Zoning Commn., 1973-74, McLean (Va.) Planning and Zoning Commn., 1975—; precinct worker in Iowa, 1946-52, N.Y., 1956-61, N.H., 1963-64, Va., 1979—; pres. I.O.W.A. Inc., Washington, 1980-81; active various community fund raising drives. Mem. AAUW, Am. Mkgt. Assn., Nat. Assn. Female Execs., Nat. Conf. State Socs. (pres. 1983); LWV, Delta Zeta. Republican. Clubs: Princeton (Washington), Normanside Country, Olympia Fields Winter, Kenilworth. Home: 707 Brier Kenilworth IL 60043

LOVE, RICHARD HENRY, art gallery executive, art historian; b. Schneider, Ind., Dec. 27, 1939; s. Glenn and Grayce L.; art history student and degrees U. Md., Europe, 1961-63, Bloom Coll., Chicago Heights, Ill., 1963-64, U. Ill., Chicago Circle, 1964-66, Northwestern U., 1967-69; independent study Villa Schifanoia, Florence, Italy; m. E. Geraldine Olson, June 30, 1962; children—Julie Renee, Jayce Christine. Owner, pres. R.H. Love Galleries, Inc., 1967—; chmn. bd. Haase-Mumm Pub. Co., 1981—, Amart Book and Catalog Distbg. Co., 1981—; pres., chmn. bd. R.H. Love Quarter Horses, Inc., 1981—, R.H. Love Paint Horses, Inc., 1983—; prof. art history Prairie State Coll., Chicago Heights, Ill., 1963-65; former art critic Star Tribune newspaper; former art commentator Stas. WEFM, WBBM, WNIB, Chgo.; weekly commentator R.H. Love on Am. Art, Sta. WCIU-TV, Chgo., 1978—; host of Am. Art Forum with Richard Love, Sta. WCIU-TV, Chgo., 1985—; chmn. 19th Century Paintings Sta. WTTW Art Auction, 1979; mem. adv. bd. Midwest Ctr., Archives Am. Art. Mem. Republican Senatorial Inner Circle. Served with U.S. Army, 1961-64. Mem. Friends Am. Art (Yale U.), U.S. C. of C., New Eng. Hist. Soc., Internat. Platform Assn. Author: John Barber, The Artist, The Man, 1981; Harriet Randall Lumis 1870-1953, 1976; William Chadwick 1879-1962, 1977; Walter Clark and Eliot Clark, 1980; Cassatt: The Independent, 1980; Theodore Earl Butler: Emergence from Monet's Shadow, 1985; co-author: A Century of American Impressionism, 1982. Office: 100 E Ohio St Chicago IL 60611*

LOVE, RICHARD REED, physician, educator, cancer prevention researcher; b. Rochester, N.Y., Feb. 28, 1945; s. George L. and Virginia (Thompson) L.; m. Carla J. Roe, June 9, 1967; children—Genevieve L., Nathaniel C. A.B., Oberlin Coll., 1966; M.D., Case Western Res. U., 1971; M.S., U. Wis., 1982. Diplomate American Bd. Internal Medicine. Intern Balt. City Hosps., 1971-72, resident, 1972-75; asst. prof. Med. Sch., U. Wis., Madison, 1980-85, assoc. prof., 1985—. Editor: Concepts in Cancer Medicine, 1984; Current Practice Letter, 1981—. Recipient preventive oncology acad. award NIH, 1980-85. Mem. ACP, Am. Soc. Preventive Oncology (sec.-treas. 1984—), Am. Soc. Clin. Oncology. Avocation: running. Home: 1234 University Bay Dr Madison WI 53705 Office: 7C 1300 University Ave Madison WI 53706

LOVEGROVE, THOMAS BERNARD, chemical company executive; b. York, Nebr., May 11, 1957; s. Bernard and Phyllis Jean (Strauss) L.; m. Kristi Jean Rasmussen, July 11, 1977; 1 child, Kati Jean. B.S. in Bus. Adminstrn., Kearney State Coll., 1980; Asst. mgr. May Seed & Nursery Co., Kearney, Nebr., 1977-80; owner, mgr. Waitin' Wear-Maternity Shop, Kearney, 1978-80; tech. sales rep. Nebr. Solvents Co., Grand Island, 1980-82; tech. sales rep. Velsicol Chem. Co., Salina, Kans., 1982-83, market mgr., Chgo., 1983-85, product mgr. Velsicol premixes, 1985—. Republican. Presbyterian. Lodge: Elks. Avocations: hunting; fishing; music. Home: 1338 Duquesne Naperville IL 60565 Office: Velsicol Chem Corp 341 E Ohio St Chicago IL 60611

LOVEJOY, LEONARD JAMES, public relations exec.; b. Topeka, Apr. 5, 1931; s. Leonard Mark and Margaret Mary (Zeller) L.; Ph.B., Marquette U., 1953; m. Julianne Rolla, May 29, 1954; children—Valerie, Christopher, Kimberly, Leslie, Julianne, Geoffrey. Writer Chgo. chpt. ARC, 1956-58; publicity mgr. U.S. Gypsum Co., Chgo., 1958-62; dir. public relations Holtzman-Kain Advt. Co., Chgo., 1962-64; account supr. Philip Lesly Co., Chgo., 1964-65; account supr. Burson-Marsteller Co., Chgo., 1965-68, client services mgr., 1968, v.p., 1969, group v.p., 1972-76, asst. gen. mgr., 1976, sr. counselor v.p., 1978-83; ptnr. Investor Relations Co., 1983—. Public relations com. Chgo. United Way, 1978—, Drake U., 1974; chmn. fund drive ARC, Westmont, Ill., 1960; agy. chmn. fund drive Girl Scouts U.S.A., Chgo., 1972; bd. dirs. Pop Warner Little Scholars, Inc., 1975—; public relations com. Marquette U., 1970-72. Served with AUS, 1953-56. Mem. Public Relations Soc. Am. (pres. Chgo. chpt. 1981-82, Silver Anvil award, 1972, 73), Publicity Club Chgo. (dir. 1970-74, Golden Trumpet awards 1973, 74, 76, 77, 81). Roman Catholic. Clubs: Headline Chgo., Chgo. Press, Union League (Chgo.); South Haven (Mich.) Country. Home: 205 S Catherine St LaGrange IL 60525 Office: 601 Skokie Blvd Northbrook IL 60062

LOVELAND, HOLLY STANDISH, information systems manager; b. Slater, S.C., Aug. 28, 1947; d. Albert C. and Lucille E. (Standish) L.; A.A., Macomb Coll., 1974; student Siena Heights Coll., 1981—. Applications analyst Burroughs Corp., Detroit, 1977-79; programmer analyst Ford Hosp., Detroit, 1979-80, project leader applications support, 1980, project mgr. applications support, 1980-82, mgr. systems services, 1982-84; dept. exec. VI, info. services Wayne County, Detroit, 1984—; computer cons. Mem. Data Processing Mgmt. Assn., Electronic Computing Health Oriented Assn. Home: 1068 Lakepointe Grosse Pointe Park MI 48230 Office: 900 W Lafayette Detroit MI 48226

LOVELL, MARY ANN, educator; b. Magnolia, Ark., May 30, 1943; d. Dezzy and Priscilla (Glover) Biddle; m. Clearence Edward Lovell, June 4, 1966 (div. 1975); children—Clearesia Ann, Delia Marie, Dezzy Aquib. B.A., U. Ark., 1965; M.S., Ouachita Bapt. U., 1972. Tchr. high sch., Stutgart, Magnolia, Arkadelphia and Eudora, Ark., 1964-75, Milw., 1981—; job service specialist CETA, Wis. Dept. Industry, 1975-76; spl. project, coordinator Milwaukee County Civil Service Commn., 1976-78. Mem. Milw. Tchrs. Edn. Assn., Milw. Inner City Arts Couchil, Inc., Milw. Area Reading Council, Educators' Politically Involved Council, Am. Mgmt. Assn. Democrat. Pentecostal. Club: Playboy (Chgo.).

LOVELY, NANCY N(ICHOL), marketing communications consultant; b. Washington, Oct. 16, 1936; d. William W. and Marjorie (Metcalfe) Nichol; m. Howard E. Lovely, Feb. 15, 1959 (div. 1982); 1 dau., Lynn Dianne. B. Journalism, U. Tex.-Austin, 1957. Editor, departmental asst. publicity dept. San Antonio C. of C., 1957-59, 60-61; freelance pub. relations cons., Chgo., 1973-77; founder, dir., owner Nancy Lovely & Assocs., Wilmette, Ill., 1977—; gen. mgr. Chgo. office McDonald Davis & Assocs., Milw., 1981—. Mem. Acad. Hosp. Pub. Relations, Pub. Relations Soc. Am., Women in Mgmt. (past pres. North Shore Chpt.), Chgo. Hosp. Pub. Relations Soc., Publicity Club Chgo., Theta Sigma Phi. Republican. Episcopalian.

LOVING, RICHARD, artist; b. Vienna, Austria, Jan. 27, 1924; s. Pierre and Faith (Maris) L.; m. Milica Nikich, 1981; children—Julia, Katherine, Zoe; m. Militza Nikich, Jan. 24, 1981. Student Bard Coll., 1945-46. Tchr. Art Inst. Chgo., 1956—, prof., 1979—, chmn. painting and drawing dept., 1971-75. One-man shows include: Jan Cicero Gallery, Chgo., 1981, Lerner-Heller Gallery, N.Y.C., 1982, Roy Boyd Gallery, Chgo., 1983, Roy Boyd Gallery, Los Angeles, 1984; exhibited in group shows: Ill. Arts Council travelling exhbn., 1984-86, Chgo.: Some other Traditions, Am. Mus. Assn., 1984; represented in permanent collections. Art Inst. Chgo., Elmhurst Coll., Corp. Collections. Bd. dirs. Ox-Bow Sch. Art, Saugatuck, Mich., 1978-81; mem. sch. bd. Fremont Dist. 79, Lake County, Ill., 1962-65. Served with U.S. Army, 1945-46. Nat. Endowment for Arts grantee, 1982. Home: 1857 W Armitage St Chicago IL 60622 Office: Sch Art Inst Chgo Columbus Dr and Jackson Chicago IL 60603

LOVY, ANDREW, osteopathic physician, psychiatrist; b. Budapest, Hungary, Mar. 15, 1935; came to U.S., 1939, naturalized, 1944; s. Joseph and Elza (Kepecs) L.; m. Madeline Rotenberg, Aug. 16, 1959; children—Daniel, Jordan, Howard, Jonathan, Elliot, Richard, Mickey. Student Wayne State U., 1956; B.S., Ill. Coll. Optometry, 1957, O.D., 1958. D.O., Chgo. Coll. Osteopathy, 1962. Intern, Mt. Clemens (Mich.) Hosp., 1962-63; resident VA Hosp., Augusta, Ga., 1971-74; practice medicine specializing in psychiatry, Detroit, 1982; prof. psychiatry, chmn. dept. psychiatry Chgo. Coll. Osteo. Medicine, 1981-82; dir. psychiat. tng. program Mich. Osteo. Med. Ctr., Detroit, 1982—; adj. prof. psychiatry W.Va. Coll. Osteo. Medicine, 1984; clin. prof. psychiatry N.Y. Coll. Osteo. Medicine, 1984. Served with M.C., U.S. Army, 1966-68; Vietnam. Decorated Air medal, Bronze Star with oak leaf cluster, Purple Heart, Army Commendation medal. Mem. Am. Osteo. Assn., Am. Psychiat. Assn., Am. Coll. Neuropsychiatry, Assn. Acad. Psychiatrists, Assn. Clin. Hypnosis, Am. Osteo. Coll. Neuropsychiatry (pres.-elect 1982-83, pres. 1983-84), Am. Med. Joggers Assn. Author: Vietnam Diary, 1971. Office: 5435 Woodward Detroit MI 48202

LOW, WALTER CHENEY, neurophysiology educator, scientist; Madera, Calif., May 11, 1950; s. George Chen and Linda Quan (Gong) L.; m. Margaret Mary Schwarz, June 4, 1983. B.S. with honors, U. Calif.-Santa Barbara, 1972; M.S., U. Mich., 1974, Ph.D., 1979. Postdoctoral fellow U. Cambridge, Eng., 1979-80, U. Vt., Burlington, 1980-83; asst. prof. neurophysiology Ind. U. Sch. Med., Indpls., 1983—. Contbr. numerous publs. to profl. jours. on brain research. Recipient Individual Nat. Research Service award Nat. Heart, Lung and Blood Inst., 1981-83, Nat. Inst. Neurol., Communicative Disorders and Stroke, 1979, Bank of Am. Lab. Scis. award, 1968; NIH grantee, 1984, 85; Rackham grantee U. Mich., 1976-78; internat. programs travel grantee Ind. U., 1984; AGAN research fellow Am. Heart Assn., 1980-81; Rotary scholar, 1968-69. Mem. Soc. for Neurosci., AAAS, Internat. Brain Research Orgn., Calif. Scholastic Fedn. (life). Avocations: tennis, cross-country skiing, sailing. Home: 4565 Broadway Indianapolis IN 46205 Office: Dept Physiology and Biophysics Ind U Sch Medicine Indianapolis IN 46223

LOWE, BARBARA LEWIS, telecommunications executive; b. Balt., Aug. 19, 1946; d. Warren Ashby and Averal Lois (Marchant) Lewis; m. Todd H. Lowe, Jan. 30, 1983. B.S., U. Ala.-Tuscaloosa, 1969; M.B.A., U. Ala.-Birmingham, 1978. Various mgmt. positions Bell System, Birmingham, Ala., N.Y.C., 1969-82; dir. planning, adminstrv. asst. Allnet Communications Services, Chgo., exec. dir., customer service, residential sales, 1982-83, exec. dir. engring., 1983-85, asst. v.p., Chgo., 1985, v.p. adminstrn., 1985—. Avocations: backgammon; student pilot; skiing. Home: 1255 Sandberg Terr #2602 Chicago IL 60610 Office: Allnet Communications Services 100 S Wacker Dr Chicago IL 60606

LOWE, CHARLES RICHARD, public utility executive, accountant; b. Champaign, Ill., Dec. 8, 1946; s. Richard Morgan and Mary Letitia (Smith) L.; m. Martha Elizabeth Coblentz, June 17, 1967; children—Leah, Richard, Brenner. B.S., So. Ill. U., 1971. C.P.A., Ill. Sr. acct. Touche Ross & Co., St. Louis, 1971-74; ptnr. in charge Charles R. Lowe, C.P.A., St. Elmo, 1974-84; sec., treas., gen. mgr. Monarch Gas Co., 1974-83, pres. 1983—; sec., treas., dir. Rainbow Farms, Inc., St. Elmo, 1983—; dir. Land No. 820, Inc., St. Elmo, 1980—; co-founder Ill. Small Utility Assn., Salem, Ill., 1980—. Mem. adminstrv. bd. St. Elmo 1st United Meth. Ch., 1978—. Recipient Outstanding Young Men of Am. award U.S. Jaycees, 1982, Loaned Exec. award St. Louis United Fund, 1972. Mem. Am. Gas Assn., Am. Inst. C.P.A.s, Ill. Inst. C.P.A.s, Ill. Gas Rate Engrs., Soc. Advancement of Mgmt. (pres. 1969-71, honor 1971), Altamont C. of C. (indsl. com. 1975-83), Jr. C. of C. Lodge: Lions (St. Elmo) (pres. 1979-81). Avocations: golfing; hunting; chess; fishing; boating. Home: 103 N Walnut St St Elmo IL 62458 Office: Monarch Gas Co 408 N Main St St Elmo IL 62458

LOWE, DOROTHY JONES, educational administrator; b. Columbus, Ohio, July 14, 1923; d. Charles Herbert and Anna Gladys (Parry) Jones; m. Donald B. Lowe, Mar. 24, 1945 (div.); children—Donald Blair III, Geoffrey David, Nancy Lowe Murphy, Steven Michael. A.A., Stephens Coll., 1943; B.S., Ohio State U., 1945, B.A., 1945; M.S., No. Ill. U., 1973. Cert. tchr., curriculum and supervision, adminstr., Ill. Tchr. Batavia (Ill.) pub. schs., 1963-70, asst. prin., curriculum supr., 1970-74; prin. Alice Gustafson Sch., Batavia, 1974—; mem. faculty Nat. Coll. Edn. Bd. dirs. Tri-City Family Project, Geneva, Ill., pres., 1980-82; bd. dirs. Furnas Found., Batavia, Ill. Mem. Kane County Elem. Prins. Orgn. (pres. 1981-82), Assn. Supervision and Curriculum Devel. Congregationalist. Office: Gustafson Sch Carlisle Rd Batavia IL 60510

LOWE, FORREST GILBERT, engineer, educator; b. Gilman City, Mo., Mar. 27, 1927; s. Forrest Ray and Alice (Mather) L.; m. Joan Blaine, Aug. 15, 1948. B.S. in Edn., N.W. Mo. State U., Maryville, 1951, B.S., 1951; M.S., Tex. Christian U., 1962. Registered profl. engr., Mo. Tchr. Maryville Sch. Dist., 1950-53, Kansas City Sch. Dist., Mo., 1953-56, Kansas City Jr. Coll., 1959-64, Met. Community Coll. Dist., Kansas City, 1964—; nuclear engr. Gen. Dynamics, Convair Div., Ft. Worth, 1956-59. Served with USCG, 1944-45. Recipient award Sci. Pioneers, 1974, 79, 84. Mem. Am. Soc. Engring. Edn., Mo. Soc. Profl. Engrs. (chmn. profl. engring. in edn. Western chpt. 1982—), Nat. Soc. Profl. Engrs., Soc. Mfg. Engrs., Am. Assn. Physics Tchrs., Mo. Acad. Sci., Robotics Internat., Sigma Phi Sigma. Republican. Baptist. Lodges: Masons, Shriners. Home: 8412 E 49th St Kansas City MO 64129 Office: Longview Community Coll 500 Longview Rd Lee's Summit MO 64063

LOWE, MARY LLOYD, lawyer, educator; b. St. Louis, Feb. 15, 1948; s. James Nelson and Mary A. (Riedemann) L. B.A., Knox Coll., 1970; M.S. in Edn., Ea. Ill. U., 1974; J.D., John Marshall Law Sch., 1980. Bar: Ill. 1980, U.S. Dist. Ct. (cen. dist.) Ill. 1980, U.S. Ct. Appeals (7th cir.) 1981. Dep. chief counsel Ill. Dept. Pub. Health, Springfield, 1980—; instr. Am. Inst. Paralegal Studies, Chgo., 1982—. Bd. dirs. Altrusa Club Springfield, Ill., 1982-84. Mem. Ill. State Bar Assn., Chgo. Bar Assn., Ill. Assn. Hosp. Attys., DAR. Presbyterian. Home: 850 S Durkin Dr #138 Springfield IL 62704 Office: Ill Dept Pub Health 525 W Jefferson St Springfield IL 62761

LOWE, ROY GOINS, lawyer; b. Lake Worth, Fla., Apr. 8, 1926; s. Roy Sereno and May (Goins) L.; A.B., U. Kans., 1948, LL.B., 1951. Admitted to Kans. bar, 1951; gen. practice, Olathe, 1951—; mem. firm Lowe, Terry & Roberts and predecessor, 1951—. Served with USNR, 1944-46. Mem. Bar Assn. State Kans., Johnson County Bar Assn., Am. Legion, Phi Alpha Delta, Sigma Nu. Republican. Presbyn. Home: 701 W Park Olathe KS 66061 Office: Colonial Bldg Olathe KS 66061

LOWE, TERRANCE ALEXANDER, food service administrator; b. Detroit, July 28, 1951; s. Theodore Marian and Cecelia Pearl (Matel) L.; B.S., Mich. State U., 1973; M.B.A. Lake Forest sch. Management, 1983; m. Cathy Joyce Linville, July 27, 1974 (div. Nov. 1980); m. 2d, Nancy Eileen Leathem, Feb. 5, 1983; 1 son, Alexander Theodore. Asst. food service dir. Wishard Meml. Hosp., Indpls. 1974-77; food service dir. Altenheim Community Home, Indpls., 1977-78, Ind. Christian Retirement Park, Zionsville, 1978; food service adminstr., also project chmn. Dial-A-Dietitian, Victory Meml. Hosp., Waukegan, Ill., 1978—; founder Famous Chef's Cuisine benefit and program; lectr. Ind. U., Indpls., 1976, Purdue U., 1976; owner Stash's Egg Co., Waukegan, 1982-84. Adv. com., vice chmn. Indpls. pub. schs. Indsl. Coop. Edn. and Training, 1975-78. Recipient, Certificate of Appreciation, Purdue U. of Indpls., 1975, Indpls. Pub. Schs., 1978, Central Nine Vocational Sch. for Services, 1978; Award for outstanding contbrs. to food ser. industry. Mem. Am. Soc. for Hosp. Food Services Adminstrs., Internat. Food Service Execs. Assn., Kappa Sigma. Roman Catholic. Contbr. articles to profl. jours. Office: 1324 N Sheridan Rd Waukegan IL 60085

LOWE, TERRY RAY, insurance company official, management educator, author; b. Bloomington, Ill., Mar. 6, 1950; s. Raymond Blaine and Helen Louise (Necessary) L. B.S. Ill. State U., 1972, M.B.A., 1977. Asst. payroll supr. Eureka Co., Bloomington, 1972-73; claim examiner State Farm Ins. Co., Bloomington, 1973-78, claims supr., 1978-81, sr. analyst, 1981-83, staff asst., 1983—; instr. mgmt. Ill. State U., Normal, 1978, Lincoln Coll., Bloomington, 1980—. Fellow Life Office Mgmt Assn.; mem. Central Ill. Soc. of Life Office Mgmt. Assn. Home: 503 Cheshire Bloomington IL 61701 Office: State Farm Ins Co 1 State Farm Plaza Bloomington IL 61701

LOWE, VICTOR BROWN, former educator, school administrator; b. Ash Grove, Mo., Aug. 26, 1908; s. Charles Cletis and Susie Queen (Brown) L.; m. Esther May Allis, Nov. 26, 1937. A.A., Ozark Wesleyan U., Carthage, Mo., 1928; B.A., Baker U., Baldwin City, Kans., 1933; M.Ed., Mo. U., 1942. Cert. sch. adminstr., Mo. Prin. high sch. Highlandville Schs., Mo., 1933-38; supt. schs. Chadwick Schs., Mo., 1938-40; county supt. schs. St. Clair County, Osceola, Mo., 1940-45; supt. schs. Ash Grove Sch. Dist., Mo., 1945-62; former counselor, sch. adminstr. Springfield Schs., Mo., 1962-68. Mem. Mo. Ret. Tchrs. Assn., Springfield Area Ret. Tchrs. (pres. 1978-80), Phi Delta Kappa. Republican. Methodist. Lodge: Masons. Avocations: traveling, reading, gardening. Home: 634 S National St Apt 206 Springfield MO 65804

LOWEN, ALLEN WAYNE, educational administrator, clergyman; b. Covington, Va., Nov. 8, 1946; s. James Ervin and Florence Maude (Taylor) L.; m. Sharon Kay Tyler, Aug. 29, 1969; children—Kristen Dawn, Kimberly Danielle, Gabrielle Brooke. B.A., Cin. Bible Coll., 1969; M.A., Cin. Christian Sem., 1971, M.Div., 1972; Ph.D. candidate U. Mo., 1985—. Ordained to ministry Christian Ch., 1969. Minister Mt. Olivet Ch. of Christ, Williamstown, Ky., 1968-70, Ch. of Christ-Delhi, Cin., 1970-73; prof. Central Christian Coll., Moberly, Mo., 1973—, acad. dean, 1976—. Editor Adam Newsletter, 1980-84. Contbr. articles to profl. jours. Committeman Chariton Council Boy Scouts Am., Moberly, 1974. Mem. Am. Assn. Higher Edn., Mo. Assn. Collegiate Registrars and Admission Officers. Club: Moberly Taerkwon-Do, Lodge: Optimist (Moberly). Home: 5 Windsor Pl Moberly MO 65270 Office: Central Christian Coll 911 Urbandale Moberly MO 65270

LOWENSTINE, JOHN ANDREW, retail company executive; b. Valparaiso, Ind., Nov. 15, 1953; s. Kenneth Bennett and Marilyn Jay (Tapocsi) Bradford L.; m. Janet Yvonne Haney, May 20, 1978 (div. 1980); 1 dau., Amy Catherine. B.A., Hanover Coll., 1975. Buyer, J. Lowenstine & Sons, Valparaiso, Ind., 1974-82, controller, 1982—. Vice-chmn. Assocs. in Downtown, Valparaiso, 1983, chmn., 1984-85. Loaned exec. United Way of Porter County, Ind., 1976-77; pres. Porter County chpt. Am. Cancer Soc., 1981; bd. dirs. Valparaiso Adult Learning Ctr., 1983—, Greater Valparaiso C. of C., 1984-87. Mem. Sigma Chi. Club: Elks. Home: 1193 Mill Pond Rd Valparaiso IN 46383 Office: J Lowenstine & Sons Inc 57 Franklin St Valparaiso IN 46383

LOWER, JOHN JOSEPH, utility company executive; b. Rushville, Ind., Nov. 24, 1921; s. John W. and Favora Francena (Goddard) L.; m. Edna D. Nixon, Nov. 26, 1942; children—Judith Elaine, Steven Joe, Mark Allen. Student Ball State U., 1939-40; cert., mgrs. internship curriculum U. Nebr., 1971; continuing edn. student Purdue U., Ohio State U., Mich. State U., Ind. U. Lineman, serviceman, power use adviser Rush County Rural Electric Coop., Rushville, Ind., 1949-59; gen. mgr. Southeastern Mich. Rural Electric Coop., Adrian, 1959-66; ins. salesman Preferred Risk Mut. Ins. Co., Huntington Woods, Mich., 1966-67; cost acct. Am. Chain & Cable Co., Adrian, 1967; mem. services dir., dept. supr. Shelby County Rural Electric Coop., Shelbyville, Ind., 1967-79; gen. mgr. Rush County Rural Electric Membership Corp., Rushville, 1979—; bd. dirs. Hoosier Energy Generation and Transmission Rural Electric Coop., 1979—, Rush County Extension Bd., 1984—, SHARES Inc., 1985—; treas. Hoosier Coop. Energy, Inc.; past pres. So. Ind. Electric Heating Inst.; area chmn. Hoosier Energy Apprenticeship Tng. Sch., 1982-83, adv. com., 1984—. Past chmn. Shelby County Extension Bd.; bd. dirs. Shelby County Assn. Retarded Citizens, 1973-79; mem. Rush County Indsl. Devel. Com., 1985—. Served with U.S. Army, 1943-46; ETO, MTO. Recipient 4-H Electric Leaders cert., 1976; Joseph F. Kennedy Jr. Found. award, 1972; outstanding service award Ind. Vocat. Clubs of Am., 1976, cert. spl. services, 1977. Mem. Internat. Assn. Elec. Inspectors (dir., pres. Ind. chpt. 1976-77), IEEE (assoc.), Food and Energy Council, Ind. Farm Electrification Council, Rush County C. of C. (bd. dirs., officer 1982-85), Ind. Member Services Assn. (past pres.), Home Builders Assn. Shelby County (dir. 1977-79). Mem. Ch. of Christ. Home: PO Box 144 Rushville IN 46173 Office: PO Box 7 Rushville IN 46173

LOWRY, ETHEL JOYCE, educational administrator; b. Crandon, Wis., Mar. 4, 1933; d. Frank Ames and Leila Emma (Feight) Butler; m. Thomas Franklin Lowry, Dec. 27, 1952; children—Genice Ann, Cheryl Lea, Dwight Thomas. M.S., Bemidji State U., 1969; postgrad., U. N.D., 1970-73, 77-84, N.D. State U., 1978-81, No. State Coll., 1984. Teaching asst. U. N.D., Grand Forks, 1970-73; reading cons. Devils Lake Pub. Sch., N.D., 1973-76; right to read coordinator N.D. Dept. Pub. Instrn., Bismarck, 1976-81, asst. dir. elem. edn., 1981-84, state dir. chpt. I, 1984—. Editor: Reading: In the Content Areas, 1980; The Answer Book: A Guide to Teaching Basic Skills K-12, 1981; Your Child and Reading, 1979. Mem. N.D. Reading Assn. (pres. 1981-83, Leadership award 1983). Avocations: reading, cross country skiing, fishing, baking. Home: 328 Lunar Ln Bismarck ND 58501 Office: ND Dept Pub Instrn State Capitol Bismarck ND 58505

LOWRY, JAMES HAMILTON, management consultant; b. Chgo., May 28, 1939; s. William E. and Camille C. L.; B.A., Grinnel Coll., 1961; M.P.I.A., U. Pitts., 1965; P.M.D., Harvard U., 1973; 1 child, Aisha. Asso. dir. Peace Corps, Lima, Peru, 1965-67; spl. asst. to pres., project mgr. Bedford-Stuyvesant Restoration Corp., Bklyn., 1967-68; sr. asso. McKinsey & Co., Chgo., 1968-75; pres. James H. Lowry & Assos., Chgo., 1975—; dir. Independence Bank. Trustee Grinnell Coll.; bd. dirs. Chgo. United, Northwestern Hosp., Goodman Theatre. John Hay Whitney fellow, 1963-65. Mem. Harvard Alumni Assn. (dir.). Clubs: Econ., Monroe, Univ. Home: 3100 Sheridan Rd Chicago IL 60657 Office: 303 E Wacker Dr Chicago IL 60601

LOWRY, JAMES JOSEPH, JR., association executive, park and recreation administrator; b. Norfolk, Va., Sept. 28, 1951; s. James Joseph and Joan (Kelly) L.; m. Cathy Benton, Mar. 17, 1979; 1 son, Samuel Benton. B.S., N.C. State U.-Raleigh, 1974. Research asst. Sea Pines Co., Hilton Head Island, S.C., 1973; recreation supr. Durham Dept. Pub. Recreation, N.C., 1974-78; exec. dir. N.C. Recreation and Park Soc., Raleigh, 1978-81; exec. dir. Ohio Parks and Recreation Assn., Columbus, 1981—. Author: Guerilla Tactics for Securing Employment in the Recreation and Park Field, 1984. Mem. Ohio Recreation and Resources Commn., 1984—; pres. Ohio Environ. Council, 1983-84. Mem. Ohio Parks and Recreation Assn., Ohio Environ. Council (pres. 1983-84, dir. 1982-83). Democrat. Episcopalian. Club: Central Ohio Fly Fishers. Avocations: fishing, boating, writing. Home: 3329 Riverside Dr Columbus OH 43221 Office: Ohio Parks and Recreation Assn 5l N High St Suite 601 Columbus OH 43215

LOWTHER, GERALD EUGENE, optometry educator; b. Lancaster, Ohio, Sept. 16, 1943; s. Richard Eugene and Mary Alice (Barr) L.; m. Andrya Gene Huffman, Dec. 26, 1965; children—Karen, Dan. B.Sc., Ohio State U., 1966, O.D., 1967, M.Sc., 1969, Ph.D., 1972. Practice optometry, Newark, Ohio, 1967-69; asst. prof. Ohio State U., Columbus, 1972-75, assoc. prof. optometry, 1975-77; prof. optometry Ferris State Coll., Big Rapids, Mich., 1977—. Author: Contact Lens Correction, 1977; Contact Lens Procedures, 1983. Editor: Internat. Contact Lens Clinic Jour., 1979—. Fellow Am. Acad. Optometry; mem. Am. Optometric Assn. Avocations: skiing; sailing; travel. Home: 18904 Winding Brook Big Rapids MI 49307 Office: College Optometry Ferris State Coll Big Rapids MI 49307

LOWTHIAN, PETRENA, college president; b. London, Feb. 10, 1931; d. Leslie Irton and Petrena Lowthian; m. Clyde Hennies (div.); children—David Lowthian, Geoffrey Lowthian. Student Royal Acad. Dramatic Art, 1949-52. Retail career with various orgns., London, Paris, 1949-57; founder, pres. Lowthian Coll. div. Lowthian Inc., Mpls., 1964—. Mem. adv. council Minn. State Dept. Edn., Mpls., 1974-82; mem. adv. bd. Mpls. Community Devel.

Agy., Mpls., 1983—; mem. Downtown Council Mpls., 1972, chmn. retail bd., 1984—; mem. Bd. Bus. Indsl. Advisors U. Wis., Stout, 1983—. Mem. Fashion Group, Inc. (regional bd. dirs. 1980). Home: 21 Turners Cross Rds Golden Valley MN 55416 Office: Lowthian Coll 84 S 10th St Minneapolis MN 55403

LUBBEHUSEN, JOHN RICHARD, educational administrator; b. Terre Haute, Ind., Mar. 2, 1941; s. John Joseph and Ruth May (White) L.; m. Jane Ellen Drew, June 22, 1963; children—John Drew, Richard Eric, Marci Jo. A.B., Ind. State U., 1962; M.S., 1966, 6th yr. cert., 1973. Tchr. English, jr. high sch., Merrillville, Ind., 1962-68; tchr. English Scott Jr. High Sch., Terre Haute, Ind., 1968-82, head dept., 1974-82; coordinator adult basic edn. Vigo County Schs., Terre Haute, 1976—, supr. adult evening sch., 1982—; dir. adult edn. Vincennes Jr. Coll., summer 1980; cons. reading Pvt. Industry Council, Terre Haute, summer 1983. Safety chmn., community service chmn. Traveler's Protective Assn., Terre Haute; team mgr. Little League, Babe Ruth Team, 1974-81. Recipient awards Travelers Protective Assn., 1976, 75, 77, 80, 81, Am. Cancer Soc., 1973; Outstanding Young Educator award Jaycees Merrillville, 1966. Mem. Ind. Council Adult Edn. Adminstrs., Vigo County Sch. Corp. Adminstrs. Assn., Ind. Council Adult Edn. Adminstrs., Am. Assn. Adult and Continuing Edn., Phi Delta Kappa. Democrat. Roman Catholic. Lodges: KC, Elks. Home: 36 Canterbury Rd PO Box 5034 Terre Haute IN 47805 Office: 961 Lafayette Ave Vigo County Sch Corp Terre Haute IN 47804

LUBBEN, CRAIG HENRY, lawyer; b. Fort Lee, Va., Aug. 10, 1956; s. George and Dorothy Marion (Vree) L.; m. Lois Beth Zylstra, June 9, 1979; children—Christina Anne, Brian Craig. B.A., Calvin Coll., 1978; J.D. cum laude, Northwestern U., 1981. Bar: Mich. 1981, U.S. Dist. Ct. (we. dist.) Mich. 1981, U.S. Ct. Appeals (6th cir.) 1984. Assoc. Miller, Johnson, Snell & Commiskey, Grand Rapids, Mich., 1981—. Pres., Alternative Directions, Grand Rapids, 1985; trustee Grand Rapids Pub. Mus. Assn., 1984-87. Mem. Order of Coif. Mem. Christian Reformed Church. Office: Miller Johnson Snell & Cummiskey 800 Calder Plaza Bldg Grand Rapids MI 49503

LUBBOCK, JAMES EDWARD, writer, photographer, publicity cons.; b. St. Louis, Sept. 12, 1924; s. Winans Fowler and Hildegard Beauregard (Whittemore) L.; B.A. in English, U. Mo., 1949; m. Charlotte Frances Ferguson, Aug. 24, 1947; children—Daniel Lawrason, Brian Wade, Kathleen Harper. Asst. editor St. Louis County Observer, 1949-51; staff writer St. Louis Globe-Democrat, 1951-53, state editor, 1954-56; mng. editor Food Merchandising mag., 1956-57; free-lance indsl. writer-photographer, cons., St. Louis, 1958—; pres. James E. Lubbock, Inc., 1981—. Bd. dirs. Practical Seminar Inst. Served with Signal Corps, U.S. Army, 1943-46. Mem. Soc. Profl. Journalists, Sigma Delta Chi, St. Louis Press Club, ACLU, Common Cause. Liberal Democrat. Home and Office: 10734 Clearwater Dr Saint Louis MO 63123

LUCAS, ALFRED MARTIN, research zoologist; b. New Albany, Ind., Oct. 16, 1900; m. Miriam Jackson Scott, June 14, 1928 (dec.); children—Carol Scott, Donald Hallowell. Student Marine Biol. Lab., Woods Hole, Mass., 1921, 22, 23; B.A., Wabash Coll., 1924; Ph.D., Washington U., 1929. Instr. dept. zoology, Washington U., St. Louis, 1924-25, Sch. of Dentistry, 1925-30; asst. prof. anatomy dept. Sch. of Medicine, 1930-33; asst. prof. zoology U. Iowa, Iowa City, 1933-34; assoc. prof. zoology Iowa State Coll., Ames, 1934-44; cytopathologist Regional Poultry Research Lab., U.S. Dept. Agr., East Lansing, Mich., 1944-56, investigation leader, 1950-54, research zoologist, project leader of the Avian Anatomy Investigations cooperative with Mich. State U., 1956-70, research prof. in animal sci., 1979-81, research prof. emeritus, 1982—; chmn. Internat. Com. of Avian Anatomical Nomenclature, 1971-73. Served to pvt., USMC, 1918-19. Recipient Superior Service award Dept. Agr. 1962; Tom Newman Meml. Internat. award (England), 1962, 1972; Borden Poultry award, 1964. Fellow Poultry Sci. Assn., Linnean Soc. London; life mem. Am. Assn. Avian Pathologists, (hon.) Mich. Allied Poultry Inds., (hon.) mem. Am. Assn. Veterinary Anatomists, Sigma Xi. Co-editor: Nomina Anatomica Avium, 1972-79; contbr. numerous articles in field to various profl. jours. Home: 6035 Grand River Dr Grand Ledge MI 48837 Office: Dept Animal Sci Anthony Hall Mich State Univ East Lansing MI 48824

LUCAS, ALFRED WINSLOW, JR., mgmt. cons. co. exec.; b. Washington, Oct. 14, 1950; s. Alfred Winslow and Mildred Elizabeth (Lawson) L.; B.A. in Sociology, Social Welfare, St. Augustine's Coll., Raleigh, N.C., 1972; M.S.W., Syracuse U., 1974; M.P.A., Roosevelt U., Chgo., 1979; m. Debra Denise DeBerry, Aug. 20, 1977; 1 son, Michael Maurice. Planner, United Way Central N.Y., 1973-74; adminstrv. asst. to dir. community devel. People's Equal Action Community Effort Inc., Syracuse, N.Y., 1972-73; research cons. Urban Inst., Washington, 1974-75; exec. dir. New Birth Community Devel., Elgin, Ill., 1975-79; pres. Razen Mgmt. Cons., Inc., Chgo., 1979—; asso. dir. Centers for New Horizons, Chgo., 1979-80; cons. in field. Chmn. bd. dirs. Kane County (Ill.) Community Action Agy., 1976-77; bd. dirs. Kane County Overall Econ. Devel. Com., 1977-78; trustee Mildred Lawson Lucas Meml. Found., 1981—. NIMH fellow, 1972-74. Mem. Am. Mgmt. Assn., Nat. Assn. Social Workers, Acad. Cert. Social Workers, Am. Soc. Public Adminstrs., Nat. Urban League, Am. Soc. Profl. Consultants, Kappa Alpha Psi. Roman Catholic. Author: Getting Funded, Grantsmanship and Proposal Development, 1982. Home: 9447 Bay Colony Dr 1S Des Plaines IL 60016 Office: 25 E Washington Chicago IL 60609

LUCAS, BARBARA DOREEN, data processing educator; b. Columbus, Ohio, Aug. 14, 1949; d. Bernard Arthur and Louella (Call) Downs; m. David Eberst Lucas, June 23, 1970 (div.); 1 child, Doreen Bethany. B.S. in Edn., Ohio U., 1970, postgrad., 1970—; M.A., Ohio State U., 1984; postgrad. Capital U. Law Sch., 1984—. Cert. edn., Ohio. Info. systems assoc. Western Electric Co., Columbus, 1970-74; systems programmer, analyst Xerox Corp., Columbus, 1974-75; safety systems analyst State Ohio Hwy. Dept., Columbus, 1975-77; sr. systems analyst State Ohio Dept. Taxation, Columbus, 1977-79; sr. data processing instr. SouthWestern City Schs., Grove City, Ohio, 1979—; lectr. Ohio State U., Columbus, 1974—; instr. Eastland Vocat. Sch., Groveport, Ohio, 1979—, Paul C. Hayes Tech. Sch., Grove City, 1979—. Mem. civilian rev. bd. SSS; vol. Girl Scouts U.S. Mem. Bus. and Profl. Women's Club (Grove City chpt. sec.), Assn. for Computing Machinery, Ohio Edn. Assn. (advisor, mem. sch. curriculum com.), S.W. Edn. Assn., Ohio Vocat. Assn. Contbr. articles to profl. jours. Home: 115 Main St Groveport OH 43125 Office: 4436 Haughn Rd Grove City OH 43123

LUCAS, CONSTANCE ELAINE, children's librarian; b. Dayton, Ohio, July 8, 1951; d. Kenneth Dunson and Rosa L. (Moon) Persons; m. Mitchell D. Lucas, Nov. 22, 1969 (div. Feb. 1979); children—Mitchell D., Lukinte. B.S. in Polit. Sci., Wright State U., 1980, B.S. in Edn., 1981; M.P.A., Central Mich. U., 1981. Library asst. I, Dayton and Montgomery Counties (Ohio), Dayton, 1969-73, library asst. II, 1973-80, children's librarian, 1981—. Speaker film: What's a Good Book-How to Select a Good Book, 1982. Mem. Republican Nat. Com., Washington, 1980—; pres. Young Reps. West, Dayton, 1981-83; 1st v.p. Ohio Rep. Council, Columbus, 1981—; del.-at-large Rep. Nat. Conv., 1984; bd. dirs. Montgomery County Rep. Central and Exec. coms., Dayton, 1977—; mem. Presdl. Task Force, 1984. Recipient Concordian cert. Nat. Rep. Com., 1980. Mem. ALA, Ohio Library Assn. (chair outreach services to ethnic communities), Dayton and Montgomery Counties Staff Assn. (spl. com., collective bargaining com.). Baptist. Lodge: Athena Chpt. #37 (corr. sec. 1980-81). Home: 2211 Ridge Creek Circle Trotwood OH 45426 Office: Madden Hills Library 2542 Germantown St Dayton OH 45408

LUCAS, FREDERICK, lawyer; b. Tehran, Oct. 28, 1954; came to U.S., 1956, naturalized, 1964; s. John and Virginia (Gevorkian) L.; m. Sandra Lee Seigneur, Apr. 25, 1981. B.A., U. Mich., 1975; J.D. cum laude, Wayne State U., 1978. Bar: Mich. 1978. Ptnr. Jameson, Pickard & Lucas, Adrian, Mich., 1978-81, Robertson, DesChenes & Lucas, P.C., Adrian, 1983-84, DesChenes, Lucas & Baker, Adrian, 1984—; sole practice, Adrian, 1981-83. Mem. Assn. Trial Lawyers Am., Mich. Trial Lawyers Assn., Mich. Bar Assn., Order of Barristers. Armenian Orthodox. Home: 349 Anthony Ct Adrian MI 49221 Office: DesChenes Lucas & Baker PC 5285 W US 223 Adrian MI 49221

LUCAS, VIRGINIA HIBBETT, teacher educator; b. Springfield, Ohio, June 18, 1930; d. Howard Scott and Maggie Ellen (Coughenhour) Hibbett; m. Rudolf Lucas, Jr., June 7, 1952; children—Scott A., Mark R. B.S., Wittenberg U., 1952; Ed.M., Miami U., Oxford, Ohio, 1968; Ph.D., Ohio State U., 1973. Cert. elem., educable mentally retarded tchr., Ohio. Elem. tchr. DeGraff Sch., Ohio, 1952-55; spl. edn. tchr. Mad River Schs., Dayton, Ohio, 1965-68; supr. Montgomery County Schs., Dayton, 1968-71; assoc. editor Zaner-Bloser, Inc., Columbus, 1973—; assoc. prof. edn. Wittenberg U., Springfield, 1978—, chmn. edn. dept., 1981—; mem. Ohio Edn. Dean's Task Force on Personnel Preparation for Handicapped, 1983—; book reviewer Prentice-Hall, Charles Merrill; mem. editorial staff Directive Tchr., Columbus, 1977—. Author: Resource Book for Kindergarten Teachers, 1980; (with others) Teaching Children Basic Skills, 1982, (textbook series) Creative Growth with Handwriting, 1979; Reading comprehension, 1981. Contbr. articles to profl. jours. Mem. adv. bd. Springview Devel. Ctr., 1983—; mem. adv. com. Springfield City Schs., 1980—. Recipient Disting. Teaching award Wittenberg U. Alumni Assn., 1982. Mem. Internat. Reading Assn., Council for Exceptional Children, Assn. of Gifted, Nat. Assn. for Edn. Young Children, Nat. Council Tchrs. of English, Omicron Delta Kappa. Republican. Methodist. Avocations: Antiques; travel; reading. Home: 4455 Redmond Rd Springfield OH 45505 Office: Wittenberg U Box 720 Springfield OH 45501

LUCEY, LAWRENCE HAYDN, investment counselor, lawyer; b. Henderson, Nev., Dec. 17, 1947; s. Lawrence Young and Elizabeth Ruth (Fischer) L.; m. Nancy Gina Scaramella, Nov. 6, 1981; 1 child, Clare Poole. B.S., Purdue U., 1969; M.B.A., U. Chgo., 1975; J.D., Loyola U., 1982. Bar: Ill. 1982; chartered fin. analyst, 1975. Vice pres. Continental Ill. Nat. Bank, Chgo., 1969-83; v.p. Chgo. Corp., 1983—. Author, editor Ready Reference of Investment Sect. Ill. Ins. Code, 1984; co-author: Investment Regulations for Illinois Insurance Agents and Brokers, 1982. Fellow Fin. Analysts Fedn.; mem. Ill. State Bar Assn., Investment Analysts Soc., Chgo., Fin. Stock Assn., Inst. Chartered Fin. Analysts, Nat. Assn. Life Cos. Republican. Roman Catholic. Club: Mid-Town Tennis (Chgo.). Office: Chgo Corp 208 S LaSalle St Chicago IL 60604

LUCHI, THOMAS ANDREW, health care executive; b. Harrisburg, Pa., Apr. 30, 1947; s. Andrew Thomas and Mary Jane (Welsh) L.; m. Dorothy Marie Bette, May 1, 1970; children—James Thomas, Elizabeth Anne. B.Arch., U. Detroit, 1971, M.Arch., 1975, M.B.A., 1982. Registered architect, Mich.; cert. Nat. Council Archtl. Registration Bds. Project mgr. LGR Assocs., Livonia, Mich., 1971-75; sr. health planner CHPC SEM, Detroit, 1975-78; dir. Horizon Health Systems, Oak Park, Mich., 1978-82; v.p. Health One Corp., Mpls., 1982-84; mgr. Laventhol & Horwath, Mpls., 1985—. Bd. dirs., sec. Home Services Assn., St. Paul, 1983-84. Mem. N.Am. Soc. Corp. Planning (bd. dirs., sec. treas. 1984—), AIA, Am Coll. Hosp. Adminstrs., Soc. Hosp. Planning and Mktg., Citizens League, Blue Key, Beta Gamma Sigma. Roman Catholic. Avocation: carpentry. Home: 991 Amble Rd Shoreview MN 55112 Office: Laventhal & Horwath 100 Washington Sq Minneapolis MN 55401

LUCKE, ROY EDWARD, research analyst; b. Oak Park, Ill., Oct. 8, 1948; s. Roy Otto and Ruth Rose (Strachan) L.; m. Linda Marie Hill, Sept. 28, 1974; 1 child, Robert Roy. B.S., Northwestern U., 1970; M.S., Nat. Coll., 1982. Officer Lake Forest Police, Ill., 1970-73; officer, adminstr. Fox Lake Police, Ill., 1973-78; instr. Traffic Inst., Northwestern U., Evanston, Ill., 1978-81, research analyst, 1981—; cons. Task Force on Driving under the Influence, N.Y., 1981-82, Chgo. Assn. Commerce, 1981—, mem. Transp. Research Bd., Nat. Acad. Sci. Contbr. articles on impaired driving. Mem. Ill. Gov's Task Force on Driving under the Influence, 1983—, Fox Lake Planning Commn., 1976-80; mem. Fox Lake Fire Dept., 1969—, asst. chief, 1985—. Mem. Internat. Assn. Chiefs Police, Nat. Registry Emergency Med. Technicians, Nat. Assn. Fire Fighters. Republican. Presbyterian. Lodge: Masons. Avocations: reading, gardening. Home: 613 Knollwood Dr S Ingleside IL 60041 Office: Traffic Inst Northwestern U PO Box 1409 Evanston IL 60204

LUDD, STEVEN OLIN, political science educator, lawyer; b. Salem, N.Y., Nov. 17, 1946; s. Edward S. and Elizabeth (Priest) L.; m. Oksana Mihaychuk, July 23, 1977. B.A., Syracuse U., 1968, J.D., 1972, Ph.D., 1976. Bar: Ohio 1981. Law clk. Onondaga Neighborhood Legal Services, 1969-72; assoc. dir. Alumni Programs Office, Syracuse U., 1976; asst. prof. polit. sci. Bowling Green (Ohio) State U., 1976—; dir. acad. advising Syracuse U., 1979-80; monitor U.S. Dist. Ct. Chmn., Bowling Green State U. Human Relations Commn., 1983-84. Served with USAR, 1969-73. Named Master Tchr., Bowling Green State U. Alumni Assn., Parents Club and Undergrad. Com., 1983; recipient Hollis Moore award for outstanding service Undergrad. Student Govt., 1983. Mem. Ohio Bar Assn., Toledo Bar Assn., Omicron Delta Kappa. Author: (with others) Outlook on Ohio, 1983. Home: 1967 Richmond Rd Toledo OH 43607 Office: Williams Hall Room 217 Bowling Green State University Bowling Green OH 43403

LUDGIN, DONALD HUGH, editor; b. Chgo., Sept. 16, 1929; s. Earle and Mary King (MacDonald) L.; m. Sue Keating Conway, Oct. 26, 1957; children—Sarah, Katherine, Peter. A.B., Oberlin Coll., 1951. Asst. editor World Book Ency., Chgo., 1953-56, sr. editor, 1956-62, editorial coordinator, London and Sydney, Australia, 1962-66, assoc. editor, Chgo., 1966-69, dir. spl. projects, 1969-83; pres. Electronic Scribe, Evanston, Ill., 1983—. Trustee Mus. Contemporary Art, Chgo., 1971-79, sec., 1974-78; mem. Joseph Jefferson Theatre Awards Com., Chgo., 1979-81. Served with U.S. Army, 1951-53. Mem. Graphic Communications Assn. (editorial bd. jour. 1978). Democrat. Roman Catholic. Home: 1022 Ridge Ave Evanston IL 60202 Office: Electronic Scribe 1022 Ridge Ave Evanston IL 60202

LUDINGTON, JOHN SAMUEL, manufacturing company executive; b. Detroit, May 7, 1928; s. Samuel and Fredda (Holden) L.; B.S. in Econs., Albion (Mich.) Coll., 1951; LL.D. (hon.), Saginaw Valley State Coll.; D.B.A. (hon.), S.D. Sch. Mines and Tech.; m. Dorothy Lamson, Feb. 14, 1953; children—Thomas, Laura, Ann. With Dow Corning Corp., Midland, Mich., chmn., chief exec. officer; dir. Comerica Bank, Midland. Trustee Albion Coll., Mich. Molecular Inst. Served with AUS. Methodist. Office: 2200 W Salzburg Rd Midland MI 48640

LUDLOW, GREGORY ALAN, advertising consultant; b. Crawfordsville, Ind., Mar. 24, 1954; s. J.L. and Gretchen Elizabeth (Drake) L.; m. Catherine Barnhart, Dec. 4, 1976; 1 child, Gregory Paul. B.S., Ind. State U., 1976. Salesman Burroughs Corp., Indpls., 1977; asst. mgr. store T-Way of Kokomo, Elwood, Ind., 1977-79; group mgr. Zayre Corp., Muncie, Ind., 1979-81; mgr. classified advtg. Elwood Pub. Co., 1981-85; advt. cons., 1985—. Contbg. author mag. Hoosier Runner, 1983. Race co-chmn. Elwood Glass Festival, 1982-85; pres. Elwood Running Club, 1983. Mem. Ind. Classified Advt. Mgrs. Assn. (bd. dirs. 1984), Gamma Epsilon Tau. Avocations: camera collecting, running. Home: 720 S A St Elwood IN 46036

LUDLOW, JOHN DUER, business management educator, consultant; b. Manistique, Mich., Mar. 8, 1924; s. Archie Carlyle and Helen Maureen (Sherman) L.; m. Patricia Jane Barrett, Dec. 31, 1949; children—Lark Carlyle, John Barrett, Barrett Campbell. B.S., U.S. Mil. Acad., 1945; M.B.A., U. Chgo., 1963; Ph.D., U. Mich., 1972. Commd. 2d lt. U.S. Army Air Force, 1945, advanced through grades to lt. col., U.S. Air Force, 1963; instr. USAF Acad., 1957-61; program mgr. Strategic Air Command Airborne Command Post, Wright-Patterson AFB, Ohio, 1963-64, system program dir. B-1 Bomber Program, 1965-67, ret., 1967; research asst. U. Mich., Ann Arbor, 1967-70, research assoc., 1970-72, lectr., 1968; asst. prof. bus. mgmt. No. Mich. U., Marquette, 1972-76, assoc. prof., 1976—; cons. bus. Vol. bus. cons. SBA SCORE/ACE; vol. football coach No. Mich. U.; mem. Republican Presdl. Task Force. Decorated Air medal with oak leaf cluster, Air Force Commendation. Clubs: U. Mich. Pres.', No. Mich. U. Pres.' Lodge: Masons. Author articles, chpt. in book. Home: 405 Lakewood Ln Marquette MI 49855 Office: No Mich U Marquette MI 49855

LUDLUM, MARY ELLEN, librarian; b. Newnan, Ga., June 2, 1953; d. Ralph Arnold and Arlene Laura (Koengeter) Dobberstein; m. Daniel Spencer Ludlum, June 28, 1975; children—David Spencer (dec.), Stephen Christian. B.A., Capital U., 1975; postgrad. Otterbein Coll., 1979-80; A.M.L.S., U. Mich., 1981. Circulation asst. Capital U. Library, Columbus, Ohio, 1972-75; periodicals librarian Otterbein Coll. Library, Westerville, Ohio, 1975-76, circulation librarian, 1976-80; reference asst. U. Mich. Grad. Library, Ann Arbor, 1980-81; young adult librarian Grandview Heights Pub. Library, Columbus, 1981-83, program coordinator, 1983-85, head of programming and publicity, 1985—; librarian Hope Luth. Ch., Columbus, 1982—. Bd. dirs. Friends of Grandview Heights Pub. Library. Faculty-alumni scholar U. Mich. Library Sch., Ann Arbor, 1981. Mem. ALA, Ohio Library Assn. (asst. coordinator jr. mems. roundtable 1982-83), AAUW, Franklin County Library Assn. (corr. sec. 1984-85, v.p. 1985-86), Capital U. Alumnae Assn., Beta Phi Mu. Lutheran. Office: Grandview Heights Pub Library 1685 W 1st Ave Columbus OH 43212

LUDOLPH, PAMELA SEARS, clinical psychologist, psychology educator; b. Montreal, Que., Can., Jan. 27, 1950; d. William Beeks and Nadine (Sandlin) Sears; m. Robert Charles Ludolph, Aug. 19, 1972. A.B., Mt. Holyoke Coll., 1971; A.M., U. Toronto, 1972; M.A., U. Mich., 1978, Ph.D., 1981. Lic. psychologist, Mich. High sch. remedial reading tchr., Great Barrington, Mass., 1972-74; asst. dir. Berkshire Learning Ctr., Pittsfield, Mass., 1974-76; clin. psychology intern Psychol. Clinic, York Woods Ctr., U. Mich. Hosp., Ann Arbor, 1977-81; postdoctoral fellow U. Mich. Hosp., 1981-82; staff psychologist U. Mich. Counseling Ctr., 1982—, lectr. dept. psychology, 1982—; pvt. practice psychology, 1982—. Dissertation grantee U. Mich., 1979-80. Mem. Am. Psychol. Assn., Sigma Xi Assocs., Phi Beta Kappa. Office: Suite 1B 122 1/2 E Liberty St Ann Arbor MI 48104

LUDWIG, ARNOLD FRANCIS, candy company executive; b. Toledo, May 30, 1934; s. Clarence J. and Helen D. (Pry) L.; B.S. (scholar), U. Wis., 1956, B.B.A., 1958; M.B.A., U. Ill., 1981; m. Betty Jean Bubolz, Dec. 31, 1958; children—Wendy Lou, Timothy Daniel. Dir. quality control Babcock Dairy Co., Toledo, 1958-60; v.p., co founder Seaway Candy Co., Toledo, 1960-69; pres., founder Ludwig Candy Co., Manteno, Ill., 1969—; co-founder, chief exec. officer Basic Computer Literacy Inc., Manteno, Ill., 1982—; dir. exec. M.B.A. program U. Notre Dame (Ind.), 1984—. also dir. Chmn. music program Manteno Bi-Centennial, 1976. Mem. U. Wis. W Club (dir.), Am. Mgmt. Assn. (pres.), U. Wis. Alumni Assn. (bd. dirs.), U. Ill. Alumni Assn., Wis. Agrl. and Life Scis. Alumni Assn. Roman Catholic. Club: Moose. Home: Rt 1 Box 45 Manteno IL 60950 Office: 395 Locust St S Manteno IL 60950

LUDWIG, JAMES CHRISTIAN OBERWETTER, architect; b. Kattowitz, Oberschlesien, Oct. 6, 1933; came to U.S. 1952, naturalized 1957; s. Georg Karl and Margarete (Oberwetter) L.; m. Joann Painchaud Stone; children—Karen, Karl, George. Registered architect, Fla., Ind., Ill., Iowa, Mich., Ohio, Wis. With Erwin G. Fredrick, Architect, Chgo., 1958-60, Werner-Donner Architects, Chgo., 1960-62, Norman R. Werner & Assocs., Chgo., 1962-67; sole practice architecture, Chgo., 1967—; cons. Urban Planning, Inc., Arlington Hts., Ill., 1974-84; lectr. Oakton Community Coll., Des Plaines, 1979—; cons. Dean Foods/Baskin Robbins, Chgo., 1968—. Com. chmn. Boy Scouts Am., St. Tarcissus, Chgo., 1968-82; comdr. CAP, Ill. Wing, 1979—. Served with U.S. Army, 1956-58. Mem. Nat. Council Archtl. Registration Bds., Architects Club. Lodge: Rotary. Home: 5806 N Newark Chicago IL 60631 Office: James C O Ludwig 6760 W Ardmore Chicago IL 60631

LUDWIG, JOHN ROBERT, wildlife research biologist, consultant; b. West Reading, Pa., Mar. 14, 1943; s. Robert Mandon and Grace Elaine (Nice) L.; m. Barbara Ann Ely, Aug. 28, 1965; children—Todd Alan, Kristen Sue. B.S., Pa. State U., 1965; M.A., So. Ill. U., 1967, Ph.D., 1976. Research asst., grad. fellow, teaching asst. So. Ill. U., Carbondale, 1965-69, 71-73; research asst. N.C. State U., 1969-71; camp dir. Youth Conservation Corps, So. Ill. U., Carbondale, 1971, 72; deer, elk, black bear staff biologist Ont. Ministry Natural Resources, 1973-76; white-tailed deer and wild turkey research biologist Farmland Wildlife Population and Research Group, Minn. Dept. Natural Resources, Madelia, 1976-84; regional dir. Ducks Unltd., Nev., 1984—. Pa. State scholar, 1961-65; grantee Pope and Young Club, 1981, 82, 83, Minn. Archery Assn., 1981, 82. Mem. Wildlife Soc., Wildlife Disease Assn., Nat. Wildlife Fedn., Nat. Wild Turkey Fedn. (grantee 1983), Nat. Rifle Assn., Nev. Orgn. for Wildlife, Nev. Rifle and Pistol Assn., Sigma Xi. Contbr. articles to profl. jours. Home and Office: Route 2 Box 981 639 Thorobred Ave Gardnerville NV 89410

LUDWIG, JOSEPH GEORGE, JR., auto company executive; b. Pitts., July 10, 1939; s. Joseph George and Dolores (Straka) L.; m. Diana Gayle Ferenc, July 31, 1970. B.S.E.E., Carnegie Mellon U., 1960; M.S.I.A., 1965. Analyst, zone mgr. Lincoln-Mercury, Ford Motor Co., Cin., 1965-67; bus. planner Ford Motor Co., Dearborn, Mich., 1967-71, mktg. mgr. Rotunda equip., Dearborn, Mich., 1971-75, strategic planner, Dearborn, Mich., 1978-80, sales planning and analysis mgr., Detroit, 1980—. Served to 1st lt. U.S. Army, 1961-63. Avocations: golf; travel. Home: 3885 Estates Ct Troy MI 48084 Office: Ford Motor Co 300 Renaissance Center PO Box 43309 Detroit MI 48243

LUEBBERS, JOSEPH ALOYSIUS, judge; b. Cin., Mar. 12, 1922; s. Joseph H. and Rose (Nether) L.; m. Dorothy Ann O'Kane, Sept. 21, 1953; children—Jeolle, Mark, Ann, Jody, John. Cert., U. Florence, Italy, 1945; A.B., Xavier U., 1946; J.D., Chase Coll., 1950. Bar: Ohio 1950. Hearing officer Bur. Workmen's Compensation, Cin., 1953-62; adminstr. Cin. Indsl. Com., 1956-62; sole practice, Cin., 1962-65; judge Hamilton County Mcpl. Ct., Ohio, 1965—. Bd. dirs. St. Aloysius Orphanage, Cin., 1965—; pres. Men of Milford, 1977—. Served to cpl. U.S. Army, 1943-46. Named Man of Yr., Bldg. Trades Union, 1971. Mem. Ohio State Bar Assn., Cin. Bar Assn., Ohio Mcpl. Judges Assn., Am. Jud. Assn., Xavier U. Alumni (Disting. Alumnus award 1984). Democrat. Roman Catholic. Mem. VFW. Lodges; KC, Eagles. Home: 3733 Donegal Dr Cincinnati OH 45236 Office: Hamilton County Mcpl Ct 22 E Central Pkwy Cincinnati OH 45202

LUEBKE, MARTIN FREDERICK, curator; b. Concord, Wis., Oct. 2, 1917; s. Frederick John and Martha (Kretzmann) L.; m. Dorothy Lorraine Kutschinski, July 5, 1947; children—Judith, Charles. B.S., Concordia Coll., 1941; M.A., U. Mich., 1952; Ph.D., U. Ill., 1966; postdoctoral Cambridge U., 1974. Tchr. Our Savior Luth. Sch., Chgo., 1938-45; prin. Immanuel Luth. Sch., Grand Rapids, Mich., 1945-58; prof., dean. Concordia Theol. Sem., Springfield, Ill., 1958-76, Ft. Wayne, Ind., 1976-80; curator Saxon Luth. Meml., Frohna, Mo., 1980—. Editor: Curriculum in Process, 1963; contbr. articles to profl. jours. Bd. dirs. Mich. Dist. Luth. Ch., Mo. Synod, 1957-58; mem. bd. parish edn. Luth. Ch., Mo. Synod, 1962-75; commr., sec. Perry County Tourism Commn., Perryville, Mo., 1983—; bd. dirs. River Heritage Assn., Cape Girardeau, Mo., 1984—. Faculty fellow Aid Assn. Luths., 1963, 73; recipient Outstanding Educators Am. award, 1972. Avocations: music; tour host. Home: Route 1 Box 17 Frohna MO 63748

LUECKE, JOSEPH E., insurance company executive. Chmn. bd., chief exec. officer, pres. Kemper Corp. Office: Kemper Corp Long Grove IL 60049*

LUEDTKE, ROLAND ALFRED, lawyer, mayor of Lincoln; b. Lincoln, Nebr., Jan. 4, 1924; s. Alfred C. and Caroline (Senne) L.; B.S., U. Nebr., 1949, J.D., 1951; m. Helen Snyder, Dec. 1, 1951; children—Larry O., David A. Admitted to Nebr. bar, 1951; practiced in Lincoln, 1951—; mem. firm Kier, Cobb & Luedtke, 1961-69, Kier & Luedtke, 1969-73, Luedtke, Radcliffe & Evans and predecessor, 1973—; dep. sec. state State of Nebr., Lincoln, 1953-60; spl. legislative liaison Nebr. Dept. State, Lincoln, 1953-60; corps and elections counsel to sec. state, Lincoln, 1960-65; state senator Nebr. Unicameral Legislature, 1967-78, speaker, 1977-78; lt. gov. Nebr., 1979-83; mayor City of Lincoln, 1983—. Exec. sec. Nebr. Gov.'s Com. Refugee Relief, 1954-58; conferee Nat. Conf. Judiciary, Williamsburg, Va., 1971, Nat. Conf. Corrections, Williamsburg, Va., 1971; del. Nat. Conf. Criminal Justice, Washington, 1973; mem. Nat. Conf. State Cts., Williamsburg, Va., 1978; mem. exec. com. Nat. Conf. Lt. Govs., chmn. Midwest region, 1982-83, mem. budget com. Council State Govts. Past pres. Lancaster County Cancer Soc., crusade chmn. Nebr. div. Am. Cancer Soc., 1981-82; dist. v.p., finance chmn. Boy Scouts Am. Treas., Nebr. Young Republicans, 1953-54; jr. pres. Founders Day Nebr. Rep. Com., 1958-59; chmn. Lancaster County Rep. Com., 1962-64. Bd. dirs. Concordia Coll. Assn., Seward, Nebr., pres., 1962-66; bd. dirs. Lincoln Luth. Sch. Assn., pres., 1964-65; bd. dirs. Immanuel Health Center, Omaha. Served with AUS, 1943-45; ETO. Decorated Bronze Star, Purple Heart; recipient Distinguished Service award Concordia Tchrs. Coll., 1975. Mem. Am., Nebr. (spl. com. corp. law revision), Lincoln bar assns., Am. Legion, Lincoln Jr. C. of C. (dir. 1955-57, v.p., 1956-57), Nat. Conf. State Legislators (chmn. criminal justice task force and consumers affairs com., mem. exec. com. 1977-78), Am. Judicature Soc., Delta Theta Phi. Lutheran (pres. ch. 1971-74). Club: Sertoma (pres. 1962-63, chmn. bd. 1963-64) (Lincoln). Office: Office of Mayor Lincoln NE 68509*

LUEGER, JAMES JOHN, osteopathic physician; b. Axtell, Kans., Aug. 4, 1951; s. Alvin Joseph and Leona Mildred (Wietharn) L.; m. Joan Marie Winkler, Aug. 17, 1974; children—Jennifer, Sarah, Matthew. B.A., Benedictine Coll., 1973; D.O., Kansas City Coll. Osteo. Medicine, 1978. Diplomate Nat. Bd. Examiners Osteo. Physicians. Intern Osteo. Hosp. Wichita, Kans., 1978-79; practice osteo. medicine, Seneca, Kans., 1979—; mem. active med. staff Nemaha Valley Community Hosp., Seneca, 1979—; county health officer Nemaha County, Seneca, 1982—; co-med. dir. Seneca Ambulance Service, 1980-85; med. dir. Crestview Manor, Seneca, 1979—. Mem. Kans. Adv. Council for Employment of Handicapped, Topeka, 1984; bd. govs. Health Care Stabilization Fund Kans., Topeka, 1984. Mem. Am. Osteo. Assn., Am. Coll.

Gen. Practitioners, Kans. Med. Soc., Kans. Assn. Osteo. Medicine, N.E. Kans. Med. Soc. (v.p. 1982, sec.-treas. 1985). Roman Catholic. Lodge: K.C. Avocations: woodworking; gardening. Home: 313 N 9th St Seneca KS 66538 Office: 713 Main St Seneca KS 66538

LUELLEN, DONALD JAY, dentist; b. Newton, Kans., Aug. 19, 1943; s. Thomas J. and W. Ruth (Epp) L.; m. Jane Ann Stevens, Sept. 3, 1971; children—Connie Ann, Maggie Ruth. Student Grinnell Coll., 1961-62; B.A. U. Kans., 1965; D.D.S., Northwestern U., 1969. Dentist Project Concern, Alpine, Tenn., 1970, Wichita Clinic, Kans., 1970—. Bd. dirs. Project Concern, Wichita, 1984, walk dir., 1985. Mem. ADA, Wichita Dist. Dental Soc., Kans. Dental Soc. Republican. Presbyterian. Club: Air Capitol Gun (pres. 1983—). Avocations: pistol shooting, tennis, sailing. Home: 246 N Battin Wichita KS 67208

LUERSSEN, FRANK WONSON, steel company executive. Chmn., chief exec. officer Inland Steel Co., Chgo., also dir. Office: Inland Steel Co 30 W Monroe St Chicago IL 60603*

LUFKIN, ORAN E. (SAM), nursing home administrator; b. Idaho Falls, Idaho, May 11, 1939; s. Ellwood J. and Wanda (Scott) L. Exec. dir. 432 Poplar Corp. Normandy House and Old Orchard Manor, Wilmette, Ill., 1971—. Served with USAF, 1961-64. Mem. Am. Coll. Health Care Adminstrs. Lodge: Rotary (pres. 1984-85). Office: Normandy House 432 Poplar Dr Wilmette IL 60091

LUGAR, RICHARD GREEN, U.S. senator; b. Indpls., Apr. 4, 1932; s. Marvin and Bertha (Green) L.; B.A., Denison U., 1954; B.A., M.A. (Rhodes scholar), Oxford (Eng.) U., 1954-56; m. Charlene Smeltzer, Sept. 8, 1956; children—Mark, Robert, John, David. With Thomas L. Green & Co., Indpls., 1960—, v.p., treas., 1960-67, sec.-treas. 1967—; treas. Lugar Stock Farm Inc., Indpls., 1960—; mayor city Indpls., 1968-75; U.S. Senator from Ind., 1977—, chmn. fgn. relations com., 1985—. Mem. Adv. Commn. on Intergovtl. Relations, 1968-75, vice chmn., 1970-75; mem. adv. council U.S. Conf. Mayors, 1969-75; pres. Nat. League Cities, 1970-71; mem. regional export expansion council Dept. Commerce, Indpls., 1967-73. Incorporator, 1st v.p. Community Action Against Poverty Bd., Indpls., 1965-67; mem. Indpls. Bd. Sch. Commrs., 1964-67, v.p., 1965; mem. Nat. Adv. Commn. on Criminal Justice Standards and Goals, 1971-72. Mem. adv. com. Marion County Republican Com., 1966—; keynoter Ind. Rep. Conv., 1968, del., 1970, 72; mem. platform com. Rep. Nat. Conv., 1968, 72, Keynote speaker, 1972, del., 1980; chmn. Nat. Rep. Senatorial Com., 1983-84; mem. exec. com. Indpls. Symphony Orch., 1964-66; trustee, vice chmn. Ind. Central U.; trustee Denison U., Indpls. Center Advanced Research, 1973-76; trustee, past mem. bldg. fund com. Westview Hosp.; mem. Nat. 4-H Service Com.; bd. visitors Joint Center for Urban Studies, Harvard-Mass. Inst. Tech. Served to lt. USNR, 1957-60. Named Outstanding Young Man, Indpls. Jr. C. of C., 1966. Mem. Washington High Sch. Men's Club (pres. 1966-68), Phi Beta Kappa, Beta Theta Pi. Methodist. Rotarian (v.p. Indpls. 1967-68). Home: 7841 Old Dominion Dr McLean VA 22102 Office: 306 Hart Senate Office Bldg Washington DC 20510

LUI, ALEC YEN NIEN, physician, researcher; b. Hong Kong, Feb. 13, 1950; came to U.S., 1969; s. Hok Wan and Kwan Hwa (Chang) L.; m. May So-Ying Sim, Dec. 31, 1971; children—Natalie Shau Bie, Bertrand Howyen. B.S., U. Minn., 1973; M.D., Med. Coll. Wis., 1977. Am. Bd. Internal Medicine, Am. Bd. Gastroenterology. Intern Ind. U. Med. Ctr., Indpls., 1977-78, resident, 1978-79; asst. prof. Ind. U. Sch. Med., 1982-85; research assoc. VA Med. Ctr., Indpls., 1984-85; staff physician Humana Hosp., Sebastian, Fla., 1985—. Recipient Career Devel. award VA, Indpls. Mem. ACP, Am. Assn. for Study Liver Diseases, Sigma Xi, Alpha Omega Alpha.

LUI, JOSEPH HON-CHIU, biologist, researcher; b. Sheung Shui, New Territories, Hong Kong, June 6, 1952; came to U.S., 1975; s. Chung-Pui and Fong (Lam) L.; m. Josephine Ding-Woei, July 8, 1978; children—Daniel Ling, Alberta Ling. B.S. in Pharmacy, Nat. Def. Med. Ctr., Taipei, Republic of China, 1975; Ph.D., U. Minn., 1980. Research fellow W. Alton Jones Sci. Ctr., Lake Placid, N.Y., 1980-81; sr. research biologist Goodyear Tire & Rubber Co., Akron, Ohio, 1981-82, sect. head, 1983—. Author: Cell Culture and Somatic Cell Genetics of Plants, 1984. Contbr. articles to profl. jours. Mem. Am. Soc. Pharmacognosy, Internat. Assn. Plant Tissue Culture, Rhochi Soc., AAAS. Avocations: contemporary printing; traveling. Home: 1613A Treetop Trail Akron OH 44313 Office: Goodyear Tire & Rubber Co 142 Goodyear Blvd Akron OH 44316

LUKE, CHU-YEN, food educator, electrical engineer; b. Chung Leo, China, July 18, 1938; came to U.S., 1948; s. Gene Soon and Sin Hong (Chin) Look; m. Pansy Wong Luke, Aug. 17, 1963; children—Ala, Asa. E.E., Ill. Inst. Tech., Chgo., 1969. Lab. engr. Skil Corp., Chgo., 1965-69; lab. mgr. No. Electric Co., Chgo., 1969-76; food educator Oriental Food Market and Cooking Sch., Chgo., 1976—; cons. Oriental Cookbook, 1977. Served with U.S. Army, 1961. Home: 2500 N Jarvis Ave Chicago IL 60645 Office: Oriental Food Market and Cooking Sch 2801 W Howard St Chicago IL 60645

LUKE, JEFFREY SCOTT, educator, consultant; b. Tucson, Jan. 3, 1951; s. Fred Graves and Victoria Mae (Hedden) L.; m. Peggy Jane Grace; children—Kavi, Mona, Victoria. B.S., U. So. Calif., 1972, M.P.A., 1974, Ph.D., 1981; cert. C.G. Jung Sch. Analytical Psychology, 1977. Project dir. Los Angeles Metro YMCA, 1970-73; asst. to dep. city mgr. City of Scottsdale, Ariz., 1973; adminstrv. analyst County of Monterey, Carmel, Calif., 1974-78; lectr. U. So. Calif., Los Angeles, 1978-81; asst. prof. U. Nebr., Omaha, 1982-84, asst. to dean, 1984—; script cons. CRM/McGraw Hill Films, Santa Monica, Calif., 1979-80; pub. mgmt. cons. city and state govts., 1978-85. Author: Job Creation in Southern California, 1981 (WGRA award 1981). Contbr. articles to profl. jours. Faculty advisor Omicron Delta Kappa Leadership Soc., Omaha, 1984. Recipient Scholar/Athlete award U. Soc. Calif., 1972, Fletcher Bowron award, 1974; HUD fellow, 1973-74. Mem. Am. Soc. Tng. and Devel., Am. Soc. Pub. Adminstrn., World Future Soc. Avocations: water skiing; hiking. Home: 9122 Pine St Omaha NE 68124 Office: U Nebr at Omaha Annex 24 Omaha NE 68182

LUKEN, THOMAS A., Congressman; b. Cin., July 9, 1925; A.B., Xavier U., 1947; postgrad. Bowling Green State U., 1943-44; LL.B., Salmon P. Chase Law Sch., 1950; m. Shirley Ast, 1947; 8 children. Admitted to Ohio bar, 1950; practiced in Cin.; city atty. City of Deer Park (Ohio), 1955-61; Fed. dist. atty., 1961-64; mem. Cin. City Council, 1964-67, 69-71, 73, mayor, 1971-72; mem. 93d, 95th-99th congresses from 2d Ohio Dist.; chmn. Cin. Law Observance Com. Served in USMC, 1943-45. Mem. Am. Legion, Jaycees (life). Lodge: K.C. Office: Room 2342 Rayburn Office Bldg Washington DC 20515*

LUKENSMEYER, CAROLYN JEAN, organizational development and human process consultant; b. Hampton, Iowa, May 13, 1945; d. Gerald William and Jean Rae (Swartz) L.; B.A. magna cum laude, U. Iowa, 1967; Ph.D., Case Western Res. U., 1974. Community organizer City of Yellow Knife (NW Ter., Can.), 1965; dir. English studies LaCandalabra, Bogota, Colombia, 1966; tng. dir. Goodwill Industries, Iowa City, 1966-67; asst. dean students U. Rochester (N.Y.), 1967-68; counselor for student life Cleve. State U., 1968-71, asst. prof. dept. social services, 1971-74; dir. planning and devel. Gestalt Inst. Cleve., 1978—; pres. Lukensmeyer Assos., Inc., work projects on boundary mgmt. in joint ventures between multinat. corps. and govts., Cleve., 1974-79. Bd. dirs. Nat. Tng. Labs., Washington, WomenSpace, Cleve.; mem. Citizen's Action Council, Mayor's Office, Cleve., 1968-69; mem. adv. council on youth YWCA, 1968-70; mem. People's Commn. of Inquiry, Vietnam, 1970-72; mem. Internat. Assembly of Christians in Solidarity with the People of SE Asia, 1970-72. Mem. Internat. Assn. Applied Social Scientists, Cert. Consultants Internat., Am. Psychol. Assn. Address: 7 Mornington Ln Cleveland Heights OH 44106

LUMAN, RONALD JOHN, architect; b. Canton, Ill., Apr. 12, 1947; s. Bernard Joseph and Lucille N. (Young) L.; m. Zalene Marie Murphy, Aug. 4, 1968; children—Christopher, Amanda, Katharine. B.Arch., U. Ill., 1975. Registered architect, Ill., Wis. Architect, Abreu & Robeson, Brunswick, Ga., 1971, RSS & G, Champaign, Ill., 1973-75, Pioneer Hi-Bred Internat., Inc., Princeton, Ill., 1975—; part-time tchr., cons. in field. Served to sgt. USMC, 1968-71. Recipient cert. merit Ill. Bicentennial Planning Commn., 1976. Republican. Methodist. Home: Sherwood Glen Princeton IL 61356 Office: Pioneer Hi-Bred Internat Inc PO Box 40 Princeton IL 61356

LUMLEY, THOMAD DEWEY, manufacturing company executive; b. Ashland, Ky., Sept. 6, 1944; s. George Francis and Cathrine Ellenor L. B.S. in Acctg., U. Ky., 1969. Plant controller Trane Co., 1967-70; mgr. customer sales and service Sikes Corp., 1971-75; v.p., owner Robert Half, Inc., Louisville, 1975-76; v.p., sec. Fire King Internat., Inc., New Albany, Ind., 1976—; mem. Domestic Export Council, U.S. Dept. Commerce. Pres. Kentuckiana World Commerce Council, 1981-82, mem., 1976—. Served to sgt. AUS, 1970-71. Mem. Nat. Acctg. Assn., Louisville Personnel Assn. (pres. 1982-83), Internat. Credit and Fin. Assn. (chmn. 1980-81), New Albany C. of C. (bd. dirs. 1981-83, pres. 1983-84). Roman Catholic. Office: 59 Indian Hills Trail Louisville KY 40207

LUMPKIN, PENNY PALMER, wholesale periodicals company executive; b. Topeka, Aug. 20; d. William H. and Vivian J. Palmer; student U. Ariz., 1957-59, U. Kans., 1959-60; m. Joseph Henry Lumpkin, Nov. 26, 1960; children—William Henry, Kelley Kathleen. Buyer, merchandiser City News & Gift Shop, Topeka, 1954-57; mgr., buyer Vivian's Gift Shop, Topeka, 1961-76; book buyer Palmer News, Inc., Topeka, 1976-79, book buyer, personnel dir., 1979-80, dir. retail ops., treas., 1980—, also dir.; sec., dir. Palmer Cos., Inc., 1983—, treas., 1984—; dir. Ultra Fund-Security Benefit Life. Bd. dirs. Mulvane Art Center, Topeka, 1968-80, Seven Step Found., Topeka, 1969-72, Topeka Civic Theatre, 1984—; bd. dirs., charter mem. Mulvane Women, Topeka, 1969; div. chmn. United Way, Topeka, 1969; chmn. King of Hills Pro/Celebrity Tennis Benefit, 1977-79; spl. events chmn. Shawnee County unit Am. Cancer Soc., Topeka, 1976-78, v.p. bd. dirs., 1977, pres. bd. dirs., 1979; mem. exec. bd. Jayhawk Area council Boy Scouts Am.; hon. chmn. holiday treasures Shawnee Country Day Sch., 1985 Named an Outstanding Woman Am., Jr. League of Topeka, 1975; recipient Outstanding Service award Am. Cancer Soc., 1976, Kans. div., 1978. Mem. Central States Periodicals Distbrs. Assn., Am. Booksellers Assn., Mid-Am. Periodicals Distbrs. Assn., Ind. Periodicals Distbrs. Assn., Topeka Friends of Zoo, Am. Heritage Assn., Kappa Kappa Gamma Alums. Republican. Episcopalian. Club: Jr. League (pres. Topeka 1971). Researcher, pub. fund-raising manual Assn. Jr. Leagues, 1974. Home: 3161 Shadow Ln Topeka KS 66604 Office: Palmer News Inc 1050 Republican Topeka KS 66604

LUMSDAINE, EDWARD, engineering educator, administrator; b. Hong Kong; Sept. 30, 1937; came to U.S., 1953; s. Clifford Vere and Miao Ying (Ho) L.; m. Monika Amsler, Sept. 8, 1959; children—Andrew, Anne Josephine, Alfred, Arnold. B.S. in Mech. Engring., N.Mex. State U., 1963, M.S. in Mech. Engring., 1964, Sc.D., 1966. Research engr. Boeing Co., Seattle, 1966-67, 68; asst. prof., then assoc. prof. S.D. State U., Brookings, 1967-72; assoc. prof., then prof. U. Tenn., Knoxville, 1972-77; prof., sr. research engr., dir. N.Mex. Solar Energy Inst., N.Mex. State U., Las Cruces, 1977-81; prof., dir. Energy Environ. and Resources Ctr., U. Tenn., Knoxville, 1981-83; dean engring., prof. U. Mich., Dearborn, 1982—; dir., cons. E&M Lumsdaine Solar Cons., Inc., Southfield, Mich., 1979—; cons. BDM Corp., Albuquerque, 1984—, Oak Ridge Nat. Lab., 1979-82. Author workshop manual: Industrial Energy Conservation for Developing Countries, 1984. Contbr. articles to profl. jours. NASA trainee, N.Mex. State U., 1964-66; NASA/ASEE fellow, 1969, 70; grantee NSF, NASA, Dept. Energy, U.S. Navy, ASHRAE, AID, Ford Motor Co. Assoc. fellow AIAA (mem. tech. com. terrestrial energy systems); mem. Am. Soc. Engring. Edn., ASME, ASTM (various coms.), Internat. Solar Energy Soc., AAUP. Presbyterian. Lodge: Rotary. Office: U Mich 4901 Evergreen Rd Dearborn MI 48128

LUMSDEN, GEORGE JAMES, communications company executive; b. Niagara Falls, N.Y., Aug. 23, 1921; s. James and Helen Jessie (Simpson) L.; m. Marjorie G. Brouwer, Apr. 15, 1944; children—James William, Nancy Lumsden Sullivan. A.B., Hope Coll., Holland, Mich., 1944; M.A., U. Mich., 1953. Tchr., adminstr. Holland Pub. Sch., Mich., 1949-54; tng. specialist Gen. Electric Co., 1954-58; acct. exec. Lindeman Advtg., Holland, 1958-62; mem. editorial staff Jam Handy Orgn., Detroit, 1962-63; mgr. sales tng. Chrysler Corp., Detroit, 1963-80; prin. Exec. Communications, Birmingham, Mich., 1980—. Author: Tips on Talks, 1962; Impact Management, 1979; Dartnell Human Resource Development Series, 1980—; Middle Management, 1982. Trustee, First Presbyterian Ch., Birmingham, Mich., 1965-68, elder, 1975-79. Served with USN, 1942-44. Mem. Am. Legion (comdr. 1946-47), Nat. Speakers Assn., Nat. Soc. Sales Tng. Execs. (editorial honor award 1974, 78, 80). Republican. Avocations: golf; reading; travel. Home and Office: 2694 Heathfield Rd Birmingham MI 48010

LUND, DAVE LEE, counseling program administrator; b. Fremont, Nebr., Sept. 25, 1949; s. Clifford Albert and Marie (Jensen) L.; m. Linda Mae (Gudgel), Aug. 16, 1970; children—Laura, Matthew, Albert. B.S., Kearney State Coll., 1971; M.S., U. Nebr., 1978. Vocat. counselor Nebr. Dept. Labor, Fremont, 1972-81; chem. dependency counselor Immanuel Med. Ctr., Omaha, 1981-82; program coordinator Immanuel Med. Ctr., 1982—; cons. Midland Luth. Coll., Fremont, 1982-83, Bergen Jr./Sr. High Sch., 1982-84, Fremont Jr.-Sr. High Sch., 1982-84. Pres., Trinity Parent Tchr. League, Fremont, 1983; project com. mem. Ad Hoc Prevention Com., Fremont, 1983; co-dir. Community Alcoholism Needs Assessment Group, 1982; facilitator Chem. Abuse Adv. Bd., Fremont, 1984; mem. Area Youth Counselors Group, 1984; defensive driving instr. Nat. Safety Council, 1984. Mem. Fremont Area Personnel Mgrs. Assn. Democrat. Lutheran. Avocations: racquetball; fishing; swimming; camping. Address: Route 1 Fremont NE 68025

LUND, EUGENE HAROLD, air force officer; b. Mpls., July 7, 1940; s. Harold A. and Esther (Ryberg) L.; m. Flory Ann Reed, Dec. 19, 1970. B.A. in Econs., St. Olaf Coll., 1965; M.B.A., U. Utah, 1974; postgrad. George Washington U., 1974-76, AF Squadron Officers Sch., 1972, Armed Forces Staff Coll., 1979. Commd. 2d lt. U.S. Air Force, 1965, advanced through grades to lt. col., 1981; officer-in-charge telecommunications ops. 91st Bombardment Wing, Glasgow AFB, Mont., 1966-67, chief communications-electronics ops., 1967, chief tactical communications, 1967-68; chief communications-electronics div. 4257th AB Squadron 1968; asst. chief sect. 4220th Air Refueling Squadron, Taiwan, 1969, chief communications maintenance, 1969-70, chief sect., 1970; chief of maintenance 2143d Communications Squadron, Zweibrucken AB, Federal Republic Germany, 1971-74; radio frequency engr. U.S. Air Force Frequency Mgmt. Office, Washington, 1975-78; asst. dir. joint interoperability communications, comdr.-in-chief Atlantic Command, Norfolk, Va., 1979-82; comdr. 1936th Communications Squadron, also dep. comdr. for communications 1605th Mil. Airlift Support Wing, asst. chief of staff for communications, Azores, Portugal, 1982-85; wing rep. Jr. Officers Council, 1966-68; project officer newspaper awards program Am. Heritage Found., 1967; mil. project officer Valley County Devel. Council, Mont., 1968; escort Pub. Land Law Rev. Commn., 1968; mil. aide to family of Vice-Pres. Walter Mondale at Presdl. Inauguration, 1977; accident prevention counselor FAA, 1977-79; escort officer, comdr.-in-chief Atlantic Command, 1979, command briefing officer, 1979-80; organizer, operator Flory Ann's of Sherman, Inc., 1974-79; cons. in field. Columnist, Glasgow Courier, Mont., 1968. Contbr. articles on bus. to publs. Mem. com. Big Sky council Boy Scouts Am., 1967-68, scoutmaster, Taiwan, 1969-70, bd. dirs. Tidewater council, 1979, asst. council commr., 1981-85; comdr. Group II, Mont. wing CAP, 1967-68, safety officer Nat. Capital wing, 1976-77, chief-of-staff Nat. Capital wing, 1977-78; pres. Protestant Men of the Chapel, Zweibrucken AB, 1973-74, chmn. chapel fund council, 1974; staff dir. No. Va. chpt Full Gospel Businessmen's Fellowship, 1974-76. Decorated Air medal, others; named Outstanding Safety Officer of Yr., CAP, 1976, 77; recipient Paul W. Turner Safety award, 1976, Grover Loening award, 1978, Paul E. Garber award, 1978, Order of Arrow, Boy Scouts Am., 1965, spl. recognition Boy Scouts Am., 1981. Mem. Air Force Assn., Aircraft Owners and Pilots Assn., Gideons Internat., Nat. Assn. Flight Instrs., Armed Forces Communications and Electronics Assn., Norfolk C. of C. (econ. affairs com. 1979-85). Lutheran. Address: 2116-A Willow Wood Ln Scott AFB IL 62225

LUND, WILMA JEAN, educational administrator; b. Greenfield, Ill., Nov. 3, 1932; d. William Frederick and Illah Marie (Elmore) Overbey; m. Keith R. Lund, Aug. 26, 1951; children—Gregory Thomas, Pamela Jean. B.S., Western Ill. U., Macomb, 1965, M.S., 1978. Social studies tchr. Community Unit Dist. No. 210, Aledo, Ill., 1964-80, gifted edn. coordinator, 1970-80, gifted edn. coordinator Ill. Bd. Edn., Springfield, 1980—; cons. in field, 1968-80; mem. exec. com. Nat. Council Social Studies, Washington, 1977-80, bd. dirs., 1977-80. Editor: Illinois Teachers Bicentennial Resource Guide, 1975. Campaign chmn. Edn. Service Region Supt. Election, Henderson, Mercer and Warren Counties, Ill., 1977. Recipient Outstanding Contbn. to Edn. award City of Aledo, 1971, Gifted Edn. Outstanding Contbns. award Region IV Gifted Area Service Ctr., 1980; named Outstanding Tchr., Ill. State Hist. Soc., 1976, Lady of Yr., Aledo Jaycees, 1978. Mem. Ill. State Hist. Soc. (chmn. bd. dirs. 1983-84, pres. 1982-83), Ill. Council Gifted Children, Nat. Assn. Gifted Children. Republican. Methodist. Lodge: Zonta Internat. Avocations: golf, bridge, writing. Office: Ill State Bd Edn 100 N 1st St Springfield IL 62777

LUNDGREN, DAVID JONATHAN, lawyer; b. Greensburg, Pa., June 6, 1947; s. Carl Russell and Mildred (Forse) L.; m. Cheryl Lynn Mueller, June 28, 1969; children—Scott, Curtis. B.A., Wittenberg U., 1969; J.D., Case Western Reserve U., 1976. Bar: Ohio 1976. Assoc. Blumenstiel and Lundgren, Alliance, Ohio, 1976-82; pros. atty. Alliance Law Dept., 1982-83; ptnr. Brown, Ogline and Lundgren, Alliance and Hartville, Ohio, 1984—. Sec. Alliance YMCA, 1979—, chmn. membership campaign, 1985; pres. Friends of Rodman Pub. Library, Alliance, 1982-85; pres. ch. council St. Paul Lutheran Ch., 1982. Served with USAF, 1969-73. Mem. ABA, Ohio Bar Assn., Stark County Bar Assn., Alliance Bar Assn. Republican. Lodge: Rotary (Rotarian of Yr. award 1980). Avocations: running; tennis; traveling; reading. Home: 307 W Simpson Alliance OH 44601 Office: Brown Ogline and Lundgren 608 Bank One Bldg Alliance OH 44601

LUNDIE, LOUISE MARIE, electric sign manufacturing company executive; b. Meeme Twp., Wis., Mar. 2, 1940; d. Henry Joseph and Irene Theresa (Salm) Schwartz; A.A., Milw. Area Tech. Coll., 1978; B.S., Carroll Coll., 1982; M.S. in Mgmt., Cardinal Stritch Coll., 1984; m. Mel A. Lundie, Oct. 2, 1976; 1 child by previous marriage, Ann Louise Mathews. Sec. to gen. mgr. St. Regis Paper Co., Milw., 1961-65; asst. to pres. Wells Badger Corp., Milw., 1966-74; sec. to v.p. mktg. Everbrite Electric Signs, South Milwaukee, Wis., 1975, nat. sales adminstr., 1976-81, mgr. mktg. adminstrn., 1981, mgr. corporate planning, advt. and market research, 1981-84, dir. customer service, 1984—. 4-H Club leader City of Cudahy (Wis.), 1977-82; pres. adult chpt. Am. Friends Service, Cudahy, Wis. Mem. Nat. Secs. Assn. (pres. Milw. chpt. 1971-73), Adminstrv. Mgmt. Soc., Am. Assn. Individual Investors, Friends of Cudahy Library, AAUW. Home: 5938 S Pennsylvania Ave Cudahy WI 53110 Office: Everbrite Electric Signs 315 Marion Ave South Milwaukee WI 53172

LUNDQUIST, JULIE ANNE, lawyer; b. Chgo., Sept. 22, 1946; d. Donald Carl and Gertrude (Kelly) L. B.A., St. Olaf Coll., 1968; J.D., John Marshall Law Sch., 1978. Bar: Ill. 1978, U.S. Dist. Ct. (no. dist.) Ill. 1978. Mem. firm Lundquist & Mitchell, Zion, Ill., 1978—; instr. law and trust div. Am. Inst. Banking, Chgo., 1980—. Pres. YWCA of Lake County, Ill., 1985; chmn. Council of YWCAs of Ill. and St. Louis, Waukegan, Ill., 1984; treas. Com. to Elect Judge Scott, Libertyville, Ill., 1984. Mem. ABA, Ill. State Bar Assn., Chgo. Bar Assn., Lake County Bar Assn. (sec. 1984—), Assn. Women Attys. (pres. 1981-83), Jr. Women's League. Republican. Episcopalian. Office: Lundquist & Mitchell 2610 Sheridan Rd Zion IL 60099

LUNDY, BARBARA JEAN, communications consultant, writer; b. Frankfurt, Germany, Aug. 1, 1953; d. Roger J. and Helen E. (Branch) L.; B.A. in Journalism, Ohio State U., 1974. Edn. specialist Ohio Hist. Soc., Columbus, 1975-76; asst. chief communications Ohio Youth Commn., Columbus, 1976-79; public info. coordinator Central Ohio Transit Authority, Columbus, 1979-81; owner B.J. Lundy Enterprises, Columbus, 1981—; communications cons. Fedn. of Community Orgns., 1980, Driving Park Area Commn., 1980, Driving Park Civic Assn., 1980, Africa: A First Experience, 1980—. Chmn. membership com. Leadership Columbus, 1980-81, mem. steering com., 1980-83, v.p. steering com., 1982-83; mem. program selection com. Columbus Area Leadership Program, 1982—; mem. Central Ohio Young Republicans Nominating Com., 1981. Mem. Public Relations Soc. Am. (public service com. 1980-81, chmn. speaker's bur. com. 1979-81), Columbus Area C. of C. Baptist.

LUNDY, PAUL ANDREW, environmental engineer; b. Sioux Falls, S.D., Aug. 30, 1944; s. Andrew Mandus and Edna Joy (Searles) L.; m. Carol Ann Barnes, Sept. 16, 1963 (div. 1967); m. Mary Ann Westergreen, Apr. 1, 1967; children—Erik Magnus Gustavus, Karl Edward. B.S. in Geol. Engring., S.D. Sch. Mines and Tech., 1967. Profl. engr., Iowa. Found. engr. Iowa Dept. Transp., Ames, 1969-71, project engr., 1971-80; environ. engr., solid and hazardous waste mgmt. Iowa Dept. Environ. Quality, Des Moines, 1980-83; water supply engr. Iowa Dept. Water, Air and Waste Mgmt., Des Moines, 1983—. Pres. Ames Council PTAs and PTSAs, 1977-78. Served with U.S. Army, 1967-69, USAR, 1969—. Decorated Humanitarian Service medal, 1980; recipient Pub. Service award Am. Radio Relay League, 1972, 79. Mem. Soc. Am. Mil. Engrs., Am. Indian Sci. and Engring. Soc. (regional gov. 1985—), AIME, Scabbard and Blade. Republican. Methodist. Clubs: Story County Amateur Radio, Encore Toastmasters (area gov. 1973-74). Home: 4316 Phoenix Ames IA 50010 Office: 900 E Grand Des Moines IA 50319

LUPKE, WALTER HERMAN, JR., insurance agency executive; b. Ft. Wayne, Ind., Sept. 25, 1922; s. Walter Herman and Lucy Viola (Bell) L.; m. G. Frances McGahey, Aug. 11, 1944; children—Karen Ann McArdle, Hans R. B.S. in Chem. Engring., Purdue U., 1942. C.L.U., chartered property casualty underwriter. Underwriter, Lupke Ins. Agy., Ft. Wayne, 1946-50, acct., 1950-51, claims mgr., 1951-52, treas., 1946-83, sales exec., 1952-83, chmn. bd., 1970—. Pres. Lupke Found.; bd. dirs. Embassy Found., St. Francis Coll. Found., Kirksville Coll. Medicine Found., Luth. Hosp., Allen Wells chpt. ARC. Served with U.S. Army, 1942-46; ETO. Mem. Ind. Ins. Agts. Assn. U.S.A., Ind. Ind. Ins. Agts. Assn., Ft. Wayne Ind. Ins. Agts., Ft. Wayne C. of C. Republican. Lutheran. Club: Kiwanis.

LUQMANI, MUSHTAQ, marketing and international business educator, consultant; b. Karachi, Pakistan, Nov. 5, 1944; came to U.S., 1967; s. Arif A. and Badar (Beg) Lukmani; m. Zahida M. Luqmani, Mar. 15, 1973. B.S. with honors, U. Karachi, 1966; B.S. in Chem. Engring., Ind. Inst. Tech., 1969; M.B.A., Mich. State U., 1971, Ph.D. in Mktg. and Internat. Bus., 1978. Ptnr., Hotel Properties, Karachi, 1963-66; mktg. mgr. Al-Afia Resorts, Karachi, 1972-73; teaching asst. Mich. State U., East Lansing, 1973-76; assoc. prof. mktg. Western Mich. U., Kalamazoo, 1977—. Mem. Am. Mktg. Assn. (pres. West Mich. chpt. 1983-84), Acad. Mktg. Sci., Acad. Internat. Bus., West Mich. World Trade Club, Beta Gamma Sigma. Lodge: Lions (Kalamazoo). Contbr. articles to profl. jours. Home: 7600 Orchard Hill Kalamazoo MI 49002 Office: 230 N Hall Western Michigan Univ Kalamazoo MI 49008

LURING, ROGER ESSELL, lawyer; b. Elmhurst, Ill., Sept. 30, 1946; s. Bert Gustave and Elizabeth (Ross) L.; m. Kathleen Ann Clark, Aug. 17, 1974; children—Jason, Sara, Andrew. A.B., Miami U., Ohio, 1968; J.D., U. of Cin., 1975. Bar: Ohio 1975, U.S. Dist. Ct. (so. dist.) Ohio 1976, U.S. Tax Ct. 1980, U.S. Ct. Claims 1980. Assoc., Miller & Schlemmer, Troy, Ohio, 1975-78; asst. prosecutor Miami County Prosecutor's Office, Troy, 1975-80; spl. counsel Office Atty. Gen. State of Ohio, Columbus, 1979; ptnr. Miller, Schlemmer & Luring, Troy, 1978; trustee in bankruptcy U.S. Bankruptcy Ct., Dayton, Ohio, 1979—. Pres. Troy Dollars for Scholars, 1976-78; mem. recreation bd. City of Troy, 1976-78, Riverside Sch. Bd., Troy, 1981—. Served to 1st lt., U.S. Army, 1968-71. Mem. Miami County Bar Assn., Ohio Bar Assn., ABA, Assn. Trial Lawyers of Am. Democrat. Methodist. Lodge: Kiwanis (pres. 1984—). Avocation: golf. Home: 1071 Maplecrest Dr Troy OH 45373

LURQUIN, JOHN HENRY, former educator; b. Green Bay, Wis., Mar. 15, 1924; s. Henry J. and Mary Odile (Beno) L.; m. Bernadette Margarite DeGroot, Aug. 7, 1948; children—Judith M., John J., James M., Joseph P., Jean A., Jerome T., Jane L., Jeffery A., Jennifer O., Jay M., Joyce E., Joel H., Jan C. B.S., U. Wis.-Stout, 1950, M.S., 1952; postgrad. Purdue U., 1965; Cert. Advanced Studies, U. Ill., 1971. Tchr. pub. schs., Marty, S.D., 1950-53, Pulaski, Wis., 1953-54; tchr., supr., adminstr., Evergreen Park, Ill., 1954-84; dir. vocat. edn. Evergreen Park (Ill.) High Sch. Dist. 231, 1981-83. Bd. dirs. Sch. Employees Credit Union, 1957-85, pres., 1971-75, chmn. bd., 1975-85. Served with U.S. Army, 1943-46. Decorated Bronze Star. Named Indsl. Educator of Yr., Indsl. Edn. Tchrs. of Northeast Ill. Round. Table 5, 1979; 25 Yr. Indsl. Educator, Ill. Indsl. Edn. Assn., 1981; Ill. Indsl. Arts Educator of Yr., Am. Indsl. Arts Assn., 1983. Mem. Am. Vocat. Assn., NEA, Ill. Indsl. Edn. Assn. (Indsl. Educator of Yr. 1983), Phi Delta Kappa. Roman Catholic. Lodge: K.C. Home: 5019 W 99th St Oak Lawn IL 60453

LURTON, ERNEST LEE, insurance broker; b. Santa Ana, Calif., Nov. 13, 1944; s. Charles Leland and Mary Crystal (McGannon) L.; m. Janet C. Edington, June 17, 1967; children—Matthew, Katherine. B.A., Ind. U., 1967, M.B.A., 1978. C.L.U. Pension cons. Edward B. Morris & Assocs., Inc., Indpls., 1971-74, sr. cons. group ins. and pension plans, 1974-77; pres. Risk Mgmt. Group, Indpls., 1977—, Benefit Concepts of Ind. Inc., Indpls., 1982—. Dir.,

Edward B. Morris & Assocs. Inc. Bd. dirs. Big Bros. Indpls. Served as capt. USAF, 1967-71. Mem. Nat. Assn. Securities Dealers, Nat. Assn. Life Underwriters, Am. Soc. C.L.U.s, Stanley K. Lacey Exec. Leadership Alumni Assn., Ind. U. Coll. Arts and Scis. Alumni Assn. (past pres.), Beta Theta Pi (past pres.). Republican. Mem. Christian Ch. (past chmn. bd. dirs.). Lodges: Masons, Shriners. Home: 7217 Allisonville Rd Indianapolis IN 46250 Office: One N Capitol Ave 8th Floor Indianapolis IN 46204

LUSSIER, ROBERT FRANCIS, federal investigator; b. Washington, Feb. 13, 1953; s. Edward Francis and Jean Joyce (Beahan) L.; m. Martha Katherine O'Malley, June 15, 1974; children—Katherine Marie, Mary Frances. B.A., U. Va., 1975; M.B.A. in Fin., DePaul U., 1983. Benefit authorizer Social Security Adminstrn., Chgo., 1976-79; officer-in-charge Fed. Maritime Commn., Chgo., 1979—. Mem. Fin. Mgmt. Assn. Nat. Honor Soc., Delta Mu Delta, Tau Kappa Epsilon (v.p. 1973-74). Home: 1030 Linden Ave Wilmette IL 60091 Office: Fed Maritime Commn 610 S Canal Suite 1117 Chicago IL 60607

LUSTGRAAF, MARY ANNE, university student union director; b. Great Falls, Mont., July 20, 1954; d. Edward Charles and Gladys Lorraine (Pepos) L. B.A., U. No. Colo., 1972; M.Ed., Mont. State U., 1980. Property appraiser James Laird Assocs., Madison, Wis., 1975-76; field dir. Girl Scouts U.S.A., Great Falls, Mont., 1976-77; student dir. orientation Mont. State U., 1978-80; grad. teaching asst., 1978-80; coordinator activities and orientation Saginaw Valley State Coll., University Center, Mich., 1980-84; dir. Meml. Union, U. N.D.-Grand Forks, 1984—. Mem. Am. Coll. Personnel Assn. (commn. II program chmn. 1983—), Nat. Assn. Women Deans (services and activities program chmn. 1983-84), Assn. Coll. Unions Internat., Nat. Assn. Campus Activities. Avocation: Community gardening organizer. Home: Route 2 Box 30 Fisher MN 56723 Office: Memorial Union Univ ND Grand Forks ND 58202

LUTES, TERRY GLENN, economic and political research analyst; b. Springfield, Ill., Dec. 29, 1948; s. Glenn Hubert and Maxine (Blessman) Lutes; m. Donna Jayne Vaught, Sept. 17, 1977; children—Jamie Lynn, Brian Marcus. B.A., Sangamon State U., 1973, M.A., 1981. Counterintelligence coordinator Def. Intelligence Agy., Bonn, W.Ger., 1968-71; chief fiscal officer Ill. Dept. Agr., Springfield, 1973-77; editor Practical Politics Mag., Springfield, 1977-79; research asst. Sangamon State U., Springfield, 1979-81; econ. and polit. research analyst Ill. Assn. Realtors, Springfield, 1981—. Treas., Walker for Gov., 1972; rural organizer Carter for Pres., 1976. Served with U.S. Army, 1968-71. Mem. Am. Polit. Sci. Assn., Am. Econs. Assn., Issue Mgmt. Assn., Polit. Psychology Assn., Am. Statis. Assn. Home: 2225 Spring St Springfield IL 62704 Office: Ill Assn Realtors 3180 Adloff Ln Springfield IL 62703

LUTH, THOMAS EDWARD, lawyer; b. Celina, Ohio, June 28, 1952; s. Ralph Edward and Eleanora Jean (Stetler) L.; m. Norma G. Weitzel, Feb. 3, 1979; children—Dylan R., Zebulun L. B.A., Wright State U., 1974; J.D., Ohio No. U., 1977. Bar: Ohio 1977. Assoc., Meikle & Tesno, 1977-81; ptnr. Meikle, Tesno & Luth, Celina, 1982—. Trustee Allen County Legal Services, Lima, Ohio, 1980. Mem. Ohio Acad. Trial Lawyers, Ohio State Bar Assn. Lodges: Moose, Fraternal Order of Police. Avocation: music. Office: Meikle Tesno & Luth 100 N Main St Celina OH 45822

LUTHER, DON PRESTON, association executive; b. Flint, Mich., Dec. 8, 1920; s. Clarence Dar and Hazel Rhea (Crandall) L.; student U. Mich., 1952; B.A., Wayne State U., 1976; m. Frances Almeda Denton, June 3, 1943; children—Darleen R. Luther Hatt, Norma O. Luther Acton. Asst. ct. reporter St. Clair County, Port Huron, Mich., 1942; sec. San Diego Employers Assn., 1946-49; exec. sec. The Economic Club Detroit, 1949-64, asst. to pres., 1964-68, exec. dir., 1968—, sr. v.p., 1980—. Co-chmn. Mich. Rendezvous at EXPO 70, 1969-70; pres. Los Buenos Vecinos de Detroit, Spanish good neighbors club, 1958-59; bd. dirs. Lula Belle Stewart Center, 1976—. Served with USNR, 1942-45. Mem. Pub. Relations Soc. Am. (bd. dirs. Detroit chpt. 1983—). Clubs: Circumnavigators (sec.-treas. Mich. chpt. 1980—), Renaissance, Detroit Press. Episcopalian. Home: 48901 Denton Rd #201 Belleville MI 48111 Office: 920 Free Press Bldg Detroit MI 48226

LUTHER, TALMAGE NELSON, rare book and art dealer, consultant; b. Leominster, Mass., May 19, 1927; s. Alfred Nelson and Evelyn Dalton (McAlpine) L.; m. Marilyn Carol Shoemaker, Feb. 20, 1959; 1 dau., Faith Elizabeth. B.A., Yale U., 1950. Personnel supr. Remington Arms Co., Inc., Independence, Mo., 1951-84; owner, operator T.N. Luther Books, Shawnee Mission, Kans., 1962—. Author: Custer High Spots, 1972; editor: Important Firsts in Missouri Imprints, 1967. Founding mem. Kansas City Soc. Western Art, Mo., 1974. Served to sgt. U.S. Army, 1945-46; ETO. Mem. Western History Assn., Kansas State Hist. Soc. (life). Avocations: Southwest Indian artifacts, Western art. Home: 8820 Delmar St Shawnee Mission KS 66207 Office: T N Luther Books Box 6083 Shawnee Mission KS 66207

LUTHIN, RICHARD EMMONS, college dean; b. Hinsdale, Ill., Aug. 8, 1929; s. Emmons F. and Ruth (Roberts) L.; m. Sally Rideout, June 28, 1952; children—Gary, Charles, Mark, Laura, David. B.A., Lawrence Coll., 1951; M.B.A., U. Chgo., 1957. C.P.A., Ill. Acct. Martin, Johnson & Bolton, Chgo., 1958-61; internal auditor Micro Switch div. Honeywell, Freeport, Ill., 1961-63, supr. cost and inventory accountancy, 1963-72; dean bus. services Highland Community Coll., Freeport, 1972—; dir. Union Loan and Savs., Freeport. Bd. dirs., asst. treas. Parkview Home for Aged, Freeport, 1970—; chmn. Stephenson County Planning Commn., 1972—; mem. budget com. Freeport United Way, 1980—; alderman Freeport City Council, 1963-71; dist. chmn. Blackhawk Council Boy Scouts Am., 1976-80; Republican precinct committeeman. Mem. Ill. Assn. Community Coll. Bus. Adminstrs. (treas. 1980-81, chmn. 1981-82), Ill. Assn. Sch. Bus. Officers. Methodist. Lodges: Kiwanis (treas. 1964-68, pres. 1971-72, Kiwanian of Yr. 1984), Elks. Home: 1508 W Empire St Freeport IL 61032 Office: Highland Community Coll Pearl City Rd Freeport IL 61032

LUTON, JOHN ROLAND, computer services company executive; b. Grand Rapids, Mich., Sept. 20, 1948; s. Harry Heatcote and Josephine Elaine (Johnson) L.; m. Aletta Ann Biersack, Oct. 5, 1973 (div. 1977). B.S., U. Mich., 1971. Statistician U. Mich., Ann Arbor, 1971-74; forest officer Office of Forests, Papua, New Guinea, Port Moresby, 1974-79, asst. dir., 1979-81; owner, operator Personalized Computer Services, Rockford, Mich., 1981—. Contbr. articles to profl. jours. Treas. South Kent Mental Health Services, Grand Rapids, 1983—. Mem. Internat. Soc. Tropical Foresters, Commonwealth Forestry Assn., Izaak Walton League (v.p. Grand Rapids 1983-84), Am. Philatelic Soc. Avocations: philately, hunting. Home and Office: 8015 9-Mile Rd Rockford MI 49341

LUTZ, JOHN THOMAS, author; b. Dallas, Sept. 11, 1939; s. John Peter and Esther Jane (Gundelfinger) L.; m. Barbara Jean Bradley, Mar. 15, 1958; children—Steven, Jennifer, Wendy. Student Meramec Community Coll., 1965. Mem. Mystery Writers Am. (Scroll 1981), Pvt. Eye Writers Am. Democrat. Author: The Truth of the Matter, 1971; Buyer Beware, 1976; Bonegrinder, 1977; Lazarus Man, 1979; Jericho Man, 1980; The Shadow Man, 1981; (with Steven Greene) Exiled, 1982; (with Bill Pronzini) The Eye, 1984; Nightlines, 1984; contbr. short stories and articles to mystery and pvt. eye mags. Home and office: 880 Providence Ave Webster Groves MO 63119

LUTZ, ROBERT ANTTHONY, automotive company executive; b. Zurich, Switzerland, Feb. 12, 1932; s. Robert H. and Marguerite (Schmid) L.; m. Heide M. Schmid, Mar. 3, 1980; children—Jacqueline, Carolyn, Catherine, Alexandra. B.Sc., U. Calif.-Berkeley, 1961, M.B.A., 1962. Research assoc. IMEDE, Lausanne, Switzerland, 1962-63; forward planning dept. Gen. Motors, N.Y.C., 1963-65; mgr. vehicle div. Gen. Motors France, Paris, 1966-69; staff asst. Adam Opel, Russelsheim, W.Ger., 1965-66, dir. sales, mgr., mem. Vorstand, 1969-71; v.p. sales Vorstand BMW-AG, Munich, W.Ger., 1971-74; gen. mgr. Ford of Germany, Cologne, 1974-76; v.p. truck ops. Ford of Europe, Warley, Eng., 1976-77, pres., 1977-79, chmn., 1979-82; v.p. Ford Motor Co., Dearborn, Mich., 1976-82, exec. v.p. Ford Internat. ops., 1982—, also dir.; dir. Ford of Europe, Inc., Ford Motor Co., Ltd. (Brit.), Ford Mid-East & Africa, Ind., Ford Asia-Pacific, Inc., Ford Motor Co. Mem. econ. policy council UN Assn. of U.S.; mem. U. Calif.-Berkeley Bus. Sch. Adv. Bd.; mem. European Adv. Council. Served to capt. USMC, 1954-59. Kaiser Found. grantee-in-aid, 1962—. Mem. Atlantic Inst. Internat. Affairs (bd. govs.), Conf. Bd. Office: Ford Motor Co American Rd PO Box 1899 Dearborn MI 48121*

LUUS, GEORGE AARNE, physician; b. Estonia, Apr. 23, 1937; s. Edgar and Aili (Poldmaa) L.; M.D., U. Toronto (Ont., Can.), 1962; m. Margit Jaanusson, Sept. 14, 1962 (div. 1983); children—Caroline Anna Elizabeth, Clyde Gregory Edgar, Lia Esther Isabelle; m. 2d, Donna Gervais Martell, Oct. 1, 1983. Intern Toronto East Gen. and Orthopaedic Hosp.; practice medicine specializing in family medicine, Sault Ste Marie, Ont., 1963—; mem. Algoma Dist. Med. Group, 1966—; sec. med. staff Gen. Hosp., 1972—, v.p., bd. dirs., 1973. Adv. bd. Can. Scholarship Trust Found., 1976-77. Mem. Algoma West Med. Acad., Acad. Medicine Toronto. Lodge: Rotary. Home: 42 Linstedt St Sault Ste Marie ON Canada Office: 240 McNabb St Sault Ste Marie ON P6B 1Y5 Canada

LUZADRE, JOHN HINKLE, obstetrician, gynecologist; b. Logansport, Ind., Dec. 4, 1921; s. John Franklin and Mary Gladys (Hinkle) L.; B.S., U. Pitts., 1942, D.D.S., 1945; M.D., Duke U., 1951; m. Barbara Louise Cary, Sept. 24, 1949; children—John Cary, Jo Ann, Robert Allan, David James, Timothy Hart. Instr., U. Pitts. Sch. Dentistry, 1947; intern Henry Ford Hosp., Detroit, 1951-52, resident in ob-gyn, 1952-55; practice medicine specializing in ob-gyn, Grosse Pointe Farms, Mich., 1955—; mem. staffs St. John Hosp., Detroit, Cottage Hosp., Grosse Pointe Farms. Served as capt. Dental Corps, U.S. Army, 1945-47; ETO. Diplomate Am. Bd. Ob-Gyn. Fellow ACS, Am. Coll. Ob-Gyn; mem. Continental Gynecologic Soc., Alpha Omega Alpha. Republican. Presbyterian. Clubs: Country of Detroit; Hillsboro (Fla.); Tennis House (Grosse Pointe Farms). Home: 1311 Devonshire Rd Grosse Pointe Park MI 48230 Office: 25599 Kelly Rd Roseville MI 48066

LUZIUS, JOSEPH WALTER, JR., pharmacist; b. St. Joseph, Minn., Apr. 17, 1953; s. Joseph Walter and Mary A. (Belgarde) L.; m. Cynthia Rae Weisman, May 14, 1981; children—Thomas, Abraham. A.A., Bemidji U., 1978; B.S. in Pharmacy, U. Minn., 1981. Lic. pharmacist, Minn. Intern, Pilot City Project, Mpls., 1979; mem. Indian Health Bd., Mpls., 1979-80; pharmacy intern VA Hosp., Mpls., 1981-82; pharmacist Walgreen's, Mpls., 1981—; pharmacy student-extern preceptor U. Minn. Coll. Pharmacy, Mpls., 1984—. Mem. Minn. Pharm. Assn., Am. Pharm. Assn., U. Minn. Alumni Assn. Avocations: tennis; fishing; hunting; racquetball; swimming. Office: 1235 E Franklin Ave Minneapolis MN 55404

LYBERG, MATTHEW LOUIS, floor covering co. exec.; b. Howell, Mich., Aug. 3, 1947; s. John King and Phyllis Jane (Long) L.; B.A., Capital U., 1969; postgrad. Evang. Luth. Theol. Sem., 1969, U. Mich., 1970; m. Mary Anne Kennedy, June 17, 1972; children—Elizabeth Jane, Sarah Anne, Basil John, Matthew Peter. Asst., Rickett Sch. for Mentally Handicapped, 1962-64; Head Start tchr. Livingston County Intermediate Sch. Dist., Howell, summers, 1962-71; tchr., dir. phys. edn. St. Joseph Sch., Howell, 1971-72; tchr., Mich. Dept. Corrections, Camp Brighton, Pinckney, 1970-75; tchr. Livingston County (Mich.) Sheriff's Dept., 1972-73; pres. Hamburg Warehouse, Inc., Hamburg, Mich., 1972—; trustee dir. Workskills Corp., Brighton, Mich., 1975—, pres., 1980—; sports announcer Sta. WHMI, 1975—. Mem. fin. and stewardship bd. Zion Luth. Ch., Ann Arbor, Mich., 1979. Mem. Am. Assn. Mental Deficiency, Retail Floor Covering Inst., Jaycees, Fellowship of Christian Athletes. Clubs: Optimist, Kiwanis. Home: 524 W Sibley St Howell MI 48843 Office: 10588 Hamburg Rd Hamburg MI 48139

LYDERSON, BJORN KENNETH, chemist; b. Bklyn., Sept. 19, 1945; s. Bjorn K. and Eleanor L. B.S., Clarkson Coll., 1967; Ph.D., Pa. State U., 1974. Research assoc. U. Colo., Denver, 1974-80; sr. scientist Corning Glass Works, N.Y., 1980-83; mgr. research KC Biol., Lenexa, Kans., 1983—. Contbr. articles to profl. jours. Mem. Tissue Culture Assn., Cell Biology Assn., Am. Chem. Soc. Office: KC Biol PO Box 14848 Lenexa KS 66215

LYDIC, FRANK AYLSWORTH, retired riverman, poet; b. Farnam, Nebr., Jan. 22, 1909; s. Robert Johnston and Lula Ethel (Aylsworth) L.; B.F.A., Kearney (Nebr.) State Coll., 1931; m. Florence Faye Meadows, July 2, 1934 (dec. 1984); children—Marcelle, Bernice Joy (dec.), Robert Norman; m. 2d, Nellie Snyder Yost, Aug. 30, 1984. Tchr. schs., Calif., 1931-56; riverman various vessels Mississippi River, from 1961; now ret.; del. Nat. Maritime Union Conv., 1966, 69, 72, 76, named union poet laureate, nat. conv., 1980. Served in U.S. Mcht. Marine, 1943-48, 56-61. Mem. Western Writers Am. (asso.), Nebr. Writers Guild, Nebr. Poets Assn. (asso.), Ill. State Poetry Soc. (pres. 1983—), Chgo. Poets and Patrons, Little Big Horn Assos. Democrat. Author: Desert Lure, 1971, 3d edit., 1984; Rhymes of a Riverman, 1973; When My Stretch on the River is Done, 1974; Nebraska! Oh Nebraska, 1975; San Francisco Revisited, 1976; At the Little Bighorn, 1976; The Far West's Race with Death, 1979; Rhymed Lines from the River, 1980; Comanche! Oh Comanche!, 1982; Custer Controversies, 1983; In Praise of Texas Jack, 1984. Home: 1505 W D St North Platte NE 69101

LYKOUDIS, PAUL S., nuclear engineering educator; b. Preveza, Greece, Dec. 3, 1926; s. Savvas Paul and Loukia (Miliaressis) L.; came to U.S., 1953, naturalized, 1964; Mech. and Elec. Engring. degree, Nat. Tech. U. Athens (Greece), 1950; M.S. in Mech. Engring., Purdue U., 1954, Ph.D., 1956. Mem. faculty Purdue U., 1956—, prof. aeros., astronautics and engring. scis., 1960-73, prof., head sch. nuclear engring., 1973—, dir. Aerospace Scis. Lab., 1968-73, Vis. prof. aero. engring. Cornell U., 1960-61; cons. RAND Corp., 1960—. NSF grantee, 1960—. Assoc. fellow AIAA (former assoc. editor jour.); mem. Am. Nuclear Soc., Am. Phys. Soc., Am. Astron. Soc., Sigma Xi. Contbr. numerous papers on fluid mechanics, magneto-fluid-mechanics, astrophysics, and fluid mechanics of physiol. systems. Office: Sch Nuclear Engring Purdue U Lafayette IN 47907

LYLE, JAMES CARL, JR., pipe line company executive, accountant; consultant; b. Belleville, Kans., May 17, 1923; s. James Carl and Mary Ann (Lipsey) L.; m. Benicia Isabell Nagle, Dec. 11, 1942; children—Ronald Dean, Marsha Faye, Rolger Kent. B.A. in Acctg., Pittsburg (Kans.) State U., 1950, M.A. in Bus. Edn., 1956. Asst. instr. acctg. Pittsburg State U., 1950-51; mgr. internal audits Nat. Gypsum Co., Parsons, Kans., 1951-56; plant controller Callery Chem. Co., Lawrence, Kans., 1956-60; mgr. system and procedures Panhandle Eastern Pipe Line Co., Kansas City, Mo., 1960-68, mgr. procedures devel., Houston, 1968-79, dir. procedures devel. and word processing, Kansas City, 1979—; cons. office automation office of future. Served with AC, U.S. Army, 1943-46. Republican. Lodges: Masons, Shriners. Home: 9618 Woodson Overland Park KS 66207

LYLE, LEON RICHARDS, immunologist, administrator; b. Ottumwa, Iowa, Nov. 28, 1941; s. Leon Richards and Prudence (Tomlinson) L.; m. Mary Jane Dueber, May 19, 1972; children—Elizabeth Anne, Daniel Carpenter. B.A., Drake U., 1963, M.A., 1965; Ph.D., Mont. State U., 1969; Nat. Inst. Allergy and Infectious Diseases postdoctoral trainee, Washington U. Sch. Medicine, St. Louis, 1970-73. Research chemist Mallinckrodt, Inc., St. Louis, 1973-75, group leader, 1975-80, mgr. hybridoma sect., 1980-84, asst. dir. in vitro assay research and devel., 1984—; indsl. rep. immunology devices panel FDA, Silver Spring, Md., 1981—. Author jour. articles; invited speaker. Recipient pres.'s award for tech. innovation Mallinckrodt, 1981. Mem. Clin. Ligand Assay Soc. (bd. St. Louis chpt. 1984—), Am. Soc. Microbiology, N.Y. Acad. Scis. Home: 1319 Webster Path Dr Webster Groves MO 63119 Office: Mallinckrodt Inc 675 McDonnell Blvd PO Box 5840 Saint Louis MO 63134

LYNAM, DAVID JOHN, lawyer; b. Fort Bragg, N.C., Sept. 23, 1951; s. Thomas Joseph and Carole Ann (Dascola) L. B.A., Loyola U., Chgo., 1973; Attended Hague Acad. Internat. Law, The Netherlands, 1977; J.D., Loyola U., Chgo., 1978. Bar: Ill. 1978, U.S. Tax Ct. 1978, U.S. Dist. Ct. (no. dist.) Ill. 1978. Assoc. Robert A. Michalak Assocs., Chgo., 1978—. Author: (with others) The Practical Guide to Ill. Preservation Law, 1984. Mem. Chgo. Bar Assn. (dir. Legal Clinic for Disabled, co-chmn. Young Lawyers Sect. architecture and law com.). Democrat. Club: Chgo. Civil War Roundtable. Home: 2012 N Cleveland St Chicago IL 60614 Office: Robert A Michalak Assocs 312 W Randolph St Suite 200 Chicago IL 60606

LYNAM, JACK, manufacturing company executive, mechanical engineer; b. Cleve., Apr. 19, 1923; s. Thomas J. and Beatrice E. (Harvey) L.; m. Dorothy E. Correll, Apr. 19, 1951; children—Patricia, Carol, Colleen, Gale, Lee. B.S., U.S. Merchant Marine, 1944. Dist. mgr. Powers Regulator Co., Pitts., 1951-68; owner, pres. Advanced Tech. Sales Inc., Cleve., 1968—, Admiral Valve Inc., Cleve., 1972—; cons. C.E., U.S. Army, Saudia Arabia, 1980, 82. Served to lt. (s.g.) USN, 1942-46, ETO and PTO. Mem. Instrument Soc. Am. (sr.), Cleve. Engring. Soc., ASHRAE, Am. Soc. Iron and Steel Engrs. Club: Edgewater Yacht. Lodges: Rotary, Order of Alhambra. Home: 4025 Meadow Gateway Broadview Heights OH 44147 Office: Advanced Tech Sales Inc 3819 Ridge Rd Cleveland OH 44144

LYNCH, BRENDA CLARK, lawyer; b. Toledo, June 10, 1954; d. Robert Ellwood and Rosalyn Jean (Meyer) Clark; m. John E. Lynch, Jr., Nov. 16, 1984. B.Ed., U. Toledo, 1975, J.D., 1978; grad. Nat. Inst. Trial Advocacy, 1983. Bar: Ohio 1978, U.S. Dist. Ct. (no. dist.) Ohio 1978, U.S. Ct. Appeals (6th cir.) 1982. Summer clk. Advs. for Basic Legal Equality, Toledo, 1976; summer assoc. Shumaker, Loop & Kendrick, Toledo, 1977; assoc. Squire, Sanders & Dempsey, Cleve., 1978-84; assoc. Porter, Wright, Morris & Arthur, Cleve., 1984—. Note and comment editor U. Toledo Law Rev., 1977-78. Mem. Ohio State Bar Assn., Greater Cleve. Bar Assn., Greater Cleve. Growth Assn. Democrat. Office: Porter Wright Morris & Arthur 1500 Huntington Bldg Cleveland OH 44115

LYNCH, RAY JOSEPH, gas pipeline company executive; b. Chgo., Oct. 10, 1922; s. Rollin John and Eva (Schoeller) L.; B.S. in Commerce, U. Ill., 1948; C.P.A.; m. Leila Mariotti, June 11, 1949; children—Dawn, Mary Joy, Tim, Cheryl, Jane, Martha, Christopher, John, Robert. With Arthur Andersen & Co., C.P.A.'s, Chgo., 1948-53, Mich. Wis. Pipe Line Co., Detroit, 1953—, treas. 1960—, v.p., 1962—, exec. v.p., 1969-73, pres., 1973-82, chmn., 1982—; dir. parent co. Am. Natural Resources Co. and affiliates, Mich. Nat. Bank Detroit. Bd. dirs. Boysville of Mich., Children's Hosp. of Mich., Bon Secours Hosp. Served as pilot USAAF, World War II. Mem. Am. Gas Assn. (dir.), Interstate Natural Gas Assn., Gas Research Inst., Midwest Gas Assn. Home: 529 Ballantyne Rd Grosse Pointe Shores MI 48236 Office: 1 Woodward Ave Detroit MI 48226

LYNCH, SHERRY KAY, community program consultant; b. Topeka, Kans., Nov. 20, 1957; d. Robert Emmett and Norma Lea Lynch. B.A., Randolph-Macon Woman's Coll., 1979; M.S., Emporia State U., 1980; postgrad. Kans. State U., 1983—. Vocat. rehab. counselor Rehab. Services, Topeka, 1980-81, community program cons., 1981—. Mem. exec. com. Sexual Assault Counseling Program, Topeka, 1983—, recruitment coordinator, 1983—, counselor, 1981—; area admissions rep. Randolph-Macon Woman's Coll., Lynchburg, Va., 1981—. Recipient Kans. 4-H Key award Extension Service of Kans. State U., 1974; named Internat. 4-H Youth Exchange Ambassador to France, 1977. Mem. Nat. Rehab. Counseling Assn. (bd. dirs. 1982—, chairperson br. devel. subcouncil 1982—), Gt. Plains Rehab. Counseling Assn. (newsletter editor 1982-85, bd. dirs. 1983—, pres. 1984-85, sec. 1986—), Gt. Plains Rehab. Assn. (bd. dirs. 1983-85, awards chairperson 1984-85), Kans. Rehab. Counseling Assn. (bd. dirs. 1983—, pres. 1984-85), Kans. Rehab. Assn. (bd. dirs. 1982-85, advt. chairperson 1983-85), Topeka Rehab. Assn. (bd. dirs. 1982-85, sec. 1982-83, pres. 1983-84), Am. Assn. Counseling and Devel., Am. Coll. Personnel Assn., Am. Rehab. Counseling Assn. Republican. Methodist. Avocation: tennis. Home: 3443 SW Burlingame 303A Topeka KS 66611 Office: Rehab Services 2700 W 6th St 2d Floor Biddle Bldg Topeka KS 66606

LYNCH, TWINK, theatre association executive, consultant, trainer; b. Washington, May 8, 1934; d. Austin Francis Sr. and Gertrude Rita (MacBride) Canfield; m. John Anthony Lynch, Nov. 26, 1960; children—Mark Andrew, Christopher Michael, Nancy Maureen, Gregory Patrick. B.A. in Drama, Catholic U. Am., 1955, M.A. in Speech Therapy, 1961; M.A. in Theatre, U. Kans., 1971, Ph.D. in Community Theatre, 1981. Box office asst. Olney Theatre, Md., 1956, box office mgr., 1957; clk., typist United Clay Products, Washington, 1957-58; speech therapist pub. schs., Prince George County, Md., 1959-61; instr. theatre Washburn U., Topeka, 1968, pub. speaking, 1974; instr. Pa. State U. Ind. Study, University Park, 1978—; exec. dir. Assn. Kans. Theatre, Topeka, 1979—; dir. Topeka Civic Theatre, 1971-77, 83—, Kans. Citizens for Arts, Topeka, 1985—. Workshop leader numerous state, regional, nat. theatre orgns., 1977—; cons., trainer various community theatres, 1979—. Author: (correspondence course text) Volunteer and Staff Development in Community Theatre, 1981. Editor correspondence courses Pa. State U., 1978—. Officer, Whitson Sch. PTA, Topeka, 1968-69; dir. Performing Arts for Children, Topeka, 1971-73, Goals for Topeka, 1972-74, Kans. Alliance Arts Edn., Topeka, 1979-83, YWCA, Topeka, 1982-83. Recipient Topeka Civic Theatre Renna Hunter award, 1968, 70; named Outstanding Community Vol., Topeka Jr. League, 1973. Mem. Am. Community Theatre Assn. (pres. 1984—), Am. Theatre Assn. (bd. dirs. 1984—, Disting. Woman award 1977), Nat. Assn. Local Arts Agys. (keynoter 1985), Assn. Coll., Univ. and Community Arts Adminstrs., Theatre Trustees Am., Assn. Vol. Adminstrs. (vol.), Assn. Vol. Action Scholars. Avocations: travel; musical events.

LYNN, MICHAEL EDWARD, III, professional football team executive; b. Scranton, Pa., May 18, 1936; s. Robert Norman and Gertrude (Smith) L.; student Pace U.; m. Jorja Swaney, July 12, 1967; children—Louisa, Robert, Michael Edward, Lucia. Mgr., Dixiemar-Corondolet, Inc., Memphis, 1965-67; pres. Mid South Sports, Inc., Memphis, 1967-74; v.p., gen. mgr. Minn. Vikings, 1974—; founder East-West All Am. Basketball Game, 1968, Mid South Prodn. Co., 1970; chief exec. officer Memphis Am. Basketball Team, 1970. Founder Morris County Theatre League and Highstown Little Theatre Group, 1961. Served with U.S. Army, 1955-58. Roman Catholic. Office: Minnesota Vikings 9520 Viking Dr Eden Prairie MN 55344*

LYNN, PATRICIA ANN, manufacturing company executive; b. Eau Claire, Wis., Dec. 11, 1939; d. Edward A. and Catherine J. (Jones) O'Connor; m. Jack A. Lynn, Aug. 31, 1963; children—Michael E., Cynthia C. Cert. bus. law, Upper Wabash Vocat. Coll., 1973, cert. acctg., 1974. Sec., Ind. Glass Products, Wabash, 1960-61; bookkeeper/receptionist Graycon Tools, Wabash, 1961-62, corp. sec., 1963-77, pres., 1978-81; v.p. Graycon div. Diehl Machines, Wabash, 1982—. Mem. Wabash Planning Commn., 1983—; Democrat precinct committeeperson, 1980—; mem. Wabash Community Service Orgn., 1983—; chair North Central Pvt. Industry Council, 1984. Mem. Wabash County Mgmt. Club (pres. 1982), Wabash C. of C. (treas. 1981), Am. Legion Aux. Democrat. Roman Catholic. Avocations: camping; gardening; reading. Home: 141 E Sheridan Dr Wabash IN 46992 Office: 981 S Wabash St Wabash IN 46992

LYNN, ROBERT WILLIAM, gas and electric utility company official; b. N.Y.C., Jan. 27, 1943; s. William Ernest and Jeannette (Reardon) L.; m. Sara E. Davis, Aug. 26, 1961 (dec. Nov. 1980) children—Robert, John, William, David, Michelle; Linda L. Marckese, Nov. 14, 1982. A.A.S. in Supervision, Purdue U., 1974, B.S. in Indsl. Engring., 1976. Engr. No. Ind. Pub. Service Co., Crown Point, 1968-77, engring. supr., Gary, 1977-79, sr. cons., Hammond, 1979-82, mgr., 1982—; lectr., advisor Purdue U.-Hammond, 1979, tech. advisor, 1980-84. Served with USN, 1960-67. Mem. Am. Inst. Indsl. Engrs. (sr. mem.; sr. project award 1976). Avocations: pen and ink on glass, sailing. Home: 443 Scarborough Rd Valparaiso IN 46383 Office: NIPSCO Mgmt System Control Dept 5265 Hohman Ave Hammond IN 46320

LYON, BRUCE WILLIAM, real estate agent; b. Huron, S.D., Nov. 18, 1947; s. William Robert and Alice Lee (Zeeck) L.; m. Darla Lynn Anderson, Oct. 10, 1970; children—Matthew Jon, William Robert. Student U. S.D., 1966-69, S.D. Sch. Mines & Tech., 1972, Black Hills State Coll., 1977. Insp., U.S. Dept. Agriculture, Rapid City, S.D., 1972-77; real estate agent Lewis & Kirkeby R.E., Rapid City, 1977—. Pres. Ducks Unlimited, Rapid City, 1981-83. Served with U.S. Army, 1970. Mem. Nat. Assn. Realtors, Black Hills Bd. Realtors (pres. 1984—), S.D. Assn. Realtors (dir. 1982—). Republican. Lutheran. Avocations: Hunting; fishing; skiing. Office: PO Box 9129 728 Jackson Blvd Rapid City SD 57709

LYON, JAMES ROBERT, utilities company executive; b. Otterville, Mo., Nov. 30, 1927; s. William H. and Laura Virginia (Eubank) L.; student Mo. Valley Coll., 1945-46; B.S.E.E., U. Mo., 1951; m. Janet Drescher, Sept. 1, 1951; children—Sally Beth, Suzanne. Engr., Bonneville Power Adminstrn., Portland, Oreg., 1951-53; with Iowa Power & Light Co., Des Moines, 1953—, v.p. ops., 1966-71, sr. v.p., 1971-73, exec. v.p., 1973-79, pres., 1979—; dir. United Central Bank. Pres. United Way, 1978-79; dir. Mercy Hosp., Des Moines; dir. Des Moines Area Community Coll. Found. Served with U.S. Army, 1945-47. Office: Iowa Power & Light Co 666 Grand Ave Des Moines IA 50303*

LYONS, DAYMON EUGENE, purchasing manager; b. Jacksonville, Ill., Nov. 5, 1948; s. Kenneth H. and Evelyn C. (Breeze) L.; m. Karen Jean Piascyk, Feb. 12, 1977; children—Stephanie Jean, Christopher Kenneth. A.A., Lincoln Land Community Coll., 1973; B.A., Sangamon State U., 1982, postgrad., 1984. Prodn. acct. Hobbs div. Stewart Warner Corp., Springfield, Ill., 1973-74, prodn. and inventory control analyst, 1974-80; buyer Dickey-John Corp., Auburn, Ill., 1980-82, supr. prodn. and inventory control, 1982-84; mgr.

procurement Hobbs div. Stewart Warner, Springfield, 1984—. Served with USAF, 1967-71. Mem. Am. Prodn. and Inventory Control Soc., Am. Legion. Democrat. Methodist. Club: Hobbs Management (Springfield). Lodge: K.P. Avocations: reading; trapshooting; hunting; cattle raising. Home: 450 S Grove St Waverly IL 62692 Office: Hobbs Div Stewart Warner Ash St and Yale Blvd Springfield IL 62703

LYONS, J. ROLLAND, civil engr.; b. Cedar Rapids, Iowa, Apr. 27, 1909; s. Neen T. and Goldie N. (Hill) L.; B.S., U. Iowa, 1933; m. Mary Jane Doht, June 10, 1924; children—Marlene Lyons Sparks, Sharon Lyons Hutson, Lynn Lyons Panichi. Jr. hwy. engr. Works Projects Adminstrn. field engr. Dept. Transp., State Ill., Peoria, 1930-31, civil engr. I-IV Central Office, Springfield, 1934-53, civil engr. V, 1953-66, municipal sect. chief, civil engr. VI, 1966-72. Civil Def. radio officer Springfield and Sangamon County (Ill.) Civil Def. Agy., 1952—. Recipient Meritorious Service award, Am. Assn. State Hwy. Ofcls., 1968; 25 Yr. Career Service award, State Ill., 1966; Certificate Appreciation, Ill. Municipal League, 1971. Registered profl. engr., Ill.; registered land surveyor, Ill. Mem. Ill. Assn. State Hwy. Engrs., State Ill. Employees Assn., Am. Pub. Works Assn., Am. Assn. State Hwy. Ofcls., Amateur Trapshooters Assn. Clubs: K.C., Sangamon Valley Radio; Lakewood Golf and Country. Address: 3642 Lancaster Rd Springfield IL 62703

LYONS, THOMAS FRANCIS, management educator; b. Detroit, Oct. 5, 1937; s. Edward Coleburke and Nell (Hamilton) L.; m. Ann Liu, June 22, 1963; children—Kathleen Liu, William Francis. B.B.A., U. Mich., 1959, M.B.A., 1960, M.A., 1964, Ph.D., 1967. Lic. psychologist, Ohio. Asst. prof. Iowa State U., Ames, 1967-70; research assoc. U. Mich. Sch. Medicine, Ann Arbor, 1970-72; asst. prof. Case Western Res. U., Cleve., 1972-74; sr. research assoc. Med. Sch., U. Mich., Ann Arbor, 1974-78; assoc. prof., chmn. dept. mgmt./mktg. Sch. Mgmt., U. Mich.-Dearborn, 1978-84, prof., chmn. dept. mgmt./mktg., 1984—. Served with U.S. Army, 1960-62. Mem. Am. Psychol. Assn. (James McKeen Cattell award 1968), Acad. of Mgmt., Am. Soc. Tng. and Devel., Sigma Xi. Roman Catholic. Author: Nursing Attitudes and Turnover, 1968; co-author: Method of Evaluation and Improving Ambulatory Medical Care, 1980; co-author: Evaluation and Improving Personal Medical Care Quality, 1976; contbr. articles to profl. jours. Home: 2155 Blaney St Ann Arbor MI 48103 Office: U Mich 4901 Evergreen St Dearborn MI 48128

LYPECKYJ, CHRISTINA ROMANA, mezzo-soprano; b. Stanyslaviv, Ukraine, Feb. 20; d. Roman and Anna (Skochdopol) Semaniuk; naturalized U.S. citizen; student Boris Goldovsky's opera workshop Oglebay Inst.; pupil of Aurelia Peralta, Marilyn Cotlow, Avery Crew, opera coaches Walter Tausig, Josef Blatt; m. Lubomyr Alexander Lypeckyj, July 9; children—Alexander Ihor, Natalia Christina. Operatic debut Mich. Opera Theatre, 1972, symphony orch. debut Warren Symphony Orch., 1977; numerous concert performances, recitals, U.S., Can., Italy; major opera roles include: Amneris in Verdi's Aida, Azucena in Verdi's Rigoletto, Charlotta in Massenet's Werther, Dorabella in Mozart's Cosi Fan Tutte, title role in Bizet's Carmen; recording for Symfonia Co., H&L Record Co. Recipient award Met. Opera Nat. Council, 1971. Mem. Met. Opera Guild. Greek Catholic. Home: 11219 Irene Dr Warren MI 48093 Office: PO Box 525 Warren MI 48090

LYTHCOTT, STEPHEN XAVIER, administrative law judge; b. Boston, Aug. 2, 1950; s. George Ignatius and Ruth Louise (Andrade) L. B.A., Antioch Coll., Yellow Springs, Ohio, 1973; J.D., U. Wis., 1978. Bar: Wis. 1978, Ill. 1978, U.S. Dist. Ct. (no. dist.) Ill. 1978. Personnel specialist Fed. Govt., Washington, 1973-75; intern So. Regional Council, Atlanta, 1976; legal research asst. Wis. Legis. Council, Madison, 1976-78; staff atty. Legal Assistance Found. Chgo., 1978-82; adminstrv. law judge Ill. Human Rights Commn., Chgo., 1982—. Del., Nat. Black Polit. Conv., Gary, Ind., 1972. Recipient Minority Alumni of Yr. award U. Wis. Law Sch., Madison, 1983; fellow Joint Ctr. Polit. Studies, Washington, 1971. Mem. Ill. Jud. Council, Am. Judicature Soc., ABA, Chgo. Bar Assn., Cook County Bar Assn. Democrat. Home: 933 W Cornelia Ave Chicago IL 60657 Office: Illinois Human Rights Commission 32 W Randolph St Suite 209 Chicago IL

LYTLE, FRED EDWARD, chemistry educator, researcher, consultant; b. Lewisburg, Pa., Jan. 13, 1943; s. Peter E. and Ethel B. (Strouse) L.; m. Marsha Jones, July 1, 1967; children—Bradley J., Megan J. B.S., Juniata Coll., 1964; Ph.D., MIT, 1968. Asst. prof. chemistry Purdue U., West Lafayette, Ind., 1968-74, assoc. prof., 1974-79, prof., 1979—; cons. govtl. and indsl. facilities; guest lectr. colls., univs., govtl. and indsl. facilities. Patentee; contbr. articles to profl. jours. Recipient Merck Co. Found. Faculty Devel. award, 1970-71; Sigma Xi grantee, 1970; Best Tchr. Sch. of Sci. award Purdue U., 1979. Mem. Am. Chem. Soc., Soc. Applied Spectroscopy, Phi Lambda Upsilon. Office: Purdue U Dept Chemistry West Lafayette IN 47907

LYTLE, JAMES MARK, manufacturing company executive, educational consultant; b. Pitts., Sept. 16, 1939; s. William Allen and Mary Elizabeth (Leahey) L.; m. Katherine Martha Rausch, Apr. 19, 1965; children—Mark, David, Susan. B.S.E.E., N.Y. Inst. Tech., 1972. Tech. writer Bendix Corp., Lanham Md., 1967-70; chief engr. McGraw Hill, Washington, 1970-79; product line mgr. Heath Co., Benton Harbor, Mich., 1979—; free lance cons. 1967—. Author numerous self-study books on electronics and computer related subjects. Served with USN, 1958-67. Avocation: computers. Home: 5780 Echo Ridge Stevensville MI 49127 Office: Heath Co Hilltop Rd St Joseph MI 49085

LYTTLE, RICHARD GIBSON, educator; b. Laramie, Wyo., Dec. 22, 1924; s. Richard G. and Jessie M. (Gillis) L.; m. Mary Beth Latson, June 18, 1950; 1 son, William George. B.A., U. Colo., 1949; M.S., Bemidji State U., 1971; postgrad. U. Alaska, 1962-67, Bemidji State U., 1973-74. Instr. history Northland Community Coll., Thief River Falls, Minn., 1967-85, chmn., 1972-75. Pres. Bd. Rio Blanco Dist. 1, Meeker, Colo., 1952-54; chmn. Sch. Dist. Reorgn., Rio Blanco County, Colo., 1957; city councilman Meeker City Council, Colo., 1952-57. Mem. Nat. Jr. Coll. Publ. Advisors, County Hist. Soc. Lodges: Masons (master 1973), Shriners. Home: 1304 N Arnold St Thief River Falls MN 56701 Office: Northland Community Coll Hwy 1 East Thief River Falls MN 56701

MAASBERG, ALBERT THOMAS, retired chemical company executive, consultant; b. Bronx, N.Y., Feb. 10, 1915; s. Albert Paul and Lillian Genevieve (Harlach) M.; m. Margaret Celeste Haley, May 31, 1941; children—Thomas Albert, Michael William. B.S. magna cum laude, Syracuse U., 1936. Tech. dir. plastics prodn. dept. Dow Chem. Co., Midland, Mich., 1954-56, dir. research and devel., 1956-63, dir. contract research, devel. and engring., 1963-79, cons., 1979-81; cons. NSF, Carnegie Mellon U., Pitts., 1975-77. Patentee (7) in cellulose ethers. Contbg. author: Cellulose and Cellulose Derivatives, 1955. Contbr. articles to profl. jours. Pres. Paul Bunyan council Boy Scouts Am., Midland, 1965-68; bd. dirs. United Community Fund Midland County, 1968-74; v.p., exec. bd. Lake Huron Area council Boy Scouts Am., Auburn, Mich., 1974—. Served with AUS, 1942-45. Decorated Army Commendation medal; recipient Trailblazer award Boy Scouts Am., 1963, Silver Beaver award, 1966. Fellow Am. Inst. Chem. Engrs.; mem. Am. Chem. Soc. (emeritus). Republican. Roman Catholic. Club: Midland Country. Lodge: Rotary. Avocations: golf; bowling; hunting; fishing; travel. Address: 3220 Noeske St Midland MI 48640

MAASS, VERA SONJA, psychologist; b. Berlin, Germany, July 6, 1931; d. Willy Ernst and Walli Elisabeth (Reinke) Keck; came to U.S., 1958, naturalized, 1970; B.A., Monmouth Coll., 1971; M.A., Lehigh U., 1974; Ph.D., U. Mo., 1978; m. Joachim A. Maass, Dec. 24, 1954. Teaching asst. Lehigh U., Bethlehem, Pa., 1971-72; tutor in adult basic edn. Teaching Assistance Orgn., Kansas City, Mo., 1973-74; grad. research asst. U. Mo., Kansas City, 1974-76; intern U. Ky. Med. Sch., Lexington, 1975-76; psychologist-therapist Dunn Mental Health Center, Richmond, Ind., 1976-80, psychologist; br. dir., Winchester, Ind., 1980—; developer, conductor workshops in rational behavior therapy, Lexington, 1975-76, Richmond, 1976-77; v.p. Vitatronics, Inc., Wall, N.J., 1969—; pres. Living Skills Inst., Inc., Indpls., 1982—. Recipient Cert. of Appreciation, Ky. Coll. Medicine, 1978; cert. sex counselor. Mem. Am. Personnel and Guidance Assn., Nat. Council Family Relations, Internat. Assn. Applied Psychology, Am. Psychol. Assn., Internat. Platform Assn., Psi Chi. Contbr. articles to profl. jours. Office: 6221 N Keystone Ave Suite 6 Indianapolis IN 46220

MAATSCH, JACK LOU, medical education research and development administrator, psychologist; b. Lansing, Mich., Aug. 26, 1925; s. Thurlow Henry and Margaret Tanner (Buehler) M.; m. Patricia Ann Gardner, Jan. 26, 1946 (div. 1971); m. Rosemarie Patricia Phelan, Oct. 27, 1971; children—Martha, Stephen, Tracy, Johnathan. B.A., Mich. State U., 1950, M.A., 1951, Ph.D., 1955. Project leader Inst. Def. Analysis, Arlington, Va., 1962-67, v.p., mgr. eastern ops. div., 1968-70; pres., chmn. bd. Serendipity, Inc., Sherman Oaks, Calif., 1970-71; prof. Office Med. Edn. Research and Devel., Coll. Human Medicine, Mich. State U., East Lansing, 1971—, also dir.; cons. Am. Bd. Emergency Medicine, East Lansing, 1976—. Contbr. chpts. in books and sci. articles to profl. jours. Served with USAF, 1943-45, PTO. Mem. Am. Assn. Med. Colls., Am. Psychol. Assn. Avocation: sailing. Home: 4790 Skyline Dr Perrinton MI 48871 Office: Med Edn Research Devel A-217 East Fee Hall East Lansing MI 48824

MABRY, BEVARS DUPRE, economics educator, educational administrator, consultant, researcher; b. Atlanta, July 7, 1928; s. Jerry Leon Mabry and Kathryn Elizabeth (Reed) Mabry Bright; m. Mary Jeanne Connelly, June 10, 1961; children—Michael D., Maria Anne. B.B.A., U. Tenn.-Chattanooga, 1950; M.S., U. Tenn.-Knoxville, 1954; Ph.D, Tulane U., 1959. Adminstrv. clerk TVA, Chattanooga and Knoxville, Tenn., 1950-54; researcher U. Tenn., Knoxville, 1954; asst. prof. econs. U. Idaho, Moscow, 1957-59; prof., chair dept. econs. Bowling Green State U., Ohio, 1959—, coordinator indsl. relations program Coll. of Bus., 1979—. Author: Labor Relations and Collective Bargaining, 1966; Economics of Manpower and Labor Market, 1973; The Development of the Labor Sector, 1979; also articles. Advisor on budget Wood County Health Dept., Bowling Green, 1977. Served with U.S. Army, 1946-47. Grantee Rockfeller Found., 1967-68, 1971-73, 76, NSF, 1979, Bowling Green State U. 1983. Mem. Midwest Econ. Assn., Indsl. Relations Research Assn., Thai Mgmt. Assn., Assn. Cultural Econs., So. Econ. Assn., Assn. Social Econs., Phi Kappa Phi, Beta Gamma Sigma. Democrat. Roman Catholic. Avocations: chess, bridge, horse raising (english hunters). Home: 1001 Napoleon Rd Bowling Green OH 43402 Office: Dept of Econs Coll of Bus Bowling Green State U Bowling Green OH 43403

MACADAMS, RICHARD JOSEPH, consulting and industrial process engineer; b. N.Y.C., Mar. 27, 1925; s. Robert John and Josephine Theresa (Ziegler) MacA.; m. Gerry M. Mitchell, Oct. 23, 1948; children—Monica MacAdams Smith, Michael R., Melanie R. B.S. in Mech. Engring., Lehigh U., 1946. Profl. engr., Ohio, Mich., Pa., N.Y., Okla., Fla. Plant engr. Pure Oil Co., Toledo, 1946-60; research and devel. tech. supr. Allied Chem. Plastics Div., Tonawanda, N.Y., 1960-62, project mgr., Toledo, 1962-65; div. mgr. SSOE, Inc., Toledo, 1965—, v.p., 1973—; sec. Tech. Found. Toledo, 1984—. Chmn. Bedford Twp. Plan Commn., Mich., 1978—; mem. Bedford Twp. Republican Club, 1960—. Mem. Nat. Soc. Profl. Engrs. (sec. Toledo 1968-70), Am. Inst. Chem. Engrs., Tech. Soc. Toledo (pres. 1980-81), Engr.-of-Yr. award 1985), Toledo C. of C. Republican. Roman Catholic. Club: Rotary. Home: 7066 Edinburgh Dr Lambertville MI 48144 Office: SSOE Inc 1001 Madison Ave Toledo OH 43624

MACCABEE, PAULA GOODMAN, lawyer; b. Mpls., Feb. 10, 1957; d. Ernest and Malka (Lotterstein) Goodman; m. Paul Fishman Maccabee, June 22, 1980; 1 child, Leora. Student Macalester Coll., 1973-75; B.A. summa cum laude, Amherst Coll., 1977; J.D., Yale U., 1981. Bar: Minn. 1981, U.S. Dist. Ct. (fed. dist.) 1981. Congl. intern Sen. Walter Mondale, Washington, 1976; fiscal policy aide Mayor George Latimer, St. Paul, 1977; law clk., lobbyist Dayton, Herman et al., Mpls., 1979-80; atty. litigation Robins, Zelle et al, St. Paul, 1981-83; sole practice Maccabee Law Offices, Mpls., 1983—; vol. atty. Chrysalis Women's Ctr., Mpls., 1983—; trademark cons. Greenpeace, San Francisco, 1979; legis. cons. Natural Resources Def. Council, Washington, 1978-79. Community organizer Clamshell Alliance, New Haven, 1978-79; writer, cons. DFL Feminist Caucus, St. Paul, 1981; treas. bd. Harriet Tubman Women's Shelter, Mpls., 1981-83; del. Democratic Farm Labor Party, Mpls, 1982, 84. John Simpson fellow, Densmore Berry Collins award Amherst Coll., 1977; Nat. Merit Scholar Nat. Merit Found., 1974. Mem. Minn. Women Lawyers, Minn. Trial Lawyers Assn., Assn. Trial Lawyers Am., Minn. Bar Assn., ABA, Phi Beta Kappa. Democrat. Jewish. Home: 2304 30th Ave Minneapolis MN 55406 Office: 525 Lumber Exchange Bldg Minneapolis MN 55402

MACCANN, RICHARD DYER, film study educator; b. Wichita, Kans., Aug. 20, 1920; s. Horace Shores and Marion (Dyer) MacC.; m. Donnarae Charlotte Thompson, Oct. 12, 1957. A.B., U. Kans., 1940; M.A., Stanford U., 1942; Ph.D. in Polit. Sci., Harvard U., 1951. Staff corr. The Christian Sci. Monitor, Los Angeles, 1951-57; asst. prof. cinema U. So. Calif., 1957-62; screenwriter MGM-TV and John Houseman Prodns., Los Angeles, 1963-64; producer Subscription TV, Inc., Santa Monica, Calif., 1964; TV producer Los Angeles County Schs., 1964-65; assoc. prof. speech and journalism U. Kans., 1965-69, prof., 1969-70; vis. prof. fine arts and visual studies Harvard U., summer 1967; prof. broadcasting and film dept. communication and theater arts U. Iowa, 1970—; adviser Nat. Film Prodn. Ctr., Republic of Korea, 1963; mem. steering com., lectr. Aspen Film Conf., 1963, 64; weekly broadcaster film criticism KANU-FM, U. Kans., 1966-68; writer-producer-host The Quiet Channel, U. Iowa Cable Channel 28, Iowa City, 1983, American Silent Film, 1984. Served with AUS 1942-45. NEH sr. fellow, 1973; co-adminstr. Rockefeller Found. grantee, 1973-76; Jerome Found. grantee, 1977. Mem. Com. Constl. System, Univ. Film and Video Assn., Soc. Cinema Studies, Authors Guild, Writers Guild Am., Phi Beta Kappa. Democrat. Christian Scientist. Author: Hollywood in Transition, 1962; Film and Society, 1964; Film: A Montage of Theories, 1966; The People's Films, 1973; The New Film Index, 1975; Cinema Examined, 1982. Editor: Cinema Jour., 1967-76; (play) Senator-at-Large, 1981; producer: Degas: Master of Motion, 1960; Murder at Best, 1981; contbr. articles to profl. jours.; contbr. poetry to Harpers Mag., Saturday Rev., Christian Science Monitor. Home: 717 Normandy Dr Iowa City IA 52240 Office: Broadcasting and Film U Iowa Iowa City IA 52242

MACCECCHINI, MARIA-LUISA, molecular biologist, research scientist; b. Bern, Switzerland, Jan. 15, 1951; came to U.S., 1980; d. Paola and Alfreda Maccecchini. Ph.D. in Biochemistry, U. Basel, 1978; vis. student Rockefeller U., 1977-78. Postdoctoral fellow Basel (Switzerland) Inst. Immunology, 1978-79, Calif. Inst. Tech., Pasadena, 1980—; group leader molecular biology IMC Corp., Northbrook, Ill., 1982—; asst. prof. molecular biology Ind. State U. Chmn. community research and study groups Leadership Terre Haute, 1983; bd. dirs. Youth Ctr., Ryves Hall, Terre Haute, 1982. Mem. AAAS, Am. Soc. Microbiology, Genetics Soc. Am., Sigma Xi (exec. bd.). Contbr. articles in biochemistry and genetics to sci. jours. Home: 3710 Salem Walk S Northbrook IL 60062 Office: IMC Corp R&D 1810 Frontage Rd Northbrook IL 60062

MACCOY, DOUGLAS MAIDLOW, veterinary surgeon; b. Washington, Aug. 15, 1947; s. Edgar Milton and Charlotte (Maidlow) MacC. B.S. in Animal Scis., Purdue U., 1969; D.V.M. magna cum laude, U. Ga., 1973. Diplomate Am. Coll. Vet. Surgeons. Intern, N.Y. State Coll. Vet. Medicine, Cornell U., Ithaca, N.Y., 1973-74, surg. resident, 1974-76, asst. prof. surgery, 1976-82; dir. avian rehab. project Coll. Vet. Medicine, U. Ill., Urbana, 1982—, asst. prof. surgery, 1982—. Mem. AVMA, Am. Animal Hosp. Assn., Assn. Avian Veterinarians, Vet. Cancer Soc., Am. Assn. Vet. Med. Records Adminstrn., Am. Assn. Vet Clinicians, Am. Motorcyclist Assn., Nat. Riflemans Assn., Raptor Research Found., Sigma Xi, Omega Tau Sigma, Phi Zeta. Home and Office: 1008 W Hazelwood Dr Urbana IL 61801

MACDONALD, EDMUND BACON, canning company executive; b. San Francisco, July 25, 1915; s. Graeme and Maria (Moore) MacD.; m. Virginia Vandever, Jan. 7, 1946; children—Reid V., Edmund B., Jr., Sidney B., Helen T. A.B., Stanford U., 1936. Mng. ptnr. MacDonald Products Co., San Francisco, 1950—; chmn., chief exec. officer Faribault Canning Co., Mpls., 1969—. Bd. dirs. Presbyn. Med. Ctr., San Francisco, 1975-83; trustee Calvary Presbyn. Ch., San Francisco. Republican.

MACDONALD, MARY CATHERINE, data processing coordinator, systems analyst, programmer; b. Midland, Mich., Oct. 1, 1958. A.S. in Bus. Studies, Delta Coll., 1978; B.S. in Bus. Adminstrn., Central Mich. U., 1980. Student cons. physics dept. Central Mich. U., Mt. Pleasant, 1979-80; asst. registrar Mercy Coll., Detroit, 1980-82; coordinator data systems Archdiocese of Detroit, 1982—. Mem. Data Processing Mgmt. Assn. Office: Archdiocese of Detroit 1234 Washington Blvd Detroit MI 48226

MACDONALD, VIRGINIA B., state senator; b. El Paso, Tex., Oct. 24, 1920; d. Wendell Holmes and Dorothy (White) Blue; m. Alan H. Macdonald, 1941; children—Susan Macdonald Van Bramer, Alan H. Mem. Ill. Senate, 1980—. Chairwoman, Cook County Republican Com., 1964-68; pres. Ill. Fedn. Rep. Women, 1972-74; sec. Ill. Rep. Ho. Rep. Caucus; del. 6th Constl. Conv., 1970; mem. Salvation Army Service Div., Mt. St. Joseph Assn. for Mentally Retarded. Recipient Commemorative Appreciation Coin, Salvation Army, 1978; Ill. Environ. Council Legis. award, 1978, 79, 80, 81; Star Mental Health award, 1982; award for service Countryside Assn. for Handicapped, 1985; named Ill. Legislator of Yr. in 83d Gen. Assembly, Ill. Dept. on Aging, 1984. Mem. Mt. Prospect Bus. and Profl. Women. Episcopalian. Lodge: Altrusa. Office: 1100 W Northwest Hwy Mount Prospect IL 60056

MAC DOUGALL, GENEVIEVE ROCKWOOD, journalist, educator; b. Springfield, Ill., Nov. 29, 1914; d. Grover Cleveland and Flora Maurine (Fowler) Rockwood; B.S., Northwestern U., 1936, M.A., 1956, postgrad., 1963—; m. Curtis D. MacDougall, June 20, 1942; children—Priscilla Ruth, Bonnie MacDougall Cottrell. Reporter, Evanston (Ill.) Daily News Index, 1936-37; asso. editor Nat. Almanac & Yearbook, Chgo., 1937-38, News Map of Week, Chgo., 1938-39; editor Springfield (Ill.) Citizens' Tribune, also area supr. Ill. Writers Project, 1940-41; reporter Chgo. City News Bur., 1942; tchr. English-social studies Skokie Jr. High Sch., Winnetka, Ill., 1956-68, coordinator TV, 1964-68; tchr. English Washburne Sch., Winnetka, 1968-81; editor Winnetka Public Schs. Jour., Winnetka Public Schs. Newsletter, 1981—; dir. Winnetka Jr. High Archeology Field Sch., 1971-83; cons., lectr. in field. Winnetka Tchrs. Centennial Fund scholar, 1964, 68. Named Tchr. of Year, Winnetka, 1976; Educator of Decade, Northwestern U. and Found. for Ill. Archeology, 1981. Mem. Winnetka Tchrs. Council (pres. 1971-72), Nat., Ill. edn. assns., Ill. Assn. Advancement Archeology, Women in Communications (pres. N. Shore alumni chpt. 1949-53), Pi Lambda Theta. Author: Grammar Book VII, 1963, 68; (with others) 7th Grade Language Usage, 1963, rev. 1968. Contbr. articles to profl. publs. Home: 537 Judson Ave Evanston IL 60202 Office: 515 Hibbard Rd Winnetka IL 60093

MACE, MONTE CLARK, publisher; b. Tulsa, Mar. 30, 1947; s. Kenneth Donaldson and Bonnie Bell (Clark) M.; m. Joyce Ann Yort, Apr. 30, 1971; 1 child, Suzanne Marie. B.A. in Journalism, U. Kans., 1969, M.A. in Journalism, 1973. Russian linguist U.S. Army Security Agy., 1969-72; editor Assoc. Press., Mpls., 1973; editor Vance Pub. Co., Lincolnshire, Ill., 1974-78, pub., 1978—; mem. editorial bd. Am. Bus. Press., N.Y.C., 1976-77. Recipient Neal award Am. Bus. Press. Roman Catholic. Avocations: sports, writing, travel. Office: Vance Pub Corp 400 Kightsbridge Pkwy Lincolnshire IL 60069

MACE, SHARON ELIZABETH, physician, educator; b. Syracuse, N.Y., Oct. 30, 1949; d. James Henry and Leona Helen (Bednarski) M. B.S., Syracuse U., 1971; M.D., Upstate Med. Ctr., 1975. Diplomate Am. Acad. Pediatrics, Am. Coll. Emergency Physicians. Pediatric intern Case Western Res. U., Cleve., 1975-77, cardiology fellow, 1977-79; research assoc. Mount Sinai Med. Ctr., Cleve., 1979-80, residency coordinator, 1983—, asst. dir. emergency dept., 1980—; mem. faculty Case Western Res. Sch. Medicine, Cleve., 1982—; mem. N.E. Ohio Council on Emergency Med. Services, Cleve., 1983—. Contbr. articles to profl. jours. Recipient Residency Sci. Day award Case Western Res. U., Cleve., 1978. Mem. Soc. Tchrs. Emergency Medicine, Univ. Assn. Emergency Medicine, Am. Coll. Emergency Physicians (bd. dirs., chmn. edn. com. Ohio chpt.). Republican. Congregationalist. Home: 5495-D Sierra Dr Willoughby OH 44094 Office: Mt Sinai Med Ctr Dept Emergency Medicine 1800 E 105th St Cleveland OH 44106

MACEDA, JAIME M., chemist; b. Pagsanjan, Laguna, Philippines, Mar. 12, 1943; came to U.S., 1968; s. Vicente Fernandez and Julieta (Maceda) M.; m. Remedios Belmonte Paat, Oct. 19, 1974; 1 child, Therese Marie-Juliet. B.S. in Chemistry, Mapua Inst. Tech., Manila, 1965. Quality control supr. Mercury Drug Co., Manila, 1965-68; quality control chemist Consol. Distilled Products, Chgo., 1968-70; supr. chemistry Rosner-Hixon Lab., Chgo., 1970-77; chief chemist Rosner-Runyon Lab., Chgo., 1977—; judge Chgo. Pub. Schs. Sci. Fair, 1971—. Mem. Assn. Vitamin Chemists, Am. Chem. Soc. Roman Catholic. Home: Morton Grove IL Office: Rosner-Runyon Labs 434 S Wabash St Chicago IL 60605

MACEDA, REMEDOIS PAAT, nurse; b. Santa Remedios, Ilocos Sur, Philippines, Jan. 19, 1943; came to U.S., 1967; d. Melquiades Palasigui and Eufrosina (Belmonte) Paat; m. Jaime M. Maceda, Oct. 19, 1974; 1 child, Therese Marie Juliet. B.S. in Nursing, U. St. Tomas, Manila, Philippines, 1965; postgrad. U. Ill., Chgo., 1970-72. Head nurse, supr. U. St. Tomas Hosp., 1965-67; staff nurse Hahneman Hosp., Phila., 1967-68; staff nurse Michael Reese Hosp., Chgo., 1968-72, adminstrv. coordinator for continuing edn., 1973-80, adminstrv. coordinator for fgn. grads., 1980-85, adminstrv. coordinator for acad. affiliations, continuing edn., and fgn. grads, 1985—. Mem. Am. Nurses Assn., Ill. Nurses Assn., Philippines Nurses Assn. Chgo. (editor gazette 1968-70). Roman Catholic. Avocations: home-making, gardening, singing, piano, writing. Office: Michael Reese Hosp and Med Ctr Lakeshore Dr at 31st St Chicago IL 60616

MACEY, EARL CHRISTOPHER, osteopathic physician and surgeon; b. Richmond, Mo., Mar. 10, 1909; s. Henry Christopher and Lucy Ann (Penny) M.; m. Dorothy Belle Gstrein, July 2, 1939; children—Martha Ann, Earl Christopher. Student Central Coll., Fayette, Mo., 1928-29; D.O., Kirksville Coll. Osteo. Medicine, Mo., 1933; postgrad. Coll. Physicians-Surgeons, Los Angeles, 1946-47, U. Mex., Mexico City, 1948, U. Nebr. Med. Sch., 1979. Intern Laughlin Hosp., Kirksville, 1933; tng. in proctology Mayo Clinic, Rochester, Minn., 1944; practice osteo. medicine and surgery, Marshall, Mo.; del. seminars, Nassau, Bahamas, 1972, Bermuda, 1974, Tokyo, 1976. Author: Poliomyelitis, 1938; Hypertension, 1940; Biblical Medicine, 1975. Mem. West-Central Mo. Assn. Osteo. Physicians and Surgeons (pres. 1941), Am. Osteo. Assn. (life), Mo. Assn. Osteo. Physicians and Surgeons (life). Democrat. Methodist. Lodges: Kiwanis (v.p. 1975), Optimist (pres. 1957). Home: 765 S Brunswick St Marshall MO 65340

MACGREGOR, LAUCHLIN WALTER SHEARER, JR., strategic planner, mechanical engineer, consultant, iridologist; b. Mt. Pleasant, Mich., Oct. 27, 1948; s. Lauchlin Walter Shearer and Bernice Pauline (Hotchkiss) MacG.; m. Mary Elizabeth Garrett, Sept. 28, 1968; children—Kristin Heather, Lauchlin Walter, III. A.A.S., Alpena Community Coll., Mich., 1968; B.S., Saginaw Valley State Coll., 1974; M.A., Central Mich. U., 1980. Registered profl. engr., Mich. Engring. technician Detroit Edison, 1968-75; supr. operational analysis Mich. Pub. Service Commn., Lansing, 1975-82, pub. utilities supr., 1982—; chmn. power plant availability, 1978—; v.p. Besser Engring. and Tech. Assn., Alpena, Mich., 1967-68. Served with U.S. Army, 1969-71. Mem. IEEE (corr., availability subcom. 1981—), ASME, Sigma Phi Zeta. Lutheran. Clubs: CMV Group (sec. 1983-84), Van Com. Ltd. (Lansing, Mich.) (treas. 1981-82). Avocations: football; coin collecting; investing; health. Home: 7299 W Hoover St Saint Johns MI 48879 Office: Mich Pub Service Commn 6545 Mercantile Way Lansing MI 48909

MACGREGOR, ROBERT, psychologist; b. Canton, Ohio, Jan. 27, 1920; s. Walter and Marion (Knapp) MacG.; m. Mary Adeline Houston, Apr. 26, 1944; children—Robert, Margaret, Donald. B.A., U. Mich., 1941, M.A., 1942; Ph.D., NYU, 1954. Diplomate Am. Bd. Profl. Psychology; registered psychologist, Ill. Clin. psychologist VA, Washington, 1946-56; research dir., from instr. to asst. prof. Youth Devel. Project, U. Tex. Med. Br., Galveston, 1956-65; chief family and group therapy State of Ill. Mental Health Ctr., 1966-68; family therapy cons. Chgo. region Ill. Dept. Mental Health, 1969-75; ptnr. in family therapy Robert and Mary MacGregor, 1982—; pres. profl. staff Chgo. Read Mental Health Ctr., 1982; dir. staff tng. Henry Horner Children's Ctr., Ill. Dept. Mental Health, Chgo., 1975-84; adj. faculty Forest Inst. Profl. Psychology, Des Plaines, Ill. Served with U.S. Army, 1942-46. Fellow Am. Psychol. Assn., Am. Orthopsychiat. Assn., Am. Group Psychotherapy Assn.; mem. Southwestern Group Psychotherapy Soc. (pres. 1963-65, award 1978), Ill. Group Psychotherapy Soc. (pres. 1971, 83), Team Family Methods Assn. (hon. dir.), Am. Family Therapy Assn. (charter). Democrat. Unitarian-Universalist. Sr. author: Multiple impact Therapy with Families, 1964; contbr. articles to profl. jours. Home and Office: 19W 155 Rochdale Circle Lombard IL 60148

MACH, ELYSE JANET, music educator, author, pianist; b. Chgo., Jan. 12, 1942; d. Theodore August and Minna Louise (Holz) M.; children—Sean, Aaron, Andrew. B.Music Edn., Valparaiso U., 1962; Mus.M., Northwestern U., 1963, Ph.D. in Music, 1965. Mem. faculty Northeastern Ill. U., Chgo.,

1964—, prof. music, 1974—; concert tours of Netherlands, Germany, Switzerland; recitalist, guest soloist; cons., book reviewer Harcourt Brace Jovanovich and Macmillan. Recipient Presdl. Merit award Northeastern Ill. U., 1978, 81; Northeastern Ill. U. Found. grantee, 1980. Mem. Am. Liszt Soc., English Liszt Soc., Music Educators Nat. Conf., Ill. Music Tchrs. Assn., Midland Soc. Authors. Author: The Liszt Studies, 1973; Contemporary Class Piano, 1976, rev., 1982; Great Pianists Speak for Themselves, 1980; The Rare and the Familiar: Twenty-eight Piano Pieces by Franz Liszt, 1982. Home: 6551 Waukesha Ave Chicago IL 60646 Office: 5500 N St Louis Ave Chicago IL 60625

MACHINIS, PETER ALEXANDER, civil engineer; b. Chgo., Mar. 12, 1912; s. Alexander and Catherine (Lessares) M.; B.S., Ill. Inst. Tech., 1934; m. Fay Mezilson, Aug. 5, 1945; children—Cathy, Alexander. Civil engr. Ill. Hwy. Dept., 1935-36 engr., estimator Harvey Co., Chgo., 1937; project engr. PWA, Chgo., 1938-40; supervisory civil engr. C.E., Dept. Army, Chgo., 1941-78; asst. to exec. dir. Chgo. Urban Transp. Dist., 1978-84; sr. civil engr. Parsons Brinckerhoff, 1985—; partner MSL Engring. Consultants, Park Ridge, Ill., 1952—. Mem. Civil Def. Adv. Council Ill., 1967—. Served with USAF, also C.E., U.S. Army, 1943-45; ETO; lt. col. Res. ret. Registered profl. engr., Ill. Fellow Soc. Am. Mil. Engrs.; mem. ASCE (life), Nat. Soc. Profl. Engrs. (life), Am. Congress Surveying and Mapping, Assn. U.S. Army, Ill. Engring. Council, Mil. Order World Wars (life). Greek Orthodox (ch. trustee). Home: 10247 S Oakley Ave Chicago IL 60643

MACHULAK, EDWARD LEON, real estate, mining and financial corporation executive; b. Milw., July 14, 1926; s. Frank and Mary (Sokolowski) M.; B.S. in Accounting, U., Wis., 1949; student spl. courses various univs.; m. Sylvia Mary Jablonski, Sept. 2, 1950; children—Edward A., John E., Lauren A., Christine M., Paul E. Pres., Commerce Group Corp., Milw., 1962—; dir. Gen. Lumber & Supply Co., Inc., San Luis Estates, Inc., San Sebastian Gold Mines, Inc., Homespan Realty Co., Inc., Universal Developers, Inc., Piccadilly Advt. Agy., Inc. Mem. nat. small bus. investment co. adv. council Small Bus. Adminstrn., 1972-74, co-chmn., 1973-74, bd. govs., 1970-74, exec. com., 1971-74, v.p., 1970-71, pres., 1971-72, sec., 1972-74; mem. Wis. Small Bus. Investment Co. Council, 1970-74, chmn., 1974; mem. Wis., Milw. bds. realtors, 1955—. Financial adv. mem. planning com. Marmion Mil. Acad., Aurora, Ill., 1967-71, lay life trustee, 1967—. Mem. adv. bd. Jesuit Retreat House, Oshkosh, Wis., 1966-68; chmn. St. John Cathedral Symphony Concert Com., Milw., 1978; sustaining mem. Met. Mus. Art, 1974—, Phila. Mus. Art, 1974—. Served with AUS, 1945-46. Mem. Nat. Assn. Small Bus. Investment Cos. (award for distinguished service to small bus. 1970, mem. exec. com., bd. govs. 1970-74), Regional Assn. Small Bus. Investment Cos. (pres. 1971-72). Clubs: K.C. (4 deg.), Senior Citizens of Wauwatosa (organizer, treas. 1958); Milwaukee Athletic, Tripoli Golf (Milw.); Met., Canadian (N.Y.C.). Home: 903 W Green Tree Rd River Hills WI 53217 Office: 6001 N 91st St Milwaukee WI 53225

MACHULAK, JOHN EDWARD, lawyer; b. Milw., Feb. 27, 1953; s. Edward L. and Silvia M. (Jablonski) M.; m. Susan Ruth Robertson, Oct. 11, 1975. A.B., U. Chgo., 1975; L.L.D., U. Wis., 1977. Bar: Wis. 1978, U.S. Dist. Ct. (we. and ea. dists.) 1978. Assoc. Jacobson, Sodos & Krings, S.C., Milw., 1978-84; sole practice, Brookfield, Wis., 1984—. Bd. dirs. S. Community Orgn., Milw., 1981-84. Mem. Wis. Bar. Assn., Assn. Trial Lawyers Am. Office: 12845 W Burleigh Rd Brookfield WI 53005

MACIAG, JOSEPH FELIX, steel service company executive; b. Buffalo, Jan. 5, 1952; s. Stanley and Josephine (Wyzykowski) M.; m. July 5, 1980, Maryann Cavanaugh; children—Karl Stanley, Rachel. B.S. in Elec. Engring., SUNY, 1974. Instrument engr. Republic Steel Corp., Buffalo, 1974-79, gen. foreman, 1979-82, fume system coordinator, Canton, Ohio, 1982; gen. foreman elec. melt shops LTV Steel, Canton, 1982-84; mgr. field ops. Steel Equipment Specialists, Alliance, Ohio, 1985—. Named Republic Steel Corp. Buffalo Dist. Total Resources Improvement Man of Yr., 1978. Vice pres. alumni bd. govs. Canisius High Sch., 1979-82. Mem. IEEE, Instrument Soc. Am., Tau Beta Pi, Eta Kappa Nu. Republican. Office: Steel Equipment Specialists 1507 Beeson St Box 2148 Alliance OH 44601

MACINTOSH, SUSAN CARYL, biochemist; b. Watertown, Wis., June 11, 1953; d. Donald James and Cynthia Ann (Stone) MacI.; m. Daniel Lee Hale, Aug. 10, 1974 (div. Dec. 1982); children—Katharine MacIntosh, Laura MacIntosh. B.A., U. Iowa, 1974. Research technician St. Mary's Health Ctr., St. Louis, 1975-77; research asst. U. Iowa, Iowa City, 1979-83; chemist Sigma Chem. Co., St. Louis, 1983—. Contbr. articles to profl. jours. Episcopalian. Office: Sigma Chem Co-Blood Products PO Box 14508 Saint Louis MO 63178

MAC INTYRE, PATRICIA NELLE, speech-language pathologist; b. E. Cleveland, Ohio, July 2, 1923; d. Robert Isadore and Blanche Esther (Schlesinger) Grossman; B.A., Western Reserve U., 1945; M.A., Case Western Reserve U., 1968; m. William James MacIntyre, Sept. 16, 1947; children—Kathleen Suzanne, Steven James. Staff mem. dept. speech pathology Soc. Crippled Children, Cleve., 1968-75, clin. dir., 1975-79; coordinator outside center services Cleve. Hearing and Speech Center, 1979—; clin. instr. dept. speech communication Case Western Res. U., 1973—; adj. asst. prof. dept. communication Cleve. State U., 1973-79; active in teaching and research with presch. children, Head Start speech-lang. services. Bd. dirs. Flora Stone Mather Coll., 1957-61. Certificate clin. competence speech pathology; Receptive-Expressive Lang. Tng. Program grantee, 1976-79. Fellow Ohio Speech and Hearing Assn.; mem. Am. Speech and Hearing Assn., Ohio Speech and Hearing Assn., Northeastern Ohio Speech and Hearing Assn. (v.p. 1973), Aphasiology Assn. Ohio, Internat. Assn. Logopedics and Phoniatrics. Home: 3108 Huntington Rd Shaker Heights OH 44120 Office: 11206 Euclid Ave Cleveland OH 44106

MACINTYRE, WILLIAM JAMES, physicist; b. Canaan, Conn., Nov. 26, 1920; s. William M. and Helen (Hoyt) MacI.; m. Patricia Nelle Grossman, Sept. 16, 1947; children—Kathleen S., Steven J. B.S. in Physics, Western Res. U., 1943, M.A. in Physics, 1947; M.S. in Physics, Yale U., 1948, Ph.D. in Physics, 1950. Prof. biophysics Western Res. U., Cleve., 1949-72; physicist, Cleve. Clinic Found., 1972—; cons. Bur. Radiol. Health, 1976—, IAEA, 1960-72, NIH, 1975—. Contbr. numerous articles to sci. pubs., chpts. to books. Fellow Am. Coll. Nuclear Physicians; mem. Soc. Nuclear Medicine (pres. 1976-77), Federated Council Nuclear Medicine Orgns. (chmn. 1978-81), Nat. Council Radiation Protection (chmn. sci. com. 1973—), Soc. Magnetic Resonance Imaging (bd. dirs. 1983—). Home: 3108 Huntington Rd Cleveland OH 44120 Office: Cleve Clinic Found 9500 Euclid Ave Cleveland OH 44106

MACK, ALAN WAYNE, interior designer; b. Cleve., Oct. 30, 1947; s. Edmund B. and Florence I. (Oleska) M. B.S. in Interior Design, Case Western Res. U., 1969. Designer interior design dept. Halle's, Cleve., 1969, 71-73; designer Nahan Co., New Orleans, 1973-75, Hemenway's Contract Design, New Orleans, 1975-76; ptnr. Hewlett-Mack Design Assocs., New Orleans, after 1976; adv. com. interior design dept. Delgado Jr. Coll., New Orleans; mktg./merchandising adv. council St. Mary's Dominican Coll., New Orleans. Served with U.S. Army, 1969-71. Co-author audiovisual presentation Nat. Home Improvement Council Conf., 1981. Mem. ASID (profl. mem., presdl. citation, 1980, treas. La. dist. chpt. 1984), Found. for Interior Design Edn. Research (standards com., 1972-76, bd. visitors 1977-80, accreditation com., 1981). Home: 922 Boston Way #7 Iowa City IA 52241

MACK, HARRY EDMUND, III, dentist; b. St. Louis, Dec. 5, 1921; s. Harry Edmund and Louella Pauline (Delvaux) M.; m. Johanna Mary Kelly, Aug. 18, 1948; chilldren—Mary Catherine, Bonacorsi, Julia Anne, Eileen Johanna, Harry Edmund, Michael Patrick. A.S., U. Mo.-Columbia, 1939-42; D.D.S., St. Louis U., 1946. Pvt. practice dentistry and dental surgery, Kirkwood, Mo., 1946—. Fellow Acad. Gen. Dentistry; mem. Am. Dental Assn., Mo. Dental Assn., St. Louis Dental Soc., Phi Gamma Delta, Delta Sigma Delta. Republican. Roman Catholic. Avocations: Golf, sailing. Office: 333 S Kirkwood Rd Kirkwood MO 63122

MACK, JONATHAN TOBIAS, trade association executive; b. Phila., Dec. 15, 1944; s. Henry S. and Jane Mack; m. Marti DeGraaf, Jan. 10, 1981. B.A. in English, Pa. State U., 1966. Vice-pres. Electronic Industries Assn., Washington, 1971-77; exec. v.p., chief exec. officer Nat. Electronic Distbrs. Assn., Chgo., 1977—. Served to lt. USN, 1966-71. Mem. Nat. Assn. Wholesalers (dir.). Republican. Home: 1516 N State St Chicago IL 60610 Office: 35 E Wacker Dr Suite 3202 Chicago IL 60601

MACK, MARY MARGARET, educator; b. Cleve., Aug. 14, 1955; d. Edward Stephen and Bernetta Ann (Stracensky) Hudak; m. Thomas Edward Mack, July 8, 1978. B.S., Cleve. State U., 1977, also postgrad. Tchr., Lulu Diehl Jr. High Sch., Cleve., 1977-78; tchr. Charles W. Eliot Jr. High Sch., 1978—, mem. project Perform proposal writing team, 1982—. Mem. Council Exceptional Children, Assn. Supervision and Curriculum Devel. Roman Catholic. Home: 1353 E 343d St Eastlake OH 44094 Office: 15700 Lotus Dr Cleveland OH 44128

MACK, RICHARD ARTHUR, edn. co. exec.; b. Bagley, Minn., Dec. 24, 1941; s. Lloyd Benton and Rose Delia (Belland) M.; B.S., U. Wis., 1968, M.S., 1974, Ph.D., 1980; postgrad. U. Wis., 1971, U. Hawaii, 1971, U. Utah, 1976; m. Gloria Jean Gooding, Oct. 6, 1965; children—John, Christopher, Elizabeth, Jennifer, Nicholas, Mary. Tech. writer McGraw-Edison, Milw., 1962-65; writer Marrow Pub., Berkeley, Calif., 1968-70; curriculum cons. Milw. public schs., 1970-72; dir. research and devel. Ramco Cons. Services, Aurora, Ill., 1972-75; gen. mgr. Nevada Mgmt. & Tng. Co., Carson City, 1975-79, now dir.; chief exec. officer Edn. Systems Co., Garfield, Minn., 1979—, Capital Systems Inc., 1982—; dir. Ramco Cons. Services, Edn. Systems Co. Served to lt. comdr. U.S. Army, 1959-62. Mem. Communications Assn. Am., Am. Correctional Assn., Tech. Edn. Assn., Christian Family Movement. Roman Catholic. Clubs: K.C., Eagles. Home: 202 Maple St Alexandria MN 56308 Office: Douglas County 82 PO Box 38 Garfield MN 56332

MACKE, JOHN GEORGE, manufacturers' representative company executive; b. St. Louis, Jan. 16, 1931; s. F. George and Isabella Antonette (Garlich) M.; m. Dorothy Jeanne Maher, July 13, 1957; children—John George, Daniel, Donna, James, Diane, Doris. B.S. in Elec. Engring., U. Mo.-Rolla, 1952; M.B.A., St. Louis U., 1960. Supr. motor sales Wagner Electric Corp., St. Louis, 1952-62; sales mgr. Fasco Industries, Inc., Rochester, N.Y., 1962-68; product sales mgr. Emerson Electric Motor Div., St. Louis, 1968-71; owner Whitehill Systems of South St. Louis, 1971-74; dist. mgr. John G. Twist Co., St. Louis, 1974-82; pres. John G. Macke Co., St. Louis, 1982—. Served to capt. USAF, 1952-60; Korea. Mem. Nat. Elec. Mfrs. Assn. (co. rep. 1963-68). Roman Catholic. Lodge: KC (dep. grand knight 1973-75). Avocation: flying. Home: 1508 Sugargrove Ct Saint Louis MO 63146 Office: John G Macke Co 11710 Administration Dr Saint Louis MO 63146

MACKE, KENNETH A., retail company executive. Chmn., chief exec. officer, chmn. exec. com., dir. Dayton-Hudson Corp., Mpls. Office: Dayton-Hudson Corp 777 Nicollet Mall Minneapolis MN 55402

MACKE, THOMAS FREDERICK, lawyer, educator; b. Ft. Wayne, Ind., Mar. 14, 1954; s. Donald M. and Mary J. Macke; m. Debra L. Wenthe, June 10, 1978. B.A., Valparaiso U., 1976, J.D., 1979; postgrad. Nat. Inst. Trial Lawyers, U. Notre Dame, 1980-81. Bar: Ind. 1979. Tchr. Ind.-Purdue U., Hammond, 1979, 80-83; assoc. Blachly, Tabor, Bozik, & Hartman, Valparaiso, Ind., 1978—. Pres. Valparaiso Jaycees, 1983-84, sec., 1982-83; sec. Valparaiso Bldg. Fund., Inc., 1984-85. Mem. ABA, Ind. Bar Assn., Porter County Bar Assn., Assn. Trial Lawyers Am., Ind. Trial Lawyers Assn. Lutheran. Office: Blachly Tabor Bozik Hartman 56 S Washington Valparaiso IN 46383

MACKENZIE, CHARLES WESTLAKE, III, pharmacology educator; b. N.Y.C., Jan. 25, 1946; s. Charles W. Mackenzie, Jr. and Mally (Carnegie) Mackenzie Echols; m. Nina Drachenfels, July 12, 1969; children—Heidi, Timothy. B.S. in Chemistry, U. of Pacific, 1968; Ph.D. in Biochemistry, U. So. Calif., 1975. Postdoctoral fellow U. Minn., Mpls., 1974-76, research specialist, 1976-78; research assoc. U. Nebr. Med. Ctr., Omaha, 1978-79, instr., 1979-81, asst. prof., 1981—. Contbr. articles to profl. jours. Grantee Am. Heart Assn., 1980-82, 83—, Am. Lung Assn., 1982-84, NIH, 1984—. Mem. AAAS, CP/M Users Group, Applesauce. Avocation: computers. Home: 5624 Pierce St Omaha NE 68106 Office: Dept Pharmacology U Nebr Med Ctr 42d and Dewey Ave Omaha NE 68105

MACKETY, CAROLYN JEAN, nurse, hospital administrator; b. Chgo., Feb. 27, 1932; d. Gerald James and Minnette (Buis) Kruyf; m. Robert J. Martin, Oct. 3, 1952 (div. 1959); children—Daniel, David, Steven, Laura. Diploma, Hackley Hosp. Sch. Nursing, 1969; B.S., Coll. St. Francis, 1977; postgrad. Exec. M.B.A. Program, Canadian Sch. Mgmt., Northland U., Toronto. Nursing coordinator operating room Grant Hosp., Columbus, Ohio, 1981-84, dir. operating room services, 1981—; pres., owner Laser Cons., Inc.; laser nurse specialist. Mem. Polit. Action Group for Nurses, Assn. Operating Room Nurses, Am. Soc. Laser Medicine and Surgery (chmn.). Republican. Mem. editorial bd. Clin. Laser Mag. Author: Perioperative Laser Nursing.

MACKEY, DAVID JOE, architect, educator; b. Oakland, Calif., Nov. 14, 1953; s. Jor Franklin and Mary Lou (Stagner) M.; m. Mary Jo Lewis, May 28, 1976; 1 child, Anne. B. Arch., Kans. State U., 1976. Registered architect, Mo., Nat. Council Archtl. Registration Bds. Architect David Mackey AIA, West Plains, Mo., 1981—; instr. So. Mo. State U., West Plains, 1983—. Co-chmn. evangelism First Christian Ch., West Plains, 1985. Mem. AIA, Tau Sigma Delta, Phi Kappa Phi. Lodge: Rotary. Avocations: philately; weight lifting. Home: Route 3 Box 526 H West Plains MO 65775 Office: David Mackey Architect 20 Ct Sq West Plains MO 65775

MACKICHAN, KENNETH ALLEN, hydrologist; b. Sanilac County, Mich., Oct. 27, 1911; s. John Allen and Anna Pearl (Brooks) MacK.; A.A., Port Huron Jr. Coll., 1932; B.S., U. Mich., 1934, M.S., 1935; m. Lois Alma Deyton, May 1, 1943; children—John, Robert, Margaret, Jr. draftsman Mich. Hwy. Dept., Lansing, 1935; civil engr. Appalachian Forest Expt. Sta., Asheville, N.C., 1935-38; hydraulic engr. U.S. Geol. Survey, Asheville, 1938-41, Charleston, W.Va., 1941-51, Washington, 1951-61, chief hydraulic studies sect. Gen. Hydrology Br., 1955-61, dist. engr. quality Water Br., Ocala, Fla., 1961-65, dist. chief Water Resources Div., Lincoln, Nebr., 1965-79; ret., 1979. Active Boy Scouts Am. Registered profl. engr., W.Va., Md. Fellow ASCE (life mem.); mem. Am. Geophys. Union, Am. Water Works Assn., Water Pollution Control Fedn., Am. Water Resources Assn. (sect. sec.-treas. 1971-72), Nebr. Acad. Sci., Nebr. Irrigation Assn., Sigma Xi. Contbr. articles to profl. jours. Home: 2570 Woods Blvd Lincoln NE 68502

MACKLIN, CROFFORD JOHNSON, JR., lawyer; b. Columbus, Ohio, Sept. 10, 1947; s. Crofford Johnson, Sr. and Dorothy Ann (Stevens) M.; m. Mary Carole Ward, July 5, 1969; children—Carrie E., David J. B.A., Ohio State U., 1969; B.A. summa cum laude, U. West Fla., 1974; J.D. cum laude, Ohio State U., 1976. Bar: Ohio 1977, U.S. Tax Ct. 1978. Acct., Touche Ross, Columbus, 1976-77; assoc. Smith & Schnacke, Dayton, 1977-81; ptnr. Porter, Wright, Morris & Arthur, Dayton, 1983—; sole practice, Dayton, 1981-82; adj. faculty Franklin U., 1977; adj. prof. U. Dayton Law Sch., 1981. Contbr. articles to profl. jours. Bd. dirs. Easter Seals, 1984—. Served to capt. USMCR, 1969-74. Mem. Dayton Bar Assn. (chmn. probate com. 1981-83), Dayton Trust & Estate Planning (pres. 1983-84), Ohio Bar Assn., ABA. Presbyterian. Home: 7333 Timbernoll Dr West Chester OH 45069 Office: Porter Wright Morris & Arthur PO Box 1805 2100 1st Nat Bank Bldg Dayton OH 45401

MACKLIN, ELIZABETH MARGARET, police officer; b. Cleve., Mar. 7, 1938; d. Lucius and Rachel (Hart) Woods; m. Moses Macklin, July 25, 1959; 1 son, Earl Allan. Student Fenn Coll., 1964-66, Case Western Res. U., 1966, Cuyahoga County Community Coll., 1969, 83. Sec., Vis. Nurse Assn., Cleve., 1957-64, Welfare Fedn., 1964-66; adminstrv. asst. Village of Woodmere (Ohio), 1967—, police officer, 1972—. Mem. declining enrollment com. Orange Schs., 1983—; mem., past officer Nat. Bapt. Conv., Ohio Bapt. State Conv. Mem. NAACP, Profl. Secs. Internat., Cuyahoga County Mayors' Secs. Assn., Woodmere Women's Civic League. Democrat. Lodges: Order Eastern Star, Dau. of Isi. Home: 3749 Brainard Rd Woodmere Village OH 44122 Office: 27899 Chagrin Blvd Woodmere Village OH 44122

MACKLING, ALVIN HENRY, Canadian government official, lawyer; b. Winnipeg, Man., Can., Dec. 31, 1927; s. John and Anne Gertrude (Williams) M.; m. Patricia Taeko Ono, Aug. 18, 1956; children—Holly Naomi, Thomas Hal. B.A., U. Winnipeg, 1953; LL.B., U. Man., 1958. Sole practice, St. James, Man., 1958-69; atty.-gen. Man. Govt., Winnipeg, 1969-73, consumer and corp. affairs minister, Winnipeg, 1969-73; chmn. Man. Motor Transport Bd., Man. Traffic Bd., Winnipeg, 1974-80; minister Ministry Natural Resources, Winnipeg, 1981-84, Ministry Labour, Winnipeg, 1985—. Councillor, City of St. James, Winnipeg, 1961-69; mem. legis. assembly Province of Man., St. James, 1969-73. Named to Queen's Counsel, Province of Man., 1969. Mem. New Democratic Party. Mem. United Ch. Lodges: Ind. Order Foresters, Pioneer Fraternal Assn. Home: Rural Route 1 Dugald MB R0E 0K0 Canada Office: Ministry Labour Room 343 Legis Bldg Winnipeg MB R3C 0V8 Canada

MACKNIN, MITCHELL HOWARD, lawyer, consultant; b. Cleve., Oct. 27, 1953; s. Reynold and Eleanore (Mintz) M. B.A. in Econs. with honors, Northwestern U., 1975, J.D. with distinction, 1978. Bar: Ill. 1978, U.S. Dist. Ct. (no. dist.) Ill. 1978, U.S. Ct. Appeals (7th cir.) 1979, Assoc. Rosenthal & Schanfield, Chgo., 1978-80; ptnr. Sperling, Slater & Spitz, Chgo., 1980—. Com. mem. Soviet Jewry, Highland Park, Ill., 1984—; campaign worker Paul Simon for U.S. Senator, Chgo., 1984. Mem. Chgo. Bar Assn., Chgo. Council Lawyers, ABA, Ill. State Bar Assn., Order of Coif, Phi Eta Sigma. Home: 444 W Fullerton Apt 906 Chicago IL 60614 Office: Sperling Slater & Spitz 55 W Monroe Chicago IL 60603

MACKOVIC, JOHN, football coach; b. Barberton, Ohio, Oct. 1, 1943; m. Arlene Francis; children—Aimee, John. B.A. in Spanish, Wake Forest U., 1965; M.Edn. in Secondary Sch. Adminstrn., Miami U., Oxford, Ohio, 1966. Various coaching positions, 1965-72; offensive backfield coach U. Ariz., Tucson, 1973-74, offensive coordinator, 1974-75, asst. head coach, 1976; asst. head coach/offensive coordinator Purdue U., West Lafayette, Ind., 1976-78; head football coach Wake Forest U., Winston-Salem, N.C., 1978-81; asst. football coach Dallas Cowboys, 1981-83; head football coach Kansas City Chiefs, Mo., 1983—. Directed Wake Forest to first-ever Nat. Ranking in 1979. Named Coll. Football Coach Yr., The Sporting News, 1979; Coach of Yr., Walter Camp Football Found., 1979, Atlantic Coast Conf., 1979; Alumnus of Yr. Wake Forest U., 1980. Office: Kansas City Chiefs One Arrowhead Dr Kansas City MO 64129

MACLAREN, DAVID SERGEANT, pollution control equipment co. exec.; b. Cleve., Jan. 4, 1931; s. Albert Sargeant and Theadora Beidler (Potter) MacL.; children—Alison, Catherine, Carolyn. A.B. in Econs., Miami U., Oxford, Ohio, 1955. Mgr. Jet, Inc., Cleve., 1958-60, chmn. bd., pres., 1961—; founder, chmn. bd., pres. Air Injector Corp., Cleve., 1958-78; founder, pres. Fluid Equipment, Inc., Cleve., 1962-72, chmn. bd., 1962-72; founder, pres. T&M Co., Cleve., 1963-71, chmn. bd., 1964-71; founder, pres. Alison Realty Co., Cleve., 1965—, chmn. bd., 1967—; founder, pres. Mold Leasing, Inc., Cleve., also chmn. bd., 1968-71; Sargeant Realty, Inc., 1979—, dir. 1978-82; dir. Gilmore Industries, 1975-77, MWL Systems, 1979—. Mem. tech. com. Nat. Sanitation Found., Ann Arbor, Mich., 1967—. Mem. Republican State Central Com., 1968-72, Cuyahoga County Rep. Central Com., 1968-72; registered legis. agt. 110th Ohio Gen. Assembly, 1973-74. Served with arty. AUS, 1955-58. Fellow Royal Soc. Health (London); mem. Nat., Ohio Environ. Health Assns., Nat. Precast Concrete Assn., Am., Ohio Pub. Health Assns., Nat. and Ohio Water Pollution Control Fedns., Am. Mgmt. Assn., Ohio Gun Collectors Assn., Defenders Wildlife, Friends of Animals, Central Taek Wondo Assn., Gullwing, Mercedes Benz Club N.Am. (pres. 1968), U.S. Martial Arts Assn. (black belt, instr.), Jiu-Jitsu/Karati Black Belt Fedn., Scottish Tartans Soc., Clan MacLaren Soc. of Scotland and N. Am., Vintage Sports Car Club, Ferrari Club Am., Cleve. Animal Protective League, Geauga County Humane Soc., Highland Heights Citizens League , SAR, Fraternal Order Police, H.B. Leadership Soc., H.B. Devel. Commn., Western Reserve Hist. Soc., Cleve. Mus. of Art, Delta Kappa Epsilon (nat. dir. 1974—; dir. chpt. assn. 1969—). Clubs: Am. Yoga Assn. (life), Mentor Harbor Yachting; Country (Cleve.), Union League (N.Y.C.), Yale (N.Y.C.), Deke (N.Y.C.), Cotillion Soc. (Cleve.). Patentee in field. Home: West Hill Dr Gates Mills OH 44040 Office: Jet Inc 750 Alpha Dr Cleveland OH 44143

MACLAUCHLAN, DONALD JOHN, JR., real estate company executive; b. S.I., N.Y., Mar. 2, 1935; s. Donald John and Alice Lucy (Macklin) MacL.; B.A. magna cum laude, Harvard U., 1957; m. Mary Eleanor Manor, Oct. 14, 1967; children—Douglas Laird, Phyllis Ann, Donald John III. Mortgage analyst Conn. Gen. Life Ins. Co., Hartford, 1957-60; mortgage broker James W. Rouse & Co., Balt., 1960-62; devel. mgr. Devel. & Constrn. Co., Inc., Balt., 1962-66; v.p. Nat. Homes Corp., Lafayette, Ind., 1966-75; pres., dir. The Criterion Group, Lafayette, 1975—; dir. Lafayette Parking, Inc., Insight Unlimited, Inc., Sagamore Food Services, Inc. Elder, Central Presbyn. Ch., Lafayette, 1971—; mem. gen. council Presbytery of Wabash Valley, 1976-78. Mem. Lafayette Bd. Realtors, Greater Lafayette C. of C., Ind. Apt. Assn. (dir. 1980—), Tippecanoe County Apt. Assn. (dir. 1977—, pres. 1980). Republican. Clubs: Lafayette Country, Romwell Foxhounds (joint master). Office: PO Box 275 Lafayette IN 47905

MACLAUGHLIN, HARRY HUNTER, Judge; b. Breckenridge, Minn., Aug. 9, 1927; s. Harry Hunter and Grace (Swank) MacL.; B.B.A. with distinction, U. Minn., 1949, LL.B., J.D., 1956; m. Mary Jean Shaffer, June 25, 1958; children—David, Douglas. With Gen. Motors Corp., Mpls., 1949-52, Minn. Mining Co., St. Paul, 1952-54; law clk. to Justice Frank Gallagher Minn. Supreme Ct., 1955-56; admitted to Minn. bar, 1956; practice law, Mpls., 1956-72; ptnr. firm MacLaughlin & Mondale, 1957-60, MacLaughlin & Harstad, 1960-72; asso. justice Minn. Supreme Ct., 1972-77; U.S. dist. judge Dist. of Minn., 1977—; lectr. U. Minn. Law Sch., 1973—; part-time instr. William Mitchell Coll. Law, St. Paul, 1958-63. Mem. Mpls. Charter Commn., 1966-72, Minn. State Coll. Bd., 1971-72, Minn. Jud. Council, 1972; nat. adv. council Small Bus. Adminstrn., 1968-70; mem. 8th Circuit Jud. Council, 1981-83. Served with USNR, 1945-46. Mem. ABA, Minn., Hennepin County bar assns., Assn. Trial Lawyers Am., Beta Gamma Sigma, Phi Delta Phi. Methodist. Bd. editors Minn. Law Rev., 1954-55. Office: US Court House Minneapolis MN 55401

MAC LEOD, RICHARD ALAN, government revenue agent; b. Flint, Mich., Dec. 7, 1947; s. Archibald Charles and Georgenia Anne (Youmans) MacL.; m. Cynthia Lou Jeziorski, Dec. 13, 1975. B.A., U. Mich.-Flint, 1973; M. Taxation, DePaul U., 1979. Internal revenue agt. U.S. Treasury Dept., Chgo., 1973—. Served to sgt. U.S. Army, 1967-69, Vietnam. Mem. Vietnam Vets. of Am. Avocations: racquetball, genealogy. Home: 990 Waverly Rd Glen Ellyn IL 60137

MACLEOD, WILLIAM CYRUS, lawyer, economist; b. Chgo., Apr. 7, 1952; s. Charles William MacLeod and Sarah Ann (Updyke) MacLeod Simitz; m. Michele Benoit, May 5, 1956; 1 child, Christine Michele. B.A., Ripon Coll., 1973; Ph.D. candidate, U. Va., 1975; J.D., U. Miami, Coral Gables, Fla., 1979. Bar: Ill. 1979, U.S. Dist. Ct. (no. dist.) Ill. 1979, U.S. Ct. Appeals (7th cir.) 1985. Instr., U. Va., Charlottesville, 1976; cons. Law and Econs. Ctr., Coral Gables, Fla., 1976-79; assoc. McDermott Will & Emery, Chgo., 1979-82; atty. advisor FTC, Washington, 1982-83, dir. Chgo. region, 1983—. Contbr. articles to profl. publs. Mem. ABA, Ill. Bar Assn. (mem. antitrust council 1983—), Chgo. Bar Assn. Office: Federal Trade Commission Chicago Regional Office 55 E Monroe St Suite 1437 Chicago IL 60603

MAC MAHON, HAROLD BERNARD, manufacturing company executive; b. Newton, Mass., Nov. 15, 1917; s. Harold A. and Alma A. (McCabe) MacM.; B.S. in Edn., Boston U., 1940; m. Mary M. Savage, Jan. 1, 1942; 1 dau., Karen D. MacMahon Levisay. Plant mgr. Bassick div. Stewart-Warner Corp., Spring Valley, Ill., 1958-66, controller Alemite and Instrument div., Chgo., 1966-73, asst. gen. mgr., 1973-74, gen. mgr. Hobbs div., Springfield, Ill., 1974—, v.p., 1976—; dir. Springfield Marine Bank. Mem. adv. council St. John's Hosp.; bd. dirs. Sangamon County Pvt. Industry Council. Served with U.S. Army, 1943-45. Mem. Soc. Automotive Engrs., Newcomen Soc. N.Am., Greater Springfield C. of C. (dir. 1978-83), Ill. C. of C., Phi Delta Kappa. Club: Sangamo (Springfield). Home: 1525 W Ash Springfield IL 62704 also 260 E Chestnut St Chicago IL 60611 Office: Hobbs Div Stewart-Warner Corp Yale Blvd and Ash St Springfield IL 62705

MACMILLAN, PETER ALAN, lawyer; b. Mpls., Apr. 10, 1955; s. John Louis and Celeste Caroline (Eggers) MacM. B.S., Mankato State U., 1977; J.D., Hamline U., 1980; postgrad. Sch. Law, U. San Diego, 1980. Bar: Minn. 1980, U.S. Tax Ct. 1980, U.S. Dist. Ct. Minn. 1981. Sole practice, Robbinsdale, Minn., 1981-84; assoc. Rosenthal & Rondoni, Ltd., Mpls., 1984-85; shareholder Rosenthal, Rondoni & MacMillan, 1985—. Mem. Minn. State Bar Assn., Hennepin County Bar Assn., Assn. Trial Lawyers Am., Am. Judicature Soc., ABA, Jaycees. Lutheran. Home: 3318 Penn Ave N Minneapolis MN 55412 Office: Rosenthal Rondoni & MacMillan Ltd 7600 Bass Lake Rd Suite 120 Minneapolis MN 55428

MACON, IRENE ELIZABETH, designer, consultant; b. East St. Louis, Ill., May 11, 1935; d. David and Thelma (Eastlen) Dunn; m. Robert Teco Macon,

Feb. 12, 1954; children—Leland Sean, Walter Edwin, Gary Keith, Jill Renee Macon Martin, Robin Jeffrey Lamont. Student Forest Park Coll., Washington U., St. Louis, 1970, Bailey Tech. Coll., 1975, Lindenwood Coll., 1981. Office mgr. Cardinal Glennon Hosp., St. Louis, 1965-72; interior designer J.C. Penney Co., Jennings, Mo., 1972-73; entrepreneur Irene Designs Unltd., St. Louis, 1974—; vol. liaison Pub. Sch. System, St. Louis, 1980-82; cons. in field. Inventor venetian blinds for autos, 1981. Committeewoman Republican party, St. Louis, 1984; vol. St. Louis Assn. Community Orgns., 1983; instr. first aid Bi-State chpt. ARC, St. Louis, 1984; block capt. Operation Brightside, St. Louis, 1984. Named one of Top Ladies of Distinction, St. Louis, 1983. Mem. Nat. Council Negro Women (1st v.p. 1984), Invention Assn. of St. Louis (subcom. head 1985), Coalition of 100 Black Women. Methodist. Club: 500 (Washington). Avocations: reading; designing personal wardrobe; modeling; horseback riding; boating. Home and office: 5469 Maple St Saint Louis MO 63112

MACPHEE, CRAIG ROBERT, economist, educator; b. Annapolis Royal, N.S., Can., July 10, 1944; came to U.S., 1950; s. Craig and Dorothy (Seney) MacP.; m. Kathleen Gray McCown, Feb. 6, 1966 (div. 1981); children—Paul, Heather, Rob; m. Andrea Joy Sime, June 26, 1983. B.S., U. Idaho, 1966; M.A., Mich. State U., 1968, Ph.D., 1970. Asst. prof., then assoc. prof. econs. U. Nebr., Lincoln, 1969—; chmn. econs. dept., 1980-83; econ. affairs officer UN, Geneva, 1975-77; internat. economist U.S. Dept. Labor, Washington, 1983-84; cons. in field. Author: Economics of Medical Equipment and Supply, 1973; Restrictions on International Trade in Steel, 1974. Mem. Am. Econ. Assn., Midwest Econ. Assn., Nebr. Econ. and Bus. Assn., Delta Sigma Pi (faculty adviser 1982—), Phi Eta Sigma, Omicron Delta Epsilon. Avocations: running, skiing, sailing, reading. Home: 6208 Tanglewood Ct Lincoln NE 68516 Office: U Nebr Coll Bus Dept Econs Lincoln NE 68588

MACRAE, DONALD ALEXANDER, emeritus business educator; b. Eldora, Iowa, Dec. 3, 1916; s. William and Mary (Stewart) MacR.; B.A., U. No. Iowa, 1943; M.A., U. Iowa, 1950, Ph.D., 1962; m. Adeline Taylor, July 8, 1943 (dec. Jan. 1963); children—Margaret Ann, Pamela, Patricia; m. 2d, Joyce M. Spooner McCrea, June 1, 1968. Prin., Solon (Iowa) High Sch., 1943-44, Riverton (Iowa) High Sch., 1944-45, 47-48; instr. U. Iowa, 1949-54; prof. bus. adminstrn. Mankato (Minn.) State U., 1954-82, prof. emeritus, 1982—. Bd. dirs. United Fund, 1971-76, Mankato Symphony Orch., 1981-84. Served with AUS, 1946-47. Mem. Am. Bus. Writing Assn., Nat. Bus. Edn. Assn., Internat. Soc. Bus. Edn., Adminstrv. Mgmt. Soc. (Merit award 1984), Clan Mac Rae Soc. N.Am., Twin Cities Scottish Club, St. Andrew's Soc. Minn., Sigma Tau Delta, Kappa Delta Pi, Pi Omega Pi, Delta Pi Epsilon, Phi Delta Kappa. Presbyterian. Home: 211 Woodshire Dr Mankato MN 56001 Office: College of Business Mankato State University Mankato MN 56001

MACY, JANET KUSKA, broadcaster, educator; b. Omaha, Nov. 9, 1935; d. Val and Marie (Letovsky) Kuska; m. Duane S. Thompson, 1982. B.S., U. Nebr., 1957; M.S., Kans. State U., 1961; M.Ed., S.D. State U., 1970; postgrad. Iowa State U., 1965-67, Colo. State U., 1965, U. Minn., 1975, U. Ariz., 1979, 80. Div. Broadcaster Sta. KSAC, Kans. State U., Manhattan, 1957-61; extension home econs. editor U. Nebr., Lincoln, 1961-62; TV specialist Iowa State U. Sta. WOI-TV, 1962-67; asst. prof. Coll. Home Econs., TV specialist Sta. KESD-TV, S.D. State U., Brookings, 1967-71; field editor Better Homes and Gardens Book div. Meredith Pub. Co., 1972-73; media cons. U.S. Consumer Product Safety Commn., Minn., 1977-79; assoc. prof. Coll. Agr., extension info. specialist, broadcaster Sta. KUOM, U. Minn., St. Paul, 1971—, extension info. specialist in alcohol edn., 1984—, assoc. prof. family/social sci. Coll. Home Econs., 1982—, mem. faculty adv. com. for women; public relations cons. Rational Emotive Edn. Center. Recipient Nutrition Communication award Am. Women in Radio and TV, 1977; Alumni Recognition award U. Nebr., 1973; Agrl. Coll. Editors Blue Ribbon awards, 1967, 68, 69, 79 Sch. Bell award Minn. Edn. Assn., 1980, 81, 82, 84, Merit award, 1983. Mem. Women in Internat. Devel., Am. Soc. for Tng. and Devel., Agrl. Communicators in Edn. (superior awards 1979, 81), Minn. Chem. Health Assn. (bd. dirs.), Gamma Sigma Delta, Phi Delta Gamma, Theta Sigma Phi, Delta Gamma. Club: Ski. Home: 5 Appletree Sq 202 Minneapolis MN 55420 Office: 299F McNeal Hall 1985 Buford Ave Saint Paul MN 55108

MADARAS, PATRIK ISTVAN, state official; b. Akron, Ohio, Oct. 29, 1948; s. George Roger and Martha Grace (McCann) M. A.B. cum laude, Alma Coll., Mich., 1970; A.M., Ind. U., 1972, postgrad., 1975. Assoc. instr. Ind. U., Bloomington, 1975; manpower specialist Ind. Office Occupational Devel., Indpls., 1975-76, MIS supr., 1976-77, assoc. dir. mgmt. analysis, 1977-81, acting dir. statewide services, 1981, dir. research and analysis, 1981—. Editor: Competency Based Training, 1985; editor jour. The Literacy Letter, 1985-86; assoc. editor jour. The Source, 1983-86. Chmn. Ind. Occupational Coordinating Com., Indpls., 1983-84; deacon Second Presbyn. Ch., Indpls., 1984-86. Henry Howe scholar, 1970; NIMH fellow, 1970-73. Mem. Am. Sociol. Assn., Ind. Econ. Forum, Ind. Employment and Tng. Assn. (sec. 1983-85), Ind. Vocat. Assn., Psychometric Soc. Republican. Avocations: basketball, bicycling, woodworking. Home: 1449 W 76th Pl Indianapolis IN 46260 Office: Ind Office Occupational Devel 150 W Market St Indianapolis IN 46204

MADDEN, CHERYL ANN, geologist; b. Kimball, Nebr., Dec. 12, 1959; d. Roy Lee and Jackie Louise (Nadeau) M. B.A., U. No. Colo., 1982. Geologist D.C. Drilling Co., Lusk, Wyo., 1982-84, Petroleum Exchange, Johnson, Kans., 1984—. Mem. Am. Assn. Petroleum Geologists. Republican. Roman Catholic. Avocations: biking, hiking; camping; needlework. Home: 403 Logan St Johnson KS 67855 Office: Petroleum Exchange Inc Johnson KS 67855

MADDEN, EDGAR ALLEN, college administrator; b. Merrill, Mich., Jan. 8, 1933; s. James Joseph and Flora Mary (Johnson) M.; m. Shirley Ann Gibson, Aug. 28, 1954; children—Denise, Mark, Thomas, David, Helen. B.A., Central Mich. U., 1955, M.A., 1960. Tchr., chmn. English dept. Merrill High Sch., Mich., 1955-64; prof. English, Northwood Inst., Midland, 1964-76, head English dept., 1968-76, assoc. dean acad. affairs, 1976-79, dean coll., 1979—, v.p. acads., 1982—. Contbr. author: Appreciating the 9 Fine, 1977; also articles. Chmn. Diocesan Pastoral Council, Saginaw, Mich., 1971-73. Dow Chem. Co. grantee, 1956; U. S.D. Fgn. Lang. Inst. grantee, 1959; recipient Am. Security Council Excellence award, 1967. Mem. Council Assessment Exptl. Learning, Am. Mgmt. Assn. Republican. Roman Catholic. Home: 16901 Gratiot Rd Hemlock MI 48626 Office: Northwood Inst 3225 Cook Rd Midland MI 48640

MADDEN, JOSHUA ROBERT, automotive company executive; b. Shamokin, Pa., Feb. 23, 1930; s. Joshua Elwood and Helen (Shremshock) M.; m. Jennie Buel Quirk, Dec. 5, 1953; children—Suzanne, Jill, Joshua E., Philip, Daniel. Student Muhlenberg Coll., 1947-49. Exptl. metallurgist, sr. engr. materials, devel. engr. Pontiac Motor div. Gen. Motors Co., Pontiac, Mich., 1954-77; exec. engr., chief engr. Volkswagen of Am., Troy, Mich., 1977—. Patentee in field. Bd. dirs. YMCA, Rochester, Mich., 1970-72, subcom. chmn. centennial com., 1969. Served to lt. U.S. Army, 1951-54. Recipient Nat. Industry award Soc. Plastics Industries, 1976-77. Mem. Soc. Automotive Engrs. (mem. gen. materials council), Detroit Rubber Group (tech. program organizer 1956—), Engring. Soc. Detroit. Episcopalian. Lodge: Kiwanis (pres. 1970, treas. 1971-81), Elks. Home: 772 Allston Dr Rochester MI 48063 Office: Volkswagen Am 888 W Big Beaver St Troy MI 48099

MADDOX, FRANKLIN DONALD, state official, civil engineer; b. St. Louis, Feb. 4, 1938; s. Ernest Adel and Agnes Elizabeth (Fagyal) M.; m. Minta Marie Shackelford, Aug. 7, 1960 (div. Feb. 1982); children—Ellen, Franklin, Richard. m. Susan Carroll Gossrau, Mar. 3, 1982; children—Jane, Nancy. B.S. in Mech. Engring., U. Cin., 1960; B.S. in Civil Engring. Ga. Inst. Tech., 1961; M.S. in San. Engring., U. Fla., 1964. Registered profl. engr., Ohio. Field engr. Rust Engring Co., Rome, Ga., 1960; staff engr., USPHS-N.Y. State Dept. Health, Albany, 1961-62; staff engr. USPHS-EPA, Cin., Washington and Chgo., 1963-71; chief air policy br. Region V, EPA, Chgo., 1972-75, chief tech. support sect., 1976-80; regional adminstr. Mo. Dept. Natural Resources, St. Louis, 1981—. Commr. Streamwood Park Dist., Ill., 1975-81; Webelo leader Pack 48, Cub Scouts Am., Streamwood, 1974-78. Mem. ASCE, Am. Waterworks Assn., Air Pollution Control Assn., Water Pollution Control Fedn., Mo. Waste Control Coalition. Baptist. Avocations: war games, do-it-yourself projects. Office: Mo Dept Natural Resources 8460 Watson Rd Saint Louis MO 63119

MADDUX, PAUL EUGENE, city official; b. Mt. Sterling, Ohio, Nov. 15, 1940; s. Harold Eugene and Opal Jane (Graham) M.; m. Ginger A. Carrol, Aug. 28, 1964; children—Dwayne K., Michael H. Student Mt. Sterling pub. schs. Class III water and wastewater lics., Ohio. Supt. water and wastewater Mt. Sterling, Ohio, 1965-74; supt. wastewater City of London, Ohio, 1974-82, dir. utilities, 1982—. Served with U.S. Army, 1962-64; Korea. Mem. Water Pollution Control Fedn., Ohio Water Pollution Control Conf., Am. Legion. Presbyterian. Avocations: Hunting; fishing. Home: 37 Birchwood St London OH 43140 Office: City of London 4080 St Rt 56 London OH 43140

MADEY, GREGORY RICHARD, mathematician; b. Cleve., June 30, 1947; s. Richard M. and Rose Madej; m. Wendy Ann Lawrence, Aug. 8, 1975; children—Candice, Gregory. B.S., Cleve. State U., 1974; M.S., 1975; M.S. in Ops. Research, Case Western Res. U., 1979, Ph.D., 1984. Instr math. Cuyahoga Community Coll., Cleve., 1975-79, asst. to dean instrn., 1975-77; ops. research analyst Gould Corp., Cleve. 1978-79; bus. planning analyst Goodyear Aerospace Corp., Akron, Ohio, 1979—. Author: (with others) College Mathematics, 1974; contbr. articles to IEEE Trans. Mem. Ops. Research Soc. Am., Inst. Mgmt. Sci. (sec. coll. on research and devel. 1982—, editor newsletter 1983—), Math. Assn. Am., Mil. Ops. Research Soc., Omega Rho, Pi Mu Epsilon. Office: Goodyear Aerospace Akron OH 44315

MADGETT, JOHN PATRICK, III, business executive; b. Hastings, Nebr., Dec. 12, 1940; s. John Patrick, Jr. and Marian Ellen (Dominy) M.; m. Jean Belli, June 15, 1966 (div. 1979); children—Kimberly, John Patrick, Robyn, David. B.A. in Math. and Physics, Carleton Coll., 1962; B.S.E.E., Columbia U., 1963; M.B.A., Stanford U., 1965. Case writer Harvard Bus. Sch., Cambridge, Mass., 1965; indsl. economist Stanford Research Inst., Palo Alto, Calif., 1965; fin. analyst Kaiser Aluminum & Chem. Corp., Oakland, Calif., 1965-68; pres., dir. Ajax Towing Co., Mpls., 1968-77, United Dock Service, Rochester, Ky., 1968-77, Ener-Tran, Inc., Mpls., 1975-81, United Barge Co., Mpls., 1968-77, Wellspring Energy Corp., Mpls., 1977—, Wellspring Fin. Corp., Mpls., 1980—; pres., dir. Wellspring Offshore Services Corp., New Orleans, 1980—; pres., chief exec. officer, dir. Wellspring Corp., Mpls., 1980—; chmn., dir. Wellspring Properties, 1984—; chmn. Wellspring Andrena Ltd., 1984—; dir. Trend Sci., Inc., Mpls., Minn. Ranch & Cattle Co., Mpls.; cons. German Pub. Utility Industry, Joint Engring. Council U.S.A. and Europe, N.Y.C., 1962. Co-author: World of Science and Technology, 1975. Trustee, Breck Sch., Mpls., 1978-81; active vol. mgmt. Mpls. United Way, 1968-76, fund raising Campus Crusade for Christ Internat., San Bernardino, Calif., 1978-84. Mem. Nat. Feed & Grain Dealers Assn., Water Transprt Assn., Young Pres. Orgn. (treas. 1973-80), Propellar Club. Republican. Episcopalian. Clubs: Marsh Lake, Five Fifty-Five, Minneapolis, Minikahda. Office: Wellspring Corp 4530 IDS Center 80 S 8th St Minneapolis MN 55402

MADIA, ASHWIN M., microbiologist; b. Lathi, Gujarat, India, Dec. 5, 1946; s. Mohanlal D. and Jakunvar (Bhayani) M.; m. Nirupama A. Shah, Feb. 20, 1973; children—Jigar, Surbhi, Virat. B.S. in Microbiology, U. Bombay, 1969; M.S. in Microbiology with honors, U. Baroda, 1971, Ph.D. in Microbiology, 1976. Research assoc. dept. biochemistry Sch. Medicine, Boston U., 1977-78, dept. nutrition and food sci. MIT, Cambridge, 1978-79; microbiologist A.E. Staley Mfg. Co., Decatur, Ill., 1979-81, sr. research microbiologist, 1981-83, sr. scientist, 1983—. Contbg. author articles to publs. India, U.S., Europe. Patentee hydrolosis of cellulose. Mem. Am. Soc. Microbiology, Soc. Indsl. Microbiology, Am. Chem. Soc. (div. microbial and biochem. tech.), Mycol. Soc. Am., Assn. Microbiologists of India. Home: 43 Eastmoreland Dr Decatur IL 62521 Office: A E Staley Mfg Co 2200 Eldorado St Decatur IL 62525

MADIGAN, CHARLES EUGENE, marketing and sales executive; b. Lincoln, Ill., Mar. 11, 1922; s. Orville E. and Virginia M. (Moak) M.; LL.B., Am. Sch. Law, 1952; m. Jane Veach, Nov. 24, 1942; children—Janet, Virginia Ann, Barbara. Regional mgr. Alcoa Steamship Co., Inc., 1945-67; regional mgr. Bahama Ministry Tourism, Chgo., 1967-71; gen. sales mgr. Pheasant Run Lodge, St. Charles, Ill., 1971-74; dir. mktg. and sales O'Hare Inn, Des Plaines, Ill., 1974-79; v.p. Olympia Resort, Oconomowoe, Wis., 1979-82; pres. Hotel/Resorts Meeting and Conv. Cons. Served to lt. U.S. Mcht. Marines, 1944-46. Recipient Sch. award Am. Legion, 1936; plaques, VFW, 1975-76, 77, 78, 79, U.S. Army, 1979, Nat. Sheriffs Assn., 1975, Kiwanis Internat., 1979, Research Inst. Am., 1978. Republican. Lodge: Masons. Home: 139 E Blodgett St Lake Bluff IL 60044 Office: 1400 E Touhy Ave Des Plaines IL 60018

MADIGAN, EDWARD R., congressman; b. Lincoln, Ill., Jan. 13, 1936; s. Earl T. and Theresa (Loobey) M.; grad. bus. Lincoln Coll., 1957; L.H.D. (hon.), Lincoln Coll., 1975, Millikin U., 1976, Ill. Wesleyan, 1978; m. Evelyn George, Sept. 1, 1954; children—Kim, Kellie, Mary. Mem. 93-99th Congresses from Ill. 15th Dist., ranking minority mem. Agr. Com., mem. energy and commerce com., ranking minority mem. subcom. on health and the environment. Mem. Ill. Ho. of Reps., 1966-72. Recipient Outstanding Legislator award Ill. Assn. Sch. Supts., Outstanding Achievement award Lincoln Coll. Alumni Assn. Named Outstanding Freshman Congressman Nat. R.R. Unions. Office: 2312 Rayburn Bldg Washington DC 20515

MADORIN, FRED L., city transportation executive; b. East Saint Louis, Ill., May 2, 1920; s. Fred E. and Frederika M. (Rottman) M.; m. Imogene Elizabeth Ernst, Oct. 21, 1944; children—Judith Elen, Freddie Jean. Student Washington U., St. Louis, 1937-41, Denver U., 1944-45. Sales staff Mobil Oil Co., St. Louis, 1939-70, sales mgr. Oil div., Chgo., 1970-71; exec. v.p. Pvt. Brand Gasoline Marketers, Indpls., 1971-73; dir. Dept. Transp., City of Indpls., 1974—. Active Service Club Indpls. Served to capt. USAAC, 1941-47. Decorated Air medal, Purple Heart; recipient award for Market St. Renovation, Ind. chpt. Am. Soc. Landscape Architects, 1982; award for Indpls. Monument Circle, Commn. for Downtown, 1982. Republican. Presbyterian. Clubs: Columbia, Rotary, Kiwanis, Masons. Home: 6325 Hythe Rd Indianapolis IN 46220 Office: Dept Transportation 2360 City County Bldg Indianapolis IN 46204

MADSEN, DOROTHY LOUISE (MEG), career counseling executive; b. Rochester, N.Y.; d. Charles Robert and Louise Anna Agnes Meyer; B.A., Mundelein Coll., Chgo., 1968; m Frederick George Madsen, Feb. 17, 1945. Public relations rep. Rochester Telephone Corp., 1941-42; feature writer Rochester Democrat & Chronicle, 1939-41; exec. dir. LaPorte (Ind.) chpt. ARC, 1964; dir. adminstrv. services Bank Mktg. Assn., Chgo., 1971-74; exec. dir. Eleanor Assn., Chgo., 1974-84; founder Meg Madsen Assocs., Chgo., 1984—; women's career counselor; founder, editor Clearinghouse Internat. Newsletter; founder Eleanor Women's Forum, Clearinghouse Internat., Eleanor Intern Program Coll. Students and Returning Women. Served to lt. col. WAC, 1942-47, 67-70. Decorated Legion of Merit, Meritorious Service award. Mem. Res. Officers Assn., Mundelein Alumnae Assn., Central Eleanor Club, Phi Sigma Tau (charter mem. Ill. Kappa chpt.). Club: Executives (Chgo.). Home and Office: 1030 N State St Chicago IL 60610

MADUZIA, GLEN ANTHONY, packaging company executive; b. Chgo., May 19, 1947; s. Norbert John and Catherine (Stanko) M.; B.S., U. Ill., 1969; M.B.A., Mich. State U., 1971. Prodn. supr. Continental Can Co., Chgo., 1969-70; prodn. supr. Am. Metal Decorating Co., Alsip, Ill., 1971-74, prodn. control mgr., 1974-78, plant supt., 1978-80; location mgr. Champion Internat. Corp., Belvidere, Ill., 1980—; teaching asst. Mich. State U., 1970-71. Mem. Belvidere C. of C., U. Ill. Alumni Assn., Mich. State U. Alumni Assn., Delta Sigma Pi. Home: 4742 Charing Dr #1 Rockford IL 61111 Office: 801 5th Ave Belvidere IL 61008

MAERKI, WALTER GEORGE, incentive travel company executive; b. Cin., Nov. 1918; s. Walter J. and Christina (Pelzel) M.; m. Wilda Marie Houer, Oct. 5, 1944; children—Kent M., Christina Maerki Gambetta. B.A., Ohio Wesleyan U., 1942, postgrad., 1946-47; postgrad., U. Cin., 1947-49. Regional mgr. Sunray Corp., Delaware, Ohio, 1946-56; sales mgr. Eureka Co., Chgo., 1957-84; pres. Spectra Incentive Corp., Cin., 1984—; dir. Fed. Real Estate Investment Trust, Cin. Mem. Pres.'s Com. for Retirees, Washington, 1982-84, Republican Nat. Com., Cin., 1984. Served with USN, 1941-45, PTO. Decorated Air medal, DFC, Silver Star; recipient sales awards Eureka Co. Mem. Ind. Mgmt. Retail Assn., VFW, Am. Legion. Clubs: Decathalon (Mpls.); Dayton Racquet (Ohio). Home: 2200 Victory Pkwy Cincinnati OH 45206 Office: Spectra Corp Suite 101 2181 Victory Pkwy Cincinnati OH 45206

MAESEN, WILLIAM AUGUST, educational administrator; b. Albertson, N.Y., May 18, 1939; s. August and Wilhelmina (Gaska) M.; B.A., Oklahoma City U., 1961, B.S. in Bus., 1961; M.A., Ind. State U., 1968; Ph.D., U. Ill., Chgo., 1979, postgrad., 1982-83; postgrad. Mich. State U., 1980-81, John Marshall Law Sch., Seabury-Western Theol. Sem.; m. Sherry Lee Jaeger, Aug. 13, 1971 (div. Jan. 1985); children—Ryan and Betsy (twins), Steven. Instr. sociology Aquinas Coll., Grand Rapids, Mich., 1967-70; assoc. prof. behavioral sci. Coll. St. Francis, Joliet, Ill., 1970-78; lectr. U. Ill., Chgo., 1974-78; asso. prof. M.S.W. program Grand Valley State Coll., Allendale, Mich., 1978-82; pres. Chgo. Inst. for Advanced Studies, 1982—; intake examiner Ill. State Psychiat. Inst., 1984—; adminstr. Chgo. div. Phila. Sch. Psychoanalysis. dir. residential treatment Cathedral Shelter of Chgo., 1982-83. Chmn., Christian social relations dept. Episcopal Diocese Western Mich., 1979-80, mem. Bishops Council, 1979-80. Served with USAFR, 1962-68. Mem. Nat. Assn. Social Workers, Am. Sociol. Assn., Clin. Sociology Assn. (exec. bd.), Community Devel. Soc., ABA, Beta Gamma, Alpha Kappa Delta. Founding Editor: Clin. Sociology Rev., 1980-81; contbr. articles to profl. jours. Home: PO Box 4380 Chicago IL 60680

MAGERS, LINDA SUE, school librarian, educator; b. Marion, Ind., Oct. 23, 1955; d. Robert Eugene Eckert and Virginia Louise (Sprinkle) E.; m. Terry Lee Magers, June 10, 1978; 1 child, Timothy Allen. B.S., Ball State U., 1978, M.L.S., 1983. Tchr. English jr. high sch. and librarian, Marion, Ind., 1978-80, sch. librarian, Ind., 1980—, tchr. writing, 1984—. activity coordinator. Leader Girl Scouts U.S.A.; sec. Grant County chpt. Ducks Unltd. Recipient 5 yr. pin Girl Scouts U.S.A., 1982. Mem. ALA, AIME, Ind. Library Assn., Delta Theta Tau. Clubs: Central Ind. Retriever, Michiana Retriever (Ind.), Bluegrass Retriever (Ky.). Home: 916 E 35th St Marion IN 46953

MAGIDSON, ERROL MICHAEL, social science educator; b. Chgo., May 15, 1943; s. Leo and Shirley (Rosenberg) M.; m. Janice Marie Wilder, June 15, 1975; 1 child, Lisa Anne. A.B. in Govt., Ind. U., 1965; M.A.T. in Social Scis., Antioch Coll., 1969; Ed.D in Curriculum and Instrn., Nova U., 1976; postgrad. U. Ill., 1972-73, Gov's State U., 1980-81, Chgo. State U., 1980-81. Vol. Peace Corps Fourah Bay Coll., Sierra Leone, 1965-67; instr. Ind. Vocat. Tech. Coll., Gary, 1970-71; coordinator computer assisted instrn. City Colls. Chgo., 1971-77; asst. prof. social sci. Kennedy-King Coll., Chgo., 1976-81, assoc. prof., 1981—, chmn. dept., 1983-85; guest lectr. Purdue U., Hammond, Ind., 1973-75; adj. prof. Nat. Coll. Edn., Lombard, Ill., 1979—; grant proposal evaluator U.S. Dept. Edn., Washington, 1981—. Contbr. articles to profl. jours. Producer videocassette Heredity and Human Devel., 1981. Fellow Antioch Coll., 1967-69. Mem. Assn. Ednl. Communications and Tech., Phi Delta Kappa. Avocations: jogging, swimming. Home: 10227 S Oakley Ave Chicago IL 60643 Office: Kennedy-King Coll Social Sci Dept 6800 S Wentworth Chicago IL 60621

MAGNAN, GEORGE AUGUSTINE, systems analyst, pharmacist; b. St. Louis, Sept. 2, 1948; s. William B. and Marcella C. (Wesselny) M.; m. Nanette Marie Herye, Jan. 31, 1969; children—John William, Dawn Michelle. B.S. in Pharmacy, St. Louis Coll. Pharmacy, 1971. Registered pharmacist, Mo. Clin. pharmacist Sisters of St. Mary's Health Ctr., St. Louis, 1971-79, systems analyst, 1979—. Bd. dirs. START Credit Union, St. Louis, 1982—, vice chmn., 1984—. Mem. Am. Soc. Hosp. Pharmacists, Mo. Soc. Hosp. Pharmacists, St. Louis Soc. Hosp. Pharmacists, Coll. Pharmacy Alumni Assn. (bd. dirs. 1978—, historian 1984—), Kappa Psi (bd. dirs. 1982—). Roman Catholic. Avocations: woodworking, mechanics, water and snow skiing, hiking. Office: Sisters of St Mary's Data Ctr 7980 Clayton Rd Saint Louis MO 63117

MAGNUSON, JAMES RUSSELL, banker; b. Lexington, Nebr., June 7, 1953; s. Donald Dean and Gail (McKee) M.; m. Marilyn Mae Meyer, May 18, 1974; children—Carrie Leigh, Peter James. Student Hastings Coll., 1971-73, U. Mo., 1973-74; B.S., U. Nebr., 1976, M.S., 1977. Loan officer Omaha Bank for Coops., 1977-83; sr. loan officer, 1984; dir. tech. services Farm Credit Banks Omaha, 1985—. Bd. dirs. Good Shepherd Luth. Ch., Gretna, 1978-84; sec. Action Team for Econ. Devel., Gretna, 1984-85; treas. Gretna Area Devel. Corp., 1985. Republican. Avocations: woodworking, gardening, camping. Home: 20104 Westridge Rd Gretna NE 68028 Office: Farm Credit Banks Omaha 206 S 19th St Omaha NE 68102

MAGNUSON, PAUL A., federal judge; b. Carthage, S.D., Feb. 9, 1937; s. Arthur and Emma Elleda (Paulson) M.; m. Sharon Schultz, Dec. 21, 1959; children—Marlene, Margaret, Kevin, John, Kara. B.A., Gustavus Adolphus Coll., 1959; J.D., William Mitchell Coll. Law, 1963. Bar: Minn. 1963. Mem. LeVander, Gillen, Miller & Magnuson, South St. Paul, Minn., 1963-81; judge U.S. Dist. Ct., St. Paul, 1981—. Bd. dirs. Met. Health Bd., St. Paul, 1970-72; legal counsel Ind. Republican Party, Minn., 1979-81. Recipient Disting. Alumnus award Gustavus Adolphus Coll., 1982. Mem. ABA, Dakota County Bar Assn., 1st Dist. Bar Assn. (pres. 1974-75), Minn. Bar Assn., Am. Judicature Soc., South St. Paul C. of C. (dir. 1963-81). Presbyterian. Clubs: Minn. (St. Paul); Mpls. Office: US Dist Court 754 Federal Bldg St Paul MN 55101

MAGOR, ROBERT BROWNING, pharmaceutical company executive; b. Charlevoix, Mich., June 30, 1936; s. Robert Browning and Alta Lynn Magor; m. Carol Prout, June 28, 1958; children—Marc Erwin, Matthew Chad. B.S., Ind. U., 1972, M.S., 1984. Personnel mgr. Assocs. Corp. N.Am., South Bend, Ind., 1958-69; with Miles Labs., Elkhart, Ind., 1969—, now personnel mgr. Mem. Am. Soc. Tng. and Devel., Am. Soc. Personnel Adminstrn., Beta Gamma Sigma. Republican. Methodist. Home: 19208 Haviland Dr South Bend IN 46637 Office: Miles Labs Inc 1127 Myrtle St Elkhart IN 46515

MAGORIAN, JAMES, author, poet; b. Palisade, Nebr., Apr. 24, 1942; s. Jack and Dorothy (Gorthey) M. B.S., U. Nebr., 1965; M.S., Ill. State U., 1969; postgrad. Oxford U., 1971, Harvard U., 1973. Author children's books: School Daze, 1978; 17%, 1978; The Magic Pretzel, 1979; Ketchup Bottles, 1979; Imaginary Radishes, 1980; Plucked Chickens, 1980; Fimperings and Torples, 1981; author numerous books of poetry, including: Ideas for a Bridal Shower, 1980; The Edge of the Forest, 1980; Spiritual Rodeo, 1980; Tap Dancing on a Tight Rope, 1981; Training at Home to Be a Locksmith, 1981; The Emily Dickinson Jogging Book, 1984; Keeper of Fire, 1984; Weighing the Sun's Light, 1985; contbr. poems to numerous publs. Address: 1225 N 46th St Lincoln NE 68503

MAGRATH, C. PETER, university president; b. Bklyn., 1933; m. Diane Skomars, 1 child: Monette; 1 child by previous marriage: Valerie. B.A. summa cum laude, U. N.H., 1955; Ph.D. in Polit. Sci., Cornell U., 1962. Mem. faculty Brown U., 1961-65, prof., 1965-68; dean Coll. Arts and Scis., U. Nebr., Lincoln, 1968-72; pres. SUNY-Binghamton, 1972-74, U. Minn., 1974-84, U. Mo. system, Columbia, Kansas City, Rolla and St. Louis, 1985—. Mem. Univ. Forum, Dept. Def. Served with U.S. Army, 1955-57. Named one of 200 Leaders for Future, Time mag., One of 100 Younger Leaders in Am. Higher Edn., Change Mag. Mem. Nat. Assn. State Univs. and Land Grant Colls. (chmn. 1984-85), Assn. Am. Univs. (vice chmn.), Am. Council Edn. (bd. dirs. commn. internat. edn.), Commn. for Excellence in Tchr. Edn. (chmn.). Author: Morrison R. Waite: The Triumph of Character; Yazoo: Law and the Politics in the New Republic, The Case of Fletcher N. Peck; Constitutionalism and Politics; Conflict and Concensus; The American Democracy. Address: 321 University Hall U Mo Columbia MO 65211

MAGUIRE, JOHN PATRICK, aerospace industry executive, lawyer; b. New Britain, Conn., Apr. 1, 1917; s. John Patrick and Edna Frances (Cashen) M.; m. Mary-Emily Jones, Sept. 8, 1945; children—Peter Dunbar, Joan Guilford. Student, Holy Cross Coll., Worcester, Mass., 1933-34, Babson Coll., Wellesly Hills, Mass., 1934-36; B.A., Princeton U., 1941; J.D., Yale U., 1943; LL.D. (hon.), St. Bonaventure U., Olean, N.Y., 1965. Bar: Conn. 1943, N.Y. 1944. Assoc. Cravath, Swaine, Moore, N.Y.C., 1944-50, 52-54; v.p. investments Forbes Pub. Co., N.Y.C., 1950-52, asst. counsel Gen. Dynamics, N.Y.C., 1954-60, v.p., sec., N.Y.C. and St. Louis, 1962—; gen. counsel, sec. Tex. Butadiene and Chem. Corp., N.Y.C., 1960-62. Mem. investment com. John Burroughs Sch., St. Louis, 1978—; trustee World Affairs Council St. Louis, 1983—; bd. dirs. Webster U., St. Louis, 1984-85. Mem. ABA, Am. Soc. Corp. Secs. Republican. Clubs: Piping Rock (Locust Valley, N.Y.); St. Louis Country, University. Home: 8 Chatfield Pl Rd Saint Louis MO 63141 Office: Gen Dynamics Corp Pierre Laclede Ctr Saint Louis MO 63105

MAHAFFEY, CHARLES LEE, dentist; b. Springfield, Mo., Aug. 15, 1946; s. Robert Lee and Francis (Lakin) M.; m. Diana Kay Mayfield, Mar. 4, 1966; children—Brian Lee, Alan Lee, Darren William. B.S., Southwest Mo. State U., 1968; D.D.S., U. Mo.-Kansas City, 1972. Practice dentistry Springfield, Mo., 1975—. Vice pres. Springfield Little League, 1979, Kickapoo Am. Legion Baseball, Springfield, 1983-84. Served to capt. USAF, 1972-75. Mem. Springfield Dental Soc. (sec., treas. 1979-81, v.p. 1982, pres. 1983), Mo. Dental Assn. (state del. 1982-85), Horizon Dental Study Club (sec. 1979, pres. 1981). Republican. Methodist. Avocations: antique cars; golf; fishing. Home: 2853

Grayrock Rd Springfield MO 65807 Office: 509 W Battlefield St Springfield MO 65807

MAHAN, GENEVIEVE ELLIS, sociologist; b. Canton, Ohio, Aug. 1, 1909; d. William and Lillian (Ellis) Mahan; A.B., Case Western Res. U., 1931, A.M., 1941; postgrad. (Ford Found. fellow) Yale, 1952, Akademie fur Politische Bildung, Tutzing, Germany, 1963. Tchr. high schs., Canton, 1937-52; research asst. dept. sociology Yale, 1953-55; lectr. sociology Walsh Coll., Canton, 1970. Participant Instns. Atlantic and European Cooperation Seminar, Coimbra, Portugal, 1970; participant World Congress of Sociology, Evian, France, 1966. Trustee, Stark County Psychiat. Found., 1961-68. Fellow Am. Sociol. Assn.; mem. Internat. Sociol. Assn., Eastern Sociol. Soc., Am. Acad. Polit. and Social Sci., Nat., Ohio (exec. bd. 1962-69, pres. 1965) councils for social studies, AAAS, AAUW (mem. exec. bd. Canton 1966-67), Ohio Acad. Sci., Ohio Soc. N.Y. Clubs: Canton Womans, Massillon Woman's, Canton College. Research in polit. caricature, 1955—. Home: 804 5th St NW Canton OH 44703

MAHAN, HAROLD DEAN, museum executive; b. Ferndale, Mich., June 11, 1931; s. Elbert Verl and Jo Ann Magdeline (Upton) M.; m. Mary Jane Gairdner, June 9, 1954; children—Michael, Eric, David, Christopher, Thomas; B.A., Wayne U., 1954; M.S., U. Mich., 1957; Ph.D., Mich. State U., 1964. Prof. biology Central Mich. U., 1957-73, dir. Center for Cultural and Natural History, 1970-72; pres. Environ. Enterprises, Inc., Mt. Pleasant, Mich., 1970-73; dir. Cleve. Mus. Natural History, 1973—; adj. prof. Case-Western Res. U., 1973—; resident scientist Museo de Historia Natural, Cali, Colombia, 1968; v.p. Midwest Museums Conf., 1974-76, pres., 1976-80. Mem. Airport Commn. Mt. Pleasant, 1965-68; pres. Mich. Audubon Soc., 1972-73; mem. Ohio Natural Areas Council, 1974-80; trustee Inst. for Environ. Edn., Shaker Lakes Regional Nature Center, Holden Arboretum (corporate bd.), Greater Cleve. Garden Center, Univ. Circle, Inc., Rapid Recovery, Inc.; v.p. SEARCH Found., Dallas, 1983—, Cleanland, 1983—. Trustee, Sea Research Found., Hartford, Conn. Recipient Outstanding Exec. of Yr. award Exec. Women Internat., 1983. Mem. Ohio Museums Assn. (pres. 1976-80), Assn. Sci. Mus. Dirs. (pres. 1980-82, sec.-treas. 1982—). Assn. Systematic Collections (v.p. 1979-81), Sigma Xi, Phi Kappa Phi, Phi Sigma, Beta Beta Beta, NSF faculty fellow Mich. State U., 1965. Clubs: Cleve. Playhouse, Rowfant; Explorers (N.Y.C.). Author: (with George J. Wallace) An Introduction to Ornithology, 1975; editor: The Jack Pine Warbler, 1965-72; Nature columnist Cleve. Press, 1973-74; book rev. editor Explorer mag., 1974—; contbr. articles to profl. jours. Office: Mus Natural History Wade Oval University Circle Cleveland OH 44106

MAHANNA, GORDON KENT, dentist; b. Norton, Kans., Apr. 30, 1938; s. Raymond Wendell and Aileen (McCartney) M.; m. Karen Marie Mowry, Aug. 23, 1959 (dec. June 1979); children—Kent Wendell, Thaine Allan, Kimberly Kay; m. Sylvia M. Braun, Aug. 18, 1984; stepchildren—Marcel J., Trent G. Student Kans. State U., 1956-59; D.D.S. with distinction, U. Mo.-Kansas City, 1963; postgrad. U. Tex. Dental Sch., 1985. Pvt. practice dentistry, Hoxie, Kans., 1963—; team leader Sino Am. Tech. Exchange Council, 1982; chief dental services Sheridan County Hosp., Hoxie, Kans., 1964—; mem. coop. research project U. Mo. Dental Sch., Kansas City, 1972-73; chief dental services Sheridan County Hosp., Hoxie, 1964—; lectr. elective enrichment program U. Mo. Sch. Dentistry, Kansas City, 1971, 72, lab. instr., endodontic asst., 1962-63; teaching asst. U. Tex. Sch. Dentistry, San Antonio, 1985. Mem. Airport Improvement Commn., Hoxie, 1967; instr. Kans. Hunter Safety Program, 1971-74, master instr., 1973; mem. Sheridan County Mental Health Assn., 1963—, pres., 1964-66; actor Neighborhood Entertainment Co., 1980—; cubmaster Tomahawk council Boy Scouts Am., 1971-73; bd. dirs. Sheridan County Cancer Soc., 1983—, med.-dental advisor, 1984. Recipient award Kans. Arts Commn., 1984. Mem. ADA, Kans. State Dental Assn. (exec. council 1980-81, fed. manpower com. 1981, impared dentist com. 1980—), N.W. Kans. Dental Assn. (sec.-treas. 1978-79, v.p. 1979-80, pres. 1980-81), Phi Beta Kappa, Omicron Kappa Upsilon, Xi Psi Chi. Clubs: Oil Belt Dental Study (pres. 1970); Gideons. Avocations: soaring; photography; snow skiing; fine arts. Home: 1500 Henry St Hays KS 67601 Office: 830 Main St Hoxie KS 67740

MAHANNA, ROBERT DEAN, pharmacist; b. Hoxie, Kans., May 8, 1925; s. Raymond Wendell and Aileen P. (McCartney) M.; m. Kathleen L. McCutcheon, June 29, 1945; children—Jan, Susan, David. B.S., U. Kans., 1950. Lic. pharmacist, Kans. Pres., pharmacist Mahanna Pharmacy, Inc., Hoxie, 1950—; pharmacy cons. Sheridan County Hosp.; mem. pharmacy adv. council U. Kans., 1972—, preceptor, 1974—; mem. Kans. State Bd. Pharmacy, 1976-79. Active Boy Scouts Am.; mem. steering com. Indsl. Devel. for Hoxie, 1974-80; bd. dirs. Three County Title 5 Program, 1972-75; treas. Greater N.W. Kans., Inc., 1968-76; trustee Hoxie Methodist Ch., 1978-82. Served with USN, 1943-46. Mem. Kans. Pharmacists Assn. (pres. 1963-64; Bowl of Hygeia award 1977), Am. Pharm. Assn., Nat. Assn. Retail Druggists, Hoxie C. of C. (pres. 1954), ISIS Clowns (pres. 1979), Clowns of Am., Pi Kappa Alpha, Kappa Psi; fellow Am. Coll. Apothecaries. Republican. Lodges: Rotary (pres. 1954, 70), Masons (past master), Order Eastern Star (past patron), Shriners, Elks (Hoxie). Avocations: clowning; antiques; furniture refinishing; gardening. Home: 1341 Sheridan Ave Hoxie KS 67740 Office: Mahanna Pharmacy 833 Main St Hoxie KS 67740

MAHANNA, SIMON ALBERT, construction management company executive; b. St. Louis, Sept. 14, 1948; s. Simon Albert and Patricia Ruth (Swift) M.; B.S., U. Mo., 1970, M.S., 1975; m. Debra Ann Brady, July 24, 1971; children—Rachele Christina, Elizabeth Brady, Simon Albert III. Civil engr. City of St. Louis, 1970-72; sr. planning engr. Bechtel Power Corp., 1973-76; project engr. McCarthy Bros. Co., St. Louis, 1976-77; sr. v.p. Escrow Mgmt., Inc., Crestwood, Mo., 1977-82, pres., 1982—, also dir.; pres. Profl. Devel. and Mgmt. Services, 1977—, also dir.; pres. Profl. Builders of St. Louis, Inc., 1979—; pres. Century Subaru, 1983—, AMG of Mo., 1983—; gen. partner Profl. Realty Assocs., 1980—; dir. Boatmen's Nat. Bank of Concord Village. Served with U.S. Army, 1969-77. Registered profl. engr., Mo., Calif., Ill. Mem. ASCE, Nat. Soc. Profl. Engrs., Am. Fedn. Scientists. Maronite Catholic. Office: PO Box 56 Chesterfield MO 63017

MAHANTI, SUBHENDRA DEV, physicist, researcher, physics educator; b. Cuttack, Orissa, India, Sept. 24, 1945; came to U.S., 1964, naturalized, 1978; s. Bhaba K. and Priyambada Mahanti; m. Joyasree Raichoudhury, Dec. 9, 1972; children—Sanjit, Smeeta. B.S. with honors, Ravenshaw Coll., Cuttack, Orissa, India, 1961; M.S., Allahabad U., 1963; Ph.D., U. Calif.-Riverside, 1968. Mem. tech. staff Bell Telephone Labs., Murray Hill, N.J., 1968-70; asst. prof. physics Mich. State U., East Lansing, 1970-77, assoc. prof. physics, 1977-82, prof. physics, 1982—; vis. assoc. prof. Inst. of Physics, Bhubaneswar, Orissa, 1976; vis. prof. U. Antwerp, Belgium, 1980; vis. scientist Max Planck Inst., Stuttgart, Fed. Republic Germany, 1980. Contbr. articles to profl. jours. Recipient Gold medal U. Allahabad, 1963; grantee NSF, Fulbright Found., 1983-84. Mem. Am. Phys. Soc., Am. Biophys. Soc. Avocations: photography, reading, travel. Home: 1165 Ramblewood Dr East Lansing MI 48823 Office: Mich State U Physics Dept East Lansing MI 48824

MAHER, DAVID WILLARD, lawyer; b. Chgo., Aug. 14, 1934; s. Chauncey Carter and Martha (Peppers) M.; A.B., Harvard, 1955, LL.B., 1959; m. Jill Waid Armagnac, Dec. 20, 1954; children—Philip Armagnac, Julia Armagnac. Admitted to N.Y. bar, 1960, Ill. bar, 1961; practiced in Chgo., 1961—; asso. Kirkland & Ellis, and predecessor firm, 1960-65, partner, 1966-78; partner firm Reuben & Proctor, 1978—; lectr. Loyola U. Sch. Law., Chgo. Bd. dirs. Chgo. Better Bus. Bur. Served to 2d lt. USAF, 1955-56. Mem. Am., Ill., Chgo. bar assns. Roman Catholic. Clubs: Bull Valley Hunt, Chicago Literary, Union League, Tavern. Home: 311 Belden Ave Chicago IL 60614 Office: 19 S LaSalle St Chicago IL 60603

MAHJOURI, FEREYDOON SABET, plastic surgeon, hand surgeon; b. Tehran, Iran, Aug. 1, 1943; came to U.S., 1969, naturalized, 1978; s. Ali and Ghamar M.; m. Sussan N. Navidi, Feb. 10, 1984. M.D., Tehran U., Iran, 1966. Diplomate Am. Bd. Plastic and Reconstructive Surgery. Intern Tehran U. Hosps., 1966-67, research fellow Cancer Inst., 1967; surg. intern Cook County Hosp., Chgo., 1969-70, resident in gen. surgery and trauma surgery, 1970-74; resident in plastic and reconstructive surgery and surgery of hand Loyola U. Med. Ctr., Cook County Hosp., Chgo., 1974-77; practice medicine specializing in plastic surgery and hand surgery, Mpls., 1977—; mem. staff Unity Med. Ctr., Fridley, Minn., Mercy Med. Ctr., Coon Rapids, Minn., North Meml. Med. Ctr., Mpls. Served with Imperial Iranian Air Force, 1967-69. Fellow ACS, Internat. Coll. Surgeons; mem. AMA (Physicians Recognition award 1977, 80, 83), Hennepin County Med. Soc., Minn. State Med. Assn., Minn. Surg. Soc., Minn. Acad. Plastic and Reconstructive Surgeons, Am. Soc. Plastic and Reconstructive Surgeons, Am. Burn Assn., Am. Soc. Abdominal Surgeons, Am. Assn. Hand Surgery, Midwestern Assn. Plastic Surgeons. Home: 1530 Tanglewood Rd Long Lake MN 55356 Office: Cosmetic Plastic and Reconstructive Surgeons PA 500 Osborne Rd Ste 110 Unity Professional Bldg Minneapolis MN 55432

MAHONEY, BILL, professional hockey coach. Coach Minn. North Stars, NHL. Office: Minn North Stars 7901 Cedar Ave S Bloomington MN 55420*

MAHONEY, PATRICIA ANN NORDSTROM, personal services company executive; b. Hastings, Minn., Apr. 13, 1939; d. Harold Edward and Mary Patricia (Ahern) Nordstrom; B.S. cum laude, U. Minn., 1961; children—Patrick Sean, Erin Mary. Tchr., head curriculum com. Hopkins (Minn.) Sr. High Sch., 1961-64; mgr. Bridal Services, Inc., Mpls., 1969-73; buyer, gen. mgr. Anderson's Wedding World Stores, Mpls., 1973-77; dir. fashion div. Nat. Bridal Service, Richmond, Va., 1975—, also dir.; mktg. and tng. specialist Minn. Dept. Edn., 1977-80; edn. cons. Mpls. Star & Tribune Newspapers, 1981-83, mgr. edn. services, 1983-85, single copy sales mgr., 1985—. Mem. Phi Beta Kappa. Home: 5604 Colfax Ave S Minneapolis MN 55419

MAHONEY, RICHARD J., chemical company executive. Pres., chief exec. officer, dir., Monsanto Co., St. Louis. Office: Monsanto Co 800 N Lindbergh Blvd Saint Louis MO 63166*

MAHONEY, ROBERT W., banking and security systems manufacturing company executive. Pres., chief exec. officer, chief operating office, dir. Diebold, Inc., Canton, Ohio. Office: Diebold Inc 818 Mulberry Rd SE Canton OH 44711*

MAHONEY, VINCENT DAVID, science educator; b. Chgo., Dec. 22, 1931; s. Vincent Patrick and Hannah (Flynn) M.; m. Betty Bollin, June 22, 1963. B.A., in English, U. Nev., 1954; M.A.T. in Sci., Mich. State U., 1963; Ph.D., U. Calif.-Berkeley, 1970. Tchr. sci. Walnut Creek, Calif., 1963-68; sci. supr. U. Calif.-Berkeley, 1968-70; dept. chmn. edn. div. Iowa Wesleyan Coll., Mt. Pleasant, 1970—; sci. cons. Harper & Row Pub., Walnut Creek, 1966-68, Sci. Found. Ctr., U. Iowa, 1977-80. Author: Individualized Physical Geology, 1979. Contbr. articles to profl. jours. Served with Signal Corps, U.S. Army, 1954-56, Korea. Mem. Nat. Sci. Tchrs. Assn. (life), Iowa Acad. Sci. Roman Catholic. Lodge: Kiwanis (pres. 1977-78, sec. 1983—). Home: 801 N Main St Mount Pleasant IA 52641 Office: Iowa Wesleyan Coll Edn Div 601 N Main St Mount Pleasant IA 52641

MAHONEY, WALTER CHARLES, JR., genetics and cell biology educator, researcher; b. Seattle, Sept. 12, 1951; s. Walter Charles Mahoney and Georgia Marie (Southwell) Franklin; m. Paula Ann Schueler, Apr. 14, 1983; children—Lindsey L.; Kristen E. B.S. in Organic Chemistry, U. Wash., Seattle, 1976; Ph.D. in Biochemistry, Purdue U., 1980. Dir. protein and nucleic acid chemistry Immuno Nuclear Corp., Stillwater, Minn., 1982-84, dir. research, 1984—; asst. prof. genetics and cell biology U. Minn., St. Paul, 1983—. Patentee in field. Mem. Am. Soc. Biol. Chemists, N.Y. Acad. Scis., Am. Chem. Soc. Avocations: sailing; flying; jazz. Home: 7628 Dunmore Dr Woodbury MN 55125 Office: Immuno Nuclear Corp 1951 Northwestern Ave Stillwater MN 55082

MAHRT, STEVEN DALE, lawyer; b. Sioux City, Iowa, Feb. 4, 1953; s. Donald Duane and Ada May (Chamberlain) M.; m. Vickie Lou Krause, Aug. 7, 1976; children—Abigail, Elizabeth. B.A. in Polit. Sci. and English, William Jewell Coll., 1975; J.D., U. Nebr., 1978. Bar: Mo. 1978, Ill. 1983. Assoc. Zahnd & Mahrt and predecessor Zahnd Law Offices, Savannah, Mo., 1978-81, ptnr., 1981-83; corp. counsel Town of Normal, Ill., 1983—. Republican nominee for pros. atty., Andrew County, Mo., 1980, 82. Mem. ABA (urban, state and local govt. law sect.), Mo. State Bar Assn., Ill. State Bar Assn. (govt. law sect.), McLean County Bar Assn. Baptist. Home: 1316 E Vernon St Normal IL 61761 Office: Town of Normal 100 E Phoenix Ave Normal IL 61761

MAI, JOETTA, banker; b. Milberger, Kans., May 30, 1937; d. Reuben and Elsie (Boxberger) Nuss; m. Howard E. Mai, Aug. 19, 1956; children—Mona L., Michelle L. Grad. High Sch., Russell, Kans., 1955. Bookkeeper, supr. Home State Bank, Russell, Kans., 1956-60; bookkeeper Russell State Bank, Kans., 1968-70, drive-in teller, 1970-71, clk., 1971-79, asst. cashier, 1979-81, asst. v.p., 1981—, personnel officer, 1985—. Advisor Community Chest, 1984—. Republican. Lutheran. Avocations: fishing; bowling; horse racing. Home: 326 Hartman Russell KS 67665

MAIANU, ALEXANDRU, soil science educator, researcher; b. Moldoveni, Romania, Jan. 8, 1931; came to U.S., 1977; s. Nedelcu and Voica (Burtea) M.; B.S., U. Bucharest (Romania), 1953, M.S., 1954, Ph.D., 1962. Research soil scientist Romanian Agr. Research Inst., 1954-63; sr. research soil scientist, head Soil Reclamation Lab., Romania, 1963-77; asst. prof. soil sci. U. Bucharest, 1963-66; assoc. prof. soil sci. N.D. State U., Fargo, 1980—; nat. supr. Romanian research programs in soil reclamation, 1969-74. Pres. Emmanuel, Inc., Christian Ministry to East European countries. Recipient Ion Ionescu de la Brad award Romanian Acad. Scis., 1966, Emil Racovitza award, 1972; award Romanian Dept. Edn., 1968. Mem. Am. Soc. Agronomy, N.D. Acad. Sci., Soil Sci. Soc. Am., Internat. Soc. Soil Sci. Author: Secondary Soil Salinization, 1964; (with A. Ghidia) Improving Soil Fertility in Greenhouses, 1974; (with G. Obrejanu) Limnology of the Romanian Sector of the Danube River, 1967, Soil Study on the Experimental Stations of Romanian Agriculture, 1958. Home: PO Box 5422 Fargo ND 58105 Office: ND State U Dept Soil Sci Waldron Hall 201 H PO Box 5575 Fargo ND 58105

MAIER, HENRY W., mayor; b. Dayton, Ohio, Feb. 7, 1918; s. Charles Jr. and Marie L. (Knisley) M.; B.A., U. Wis., 1940; M.A., U. Wis.-Milw., 1964; m. Karen Lamb, May 8, 1976; children by previous marriage—Melinda Ann Maier Carlisle, Melanie Marie. Mem. Wis. Legislature, 1950-60, minority floor leader for Senate, 1953, 55, 57, 59; mayor of Milw., 1960—. Served as lt. USNR, World War II; PTO. Named 1 of 60 most influential men in Am., U.S. News and World Report, 1975, 76; Disting. Urban Mayor, Nat. Urban Coalition, 1979; recipient City Livability award 1980. Mem. U.S. Conf. Mayors (pres., 1971-72, now mem. exec. com.; Disting. Pub. Service award 1983), Nat. Conf. Dem. Mayors (past pres.), Nat. League of Cities (dir., past pres.). Democrat. Author: Challenge to the Cities, 1966; Strategic Budgeting and Resource Management: A System, 1982. Home: 1324 W Birch St Milwaukee WI 53209 Office: City Hall Milwaukee WI 53202

MAIER, NORMAN RAYMOND, trade association executive; b. Thorp, Wis., Feb. 23, 1928; s. John Capser and Helen Catherine (Schmidt) M.; m. Mary Lee, Sept. 28, 1933; children—Susan, Sharon. B.S. in Dairy Tech., U. Wis., 1954. Supr. prodn. Sealtest Foods, Milw. and Chgo., 1954-63; with Nat. Flavors, Indpls., 1963-77; exec. dir. Wis. Dairy Products Assn., Madison, 1977—; lobbyist dairy industry, and dairy processors, 1977—. Served with USAF, 1946-49, 50-51. Mem. Dairy Assn. Execs. Conf., Wis. Soc. Assn. Execs., Wis. Assn. Lobbyists. Roman Catholic. Club: Toastmasters (bd. dirs. 1974-76).

MAILE, MARIE HENNINGER, biostatistician; b. McKeesport, Pa.; d. William Beuscher and Caroline Florentine (Graf) Henninger; m. James Paul Maile, Jan. 17, 1970; children—Carolyn, John, Judy, Sara. B.S., Samford U., Birmingham, Ala., 1964; M.S., Fla. State U., 1966. Assoc. biostatistician I, Upjohn, Co., Kalamazoo, Mich., 1966-70, assoc. biostatistician II, 1970-73, biostatistician I, 1973—. Contbr. articles to profl. publs. Leader 4-H, Galesburg, 1983—. Mem. Am. Statis. Assn. (sec.-treas. southwest Mich. chpt. 1983—). Congregationalist. Home: 9799 E G Ave Galesburg MI 49053

MAIN, PAUL KEITH, health planner; b. Greenfield, Ind., May 22, 1931; s. Clarence B. and Ruth (Elnora) M.; m. Barbara Esther Pomeranz, Mar. 23, 1980; children—Timothy, Michal. B.A., Hanover Coll., 1953; B.D., Louisville Presbyn. Theol. Sem., 1956; postgrad. U. Edinburgh (Scotland), 1956-58; M.Community Planning, U. Cin., 1970; Ed.D., Ind. U., 1978. Pastor North Fairmount Presbyn. Ch., Cin., 1958-68; assoc. dir. Tri-State Area Health Planning Council, Evansville, Ind., 1970-76; sr. health planner Ind. State Bd. Health, Indpls., 1978—; adj. prof. Bur. Studies Adult Edn., Ind. U., 1978—. Mem. community adv. com. Multipurpose Arthritis Ctr., Ind. U. Patterson scholar, 1949-56; Patterson fellow, 1956-58; USPHS trainee, 1968-70. Mem. Am. Assn. Adult Edn., Am. Planning Assn., World Future Soc. Presbytery of the Ohio Valley. Contbr. articles to profl. jours. Home: 371 E Westfield Blvd Indianapolis IN 46220 Office: 1330 W Michigan St Indianapolis IN 46206

MAIN, ROBERT PEEBLES, hospital administrator; b. Buffalo, Nov. 13, 1943; s. Andrew and Jane (Neary) M.; m. Cleta Miller, June 13, 1964; children—Kelly Ann, Thomas. B.S. in Edn., SUNY-Buffalo, 1965; M.A. in Hosp. and Health Adminstrn., U. Iowa, 1973. Coordinator rehab. medicine services for psychiat. service and drug treatment unit VA Hosp., Iowa City, 1971-72, staff asst. to hosp. dir., 1972-74, asst. to chief staff, Oklahoma City, 1974-76; adj. asst. prof. health care adminstrn. U. Okla. Coll. Health, Oklahoma City, 1975-76; asst. hosp. dir. trainee VA Hosp., Memphis, 1976-77; assoc. hosp. dir. VA Lakeside, Chgo., 1977-79; exec. v.p. Marianjoy Rehab. Ctr., Wheaton, Ill., 1979—. Chmn. fund raising activity Ch. of Holy Spirit, Schaumburg, Ill., 1979-85. Mem. Am. Coll. Hosp. Adminstrs., Am. Hosp. Assn., Chgo. Health Execs. Forum (sec., treas. 1981-82), Ill. Regents Adv. Council, DuPage Subarea Adv. Council, Health Systems Agy., Oklahoma City Met. Hosp. Council. Home: 212 Continental Ln Schaumburg IL 60194

MAIN, STANLEY ROBERT, financial analyst, market researcher; b. Indpls., Feb. 24, 1945; s. Robert Earnest and Clarice (Hitch) M.; m. Carla Ann Harton, June 19, 1966 (div. 1972); 1 child, Michael; m. Kathleen Susanna Murrell, June 9, 1973; children—Susanne, Jennifer, Lauren, Matthew. B.S. in Bus., U. Evansville, 1968; M.B.A. in Fin., Mich. State U., 1969. Auditor, Outboard Marine Corp., Waukegan, Ill., 1969-70, budget analyst, 1970-72, fin. analyst, 1972-75, mgr. fin. analysis, 1975-78, mgr. market research, 1978-80, mgr. fin. analysis, market research, 1980-85, dir. fin. and sales analysis, 1985—. Mem. Nat. Assn. Bus. Economists. Republican. Methodist. Avocations: running, backgammon, computers. Home: 310 Cypress Ln Libertyville IL 60048 Office: Outboard Marine Corp 100 Sea Horse Dr Waukegan IL 60085

MAIN, STEPHEN PAUL, biology educator; b. Iowa City, Aug. 26, 1940; s. Clarence Ervin and Margaret (Paul) M.; m. Elaine Carol Blum, Aug. 3, 1963. B.S., Valparaiso U., 1962, M.A. L.S., 1965; Ph.D., Oreg. State U., 1972. Tchr. Crescent Iroquois Community High Sch., Crescent City, Ill., 1962-63; lab. instr. Valparaiso U., Ind., 1963-65; tchr. Santiam High Sch., Mill City, Oreg., 1965-69; asst. prof. biology Wartburg Coll., Waverly, Iowa, 1971-79, assoc. prof., 1979—. Contbr. articles to profl. jours. Mem. Am. Inst. Biol. Sci., Nat. Assn. Biology Tchrs., Bot. Soc. Am., Phycol. Soc. Am., Ecol. Soc. Am., Iowa Acad. Sci., Sigma Xi. Lutheran. Office: Wartburg Coll Waverly IA 50677

MAINE, LUCINDA LOUISE, pharmacist, educator; b. New London, Conn., Aug. 11, 1956; d. Richard Prentice Maine and Marilyn Agnes (Tripp) Austin. B.S. in Pharmacy, Auburn U., 1980; Ph.D., U. Minn., 1984. Pharmacist Mobile Infirmary, Ala., 1980; research asst. Minn Ho. of Reps., 1981-82; fellow U. Minn., Mpls., 1981-84; asst. prof. U. Minn. Park Nicollet Med. Ctr., Mpls., 1984—. Editor newsletter Grapevine, 1980-83. Vol. Durenberger for U.S. Senate, Mpls., 1982. Recipient research achievement award Kellogg Pharm. Clin. Scientist Program, 1983. Mem. Am. Pharm. Assn. (policy com. on ednl. affairs policy com. on profl. affairs, vice speaker ho. of dels. 1985-86), Minn. Pharm. Assn. (vice speaker ho. of dels., dir. 1984-85, dir. task force on women in pharmacy 1981-82), Gerontol. Soc. Am., Am. Soc. Hosp. Pharmacists. Republican. Presbyterian. Club: Women's (Mpls.) Avocations: skiing, sailing, reading. Home: 4418 W Lake Harriet Pkwy Apt 202 Minneapolis MN 55410 Office: Park Nicolle Med Ctr 5000 W 39th St Minneapolis MN 55416

MAIWALD, DIANE CECILE, dermatologist; b. Huntington, L.I., N.Y., Apr. 4, 1947; d. Ernest John and Cecelia Ann (Kuskowski) M. B.A., Fordham U., 1969; M.D., Emory U., 1975. Diplomate Am. Bd. Dermatology. Intern, Stonybrook U. Affiliated Hosps., N.Y., 1975-76; resident Louisville Med. Sch. Assoc. Hosps., 1976-78, Wayne State U., 1978-79; practice medicine specializing in dermatology, Toledo, Ohio, 1979—. Bd. dirs. Goodwill Industries, Toledo, 1983. Mem. Am. Acad. Dermatology. Mem. Soc. Friends. Office: 3450 W Central Ave Suite 118 Toledo OH 43606

MAJOR, SCHWAB SAMUEL, aerospace company manager; b. Windsor, Mo., July 2, 1924; s. Schwab Samuel and Meda Anne (Fultz) M.; m. Wilma Jean Briscoe, June 10, 1951; children—Schwab Samuel III, Karen Lee, Karl Bruce. B.A., Wichita State U., 1949; M.S., Kans. State U., 1953, Ph.D., 1967. Staff engr. Boeing Co., Wichita, Kans., 1951-53; instr. physics Southwestern Coll., Winfield, Kans., 1953-55; asst. prof. Midland Coll., Fremont, Nebr., 1955-59; prof. U. Mo., Kansas City, 1959-81; adminstr. tech. devel. Allied Corp., 1981—. Author: Introduction to Quantum Mechanics, 1976. Contbr. articles to profl. jours. Served with U.S. Army, 1943-46. Mem. AIAA. Avocations: flying, photography, backpack hiking, shooting. Office: Bendix Kansas City Div PO Box 1159 Kansas City MO 64141

MAJOR, TERRY CHARLES, cardiovascular physiologist, pharmacology researcher; b. Ludington, Mich., May 6, 1952; s. Charles Fredrick and Joyce Eleanor (Petersen) M.; m. Suzanne Kay Nelson, July 1, 1978; 1 dau., Katherine Grace. B.A., Hope Coll., 1974; M.S., Mich. State U., 1977; M.S., U. Mich., 1985. Nuclear med. technician Blodgett Meml. Hosp., Grand Rapids, Mich., 1977-78; research scientist Oak Ridge Nat. Lab., 1978-80; assoc. scientist Warner Lambert, Ann Arbor, Mich., 1980—. NIH grantee 1977. Avocations: computer programming; model railroading. Office: Warner Lambert/Parke Davis 2800 Plymouth Rd Ann Arbor MI 48105

MAKAR, FAROUK TAKLA, family practice physician; b. Cairo, Egypt, July 1, 1930; s. Takla and Wadiaa Abd (El Malek) M.; m. Marguerite Emile Wassef, Jan. 9, 1965; children—Nevine, Simon. M.B.B.Ch., Cairo U., 1954; D.P.H., High Inst. Pub. Health, 1963. Diplomate Am. Bd. Family Practice, 1978. Rotating intern, Egypt, 1955-56; rural health officer, 1956-61, 61-65; chief med. and health officer rural ctrs., resident in chest disease, Abhasia, Cairo, 1965-67; resident in pulmonary medicine Univ. Hosp., Cairo, 1967-68; staff physician Abhassia Hosp., 1968-70, dir., mem. bd. adminstrn., 1970-71; with Edge Water Lab., 1971-73; pulmonary fellow Wayne County Health Dept., 1973-74; rotating intern, Highland Park, Mich., 1974-75; resident in internal medicine Sinai Hosp., Detroit, 1975-76; physician specialist respiratory disease control Wayne County Dept. Health, Birmingham, Mich., 1976—; mem. staff family practice Holy Cross Hosp.; assoc. staff dept. medicine St. Joseph Mercy Hosp., Detroit. Coptic Orthodox. Office: 751 Chestnut St Suite 203 Birmingham MI 48008

MAKI, ALBERT JOHN, mechanical engineer; b. Hancock, Mich., Aug. 28, 1920; s. Alexander Edward and Olga Matalda (Tossava) M.; m. Beatris Loraine Ingraham, Oct. 10, 1941. B.S.M.E., Mich. Tech. U., 1948; postgrad. Union Coll., 1948, U. Cin., 1949, UCLA, 1951-52. Registered profl. engr., Mass. Engr., Aircraft and Gas Turbine div. Gen. Electric Co., Evendale, Ohio, 1948-53; asst. to v.p. mfg. Rockwell Internat., El Segundo, Calif., 1953-55; v.p., asst. to pres. Avco Corp., Wilmington, Mass., 1955-73; plant mgr. Centex Corp., St. Charles, Ill., 1973-75; plant mgr. Def. div. Brunswick, Corp., Willard, Ohio, 1975—; treas., dir. Pelham Bank & Trust Co. (N.H.). Mem. N.H. Gov.'s Council Adv. Com., Concord, 1967-69; bd. dirs. ARC, Lowell, Mass., 1967-69; chmn. United Fund, Pelham, 1961-71; one of founders Cin. Jr. Achievement, 1949; mem. State of N.H. Republican Com., 1982-83; trustee Willard Area Hosp. (Ohio); mem. Nat. Republican Com., 1982; life trustee Mich. Tech. Fund. Served with USN, 1942-46. Recipient Mich. Tech. U. Silver medal, 1969. Mem. AIAA, Navy League of U.S., Air Force Assn. Republican. Lutheran. Clubs: Pres.'s (charter mem.), Lions (past pres., past dep. dist. gov. N.H.). Contbr. articles to profl. jours. Home: 715 Maplewood St Willard OH 44809 Office: 302 Conwell St Willard OH 44890

MAKOWSKI, DONNA BIRUTE, lawyer, educator; b. Chgo., Oct. 11, 1954; d. Charles J. and Jean V. (Kriauciunas) M. B.A. with honors, U. Ill.-Chgo., 1976; J.D., John Marshall Sch. Law, 1983. Bar: Ill. 1984, U.S. Dist. Ct. (no. dist.) Ill. 1984, U.S. Ct. Appeals (7th cir.) 1984. Mgr. Jewel Food Corp., Chgo., 1972-76; tchr. fgn. lang. U. Ill.-Chgo., 1976-77, Chgo. Pub. Schs., 1976-83; course/seminar coordinator John Marshall Law Sch., Chgo., 1983-84; sole practice, Chgo., 1984—; mem. Mayor's Adv. Com. on Women's Affairs, Chgo., 1984—; of counsel John De Leon, Chgo. pro bono advocate Chgo. Vol. Legal Services. Aide Sen. Carroll Democratic Orgn., Chgo., 1981-82. Fellow Kosciusko Found., N.Y., 1983. Mem. ABA, Ill. Bar Assn., Chgo. Bar Assn. (sec. young lawyers div. 1982-83), Women's Bar Assn., Ill. Trial Lawyers Assn., Advocates Soc. Phi Kappa Phi, Phi Delta Phi. Roman Catholic. Home: 6231 N Francisco Ave Chicago IL 60659 Office: 3827 N Lincoln Ave Chicago IL 60613 also 134 N La Salle St Suite 306 Chicago IL 60602

MAKRIDIS, IRENE KAFANTARIS, lawyer; b. Chios, Greece, May 16, 1956; came to U.S., 1966, naturalized, 1972; d. Nicholas G. and Evelyn (Frangias) Kafantaris; m. Nicholas G. Makridis, Aug. 21, 1982. B.S., Youngstown State U., 1977; J.D., U. Toledo, 1980. Bar: Ohio, U.S. Dist. Ct.

(no. dist.) Ohio. Sole practice, Warren, Ohio, 1981—; pub. defender County of Trumball, Warren, 1984—. Mem. Trumbell County Bar Assn., Ohio Bar Assn., Ohio Acad. Trial Lawyers. Office: 183 W Market St Warren OH 44481

MAKUPSON, AMYRE ANN PORTER, television executive; b. River Rouge, Mich., Sept. 30, 1947; d. Rudolph Hannibal and Amyre Ann (Porche) P.; B.A., Fisk U., 1970; M.A., Am. U., Washington, 1972; m. Walter H. Makupson, Nov. 1, 1975; children—Rudolph Porter, Amyre Nisi. Public relations dir. Mich. HMO Plans, Detroit, 1973-75; asst. news dir. WGPR TV, Detroit, 1975-76; public relations dir. Kirwood Hosp., Detroit, 1977; news and public affairs mgr. WKBD TV, Southfield, Mich., 1977—. Mem. exec. com. March of Dimes. Recipient Outstanding Public Service awards Arthritis Found. Mich., 1979, Mich. Mechanics Assn., 1980, Afro Am. Mus.; Service Appreciation award Salvation Army, 1980; Humanitarian Service award DAV, 1981; Community Service award Jr. Achievement; Service award Cystic Fibrosis Found., 1981; Disting. Service award City of Detroit; named Outstanding Woman of Year, Prince Matchabelli, 1980. Mem. Women in Communications, Am. Women in Radio and TV (award for Outstanding Achievement 1981), Public Relations Soc. Am., Nat. Acad. TV Arts and Scis., Detroit Press Club, Adcraft, Wheelchair Athletic Assn. (bd. dirs.). Roman Catholic. Office: 26955 W 11 Mile Rd Southfield MI 48037

MALAMUD, ERNEST I., physicist; b. N.Y.C., May 8, 1932; s. Nathan and Rita (Kayser) M. A.B. in physics with highest honors, U. Calif.-Berkeley, 1954; Ph.D. in Physics, Cornell U., 1959. Pvt. docent U. Lausanne, Switzerland and CERN fellow, Geneva, 1960-64; asst. to assoc. prof. U. Ariz., Tucson, 1964-65; assoc. prof. UCLA, 1966-67; physicist Fermilab, Batavia, Ill., 1968—, dept. head Meson Dept., 1978-81, leader program of joint Soviet-Am. expts. in small angle elastic scattering, 1972-78; cons. Exploratorium, San Francisco, 1982. Contbr. articles to profl. jours. Mem. Sesquicentennial Commn., City of Warrenville, 1983-84. Mem. IEEE, Am. Phys. Soc. Club: Swiss Alpine. Avocations: mountaineering; skiing. Home: 3S710 River Rd Warrenville IL 60555 Office: Fermilab Box 500 Batavia IL 60510

MALAND, ROBERT ARTHUR, management consulting company executive, consultant; b. Story City, Iowa, Oct. 2, 1940; s. Lloyd and Mildred Ardys (Nelson) M.; m. Dawn Marie Korn, Sept. 21, 1961 (div. 1972); children—Daniel, Roxanne, Rhonda, Leonard, Eric; m. 2d, Michelle Noreen Molberg, Sept. 22, 1979. A.A., U. Wis.-Barron County, 1975; B.S., U.Wis.-Whitewater, 1977. Enlisted U.S. Air Force, 1961, advanced through grades to staff sgt., 1963, served Pentagon, Washington, ret., 1969; founder, pres., chmn. bd. Maland Mgmt. Cons., Ltd., Marshfield, Wis., 1977—; adj. prof. Milton Coll. (Wis.), 1981-82; instr. Vocat. Sch., Marshfield, 1980-81. Republican Party candidate state senate 24th dist., 1980; sr. warden St. Alban's Episcopal Ch., Marshfield, 1983, 84; mem. Nat. Rep. Congl. Com., 1981-83. Served with USAFR, 1969-76. Recipient Presdl. Achievement award Republican Nat. Com., 1980. Mem. Am. Entrepreneurs Assn., Internat. Entrepreneurs Assn., Nat. Fedn. Ind. Businessmen, Am. Legion, DAV (Comdr.'s Club). Clubs: Friday Night Dance (pres. 1983—), Toastmasters. Home: 427 Parkview Terr Marshfield WI 54449 Office: Maland Mgmt Cons Ltd 110 W 2nd St Suite 1 PO Box 802 Marshfield WI 54449

MALANY, BARBARA BUMGARDER, special education and learning disabilities educator, consultant businesswoman; b. Waco, Tex., Aug. 20, 1943; d. James McNabb and Helen (Welker) Bumgardner; m. LeGrand Lynn Malany, June 27, 1965; children—LeGrand Karl, Siobhan, Carlieen. B.A. in English with honors, U. Ill., 1965, M.Ed. in Spl. Edn., 1972. Coordinator reading lab. Urbana High Sch., Ill., 1968-70; spl. needs tchr. Jefferson Middle Sch., Springfield, Ill., 1973-74; commr. Ill. Commn. on Children, 1974-85; instr. Lincoln Land Community Coll., Springfield, 1977-79; hearing officer Ill. State Bd. Edn., Springfield, 1980—; dir. Childrens' Edn., Central Bapt. Ch., Springfield, 1981—; pres. Flowers Le Grand Ltd., Flowers and Gift Shop, Springfield, 1985—; v.p. Ill. Foster Parent Assn., Springfield, 1970-83; foster parent tng. commr. Ill. Dept. Children and Family Services, Springfield, 1978-79; mem. Ill. White House Com. on Children, 1980; dir. Rutledge Found., Springfield, 1982—, pres., 1983-84; research asst. Inst. Research on Exceptional Children, Urbana, 1971-72. Editor quar. newspaper The Foster Parent, 1976-82. Foster parent to over 15 children Ill., 1968—; active LWV, 1970—, Girl Scouts Am., 1981-82. Fellow U.S. Office Edn., 1971. Mem. Nat. Foster Parents Assn., Women in Mgmt., Ill. Foster Parents Assn., Sangamon Foster Parents Assn., Council for Exceptional Children. Home: 600 S Rosehill Springfield IL 62704 Office: Central Bapt Ch 4th and Jackson Springfield IL 62701 also Flowers Le Grand The Hilton Plaza 7th and Adams Springfield IL 62701

MALARKEY, WILLIAM B., medical educator, physician; b. Pitts., Apr. 9, 1939. B.S., U. Pitts., 1961, M.D., 1965. Intern, Ohio State U. Hosps., Columbus, 1965-66, resident in medicine, 1966-67; fellow in endocrinology Washington U., St. Louis, 1969-71, U. Colo. Med. Ctr., Denver, 1971-72; asst. prof. medicine Ohio State U., 1972-76, assoc. prof. endocrinology and metabolism, 1976-80, mem. staff Ohio State U. Cancer Ctr., 1977—, program dir. Clin. Research Unit, 1978—, prof. endocrinology and metabolism, 1980—, mem. Clin. Research Ctr. adv. and protocol com., 1978—, grant reviewer Cancer Ctr. Core Grant, 1978—; ad hoc grant reviewer Am. Cancer Soc., NSF, 1979—; mem. ad hoc grant rev. com. Nat. Cancer Inst., 1980; mem. NIH study sect. on epidemiology, 1981-82; cons. Brookhaven Nat. Lab., Marshall Island Project, VA Hosp., Dayton, Wright Patterson AFB Hosp., Dayton, Kettering Meml. Hosp., Ohio. Reviewer Jour. Clin. Endocrinology and Metabolism, Annals of Internal Medicine, Archives of Internal Medicine, Clin. Chemistry, Endocrinology and Metabolism, Procs. Soc. Exptl. Medicine, Life Scis., mem. editorial bd. Jour. Clin. Endocrinology and Metabolism. Recipient Landacre Soc. award, 1978. Fellow Am. Coll. Physicians; mem. Am. Soc. Clin. Investigation, Am. Fedn. Clin. Research, AAAS, Columbus Soc. Internal Medicine, Central Soc. Clin. Research, Endocrine Soc., Med. Symposium, Physicians for Social Responsibility.

MALCOLM, DANIEL DWAYNE, industrial educator; b. Herrin, Ill., Oct. 14, 1942; s. Wayne Edward and Geraldine May (Chitty) M.; m. Nancy Aileen Jones, Aug. 21, 1965; 1 dau., Cara Dyanne. B.S. in Indsl. Arts, Ill. State U., 1965, M.S., 1968, postgrad., 1968—. Cert. vocat. tchr., Ill. Tchr. auto mechanics Irving Crown High Sch., Carpentersville, Ind., 1965-66; tchr. power mechanics Richwoods High Sch., Peoria, Ill., 1966-68; coordinator indsl. edn. Bloomington (Ill.) Area Vocat. Ctr., 1968—; mem. Ill. Indsl. Edn. Assn. Bd., 1971-79. Mem. Am. Vocat. Assn., Ill. Vocat. Assn., Ill. Indsl. Edn. Assn., Ill. Coordinators Assn., Vocat. Indsl. Clubs Am., Kappa Delta Pi. United Methodist. Office: 1202 E Locust Bloomington IL 61701

MALCOLM, RONALD ALAN, insurance company executive; b. Chgo., Aug. 15, 1946; s. Robert and Lula Frances (Westenberger) M.; m. Gloria Jean Burns, May 29, 1977; children—Brandi Leigh, Ali Dawn. B.J., U. Mo., 1968, postgrad., 1970-71, 77-78. Mktg. specialist Mid-Continent Aviation, North Kansas City, Mo., 1972-73; supt. mktg. communications Aetna Life & Casualty, Hartford, Conn., 1973-75; gen. mgr. Response Mktg., Kansas City, Mo., 1975-77; advt. mgr. Kansas City Life, Mo., 1977—. Served with U.S. Army, 1968-70. Decorated Bronze Star, Army Commendation medal. Mem. North Central Round Table, Life Communicators Assn. Republican. Avocations: running; handball. Home: 43 E 52d St Kansas City MO 64112 Office: Kansas City Life Ins Co 3520 Broadway Kansas City MO 64111

MALE, MICHAEL J(OHN), veterinarian; b. DeKalb, Ill., May 3, 1952; s. Laverne P. and Betty J. (Flusch) M.; m. Barbara K. Feuerbach, Aug. 10, 1974; children—Kristine Marie, Brandon Michael. B.S., U. Ill., 1975, D.V.M., 1977. Pvt. practice vet. medicine Junction Vet. Clinic, Wilton, Iowa, 1977—. Mem. AVMA, Iowa Vet. Med. Assn., Soc. Theriogenology, Am. Assn. Swine Practitioners. Republican. Home: Box 117 RR 2 Wilton IA 52778 Office: 1015 W 5th St Wilton IA 52778

MALECKI, DAVID MICHAEL, airport manager, aerial observer; b. Ft. Leavenworth, Kans., Sept. 10, 1948; s. John Adam and Marylee Kathryn (Fogle) M.; m. Janice Adele Mayse, Sept. 2, 1972; 1 child, Joshua Gerald. B.S., Central Mo. State U., Warrensburg, 1973; M.P.A., U. Mo.-Kansas City, 1977. Lic. pvt. pilot FAA. Probation and parole officer Mo. Bd. Probation and Parole, Independence, 1973-76; research asst. budget and systems office City of Kansas City (Mo.), 1976-77, budget analyst, 1977-80, adminstrv. officer, asst. airport mgr. aviation dept. Richards-Gebaur Airport, 1980—. Mem. Independence Neighborhood Council, 1974-75. Served with U.S. Army, 1969-71, to staff sgt. Army NG, 1972—. Decorated Army Commendation Medal, Army Res. Achievement Medal with oak leaf clusters (2). Mem. N.G. Assn., Mo. N.G. Assn., Aircraft Owners and Pilots Assn., Pi Sigma Alpha. Home: 5009 Byrams Ford Rd Kansas City MO 64129 Office: 104 Maxwell St Richards Gebaur Airport Kansas City MO 64147

MALEMUD, CHARLES J., biologist, researcher; b. Bklyn., Nov. 5, 1945; s. Irving and Adele (Silvermond) M.; children—Franklin, Rachel. B.S., L.I. U., 1966; Ph.D., George Washington U., 1973. Biologist, NIH, 1968-73; instr. pathology SUNY-Stony Brook, 1973-77; asst. prof. medicine, developmental genetics and anatomy Case Western Res. U., Cleve., 1978-82, assoc. prof., 1982—. Cons., CIBA-Geigy Corp.; mem. study sect. NIH. Nat. Inst. Aging grantee, 1980—; Kroc Found. grantee, 1980-82; Arthritis Found. grantee, 1978-79. Mem. Am. Soc. Cell Biology, Orthopedic Research Soc., Soc. Exptl. Biology and Medicine, N.Y. Acad. Scis., Am. Rheumatism Assn., Sigma Xi. Democrat. Jewish.

MALENICK, DONAL, metals processing company executive. Pres., dir. Worthington Industries Inc., Columbus, Ohio. Office: Worthington Industries Inc 1205 Dearborn Dr Columbus OH 43085*

MALENKE, NORMAN JOHN, computer company business analyst; b. Rochester, Minn., Mar. 10, 1949; s. Glen C. and Bernice R. (Rotermund) M.; m. Glenda Diane Windisch, Nov. 24, 1973; children—Rebecca, Corinna, Andrew. Mus.B. cum laude, U. Idaho, 1972; Mus.M., St. Cloud State U., 1976. Cert. systems profl. Tchr., Rochester pub. schs., 1972-77; asst. v.p., mgr. mortgage loan service dept. United Fin. Savs., 1977-83; product analyst Fin. Info. Trust, Des Moines, 1983—; student affairs cons. Assoc. Systems Mgmt., 1984—; workshop clinician Inst. Fin. Edn., 1985—. Active performer and supporter Rochester Civic Music, 1972-83. Minn. State Dept. Edn. grantee, 1976. Mem. Assn. Systems Mgmt., Phi Kappa Phi. Avocations: active professional cellist, private studio teacher. Home: 3921 73d St Des Moines IA 50322 Office: Fin Info Trust 907 Walnut St Des Moines IA 50309

MALES, HOWARD EDWARD, management consultant, psychologist; b. N.Y.C., Aug. 18, 1954; s. Kenneth Lewis and Adele Esther (luers) M. B.A., Drew U., 1976; M.A. U. Chgo., 1977, Ph.D., 1981. Cons. Booz, Allen and Hamilton, Inc., Chgo., 1979-80, Ernst and Whinney, Chgo., 1982-84; pres. Research Pros, Inc., Chgo., 1985—. Cons. orgnl. devel. activities univs. and hosps. Asst. chmn. DePaul U. Coll. Commerce Anniversary Com., 1982-83; chmn. grad. intern adv. bd. U. Chgo., 1983-85. Mem. Am. Psychol. Assn., Greater Chgo. Assn. Indsl./Orgnl. Psychologists. Clubs: U. Chgo. (steering com. 1981—), Quadrangle. Home: 1642 E 56th St Chicago IL 60637

MALEY, CHARLES DAVID, lawyer; b. Highland Park, Ill., Aug. 18, 1924; s. Lyle West and Irene (Davis) M.; A.B., State U. Iowa, 1948; J.D., De Paul U., 1952; m. Mildred J. Tobin, Apr. 27, 1957; 1 dau., Annabel Irene. Bar: Ill. 1952, U.S. Supreme Ct. 1956. Assoc. firm Friedlund, Levin & Friedlund, Chgo., 1952-58; pvt. practice law, Chgo., 1958-68, Lake Bluff, Ill., 1966-72, Lake Forest, Ill., 1972-83; mem. firm Ori, Tepper, Fox, Maley & Gilleran-Johnson & Waldeck, Waukegan, Ill., 1983—; pub. adminstr. Lake County, 1971-74. Asst. dist. commr. Boy Scouts Am., 1963-65; trustee Lake County Mus. Assn., 1978-79, Lake Forest-Lake Bluff Hist. Soc., 1979-81; bd. dirs. Petite Ballet, 1975-80. Mem. Lake County Republican Central Com., 1967-72, 76—, Rep. State Com., 1971-74; bd. govs. Lake County Rep. Fedn., 1980-83. Served with AUS, 1943-46, Decorated Purple Heart with oak leaf cluster, Bronze Star. Mem. ABA, Seventh Circuit, Ill., Chgo., Lake County bar assns., Am. Judicature Soc., SAR, Am. Legion (post comdr. 1967-68, 74-81, service officer 1968-69, adj. 1982-84, chaplain 1984—), Am. Arbitration Assn. (mem. panel 1965-67), Phi Gamma Delta, Phi Alpha Delta. Republican. Presbyn. Kiwanian (bd. govs. 1976-80). Clubs: Capitol Hill (Washington); Tower (Chgo.). Home: 241 W Washington St Lake Bluff IL 60044 Office: 301 W Washington St Suite 100 Waukegan IL 60085

MALIK, FAZLEY BARY, physics educator; b. Bankura, India, Aug. 16, 1934; came to U.S., 1960; s. Malik Abdul and Feroza (Joader) Bary. B.Sc. with honors, Calcutta U., 1953; M.Sc., Dhaka U., Bangladesh, 1955; Ph.D., Göttingen U., Fed. Republic Germany, 1958. Research assoc. Max Planck Inst., Munich, Fed. Republic Germany, 1958-60, Princeton U., N.J., 1960-63; asst. prof. physics Yale U., New Haven, 1964-68; assoc. prof., then prof. Ind. U., Bloomington, 1968-80; prof., So. Ill. U., Carbondale, 1980—, chmn. dept., 1980-85; chmn. organization com. IX Internat. Workshop on Condensed Matter Theories, 1984-85; mem. Gov.'s Task Force on Fusion, Ill., 1983—; mem. internat. adv. com. Internat. Workshop on Condensed Matter Theories, 1985—; hon. prof. Northwest Norman U., Chang Chun, China, 1984; vis. prof. Tech. U. Karlsruhe, 1965, Tech. U. Darmstadt, 1967, U. Geneva, U. Lausanne, U. Neuchatel, 1971-72, U. Frankfurt, 1971, U. Helsinki, U. Jyvankyla, Abo Acad., 1983, U. Tübingen, 1985-86; adj. assoc. prof. Fordham U., 1961-63, Australia Nat. U., 1966 cons. in field; speaker in field; mem. select com. on synchronization source U. Chgo., 1985—; councilor Oak Ridge Assoc. U., 1985. Editor: Condensed Matter Theories, 1985. Contbr. articles to profl. publs. Named hon. citizen state of Tenn. Mem. Am. Phys. Soc., Sigma Xi. Lodge: Rotary. Avocations: tennis, mountaineering, travel. Home: 200 Emerald Ln Carbondale IL 62901 Office: So Ill U Neckers Bldg 483A Carbondale IL 62901

MALL, SHANKAR, engineering mechanics educator, researcher; b. Varanasi, India, June 10, 1943; came to U.S., 1974; s. Hari Das and Methul Mall; m. Raj Kumari, Dec. 2, 1965; 1 child, Sharal. B.S. in Mech. Engring., Banaras Hindu U. (India), 1964, M.S., 1966; Ph.D., U. Wash., 1977. Engr. in trng. Kisha Seizo Kaisha, Osaka, Japan, 1966-67; lectr. mech. engring. Banaras Hindu U., Varanasi, 1967-74; research asst. U. Wash., Seattle, 1974-77; asst. prof. U. Maine, Orono, 1978-81, assoc. prof., 1981-83; assoc. prof. U. Mo.-Rolla, 1983—; research engr. NASA Langley Research Ctr., Hampton, Va., 1981-82. Contbr. articles to profl. jours. Grantee U.S. Forest Products Lab., 1979-81, NASA, 1982—. Mem. Am. Soc. Engring. Edn., ASME, Am. Acad. Mechanics, Sigma Xi, Tau Beta Pi. Home: 1953 Malibu Ct Rolla MO 65401 Office: Dept Engring Mechanics Univ Missouri Rolla MO 65401

MALLANEY, CAROLYN JEAN, recreation agency administrator; b. Kankakee, Ill., Apr. 22, 1953; d. James F. and Gloria J. (LaMarre) M. B.S., Ill. State U., 1975. Dir. social services Shamel Manor Nursing Home, Normal, Ill., 1975-76; activity therapist Galesburg Mental Health Ctr., Ill., 1976-77; dir. Spl. Olympics and Recreation, Bloomington, Ill., 1977-81; supt. No. Suburban Spl. Recreation Assn., Highland Park, Ill., 1982-84, exec. dir., 1984—; therapeutic recreation cons. McLean County Nursing Home, Shamel Manor Nursing Home, 1979-81; instr. Ill. State U., Normal, 1979; area coordinator Ill. Spl. Olympics, 1977-81. Bd. dirs. McLean County Mental Health Assn., 1979-80, Lake County Marathon, 1984—. Recipient Dr. Martin Luther King Jr. Human Relations award Human Relations Commn. of Bloomington, 1981; nominee Career Woman of Yr., City of Bloomington, 1981; named Outstanding Young Women of Am., 1981. Mem. Ill. Therapeutic Recreation Sect. (dir. 1984—, bd. dirs. 1982-84, sec. 1979-80). Roman Catholic. Home: 574 Fairway View Dr #2K Wheeling IL 60090 Office: No Suburban Spl Recreation Assn 636 Ridge Rd Highland Park IL 60035

MALLEN, GARY PATRICK, newspaper executive; b. Kansas City, Mo., Feb. 19, 1949; s. Arthur Louis and Annebell (Putney) M.; student U. Mo., Kansas City, 1967-69; B.F.A., Kansas City Art Inst., 1973. Art dir. Travis/Walz/Lane Advt., Overland Park, Kans., 1973-74; v.p. Mid-Continent Advt. and Public Relations, Kansas City, Mo., 1975-76; pres. Gary Mallen Design Cons., Kansas City, Mo., 1975—; creative dir. Galvin/Farris/Ross Advt., Kansas City, Mo., 1976-78; mgr. creative services Kansas City (Mo.) Times and Star (Kansas City Star Co.), 1978-82, mktg. creative dir., 1982, promotions mgr., 1983, v.p., nat. creative dir. Am. City Bus. Jours., 1983—. Bd. dirs. Bishop Hogan High Sch., 1978-79, chmn. public relations com., 1979. Winner Kimberly Clark Bi-Centennial Design Competition, 1977; recipient 40 local Addy awards, 8 regional Addy awards, N.Y. Art Dirs. Club award, Dallas Soc. Visual Communications award. Mem. Kansas City Art Dirs. Club (12 awards), Ad Club of Kansas City (chmn. Addy awards com., 1981, 83). Mem. Christian Church. Clubs: Country, Kansas City. Designer books: Historic Kansas City Architecture, 1974, The Star: The First 100 Years, 1980; Folly Theatre Commemorative Book, 1981. Office: 3535 Broadway Kansas City MO 64111

MALLENBY, DOUGLAS WAYNE, business educator; b. Toronto, Mar. 4, 1944; s. Thomas Todd and Anita Mary (Nowlan) M.; m. Micki Lee Deeds, Aug. 24, 1979; children—Courtney, Whitney. B.A., U. Toronto, 1967; M.S., U. Man., 1972; Ph.D., Colo. State U., 1977; M.B.A., U. Nebr., 1980. Systems analyst IBM, Toronto, 1967; mem. faculty St. Francis Xavier U., Antigonish, N.S., Can., 1968-70, U. Man., Winnipeg, 1971-72, Nebr. U., Lincoln, 1975-79; asst. prof. Gonzaga U., Spokane, 1979-82; assoc. prof. Creighton U., Omaha, 1982—; cons. to City Mgr. of Spokane, 1980-81. Contbr. articles to profl. jours. Mem. Am. Statis. Assn. (pres. Omaha 1984-85), Am. Inst. Decision Scis., Inst. Mgmt. Sci., Internat. Bus. Schs. Computer Users Group, Inst. Advancement Decision Support Systems, Mu Sigma Rho. Avocation: dancing. Office: Coll Bus Adminstrn Creighton U Omaha NE 68178

MALLERS, GEORGE PETER, lawyer; b. Lima, Ohio, Apr. 28, 1928; s. Peter G. and Helen (Daskalakis) M.; B.S., Ind. U., 1951; J.D., Valparaiso U., 1955; m. Rubie Loomis, Feb. 2, 1950; children—Peter G. II, William G., Elaine. Admitted to Ind. bar, 1955; practiced in Ft. Wayne, 1955—; mem. Beers, Mallers, Backs, Salin & Larmore, 1955—; county atty., Allen County, Ind., 1964-73; pres. Mallers Theatres, Ft. Wayne, 1949—, Holiday Theatres, Inc., Mallers Mgmt., 1964—, Lansing Theatres, Inc., 1968—, Mallers & Spirou Enterprises, Inc., 1971—, Georgetown Square Theatres I & II, 1971—, Stage Door, Inc., 1972—, M-S Amusement Corp., 1972—, Georgetown Lounge & Restaurant, Inc., 1972—; Mallers-Spirou Mgmt. Corp., 1973—, Georgetown Bowl, Inc., 1976—. Pres., Village Little League, Ft. Wayne, 1962-64, Hoevelwood Civic Assn., 1959-61; mem. Allen County Police Merit Bd., 1967-77. Pres., Allen County Young Republican Club, 1956-58; asst. to Rep. county chmn. Allen County, 1958—; chmn. City-County Bd. Health, 1980—. Fellow Ind. Bar Found.; mem. ABA, Ind., Allen County (sec., dir. 1961-63) bar assns., Am. Judicature Soc., Valparaiso U. Law Sch. Alumni Assn. (nat. pres. 1978-80), Phi Alpha Delta. Office: Ft Wayne Nat Bank Bldg Fort Wayne IN 46802

MALLIN, MORTON LEWIS, microbiology educator; b. Phila., Feb. 13, 1926; s. Benjamin Isaac and Dora (Feldman) M.; m. Roberta Rae Levinthal, Oct. 9, 1960; children—Michael Lee, Diana Faye. B.S., Phila. Coll., 1950; M.S., Hahnemann Med. Coll., 1952; Ph.D., Cornell U., 1956. Research scientist, dept. bacteriology Ind. U., Bloomington, 1952-53; postdoctoral fellow biochemistry Johns Hopkins U., Balt., 1956-57, Brandeis U., Waltham, Mass., 1957-59; biochemist May Inst. Med. Research Jewish Hosp., Cin., 1959-64; assoc. prof. microbiology Ohio No. U., Ada, 1964-70, prof., 1970—; cons. ITT. Contbr. articles to profl. jours. Served with inf. U.S. Army, 1944-46, ETO, Philippines. Research grantee USPHS, 1962-65, Central Ohio Heart Assn. 1966-70, Mead Johnson, 1967, Eli-Lilly, 1969; sabbatical research in enzymology U. Mich. Sch. Medicine, 1976, research in plasmid biology Bowling Green State U., Ohio, 1983. Home: 2904 Hanover Dr Lima OH 45805 Office: Ohio Northern Univ Coll Pharmacy Bldg Ada OH 45810

MALLON, JAMES HOWARD, magazine advertising executive; b. Milw., May 26, 1929; s. J. Howard and Kathryn (Carney) M.; m. Joyce Mary Russo, Sept. 22, 1956; children—James Howard III, Paul A., David C. B.S. in Bus. Adminstrn., Marquette U., 1955. Gen. sales mgr. Naegele Outdoor Advt. Co. of Wis., Milw., 1955-63, v.p., nat. sales mgr. Naegele Advt. Cos. Inc., Chgo., 1963-69; with advt. sales dept. Forbes Mag., Chgo., 1969-80, mgr. midwest sales, 1980—. Mem. Republican Nat. Com. Mem. Advt. Fedn. of Minn., Nat. Assn. Ry. Advt. Mgrs., Delta Sigma Pi (life mem.). Clubs: 1200 of Ill.; Chgo. Athletic, Mid Am., Agate of Chgo.; Mpls. Athletic; Meadow. Office: 435 Michigan Ave Suite 1729 Chicago IL 60611

MALLORY, ARTHUR LEE, state education official; b. Springfield, Mo., Dec. 26, 1932; s. Dillard A. and Ferrell (Claxton) M.; B.S. in Edn., S.W. Mo. State Coll., 1954; M.Ed., U. Mo. at Columbia, 1957, Ed.D., 1959; L.H.D., S.W. Bapt. Coll., 1972; m. Joann Peters, June 6, 1954; children—Dennis Arthur (dec.), Christopher Lee, Stephanie Ann, Jennifer Lyn. History supr. U. Mo. Lab. Sch., Columbia, 1956-57; asst. to supt. schs. Columbia Pub. Schs., 1957-59; asst. supt. schs. Pkwy. Sch. Dist., St. Louis County, Mo., 1959-64; dean U. Mo. at St. Louis, 1964; pres. S.W. Mo. State Coll., Springfield, 1964-70; commr. edn. Dept. Edn., Jefferson City, Mo., 1971—. Pres., Great Rivers council Boy Scouts Am., 1971-73; bd. dirs. N. Central Region, 1984—; Bd. dirs. ARC Cole County; mem. adv. com. Mo. 4-H Found., 1974; mem. Gov.'s Council on the Arts, 1965-66; mem. St. Louis Ednl. TV Comm. Bd.'s Adv. Council KETC-TV, Mo. Law Enforcement Assistance Council, Juvenile Delinquency Task Force, Edn. Commn. States; chmn. bd. trustees Mo. Council on Econ. Edn.; mem. Commrs. Com. on Parents as Tchrs.; chmn. com. bds. So. Bapt. Conv., 1973, mem. exec. bd. Mo. Bapt. Conv., 1972-75, 77-80. Bd. dirs. Midwestern Bapt. Theol. Sem., 1968-72, Internat. House, U. Mo., 1956-59, trustee Meml. Hosp., Jefferson City; bd. regents William Jewell Coll., 1972-74. Mem. Am., Mo., S.W. Mo. assns. sch. adminstrs., NEA, Mo. State Tchrs. Assn., Mo. Congress Parents and Tchrs. (hon. life). Baptist (deacon). Lodges: Masons (33 deg.), Rotary. Office: 100 E Capitol Ave Jefferson City MO 65101

MALLORY, DENNIS IVAN, osteopathic physician and surgeon; b. Council Grove, Kans., Mar. 1, 1940; s. Victor A. and Caris Gwendolyn (Nutt) M.; m. Judi Ann Deardorff, Nov. 27, 1959 (div.); children—Sean Dean, Daryn Joseph; m. 2d Yvonne Frances Grimm, Mar. 16, 1974; children—Heather Laney, Ian Dennis. A.A., Wentworth Mil. Acad., 1959; B.S. in Edn., U. Kans., 1961; D.O., Coll. Osteo. Medicine and Surgery, Des Moines, 1973. Intern Stevens Park Osteo. Hosp., Dallas, 1973-74; gen. practice osteo. medicine, Dallas, 1974-75; owner, dir. Mallory Med. Ctr., Toledo, Iowa, 1975—; mem. staff Marshalltown Area Community Hosp.; dir. Tama County Emergency Med. Service; med. advisor Tama-Toledo Ambulance Services; dep. med. examiner Tama County. Served to 1st lt. U.S. Army, 1964-66; to lt. comdr. USPHS, 1975-77. Mem. AMA, Am. Coll. Emergency Physicians, Am. Coll. Gen. Practitioners Osteo. Medicine and Surgery, Tama County Med. Soc., Iowa Med. Soc., Am. Osteo. Assn. Med. editorial writer Toledo Chronicle, Tama News Herald. Office: Mallory Med Ctr 104 W State St Toledo IA 52342

MALLORY, THOMAS HOWARD, orthopaedic surgeon, educator; b. Ohio, Jan. 10, 1939; s. Guy Howard and Freada (Shepherd) M.; m. Kelly Lynn Smith, Dec. 31, 1964; children—Scot Thomas, Thomas Howard, Jr., Charles Christian. A.B., Miami U., Oxford, Ohio, 1961; M.D., Ohio State U., 1965. Diplomate Am. Bd. Orthopaedic Surgery. Intern, Ohio State U. Hosp., Riverside Methodist Hosp., Columbus, 1965-66; orthopaedic resident Ohio State U. Hosp., Columbus, 1966-70; fellow in hip surgery Harvard Med. Sch., Mass. Gen. Hosp., Boston, 1970-71; tchg. fellow Harvard Med. Sch., Tufts U., Boston, 1970; clin. instr. orthopaedic surgery Ohio State U., Riverside Methodist Hosp., Columbus, 1977—, Ohio State U., 1977—; mem. joint med. study group, orthopaedic adv. panel, Ethicon, Richards Med. Co.; editorial adv. bd. Profl. Educ. Programs, Inc. Mem. editorial bd. Clin. Orthopaedics and Related Research. Contbr. articles to profl. jours. Served to maj. USAR, 1965-72. Mem. Am. Acad. Orthopaedic Surgeons, ACS, AMA, Assn. Bone and Joint Surgeons, Hip Soc., Knee Soc., Sir John Charnley Soc., Ohio State Med. Soc., Ohio Orthopaedic Soc., Columbus Orthopaedic Soc., Columbus Acad. Med., Mid-Am. Orthopaedic Assn., Med. Forum, Christian Med. Soc., Fellowship of Christian Athletes. Avocations: jogging, riding, polo. Office: Joint Implant Surgeons Inc 380 E Town St Columbus OH 43215

MALLORY, TROY L., accountant; b. Sesser, Ill., July 30, 1923; s. Theodore E. and Alice (Mitchell) M.; student So. Ill. U., 1941-43, Washington and Jefferson Coll., 1943-44; B.S., U. Ill., 1947, M.S., 1948; m. Magdalene Richter, Jan. 26, 1963. Staff sr., supr. Scovell, Wellington & Co., C.P.A.s, Chgo., 1948-58; mgr. Gray Hunter Stenn, C.P.A.s, Quincy, 1959-62, partner, 1962—. Mem. finance com. United Fund, Adams County, 1961-64. Bd. dirs. Woodland Home for Orphans and Friendless, 1970—, v.p., 1978-81, pres., 1981-84. Served with 84th Inf. Div. AUS, 1942-45. Decorated Purple Heart, Bronze Star. Mem. Quincy C. of C. (dir. 1970-76), Am. Inst. C.P.A.s, Ill. C.P.A. Soc. Clubs: Rotary (dir. Quincy 1967-70, pres. 1978-79), Shriners (dir. Quincy 1982—). Home: 51 Wilmar Dr Quincy IL 62301 Office: 200 Am Savs Bldg Quincy IL 62301

MALLOY, JAMES MATTHEW, hospital administrator; b. N.Y.C., Aug. 26, 1939; s. Peter Joseph and Catherine (Cunningham) M.; m. Joan Wagner, Sept. 9, 1967; children—Stephen, Christopher. B.S., Manhattan Coll., 1961; M.P.H., Yale U., 1967. Asst. to dir. Yale New Haven Hosp., 1967-68; assoc. adminstr. Waterbury Hosp. (Conn.), 1969-75; exec. dir., chief exec. officer Jersey City Med. Ctr. 1975-77; hosp. dir., chief exec. officer U. Conn. Hosp., Farmington, 1977-82, U. Ill. Hosp., Chgo., 1982—; cons. Nat. Heart, Lung and Blood Inst., Bethesda, Md., 1976-84; dir., Chgo. Metrocare, Chgo., 1983-84. Bd. dirs. Capitol Area Health Consortium, Hartford, Conn., 1978-82, Consortium for Study of Univ. Hosps., 1983-84. Yale U. fellow, 1982; USPHS fellow, 1965-67; Am. Coll. Hosp. Adminstrn. fellow, 1975-84. Roman Catholic. Club: Yale

(Chgo.). Mem. Conf. Teaching Hosps., Hosp. Adminstrs. Club of N.Y. Home: 666 Sheridan Rd Winnetka IL 60093 Office: Office of Dir U Ill Hosp-Clinics 1740 W Taylor St Chicago IL 60612

MALLOY, JOHN BERNARD, oil company executive; b. Chgo., May 6, 1928; s. John Edward and Clara (Trossen) M.; m. Nancy Bryce Roberts, Feb. 14, 1953; children—Philip A., Beth E. B.S., MIT, 1950, M.S., 1951; M.B.A., U. Chgo., 1960. Group leader Amoco Oil Research Co., Whiting, Ind., 1954-62, mgr. long range planning Amoco Chems., Chgo., 1962-74; dir. chem. industry analysis Amoco Corp., Chgo., 1974—. Contbr. articles to profl. jours. Mem. Chem. Mktg. Research Assn., Am. Inst. Chem. Engrs., Am. Chem. Soc. Avocations: quartet singing, music arranging, show production. Office: Amoco Corp 200 E Randolph Chicago IL 60601

MALONE, DONALD JOSEPH, geologist; b. Wichita, Kans., Mar. 2, 1931; s. Harold Herman and Monica Magdalen (Flakus) M.; m. Rosemary Helen Peak, Apr. 24, 1954; children—Monica Marie, Theresa Lynn, Donald Joseph, Jr., Susan Kathleen, Maria Elizabeth, Stephen Matthias. B.S. in Geology, U. Kans., 1954; M.S. in Geology, Wichita State U., 1962. Staff mem., mng. geologist with various oil and gas cos., Wichita, 1959-77; cons., Wichita, 1977—; mem. geology adv. bd. Wichita State U., 1982—. Served to 1st lt. USAF, 1954-57. Mem. Am. Assn. Petroleum Geologists, Kans. Geol. Soc., Am. Inst. Profl. Geologists, Soc. Ind. Earth Scis. (pres. local chpt.). Republican. Roman Catholic. Avocations: golf, woodworking, gardening, barbershop quartet singing. Home: 164 S Fountain St Wichita KS 67218 Office: Donald J Malone Geologist 919 Century Plaza Bldg Wichita KS 67202

MALONE, FRANCIS EDWARD, accountant; b. Kempton, Ill., Jan. 18, 1907; s. Frank Mark and Julia Kathern (Walgenback) M.; A.A. in Commerce, Springfield Coll. Ill., 1954; B.S.C., U. Notre Dame, 1956. Mgr., Walgenback-Walker Farm, near Kempton, 1930-42; chief statis. clk. U.S. War Dept., McCook Army Air Field, McCook, Nebr., 1945-46; bookkeeper and office mgr. Tombaugh-Turner Hybrid Corn Co., Pontiac, Ill., 1946-47; safety responsibility evaluator Ill. Div. Hwys., Springfield, 1947-49; agrl. statistician U.S. Dept. Agr. Bur. Agrl. Econs., Springfield, 1949-53; sr. accountant Raymond E. Rickbiel, C.P.A., 1955-61, Ernst & Ernst, Springfield, 1961-62; pvt. practice pub. accounting, Springfield, 1963—. Served to sgt. USAAF, 1942-45. Mem. Am. Accounting Assn., Air Force Assn., Am. Legion (adj. post 1973—), Alumni Assn. U. Notre Dame, Te Deum Internat. (sec.-treas. Ill. chpt. 1962-65), Thomist Assn. (chmn. Ill. chpt. 1957-62), K.C. Home and office: One Maple Ln Kempton IL 60946

MALONE, JEAN HAMBIDGE, university administrator; b. South Bend, Ind., Nov. 23, 1954; d. Craig Ellis and Dorothy Jane (Piechorowski) Hambidge; B.S. in Edn., Butler U., 1976, M.S. in Edn., 1977; m. James Kevill Malone, July 8, 1978. Tchr., Indpls. Public Schs., 1977-78; dir. student center and activities Butler U., Indspl., 1978—; Eisenhower Meml. scholarship trustee, 1977-80. Bd. dirs. Campfire of Central Ind., 1980-84, Heritage Pl. of Indpls., 1983—. Recipient Outstanding Faculty award, Butler U., 1980. Mem. Ind. Assn. Women Deans, Adminstrs. and Counselors (state bd. dirs. 1982-84), Ind. Assn. Coll. Personnel Adminstrs., Nat. Assn. Women Deans, Adminstrs. and Counselors, Kappa Delta Pi, Phi Kappa Phi, Alpha Lambda Delta (nat. liaison officer), Mortar Bd. (nat. liaison officer), Kappa Kappa Gamma (Mu house corp. bd. 1981-82). Roman Catholic. Office: 4600 Sunset Ave Indianapolis IN 46208

MALONE, ROBERT ROY, art educator, painter, printmaker; b. McColl, S.C., Aug. 8, 1933; s. Robert Roy and Anne (Matthews) M.; m. Cynthia Enid Taylor, Feb. 22, 1956; 1 child, Brendan. Student, Furman U., 1951-53; B.A., U. N.C., 1955; M.F.A., U. Chgo., 1958; postgrad. U. Iowa, 1959. Instr. art Union U., Jackson, Tenn., 1959-60, Lambuth Coll., Jackson, 1959-61; asst. prof. Wesleyan Coll., Macon, Ga., 1961-67, assoc. prof., 1967-68; assoc. prof. W.Va. U., Morgantown, 1968-70; prof. art So. Ill. U., Edwardsville, 1970—. Exhibited one-man shows including: U. Wis.-Madison, 1968, Contemporary Art Ctr., Oklahoma City, 1968, Gallerie Illien, Atlanta, 1969, U. Maine, Orono, 1971, Kenyon Coll., 1973, Ill. State Mus., 1974, U. Del., Newark, 1978, Elliot Smith Gallery, St. Louis, 1985, Merida Gallery, Louisville, 1985; group exhbns. include: Bklyn. Mus. Art, 1966, Assoc. Am. Artists, N.Y.C., 1968, Calif. State Coll.-Long Beach, 1969, Musee d'Art Moderne, Paris, 1970, U.S. Pavillion, World's Fair, Osaka, Japan, 1970, Silvermine Guild Artists, 1973, Krannert Art Mus., 1980, Greenwich Printmakers Assn., London, 1981, St. Louis Art Mus., 1985; represented in pub., pvt. collections. Recipient various awards including Sr. Research Scholar award So. Ill. U. Grad. Sch., 1976, 84; Ford Found. fellow, 1976. Republican. Avocations: running, swimming, photography. Home: 600 Chapman St Edwardsville IL 62025 Office: Dept Art and Design Sch Fine Arts and Communications So Ill U Box 74 Edwardsville IL 62026-1001

MALONE, WILLIAM FRANCIS, dentist; b. Chgo., Sept. 18, 1930; s. Francis J. and Ruth I. (Lingen) M.; student John Carroll U., 1948-51; D.D.S., Northwestern U., 1955, Ph.D., 1973; cert. U. Ill. Coll. of Dentistry, 1963; M.S., U. Ill., 1964; m. Mary Ellen Wrenn, Aug. 8, 1953; children—William, Patrick, Timothy, Robert, Mary Ruth, Maureen, Christine. Practice dentistry, Chgo., 1958-75, Palos Heights, Ill., 1975—; instr. dept. operative dentistry Dental Sch., Northwestern U., Chgo., 1957-58, now prof. advanced prosthodontics; asst. prof. dept. fixed partial prosthodontics U. Ill., Chgo., 1963-65, chmn. dept. operative dentistry, 1966-69; chmn. dept. fixed prosthodontics Loyola U., Maywood, Ill., 1969-76, dir. grad. prosthodontics, 1976-80; lectr. radio and TV programs, 1967-68. Served to maj. U.S. Army, 1955-62. Recipient Nell Snow Talbot All Sch. award, 1965-68. Mem. Am. Dental Assn., Ill. Dental Soc., Chgo. Dental Soc., Am. Acad. Crown and Bridge Prosthodontics, Am. Prosthodontic Soc., Am. Coll. Dentists, Sigma Xi, Omicron Kappa Upsilon. Contbr. articles on prosthodontics to profl. jours.; author: (with T.K. Barber, Howard Redmann) Teenage Dentistry, 1969; Electrosurgery, 1973; co-author: Tylman's Fixed Prosthodontics, 1978; sect. editor Jour. Prosthetic Dentistry, 1980—. Home: 13009 S 83d Ct Palos Park IL 60464

MALONEY, GARY LEE, psychologist, reality therapist; b. Casper, Wyo., Nov. 4, 1944; s. Walter Leo and Betty May (Opfer) M.; m. Sandra Ann Hawthorne, Mar. 2, 1968; children—Travis Alan, Derek Bryan. A.A., Butler County Community Coll., El Dorado, Kans., 1971; B.A. in Psychology, Emporia State Coll., 1973, M.S. in Psychology, 1975. Cert. reality therapist, Kans. Psychologist Sedgwick County Drug Treatment Ctr., Wichita, Kans., 1975-79, South Mental Health Ctr., 1979—; lectr., cons. reality therapy; faculty assoc., practicum supr. levels I and II, Inst. for Reality Therapy. Served to 1st lt. U.S. Army, 1966-69. Decorated Bronze Star. Lutheran. Home: 1050 North Edgemoor St Wichita KS 67208 Office: 3620 East Sunnybrook St Wichita KS 67210

MALONEY, MICHAEL JAMES, research scientist; b. Madison, Wis., Aug. 29, 1942; s. James Edward and Wanda Marie (Berry) M; m. Diane Lois Best, Apr. 20, 1962; children—Lance, Robin, Tracy, Scott. Staff scientist Bjorksten Research Labs., Inc., Madison, Wis., 1962-79, v.p., 1979-84, pres., 1984—. Inventor in field. Contbr. articles to profl. jours. Chmn., Fitchburg Parks Commn., Wis., 1972—; mem. Fitchburg Planning Commn., 1972—. Mem. Soc. Plastics Engrs., ASTM. Roman Catholic. Office: Bjorksten Research Lab Inc PO Box 9444 Madison WI 53715

MALOOLEY, DAVID JOSEPH, electronics and computer technology educator; b. Terre Haute, Ind., Aug. 20, 1951; s. Edward Joseph and Vula (Starn) M. B.S., Ind. State U., 1975; M.S., Ind. U., 1981, doctoral candidate. Supr., Zenith Radio Corp., Paris, Ill., 1978-79; assoc. prof. electronics and computer tech. Ind. State U., Terre Haute, 1979—; cons. in field. Served to 1st lt. U.S. Army, 1975-78. Mem. Soc. Mfg. Engrs., Nat. Assn. Indsl. Tech., Am. Vocat. Assn., AAAS, Phi Delta Kappa, Pi Lambda Theta, Epsilon Pi Tau. Democrat. Christian. Home: 6411 N 30th St Terre Haute IN 47805 Office: Ind State U Terre Haute IN 47809

MALOON, JERRY LEE, physician, lawyer, medicolegal cons.; b. Union City, Ind., June 23, 1938; s. Charles Elias and Bertha Lucille (Creviston) M.; B.S., Ohio State U., 1960, M.D., 1964; J.D., Capital U. Law Sch., 1974; children—Jeffrey Lee, Jerry Lee II. Intern, Santa Monica (Calif.) Hosp., 1964-65; tng. psychiatry Central Ohio Psychiat. Hosp., 1969, Menninger Clinic, Topeka, 1970; clin. dir. Orient (Ohio) Developmental Ctr., 1967-69, med. dir., 1971-83; asso. med. dir. Western Electric, Inc., Columbus, 1969-71; pvt. practice law, Columbus, 1978—; medicolegal cons., 1972—. Guest lectr. law and medicine Orient Developmental Ctr. and Columbus Developmental Ctr., 1969-71; dep. coroner Franklin County (Ohio), 1978-84. Served to capt. M.C., AUS, 1965-67. Fellow Am. Coll. Legal Medicine; mem. AMA, Columbus and Franklin County Acad. Medicine, Ohio State Med. Assn., ABA, Ohio, Columbus bar assns., Am., Ohio, Columbus trial lawyers assns., Ohio State U. Alumni Assn., U.S. Trotting Assn., Am. Profl. Practice Assn. Club: Ohio State U. Pres.'s. Home: 501 S High St Columbus OH 43215 Office: Courthouse Sq 501 S High St Columbus OH 43215

MALOTT, ROBERT H., manufacturing company executive; b. Boston, Oct. 6, 1926; s. Deane W. and Eleanor (Thrum) M.; A.B., Kans. U., 1948; M.B.A., Harvard, 1950; student N.Y. U. Law Sch., evenings 1953-55; m. Elizabeth Harwood Hubert, June 4, 1960; children—Elizabeth Hubert, Barbara Holden, Robert Deane. Asst. to dean Harvard Grad. Sch. Bus. Adminstrn., 1950-52; with FMC Corp., 1952—, v.p., mgr. film ops. div. Am. Viscose div., 1966-67; exec. v.p., mem. pres.'s office, 1967-70, mgr. machinery divs., 1970-72, pres. corp., 1972-77, chief exec. officer, 1972—, chmn. bd., 1973—; dir. FMC Corp., Chgo., Continental Ill. Bank, Chgo., Continental Ill. Corp., Standard Oil Ind., Bell & Howell, United Technologies Corp. Trustee Kans. Endowment Assn., U. Kans. Served with USNR, 1944-46. Mem. Machinery and Allied Products Inst. (exec. com.), Bus. Council, Explorers Club, Phi Beta Kappa, Beta Theta Pi, Alpha Chi Sigma. Clubs: Indian Hill (Kenilworth, Ill.); Links (N.Y.C.); Economic, Mid-Am. (Chgo.). Office: FMC Corp 200 E Randolph Dr Chicago IL 60601*

MALSCH, LAWRENCE H., police chief; b. Geneva Township, Wis., Mar. 8, 1944; s. Lloyd Lawrence and Elenna Dorothy (Beach) Malsch Swanke; m. Judith Mary Yant, Jan. 8, 1966; children—David Lawrence, Eric Philip, Lori Ann. Student in Police Adminstrn. U. Wis. Extension-Milw., 1976; grad. So. Police Inst., Louisville, 1977; postgrad. Northwestern Traffic Inst., Evanston, Ill., 1978. Cert. FBI Nat. Acad., 1982. Police officer City of Delavan, Wis., 1965—, police chief, 1982—. Coordinator deaf warning systems. Committeeman Sinnissippi council Boy Scouts Am.; mem. Selective Service Bd. Walworth County, Wis. Served with USNR, 1962-68. Named Outstanding Young Adult, Delavan Jaycees, 1979. Mem. Wis. Chiefs of Police Assn., Walworth County Chiefs of Police (sec.-treas. 1982—), Internat. Chiefs of Police Assn., Am. Legion (comdr. Post 95 Delavan). Lodge: Lions (v.p. Delavan 1983-84). Avocations: bowling, fishing and hunting. Home: 520 S 3d St Delavan WI 53115 Office: City of Delavan Police Dept 123 S 2d St Delavan WI 53115

MAMMEL, RUSSELL NORMAN, food distribution company executive; b. Hutchinson, Kans., Apr. 28, 1926; s. Vyvian E. and Mabel Edwina (Hursh) M.; m. Betty Crawford, Oct. 29, 1949; children—Mark, Christopher, Elizabeth, Nancy. B.S., U. Kans., 1949. Sec.-treas. Mammel's Inc., Hutchinson, 1949-57, pres., 1957-59; retail gen. mgr. Kans. div. Nash Finch Co., Hutchinson, 1959-61, retail gen. mgr. Iowa div., Cedar Rapids, 1961-66, dir. store devel., Mpls., 1966-75, v.p., 1975-83, exec. v.p., 1983—, also dir. Served with AUS, 1944-46. Home: 6808 Cornelia Dr Edina MN 55435 Office: 3381 Gorham Ave Saint Louis Park MN 55426

MANASEK, FRANCIS JOHN, biology educator; b. N.Y.C., July 22, 1940; s. Francis William and Marie M.; m. Gretel Braidwood, Dec. 27, 1965 (div. 1981); 1 child, Jared. A.B., NYU, 1961; D.M.D. cum laude, Harvard U., 1966. Vis. investigator Carnegie Instn., Balt., 1968; asst. prof. Harvard U. Med. Sch., Boston, 1971-74; assoc. prof. devel. biology U. Chgo., 1975—; rare book dealer-cons., dir. G.B. Manasek, Inc., Chgo., also Norwich, Vt., 1981—. Contbr. chpts. and articles to sci. and tech. publs. Research grantee NIH, 1969—; travel grantee NSF, Santander, Spain, 1985—. Mem. Biophys. Soc., Internat. Soc. Heart Research, Antiquarian Booksellers Assn. Am., Internat. League Antiquarian Booksellers. Clubs: Harvard, Quadrangle (Chgo.). Avocation: collecting art. Home: 5805 S Dorchester Ave Chicago IL 60637 Office: Univ of Chgo 1025 E 57th St Chicago IL 60637

MANASSE, HENRI RICHARD, JR., college dean, pharmacy administration educator; b. Amsterdam, Netherlands, Nov. 27, 1945; came to U.S., 1954, naturalized, 1963; s. Henri David and Janny Lynn (Borst) M.; m. Arlynn Hem, Aug. 9, 1969; children—Bryan, Sheralynn. B.S. in Pharmacy, U. Ill.-Chgo., 1968; M.A., Loyola U., Chgo., 1972; Ph.D., U. Minn., 1974. Lic. pharmacist, Ill. Research pharmacist Xttrium Labs., Chgo., 1968-69; asst. to dean Coll. Pharmacy, U. Ill.-Chgo., 1969-72, asst. prof. pharmacy adminstrn., 1974-77, assoc. dean, 1977-80, acting dean, 1980-81, dean, prof., 1981—; instr. U. Minn., Mpls., 1972-74; mem. Ill. Bd. Pharmacy, Springfield, 1982-87; pub. mem. Am. Soc. Hosp. Pharmacists Commn. on Credentialing, Bethesda, Md., 1984-86. Contbr. chpts. to books, articles to profl. jours. Pres. Downers Grove Sch. Bd. Caucus, Ill., 1984-85; bd. dirs. med service Westside Holistic Ctr., Chgo., 1979—. Recipient Lederle Faculty award Lederle Pharm. Co., 1975; named Alumnus of Yr., U. Ill. Alumni Assn., 1983. Mem. Am. Assn. Colls. Pharmacy (adminstrv. bd. 1982-86, bd. dirs. 1984-86), Ill. Pharmacists Assn., Am. Pharm. Assn. Baptist. Avocations: computers; international travel. Home: 107 56th Ct Downers Grove IL 60516 Office: U Ill Coll Pharmacy m/c 874 Box 6998 Chicago IL 60680

MANATT, KATHLEEN GORDON, publishing company executive; b. Boone, Iowa, June 3, 1948; d. Richard Condon and Lewise Ryan (Gordon) M.; B.A., Coll. Wooster, 1970. Prodn. coordinator Scott, Foresman & Co., Glenview, Ill., 1970-73, editor, 1973-81, product mgr., 1981—. Mem. Nat. Council Social Studies, Ill. Council Social Studies, Nat. Assn. Bilingual Educators, Am. Council Tchrs. Fgn. Langs., Common Cause, So. Poverty Law Ctr., Chgo. Council Fgn. Relations. Presbyterian. Home: 3270 N Lake Shore Dr Chicago IL 60657 Office: Scott Foresman & Co 1900 E Lake Ave Glenview IL 60025

MANCUS, DIANE SIRNA, teacher educator, administrator; b. Cumberland, Md., Apr. 21, 1946; s. Michael James and Vera Devore (Whitman) Sirna; m. Henry Vincent Mancus, Aug. 12, 1967 (div. Aug. 1980); children—Philip Michael, Gibran Christian; m. Curtis Keith Carlson, Mar. 5, 1981; 1 child, Catherine Elizabeth. A.A., Potomac State Coll., 1966; B.A., Frostburg State Coll., 1971, M.S. in Reading Edn., 1973; Ed.D. in Ednl. Psychology, U. Mass., 1978. Tchr. pub. schs. Keyser, W.Va., and Cumberland Md., 1966-76; teaching assoc. U. Mass., Amherst, 1976-78; coordinator elem. edn. N.Mex. State U., Las Cruces, 1978-79; asst. prof. Coll. of V.I., St. Thomas, 1979-81; dir. grad. studies, Sioux Falls Coll., S.D., 1981—, inst. rep. Univ. Grad. Ctr., 1982-85; vis. team leader S.D. Dept. Elem. and Secondary Edn., 1985; bd. regents task force State Bd. Edn., 1984—; chmn. subcom. on prepartation of math. tchrs., 1984—. Contbr. articles to profl. jours. Visitor Republic of Iraq, 1981. Mem. Internat. Reading Assn., S.D. Assn. Colls. of Tchr. Edn. (exec. com. 1984-85), Am. Assn. Colls. of Tchr. Edn. (inst. rep. 1982-85), Democrat. Roman Catholic. Avocations: gardening, sewing, writing poetry. Office: Sioux Falls Coll 1501 Prairie Ave Sioux Falls SD 57105 1699

MANCUSO, PAUL ROBERT, lawyer; b. Flushing, N.Y., Dec. 11, 1952; s. Paul S. and Pauline J. (Mandra) M.; m. April Lynn Sheibar, June 26, 1977. B.A., Queen's Coll., 1974; J.D., Gonzaga U., 1977. Bar: Ohio 1977. Assoc., Wilcox Schlosser & Mirrass, Columbus, Ohio, 1977; assoc. Barkan & Neff, Columbus, 1978-81, jr. ptnr., 1981-85; ptnr. Chorpening, Good & Mancaso, Columbus, 1985—. Mem. Assn. Trial Lawyers Am., Ohio Acad. Trial Lawyers, ABA, Ohio Bar Assn., Columbus Bar Assn. Home: 259 N Remington Rd Bexley OH 43209 Office: Chorpening Good & Mancaso Co LPA 533 S Third St Columbus OH 43215

MANCUSO, ROBERT POPE, automobile dealer; b. Chgo., Feb. 2, 1951; s. James Vincent and Clarissa Rosary (Pope) M.; A.B. in Psychology, Princeton U., 1973. Vice pres. Mancuso Chevrolet, Inc., Skokie, Ill., 1969—; pres. Mancuso Cadillac Honda Inc., Barrington, Ill., 1974—, also RPM Systems, Inc., Consumer Concepts, Ltd. Career advisor Barrington Bd. Edn.; mem. Princeton Alumni Com., 1980—, Hundred Club Cook County, 1980—; mem. exec. com. Americas Marathon Chgo., 1982—; chmn. Barrington Lifeline Program, 1981-82; mem. Barrington Vol. Speakers Bur., 1979—. Recipient Nat. Auto Dealers Edn. award, 1977. Mem. Nat., Barrington (past pres.) auto dealers assns., Chicagoland Cadillac Dealers Assn. (exec. com. 1979—, chmn. advt. com.), Chicagoland Honda Dealers Assn. (exec. com. 1979—, pres. 1981-82), Barrington C. of C. (treas. 1976-77, v.p. 1977-79, pres. 1979—), Chgo. Auto Trade Assn. Roman Catholic. Club: Rotary (chpt. dir., pres. 1981-82). Office: 1445 S Barrington Rd Barrington IL 60010

MANDEL, BRUCE PHILIP, lawyer; b. Cleve., Mar. 16, 1951; s. Harold and Harriet (Stotsky) M.; m. Rita Lena Friedman, Aug. 19, 1973; children—Joshua Aaron, Rachel Elizabeth. B.S. in Edn. summa cum laude, Ohio State U., 1973; J.D., Case Western Res. U., 1976. Bar: Ohio 1976, U.S. Supreme Ct. 1985. Ptnr. Ulmer, Berne, Laronge, Glickman & Curtis, Cleve., 1976—. Trustee Cleve. Hillel Found., 1984—, N.E. Ohio Arthritis Found., Cleve., 1982—; chmn. young bus. and profl. div. Cleve. Jewish Community Fedn., 1983-85, mem. archives and history com., 1983—; founding mem., trustee Congregation Bethaynu, Cleve., 1979-82, mem. Citizens League Greater Cleve., 1985—. Mem. ABA, Ohio Bar Assn., Bar Assn. Greater Cleve., Nat. Order Barristers. Democrat. Avocations: Athletics; stamp collecting. Home: 4338 Groveland Rd University Heights OH 44118 Office: Ulmer Berne Laronge Glickman & Curtis 900 Bond Court Bldg Cleveland OH 44114

MANDEL, KARYL LYNN, accountant; b. Chgo., Dec. 14, 1935; d. Isador J. and Eve (Gellar) Karzen; student U. Mich., 1954-56, Roosevelt U., 1956-57; A.A. summa cum laude, Oakton Community Coll., 1979; m. Fredric H. Mandel, Sept. 29, 1956; children—David Scott, Douglas Jay, Jennifer Ann. Pres., nat. bd. mem. Women's Am. Orgn. for Rehab. through Tng., 1961-77; pres. Excel Transp. Service Co., Elk Grove, Ill., 1958-78; tax mgr. Chunowitz, Teitelbaum & Baerson, C.P.A.s, Northbrook, Ill., 1981-83, tax ptnr., 1984—; sec-treas. Trimark of Chgo. Recipient State of Israel Solidarity award, 1976. C.P.A., Ill. Mem. Am. Inst. C.P.A.s, Am. Soc. Women C.P.A.s, Women's Am. ORT, Ill. C.P.A. Soc. (vice chmn. estate and gift tax com., mem. legis. contact com. 1981-82, pres. North Shore chpt., award for excellence in acctg. edn.), Chgo. Soc. Women C.P.A.s, Chgo. Estate Planning Council. Contbg. author: Wiley Federal Tax Manual. Office: 401 Huehl Rd Northbrook IL 60062

MANDEL, TERRY JAY, physician; b. Chgo., Aug. 7, 1953; s. Seymour L. and Beverly (Sklare) M. Student Drake Coll. Pharmacy, Des Moines, 1971-75; D.O., Chgo. Coll. Osteo. Medicine, 1979. Practice family medicine, Indpls., 1980—; chief family practice div. Westview Hosp., Indpls., 1983, chief infection control, 1984-85, mem. exec. com., 1984-85, mem. intern tng. com., 1984-85, chief of staff, 1985—. Mem. Am. Osteo. Assn., Am. Coll. Gen. Practitioners Osteo. Medicine, Ind. Assn. Osteo. Physicians, Rho Chi, Phi Eta Sigma, Sigma Sigma Phi. Jewish. Avocations: antiques; coin collecting; photography; political items and history. Office: 4006 N High School Rd Indianapolis IN 46254

MANDERS, DANIEL NORBERT, hospital administrator; b. Green Bay, Wis., Nov. 15, 1949; s. Norbert G. and Bette (Calaway) M.; m Kathleen T. Farrell, Aug. 19, 1972; children—Michelle, Michael, John. B.B.A., U. Wis.-Whitewater, 1972. Sr. auditor Blue Cross, Milw., 1972-74; controller Hess Meml. Hosp., Mauston, Wis., 1974-78, assoc. adminstr., 1978-81, adminstr., 1981—; adminstr. Fair View Nursing Home, Mauston, 1981—. Chmn., Juneau County Health Resources Com., Mauston, 1978-79. Mem. Wis. Hosp. Assn. (bd. dirs. 1985—), Mauston C. of C. (bd. dirs. 1979-81), Health Care Fin. Mgmt. Assn. Republican. Roman Catholic. Lodge: Lions (sec. 1978-79) (Mauston). Avocations: golf, hunting, fishing, skiing, boating. Office: Mile Bluff Med Ctr 1050 Division St Mauston WI 53948

MANDERS, KARL LEE, neurological surgeon; b. Rochester, N.Y., Jan. 21, 1927; s. David Bert and Frances Edna (Cohan) Mendelson; student Cornell U., 1946; M.D., U. Buffalo, 1950; m. Ann Laprell, July 28, 1969; children—Karlanna, Maidena; children by previous marriage—Karl, Kerry, Kristine. Intern, U. Va. Hosp., Charlottesville, 1950-51, resident in neurol. surgery, 1951-52; resident in neurol. surgery Henry Ford Hosp., Detroit, 1954-56; practice medicine specializing in neurol. surgery, Indpls., 1956—; med. dir. Community Hosp. Rehab. Center for Pain, 1973—; chief hosp. med. and surg. neurology Community Hosp., 1983; coroner Marion County (Ind.), 1977-84, chief med. dep. coroner, 1985—; pres. Manders-Marks, Inc., Hyperbaric Oxygen Inc. Served with USN, 1952-54; Korea. Recipient cert. achievement Dept. Army, 1969. Diplomate Am. Bd. Neurol. Surgery, Nat. Bd. Med. Examiners, Am. Bd. Clin. Biofeedback. Fellow A.C.S., Internat. Coll. Surgeons; mem. AMA, Am. Assn. Neurol. Surgery, Congress Neurol. Surgery, Am. Acad. Neurology, Internat. Assn. Study of Pain, Am. Assn. Study of Headache, N.Y. Acad. Sci., Am. Coll. Angiology, Am. Soc. Contemporary Medicine and Surgery, Am. Holistic Med. Assn. (a founder), Undersea Med. Soc., Am. Acad. Forensic Sci., Am. Assn. Biofeedback Clinicians, Soc. for Cryosurgery, Pan Pacific Surg. Assn., Biofeedback Soc. Am., Acad. Psychosomatic Medicine, Pan Am. Med. Assn., Am. Soc. for Stereotaxic and Functional Neurosurgery, Soc. for Computerized Tomography and Neuroimaging, Ind. Coroners Assn. (pres. 1979), Royal Soc. Medicine, Am. Pain Soc., Midwest Pain Soc., Central Neurol. Soc., Interurban Neurosurg. Soc., Pan Am. Med. Assn., Internat. Soc. Aquatic Medicine: Clubs: Brendonwood Country, Highland Country, Indpls. Athletic. Home: 5845 Highfall St Indianapolis IN 46226 Office: 5506 E 16th St Indianapolis IN 46218

MANDEVILLE, GEOFFREY H(AMILTON), rubber company executive; b. Sao Paulo, Brazil, Oct. 15, 1948; came to U.S., 1968; s. Ernest Wycoff, Jr. and Olga Florence (Hamilton) M.; m. Penelope Meyer, Aug. 1, 1970; children—Geoffrey H., Elizabeth, Joseph. B.A. in Fgn. Careers, Lehigh U., 1971; M.A. in Ibero-Am Studies, U. Wis.-Madison, 1972. Controller, Mykroy Ceramics Corp. affiliate Alco Standard Corp., Ledgewood, N.J., 1974-76, ops. adv. Alco Standard Corp., Valley Forge, Pa., 1976-79, exec. v.p. Sperry Rubber & Plastics affiliate, Brookville, Ind., 1979-80, pres., 1980—. Mem. Rubber Mfrs. Assn. Democrat. Episcopalian. Home: 1292 Sweetwater Dr Cincinnati OH 45215 Office: Sperry Rubber & Plastics RR 2 Box 42 Brookville IN 47012

MANDICH, DONALD RALPH, See *Who's Who in America,* 43rd edition.

MANDLE, EARL ROGER, mus. adminstr.; b. N.J., May 13, 1941; s. Earl and Phyllis Key (O'Berg) M.; B.A. cum laude, Williams Coll., 1963; M.A., N.Y. U., 1967, also postgrad.; m. Gayle Wells Jenkins, July 11, 1964; children—Luke Harrison, Julia Barnes. Intern, Met. Mus. Art, N.Y.C., Victoria and Albert Mus., London, 1966-67; assoc. dir. Mpls. Inst. Arts, 1967-74; assoc. dir. Toledo Mus. Art, 1974-76, dir., 1977—; mem. vis. com. Williams Coll. Mus. Art; mem. Spanish Found. for the Restoration of Toledo; mem. U.S. Com. for Restoration of Toledo (Spain); mem. adv. council Nat. Mus. Act; mem. Am. Arts Alliance Policy Com., Nat. Inst. of Conservation Alliance. Chmn. youth commn. ARC, 1967; chmn. internat. service com. Rotary, 1978-79; trustee Toledo Arts Commn., Art Interests, Toledo Hosp.; mem. Toledo Econ. Planning Council, Toledo Exec. Forum, Toledo 1% for the Arts, Toledo Trust Corp. Bd.; mem. Riverside Hosp. Centennial Commn.; mem. exec. com. Intermuseum Conservation; mem. adv. com. J. Paul Getty Trust. Recipient Ednl. award Am. Hellenic Assn.; Disting. Citizens award Ohio Art Edn., 1983; Gov.'s award State of Ohio, 1983; Andover Teaching fellow, 1963, Ford Found. fellow, 1966, Nat. Endowment for the Arts fellow, 1974. Mem. Am. Assn. Mus., Art Mus. Assn. Am. (pres.), Mus. Mgmt. Inst., Am. Assn. Art Mus. Dirs., Coll. Art Assn., Internat. Council Mus., Ohio Found. for Arts, Ohio Art Council (council), Young Pres.'s Orgn. Clubs: Toledo, Carranor Hunt & Polo, Catawba Island Yacht, Tile. Contbr. articles to profl. jours. Office: 2445 Monroe St Toledo OH 43697*

MANELLI, DONALD DEAN, writer, producer motion pictures; b. Burlington, Iowa, Oct. 20, 1936; s. Daniel Anthony and Mignon Marie M.; B.A., U. Notre Dame, 1959; children by former marriage—Daniel, Lisa. Communications specialist Jewel Cos., 1959; script writer Coronet Films, Chgo., 1960-62; freelance writer, 1962-63; creative dir. Fred A. Niles Communications Centers, Chgo., 1963-67; sr. writer Wild Kingdom, NBC-TV network, also freelance film writer, 1967-70; pres. Donald Manelli & Assos., Inc., Chgo., 1970—. Recipient internat. film festival and TV awards. Mem. Writers Guild Am., Nat. Acad. TV Arts and Scis. Am. Home: 100 E Bellevue Pl Chicago IL 60611 Office: 1 E Erie St Chicago IL 60611

MANFRE, THOMAS STEVEN, air freight transportation company executive, banking executive, financial management consultant; b. Chgo., Dec. 21, 1942; s. Thomas and Cecelia (Kwiatkowski) M.; m. Sharon L. Jozwiak, July 24, 1965; children—Susan, Karen, Thomas Steven III. Student, De LaSalle Inst., Chgo., 1956-60, Coll. Advanced Traffic, Chgo., 1965-67, Loyola U., Chgo., 1967-72. Mgr. customer service and claim Terminal Transport, Chgo., 1963-65; mgr. internat. service dept. Consol. Freightways, Chgo., 1967-68; asst. term mgr. CF Package Div., Chgo., 1967-69; ops. mgr. CF Air Freight Div., Chgo., 1969-70; owner, dir. Internat. Air Service Ltd., Chgo., 1970-71; owner, pres., dir., chmn. bd. Performance By Air, Inc., Chgo., 1971—; organizer, dir., chmn. bd. First Nat. Bank Roselle, Ill., 1983—; cons. Birks Transport Co., Arlington Heights, Ill., 1982—. Served with U.S. Army, 1965-67, Vietnam. Mem. Air Freight Forwarder Assn., Internat. Air Transport Assn. Roman Catholic. Home: 732 Tomlin Dr Burr Ridge IL 60521 Office: Performance By Air Inc PO Box 66397 Chicago IL 60666

MANFRO, PATRICK JAMES (PATRICK JAMES HOLIDAY), radio artist; b. Kingston, N.Y., Dec. 30, 1947; s. Charles Vincent and Anna Agnes (Albany) Manfro; Asso. Sci. in Acctg., Ulster Coll., 1968; diploma Radio Electronics Inst., 1969; student St. Clair Coll., 1974—; m. Janice Lynn Truscott, July 5, 1975; 1 son, Wesley Patrick. Program dir., radio artist WKNY, Kingston, 1966-70; radio artist WPTR, Albany, N.Y., 1970, WPOP, Hartford, Conn., 1970, CKLW, Detroit, 1970-71, WOR-FM, N.Y.C., 1971-72; radio artist CKLW Radio, Detroit, 1972—, asst. program dir., 1978-80, program dir., 1980-83; v.p. programming CKLW/CFXX, Detroit, 1983—; pres. Musicom Inc., audio-visual prodn. co., Detroit; pres., chief exec. officer Internat. Data Corp., Wilmington, Del.; adviser New Contemporary Sch. Announcing, Albany, 1973—; comml. announcer radio, television, 1970—. Judge, Miss Mich. Universe Pageant, 1970. Mem. N.Y. State N.G., 1968-74. Recipient 5 Year Service ribbon N.Y. State, 1973; named Runner-up Billboard Air Personality awards, 1971. Mem. AFTRA, Screen Actors Guild, Internat. Platform Assn., Smithsonian Assos., BMI Songwriters Guild. Club: Dominion Golf and Country. Home: 3466 Wildwood St Windsor ON N8R 1X2 Office: PO Box 1142 Dearborn MI 48121

MANGE, FRANKLIN EDWIN, chemical executive; b. St. Louis, Feb. 12, 1928; s. Clarence E. and Janet (Purvin) M.; m. Barbara I. Kling, July 25, 1954; children—Lawrence, Joyce, Martin, Emily. B.S., MIT, 1948; Ph.D., U. Ill.-Urbana, 1951. Research chemist Petrolite Corp., St. Louis, 1951-60, group leader, 1960-63, sect. mgr., 1963-67, dir. research and devel. Tretolite div., 1967-80, v.p. research and devel., 1982-85, dir. corp. devel., 1985—. Patentee in field. Contbr. articles to profl. jours. Mem. Am. Chem. Soc. (sect. chair 1971), Sigma Xi. Avocations: tennis, skiing, sailing. Home: 18 Granada Way Saint Louis MO 63124 Office: Petrolite Corp 100 N Broadway Saint Louis MO 63102

MANGELS, DONALD KEITH, banker; b. Durant, Iowa, June 9, 1929; s. Leonard Lester and Evelyn Anna (Ruhser) M.; m. Verlene Mary Dow, Apr. 4, 1953; children—Kristen, Lisa, Eric. B.S. in Commerce, U. Iowa, 1950; M.A. in History, U. Okla., 1966. Trainee, Internat. Harvester, E. Moline, Ill., 1950-52; asst. v.p. First Nat. Bank, Ames, Iowa, 1982—; dir. Ames Found., 1982—; commd. U.S. Air Force, 1952, advanced through grades to col., 1973, ret., 1977. Mem. C. of C. (membership chmn.). Republican. Episcopalian. Advocation: outdoor sports. Home: Route 4 Ames IA 50010 Office: PO Box 607 5th and Burnett Ames IA 50010

MANGOLD, WAYNE J., tractor company executive; b. Lincoln, Ill., Aug. 11, 1944; s. Wilbur James and Rose Belle M.; m. Hanne Vessel, Dec. 4, 1962; children—Angela, Malene, Kristin, Mark. B.S. in Bus. Adminstrn., Bradley U., 1976. Computer programmer Caterpillar Co., East Peoria, Ill., 1966-68, sr. analyst, 1968-71, computer ops. supr., 1971-73, staff asst. parts distbn. systems, 1973-77, tech. graphics supr., 1977—; tchr. Midstate Bus. Coll., 1962-63. Mem. Tri-County Drug Abuse Counsel, 1970. Mem. Nat. Microfilm Assn., Nat. Computer Graphics Assn. Republican. Unitarian. Home: 903 Parkway Dr East Peoria IL 61611 Office: 600 SW Washington St East Peoria IL 61630

MANGUM, RONALD SCOTT, lawyer; b. Chgo., Nov. 14, 1944; s. Roy Oliver and Marjorie Wilma (Etchason) M.; m. Kay Lynn Booton, July 14, 1973 (div. July 1983); children—Scott Arthur, Katherine Marie. B.A., Northwestern U., 1965, J.D., 1968. Bar: Ill. 1968. Asst. univ. atty. Northwestern U., 1968-73; assoc. Lord, Bissell & Brook, Chgo., 1974-76; ptnr. Liss, Mangum & Beeler, Chgo., 1976-80, Mangum, Beeler, Schad & Diamond, Chgo., 1980-82, Azar, Mangum & Jacobs, Chgo., 1982-84, Mangum, Smietanka & Johnson, Chgo., 1984—; lectr. Northwestern U., 1972-74, NYU Inst. Fed. Taxation, 1980; lectr. on health care topics to profl. groups; faculty Healthcare Fin. Mgmt. Assn. Ann. Nat. Inst., Boulder; pres. Planned Giving, Inc., 1978—, 1426 Chicago Ave Bldg Corp., 1975-76, Parkinson Research Corp., 1970-74. Commr. Evanston Preservation Commn., 1981-83; chmn. Am. Hearing Research Found., 1977-79, v.p., 1972-77; bd. dirs. Episcopal Charities, 1978-80; trustee Evanston Art Ctr., 1977-78; mem. health care subcom. Nat. Fire Protection Assn., 1980-82. Recipient cert. of appreciation Ill. Inst. Continuing Legal Edn., 1972. Mem. Chgo. Bar Assn., Ill. Bar Assn., ABA, Nat. Assn. Coll. and Univ. Attys., Chgo. Estate Planning Council, Art Inst. Chgo. (life), Nat. Rifle Assn. (life), Nat. Soc. Fund Raising Execs., Psi Upsilon. Clubs: Union League (Chgo.); John Evans (bd. dirs. Evanston, Ill.). Author: (with R. M. Hendrickson) Governing Board and Administrator Liability, 1977; Tax Aspects of Charitable Giving, 1976. Contbr. articles to legal jours. Home: 1426 Chicago Ave Evanston IL 60201 Office: 35 E Wacker Dr Chicago IL 60601

MANHART, JAMES WESLEY, physician; b. Effingham, Ill., May 19, 1940; s. Edwin Ray and Ruth Foster (Anderson) M.; m. Oksana Mensheha, May 8, 1971; children—Mark Mensheha, Ingrid Oksana, Peter James. B.A., Knox Coll., 1962; M.D., Stanford U., 1967. Diplomate Am. Bd. Internal Medicine, Am. Bd. Hematology, Am. Bd. Med. Oncology. Resident medicine Kings County Hosp., Bklyn., 1968-69; resident medicine U. Wis., Madison, 1969-70, fellow hematology, 1970-71; fellow hematology U.S. Naval Hosp., Phila., 1973-74; staff physician U.S. Naval Hosp., Great Lakes, Ill., 1971-77, asst. chief dept. medicine, 1974-77; practice medicine specializing in oncology and hematology, Libertyville, Ill., 1977—; med. dir. S.T.A.R. Hospice, Waukegan, Ill., 1980—; chmn. dept. medicine Lake Forest Hosp. (Ill.), 1983-84; cons. Ill. Cancer Council, Chgo., 1979-81. Contbr. articles to med. jours. Substitute organist Grace Lutheran Ch., Libertyville, 1976—; bd. dirs. Am. Cancer Soc., Lake County, Ill., 1980—. Served to comdr. USN, 1971-77, capt. Res. Mem. ACP, Lake County Med. Soc., Ill. Med. Soc., AMA, Eastern Coop. Oncology Group, Sierra Club, Audubon Soc., Phi Beta Kappa. Avocations: music, gardening, travel, sailing, reading. Office: 1117 S Milwaukee Ave Libertyville IL 60048

MANIA, ROBERT CHESTER, JR., physics educator; b. Mt. Clemens, Mich., May 19, 1952; s. Robert Chester and Patricia Dawn (Jobse) M.; m. Cathy Gayheart, Oct. 17, 1980; children—Tracey Anne, Robert Alan. B.S. in Physics, Mich. Tech. U., 1974, M.S. in Physics, 1976; Ph.D. in Physics, Va. Tech. U., 1981. Grad. teaching asst. Va. Tech. Inst., Blacksburg, 1976-79, grad. research asst., 1979-80; instr. Alice Lloyd Coll., Pippa Passes, Ky., 1980-81, asst. prof., 1981-84, assoc. prof. physics, 1984—. Mem. Am. Phys. Soc., Am. Nuclear Soc., Sigma Si (assoc.). Home and Office: Alice Lloyd Coll Pippa Passes KY 41844

MANIGAULT, JUAN ALEJANDRO, human resources executive, consultant; b. Charleston, S.C., Oct. 7, 1952; s. Nathaniel Lomax and Marion Pearl (Waterman) M.; m. Kimberly Ann Kurka, July 14, 1980. A.B., U. Notre Dame, 1974; M.B.A., Ind. U.-Gary, 1984. Assoc. tennis pro Mansard Raquet Club, Griffith, Ind., 1975-77; planner Lake County Employment and Tng. Adminstrn., Crown Point, Ind., 1977-79; dir. Office Career Edn., Hobart, Ind., 1979-84; dir. devel. Kids Alive Internat., Valparaiso, Ind., 1984—; mem. State Ind. Career Edn. Adv. Com., Indpls., 1981-83; participant Leadership Calumet, Gary, Ind., 1982-83. Assoc. pub. Our Town Michiana mag. Sec. bd. dirs. Christian Haven Homes, Inc., Wheatfield, Ind.; bd. dirs. Am. Cancer Soc., Indpls.; chmn. human resource, job tng. subcom. Calumet Forum, Merrillville, Ind.; pres. Indigan Corp. Recipient Holy Cross award U. Notre Dame, 1971. Mem. U.S. Profl. Tennis Assn., Am. Soc. Pub. Adminstrn. Home: 508 Albert St Valparaiso IN 46383 Office: Kids Alive Internat 2507 Cumberland Dr Valparaiso IN 46383

MANILLA, JOHN ALLAN, office furniture company executive; b. Sharon, Pa., July 17, 1941; s. Vito John and Helen Elizabeth (Papai) M.; B.S., Youngstown State U., 1966; postgrad. Duquesne U., 1967-68; M.S. in Mgmt., Aquinas Coll., 1984; m. Paula Gale Jurko, Nov. 26, 1960; children—Jacqueline Lee, John Paul, Paul Allan, Bradley James. Sr. staff asst. Elevator Co., Westinghouse Electric Corp., Pitts., 1966-68, salesman I, 1968-70, salesman II, Union, N.J., 1971, Miami, Fla., 1971-72, dist. mgr., Indpls., 1973-77, regional mgr. archtl. and furniture systems div., Grand Rapids, Mich., 1977-79, nat. field sales mgr., 1979-81; mgr. strategic programs Herman Miller, Inc., Zeeland, Mich., 1981, group mktg. mgr., 1981, dir. mktg., 1981-83, dir. corp. distbn. resources, 1984—; dir. sales and mktg. Gen. Office Equipment Co., Inc., Saddle Brook, N.J., 1984—; v.p. Yankee Lake Amusement Co., Yankee Lake Village, Ohio, 1961-66, 70-71; elevator cons. architects, engrs., bldg. mgr., contractors. Chief, YMCA Indian Guides, Allison Park, Pa., 1970; asst. scoutmaster Boy Scouts Am., Dania, Fla., 1971-72; asst. to Boys Scouts Am., Ind. Sch. for Blind, Indpls., 1973; jr. high sch. prin., instr. Christian Doctrine, St. Ursula Ch., Allison Park, 1968-70, St. Sabastion Ch., Masury, Ohio, 1970-71; pres. bd. edn. Our Lady of Mt. Carmel Sch., Carmel, Ind., 1973-76; mem. Carmel Dad's Club, 1973-74; pres. Princeton Estates Homeowners Assn., 1982; co-chmn. capital endowment campaign-continuing edn. div. Aquinas Coll., 1982, mem. master's program scholarship fund com., 1983-84; active Grand Rapids Bishop's Service Appeal, 1982, Grand Rapids Arts Council, 1980; mem. fin. and bldg. fund cons. St. Mary Magdalen Ch., 1984—; exec. com. Kentwood High Sch. Acad. Boosters, Mich., 1984. Recipient First in Performance award Westinghouse Electric Corp., 1972, 120 Club Honor Roll, 1968, 69, 70, 71, 72. Mem. Bldg. Owners and Mgrs. Assn., Constrn. Specification Inst., Assn. Gen. Contractors Ind., Am. Water Ski Assn., Mich. Water Ski Assn., West Mich. Water Ski Assn. Clubs: Rotary, Indpls. Athletic; Yankee Lake (Ohio) Water Ski (pres.); Renaissance (Detroit). Home: 1924 Lockmere SE Kentwood MI 49508 Office: Gen Office Equipment Co Inc 381 Market St Saddle Brook NJ 07662

MANLEY, DAVID THOMAS, employment benefit plan administration company executive; b. Youngstown, Ohio, Apr. 13, 1938; s. Harry T. and Margaret M. (Stein) M.; m. Virginia Borcik, Sept., 1961 (div. 1975); children—Kelly A., Scott D., Lynne M., Brian D., Leslie; m. 2d Ruth Ann Osterhage, Dec. 31, 1975; children—David Louis, Mollie O. Student Youngstown U., 1956-60. Dist. sales mgr. Res. Life, Dallas, 1960-63, Guarantee Res. Life, Hammond, Ind., 1963-64; mgr. brokerage CNA Ins. Group, Chgo., 1964-68; pres. Greater Del. Corp., Dover, 1981—; pres. Variable Protection Adminstrn., Cleve., 1968—, also dir.; dir. Del. Nat. Life, Greater Del. Corp., Fla. Employee Benefits, Orlando, Fla. Precinct committeeman Republican Com., 1966-72, ward leader, 1970-72, mem. Cuyahoga County Republican Com., 1970-72. Mem. Soc. Profl. Benefit Adminstrs., Mass Market Ins. Inst., Internat. Found. Employee Benefits, Am. Mgmt. Assn. Republican. Roman Catholic. Lodge: KC. Home: 2485 Bethany Ln Hinckley OH 44233 Office: Variable Protection Adminstrs Inc 7123 Pearl Rd Suite 300 Cleveland OH 44130

MANLY, CHARLES M., III, lawyer; b. Spencer, Iowa, July 18, 1950; s. Charles M. and B.A. (Lippold) M.; m. Debra Jo Yellick, May 22, 1982. B.A., Simpson Coll., 1972; J.D., Hamline U., 1976. Bar: Iowa 1976. Gen. practice law, Grinnell, Iowa, 1976—; ptnr. Manly Law Firm. Mng. editor Iowa Trial Lawyer, 1982—. Trustee Simpson Coll., Indianola, Iowa, 1984—. Chmn. Robert Ray for Gov. Campaign, Poweshiek County, 1978; pres. Grinnell Area Arts Council, 1982-83. Mem. ABA, Poweshiek County Bar Assn. (pres. 1978-79), Assn. Trial Lawyers Am., Assn. Trial Lawyers Iowa (bd. govs. 1981—), Simpson Coll. Alumni Assn. (pres. 1984—). Club: Okoboji Yacht. Avocations: reading, sailing, sports. Home: 917 10th Ave Grinnell IA 50112 Office: 720 4th Ave Grinnell IA 50112

MANLY, WILLIAM DONALD, special metals company executive; b. Malta, Ohio, Jan. 13, 1923; s. Edward J. and Thelma M. (Campbell) M.; m. Jane Wilden, Feb. 9, 1949; children—Hugh, Ann, Marc, David. B.S., U. Notre Dame, 1947, M.S., 1949; postgrad. U. Tenn., 1950-55. Metallurgist, mgr. Oak Ride Nat. Labs., 1949-64; mgr. UCC, N.Y.C., 1964-65; gen. mgr. Union Carbide Corp., Kokomo, Ind., 1967-69, v.p., 1969-70; v.p. Cabot Corp., Kokomo, 1970-74, sr. v.p., 1974-84, exec. v.p., 1984—, also dir.; dir. Boston Edison Co., Union Bank & Trust Co., Kokomo. Served with USMC, 1943-46. Recipient Honor award U. Notre Dame, 1974. Fellow Am. Soc. Metals (pres. 1972-73); mem. Am. Nuclear Soc., Nat. Acad. Engring., Nat. Assn. Corrosion Engrs. Presbyterian. Home: 5610 Princeton Pl Kokomo IN 46902 Office: Cabot Corp 1020 W Park Ave Kokomo IN 46901

MANN, BARBARA L., statistics educator; b. Asheville, N.C., Mar. 14, 1941; d. E. Ray and Marjorie (Hieber) Mann; A.B., U. Tenn., 1962; M.S. in Math., Tulane U., 1965; M.S., Va. Poly. Inst. and Tech. U., 1975, Ph.D., 1979. Instr. math Concord Coll., Athens, W.Va., 1966-69, asst. prof., 1969-75; instr. stats. Wright State U., Dayton, 1977-79, asst. prof., 1979-84, assoc. prof., 1984—, dir. Statis. Cons. Ctr., 1982—. Contbr. articles to profl. jours. Trustee, Glen Helen Assn., Yellow Springs, Ohio, 1979—. NSF fellow, 1975-76. Mem. Biometric Soc., Am. Statis. Assn., Assn. Women in Math. Avocations: Early music, harpsichord, recorder. Office: Dept Math and Stats Wright State U Dayton OH 43435

MANN, CHRISTIAN JOHN, geology educator, consultant; b. Junction City, Kans., Oct. 16, 1931; s. Chris J. and Vaughnie Jean (Waynick) M.; m. Diane K. Messmann, Feb. 1961; children—Chris J. III, Anna M., Vaughn, Katrina E. B.S. in Geol. Engring., Kans. U., 1953, M.S. in Geology, 1957; Ph.D. in Geology, Wis. U.-Madison, 1960. Geologist Gulf Oil Corp., Marfa, Tex., 1953, Calif. Oil Co., Jackson, Miss., 1957-58, 61-64; sr. scientist Hazelton Nuclear Sci., Palo Alto, Calif., 1964-65; prof. geology U. Ill., Urbana, 1965—; ptnr. Lanman Assocs., Urbana, 1976—. Author tech. papers. Served to lt. U.S. Army, 1953-55. Fellow Geol. Soc. Am., AAAS; mem. Internat. Assn. Math. Geologists (editor 1984—, best paper award 1978), Math. Geologists U.S. (pres. 1976-78), Nat. Com. Math. Geologists. Avocations: woodworking; camping. Office: U Ill Dept Geology 1301 W Green St Urbana IL 61801

MANN, MICHAEL DAVID, neurobiologist, researcher, educator; b. Gold Beach, Oreg., May 20, 1944; s. Merrill Gordon and Geraldine Avis (Erickson) M.; m. Sally Lee Pingleton, Aug. 19, 1966; children—Koren Kathleen, Aaron Michael. A.B., U. So. Calif., 1966; Ph.D., Cornell, U., 1971. Asst. prof. physiology U. Nebr. Med. Ctr., Omaha, 1973-77, assoc. prof., 1977—. Author: The Nervous System and Behavior, 1981. Contbr. articles to profl. jours. Vol. tchr. Omaha Pub. Schs., 1975—, mem. curriculum rev. com., 1975—. Grantee NSF, 1976-82, NIMH, 1976-77. Mem. Am. Physiol. Soc., Soc. for Neurosci., Cajal Club. Democrat. Avocations: stained glass leading; gardening; woodworking. Office: Dept Physiology Univ Nebr Med Ctr 42nd and Dewey Ave Omaha NE 68105

MANN, THOMAS JAMES, JR., lawyer, state senator; b. Haywood County, Tenn., Dec. 15, 1949; s. Thomas James and Flossie Lou (Maclin) M.; m. Leala Ann Salter, July 24, 1976; 1 dau., Nari. B.S. in Polit. Sci., Tenn. State U.-Nashville, 1971; J.D., U. Iowa, 1974. Bar: Iowa 1974. Asst. atty. gen. State of Iowa, 1974-76, 80-82; exec. dir. Iowa Civil Rights Commn., 1976-79; mem. Iowa Senate, 1982—, vice chmn. judiciary com., 1983-84. Dir., chmn. polit. action com. Des Moines br. NAACP; mem. Iowa Democratic Party Central Com.; former bd. dirs. Central Iowa chpt. ARC. Named Outstanding Young Iowan, Iowa Jaycees, 1979. Mem. Nat. Bar Assn., Omega Psi Phi. Home: 4049 Lower Beaver Rd Des Moines IA 50310 Office: 4921 Douglas Ave Suite 4 Des Moines IA 50310

MANN, WILLIAM ROBERT, educational administrator, consultant; b. 1950. B.S. in Edn., Chadron State Coll., 1973, Ed.M., 1980. Cert. adminstrv., supervisory, Nebr. Tchr., St. Patrick's Sch., Sidney, Nebr., 1973-76; grad. asst. Chadron State Coll., Nebr., 1977-80; guidance counselor Alliance Pub. Schs., Nebr., 1979-80, Sioux County High Sch., Harrison, Nebr., 1980-82; county supt. schs., Harrison, Nebr., 1982—; adminstr. Dawes-Sioux County Ednl. Services, Coop., Harrison, 1984—; cons. tchr. evaluation, in-service. Chmn. Harrison Community Club, Inc., Nebr., 1982-85, creator, coordinator community celebrations, 1983-84; chmn. trustees Meml. United Methodist Ch., Harrison, 1982-84; com. mem. regional hist. celebrations, 1983-85. Mem. Phi Delta Kappa. Avocations: Community development projects. Home: PO Box 115 Harrison NE 69346 Office: Sioux County Courthouse PO Box 247 Harrison NE 69346

MANNEY, RUSSELL FIELD, JR., clergyman; b. Detroit, Oct. 11, 1933; s. Russell Field and Mildred Allison (Lamb) M.; m. Mary Janet Fairbanks, June 9, 1955; children—Russell III, Timothy, Thomas. B.B.A., U. Detroit, 1959; student Trinity Coll., 1950-51; postgrad. Mich. Sch. Theology, 1963-68, Seabury Western Theol. Sem., 1981-82. Ordained priest Episcopal Ch., 1983. Controller, City of Troy, Mich., 1959-61, City of Grosse Pointe Woods, Mich., 1961-64; city mgr. Harper Woods, Mich., 1964-68; pres. Prescot Press Inc., East Detroit, Mich., 1968-81; acct., 1959-81; treas., dir. Metamora Hills Inc., Metamora, Mich., 1965-81; vicar St. Matthew's Episcopal Ch., Flat Rock, Mich., 1982-84; treas. chpt. Cathedral Ch. St. Paul, Detroit, 1978-83, provost, 1984—; bd. dirs. Cathedral Found., 1981—, Cathedral Bookstore, 1981—; instr. Wayne State U., 1971-72. Leader, Boy Scouts Am., Harper Woods, 1973-76; bd. dirs. Harper Woods Citizens for Good Govt., 1969-70. Mem. Roseville C. of C. (sec., bd. dirs. 1973-78). Home: 18987 Huntington St Harper Woods MI 48225 Office: Cathedral Ch St Paul 4800 Woodward Ave Detroit MI 48201

MANNING, HELEN HARTON, speech communication and theater educator; b. Albion, Mich., June 7, 1921; d. William C. and Mildred B. (Brown) Harton; m. George A. Manning, Mar. 21, 1959 (dec. May 1979); 1 child, Lora Annette. B.A., Albion Coll., 1943; M.A., Northwestern U., 1950, Ph.D., 1956. Dir. theater Hope Coll., Holland, Mich., 1950-53, chmn. speech dept., 1954-55; teaching fellow Northwestern U., Evanston, Ill., 1953-54, 55-56; faculty Albion Coll., 1956—, prof. speech communication and theater, 1966—, chmn. dept., 1970—. Editor: A Guide to Environment Theater, 1974. Founder, Albion Community Theater, 1967; mem. Sesquicentennial Com. Albion, 1982—, div. chmn., 1982-85; lay leader United Meth. Ch., Albion, 1983—; mem. adv. bd. N.Y. Arts Program, N.Y.C., 1976—. Recipient Community Service award City of Albion, 1984; Mellon research grantee Albion Coll., 1983. Mem. Speech Communication Assn., Mich. Speech Communication Assn. (sec.-treas. 1957-61, Disting. Service award 1984), AAUW (v.p. 1970-73), Theta Alpha Phi (advisor 1956—), Delta Sigma Rho. Clubs: Emitte Lucem Tuam (v.p. 1985—), United Methodist Women (v.p. 1983-84, 85-86), Review (Albion). Avocations: collecting local oral history; knitting. Home: 415 Brockway Pl Albion MI 49224 Office: Dept Speech Communication and Theater Albion College E Porter St Albion MI 49224

MANNING, HENRY EUGENE, hospital administrator; b. Moresburg, Tenn., May 19, 1935; s. Henry Barnett and Lillian Pearl (Spradling) M.; m. Edna Magda (div. 1976); 1 child, Henry Eugene; m. Hope Snider Heneke, Aug. 3, 1976. B.S. in Bus. Adminstrn., L.I. U., 1960; M.S. in Hosp. Adminstrn., Columbia U., 1962. Asst. adminstr. Cumberland Hosp.; dep. commr. N.Y.C. Dept. Hosps., 1967-70; pres. Cuyahoga County Hosp. System, Cleve., 1970—; lectr. Sch. Pub. Health and Adminstrv. Medicine, Columbia U., N.Y.C., 1970-74; adj. instr. health care adminstrn., health adminstrn. and planning program Washington U. Sch. Medicine, 1983-84; asst. prof. dept. epidemiology and community health Case Western Res. U., 1970-84, asst. prof. dept. medicine, 1984—. Contbr. articles to profl. jours. Mem. adv. com., physicians assisting program Cuyahoga Community Coll., 1978-80; hosp. adv. bd. Blue Cross of Northeastern Ohio; bd. dirs. Greater Cleve. Coalition on Health Care Cost Effectiveness, 1977-82; mem. acute care adv. com. Met. Health Planning Corp.; bd. govs., mem. vis. coms. Case Western Res. U.; mem. study team for Cleve. regional jetport Lake Erie Regional Transp. Authority. Served with USAF, 1950-58. Named Alumnus of Yr., Alumni Assn. Columbia U. Sch. Pub. Health, 1977. Library fund established in his name Brittingham Meml. Library, Cuyahoga County Hosp., 1981. Mem. Am. Hosp. Assn. (del.-at-large 1972-74, 82-84, chmn. governing council, pub.-gen. hosps. sect. 1972-73, commn. on pub.-gen. hosps., regional adv. bd., governing council met. hosp. sect. 1984-85), Assn. Am. Med. Colls. (assembly), Ohio Hosp. Assn. (congl. action com. 1984-85, govt. liaison com.), Greater Cleve. Hosp. Assn. (trustee, various coms.). Office: Cuyahoga County Hosp System 3395 Scranton Rd Cleveland OH 44109

MANNING, JAMES HALLISSEY, JR., music pub. co. exec., fiber broker; b. Cornell, Ill., May 2, 1934; s. James H. and Lucille Myrtle (Robertson) M.; grad. high sch.; children—James Hallissey III, Ken Neal, Raymond James, Monica Frances. Sales rep. Lissner Paper Grading Co., Chgo., 1960-66, Royal Typewriter Co., Chgo., 1966-69, Curtis 1,000, Inc., Rolling Meadows, Ill., 1969—; co-owner, v.p. GiGi-Dor Music Co., Chgo., 1969—; account exec. Consol. Fibres, 1972—; pres., owner Chgo. Global Fibres Co., 1975—. Instr., cons. graphoanalysis, 1964—. Served with USAF, 1952-56. Recipient Hon. graphoanlysis degree St. Dominics, St. Charles, Ill., 1964. Mem. Internat. Platform Assn. Club: Western Irish Setter. Author adult and juvenile fiction. Home and Office: 2332 W Superior St Chicago IL 60612

MANNING, KENNETH PAUL, chocolate company executive; b. N.Y.C., Jan. 18, 1942; s. John Joseph and Edith Helen (Hoffmann) M.; m. Maureen Lambert, Sept. 12, 1964; children—Kenneth J., John J., Elise, Paul, Caroline, Jacqueline. B.Mech.Engring., Rensselaer Poly. Inst., 1963; postgrad. in Statistics George Washington U., 1965-66; M.B.A. in Ops. Research, Am. U., 1968. With W.R. Grace & Co., N.Y.C., since 1973—, v.p. European consumer div., 1975-76, pres. ednl. products div., 1976-79, pres. real estate div., 1979-81, v.p. corp. tech. group, 1981-83, pres., chief exec. officer Ambrosia Chocolate Co. div., Milw., 1983—. Mem. adv. council Marquette U.; Trustee Rensselaer Newman Found., Troy, N.Y. Served as lt. USN, 1963-67, Caribbean. Decorated Nat. Def. medal, Armed Forces Res. medal. Mem. Chocolate Mfrs. Assn. (chmn. 1985-86), Greater Milw. Com. Republican. Roman Catholic. Clubs: Union League (N.Y.C.); Univ. (Milw.). Home: 2914 E Newberry Blvd Milwaukee WI 53211 Office: Ambrosia Chocolate Co Div WR Grace & Co 1133 N 5th St Milwaukee WI 53203

MANNINO, THOMAS ANTHONY, physicist; b. Bridgeport, Conn., Nov. 17, 1945; s. Thomas P. and Mary E. Mannino; B.S. in Physics, U. New Haven, 1972; M.S., Drexel U., 1974; m. Donna Lee Keller, Mar. 22, 1974; children—Michele, Thomas. Instrumentation flight test engr. Sikorsky Aircraft, Stratford, Conn., 1974-76; prin. engr. Sperry Flight Systems, Phoenix, 1976-81, Rosemount, Inc., Eden Prairie, Minn., 1981—; instr. physics Phoenix Coll. Research in pressure sensing.

MANNIS, VALERIE SKLAR, lawyer; b. Green Bay, Wis., May 26, 1939; d. Phillip and Rose (Aaron) Sklar; m. Kent Simon Mannis, Dec. 28, 1958; children—Andrea, Marci. B.S., U. Wis., 1970; J.D., 1974. Bar: Wis. 1974. Staff atty. Legis. Council, Madison, Wis., 1975; gen. practice, Madison, 1975-84; asst. to pres. Bank of Shorewood Hills (Wis.), 1984—; founding mem. Legal Assn. for Women, Madison, 1975—. Pres. Nat. Women's Polit. Caucus Dane County, Madison, 1984; bd. dirs. Madison Estate Planning Council, 1980-84, bd. dirs. Madison Jewish Community Council, 1975-79, 82-84. Mem. ABA (family law sect.), Dane County Bar Assn. (chmn. property com. 1978—), State Bar. Wis. (gov. 1980-84), Nat. Assn. Banking Women. Democrat. Jewish. Club: Hadassah. Office: Asst to Pres Bank of Shorewood Hills Madison WI 53705

MANNISTO, RALPH AXEL, violinist, music educator; b. Phoenix, Mich., Mar. 23, 1919; s. Gust and Hilda (Huhta) M.; m. Ruth Edna Siira, Mar. 29, 1948; children—Keith, Dennis, Eliisa, Mark. Diploma U.S. Sch. Music, 1938; pvt. studies in violin, 1931-33; student Detroit Conservatory of Music, 1947-48, Detroit Inst. Mus. Arts, 1949; pvt. studies violin Carl Christensen, Rochester (N.Y.) Symphony, accordion Lloyd Lavaux and Lauri Holzhauer, Edio DiCiantis. Instrumental musician, entertainer, amateur actor Eddie Dowling for Spic and Spam Rev., Eng., 1944; with spl. services shows, World War II. pvt. tchr., 1934-83; with Burroughs Corp., 1947-56; theater projectionist Internat. Alliance of Theatrical Stage Employees and Moving Picture Machine Operators of U.S. and Can.; active in preserving Finnish and Scandinavian music heritage since 1960's; accompanist Internat. Finnish Folk Dance Group; performs for weddings and pvt. parties and Scandinavian festivals; accompanist for singer at sr. citizens homes; active with ethnic folk music group Mannisto Pelimannit; performer Northville (Mich.) Ethnic Festival. Served to cpl., USAAF, 1942-46. Finnish Center Assn. grantee, 1980; recipient 1st prize Farmington (Mich.) Meml. Day Parade, 1976, 2d prize, 1979. Mem. Detroit Fedn. Musicians, Finnish Center Assn., Detroit Finnish Summer Camp Assn. Home: 19659 Fry Rd Northville MI 48167

MANOHARAN, KALIAMOORTHY, cancer biologist; b. Tiruchy, India, May 20, 1955; came to U.S., 1983. s. Kaliamoorthy Appavoo and Valliammal Subbarayan; m. Balaparvati Manoharan Dec. 10, 1982; 1 child, Vivek Saravanan. B.S., U. Madras, India, 1975; M.S., 1977; M. Phil., Jawaharlal Nehru U., New Delhi, 1979, Ph.D., 1982. Asst. prof. Vivekananda Coll., Madras, India, 1982-83; postdoctoral research assoc. U. Nebr., Lincoln, 1983—. Author research publs. on chem. and horomonal interaction in cancer. Avocation: popular science. Home: 3401 Starr St Lincoln NE 68503 Office: 201 Lyman Hall Tumor Biology Lab U Nebr Lincoln NE 68588

MANOS, JOHN M., judge U.S. Dist. Judge Sixth Cir., No. Ohio. Office: US Dist Ct 256 US Courthouse Cleveland OH 44114*

MANSFIELD, BONNIE LOU, educator; b. Silver City, Iowa, June 25, 1932; d. Ed C. and Mildred L. Kruse; m. Roy Dean Mansfield, Feb. 16, 1957; children—Barbara Michelson, Bob. Cert., U. No. Iowa, 1951, M.A., 1979; B.S., U. Nebr., 1957, M.S., 1961. Tchr., Shenandoah, Iowa, 1951-53; tchr., Omaha, 1953-60; substitute tchr., Malvern, Iowa, 1960-70, aide, tchr. spl. class, 1971-75; grad. asst. U. No. Iowa, 1976-82, adj. instr., 1981-82; tchr. spl. edn. multi-categorical elem. resource room Malvern Sch., 1975—. Leader, Girl Scouts U.S.A., 1967-71; bd. dirs. Day Camp, 1970; Sunday Sch. supt. Meth. Ch., 1963-73; chmn. Bloodmobile, 1970, pres. adv. bd., 1968. Named Reading Tchr. of Yr., Iowa Reading Conf., 1983. Iowa Dept. Pub. Instrn. Tchr. Incentive grantee, 1982-83. Mem. Internat. Reading Assn., Assn. Supervision and Curriculum Devel., Am. Council Learning Disabilities, Midlands of Iowa Reading Council (past pres.), Iowa State Edn. Assn., Council for Exceptional

Children, Profl. Educators Iowa, Phi Delta Kappa. Democrat. Methodist. Clubs: Methodist Circle, Book. Home: 809 Kearney St Malvern IA 51551 Office: 409 E 9th St Malvern IA 51551

MANSFIELD, MARC RAYMOND, town official; b. Muncie, Ind., Apr. 13, 1949; s. Walter R. Mansfield, Jr. and Jayne (Benbow) Mansfield Falls; m. Cynthia Ann Campbell, July 11, 1970. B.S., Ball State U., 1971, M.A., 1977. Tchr. Monroe Schs., Cowan, Ind., 1973-75, St. Mary's Schs., Muncie, 1975-77; spl. rep. Franklin Life Ins. Co., Muncie, 1977-79; econ. devel. planner Planning Dept., Anderson, Ind., 1979-81; town mgr. Town of Yorktown, Ind., 1981—. Active Acad. Pub. Service, Indpls., Tech. Adv. Com., Muncie. Served with USMC, 1971-73. Recipient cert. Acad. Pub. Service, 1983, Ind. Econ. Devel. Acad., 1984. Mem. Internat. City Mgmt. Assn., Ind. Municipal Mgmt. Assn., C. of C. (bd. dirs. 1984—). Avocations: golf; running; reading; watching baseball. Home: 5600 N Fox Run Ln Muncie IN 47302 Office: Town of Yorktown 720 W Smith Yorktown IN 47396

MANSHIP, JOHN HARVEY, JR., land surveyor; b. Hancock County, Ind., Aug. 31, 1927; s. John Harvey, Sr. and Easter Lillian (Mock) M.; m. Helen Lorraine Steele, June 8, 1947; children—Larry Eugene, Linda Jane, Patrick Jay, Teena Marie. Grad. Pendleton Sch., Ind., 1945. Registered land surveyor, Ind. Dep. surveyor Madison County, Ind., 1949-60, county surveyor, 1971-72; asst. city engr. City of Anderson, Ind., 1973-76; county surveyor Madison County, 1977—. Mem. Democratic Com., Madison County; mem., deacon Whetstone Ch. Mem. Ind. Soc. Profl. Land Surveyors, Am. Congress Surveying and Mapping, Ind. County Surveyors Orgn. (pres. 1970). Democrat. Lodges: Lions, Elks, Masons, Order Eastern Star. Avocations: bowling; sports spectator. Home: 3140 Meadowcrest Dr Anderson IN 46011 Office: John H Manship & Assocs 626 Jackson St Anderson IN 46016

MANSON, BRUCE MALCOLM, construction company executive; b. Chgo., July 16, 1944; s. William Donald and Evelyn Florence (Drinnen) M.; m. Mary Jane Romans, July 30, 1966; children—Jennifer Lyn, Scott Lindsay. C.E., Bradley U., 1966. Field engr. E.W. Corrigan Constrn. Co., Chgo., 1966-68, estimator, 1968-73; project mgr. Pepper Constrn. Co., Chgo., 1973-77, v.p. div., 1977-78, v.p. engrng., 1978-80, exec. v.p., 1980-85; exec. v.p., chief operating officer Inland Constrn. Co., Chgo., 1985—; cons. Carlson Reports, Mt. Prospect, 1983. Served with AUS, 1966-71. Mem. Internat. Council Shopping Ctrs. Builders Assn. Chgo., Assoc. Gen. Contractors, Barrington C. of C. Contbr. articles to profl. jours. Club: Chgo. Athletic Assn. Office: Inland Constrn Co 640 N LaSalle St Chicago IL 60610

MANSUR, CHARLES ISAIAH, geotechnical engineering consultant; b. Kansas City, Mo., Dec. 22, 1918; s. Isaiah and Florence (Cramer) M.; children—Richard C., Cheryl Ann; m. Betty Jo Sauer, Nov. 26, 1960. B.S. in Civil Engrng., U. Mo., 1939; M.S. in San. Engrng., Harvard U., 1941. Registered profl. engr., Miss., La., Kans., Mo. Chief design sect. Waterways Express Sta., Vicksburg, Miss., 1941-43, asst. chief, 1946-56; san. engr. USPHS, Washington, 1943-46; chief Lower Miss. Valley div. C.E., U.S. Army, Miss., 1957-57; v.p. then pres. Fruco & Assoc., Mo., 1959-69; sr. v.p., cons. McClelland Engrs., St. Louis, 1969-84, sr. engring. cons., 1984—. Author: (with others) Foundation Engineering, 1962. Editor: Malaria Control on Impounded Water, 1946. Mem. planning com. City of Frontenac, Mo., 1967-69, mem. com. on bldgs., 1972. Served to maj. USPHS, 1943-46. Gordon McKay fellow, 1939-41. Fellow ASCE (Thomas F. Rowland prize 1958, Thomas A. Middlebrook award 1957, J.James R. Cross medal 1959); mem. St. Louis Engrs. Club. Presbyterian. Avocations: farming, wood working. Home: 1715 N Geyer Rd Saint Louis MO 63131 Office: McClelland Engrs Inc 744 Office Pkwy Saint Louis MO 63141

MANTICA, JOHN FRANCIS, hospital administrator; b. Turin, Italy, July 27, 1958; came to U.S., 1959, naturalized, 1964; s. John Louis and Betty Marie (Fortunato) M. B.A., Marietta Coll., 1980; M.B.A., U. Steubenville, 1982. Admissions intern U. Steubenville (Ohio), 1980; personnel generalist St. John Med. Ctr., Steubenville, 1981—, asst. dir. personnel, 1981—. Bd. dirs. Am. Cancer Soc.; football coach; mem. Republican Nat. Com. Club: K.C. (officer). Home: 113 Teresa Dr Steubenville OH 43952 Office: St John Med Center St John Heights Steubenville OH 43952

MANUEL, EDWARD, utility company executive; b. Raleigh, N.C., Aug. 8, 1949; s. George Edward and Eloise (Morton) M.; m. Marilyn Kaye Moore, July 23, 1982; children—Leya, Aaron, Tasha. B.S., U. Wis.-Platteville, 1971; M.A., U. Wis., Madison, 1975, Ph.D., 1979. Tchr. Madison Met. Sch. Dist., Wis., 1971-79, chmn. dept., 1975-79, adminstrv. intern, 1979; community relations coordinator Madison Gas and Electric Co., 1980—. Bd. dirs. ARC, 1984—, Dane County Area Youth Football League, 1983, Black History Inc., 1981-82; mem. United Way Dane County, 1984. Mem. Am. Assn. Blacks in Energy, Am. Gas Assn. (urban affairs com. 1984—), Edison Electric Inst. (consumer affairs com. 1984—), Kappa Alpha Psi. Democrat. Lodge: Rotary (bd. dirs. 1983—). Avocations: racquetball, weightlifting. Home: 206 N Gammon Rd Madison WI 53717 Office: Madison Gas and Electric Co 133 Blair St Madison WI 53703

MAPA, HELOUISE CULANCULAN, pediatrician; b. Katipunan, Zamboanga del Norte, Philippines, Jan. 3, 1944; came to U.S., 1967; s. Alfonso Emia and Bienvenida (Cadavedo) Culanculan; m. Manolo P. Mapa, Dec. 24, 1968; children—Michael, Marissa, Mimi, Mohmoi. M.D., U. St. Thomas, Manila, 1967. Diplomate Am. Bd. Pediatrics. Rotating intern St. Luke's Hosp. and Children's Med. Ctr., 1968-69; resident Kings Country Hosp. Ctr., Bklyn., 1969-71, asst. instr., K H 1970-74; med. dir. East N.Y. Med. Ctr., Bklyn., 1973-74; attending physician East Liverpool City Hosp. Ohio, 1974-83, chief pediatrics, 1983—; practice medicine specializing in pediatrics East Liverpool, 1974—. Fellow Am. Acad. Pediatrics; mem. Assn. Practicing Philippine Physicians in Am., Am. Assn. Clin. Immunology and Allergy, Ohio Valley Philippine Med. Assn., Ohio State Med. Assn., Bus. and Profl. Women's Assn. Roman Catholic. Home: Box 250 Casa Mapa Laurel Farms Chester WV 26034

MAPES, ROGER ALLEN, pharmacist; b. Lafayette, Ind., July 17, 1951; s. Herschel E. and Marjorie Ann (Brown) M.; m. Peggy Ann Holt, June 21, 1975; children—Gregory Scott, Amanda Suzanne. B.S., Purdue U., 1976. Registered pharmacist, Ind. Asst. mgr., pharmacist Hook Drugs, Connersville, Ind., 1976-77, mgr., pharmacist, Kentland, Ind., 1977—; nursing home cons. pharmacist, 1985—. Vol. basketball coach South Newton Jr.-Sr. High Sch., Kentland, 1981—; mem. Newton County Bd. Health, 1985—. Recipient awards Hook Drugs, 1980, 82, 83, 84. Mem. Purdue U. Pharmacy Alumni Assn. (exec. com. 1984), Kentland Jaycees (charter). Methodist. Avocation: running. Home: 311 E Iroquois Dr Kentland IN 47951 Office: Hook Drugs 512 E Seymour St Kentland IN 47951

MAPLE, FRANCIS MARION, physician, consultant; b. Spiceland, Ind., Mar. 28, 1922; s. Frederick Marion and Dora Belle (Wagoner) M.; m. Margaret Ruth Feeny, July 28, 1946; children—John Frederick, Margaret Anne, Louis Kay, Thomas Edward. Student Earlham Coll., 1940-41, Ball State U., 1942-43, U. Mich., 1943-44; B.S., Ind. U., 1947, M.D., 1950. Diplomate Am. Bd. Internal Medicine. Intern, then resident U. Wash., Seattle, 1950-54; cons. gastroenterology and internal medicine Smith-Glynn-Callaway Clinic, Springfield, Mo., 1954—; cons. gastroenterology U.S. Med. Ctr., Springfield, 1970—; chief of staff St. John's Hosp., Springfield, 1969-71, chmn. gastroenterology sect., 1972—; lectr. U. Mo.-Kansas City; med. missionary to Egypt. Pres. Christian Guidance Fellowship. Served to lt. (j.g.) USNR, 1944-54. Fellow ACP, Am. Coll. Gastroenterology, Royal Soc. Medicine; mem. AMA, Mo. State Med. Assn., Greene County Med. Soc., Mo. Health Data Corp. (pres. 1975-82), Springfield Area Council Chs. (pes. 1970-72). Republican. Episcopalian. Club: Hickory Hills Country (Springfield). Lodge: Kiwanis (pres. Springfield 1959). Home: 2115 E Edgewood Ave Springfield MO 65804 Office: Smith Glynn Callaway Clinic 3231 S National St Springfield MO 65807

MAPLE, KARL EDWARD, political science educator, consultant; b. Carbondale, Ill., Mar. 23, 1945; s. June and Vivian (Robinson) M.; married; 1 child, Mark Edward. B.S., So. Ill. U., 1967, M.S., 1968, Ph.D., 1980. Research asst. So. Ill. U., Carbondale, 1968-69; instr. Southeastern Ill. Coll., Harrisburg, 1969; instr. John Logan Coll., Carterville, Ill., 1970—, chmn. dept. social scis., 1979—; dist. asst. Congressman Paul Simon, Washington, 1981-84. Bd. dirs. Prison Family Support, Carbondale, 1970—; councilman Elkville City, Ill., 1972—. Named Outstanding Young Educator, Ill. Jaycees, 1974; disting. faculty Logan Student Body, 1982. Mem. NEA, Ill. Edn. Assn., Kappa Delta Pi, Phi Kappa Phi, Phi Delta Kappa. Democrat. Baptist. Avocations: skiing; photography. Home: 1 Maple Acres Elkville IL 62932 Office: John Logan College Carterville IL 62918

MAPLES, STEPHEN SEVEDUS, automation company executive; b. Tecumseh, Mich., June 18, 1950; s. Sevedus Allister and Janet Ellen (Wilcox) M.; m. Cathy Ann Beevers, Aug. 11, 1979; children—Titian Elizabeth, Kirsten Katherine. Student Eastern Mich. U., 1975-78, Ind. Vocat. Tech. U., 1978-79. Product checker Ford Motor Co., Saline, Mich., 1972-73; teaching asst. dept. chemistry Eastern Mich. U., Ypsilanti, 1975-78; application engr. Control Gaging Co., Ann Arbor, Mich., 1979-82; pres., chief engr. Acer Automation Corp., Adrian, Mich., 1982-85; chief engr. Air Hydraulics, Inc., Jackson, Mich., 1985—; metrology cons. Molden Assocs., Michigan City, Ind.; gaging cons. Lyon Machine & Tool Co., Muskegon, Mich. Served with U.S. Army, 1969-72. Mem. Phi Kappa Phi. Inventor gaging apparatus.

MAPPA, PHILIP IRWIN, real estate developer, accountant; b. Chgo., May 2, 1944; s. Samuel and Anne E. (London) M.; m. Susan Posner, Aug. 16, 1964; children—Steven Andrew, Jacqueline Suzanne. Student U. Ill., 1962-66. C.P.A., Ill. Mgr. tax Arthur Andersen & Co., Chgo., 1966-73; exec. v.p. Farnsworth, McKoane & Co., Chgo., 1973-83; pres., owner Philip I. Mappa Interests, Des Plaines, Ill., 1984—; lectr. in field. Editor: Fed. Taxes Affecting Real Estate, 1976. Contbr. articles to profl. jours. Mem. Am. Inst. C.P.A.s, Ill. C.P.A.s. Republican. Jewish. Club: Idlewild Country (Flossmoor) (bd. dirs. 1978-83). Avocations: 12— softball; tennis; racquetball; golf. Office: 1350 E Touhy Ave Des Plaines IL 60018

MARAKAS, JOHN LAMBROS, insurance company executive; b. Connellsville, Pa., July 16, 1926; s. Gust John and Elizabeth Hamilton (Cutler) M.; A.B., U. Mich., 1949; m. Alice Dixon, Dec. 26, 1948; children—Andy, Nancy, Donna. Actuarian asst. Acacia Mut., Washington, 1949-50; actuary Continental Assurance, Chgo., 1950-53; v.p., actuary, exec. v.p., pres. Res. Life Ins. Co., Dallas, 1953-70; v.p., then pres. Nationwide Corp., Columbus, Ohio; dir. Gates, McDonald & Co., Gulf Atlantic Life, Mich. Life, Nat. Casualty Co., Nat. Services, Inc., Nationwide Community Urban Redevelopment Corp., Nationwide Funding, Nationwide Life, Nationwide Profl. Services Corp., Nationwide Properties, Pacific Life, West Coast Life; trustee Nationwide Real Estate Services, Real Estate Investors, Heritage Securities Inc. Bd. dirs. Mt. Carmel Med. Center, Planned Parenthood, Capital U. Served with U.S. Army, 1946-47. Mem. Am. Acad. Actuaries. Office: Nationwide Life Ins Co One Nationwide Plaza Columbus OH 43216

MARCH, DON FRANCIS, educator; b. Denver, Sept. 27, 1951; s. Francis Milton and Wanda May (Jacoby) M.; B.A., Ill. Coll., 1973; m. Joanne Margaret Dunbar, June 21, 1975; children—Roger Arnold, Phillip Ray, Jesica Lyn. Tchr. English, asst. football coach, head wrestling coach, head track coach Shelbyville (Ill.) Unit Dist. 323, 1973-78; tchr. journalism and reading, asst. varsity football coach and defensive coordinator, head wrestling coach Johnsburg Sch. Dist. 12, McHenry, Ill., 1978-83; asst. wrestling coach McHenry Sch. Dist. 156, 1983—, head McHenry Wrestling Club, 1983—. Youth leader Presbyterian Ch. Democrat. Home: 1205 Bonnie Brae McHenry IL 60050

MARCH, EDMUND SIMON, communications exec.; b. Phila., Apr. 7, 1941; s. Edmund S. and Sylvia S. (Olack) M.; B.S., Tampa Coll., 1973; m. Kay Batdorf, Nov. 1, 1978. Computer technician Honeywell, Inc., St. Petersburg, Fla., 1966-72, computer ops. analyst, Mpls., 1972-76, communications computer analyst, 1976—. Served with USAF, 1958-60. Mem. Assn. Timesharing Users, Computer Security Inst., Assn. Data Communications Users, Honeywell Engrng. Club. Republican. Roman Catholic. Home: 3112 Wilson St Saint Anthony MN 55418 Office: Honeywell Plaza Minneapolis MN 55408

MARCH, JACQUELINE FRONT, chemist, consultant; b. Wheeling, W.Va., July 10, 1914; d. Jacques Johann and Antoinette (Orenstein) Front; B.S., Case Western Res. U., 1937, M.A., 1939; Wyeth fellow med. research U. Chgo., 1940-42; postgrad. U. Pitts., 1945, Ohio State U., 1967, Wright State U., 1970-76; m. Abraham W. Marcovich, Oct. 7, 1945 (dec. 1969); children—Wayne Front, Gail Ann. Chemist, Mt. Sinai Hosp., Cleve., 1934-40; med. research chemist U. Chgo., 1940-42; research analyst Koppers Co., also info. scientist Union Carbide Corp., Mellon Inst., Pitts., 1942-45; propr. March. Med. Research Lab., etiology of diabetes, Dayton, Ohio, 1950-79; guest scientist Kettering Found., Yellow Springs, Ohio, 1953; Dayton Found. fellow Miami Valley Hosp. Research Inst., 1956. mem. chemistry faculty U. Dayton, 1959-69, info. scientist Research Inst., 1968-79; prin. investigator Air Force Wright Aero. Labs., Wright-Patterson AFB Tech. Info. Center, 1970-79; chem. cons.; div. tech. services Nat. Inst. Occupational Safety and Health, Health and Human Services, Cin., 1979—, guest lectr. on info. retrieval, tng. div., 1981—; mem. toxic chems. rev. com. Am. Conf. Govtl. Indsl. Hygienists; pres. JFM Cons.; designer info. systems, speaker in field. Treas. Fairway 11, Village 3 Condo Assn., 1985. Recipient Recognition cert. U. Dayton, 1980. Mem. Am. Soc. Info. Sci. (treas. South Ohio 1973-75), Am. Chem. Soc. (pres. Dayton 1977, selection com. Patterson-Crane award 1981—, nat. councillor 1983-85, fin. investment com. for Cin. endowment 1985), Soc. Advancement Materials and Process Engring. (editor nat. tech. seminar publ. 1976, pres. Midwest chpt. 1977-78, nat. dir. for Midwest 1979), Affiliated Tech. Socs. (Outstanding Scientist and Engr. award 1978), AAUP (exec. bd.), Sigma Xi (treas. Dayton 1976-79, Straub lectr., Cin. 1982, v.p., pres.-elect Cin. fld. chpt. 1985). Club: Royal Oak Hunt and Country (Cin.). Contbr. articles to profl. publs. Office: 4676 Columbia Pkwy Cincinnati OH 45226

MARCHESSEAULT, PAUL JOSEPH, realtor; b. Worcester, Mass., July 3, 1932; s. Henry Arthur and Mary Florence M.; m. Karen Elizabeth Ruble, Jan. 26, 1974; children—Marcus, Jeffrey, Michelle. B.S. in Edn., State Coll., Worcester, 1966; M.Ed., 1957; postgrad Grad. Sch. Bus., Ind. U., 1976-78. Tchr. pub. schs., Worcester, 1955-63; tng. dir. Sci. Research Assocs., Chgo., 1964-68; dir. sales Sch. div. Bobbs Merrill Co., Indpls., 1968-76, dir. spl. services, 1976-80, dir. product devel. and mgmt., 1980-84; realtor F.C. Tucker Co., 1984—. Chmn. fin. Republican Precinct Com., 1978. Served with U.S. Army N.G., 1950-59. Mem. Am. Assn. Higher Edn., Am. Soc. Tng. and Devel., Met. Indpls. Bd. Realtors. Club: Eagle Creek Sailing. Lodge: Kiwanis. Home: 1204 Darby Ln Indianapolis IN 46260 Office: 3405 E 86th St Indianapolis IN 46240

MARCIAL, ROGELIO GENEROSO, physician; b. Manila, Philippines, Apr. 19, 1925; came to U.S., 1953; s. Jesus Fernandez Marcial and Consuelo (Generoso) Inayan; m. Gail Jean Walker, July 29, 1955; children—Diane, Deborah, Doreen, Michael, Melanie, Melita, Matthew. A.A., U. Santo Tomas, Manila, 1947, B.S., 1950, M.D., 1952. Diplomate Am. Bd. Family Practice. Pres. Portage County Med. Soc., Ravenna, Ohio, 1970-71, Portage County chpt., Ohio Acad. Family Practice, Ravenna, 1983-84; physician The Windham Clinic, Inc., Ohio, 1984—. Republican. Roman Catholic. Lodge: KC. Home: 9622 Wisteria St Windham OH 44288 Office: 9250 N Main St Windham OH 44288

MARCINCAVAGE, MARIE CREWS, educator; b. Lerona, W.Va., July 25, 1944; d. John W. and Fannie Esther (Caudill) Crews; m. Gerald Lee Mullins, June 13, 1965; m. 2d, Stephen Paul Marcincavage, Aug. 2, 1980. B.S. in Edn., Concord Coll., Athens, W.Va., 1965; M.S. in Edn., U. Akron, 1980; postgrad. Kent State U., 1981-82. Tchr. English, Green Bank High Sch. (W.Va.), 1965, Iaeger High Sch (W.Va.), 1965-66, Talcott High Sch. (W.Va.), 1966-67, Cuyahoga Falls City Schs. (Ohio), 1967-70; tchr. English, dept. head Jackson High Sch., Massillon, Ohio, 1970-80; cons. lang. arts and gifted edn. Stark County Dept. Edn., Louisville, Ohio, 1981—. Mem. Am. Soc. Tng. and Devel., Nat. Council English Tchrs., Assn. for Supervision and Curriculum Devel., Northeastern Ohio Sch. Suprs. Assn., Stark County Assn. Elem. Sch. Prins., Consortium of Ohio Coordinators for Gifted, Ohio Assn. Gifted Children, Phi Delta Kappa. Democrat. Methodist. Home: 4331 Meadowlark Trail Stow OH 44224 Office: 7800 Columbus Rd NE Louisville OH 44641

MARCINKOSKI, ANNETTE MARIE, educator; b. Akron, Ohio, Aug. 2, 1933; d. Frank J. and Barbara (Popielarczyk) Marcinkoski; B.S., U. Akron, 1955; M.A., U. Mich., 1959. Tchr. Flint (Mich.) Pub. Schs., 1955-63, tng. tchr. Coop. Tchr. Edn. Program, 1963-69, elementary tchr., 1969—. Active Big Sister program; sponsor Jr. Red Cross, 1959-63; tchr. Confraternity of Christian Doctrine. Mem. United Tchrs. of Flint (del. rep. assembly), Mich. Edn. Assn. (bd. dirs. 1978—, pres. Region X, 1976-77), NEA (regional dir. 1973-78), Elementary, Kindergarten and Nursery Educators, Mich. (treas. 1970-72, pres. 1973-75), Flint (sec. 1959-62) assns. childhood edn., Assn. Childhood Edn. Internat., AAUW (v.p. 1967-69, area rep. in edn. 1969-72), Theta Phi Alpha (adviser Gen. Motors Inst. chpt. 1973—, chmn. bd. dirs. 1973-79, sec. Founders Found. 1978-80, nat. treas. 1980-82), Cath. Bus. Women (sec. 1970-72, del. council state orgns. 1974-76), Flint Area Reading Council, Mich. Reading Assn., Flint Community Schs. Edn. Fund (bd. govs. 1984-86), Delta Kappa Gamma, Phi Delta Kappa (del. 1981-84). Home: 1911 Laurel Oak Dr Flint MI 48507 Office: 1402 W Dayton St Flint MI 48504

MARCO, HOWARD CLARENCE, business consultant; b. Chgo., June 30, 1928; s. Clarence S. and Martha (Gutfreund) M.; m. Constance Elizebeth Ebener, July 25, 1959; children—Frederick H., Martha Elizebeth. Student U. Iowa, 1947, Drake U., 1948. Mfr.'s rep. Futorian Stratford Furniture Co. (name now Mahasko Industries), Kansas City, Mo., 1957-60; ptnr. H&R Block, Des Moines, 1963-69; v.p. CenCor, Inc., Kansas City, 1969-72; cons. Gen. Bus. Services, Prairie Village, Kans., 1974—, regional dir., recruiter, 1969—. Bd. dirs. Turner House Inc., Kansas City, 1978—, treas., 1980-83. Served with USAF, 1951-52. Republican. Episcopalian. Home: 4811 W 80th St Shawnee Mission KS 66208 Office: Gen Bus Services 4200 Somerset Dr Suite 200 Shawnee Mission KS 66208

MARCOUX, CHARLES ROSS, JR., transp. co. exec., lawyer; b. Bristol, Conn., July 14, 1935; s. Charles Ross and Barbara (Johnston) M.; B.A. cum laude, Niagara U., 1956; LL.B., Georgetown U., 1962; m. Mary Kathryn Chartier, Oct. 10, 1959; children—Susan, Michele, Edward, Christopher. Admitted to Va. bar, 1962; atty. SEC, Washington, 1961-65; gen. counsel Leaseway Transp. Corp., Cleve., 1966-75, vice chmn., dir., 1975-81, exec. v.p., dir., 1981—, pres., dir., 1982—; chmn. bd. Signal Delivery Service, Inc., 1968—. Served to 1st lt. AUS, 1956-58. Mem. Va. Bar Assn. Home: 10010 Mitchell's Mill Rd Chardon OH 44024 Office: 3700 Park East Dr Cleveland OH 44122

MARCUM, JOSEPH LARUE, See *Who's Who in America,* 43rd edition.

MARCUS, DANIEL ROBERT, stockbroker; b. N.Y.C., June 12, 1931; s. Ralph S. and Alice R. Marcus; m. Florence R. Marzano, May 19, 1960; children—Amy B., Grant R. B.S., Northwestern U., 1955. With Bear Stearns & Co., Chgo., 1949-55, Gofen & Glossberg, Chgo., 1956-70, Freehling & Co., Chgo., 1970, Drexel Burnham Lambert, Inc., Chgo., 1971—. Vice-pres. Evanston Boys Hockey Assn., Ill., 1977-83; bd. dirs. Met. High Sch. Hockey League, Northbrook, Ill., 1980-83; mem. dist. com. Amateur Hockey Assn. Ill., 1982—. Fellow Fin. Anlysts Fedn.; mem. Midwest Communications Assn., Security Traders Chgo., Internat. Facilty Mgrs. Assn., Chgo. Anlysts Soc. Republican. Home: 904 Michigan Evanston IL 60202 Office: Drexel Burnham Lambert One S Wacker Dr 14th Floor Chicago IL 60606

MARCUS, MARY DONNA, osteopathic physician; b. Germany, Mar. 16, 1945; came to U.S., 1949; d. John and Donna (Budras) M. B.S., U. Detroit, 1968; D.O., Chgo. Coll. Osteo. Medicine, 1973. Intern Chgo. Osteo. Hosp., 1973-74, resident, 1974-78, now staff; fellow in pathology Chgo. Coll. Osteo. Medicine, 1972-73; practice medicine specializing in ob-gyn, Tinley Park, Ill., 1979—; asst. prof. ob-gyn Chgo. Coll. Osteo. Medicine, 1978—; staff physician Olympia Field Hosp. Mem. Ill. Assn. Osteo. Physicians and Surgeons, Coll. Ob-Gyn, Am. Osteo. Assn., Am. Soc. Colposcopy, Alumni Assn. Chgo. Coll. Osteo. Medicine, Ill. Osteo. Assn. (chmn. ethics com.). Office: 20303 S Crawford Ave Olympia Fields IL 60461

MARCY, BONNIE LOU, pharmacist; b. Gary, Ind., Oct. 24, 1954; d. Donald Ivan and Marie Maxine (Ritenour) Phillips; m. Randy Michel Marcy, Oct. 28, 1978. B.S. in Pharmacy, Purdue U., 1978. Staff pharmacist Lakeview Med. Ctr., Danville, Ill., 1978-79; relief pharmacist Harding Pharmacy, Danville, 1979; asst. pharmacy mgr. Kroger Co., Terre Haute, Ind., 1979-84; staff pharmacist Peoples Drug, Indpls., 1984—. Mem. Am. Pharm. Assn., Ind. Pharmacists Assn., DAR, Kappa Epsilon. Republican. Presbyterian. Avocations: reading, organ playing, needlework. Home: PO Box 26494 Indianapolis IN 46226 Office: Peoples Drug 5025 8317 Pendleton Pike Indianapolis IN 46226

MARDIGIAN, EDWARD STEPHAN, machine tool company executive; b. Stambul, Turkey, Oct. 25, 1909; s. Stephan and Agavine (Hagopian) M.; came to U.S., 1914, naturalized, 1929; student Wayne U., 1932-34; m. Helen Alexander, June 5, 1938; children—Marilyn, Edward, Robert. Asst. tool engr. Briggs Mfg. Co., Detroit, 1935-37, chief tool engr., Eng., 1937-45, chief project engr., 1945; owner, operator Mardigian Corp., Warren, Mich., 1948-69, Marco Corp., Warren, 1954, bought Buckeye Aluminum Co., Wooster, Ohio, 1956, Mardigian Car Corp., Warren, 1966—; pres. Hercules Machine Tool & Die Co., Warren, 1973—; chmn. bd. Central States Mfg. Co., Warren, 1973—. Pres. Armenian Gen. Benevolent Union Am., 1972—; chmn. Chief Exec. Orgn., Warren, 1974, Chief Exec. Orgn. Internat. Decorated medal St. Gregory by Vasken 1st Supreme Patriarch of All Armenians, 1966; named Man of Year Diocese Armenian Ch. N.Am., 1977. Home: 1525 Tottenham Rd Birmingham MI 48009 Office: Hercules Machine Tool & Die Co 13920 Address: E Ten Mile Rd Warren MI 48089

MARE, WILLIAM HAROLD, Bible educator, talk show host; b. Portland, Oreg., July 23, 1918; s. Scott Creighton and Sallie Gertrude (Knight) Brown, m. Clara Elizabeth Potter, Mar. 23, 1945; children—Myra Ann, Sally Elizabeth, Nancy Lee, William Harold, Jr., Judith Eileen. B.A. (hon. soc.), Wheaton Coll., 1941; B.D., Faith Theol. Sem., 1945; M.A., Wheaton Coll., 1946; Ph.D., U. Penn., 1961. Ordained to ministry Presbyterian Ch., 1945. Grad. fellow, tchr. Wheaton Coll., Ill., 1941-42; tchr. Faith Theol. Sem., Wilmington, Del., 1946-53, pastor Presbyn. Chs., Denver, Charlotte, N.C., 1953-63, prof. classics Covenant Coll. St. Louis, 1963-64; prof. N.T., Covenant Theol. Sem., St. Louis, 1963—; dir. Near East Sch. of Archaeology, Jerusalem, 1962, 64; archaeologist Jerusalem, Raddana, Heshbon, Moab, summers 1970, 72, 74, 76, 79; dir. Abila of Decapolis Excavation, No. Jordan, 1980—. Contbr. articles to profl. jours. Author: First Corinthians Expositors Bible Commentary, 1976; Mastering New Testament Greek, 1977; Archaeology of the Jerusalem Area, 1986. Treas. Mo. Roundtable, St. Louis, 1981—. Mem. Archeol. Inst. Am. (pres. 1978-80), Nr. East Archeol. Soc. (pres. St. Louis chpt. 1971-80), Evang. Theol. Soc., Am. Schs. Oriental Research, Soc. Bibl. Lit. Republican. Club: Classical (St. Louis) (pres. 1977-79). Avocation: photography. Home: 978 Orchard Lakes Dr St Louis MO 63146 Office: Covenant Theol Sem 12330 Conway Rd St Louis MO 63141

MARGARITONDO, GIORGIO, physics educator; b. Rome, Aug. 24, 1946; came to U.S. 1978; s. Giuseppe and Maria Luisa (Averardi) M.; m. Marina Savalli, Sept. 1, 1971; children—Laura, Francesca. Ph.D. in Physics, U. Rome, 1969. Staff scientist Italian Nat. Research Council, Rome, 1971-78; resident visitor Bell Labs., Murray Hill, N.J., 1975-77; from asst. prof. to assoc. to prof. physics U. Wis., Madison, 1978—, assoc. dir. Synchrotron Radiation Ctr., 1984—. Contbr. articles to profl. jours. Served to 2d lt. Italian Army, 1972-73. Romnes Found. fellow, 1983. Mem. Am. Phys. Soc., Am. Vacuum Soc. Roman Catholic. Avocations: classical music, tennis. Home: 2728 Tami Trail Madison WI 53711 Office: Dept Physics U Wis Madison WI 53706

MARGOLIS, BERNARD ALLEN, library administrator, antique book merchant, appraiser of rare books; b. Greenwich, Conn., Oct. 2, 1948; s. Sidney S. and Rose (Birkenfeld) M.; m. Amanda Batey, Nov. 2, 1973. B.A. in Polit. Sci., U. Denver, 1970, M.A. in Librarianship, 1973. Cert. librarian, Mich. Library asst. Denver Pub. Library, 1970-72; br. head Virginia Village Library, Denver Pub. Library, 1972-73; dep. dir. Monroe County Library System, Mich., 1973-75; dir. Raisin Valley Library System, Monroe, 1976-78, S.E. Mich. Regional Film Library, Monroe, 1976—, Monroe County Library System, 1976—; cons. in library pub. relations, 1976—; lectr. Western Mich. U., Kalamazoo, 1978-81; appraiser rare books, Monroe, 1970—. Contbr. articles to profl. jours. Bd. dirs. Monroe Sen. Citizens Ctr., 1976-80, Monroe Fine Arts Council, 1978-81; chmn. Blue Cross-Blue Shield Consumer Council, Detroit, 1984—; mem. adv. bd. Mercy Meml. Hosp., Monroe, 1984—. Recipient Mayoral Cert. Commendation award Denver, 1972, 73. Mem. ALA (cons. annual swap and shop 1979-84; John Cotton Dana award 1977, Library Awareness Idea Search award Washington 1982), Library Adminstrv. Mgmt. Assn., Pub. Library Assn., Library Pub. Relations Council. Democrat. Jewish. Home: 1565 Arbor Ave Monroe MI 48161 Office: Monroe County Library System 3700 S Custer Rd Monroe MI 48161

MARGOLIS, FRED SHELDON, pediatric dentist, educator; b. Lorain, Ohio, Mar. 31, 1947; s. Benjamin Barnett and Zelma (Bordo) M.; m. Susan Kreiter, Sept. 12, 1971; children—David S. and Adam R. B.S., Ohio State U., 1969,

D.D.S., 1973; cert. pediatric dentistry U. Ill.-Chgo., 1976. Dental intern Mount Sinai Hosp., Chgo., 1973-74; practice dentistry North Suburban Dental Assocs., Skokie, Ill., 1974-84; practice dentistry, Arlington Heights, Ill., 1979—; asst. prof. pediatric dentistry Loyola U. Dental Sch., Maywood, Ill., 1982-83, guest lectr. pediatric dentistry, 1983-85; dental cons. Delta Dental Plan, Chgo., 1983—. Contbr. articles to profl. publs. Cubmaster N.E. Ill. council Boy Scouts Am., 1984. Mem. Am. Dental Assn., Am. Acad. Pediatric Dentistry, Ill. State Dental Soc., Am. Soc. Dentistry for Children, Chgo. Dental Soc., Alpha Omega. Jewish. Lodge: B'nai B'rith. Avocations: photography; golfing; stained glass. Office: 3419 N Arlington Heights Rd Arlington Heights IL 60004

MARGULIS, FRANCINE MARJORIE, interior designer, consultant; b. N.Y.C., Jan. 17, 1926; d. Jacob S. and Dorothy (Frieder) Kopell; m. Martin Margulis, Sept. 11, 1949; children—Barbara (dec.), Barry. B.A., NYU, 1946; M.A. in Psychology, L.I.U., 1949. Pres. Mark Interior Designers, Dayton, Ohio, 1951-74; dir. interior design Elder-Beerman Corp., Dayton, 1974-81; owner, pres. Francine Margulis A.S.I.D. Interiors, Dayton, 1981—; pres. Mega Systems Research, Dayton, 1982—; instr., developer interior design program Sinclair Coll., Dayton, 1974-81; instr. U. Dayton, 1981—. Contbr. articles to profl. jours. Panelist Ohio Women's Conf., Columbus, 1982. Recipient Merit award Sinclair Coll., 1979, Achievement award U. Dayton, 1982. Mem. Am. Soc. Interior Designers (advisor), Nat. Soc. Interior Designers (founder). Jewish. Lodge: Hadassah, Miami Valley Golf. Avocation: reading. Home: 4180 Cedar Bluff Dayton OH 45415

MARI, REGINALD R., JR., civil engr., city ofcl.; b. Springfield, Ill., June 18, 1931; s. Reginald and Rose (Colantino) M.; B.S., U. Ill., 1955. Foreman, pipe mill Youngstown Sheet & Tube Co., Indiana Harbor, Ind., 1955-57; field supr. constrn. elevated hwys., sewers, sts., tunnels, dock walls and airport facilities City of Chgo., 1957-76, head constrn. subsect. airport programs Bur. Engring., 1976—. Registered profl. engr., Ill. Mem. ASCE, Internat. Platform Assn., Mid Am. Commodity Exchange. Home: 5241 NE River Rd Chicago IL 60656 Office: City of Chgo Bur Engring 320 N Clark St Chicago IL 60610

MARICK, MICHAEL MIRON, lawyer; b. Chgo., Nov. 20, 1957; s. Miron Michael and Geraldyne Marilyn (Lid) M. B.A., Denison U., 1979; J.D., Ill. Inst. Tech./Chgo.-Kent Coll. Law, 1982. Bar: Ill. 1982, U.S. Dist. Ct. (no. dist.) Ill. 1982, Fla. 1983. Mem. firm Hinshaw, Culbertson, Moelmann, Hoban & Fuller, Chgo., 1982-85; mem. Phelan, Pope & John, Chgo., 1985—; instr. Ill. Inst. Tech./Chgo.-Kent Coll. Law, 1983-84; comml. arbitrator Am. Arbitration Assn., Chgo., 1983—. Treas., exec. com. 42d Ward Rep. Orgn., 1984—. Econs. fellow Denison U., Granville, Ohio, 1978; Govs. fellow State of Ill., Springfield, 1978. Mem. ABA (exec. com., com. on legis. action young lawyers div. 1983-84), Ill. Bar Assn., Fla. Bar Assn., Collier County (Fla.) Bar Assn., Chgo. Bar Assn., Omicron Delta Upsilon, Pi Sigma Alpha, Alpha Tau Alpha. Republican. Presbyterian. Clubs: East Bank, Trial Lawyers, Executives, City (Chgo.). Contbr. articles on ins. law and litigation to profl. jours.; mem. writing staff Ill. Inst. Tech./Chgo.-Kent Law Rev., 1980-82. Home: 235 W Eugenie Apt G-7 Chicago IL 60614 Office: Phelan Pope & John 180 N Wacker Dr Suite 500 Chicago IL 60606

MARIETTA, KARL EDWARD, electrical engineer, administrator; b. Ligonier, Pa., Nov. 10, 1949; s. Melvin Grey and Ada (Betz) M.; m. Deborah Lynn Koerner, June 7, 1975; children—Andrew Rockwell, Geoff Eckman. B.S.E.E., Carnegie-Mellon U., 1971. Registered profl. engr., Minn., Pa. Elec. engr. Hershey Elec. Co., Pa., 1971-74, operating supt., 1974-77; elec. distbn. supt. Hibbing Pub. Utilities, Minn., 1977-80, asst. gen. mgr., 1980-81, gen. mgr., 1981-85; sr. cons. Henningson, Durham & Richardson, Inc., 1985—; dir. Western Fuels Assn., Washington, others. Mem. Nat. Soc. Profl. Engrs., Minn. Soc. Profl. Engrs., Am. Pub. Power Assn., Minn. Mcpl. Utilities Assn., IEEE. Republican. Presbyterian. Lodge: Rotary. Avocations: golf, hunting, fishing, sports. Home: 10101 Johnson Ave S Bloomington MN 55437 Office: HDR Inc 300 Parkdale Bldg 5401 Gamble Dr Minneapolis MN 55416

MARIKOS, MARK ALAN, geologist; b. St. Louis, Mar. 20, 1954; s. Theodore Virgil and Rose Mae (Pointer) M. B.S. in Geology and Geophysics, U. Mo., 1976; M.S., 1984. Lab technician Mo. Dept. Natural Resources, Rolla, Mo., 1976; grad. teaching asst. U. Mo., Rolla, 1976-77; research asst. U. Mo., Rolla, 1977-78; geologist Mo. Dept. Natural Resources, Rolla, 1978—. Contbr. articles to profl. jours. Bd. dirs. Christian Encounter Ranch, Bunker, Mo., 1982; bd. dirs. Birthright Rolla, 1984; deacon First Christian Ch., Rolla, 1984; tchr. Bible study for Chinese students, Rolla, 1984. Served to 2nd lt. USAF, 1976. Mem. Soc. Econ. Geologists (assoc.), Am. Assn. Petroleum Geologists, Geochem. Soc., Assn. Mo. Geologists. Avocations: Bible study; mineral collecting; photography; gardening; landscaping. Home: 11 Rolla Gardens Rolla MO 65401 Office: Dept Natural Resources PO Box 250 Rolla MO 65401

MARINE, JAMES, educational adminstrator; b. Knoxville, Tenn., Oct. 9, 1934; s. Harry Hobart and Delia Idelle (LaRue) M.; m. Marjorie May Butler, Aug. 29, 1959 (div. Dec. 1975); children—Cynthia Ann, Susan Beth; m. Judith Marian Gunning, May 27, 1977. B.S., U. Tenn., 1956; M.A., Columbia U., 1957, Ed.D., 1960. Asst. dean of students SUNY-Oneonta, 1960-62; dean of men Miami-Dade Community Coll., 1962-64; asst. dean student programs Ball State U., Muncie, Ind., 1964—. Contbr. chpts. to books, articles to profl. jours. Bd. dirs. Planned Parenthood East Central Ind., 1969-71; treas. Meals on Wheels, Inc., 1980-82; precinct committeeman Democratic Party, Muncie, 1973-75. Danforth fellow, 1956; Fellow Soc. Values in Higher Edn.; mem. Am. Coll. Personnel Assn. (chmn. commn. 1968-70, commn. publs. bd. 1970-74, chmn. conv. 1972, 74, mem. media bd. 1983—, editorial bd. 1978—). Served to capt. U.S. Army, 1957-58. Methodist. Home: 404 Skyway Dr Muncie IN 47303 Office: Ball State U Office of Student Programs Muncie IN 47306

MARINELLI, ARTHUR JOSEPH, law educator, lawyer; b. Youngstown, Ohio, July 17, 1942; m. Kathleen Cannon; children—Kristin Ann, Brent Arthur. B.A., Ohio U., 1964; J.D., Ohio State U., 1967. Asst. prof. Ohio U., Athens, 1967-71, assoc. prof., 1971-75, prof., 1976—. Vice pres. Athens Found., 1984—. Contbr. articles to profl. jours. City atty., solicitor Athens, 1977; city prosecutor and asst. solicitor, Athens, 1973; sec. bd. zone appeals, Athens, 1968-70. Mem. ABA, Ohio State Bar Assn., Tri-State Bus. Law Assocs. (pres. 1983-84), Athens County Bar Assn. (pres. 1984), Omicron Delta Kappa, Phi Alpha Theta, Phi Gamma Mu. Home: 24 Cable Ln Athens OH 45701

MARINO, JOHN ANTHONY, management educator, marketing management consultant; b. Youngstown, Ohio, Dec. 30, 1945; s. John Anthony and Betty Jane (Anzivino) M.; m. Lucille Ann D'Onofrio, Sept. 5, 1970; children—Jacqueline, Elizabeth. Student Ohio State U., 1963-64; B.S. in Bus. Adminstrn., Youngstown State U., 1969; M.B.A., Suffolk U., 1976. Div. mgr. Sears Roebuck & Co., Youngstown, 1966-73; tech. rep. E.I. DuPont, Wilmington, Del., 1973-76; tech. mktg. rep. Polaroid Corp., Cambridge, Mass., 1976-77; asst. prof. Jefferson Tech. Coll., Steubenville, Ohio, 1977-80, Kent State U., Warren, Ohio, 1980—; cons. U.S. SBA, Youngstown, 1980—; advisor Gordon James Career Ctr, 1980—, Eastgate Devel. and Transp. Agy., 1982—; cons. various cos. Contbr. articles to profl. jours. Served to maj. U.S. Army, 1969—. Democrat. Roman Catholic. Avocation: Classic automobiles. Home: 7609 Jaguar Pl Buardman OH 44512 Office: Kent State U-Trumbell 4314 Mahoning Ave NW Warren OH 44512

MARION, DANIEL J(OSEPH), hospital executive; b. N.Y.C., Aug. 19, 1947; s. Sidney and Mildred (Eichenbaum) M.; m. Nancy Vogel, Oct. 5, 1974; 1 dau., Stacey Frances. B.S., Cornell U., 1969, M.H.A., 1974; M.S., Syracuse U., 1972. Lic. nursing home adminstr., Ill. Adminstrv. resident Fairfield Hills Hosp., Newtown, Conn., 1973; adminstrv. asst. Oak Forest (Ill.) Hosp., 1974-75; adminstr. Louise Burg Hosp., Chgo., 1975-77; asst. adminstr. Community Hosp. Ottawa (Ill.), 1977-81; exec. dir. Gibson Community Hosp., Gibson City, Ill., 1981—; mem. Ill. Provider Trust Bd.; mem. Ill. Compensation Trust. Mem. Ford County (Ill.) Mental Health Bd.; mem. Champaign/Ford County Emergency Med. Services Bd. Mem. Am. Coll. Hosp. Adminstrs., Am. Hosp. Assn., Central Ill. Hosp. Personnel Mgmt. Assn., Gibson City C. of C. Club: Lions (Gibson City). Office: Gibson Community Hosp 1120 N Melvin St Gibson City IL 60936

MARITZ, WILLIAM E., communications company executive; b. St. Louis; m. Phyllis Mesker; 4 children. Grad., Princeton U., 1950. With Maritz Inc., St. Louis, now chief exec. officer. Bd. dirs. Community Sch., John Burroughs Sch., Princeton U., Sta. KETC, Mo. Bot. Garden, St. Luke's Hosp., Washington U., Brown Group, Am. Youth Found., Camping and Edn. Found., Cystic Fibrosis, others; founder, chmn. bd. Laclede's Landing Devel. Corp., St. Louis; chmn. bd. VP Fair Found. Recipient Levee Stone award Downtown St. Louis; Right Arm of St. Louis award, Regional Commerce and Growth Assn. Served with USN. Home: #10 Upper Ladue Rd Saint Louis MO 63124 Office: Maritz Inc 1375 N Highway Dr Fenton MO 63026

MARK, JOANN LOUISE, educational administrator, nun; b. Platte Center, Nebr., Nov. 21, 1940; d. Gilbert J. and Evelyn Adelaid (Schroeder) M. B.A., Kans. Newman Coll., 1962; M.S., Okla. State U., 1968, Ed.D., 1975. Joined Order of Adorers of the Blood of Christ, Roman Catholic Ch., 1959. Asst. prof. math. Kansas Newman Coll., Wichita, 1975-77, assoc. prof. math./computer sci., 1977-81, acad. dean, 1981-83, v.p., acad. dean, 1983—; grant reader, reviewer NSF. Pres. Cath. Bus. and Profl. Women, Wichita, 1979-80; mem. Social Justice Com., Wichita, 1981-83; mem. Danforth Nat. Adv. Council. NSF grantee, 1978-82; recipient Commisen Recognition award Kansas Newman Coll., 1980. Office: Kansas Newman Coll 3100 McCormick Wichita KS 67213

MARKEL, CHARLES ELWIN, farmer; b. Garden City, Kans., Sept. 30, 1947; s. Walter Ray and Martha Josephine (Henderson) M.; m. Kristin Hill Gurtner, Aug. 17, 1968; 1 child, Jonathan. A.A., Dodge City Community Coll., 1967; B.S. in Agr., Kans. State U., 1970. Insp., DeKalb Agrl. Research, Ulysses, Kans., 1969-71, Dumas, Tex., 1971-73; owner, operator farm Cimmarron, Kans., 1973—; bd. dirs. Farm Mgmt. Assn., Garden City, 1980-82. Mem. United Sch. Dist. 102 Sch. Bd., Cimarron, 1981-82, pres., 1983—. Methodist. Avocation: hunting. Home: Rural Route Box 9 Cimarron KS 67835

MARKER, EVELYN LUCINDA, hospital executive; b. Westerville, Ohio, Jan. 5, 1951; d. Forrest H. and Mary Louise (Mikesell) Schar; m. Michael R. Prenzlin, Mar. 24, 1972 (div. Feb. 1981); children—Matthew Eric, Mark Andrew; m. Wayne L. Marker, Jr., Sept. 14, 1985. B.A. in English, Heidelberg Coll, 1982. Dir. devel. and pub. relations Mercy Hosp., Tiffin, Ohio, 1980—. Author: (with others) Drug Abuse Prevention for Children workbook, 1980. Bd. dirs. Sandusky Valley Substance Abuse Prevention, Tiffin, 1980-82, Northwest Ohio Health Planning Agy., Toledo, Ohio, 1978-81, United Services for Alcoholism, Tiffin, 1983—; v.p. Community Council, Tiffin, 1984—. Mem. Nat. Assn. for Hosp. Devel. (cert.), Ohio Assn. for Hosp. Devel. (regional v.p. 1984—), Northwest Ohio Hosp. Council, Tiffin C. of C. Republican. Methodist. Avocation: coaching youth soccer. Office: Mercy Hosp 485 W Market St Tiffin OH

MARKERT, RONALD JAMES, medical educator; b. Renovo, Pa., Dec. 31, 1944; s. John William and Elsie Jane (Lucas) M.; m. Deborah Ann Dayspring, June 27, 1981; children—Brigetta, Ashley. B.S., Mansfield State Coll., 1966; M.A., Mich. State U., 1972, Ph.D., 1976. Asst. prof. med. edn. Mich. State U., East Lansing, 1976-78, Tex. Coll. Osteo. Medicine, Fort Worth, 1978-80; assoc. prof. Wright State U., Dayton, Ohio, 1980—; cons. in field; researcher in field. Author med. edn. studies. Mem. Assn. Am. Med. Colls., Am. Ednl. Research Assn., Nat. Council Measurement in Edn., Am. Statis. Assn., Midwestern Ednl. Research Assn. Avocation: Running. Home: 51 Temple Dr Xenia OH 45385 Office: Wright State U Dept PMCE PO Box 927 Dayton OH 45401

MARKGRAF, DAVID ANDREW, electronic manufacturing company executive; b. Sheboygan, Wis., Apr. 20, 1938; s. David and Vernetta Johanna (Lau) M.; m. Judith Ann Herber, Feb. 7, 1959; children—David, Michael, Maria, Deanna. Student, U. Wis., 1956-58; A.B., Milw. Tech. Coll., 1972. Regional sales mgr. Winthrop Lab. div. Sterling Drug, Cleve., 1960-72; dir. mktg. ITT Service Ltd., Cleve., 1972-76; sales mgr. Ametek Plymouth Products, Sheboygan, 1976-79, Consoer Equipment Co., New Berlin, Wis., 1979-81; mktg. mgr. Enercon Industries Corp., Menomonee Falls, Wis., 1981—. Contbr. articles to profl. jours. Mem. TAPPI (vice chmn. extrusion com. 1984), Converting Equipment Machinery Assn. (chmn. membership com. 1984). Republican. Roman Catholic. Clubs: Sheboygan Stamp (v.p. 1984), Scandinavian Stamp Collectors. Avocation: Stamp collecting. Office: Enercon Industries Corp W140 N9572 Fountain Blvd Menomonee Falls WI 53051

MARKHAM, CONSTANCE DENZINGER, financial executive; b. Evanston, Ill., June 7, 1955; d. Norman and Catherine (Bensko) Denzinger; m. James Edward Markham, Aug. 20, 1983. Student U. Denver, 1973; B.B.A., U. Tex., 1977; M.B.A., Keller Grad. Sch. Bus., 1985. Acct. Clegg/Austin, Austin, Tex., 1977-78, Centex Materials, Austin, 1978-80; cost acct., Tracor, Inc., Austin, 1980-82; budget and standards supr. Griffith Labs., Alsip, Ill., 1982—; pres. Denmark, Orland Park, Ill. 1984—. Mem. Nat. Assn. Accts. (assoc. dir. profl. devel. 1982, term commendation 1982-83). Avocations: skiing; bicycling; soccer; soccer referee. Office: Griffith Labs One Griffith Ctr Alsip IL 60658-3495

MARKHAM, JACK EDWARD, telephone company executive; b. Willard, Ohio, Jan. 7, 1934; s. Aubrey Lynn and Luella C. (Miller) M.; m. Sally Sue Hassinger, Dec. 19, 1954; children—Michelle Lynn, Jodie Sue. B.S., Miami U., Oxford, Ohio, 1956. Mgmt. trainee Reliance Elec. and Engring., Cleve., 1956; mgr. advt. and communications Ideal Electric Co., Mansfield, Ohio, 1957-65; sales mgr. Mansfield Printing, 1965-68; community relations mgr. United Telephone Co. Ohio, Mansfield, 1968-70, pub. relations dir., 1970-80; v.p. pub. relations United Telephone System, Inc., Kansas City, Mo., 1980—. Bd. dirs. Friends of Kansas City Zoo, Downtown YMCA. Mem. U.S. Ind. Telephone Assn. (chmn. pub. relations com.), Pub. Relations Soc. Am. Republican. Lutheran. Clubs: Optimists, Kiwanis.

MARKHAM, MARILYN JEAN, librarian; b. Lancaster, Calif., July 15, 1956; d. Keith George and Lela Ruth (Hartley) M. A.A., Antelope Valley Jr. Coll., 1976; B.A., Brigham Young U., 1979; M.L.S., Brigham Young U., 1982. Librarian, Findlay-Hancock County Pub. Library, Findlay, Ohio, 1982—. Mem. ALA, Bus. and Profl. Women's Club, Ohio Geneal. Soc., Alpha Gamma Sigma. Republican. Mormon. Home: 500 W Lincoln St Apt 1 Findlay OH 45840 Office: Findlay-Hancock County Pub Library 206 Broadway Findlay OH 45840

MARKHAM, MARION M., writer; b. Chgo., June 12, 1929; d. William Joseph and Marion (Dammann) Bork; b. Robert Bailey Markham, Dec. 30, 1955; children—Susan Markham Andersen, Jane Markham Madden. B.S. in Speech, Northwestern U., 1953. Continuity dir. Sta. WTVP, Decatur, Ill., 1953-54; TV bus. mgr. Earle Ludgin Advt. Co., Chgo., 1955-58; free-lance writer, Northbrook, Ill., 1967—. Novels include: Escape from Velos, 1981; The Halloween Candy Mystery, 1982; The Christmas Present Mystery, 1984; contbr. articles and short stories to mags. and jours. Bd. dirs. Northbrook Pub. Library, 1976—, pres. bd., 1981-83. Mem. Soc. Children's Book Writers, Sci. Fiction Writers Am., Authors Guild, Mystery Writers Am. (midwest regional v.p. 1977-78, dir. 1983—), Soc. Midland Authors (dir. Chgo. 1983—). Home and office: 2415 Newport Rd Northbrook IL 60062

MARKING, T(HEODORE) JOSEPH, JR., transportation and urban planner; b. Shelbyville, Ind., June 28, 1945; s. Theodore Joseph and Alvena Cecelia (Thieman) M.; B.A., So. Ill. U., 1967, M. City and Regional Planning, 1972; m. Kathy K. Hagerman, Nov. 25, 1969. Intelligence research specialist Def. Intelligence Agy., Washington, 1967-68; planner I, St. Louis City Plan Commn., 1970; transp. planner Alan M. Voorhees & Assocs., St. Louis, 1970-74, sr. transp. planner, 1974-78, assoc., 1978; sr. transp. planner Booker Assocs., Inc., St. Louis, 1978-80, chief traffic and transp. sect., 1980-85; mgr. transit planning East-West Gateway Coordinating Council, St. Louis, 1985—; planner-in-charge, Mo.; guest lectr. St. Louis Community Coll. Dist., Webster U. Mem. Am. Inst. Cert. Planners (charter), Am. Planning Assn. (charter; past pres. St. Louis sect.), Inst. Transp. Engrs., Traffic Engrs. Assn. Met. St. Louis (v.p.). Office: 100 S Tucker Blvd Saint Louis MO 63102

MARKLEY, JOHN LUTE, biochemistry educator; b. Denver, Mar. 6, 1941; s. Miles Russell and Winnifred Farrar (Lute) M.; m. Diane Sheehan, Aug. 9, 1975; children—Jessamyn Sheehan, Andrew Lute. B.A., Carleton Coll., 1963; student U. Munich, Fed. Republic Germany, 1960-61; Ph.D., Harvard U., 1969. Sr. research chemist Merck Inst., Rahway, N.J., 1966-69; NIH postdoctoral fellow U. Calif.-Berkeley, 1970-71; asst. prof. biochemistry Purdue U., West Lafayette, Ind., 1972-75, assoc. prof., 1975-81, prof., 1981-84, adj. prof., 1984—; dir. Biochem. Magnetic-Resonance Lab., 1975-84; prof. biochemistry U. Wis.-Madison, 1984—, dir. Nuclear Magnetic Resonance Facility, 1984; mem. adv. com. Resource for Biomed. Nuclear Magnetic Resonance Spectroscopy, Carnegie-Mellon U., 1975—, Metabolic Research Ctr., U. Pa. Sch. Medicine, 1984—. Mem. editorial bd. Bull. Magnetic Resonance, 1983—. Contbr. research articles to profl. jours. Recipient Research Career Devel. award USPHS, 1975-80; sr. Fogarty fellow USPHS, Montpellier, France, 1980-81; grantee USPHS, U.S. Dept. Agr., NSF. Mem. Soc. Magnetic Resonance in Medicine, Internat. Soc. Magnetic Resonance, Am. Chem. Soc., Am. Assn. Biol. Chemistry, Biophys. Soc., Phi Beta Kappa, Sigma Xi. Avocations: travel; gardening; photography. Home: 3452 Crestwood Dr Madison WI 53705 Office: Dept of Biochemistry U Wis 420 Henry Mall Madison WI 53706

MARKMAN, RONALD, artist, educator; b. Bronx, N.Y., May 29, 1931; s. Julius and Mildred (Berkowitz) M.; m. Barbara Miller, Sept. 12, 1959; 1 child, Ericka Elizabeth. B.F.A., Yale U., 1957, M.F.A., 1959. Instr. Art Inst. Chgo., 1960-64; prof. fine arts Ind. U., 1964—; color cons. Hallmark Card Co., 1959-60. One-man shows include Kanegis Gallery, 1959, Reed Coll., 1960, Terry Dintenfass Gallery, 1966, 68, 70, 76, 79, 82, '84, The Gallery, Bloomington, Ind., 1972, 79, Indpls. Mus., 1974, Tyler Sch. Art, Phila., 1976, Franklin Coll., 1980, Dart Gallery, Chgo., 1981, Patrick King Gallery, Indpls., 1983; exhibited in group shows at Kanegis Gallery, Boston, 1958, 60, 61, Boston Arts Festival, 1959, 60, Mus. Modern Art, 1959, 66, Whitney Mus., N.Y.C., 1960, Art Inst. Chgo., 1964, Gallery 99, Miami, Fla., 1966, Ball State Coll., Butler Inst., 1967, Indpls. Mus., 1968, 69, 72, 74, Phoenix Gallery, N.Y.C., 1970, Harvard U., 1974, Skidmore Coll., 1975, Am. Acad. Arts and Letters, 1977, Tuthill-Gimprich Gallery, N.Y.C., 1980, others; represented in permanent collections Met. Mus. Art, Mus. Modern Art, Art Inst. Chgo., Library of Congress, Cin. Art Mus., Bklyn. Mus., Ark. Art Ctr., Worcester Mus. Fine Arts, Bklyn. Man., Ind. U. Mus. Art, others. Served with U.S. Army, 1952-54. Fulbright grantee, Italy, 1962. Home: 719 S Jordan St Bloomington IN 47401 Office: Dept Fine Arts Ind U Bloomington IN 47401

MARKOVITZ, ALVIN, molecular biologist, geneticist, educator; b. Chgo., May 30, 1929; s. Raymond and Fannie (Rudich) M.; m. Harriet June Porter, Aug. 24, 1952; children—Paula, Ellen, Nancy. B.S., U. Ill., 1950, M.S., 1952; Ph.D., U. Wash., 1955. Instr., U. Chgo., 1957-59; asst. prof., 1959-64, assoc. prof. microbiology, 1964-74, prof. microbiology, 1974-84, prof. biochemistry and molecular biology, 1984—. Contbr. articles to sci. publs. Mem. Am. Soc. for Microbiology, Am. Soc. Biol. Chemists, AAAS. Jewish. Avocations: piano, sports.

MARKS, DAVID ALAN, architect; b. Chgo., Dec. 19, 1934; s. Maurice Lawrence and Leonore Bernita (Gale) M.; m. Lois Jean Stern, Mar. 5, 1961; children—Susan Meridith, Ellen Leslie, Jami Beth. B.Arch., U. Ill., 1958. Registered architect, Ill. Draftsman, Mark D. Kalisher, Chgo., 1958-59, Joel Hillman, Chgo., 1959; architect Loebl Schlossman & Bennett, Chgo., 1966, assoc. ptnr. Loebl Schlossman Bennett & Dart, 1966-74, prin. Loebl Schlossman & Hackl, 1974—; guest critic U. Ill. Sch. Architecture, 1974, 76, U. Notre Dame, 1981. Mem. Deerfield Ill. Plan Commn., 1981—, chmn., 1984—. Served with U.S. Army, 1961. Mem. AIA. Project architect for numerous public bldgs. and instns. Home: 723 Byron Ct Deerfield IL 60015 Office: 845 N Michigan Ave Suite 804 Ci Chicago IL 60611

MARKS, ELAINE, language educator, university administrator; b. N.Y.C., Nov. 13, 1930; d. Harry and Ruth (Elin) Marks. B.A., Bryn Mawr Coll., 1952; M.A., U. Pa., 1953; Ph.D. (Fulbright award France 1956), NYU, 1958. Asst. prof. French, NYU, N.Y.C., 1958-60; assoc. prof. U. Wis., Milw., 1963-65, prof., Madison, 1967-68, prof. French, Italian and women's studies, 1980—; dir. Women's Studies Research Ctr., 1977-85; prof. French U. Mass., Amherst, 1965-66. Mem. MLA, Midwest Modern Lang. Assn., Am. Assn. Tchrs. French, Nat. Women's Studies Assn. Author: Colette, 1960, 2d edit., 1981; Simone de Beauvoir: Encounters with Death, 1973. Co-editor Homosexualities and French Literature, 1979; New French Feminisms, 1980, 81. Home: 2040 Field St Madison WI 53713

MARKS, PETER AMASA, technical company administrator; b. Passaic, N.J., Dec. 5, 1948; s. Amasa A. and Eunice L. (Irwin) M.; B.S. in Design Engring., U. Cin., 1972, M.A. in Media Communications, 1973, postgrad. in human factors engring. Research asst. dept. mech. engring. U. Cin., 1972; sr. engr. Ford Motor Co., Sharonville, Ohio, 1972-75; prin. Design Insight Cin., 1976—; mng. dir. SDRC TEC Services, Milford, Ohio, 1979-81, dir. product planning and devel., SDRC, Inc., Milford, 1981—; lectr., cons. on product design tech. implementation, U.S., Japan, Europe, also for Am. Mgmt. Assns. Grad. fellow; Gen. Motors grantee in design, 1970; winner nat., internat. competitions for audiovisual programs. Mem. ASME, Soc. Mfg. Engrs., Soc. for Tech. Communication, AAAS, Mensa. Author books, articles and films in field. Home: 1 Skynotch Ln PO Box 80 Milford OH 45150 Office: 2000 Eastman Dr Milford OH 45150

MARKS, RENEE LEE, educator; b. Chgo., Nov. 20, 1936; d. Sol and Celia (Freund) Kaplan; B.S.J., Northwestern U., 1958, postgrad. (Chgo. Bd. Edn. scholar), summer 1978; B.J.S., Spertus Coll., 1972; M.A., Mundelein Coll., 1975; M.Ed. with distinction, De Paul U., 1981; postgrad. in ednl. adminstrn. Northeastern Ill. U., 1980-81; cert. in adminstrn. and supervision Nat. Coll. Edn., Evanston, Ill., 1982, postgrad., 1985—; postgrad. in computer sci. U. Ill.-Chgo., 1982-85; doctoral student in instrnl. leadership Nat. Coll. of Edn., 1984—; m. Donald Norman Marks, June 22, 1958; children—Robin Debra Marks Dombeck, Steven Michael, Jody Ilene. Tchr. Chgo. Bd. Edn., 1976—; lectr. on Holocaust. Mem. Nat. Council for Social Studies, Chgo. Council for Social Studies, Assn. for Supervision and Curriculum Devel., Am. Ednl. Research Assn., Nat. Soc. for Study of Edn., Phi Delta Kappa. Jewish. Author, Holocaust curriculum for Chgo. Bd. Edn., 1980. Home and Office: Kelvyn Park High Sch 4343 W Wrightwood Chicago IL 60639

MARKS, RONNIE FAIN, manufacturers representative, consultant; b. Detroit, May 2, 1953; s. Roger Campbell and Helen Lucille (Saunders) M.; m. Clara Helen Salisbury, June 14, 1975; children—Jennifer Marie, Ronald Austin. Student Henry Ford Coll., Dearborn, Mich., 1972-75; B.B.A., U. Detroit, 1978, M.B.A., 1981. Indsl. engr. Demco, Detroit, 1973-75, sales engr., 1975-77, asst. to v.p., 1977, mfg. mgr., 1978; account mgr. GRM Industries, Grand Rapids, Mich., 1978-85; mfrs. rep. T.S. Maentz, Inc., Troy, Mich., 1983—; pres. Marks Mgmt. Services, Inc., Bloomfield Hills, Mich., 1985—. Fund raiser Republican Party, Canton, Mich., 1982. Named hon. Ky. col. Fellow Am. Mktg. Assn.; mem. Assn. M.B.A. Grads., Nat. Assn. Bus. Economists, Indsl. Mktg. Group, Detroit Assn. Bus. Economists, Delta Sigma Pi (treas. 1976-78), Alpha Sigma Lambda. Republican. Clubs: Fairlane (Dearborn); Pine Lake Country (Orchard Lake, Mich.). Home: 5390 Vincennes Dr Bloomfield Hills MI 48013 Office: Thomas S Maentz Inc 2075 W Big Beaver St Suite 300 Troy MI 48084

MARKSTROM, PAUL RAGNVALD, clergyman; b. Skanninge, Sweden, May 30, 1921; came to U.S., 1922, naturalized, 1970; s. Gustaf Eric and Elsa Marie (Markstrom) Karlson; student Zion Bible Inst., 1940-41, Central Bible Coll. and Sem., Springfield, Mo., 1941-44, So. Methodist U., 1948, Southwestern State Coll., 1961-62, Am. Clin. Pastoral Assn., 1962-63; m. Berniece Elva Hoehn, June 1, 1944; children—Paul Eugene, Sondra Kay Markstrom Todd. Ordained to ministry Assemblies of God Ch., 1947; pastor Assembly of God Ch., Ely, Nev., 1944-46, Newburgh, N.Y., 1946-49, Bucklin, Kans., 1950-57, Coldwater, Kans., 1958-63; instr. Central Bible Coll. and Sem., 1966-72; dir. Instl. Chaplaincies of Assemblies of God, Springfield, Mo., 1963—, dir. spl. ministries, 1974-80; dir. Am. Indian Bible Coll., Phoenix, 1974-80. Mem. Nat. Assn. Evangelicals (chmn. spl. ministries com. 1967-80), Am. Protestant Correctional Chaplains Assn. (dir. 1963, pres. central region 1974, sec. 1983—), Ministerial Assn. (pres. 1953-60). Republican. Club: Lions. Author: Bible Basics, 1964; The Book of Acts, 1965; The Five Books of Moses, 1965; The Four Gospels, 1966; Outstanding Bible Profiles, 1967; Summary of The Old Testament, 1966. Volunteers in Corrections, 1977; Chaplains Manual, 1973. Contbr. articles to profl. jours. Home: 1520 Devon St Springfield MO 65804 Office: 1445 Boonville St Springfield MO 65802

MARKUS, CAROLE JEAN, glass etching company executive; b. Austin, Minn., June 5, 1946; d. Lawrence Matt and Genevieve Mary (Majerus) Weber; m. Gregory Robert Markus, May 4, 1980. Student Coll. St. Teresa, 1964-67; B.S., Mankato State U., 1969. Tchr. Benilde High Sch., St. Louis Park, Minn., 1970-74; owner, pres. CW Design, Inc., Mpls., 1974—; tchr. Henn County Vo-Tec, 1975-80; ptnr. Schrunk Studio, Inc., 1985—. Mem. Am. Soc. Interior Designers Industry Found. Roman Catholic. Avocations: music; tennis; travel.

Home: 468 Marshall Ave Saint Paul MN 55102 Office: CW Design Inc 1618 Cental Ave NE Minneapolis MN 55413

MARKWOOD, STEPHEN ERNEST, educator, college dean; b. Glasgow, Ky., Nov. 26, 1942; s. Chester Ray and Mary (Tandy) M.; m. Susan Hendee, Dec. 26, 1965; children—Christopher M., Kathryn M. B.S. in Edn., Bowling Green U., 1964, M.A., 1968, D.Ed., Pa. State U., 1983. Asst. dean student life Waynesburg Coll., Pa., 1968-70; assoc. dean students Dickinson Coll., Carlisle, Pa., 1970-77; dean student devel. Rio Grande Coll., Ohio, 1977-80; dean students Marietta Coll., Ohio, 1980—. Contbr. articles to prof. jours. Served to capt. U.S. Army, 1964-66. Mem. Nat. Assn. Student Personnel Adminstrs., Am. Coll. Personnel Assn. (commn. 1983-84), Ohio Coll. Personnel Assn. (pres. 1983-84, outstanding leadership 1984), Ohio Assn. Student Personnel Adminstrs. Lodges: Kiwanis. Avocation: golf, running. Office: Marietta Coll 5th St Marietta OH 45750

MARNELL, RICHARD THOMAS, physician, consultant; b. Hoboken, N.J., May 25, 1927; s. Francis Xavier and Mabel (Fitzpatrick) M.; m. Maria Adele Strong, Aug. 28, 1954; children—Francis, Mary, Stephen, Chris, David, Sean, Nichole. B.S., St. Peter's Coll., Jersey City, 1946-50; M.D., SUNY-Bklyn., 1955. Diplomate Am. Bd. Internal Medicine. Intern, Hosp. of St. Raphael, New Haven, 1955-56, resident, 1956-59; NIH research fellow U. Cin., 1959-62; assoc. prof. medicine, 1962-67; practice specializing in endocrinology and internal medicine, Cin., 1967—; cons. in endocrinology Childrens, Christ, Bethesda hosps.; assoc. attending Jewish Hosp.; sr. attending Good Samaritan Hosp.; med. cons. Union Central Life Ins. Co., Cin., 1982—. Served with USN, 1945-47. Avocations: tennis, sailing, backpacking, painting. Home: 359 Warren Cincinnati OH 45220 Office: 3333 Vine St Cincinnati OH 45220

MAROHL, DAVID WILLIAM, lawyer; b. Beaver Dam, Wis., Jan. 25, 1955; s. John Ralph and Mary Elizabeth (Knop) M. B.A., U. Wis.-Madison, 1976; J.D., DePaul U., 1980. Bar: Ill. 1980, U.S. Dist. Ct. (no. dist.) Ill. 1980, Wis. 1984. Editor Commerce Clearing House, Chgo., 1980; assoc. counsel Ill. State Bar Assn., Springfield, 1980; staff atty. Nat. Bus. Inst. Mem. Wis. Bar Assn., Chgo. Bar Assn., Ill. State Bar Assn., ABA, Am. Judicature Assn. Republican. Lutheran. Home: 708 S Farwell St Eau Claire WI 54701

MAROHL, RUDOLPH OTTO, manufacturing executive, mechanical engineer; b. Hankinson, N.D., May 22, 1938; s. Emil W. and Lily (Henke) M.; m. Mary Beth Wipperman, Aug. 26, 1961; children—Beth Marie, Michael Anthony. B.S.M.E., U. N.D., 1962; A.S., N.D. State Sch. Sci., 1960. Mem. tech. staff Westinghouse Corp., Idaho Falls, 1962-69; v.p. Nuclear Pacific Inc., Seattle, 1970-75; pres. Central Research div. Sargent Industries, Red Wing, Minn., 1976—. Author/editor: Remote Manipulation, 1984. Bd. dirs. St. Paul's Found., Red Wing, 1984—, Red Wing Hockey Assn., 1979-81; pres. Red Wing Mfg. Assn., 1981, advisor, 1982-83. Served with U.S. Army, 1956-58; Korea. Recipient Meritorious Service award Westinghouse Corp., 1966, ASME, 1970. Mem. ASME (vice-chmn. 1969), Am. Nuclear Soc., Soc. Mfg. Engrs., Robotics Internat. (sr.), Pres. Assn. Lutheran. Lodge: Elks (Red Wing). Avocations: golf; carpentry.

MAROTTA, RICHARD NATHAN, engineer; b. Rockford, Ill., Sept. 1, 1941; s. Sam and Angelina (Cremi) M.; m. Linda Sue Welsby, July 24, 1968; children—Jeffery, Cynthia. Student Rockford Coll., 1962, Milw. Sch. Engring., 1964, R.C.A., 1965-68. Control engr. Ingersoll, Rockford, 1964-72; project engr. Beloit Corp., Wis., 1972-74; chief control engr. Feldmanan Inc., Rockford, 1974—; pres., owner Control Ltd., Rockford, 1974—. Patentee temperature controller, 1973, constant-speed drive, 1974. Mem. Fluid Power Soc. (pres. 1977-78). Republican, Lutheran. Avocation: electronics. Home: 1123 Prestwick Pkwy Rockford IL 61107 Office: 4902 Hydraulic Dr

MAROUS, JAMES EDWARD, JR., banker; b. Cleve., Mar. 29, 1954; s. James Edward and Jean (Michell) M.; m. Linda Booth, July 26, 1980. B.S. in Fin. and Acctg., Miami U., Oxford, Ohio, 1976; M.B.A. in Fin., Cleve. State U., 1978; grad. Sch. Bank Mktg., Boulder, Colo., 1983. Mgmt. trainee Nat. City Bank, Cleve., 1976-79, bus. devel. officer, 1979-81; mktg. dir. Women's Fed. Savs. Bank, Cleve., 1981-84; sr. v.p. Mid-Am. Fed. Savs. and Loan, Columbus, Ohio, 1984—; dir. Fin. Instn. Marketers Ohio, Cleve., 1981-84, pres., 1984-85, 85-86. Vice pres. Nat. Jr. Tennis League, Cleve., 1980-82; chmn. Mayoral Campaign, Shaker Heights, Ohio, 1983. Mem. Bank Mktg. Assn., Cleve. Jaycees, Planning Execs. Inst. Avocations: Coin collecting, cycling. Home: 1021 Cross Country Worthington OH 43085 Office: Mid-Am Fed Savs and Loan 175 S 3d St Columbus OH 43215

MAROUS, RICHARD SAYLE, tennis league administrator; b. Shaker Heights, Ohio, Mar. 13, 1922; s. James Edward and Mona (Sayle) M.; m. Janet Marie Cox, Nov. 25, 1948; children—Richard, James, Don. A.B. in Econs. and Phys. Edn., Baldwin-Wallace Coll., 1949; postgrad. Bowling Green State U., 1949-50. Tchr. pub. schs., Shaker Heights, 1950-57; dir. parks and adult edn. City of Shaker Heights, 1957-80; dir. parks, recreation and properties City of Cleve., 1980-83; exec. dir. Greater Cleve. chpt. Nat. Jr. Tennis League, 1983—; cons. in field. Mem. allocation com. United Appeal; mem. Greater Cleve. council Boy Scouts Am.; mem. fine arts com. Cleve. Mus. Art; bd. dirs. YMCA. Served with USN, 1943-46. Recipient Order of Merit, Greater Cleve. council Boy Scouts Am., 1970, Pres. Citation, 1975. Mem. Nat. Recreation and Park Assn. (outstanding contbn. award 1976), Ohio Parks and Recreation Assn. (pres. 1973-74). Methodist. Club: Shaker Heights Country. Lodge: Rotary (pres. 1967-68). Contbr. articles to profl. jours. and mags. Home and office: 3295 Kenmore Rd Shaker Heights OH 44122

MAROVITZ, SANFORD E., English language and literature educator; b. Chgo., May 10, 1933; s. Harold and Gertrude (Luster) M.; m. Eleonora Dimitsa, Sept. 1, 1964. B.A. with honors, Lake Forest Coll., 1960; M.A., Duke U., 1961, Ph.D., 1968. Instr. English, Temple U., 1963-65; Fulbright instr. U. Athens (Greece), 1965-67; asst. prof. English, Kent State U. (Ohio), 1967-70, assoc. prof., 1970-75, prof., 1975—; vis. prof. English, Shimane U., Matsue, Japan, 1976-77. Served with USAF, 1953-57. Woodrow Wilson fellow, 1960-61. Mem. MLA, N.E. MLA, Am. Studies Assn., Melville Soc., Hawthorne Soc., Western Lit. Assn., Henry James Soc., Coll. English Assn., Phi Beta Kappa. Democrat. Jewish. Co-editor: Artful Thunder: Versions of Romanticism in American Literature in Honor of Howard P. Vincent, 1975; co-author: Bibliographical Guide to the Study of the Literature of the U.S.A., 1984; contbr. articles, chpts. to profl. jours., collections. Home: 1155 Norwood St Kent OH 44240 Office: Dept English Kent State U Kent OH 44242

MAROVITZ, WILLIAM A., state senator, lawyer; b. Chgo., Sept. 29, 1944; s. Sydney Robert and Jane (Chulock) M.; B.A., U. Ill., 1966; J.D., DePaul U., 1969. Admitted to Ill. bar, 1970; tchr. Chgo. Bd. Edn., 1969-70; partner firm Marovitz, Powell, Pizer & Edelstein, Chgo., 1970-82; asst. corp. counsel City of Chgo., 1973-74; mem. Ill. State Ho. of Reps., 1975-80; mem. Ill. State Senate, 1981—. Mem. Young Men's Jewish Council; chmn. Spanish Speaking Peoples' Study Commn. in Ill., 1976—, High-Rise Fire Commn. Mem. Ill. Bar Assn., Chgo. Bar Assn., Decalogue Soc. Lawyers. Recipient Chgo. Met. Outstanding Citizen award, 1976; named Best Freshman Legislator, Ill. Young Democrats, 1975; Best Freshman Senator, 1981, Chgo. Jaycees, 1976 (Young Citizens award). Jewish. Office: Marovitz Powell Pizer & Edelstein 134 N LaSalle St Chicago IL 60602

MARQUART, STEVEN LEONARD, lawyer; b. Georgetown, Minn., Feb. 2, 1954; s. Leonard Matthew and Gladys Viola (Mahre) M.; m. Cynthia Lou Smerud, June 21, 1975; children—Stephanie Lynn, Angela Marie. B.A. in Polit. Sci., Moorhead State U., 1976; J.D. with distinction, U. N.D., 1979. Bar: Minn. 1979, N.D. 1979, U.S. Dist. Ct. N.D. 1979, U.S. Dist. Ct. Minn. 1981, U.S. Ct. Appeals (8th cir.) 1981. Law Clk. U.S. Dist. Ct. N.D., Fargo, 1979-81; assoc. Cahill, Jeffries & Maring, Moorhead, Minn., 1981-85, ptnr., dir., 1985. Mem. ABA, Minn. Bar Assn., N.D. Bar Assn., Order of Coif. Roman Catholic. Home: 1913 S 23d St Fargo ND 58103 Office: Cahill Jeffries & Maring PA 403 Center Ave Moorhead MN 56560

MARQUETTE, ANDREW DELBERT, market research executive; b. Oak Park, Ill., Sept. 9, 1946; s. Delbert Webster and Mary Edith (Weith) M.; m. Audrey Jean Walton; children—Emily, Jill. B.S. in Bus. Adminstrn., DePaul U., 1974, M.B.A., 1975. Mktg. cons. Ernst & Whinney, Chgo., 1975-78; market research mgr. Wickes Furniture, Wheeling, Ill., 1978-81; dir. market research DeVry Inc. div. Bell & Howell, Evanston, Ill., 1981—. Bd. dirs. Edison Park Youth Club, Chgo., 1979—. Served with U.S. Army, 1966-68, Viet Nam. DePaul U. grad. fellow, 1975. Mem. Am. Mktg. Assn. (v.p. edn. div. Chgo. chpt. 1980-82), World Future Soc. Roman Catholic. Avocation: coaching organized youth sports. Home: 7762 W North Shore Ave Chicago IL 60631 Office: DeVry Inc a Bell & Howell Co 2201 W Howard St Evanston IL

MARQUETTE, JESSE FRANK, political science educator, researcher; b. Paterson, N.J., Sept. 4, 1945; s. Jesse Aloysius and Ruth Rosalie (Gesch) M.; m. Roberta Penny Katz, Apr. 23, 1967; 1 child, Michael Carlos. B.A., U. Fla., 1967, M.A., 1968, Ph.D., 1971. Teaching fellow U. Fla., Gainesville, 1968-69; asst. prof. polit. sci., U. Akron, Ohio, 1971-75, assoc. prof., 1975-82, prof., head dept., 1982—; cons. in field of survey research. Contbr. articles to profl. jours. NDEA fellow, 1969-71. Mem. Am. Polit. Sci. Assn., Am. Sociol. Assn., So. Polit. Sci. Assn., Midwest Polit. Sci. Assn., Southwestern Social Sci. Assn., Am. Statis. Assn. Avocations: flying, stained glass. Office: Univ Akron Dept Polit Sci Akron OH 44325

MARQUIS, GERALDINE MAE HILDRETH (MRS. FORREST W. MARQUIS), educator; b. Ankeny, Iowa, Aug. 8; d. Vernon Otto and Alma Leona (Woods) Hildreth; student U. No. Iowa; M.A., Drake U., 1972; m. Forrest William Marquis; 1 son, Robert William. Elementary tchr., Ankeny and Ft. Dodge, Iowa, 1944-49, 56—; organizer Ft. Dodge Coop. Nursery Sch. Mem. NEA, Iowa, Ft. Dodge edn. assns., Assn. Childhood Edn. Internat. (Ia. pres. 1974-77), Nat. Assn. Edn. Young Children, Civic Music Assn., TTT Nat. Soc. (pres. chpt.), Delta Kappa Gamma (local pres. 1974-77), Phi Sigma Alpha. Republican. Methodist. Home: 2602 Williams Dr Fort Dodge IA 50501 Office: 615 N 16th St Fort Dodge IA 50501

MARQUIS, WILLIAM OSCAR, lawyer; b. Fort Wayne, Ind., Feb. 26, 1944; s. William Oscar Marquis and Lenor Mae (Gaffney) Marquis Jensen; m. Mary Frances Funderburk, May 11, 1976; children—Lenor, Kathryn, Timothy Patrick, Daniel. B.S., U. Wis.-Madison, 1973; J.D., South Tex. Coll. Law, 1977. Bar: Wis. 1979, U.S. Dist. Ct. (we. dist.) Wis. 1979, U.S. Dist. Ct. (ea. dist.) Wis. 1982, U.S. Tax Ct. 1983. With Wis. Dept. Vet. Affairs, Madison, 1977-79; corp. counsel Barron County, Wis., 1979-80; assoc. Riley, Bruns & Riley, Madison, 1980-81; assoc. Jastroch & LaBarge, S.C., Waukesha, Wis., 1981-84; ptnr. Groh, Hackbart, Lichter & Marquis, 1984—. Served to sgt. USAF, 1966-70. Mem. Assn. Trial Lawyers Am., Wis. Trial Lawyers Assn., Waukesha Bar, Milw. Bar, ABA, Wis. Bar. Office: 6525 W Bluemound Milwaukee WI 53213

MARR, RICHARD GREEN, dentist; b. Detroit, Oct. 31, 1944; s. Carl Bonning and Cora Marr. Student, Coll. of Wooster, 1963; B.S., Mich. State U., 1967; D.D.S., U. Detroit, 1973; postgrad. U. Mich., 1975—. Biochemist, Pontiac Gen. Hosp., Mich., 1967-69; systems analyst Med. Data Systems, Detroit, 1969-72; biochemist Childrens Hosp., Detroit, 1972-73; gen. practice dentistry, Traverse City, Mich., 1973—; pres. Synergistic Systems, Traverse City, 1979—; cons. Am. Assn. Dental Cons., 1982—; lectr. Northwestern Mich. Coll., Traverse City, 1975—. Alpine patroler Nat. Ski Patrol, Sugar Loaf, 1982—. Fellow Acad. Gen. Dentistry; mem. ADA, Mich. Dental Assn., Resort Dental Assn., Chgo. Dental Assn. Republican. Clubs: Grand Traverse Athletic, Long Lake Yacht (pres. 1985). Lodge: Elks. Avocations: sailing, skiing, astronomy, hunting, falconry. Home: 1651 S Long Lake Traverse City MI 49684 Office: Synergistic Systems Corp PO Box 913 Traverse City MI 49685

MARRERO, MICHAEL ALVIN, lawyer; b. South Bend, Ind., July 8, 1953; s. Alvin Clarence and Jean Helen (Udelhofen) M.; m. Deborah DeLong, Jan., 12, 1981; children—Amelie DeLong, Samuel Prentice. A.B., Xavier U., 1974; J.D., U. Mich., 1977. Bar: Ohio 1977. Law clk. U.S. Dist. Ct., Cin., 1977-79; assoc. Paxton & Seasongood Co. L.P.A., Cin., 1979-82; sr. staff atty. Drackett Co., Cin., 1982—. Bd. dirs., legal counsel Downtown Montessori, Inc., Cin., 1984—; mem. corp. sponsorship com. Heart mini-marathon Ohio Southwest chpt. Am. Heart Assn., 1983—. Mem. ABA, Cin. Bar Assn., Ohio State Bar Assn., Chemical Specialties Mfrs. Assn. (com. hazardous cargo transp. 1983—), Soc. Am. Baseball Research. Democrat. Roman Catholic. Club: Clifton Track (pres. 1981—). Home: 197 Green Hills Rd Cincinnati OH 45208 Office: 201 E 4th St Cincinnati OH 45202

MARRINER, NEVILLE, orchestral director; b. Lincoln, Eng., Apr. 15, 1924; s. Herbert Henry and Ethel May (Roberts) M.; ed. Royal Coll. Music, Paris Conservatory; m. Diana Margaret Carbutt, May 10, 1949 (div. 1957); m. 2d, Elizabeth Sims, Dec. 20, 1957; children—Susan Frances, Andrew Stephen. Prof., Eton Coll., 1947, Royal Coll. Music, 1952; violinist Martin String Quartet, 1946-53, Virtuoso String Trio, 1950, Jacobean Ensemble, 1952, London, Philharmonia, 1952-56, London Symphony Orch., from 1956; condr. Los Angeles Chamber Orch., 1969-77; music dir., condr. Minn. Orch., 1979—; music dir. Suddeutches Rundfunk Orch., 1983—; dir. South Bank Festival of Music, 1975-78, Meadowbrook Festival, Detroit, 1979-83. Bd. dirs., founder Acad. of St. Martin-in-the Fields, 1959—. Decorated comdr. Brit. Empire; recipient Grand prix du Disque, Edison award, Mozart Gemeinde prize, Tagore prize, others. Office: Minn Orch 1111 Nicollet Mall Minneapolis MN 55403

MARRS, STEVE BARTON, music educator; b. South Whitley, Ind., Dec. 16, 1940; s. Barton Edwin and Hannah Belle (Thomson) M.; m. Barbara June Lykins, Aug. 4, 1962 (div. 1981); children—Douglas Barton, Kelly Suzanne, Jill Dianne; m. Carolyn Galbreath Graham, Apr. 15, 1981; 1 child, Kenneth Edward; stepchildren—Eric Sean, Todd Heston, Misty Allison. B.A., Morehead State U., 1962; Mus.M., Ball State U., 1966; M.S. in Music Edn., Butler U., 1972-74. Band and choir dir. Morgan County Schs., West Liberty, Ky., 1962-63; tchr. music Decatur County Schs., Greensburg, Ind., 1963-67; choir dir. Presbyn. Ch., Greensburg, 1963-74; jr. and sr. high sch. band dir. Greensburg Schs., 1967-74; instr. music Olney Central Coll., Ill., 1974—. Mem. Nat. Assembly Local Arts Agys., Ill. Arts Alliance, Phi Mu Alpha Sinfonia. Democrat. Presbyterian. Lodges: Elks, Optimist, Gideons. Avocation: woodworking. Home: 112 Holly Rd Olney IL 62450 Office: Olney Central Coll 305 N West St Olney IL 62450

MARS, HAROLD, neurologist; m. Montreal, Que., Can., Mar. 21, 1935; came to U.S., 1970; s. Bernard and Florence (Silver) M.; m. Suzanne Pevaroff, Sept. 2, 1965; children—Lee Michael, Deborah Ann. B.Sc. with honors in Physics and Physiology, McGill U., Montreal, 1956, M.D., C.M., 1960. Intern, Jewish Gen. Hosp., Montreal, 1960-61; resident Montreal Gen. Hosp., Cleve. clinic, 1961-67; asst. clin. prof. neurology Case Western Res. U., Cleve., 1974—; staff neurologist Univ. Hosp., Cleve., 1970—, Mt. Sinai Hosp., Cleve., 1970—, Suburban Community Hosp., Cleve., 1978—, Hillcrest Hosp., 1980—; v.p. United Parkinson's Found., Chgo., 1978—. Contbr. articles to profl. jours., chpts. to books. Fellow Am. Acad. Neurology; mem. Royal Coll. Physicians and Surgeons Can., Can. Neurol. Soc., Cleve. Acad. Medicine, Ohio State Med. Assn. Avocations: photography, music. Office: 3690 Park East Beachwood OH 44122

MARSCHALL, CHARLES WALTER, metallurgist, researcher; b. Rosendale, Wis., Sept. 25, 1930; s. Walter Conrad and Esther Ruth (Haberkorn) M.; m. Bette Ann Williams, June 22, 1952; children—Mark, Gwynette, Elizabeth, David, Catherine. B.S. in Metall. Engring., U. Wis., 1953, M.S., 1957; Ph.D. in Metallurgy, Case Inst. Tech., 1960. Registered profl. engr., Wis. Instr. metallurgy U. Wis., Madison, 1955-57; grad. asst. Case Inst. Tech., Cleve., 1957-59; sr. metallurgist Battelle Columbus Labs., Columbus, Ohio, 1959-66; asst. prof. U. Wis.-Milw., 1966-67; assoc. mgr. Battelle Columbus Labs., 1967-76, prin. research scientist, 1976-85, sr. research scientist, 1985—; cons. Woodward Gov. Co., Rockford, Ill., 1966-67. Contbr. articles to profl. jours. Chmn. Citizens Adv. Council to Sch. Bd., Westerville, Ohio, 1975-76; com. mem. Westerville Methodist Ch. of the Messiah, 1978-82. Served to 1st lt. USAF, 1953-55. Research fellow Battelle Meml. Inst., Seattle, 1973. Mem. ASTM, Am. Soc. for Metals, Am. Inst. of Mining, Metall. and Petroleum Engrs. Democrat. Avocations: tennis; handball; basketball; golf; oil painting. Home: 3401 Paris Blvd Westerville OH 43081 Office: Battelle Columbus Labs 505 King Ave Columbus OH 43201

MARSCHALL, MARLENE ELIZABETH, hospital administrator, nurse; b. St. Paul, Nov. 20, 1936; d. Bruno and Adelheid A. Mirsch; m. George Marschall, June 8, 1973. Diploma, Ancker Hosp. Sch. Nursing, 1958; B.S. cum laude in Biol. Scis./Nursing, Viterbo Coll., 1965; M.A. in Nursing Service Adminstrn., U. Iowa, 1972. With Ancker Hosp., St. Paul, 1958-60, Ancker Hosp. Sch. Nursing, St. Paul, 1960-61, St. Frances Sch. Nursing, LaCrosse, Wis., 1964-68; dir. nursing edn. St. Paul-Ramsey Med. Ctr., 1969-71, asst. dir. nursing, 1971, assoc. dir. nursing services, 1972-76, dir. nursing services, 1976-77, assoc. dir., 1977-80, sr. assoc. dir., 1980—; preceptor, lectr., clin. faculty mem. U. Minn. Advisor, Congl. Awards Program. Recipient Air Nat. Guard recognition for Bus. and Industry Leaders in U.S., 1977. Mem. Am. Coll. Hosp. Adminstrs., Twin City Area Soc. Nursing Service Adminstrs., Nat. League for Nursing, Sigma Theta Tau. Roman Catholic. Contbr. articles to med. jours. Office: St Paul Ramsey Med Ctr 640 Jackson St Saint Paul MN 55101

MARSEE, CHARLES DEWEY, educational administrator; b. Nashville, Sept. 30, 1942; s. Dewey Marion and Essie Corina (Bolton) M.; m. Jerri Wade, Nov. 25, 1961; children—Sharon, Linda. Student, Lincoln Meml. U., 1960-62; B.S., U. Tenn., 1964; M.S., Fla. State U., 1968, postgrad., 1973. Tchr. sci. Dixie County High Sch., Cross City, Fla., 1964-66, Leon County High Sch., Tallahassee, 1966-68; chmn. sci. dept. Hawken Sch., Gates Mills, Ohio, 1968-80; headmaster The Andrews Sch., Willoughby, Ohio, 1980—. Trustee, Willoughby Sch. Fine Arts, 1980—. Recipient Bole award Hawken Sch., 1980. Mem. Nat. Assn. Prins. Schs. for Girls, Nat. Assn. Secondary Sch. Prins., Assn. Secondary Curriculum Dirs, Ohio Assn. Secondary Sch. Adminstrs., Cleve. Regional Council Sci. Tchrs. (pres., dir.). Republican. Mem. Evangelical Free Ch. Club: Rotary (Willoughby, Ohio). Home and Office: 38588 Mentor Ave Willoughby OH 44094

MARSH, CLAYTON EDWARD, army officer; b. Worthington, Minn., Jan. 24, 1942; s. Cecil Eugene and Edna Luella (Clausen) M.; m. Carol Ruth Lundmark Franz, June 30, 1962 (div. 1979); children—Tracey Diane, Julie Doreen, Leslie Dawn, Lori Dion; m. Kyong Hui Yi, Aug. 28, 1979. B.A., St. Cloud State U., 1974; M.S., U. So. Calif., 1979. Commd. 2d lt. U.S. Army, 1967, advanced through grades to lt. col., 1985; chief Info. Systems Div., DECCO, Scott AFB, Ill., 1985—. Decorated D.F.C., Bronze Star, Army Commendation medal, Air medal. Mem. Internat. Assn. Approved Basketball Ofcls., Ill. High Sch. Assn., S.W. Athletic Ofcls. Assn. Republican. Mem. Ch. of Christ. Home: 47 Innsbruck Ln Belleville IL 62221 Office: Defense Comml Communications Office Bldg 3189 Scott AFB IL 62225

MARSH, DON E., supermarket executive; b. Muncie, Ind., Feb. 2, 1938; s. Ermal W. and Garnet (Gibson) M.; B.A., Mich. State U., 1961; m. Marilyn Faust, Mar. 28, 1959; children—Don Ermal, Arthur Andrew, David Alan, Anne Elizabeth, Alexander Elliott. With Marsh Supermarkets, Inc., Yorktown, Ind., 1961—, pres., chief exec. officer, 1966—, also dir.; dir. Mchts. Nat. Bank Muncie, Village Pantry, Inc.; officer Kokomo Land, Inc. Bd. dirs. Ball State U. Found., St. Vincent Hosp. Found., Indpls.; officer, bd. dirs. Ind. Retail Council, Food Industry Good Govt.; mem. Nat. Republican Senatorial Com., Rep. Fin. Com.; mem. adv. council Indpls. Civic Theatre, Connor Prairie Pioneer Settlement, Noblesville, Ind. Mem. Ind. C. of C. (dir.), Delaware County C. of C., Newcomen Soc. N.Am., Internat. Assn. Food Chains, Ind. Retail Grocers Assn. (bd. dirs.), Nat. Assn. Convenience Stores, Am. Mgmt. Assn. (gen. mgmt. council), Young Pres.'s Orgn., Food Merchandisers Edn. Council, Food Mktg. Inst., Ind. Soc. Chgo., Am. Bus. Club, Phi Sigma Epsilon, Lambda Chi Alpha. Presbyterian. Clubs: Columbia (Indpls.); Indpls. Athletic, Ind. U. Varsity; Crooked Stick Country (Carmel, Ind.); Delaware Country (Muncie); Rotary, Masons, Elks. Home: 2042 St Andrews Circle Carmel IN 46032 Office: Marsh Supermarkets Inc 501 Depot St Yorktown IN 47396

MARSH, DORIS ELAINE, ballet teacher, choreographer; b. Saginaw, Mich., Sept. 14, 1931; d. William Henry and Elizabeth Ann (Bates) M. B.A., U. Mich., 1953, M.A., 1956. Tchr. Saginaw pub. schs., 1956-70; tchr. ballet, Saginaw, 1956—; dir. Summer Sch. Dance, Delta Coll., University Ctr., 1964-84; artistic dir. Saginaw Valley Dancers, 1964—. Choreographer ballets: Summer, 1981; The Nutcracker, 1982; Five Lyric Pieces, 1983; Si Re Do, 1983. Bd. dirs. Community Concert Assn., Saginaw; mem. program com. Temple Theatre Arts Assn., Saginaw, 1980—; pres. Saginaw Valley Dance Council, Mid-Mich. area, 1971-73. Mem. Imperial Soc. Tchrs. Dancing (London), Saginaw Valley Dance Council (bd. dirs., pres. 1971-73), Saginaw Valley Dancers (pres. 1975—). Avocations: photography; writing; cross-country skiing; hiking; canoeing. Home: 2701 Willard St Saginaw MI 48602

MARSH, R. BRUCE, advt. agy. exec.; b. Milw., Aug. 31, 1929; s. Lester B. and Margaret (Hermsen) M.; B.A. in Econs., State U. Iowa, 1951; m. Margaret Ross, Oct. 11, 1952; children—Marilyn Elaine, Robert Ross, Gregory Bruce; m. 2d, Gayle Johnson, June 14, 1981. Profl. baseball pitcher, 1951-52; indsl. sales rep. 3M Co., 1952-55; advt. sales rep. Curtis Publishing Co., 1955-56; advt. sales rep., then nat. sporting goods sales mgr. Sports Illus. mag., Chgo., 1956-64; v.p., account supr. Campbell Mithun Inc., Chgo., 1964-67; pres. R. Bruce Marsh, Inc., pubs. reps., Chgo., 1967-70, R. Bruce Marsh, Inc., real estate, Chgo., 1970-71; v.p. mktg. Johnson & Quin, Inc., printers, Chgo., 1971-72; Midwest mktg. mgr. Project Health div. G.D. Searle & Co., Chgo., 1972-73; v.p., account supr. Fuller, Smith & Ross Advt., Chgo., 1974-75; sr. v.p. Frank C. Nahser, Inc./Advt., Chgo., 1975—. Dir. SERMAC Industries Inc. Coach, Northfield (Ill.) Boys Baseball Assn., 1968-78, pres., 1972-76, bd. dirs., 1970—; chmn. North Suburban chpt. Fellowship Christian Athletes, 1980-83; area chmn. United Fund Northfield, 1963-65; speaker Ill. Prison Ministries. Recipient spl. recognition award contbn. to youth Community of Northfield. Mem. Internat. Platform Assn. Mem. Bible Ch. Clubs: Sunset Ridge Country (Northbrook, Ill.); University (Chgo.). Address: 346 Crooked Creek Ln Northfield IL 60093

MARSH, ROBERT CHARLES, writer, music critic; b. Columbus, Ohio, Aug. 5, 1924; s. Charles L. and Jane A. (Beckett) M.; B.S., Northwestern U., 1945, A.M., 1946; Sage fellow Cornell U., 1946-47; postgrad. U. Chgo., 1948; Ed.D., Harvard U., 1951; postgrad. U. Oxford, 1952-53, U. Cambridge, 1953-56; m. Kathleen C. Moscrop 1956 (div. 1985). Instr. social sci. U. Ill., 1947-49; lectr. humanities Chgo. City Jr. Coll., 1950-51; asst. prof. edn. U. Kansas City, 1951-52; vis. prof. edn. SUNY, 1953-54; humanities staff U. Chgo., 1956-58, lectr. social thought, 1976; music critic Chgo. Sun-Times, 1956—; mem. nat. adv. com., project for tng. music critics U. So. Calif., 1964-72; dir. Chgo. Opera project Newberry Library, 1983—. Co-recipient Peabody award; Ford Found. fellow, 1965-66. Episcopalian. Club: Press (Chgo.). Author: Toscanini and the Art of Orchestral Performance, 1956, rev. edit., 1962; The Cleveland Orchestra, 1967; Ravinia, 1985. Editor: Logic and Knowledge, 1956. Home: 1825 N Lincoln Plaza Apt 309 Chicago IL 60614 Office: Chgo Sun-Times 401 N Wabash Ave Chicago IL 60611

MARSHAK, MARVIN LLOYD, physicist, educator; b. Buffalo, Mar. 11, 1946; s. Kalman and Goldie (Hait) M.; m. Anita Sue Kolman, Sept. 24, 1972; children—Rachel Kolman, Adam Kolman. A.B. in Physics, Cornell U., 1967; M.S. in Physics, U. Mich., Ph.D. in Physics, 1970. Research assoc. U. Minn., Mpls., 1970-74, asst. prof., 1974-78, assoc. prof., 1978-83, prof. physics, 1983—, dir. grad. studies in physics, 1983—, prin. investigator high energy physics, 1982—. Contbr. articles to profl. jours. Mem. Am. Phys. Soc. Home: 2855 Ottawa Ave S Minneapolis MN 55416 Office: U Minn Physics Dept 116 Church St SE Minneapolis MN 55455

MARSHALL, AUSTIN SCOTT, civil engineer; b. Providence, Aug. 5, 1952; s. George L. and Marion V. (Scotti) M.; m. Cynthia Gail Humphreys, Aug. 18, 1972; children—Adam, Garrett. B.S.C.E., Cornell U., 1974; M.S.C.E., U. Mich., 1975; J.D., U. Detroit, 1986. Registered profl. engr., Mich., Fla., Ill., Ohio. Soil engr. Neyer, Tiseo, Farmington, Mich., 1974, Woodward-Clyde, Denver, 1975-78; project engr. Bechtel Corp., Ann Arbor, Mich., 1978-81; gen. mgr. Millgard Corp., Livonia, Mich., 1981-85; pres. Marshall, Halpert, Birmingham, Mich., 1985—; adj. prof. U. Detroit, 1984—; cons., dir. Scott, Orlin Assocs., Northville, Mich., 1981—. Bd. dirs. Denver YMCA, 1977; arbitrator Am. Arbitration Assn., 1984. Mem. ASCE (com.), Deep Founds. Inst. (bd. dirs. 1982—), Assn. Engring. Geologists, Am. Concrete Inst. (com.), ABA, Detroit Engrs. Club. Club: Cornell (Detroit). Avocations: basketball; golf; camping; mineral collecting. Home: 41130 Croydon Ct Northville MI 48167 Office: 6735 Telegraph Suite 35 Birmingham MI 48010

MARSHALL, BENJAMIN FRANKLIN, IV, lawyer; b. Cape Girardeau, Mo., May 19, 1957; s. Benjamin Franklin and Elizabeth Claire (Anderson) M.; m. Mary Margaret Walsh, Jan. 3, 1981; 1 child, Benjamin Franklin. B.S., Regis Coll., 1979; J.D., St. Louis Univ., 1982. Bar: Mo. 1982. Assoc., Blanton, Rice, Sidwell and Ottinger, Sikeston, Mo., 1982—; dir. Oran State Bank, Mo., 1984—. Vice pres. Scott County Young Democrats, Sikeston, 1984; pres. Scott Unit, Am. Cancer Soc. Named to Outstanding Young Men Am. U.S. Jaycees, 1983. Mem. Mo. Bar Assn., ABA, Scott County Bar Assn. (treas. 1984—), Sikeston Jaycees, Alpha Sigma Nu. Roman Catholic. Avocations: Woodworking; photography; gardening. Home: 510 N Kings Hwy Sikeston MO 63801

Office: Blanton, Rice, Sidwell and Ottinger 219 S Kings Hwy Sikeston MO 63801

MARSHALL, FINLEY D., biochemistry educator; b. Rochester, N.Y., Aug. 1, 1930; s. F. D. and Eva M. (Scharf-Keene) M.; m. Jean Y. Kido, Jan. 31, 1959; children—Jeffrey, Kimberly, Kenna. B.S., Bucknell U., 1952; M.S., U. Mo., 1959, Ph.D., 1961. Research chemist Olin-Mathieson Chem. Co., Niagara Falls, N.Y., 1952-56; research assoc. Sterling-Winthrop Research Inst., Rensselaer, N.Y., 1961-62, U. Iowa, Iowa City, 1962-64; prof. biochemistry U. S.D., Vermillion, 1964—. Contbr. articles to profl. jours. Nat. cert. swimming ofcl., Indpls., 1975—. Research grantee NIH, 1965—, Huntington's Chorea Found., 1973-76. Mem. Am. Soc. Biol. Chemists, Am. Soc. Neurochemistry, Am. Soc. Neurosci. Office: Univ SD Biochemistry Dept Sch Medicine Vermillion SD 57069

MARSHALL, HARRY DWIGHT, machine tool company executive; b. Grand Rapids, Mich., Aug. 26, 1915; s. Harry Dwight and Edith Lenore (Butler) M.; m. Judy Corrigan, Dec. 26, 1942; children—Nancy Marshall Taylor, John Stephen. B.S. in Mech. and Indsl. Engring., U. Mich., 1939. Cost engr. Eastman Kodak Co., Rochester, N.Y., 1939-40; asst. to v.p. mfg. Gallmeyer & Livingston Co., Grand Rapids, 1940-52, dir., 1951—, v.p., 1952—, treas., 1959—; dir. Mut. Home Fed. Savs. Bank, Grand Rapids, 1954—. Bd. dirs. Employers' Assn. Grand Rapids, 1956—, pres., 1956-60; bd. dirs. Kent County chpt. ARC, Grand Rapids, 1960-69. Mem. ASME (life), Tau Beta Pi, Phi Kappa Phi. Republican. Presbyterian. Clubs: University, Peninsular. Lodge: Rotary (dir. 1969-71, v.p. 1969-70). Home: 1661 Fisk Rd SE Grand Rapids MI 49506 Office: Gallmeyer & Livingston Co 336 Straight Ave SW Grand Rapids MI 49504

MARSHALL, JOHN CROOK, internal medicine educator, researcher; b. Blackburn, Lancashire, Eng., Feb. 28, 1941; came to U.S., 1976; s. Albert Acey and Marion Miller (Crook) M.; m. Marilyn Dallas Parry, Sept. 20, 1969; children—Samantha Jane, Susannah Crook. B.S., Victoria U., Manchester, Eng., 1962, M.B., Ch.B., 1965, M.D., 1973. Diplomate Am. Bd. Internal Medicine, Am. Bd. Endocrinology and Metabolism. Intern Manchester Royal Infirmary, 1965-66; resident Brompton Hosp., Nat. Heart Hosp., London, 1966-69; resident Hammersmith Hosp., 1966-69, research fellow, London, 1969-72; lectr. U. Birmingham, Eng. 1972-76; assoc. prof. internal medicine U. Mich., Ann Arbor, 1976-79, prof., 1979—; sci. counselor NIH, Bethesda, Md., 1983—. Editor Endocrinology Jour., 1979-83. Contbr. articles to profl. jours. NIH grantee 1977-84. Fellow Royal Coll. Physicians, Royal Soc. Medicine, ACP; mem. Central Soc. for Clin. Research (council 1983—), Am. Soc. for Clin. Investigation. Anglican. Avocations: vintage racing cars; golf; tennis. Office: Dept Internal Medicine Univ Michigan Univ Hosp Ann Arbor MI 48109

MARSHALL, KEITH MACDONALD, anthropology educator, administrator; b. San Francisco, Oct. 12, 1943; s. Walter Leslie and Alice Marie (Hitch) M.; m. Leslie Joanne Brusletten, Aug. 21, 1965; 1 child, Kelsey Andrew. B.A., Grinnell Coll., 1965; M.A., U. Wash.-Seattle, 1967, Ph.C., 1969, Ph.D., 1972. Asst. prof. anthropology U. Iowa, 1972-76, assoc. prof., 1976-80, prof., 1980—, chmn. dept., 1982-85; vis. sr. research fellow Papua New Guinea Inst. Applied Social and Econ. Research, Boroko, 1980-81. Bd. editors Micronesica, 1975—; editor: Beliefs, Behaviors and Alcoholic Beverages, 1979; Siblingship in Oceania, 1981; Through a Glass Darkly: Beer and Modernization in Papua New Guinea, 1982; author: Weekend Warriors: Alcohol in a Micronesian Culture, 1979. USPHS-NIMH research grantee, 1969-72; WHO research grantee, 1981; NSF research grantee, 1985-86. Fellow Am. Anthropol. Assn. (newsletter editor alcohol and drug study group 1984—), Assn. Social Anthropology in Oceania, Royal Anthropol. Inst. Gt. Britain and Ireland; mem. Pacific Sci. Assn., Polynesian Soc., Research Soc. on Alcoholism, Sierra Club. Democrat. Unitarian-Universalist. Avocations: gardening, camping and hiking, swimming, traveling. Office: Dept Anthropology U Iowa Iowa City IA 52242

MARSHALL, LINDA RAE, cosmetic company executive; b. Provo, Utah, Aug. 1, 1940; d. Arvid O. and Tola V. (Broderick) Newman; children—James, John. Student Brigham Young U., 1958-59, U. Utah, 1960-61. Buyer, Boston Store, 1961-62; sec. Milw. Gas & Light Co., 1962-64; mktg. rep. Elysee Cosmetics, Madison, Wis., 1971-75, pres., 1975—. Pres. Falk Sch. PTA, Madison. Mem. Aestheticians Internat. Assn. (adv. bd.), Cosmetic, Toiletry and Fragrance Assn. (exec. com., bd. dirs., chmn. voluntary program, chmn. small cosmetic com., membership com. task force). Club: Dental Wives. Author: Discover the Other Woman in You; monthly beauty columnist Beauty Fashion Mag.; contbg. author Cosmetic Industry Sci. and Regulatory Found., 1984. Address: Box 4084 Madison WI 53711

MARSHALL, LONNIE LOU, psychiatrist; b. Des Moines, June 28, 1953; s. Adam and Betty (Shupe) M. B.S., Northeast Mo. State U., 1974; D.O., Kirksville Coll. Osteo. Medicine, 1978. Intern Doctors Hosp., Erie, Pa., 1978-79; resident U. Mo.-Columbia, 1982-85, mem. staff dept. psychiatry, 1985—; practice osteo. medicine specializing in psychiatry, Columbia, Mo.; instr. emergency medicine Hamot Med. Ctr., Erie, Pa., 1979-80; assoc. clin. instr. psychiatry U. Mo., Columbia, 1984-85. Mem. Am. Psychol Assn., Am. Osteo. Assn., Am. Psychiat. Assn. Avocations: skiing, diving.

MARSHALL, MARK FRANCIS, lawyer; b. Huron, S.D., Sept. 21, 1954; s. Merle William and Alice Donaline (Pierce) M.; m. Laurel Ann Housiaux, Dec. 31, 1976; 1 child, Kay Lynn. B.S., U. S.D., 1977, J.D., 1981. Bar: S.D. 1981, U.S. Ct. Appeals (8th cir.) 1981, U.S. Dist. Ct. S.D. 1981, U.S. Supreme Ct. 1984. Intern Dana, Golden, Moore & Rasmussen, Sioux Falls, S.D., summer 1980; staff atty. Davenport, Evans et al, Sioux Falls, summer 1981; law clk. to sr. judge U.S. Dist. Ct., Sioux Falls, 1981-83; assoc. Bangs, McCullen, Butler, Foye & Simmons, Rapid City, S.D., 1983—. Asst. editor: Agricultural Law, 1982; contbr. articles to profl. jours. Kelton Lynn scholar, 1980; Marshall McKusick scholar, 1982; recipient J.N. Spencer Writers award S.D. Law Rev., 1982. Mem. ABA, State Bar S.D., Assn. Trial Lawyers Am., Phi Alpha Delta (treas. 1980). Democrat. Presbyterian. Home: 2507 Tomahawk Dr Rapid City SD 57702 Office: Bangs McCullen Butler Foye & Simmons 818 St Joseph St Rapid City SD 57701

MARSHALL, PRENTICE H., judge; b. 1926; B.S., J.D., U. Ill.; Admitted to Ill. bar, 1951; now judge U.S. Dist. Ct. for No. Ill. Office: US Courthouse 219 S Dearborn St Chicago IL 60604*

MARSHALL, TARI BETH, public relations executive; b. Kankakee, Ill., Nov. 4, 1955; d. Jerome and Joan Sue Marshall. B.A. in Journalism, Drake U., 1977. Pub. info. officer Ill. Info. Service, Springfield, 1978-79; account exec. Pub. Relations Bd. Inc., Chgo., 1979-80, account supr., 1980-84; pub. relations dir. Nat. PTA, 1984—. Mem. Pub. Relations Soc. Am. (Silver Anvil 1982), Publicity Club Chgo. (merit award 1982), Women in Communications. Office: 700 N Rush St Chicago IL 60611

MARSIK, FREDERIC JOHN, clinical microbiologist; b. Camden, N.J., June 22, 1943; s. Ferdinand Vincent and Helen (Reidl) M.; children—Terri Jean, Kristi Ann. B.A., Lebanon Valley Coll., 1965; M.S., U. Mo., 1970, Ph.D., 1973. Diplomate Am. Acad. Microbiology; cert. Agy. Clin. Lab. Mgmt. Research assoc. Sloan Kettering, N.Y.C., 1965-66; research asst. Merck Inst. Therapeutic Research, Rahway, N.J., 1966-68; teaching and research asst. U. Mo., Columbia, 1968-74; postdoctoral trainee microbiology Hartford (Conn.) Hosp., 1974-76; asst. prof. pathology U. Va., Charlottesville, 1976-80; tech. dir. immunology and microbiology Milw. Children's Hosp., 1980-84; assoc. prof. microbiology and internal med., dir. Infectious Disease Research Lab., Oral Roberts Sch. of Med., 1984—; cons., tchr. Mem. Germantown Vol. Fire Dept. Served to maj., USAR, 1965—. Recipient Microbiology Student award U. Mo., 1973, Outstanding Clinical Microbiology Research Southwestern Assn. for Clinical Microbiology, 1984. Mem. Am. Soc. Microbiology, Am. Soc. Med. Tech., N.Y. Acad. Scis., Res. Officers Assn., Sigma Xi. Congregationalist. Contbr. articles profl. jours., chpts. in book.

MARSNIK, NADINE ALICE, English and speech communication educator, consultant; b. Clontarf, Minn., Sept. 5, 1931; d. Ellard Dennis and Alice Edna (Johnson) Chamberlain; m. George Michael Marsnik, Aug. 14, 1954; children—Anne, Susan, Peter, Catherine, Adam, Sara. B.A., Coll. of St. Catherine, 1953; M. Ed., U. Minn.-Duluth, 1974. Tchr. Foley High Sch., Minn., 1953-54, Holdingford High Sch., Minn., 1954-57; pres. Info. Systems, Ely, Minn., 1984—; instr. Vermilion Coll., Ely, 1966—; adj. prof. Bemidji State U., Minn., 1984—; listening cons. Boston State Coll., 1982-83; communications cons. Minn. Dept. Edn., St. Paul, 1984—. Author: (with others) Perceptive Listening, 1983. Vol. Hospice Vols., Ely, 1983, cons., 1984; cons. East Range Women's Advs., Eveleth, Minn., 1982. Mem. Internat. Listening Assn. (founder, pres. 1985), Speech Communication Assn., Central States Speech Assn., Nat. Council Tchrs. of English, Midwest Regional Conf. Tchrs. of English, AAUW, Phi Beta Kappa, Pi Epsilon Delta Delta Phi Lambda. Roman Catholic. Office: Vermilion Community Coll 1900 E Camp St Ely MN 55731

MARSTON-FOUCHER, CAROL LYNN, optometrist; b. Detroit, July 14, 1956; d. George Marion and Genevieve Agnes (Godzisz) Marston; m. Mark Jay Foucher, Jan. 5, 1985. Student, U. Mich., 1974-76; O.D., Ferris State Coll., 1980. Pvt. practice optometry, Livonia, Mich., 1980—; clin. instr. Ferris State Coll. Optometry, Detroit, 1981—. Trustee Detroit Hearing and Speech Ctr., 1984. Mem. Livonia C. of C., Wayne County Soc. Optometrists (pres. 1985-86), Met. Detroit Optometric Soc. (bd. dirs.), Mich. Optometric Assn., Optometric Inst. and Clin. Detroit (trustee). Avocations: skiing; golfing. Office: 32037 Plymouth Rd Livonia MI 48150

MARTAN, JOSEPH RUDOLF, lawyer; b. Oak Park, Ill., Mar. 28, 1949; s. Joseph John and Margarete Paulina (Rothenbock) M.; B.A. with honors, U. Ill., Champaign-Urbana, 1971; J.D. with honors, Ill. Inst. Tech./Chgo.-Kent Coll. Law, 1977. Admitted to Ill. bar, 1977, U.S. dist. ct. for No. dist. Ill., 1977; assoc. firm V. C. Lopez, Chgo., 1978-80; litigation counsel Goldblatt Bros., Inc., Chgo., 1980-81; br. counsel Ill. br. Am. Family Ins. Group, Rolling Meadows, 1981—. Mem. West Suburban Community Band, Inc., Western Springs, Ill., 1975—, pres., 1979-81. Served with U.S. Army, 1972-74, to capt. USAR, 1974—. Decorated Army Commendation medal. Mem. Ill. State Bar Assn., Chgo. Bar Assn., Du Page County Bar Assn. (mem. civil practice com.), Bohemian Lawyer's Assn. Chgo., Def. Research Inst., Assn. Trial Lawyers Am., Res. Officer's Assn., Assn. U.S. Army, Met. Opera Guild, Pi Sigma Alpha. Home: 4056 Gilbert Ave Western Springs IL 60558 Office: 1501 Woodfield Rd Suite 200 W Schaumburg IL 60195

MARTEL, IRA, marketing executive; b. Bronx; m. Ruth Saffati, Dec. 25, 1978; children—Josef Nissim, Eliahu Zvi, Shoshana. Student U. Mo., 1967; B.A., William Penn Coll., 1968; postgrad. U. Ariz., 1968; tchr. cert. Augustana Coll., 1970; M.S., Mont. State U., 1971; postgrad. U. S.D., 1971; Ph.D. (grad. teaching asst.), Oreg. State U., 1974. Salesman, Martel Products, Bronx, 1953-63; numis. salesman M. Geiger, Rare Coins, N.Y.C., 1959-62; sales clk. E.J. Korvette, Scarsdale, N.Y., summer 1963; pressroom asst. N.Y. Sch. Printing Pressmen, N.Y.C., 1962-64; demonstrator Tower Products Corp., Bklyn., 1965; dir. World Wide Fashions of Sioux Falls (S.D.), 1970-72; salesman Van Zee Motors, Oskaloosa, Iowa, 1966-67, Stoner Piano Co., Ottumwa, Iowa, 1967, Sears, Roebuck & Co., Sioux Falls, 1970-71; instr. Mont. State U., summer 1971; tchr. coordinator distributive edn. Sioux Falls Pub. Schs., 1968-72; research/devel. specialist Ohio State U., Columbus, 1972-73; sales/promotion specialist Vita-Mix Corp., Cleve., 1965; asst. prof. bus. and distributive edn. Emporia (Kans.) State Coll., 1974-77; assoc. prof. mktg./internat. bus. Baldwin Wallace Coll., Berea, Ohio, 1979-81; assoc. prof. mktg. and internat. bus. Lake Erie Coll., Painesville, Ohio, 1981-82; mktg. v.p. Vita-Mix Corp., Cleve., 1977—. Mem. Am. Mgmt. Assn., Assn. Home Appliance Mfrs. (internat. trade com.), Nat. Assn. Distributive Edn. Tchrs., Direct Mail Mktg. Assn., NEA, Am. Vocat. Assn., Direct Mktg. Assn., Aircraft Owners and Pilots Assn., Internat. Platform Assn. Contbr. articles to profl. jours. Home: 8710 Root Rd North Ridgeville OH 44039

MARTENIUK, JUDITH VIOLA, veterinarian, educator; b. Yorkton, Sask., Can., June 14, 1951; d. Nick K. and Violet M. (Ironside) Marteniuk; m. Kent Roswell Refsal, July 22, 1976. D.V.M., Western Coll. Vet. Medicine, Saskatoon, Sask., 1975; M.S., Mich. State U., 1984. Intern, Western Coll. Vet. Medicine, Saskatoon, 1975-76, resident Mich. State U., East Lansing, 1978-80, asst. prof., 1980—; gen. practice vet. medicine, Mora, Minn., 1976-78. Home: 6905 Friegel Rd Laingsburg MI 48848 Office: Michigan State U VCC LCS Bogue St East Lansing MI 48824

MARTENS, TED WILLIAM, consumer products manufacturing executive; b. Darlington, Wis., Feb. 5, 1938; s. Walter Wilmer and Geraldine Loretta (McWilliams) M.; m. Nancy Claire Johnson, Jan. 28, 1961; 1 child, Ryan Arthur. B.S. in Chem. Engring., U. Wis., 1961, B.S. in Naval Sci., 1961; M.S. in Engring. Adminstrn., George Washington U., 1964. Mfg. dept. mgr. Procter & Gamble, Sacramento, 1964-68, mfg. ops. mgr., Lima, Ohio, 1968-71, N.Y.C., 1971-79, mfg. planning mgr., Cin., 1979-83, mfg. plant mgr., Iowa City, Iowa, 1983—. Indsl. chmn. United Way, Boy Scouts Am., 1984. Served to lt. USN, 1961-64. Mem. Iowa City C. of C. Republican. Roman Catholic. Lodge: Rotary. Avocations: sailing; tennis. Home: 49 Lakeview Pl N Iowa City IA 52240 Office: Procter & Gamble Mfg Co 2200 Lower Muscatine Rd Iowa City IA 52240

MARTENSON, DENNIS RAYMOND, civil engineer; b. Eau Claire, Wis., Oct. 15, 1942; s. Raymond R. and Elinor L. (Aaserude) M.; m. Catherine Marie Thompson, Sept. 15, 1962; children—Annemarie Lynn, Amy Elizabeth. B.C.E., U. Minn., 1967, M.S., 1968. Registered profl. engr., Minn. Research asst. U. Minn., Mpls., 1967; plant engr. Western Electric Co., Inc., N.Y.C., 1968-69; process control engr. Met. Sewer Bd., St. Paul, 1969-71; project engr. Pfeifer & Shultz, Inc., Mpls., 1971-72; chief san. engr. Watermation, Inc., St. Paul, 1972-75; project mgr./assoc. mem. firm Toltz, King, Duvall, Anderson & Assocs., Inc., St. Paul, 1975—. USPHS fellow, 1967; named Minn.'s Young Civil Engr. of Yr., Minn. sect. ASCE, 1975. Mem. ASCE (pres. 1976-77), Am. Water Works Assn., Instrument Soc. Am., Nat. Assn. Corrosion Engrs., Water Pollution Control Fedn. Lutheran. Contbr. articles to profl. jours. Home: 8140 46 1/2 Ave N Minneapolis MN 55428 Office: 2500 American National Bank Bldg Saint Paul MN 55101

MARTI, PAUL EDGAR, JR., architect, educator; b. Wichita, Kans., Sept. 7, 1929; s. Paul Edgar and Edna Clareen (Conley) M.; m. Audrey Lee Marti, Mar. 15, 1933; children—Dane Eric, Kara Lynn. B.Arch., Kans. State U., 1953; M.A., U. Calif.-Berkeley, 1958. Architect, Murphy-Mackey, St. Louis, 1955-57, Hellmuth-Obata-K, St. Louis, 1958-62; v.p. Smith-Entzeroth, Clayton, Mo., 1962—; juror Am. Plywood Assn. awards, Seattle, 1973; instr. archtl. tech. Washington U., St. Louis, 1979—. Contbr. articles in field to profl. jours. Chmn. Bd. Adjustment, Oakland, Mo., 1983-84. Served with USAF, 1953-55. Recipient 3d Prize, Kirkwood Civic Ctr. Competition, 1967; citation of merit Am. Plywood Assn., 1978. Mem. AIA (award of merit St. Louis 1970), Alpha Tau Omega. Club: Optimist (pres. 1968) (Clayton, Mo.). Home: 105 Minturn St Oakland MO 63122 Office: Smith-Entzeroth Architects 7701 Forsyth St Clayton MO 63105

MARTIA, DOMINIC FRANCIS, university administrator; b. Canton, Ohio, May 9, 1935; s. Joseph James and Anita (Cimadevilla) M.; m. Roberta Christine Abel, Feb. 13, 1954; children—Laura Ann, Paul Abel. B.A., Roosevelt U., 1962; M.A., U. Chgo., 1963; Ph.D., Loyola U.-Chgo., 1972. Assoc. prof. English, Roosevelt U., Chgo., 1972—, asst. to pres., 1972-76, dean grad. div., 1976-79, v.p. student services, 1979—. Author: Getting Verse, 1985; contbr. articles to profl. jours., poems to anthologies. Served with U.S. Army, 1954-56. Bd. dirs., chmn. med. award com. The Gavin Found., Park Forest, Ill., 1981—; mem. scholarship com. Stone Found., Chgo., 1981—. Woodrow Wilson Found. fellow, 1962. Mem. Nat. Assn. Student Personnel Adminstrs., Assn. Bus. Communicators, Ill. Tng. and Devel. Assn., Council for Advancement and Support Edn. Lodge: Toast-masters. Avocation: writing light verse. Home: 20 E Rocket Circle Park Forest IL 60466 Office: Roosevelt U 430 S Michigan Chicago IL 60605

MARTIEN, HARRY L., JR., electrical contracting company executive; b. Cleveland Heights, Ohio, Sept. 11, 1916; s. Harry L. and Iona Mary (Parsons) M.; m. Barbara Ruth Smith, Nov. 27, 1948; children—Melissa Martien Driscoll, Robert G., Katherine Martien MacMillan, Barbara, Richard. B.S.A.E./E.E., Cornell U., 1938. With Gen. Cable Corp., Cleve., Cin., N.Y.C., 1938-46; with Navy Dept. Bur. Ships, Clearfield, Utah, 1943-45; with Martien Electric Co., Cleve., 1946—, pres., 1970—. Mem. Greater Cleve. Growth Assn., United Way; pres. Cornell U. class of 1938. Mem. Nat. Elec. Contractors Assn. (past pres., dir. 1978-83), Builders Exchange (past pres., dir. 1978-83). Republican. Episcopalian. Clubs: Mayfield Country, Cleve. Skating, Hermit, Rotary, Midday. Home: 2720 Cranlyn Rd Shaker Hts OH 44122 Office: Martien Electric Co 3328 Carnegie Ave Cleveland OH 44115

MARTIN, ALPHADINE ELSIE, physical education educator; b. W.Va., Mar. 21, 1928; d. James Mark and Beulah Elsie (Bell) M. B.S., Bridgewater Coll. (Va.), 1950; M.A., George Peabody Coll., Nashville, 1954; Ph.D., Iowa U., 1966. Cert. tchr., Va. Tchr. Montevideo High Sch. (Va.), 1950-54; Central Mo. State U., Warrensburg, 1954—. Mem. AAHPER, Mo. Assn. Health, Phys. Edn. and Recreation, Central Assn. Phys. Edn. in Higher Edn. Home: Route 5 Green Acres Warrensburg MO 64093 Office: Central Mo State U Warrensburg MO 64093

MARTIN, ARLENE PATRICIA, pathology and biochemistry educator and researcher; b. Binghamton, N.Y., June 30, 1926; d. Edward J. and Helena F. (Hogan) M. B.A., Cornell U., 1948; M.N.S., 1952; Ph.D., U. Rochester, 1957. Postdoctoral fellow U. Rochester, N.Y., 1957-58, instr. biochemistry, 1958-65; asst. prof. radiology Jefferson Med. Coll., Phila., 1965-68, asst. prof. biochemistry, 1966-68; assoc. prof. biochemistry U. Mo., Columbia, 1968-74, prof. biochemistry/pathology, 1974—. Contbr. articles to profl. jours. Fellow AAAS; mem. Am. Soc. Biol. Chemists, Am. Chem. Soc., Am. Soc. Cell Biology, Sigma Xi. Avocations: sports; gardening. Home: 6417 Locust Grove Dr Route 6 Columbia MO 65202 Office: U Mo Dept Pathology Sch Medicine Columbia MO 65212

MARTIN, BARBARA NELL, elementary principal; b. Independence, Mo., Oct. 26, 1952; d. Harold and Mary Ida (Ropp) Martin. B.S., U. Mo., 1974, M.S., 1975, Ed.D., 1983. EMR classroom tchr., North Kansas City, Mo., 1974-77; EMR resource tchr., Blue Springs, Mo., 1977-78; dir. spl. service, Excelsior Springs, Mo., 1979-81; elem. prin. Franklin Sch., Liberty, Mo., 1981—; developer pub. sch. workshops relating to spl. services; coordinator Spl. Olympics; mem. North Central Evaluation Com., 1977-79. Chmn. Council Prevention Child Abuse, 1979—; active PTA. Mem. AAUW, Nat. Assn. Elem. Sch. Prins., Mo. Assn. Elem. Sch. Prins., Mo. Tchrs. Assn., Council for Exceptional Children, Assn. for Supervision and Curriculum Devel., Pi Lambda Theta, Phi Delta Kappa. Democrat. Baptist. Home: 14700 E 39th Terrace Independence MO 64055 Office: 201 W Mill St Liberty MO 64068

MARTIN, BRUCE LAWRENCE, biochemist; b. Balt., Jan. 18, 1959; s. John Aloysius and Aura (Ruiz) M. B.S. in Chemistry, U. Notre Dame, 1981. Grad. asst. dept. biochemistry Iowa State U., Ames, 1981—. Mem. AAAS, Am. Chem. Soc. Avocations: reading, athletics. Office: Iowa State U A321 Gilman St Ames IA 50011

MARTIN, CLARENCE JOSEPH, educational administrator, counselor, psychology educator; b. Durand, Mich., Aug. 3, 1931; s. H. Ward and Bernice I. (Benton) M.; m. Shirley J. Pletcher, May 5, 1951; children—Starley J. Tomchik, Scott A. Martin. B.A., Bethel Coll., 1957; B.D., Goshen Coll. Bibl. Sem., 1960, M.R.E., 1965; M.A., St. Mary's Coll., South Bend, Ind., 1968; D.Min., Union Theol. Sem., 1975. Lic. profl. counselor. Tchr., prin. Belvue Christian Schs., Albuquerque, 1961-63; instr. Bible, acting bus. mgr. Coll. of Southwest, Hobbs, N.Mex., 1963-64; dairyman, supr. Maple J. Farms, Goshen, Ind., 1964-68; spl. reading tchr. Wa-Nee Community Schs., Wakarusa, Ind., 1966-68; dir. career and personal counseling ctr., asst. prof. psychology Davis and Elkins Coll., W.Va., 1968-80; dir. student devel., asst. prof. psychology Bethel Coll., Mishawaka, Ind., 1980-82, v.p. student affairs, assoc. prof. psychology, 1982—. Co-author: Life Career Planning, 1978. Minister Belvue Baptist Ch., Kermit, Tex., 1963-64; interim pastor various other chs.; chmn. Randolph County Assn. for Retarded Citizens (W.Va.), 1972-74, W.Va. Assn. for Retarded Citizens, 1974-75; mem. leadership tng. program Pres's. Commn. on Mental Retardation. Mem. Am. Assn. for Counseling and Devel., Nat. Vocat. Guidance Assn., Am. Coll. Personnel Assn. Republican. Baptist. Avocation: farming. Home: 128 S 33d St South Bend IN Office: Bethel Coll 1001 W McKinely Ave Mishawaka IN 46545

MARTIN, DAVID K., health care administrator; b. Pelican Rapids, Minn., Aug. 10, 1953; s. Chauncey R. and Mildred M. Martin; m. Donna M. Knudson, July 19, 1975. B.S., Moorhead State U., 1976; M.Ed., Colo. State U., 1980. Health edn. coordinator Alexandria pub. schs., Minn., 1976-78; asst. dir. housing Trinity U., San Antonio, 1980-81; dean of students Dana Coll., Blair, Nebr., 1981-82; coordinator corp. support services Lutheran Health Systems, Fargo, N.D., 1982-84, dir. adminstrv. services, 1984—. Mem. budget com. United Way Cass-Clay, Fargo, 1984—; acting chmn. bd. Trinity Caring Ctr., Moorhead, Minn., 1984—; vol. instr. F.M. Heart Health Program, Moorhead, 1984—. Mem. Am. Mgmt. Assns., Am. Soc. Healthcare Edn. and Tng. Lutheran. Avocations: sports; travel. Office: PO Box 2087 Fargo ND 58107

MARTIN, DONALD CREAGH, surgeon; b. Port Chester, N.Y., Mar. 7, 1937; s. Donald Creagh and Margaret Eleanor (Dobson) M.; m. Jacqueline Anne Poole, Sept. 25, 1965; children—Samuel, Joseph. B.A. in Econs., Yale U., 1958; M.D., U. Pa., 1962. Diplomate Am. Bd. Surgery. Intern, Pa. Hosp., Phila., 1962-63, resident in gen. surgery and pathology, 1965-67, 70-71, 72-74, instr. anatomy, 1968-69, 71-72; practice gen. surgery, White Plains, N.Y., 1974-78, Toledo, 1978—; research asst. dept. surgery Guy's Hosp., London, 1967-68; mem. staff Toledo, Mercy, Riverside, St. Charles hosps.; clin. asst. prof. Med. Coll. Ohio, Toledo, 1980—. Bd. dirs. Lucas County chpt. Am. Cancer Soc., 1983. Served with M.C., USNR, 1963-65. Mem. AMA, Toledo Surg. Soc., N.Y. Acad. Scis., Am. Soc. Enteral and Parenteral Nutrition, Internat. Platform Assn., AAAS. Republican. Episcopalian. Clubs: Yale of N.Y.C.; Shadow Valley. Contbr. articles to med. jours. Home: 4456 W Bancroft St Toledo OH 43615 Office: 3939 Monroe St Suite 319 Toledo OH 43606

MARTIN, EDWARD OTTO, osteopathic physician, surgeon; b. Wingate, Ind., Mar. 7, 1914; s. Otto Tevis and Maria (Huffman) M.; m. Dorothy Katherine Rinne, Dec. 30, 1939 (div.); children—Rinne Tevis, Debra Jean. B.S. in Medicine, Ind. U., 1938; D.O., Kirksville Coll. Osteo. Medicine, 1942. Diplomate Am. Acad. Osteo. Surgeons. Intern, Derfelts Osteo. Hosp., Joplin, Mo., 1943-44, resident, 1944-47; practice osteo. medicine specializing in gen. surgery, Joplin; chmn. dept. surgery Oak Hill Osteo. Hosp., Jane Chinn Meml. Hosp., 1978—; mem. teaching staff intern tng. Oak Hill Hosp.; chmn. Osteo. Bd. Cert. Mem. Joplin Airport Bd. Served with U.S. Army, 1943. Fellow Am. Acad. Osteo. Surgeons (Surgeon of Yr. award 1982; founder) mem. Mo. Assn. Osteo. Physicians and Surgeons (pres. 1967-68), Am. Osteo. Assn., Aircraft Owners and Pilots Assn. Republican. Methodist. Clubs: Elks, Masons, Shriners. Home: 2202 Connecticut St Apt 2 Joplin MO 64801 Office: 908 E 7th St Joplin MO 64801

MARTIN, EDWARD PHILIP, data processing consultant; b. N.Y.C., Aug. 18, 1956; s. Philip Edward and Eileen F. (Higgins) M. B.S. in Bus. Adminstrn., Ohio State U., 1978, M.B.A., 1982. Programmer analyst Xerox Corp., Columbus Ohio, 1978-82; cons. Arthur Young & Co., Columbus, 1982—. Treas. condominium assn., 1982—; mem. Cath. Com. on Scouting, 1980—; cubmaster Boy Scouts Am., Columbus, 1983—. Mem. Assn. Systems Mgmt., Assn. Computing Machinery. Republican. Roman Catholic. Avocations: softball, soccer, hiking, jogging. Home: 2400 Briers Dr Columbus OH 43209 Office: Arthur Young & Co 100 E Broad St Columbus OH 43215

MARTIN, FLOYD EDWARD, manufacturing company executive; b. Waterbury, Conn., May 12, 1926; s. Floyd E. and Minnie G. (Hibbard) M.; m. Jean P. Colby, Sept. 25, 1948; children—Dawn, Colby, Georgia, Douglas. B.A., U. Conn., 1950. Vice-pres. ops. Coleman Cable Corp., River Grove, Ill., 1971-72; plant mgmt. staff, metal container div. Nat. Can Corp., Chgo., 1973-77, mfg. mgr. closure div., Bedford Park, Ill., 1978—. Served with USAF, 1944-46, NATOUSA, ETO. Avocation: golf. Office: Nat Can Corp 7300 S Narragansett Bedford Park IL 60638

MARTIN, FRANCES HUGHSON, lawyer; d. Donald T. and Frances Kathryn (Gramling) Hughson; m. Peter Alan Martin, Nov. 10, 1962; children—Kathryn F., Wrye P. B.S., U. Wis.-Madison, 1966; M.S., U. Wis.-Milw., 1974; J.D. cum laude, Marquette U., 1980. Bar: Wis. 1980, U.S. Dist. Ct. (ea. dist.) Wis. 1980, U.S. Dist. Ct. (we. dist.) Wis. 1980. Instr. biology U. Wis.-Parkside, Kenosha, 1975-77; assoc. Churchill Duback & Smith, Milw., 1980—. Mem. Wis. Bar Assn., Assn. Women Lawyers Milw. Bar Assn. (vice chmn. probate sect. 1983-84, chmn. probate sect. 1984-85). Democrat. Office: Churchill Duback & Smith 780 N Water St Milwaukee WI 53202

MARTIN, GRENVILLE WHITNEY, lumber company executive; b. Bancroft, Ont., Can., July 30, 1936; s. Whitney Lloyd and Nellie Pearl (Martin) M.; m. Ruby Fay Sarginson, May 10, 1957 (div. 1978); children—Kim, Kathy, Kelly, Kenton. Grad. high sch. Pres., gen. mgr. G.W. Martin Lumber Ltd., 1958—, G.W. Martin Wood Products Ltd., Tweed, Ont., 1958—, G.W. Martin Veneer Ltd., 1958—, G.W. Martin Logging Ltd., 1961—, G.W. Martin Forest Products Ltd., North Bay-Rutuglen, Tweed, Ont., 1982—, Martin Four Holdings Ltd., 1980—, Sawyer-Stoll Lumber Co. Ltd., Mattawa, Ont., 1960—. Served with Royal Can. Army Res. Mem. Ont. Forestry Assn., Can. Lumberman's Assn. Club: Rotary (Haliburton, Ont., Can.). Office: Box 49 Harcourt ON K0L 1X0 Canada

MARTIN, JAMES DAVID, marketing communications executive; b. Madison, Wis., May 7, 1943; s. Ruscal Wendel and Phyllis (Edwards) M.; B.S. in Sociology, U. Wis., 1968; postgrad. Northeastern U., Chgo., 1970-72; m. Melinda Robinson, July 17, 1968; children—James Richard Lawrence, Geoffrey Michael. Freelance writer, 1971—; staff writer, editorial asst. Chicogan mag., 1973-74; staff writer Ill. Div. Tourism, 1974-75, also owner of public relations firm; speechwriter for gov. Ill., 1975-77; speechwriter, staff writer Gould, Inc., Rolling Meadows, Ill., 1977-79; editor Chicagoland mag., 1977-79; dir. communications Portec Inc., Oak Brook, Ill., 1979-84; pres. James D. Martin & Assocs., Evanston, Ill., 1984—; author: The Gould Charge Coloring Book, 1977; co-author feature film The Last Affair, 1975; writer, co-producer film Where Total Systems Responsibilities Means Everything (Silver award N.Y. Internat. Film Festival), 1979; vis. prof. film Columbia Coll., Chgo., 1973; bd. dirs. Chgo. Internat. Film Festival, 1972-77. Mem. Am. Film Inst., Assn. R.R. Advt. and Mktg., R.R. Public Relations Assn., Internat. Assn. Bus. Communicators, Ry. Progress Inst. (chmn. public relations com. 1981-83). Club: Chgo. Press. Home: 2623 Prairie Ave Evanston IL 60201

MARTIN, JAMES DAVID, architectural project administrator, computer programmer; b. Lyman, S.C., Oct. 16, 1933; s. Cornelius Benson Jr. and Geneva (James) Martin; m. Marie Austin, Dec. 28, 1955; children—James Eric, David Brian. B.S. in Agrl. Engring., Clemson U., 1955; B.S. in Archtl. Engring., U. Okla., 1962; M.Arch., Okla. State U., 1966. Research asst. U.S. Dept. Agr., Clemson, S.C., 1955; commd. officer U.S. Air Force, 1955, advanced through grades to lt. col., 1972; maintenance staff, Langley AFB, Va., 1955-60; archtl. engr., 1960-80, ret., 1980; archtl. project mgr. HOK Architects, St. Louis, 1980—. Scoutmaster Boy Scouts Am., Lyman, 1954. Mem. AIA, Am. Mgmt. Assn., Constrn. Specifications Inst., Project Mgmt. Assn., Tau Beta Pi. Republican. Methodist. Home: 823 Samone Ct Manchester MO 63021 Office: HOK Architects Inc 100 N Broadway Saint Louis MO 63102

MARTIN, JAMES MERWYN, automotive safety administrator; b. Milton, Wis., Nov. 19, 1933; s. Merwyn Arthur and Mary Josephine (Finnane) M.; m. Elizabeth Ann Tomazewski, Aug. 27, 1960; children—Michael James, James Patrick, Mary Elizabeth. B.S., U. Wis.-Stevens Point, 1961. With Fisher Body div. Gen. Motors Corp., Janesville, Wis., 1953-61, trainee Chevrolet Motor div., 1961-62, truck prodn. foreman, 1963, safety engr. Janesville, Wis., 1964-68, safety supr. Assembly div., 1968-73, sr. adminstr. safety, Warren, Mich., 1973—; cons. in field. Served with U.S. Army, 1953-55. Mem. Am. Soc. Safety Engrs., Nat. Safety Council, Mich. Safety Council. Republican. Roman Catholic. Author manuals. Office: 30009 Van Dyke Ave Warren MI 48090

MARTIN, JAMES ORVILLE, gas company executive; b. Grandview, Ind., Jan. 29, 1922; s. Orville and Gladys Heath (Craig) M.; m. Theresa Louise Swinney, June 30, 1946; children—Joan Elizabeth, Susan Louise, Theresa Ellen, Karen Marie. B.S. in Elec. Engring., Purdue U., 1942; diploma Harvard U., 1943; postgrad. MIT, 1943. Equipment engr. Western Electric Co., Chgo., 1946-48; aircraft antenna designer Electronics Research Lab., Evansville, Ind., 1948-52; with Lincoln Natural Gas Co., Rockport, Ind., 1957—, pres., 1985—; with Martin-Serrin Co., Inc., Rockport, Ind., 1953—, treas., 1985—. Sr. mem. president's council Purdue U., 1980—, mem. dean's adv. com. Sch. Consumer and Family Scis., 1980-81. Served to capt. USAF, 1942-46; PTO. Mem. Am. Legion (comdr.). Methodist. Lodge: Masons (master). Home: RR 1 Rockport IN 47635 Office: 317 Main St Rockport IN 47635

MARTIN, JEFFREY JON, comptroller; b. Waukon, Iowa, July 29, 1959; s. Francis Anthony and Janet Iona (Schmidt) M.; m. Lori Ann Lyons, Nov. 24, 1984 Assoc. Applied Sci., Northeast Iowa Tech. Inst., 1979. Staff acct. Thomas Sanger, C.P.A., Waukon, 1979-80, Dee, Gosling & Co., Waukon, 1980-84; comptroller Leadfree Enterprises, Inc., Waukon, 1984—. Mem. adv. com. Northeast Iowa Tech. Inst. Accounting Program, Calmar, 1978-79. Mem. Waukon Jaycees. Republican. Roman Catholic. Avocations: softball; basketball. Home: 21 2nd Ave SE Waukon IA 52172 Office: Leadfree Enterprises Inc Elon Rd Waukon IA 52172

MARTIN, JERRY, III, university administrator; b. Pitts., July 26, 1942; s. Jerry and Jean (Quash) M.; m. Rita C. Lane, Feb. 28, 1964 (div. Aug. 1969); children—Danielle Renee, Trent Otis; m. Carol Moore, Mar. 27, 1972; children—Lea-Jeanne, Kara Faithe. A.A., Kennedy-King Coll., 1970; B.S., Chgo. State U., 1972; M.A., Governors State U., 1976. Salesman, Sci. Research Assocs., Chgo., 1973-80, Prescription Learning Corp., Chgo., 1980-81; tchr. Chgo. Bd. Edn., 1980-82; tchr. City Colls. of Chgo., 1980-82, admistr., 1982—. Chgo. State U. scholar, 1970; mem. 100% Club Sci. Research Assocs., 1978. Mem. Nat. Alliance Black Sch. Educators. Democrat. Presbyterian.

MARTIN, JOHN AUGUSTINE, III, physical education educator, athletic director; b. Boston, Dec. 9, 1948; s. John Augustine and Jean (Murphy) M.; m. JoAnn Bamford, June 20, 1980; 1 child, Ryan Patrick. B.S., Springfield Coll. (Mass), 1971; M.A., Ohio State U., 1974, Ph.D., 1979. Dir. sports Munich YMCA, (Fed. Republic Germany), 1971-73; athletic dir. Am. Sch., Dusseldorf, Fed. Republic Germany, 1974-76; prof. Ohio Wesleyan U., Delaware, 1978—, athletic dir., chmn. phys. edn., 1978—. Mem. exec. bd. Parks and Recreation Dept., Delaware, 1982—. Named Coach of Yr., Midwest Lacrosse Assn., 1977-79; Outstanding Young Man, Am. Jaycees, 1981; Coach of Yr.-soccer Nat. Soccer Coaches, 1981, 82, 83. Mem. Nat. Soccer Coaches (exec. bd. 1977), Nat. Lacrosse Coaches (exec. bd.). Avocations: Reading, travel. Home: 101 Montrose Delaware OH 43015 Office: Edwards Gym Sandusky St Delaware OH 43015

MARTIN, JOHN BRUCE, chemical engineer; b. Auburn, Ala., Feb. 2, 1922; s. Herbert Marshall and Lannie (Steadham) M.; m. Mildred Jane Foster, Aug. 7, 1943 (dec. Nov. 1960); children—Shirlie Martin Briggs, John Bruce; m. Phyllis Barbara Rodgers, June 25, 1963; children—Richard Kipp. B.S., Ala. Poly. Inst., 1943; M.Sc., Ohio State U., 1947, Ph.D., 1949. Registered profl. engr., Ohio. With Procter & Gamble Co., Cin., 1949-82, coordinator orgn. devel., research and devel., 1967-77, mgr. indsl. chem. market research, 1977-82; sr. assoc. Indumar, Inc., Cin., 1982—, dir., 1984—; adj. assoc. prof. Auburn U., 1983—; lectr. U. Cin., 1982—. Served with AUS, 1943-46. Decorated Air Medal, Bronze Star with oak leaf cluster. Recipient Disting. Alumnus award Coll. Engring. Ohio State U., 1970, Disting. Engr. award Tech. Socs. Council Cin., 1982. Fellow Am. Inst. Chem. Engrs. (Chem. Engr. of Yr., Ohio Valley 1971; dir. 1968-70, vice chmn. mktg. div. 1983-84, chmn. 1985); Engring. Soc. Cin. (pres. 1972-73), Tech. and Sci. Socs. Cin. (pres. 1972-73), Chem. Mktg. Research Assn., Am. Soc. Engring. Edn., Am. Chem. Soc., Sigma Xi, Tau Beta Pi, Phi Kappa Phi, Phi Lambda Upsilon. Republican. Mem. Disciples of Christ Ch. Club: Clifton Track. Patentee in field; contbr. articles to profl. jours. Home: 644 Doepke Ln Cincinnati OH 45231 Office: 4164 Crossgate Dr Cincinnati OH 45333

MARTIN, JOHN WILLIAM, educator, antiquarian bookseller; b. Palo Alto, Calif., Feb. 21, 1946; s. Norman J. and Betty G. (Fawcett) M.; m. Diane Elizabeth Hirsch, Dec. 29, 1968; children—Molly E., Jamie S. B.A., U. Minn., 1968; M.A., U. Oreg., 1972, D.A. in English, 1973. Instr., U. Oreg., Eugene, 1972; mem. faculty Moraine Valley Coll., Palos Hills, Ill., 1972—, prof., 1985—; owner/mgr. John Wm. Martin--Bookseller, La Grange, Ill., 1973—; tech. writing cons., 1972—; lit. property appraiser, 1973—. Co-author: Township Trustees, 1980. Contbr. articles to profl. jours. Trustee LaGrange Pub. Library Bd., 1982—. Mem. Bibliog. Soc. Am., William Morris Soc., Pvt. Libraries Assn., MLA. Unitarian. Avocations: travel; hiking. Office: 437 S 7th Ave LaGrange IL 60525

MARTIN, JOSEPH CLAIR, medical clinic administrator; b. Huron, S.D., Dec. 10, 1939; s. Clair Francis and Mary Alice (Brinkman) M.; m. Sandra Kathleen Stadheim, Apr. 1, 1967; children—Christine Mary, Nicholas Joseph. B.A., Huron Coll., 1961; M.B.A., U. S.D., 1963. Tchr., Wash. and S.D., 1961-62, 64-66; adminstr. Mayo Clinic, Rochester, Minn., 1967—. Republican. Roman Catholic. Home: 2515 4th Ave NW Rochester MN 55901 Office: Mayo Clinic 200 SW 1st Ave Rochester MN 55905

MARTIN, KENNETH WAYNE, state transportation administrator; b. Carmi, Ill., Mar. 4, 1955; s. Lawrence Eugene and Ina Joyce (Pollard) M.; m. Jane Maria Kettelkamp, Feb. 25, 1978; 1 child, Joshua Paul. B.A. with honors, Eastern Ill. U., 1977; M.A., U. Ill., 1983. Project mgr. Ill. Dept. Transp., Springfield, 1978-81, team leader, 1984—. Mem. cons. team U. Ill., Champaign., 1983; deacon, bd. dirs. Southside Christian Ch., Springfield, 1980-81; chmn. evangelism dept. Webber St. Ch. of Christ, Urbana, Ill., 1983-84. Avocations: woodworking, running, basketball, camping, racquetball. Office: Ill Dept Transp 2300 S Dirksen Pkwy Springfield IL 62764

MARTIN, LAWRENCE, physician, educator; b. Savannah, Ga., Sept. 12, 1943; m. Ruth S. Martin, July 4, 1970; children—Joanna, Rachel, Amy. M.D. U. Fla., 1969. Diplomate Am. Bd. Internal Medicine, Am. Bd. Pulmonary Disease. Intern Kings County Hosp. Downstate Med. Ctr., Bklyn., 1969-70. resident in medicine, 1970-71; resident Albert Einstein Coll. Medicine, Bronx, N.Y., 1973-74, fellow in pulmonary disease, 1974-76; chief pulmonary div. Mt. Sinai Med. Ctr., Cleve., 1976—; assoc. prof. medicine Case Western Res. U. Sch. Medicine, Cleve., 1976—. Author: Breathe Easy: A Guide to Lung and Respiratory Diseases for Patients and Their Families, 1984. Recipient Goodman Teaching award Mt. Sinai Med. Ctr., 1983. Fellow ACP, Am. Coll. Chest Physicians; mem. Am. Thoracic Soc. Home: 3980 E Meadow Ln Orange Village OH 44122 Office: Pulmonary Div Mt Sinai Med Center Cleveland OH 44106

MARTIN, LEE EDWIN, architect, state official; b. Lakewood, Ohio, Sept. 19, 1948; s. Ira Paige and Helen P. (Livingston) M.; m. Charlene Ann Hunt, Nov. 30, 1968; 1 child, Jeffrey Allen. Student Capital U., 1966-67; B.S. in Architecture, Ohio State U., 1975. Cert. energy auditor. Designer/draftsman J.E. Bletzacker, Architect, Lancaster, Ohio, 1975-76, Crooks & George, Architects, Inc., Columbus, Ohio, 1976-78; project mgr. Jane Shapiro, Architect, Columbus, 1978; intern architect Kellam & Smith, Columbus, 1978-79; design technician Office of State Architect and Engr., Columbus, 1979-80, asst. chief project rep., 1980-82, acting chief project control sect., 1982-83, state architect, 1983-85. Pres., Tribute to Vietnam Vets., Inc., Columbus, 1984; bd. dirs. Friends of Gov.'s Residence, Columbus, 1984; mem. Maple Grove United Methodist Ch., Columbus; rep. Columbus PTA Council. Served with USAF, 1968-72. Mem. AIA (contbg. editor chpt. newsletter), VFW. Club: Governor's (Columbus). Avocations: architectural photography; scuba diving. Home: 718 E Weisheimer Rd Columbus OH 43214 Office: 4401 Indianaola Ave Columbus OH 43214

MARTIN, LYNN MORLEY, congresswoman; b. Chgo., Dec. 26, 1939; d. Lawrence William and Helen (Hall) Morley; B.A., U. Ill., 1960. Tchr. pub. schs., DuPage-Winnebago County, 1963-69; mem. Winnebago County Bd., 1972-76; mem. Ill. Ho. of Reps., 1976-78, Ill. Senate, 1978-80; mem. 97th-98th congresses from Ill. Mem. Phi Beta Kappa. Republican. Office: 416 E State St Rockford IL 61104

MARTIN, MARY LENORE, history educator, nun; b. Butte, Mont., Nov. 15, 1925; d. William Henry and Mary Ann (Sullivan) M. B.A. cum laude; St. Mary Coll., Leavenworth, Kans., 1947, M.S. in Edn., 1958; M.A.T., St. Louis U., 1966, D.A., U. Miami, 1982. Joined Order Sisters of Charity, Leavenworth, 1947, mem. governing body gen. chpt., 1968, 70, mem. gen. forum, 1976-78; tchr. high sch., Mont., Kans., Mo., 1949-59; prin. Billings Central High Sch., Mont., 1959-66; faculty dept. history St. Mary Coll., Leavenworth, 1969—, prof., 1983—, chmn. dept., 1981—; cons. St. Pius X High Sch., Kansas City, Mo., 1969-75. Author: (course of study) Introduction to International Affairs, 1983. Sec., Leavenworth Hist. Soc., 1979—. Named Outstanding Educator, St. Mary Coll., 1975; Danforth assoc., 1976. Mem. Orgn. Am. Historians, Am. Hist. Assn., Kans. Hist. Assn., Acad. Polit. Sci., Phi Alpha Theta, Delta Epsilon Sigma, Kappa Gamma Phi. Avocations: music; reading; sewing; craft activities. Home and Office: Dept History Saint Mary Coll 4100 S 4th St Trafficway Leavenworth KS 66048

MARTIN, PAUL WILLIAM, JR., dentist, volunteer fire chief; b. Cleve., Aug. 13, 1934; s. Paul William and Ethel (Geren) M.; m. Susan Marie Nosker, Dec. 11, 1975; children—Mark Wallace, Lynn Roberta, Kurt William. B.A. in History, Coll. Wooster, 1956; D.D.S., Western Res. U., 1960; A.A.S. in Fire Sci. Tech., U. Akron, 1978. Lic. dentist, Ohio; cert. emergency med. technician, fire safety insp., Ohio. Gen. practice dentistry, Hudson, Ohio, 1960—; vol. firefighter Hudson Fire Dept., 1962-71, lt., 1971-75, capt., 1975-77, asst. chief, 1977-82, chief, 1982—; fire sci. advisor U. Akron, Ohio, 1979—. Mem. charter rev. com. Village of Hudson, 1971, 81. Served to capt. with USNR, 1961-82. Recipient Outstanding Young Men of Am. award, Hudson, 1970, Fireman of Yr. award Hudson Fire Dept., 1972, Community Service award Hudson Jaycees, 1982; fellow Acad. Gen. Dentistry Am. Dental Assn., 1981. Fellow Acad. Gen. Dentistry; mem. ADA, Ohio Dental Soc., Cleve. Dental Soc., Am. Soc. Dentistry for Children, Ohio Fire Chiefs Assn. (pres. 1980-81, asst. sec., treas. 1982—). Republican. Lodges: Masons, Rotary (pres. 1967-68). Avocations: photography; hiking; golfing; fishing. Home: 20 Owen Brown St Hudson OH 44236 Office: 201 N Main St Hudson OH 44236

MARTIN, RAYMOND BRUCE, plumbing equipment manufacturing company executive; b. N.Y.C., Oct. 23, 1934; s. Raymond M. and Margaret (Lennon) M.; m. Suzanne Ruth Longpre, Sept. 3, 1960; 1 son, Christopher Haines. A.B., Villanova U., 1956. With Corning Glass Works (N.Y.), 1956-68, nat. plumbing sales mgr., 1966-68; v.p. mktg. Briggs Mfg. Co., Warren, Mich., 1968-69, v.p., gen. mgr. plumbing fixture div., 1969-72; pres., chief exec. officer Water Control Internat. Inc., Troy, Mich., 1972—; dir. Internat. Tech. Corp., Cash Control Products Inc. Served with AUS, 1957-58. Mem. Am. Soc. Plumbing Engrs., Plumbing Mfrs. Inst. (chmn. HUD Task Group 1981-82, chmn. communications com. 1983—), Am. Nat. Standards Inst., Am. Soc. Sanitary Engrs., ASME (panel 19), Republican. Roman Catholic (trustee 1982—). Clubs: Orchard Lake Country, L'Arbre Croche. Patentee in field. Office: 2820-224 W Maple Rd Troy MI 48084

MARTIN, RICHARD EDWARD, educational administrator; b. Paris, Ill., July 28, 1941; s. Alwyn Hamilton and Mabel Florence (Rhoads) M.; m. Elaine Anne Schultz, Apr. 7, 1963; children—Michelle Anne, Cynthia Lynne, Chandra Sue, Richard Edward. B.A., Ind. Central Coll., 1963; M.A., No. Ill. U., 1966; Ph.D., Purdue U., 1972. Research asst. Nat. Opinion Research Ctr., Chgo., 1964-65; vis. lectr. Ind. U., Gary, 1965; from instr. to prof. sociology Butler U., Indpls., 1965—, dean extended programs, 1982—; research cons. Child Birth Edn., Indpls., 1976-78, Ctr. Law Related Edn., Indpls., 1973-76. Mem. Am. Sociol. Assn., North Central Sociol. Assn., So. Sociol. Soc., Assn. Continuing Higher Edn., Ind. Council Continuing Edn. (chmn. 1984—). Home: 1418 Sandi Dr Indianapolis IN 46260 Office: Butler U 4600 Sunset Ave Indianapolis IN 46208

MARTIN, RICHARD LYNN, sales executive; b. Harriman, Tenn., Oct. 18, 1943; s. Harlan Henry and Mary Grace (Morgan) M.; m. Linda Bernadette Cox, Oct. 28, 1967; children—Sidney Keith, Caroline Bernadette. Student, Oakland Community Coll., 1972. Lab asst. Stover, Inc., Bloomfield Hills, Mich., 1967-68; machinist Lebow Assocs., Troy, Mich., 1968-69, service technician, 1969-70, service mgr., 1971-72, supr. service and calibration, 1972-74, sales engr., 1975-76, nat. sales mgr., 1977; sales engr. MTS Systems, Bloomfield Hills, 1977-81, area sales mgr. prodn. line group, 1982, regional sales mgr. machine controlls div., 1983—. Author service manual. Served with USN, 1962-67. Mem. Am. Motorcycle Assn., Soc. Mfg. Engrs., Soc. Exptl. Stress Analysis (sec. 1981-82). Republican. Club: Bunnyrun Country. Avocations: woodworking, metalworking, motorcycle mechanics, motorcycle racing. Home: 740 Camilla St Lake Orion MI 48035 Office: MTS Systems Corp 2600 Telegraph St Suite 140 Bloomfield Hills MI 48103

MARTIN, ROBERT ALLEN, industrialist; b. Alburnett, Iowa, Jan. 13, 1939; s. Robert William and Evelyn Elaine (Helbig) M.; B.A., B.S. in Elec. Engring., U. Iowa, 1962; M.B.A., Northwestern U., 1964; m. Margaret Ann Cunningham, Dec. 26, 1964; children—Robert William, William Allen. With Motorola Communications and Electronics Chgo., 1962-65, mgr. tech. computer ops., 1964-65; with Syntronic Instruments, Inc., Addison, Ill., 1964-68, v.p. engring., dir. operations, 1967-68; founder, pres., chmn. bd. Nationwide Electronic Systems, Inc., Streamwood, Ill., 1968—, chief exec. com., 1970—; founder, chmn. bd. Martin's Marine, Door County, Wis., 1970—; founder, chmn. bd. Engring. Devel. Corp., Chgo., 1972-83; founder, chmn. bd., pres. Internat. Investments, Inc., Chgo., 1973—; founder, pres., chmn. bd. Martin Communication Corp., Dallas, 1974—; founder, pres., chmn. bd. Martin Devel. Corp., Chgo., 1974—; founder, pres., chmn. bd. Martin Farms, Cedar Rapids, Iowa, 1975—. Committeeman Republican Party, DuPage County, Ill., 1970-74; active Boy Scouts Am., 1963—; mem. adv. bd., fin. bd. Ill. Retired Folks Found., 1970-74; dir. Ill. Found. Boys Clubs, 1974—; pres. Sr. Citizens Help Group, 1971-73, dir., 1973—; founder, exec. dir. Equipment for the Blind Found., 1972. Recipient numerous civic, shooting and rifleman, bus. awards latest including Achievement award Advt. Assn. Am., 1974, Gold medal Assn. Commerce and Industry, 1975, Grand Entrepreneur Gold medal Am. Assn. Entreprenuers, 1975, White Hat award Mchts. Council Cedar Rapids, 1975, Pub. Service award Ill. Indsl. Assn., 1976. Mem. IEEE (past chmn. regional sect.), Am. Vacuum Soc., Internat. Physics Soc., Instrument Soc. Am., Fin. Execs. Assn., Am. Mgmt. Assn. (mem. adv. bd.), Interstate Bus. Assn. (trustee), Great Lakes Assn. (dir.), and others. Clubs: Ephraim (Wis.) Yacht, Beaver Island Yacht, Chgo. Yacht, Lions, Barrington Archery and Gun. Patentee in field. Author: The Best There Is; No Second Fastest Gunfighters; Real Truth in Accounting; There Is No Such Thing as a Good Loser; Who's Watching the Watchers?; Real Research or Repeat?; The Young Are Intelligent, The Old Are Experienced. Contbr. articles to jours., mags. Office: 1536 Brady Pkwy Streamwood IL 60103

MARTIN, SANDY JEAN, advertising executive; b. St. Louis, Jan. 29, 1949; d. Frank John and Vivian Florine (Rathbone) M.; B.S., U. Mo., 1969; postgrad. Meramac Coll., 1969-70. Music dir., program dir., producer Sta.-KMOX, St. Louis, 1965-70; sta. mgr. Sta. KGRV/KKSS, St. Louis, 1970-75; gen. mgr., dir. ops. Sta.-KUDL-AM-FM, Kansas City, Mo., 1975-77; ptnr., v.p. Pasternak-Higbee Advt., Kansas City, Mo., 1977-81; sr. account supr. Bernstein-Rein Advt., 1983—. Bd. dirs. Theatre League Assn., Kansas City, Lyric Opera, Kansas City, Cystic Fibrosis, Kansas City, Am. Film Inst. Recipient Outstanding Achievement award Cystic Fibrosis Found., 1980, Heart Assn., 1981; Service award Cystic Fibrosis, 1980, 81; Alsac Hnor award St. Jude Hosp., 1971. Mem. Am. Women in Radio and TV (Hall of Fame 1983; (dir. 1977-80, Account Exec. of Yr. 1980, 81), Kansas City Advt. Club, St. Louis Advt. Club, Media Exchange, Am. Mktg. Assn., Am. Notary Assn., Internat. Platform Assn., Am. Bus. Women Assn., Fashion Group, Am. Soc. Notaries, Mo. Broadcasters Assn., Kansas City C. of C. Jewish. Office: 7720 Ward Pkwy Kansas City MO 64114

MARTIN, STEPHEN DAVID, lawyer; b. Paducah, Ky., May 14, 1947; s. Guy Francis and Hazel O. (Davis) M.; m. Deborah Sue Brown, Aug. 2, 1974; 1 child, Gary Alan. B.A., Rutgers U., 1969; J.D., Capital U., 1973. Bar: Ohio 1974. Personnel supr. Janitrol, Columbus, Ohio, 1969-72; labor relations supr. Celanese Plastics, Columbus, 1972-74; govt. services atty. Ohio Edn. Assn., Columbus, 1974-76; ptnr. firm Martin, Eichenberger & Baxter, Columbus, 1976—. Mem. ABA, Nat. Assn. Tchr. Attys., Ohio Bar Assn., Ohio Council Sch. Bd. Attys., Columbus Bar Assn. Democrat. Lodge: Kiwanis. Home: 4785 Bayhill Dr Powell OH 43065 Office: Martin Eichenberger & Baxter 6641 N High St Worthington OH 43085

MARTIN, STEVEN DEAN, civic worker; b. Richmond, Ind., Jan. 2, 1952; s. Howard and Ruth Ellen (Wiles) M.; m. Lois Iva Lindsey, Mar. 3, 1973. Grad. high sch., Centerville, Ind. Bd. dirs., past pres. Wayne County Easter Seal Soc., Richmond, 1976—; bd. dirs. Ind. State Easter Seal Soc., Indpls., 1979—; pres., bd. dirs. Citizens Against Annexation, Richmond, 1979—; bd. dirs. Community Council on Disability Awareness, Richmond, 1984—; treas. Elmer Toschlog for Wayne County Commr., Richmond, 1984. Democrat. Methodist. Avocations: baseball, basketball, football, card and board games. Home: 3229 College Corner Rd Richmond IN 47374

MARTIN, TERRY JEFFREY, electronics manufacturing company executive; b. Stevens Point, Wis., Jan. 5, 1947; s. Frederick Dickinson and Dorothy Fern (Kinney) M.; m. Carol Anne Sprada, Dec. 22, 1966; children—Deanna Rae, Vikki Carol. A.A. in Electronics, U.S. Army, 1967. Gen. foreman GTE Automotive Electronics Co., Huntsville, Ala., 1977-80; mgr. thick film-hybrid prodn. GTE Communications Systems, Genoa, Ill., 1980-82, mgr. mfg. ops., 1982-83, mgr. Genoa ops., 1983-84, mgr. br. plant ops., 1984—, also staff mfg. electronics div., 1980—. Served with U.S. Army, 1966-69, Vietnam. Decorated Commendation medal. Mem. Internat. Soc. Hybrid Microelectronics, Am. Prodn. Inventory Control Soc. Republican. Roman Catholic. Avocations: guitar; softball; tennis; skiing. Home: 6310 Dornock St Caledonia IL 61011 Office: GTE Communications Systems 333 E 1st St Genoa IL 60135

MARTIN, THOMAS JOHN, banker; b. Chgo., July 3, 1925; s. John and Rose (Barranco) M.; m. Carol Lorraine Klima, June 30, 1951; children—John Charles, Lawrence Thomas, Sylvia Rose, Donald, Marjorie, Celeste. Student Wright Jr. Coll., 1946; B.A., Beloit Coll., 1950; postgrad. Northwestern U., 1950; standard diploma Am. Savs. and Loan Inst.-Chgo., 1958, grad. diploma, 1959, grad. sch. diploma and key, 1967. Agt., Fidelity Mut. Life Ins. Co., Phila., Chgo., 1950-51; sec., treas., dir. Klima Ins. Agy., Inc. (Celkay Enterprises Inc.), North Riverside, Ill., 1951—; with Clyde Savs. & Loan Assn., 1951—, v.p., 1964-71, sr. v.p., 1971-74, exec. v.p., dir., 1974—; pres., dir. Clyde Service Corp., 1971—. Mem. gen. occupation adv. com. Morton Coll., Cicero, 1973—. Served with Signal Corps, AUS, 1943-46. Mem. Soc. Real Estate Appraisers, Czechoslovak Savs. and Loan Inst., Am. Savs. and Loan Inst., Ill. Savs. and Loan League (dir. 1978—), Ill. League Savs. Instns. (chmn. 1984—), Savs. Instns. Mktg. Soc. Am., Inst. Fin. Edn., Cermak Rd. Bus. Assn. Republican. Roman Catholic. Home: 4721 Howard Ave Western Springs IL 60558 Office: Clyde Fed Savs & Loan Assn 7222 W Cermak Rd North Riverside IL 60546

MARTIN, WAYNE MALLOTT, lawyer, real estate company executive; b. Chgo., Jan. 9, 1950; B.A., Drake U., 1972; J.D., De Paul U., 1977; m. JoAnn Giordano, Mar. 1978; 1 son, Bradley. Bar: Ill. 1978. Loan officer Clyde Savs. & Loan Assn., Chgo., 1972-75, Am. Nat. Bank, Chgo., 1976-77; sales dir., atty., financing Inland Real Estate Corp., Chgo., Oak Brook, then Palatine, Ill., 1977-83; pres. Inland Property Sales, Inc., Palatine, 1983-84, Oak Brook, Ill., 1984—. Mem. ABA, Ill., Chgo. bar assns., Nat., Ill., N.W. Suburban assns. realtors, Northside Bd. Realtors, Westside Bd. Realtors (dir. 1983-84, pres. 1984—). Home: 1618 RFD Picardy Ct Long Grove IL 60047 Office: Inland Property Sales Inc 2100 Clearwater Dr Oak Brook IL 60521

MARTIN, WESLEY GEORGE, electrical engineer; b. Chgo., Apr. 15, 1946; s. Chester W. and Marie L. (Seifarth) M.; m. Margaret Rose Kowach, Aug. 17, 1968; children—Patrick, Christopher. B.S., Milw. Sch. Engring., 1969; cert. Alexander Hamilton Inst., N.Y.C., 1976. Registered profl. engr., Ill., Ind., Wis. Elec. engr. and estimator The Austin Co., Des Plaines, Ill., 1969-78; elec. estimator Skidmore, Owings & Merrill, Chgo., 1978-83; elec. engr. Holabird & Root, Chgo., 1983—; owner W.G. Martin & Assocs., cons., Palatine, Ill., 1978—. Contbr. articles to profl. jours. Democratic precinct capt., Palatine, 1979-82. Recipient award of Merit, Chgo. Lighting Inst., 1981, 82, 83. Mem. Nat. Soc. Profl. Engrs., Ill. Soc. Profl. Engrs., Nat. Eagle Scout Assn. Roman Catholic. Home: 918 W Colfax St Palatine IL 60067 Office: Holabird & Root 300 W Adams St Chicago IL 60606

MARTIN, WILFRED SAMUEL, management consultant; b. Adamsville, Pa., June 11, 1910; s. Albert W. and Elizabeth (Porter) M.; B.S., Iowa State U., 1930; M.S., U. Cin., 1938; m. Elizabeth Myers, July 9, 1938; children—Peter, Judith (Mrs. Peter Kleinman), Nancy (Mrs. Richard Foss), Paula (Mrs. Dale Birdsell). Chem. engr. process devel. dept. Procter & Gamble Co., Cin., 1930-50, mgr. drug products mfg., 1950-51, asso. dir. chem. div., 1952-53, dir. product devel., soap products div., 1953-63, mgr. mfg. and products devel. Food Products div., 1963-71, sr. dir. research and devel., 1971-75; mgmt. cons., 1975—. Mem. Wyoming (Ohio) Bd. Edn., 1961-69, pres., 1965-68. Bd. dirs. Indsl. Research Inst., 1964-68, v.p., 1968-69, pres., 1970-71; chmn. trustee Ohio Presbyn. Homes, Columbus, Ohio, 1959-69, 73-77; vice chmn. bd. trustees Pikeville (Ky.) Coll., 1973-76, 80—, chmn. bd. trustees, 1976-78, 83-84, mem., 1980-84. Adv. council Clarkson Coll., Potsdam, N.Y., 1975-81. Fellow AAAS; mem. Am. Chem. Soc., Am. Inst. Chem. Engrs., Soc. Chem. Industry, Am. Oil Chemist Soc., Engring. Soc. Cin. (dir. 1972-75), N.Y. Acad. Scis., Am. Mgmt. Assn. (research devel. council 1974-81), Soc. Research Adminstrs. Club: Wyoming Golf (Cin.). Home: 504 Hickory Hill Ln Cincinnati OH 45215

MARTIN, WILLIAM BRYAN, college president, clergyman, lawyer; b. Lexington, Ky., Apr. 11, 1938; s. William Stone Martin and Alice Bryan (Spiers) O'Connell; m. Marilyn Jenrose Morgan, June 15, 1962 (div. 1972); 1 child, Chawley Morgan; m. Mary Ellen Matson, Aug. 11, 1973; children—Matson Bryan, Evan Andrew. A.B., Transylvania U., 1960; J.D., U. Ky., 1964; LL.M., Georgetown U., 1965; M.Div., Candler Sch. Theology, Emory U., 1979. Bar: Ky., D.C.; ordained to ministry Christian Ch. (Disciples of Christ). Pub. defender Georgetown U. Law Ctr., Washington, 1964-65; asst. U.S. atty. Western Dist. Ky., Louisville, 1965-67; assoc. McElwain, Denning, Clarke & Winstead, Louisville, 1967-69; asst. atty. gen. Commonwealth of Ky., Frankfort, 1969-71; prof. law Sch. Law U. Louisville, 1971-81; dean Sch. Law Oklahoma City U., 1981-83; pres. Franklin Coll. of Ind., 1983—. Contbr. articles to legal publs. Candidate Democratic nomination county exec. Jefferson County, Ky., Louisville, 1969. Home: 253 S Forsythe Franklin IN 46131 Office: President's Office Franklin Coll Franklin IN 46131

MARTIN, WILLIAM COURTNEY, III, lawyer; b. Gallipolis, Ohio, Sept. 25, 1947; s. William Courtney and Elizabeth Rose (Lee) M.; m. Agnes Kathryn Ice, May 28, 1969; 1 child, John Ice. B.A. summa cum laude, Ohio State U., 1969, B.S. in Edn. summa cum laude, 1969; J.D. cum laude, Harvard U., 1974. Bar: Ohio 1974. Assoc. Smith & Schnacke, Dayton, Ohio, 1974-78; sole practice, Jackson, Ohio, 1978—; dir. law City of Jackson, 1980—. Author: Foul Deeds Will Rise, Citizens Against Hazardous Waste Disposal in Ohio, 1985. Pres. Voting Ohioans Initiating Clean Environment, Columbus, Ohio, 1984—; trustee Buckeye Community Services Inc., Jackson, 1984, Oak Hill Community Med. Ctr., Oak Hill, Ohio, 1984—, Jackson County Alcohol Program, 1984—. Served with U.S. Army, 1969-71. Recipient, Environ. Recognition award Ohio Environ. Council, 1984. Republican. Office: William C Martin PO Box 926 259 Main St Jackson OH 45640

MARTIN, WILLIAM J., judge; b. Canton, Ohio, Feb. 19, 1947; s. John William and Sarah Elizabeth (Nichols) M.; m. Kristine S. Knudson, Aug. 16, 1969 (div. Nov. 1974); m. Barbara Jean Dennis, June 21, 1975; 1 child, Erin Beth; 3 stepchildren. B.A., Ohio State U. 1969; J.D., Case-Western Res. U., 1972. Bar: Ohio, U.S. Dist. Ct. (no. dist.) Ohio, U.S. Supreme Ct. Ptnr. Saltsman, Heflin & Martin, Carrollton, Ohio, 1972-83; asst. prosecutor Carroll County, Carrollton, 1973-81; judge Common Pleas Ct., Carrollton, 1983—; adj. lectr. law U. Akron, Ohio, 1985—; lectr. Minerva Police Acad., Ohio, 1984—. Law dir. Village Dellroy, Ohio, 1980-83; deputy sheriff (reserve) Carroll County, Carrollton, 1975-83; mem. Carroll County Airport Auth., Carrollton, 1980-83, Deford Scholarship Selection com., Carrollton, 1979-82. Recipient Excellent Jud. Service award Ohio Supreme Ct., 1983. Mem. Ohio State Bar Assn., Ohio Common Pleas Judges' Assn., Ohio Jud. Conf., Carroll County Bar Assn. (v.p. 1978-83). Republican. Presbyterian. Avocation: military and world history. Office: Common Pleas Court Carroll County Courthouse Carrollton OH 44615

MARTIN, WILLIAM THOMAS, ophthalmologist; b. Warsaw, Ohio, Feb. 18, 1936; s. John Thomas and Myra (Rauenzahn) M.; m. Mildred Louise Decker, June 20, 1965; children—John Thomas, Michael Thomas. B.S. in Mech. Engring., Case Inst. Tech., 1959; M.D., Ohio State U., 1965. Diplomate Am. Bd. Ophthalmology. Intern, Riverside Meth. Hosp., Columbus, Ohio; resident Ohio State U. Hosps.; practice medicine, specializing in ophthalmology, Massillon, Ohio, 1971—. Served to capt. AUS, 1966-68. Fellow ACS; mem. Stark County Med. Soc. Club: Rotary. Avocations: Golfing; bowling; skiing. Home: 2113 Darby Dr NW Massillon OH 44646 Office: 845 8th St NE Massillon OH 44646

MARTINAZZI, TONI, educational media specialist, consultant; b. Portland, Oreg., Apr. 27, 1936; d. Arthur Julius and Ann (Chapman) M.; m. Robert Eugene Leber, Nov. 6, 1954 (div. June 1970); children—Michael Jene, Donna Loyce Leber Conroy, Max Arthur, Rhonda Carol; m. 2d Joseph John Kinzig, March 2, 1984. B.A. in English, Portland State U., 1969, M.A. in Teaching, 1975; postgrad. in edn. Northeastern Ill. U., 1983. Cert. tchr., media specialist, Ill.. Head librarian Scappoose High Sch. (Oreg.), 1969-73; head media specialist Grant High Sch., Portland, Oreg., 1975-80; librarian, High Sch. Dist. 214, Ill., 1984-85; media specialist Dist. 62, Ill., 1985—; cons. ednl. media, Chgo., 1982—; chairperson charter task force Tualatin Pub. Library (Oreg.), 1976-77, 78-79, charter chairperson adv. bd., 1977-79. Reviewer media library and ednl. jours., 1975—. Recipient commendation City of Tualatin, 1978. Mem. Gregorians, Ill. Assn. for Media in Edn., ALA, Am. Assn. Sch. Librarians, Internat. Assn. Sch. Librarians, Nat. Trails Council, Appalachian Trail Council, Am. Hiking Soc. (transcontinental backpacker 1980-81). Republican. Roman Catholic. Club: Mazamas, Mountaineers. Home: 3802 N Seeley Ave Chicago IL 60618

MARTINEC, EMIL LOUIS, research administrator; b. Chgo., July 28, 1927; s. Emil James and Emily (Sebek) M.; m. Barbara Katherine Wolter, Nov. 6, 1954; children—Beatrice Emily, Emil John, James Edward. B.S. in M.E., IIT, Chgo., 1950; M.S. in M.E., U. Idaho, 1957; M.B.A. in Fin., Northwestern U., 1965; D.Sc. (hon.), Midwest Coll. Engring., Lombard (Ill.), 1973. Registered profl. engr., Ill.; cert. quality engr. Mech. engr. Standard Oil Co. of Ind., Whiting, 1952-55; mech. engr. Argonne (Ill.) Nat. Lab., 1955-65, asst. project mgr., 1965-70, div. mgr. quality assurance, 1970-73, asst. div. dir., 1973-79, dir. program adminstrn., 1979—; prof. Midwest Coll. Engring., Lombard, Ill., 1969—, v.p., 1982—, trustee, 1984—. Assoc. editor: Engineering Management International, Amsterdam, Netherlands, 1984—. Contbr. articles to profl. jours. Served with AUS, 1945-47. Fellow ASME (chmn. mgmt. div. 1980-81, chmn. bd. profl. devel. 1980, sect. chmn. 1965, 70); mem. Am. Soc. Quality Control, Am. Soc. Engring. Edn., Am. Soc. Engring. Mgmt. (treas. 1984—), North Central Assn. Colls. and Schs. (mem. accreditation team 1984). Club: Argonne Radio. Avocations: Woodworking, gardening, running. Home: 5725 Brookbank Rd Downers Grove IL 60516 Office: Argonne Nat Lab Bldg 205 9700 S Cass Ave Argonne IL 60439

MARTINEK, ROBERT GEORGE, clinical biochemist; b. Chgo., Nov. 25, 1919; s. Anton and Agnes (Simon) M.; m. Lydia Mildred Chab, July 12, 1952. B.S. in Pharmacy, U. Ill., 1941, B.S. in Medicine, 1945, M.S. in Biochemistry, 1943; Pharm.D., U. So. Calif., 1954. Research analytical chemist AMA, Chgo., 1950-55; sr. chemist Jead Johnson & Co., Evansville, Ind., 1955-56; sr. prof. asst. biochemistry Butterworth Hosp., Grand Rapids, Mich., 1956-58; clin. chemist Iowa Meth. Hosp., Des Moines, 1958-62, Chgo. Dept. Health, 1962-65; with Ill. Dept. Pub. Health, Chgo., 1965—, chief lab. improvement sect., 1965—. Editorial cons. Med. Electronics, Pitts., 1968—; lectr. Dept. Preventive Medicine Community Health, U. Ill., Chgo., 1969—; cons. Lab-Line Instruments, Inc., Melrose Park, Ill., 1971—, mem. bd. dirs., 1973—. Author: Technical Characteristics of Clinical Laboratory Instruments, 1967; MED Equipment Buyers Guide, 1974, Practical Mathematics for Clinical Laboratory Personnel: Home Study Guide, 1980, 3d edit., 1984. Contbr. articles to profl. publs. Served to 1st lt. U.S. Army, 1951-52. Recipient Ebert award U. Ill. Coll. Pharmacy, 1941; Pub. Health Service award Ill. Assn. Clin. Labs., Chgo., 1970. Mem. AAAS, Am. Inst. Chemists, AMA, Am. Pharm. Assn., Nat. Geog. Soc., Am. Inst. Econ. Research, USPHS (scientist dir. 1980), Rho Chi, Sigma Xi, Phi Kappa Phi. Office: Ill Dept Pub Health Labs 2121 W Taylor St Chicago IL 60612

MARTINSEN, BLAINE LEE, financial manager, administrator; b. Salt Lake City, Oct. 4, 1937; s. Henry Wilford and Aslaug Marie (Samuelsen) M.; m. Dianne Woodruff, June 4, 1966; children—Rebeccah, Matthew, Daniel, Jonathon, Steven. B.S. in Acctg., Brigham Young U., 1967; M.B.A., Syracuse U., 1984. Sr. acct. Fitzsimmons Army Med. Ctr., Aurora, Colo., 1974-76; jr. auditor Tooele Depot, Utah, 1976-78; sr. auditor Hawthorne Army Ammunition Plant, Nev., 1978-79; chief internal rev., Ft. Lewis, Wash., 1979-83; fin. mgr. Ft. Sheridan, Ill., 1984—. Active Boy Scouts Am., 1984-85. Served to capt. USAR, 1978—. Recipient Outstanding Performance award, Ft. Lewis, 1980, 82, Fitzsimmons Army Med. Ctr., 1976. Mem. Am. Soc. Mil. Comptrollers, Inst. Internal Auditors (bd. dirs. 1980-83). Republican. Mormon. Avocations: woodworking, fishing. Home: 2426 Highland Circle Lindenhurst IL 60046 Office: Fin Mgmt Div DCSRM 4th US Army Fort Sheridan IL 60037

MARTINSON, MELISSA SCHULTHEIS, statistician; b. Phila., June 2, 1956; d. Carl Francis and Ella Ruth (Katkowski) Schultheis; m. Noel Gordon Martinson, July 25, 1981; 1 child, Adam Redmond. B.A. in Biology, Swathmore Coll., Pa., 1978; M.S. in Stats., U. Minn., Mpls., 1983. Sr. biometrician Medtronic, Inc., Mpls., 1982—. Mem. Am. Statis. Assn. Home: 2420 179th Ave NW Andover MN 55304 Office: Medtronic Inc 6951 Old Central St Minneapolis MN

MARTINSON, TIMOTHY PAUL, oil company exeuctive; b. Beaver Dam, Wis., July 9, 1951; s. Virgil Oscar and Anabelle (Lawrence) M.; m. Lois Lynn Poppy, Nov. 30, 1974; children—Erik Paul, Krista Lynn, Nicholas Paul. B.S., U. Wis.-Parkside, Kenosha, 1973; M.S., U. Wis.-Milw., 1977. Lectr., U. Wis.-Milw., 1977; petroleum geologist Conoco, Houston, 1977-80; exploration mgr. Dart Oil & Gas Corp., Mason, Mich., 1980-84, No. Mich. Exploration Co., Jackson, 1984—. Mem. Mich. Basin Geol. Soc. (v.p. Lansing 1984-85, pres. 1985-86), Am. Assn. Petroleum Geologists, Soc. Exploration Geophysicists, Houston Geol. Soc. Avocations: golf; flying. Home: 1575 Menominee Dr Mason MI 48854 Office: Northern Michigan Exploration Co 1 Jackson Sq Jackson MI 49204

MARTINY, KIM REITH, advertising agency executive; b. Neenah, Wis., Jan. 13, 1940; s. Keith C. and Marion O. (Ott) M.; m. Lynn Anne Spicer, Mar. 6, 1971; children—Lauren, Ryan. B.S. in Bus. Adminstrn., Carroll Coll., 1962. Mgr. spl. accounts Container Corp. Am., Chgo., N.Y.C., Cin., 1966-75; account exec. Baer, Kemble & Spicer, Inc., Cin., 1975-78, pres., 1978-80; pres., chief exec. officer Martiny & Co., Inc., Cin., 1981—; dir. Telephone Directory Advt. Mem. Southwestern Ohio chpt. Arthritis Found., 1976—, pres., 1979-81. Recipient Nat. Vol. Service citation Ohio chpt. Arthritis Found., 1978. Mem. Mut. Advt. Agy. Network, Am. Assn. Advt. Agys. Republican. Episcopalian. Club: Bankers (Cin.). Home: 6750 N Clippinger Dr Indian Hill OH 45243 Office: Martiny & Co Inc 2260 Francis Ln Cincinnati OH 45206

MARTOSELLA, PETER A., JR., diversified holding company executive. Pres., dir. Baldwin-United Corp., Cin. Office: Baldwin-United Corp 1801 Gilbert Ave Cincinnati OH 45202*

MARTSCHINKE, JUDITH ANN, educator, consultant; b. Chgo., Jan. 31, 1947; d. John A. and Leta Moorhead; m. Charles E. Martschinke, July 12, 1969. Student Ill. State U., 1965-66; B.S., So. Ill. U., 1969; M.Ed., U. Ill., 1979. Teaching certs., adminstrv. cert., Ill. Tchr. math. Conrady Jr. High Sch., Dist. 117, Hickory Hills, Ill., 1969-79, 82-84, project coordinator Dist. 117, 1979-82; curriculum specialist Evanston Elem. Schs. Dist. 65, Ill., 1984—; adj. prof. math. edn. Nat. Coll. of Edn., Evanston, Ill., 1981—; workshop leader, cons. Kohl Tchr. Ctr., Wilmette, Ill.; cons. to elem. sch. dists., pub. co. Bldg. rep. Winston Village Homeowners Assn., 1974—. Mem. Nat. Council Tchrs. Math., Assn. for Supervision and Curriculum Devel., Ill. Women in Adminstrn., Ill. Council Tchrs. Math., Met. Math. Club of Chgo., Am. Legion Aux., Kappa Delta Pi. Home: PO Box 1183 Bolingbrook IL 60439 Office: Evanston Dist 65 1314 Ridge Ave Evanston IL 60201

MARTUCCIO, JOSEPH, lawyer; b. Youngstown, Ohio, Apr. 21, 1953; s. Vincent and Mary (Zeolla) M.; m. Pamela Ann Michaels, June 17, 1977; 1 child, Maria. B.A., Youngstown State U., 1976; J.D., Gonzaga U., 1980. Bar: Ohio 1981, U.S. Dist. Ct. (no. dist.) Ohio 1981, U.S. Ct. Appeals (6th cir.) 1982. Legal intern Spokane County Pub. Defender, 1979-80; law clk. Youngstown City Law Dept., 1980-81; staff atty. Stark County Pub. Defender, Canton, Ohio, 1981-83, asst. dir., 1983-84, pub. defender, dir., 1984—. Actor North Canton Playhouse, 1982, Players Guild, Canton, 1984. Recipient cert. of appreciation Victim/Witness div. Stark County Prosecutor Office, 1983. Mem. ABA, Ohio State Bar Assn., Stark County Bar Assn., Assn. Trial Lawyers Am. Democrat. Club: Eckankar. Home: 923 Spangler NE Canton OH 44714 Office: Stark County Pub Defender 903 Renkert Bldg 306 Market Ave N Canton OH 44702

MARTY, MYRON AUGUST, historian, educator; b. West Point, Nebr., Apr. 10, 1932; s. Emil Adolph and Anna Louise (Wuerdemann) M.; m. Shirley Lee Plunk, July 31, 1954; children—Miriam, Timothy, Elizabeth, Jason. B.S., Concordia Coll., River Forest, Ill., 1954; M.A. in Edn., Washington U., St. Louis, 1960; M.A., St. Louis U., 1965; Ph.D. in History, 1967. Tchr. Trinity Luth. Sch., Ft. Wayne, Ind., 1954-57, Luth. High Sch., St. Louis, 1957-65; prof. history, adminstr. Florissant Valley Community Coll., St. Louis, 1966-80; dep. dir. div. edn. programs NEH, Washington, 1980-84, acting dir., 1981, cons., 1977-80; dean Coll. Liberal Arts and Scis., prof. history Drake U., Des Moines, 1984—; mem. com. Coll. Bd. and Ednl. Testing Service, 1967-76; accreditation cons., evaluator N. Central Assn., 1969-80, mem. exec. bd. Commn. on Instns. Higher Edn., 1977-80. Author: Lutherans and Roman Catholicism: The Changing Conflict, 1968; Retracing Our Steps: Studies in Documents from the American Past, 1972; co-author: Nearby History: Exploring the Past Around You, 1982; Your Family History: A Handbook for Research and Writing, 1978. Book reviewer St. Louis Post-Dispatch, 1969—. Pres. Normandy Area Hist. Assn., St. Louis, 1979-80, NEH fellow, 1972-73; Newberry Library fellow, 1979. Mem. Orgn. Am. Historians (exec. bd. 1985—), Am. Hist Assn., Soc. History Edn., Am. Soc. Ch. History, Am. Assn. State and Local History, Nat. Trust for Hist. Preservation, Nat. Book Critics Circle, Community Coll. Humanities Assn., Phi Beta Kappa. Democrat. Lutheran. Home: 917 41st St West Des Moines IA 50265 Office: Coll Liberal Arts and Scis Drake U Des Moines IA 50265

MARTY, STEWART PARNELL, printing company executive, marketing consultant, photofinishing consultant; b. Bloomington, Ill., Sept. 21, 1950; s. Stewart Parnell and Aileen Alice (Tobiassen) M.; m. Karen Sue Hadley, Aug. 14, 1970 (div. July 1976); 1 child, Angela Marie; m. Karen Sue Hocking, Oct. 22, 1977; children—Jennifer Lynn, Elizabeth Nichole. Student Parkland Jr. Coll., Champaign, Ill., 1969, Ill. State U., Normal, 1970. Mgr. pro lab. div. Colorcraft Corp., Rockford, Ill., 1975-78; v.p., ptnr. Oaktree Advt. Agy., Bloomington, Ill., 1978-79; corp. v.p. Bruce-Green Advt. Ltd., Bloomington, 1979-83; account exec. Hagerty, Lockenvitz, Cinzkey & Assocs., Bloomington, 1983-84; pres. Kro-Mar Advt. div. Kro-Mar Industries, Normal, Ill., 1984—; pres. Wright Printing Co., Bloomington, Ill., mktg. and prodn. cons. for photofinishing firms. Bd. dirs. McLean County chpt. ARC, Ill., 1982—, mem. exec. com., 1983—, chmn. pub. relations com., 1982—; mem. cast The Am. Passion Play, Bloomington, 1981—. Recipient Spl. Service award ARC, 1983, 85. Mem. Soc. Photofinishing Engrs., (cert.), Photo Mktg. Assn., Comedy Writers Guild. Republican. Presbyterian. Club: Bloomington Ad. Lodge: Masons. Home: 23 Delaine Dr Normal IL 61761 Office: 1106 E Bell Bloomington IL 61701

MARTYNIAK, RAY, retail food executive; b. Detroit, Dec. 28, 1932; s. Ignatious and Jean (Paszkowski) M.; m. Rosemarie McClatcher, July 9, 1953 (div. July 1983); children—Raymond, Sherry, Dawn, Scott, Brent. Student Mich. State U., 1965-67, Henry Ford Community Coll., 1979-81, U. Mich.-Detroit, 1982. Mgr. meat Victor's Market, Allen Park, Mich., 1953-57; mgr. store Ray's Choice Meats, Allen Park, Mich., 1957-61; gen. mgr., owner Ray's Prime Meats, Inc., Trenton, Taylor, Mich., 1961—. Bd. dirs. Comml. Indsl. Devel. Com., Trenton, 1975. Mem. So. Wayne County C. of C. (pres. 1971), Associated Food Dealers (pres. 1974), Am. Assn. Meat Processors. Clubs: Downriver Racquet (Riverview), Vic Tanny Health (Woodhaven). Lodge: Trenton Rotary (pres. 1968-69). Avocations: running; tennis; water and snow skiing; travel; aerobics; volleyball; ice hockey. Office: Ray's Prime Meats Inc 3695 West Road Trenton MI 48183

MARTYN-NEMETH, PAMELA ANN, nurse; b. Chgo., Jan. 13, 1956; d. Leonard M. and Kyra V. (Hitz) M.; m. John P. Nemeth, Nov. 27, 1982. B.S., St. Xavier Coll., Chgo., 1976; M.S., U. Mich., 1982. R.N., Ill. Research assoc. U. Mich., Ann Arbor, 1980-81; mem. clin. faculty Northwestern U., Evanston, Ill., 1982-84; clin. specialist Northwestern Meml. Hosp., Chgo., 1982—; speaker to nursing orgns., Chgo., Dallas, Los Angeles, 1982—. Mem. Am. Nurses Assn., Am. Soc. Parental and Enteral Nutrition, Sigma Theta Tau.

MARTZ, FREDIC ALLEN, research animal scientist, nutrition educator; b. Whitley County, Ind., May 24, 1935; s. Joseph Clemont and Dora Belle (Barnes) M.; m. Donna Joan Wilkinson, Jan. 25, 1959; children—Erich, Kile, Connie, Kevin, Kathy. B.S., Purdue U., 1957, M.S., 1959, Ph.D., 1961. From asst. prof. to prof. dairy sci. U. Mo., Columbia, 1961-82, chmn. dept., 1978-82; research animal scientist U.S. Dept. Agr., Columbia, 1982—. Contbr. articles to profl. jours. Leader 4-H Club. Recipient Outstanding Young Scientist award Gamma Sigma Delta, 1972. Mem. Am. Forage and Grassland Assn. (merit cert. 1978, bd. dirs. 1983—), Am. Dairy Sci. Assn., Am. Soc. Animal Sci., Am. Inst. Nutrition. Home: Rural Route 8 Box 81 Columbia MO 65202 Office: US Dept Agr S-142 ASRC Columbia MO 65211

MARTZ, LEONARD JOHN, college administrator, consultant; b. Sioux Rapids, Iowa, Nov. 5, 1929; s. Leonard J. and Gladys O. (Brekke) M.; m. Louise Turner, Jan. 8, 1965; children—Carrie E., Anne E. B.A., U. Iowa, 1950; A.M., U. S.D., 1952; Ed.D., U. Nebr., 1965. Instr. English, Emmetsburg Community Coll., Iowa, 1952-54; dir. secondary edn. Community Sch. Dist. Emmetsburg, 1954-66; prof., div. chair No. State Coll., Aberdeen, S.D., 1966-67; prof., div. chair Buena Vista Coll., Storm Lake, Iowa, 1967-76, prof., asst. to pres., 1976-79, prof., dean continuing edn., 1979—. Author: (with others) English for the Academically Talented Student, 1969. Pres. bd. edn., Alta, Iowa, 1984—; bd. dirs. Alta Meml. Hosp., 1984—. Mem. Nat. Council Tchrs. English, NEA, Phi Delta Kappa, Sigma Tau Delta, Phi Mu Alpha. Lutheran. Lodge: Lions (pres. 1963-64). Avocations: flying; music; sports. Home: 602 Peterson St Alta IA 51002 Office: Buena Vista Coll College at 4th Storm Lake IA 50588

MARUSKA, EDWARD JOSEPH, zoo director; b. Chgo., Feb. 19, 1934; s. Edward M.; student Wright Coll., Chgo., 1959-61; m. Nancy; children—Donna, Linda. Keeper hoofed animals Lincoln Park Zoo, Chgo., 1956-62, head keeper Children's Zoo, 1959-62; gen. curator Cin. Zoo, 1962-68, dir., 1968—; lectr. biol. sci. U. Can.; numerous TV appearances. Recipient Cin. Conservation Man of Year award, 1973, Ambassador award Cin. Conv. and Visitors Bur., 1974. Fellow Am. Assn. Zool. Parks and Aquariums (pres. 1978-79); mem. Am. Soc. Ichthyologists and Herpetologists, Whooping Crane Conservation Assn., Am. Assn. Zool. Parks and Aquariums (pres. 1978-79), Internat. Union Zoo Dirs., Cin. Naturalists Soc., Langdon Club. Lodge: Rotary of Cin. Office: Cincinnati Zoo 3400 Vine St Cincinnati OH 45220

MARUYAMA, GEORGE M(ASAO), bioanalyst, laboratory director; b. Las Animas, Colo., June 15, 1918; s. Masakuni and Umeyo (Amino) M.; m. Helen Elizabeth Purnell-Edwards, Apr. 13, 1946; children—Geoffrey Mark, Tani Kathleen. B.A., Western State Coll. Colo., 1941; M.S., U. Wis.-Madison, 1948. Registered clin. chemist, bioanalyst, lab. dir. Asst. dir. lab. Med. Assocs. Clinic, P.C., Dubuque, Iowa, 1948—. Evaluator: Chemical Procedure in Medicine, 1979; contbr. articles to jour. Mem. Dubuque County Equal Employment Opportunity Com., 1976-84, chmn., 1982-83; Med. Assocs. chmn. United Fund, Dubuque, 1954-75. Served with U.S. Army, 1941-46, Caribbean. Fellow Am. Inst. Chemists; mem. Am. Assn. Clin. Chemistry (pres. Midwest sect. 1957), Am. Assn. Bioanalysts (nat. pres. 1967-68), Am. Chem. Soc. Republican. Presbyterian. Clubs: Dubuque, Kiwanis (pres. Dubuque 1959). Lodge: Masons (master Dubuque Lodge 3 1960), K.T. Avocations: sports, bridge, photography. Home: 1650 Atlantic St Dubuque IA 52001 Office: Med Assocs Clinic PC 1000 Langworthy Dubuque IA 52001

MARVIN, JAMES CONWAY, librarian; b. Warroad, Minn., Aug. 3, 1927; s. William C. and Isabel (Carlquist) M.; B.A., U. Minn., 1950, M.A., 1966; m. Patricia Katharine Moe, Sept. 8, 1947; children—Heidi C., James Conway, Jill C., Jack C. City librarian, Kaukauna, Wis., 1952-54; chief librarian, Eau Claire, Wis., 1954-56; dir. Cedar Rapids (Iowa) Pub. Library, 1956-67, Topeka Pub. Library, 1967—; Am. Library Assn.-Rockefeller Found. vis. prof. Inst. Library Sci. U. Philippines, 1964-65; vis. lectr. dept., librarianship Emporia (Kans.) State U., 1970—; chmn. Kans. del. to White House Conf. on Libraries and Info. Services; chmn. Gov.'s Com. on Library Resources, 1980-81. Served with USNR, 1945-46. Mem. Am., Iowa (past pres.), Kans., Philippine (life) library assns., Mountain Plains Library Assn. Rotarian. Home: 40 Pepper Tree Ln Topeka KS 66611 Office: 1515 W 10th St Topeka KS 66604

MARWAHA, JOE, neurobiologist, educator; b. Uganda, May 27, 1952; came to U.S., 1978, naturalized, 1984; s. Suraj and Kamla (Kapur) M.; m. Carmen Kim Fonkalsrud, Dec. 20, 1978. B.Sc. with honors, U. London, 1974; Ph.D., U. Alta. (Can.), 1977; postgrad. U. Colo., 1979, Yale U., 1981. Research scientist U. Colo., Denver, 1978-80, Yale U., New Haven, 1980-82; prof. pharmacology and physiology Ind. U.-Terre Haute, 1982—; prof. anthropology U. Medicine and Dentistry N.J., 1985—; cons. in field. Recipient A.E. Bennett award for neuropsychiatric research, Soc. Biol. Psychiatry, 1981. Mem. Am. Soc. Pharmacology and Exptl. Therapeutics, Am. Physiol. Soc., Soc. Neurosci., N.Y. Acad. Sci. Contbr. articles to profl. jours. Home: 7595 Carlisle Rd Terre Haute IN 47802 Office: Indiana State Univ 135 Holmstedt Hall Terre Haute IN 47809

MARX, GEORGE DONALD, animal science educator; b. Antigo, Wis., Apr. 30, 1936; s. Joseph C. and Mildred T. (Welch) M.; m. Elizabeth P. Clarke, May 22, 1964; children—Christina, Jeremy. B.S., U. Wis.-River Falls, 1958; M.S., S.D. State U., 1960; Ph.D., U. Minn., 1964. Prof. U. Minn-Crookston, 1964—. Contbr. articles to profl. jours. Key leader Four Corners 4-H Club; mem. Polk County Hist. Soc., Crookston Community Blood Bank, Northwest Ednl. Improvement Assn., Crookston Conservation Club; treas. PTA. Recipient dairy award Honorable Order of Gopatis, Royal Order Oxcart; named Minn. Dairy Person of the Yr. award. Mem. Am. Dairy Sci. Assn. (bd. dirs. Red River Valley div., chmn. various coms.), Am. Soc. Animal Sci., Nat. Assn. Colls. Tchrs. Agr., Nat. Dairy Shrine Club, Holstein Friesian Assn. Am., Dairy Herd Improvement Assn., N.W. Minn. Dairy Assn. (chmn. com. dairy day), Gamma Sigma Delta, Delta Theta Sigma, Kappa Delta Pi, Gamma Alpha. Home: 401 Jefferson Ave Crookston MN 56716 Office: U Minn Crookston MN 56716

MARX, GERALD VINCENT, training and development executive; b. Westbury, N.Y., July 23, 1926; s. Francis John and Mildred (Keller) M.; B.A., U. Buffalo, 1948; m. Mildred Rieman, Sept. 11, 1948; children—Barbara M., Gerald Vincent, Diane R. Field sales rep. William Wrigley Jr. Co., Buffalo, 1948-52, regional sales mgr., St. Louis, 1956-68, nat. mktg. mgr., Toronto, Ont., Can., 1968-72, Midwest area sales mgr., Chgo., 1972-79, dir. sales tng., Schaumburg, Ill., 1979-84; pres. Gamma Presentations, 1982—. Served with USN, 1944. Mem. Am. Soc. for Tng. and Devel. (regional v.p. sales tng. div. 1980-81), Nat. Soc. Sales Tng. Execs., Nat. Speakers Assn. Roman Catholic. Clubs: Lions, Rotary, Toastmasters (v.p. adminstrn. 1980-81, pres. 1984—). Office: 210 W Coventry Pl Mount Prospect IL 60056

MARX, THOMAS GEORGE, economist; b. Trenton, N.J., Oct. 25, 1943; s. George Thomas and Ann (Szymanski) M.; B.S. summa cum laude, Rider Coll., 1969; Ph.D. in Econs., Wharton Sch., U. Pa., 1973; m. Arlene May Varga, Aug. 23, 1969; children—Melissa Ann, Thomas Jeffrey. Fin. analyst Am. Cyanamid Co., Trenton, N.J., 1968-68; economist FTC, Washington, 1973; econ. cons. Foster Assocs., Inc., Washington, 1974-77; sr. economist Gen. Motors, Detroit, 1977-79, mgr. indsl. econs., 1980-84, dir. econ. policy studies, 1981-84, dir. plans consolidation, corp. strategic planning group; mem. faculty Temple U., U. Pa., 1972-73; adj. prof. Wayne State U., 1981; co-founder Ctr. Study of Bus., Labor and Community, U. Detroit, 1983. Served with USAF, 1961-65. Mem. Nat. Economist Club, Am. Econ. Assn., Nat. Assn. Bus. Economists, Detroit Area Bus. Economists, Econ. Soc. Mich., So. Econ. Assn., Western Econ. Assn., Pi Gamma Mu, Beta Gamma Sigma. Roman Catholic. Author text; assoc. editor Bus. Econs., 1980—; editorial bd. Akron Bus. and Econ. Rev., 1981—; contbr. articles to profl. jours. Home: 4100 Shore Crest Dr West Bloomfield MI 48033 Office: GM Tech Ctr Warren MI 48090

MARZOLF, JOHN EDWARD, geologist, educator; b. Columbus, Ohio, Aug. 26, 1938; s. Stanley S. and Helen M. (Gooding) M.; m. Mary Farmer, May 4, 1968 (div. 1979); 1 child, Zachary John Arthur. B.A., Wittenberg U., 1960; Ph.D., UCLA, 1970. Phys. sci. technician U.S. Geol. Survey, 1962-65; research asst. Antarctic Expdn., UCLA, 1967-68; prin. investigator Earth Sci. Research Corp., Santa Monica, Calif., 1969-70; asst. prof. geology Calif. State U., Los Angeles, 1970-71; assoc. prof. geology East Los Angeles Coll., 1971-81; assoc. prof. geology U. Nev., Las Vegas, 1981-82, So. Ill. U., 1982—. Contbr. articles to profl. jours. Mem. Geol. Soc. Am., Soc. Econ. Paleontologists and Mineralogists, Internat. Assn. Sedimentologists, Sigma Xi. Lutheran. Office: So Ill U Dept Geology Carbondale IL 62901

MARZOLF, STANLEY S(MITH), educator; b. Aurora, Ill., Oct. 18, 1904; s. George E. and Cora E. (Smith) M.; A.B., Wittenberg U., 1926; M.A., Ohio State U., 1930, Ph.D., 1937; m. Helen M. Gooding, Mar. 1, 1934; children—George Richard, John Edward. Tchr. chemistry Bucyrus High Sch. (Ohio), 1926-30; psychologist Ohio Dept. Pub. Welfare, Columbus, 1930-35; asst. prof. psychology Ill. State U., Normal, 1937-42, assoc. prof., 1942-46, prof., 1946-68, Disting. prof., 1968-72, prof. emeritus, 1972—. Sec.-treas. Ill. Bd. Examiners in Psychology, 1958-61. Fellow Am. Psychol. Assn.; mem. Ill. Psychol. Assn. (pres. 1954), Am. Assn. Psychol. State Bds. (pres. 1962). Author: Studying the Individual, 1941; Psychological Diagnosis and Counseling in the Schools, 1956. Contbr. to profl. jours., psychol. textbooks. Home: 806 Hester Ave Normal IL 61761

MASAR, EDWARD JOHN, coatings laboratory executive; b. Cleve., June 26, 1943; s. Joseph C. and Elizabeth (Vicarchek) M.; m. Sherry Lynn Patterson, Oct. 17, 1964; children—Joycelyn Marie, Jacquelyn Michelle. B.S., U. Toledo, 1973, M.B.A., 1983. Group leader Inmont, Detroit, 1966-70, new product devel., 1970-72, chemist, automotive research dept., 1972-78, lab. supr.,

Detroit, 1978—. Served with U.S. Army, 1963-66. Mem. Nat. Paint and Coatings Assn., Assn. Finishing Processes Soc. Mfg. Engrs., Soc. Automotive Engrs. Club: Jolly Roger Sailing. Patentee in field. Office: 5935 Milford Ave Detroit MI 48210

MASCHOFF, JANET BRANDT, educational adminstr.; b. St. Louis, Aug. 24, 1937; d. Oliver William and Esther Rose (Koehler) Brandt; B.S. in Edn., Concordia Tchrs. Coll., River Forest, Ill., 1959, M.A. in Edn., 1967; Edn. Specialist, So. Ill. U., 1981; m. Karl Edgar Maschoff, June 10, 1967. Tchr., prin. Lutheran Schs., N.J. and Mo., 1959-66; with Hazelwood Sch. Dist., St. Louis County, 1967—, instructional specialist, 1971-78, prin., 1981—. Mem. Assn. Supervision and Curriculum Devel., Internat. Reading Assn., Nat. Council Tchrs. Math., Nat. Council Tchrs. English, Nat. Assn. Elem. Sch. Prins., Delta Kappa Gamma, Phi Delta Kappa, Kappa Delta Pi. Lutheran. Contbr. to ednl. materials. Home: 2280 Derhake Rd Florissant MO 63033 Office: 2324 Redman Ave Saint Louis MO 63136

MASCIOLI, DEBORAH WYGAL, biology educator, microbiologist; b. Middlesboro, Ky., Oct. 4, 1951; d. Samuel Terrell and Vivian (Bailey) Wygal; m. Stephen Ralph Mascioli, Aug. 13, 1977; children—Nicholas Todd and Matthew Dean (twins). A.B., Stanford U., 1973; Ph.D., Brandeis U., 1980. Postdoctoral fellow in genetic toxicology, MIT, Cambridge, 1979-80; research assoc. U. Minn., Mpls., 1980-83; asst. prof. biology Coll. of St. Catherine, St. Paul, 1983—. Author jour. articles. Mem. Am. Soc. Microbiology, AAAS, Sigma Xi. Democrat. Presbyterian. Avocations: Running; tennis. Home: 4204 Alden Dr Edina MN 55416 Office: Coll of St Catherine 2040 Randolph Ave Saint Paul MN 55105

MASEK, RAYMOND JOHN, lawyer; b. Cleve., Sept. 1, 1946; s. Raymond Clement and Rita Ann (Kalous) M.; B.B.A., Cleve. State U., 1969, J.D., 1975. Internal auditor, asst. to acctg. mgr. Procter & Gamble Co., Balt. and Cin., 1969-71; cost/fin. analyst Ford Motor Co., Toledo and Cleve., 1971-75; corp. auditor Harris Corp., Cleve., 1975-77; sr. corp. auditor Midland-Ross Corp., Cleve., 1977-78; mgr. internat. audits, corp. counsel Reliance Electric Co., Cleve., 1978—; admitted to Ohio bar, 1977. Named Outstanding Coop. Edn. Student in Sch. Bus., Cleve. State U., 1969. Mem. Cleve. State U. Bus. Alumni Assn. (dir. 1979-82), Bar Assn. of Greater Cleve., Ohio Bar Assn., Inst. Internal Auditors, ABA (internat. law sect.). Home: 2250 Par Ln Willoughby Hills OH 44094 Office: 29325 Chagrin Blvd Pepper Pike OH 44122

MASI, ALFONSE THOMAS, physician, educator; b. N.Y.C., Oct. 29, 1930; s. Antonio and Mary (Genese) M.; m. Nancy Ann Bouton, Aug. 27, 1960; children—Anthony Mark, Christopher Maurice, Maria Lisa, Amy Elizabeth. B.S., CUNY, 1951; M.D., Columbia Coll. Physicians and Surgeons, 1955; Dr. P.H., Johns Hopkins U., 1963. Diplomate Am. Bd. Internal Medicine. Intern Johns Hopkins Hosp., Balt., 1955-56, resident, 1958-59; resident UCLA Med. Ctr., Los Angeles, 1959-60; asst. prof. epidemiology Johns Hopkins Sch. Hygiene, Balt., 1963-65, assoc. prof. epidemiology, 1965-67; prof. medicine, dir. div. connective tissue disease U. Tenn.-Memphis, 1967-78; prof., head dept. medicine U. Ill. Coll. Medicine, Peoria, 1978—; cons. NIH, 1971-78, NRC, 1972, 75. Contbr. articles to med. jours. Bd. dirs. Peoria Civic Opera Co., Inst. Phys. Medicine and Rehab. Russell L. Cecil fellow Am. Rheumatism Assn., 1970-71; United Scleroderma Found. research grantee, 1980. Fellow ACP; mem. AMA, Am. Coll. Epidemiology, Am, Fedn. Clin. Research, Central Soc. Clin. Research, Peoria C. of C. Avocations: traveling, swimming, dancing, reading. Home: 6710 N Skyline Dr Peoria IL 61614 Office: Dept Medicine U Ill Coll Medicine PO Box 1649 Peoria IL 61656

MASIELLE, RICHARD, township police executive; b. Cleve., June 30, 1937; s. Michael and Rose M.; m. Karol Ann V. Jakupca, Oct. 20, 1979. Grad. Cuyahoga County (Ohio) Sheriff's Dept. Sch., 1968, Am. Inst. for Paralegal Studies, 1984. Quality control insp. TRW Inc., Cleve., 1955-65; mem. Cuyahoga County Sheriff's Dept., 1968; with Olmsted Twp. (Ohio) Police Dept., 1969—, chief of police, 1972—. Served with U.S. Army, 1960-62. Mem. Cuyahoga County Chiefs of Police Assn., Ohio Assn. Chiefs of Police, Frat. Order Police, Met. Crime Bur., Internat. Personnel Mgmt. Assn., Nat. Assn. Legal Assts. Home: 15657 Hickox Blvd Middleburg Heights OH 44130 Office: 26900 Cook Rd Olmsted Township OH 44138

MASKREY, JOYCE ELOISE, real estate company executive; b. Des Moines, Apr. 11, 1944; d. Earl Raymond and Bernice Elizabeth (Taylor) Wagner; B.A. in Journalism, Drake U., 1967; M.S.T., Drake U., 1970; m. Richard Maskrey, Apr. 11, 1970; children—Chris, Chad, Natalie Jo. Advt. copywriter Sta. KCBC, Des Moines, 1967-68; writer Iowa Credit Union League, Des Moines, 1968; tchr. Fed. Tchr. Corps Program, 1968-69; tng. officer, manpower coordinator, employee counselor Greater Opportunities, 1969-73; pharm. sales rep. Lederle Labs., Des Moines, 1973-75; pharm. salesman Rachelle Labs., Des Moines, 1975-81; pres., broker So. Realty, Des Moines, 1977—; owner, pres. R & J Enterprises, R & J Trucking, R & J Snow Removal, R & J Lawn Aid (all Des Moines). Active local PTA, Des Moines; Mem. Drug Travelers Assn., Homebuilders Assn., Iowa Assn. Realtors, South Des Moines C. of C. Office: 1135 SW Army Post Rd Des Moines IA 50315

MASON, CAROLYN, automobile club executive, psychotherapist, consultant; b. Buffalo, July 1, 1927; children—Gilbert D. Sylva, Nickolas A. Sylva, Christopher D. Mason. B.A., George Williams Coll., 1976, M.S.W., 1978; Ph.D., Southeastern U., 1980. Cert. clin. social worker. Pvt. practice psychotherapist, Oakbrook Terrace, Ill., 1973-79; v.p. human resources AAA/Chgo. Motor Club, Chgo., 1980—; cons. Chgo., Milw., 1975—. Author: Synthesis of Physiology and Psychology: Toward Wholism, 1978; artist retrospective aquatints (1st place Ill. Sesquicentennial, 1976). Co-founder All the Way House, Lombard, 1970. AAUW scholar, 1978, Hinsdale Bus. and Profl. Womens Assn. scholar, 1978; winner 1st place Oakbrook Artists Invitational, 1977. Mem. Am. Mgmt. Assn., Am. Assn. Tng. and Devel., AAUP. Democrat. Roman Catholic. Office: AAA Chicago Motor Club 66 E South Water St Chicago IL 60601

MASON, DAVID JOHN, insurance agent; b. Anoka, Minn., Aug. 31, 1937; s. Leslie B. and Evelyn G. (Brown) M.; m. Joan Clare Bourassa, Sept. 15, 1962; children—Thomas Curtis, Timothy Patrick. Student U. Minn., 1960-63. Ins. agt. Farmers Insurance Group, Mpls., 1971-84; dist. mgr. Am. Family Assurance Co., Mpls., 1983-84; sales rep. Sentry Insurance Co., Mpls., 1984—. Served with U.S. Air Force, 1956-60. Mem. Nat. Assn. Life Underwriters, Alpha Kappa Psi, Delta Psi Omega. Republican. Roman Catholic. Clubs: Anoka Band Parents (pres. 1980-81), Anoka Halloween (dir.). Avocation: flying. Home: 4050 147th Ln Box 821 Anoka MN 55303 Office: Sentry Insurance Co 1660 S Highway 100 Minneapolis MN 55440

MASON, EARL JAMES, JR., physician; b. Marion, Ind., Aug. 26, 1923; s. Earl James and Grace A. (Leer) M.; student Marion Coll., 1940-41; B.S. in Medicine, Ind. U., 1944, A.B. in Chemistry, 1947, M.A. in Bacteriology, 1947; Ph.D. in Microbiology, Ohio State U., 1950; M.D., Western Res. U., 1954; m. Eileen Gursansky, Dec. 2, 1967. Teaching asst. dept. bacteriology Ind. U., 1945-47; research fellow depts. ophthalmology and bacteriology Ohio State U., Columbus, 1947-48, teaching asst. dept. bacteriology, 1948-50; Crile research scholar Western Res. U., Cleve., 1951-53; Damon Runyon cancer research fellow dept. pathology Western Res. U.-Cleve. City Hosp., 1951-56; dept. chief dept. pathology USPHS Hosp., San Francisco, 1956-58; fellow pathology U. Tex. Postgrad. Sch. Medicine, M.D. Anderson Hosp. and Tumor Inst., Houston, 1958-59; asst. prof. dept. pathology Baylor U. Coll. Medicine, 1959-60; asst. pathologist Jefferson Davis Hosp., 1959-60; asst. pathologist Michael Reese Hosp. and Med. Center, Chgo., 1960-61; asso. dir. dept. pathology, dir. dept. biol. scis. Mercy Hosp., 1960-65; dir. labs. St. Mary Med. Center, Gary and Hobart, Ind., 1965—; asso. prof. pathology Chgo. Med. Sch., 1966—; clin. prof. pathology Ind. U. Med. Sch., 1976—. Diplomate Am. Bd. Pathology in anat. and clin. pathology, radioisotopic pathology and dermatopathology, Am. Bd. Nuclear Medicine. Mem. Coll. Am. Pathologists, Am. Assn. Pathologists and Bacteriologists, Am. Soc. Clin. Pathologists, Internat. Acad. Pathologists, Am. Soc. Exptl. Pathology, Am. Assn. Cancer Research, Am. Assn. Blood Banks, Am. Soc. Hematology, Am. Acad. Dermatology, Soc. Nuclear Medicine, Lake County Med. Soc., Am. Soc. Cytology, Sigma Xi. Research on cellular origin of antibodies and virus-cell interactions. Home: PO Box 485 7 Summit Rd Ogden Dunes Portage IN 46368 Office: 540 Tyler St Gary IN 46402

MASON, EARL SEWELL, engineering educator; b. Grand Forks, N.D., June 9, 1935; s. Sewell Luverne and Margaret Jean (Lovell) M.; m. Sandra Jean Smith, June 21, 1958; children—Kristen, Karl, Mark. B.S. in Civil Engring., U. N.D., 1957, J.D., 1973; Ph.D., Utah State U., 1965. Registered profl. engr., N.D. Bar: N.D. 1974. Asst. prof. U. Utah, Salt Lake City, 1964-68; faculty U. N.D., Grand Forks, 1968—, prof. civil engring., 1978—; assoc. dir. N.D. Water Resource Research Inst., 1975—. Contbr. articles to profl. jours. Served with USAF, 1957-85, lt. col. Res. Mem. Nat. Soc. Profl. Engrs., Am. Soc. Engring. Edn., ASCE. Presbyterian. Avocations: skiing; flying; sailing; amateur radio. Home: 2211 4th Ave N Grand Forks ND 58201 Office: UND Box 8115 Univ Sta Grand Forks ND 58202

MASON, JON DAVID, bookseller; b. Jeffersonville, Ind., Feb. 13, 1942; s. Carlyle Lyman and Mildred (Whitenack) M.; widowed; children—Jenny Leigh, David Stephen. B.A., U. Evansville, 1965; M.A., Pa. State U., State College, 1966. Owner, operator Mason's Rare and Used Books, Wabash, Ind., 1975—. Mammonite. Avocations: reading, forestry. Office: Mason's Rare and Used Books 264 S Wabash St Wabash IN 46992

MASON, JOSEPH L., real estate executive; m. Sandra Jean Duenke; children—Joseph W., Monica L. With J.L. Mason Group, Inc., St. Louis, now pres., chief exec. officer; pres. J.L. Mason of Fla., Inc., J.L. Mason of Mo., Inc., J.L. Mason of Colo., Inc., J.L. Mason Realty & Investment, Inc.; gen. ptnr. Conway Meadows Venture, Glen Park Properties, Security Storage Systems, Storage Properties '79 Ltd., Sundance Valley Venture, Barrington Oaks E. Venture, Bryn Mawr Venture; owner, dir. Brentwood Bancshares; dir., major shareholder Micro Term, Inc.; chmn. bd. Community Mortgage Trust. Bd. dirs., exec. com. St. Louis Home Builders Assn.; bd. dirs. St. Louis Home Bldg. Industry Fund; mem. bd. police commrs. St. Louis County, Mo.; mem. tech. adv. com. St. Louis County Planning Commn.; mem. St. Louis County Hwy. Funding Task Force, others. Mem. Nat. Assn. Home Builders (dir.). Address: 1215 Fern Ridge Pkwy Saint Louis MO 63141

MASON, LINDA, softball and basketball coach; b. Indpls., Jan. 29, 1946; d. Harrison Linn and Hazel Marie (Bledsoe) Crouch; m. Robert Mason, Aug. 20, 1967; children—Cassandra, Andrew. B.S., Ind. U., 1968, M.S., 1977. Cert. phys. edn. tchr., K-12, Ind. Tchr. phys. edn. Woodview Jr. High Sch., Indpls., 1968-71; tchr. phys. edn., coach Ind. U.-Purdue U. of Indpls., 1972-76; basketball coach Butler U., Indpls., 1976-84; head softball coach, asst. basketball coach Westfield Washington High Sch., Westfield, Ind., 1985—; head coach Ind. Girls' High Sch. All-Stars, Indpls., 1980. Named Coach of Yr. Dist. 4, Nat. Collegiate Athletic Assn., 1983. Mem. Delta Psi Kappa.

MASON, MILO CHARLES, lawyer; b. Palestine, Ill., Oct. 25, 1950; s. Mack Henry and Marcella (Anspach) M.; m. Marianne Dise, July 2, 1983; 1 child, Luke Henry. B.A., Cornell U., 1973; M.A., Stanford U., 1977; J.D., Harvard U., 1979. Bar: Ill. 1979, D.C. 1982, U.S. Dist. Ct. (cen. dist.) Ill. 1983, U.S. Ct. Appeals (D.C. cir.) 1982. Vice-pres. Mason Gas Co., Oblong, Ill., 1972—; teaching fellow Stanford U., 1974-77; atty.-advisor U.S. Dept. Interior, Office of the Solicitor, Washington, 1979—. Mem. Winchester on the Severn Assn., Annapolis, Md., 1984. Mem. Ill. Bar Assn., D.C. Bar Assn. Episcopalian. Clubs: Severn Sailing (Annapolis, Md.); Harvard (Washington).

MASON, NORMAN RONALD, neuroscientist; b. Rochester, Minn., Nov. 20, 1929; s. Harold Lawrence and Maude (McKenzie) M.; m. Nancy Mae Bumgarner, June 24, 1953; children—Charles Norman, Susan Elizabeth. B.A., U. Chgo., 1950, B.S., 1953; M.A., U. Utah, 1956, Ph.D., 1959. Instr., U. Miami, Fla., 1959-60, research asst. prof., 1960-64; investigator Howard Hughes Med. Inst., Miami, 1959-64; sr. scientist Eli Lilly and Co., Indpls., 1964—. Contbr. articles on gonadotrophin action, gonadal function, steroid immunoassay, serotonin receptors to sci. jours. Mem. Endocrine Soc., Am. Chem. Soc., AAAS, Soc. Neurosci. Methodist. Avocations: gardening; woodworking; racquetball. Home: 7301 Steinmeier Dr Indianapolis IN 46250 Office: Lilly Research Labs Lilly Corporate Ctr Indianapolis IN 46285

MASON, STEVEN CHARLES, business executive; b. Sarnia, Ont., Can., Feb. 22, 1936. B.S., MIT, 1957. With Mead Corp., Dayton, Ohio, dir. corp. research, 1973-75, exec. v.p. paperboard group, 1975-76, pres. paperboard div., 1976-78, group v.p. paperboard, 1979, group v.p. paper, 1980, sr. v.p. ops., 1981, pres., chief operating officer, 1982—; bd. dirs. Am. Productivity Ctr. Mem. Inst. Paper Chemistry, TAPPI. Office: Courthouse Plaza NE Dayton OH 45463

MASON, THEODORE MOYER, dentist; b. Dixon, Ill., Mar. 4, 1927; s. Theodore Remington and Fern Marie (Buzzard) M.; 1 child, Marcia Anne. Student North Central Coll., 1946-48; D.D.S., U. Ill.-Chgo., 1952. Gen. practice dentistry Dixon, Ill., 1952—; tchr. Cert. Dental Assts., Dixon, Sterling, Ill., 1957-59, also lectr. Mem. Lee County Cancer Soc., 1953-57, del., 1957-60; mem. City of Dixon Park Bd., 1969-79, pres., 1974-75; mem. Lee County Bd. Health, 1968-78, pres., 1976-78; mem. governing bd. Dixon YMCA, 1954-56. Served with USN, 1944-46. Recipient Dedication award Lee County Health Dept., Dixon, 1978. Mem. ADA, Lee-Whiteside County Dental Soc. (sec. 1960-62, pres. 1963, del. 1963), Acad. Gen. Dentistry, Am. Legion (Excellence award 1940); fellow Ill. State Dental Soc. Republican. Episcopalian. Clubs: Toastmasters (Dixon); Western Lawn Tennis Assn. (Indpls.), No. Ill. So. Wis. Tennis Assn. (Janesville, Wis.). Avocations: collecting coins, Rockwell plates; tennis; bicycling; fishing. Home and Office: 315 Crawford Ave Dixon IL 61021

MASON, THOMAS RICHARD, higher education planner, researcher; b. Trinidad, Colo., Apr. 17, 1930; s. Abraham Gartin and Ethel Arlene (Jackson) M.; m. Margaret Marie Emma Bartram, Aug. 11, 1950 (div. 1979); m. 2d, Mary Lucille Coghlan, Aug. 2, 1980. A.B. magna cum laude, U. Colo., 1952, M.A. (Rotary Found. fellow), 1955; postgrad. London Sch. Econs. and Polit. Sci., 1952-53; Ph.D. (Ford Found. fellow), Harvard U., 1963. News writer, announcer Sta. KBOL, Boulder, Colo., 1948-53; asst. to pres. U. Colo.-Boulder, 1955-56, planning officer, 1959-64; dir. planning U. Rochester, N.Y., 1964-68; dir. instl. research U. Colo.-Boulder, 1968-72, dir. spl. studies, planning, Denver, 1972-74, dir. spl. studies, Boulder, 1975-76; pres. MIRA Inc., Mpls., 1977—. Author: (with others) Higher education Facilities Planning and Management Manuals, 1971; (with Paul L. Dressel & Assocs.) Institutional Research in the University, 1971; editor: Assessing Computer-Based Systems Models, 1976; contbr. numerous papers in field to profl. jours. Mem. Zoning Rev. Com., City of Boulder (Colo.), 1959, Com. on Utility Ownership Study, 1969-70, Com. on Analysis of Growth, 1971-72. Recipient Outstanding Young Men of Am. award, 1965. Mem. Assn. for Instl. Research (pres. 1969-70), Soc. Coll. and Univ. Planning, World Futures Soc., Phi Beta Kappa. Mem. Democratic Farm Labor Party. Roman Catholic. Home: 4526 Blaisdell Ave S Minneapolis MN 55409 Office: MIRA Inc 3112 Hennepin Ave Minneapolis MN 55408

MASON, THOMAS WILLIAM, economics educator, university official; b. New Brighton, Pa., Aug. 20, 1946; s. Wilfred Wayne and Sara Jean (Dunlap) M.; m. Sandra Lee Mascari, Sept. 17, 1965; children—Gary T., Jennifer L. B.A., Geneva Coll., 1968; M.A., U. Pitts., 1970, Ph.D., 1972. NSF trainee, 1968-72; asst. prof. Rose-Hulman Inst. Tech., Terre Haute, Ind., 1972-75, assoc. prof., 1975-79, prof. econs., 1979-83, chmn. div. humanities, social and life scis., 1975-83, v.p. for adminstrn. and fin., 1983—; assoc. dir. Ctr. for Tech. and Policy Studies, Terre Haute, 1973—; dir. Applied Computing Devices, Terre Haute. Contbr. articles to profl. jours. Mem. com. on edn. and high tech. industry Ind. Dept. Commerce, Indpls., 1984—. U.S. Dept Energy grantee, 1978. Mem. Am. Econs. Assn., Midwest Econs. Assn., Ind. Acad. for Social Scis., Internat. Assn. for Impact Assessment (revs. editor 1981—), Nat. Assn. Coll. and Univ. Bus. Officers, Vigo County Hist. Soc., Alpha Tau Omega (hon.). Lodge: Rotary. Office: Rose-Hulman Inst Tech 5500 Wabash Ave Terre Haute IN 47803

MASSENGALE, MARTIN ANDREW, agronomist, university chancellor; b. Monticello, Ky., Oct. 25, 1933; s. Elbert G. and Orpha (Conn) M.; B.S., Western Ky. U., 1952; M.S., U. Wis., 1954, Ph.D., 1956; m. Ruth Audrey Klingelhofer, July 11, 1959; children—Alan Ross, Jennifer Lynn. Research asst. agronomy U. Wis., 1952-56; asst. prof. asst. agronomist U. Ariz., 1958-62, asso. prof., asso. agronomist, 1962-65, prof., agronomist, from 1965, head dept., 1966-74, asso. dean Coll. Agr., asso. dir. Ariz. Agr. Expt. Sta., 1974-76; vice chancellor for agr. and natural resources U. Nebr., 1976-81, chancellor U. Nebr.-Lincoln, 1981—; past chmn. pure seed adv. com. Ariz. Agrl. Expt. Sta.; past chmn. bd., pres. Midam. Internat. Agrl. Consortium; mem. EPA-Dept. Agr. Land Grant Univ. Coordinating Com. Environ. Quality; past chmn. Am. Registry Cert. Profls. in Agronomy, Crops and Soils. Bd. dirs. Council on Agrl. Sci. and Tech., 1982—, mem. editorial bd., 1982—; bd. dirs. Nat. Merit Scholarship Bd., 1982—; mem. NASULGC Water Resources Commn., 1982—. Served with AUS, 1956-58. Named One of Outstanding Educators Am., 1970; Faculty Recognition award Tucson Trade Bur., 1971. Cert. profl. agronomist, profl. crop scientist. Fellow Am. Soc. Agronomy (dir.), AAAS (past sect. chmn.); mem. Am. Grassland Council, Ariz. Crop Improvement Assn. (dir.), Crop Sci. Soc. Am. (past dir., pres. 1972-73), Am. Soc. Plant Physiology, Nat. Assn. Colls. and Tchrs. of Agr., Ariz. Acad. Sci., Nebr. Acad. Sci., Agrl. Council Am. (dir. mem. issues com.), Sigma Xi, Phi Kappa Phi, Gamma Sigma Delta, Alpha Zeta, Phi Sigma, Gamma Alpha, Alpha Gamma Rho. Pioneer in floral initiation and photoperiodism in alfalfa, photosynthate prodn. and use in alfalfa and water-use efficiency in forage crops. Office: U Nebr Office of Chancellor 14th and R Sts Lincoln NE 68588

MASSENGALE, ROBERT AMES, forester; b. St. Louis, Jan. 13, 1933; s. George P. and Emily (Ames) M.; m. Betty Jo Miller, Dec. 15, 1962; children—David, Debra. B.S. in Forestry, U. Mo., 1956, M.S. in Forestry, 1970. Farm forester Mo. Conservation Dept., Hannibal, 1958-61, forest products specialist, Jefferson City, 1961-77, staff asst. for adminstrn., 1977-81, staff asst. for utilization, 1981—; cons. U.S. Forest Service, Portland, Oreg., 1973; mem. adv. council Sch. Forestry, Fisheries and Wildlife, U. Mo., 1970—, membership chmn., 1982, vice chmn., 1983, chmn. adv. council, 1983-84. Author 14 directories on forest products, 1962-77. Chmn. adminstrn. bd. 1st United Methodist Ch., Jefferson City, 1984: bd. govs. Meml. Community Hosp., 1981—, mem. fin. com., 1984-86. Served with U.S. Army, 1956-58. Recipient Forest Conservationist award Conservation Fedn., 1974; Outstanding Service award Mo. Forest Products Assn., 1974; Outstanding Service award U.S. Forest Service, 1976. Mem. Soc. Am. Foresters (continuing edn. com. 1985-86), Forest Products Research Soc., Mo. Soc. Am. Foresters (chmn. edn. com. 1982-85), Internat. Wood Collectors Soc., Midwest Woodworkers. Avocations: woodworking; windmills. Home: 914 Westwood Dr Jefferson City MO 65101 Office: Forestry Div Mo Conservation Dept PO Box 180 Jefferson City MO 65101

MAST, ALAN G(EORGE), water conditioning company executive, consultant; b. Milw., Mar. 6, 1953; s. Glenn L. and Elizabeth A. (Hahn) M.; m. Joanne L. Lowry, Jan. 4, 1975; children—Tracy, Travis. B.S.I.E., with honors, U. Wis., 1975; M.B.A., Marquette U., 1981. Registered profl. engr., Wis.; cert. water conditioning dealer. Process engr. Falk Corp., Milw., 1976-79; engring. mgr. Watercare Corp., Manitowoc, Wis., 1979-81; v.p., mgr. Mast & Co., Inc., Cuba City, Wis., 1981—; cons. engring. Mem. Water Quality Assn., Wis. Water Quality Assn., Cuba City (Wis.) C. of C. (v.p.), Platteville (Wis.) C. of C. (com. chmn.). Club: Rotary (sgt. at arms) (Platteville). Home: 910 Hillcrest Circle Platteville WI 53818 Office: 108 S Main St Cuba City WI 53807 also 250 E Main Platteville WI 53818

MAST, PAUL, radio and TV transmitting industry executive. B.S.E.E., M.S.E.E., Purdue U. With ITT, Ft. Wayne, Ind., 1955—, v.p., dir. engring., pres., gen. mgr. Aerospace/Optical div., 1980—. Chmn. The Com. of 24, Ft. Wayne; vice chmn. area ops. Jr. Achievement; bd. dirs. YMCA, Ft. Wayne; mem. Ft. Wayne Urban League. Mem. Sigma Xi, Tau Beta Pi, Eta Kappa Nu. Club: Nat. Space (governing bd.). Address: ITT Aerospace Optical Div 3700 E Pontiac St PO Box 3700 Fort Wayne IN 46801

MASTERMAN, JACK VERNER, See *Who's Who in America,* 43rd edition.

MASTERS, WILLIAM HOWELL, physician, educator; b. Cleve., Dec. 27, 1915; s. Francis Wynne and Estabrooks (Taylor) M.; m. Virginia Johnson; children by previous marriage—Sarah Masters Worthington, William Howell. B.S., Hamilton Coll., 1938, Sc.D. (hon.), 1973; M.D., Rochester, U., 1943. Diplomate Am. Bd. Ob-Gyn. Intern, St. Louis Maternity Hosp., 1943, asst. resident in ob-gyn and pathology, 1944, resident in obstetrics, 1945-46; intern Barnes Hosp., St. Louis, 1943, 45, asst. resident in ob-gyn and pathology, 1944, resident in gynecology, 1944, 46-47; intern dept. pathology Washington U., St. Louis, 1944, asst. in ob-gyn, 1944-47, instr., 1947-49, asst. prof., 1949-51, assoc. prof., 1951-64, assoc. prof. clin. ob-gyn, 1964-69, prof., 1969—, lectr. human sexuality in psychiatry, 1981—, dir. div. reproductive biology, 1960-63; assoc. obstetrician and gynecologist St. Louis Maternity Hosp., Barnes Hosp., Washington U. Clinics; assoc. gynecologist St. Louis Children's Hosp.; asst. attending obstetrician and gynecologist Jewish Hosp. St. Louis; cons. gynecologist St. Louis City Infirmary; dir. Reproductive Biology Research Found., St. Louis, 1964-73; co-dir. Masters and Johnson Inst., St. Louis, 1973-80, chmn. bd., 1981—; Served to lt. (j.g.) USNR, 1942-43. Fellow Am. Coll. Ob-Gyn (founding); mem. AAAS, Am. Assn. Sex Educator, Counselors and Therapists (cert., award 1978), Am. Fertility Soc., Am. Geriatrics Soc. (Edward Henderson lectr. 1981), AMA, Am. Soc. Andrology, Am. Soc. Cytology (cert.), Eastern Assn. for Sex Therapy (life), Endocrine Soc., Internat. Acad. Sex Research, Mo. State Med. Assn., N.Y. Acad. Scis., Pan Am. Cancer Cytology Soc., Pan Am. Med. Assn., Sex info. and Edn. Council U.S., St. Louis Gynecol. Soc., St. Louis Met. Med. Soc., Soc. Sci. Study of Sex, Soc. Study of Reprodn., Washington U. Med. Ctr. Alumni Assn., Internat. Acad. Profl. Counseling and Psychotherapy, Colombian Sexological Soc. (hon.), Eastern Mo. Psychiat. Soc. (hon.), Sigma Xi, Alpha Omega Alpha, Alpha Sigma Lambda, Alpha Delta Phi. Episcopalian. Clubs: St. Louis, Racquet. Author: Sex in Our Culture, 1955; (with V.E. Johnson) Human Sexual Response, 1965, Human Sexual Inadequacy, 1970, The Pleasure Bond, 1975, Homosexuality In Perspective, 1979; (with V.E. Johnson and R.C. Kolodny) Ethical Issues in Sex Therapy and Research, 1977, Textbook of Sexual Medicine, 1979, Human Sexuality, 1982, 2d edit., 1985; (with V.E. Johnson, R.C. Kolodny, and M.A. Biggs) Textbook of Human Sexuality for Nurses, 1979; (with V.E. Johnson, R.C. Kolodny, and S.M. Weems) Ethical Issues in Sex Therapy and Research, vol. 2, 1980; contbr. chpts. to profl. books, articles to profl. jours; mem. editorial bd. Contraceptive Tech. Update Jour.; cons. editor: Sexuality and Disability. Office: 24 S Kingshighway Saint Louis MO 63108

MASTERSON, WILLIAM LLOYD, management consultant, grain company executive; b. Chgo., Aug. 19, 1949; s. Lawrence and Lorraine Mae (Shaw) M. Student public schs., Chgo. Organiser, United Farm Workers, various locations, 1968-72; innkeeper Holiday Inns, Skokie, Ill., 1973-74; sec. Ill. Racing Bd., Chgo., 1974-79; gen. mgr. Maywood Park (Ill.) Race Track, 1979-83; pres. N.Am. Grain Co., Chgo.; gen. mgr. Racing Assn. Central Iowa. Recipient Outstanding Achievement award Chgo. div. Horsemen's Benevolent and Protective Assn., 1976. Mem. Nat. Assn. State Racing Commrs. (hon. life), Amnesty Internat., Harness Tracks of Am. (dir. 1979-83), Lincoln Park Zool. Soc., Am. Horse Council, Chgo. Symphony Soc., Irish Am. Cultural Inst., Art Inst. Chgo. Democrat. Lutheran. Club: Irish Fellowship (Chgo.). Home: 3100 Grand Ave Des Moines IA 50312

MATCHETT, HUGH MOORE, lawyer; b. Chgo., Apr. 24, 1912; s. David Fleming and Jennie E. (Moore) M.; A.B., Monmouth (Ill.) Coll., 1934; J.D., U. Chgo., 1937; m. Ilo Venona Wolff, May 12, 1956. Bar: Ill. 1937. Practice, Chgo., 1937—. Served with USNR, 1942-46; MTO, PTO; lt. comdr. JAGC, USNR. Mem. Fed. Bar Assn. (chmn. mil. law com. Chgo. chpt. 1954-55, mem. com. 1960-61), ABA, Ill. Bar Assn. (mem. assembly 1980—), Chgo. Bar Assn., Judge Advs. Assn., Tau Kappa Epsilon, Phi Alpha Delta. Republican. Presbyterian. Counsel in litigation establishing rule that charitable instns. are liable in tort to extent of their non-trust funds. Home: 5834 S Stony Island Ave Chicago IL 60637 Office: 10 S La Salle St Chicago IL 60603

MATCHETTE, PHYLLIS LEE, editor; b. Dodge City, Kans., Dec. 24, 1921; d. James Edward and Rose Mae (McMillan) Collier; A.B. in Journalism, U. Kans., 1943; m. Robert Clarke Matchette, Dec. 4, 1943; children—Marta Susan, James Michael. Reporter, Dodge City Daily Globe, 1944; tchr. English, Dode City Jr. High Sch., 1944-45; asst. instr. Coll. Liberal Arts, U. Kans., Lawrence, 1945-47; dir. Christian edn. Southminster United Presbyn. Ch., Prairie Village, Kans., 1963-65; editor publs., dir. communications, supr. in-plant printing Village United Presbyn. Ch., Prairie Village, 1965—. Hon. mem. Commn. of Ecumenical Mission and Relations, hon. mem. Program Agy., United Presbyn. Ch., U.S.A.; ordained elder Village United Presbyn. Ch., 1964. Mem. Women in Communications, Kans. U. Dames (pres. 1946), Kansas City Young Matrons, Alpha Chi Omega (pres. edn. found. Phi chpt. 1951). Republican. Club: Order of Eastern Star. Home: 7405 El Monte Rd Prairie Village KS 66208 Office: 6641 Mission Rd Prairie Village KS 66208

MATERA, RAYMOND AMBROSE, national guard official; b. Rock Falls, Ill., Jan. 9, 1925; s. Rocco and Josephine (Cappatelli) M.; student St. Mary's

Coll., 1946-48, Air U., 1952, U. Wis., 1959, Air War Coll., 1972; m. Janet Lee Silliman, Aug. 11, 1952; children—Terry Joan Gopman, Eugene Rocco, Rae Anne Matera, Steven Lee. Air ops. officer, squadron comdr., group ops. officer Wis. Air NG, 1954-61; sales mgr. Madison Kipp Corp. (Wis.), 1961-79; adj. gen. State of Wis., Madison, 1979—. Served with USMC, 1943-45; with USAF, 1948-54. Decorated Legion of Merit, D.F.C., Air medal with clusters. Mem. N.G. Assn. U.S. (pres.), Air Force Assn., Am. Legion, VFW, Wis. N.G. Assn. Office: 3020 Wright St Madison WI 53704

MATHEIN, JAMES DANIEL, health promotion company executive; b. Evanston, Ill., Jan. 31, 1943; s. Edward Lawrence and Isabel (Wynn) M.; B.S., U. Ill., 1968; postgrad. Forest Inst. Profl. Psychology, 1979-80; children—Adam Scott, Jason Daniel. Lab. automation cons. Am. Hosp. Supply, Chgo., 1969-71, support service supr., Dallas, 1971, ops. mgr., Mpls., 1971-73, dir. tech. support, Chgo., 1974-78; area ops. mgr. Can. Lab. Supply Ltd., Toronto, Ont., 1973-74; v.p. community relations, exec. dir. personal mgmt. systems Forest Hosp. and Found., Des Plaines, Ill., 1978—. Mem. Am. Soc. Tng. and Devel., Am. Soc. Health Manpower Edn. and Tng., Internat. Platform Assn., Nutrition for Optimal Health Assn. Author: The Personal Management System, 1979; How to Make Decisions That Pay Off, 1982; contbr. articles to profl. jours. Home: 448 Prairie Ave Libertyville IL 60048 Office: 555 Wilson Ln Des Plaines IL 60016

MATHER, MERRILIE, educator; b. Melrose, Mass., Mar. 28, 1921; d. Thomas Ray and Ruth Evelyn (Hutchins) Mather; A.B., Boston U., 1942, M.A., 1943, Ph.D., 1950. Teaching fellow, Sargent Coll., Boston U., 1943-44; children's room, Dorchester Br., Boston Pub. Library, 1946-47; instr., Morningside Coll., Sioux City, Iowa, 1947-51; prof. English and children's lit. Eastern Ill. U., Charleston, 1951—; speaker, teller children's stories, writer, reader poetry for children. Vol. children's school camp, Ont., Can. Mem. Phi Beta Kappa, Delta Kappa Gamma. Theistic Unitarian-Universalist. Office: English Dept Eastern Ill Univ Charleston IL 61920*

MATHERS, JAMES BRADLEY, insurance company salesman; b. Elyria, Ohio, Nov. 17, 1936; s. Theodore Kenneth and Grace Rhea (Dawson) M.; m. Joan Kay Landahl, June 28, 1955 (div. 1970); children—James Bradley Jr., Jill, Joel, Jeff, Joni; m. Marty Lou Young, Mar. 10, 1971; children—Jeff, Jay. Student Franklin U., 1958-60. Underwriting supt. Buckeye Union, Columbus, Ohio, 1956-73; sales rep. Aetna Ins., Rocky River, Ohio, 1973-75; sr. sales rep. Midwestern Indemnity Co., Milford, Ohio, 1975—. Bd. dirs. Walnut Twp. Zoning Bd., Ashville, Ohio, 1984; fin. chmn. Village Methodist Ch., Ashville, 1984. Mem. Profl. Ins. Agts. Assn. (mem. com. 1982—, licensing instr. 1984—, co. rep. of yr. 1980), Ohio 1752 Club (pres. 1982-83), Ohio Speakers Bur. Republican. Lodges: Kiwanis (local v.p. 1984), Shriners (local pres-elect), K.P., Masons. Avocations: music, golf, fishing. Home: 16523 Lockbourne Eastern Rd Ashville OH 43103 Office: Midwestern Indemnity Co 1700 Edison Dr Milford OH 45150

MATHERS, THOMAS NESBIT, investment counselor; b. Bloomington, Ind., Apr. 22, 1914; s. Frank Curry and Maud Esther (Bowser) M.; m. Helen M. Curtis, Oct. 23, 1943 (dec. 1981); children—Mary, Abigail. A.B., Ind. U., 1936, LL.B., 1939; M.B.A., Harvard U., 1941. Bar: Ind. 1939. Research asst. No. Trust Co., 1941-43; legal asst. Chgo. Ordnance Dist., 1943-44; employee to ptnr. Woodruff Hays & Co., Chgo., 1944-51; pres. Security Counselors, Inc., Chgo., 1951-62, Mathers & Co., 1962-75, chmn. bd., 1975—; dir. Lincoln Nat. Direct Placement Fund; pres. Mathers Fund, 1965-75, chmn. bd., 1975—. Trustee Beloit Coll., 1970—. Recipient Disting. Alumni Service award Ind. U., 1979, pres. 1983-85. Mem. Investment Analysts Club Chgo. (pres. 1958-59). Republican. Presbyterian. Clubs: Union League, Econ. of Chgo., Westmoreland Country, Mich. Shores, Execs. Home: 115 Bertling Ln Winnetka IL 60093 Office: 125 S Wacker Dr Chicago IL 60606

MATHESON, GORDON H., agricultural industry executive; Chmn. bd. Harvest States Coops., Falcon Heights, Minn. Office: 1667 N Snelling Ave Falcon Heights MN 55108

MATHESON, GORDON KEITH, anatomy educator; b. Chgo., Apr. 22, 1934; s. William John and Dorothy Fletcher (Taylor) M.; m. Linda Nan Olsen, Dec. 19, 1958: children—Mark, Paul, Jan, Jean. B.S., Brigham Young U., 1962, M.S., 1964; Ph.D., U. Wash., 1968. Postdoctoral fellow UCLA-Brain Research Inst., Los Angeles, 1968-69; asst. prof. anatomy Loyola U. Chgo., Maywood, Ill., 1969-74; assoc. prof. anatomy Ind. U.-Evansville, 1974—. Contbr. articles to profl. jours. Served with U.S. Army, 1958-60. Mem. AAAS, Soc. for Neurosci., Am. Assn. Anatomists, Sigma Xi. Office: Ind U Sch Medicine 1800 Lincoln Ave Evansville IN 47714

MATHESON, WILLIAM ANGUS, JR., farm machinery company executive; b. Oregon City, Oreg., Dec. 6, 1919; s. William Angus and Maude (Moore) M.; B.S. in Bus. Adminstrn., Lehigh U., 1941; m. Jeanne Elyse Manley, Feb. 14, 1942; children—Jeanne Sandra, Susan Manley, Bonnie Ann. Procurement engr. Office Chief of Ordnance, 1942-43; mgr. contract sales Eureka-Williams Corp., Bloomington, Ill., 1946-49; dist. sales mgr. Perfex Corp., Milw., 1949-51; v.p. sales Internat. Heater Co., Utica, N.Y., 1951-53; sales mgr. heating div. Heil Co., Milw., 1953-55; v.p. sales, dir. Portable Elevator Mfg. Co., Bloomington, 1955-70; exec. v.p. portable elevator div. Dynamics Corp. Am., 1971-75, pres., 1975-84, dir., 1971-85. Bd. dirs. Jr. Achievement Central Ill., 1959-71, pres. Bloomington dist., 1964. Served from pvt. to 1st lt. AUS, 1943-46. Mem. Farm Equipment Mfrs. Assn. (dir. 1961-80, pres. 1969, treas. 1970-80), Ill. C. of C. (dir. 1978-84, vice chmn. 1984), McLean County Assn. Commerce and Industry (pres. 1974), Truck Equipment and Body Distbrs. Assn. (co-founder 1963), Am. Legion, Flying Farmers, Nat. Pilots Assn., Chi Phi. Republican. Presbyterian. Clubs: Rotary, Bloomington Country, Masons, Shriners, Elks. Home: 1404 E Washington St Bloomington IL 61701 Office: 105 W Market St Bloomington IL 61701

MATHEWS, HERBERT LESTER, immunology educator; b. Johnstown, Pa., Oct. 5, 1949; s. Ronald Lester and Emma Jane (Daly) M.; m. Diane Lee Bourbouse, May 19, 1973; children—Jill Leigh, Aaron Richard, Ryan Adam. B.A., Washington and Jefferson Coll., 1971; M.S., W.Va. U., 1974, Ph.D., 1977. Predoctoral fellow W.Va. U., Morgantown, W.Va., 1972-77, Nat. Jewish Hosp., Denver, 1977-78; NIH postdoctoral fellow, 1978-80; asst. prof. immunology Loyola U. of Chgo., Maywood, Ill., 1980—; sci. reviewer Am. Osteo. Assn., Chgo., 1984. Contbr. sci. articles to profl. jours. Coach Am. Youth Soccer Orgn., Elmhurst, Ill., 1983-84. Research grantee NIH, Bethesda, Md., 1981, 84, Am. Cancer Soc., Chgo., 1984, Chgo. Community Trust, 1982. Mem. Am. Assn. Immunologists, Chgo. Assn. Immunologists, Am. Soc. Microbiology, Fedn. Am. Socs. Exptl. Biology, Phi Kappa Phi. Republican. Presbyterian. Home: 291 Fair Ave Elmhurst IL 60126 Office: Dept Microbiology Stritch Sch Medicine 2160 S 1st Ave Maywood IL 60153

MATHEWS, JUDY CAROL, reporting service executive, consultant; b. Chgo., Sept. 29, 1957; d. Elliott A. and Jacqueline V. (Carter) M. B.A., Eastern Ill. U., 1978. Researcher James Lowry and Assocs., Chgo., 1977-78, cons., 1982—; intern U.S. C. of C., Washington, 1978; cons. Capitol Personnel, Washington, 1979-80; co-owner, prin. Carter Reporting Service, Chgo., 1980—; cons. James H. Lowry & Assocs., 1982—; profl. newsletter editor. Active, Chgo Urban League, NAACP, Young Dems., Citizens Choice, Washington. Mem. Nat. Assn. Female Execs. Roman Catholic. Office: Carter Reporting Service 179 W Washington St Chicago IL 60602

MATHEWS, KENNETH PINE, physician, medical researcher, teacher; b. Schenectady, N.Y., Apr. 1, 1921; s. Raymond and Marguerite Elizabeth (Pine) M.; m. Alice Jean Elliot, Jan. 26, 1952 (dec.); children—Susan Kay, Ronald Elliott, Robert Pine; m. Winona Beatrice Rosenburg, Nov. 8, 1975. A.B., U. Mich., 1941, M.D., 1943. Diplomate Am. Bd. Internal Medicine, Am. Bd. Allergy and Immunology. Asst. prof. U. Mich. Med. Sch., Ann Arbor, 1951-55, assoc. prof., 1955-61, prof., 1961—, head, div. of allergy, 1967-83; cons. in allergy, Ann Arbor VA Med. Ctr. Author: (with others) Manual of Clinical Allergy, 1953, 2d edit., 1967. Editor: Jour. Allergy, 1968-72. Served to capt. AUS, 1946-48. Recipient Disting. Service Award, Am. Acad. Allergy, 1976. Fellow Am. Acad. Allergy and Immunology (pres. 1964-65), ACP; mem. Am. Assn. Immunologists, Am. Thoracic Soc., Mich. Allergy Soc. (pres. 1956-57), County Med. Soc. Avocations: bird watching; music. Home: 1145 Aberdeen Dr Ann Arbor MI 48104 Office: U Mich Med Ctr Box 027 Ann Arbor MI 48109

MATHIS, JACK DAVID, advertising executive; b. La Porte, Ind. Nov. 27, 1931; s. George Anthony and Bernice (Bennethum) M.; student U. Mo., 1950-52; B.S., Fla. State U., 1955; m. Phyllis Dene Hoffman, Dec. 24, 1971; children—Kane Cameron, Jana Dene. With Benton & Bowles, Inc., 1955-56; owner Jack Mathis Advt., 1956—; cons. films, including That's Action!, 1977, Great Movie Stunts: Raiders of the Lost Ark, 1981, The Making of Raiders of the Lost Ark, 1981, An American Legend: The Lone Ranger, 1981; Heroes and Sidekicks: Indiana Jones and the Temple of Doom, 1984. Mem. U.S. Olympic Basketball Com. Recipient citation Mktg. Research Council N.Y. Mem. Alpha Delta Sigma. Author: Valley of the Cliffhangers. Office: Forum Sq 1117 S Milwaukee Ave Libertyville IL 60048

MATHIS, JOHN SAMUEL, astronomy educator; b. Dallas, Feb. 7, 1931; s. Forrest and Mattie (Godbold) M.; m. Carol Simpelaar, Sept. 11, 1954; children—Matthew, Alice, Jeffrey, Emily, Sarah. B.S. in Physics, MIT, 1953; Ph.D. in Astronomy, Calif. Inst. Tech., 1956. Postdoctoral fellow Yerkes Cbs., Williams Bay, Wisc., 1956-57; asst. prof. Mich. State U., East Lansing, 1957-59; from asst. prof. to assoc. prof. astronomy U. Wis., Madison, 1959-64, prof., 1968—; cons. Los Alamos Nat. Lab., 1965-82. Contbr. articles to profl. jours. Trustee Meadville/Lombard Theol. Sch., Chgo., 1983—. Recipient U.S. sr. scientist award Alexander Humboldt Found., 1975. Mem. Am. Astron. Soc., Internat. Astron. Union, Astron. Soc. Pacific. Home: 1639 Norman Way Madison WI 53705 Office: Dept Astronomy Univ Wis 475 N Charter St Madison WI 53706

MATHIS, PATRICK BISCHOF, lawyer; b. Pinckneyville, Ill., Feb. 1, 1952; s. John Archibald and Theresa Ann (Bischof) M. B.A. in Chemistry, St. Louis U., 1973; M.B.A., Washington U., St. Louis, 1978, J.D., 1978, LL.M. in Taxation, 1979. Bar: Mo. 1978, Ill. 1979, U.S. Tax Ct. 1979, U.S. Dist. Ct. (so. dist.) Ill. 1980, U.S. Ct. Appeals (7th cir.) 1980, U.S. Ct. Claims 1980, U.S. Supreme Ct. 1982. Assoc. John J. Vassen, P.C., Belleville, Ill., 1979-84; ptnr. Mathis, Marifian & Richter, Ltd., Belleville, 1984—. Mem. ABA (domestic relations tax problems com., vice chmn. subcom. alimony issues), Ill. Bar Assn. (fed. taxation sect. council, chmn. corp. div.), St. Clair County Bar Assn., Bar Assn. Met. St. Louis. Roman Catholic. Club: Mo. Athletic. Home: 46 Glenview Belleville IL 62223 Office: Mathis Marifian & Richter Ltd 7705 W Main St Suite 15 Belleville IL 62223

MATHIS, WILLIAM ERVIN, music educator, consultant, clinician; b. Price, Utah, Aug. 2, 1931; s. George Macfarlane and Anna Frances (Stoker) M.; m. Ann Bunnell, Aug. 22, 1957; children—William Bunnell, Marcy Ann Mathis Matheson. A.S., Coll. E. Utah, 1955; B.S., Brigham Young U., 1957, M.S., 1961; Ph.D., U. Mich., 1969. Tchr. music jr. high schs., Provo and Orem, Utah, 1957-61, Clearfield High Sch., Utah, 1961-62; instr. music Brigham Young U., Provo, 1962-66; teaching fellow U. Mich., Ann Arbor, 1966-68; coordinator grad. studies Wichita State U., Kans., 1969-81, prof., chmn. music dept., 1971—. Contbr. articles to profl. jours. Adj. clinician Kans. State Music Festivals, 1970—; condr. youth symphony Wichita Symphony Soc., 1976—; guest Condr. Hutchinson Symphony, Kans., 1977, 82; pres. Univ. Senate Wichita State U., 1982-83. Served with USN, 1951-54. Mem. Coll. Music Soc., Kans. Music Educators Assn. (bd. dirs. 1972-80), Utah Music Educators Assn. (v.p. 1958-64, treas. 1964-66), Music Educators Nat. Conf. (chmn. nat. council students 1976-82), Blue Key, Phi Kappa Phi, Phi Kappa Lambda, Omicron Delta Kappa. Mormom. Avocations: graphics; travel. Home: 2343 Hathway Circle Wichita KS 67226 Office: Wichita State U Div Music 1845 Fairmount Ave Wichita KS 67208

MATHISON, IAN WILLIAM, dean, medicinal chemistry educator; b. Liverpool, England; Apr. 17, 1938; s. William and Grace (Almond) M.; m. Mary Ann Gordon, July 20, 1968; children—Mark W., Lisa A. B. Pharm., U. London Sch. Pharmacy, Eng., 1960, Ph.D., 1963, D.Sc., 1976. From asst. prof. to prof. medicinal chemistry U. Tenn. Center for Health Scis., Memphis, 1965-76; dean, prof. Ferris State Coll. Sch. of Pharmacy, Big Rapids, Mich., 1977—; mem. Mich. Dept. Mental Health Drug Quality Assurance Com., 1984—. Contbr. articles to profl. jours. and books. Patentee in field. Recipient numerous grants for research, 1965—. Mem. Chem. Soc. London, Pharm. Soc. Great Britain, Am. Pharm. Assn., Acad. Pharm. Scis., Am. Chem. Soc., Royal Inst. Chemistry, Am. Assn. Colls. Pharm., Mich. Pharm. Assn., Am. Soc. Hosp. Pharmacists. Episcopalian. Home: 820 Osburn Circle Big Rapids MI 49307 Office: Sch Pharmacy Ferris State Coll 901 S State Big Rapids MI 49307

MATHIS-TOLF, REBECCA JANE, marketing company executive; b. Peoria, Ill., Dec. 31, 1956; d. Wayne Harold and Cleo Pauline (Wilcoxen) Mathis; m. Randall Robert Tolf, Nov. 17, 1979; 1 dau., Amy Jo. B.A. in Polit. Sci., Ill. State U., Normal, 1978; J.D., U. Ill., 1984. Dir. mktg. Lee Creative Mktg., Peoria, 1978-79; pres. Marbeck Mktg., Inc., Peoria, 1980—; small bus. mktg. cons. Econ. Devel. Assn., Peoria. Mem. Delta Theta Phi. Republican. Presbyterian. Clubs: Jr. League, Creve Coeur (Peoria). Office: 100 NE Crescent St Peoria IL 61606

MATHUR, PRACHEESHWAR SWAROOP, metallurgist; b. Shahjahanpur, India, Dec. 19, 1945; came to U.S., 1967; s. Parmeshwar and Gopal Rani M.; B.Sc., Agra Coll. (India), 1962; B.Tech., Indian Inst. Tech., Kanpur, 1967; S.M., M.I.T., 1968, Sc.D., 1972; m. Meena Mathur, Dec. 27, 1976; children—Shashank, Nishant. Metall. cons., 1969-71; research asst. M.I.T., Cambridge, 1969-72, research asso., 1968-69; mech. metalworking engr. aircraft engine group Gen. Electric Co., Lynn, Mass., 1972-78, mgr. metals processing, Cin., 1978-80, mgr. customer support, 1980—. Recipient numerous awards Gen. Electric Co. Mem. Am. Soc. Metals, AIME, ASME, Metals Soc. Eng. Contbg. author: Superalloys—Processing, 1981. Patentee in field (5).

MATHWIG, JOHN, environmental educator, consultant; b. Oshkosh, Wis., Mar. 18, 1944; s. Robert John and Ruth Dorothy (Kath) M.; m. Bonnie Lou Masik, Oct. 17, 1965; children—Jill Leslie, Jonathan Tyler. B.S., U. Wis.-Madison, 1966; Ph.D., Kans. U., 1971. Mem. faculty Coll. of Lake County, Grayslake, Ill., 1970—, prof. biology, 1976—, asst. chmn. Biol. and Health Scis. Div., 1979-83, curator insect collection, 1970—; dir. Entomology Research Lab., Lake Villa, Ill., 1982—; mosquito control cons., dir. quality control and environ. assessment Protection Unlimited, Lake Villa, 1982—; co-owner, mgr. WillowPoint Industries, Grayslake, 1984—; prin. investigator-mosquitos Des Plaines River Wetlands Demonstration Project, U.S. Fish and Wildlife Service Research Program, 1985—; aquatic cons., 1975—. Author: Biology Lab Manual, 1973; Environmental Biology, 1977. Writer, editor The Environ Newsletter, 1982—. Contbr. articles in field to newspapers. Named Outstanding Coll. Tchr., Coll. of Lake County, 1973. Mem. Nat. Assn. Biology Tchrs., Am. Assn. Mosquito Control, Ill. Mosquito Control Assn. Presbyterian. Avocations: fishing; hunting; stamp collecting; art collecting; skiing. Home: 535 Midlothian St Mundelein IL 60060 Office: Coll of Lake County 19351 Washington St Grayslake IL 60030

MATIASKA, ERNEST ALLAN, instruments and controls engring. co. exec.; b. Cleve., Nov. 20, 1930; s. Charles A. and Emma (Hanzlik) M.; B.M.E., Cleve. State U., 1963; m. Barbara Ann Yonchak, Sept. 23, 1967; children—Douglas, Carla. Devel. project engr. Bailey Meter Co. div. Babcock & Wilcox (name now Bailey Controls Co.), Wickliffe, Ohio, 1959-63, mgr. engring. test lab., 1963-66, mgr. product reliability and testing, 1966-69, mgr. product engring., 1969-80, mgr. internat. tech., 1980—; U.S.A. expert to Internat. Electrotech. Commn., 1976—. Served with USAF, 1951-55; Korea. Mem. ASME, Instrument Soc. Am., Am. Nat. Standards Inst., Sci. Apparatus Makers Assn. Home: 21990 Roberts Ave Euclid OH 44123 Office: 29801 Euclid Ave Wickliffe OH 44092

MATLACK, ARDENA LAVONNE, state legislator; b. Carlton, Kans., Dec. 20, 1930; d. Walter D. and Bessie B. (Major) Williams; student Kans. Wesleyan U., 1948, Kans. State U., 1949-51, Washburn U., 1955; B.A. cum laude, Wichita State U., 1969; m. Don Matlack, June 10, 1951; children—Lucinda Donn, Roxanne, Terry Clyde, Rex William, Timothy Alan. Tchr., Carlton Grade Sch., 1948-49; substitute tchr. Clearwater (Kans.) Schs., 1969-74; part-time music tchr., 1960-72; mem. Kans. Ho. of Reps., 1974—; arts council mem. Kans. Arts Commn., 1985—. Democratic precinct committeewoman, 1966-68; mem. Dem. State Com., 1974-78; pres. Kans. State Dem. Club, 1978; chmn. Clearwater March of Dimes, 1980, Clearwater Area United Fund, 1980, 83; choir dir. United Meth. Ch., 1984—; project leader 4-H, 1962-71. Recipient Gold Star Legis. award Assn. for legis. action by Rural Mayors, 1981. Mem. Clearwater United Methodist Women (hon. life; pres. 1972), Dist. United Meth. Women (hon. life, dist. coordinator social involvement 1975-76), Kans. Press Women's Assn. (hon.), Gold Key, Alpha Xi Delta, Mu Phi Epsilon. Clubs: Clearwater Federated Women's Study (pres. 1966-67); Kans. Federated Women's Dem. (Disting. Achievement award 1977), Clearwater Bus. and Profl. Women's (pres. 1985-86), West Side Dem., South Side Dem., Sedgwick County Federated Women's Dem. (pres. 1985-86). Home: 615 Elaine St Clearwater KS 67026 Office: State Capitol Bldg Topeka KS 66612

MATOCHA, GEORGE RICKY, architectural engineer; b. Hinsdale, Ill., Mar. 7, 1951; s. George R. and Barbara (Dehr) M.; m. Linda Kaye Huff, Dec. 28, 1974; children—George Ryan, Krystal Lynn. B.S., U. Kans., 1975. Registered architect, Ill. Draftsman, Wes Engring., Western Springs, Ill., 1975-76; asst. dir. planning and constrn. Rush Presbyn. St. Lukes Med. Ctr., Chgo., 1976-81; pres., owner Matocha Assocs., Clarendon Hills, Ill., 1981—. Prin. works include Evergreen I, Chgo. (hon. beautification award 1982). Mem. archtl. adv. bd. City of Clarendon Hills. Mem. AIA, Constrn. Specification Inst., Assn. Energy Engrs., Am. Soc. Hosp. Engring., Ill. Solar Energy Assn. (sec., treas., pres. 1980-85), Sigma Nu. Republican. Presbyterian. Avocations: computers; fishing; hunting. Home: 16 Mohawk Dr Clarendon Hills IL 60514 Office: 4 S Walker St Clarendon Hills IL 60514

MATRANGA, LUKE FRANCIS, JR., dentist, air force officer; b. Rockford, Ill., Nov. 6, 1942; s. Luke Francis and Rena Lucy (Toti) M.; m. Cheryl Ann Fennig, Sept. 5, 1966; 1 child, Lisa Maria. D.D.S., Marquette U., 1966; M.S., U. Tex.-Houston, 1973. Diplomate Fed. Services Bd. Gen. Dentistry. Commd. officer U.S. Air Force, 1966, advanced through grades to col., 1979; dental officer, Langley AFB, Va., 1966-67, Phan Rang AFB, Viet Nam, 1967-68; preventive dental officer, San Vito AS, Italy, 1968-71; resident in gen. dentistry, Lackland AFB, Tex., 1971-73; chmn. dept. gen. dentistry, Scott AFB, Ill., 1973-79; base dental surgeon, Andersen AFB, Guam, 1979-81; officer-in-charge dental clinic, Bolling AFB, Washington, 1981-83; command dental surgeon Strategic Air Command, Offutt AFB, Nebr., 1983—; cons. in gen. dentistry to U.S. Air Force Surgeon Gen. Contbr. articles to profl. jours. Pres. Normanni Little Theater Workshop, San Vito, 1970. Decorated Bronze Star medal, 1967, Meritorious Service medal, 1979, 81; Air Force Commendation medal, 1967, Outstanding Unit award with Valor Device, 1967; Republic of Vietnam Gallantry Cross with Palm, 1967. Mem. Acad. Gen. Dentistry (master, nat. dir. region XVII 1985-88), ADA. Republican. Roman Catholic. Lodge: K.C. Avocations: sailing; skiing; racquetball. Home: 20829 Paddock Circle Elkhorn NE 68022 Office: HQ SAC/SGD Offutt AFB NE 68113

MATSESHE, JOHN WANYAMA, gastroenterologist; b. Kakamega, Kenya, June 5, 1941; s. James K. and Anyachi S. (Nyikuli) M.; came to U.S., 1970; M.D., Makerere U., Kampala, Uganda, 1969; m. Rebecca Z. Wazome, Mar. 14, 1970; children—Lily, Carolyn, Lynn, Andrew. Intern, Stamford (Conn.) Hosp., 1971-72; resident in medicine Northwestern U. Hosps., 1972-74; fellow in gastroenterology Mayo Clinic, Rochester, Minn., 1974-77, cons. in medicine and gastroenterology, 1977-78; instr. medicine Mayo Med. Sch., 1976-78, asst. prof., 1978; practice medicine specializing in gastroenterology, Libertyville, Ill., 1978—; asst. prof., Chgo. Med. Sch., U. of Health Scis., 1981; cons. Condell Meml. Hosp., St. Therese Hosp., Waukegan, VA Hosp., North Chicago. Diplomate Am. Bd. Internal Medicine (gastroenterology). Mem. AMA, A.C.P., Am. Gastroent. Assn., Am. Soc. Gastrointestinal Endoscopy, Sigma Xi. Address: 890 Garfield St No 210 Libertyville IL 60048

MATTEN, LAWRENCE CHARLES, biology educator; b. Newark, Sept. 1, 1938; s. Bernard and Florence (Law) M.; m. Marlene Alice Rotbart, Sept. 6, 1959; children—Sharlene Ruth, Alan Howard, Sharon Jeanne, Ronald Thomas. Student U. Mich., 1955-57, Bloomfield Coll., 1957-58; A.B., Rutgers U., 1959; Ph.D., Cornell U., 1965. Tchr. gen. sci. Woodstown High Sch., N.J., 1959-60; research and teaching asst., extension coordinator Cornell U., Ithaca, N.Y., 1960-64; instr. biology SUNY-Cortland, 1964-65; asst. prof. botany So. Ill. U., Carbondale, 1965-69, assoc. prof., 1969-77, prof., 1977—. Author: (with others) Laboratory Manual for General Botany, 1981, Syllabus and Study Guide for General Botany, 1984. Assoc. editor Palaeontographica, 1981—. Contbr. articles to profl. jours. NSF grantee, 1981—; Am. Philos. Soc. grantee, 1982-83. Fellow Linnean Soc. (London); mem. Internat. Orgn. Paleobotany, Internat. Assn. Plant Taxonomy, Paleontol. Soc., Bot. Soc. Am., Torrey Bot. Club. Avocations: music; computers. Office: Dept Botany So Ill U Carbondale IL 62901

MATTER, MICHAEL CARL, pharmacist; b. Williamsport, Pa., Sept. 25, 1945; s. Paul H. and Mary L. (Gladewitz) M.; B.Sc. in Pharmacy, Temple U., 1968; M.B.A., Ohio U., 1984; m. Pamela Sue Gault, Feb. 9, 1974; 1 son, Drew Michael-Paul. Resident in hosp. pharmacy Bethesda Hosp., Zanesville, Ohio, 1968-69, spl. project pharmacist, 1969; dir. pharmacy services Med. Center Hosp., Chillicothe, Ohio, 1970—; evening instr. pharmacology Hocking Tech. Coll., Chillicothe, 1977-82. Mem. Am. Soc. Hosp. Pharmacists (preceptor; accredited residency in hosp. pharmacy), Ohio Soc. Hosp. Pharmacists (treas. 1979-85), Central Ohio Soc. Hosp. Pharmacists, Nat. Order Symposiarchs (past pres. Zeta chpt.). Home: 204 Vine St Chillicothe OH 45601 Office: Med Center Hosp 272 Hospital Rd Chillicothe OH 45601

MATTES, DAVID DWIGHT, judge; b. Springfield, Ohio, Feb. 17, 1937; s. Paul Gotlieb and Edith Irene (Burr) M.; m. Linda Lee Thomas, Sept. 9, 1961; children—Polly L., Matthew T. B.A., Wittenberg Coll., 1959; J.D., Ohio State U., 1962. Bar: Ohio 1962. Spl. agt. FBI, 1962-66; assoc. Cole, Cole & Harmon, Springfield, 1966-73; judge Springfield Mcpl. Ct. (Ohio), 1973-79; judge juvenile div. Clark County Probate Ct., 1979—; judge juvenile-probate div. Clark County Common Pleas Ct. Address: 101 E Columbia St Springfield OH 45502

MATTESON, RICHARD ARTHUR, JR., public affairs specialist; b. Lock Haven, Pa., Dec. 26, 1950; s. Richard Arthur and Jeanne (Keeler) M.; B.S. with high honors, U. Fla., 1973; postgrad. Central Mich. U., 1973-75; m. Sue A. Cornell, Aug. 12, 1972; children—Sandra Rene, Jonathon Richard. Copy editor Midland (Mich.) Daily News, 1973-74, city editor, 1975-76; copy editor Oakland Press, Pontiac, Mich., 1976-77, copy desk chief, 1977-78, city editor, 1978; mng. editor Cadillac (Mich.) Evening News, 1978-79, exec. editor, 1979-81; dir. publs. and exec. communication Consumers Power Co., Jackson, Mich., 1981—. Mem. bd. edn. St. Ann's Parish, 1980-81; bd. dirs. Jackson County Rose Festival, Inc. Mem. Sigma Delta Chi, Kappa Tau Alpha, Phi Kappa Phi. Roman Catholic. Home: 1020 Maple Grove Rd Jackson MI 49201 Office: 212 W Michigan Ave Jackson MI 49201

MATTHEWS, DWIGHT EARL, medical educator, consultant; b. Greencastle, Ind., Sept. 10, 1951; s. Robert Earl and Madeline Vivian (Huber) M.; m. Ellen Lee Keller, Aug. 12, 1972; children—Thomas Earl, Benjamin Earl. B.A., DePauw U., 1973; Ph.D., Ind. U., 1977. Instr. Washington U. Sch. Medicine, St. Louis, 1977-80, asst. prof., 1980—; v.p. Prevo's Inc., Greencastle, 1975—. Contbr. articles to profl. jours., chpts. to textbooks. Grantee NIH, 1979—, Nat. Livestock and Meat Bd., 1979—. Mem. Am. Inst. Nutrition, Am. Soc. Clin. Nutrition, Am. Soc. Parenteral and Enteral Nutrition, Am. Soc. Mass Spectrometry, Am. Chem. Soc. Avocations: photography; cycling; backpacking. Home: 6309 Pershing Ave University City MO 63130 Office: Metabolism Div Washington U Sch Medicine 660 S Euclid Ave Saint Louis MO 63110

MATTHEWS, GERTRUDE ANN URCH, retired librarian, writer; b. Jackson, Mich., July 16, 1921; d. Charles P.A. and Amy (Granville) Urch; student Albion Coll., 1940-41; A.A., Jackson Jr. Coll., 1939; B.S., M.S. in Library Arts, U. Mich., 1959; m. Geoffrey Matthews, June 30, 1942 (dec.). Adult services librarian Jackson, Mich., 1959-63; asst. dir., librarian Franklin Sylvester Library, Medina, Ohio, 1963-81, now vol. older adults facility library. Pres., Hist. Soc., 1966-67; active Dollars for Scholars Com., 1966—; mem. Bicentennial Com.; officer diocesean leval Episcopal Ch.; mem. vestry St. Paul's Ch., Medina, 1981-84. Mem. ALA, Ohio Library Assn., AAUW (dir., Community Service award 1985, Woman of Yr.), LWV (dir.). Republican. Contbr. articles to profl. and popular publs.; weekly newspaper columnist, 1958-81; bookreviewer The Nat. Librarian. Home: 750 Weymouth Medina OH 44256

MATTHEWS, JOHN EDWARD, dentist; b. Indpls., Feb. 17, 1923; s. Edward Michael and Elizabeth (Bethel) M.; m. Willa Jean Trout, June 5, 1948; 1 child, Stepheny. B.S., Ind. U., 1948, D.D.S., 1956. Acct., Eli Lilly Internat. Corp., 1948-52; practice dentistry, Indpls., 1956—. Served with USMC, 1943-46. Mem. ADA, Ind. Dental Assn., Indpls. Dist. Dental Soc., Delta Sigma Delta, Delta Sigma Pi, Alpha Tau Omega. Republican. Roman Catholic. Lodge: K.C. Avocations: fishing; woodworking; bicycling; boating. Home: 9419 Hague Rd Indianapolis IN 46256 Office: John E Matthews DDS 6515 E 82d St Suite 210 Indianapolis IN 46250

MATTHEWS, JOHN L., manufacturing company executive; b. Atkins, Ark., 1914; s. John Jefferson and Naomi L. (Gipson) M.; B.S. in Banking and Fin., U. Ark., 1932; m. Mary Beth Higby, June 13, 1939; children—John Lannes, Nancy D., Jill K. Mgr., S.H. Kress Co., Oklahoma City, 1932-34; nat. sales mgr. Sears Roebuck, Chgo., 1937-40; owner Matthews Constrn. Co., Kansas City, Mo., 1945-49; pres. Van Brunt Machinery, Kansas City, 1946-49; pres. Airosol Co., Inc., Neodesha, Kans., 1949—; dir. Merc. Bank and Trust, Kansas City-St. Louis, Racon Co., Wichita, Kans. Served with U.S. Army, 1941-45; ETO. Decorated Legion of Merit, Bronze Star; Croix de Guerre with gold star. Mem. Nat. Aerosol Packers Assn. (pres. 1976-80), Chem. Spltys. Mfg. Assn. Republican. Methodist. Clubs: Kansas City, Independence, Kansas Country, Elks, Masons, Shriners. Home: 1100 N 5th St Neodesha KS 66757 Office: 525 N 11th St Neodesha KS 66757

MATTHEWS, RICHARD DAVID, clergyman, religious association executive; b. Van Wert, Ohio, May 16, 1933; s. Dale T. and Evelyn (Riley) Matthews Kear; m. Marie Elvira Manera, Feb. 13, 1954; children—Evi Marie, David Salvator, Thomas Joe, John Wesley. B.D., Luther Rice Sem., Fla., 1980; Th.D., Clarksville Sch. Theology, Tenn., 1976. Ordained to ministry Ind. Baptist Ch., 1962. Pastor Chs. in Wis., 1959-65; missionary evangelist Overseas Crusades, Inc., Santa Barbara, Calif., 1965-70, Gospel Missionary Union, Kansas City, Mo., 1970-76; gen. dir. Mission Outreach Soc., Oregon, Wis., 1970-82; exec. dir. Assn. N.Am. Missions, Madison, Wis., 1982—; cons. Author: From Whence Cometh My Help, 1976; also articles. Editor Roundtable mag., 1982—. Served with USAF, 1951-56; Korea. Republican. Club: Optimists (Oregon). Avocations: amateur radio; gardening; clock repair; camping; hunting. Office: PO Box 9710 Madison WI 53715

MATTHEWS, ROBERT WILLIAM, JR., office equipment company executive, consultant; b. Chgo., Mar. 4, 1944; s. Robert William and Kathleen Josephine (Johnson) M.; m. Linda Valory Appleby, Feb. 14, 1970 (div. 1972); 1 dau., Jennie Lin; m. Patricia Anne McKenzie, Dec. 22, 1973; children—Victoria Elizabeth, Veronica Ellen. B.S. in Am. Studies, Roosevelt U., 1976, M.A. in Am. Lit., 1977. Cert. Am. Records Mgmt. Assn. Mktg. rep. Xerox Corp., Mpls., 1968-70, product mktg. mgr., Ann Arbor, Mich., 1971-75; spl. account rep. Minn. Mining and Mfg. Co., Chgo., 1976-79, area mktg. specialist, 1979-81; midwest regional mgr. Canon U.S.A., Inc., Chgo., 1981—; dir. JVP Machine Co. Inc.; records mgmt. cons. Active Chgo. Commons Assn., Lyric Opera Guild. Served with USCGR, 1966-72. Mem. Assn. Info. and Image Mgmt., Am. Mgmt. Assn., Nat. Office Machine Dealers Assn., Mensa. Republican. Roman Catholic. Clubs: Theodore Roosevelt Assn., Safari Club Internat., Game Conservation Internat., K.C., Hemingway Soc. Author: Hemingway and the Blood Sports, 1977. Office: 140 Industrial Dr Elmhurst IL 60126

MATTHEWS, ROWENA GREEN, biological chemistry educator; b. Cambridge, Eng., Aug. 20, 1938 (parents Am. citizens); d. David E. and Doris (Cribb) Green; m. Larry Stanford Matthews, June 18, 1960; children—Brian Stanford, Keith David. B.A., Harvard U., 1960; Ph.D., U. Mich., 1969. Instr. U. S.C., Columbia, 1964-65; postdoctoral fellow U. Mich., Ann Arbor, 1970-75, asst. prof., 1975-81, assoc. prof. biol. chemistry, 1981—; mem. phys. biochemistry study sect. NIH, 1982-86. Editorial adv. bd. Biochem. Jour., 1984-85. Contbr. articles to profl. jours. Recipient Faculty Recognition award U. Mich., 1985; NIH grantee, 1978—. Mem. AAAS, Am. Soc. Biol. Chemists, Am. Chem. Soc. (program chmn. biol. chemistry div. 1985), Phi Beta Kappa, Sigma Xi. Avocations: bicycling, snorkeling, cross country skiing, cooking. Home: 1609 S University St Ann Arbor MI 48104 Office: U Mich Biophysics Research Div 2200 Bonisteel Blvd Ann Arbor MI 48109

MATTHEWS, TOMMY REED, fire chief; b. Massillon, Ohio, Apr. 20, 1942. Firefighter Massillon Fire Dept., 1966-74, fire capt., 1974-79, asst. fire chief, 1979-81, fire chief, 1981—. Served with U.S. Army, 1964-66, Korea. Mem. Internat. Assn. Fire Chiefs, Ohio Fire Chiefs, Stark County Fire Chiefs, Internat. Assn. Firefighters. Lodges: Moose, Masons. Home: 220 Hawthorne Ave NE Massillon OH 44646 Office: Massillon Fire Dept 233 Erie St South Massillon OH 44646

MATTHIAS, JOHN EDWARD, English literature educator; b. Columbus, Ohio, Sept. 5, 1941; s. John Marshall and Lois (Kirkpatrick) M.; m. Diana Clare Jocelyn, Dec. 27, 1967; children—Cynouai, Laura. B.A., Ohio State U., 1963; M.A. Stanford U., 1966; postgrad. U. London, 1967. Asst. prof. dept. English, U. Notre Dame (Ind.), 1966-73, assoc. prof., 1973-80, prof., 1980—; vis. fellow Clare Hall, Cambridge U., 1966-77, assoc., 1977—; vis. prof. dept. English, Skidmore Coll., Saratoga Springs, N.Y., 1975, U.Chgo., 1980; Woodrow Wilson fellow, 1963; Fulbright grantee, 1966; recipient Columbia U. Transl. award, 1978; Swedish Inst. award, 1981; Poetry award Soc. Midland Authors, 1984. Mem. AAUP, Poets and Writers, London Poetry Secreariat, PEN Author: Bucyrus, 1971; Turns, 1975; Crossing, 1979; Five American Poets, 1980; Introducing David Jones, 1980; Contemporary Swedish Poetry, 1980; Bathory and Lermontov, 1980; Northern Summer: New and Selected Poems, 1984. Office: Dept English U Notre Dame Notre Dame IN 46556

MATTHIES, DONNA K., librarian; b. Reedley, Calif., Apr. 21, 1957; d. David Glenn and Ruth Ann (Dettweiler) Kope; m. Mark Alan Matthies, Aug. 18, 1979. B.A., Bethel Coll., 1979; M.L.S., Emporia State U., 1982. German tchr. Unified Sch. Dist. 418, McPherson, Kans., 1979-80, jr. high art tchr., 1980-81; library media specialist Unified Sch. Dist. 259, Wichita, Kans., 1982-84. Mem. ALA, Kans. Assn. Sch. Librarians, Kans. Library Assn., Wichita Assn. Sch. Librarians, Beta Phi Mu. Democrat. Mennonite. Home: 601 E 7th #4 Davis CA 95616 Office: Fairview Elementary School 830 First St Fairview CA 94533

MATTHIES, FREDERICK JOHN, architectural and engineering firm executive; b. Omaha, Oct. 4, 1925; s. Fred John Matthies and Charlotte (Leota) Matthies Metz; m. Carol Mae Dean, Sept. 14, 1947; children—John Frederick, Jane Carolyn Matthies Goding. B.S. in Civil Engring., Cornell U., 1947; postgrad. U. Nebr., 1954-56. Civil engr. Henningson, Durham & Richardson, Omaha, 1947-50, 52-54; sr. v.p. Leo A. Daly Co., Omaha, 1954—; lectr. on doing bus. with fed. govt., 1980, on export of services, 1982. Sec. Orange County Luth. Hosp. Assn., Calif., 1961-62; regent Augustana Coll., Sioux Falls, S.C., 1976—; mem. Douglas County Republican Central Com., Nebr., 1968-72; trustee Luth. Med. Ctr., Omaha, 1978-82. Served to 1st lt. USMCR, 1943-46, 50-52; Korea. Fellow ASCE, Instn. Civil Engrs. (U.K.); mem. Am. Waterworks Assn. (life), Nat. Soc. Profl. Engrs., Air Force Assn. Lutheran. Club: Happy Hollow Country (Omaha). Avocations: golf; stamp collecting; coin collecting; travel; volunteer work. Home: 337 S 127th St Omaha NE 68154 Office: Leo A Daly Co 8600 Indian Hills Dr Omaha NE 68154

MATTILA, EDWARD CHARLES, music educator; b. Duluth, Minn., Nov. 30, 1927; s. Edward H. and Ellen M. (Matson) M.; m. Nancy Ann Norton, Oct. 12, 1956; children—Amy Lara, Edward Norton. B.A. in Music, U. Minn., 1950, Ph.D. in Music Theory and Composition, 1963; M.Mus., New Eng. Conservatory, 1956. Instr. Concordia Coll., St. Paul, 1958-62; asst. prof. Bishop Coll., Dallas, 1962-64; faculty U. Kans., Lawrence, 1964—, prof. music, 1975—, producer, host program contemporary music Sta. KANU, 1971—. Served with Signal Corps, U.S. Army, 1952-53. Grantee in field. Mem. Am. Soc. Univ. Composers, Coll. Music Soc., Am. Music Ctr. Composer: Symphony No. 1, Theme and Variations for 2 pianos; Partitions for String Orch.; 6 arrays for piano; Repercussions for Tape; Movements for Computer and Dancers. Office: Sch of Fine Arts U Kans Lawrence KS 66045

MATTINGLY, THOMAS PAUL, ophthalmologist; b. Evansville, Ind., Nov. 19, 1949; s. Paul Thedus and Genevieve Catherine (Devoy) M.; m. Margarita Sylvia Lopez-Silvero, May 11, 1973; children—Christine Elise, David Thomas, Ann Elizabeth. B.A. Ind. U., 1971, M.D., Indpls., 1975. Diplomate Am. Bd. Ophthalmology. Intern Methodist Hosp., Indpls., 1975-76; resident in ophthalmology Shands Teaching Hosp., Gainesville, Fla., 1976-79; ophthalmologist Arnett Clinic, Lafayette, Ind., 1979—; clin. asst. prof. Ind. U. Sch. Med., 1980. Author Home Study Course, 1982. Contbr. articles to profl. jours. Fellow Am. Acad. Ophthalmology; mem. AMA. Republican. Roman Catholic. Club: Sierra. Lodges: Rotary, Elks. Avocations: piano, astronomy, reading, boating. Office: 2600 Greenbush St Lafayette IN

MATTISON, DONALD CHARLES, dentist; b. Chgo., Oct. 22, 1928; s. Donald Charles and Margaret (Munger) M.; m. Helen Manson, Sept. 6, 1952; children—Susan, Thomas, Sandra; m. Diane Schulte, June 17, 1975. Practice dentistry, Wheaton, Ill., 1956—. Founder/mgr. Wheaton Summer Symphony; personnel mgr. Wheaton Mcpl. Band, 1964. Served to capt. U.S. Army, 1954-56. Mem. Chgo. Fedn. Musicians. Lodge: Lions (Wheaton) (sec. 1959-60). Avocations: orchestra management; music; fishing. Office: 1600 E Roosevelt Rd Wheaton IL 60187

MATTSON, PETER ROLAND, electric company official; b. Oakland, Calif., Apr. 15, 1931; s. Edward Carl and Anna Christina (Gustavson) M.; m. Roberta Mae Francine, Jan. 17, 1954; children—Pamela, Bruce. B.S. in Marine Engring., Calif. Maritime Acad., 1953; postgrad. San Jose State Coll., 1956. With Gen. Electric Co., Oak Brook, Ill., 1956—, dist. mgr. generation equipment sales, 1969—. Served to lt. (j.g.) USN, 1953-55. Mem. ASME, Am. Nuclear Soc., Western Soc. Engrs. (trustee 1976-77). Republican. Methodist. Club: Union League (Chgo.). Home: 1333 Glenwood Ave Glenview IL 60525 Office: Gen Electric Co 2015 Spring Rd Suite 301 Oak Brook IL 60522

MATTSON, ROBERT W., state official. Treas. State of Minn., St. Paul, 1983—. Office: Office of Treas 50 Sherburne Ave Saint Paul MN 55155*

MATUSZEWSKI, STANLEY, clergyman; b. Morris Run, Pa., May 4, 1915; s. Andrew and Mary (Czekalski) M.; grad. St. Andrew's Prep. Sem., Rochester, N.Y.; student La Salette Coll., Hartford, Conn., Scholastic Sem., Altamont, N.Y. Ordained priest Roman Catholic Ch., 1942; disciplinarian, prof. classics, La Salette Sem., Olivet, 1942-46, dir., 1948—; superior Midwest province LaSalette Fathers; founding editor Our Lady's Digest, 1946—; exec. bd. Nat. Catholic Decency in Reading Program; faculty adv. Midwest Conf. of Internat. Relations Clubs sponsored 1944 in Chgo. by Carnegie Endowment for Internat. Peace. Trustee Nat. Shrine of Immaculate Conception, Washington. Honored by Rochester, N.Y. Centennial Com. 1934 as Monroe County (N.Y.) orator. Mem. Mariological Soc. Am. (1954 award), Missionaries of Our Lady of La Salette, Catholic Press Assn., Canon Law Soc., Catholic Broadcasters' Assn., Religious Edn. Assn., Polish-Hungarian World Fedn. (trustee). K.C. Author: Rochester Centennial Oration; Youth Marches On. Home: Box 777 Twin Lakes WI 53181

MATZ, MILTON, clinical psychologist, management relations consultant, rabbi; b. N.Y.C., June 30, 1927; s. Joshua E. and Sonja (Kviat) Matz; m. Anne L. Jaburg, June 20, 1952; children—Deborah, David. B.A., Yeshiva U., 1947; M.H.L., rabbinic ordination, Hebrew Union Coll., 1952, D.D. (hon.), 1977; Ph.D., U. Chgo., 1966. Cert. Ohio Psychol. Assn. Bd. Examiners Psychologists, 1966; lic. Ohio Bd. Psychology, 1973. First lt. USAF, 1952-54; asst. rabbi Kehilath Anshei Maariv Temple, Chgo., 1954-57; rabbi Congregation B'nai Jehoshua, Chgo., 1957-59; dir. pastoral psychology, asso. rabbi The Temple, Cleve., 1959-66; sr. staff psychologist Fairhill Psychiat. Hosp., Cleve., 1966-69; adj. prof. Cleve. State U., 1966-70; clin. instr. Case-Western Res. Sch. Medicine, 1966-73, asst. clin. prof., 1973—, dir. Pastoral Psychology Service Inst., 1973—, clin. dir. bereavement project, 1978—; pvt. practice clin. psychology, Beachwood, Ohio, 1966—; mng. ptnr. Matz Assocs., Beachwood, 1966—; cons. dir. Erie Pastoral Psychology Inst., 1977—; mng. ptnr. Mgmt. Relations Cons. div. Matz Assocs., Beachwood, 1984—; cons. dir. pastoral tng. project Central Conf. Am. Rabbis, 1978-79; lectr. mgmt. relations, negotiation and mediation skills. Sec., v.p. Greater Cleve. Bd. Rabbis, 1964-66; bd. mem. Jewish Children's Bur. and Bellefaire Jewish Community Ctr., Cleve., 1952-64; advisory bd. Div. Child Welfare, Cuyahoga County, Ohio, 1962-66; founding mem. Cuyahoga County Community Mental Health and Retardation Bd., Cleve., 1967-71, chmn., 1972-73; chmn. Central Conf. Am. Rabbis Com. on Judaism and Health, N.Y.C., 1975-79. Diplomate Am. Assn. Pastoral Counselors; mem. Am., Ohio psychol. assns., Soc. for Indsl. and Orgnl. Psychology, Am. Assn. Pastoral Counselors, Ohio Acad. Profl. Psychology (trustee 1984—). Author numerous papers and articles on interpersonal communication, dispute resolution, treatment of marital conflict and grief, primary prevention of mental illness, psychology and religion, and pastoral tng.; recipient commendation for outstanding leadership in mental health Bd. Commrs. of Cuyahoga County, 1973. Home: 3346 Stockholm Rd Cleveland OH 44120 Office: 3609 Park East Beachwood OH 44122

MAUGANS, JOHN CONRAD, lawyer; b. Miami County, Ind., May 10, 1938; s. Willis William and Evelyn Jeannette (Mills) M.; A.B., Manchester Coll., 1960; LL.B. with distinction (Krannert scholar), Ind. U., 1962, J.D., 1970; m. Judith M. Gallagher, Jan. 24, 1960 (dec. June 1984); children—Lisa Denise, Stacy Erin, Kristen Cherie; m. Jo Ella Middlekauff, June 7, 1985. Admitted to Ind. bar, 1962; with firm Barnes, Hickam, Pantzer & Boyd, Indpls., 1962-63; practice in Kokomo, 1966—; ptnr. firm Bayliff, Harrigan, Cord & Maugans, P.C., 1969—; guest lectr. Coll. Bus., Manchester Coll., 1966-80. Chmn. Howard County fund dr. Manchester Coll., 1971; bd. dirs. Tribal Trails council Girl Scouts U.S.A., 1977—, Vols. in Community Service, 1978-84, Home Health Care of Central Ind., Inc., 1983—. Served to capt. AUS, 1963-66. Mem. Am., Ind., Howard County bar assns., Am., Ind. trial lawyers assns., Manchester Coll. Alumni Assn. (chmn. area chpt. 1970), Manchester Coll. M. Alumni Assn. (pres. 1972), Order of Coif, Phi Delta Phi. Lutheran. Contbr. articles to legal jours. Home: 1890 S 820 W Russiaville IN 46979 Office: Box 2249 123 N Buckeye Kokomo IN 46902

MAUL, GARY PIERRE, engineering educator, consultant, researcher; b. Sharon, Pa., June 27, 1947; s. David H. and Liliane M. Maul; m. Linda S. Koch, May 6, 1972; children—Hayden B., Allison R. B. Engring., Youngstown State U., 1970; M.S. in Indsl. Engring., Purdue U., 1976; Ph.D., Pa. State U., 1982. Profl. engr., Pa., Ohio. Indsl. engr. Packard Electric div. Gen. Motors, Warren, Ohio, 1972-77; asst. prof. Youngstown (Ohio) State U., 1977-79; instr. Pa. State U., University Park, 1979-82; asst. prof. indsl. engring. Ohio State U., Columbus, 1982—; active automation research and devel.; cons. to Midwest industry. Adv. to vocat. programs, Rehab. div. Ohio Indsl. Commn. Mem. Inst. Indsl. Engrs. (award Youngstown chpt. 1970), Alpha Pi Mu, Phi Kappa Phi. Contbr. article to profl. publ., paper to profl. conf. Home: 7548 Sagewood Ct Worthington OH 43085 Office: 1971 Neil Ave Columbus OH 43210

MAUL, JAMES ROBERT, optometrist; b. Mansfield, Ohio, June 18, 1953; s. John and Sara Elizabeth (Scott) M.; m. Peggy Ann Harpster, June 24, 1978; children—Courtney Harpster, Alissa Lauren. B.Sc. in Indsl. Engring., Ohio State U., 1976, O.D., 1982. Lic. optometrist, Ohio. Engr., mgmt. trainee Allis Chalmers, York, Pa. and Cin., 1976-78; engr. Schuler, Columbus, Ohio, 1978-82; owner, pres. Firelands Optical Ctr., Norwalk, Ohio, 1982—. Mem. Am. Optometric Assn. (zone sec.), Norwalk C. of C., Beta Sigma Kappa. Lutheran. Avocations: vollyball; racquetball. Office: Firelands Optical Ctr 112 Benedict Ave Norwalk OH 44857

MAUL, THOMAS MARTIN, lawyer; b. Kearney, Nebr., Nov. 28, 1952; s. M.G. and Adalynne (Symonds) M.; m. Mary Elizabeth Schulte, Aug. 11, 1979; children—Leslie, Lauren. Student Kearney State Coll., 1971-72; B.S. in Bus. Adminstrn., U. Nebr., 1977, J.D., 1980. Bar: Nebr. 1980. Ptnr., Leininger, Grant, Rogers & Maul, Columbus, Nebr., 1980—. Served with U.S. Army, 1972-74. Mem. Nebr. State Bar Assn. (exec. com. Young Lawyers Div. 1984), Columbus C. of C. (pub. relations com. 1982—, membership chmn. 1984), Beta Sigma Psi. Republican. Lutheran. Lodge: Elks. Office: Leininger Grant Rogers & Maul 1465 27th Ave Columbus NE 68601

MAULDIN, WILLIAM H., cartoonist; b. Mountain Park, N.Mex., Oct. 29, 1921; s. Sidney Albert and Edith Katrina (Bemis) M.; ed. pub. schs., N.Mex. and Ariz.; student art Chgo. Acad. Fine Arts; M.A. (hon.), Conn. Wesleyan U., 1946; L.H.D. (hon.), Lincoln Coll., 1970; Litt.D. (hon.), Albion Coll., 1970, N.Mex. State U. at Las Cruces, 1972, U. Mich., 1973, Washington U., St. Louis, 1982; m. Norma Jean Humphries, Feb. 28, 1942 (div. 1946); children—Bruce Patrick, Timothy; m. 2d, Natalie Sarah Evans, June 27, 1947 (dec. Aug. 1971); children—Andrew, David, John, Nathaniel; m. 3d, Christine Ruth Lund, July 29, 1972; 1 dau., Kaja Lisa. Cartoonist, St. Louis Post-Dispatch, until 1962, Chgo. Sun-Times, 1962—; tech. adviser, actor in movie Teresa, 1950; actor The Red Badge of Courage, 1950. Served with AUS, 1940-45; with 45th Div. (worked part time on div. newspaper); transferred to Mediterranean edit. Stars and Stripes, 1943; participated in campaigns, Sicily, Italy, France, Germany. Decorated Purple Heart, Legion of Merit; recipient Pulitzer prize for cartoons, 1944, Pulitzer prize for satiric comment on plight of Boris Pasternak, 1958; Sigma Delta Chi journalism award for cartoons, 1964, 70, 72, Distinguished Service award, 1969; Prix Charles Huard de dessin de presse Found. Pour L'Art et la Recherche, 1974. Fellow Sigma Delta Chi. Author, cartoonist: Up Front (Book of the Month Club selection), 1945; Back Home (Book of the Month selection), 1947; cartoonist: Star Spangled Banter, 1941; Sicily Sketch Book, 1943; Star Spangled Banter (separate collection of cartoons), 1944; Mud, Mules and Mountains (Italy), 1944; This Damn Tree Leaks (Italy) 1945; A Sort of a Saga, 1949; Bill Mauldin's Army, 1951; Bill Mauldin in Korea, 1952; What's Got Your Back Up?, 1961; I've Decided I Want My Seat Back, 1965; The Brass Ring, 1972 (Book of Month Club selection); Mud and Guts, 1978. Address: care Chgo Sun-Times Chicago IL 60611

MAUPIN, STEPHANIE ZELLER, French teacher; b. St. Louis, Apr. 16, 1946; d. Robert H. and Pernelle (Santhuff) Zeller; 1 child, Britt. B.S.Ed., U. Mo., 1967; M.A.T. in Communication Arts, Webster Coll., St. Louis, 1977, postgrad., 1979-82. Cert. tchr., Mo. Tchr. Mehlville Sch. Dist., St. Louis County, 1967—; tchr. French and English, Oakville High Sch., Mehlville Sch. Dist., 1971-84; adj. faculty Webster Coll., St. Louis, 1980, St. Louis U., 1982—. Dir. in charge exchange program St. Louis-Lyon Sister Cities Corp. NEH Fellow. Mem. Am. Assn. Tchrs. French (dir.), NEA, Assn. Supervision and Curriculum Devel., Internat. Edn. Consortium, Webster Coll. Alumni Assn. Home: 9641 Chancellorsville Dr Saint Louis MO 63126 Office: 5557 Milburn Rd Saint Louis MO 63129

MAURER, DONALD DELBERT, medical device manufacturer; b. Lead, S.D., July 17, 1937. A.A.S., Milw. Sch. Engring., 1960; B.S. in Elec. Engring., S.D. State U., 1965; M.S. in Biomed. Engring., Iowa State U., 1971. With Univac Co., 1960-62; prodn. design engr. Control Data, Inc., Mpls., 1965-66; cons. engr., mgr. spl. external pacing project Medtronic, Inc., Mpls., 1966-71, research engr., 1971-74, dir. Neurol. research and engring., 1974-77, co-founder neurol. rehab. div., 1974-77; research asst. Iowa State U., 1969-71; founding dir. rehab. engring. program Courage Ctr., Golden Valley, Minn., 1977-79; chmn. EMPI, Inc., Mpls., 1977-79, pres., chief exec. officer, 1979—. Contbr. articles to profl. jours. and book. Patentee in field. Mem. Health Industry Mfrs. Orgn., Am. Assn. Med. Instrumentation, IEEE, Internat. Assn. Study Pain, Am. Congress Rehab. Medicine, Neuroelectric Soc., Am. Mgmt. Assn., Am. Acad. Sci., Electrostatic Soc. Am., Eta Kappa Nu. Home: 2020 Shaw St Anoka MN 55303 Office: 261 S Commerce Circle Minneapolis MN 55432

MAURER, STEPHEN VEITH, optometrist; b. Dover, Ohio, Aug. 13, 1954; s. John Frederick and Phyllis Ann (Ball) M.; m. Claudia Lynne Coggeshall, Aug. 27, 1977; children—Christopher, Justin, Stephanie. B.S. in Biol. Scis., Ohio State U., 1976, O.D., 1980. Gen. practice optometry, New Philadelphia, Ohio, 1980—. Mem. Am. Optometric Assn., Contact Lens Soc., Ohio Optometric Assn., Jaycees, Ohio U. Alumni Assn. (pres. 1984—). Republican. Methodist. Avocations: tennis, camping. Home: 818 3d St NW New Philadelphia OH 44663 Office: 161 W High St New Philadelphia OH 44663

MAURER, STEVEN DOUGLAS, state official; b. Sidney, Ohio, July 20, 1947; s. Walter and Patsy M.; m. Amy Lowers, July 4, 1978; 1 child, Jennifer. B.S. in Social Studies, Ohio State U. Mayor, clk./treas. City of Botkins (Ohio); tchr. Botkins High Sch., New Knoxville High Sch.; mgr. Maurer Oil Co.; mem. Ohio Senate, 1980-84, chmn. agr., small bus. and econ. devel. com.; asst. dir. agr. State of Ohio, 1985—; mem. Ohio Gov's Adv. Council on Travel and Tourism, Capital Planning and Improvements Adv. Bd. Mem. Shelby County Democratic Central Com., Civilian Conservation Adv. Council, Served with U.S. Army, 1969-71. Decorated Army Commendation medal with double oak leaf cluster, Bronze Star; recipient Distiing. Service award State VFW, 1983. Mem. Botkins Hist. Soc., Am. Legion, VFW. Lutheran. Club: Botkins Area Community. Lodge: Kiwanis. Office: Ohio Dept Agr 65 S Front St 6th Floor Columbus OH 43215

MAURICE, ALFRED PAUL, artist, art educator; b. Nashua, N.H., Mar. 11, 1921; s. Paul and Gertrude (Martel) M.; m. J. Dolores Robson, Feb. 26, 1946. Student U. N.H., 1940-42; B.A., Mich. State U., 1947, M.A., 1950. Instr. Macalester Coll., St. Paul, 1947-49; asst. prof., assoc. prof. SUNY-New Paltz, 1950-57; exec. dir. Md. Inst., Balt., 1957-59; dir. Kalamazoo Inst. Arts, Mich., 1959-65; prof. U. Ill., Chgo., 1965—, chmn. art dept., 1965-67, assoc. dean faculties, 1969-72, dean coll. of art, 1975-77. Exhibited in solo exhbns., numerous group exhbns., 1981-84. Contbr. articles to profl. jours. Mem. Mercy Hosp., Instl. Rev. Bd., Chgo., 1979—, gov. Mich. council on Arts, 1964-65. Served with U.S. Army, 1943-46. Recipient Medal of Honor Graphics award Audubon Artists. Mem. Nat. Soc. Painters in Casein and Acrylic (Dr. David Soletsky award 1983), Pastel Soc. Am. Home: 2725 A South Michigan Ave Chicago IL 60616 Office: U Ill Chicago Box 4348 Chicago IL 60680

MAUZEY, ARMAND JEAN, physician; b. Findlay, Ill., Apr. 18, 1905; s. George Washington and Catherine E. (Cloos) M.; B.S., Eureka (Ill.) Coll., 1928; B.S., U. Ill., 1931, M.D., 1932; postgrad. U. Pa., 1937-38, M.Sc., 1940, D.Sc., 1948; m. Virginia E. Tompkins, May 25, 1945; children—Katherine E., John M., Suzanne R. Surveyman, U.S. C.E., East St. Louis, Ill., Coal Creek, Tenn. and Fairfax County, Va., summers 1925-30; intern St. Luke's Hosp., Chgo., 1932-33; gen. practice medicine, Shelbyville, Ill., 1934-37; resident in ob-gyn U. Ill. Coll. Medicine, Chgo., 1938-40, to clin. assoc. prof.; practice medicine specializing in ob-gyn, Elmhurst, Ill.; cons. gynecologist Cook County Hosp., Chgo., 1946-49, Elgin (Ill.) State Hosp., 1949-52, Booth Meml. Hosp., Chgo., 1952-58; chmn. dept. ob-gyn Elmhurst Meml. Hosp., 1954-58, 66-67; pres. med. staff Meml. Hosp., DuPage County, Elmhurst, 1968-69. Bd. dirs. Elmhurst YMCA. Recipient 25 Year Teaching award U. Ill. Coll. Medicine, 1963; Achievement Citation award Eureka Coll., 1968; named to Athletic Hall of Fame, Eureka Coll., 1970. Served from 1st lt. to maj. M.C., AUS, 1941-46; ETO. Recipient Asso. Prof. Emeritus citation U. Ill. Coll. Med., 1976; diplomate Am. Bd. Obstetrics and Gynecology. Fellow ACS; mem. AMA, Ill. Med. Soc., (chmn. sect. ob-gyn 1951-52), Du Page County Med. Soc., Am. Coll. Ob-Gyn, Internat. Coll. Surgeons, Chgo. Gynecol. Soc., N.Y. Acad. Scis., Huguenot Soc. S.C., Nat. Huguenot Soc., Va. Hist. Soc., S.C. Hist. Soc., SAR, Huguenot Soc. London, Lambda Chi Alpha, Alpha Kappa Kappa. Republican. Episcopalian. Mason (50 Yr. Membership citation Findlay 1979). Author: The Mauzey-Mauzy Family-From the Crusades to Colonial America. Contbr. articles to med. jours. and hist. mags. Home: 21 Spinning Wheel Rd Apt 6A Hinsdale IL 60521

MAVEL, MARY ANN, foundation administrator; b. LeRoy, Wis., June 1, 1935; d. James Joseph and Marie Ann (Bauer) Weinberger; m. Gerald George Davel, June 21, 1958 (dec. 1963); children—Elizabeth, David, Ann, Amy. B.S., St. Norbert Coll., 1957. Traffic coordinator Sta. WTMJ-TV, Milw., 1966-71; ptnr. Maier, Richman & Costello Advt., Inc., Milw., 1971-75; pub. relations specialist Milw. Area Tech. Coll., 1975-77; exec. dir. Milw. Area Tech. Coll. Found., Inc., 1977—. Mem. Nat. Soc. Fund Raising Execs. (Wis. chpt.). Avocations: biking; sailing; cross-country skiing; gardening; needlecraft. Home: 1420 Lone Oak Ln Brookfield WI 53005 Office: Milw Area Tech Coll Found Inc 1015 N 6th St Milwaukee WI 53005

MAVRELIS, WILLIAM PETER, physician, surgeon; b. Waterloo, Iowa, Jan. 12, 1912; s. Peter L. and Amelia (Commandros) M.; student Iowa State Tchrs. Coll., 1930-32; B.S., U. Minn., 1934, M.D., 1937; m. Cornelia MacDonald, Mar. 1, 1938; children—Penelope, Amy, Peter. Intern, St. Francis Hosp., Peoria, Ill., 1936-37, resident, 1937-38; jr. pathology resident Cook County Hosp., Chgo., 1938-42, sr. pathology resident, 1942, sr. pathologist, 1946-50; pathologist, clin. pathologist Ill. Central Community Hosp., 1950-77; asst. prof. Northwestern Med. Sch., 1946-81; police surgeon, Chgo., 1957-81. Sec. bd. dirs. Ill. Central Community Hosp., 1974—, Hyde Pk. Community Hosp. Served to lt. col. U.S. Army, 1942-46. Diplomate Am. Bd. Path. Anatomy. Mem. AMA, Am. Assn. Rwy. Surgeons, Assn. Practitioners and Infection Control, Am., Ill. assns. blood banks, Ill., Chgo. med. assns., Chgo. Path. Soc., Chgo. Gas Chromotography, Chgo. Mycol. Soc., Hellenic Med. Soc. Greek Orthodox. Clubs: Beverly Hills Tennis; Chgo. Athletic Assn. Home: 614 S Lombard Ave Oak Park IL 60304 Office: 5800 Stony Island Ave Chicago IL 60637

MAWER, WILLIAM THOMAS, lawyer; b. Toledo, May 11, 1948; s. Clifford M. and Mary E. (Avey) M.; m. Catherine M. Greenler, Aug. 16, 1969; children—Jennifer M., Melinda J., Ryanne E. B.S., U. Toledo, 1970; J.D., Ohio No. U., 1973. Bar: Ohio 1973. Ptnr. FHM&D Co., L.P.A., Eaton, Ohio, 1973—; instr. Sinclair Coll., Dayton, Ohio, 1975-82; judge pro tem Eaton Municipal Ct., 1975-83. Trustee West Central Ohio council Boy Scouts Am., 1973-78; active Republican Central Com., Eaton, Ohio, 1980-84; pres. Rural Legal Aid Soc., Eaton, 1982-83; active Eaton Bd. Edn., 1984. Recipient Outstanding Jaycees award Eaton Jaycees, 1974; award of Merit, Boy Scouts Am., 1977. Mem. Ohio State Bar Assn. (taxation com.), ABA, Preble County Bar Assn. (pres. 1984-85). Lutheran. Lodges: Masons (chaplain 1974-75), Rotary. Avocations: downhill skiing; woodworking. Home: 1409 East Ave Eaton OH 45320 Office: FHM&D Co LPA 111 S Barron St Eaton OH 45320

MAXFIELD, KENNETH WAYNE, transportation company executive; b. Leo, Ind., Oct. 26, 1924; student Loyola U., Chgo., 1946-48; LL.B., De Paul U., 1950; m. Jean; 2 children. Admitted to Ind., Ill. bars, 1950; with N.Am. Van Lines Inc., 1950—, exec. v.p. corp. world hdqrs., Fort Wayne, Ind., 1966-77, pres., chief operating officer, chmn. bd., 1977—. Pres. bd. Jr. Achievement, Ft. Wayne, 1976-77. Served with U.S. Army, 1943-46; Aleutians. Mem. Ft. Wayne C. of C. (pres. 1974). Club: Summit (dir.). Lodge: Rotary (Ft. Wayne). Office: North Am Van Lines Inc 5001 US Hwy 30 W Fort Wayne IN 46801

MAXON, PAUL QUIRK, business executive; b. Elgin, Ill., Oct. 11, 1947; s. Don C. and Mary (Quirk) M.; m. Ellen Turner, Oct. 14, 1972; children—Mathew, David, Jason, Christina. Student in Econs., U. Ariz., 1972. Pres. Wilderness Log Homes, Plymouth, Wis., 1972—, Christian Foster Fund, Plymouth, 1980—. Author: Wilderness Log Homes Brochure/Plann Book, annually. Mem. Sheboygan County Republican Party; active St. Paul's Episcopal Ch., Plymouth. Recipient Cert. Commendation, Wis. Dept. Correction, 1983. Mem. Young Pres.' Orgn. Avocations: racquetball; skiing; guitar; bicycling; golf. Home: Rt 2 Ridge Rd Plymouth WI 53703 Office: Wilderness Log Homes Inc Rt 2 Plymouth WI 53073

MAXSON, ALBERT LEROY, airline executive; b. Erie, Pa., Dec. 27, 1935; s. Walter LeRoy and Emily M. (Sabol) M.; m. Linda Kay Kiger, Apr. 18, 1964; children—Barbara, Janet, Patricia. B.S., Pa. State U., 1957; M.B.A., Ga. State U., 1973; postgrad. advanced mgmt. program Harvard U., 1976. C.P.A., W.Va. With Price Waterhouse & Co., Pitts., 1957-66; v.p. fin., treas. So. Airways, Atlanta, 1966-79; v.p., treas. Republic Airlines, Mpls., 1979-80, sr. v.p. fin., 1980—. Mem. Fin. Execs. Inst., Am. Inst. C.P.A.s, Nat. Assn. Accts., Nat. Assn. Corp. Dirs. Home: 5848 Long Brake Trail Edina MN 55435 Office: Republic Airlines Inc 7500 Airline Dr Minneapolis MN 55450

MAXSON, JOHN EUGENE, land surveyor; b. Jackson, Mich., Dec. 8, 1945; s. John Wilbur Maxson and Betty Jane (Eash) Maxson Crisenbery; m. Gail Marie Poole, Aug. 8, 1966 (div. 1972); children—John Leonard, Karri Marie; m. Edna Lydia Krutsch, Dec. 6, 1975 (dec. Sept. 1984). Student Jackson Community Coll., 1964-66 cert. Internat. Corr. Schs., 1974. Registered land surveyor, Mich., Alaska, Wis., N.D., S.D., Miss. Draftsman Commonwealth Assocs., Jackson, 1964-69, designer, 1969-73, surveyor, 1973-79; project coordinator Gilbert/Commonwealth, Jackson, 1979-82, project mgr., 1982—. Pres. Mirror Lake Property Owners Assn., Jerome, Mich., 1980—. Mem. Mich. Soc. Registered Land Surveyors (sec. central chpt. 1981-82, pres. 1984—), Am. Congress Surveying and Mapping, Alaska Soc. Profl. Land Surveyors. Republican. Baptist. Avocations: hunting, fishing, trapping. Home: 224 Eaglehurst Dr Jerome MI 49249 Office: Gilbert/Commonwealth 209 E Washington Ave Jackson MI 49201

MAXTON, JULIA CURTNER, marketing manager; b. Dayton, Ohio, Feb. 8, 1940; d. Clifford Rome and Hilda Ione (Sloat) C.; m. Timothy C. Pitstick, Nov. 4, 1985; children by previous marriage—Kelly Michele, Elizabeth. B.A., Miami U., Ohio, 1961; postgrad. Sinclair Community Coll., 1980. Lic. real estate sales, Ohio, 1980. Dir. mktg. and leasing Arcade Sq., 1977-80; dir. mktg. and press Bobby Brown Racing, 1982—; dir. mktg., leasing and sales The Tipton Group, Inc., Dayton, 1982—; cons., Halcyon Ltd., Hartford, Conn.; speaker. Bd. dirs. Good Samaritan Hosp. Named Marketeer of Yr., Dayton chpt. Am. Mgmt. Assn., 1980. Mem. Dayton Area C. of C. (adv. bd.), Am. Horse Show Assn., Tri State Horse Assn., Downtown Dayton Assn. Republican. Clubs: Sports Car of Am., Corvette Troy (Dayton). Home: 8080 Condor Ct Dayton OH 45459 Office: 124 E 3d St Dayton OH 45402

MAXWELL, ALAN DAVID, systems analyst; b. Cookeville, Tenn., Feb. 11, 1957; s. John L. and Christine Evelyn (Lynn) M.; m. Malissa LeAnne Mason, Mar. 16, 1984. B.S. in Acctg., Tenn. Tech. U., 1979; postgrad. in bus. adminstrn., U. Dayton, 1984—. Mktg. applications rep. Triad Systems Corp., Nashville, 1979-81; gen. mgr. U.C. Craft Ctr., Cookeville, Tenn., 1981-83; cost estimator Duriron Co., Inc., Cookeville, 1983-84, systems analyst, Dayton, Ohio, 1984—. Mem. Cookeville Jaycees, (v.p. 1982). Mem. Ch. of Christ. Avocations: racquetball; running; skiing. Home: 311 W Dorothy Ln Kettering OH 45429

MAXWELL, DONALD ROBERT, pharmaceutical company executive; b. Paris, Mar. 30, 1929; s. Titus B. and Helen Maxwell; m. Catherine Billon, Aug. 16, 1956; children—Monica, Nicholas, Christopher, Caroline, Denis, Dominic, Marie-Claire, Philip. B.A., U. Cambridge, Eng., 1952, Ph.D., 1955, M.A., 1956. Attaché de recherche Inst. Pasteur, Paris, 1956-57; researcher Pharmacologist Research Labs., May and Baker Ltd., Eng., 1957-74; dir. preclin. research Warner-Lambert Co., Morris Plains, N.J., 1974-77; v.p. preclin. research Warner-Lambert/Parke Davis, Ann Arbor, Mich., 1977—. Contbr. articles to profl. jours. Fellow Royal Soc. Medicine; mem. Am. Soc. Pharmacology and Exptl. Therapeutics, Brit. Pharm. Soc., Physiol. Soc. Eng., Biochem. Soc. Eng. Avocation: long distance running. Office: Warner-Lambert/Parke-Davis Pharm Div 2800 Plymouth Rd Ann Arbor MI 48105

MAXWELL, FLORENCE HINSHAW, civic worker; Nora, Ind., July 14, 1914; d. Asa Benton and Gertrude (Randall) Hinshaw; B.A. cum laude, Butler U., 1935; m. John Williamson Maxwell, June 5, 1936; children—Marilyn, William Douglas. Coordinator, bd. dirs. Sight Conservation and Aid to Blind, 1962-73, nat. chmn., 1969-73; active various fund drives; chmn. jamboree, hostess coms. North Central High Sch., 1959, 64; Girl Scouts U.S.A., 1937-38, 54-56; mus. chmn. Sr. Girl Scout Regional Council, 1956-57; scorekeeper Little League, 1955-57; bd. dirs. Nora Sch. Parents' Club, 1958-59, Eastwood Jr. High Sch. Triangle Club, 1959-62, Ind. State Symphony Soc. Women's Com., 1965-67, 76-79, Symphoguide chmn., 1976-79; vision screening Indpls. inner-city pub. sch. kindergartens, pre-schs., 1962-69, also Headstart, 1967—; asst. Glaucoma screening clinics Gen. Hosp., Glendale Shopping Center, City County Bldg., Am. Legion Nat. Hdqrs., Ind. Health Assn. Conf., 1962-73; chmn. sight conservation and aid to blind Nat. Delta Gamma Found., Indpls., Columbus, Ohio, 1969-73; mem. telethon team Butler U. Fund, 1964; symphoguide hostess Internat. Conf. on Cities, 1971, Nat. League of Cities, 1972; mem. health adv. com. Headstart, 1976—, assessment team of compliance steering com., 1978-79, 84, appreciation award, 1983; founder People of Vision Aux., 1981. Recipient Cable award Delta Gamma, 1969, Outstanding Alumna award, 1973, scholarship honoree, 1981; Key to City of Indpls., 1972, those Spl. People award Women in Communication, 1980. Mem. Nat., Ind. (dir. 1962—, exec. com. 1971—, v.p. 1983—, sec., 1971-83, Ind. del. to nat. 3-yr. program planning conf. 1985, Sight Saving award 1974, life hon. v.p. 1983—) socs. to prevent blindness, Delta Gamma (chpt. golden anniversary celebration decade and communication chmn. 1975, treas. Alpha Tau house corp. 1975-78, nat. chmn. Parent Club Study Com. 1976-77; Service Recognition award 1977, Shield award 1981). Republican. Address: 1502 E 80th St Indianapolis IN 46240

MAXWELL, HERBERT GEORGE, aeronautical engineering company executive; b. Avellaneda, Argentina, Aug. 4, 1939; came to U.S., 1958; s. Juan Samuel and Maria Sara (Rodriguez) M.; m. Marta Emilse Gaton, Mar. 31, 1982. B.S. in Aero. Engring., Northrop U., 1961. Assoc. engr. Aero Commander, Santa Monica, Calif., 1962-63; ptnr. Maxwell & Assoc., Buenos Aires, Argentina, 1964-79; mgr. engring. Tensa-Cessna, Buenos Aires, 1979-80; chief program evaluation Fuerza Aerea Argentina, Buenos Aires, 1980-83; pres. Aerotechnics Ltd., Wichita, Kans., 1983—; design supr. AVEX Exptl. Aircraft, Buenos Aires, 1969-74; dir. Tea S.Am., Buenos Aires, 1981-83, Bonding S.Am., Buenos Aires, 1981-83. Patentee in field. Recipient Ambassador's Prize Brit. Embassy, 1964. Mem. AIAA, Centro Argentino De Ingenieros. Avocations: flying, sailing, photography. Home: 2208 Bullinger Wichita KS 67277 Office: Aerotechnics LTD Wichita KS

MAXWELL, PATRICIA JOY, association executive; b. Belle Plaine, Iowa, Feb. 7, 1937; d. Verne Edwin and Julia Inez (Beem) M.; student Pepperdine Coll., 1954-55; B.S., Iowa State Tchrs. Coll., 1958; M.P.A., Roosevelt U., 1982; m. Martin E. Sodetz, Jan. 21, 1984. Dir. resource devel. Boys Clubs Am., 1978-81; exec. dir. Westlake Health Services Found., 1981-84; dir. devel. and alumni affairs U. Ill. Coll. Medicine, 1984—; dir. profl. services Ency. Britannica Ednl. Corp.; cons. Prentice Hall Inc., U.S. State Dept. Mem. Am. Mktg. Assn., Chgo. Area Pub. Affairs Group, City Club of Chgo., Women Health Execs. Office: 1130 S Michigan Ave Chicago IL 60605

MAXWELL, ROBERT OLIVER, insurance executive; b. Sioux City, Iowa, Sept. 23, 1940; s. Lyle Charles and Corinne Zenobia (Knudson) M.; m. Carol Marie Lejchar, June 23, 1973; 1 son, Todd Robert. B.S., Drake U., 1962. Home officer mgr. Occidental Life Co., Los Angeles, 1962-68; salesman William Volker & Co., Los Angeles, 1968-70; mgr. sales office State Farm Ins. Co., Palos Verdes, Calif., 1970-71; v.p. group div. Security Life Ins. Co., Mpls., 1971—; dir. Congress Life Ins. Co., Phoenix, 1978—; v.p., sec. Security Am. Fin. Enterprises, Mpls., 1981—, trustee pension plan, 1975—. Fellow C.L.U.s, Life Office Mgmt. Assn. Republican. Club: Hazeltine Nat. Golf (Chaska, Minn.). Home: 7269 Tartan Curve Eden Prarie MN 55344 Office: Security Life Ins Co 6681 Country Club Dr Minneapolis MN 55427-4698

MAXWELL, VIRGIL ALLEN, savings and loan executive; b. Yarmouth, Iowa, Aug. 22, 1933; s. Guy Emory and Grace Marie (Keitzer) M.; B.B.A., Drake U., 1955; grad. Ind. U. Grad. Sch. Savs. and Loans, 1966-68; postgrad. U. So. Calif., 1978; m. Margaret Ann Wickard, Mar. 9, 1963; children—Pamela Sue, Todd Dwight, Scott Allen. Trainee, Farmers Casualty Co., Des Moines, 1953-55; with Midland Fin. Savs. & Loan, and predecessor, Des Moines, 1958-76, sr. v.p., until 1976; pres., chief exec. officer Ames Savs. & Loan Assn. (Iowa), 1976—, also dir.; chmn. adv. com. State Auto & Casualty Co.; dir. Farmers Casualty Co. Chmn. Ames Electric Ops. Rev. and Adv. Bd.; bd. dirs. Youth and Shelter Services; mem. fin. com. Story County Republican Com., 1981-82. Served with USAF, 1955-58; ret. col. Iowa Air N.G. Named Des Moines Jaycee's Boss of Yr., 1976-77. Mem. Inst. Fin. Edn. (pres. 1978-79), Fin. Info. Trust (formerly Savs. and Loan Computer Trust of Des Moines) (trustee), Iowa Savs. and Loan League (dir.), Alpha Tau Omega. Republican. Congregationalist. Clubs: Rotary (pres.), Ames Golf and Country (fin. com.), Embassy. Home: 1706 Amherst Dr Ames IA 50010 Office: 424 Main St Ames IA 50010

MAXWELL, WILLIAM HALL CHRISTIE, civil engineering educator; b. Coleraine, Londonderry, No. Ireland, Jan. 25, 1936; came to U.S., 1958, naturalized, 1967; s. William Robert and Catherine Dempsey (Christie) M.; m. Mary Carolyn McLaughlin, Sept. 28, 1960; children—Katrina, Kevin, Wendy, Liam. B.Sc., Queen's U., Belfast, No. Ireland, 1956; M.Sc., Queen's U., Kingston, Ont., Can., 1958; Ph.D., U. Minn., 1964. Registered profl. engr., Ill. Site engr. Motor Columbus AG, Baden, Switzerland, 1956; teaching asst. Queen's U., 1956-58; research asst. to instr. U. Minn., Mpls., 1959-64; asst. prof. civil enging. U. Ill., Urbana, 1964-70, assoc. prof., 1970-82, prof., 1982—. Editor: Water Resources Management in Industrial Areas, 1982; Water for Human consumption, Man and His Environment, 1983; Frontiers in Hydrology, 1984. Vestryman, Emmanuel Meml. Episcopal Ch., Champaign, Ill., 1977-80. State exhibitor Ministry Edn., Stormont, No. Ireland, 1953-56; Queen's U. Found. scholar, Belfast, 1954-56; R.S. McLaughlin travelling fellow Queen's U., 1958-59; NSF grantee, 1966. Fellow ASCE (com. chmn. 1982-83); mem. Internat. Water Resources Assn. (tech. editor Water Internat. 1976—, mem. publs. com. 1980—), Internat. Assn. for Hydraulic Research, Am. Geophys. Union. Avocations: camping; fishing; home construction; oil painting. Home: 804 Westfield Dr Champaign IL 61821-4135 Office: Dept Civil Engring Univ Illinois 208 N Romine St Urbana IL 61801

MAY, ALAN ALFRED, lawyer; b. Detroit, Apr. 7, 1942; s. Alfred Albert and Sylvia (Sheer) M.; m. Elizabeth Miller; children—Stacy Ann, Julie Beth. B.A., U. Mich., 1963, J.D., 1966. Bar: Mich. 1967, D.C. 1976; registered nursing home adminstr., Mich. Ptnr. May and May, Detroit, 1967-79, pres. May & May, P.C., 1979—; spl. asst. atty. gen. State of Mich., 1970—; of counsel Charfoos, Christensen & Archer, P.C., Detroit, 1970—; pres., instr. Med-Leg Seminars, Inc., 1978; lectr. Wayne State U., 1974; instr. Oakland U., 1969. Chmn. Republican 18th Congl. Dist. Com., 1983—; chmn. 19th Congl. Dist. Com., 1981-83; mem. Mich. Rep. Com., 1976-84; del. Rep. Nat. Conv., 1984; former chmn. Mich. Civil Rights Commn.; mem. Mich. Civil Service Commn.; trustee NCCJ; mem. Electoral Coll.; bd. dirs. Detroit Round Table, Charfoos Charitable Found., Temple Beth El, Birmingham, Mich. Mem. Detroit Bar Assn. Clubs: Victors, Franklin Hills Country (bd. dirs.), Presidents (trustee). Contbr. article to profl. jours. Home: 4140 Echo Rd Bloomfield Hills MI 48013 Office: 3000 Town Center Suite 2600 Southfield MI 48075

MAY, AVIVA RABINOWITZ, educator, linguist, musician; b. Tel Aviv; naturalized, 1958; d. Samuel and Paula (Gordon) Rabinowitz; B.A., in Piano Pedgogy, Northeastern Ill. U., 1979; m. Stanley Lee May, children—Rochelle, Alan, Risa, Ellanna. Tchr., pianist, 1948—; tchr. adult B'nai Mitzva, 1973; tchr., music, dir. McCormick Health Ctrs., Chgo., 1978-79, Cove Sch. Perceptually Handicapped Children, Chgo., 1978-79; prof. Hebrew and Yiddish, Spertus Coll. Judaica, Chgo., 1980—; tchr. continuing edn. Northeastern Ill. U., 1978-80, also Jewish Community Ctrs.; with Office Spl. Investigations, Dept. Justice, Washington; folksinger, guitarist, 1962—; composer classical music for piano, choral work, folk songs. Recipient Magen David Adom Pub. Service award, 1973; awards from women's programs Oakton Community Coll., 1976, 78; Adults Returning to Sch. award Northeastern Ill. U.-Chgo. Ill. State grantee, 1975-79; Ill. Congressman Woody Bowman grantee, 1978-79. Mem. Music Tchrs. Nat. Assn., North Shore Music Tchrs. Assn. (a founder, charter mem., sec.), Ill. Music Tchrs. Assn., Organ and Piano Tchrs. Assn., Am. Coll. Musicians, Ill. Assn. Learning Disabilities, Sherwood Sch. Music, Friends of Holocaust Survivers, Nat. Yiddish Book Exchange, Nat. Ctr. for Jewish Films, Chgo. Jewish Hist. Soc., Oakton Community Coll. Alumni Assn., Northeastern Ill. U. Alumni Assn. Democrat. Contbr. articles to profl. jours. Address: 3600 N Lake Shore Dr Chicago IL 60613 Studio: Fine Arts Bldg 410 S Michigan Ave Chicago IL

MAY, DANIEL FRANCIS, airline executive; b. Rainier, Oreg., Feb. 8, 1930; s. Alfred and Frances L. (Kelly) M.; m. Radona Ashman, 1969; children—Gary, Steven, Kathleen May Rudkin. Grad. Multnomah Coll., 1951; postgrad. U. Minn., 1956-58; LL.B., LaSalle Extension U., 1971. C.P.A., Minn. Acct., May Agy., Rainier, 1947-51, Webster Lumber Co., Mpls., 1954-56; acct. North Central Airlines, Inc., Mpls., 1956-62, asst. treas., 1962-63, treas., 1963-67, v.p., treas., 1967-71, v.p. fin., 1971-79; sr. v.p. fin. Republic Airlines, Inc. (formerly North Central Airlines), Mpls., 1979-80, exec. v.p., 1980, pres., 1980-82, pres., chief exec. officer, 1982-84, chmn. bd., chief exec. officer, 1984-85, chmn. bd., 1985—; dir. Republic Energy Inc., Twin City Fed. Savs. and Loan Assn., Cherne Industries Inc., Rexnord Inc., Young Life. Elder, Hope Presbyn. Ch., Mpls. Mem. Minn. Assn. Commerce and Industry (dir.). Club: Rotary. Office: Republic Airlines Inc 7500 Airline Dr Minneapolis MN 55450

MAY, DAVID L., chamber of commerce executive. Pres., Independence C. of C., Independence, Mo. Office: Independence C of C 213 S Main PO Box 147 Independence MO 64051*

MAY, GARY WENTWORTH, dentist; b. Valentine, Nebr., Apr., 17, 1945; s. William T. May and Boneda Irene (Walton) Hoisington; m. Mary Beth Kreuch, Aug. 27, 1966; children—Christophe, Nicholas. Student Wayne State U., 1963-65; D.D.S., U. Nebr., 1969. Dentist, Lauren Teutch, Pedodontist, Omaha, 1971-72; dir. dentistry M&I program U. Nebr. Med. Ctr., Omaha, 1972-75; practice dentistry, Fremont, Nebr., 1972—. Mem. Fremont Citizens Adv. Com., 1974-78. Served to lt. USN, 1969-71. Mem. ADA, Nebr. Dental Assn., Omaha Dist. Dental Soc. (del. 1978), Tri Valley Soc. (pres. 1974). Republican. Lutheran. Avocations: skiing; boating; bridge. Home: 2123 Teakwood Dr Fremont NE 68025 Office: 2350 N Clarkson St Fremont NE 68025

MAY, JAMES MICHAEL, classics educator; b. Youngstown, Ohio, Sept. 2, 1951; s. John Lawrence and Ann (Pavlik) M.; m. Donna M. Fialko, July 20, 1974; 1 child, Joseph Alexander. B.S. in Edn., Kent State U., 1973; Ph.D., U. N.C., 1977. Instr., asst. prof., then assoc. prof. classics, St. Olaf Coll., Northfield, Minn., 1977—. Author: Ethos: A Study in Ciceronian Oratory. Contbr. articles and revs. to scholarly publs. Chmn. budget and fin. com. Northfield United Way, 1983-84. NEH fellow, 1983-84. Mem. Classical Assn. Minn. (pres. 1984-86), M. Philol. Assn., Classical Assn. Middle West and South (exec. com. 1981-85). Roman Catholic. Avocations: harpsichord and fine furniture building; tournament handball playing. Home: 1509 Lia Dr Northfield MN 55057 Office: Dept Classics St Olaf Coll Northfield MN 55057

MAY, PHYLLIS JEAN, businesswoman; b. Flint, Mich., May 31, 1932; d. Bert A. and Alice C. (Rushton) Irvine; grad. Dorsey Sch. Bus., 1957; cert. Internat. Corr. Schs., 1959, Nat. Tax Inst., 1978; M.B.A., Mich. U., 1970; m. John May, Apr. 24, 1971; children—Phillip, Perry, Paul. Office mgr. Comml. Constrn. Co., Flint, 1962-68; bus. mgr. new and used car dealership, Flint, 1968-70; controller 6 corps., Flint, 1970-75; fiscal dir. Rubicon Odyssey Inc., Detroit, 1976—; acad. cons. acctg. Detroit Inst. Commerce, 1980-81; pres. small bus. specializing in adminstrv. cons. and acctg., 1982—; supr. mobile service sta., upholstery and home improvement businesses; owner retail bus. Pieces and Things; notary public, 1968—; also real estate broker. Pres. PTA Westwood Heights Schs., 1972; vol. Fedn. of Blind, 1974-76, Probate Ct., 1974-76. Recipient Meritorious Service award Genesee County for Youth, 1976, Excellent Performance and High Achievement award Odyssey Inc., 1981. Mem. Am. Bus. Women's Assn. (treas. 1981, rec. sec. 1982, v.p. 1982-83, Woman of Yr. 1982), Nat. Assn. Profl. Female Execs. (bd. dirs.), Internat. Platform Assn., Pi Omicron (officer 1984-85). Baptist. Home: 12050 Barlow St Detroit MI 48205 Office: Rubicon Odyssey Inc 7441 Brush St Detroit MI 48202

MAY, RONALD CHARLES, manufacturing company official; b. Corpus Christi, Oct. 4, 1945; s. Warren Charles and Kathryn Marie (Mange) M.; m. Sharon J. Denniger, May 21, 1983. B.S., U. Mo., 1973; M.B.A., So. Ill. U., 1978. Draftsman, Sterling div. Fed. Mogul Corp., St. Louis, 1964-67; buyer Wagner div. McGraw Edison Co., St. Louis, 1973-74, asst. purchasing agt., 1974-75, purchasing agt., 1975-76, mgr. purchases, brake products, 1976-80, mgr. corp. purchases, automotive parts, 1980-81; dir. purchasing Hussmann Refrigerator div. IC Industries, St. Louis, 1981-84; dir. material Hunter Engring. Co., St. Louis, 1984—. Served with USAF, 1967-71. Mem. Nat. Assn. Purchasing Mgmt., Am. Foundrymen's Soc., Assn. M.B.A. Execs., Soc. Automotive Engrs. Home: 709 Paschon Ct Florissant MO 63034 Office: 12999 Saint Charles Rock Rd Bridgeton MO 63044

MAYBERRY, ALAN REED, assistant prosecuting attorney; b. Akron, Ohio, Mar. 15, 1954; s. Franklin Reed Mayberry and Mary K. (Kissane) Mayberry Alexander; m. Lisa Renee Rush, Dec. 19, 1982. B.S. in Edn., Bowling Green State U., 1975; J.D., U. Toledo, 1978. Asst. prosecutor Wood County Pros. Atty.'s Office, Bowling Green, Ohio, 1980-81, chief criminal div., asst. pros. atty., 1981—; small claims ct. referee Bowling Green Mcpl. Ct., 1981. Mem. Bowling Green City Council, 1984—; chmn. Bowling Green Planning, Zoning and Econ. Devel. Com., 1984. Named to Outstanding Young Men Am., U.S. Jaycees, 1983, 84. Mem. Bowling Green Jaycees (bd. dirs. 1983—). Republican. Presbyterian. Lodges: Fraternal Order Police, Optimists (local program chmn.). Office: Wood County Pros Atty's Office Courthouse Bowling Green OH 43402

MAYE, RICHARD BOYKIN, clergyman; b. Uniontown, Ala., Oct. 25, 1933; s. Johnny and Frances (May) Boykin; B.A., Sangamon State U., Springfield, Ill., 1972, M.A., 1972; m. Rose Owens, June 24, 1978; children—Darryl Kermit, Byron Keith. Juvenile parole agt. Ill. Dept. Corrections, Chgo., 1967-70, adminstrv. asst., Springfield, 1970-72; lectr. polit. sci. Ill. State U., Normal, 1973-77; ordained to ministry Baptist Ch., 1960; pastor Pleasant Grove Bapt. Ch., Springfield, 1970—; mem. faculty Chgo. Bapt. Inst., 1968-70. Mem. Springfield Civil Service Comn., 1979—; mem. sch. integration commn., Springfield, 1977-79; bd. dirs. Morgan-Washington Home Girls, Springfield, 1977, Lincoln Library, Springfield, 1975-76, Springfield Area Arts Council; mem. grad. council So. Ill. U., 1975-76; mem. citizen's adv. com. Ill. Dept. Children and Family Services, Springfield, 1980-81, now chairperson com.; chmn. bd. dirs. Access to Housing, Springfield, 1981-83. Served with AUS, 1954-56. Grad. fellow U. Iowa, 1977-78, 79-80; grad. dean fellow So. Ill. U., 1975-76; recipient Citizen of Year award Springfield NAACP, 1976, Public Service award U.S. Dist. Ct., Springfield, 1978. Mem. Nat. Polit. Sci. Assn., Greater Springfield Interfaith Assn. (v.p.).

MAYER, BEATRICE CUMMINGS, civic worker; b. Montreal, P.Q., Can., Aug. 15, 1921; came to U.S., 1939, naturalized, 1944; d. Nathan and Ruth (Kellert) Cummings; B.A. in Chemistry, U. N.C., 1943; postgrad. U. Chgo., 1946; L.H.D. (hon.), Spertus Coll. Judaica, 1983; m. Robert Bloom Mayer, Dec. 11, 1947 (dec.); children—Robert N., Mrs. Stephen P. Durchslag. Mem. vis. com. Sch. Social Service Adminstrn. U. Chgo., 1964—, dept. art, 1972; dir. women's bd., 1973—; governing life mem. Art Inst. Chgo., also mem. women's bd.; trustee Michael Reese Hosp. and Med. Ctr., Chgo., 1974-81; bd. dirs. Michael Reese Hosp. and Med. Ctr. Corp., 1981—; bd. dirs. Spole to Festival, 1980; trustee Kenyon Coll., Gambier, Ohio, 1976—; bd. fellows Brandeis U., Waltham, Mass., 1977—; mem. womens bd. Northwestern U., 1978—; trustee Anshe Emet Synagogue, Chgo., 1974—, v.p., 1978—; trustee Mus. Contemporary Art, Chgo., 1974—, v.p., 1978—; dir. Consol. Foods Corp. Recipient Brandeis U. Disting. Community Service award, 1972; Am. Jewish Com. Human Rights medallion, 1976; Outstanding Achievement award in the Arts, YWCA Met. Chgo., 1979. Clubs: Tavern, Standard (Chgo.); Lake Shore Country (Glencoe, Ill.). Home: 175 E Delaware Pl Apt 7403 Chicago IL 60611

MAYER, JAMES LAMOINE, liturgical consultant, evangelist, bible educator; b. Eau Claire, Wis., Oct. 7, 1951; s. Harold L. and Eleanor C. (Williams) M. B.A., U. Wis.-Eau Claire, 1973; M.Div., Bethel Theol. Sem., 1976. Dir. communications media Bethel Theol. Sem., St. Paul, 1976-78; night chaplain coordinator Sacred Heart Hosp., Eau Claire, 1979-80, coordinator pastoral care TV ministries Sacred Heart Hosp., 1978-82; Christian edn. and liturgical cons. Shepherd of Love, Eau Claire, Wis., 1983-85; sr. pastor, rector Pilgrim Congl. Parish, Durand, Wis., 1985—; coordinator communications Lake St. United Meth. Ch., Eau Claire. Chmn. bd. Am. Heart Assn., 1984—; pres. Eau Claire Clergy Assn., 1982; bd. dirs. Am. Cancer Soc., 1982-83. Recipient Excellence in Christian Edn. award Baptist Gen. Conf., 1976; Awana Leadership award First Baptist Ch. Awana, 1980. Mem. Eau Claire Clergy Assn., Upper Midwest Area Gifted Assn., Christian Booksellers Assn. Democrat. Club: Triniteam. Avocations: cross country skiing; bowling; golf; photography. Office: Pilgrim Rectory 412 1st Ave E Durand WI 54736

MAYER, RAMONA ANN, quality assurance executive; b. Algona, Iowa, May 9, 1929; d. William John and Esther (Wolf) M. B.A. in Chemistry, State U. Iowa, 1956. Library asst. State U. Iowa, Iowa City, 1954-56; info. specialist Battelle, Columbus, Ohio, 1956-59, research scientist, 1959-77, quality assurance dir., 1977—; lab. asst. U. Iowa Tb Hosp., Iowa City, 1952-53; abstractor Chem. Abstract Services, Columbus, 1958-79. Contbr. articles to profl. jours. Recipient Achievement award NASA Research Project, 1970. Fellow Am. Inst. Chemists; mem. Am. Soc. Quality Control (vice chmn. Columbus sect. 1982-84, Saddoris chmn. 1984-85), ASTM (chmn. com. 1984-86), Am. Chem. Soc., Soc. Quality Assurance (bylaws com. 1985). Avocations: golf; crafts; travel. Office: Battelle-Columbus 505 King Ave Columbus OH 43201

MAYER, ROBERT NATHAN, food company executive; b. Chgo., May 21, 1949; s. Robert Bloom and Beatrice Violet (Cummings) M.; m. Debra Ellyn Weese, June 17, 1976; children—Jennifer Robyn, Jaimie Ariel. A.B., Kenyon Coll., 1971; M.B.A., U. Chgo., 1973; Ph.D., Northwestern U., 1985. Cons. Ernst & Whinney, Chgo., 1973-76; supr. employee relations R.R. Donnelley & Sons, Chgo., 1976-78, mgr. employee relations, 1978-80; dir. orgn. planning and devel. Superior Coffee, Chgo., 1980-81; mgr. corp. human resources planning and devel. Sara Lee Corp., Chgo., 1981-84, sr. mgr. mgmt. resources, 1984—. Trustee Mus. Contemporary Art, Chgo., 1983—, Rothschild Found., Chgo., 1983—; chmn. U. Chgo., Vis. Com., 1980-83. Mem. Am. Soc. Personnel Adminstrn., Am. Soc. Tng. and Devel., Human Resources Planning Soc. Clubs: Standard, Lake Shore Country (Chgo.). Avocations: contemporary art; numismatics. Office: Sara Lee Corp 3 First Nat Plaza Chicago IL 60602

MAYER, STEPHEN EDWARD, respiratory therapist; b. St. Louis, Aug. 5, 1954; s. Marvin Edward and Viola Geraldine (Jack) M.; m. Susan Helen De Neui, Aug. 26, 1978; children—Holly, Bethany, Valerie. B.S., Iowa State U., 1977. Respiratory therapist Iowa Methodist Med. Ctr., Des Moines, 1978-80, supr. pediatric respiratory care, 1980-82, dir. respiratory care, 1982—; chmn. blood donor drive, 1984-85. Mem. adv. com. Des Moines Area Community Coll., 1982—, chmn., 1985. Mem. Iowa Soc. Respiratory Therapy (bd. dirs. 1984-85). Republican. Mem. Assembly of God. Avocations: golf; hunting; fishing; outdoors; hockey. Office: Iowa Meth Med Center 1200 Pleasant St Des Moines IA 50308

MAYER, STEVEN CHARLES, lawyer; b. Alliance, Ohio, June 1, 1955; s. Dean Lowell and Marjorie (Gorman) M.; m. Teresa Jean Oliver, Sept. 6, 1980. B.S., Kent State U., 1977; J.D., Ohio State U., 1980. Bar: Ohio 1981, U.S. Dist. Ct. (no. dist.) Ohio 1982. Hearing officer Columbus Night Prosecutor (Ohio), 1980-81; estate planner Aetna Life & Casualty Co., Columbus, 1981; assoc. Stephen Enz, Columbus, 1981-82; atty. Hyatt Legal Services, Euclid, Ohio, 1982-84, mng. atty., 1984—. Mem. Alpha Phi Sigma, Phi Delta Phi. Republican. Mem. Assembly of God Ch. Home: 19568 Meredith Ave Euclid OH 44119 Office: Hyatt Legal Services 22802 Lake Shore Blvd Euclid OH 44123

MAYFIELD, JEAN ERNST, school administrator; b. Detroit, May 7, 1931; s. Clifford and Edna (Speed) Ernst; m. Rutledge R. Mayfield, Oct. 9, 1949; children—Rutledge, Shannon, Gina, Martin. B.S. in Elem. Edn., Mich. State Normal Coll., 1954; M.A. in Ednl. Guidance and Counseling, Wayne State U., 1969, Ed.D., 1983. Tchr. Detroit pub. schs., 1954-69; adminstr. 1969—, now spl. projects personnel adminstr.; supr. Head Start, Detroit, 1965, lang. devel. specialist, 1969; dir. Pub. Service Careers, 1970-74, producer, dir. TV show FACTS Factory, 1974-77, adminstr. state funded Article 3 Programs, region 3 Detroit pub. schs., 1977-83; instr. Wayne State U., Wayne Community Coll., 1969—; mgmt. tng. specialist D.P.S. Mgmt. Acad., 1983-84; cons. Active Nat. Council Negro Women, NAACP, Big Sisters of Tabernacle, Westside Clubs, Ave. of Fashion Mchts. Recipient Profl. Devel. award Wayne Commmunity Coll., 1979; merit award Mich. Assn. Suprs. Curriculum Devel., 1980. Mem. Orgn. Suprs. and Adminstrs., Assn. Supervision and Curriculum Devel., Nat. Assn., Edn. Young Children, Met. Detroit Assn. Black Sch. Adminstrs., Profl. Women's Network, Internat. Assn. Transactional Analysis, Am. Fedn. Coll. Tchrs.; Alpha Kappa Alpha. Baptist. Contbr. articles to profl. jours.

MAYL, JACK JOSEPH, lawyer; b. Dayton, Ohio, June 21, 1930; s. Eugene Aloysius and Helen Irene (Cooper) M.; B.S. cum laude, U. Notre Dame, 1952; J.D., Georgetown U., 1958; m. Gay Reddig, Apr. 8, 1972. Admitted to Ohio bar, 1960; ptnr. firm Murphy & Mayl, Dayton, 1960—; dir. Central Pharms., Inc., Seymour, Ind., R.L. Consol. Inc., Canton, Ohio, White Engines, Inc., Canton. Served to lt. USNR, 1952-56. Mem. ABA, Internat., Inter-Am., Ohio, Dayton bar assns., Antique Automobile Club Am., Rolls Royce Owners Club, Packards Internat., Classic Car Club Am., Phi Alpha Delta. Clubs: Lawyers, Dayton Bicycle, Dayton Country, Dayton Racquet; Union (Cleve.). Home: Plantation Ln Kettering OH 45419 Office: 32 N Main St Dayton OH 45402

MAYNARD, JERRY ALLEN, anatomist; b. Reedsburg, Wis., Apr. 22, 1937; s. Paul Richard and Hazel Irene (Nelson) M.; m. Marilyn Rochell Tritle, June 15, 1957; children—Doreen Renee, Susan Carol. B.A., No. Iowa U., 1958; M.S., Ind. U., 1961; postgrad. U. Wis., 1961-62; Ph.D., U. Iowa, 1970. Teaching asst. U. Iowa, Iowa City, 1965-68, research fellow, 1969-71, research assoc., 1971-72, asst. prof. depts. orthopaedic surgery and exercise sci. and phys. edn., 1972-76, assoc. prof., 1976-81, prof., 1981—. Contbr. articles to profl. jours. Mem. AAUP, Anatomical Soc. Great Britain and Ireland, Orthopaedic Research Soc. Methodist. Home: 26 Montrose Ave Iowa City IA 52240 Office: U Iowa Dept Orthopaedic Surgery 178 Medical Labs Iowa City IA 52242

MAYNARD, JOHN RALPH, lawyer; b. Seattle, Mar. 5, 1942; s. John R. and Frances Jane (Mitchell) Maynard Kendryk; m. Mary Ann Mascagno, May 1, 1945; children—Bryce James, Pamela Ann. B.A., U. Wash., 1964; J.D., Calif. Western U., San Diego, 1972; LL.M., Harvard U., 1973. Bar: Calif. 1972, Wis. 1973. Assoc. firm Whyte & Hirschboeck, Milw., 1973-78, firm Minahan & Peterson, Milw., 1979—. Bd. dirs. Am. Heart Assn. of Wis., Milw., 1979-82. Served to lt. USN, 1964-69. Mem. ABA, Wis. Retirement Plan Profls. Republican. Club: University (Milw.). Home: 9449 N Waverly Dr Milwaukee WI 53217 Office: Minahan & Peterson SC 411 E Wisconsin Ave Milwaukee WI 53202

MAYNE, LUCILLE STRINGER, finance educator; b. Washington, June 6, 1924; d. Henry Edmond and Hattie Benham (Benson) Stringer; children—Patricia Anne, Christine Gail, Barbara Marie. B.S., U. Md., 1946; M.B.A., Ohio State U., 1949; Ph.D., Northwestern U., 1966. Instr. fin. Utica Coll., 1949-50; analytical statistician Air Materiel Command, Dayton, Ohio, 1950-52; lectr. fin. Roosevelt U., Chgo., 1961-64, Pa. State U., 1965-66, asst. prof., 1966-69, assoc. prof., 1969-70; assoc. prof. banking and fin. Case Western Res. U., 1971-76, prof., 1976—, grad. dean, 1980-84; sr. economist, cons. FDIC, 1977-78; cons. Nat. Commn. Electronic Fund Transfer Systems, 1976; research coms. Am. Bankers Assn., 1975, Fed. Res. Bank Cleve., 1968-70, 73; cons. Pres.'s Commn. Fin. Structure and Regulation, 1971, staff economist, 1970-71; expert witness cases involving fin. instns., 1968—; dir. Cleve. Citywide Devel. Corp., Horizon Savs. Assoc. Editor: Jour. Money, Credit and Banking, 1980-83, Bus. Econs., 1980-83. Contbr. articles to profl. jours. Home: 3723 Normancy Rd Shaker Heights OH 44120

MAYNERT, EVERETT WILLIAM, pharmacologist; b. Providence, R.I., Mar. 18, 1920; s. William Wiegand and Anna Emma (Erler) M. Sc.B. in Chemistry, Brown U., 1941; Ph.D. in Chemistry, U. Ill., 1945; M.D., Johns Hopkins U., 1957. Group leader Interchem. Corp., N.Y.C., 1945-47; asst. prof. pharmacology Columbia U., N.Y.C., 1947-52; Am. Cyanamid fellow Johns Hopkins U., Balt., 1952-57, assoc. prof., pharmacology, 1957-65; prof. pharmacology, U. Ill., Chgo., 1965—; mem. psychopharmacology study sec. NIH, Bethesda, Md., 1962-67; mem., chmn. pharmacology study sec. NIH, Bethesda, Md., 1968-72, dir. symposia and workshops Internat. Brain Research Orgn., 1968-74. Contbr. articles to profl. jours. Recipient Lederle Labs. Med. Faculty award, 1957-60, Career Devel. award USPHS, 1960-63; vis. prof. Japan Soc. Promotion Scis., 1974. Fellow AAAS; mem. Am. Chem. Soc., Am. Soc. Pharmacology and Exptl. Therapeutics, Harvey Soc., Alpha Chi Sigma Home: 339 Barry Ave Chicago IL 60657 Office: Dept Pharmacology Coll Med U Ill PO Box 6998 Chicago IL 60680

MAYO, WILLIAM EDWARD BARRY, orthopaedic surgeon; b. Ottawa, Ont., Can., Apr. 1, 1930; s. Reginald Sidney and Verena Mary (Haney) M.; m. Helene Puskas, June 21, 1958; children—David, Ilona, Robert, Paula. M.D., U. Western Ont., 1958. Diplomate Am. Bd. Orthopaedic Surgery. Resident, Latter Day Saints Hosp., Salt Lake City, 1958-60, Primary Childrens Hosp., Salt Lake City, 1960-61, Henry Ford Hosp., Detroit, 1961-64; practice medicine specializing in orthopaedic surgery, arthroscopy and arthroscopic surgery, Royal Oak, Mich., 1964—; mem. staff William Beaumont Hosp., Royal Oak; dir. Sports Medicine Clinic; dir. Mich. Nat. Bank, Farmington, 1979-85. Pres., Bloomfield Hills Mich. Stake, Latter Day Saints Ch., 1980-85; mem. exec. bd. Detroit Area council Boy Scouts Am., 1980-85. Recipient Silver Beaver award Boy Scouts Am. Mem. ACS, Internat. Arthroscopy Assn., Royal Soc. Medicine, Am. Acad. Orthopaedic Surgery, Arthroscopy Assn. N.Am., Sportopaedics (pres. 1985). Home: 4387 Barchester Dr Bloomfield Hills MI 48013 Office: 2338 N Woodward St Royal Oak MI 48013

MAYSE, MICHAEL CARL, youth organization administrator; b. Detroit, May 29, 1954; s. Carl and JoAnne (Stapleton) M., m. Connie Jean Lemons; 1 child, Franklin Stuart. B.S., Central Mich. U., 1977. Dist. exec. Detroit Area council Boy Scouts Am., 1977-78, exploring exec., 1978-81, exploring exec. Bay-Lakes council, Menasha, Wis., 1981-82, exploring dir., 1982-83, fin. dir., 1983—, nat. law enforcement conf. dir., Dallas, 1983-84. Editor Bay-Lake News, 1983-85. Res. officer Detroit Police Dept., 1978-81. Recipient Eagle Scout award Boy Scouts Am., 1970. Mem. Soc. Am. Mil. Engrs., Sigma Chi (Life Loyal Sig award 1976). Republican. Methodist. Clubs: Optimists (sec. 1982-83), Rotary. Avocations: photography; swimming; golf. Home: 1109 Thorndale St Green Bay WI 53404 Office: Bay-Lakes Council Boy Scouts Am PO Box 516 Menasha WI 54952

MAYSTEAD, SUZANNE RAE, optometrist; b. Hillsdale, Mich., Sept. 30, 1955; d. Marvin Charles and Helen Alberta (Glendenning) Patrick; m. Ivan Karl Maystead, III, June 4, 1977. O.D., Ferris State Coll. Optometry, 1979. Research asst. to optometrist, Big Rapids, Mich., 1979-80; clin. assoc. Ferris State Coll. Optometry, Big Rapids, 1979-84; pvt. practice optometry, Portland, Mich., 1980—. Recipient Contact Lens Achievement award Bauch & Lomb, 1979. Mem. Mich. Optometric Assn., Nat. Bus. Assn., Portland C. of C. Avocations: indoor gardening, interior decorating. Home: 7667 Peckins Rd Lyons MI 48851 Office: 1311 E Bridge St Portland MI 48875

MAZUR, DEBORAH JOAN, financial services executive; b. Highland Park, Mich., Apr. 22, 1958; d. Frank J. and Joan A. (Cader) Mazur. B.S., Western Mich. U., 1981. Spl. edn. resource room tchr. Capac Community Schs., Mich., 1981-82; supr. group home Blue Water Developmental Housing, Port Huron, Mich., 1982-83; unit adminstr. group home Luth. Social Services of Mich., Detroit, 1983-85; account rep. Fin. Services of Am., Inc., Berkeley, Mich., 1985—. Mem. Council Exceptional Children (sec.), Am. Behavioral Assn., Western Mich. U. Alumni Assn. (bd. dirs.). Home: 27663 Ryan Rd Warren MI 48092 Home: 2185 Kipling St Berkeley MI 48072

MAZUR, JOHN BERNARD, neurological surgeon; b. Fargo, N.D., Dec. 11, 1947; s. Bernard Alexander and Gertrude Isobel (Parry) M.; m. Lynda Rose Abbink, Feb. 12, 1972. B.S. in Chemistry, U. Notre Dame, 1968; B.S. in Medicine, U.N.D., 1970; M.D., Northwestern U., 1972. Diplomate Am. Bd. Neurol. Surgery. Intern in gen. surgery Wesley Meml. Hosp., Chgo., 1972-73; physician in adult medicine Chgo. Bd. Health, 1973-74; resident in neurol. surgery U. Ill. and affiliated hosps., Chgo., 1974-78; attending staff physician Mercy Ctr. Copley Meml. Hosp., Aurora, Ill., 1978—; cons. physician Kishwaukee Community Hosp., DeKalb, Ill., 1980—, Delnor Hosp., St. Charles, Ill., 1972—, Geneva Community Hosp., Ill., 1972—. Mem. AMA, Am. Assn. Neurol. Surgeons, Congress of Neurol. Surgeons, Soc. Neurovascular Surgery, Ill. State Med. Soc. Avocations: skiing; boardsailing. Office: Fox Valley Neurol Inst 1300 North Highland Aurora IL 60506

MAZUR, MICHAEL JAMES, JR., international fraternity executive; b. Trenton, N.J., June 4, 1952; s. Michael James and Sophia P. (Dziak) M. B.B.A., Ga. State U., 1974. Staff acct. United Family Life, Atlanta, 1974-78; sr. staff acct. Am. Heritage Life, Jacksonville, Fla., 1978-79; dir. internal audit United Family Life, Atlanta, 1979-81; exec. dir. Internat. Fraternity of Delta Sigma Pi, Oxford, Ohio, 1981—. Editor: The Deltasig of Delta Sigma Pi, 1981— (Coll. Fraternity Editors' Assn. award 1982, 83). Mem. Am. Soc. Assn. Execs., Oxford, Ohio Jaycees (treas. 1983-84), Profl. Frat. Assn. (treas. 1983-85), Cin. Assn. Execs. Roman Catholic. Avocations: photography; travel. Home: Rural Route 1 Box 70 Cedar Grove IN 47016 Office: Internat Fraternity of Delta Sigma Pi 330 S Campus Ave Oxford OH 45056

MAZUREK, DIANE JONUSAS, utility company executive; b. Munster, Fed. Republic Germany, June 24, 1949; came to U.S., 1951; d. Petras and Jadvyga Jonusas; m. Steve Paul Mazurek, Aug. 28, 1970. A.S., Grand Rapids Jr. Coll., 1969; B.S., Mich. State U., 1971. Engring. clerical asst. Stow-Davis Furniture Co., Grand Rapids, Mich., 1972-73; med. technician nuclear physics Butterworth Hosp., Grand Rapids, 1973-76; paralegal, Grand Rapids, 1976-77; tech. tng. assoc. Bell System Tng. Ctr., Dublin, Ohio, 1977-80; staff supr. Mich. Bell Telephone Co., Southfield, Mich., 1980—; task force mem. for digital tech. Bell Communications Research, 1983—. Author: (pamphlet) Guideline for Hosting a Car Convention, 1985. Mem. N.Am. MGA Register (membership chmn. 1976, co-chmn. 1977-80; events coordinator nat. 1982—). Avocations: piano; travel; biking; MGA cars. Office: Mich Bell Telephone Co 29777 Telegraph Rd Room 3500D Southfield MI 48034

MAZZOLA, MICHAEL LEE, foreign language educator; b. Frankfort, N.Y., Jan. 19, 1941; s. Dominick Frank and Mary Ann (Galvano) M. A.B., LeMoyne Coll., 1962; M.A., Middlebury Coll., 1964; Ph.D., Cornell U., 1967. Lectr. Cornell U., Ithaca, N.Y., 1965-66, asst. prof., 1966-68; asst. prof. Ind. U., Bloomington, 1968-74; asst. prof. fgn. langs. No. Ill., DeKalb, 1975-79, assoc. prof., 1979—, dir. French and Italian, 1983—. Author: Proto-Romance and Sicilian, 1976. Recipient Summer Seminar award NEH, Cambridge, Mass., 1982, Summer Inst., Washington, 1984. Mem. Linguistic Soc. Am., MLA. Home: 115 Tilton Park Dr DeKalb IL 60115 Office: Dept Foreign Langs and Literatures Northern Ill U DeKalb IL 60115

MAZZOLA, ROBERT ANTHONY, automotive company executive; b. Detroit, Mar. 31, 1942; s. Samuel A. and Mary Grace (Ciaramitaro) M.; m. Marlene Lenore Pomaski, May 9, 1964; children—Robert L., Michele R., James S. B.S. in Elec. Engring., U. Detroit, 1965; M.E.E., Iowa State U., 1967. Project engr. Collins Radio Co., Cedar Rapids, Iowa, 1965-67; devel. engr. Ford Motor Co., Dearborn, Mich., 1967-75, product planner, 1976-80; product planning mgr. TRW, Inc., Cleve., 1980-82, dir. planning, 1983—. Contbr. articles to profl. publs. Officer Golview Manor Civic Assn., Dearborn Heights, Mich., 1970. Mem. IEEE (bd. dirs. vehicular tech. soc. 1968-72; bd. dirs. 1982—, Avant Garde award 1982, Centennial award 1984), Soc. Automotive Engrs. Republican. Roman Catholic. Avocations: tennis, photography. Home: 19910 S Woodland Rd Shaker Heights OH 44122 Office: TRW Inc 30000 Aurora Rd Solon OH 44139

MCABOY, LOUIS, oil company executive; b. Mobile, Ala., July 29, 1950; s. Lorenzo Johnson and Consuelo (McLeod) McAboy Todd; m. Sherrelyn Y. Williams, Sept. 15, 1979. B.S. in Mktg., Grambling Coll., 1972; student in mktg. St. Louis U., 1969. Planner, subcontractor McDonnell Douglas Aircraft, St. Louis, 1972; with Shell Oil Co., 1972—, devel. rep., Cleve., 1978-80, packaged product specialist, Detroit, 1980-83, sr. retail tng. instr., Chgo., 1983—. Usher St. Francis D'Sales Catholic Ch., Detroit, 1974-76, pres. Archdiocese Devel. Fund, 1976. Mem. Kappa Alpha Psi (sec. chpt. 1971-72). Home: 4520 Bicek Ct Hoffman Estates IL 60195 Office: Shell Oil Co 1139 N Tower Ln Bensenville IL 60106

MCAFEE, CHARLES FRANCIS, architect; b. Los Angeles, Dec. 25, 1932; s. Arthur James and Willie Anna (Brown) McA.; m. Gloria Myrth Winston, 1955; children—Cheryl Lynn, Pamela Anita, Charyl Frena. B. Arch., U. Nebr., 1958. Registered architect, Kans., Mo., Nebr., Calif., Mass., Ga., Fla., Okla., Tex. Prin., pres. Charles F. McAfee FAIA, NOMA Architects Engrs. Planners, Wichita, Kans., 1963—, Kansas City, Mo., 1970—, Atlanta, 1975—. Served with U.S. Army, 1953-55. Recipient design awards Wichita Eagle & Beacon Pub. Co. 1971, McKnight Art Ctr., Ulrich Mus., Wichita State U., 1975, Vulcan Control Lab., 1980, Calvary Bapt. Ch. Volks Homes, 1980. Mem. AIA, Nat. Orgn. Minority Architects. Home: 16 Crestview Lakes Wichita KS 67220 Office: 2600 N Grove St Wichita KS 67219

MCANELLY, JAMES ROBERT, business administration educator, author, researcher, consultant; b. Bloomington, Ill., Mar. 16, 1932; s. Clyde Thomas and Virginia Sue (Jett) McA.; m. Patricia Lynne Staas, July 22, 1980; children—Michael L., Robert A. B.S., U. Colo., 1956; M.S. in Edn., No. Ill. U., 1963, Ed.D., 1978. Ins. investigator, claims adjustor Kemper Ins. Co., Chgo., 1956-59, Allstate Ins. Co., Chgo., 1956-59; faculty Haines Jr. High Sch., St. Charles, Ill., 1959-63; faculty, dist. edn. coordinator Aurora E. High Sch., Ill., 1963-67; grad. asst. No. Ill. U., DeKalb, 1974-75; prof. bus. adminstrn. Waubonsee Community Coll., Sugar Grove, Ill., 1967—, chmn. mktg. com., 1979-83, dir. fgn. studies, 1975—; cons., pres. McAnelly & Assocs., Aurora, 1976—. Author: (textbook study guide) Fundamentals of Retailing, 1973—; (textbook) Business Math for College, 1985. Chmn. Waubonsee Community Coll. FAC PAC, 1983—; mktg. consumer City of Yorkville, Ill., 1980; consumer advocate Health Systems Agy., Kane County, Ill., 1980-82; mktg. researcher Ill. Hosp. Assn., Oak Brook, 1979; mktg. consumer St. Planning & Services, Geneva, Ill., 1979. Recipient Distributive Edn. Coordinator's award, 1967; named to Hall of Fame Mooseheart Alumni Assn., 1972. Mem. Am. Bus. Law Assn., Nat. Bus. Edn. Assn., Ill. Community Coll. Mktg. Mgmt. Assn. (regional v.p.), Delta Pi Epsilon. Home: 1334 W Downer Pl Aurora IL 60506 Office: Waubonsee Community Coll Route 47 at Harter Rd Sugar Grove IL 60554

MCARDLE, RICHARD JOSEPH, university dean; b. Omaha, Mar. 10, 1934; s. William James and Abby Marie (Menzies) McA.; m. Katherine Ann McAndrew, Dec. 27, 1958; children —Bernard, Constance, Nancy, Susan, Richard. B.A., Creighton U., 1955, M.A., 1962; Ph.D., U. Nebr., 1969. Cert. tchr., Nebr. Tchr. high schs., Nebr., 1955-65; instr. U. Nebr., Lincoln, 1965-69; asst. prof. Cleve. State U., 1969-71, dean Coll. Edn., 1975—; dept. chmn. U. North Fla., Jacksonville, 1971-75; facilitator Cleve. Bd. Edn., Danforth Sch. Bd. Project, 1984-85. Author: (tng. manual) Interaction Analysis for Foreign Language Teachers, 1969; co-author (tech. reports) The Use of Computers in Education, 1984, Merit Pay-Issues and Concerns, 1984; also articles. Bd. dirs. Greater Cleve. Ednl. Devel. Ctr., 1983—. Martha Holden Jennings Found. grantee for establishment ctr. for study computers in edn., 1982-84. Mem. Am. Assn. Colls. for Tchr. Edn., Am. Assn. Tchr. Educators, Am. Council on Teaching Fgn. Langs., Tchr. Edn. Council State Colls. and Univs. (pres. 1982-83), Phi Delta Kappa. Roman Catholic. Avocations: sports; reading. Home: 28276 Gardenia St North Olmsted OH 44070 Office: Cleve State U 24th St at Euclid Ave Cleveland OH 44115

MCATEE, JOSEPH G., law enforcement official. Police chief City of Indpls. Office: Indianapolis Police Dept Office of the Police Chief Indianapolis IN 46204*

MC AULIFFE, CORNELIUS (CONNIE), bookstore manager; b. Castleisland Kerry, Ireland, Nov. 24, 1932; came to U.S., Dec. 16, 1953, naturalized, 1955; s. David Joseph and Katherine (Murphy) Mc A.; m. Jane Mangan, Aug. 23, 1958; children—Mary, Ann, Kathleen, David. Student Lansing Bus. U., 1956-59. Asst. mgr., buyer McElligotta Castleisland, Ireland, 1949-53; telephone service rep. Mich. Bell Telephone Co., Lansing, 1954-59; bus. mgr. union Mich. State U., East Lansing, 1959-66, chief acct., asst. mgr. bookstore, 1966-83, mgr., 1983—. Served to sgt. U.S. Army, 1954-56. Recipient Community Service award Mich. State U. Womens Sports Booster Club, 1983. Mem. Nat. Assn. Accts., Nat. Assn. Coll. Stores, Mich. Assn. Coll. Stores (treas. 1984—), Am. Numismatic Soc., Adminstrn. and Profl. Employees Assn. (bd. dirs. 1979-82). Democrat. Roman Catholic. Clubs: Civitan (treas. 1974-78), Lansing Skating (treas. 1976-80), Trojan Hockey (treas. 1983), University. Avocations: collecting Irish coins; golf; sports, especially hockey, football. Home: 1854 Cahill Dr East Lansing MI 48823 Office: Mich State U Bookstore East Lansing MI 48824

MCBAIN, ROBERT PRINCE, lawyer, accountant; b. Grand Rapids, Mich., Aug. 25, 1942; s. Robert James and Inez Marie (Prince) McB.; m. Gwendolyn Greene, Aug. 1, 1964; children—Robert Scott, James Kent. B.A., Mich. State U., 1964; J.D., U. Mich., 1966. Bar: Mich. 1968; C.P.A., Mich. Prin. Robert J. McBain & Co., P.C., Grand Rapids, Mich., 1967—; atty., cert. pub. acct., 1971—, exec. v.p., 1977—. Co-chmn. subcom. United Way of Kent County, 1974-77; treas. Goodwill Industries of Grand Rapids, 1974-79. Mem. ABA, Mich. Bar Assn., Grand Rapids Bar Assn., Am. Inst. C.P.A.s, Mich. Assn. C.P.A.s, Am. Assn. Atty.-C.P.A.s, Mich. Assn. Atty.-C.P.A.s (v.p.). Republican. Congregationalist. Lodge: Rotary.

MCBRAYER, JAMES DONALD, university dean; b. Pueblo, Colo., July 7, 1936; s. Benjamin Edgar and Helene (Leutenegger) McB.; m. June Ann Reiss, Aug. 2, 1958; children—Kenneth (dec.), Timothy, Theresa. B.S. in Aero. Engring., Parks Coll./St. Louis U.-Cahokia, Ill., 1957; M.S., St. Louis U., 1962; diploma with distinction VonKarman Inst., Brussels, 1963; D.Sc., Washington U., 1967. Registered profl. engr., Mo., Ohio. Aerodynamics engr. Emerson Electric Co., St. Louis, 1957-62, sr. aerodynamics engr., 1963-64; assoc. prof. mech. engring. U. Mo.-Rolla, 1967-70; dean faculty Parks Coll., Cahokia, 1970-74; dean coll. Central Methodist Coll., Fayette, Mo., 1974-77; dean Franklin U., Columbus, Ohio, 1977—. Vice commr. Central Ohio council Boy Scouts Am., 1980-83, asst. dist. commr., 1984—; mem. pastor-parish com. Worthington U. Meth. Ch., 1981-84. Von Karman scholar, 1962-63; recipient 100% award Central Ohio council Boy Scouts Am., 1982, Bridgebuilder award Olentangy Dist., Boy Scouts Am., 1982, 84. Fellow AIAA (assoc.); mem. ASME (exec. com. 1980-83), Columbus Tech. Council (pres. 1982-83), Am. Soc. Engring., Edn. (nat. sec. 1984-85 engring. tech. div.), Ohio Soc. Profl. Engrs. (trustee 1983—, trustee Franklin County chpt. 1979—, state chmn. profl. engr. in edn. 1983—), Engrs. Found. Ohio (trustee 1979—), Sigma Xi (mem. at large), Tau Alpha Pi (faculty adviser Franklin U. 1978—). Lodge: Rotary. Home: 202 Greenglade Ave Worthington OH 43085 Office: Franklin U 201 S Grant Ave Columbus OH 43215

MCBRIDE, ARTHUR WILBERT, insurance company executive; b. Youngstown, Ohio, May 5, 1927; s. James Henry and Gladys (Haag) M.; m. Pauline R. Wagner, Nov. 1, 1956; children—Tammie Lynn, Jeffrey Allen; m. 2d, Barbara R. Schinke, Nov. 6, 1971. B.C.E., Youngstown State U., 1952. Registered profl. engr., Calif.; cert. defensive driving instr., Nat. Safety Council; cert. hazard control mgr. (master level; cert. hazardous materials mgmt. (sr. level). Field insp. Ins. Services Office of Ohio, Youngstown, 1952-70; sr. loss control rep. Continental Ins. Cos., Cleve., 1970—; driving instr., vehicle safety employee tng.; participant mcpl. safety programs; lectr. profl. engring. and safety groups; coordinator vehicle safety program, bd. control Greater Cleve. Safety Council. Served with USN, 1945-46. Mem. Nat. Soc. Fire Protection Engrs., Am. Soc. Safety Engrs., Vets. Safety Internat., Internat. Hazard Control Mgmt., Audubon Soc., Western Res. Hist. Soc., 8th Air Force Hist. Soc., Air Racing Soc. Democrat. Roman Catholic. Office: care Cleve Safety Council One Playhouse Sq 1375 Euclid Ave Suite 417 Cleveland OH 44115

MCBRIDE, BEVERLY JEAN, lawyer; b. Greenville, Ohio, Apr. 5, 1941; d. Kenneth Birt and Glenna Louise (Ashman) Whited; m. Benjamin Gary McBride, Nov. 28, 1964; children—John David, Elizabeth Ann. B.A. magna cum laude, Wittenberg U., 1963; J.D. cum laude, U. Toledo, 1966. Bar: Ohio 1966. Intern Ohio Govs.' Office, Columbus, 1962; asst. dean of women U. Toledo, 1963-65; assoc. Title Guarantee and Trust Co., Toledo, 1966-69; spl. counsel Ohio Atty. Gen.'s Office, Toledo, 1975; assoc. Cobourn, Smith, Rohrbacher and Gibson, Toledo, 1969-76; sr. counsel The Andersons, Maumee, Ohio, 1976—. Exec. trustee, bd. dirs. Wittenberg U., Springfield, Ohio, 1980—; trustee Anderson Found., Maumee, 1981—; chmn. Sylvania Twp. Zoning Commn., Ohio, 1970-80; candidate for judge, Sylvania Mcpl. Ct., 1975; trustee Goodwill Industries, Toledo, 1976-82, Sylvania Community Services Ctr., 1976-78; founder Sylvania YWCA Program, 1973; active membership drives Toledo Mus. Art, 1977—. Recipient Toledo Women in Industry award YWCA, 1979; Outstanding Alumnus award, Wittenberg U., 1981. Mem. ABA, Ohio Bar Assn. Toledo Bar Assn. (treas. 1979-84, chmn., sec. various coms.), Toledo Women Attys. Forum (exec. com. 1978-82), AAUW. Club: Presidents (U. Toledo) (exec. com.). Home: 5274 Cambrian Rd Toledo OH 43623 Office: The Andersons 1200 Dussel Dr Maumee OH 43537

MCBRIDE, JACK J., financial services company executive; b. Orient, Iowa, June 24, 1936; s. Marvin Clair and Ruth (Jones) McB.; m. Mary Ann Garden, June 16, 1957; children—Jeffry J., Beth Ann, Kelley Lynn, Grant G. B.A., Simpson Coll., Indianola, Iowa, 1958. Spl. agt. Bankers Life Co., Des Moines, 1958-60; agy. supr. Aetna Life, Annuity, Fin. Services Inc., Hartford, Conn., 1960-65, gen. agt., Springfield, Ill., also Milw., 1972-82; agy. mgr. Equitable Life Iowa, Davenport, Iowa, 1965-72, E.I. Sales, Inc., Omaha, also Davenport; supt. Personal Fin. Security Div., Aetna Life & Casualty Co., Chgo., 1982-84; instr. Life Underwriters Tng. Council, Davenport, 1968-69; guest lectr. univs. and colls. Contbr. articles to profl. jours. Chmn. friends bd. So. Ill. U. Med. Sch., 1973-77; co-chmn. 1st Day Care Ctr., Springfield, Ill., 1973-77; charter chmn. stewardship St. Luke's Ch., Omaha, 1966-68; mem. Union Ch. of Hinsdale, Ill.; mem. steering com. devel. council Simpson Coll. Mem. Nat. Assn. Life Underwriters (past co-chmn. edn. com., chmn., dir. Iowa State com.), Gen. Agts. and Mgrs. Assn. (past pres., dir.), Sangamon Estate Planners Council (charter mem.), Am. C.L.U. Soc., Adminstrv. Mgmt. Soc., Quad City C. of C. (Speakers Bur.), Scottish Cultural Soc. Republican. Lodge: Masons (Scottish Rite). Office: Aetna Life and Casualty 230 W Monroe St Chicago IL 60606

MCBRIDE, PETER S., insurance agent; b. Chgo., Nov. 18, 1940; s. Thomas J. and Margaret Katherine (Simon) M.; m. Therese J. Van Der Bosch, Aug. 30, 1969; children—Katherine O'Neill, Elizabeth Clare. B.S., DePaul U., 1967. C.L.U. 1976; chartered fin. cons., 1984. Regional credit mgr. Sinclair Oil Co., 1968-69; ins. agt. N.Y. Life Ins. Co., Niles, Ill., 1969—; instr. C.L.U. studies Grad. Sch. Bus., DePaul U. Served with USMC, 1958-59. Recipient numerous achievement awards New York Life Ins. Co. Mem. Nat. Assn. Life Underwriters, Chgo. Assn. Life Underwriters, Chgo. Assn. Commerce and Industry. Roman Catholic. Club: K.C. Home: 2307 Woodlawn Rd Northbrook IL 60062 Office: 8410 W Bryn Mawr Ave Suite 300 Chicago IL 60631

MCBURNEY, JAMES BERNARD, consulting company executive; b. Washington, Pa., May 17, 1927. s. Bernard Reckers and Marion Laura (Perkins) McB.; m. Carolyn Martha Keathley, Apr. 1, 1973; children—Karen L., Steven B., James R. (dec.), Brenda, Susan, William, Faith. B.A., Washington and Jefferson Coll., 1948; postgrad. U. Miami Grad. Sch. Bus., 1949-51. With Sears Roebuck & Co., 1950-75, successively personnel trainee, div. mgr. sales, Miami, Fla., personnel mgr., Chattanooga, service mgr., St. Petersburg, Fla., personnel mgr., Coral Gables, Fla., asst. store mgr., Ft. Myers Fla., service staff asst., Atlanta, sales promotion mgr., nat. sales mgr. service and parts, mktg. mgr. home laundry sect., Chgo., exec. v.p., pres. Markoa Corp., Lincolnshire, Ill., 1975—. Named Boss of Yr., Bus. Women's Assn. of Am., 1964. Mem. Midwest Soc. Profl. Cons., Soc. Personnel Adminstrs., Sales/Mktg. Execs. of Chgo., Sales/Mktg. Execs. Internat., Chgo. Sales Tng. Assn., Chgo. Assn. Commerce and Industry, Phi Gamma Delta. Republican. Presbyterian. Avocations: music; auto and home restoration. Home: 3825 Maple Ave Northbrook IL 60062 Office: Markoa Corp 175 Olde Half Day Rd Suite 20 Lincolnshire IL 60069

MC CABE, ARTHUR LEE, consultant; b. Otsego, Mich., Dec. 18, 1937; s. Arthur Lee and Florence Gertrude (Mollison) McC.; student Kalamazoo Coll., 1956-58, Western Mich. U., 1958-59; m. Nancy Lee Smith, June 26, 1959; children—Janet Lee, William Arthur, Sherry Linn, Arthur Lee, Elizabeth Ann, Susan Faye. Asst. mgr. D & C Stores, Kalamazoo, 1959-60; asst. fleet supt. McNamara Motor Express Co., Kalamazoo, 1960-61; with Upjohn Co., Kalamazoo, 1961-63; chemistry technician Consumers Power Co., Kalamazoo, 1963-66, sr. chemistry technician, 1966-73, sr. radiation protection technician Palisades plant, Covert, Mich., 1973-74, chemistry supr., Palisades Nuclear Plant, 1974-78, fossil fuels specialist, Jackson, Mich., 1978-79, fuel transp. adminstr., 1979—; pres. Fuels Technology Co. Inc., 1983—. Dist. commr.

Southwestern Mich. council Boy Scouts Am., 1973-74. Republican. Inventor in field. Home and office: PO Box 84 215 Hanover St Concord MI 49237

MCCABE, CHARLES KEVIN, lawyer, author; b. Springfield, Ill., Nov. 2, 1952; s. Charles Kenneth and Betty Lou (Williams) McC. B.S. in Aero. and Astronautical Engring. magna cum laude, U. Ill., 1975; J.D., U. Mich., 1978. Bar: Ill. 1978, U.S. Dist. Ct. (no. dist.) Ill. 1978, U.S. Ct. Appeals (7th cir.) 1980. Engring. co-op. student McDonnell Aircraft, St. Louis, 1972-74; chief aerodynamicist Vetter Fairing Co., Rantoul, Ill., 1974-75; assoc. Lord, Bissell, & Brook, Chgo., 1978—. Author: Qwiktran: Quick FORTRAN, 1979; FORTH Fundamentals, 1983; co-author: 32 BASIC Programs, 1981. Contbr. articles on aviation, computers to various mags., 1974—. Nat. Merit scholar U. Ill., Urbana, 1970. Mem. ABA, Ill. State Bar Assn., Chgo. Bar Assn. Office: Lord Bissell & Brook 115 S LaSalle St Chicago IL 60603

MCCABE, MILO FRANCIS, economist, educator; b. Oconomowoc, Wis., Apr. 5, 1931; s. Milo John and Mary Catherine (Anglesberg) McC.; B.S. in Sociology, Marquette U., 1956; M.A. in Econ. Edn., Ohio U., 1968; M.S. in Econs., U. Ill., 1968; m. Jeanne E. Schraa, Aug. 25, 1956; children—James, Jeanne Marie, Timothy, Margaret. Tchr., Pius XI High Sch., Milw., 1956-64, Kenosha (Wis.) Tremper High Sch., 1964-69, Lake Forest (Ill.) High Sch., 1969-70; supervising tchr. sociology, econs., history for practice tchrs. Alverno Coll., Milw., 1963-64; supervising tchr. Am. history Carthage Coll., Kenosha, Wis., 1966-69; instr. Upward Bound program U. Wis.-Whitewater, 1966-67; mem. faculty U. S.D., Vermillion, 1970—, asso. prof. econs., dir. Henry T. Quinn Center Econ. Edn., 1970—; exec. dir. S.D. Council Econ. Edn., 1978—. Served with AUS, 1951-53; Korea. Recipient Tchr. of Yr. award U. S.D., 1976-77; summer fellow Gen. Electric Co., NSF, NDEA, Libby Found., others. Mem. Am. Econ. Assn., Am. Acad. Polit. and Social Scis., Nat. Assn. Bus. Economists, Nat. Council Social Studies, Nat. Bus. Edn. Econ. Assn., Assn. Supervision and Curriculum Devel., Midwest Econ. Assn., S.D. Council Social Studies, S.D. Bus. Edn. Tchrs. Assn., Beta Gamma Sigma, Delta Sigma Pi, Omicron Delta Epsilon. Clubs: K.C., Lions (treas. 1976—). Author curriculum materials, articles in field. Home: 933 Eastgate Dr Vermillion SD 57069 Office: 218 Patterson Hall Sch Bus Vermillion SD 57069

MCCALL, JOHN THOMAS, home furnishing representative; b. Kansas City, Mo., Jan. 3, 1932; s. Jim John and Ruth Mae (Clark) McC.; m. Marilyn Marie Rigby, Feb. 14, 1958; children—Julianne Marie, Cheryl Ann, John Justin. B.B.A. in Mktg., North Tex. State Coll., 1957. With Foleys' Dept. Store div. Federated Dept. Stores, Houston, 1957-65, buyer, 1960-65; with Westwood Lighting, 1965-84, regional sales mgr. Midwest and Can., 1972-76, sr. regional sales mgr., 1976-80, nat. dir. sales shades and accessories div., 1980-81, regional sales mgr. Midwest, 1981-83, decorative accessories sales rep. for Wis. and Ill., Glen Ellyn, Ill., 1983-84, Bloomingdale, Ill., 1983-85; ind. home furnishings rep., Wis., Ill., Mo., Minn., 1984—. Mem. nat. adv. bd. Am. Security Council; mem. Republican Nat. Com. Served with USN, 1951-54; Korea. Mem. Am. Mgmt. Assn., Internat. Entrepreneurs Assn., Mail Order Bus. Bd., Ill. Conf. Police (assoc.), Ill. Sheriffs Assn., U.S. Senatorial Club, Am. Revenue Assn., Am. Philatelic Assn. Club: Aloha Vacations. Home and Office: 259 Sutton Ct Bloomingdale IL 60108

MCCALL, JULIEN LACHICOTTE, banker; b. Florence, S.C., Apr. 1, 1921; s. Arthur M. and Julia (Lachicotte) McC.; B.S., Davidson Coll., 1942; M.B.A., Harvard U., 1947; m. Janet Jones, Sept. 30, 1950; children—Melissa, Alison Gregg, Julien Lachicotte. With First Nat. City Bank, N.Y.C., 1948-71, asst. mgr. bond dept., 1952-53, asst. cashier, 1953-55, asst. v.p., 1955-57, v.p., 1957-71; 1st v.p. Nat. City Bank, Cleve., 1971-72, pres., 1972-79, chmn. bd., chief exec. officer, 1979—, also dir.; chmn. bd., chief exec. officer Nat. City Corp.; dir. Atlas Copco-Jarva, Inc., Progressive Corp., Russell Burdsall & Ward Corp. Trustee, St. Luke's Hosp., Greater Cleve. Roundtable, Cleve. Tomorrow, Case Western Res. U., Greater Cleve. council Boy Scouts Am., Playhouse Sq. Found., Mus. Arts Assn., United Way Services, Cleve. Mus. Natural History. Served from 2d lt. to 1st lt. Ordnance Dept., AUS, 1942-46; Africa, ETO. Episcopalian. Clubs: Union, Pepper Pike, Tavern, Chagrin Valley Hunt (Cleve.); Kirtland; Rolling Rock (Ligonier, Pa.). Home: Arrowhead County Line Rd Hunting Valley OH 44022 Office: Nat City Corp 1900 E 9th St Cleveland OH 44114

MC CALLUM, CHARLES EDWARD, lawyer; b. Memphis, Mar. 13, 1939; s. Edward Payson and India Raimelle (Musick) McC.; B.S., M.I.T., 1960; Fulbright scholar U. Manchester (Eng.), 1960-61; J.D., Vanderbilt U., 1964; m. Lois Temple, Nov. 30, 1985; children—Florence Andrea, Printha Kyle, Chandler Ward Payson. Bar: Mich. 1964. Assoc. Warner, Norcross & Judd, Grand Rapids, Mich., 1964-69, ptnr., 1969—; rep. assemblyman State Bar of Mich., 1973-78; lectr. continuing legal edn. programs. Chmn. Grand Rapids Area Transit Authority, 1976-79, mem., 1972-79; regional v.p. Nat. Mcpl. League, 1978—, mem. council, 1971-78; pres. Grand Rapids Art Mus., 1979-81, trustee, 1976-83; chmn. Butterworth Hosp., 1979—, trustee, 1977—; vice chmn. Citizens Com. Consolidation of Govt. Services, 1981-82, chmn. cultural services consol. com., 1984—; ednl. counselor MIT, 1974—; nat. chmn. Vanderbilt Law Sch. Devel. Com., 1977-78; trustee Kent Med. Found., 1979-82; dir. Vol. Trustees of Not-for-Profit Hosps., 1973—. Woodrow Wilson fellow, 1960-61. Mem. Am., Tenn., Mich., Grand Rapids bar assns., Grand Rapids C. of C. (pres. 1975, dir. 1970-76), Order of Coif, Sigma Xi. Clubs: Kent Country, Grand Rapids Athletic, Peninsular, University. Home: 1346 Cornell Ave SE Grand Rapids MI 49506 Office: 900 Old Kent Bldg 1 Vandenberg Center Grand Rapids MI 49503

MCCANN, MARY KATHLEEN, lawyer; b. Milw., Dec. 4, 1944; d. Ray Thomas and Annetta (O'Connor) McC. B.A. in Psychology, U. Wis.-Madison, 1967, M.S. in Counseling and Guidance, 1970; J.D., Marquette U., 1981. Bar: U.S. Dist. Ct. (we. dist.) Wis. 1981, U.S. dist. Ct. (ea. dist.) Wis. 1981, Wis. 1981. Social worker Milw. Dept. Social Services, 1971-79; assoc. Leonard & Loeb, S.C., Milw., 1981—. Office: Leonard & Loeb SC 111 E Wisconsin Suite 1716 Milwaukee WI 53202

MCCANN, ROBERT WALTER, lawyer; b. Evanston, Ill., Dec. 11, 1951; s. Walter Robert and Reba Marie (York) McC.; m. Mona M. Signer, Aug. 30, 1982; children—Harrison Scott, Laura Frances. A.B., Miami U., Oxford, Ohio, 1973; M.H.A., U. Mich., 1975, J.D., 1978. Bar: Ill. 1980, U.S. Supreme Ct. 1983. Adminstrv. resident W. K. Kellogg Found., Battle Creek, Mich., 1974; research asst. U. Mich., Ann Arbor, 1974-77; mgmt. cons. Health Mgmt. Advisors, Ann Arbor, 1976-78; v.p., assoc. gen. counsel Am. Hosp. Assn., Chgo., 1978—. Mem. Chgo. Bar Assn., Ill. State Bar Assn., Am. Acad. Hosp. Attys., Phi Beta Kappa. Home: 344 W Wisconsin Chicago IL 60614 Office: Am Hosp Assn 840 N Lake Shore Dr Chicago IL 60611

MCCANNA, WILLIAM JOSEPH, food company executive; b. Pittston, Pa., Jan. 21, 1940; s. James Gerald and Agnes Rita (Leonard) McC.; m. Patricia Ellen Shockey, Dec. 28, 1963; children—William J., Thomas M. B.S.E.E., Pa. State U., 1965; postgrad., Harvard U., 1982. Unit mgr. Gen. Electric Co., Louisville, 1965-70; plant mgr. Phelps Dodge Co., Newark, Ohio, 1970-74; gen. mgr. Emerson Electric Co., Napanee, Ont., Can., 1974-76; pres., dir. gen. Allis Chalmer-Europe, Paris, 1976-82; exec. v.p. Universal Foods Corp., Milw., 1983—, dir., 1985—. Mem. exec. bd. Milwaukee County council Boy Scouts Am., 1984; bd. dirs. Newark United Way, 1974. Served with U.S. Marine Corps, 1958-61. Club: Athletic (Milw.). Avocations: running; tennis. Office: Universal Foods Corp 433 E Michigan St Milwaukee WI 53201

MCCARTHY, DEBORAH JANE, telephone company executive; b. St. Louis, Sept. 4, 1957; d. Gerard Francis and Almaretta Maxine (Hutchings) Bedford; m. Kevin Joseph McCarthy, Oct. 23, 1982. B.S., U. Mo., 1979. Yellow pages sales rep. Southwestern Bell, St. Louis, 1980-81, yellow pages sales trainer, 1981-82, computer aided trainer, 1982-84; supr. sales tng. and course devel. Southwestern Bell Publs., St. Louis, 1984—. Mem. Am. Soc. Tng. and Devel. Republican. Roman Catholic. Avocation: antique collecting. Office: Southwestern Bell Publs 1625 Des Peres Room 200 Saint Louis MO 63131

MCCARTHY, GEORGE JOSEPH, corporate planner; b. St. Louis, Dec. 17, 1950; s. George Gerald and Leona Rose (Hotop) McC.; m. Barbara Jean Lowery, Mar. 31, 1978; 1 child, Ashley Danielle. A.A. in Bus. Adminstrn., Florissant Valley Community Coll., 1972, A.A. in Liberal Arts, 1973; B.S. in Bus. Adminstrn., U. Mo.-St. Louis, 1975; M.B.A., Southwest Mo. State U., 1976. Sr. planner McDonnell Douglas Co., St. Louis, 1976-80; fin. dir. Midwest Health Plan, Inc., St. Louis, 1980-82; corp. planning specialist Gen. Dynamics Co., St. Louis, 1982—. Mem. Selective Service Bd. 17, St. Charles, Mo., 1981—; bd. dirs. Greater St. Louis Health Systems Agy., 1981-82. Served with U.S. Army, 1969-71, Vietnam. Roman Catholic. Avocation: travel. Home: 4208 Weatherton Pl Saint Charles MO 63303 Office: General Dynamics DSD 12101 Woodcrest Executive Dr Saint Louis MO 63141

MCCARTHY, JAMES BRYAN, management consultant; b. Evergreen Park, Ill., May 26, 1951; s. Martin Joseph and Margaret (McNeill) McC.; m. Cheryl Sleepeck McCarthy, June 3, 1978; children—James Bryan Jr., William M., Kelly Ann. B.A., U. Notre Dame, 1973; M.B.A., Keller Grad. Sch. Mgmt., Chgo., 1977; J.D., Loyola U., Chgo., 1983. Planning analyst 3M Co. Med. Products div., Hinsdale, Ill., 1973-78; asst. to pres. The Cameron Group, Addison, Ill., 1978-81; assoc. Heidrick & Struggles, Inc., Chgo., 1981-83; v.p., gen. mgr. Ferris Med. Systems, Inc., Burr Ridge, Ill., 1983-85; v.p. Paul R. Ray and Co., Inc., 1985—. Bd. dirs. United Way Hinsdale/Oak Brook, 1983—, pres., 1985-86; mem. adv. council Keller Grad. Sch. Mgmt., 1983—; mem. bd. assocs. Rush-Presbyn.-St. Luke's Med. Ctr. Mem. Assn. M.B.A. Execs., Assn. Advancement Med. Instrumentation (govt. relations com.), Chgo. Council Fgn. Relations, Chgo. High Tech. Assn. Club: Mid America (Chgo.). Home: 418 S Park Ave Hinsdale IL 60521 Office: Paul R Ray and Co Inc 200 S Wacker Dr Suite 3820 Chicago IL 60606

MC CARTHY, JEAN JEROME, physical education educator; b. St. Paul, Sept. 11, 1929; s. Joseph Justin and Florence (Quirin) McC.; m. Norma Louise Shermer, July 30, 1955; children—Patrick J., Anne L., Kevin M. B.S., U. Minn., 1956; M.S., Wash. State U., 1958; grad. student U. Minn., 1979—. Teaching asst. Wash. State U., 1956-57, U. Minn., 1957-59, adminstrv. asst., 1959-60; asst. prof. phys. edn. U. South Fla., 1960-62; asst. prof. phys. edn. Mankato State U., 1962-71, assoc. prof., 1971—, baseball coach, 1962-77. Cons., AAU. Mem. Minn. Gov.'s Phys. Fitness Adv. Com. Served with USAF, 1950-54. Recipient Outstanding Faculty award Mankato State U., 1979; named Region 2 Coach of Yr., NCAA, 1971; U. Minn. Grad. Sch. fellow, 1959-60; Lilly Found. scholar, 1974—; Research Consortium fellow. Mem. AAHPER, Minn. Assn. Health, Phys. Edn. Recreation and Dance, Phi Delta Kappa, Phi Epsilon Kappa (scholarship award 1972). Roman Catholic.

MCCARTHY, ROBERT ELMER, research immunologist, immunology educator; b. Washington, May 19, 1926; s. John Albin and Irene Sarah (Raum) McC. B.S., U. Md., 1951, M.S., 1953; Ph.D., Brown U., 1956. Research assoc. in pathology Children's Hosp., Boston, 1959-70; chief lab. immunology Children's Cancer Research Found., Boston, 1968-69; assoc. pathology Harvard Med. Sch., Boston, 1969-70; assoc. oral pathology Harvard Dental Sch., Boston, 1969-70; assoc. prof. U. Nebr. Med. Ctr., Omaha, 1970—; cons. Norden Lab., Lincoln, Nebr., 1971-75. Contbr. articles to profl. jours. Mem. Am. Assn. Immunologists, Am. Assn. Pathologists, Am. Assn. Cancer Research. Office: U Nebr Med Ctr 42nd and Dewey Ave Omaha NE 68105

MCCARTHY, THOMAS WILLIAM, II, state senator, lawyer; b. St. Louis, Sept. 26, 1945; s. Thomas William and Jonell (Coburn) McC.; m. Linda Tobin, 1971; children—Erin Colleen, Thomas William. Grad. St. Louis U., 1967, J.D., 1973. Bar: Mo. Ptnr. firm Harris, Dowell, Fisher, McCarthy & Kaemmerer; mem. Mo. Ho. of Reps., 1981-82, Mo. Senate, 1983—. Mem. ABA, Mo. Bar Assn., St. Louis Bar Assn., St. Louis County Pachyderms, Alpha Delta Gamma. Republican. Office: Senate PO State Capital Jefferson City MO 65101

MCCARTHY, WALTER JOHN, JR., electric utility company executive; b. N.Y.C., Apr. 20, 1925; s. Walter J. and Irene (Trumbland) McC.; B.M.E., Cornell U., 1949; postgrad. Oak Ridge Sch. Reactor Tech., 1951-52; D.Eng. (hon.), Lawrence Inst. Tech., 1981; D.Sc. (hon.), Eastern Mich. U., 1983; L.H.D. (hon.), Wayne State U., 1984; m. Alice Anna Ross, Sept. 3, 1947; children—Walter, David, Sharon, James, William. Engr., Public Service Electric & Gas Co., Newark, 1949-56; sect. head Atomic Power Devel. Assos., Detroit, 1956-61; gen. mgr. Power Reactor Devel. Co., Detroit, 1961-68; project mgr. Detroit Edison Co., 1968-71, mgr. engring., 1971-73, mgr. ops., 1973-74, v.p. ops., 1974-75, exec. v.p. ops., 1975-77, exec. v.p. divs., 1977-79, pres., chief operating officer, 1979-81, chmn. bd., 1981—, also dir.; dir. Comerica, Inc., Fed.-Mogul Corp., Perry Drug Stores. Bd. dirs. Cranbrook Inst. Sci., Detroit Econ. Growth Corp., Detroit Symphony Orch., Detroit Renaissance, Econ. Alliance Mich., Edison Electric Inst., Inst. Nuclear Power Ops., Met. Affairs Corp., United Found., Gov.'s Exec. Corp.; trustee New Detroit, Harper-Grace Hosps., Interlochen Ctr. for Arts, Rackham Engring. Found., Thomas Alva Edison Found. Named One of 5 Outstanding Young Men in Mich., Mich. Jr. C. of C., 1958. Fellow Am. Nuclear Soc., Engring. Soc. Detroit; mem. Nat. Acad. Engring., ASME. Methodist. Clubs: Detroit Athletic, Detroit, Renaissance (Detroit). Contbr. numerous articles on nuclear and power system engring. to profl. jours. Office: 2000 2d Ave Detroit MI 48226

MCCARTHY, WILLIAM ROBERT, clergyman; b. Tacoma, Wash., Nov. 17, 1941; s. Denward Sylvester and Florence Elizabeth (Lohan) McC.; m. Bernice Bigler, Apr. 22, 1962; children—Brian Edward Earl, Sean David. B.S., Oreg. State U., 1966; M.Div., Nashotah House, 1975. Ordained deacon Episcopal Ch., 1975, priest, 1975. Sales rep. Chevron Chem. Co., Greeley, Colo., 1965-67; tech. sales rep., Des Plaines, Ill., 1967-72; curate St. Michael's Ch., Barrington, Ill., 1975-77; vicar St. Anselm's Ch., Park Ridge, Ill., 1977-81; rector Christ Ch. Parish, Waukegan, Ill., 1981—; diocesan cursillo officer Diocese Chgo., 1977—; spiritual dir. Ecumenical Cursillo Community, Chgo., 1977-83; mem. steering com. Happenings in Christianity, Chgo., 1978-80; chmn. Bishop's Adv. Commn. on Renewal and Evangelism, Chgo., 1983—. Contbr. articles to profl. jours. Bd. mem. Waukegan Area Crime Stoppers, 1982-85; charter bd. dirs. Waukegan Downtown Assn., 1983—. Served with USNR, 1962-65. Mem. Waukegan Downtown Ministries (coordinator 1983—), Acad. Parish Clergy (assoc.), Assn. for Psychol. Type, Internat. Platform Assn., Phi Sigma Kappa. Lodge: Masons. Office: Christ Ch Parish 410 Grand Ave Waukegan IL 60085

MCCARTNEY, MICHAEL JERRY, lawyer; b. Antigo, Wis., Feb. 14, 1949; s. Clayton Fred and Joyce (Tesch) McC.; m. Mary Jean Exner, Oct. 3, 1969; children—Molly, Thomas, Maureen. Student U. of N.D., 1967-70; B.B.A., Troy State U., 1974; J.D., South Tex. Coll. Law., 1976. Bar: Tex. 1976, Minn. 1977, U.S. Dist. Ct. Minn. 1978. Title analyst Tenneco Oil Co., Houston, 1976-77; sole practice, Breckenridge, Minn., 1977—. Appeared in Community Theatre play The Night of January 16th, 1980. Pres., head Red United Way, Breckenridge-Wahpeton, 1981; pres. St. Mary's Ch. Council, Breckenridge, 1981-82, Richland-Wilkin Alphaen Male Chorus, Breckenridge, 1983-84; mem. adv. com. Lake Aggasiz chpt. Compasionate Friends, Breckenridge, 1983—; chmn. Wilkin County Group Home, Inc., Breckenridge, 1984-85. Served with U.S. Army, 1971-73. Mem. ABA, Am. Acad. Hosp. Attys., Minn. Soc. Hosp. Attys., Minn. Sch. Bds. Assn. Council Sch. Attys. Club: Bois de Sioux Golf (pres. 1984), Toastmaster's (pres. 1981). Lodge: Lions (pres. 1981). Home: 809 N Fifth St Circle Breckenridge MN 56520 Office: 110 N Sixth St Breckenridge MN 56520

MC CARTNEY, RALPH FARNHAM, lawyer, district judge; b. Charles City, Iowa, Dec. 11, 1924; s. Ralph C. and Helen (Farnham) McC.; J.D., U. Mich., 1950; B. Sci., Iowa State U., 1972; m. Rhoda Mae Huxsol, June 30, 1950; children—Ralph, Julia, David. Bar: Iowa 1950. Mem. firm Miller, Heuber & Miller, Des Moines, 1950-52, Frye & McCartney, Charles City, 1952-73, McCartney & Erb, Charles City, 1973-78; judge Dist. Ct. Iowa, Charles City, 1978—; mem. jud. coordinating com. Iowa Supreme Ct. Chmn., Iowa Republican Conv., 1972, 74; chmn. Supreme Ct. Adv. Com. on Adminstrn. of Clks. Offices; mem. Iowa Ho. of Reps., 1967-70, majority floor leader, 1969-70; mem. Iowa Senate, 1973-74. Bd. regents U. Iowa, Iowa State U., U. No. Iowa, Iowa Sch. for Deaf, Iowa Braille and Sight Saving Sch. Served with AUS, 1942-45. Mem. Am., Iowa bar assns., Iowa Judges Assn. Home: RFD 1 Charles City IA 50616 Office: Ct Chambers Courthouse Charles City IA 50616

MCCARTY, LESLIE PAUL, pharmacologist, chemist; b. Detroit, May 30, 1925; s. Leslie Evart and Ruth Winifred (Clouse) McC.; m. Marie-Jeanne Beullay, May 8, 1976; children—Michael, Patricia, Maureen, Brian. B.S., Salem Coll., 1947; M.Sc., Ohio State U., 1949; Ph.D., U. Wis., 1960. Diplomate Am. Bd. Toxicology. Research chemist Upjohn Co., Kalamazoo, 1949-55; research leader Dow Chem. Co., Midland, Mich., 1960—. Contbr. articles to profl. jours. Patentee in field. Served with USNR, 1943-45. Mem. Am. Soc. Pharmacology and Exptl. Therapeutics, AAAS, Sigma Xi. Avocations: amateur radio; gardening; woodworking. Home: 4588 S Flavjole Rd Midland MI 48640 Office: Dow Chem Co Bldg 1803 Midland MI 48674

MCCARTY, THEODORE MILSON, manufacturing company executive; b. Somerset, Ky., Oct. 10, 1909; s. Raymond Andrew and Jennie (Milson) McC.; m. Elinor H. Bauer, June 14, 1935; children—Theodore F., Susan McCarty Davis. Comml. Engr., U. Cin., 1933, postgrad., 1934-35. Asst. store mgr. Wurlitzer Co., Rochester, N.Y., 1936-38, mgr. real estate div., Cin. and Chgo., 1939-41, dir. procurement, DeKalb, Ill., 1942-44, mdse mgr. retail div., Chgo., 1945-48; pres., gen. mgr., dir. Gibson, Inc., 1948-66; owner, pres., treas., dir. Bigsby Accessories, Inc., Kalamazoo, 1966—; owner, pres., dir. Flex-Lite, Inc.; v.p., dir. Command Electronics, Kalamazoo. Bd. dirs. Glowing Embers council Girl Scouts U.S.A., 1968-74; mem. Pres. Reagan's Task Force, 1982—. Mem. Am. Music Conf. (pres., adminstr. 1961-63, 70-77, dir. 1956—, hon. life dir.), Guitar and Accessory Mfrs. Assn. (past pres., hon. life dir.), Kalamazoo Symphony Soc. (past pres.), SAR (charter mem.), Alpha Kappa Psi, Alpha Tau Omega, Omicron Delta Kappa. Presbyterian. Clubs: Masons, Rotary (past pres.), Kalamazoo Country (past pres.), Park. Patentee in music field. Home: 1028 Essex Circle Kalamazoo MI 49008 Office: Bigsby Accessories Inc 3521 E Kilgore Rd Kalamazoo MI 49008

MCCARTY, WILLIAM DENNIS, state senator, lawyer; b. Anderson, Ind., July 11, 1943; s. Harold Lee and Mary Elizabeth (Dill) McC.; m. Gwendolyn Jo Rudd, 1972; children—Stacia Crick, Matthew Crick. B.A., Wabash Coll., 1965; M.A., Johns Hopkins U., 1967; J.D., Ind. U., 1979. Bar: Ind. 1979. Sole practice, Anderson, 1979—; mem. staff Sec. State Larry A. Conrad, 1971, to Mayor Robert Rock, 1972-80, to Sen. Birch Bayh, 1973-74; mem. Ind. Senate, 1982—. Mem. ABA, Ind. Bar Assn., Madison County Bar Assn., Phi Beta Kappa, Phi Gamma Delta. Lodge: Optimists. Office: 903 Forest Dr Anderson IN 46011

MCCHESNEY, KATHRYN MARIE (MRS. THOMAS DAVID MCCHESNEY), educator; b. Curwensville, Pa., Jan. 14, 1936; d. Orland William and Lillian Irene (Morrison) Spencer; B.A., U. Akron, 1962; M.L.S., Kent State U., 1965, postgrad., 1971—; m. Thomas David McChesney, June 12, 1954; 1 son, Eric Spencer. Tchr. English, Springfield Local High Sch., Akron, Ohio, 1962-63, librarian, 1963-64, head librarian, 1965-68; asst. to dean, instr. Kent (Ohio) State U. Sch. Library Sci., 1968-69, asst. dean, 1969-77, asst. prof., 1969—. Rep. Uniontown Community Council, 1964-66. Mem. Am., Ohio (chmn. Library Edn. Roundtable 1971-72, exec. council Div. VI Library Edn. 1972—) library assns., AAUP, Am., Ohio assns. sch. librarians, Beta Phi Mu, Phi Sigma Alpha, Phi Alpha Theta, Sigma Phi Epsilon. Club: Uniontown Jr. Womans (pres. 1965-66). Co-author: The Library in Society, 1984. Contbr. articles, book revs. to profl. periodicals. Home: 3611 Edison St NW Uniontown OH 44685 Office: Kent State U Kent OH 44242

MCCLAIN, SHIRLA ROBINSON, educator; b. Akron, Ohio, Feb. 4, 1935; d. Dumas Defoe and Marcella Carolyn (Macbeth) Robinson; B.S. in Edn. with distinction, U. Akron, 1956, M.S. in Edn., 1970, Ph.D. in Edn., 1975; m. Henry Lee McClain, Apr. 6, 1957; children—Kelli Jesselyn, Scott Jay. Tchr. Akron Pub. Schs., 1956-65, remedial tchr., 1966-71, ednl. specialist, 1971-76; asst. prof. edn. Kent (Ohio) State Univ., 1976-81, asso. prof. edn., 1981—; multicultural edn. cons. Gt. Rivers council Girl Scout U.S.A., 1981-82; mem. State of Ohio Library Bd., 1979—, v.p., 1983—; bd. dirs. Summit County Hist. Soc., 1981—, 2d v.p., 1982—; mem. City of Akron Human Relation Commn., 1982—; bd. trustees Akron Urban League, 1980—; mem. WAKR Community Relations Bd., 1976-81. Recipient Black Applause award for outstanding achievement in edn., Phi Beta Sigma, 1980; Achievement award Akron Urban League, 1975. Mem. Nat. Council Social Studies, (publs. bd.), Am. Assn. Colls. for Tchr. Edn. (multicultural task force), Phi Delta Kappa. Episcopalian. Home: 865 Packard Dr Akron OH 44320 Office: 404 White Hall College of Edn Kent State Univ Kent OH 44242

MCCLAIN, WILLIAM H., molecular biology educator; b. Middletown, Ohio, Mar. 29, 1942; s. William H. and Emma (Brittingham) McC., Sr.; m. Lucinda Lewis; children—Carin, Gary, Patricia, Susan. B.S., Iowa Wesleyan Coll., 1964; Ph.D., Purdue U., 1967. Postdoctoral fellow Med. Research Council Lab. Molecular Biology, Cambridge, Eng., 1969-71; asst. prof. U. Wis.-Madison, 1971-74, assoc. prof., 1974-77, prof., 1977—. Mem. editorial bd. Nucleic Acid Research, 1980—. Contbr. articles to profl. jours. Recipient USPHS Research Career Devel. award NIH, 1976-81; NIH grantee, 1971—. Office: U Wis 1550 Linden Dr Madison WI 53706

MCCLANAHAN, BETTY COLLEEN, publishing company executive; b. Altoona, Iowa, Jan. 19, 1924; d. Ezra Guy and Minnie (Hersbergen) Plummer; m. Willard Dale McClanahan, Oct. 7, 1944; children—Bonnie Sue McClanahan Hosler, Nancy Jo McClanahan Miller, Sarah Jane McClanahan Valenti. Student Altoona, Iowa schs. With Denniston & Partridge Lumber Co., Altoona, 1942-46; farm bookkeeper, Bondurant, Iowa, 1944—; owner, mgr. Hiawatha Book Co., Bondurant, 1980—; mem. Farmers Elevator Co.; rep. Ramsey Meml. Home Guild, 1978-84; mem. steering com. Spiritual Frontiers Fellowship, Des Moines, 1978—. Adaptor psalms to music. Mem. Builders of the Adytum, Assn. Research and Enlightenment, Huna Assoc. Mem. Ch. Disciples of Christ. Avocations: stamp collecting, astrology, I Ching, Tarot, esoteric philosophies, piano. Home: 7783 NE 102 Ave Bondurant IA 50035 Office: Hiawatha Book Co 7567 NE 102 Ave Bondurant IA 50035

MCCLANAHAN, HARRY ALLEN, III, training coordinator, radio producer; b. Ypsilanti, Mich., Mar. 30, 1949; s. Harry Allen and Ann Mary (Micheletti) McC.; m. Jo Ann Shroyer, Nov. 15, 1969 (div. Dec. 20, 1982); children—Peter Jason, Claire Marie; m. Naomi Ruth Johnson, May 10, 1984; 1 child, Briana Michelle. B.A., St. Mary's Coll., 1971. Tchr. St. Bede Acad., Peru, Ill., 1972-78, Ind. Sch. Dist. 719, Prior Lake, Minn., 1978-83; producer, host Sta. WCAL-FM, Northfield, Minn., 1979—; tng. and media devel. group mgr. Lawson Assocs., Mpls., 1983—. Mem. Am. Soc. Tng. and Devel., Programming, Analysis and Computer Trainers Assn. Roman Catholic. Avocation: amateur radio. Home: 4800 Hwy 7 Apt 206 Saint Louis Park MN 55416 Office: Lawson Assocs 2021 E Hennepin Ave Minneapolis MN 55413

MCCLAREN, H. BRUCE, real estate syndicator; b. Pitts., Dec. 18, 1942; s. William Wilson and Katharine (Knox) M.; m. Adele C. Richter, June 28, 1968 (div. 1983); children—Kaye, John. B.A. in Fin., Lehigh U., 1964; M.A. in Fin., Columbia U., 1966. Cert. property mgr., specialist in real estate securities. Founding ptnr. Partnership Concepts, Hinsdale, Ill., 1971—; dir. 1st Security Bank of Aurora, Ill.; instr. Real Estate Securities and Syndication Inst. Served to lt. USNR, 1966-71. Mem. Real Estate Securities and Syndication Inst., Inst. of Real Estate Mgmt. Home: 511 S Oak St Hinsdale IL 60521 Office: 210 E Ogden Ave Suite 26 Hinsdale IL 60521

MCCLARNON, KEITH JOE, mayor; b. Charlottsville, Ind., Nov. 29, 1929; s. David Russell and Mary E. (Williams) McC., m. Joanne Carr, June 28, 1950; children—Kevin C., Keith S., Kelly J., Marcia Ann McClarnon Richardson, Kathleen McClarnon Book. Student Butler U., 1952. With antibiotic dept. Eli Lilly Co., Indpls., 1949-53; v.p. Carr Mac's Inc., Greenfield, Ind., 1953-76; mayor City of Greenfield, 1976—. Mem. Hancock County Council, Ind., 1964-68; del. Ind. Democratic Conv., 1962-84; commr. Ind. Mcpl. Power Agy., 1985—; pres. Bradley Meth Men, 1962. Served with Ind. N.G., 1949-54. Mem. Hancock County Home Builders Assn., Am. Water Works Assn., Ind. Water Pollution Control Fedn., Ind. Assn. Police Chiefs, Wabash Valley Assn., Ind. Assn. City-Town Execs., South Central Mayors Roundtable Assn. (pres. 1985). Lodges: Kiwanis (past pres.), Elks (past exalted ruler). Avocations: golf, bowling, hiking, philately, skiing. Home: 212 E North St Greenfield IN 46140 Office: 110 S State St Box 456 Greenfield IN 46140

MCCLEAN, VINCENT C., educational consultant; b. Rock Island, Ill., May 14, 1940; s. C.W. and Mary Agnes (Kerwin) M. B.A. in English and History, St. Mary's Coll., Winona, Mich., 1964; M.A. in Guidance and Counseling, Roosevelt U., 1972; Ed.D., No. Ill. U., 1978. Instr. English and Philosophy De LaSalle High Sch., Chgo., 1963-64; instr. English, Bennett (Iowa) High Sch., 1964-65; instr. lang. arts Morton West High Sch., Berwyn, Ill., 1966—; dir. McClean & Assocs., DeKalb, Ill., 1981—; field supr. Roosevelt U.; test analyst Ill. correctional instns.; cons. Riverside (Ill.) Nat. Bank. Mem. Nat. Council Tchrs. English, Assn. for Supervision and Curriculum Devel., Nat. Guidance Counselors Assn. Democrat. Roman Catholic. Clubs: University, Knights of Malta. Contbr. poems to profl. jours.

MCCLEARY, PAUL FREDERICK, relief agency executive; b. Bradley, Ill., May 2, 1930; s. Hal C. and Pearl (Aeicher) McC.; A.B., Olivet Nazarene Coll., Kankakee, Ill., 1952; M.Div., Garrett-Evang. Sem., Evanston, Ill., 1956; M.A., Northwestern U., 1972; D.D., MacMurray Coll., Jacksonville, Ill., 1970; m.

Rachel Timm, Jan. 26, 1951; children—Leslie Ann, Rachel Mary, John Wesley, Timothy Paul. Ordained to ministry United Methodist Ch., 1956; missionary in Bolivia, 1957-68; exec. sec. structure study commn. United Meth. Ch., 1969-72, asst. gen. sec. to Latin Am., 1972-75; exec. dir. Ch. World Service, N.Y.C., 1975-84; assoc. gen. sec. for research Gen. Council on Ministries, United Meth. Ch., 1984—; mem. exec. com., bd. dir. Overseas Devel. Council; mem. com. on interch. aid World Council Chs.; mem. com. on African Devel. Strategies; mem. Com. on Dialogue and Devel.; mem. Bretton Woods Com. Mem. Am. Soc. Missiology, Hastings Center, AAAS, Acad. Polit. Sci., N.Y. Acad. Scis., Latin Am. Studies Assn., Alpha Kappa Lambda. Democrat. Club: Masons. Author: Global Justice and World Hunger, 1978; co-author: Quality of Life in a Global Society, 1978; contbr. articles to mags. Home: 2001 Tiara Ct Dayton OH 45459 Office: 601 W Riverview Ave Dayton OH 45406

MCCLELLAN, WALTER FRITZ, land management engineer; b. Salem, Ind., June 21, 1936; s. Lawrence Oral McClellan and Samantha Bernice (Wolfe) McKnight; m. Linda Sue Hattabaugh, Apr. 7, 1962; children—Jeffery, Jill. Student Chgo. Tech. Coll., 1960-63, Cooperative Agrl. Sch., 1975-77. With cabinet assembly dept. Willetts Cabinet Co., New Albany, Ind., 1961-62; draftsman Ferraloy, Inc., Salem, Ind., 1962-64; machine operator Bata Shoe Co., Salem, 1964; draftsman, engr. Olin Corp., Charlestown, Ind., 1964-72; engr. land mgmt. Imperial Chem. Industries Inc., Charlestown, 1972—. Served to E-3 USAF, 1955-59, to master sgt. USAFR, 1983. Republican. Baptist. Avocations: breeding, raising and showing quarter horses. Office: Ind Army Ammunition Plant Highway 62 Charlestown IN 47111

MCCLELLAND, ROBERT CRAIG, lawyer; b. Lakewood, Ohio, Dec. 27, 1952; s. Joseph Bitner and Sara Louise (Puleio) McC.; m. Barbara Ann Peterson, July 24, 1976; children—Sara Elizabeth, Andrew Stephen. B.A. in Speech Communications, Denison U., 1975; J.D., Cleve. State U., 1980. Bar: Ohio 1980, U.S. Dist. Ct. (no. dist.) Ohio 1980, U.S. Ct. Appeals (6th cir.) 1983. Tchr. Berea City Schs., Ohio, 1975-77, Strongsville City Schs., Ohio, 1977-79; assoc. Petro & Troia, Cleve., 1980-84; ptnr. Petro, Rademaker, Matty & McClelland, 1984—; asst. law dir. City of Westlake, Ohio, 1982—. Mem. Ohio State Bar Assn., Cuyahoga county Bar Assn., Ohio Acad. Trial Lawyers. Republican. Office: Petro Rademaker Matty & McClelland 33 Pub Sq Suite 510 Cleveland OH 44113

MCCLENAHAN, GREGORY ALAN, lawyer; b. Belmond, Iowa, July 14, 1951; s. Guy Edwin and Betty Jane (Frye) M.; m. Melissa Jane Warner, Apr. 15, 1984. B.S. in Psychology, U. Iowa, 1974, M.B.A., J.D., 1979. Bar: Iowa 1979, Minn. 1982, U.S. Dist. Ct. (no. dist.) Iowa 1979, U.S. Ct. Appeals (8th cir.) 1979, U.S. Dist. Ct. Minn. 1983. Staff atty., corp. counsel Iowa Elec. Light & Power Co., Cedar Rapids, Iowa, 1979-83; sole practice, Mpls., 1983—. Contbr. articles to profl. jours. Mem. Iowa Bar Assn., Minn. State Bar Assn., Hennepin County Bar Assn. (lawyer referral com., environ. law com.), ABA (sect. on litigation and natural resources), Assn. Trial Lawyers Am., Minn. Mcpl. Utilities Assn. Home: 7020 James Ave S Richfield MN 55423 Office: 808 1st Bank Pl W Minneapolis MN 55402

MCCLENDON, JOHN HADDAWAY, plant physiologist, educator; b. Mpls., Jan. 17, 1921; s. Jesse Francis and Margaret (Stewart) McC.; m. Betty Virginia Morgan, June 27, 1947; children—Susan, Lise Ann, Natalie. B.A., U. Minn., 1942; Ph.D., U. Pa., 1951. Research assoc. Stanford U., Pacific Grove, Calif., 1951-52, U. Minn., Mpls., 1952-53; asst. prof. physiology U. Del., Newark, 1953-64; assoc. prof. plant physiology U. Nebr., Lincoln, 1965—. Contbr. articles to sci. jours. Mem. Lincoln Planning Citizens' Com., 1970—; pres. local chpt. Zero Population Growth, Lincoln, 1970—, Nebr. Environ. Coalition, 1971-73. NSF grantee, 1959-64, 65-68. Mem. AAAS, Am. Inst. Biol. Scis., Am. Soc. Plant Physiologists, Bot. Soc. Am., Sigma Xi. Democrat. Avocations: bird watching, photography. Home: 1970 B St Lincoln NE 68502 Office: U Nebr Sch Biol Scis Lincoln NE 68588

MCCLOSKEY, FRANK, congressman; government official; b. Phila., June 12, 1939; s. Frank and Helen (Warner) McC.; m. Roberta Ann Barker, Dec. 23, 1962; children—Helen-Marie, Mark. A.B. in Govt., Ind. U., 1968, J.D., 1971. News reporter City of Chgo. News Bur., 1960-61, Ind., 1963-69; mayor City of Bloomington (Ind.), 1971-82; mem. 98th-99th U.S. Congresses from 8th Dist. Ind. Served with USAF, 1957-61. Mem. Ind. Assn. Cities and Towns (pres. 1981-82). Democrat. Roman Catholic. Office: 116 Cannon House Office Bldg Washington DC 20515*

MCCLOSKEY, JACK, professional basketball team executive; m. Anita McCloskey. Basketball coach U. Pa., 1956-66, Wake Forest Coll., 1966-72; head coach Portland (Oreg.) Trail Blazers, 1972-80; gen. mgr. Detroit Pistons, 1980—. Address: Detroit Pistons Pontiac Silverdome 1200 Featherstone St Pontiac MI 48057*

MCCLOSKEY, KEITH RICHARD, physician; b. Lock Haven, Pa., Apr. 10, 1939; s. Richard K. and Gwendolyn I. (Stringfellow) McC.; B.S. with highest distinction in Chemistry, U. Ill., 1960; M.D., Johns Hopkins U., 1964; m. Apr. 20, 1963; children—Patricia, Gordon. Research asso. life scis. dept. Martin-Marietta Corp., Balt., 1962; intern pediatrics Johns Hopkins Hosp., Balt., 1964-65, asst. resident pediatrics, 1968-69; chief resident pediatrics Sinai Hosp., Balt., 1968, Balt. City Hosps., 1969; fellow child psychiatry Johns Hopkins Hosp. and U., 1969-70; practice medicine specializing in pediatrics, Arlington Heights, Ill., 1970-73; practice medicine specializing in behavior and learning disorders in children, adolescents and adults, Arlington Heights, 1973—; psychiatry resident U. Chgo., 1976-78; vis. physician pediatric out-patient services Balt. City Hosps., 1969-70; mem. courtesy staff Northwest Community Hosp., Arlington Heights, 1970-73; attending physician Children's Meml. Hosp., Northwestern U., Chgo., 1970-73; mem. med. adv. bd. Samuel A. Kirk Devel. Tng. Center, Palatine, Ill., 1971-74; vis. lectr. dept. spl. edn. No. Ill. U., 1976, So. Ill. U., Carbondale, 1978; research asso. dept. psychiatry U. Chgo., 1973—; cons. and mem. faculty minimal brain dysfunction Abbott Labs., 1975—; mem. faculty Speakers Bur., CIBA, 1976—, Nat. Coll. Juvenile Justice Inst., 1976; mem. cons. med. staff dept. pediatrics Northwest Community Hosp., 1973—. Mem. adv. council pre-sch. program for handicapped children Sch. Dist. 57, Mt. Prospect, Ill., 1972-74; mem. bd. govs. Northwest Suburban Council of Understanding Learning Disabilities, 1972-74. Served to capt. M.C., U.S. Army, 1965-67. Diplomate Am. Bd. Pediatrics. Fellow Am. Acad. Pediatrics, Am. Acad. Cerebral Palsy; mem. N.Y. Acad. Scis., Assn. Children with Learning Disabilities, AAAS, Johns Hopkins Med. Soc., Northwest Suburban Council on Understanding Learning Disabilities (chmn. adv. bd.), Sigma Xi, Phi Beta Kappa, Phi Alpha Mu (pres. 1959-60), Phi Eta Sigma, Phi Kappa Phi, Omega Beta Pi (pres. 1959-60). Contbr. articles to med. and psychiat. jours. Office: 1011 S Evergreen Ave Arlington Heights IL 60005

MCCLOW, THOMAS ALAN, lawyer; b. Detroit, Apr. 25, 1944; s. Kenneth Ray and Rita Beatrice (Periard) McC.; B.S., Mich. State U., 1966; J.D., Loyola U., 1969; m. Diana L. McClow, Oct. 16, 1982; children—Amy Christine, Adam Andrew. Bar: Ill. 1969, U.S. Supreme Ct. 1973. Assoc. Douglas F. Comstock, Geneva, Ill., 1970-73, John L. Nickels, Elburn, Ill., 1973-78; ptnr. Nickels & McClow, Elburn, 1978-82; ptnr. McClow & Britz, Elburn, 1982-84; prin. Law Offices of Thomas A. McClow, Geneva, Ill., 1985—; pub. conservator, guardian, adminstr. Kane County, 1975-78. Bd. dirs. Kane County Council Econ. Opportunity, 1st vice chmn., 1971-73; bd. dirs. Tri City Youth Project, 1972-73; faculty dean Parent Edn. Center, 1974-76. Mem. ABA, Ill. Bar Assn., Chgo. Bar Assn., Kane County Bar Assn. (chmn. membership and admissions com. 1979-84), Am. Judicature Soc., Fox Valley Estate Planning Council, Mensa. Home: 919 Arbor Ave Wheaton IL 60187 Office: PO Box 721 Geneva IL 60134

MCCLURE, ARTHUR FREDERICK, II, history educator, archivist; b. Leavenworth, Kans., Jan. 24, 1936; s. Arthur Frederick and Dorothy Louise (Davis) McC.; m. Judith Hallaux, Jan. 20, 1959; children—Allison, Arthur Kyle, Amy Louise, Steven Anderson. B.A., U. Kans., 1958; Ph.D., 1966; M.A., U. Colo., 1960. Asst. prof. history Central Mo. State U., Warrensburg, 1965-69, assoc. prof., 1969-72, prof., 1972—, chmn. dept. history, 1971-81, chmn. dept. history and anthropology, 1981—, univ. archivist, 1985—. Author: The Truman Administration and the Problems of Postwar Labor, 1945-48, 1969; The Versatiles: A Study of Supporting Players in the American Motion Picture, 1930-55, 1969; The Films of James Stewart, 1970; The Movies: An American Idiom, Readings in the Social History of the American Motion Picture, 1971; Heroes, Heavies, and Sagebrush: A Pictorial History of the "B" Western Player, 1973; Hollywood at War: The American Motion Picture and World War II, 1939-1945, 1973; The Fulbright Premise: Senator J. William Fulbright and Presidential Power in Foreign Policy, 1973; Star Quality: Screen Actors from the Golden Age of Film, 1974; Character People: Supporting Players in the American Motion Picture, 1976; Remembering Their Glory: Sports Heroes of the 1940s, 1977; Character People: Supporting Players in the American Motion Picture, 1979; International Film Necrology, 1981; William Inge: A Bibliography, 1982; Research Guide to Film History, 1983; More Character People: Supporting Players in the American Motion Picture, 1984, Education for Work: The Historical Evolution of Vocational and Distributive Education in America, 1985. Contbr. articles to profl. jours. Mem. film adv. com. Mo. Council on Arts, 1972-73; hon. commr. Mo. Am. Revolution Bicentennial Commn., 1975; mem. Mo. Health Coordinating Council, 1976-79; mem. Mo. Health Facilities Rev. Com., 1981-82; mem. Mo. Commn. on Status of Women, 1982—; mem. nat. adv. com. William Inge Collection, Independence Community Coll., Kans., 1982—; mem. Mo. Com. for Humanities, 1984. bd. dirs. Warrensburg Youth Services, Inc., 1982—; mem. community adv. bd. Sta. KMOS-TV, 1980—. Served with U.S. Army, 1958. Recipient Disting. Faculty award Sch. Arts and Scis., Central Mo. State U., 1979; grantee Harry S. Truman Library Inst., 1964, 71, Kansas City Regional Council for Higher Edn., 1969-70; hon. fellow Harry S. Truman Library Inst. Nat. and Internat. Affairs, 1970; NEH grantee Northwestern U., 1979; Herbert Hoover scholar, 1980, Moody grantee, 1980-81. Mem. Soc. Am. Archivists (audio-visual records com. 1971-73), Popular Culture Assn., Nat. Film Soc., Am. Film Inst., Soc. Cinema Studies, State Hist. Soc. Mo., Orgn. Am. Historians, Am. Hist. Assn., Phi Kappa Phi. Republican. Episcopalian. Avocation: history of motion pictures. Home: 304 Jones Ave Warrensburg MO 64093 Office: Dept History and Anthropology Central Mo State U Warrensburg MO 64093

MCCLURE, CHARLES RICHARD, advertising agency executive; b. Dayton, Ohio, June 3, 1947; s. Richard Allison and Mary Lois McC.; B.A., Ohio State U., 1969; m. Patricia Ann Stridsberg, Apr. 4, 1969; children—Lisa Marie, Richard Ryan. News reporter Sta. WBNS-TV-Radio, Columbus, Ohio, 1967-70; asst. dir. public relations Ohio State U., Columbus, 1970-73; communications dir. Columbus Devel. Dept., 1973-75; account exec. Paul Werth Assos., 1975-78; account exec., public relations mgr. Howard Swink Advt., 1978-82; v.p. Shelly Berman Communicators, 1982—; mem. mktg. faculty Ohio State U., 1979—. Served to 1st lt. Army N.G., 1969-73. Mem. Am. Mktg. Assn., Public Relations Soc. Am., Columbus Advt. Fedn., Ohio Press Club. Episcopalian. Clubs: Athletic, Ohio State U. Faculty. Office: Shelly Berman Communicators 1070 Morse Rd Columbus OH 43229

MCCLURE, DONALD JOHN, lawyer; b. Pitts., Mar. 31, 1940; s. Edward L. and Anna McC.; m. Judith Linda Richards, Sept. 2, 1961; children—Ian J., Sean M. Student El Dorado Jr. Coll., Kans., 1958-60; B.A., U. Denver, 1964, J.D., 1966. Bar: Colo. 1967, Ill. 1973, Tex. 1978, Kans. 1985. Ptnr. Robert J. Flynn Assocs., Englewood, Colo., 1967-68; with law dept. PepsiCo., Inc., 1968—, v.p., div. counsel Wilson Sporting Goods div., River Grove, Ill., 1972-77, v.p., div. counsel Frito-Lay, Inc. div., Dallas, 1977-84, Pizza Hut, Inc. div., 1984—; adv. bd. Internat. and Comparative Law Ctr. of Southwestern Legal Found. Mem. Dallas Bar Assn. (chmn. council antitrust and trade regulation sect.), ABA, Tex. Bar Assn., Colo. Bar Assn., Ill. Bar Assn., Denver Bar Assn., Chgo. Bar Assn., Kans. Bar Assn., Wichita Bar Assn. Home: 14330 Donegal Circle Wichita KS 67230 Office: PO Box 428 Wichita KS 67201

MCCLURE, JAMES ALLAN, public relations executive; b. Oak Park, Ill., Aug. 22, 1943; s. M. Allan and Vilma Laura (Gasperik) McC.; m. Kathleen Jameson, June 1, 1966; children—Steven Allan, Wendy Marie. B.S. in Journalism, Northwestern U., 1964. Reporter, Pioneer Newspapers, 1961-64; pub. relations asst. Ill. Bell, Chgo., 1968-72; sr. pub. relations specialist Western Electric Co., 1973-76; mgr. pub. relations Ill. Bell, Chgo., 1976-79, dist. mgr. corp. communications, 1979—. Bd. dirs. Oak Park Devel. Corp. (Ill.), 1982—. Served to capt. USNR, 1964—. Mem. Pub. Relations Soc. Am. (accredited; bd. dirs. Chgo. chpt.), Chgo. Press Vets. Assn. Home: 522 S Elmwood St Oak Park IL 60304 Office: Ill Bell 225 W Randolph St Chicago IL 60606

MC CLURE, MICHAEL DESTEWART, professional baseball team marketing executive; b. Chgo., Jan. 23, 1942; s. Charles F. and Janette L. (Lawler) McC.; B.A., DePauw U., 1964; m. Brenda G. Jones, Oct. 24, 1964; children—Michael C., Matthew D. Reporter, City News Bur., Chgo., 1964-65, Chgo. Tribune, 1965-66; public relations cons. Peoples Gas Co., Chgo., 1966-69; sports dir. Sta. WLFI-TV, Lafayette, Ind., 1969-70; service bur. dir. Big Ten Conf., 1970-73; dir. public relations and mktg. Chgo. Bulls, 1973-78; v.p. public relations and mktg. Houston Oilers, 1978-81; v.p. mktg. Chgo. White Sox, 1981—; v.p. Houston Oilers Publs., Inc., Houston Oilers Dancers, Inc.; dir. NFL Properties; founder Luv Ya Blue!, lic. program; chmn. Am. League Licensing Com. Mem. Chgo. Baseball Cancer Charities Com. Recipient Best in Nation awards Cosida, 1972, 73; Matrix award Houston chpt. Women in Communication, 1981; Maj. League Baseball Mktg. Excellence award, 1982; Maj. League Baseball's Top Mktg. Excellence award, 1983; named One of 10 Outstanding Young Citizens, Chgo. Jaycees, 1974. Mem. Houston Advt. Fedn., Houston Sportswriters and Sportscasters Assn., DePauw U. Alumni Assn., Am. Mktg. Assn., Am. Legion, Purdue Coaches Club, Sigma Delta Chi, Sigma Chi. Presbyterian. Editor Big Ten Records Book, 1970-73; editor Houston Oilers Pro mag., 1979. Home: 617 W Elm St Wheaton IL 60187

MCCLURE, NORMA LEE, village official; b. Scottsbluff, Nebr., Feb. 13, 1929; d. Byron E. and G. Irene Logan; m. Glen Arnold Stoeger, Sept. 27, 1947 (dec. Apr. 30, 1960); children—Glenda, Charles, Dale L.; m. Lawrence F. McClure, Mar. 4, 1961. Grad. Lyman High Sch.; grad. U. Lincoln Clerk's Sch., 1979. Dep. clk. Village of Lyman, Nebr., 1973-74, village clk., 1974-80, village clk., treas., 1980—, village clk., treas., grant adminstr., 1983—. Contbr. articles to profl. jours. Recipient Nebr. Village Clk. of Yr. award, 1985. Mem. Internat. Inst. Mcpl. Clks. (cert.), Nebr. Clks. Assn. (mem. auditing com. 1983-84), N.W. Clks. Assn. (sec., treas. 1983-85). Methodist. Lodge: Belle Rebekah (dist. dep. pres. 1960). Avocations: sewing; scrap books. Home: Box 192 Lyman NE 69352-0192 Office: Village Lyman 414 Jeffers Ave Lyman NE 69352-0301

MCCLURE, PHILIP EUGENE, aviation company executive; b. Marion, Ind., June 22, 1939; s. Donald Robert and Dorothy (Guhl) McC.; m. Jean Joyce Theiss, June 4, 1960; children—Roger, Donna J., Martin P. Maintenance technician Remmert Werner Corp., St. Louis, 1964-66; maintenance technician Assocs. Corp., South Bend, Ind., 1966-67; pres., owner Ni-Cad, Inc., South Bend, 1970—; cons. Facet Aerospace, Jackson, Tenn., 1981—. Designer engine filter systems for helicopters. Lutheran. Avocations: flying; tennis; golf. Home: 21885 Auten Rd South Bend IN 46628 Office: Ni-Cad Inc 4715 Progress Dr South Bend IN 46628

MCCLURG, CHARLES ROBERT, musician, drum shop owner; b. Galesburg, Ill., Aug. 27, 1948; s. Harry D. and Eileen L. (Dickerson) McC.; m. Linda K. Dana; 1 child, Robert Dale; m. 2d. Karen Steele, Nov. 27, 1974; children—Jason Daniel, Kristin Lynn. A. in Archtl. Drafting, Inst. Drafting and Tech., Morrison, Ill., 1968. Performed as percussionist with symphonies, recording jazz groups and dance bands in Midwest, 1970—; owner, operator Chuck's Drum Shop, Galesburg, Ill., 1975—; originator Libra Drumsticks, 1984—. Mem. AFL-CIO, past pres., trustee Musicians local). Republican. Methodist. Office: Chuck's Drum Shop Weinberg Arcade Lower Level 17 Galesburg IL 61401

MCCLURG, JAMES EDWARD, research laboratory executive; b. Bassett, Nebr., Mar. 23, 1945; s. Warren James and Delia Emma (Allyn) McC. B.S., N.E. Wesleyan U., 1967; Ph.D., U. Nebr., 1973. Instr., U. Nebr. Coll. Medicine, Omaha, 1973-76, research instr., 1973-76, clin. asst. prof. Med. Ctr., 1984—, mem. dean's adv. council Sch. Pharmacy, 1984—; v.p., tech. dir. Harris Labs., Inc., Lincoln, Nebr., 1976-82, exec. v.p., 1982-84, pres., 1984—; dir. Streck Labs., Inc., Omaha. Mem. editorial bd. Clin. Research Practices and Drug Regulatory Affairs, 1984. Contbr. articles to profl. jours. Mem. Commn. on Human Rights, Lincoln, 1982-85; com. mem. Nebr. Citizens for Study Higher Edn., Lincoln, 1984. Recipient ann. research award Central Assn. Obstetricians and Gynecologists, 1982. Mem. Am. Assn. Lab. Accreditation (bd. dirs.). Republican. Clubs: Century (pres. Nebr. Wesleyan U. 1983-84), Nebraska (Lincoln). Lodge: Rotary. Avocation: boating. Office: Harris Laboratories Inc Box 80837 624 Peach St Lincoln NE 68501

MCCLUSKEY, WALTER HAROLD, steel mills executive, metallurgical engineer; b. Herrin, Ill., Aug. 18, 1939; s. Walter Ralph and Evelyn Maye (Gamble) McC.; m. Eulajean Evelyn York, Nov. 23, 1961; children—Christopher Wayne, Michael Andrew, Kelly Jean. B.S. in Metall. Engrng. and Nuclear Ops., U. Mo.-Rolla, 1962. Metall engr. Wheeling Steel/Republic Steel, Steubenville and Canton, Ohio, 1962-68; gen. foreman ops. Republic Steel Corp., Canton, 1968-72, melt shops/caster supt./asst., 1973-81, gen. supt. tech. devel., 1981, dist. mgr. C.A.D., Canton and Massillon, Ohio, 1983-84; gen. mgr. ops. LTV Steel Co., Canton, 1984—. Contbr. articles to profl. jours. Served to 1st lt. C.E., U.S. Army, 1962-64. Mem. Am. Soc. for Metals, AIME, Am. Iron and Steel Engrs. (trustee 1983—), Am. Iron and Steel Inst. corp. rep. 1981-84. Electric Furnace Metal Makers Guild, Greater Canton C. of C. (trustee 1983). Republican. Avocations: fishing; hunting; ball sports; radio control planes. Office: LTV Steel Co Inc 8th St NE Canton OH 44701

MC COIN, JOHN MACK, social worker; b. Sparta, N.C., Jan. 21, 1931; s. Robert Avery and Ollie (Osborne) McC.; B.S., Appalachian State Tchrs. Coll., Boone, N.C., 1957; M.S. in Social Work, Richmond (Va.) Profl. Inst., 1962; Ph.D., U. Minn., 1977. Social service worker Broughton State Hosp., Morganton, N.C., 1958-59, John Umstead State Hosp., Butner, N.C., 1960-61; clin. social worker Dorothea Dix State Hosp., Raleigh, N.C., 1962-63; child welfare case worker Wake County Welfare Dept., Raleigh, 1963-64; psychiat. social worker Toledo Mental Hygiene Clinic, 1964-66; sr. psychiat. social worker N.Y. Hosp.-Cornell U. Med. Center, 1966-68; social worker VA Hosp., Montrose, N.Y., 1968-73, also vol. mental health worker Westchester County Mental Health Assn. and Mental Health Bd., White Plains, N.Y.; seminar instr. Grad. Sch. Social Work, U. Minn., Mpls., 1973-74; social worker F.D.R. VA Health Care Facility, Montrose, 1975-77; asst. prof. social work U. Wis., Oshkosh, 1977-79, chmn. dept. community liaison com., 1978-79; asso. prof. social work Grand Valley State Colls., Allendale, Mich., 1979-81; social worker VA Med. Ctr. Battle Creek, Mich., 1981-83; supr. social worker VA Med. Ctr., Leavenworth, Kans., 1983—; cons. 44th Gen. Hosp., USAR, Menasha, Wis., 1978-79, 5540th Support Command, USAR, Grand Rapids, Mich., 1979-83; cons. in field. Served with USMC, 1948-52; USMCR, 1957-72; lt. col. USAR, 1972—. Recipient Outstanding Performance award VA, 1971, Superior Performance award, 1982, Outstanding Performance award, 1983; grantee NIMH, 1974; cert. social worker, N.Y. Mem. Nat. Assn. Social Workers (social action com. W. Mich. br. 1980-81), Acad. Cert. Social Workers, Council Social Work Edn., Res. Officers Assn. U.S., Am. Soc. Pub. Adminstrn., Alpha Delta Mu. Democrat. Baptist. Author: Adult Foster Homes, 1983. Home: 310B Kiowa St Leavenworth KS 66048

MCCOLLOUGH, FRED, JR., chemistry educator; b. Crawfordsville, Ind., July 19, 1928; s. Fred and Dorothea Lucile (Weidner) McC.; m. Elizabeth Ruth Hall, Aug. 24, 1952; children—Bruce Stanley, Lynn Elizabeth McCollough Coehoorn. A.B., Wabash Coll., Crawfordsville, Ind., 1950; M.S., U. Ill., 1952, Ph.D., 1955. Research chemist Stauffer Chem. Co., Chicago Heights, Ill., 1955-64; assoc. prof. chemistry MacMurray Coll., Jacksonville, Ill., 1964-71, prof., 1971—, chmn. dept. chemistry, 1969—. Contbr. articles to profl. jours. Patentee in field. Bd. dirs. Jacksonville Symphony Soc., 1980-85, treas., 1983-85. Mem. Midwest Assn. Chemistry, Tchrs. in Liberal Arts Coll., Phi Beta Kappa, Sigma Xi. Republican. Avocations: music, computers. Home: 407 Sandusky St Jacksonville IL 62650 Office: Dept Chemistry MacMurray Coll Jacksonville IL 62650

MCCOLLOUGH, PATRICK HANNA, lawyer, state senator; b. Detroit, May 19, 1942; s. Clarence Lindsay and Lucille (Hanna) McC.; m. Sylvia Jean Chappell, Jan. 4, 1975; 1 child, Alexander Patrick. A.A., Henry Ford Community Coll., 1962; B.A., Mich. State U., 1964; M.A., U. Mich., 1967; J.D., Detroit Coll. Law, 1970. Bar: Mich. 1970, U.S. Dist. Ct. Mich. 1970. Mem. Mich. Senate, Lansing, 1971-78, 83—; dir. Region V, U.S. Def. Civil Preparedness Agy. 1979-80; dir. Region V, Fed. Emergency Mgmt. Agy. for Plans and Preparedness; sole practice, Dearborn, Mich. Named Conservation Legislator of Yr., Mich. United Conservation Club, 1973. Democrat. Presbyterian. Home: 7511 Kentucky St Dearborn MI 48126 Office: State Capitol PO Box 30036 Lansing MI 48909

MCCOMAS, JAMES DOUGLAS, university president; b. Prichard, W.Va., Dec. 23, 1928; s. Herbert and Nell (Billips) McC.; m. Frances Adele Stoltz, May 11, 1961; children—Cathleen, Patrick. B.S., W.Va. U., 1951, M.S., 1960; Ph.D., Ohio State U., 1962. High sch. tchr., 1951-54, 56-60; from asst. prof. to prof., head dept. agrl. and extension edn., prof. edml. adminstrn., head dept. elem. and secondary edn. N.Mex. State U., 1961-67; dean coll. edn. Kans. State U., 1967-69; dean U. Tenn., 1969-76, also prof. continuing and higher edn.; pres. Miss. State U., 1976-85, U. Toledo, 1985—; field reader U.S. Office Edn.; chmn. Southeastern Manpower Adv. Com.; mem. exec. com. Southeastern Conf.; mem. appeals bd. Nat. Accreditation Council for Agys. Serving the Blind; mem. exec. com. Land Grant Deans Edn.; chmn. com. equal opportunity Nat. Assn. Land Grant Colls. and State Univs.; assoc. mem. Nat. Manpower Adv. com. Gov.'s Manpower Adv. Com.; chmn. Council of Pres. State Univs. Miss.; pres. So. Land Grant Colls. and Univs.; chmn. Tenn. Council Deans Edn.; mem. Miss. Jr. Coll. Commn. Pres., Belmont West Community Assn., Miss. Econ. Council, East Miss. Council; mem. Am. Council Ednl. Community Leadership Devel. and Acad. Adminstrn.; civilian aide Sec. of Army. Served with USMC, AUS, 1954-56. Mem. Am. Sociol. Assn., Am. Higher Edn. Assn., Am. Acad. Polit. and Social Sci., Kappa Delta Pi, Gamma Sigma Delta, Alpha Zeta, Omicron Delta Kappa, Phi Kappa Phi, Beta Gamma Sigma. Home: 3425 W Bancroft St Toledo OH 43606

MCCOMB, THOMAS VICTOR, insurance company executive; b. Ft. Wayne, Ind., Oct. 19, 1936; s. John H. and Margaret E. (Ridley) McC.; m. Norma Jean Born, Feb. 9, 1957; children—Bethany Ann, Kenneth Alan, Susan Marie Stephanie Jo. B.S., Ind. U., 1959; J.D., Ind. U., 1974. Pres. Profl. Design Ins. Mgmt. Corp., Indpls., 1979—; mgmt. cons. Mem. Ind. Ho. of Reps., 1966-70, Ind. State Senate, 1970-74. Recipient Disting. Service award Ft. Wayne Jaycees, 1963. Mem. Ind. Ins. Agts. Assn., Am. Soc. Assn. Execs. (cert. assn. exec.). Republican. Methodist. Clubs: Columbia, Ind. Soc. of Chicago. Lodges: Masons, Shriners. Author: Loss Prevention and Control for Design Professionals, 1981. Home: 7406 N Layman Ave Indianapolis IN 46250 Office: 222 N New Jersey Suite 200 Indianapolis IN 46204

MC COMBS, SHERWIN, oil and gas co. exec.; b. Sterling, Ill., Jan. 27, 1934; s. C. Vernon and Helen (Jennings) McC.; grad. Palmer Chiropractic Coll., 1956-60; m. Rita J. Page, Feb. 8, 1957; children—Kim, Kelly, Jeff, Terry. Owner McCombs Chiropractic Clinic, Sterling, Ill., 1960—, McCombs Petroleum Prodns., Sterling, 1966—; v.p., dir. Coyote Oil & Gas Corp., Casper Wyo., 1968-75, exec. v.p., dir., 1975—; v.p., dir. Coyote Assos., Inc., Ankeny, Iowa, 1970-72; pres., dir. Coyote Oil & Gas Programs, Inc., Ankeny, 1970-72; with McCombs-Conrad & Barrett Oil & Gas Properties, Sterling, Ill., 1972-82. Served with USNR, 1952-54. Mem. Internat., Prairie, Whiteside County chiropractic assns., Internat. Chiropractic Honor Soc. Home: 1808 Thome Dr Sterling IL 61081 Office: 507 W 3d St Sterling IL 61081

MCCONNAUGHAY, SHIRLEY MARIE, nursing education coordinator; b. Centralia, Ill., Sept. 27, 1937; d. Clyde Elmer and Bessie Gladys (Presgrove) McC. Diploma Rockford Meml. Sch. Nursing, Ill., 1958; A.A., Sauk Valley Coll., 1967; B.S. in Nursing, No. Ill. U., 1968; M.A. in Nursing Services Adminstrn., U. Iowa, 1970. Staff nurse hosps. in Rockford, Dixon, DeKalb and Highland Park, Ill., 1958-68; instr. ADN program Carl Sandburg Coll., Galesburg, Ill., 1970-73; asst. dir. nursing Rockford Meml. Hosp., 1973-75; Instr. ADN Program Lincoln Land Community Coll., Springfield, Ill., 1975-79; coordinator Capital Area Sch. Practical Nursing, Springfield, 1979—. Mem. Springfield Mcpl. Choir, 1975-81, 3d Presbyterian Ch. Choir, Springfield, 1978—; usher Sangamon State U. Usher Orgn., Springfield, 1984—. Mem. Ill. Nurses Assn. (bd. dirs. 9th dist. 1980-82, sec. 1982—), Am. Nurses Assn., Nat. League for Nursing, Ill. Vocat. Assn., Am. Vocat. Assn., Springfield Theatre Guild Springfield Mcpl. Opera, Phi Theta Kappa. Avocations: music; theatre; crafts. Home: 3500 N Dirksen Parkway Apt 27 Springfield IL 62702 Office: Capital Area Sch of Practical Nursing 2201 Toronto Rd Box 3427 Springfield IL 62708

MCCONNAUGHHAY, JOHN GERALD, special education educator; b. Larned, Kans., Mar. 23, 1926; s. Sidney Gerald and Faye Elizabeth (Nelson) McC.; m. June Maurine Gilbert, July 31, 1954; children—Jayne Marie, John Jerald, Janet Faye, Judith Ann, Jill Susanne. B.S., Fort Hays State U., 1951, M.S., 1972. Elem. prin. Luray (Kans.) pub. schs., 1951-52; tchr. 6th grade Larned (Kans.) Pub. Schs., 1952-53, tchr. jr. high, 1953-57, tchr. high sch., 1957-70, tchr. mentally retarded, 1970-77; tchr. dist. 495 Larned State Hosp., 1977-82; tchr. mentally retarded Dist. 495, Larned, 1982—; cons. Larned State Hosp., 1980-82; pres. Pawnee Savs. Credit Union, Larned, 1970, dir., 1982. Pres., Pawnee County Mental Health Assn., Larned, 1977. Mem. Council Exceptional Children, Kans. NEA (local pres. 1956). Democrat. Methodist.

Club: Lions (pres. 1976-77, zone chmn. 1977-78) (Larned). Lodge: Masons. Office: Larned High Sch 815 Corse Larned KS 67550

MCCONNELL, ALBERT LYNN, army officer; b. Springfield, Ohio, Oct. 20, 1946; s. Jack Pershing and Betty Ann (Venema) McC.; m. Tamara N. Robinson, Feb. 9, 1983; 1 stepson, L. Anthony Hudson. B.A., Central State U., Wilberforce, Ohio, 1969; M.A., Webster U., 1983. Commd. 2d lt. U.S. Army, 1969, advanced through grades to maj., 1980; served as infantry co. comdr., 1971, intelligence analyst Mil. Asst. Command, Vietnam, 1972-73, instr. Intelligence Sch., Ft. Huachuca, Ariz., 1973-77, advanced individual tng. co. comdr., 1977-78, electronic warfare officer/asst. plans officer, 3rd Armored Div., W.Ger., 1978-79, dep. G-2, 1980-81, Airland Battle 2000 Project Officer, Ft. Leavenworth, Kans., 1981-83, comdr. spl. security detachment, 1983-84; dep. G-2, 193d Inf. Brigade, Panama, 1984-85; bn. xo 29th MI Bn., 1985—; grad. U.S. Army Armor Sch. Officer Basic Course, U.S. Army Intelligence Basic and Advanced Courses, NATO Electronic Warfare Course, U.S. Army Command and Gen. Staff Coll. Decorated Bronze Star. Mem. Assn. U.S. Army, Air Force Assn., Mil. Intelligence Assn. Republican. Presbyterian. Home: PSC Box 32 APO Miami FL 34005 Office: Room 2 Bldg 70 Fort Davis Republic of Panama

MC CONNELL, JOHN HENDERSON, steel company executive; b. New Manchester, W.Va., May 10, 1923; s. Paul A. and Mary Louise (Mayhew) McC.; B.A., Mich. State U., 1949; m. Margaret Jane Rardin, Feb. 8, 1946; children—Margaret Louise, John Porter. With blooming mill Weirton Steel Co. (W.Va.), 1941-43, with sales dept., 1950-52; with sales dept. Shenango Steel Co., Farrell, Pa., 1953-55; founder, chmn., chief exec. officer Worthington Steel Co. (Ohio) (name changed to Worthington Industries, 1971), 1955—; dir. Anchor-Hocking Corp., Nat. City Corp. Bank. Bd. dirs. Pilot Dogs Inc., Columbus, Ohio; trustee Children's Hosp., Columbus, Ashland (Ohio) Coll. Served with USNR, 1943-46. Recipient Gov.'s award State of Ohio, 1980; Am. Acad. Achievement award, 1982; Horatio Alger award, 1983; named Central Ohio Mktg. Man of Year, 1975. Mem. Columbus C. of C. (dir., chmn. aviation com., vice chmn. 1977, chmn. 1978), Columbus Indsl. Assn. (dir.), Mich. State U. Bus. Alumni Assn. (dir.). Republican. Presbyn. (past trustee). Mason (Shriner, 32 deg.). Clubs: Columbus Athletic, Columbus; The Golf (New Albany, Ohio); Brookside Country (Worthington); Muirfield Village Golf (Dublin, Ohio); Bob O' Link Golf (Chgo.); Sea Pines (Hilton Head, S.C.); Waialae Country (Honolulu); Laurel Valley Golf (Ligonier, Pa.); Pine Valley Golf; Keenland (Lexington, Ky.). Office: Worthington Industries Inc 1205 Dearborn Dr Columbus OH 43085

MCCONNELL, JOHN THOMAS, newspaper publisher; b. Peoria, Ill., May 1, 1945; s. Golden A. and Margaret (Lyon) McC.; B.A., U. Ariz., 1967; m. Elizabeth Jean Slane, Aug. 14, 1971; 1 son, Justin. Mgr., Fast Printing Co., Peoria, 1970-71; mgmt. trainee Quad-Cities Times, Davenport, Iowa, 1972-73; asst. gen. mgr., then v.p., gen. mgr. Peoria Jour. Star, 1973-81, pub., 1981—. Bd. dirs. Peoria Downtown Devel. Council, Peoria Devel. Corp.; past trustee Methodist Hosp., Peoria, Econ. Devel. Council; mem. Gov.'s Commn. on Election Reform. Served with USAR, 1967-69. Named Young Man of Year, Peoria Jaycees, 1979. Mem. Peoria Advt. and Selling Club, Peoria C. of C. Congregationalist. Club: Peoria Country. Office: 1 News Plaza Peoria IL 61643

MCCONNELL, STEPHEN CLARK, educator; b. Washington, Mar. 15, 1946; s. Frank S. and Madge K. (Kennerley) McC.; m. Johanna R. Young, June 18, 1971; children—Westen Young, Eleni Young. B.A., Bucknell U., 1968; M.A., Ind. U., 1971; Psy.D., Baylor U., 1976. Diplomate Am. Bd. Profl. Psychology. Lic. psychologist, Ohio; in Nat. Register Health Service Providers in Psychology. Asst. dir. human relations dept. Tulsa pub. schs., 1972-73; staff psychologist Smoky Mountain Mental Health, Marble, N.C., 1976-79; prof. Sch. Profl. Psychology, Wright State U., Dayton, Ohio, 1979—; cons. in field. Recipient H. Boardman Hopper Acad. prize Bucknell U., 1968. Mem. Am. Psychol. Assn., Assn. for Advancement Psychology, Midwestern Psychol. Assn., Common Cause, Nat. Peace Acad., Psi Chi. Clubs: Triumph Sports Car, U.S. Golf Assn. Contbr. articles to profl. jours. Home: 4398 E Entrada Dr Beavercreek OH 45431 Office: Sch Profl Psychology Wright State U Dayton OH 45435

MCCORMACK, LAWRENCE RALPH, gastroenterologist; b. San Antonio, Dec. 31, 1946; s. Lawrence John and Dorothy Mae (Rice) McC.; m. April Lee Geis, Nov. 17, 1977; children—Lawrence John, Dona Lou, Constance Jeanne. B.A., Coll. of Wooster, 1969; M.D., Ohio State U., 1972. Intern and resident in medicine Mayo Clinic, Rochester, Minn., 1972-75; fellow in gastroenterology Scripps Clinic, La Jolla, Calif., 1975-77; research fellow Scripps Research Found., La Jolla, 1977-78; practice medicine specializing in gastroenterology, Sandusky, Ohio, 1978—; pres. med-staff Good Samaritan Hosp., Sandus Ky; clin. asst. prof. Med. Coll. Ohio, Toledo, 1982-83. Contbr. articles to med. publs. Mem. AMA, Ohio Med. Assn., Erie County Med. Soc. (pres. 1984—), Am. Soc. Gastrointestinal Endoscopy, Ohio Soc. Internal Medicine, Bockus Internat. Soc. Gastroenterology, Sandusky C. of C. Republican. Club: Plumbrook. Home: 217 Marshall Ave Sandusky OH 44870 Office: 1410 Milan Rd Sandusky OH 44870

MCCORMICK, EDWARD JAMES, JR., lawyer; b. Toledo, May 11, 1921; s. Edward James and Josephine (Beck) McC.; m. Mary Jane Blank, Jan. 27, 1951; children—Mary McCormick Krueger, Edward James III, Patrick William, Michael J. B.S., John Carroll U., 1942; J.D., Western Res. U., 1948. Bar: Ohio 1948, U.S. Supreme Ct. 1980. Ptnr., office mgr. McCormick & Pommeranz, Toledo; mem. teaching staff St. Vincent Hosp. Sch. Nursing, 1951-67. Trustee Toledo Small Bus. Assn., 1950-75, pres., 1954-55, 56-58, 67-68; trustee Goodwill Industries Toledo, 1961-74, chmn. meml. gifts com., mem. exec. com., 1965-70; trustee Lucas County unit Am. Cancer Soc., 1950-61, sec., 1953, v.p., 1954-56, pres., 1957-58; founder, incorporator, sec., trustee Cancer Cytology Research Fund Toledo, Inc., 1956-79; trustee Ohio Cerebral Palsy Assn., 1963-70; incorporator, sec., trustee N.W. Ohio Clin. Engring. Ctr., 1972-74; trustee Friendly Ctr., 1973-83, Ohio Blind Assn., 1970-79; founder-incorporator, trustee, sec. Western Lake Erie Hist. Soc., 1978-85; mem. Toledo Deanery Diocesan Council Catholic Men; asst. gen. counsel U.S. Power and Sail Squadrons. Named Outstanding Young Man of Yr., Toledo Jr. C. of C., 1951; Man of Nation, Woodmen of World, Omaha, 1952. Mem. ABA (corp., banking and bus. law sect.), Ohio Bar Assn. (chmn. Am. citizenship com. 1958-67, mem. pub. relations com. 1967-72), Toledo Bar Assn. (chmn. pub. relations com. 1979, mem. grievance com. 1975-85), Lucas County Bar Assn. (chmn. Am. citizenship com.), Assn. Trial Lawyers Am., Am. Judicature Soc., Am. Arbitration Assn., Conf. Pvt. Orgns. (sec.-treas.), Toledo C. of C. Clubs: Toledo Torch, Toledo, Blue Gavel. Lodges: Elks (grand esteemed leading knight 1964-65, mem. grand forum 1965-70), Lions (trustee, legal advisor Ohio Eye Research Found. 1956-70; pres. 1957-58, chmn. permanent membership com. 1961-85, hon. mem. 1984), KC. Office: Nat Bank Bldg Suite 824 Toledo OH 43604

MCCORMICK, JOHN FRANCIS, life insurance company executive; b. Detroit, Feb. 22, 1933; s. John Joseph and Mary Adelaide (Devine) McC.; m. Janet Rose Ungelbach, Sept. 8, 1956; children—Jacqueline Ann, Jayne Mary, John Gerald. B.S. in Indsl. Mgmt., U. Detroit, 1956. Chartered fin. analyst. Investment analyst Mfrs. Nat. Bank Detroit, 1956-63, asst. trust officer, 1964-66; sr. investment analyst Nationwide Ins. Co., Columbus, Ohio, 1963-64; investment mgr. Maccabees Mut. Life Ins. Co., Southfield, Mich., 1966-76, v.p., treas., 1976—; dir. Omni Petroleum Co., Allegan, Mich. Pres. Franklin Corners Homeowners Assn., West Bloomfield, Mich., 1984; mem. investment com. Met. Detroit council Boy Scouts Am., 1982—; fundraiser Mich. Colls. Found., Detroit, 1981-84, Mich. Opera Theatre, Detroit, 1984. Mem. Fin. Analysts Soc, Detroit (pres. 1973-74). Republican. Roman Catholic. Club: Economic (Detroit). Avocations: classical music; play guitar; harmonica; dulcimer; jogging. Home: 5176 Corners Dr West Bloomfield MI 48033 Office: Maccabees Mutual Life Ins Co 25800 Northwestern St Southfield MI 48075

MCCORMICK, MARK, state justice Iowa; b. Ft. Dodge, Iowa, Apr. 13, 1933; s. Elmo Eugene and Virgilla (Lawler) McC.; A.B., Villanova U., 1955; LL.B., Georgetown U., 1960; m. Marla Rae McKinney, June 11, 1966; children—Marcia, Michael, Paul. Admitted to Iowa bar, 1960; law clk. to judge U.S. Ct. Appeals, 1960-61; practice law, Ft. Dodge, 1961-68; asst. county atty. Webster County, 1963-67; judge 11th and 2d jud. dists., 1968-72; justice Iowa Supreme Ct., Des Moines, 1972—. Served with USN, 1955-58. Mem. ABA, Iowa Bar Assn., Am. Judicature Soc. Office: Capitol Bldg Des Moines IA 50319*

MCCORMICK, RICHARD EARL, engineering company executive; b. Mt. Vernon, Ohio, Mar. 11, 1946; s. Earl R. and Beulah (Snow) McC.; m. Linda L. Lehmann, June 6, 1970; children—Erin, Pearce. B.S. in Mech. Engring., U. Cin., 1969, M.B.A., 1975. Registered profl. engr., Colo. Process control engr. Monsanto Corp., Pensacola, Fla., 1969-72; industry mgr. Structural Dynamics Research Corp., Cin., 1972-76; mng. dir. SDRC Engring. Services, Ltd., Hitchin, Herts., Eng., 1976-81; pres. SDRC, Inc., Milford, Ohio, 1981-83; gen. mgr. robotics div. Nordson Corp., Amherst, Ohio, 1983-84; pres. MB Dynamics, Inc., Cleve., 1984—. Mem. Jaycees, Pensacola, 1971. Mem. Robotics Internat. (So. Mech. Engrs.), Pres.' Assn. of Am. Mgmt. Assn., Omicron Delta Kappa, Pi Tau Sigma, Delta Tau Delta. Republican. Episcopalian. Home: 329 Kenmore Bay Village OH 44140 Office: MB Dynamics Inc 25865 Richmond Rd Cleveland OH 44146

MC CORMICK, WILLIAM EDWARD, corporation executive, consultant; b. Potters Mills, Pa., Feb. 9, 1912; s. George H. and Nellie (Mingle) McC.; B.S., Pa. State U., 1933, M.S., 1934; m. Goldie Stover, June 6, 1935; children—John F. (dec.), Kirk W. Tchr., Centre Hall (Pa.) High Sch., 1934-37; chemist Willson Products, Inc., Reading, Pa., 1937-43; indsl. hygienist Ga. Dept. Pub. Health, Atlanta, 1946; mgr. indsl. hygiene and toxicology B.F. Goodrich Co., Akron, Ohio, 1946-70, mgr. environ. control, 1970-73; mng. dir. Am. Indsl. Hygiene Assn., Akron, 1973-83; exec. sec. Soc. Toxicology, 1976-83; pres. Am. Indsl. Hygiene Found., 1983-84; chmn. Envirotox Mgmt., Inc., 1983—. Mem. exec. com., rubber sect. Nat. Safety Council, 1955-73; mem. environ. health com. Chlorine Inst., 1968-73; mem. food, drug and cosmetic chems. com. Mfg. Chemists Assn., 1960-73, chmn., 1967-69, also mem. occupational health com., 1965-73; mem. adv. com. on heat stress U.S. Dept. Labor, 1973; mem. Nat. Adv. Com. on Occupational Safety and Health, Dept. Labor, 1983—. Served to capt. Adv. Com. USPHS, 1943-46. Mem. Chem. Soc., Soc. Toxicology, AAAS, Am. Indsl. Hygiene Assn. (pres. 1964, hon. mem.), Indsl. Hygiene Roundtable, Am. Acad. Indsl. Hygiene. Republican. Episcopalian. Clubs: Masons (32 deg.), Shriners. Contbr. articles to profl. jours. Home: 419 Dorchester Rd Akron OH 44320 Office: EMI 149 N Prospect St Ravenna OH 44266

MCCORMICK, WILLIAM THOMAS, JR., gas company executive; b. Washington, Sept. 12, 1944; s. William Thomas and Lucy Valentine (Offutt) McC.; B.S., Cornell U., 1966; Ph.D., M.I.T., 1969; m. Ann Loretta du Mais, June 13, 1969; children—Christopher, Patrick. Mem. staff Inst. for Def. Analysis, Arlington, Va., 1969-72; mem. staff Office of Sci. and Tech., Exec. office of the Pres., Washington, 1972-73; sr. staff mem. Energy Policy Office, The White House, 1973-74; chief sci. and energy tech. br., Office Mgmt. and Budget, Exec. Office of the Pres., 1974-75; dir. commercialization U.S. Energy Research and Devel. Adminstrn., 1975-76; v.p. policy and govt. relations Am. Gas Assn., 1976-78; v.p., asst. to chmn. Am. Natural Resources Co., Detroit, 1978-80; exec. v.p. Mich. Wis. Pipeline Co., Am. Natural Resources System, Detroit, 1980-81; pres. Am. Natural Resources, 1981-85, chmn., chief exec. officer, 1985—. Bd. dirs. United Fund, St. John Hosp., Detroit Symphony, Detroit Econ Growth Corp. Alfred P. Sloan scholar, 1962-66. Mem. AAAS, Ops. Research Soc. Am., Am. Gas Assn. Roman Catholic. Clubs: Cosmos (Washington); Detroit Athletic, Country of Detroit, Detroit. Prin. author, editor: Commercialization of Synthetic Fuels in the U.S., 1975. Home: 166 Ridge Rd Grosse Pointe Farms MI 48236 Office: 1 Woodward Ave Detroit MI 48226

MCCOSKEY, LUCY, computer scientist; b. Rochester, N.Y., May 8, 1940; d. Lester Joseph and Julia (Michel) Berlove; m. Lowell McCoskey, July 12, 1968. B.A., Goucher Coll., 1962. System analyst city, state and fed. govt., Washington and Indpls., 1962-70; user liaison, project mgr. Ind. U., Bloomington, 1970-80; data processing officer, project mgr. Am. Fletcher Nat. Bank, Indpls., 1980—. Mem. Assn. Systems Mgmt. (cert. systems profl.; pres. 1985-86, Systems Profl. of Yr. award 1984). Club: Economic (Indpls). Avocation: bicycling.

MCCOWEN, MAX CREAGER, research scientist; b. Sullivan, Ind., July 4, 1915; s. Roy E. and Ethel G. (Creager) McC. B.S., Ind. State U., 1937, M.S., 1938; postgrad. U. Buffalo, 1939, U. Chgo., 1940. Head sci. dept. Edison High Sch., Hammond, Ind., 1938-42; research assoc. Eli Lilly & Co., Indpls., 1946-47, asst. chief parasitology research dept., 1947-48, sr. parasitologist, 1958-65, head parsasitology research Lilly Research Centre Ltd., Windlesham, Eng., 1965-70, research scientist Lilly Research Labs., Greenfield, Ind., 1970—; lectr. Marion County Gen. Hosp., Indpls., 1959-70, Ind. U. Sch. Medicine, 1960-70. Elder, First Presbyn. Ch. and First Meridian Heights Presbyn. Ch.; commr. synod assembly United Presbyn. Ch. USA, 1976. Recipient Disting. Alumni award Ind. State U., 1977. Served to lt. USN, 1942-46, to comdr. Res. ret., 1975. Fellow Royal Soc. Tropical Medicine and Hygiene; mem. Internat. Coll. Tropical Medicine, Am. Soc. Tropical Medicine and Hygiene, AAAS, Am. Soc. Parasitologists, Brit. Soc. Parasitologists, Sociedad Mexicana de Parasitologia, Soc. Protozologists, Aquatic Plant Mgmt. Soc. (dir. 1978-81, chmn. local chpts. com. 1979-82, v.p. 1982-83, pres. 1984-85), English Speaking Union, Sigma Xi, Alpha Phi Omega, Am. Legion. Clubs: Lilly Putian (sec. 1977-78), Torch (pres. 1962-63, dir. 1975-77) (Indpls.); Contemporary (dir. 1975-76), Indpls. Literary (3d v.p. 1981-82). Lodges: Masons, Shriners. Home: 3916 Rue Renoir Indianapolis IN 46220 Office: Lilly Research Labs Greenfield IN 46140

MCCOWEN, THOMAS ALAN, university official; b. Kansas City, Mo., July 15, 1934; s. Roy Alan and Irene (Doidge) McC.; m. Janet Elaine Anderson, July 17, 1954 (div. Feb. 1972); children—Carole, Kimberly; m. Nancy Jane Hartz, Aug. 5, 1972; children—Andrew, Kathleen. B.S. in Indsl. Adminstrn., U. Ill., 1958, B.S. in Econs., 1959, M.S. in Econs., 1974. Asst. dir. AID project, U. Ill., Urbana, 1962-68, dir. overseas project, 1968-70, assoc. dir. overseas project and fgn. visitors, 1970-75, asst. dir. internat. agr., 1975—. Author: (with others) (manual) Guideline for Universities in Negotiating Contracts with the Agency for International Development Projects, 1984. Mem. Assn. U.S. Univ. Dirs. of Internat. Agr. Programs (bd. dirs., sec., treas., 1983—), Assn. Internat. Edn. Adminstrs. Democrat. Lutheran. Office: Office of Internat Agr Univ Ill 113 Mumford Hall 1301 W Gregory Dr Urbana IL 61801

MCCOWN, FRANK J., lawyer, educator; b. Ironton, Ohio, Feb. 6, 1940; s. Henry Anderson and Adrienne (Tucker) McC.; m. 2d, Tyna L. Dilley, Mar. 3, 1979; 1 son, Brigham A. B.S. in Bus. Adminstrn., Miami U., 1962; J.D., Ohio State U., 1964. Bar: Ohio 1965. Ptnr., Crowe & McCown, Ironton, 1965—; atty. City of Ironton, 1966-82; asst. atty. gen. State of Ohio, 1971-81; instr. law Shawnee State Coll., Ohio U.-Ironton, 1971—. Mem. Democratic Exec. Com., Lawrence County, Ohio, 1965—; former Dem. candidate for Ohio Ho. of Reps.; campaign chmn. United Way of Lawrence County, 1981-82; past pres. Ironton Jaycees. Recipient Disting. Service award Ohio State U., 1967; Lawrence County Assocs. award Lawrence County Bd. Realtors, 1981; named several times Outstanding Lawyer, Lawrence County Legal Secs. Mem. Ohio State Bar Assn., Lawrence County Bar Assn. (past pres.), Am. Arbitration Assn., Ohio Land Title Assn., Phi Alpha Delta (pres. 1978-80, chmn. bd. 1980-82). Methodist. Club: Mason. Home: 1235 Shawnee Trail Ironton OH 45638 Office: Crowe and McCown 311 Park Ave Ironton OH 45638

MCCOY, GAYLE ANDERSON, association executive, audiovisual program administrator; b. Lexington, Ky., Oct. 3, 1917; s. Harry Strange and Viola Elizabeth (Hunter) McC.; m. Sara Mae Bryant, Aug. 15, 1947; children—David Anderson, Mary Elizabeth. B.A. in Advt. and Illustration, Woodbury Coll., 1949. Advt. mgr. Hymson's Tots and Teens, Lexington, 1951-54, Rothchilds Dept. Store, Rock Island, Ill., 1954-55, Hill's Dept. Store, Davenport, Iowa, 1955-58; sr. indsl. illustrator J.I. Case Co., Bettendorf, Iowa, 1958-62; audiovisual program mgr. U.S. Govt., Rock Island, 1962-80; adminstr. Deaf Missions, Council Bluffs, Iowa, 1980—; lectr. in field. Author: Effective Oral Presentation (commendation award 1969), 1969; Clearing in The Forest, 1980; also articles. Bd. dirs. George Davenport Hist. Found., Rock Island, 1979-80; active Davenport Arts Council, 1969-80; co-founder Rock Island Arsenal Hist. Found., 1970; speaker Rock Island Arsenal Speakers Bur., 1970-82. Served with U.S. Army, 1941-45. Recipient Toastmaster of Yr. award, 1974. Republican. Mem. Christian Ch. Avocations: travel; stage design. Home: Bennett & Franklin Aves Greenbriar Apt 57 Council Bluffs IA 51501 Office: Deaf Missions RR 2 Box 26 Council Bluffs IA 51501

MCCOY, JOHN BONNET, banker. Pres., chief exec. officer, chief operating officer Banc One Corp., Columbus, Ohio, also dir. Office: Banc One Corp 100 E Broad St Columbus OH 43215*

MCCRACKEN, DENNIS WAYNE, corporate controller; b. East St. Louis, Ill., May 18, 1951; s. Ronald W. and Dorothy (Metzger) McC.; m. Jo Ellen Niebrugge, Oct. 2, 1976; children—Thomas A., Kara A. B.S., So. Ill. U., 1973, M.B.A., 1976. Jr. accountant Rexall Drug Co., St. Louis, 1973-74, sr. acct., 1974-75, acctg. supr., 1975-77; sr. acct. ITT Fin. Corp., St. Louis, 1977-80; asst. controller Hasco Internat., St. Charles, Mo., 1980-81, corp. controller, 1981—. Chmn. fin. com. Maryland Heights Citizens Coalition, 1984. Mem. Nat. Assn. Accts. Roman Catholic. Club: So. Ill. U. Alumni Assn. Home: 2390 Meadow Park Ct Maryland Heights MO 63043 Office: Hasco Internat Inc 3613 Mueller Rd Saint Charles MO 63301

MCCRACKEN, L. SCOTT, engineering construction company executive; b. St. Joseph, Mo., Apr. 8, 1928; s. Dwight Taylor and Mary Esther (Scott) McC.; m. Betsy Nichols, Feb. 4, 1950; children—Scott Bruce, Robert Glen, Richard Curtis, Janet Susan. B.S., Iowa State U., 1949. Design engr. Economy Forms Corp., Des Moines, 1949-55, mgr. spl. forms dept., 1955-68, chief engr., 1968-76, v.p. engring., 1976-80, v.p., regional mgr. Central U.S. and S.Am., 1980—; v.p. Constrn. Products Inc., Des Moines, Metal Products Mfg., Ames, Iowa; engring. rep. Scaffolding, Shoring and Forming Inst. Mem. Sigma Alpha Epsilon. Republican. Mem. United Ch. of Christ. Patentee in field.

MCCRACKEN, ROBERT EUGENE, SR., cemetery company executive, funeral director; b. Kansas City, Mo., Jan. 29, 1930; s. Eugene Emerson and Lelia Mabel (Meeker) McC.; m. Ada Margaret Watson, June 7, 1952; children—Robert Mark, Cherie Ann, Robert Eugene. A.B. in Econs., Washburn U., 1952; M.S. in Mortuary Sci., Dallas Inst. Mortuary Sci., 1956; grad. Nat. Found. Funeral Service Sch. Mgmt., 1957. Lic. funeral dir., Kans. Tchr., coach, acting prin., Auburn, Kans., 1954-55; bus. mgr. Penwell-Gabel Funeral Home, Topeka, Kans., 1956-67, exec. v.p., 1967-70, pres., 1970-78; exec. sec. Kans. State Bd. Embalming, Topeka, 1978-79; gen. mgr. Mt. Hope Cemetery, Topeka, 1983—; pres. McCracken Assocs., Topeka, 1979-83; v.p., dir. Kans. Funeral Ins. Agy., 1967-78. Served to 1st lt. USAF, 1952-54; Korea. Mem. Kans. Cemetery Assn. (bd. dirs. 1984—). Methodist. Club: Topeka Country. Lodges: Kiwanis (pres. 1964), Moose. Avocation: classic car collecting. Home: 1401 SW Westover Rd Topeka KS 66604 Office: Mt Hope Cemetery Co 4700 W 17th St Topeka KS 66604

MCCRAW, RONALD KENT, psychologist, air force officer, b. Houston, Dec. 6, 1947; s. Leon Frank and Lorna Mae (Bailey) McC. B.A., U. Tex., 1970; M.A., U. Tex. Med. Br., Galveston, 1972; Ph.D., U. South Fla., 1981; postgrad. Squadron Officers Sch., Air U., 1982-83, Air Command and Staff Coll., 1985—. Cert. instr. ARC. Research asst. div. child and adolescent psychiatry U. Tex. Med. Br., 1972-74; grad. asst. div. neuropsychology Fla. Mental Health Inst., Tampa, 1975-76; resident in clin. psychology U. Tex. Health Scis. Ctr., San Antonio, 1977-78; psychometrician Hillsborough Community Mental Health Ctr., Tampa, Fla., 1978-79; clin. psychologist U.S. Air Force Hosp., Chanute AFB, Ill., 1982—. Film and book reviewer for AAAS Sci. Books and Films, 1977—, Birth, 1983—, Jour. Nurse-Midwifery, 1985—; editorial bd. Birth Psychology Bull., 1984—, Health Care of Women Internat., 1984—; abstractor Psychosomatics; contbr. articles to sci. jours. Coach Baytown Girls Softball Assn. (Tex.), 1980-82, Rantoul Ponytail Softball League (Ill.), 1983-85, Men's Varsity Softball Team, Chanute AFB, Ill., 1983-84, U.S. Slo-Pitch Softball Assn. State and Div. Qualifying Team, 1984. Served to capt. USAF, 1982—. Fellow Am. Orthopsychiat. Assn.; mem. Am. Psychol. Assn., Ill. Psychol. Assn., AAAS, Soc. Air Force Clin. Psychologists, Am. Acad. Behavioral Medicine, Assn. for Advancement Behavior Therapy, Assn. for Birth Psychology, Internat. Childbirth Edn. Assn. (alt. hour rev. subcom. 1985—), Acad. Psychosomatic Medicine, Soc. Behavioral Medicine, Soc. for Personality Assessment, U. Tex. Ex-Students Assn. (life), N.Y. Acad. Scis., Sigma Xi, Psi Chi, Omicron Delta Kappa, Nu Sigma Nu. Methodist. Lodges: Order DeMolay (chevalier), Masons. Home: PSC Box 1429 Chanute AFB IL 61868 Office: SGHMA USAF Hosp Chanute AFB IL 61868

MCCRAW, SAMMY TIMOTHY, cost/schedule planning specialist; b. Memphis, Jan. 23, 1946; s. Richard Clarence and Susie (Wright) McC.; m. Patricia Pompey, Oct. 30, 1982; 1 son, Jules Singer. B.A. in Econs., Memphis State U., 1972; M.S. in Ops. Mgmt., Northrop U., Inglewood, Calif., 1975, M.B.A., 1976. Purchasing asst. Memphis State U., 1965-68; distbn. clk. Memphis Post Office, 1971-72; program adminstr. Rockwell Internat., Los Angeles, 1972-77; schedule planning specialist Battelle Meml. Inst., Columbus, Ohio, 1977—; adj. asst. prof. Central Washington U.; instr. Columbia Basin Coll. Active Riverside Hills Civic Assn. Served to capt. USAR, 1968—. Decorated Bronze Star, Army Commendation medal. Recipient cert. of appreciation Project Mgmt. Inst., 1980; hon. teaching cert. Los Angeles Unified Sch. Dist., 1976. Mem. Project Mgmt. Inst., Res. Officers Assn., Inst. Cert. Profl. Mgrs., Am. Mgmt. Assn. Democrat. Contbr. articles to profl. jours. Home: 3204 Needham Dr Dublin OH 43017 Office: 505 King Ave Columbus OH 43201

MC CRAY, BILLY QUINCY, former state senator, real estate broker; b. Geary, Okla., Oct. 29, 1927; s. John Joel and Ivory Beatrice (Jessie) McC.; m. Wyvette M. Williams, Oct. 12, 1952; children—Frankie Leen Conley, Anthony, Melody McCray Miller, Kent. Mem. Kans. Ho. of Reps., Wichita, 1967-72, Kans. Senate, 1973-84; real estate broker; dir. minority bus. div. Kans. Dept. Econ. Devel., 1984—. Mem. Human Relations Comm., 1961-63; mem. Mayor's Adv. Com., 1964—. Served with USAF, 1947-51. Mem. African Methodist Episcopal Ch. Democrat. Mason. Home: 1532 N Ash St Wichita KS 67214 Office: 3712 W 29th St Suite 513 Topeka KS 66614

MCCREARY, WILLIAM NORTH, JR., brass mill executive; b. Pitts., June 12, 1948. Student U. Cin., 1966-68; B.S.Ch.E., U. Toledo, 1971, M.A. in Econs., 1973, M.S. in Math., 1974, M.B.A., 1974; postgrad. U. Mich., 1974. Mgr. mfg. EOD div. Owens Ill. Inc., 1971-73, mgr. corp. mktg., 1973-74, sr. corp. planner, 1974-76, nat. account mgr., sales, 1976-78; dir. mktg. Chase Brass div. Standard Oil of Ohio, Solon, 1978-79, dist. sales mgr., 1979, venture mgr., 1979-80, gen. mgr. narrow strip div., 1981—. Mem. Copper Devel. Assn., Cooper Club, Am. Soc. Metals, Copper and Brass Fabricators.

MCCRYSTAL, JAMES LINCOLN, JR., lawyer; b. Sandusky, Ohio, Nov. 6, 1948; s. James Lincoln and Elizabeth (Ernst) McC.; m. Gayle Ann Newman, Oct. 5, 1985. B.A., John Carroll U., 1970; J.D., U. Notre Dame, 1973. Bar: Ohio 1973, U.S. Dist. Ct. (no. dist.) Ohio 1974, U.S. Ct. Appeals (6th cir.) 1977, U.S. Supreme Ct. 1979. Assoc. Weston, Hurd, Fallon, Paisley & Howley, Cleve., 1974-79, ptnr., 1980—. Chmn. Friends of Western Res. Hist. Soc. Library, Cleve., 1984—. Mem. Erie County Bar Assn., Greater Cleve. Bar Assn., Ohio State Bar Assn. (jud. adminstrn. com., legal reform com.), ABA, Def. Research Inst., Ohio Assn. Civil Trial Attys., John Carroll U. Alumni Assn. (nat. pres. 1983—). Democrat. Roman Catholic. Avocation: sailing. Home: 2301 Chatfield Dr Cleveland Heights OH 44106

MCCUBBREY, DAVID RAYMOND, physician; b. Windsor, Ont., Can., Dec. 15, 1928; came to U.S., 1929, naturalized, 1937; s. David Dunlop and Ann (Zayots) McC.; m. Claire Ward Lambert, Mar. 25, 1950; children—David, Douglas, Doris. M.D., U. Mich., 1953. Diplomate Am. Bd. Surgery. Intern, Albany Med. Ctr., N.Y., 1953-54; resident in surgery St. Joseph Hosp., Ann Arbor, 1957-61; Practicing medicine, Plymouth, Mich., 1961—. Served to capt. U.S. Army, 1955-57. Fellow ACS. Presbyterian. Office: 990 W Ann Arbor Trail Suite 200 Plymouth MI 48170

MCCUISTION, ROBERT WILEY, hospital adminstrator, lawyer; b. Wilson, Ark., June 15, 1927; s. Ed Talmadge and Ruth Wiley (Bassett) McC.; m. Martha Virginia Golden, June 11, 1949; children—Martha Elizabeth, John Daniel, James Edward. A.B., Hendrix Coll., 1949; J.D., U. Ark., 1952. Bar: Ark. 1952. Sole practice, Dermott, Ark., 1952-57; adminstr. Stuttgart Meml. Hosp., Ark., 1957-60, Forrest Meml. Hosp., Forrest City, Ark., 1960-68; assoc. adminstr. St. Edward Mercy Hosp., Fort Smith, Ark., 1968-70; pres. Meml. Med. Ctr., Corpus Christi, Tex., 1970-79; adminstr. Meth. Hosp., Mitchell, S.D., 1979—; cons. Ark. Constl. Conv., 1969; preceptor, mem. adj. faculty Trinity U., San Antonio, 1970-79, Washington U., St. Louis, 1971-79, Ga. State U., Atlanta, 1970-79. Served with USAAF, 1944-47. Recipient Eminent Leadership award Desoto area council Boy Scouts Am., Ark., 1956. Mem. ABA, Am. Coll. Hosp. Adminstrs., Am. Assn. Hosp. Accts. (pres. Ark. chpt. 1959), Ark. Hosp. Assn. (pres. Forrest City 1964-65), Ark. Adminstrs. Forum (pres. 1962), Ark. Conf. Cath. Hosps. (pres. 1970). Methodist. Lodge: Rotary (pres. 1964-65). Avocations: swimming; golf; bowling; skiing; woodworking. Home: Rural Route 3 Box 320 Mitchell SD 57301 Office: Meth Hosp 909 S Miller St Mitchell SD 57301

MCCULLOUGH, NANCY CAMP, public relations executive; b. Honolulu, Sept. 14, 1948; d. Joseph Martin and Elizabeth Hyers (Reitz) Camp. B.F.A., Ill. Wesleyan U.-Bloomington, 1971; M.S. in Info. Scis., Ill. State U.-Normal, 1974. Mem. faculty Ill. Wesleyan U., 1971-72; cons. social rehab. Schultz & Assocs., Bloomington, Ill., 1972-74; mem. faculty Ill. State U., 1974-76; communications specialist Mennonite Health Care Assn., Bloomington, 1976-79; dir. pub. relations Ill. Agrl. Assn., Bloomington, 1979-85; founder McCullough Pub. Relations, 1985—. Chmn. pub. relations McLean County United Way, 1981; chmn. McLean County residential crusade Am. Cancer Soc., 1981-82. Mem. McLean County Dance Assn. (co-founder 1976, bd. dirs. 1976-80), Agrl. Relations Council Am., Public Relations Soc. Am. (accredited mem.), Nat. Assn. Female Execs. Author: Farm In The School, 1981; contbr. articles, photog. studies to profl. pubs. Home: Route 2 Box 71 Eureka IL 61530

MCCULLOUGH-WIGGINS, LYDIA STATORIA, pharmacist, consultant; b. Chgo., May 14, 1948; d. George Robert and Isabell (King) Boulware; m. Robert Dale McCullough, Aug. 1, 1970 (div. Oct. 1977); m. 2d, James Calvin Wiggins, Nov. 3, 1979. Student Wis. State U.-Whitewater, 1966-69; B.S. in Pharmacy, U. Ill.-Chgo., 1972; cert. UCLA, 1976-78. Registered pharmacist, Ill. Registered pharmacy apprentice Lefel Drugs, Chgo., 1971-72; pharmacy mgr. Fernwood Pharmacy, Chgo., 1972-73, Sapstein Bros. Pharmacy, Chgo., 1973-74; dir. pharmacy Martin Luther King Neighborhood Health Ctr., Chgo., 1974-80; pharmacist in charge Walgreens, Chgo., 1980—. Author: M.L.K. Drug Formulary, 1978. Recipient Cert. of Leadership, YMCA Met. Chgo., 1979; Kizzy award 1980 Black Women Hall of Fame Found., Chgo., 1981; Ann. Med. Achievement award Greater Chgo. Met. Community, 1981. Mem. Chgo. Pharmacists Assn., Am. Pharm. Assn., Ill. Pharm. Assn., Nat. Assn. Female Execs., U. Ill. Alumni Assn. Democrat. Baptist. Club: Christian Novice (pres. 1977-78) (Chgo.). Office: Walgreens 1650 W Chicago St Chicago IL 60622

MCCURDY, DAVID WHITWELL, anthropology educator, author; b. N.Y.C., Sept. 30, 1935; s. Henry Benson and Theodora (Wilson) McC.; m. Carolyn Durham, July 26, 1957; children—Victoria W., David D., Alexander M., Heather W. B.A., Cornell U., 1957, Ph.D., 1964; M.A., Stanford U., 1959. Asst. prof. anthropology Colo. State U., Fort Collins, 1964-66; prof. anthropology Macalester Coll., St. Paul, 1966—. Co-author: The Cultural Experience, 1972; Anthropology: The Cultural Perspective, 1975, 2d rev. edit., 1980. Co-editor: Conformity and Conflict, 1971, 5th rev. edit., 1984; Issues on Cultural Anthropology, 1979. Mem. Democratic Farmer-Labor State Central Com., Minn., 1968. Served to 1st lt. U.S. Army, 1958. Ford Found. fgn. area tng. fellow, India, 1961-63; Hill Found. anthropology devel. grantee, 1966-69; Bush Found. grantee, India, 1985. Fellow Am. Anthropol. Assn.; mem. Am. Ethnological Soc., Central States Anthropol. Soc., Med. Anthropol. Soc., Soc. for Anthropology and Edn., Am. Fedn. Musicians, United Sidecar Assn., Gold Wing Rd. Riders Assn. Phi Kappa Phi, Phi Kappa Psi. Democrat. Home: 1731 Princeton Ave Saint Paul MN 55105 Office: Dept Anthropology Macalester Coll St Paul MN 55105

MCCURDY, SUSAN REPLOGLE, tax and accounting practitioner; b. Marshalltown, Iowa, Feb. 12, 1949; d. Paul Gilmore and Doris Mae (Schulz) Replogle; m. John William McCurdy, Dec. 21, 1968; children—William (dec.), Kathryn, Elizabeth. A.A., Marshalltown Community Coll., 1969, B.A., U. No. Iowa, Cedar Falls, 1970; postgrad. Iowa State U., Ames, 1980—, M.A., U. No. Iowa, 1983. With McCall Monument Co., Oskaloosa, Iowa, 1968-72; sr. sec. Grace United Meth. Ch., Marshalltown, 1971-72; exec. sec. Elim Luth. Ch., Marshalltown, 1977-80; founder, ptnr. Su McCurdy Bus. Alternatives, Marshalltown 1978—; faculty Marshalltown Community Coll., 1983—. Permanent mem. Iowa Jr. Coll. Honor Soc., 1969; recipient Fisher Gov. Found. scholarship, 1968-69. Mem. Nat. Assn. Tax Practitioners; Nat. and Iowa Bus. Edn. Assns., Accts. Assn. Iowa, Marshalltown C. of C., Nat. Assn. Female Execs., Am. Bus. Communicators Assn., Kappa Delta Pi, Delta Pi Epsilon. Baptist. Home: 405 E South St Marshalltown IA 50158 Office: 7 Westwood Dr Suite A Marshalltown IA

MCDANIEL, DREW OVERTON, university official, educator; b. Ontario, Oreg., Sept. 15, 1941; s. James Allen and Maudie Louise (Drewrey) McD.; m. Nancy Louise Balkema, Aug. 18, 1979; children—Sean Michael, Patrick. B.A., U. Idaho, 1963; M.A., U. Denver, 1963; Ph.D., Ohio U., 1970. Producer Sta. KHQ, Spokane, Wash., 1965-67, Sta. KING, Seattle, 1967-68; prof. Ohio U., Athens, 1969—, dir. Sch. Telecommunications, 1976—; cons. USIA, Washington, 1981—, Arab States Broadcasting Union, Damascus, Syria, 1983—; participant Nat. Telecommunications Policy Conf., Annapolis, Md., 1982-83, chmn. telecommunications adv. com. Athens City Council, 1980-82; Mem. editorial bd. Advances in Telematics, Oxford, Eng., 1983—. Contbr. articles to profl. jours. Nqmed Outstanding Mem. Grad. Faculty, Ohio U., 1982; recipient Internat. Understand award Ohio U., 1984. Mem. Internat. Inst. Communication, Broadcast Edn. Assn. (instl. rep., chmn. internat. com. 1977-79, 94—), Am. Radio Relay League. Club: Porsche of Am. Avocations: amateur radio; skiing; sports cars. Home: 47 Charles St Athens OH 45701 Office: Sch Telecommunications Ohio U Athens OH 45701

MCDANIEL, ROSE LEE, educator; b. Norcross, Ga., June 26, 1929; d. Frank Lee and Mary Pearl Bower; m. Charles William McDaniel, Mar. 4, 1949; children—Deborah D. McDaniel Roberts, Charles F., Reginael D. Student Wilkins Sch. Cosmetology, 1947; B.Edn., Toledo U., 1964, M.Ed., 1971, Ed.S., 1975. Cosmetologist, 1947-60; tchr. elem. sch., Toledo, 1964-67, resource tchr., 1968-69, team leader Tchr. Corps, 1969-71, elem. tchr., 1971, adminstrv. intern, 1972, ednl. specialist, 1972-80; tchr. elem. sch. Fulton County (Ga.), Atlanta, 1980-81; asst. prin. Sherman Elem. Sch., Toledo, 1981-84; prin. Reynolds Elem. Sch., Toledo, 1984—. Supt. Sunday sch. Bapt. Ch., 1975-78, dir. Christian Edn., 1978-84; sec. Matrons Conv. N.W. Ohio Bapt. Assn., 1979. Recipient service cert. Family Life Edn. Ctr., 1980, Nat. Appreciation award Soc. Disting. Am. High Sch. Students, 1978. Mem. Assn. Supervision and Curriculum Devel., Internat. Reading Assn., U. Toledo Alumni Assn., Phi Delta Kappa, Alpha Chi Pi Omega (pres. 1967-69, Woman of Yr. award 1970). Democrat.

MCDAVID, GLENN TRUXTUN, computer systems analyst, consultant; b. Ithaca, N.Y., May 14, 1951; s. Raven Ioor and Virginia (Glenn) McD.; m. Mia Ellen Fagerstrom, July 15, 1978. B.A., Carleton Coll., 1972; M.S. in Applied Physics, Stanford U., 1974, M.S. in Stats., 1976. Programmer, analyst 1st Nat. Bank Chgo., 1977-79; list services analyst Signature Fin. Mktg. Co., Evanston, Ill., 1979-80; sr. programmer, analyst Harris Bank, Chgo., 1980-81; system cons. I.P. Sharp Assocs., Chgo., 1981-83, Harris Bank, Chgo., 1983—. Mem. Assn. Computing Machinery, Am. Statistical Assn., Soc. Indl. and Applied Math., Am. Assn. Physic Tchrs., British Interplanetary Soc. Episcopalian. Avocations: philately; history; sci. fiction; home brewed beer. Home: 1791-A W Greenleaf St Chicago IL 60626 Office: Harris Trust and Savs Bank PO Box 755 Chicago IL 60690

MCDERMED, RONALD DEAN, educational administrator; b. Muskegon, Mich., Aug. 12, 1951; s. Harold Walter and Frances May (Ervin) McD.; m. Irene Presnikovs, Nov. 20, 1976; children—Alina Michele, Michael Walter. B.A., Western Mich. U., 1974; M.A., Mich. State U., 1978, Ed.S., 1983, doctoral candidate, 1983—. Tchr., Portland (Mich.) Pub. Schs., 1974-79, dir. fed. programs, 1980—, reading cons. elem., 1979-80. Trustee scholar Western Mich. U., 1971-74. Mem. NEA, Mich. Edn. Assn., Mich. Assn. State and Fed. Program Specialists, Assn. Supervision and Curriculum Devel., Portland Community Theatre, Phi Delta Kappa. Congregationalist. Lodge: Lions.

MCDONALD, ARLINE MARGARET, researcher, nutrition educator; b. Chuquicamata, Chile, Jan. 8, 1953; came to U.S., 1953; s. Robert Emmett and Barbara Ann (Gehres) McD. B.S., U. Ky., 1974; M.S., U. Tenn., 1976, Ph.D., 1978. Postdoctoral research fellow Northwestern U. Med. Sch., Chgo., 1978-81, asst. prof. community health and preventive medicine, 1982—; asst. prof. nutrition and med. dietetics U. Ill., Chgo. Health Scis. Center, 1981—. Mem. Chgo. Heart Assn. Recipient Chancellor's Citation, U. Tenn., 1978; Research Career Devel. award Nat. Heart, Lung and Blood Inst., NIH, 1982-87. Mem. Sigma Xi. Roman Catholic. Home: 1219 Hull Terrace Evanston IL 60202 Office: 303 E Chicago Ave Chicago IL 60611

MCDONALD, CHARLES OLIVER, county official; b. Batavia, Ill., Nov. 22, 1929; s. Thomas William and Mary Isabel (Morrison) McD.; m. Shirley Ann Knur, Nov., 20, 1948; children—Randy Charles, Ricky William, Rojean Lynn, Rodney John. Ticket agt. railroad, Batavia, Ill., 1947-48; truck driver, Aurora, Ill., 1948-51; construction worker T. W. McDonald Constn. Batavia, 1951-54, plastering contractor, Aurora, 1954-60; patrolman Aurora Police Dept., 1960-80; sheriff Kendall County, Yorkville, Ill., 1982—. Mem. Ill. Police Assn. (state auditor 1983—), No. Ill. Sheriff's Assn. (pres. 1983-84). Republican. Roman Catholic. Clubs: Tiger, Eagle (Aurora). Lodges: Moose, Eagles. Avocations: Camping, mechanical repair, golf. Office: Kendall County Sheriff's Dept Main and Madison Sts PO Box 190 Yorkville IL 60560

MCDONALD, DANIEL J(OSEPH), police official; b. Cin., Sept. 3, 1947; s. Raymond C. and Patricia A. (Senft) McD.; m. Penny J. Haines, Nov. 30, 1968; children—Michelle, Daniel J., Brian. B.S., U. Cin., 1969. Lic. pvt. pilot single engine; lic. forensic hypnosis, Ohio. Police lt. City of Cin., 1966—, relief comdr., 1982—. Active World Wings Assn., Cin. Police Holy Name. Mem. Cin. Police Suprs. Assn., Ohio Assn. Forensic and Investigative Hypnosis, Internat. Police Assn. Republican. Roman Catholic. Lodge: Fraternal Order Police. Office: 1012 Ludlow Ave Cincinnati OH 45223

MCDONALD, DONALD BURT, environmental engineering educator, consultant; b. Salt Lake City, Utah, Mar. 5, 1932; s. Donald T. and Dorthea (Miller) McD.; m. Marilyn Pratt, June 19, 1954 (div. 1967); children—Barbara, Karen, Donald; m. Ardis J. Brower, July 23, 1977. B.S., U. Utah, 1954, M.S., 1956, Ph.D., 1962. Project dir. Utah Fish & Game Dept., Salt Lake City, 1958-60; instr. Carbon Coll., Price, Utah, 1960-62; prof. U. Iowa, Iowa City 1962—; cons. various utilities and engring. firms. Served to sgt. U.S. Army, 1949-52, Korea. Mem. Water Pollution Control Fedn., Am. Water Works Assn., Am. Soc. Testing Materials. Avocations: Skiing; Backpacking. Home: Route 1 Box 36 Iowa City IA 52240 Office: Dept Environ Engring U Iowa Iowa City IA 52242

MCDONALD, JOHN WILLIAM, chemist; b. Decatur, Ill., Mar. 29, 1945; s. John William and Blanche Margaret (Longbons) McD.; m. Mary Helen Melison, Nov. 4, 1972; children—John William, Nicholas Michael. B.A., Grinnell Coll., 1967; Ph.D., Northwestern U., 1972. Sr. research assoc. C.F. Kettering Research Lab. (name now Battelle Kettering Research Lab.), Yellow Springs, Ohio, 1971-73, staff scientist, 1973-78, investigator, 1978-84, prin. research scientist, 1984—. Contbr. articles to profl. jours. NASA fellow; Northwestern U. fellow 1967-68, 69-71; NIH fellow. Mem. Am. Chem. Soc. Avocations: fishing, camping. Home: 606 Sharon Dr Fairborn OH 45324 Office: Battelle Kettering Research Lab 150 E S College St Yellow Springs OH 45387

MCDONALD, MARVIN LEROY, school administrator, real estate salesman; b. Pana, Ill., Apr. 1, 1936; s. Harry C. and Norma V. (Baker) McD.; m. Mary Jo Dunauan, Dec. 27, 1960; children—Scott, Karen. B.S. in Vocat. Agr., U. Ill., 1958, M.S. in Endl. Adminstrn., 1963; adv. cert. Ill. State U., 1972. Vocat. agr. tchr. Henning High Sch., Ill., 1958-59; vocat. agr., biology tchr., then prin. Chrisman High Sch., Ill., 1959-64; biology tchr., prin., asst. supt. Manteno High Sch., Ill., 1964-69; prin., transp. dir. Chenoa High Sch., Ill., 1969-82; real estate sales man Century 21, Pontiac, Ill., 1976-82; prin. Bismarck-Henning High Sch., Ill., 1982—. Lay leader Methodist Ch., Chenoa, Ill., 1979-80. Named Boss of Yr. Secretaries Club McLean County, Ill., 1978. Mem. Ill. Prins. Assn. (sec. Region IV 1974, pres., 1975—), Ill. Athletic Dirs. Assn., Chenoa Jaycees (pres. 1970-71). Lodge: Lions (v.p. Chrisman chpt. 1959-64, mem. Bismarck chpt. 1983—). Avocations: camping; spectator sports; fishing; working on home.

MCDONALD, MERLE HARRY, JR., nursing home administrator; b. Christchurch, N.Z., Dec. 16, 1944; came to U.S., 1945; s. Merle Harry and Stella Nairn (Neylon) McD.; m. Sandra Kay Wade, June 11, 1966; children—Christine, Maureen. B.A., Carthage Coll., Kenosha, Wis., 1966; M.S., U. Wis.-Milw., 1972. Adminstrv. asst. U.S. Senator George McGovern, Washington, 1971-72; asst. adminstr. Luther Manor, Wauwatosa, Wis., 1972-73; exec. adminstr. Office Lt. Gov., Madison, Wis., 1973-74; assoc. adminstr. Lutheran Home for Aging, Milw., 1974-77; pres. Marian Catholic Home, Milw., 1977—. Treas. Wis. McGovern for Pres. Com., Milw., 1972; bd. dirs. Wis. S. Action Coalition, Milw., 1974-78, Independent Living, Inc., Madison, 1973; co-chmn. Wis. Carter for Pres. Com., Milw., 1976; pres. Milw. Symphony Knights, 1978-83; dep. dir. Dem. Conv., N.Y.C., 1980; bd. dirs. Wis. Conservatory Music, Milw., 1985. Named Outstanding Young Man Am., Jaycees, 1974; recipient Achievement award United Way, 1975, Goodwill Industries, 1973. Served to sgt. U.S. Army, 1968-70. Mem. Am. Assn. Homes for Aging, Wis. Assn. Homes for Aging (bd. dirs. 1982—), Am. Coll. Health Care Adminstrs. Lutheran. Club: Wis. (Milw.). Avocations: tennis, reading. Home: 1738 Alta Vista Ave Wauwatosa WI 53213 Office: Marian Catholic Home Inc 3333 W Highland Blvd Milwaukee WI 53208

MCDONALD, OZZIE HORACE, II, psychologist, consultant; b. Belle Glade, Fla., Feb. 20, 1941; s. Sammie and Louise McD. A.A., Highland Kans. Community Jr. Coll., 1973; B.A., U. Kans., 1975; M.A., Miami U. (Ohio), 1977; Ph.D., U. Cin., 1981. Psychologist, chief exec. officer McDonald & Assocs., Cin., 1981—. Home: 2478 Mustang Dr Cincinnati OH 45219 Office: 2650 Burnet Ave Cincinnati OH 45219

MCDONALD, ROBERT DELOS, manufacturing and wholesale distributing company executive; b. Dubuque, Iowa, Jan. 30, 1931; s. Delos Lyon and Virginia (Kolck) McD.; m. Jane M. Locher, Jan. 16, 1960 (div. 1970); children—Jean, Patricia, Maria, Sharon, Rob; m. 2d Marilyn I. Miller, July 4, 1978. B.A. in Econs. U. Iowa, 1953. Salesman, A.Y. McDonald Mfg. Co., Dubuque, 1956-60, sales mgr., 1961-64, dir., 1964—, mgr. Dubuque Wholesale br., 1965-72, v.p., 1971-72, v.p., corp. sec., 1972-82, sr. v.p., corp. sec., 1983-84, pres., 1985—; dir. Brock-McVey Cos., Ky.; pres. A.Y. McDonald Mfg. Co. Charitable Found.; bd. dirs. Dubuque Area Indsl. Devel. Corp., Stonehill Care Ctr.; trustee Iowa Hist. Mus. Found. Served with USNR, 1953-56. Mem. Am. Mgmt. Assn., Am. Supply Assn., Dubuque Area C. of C., Am. Legion, Dubuque Shooting Soc., U. Iowa Alumni Assn. Sigma Alpha Epsilon. Republican. Roman Catholic. Clubs: Dubuque Golf and Country, Presidents (life), Golden Hawks, U. Iowa. Lodge: Elks. Home: 3055 Powers Ct Dubuque IA 52001 Office: 4800 Chavenelle Rd PO Box 508 Dubuque IA 52004-0508

MC DONALD, SHIRLEY PETERSON, social worker; b. Indpls., July 7, 1934; d. Harry and Marcella Iona (Kober) Peterson; B.A., Denison U., 1956; teaching credentials Chgo. State U., Nat. Coll. Edn., Prairie State U.; M.S.W., U. Ill., 1976; cert. mediator ednl. disputes, Ill. State Bd. Edn.; m. Stanford Laurel McDonald, Apr. 26, 1964; children—Stacia Elizabeth Virginia, Jeffrey Jared Stern, Kathleen Shirley, Patricia Marie. Tchr., Chgo. Public Schs., 1962-64, Flossmoor, Ill., 1972-74; communication devel. program social worker S. Met. Assn., Harvey, Ill., 1976-79; sch. social worker S.W. Cook County Coop. Spl. Edn., Oak Forest, Ill., 1979—. Religious edn. dir. All Souls Unitarian Ch., 1968-71; religious edn. dir. Unitarian Community Ch., Park Forest, 1975-79, bd. dirs., 1978-81, chmn. bldg. feasibility com., 1981, chmn. bldg. com., 1981-82, also adv. to bd. Mem. Acad. Cert. Social Workers, Nat. Assn. Social Workers, Ill. Assn. Sch. Social Workers (area rep.; mem. com. consultation service, program com. state conf. 1981, adv. 1981-83, pres.-elect 1982-83, pres. 1983-84), Kappa Kappa Gamma, Women's Internat. League Peace and Freedom (past chpt. pres.), Pi Sigma Alpha. Home: 255 Rich Rd Park Forest IL 60466

MCDONALD, W. R., employee-benefits consultant, developer; b. Mt. Vernon, Ill., Nov. 1, 1929; s. Archie R. and Vernadean Pearl (Bailey) McD.; B.S., Ind. State U., 1953; m. Dec. 26, 1953 (div. 1967). Pres., Youth, Inc., Terre Haute, Ind., 1947; dist. mgr. New Eng. Life Ins. Co., Sacramento, 1958-62; v.p. Sutter Sq., Inc., Sacramento, 1960-62, Southland Trust Co., Tucson, 1963-65, Am. Equity Group, Inc., Indpls., 1966-68; sr. ptnr. Ins.-Investors' Guidance Systems, Mt. Vernon, 1972—; pres. Interstate Investors & Growers Syndicate, Inc., Indpls., 1975—; mng. ptnr. Halia Crest Land Trust, Mt. Vernon, 1977-79; pres. Intermed. Self-Ins. Group, Mt. Vernon, 1979—; sr. gen. ptnr. Interstate Investors Golf and Garden Solar Lodges, 1980—, Investors Strategies Group, St. Louis, 1982—, Internat. Benefits Adv. Group, St. Louis, 1984; dir. Southland Trust Life Ins. Co., Phoenix, 1964; cons. So. Ill. U., Carbondale, 1973, 84—. Chmn. United Crusade, Sacramento, 1960; pres. Civitan Internat., Sacramento, 1961; chmn. bd. dirs. Salvation Army, Sacramento, 1961; bd. dirs. USO, 1962. Served with USAF, 1951-57. Recipient Outstanding Flight Officer Achievement cert. USAF, 1957; named Disting. Grad., Aviation Cadets, 1953; U.S. Rookie of Year, New Eng. Life Ins. Co., 1959. Mem. Mt. Vernon C. of C. Republican. Office: PO Box 946 Mount Vernon IL 62864 also 11 S Meridian Suite 810 Indianapolis IN 46204

MCDONELL, ROBERT MICHAEL, computer company executive; b. Monticello, Iowa, Apr. 7, 1950; s. William Francis and Patricia Ann (Oswald) McD.; m. Mary Lynn Jacobson, Sept. 6, 1975; children—Molly, Seth. B.A. in Psychology, Loras Coll., 1972; M.S. in Psychology, Miss. State U., 1974; M.B.A., Nova U., 1983. Staff psychologist Famco, Inc., Dubuque, Iowa, 1974-76; juvenile probation officer Linn County Juvenile Probation, Cedar Rapids, Iowa, 1976-78; market research mgr. Norand Corp., Cedar Rapids, 1978-81, mgr. corporate communications, 1981—; mem. adj. faculty Nova U., Ft. Lauderdale, Fla., 1983—. Mem. Nat. Mgmt. Assn. (Outstanding Service award 1981). Democrat. Roman Catholic. Club: Civitan. Home: 6904 Chelsea Dr NE Cedar Rapids IA 52402 Office: Norand Corp 550 2d St SE Cedar Rapids IA 52401

MCDONNELL, JOHN FINNEY, aviation manufacturing company executive; b. 1938. B.S. in Aero. Engring., Princeton U., 1960, M.S. in Aero. Engring., 1962; postgrad. Washington U. Grad. Sch. Bus. Adminstrn., St. Louis. With McDonnell Douglas Corp., St. Louis, 1957—, contract coordinator and adminstr., 1957-68, asst. to v.p. fin., 1968-72, then v.p. McDonnell Douglas Fin. Corp. subs., staff v.p. fiscal McDonnell Douglas Corp., corp. v.p. fin. and planning, 1972-75, corp. v.p. fin. and devel., 1975-77, corp. exec. v.p., 1977-80, pres., dir., 1980—. Office: McDonnell Douglas Corp PO Box 516 Saint Louis MO 63166*

MC DONNELL, SANFORD NOYES, aircraft company executive; b. Litte Rock, Oct. 12, 1922; s. William Archie and Carolyn (Cherry) McD.; B.A. in Econs., Princeton U., 1945; B.S. in Mech. Engring., U. Colo., 1948; M.S. in Applied Mechanics, Washington U., St. Louis, 1954; m. Priscilla Robb, Sept. 3, 1946; children—Robbin McDonnell MacVittie, William Randall. With McDonnell Douglas Corp. (formerly McDonnell Aircraft Corp.), St. Louis, 1948—, v.p., 1959-66, pres. McDonnell Aircraft div., 1966-71, corp. exec. v.p., 1971, corp. pres., 1971-80, corp. chmn., 1980—, chief exec. officer, 1972—, also dir.; dir. Centerre Bancorp., St. Louis. Active St. Louis United Way; exec. bd. St. Louis council Boy Scouts; nat. pres. Boy Scouts Am.; bd. dirs. Ethics Resource Center. Fellow AIAA; mem. Aerospace Industries Assn. (gov.), Navy League U.S. (life), Air Force Assn., C. of C. U.S., Armed Forces Mgmt. Assn., Nat. Def. Transp. Assn., Am. Security Council, Nat. Aero. Assn., Tau Beta Pi. Presbyterian (trustee, elder). Office: McDonnell Douglas Corp PO Box 516 Saint Louis MO 63166

MC DONOUGH, GERALD CLYDE, transportation leasing company executive; b. Cleve., 1928. B.B.A., Case Western Res. U., 1953. Treas. Molded Fiberglass Co., 1964-69, Rexnord Inc., 1969-74; v.p. and treas. Reliance Electric Co., 1974-79; exec. v.p., dir. Leaseway Transp. Corp., Cleve., 1979-82, chmn. and chief exec. officer, 1982—, acting pres., chief operating officer, 1985—; dir. AmeriTrust Corp., Brush Wellman Inc. Office: Leaseway Transp Corp 3700 Park East Dr Cleveland OH 44122*

MCDONOUGH, JAMES FRANCIS, civil engineer, educator; b. Boston, June 7, 1939; s. John Joseph and Blanche Cecelia (Murphy) McD.; m. Joanna Marie DiPasquale, Aug. 11, 1963 (div. 1982); children—John, James, Jennifer; m. Kathryn Ann Hilver, Mar. 9, 1985. B.S. in Civil Engring., Northeastern U., 1962, M.S. in Civil Engring., 1964; Ph.D., U. Cin., 1968, M.B.A., 1981. Registered profl. engr., Ohio. Project engr. Fay, Spofford & Thorndike, Boston, 1962; teaching asst. Northeastern U., 1962-64; teaching asst. U. Cin., 1965, instr., 1965-68, asst. prof., 1968-74, assoc. prof., 1974-78, William Thoms prof. civil engring., chmn. dept. civil and environ. engring., 1978—; vis. prof. faculty engring. Kabul U. (Afghanistan), 1969-71; vis. prof. N.C. State U., 1971. Pres. Greenhills Winton Sports Assn., 1981-83, treas., 1977-81. Recipient Teaching Excellence award U. Cin., 1973-75, Dow Chem. Outstanding Young Faculty award Am. Soc. for Engring. Edn., 1975, Outstanding Engring. Educator award Am. Soc. Engring. Edn.-Western Electric, 1977, Profl. Accomplishment award Acad.-Tech. and Sci. Council Cin., 1979; Niel Wandmacher Teaching award, 1985. Mem. Am. Soc. Engring. Edn. (v.p. elect 1983, chmn. sect. 1982, 83), ASCE (zone sec. 1983, sect. pres. 1982), Nat. Soc. Profl. Engrs., Ohio Soc. Profl. Engrs., Sigma Xi, Tau Beta Pi, Chi Epsilon, Beta Gamma Sigma. Roman Catholic. Contbr. articles to profl. jours. Home: 3308 Bishop St Cincinnati OH 45220 Office: Mail Location 71 U Cincinnati Cincinnati OH 45221

MCDOUGAL, ROBERT ALAN, pathologist, pathology educator; b. Kalamazoo, Mich., June 22, 1928; s. Russell Prescott and Helen Ernestine (Albert) McD.; m. Lee McCall, Dec. 25, 1955; children—Della Lee, James Alan, Bruce William. Student, Ind. State U., 1945-48; B.S., Ind. U., 1949, M.D., 1952. Diplomate Am. Bd. Nuclear Medicine, Diplomate Am. Bd. Pathology. Intern City Hosp., Akron, Ohio, 1952-53; resident Ind. U., 1953-54, City Hosp., Akron, 1954-55, Marion County Gen. Hosp., Indpls., 1955-57; clin. pathologist City Hosp., Akron, Ohio, 1957-59; pathologist Meml. Hosp., Marietta, Ohio, St. Josephs Hosp., Parkersburg, W. Va., 1959-65; dir. lab. and nuclear medicine Winona Meml. Hosp., Indpls., 1966-76; dir. lab. Hendricks County Hosp., Danville, Ind., 1976—; pres. Blood Research Ednl. Found., Indpls., 1984—; pres., dir., med. advisory com., mem. Central Ind. Regional Blood Ctr., Indpls., 1967—; assoc. clin. prof. pathology Ind. U. Sch. Medicine, Indpls., 1966—. Contbr. articles to profl. jours. Dir. Marion County Cancer Soc., Indpls., 1968-74; cabinet mem., profl. chmn. Hendricks County United Way Greater Indpls., 1983—. Fellow Am. Soc. Clin. Pathologists, Coll. Am. Pathologists; mem. Ind. Assn. Pathologists (dir.), N.Y. Acad. Scis. Republican. Avocations: swimming, genealogy. Home: 1209 Vestal Rd Plainfield IN 46168 Office: Hendricks County Hosp PO Box 409 Danville IN 46122

MCDOWELL, ALMA SUE, financial executive; b. Bedford, Ind., Oct. 16, 1942; d. Claude Edward and Lydia Helen McD.; B.S., Ind. U., 1978, also postgrad. Calculating clk., assigned risk examiner Grain Dealers Mut. Ins. Co., Indpls., 1960-62; with Keach & Grove Ins. Agy., Inc., Bedford, 1962-65; account clk., acctg. mgr. Purdue U., Indpls., 1965-71; fin. asst. to dean adminstrv. affairs Ind.-Purdue U., Indpls., 1971-75; asst. bus. mgr. Ind. U.-Purdue U., Indpls. Center Advanced Research, Inc., from 1975, controller, dir. central adminstrv. services, 1975-81; auditor U.S. Army Fin. & Acctg. Center, 1981—. Asst. treas. E. 38th St. Christian Ch.; vol. VA Hosp. Mem. Nat. Assn. Accts., Assn. Govt. Accts., Am. Soc. Mil. Comptrollers (treas.). Republican. Club: Internat. Toastmistress. Home: 5402 E 20th Pl Indianapolis IN 46218 Office: 1219 W Michigan St Indianapolis IN 46202

MCDOWELL, DANIEL QUINCE, airline executive; b. Bklyn., Dec. 6, 1949; s. Daniel Quince and Amelia (DeFreese) McD.; m. Lesa Belle Wurmnest, July 5, 1980. Assoc. in Sci., Ill. Central U., 1977; B.S., Bradley U., 1979; diploma U.S. Air Force Regional Staff Coll., Colorado Springs, Colo., 1984; cert. Air Force Corp. Learning Course, Mpls., 1984. Sr. ground services rep. Overseas Nat. Airways, JFK Airport, N.Y., 1967-70; asst. carrier U.S. P.O., Roosevelt, N.Y., part-time 1969-70; sta. agt. Ozark Air Lines, Peoria, Ill., 1971-81, Mpls., 1981—; dual aux. video bd. design cons. TriImage Tactical Systems, Sacramento, 1982—. Author: The Sign of the Eagle, 1982. Squadron comdr. CAP/U.S. Air Force Aux., Peoria, 1980-82, group staff officer, Mpls., 1983—. Served with USAF, 1970-71. Recipient Outstanding Achievement award Ozark Air Lines, 1984, Execptional Service medal U.S. Air Force Aux.-CAP, 1984, Grover Loening Aerospace, Aerospace Edn. awards, 1985. Mem. Res. Officers Assn., Am. Def. Preparedness Assn., Am. Aerospace Educators Assn., Air Force Assn. (life), Associated Photographers Internat., Am. Legion (Aviation Post 511). Avocations: creative writing; reading; freelance photography; listening to classical music; travel. Office: Ozark Air Lines Twin Cities Internat Airport Saint Paul MN 55101

MCDOWELL, RICHARD WILLIAM, college president; b. McDonald, Pa., Aug. 20, 1936; s. William Murdock and Cora Josephine (Brackman) McD.; m. Ann Brammer, May 27, 1961; children—Susan, Kathleen, Karen. B.S., Indiana U. of Pa., 1960, M.Ed., 1962; M.S., Purdue U., 1967, Ph.D., 1969. Cert. tchr., Pa. Tchr. Penn Hills Sch. Dist., Pa., 1960-67; div. chmn. Community Coll. Allegheny County, West Mifflin, Pa., 1969-71; dean, acting pres. Community Coll. Beaver County, Monaca, Pa., 1971-72; exec. dean Community Coll. Allegheny County, Monroeville, Pa., 1972-80; v.p. strategic planning Community Coll. Allegheny County, Pitts., 1980-81; pres. Schoolcraft Coll., Livonia, Mich., 1981—; mgmt. cons., Pa. and Ill., 1975-80; chmn., mem. evaluation team Middle States Assn., Phila., 1972-80; trainer workshop leaders Higher Edn. Mgmt. Inst., Washington, 1976-77. Served with USMC, 1954-56. Recipient Outstanding Tchr. award Spectroscopy Soc., Pitts., 1966; Edn. award Plymouth C. of C., Mich., 1982. Mem. Am. Assn. Community and Jr. Colls., Mich. Community Coll. Assn. (bd. dirs. exec. com.), Southeast Mich. League Community Colls. (chmn.), North Central Assn., Assn. Community Coll. Trustees. Office: Schoolcraft Coll 18600 Haggerty Rd Livonia MI 48152

MCDOWELL, ROBERT JOSEPH, metal finishing company executive; b. Elkhart, Ind., Aug. 4, 1951; s. Robert Manson and Doris Elizabeth (Mealor) M.; m. Carol McCullough Watters, June 28, 1975; children—Robert Joseph, Jacqueline Rose. A.B. in Polit. Sci., Ind. U., 1973. Claims rep. Crawford & Co., Atlanta, 1973-75, Crum & Forsler, Knoxville, Tenn., 1975-78; real estate salesman Crossroads Real Estate, Knoxville, 1978-79; chmn., pres. chief exec. officer South Side Plating Works, Elkhart, Ind., 1979—; chmn., chief exec. officer, pres., treas. McDowell Enterprises, Elkhart, 1980—. Bd. dirs. Legal Aid, Elkhart, 1981-84. HUD grantee, 1983. Mem. Am. Electroplaters Soc. (v.p. 1982-83), Ind. Assn. Metal Finishers (pres. 1984—), Ind. U. Alumni Assn. (pres. 1984—), Alpha Sigma Phi (pres. 1977-78). Lodge: Elks. Avocations: photography; sailing. Office: PO Box 846 2010 Superior St Elkhart IN 46515

MCEACHEN, RICHARD EDWARD, banker; b. Omaha, Sept. 24, 1933; s. Howard D. and Ada (Baumann) M.; m. Judith Gray, June 28, 1969; children—Mark, Neil. B.S., U. Kans., 1955; J.D., U. Mich., 1961. Assoc., Hillix, Hall, Hasburgh, Brown & Hoffhaus, Kansas City, Mo., 1961-62; sr. v.p. First Nat. Bank of Kansas City (Mo.), 1962-75; sr. v.p. Commerce Bank of Kansas City (Mo.), 1975-80, exec. v.p., 1980-85; exec. v.p., trust mgr. Centerre Bank of Kansas City, Mo., 1985—. Bd. dirs. Truman Medical Center, 1974—, exec. com., fin. com., retirement com., treas., 1979-84, asst. treas., 1984—; trustee United Community Services; adv. bd. Urban Services YMCA, 1976-83; trustee Clearinghouse Midcontinental Founds., 1980—; bd. govs. Am. Royal Livestock and Horse Show Assn., 1970—; vice-chmn. fin. Kanza dist. Boy Scouts Am., 1982-84; bd. dirs. Greater Kansas City Mental Health Fedn., 1963-69, treas., 1964-69, v.p., 1967-69; mem. adv. com. legal asst. program Avila Coll., 1978-80; hon. bd. dirs. Rockhurst Coll., 1983—. Served as lt. USAF, 1955-58. Mem. ABA, Am., Mo., and Kansas City Bar Assn., Lawyers Assn. Kansas City, Kans. Bar Assn., Estate Planning Council, Estate Planning Assn. (pres. 1974-75), Corp. Fiduciaries Assn. Kansas City (pres., 1979-80), Mo. Bankers Assn. (trust services com. 1977-81), Am. Inst. Banking, Delta Tau Delta (v.p. Kansas City alumni 1978, 79). Clubs: Kansas City, Indian Hills Country. Home: 9100 El Monte Prairie Village KS 66207 Office: PO Box 666 Kansas City MO 64141

MCEACHERN, BARBARA ANN, speech communications educator; b. Bklyn., Jan. 3, 1952; d. Daniel Robert and Mary Minnie (Cunningham) McEachern; m. Morton Vogel Smith Jr., Sept. 30, 1976; children—Diambu Kibwe, Tor Yohance. B.A., Ohio Wesleyan U., 1974; M.A., Bowling Green State U., 1975; postgrad. Cleve. State U., 1979. Instr. speech communications Lakeland Community Coll., 1976-80, asst. prof., 1980-82, assoc. prof., 1982—. Mem. NEA, Ohio Educators Assn., Community Coll. Humanities Assn., Ohio Speech Assn., NAACP, Nat. Assn. Dramatic and Speech Arts, Black Women's Polit. Action Com., Afro-Am. Cultural and Hist. Soc. Mus., Theta Alpha Phi. Office: Lakeland Community College Mentor OH 44060

MCEACHRON, KARL BOYER, JR., retired university official; b. Ada, Ohio, June 27, 1915; s. Karl Boyer and Leila Emily (Honsinger) McE.; m. Marjorie Blalock, Mar. 20, 1937; children—Norman Bruce, Lawrence Karl, Linda Louise, Donald Lynn. B.S. in Elec. Engring., Purdue U., 1937. With Gen. Electric Co., 1937-55, project engr., 1952-55; mem. faculty Case Inst. Tech., 1955-57, dean instrn., 1957-64, vice provost, 1964-67, dean Case Inst. Tech. of Case Western Res. U., Cleve., 1967-72, dir. admissions and fin. aid, 1972-74, dean undergrad. affairs, 1974-80. Contbr. articles to profl. jours. Named Disting. Alumnus Purdue U., 1964. Fellow IEEE (chmn. edn. com. 1959-61, chmn. Cleve. chpt. 1961-62); mem. Am. Soc. Engring. Edn. (v.p. 1967-69), Engrs. Council Profl. Devel. (com. edn. and accreditation 1956-61, exec. com. 1964-65), Nat. Soc. Profl. Engrs., Cleve. Soc. Profl. Engrs. (pres. 1975-76), Sigma Xi, Tau Beta Pi, Eta Kappa Nu. Republican. Methodist. Home: 8300 Deepwood Blvd 2 Mentor OH 44060 Office: 2040 Adelbert Rd Cleveland OH 44106

MCELDOWNEY, TODD RICHARD, lawyer; b. Rhinelander, Wis., Apr. 7, 1955; s. Russell James and Donna Jo (Stoll) McE.; m. Margaret Lee Peterson, Mar. 29, 1985. B.S. with highest honors, U. Wis.-Stevens Point, 1977; J.D., Marquette U., 1980. Bar: Wis. 1980, U.S. Dist. Ct. (ea. dist.) Wis. 1980, U.S. Dist. Ct. (we. dist.) Wis. 1980. Assoc. O'Melia, Eckert, McEldowney & Mangerson, Rhinelander, 1981-85; ptnr. O'Melia & McEldowney, S.C., 1985—. Commr., Rhinelander Basketball league, 1976—; mem., sec. Rhinelander Police and Fire Commn., 1982—; mem. Oneida County Hwy. Safety Commn., Rhinelander, 1983—. Mem. Oneida-Vilas-Forest County Bar Assn. Congregationalist. Lodge: Optimists (pres. local club 1981—). Home: 1421-A Elizabeth St Rhinelander WI 54501 Office: O'Melia & McEldowney SC Bldg PO Box 797 Rhinelander WI 54501

MCELRATH, KAY PAULA, performing arts administrator, stage manager, lighting designer; b. Cedar Rapids, Iowa, Aug. 20, 1954; d. Paul L. and Olive M. (Cannell) Bassett; m. William W. McElrath IV, July 9, 1979. Student Ia. State U., 1972-77. Prodn. mgr. Meml. Union Theater, Ames, Iowa, 1975-76; stage foreman Iowa State Ctr., Ames, 1975-78; gen. mgr., tech. dir. Des Moines Ballet Co., 1978—; stage mgr. Iowa Arts Council, Des Moines, 1979-85, Pioneer Hi-Bred Indsl., Des Moines, 1984; set designer Ingersoll Dinner Theater, Des Moines, 1979-80; lighting designer various projects. Mem. Assn. Coll., Univ. and Community Arts Adminstrs., Internat. Alliance Theatrical Stage Employees 67 (stagehand), Gamma Gamma. Office: Des Moines Ballet 4333 Park Ave Des Moines IA 50321

MCEUEN, EVERETT RANDAL, safety engineer; b. Marion, Ky., June 18, 1936; s. James Everett and Lorene Agnes (Fritts) McE.; m. Sharon Lee Marshall, June 20, 1959; children—Scott, Shari, Shawn, Patrick. Laborer, warehouse supr., steel inspector/supr. U.S. Steel Co., Gary, Ind., 1955-74, safety engr., 1974-84; safety engr. P.C.L. Constrn., Denver, 1984—. Pres. bd. dirs. Hobart Swin and Play Ctr., Ind., 1970, Sch. City of Hobart, 1979—; bd. dirs. Selective Service, Hobart, 1981—. Served with U.S. Army, 1958-64. Democrat. Presbyterian. Lodge: Masons. Avocation: Camping. Home: 1419 1st Pl Hobart IN 46342 Office: PCL Constrn 359 N Clark Chicago IL 60610

MCEVOY, WILLIAM MICHAEL, pharmacist; b. Davenport, Iowa, June 10, 1952; s. William Ernest and Margaret Elizabeth (Tigue) McE.; m. Patricia Sue Low, July 27, 1980. B.S. in Pharmacy, U. Iowa, 1976. Registered pharmacist, Iowa, Ill. Staff pharmacist Glenbrook Hosp., Glenview, Ill., 1979—, HPI Hosp. Pharmacies, Chgo., 1976-79. Mem. Am. Soc. Hosp. Pharmacists, Ill. Council Hosp. Pharmacists, No. Ill. Soc. Hosp. Pharmacists. Roman Catholic. Lodge: Masons. Avocations: photography; computer programming. Home: 11 A Dundee Quarter Unit 107 Palatine IL 60074 Office: Glenbrook Hosp 2100 Pfingsten Rd Glenview IL 60025

MCEWEN, BOB, Congressman; b. Hillsboro, Ohio, Jan. 12, 1950; B.B.A. in Econs., U. Miami, 1972; m. Liz McEwen, 1976; children—Meridith Evans, Jonathan David, Robert Winston, Elizabeth Morgan. Vice pres. Boebinger, Inc.; mem. 97-99th Congresses from 6th Ohio Dist.; mem. Ohio Ho. of Reps., 1974-80. Mem. Farm Bur., Gideons, Grange, Jaycees, Sigma Chi. Republican. Clubs: Optimist, Rotary. Address: Room 329 Cannon House Office Bldg Washington DC 20515

MCEWEN, MILDRED K. BROWN, data processing co. consultant; b. St. Croix Falls, Wis., June 24, 1911; B.A., Met. U., Mpls., 1978; M.A. in Edn., Villanova U., 1984. Local dir. Camden and Union Counties (N.J.), Girl Scouts U.S.A., regional trainer, Minn., S.D., N.D., 1932-42; retail buyer Hahne & Co., Newark, 1942-47; occupations adv. Pa. Hosp., Phila., 1947-52, coordinator devel., 1966-67, mgr. Frigate Book Shops, Phila., 1952-53; prin. sec. dept. phys. medicine U. Minn., Mpls., 1954-55; dir. exec. placement Lit Brothers Co., Phila., 1955-65; dir. manpower edn. and tng. Twin City Hosp. Assn., Mpls., 1967-72; coordinator Richmond Area (Va.) Va. Regional Med. Program, 1972-74; ednl. developer Control Data Corp., Arden Hills, Minn., 1974-77, adminstr. tng. human resources div., 1977-78, adminstr. field ops. div., 1978-79, mgr. courseware implementation U.S. Learning Center Network, 1979-82, cons., facilitator, 1982—; v.p., treas. DMB Specialists, Inc., cons. firm. Water safety instr. ARC, 1937-47; capt., Cancer Assn. Campaign, 1950-60; mem. task force clin. service for health manpower Health Manpower Commn., Washington, 1972-73; mem. prodn. com. theatre group Stagecrafters of Chestnut Hill. Mem. Am. Soc. Tng. and Devel., Am. Soc. Health, Manpower, Tng. and Edn., AAUW. Club: Tarpon (Control Data Pres.'s award 1978). Editor, chief scriptwriter Taped Health Info. Service, 1970-72. Mpls. city champion women's archery. Home: 200 N Wynnewood Ave Wynnewood PA 19096 Office: Control Data Corp 8100 34th Ave S Minneapolis MN 55440

MCFADDEN, JOSEPH MICHAEL, university president; b. Joliet, Ill., Feb. 12, 1932; s. Francis McF.; m. Norma Mae Cardwell, Oct. 11, 1958; children—Timothy, Colleen, Jon. B.A., Lewis Coll., 1954; M.A., U. Chgo., 1961; Ph.D., No. Ill. U., 1968. Mem. staff history dept., chmn. dept., dean coll. Lewis Coll., 1960-70; dean Sch. Natural and Social Scis. Kearney State Coll. (Nebr.), 1970-74; dean Sch. Social and Behavioral Scis. Slippery Rock State Coll. (Pa.), 1974-77; pres. No. State Coll. (S.D.), 1977-82; pres. U. S.D., 1982—. Served to lt. USNR, 1954-56. Mem. Phi Beta Kappa. Roman Catholic. Office: U SD Vermillion SD 57069

MCFADIN, ROBERT J., heating and cooling systems company executive. Pres., dir. Marley Co., Mission Woods, Kans. Office: Marley Co 1900 Johson Dr Mission Woods KS 66205*

MCFARLAND, DAVID E., university provost; b. Enid, Okla., Sept. 25, 1938; s. Eugene James McF. and Lydia May (Catlin) Lawson; m. Marcia Ruth Lake, Nov. 27, 1958 (div. 1978); children—Jennifer, Jeffrey, Jon, Julie; m., Susan Kaye Siler, Mar. 3, 1979; 1 child, Matthew Chapple. B.S., Wichita State U., 1961, M.S., 1964; Ph.D., U. Kans., 1967. Stress analysis engr. Boeing Co., Wichita, Kans., 1957-64; instr. U. Kans., Lawrence, 1964-67; asst. v.p., dean Wichita State U., 1967-81; dean. sch. tech., Pittsburgh State U., Kans., 1981-85; provost, v.p. acad. affairs Central Missouri State U., 1985—. Author: Mechanics of Materials, 1977; Analysis of Plates, 1972. Contbr. articles to tech. jours. Vice pres. Mid-Am., Inc., Parsons, Kans., 1984; active Pittsburg United Way, YMCA. Mem. Am. Assn. of Higher Edn., Am. Soc. of Engring. Edn., Soc. of Mech. Engrs. Republican. Methodist. Home: Warrensburg MO 64093 Office: Central Missouri State U Warrensburg MO 64093

MCFARLAND, KAY ELEANOR, state justice Kans.; b. Coffeyville, Kans., July 20, 1935; d. Kenneth W. and Margaret E. (Thrall) McF.; B.A. magna cum laude, Washburn U., Topeka, 1957, J.D., 1964. Admitted to Kans. bar, 1964; pvt. practice, Topeka, 1964-71; probate and juvenile judge Shawnee County, Topeka, 1971-73; dist. judge, Topeka, 1973-77; justice Kans. Supreme Ct., 1977—; owner, operator Quilts by Kay McFarland, Topeka, 1961-64. Mem. ABA, Kans., Topeka bar assns. Office: Supreme Ct Kansas State House Topeka KS 66612*

MCFARLAND, MICHAEL CLARK, geologist; b. St. Louis, Oct. 21, 1948; s. Clark Charles and Elvira Antoinette (Toni) McF.; m. Vicki Lynn Dosing, Apr. 17, 1971; children—Stephen Michael, Shannon Victoria. Student Florissant Valley Community Coll., 1967-69; B.S. in Geology and Geophysics, U. Mo.-Rolla, 1978. Geologist, dept. natural resources Div. Geology State of Mo., Rolla, 1979-85. Baseball coach Optimists Club, Rolla, 1979-85; vol. Spl. Olympics, Rolla, 1984. Mem. Am. Assn. Petroleum Geologists, Geol. Soc. of Am., AAAS. Avocations: team sports, audiophile. Home: 1019 W 14th St Rolla MO 65401 Office: Division of Geology 111 Fairgrounds Rd Rolla MO 65401

MCFARLAND, PAUL GEREN, educational administrator; b. Victoria, Tex., Oct. 7, 1942; s. Drew Pate and Reba Mary (Wallace) McF.; m. Sara Stuckey, Aug. 10, 1974. B.A., Vanderbilt U., 1964; M.B.A., U. N.C., 1967. Aerospace technologist NASA, Hampton, Va., 1964-65; aerospace engr. AVCO Corp., Nashville, 1965-67; mktg. rep. IBM, Nashville, 1967-71, XEROX, Nashville, 1971-74; asst. v.p. Vanderbilt U. Med. Ctr., Nashville, 1974-78; v.p. health affairs Tulane U., New Orleans, 1978-80, v.p. bus. and fin., 1980-81; v.p. fin. Loyola U., Chgo., 1981—. Served with USAF, 1960-62. Mem. Hosp. Fin. Mgmt. Assn., Nat. Assn. Coll. and Univ. Bus. Officers. Republican. Presbyterian. Avocations: golf, boating, sports. Office: Loyola U Chgo 2160 S 1st Ave Maywood IL 60153

MCFARLAND, ROBERT HAROLD, physicist, educator, researcher; b. Severy, Kans., Jan. 10, 1918; s. Robert Eugene and Georgia Ellen (Simpson) McF.; m. Twilah Mae Seefeld, Aug. 28, 1940; children—Robert Alan, Rodney Jon. B.S., B.A., Kans. State Tchrs. Coll., Emporia, 1940; Ph.M., U. Wis.-Madison, 1943, Ph.D., 1947. Tchr. sci., coach Chase High Sch., Kans., 1940-41; instr. Navy Radio Sch. U. Wis., Madison, 1943-44; sr. engr. Sylvania Elec. Corp., Salem, Mass., 1944-46; mem. faculty Kans. State U., Manhattan, 1947-60, prof. physics, 1954-60, dir. Nuclear Labs., 1958-60; physicist U. Calif. Lawrence Radiation Lab., Livermore, 1960-69; dean grad. sch. U. Mo., Rolla, 1969-79, dir. instl. analysis and planning, 1979-82, prof. physics, 1969-85, prof. emeritus, 1985—; acting v.p. for acad. affairs U. Mo. System, Columbia, 1974-75; vis. prof. U. Calif., Berkeley, 1980-81; intergovernmental personnel act appointee U.S. Dept. Energy, Germantown, Md., 1982-84; cons. in field. Contbr. articles to profl. jours. Patentee in field. Active Boy Scouts Am., 1952—, mem. exec. bd. San Francisco Bay Area council, 1964-68; chmn. Livermore Library Bond Dr., 1964. Recipient Community Service award C. of C. Livermore, 1965; Silver Beaver award Boy Scouts Am., 1968; Disting. Alumnus award Kans. State Tchrs. Coll., 1969; Mendenhall fellow U. Wis., 1943; Wis. Alumni Research Found. fellow, 1946-47; grantee in field. Fellow Am. Phys. Soc., AAAS; mem AAUP (chpt. pres. 1956-57), Mo. Acad. Scis., Sigma Xi, Phi Kappa Phi, Lambda Delta Lambda, Xi Phi, Kappa Mu Epsilon, Kappa Delta Pi, Pi Mu Epsilon, Gamma Sigma Delta. Club: Kiwanis Internat. (lt. gov. Mo.-Ark. dist. 1984-85). Home: 309 Christy Dr Rolla MO 65401 Office: Dept Physics Univ Missouri Rolla MO 65401

MCFARLANE, DORIS JEAN, educator; b. Eau Claire, Wis., July 10, 1943; d. Phillis Marie (Petrick) McFarlane May. B.S., Wis. State U., 1965; M.S., U. Wis.-LaCrosse, 1970. Tchr. pub. schs., Oconomowoc, Wis., 1965-68, dept. head, 1967-68; tchr. pub. schs., Watertown, Wis., 1969—, varsity head tennis coach, 1971—, varsity head softball coach, 1976—; tennis instr. City of Eau Claire, 1963-72. Mem. choir Our Saviors Luth. Ch., Oconomowoc, 1966—. U. Wis. fellow, 1968; winner Yard of Month award Oconomowoc Women's Club, 1983; named Coach of Yr., 1985; numerous coaching championships, 1970—. Mem. Wis. Edn. Assn., So. Wis. Edn. Assn., NEA, Wis. Fedn. Coaches, United Lakewood Educators, Delta Psi Kappa. Lutheran. Office: Riverside Jr High Sch 131 Hall St Watertown WI 53094

MC GADY, DONALD LAWRENCE, elec. engr.; b. Chgo., July 22, 1947; s. David Lawrence and Irene Veronica (O'Connor) McG.; B.S. in Elec. Engring., Chgo. Tech. Coll., 1974; m. Joan May Bachman, Sept. 5, 1970; children—Jody Katherine, Donald Lawrence Carlson, Noel Veronica-Clare, Ryan David. Elec. supr. Mercy Hosp. and Med. Center, Chgo., 1969-73, mng. elec. engr., 1973-76, asst. dir. engring., 1976-78; asst. dir. engring. Ill. Masonic Med. Center, Chgo., 1978-80, dir. engring., 1980—. Mem. IEEE, Bio-med. Engring. Group, Industry Application Soc., Elec. Maint. Engrs., Ill. Fire Chiefs Assn., Internat. Assn. Elec. Inspectors, Am. Soc. for Hosp. Engring. of Am. Hosp. Assn., Kappa Sigma Kappa. Roman Catholic. Inventor in field of computerized monitoring, data logging and control system for hosp. sterilization equipment. Home: 7827 Pine Pkwy Darien IL 60559 Office: 836 W Wellington Chicago IL 60657

MCGAHAN, JAMES EUGENE, educator; b. Wallace, Nebr., Feb. 8, 1944; s. William Conrad and Mildred Marie (Nelson) McG.; m. Martha Ida Willhoft, Dec. 28, 1966; children—Ellen Jane, Steven John. B.S., Kearney State Coll., 1966; M.S., Emporia State U., 1971; Ed.D., U. No. Colo., 1978. Cert. tchr., Nebr. Phys. sci. tchr. Central City Pub. Schs., Nebr., 1966-68; physics, chemistry tchr. Northwest High Sch., Grand Island, Nebr., 1968-75, tchr. physics, chemistry, computers, 1977—; sci. cons. Nebr. Dept. Edn., Lincoln, 1976; peer reviewer Nebr. Profl. Practices Commn., Lincoln, 1980—. Precinct capt. Hall County Democratic party, 1980-82; del. county Dem. convs., 1980, 84; del. Nebr. Dem. Conv., 1984; bd. dirs. Grand Island 2M Coordinating Council; commr. Profl. Rights, Relations and Responsibilities Commn., Lincoln, 1984—. Named Outstanding Young Educator, Grand Island Jr. C. of C., 1976, Disting. Educator, U. Nebr., Omaha, 1984, Outstanding Chemistry Tchr., Nebr. sect. Am. Chem. Soc., 1984. Mem. Greater Nebr. Assn. Sci. Tchrs. (bd. dirs.), Nat. Sci. Tchrs. Assn., Nebr. Assn. Ednl. Data Systems (bd. dirs., Computer Tchr. of Yr. 1984), NEA, Nebr. Edn. Assn. (commr. 1984-86), Northwest Edn. Assn. (polit. action chmn. 1980—). Roman Catholic. Avocations: gardening; photography; music; computers. Home: 1205 N Howard Ave Grand Island NE 68803 Office: Northwest High Sch 2710 North Rd Grand Island NE 68803

MC GARR, FRANK J., federal judge; b. 1921; A.B., J.D., Loyola U., Chgo. Admitted to Ill. bar, 1950; now chief judge U.S. Dist. Ct. for No. Ill. Office: US Dist Ct US Courthouse 219 S Dearborn St Chicago IL 60604*

MCGARRY, KEVIN VINCENT, newspaper company executive; b. Bayside, N.Y., May 18, 1929; s. John James and Julia (McCarthy) McG.; m. Anne Pritchard, Sept. 15, 1956; children—Elizabeth Moore, John Manion, Kevin Vincent, Peter Thomas, Anne Julia. B.S., Fordham U., 1952; postgrad. Wharton Sch., U. Pa., 1954-55. With IBM, 1955-56, Honeywell Corp., 1956-59; advt. mgr. Wall St. Jour., Mpls., 1959-67; advt. mgr. Nat. Observer, Detroit, 1967-73; assoc. Midwest advt. mgr. Wall St. Jour., Chgo., 1973-78; Midwest advt. mgr. Wall St. Jour., Chgo., 1978—. Served to 1st lt., arty. AUS, 1952-54. Mem. Detroit Advt. Assn., Am. Mktg. Assn., Delta Sigma. Republican. Roman Catholic. Clubs: Chgo. Advertising, AdCraft, Tavern (Chgo.); Westmoreland Country (Wilmette, Ill.); University (Detroit).

MCGARRY, ROBERT GEORGE, safety engineer; b. Mpls., Jan. 4, 1917; s. Emmett Frank and Ethel Florence (Bryant) McG.; m. Evelynne Anne Kubik, Oct. 28, 1968; children—Mary Kathleen, Nancy Margaret, Susan Elaine, Kevin Robert. B.S. in Indsl. Engring., U. Minn., 1939; M.S. in Safety Engring., Ga. Inst. Tech., 1947. Sr. safety engr. U.S. Fidelity & Guaranty Co., Atlanta, Mpls., 1950-63; Bechtel Corp., San Francisco, 1963-77; corp. safety engr. Burns & McDonnell Engrs., Cons., Kansas City, Mo., 1977-82; con. safety engr., Lee's Summit, Mo., 1982—; adj. instr. safety engring. Sch. Mgmt. Devel., U. Mo., Kansas City. Served with USN, 1942-46. Registered profl. engr., Calif.; cert. safety profl. Recipient Minn. Gov.'s Outstanding Safety Achievement award, 1969. Mem. Am. Soc. Safety Engrs. (chmn. engring. com.), Vets. of Safety Internat. (dir.-at-large), Nat. Soc. Profl. Engrs., Mo. Soc. Profl. Engrs., Profl. Engrs. in Pvt. Practice, Am. Arbitration Assn. (arbitrator. Lodges: Masons, Shriners. Home and Office: 818 E Langsford Rd #102 Lees Summit MO 64063

MC GARY, THOMAS HUGH, lawyer; b. Milburn, Ky., Mar. 6, 1938; s. Ollie James and Pauline Elizabeth (Tackett) McG.; A.B., Elmhurst Coll., 1961; J.D., U. Chgo., 1964; m. Madalyn Maxwell, July 4, 1968. Admitted to Ill. bar, 1964; asst. atty. gen. State of Ill., 1965-67, supr. consumer credit, 1967-71; ind. practice law, Springfield, Ill., 1971—; v.p., dir. Citizens Bank of Edinburg (Ill.), 1971—, Bank of Kenney (Ill.), 1977—, Bank of Springfield; instr. Lincolnland Coll., 1970-73; asso. prof. med. humanities So. Ill. U. Sch. Medicine. Mem. Ill. Spl. Com. on Uniform Credit Code, Springfield Art Assn., Springfield Symphony Assn.; mem. Springfield Election Commn.; mem. Ill. Adv. Commn. on Group Ins.; bd. dirs. Central Ill. Youth Services Bur.; vestryman St. Paul's Cathedral. Mem. Am., Ill., Sangamon County bar assns., Am. Judicature Soc., 3d House, Sangamon County Hist. Assn., Chgo. Council on Fgn. Relations, Chaine de Rotisseurs. Democrat. Clubs: Sangamo (Springfield); Oakcrest Country. Home: 2018 Briarcliff Dr Springfield IL 62704 Office: 600 S 4th St Springfield IL 62703

MCGEE, GEORGE WILLIAM, farmer; b. Logan County, Ill., Apr. 12, 1921; s. William Roy and Maurine Ellen (Lucas) McG.; student Bradley Poly. Inst., 1939-40; m. Gloria Faye Lewis, Sept. 7, 1947 (dec. May 1982); children—Mark William, Sara Faye. Farmer, Mt. Pulaski, Ill., 1940—; part-owner, operator cash grain farm, Mt. Pulaski, 1953—; dir. 1st Nat. Bank of Mt. Pulaski. Mem. Mt. Pulaski Sch. Bd., 1958-67, pres., 1965-66; mem. Logan County Extension Council, 1978-80. Mem. Logan County Farm Bur. (dir. 1969-78), Land of Lincoln Soybean Assn., Ill. Corn Growers Assn. Republican. Clubs: Masons, Shriners. Home and office: Route 2 Mount Pulaski IL 62548

MCGEE, ROBERT DAVID, wholesale beer company executive; b. Elmhurst, Ill., Sept. 15, 1948; s. Harry Francis and Winifred Virginia (Schroeder) McG.; m. Kathy Lyn Kassnel, Aug. 30, 1969; children—Ryan David, Amanda Kay. B.S., No. Ill. U., 1970. C.P.A., Ill. Asst. mgr. payroll Brand Insulations, Chgo., 1974-76; mgr. data processing Quad County Distbg. Co., Geneva, Ill., 1976-77, contoller, 1977-78, v.p. adminstrn., St. Charles, Ill., 1978—. Served with USCGR, 1970-74. Republican. Congregationalist (treas. 1979-83, moderator-elect 1983). Office: Quad County Distbg Co Inc 248 N Randall Rd Saint Charles IL 60174

MCGEHEE, H. COLEMAN, JR., clergyman. Bishop, Episcopal Ch., Detroit. Office: 4800 Woodward Ave Detroit MI 48201*

MCGEOUGH, ROBERT SAUNDERS, lawyer; b. Chgo., Aug. 30, 1930; s. Edward James and Florence Isabelle (Saunders) McG.; m. Janet James, Nov. 24, 1961; children—Maureen, Michael, Molly. A.B., Duke U., 1952; J.D., U. Mich., 1959. Assoc. Hoppe, Frey, Hewitt & Milligan, Warren, Ohio, 1965-70, ptnr., 1970—; dir. First Fed. Savs. and Loan Assn., Warren. State trustee Jaycees, Warren, 1963; pres. Warren Exchange Club, 1965; pres. Children's Rehab. Ctr. Found., Warren, 1979, trustee, 1983—. Served to lt. USN, 1952-56. Recipient award of merit Ohio Legal Ctr. Inst., 1978. Mem. ABA. Republican. Home: 3264 Cresent Dr NE Warren OH 44483 Office: Hoppe Frey Hewitt & Milligan 500 Second Nat Tower Warren OH 44481

MCGILL, BOB, technical services company executive; b. Smackover, Ark., Jan. 9, 1930; s. Willie Floyd and Minnie Ola (Anders) McG.; m. Karen Sue Schluens, June 11, 1976; children—Matt, Clay. B.A., U. Tex., Austin, 1959; M.A., So. Meth. U., 1972. Mgr. contracts Baifield Industries, Carrollton, Tex., 1960-65; cons. Comprehensive Designers, Atlanta, 1965-68; dir. purchasing Royal Coach Hotels, Dallas, 1968-70, RSR Corp., Dallas, 1970-74; cons. Intercon Mgmt. Systems, Tulsa, also Baton Rouge, 1975-80; pres. Sunbelt Tech. Services, Mt. Vernon, Mo., 1980—; cons. Skytop Brewster, Houston, 1976. Served with AUS, 1946-52. Mem. Nat. Assn. Purchasing Mgrs., Am. Nuclear Soc., Nat. Tech. Services Assn. Republican. Lodge: Rotary. Office: Sunbelt Tech Services Inc PO Box 448 South Side of Sq Mount Vernon MO 65712

MCGILL, KATHLEEN ANN, human resources manager; b. Columbus, Ohio, Oct. 16, 1952; d. James Dawn and Madolin Rose (Gardner) McG.; B.Sc. in Biology-Chemistry, Bowling Green State U., 1974; postgrad. Western State Coll., 1974-75, U. Colo., 1977-79, Capital U., Columbus 1981—. Tutor biology Bowling Green State U. 1971-74; grad. teaching asst. Western State Coll. 1974-75; sales agt., office mgr. Heritage Mt. Homes, Inc., Woodland Park, Colo. 1976-80; mgr. human resources United McGill Corp., Inc., Columbus, Ohio, 1980—. Docent Columbus Zoo, 1982—. Lic. real estate salesperson, Colo. Mem. Am. Soc. Personnel Adminstrs., Central Ohio Personnel Assn., Midwest Coll. Placement Council, Colo. Assn. Cert. Closers, Am. Compensation Assn., Tri-Beta, Delta Phi Alpha. Republican. Clubs: Alaskan Malamute Am., Southwestern Ohio Alaskan Malamute Fanciers Assn., Nat. Audubon Soc., Columbus Audubon Soc. Home: 6725 Lithopolis-Winchester Canal Winchester OH 43110 Office: 1 Mission Park PO Box 7 Groveport OH 43125

MCGILLEN, TIMOTHY HEATON, optometrist, electrical engineer; b. Chgo., Nov. 5, 1953; s. Vincent Patrick and Charlotte (Heaton) McG.; m. Brenda Ann Simons, Sept. 29, 1979. Assoc. B.S. in Elec. Engring. Tech., Purdue U., 1973; B.S. in Optometry, Ind. U., 1976, O.D., 1977. Gen. practice optometry South Holland, Ill., 1977-78, Merrillville, Ind., 1979—; staff optometrist Ill. Coll. Optometry, Chgo., 1977-78; ptnr. Greenspan Assocs., Harvey, Ill., 1978-79. Treas. Pine Island Community Assn., Schererville, Ind., 1982, v.p., 1983, pres., 1984. Mem. Merrillville C. of C. Avocations: amateur radio, astronomy, scuba diving, automobile restoration, windsurfing.

MCGILLEY, MARY JANET, college president, nun; b. Kansas City, Mo., Dec. 4, 1924; d. James P. and Peg (Ryan) McG. B.A., St. Mary Coll., 1945; M.A., Boston Coll., 1951; Ph.D., Fordham U., 1956; postgrad. U. Notre Dame, 1960, Columbia U., 1964. Joined Sisters of Charity of Leavenworth, Roman Catholic Ch., 1946; social worker Catholic Welfare Bur., Kansas City, Mo., 1945-46; tchr. Hayden High Sch., Topeka, 1948-50, Billings Central High Sch., Mont., 1951-53; English faculty St. Mary Coll., Leavenworth, 1956-64, pres. coll., 1964—; Archdiocese bicentennial coordinator, 1974-75; commr. North Central Assn. Colls. and Schs. Commn. on Higher Edn., 1980—, exec. bd., 1985—, v.p. 1985—; Roman Cath. denom. del. Nat. Congress on Ch.-Related Colls. and Univs., 1979; bd. dirs. Kansas City Regional Council for Higher Edn., 1964—, sec. exec. com., 1968-70, 84-85, chmn. acad. affairs com., 1968-72, sec.-treas. exec. com., 1984-85. Contbr. poetry, articles, short stories, addresses to nat. jours., lit. mags. Bd. dirs. United Way of Leavenworth, 1966-85; mem. Leavenworth Mayor's Citizens Adv. Com., 1967-72, Leavenworth Planning Council, 1977-78. Recipient Disting. Service award Baker U., 1981; Danforth fellow ACE Pres.'s Inst., 1966. Mem. Nat. Assn. Ind. Colls. and Univs. (bd. dirs. 1982-85), Assn. Am. Colls. (mem. commn. on liberal learning 1970-73, commn. on curriculum and faculty devel. 1979-82), Am. Council on Edn. (commn. on women in higher edn. 1980-83), Kans. Ind. Coll. Assn. (treas. 1982-84, v.p. 1984-85, pres. 1985-86), Kans. Ind. Coll. Fund dir., pres. 1972-74), Nat. Council Tchrs. English, Am. Assn. Higher Edn., AAUW, St. Mary Alumnae Assn. (hon. pres. 1964—, Ancilla award 1969), Leavenworth C. of C. (dir. 1983-85), Delta Epsilon Sigma. Home and Office: Office of Pres Saint Mary College Leavenworth KS 66048

MCGILLIVRAY, DONALD DEAN, seed company executive, agronomist; b. Muscatine, Iowa, Aug. 28, 1928; s. Walter C. and Pearl E. (Potter) M.; m. Betty J. Anderson, June 24, 1951; children—Ann E., Jean M. B.S. in Agronomy, Iowa State U., 1950. Asst. mgr. Iowa, Minn., Wis. sect. Funk Seeds Internat., Belle Plaine, Iowa, 1965-69, mgr., 1969-70, mgr. hybrid corn ops., Bloomington, Ill., 1970-75, v.p. ops., 1976-82, pres., 1982—; dir. U.S. Feed Grains Council, Washington, D.C., 1984—. Bd. dirs. Ill. Agrl. Leadership Found., Macomb, Ill., 1985. Served to sgt. U.S. Army, 1951-53, Mem. Am. Seed Trade Assn. (bd. dirs. 1978-84, div. chmn. 1978-79), Am. Seed Research Found. (bd. dirs. 1982-85, pres. 1984-85), McLean County C. of C. (com. mem. 1984). Lodge: Masons. Office: Funk Seeds Internat PO Box 2911 Bloomington IL 61701

MCGIMPSEY, EARL RAYNOR, lawyer; b. Cleve., Sept. 6, 1941; s. John Earle and Muriel Naomi (Heasley) McG.; m. Susan Lamar Webster, Apr. 25, 1964; children—David, Susanna, Kathleen. B.A., Wabash Coll., 1963; J.D., U. Washington, 1971. Bar: Ohio 1982. Law clk. to justice Wash. Supreme Ct., Olympia, 1971-72; asst. atty. gen. State of Wash., Olympia, 1972-81; ptnr. Carpenter & Paffenbarger, Norwalk, Ohio, 1981—. Editor Jour. Wash. Law Rev., 1970-71. Bd. dirs., pres. Puget Sound Legal Services Corp., Tacoma, 1976-81; mem. dist. com. Firelands council Boy Scouts Am., Norwalk, 1982—; bd. dir. Huron County Alcoholism Ctr., Norwalk, 1984—, Norwalk City Library Bd., 1984—. Recipient Dist. Merit award Boy Scouts Am., 1984. Mem. ABA, Ohio Bar Assn., Huron and Erie Counties Bar Assn. (treas. 1983-84), Ohio Assn. Civil Trial Attys., Def. Research Inst., Order of Coif. Episcopalian. Lodge: Kiwanis (chmn. fund raising Norwalk 1983—). Avocations: camping; fishing; woodworking. Home: 17 Milan Manor Dr Milan OH 44846 Office: Carpenter Paffenbarger & McGimpsey PO Box 737 Norwalk OH 44857

MCGINLEY, DONALD FRANCIS, state official; b. Keystone, Nebr., June 30, 1920; s. George and Margaret Ellen (Thalken) McG.; m. Nancy Halligan Childs, May, 1977. A.B., Notre Dame U., 1942; J.D., Georgetown U., 1949. Judge, Commn. of Indsl. Relations Nebr., 1976-80; mem. Nebr. Legislature, 1955-59, 63-65; mem. U.S. Ho. of Reps., 1959-60; lt. gov. Nebr., 1983—. Trustee, Mid Plains Community Coll., North Platte, McCook Schs., State Community Coll. System. Served with USAAF, 1943-45. Mem. Am. Legion, VFW. Democrat. Roman Catholic. Clubs: Elks, KC. Office: State Capitol Room 2315 Lincoln NE 68509

MCGINN, DAVID FRANCIS, furniture sales executive; b. New Hampton, Iowa, Sept. 9, 1948; s. Philip Joseph McGinn and Rebecca Jean (Murphy) Ransom; m. Virginia Rae Midness, June 6, 1970; children—Matthew David, Erin Eileen. A.A., Mason City Jr. Coll. (Iowa), 1968; B.S. in Radio and TV, Mankato State Coll. (Minn.), 1970. Salesman, Conwed Corp., Phila., 1970-76, corp. mgmt. trainee, Phila., 1976-77, mktg. research analyst, St. Paul, 1977-78, regional sales mgr., officer interiors, 1978, nat. sales mgr., 1978-82, mktg. mgr., 1982, eastern sales mgr., St. Paul, 1982—. State advisor U.S. Congl. adv. bd., Washington, 1983, 84; coach Mounds View Parks and Recreation Dept. (Minn.), 1981, 82, 83; Leukalpheresis donor ARC, St. Paul, 1981, 82, 83. Recipient Eagle Scout award Boy Scouts Am., 1962, Order of the Arrow, 1963. Mem. Internat. Assn. Platform Assn., Minn. Council for the Gifted and Talented. Republican. Methodist. Club: Arden Hills (Minn.). Office: Conwed Corp 444 Cedar St Saint Paul MN 55164

MCGINNESS, JOYCE NOLLE, computer software company owner, consultant; b. St. Louis, Jan. 15, 1955; d. Ernest W. and Norma (Patton) Nolle; m. David S. McGinness, Nov. 24, 1977. B.S., Drake U., 1976. Store mgr. Jean Nicole Stores, West Des Moines, 1977-78; programmer Computer Applications Team, Des Moines, 1978-79, payroll clk. Corn State Metal Fabrications, 1979-80, analyst, programmer F.A.C.T.S. Data Services, Inc., 1980-83; owner, system analyst McGinness Computer Consulting & Programming, Inc., 1983—. Vol. for Iowa Senate Harkin, 1984. Mem. Assn. System Mgrs., Nat. Assn. Female Execs. Democrat. Clubs: Women's Exchange Breakfast, Metro Womens Network. Avocations: sewing; jogging; camping; traveling. Home and Office: McGinness Computer Consultant & Programming Inc 4118 Cottage Grove Des Moines IA 50311

MC GINNIS, JAMES EDWARD, accountant; b. Oxford, Mass., July 31, 1917; s. John James and Jennie Catherine (Fenner) McG.; A.B., Youngstown (Ohio) Coll., 1950; m. Catherine Irene Cronk, July 12, 1941; children—Barbara McGinnis Cash II, Kathleen, Patricia McGinnis Vavrinak, James Brian, John Edward, Robert Michael. Accountant, W.L. Reali, Pub. Accountant, Youngstown, 1945-50; pvt. practice pub. accounting, Youngstown, 1950-80; office mgr. Patterson Buckeye, Inc., North Lima, Ohio, 1950-80, also dir.; exec. v.p., treas. Patterson Buckeye, Inc., 1980—; dir., gen. mgr., exec. v.p., treas. Wolf Food Distbrs., 1980—; moderator Veteran's Show, Sta. WBBW, Youngstown, 1973-85. Chmn. Vets. Day Parade, Youngstown, 1970—, chmn. Meml. Day parade, 1971—; chmn. Mahoning County (Ohio) Grave Decorating Com., 1969-85, mem. Civic Day Com., 1970—; Ohio Bicentennial Com., 1974-75, Mahoning County Soldiers and Sailors Relief Commn., 1980-86; mem. legis. com. Ohio Assn. of Soldiers Relief Commn., 1982—. Served to sgt. AUS, 1940-45; PTO. C.P.A., Ohio Mem. Amvets (past comdr.), V.F.W., 37th Div. Vets. Assn., D.A.V., United Vets. Council of Mahoning County (comdr. 1972, Vet. of Yr. award 1982), Nat. Soc. Pub. Accts., Public Accountants Soc. Ohio, Mahoning Valley Gaelic Soc., Irish Nat. Caucus, Irish Am. Cultural Inst., Youngstown U. Alumni Assn., Internat. Platform Assn., Ancient Order Hibernians. Sigma Kappa Phi. Roman Catholic. K.C. (3 deg.). Home: 3821 Frederick St Youngstown OH 44515 Office: 550 W Pine Lake Rd North Lima OH 44452

MC GIVERIN, ARTHUR A., justice Supreme Court Iowa; b. Iowa City, Nov. 10, 1928; s. Joseph J. and Mary B. McG.; B.S.C. with high honors, U. Iowa, 1951, J.D., 1956; m. Mary Joan McGiverin, Apr. 20, 1951; children—Teresa, Thomas, Bruce, Nancy. Admitted to Iowa bar, 1956; practice law, Ottumwa, Iowa, 1956; alt. mcpl. judge, Ottumwa, 1960-65; judge Iowa Dist. Ct. 8th Jud. Dist., 1965-78; assoc. justice Iowa Supreme Ct., Des Moines, 1978—. Mem. Am. Law Inst. Served to 1st lt. U.S. Army, 1946-48, 51-53. Mem. Iowa Bar Assn. Roman Catholic. Office: Supreme Ct of Iowa Capitol Bldg 10th and Grand Des Moines IA 50319*

MCGIVNEY, GLEN PERRY, prosthodontist, consultant; b. Dillon, Mont., Aug. 3, 1937; s. Lawrence Bowen and Leota Victoria (Hughes) McG.; m. Lydia Lee Capettini, Mar. 23, 1963; children—Megan, Gregory, Erin. B.S., Mont. State U., 1958; D.D.S., Northwestern U., 1962, postgrad. cert in prosthetic dentistry, 1967. Diplomate Am. Bd. of Prosthodontics, 1970. Gen. practice medicine, Salmon, Ida., 1962, 1966—; asst. prof. Northwestern U. Dental Sch., Chgo., 1966-70; acting chmn. dept. prosthodontics, 1969-71; assoc. prof. of prosthodontics, Marquette U. Sch. of Dentistry, Milw., 1971-75, chmn. dept. removable prosthodontics, 1974—, prof. prosthodontics, 1975—; cons. Downey VA Hosp., Downey, Ill., 1968-80. Author: (with others) McCracken's Removable Partial Prosthodontics, 1984; lectr.-clinician on prosthetic dentistry Marquette U. Dental Sch., 1971—. Bd. dirs. Y.M.C.A., Oconomowoc, Wis., 1976-82. Served to lt. USN, 1962-69. Fellow Am. Coll. of Dentists, Acad. of Denture Prosthetics; mem. ADA, Am. Soc. of Geriatric Dentistry, Am. Coll. of Prosthodontics, Midwest Acad. of Prosthodontics, Am. Assn. of Dental Schs., Fedn. of Prosthodontics Org., Omiaron Kappa Upsilon. Republican. Episcopalian. Clubs: Oconomowoc Golf, Bear Paw Affiliate of Inter-Collegiate Knights. Avocations: sports. Office: 5726 W National West Allis WI 53219

MCGLONE, MARY ELLEN, business school official, columnist, fashion consultant; b. Cin., Jan. 2, 1943; d. Morris S. and Rose Caroline (Fremmel) Hermann; m. Samuel D. McGlone, Nov. 4, 1967; children—Michael, Molly, Michelle. B.A., Barat Coll., 1964; postgrad. U. Minn., Mankato State U., Troy State U., Northeastern Ill. State U. Freelance fashion coordinator, cons., model, 1967—; asst. dir. fashion merchandising and self-improvement Lowthian Coll. (formerly Patricia Stevens Sch.), Mpls., 1968-70; mgr. Patricia Stevens Modeling Agy., Mpls., 1970; instr., dir. fashion merchandising ITT-Minn. Sch. Bus., Mpls., 1971-81, asst. dir. placement, 1981-82, student services coordinator, 1982—; columnist Skyway News, Mpls., 1978—; originator Reach Out & Touch Me, ann. fashion for blind and handicapped. Bd. dirs. Minn. Heart Assn., 1970-71; publicity chmn. cookie drive Girl Scouts U.S.A., 1983. Barat scholar, 1960-64; Ill. State scholar, 1960-64; NDEA fellow, 1965. Mem. Minn. Press Club, Fashion Group (dir., program chmn. 1982-83, past treas.), Sales and Mktg. Execs. Club: N.W. Pilots Wives (past pres.). Author: (with others) The Person You Are, 1978, 2d edit., 1985; (with Mayer) Kids' Chic, 1984; columnist Entourage, Rapport; guest editor MSB News, Minn. Fashion Group News, Placement World; contbr. articles to Woman's World, Creative Service, WITT's. Home: 4457 Gaywood Dr Minnetonka MN 55343 Office: ITT-Minn Sch Bus 11 S 5th St Minneapolis MN 55402

MCGOLDRICK, JAMES EDWARD, historian, educator; b. Phila., Jan. 5, 1936; s. James Edward and Bernardine Estelle (Glenn) McG. B.S., Temple U., 1961, M.A., 1964; Ph.D., W.Va. U., 1974. Asst. prof. history John Brown U., Siloam Springs, Ark., 1966-70; instr. W.Va. U., Morgantown, 1970-73; prof. Cedarville Coll., Ohio, 1973—. Author: Luther's English Connection, 1979. Named Faculty Mem. of Yr., Cedarville Coll., 1976. Mem. Am. Soc. Church History, Conf. Brit. Studies, Am. Soc. for Reformation Studies. Avocations: flag collecting, raising cats. Home: Box 601 Cedarville OH 45314 Office: Cedarville Coll Dept History Cedarville OH 45314

MCGONAGLE, JACK WILSON, optometrist; b. New Lexington, Ohio, Nov. 12, 1923; s. Urban S. and Hazel (Wilson) McG.; m. Rita S. Steiner, Apr. 17, 1950 (dec. 1983); children—Mike, Pat, Tim, Molly, Kathy; m. Helen L. Grieve, Nov. 25, 1983. Student, Xavier U., Cin., 1941-43, Ohio U., 1946—; O.D., Ill. Coll. Optometry, Chgo., 1949. Practice optometry, Lancaster, Ohio, 1950—. Served with AUS, 1943-46. Mem. Am. Optometric Assn., Ohio Optometric Assn., Lancaster C. of C., Am. Legion. Republican. Roman Catholic. Club: Symposiarchs, Elks. Lodge: KC. Avocations: Golf; tennis; fishing. Office: 404 E Main St Lancaster OH 43130

MCGONIGAL, PEARL, lieutenant governor of Manitoba; b. Melville, Sask., Can., June 10, 1929; d. Fred and Kathryne Kuhlman; ed. in Melville, Sask.; LL.D. (hon.), U. Man.; m. Marvin A. McGonigal, Nov. 3, 1948; 1 dau., Kimberly Jane. Formerly engaged in banking; then mdse. rep.; mem. St. James-Assiniboia (Man.) City Council, 1969-71; mem. Greater Winnipeg (Man.) City Council, 1971-81, chmn. com. on recreation and social services, 1977-79, dep. mayor and chmn. exec. policy com., 1979-81; lt. gov. Man., 1981—. Bd. dirs. Winnipeg Conv. Centre, 1975-77, Red River Exhbn., 1975-81, Rainbow Stage, 1976-81; ex-officio mem. Man. Theatre Centre, 1977-81; mem. Winnipeg Conv. and Visitors Bur., 1973-75, Man. Environ. Council, 1974-76, Man. Aviation Council, 1974-77; mem. selection com. Faculty Dental Hygiene, U. Man., 197-80; bd. mgmt. Winnipeg Home Improvement Program, 1979-81; chmn. adv. com. Sch. Nursing, Grace Gen. Hosp., 1972—; past chmn. St. James-Assiniboia Inter-faith Immigration Council; former mem. vestry St. Andrew's Anglican Ch.; former vol. Lions Manor, Sherbrook Day Centre. Decorated Dame of Grace, Order of St. John; recipient award Dist. 64 Toastmasters, 1974, Winnipeg lodge Elks, 1975, Nat. Humanitarian award B'nai B'rith, 1984, Silver medal Con. Corps Commissionaires, 1984; named hon. col. 735th Communications Regt. Liberal. Club: Winnipeg Winter. Author: Frankly Feminine Cookbook, 1975; weekly columnist Reliance Press Ltd. Newspapers, 1970-81. Home: 10 Kennedy St Winnipeg MB R3C 1S4 Canada Office: Rm 235 Legislative Bldg Winnipeg MB R3C 0V8 Canada

MCGONIGAL, WILLIAM MICHAEL, marketing executive; b. St. Paul, June 27, 1928; s. Thomas Joseph and Marie E. (Maher) McG.; m. Joan Lee Moilanen, Feb. 7, 1959; children—Thomas J., Kevin C., Elizabeth A., Molly K. B.A., Coll. St. Thomas, 1952. Dir. sales and mktg. Donnay Homes, Mpls., 1954-74, 84—; dir. sales and mktg. Skyline, Mpls., 1974-81; dir. condominium mgmt. Community Mgmt. Co., 1981-84; dir. sales and mktg. Developer Services Inc., Mpls., 1981-84. Contbr. articles to profl. jours. Bd. dirs. Bklyn. Hist. Soc., Mpls., 1977—. Served to 1st lt. USAF, 1952-62. Recipient Nat. Idea of Yr. awards Nat. Assn. Home Builders, 1974, 80, named Nat. Sales Mgr. of Yr., 1975. Mem. Community Assns. Inst. (mem. bd., past pres.), Nat. Assn. Home Builders (mem. mktg. com. 1970—, pres. sales and mktg. council), Inst. Residential Mktg. (membership com. 1982—). Roman Catholic. Club: Little People of Am. Avocation: Music. Home: 4806 Howe Ln Minneapolis MN 55429

MCGRAIL, SUSAN KING, travel agency executive, accountant; b. Richmond, Va., Mar. 7, 1952; d. William Jr. and Anne Winn (Gibson) King; m. John Patrick McGrail, Jr., June 2, 1979; 1 child, Katharine Anne. B.B.A., Coll. William and Mary, 1974. C.P.A., Va. Employment counselor Avante Gard of Richmond, Inc., 1970-73; staff acct. Touche Ross & Co., Washington, 1974-75, Richmond, 1975-78; controller Continental Cablevision, Richmond, 1978-81; v.p. fin. Warner Amex Cable Communications, Cin., 1981-85; prin. Travel Agts. Internat., Cin., 1985—; sec., treas. Warner Amex Minority Loan Fund, Cin., 1981-85. Alumni career adviser Coll. William and Mary, Williamsburg, Va., 1982—, fund raiser ann. fund, 1984—. Fellow Am. Inst. C.P.A.s, Va. Soc. C.P.A.s; mem. Women in Cable, Nat. Assn. Female Execs. Republican. Episcopalian. Avocations: scuba diving; snorkeling; reading. Home: 2207 Spinningwheel Ln Cincinnati OH 45244 Office: Travel Agts Internat Montgomery 10778 Montgomery Rd Cincinnati OH 45242

MCGRANE, JAMES JOHN, JR., dentist, educational administrator; b. Balt., July 27, 1948; s. James John McGrane and Jean (Lesczenski) Pfeiffer; m. Cheryl Ann Lapp, May 30, 1981. B.S., Nebr. Wesleyan U., Lincoln, 1970; D.D.S., U. Nebr.-Lincoln, 1974; M.P.H., U. Minn., 1980. Dental officer Royal Dental Hosp., Melbourne, Victoria, Australia, 1974-77; dental dir. Normandale Community Coll., Bloomington, Minn., 1979—. Chmn. Manor Homes of Edina, Minn., 1982. Ak-Sar-Ben Scholor, 1972. Mem. Am. Assn. Pub. Health Dentists, ADA, Minn. Dist. Dental Soc. (chmn. dental health edn. com. 1984), Minn. Dental Assn., Am. Pub. Health Assn. Methodist. Home: 6879 Langford Dr Edina MN 55436 Office: Normandale Community Coll 9700 France Ave S Bloomington MN 55431

MCGRATH, PATRICK JOSEPH, osteopathic physician; b. Milw., Apr. 24, 1948; s. Joseph Eugene and Margaret Anne (Kenny) McG.; m. Nancy Anne Benninghouse, July 10, 1982. B.S. in Biol. Sci., Mich. Technol. U., 1977; D.O., Mich. State U., 1982. Registered profl. engr., Mich. Hwy. engr. State of Wis., 1970-71; intern Lansing Gen. Hosp. (Mich.), 1981-82; gen. practice osteo medicine, East Troy, Wis., 1982-83; family practice resident St. Michael Hosp., Milw., 1984—. Served to lt. USN, 1971-74. Mem. Am. Osteo. Assn., Am. Acad. Family Practice. Roman Catholic.

MCGRATH, PATRICK RICHARD, college dean; b. Ottawa, Ill., May 21, 1944; s. Burdette James and Anita Cecilia (Scherer) McG.; m. Denise Hertz, Nov. 14, 1970; children—Justin Teague, Zachary Choe. A.B in Psychology, U. Ill.-Chgo. Circle, 1969; M.S. in Community Mental Health, Northern Ill. U., 1970; postgrad. U. Alaska-Anchorage, 1971; postdoctoral Norther Ill. U. Adminstr. Psychiatric Halfway Hse., Chgo., 1967-68; asst. adminstr. Adult Day Care Shelter, Chgo., 1968-69; mental health program coordinator U. Alaska-Anchorage, 1971-72; div. chmn. human services U. Bridgeport, Conn., 1972-79; dean health and human services Nat. Coll. of Edn., Evanston, Ill., 1979—; lecturer Cambridge U., England, 1984; cons. NIMH, Rockville, Md., 1984. Bd. dirs. New Trier Township Commn. on Youth, Winnetka, Ill., 1983—. Served to specialist 4 with U.S. Army, 1965-67, Viet Nam. Grantee NIMH, 1972-79, Adminstrn. on Aging, 1975. Mem. Nat. Orgn. of Human Services Educators (v.p. 1982—), Am. Assn. Counseling and Devel.; mid-west rep. Council for Standards in Human Service Edn., 1984—. Democrat. Roman Catholic. Avocation: home remodeling. Home: 1069 Chatfield Rd Winnetka IL 60093 Office: Nat Coll Edn Dept Health and Human Services 2840 Sheridan Rd Evanston IL 60201

MCGRAW, JAMES JOSEPH, JR., lawyer; b. Cin., Sept. 4, 1949; s. James Joseph and Marjorie (Hines) McG.; m. Anne Scheidler, July 1, 1972; children—Carey A., Lauren M., Jennifer M., Courtney S. B.B.A. in Acctg., U. Notre Dame, 1971; J.D., U. Akron, 1974. Bar: Ohio 1974, Ky. 1983, U.S. Dist. Ct. (so. dist.) Ohio 1974, U.S. Ct. Mil. Appeals 1975, U.S. Supreme Ct. 1980. Assoc. Carroll, Bunke, Henkel, Haverkamp & Smith, Cin., 1979-81; rate counsel Cin. Gas & Electric Co., 1981—. Articles editor: Akron Law Rev., 1973-74. Bd. dirs. Hildebrandt for Judge Com., Cin., 1984; pres., chmn. bd. Mt. Lookout Civic Club, Cin., 1982—; bd. advisors Neighborhood Support Program, Cin., 1982-83; chmn. United Way 2750th Air Base Wing, Wright-Patterson AFB, Ohio, 1978. Served as capt. JAG, USAF, 1975-79, USAFR, 1979-82. Recipient award of Yr. U. Notre Dame Alumni Assn., 1983; U. Akron U. Bd. Trustees scholar, 1973-74. Mem. Cin. Bar Assn. (coms. 1979—, participant Vol. Lawyers for Poor Found. 1984—), Ohio State Bar Assn., Fed. Bar Assn., Ky. Bar Assn. Notre Dame Alumni (Cin.) (pres. 1981-82, bd. dirs. 1981—). Republican. Roman Catholic. Avocations: golf; racquetball; tennis. Home: 3321 Mannington Ave Cincinnati OH 45226 Office: Cincinnati Gas and Electric Co Legal Dept 139 E Fourth St Cincinnati OH 45202

MCGRAW, PATRICK ALLAN, lawyer; b. Radford, Va., Aug. 26, 1942; s. Delford Armstrong and Virginia Elizabeth (Ramsey) McG.; m. Martha Jane Schrock, June 22, 1968; children—Katherine Martha, Michael Patrick. A.B., Kenyon Coll., 1963; J.D., Harvard U., 1966. Bar: Ohio 1966; U.S. Dist. Ct. (no. dist.) Ohio 1967, U.S. Ct. Appeals (6th cir.) 1983, U.S. Supreme Ct. 1978. Assoc. Fuller and Henry, Toledo, 1967-72, ptnr., 1972-84; trustee Bell and Beckwith Liquidation, Toledo, 1983—; prin. VR Fin. Services, The Toledo Group, Inc., Toledo, 1985—; adv. coms. to Commnr. Securities, Sec. State of Ohio. Trustee Knoxville Coll., Tenn., 1981-83. Served with USAR, 1966-72. Mem. ABA (fed. regulation of securities com.), Ohio State Bar Assn. (corp. law com.), Am. Judicature Soc., Fed. Bar Assn., Bar Assn. Greater Cleve., Toledo Bar Assn., Kenyon Coll. Alumni Assn. (pres. 1980), Phi Beta Kappa. Democrat. Home: 2530 Manchester Dr Toledo OH 43606

MCGREEVEY, KATE ANN DEMAIN, nurse; b. Washington, Pa., Apr. 8, 1947; d. Charles Frances and Elsie Louise (Schievenin) Gorby; m. Anthony Edward DeMain, Jr., Sept. 7, 1968; children—Anthony III, Michael, Kevin; m. 2d, John F. McGreevey, Jr., Oct. 23, 1982. Student Youngstown State U., 1965-66; diploma in nursing Sch. Nursing Youngstown Hosp. Assn., 1968. R.N., Ohio. Staff and charge nurse North Side Hosp., Youngstown, Ohio, 1968, Wood County Hosp., Bowling Green, Ohio, 1968-72; nurse coronary care unit St. Vincent Hosp., Toledo, 1972-75, coronary care unit Med. Coll. Ohio, Toledo, 1975-78; head nurse coronary care unit med. intensive care unit, 1978-82, dir. heart station dept., 1982—; tchr. cardiac related topics; CPR instr., trainer. Mem. Am. Nurses Assn., Ohio Nurses Assn., Am. Assn. Critical Care Nurses. Home: 819 Lamonde St Maumee OH 45537 Office: Med Coll Ohio 3000 Arlington St CS 10008 Toledo OH 43699

MCGREW, LEROY ALBERT, chemistry educator; b. Galva, Ill., Nov. 1, 1938; s. Leroy Edwin and Irene Elizabeth (Youngberg) McG.; m. Carol Joyce Brown, June 2, 1963; children—Clark Edwin, Laura Ann, LeRoy Andrew. B.A., Knox Coll., 1960; M.S., U. Iowa, 1963, Ph.D., 1964. Prof. chemistry Ball State U., Muncie, Ind., 1964-77, prof. chemistry U. No. Iowa, Cedar Falls, Iowa, 1977—, head dept. chemistry, 1977—. Contbr. articles to profl. jours.; lectr. profl. mtgs. Ethyl Corp. fellow U. Iowa, 1963. Mem. Am. Chem. Soc. (div. Chem. Educ.), Iowa Acad. Sci., Sigma Xi, Phi Beta Kappa, Phi Lambda Upsilon. Lutheran. Avocations: piano, computer programming, motorcycle mechanics. Office: Dept Chemistry Univ No Iowa Cedar Falls IA 50614

MCGRUDER, SANDRA ANN, air force personnel administrator; b. Dayton, Ohio, Mar. 29, 1953; d. William David and Irene (Smith) Patterson; m. Leonard Nathaniel McGruder, Nov. 27, 1982; stepchildren—Lisa, Euna. B.S. summa cum laude, Tenn. State U., 1976; postgrad. U. Dayton, 1981—. Coop. student Wright-Patterson AFB, Ohio, 1972-76, classification specialist, 1976-79, dir. coop. edn., 1979-81, employee devel. specialist Directorate Civilian Personnel, 1981—; mem. adv. bd. for student programs, 1984-86. Sec. Blacks in Govt., Dayton, 1980; mem. NAACP, Dayton, 1984-85, Dayton Urban League, 1984, Humane Soc., Dayton, 1984, Tabernacle Baptist Ch. Unity Club, 1984-85, and Boosters Club. Recipient Spl. Act award Civilian Personnel Office, Ohio, 1984, Sustain Supr. Performance award Wright-Patterson AFB, 1984; named one of Top Ten Outstanding Women of Fed. Govt., Wright-Patterson AFB, 1977. Mem. Tenn. State U. Alumnae Assn. (sec. 1976-78), Am. Soc. Trainers and Developers, Internat. Personnel Mgmt. Assn., Delta Sigma Theta (1st v.p. 1975-76, life). Baptist. Avocations: skating; knitting; dancing; reading. Home: 4625 Knollcroft Rd Dayton OH 45426Office: US AFB 2750 ABW DPCT Wright Patterson AFB OH 45433

MC GUIGAN, JOHN ROBERT, univ. information systems adminstr.; b. Phila., Dec. 16, 1923; s. John Joseph and Margaret Mary (Maher) M.; B.S., Washington U., St. Louis, 1959; m. Grayce Dorothy Rosegrant, Feb. 10, 1948; children—Cecilia Anne McGuigan Yeager, Margaret Mary McGuigan Sisk, A. John, Grayce Byrne. Systems mgr. UNIVAC, Washington, 1963-64; corporate systems mgr. Am. Motors Corp., Detroit, 1964-66, corporate dir. info. systems, 1966-75; dir. info. systems St. Louis U., 1975—. Served to maj. USMC, 1942-63. Decorated Bronze Star. Home: 3939 Canterbury Dr Pasadena Hills MO 63121 Office: 3690 W Pine St Saint Louis MO 63108

MCGUIRE, JAMES HORTON, physics educator; b. Canandaigua, N.Y., July 6, 1942; s. Horton Ellis and Kardyn (Wright) McG.; m. V. Jane Rasmussen, Oct. 10, 1981; children—Marti, Carrie, Hobie, Brooke. B.S., Rensselaer U., 1964; M.S., Northeastern U., 1966, Ph.D., 1969. Assoc. prof. Kans. State U., Manhattan, 1976-81, prof. physics, 1982—; vis. scientist Hahn Meitner Inst., Berlin, 1980-81. Contbr. articles to profl. jours. Office: Physics Dept Kans State U Manhattan KS 66506

MCGUIRE, MAUREEN ANN, lawyer; b. Chgo., June 7, 1956; d. James Browne and Mary Margaret (Egan) M.; m. Ira N. Helfgot, Jan. 23, 1983. Student Loyola U., Rome, 1976; B.A., Loyola U., Chgo., 1978; J.D., DePaul U., 1981. Bar: Ill. 1981, U.S. Dist. Ct. (no. dist.) Ill. 1981. Legal asst. Am. Judicature Soc., Chgo., 1978; paralegal-intern Cook County States Atty., Chgo., 1981; assoc. Gorham, Metge, Bowman & Hourigan, Chgo., 1981—. Mem. Ill. Trial Lawyers Assn., Assn. Trial Lawyers Am., ABA, Chgo. Bar Assn., Ill. Bar Assn., Women's Bar Assn. Ill. Democrat. Roman Catholic. Office: Gorham Metge Bowman & Hourigan 33 N LaSalle St Suite 3500 Chicago IL 60602

MCGUIRE, WILLIS CLARK, veterinary entomologist, parasitologist, research consultant; b. Fairfield, Iowa, May 24, 1923; s. Roy Alvin and Lulu Agnes (Seaman) McG.; m. Charlotte Maxine Waller, Aug. 20, 1945; 1 child, Matthew Mark B.A., U. Iowa, 1948, M.S., 1949. Mgr. parasitology research Salsbury Labs., Charles City, Iowa, 1949-64; supr. animal health research Stauffer Chem. Co., Richmond, Calif., 1964-70; dir. chemotherapy research Philips Roxane Inc., St. Joseph, Mo., 1970-82; dir. tech. affairs Boehringer Ingelheim Animal Health Inc., St. Joseph, 1982—; ind. research cons., St. Joseph, 1985—. Patentee Control of Histomoniasis, 1951; Control of Hexamithiasis, 1955; Carbamate Insecticides, 1970; Cattle Insecticidal Ear Tag, 1984. Pres. Young Republicans Floyd County, Charles City, 1962. Served with U.S. Army, 1942-45. Mem. Am. Soc. Parasitologists, Am. Soc. Protozoologists, Livestock Insect Workshop, Entomol. Soc. Am., Sigma Xi. Democrat. Presbyterian. Club: Moila Country (St. Joseph). Lodge: Masons. Avocations: golf; antique furniture; art. Home: 1102 49th Terr Saint Joseph MO 64506

MCHALE, VINCENT EDWARD, political science educator; b. Jenkins Twp., Pa., Apr. 17, 1939; m. Ann Barbara Cotner, Nov. 8, 1963; 1 child, Patrick James. A.B., Wilkes Coll., 1964; M.A., Pa. State U., 1966, Ph.D. in Polit. Sci., 1969. Asst. prof. polit. sci. U. Pa., Phila., 1969-75, dir. grad. studies, 1971-73; assoc. prof. Case Western Res. U., Cleve., 1975-84, prof., 1984—, chmn. dept. polit. sci., 1978—; vis. lectr. John Carroll U., summer 1980, Beaver Coll., spring 1975. Author: (with A.P. Frognier and D. Paranzino) Vote, Clivages Socio-politiques et Developpement Regional en Belgique, 1974. Co-editor; contbr.: Evaluating Transnational Programs in Government and Business, 1980; Political Parties of Europe, 1983. Contbr. chpts. to books, articles to profl. jours. Project cons. Council Econ Opportunity in Greater Cleve., 1978-81; mem. Morris Abrams Award Com., 1977—. NSF grantee, 1971-72; HEW grantee, 1976-78; Woodrow Wilson fellow, 1968, Ruth Young Boucke fellow, 1967-68; All-Univ. fellow, 1967-68. Mem. Phi Kappa Phi. Home: 3070 Coleridge Rd Cleveland Heights OH 44118 Office: Case Western Res U Cleveland OH 44106

MCHARRIS, WILLIAM CHARLES, chemistry and physics educator; b. Knoxville, Tenn., Sept. 12, 1937; s. Garrett Clifford and Margaret Alice (Zimmerman) McH.; m. Orilla Ann Spangler, Aug. 27, 1960; 1 child, Louise Alice. B.A., Oberlin Coll., 1959; Ph.D., U. Calif., 1965. Summer trainee Oak Ridge Nat. Lab., 1957-59; research student Lawrence Berkeley Lab., Calif., 1959-65; cons. Argonne Nat. Lab., 1965—; asst. prof. Mich. State U., East Lansing, 1965-68, assoc. prof., 1968-70, prof. chemistry, physics, 1970—; vis. prof., scientist Lawrence Berkeley Lab., 1970-71, 81—. Author: (sci. fantasy) Into the Atom, 1985. Contbr. sci. articles to profl. jours. and popular mags. Composer organ and choral works. Alfred E. Sloan fellow, 1971-75. Mem. Am. Chem. Soc., Am. Phys. Soc., Sigma Xi (Jr. Sci. award 1972). Congregationalist. Avocation: music. Home: 512 Beech St East Lansing MI 48823 Office: Nat Superconducting Cyclotron Lab Michigan State Univ East Lansing MI 48824

MCHENRY, DALE EDWARD, educational administrator; b. Beardstown, Ill., Aug. 2, 1937; s. Edward and Mabel Edith (Blake) McH.; m. Frankie Ann Smith, Nov. 23, 1958; children—Marcia Jill, Cheryl Lynn, Caren Gayle, Todd Edward. B.S., Bradley U., 1959; M.S., U. So. Calif., 1962; Ph.D., U. Denver, 1974. Commd. 2d lt., 1959, advanced through grades to lt. col., 1982; chief vocat. tng. Hdqts. SAC, Omaha, 1963-67; dir. educl. research USAF Acad., Colorado Springs, Colo., 1967-71; dir. degree programs AF Inst. Tech., Dayton, Ohio, 1971-74; chief profl. educ. Hdqtrs. USAF, Washington, 1974-79; v.p. Community Coll. of AF, Maxwell AFB, Ala., 1979-82; chmn. bus. div. Metro Tech. Community Coll., Omaha, 1982—; cons. Univ. Computing Co., Dallas, 1969-70; adj. prof. psychology Park Coll., Kansas City, Mo., 1975-78; adj. prof. mgmt. Troy State U., Montgomery, Ala., 1979-82; dir. Mini Homes Corp., Papillion, Nebr. Contbr. articles to profl. jours. Decorated M.S.M. with two oak leaf clusters; Nebr. Dept. Educ. grantee, 1983-84, 85-86. Mem. Phi Delta Kappa, Greater Omaha C. of C. (south council exec. com. 1982—). Home: 310 Forest Dr Bellevue NE 68005 Office: Metro Tech Community Coll PO Box 3777 Omaha NE 68103

MC HENRY, MARTIN CHRISTOPHER, physician; b. San Francisco, Feb. 9, 1932; s. Merl and Marcella (Bricca) McH.; student U. Santa Clara (Calif.), 1950-53; M.D., U. Cin., 1957; M.S. in Medicine, U. Minn., Mpls., 1966; m. Patricia Grace Hughes, Apr. 27, 1957; children—Michael, Christopher, Timothy, Mary Ann, Jeffrey, Paul, Kevin, William, Monica, Martin Christopher. Intern, Highland Alameda County (Calif.) Hosp., Oakland, 1957-58; resident, internal medicine fellow Mayo Clinic, Rochester, Minn., 1958-61, spl. appointee in infectious diseases, 1963-64; staff physician infectious diseases Henry Ford Hosp., Detroit, 1964-67; staff physician Cleve. Clinic, 1967-72, head dept. infectious diseases, 1972—. Asst. clin. prof. Case Western Res. U., 1970-77, assoc. clin. prof. medicine, 1977—; asso. vis. physician Cleve. Met. Gen. Hosp., 1970—; cons. VA Hosp., Cleve., 1973—. Chmn. manpower com. Swine Influenza Program, Cleve., 1976. Served with USNR, 1961-63. Named Distinguished Tchr. in Medicine Cleve. Clinic, 1972; recipient 1st ann. Bruce Hubbard Stewart award Cleve. Clinic Found. for Humanities in Medicine, 1985. Diplomate Am. Bd. Internal Medicine. Fellow Infectious Diseases Soc. Am., A.C.P., Am. Coll. Chest Physicians (chmn. com. cardiopulmonary infections 1975-77, 81-83); mem. Am. Soc. Clin. Pharmacology and Therapeutics (chmn. sect. infectious diseases and antimicrobial agts., 1970-77, 80-85, dir.), Am. Thoracic Soc., Am. Soc. Clin. Pathologists, Royal Soc. Medicine of Great Britain (asso.), Am. Fedn. Clin. Research, Am. Soc. Tropical Medicine and Hygiene, Am. Soc. Microbiology, N.Y. Acad. Scis. Contbr. numerous articles to profl. jours., also chpts. to books. Home: 2779 Belgrave Rd Pepper Pike OH 44124 Office: 9500 Euclid Ave Cleveland OH 44106

MCHUGH, MARY LYNN, health researcher consultant; b. Rockford, Ill., Sept. 7, 1948; d. James Paul and Helen Evelyn (Pittman) McH.; m. Dennis W. Gumieny, Dec. 23, 1982. B.S.N., Wichita State U., 1973; M.S., U. Mich., 1978, postgrad., 1981. Instr. Med. Coll. Toledo, Ohio, 1974-76; supr. ICU, Chelsea Hosp., Mich., 1978-79; research assoc. U. Mich., Ann Arbor, 1979-82; v.p. Cybernetic Health Systems Corp., Ann Arbor, 1983—; researcher Catherine McAuley Health Corp., Ann Arbor, 1982—; cons. Hosp. Corp. Am., Nashville, 1983. Contbr. articles to profl. jours. Profl. nurse trainee HEW, 1976-78, predoctoral fellow HHS, U. Mich., 1979-82; Small Bus. Innovation grantee, 1985. Mem. Am. Statis Assn., Am. Nurses Assn., Assn. Computing Machinery, Council on Computers in Nursing, Sigma Theta Tau, Psi Chi. Democrat. Avocations: horseback riding, interior decorating, tailoring, aerobics, camping. Office: Cybernetic Health Systems Corp PO Box 1185 Ann Arbor MI 48106

MCINNES, DONALD GORDON, railroad executive; b. Buffalo, Nov. 6, 1940; s. Milton Gordon and Blanche Mae (Clunk) McI.; m. Betsy Campbell, Mar. 18, 1967; children—Campbell Gordon, Cody Milton. B.A., Denison U., 1963; M.S., Northwestern U., 1965; certificatein transp. Yale U., 1965. Budget mgr. operating AT&SF R.R. Co., Chgo., 1969-71, asst. trainmaster, San Bernardino, Calif., 1971-73, trainmaster, Temple, Tex., 1973-76, asst. supt., Carlsbad, N.M., 1976-77, supt. eastern div., Emporia, Kans., 1977-79, supt. Los Angeles div., San Bernardino, Calif., 1979-81, asst. to exec. v.p., Chgo., 1981-82, gen. supt. transp., 1983—; dir. Santa Fe Terminal Services Co.; mem. transp. adv. com. Trailer Train Co., 1983—, mem. intermodal adv. com., 1983—. Served to 2d lt., USAF, 1965-67; capt. U.S. Army, 1967-69. Decorated Bronze Star. Republican. Episcopalian. Clubs: Traffic, Union League (Chgo.); Cress Creek Country. Home: 1651 White Pines Ct Naperville IL 60540 Office: AT&SF Railway Co 80 E Jackson Blvd Chicago IL 60604

MCINNES, GILBERT, III, agricultural manufacturing company executive; b. Pitts., Mar. 3, 1946; s. Gilbert and Florence (Heinlein) McI.; m. Vera Ellen Kovalich, Sept. 25, 1971. B.S. in Bus. Adminstrn., Pa. State U., 1968, M.B.A., 1971. Programming cons. Pa. State U., State College, 1968, programmer, analyst, grad. asst., 1970-71; traffic analyst Procter and Gamble Co., Cin., 1971-73; logistics info. systems mgr. Massey-Ferguson Ltd., Toronto, Ont., Can., 1973-77; projects mgr.-comptrollers Massey-Ferguson, Inc, Des Moines, 1977-79, fin. systems mgr., 1979, gen. bus. systems mgr., 1979-82, gen. systems devel. mgr. N.Am., 1982—. Served with U.S. Army, 1968-70. Republican. Avocations: travel; biking; tennis; swimming. Home: 1035 22d St West Des Moines IA 50265 Office: Massey-Ferguson Inc 1901 Bell Ave Des Moines IA 50315

MCINTIRE, MURIEL ELAINE, dietitian; b. Saskatoon, Sask., Can.; d. Stafford Lenox and Nellie Susan (Whitehead) Osborne; came to U.S., 1915, naturalized, 1922; B.S., Lewis Inst. Tech., 1938; m. Claude Vernon McIntire, Nov. 23, 1941; children—Patricia Anne McIntire Maker, Susan Elaine McIntire Beranek. Intern, Walter Reed Hosp., Washington, 1940; head dietitian Sta. Hosp., Ft. Sheridan, Ill., 1939-40, Regional Hosp., Scott Field, Ill., 1940-43; therapeutic dietitian Barnes Hosp., St. Louis, 1948; head dietitian Hines (Ill.) Hosp., 1956-57; staff dietitian Ohio State U. Hosp. and Health Center, 1957-59; staff dietitian Oak Forest (Ill.) Hosp., 1960-61, exec. dietitian, 1961-69; chief dietitian Little Company of Mary Hosp., Evergreen Park, Ill., 1980. 1971-77, therapeutic dietitian, 1977-84. Served to 1st lt. USAAF, 1943-45. Named Employee of Yr., Little Company of Mary Hosp., 1980. Mem. Am. Dietetic Assn., Am. Home Econs. Assn., Soc. for Nutrition Edn., Chgo. Nutrition Assn. Co-author: Manual of Clinical Dietetics, 1975. Home: 7144 S Fair Elms Ave La Grange IL 60525

MCINTOSH, JOHN EDWIN, greeting card company executive; b. Pitts., June 13, 1944; s. Ralph Oscar and Rosamond Virginia (Petty) McI.; m. Katharine Louise Weaver, Dec. 28, 1967; 1 child, Heather Rebecca. B.S. in Econ. Physics, Otterbein Coll., 1966; postgrad. U. Mich., 1966-67; M.S. in Indsl. Mgmt., Clarkson Coll. Tech., 1970. Indsl. engr. Alcoa, Massena, N.Y., 1967-70; economist, statistical analyst State of N.Y., N.Y.C., 1970-75; statistical analyst Great Adventure Inc., Jackson, N.J., 1975-77; mkt. researcher, retail test planner Am. Greetings Corp., Cleve., 1977-79, forecasting specialist, 1979-84, strategic planning mgr., 1984—. Pres. Cleve. Bus. Economist Club, 1983-84, pres. bd. trustees Bay Presbyterian Ch., Bay Village, Ohio, 1983. Democrat. Avocations: sailing, tennis, automobiles. Home: 574 Oakmoor Bay Village OH 44140 Office: Am Greetings Corp 10500 American Rd Cleveland OH 44144

MC INTURF, FAITH MARY, engineering company executive, thoroughbred harness racing executive; b. Grand Ridge, Ill., Aug. 22, 1917; d. Lynne E. and Margaret (Garver) McInturf; grad. high sch. With The J.E. Porter Corp., Chgo., 1963-65, v.p., 1951-65, sec., 1951-65, also dir.; v.p., sec. Potomac Engring. Corp., 1941—; sec.-treas., dir. Chgo. Harness Racing Inc., also Balmoral Jockey Club, Inc., 1967-72, sec., dir., 1974-78; sec., treas., dir. Balmoral Park Trot, Inc., 1969-72; sec., dir. Horse Racing Promotions, Inc., 1974-77. Roman Catholic. Home: 1360 Lake Shore Dr Chicago IL 60610 Office: 919 N Michigan Ave Chicago IL 60611

MCINTYRE, GARY NOEL, educator; b. Elmo, Mo., June 29, 1947; s. Bobby Noel and Marie Margaret (Davis) McI.; m. Janice Lee Thornton, June 5, 1970 (div.); 1 dau., Amy Christine. B.S. in Bus. Edn., N.W. Mo. State U., 1969; B.S. in Elem. Edn., Central Mo. State U., 1973; M.S. in Elem. Adminstrn., U. Mo.-Kansas City, 1977. Cert. tchr., elem. adminstr., Mo. Tchr. pub. schs., Adel, Iowa, 1969-71, Kansas City, Mo., 1971-78; child devel. specialist/counselor Kansas City (Mo.) pub. schs., 1978-79, sci./math. facilitator, 1979—, outdoor edn. tchr., 1979—. Mem. Am. Fedn. Tchrs., Nat. Council Tchrs. Math., Nat. Sci. Tchrs., Assn., Nat. Wildlife Assn., NAACP, Phi Delta Kappa. Democrat. Episcopalian.

MCINTYRE, RUSSELL THEODORE, research administrator; b. Alexis, Ill., Mar. 20, 1925; s. Russell Howard and Marie Elizabeth (Cook) M.; m. Rhoda M. Cooper, June 14, 1948; children—Margaret, Nancy. B.S., Monmouth Coll., 1949; M.S., Kans. State U., 1950, Ph.D., 1952. Asst. prof. biochemistry La. State U., Baton Rouge, 1952-54; research dir. Haynie Products Co., Wildwood, N.J., 1954-60; dir. spl. products research Capital City Products Co., Columbus, Ohio, 1960-85, spl. products dir. mktg., 1985—. Contbr. articles to profl. jours. Patentee tire cord lubricants, 1983. Served to sgt. U.S. Army, 1943-46, ETO. Mem. Am. Oil Chemists Soc. Republican. Presbyterian. Lodge: Kiwanis (lt. gov. 1979-80). Avocations: reading, travel, camping, gardening. Office: Capital City Products Co 525 W 1st Ave Columbus OH 43215

MCINTYRE, WILLIAM DAVIS, JR., business executive; b. Monroe, Mich., Dec. 5, 1935; s. William D. and Prudence A. (Harrington) M.; m. Susan Lenhart, May 3, 1963; children—Michael, Molly, Frank, Ann Marie. Student U. Notre Dame, 1955-59, U. Detroit, 1954-55, participant advance mgmt. program Harvard U., 1976. With Monroe Auto Equipment Co., Monroe, 1959-80, dir. export ops., 1960-64, v.p. internat. ops., 1964-66, exec. v.p. internat. ops., 1966-80; pres. Mich. Tech. Investors Inc., Monroe, 1980—, also dir.; pres. Environ. Dynamics, Inc., Ann Arbor, Mich., 1981—; ptnr., dir., v.p. Mich. Mineral Investors Ldt., Traverse City, 1981—; dir. Monroe Bank, Trust Co., Q.E.D. Environ. Systems, Ann Arbor, Mich., Am. Cycloidal Gear Corp., Chagrin Falls, Ohio; Pres. bd. dirs. Monroe County United Way, 1982-83, gen. campaign chmn. 1980, 81; gen. campaign chmn. Monroe Family YMCA Capital Funds drive, 1983; past pres. bd. dirs. Mercy-Meml. Hosp. Corp; past chmn. Monroe County chpt. ARC; past pres. St. John's Sch. Bd. Recipient Monroe Catholic Central Alumnus of Yr. award, 1982 United Way Outstanding Citizens' award, 1981 City Monroe Minuteman award, 1981, Gov. Mich. Minuteman award. Mem. Young Pres. Orgn., Soc. Automotive Engrs., Automotive Orgn. Team Inc., Monroe C. of C. (chmn. 1984, 85). Republican. Roman Catholic. Clubs: Monroe Golf, Country, Monroe Rod, Gun, Monroe, Otsego Ski (Gaylord, Mich.).

MCKANE, TERRY JOHN, mayor; b. Lansing, Mich., July 9, 1941; s. Kenneth Bernard and Mary Ella (Hill) McK.; m. Virginia Lee Amundsen, Nov. 23, 1968; children—Heather Anne, John Thorsen, Katherine Maureen. B.A., Mich. State U., 1963, M.A., 1968. Cert. secondary tchr., Mich. Secondary tchr. Lansing Sch. Dist., 1967-82; city councilman, Lansing 1971-82; mayor City of Lansing, 1982—; chmn. bd. dirs. Tri-County Aging Consortium, Lansing, 1985—; bd. dirs. Tri-County Manpower Adminstrn., 1974—. Div. chmn. United Way Campaign, Lansing, 1982—; bd. dirs. Friends of Gov.'s Residence, Lansing, 1984—, Ingham-Eaton Emergency Food and Shelter, Lansing; lay speaker United Methodist Ch., Lansing. Served to 1st lt. U.S. Army, 1964-66, to 1st lt. USNG, 1966-69. Named Outstanding Govt. Official, Mich. Rehab. Assn., 1984. Mem. Mich. Soc. Mayflower Descs. (dep. gov. 1984—), SAR, U.S. Conf. Mayors, Nat. League of Cities, Mich. Mcpl. League (v.p. 1984—), Am. Legion. Clubs: City, University (Lansing). Home: 3300 Ginger Snap Ln Lansing MI 48910 Office: Office of Mayor 9th Floor City Hall Lansing MI 48933

MCKAY, JAMES EDGAR, banker; b. Ludington, Mich., Mar. 24, 1939; s. James Henry and Beatrice Delia (Cowell) McK.; m. Judith Ann Robinson, June 26, 1961; children—Robin Lee, Michael James, Amy Lynne. A.C., Grand Rapids Jr. Coll., 1961; B.B.A., Aquinas Coll., 1982; cert. banking U. Mich., 1982-83. Asst. v.p. Union Bank, Grand Rapids, Mich., 1966-73, v.p., 1973-81, sr. v.p., 1981—. Bd. dirs. Am. Cancer Soc., Grand Rapids, 1980—; pres. Grand Rapids Jr. Achievement, 1981; v.p. planning United Way of Kent County, Grand Rapids, 1983-84; exec. v.p. John Ball Zoological Soc., Grand Rapids, 1984—. Recipient Leadership award Jr. Acheivement of Am., 1981, Leader award Close Up Found., 1983, Chmn. award PAC, 1984. Mem. Mich. Bankers Assn., Mich. Bankers Political Action Com. (chmn. award 1984, chmn. 1984—), Am. Bankers Political Action Com. (state rep.). Club: Blythefield Country (Belmont) (treas. 1984—), Peninsular. Avocations: golf, running. Home: 2245 Shawnee SE Grand Rapids MI 49506 Office: Union Bank & Trust Co NA 200 Ottawa NW Grand Rapids MI 49503

MCKAY, LARRY MICHAEL, architect; b. Hot Springs, S.D., Aug. 18, 1942; s. Lawrence George and Beulah Ioan (Petro) McK.; m. Alyce Gilman, Apr. 13, 1968; children—Heather Lynn, Larry Tyler Arthur. Student S.D. Sch. Mines and Tech., 1960-61; B.S. in Architecture, Idaho State U., 1965, postgrad., 1966-67. Cert. architect, S.D., Colo., Nebr., Wyo. Designer Ken E. Douglas & Assocs., Pocatello, Idaho, 1965-66; architect Brady Cons., Spearfish, S.D., 1966-69, Hengel Assocs., Rapid City, S.D., 1969-70, Shaver Partnership, Michigan City, Ind., 1970-72, Bell Galyardt & Wells, Rapid City, 1972-75; pvt. practice architecture, Rapid City, 1975-81; ptnr. McKay/McConnell, Rapid City, 1981—. Pres. Girls Club Rapid City, 1981-82; bd. dirs. Pennington County (S.D.) chpt. Am. Cancer Soc., 1978—, v.p., 1980-81; mem. Leadership 1982, Rapid City. Recipient Lighting Design award Illuminating Engring. Soc., 1978, Herb Martalon award Episcopal Ch., 1980. Mem. AIA, Black Hills Architects, Nat. Council Archtl. Registration Bds. Republican. Episcopalian. Club: Cosmopolitan. Lodge: Elks. Ink prints and landscapes pub. in ltd. editions, 1978-83. Home: 2215 Alamo Dr Rapid City SD 57702 Office: 2100 S 7th St Rapid City SD 57702

MCKAY, NEIL, banker; b. East Towas, Mich., Aug. 9, 1917; s. Lloyd Garrison and Rose Martha (McDonald) McK.; m. Olive Baird, Nov. 11, 1950; children—Julia Lynn, Hunter. A.B., U. Mich., 1939, J.D. with distinction, U. Mich., 1946. Bar: Mich. 1946, Ill. 1946. Assoc. Winston & Strawn, Chgo., 1946-53, ptnr., 1953-63; head lending div. to heavy industry 1st Nat. Bank Chgo., 1965-68, gen. mgr. London br., 1968-70, cashier, 1970-82, head various depts. including retail, trust, personnel and exec., 1978-79, vice chmn. bd., 1975-83, also dir.; sec. 1st Chgo. Corp., 1970-82, vice chmn., dir., 1975-83; ret., 1983; dir. Morton Thiokol Inc., Kerr McGee Corp., Baird & Warner, Inc. Founding bd. dirs. Student Loan Mktg. Assn.; bd. dirs. Chgo. Hort. Soc.; trustee Morton Arboretum, Ill. Inst. Tech. Served to lt. USNR, 1942-46. Mem. ABA, Ill. Bar Assn., Chgo. Bar Assn., Order of Coif. Clubs: Chicago, Mid-Day, Geneva Golf (Ill.). Sr. editor Mich., Law Rev. Home: 906 Sunset Rd Geneva IL 60134 Office: Suite 2538 One First Nat Plaza Chicago IL 60670

MCKAY, WILLIAM, educational facility administrator, accountant; b. Wessington, S.D., July 22, 1923; s. Milton Runnels and Edythe Mae (Boller) McK.; m. Irene Florence Juderjahn, Apr. 23, 1948 (div. 1978); children—Janet McCart, Karen Samstad, Peggy. B.S. with distinction, U. Nebr., 1949. C.P.A., Minn. Staff acct. Arthur Andersen & Co., Mpls., 1949-52; sole practice, Mpls., 1952-56; pres. McConnell Travel Sch., Mpls., 1956—. Dir., Self Help for Hard of Hearing People, Inc., Bethesda, Md., 1982—. Served to sgt. U.S. Army, 1943-46. Mem. Am. Inst. Accts., Minn. Soc. C.P.A.s, Nat. Assn. Trade and Tech. Schs. Republican. Methodist. Lodge: Century. Avocations: boating; golf; travel; reading. Home: 2950 Dean Pkwy Unit 2205 Minneapolis MN 55416 Office: McConnell Sch Inc 831 2d Ave S Minneapolis MN 55402

MCKAY, WILLIAM PAUL, media management company executive; b. Los Angeles, Jan. 21, 1951; s. William R. and Marjorie E. (Bostrom) McK.; m. Janet Broderick, May 13, 1978; 1 child, Grant Broderick. A.A., Mt. San Antonio Coll., 1970; B.S., So. Calif. Coll., 1971. Vice-pres., Estey-Hoover, Inc., Irvine, Calif., 1978-80; pres. Am. Resource Bur., Wheaton, Ill., 1980—; chmn. bd. McKay-Doerschuk & Co., Wheaton, 1981—, Gabriel Distbn. Co., Wheaton, 1983—. Co-author: Vital Signs, 1984. Mem. UN Assn. Los Angeles, 1976. Mem. Am. Mktg. Assn., Religion in Media (Angel award 1983). Republican. Mem. Assemblies of God Ch. Home: 7S131 Vale Ct Downers Grove IL 60515 Office: Am Resource Bur 1135 Wheaton Oaks Ct Wheaton IL 60515

MCKEE, CHARLES CLIFTON, conservationist; b. Telford, Tenn., Apr. 18, 1926; s. Wallace D. and Mae (Keplinger) McK.; m. Norma Jean Schurmeier, Jan. 14, 1951; children—Diane Rae, Gary Lee. Student East Tenn. State Coll., 1947-48; B.S., U. Tenn., 1950; M.S., Purdue U., 1961. Vocat. agr. tchr., Mackey, Ind., 1951-52; soil conservationist U.S. Dept. Agr.-Soil Conservation Service, Princeton, Ind., 1953-54, Petersburg, Ind., 1954-55; extension soil conservationist Coop. Extension Service, Purdue U., West Lafayette, Ind., 1955-64; exec. sec. Ind. Soil and Water Conservation Com., West Lafayette, 1964—. Served with USNR, 1944-46. Mem. Soil Conservation Soc. Am. (chpt. pres. 1960, merit award 1984), Extension Specialists Assn., Nat. Assn. State Conservation Adminstrs. (pres. 1977-78), Epsilon Sigma Phi. Republican. Methodist. Lodge: Masons. Home: 2531 State Rd 26 W West Lafayette IN 47906 Office: State Soil and Water Conservation Com Room 7 AGAD Bldg Purdue U West Lafayette IN 47907

MC KEE, DALE, promotions, premiums and incentives co. exec.; b. Ironton, Ohio, May 24, 1938; s. Frank and Eloise McK.; B.S., U. Dayton, 1966; student Sinclair Community Coll., 1975; m. Barbara Jean Robinson, June 15, 1957; children—Dale, Jeffery Scott. Pres., McKee & Parrish Bldg. Contractors, Miamisburg, Ohio, 1968-72; pres. McKee & McKee Bldg. Contractors, Miamisburg, Ohio, 1972-79; pres., treas. World Wide Crusade, Inc., Miamisburg, 1978—; pres. Del Diablo Recording, Miamisburg, 1978-79; pres. Del Diablo Pub. Co., Miamisburg, 1978-79; asso. realtor Joe McNabb Realtor, Miamisburg, 1978-79; announcer WCXL & WQRP Radio F.M., 1978-79; v.p., dir. Bar Del, Inc., Miamisburg, 1974—; supr. Frigidaire div. Gen. Motors Corp., Dayton, 1956—. Mem. Am. Ind. Party Central Com., 1973-74; scoutmaster Sequoia council, Boy Scouts Am., 1971-73. Mem. IEEE, Dayton Area Bd. Realtors, Ohio Bd. Realtors, Internat. Platform Assn., Country Music Assn., Nashville Songwriters Assn. Internat., Am. Fedn. Musicians. Democrat. Roman Catholic. Clubs: Foremans' Club of Dayton, Moose. Composer: Ten Days I'll Be Getting Out of Prison, 1978; The Bottle Almost Empty, 1978. Home: 1232 Holly Hill Dr Miamisburg OH 45342 Office: Kettering Blvd Dayton OH 45439

MC KEE, DONALD DARRELL, real estate broker; b. Highland, Ill., July 20, 1932; s. Earl Michael and Leta Evelyn (Dresch) McK.; grad. high sch.; m. Emma A. Becker, Aug. 28, 1956; children—Dale Michael, Gail Ann. Sales clk. C. Kinne & Co., Highland, 1952-63; salesman Lowenstein Agy., Inc., Highland, 1963-69; owner Don McKee Ins., 1970-77; owner Don McKee Realty, Highland, 1969-73; owner Century 21-McKee Realty, Highland; owner Key Antiques, Key Sales Co. Tchr. real estate So. Ill. U., Edwardsville, 1974-81, Lewis and Clark Community Coll., Godfrey, Ill., Belleville (Ill.) Area Coll.; pres. Real Estate Inst., 1973-79; exec. officer Edwardsville-Collinsville Bd. Realtors, 1975-76; pres. So. Ill. Conf. Real Estate. Mem. So. Ill. Tourism Council, 1969-79; mem. adv. bd. Friends of Lovejoy Library, So. Ill. U.-Edwardsville Mem. So. Ill. Independent Ins. Agts. (pres. 1974-75), Edwardsville-Collinsville Bd. Realtors (pres. 1974), Nat., Ill. (v.p. dist. 1977) assns. Realtors, Highland C. of C., Highland Hist. Soc. (dir.), Helvetia Sharpshooters Soc., St. Louis Art Mus., Ill. Real Estate Educators, Nat. Real Estate Educators. Club: Highland Country. Contbr. articles to profl. jours. Home: 1403 Pine St Highland IL 62249 Office: 825 Main St Highland IL 62249

MC KEE, GEORGE MOFFITT, JR., consulting civil engineer; b. Valparaiso, Nebr., Mar. 27, 1924; s. George Moffitt and Iva (Santrock) McK.; student Kans. State Coll. Agr. and Applied Sci., 1942-43, Bowling Green State U., 1943; B.S. in Civil Engring., U. Mich., 1947; m. Mary Lee Taylor, Aug. 11, 1945; children—Michael Craig, Thomas Lee, Mary Kathleen, Marsha Coleen, Charlotte Anne. Draftsman, Jackson Constrn. Co., Colby, Kans., 1945-46; asst. engr. Thomas County, Colby, 1946; engr. Sherman County, Goodland, Kans., 1947-51; salesman Oehlert Tractor & Equipment Co., Colby, 1951-52; owner, operator George M. McKee, Jr., cons. engrs., Colby, 1952-72; sr. v.p. engring. Contract Surety Consultants, Wichita, Kans., 1974—. Adv. rep. Kans. State U., Manhattan, 1957-62; mem. adv. com. N.W. Kans. Area Vocat. Tech. Sch., Goodland, 1967-71. Served with USMCR, 1942-45. Registered profl. civil engr., Kans., Okla., registered land Surveyor, Kans. Mem. Kans. Engring. Soc. (pres. N.W. profl. engrs. chpt. 1962-63, treas. cons. engrs. sect. 1961-63), Kansas County Engr's. Assn. (dist. v.p. 1950-51), Northwest Kans. Hwy. Ofcls. Assn. (sec. 1948-49), Nat. Soc. Profl. Engrs., Kans. State U. Alumni Assn. (pres. Thomas County 1956-57), Am. Legion (Goodland 1st vice comdr. 1948-49), Colby C. of C. (v.p. 1963-64), Goodland Jr. C. of C. (pres. 1951-52). Methodist (chmn. ofcl. bd. 1966-67). Mason (32 deg., Shriner); Order Eastern Star. Home: 34 Lakeview Circle Route 1 Towanda KS 67144 Office: 6500 W Kellogg Wichita KS 67209

MCKEE, JAMES LEE, publisher, merchant retail books, author, historian; b. Lincoln, Nebr., Dec. 12, 1940; s. E. S. and Charlotte Arline (Smith) McK.; m. Linda Lee Hillegass, June 9, 1978; 1 child, Laura Jane. B.A., B.S., U. Nebr., 1963. Pres., J & L Lee Corp., Lincoln, 1980—; corp. sec., treas. Bailey, Lewis & Assocs., Lincoln, 1969—; cons. Lincoln Pub. Schs., 1967—; prof. history Southeast Community Coll., Lincoln, 1972—. Author: Nebraska Wildcat Banks, 1969, Lincoln: A Photo History, 1977, Lincoln The Prairie Capital, 1984. Contbr. articles on history to profl. jours. Organizer, Lincoln Host Family Assn., 1967, Lincoln, Lancaster Landmarks Soc., 1978; bd. dirs., treas. The Lincoln Found., 1975-81; bd. dirs. Lincoln, Lancaster Hist. Assn.; mem. Lincoln Hist. Preservation Commn., 1985. Served to sgt. U.S. Army, 1963-69. Recipient Numismatic Ambassador award Numismatic News, 1984. Mem. Nebr. Numismatic Assn. (life, editor 1955—); mem. Am. Booksellers Assn., Nebr. Writers Guild, Central States Numismatic Soc., Am. Numismatic Soc. Presbyterian. Clubs: Sertoma (bd. dirs.) Lincoln Coin (sec. 1958—). Avocations: numismatics; history; swimming; reading; book collecting. Home: 3425 Otoe St Lincoln NE 68506 Office: J & L Lee Corp PO Box 5575 281 E Park Plaza Lincoln NE 68505

MCKEE, THOMAS FREDERICK, lawyer; b. Cleve., Oct. 27, 1948; s. Harry Wilbert and Virginia (Light) McK.; m. Linda Miller, Aug. 22, 1970. B.A. with high distinction, U. Mich., 1970; J.D., Case Western Res. U., 1975. Bar: Ohio 1975, U.S. Dist. Ct. (no. dist.) Ohio 1975, U.S. Supreme Ct. 1979. Assoc. firm Calfee, Halter & Griswold, Cleve., 1975-81, ptnr., 1982—. Contbg. editor Going Public, 1985. Mem. ABA (com. fed. regulation securities law sect.), Bar Assn. Greater Cleve., Order of Coif. Clubs: Hermit, Country (Cleve.). Office: 1800 Central Nat Bank Bldg Cleveland OH 44114

MCKEEHAN, CHARLES WAYNE, pharmaceutical company executive; b. Greencastle, Ind., Nov. 16, 1929; s. Frank Theodore and Edna Ruth (Arnold) McK.; m. Helen Christine Fletcher, June 1, 1953; children—Karen D., Stuart N., Mark W., Brian D. B.S. in Pharmacy, Purdue U., 1951, M.S. in Pharm. Chemistry, 1953, Ph.D., 1957. Registered pharmacist, Ind. Sr. pharmacy chemist Eli Lilly & Co., Indpls., 1957-62, corp. trainee, 1962-64, project mgr., 1965-67, head parenteral pilot plant, 1968, head pharm. research, 1969-72, head product devel., 1972—; mem. revision subcom. U.S. Pharmacopeia, Washington, 1975. Patentee in field. Vice-chmn. maintenance fund Indpls. Symphony, 1968-70; sec. Indpls. Jr. Soccer League, 1973-74. Served with AUS, 1953-55. Mem. Am. Chem. Soc., Am. Pharm. Assn., Am. Men of Sci., Sigma Xi, Rho Chi, Phi Lambda Upsilon. Lodge: Masons, Shriner. Avocations: photography, camping. Home: 304 Daffon Dr Indianapolis IN 46627 Office: Eli Lilly & Co Lilly Corp Ctr Indianapolis IN 46285

MCKEEHAN, M. RICKY, pharmacist, pharmacy consultant; b. Evansville, Ind., Oct. 20, 1949; s. William M. and Amile (Tapp) McK.; m. Linda Susan Lampton, Jan. 23, 1972. B.S. in Pharmacy, Butler U., 1972. Pharmacy mgr. Scales Pharmacy, Boonville, Ind., 1972-78; asst. dir. pharmacy Meml. Hosp., Jasper, Ind., 1978-81; pharmacy asst. mgr. Peoples Pharmacy, Evansville, 1981-88, Schnucks, Evansville, 1982-84; pharmacy mgr. K-Mart, Evansville, 1984—; nursing home pharmacy cons. Miller's Merry Manor, Rockport, Ind., 1983—. Mem. Rho Chi, Phi Kappa Phi. Republican. Baptist. Club: Baptist Youth Basketball (Tennyson, Ind.) (capt. 1984). Avocations: baseball, basketball, coin collecting. Office: K Mart 2300 Morgan Ave Evansville IN 47711

MCKENNA, ALVIN JAMES, lawyer; b. New Orleans, Aug. 17, 1943; s. Dixon N. and Mabel M. (Duplantier) McK., Sr.; m. Carol Jean Windheim, 1963; children—Sara, Alvin, Jr., Martha, Andrea, Erin, Rebecca. A.B., Canisius Coll., 1963; J.D., Notre Dame Law Sch., 1966. Law clk. U.S. Dist. Ct., So. Dist. Ohio, Columbus, 1966-68; asst. U.S. atty. U.S. Dist. Ct. (so. dist.) Ohio, Columbus, 1968-70; ptnr. Alezander, Ebinger, Fisher, McAlister & Lawrence, Columbus, 1970—; mem. com. revision rules practice U.S. Dist. Ct. (so. dist.) Ohio, 1973-74, 80—, mem. bar examining com., 1973-76, 81—. Council mem. City of Gahanna, Ohio, 1972-80, 82-84, chmn. charter rev. com., 1981; bd. trustees Community Urban Redevel. Corp., Gahanna, 1984—; chmn. Mayor's Capital Improvements Task Force, Gahanna, 1980. Named one of the Outstanding Young Men in Columbus Jaycees, 1974. Mem. ABA, Fed. Bar Assn. (pres. Columbus chpt. 1973), Ohio Bar Assn., Columbus Bar Assn. (chmn. fed. ct. com. 1973-74). Home: 202 Academy Ct Gahanna OH 43230 Office: Alexander Ebinger Fisher McAlister & Lawrence 1 Riverside Plaza 25th Floor Columbus OH 43215

MCKENNA, ANDREW JAMES, distribution and printing executive, baseball executive; b. Chgo., Sept. 17, 1929; s. Andrew James and Anita (Fruin) McK.; m. Mary Joan Pickett, June 20, 1953; children—Suzanne, Karen, Andrew, William, Joan, Kathleen, Margaret. B.S., U. Notre Dame, 1951; J.D.,

DePaul U., 1954. Bar: Ill. 1955. Pres. and chief exec. officer Schwarz Paper Co., Morton Grove, Ill., 1964—; dir. Chgo. Nat. League Ball Club Inc., Combined Internat. Corp., Dean Foods Co., Lake Shore Nat. Bank, Sargent-Welch Sci. Co., Skyline Corp., Tribine Co., Mohican Corp., Chgo. Bears. Trustee U. Notre Dame, La Lumiere Sch., La Porte, Ind., past chmn.; bd. dirs. Cath. Charities of Chgo., Nat. Found. March of Dimes, Chgo. chpt., St. Francis Hosp. of Evanston (Ill.), Woodlands Acad. Mem. Ill. Bar Assn., Young Pres. Orgn. Clubs: Chicago, Commercial, Economic, Chicago Athletic Assn. (Chgo.); North Shore (Glenview, Ill.); Glen View (Golf, Ill.). Office: Schwarz Paper Co 8338 N Austin Ave Morton Grove IL 60053

MCKENNA, RICHARD HENRY, hospital executive; b. Covington, Ky., Dec. 19, 1927; s. Charles Joseph and Mary Florence (Wieck) McK.; B.S. in Commerce, U. Cin., 1959; M.B.A., Xavier U., 1963; m. Patricia Ann Macdonald, Jan. 6, 1979; children—Linda Ann, Theresa K., Joan Marie. Accountant, Andrew Jergens Co., Cin., 1947-55; treas., dir. Ramsey Bus. Equipment, Inc., Cin., 1955-59; with Oakley Die & Mfg. Co., also Electro-Jet Tool Co., Cin., 1959-60; pvt. practice accounting, No. Ky. and Cin., 1960-62; bus. mgr. St. Joseph Hosp., Lexington, Ky., 1962-66; asst. adminstr. fin. U. Ky. Hosp., Lexington, 1966-70; v.p., chief fin. officer St. Lawrence Hosp., Lansing, Mich., 1970—; adj. faculty Aquinas Coll., Grand Rapids, Mich., 1980—; chmn. bd. McKenna & McKenna Assocs., Inc., 1983—. Former mem. adv. com. to commr. of finance State of Ky.; chmn. cath. div. Oak Hills Bus. Com.; mem. speakers com. Oak Hill Sch. Dist. Served with U.S. Mcht. Marine, 1945-47, U.S. Army, 1948-51. C.P.A., Ohio, Ky. Mem. Hosp. Fin. Mgmt. Assn. (Follmer award, past dir. Ky. chpt.), Am. Mgmt. Assn., Am. Inst. C.P.A.s, Ky. Soc. C.P.A.s, Mich. Hosp. Assn. (former mem. com. on reimbursement), Delta Mu Delta, Alpha Sigma Lambda. Home: 1444 Cambridge Rd Lansing MI 48910 Office: 1210 W Saginaw St Lansing MI 48914

MCKENNA, WILLIAM J., textile products manufacturing company executive; b. N.Y.C., Oct. 11, 1926; s. William T. and Florence (Valis) McK.; m. Jean T. McNulty, Aug. 27, 1949 (dec. 1985); children—Kevin, Marybeth, Peter, Dawn. B.B.A., Iona Coll., 1949; M.S., NYU, 1950. Vice pres. Hat Corp. Am., N.Y.C., v.p. mktg., 1961-63; exec. v.p., 1963-67; pres. Manhattan Shirt Co., N.Y.C., 1967-74; pres. Lee Co., Inc., Shawnee Mission, Kans., 1974-82; pres. Kellwood Co., St. Louis, Mo., 1982—, chief exec. officer, 1984—, also dir.; dir. Genovese Drug Stores, United Mo. Bancshares. Served with USN, 1944-46; PTO. Roman Catholic. Clubs: St. Louis; Metropolitan (Chgo.). Office: Kellwood Co 600 Kellwood Pkwy Saint Louis MO 63017*

MCKENZIE, GREGORY ALLEN, sanitary supply company executive; b. Covington, Ky., June 30, 1949; s. William H. and Jane C. (Bradford) McK.; m. Barbara Lynn Wyatt, Jan. 30, 1971 (div. Aug. 1980); children—Carrissa, Ian; m. 2d Christine Clair Kienzle, Oct. 1, 1983. B.A., No. Ky. U., 1971. Dist. sales mgr. Rubbermaid Comml. Products. Co., Winchester, Va., 1972-80; sales mgr. Drackett Profl. Products Co., Cin., 1980—. Contbr. articles to san. supply industry publs. Mem. Am. Mgmt. Assn., Young Execs. Soc. (dist. dir. 1984—). Avocations: sports, music. Home: 2713 Hurstland St Crestview Hills KY 41017 Office: Drackett Profl Products Co 5020 Spring Grove Ave Cincinnati OH 45232

MCKENZIE, RONALD PAUL, newspaper executive; b. Mpls., May 5, 1932; s. Leonard Francis and Margaret Catherine (Riley) McK.; m. P. Ann Devoy, Apr. 30, 1960; children—Angela, Ronald Paul, Gregory, Mark. B.A., U. Minn., 1955; M.B.A., U. Wis., 1976. Copywriter, Star & Tribune, Mpls., 1960-65; dir. promotion and research Press-Gazette, Green Bay, Wis., 1965—. Served to 1st lt. USAF, 1955-57. Mem. Internat. Newspaper Promotion Assn., Advt. Fedn. Green Bay, Newspaper Research Council. Roman Catholic. Club: Windjammers Sailing (commodore 1985—). Advocations: sailing, skiing, photography, acting. Home: 516 Arrowhead Dr Green Bay WI 54301 Office: Green Bay Press Gazette 435 E Walnut St Green Bay WI 54307

MCKEOUGH, WILLIAM DARCY, gas utility executive; b. Chatham, Ont., Can., Jan. 31, 1933; s. George Grant and Florence Sewell (Woodward) McK.; B.A., U. Western Ont., 1954; LL.D. (hon.), 1979; LL.D. (hon.), Wilfrid Laurier U., 1980; m. Margaret Joyce Walker, June 18, 1965; children—Walker Stewart, James Grant. Chmn., chief exec. officer Union Gas Ltd., Chatham, 1979—, chmn., 1984-85; chmn., pres., chief chief exec. officer Union Enterprises, Chatham, 1985—; chmn. Redpath Industries Ltd.; dir. Algoma Central Ry., Can. Imperial Bank of Commerce, Precambrian Shield Resources Ltd., McKeough Sons Co. Ltd., Noranda Mines Ltd., Numac Oil & Gas Ltd. Former mem. exec. com. Anglican Diocese of Huron; former mem. Gen. Synod, Anglican Ch. Can.; mem. Chatham City Council, 1960-63, also mem. Planning Bd. and Lower Thames Valley Conservation Authority; former mem. Chatham-Kent adv. bd. Can. Nat. Inst. of the Blind; former bd. dirs. Chatham YMCA, Chatham Little Theatre; bd. govs. Ridley Coll., Wilfrid Laurier U.; mem. Can. group Trilateral Commn.; mem. Ont. Legislature, 1963-78, minister without portfolio, 1966, minister mcpl. affairs, 1967, treas. and minister of econs., also chmn. Treasury Bd., 1971-72, minister mcpl. affairs, 1972, treas. and minister of econs. and intergovtl. affairs, 1972, parliamentary asst. to premier Ont., 1973, minister of energy, 1973-75, treas. and minister econs. and intergovtl. affairs, 1975-78. Office: Union Enterprises Ltd PO Box 2001 50 Keil Dr N Chatham ON N7M 5M1 Canada

MC KEOWN, MARY ELIZABETH, educational administrator; d. Raymond Edmund and Alice (Fitzgerald) McNamara; B.S., U. Chgo., 1946; M.S., DePaul U., 1953; m. James Edward McKeown, Aug. 6, 1955. Supr. high sch. dept. Am. Sch., 1948-68, prin., 1968—, trustee, 1975—, v.p., 1979—. Mem. Nat. Assn. Secondary Sch. Prins., Central States Assn. Sci. and Math Tchrs. Nat. Council Tchrs. Math., Assn. for Supervision and Curriculum Devel., Adult Edn. Assn., LWV. Author study guides for algebra, geometry and calculus. Home: 1469 N Sheridan Rd Kenosha WI 53140 Office: 850 E 58th St Chicago IL

MCKIBBIN, SAMUEL MCKAY, II, radio news director; b. Youngstown, Ohio, May 24, 1938; s. Raymond Johnson and Martha Elizabeth (Cash) McK.; m. Jeanette Marie Burnette, July 27, 1968. B.Sc. in Communications, Ohio U., 1972. With WPAY, Portsmouth, Ohio, 1960-62, WNXT, Portsmouth, 1962-67, WSAZ Radio, Huntington, W.Va., 1967, WNXT Radio, Portsmouth, 1968-71, WATH Radio, Athens, Ohio, 1972; news dir. WPAY, 1972—; instr. mass communication/journalism Shawnee State Coll., Portsmouth, 1983—. Pres. Portsmouth Conv. and Visitors Bur., 1983—; treas. Portsmouth Area Recognition Soc. Served with USAF, 1956-60. Mem. Ohio AP Broadcasters (pres.), AP Broadcasters, Radio-TV News Dirs. Assn., Ohio Sportscasters Assn., Ohio U. Alumni Assn. Republican. Christian Ch. Contbr. articles to profl. jours. Office: 1009 Gallia St Portsmouth OH 45662

MCKILLIP, WILLIAM JAMES, chemical company executive, research executive; b. LaCrosse, Wis., Jan. 13, 1935; s. James William and Helen Marie (Sieger) McK.; m. Elizabeth Catherine Poehling, Jan. 8, 1957; children—Mary, Robert, Teresa, Ann, Susan, Martha. B.S., Loras Coll., 1957, Ph.D., U. Iowa, 1962. Sr. research chemist Archer Daniels Midland, Mpls., 1962-67, group leader; mgr. research Ashland Chem. Co., Dublin, Ohio, 1967-74; assoc. dir. research to v.p. mktg. and research QO Chemicals Inc. (previously Quaker Oats Co.), Chgo., 1974—, sr. v.p., 1984—. Contbr. articles to profl. jours. Patentee in field. Mem. Am. Chem. Soc., Am. Foundry Soc., Comml. Devel. Assn., Sigma Xi, Lambda Phi Upsilon. Democrat. Roman Catholic. Avocations: reading, classical music, golf. Office: QO Chemicals Inc 823 Commerce Dr Chgo IL 60521

MC KILLIP, WILLIAM JOHN, data processing supply co. exec.; b. Chgo., Sept. 24, 1942; s. Hugh Anthony and Helen Jane (Graham) McK.; B.S.A., Walton Sch. Commerce, Chgo., 1962; m. Antonette Marie Wyrwicki, Nov. 12, 1966; children—Gwen, Sandra, Melissa, Vanessa, William Anton. Sr. acct. Harry B. Bernfield and Co., C.P.A.s, Chgo., 1962-67; corp. controller Pryor Corp. (formerly Info. Supplies Corp.), Chgo., 1967-77, corp. treas., 1977—. Mem. Ill. Mfrs. Assn. (exec. bd.), Fin. Mgmt. Assn., Am. Inst. Corp. Controllers. Office: 400 N Michigan Ave Chicago IL 60611

MCKILLIPS, GARY WILLIAM, telecommunications executive, broadcaster, writer; b. Cleve., Jan. 10, 1945; s. Alfred George and Cecelia Grace (Duignan) McK.; m. Judy Stadnick, Aug. 19, 1967; children—Robert, David, Brian. B.A. in English, John Carroll U., Cleve., 1967. Pub. affairs programs mgr. Gen. Telephone Co. Upstate N.Y., 1970-77; dir. pub. affairs Continental Telephone of Upstate N.Y., 1977-81; asst. v.p. pub. affairs Contel Service Corp., St. Louis, 1981—; sports commentator Sta. WTRY. Mem. exec. com. Continetal Telecom Polit. Action Com., 1979—. Served to capt. U.S. Army, 1967-70. Decorated Bronze Star (2), Army Commendation Medal. Mem. Pub. Relations Soc. Am., Internat. Assn. Bus. Communicators, Advt. Club St. Louis. Roman Catholic. Club: St. Louis Press. Office: Continental Telephone Service 600 Mason Ridge Center Saint Louis MO 63141

MCKINLEY, MICHAEL ROBERT, judge; b. Ashland, Ohio, Nov. 13, 1936; s. Robert Steele and Amy Louise (Snyder) M.; m. Norma Elizabeth Anderson, June 8, 1959; 1 child, Scott. B.A., Ohio U., 1959; J.D., Ohio State U., 1962. Bar: Ohio 1962, U.S. Supreme Ct. 1973, U.S. Dist. Ct. (no. dist.) Ohio 1975. Dir. law City of Ashland, 1964-75; sole practice, Ashland, 1963-73; ptnr. Scheaffer & McKinley, Loudonville, Ohio, 1974-80; judge probate and juvenile divs. Ct. of Common Pleas, Ashland County, 1981—; dir. instl. research Ashland Coll., 1968-73. Pres. Ashland Nat. Little League, 1965-66; chmn. bd. trustees 1st Presbyterian Ch. of Ashland, 1970. Recipient Superior Jud. Service award, Ohio Supreme Ct., 1981, 82, 83, 84, Cert. of Distinction, Ohio State U., 1983. Mem. Ohio Mcpl. Attys. Assn. (pres. 1975-76), Ashland County Bar Assn. (pres. 1976-77), Ohio State Bar Assn. (chmn. local law com. 1978-80), ABA, Ohio Assn. Probate Judges (chmn. edn. com. 1983), Ohio Juvenile Judges Assn. Republican. Presbyterian. Avocations: golf; boating; swimming; traveling. Home: 404 Lake Shore Rd RFD 4 Ashland OH 44805 Office: Ashland County Courthouse W 2d St Ashland OH 44805

MCKINLEY, ROBERT CHARLES, printing company executive; b. Cin., Sept. 16, 1915; s. Charles J. and Lida (White) McK.; children—Bruce, Teri. Student Kansas City U., 1934-37. With Ashcraft, Inc., Kansas City, Mo., 1946—, chmn. bd., 1968-83, chmn. bd., 1983—. Served to 2d lt. USAAF, 1943-46. Mem. Printing Industry Am. (Kansas City Man of Yr. 1972), C. of C. Republican. Clubs: Kansas City, Mission Hills Country, Carriage, Jesters, Masons, Shriners. Office: 405 E 8th St Kansas City MO 64106

MCKINNEY, DALE JOHN, safety engineer; b. Shelby, Ohio, Mar. 5, 1922; s. John D. and Mary R. (Sprague) McK.; m. Elizabeth Marie Lawrence, Mar. 13, 1943; 1 son, Loren J. Student pub. schs., Shelby, Ohio. Plastering and masonry, 1947-50; asst. foreman forging Ohio Seamless Tube Co., 1950-53; shipping clk. transp. Govt. Supply Depot, 1953-56; auditor, safety engr. Shelby Mut. Ins. Co., 1956—. Bd. dirs. YMCA, 1970-80, pres., 1972-79; chmn. Ch. Bd. Served with U.S. Army, 1942-45, 50-53. Mem. Am. Soc. Safety Engrs., Jaycees (past pres.). Club: Sertoma (past pres.).

MCKINNON, ROBERT HAROLD, insurance company executive; b. Holtville, Calif., Apr. 4, 1927; s. Harold Arthur and Gladys Irene (Blanchar) McK.; B.S., Armstrong Coll., 1950, M.B.A., 1952; m. Marian Lois Hayes, Dec. 18, 1948; children—Steven Robert, Laurie Ellen, David Martin. Regional sales mgr. Farmers Ins. Group, Austin, Tex., 1961-66, Aurora, Ill., 1966-68; dir. life sales Farmers New World Life, Los Angeles, 1968-75; v.p. mktg. Warner Ins. Group, Chgo., 1975-82; mem. Canners Exchange Dairy Adv. Com., 1977-82; sr. v.p. mktg. The Rural Cos. Scoutmaster Boy Scouts Am., 1971-72. Served with U.S. Army, 1944-45. Mem. Am. Soc. C.L.U.s, Soc. C.P.C.U.'s, Internat. Ins. Seminars. Episcopalian. Clubs: Anvil (East Dundee, Ill.); Nakoma Golf (Madison, Wis.). Home: 402 Walnut Grove Dr Madison WI 53717 Office: 7010 Mineral Point Rd Madison WI 53705

MCKINSTRY, KEVIN LEE, insurance executive; b. Salem, Ohio, Mar. 1, 1955; s. George Thomas and Charlene Elizabeth (Davis) McK.; m. Ruby Kay Coppock, May 18, 1984; stepchildren—Leslie Brittain, Tracy Brittain. B.S. in Bus., Maryville Coll., 1977. Tax rep. H&R Block, Lenoir City, Tenn., 1978; ins. salesman McKinstry and Assocs., East Palestine, Ohio, 1978—. Dir. Pony Little League Baseball, 1983, 84; bd. dirs. East Palestine Athletic Boosters, 1984-85. Mem. Youngstown Assn. Life Underwriters (bd. dirs. 1982-84, treas. 1984—), East Palestine Jaycees (pres. 1981, 82, bd. dirs. 1984). Republican. Presbyterian. Avocations: volleyball and basketball officiating; basketball coach; reading; working with children. Home: 176 E Martin St East Palestine OH 44413 Office: McKinstry and Assocs 566 Alice St PO Box 351 East Palestine OH 44413

MCKINSTRY, ROGER LEE, pharmacist; b. Wooster, Ohio, Nov. 22, 1953; s. Clyde A. and Wanda M. (Thorley) McK.; m. Lesley E. Stambaugh, Aug. 13, 1977; children—Mark Alan, Gregory Lee. B.S. in Pharmacy, Ohio No. U., 1977. Staff pharmacist Akron Gen. Med., Ohio, 1977-81; dir. of pharmacy Lodi Community Hosp., Ohio, 1981-83, Molly Stark Hosp., Louisville, Ohio, 1983—; cons. pharmacist J. T. Nist Geriatric, Louisville, 1983—, Stark Surg. Co., 1984—. Mem. Ohio State Pharmacy Assn., Akron Soc. Hosp. Pharmacists. Democrat. Lutheran. Avocations: camping, boating, swimming, gardening. Home: 1055 Canyon St NW Uniontown OH 44685 Office: Molly Stark Hosp 7900 Columbus Ave Louisville OH 44632

MCKNIGHT, ROBERT ALLEN, marketing and business consultant; b. Detroit, Apr. 24, 1943; s. L. Allen and Mildred Mary (Schwartz) McK.; m. Jacqueline Sue Estes, Nov. 23, 1966. Student Miami U., Oxford, Ohio, 1961-63; B.A., Ohio State U., 1966, M.A., 1968. Copy writer Terra Advt. Co., Columbus, Ohio, 1965; pub. info. officer Ohio Dept. Liquor Control, Columbus, 1966-68; research and pub. relations dir. Ohio Rep. Hdqrs., Columbus, 1968-71; with Columbus Air Conditioning Corp., 1971-82, pres., chmn., 1979-82; ptnr. Prime Asset Mgmt., Columbus, 1982—, These Are My Jewels, 1982—; owner Misc., Inc., Columbus. . Pres., Pilot Dogs, Inc., 1981-84; bd. dirs. Better Bus. Bur., 1981—. Mem. Heating and Air Conditioning Assn. Ohio (pres. 1979-81), Carrier Midwest Dealer Council (chmn. 1980-82). Republican. Lutheran. Lodges: Mason, Shriners (exec. sec. 1984—), Rotary. Home: 4540 Tetford Rd Upper Arlington OH 43220 Office: 691 S 5th St Columbus OH 43206 also 34 N 4th St Columbus OH 43215

MCKNIGHT, ROBERT LORNE, marketing executive, investor; b. Wichita, Kans., Feb. 23, 1947; s. Philip Charles and Margaret Catherine (McClymonds) McK.; m. Caroline King Hampton, July 29, 1972; children—Margaret Hampton, Elizabeth King. Student U. Kans., 1965-67, 68-70, Wichita State U., 1967-68. Writer Barickman Advertising, Kansas City, Mo., 1971-73; project creative dir. Rickey & Biederman, Shawnee Mission, Kans., 1973-75; pres. McKnight & Assocs., Shawnee Mission, 1975-79; mag. pub. Sosland Publishing Co., Kansas City, 1979-84; pres. Ceres Group, Overland Park, Kans., 1984—, AMERIND, Overland Park, 1985—; dir. Sugarloaf Mountain Wood Works, Hartford, Ark., 1983—. Author: Creative Services-Kansas City, 1974. Captions Author: Return to Kansas, 1984. Purple Mountains Majesties, 1986. Co-founder, pres. Park & Recreation Found. Johnson County, Overland Park, Kans., 1979—; bd. dirs. Friends of the Zoo, Kansas City, 1974-77, Planned Parenthood, Kansas City, 1975-78. Recipient various awards Kansas City Advertising Club, Art Directors Club. Fellow Stephen Duck Soc.; mem. Grain Elevator and Processing Soc., Nat. Grain and Feed Assn., Kansas Grain and Feed Dealers, Am. Mktg. Assn., Internat. Trade Club, Am. Cons. League, Am. Soc. Agrl. Cons. Avocations: travel; flying. Office: Ceres Group 5443 W 100th Terrace Overland Park KS 66207

MC KNIGHT, VAL BUNDY, engineering consultant; b. Budapest, Hungary, Sept. 14, 1926; s. Valentine B. and Maria E. (Heray) Mariahegyi; came to U.S., 1966, naturalized, 1971; student Inst. Tech., Budapest; M.E.E., Tech. U. Budapest, 1954; postgrad. Bradley U., 1966-68; m. Ruby P. Fulop, Aug. 9, 1947; children—Bela, Suzy. Mgr. engring. Ministry of Constrn. Industry, Budapest, 1955-57; supervising engr. Canadian Brit. Aluminum Co., Baie Comeau, Que., 1958-66; utilities cons. Caterpillar Tractor Co., Peoria, Ill., 1966—. Mem. Republican Nat. Com., Presdl. Task Force; radio communication advisor Civil Def. System, 1969-76; nat. adv. bd. Am. Security Council, 1975-77; deacon Westminster Presbyterian Ch. Served to lt., Budapest Mil. Acad., 1954-55. Named Innovator of Yr., 1955; knighted, Order of Knights, 1942; cert. plant engr.; registered profl. engr., Que. Mem. Am. Inst. Plant Engrs. (plant engr. of year 1976-77, 77-78, pres. chpt. 93, 1979-80, del. dir. 1981—), Nat., Ill. (govt. relations and public affairs com. 1977-80, planning resources com. 1982—) socs. profl. engrs., Corp. of Profl. Engrs. of Que., IEEE (liquid dielectric com.), Illuminating Engring. Soc., Nat. Assn. Bus. Ednl. Radio, NAM (policy com.), Engring. Inst. Can., Mfrs. Radio Frequency Adv. Council (dir. 1978—, v.p.), Assn. Energy Engrs., Nat. Machine Tool Builders Assn. (joint indsl. council), Am. Assn. Engring. Socs. (internat. affairs council), Ill. State C. of C. (energy task force). Clubs: Masons, Shriners. Home: 6831 N Michele Ln Peoria IL 61614 Office: 100 NE Adams St Peoria IL 61629

MC KONE, DON T., corporate executive; b. Jackson, Mich., 1921; grad. U. Mich., 1947. Chmn. bd., chief exec. officer, dir. Libbey-Owens-Ford Co., Toledo; dir. Ohio Citizens Bancorp, Inc., Ashland Oil Co., Consumers Power Co., Nat. Bank Detroit. Office: Libbey-Owens-Ford Co 811 Madison Ave Toledo OH 43695

MCKOWEN, DOROTHY KEETON, librarian; b. Bonne Terre, Mo., Oct. 5, 1948; d. John Richard and Dorothy (Spoonhour) Keeton; m. Paul Edwin McKowen, Dec. 19, 1970; children—Richard James, Mark David. B.S., Pacific Christian Coll., 1970; M.S. in Library Sci., U. So. Calif., 1973; M.A. in English, Purdue U., 1985. Librarian-specialist Doheny Library, U. So. Calif., 1973-74; asst. librarian Pacific Christian Coll., 1974-78; serials cataloger Purdue Univ. Libraries, 1978—. Mem. ALA (resources and tech. services div. council of regional groups 1983—), Ind. Library Assn. (vice chmn. tech. services div. 1983-84, chmn. 1984-85), Ohio Valley Group Tech. Services Librarians (vice chmn. 1984-85, chmn. 1985-86). Republican. Home: 7625 Summit Ln Lafayette IN 47905 Office: Purdue Univ Libraries West Lafayette IN 47907

MCLAREN, RICHARD WELLINGTON, JR., lawyer; b. Cin., May 15, 1945; s. Richard Wellington and Edith (Gillett) McL.; m. Ann Lynn Zachrich, Sept. 4, 1974; children—Christine, Richard, Charles. B.A., Yale U., 1967; J.D., Northwestern U., 1973. Bar: Ohio 1973, U.S. Dist. Ct. (no. dist.) Ohio, 1973, U.S. Ct. Appeals (6th cir.) 1978, U.S. Supreme Ct. 1981. Assoc. Squire, Sanders & Dempsey, Cleve., 1973-82, ptnr., 1983—. Served to 1st lt. U.S. Army, 1967-70. Mem. ABA (litigation and pub. utilities sect.), Ohio Bar Assn. (pub. utilities com.), Defense Research Inst. Club: Cleve. Athletic. Office: Squire Sanders & Dempsey 1800 Huntington Bldg Cleveland OH 44115

MCLATCHIE, LOIS REEDER, psychologist, educator; b. Camden, N.J., Sept. 27, 1931; d. Amos Smith and C. Inez (Landis) Reeder; m. William Richmond Locky McLatchie, June 4, 1955; children—Ruth, John, David, Elizabeth, Willa. B.A., U. Alta. (Can.), 1974; M.S., Pa. State U., 1977, Ph.D., 1981. Lic. psychologist, Ohio. Instr. psychology Pa. State U., 1976-77; psychology intern Cleve. VA Hosp., 1978-79; psychologist HMO Health-Ohio, Cleve.-West, 1984—; psychologist Western Res. Psychiat. Habilitation Ctr., Northfield, Ohio, 1979-84; adj. clin. instr. Case Western Res. U., Cleve., 1982-84; pres. Clearfield-Jefferson Mental Health Assn., 1977-78. Bd. dirs. Mental Health Assn. Pa., 1976-78. Recipient Disting. Service award Mental Health/Alta., 1973. Mem. Am. Psychol. Assn., Ohio Psychol. Assn., State Assn. Psychology, Psychol. Assn. Western Res., Republican. Baptist. Home: 1711 Lander Rd Mayfield Heights OH 44124 Office: HMO Health-Ohio Cleve West 4330 W 150th St Cleveland OH 44135

MCLAUCHLIN, LON ROYCE, telephone company official; b. Hutnsville, Tex., Dec. 9, 1934; s. Aubrey Royce and Ara Lee (Cockrell) McL.; m. Glenda Lou Porter, Sept. 6, 1955; children—Lon, Kevin, Kimberly. B.B.A., N. Tex. State U., 1957. Mgr., Southwestern Bell Telephone Co., Uvalde, Tex., 1958, Houston, 1959-68, dist. mgr., 1968-69, div. supr., Kansas City, Mo., 1969-72, div. mgr., Springfield, Mo., 1972-83, div. staff mgr., St. Louis, 1983—; dir. Centerre Bank, Springfield. Bd. dirs. Jr. Achievement, Springfield, 1972-83, Boy Scouts Am., 1974-78, St. John's Hosp., Springfield, 1975-80, Community Found., 1980-83, Better Bus. Bur., 1982-83; pres. Downtown Springfield Assn., 1982-83; pres., organizer Safety Council S.W. Mo., 1983. Named Boss of Yr., Am. Bus. Women's Assn. Springfield, 1973; recipient Caring award Springfield council Girl Scouts U.S.A., 1976. Mem. Springfield Area C. of C. (pres. 1977). Republican. Methodist. Club: Twin Oaks Country (Springfield). Lodge: Rotary (Springfield). Avocations: golf; camping. Home: 370 Greentrails Dr S Chesterfield MO 63017 Office: Southwestern Bell Telephone One Bell Ctr Saint Louis MO 63101

MCLAUGHLIN, JOHN FRANCIS, engineering educator, consultant; b. N.Y.C., Sept. 21, 1927; s. William and Anne (Goodwin) McL.; m. Eleanor Thomas Trethewey, Nov. 22, 1950; children—Susan, Donald, Cynthia, Kevin. B.S. in Civil Engring., Syracuse U., 1950; M.S. in Civil Engring., Purdue U., 1953, Ph.D., 1957. Registered profl. engr., Kans. From asst. prof. to prof. Purdue U., West Lafayette, Ind., 1957—, head sch. civil engring., 1968-78, now assoc. dean engring. Fellow ASTM (bd. dirs. 1984-86, award of merit 1984), ASCE; hon. mem. Am. Concrete Inst. (pres. 1979-80); mem. Nat. Soc. Profl. Engrs., Am. Soc. Engring. Edn. Home: 112 Sumac Dr West Lafayette IN 47906 Office: Purdue U Sch Civil Engring West Lafayette IN 47907

MC LAUGHLIN, WILLIAM GAYLORD, metal products manufacturing company executive; b. Marietta, Ohio, Sept. 28, 1936; s. William Russell and Edna Martha (Hiatt) McL.; B.S. in Mech. Engring., U. Cin., 1959; M.B.A., Ball State U., 1967; children—Debora, Cynthia, Leslie, Teresa, Kristin, Jennifer; m. 2d, Karen Davis Newhouse, Apr. 16, 1983; stepchildren—Marcina Newhouse, David Newhouse. Plant engr. Kroger Co., Marion, Ind., 1959-62; with Honeywell, Inc., Wabash, Ind., 1962-75, mgr. metal products ops., 1971-72, gen. mgr. ops., 1972-75; pres. MarkHon Industries Inc., Wabash, 1975—. Pres. Wabash Assn. for Retarded Children, 1974-75; gen. chmn. United Fund Drive, 1971; mem. Wabash County Arts Council; pres. Wabash Valley Dance Theater; North Central Ind. Pvt. Industry Council, 1983-84; mem. bus. adv. bd. Manchester Coll. Treas., Young Republicans., Wabash, 1968-70. Bd. dirs. Youth Service Bur., Sr. Citizens, Jr. Achievement. Recipient Ind. Jefferson award for public service, 1981; Disting. Citizen award Wabash, 1981; named Outstanding Young Man of Year, Wabash Jr. C. of C., 1972. Mem. Indsl. (pres. 1973-74), Wabash Area (pres. 1976) chambers commerce, Am. Metal Stamping Assn. (chmn. Ind. dist. 1978, chmn. metal fabrication div.), Ind. Mfg. Assn. (dir.), Young Presidents Orgn., Cincinnatus Soc. Rotarian (pres. 1970-71, dist. youth exchange officer 1974-77, dist. gov. 1979-80). Methodist (mem. ofcl. bd. 1966-71, pres. Methodist Men 1975-77). Clubs: Wabash Country (v.p. 1972-76), Masons. Patentee design electronic relay rack cabinet. Home: 141 W Maple St Wabash IN 46992 Office: 200 Bond St Wabash IN 46992

MCLAUGHLIN, WILLIAM HARRIS, chem. engr.; b. San Antonio, June 21, 1927; s. Harris M. and Viola (Essen) McL.; B.S. in Chem. Engring., Northwestern U., 1949; m. Jean Trangmar, Aug. 21, 1954; children—Thomas H., Karen J. Process engr. Abbott Labs., North Chicago, Ill., 1949-60; mgmt. sci. mgr. Monsanto Co., St. Louis, 1960-76, gen. engr., 1977—; gen. mgr. The Hugo Essen Farms, St. Louis County, 1968—. Trustee, gen. mgr. Hiram Cemetery, Creve Coeur, Mo., 1964—; pres. Graeler Park Assn., St. Louis County, 1966-68. Served with U.S. Army, 1945-46. Mem. Nat. Assn. Cemeteries, Assn. Cemeteries of Mo., Associated Cemeteries of St. Louis (bd. dirs. 1983-84), Sigma Xi, Triangle. Clubs: Masons, Shriners. Patentee in field. Home: 7 Gandy Dr Creve Coeur MO 63146 Office: 800 N Lindbergh Blvd Saint Louis MO 63166

MCLEAN, E(DWARD) BRUCE, biology educator, university administrator, ecology, behavior researcher; b. Washington Ct. House, Ohio, Jan. 10, 1937; s. Richard H. and Nell (Whitmer) McL.; m. Talia Sue Korn, Aug. 25, 1968 (div. Jan. 4, 1985); children—Scott Walter, Hillary Beth, Jeremy Ryan. B.S., Ohio State U., 1958, M.S., 1963, Ph.D., 1968. Asst. prof. biology So. U., Baton Rouge, La., 1968-70; asst. prof. to prof. biology John Carroll U., Univ. Heights, Ohio, 1970-81, prof., chmn. dept. biology, 1981—; ecol. cons. to various agencies, 1973—. Contbr. articles to profl. jours. Adv. trustee Shaker Lakes Regional Nature Ctr., Shaker Heights, Ohio, 1976—; various positions Boy Scouts Am., Girls Scouts Am., Univ. Heights, 1979-82. Served with U.S. Army Med. Corps, 1958-60. Grantee So.. Univ. Research Found., 1969, Ohio Biol. Survey, 1980. Fellow Ohio Acad. Sci. (v.p. 1982-83); mem. Am. Ornithologists' Union, Wilson Ornithological Soc.; institution rep. Ohio Biol. Survey (mem. exec. com. 1979-82). Avocations: birding; camping; fishing; hunting. Office: Dept Biology John Carroll Univ University Heights OH 44118

MCLEAN, MALCOLM, college president; b. Duluth, Minn., Apr. 23, 1927; s. Charles Russell and Mildred (Washburn) M.; m. Wendy Heaton, May 20, 1956; children—Ian, Hugh, Christopher Russell. B.A. in English Lit., Yale U., 1948; M.S. in Internat. Relations, George Washington U., 1967; L.H.D., Coll. of St. Scholastica, 1973. Advt. rep. Bemidji Daily Pioneer, Minn., 1950-53; advt. mgr. H.B. Fuller Co., St. Paul, 1953-55; mem. staff USIA, 1955-71, pub. affairs officer U.S. Embassy, Guatemala City, 1969-71; pres. Northland Coll., Ashland, Wis., 1971—; mem. adv. bd. Sigurd Olson Environ. Inst.; bd. dirs. Lake Superior Dist. Power Co., No. States Power Co.-Wis., Chippewa Industries. Chmn., Council for Higher Edn., United Ch. of Christ, 1976-77; chmn. Wis. Arts Bd., 1983-84. Served with USN, 1944-46, U.S. Army, 1950-52, Korea. Mem. Lake Superior Assn. Colls. and Univs. (bd. trustees), Wis. Assn. Ind. Colls. and Univs. (pres. 1975-77), Wis. Acad. Scis. Arts and Letters (governing council 1977-80) Office: Northland Coll Ashland WI 54806

MCLEAN, ROBERT ALEXANDER, educator, consulting economist; b. Denton, Tex., Aug. 7, 1949; s. Billy Bob and Cora Alice (Guenther) McL.; m. Sharon Rose Noftz, Feb. 17, 1979; 1 child, Robert Alexander Jr. B.A., U. Tex.-Austin, 1971, M.A., 1973; Ph.D., Cornell U., 1976. Instr. Hobart Coll., Geneva, N.Y., 1975; asst. prof. U. Wis.-Milw., 1975-78; research assoc. AMA, Chgo., 1978-79; asst. prof. U. Kans., Lawrence, 1979-83, assoc. prof., 1983—; pres. Robert A. McLean, Cons. Economist, Lawrence, 1981—. Contbr. articles to profl. jours. Recipient Faculty scholarship U. Kans., 1983. Fellow Fin. Analysts Fedn.; mem. Am. Econ. Assn., Am. Fin. Assn., Inst. Chartered Fin. Analysts, Kans. Econ. Assn. (dir. 1984-85, v.p. 1985—), Phi Beta Kappa, Omicron Delta Kappa, Phi Kappa Phi. Democrat. Presbyterian. Home: 3224 Tomahawk Dr Lawrence KS 66044 Office: U Kans Sch Bus Lawrence KS 66045

MCLELLAN, EDWARD GEORGE, university adminstrator; b. Pawtucket, R.I., Dec. 24, 1946; s. Robert and Mildred Lyvonia (Doran) McL.; m. Raverne Eloise Scott, Nov. 15, 1967; 1 dau., Melissa Rae. B.A., U. R.I., 1972; M.B.A., Nat. U., 1980. Mgmt. specialist San Diego Gas & Electric Co., 1978-80; v.p. adminstrn. Seabury-Western Theol. Sem., Evanston, Ill., 1980—. Served with USMC, 1964-68, 73-77. Decorated Purple Heart. Mem. Nat. Assn. Coll. and Univ. Bus. Offices, Central Assn. Coll. and Univ. Bus. Offices. Republican. Episcopalian. Home: 2750 Lawndale Ave Evanston IL 60201 Office: 2122 Sheridan Rd Evanston IL 60201

MC LENDON, HENRY LEWELLYNN, real estate broker; b. Valdosta, Ga., Feb. 16, 1908; s. Henry Kirk and Lila (Sharp) McL.; student U. Miami, 1927, U. Ky., 1928-29; m. Mary Louise Plummer, May 27, 1938; children—Vicky Lu, Judy, James Clifford. Sec., treas. Zanesville Devel. Co., 1947—. Mem. Zanesville Exchange Club. Home: 3058 Lookout Dr Zanesville OH 43701 Winter: 615 Rabbit Rd Sanibel Island FL Office: 330 Main St Zanesville OH 43701

MCLEOD, DEBRA ANN, librarian, mail order book company executive; b. St. Louis, Apr. 21, 1952; d. Frank Joseph and Virginia Veronica (Jasso) Osterloh; m. Bradley J. McLeod, June 24, 1977; 1 dau., Catherine Rose. B.A. in History, U. Mo.-St. Louis, 1974; M.S.L.S., U. Ill., 1975. Research asst. Grad. Sch. Library Sci., U. Ill., Urbana, 1974; children's librarian St. Louis Pub. Library, 1976-77, Kent County Library System, Grand Rapids, Mich., 1977-81; children's specialist Johnson County Library, Shawnee Mission, Kans., 1981-83, coordinator children's collections, 1983—; mng. ptnr. The Book Tree, Lenexa, Kans., 1982—; library cons. Family Services of Kent County (Mich.), 1977-79. Mem. ALA, Assn. for Library Service to Children (Scribner award 1980, Newbery award com. 1983), Shawnee Jaycee Women (pres. 1982-83). Roman Catholic. Home: 9134 Twilight Ln Lenexa KS 66219 Office: Johnson County Library System 8700 W 63d St Shawnee Mission KS 66201

MCLIN, NATHANIEL, JR., educator; b. Chgo., June 19, 1928; s. Nathaniel and Anna (Polk) McL.; m. Lena Mae, July 18, 1952; children—Nathaniel Gerald, Beverly Jane. Student Wilson Jr. Coll., Chgo., 1946-50, Roosevelt U., 1950-52; M.A. Govs. State U.; postgrad. (fellow), Walden U., 1976. Technician, Michael Reese Hosp., 1951-52, U. Chgo. Goldblatt Clinic, 1952-53; bus driver Chgo. Transit Authority, 1953-64; pub. relations dir. Opera Theater of Chgo., 1959-60; mgr. McLin Opera Co., Chgo., 1960-71; salesman Watkins Products Co., 1964-65; tchr. Chgo. Com. on Urban Opportunity, 1965-71; soloist Park Dist. Opera Guild, Chgo., 1964-68. Active Beatrice Caffrey Found., Chgo.; dir. Trinity United Ch. Mens Chorus, Chgo., 1962-66; active fund raising campaign pub. relations YMCA, 1963-64; cultural coordinator, dir. Halsted Urban Progress ctr., Chgo., 1966-71; dir. Faces of Crime Symposium All Souls Ch., Chgo., also lay leader, 1980—. Served with U.S. Army, 1946-47. Recipient Wheelers Social Club citation for efforts in nations cultural devel., 1962. Lodge: Fraternal Order of Police (pres. lodge 83 1980-81). Author: Parole: The Ex-offender's Last Hope, 1983. Home and Office: 7630 S Hoyne St Chicago IL 60620

MCLIN, RHINE LANA, funeral director, educator; b. Dayton, Ohio, Oct. 3, 1948; d. C. Josef, Jr., and Bernice (Cottman) McL. B.A. in Sociology, Parsons Coll., 1969; M.Ed., Xavier U., Cin., 1972; postgrad. in law U. Dayton, 1974-76. Lic. funeral dir. and notary pub.; cert. tchr., Ohio. Tchr. Dayton Bd. Edn., 1970-72; divorce counselor Domestic Relations Ct., Dayton, 1972-73; law clk. Montgomery Common Pleas Ct., Dayton, 1973-74; v.p., mgr. McLin Funeral Homes, Dayton, 1972—; instr. Central State U., Wilberforce, Ohio, 1982—; speaker Dayton Pub. Schs., 1980—. Author 6-series article: Death and Dying, 1980. Adv. bd. Dayton Contemporary Dance Co., 1977, Montgomery County Welfare and Social Services, Dayton, 1983, Nat. Council on Women's Edn. Programs, 1980; mem. Democratic Voters League, Dayton, 1969; mem. Ohio Lottery Commn., 1983—; trustee Greater Dayton Sr. Citizens, 1984. Recipient Friendship award St. Mark's Masonic Lodge 165, 1980, Brotherhood award Upshaw African Meth. Episcopal Ch., 1983, Recognition award Fed. Women's Program, Dayton, 1981; One in a Million award Columbus 10-City Rally of Nat. Council Negro Women, 1984. Mem. Nat. Funeral Dirs. Assn., Ohio Funeral Dirs. Assn., Montgomery County Funeral Dirs. Assn., Women Bus. Owners Assn., NAACP (life), Nat. Council Negro Women (life), Delta Sigma Theta (recognition award 1981). Home: 1130 Germantown St Dayton OH 45408 Office: McLin Funeral Home Inc 1130 Germantown St Dayton OH 45408

MCLOUGHLIN, CAVEN SEAN, education and psychology educator; b. London, Nov. 11, 1948; came to U.S., 1976; m. Patricia J. Bracey. B.A., Open U., Eng., 1976; M.A., Calif. Poly. U., 1977; Ph.D., U. Utah, 1981. Asst. prof. edn. and psychology Kent State U., Ohio, 1981—. Editor, contbg. author: Educators, Children and the Law, 1985. Contbr. articles to profl. jours. Home: 617 N Willow Kent OH 44240 Office: Kent State U 412 White Hall Kent OH 44242

MCMAHAN, GARY LYNN, medical foundation executive; b. Kansas City, Mo., Mar. 2, 1948; s. Stanley Owen and Edith Evelena (Shannon) McM.; m. Kathy Sue Brockman, Mar. 28, 1970 (div. 1974); m. 2d, Mary Garold Hearn, Aug. 20, 1976; 1 dau., Terri Lee. B.A., U. Mo., 1970, M.P.A., 1973. Sr. program planner Bendix Corp., Kansas City, Mo., 1971-73; project adminstr. U. Mo., Kansas City, 1973-79; exec. v.p. Acad. Health Profls., 1979-80, Family Health Found. Am., 1980—. Bd. sec. AAFP-MDIS Inc., 1981—. Author: An Evaluation Profile: Summary of the Evaluation Activities of the Individual Area Health Education Centers, 1977. Mem. task force Mo. Govs. Task Force on Rural Health, Jefferson City, 1978; bd. dirs., treas. Jackson County Bd. Services for the Developmentally Disabled, Kansas City, 1981—, pres., 1985. Mem. Mid Am. Soc. Assn. Execs., Soc. Tchrs. Family Medicine, N.Am. Primary Care Research Group, Nat. Soc. Fund Raising Execs. Home: 805 Burning Tree Lee's Summit MO 64063 Office: Family Health Found Am 1740 W 92d St Kansas City MO 64114

MCMAHEL, DONALD EUGENE, music educator; b. New Albany, Ind., Feb. 25, 1930; s. Lawrence and Gertrude (Denison) McM.; m. Elizabeth Hadley, Sept. 3, 1950; children—Donna, Brian. B.A. in Music, Ind. U., 1952, M.A. in Music, 1957. Instr. music Western Ky. U., Bowling Green, 1952-56, Tex. A&I U., Kingsville, 1957-59; tchr. New Albany Sch. Corp, Ind., 1959—; mem. orch. Corpus Christi Symphony, Tex., 1957-59; adj. faculty Ind. U., New Albany, 1961-83; co-dir. Southern Ind. Orch. New Albany, 1963-70; Floyd County Youth Orch. New Albany, 1974-84; asst. dir. Louisville Youth Orch., 1961-73; music cons. Ministry of Edn., Singapore, 1972, 74, 83. Contbr. articles to profl. jours. Recipient Tchr. of Yr. award Ind. U., 1975. Mem. NEA, Ind. State Tchrs. Assn., Am. Fedn. Musicians. Avocations: photography, travel, gardening. Home: 1 Oxford Dr New Albany IN 47150 Office: New Albany Sch Corp 802 E Market St New Albany IN 47150

MCMAHON, FRANKLIN, artist, reporter; b. Oak Park, Ill., Sept. 9, 1921; s. William Francis and Elizabeth (Franklin) McM.; m. Irene Mary Leahy, July 28, 1945; children—William Franklin, Mark, Mary, Deborah, Patrick, Hugh, Margot, Michelle, Michael. Student Art Inst. Chgo., 1940-42, Inst. Design, Chgo., 1946-50, Am. Acad. Fine Arts, Chgo., 1939-40; D.F.A. (hon.) Chgo. Acad. Fine Arts, 1973, Lake Forest Coll., 1977; L.H.D. (hon.) Loyola U., 1985. Freelance artist, Chgo., 1939—; freelance artist-reporter, Chgo., 1960—. Works pub. in various mags. and newspapers including: Life, Look, Sports Illustrated, Fortune, N.Y. Times, Chgo. Tribune, Chgo. Sun Times, U.S. Catholic, Chgo. Mag. Author, artist: This Church, These Times, 1980; author art documentaries Stas. PBS-TV and CBS-TV. Bd. dirs. Lake Forest High Sch. Served to 2d lt. USAF, 1942-45. Named Artist of Yr., Artists Guild N.Y.; recipient 3 Emmys, 1 Peabody and other art awards. Mem. Soc. Typog. Arts (hon.), Artists Guild Chgo. (hon.), Arts Club Chgo. Roman Catholic. Office: Aerie Gallery 501 N Wells St Chicago IL 60610

MCMAHON, JIM (JAMES ROBERT), professional football player. Quarterback, Chgo. Bears, NFL. Office: Chgo Bears 55 E Jackson Blvd Suite 1200 Chicago IL 60604*

MCMAHON, JOHN ALEXANDER, association executive; b. Monongahela, Pa., July 31, 1921; s. John Hamilton and Jean (Alexander) McM.; m. Betty Wagner, Sept. 14, 1947; m. 2d, Anne Fountain Willets, May 1, 1977; children—Alexander Talpey, Sarah Francis, Elizabeth Wagner, Ann Wallace. A.B. magna cum laude, Duke U., 1942; J.D., Harvard U., 1948; LL.D., Wake Forest U., 1978. Bar: N.C. 1950. Prof. pub. law and govt. U. N.C., Chapel Hill, asst. dir. Inst. Govt., 1948-59; gen. counsel, sec.-treas. N.C. Assn. County Commrs., Chapel Hill, 1959-65; v.p. spl. devel. Hosp. Savs. Assn., Chapel Hill, 1965-67; pres. N.C. Blue Cross and Blue Shield, Inc., Chapel Hill, 1968-72; pres. Am. Hosp. Assn., Chgo., 1972—; dir. 3M. Mem. council of mgmt., past pres. Internat. Hosp. Fedn.; chmn. bd. trustees Duke U., 1971-83, chmn. emeritus, 1983—; vice chmn. bd. dirs. Nat. Ctr. Health Edn.; mem. U.S. C. of C. health care com.; mem. Pres.'s Commn. Health Edn., 1971-72; mem. adv. council Northwestern U. Served as col. USAAFR, 1942-46. Mem. Inst. of Medicine. Presbyterian. Clubs: Chapel Hill Country; Hope Valley, Durham Dunes Golf and Beach (Myrtle Beach); Carlton (Chgo.). Home: 1150 N Lake Shore Dr Chicago IL 60611 Office: 840 N Lake Shore Dr Chicago IL 60611

MCMAHON, TIMOTHY T., optometrist, educator, researcher; b. Milw., Apr. 27, 1954; s. David James and Carla (Tiernam) McM; m. Kay Ellen Lillie, July 28, 1979; 1 child, Ryan Andrew. Student, U. of Wis.-Madison, 1972-76; B.S., Ill. Coll. Optometry, 1977, O.D., 1980. Resident Kansas City VA Hosp., 1980-81; optometrist Abraham Lincoln Sch. Medicine, Chgo., 1981—; asst. prof. U. Ill. Chgo., 1981—. Contbr. articles to profl. jours. Nikon scholar, 1976; recipient William Feinbloom Low Vision award Designs for Vision Inc., 1980. Fellow Am. Acad. Optometry; mem. Assn. Research in Vision and Ophthalmology Ill. Low Vision Soc. (sec. 1983—), Am. Optometric Assn. (charter mem. low vision sect.), Ill. Optometric Assn., South Suburban Optometric Assn. (v.p. 1984—), Gold Key Honor Soc., Beta Sigma Kappa. Office: Eye and Ear Infirmary U Ill at Chgo 1855 W Taylor Suite 3164 Chicago IL 60612

MCMANAMAN, RAYMOND, brother, theology educator; b. Waukegan, Ill., July 14, 1929; s. Raymond John and Fraces (Tonigan) McM. M.A., St. Mary's Coll., Winona, Minn., 1956; M.A., Seattle U., 1972; D.Min., Aquinas Inst. Theology, 1977; S.T.D., San Francisco Theol. Sem., 1981. Joined Christian Brothers, Roman Catholic Ch., 1947. Prin. St. Francis High Sch., Wheaton, Ill., 1963-66, La Salle High Sch., Cin., 1966-68, St. Paul High Sch., Chgo., 1968-70; dean students Lewis U., Romeoville, Ill., 1960-63, tchr., 1961-63, 72—, chmn. religious studies dept., 1974-77, 79—; bd. dirs. Commn. for Catholic Impact, Lockport, Ill., 1974-75; Ednl. Policies Com., Romeoville, 1974-76, profl. status com., 1977-84; dir. Inst. for Parish Ministry, Joliet, Ill., 1974-77. Author: The Seven Sacraments, 1981. Mem. Coll. Theology Soc., Nat. Catholic Evangelization Assn., Theta Alpha Kappa (treas. 1093—). Avocations: hiking, swimming, reading. Home and Office: Lewis U Romeoville IL 60441

MCMANAMON, JOHN THOMAS, management consultant; b. Cleve., Dec. 14, 1938; s. John J. and Cathrine B. (Bauman) McM.; m. Donna M. Pahoresky; children—Daniel, Patricia, Mary, Timothy. B.S., John Carroll Coll., 1961; grad. in Bus., Western Reserve Sch., 1964. Mfg. co-ordinator Sherwin Williams, Cleve., 1966-68; cons. Peat, Marwick & Mitchell, Cleve., 1968-69; Datalogics, Cleve., 1969-70; dir. mgmt. info. systems Mid-continent Telephone, Hudson, Ohio, 1970-83, v.p. cons. Alltel Corp., Hudson, 1983—, dir. Alltel Middle East, Dammam, Saudi Arabia, 1984—. Republican. Roman Catholic. Avocations: boating; traveling. Home: 148 Bayberry Dr Northfield OH 44067 Office: Alltel Corp 100 Exec Pkwy Hudson OH 44236

MCMANUS, DARCY DIANE EDGERTON, lawyer; b. Waterloo, Iowa, Mar. 27, 1951; d. Edward Keith Edgerton and Margaret Miriam (Frost) Edgerton Morton; m. Douglas Brien McManus, Aug. 12, 1972; children—Matthew Keith, Bradley David, Daniel Burton. B.A., Macalester Coll., 1972; J.D. with honors, U. S.D., 1975. Bar: S.D. 1976, U.S. Dist. Ct. (ea. dist.) S.D. 1976, Wis. 1978. Law clk. S.D. 2d Cir. Ct., Sioux Falls, 1976-77; assoc. Morton D. Newald, S.C., Milw., 1978-84, Grady Law Office, Port Washington, 1984—. Bd. dirs., treas. Community Learning Cr., Inc., Port Washington, Wis., 1981-83; treas. First Congl. Ch., United Ch. of Christ, Port Washington, 1982-84; bd. dirs. United Way of Port Washington-Saukville, 1984—. Nat. Merit scholar Macalester Coll., 1969. Mem. State Bar S.D., State Bar Wis., ABA, Ozaukee County Bar Assn., LWV, P.E.O. Democrat. Home: 308 E Whitefish Rd Port Washington WI 53074 Office: Grady Law Office 114 E Main Port Washington WI 53074

MCMANUS, EDWARD J., judge. U.S. Dist. Judge Eighth Cir., No. Iowa, now chief judge. Office: US Dist Ct PO Box 4815 Cedar Rapids IA 52407*

MC MANUS, ROBERT LEE, marketing services executive; b. Carmi, Ill., Dec. 3, 1922; s. Merle LeRoy and Laura Marie (Dissman) McM.; B.A., U. Ill., 1950; children—Laurie Ann McManus Kammerer, Katharine Sue, Bridgit Kathleen. Sales engr. James L. Lyon Co., Chgo., 1951-56; pres., R.L. McManus & Co., Peoria, Ill., 1956-65; dir. project devel. John Hackler & Co., architects, Peoria, Ill., 1966-80; specifications mgr. Beling Consultants Inc., 1980—; treas. Prairie State Legal Services Corp., 1977-79, v.p., 1979-80, pres., 1980-81. Pres., Greater Peoria (Ill.) Legal Aid Soc., 1972-74, Central Ill. Agy. on Aging, 1972-75; chmn. Comprehensive Geriatric Treatment Service, 1972-75; chmn. Mayor's Commn. on Aging, 1975—; pres., Sr. Citizens Found., Inc., 1972-78. Served with USAAF, 1941-43. Fellow Constrn. Specifications Inst. (bd. dirs., region dir., pres. Central Ill. chpt. 1973-75, chmn. inst. tech. documents com., v.p. 1984-85, Tech. Excellence in Specification Writing award 1973, Honor award 1978, 84); mem. U. Ill. Alumni Assn. (life). Club: Creve Coeur (Peoria, Ill.). Home: 7133 N Terra Vista #202 Peoria IL 61614 Office: 7620 N University Suite 2200 Peoria IL 61614

MCMASTERS, DONALD WARD, architect; b. Chgo., Oct. 19, 1933; s. Ward H. and Mary E. (Rabson) M.; m. Helen D. Russell, June 21, 1958; children—Dale R., Laura L., Peter B. B.Arch. U. Ill., 1957. Lic. architect., Ill., Mich., Wis., Nat. Council Archtl. Registration Bds. Architect, Henchien-Everds-Crombie, Chgo., 1953-54, W.B. Cohen, Chgo., 1957-59, Fridstein-Fitch, Chgo., 1959-61, H. Johnson Constrn., Co., Evanston, Ill., 1961-63; pvt. practice architecture, Libertyville, Ill., 1963—. Chmn., Park Bd., Village of Fontanta, Wis.; mem. Planning Commn., Fontana. Served with USAR, 1957-63. Recipient SARA Nat. Residence design award 1978. Fellow Soc Am. Registered Architects (past dir.). Republican. Presbyterian (elder). Office: 150 E Cook St Libertyville IL 60048

MCMENAMIN, MICHAEL TERRENCE, lawyer, author; b. Akron, Ohio, Nov. 11, 1943; s. John Joseph and Maxine Ann (Lipp) McM.; m. Carol Anne Breckenridge, June 27, 1967; children—Kathleen Heather, Colleen Cara, Patrick Rankin. B.A. with honors in Polit. Sci., Western Res. U., 1965; LL.B., U. Pa., 1968. Bar: Ohio 1968, U.S. Dist. Ct. (no. dist.) Ohio 1969, U.S. Ct. Appeals (6th cir.) 1971, U.S. Supreme Ct. 1981. Assoc. Walter, Harverfield, Buescher & Chockley, Cleve., 1968-74, ptnr., 1975—. Author: Milking the Public: Political Scandals of the Dairy Lobby from LBJ to Jimmy Carter, 1980. Contbg. editor Inquiry Mag., 1980-84, Reason Mag., 1983—. Trustee Fairmont Montessori Assn., 1979—, sec., 1979-80, 81-82, treas., 1980-81, pres., 1982—; trustee, sec. Inst. for Child Advocacy, 1977-80; active Citizens League Greater Cleve., 1968—, Council for a Competitive Economy, 1981—. Served to 1st lt. USAR, 1968-74. Mem. ABA, Ohio State Bar Assn., Greater Cleve. Bar Assn. Home: 3386 Ingleside Rd Shaker Heights OH 44122 Office: 1215 Terminal Tower Cleveland OH 44113

MCMICHAEL, JEANE CASEY, real estate corporation executive; b. Jeffersonville, Ind., May 7, 1938; d. Emmett Ward and Carrie Evelyn (Leonard) Casey; m. Norman Kenneth Wenzler, Sept. 12, 1956 (div. 1968); m. Wilburn Arnold McMichael, June 20, 1978. Student Ind. U. Extension Ctr., Bellermine Coll., 1972-73, Ind. U. S.E., 1973—, Kentuckiana Metroversity, 1981—; Grad. Realtors Inst., Ind. U., 1982. Lic. real estate salesman, broker, Ind.; real estate broker, Ky. Owner, pres. McMichael Real Estate, Inc., Jeffersonville, 1979—; mgr., broker Bass & Weisberg Realtors, Jeffersonville, Ind., 1984—. Pres., Mr. and Mrs. class St. Mark's United Ch. of Christ; chmn. social com. Republican party Clark County (Ind.). Recipient cert. of appreciation Nat. Ctr. Citizen Involvement, 1983; award Contact Kentuckiana Teleministries, 1978. Mem. Nat. Assn. Realtors, Ind. Assn. Realtors (hon.), Nat. Women's Council Realtors (pres. chpt., chmn. coms.; state rec. sec., 1984, state pres. 1985-86, chmn. Achievement award 1982, nat. award winner 1982, 83, 84), Ky. Real Estate Exchange, So. Ind. Bd. Realtors, Psi Iota Xi. Democrat. Office: Bass & Weisberg Realtors 1713 E 10th St Jeffersonville IN 47130

MCMILLAN, DONALD ANDREW, technical service company executive; b. Cleve., May 15, 1936; s. Andrew Montgomery and Anna (Maloney) McM.; m. Carol Bernadette Flowers, Aug. 29, 1959 (div. 1978); children—Donna Marie, Diana Lynn, Andrew Francis, Danielle, Donald Andrew, II; m. Cheryl Ann Eger, Apr. 23, 1983. B.S., John Carroll U., 1959; postgrad. Case Western Res. U., 1959-60. Spl. caseworker Cuyahoga County, Cleve., 1960-61; acct. rep. Salada Foods, Cleve., 1961-64; tech. rep. Picker Internat., Cleve., 1964-82; regional sales mgr. Elscint Inc., Boston, 1982-84; v.p., treas. Ultrasound Tech. Services, Chgo., 1984—, corp. bus. mgr., Woodridge, Ill., 1980—; tech. cons. to authors of ultrasound books. Bd. dirs. Willow Creek Sch., Woodridge, 1976-77, St. Joan of Arc Sch., Lisle, Ill., 1977-78; audio visual specialist St. Joan of Arc Sch., 1976-77. Mem. Am. Inst. Ultrasound in Medicine, Soc. Diagnostic Med. Sonographers, Chgo. Ultrasound Soc. (cert. 1982), Chgo. Echocardiography Soc., Chgo. Radiol. Engring. Soc. Republican. Roman Catholic. Avocations: golf; camping; photography; racquetball; travel. Home and Office: PO Box 17070 17054 Calle Del Oro Fountain Hills AZ 85268

MCMILLAN, FRED LEROY, educational administrator; b. Argonia, Kans., Feb. 17, 1933; s. Roy Owen and Cleo (Covell) McM.; m. Barbara J. Shinn, July 3, 1956; children—Pamela, Phyllis, Paula. B.A., Ark. Tech. U., 1960; M.A., Wichita State U., 1969. Tchr. Sci. pub. schs., Atlanta, Kans., 1960-69; prin. pub. schs., Bueden, Kans., 1969-75, Leon, Kans., 1976—. Served with U.S. Army, 1953-55. Mem. Nat. Prins. Assn., Kans. State Prins. Assn., VFW, Am. Legion. Democrat. Lodge: Masons (32 degree). Avocation: golf. Home: 1704 Fairway Dr Augusta KS 67010 Office: Dist 205 Box 8 Leon KS 67074

MCMILLAN, JAMES ALBERT, electronics engr., educator; b. Lewellen, Nebr., Feb. 6, 1926; s. William H. and Mina H. (Taylor) McM.; B.S. in Elec. Engring., U. Wash., 1951; M.S. in Mgmt., Rensselaer Poly. Inst., 1965; m. Mary Virginia Garrett, Aug. 12, 1950; children—Michael, James, Yvette, Ramelle, Robert. Commd. 2d lt. U.S. Air Force, 1950, advanced through grades to lt. col., 1970; jet fighter pilot Columbus AFB, Miss., Webb AFB, Tex., 1951-52, Nellis AFB, Nev., 1953, McChord AFB., Wash., 1953-54; electronic maintenance supr. Lowry AFB, Colo., 1954, Forbes AFB, Kans., 1954-56, also in U.K., 1956-59; electronic engr., program dir. Wright-Patterson AFB, Ohio, 1959-64; facilities dir. Air Force Aero Propulsion Lab., Wright-Patterson AFB, 1965-70, ret., 1970; instr. div. chmn. Chesterfield-Marlboro Tech. Coll., S.C., 1971-75; asso. prof., chmn. indsl. programs Maysville (Ky.) Community Coll., 1976—; cons. mgmt. and electronic maintenance, 1970—. Served with U.S. Army, 1943-45. Mem. IEEE (sr.), Soc. Mfg. Engrs. (sr.), Nat. Rifle Assn. (life), Sigma Xi (life). Republican. Presbyterian (elder). Clubs: Rotary, Masons (32 deg.), Shriners. Author: A Management Survey, 1965. Home: 6945 Scoffield Rd Ripley OH 45167 Office: Maysville Community College Maysville KY 41056

MCMILLAN, S. STERLING, economist, horse breeder; b. Cleve., June 28, 1907; s. S. Sterling McMillan and Ruth McMillan Strong; m. Elizabeth Harman Mather, Oct. 9, 1937; children—S. Sterling, Madeleine McMillan Offutt, Elizabeth, Katharine McMillan Farrand. A.B., Princeton U., 1929; M.B.A., Harvard U., 1932; Ph.D., Ind. U., 1948. Security analyst No. Trust Co., Chgo., 1933-35; sec.-treas., dir., Strong, Cobb and Co., Cleve., 1935-42; regional prince economist, Washington, 1942, Chgo., 1942-45; instr. Ind. U., Bloomington, 1945-47; from asst. prof. to prof. Western Res. U., Cleve. (name Case Western Res. U. 1967), 1947-69; dir. indsl. econs. div. Nat. Prodn. Authority, Washington, 1951-52; founder, chmn. bd., dir. Predicasts, Inc., Cleve., 1960-81; farmer, horsebreeder Mountain Glen Farm, Stable, Mentor, Ohio, 1961—; chmn. Cleve. Forum Community Devel., 1964-65; mem. Ohio Crime Commn., 1967-69; cons. Nat. Planning Assn., NSF Oceanics Project, 1967-68. Active Children's Aid Soc., 1953—, Ctr. Human Services, Cleve., 1970—, Welfare Fedn. Cleve. Fedn. for Community Planning, United Way, Cleve., others. Recipient Vol. of Yr. award United Torch Services, 1974. Mem. Am. Econs. Assn., Royal Econs. Soc., Am. Fin. Assn., Midwest Econs. Assn. (v.p. 1954-55), Nat. Assn. Bus. Economists, AAUP (past officer), Beta Gamma Sigma. Episcopalian. Clubs: Union, Rowfant (Cleve.); Kirtland Country (Willoughby, Ohio); Rolling Rock (Ligonier, Pa.). Author: Individual Firm Adjustments under OPA, 1949; The Growth of Civilian Atomic Energy, 1968; Case Studies of Government Cooperation in Founding New Industries, 1970; contbr. articles to profl. jours. Home and office: Mountain Glen Farm RD Route 1 Mentor OH 44060

MCMILLAN, VIRGINIA KAY, educational researcher; b. West Plains, Mo., Oct. 1, 1940; s. Glen W. and Helen (McCallon) Moore; m. R. Bruce McMillan, Sept. 30, 1961; children—R. Gregory, Michel D., Lynn K. B.A., Sangamon State U., 1976, M.A., 1978. Vis. instr. So. Ill. U. Med. Sch., Springfield, 1976-81; info. devel. specialist Eastern Ill. U., Charleston, 1981-83; assoc. dir. research Ill. Community Coll. Bd., Springfield, 1983—; mem. health occupations adv. council So. Ill. U. Vocat. Edn. Studies, Carbondale, 1982—. Author: Health Care Information Needs, 1979; Health Occupations in Illinois, 1981; A Guide to Health Occupations, 1981; Illinois Employment Demand and Vocational Education, 1983. Ill. Bd. Edn. grantee, 1979, 80-81, 83. Mem. Ill. Assn. Allied Health Professions (bd. dirs. 1983—), Ill. Assn. Instl. Research, Ill. Employment and Tng. Assn., Am. Statis. Assn., Ill. State Mus. Soc., Springfield Art Assn. Home: 2844 E Lake Dr Springfield Il 62707 Office: Ill Community Coll Bd 509 S 6th St Springfield IL 62701

MC MILLEN, THOMAS ROBERTS, judge; b. Decatur, Ill., June 8, 1916; s. Rolla C. and Ruth (Roberts) McM.; A.B., Princeton, 1938; LL.B., Harvard, 1941; m. Anne Ford, Aug. 16, 1946; children—Margot F. (Mrs. James Roberson), Patricia R., Anne C. (Mrs. Steven Scheyer). Admitted to Ill. bar, 1941; practiced in Chgo., 1946-66; mem. firm Bell, Boyd, Lloyd, Haddad & Burns, 1946-66; judge Cook County, Ill., 1966-71, U.S. Dist. Ct., No. Dist. Ill., Chgo., 1971—. Bd. govs. United Republican Fund Ill., 1950-66. Served to maj. CIC, AUS, 1941-45. Decorated Bronze Star medal; Croix de Guerre. Mem. ABA, Chgo. Bar Assn. (bd. dirs. 1964-66), Fed. Bar Assn. (bd. dirs 1982—), CIC Assn., Phi Beta Kappa. Club: Indian Hill Country (Winnetka, Ill.). Office: Everett M Dirksen Bldg S Dearborn St Chicago IL 60604

MCMILLIAN, THEODORE, judge; b. St. Louis, Jan. 28, 1919; B.S., Lincoln U., 1941, H.H.D. (hon.), 1981; J.D., St. Louis U., 1949; H.H.D. (hon.), U. Mo., St. Louis, 1978; m. Minnie E. Foster, Dec. 8, 1941. Asst. circuit atty. U.S. Eighth Circuit, St. Louis, 1953-56, U.S. circuit Judge U.S. Ct. Appeals (8th cir.), 1978—; judge Circuit Ct. for City St. Louis, 1956-72; judge Eastern div. Mo. Ct. Appeals, 1972-78; assoc. prof. adminstrn. justice U. Mo., St. Louis, from 1970; assoc. prof. Webster Coll. Grad. Program, from 1977; mem. faculty Nat. Coll. Juvenile Justice, U. Nev., from 1972. Served to 1st lt. Signal Corps, U.S. Army, 1942-46. Recipient Alumni Merit award St. Louis U., 1965. Mem. Lawyers Assn., Mound City Bar Assn., Am. Judicature Soc., Phi Beta Kappa, Alpha Sigma Nu. Office: 1114 Market St Room 526 Saint Louis MO 63101

MCMULLEN, FRANCIS LEE, secondary school principal; b. Cumberland, Iowa, Apr. 20, 1926; s. William Eugene and Mary (Eblen) McM.; m. Ann Bernice Bequette, Dec. 31, 1945; children—Mary Ann, Cheryl Lee. B.A., Bethany Coll., 1963; M.A., U. Mo., St. Louis, 1973, M.A., 1975, 77, advanced cert., 1976. Cert. tchr., guidance counselor, prin., supt., Mo. Commd. 2d lt. U.S. Air Force, 1944, advanced through grades to lt. col., 1970; pilot, navigator, 1954-70, ret., 1970; tchr. Allan Hancock Jr. Coll., Vandenburg AFB, Calif., 1966-67, Ft. Zumwalt Sr. High Sch., O'Fallon, Mo., 1970-76; prin. Pacific (Mo.) Sr. High Sch., 1976—. Decorated Silver Star (3), D.F.C. (8), Air medal with 16 oak leaf clusters. Mem. Nat. Assn. Secondary Sch. Prins., Mo. Assn. Secondary Sch. Prins., Assn. Supervision and Curriculum Devel., Am. Legion, VFW. Roman Catholic. Clubs: Masons, Eagles. Office: Route 4 Ude Dr Pacific MO 63069

MCMULLEN, JAMES ROBERT, research microbiologist; b. Clinton, Ind., May 22, 1942; s. Robert LeRoy and Elsie Pauline (Buckler) McM.; m. Suetta Rae Brown, July 24, 1964; 1 son, Patrick James. B.S., Ind. State U., Terre Haute, 1964; M.S., U. Wis., 1966. Microbiologist, Comml. Solvents Corp., Terre Haute, summer 1964, research microbiologist, 1966-75; research microbiologist Internat. Minerals and Chem. Corp., Terre Haute, 1975—. Adviser, Jr.

Achievement Wabash Valley, 1970; bd. dirs. v.p. Internat. Minerals and Chem. Fed. Credit Union, 1978-84. Mem. Am. Soc. Microbiology, Sigma Xi. Republican. Methodist. Club: Lost Creek Conservation. Lodges: Elks, Masons. Contbr. articles to profl. jours.; patentee process for producing zearalenone, 1972, microbiol. reduction of zearalenone, 1977. Home: 236 Van Buren Blvd Terre Haute IN 47803 Office: 1331 S 1st St Terre Haute IN 47808

MCMULLIN, CRAIG STEPHEN, accountant; b. Fort Dodge, Iowa, Apr. 5, 1957; s. Eugene Baker and Delores Joan (Lark) McM.; m. Marilyn Kay Brandhof, Aug. 16, 1975; children—Matthew, Megan. B.S., Iowa State U., 1979. C.P.A., Iowa. Supr. audit Ernst & Whinney, Des Moines, 1979-83; asst. treas. Des Moines Register and Tribune Co., 1983—. Recipient McGaldery Hendrickson award, 1979. Mem. Iowa Soc. C.P.A.s, Am. Inst. C.P.A.s, Am. Mgmt. Assn. Avocations: skiing, fishing, camping. Office: Des Moines Register and Tribune Co 715 Locust St Des Moines IA 50309

MCMURRY, PETER HOWARD, mechanical engineering educator; b. Palmerton, Pa., July 5, 1947; s. Howard V. and Margaret A. (Gifford) McM.; m. Pamela S. Schain, May 10, 1969; children—Timothy, Nathaniel. B.A. in Physics, U. Pa., 1969; M.S. in Environ. Engring Sci., Calif. Inst. Tech., 1973, Ph.D. in Environ. Engring Sci., 1977. Asst. prof. Univ. Minn., Mpls., 1977-83, assoc. prof. mech. engring., 1983—. Contbr. articles to profl. jours. Mem. Am. Assn. Aerosol Research, Am. Chem. Soc., AAAS, Air Pollution Control Assn., ASME, Sigma Xi. Office: Univ Minn Dept Mech Engring 111 Church St SE Minneapolis MN 55455

MCMURRY, WILLIAM SCOTT, allied health educator; b. Poteau, Okla., Apr. 10, 1921; s. Ulysses Scott and Syntha Alice (McDonald) McM.; m. Kathryn Elizabeth Robison, Feb. 2, 1946. B.S., N.E. U., Okla., 1942; D.D.S., U. Mo., 1950, M.S., 1966; Ph.D., Columbia Pacific U., 1983. Commd. 2d lt., U.S. Air Force, 1941, advanced through grades to lt. col., 1963; ret., 1969; assoc. chief of staff edn. VA, Dayton, Ohio, 1973-79; asst. dean veterans affairs Wright State Med. Sch., 1975-79; ret., 1979; adj. prof. Ohio State U., 1973-79; assoc. prof. allied health So. Ill. U., 1979—. Fellow Am. Assn. Oral and Maxillofacial Surgeons, Internat. Assn. Oral and Maxillofacial Surgeons; mem. Council Occupational Edn., Midwestern Oral Surgeons, Okla. State Dental Assn., Ill. Police Assn., Ret. Officers Assn., Assn. Mil. Surgeons, Assn. Ret. Fed. Employees, Air Force Assn. Republican. Lodges: Masons, Lions, Elks. Contbr. articles to profl. jours. Office: So Ill U STC Bldg Suite 118-A Carbondale IL 62901

MCNABB, NANCY ELAINE, metals company executive, investments company executive; b. Kendallville, Ind., Jan. 30, 1943; d. Otis Daye and Valda Belle (Simon) Brown; m. Robert Leroy McNabb, Oct. 14, 1967; children—Nathan Ray, Colleen Sue, Kevin Leith. Student Ind. U., 1961-64. Office mgr. Nat. Magnesium & Aluminum Foundry, Inc., Ft. Wayne, Ind., 1964-70; office mgr. Sturgis Light Metals Foundry, Inc., 1964-70, v.p., 1970—; office mgr. Otis Brown Investments, Inc., 1964-70, v.p., 1970—. Bd. sch. trustees DeKalb County Central United Sch. Dist., Auburn, Ind., 1976—, v.p., 1976-78, 81-83, sec. 1979-80, pres., 1984. Active lay leader First United Methodist Ch., Auburn, 1976—; chmn. Internat. Christian Leadership DeKalb County Women's Prayer Breakfast, 1975; sec., treas. Ind. State Young Mothers Council Service, 1976; sec., bd. dirs. United Way of DeKalb County, 1976; mem. McKenney-Harrison Elem. Sch. PTO, Auburn Community Theatre. Recipient cert. appreciation Auburn Kiwanis Club, 1980, Auburn Optimist Club, 1983, McDonald's Hon. Crew Mem. award, 1980, Duesey award Auburn Community Theatre, 1982; named 1st Young Mother of the Year St. Ind., 1976. Mem. The Am. Mothers' Com. Inc., the Nat. Young Mothers' Council, Ind. Sch. Bds. Assn., Nat. Sch. Bds. Assn. (cert. of recognition 1979), Gen. Fedn. Women's Clubs. Republican. Clubs: Hamilton Fish and Game, Hamilton Lake Assn.; Greenhurst Country, Ladies' Literary (Auburn). Lodge: Ladies of Moose. Avocations: vocalist, guest lecturer on history of hats. Home: 4488 County Rd No 68 Auburn IN 46706 Office: Nat Magnesium and Aluminum Foundry Inc 4817 Industrial Rd Ft Wayne IN 46825

MCNALL, SCOTT GRANT, sociology educator; b. New Ulm, Minn., Jan. 16, 1941; s. Everett Herman and Dorothy Grant (Brown) McN.; m. Sally Anne Allen, Oct. 11, 1960; children—Miles Allen, Amy Ellen. B.A., Portland State U., 1962; Ph.D., U. Oreg., 1965. Instr. U. Oreg., Eugene, 1964-65; asst. prof. U. Minn., Mpls., 1965-70; assoc. prof. to prof. Ariz. State U., Tempe, 1970-76; prof. sociology, chmn. dept. sociology U. Kans., Lawrence, 1976—; Fulbright lectr. Pierce Coll., Athens, Greece, 1968-69. Author books, including: The Sociological Experience, 1974; The Greek Peasant, 1974; Career of A Radical Rightist, 1975; Social Problems Today, 1975; (with Sally A. McNall) Plains Families: Exploring Sociology Through Social History, 1983; also numerous articles, revs. Editor books, including: The Sociology Perspective, 1977; Theoretical Perspectives in Sociology, 1979; Political Economy, 1981. Fulbright grantee, New Zealand, 1983. Mem. Midwest Sociol. Soc. (pres. 1982-83), Pacific Sociol. Soc. Am. Sociol. Assn. (various past sect. positions), Inter-Univ. Seminar on Armed Forces and Society, others. Democrat. Home: 3026 Riverview Dr Lawrence KS 66044 Office: U Kansas Dept Sociology Lawrence KS 66045

MCNALLY, ANDREW, III, printer, publisher; b. Chgo., Aug. 17, 1909; s. Andrew and Eleanor (Vilas) McN.; A.B., Yale U., 1931; m. Margaret Clark MacMillin, Nov. 20, 1936 (dec.); children—Betty Jane, Andrew, Edward Clark. With Chgo. factory Rand McNally & Co., 1931, N.Y. sales office v.p., dir., 1933, pres., 1948-74, chmn. bd., 1974—. Past pres. Graphic Arts Tech. Found. Served as capt., C.E. Army Map Service, 1942-45. Mem. Chgo. Hist. Soc. (past pres., trustee). Office: Rand McNally & Co 8255 N Central Park Skokie IL 60076

MCNALLY, MICHAEL FRANCIS, engineer; b. Flemington, N.J., Aug. 27, 1954; s. Thomas Kevin and Yone (Elder) McN.; m. Stephanie Ann Ramian, Aug. 2, 1975; 1 child, Lauren Michelle. B.A. in Biology, Hiram Coll., 1976; M.B.A., Kent State U., 1984. Lab. analyst Akron Health Dept., Ohio, 1975-78, field tech., 1978-80; sr. field engr. Enviroplan, Inc., West Orange, N.J., 1980—. Fellow U.S. EPA, 1977. Mem. Air Pollution Control Assn. Avocations: personal computing; photography; home remodeling; golf. Office: Enviroplan Inc PO Box 325 Akron OH 44309

MCNAMARA, DAVID JOSEPH, financial and tax planning executive; b. Osceola, Iowa, Feb. 6, 1951; s. Loras Emmett and Nadine Evelyn (DeLancey) McN.; m. Ruth Ellen Hanken, Oct. 4, 1974; children—Benjamin, Shawna. B.G.S., U. Iowa, 1974. Cert. fin. planner Coll. Fin. Planning, 1985; registered investment advisor; registered prin. Nat. Assn. Securities Dealers. Bus. mgr. Cost Comparison Inc., Des Moines, 1975; exec. dir. Story County R.S.V.P., Story City, Iowa, 1975-77; communications asst. United Way Central Iowa, Des Moines, 1977, staff assoc., 1977-78, asst. campaign dir., 1979-81, assoc. exec. dir., 1982-85; pres. Integrated Tax and Fin. Planning Services, 1985—; pres. Iowa Assn. RSVP Execs., Des Moines, 1975-76; cons. ACTION, Washington, 1976; cons. Story County Council on Aging, Nev., 1975-76; dir. Central Investments Ltd., Des Moines. Mem. Nat. Soc. Fund Raising Exec., Inst. Cert. Fin. Planners, Internat. Assn. Fin. Planners (bd. dirs. Iowa chpt. 1984—). Republican. Lutheran. Lodge: Kiwanis. Author: Wisdom and Aging, 1976; Crisis is Really Opportunity, 1977; Key Person Institute, 1980. Home: 3119 Lawnview Dr Des Moines IA 50310 Office: Integrated Tax and Fin Planning Services 3520 Beaver Ave Suite B Des Moines IA 50310

MC NAMARA, EDWARD HOWARD, mayor; b. Detroit, Sept. 21, 1926; s. Andrew Kurcina and Ellen Gertrude (Bennett) McN.; Ph.B, U. Detroit, 1959, postgrad. in law; m. Lucille Yvonne Martin, June 26, 1948; children—Colleen, Michael, Nancy, Kevin, Terence. Councilman, City of Livonia, 1962-70, pres. council, 1968-70, mayor, 1970—; pres. Dearborn Twp. Sch. Bd., 1954; mem. Wayne County Bd. Suprs., 1964; mem. Mich. Gov.'s Spl. Com. Land Use, 1971; pres. Mich. Conf. Mayors, 1975-76; chmn. South Eastern Mich. Transp. Authority, 1978-79; pres. Mich. Mcpl. League, 1974-75; mem. Livonia Meadows Civic Assn.; chmn. Sunset dist. Detroit Area council Boy Scouts Am.; mem. Mich. Dem. Com. Served with USN, 1944-46. Club: K.C. Office: Office of Mayor City Hall Livonia MI 48150*

MCNAMARA, JOHN RICHARD, county official; b. Brockton, Mass., Aug. 18, 1940; s. Edward Joseph and Agnes Loretta (Ervin) McN.; m. Carol Ann Hood, Nov. 17, 1962; children—Kevin, Patrick, Megan, Kelly, Kerry. B.S. in Civil Engring., Notre Dame U., 1965. Registered profl. engr., Ind.; profl. land surveyor. Survey party chief Engring. Planning Service, Mishawaka, Ind., 1962-66; hwy. engr. Brighton Engring., Little Rock, 1966-67; asst. chief engr. Engring. Planning Service, 1967-72; county engr. St. Joseph County, South Bend, Ind., 1972-72, county surveyor, 1973—; chmn. Kankakee River Basin, Highland, Ind., 1984—, Area Plan Commn. Plat Com., South Bend, 1983—; chmn. ann. conv. Ind. Soc. Profl. Land Surveyors, 1984—. Bd. dirs. United Religious Community, South Bend, 1980-82, Michiana Watershed, South Bend, 1977-81, Penn High Bldg. Trades, Mishawaka, 1977-81; pres. Marian High Boosters Club, 1983. Recipient award for dedication and service Marian High Sch. Athletic Dept., 1984; George award, Mishawaka Enterprise Newspaper. 1980; Outstanding County Ofcl., Assn. Ind. Counties, 1983. Mem. ASCE, County Surveyors Assn. (sec.-treas. 1979—), Am. Congress Surveying and Mapping, Ind. Soc. Profl. Land Surveyors (dir.), Surveyors Hist. Soc. Democrat. Roman Catholic. Club: Men's (pres. 1980-81). Avocations: softball; tennis. Home: 10679 Jefferson Rd Osceola IN 46561 Office: 1100 County City Bldg South Bend IN 46601

MCNAMEE, JAMES, municipal official. Fire chief City of Cleve. Office: Cleveland Fire Dept Office of the Fire Chief Cleveland OH 44113*

MCNARY, GENE, county official; b. Muncie, Ind., Sept. 14, 1935; m. Ina Risch, 1959; children—Mark, Cole, Wade. B.S. in Fin., Ind. U., 1957; J.D., Ind. U., 1960. Bar: Mo. Mem. firm Lashly, Lashly and Miller, St. Louis, 1961-63; asst. pub. defender St. Louis County, 1963-66, prosecuting atty., 1966-74, chief exec., 1974—. Bd. dirs. East-West Gateway Coordinating Council; chmn Mo. Pres. Ford Com., 1975-76. Served with U.S. Army, 1960-66. Mem. Mo. Assn. Counties, Regional Commerce and Growth Assn. (dir.), Mo. Assn. Prosecuting Attys. (pres.). Address: 10 Fox Meadows Sunset Hills MO 63127

MCNEAL, JAMES HECTOR, JR., See *Who's Who in America,* 43rd edition.

MC NEER, CHARLES SELDEN, utility executive; b. Gilbert, W.Va., Apr. 8, 1926; s. Richard Mason and Bertie May (Sparks) McN.; student Berea Coll., 1943-44, 46-47, U.S. Mcht. Marine Acad., 1944-46; B.S. in Elec. Engring., Northwestern U., 1950; m. Ann Campbell Bishop, Mar. 20, 1949; children—Charles William, Robert Lee, Thomas Richard. With Wis. Electric Power Co., Milw., 1950—, mgr. elec. engring., 1961-65, research engr. Operating Research Bur., 1965-67, asst. v.p., 1967, v.p. adminstrn., 1968, sr. v.p., 1969-73, exec. v.p., 1973-75, pres., 1975-82, chmn., chief exec. officer, 1982—; chmn., dir. Wis. Natural Gas Co.; pres., dir. Badger Service. Chmn. exec. com. Wis.-Upper Mich. Systems; mem. exec. com. Mid-Am. Interpool Network; mem. council Operation ACTION UP; bd. dirs. Competitive Wis., Inc., Forward Wis., Inc., Milw. Innovation Ctr., Inc., Wis. Electric Utilities Research Found., Milw. Redevel. Corp., Greater Milw. Com., YMCA of Met. Milw., Nat. Soc. to Prevent Blindness; mem. adv. council U. Wis. Sch. Bus. Adminstrn.; mem. council Med. Coll. Wis.; bd. govs. Jr. Achievement. Served with USNR, 1946-47. Registered profl. engr., Wis. Mem. Wis. Utilities Assn. (dir.), Met. Milw. Assn. Commerce (dir.), Edison Electric Inst. (policy com. on environ. affairs), N.Am. Elec. Reliability Council (trustee), Wis., Nat. socs. profl. engrs., Sigma Xi, Eta Kappa Nu, Tau Beta Pi, Sigma Pi Sigma, Pi Mu Epsilon. Lodge: Kiwanis. Home: 6520 Washington Circle Wauwatosa WI 53213 Office: 231 W Michigan St Milwaukee WI 53201

MC NEESE, WILMA WALLACE, social worker; b. Chgo., Apr. 30, 1946; d. Nettie Fletcher Wallace; student Wilson City Coll., 1964-66; B.A., So. Ill. U., 1969; M.S.W., Loyola U., Chgo., 1976; m. Mose D. McNeese, Dec. 27, 1969; children—Derrick, Christina. Program coordinator Intensive Tng. and Employment Program, East St. Louis, Ill., 1970-71; methods and procedures adviser Ill. Dept. Pub. Aid, Chgo., 1972-73; social work intern Robbins (Ill.) Presch. Center, 1974; with U.S. Probation Office, Chgo., 1975; officer U.S. Pretrial Services Agy., Chgo., 1976—; fieldwork instr. Aurora Coll., 1981, Chgo. State U., 1981-82. Recipient Community Service award Village of Robbins, 1975; advanced tng. cert. Fed. Jud. Center.; cert. social worker, Ill. Mem. Nat. Assn. Social Workers, Acad. Cert. Social Workers, Fedn. Probation Officers Assn. Baptist. Home: 209 Todd St Park Forest IL 60466 Office: 219 S Dearborn St Room 1100 Chicago IL 60604

MCNEILL, ROBERT PATRICK, investment counselor; b. Chgo., Mar. 17, 1941; s. Donald Thomas and Katherine (Bennett) McN.; m. Martha Stephan, Sept. 12, 1964; children—Jennifer, Donald, Victoria, Stephan, Elizabeth. B.A. summa cum laude, U. Notre Dame, 1963; M.Letters, Oxford U., 1967. Chartered investment counselor. Assoc. Stein Roe & Farnham, Chgo., 1967-72, gen. ptnr., 1972-77, sr. ptnr., 1977—; underwriting mem. Lloyds of London, 1980—; dir. Comml. Chgo. Corp.; vice chmn. bd. Hill Internat. Prodn. Co., Houston, 1982—; dir., adv. bd. Touche Remnant Investment Counselors, London, 1983—. Voting mem., sec. Ill. Rhodes Scholarship Selection Com.; voting mem., Ill. rep. Great Lakes Dist. Rhodes Scholarship Selection Com.; bd. dirs. Kennedy Sch. for Retarded Children, Palos Park, Ill., 1972—, Winnetka United Way, Ill., 1984—, Division St. YMCA, Chgo., 1972—; assoc. Rush-Presbyn.-St. Lukes Med. Ctr., Chgo., 1975—. Rhodes scholar, 1963. Fellow Fin. Analysts Fedn.; mem. Chgo. Council on Fgn. Relations (bd. dirs., treas. 1975—), Inst. European Studies (bd. govs., treas. 1981—), Investment Analysts Soc. Chgo. (Chgo. com., com. on fgn. affairs, com. on internat and domestic issues). Clubs: Sunset Ridge Country (Northfield, Ill.) (bd. dirs. 1983—); Chicago; Econ. of Chgo. Avocations: coin collecting; bridge; golf; skiing; reading; art. Home: 700 Rosewood Ave Winnetka IL 60093 Office: Stein Roe & Farnham 1 S Wacker Dr Chicago IL 60606

MCNEILL, WILLIAM JAMES, insurance company executive; b. Atlanta, Feb. 24, 1945; s. Arland Stiver and Helen Lorraine (Hawk) McN.; m. Cynthia Alice Meyer, June 17, 1967; children—Andrea Lynne, William John. A.A., Black Hawk Coll., 1965; B.A., St. Ambrose Coll., 1971. With Internat. Harvester Co., East Moline, Ill., 1971-82, compensation mgr., 1981-82; mgr. tng. and devel., mgmt. planning and devel. Mut. of Omaha, Nebr., 1982—. Vice chmn. United Way, Rock Island, 1981, 82. Served with USN, 1966-71; Vietnam. Mem. Am. Soc. Tng. and Devel., Human Resource Planning Soc. Republican. Lutheran. Office: Mutual of Omaha Mutual of Omaha Plaza Omaha NE 68175

MC NELLY, FREDERICK WRIGHT, JR., psychologist; b. Bangor, Maine, Apr. 14, 1947; s. Frederick Wright and E. Frances (Cutter) McN.; 1 adopted son, Roger; foster children—Joseph, Ronald, Michael, Jeffrey. B.A. magna cum laude, U. Minn., 1969; M.A., U. Mich., 1971, Ph.D., 1973. Lic. foster parent, Ill. USPHS trainee, 1969-70, 72. Research coordinator NSF project U. Minn., Morris, 1968-69, lab. instructor, 1969; teaching fellow psychology U. Mich., 1970-72; ednl. examiner Ann Arbor (Mich.) Public Schs., 1971; dir. psychol. services Children Devel. Center, Rockford, Ill., 1972-82, program dir., 1982—; lectr. Rock Valley Coll., Rockford, 1974-75; part-time pvt. practice psychology, Rockford and Belvidere, Ill., 1980—, Beloit, Wis., 1985—; mental health cons. Rockford Head Start, 1982—, mem. health services adv. com., 1985—; presenter state and regional workshops and confs. Active Boy Scouts Am.; chmn. spl. edn. regional advisory com. Bi-County Office of Edn., Rockford, 1976-78; mem. Nat. and Ill. Com. on Child Abuse; co-chmn. Winnebago County Child Protection Assn., 1980; elder Willow Creek United Presbyn. Ch., Rockford, 1980—; mem. stronghold renovation session com. Presbytery of Blackhawk, Oregon, Ill., 1985. Registered clin. psychologist Ill.; named U.S. Jaycees Outstanding Young Man of 1977. Mem. Am., Midwestern, Ill. No. Ill. (chmn. 1976-77) psychol. assns., Soc. Research in Child Devel., Nat., Ill. assns. retarded citizens, Am. Humane Assn. (children's div.), Nat. Register Health Service Providers in Psychology, Nat., Ill. Foster parents assns. Contbr. articles to profl. jours. Home: 11591 Beverly Ln Belvidere IL 61008 Office: Childrens Devel Center 650 N Main St Rockford IL 61103 also 995 N Main St Rockford IL 61103

MCPHAIL, DOUGLAS JAMES, business executive; b. Arcadia, Fla., Oct. 26, 1944; s. Clayton James and Gladys Mary (Gracyalny) McP.; m. Helen Dorothy White, Mar. 31, 1969; 1 son, Steven James. B.A., U. Toledo, 1967. Regional sales mgr. Polaroid Corp., Cambridge, Mass., 1967-72; br. mgr. A. Bruce Crock, Columbus, Ohio, 1972-75; chmn., chief exec. officer Ind. Records Mgrs., Inc., Indpls., 1975—; pres., Productive Bus. Interiors, Inc., Ft. Wayne, Ind., 1982—. Mem. Assn. Records Mgrs. and Adminstrs. (past pres.). Republican. Roman Catholic. Clubs: Carmel Racquet, Woodland Country (Carmel, Ind.). Home: 5055 Sun Briar Ct Carmel IN 46032 Office: Indiana Records Managers Inc 6886 Hawthorn Park Dr Indianapolis IN 46220

MCPHAIL-KOHR, DOREEN, public relations agency executive; b. Detroit, Jan. 4, 1933; d. Harry H. and Myrtle A. (Schilke) Fante; m. Donald R. McPhail, Nov. 30, 1957 (div. 1976); children—Dean Bruce, Scott Harry. B.A., Mich. State U., 1954. Asst. dir. Detroit Town Hall, 1975-76; devel. and pub. relations dir. Grosse Pointe Acad. (Mich.), 1976-78; asst. dir. pub. relations Detroit Plaza Hotel, 1979-80; spl. events pub. relations dir. Detroit Renaissance, 1980-84, including Detroit Grand Prix, Internat. Freedom Festival, Montreux Detroit Kool Jazz Festival; account supr. Anthony M. Franco, Inc., Detroit, 1984—; panelist U. Mich. mktg. seminar, 1982. Prodn. floor supr., personnel chmn. for art auction Sta. WTVS, 1971-75; bd. dirs. Sr. Ctr., Inc., 1960-70; mem. Grosse Pointe Human Relations Council. Mem. Pub. Relations Soc. Am. (seminar panelist 1983), Kappa Alpha Theta. Clubs: Grosse Pointe Hunt, Jr. League of Detroit. Guest speaker profl. confs. Home: 925 Three Mile Dr Grosse Pointe Park MI 48230 Office: 400 Renaissance Center Suite 600 Detroit MI 48243

MCPHEE, MALCOLM CLINTON, physician; b. Tisdale, Sask., Can., July 11, 1939; s. Clinton A. and Edna (Loucks) McP.; m. Corinne Petrusia Greschuk, July 10, 1965; children—Neil Edward, Charlene Ann, Kelly Lynn. M.D., U. Sask., Can., 1964. Diplomate Am. Bd. Phys. Medicine and Rehab., Royal Coll. Physicians Can. Intern, McLaren Hosp., Flint, Mich., 1964-65; resident U. Mich. Hosps., Ann Arbor, Mich., 1965-69; asst. dir. phys. medicine and rehab. dept. Calgary Gen. Hosp., 1969-73; dir. phys. medicine and rehab. dept. Colonel Belcher Hosp., Calgary, Alta., Can., 1970-73; cons. phys. medicine and rehab. dept. Mayo Clinic, Rochester, Minn., 1973—, chmn. dept., 1981—; mem. cons. staff Alta. Children's Hosp., Calgary, Alta., Can., 1970-73; cons. physiatrist Foothills Gen. Hosp., Calgary, 1971-73, Rochester Meth. Hosp., 1973—, St. Mary's Hosp., Rochester, 1973—. Inventor electrode placement device. Chmn. award subcom., troop com. Gamehaven council Boy Scouts Am., 1981-83. Fellow Am. Acad. Phys. Medicine and Rehab.; mem. AMA, Am. Assn. Electromyography and Electrodiagnosis, Am. Spinal Injury Assn., Assn. Academic Physiatrists. Avocations: horticulture, photography, computers. Office: Mayo Clinic 200 First St SW Rochester MN 55905

MCPHERSON, EUGENE VIRGIL, broadcasting executive; b. Columbus, Ohio, Aug. 29, 1927; s. Arthur Emerson and Emma (Scott) McP.; B.A., Ohio State U., 1950; m. Nancy Marie Clark, June 13, 1953; children—Lynne, Scott. Prodn. exec. WBNS-TV, Columbus, 1952-62; exec. producer documentary unit WLWT-TV, Cin., 1962-64; dir. news and spl. projects WLWT-TV, Cin., 1964-66; v.p. news and spl. projects AVCO Broadcasting Co., Cin., 1966-69, v.p. programming, 1969-73; v.p., gen. mgr. WLWI-TV, Indpls., 1973-75; now pres. McPherson Media, Inc.; owner, operator WVLN, WSEI-FM. Served with AUS, 1946-47. Recipient creative writer producer award Alfred P. Sloan, 1966; Chris award Columbus Film Festival, 1960, 61, 62, 64, 71; Nat. Assn. TV Execs. Program award, 1968; Ohio State award, 1960, 63, 64; Freedom's Found. award, 1963, Regional Emmy, 1977; Cine Golden Eagle award, 1982; Blue Ribbon, Am. Film Festival, 1985. Mem. Broadcast Pioneers, Ill. Broadcasters Assn. (pres.). Author: (with Bleum and Cox) Television in the Public Interest, 1961. Writer, producer, dir. films The Last Prom, 1963, Death Driver, 1968, Citizen, 1962, Birth by Appointment, 1960, Diagnostic Countdown, 1962, Veil of Shadows, 1961, Rails in Crisis, 1963, Palm Trees and Ice Bergs, 1977, Tinsel Town and the Big Apple, 1979, Goodbye Carnival Girl, 1980, Atomic Legs, 1981, The Edison Adventures, 1981, The Championship, 1982, Little Arliss, 1984; Umbrella Jack, 1984; Buddies, 1985; That Funny Fat Kid, 1985; Zerk the Jerk, 1985; My First Swedish Bombshell, 1985. Office: Radio Tower Rd Box L Olney IL 62450

MCPHERSON, JAMES ALAN, writer, educator; b. Savannah, Ga., Sept. 16, 1943; s. James and Mable (Smalls) McP.; 1 child, Rachel Alice. B.A., Morris Brown Coll., 1965; LL.B., Harvard U., 1968; M.F.A., U. Iowa, 1971. Asst. prof. lit. U. Calif., Santa Cruz, 1969-76; assoc. prof. English, U. Va., Charlottesville, 1976-81; prof. English U. Iowa, Iowa City, 1981—; contbg. editor Atlantic Monthly, Boston, 1969; mem. lit. panel Nat. Endowment Arts, 1977-80. Author: (short stories) Hue and Cry, 1969; Railroad, 1976; Elbow Room, 1977 (Pulitzer prize 1978); stories selected for O'Henry Collection and Best Am. Short Stories, 1969-73. Atlantic grantee, 1968; recipient lit. award Nat. Inst. Arts and Letters, 1970; MacArthur Found. award, 1981; Guggenheim fellow, 1972-73. Mem. Authors League, ACLU. Office: Dept English Iowa U Iowa City IA

MC REE, EDWARD BARXDALE, hospital administrator; b. Pauls Valley, Okla., Oct. 20, 1931; s. Henry Barxdale and Mary (Shumate) McR.; B.A., Okla. City U., 1953; student U. Okla., 1953; student Central State Coll., 1954-55; m. Jan Bryant, Aug. 23, 1953; children—Scott, Kent, Chad. Adminstr. Eaton Rapids (Mich.) Community Hosp., 1957-61; pres. Ingham Med. Center, Lansing, Mich., 1961—; dir. Grad. Med. Edn., Inc., 1970—, treas., 1978-79, pres., 1979-81; pres. Mid-Mich. Emergency Services Council, 1978-81; dir. Kent Bank & Trust, Lansing, N.A., Olo Kent Bank of Lansing. Mem. Eaton Rapids (Mich.) Bd. Edn., 1964-71, treas., 1968-71. Pres., Tri-County Emergency Med. Services Council, 1974—, also mem. bd. dirs.; bd. dirs. Blue Cross Mich., 1974-75; bd. dirs. Hosp. Purchasing Service Mich., 1973—, pres., 1976-77; bd. dirs. Mid-Mich. chpt. ARC, 1979—, treas., 1980—, chmn., 1981-83; bd. dirs. Lansing Symphony Assn., 1984—. Served with AUS, 1955-57. Mem. Mich. (v.p. 1965-68), Southwestern Mich. (pres. 1968) hosp. assns., Am. Coll. Hosp. Adminstrs., Am. Hosp. Assn., Lambda Chi Alpha. Beta Beta Beta. Methodist (mem. West Mich. Conf. Bd. Finance 1972—). Club: Rotary. Contbr. articles to profl. jours. Home: 123 N East St Eaton Rapids MI 48827 Office: 401 W Greenlawn Ave Lansing MI 48910

MCREYNOLDS, DOUGLAS JOHN, English educator, author; b. Shreveport, La., June 5, 1946; s. John Wilson McR. and Mary Jane (Zagst) McR. Roden; m. Carol Susan Ghio, Mar. 7, 1969 (div. 1979); children—Roland, Quentin, Stabler; m. Barbara Jean Kirkpatrick Lips, Dec. 2, 1980. B.A., U. Mo., 1967, M.A., 1969; Ph.D., U. Denver, 1977. Instr. East Carolina U., Greenville, N.C., 1970-74; guard Colo. Nat. Bank, Denver, 1974-77; foreman Bar None Builders, Denver, 1977-79; research assoc. U. Mo., Columbia, 1979-80; asst. prof. English, Upper Iowa U., Fayette, 1980-84, assoc. prof. English, 1984-85, Bissell prof. English, head div. arts and humanities, 1985—. Contbr. articles to profl. jours. Recipient Sam Ragan Poetry Prize, Atlantic Christian Coll., 1972; NEH fellow, 1981, U. Denver fellow, 1974-77. Mem. Modern Lang. Assn., Rocky Mountain Modern Lang. Assn. Democrat. Roman Catholic. Lodge: Lions. Avocations: photography; cooking; entomology. Home: 405 S Main St Fayette IA 52142 Office: Dept English Upper Iowa U Fayette IA 52142

MCVAY, PATRICIA MARIE, travel agency executive; b. Indpls., Feb. 14, 1946; d. Charles and Marcella (Hadjieff) Nicholas; m. Edwin L. McVay, Mar. 21, 1969 (div. 1981); 1 son, Brian Hollingsworth. B.A., Aquinas Coll., 1968; teaching cert., Marion Coll., 1969; postgrad. Ind. U., 1970. Tchr. Sch. Bus., Indpls., 1969-70; with real estate sales Meridian Realty, Indpls., 1970-74; tchr. acctg. Clark Coll., Indpls., 1974-77; pres., chief exec. officer Fifth Season Travel Inc., 1977—. Mem. Indpls. C. of C. Office: Fifth Season Travel Inc 4930 N Pennsylvania St Indianapolis IN 46205

MCVEY, JAMES W., meat products company executive. Pres. Oscar Mayer & Co., Madison, Wis. Office: Oscar Mayer & Co PO Box 7188 Madison WI 53707*

MCVEY, WILLIAM MOZART, sculptor; b. Boston, July 12, 1905; s. Silas R. and Cornelia (Mozart) McV.; m. Leza Marie Sullivan, Mar. 31, 1932. Grad. Cleve. Sch. Art, 1928; student Rice Inst., 1923-25, Acadamie Colarossi and Acadamie Scandinave, Paris, 1929-31; pupil of Dispiau, Paris, 1929-31; Tchr. Cleve. Mus., 1932, Houston Mus., 1936-38, U. Tex., Austin, 1939-46, Ohio State U., Columbus, summer 1946, Cranbrook Art Acad., Bloomfield Hills, Mich., 1946-53; head sculpture dept. Cleve. Inst. Art, 1953-67; vis. sculptor Sch. Fine Arts, Ohio State U., Columbus, 1963-64. Represented in permanent collections IBM, Univ. Mus., Pomona, Calif., Wichita Art Mus., Cleve. Mus., Houston Mus., Syracuse Mus., Cranbrook Mus., Harvard Library, Smithsonian Inst., Yale Library, Nat. Cathedral, Washington, Ariana Mus., Geneva, others; publicly owned works include heroic reliefs and doors San Jacinto Monument, Tex., door FTC, Washington, doors and reliefs Tex. Meml. Mus., reliefs Lakeview Terrace Housing Project, Cleve., heroic grizzly Nat. Hist. Mus., figure Abercrombie Lab., Rice Inst., monument to Davy Crockett, Ozonz, Tex., to James Bowie, Texarkana, Tex.; 9 foot bronze of Winston Churchill, British Embassy, Washington; St. Margaret of Scotland and Jan Hus at Washington Cathedral, St. Olga of Russia, Simon de Monfort, Stephen Langton, Sir Edward Coke, Churchill Bay of Nat. Cathedral heroic U.S. Shields Fed. Bldg., Cleve., Jennings Meml., Univ. Circle, Cleve., granite hippo (with Victor Gruen) Eastgate Shopping Ctr., Detroit, 5-ton whale Lincoln Ctr., Urbana, Ill., bronze hippo Cleve. Heights Children's Library, Bell Tower, Hiram Coll., Berry Monument bronze Cleve. Hopkins Airport, panels (with

Eero Saarinen) Christ Lutheran Ch., Mpls., bronze of George Washington at Severance Hall, Univ. Circle, Cleve., head of Churchill, Chartwell, Eng., stainless steel and bronze B clef logo Blossom Music Ctr., numerous others; exhibited honor ct. Paris Grand Salon, 1930, Salon d'Automne, 1931. Chmn. Nat. screening com. Fulbright grants. Served to maj. USAF, World War II. Recipient numerous awards Nat. Sculpture Show, Ceramic Nat., Nat. Archtl. Ceramic, Mich. Acad. Sci. Arts and Letters, Internat. Cultural Exchange Ceramic Exhibit. Fellow Nat. Sculpture Soc.; mem. Coll. Art Assn., Am. Soc. Aesthetics, Internat. Platform Assn., NAD (assoc.). Papers in Archives Am. Art, Smithsonian Inst. Home and Office: 18 Pepper Ridge Rd Cleveland OH 44124

MCVICKER, MARY ELLEN HARSHBARGER, museum director, art history educator; b. Mexico, Mo., May 5, 1951; d. Don Milton and Harriet Pauline (Mossholder) Harshbarger; m. Wiley Ray McVicker, June 2, 1973; children—Laura Elizabeth, Todd Michael. B.A. with honors, U. Mo., 1973, M.A., 1975, postgrad. Adminstrv. sec. Engring. Surveys, Columbia, Mo., 1976-77; instr. Columbia U., Mo., 1977-78, Central Methodist Coll., Fayette, Mo., 1978—; mus. dir. Central Methodist Coll., Fayette, 1980—; project dir. Mo. Com. for Humanities, Fayette, 1981—, Mo. Dept. Natural Resources Office Hist. Preservation, 1978-79. Author: History Book, 1984. Vice pres. Friends Hist. Boonville, Mo., 1982-84; bd. dirs. Mus. Assocs. Mo. U., Columbia, 1981-83, Mo. Meth. Hist. Soc., Fayette, 1981-84; chmn. Bicentennial Celebration Methodism, Boonville, Mo., 1984. Mem. Mo. Heritage Trust (charter mem.), AAUW (treas. 1977-79), Am. Assn. Museums, Centralia Hist. Soc. (project dir. 1978), Mus. Assocs. United Methodist Ch. (charter mem., bd. dir. 1981-83), Phi Beta Kappa, Mortar Bd. Democrat. Clubs: Women's (treas. 1977-79), United Methodist Women's Group (charter mem.). Avocations: collecting antiques; gardening; family farming; singing; travelling. Home: 813 Christus Dr Boonville MO 65233 Office: Central Methodist Coll 411 CMC Square Fayette MO 65248

MCWHORTER, JOHN FRANCIS, manufacturing engineer; b. Cleve., June 20, 1941; s. John Francis and Daisy Alice (Morrell) M. B.S. in Mgmt. Sci., Case Inst. Tech., 1963. With TRW Inc., Cleve., 1963—, process planning engr., 1963-64, tool evaluation engr., 1964-67, computer applications engr., 1967—, prodn. engr., 1972—, mem. info. systems conf., 1982. Chmn. Cuyahoga County Youth for Goldwater, 1964; Republican precinct Committeeman, 1964-68; mem. Shaker Heights (Ohio) Rep. Club, 1964-72, sec., 1970; coordinator Ward 32 Cleve. Mayoral Campaign; 1969; mem. ARC Gallon Club, 1971. Mem. Kirley Investment Club (pres. 1982), English Speaking Union (dir. Cleve. br. 1980—), Sigma Nu. Developer more than 200 computer software applications for company. Home: 20900 Claythorne Rd Shaker Heights OH 44122 Office: TRW Valve Div 1455 E 185 St Cleveland OH 44110

MEAD, GEORGE WILSON, II, See *Who's Who in America,* 43rd edition.

MEAD, IRENE MARIE, lawyer, educator; b. Gary, Ind., Aug. 3, 1952; d. Robert R. and Marian F. (Eister) M.; m. Thomas R. Broadbent, Sept. 5, 1981. B.S.C.E., Mich. State U., 1975; J.D. cum laude, T.M. Cooley Law Sch., 1980. Bar: Mich. 1980, U.S. Dist. Ct. (we. dist.) Mich. 1980, U.S. Ct. Appeals (6th cir.) 1985. Transp. engr. Mich. Dept. Transp., Lansing, 1975-80, litigation coordinator, 1981-83; research atty. Mich. Ct. Appeals, Lansing, 1980; sole practice, Haslett, Mich., 1981-83; asst. atty. gen. Office Mich. Atty. Gen., Lansing, 1983—; adj. prof. civil engring. Mich. State U., East Lansing, 1980—; cons. engring., spl. project, Hwy. Safety Office, Mich. State U., East Lansing Mem. Soc. for Women in Transp. (founding pres. 1977-78), Women in State Govt., Inst. Transp. Engrs., Ingham County Bar Assn. (exec. council young lawyers sect. 1980-81), Assn. Asst. Attys. Gen. Mich. Home: 7030 N River Rd Grand Ledge MI 48837 Office: Dept Atty Gen Room 35 Plaza 1 Bldg Lansing MI 48913

MEADOR, CARL EDWARD, JR., lawyer; b. Akron, Ohio, Nov. 19, 1935; s. Carl E., Sr. and Clara Helen (Warren) M.; m. Lucinda Greig, June 8, 1963; children—Julia Ann, Carle E., III, Melinda. B.S. in Labor Relations, U. Akron, 1959, J.D., 1966. Bar: Ohio 1966, U.S. Dist. Ct. Ohio 1968. Asst. prosecutor City of Akron, 1966-68; assoc. Chuparkoff Law Firm, Akron, Ohio, 1968-70, Kalavity & Meador Law Firm, Akron, 1970-80; ptnr. Meador & Corzin Law Firm, Akron, 1980—; spl. counsel Atty. Gen. State of Ohio, 1970—. Served to 1st lt. U.S. Army, 1959-62. Mem. Akron Bar Assn., Ohio Bar Assn., ABA, Am. Judicature Soc. Home: 4171 Derrwood Dr Akron OH 44313

MEADOR, RICHARD ESTEN, furniture manufacturing company executive; b. Balt., May 12, 1945; s. Francis Xavier and Doris Virginia (Hardy) M.; m. Cynthia Marie Bailey, June 6, 1970 (div. 1981). B.S. in Furniture Mfg. and Mgmt., N.C. State U.-Raleigh, 1968; M.B.A., U. N.C., 1970. With DMI Furniture, Inc., 1971—, v.p. mfg., 1978-80, exec. v.p. ops., 1980-83, pres., chief operating officer, 1983—, also dir. Pres., chmn. bd. Hardwood Research Council, Asheville, N.C., 1983-85; sustaining mem. Republican Nat. Com., 1982—. Served to capt. Ind. Army N.G., 1968-76. Mem. Am. Furniture Mfrs. Assn. (dir. prodn. div. 1983—), Young Pres.'s Orgn. Clubs: Christmas Lake Golf and Tennis (Santa Claus, Ind.). Editor: Production Woodworking Machinery, 1968; Furniture Construction, 1968. Home: 4121 Browns Ln B-12 Louisville KY 40220 Office: 10400 Linn Station Rd Suite 100 Louisville KY 40223

MEADORS, JERREL E., manufacturing company executive; b. Jasper, Ind., June 11, 1934; s. Ferrel E. and Marie M. (Brittian) M.; m. Barbara Lauren Bridgewater, May 11, 1957; 1 dau., Terry Lynn. B.S., Ind. U., 1959. C.P.A., Ind. Pres., chmn. Perry Mfg. Inc., Indpls., 1968—; sec., treas. Indy Leasing & Realty, Inc., Indpls., 1976—, also dir.; owner J.E. Meadors P.A., Mgmt. Cons. to Physicians, Indpls.; ptnr. CMW Aviation, Indpls. Mem. Am. Soc. Pub. Accts., Scaffolding and Shoring Inst., Wall and Ceiling Contractors Assn. Republican. Methodist. Home: 6843 Shadow Brook Ct Indianapolis IN 46224 Office: 2535 Burton Ave Indianapolis IN 46208

MEADOWS, MICHAEL LEON, environmental engineer; b. Kansas City, Mo., Sept. 18, 1949; s. Harold Leon and Julia Ann (Harris) M.; m. Catherine Ann Benson, Jan. 9, 1972; children—Adam Leon, Stephen Michael. B.S. in Mech. Engring., U. Mo., 1972, M.S. in San. Engring., 1973. Registered profl. engr., Kans. Pollution control engr. Va. State Water Control Bd., Virginia Beach, 1973-76; mech. and environ. engr. Black & Veatch Engrs. and Architects, Kansas City, Mo., 1976—. Mem. ASME (performance test code desulfurization com. 1984). Club: Toastmasters (Kansas City). Office: Black & Veatch Engrs and Architects PO Box 8405 Kansas City MO 64114

MEANS, CHARLES LEE, university administrator; b. Holly Springs, Miss., Sept. 6, 1942; s. Charles Elias and Odessa Louise (Ruff) M.; B.S. in Polit. Sci., So. Ill. U., 1967; M.S. in Social Sci., Webster Coll., 1969; Ph.D. in Urban Edn., St. Louis U., 1973; m. Robin Williams; 1 son, Chuck Means III; 1 dau. by previous marriage, J. Markelle. Community relations specialist Job Corps, 1966; dir. relocation City of East St. Louis (Ill.), 1967, exec. dir. Urban renewal, 1968-72; exec. dir. community devel., 1972-74; vice provost for minority affairs Bowling Green State U., 1974, vice provost for acad. services, 1975-78, vice provost edn1. devel., 1978-83; asst. v.p. acad. affairs U. No. Iowa, Cedar Falls, 1983—. Mem. Waterloo (Iowa) Planning, Programming and Zoning Commn., Iowa Council Children and Families; pres. Waterloo-Cedar Falls Community Cultural Assn. Recipient award for effort in completion, Mary E. Brown Community Center, Ill. Ho. of Reps., 1976. Mem. Am. Assn. Univ. Adminstrs., Am. Assn. Higher Edn., Am. Assn. State Colls. and Univs., Ohio Assn. Ednl. Opportunity Program Personnel, Mid-Am. Assn. Ednl. Opportunity Program Personnel, Soc. Coll. and Univ. Planning, Internat. Reading Assn., Phi Delta Kappa. Democrat. Baptist. Editor conf. procs. 4th Ann. Ohio Devel. Edn. Conf., Bowling Green, 1976. Office: Room 200 Gilchrist Hall U No Iowa Cedar Falls IA 50614

MECKLENBURG, JOHN ROBERT, educational administrator; b. Gary, Ind., Mar. 20, 1948; s. John August and Margaret Elizabeth (Armagest) M.; m. Kathy Kay Shipman; children—David Mark, Brian Wade. B.S. in Edn., Troy State U., 1970; M.A., No. Ill. U., 1979. Dir. univ. relations Troy State U. 1970-73, No. Ill. U., DeKalb, 1973-79, Culver-Stockton Coll., Canton, Mo., 1979-80, Rockford Coll., Ill., 1981—; ednl. pub. relations cons., 1975—; sec. Ill. Coll. Relations Conf., 1978-79; dir. seminars in field, 1982—. Author: Publications Policies and Procedures at Four-Year, State-Supported Institutions of CASE in District V in the United States, 1979. Editor mag. Rockford Report, 1981—. Bd. dirs. Rockford Urban League, 1981-83, Blackhawk council Boy Scouts Am., 1981-83; soccer coach AYSO, Rockford, 1982—. Recipient All-Am. award Nat. Assn. Intercollegiate Athletics, 1971-72, 79, Golden Quill award Internat. Assn. Bus. Communications, 1977, award for publication Council for the Advancement and Support of Edn., 1975-76. Baptist. Avocation: coaching youth sports. Home: 5852 Pepper Dr Rockford IL 61111 Office: Rockford Coll 5050 E State St Rockford IL 61108-2393

MEDARIS, FLORENCE ISABEL, osteopathic physician and surgeon; b. Kirksville, Mo.; d. Charles Edward and Nellie (Finley) Medaris; B.A., Coll. Wooster, 1932; D.O., Kirksville Coll. Osteopathy and Surgery, 1939; postgrad. U. Wis., Marquette U. Pvt. practice osteo. medicine and surgery, Milw., 1940—. Active Milwaukee County Mental Assn., Milw. Art Center, Friends of Art; mem. med. bd. dirs. Milw. Soc. Multiple Sclerosis Soc., 1973—; mem. Mayor's Beautification Com., 1968—. Dir. Zonta Manor, 1957-67, Brace Fund Bd. of Advt. Women of Milw., 1958-64, pres. bd., 1962-63, 77—; bd. mem. Bookfellows Milw.; finance com. Coll. Womens Club Found., 1971-78. Mem. Am. Osteo. Assn. (com. mental health 1964), Wis. Assn. Osteo. Physicians and Surgeons, Milw. Dist. Soc., Osteo. Physicians and Surgeons, Am. Coll. Gen. Practitioners, Applied Acad. Osteopathy, Am. Assn. U. Women, Inter-Group Council Women (pres. 1947-49, dir.), Wis. Pub. Health Assn., Council for Wis. Writers, Photog. Soc. Am., Wis. Acad. Scis., Arts and Letters, Delta Omega (nat. pres. 1952-53). Presbyn. Club: Zonta (bd. mem. Milw. 1968-69). Home: 1121 N Waverly Pl Milwaukee WI 53202 Office: 161 W Wisconsin Ave Milwaukee WI 53203

MEDINA, BILL STEVENS, construction company executive; b. Lajes Field Naval Base, Azores, Portugal, Aug. 20, 1956; came to U.S., 1962; s. Abel and Renee Denise (Boniface) M.; m. Peggy Eileen Lewis, Mar. 18, 1978; children—Dustin Daniel, Dylan Michael. Student pub. schs., Salina, Kans. Motorcycle mechanic Road & Trail, Salina, Kans., 1972; landscaper Kline's Landscaping Co., Salina, 1972-73; carpenter Bradshaw Constrn. Co., Salina, 1974-76, Umphrey Builders, Salina, 1976, Abbott Constrn. Co., Salina, 1976-77; pres. Bill Medina Constrn. Co., Salina, 1977—. Mem. Salina Builders Assn., Associated Gen. Contractors of Am. Republican. Avocations: fishing; karate. Home: 537 Aullwood Salina KS 67401 Office: Bill Medina Constrn Co PO Box 141 Salina KS 67402

MEECE, DAVID CHARLES, advanced systems development manager; b. Somerset, Ky., July 4, 1953; s. Charles Franklin and Shirley Ann (Chaney) M.; m. Marsha Kay Wells, Oct. 14, 1978; children—Sarah Noelle, Christopher Charles. B.A., Campbellsville Coll., 1975; M.B.A., Ind. Central U., 1979. Mgmt. analyst Ind. Nat. Bank, Indpls., 1975-82; info. systems specialist Marble Hill Nuclear Generating Sta., Pub. Service of Ind., New Washington, 1982-85; mgr. advanced systems devel. Bank of Louisville, 1985—. Youth dir. Marwood Baptist Ch., Indpls., 1975-78, Sunday sch. dir., 1979-81; youth dir. Calvary Bapt. Ch., Indpls., 1982; Sunday sch. dir. First Bapt. Ch., Sellersburg, Ind., 1982—, deacon, 1983—. Campbellsville Coll. scholar, 1971-72, 73-75. Republican. Home: 7702 Stone Creek Circle Charlestown IN 47111 Office: Bank of Louisville 500 W Broadway Louisville KY 40202

MEEK, JOSEPH CHESTER, JR., physician, educator; b. Hiawatha, Kans., July 16, 1931; s. Joseph Chester and Florence Mildred (Eicholtz) M.; A.B., U. Kans., 1954, M.D., 1957; m. Bette Ewing, June 5, 1954; children—Thomas, Nancy, Katherine. Intern San Diego County Gen. Hosp., 1957-58; resident U. Kans. Med. Ctr., Kansas City, 1958-60; instr. medicine U. Kans., 1964-65, asst. prof., 1965-69, assoc. prof., 1969-75, prof., 1975—, vice chancellor acad. affairs, 1981—. Mem. adminstrv. bd. Asbury United Meth. Ch., 1982—. Served with USNR, 1960-62. Mem. Am. Fedn. Clin. Research, AMA, Wyandotte County Med. Assn., Kans. Med. Soc., Am. Diabetes Assn., Endocrine Soc., Central Soc. Clin. Research, Am. Thyroid Assn., Soc. Med. Coll. Dirs., Am. Heart Assn., Phi Beta Kappa, Alpha Omega Alpha. Contbr. articles to profl. jours. Home: 10071 Hemlock St Overland Park KS 66212 Office: University of Kansas Medical Center 39th St and Rainbow Blvd Kansas City KS 66103

MEEK, LEROY RICHARD, watchmaker, jeweler; b. Pleasant Lake, Ind., Feb. 15, 1932; s. Joseph Nathan and Beulah Naomi (Dreher) M.; m. Julia Ann Perry, Nov. 21, 1969; children—Leroy M., Sheila C. B.A. in Horology, Bradley U., 1957. Cert. master watchmaker. Watchmaker, jeweler Liechty Jewelry, Angola, Ind., 1958-62; owner, watchmaker, jeweler Meek's Jewelry, LaGrange, Ind., 1962—; guest watchmaker Watchmakers Assn. of Switzerland, Berne, 1970, Bulova Watch Co., Berne, 1970. County Vets. Service officer VA, LaGrange, 1977—. Served with USN, 1951-55, FPO, Korea. Mem. Watchmakers Assn. of Ind. (cert.), Am. Watchmakers Inst. (cert.), Northeastern Ind. Horology Guild, Ind. Jewelers Assn., VFW, Am. Legion, LaGrange C. of C. (bd. dirs. 1982—). Club: LaGrange Country (social dir. 1984). Lodges: Loyal Order of Moose (1st gov. 1976, fellowship degree 1978), Masons. Avocations: bowling; golf; fishing. Office: Meek's Jewelry 111 S Detroit St LaGrange IN 46761

MEEKER, BARBARA MILLER, art educator, artist, painter; b. Peru, Ind., Dec. 31, 1930; d. George Curtis Jr. and Ruth Mae (Burton) Miller; m. William F. Meeker, Aug. 10, 1952; children—David George, Stephen George. A.B., DePauw U., 1952. Art tchr. Hammond Pub. Schs., Ind., 1952-57, B&B Designs, Munster, Ind., 1958-65; mem. faculty dept. drawing, painting and archtl. rendering Purdue U. Calumet, Hammond, Ind., 1965—, assoc. prof., 1979—; art advisor North Ind. Art Assn., Munster, 1970—; art gallery coordinator Purdue U. Calumet, 1976—. Author: Freehand Drawing Man, 1972, 3rd edit. 1980; designed courses of study of imagination and drawing, 1965-85. Recipient 2nd prize and Purchase prize Artists Guild Chgo., 1980, jury prize distinction Hoosier Salon, Indpls., 1983, 84, various prizes at juried art exhibitions throughout tri-state area. Mem. Midwest Watercolor Soc. (bd. dirs. 1983-85), Artists Equity, San Antonio Water Color Group, Ind. Artists Assn., Kappa Kappa Gamma Alumni Group (pres. 1969-61), Pan Hellenic (pres. Highland, Ind. chpt. 1960-61). Methodist. Avocations: gardening; flowers; teaching children. Home: 8314 Greenwood Ave Munster IN 46321 Office: Purdue Univ Calumet 2233 171st St Hammond IN 46323

MEEKS, CORDELL DAVID, JR., state judge; b. Kansas City, Kans., Dec. 17, 1942; s. Cordell David and Cellastine Dora (Brown) M.; m. Mary Ann Sutherland, July 15, 1967; 1 child, Cordell D. III. B.A., U. Kans., 1964, J.D., 1967; postgrad., U. Pa., 1968. Bar: Kans. 1968, U.S. Dist. Ct. Kans. 1968, U.S. Mil. Ct. Appeals 1971, U.S. Ct. Appeals (10th cir.) 1971, U.S. Supreme Ct. 1971. Staff counsel Wyandotte County Legal Aid Soc., Kansas City, Kans., 1968-70; spl. asst. atty. gen. State of Kans., Kansas City, 1975; sr. ptnr. Meeks, Sutherland, and McIntosh, Kansas City, 1972-81; judge Mcpl. Ct. Kansas City, 1976-81; dist. ct. judge 29th Judicial Dist. Kans., Kansas City, 1981—; mem. govs. com. crime prevention, Kans., 1984—; mem. Kans. adv. com. overcrowded prisons, 1983-84; pres. Wyandotte County Law Library Com., 1982-83; staff judge adv. 35th Inf. Div. Kans. N.G., 1984—. Vice pres. Jr. Achievement Greater Kansas City, 1975- 76; pres. Wyandotte County chpt. ARC, 1971-73, Mental Health Assn., 1981-83, Legal Aid Soc., 1971-73, Econ. Opportunity Found., Inc., Kansas City, 1981-83; bd. dirs. Family and Childrens Service, 1983—; pres. Substance Abuse Ctr. Eastern Kans., 1985—; mem. exec. com. NCCJ, Kansas City, 1984—. Recipient Outstanding Service award Kansas City United Way, 1979. Mem. Kans. Mcpl. Judges Assn. (pres. 1980-81), U. Kans. Law Soc. (pres. bd. govs. 1984—), Nat. Conf. State Trial Judges (ethics and profl. responsibility com.), Am. Judicature Soc., Am. Judges Assn., ABA, Kans. Bar Assn., Am. Royal Assn. (bd. govs. 1981—). Democrat. African Methodist Episcopalian. Lodge: Optimists (bd. dirs. 1977). Avocations: jazz piano; table tennis; swimming. Home: 7915 Walker Kansas City KS 66112 Office: Wyandotte County Courthouse 701 N 7th St Kansas City KS 66101

MEENGS, WILLIAM LLOYD, cardiologist; b. Zeeland, Mich., Dec. 23, 1942; s. Lloyd Stanley and Gertrude (Wyngarden) M.; A.B., Hope Coll., 1964; M.D., U. Mich., 1968; m. Helen Delores Van Dyke, June 10, 1964; children—Michelle Rene, William Lloyd, Lisa Ann. Intern in internal medicine Univ. Hosp., Ann Arbor, Mich., 1968-69, resident in internal medicine, 1971-73, fellow in cardiology, 1973-75; practice medicine specializing in cardiology, Petoskey, Mich., 1975—; cardiologist Burns Clinic Med. Center, Petoskey, 1975—, chmn. dept. cardiology and cardiac surgery, 1978—; cardiologist Little Traverse Hosp., Petoskey, 1975—, dir. coronary care unit, 19—. Trustee Mich. Heart Assn., 1979—. Served as surgeon USPHS, 1969-71. Fellow Am. Coll. Cardiology; mem. A.C.P., Am. Heart Assn., Alpha Omega Alpha. Home: 1052 Lindell St Petoskey MI 49770 Office: Burns Clin Med Center 560 W Mitchell St Petoskey MI 49770

MEERSCHAERT, JOSEPH RICHARD, physician; b. Detroit, Mar. 4, 1941; s. Hector Achiel and Marie Terese (Campbell) M.; m. Jeanette Marie Ancerewicz, Sept. 14, 1963; children—Eric, Amy, Adam. B.A., Wayne State U., 1965, M.D., 1967. Diplomate Am. Bd. Phys. Medicine and Rehab. Intern, Harper Hosp., Detroit, 1967-68; resident in phys. medicine and rehab. Wayne State U. Rehab. Inst., Detroit, 1968-71; chief div. phys. medicine Naval Hosp., Chelsea, Mass., 1971-73; attending physician William Beaumont Hosp., Royal Oak, Mich., 1973—, med. dir. rehab. unit, 1979—; pvt. practice medicine specializing in phys. medicine and rehab., Royal Oak, 1973—; mem. med. adv. bd. Nat. Wheelchair Athletic Assn., 1973—, examining physician Nat. Wheelchair Athletic Games, Marshall, Minn., 1982, U.S. team physician VII World Wheelchair Games, Stoke Mandeville, Eng.; clin. instr. Wayne State U., 1973-83, clin. asst. prof. phys. medicine and rehab., 1983—; mem. Mich. Dept. Licensing and Regulation State Bd. Phys. Therapy, 1978-81. Served with M.C., USN, 1971-73. Recipient John Hussey award Mich. Wheelchair Athletic Assn., 1981. Mem. Am. Acad. Phys. Medicine and Rehab. (reviewer, presenter), Am. Congress Rehab. Medicine, Mich. Phys. Medicine and Rehab. Soc., Am. Geriatrics Soc., Am. Assn. Electromyography and Electrodiagnosis, Mich. Rheumatism Soc., Mich. Acad. Phys. Medicine and Rehab. (chmn. program com. 1977-78, trustee 1980—, del. 1982), Oakland County Med. Soc. (alt. del. 1979-81), Met. Soc. Crippled Children and Adults (bd. dirs. 1979-82, pres. 1981-82), Alpha Omega Alpha. Roman Catholic. Contbr. articles to profl. jours. Office: 3535 W Thirteen Mile Rd Royal Oak MI 48072

MEESE, ERNEST HAROLD, thoracic and cardiovascular surgeon; b. Bradford, Pa., June 23, 1929; s. Ernest D. and Blanche (Raub) M.; B.A., U. Buffalo, 1950, M.D., 1954; m. Margaret Eugenia McHenry, Oct. 4, 1952 (dec. May 7, 1984); children—Constance Ann, Roderick Bryan, Gregory James. Resident in gen. surgery Millard Fillmore Hosp., Buffalo, 1955-59; resident in thoracic surgery U.S. Naval Hosp., St. Albans L.I., N.Y., 1961-63; group practice thoracic and cardiovascular surgery, Cin., 1965—; asst. clin. prof. surgery Cin. Med. Center, 1972—; head sect. thoracic and cardiovascular surgery St. Francis-St. George Hosp., Deaconess Hosp.; mem. staff Good Samaritan, Bethesda, Christ, Providence, Childrens, Epp Meml. and St. Luke hosps., Cin. Pres. bd. dirs., chmn. service com. Cin.-Hamilton County unit Am. Cancer Soc., trustee, mem. exec. bd. Ohio div.; trustee, exec. bd. Southwestern Ohio chpt. Am. Heart Assn. Served to comdr. M.C., USN, 1959-65. Diplomate Am. Bd. Surgery, Am. Bd. Thoracic Surgery. Fellow A.C.S., Internat. Coll. Surgeons; mem. Soc. Thoracic Surgeons, Am. Coll. Chest Physicians, Am. Coll. Angiology, Cin. Surg. Soc., Am. Coll. Cardiology; mem. Gibson Anat. Hon. Soc., AMA, Am. Thoracic Soc., Assn. Mil. Surgeons U.S., Acad. Medicine Cin., Assn. Advancement Med. Instrumentation, N.Am. Soc. Pacing and Electrophysiology, Phi Beta Kappa, Phi Chi (treas. 1952-54). Clubs: Western Hills Country, Queen City, Masons, Mediclub (pres. 1983-85) (Cin.). Contbr. articles to profl. jours. and textbooks. Home: 174 Pedretti Rd Cincinnati OH 45238 Office: 311 Howell Ave Cincinnati OH 45220 also 5049 Crookshank Cincinnati OH 45211

MEGEL, HERBERT, toxicologist, researcher; b. Newark, N.J., Nov. 10, 1926; s. Benjamin Abraham and Anna Ruth (Geller) M.; m. Eleanor Sitzman, Jan. 20, 1951; children—Diana Lynn, Joseph Lawrence. B.A., NYU, 1948, M.S., 1950, Ph.D., 1954. Diplomate Am. Bd. Toxicology. Dir. bioassay Princeton Labs., N.J., 1954-50; physiologist Boeing Co., Seattle, 1959-62; sr. research toxicologist Merrell Dow Pharms., Cin., 1962—. Contbr. articles to profl. jours. and books. Fellow N.Y. Acad. Scis.; mem. Am. Assn. Immunology, Am. Soc. Pharmacology and Exptl. Therapeutics, Soc. Toxicology, Soc. Exptl. Biology and Medicine, Internat. Union Pharmacology. Avocations: photography, gardening, bridge, numismatics. Home: 1250 Forest Ct Cincinnati OH 45215 Office: Merrell Dow Pharms 2110 E Galbraith Rd Cincinnati OH 45215

MEGEL, ROBERTA JEAN PENNING, lawyer; b. Omaha, Sept. 24, 1953; d. Robert Joseph and Zora Daisy (Huisman) Penning; m. Terry Michael Megel, May 18, 1974. B.A. magna cum laude, U. Nebr., Omaha, 1975; J.D., Creighton U., 1979. Bar: Iowa 1979, U.S. Dist. Ct. (so. dist.) Iowa 1979, Nebr. 1981, U.S. Dist. Ct. Nebr. 1981. Sole practice, Council Bluffs, Iowa, 1981—. Author poetry. Camp mem. Vol. Lawyer's Project, Iowa, 1982, 83, 84; leader Nishnabotna council Girl Scouts U.S., 1983-84. Recipient Appreciation award Nishnabotna council Girl Scouts, 1984. Mem. ABA, Iowa State Bar Assn., (com. on alternative dispute resolutions), Nebr. State Bar Assn., Am. Jucicature Soc., Assn. Trial Lawyers Am. Democrat. Roman Catholic. Clubs: Westroads (Omaha), Ronnie McDowell Fan (Atlanta). Office: Megel Law Firm 409 S 8th St Council Bluffs IA 51501

MEHL, EDWARD JEROME, hospital administrator; b. Breckenridge, Minn., Aug. 21, 1945; s. Edward G. and Alma H. (Anderson) M.; m. Gail Marie Mikkelson, June 25, 1966; children—Jeffrey, Christopher, Joseph, Jacqueline. Assoc. Sci., N.D. State, Sch. Sci. 1965; B.A., Moorhead State U., 1967; M.H.A., U. Minn., 1980. Adminstr. Lake Region Hosp. Corp., Fergus Falls, Minn. Mem. Planning Commn., City of Fergus Falls, Minn., 1978-83. Roman Catholic. Avocations: hunting; fishing; sports; kids. Office: Lake Region Hosp Corp 712 S Cascade St Fergus Falls MN 56537

MEHRLE, PAUL MARTIN, JR., biochemist; b. Caruthersville, Mo., Dec. 13, 1944; s. Paul Martin and Hazel (Marshal) M.; m. Frankye Sue Long, Dec. 22, 1964; children—Fran, Betsy. B.A., Southwestern U., Memphis, 1967; M.A., U. Mo., 1969, Ph.D., 1971. Physiologist, Nat. Fishery Research Lab, Columbia, Mo., 1971-81, chief biologist, 1981—. Co-author sci. publs. and books on environ. toxicology. Chmn. Zoning Adjustment Bd., 1981-82; mem. Mayor of Columbia Task Force on Drug Abuse, 1983—. Recipient Spl. Achievement award, U.S. Dept. Interior, 1975, 77, 78, 81. Mem. Am. Fishery Soc. (editor water quality reports 1981—, assoc. editor transactions 1981-83), Am. Chem. Soc., Soc. Environ. Toxicology and Chemistry. Presbyterian. Lodge: Rotary. Avocation: tennis. Home: 1804 W Broadway St Columbia MO 65203 Office: Nat Fishery Research Lab US Dept Interior Fish and Wildlife Service Columbia MO 65201

MEHTA, INDER S., housewares manufacturing company executive; b. India, Jan. 28, 1939; came to U.S. 1968, naturalized, 1985; s. Harnath and Sajjan Kumari (Chajjer) M.; m. Sudha Saklecha, Feb. 6, 1965; children—Sandeep, Rajeev. M.A., U. Delhi-India, 1960; M.B.A., Marquette U., 1970. With Regal Ware, Inc., Kewaskum, Wis., 1971—, now product dir. cookware and dir. internat. sales. Mem. Cookware Mfrs. Assn. Am. (chmn. statis. com. 1977-79). Avocations: bridge; tennis. Office: Regal Ware Inc 1675 Reigle Dr Kewaskum WI 53209

MEIDINGER, R. E., state education official. Pres., State Bd. of Higher Edn., N.D. Office: State Bd Higher Edn Jamestown ND 58402*

MEIER, BEN, secretary of state of North Dakota; b. Napoleon, N.D., Aug. 1, 1918; s. Bernhardt and Theresia (Helzenderger) M.; diploma Dakota Bus. Coll., Fargo, N.D.; student U. Wis. Sch. Banking; m. Clara Kaczynski, Dec. 30, 1944; 1 son, Bernie. With Stock Growers Bank, Napoleon, 1943-45, Bank of Gackle (N.D.), 1945-47; v.p. Bank of Hazelton (N.D.), 1947-50; oil broker, real estate exec., ins. salesman, Bismarck, N.D., 1950-54; pres., owner Mandan Security Bank (N.D.), 1957-74; pres. Bismarck State Bank, 1977-81; sec. of state State of N.D., 1955—. Mem. Nat. Assn. Secs. State (past pres.), Nat. Assn. State Contractor Lic. Registars (past pres.). Republican. Roman Catholic. Lodges: Elks, Moose. Office: Capitol Bldg Bismarck ND 58501*

MEIER, KAREN LORENE, educator; b. Davenport, Iowa, Aug. 17, 1942; d. Charles Frank and Minnie Louise (Arp) Meier; B.A., U. Iowa, 1963, M.A., 1974. Tchr., librarian Plano (Ill.) High Sch., 1963-67; tchr. social studies Moline (Ill.) High Sch., 1967—, also Secondary Social Studies Coordinator. Bd. dirs. Quad-City World Affairs Council; active LWV. Recipient regional award Ill. State Hist. Soc. Mem. Nat. Council Social Studies Ill. Council Social Studies (sec. 1973-74, v.p. 1974-75, bd. dirs. 1982-83, treas. 1984—), Iowa Council Social Studies, NEA, Ill. Edn. Assn. (sec.-treas. regional council 1975-79, legis. chairperson 1980-81), Moline Edn. Assn. (pres. 1977-78), Am. Soc. Profl. and Exec. Women, Social Studies Suprs. Assn., Assn. Supervision and Curriculum Devel., AAUW, Women in Ednl. Adminstrn., (dir. 1985, pres. 1985-86), Iowa Women in Ednl. Leadership, Alpha Delta Kappa. Home: 1855 14th St Bettendorf IA 52722 Office: 3600 23d Ave Moline IL 61265

MEIER, ROBERT H(ALLING), mining company executive; b. New Salem, N.D., May 26, 1930; s. Archibald Stevens and Mabel (Halling) M.; m. Bettye Louise Kerr, Oct. 18, 1958; children—Anne Kerr, John Edward. B.S., U. Colo., 1954; M.B.A., Tulsa U., 1969. C.P.A., Okla. Staff acct. Amoco Prodn. Co., Tulsa, 1965-68, acctg. research analyst, 1968-73; sr. staff research acct.

Standard Oil Co., Chgo., 1973-81; supr. acctg. procedures Amoco Minerals Co., Englewood, Colo., 1981-83, mgr. acctg. systems and procedures 1983—; research staff FASB Extractive Industry Study, 1974. Mem. vestry, treas. St. John's Episcopal Ch., Naperville, Ill., 1974-78. Served with U.S. Army, 1950-52. Recipient Acctg. Adv. Council award Colo. U., 1984. Mem. Am. Mining Congress, Nat. Coal Assn. (conf. chmn. acctg. com. 1984). Avocation: skiing. Home: 7894 S Locust Ct Englewood CO 80112 Office: Amoco Minerals Co 7000 S Yosemite St Englewood CO 80155

MEIERHENRY, MARK V., attorney general of South Dakota; b. Gregory, S.D., Oct. 29, 1944; s. Vernon and Mary (Casey) M.; B.A., U. S.D., 1966, J.D., 1970; m. Judith Knittel, May 14, 1961; children—Todd, Mary. Admitted to Nebr. bar, 1970, S.D. bar, 1971; assoc. firm Camerer, Meierhenry and Tabor, Scottsbluff, Nebr., 1970-71; dir. S.D. Legal Services, Mission, 1971-74; ptnr. Meierhenry, DeVany & Krueger, Vermillion, S.D, 1974-78; atty. gen. State of S.D., Pierre, 1978—. Mem. Sch. Bd. Vermillion, 1976-78. Mem. S.D. State Bar Assn., S.D. Trial Lawyers Assn. Republican. Office: Office of the Atty Gen State Capitol Pierre SD 57501-5090*

MEIERS, RUTH L., state official. Lt. gov. State of N.D., 1985—. Office: Office of Lt Gov Capitol Bldg Bismarck ND 58505*

MEIJER, FREDERIK, retail company executive; b. 1919. With Meijer, Inc., Grand Rapids, Mich., now chmn. bd., dir. Office: Meijer Inc 2727 Walker Ave NW Grand Rapids MI 49501*

MEIKLE, WILLIAM MACKAY, lawyer; b. Wilkinsburg, Pa., July 13, 1933; s. William and Martha (Bohlender) M.; m. Mary Eileen Luth, Mar. 12, 1966; children—Elizabeth Ellen, Martha Pauline. B.B.A., U. Mich., 1955, J.D., 1959. Bar: Ohio 1959. Sole practice, Celina, Ohio, 1959-63; ptnr. Knapke & Meikle, Celina, 1964-76; ptnr. Meikle & Tesno, Celina, 1977-81; ptnr. Meikle, Tesno & Luth, Celina, 1982—; also asst. pros. atty. Mercer County (Ohio) 1959-74, pros. atty., 1975-76; sec., treas. Mercer County Civic Found., 1961-82. Vice pres. Mercer County Health Care Found., 1980—; sec. Western Ohio Ednl. Found., 1975—; trustee Auglaize County Family Y Inc., 1981-84. Served to capt. USAR, 1959. Mem. Ohio State Bar Assn., Ohio Assn. Civil Trial Attys. Democrat. Methodist. Home: 209 Mercer St Celina OH 45822 Office: 100 N Main St Celina OH 45822

MEININGER, ROBERT ALLEN, languages educator; b. Torrington, Wyo., Mar. 29, 1938; s. Victor E. and Anne C. (Pelz) M.; m. Genevieve Marie Proot, Jan. 16, 1963 (div. Mar. 1969); 1 child, Jean-Paul. B.A. cum laude, U. Wyo., 1961; M.A., U. Nebr., 1964, Ph.D., 1970. Instr., U. Nebr., Lincoln, 1966-68; asst. prof. Nebr. Wesleyan U., Lincoln, 1968-72, assoc. prof., 1972-79, prof. langs., 1979—, head fgn. lang. dept., 1968—, chmn. humanities div., 1979-83; mem. Fulbright selection com. Inst. Internat. Edn., Chgo., 1979-82. Contbr. articles to profl. jours.; translator. Fulbright fellow, Belgium, 1961-62; NEH grantee, 1976; Goethe Inst. grantee, 1982. Mem. Am. Assn. Tchrs. of French (treas. 1976-80), Am. Assn. Tchrs. of German, Nebr. Fgn. Lang. Tchrs. Assn., Am. Legion, Am. Hist. Soc. of Germans from Russia (charter), Phi Beta Kappa, Phi Kappa Phi. Home: 5011 L St Lincoln NE 68510 Office: Nebr Wesleyan U Lincoln NE 68504

MEINKE, DARREL MYRON, university administrator; b. Plymouth, Nebr., June 19, 1929; s. Elmer Enno and Leila Hilda (Diekmann) M.; m. A. Lois Koenig, Aug. 1, 1952; children—Lance, Doreen, Russ, Troy. B.Sc. in Edn., U. Nebr., 1951, M.Ed., 1955; M.A., Denver U., 1959; D.Ed., U. Nebr., 1966. Prin. Grace Luth. Sch., Platte Center, Nebr., 1951-54; librarian Concordia High Sch., Seward, Nebr., 1954-60; dir. library Concordia Coll., Seward, 1960-70, assoc. dean; 1970-72; dean instructional research Moorhead State U., Minn., 1973—. Mem. ALA, Minn. Library Assn. Republican. Lutheran. Avocations: golf, bowling, fishing, acting. Office: Livingston Lord Library Moorhead State U Moorhead MN 56560

MEIRINK, THOMAS PAUL, orthopedic surgeon; b. St. Louis, Mar. 16, 1936; s. Paul H. and Cornelia (St. Eve) M.; m. Suzanne Macdonald, Apr. 16, 1966; children—William Charles, Stephanie Regnier, Thomas Paul. B.S., U. Notre Dame, 1958; M.D., Loyola U., Chgo., 1962. Diplomate Am. Bd. Orthopaedic Surgeons. Intern, St. John's Hosp., St. Louis, 1962-63; resident St. Louis U., 1963-68; practice medicine specializing in orthopedic surgery, Belleville, Ill., 1968—; mem. staff St. Elizabeth's Hosp., Belleville Meml. Hosp., Firmin Desloge Hosp., St. Louis, Cardinal Glennon Hosp., St. Louis; clin. instr. St. Louis U., 1968—; with Ill. Services for Crippled Children, U. Ill., Belleville, 1968—. Contbr. articles to profl. jours. Bd. dirs. Med. Utilization Review Com. for So. Ill., 1980—; Ill. Council of Continuing Med. Edn., 1983—. Fellow ACS, Internat. Coll. Surgeons, Am. Acad. Orthopaedic Surgeons; mem. AMA, Am. Trauma Soc., Am. Fracture Assn., Ill. Med. Soc. (trustee 1981—), Ill. Orthopaedic Soc., Clin. Orthopaedic Soc., So. Ill. Med. Assn. (pres. 1981-82), St. Clair County Med. Assn. (pres. 1981), St. Louis Orthopaedic Soc., St. Louis Surg. Soc., St. Louis Rheumatism Soc., Phi Chi. Home: 41 Country Club Pl Belleville IL 62223 Office: Assoc Orthopedic Surgeons 8601 W Main St Belleville IL 62223

MEIS, NANCY R., marketing and fundraising executive; b. Iowa City, Aug. 6, 1952; d. Donald J. and Theresa (Dee) M.; m. Paul L. Wenske, Oct. 14, 1978; children—Alexis Meis, Christopher Meis. B.A., Clarke Coll., 1974; M.B.A., U. Okla., 1981. Cultural program supr. City of Dubuque, Iowa., 1974-76; community services dir. State Arts Council of Okla., Oklahoma City, 1976-78, program dir., 1978-79; mgr. Cimarron Circuit Opera Co., Norman, Okla., 1979-82, bd. dirs., 1982—; account exec. Bell System, Kansas City, Mo., 1982; mgr. special services Holy Land Christian Mission, Internat., Kansas City, 1983—. Named Outstanding Young Woman in Am., 1977, 78. Mem. fund raising com. St. Peters Ch., Kansas City, 1983, Interfaith Peace Alliance, Kansas City, 1984. Mem. Nat. Soc. Fund Raising Exec. (Kansas City chpt. program com. 1985), Nat. Network Bus. Sch. Women (rep. 1980), Greater Kansas City Chpt. Council on Philanthropy. Roman Catholic.

MEISER, JOHN HENRY, chemistry educator; b. Cin., Nov. 21, 1938; s. Paul M. and Mildred P. (Turck) M.; m. Enya P. Flores, Aug. 12, 1967; children—Maria Cristina, Maria Teresa, Maria Katharina. B.S., Xavier U., 1961; Ph.D., U. Cin., 1966. Asst. prof. Univ. Dayton, Ohio, 1966-69; from asst. prof. to assoc. prof. Ball State Univ., Muncie, Ind., 1969-1980, prof., 1980—. Author: (with K.J. Laidler) Physical Chemistry, 1980; (with others) Problems and Solutions, 1984. Fellow Ind. Acad. Sci. (sec. 1980-83); Fulbright grantee, 1985-86; mem. Soc. Applied Spectroscopy (chmn. 1984—), Am. Chem. Soc., Am. Phys. Soc. Roman Catholic. Avocation: flying. Home: R R 12 Box 34 Muncie IN 47302 Office: Ball State Univ Dept Chmistry Muncie IN 47302

MEISSE, GUNTHER SAGEL, radio station executive; b. Mansfield, Ohio, Nov. 28, 1942; s. Louis Albert and Barbara Marka (Sagel) M.; grad. high sch., Mansfield; m. Jeanne H. Robinson, Jan. 15, 1983; children by previous marriage—Marka, Melinda, Gunther Sagel II, Robert; stepchildren—Steve, Russell. Salesman Service Audio Cons., 1956-61; part-time engring. radio stas. WMAN and WCLW, Mansfield, 1956-60; one of founders Johnny Appleseed Broadcasting Co. and radio sta. WVNO, Mansfield, 1961—, gen. mgr., v.p., 1962-74, pres., 1974—; pres. GSM Media Corp., 1976—; pres. Mid State Media Corp. (WWWY Radio), Columbus, Ind.; mem. adv. bd. Richland Trust Co., 1972—. Bd. dirs. Planned Parenthood, 1973, Renaissance Theatre, 1980—; bd. dirs., mem. exec. com. Richland Econ. Devel. Corp. Mem. Mansfield Area C. of C. (dir. 1970-75), Advt. Club (past dir.), North Central Ohio Marketing Club (past dir.), Nat. Assn. FM Broadcasters (dir. 1964-73, 75-76), FM Broadcast Pioneers (charter), Ohio Assn. Broadcasters (dir. 1980-83, v.p. 1977-78). Rotarian. Home: Bell Rd Mansfield OH 44904 Office: 2900 Park Ave W Mansfield OH 44906

MEISTER, RICHARD J., educational administrator, history educator; b. Gray, Ind., Sept. 22, 1938; s. Edward J. and Lillian A. (Jones) M.; m. Joan Marie Costanza, Apr. 4, 1964; children—Christopher B., Erica A., Jonathan R. B.A., St. Joseph's Coll., 1960; M.A., U. Notre Dame, 1962, Ph.D., 1967. Asst. prof. history Xavier U., Cin., 1965-69; from asst. prof. to prof. U. Mich.-Flint, 1969-81; prof., dean coll. liberal arts and scis. DePaul U., Chgo., 1981—. Co-author: Cities in Transition, 1979. Editor: Black Ghetto: Promised Land or Colony, 1972; Race and Ethnicity in America, 1974. Vice-chmn. Civil Service Commn., Flint, 1979-81; v.p. Genesee County Hist. Soc., Flint, 1980-81. Roman Catholic. Home: 838 N Kenilworth Oak Park IL 60302 Office: DePaul U Dean's Office 2323 N Seminary Chicago IL 60614

MEISTER, THOMAS NEAL, pharmacy services administrator; researcher; b. St. Cloud, Minn., July 20, 1952; s. Neal Walter and Lois Mae (Nelson) M.; m. Gail Marian Jasmer, June 7, 1975; children—Andrew Neal, Maren Gail. B.S., N.D. State U., 1975; M.S., U. Minn., 1984. Regis. pharmacist, Wis., Minn., N.D. Pharmacy intern St. Mary's Hosp., Detroit Lakes, Minn., 1974-75, San Diego VA Hosp., LaJolla, Calif., 1975-76; pharmacy residency Mpls. VA Hosp., 1976-78; dir. pharmacy services St. Croix Valley Meml. Hosp., Wis., 1978—; preceptor pharmacy technician tng. program Area Vocat. Tech. Inst., White Bear Lake, Minn., 1983—. Contbr. articles to profl. jours. Recipient Merck-Sharp-Dohme Corp. Scholarship award, 1975. Mem. Am. Soc. Hosp. Pharmacists, Wis. Soc. Hosp. Pharmacists, Kappa Psi (pres. N.D. chpt. 1973-74), Rho Chi, Phi Kappa Phi. Republican. Lutheran. Club: Ducks Unltd. (chmn. 1983—). Avocations: fishing; hunting; cross-country skiing. Home: Route 1 Box 1C St Croix Falls WI 54024

MEITES, SAMUEL, clinical chemist, educator; b. St. Joseph, Mo., Jan. 3, 1921; s. Benjamin and Frieda (Kaminsky) M.; m. Lois Pauline Maranville, Mar. 11, 1945; 1 child, David Russell. A.S., St. Joseph Jr. Coll., 1940; A.B., U. Mo., 1942; Ph.D., Ohio State U., 1950. Diplomate Am. Bd. Clin. Chemistry. Clin. biochemist VA, Poplar Bluff, Mo., 1950-52, Toledo Hosp., 1953-54, Children's Hosp., Columbus, Ohio, 1954—; prof. dept. pediatrics Ohio State U. Coll. Medicine, Columbus, 1972—, prof. dept. pathology, 1974—; cons. Brown Labs., Columbus, 1968-83, VA, Chillicothe, Ohio, 1980-84. Co-author: Manual of Practical Micro and General Procedures in Clinical Chemistry, 1962. Editor: Standard Methods of Clinical Chemistry, Vol. 5, 1965; Pediatric Clinical Chemistry, 1977, 2d edit., 1981; co-editor: Selected Methods for the Small Clinical Chemistry Laboratory, 1982. Contbr. articles to profl. jours. Served to 1st lt. U.S. Army, 1942-46. Fellow AAAS; mem. Am. Chem. Soc., Am. Assn. Clin. Chemistry (sec. 1975-77, Bernard Katchman award Ohio Valley sect. 1971, Fisher award 1981, chmn. com. on archives, 1982—). Democrat. Jewish. Avocations: gardening, history of clinical chemistry. Office: Childrens Hosp 700 Childrens Dr Columbus OH 43205

MEJIA, PAUL ROMAN, See *Who's Who in America*, 43rd edition.

MELANCON, MARK JOHN, pharmacologist educator, researcher; b. Chgo., Sept. 17, 1939; s. Mark John and Margaret (Pleiss) M.; m. Janet Kathleen, Jan. 16, 1966; children—Mark John, Mary Margaret, Paul Matthew. B.A., St. Mary's Coll., 1961; M.S., Loyola U., 1964, Ph.D., 1966. Instr. Loyola U., Chgo., 1966; research assoc. U. Wis.-Madison, 1968-70, asst. prof., U. Wis., Milw., 1970-74; research assoc. Med. Coll. Wis., Milw., 1974-83, adj. asst. prof., 1979—; assoc. scientist, U. Wis. Med. Sch. at Mt. Sinai Med. Ctr., Milw., 1983—. Contbr. chpts. to books, articles to profl. jours. Postdoctoral fellow NIH, U. Wis.-Madison, 1966-68. Grantee Wis. Sea Grant Program, 1973-74, 80-82, U.S. EPA, 1984-86. Mem. AAAS, Am. Chem. Soc., Am. Soc. Pharmacology Exptl. Therapeutics, Sigma Xi. Avocations: gardening, fishing, woodworking. Home: 2941 N Farwell Milwaukee WI 53211 Office: Mt Sinai Med Ctr 950 N 12th St Milwaukee WI 53233

MELCER, IRVING, research chemist; b. Havana, Cuba, Nov. 15, 1931; came to U.S., 1946, naturalized, 1952; s. David and Sylvia (Sherman) M.; m. Arlene Lee Glassman, Nov. 23, 1954; children—David, Sylvia Lisa, Allen G., Marshall Sim. Rachel Rebecca. B.S. in Pharmacy, Wayne State U., 1953, Ph.D., 1958. Postdoctoral fellow Yale U., New Haven, 1958-59; research chemist Wilson Labs., Chgo., 1959-64; from research chemist to mgr. Griffith Labs USA Inc., Alsip, Ill., 1965—. Patentee in field of food processing. Mem. Inst. Food Technologists. Avocations: bridge, golf. Home: 10 Wilson Ct Park Forest IL 60466 Office: Griffith Labs USA Inc 1 Griffith Ctr Alsip IL 60658

MELE, JOANNE THERESA, dentist; b. Chgo., Dec. 5, 1943; d. Andrew and Josephine Jeanette (Calabrese) M. Diploma, St. Elizabeth's Sch. Nursing, Chgo., 1964; diploma in Dental Hygiene, Northwestern U., 1977; A.S., Triton Coll., 1979; D.D.S., Loyola U., 1983. Registered nurse, dental hygienist. Staff nurse in medicine/surgery St. Elizabeth's Hosp., Chgo., 1964-66, operating room nurse, 1966-67; head nurse operating room Cook County Hosp., Chgo., 1967-76, head nurse ICU, 1976-77; dental hygienist Mele Dental Assocs., Ltd., Oakbrook, Ill., 1977-79, practice dentistry, 1983—. Recipient Northwestern U. Dental Hygiene Clinic award, 1977; Dr. Duxler Humanitarian award scholar Loyola U., 1982. Mem. Chgo. Dental Soc., Ill. State Dental Soc., Acad. Gen. Dentistry, Am. Assn. Women Dentists, Psi Omega (Kappa chpt.). Roman Catholic. Avocations: reading; music; golfing; jogging; skiing.. Office: Mele Dental Assocs Ltd 120 Ctr Mall Suite 610 Oakbrook IL 60521

MELECKI, RICHARD GEORGE, training and performance specialist; b. Cleve., Dec. 18, 1948; s. George William and Frances Ann (Cooper) M.; m. Susan Estelle Greathouse. B.A. in English, U. Akron, 1970, M.A. in English, 1973; M.P.A., Kent State U., 1982. Teaching grad. asst. U. Akron, Ohio, 1971-72; asst. workshop dir. Summit County, Tallmadge, Ohio, 1972-80; mgmt. devel. specialist Robinson Meml. Hosp., Ravenna, Ohio, 1980-84; coordinator mgmt. devel. Univ. Hosp., Cleve., 1984—; part-time faculty Kent State U., Ohio, 1983-84. Mem. Nat. Soc. Performance and Instrn., Am. Soc. Tng. and Devel., Phi Eta Sigma, Phi Sigma Alpha, Phi Alpha Alpha. Avocations: maritial arts; photography; cross-country skiing. Office: Univ Hosps of Cleveland 2074 Abington Cleveland OH 44106

MELGAARD, HANS LELAND, manufacturing company executive, inventor; b. Mpls., Jan. 3, 1940; s. Harold L. and Josepha (Knutson) M.; m. Marcia R. Peterson, Mar. 20, 1962 (div. Feb. 1974); children—Rebecca, Christine, Hans, Timothy; m. Ilona L. Sjovall, May 28, 1977; 1 child, Andrew. B.S., U. Minn., 1971, M.B.A., 1978. Research mgr. Despatch Industries, Inc., Mpls., 1964-67, research dir., 1967-69, v.p. devel., 1969-72, exec. v.p., 1972-74, v.p. research and devel., 1975-79, v.p. research and engring., 1979—. Patentee in field. Author books and articles, 1966—. Recipient Hanson award for editorial excellence for best tech. article Plant Engring. Publ., 1982. Mem. Internat. Microwave Power Inst. (treas. 1982, pres. 1983-85), Indsl. Heating Equipment Assn. (energy com. 1981-84, chmn. drying and coating seminar 1982-84), Am. Gas Assn. Club: Mpls. Athletic. Lodge: Sons of Norway. Avocations: Skiing, sailing, hunting, farming. Home: 3804 Washburn Ave S Minneapolis MN 55410 Office: Despatch Industries Inc PO Box 1320 Minneapolis MN 55440

MELLER, ROBERT LOUIS, JR., lawyer; b. Mpls., Apr. 24, 1950; s. Robert Louis and June Louise (Grenacher) M. B.A., Carleton Coll., 1972; J.D., Cornell U., 1975. Atty., Best & Flanagan, Mpls., 1977—, ptnr., 1982—. Mem. ABA, Minn. State Bar Assn., Phi Beta Kappa, Sigma Xi. Republican. Episcopalian. Club: Mpls. Home: 3102 Dean Ct Minneapolis MN 55416 Office: Best and Flanagan 4040 IDS Center Minneapolis MN 55402

MELLETT, WILLIAM BREWER, metal working company executive; b. Newark, Mar. 10, 1930; s. William Joseph and Ruth Ellen (Brewer) M.; m. Marianne Schweikart, Dec. 27, 1957 (div. 1971); children—Celeste Marie, Michele Marie; m. Ellen Margret Foley, June 30, 1971; children—Thomas William O'Leary, Joseph William O'Leary, Matthew William. B.B.A., Seton Hall U., 1959; postgrad. Newark Coll. Engring., 1959-62, Ill. Inst. Tech., 1968-70, Thornton Community Coll., 1982-83. Mem. sales staff Monsanto, Kenilworth, N.J., 1959-63; sr. sales div. mgr. Tenneco, Piscataway, N.J., 1963-70; regional mgr. Matador Chem. Co., Houston, 1970-74, Bolton-Emerson Co., Lawrence, Mass., 1974-77, Newcor, Inc., Bay City, Mich., 1977—. Assisted on patent for oxygen-hydrogen catalist for rockets, 1963-70. Block capt. Democratic Party, Dolton, Ill., 1972-80; precinct capt. Concerned Party, Dolton, 1985; mem. zoning bd. Village Dolton, 1985. Served with USN, 1950-55, Korea. Mem. Am. Welding Soc., Soc. Mfg. Engrs. (sr.), Soc. Plastic Engrs., Am. Def. Preparedness Assn., V.F.W., Am. Legion. Roman Catholic. Office: Newcor Inc 5251 W 147th St Oak Forest IL 60452

MELLIJOR, ALFONSO VELOSO, surgical oncologist; b. Philippines, May 15, 1946; came to U.S., 1975; s. Camilo Saab and Eufrosina (Veloso) M. M.D., Cebu Inst. Medicine, Philippines, 1972. Diplomate Am. Bd. Surgery. Intern, St. John's Episc. Hosp., Bklyn., 1975-76, resident, 1976-80, chief resident, 1979-80; fellow in surg. oncology Downstate Med. Ctr., Bklyn., 1980-81; attending cons. Am. Internat. Hosp., Zion, Ill., 1981—, attending oncology service, 1981—, chmn. tumor restry service, 1982—, chmn. dept. surgery, 1982—, chmn. cancer com., 1982—. Home: 2215 11th St Winthrop Harbor IL 60096 Office: Am Internat Hosp Emmaus St Zion IL 60099

MELLON, JAMES ISAAC, statistician, consultant; b. Aurora, Ill., Dec. 6, 1943; s. Leonard Baker and Almira Louise (Hoskin) M.; m. Carol Cornelia Warner, July 11, 1970; children—Heather Lynne, Brian Douglas. B.S., Iowa State U., 1966, M.S., 1968, postgrad., 1973. Quality control engr. Eastman Kodak, Rochester, N.Y., 1966; research assoc. U.S. Dept. Agr., Iowa State U., Ames, 1966-73; research statistician Swift & Co., Oak Brook, Ill., 1973-81; sr. statistician Travenol Labs., Round Lake, Ill., 1981-84, sr. prin. statistician, 1984-85, research statistician, 1985—. Reviewer: Introduction to Statistical Time Series, 1976. Coach ch. softball league, Yorkville, Ill., 1976-79; deacon Oswego Presby. Ch., Ill., 1980—; coach Little League, Gagewood, Ill., 1983-84. Served to 1st lt. U.S. Army, 1972-72. Recipient Tech. Achievement award Travenol Labs., Inc., 1983. Mem. Am. Statis. Assn., (chmn. awards com. 1985—) Sigma Xi (assoc.), Gamma Sigma Delta. Republican. Presbyterian. Avocations: music; history; sports. Home: 17465 W Winnebago Dr Wildwood IL 60030 Office: Travenol Labs Inc PO Box 490 Round Lake IL 60073

MELLOR, FREDERIC WALTER, JR., aerospace company executive; b. New Haven, Conn., Mar. 22, 1921; s. Frederic Walter and Katherine Carolyn (Vogler) M.; m. Hjordis Ester Janson, Dec. 12, 1947; children—Frederic Walter, Donald Haywood, Pamela Ann. Student, Wesleyan U., 1939-42, U. N.C.-Chapel Hill, 1943. Capt., PAA-Panagra Airlines, Miami, Fla., 1946-47, Scandinavian Airlines, Stockholm, Sweden, 1947-53; dir. field ops. Goodyear Aerospace Corp., Akron, Ohio, 1953—. Contbr. articles to profl. jours. Patentee in field. Pres. Area V, East Central Region, Boy Scouts Am., 1985—. Served to lt. comdr., USN, 1942-46. Recipient Silver Beaver award, Boy Scouts Am., 1972. Mem. SAE, AIAA, Nat. Soc. Indsl. Assn., Assn. Old Crows, Navy League U.S. Clubs: Turkeyfoot Island, Akron City. Lodge: Masons. Avocations: golf; tennis; stamp collecting. Home: 141 Melbourne Ave Akron OH 44313 Office: Goodyear Aerospace Corp 1210 Massillon Rd Akron OH 44315

MELLOTT, ROBERT VERNON, radio/TV advertising executive; b. Dixon, Ill., Jan. 1, 1928; s. Edwin Vernon and Frances Rhoda (Miller) M.; m. Carolyn Frink, June 11, 1960; children—Lynn Lorraine, Susan Michelle, David Robert. B.A., DePauw U., 1950; postgrad. Ind. U., 1950-51, Law Sch., 1959-61, M.A., 1983. TV producer, dir. Jefferson Standard Broadcasting Co., Charlotte, N.C., 1951-59; asst. dist. mgr. Gen. Motors Corp., Flint, Mich., 1961-62; TV radio comml. supr. N.W. Ayer & Son, Chgo., 1962-65; TV radio producer FCB, Chgo., 1965-67, mgr. midwest prodn., 1967-69, mgr. comml. coordination, 1969-74, v.p., mgr. comml. services, Chgo., 1974—. Mem. media adv. com. Coll. of Dupage, Glen Ellyn, Ill., 1971-82; chmn. Cub Scout com., Wheaton, Ill., 1978-79; bd. dirs. Chgo. Unltd., 1969-71. Mem. Am. Assn. Advt. Agencies (broadcast adminstrn. policy com., broadcast union relations policy com.), Phi Delta Phi, Alpha Tau Omega. Republican. Clubs: Chgo. Farmers, Chgo. Advt., Ind. U. Alumni. Home: 26 W 130 Tomahawk Dr Wheaton IL 60187 Office: Foote Cone & Belding Advt 401 N Michigan Ave Chicago IL 60611

MELOY, HAROLD H., lawyer; b. Waldron, Ind., Nov. 29, 1913; s. James Henry and Pearl (Haymond) M.; LL.B., Ind. U., 1939; m. Loretta Marie Schrader, Sept. 9, 1951. Bar: to Ind. 1939, U.S. Supreme Ct. 1951. Practice law, Shelbyville, Ind., 1939—; historian Mammoth Cave, 1960—; lectr. on history, legends and folklore of Mammoth Cave. Pros. atty. for 16th Jud. Circuit Ct. of Ind., 1945-50; city judge, Shelbyville, 1956. Bd. dirs. Major Hosp. Found., Shelbyville, pres., 1976—; mem. adv. bd. Shelbyville Salvation Army, chmn., 1971-72; Served with AUS, 1941-43. Fellow Nat. Speleol. Soc.; mem. Am. Spelean History Assn. (dir. 1968—), Shelby County Bar Assn. (pres. 1958), Cave Research Found., Mammoth Cave Nat. Park Assn. (dir. 1974—). Democrat. Methodist. Mason (Shriner). Elk. Author: Mummies of Mammoth Cave, 1968, 8th edit., 1984; The Stephen Bishop Story, 1974. Contbr. numerous articles on history of Mammoth Cave to various jours. Home: PO Box 454 Shelbyville IN 46176 Office: 302 Methodist Bldg PO Box 454 Shelbyville IN 46176

MELROY, LUELLA ELIZABETH, ins. agy. exec.; b. Churchs Ferry, N.D., May 22, 1920; d. Roy Arthur and Grace Alma (Dingman) Noltimier; student Dakota Bus. Coll., 1938-39; m. Richard Melroy, May 25, 1957. Cert. mgr. With various ins. offices, Fargo, N.D., 1939-51, Mpls. and St. Paul, 1951-53, Toledo, 1953-61; with Manhattan Ins. Service, Inc., Toledo, 1961—, pres., owner, 1971—. Bd. dirs. Toledo YWCA, 1963-76, pres., 1973-75; bd. dirs., treas. Girls Club of Toledo, 1981-82; chmn. Community Planning Council Com. on Battered Women; bd. dirs., treas. Rescue-Crisis Bd., 1979-81. Named Woman of Yr., Toledo chpt. Nat. Mgmt. Assn., 1975; Bus. Woman of Yr., Dist. 2 Bus. and Profl. Women, 1978; Ins. Woman of Yr., Toledo Assn. Ind. Ins. Agts., 1967. Mem. Ohio Assn. Profl. Ins. Agts. (dir. 1980-83, membership chmn. 1981-83), Toledo Assn. Ind. Ins. Agts. (pres. 1980-81, dir. 1973-82), Nat. Assn. Ins. Women (v.p. 1978-79, regional dir. 1976-77), Women Bus. Owners, Nat. Mgmt. Assn. (nat. dir. 1982—, vice chmn. midwest area 1984—), Women Involved in Toledo. Republican. Office: 709 Madison Ave Toledo OH 43624

MELTON, ARTHUR RICHARD, health care executive; b. Ysleta, Tex., Apr. 28, 1943; s. Francis Charles and Jean (Graham) M.; m. Frances Bay, Aug. 19, 1965; children—David Bay, Amy Elizabeth. B.S., U. Utah, 1969; M.P.H., U. N.C., 1974, Dr. Pub. Health, 1976. Microbiologist Utah Dept. Health, Salt Lake City, 1970-73; dir. labs. S.D. Dept. Health, Pierre, 1976—. Mem. Am. Pub. Health Assn. (governing council 1980-83), S.D. Pub. Health Assn. (pres. 1980-81). Mormon. Home: 1127 N Oneida Pierre SD 57501 Office: South Dakota Health Lab 600 E Capitol Pierre SD 57501

MELTON, EMORY LEON, lawyer, publisher, state legislator; b. McDowell, Mo. June 20, 1923; s. Columbus Right and Pearly Susan (Wise) M.; student Monett Jr. Coll., 1940-41, S.W. Mo. State U., 1941-42; LL.B., U. Mo., 1945; m. Jean Sanders, June 19, 1949; children—Stanley Emory, John Russell. Admitted to Mo. bar, 1944; individual practice law, Cassville, Mo., 1947—; pres. Melton Publs., Inc., pub. 4 newspapers, 1959—; pros. atty. Barry county (Mo.), 1947-51; mem. Mo. Senate, 1973—. Chmn., Barry County Republican Com., 1964-68. Served with AUS, 1945-46. Recipient award for meritorious public service St. Louis Globe-Democrat., 1976. Mem. Mo. Bar Assn. Baptist. Clubs: Lions, Masons. Office: 201 W 9th St Cassville MO 65625

MELTON, JOHN LESTER, English educator; b. Walsenburg, Colo., Aug. 11, 1920; s. Harry W. and Elizabeth (Cahalan) M.; m. Virginia Anne Cadmus. B.A., U. Utah, 1948, M.A., 1949; Ph.D., Johns Hopkins U., 1955. Instr. Johns Hopkins U., Balt., 1950-55; from instr. to prof. John Carroll U., Cleve., 1955-68; assoc. prof. St. Cloud State U., Minn., 1968-69, prof. 1969—; cons. linguistics Western Res. U., Cleve., 1957-64. Author (TV series) Literature of the Am. Frontier, 1970. Editor: Semantic Code Dictionary, 1958. Contbr. articles to profl. jours. Mem. Home Rule Charter Commn., St. Cloud, 1970-79. Served to maj. U.S. Army, 1936-46. Mem. Internat. Arthurian Soc., Oreg. and Calif. Trails Assn., MLA, Coll. English Assn., Minn. Council Tchrs. English, Sierra Club, Phi Beta Kappa, Alpha Sigma Lambda, Lambda Iota Tau. Avocations: camping, photography, travel. Home: 3040 Santa Fe Trail Saint Cloud MN 56301 Office: Saint Cloud State U Saint Cloud MN 56301

MELTZER, KRIS, lawyer; b. Shelbyville, Ind., Oct. 31, 1955; s. Phillip E. and Charlene (Jordan) M.; m. Sandra Everitt, Aug. 16, 1979; 1 child, Trent Everitt. B.S., Ball State U., 1976; J.D., Ind. U., 1980. Bar: Ind. 1980, U.S. Dist. Ct. (so. dist.) Ind. 1980, U.S. Supreme Ct. 1984. Assoc. Shoshnick, Bate & Harrold, Shelbyville. 1980—. Bd. dirs. Shelby County Youth Shelter, Shelbyville, 1982—. Mem. ABA, Assn. Trial Lawyers Am., Ind. State Bar Assn., Ind. Trial Lawyers Assn., Shelby County Bar Assn. (chmn. Law Day activities 1983, 84), Shelby County Jaycees (legal adviser 1982). Democrat. Roman Catholic. Lodge: Sertoma (pres. local club 1984). Home: 230 W Mechanic St Shelbyville IN 46176 Office: Soshnick Bate & Harrold 24 W Broadway St Shelbyville IN 46176

MELUM, MARA MINERVA, health corporation officer; b. Mpls., June 21, 1951; d. Dan and Phyllis (Mondshein) Minerva; B.A., Princeton U., 1973; M.P.A., Syracuse U., 1974; m. Eric Melum, June 12, 1971. Adminstrv. resident Blue Cross/Blue Shield Central N.Y., Syracuse, 1973; asst. dir. Health Services Assn., Syracuse, 1973-74; cons., policy analyst InterStudy, Mpls., 1974-75; v.p. Minn. Hosp. Assn., Mpls., 1975-82; v.p. corp. devel. Met. Med. Ctr., Mpls., 1982-83; now sr. v.p. HealthOne Corp.; adj. faculty U. Minn. Sch. Hosp. and Health Care Adminstrn., dept. health adminstrn. U. N.C.; tchr. health facilities mgmt. program St. Mary's Coll.; cons. Region VI Center for Health Planning, HEW. Recipient DeWitt Clinton Poole Meml. prize Princeton U., 1973. Goldman Health Care Delivery scholar, 1973-74. Mem. Am. Hosp. Assn. (adv. panels on planning and on privacy and confidentiality of med. records), Am. Health Planning Assn., Soc. Hosp. Planning (past pres.). Author: Assessing the Need for Hospital Beds: A Review of Current Criteria, 1975; Model to be Used to Determin Optimal Premium Rates for HMOs, 1975; An Analysis of the

Claims Processing and Payment System Employed by the Central State SE and SW Areas Health and Welfare Fund, 1975; Criteria for Plan Evaluation, 1978; The Hospital Industry in Transition: New Roles and Service Diversification, 1980; The Changing Role of the Hospital: Options for the Future, 1980. Home: 22 Dellwood Ave White Bear Lake MN 55110 Office: 2100 IDS Center Minneapolis MN 55402

MELVOLD, ROGER WAYNE, microbiology-immunology educator; b. Henning, Minn., Mar. 21, 1946; s. Sam Reder and Palma (Ronning) M. B.S., Moorhead State U., 1968; Ph.D., U. Kans.-Lawrence, 1973. Assoc. radiation therapy Harvard U., 1972-76, prin. research assoc., 1976-79; asst. prof. medicine and microbiology-immunology Northwestern U., 1979-82, asst. prof. microbiology-immunology, 1982-83; assoc. prof. 1983—. Contbr. articles to profl. jours. NIH grantee, 1979—. Mem. Am. Assn. Immunologists, Transplantation Soc., Sigma Xi. Democrat. Home: 517 S Clarence St Oak Park IL 60304 Office: Dept Microbiology-Immunology Northwestern Univ Med Sch 303 E Chicago Ave Chicago IL 60611

MENA, JUDY LYNN, nursing administrator, educator; b. East St. Louis, Ill., Sept. 30, 1946; d. Winfurd Louis and Dorothy Louise (Fitzgerald) Thurman; m. Terry Gene Quate, Dec. 18, 1966; m. 2d, Jorge Mena, Apr. 11, 1982. B.S. in Nursing, St. Louis U., 1975; M.Nursing, La. State U., 1980. Cert. nurse adminstr. Am. Nurses Assn. Asst. dir. nursing Christian Welfare Hosp., East St. Louis, 1967-75; coordinator nursing systems and research Hotel Dieu Hosp., New Orleans, 1975-79; asst. dir. nursing West Bank Med. Ctr., New Orleans, 1979-81; mem. faculty Nichols State U., Thibedeaux, La., 1980-81; mem. adj. faculty Washburn U., Topeka, 1982-83; v.p. Stormont-Vail Regional Med. Ctr., Topeka, 1983—; mem. adj. faculty, mental health adv. com. Kans. U. Med. Ctr.; mem. profl. liaison com. Sch. Grad. Nursing Topeka Hospice, 1982. Mem. Am. Nurses Assn., Am. Soc. Nursing Service Adminstrs., Sigma Theta Tau. Club: Soroptimist. Home: 3602 SW Oak Pkwy Topeka KS 66614 Office: Stormont-Vail Regional Med Ctr 1500 W 10th St Topeka KS 66606

MENADUE, JUDITH GEORGETTE, lawyer; b. Milw., June 29, 1944; d. George R. Retzlaff and Kay L. Retzlaff Curry; m. Bock Ki Kim, Jan. 22, 1966 (div. 1973); children—Mike, Jeff; m. Jerry R. Menadue, July 20, 1974 (div. 1979); 1 child, Joseph; m. Sanford N. Boshart, May 21, 1983. B.S., U. Wis.-Milw., 1966, M.A., 1968; Ph.D., U. Wis.-Madison, 1974; J.D., U. Iowa, 1980. Bar: Minn. 1980, U.S. Dist. Ct. Minn. 1980. Asst. prof. Spanish, Loras Coll., Dubuque, Iowa, 1972-78; spl. asst. atty. gen. Minn. Atty. Gen.'s Office, St. Paul, 1980-83; assoc. Felhaber, Larson, Fenlon & Vogt, P.A., St. Paul, 1983—; instr. Coll. Law, U. Iowa, Iowa City, summers 1981, 82. Mem. Minn. State Bar Assn., Ramsey County Bar Assn. Mem. Democratic-Farm-Labor Party. Mennonite. Home: 1897 Field Ave Saint Paul MN 55116 Office: Felhaber Larson Fenlon & Vogt PA 900 Conwed Tower 444 Cedar St Saint Paul MN 55116

MENARD, CHARLES WALTER, JR., envelope company executive; b. Chgo., Apr. 15, 1929; s. Charles Walter and Hazel (Froehde) M.; m. Helen Bernice Ligas, May 14, 1955; children—Charles, Christopher, Juliette, C. Timothy, Jennifer. B.S. in Commerce, DePaul U., 1954. Various positions to controller St. Joseph Hosp., Chgo., 1962-64; controller, sec. Continental Envelope Corp., Chgo., 1965—. Mem. Dist. 231 Bd. Edn., Evergreen Park, Ill.; treas., bd. dirs. Evergreen Park AquaPark; treas. scholarship bd. Evergreen Park Community High Sch. Democrat. Roman Catholic. Lodge: Lions (dir. Evergreen Park). Home: 2941 W 100th St Evergreen Park IL 60642 Office: 1301 W 35th St Chicago IL 60609

MENCHIN, ROBERT STANLEY, board of trade executive; b. Kingston, N.Y., Oct. 31, 1923; s. Abraham H. and Gertrude (Gorlin) M.; B.A., N.Y. U., 1948; m. Marylin Barsky, Dec. 26, 1949; children—Jonathan, Scott. Account exec. DKG Advt., N.Y.C., 1949-51; dir. spl. projects Am. Visuals Corp., N.Y.C., 1952-59; dir. advt. and public relations Arthur Wiesenberger & Co., N.Y.C., 1959-65; pres. Wall St. Mktg. Communications, Inc., N.Y.C., 1967-77; dir. mktg. communications Chgo. Bd. Trade, 1977-83, v.p. communication and member relations, 1983—. Served with AUS, 1942-45. Mem. Public Relations Soc. Am., Fin. Planners Assn. Author: The Last Caprice, 1964; Where There's a Will, 1977; editor: The Financial Futures Professional, 1977—. Home: 1313 Ritchie Ct Chicago IL 60610 Office: Chgo Bd Trade LaSalle and Jackson Sts Chicago IL 60604

MENDELSON, RALPH RICHARD, water heater manufacturing company executive, consultant; b. Cleve., July 11, 1917; s. Louis Ralph and Ruth Margaret (Cohen) M.; m. Mary Adelaide Jones, Feb. 22, 1941 (div. 1984); children—Walton, Philip. B.S. in M.E., U. Mich., 1939. With The Hotstream Heater Co., Cleve., 1941-61, v.p., 1948-59, pres, 1959-61; pres. The Glass-Lined Water Hearter Co., Lakewood, Ohio, 1961-82; cons. heating equipment design, Lakewood, 1982—. Bd. dirs. Urban League of Cleve., 1957-61; bd. dirs. Merrick House, Cleve., 1972-85, pres., 1980-82; vis. com. Case Western Res. U., 1972-80. Served to lt. USAAF, 1942-46. Mem. Assn. Energy Engrs., Heights C. of C. (dir. 1953-60), Oil Heat Inst. No. Ohio (dir. 1966-73, pres. 1969-70). Democrat. Jewish. Club: Cleve. Play House. Author: Solar Energy, 1978; patentee water heater, infra-red heater. Office: 13000 Athens Ave Lakewood OH

MENDENHALL, ELTON BRUCE, educational administrator, researcher; b. Hay Springs, Nebr., Feb. 25, 1936; s. Floyd Elton and Celine F. (Barnett) M.; m. Ardyth Jean Haverkamp, Mar. 21, 1937; children—Ardene, Allan. B.S. in Edn., Chadron State Coll., 1965; M.Ed., Colo. State U., 1967; Ph.D., U. Nebr., 1978. Secondary sch. tchr. Colorado Springs, Colo., 1966-68; prof. indsl. edn. Kearney (Nebr.) State Coll., 1968-70; dir. Nebr. Research Coordinating Unit for Vocat. Edn., Lincoln, 1971-84; dir. Nebr. Career Info. Systems, Lincoln, 1976-85; pres. Incentive Devel. Cons., Lincoln, 1985—; tchr. indsl. edn.; developer career info. system; adminstr. Served with U.S. Army, 1955-57. U.S. Office Edn. grantee, 1974-76; Nat. Occupation Info. Coordinating com. grantee, 1979-82. Mem. Am. Vocat. Assn., Am. Soc. Tng. and Devel., Am. Edn. Research Assn., Phi Delta Kappa, Iota Lambda Sigma. Methodist. Contbr. articles to profl. jours. Home and Office: 721 Rockhurst Dr Lincoln NE 68510

MENDENHALL, GEOFFREY NORMAN, electronics company executive; b. Johnstown, Pa., May 12, 1947; s. Norman E. and Johanna (Krauss) M.; m. M. Nike Cotchen, July 4, 1978; 1 child, Merideth. B.S.E.E., Ga. Inst. Tech., 1969. Registered profl. engr., Ill. Sr. project engr. Harris Corp., Quincy, Ill., 1971-78; engring. mgr. Broadcast Electronics, Inc., Quincy, 1978-81, v.p. engring., 1981—. Contbr. chpt. to FM Transmitters NAB Engring. Handbook, 1985. Patentee in electronics, 1970. Mem. fin. bd. Soc. Fine Arts, Quincy, 1983; trustee John Wood Community Coll., Quincy, 1984—. Recipient 1st Place award Underwater Soc. Am., 1972; mem. IEEE, Amateur Radio Club (past officer), Astronomical Soc. Quincy. Unitarian. Avocations: underwater photography; videophile; audiophile; canoeing. Office: Broadcast Electronics Inc N 24th St Quincy IL 62301

MENDIRATTA, VEENA BHATIA, telecommunications research engineer; b. New Delhi, India, Oct. 21, 1948; came to U.S., 1976; f. Jaman Lal and Dharam (Devi) Bhatia; m. Shiv S. Mendiratta, Apr. 13, 1974; 1 son, Arjun. B.Tech., Indian Inst. Tech., 1970; M.C.P., Ohio State U., 1971, M.S. in Civil Engring., 1972; Ph.D., Northwestern U., 1981. Asst. prof. Sch. of Planning, Ahmedabad, India, 1972-74; asst. town planner State Planning Dept., Chandigarh, India, 1975-76; research engr. U. Ill.-Chgo., 1976-78; systems engr. Argonne Nat. Lab., 1981; mgr. computer modeling and simulation Ill. Central Gulf R.R., Chgo., 1981-84; mem. tech. staff AT&T Bell Labs., Naperville, Ill., 1984—; adj. prof. Elmhurst (Ill.) Coll., 1984—. Bd. dirs.: Chambord Homeowners Assn. Mem. Ops. Research Soc. Am., Inst. Mgmt. Scis. Club: Chgo. Health. Hindu. Home: 18W758 Chateaux N Oak Brook IL 60521 Office: Ill Central Gulf RR 233 N Michigan Ave Chicago IL 60601

MENG, DOROTHY SMITH, nurse, administrator; b. Oak Creek, Colo.; d. William M. and Nellie (Berere) Smith; m. Ernest Meng, 1946; children—Terese, Adrienne, Marilyn, Carter, Kevin, Brian, Eric. A.A. with honors, Daley Coll., 1976; B.A. with honors, Roosevelt U. Staff nurse Michael Reese Hosp., Chgo., 1977; Rush-Presbyn. St. Luke's Hosp., Chgo., 1979—; registry nurse Staff Builders, Inc., 1977-80. Active Christian Family Movement. Mem. Internat. Flying Nurses Assn., Daley Coll. Nursing Alumni (editor 1980-84). Home: 6039 S Mobile Ave Chicago IL 60638 Office: Rush Presbyterian St Lukes Med Ctr 1753 W Congress Pkwy Chicago IL 60612

MENGARELLI, MARCIA ANGLEMIER, farm equipment company executive; b. Hinsdale, Ill., Nov. 22, 1953; s. Orville Wellington and Arlene (Butler) Anglemier; m. Robert Jay Mengarelli, July 19, 1975. A.A., Coll. of Dupage, 1977; student Elmhurst Coll., 1978—. Various positions Internat. Harvester, Chgo., 1972-78, supr. adminstrv. services, 1978-80, Hinsdale, Ill., 1981-83, supr. materials control, 1983-84, purchasing supr., 1984-85; mgr. purchasing J.I. Case Co., 1985—. Asst. clerk Hinsdale Baptist Ch., Ill., 1983-85. Mem. Internat. Harvester Exec. Club (pres. 1984), Internat. Order Foresters (asst. editor 1983-85). Home: 326 69th St Darien IL 60559

MENGEL, PAULA PADGETT, rental property administrator; b. Independence, Mo., Sept. 24, 1948; d. Darius Curtis and Rose Marie (Clemens) Padgett; m. Charles Edmund Mengel, June 5, 1978; 1 child, Michael Daniel. B.A., U. Mo.-Kansas City, 1970; M.Ed., U. Mo., 1979. Cert. tchr., Mo. Tchr. Kansas City Pub. Schs., 1970-72; adminstrv. sec. U. Mo. Health Scis. Ctr., Columbia, 1973-78; editorial asst. Jour. Lab. and Clin. Medicine, Columbia, 1980-82; sec. treas. Editorial Process, Inc., Columbia, 1980-82; adminstr. CPMC Apts., Moberly, Mo., 1984—. Republican. Roman Catholic. Office: CPMC Apts 1364 Overland Ln Moberly MO 65270

MENIKHEIM, MARIE-LOUISE LOLAND, educator, nurse; b. St. Charles, Ill., Mar. 30, 1939; d. Harold John and Inger Astrid (Petersen) Loland; B.S., Case Western Res. U., 1963; M.S., Cath. U. Am., 1968; postgrad. U. Minn., 1975—; m. Douglas Karl Menikheim, Nov. 2, 1963; children—Maureen, Mary-Katherine, Molly. Instr., Southwestern Coll., San Diego, 1969-71, Sch. Nursing, U. Hawaii, Honolulu, 1971-72; lectr. Sch. Nursing U. Minn., Mpls., 1976-78; instr. Met. Comml. Coll., 1973-75; coordinator upper div. nursing curriculum Met. State U., St. Paul, 1978-81, asso. dean, 1981—. Bd. dirs. Neighborhood Involvement Program, Mpls., 1974-77; mem. adv. bd. Normandale Community Coll., Edina, Minn., 1976—; bd. dirs. Contact Twin Cities, 1979—, chmn.-elect, 1981, chmn., 1982-83; bd. dirs. 1st Call For Help United Way, 1981. Mem. AAUW, AAUP, Am. Nurses Assn., Minn. Nurses Assn. (dir. 1981—, v.p. 1983—), Nat. League Nursing, NOW. Episcopalian. Club: Woman's (Mpls.). Home: 2901 Benton Blvd Minneapolis MN 55416 Office: Metropolitan State Univ 121 Metropolitan Sq Bldg Saint Paul MN 55101

MENK, MARTIN C., engineering company executive; b. St. Peter, Minn., May 21, 1923; s. Martin T. and Amelia (Gerholz) M.; m. Carol Johnson, Apr. 5, 1951; children—M. Pell, Robert T., Margaret C. B.S. in Civil Engring., Wash. State U., Pullman, 1949. Profl. engr., Minn. With Bolton & Menk, Inc., Mankato, Minn., 1949—, pres., 1965—; evaluator civil engring. tech. programs Minn. Vocat. Tech. Schs., 1973-76; speaker profl. seminars; mem. State Bd. of Registration for Architects, Engrs., Land Surveyors and Landscape Architects. Author: Requirements for Land Surveyor Registration Summaries by State, 1981. Bd. dirs. St. Peter Devel. Corp., Mankato Old Town Devel. Corp., 1978—; com. mem. Twin Valley council Boy Scouts Am., 1965-70; mem. vestry Ch. of Holy Communion, St. Peter, 1955-70, lay reader, Sunday sch. tchr., 1956-59, sr. warden, 1970-78; Episcopal rep. to Regional chpt. Minn. Council Chs., 1979-81; mem. St. Peter Planning Commn., 1955—. Served with submarine service USN, World War II. Recipient Boss of Yr. award Mankato chpt. Am. Bus. Women, 1971, Good Neighbor award, Sta. WCCO, 1977, Constrn. Award of Yr., Mankato Builders Exchange, 1980. Mem. Am. Water Works Assn., City Engrs. Assn. Minn. (active coms.), Cons. Engrs. Council (bd. dirs. 1967-68, arbitration com. 1981-82), Am. Pub. Works Assn., Am. Arbitration Assn. (arbitrator civil engring. problems), Minn. Land Surveyors Assn. (bd. dirs. 1958-61, 78-83, state v.p. 1960, state pres. 1961, Minn. del. to Am. Congress Surveying and Mapping 1978-85, Minn. rep. to Gt. Lakes Council 1978-85, nat. legis. action com. 1980, candidate for nat. dir. 1983, chmn. coms., Land Surveyor of Yr. award 1977, William S. Kelley award 1981), Nat. Soc. Profl. Surveyors (nat. pub. relations com. 1981), Minn. Soc. Profl. Engrs. (pres. Traverse Des Sioux chpt. 1960, founder student chpt. Mankato State Coll. 1960, Engr. of Yr. award 1983), St. Peter C. of C., VFW (comdr. 1951), U.S. Submarine Vets. Club: G-1000 (Gustavus Adolphus Coll.). Lodges: Lions, Rotary. Home: 513 N 7th St Saint Peter MN 56082 Office: Bolton & Menk Inc 515 N Front St Mankato MN 56001

MENKES, JEFFREY S., emergency physician, administrative consultant; b. East Orange, N.J., Apr. 1, 1947; s. Fred and Rae (Daneshefsky) M. B.A. in Psychology, Yale U., 1968, M.D., 1972. Diplomate Am. Bd. Emergency Medicine. Resident in orthopedic surgery U. Minn., Mpls., 1972-74, U. Conn., Farmington, 1975-76; resident in emergency medicine U. Chgo., 1976-78; med. dir. of emergency services Holy Cross Hosp., Chgo., 1978—; clin. instr. U. Ill., Chgo., 1980, clin. asst. prof. emergency medicine, 1984—; guest faculty Cook County Grad. Sch., Chgo., 1981—; oral examiner Am. Bd. Emergency Medicine, E. Lansing, Mich., 1982—. Recipient Recognition award AMA, 1983. Fellow Am. Coll. Emergency Physicians, Alpha Omega Alpha. Avocations: video collections; guitar.

MENNING, LARRY L., optometrist; b. Parkston, S.D., May 18, 1948; s. Lloyd G. and Bernice D. (Plooster) M.; m. Linda L. Denbeste, Dec. 23, 1970 (div.); children—Chad, Trent. B.S., Ill. Coll. Optometry, Chgo., 1972, D. Optometry, 1972. Pvt. practice optometry, Chamberlain, S.D., 1972—. Mem. S.D. Optometric Soc. (pres. S.E. dist. 1979), Am. Optometric Assn. Republican. Office: Box 490 103 E Lawler Chamberlain SD 57325

MENSER, MICHAEL MILLS, jewelry store executive; b. Louisville, Oct. 9, 1946; s. Charles Dudley and Clara (Foster) M.; m. Joan Foster, July 9, 1967; children—Monica Meredith, Michael Mills. Jr. B.B.A., U. Ga., 1968; postgrad. Gemological Inst. Am., 1970-71. Vice pres. Foster's Jewelers Inc., Athens, Ga., 1968-71; pres. Menser & Co., Inc., Buchroeder's, Columbia, Mo., 1971—, Mintz Jewelers, Inc., Gainesville, Ga., 1985—; dir. First Nat. Bank, Columbia. Bd. dirs. Rusk Rehab. Ctr., Columbia, 1981-84. Mem. Am. Gem Soc. (mktg. com. 1972-74), Columbia C. of C. Republican. Methodist. Lodge: Rotary. Avocations: scuba diving; snow skiing; horseback riding. Home: 200 W Brandon Rd Columbia MO 65201 Office: Buchroeder's Jewelers 1021 E Broadway Columbia MO 65201

MENTZER, MERLEEN MAE, adult education educator; b. Kingsley, Iowa, July 25, 1920; d. John David and Maggie Marie (Simonsen) Moritz; m. Lee Arnold Mentzer, June 1, 1944. Student Westman Coll., 1939, Wayne State U., Nebr., 1942, Bemidji State U., 1950, Mankato Coll., 1978, U. Minn.-St. Paul, 1979. Tchr., Kingsley, Iowa, 1938-41; owner, mgr. Mentzer's Sundries, Hackensack, Minn., 1946-76, House of Mentzers, Pine River, Minn., 1974-77; instr. Hennepin Tech., Eden Prairie, Minn., 1978—. Mem. Mpls. C. of C., Hackensack C. of C., (v.p. 1970-76), Northern Lights Federated Woman's Club (pres. 1958-59). Republican. Lutheran. Avocations: dancing; bowling; reading; theatre; seminars. Home: 6781 Tartan Curve Eden Prairie MN 55344

MENTZER, WILLIAM FREDERICK, JR., health administrator, planning and research consultant; b. Carlisle, Pa., Sept. 4, 1951; s. William Frederick and Lena Margaret (Anderson) M.; m. Joan Ann Hoeschele, Aug. 18, 1973; children—Laura Katherine, Jeffrey Daniel. B.A. in Govt., Franklin and Marshall Coll., 1973; M.P.A., Pa. State U., 1983. Accounts mgr. Dun & Bradstreet Inc., Harrisburg, Pa., 1973-76; student intern Harrisburg Hosp. Mental Health/Mental Retardation Ctr., 1977; evaluation specialist Ashtabula County Community Mental Health Bd., Ohio, 1977-85, dep. dir., 1985—; planning cons. Ashtabula County Health Dept., Jefferson, Ohio, 1984—; mem. exec. com. Ohio Evaluators Group, Columbus, 1983—. Mem. Ashtabula Area Devel. Assn., 1984—, Ashtabula County Dist. Library, 1984—, Ashtabula Arts Ctr., 1984—; vol. Ashtabula County Dist. Library-project OASIS, 1984—. Mem. Am. Soc. for Pub. Adminstrn., Ohio Program Evaluator's Group, Ohio Alliance for Child Advocates, Evaluation Research Soc., Evaluation Network, Am. Consultants League, Policy Studies Orgn. Democrat. Lutheran. Club: Ashtabula Exchange. Avocations: photography; hiking; camping; personal computing; bicycling.

MERANUS, LEONARD STANLEY, lawyer; b. Newark, Jan. 7, 1928; s. Norman and Ada (Binstock) M.; m. Ann Moss, Sept. 5, 1953; children—Norman, James M., David. Litt.B., Rutgers U., 1948; LL.B., Harvard U., 1954. Bar: Ohio 1954. Assoc. Paxton & Seasongood, Cin., 1954-59, ptnr., 1959-77, shareholder, 1977—. Co-editor: Law and the Writer, 1978. Chmn. bd. dirs. Jewish Hosp., 1982—; trustee Andrew Jergens Found., 1962—. Mem. ABA, Ohio Bar Assn., Internat. Bar Assn., Cin. Bar Assn., Union Internationale Des Avocats. Home: 25 Dorino Place Cincinnati OH 45215 Office: Paxton & Seasongood 1700 Central Trust Tower Cincinnati OH 45202

MERCER, ROBERT E., rubber company executive; b. Elizabeth, N.J., 1924; grad. Yale U.; married. With Goodyear Tire & Rubber Co., Akron, Ohio, 1947—, mgr. indsl. products ops., 1963-66, div. gen. sales mgr., 1966-68, div. gen. mgr., 1968-73, asst. to pres., 1973-74, pres. Kelly-Springfield Tire Co. subs., 1974-76, exec. v.p. parent co., 1976-78, pres., chief operating officer, 1978-82, vice chmn., chief exec. officer, 1982, chmn., chief exec. officer, 1983—, also dir. Office: Goodyear Tire & Rubber Co 1144 E Market St Akron OH 44316

MERCER-KLIMOWSKI, JENIFER LEA, insurance adjuster; b. Des Moines, Nov. 10, 1953; d. Forrest Carey and Veva Verna (Moore) Mercer; m. Kevin Michael Klimowski, Dec. 18, 1982. B.A., Wellesley Coll., 1976; J.D., Drake U., 1979. Bar: Iowa 1979, U.S. Dist. Ct. (so. and no. dist.) Iowa 1979. Sole practice Des Moines, 1979-81; claims adjuster Employers Mutual Cos., Des Moines, 1981—. Mem. cast and crew Tatterdemalion Prodns., Des Moines, 1980—, Des Moines Community Playhouse, 1979—. Mem. Nat. Soc. Arts & Letters (pres. Iowa chpt.). Republican. Presbyterian. Club: Des Moines Women's. Office: Employers Mutual Cos Box 884 Des Moines IA 50304

MERCURIO, MARK ANDREW, home builder, land developer; b. Cin., July 5, 1948; s. Vincent Marrian and Peggy (Foppe) M.; m. Jane Liggett, July 19, 1980; children—Andrew, Graham. B.B.A. in Mktg., U. Cin., 1971. Field supr. Crest Communities, Cin., 1971-75; pres. Hercurio Homes, Cin., 1976—; v.p. Cin. Environs Corp., 1976—; co-chmn. Homearama, 1980; mem. Concorama Site Com., 1983. Recipient One Million Dollar award Crest Communities, 1973, Cert. Appreciation, Easter Seals, 1977, award of Excellence, Landen Devel. Co., 1983, award Am. Wood Council, 1984. Mem. Cin. C. of C., Home Builders Assn. (mktg. com. Greater Cin. chpt. 1979-80, bd. dirs. 1979-83, v.p. 1983—, chmn. bldg. code com. 1983-84, exec. com. 1983—, treas. 1984-85, chmn. constn. and by-laws com. 1984, mem. nominating com. 1984—), Nat. Assn. Home Builders (bd. dirs. 1984—). Clubs: C-Club, Build-Pac (Cin.). Home: 2555 Observatory Dr Cincinnati OH 45208 Office: Mercurio Homes Inc 4144 Crossgate Dr Cincinnati OH 45236

MEREDITH, EDWIN THOMAS, III, publishing company executive; b. Chgo., Feb. 7, 1933; s. Edwin Thomas, Jr. and Anna (Kauffman) M.; student U. Ariz., 1950-53; m. Katherine Comfort, Sept. 4, 1953; children—Mildred K., Dianna M., Edwin Thomas. With Meredith Corp., Des Moines, 1956—, dir., 1966—, v.p., 1968-71, pres., chief exec. officer, 1971-73, chmn. bd., 1973—; dir., mem. exec. com. Bankers Trust Co., Des Moines; dir. Mut. of Omaha. Bd. dirs. Nat. Merit Scholarship Corp., Evanston, Ill.; trustee Iowa Methodist Med. Center, Drake U., Des Moines, Iowa 4-H Found., Ames. Served with U.S. Army, 1953-56. Clubs: Chgo.; Wakonda, Des Moines (Des Moines). Office: 1716 Locust St Des Moines IA 50336

MERENSKI, PAUL, marketing educator; b. Greenwich, Conn., Oct. 13, 1939; m. Frances M. Schaffner, Aug. 31, 1963; children—Dara, Dawn. B.S. summa cum laude in Bus. Adminstrn., Wright State U., 1971, M.B.A., 1972; Ph.D., U. Cin., 1982. Stress analyst Titan Project Office, Am. Machine and Foundry Co., Stamford, Conn., 1960-62; instr. Wright State U., Dayton, Ohio, 1972-73; account exec. No. Securities Co., Dayton, 1973-74; dist. mgr. Church's Fried Chicken Inc., Dayton, 1974-76; asst. prof. mktg. U. Dayton, 1976—; cons. in field. Contbr. numerous articles to profl. jours. Served as officer USAF, 1962-69. Mem. Am. Mktg. Assn., Assn. Consumer Research, Am. Acad. Advt., Acad. Mktg. Sci., Inst. Mgmt. Sci., Am. Inst. Decision Scis., Mensa, Mu Kappa Tau. Address: 416 Falcon Dr New Carlisle OH 45344

MERGLER, H. KENT, investment counselor; b. Cin., July 1, 1940; s. Wilton Henry and Mildred Amelia (Pulliam) M.; B.B.A. with honors, U. Cin., 1963, M.B.A., 1964; m. Judith Anne Metzger, Aug. 17, 1963; children—Stephen Kent, Timothy Alan, Kristin Lee. Portfolio mgr. Scudder, Stevens & Clark, Cin., 1964-68, v.p. investments, Chgo., 1970-73; v.p. Gibraltar Research and Mgmt., Ft. Lauderdale, Fla., 1968-70; portfolio mgr., ptnr. Stein Roe & Farnham, Ft. Lauderdale, 1973—, also mem. investment policy com., chmn. account dept.; v.p. Stein Roe & Farnham, Capital Opportunities Fund, Inc.; arbitrator Nat. Assn. Security Dealers, Inc. Chmn. adminstrv. bd. Christ United Meth. Ch., Ft. Lauderdale, 1981-83; chmn. fin. com., bd. dirs. Pine Crest Prep. Sch., 1982-84; bd. dirs. Coral Ridge Little League, 1976-84, pres., 1980-81; fin. adv. to Jr. League Ft. Lauderdale, 1978-83. Chartered fin. analyst; chartered investment counselor. Mem. Fin. Analysts Soc. S. Fla. (pres. 1975-76, dir. 1974-78), Bond Club Ft. Lauderdale (v.p. 1980-81, dir. 1978-82), Inst. Chartered Fin. Analysts. Republican. Clubs: Coral Ridge Country, Sea Ranch Lakes Beach, Tower, Touchdown, University (Milw.); Bankers (San Juan, P.R.). Home: 924 Pine Tree Ln Winnetka IL 60093 Office: One S Wacker Dr Chicago IL 60606

MERILAN, MICHAEL PRESTON, astrophysicist, educator; b. Columbia, Mo., Jan. 5, 1956; s. Charles Preston and Phyllis Pauline (Laughlin) M. B.S. summa cum laude in Physics, U. Mo.-Columbia, 1978, M.S., 1980; Ph.D. in Astronomy, Ohio State U., 1985. Teaching asst. dept. physics and astronomy U. Mo.-Columbia, 1976-78, grad. teaching asst., 1978-80; grad. teaching assoc., instr. dept. astronomy Ohio State U., 1980-85; asst. prof. dept. physics SUNY, Oneonta, 1985—; astron. cons. Ohio Dept. Natural Resources, 1982-83. O.M. Stewart fellow, 1979; U. Mo. Curators scholar, 1974-78; Mahan Writing award, 1975. Mem. Am. Astron. Soc., Astron. Soc. Pacific, AAAS, Sigma Xi, Phi Eta Sigma, Phi Kappa Phi, Phi Beta Kappa, Pi Mu Epsilon. Contbr. articles in field. Home: 1509 Bouchelle Ave Columbia MO 65201 Office: Dept Physics State U NY Oneonta NY 13820

MERKEL, EDWARD WAGNER, JR., lawyer; b. Cin., Feb. 18, 1943; s. Edward Wagner and Ellen (Taylor) M.; m. Jayne Silverstein, Aug. 7, 1965; children—Mary and Jane. B.A., Wesleyan U., 1965; J.D., U. Mich., 1968. Bar: Ohio, U.S. Dist. Ct. (so. dist.) Ohio, U.S. Ct. Appeals (6th cir.). Assoc., Dinsmore & Shohl, Cin., 1968-74, ptnr., 1975—. Mem. Cin. Bar Assn., ABA, Ohio State Bar Assn. Home: 1908 Dexter Ave Cincinnati OH 45206 Office: Dinsmore & Shohl 511 Walnut St Cincinnati OH 45202

MERKEL, JAYNE SILVERSTEIN, architecture critic, art historian; b. Cin., Sept. 28, 1942; d. Elmore Herman and Ruth Dell (Feiler) Silverstein; m. Edward W. Merkel Jr., Aug. 7, 1965; children—Mary Feiler, Jane Scranton. B.S. in Eng. Lit., Simmons Coll., 1964; M.A. in Art History, Smith Coll., 1965. Curator, Contemporary Arts Ctr., Cin., 1968-69; instr. art history Art Acad. of Cin., 1973-78; vis. lectr. art history Miami U., Oxford, Ohio, 1978-79, 81-82; freelance writer and critic, 1969—; architecture critic Cin. Enquirer, 1977—; curator "In Its Place" exhbn., Contemporary Arts Ctr., winter 1985; Cons. Cin. Art Mus., 1984, dept. history U. Cin., Spring Grove Cemetery Research Project, 1984-85. Author: Michael Graves and the Riverhead Music Center, 1985; In Its Place, the Architecture of Carl Strauss and Ray Roush, 1984. Lectr. in field. Mem. editorial bd. Dialogue Mag., 1981-82. Mem. Coll. Art Assn., Ohio Arts Council (panel mem.) Clubs: Cin. Tennis, Women's City (Cin.). Home: 1908 Dexter Ave Cincinnati OH 45206

MERKEL, JOANN KAYE, personnel services executive; b. Bottineau, N.D., Jan. 18, 1949; d. Kenneth Harlan and Joyce Suzanne (Larson) Kornkven; m. Donevan A. Mortenson, May 28, 1971 (div. Mar. 1978); children—Alexia, Ryan; m. 2d, Arnold Elroy Merkel, May 29, 1980; children—Brian, Brad, Barry. Student U. N.D., 1967-68, N.D. State U., 1968-69, N.D. State U., 1970, Minot State Coll., 1970-71, Moorhead State U., 1981—. Adminstrv. asst. Involved, Inc., Minot, N.D., 1973-75; coll. placement specialist Job Service N.D., Minot, 1975-81; owner, mgr. Personnel Service Systems, Minot, 1982—. Bd. dirs. Minot Winterfest Assn., 1983—, Minot Art Gallery, 1984—, Friends of Minot Art Gallery, 1983—; active fund raising campaign Dakota Northwestern U.; sec. North Hill Sch. PTA, 1984-86; Summer Youth Employment Com., 1984-86; v.p. Easter Seal Campaign, 1984. Mem. Am. Soc. Personnel Adminstrs., Minot Area Personnel Assn., Minot C. of C. (ambassador com. 1982—), United Fund of Greater Minot (bd. dirs.) Republican. Lutheran. Club: Quota (Minot) (bd. dirs.). Home: 1812 Highland Dr Minot ND 58701 Office: Personnel Service Systems 1542 S Broadway Minot ND 58701

MERKLE, HELEN LOUISE, hotel executive; b. Carrington, N.D., May 23, 1950; d. Orville F. and Lillian M. (Argue) M.; B.S., N.D. State U., 1972. Asst. dir. food mgmt. Stouffer's Atlanta Inn, Atlanta, 1972-74; dir. food mgmt. Stouffer's Indpls. Inn, 1974-78; adminstrv. dir. food mgmt. Stouffer's Riverfront Towers, St. Louis, 1978-80; food mgmt. cons. Fraser Mgmt., Westlake, Ohio, 1980-83; exec. chef Marriott Hotel, Cleve., 1983—. Recipient First Place award for soups Taste of Indpls., 1976. Mem., Am. Culinary Fedn., Cleve. Culinary Assn., Food Service Execs. Assn., Nat. Assn. Female Execs.

Democrat. Lutheran. Home: 27618 B Caroline Circle Westlake OH 44145 Office: Marriott Hotel 4277 150th St Cleveland OH 44135

MERRICK, DWAYNE PAUL, diagnostic medical equipment company executive; b. Youngstown, Ohio, June 10, 1955; s. Stephen Clarence and Lois Marie (Berlin) M.; m. Victoria Lynn Surridge, Aug. 21, 1976. A.E.E.T., Ohio Inst. Tech., 1976; postgrad. Youngstown State U. Field service engr. Technicare Corp., Solon, Ohio, 1976-77, systems service engr., 1977-79, tech. support specialist, 1979-81, quality assurance supr., 1981-82, coordination mgr., 1982-83, project mgr., 1983—. Recipient prizes for photography. Chmn. Technicare United Way campaign, Solon, 1983. Mem. Photography Soc. Republican. Lutheran. Office: Technicare Inc 29100 Aurora Rd Solon OH 44139

MERRIHEW, MARK WALTER, educational administrator; b. Alliance, Nebr., July 3, 1953; s. Walter Earl and Barbara Ann (Schauda) M.; m. Constance Sue Anderson, July 6, 1974; children—Gabriel Marc, Chalin Christopher. A.S., Nat. Coll., Rapid City, S.D., 1973. Programmer, NCR Corp., Mpls., 1973-74, systems analyst, Omaha, 1974-76, systems engr., Lincoln, Nebr., 1976-79; data processing dir. Seward County Community Coll., Liberal, Kans., 1979—. Republican. Episcopalian. Avocations: sports, especially tennis, basketball; science fiction. Home: 1030 S Holly Dr Liberal KS 67901 Office: Seward County Community Coll 1801 North Kansas Liberal KS 67901

MERRILL, JOHN MOORE, oncologist; b. Seattle, Mar. 27, 1946; s. John Moore and Elizabeth (Jensen) M.; m. Nancy Louise Hexter, July 12, 1968; children—Deborah, Daniel. B.A. cum laude, Stanford U., 1968; M.D., U. Wash., 1972. Diplomate Am. Bd. Internal Medicine, Am. Bd. Med. Oncology. Intern U. Chgo., 1972-73, resident, 1973-74; fellow Nat. Cancer Inst., 1974-76; assoc. prof. Northwestern U., 1976—; mem. staff Northwestern Meml. Hosp., VA Lakeside Hosp., 1976—; mem. staff, coordinator Fox Cancer Care Unit, Northwestern Meml. Hosp., Chgo., 1978—; trustee Cook County Grad. Sch. Medicine, Chgo., 1981—. Author cancer research papers. Bd. dirs. Y-Me (breast cancer support group), Homewood, Ill., 1983—. Served to surgeon USPHS, 1974-76. Recipient George H. Joost award Northwestern U. Med. Sch., 1983; Internat. fellow Am. Assn. Med. Colls.; Am. Cancer Soc. fellow. Mem. ACP, AMA, Am. Soc. Clin. Oncology, Am. Assn. Cancer Edn. Avocations: sports; music. Office: Hematology-Oncology Assocs 676 N Saint Clair Suite 2140 Chicago IL 60611

MERRILL, LOIS JEAN, university dean, nursing educator; b. New Haven, Aug. 3, 1932; d. Robert Warner and Lydia Mabel (Crook) M.; B.S., U. Conn.-Storrs, 1955; M.S., U. Colo., 1960; Ph.D., U. Nebr.-Lincoln, 1978. Instr. nursing Syracuse U., N.Y., 1960-63; assoc. prof. U. Ky., Lexington, 1963-69; assoc. prof., assoc. dean, U. Nebr., Lincoln, 1969-76; prof., dean of nursing U. Evansville, Ind., 1978—. Contbr. articles to profl. jours. Mem. adv. bd. Evansville-Vanderburg County Health Occupations Programs, 1978—, Evansville-Vanderburg County Sch. of Practical Nursing. Mem. Am. Nurses Assn., Nat. League for Nursing, Am. Edn. Research Soc., Midwest Nursing Research Soc. Home: 809 Meadow Brook Dr Evansville IN 47712 Office: U Evansville Sch Nursing and Health Sci PO Box 329 Evansville IN 47702

MERRITT, DEBRA ANN, transportation executive; b. Lincoln, Nebr.; d. William E. and Nancy Lea (Kryger) Dolezal; m. Michael Ray Merritt, May 27, 1972 (div.); 1 dau., Anna Lea. Grad. high sch. Mgr., Off Broadway Enterprizes, Council Bluffs, Iowa, 1979—; pres. Wings Transp., Inc., Omaha, 1982—. Mem. Nat. Right to Work Com., Nat. Republican Congressional Com. Served in USN, 1971-73. Mem. Am. Entrepreneurs Assn., Am. Mgmt. Assn., Working Woman's Assn. Office: 717 S 9th St Omaha NE 68102

MERRITT, JOHN STEPHENS, JR., university administrator; b. Indpls., Dec. 22, 1935; s. John Stephens and Dorothy Grace (Hess) M.; m. Brenda Joyce Piercy, Dec. 28, 1963; children—Stephen Bradley, Christopher Alan. B.S., Ind. U.-Bloomington, 1969, M.S. in Pub. Affairs, 1977. Mgr. Crown Finance Co., Indpls., 1958-61; police officer Marion County, Indpls., Ind., 1961-66; assoc. dir. Inst. Research & Pub. Safety, Bloomington, 1968-75; dir. external affairs, Ind. U.-Bloomington, 1975-80, dir. devel., 1980—; cons. State of Ind., Indpls., 1975-80, Ind. Local Govt., 1975-80, Boys Clubs Am., Chgo., 1980-84. Chmn., Ind. Area Council Boys Clubs, 1982-84; pres. Bloomington Boys Club, 1980. Served with USNR, 1954-57. Mem. Soc. Research Adminstrs. (pres. Midwest chpt. 1980-81), Soc. Pub. Adminstrn., Internat. Personnel Mgmt. Assn., Coll. Placement Council, Internat. City Mgmt. Assn. Club: Lions (past pres.). Avocations: golf, fishing. Home: 4825 Yorkshire Ct Bloomington IN 47401 Office: Sch Pub and Environ Affairs Ind Univ Bloomington IN 47405

MERRITT, MELODY BETH, osteopathic physician; b. Muscatine, Iowa, Jan. 26, 1953; d. Ernest Everett and Elizabeth (Townsley) James; m. Robert Eugene Merritt, Apr. 16, 1983; 1 child, Harlie James. B.S. in Biology magna cum laude, Iowa Wesleyan Coll., 1975; M.S., U. Iowa, 1976; D.O., Coll. Osteo. Medicine and Surgery, 1980. Diplomate Nat. Bd. Examiners Osteo. Physicians and Surgeons. Accident investigator Consumer Product Safety Commn., Iowa City, 1976; intern Riverside Osteo. Hosp., Trenton, Mich., 1980-81; gen. practice osteo. medicine, Seymour, Iowa, 1981—; mem. staff Wayne County Hosp.; mem. courtesy staff St. Joseph Hosp.; founder, med. dir. Seymour 1st Responder Emergency Team. Bd. dirs. Wayne County Bd. Health; mem. adv. com. Pub. Health Nursing. Recipient Disting. Service award Nat. Health Service Corp., 1983. Mem. Am. Osteo. Assn., Am. Coll. Gen. Practice Physicians, Iowa Acad. Osteopathy, Beta Beta Beta (pres. 1974-75). Roman Catholic. Home: 206 Lee St Seymour IA 52590 Office: 102 N 4th St Seymour IA 52590

MERRITT, RICHARD WILLIAM, entomology educator; b. San Francisco, July 26, 1945; s. Robert Edward and June Adele (Reynolds) M.; m. Pamela Ann Hamlin, Sept. 2, 1967; children—Brett, Scott. B.A., Calif. State U.-San Jose, 1968; M.S., Wash. State U., 1970; Ph.D., U. Calif., 1974. Grad. research trainee U. Calif., Berkeley, 1970-74, asst. research entomologist, 1974; faculty Mich. State U., East Lansing, prof. entomology, 1984—. Editor: An Introduction to the Aquatic Insects of North America, 1978, 84; assoc. editor: Am. Midland Naturalist, 1976-80, Freshwater Invertebrate Biology, 1980-85. Contbr. articles to profl. jours. Mem. Entomol. Soc. Am., N.Am. Benthological Soc. (pres. 1984-85), Am. Inst. Biol. Scis., Sierra Club, Phi Beta Kappa, Phi Kappa Phi. Office: Dept Entomology Mich State Univ 243 Natural Sci Bldg East Lansing MI 48824

MERRITT, ROSE BILLINGSLEY, bank executive; b. Pitts., May 10, 1936; d. Harold James and Rose Stephanie (Sladack) Billingsley; student Mt. Mercy Coll., Pitts., 1952-53, Coll. Notre Dame, San Mateo, Calif., 1968, Met. Coll., Denver, 1972-74; B.A. in Acctg., Golden Gate U., San Francisco, 1978; 1 son, William Paul. Owner, operator Southway Lodge, Grand Lake, Colo., 1969-72; controller CBISF, San Francisco, 1974-79; controller U.S. group Chem. Bank, N.Y.C., 1979-82; v.p. bus. devel. Chem. Bank, Chgo., 1982—. speaker at colls. and univs., profl. groups. Choral dir. various secular and religious groups, 1960-75; a founder, coordinator vol. classroom and assistance program, Grand County, Colo., 1970-71; sec. Calif. Assn. Neurologically Handicapped Children, 1968-69; pres. Colo. Assn. Children With Learning Disabilities, 1972. Mem. Am. Bankers Assn., Fin. Womens Club San Francisco, Fin. Women's Assn. N.Y. Editor: (with L. Anderson and others) Helping the Adolescent With The Hidden Handicap, 1969. Home: 1540 N State Pkwy 4C Chicago IL 60610 Office: 3 First Nat Plaza 70 W Madison St Chicago IL 60602

MERRY, CARROLL EUGENE, manufacturing company communications exec.; b. Richland Center, Wis., Jan. 8, 1948; s. Elmo Carroll and Helen Evelyn (Peaslee) M.; B.S. in Journalism, U. Wis., Oshkosh, 1973; M.S. in Mgmt., Cardinal Stritch Coll., Milw., 1983; m. Amy Jo Sweet, Oct. 21, 1967; children—JaNelle Paulette, Jennifer Erin. Bur. chief Oshkosh Daily Northwestern, Berlin, Wis., 1973-74; advt. coordinator J I Case Outdoor Power Div., Winneconne, Wis., 1974-76; advt. mgr. Gehl Co., West Bend, Wis., 1976-78, mktg. communications mgr., 1978—. Mem. editorial adv. bd. Agri-Mktg. mag., 1983. Chmn. communications com. St. Joseph's Community Hosp., West Bend, 1980-85; v.p. Washington County 4-H Leaders Assn., 1981. Served with USAF, 1968-72. Recipient Outstanding Young Man Civic award, 1979. Mem. Nat. Agri-Mktg. Assn. (dir., sec. Badger chpt.). Office: 143 Water St West Bend WI 53095

MERTINS, GUILBERT EUGENE, sales executive; b. Racine, Wis., May 15, 1929; s. William Alexander and Anna Evangeline (Petersen) M.; m. Vicky Doris Jensen, Mar. 14, 1953; children—Scott, Kimberly. B.A. in Bus. Adminstrn., U. Wis.-Milw., 1948; B.S. in Mech. Engring., U. Wis.-Madison, 1952. Dist. mgr. Harnischfeger Corp., 1952-57, Hunter Machy, Milw., 1957-66; sales mgr. Hertz Corp., Chgo., 1966-68; nat. accounts mgr. Wacker Corp., Milw., 1968-70; br. mgr. Koehring Co., Syracuse, N.Y., 1970-74; nat. sales mgr. Master Appliance Corp., Racine, 1974—. Mem. Am. Mgmt. Assn. Republican. Lutheran. Avocations: sailing, golf, hunting, fishing. Home: 1036 Illinois St Racine WI 53405 Office: Master Appliance Corp 2420 18th St Racine WI 53403

MERULLA, EM EVANS, learning disabilities specialist; b. Waukon, Iowa, Apr. 12. B.A., U. Iowa, M.A., Ed.S. Tchr., cons. Cedar Rapids Schs., Iowa, 1969—. Mem. Phi Delta Kappa (del. 1984—), Sierra Club (Cedar-Wapsie group chmn., publicity chmn. 1981—, Iowa chpt. vice chmn. 1984—, council del. 1984—). Avocation: environmental activist.

MESAROS, MARSHALL GEORGE, dentist; b. Dearborn, Mich., Feb. 23, 1946; s. George and Edna A. M.; m. Bonny K. Reimer; children—Melanie, Lauren. B.S., U. Detroit, 1967, D.D.S., 1971. Prefellowship Gen. Dentistry. With dental div. Detroit Health Dept., 1971-74; gen. practice dentistry, Wayne, Mich., 1972-74, Farmington Hills, Mich., 1973—. Pres. Commerce Area Hist. Soc., Mich., 1983-84. Mem. ADA, Mich. Dental Assn., Oakland County Dental Assn., R.W. Bunting Periodontal Study Club, Acad. Gen. Dentistry. Avocations: photography; creative writing. Home: 3155 GlenIris Dr Milford MI 48042 Office: Halsted Hills Dental Office 37325 W 12 Mile Rd Farmington Hills MI 48018

MESCHEFSKE, DANIEL ALBIN, insurance company executive; b. Wausau, Wis., Apr. 2, 1954; s. John and Carolyn Mae (Borman) M. A.A. in Bus. Adminstrn., North Central Tech. Inst., Wausau, 1974. With Continental Ins. Cos., 1974—, sr. underwriter, Milw., Wausau, 1980-81, supr. property and casualty personal lines underwriting, office mgr., Wausau, 1981—, condr. product seminars, 1980—, auditor, 1980—; participant state ins. convs., 1982—; mem. ins. adv. bd. North Central Tech. Inst., Wausau, 1982—. Mem. Am. Mgmt. Assn. Lutheran. Lodge: Elks. Home: Apt 3 3738 Troy St Wausau WI 54401 Office: Continental Ins Cos Suite 200 2800 Westhill Dr Wausau WI 54401

MESERVE, WALTER JOSEPH, JR., drama educator; b. Portland, Maine, Mar. 10, 1923; s. Walter Joseph and Bessie Adelia (Bailey) M.; A.B., Bates Coll., 1947; M.A., Boston U., 1948; Ph.D., U. Wash., 1952; m. Mollie Ann Lacey, June 18, 1981; children—Gayle Ellen, Peter Haynes, Jo Alison, David Bryan. Instr., U. Kans., 1951-53, asst. prof. English, 1953-58, assoc. prof., 1958-63, prof., 1963-68; prof. theatre and drama Ind. U., Bloomington, 1968—, assoc. dean Office Research and Grad. Devel., 1980-83, dir. Inst. Am. Theatre Studies, 1983—; vis. lectr. Victoria U., Manchester, Eng., 1959-60; vis. prof. U. Calif., Santa Barbara, 1967-68; Rockefeller scholar, Bellagio, Italy, 1979. Served with AC, U.S. Army, 1943-46. Nat. Endowment for Humanities fellow, 1974-75, 83-84; Guggenheim fellow, 1984-85. Mem. Am. Soc. Theatre Research, Dramatists Guild, Am. Theatre Assn., Author's Guild, Am. Studies Assn. Club: Cosmos. Author five books, including: An Emerging Entertainment: The Drama of the American People to 1828, 1977; American Drama to 1900, 1980; editor seven books, including: The Complete Plays of W.D. Howells, 1960; mem. editorial bd. Modern Drama, 1960-82, Studies in Am. Drama, 1945-80, 1984—; assoc. editor Theatre Jour., 1982—. Office: Inst Am Theatre Studies Ind U Bloomington IN 47405

MESSERLE, JUDITH ROSE, medical librarian, public relations director; b. Litchfield, Ill., Jan. 16, 1943; d. Richard Douglas and Nelrose B. (Davis) Wilcox; m. Darrell Wayne Messerle, Apr. 26, 1968; children—Kurt Norman, Katherine Lynn. B.A. in Zoology, So. Ill. U., 1966; M.L.S., U. Ill., 1967. Cert. med. librarian. Librarian, St. Joseph's Sch. Nursing, Alton, Ill., 1967-71, dir. med. info. ctr., 1971-76, dir. info. services, 1976-79, dir. ednl. resources and community relations, 1979—; instr. Lewis and Clark Coll., 1975; con. 1973—; instr. Med. Library Assn. Bd. dirs. Family Services and Vis. Nurses Assn., Alton, 1976-79. Mem. Med. Library Assn. (dir. 1981-84, search com. for exec. dir. 1979), Ill. State Library Adv. Com., Midwest Health Sci. Library Network (dir. health sci. council), St. Louis Med. Librarians, Hosp. Pub. Relations Soc. of St. Louis. Club: PR and Ad (Alton). Office: St Josephs Hosp 915 E 5th St Alton IL 62002

MESSERSCHMIDT, JAMES WARREN, sociology and criminal justice educator; b. Chgo., Jan. 21, 1951; s. George Gus and Joan May (Chapman) M.; m. Ulla Kristina Eurenius, July 23, 1977; children—Erik Eurenius, Jan Eurenius. B.A., Portland State U., 1973; M.A. with honors, San Diego State U., 1976; Ph.D., U. Stockholm, 1979. Asst. prof. sociology and criminal justice Moorhead State U., Minn., 1979—. Author: The Trial of Leonard Peltier (nominated for C. Wright Mills award 1984), 1983. Research grantee Nat. Swedish Council for Crime Prevention, Nat. Swedish Soc. Sci. Research Council, 1975. Mem. Am. Sociol. Assn., Am. Soc. Criminology, Western Soc. Criminology, Soc. Study Social Problems, European Group for Study Deviance and Social Control. Home: 508 32d Ave S Apt 21 Moorhead MN 56560 Office: Moorhead State U Dept Sociology Moorhead MN 56560

MESSINEO, ANTHONY ONOFRIO, JR., restaurant executive; b. Lincoln, Nebr., Jan. 24, 1941; s. Anthony Onofrio and Josephine M.; B.S., U. Nebr., Lincoln, 1965; m. Carmen Monaco, Apr. 20, 1963; children—Deborah, Michael, Anthony Onofrio III. Mgr., Tony and Luigi's Restaurant, Lincoln, 1965-71, chmn. bd., 1978—, pres., 1978—; owner, chmn. bd., pres. Valentino's Pizza, Lincoln, 1971—, Valentino's of Am., Lincoln, 1978—. Mem. Young Pres. Orgn. Republican. Roman Catholic. Clubs: Sertoma, Rotary. Home: 7535 S Hampton St Lincoln NE 68506 Office: 201 N 8th St Lincoln NE 68501

MESSING, RITA BAILEY, pharmacology educator; b. Bklyn., July 7, 1945; d. Max and Kate (Katkin) Zimmerman; m. William Messing, June 20, 1965; 1 child, Charles. B.A., CUNY, 1966; Ph.D., Princeton U., 1970. Asst. prof. Rutgers U., Camden, N.J., 1969-72; research assoc. MIT, Cambridge, 1973-75; asst. then assoc. research psychobiologist U. Calif.-Irvine, 1976-81; research assoc. U. Minn.-Mpls., 1981-83, asst. prof. pharmacology, 1983—; research fellow Organon Pharms., The Netherlands, 1980. Editor: Endogenous Peptides and Learning and Memory Processes, 1981. Contbr. articles to profl. jours. Patentee process for promoting analgesia. USPHS grantee, 1983-86; Med. Found. fellow, 1974-75; NSF fellow, 1966-69. Mem. AAAS, Soc. Neurosci., Am. Soc. Pharmacology and Exptl. Therapeutics, Phi Beta Kappa. Home: 735 Goodrich Ave Saint Paul MN 55105 Office: 435 Delaware St SE Minneapolis MN 55455

MESSMAN, WILBUR WALLACE, accountant, consultant, educator; b. Dakota, Ill., June 25, 1906; s. David Frederick and Edith Jane (Hutchison) M.; m. Isabel Harrison, July 28, 1950. B.A., Cornell Coll., 1930; postgrad. U. Wis.-Milw., 1933, Marquette U., 1935, Milw. Area Tech. Coll., 1936. Bookkeeper, teller Dakota State Bank, 1925-26; bookkeeper Cornell Coll., Mount Vernon, Iowa, 1928-30; acct. Wis. Telephone, Milw., 1930-37; semi-sr. auditor Arthur Young & Co., Milw., 1937-40; chief acct., office mgr. FMC Corp., Port Washington, Wis., 1940-71; acctg. instr. Milw. Area Tech. Coll., Port Washington, 1971-76. Clk. First Congregational Ch., Port Washington, 1944-51, 63-79, moderator, 1979—; pres. Mental Health Assn. Ozaukee County, 1977-79; v.p. Orgn. Mental Health Assns. State of Wis., Madison, 1980—. Named Regional Vol. of Yr., Mental Health Assn. Wis., 1980. Republican. Mem. United Church of Christ. Lodge: Masons. Avocations: singing in regional chorus and church choir. Home: 5819 W Cedar Sauk Rd Saukville WI 53080

MESSNER, RONALD PIERCE, medicine educator; b. Chgo., July 15, 1935; m. Christine Simonelli. B.A., Oberlin Coll., 1957; M.D., U. Chgo., 1961. Diplomate Am. Bd. Internal Medicine. Intern U. Hosps. Cleve., 1961-62; resident in internal medicine U. Minn., Mpls., 1962-63, 65-66; fellow in rheumatology U. Minn. Hosps., 1966-67; instr. in medicine U. Minn. Med. Sch., Hennepin County Gen. Hosp., 1967-68; asst. prof. medicine U. Minn. Med. Sch., Arthritis Unit U. Hosps., 1968-69; asst. prof. medicine, dir. sect. rheumatology U. N.Mex. Sch. Medicine, Albuquerque, 1969-72, assoc. prof. medicine, dir. sect. rheumatology, 1972-76, prof. medicine, dir. sect. rheumatology, 1976-79; dir. U. N.Mex. Arthritis Found. Clin. Research Ctr., 1969-79; prof. medicine, dir. sect. rheumatology/clin. immunology U. Minn. Med. Sch., 1979—. mem. state precert. com. N.Mex. Profl. Service Rev. Orgn., 1972-77; med. dir. N.Mex. Regional Med. Program Arthritis Project, 1973-76; mem. U. N.Mex. N.Mex. Profl. Service Rev. Orgn. Com., 1974-77; mem. immunologic sci. study sect. NIH, 1977-81; mem. med. adv. com. Minn. Arthritis Found., 1979—; dir. U. Minn. Arthritis Found. Clin. Research Ctr., 1980—; pres. med. adv. bd. Minn. Lupus Found., 1982—. Assoc. editor Jour. Lab. Clin. Medicine, 1983—. Recipient research award U. Minn., 1967-68, research award Minn. Arthritis Found., 1968-69, career devel. award Nat. Inst. Arthritis, Metabolism and Digestive Diseases, 1972-77; named vis. investigator Scripps Clinics and Research Found., 1977-78, Minn. Arthritis Found. Research Prof., 1979—; postdoctoral fellow Arthritis Found., 1969-72; fellow ACP. Mem. N.Y. Acad. Sci., AAAS, Soc. Exptl. Biology and Medicine, Am. Assn. Immunologists, Am. Fedn. Clin. Research (counselor western sect. 1971, chmn., 1974), Am. Rheumatism Assn. (chmn., mem. various coms.), Western Soc. Clin. Research, Central Soc. Clin. Research, Am. Soc. Clin. Investigation, Alpha Omega Alpha. Office: Mayo Meml Bldg Box 108 Minneapolis MN 55455

METCALF, ALLAN ALBERT, English educator, b. Clayton, Mo., Apr. 18, 1940; s. George Joseph and Mary Ellen (Stephens) M.; m. Teri Flynn, Dec. 20, 1966; children—Stephen, David, Michael, Sara. B.A., Cornell U., 1961; postgrad. Free U., Berlin, 1961-62; M.A., U. Calif.-Berkeley, 1964, Ph.D., 1966. Asst. prof. English U. Calif.-Riverside, 1966-73; assoc. prof. English MacMurray Coll., Jacksonville, Ill., 1973-81, prof., 1981—, chmn. English dept., 1973-83; co-dir. Calif. summer program linguistics U. Calif.-Santa Cruz, 1973, mem. faculty, 1971-72. Author: Riverside English: The Spoken Language of a Southern California Community, 1971; Poetic Diction in the Old English Meters of Boethius, 1973; Chicano English, 1979. Editor-in-chief Cornell Daily Sun, 1960-61. Mem. MLA, Commn. on English Lang., Nat. Council Tchrs. English, Linguistic Soc. Am., Conf. Secs., Am. Council Learned Socs., Medieval Acad. Am., AAUP, Am. Dialect Soc. (exec. sec. 1981—), Phi Beta Kappa, Phi Kappa Phi. Home: 713 S Main St Jacksonville IL 62650 Office: English Dept MacMurray Coll Jacksonville IL 62650

METCALFE, DAVID STAFFORD, medical laboratory administrator; b. Kansas City, Mo., Dec. 28, 1936; s. Donald Catron and Mildred Stafford (McKnight) M.; m. Sharon Ruth Cunningham, Sept. 18, 1965; children—Lisa Gaye Murray, Elizabeth Marie. B.S. in Chemistry, U. Mo., 1958, M.S. in Med. Microbiology, 1961. Cert. specialist in clin. microbiology. Tchr. supr. Physicians' Clin. Lab., Cape Girardeau, Mo., 1960-63; dir. microbiology St. John's Hosp., St. Louis, 1963-68; tech. dir. Allen Med. Labs., St. Louis, 1963-68; coordinator labs. Pasco Labs., Hinsdale, Ill., 1968-69; lab. dir. Riverside Med. Ctr., Kankakee, Ill., 1969—; lab. cons. Deaconess Hosp., St. Louis, 1964-68, Riverview Lab., Kankakee, 1980—; mem. inspection team Coll. Am. Pathologists, Chgo., 1978. Contbr. articles to profl. lit. Pres., Cape Girardeau Republican Party, 1962-63; campaign chmn. United Way, Kankakee, 1975, YMCA fund drive, Kankakee, 1977; pres. bd. dirs. Mills Scholarship Found., U. Mo.-Columbia, 1981—. Research grantee NIH, 1961. Mem. N.Y. Acad. Sci., Am. Assn. for Clin. Chemists (mem. citizens ambassador program to China 1985), Clin. Lab. Mgmt. Assn., Am. Soc. Microbiology, Am. Soc. Clin. Pathology. Clubs: Kiwanis (Kankakee); Univ. Singers (Columbia) (pres. 1980—). Avocations: music, choral singing, astronomy, fishing, bicycling. Home: 813 S McKinley Ave Kankakee IL 60901 Office: Riverside Med Ctr 350 N Wall St Kankakee IL 60901

METRY, MARK SALEEM, lawyer; b. Detroit, Aug. 13, 1953; s. Gilbert Elias and Eva (Albert) M.; m. Kyle Elizabeth Sly, Feb. 14, 1981; children—Sean Gilbert, Christopher Mark. B.S., Central Mich. U., 1975; J.D., Detroit Coll. Law, 1978. Bar: Mich. 1978. Magistrate per diem Detroit Recorders Ct., 1979—; assoc. Metry Metry & Sanom, Detroit, 1978—; lectr. Macomb Coll., Madonna Coll., Wayne County, Mich., 1984. Coach Little League Basketball, Baseball, Grosse Pt., Mich., 1977-84. Mem. Mich. Trial Lawyers Assn., ABA, Am. Arbitration Assn., Detroit Bar Assn., Phi Kappa Phi. Republican. Greek Orthodox. Home: 28880 Jefferson St Clair Shores MI 48081 Office: Metry Metry & Sanom 3800 Cadillac Tower Detroit MI 48226

METSCHER, RODNEY STEVEN, agriculture educator; b. Cole Camp, Mo., Oct. 8, 1952; s. Norman Henry and Ora Ruth (Baldwin) M.; m. Barbara Ann T. McQuade, Aug. 11, 1973. B.S., U. Mo.-Columbia, 1974, M.S., 1980. Vocational agr. instr. Adrian (Mo.) R-3 Sch., 1975-76, Benton County R-1 Sch., Cole Camp, Mo., 1976-80; agr. instr. State Fair Community Coll., Sedalia, Mo., 1980—, chmn. dept., 1984—, youth coordinator Agr. Club, 1974-75. Bd. dirs. Cole Camp Fair, 1976—, Nat. Post-Secondary Agr. Student Orgn., 1983—. Mem. Am. Vocat. Assn., Nat. Vocat. Agr. Tchrs. Assn., Mo. Vocat. Agr. Tchrs. Assn., Mo. Vocat. Assn., Mo. Assn. Community and Jr. Colls., Cole Camp Jr. C. of C. Lutheran. Home: Route 2 Cole Camp MO 65325 Office: Agr Dept 1900 Clarendon Rd State Fair Community Coll Sedalia MO 65301

METTLER, RUBEN FREDERICK, electronics and engineering company executive; b. Shafter, Calif., Feb. 23, 1924; s. Henry Frederick and Lydia M.; student Stanford U., 1941-43; B.S. in Elec. Engring., Calif. Inst. Tech., 1944, M.S., 1947, Ph.D. in Elec. and Aero. Engring, 1949; L.H.D. (hon.), Baldwin-Wallace Coll., 1980; m. Donna Jean Smith, May 1, 1955; children—Matthew Frederick, Daniel Frederick. Asso. div. dir. systems research and devel. Hughes Aircraft Co., 1949-54; spl. cons. to asst. sec. def., 1954-55; asst. gen. mgr. guided missile research div. Ramo-Wooldridge Corp., 1955-58, pres., dir. Space Tech. Labs., Inc., Los Angeles, 1962-68; exec. v.p., dir. TRW Inc. (formerly Thompson Ramo Wooldridge, Inc.), 1965, asst. pres., 1968-69, pres., 1969-77, chmn. bd., chief exec. officer, 1977—; dir. Bank Am. Corp., Goodyear Tire & Rubber Co., Merck & Co.; past vice-chmn. Ind. adv. council Dept. Def. Adv. com. United Negro Coll. Fund, nat. campaign chmn., 1980; mem. bd. advisers Council for Fin. Aid to Edn., Case Western Res. U.; chmn. Pres.'s Sci. Policy Task Force, 1969; mem. Emergency Com. for Am. Trade; nat. chmn. Nat. Alliance Businessmen, 1978-79; bd. dirs. Greater Los Angeles Urban Coalition; trustee Calif. Inst. Tech., 1969—, mem. Caltech Assos., 1963—; mem. council Rockefeller U.; trustee, research policy com. Com. Economic Devel.; trustee Nat. Safety Council, Cleve. Clinic Found., Nat. Fund Minority Engring. Students; aerospace chmn. U.S. Ind. Payroll Savs. Commn.; mem. bd. Smithsonian Nat. Assos. Served with USNR, 1943-46. Registered profl. engr., Calif. Named 1 of ten Outstanding Young Men of Am., U.S. Jr. C. of C., 1955; recipient Meritorious Civilian Service award Dept. Def., 1969. named Engr. of Yr., Engring. Socs. So. Calif., 1964; Alumni Disting. Service award Calif. Inst. Tech., 1966; Nat. Human Relations award NCCJ, 1979; Excellence in Mgmt. award Industry Week mag., 1979. Fellow IEEE, AIAA; mem. Sci. Research Soc. Am., Calif. Inst. Tech. Alumni Assn. (dir.), Nat. Acad. Engring., James Smithson Soc., Sigma Xi, Eta Kappa Nu (named nation's outstanding young elec. engr. 1954), Tau Beta Pi, Theta Xi. Clubs: Cosmos (Washington); Union, 50 (Cleve.). Author reports airborne electronic systems. Patentee interceppto r fire control systems. Office: TRW Inc 1 Space Park Redondo Beach CA 90278 also 23555 Euclid Ave Cleveland OH 44117

METZ, CHARLES EDGAR, radiology educator; b. Bayshore, N.Y., Sept. 11, 1942; s. Clinton Edgar and Grace Muriel (Schienke) M.; m. Maryanne Theresa Bahr, July 1, 1967; children—Rebecca, Molly. B.A., Bowdoin Coll., 1964; M.S., U. Pa., 1966, Ph.D., 1969. Instr., U. Chgo., 1969-71, asst. prof. radiology, 1971-75, assoc. prof., 1976-80, prof., 1980—, prof. structural biology, 1984—, dir. grad. programs in med. physics, 1979—. Contbr. articles to sci. jours. Mem. Phi Beta Kappa, Sigma Xi. Office: Box 225 U Chgo 5841 S Maryland Ave Chicago IL 60637

METZENBAUM, HOWARD MORTON, senator; b. Cleve., June 4, 1917; s. Charles I. and Anna (Klafger) M.; B.A., Ohio State U., 1939, L.L.D., 1941; m. Shirley Turoff, Aug. 8, 1946; children—Barbara Jo, Susan Lynn, Shelley Hope, Amy Beth. Chmn. bd. Airport Parking Co. Am., 1958-66, ITT Consumer Services Corp., 1966-68; chmn. bd. Com Corp., 1969-74, after 1975; U.S. senator from Ohio, 1974, 77—. Mem. War Labor Bd., 1942-45, Ohio Bur. Code Rev., 1949-50, Cleve. Met. Housing Authority, 1968-70, Lake Erie Regional Transit Authority, 1972-73. Mem. Ohio Ho. of Reps., 1943-46, Ohio Senate, 1947-50; now mem. U.S. Senate from Ohio; mem. Ohio Democratic Exec. Com., 1966; mem. Ohio Dem. Finance Com., from 1969. Trustee Mt. Sinai Hosp., Cleve., 1961-73, treas., 1966-73; bd. dirs. Council Human Relations, United Cerebral Palsy Assn., Nat. Council Hunger and Malnutrition, Karamu House, St. Vincent Charity Hosp., Cleve., St. Jude Research Hosp., Memphis; nat. co-chmn. Nat. Citizens' Com. Conquest Cancer; vice-chmn. fellows Brandeis U. Mem. ABA, Ohio Bar Assn., Cuyahoga Bar Assn., Cleve. Bar Assn., Am. Assn. Trial Lawyers, Order of Coif, Phi Eta Sigma, Tau Epsilon Rho. Office: 140 Russell Senate Office Bldg Washington DC 20510*

METZLER, JEAN MARIE, consulting geologist, lecturer; b. Akron, Ohio, Mar. 9, 1942; d. Robert Andrew and Mary Rita (Welsh) M. B.S. in Geology, Kent State U., 1965, M.A. in Geology, 1967. Tchr. sci. Col. Crawford High Sch., N. Robinson, Ohio, 1967-69; asst. prof. Kent State U., Canton, Ohio, 1969-76; sales mgr. T.K. Harris Agy., Canton, 1976-81; research geologist Lomak Petroleum, Hartville, Ohio, 1981-84; consulting geologist Metzler Enterprises, Canton, 1984—. Recipient Outstanding Grad. Sr. award Kent State U. Mem. Am. Assn. Petroleum Geologists, Ohio Geol. Soc., Ohio Assn. Oil and Gas., Am. Mensa Ltd. Club: Health and Fitness (Canton). Avocations: running; swimming; classical music. Home: 3521 Culver Dr NW Canton OH 44709

MEUSE, ANN TERRELL, insurance company official; b. Massillon, Ohio, Jan. 16, 1943; d. Douglass Fuqua and Jane (Chidester) Terrell; B.A. magna cum laude, Coll. White Plains (N.Y.), 1974; diploma paralegal edn. N.Y. U., 1975; m. Lewis Andrew Meuse, Apr. 16, 1960; children—Ann W., Laura A. Corp. sec., compliance dir. Gerber Life Ins. Co., White Plains, 1974-78; dir. legis. and policy research services Colonial Penn Group, Inc., Phila., 1978-82; asst. v.p. product devel. Montgomery Ward Life Ins. Co., Chgo., 1982—. Mem. Chgo. Assn. Direct Marketers, Sigma Delta Chi. Women's Direct Response Group of Chgo. Club: Toastmasters. Office: 200 Martingale Rd Schaumburg IL 60194

MEYER, BETTY ANNE (MRS. JOHN ROLAND BASKIN), lawyer; b. Cleve.; d. William Henry and Monica (McSherry) Meyer; student Denison U., 1941-43; A.B., Flora Stone Mather Coll., Western Res. U., 1946, LL.B., 1947; m. John Roland Baskin, May 12, 1967. Admitted to Ohio bar, 1947; asst. to dean Adelbert Coll., Western Res. U., 1948-49; asso. firm Kiefer, Waterworth, Hunter & Knecht, Cleve., 1965-74; mem. firm Knecht, Rees, Meyer, Mekedis & Shumaker, Cleve., 1974—. Mem. Alpha Phi. Home: 2679 Ashley Rd Shaker Heights OH 44122 also Key Largo FL also East Corp Martha's Vineyard MA Office: Terminal Tower Cleveland OH 44113

MEYER, BETTY JANE, former librarian; b. Indpls., July 20, 1918; d. Herbert and Gertrude (Sanders) M.; B.A., Ball State Tchrs. Coll., 1940; B.S. in L.S., Western Res. U., 1945. Student asst. Muncie Public Library (Ind.), 1936-40; library asst. Ohio State U. Library, Columbus, 1940-42, cataloger, 1945-46, asst. circulation librarian, 1946-51, acting circulation librarian, 1951-52, adminstrv. asst. to dir. libraries, 1952-57, acting asso. reference librarian, 1957-58, cataloger in charge serials, 1958-65, head serial div. catalog dept., 1965-68, head acquisition dept., 1968-71, asst. dir. libraries, tech. services, 1971-76, acting dir. libraries, 1976-77, asst. dir. libraries, tech. services, 1977-83, instr. library adminstrn., 1958-63, asst. prof., 1963-67, asso. prof., 1967-75, prof., 1975-83; library asst. Grandview Heights Public Library, Columbus, 1942-44; student asst. Case Inst. Tech., Cleve., 1944-45; mem. Ohio Coll. Library Center Adv. Com. on Cataloging, 1971-76, mem. adv. com. on serials, 1971-76, mem. adv. com. on tech. processes, 1971-76; mem. Inter-Univ. Library Council, Tech. Services Group, 1971-83; mem. bd. trustees Columbus Area Library and Info. Council Ohio, 1980-83. Ohio State U. grantee, 1975-76. Mem. ALA, Assn. Coll. and Research Libraries, AAUP, Ohio Library Assn. (nominating com. 1978-81), Ohioana Library Assn., Ohio Valley Group Tech. Services Librarians, No. Ohio Tech. Services Librarians, Franklin County Library Assn., Acad. Library Assn. Ohio, PEO, Beta Phi Mu, Delta Kappa Gamma. Club: Ohio State U. Faculty Women's. Home: 970 High St Unit H2 Worthington OH 43085

MEYER, CHARLES HOWARD, lawyer; b. St. Paul, Aug. 1, 1952; s. Howard Joseph and Helen Evangeline (Ericson) M.; m. Patti Jo Graf, Sept. 11, 1981. B.S.B. with high distinction, U. Minn., 1974; J.D. magna cum laude, Harvard U., 1977. Bar: Minn. 1977, U.S. Dist. Ct. Minn. 1977, U.S. Ct. Appeals (8th cir.) 1981; C.P.A., Minn. Staff acct. Deloitte Haskins & Sells, Mpls., 1974, 75; ptnr. Oppenheimer Law Firm, St. Paul/Mpls., 1976, 77-85; sr. tax atty. Cargill, Inc., Mpls., 1985—; lectr. continuing legal edn. seminars. Mem. ABA, Minn. State Bar Assn., Hennepin County Bar Assn., Harvard Law Sch. Assn., Am. Inst. C.P.A.s (Elijah Watt Sells gold medal), Nat. Accts. Assn., Am. Accts. Assn., Minn. Soc. C.P.A.s (Harold C. Utley award 1974). Lutheran. Club: Harvard (Minn.). Home: 5879 Royal Oaks Dr Shoreview MN 55126 Office: Law Dept No 24 Cargill Inc Box 9300 Minneapolis MN 55440

MEYER, CLIFFORD ROBERT, manufacturing company executive; b. Cin., Sept. 25, 1923; s. Clifford Robert and Minerva (Sauer) M.; m. Maxine Laberheier, Aug. 12, 1948; 1 child, Judith Ann Meyer Biggs. B.B.A., U. Cin., 1948. Vice pres., gen. mgr. Morris Machine Tool Co., Cin., 1948-56; with Cin. Milacron, 1956—, v.p. machine tools, 1970-76, exec. v.p., 1976-81, pres., chief operating officer, 1981—; dir. AMCAST, Dayton, Ohio, Union Central Life Assurance Co., Cin., Senco Products, Cin., Central Trust Bank N.A. Bd. dirs. Cin. Port Authority, 1981-84; adv. council Coll. Bus. Adminstrn., U. Cin., 1980-84; chmn. Hamilton County Park Tax Levy campaign, 1982. Served to lt. j.g. USN, 1942-46. Mem. Soc. Engrs. and Scientists Cin. Clubs: Comml., Queen City, Hyde Park (Cin.); Masons, Shriners. Office: 4701 Marborg Ave Cincinnati OH 45208

MEYER, DAVID CLARENCE, publisher, writer; b. Hammond, Ind., Dec. 25, 1943; s. Clarence and Marie G. (Reilly) M. B.A., Cornell Coll., 1967. Freelance writer, 1971-74; mgr. Ind. Bot. Gardens, Hammond, 1974-76, bd. dirs., 1980—; pub. Meyerbooks, Glenwood, Ill., 1976—; dir. Calumet Nat. Bank, Hammond. Editor: 50 Years of Herbalist Almanac, 1977. Author: Wanting Jolinda, 1970; contbr. articles to mags. Served at 1st lt. U.S. Army, 1969-71, Vietnam. Writing fellow Book of Month Club, 1967. Clubs: Caxton (mem. council 1983-85) (Chgo.); Magic Circle (London). Avocation: collecting books. Office: Meyerbooks Publisher PO Box 427 Glenwood IL 60425

MEYER, DWAINE FREDRIC, lawyer, broadcasting; b. Dallas Center, Iowa, Nov. 16, 1929; s. Fredrick William and Dorothy (Cook) M.; m. Dorothy Fujii, June 23, 1956; children—David, Doraine, Darrin, Dorilee. B.S., Iowa State U., 1952; J.D. Drake U., 1957. Bar: Iowa. Sole practice, Pella, Iowa, 1956—; editor, producer, narrator broadcast interview shows, 1976—; jud. magistrate, Pella, 1974-78. Mem. Iowa State Bar Assn., Marion County Bar Assn., Am. Legion (comdr. 1980). Baptist. Lodge: Masons. Office: Meyer Law Office 810 Main St Pella IA 50219

MEYER, F(RANK) RICHARD, III, corporate financial consultant; b. University City, Mo., May 12, 1920; s. Frank Richard, Jr. and Laura (Hamilton) M.; m. Geraldine Schloerb, Sept. 5, 1942; children—Suzanne Meyer Perry, Charles Robert, John Hamilton. B.S., MIT, 1942. Asst. to v.p. electric div. Stewart Warner, Chgo., 1947-50; mem. sr. mgmt. com., asst. to pres. Acme Steel Corp., Chgo., 1950-56; corp. fin. cons., Chgo., 1956—; dir. Nibco, Inc., Elkhart, Ind., Wes-Tech, Inc., Buffalo Grove, Ill., Eastman & Beaudine, Inc., Chgo. Former trustee MIT; trustee George Williams Coll., Downers Grove, Ill., West Suburban Hosp., Oak Park, Ill., Vol. Trustees of Not-for-Profit Hosps., Washington; elder Presby. Ch.; past pres. River Forest Bd. Edn., Ill., Oak Park YMCA, Chgo. Jr. Assn. Commerce. Served to capt. USAAC, 1942-46. Republican. Clubs: Union League, Oak Park Country, River Forest Tennis, Economic (Chgo.). Avocations: flying; sports; photography. Home: 1211 Monroe Ave River Forest IL 60305 Office: 115 S LaSalle St Suite 2505 Chicago IL 60603

MEYER, FRED PAUL, research adminstrator, fish pathologist; b. Holstein, Iowa, Aug. 15, 1931; s. Rudolph F. and Anna M. (Weber) M.; m. Mary Lou Polk; children—Diane, James, Richard. B.A. in Biology and Math., U. No. Iowa., 1953; M.S. in Parasitology, Iowa State U., 1957, Ph.D. in Parasitology and Fish Biology, 1960. Cert. Fishery Sci. Research asst. Iowa State Tchrs. Coll., 1952-53; high sch. tchr. biology, physics, advanced math., Spirit Lake, Iowa, 1953-56; chief exploratory fishing crew Upper Miss. River, Iowa Dept. Conservation, summer 1956; research cons. U.S. Fish & Wildlife Service Brooks Lake, Alaska Research Sta., summer 1957; grad. research asst. zoology-entomology Iowa State U., 1956-58, instr. zoology, 1959-60; part-time instr. biology Little Rock U., 1961-62; parasitologist Fish Farming Exptl. Sta., Stuttgart, Ark., 1960-73, chief, 1965-71; asst. dir. Warmwater Fish Cultural Lab., Stuttgart, 1971-73; dir. Nat. Fishery Research Lab., LaCrosse, Wis., 1973—. Author: A Guide to Integrated Fish Health Management in the Great Lakes Basin, 1983; Parasites of Freshwater Fishes: A Review of Their Control and Treatment, 1974; Second Report to the Fish Farmers, 1973. Contbr. articles to profl. jours. Recipient Meritorious Service award U.S. Dept. Interior, 1983; fellow NSF; Thomas H. MacBride scholar, 1954-55, 58, Ira Merchant, 1954, 59. Mem. Am. Fisheries Soc. (fish health sect., fishery adminstrs. sect., S.F. Snieszko Disting. Service award 1984), Am. Soc. Parasitologist, Sigma Xi, Phi Kappa Phi, Gamma Sigma Delta, Kappa Delta Pi, Beta Beta. Lodges: Lions, Kiwanis, Rotary. Avocations: hunting; fishing; gardening. Office: Nat Fishery Research Lab PO Box 818 LaCrosse WI 54602-0818

MEYER, FRED WILLIAM, JR., memorial parks exec.; b. Fair Haven, Mich., Jan. 7, 1924; s. Fred W. and Gladys (Marshall) M.; A.B., Mich. State Coll., 1946; m. Jean Hope, Aug. 5, 1946; children—Frederick, Thomas, James, Nancy. Salesman Chapel Hill Meml. Gardens, Lansing, Mich., 1946-47; mgr. Roselawn Meml. Gardens, Saginaw, Mich., 1947-49; dist. mgr. Sunset Meml. Gardens, Evansville, Ind., 1949-53; pres., dir. Memory Gardens Mgmt. Corp., Indpls., Hamilton Meml. Gardens, Chattanooga, Covington Meml. Gardens, Ft. Wayne, Ind., Chapel Hill Meml. Gardens, Grand Rapids, Mich., Forest Lawn Memory Gardens, Indpls., Lincoln Memory Gardens, Indpls., Sherwood Meml. Gardens, Knoxville, Tenn., Chapel Hill Meml. Gardens, South Bend, Ind., Tri-Cities Meml. Gardens, Florence, Ala., White Chapel Meml. Gardens, Springfield, Mo., Nebo Meml. Park, Martinsville, Ind., Mission Hills Meml. Gardens, Niles, Mich., Mercury Devel. Corp., Indpls., Quality Marble Imports, Indpls., Quality Printers, Indpls., Am. Bronze Craft, Inc., Judsonia, Ark., Am. Granite & Marble Co., Indpls. Mem. C. of C., A.I.M., Am. Cemetery Assn., Sigma Chi, Phi Kappa Delta. Elk. Clubs: Nat. Sales Executives, Athenaem Turners, Columbia, Meridian Hills Country, Woodland Country. Home: 110 E 111th St Indianapolis IN 46280 Office: 3733 N Meridian St Indianapolis IN 46208

MEYER, HERBERT ALTON, III, editor, publisher; b. Kansas City, Mo., June 15, 1947; s. Herbert Alton, Jr. and Mary Janet (McDonald) M. B.S. in Bus. Adminstrn., U. Kans., 1969; m. Dorothy Dianne Eddins, June 3, 1969; children—Herbert Alton IV, Scott William. Courthouse reporter Lawrence (Kans.) Daily Jour.-World, 1969-71; editor, pub. Independence (Kans.) Daily Reporter, 1971—. Mem. Governmental Ethics Commn. State Kans., 1974-78. Trustee William Allen White Found., U. Kans.; bd. dirs. Mercy Hosp., 1975-81, chmn., 1977; bd. dirs. Mid-Am., Inc., Independence Community Chest, 1979-82, Independence Industries, Inc., 1972—, v.p. Jr. Achievement of Mid-Am., Inc., 1979-81, Celebrity Golf Classic Inc., 1984—. Served with AUS, 1969-70. Mem. Kans. Press Assn. (dir. 1976), Independence C. of C. (dir. 1983—), Sigma Chi. Republican. Episcopalian. Elk, Rotarian. Home: 912 Birdie Dr Independence KS 67301 Office: 320 N 6th St Independence KS 67301

MEYER, HOWARD STUART, chemical engineer, researcher; b. Chgo., Dec. 19, 1949; s. Sam and Melaine (Seldin) M.; m. Carol Renee Lewis, Sept. 5, 1972; children—Amanda Nicole, Sarah Gabrielle. B.S. in Chem. Engring., U. Ill., 1972; M.S. in Chem. Engring., U. Idaho, 1978. Chem. engr. Bee Chem. Co., Lansing, Ill., 1972-74; group leader Exxon Nuclear Idaho, Idaho Falls, 1974-80; mgr. Gas Research Inst., Chgo., 1980—. Mem. Am. Inst. Chem. Engrs. (Idaho sect. treas. and vice chmn. 1978-80, Chgo. sect. constn. and publicity chmn. 1982—, vice chmn. program), Am. Chem. Soc. (Glen award, fuel chemistry div. 1981). Office: Gas Research Inst 8600 W Bryn Mawr Ave Chicago IL 60631

MEYER, JERRY, state senator. Mem. N.D. State Senate, 1983—. Democrat. Office: PO Box 306 Berthold ND 58718*

MEYER, LEON JACOB, wholesale co. exec.; b. Chgo., Nov. 12, 1923; s. Joseph and Minnie (Lebovitz) M.; student Lake Forest Coll., 1941-43; B.S., UCLA, 1948; m. Barbara Gene Bothman, Oct. 17, 1948; children—Charles Scott, John Mark, Ellen Renee. Owner, operator Christopher Distbg. Co., Santa Monica, Calif., 1951-53; pres. J. Meyer & Co., Waukegan, Ill., 1953-80, Western Candy & Tobacco Co., Carpentersville, Ill., 1970-78, Ill. Briar Pipe & Sundry Co., Waukegan, 1963-78; chmn. bd. Phillips Bros. Co., Kenosha, Wis., 1975—, Ill. Wholesale Co., 1976—. Served with U.S. Army, 1943-46; PTO. Named Sundry Man of Year, 1976, Candy Distbr. of Yr., 1976; recipient Alex Schwartz Meml. award, 1978. Mem. Nat. Assn. Tobacco Distbrs. (trustee), Ill. Assn. Candy-Tobacco Distbrs. (past chmn. bd.), Federated Merchandising Corp. (past pres.), Internat. Tobacco Wholesaler Alliance (past chmn. bd.), Nat. Automatic Merchandisers Assn., Nat. Candy Wholesalers Assn., UCLA Alumni Club, Waukegan/Lake County C. of C. Clubs: Elks, Eagles. Home: 3444 University Ave Highland Park IL 60035 Office: 4700 Industrial Dr Springfield IL 62708

MEYER, MARK EDWARD, financial analyst; b. Elgin, Ill., Mar. 5, 1960; s. Robert E. and Janet Merry (Arseneau) M. B.A., Augustana Coll., Ill., 1982; postgrad. Northwestern U., 1984—. Credit analyst Fullerton Metals Co., Northbrook, Ill., 1982-83; fin. analyst R&D div. Am. Can Co., Barrington, Ill., 1983—. Youth adv. St. Matthew Lutheran Ch., Barrington, 1982—, chmn. youth bd., 1984. Avocations: music; electronic equipment; basketball; baseball; football. Home: 21153 N 19th St Barrington IL 60010 Office: Am Can Co 433 N Northwest Hwy Barrington IL 60010

MEYER, RALPH ROGER, biological sciences educator; b. Milw., Feb. 18, 1940; s. Ralph George and Geneva Lorna (Schmidt) M.; m. Marjorie Kathleen Stark, Sept. 24, 1960 (div. 1971); children—Christine Lynn, Gregory John, Lauren Jean; m. Diane Carla Rein, Oct. 26, 1974; 1 child, Jocelyn Ann. B.S., U. Wis., 1961, M.S., 1963, Ph.D., 1966. NSF predoctoral fellow U. Wis., 1961-66; postdoctoral fellow Yale U., New Haven, 1966-67; NIH postdoctoral fellow SUNY, Stonybrook, 1967-69; asst. prof. biol. sci. U. Cin., 1969-75, assoc. prof., 1975-79, prof., 1979—. Contbr. articles to profl. jours. Mem. Am. Soc. Biol. Chemists, Am. Soc. for Cell Biology, Am. Soc. Microbiology, Ohio Acad. of Sci., AAAS, Sigma Xi. Home: 4067 Ridgedale Dr Cincinnati OH 45247 Office: U Cincinnati Dept Biol Scis Cincinnati OH 45221

MEYER, RICHARD ALLEN, JR., lawyer; b. Wayne, Mich., Nov. 17, 1954; s. Richard Allen and Donna Jean (Sader) M.; m. Diane Marie Smith, Sept. 6, 1975. B.A., U. Toledo, 1975, J.D., 1979. Bar: Ohio 1979, U.S. Dist. Ct. (no. dist.) Ohio 1980, Mich. 1982. Sole Practice, Toledo, 1979—. Mem. Ohio Bar Assn., Toledo Bar Assn., Mich. Bar Assn., Assn. Trial Lawyers Am., ABA, Phi Kappa Phi. Democrat. Home: 5753 Pheasant Hollow Toledo OH 43615 Office: 359 Spitzer Bldg Toledo OH 43604

MEYER, RUSSELL WILLIAM, JR., aircraft company executive; b. Davenport, Iowa, July 19, 1932; s. Russell William and Ellen Marie (Matthews) M.; m. Helen Scott Vaughn, Aug. 20, 1960; children—Russell William III, Elizabeth Ellen, Jeffrey Vaughn, Christopher Matthews, Carolyn Louise. B.A., Yale U., 1954; LL.B., Harvard U., 1961. Bar: Ohio 1961, Kans., 1975. Mem. firm Arter & Hadden, Cleve., 1961-66; pres., chief exec. officer Grumman Am. Aviation Corp., Cleve., 1966-74; exec. v.p. Cessna Aircraft Co., Wichita, Kans., 1974-75, chmn. bd., chief exec. officer, 1975—; dir. Fourth Nat. Bank & Trust Co., Wichita, Kans. Gas & Electric Co. Bd. dirs. Cleve. Yale Scholarship Com., 1962-74., United Way Wichita and Sedgwick County, 1975—; trustee Wichita State U. Endowment Assn., 1975—, Wesley Hosp. Endowment Assn., 1977—. Served with USAF, 1955-58. Mem. ABA, Ohio Bar Assn., Cleve. Bar Assn., Kans. Bar Assn., Gen. Aviation Mfrs. Assn. (chmn. bd. 1973-74), Wichita C. of C. (dir. 1975—). Clubs: Wichita, Wichita Country. Home: 600 Tara Ct Wichita KS 67206 Office: Cessna Aircraft Co Wichita KS 67201

MEYER, STEVEN MICHAEL, opthalmologist, surgeon, lawyer, business consultant; b. Chgo., Feb. 3, 1946; s. Fred Bernard and Lucille (Hanson) M. Student Lake Forest Coll., 1964-66; M.D., U. Ill.-Chgo., 1970; J.D., Notre Dame U., 1982. Diplomate Nat. Bd. Med. Examiners, Am. Bd. Ophthalmology. Intern dept. surgery Case-Western Res. U., 1970-71; chief resident dept. ophthalmology U. Chgo., 1973-76; pvt. practice medicolegal cons., South Bend, Ind., 1982—; pvt. practice bus. cons., South Bend, 1982—; practice medicine specializing in ophthalmology, South Bend, 1976—; chief exec. officer Nat. Ophthalmic Mgmt., Inc., 1985—. Author: Medical Malpractice Bases of Liability, 1985. Contbr. articles to profl. jours. Patentee in field. Bd. dirs. Ind. Soc. for Prevention of Blindness, Indpls., 1983—, med. adv. council, 1982—. Served with USPHS, 1971-73. Fellow Am. Acad. Opthalmology; mem. AMA, Ind. Acad. Ophthalmology, Ind. State Med. Assn., St. Joseph County Med. Soc. Avocations: video and film production; television; photography. Office: 513 N Michigan St South Bend IN 46601

MEYER, THERESA MAURINE, nurse, transcutaneous electrical nerve stimulation consultant; b. Blue Earth, MN, June 27, 1939; d. Francis Joseph and Maurine Agnes (Mongeau) Bleess; m. Roger Louis Meyer, Sept. 3, 1960; children—Daniel, Kathleen, David. Grad. St. Mary's Sch. Nursing, Rochester, Minn., 1960. R.N., Minn. Staff nurse in medicine/surgery, Miller Hosp., St. Paul, 1960-61; staff nurse in orthopedics Sharp Hosp., San Diego, Calif., 1979; transcutaneous electrical nerve stimulation consultant PainCare (formerly Midwest Pain Control), Golden Valley, Minn., 1979-85, with sales office, Mpls., 1985—. Contbr. articles to Nursing Magazine. Del., Polit. Convention Fridley, Minn., 1974. Mem. Midwest Pain Soc. Clubs: (Mpls.) (sec. 1984), Sun Harborettes (San Diego) (sec. 1978). Avocations: barbershop singing auxilliary. Home: 8331 Red Rock Rd Eden Prairie MN 55344 Office: PainCare Div of Med Wellness Technologies Minneapolis MN

MEYER, WILLIAM CHARLES, aeronautical company executive; b. Bronxville, N.Y., Jan. 22, 1946; s. William Charles August and Sarah MacDonald (Hanna) M.; m. Penny Edith Hudson, Dec. 27, 1969; children—William Jason August, William Ethan August. B.S. in C.E., Bucknell U., 1968; M.B.A., Cornell U., 1973. Registered profl. engr., Kans. Cost engr. Procon Inc., Pointe-Aux-Trembles, Que., Can., 1974-75; field engr. Arthur G. McKee, Nanticoke, Ont., Can., 1975; sr. field engr. R.M. Parsons Co., Sar-Cheshmeh, Iran, 1976-77, Dateland, Ariz., 1977-79; coordinator contracts Boeing Mil. Airplane Co., Wichita, Kans., 1979-84, constrn. mgr., 1984—. Mem. City Council Traffic Task Force, Mulvane, Kans., 1983; leader Quivira council Boy Scouts Am., 1982-85. Served to lt. (j.g.) USNR, 1968-71, Vietnam. Avocations: woodworking, sailing, cross-country skiing. Home: 225 Centennial Mulvane KS 67110 Office: Boeing Mil Airplane Co K78-01 Wichita KS 67227-7730

MEYERING, RALPH A., psychology educator; b. Istanbul, Turkey; s. Harry R. and Fern I. (Awrey) M.; m. Joan B. Bereiter, June 14, 1956; 1 child, Ann Elizabeth. B.S., Mankato State U., 1952; M.A., Northwestern U., 1956; Ph.D., U. Iowa, 1961. Registered psychologist; cert. counselor. Tchr., counselor Am. Sch., Talas, Turkey, 1952-55; tchr., coach Central High Sch., Battle Creek, Mich., 1956-58; from assoc. prof. to prof. psychology Ill. State U., Normal, 1961—; Fulbright lectr. Chiengmai U., Thailand, 1967-68, Srinakharinwirot U., Dhitsanulok, Thailand, 1985-86; vis. prof. U. Sydney, Australia, 1968, Wayne State U., Detorit, 1972, U. Colo., Boulder, 1970, 78-79. Author: Uses of Test Data in Counseling, 1968; also articles. Mem. Am. Psychol. Assn., Am. Assn. Counseling and Devel., Am. Assn. Sex Educators, Counselors and Therapists, Am. Assn. Human Service Educators, Am. Orthopsychiat. Assn. Avocations: skiing, sailing. Home: 215 Parkview Dr Bloomington IL 61701 Office: Ill State U Normal IL 61761

MEYERLAND, HARRY, accountant; b. Chgo., Sept. 11, 1930; s. Max and Hilda (Retick) M.; m. Maxine Ida Rosenfeld, Nov. 10, 1968. B.S., Roosevelt U., 1956; diploma U.S. Treasury Law Enforcement Sch., 1963. C.P.A., Ill.; real estate broker, Ill. Spl. agt. IRS, No. Dist. Ill., 1963-64; ednl. dir. Bryant & Stratton Coll., Chgo., 1966-70; acctg. faculty MacCormac Jr. Coll., Chgo., 1971-72, Ill. Sch. Commerce, Chgo., 1978, 82-84. Bd. dirs. young people's div. Jewish Fedn. Met. Chgo., 1960. Served with U.S. Army, 1952-54, USAR, 1960. Mem. Am. Inst. C.P.A.s. Democrat. Jewish. Contbr. articles to profl. jours. Office: 6354 N Oakley St Chicago IL 60659

MEYERS, JAN, congresswoman; b. Superior, Nebr.; m. Louis Meyers; children—Valerie, Philip. A.A. with honors, William Woods Coll., 1948; B.A. in Communications with honors, U. Nebr., 1951. Mem. 99th Congress from 3d Kans. Dist.; mem. sci. and tech. com., small bus. com., select com. on aging, Rep. policy com., Rep. research com., others; mem. Kans. State Senate, 1972-84, chair pub. health and welfare com., chair local govt. com.; mem. Overland Park City Council, Kans., 1967-72, pres., 2 yrs.; past bd. dir. Nat. League Cities; past pres. League Kans. Municipalities. Founding mem. Johnson County Community Coll. Found.; past bd. dirs. Johnson County Mental Health Assn.; past pres. Shawnee Mission LWV. Recipient Woman of Achievement Matrix award Women in Communications; Disting. Service award Bus. and Profl. Women Kansas Cit, Kans., United Community Services; Disting. Legislator award Kans. Assn. Community Colls., Jonson Conty Assn. Retarded Citizens; numerous others. Office: 204 Federal Bldg Kansas City KS 66101 also 1407 Longworth House Office Bldg Washington DC 20515*

MEYERS, JOSEPH KENT, industrial engineer, manufacturing company executive; b. Kokomo, Ind., May 22, 1936; s. Lunda M. and Mercedes O. (Benham) M.; m. Cora Lee Derringer, Mar. 21, 1981; children—Cynthia K., Alicia C. B.S., Ind. U., 1966; M.B.A., U. Mo., 1970. Engring. draftsman Union Carbide, Kokomo, Ind., 1960-64; prodn. mgr. Hallmark Cards, Kansas City, Mo., 1966-71; plant mgr. Fulton Instrument Co., N.Y., 1971-73; plant engring. mgr. Gen. Housewares, Terre Haute, Ind., 1973-82; plant mgr. Kawneer Co., Franklin, Ind., 1982—. Served with USN, 1956-60. Mem. Am. Prodn. and Inventory Control Soc., Am. Mgmt. Assn., Am. Inst. Indsl. Engrs., Ind. U. Alumni Assn. Republican. Methodist. Avocations: community theater, tennis, reading.

MEYERS, MITCHELL SIDNEY, real estate company executive; b. Cin., July 3, 1934; s. Sidney and Claire Maxine (Baum) M.; m. Jacqueline P. Meyers, July 1, 1957; children—Pamela A. Meyers Margaritis, Barry, Eliot. B.A., Cornell U., 1956, M.B.A. with distinction, 1957. Various exec. positions Mehl Mfg. Co., Cin., 1957-63; pvt. practice real estate developer, 1963-64; v.p. East & Co., 1964-72; prin. Mitchell S. Meyers, developer and investor, 1972—. Pres., Cin. Housing for the Aged, Inc., 1979-83. Mem. Cin. Real Estate Bd., Ohio Verse Writers Guild, Greater Cin. Writers League (pres. 1982—), Phi Kappa Phi. Republican. Club: Losantiville Country. Contbr. poems to anthologies. Office: Meyers Found 105 E 4th St Clopay Tower Suite 1114 Cincinnati OH 45202

MEYERS, PHILIP ALAN, educator geochemistry, researcher; b. Hackensack, N.J., Mar. 3, 1941; s. Harold Grove and Gertrude Myra (Smith) M.; m. Judith Arlene Brown, May 15, 1965; children—Shelley, Suzanne, Christopher. B.S., Carnegie-Mellon U., 1964; Ph.D., U. R.I., 1972. Research chemist Inmont Corp., Clifton, N.J., 1967-68; prof. U. Mich., Ann Arbor, 1972—; cons. Marathon Oil Co., BP Oil Co., Chevron Oil Co., Cities Service Oil Co., 1980—; dir. Gt. Lakes and Marine Waters Ctr., U. Mich., 1982—. Contbr. articles to profl. jours. Served to lt. j.g. USNR, 1964-67. Recipient Disting. Service award U. Mich. Class of 1938 Engring., 1976; Vis. Scientist award Ind. U., 1979-80; NOAA Summer fellow, 1981. Fellow Geol. Soc. Am.; mem. Am. Geophys. Union, Geochem. Soc., AAAS, Am. Assn. Limnology and Oceanography, Internat. Assn. Gt. Lakes Research, European Assn. Organic Geochemists, Am. Assn. Petroleum Geologists. Club: Ann Arbor Country. Avocations: tennis; travel; photography. Office: 2455 Hayward Ave Ann Arbor MI 48109

MEYERS, SANDY R., elementary school administrator; b. Mobridge, S.D., July 20, 1947; d. Ray H. and Esther (Buchholtz) Palmer; m. Richard K. Meyers, May 3, 1968 (div.); children—Donna E., Kathryn A. A.A., Rochester Jr. Coll., 1967; B.S., U. Minn., 1970, M.A., 1975, postgrad., 1976—. Cert. teaching specialist, Minn. Tchr. Anoka-Hennepin Schs. (Minn.), 1971-75, adminstr. Jackson Jr. High Sch., 1979—; adminstr. Northfield Schs. (Minn.), 1975-76; adminstr. Elk River Schs. (Minn.), 1976-79; instr. extension div. St. Thomas Coll., 1982—. Mem. Assn. Supervision and Curriculum Devel., Minn. Assn. Secondary Sch. Prins., Nat. Assn. Secondary Sch. Prins., Anoka Hennepin Elem. Sch. Prins. Assn. Roman Catholic. Office: 6000 109th Ave N Champlin MN 55316

MEYLOR, COLLEEN BETH, foundry product specialist, educator; b. Milw., Nov. 29, 1957; d. Michael Bernard and Karole Joan (Kabbeck) M. B.S. in Chem. Engring., U. Wis.-Madison, 1979. Devel. engr. Foseco, Inc., Cleve., 1980-82, product specialist, 1982—; instr. Cast Metals Inst., Am. Foundry Soc., Chgo., 1984—. Engr.-in-Tng., Profl. Engring. Soc. Mem. Am. Foundryman's Soc., Am. Women in Metal Industries, Nat. Assn. Female Execs., U. Wis. Alumni Assn. Avocations: piano; sports. Home: 32747 Willowbrook Ln North Ridgeville OH 44039 Office: Foseco Inc 20200 Sheldon Rd Cleveland OH 44142

MEZOFF, JOHN GALL, engineer; b. Chester, Pa., Nov. 10, 1920; s. John Ralph and Mary Jane (Gall) M.; m. Marian Elizabeth Marshall, June 24, 1944; children—John Marshall, Carl Roy, Mary Lou. B.S.Met.E., Purdue U., 1942. Registered profl. engr., Okla. Vice-pres., gen. mgr. Alumicast Corp., Chgo., 1948-51; mgr. metals tech. service and devel. Dow Chem. Co., Midland, Mich., 1951-65, bus. devel. mgr. metals Zurich, Switzerland, 1965-68; v.p. mktg. Am. Magnesium Co., Tulsa, 1968-81; adv. to gen. mgr. magnesium div. Norsk Hydro a.s., Oslo, 1981—. Contbr. articles to profl. jours. Patentee in field. Recipient cert. Am. Foundrymen's Soc., 1961. Mem. Internat. Magnesium Assn. (pres., dir. 1976-78), Internat. Magnesium Club (pres. 1974-76), ASTM (com. mem. 1968—), Am. Soc. Metals, Am. Inst. Metall. Engrs. Republican. Lutheran. Avocations: handweaving; woodworking.

MICELI, JOSEPH N., pharmacology, toxicology educator, researcher; b. N.Y.C., Jan. 13, 1945; s. Salvatore and Jean (Ipolitto) M.; divorced; 1 child, Laura Marie. B.S., Pace U., 1966; M.S., U. Detroit, 1971, Ph.D., 1971. Lic. lab. dir., Mich. Assoc. research scientist NYU Sch. Medicine, N.Y.C., 1971-74; adj. asst. prof. Pace U., N.Y.C., 1972-74; sr. research scientist U. Mich., Ann Arbor, 1974-75; dir. pharmacology, toxicology labs. Children's Hosp. Mich., Detroit, 1975—; asst. prof. Wayne State U., Detroit, 1975-79, assoc. prof., 1979—. Founder Romulus Substance Abuse Council, Mich., 1984. Mem. Am. Soc. Pharmacology and Exptl. Therapeutics, Am. Acad. Clin. Toxicology, Soc. Pediatric Research, Am. Assn. Clin Chemistry. Office: Children's Hosp Mich 3901 Beaubien Blvd Detroit MI 48201

MICHAEL, HAROLD LOUIS, civil engineering educator, consultant; b. Columbus, Ind., July 24, 1920; s. Louis Edward and Martha (Armuth) M.; m. Elsie Marie Ahlbrand, Aug. 15, 1943 (dec. Sept. 1951); m. Elizabeth Annette Welch, Dec. 12, 1954; stepchildren—Betty, Ellen, Harold, Thomas William; 1 child, Edward Michael. B.S. in Civil Engring. with highest distinction, Purdue U., 1950, M.S. in Civil Engring., 1951. Registered profl. engr., Ind. Grad. asst. Purdue U., 1950-51; dir. urban transp. studies Ind. State Hwy. Commn., 1951-54; research asst., instr. Purdue U., West Lafayette, Ind., 1952-54, asst. prof. hwy. engring., asst. dir. joint hwy. research project, 1954-56, assoc. prof. hwy. engring., assoc. dir. joint hwy. research project, 1956-61, prof. hwy. engring., head transp. and urban engring., assoc. dir. joint hwy. research project, 1961-78, head Sch. Civil Engring., prof. hwy. engring., dir. joint hwy. research project, 1978—; chmn. exec. com. Transp. Research Bd., Nat. Acad. Scis., 1976, mem. exec. com., 1973-79, chmn. or mem. adv. panels for Nat. Coop. Hwy. Research Programs, 1971-79; mem. adv. bd. Hwy. Extension and Research Program for Ind. Counties, 1971-75; chmn. Nat. Com. on Uniform Traffic Control Devices, 1971-74, mem., 1969—; vice-chmn. com. on ops. Nat. Com. on Uniform Traffic Laws and Ordinances, 1973—; mem. adv. panel on nat. accident sampling system Nat. Hwy. Traffic Safety Adminstrn., 1978-80; mem. exec. res. U.S. Dept. Transp., 1967-83; chmn. com. on transp. NRC, 1976-80; mem. bd. cons. Eno Found. Transp., 1978-82; chmn. Traffic Commn., West Lafayette, Ind., 1956—, chmn. transp. tech. com., 1965—. Served to capt. U.S. Army, 1942-46, ETO. Decorated Bronze Star; recipient citation for Disting. Service State Ind., 1967, Service award Ind. Soc. Profl. Engr., 1969, Disting. Service award Transp. Research Bd., 1976, Roy W. Crum award Transp. Research Bd., 1978, award in recognition of disting. service Ind. Soc. Profl. Engrs., 1978, Theodore M. Matson award, 1979, George S. Bartlett award Am. Assn. Hwy. and Transp. Ofcls., Am. Rd. and Transp. Builders Assn. and Transp. Research Bd., 1982; named Engr. of Yr., Ind. Soc. Profl. Engrs., 1972. Fellow Inst. Transp. Engrs. (pres. 1974-75, Marsh award 1984), ASCE (mem. engring. visitors com. 1978-83, G. Brooks Earnest Lecture award Cleve. sect. 1981, Laurie Prize 1981); mem. Nat. Acad. Engring., Nat. Soc. Profl. Engrs. (nat. dir. 1964-78, Engr. of Yr. 1972), Am. Rd. and Transp. Builders. Assn. (vice chmn. 1978-80, chmn. hwys. adv. council 1981—, Bartlett award 1982), Ind. Constructors, Inc. (hon. life), Am. Hwy. Engring. Assn. (chmn. subcom. hwys. 1970—), Am. Soc. Engring. Edn., Am. Pub. Works Assn. (trustee Research Found. 1976-79), Inst. Transp. Engrs. (hon.), Theta Xi. Lodge: Rotary (dist. gov.). Avocations: gardening; golf; stamp collecting; coin collecting. Home: 1227 N Salisbury St West Lafayette IN 47906 Office: Civil Engring Bldg Purdue U West Lafayette IN 47907

MICHAEL, R(ANDALL) BLAKE, religion educator, writer, clergyman; b. Lexington, N.C., Aug. 17, 1948; s. Flynn Leonard and Dorothy Lee (Koontz) M.; m. Marlyn Compton Albright, July 25, 1970; 1 child, Meredith Cameron. B.A. with highest honor in Sociology, U. N.C., 1970; M.Div. magna cum laude, Harvard U., 1972, A.M. in Comparative Religion, 1975, Ph.D. in Comparative Religion, 1979; student Mysore U., India, 1975-76. Teaching fellow in history of religion Harvard U., Cambridge, Mass., 1974-75, 76; teaching asst. in religious studies Brown U., Providence, 1976-78; instr. religion Ohio Wesleyan U., Delaware, 1978-79, asst. prof., 79-84, Swan-Allan-Collins assoc. prof., 1984—, chmn. dept. religion, 1981—, dir. off-campus programs, 1984—; adj. asst. prof. Meth. Theol. Sch., Delaware, 1983—. Author: Types of Religious Association in Virasaivism, 1985—. Contbr. articles to profl. jours. Rotary Internat. Travelling fellow, Mysore, 1976; research grantee NEH, 1982, faculty devel. grantee Ohio Wesleyan U., 1983. Mem. Am. Acad. Religion, Am. Oriental Soc., Assn. Asian Studies, Ohio Acad. Religion, Phi Beta Kappa. United Methodist. Avocations: camera collection; soccer; swimming. Office: Ohio Wesleyan Univ Dept Religion 50 S Henry St Delaware OH 43015

MICHAK, HELEN BARBARA, educator, nurse; b. Cleve., July 31; d. Andrew and Mary (Patrick) Michak; Diploma Cleve. City Hosp. Sch. Nursing, 1947; B.A., Miami U., Oxford, Ohio, 1951; M.A., Case Western Res. U., 1960. Staff nurse Cleve. City Hosp., 1947-48; pub. health nurse Cleve. Div. Health, 1951-52; instr. Cleve. City Hosp. Sch. Nursing, 1952-56; supr. nursing Cuyahoga County Hosp., Cleve., 1956-58; pub. information dir. N.E. Ohio Am. Heart Assn., Cleve., 1960-64; dir. spl. events Higbee Co., Cleve., 1964-66; exec. dir. Cleve. Area League for Nursing, 1966-72; dir. continuing edn. nurses, adj. asso. prof. Cleve. State U., 1972—. Trustee N.E. Ohio Regional Med. Program, 1970-73; mem. adv. com. Dept. Nursing Cuyahoga Community Coll., 1967—; mem. long term care com. Met. Health Planning Corp., 1974-76, plan devel. com. 1977—; mem. policy bd. Center Health Data N.E. Ohio, 1972-73; mem. Rep. Assembly and Health Planning and Devel. Commn., Welfare Fedn. Cleve., 1967-72; mem. Cleve. Community Health Network, 1972-73; mem. United Appeal Films and Speakers Bur., 1967-73; mem. adv. com. Ohio Fedn. Licensed Practical Nurses, 1970-73; mem. tech. adv. com. TB and Respiratory Disease Assn. Cuyahoga County, 1967-74; mem. Ohio Commn. on Nursing, 1971-74; mem. Citizens com. nursing homes Fedn. Community Planning, 1973-77; mem. com. on home health services Met. Health Planning Corp., 1973—. Mem. Nat. League Nursing (mem. com. 1970-72), Am. Nurses Assn. (accreditation visitor 1977-78, 83-85) Ohio Nurses Assn., (com. continuing edn. 1974-79, 82-84, chmn. 1984-85), Greater Cleve. (joint practice com. 1973-74, trustee 1975-76) Nurses Assn., Cleve. Area Citizens League for Nursing (trustee 1976-79), Am. Soc. Tng. and Devel., Am. Assn. Univ. Profs. Zeta Tau Alpha. Home: 4686 Oakridge Dr North Royalton OH 44133 Office: Cleve State Univ 2344 Euclid Av Cleveland OH 44115

MICHALAK, EDWARD M., manufacturing company executive; b. Milw., Oct. 1, 1924; s. Michael and Emily S. (Bulak) M.; m. Rita Y. Glazewski, May 23, 1953; children—Barbara, Mary, Cynthia, Jean. B.S. in Gen. Engring., U.S. Mil. Acad., 1945; B.S.E.E., U. Wis.-Madison, 1952; M.B.A., U. Wis.-Milw., 1976. Registered profl. engr., Wis. Devel. engr. Cutler Hammer & Globe Union, Milw., 1952-57; solid state engr. Allen Bradley Co., Milw., 1958-67, dir. elec. engring., 1967-69, dir. product mgmt., 1969-73, corp. v.p., 1973—; engring. advisor Marquette U., Milw., 1980—; mem. engring. adv. com. Milw. Sch. Engring., 1984—. Bd. dirs. Internat. Inst. Milw., 1984—, 1st v.p., 1984-85; mem. Kosciuszko Found., N.Y.C., 1963—. Served with U.S. Army, 1945-49, PTO. Mem. IEEE, Am. Soc. Quality Control, Indsl. Research Inst. (prin. rep. 1978—, program chmn. 1984-85), Wis. Assn. Research Mgmt. (chmn. 1984-85). Roman Catholic. Avocations: swimming; skiing; photography. Home: 3414 W Poe St Milwaukee WI 53215 Office: Allen Bradley Co 1201 S 2d St Milwaukee WI 53215

MICHAM, NANCY SUE, senior systems analyst; b. Toledo, May 15, 1956; d. Charles Edward and Dorothy Ruth (Bittner) Linker; m. Donald Thomas Kerner, June 20, 1975 (div. June 1980); m. Ray David Micham, III, May 19, 1984. A.S. with high honors, U. Toledo, 1980; B.S.M. cum laude, Pepperdine U., 1983. Cert. systems profl. Programmer, Owens-Ill., Toledo, 1973-80; programmer analyst Smith Tool Co., Irvine, Calif., 1980-82; systems analyst Denny's, Inc., La Mirada, Calif., 1982-83; sr. corp. systems analyst Libbey-Owens-Ford Co., Toledo, 1983—; cons. personal computer implementations Seabloom, Inc., 1983—. Mem. Nat. Mgmt. Assn., Assn. Systems Mgmt., Nat. Assn. Female Execs. Republican. Roman Catholic. Avocations: running, travel, backpacking, bicycling, racquetball.

MICHEL, ROBERT HENRY, congressman; b. Peoria, Ill., Mar. 2, 1923; s. Charles and Anna (Baer) M.; B.S., Bradley U., 1948; L.H.D. (hon.), Lincoln Coll.; LL.D. (hon.), Bradley U.; m. Corinne Woodruff, Dec. 26, 1948; children—Scott, Bruce, Laurie, Robin. Adminstrv. asst. Congressman Harold Velde, 1949-56; mem. 85th-99th Congresses, 18th Dist. Ill., house minority whip 94th-96th Congresses, minority leader 97th and 98th Congresses. Vice pres. Towne House Inn, Inc. Del., Republican Conv., 1964, 68, 72, 76, 80, 84; trustee Bradley U. Served with inf. AUS, World War II; ETO. Decorated Bronze Star Medal (2), Purple Heart; recipient Distinguished Alumnus award Bradley U., 1961. Mem. Am. Legion, V.F.W., D.A.V., Amvets, Cosmopolitan Internat. Office: 2112 Rayburn House Office Bldg Washington DC 20515

MICHENER, DWIGHT WARREN, agricultural engineer, civil engineer, farmer; b. Waynesville, Ohio, June 29, 1932; s. Charles Edward and Mary Alice (Crawford) M.; m. Anita Dee Wills, Sept., 1955 (div. 1968); children—Wendy, Eric, Sara; m. 2d, Glenna Mary Witters, May 26, 1978. B.S. in Agr., Ohio State U., 1954, B.S. in Agrl. Engring., 1962. Registered profl. engr., Nev., Ohio. Agrl. engr. Soil Conservation Service, U.S. Dept. Agr., Moses Lake and Sunnyside, Wash., 1963-66, researcher Agrl. Research Service, Reno, 1966-70; sr. engr., farm devel., advisor to Toprak-su (Turkey Soil and Water Conservation Service) Engring. Cons. Inc., Denver, 1970-71; engr. Ada Devel. Project, Ethiopia, Clapp & Mayne, Inc., San Juan, P.R., 1972-74; irrigation/drainage engr. Pakistan Water and Power Devel. Authority, Harza Engring Co. Internat., Chgo., 1975-77; drainage researcher Soil Conservation Service, U.S. Dept. Agr., agrl. engring. dept. Ohio State U., Columbus, 1977-78; irrigation/-drainage engr. FAO, Bagdad, Iraq, 1978; agrl. engr. Soil and Water Conservation Dists., Ohio Dept. Natural Resources, Columbus, 1979; farmer, Waynesville, Ohio, 1979—. Served to 1st lt. U.S. Army, 1955-56. Mem. ASCE, Am. Soc. Agrl. Engrs., Soil Conservation Soc., Farmer's Grange 13, Waynesville (Ohio) C. of C. Republican. Christian Scientist. Contbr. articles to profl. jours.; patentee in drainage field. Home and Office: 4980 Old State Rt 73 Waynesville OH 45068

MICHENER, H. ANDREW, sociology educator, researcher; b. N.Y.C., Dec. 1, 1940; s. Howard Perry and Rosemary (McCabe) M. B.A., Yale U., 1963; M.A., U. Mich., 1964, Ph.D., 1968. Asst. study dir. Inst. Social Research U. Mich., Ann Arbor, 1966-68; asst. prof. sociology U. Wis.-Madison, 1968-72, assoc. prof., 1972-75, prof., 1975—. Contbr. numerous articles to profl. jours. NSF grantee, 1975-77, 78-80, 81-84, 84-85, others. Mem. Am. Psychol. Assn., Am. Sociol. Assn., Am. Statis. Assn., Ops. Research Soc. Am., Soc. Exptl. Social Psychology. Office: Dept Sociology Univ Wis Madison WI 53706

MICKELSON, LAURA CHRISTINE, lawyer, computerized legal research system researcher and developer; b. St. Paul, Aug. 26, 1951; d. Richard Carl and Jo Ann Clarice (Davies) M. B.A. cum laude, U. Minn., 1973; J.D. cum laude, William Mitchell Coll. Law, 1978. Bar: Minn. 1978. Law clk. Ramsey County Atty.'s Office, Minn., 1976-78; WESTLAW trainer West Pub. Co., St. Paul, 1979-81, WESTLAW ednl. supr., 1981-83, WESTLAW researcher and developer, 1983—. Author: WESTLAW Character Mode Manual, 1983; EUROLEX Reference Manual, 1983; author, editor: WESTLAW Users Manual, 1984. Mem. Minn. Arabian Horse Assn., Phi Beta Kappa, Phi Alpha Delta. Democrat. Roman Catholic. Home: 866 Allen Ave West Saint Paul MN 55107 Office: West Pub Co 50 W Kellogg Blvd St Paul MN 55102

MICKEY, ROSIE CHEATHAM, educational administrator; b. Indpls.; d. Smith Henry and Anna Rivers (Halyard) Cheatham; m. Gordon Eugene Mickey, June 10, 1962; children—Miguel Eugene, Madganna Mae. B.S., Ind. U., 1970; M.S., U. Akron, 1979, Ed.D., 1983. Cert. supt., prin., supr., tchr., Ohio. Tchr. bus. edn. New Castle (Del.) Sch. Dist., 1971-74, Newark (Del.) Sch. Dist., 1974-76; tchr. bus. Lorain (Ohio) City Schs., 1976-78; grad. asst. U. Akron, 1978-80, asst. high sch. prin. Mansfield (Ohio) City Schs., 1980-83; asst. to dean, asst. prof. Community and Tech. Coll., U. Akron. Vice pres. women's aux. Frontiers Internat., Akron, Ohio; gen. chairperson Vitiligo Symposium, Beautillion Militaire, Akron chpt. Jack and Jill. Recipient Service award Frontiers Internat., 1981. Mem. Assn. Acad. Affairs Adminstrs., Ohio Assn. Women Deans, Counselors and Adminstrs., AAUW, Assn. Supervision and Curriculum Devel., Jack and Jill Am., Inc. (past v.p.), PTA, Pi Lambda Theta, Phi Delta Kappa. Clubs: Akron Yokettes; Neal-Marshall Alumni (Ind. U.). Office: Dean's Office Community and Tech Coll U Akron Akron OH 44325

MICKLE, JAMES LOWELL, private investigator and security executive; b. July 11, 1935; s. James M. and Lera V. (Ragland) M.; m. Martha L. Dennis, June 11, 1955; children—Greg, Janet, Pamela. Grad., Detroit Bus. Inst., 1961. Cert. protection profl. With Pinkerton's, Inc., Detroit and Southfield, Mich., 1960-70; with World Investigations & Security Engrs., Inc., Southfield, 1971—, pres., chief exec. officer, 1971—; speaker seminars. Served with U.S. Army, 1958-60. Mem. World Assn. Detectives (pres. 1984-85), Nat. Council Investigations and Security Services (pres. 1983-84), Mich. Assn. Pvt. Detectives and Security Agys. (pres. 1977-78). Office: World Investigations & Security Engrs Inc 21819 W 9 Mile Rd Southfield MI 48075

MICKLEY, RICHARD STROUD, lawyer; b. Marion, Ohio, Apr. 21, 1939; s. Henry Arthur and Miriam Laura (Stroud) M.; m. Carolyn Latham, Sept. 6, 1964; children—Bruce Latham, Andrew Kenneth. B.A., Coll. Wooster, 1961; J.D., Ohio State U., 1970. Bar: Ohio 1971, U.S. Dist. Ct. (so. dist.) Ohio 1973, U.S. Dist. Ct. (no. dist.) Ohio 1980, U.S. Tax Ct. 1975. Assoc., Grigsby & Allen, Marysville, Ohio, 1971-73; sole practice, Marysville, 1973-77, 79; asst. county prosecutor Union County (Ohio), 1973-75, 78; ptnr. Mckinley & Mickley, 1978, Mickley & McNemar, Marysville, 1980—; city law dir. City of Marysville, 1982—. Pres. Serve Inc., 1981, 84—. Served to capt. USAF, 1962-68. Mem. Union County Bar Assn. (pres. 1973), Ohio State Bar Assn., Ohio Acad. Trial Lawyers, Nat. Inst. Mcpl. Legal Officers. Republican. Presbyterian. Lodges: Lions (pres. 1979), Masons (master 1977). Avocations: church committee work; woodworking; gardening. Home: 891 Catalpa Pl Marysville OH 43040 Office: Mickley & McNemar 128 N Main St PO Box 310 Marysville OH 43040

MIDDAUGH, ROBERT BURTON, artist, corporate art consultant; b. Chgo., May 12, 1935; s. John B. and Mae Knight (Crooks) M. B.F.A., Sch. Art Inst. Chgo., 1964. Asst. to curator of art collection 1st Nat. Bank Chgo., 1971-78, curator, 1979-84. One-man shows include: Covenant Club, Chgo., 1966, Barat Coll., Lake Forest, Ill., 1970, Deson-Zaks Gallery, Chgo., 1974, Fairweather Hardin Gallery, Chgo., 1977, 80, 83, 85, Evanston Art Ctr., Ill., 1982, Fine Arts Forum, Chgo., 1982, Lake Forest Coll., 1982, St. Mary's Coll., Notre Dame, Ind., 1975, U. Wis.-Marinette, 1982, U. Wis.-Milw., 1976, Wustum Mus., Racine, Wis., 1980; group shows include: Am. Acad. Arts and Letters (Purchase prize), N.Y.C., 1975, Art Inst. Chgo., 1964, (Mcpl. Art League prize) 1966, 73, 78, 79, Ball State U., Muncie, Ind., (hon. mention), 1965, Des Moines Art Ctr., Iowa, 1967, Ill. State Mus., Springfield, 1966, 68, 69, 71, Joslyn Art Mus., Omaha, 1968, Krannert Art Mus., Urbana, Ill., 1965, Mitchell Mus., Mt. Vernon, Ill., 1980, New Eng. Conservatory of Music, Boston, 1970, No. Ill. U., DeKalb, 1983, Pa. Acad. Fine Arts, Phila., 1967, Portsmouth Community Arts Ctr. (Purchase prize), Va., 1980, Renaissance Soc. Chgo., 1971, U. Chgo., 1967, 68, 75, U. Notre Dame, Ind., 1969, U. Wis., 1981, Va. Mus. Fine Arts, Richmond, 1966; represented in permanent collections: Art Inst. Chgo., Boston Mus. Fine Arts, Davenport Mcpl. Art Mus., Iowa, Des Moines Art Ctr., Ill. State Mus., Fine Art Mus. of South, Mobile, Ala., Los Angeles County Mus., Mary Inst., St. Louis, No. Ill. U., Phoenix Art Mus., Portsmouth Community Arts Ctr., Va., Worcester Art Mus., Mass. Served with U.S. Army, 1958-60. Home: 1318 W Cornelia Chicago IL 60657

MIDLARSKY, ELIZABETH, psychologist educator; b. Brooklyn; d. Abraham Allan and Frances Lucille Rae (Wiener) Steckel; m. Manus Issachar Midlarsky, June 25, 1961; children—Susan Rachel, Miriam Joyce, Michael George. B.A., CUNY, 1961; M.A., Norhtwestern U., 1966, Ph.D., 1968. Lic. psychologist, Colo., Mich. Asst. prof. psychology U. Denver, 1968-73; dir. research and evaluation Park East Mental Health Ctr., Denver, 1973-75; assoc. prof., dir. psychology training prog. Met. State Coll., Denver, 1975-77; chmn. dept. psychology U. Detroit, 1978-81, dir. ctr. for study devel. aging, 1981—, assoc. prof., 1977-83, prof. psychology, 1983—; initial rev. group mem. NIMH, Bethesda, Md., 1976-82; mem. site rev. groups NHLBI, Bethesda, 1985. Editor: Acad. Psychology Bull., 1972—; co-editor: Humboldt Jour. of Social Relations, 1985. Contbr. articles to profl. jours. 1980, Nat. Inst. Aging, 1982-85, AARP Andrus Found., 1982-83; AAUW fellow, 1974-75. Fellow Am. Psychol. Assn.; mem. Gerontol. Soc. Am. (exec. com. of prog. com. 1983-84), Soc. Psychol. Study Social Issues, Am. Orthopsychiatric Assn., Mich. Psychol. Assn. (exec. council mem). Jewish. Avocations: singing; playing piano; writing poetry; walking; riding horses.

MIEDEMA, LAWRENCE RAY, real estate brokerage executive, investment consultant; b. Gary, Ind., Sept. 16, 1946; s. Nicholas and Agnes M.; m. Barbara Jane Branson, Aug. 2, 1980; 1 child, Jeffrey Branson. B.A., Eastern Ill. U., 1972; B.B.A., Governors State U., 1984. Registered real estate broker, Ill. Pres., Miedema & Assocs., Inc., Kankakee, Ill. Named Million Dollar Master, Chgo. Title Ins. Co., 1978. Mem. Nat. Assn. Realtors, Ill. State Assn. Realtors, Kankakee County Bd. Realtors (past chmn. edn.). Republican. Methodist. Office: Miedema & Assocs Inc PO Box 22 Kankakee IL 60901

MIERENDORF, ROBERT CHARLES, JR., molecular biologist, reseacher; b. Milw., Apr. 18, 1952; s. Robert Charles and Adrienne Lorraine (Schmidt) M.; m. Jeannie Ann Wampole, July 6, 1974; children—Michael Robert, Elizabeth Jane. B.S., U. Wis., 1974, Ph.D., 1980. Postdoctoral fellow McArdle Lab., Madison, Wis., 1980-81; project assoc. bacteriology U. Wis., Madison, 1981-84; sr. scientist Promega Biotec, Madison, 1984—. Contbr. articles to profl. jours. Avocations: photography; music; basketball; softball; skiing.

MIGAL, CLIFFORD ANTHONY, educational administrator; b. Alliance, Ohio, Oct. 14, 1946; s. Frank and Gloria Pearl Agnes (Dono Frio) M.; m. Gloria Jean Smith, Jan. 20, 1979; children—Michelle, Toni Marie. B.S. in Bus., Bowling Green State U., 1968; M. Ed., Wright State U., 1972; postgrad. U. Cin. Cert. vocat. dir., supr., supt. Tchr./coordinator Springfield Clark County (Ohio) Joint Vocat. Sch. Dist., 1968-72, vocat. supr., 1972-73, asst. dir., 1973-74, vocat. adult dir., 1974-75, vocat. dir., 1975-79; adminstrv. specialist Great Oaks Joint Vocat. Sch. Dist., Cin., 1979-83, assoc. supt., 1983—; peer leadership dir. Ohio Dept. Edn., 1979; mem. State of Ohio Blue Ribbon Panel on Vocat. Edn., 1983. U. Cin. grant scholar, 1982. Mem. Am. Vocat. Assn., Ohio Vocat. Assn., Buckeye Assn. Sch. Adminstrs., Ohio Vocat. Dirs. Assn. (pres.), Nat. Council Local Adminstrs. Roman Catholic. Writing cons. Nat. Ctr. Research Vocat. Edn., Ohio Dept. Vocat. Edn. Office: 3254 E Kemper Cincinnati OH 45241

MIGALA, LUCYNA, broadcaster, journalist, radio station executive; b. Krakow, Poland, May 22, 1944; d. Joseph and Estelle (Suwala) M.; came to U.S., 1947, naturalized, 1955; student Loyola U., Chgo., 1962-63, Chicago Conservatory of Music, 1963-70; B.S. in Journalism, Northwestern U., 1966. Radio announcer, producer sta. WOPA, Oak Park, Ill., 1963-66; writer, reporter, producer NBC news, Chgo., 1966-69, 1969-71, producer NBC local news, Washington, 1969; producer, coordinator NBC network news, Cleve., 1971-78, field producer, Chgo., 1978-79; v.p. Migala Communications Corp., 1979—; program dir., on-air personality Sta. WCEV, Cicero, Ill., 1979—; lectr. City Colls. Chgo., 1981. Columnist Logan Sq. Free Press, Chgo., 1984—. Soloist, mgr. Lira Singers, Chgo., 1965—; mem., chmn. various cultural coms. Polish Am. Congress, 1970—; bd. dirs. Nationalities Services Center, Cleve., 1973-78; bd. dirs., exec. com. Ill. Humanities Council, 1983—; bd. dirs., v.p. Cicero-Berwyn Fine Arts Council, Cicero, Ill.; v.p. Chgo. chpt. Kosciuszko Found., 1983—; bd. dirs. Polish Women's Alliance Am., 1983—; gen. chmn. Midwest Chopin Piano Competition, 1984—; mem. ethnic and folk arts com. Ill. Arts Council, 1984—. Washington Journalism Center fellow, spring 1969. Mem. Sigma Delta Chi. Office: Sta WCEV 5356 W Belmont Ave Chicago IL 60641

MIGDAL, STANLEY BENJAMIN, lawyer; b. Akron, Ohio, Mar. 12, 1932; s. Joseph and Sarah (Grubman) M.; m. Rhoda D. Mirman, June 6, 1954; children—Keith, Kyle, Kirk, Kerry. B.Sc., Ohio State U., 1954, LL.D., 1956. Bar: Ohio 1956. Assoc., Hinton & Landi, Akron, 1964—. Trustee Akron Jewish Ctr., 1969-70. Mem. Akron Bar Assn. (exec. com.), Ohio State Bar Assn. Home: 1769 Brookwood Dr Akron OH 44313 Office: 2500 1st Nat Tower 106 S Main St Akron OH 44308

MIHAILOVIC, BETTY LOU BONWELL, nurse educator; b. Chrisman, Ill., Nov. 17, 1937; d. Robert Bertram Bonwell and Katherine Carol (Hess) Bonwell Buchanan; m. Vladimir Mihailovic, Jan. 27, 1968 (div. May 1970); children—Jill Anne Thompson, Nena Carol. Diploma, LakeView Hosp., Danville, Ill., 1958; B., U. Ill.-Chgo., 1966; M., DePaul U., 1970. Registered nurse, Ill. Staff nurse LakeView Hosp., Danville, Ill., 1958-63; instr. nursing Danville Jr. Coll., 1963-65; tchr. nursing Chgo. Pub. Schs., 1966-68; instr. Mt. Sinai Hosp., Chgo., 1970; prof. nursing Kennedy King Coll., Chgo., 1970—, chmn. dept. nursing, 1983—. Served to maj. USAFR. Recipient Chief Nurse award USAF, 1975, Sr. Flight Nurse award USAF, 1984. Mem. Am. Nurses Assn., Nat. League Nursing, Res. Officers Assn. (treas. 1980), U. Ill. Alumni Assn., Aerospace Med. Assn., Assn. Mil. Surgeons of U.S., Air Force Assn. Republican. Mem. Soc. of Friends. Lodge: Order Eastern Star. Avocation: golf. Home: 1 Heatherwood Ct Indian Head Park IL 60525 Office: Kennedy King Coll 6800 S Wentworth Ave Chicago IL 60621

MIHALEVICH, LAWRENCE JAMES, pharmacist; b. Kansas City, Mo., Aug. 3, 1951; s. Doctor Richard Anthony Mihalevich and Cheryl Kathryn (Dillon) Goodnight; m. Christine Louise Smith, Oct. 23, 1976; children—Jamie Leigh, Nickolas Anthony. B.S. in Biology, Northeast Mo. State U., 1975; B.S. in Med. Tech., Kirksville Osteo. Hosp., 1976; B.S. in Pharmacy, U. Mo.-Kansas City, 1980. Lic. pharmacist, Iowa, Mo. Med. technologist Kirksville-Osteo. Hosp., Mo., 1976-77; pharmacist, mgr. The Medicine Store, Mt. Pleasant, Iowa, 1980-84; pharmacist, asst. mgr. K Mart Pharmacy, Burlington, Iowa, 1984-85; pharmacist mgr. Wal-Mart Pharmacy, Mt. Pleasant, Iowa, 1985—. Vice pres. Mt. Pleasant Jaycees, 1982-84, bd. dirs., 1981-82; bd. dirs. Nat. Kidney Found. of Iowa, 1982—. Mem. Nat. Assn. Retail Druggists, Iowa Pharmacy Assn. (del. 1983, 84) legis. com. 1983, 84), Mo. Acad. Sci. Presbyterian. Avocations: track sports; travel. Home: 910 Hill Ave Mt Pleasant IA 52641 Office: Wal-Mart Pharmacy US 218 and Maple Leaf Dr Mount Pleasant IA 52641

MIHALY, JANET LOUISE, entrepreneur; b. Camp Blanding, Fla., July 13, 1945; d. Harry Raymond and Mary Elizabeth (Rawdon) Harris Doyle; m. Robert Andrew Mihaly, Mar. 6, 1965 (div. July 1974); children—Elizabeth, Robert, September, Tara. B.A., Capital U., 1981. Owner Pandora Restaurant, Akron, Ohio, 1969-72; co-owner Mihaly Hauling Service, Akron, 1965-74, A.J. Rubbish Service, Akron, 1975-77; co-owner Green Mansions Statuary, Akron, 1975-81; sr. sales service coordinator for Cavalier, B.F. Goodrich, Akron, 1977—, co-instr. B.F. Goodrich Learning Ctr., Akron, 1980—; resume writer, career counselor, Akron, 1980—. Mem. Am. Mktg. Assn. (newsletter editor 1982-83). Home: 2116 Lee Dr Akron OH 44306 Office: BF Goodrich Bldg 25C Dept 0611 500 S Main St Akron OH 44306

MIHLBAUGH, ROBERT HOLLERAN, lawyer; b. Lima, Ohio, June 17, 1932; s. Edward P. and Mary Elizbeth May (Holleran) M.; m. Barbara Lee Synck; children—Robert E. H., Michael Patrick. A.B., Notre Dame U., 1954, J.D., 1957. Bar: Ohio, 1957. Legal asst. fed. judge, South Bend, Ind., 1957-59; trial lawyer Marathon Oil Co., Findlay, Ohio, 1959-64; sole practice, Lima, Ohio, 1964—. Author: Marketing Manual, 1960; Sale Leaseback Financing, 1961. Dem. state central committeeman, Ohio, 1966-80; sec. Ohio Dem. party, 1976; mem. nat. adv. bd. SBA, Washington, 1965. Mem. ABA, Am. Arbitration Assn., Ohio State Bar Assn. (life). Roman Catholic. Avocation: lectr. Queen Elizabeth II. Home: 1471 W Market Blvd Lima OH 45805 Office: Mihlbaugh Bldg Lima OH 45802

MIHM, MICHAEL M., judge U.S. Dist. Ct. (7th cir.) Ill., Peoria, 1982—. Office: US Dist Ct 216 Fed Bldg 100 NE Monroe Peoria IL 61602*

MIKKELSEN, NANCY RUSSELL, physician; b. Louisville, June 12, 1953; d. Earl Dessieux and Wilma Jean (Wagner) Russell; m. William Christian Mikkelsen, Dec. 31, 1977; 1 son, Michael Christian. B.A. in Psychology, U. Mo.-Kansas City, 1974, M.D., 1978. Intern, Truman Med. Ctr., Kansas City, Mo., 1979, resident, 1980-81; practice medicine specializing in internal medicine, North Kansas City, Mo., 1982—; mem. staff N. Kansas City Meml. Hosp. Mem. ACP, Mo. State Med. Assn., Clay-Platte County Med. Soc., Greater Kansas City Soc. Internists, Gladstone C. of C. Mem. Christian Ch. (Disciples of Christ). Home: 3905 NE 59th St Gladstone MO 64119 Office: 1500 NE Parvin Rd Kansas City MO 64117

MIKKELSON-LEE, RUTH ELAINE, university administrator; b. Pitts., Mar. 2, 1936; d. Eric Carl and Amelia Suzanne (Agle) Malte; children—Greg, Rick, Jeff. B.A., Allegheny Coll., 1958; M.A., U. Wis., 1963; Edn. Specialist, U. Kans., 1983. Tchr. Lutheran West High Sch., Rocky River, Ohio, 1958-61, Madison West High Sch., Wis., 1963-65; instr. English U. Kans., Lawrence, 1975-78, assoc. dir. residential programs, 1978—. Author: Contemporary Literature/Contemporary Problems 1973. Editor: Staff Resource Book, 1979—. Editor newsletter Hallways, 1979—. Pres. Good Shepherd Luth. Ch., Lawrence, 1971-72, 1974-75, PTA, Lawrence, 1978-79; den mother Cub Scouts, Lawrence, 1970-74. Recipient Pan-Hellenic Service award 1958. Mem. Am. Assn. Counseling & Devel., AAUW (Outstanding Sr. Woman 1958), Nat. Assn. Student Personnel Adminstrs., Kans. Assn. Student Personnel Adminstrs., Phi Delta Kappa.

MIKLICH, THOMAS ROBERT, paints and drugs company executive; b. Cleveland, Apr. 17, 1947; s. Joseph J. and Josephine (Kmet) M.; m. Patricia Ann Perhavec, Oct. 4, 1969; children—Jeffrey, Amy, Christopher, Mary Beth. B.S., Cleve., 1969, J.D., 1973. Bar: Ohio 1974; C.P.A., Ohio. Tax acct., various positions Sherwin-Williams Co., Cleve., 1969-75, corp. dir. of taxes, 1975-78, corp. sec., 1978-79, treas., 1979—. Treas. High Point Homeowners Assn., Strongsville, Ohio, 1984—. Mem. ABA, Ohio State Bar Assn., Ohio Soc. C.P.A.s, Am. Soc. C.P.A.s, Greater Cleve. Growth Assn., Cleve. Treas. Club, Fin. Execs. Inst., Nat. Assn. Corp. Treas. Republican. Roman Catholic. Clubs: Cleve. Athletic, Clevelander. Office: Sherwin Williams Co 101 Prospect Ave NW Cleveland OH 44115

MIKLOS, ATHENA PAULINE, business educator, property management company executive; b. Athens, Ohio, May 13, 1950; d. Mike J. and Rallia (Psaltakis) Chakiris; m. Robert R. Miklos, June 18, 1983. B. in Gen. Studies, Ohio U., 1972. Display coordinator Lerner Shops, Pitts., 1972-75, tng. supr., 1976-78; mgr. Ups and Downs, Pitts., 1975-76; city planner City of Athens, 1980-82; mem. faculty Hocking Tech. Coll., Nelsonville, Ohio, 1982—; property mgr. Phil Chakiris, Athens, 1982—, Cathy Antonopoulos, Athens, 1982-83; bus. adviser Beaver Industries, Nelsonville, 1983—; instr. Hocking Correctional Facility, Nelsonville, 1984—; guest lectr. Methodist Ch., The Plains, Ohio, 1985. Trustee, Athens County Tourism Bur., 1982—. Grantee Ohio Hist. Soc., 1981. Mem. Ohio Mktg. Mgmt. Educators, Beta Sigma Phi. Greek Orthodox. Avocations: photography; interior design; reading; antiques; auctions. Office: Hocking Tech Coll Route 1 Nelsonville OH 45764

MIKRUT, JOHN JOSEPH, JR., labor arbitrator, educator; b. Erie, Pa., Mar. 23, 1944; s. John Joseph and Helen Frances (Dorobiala) M.; B.S., Edinboro Coll., 1966; postgrad. U. Mass., 1966-68; Ed.D., U. Mo., Columbia, 1976; m. Lois Ann Leonard, Aug. 26, 1968. Intern edn. dept. United Steelworkers Am., Pitts., 1967-68; instr. labor studies Pa. State U., 1968-69; labor specialist, asso. prof. labor edn. U. Mo., Columbia, 1969—; labor arbitrator Nat. Rail Adjustment Bd.; mem. labor arbitration panels Fed. Mediation Conciliation Service, Nat. Mediation Bd., Am. Arbitration Assn. Chmn., City of Columbia Personnel Adv. Bd., 1976—; chmn. Columbia Mayor's Spl. Labor Negotiations Rev. Com. Mem. Nat. Acad. Arbitrators, Soc. Profls. Dispute Resolution, Iowa Pub. Employee Relations Bd., Kans. Pub. Employee Relations Bd., Ill. Edn. Employee Relations Bd., Univ. and Coll. Labor Edn. Assn., Indsl. Relations and Research Assn. Contbr. articles to profl. jours. Home: 2236 Country Ln Columbia MO 65201 Office: Dept Labor Edn Univ MO Columbia MO 65211

MILAM, HUGH HENRY, public relations executive, educator; b. Houston, Mar. 17, 1941; s. Hugh Henry and Rosalie Cornelia (McClamrock) M.; m. Carol Ann Marsh, Mar. 3, 1941; children—Melanie Lyn, Tod Warner. B.S., U. Houston, 1965; M.S., East Tex. State U., 1969; Ph.D., Tex. A&M U., 1975. Editor, Fort Bend Mirror, Rosenberg, Tex., 1962-65; pub. relations exec. LTV Electrosystems, Inc., Greenville & Dallas, 1967-71; dir. pub. relations Bee County Coll., Beeville, Tex., 1971-73; researcher Tex. A&M U., College Station, 1973-75; dir. pub. relations Dundalk Community Coll., Balt., 1975-76; asst. prof. journalism Ball State U., Muncie, Ind., 1976-79; assoc. dean, assoc. prof. journalism and mass communication Drake U., Des Moines, 1979—; v.p. Directions, Inc., 1980—; dir. Communications Research, LKC, Inc. Mem. Public Relations Soc. Am., Internat. Assn. Bus. Communicators, Am. Mktg. Assn. Methodist. Home: 4026 Kingman Blvd Des Moines IA 50311 Office: Dept Journalism Drake U Des Moines IA 50311

MILANOWSKI, HENRY MAX, guidance director, educator; b. East Detroit, Sept. 27, 1927; s. Paul George and Elizabeth Sophia (Doerflinger) M.; m. Carol Mae Anderson, July 23, 1955; children—Joel David, Susan Carol, James Henry. B.A. cum laude, Seattle Pacific U., 1959; M.A., Mich. State U., 1960. Staff customer service Detroit Edison Co., 1944-55; dir. of guidance, prof. Detroit Coll. Bus., Dearborn, Mich., 1962—; dir. family life Guardian Lutheran Ch., Dearborn, 1980—. Mem. Am. Assn. Counseling Devel., Mich. Edn. Assn., NEA, PTA (v.p. 1977-78, pres. 1979-80), Phi Theta Pi. Republican. Avocations: gardening; stamps; playing piano; traveling. Home: 710 Patterson Ct Inkster MI 48141

MILDREXLER, DONALD JOE, college dean; b. Cawker City, Kans., Dec. 17, 1934; s. Jospeh S. and Katherine B. (Smith) M.; m. Mella J. Zieganbalg, June 25, 1935; children—Donella J., Janella D. B.S., Ft. Hays State U., 1956, M.A., 1960. Dean of instrn. Colby Community Coll., Kans., 1976-79, dean admissions, 1979-81, dean community services, 1981—. Mem. Kans. Bd. Nursing, 1977-80. Mem. Kans. Adult Edn. Assn. (pres. 1981), Missouri Valley Adult Edn. Assn. (del. 1984), Am. Assn. Adult and Continuing Edn. Republican. Roman Catholic. Lodges: Lions, KC (Colby). Avocations: fishing; cards. Home: 1765 W 5th St Colby KS 67701 Office: 1255 S Range St Colby KS 67701

MILENKI, JANET CHESTELYNN, financial broker; b. Albany, Ky., Nov. 24, 1953; d. Kathleen (Stearns) Conner. Student, Purdue U. Vice pres. mktg. Brandon Polo Club, Fla., 1981-82; asst. Puller Mortgage, Indpls., 1982-83; pres., owner Excalibur Fin., New Castle, Ind., 1983—. Appointed mem. Ind. Venture Capital Conf., Indpls., 1983. Named Hon. Lt. Gov., Lt. Gov. Mutz of Ind., 1983. Mem. Nat. Assn. Women Bus. Owners, Network Women in Bus., Nat. Assn. Sec. Services, Internat. Enterpreneurs Assn., Delta Sigma Pi. Republican. Methodist. Clubs: Brandon Polo (Fla.); Ind. Sanyo Users (Chmn.) (Indpls.). Avocations: polo, business, fox-hunting, computers, airplanes. Home: PO Box 48 New Castle IN 47362 Office: 9247 N Meridian Suite 245 Indianapolis IN 46260

MILER, RONALD ORVAL, nursing administrator; b. Cherokee, Iowa, Apr. 1, 1947; s. Ronald O. and Frances Darlene (Shove) M.; m. Delight Miriam Vogel, Dec. 3, 1966; children—Ronald, Perry, Todd. Diploma, Jewish Hosp. Sch. Nursing, Cin., 1971; B.S. in Mgmt., Thomas More Coll., 1976; M.S. in Health Adminstrn., U. Cin., 1984. Staff devel. instr. Jewish Hosp. Cin., 1974-77, coordinator dept. edn. and staff devel., 1977-78, dir. med. and psychiat. nursing, 1978-81; v.p. patient care Good Samaritan Med. Ctr., Zanesville, Ohio, 1981—. Vice pres. Muskingum County chpt. Nat. Kidney Found., 1982-83, pres., 1983-84; bd. dirs. Nat. Council on Alcoholism Ohio, 1981-84; mem. St. Thomas Sch. Bd. Served with AUS, 1966-69; Vietnam. Mem. Am. Orgn. Nurse Execs., Ohio Soc. Hosp. Nursing Service Adminstrs., Am. Hosp. Assn., Ohio Hosp. Assn., Am. Coll. Hosp. Adminstrs., VFW. Lodges: Kiwanis, K.C. Office: 800 Forest Ave Zanesville OH 43701

MILES, ALFRED LEE, educator; b. Eaton, Ohio, Aug. 4, 1913; s. James Sampson and Grace Blanche (Bittner) M.; student Ohio State U., 1930-33, Sinclair Coll., 1945, Miami-Jacobs Coll., 1954-56; m. Margaret Lucille Saul, Mar. 18, 1936 (div. Mar. 1949); children—Ronald Lynn, Walter Whitney; m. 2d, Virginia Null Engelman, Feb. 24, 1951; children—Victoria Ellen, Kimber Lee, Bethany Laine, Christopher Kent; stepchildren—Dianne Engelman (Mrs. M. Douglas Fogle), Norbert Nicholas Engelman, Jr. Instr. pvt. courses in real estate prins. and real estate law, Dayton, Ohio, 1949—; instr. real estate Miami Jacobs Jr. Coll. Bus., 1983-85; instr. short courses Spl. Sessions Div. U. Dayton, 1971-77. Violinist, Dayton Civic Orch., 1927-29, Ohio State U. Symphony, 1930-33, Columbus Symphony, 1930-33. Named Ky. col. Mem. Internat. Platform Assn. Republican. Methodist. Club: Cincinnati. Home: 1629 Far Hills Ave Dayton OH 45419 Office: 2185 S Dixie Ave Dayton OH 45409

MILES, JAMES RICHARD, air force officer, lawyer; b. Dayton, Ohio, June 25, 1937; s. James Nelson and Bertha Marie (Grisso) M.; m. Peggy Ann Bandy, Sept. 19, 1959; 1 child, Elizabeth Ann. B.A., Ohio State U., 1959, J.D. summa cum laude, 1961; LL.M., U. Mich., 1973. Bar: Ohio 1961, U.S. Supreme Ct. 1980. Commd. 1st lt. U.S. Air Force, 1962, advanced through grades to col., 1981; judge advocate, Edwards, Calif., London, 1962-66, Nebr., Okinawa, Washington, 1968-78; staff judge advocate, Ankara, Turkey, 1978-79; sr. appellate judge Ct. of Review, Washington, 1979-82; staff judge advocate 13th Air Force, Clark, Philippines, 1982—; atty. Smith & Schnacke, Dayton, Ohio, 1966-68. Author: International Law-Conduct of Armed Conflict and Air Operations, 1976. Contbr. articles to profl. jours. Mem. Am. Soc. Internat. Law, Fed. Bar Assn., Ohio Bar Assn. Office: 13th Air Force PACAF APO San Francisco CA 96408

MILES, KIMBERLY COLGATE, law educator; b. Wilmington, Del., Oct. 4, 1954; d. Paul A. and Betty S. (Adams) C.; m. Gordon J. Miles, Nov. 4, 1947; children—Rodney J., Cheryl A. B.A., Mich. State U., 1975; J.D., Cooley Law Sch., 1978; postgrad. Wayne State U., 1984—. Bar: Mich. 1979, U.S. Tax Ct. 1980. Staff atty. Brown & Winckler, Lansing, Mich., 1978-79; tax atty. Kimberly C. Miles P.C., Dimondale, Mich., 1979-83; adj. prof. Cooley Law Sch., Lansing, Mich., 1980-83, asst. prof., 1983—. Recipient Am. Jurisprudence awards, 1977, 78. Republican. Methodist. Home: 750 Waverly Rd Dimondale MI 48821 Office: Cooley Law Sch 217 S Capitol St Lansing MI 48933

MILES, MICHAEL ARNOLD, food company executive; b. Chgo., June 22, 1939; s. Arnold and Alice (Morrissey) M.; m. Pamela L. Miles; children—Michael Arnold, Christopher. B.S., Northwestern U., 1961. Various mgmt. positions to v.p., account supr. Leo Burnett Co., Inc., 1961-71; with Heublein, Inc., 1971-82, sr. v.p. mktg. Ky. Fried Chicken, 1971-72, v.p. group exec. grocery products, 1972-75, internat., 1975-77, v.p. group exec., chmn. foodservice and franchise group Ky. Fried Chicken, 1977-81, sr. v.p. foods, Louisville, 1981-82; pres., chief operating officer Kraft, Inc., Glenview, Ill., 1982—; dir. Capital Holding Corp., Citizens Fidelity Corp., Dart & Kraft, Inc. Bd. dirs. Lyric Opera Chgo.; mem. adv. council J.L. Kellog Grad. Sch. Mgmt., Northwestern U., Evanston. Office: Kraft Inc Kraft Ct Glenview IL 60025

MILES, RUSSELL THEODORE, JR., life insurance company executive; b. St. Louis, Mar. 8, 1937; s. Russell Theodore and Lillie Josephine (Gutman) M.; m. Mary Magdalene Rice, Oct. 31, 1958; children—Douglas Franklin, Daniel Evans. B.S.B.A., U. Ark., 1959; M.B.A., Harvard U., 1961. Supr. policy claims Mut. Benefit Ins. Co., Newark, 1961-66; asst. to v.p. claims Am. Nat. Ins. Co., Galveston, Tex., 1966-69; v.p. Quaker Life Ins. Co., Tulsa, 1969-79; sr. v.p. adminstrn. Cologne Life Reins. Co., Stamford, Conn., 1979-83; exec. v.p. Charter Nat. Life Ins. Co., St. Louis, 1983—. Served with USNR, 1955-63. Mem. Ins. Accts. and Statis. Assn., Internat. Claims Assn., Am. Soc. Personnel Adminstrs. Republican. Presbyterian. Office: Charter Nat Life Ins Co 8301 Maryland Ave Saint Louis MO 63105

MILES, SUE, childhood development educator, guidance consultant; b. Henderson, Tex., Oct. 5, 1940; d. Charles W. and Clara W. Kelty; m. George D. Miles, Aug. 26, 1961 (div. July 1973); 1 son, Joel Scott; m. Roger Kern, Jan. 1985. B.S. in Edn., Sam Houston U., 1961; M.Ed., U. Houston, 1964; postgrad. Tex. A&M U., 1967, No. Ill. U., 1976—, Northwestern U., 1975, Harvard U., 1977. Cert. tchr., Tex., Ill. Elem. tchr. Deepwater Sch., Deer Park Sch. Dist., Pasadena, Tex., 1961-63, 68-73, substitute tchr., 1963, 64; part-time instr. Lamar U., Beaumont, Tex., 1972-73; tchr. 1st and 2d grades Hinsdale (Ill.) Sch. Dist. 181, 1973-75; coordinator, instr. early childhood devel. program Waubonsee Community Coll., Sugar Grove, Ill., 1975—, coll. mgr. Waubonsee Coll. Lab. Sch., sponsor student service club; mem. Mid-Valley Vocat. Adv. Com.; mem. adv. com. Waubonsee Child Devel. Ctr.; cons. in field. Mem. adv. com. Family Focus, Indian Valley Vocat. Ctr., Aurora Home Econs. Adv. Bd.; mem. child care com. United Way. Recipient Outstanding Service awards Waubonsee Community Coll. Child Devel. Club, 1975-79. Mem. Nat. Assn. for Edn. of Young Children, Chgo. Assn. for Edn. of Young Children, Am. Fedn. Tchrs., Tex. State Tchrs. Assn., Fox Valley Child Care Com., Nat. Orgn. Future Women, Downers Grove (Ill.) Jaycee-ettes, Zeta Tau Alpha. Episcopalian. Author several booklets in field. Home: 959 Meadowlawn St Downers Grove IL 60516 Office: Waubonsee Community Coll Rt 47 at Harter Rd Sugar Grove IL 60554

MILES, WENDELL A., federal judge; b. Holland, Mich., Apr. 17, 1916; s. Fred T. and Dena Del (Alverson) M.; A.B., Hope Coll., 1938; M.A., U. Wyo., 1939; J.D., U. Mich., 1942; m. Mariette Bruckert, June 8, 1946; children—Lorraine Miles Rector, Michelle Miles Kopinski, Thomas Paul. Admitted to Mich. bar; partner firm Miles & Miles, Holland, 1948-53, Miles, Mika, Meyers, Beckett & Jones, Grand Rapids, Mich., 1961-70; pros. atty. County of Ottawa (Mich.), 1949-53; U.S. dist. atty. Western Dist. Mich., 1953-60, U.S. dist. judge, 1974—, chief judge, 1979—; circuit judge 20th Jud. Circuit Ct. Mich., 1970-74; instr. Hope Coll., 1948-53, adj. prof., from 1981; instr. Am. Inst. Banking, 1953-60; mem. Mich. Higher Edn. Commn., from 1978. Pres., Holland Bd. Edn., 1952-63. Served to capt. U.S. Army, 1942-47. Fellow Am. Bar Assn.; mem. Mich., Fed., Ottawa County bar assns., Am. Judicature Soc. Lodges: Rotary, Torch, Masons. Office: US Dist Ct 482 Fed Bldg 110 Michigan St NW Grand Rapids MI 49503*

MILIN, ELAINE LOIS, jewelry business executive; b. Chgo., July 20, 1930; d. Philip K. and Rose (Beskin) Weisman; m. Norman Zeff Milin, Oct. 21, 1950; children—Michael J., Sandra G. Milin Charak, Kenneth N., Steven R. Student U. Ill., 1948-50, Roosevelt U., 1950. Owner, operator The Consortium, Chgo.; midwest cons. on antique jewelry appraisals Internat. Soc. Appraisers, 1983—. Mem. Nat. Assn. Dealers in Antiques. Jewish. Avocation: jewelry design. Office: The Consortium 5 S Wabash Suite 1210 Chicago IL 60603

MILKS, DONALD EARLE, civil engineering educator; b. Dunkirk, N.Y., June 15, 1932; m.; 2 children. B.C.E., Clarkson Univ., 1954; M.S., U. Ariz., 1964, Ph.D., 1966. Registered profl. engr., Ariz., Ohio. Structural designer Am. Bridge, Elmira, N.Y., 1954-55; project engr. on climatic testing U.S. Army Ordnance Corps, Yuma, Ariz., 1955-57; grad. asst., instr. U. Ariz., Tucson, 1957-65; prof., chmn. dept. civil engring. Ohio No. U., Ada, 1965—; cons. Ridge and Assocs., Findlay, Ohio, Kenton Structural, Kenton, Rasinger Engring., Lima, Ohio, Rust Engring., Pitts., Kohli & Kaliher, Lima, Brewer and Assocs., Lima, Internat. Car, Kenton, New Knoxville Tile and Cement, Ohio, Auglaize County Engr., Wapokoneta, Ohio, Medlaw, Ottawa, Ohio. Precinct committeeman Rep. party, 1976—. Danforth assoc., 1978; Exxon Found. grantee, 1976-77. Mem. ASCE (pres. Toledo sect., pres. Ohio council, engr. of yr. Toledo sect.), Am. Soc. Engring. Edn., Am. Concrete Inst., Am. Inst. Steel Constrn., Lima Soc. Profl. Engrs., Sigma Xi, Chi Epsilon, Tau Beta Pi, Omicron Delta Kappa, Phi Eta Sigma. Avocations: handball; golf; tennis. Home: 701 S Main St Ada OH 45810 Office: Dept Civil Engring Ohio No U Ada OH 45810

MILLAR, ALLEN ROBERT, college adminstrator; b. Ravinnia, S.D., Dec. 5, 1922; s. George Howard and Beulah Lavonne (Wilhelm) M.; m. Edith Caroline Andrews; children—Thomas Allen, Carolyn Edith. B.S., Chadron State Coll., 1947; M.A., U. No. Colo., 1951; Ed.D., U. Nebr., 1956. Pres. So. State Coll., Springfield, S.D., 1962-71, Dakota State Coll., Madison, 1971-72; prof. edn. U. S.D., Vermillion, 1972-74; cons. U. Nebr., Lincoln, 1974-78; dean instrn. McCook Community Coll., Nebr., 1978—. Contbr. articles to profl. jours. Served to 1st lt. U.S. Army, 1941-46. Mem. NEA, Assn. Higher Edn., Am. Assn. Sch. Adminstrs., Nebr. Sch. Adminstrs. Assn., McCook C. of C., Phi Delta Kappa. Republican. Methodist. Club: Kiwanis (pres. 1981-82). Lodges: Masons (master 1953-54), Eastern Star (assoc. patron 1952-53). Avocations: hunting, fishing, classical, semi-classical and country music. Home: 910 W 10th St McCook NE 69001 Office: McCook Community Coll 1205 E 3d St McCook NE 69001

MILLARD, CHEEDLE WILLIAM, management educator, former computer company executive; b. Heavener, Okla., Sept. 22, 1937; s. Cheedle O. and Ocie E. (Ollar) M.; children—David C., Jeffrey L. B.A., Eastern Mont. Coll., 1969; M.A., U. Oreg., 1970; Ph.D., U. Nebr., 1974. Instr. mgmt. Idaho State U., Pocatello, 1970-72, U. Nebr., Lincoln, 1972-74; asst. prof. U. Tex., Dallas, 1974-77; assoc. prof., chmn. mgmt. Iowa State U., Ames, 1977-82; vis. assoc. prof. U. Hawaii, Honolulu, 1983; prof. So. Meth. U., 1983—; cons. in mgmt., 1970—. Served to sgt. USAF, 1955-59. U.S. Dept. Labor grantee, 1972-74. Mem. Acad. Mgmt., Am. Inst. Decision Scis., Am. Psychol. Assn. Contbr. articles to profl. jours.

MILLER, ANGELA PEREZ, school administrator; b. Chgo., Oct. 1, 1936; d. Jesse and Emily (Ibarra) P.; m. John F. Miller, May 6, 1961 (div.); 1 son, Dion. B.A., U. Ill., 1958; M.A., Northeastern Ill. U., 1975; M.Ed., De Paul U., 1984. Cert. elem. tchr., Ill. Tchr. Chgo. pub. schs., 1962-70; exchange tchr. Mexico City schs., 1970-71; asst. prin. Burns Elem. Sch., Chgo., 1972-77; asst. prin. Benito Juarez High Sch., Chgo., 1977—. Mem. ELValor, Inc., De Paul U. adv. com. on Hispanic affairs. Mem. Assn. Supervision and Curriculum Devel., Am. Ednl. Research Assn., Hispanic Alliance for Career Enhancement. Office: 2150 S Laflin Chicago IL 60608

MILLER, ARTHUR HAWKS, JR., librarian, consultant; b. Kalamazoo, Mar. 15, 1943; s. Arthur Hawks and Eleanor (Johnson) M.; m. Janet Carol Schroeder, June 11, 1967; children—Janelle Aileen, Andrew Hawks. A.B., Kalamazoo Coll., 1965; student U. Caen, Calvados, France, 1963-64; A.M. in English, U. Chgo., 1966, A.M. in Librarianship, 1968; Ph.D., Northwestern U., 1973. Reference librarian Newberry Library, Chgo., 1966-69, asst. librarian pub. services, 1969-72; coll. librarian Lake Forest (Ill.) Coll., 1972—; mem. Ill. Library Computer System Policy Council, Chgo., 1982—. Pres. Lake Forest-/Lake Bluff Hist. 1982-85; pres. Lake County Hist. Soc., 1985—. Mem. ALA (chmn. history sect. 1982-83), chmn.-elect coll. sect. 1985—), Melville Soc. Am., Ill. Library Assn., U. Chgo. Grad. Library Sch. Alumni Assn. (pres. 1983-85). Presbyterian. Club: Caxton (pres. 1978-80) (Chgo.). Home: 169 Wildwood Rd Lake Forest IL 60045 Office: Lake Forest Coll Donnelley Library Lake Forest IL 60045

MILLER, BEN, justice Illinois Supreme Court; b. Springfield, Ill., Nov.5, 1936; s. Clifford and Mary (Luthyens) M. B.A., So. Ill. U., 1958; J.D., Vanderbilt U., 1961. Bar: Ill. Ptnr., Olsen, Cantrill & Miller, Springfield, 1961-72; sole practice, Springfield, 1972-76; judge Circuit Ct. 7th Jud. Circuit, Springfield, 1976-82, presiding judge criminal div., 1976-81, chief circuit judge, 1981-82; judge Appellate Ct. Ill. 4th Dist., 1982-84; justice Ill. Supreme Ct., 1984—; adj. prof. So. Ill. U. Sch. Medicine, 1974—; mem. Gov.'s Adv. Council Crimnial Justice Legis., 1977—. Mem. editorial rev. bd. Illinois Civil Practice Before Trial, Illinois Civil Trial Practice. Pres. Springfield Mental Health Assn., 1969-71; bd. dirs. Aid to Retarded Citizens, 1977-80; mem. Gov.'s Ann. Prayer Breakfast Com., 1976—. Served to lt. USNR, 1966-69. Mem. ABA, Am. Judicature Soc., Ill. Bar Assn., Ill. Judges Assn., Sangamon County Bar Assn., Greater Springfield C. of C. (pres. 1973-74), Am. Bus. Club. Republican. Office: 509 S 6th St Suite 435 Springfield IL 62701

MILLER, BUCK LEE, photographer; b. Freeport, Ill., Nov. 19, 1937; s. Roy and Ruth (Giesey) M.; m. Beverley Jo Gross, Feb. 28, 1960; 1 dau., Lori Jo. B.S., So. Ill. U., 1964; postgrad. Marquette U., U. Wis., 1975. Photographer, Milw. Jour.-Sentinel, 1964-76; freelance photographer, Milw., 1976—; photographs appearing in Life, Time, Newsweek, Fortune, Forbes; now working in corp. and advt. photography. Instr. So. Ill. U., Carbondale, summer 1975, Milw. Area Tech. Coll., 1976. Served with USAF, 1955-59. Recipient award UN Environ. Contest, 1975; 1st place feature photography award Nat. Press Photographers Assn., 1973; photography awards Milw. Press Club, 1971-77; Honor award Indsl. Photography, 1985; Milw. Ad Club award, 1985. Mem. Am. Soc. Mag. Photographers, Wis. News Photographers. Democrat. Photographic murals St. Francis Hosp., Milw., Northwestern Mut. Life, Milw. Office: PO Box 33 Milwaukee WI 53201

MILLER, CALLIX EDWIN, manufacturing company executive; b. South Bend, Ind., Mar. 27, 1924; s. Callix Edwin and Marguerite Cash (Sweeney) M.; m. Theresa Ann Pirchio, June 25, 1949; children—Madeline, Callix, John, David, Thomas. B.S. in Archtl. Engring., U. Notre Dame, 1949. Mgr. engring. Internat. Mining and Chem. Corp., Chgo., 1951-61; exec. dir. Sperry Rand Corp., N.Y.C., 1961-64; v.p. Internat. Minerals & Chem. Corp., Chgo., 1964-72; v.p. Assocs. Corp. N.Am., Dallas, 1972-78; corp. v.p. tech. resources Clark Equipment Co., Buchanan, Mich., 1978—. Bd. dirs. Chgo. Area council Boy Scouts Am., 1967-70, Alexian Bros. Hosp., Chgo., 1966-68. Served with USNR, 1943-45. Mem. AIA, ASCE, Soc. Am. Mil. Engrs., Am. Concrete Inst. Republican. Roman Catholic. Clubs: Knollwood Country; Northbrook (Ill.) Sport; Faculty (U. Notre Dame). Lodges: Elks, K.C. Home: 16174 Baywood Ln Granger IN 46530 Office: Corp Office Circle Dr Buchanan MI 49107

MILLER, CECELIA ELEANOR LOTKO (MRS. GEORGE E. CHAMBERS), physician; b. Chgo., Oct. 24, 1917; d. Joseph S. and Zofia H. (Baizer) Lotko; student Northwestern U., 1945-47; B.S., U. Ill., 1949, M.D., 1951; m. James R. Miller, Sept. 3, 1938 (div. 1958); 1 dau., Josephine Ann (Mrs. John E. Mitchell); m. 2d, George E. Chambers, Dec. 5, 1970; stepchildren—Ronald, Lawrence, Leon, Marilyn (Mrs. John Raglione). Intern, Cook County Hosp., Chgo., 1951-52, resident, 1952; resident Hines (Ill.) VA Hosp., 1953-54; practice medicine, specializing in anesthesiology medicine, Hammond, Ind., 1955, Chgo., 1956-77, specializing in phys. medicine, Oak Lawn, Ill., 1982—; med. adviser Argonaut Ins. Co., Chgo., 1976-82. Mem. Field Mus. Natural History, Art Chgo., Chgo. Zool. Soc. Chgo.; mem. president's council U. Ill., 1983—. Fellow Am. Coll. Anesthesiologists (ret.); mem. AMA (ret.), Am. Med. Women's Assn., Ill., Chgo. med. socs., Am., Ill., Chgo. socs. anesthesiologists, Hines Surg. Soc., Cook County Hosp. Interns and Residents Alumni Assn., U. Ill. Alumni Assn., Dean's Club U. Ill. Coll. Medicine (charter), Alpha Epsilon Iota, Alpha Sigma Lambda. Home: 3464 Golfview Dr Hazel Crest IL 60429 Office: 10522 S Cicero Ave Oak Lawn IL 60453

MILLER, CHARLES PETER, state senator Iowa; b. Harbor Beach, Mich., Apr. 29, 1918; s. William H. and Anna (Eppenbrock) M.; student Burlington (Iowa) Community Coll., 1947-48; grad. Palmer Coll. Chiropractic, Davenport, Iowa, 1952; m. Virginia Mae Ferrington, Aug. 3, 1946; children—Charles, David, Steven, Dennis, Evelyn, Scot. Practice chiropractic, Burlington, 1952—; mem. Iowa Ho. of Reps. from Des Moines County, 1962-70, speaker pro-tem, 1965-66; mem. Iowa Senate from 30th Dist., 1970—, pres. protem, 1983-85. Mem. exec. bd. S.E. Iowa council Boy Scouts Am., 1956—. Served with USNR, 1940-46. Recipient Fellow award Palmer Acad. Chiropractic, 1966; Silver Beaver award Boy Scouts Am., 1958. Mem. Internat. Chiropractors Assn. (1st v.p. 1965; Fellowship award 1969), Chiropractic Soc. Iowa (pres. 1956-60, mem. bd. 1960-76), Am. Legion, VFW. Democrat. Lion, Eagle, Elk, K.C. Home: 801 High St Burlington IA 52601 Office: 701 Jefferson St Burlington IA 52601

MILLER, CLARENCE E., congressman; b. Lancaster, Ohio, Nov. 1, 1917; hon. degree Rio Grande Coll.; m. Helen M. Brown; children—Ronald, Jacqueline (Mrs. Thomas Williams). Mem. City Council, Lancaster, 1957-63; mayor, Lancaster, 1963-65; mem. 90th to 99th congresses from 10th Ohio Dist. Bd. dirs. Fairfield County chpt. A.R.C., YMCA. Hon. mem. Ohio Valley Health Services Found.; hon. alumnus Ohio U. mem. coms. on appropriations. Republican. Methodist. Lodge: Elks. Address: 2208 Rayburn House Office Bldg Washington DC 20215*

MILLER, CLIFFORD HARRY, dentist, educator, administrator; b. Chgo., Dec. 9, 1932; s. James V. and Hazel (Smith) M.; m. Ann Cannon, Mar. 29, 1974; children—James, Celia. D.D.S., Northwestern U., 1957. Lic. dentist, Ill. Instr., Northwestern U. Dental Sch., Chgo., 1959-60, asst. prof., 1960-62, assoc. prof., 1962-65, prof., 1965—, assoc. dean adminstrv. affairs, 1972—, dir. dental aux. utilization program, 1967-71, chmn. dept. operative dentistry, 1969-72; former mem. bd. exam. dentists for Civil Service Appt., former counselor Chgo. Dental Assts. Assn., former cons. Operative Sect., Nat. Bd. Dental Examiners, 1969-75; past chmn. Operative sect. ADA Council on Sci. Sessions; mem. subcom. MD 156 Council on Dental Materials, Instruments and equipment; mem. expert panel Prepaid Programs Dept. Pub. Aid. Former editor Dental Students Mag.; assoc. editor Jour Operative Dentistry; mem. editorial bd. Jour. Dental Edn.; cons. Jour. ADA. Contbr. articles to profl. jours. Served to lt. USN, 1957-59. Recipient Northwestern Alumni Service award, 1970; Northwestern Merit award, 1980. Fellow Am. Coll. Dentists, Internat. Coll. Dentists; mem. ADA, Ill. State Dental Soc., Chgo. Dental Soc., Am. Acad. Restorative Dentistry, Acad. Operative Dentistry (bd. dirs., membership com.), Am. Acad. Gold Foil Operators (pres. 1974, mem. editorial bd.), Internat. Assn. Dental Research, G.V. Black Soc. (pres. 1975), Dental Alumni Assn. (sec.-treas. 1966-69), John Evans Soc., Odontographic Soc., Am. Assn. Dental Schs. (chmn. operative sect. 1980-81), Am. Assn. Dental Insultants, Omicron Kappa Upsilon, Xi Psi Phi. Lodges: Masons, Rotary. Office: Northwestern Univ Dental Sch 240 E Huron St Chicago IL 60611

MILLER, CURTIS WAYNE, biomedical engineer; b. Vancouver, Wash., Dec. 11, 1948; s. Eldon W. and Ruth Miller; m. H. Melinda Garcia, Apr. 16, 1977; 1 son, Adrian Alan. Student Area Eleven Community Coll., Ankeny, Iowa, 1974-76. Owner, mgr. Celestial Leather, Des Moines, 1973-74; mgr. Blind Munchies Deli, Des Moines, 1973-74; dialysis technician Iowa Luth. Hosp., Des Moines, 1974-76; dir. tech. services West Suburban Kidney Ctr., Oak Park, Ill., 1977—; asst. v.p. Continental Health Care Ltd., Oak Park, 1981—; lectr. in field. Mem. Nat. Assn. Nephrology Technologists (pres.), Assn. Advancement of Med. Instrumentation. Contbr. articles to profl. jours.; designer in field.

MILLER, DAN LEE, educational administrator, writer; b. Aurora, Ill., July 6, 1948; s. Paul Albert and Shirley May (Beatus) M.; m. Maria Regina Montopoli, Aug. 13, 1978; children—Derek Joseph, Adam Paul. B.S., Northwestern U., 1970; M.S., Northern Ill. U., 1972, Ed.D., 1982. English tchr. Sch. Dist. #200, Wheaton, Ill., 1970-77; dean of students Sch. Dist. #219, Skokie, Ill., 1977-79; asst. prin. Sch. Dist. U-46, Elgin, Ill., 1979-82; prin. Sch. Dist. #60, Waukegan, Ill., 1982—. Author: Truancy: The First Step Toward Failure, 1982, Snowballs and Sinners, 1984. Mem. Nat. Assn. of Secondary Sch. Prins., Nat. Org. of Legal Problems of Edn., Assn. for

Supervision and Curriculum Devel., Assn. of Ill. Sch. Prins., Ill. High Sch. Assn. Lodge: Moose. Avocations: reading; writing; educational research; officiating wrestling; racquetball. Home: 1032 Borden Dr Roselle IL 60172 Office: Thomas Jefferson Jr High Sch 600 S Lewis Ave Waukegan IL 60085

MILLER, DAVID PAUL, insurance company executive; b. Buffalo, July 26, 1947; s. Alfred and Edythe Clara (Nevinger) M.; m. Georgianna Losaw, June 8, 1969. A.A., Jr. Coll. Albany, 1969; B.A. in Polit. Sci., SUNY-Albany, 1971; M.S. in Spl. Edn., Rehab., U. Tenn., 1974. Cert. disability examiner. Claim adjudicator State N.Y., N.Y.C., 1971-73, trainer, supr., 1973-75; quality assurance supr., State of Wis., Madison, 1975-78; supr., systems analyst Allstate Ins. Co., Northbrook, Ill., 1978-81; systems analyst Zurich Ins., Schaumburg, Ill., 1981-83, asst. mgr., 1983—. Collector, Palatine Twp., 1985—; sch. trustee Palatine Twp. Sch., Palatine, Ill., 1981—; precinct capt. Palatine Twp. Republicans, Rolling Meadows, Ill., 1980—; alderman candidate Madison City Council, 1977. Named Profl. of Yr., Empire State Assn. Disability Examiners, 1974. Mem. Assn. Systems Mgmt. (treas. 1983—), Nat. Assn. Disability Examiners, Chgo. Claim Assn. (conf. sem. chmn. 1981-82). Club: Ro-Meds (Rolling Meadows)(v.p. 1981—). Lodge: Masons (worshipful master 1984—). Avocations: bowling, gardening. Home: 2306 Sigwalt Rolling Meadows IL 60008 Office: Zurich Ins Cos 231 Martingale St Schaumburg IL 60196

MILLER, DONALD CLINTON, international marketing executive; b. Covington, Ky., Jan. 31, 1945; s. Martin William and Margaret Evelyn (Davis) M.; m. Johanna Maginn, July 1, 1972; 1 child, Geoffrey Denzil. B.S. in Chemistry, U. Cin., 1967, M.S. in Analytical Chemistry, 1970; M.B.A. in Mktg., Xavier U., Cin., 1975. Analytical chemist Emery Industries (now Emery Chems. div. Nat. Distillers and Chem. Corp.), Cin., 1967-70, tech. service rep., 1970-73, group leader resins research and devel., 1973-75, customer service and devel. exec. for resins, profit and loss group, 1975-77, area mgr. Europe, Africa, Near and Middle East, Australia, N.Z., 1977—. Pres., bd. dirs. Today Homes Homeowners Assn., Fairfield, Ohio, 1977-83; sec. bd. dirs. Emery Employees Fed. Credit Union, Cin., 1983—. Republican. Presbyterian. Avocations: snow skiing, cmputer programming, tutoring. Home: 7367 Lake Lakota Circle West Chester OH 45069 Office: Emery Chems Div Nat Distillers and Chem Corp 11501 Northlake Dr Cincinnati OH 45249

MILLER, EDWIN ERNEST, school administrator, athletic coach; b. Bonilla, S.D., Aug. 20, 1942; s. Glenn Harry and Vera Bella (Smith) M.; m. Paulette Marie Jablenski, Jan. 20, 1968; children—Susan, Tracey, Stephan, Mary. B.S., Valley City State Coll., 1965; M.S., No. State Coll., 1969, M.S., 1971. Cert. sch. adminstr. Tchr., coach Beach High Sch., N.D., 1965-68; counselor, coach Ipswich High Sch., S.D., 1968-71, prin., coach, 1971—. Recipient Nominee: Man of Year award Comml. Club, 1984. Mem. S.D. Assn. Secondary Sch. Prins. (state regional dir. 1982-84), S.D. High Sch. Coaches Assn. (state basketball dir. 1983-84, Nominee: Coach of Year 1983, 84, Nominee: Dist. VI Coach of Year 1984), Nat. Fedn. Interscholastic Coaches Assn. Republican. Methodist. Club: Country (Ipswich) (bd. dirs.). Lodges: Elks (ambassador), Lions (v.p. 1980—). Avocations: hunting, fishing. Home: 209 11 Ipswich SD 57451 Office: Ipswich High Sch Box 306 Ipswich SD 57451

MILLER, ELIZABETH CAVERT, oncology educator, research laboratory administrator; b. Mpls., May 2, 1920; d. William Lane and Mary Elizabeth (Mead) Cavert; m. James Alexander Miller, Aug. 30, 1942; children—Linda Ann, Helen Louise. B.S., U. Minn., 1941; M.S., U. Wis., 1943, Ph.D., 1945; D.Sc. (hon.), Med. Coll. Wis., 1982. Instr. to assoc. prof. oncology U. Wis. Med. Ctr., 1946-69, prof., 1969—; assoc. dir. McArdle Lab. for Cancer Research, U. Wis., Madison, 1973—; Wis. Alumni Research Found. prof. oncology U. Wis., 1980—, Van Rensselaer Potter prof. oncology, 1982—. Assoc. editor Cancer Research, 1957-62. Contbr. articles on chem. carcinogenesis and microsomal oxidations to profl. jours. Recipient (with J.A. Miller) Langer-Teplitz award for Cancer Research Ann Langer Cancer Research Found., 1962, Lucy Wortham James award for Cancer Research James Ewing Soc., 1965, Bertner award M.D. Anderson Hosp. and Tumor Inst., 1971, Wis. div. award Am. Cancer Soc., 1973, Outstanding Achievement award U. Minn., 1973, Papanicolaou award for Cancer Research Papanicolaou Cancer Research Inst., Miami, Fla., 1975, Rosenstiel award for Basic Med. Scis. Brandeis U., 1976, Nat. award Am. Cancer Soc., 1977, Bristol-Myers award in Cancer Research, 1978, Gairdner Found. Ann. award, 1978, Founders award Chem. Industry Inst. Toxicology, 1978, Prix Griffuel Assn. pour Developpement de Recherche sur Cancer, 1978, 3M Life Sci. award Fedn. Am. Socs. Exptl. Biology, 1979, Freedman award N.Y. Acad. Sci., 1979, Mott award Gen. Motors Cancer Research Found., 1980. Fellow Am. Acad. Arts and Scis., Wis. Acad. Scis., Arts and Letters; mem. Nat. Acad. Sci., Am. Assn. Cancer Research, Am. Soc. Biol. Chemists, Japanese Cancer Soc. (hon.). Home: 5517 Hammersley Rd Madison WI 53711 Office: U Wis McArdle Lab Madison WI 53706

MILLER, ELIZABETH JANE, material administrator; b. French Lick, Ind., Sept. 11, 1951; d. John Thomas and Mary Inez (Stewart) Rector; m. Steven Craig Miller, Apr. 17, 1971 (div.); children—Heidi, Heath. Student pub. schs., Richmond, Ind. Aide, Reid Mem. Hosp., Richmond, 1970-71; nurse's aide Colonial Manor Nursing Home, Bowling Green, Ky., 1971-72; inst. technician St. Anthony Hosp., St. Petersburg, Fla., 1973-75; technician Met. Gen. Hosp., St. Petersburg, 1977; sr. inst. technician Med. Ctr. Hosp., Largo, Fla., 1978-81; sterile supply supr. Terre Haute (Ind.) Regional Hosp., 1981-84; materials mgr. Rector Engring. and Devel. Corp., New Castle, Ind., 1984—. Mem. Am. Soc. Hosp. Central Service Personnel. Home: 3004 Hillcrest Dr New Castle IN 47362 Office: Rector Engring and Devel Corp 1851 Troy Ave New Castle IN 47362

MILLER, ERIC ARNOLD, music educator; b. Knoxville, Tenn., Mar. 5, 1943; s. Arthur A. and Florence J. (Gattis) M. B.S. in Music Edn., N.E. Mo. State U., 1965, M.A. in Music, 1966. Dir. vocal music Beecher Jr. High Sch., Hazel Park, Mich., 1965-68, Wilfred Webb Jr. High Sch., Ferndale, Mich., 1968-72, Hazel Park (Mich.) High Sch., 1972-77, United Oaks and Lee O. Clark Elem. Schs., Hazel Park, 1978—. Named Outstanding Young Educator, Hazel Park Jaycees, 1975. Mem. Assn. for Supervision and Curriculum Devel., Mich. Edn. Assn., Hazel Park Edn. Assn. (mem. exec. bd. 1979—), Mich. Music Edn. Assn., Mich. Vocal Dirs. Assn., NEA. Presbyterian. Composer: (choral) Our Time Will Come, 1975. Home: 1717 Gardenia Apt 4 Royal Oak MI 48067 Office: 23126 Hughes St Hazel Park MI 48030

MILLER, EUGENE, corporation executive, educator; b. Chgo., Oct. 6, 1925; s. Harry and Fannie (Prosterman) M.; B.S., Ga. Inst. Tech., 1945; A.B. magna cum laude, Bethany Coll., 1947, LL.D. (hon.), 1969; diploma Oxford (Eng.) U., 1947; M.S. in Journalism, Columbia, 1948; M.B.A., NYU, 1959; m. Edith Sutker, Sept. 23, 1951 (div. Sept. 1965); children—Ross, Scott, June; m. Thelma Gottlieb, Dec. 22, 1965; stepchildren—Paul Gottlieb, Alan Gottlieb. Reporter, then city editor Greensboro (N.C.) Daily News, 1948-52; S.W. bur. chief Bus. Week mag., Houston, 1952-54, assoc. mng. editor, N.Y.C., 1954-60; dir. pub. affairs and communications McGraw-Hill, Inc., 1960-63, v.p., 1963-68; v.p. pub. relations and investor relations, exec. com. N.Y. Stock Exchange, N.Y.C., 1968-70; sr. v.p., 1970-73; sr. v.p. CNA Fin. Corp., Chgo., 1973-75; v.p. USG Corp., 1977-82, sr. v.p., 1982-85, exec. v.p., chief fin. officer, 1985—, mem. mgmt. com.; cons. to sec. commerce, 1961-66; adj. prof. mgmt. Grad. Sch. Bus. Adminstrn., NYU, 1963—; prof. bus. adminstrn. Fordham U. Grad. Sch. Bus. Adminstrn., 1969—; chmn., prof. finance Northeastern Ill. U., 1975—. lectr. econs. pub. relations to bus. and sch. groups; author syndicated bus. column, 1964—; dir. Exchange Nat. Bank, USG Corp., Chgo., USG Industries Corp., Chgo., L&W Supply Corp., P.O.B. Pub. Co., Ann Arbor, Mich., A.P. Green Refractories Co., Mexico, Mo., Rodman & Renshaw, Co., Chgo., Masonite Corp., Chgo., Coleman Cable Co., North Chicago, Ill.; pres. U.S. Gypsum Found., 1979—. Alumni dir., trustee Bethany Coll.; mem. alumni bd. Columbia Sch. Journalism. Served to ensign USNR, World War II; comdr. Res. Mem. Am. Econs. Assn., Am. Finance Assn., Nat. Assn. Bus. Economists, Soc. Am. Bus. Writers, Pub. Relations Soc. Am., Newcomen Soc., Fin. Analyst Soc., Sigma Delta Chi, Alpha Sigma Phi. Clubs: Mid-Am., River (Chgo.); Green Acres Country, NYU (N.Y.C.); Inverrary Country (Ft. Lauderdale, Fla.). Author: Your Future in the Securities Business, 1974; Barron's Guide to Graduate Business Schs., 1977, 4th edit., 1984. Contbg. editor: Public Relations Handbook, 1971, 3d edit., 1983. Home: 376 Sunrise Circle Glencoe IL 60022 Office: 101 S Wacker Dr Chicago IL 60606

MILLER, EUGENE ALBERT, See *Who's Who in America,* 43rd edition.

MILLER, GAIL FRANKLIN, lawyer; b. Mansfield, Ohio, Mar. 24, 1938; s. James William and Dorothy (Franklin) M.; m. Carolyn Jean Baker, Sept. 26, 1964; children—Geoffrey Franklin, Bryan Alexander. B.A., Columbia U., 1960; J.D., U. Mich., 1963. Bar: Ohio 1963. Mem. firm Dinsmore & Shohl, Cin., 1963—. Trustee, v.p., zoning chmn. Clifton Town Meeting, 1968—, pres., 1985—; squadron comdr. CAP. Mem. Ohio Bar Assn. Club: Columbia U. Alumni of Cin. (trustee 1965—). Avocations: aviation; antique autos. Home: 545 Evanswood Pl Cincinnati OH 45220 Office: Dinsmore & Shohl 2100 Fountain Sq Plaza Cincinnati OH 45202

MILLER, GARY ALAN, software engineer, systems analyst, communications programmer; b. Ft. Wayne, Ind., June 30, 1953; s. Raymond Eugene and Patsy Ann (Welty) M. Cert. computer ops. and programming Am. Automation, 1976; certs. IBM info systems, 1982-84. B.S., Ind. U.-Gary, 1985. Computer operator Unitog, Kansas City, Mo., 1976-78, Milgrims Foods Inc., Kansas City, 1978-79; programmer, analyst Marley Corp., Mission, Kans., 1979-81; data processing mgr. Weil McLain, Michigan City, Ind., 1981-84; IBM Systems 38 software engr., security systems analyst, communications programmer Sullair, Michigan City, 1985—. Served to sgt. USAF, 1971-74. Home: 311 E Ben St Box 379 New Carlisle IN 46552 Office: Sullair Corp 3700 E Michigan Blvd Michigan City IN 46360

MILLER, GARY ARTHUR, medical technology educator; b. Mount Clemens, Mich., Nov. 7, 1950; s. George Stephen and Wilma Ielene (Hicks) M.; m. Paula Marvene Simmons, May 19, 1972; children—Shannon Noelle, Todd Andrew. B.A., Spring Arbor Coll., 1972; M.S. in Adminstrn., Central Mich. U., 1981; Ph.D., U. Nebr. Med. technologist Mercy Hosp., Bay City, Mich., 1972-73; blood bank supr. Midland Hosp., Mich., 1973-76; program coordinator Mid Mich. Community Coll., Harrison, 1976-81; program dir., asst. prof. med. tech. Nebr. Wesleyan U., Lincoln, 1981—. Contbr. articles to profl. jours. Music dir. Bible Baptist Ch., Lincoln; dir. youth soccer camp YMCA, Lincoln, 1984. Recipient Gt. Teaching Prof. award Nebr. Wesleyan U., 1982. Mem. Nebr. Soc. Med. Technologists (chmn. sci. assembly), Am. Soc. Med. Technologists, Tri-County Council Med. Tech. Educators, Am. Soc. Clin. Pathologists, Assn. for Study Higher Edn., Lambda Tau. Republican. Avocations: scuba diving; soccer refereeing. Home: 2029 Booth Circle Lincoln NE 68521 Office: Nebr Wesleyan U 50th and Saint Paul Lincoln NE 68504

MILLER, GEORGE MILTON, lawyer; b. Cleve., May 30, 1943; s. George Henry and Laverne Rose (Hiller) M.; m. Carol Ann Freed, Jan. 9, 1971; 1 child, David. B.A., Ursinus Coll., 1965; J.D., Case Western Res. U., 1968. Bar: Ohio 1968. Law clk. Cuyahoga County Common Pleas Ct., Cleve., 1970-72; staff atty. Summit City Legal Aid Soc., Akron, Ohio, 1972-75; referee Summit City Domestic Relations Ct., Akron, 1976-84; sole practice, Akron, 1984—. Served with U.S. Army, 1968-70; Vietnam. Decorated Bronze Star. Mem. Ohio State Bar Assn. (chmn. family law com. 1985—), Akron Bar Assn. Democrat. Mem. United Ch. of Christ. Club: Stow Mens Garden. Avocations: stamp and coin collecting; reading; baseball. Home: 3391 Charring Cross Dr Stow OH 44224 Office: 430 Centran Bldg Akron OH 44308

MILLER, H. RICHARD, chemical company executive; b. St. Louis Mo., Apr. 30, 1941; s. Herman C. and Grace (Novy) M.; m. Ann Wise Averill, June 15, 1967; children—Rick, Greg, Brad, Peg. B.S. in Chem. Engring., Mo. Sch. Mines and Metallurgy, 1963. Research chemist Monsanto, St. Louis, 1963-67, sales engr., Los Angeles, 1967-69; regional mgr. Edwin Cooper, Los Angeles, 1969-73; sales mgr. Ethyl Corp., St. Louis, 1975-80; pres. C.T.I., Enclid, Ohio, 1983—. Served to 1st lt. USAR, 1963-65. Mem. Soc. Automotive Engrs., ASTM, Assn. Asphalt Paving Technologists. Roman Catholic. Office: C.T.I. 29400 Lakeland Blvd Wickliffe OH 44092

MILLER, IRVING FRANKLIN, university dean; b. N.Y.C., Sept. 27, 1934; s. Sol and Gertrude (Rochkind) M.; m. Baila Hannah Milner, Jan. 28, 1962; children—Eugenia Lynne, Jonathan Mark. B.Chem.E., NYU, 1955; M.S., Purdue U., 1956; Ph.D., U. Mich., 1960. Registered profl. engr., N.Y. Research Scientist United Aircraft Corp., Hartford, Conn., 1959-61; prof. chem. engring. Bklyn. Polytech. Inst., 1961-72, head dept. chem. engring., 1970-72; dept. head bioengring. U. Ill., Chgo., 1973-79, dean, assoc. vice chancellor research, 1979—; cons. in field. Contbr. articles to profl. jours. Patentee in field. Grantee NIH, NSF. Fellow AAAS, Am. Inst. Chem. Engrs.; mem. Am. Chem. Soc., Am. Soc. Artificial Internal Organs, Fedn. Am. Scientists, N.Y. Acad. Sci., Soc. Research Adminstrs., Research Dirs. Assn. Chgo., Nat. Council Univ. Research Adminstrs., Sigma Xi, Phi Kappa Phi, Phi Lambda Upsilon, Omega Chi Epsilon, Tau Beta Pi. Home: 2600 Orrington Evanston IL 60201 Office: U Ill PO Box 4348 Chicago IL 60680

MILLER, J. F., bank executive. Sr. exec. v.p. Ameritrust Co., Cleve. Office: Ameritrust Co 900 Euclid Ave Cleveland OH 44101*

MILLER, JAMES ALEXANDER, oncologist; b. Dormont, Pa., May 27, 1915; s. John Herman and Emma Anna (Stenger) M.; m. Elizabeth Cavert, Aug. 30, 1942; children—Linda Ann, Helen Louise. B.S. in Chemistry, U. Pitts., 1939; M.S., U.Wis., 1941, Ph.D. in Biochemistry, 1943; D.Sc. (hon.), Med. Coll. Wis., 1982. Finney-Howell fellow in cancer research U. Wis., Madison, 1943-44, instr. to assoc. prof. oncology, 1944-52, prof., 1952—, Wis. Alumni Research Found. prof. oncology, 1980-82, Van Rensselaer Potter prof. oncology, 1982—; mem. adv. coms. Nat. Cancer Inst., Am. Cancer Soc., 1950—. Contbr. articles on chem. carcinogenesis and microsomal oxidations to profl. jours. Recipient awards (with E. C. Miller) Langer-Teplitz award Ann Langer Cancer Research Found., 1962, Lucy Wortham James award James Ewing Soc., 1965, G.H.A. Clowes award Am. Assn. Cancer Research, 1969, Bertner award M.D. Anderson Hosp. and Tumor Inst., 1971, Papanicolaou award Papanicolaou Inst. Cancer Research, 1975, Rosenstiel award Brandeis U., 1976, award Am. Cancer Soc., 1977, Bristol-Myers award in Cancer Research, 1978, Gairdner Found. Ann. award, Toronto, 1978, Founders award Chem. Industry Inst. Toxicology, 1978, 3M Life Sci. award Fedn. Am. Socs. Exptl. Biology, 1979, Freedman award N.Y. Acad. Sci., 1979, Mott award Gen. Motors Cancer Research Found., 1980. Fellow Am. Acad. Arts and Scis.; mem. Am. Assn. Cancer Research, Am. Soc. Biol. Chemists, AAAS, Japanese Cancer Soc. (hon.), Am. Chem. Soc., Soc. Toxicology, Soc. Exptl. Biology and Medicine, Nat. Acad. Scis. Home: 5517 Hammersley Rd Madison WI 53711 Office: McArdle Lab U Wis Madison WI 53706

MILLER, JEAN DIENER, training coordinator; b. Chgo., Feb. 20, 1926; d. Eugene Irl and Marian Roberts (Wentworth) Diener; m. Richard Paul Miller, June 21, 1947; children—Timothy E., Patrick R., Thomas E., Peter D., Leslie Anne. B.S., Northwestern U., 1947; M.A. in Teaching, U. Notre Dame, 1967. Cert. secondary tchr., Ind., systems profl. Quality analyst asst. Miles Labs., Inc., Elkhart, Inds., 1943-47, sec. to chief chemist, 1947-48, tech. writer, 1979-80, tng. coordinator, 1980—; sci. tchr. Elkhart Community Schs., 1966-79. Bd. dirs. Elkhart YMCA, 1955-60, Elkhart Family Counseling, 1962-66, Elkhart Mental Health Assn., 1960-62; sec., treas. Trucker's Helper, Inc., 1979—. Nolan scholar, 1946-47. Mem. Assn. Systems Mgmt.; Kappa Kappa Kappa, Delta Zeta (sec. 1946-47). Republican. Methodist. Avocations: backpacking, music, gardening. Home: 51585 Winding Waters Ln Elkhart IN 46514 Office: Miles Labs Inc 1127 Myrtle St Elkhart IN 46515

MILLER, JOAN SUE, college administrator, nun; b. Kansas City, Kans., Nov. 2, 1938; d. Clyde Leo Miller and Helen (Wetherwax) Miller Blackburn. B.S., St. Mary Coll., Leavenworth, Kans., 1964; M.S., U. Wis., 1965, Ph.D., 1967. Joined Sisters of Charity of Leavenworth, 1956. Tchr. elem. and jr. high sch. Sisters of Charity of Leavenworth, Laramie, Wyo., Helena, Mont. and Oklahoma City, 1958-62; assoc. prof., chmn. dept. home econs. St. Mary Coll., Leavenworth, 1968-74, acad. dean, prof., 1974—; mem. personnel bd. Sisters of Charity, Leavenworth, 1974—, long-range planning com., 1982-84. Mem. adv. council Leavenworth Agy. on Aging, 1981-84; bd. dirs. St. John Hosp., Leavenworth. Textile design research grantee Kansas City Regional Council Higher Edn., 1969, study tour grantee textile industry, 1970; exchange scholar Asian studies Sophia U., Tokyo, 1973; Am. Council on Edn. fellow profl. devel., 1975-76. Mem. Am. Assn. for Higher Edn., Am. Home Econs. Assn. Democrat. Address: Saint Mary College 4100 S 4th St Trafficway Leavenworth KS 66048

MILLER, JOHN BRUCE, hematology and oncology educator, researcher; b. Melrose Park, Ill., Oct. 8, 1943; s. John Bryant and Marjorie (Roberts) M.; m. Lois Carraro, Feb. 24, 1968. A.B., Harvard U., 1965, M.D., 1969. Diplomate Am. Bd. Internal Medicine, Am. Bd. Hematology, Am. Bd. Med. Oncology. Intern, then resident U. Chgo., 1969-71, fellow in hematology and oncology, 1971-73, instr., then asst. prof. Sch. Medicine, 1973-83; asst. chief of medicine Hines VA Hosp., Ill., 1983—; assoc. prof. hematology and oncology Loyola U. Sch. Medicine, Maywood, Ill., 1983—. Contbr. articles to med. jours. Mem. Am. Fedn. Clin. Research, Am. Soc. Clin. Oncology, Am. Soc. Hematology. Office: Loyola U Sch Medicine 2160 S 1st Ave Maywood IL 60153

MILLER, JOHN JERROLD-LARRAIN, magazine editor; b. Los Angeles, Aug. 25, 1951; s. Fred Thomas and Nona Mae (Bronner) M.; m. Joanne Elizabeth Edwards, Aug. 16, 1975; 1 dau., Genevieve. B.A., Albion Coll., 1973; postgrad. Western Mich. U., 1972; M.A., Adelphi U., 1974. Dramatic program dir. Albion (Mich.) Coll., 1972-75; lang. arts tchr. Maumee Valley C.D.S., Toledo, 1975-76; mag. editor United Kennel Club, Inc., Kalamazoo, 1976—. Mem. Dog Writers Assn. Am., Theta Alpha Phi, Lutheran. Club: Park. Contbr. articles to profl. jours. Home: 154 Bulkley St Kalamazoo MI 49007 Office: United Kennel Club Inc 100 E Kilgore Rd Kalamazoo MI 49001

MILLER, JOHN ROBERT, petroleum company executive; b. Lima, Ohio, Dec. 28, 1937; s. John O. and Mary L. (Zickafoose) M.; B.S. in Chem. Engring. with honors, U. Cin., 1960, D.Comml. Sci. (hon.), 1983; m. Karen A. Eier, Dec. 30, 1961; children—Robert A., Lisa A., James E. With Standard Oil Co. (Ohio), Cleve., 1960—, dir. fin., 1974-75, v.p. fin., 1975-78, v.p. transp., 1978-79, sr. v.p. tech. and chems., 1979-80, pres., chief operating officer, 1980—, also dir.; dir. Nat. City Corp., Eaton Corp., White Consol. Industries, Inc. Trustee Univ. Hosps. Cleve.; trustee, chmn. Greater Cleve. Roundtable; gen. chmn. Greater Cleve. Area Negro Coll. Fund; trustee, mem. exec. com. Nat. Urban League; mem. bus. adv. council Grad. Sch. Indsl. Adminstrn., Carnegie-Mellon U. Mem. Am. Petroleum Inst. (bd. dirs.), Beta Gamma Sigma, Tau Beta Pi. Clubs: Pepper Pike, Union, Fifty, Chagrin Valley Hunt. Office: Standard Oil Co (Ohio) Midland Bldg 101 Prospect Ave Cleveland OH 44115

MILLER, JONH FRANKLIN, foundation administrator; b. Hagerstown, Md., June 4, 1940; s. Roger F. and Leola V. (Ebersole) M. B.A., St. John's Coll., Md., 1962; B.D., Yale U., 1965, M.Div., 1967; postgrad. U. Md., 1969-73. Curator/adminstr. Hampton Nat. Hist. Site, Towson, Md., 1973-79; dir. edn. Stan Hywet Hall and Gardens, Akron, Ohio, 1979-81, exec. dir., 1981—; mem. faculty Montgomery Coll., Rockville, Md., 1977-78. Editor newsletter Stan Hywet Hall Found., 1982-84; Guide to Collections, 1982. Trustee, Music from Stan Hywet, Akron, 1983—, Inter-Mus. Conservation Assn., 1981. U. Md. fellow, spring 1970. Mem. nat. Trust Hist. Preservation, Am. Assn. State and Local History, Soc. Preservation of Md. Antiquities, Washington County Hist. Soc. (life), Md. Hist. Soc., Yale U. Alumni Assn. (alumni schs. com. 1984-85), SAR (mgr. chpt. 1978). Republican. Episcopalian. Avocations: gardening; military miniatures. Home: 310 Sundale Rd Akron OH 44313 Office: 714 N Portage Path Akron OH 44303

MILLER, JOSEPH IRWIN, manufacturing company executive; b. Columbus, Ind., May 26, 1909; s. Hugh Thomas and Nettie Irwin (Sweeney) M.; A.B., Yale, 1931, M.A. (hon.), 1959, L.H.D. (hon.), 1979; M.A., Oxford (Eng.) U., 1933; LL.D., Bethany Coll., 1956, Tex. Christian U., 1958, Ind. U., 1958, Oberlin Coll., 1962, Princeton U., 1962, Hamilton Coll., 1964, Case Inst. Tech., 1966, Columbia U., 1968, Mich. State U. 1968, Dartmouth Coll., 1971, U. Notre Dame, 1972, Ball State U., 1972; Hum.D. (hon.), Manchester U., 1973, Moravian Coll., 1976; L.H.D., U. Dubuque, 1977; m. Xenia Ruth Simons, Feb. 5, 1943; children—Margaret Irwin, Catherine Gibbs, Elizabeth Ann Garr, Hugh Thomas II, William Irwin. With Cummins Engine Co., Inc., Columbus, Ind., 1934—, v.p., gen. mgr., 1934-42, exec. v.p., 1944-47, pres. 1947-51, chmn. bd. 1951-77, chmn. exec. and fin. com., 1977—; pres. Irwin-Union Bank & Trust Co., 1947-54, dir., 1937—, chmn., 1954-75, chmn. exec. com., 1976—. Chmn., Pres.'s Spl. Com. East-West Trade Relations, 1965; mem. Pres.'s Commn. Postal Orgn., 1967-68, Com. Urban Housing, 1967-68; mem. Commn. Money and Credit, 1958-61, also Bus. Council; chmn. Nat. Adv. Commn. for Health Manpower, 1966-67; vice chmn. UN Com. Multinat. Corps., 1973-74; mem. adv. council Dept. Commerce, 1976-77. Pres. Nat. Council Chs. Christ in U.S.A., 1960-63; mem. U.S. Study Com. on So. Africa, 1979-81; mem. Nat. Indsl. Conf. Bd.; trustee Mayo Found., 1979-82, Yale Corp., 1959-77, Nat. Humanities Center. Fellow Branford Coll., Balliol Coll., Oxford. Served lt. USNR, aboard U.S.S. Langley, 1942-44. Recipient Rosenberger medal U. Chgo., 1977. Fellow Am. Acad. Arts and Scis.; mem. Am. Philos. Soc., AIA (hon.), Phi Beta Kappa, Beta Gamma Sigma. Mem. Christian Ch. (elder). Clubs: Yale, Century, Links (N.Y.C.); Chicago; Indianapolis Athletic, Columbia (Indpls.). Home: 2760 Highland Way Columbus IN 47201 Office: 301 Washington St Columbus IN 47201

MILLER, LARRY THOMAS, accountant; b. Omaha, Oct. 24, 1940; s. Elmer Thomas and Lucile Valentine (Hammon) M. Student U. Omaha, 1958-63. With accounting dept. Union Pacific R.R. Co., Omaha, 1959—, tax acct., 1969—. Mem. nat. adv. bd. Am. Security Council. Served with U.S. Army, M.P., 1965-67. Mem. Am. Acctg. Assn. Republican. Office: Union Pacific Railroad Co 1416 Dodge St Omaha NE 68179

MILLER, MABREY LEE, college administrator; b. Newark, Ark., Sept. 28, 1922; s. Earl Charles and Mattie Lou (Cooper) M.; m. Madge Dennis Black, May 30, 1944; children—Wanda, Ramona, Bryan, Keith, Kirk. B.A., Harding Coll., 1943; M.A., George Peabody Coll., 1953; Ed.D., U. Nebr., 1960. Math. tchr., basketball coach Parkin High Sch., Ark., 1947-53; prin. Batesville High Sch., Ark., 1953-56; registrar, asst. prof. edn. York Coll., Nebr., 1956-58, academic dean, registrar, 1958-79, v.p. academic affairs, 1979—; evaluator North Central Assn. Colls. and Schs., Chgo., 1978—, commr., 1984—. Author, editor York Coll. Catalog (yearly), 1959—. Contbr. religious articles to profl. jours. Elder, preacher Ch. of Christ, York, 1961—. Mem. NEA, Phi Delta Kappa. Lodge: Sertoma (pres. 1973-74). Avocations: reading; tennis; golf; parenting; socializing. Mabrey L. Miller Student Ctr. named in his honor York Coll., 1982. Home: 1010 Kiplinger York NE 68467 Office: York College 10th & Kiplinger York NE 68467

MILLER, MABRY BATSON, educator; b. Birmingham, Ala.; d. Ezra Orestes and Mabry Ward (Arnold) Batson; B.A., Athens (Ala.) Coll., 1937; grad. North Ala. Coll. Commerce, 1958; M.B.A., Ala. A&M U., 1974; Ph.D. (Anna M. Dice fellow), Ohio State U., 1981; m. Harry Edward Miller, Oct. 10, 1937; children—Harry Edward, Mabry Miller O'Donnell. Instr. French, Athens Coll., 1938; tchr. music, high sch. choral dir., pub. schs., South Pittsburg, Tenn., 1942-43; staff asst. dept. engring., missile div. Chrysler Corp., Huntsville, Ala., 1958-61; grad. asst. Coll. Adminstrv. Sci., Ohio State U., 1977-80; asst. prof. mgmt. Drake U., 1980—; cons., lectr., condr. workshops in field. Recipient Virginia Hammill Simms award Community Ballet Assn., Huntsville, 1971, cert. for patriotic civilian service Dept. Army, 1972; citation of merit City of Huntsville, 1972, County of Madison (Ala.), 1972. Mem. Acad. Mgmt., AAUW, Nat. Fedn. Music Clubs (life; dist. pres.), Phi Theta Kappa. Home: 1235 66th St Apt 36 Des Moines IA 50311 Office: Aliber Hall Drake U Des Moines IA 50311

MILLER, MARVIN MYRON, agricultural specialist; b. Wabash, Ind., Sept. 28, 1947; s. Kenneth Albert and Ruth Marie (Sells) M.; m. Marilyn Beth Faust, Dec. 22, 1968; children—Mikel Myron, Mark Marvin, Matthew Mac. Student pub. schs., Manchester, Ind. Cert. pesticide applicator, Ind. Farmer, Urbana, Ind., 1966-68; woodworker Cyclone Seeder Co., Inc., Urbana, 1969; asst. mgr. Sohigro, Urbana, 1969-71; custom applicator Custom Farm Service, Urbana, 1971-73; part owner, mgr. Crop Fertility Specialists, Inc., Urbana, 1973—. Fireman, reporter Urbana Vol. Fireman, 1978-83; mem. Ind. Vol. Firemen's Assn. Inc., Urbana, 1978-83. Served with Army N.G., 1967-73. Mem. Inst. Plant Food and Agrl. Chems. Assn., Wabash Jaycees (dir. 1972-73). Lodge: Lions (dir. Urbana 1980-81), Masons. Home: Rural Route 1 PO Box 51 Wabash IN 46992 Office: Crop Fertility Specialists Inc PO Box 86 Urbana IN 46990

MILLER, MARY SUE MONSEES, education educator; b. Pettis County, Mo., Dec. 30, 1928; d. Seltzer Gilbert and Waneta (Allcorn) Monsees; student U. Mo., Columbia, 1946-50; B. B.S., Eastern Conn. State Coll., 1964, M.S., 1967; Ph.D., U. Mo., Kansas City, 1974; m. Eldridge L. Miller, Dec. 24, 1950; children—Vonda Sue, Myra Lou, Gilbert Lee, Lesley Ann. Tchr., prin. pub. schs., Pettis County, Mo., 1947-51; tchr. pub. schs., Macomb County, Mich., 1957-59, Montville, Conn., 1960-62, Colchester, Conn., 1962-66; instr., supr. Eastern Conn. State Coll. Lab. Sch., Willimantic, 1966-67; asst. prof. edn. William Jewell Coll., Liberty, Mo., 1967-76, asso. prof. edn., 1976-80; dir. secondary edn. Stephens Coll., Columbia, Mo., 1980-82; asso. prof. edn. Columbia (Mo.) Coll., 1982—. Recipient Achievement award U. Mo.-Kansas

City Women Alumni, 1974. Mem. Council of Mo. Orgns. for Tchr. Edn. (organizer, pres.), Assn. of Tchr. Educators (mini-clinic coordinator, mem. conv. planning com. 1980, coordinator specialized topics seminars 1976, exec. bd. 1980—, past pres., exec. sec. Mo. unit), Assn. Supervision and Curriculum Devel., Nat. Council Social Studies, Nat. Council Tchrs. Math., Mo. Council Geog. Edn., Mo. Council Social Studies, Mo. Assn. Colls. Tchr. Edn. (coll. rep., mem. exec. bd.), AAUW, Kappa Delta Pi, Phi Delta Kappa, Pi Lambda Theta. Baptist. Office: 216 St Clair Columbia MO 65216

MILLER, MASON FERRELL, electrical engineer; b. Rockford, Nebr., Nov. 5, 1919; s. Martin Robertson and Bertha Luella (Story) M.; B.S., U. Nebr., 1940; M.S., MIT, 1941; m. Irene Elizabeth Westerman, Sept. 25, 1942; children—Paul Martin, James Mason, Marianne. Student engr. AT&T, N.Y.C., 1941; jr. engr. U.S. Navy, Bath, Maine, 1941; with NASA, Langley AFB, Va., 1941-51, aero. research scientist, 1948-51, Cleve., 1951-55; engr. specialist AiResearch Mfg. Co., Phoenix, 1955-57; preliminary design engr. Allison div. Gen. Motors Co., Indpls., 1957-61; sr. engring. specialist, supr. N. Am. Rockwell, Columbus, Ohio, 1961-69; performance engr. Gen. Electric Co., Aircraft Engine Bus. Group, Evendale, Ohio, 1969-82, part-time, 1982—; teaching advisor Gen. Motors Inst., 1960. Mem. Washington Twp. Sch. Planning Com., Indpls., 1961; asst. scoutmaster Boy Scouts Am., Berea, Ohio, 1954-55, pack treas., Phoenix, 1956-57, cubmaster, com. chmn., Indpls., 1959-61. U. Nebr. Regent's scholar, 1936; Mass. Inst. Tech. scholar, 1940; recipient NASA Merit Service award, 1948; Cleve. City and Plain Dealer award ARC program, 1953. Mem. Am. Def. Preparedness Assn., AIAA, Internat. Platform Assn., Pi Mu Epsilon, Sigma Tau. Presbyterian (deacon). Club: Order of DeMolay. Contbr. articles in field to profl. jours. Home: 6611 Franklin Street Lincoln NE 68506 Office: 6611 Franklin Street Lincoln NE 68506

MILLER, MERLYNN ALBERT, rural letter carrier, fire chief; b. Sheldon, Iowa, Aug. 31, 1927; s. Lester Ray and Florence Elizabeth (Wilson) M.; m. Mary Patricia Toal, Aug. 31, 1950; children—David, Dianne, Susan. Student pub. schs., Sheldon, Iowa. Feed driver Moorman's Feeds, Sheldon, Iowa, 1954-68; police officer City of Sheldon, 1968-80; rural letter carrier U.S. Post Office, Sheldon, 1980—; dist. coordinator Fire Assn., 1981—; fire chief City of Sheldon. Served with USN, 1945-46, PTO. Mem. Nat. Rural Letter Carriers, Internat. Assn. Arson Investigators, Iowa Rural Letter Carriers, Iowa Fire Assn., VFW (past comdr., life). Methodist. Club: Sanborn Country (Iowa). Lodge: Eagles (comdr.). Avocations: golf; bowling; fishing. Home: 622 9th St Sheldon IA 51201

MILLER, MICHAEL GARTH, city official; b. Oneonta, N.Y., Dec. 2, 1936; s. John A. and Robin L. (Robinson) M.; m. Janet A. Miller, Sept. 28, 1974. A.B., St. Lawrence U., 1959; M.Public Adminstrn., U. Kans., 1961. City mgr. City of Slater (Mo.), 1962-66, City of Vermillion (S.D.), 1966-70, City of Maplewood (Minn.), 1970-78, City of Council Bluffs (Iowa), 1978—. Mem. Internat. City Mgmt. Assn., Iowa City Mgmt. Assn. Lutheran. Club: Rotary. Home: 139 Upland Dr Council Bluffs IA 51501 Office: City Hall 209 Pearl St Council Bluffs IA 51501

MILLER, MICHAEL RAY, electrical contractor; b. Lafayette, Ind., Apr. 22, 1955; s. Raymond Howard and Roberta JoAnn (Gunion) M.; m. Cheryl Jean Marie Jepma, June 29, 1974; 1 son, Shawn Michael. With Rick Electric, Moorehead, Minn., 1973; Hi-Lite Electric of Fla., Orlando, 1974-76, Kelly Electric, Winter Park, Fla., 1976-80; owner, mgr. Miller Electric, Hancock, Minn., 1981—. Republican. Roman Catholic. Address: 758 Atlantic Ave Hancock MN 56244

MILLER, MILFORD MORTIMER, JR., lawyer; b. Evansville, Ind., Mar. 20, 1937; s. Milford Mortimer and Dorothy (Welborn) M.; A.B., Dartmouth Coll., 1959; J.D. with distinction, Ind. U., 1962; m. Mary Elizabeth Patterson, Aug. 17, 1963; children—Milford Mortimer III, John Patterson, Calvert Sterling, Rebecca Welborn. Bar: Ind. 1962, U.S. Dist. Ct. (no. dist.) Ind., U.S. Ct. Appeals (7th cir.), U.S. Supreme Ct. Assoc., Livingston, Dildine, Haynie & Yoder, Ft. Wayne, Ind., 1962-67, partner, 1967-78, mng. partner, 1978—; mem. com. on character and fitness Ind. Supreme Ct. Bd. Law Examiners, 1980—. Bldg. chmn. Center of Performing Arts, Ft. Wayne, 1967-73. Pres., bd. dirs. Ft. Wayne Civic Theatre, 1963-79; bd. dirs., mem. exec. com. Ft. Wayne Fine Arts Found.; pres. bd. dirs. Legal Aid of Ft. Wayne. Fellow Ind. Bar Found., Am. Coll. Trial Lawyers; mem. Allen County (chmn. grievance com. 1970-72, mem. jud. selection and tenure com. 1968-74, trustee 1974-76, law med. rev. panel 1977-82, chmn. jud. liaison com. 1978-80), Ind., Am., 7th Circuit bar assns., Am. Judicature Soc., Ind. Trial Lawyers Assn., Def. Research Inst., Order of the Coif, Sigma Nu. Republican. Presbyterian. Clubs: Dartmouth Alumni Club of Ft. Wayne, Ft. Wayne Country. Bd. editors Ind. Law Rev. Jour. Home: 4220 Old Mill Rd Fort Wayne IN 46807 Office: 1400 One Summit Sq Fort Wayne IN 46802

MILLER, MYRON GEORGE, retired pharmacist; b. Indpls., Sept. 11, 1909; s. William George and Anna Christina (Schier) M.; m. Edythe Louise Marquess, Aug. 21, 1937; 1 child, Allan Marquess. Pharm. Chemist, Ind. Sch. Pharmacy, 1929. Lic. pharmacist. Asst. mgr. Kerr's Pharmacy, Indpls., 1931-38, Clark's Pharmacy, Indpls., 1938-39; mgr. Harbison's Pharmacy, Indpls., 1939-49; owner, operator Miller Pharmacy, Indpls., 1949-61; asst. mgr. Vovidas Pharmacy, Indpls., 1961-66, Holder Pharmacy, Monticello, Ind., 1966-73; chief pharmacist White County Meml. Hosp., Monticello, 1973-82. Mem. Nat. Assn. Retail Druggists, 1949-61, Indpls. Assn. Retail Druggists, 1949-61; v.p. White County Food Pantry, Monticello, Ind., 1984—. Recipient 50 Year Gold Award of Pharmacy, Butler Coll. Pharmacy, Indpls., 1980. Republican. Baptist. Lodges: Mason (Grand Lodge Gold award 1981), Shriners. Avocations: motor boating; fishing; traveling. Home: Rural Route 3 Box 679 Monticello IN 47960

MILLER, NORMAN SAMUEL, bank executive, lawyer; b. Detroit, Dec. 11, 1943; s. Morton and Helene (Resh) M.; m. Paula Ruth Goldman, May 18, 1980; children—Karen, Deborah. B.B.A., U. Mich., 1965, M.B.A., 1966; J.D., Wayne State U., 1969. Bar: Mich. 1969. Ct. clerk Oakland County Probate Ct., Pontiac, Mich., 1969-70; trust officer Mfrs. Nat. Bank of Detroit, Dearborn, 1970—. Mem. Mich. State Bar Assn., Oakland County Bar Assn., Southfield Bar Assn., Tau Epsilon Rho. Republican. Jewish. Office: Mfrs Nat Bank of Detroit 16150 Michigan Ave Dearborn MI 48126

MILLER, PATRICIA LYNN, clinical psychologist, consultant; b. Chgo., Jan. 27, 1938; d. Joseph L. and Gertrude R. (Kontek) Lynn; m. Eric E. Miller, Feb. 27, 1960; children—Kurt, Nathan C., Peter J. Student Carleton Coll., 1955-56; A.B., U. Chgo., 1958; M.S., Ill. Inst. Tech., 1971, Ph.D., 1979. Pub. relations dir., dist. dir. Chgo. Area council Camp Fire Girls, 1958-66, asst. exec. dir., 1966-68; task force tchr. Assessment Team for 45-15 Year 'Round Sch. Plan, Valley View Sch. Dist., Romeoville, Ill., 1968-70; sch. psychologist Lockport (Ill.) Area Spl. Edn. Coop., 1971-80; pvt. practice psychology, Joliet, Ill., 1977—; instr., cons. sch. psychology program Ill. Inst. Tech., Chgo., 1975-77; field supr. Chgo. Sch. Profl. Psychology, 1981-82. Mem. Citizen's Com. for Wider Use of Schs., Mayor Daley's Youth Commn., Tribune Charities Youth Com., Chgo., 1958-68; mem. Women's Network for ERA, 1970s. State of Ill. grad. fellow, 1970. Mem. Am. Psychol. Assn., Internat. Neuropsychol. Soc., Nat. Assn. Sch. Psychologists, Ill. Sch. Psychologists Assn., Ill. Psychol. Assn., Sigma Xi. Club: Zonta. Office: 310 N Hammes Ave Joliet IL 60435

MILLER, PAUL DEAN, breeding company executive, geneticist, educator; b. Cedar Falls, Iowa, Apr. 4, 1941; s. Donald Hugh and Mary (Hansen) M.; m. Nancy Pearl Huser, Aug. 23, 1965; children—Michael, Steven. B.S., Iowa State U., 1963; M.S., Cornell U., 1965, Ph.D., 1967. Asst. prof. animal breeding Cornell U., Ithaca, N.Y., 1967-72; v.p. Am. Breeders Service, DeForest, Wis., 1972—; adj. prof. U. Wis.-Madison, 1980—. Contbr. articles to profl. jours. Mem. Beef Improvement Fedn. (disting. service award 1980), Am. Soc. Animal Sci., Am. Dairy Sci. Assn., Nat. Assn. Animal Breeders (dir. 1983). Republican. Home: 6688 Highland Dr Windsor WI 53598 Office: Am Breeders Service PO Box 459 DeForest WI 53532

MILLER, PAUL JOSEPH, hospital pharmacy administrator; b. Dodge, Nebr., Oct. 24, 1941; s. Emil John and Leona Elizabeth (Sellhorst) M.; m. Martha Burke, Sept. 4, 1965; children—Michelle Kristine, Kevin Burke. B.S. in Pharmacy, Creighton U., 1964; M.S., U. Iowa, 1966. Lic. pharmacist, Calif., Iowa, Minn. Project supr. Meml. Hosp. Med. Ctr., Long Beach, Calif., 1966-67; asst. dir. pharmacy USPHS Hosp., Boston, 1967-69; asst. dir. pharmacy U. Tex. at Houston, M.D. Anderson Hosp., 1969-71; clin. asst. prof. U. Ill. Hosps., Chgo., 1971-73; dir. pharmacy St. Mary's Hosp., Rochester, Minn., 1973-84; dir. pharmacy Tawam Hosp., Al-Ain, Abu Dhabi, United Arab Emirates, 1984—; cons. Baxter-Travenol Labs., Chgo., 1982-84. Co-author: Nomograms to Calculate Potent Inotropic Drugs, 1983. Editor Ill. Hosp. Pharmacists jour., 1972-73. Mem. sch. bd. nominating com. Community Caucus, Hinsdale, Ill., 1972-73. Served to lt. USPHS, 1967-69. Mem. Am. Soc. Hosp. Pharmacists (Best Contbn. to Pharmacy Lit. award 1969), Am. Pharm. Assn., Nat IV Therapists Assn., Minn. Soc. Hosp. Pharmacists (bd. dirs. 1981-83, Best Research Project award 1982), Minn. Pharm. Assn. (coms.), So. Minn. Soc. Hosp. Pharmacists (pres. 1981-83). Roman Catholic. Lodge: Rotary. Avocations: tennis; windsurfing; antique autos; reading; antiques. Home: 421 SW 15th Ave Rochester MN 55902 Office: Tawam Hosp PO Box 15258 Al-Ain Abu Dhabi United Arab Emirates

MILLER, PAUL MCGRATH, JR., executive search consulting company executive; b. Bowling Green, Ky., Oct. 31, 1935; s. Paul McGrath and Lena D. (Carr) M.; m. Charlene F. Russnak, Sept. 12, 1970 (div.); children—Andrew McGrath, Christopher Paul. B. Mech. Engring., Cornell U., 1958; M.B.A., Harvard U., 1966. Foreman, Procter & Gamble, Cin., 1958-60; market analyst United Aircraft Co., Sunnyvale, Calif., 1963-64; asst. to chmn. bd. Boise Cascade Corp. (Idaho), 1966, gen. mktg. mgr. Insulite div., 1966-67, nat. sales mgr. Lumber and Plywood, 1967-68, asst. to exec. v.p. Paper Group, 1968-69; group dir. mktg. Am. Standard, Inc., N.Y.C., 1969-71; dir. corp. communications Indian Head, Inc., N.Y.C., 1971-74; v.p. mktg. Ball & Socket Mfg. Co., Cheshire, Conn., 1975; v.p. mktg. Cory Coffee Service, Chgo., 1976, v.p., gen. mgr., 1977-80; v.p., ptnr. Korn/Ferry Internat., Chgo., 1980—. Mem. Winnetka Caucus (Ill.), 1980. Served to capt. USAF, 1960-63. Episcopalian. Clubs: Racquet Chgo., Harvard N.Y.C., Harvard Bus. Sch. Chgo. (dir.). Office: Korn/Ferry Internat 120 S Riverside Plaza Suite 918 Chicago IL 60606

MILLER, PETER LANCE, magazine executive; b. N.Y.C., July 21, 1956; s. Robert J. and Betty E. (Schwartz) M. B.A., Glassboro State Coll., 1979. Tchr., Hillsdale (N.J.) Pub. Schs., 1978, also coach football and baseball; account mgr. Good Housekeeping Mag., Hearst Corp., N.Y.C., 1979, sales/mktg. rep., Chgo., 1980-82, midwestern mgr. Country Living Mag., Chgo., 1982—. Mem. Chgo. Advt. Club, Chgo. Agate Club, N.Y. Advt. Club. Clubs: Internat. (Chgo.); Mpls. Athletic. Home: 71 E Division St Apt 802 Chicago IL 60610 Office: 1 N Wacker Dr Suite 618 Chicago IL 60606

MILLER, PETER NORMAN, trust company executive; b. Racine, Wis., Mar. 27, 1955; s. Frank N. and Dolores (Marchant) M.; m. Kathleen S. Eifler, Dec. 29, 1979. B.A., U. Wis., 1979. Retirement plan specialist Wausau Ins. Co., Wis., 1978-82, retirement plan rep., Mpls., 1982-83; asst. v.p. IDS Trust Co., Mpls., 1983—. Mem. Midwest Pension Conf., Internat. Found. Employee Benefit Plans (cert. employee benefit cons.). Avocations: sailing; skiing. Home: 5520 14th Ave S Minneapolis MN 55417 Office: IDS Trust Co IDS Tower Minneapolis MN 55402

MILLER, RAY, professional baseball executive. Mgr. Minn. Twins. Office: Minn Twins Humphrey Metrodome 501 Chicago Ave S Minneapolis MN 55415*

MILLER, RAYMOND S., manufacturing company executive; b. Constantine, Mich., May 8, 1943; s. Simon B. and Lydia M. (Miller) M.; m. Odessa Sue Miller, Feb. 23, 1963; children—Debbie Jo, Rocky Devon, Trisha Lynne. Constrn. worker Smiley Lumber Co., Denver, 1961-62; prodn. worker Weyerhauser Inc., Middlebury, 1962-64; dept. head Regent Homes, Middlebury, Ind., 1964-66, Acad. Mobile Homes, Howe, Ind., 1966-69; purchasing agent Schult Mobile Homes, Middlebury, 1969-70; div. mgr. Olwien Chem. Co. (Iowa), 1970-72, sales mgr. Gerring Ind. Inc., Shipshewana, Ind., 1972-76; owner, gen. mgr. Double Eagle Ind. Inc., Shipshewana, 1976—. Republican. Mennonite. Lodges: Moose, Eagles (sec. 1966). Office: Double Eagle Industries Inc Rd 5 S Shipshewana IN 46565

MILLER, RICHARD A., utility company executive. Pres., Cleveland Electric Illuminating Co. Office: Cleveland Electric Illuminating Co 55 Public Square Cleveland OH 44113*

MILLER, RICHARD CLARK, lawyer; b. St. Joseph, Mo., Oct. 21, 1955; s. Richard Ridley and Bonita Ray (Clark) M.; m. Leslie Ann Sullens, Dec. 29, 1978. B.A. in Math., U. Mo., 1977, B.S. in Edn., 1978, J.D., 1981. Bar: Mo. 1981, U.S. Dist. Ct. (we. dist.) Mo. 1981, U.S. Ct. Appeals (8th cir.) 1981. Assoc. Woolsey, Fisher, Whiteaker, McDonald and Ansley, Springfield, Mo., 1981—; atty. S.W. Mo. Legal Aid, Springfield, 1981—. Legal advisor Springfield Jaycees, 1984; chmn. bd. advocates U. Mo., Columbia, 1981. Mem. Mo. Bar Assn., ABA, Assn. Trial Lawyers Am., Mo. Assn. Trial Attys., Am. Judicature Soc., Springfield Claims Assn., Delta Upsilon (treas. alumni assn. 1981—, named alumni yr. 1982). Office: Woolsey Fisher Whiteaker McDonald and Ansley 300 S Jefferson Suite 600 Centerre Bank Bldg Springfield MO 65806

MILLER, RICHARD HAMILTON, lawyer, broadcasting company executive; b. Cleve., July 18, 1931; s. Ray Thomas and Ruth (Hamilton) M.; m. Susan Elizabeth Klimcheck, June 27, 1953; children—James M., Suanne R., Elizabeth M., Judith K., William P., Matthew W. A.B., U. Notre Dame, 1953, J.D., 1955. Bar: Ohio, 1955. Ptnr. Miller & Miller, Cleve., 1955—; asst. prosecutor, Cuyahoga County, Ohio, 1957-60; pres. Cleve. Broadcasting, Inc., 1966-70, Searles Lake Chem. Corp., Los Angeles, 1966-69, Miller Broadcasting Co., Cleve., 1970—, Hollywood Bldg. Systems, Inc., Meridian, Miss., 1974—; mng. ptnr. Miller & Co., Cleve., 1974—; owner, dir. Cleve. Profl. Basketball Co., Cleve. Baseball, Inc. Gen. chmn. N.E. Ohio March of Dimes, 1971-73; adv. council Catherine Horstman Home Retarded Children, 1969-73; mem. Cuyahoga Democratic Exec. Com., 1955-66. Served to capt. U.S. Army, 1956-57. Mem. Ohio Bar Assn., Cuyahoga County Bar Assn., Cleve. Bar Assn., Cleve. Citizens League. Clubs: Variety, Notre Dame (Cleve.) (pres. 1964-65), Cleve. Athletic (bd. dirs. 1971-74); Shaker Heights Country (Ohio). Lodge: K.C. Home: 2245 Stillman Rd Cleveland Heights OH 44118 Office: Park Suite 20 TE 1700 E 13th St Cleveland OH 44114

MILLER, RICHARD LAWRENCE, marketing executive; b. Pontiac, Mich., Mar, 12, 1947; s. Norwood Sterling and Muriel (Kelly) M.; m. Karen Lynne Richter, May 24, 1980; children—Scott Sterling, Elizabeth Lynne. B.S. Econs. and Math, Mich. State U., 1969. Dir. MarPlan div. Mc Cann Erickson, Detroit 1969-72; sr. dir. Survey Data Research, Birmingham, Mich., 1972-77; pres. Consumer Pulse, Inc., Birmingham, 1977—. Author, interviewer tng. film. Mem. Mktg. Research Assn. (pres.'s award 1981), Am. Mktg. Assn. Republican. Presbyterian. Home: 3380 Morningview Terr Birmingham MI 48010 Office: 725 S Adams Suite 185 Birmingham MI 48011

MILLER, RICHARD MELVIN, alcoholism treatment center director; b. Akron, Ohio, May 12, 1923; s. Charles Henry and Alice Lillian (Ritter) M.; m. Betty Leigh Murphy, June 16, 1974; children—Dawn M., Dean C., Donna L., Glenn A., Angie D. B.S., U. Akron, 1949; M.S.W., George Williams Coll., 1951. Asst. adult program dir., asst. phys. edn. dir. Rochester (N.Y.) YMCA, 1951-55; dir. central br. program Houston YMCA, 1955-65; assoc. dir. Ill. area, assoc. exec. dir. region 1 Nat. Council YMCA, 1965-70; account mgr., adminstrv. dept. mgr. Mgmt. Recruiters, Internat., Chgo., 1970-73; mgmt. cons. Info. Cons., Chgo., 1973-75; dir. Northwestern Alcoholism Treatment Ctr., Chgo., 1975—; instr. alcoholism program Nat. Coll. Edn., Chgo., 1978—. Served with U.S. Army, 1943-46. Mem. Assn. Ill. Detox Dirs. (pres. 1981—), Ill. Alcoholism and Drug Dependence Assn., Ill. Alcoholism Counsel Certification Bd., Met. Chgo. Detox Dirs. Assn. (chmn. 1977—). Republican. Presbyterian. Contbr. articles to profl. jours. Home: 123 Acacia Dr Apt 207 Indian Head Park IL 60525 Office: 30 W Chicago Ave Chicago IL 60610

MILLER, ROBERT CARL, physicist; b. Chgo., Oct. 26, 1938; s. Carl and Violet (Nelson) M.; B.S. in Physics, Ill. Inst. Tech., 1961; M.S. in Physics, No. Ill. U., 1965, Certificate Advanced Study in Physics, 1972; m. Mary Kay Ball, Sept. 3, 1969. Researcher particle accelerator div. Argonne (Ill.) Nat. Lab., 1961-66, researcher high energy physics div., 1966—. Registered profl. engr., Ill. Mem. Am. Phys. Soc., Am. Nuclear Soc., IEEE, Nat. Soc. Profl. Engrs., Soc. Certified Data Processors, Instrument Soc. Am., Am. Inst. Aero. and Astronautics, Mensa, Internat. Soc. for Philos. Enquiry, Mega Soc. Sigma Xi, Sigma Pi Sigma. Contbr. articles to profl. jours. Home: 1105 Elizabeth Ave Naperville IL 60540 Office: High Energy Physics Div Argonne Nat Lab Bldg 362 Room E-289 9700 S Cass Ave Argonne IL 60439

MILLER, ROBERT DAVID, engineer; b. Kansas City, Mo., Aug. 2, 1958; s. Oda Charles and Winona Virginia (McCorkle) M.; m. Valerie Jean Shelton, Apr. 13, 1981. B.S. in Engring., U. Mo., 1980. Registered profl. engr., Mo. Environ. engr. Mo. Dept. of Natural Resources, Jefferson City, 1981-83; engr. Union Electric Co., St. Louis, 1983—; mem. adv. bd. Electric Power Research Inst. Mem. ASCE, Air Pollution Control Assn., Greater St. Louis Air Pollution Control Assn. (bd. dirs. 1984-86, membership chmn. 1984-85), Chi Epsilon, Tau Beta Pi. Republican. Methodist. Office: Union Electric Co Box 149 MC 602 St Louis MO 63166

MILLER, ROBERT GLASGOW, ophthalmologist; b. Mt. Sterling, Ill., Sept. 7, 1926; s. Walter P. and Edna B. Miller. B.S., U. Ill., 1949, M.D., 1953. Intern King County Hosp., Seattle, 1953-54; resident Northwestern U. Med. Sch., Chgo., 1955-57; practice medicine specializing in ophthalmology, Chgo., 1958—; mem. staff Northwestern Meml. Hosp., Chgo., Children's Meml. Hosp., Chgo., Rehab. Inst., Chgo. Served with USN, 1944-46. Fellow ACS, Am. Acad. Ophthalmology. Home: 20 E Cedar St Chicago IL 60611 Office: Robert G Miller MD Ltd 645 N Michigan Ave Chicago IL 60611

MILLER, ROBERT HASKINS, state supreme court justice; b. Columbus, Ohio, Mar. 3, 1919; s. George L. and Marian Alice (Haskins) M.; student Ohio State U., 1936-37; A.B., Kans. U., 1940; LL.B., 1943; grad. Nat. Coll. State Trial Judges, Phila., 1967; m. Audene Fausett, Mar. 14, 1943; children—Stephen F., Thomas G., David W., Stacey Ann. Admitted to Kans. bar, 1943; practiced law, Paola, Kans., 1946-60; judge 6th Jud. Dist., Paola, 1961-69, U.S. Magistrate Dist. Kans., Kansas City, 1969-75; justice Kans. Supreme Ct., 1975—. Served with U.S. Army, 1942-46. Mem. ABA, Kans. Bar Assn., Shawnee County Bar Assn., Am. Legion, Phi Gamma Delta, Phi Delta Phi. Presbyterian. Club: Masons. Author: (with others) Pattern (Civil Jury) Instructions for Kansas, 1966, 69. Office: Kans Judicial Center Topeka KS 66612

MILLER, ROBERT JOSEPH, environmental manager; b. Mankato, Minn., Dec. 13, 1942; s. Andrew B. and Ann Marie (Wolf) M.; m. Mary Ann Kirsch, Oct. 31, 1964; children—Stephen, Cherly, David, Melissa. B.S. in Chemistry, Coll. St. Thomas, 1964; M.P.H. in Environ. Health, U. Minn., 1970. Registered profl. engr., Ill.; cert. indsl. hygienist. Water chemist City of St. Paul, 1964-66; environ. engr. Northwestern Oil, St. Paul Park, Minn., 1966-71; sr. environ. engr. Mobil Oil Corp., Joliet, Ill., 1971-72; environ. mgr. Bruce Lake Co., Coatsville, Pa., 1972-73; sr. environ. engr. Borg Warner Chemicals, Ottawa, Ill., 1973-77, environ. mgr., 1977—; lectr. in field. Mem. State Commn. on Hazardous Waste Adv. Council, State of Ill., 1985—. Mem. exec. com. St. Paul Park Jaycees, 1970-72; cubmaster Grand Ridge Pack, 1973-77; mgr. Grand Ridge Little League, 1974-78; village councilman Grand Ridge, 1979—. Mem. Ill. Mfrs. Assn. (state chmn. 1981-84), Ill. Environ. Concensus Forum (state exec. com. 1982—), Ill. State C. of C. (environ. com. 1978—), Am. Acad. Indsl. Hygiene, Soc. Profl. Engrs., Air Pollution Control Assn., Am. Bd. Ind. Engrs. (diplomat), Water Pollution control Fedn., Am. Chem. Soc. Roman Catholic. Avocations: golf; woodworking; martial arts.

MILLER, ROBERT STERLING, manufacturing executive; b. Millersburg, Ohio, Oct. 20, 1926; s. Roscoe C. and Evelyn M. Miller; m. Norma Jean Bird, June 12, 1948; children—Lee H., Sallie Jane. B.Sc. in Bus. Adminstrn., Ohio State U., 1951; M.B.A., Ohio U., 1981. Indsl. sales mgr. Miracle Adhesives Corp., New Philadelphia, Ohio, 1953-58; sales mgr. Buehler Bros. Co., Dover, Ohio, 1958-68; v.p. sales consumer div. Franklin Chem. Industries, Columbus, Ohio, 1968—. Served with USAAF, 1945. Recipient Outstanding Citizen award, Dover, 1968. Methodist. Author: Adhesives and Glues-How to Choose and Use Them, 1980; Home Construction Projects: With Adhesives and Glues, 1983, Energy Conservation with Adhesives and Sealants, 1985. Home: 4208 Greensview Dr Upper Arlington OH 43220 Office: 2020 Bruck St Columbus OH 43207

MILLER, RONALD HARRY, optometrist, educator; b. Cin., Jan 26, 1943; m. Madelaine Mitchel Miller, Aug. 15, 1965; children—Deena, Tamara. B.S., U. Cin., 1965; O.D., Ohio State U., 1970. Resident in orthoptics, Optometric Ctr. N.Y., N.Y.C., 1970; resident in primary care Rockland State Hosp., Orangeburg, N.Y., 1971; pvt. practice optometry, Columbus, Ohio, 1972—; clin. instr. electrodiagnostics, pediatrics, disease evaluation Ohio State U. Coll. Optometry, 1983—. Mem. Am. Optometric Assn. (Optometric Recognition award 1983, 84), Ohio Optometric Assn. Office: 17 E Gay St Columbus OH 43215

MILLER, RONALD LEE, manufacturing and entertainment company executive; b. Columbus, Ohio, Aug. 17, 1940; s. Bruce Eugene and Opal Maxine (Boss) M.; B.S. in Mech. Engring., Ohio Tech. U., 1966; M.B.A., U. Beverly Hills, 1977, Ph.D., 1979; children—Kellie Ann, Christina Lynn, Erin Nichole. Corp. engr. chems. div. U.S. Steel Corp., Circleville, Ohio, Pitts., 1970-72; owner Quality Mold, Grand Rapids, Mich., 1972-73; v.p. Nika Plastics, Grand Rapids, 1973-75; pres. Internat. Prototypes, Grand Rapids, 1975-79; founder, chief exec. Nat. Prototypes, Grand Rapids, 1977-79; pres. Hilco Plastics, Grand Rapids, 1977—; pres., founder Position Inc., Grand Rapids, 1980—, RLM Prodns., Hollywood, 1980—; pres. Hilco House, Inc., 1982—; cons. product devel. Mem. ednl. adv. com. Grand Rapids Area Colls.; mem. U.S. Senatorial Adv. Com. Served with USMCR, 1957-58. Mem. Soc. Plastics Engrs., N.Y. Acad. Scis., Am. Mgmt. Assn. Republican. Roman Catholic. Author texts in field. Office: 4172 Danvers Ct Kentwood MI 49508

MILLER, SARA BILLOW, hospital administrator; b. Seattle, Oct. 11, 1948; d. William Pierce Billow and Nancy (Kimball) Heppe; m. Geoffrey Miller, Sept. 5, 1981; children—Elizabeth Louise, Robert Richard. A.A.S., Kirkwood Community Coll., 1974; B.A. cum laude, Coe Coll., 1977. Dir. respiratory therapy St. Luke's Hosp., Cedar Rapids, Iowa, 1976-81, adminstr. Anamosa (Iowa) Community Hosp. through mgmt. contract with St. Luke's Hosp., 1981—. Bd. dirs. Jones County Heart Assn., Anamosa Ambulance. Named Alumnus of Yr., Kirkwood Community Coll., 1979. Mem. Am. Assn. Respiratory Therapy, Iowa Soc. Respiratory Therapy (Lit. Achievement award 1978), Am. Coll. Hosp. Adminstrs., Am. Soc. for Hosp. Personnel Adminstrs., Iowa Personnel Mgmt. Assn. Office: 104 Broadway Pl Anamosa IA 52205

MILLER, SARABETH, educator; b. Kouts, Ind., Apr. 6, 1927; d. Clayton Everett and Eva Margaret (Noland) Reif; m. Lloyd Melvin Miller, Dec 2, 1944; children—Virginia, Shirley, Judith, John, Nola, Steven. B.A., Valparaiso U., 1972, M.A. in L.S., 1977. Lic. tchr., Ind. Office employee Porter County Herald, Hebron, Ind., 1954-55, Little Co. of Mary Hosp. and Home, San Pierre, Ind., 1960-65, Jasper County Co-op, Tefft, Ind., 1965-69; tchr. art DeMotte (Ind.) elem. sch., 1972-76, Kankakee Valley High Sch., Wheatfield, Ind., 1976—. Leader 4-H Club, Kouts; mem. session Kouts Presbyn. Ch. Recipient various prizes Lake Central Fair (Ind.), 1975, 80; photography award Ind. Dept. Tourism, 1976. Mem. NEA, Nat. Art Edn. Assn., Ind. Tchrs. Assn., Ind. Art Edn. Assn., Kankakee Valley Tchrs. Assn. Republican. Presbyterian. Contbr. articles and photographs to various local publs. Home: 1378 S County Rd 500 E Kouts IN 46347

MILLER, STEWART CRAIG, insurance company executive; b. Lafayette, Ind., Apr. 20, 1946; s. Alfred Craig and Betty Jane (Stewart) M.; m. Mary Lou Moody, Nov. 22, 1970; children—Jennifer, Amanda, Erik, Mary Kathryn. B.A. in Sci., Ball State U., 1968. Sci. tchr., coach Marion High Sch., Ind., 1968-73; sec. bd. Union Labor Underwriters, Lafayette, 1973-80; pres. Adminstrs. & Benefit Cons., Lafayette, 1980—, Health Care Cons., 1984—; cons. in field. Author: Group Health Stabilization Trusts. Mem. Lafayette C. of C., Internat. Found. Employee Benefit Funds. Republican. Episcopalian. Clubs: YMCA (pres. 1982-83), Lafayette Country, Optimist (v.p. 1978-79). Avocations: biking; golfing; swimming; running; reading. Home: 1521 S 9th St Lafayette IN 47905 Office: Adminstrs & Benefit Cons 731 Main St Lafayette IN 47901

MILLER, SUSAN DALTON, marriage, family and chemical dependency counselor; b. St. Louis, May 8, 1943; d. George L. and Wilma Pearl (Johnston) Davis; m. Bill J. Dalton, Apr. 19, 1962; children—Cynthia Lynn, Steven Joseph; m. 2d, John Timothy Miller, July 26, 1977; 1 dau., Christine Ryann. B.S. in Edn., U. Mo.-St. Louis, 1975, M.Ed., 1982; postgrad. Purdue U., N.E. Mo. U., Webster Coll., Ohio State U. Cert. spl. edn. tchr., vocat. guidance counselor, tchr. ortho handicapped, sch. counselor, alcoholism counselor. Career edn. tchr., coordinator Ferguson-Florissant Dist., St. Louis, 1975-77; resource coordinator, tchr. retarded and handicapped J.E.S.S.E. Corp., Plymouth, Ind., 1977-79, tchr. adolescent multiple handicapped, 1978-79; tchr.

severe adolescent behavioral problems, Logos, St. Louis, 1979-80; counselor spl. needs program, coordinator career resources center, counselor spl. needs program University City Dist., St. Louis, 1980-81; mem. writing and research team, St. Louis U., 1981; counselor, edn. coordinator chemical dependency Tri-Counseling Center, Columbus, Ohio, 1981-82; program coordinator, family therapist alcoholism and drug abuse, coordinator smoking cessation program Smoke Busters, Inc. Columbus Health Dept., 1982—; cons. St. Louis U., University City Vocat. Assessment Ctr., other schs. and orgns. Mem. Am. Assn. Counseling and Devel., Nat. Vocat. Guidance Assn. (commn. on occupational status of women), Mo. Vocat. Guidance Assn. (inter-profl. communications liaison), Ferguson-Florissan Dist. Vocat. Edn. Adv. Com., Omicron Tau Theta. Author books and articles in field. Home: 101 Forest Ridge Ct Worthington OH 43085

MILLER, SUSAN HEILMANN, newspaper publishing executive; b.Yuba City, Calif., Jan. 13, 1945; d.Paul Clay and Helen Christine (Sterud) Heilmann; m. Allen Clinton Miller III, June 24, 1967. B.A., Stanford U., 1966; M.S., Columbia U., 1969; Ph.D., Stanford U., 1976. Info. officer Montgomery County Schs., Rockville, Md., 1970-71, Palo Alto Schs., Calif., 1969-70, 71-73; news-features editor Bremerton Sun, Wash., 1976-80; night city editor Peninsula Times Tribune,Palo Alto, 1980-81; exec. editor News-Gazette, Champaign, Ill., 1981-85; dir.editorial devel. Scripps Howard Newspapers, Cin., 1985—. Contbr. articles to profl. jours. Bd. dirs. Vol. Illini Projects, U. Ill., 1983-85. Mem. Am. Soc.Newspaper Editors (bd. dirs. 1985—), Assoc. Press Mng. Editors (bd. dirs.1984—), Ill. AP Mng. Editors (bd. dirs. 1984-85). Club: Executive (Champaign, Ill.)(bd.dirs. 1984-85). Office: Scripps Howard Newspapers 1100 Central Trust Tower Cincinnati OH 45202

MILLER, TERRANCE MICHAEL, lawyer; b. Fostoria, Ohio, Jan. 13, 1947; s. Robert Paul and Joan Margaret (McKivett) M.; m. Bonnie J. Price, Aug. 9, 1969; children—Kelly Anne, Robert Penn. B.A., Hobart Coll., 1969; J.D., U. Va., 1972. Bar: Ohio 1972. Ptnr. Porter, Wright, Morris & Arthur, Columbus, Ohio, 1972—. Contbr. book chpt. to Deposition Strategy, Law and Forms, 1981. Dir. membership Boy Scouts Am., Columbus, 1978-80; coach Upper Arlington Youth Football, 1984. Recipient Top Dist. Membership Achievement award Boy Scouts Am., 1980. Mem. Ohio State Bar Assn., Ohio Assn. Civil Trial Attys. (exec. com. 1982), Columbus Def. Assn. (pres. 1982-83), Def. Research Inst., Fedn. Ins. Counsel. Roman Catholic. Club: Athletic (Columbus). Home: 1306 Carron Dr Columbus OH 43220 Office: Porter Wright Morris & Arthur 37 W Broad St Columbus OH 43215

MILLER, THELMA TALLEY, nursing administrator; b. Chgo., Mar. 17, 1924; d. Lemuel and Tennie (Hawkins) Talley; m. Ernest Miller, Aug. 11, 1946 (div. 1982); children—Ernest Lemuel, Michael Eugene, Cheryl Lynn Miller Smith. Assoc. degree in Nursing, Amundsen-Mayfair 1967; B.S. in Nursing, Gov.'s State U., 1975, M. Nursing Adminstrn., 1977; postgrad. No. U. Ill., 1978. Staff nurse Cook County Sch. Nursing, Chgo., 1954-69, head nurse emergency room, 1969-74, inservice instr., 1975-76, sr. instr., 1976-80; dir. nursing recruiting Cook County Hosp., Chgo., 1980—. Nurse Mt. Calvary Baptist Ch., Chgo.; active Operation PUSH, ARC, NAACP. Named Best Instr., Cook County Sch. Nursing, 1979. Mem. Am. Nurse Assn., Ill. Nurse Assn., Nat. League for Nursing, Nat. Black Nurses Assn. (pres. Chgo. chpt. 1978-80), Lambda Pi Alpha. Home: 3651 W 177th St Country Club Hills IL 60477 Office: Cook County Hosp 1835 W Harrison Chicago IL 60612

MILLER, THOMAS J., attorney general of Iowa; b. Dubuque, Iowa, Aug. 11, 1944; s. Elmer John and Betty Maude (Kross) M.; B.A., Loras Coll., Dubuque, 1966; J.D., Harvard U., 1969; m. Linda Cottington, Jan. 10, 1981. Admitted to Iowa bar, 1969; with VISTA, 1969-70; legis. asst. to U.S. congressman, 1970-71; legal edn. dir. Balt. Legal Aid Bur., also mem. part-time faculty U. Md. Sch. Law, 1971-73; pvt. practice, McGregor, Iowa, 1973-78; city atty., McGregor, 1975-78; atty. gen. of Iowa, 1978—. Pres. 2d Dist. New Democratic Club, Balt., 1972. Mem. ABA, Iowa Bar Assn., Common Cause. Roman Catholic. Office: Hoover Bldg 2nd Floor Des Moines IA 50319*

MILLER, THOMAS WILLIAMS, music educator; b. Pottstown, Pa., July 2, 1930; s. Franklin Sullivan and Margaret (Williams) M.; m. Edythe Edwards, Dec. 20, 1952; children—Theresa, Thomas, Christine, Stefanie. B.S., West Chester State Coll., 1952; M.A., East Carolina U., 1957; D.Mus. Arts, Boston U., 1964. Dir. instrumental music Susquenita High Sch., Pa., 1955-56; instrumental trumpet tchr. East Carolina U., Greenville, N.C., 1957-61; asst. dean, 1962-68, dean Sch. Music, 1969-71; dean Sch. Music, Northwestern U., Evanston, Ill., 1971—. Contbr. articles to profl. jours. Served with AUS, 1952-55. Mem. Nat. Assn. Schs. Music (pres. 1982—), Music Educators Nat. Conf., Phi Mu Alpha, Pi Kappa Lambda (pres. 1976-79). Home: 2103 Orrington Ave Evanston IL 60201 Office: Northwestern U Sch Music 711 Elgin Rd Evanston IL 60201

MILLER, TIMOTHY NICHOLAS, public relations executive; b. Evansville, Ind., Dec. 14, 1946; s. Herdis and Mary Ellen (Grant) M. B.S. in Journalism, U. Evansville, Ind., 1980. Prodn. asst. Sta. WTVW-TV, Evansville, Ind., 1968-69; gen. mgr. cable TV program origination facilities Telesis Corp., Evansville, 1971-72; exec. dir. graphic products Adfax Agy., Indpls., 1972—; dist. circulation mktg. mgr. Evansville Printing Corp., 1976-77; pub. relations exec. Ind. Employment Security Div., Vets. Employment Service, Evansville, 1978-81; pub. affairs officer 123D U.S. Army Res. Command for Ind. and Mich., Ft. Benjamin Harrison, Ind., 1981—. Project officer Met. Indpls. United Way Campaign; former v.p. Muscular Dystrophy Assn. Am.; former chmn. Jerry Lewis Labor Day Telethon, Muscular Dystrophy Campaign Fund Southwest Ind. and Western Ky., Salvation Army Christmas Shopping Tour for Underprivileged Children. Served with U.S. Army, 1966-68. Decorated Purple Heart Medal, Bronze Star (4); Vietnamese medals; recipient Fourth Estate award for journalistic excellence. Mem. Internat. Assn. Bus. Communicators, Pub. Relations Assn. Am., Praxis, Armed Forces Broadcasters Assn., Assn. U.S. Army (exec. council Ind. chpt., nat. Best Chpt. Newsletter award, 1982), Indpls. Press Club, Press Club of Evansville, Inc., Evansville C. of C. (past bd. dirs.; Key Man, Presdl. Honor awards), Indpls. C. of C. (nat. def. com.), VFW, DAV, Tau Kappa Epsilon. Republican. Roman Catholic. Club: U. Evansville Varsity. Writer, producer, dir. 1st cablevision coverage Orange Bowl Football Classic, 1970. Home: PO Box 16246 Indianapolis IN 46216 Office: PO Box 16501 Fort Benjamin Harrison IN 46216

MILLER, VERNON RICHARD, state senator, nursing home executive; b. Des Moines, July 27, 1939; s. Wallace Thomas and Enid Lillian (Conklin) M.; B.S., Purdue U., 1963; M.S. in Bus. Adminstrn., Ind. U., South Bend, 1973; m. Jane Kay Rothrock, Aug. 19, 1961; children—Vernon Richard, II, Pamela Sue. Dept. foreman Jomac North Ltd., Warsaw, Ind., 1959-61; lab. technician Purdue U., 1963-64; microbiologist Pabst Brewing Co., Peoria Heights, Ill., 1964-65; dept. mgr. Ocean Spray Cranberries, North Chicago, Ill., 1965-67; exec. Miller's Merry Manor, Inc., Plymouth, Ind., 1967—; mem. State of Ind. Senate, 1976—, chmn. majority caucus, 1982—, chmn. health welfare and aging com., 1980-84, chmn. appointments and claims com., 1983—. Chmn. Marshall County Ind. March of Dimes, 1973-76; blood chmn. Marshall County Red Cross, 1970-74. Mem. Am. Coll. Nursing Home Adminstrs. Republican. Methodist. Clubs: Plymouth Country, Kiwanis (pres. 1972, lt. gov. 1975), Mason, Shriner, Order Eastern Star. Office: PO Box 498 Plymouth IN 46563

MILLER, WILBUR CASTEEL, university president; b. Des Moines, Aug. 26, 1923; s. Cecil S. and Laura M. (Kesterson) M.; student Drake U., 1941-43, St. Louis U., 1943-44; B.S. in Bus. Adminstrn., U. Denver, 1948, M.A., 1949, Ph.D., 1953, LL.D., 1972; m. Viretta A. Shaw, Mar. 30, 1946; children—W. Kent, Jill M. Faculty dept. psychology U. Denver, 1949-72, prof., 1963-72, dean Grad. Sch., 1964-65, vice chancellor acad. affiars, dean faculty, 1965-72, acting chancellor, 1966-67; pres. Drake U., Des Moines, 1972—; cons. USAF Acad., 1957; co-dir. research project in maladaptive behavior U. Colo. Med. Sch., 1960-72; Ford Found. cons. to Venezuela, 1968-69. Served with AUS, 1943-46. U. Mich. postdoctoral fellow, 1963-64. Fellow Am. Psychol. Assn.; mem. Colo. (past pres.), Rocky Mountain (past pres.) psychol. assns., Phi Beta Kappa, Sigma Xi. Author: Personality Social Class and Delinquency, 1966; contbg. author: New Viewpoints in the Social Sciences, 1958; Readings in Child Development and Personality, 1970. *

MILLER, WILLIAM CHARLES, librarian; b. Mpls., Oct. 26, 1947; s. Robert Charles and Cleithra Mae (Johnson) M.; m. Brenda Kathleen Barnes, July 24, 1969; children—Amy Renee, Jared Charles. B.A., Marion Coll. (Ind.), 1968; M.L.S., Kent State U. (Ohio), 1974, Ph.D., 1983. Library technician Kent State U., 1972-74; catalog librarian Mt. Vernon Nazarene Coll. (Ohio), 1974-76; catalog and acquisitions librarian, 1976-78; library dir. Nazarene Theol. Sem., Kansas City, Mo., 1978—; adj. research assoc. U. Kans., 1984-85; cons. Mid-Am. Nazarene Coll., Olathe, Kans., 1983. Served with U.S. Army, 1968-72. Mem. Assn. Study of Higher Edn., ALA, Am. Theol. Library Assn. (bd. dirs. 1985—), Wesleyan Theol. Soc., Assn. Coll. and Research Libraries, Library Adminstrn. and Mgmt. Assn., Beta Phi Mu. Home: 14405 S Cottonwood Olathe KS 66062 Office: Nazarene Theol Sem 1700 E Meyer Blvd Kansas City MO 64131

MILLER, WILLIAM EDWARD, educational administrator; b. Sebree, Ky., Dec. 29, 1931; s. Troy Edward Miller and Daisy Vivian Miller Shelton; m. Mattie Sherryl Washington, Sept. 19, 1953; 1 child, Kori Edwin. B.A., Evansville Coll., 1965; M.A., U. Evansville, 1970; student Tuskegee Inst., 1951-53. Cert. educational adminstr., Ind. Tchr. indsl. arts Plaza Park Elem. Sch., 1966-76; asst. prin. Thompkins & Cynthia Heights Schs., Evansville, Ind., 1976-77, Washington & Thompkins Schs., Evansville, 1977-78; prin. Culver Sch., Evansville, 1978-83, McGary Sch., Evansville, 1983—; adult edn. tchr. Evansville Vanderburgh Sch. Corp. 1967-76. Adminstr. Conceptual design new ednl. facility, 1981-83, design new ednl. structure, 1983-84. Vice pres. Bd. Pub. Safety, Evansville, 1984; pres., 1982-84; pres. Vanderburgh County Council, Evansville, 1970. Served with U.S. Army Airborne Div., 1953-55. Named Indsl. Arts Tchr. of Yr. Ind. Indsl. Arts Assn., 1970. Mem. Nat. Assn. Elem. Prins., Ind. Assn. Elem., Middle Sch. Prins., Internat. Reading Assn., Phi Delta Kappa, Kappa Alpha Psi (provincial v.p. 1974-78). Democrat. Avocations: water and snow skiing; wood carving. Home: 517 S Boeke Rd Evansville IN 47714 Office: McGary Middle Sch 1535 S Joyce St Evansville IN

MILLIGAN, EDITH, financial services executive; b. Evansville, Ind., Oct. 22, 1958; d. William West and Suzanne (Crimm) M.; m. Paul Alan Delphia, Sept. 1, 1984. B.A., Tulane U., 1980. C.L.U. Adminstrv. asst. Bryan Wagner, C.L.U., New Orleans, 1977-80; sec.-treas. Life Mktg. of La., New Orleans, 1980-81; dist. mgr. Creative Fin. Concepts, Columbus, Ohio, 1981-82; pres. Keeping Track, Inc., Columbus, 1982—. Author: Licensing Study Guide, 1982; Track Records, 1983. Field coordinator Fair and Impartial Redistricting Commn., Columbus, 1981; mem. steering com. Pres. Ford Com., New Orleans, 1976. Mem. Internat. Assn. Fin. Planning, LWV, Mensa. Republican. Home: PO Box 14453 Columbus OH 43214 Office: Keeping Track Inc PO Box 14468 Columbus OH 43214

MILLIGAN, FREDERICK JAMES, lawyer; b. Upper Sandusky, Ohio, Nov. 14, 1906; s. William G. and Grace (Kuenzli) M.; B.A., Ohio State U., 1928; LL.B., Franklin U., 1933; J.D., Capital U., 1966; m. Virginia Stone, June 30, 1934; children—Frederick James, David Timothy. Asst. nat. sec. Phi Delta Theta, 1928; asst. dean of men Ohio State U., 1929-33; admitted to Ohio bar, 1933; asst. atty. gen. State of Ohio, 1933-36; pvt. practice, Columbus, Ohio, 1937—; exec. sec. Adminstrv. La. Commn. of Ohio, 1940-42; exec. sec. to Gov. of Ohio, 1947; dir. commerce State of Ohio, 1948; sec. Louis Bromfield Malabar Farm Found., 1958-60. Pres. Central Ohio council Boy Scouts Am.; trustee Columbus Town Meeting; asst. dir. Pres.'s Commn. on Inter-govt. Relations, 1953; pres. Ohio Information Com., Inc., 1966-83; chmn. Blendon Twp. Bicentennial Commn., 1974-77. Mem. athletic council Ohio State U., 1958-64; trustee Blendon Twp., 1971-78. Served from 1st lt. to maj. USAAF, 1942-45. Decorated Legion of Merit; recipient Silver Beaver award Boy Scouts Am., 1949; Ann. History award Franklin County Hist. Soc., 1957; D.A.R. Citizenship award, 1958; Distinguished Service citation Ohioana Library Assn., 1970. Mem. Am., Ohio, Columbus bar assns., Columbus Jr. C. of C. (hon. life mem.; pres. 1934), Ohio (trustee 1952-77, pres. 1963-65, Franklin County (pres. 1954-56) hist. socs., Ohio State U. Assn. (trustee 1952-55), Amvets (state comdr. 1949). Am. Legion, S.A.R., League of Young Republican Clubs of Ohio (pres. 1941-42). Presbyn. Clubs: University (trustee 1956-58), Ohio State U. Faculty (Columbus). Home: 3785 Dempsey Rd Westerville OH 43081 Office: 3791 Dempsey Rd Westerville OH 43081

MILLIGAN, ROBERT LEE, JR., computer company executive; b. Evanston, Ill., Apr. 4, 1934; s. Robert L. and Alice (Connell) M.; B.S., Northwestern U., 1958; m. Susan A. Woodrow, Mar. 23, 1957; children—William, Bonnie, Thomas, Robert III. Account rep. IBM, Chgo., 1957-66; sr. cons. L.B. Knight & Assocs., Chgo., 1966-68; v.p. mktg. Trans Union Systems Corp., Chgo., 1968-73; sr. v.p. sales mktg., sec. Systems Mgmt. Inc., Rosemont, Ill., 1973—, dir., 1980—; treas. Systems Mgmt. Inc. Service Corp.; dir. Nanofast, Inc., Chgo., 1982-84. Div. mgr. N. Suburban YMCA Bldg., 1967; area chmn. Northfield Twp. Republican Party, 1965-71. Bd. dirs. United Fund, Glenview, Ill., 1967-69, Robert R. McCormick Chgo. Boys Club, 1974—; pres. bd. mgrs. Glenview Amateur Hockey Assn., 1974-79, gen. mgr. Glenbrook South High Sch. Hockey Club, 1973-78. Served with AUS, 1953-55. Mem. Data Processing Mgmt. Assn., Consumer Credit Assn. (dir., sec. 1969-70), Phi Kappa Psi. Presbyterian. Clubs: Northwestern (dir. 1973-75) (Chgo.); Glen View (Ill.). Home: 1450 Lawrence Ln Northbrook IL 60062 Office: 6300 N River Rd Rosemont IL 60018

MILLION, ROWE BURRELL, educational volunteer; b. St. Paul, Aug. 22, 1913; s. Roy Burrell and Elizabeth Melvina (Rowe) M.; m. Eva Mae Rushbrook, Sept. 8, 1937; children—Charles Irving, James Rowe, Lee Rushbrook. B.A., Macalester Coll., 1935, L.H.D. (hon.), 1978; B.D., Colgate-Rochester Div. Sch., 1938; M.A., U. Minn., 1953. Ordained to ministry Baptist Ch., 1938. Minister First Bapt. Ch., Grand Fork, N.D., 1938-42, Bozeman, Mont., 1943-44; tchr. pub. sch., Jasper and Red Wing, Minn., 1946-75; radio reporter Sta. KCUE-AM, Red Wing, 1975-83; vol. spl. radio programs Red Wing Pub. Schs., 1983-85; creator, producer U.S.A. bi-centennial pageant Red Wing Remembers, 1976; dir. high sch. and community plays, hist. pageants. Mem. auditorium bd. City of Red Wing, 1966-77; mem. exec. bd. Y-Pals, YMCA, Red Wing, 1976-83, Lake City Area Arts Council, Minn., 1983-85. Served to lt. (chaplain) USNR, 1944-46, PTO. Recipient Service award Red Wing City, 1977, Disting. Service award Red Wing Jaycees, 1976; named Ptnr. for Ednl. Excellence, Red Wing Bd. Edn., 1983. Mem. Minn. Edn. Assn. (hon. life), Speech Assn. Minn. (sec.-treas., Service award 1975, hon. life). Unitarian-Universalist. Clubs: Retired Educators (Red Wing and Lake City) (pres. 1980-84); Toastmasters (Red Wing) (adminstrv. v.p. 1985, Service award 1975). Avocations: music; reading; vol. radio work. Home: Route 2 Box 279 Lake City MN 55041

MILLIS, HARRY WARD, financial analyst; b. Appleton, Wis., Mar. 22, 1937; s. John Schoff and Katherine (Wisner) M.; m. Lee Gallagher, Nov. 22, 1961. B.A., Wesleyan U., Middletown, Conn., 1959; postgrad. Case Western Res. U., 1959-61. Chartered fin. analyst. Investment research officer Nat. City Bank, Cleve., 1961-66; ptnr. Prescott, Ball & Turben, Cleve., 1966-79; 1st v.p. McDonald & Co. Securities, Inc., Cleve., 1979—; dir. Lorain Dock Co., Ohio. Econs. editor Rubber World mag., 1978-80. Mem. investment bd. Case Western Res. U., Cleve., 1979-82. Named to Instl. Investor All-Am. Research Team, 1974-82, 84. Mem. Fin. Analysts Fedn., Cleve. Soc. Security Analysts (sec. 1973-74, mem. exec. com. 1973-75), Inst. Chartered Fin. Analysts. Republican. Episcopalian. Club: Kirtland Country (Ohio). Avocations: golf; tennis; swimming; bridge. Home: 7361 Markell Rd Waite Hill OH 44094 Office: McDonald & Co Securities Inc 2100 Central Nat Bank Bldg Cleveland OH 44114

MILLOY, FRANK JOSEPH, JR., physician; b. Phoenix, June 26, 1924; s. Frank Joseph and Ola (McCabe) M.; student Notre Dame U., 1942-43; M.S., Northwestern U., 1949, M.D., 1947. Intern, Cook County Hosp., Chgo., 1947-49, resident, 1953-57; practice medicine, specializing in surgery, Chgo., 1958—; asso. attending staff Presbyn.—St. Lukes Hosp.; attending staff Cook County Hosp.; mem. staff U. Ill. Research Hosp.; clin. asso. prof. surgery, U. Ill. Med. Sch.; asso. prof. surgery Rush Med. Sch. Cons. West Side Vet. Hosp. Served as apprentice seaman USNR, 1943-45; lt. M.C., USNR, 1950-52; PTO. Diplomate Am. Bd. Surgery and Thoracic Surgery. Mem. A.C.S., Chgo. Surg. Soc., Internat. Soc. Surgery, Am. Coll. Chest Physicians, Soc. Thoracic Surgeons, Phi Beta Pi. Clubs: Metropolitan, University (Chgo.). Home: 574 Jackson Ave Glencoe IL 60022 Office: 800 Westmoreland Lake Forest IL 60045

MILLS, ARLYN ALFRED, health care administrator; b. Neillsville, Wis., Dec. 6, 1939; s. Calvin B. and Elnora L. (Uhlman) M.; m. Mary Loris, Aug. 31, 1962; children—Suzanne, David. B.S., U. Wis., 1962, M.S., 1966. Tchr., No. Ctr. for Developmentally Disabled, Chippewa Falls, Wis., 1962-64; supr. vocat. tng., 1964-66; asst. adminstr. Clark County Health Care Center, Owen, Wis., 1966-70, adminstr., 1970—; guest lectr., cons. U. Wis.-Eau Claire, 1982—, adj. instr., 1981-82; advisor, 1972—. Contbr. articles to various publs. Advisor Future Bus. Leaders Am., Owen-Withee Sr. High Sch., Owen, Wis., 1978—. Mem. Am. Coll. Health Care Adminstrn., Am. Assn. Mental Deficiency, Wis. Assn. County Homes (chmn. com.). Intercare. Roman Catholic. Office: Clark County Health Care Center Route 2 Box X Owen WI 54460

MILLS, DOUGLAS NYE, balloonest, balloon repairman; b. Grand Rapids, Mich., July 2, 1945; s. Fredric Harold and Barbara Joan (Nye) M.; m. Karen L. Demory, July 24, 1968; 1 child, Jason Leonard. Student, Ferris State Coll., 1966-67. Sales person Gerber Products, North Grand Rapids, Mich., 1967-72; owner, operator, pilot, repairman Sky High Hot Air Balloons, Caledonia, Mich., 1972—. Builder hot air balloons. Recipient 8th Pl. award U.S. Nats. Hot Air Balloon Championships, 1974, 5th Pl. award U.S. Nats. Hot Air Balloon Championships, 1976, U.S. Competition award World Championship World Hot Air Balloon, York, Eng., 1977, 6th Pl. award U.S. Nats. Hot Air Balloon Championships, 1978. Mem. Balloon Fedn. Am., W. Mich. Balloon Assn. Repbulican. Presbyterian. Avocation: travelling. Home and Office: Sky High Hot Air Balloons 6087 100th St Caledonia MI 49316

MILLS, JAMES MYRON, dentist, farmer; b. Cadiz, Ohio, Aug. 22, 1927; s. Edwin Lewis and Olive Jane (Moorhead) M.; m. Marilyn Joanne Mattern, June 20, 1959; children—Alison Jane, James Andrew, John Edwin, Meredith Lee. Student Denison U., 1945, Union Coll., 1946; B.B.A., Ohio State U., 1949, D.D.S., 1957. Gen. practice dentistry, Cin., 1957-59, Marietta, Ohio, 1960—; also farmer. Mem. Pres.'s Club, Ohio State U., Columbus, 1979. Served as midshipman USN, 1945-47. Fellow Acad. of Gen. Dentistry; mem. ADA, Ohio Dental Soc., Muskingum Valley Dental Soc. (pres. 1982-83), Ohio State U. Dental Alumni Assn., Am. Forestry Assn. (life), Ohio Forestry Assn. (life). Republican. Presbyterian. Club: Marietta Toastmasters (pres. 1984—). Avocations: flying, sailing, golf. Office: 103 Seneca Dr Marietta OH 45750

MILLS, MORRIS HADLEY, state senator, farmer; b. Indpls., Sept. 25, 1927; s. Howard S. and Bernice H. (Sellars) M.; m. Mary Ann Sellars, 1954; children—Douglas, Fred, Gordon. B.A. in Econs., Earlham Coll., 1950; M.B.A., Harvard U., 1952. Treas., Maplehurst Farms, Inc., Indpls., 1952-62; ptnr. Mills Bros. Farms, Indpls., 1962—, treas., 1972—, also dir.; chmn. bd. AMSCOR, Indpls., 1982—; dir. Maplehurst Group, Ind. Ho. of Reps., 1970-72, mem. Ind. Senate (asst. pres. pro tem, chmn. budget subcom. fin., chmn. commerce and consumer affairs com.), 1972—; mem. Pres. Reagan's adv. council on continuing edn., Washington, 1982—. Mem., Greater Indpls. Progress Com., Conner Prairie Settlement Adv. Council; bd. dirs. Corp. Sci. and Tech., Marion County Farm Bur.; asst. treas. Valley Mills Friends Ch. Served with U.S. Army, 1946-47. Recipient Spl. award Ind. Vocat. Assn., 1976; Spl. award Ins. State Tchrs. Assn., 1978. Republican. Quaker. Club: Decatur Township Republican. Lodge: Lions. Office: Indiana State Senate Statehouse Indianapolis IN 46204

MILLS, NATHANIEL CRAIN, molecular biologist, medical research, educator; b. Bowling Green, Ky., June 3, 1948; s. Aubrey Robert and Laura Zelda (Cowles) M.; m. Teresa Martine Logsdon, Aug. 2, 1968; children—Matthew David, Jonathan Crain. B.S., Western Ky. U., 1969; M.S., Vanderbilt U., 1972, Ph.D., 1975. Postdoctoral fellow Pa. State U., 1975-78; research scientist VA Med. Ctr., Cleve., 1979-81; mem. faculty, sr. research assoc. Case Western Res. U., 1981—. Contbr. articles to sci. jours. Mem. AAAS, Endocrine Soc. Avocations: special effects photography, softball. Home: 3352 E Fairfax Rd Cleveland Heights OH 44118

MILLS, NELLY ELIZABETH, cosmetology educator; b. Concord, Ohio, July 10, 1915; d. Bernardus and Adriana Helena (Van Aartsen de Melker); m. Vane James Mills, Aug. 19, 1939 (dec.); children—Jane Ann Mills Schwab, James Vane. Student Youngstown Sch. Cosmetology, Kent State U. Beautician Geneva True Temper Corp. (Ohio), 1935-39, Marie's House of Hair Fashions, Hartsgrove, Ohio, Your Beauty Salon, Ashtabula, Ohio, 1958-70; tchr. Ashtabula County Joint Vocat. Sch., 1970—; advisor Vocat. Indsl. Clubs of Am. Mem. Am. Vocat. Assn., Ohio Vocat. Assn. Methodist. Lodge: Eastern Star. Home: 183 Elm St Geneva OH 44041 Office: Jefferson OH 44047

MILLS, NORMAN THOMAS, steel company executive; b. Hammond, Ind., Jan. 16, 1932; s. Arnold Nathan and Elsie Anna Paula (Radloff) M.; m. Helen McLaughlin, Aug. 30, 1958; children—David, Steven, Douglas, Laura, Paula, Carol. B.S. in Chem. Engring., Purdue U., 1959; M.S. in Chem. Engring., U. Del., 1961. Research engr. Standard Oil Co. of Ind., Whiting, Ind., 1959-60, Linde div. Union Carbide Corp., Speedway, Ind., 1960-64, Allison div. Gen. Motors Corp., Indpls., 1964-66; mgr. materials devel. Inland Steel Co., Chgo., 1966—. Contbr. articles to sci. jours. Patentee in field. Sci. advisor schs. Town of Highland, Ind., 1979. Served with USN, 1950-54. Mem. AIME (pres. 1984-86, disting. mem. Iron and Steel Soc., pres. of Soc. 1980-82), Assn. Iron and Steel Engrs., Am. Assn. Engring Socs. (mem. bd. govs., exec. com.), Sigma Xi, Tau Beta Pi, Omega Chi Epsilon, Phi Lambda Upsilon. Roman Catholic. Avocations: sports; reading; music. Home: 3537 41st Pl Highland IN 46322 Office: Inland Steel Co 30 W Monroe St Chicago IL 60603

MILLS, REBECCA ANN, advertising executive; b. Storm Lake, Iowa, May 11, 1950; d. Omer H. and Awanda Lucille (Mathison) Roth; student Northwestern U., summers 1968, 70; B.S. in Journalism with honors, Drake U., 1972; m. Timothy Lemar Mills, Dec. 22, 1973; children—Sarah Rebecca, Abby Elizabeth. Editor house organ Des Moines Register & Tribune, 1972-73; coordinator Mktg. Services Corp. of Iowa Credit Union League, Des Moines, 1973-74; account exec. Prescott Co., Denver, 1974-75; co-owner, pres. Mills Agy., Storm Lake, 1975—; guest lectr. Buena Vista Coll.; featured speaker Iowa Bank Mktg. Conf., 1979, 82, Internat. Telephone Credit Union Assn. conv., Dallas, 1978. Parents adv. bd. Day Care Center; v.p. Lake Creek Ladies Bd. Recipient numerous ADDY awards for excellence in advt., 1st place award in nat. bank ad news, 1984. Mem. Am. Soc. Profl. and Exec. Women, Women in Communications, Advt. Club Sioux Cities, Nat. Fedn. Ind. Bus., Des Moines Advt. Club (past chmn. edn. com.), AAUW (dir. Lake Creek 1983-86), Storm Lake C. of C. (dir., pres. 1983), Lake Creek Country (pres. 1985-86), DAR (regent Buena Vista chpt. 1981-82), Republican. Presbyterian. Clubs: Keystone (sec., pres.), Eastern Star (past officer), Faith Hope and Charity (dir. 1982—, v.p.). Home: 131 N Emerald Dr Storm Lake IA 50588 Office: 612 Seneca St Storm Lake IA 50588

MILLS, REESE FERRIS, lawyer; b. Mansfield, Ohio, Oct. 28, 1946; s. Reese and Charlotte Gorman (Ferris) M.; m. Victoria M. Voegele, Aug. 5, 1978. B.A., Denison U., 1968; J.D., U. Mich., 1974. Bar: Ohio 1975. Tchr. pub. schs., Mansfield, 1970-73; solicitor Village of Ontario (Ohio), 1977-79; ptnr. firm Mabee, Meyers & Mills, Mansfield, 1979—; law dir. City of Mansfield, 1980—. Trustee Mansfield YMCA, 1977—; 2d v.p. Richland County Republican Exec. Com. (Ohio). Mem. Ohio State Bar Assn., Richland County Bar Assn. Presbyterian. Clubs: Kiwanis, University (Mansfield), Elks. Home: 624 Overlook Rd Mansfield OH 44907 Office: Mabee Meyers Mills 24 W 3d St Suite 300 Mansfield OH 44902

MILLS-FISCHER, SHIRLEY, association executive; b. Shelbyville, Tex., Jan. 19, 1936; d. John Bailey and Ruby Elaine (Kay) Collum; m. Keith A. Mills, June, 1955, (div. Apr. 1975); m. Eugene Thomas Fischer, Aug. 9, 1980. B.S., La. State U., 1971, M.S., 1972. Asst. librarian Raleigh County Pub. Library, Beckley, W.Va., 1972-74; dir. Miracle Valley Regional Library Systems, City-County Pub. Library, Moundsville, W.Va., 1974-78; exec. dir. Pub. Library Assn., Chgo., 1978—; mem. adv. com. Gov. W.Va. Conf. Libraries and Info. Services, 1978. Mem. editorial staff: Southeastern Libraries, 1975-77. Mem. Am. Library Assn., Am. Soc. Assn. Execs. Democrat. Episcopalian. Home: 4343 Baring East Chicago IN 46312 Office: Pub Library Assn 50 E Huron St Chicago IL 60611

MILNE, GEORGE RICHARD ALOYSIOUS, manufacturing company official; b. Cin., Jan. 10, 1936; s. James A. and Elizabeth (Padur) M.; m. Lorraine V. Kraus, Sept. 21, 1963 (div.); children—James R., John E.; m. Mary Ruth Jenkins, Mar. 20, 1982. Student in commerce U. Cin., 1959-62, NOMA grad. fellow cert. in mgmt. adminstrv. services; B.S. in Bus. and Commerce, U. Louisville, 1963. Supr. engring. services and records Am. Radiator and Standard San. Corp., Cin., 1958-60, product liaison engr., 1960-61, ops. supr., 1961-62, buyer, Louisville, 1962-64, supr. purchases and services, 1964, purchasing agt., 1965; purchasing agt. Mascon Toy Co. div. Masco Corp., Lorain, Ohio, 1966-69, mgr. purchasing youth and recreational products div. Leisure Group, Inc. (formerly Masco Corp.), 1969-70; purchasing agt. plumbing products div. Delta Faucet Co., Taylor, Mich. and Greensburg, Ind., 1970-75, divisional purchasing agt., 1975-76, divisional purchasing mgr.,

Indpls., 1976-78, divisional mgr. purchasing internat., 1978—. Lectr. purchasing and economy. Bd. dirs. YMCA; active Nat. Alliance Businessmen. Served with USAF, 1955-58. Mem. Nat. Assn. Purchasing Mgmt. (Devel. Man of Yr. 1974-75, pres. 1979-82), Purchasing Mgmt. Assn. Indpls., Copper Club. Republican. Roman Catholic. Lodge: Fraternal Order of Foresters. Contbr. articles to profl. jours. Home: 9635 Greentree Dr Carmel IN 46268 Office: 55 E 111th St Indianapolis IN 46280

MILNE, ROBERT DAVID, investment management company executive; b. East Grand Rapids, Mich., Dec. 28, 1930; s. Robert Kenneth and Alice Elfrieda (Youngberg) M.; m. Alma Jean Zimmerman, Dec. 15, 1960; children—R. John, Thomas D., Ruth J., Mary E. B.A., Baldwin-Wallace Coll., Berea, Ohio, 1952; J.D., Cleve. State U., 1957. Analyst, Boyd, Watterson & Co., Cleve., 1952-54, portfolio mgr., 1954-79; pres. Duff and Phelps Investment Mgmt. Co., Cleve., 1979—. Editor: Investment Values in a Dynamic World, 1974. Assoc. editor Fin. Analysts Jour., 1966-83. Served with USAF, 1949-50. Mem. Inst. Chartered Fin. Analysts (pres. 1974-75, C. Stewart Sheppard award 1978), Cleve. Soc. Security Analysts (pres. 1962-63), Greater Cleve. Bar Assn. Clubs: Union, Print of Cleve. (chmn. aquisitions 1974—). Avocation: Boston Marathon. Home: 4455 Valley Forge Dr Fairview Park OH 44126 Office: Duff and Phelps Investment Mgmt Co 710 Ohio Savings Plaza Cleveland OH 44114

MILNER, HAROLD LEON, state public affairs administrator, journalist; b. Breese, Ill., Feb. 25, 1946; s. Shirley Logan and Dorena Doris (Burkett) M.; m. Cynthia Marie Young, Nov. 30, 1974; children—Leanne Marie, James Logan. B.S. in Communications, So. Ill. U., 1968; M.A. in Pub. Adminstrn., Sangamon State U., 1977; post grad. MacMurray Coll., 1971. Photo journalist Effingham Daily News, Ill., 1968; asst. dir. pub. relations MacMurray Coll., Jacksonville, Ill., 1971; dir. photo and audio-visual dept. Meml. Med. Ctr., Springfield, Ill., 1971-73; spl. asst. to U.S. Congressman George Shipley of Ill., Washington, 1974-75; speaker's press sec. Ill. Ho. of Rep., Springfield, 1975-79; spl. asst. for pub. affairs Ill. State Bd. Edn., Springfield, 1979—; pres. State Pub. Info. Officers' Roundtable, Springfield, 1981-83; chmn. Ill. State Employees Credit Union, Springfield, 1983—; mem. Gov.'s Task Force on Fin. Services, 1985-86. Mem. adv. com. Am. Heart Assn., Springfield, 1981—. Served with U.S. Army, 1968-70. Mem. Nat. Sch. Pub. Relations Assn., Nat. Assn. State Edn. Dept. Info. Officers (treas. 1985), Jaycees. Methodist. Office: Ill State Bd Edn 100 N 1st St Springfield IL 62777

MILNER, IRVIN MYRON, lawyer; b. Cleve., Feb. 5, 1916; s. Nathan and Rose (Spector) M.; m. Zelda Winograd, Aug. 15, 1943. A.B. cum laude, Western Res. U. (now Case Western Res. U.), 1937, J.D., 1940, LL.M., 1970. Bar: Ohio 1940, U.S. Dist. Ct. (no. dist.) Ohio 1946. Sole practice, Cleve., 1940-41, 46—; exec. sec., counsel Men's Apparel Club Ohio, Cleve., 1947-48; adj. instr. Sch. Law, Case Western Res. U., 1965-66; spl. counsel Ohio Office Atty. Gen., 1963-70; legal counsel Korean Assn. Greater Cleve., 1972—. Mem. Cleve. Fgn. Consular Corps, 1970—, hon. consul Republic Korea for Cleve., 1970—; bd. dirs. Internat. Human Assistance Programs, Inc., 1973-81, corp. mem., 1981—; bd. dirs. Cuyahoga County Bar Found., 1980—, sec.-treas., 1980-84; mem. adv. bd. internat. bus. program Notre Dame Coll. Ohio, 1983—; mem. Consular Corps Coll., 1984—; mem. nat. adv. bd. Am. Security Council. Served with U.S. Army, 1941-45; ETO. Decorated Order Diplomatic Service Merit-Heung-in medal (Korea); recipient award of Merit Cuyahoga County (Ohio) Council VFW, 1958, Merit award Greater Cleve. Vets. Council, 1983; named to Disting. Alumni Hall of Fame, Cleveland Heights (Ohio) High Sch., 1983. Fellow Ohio Bar Found., Internat. Consular Acad.; mem. Cleve. Bar Assn., Cuyahoga County Bar Assn. (pres. 1975-76, award of Spl. Merit 1976), Cuyahoga County Bar Found. (sec.-treas. 1980-84, bd. dirs. 1980—), Ohio State Bar Assn. (council dels. 1976—), ABA, Tau Epsilon Rho, Delta Phi Alpha. Republican. Jewish. Clubs: Rotary, Cleve. City, Masons (Cleve.). Office: 526 Superior Rd NE Leader Bldg Suite 711 Cleveland OH 44114

MIN, KYUNG-WHAN, pathologist; b. Seoul, Dem. Rep. of Korea, May 5, 1937; came to U.S., 1964; s. Jungki and Inyoung (Lee) K.; m. Young J., May 28, 1966; children—Kwanhong Christopher, Wonhong David. M.D., Seoul Nat. U., 1962. Diplomate Am. Bd. Pathology. Resident pathologist Balt. Cit-Hosp., 1964-65, Baylor U. Coll. Medicine, Houston, 1965-69, asst. prof., 1971-78; assoc. pathologist Chosun U. Med. Sch., Kwanjoo, Korea, 1970-71; pathologist Mercy Hosp. Med. Ctr., Des Moines, 1978—. Author: Diagnostic Electron Microscopy for Clinical Medicine, 1980. Pres., Korean Soc. Iowa, 1982-84. Fellow ACP, Am. Coll. Pathologists, Am. Soc. Clin. Pathologists; mem. Internat. Acad. Pathology, Am. Assn. Pathologists. Home: 5109 Aspen Dr West Des Moines IA 50265 Office: Mercy Hosp Med Ctr Des Moines IA 50314

MIN, LEO YOON-GEE, university administrator; b. Seoul, Korea, Nov. 1, 1933; came to U.S., 1965; naturalized, 1982; s. Byungchan and Kyungsoon M.; m. Linda Schlag, July 19, 1981; children—Richard, Sarah, Victoria. B.A., Seoul Nat. U., 1956, M.Ed., 1966; M.S., Stanford U., 1968, Ph.D., 1970. Mathematician, computer programmer Stanford Research Inst., Menlo Park, Calif., 1968-70; asst. prof. Cath. U. Am., Washington, 1970-76; dir. research and evaluation Model Secondary Sch. for Deaf, Gallaudet Coll., Washington, 1976-79; dir. computing facilities U. Mich.-Flint, 1980-83; dir. computing affairs So. Ill. U., Carbondale, 1983—. Home: Route 8 Box 174 #118 Carbondale IL 62901 Office: So Ill Univ Carbondale IL 62901

MINAMYER, WILLIAM ERIC, lawyer; b. Salem, Ohio, June 26, 1953; s. Kenneth Dean and Donna Lou (Whitehouse) M.; m. Colleen Ann Moore, Aug. 11, 1979; children—Jennifer Dale, Lisa Colleen. B.A., U. Akron, 1975; J.D., Am. U., 1978; L.L.M. in Labor Law, Georgetown U., 1982. Bar: Ohio 1979, U.S. Dist. Ct. (so. dist.) Ohio 1983, U.S. Ct. Appeals (6th cir.) 1984, U.S. Supreme Ct. 1984. Spl. asst. to Congressman Charles W. Whalen, Washington, 1975-76; assoc. Porter, Wright, Morris & Arthur, Dayton, Ohio, 1983—. Chmn. sign com. Donna Moon, Dayton, 1984; campaign coordinator Whalen for Congress, Dayton, 1976; active Young Republicans, Dayton, 1983—. Served to lt. JAGC, USN, 1979-83, USNR, 1983—. Decorated Navy Achievement medal, Meritorious Unit commendation; recipient Nat. Sojourner's award USAFR, 1974. Mem. Dayton Bar Assn., Butler County Bar Assn., Ohio Bar Assn., Fed. Bar Assn., ABA. Presbyterian. Lodge: Rotary. Home: 9146 S Normandy Ln Centerville OH 45459 Office: Porter Wright Morris & Arthur 2100 First Nat Bank PO Box 1805 Dayton OH 45402

MINARD, THOMAS MICHAEL, strategic planner, consultant; b. St. Charles, Ill., Dec. 31, 1944; s. Clarence Scott and Ruth L. (Larson) M. Cert., Coll. Advanced Traffic, Chgo., 1964. Gen. mgr. Iowa Terminal R.R. Co., Mason City, 1968-70; mgr. quality control C & NW Ry. Co., Chgo., 1970-73; pres. Great Plains Ry. Co., Seward, Nebr., 1973-76; mgr. railroad sales and procurement L.B. Foster Co., Des Plaines, Ill., 1976-80, project coordinator, 1981-83, transp. cons., Chgo., 1983; co-founder, v.p. Railmode, Inc., Chgo., 1984—. Mem. Chgo. Council Fgn. Relations, Chgo. Maintenance of Way, Coll. Advanced Traffic Alumni Assn., Delta Nu Alpha. Home: 450 W Briar Pl Chicago IL 60657 Office: 53 W Jackson Blvd Chicago IL 60604

MINARIK, KATHY DOME, educator; b. Cleve., Oct. 24, 1951; d. Wilfred John and Agnes Frances (Osicka) Dome; m. Christopher Mark Minarik, Aug. 26, 1972; 1 child, Shannon. B.A., Cleve. State U., 1973; M.Ed., Kent State U., 1979. Cert. tchr. Ohio. Tchr. Parma City Schs., Ohio, 1973—; curriculum writer Parma City Schs., 1979, 80, reading materials com., 1983-84. Mem., v.p., pres. Brunswick Bd. Edn., Ohio, 1982—; PTA. Named Outstanding Young Woman Jaycees, 1981. Mem. Medina County Vocat. Bd., Ohio Sch. Bd. Assn., Nat. Edn. Assn., Ohio Edn. Assn., Northeast Ohio Edn. Assn., Parma Edn. Assn. Roman Catholic. Avocations: traveling; reading. Office: Brunswick Sch Bd PO Box 338 Brunswick OH 44212

MINES, DUANE HERMAN, pharmacist, consultant; b. Fremont, Nebr., June 25, 1928; s. Robert A. and Gladys Margaret (Hastings) M.; m. Mary Theresa Pupkes, June 16, 1951; children—Robert, Terri Ann, Mary, Michael, Kelly. B.S. in Pharmacy, Creighton U., 1952. Grad. pharmacist Immanuel Hosp., Omaha, 1950-52; pharmacist Dodge Pharmacy, Nebr., 1953, Walgreen Co., Lincoln, Nebr., 1953-54; pharmacist, owner Mines Drug Store, Hooper, Nebr., 1954—; pharm. cons. Hooper Care Ctr., 1972—, Terrace Hill Manor, Emerson, Nebr., 1977-81, Fremont Care Ctr., 1974—. Mem. Nebr. Bd. Health, Lincoln, 1979-83, Dodge County Bd. Adjustment, Fremont, 1974—; chmn. Dodge County Comprehensive Plan, Fremont, 1972—, Hooper Planning Commn., 1964-79, Creighton U. Adv. Council, 1972—; Nebr. Coll. Pharmacy Adv. Council, 1974-82; mem. Nebr. Council Continuing Educ., 1978—. Recipient Alumni Merit award Creighton U., 1984, Disting. Service to Pharmacy award U. Nebr. Med. Ctr., 1984; named Preceptor of Yr. U. Nebr.-Syntex Corp., 1982. Served with USN, 1946-68, PTO. Mem. Nebr. Pharmacist Assn. (pres.-elect 1984—, Bowl of Hygeia award A.H. Robbins Co. 1981), Nebraska Pharmacist Assn. (bd. dirs. 1972). Roman Catholic. Club: Hooper Commercial (pres. 1975-78). Avocations: painting; flying; golf. Office: Mines Drug Store 202 North Main Hooper NE 68031

MINHAS, JASJIT SINGH, educator; b. Jalandhar, India, Mar. 22, 1933; came to U.S., 1965, naturalized, 1975; s. Charan Singh and Chaman (Kaur) M.; m. Surjit Kaur, June 19, 1960; children—Jasdip Singh, Sandip Singh. B.A., Punjab U., 1955, B.Ed., 1957; M.A., Cath. U., 1981, Ph.D., 1984. Tng. mgr. B.P. Oil Co., Washington, 1970-73; program cons. Applied Sci., Inc., McLean, Va., 1973-74; project specialist Dickinson Pub. Schs., N.D., 1975-77; dean, v.p. edn. United Tribes Ednl. Tech. Ctr., Bismarck, N.D., 1978—. Mem. Am. Vocat. Assn., Am. Mgmt. Soc., Assn. Communicational Tech. Democrat. Lodge: Elks. Home: 428 W Brandon Dr Bismarck ND 58501 Office: United Tribes Ednl Tech Ctr Bismarck ND 58501

MINICH, MARLIN DON, civil engineering educator; b. Orange, Calif., Aug. 13, 1938; s. Harry Elden and Selvestas Magdelene (Krichbaum) M.; m. Lorna Dollins Perrine, Sept. 10, 1960; children—Daniel, Thomas, Susan, Christine, Jennifer. B.S. in Civil Engring., Fenn Coll., Cleve., 1961; M.S. in Engring. Mechanics, Case Western Res., 1964, Ph.D. in Civil Engring., 1968. Registered profl. engr., Ohio. Asst. prof. to assoc. prof. Cleve. State U., 1967-79; prof. civil engring. Ohio No. U., Ada, 1979—. Chmn. Harco Industries, Kenton, Ohio, 1982-85. Mem. Am. Soc. Engring. Educators. Home: 601 W North Ada OH 45810 Office: Ohio No U Biggs Engring Bldg Ada OH 45810

MINKIN, HARVEY, radiologist, osteopathic physician; b. Bklyn., Aug. 16, 1944; s. Abraham and Evelyn (Buchman) M.; m. Elaine Eiges, Dec. 26, 1965; children—Kimberley Anne, Nicole Alyse. B.A., U. Rochester, 1965; D.O. with honors, Chgo. Coll. Osteo. Medicine, 1969. Diplomate Am. Osteo. Bd. Radiology. Intern, Detroit Osteo. Hosp. Corp., 1969-70, resident in radiology, 1970-73; attending radiologist Lapeer County Hosp., Lapeer, Mich., 1973-76, dir. med. edn., 1974-76; attending radiologist N.W. Gen. Hosp., Detroit, 1973-75, McKenzie Hosp., Sandusky, Mich., 1975-82; dir. edn. Mich. Assn. Osteo. Radiologists, Pontiac, 1983—, chmn. radiology dept. Saginaw (Mich.) Osteo. Hosp., 1983—, dir. radiology residency program, 1981—, chmn. intern-resident tng. com., 1985—; chmn. radiology dept. Yale (Mich.) Community Hosp., 1983—, Marlette (Mich.) Community Hosp., 1983—; asst. clin. prof. radiology Mich. State U., East Lansing, 1983—; clin. instr. nuclear medicine Ferris State Coll., Big Rapids, Mich., 1983—. Mem. Am. Osteo. Coll. Radiology, Am. Osteo. Assn., Mich. Assn. Osteo. Physicians, (del.), Saginaw County Osteo. Assn., Am. Inst. Ultrasound in Medicine (sr. mem.), Soc. Nuclear Medicine, Mich. Coll. Nuclear Medicine Physicians. Contbr. articles to profl. publs. Home: 1639 Apple Ln Bloomfield Hills MI 48013 Office: 515 N Michigan Ave Saginaw MI 48602

MINNEFIELD, ARTHUR LEE, automotive manufacturing company official; b. Anderson, Ind., Oct. 21, 1935; s. Arthur Minnefield and Hazel (Myers) M.; m. Rosetta Venters, May 11, 1956 (div. Sept. 1980); children—Rosetta, Arthur, Jerry, Veronica, Angela, Renee; m. Patricia Elaine Wells, Feb. 20, 1981; children—Mathis, Martan. B.Gen. Studies, U. Nebr.-Omaha, 1971. Enlisted in U.S. Army, 1952, commd. 2d lt., 1965, advanced through grades to maj., 1975; served in Korea, 1952-53, Japan, 1953-56, Europe, 1959-60, 73-75, Vietnam, 1965, 68; ret., 1975; quality control coordinator Delco Remy div. Gen. Motors Corp., Anderson, 1975—. Asst. to mayor for community affairs, Anderson, 1981—; chmn. Anderson Bd. Pub. Safety, 1980-81; mem. Ind. State Coordinating Com., 1983—; chmn. Madison Grant Pvt. Industry Council, Anderson, 1983—. Decorated Silver Star, Bronze Star (4), Purple Heart (2), Air medal. Republican. Methodist. Avocations: racquetball; jogging. Home: PO Box 266 Anderson IN 46015 Office: Delco Remy 2401 Columbus Ave Anderson IN 46011

MINNESTE, VIKTOR, JR., electronic company executive; b. Haapsalu, Estonia, Jan. 15, 1932; s. Viktor and Alice (Lembra) M.; B.S. in Elec. Engring., U. Ill., 1960. Electronic engr. Bell & Howell Co., 1960-69, microstatics div. SCM Co., 1969-71, Multigraphics div. A-M Co., 1972-73; electronic engr. bus. products group Victor Comptometer Co. (merged with Walter Kidde Corp. 1977), Chgo., 1973-74, service mgr. internat. group, 1974-75, then supr. electronics design group, to 1982; project engr. Warner Electric, 1982-84; systems engr. Barrett Electronics, 1984—. pub. Motteid/Thoughts, 1962-68; chmn., Estonian-Ams. Polit. Action Com., 1968-72. Served with AUS, 1952-54. Home: 3134 N Kimball Ave Chicago IL 60618 Office: 2933 MacArthur Blvd Northbrook IL 60062

MINNICK, EDWIN ROYCE, college dean, farm agent; b. Cambridge, Nebr., Jan. 21, 1926; s. Richard D. and Alice (Capps) M.; m. Alta M. Hubbert, Dec. 19, 1950; children—Edwin, Richard, Rebecca, Christine. B.A. in Edn., Kearney State Coll., 1951; M.Edn., Colo. State U., 1967. Cert. secondary tchr., Nebr. Tchr., coach McCook Pub. Schs., Nebr., 1951-52; coordinator pub. schs., Kearney, Nebr., 1958-65; prin. adult high sch. Lincoln Pub. Schs., Nebr., 1965-66; dean of students Central Community Coll., Hastings, Nebr., 1966—; bd. dirs. Mid Nebr. Community Service, Kearney, 1980—; coop. cons. Cloud County Community Coll., Concordia, Kansas, 1981-82; reader proposals Title VIII Higher Edn. Washington, 1983-84. Com. mem. Planning and Zoning Commn., Hastings, 1977-81; mem. bd. Econ. Devel. Corp., Hastings, 1979-83; co-chmn. United Way, Hastings, 1984. Mem. Coop. Edn. Assn. Lodge: Kiwanis (past pres., recipient pres.'s award, 1981). Avocations: picture framing; creative woods Office: Central Community Coll PO Box 1024 Hastings NE 68901

MINOR, CARL ALLEN, banker, insurance executive; b. DeKalb County, Mo., Feb. 17, 1917; s. Earle and Edna Alice (Heimbaugh) M.; m. Dorothy Ann Jarrett, Jan. 3, 1941; children—Allen R., Sue Ann Perkins. A.B., William Jewell Coll., 1938; M.A., U. Mo.-Kansas City, 1956. Counseling psychologist VA, Kansas City, 1945-61; with Farmers Bank of Maysville, Mo., 1961—, pres., chief exec. officer, 1982-83, chmn., 1983—, also dir.; dir. DeKalb County Indsl. Co., DeKalb County Health Services, Inc. Active Maysville Methodist Ch., 1961—; trustee Cameron Community Hosp., 1963-78, treas, 1970-78; treas. R-1 Sch. Dist., 1982—; mem. dist. com. Pony Express Boy Scouts Am., 1965; bd. dirs. Community Scholarship Fund, 1980—. Served to lt. comdr. USN, 1942-45, 50-52. Mem. Am. Assn. Individual Investors, Am. Legion (treas. 1980—), VFW. Democrat. Lodges: Rotary (pres. 1965), Masons, Shriners. Avocations: investments, farming, golf, travel, antique bicycles. Home: PO Box 4 Maysville MO 64469

MINTON, J. D., insurance company executive; b. 1925. Pres., dir. Mut. of Omaha Ins. Co. Office: Mutual of Omaha Ins Co Mutual of Omaha Plaza Omaha NE 68175*

MINTON, JOHN PETER, surgeon; b. Columbus, Ohio, Nov. 29, 1934; s. Harvey Allen and Elsie (Steiger) M.; B.Sc., Ohio State U., 1956, M.D., 1960, M.Med. Sci., 1966, Ph.D. in Microbiology, 1969; m. Janice Arlene Gurney, Aug. 29, 1958; children—Cathryn Anne, Elizabeth Ellen, Cynthia Jane, Christina Lynn. Intern, Ohio State U., 1960-61; clin. asso. surgery Nat. Cancer Inst., Bethesda, Md., 1962-65; resident in surgery Univ. Hosp., Ohio State U., Columbus; asst. prof. surgery Ohio State U., Columbus, 1969-73, asso. prof., 1973-77, prof., 1977—, Am. Cancer Soc. prof. clin. oncology, 1979—; mem. grant rev. com. Nat. Cancer Inst., Am. Cancer Soc. Served with USPHS, 1962-65. Mem. ACS (Ohio State U. field liaison chmn.), Ohio State Med. Soc., Columbus Surg. Soc., Soc. Univ. Surgeons, Am. Assn. Acad. Surgeons, Am. Assn. Cancer Edn., Am. Soc. Clin. Oncology, Internat. Fedn. Surgeons. Republican. Presbyterian. Clubs: Columbus Rose (pres. 1979), Central Ohio Rose Soc., Am. Rose Soc., Lido Soc. Contbr. articles to med. jours. Office: 410 W 10th Ave Columbus OH 43210

MIRANDA, CARLOS SA, business executive; b. Fall River, Mass., Nov. 16, 1929; s. Carlos Sa and Annette (Pratt) M.; m. Natalie Cardoso, Jan. 5, 1949; children—Carla, Lucy, John. B.S. in Mech. Engring., Marquette U., 1956. With internat. div. Kellogg Co., Battle Creek, Mich., 1964-65, gen. mgr., Brazil, 1965-80, gen. mgr. Kellogg's Spain, 1983, v.p. Kellogg Internat., Battle Creek, 1980—. Recipient Pero Vaz Caminha award, Brazil, 1976. Mem. ASME. Republican. Roman Catholic. Office: 235 Porter St Battle Creek MI 49016

MIRANDA, DANIEL FRANK, lawyer, real estate executive; b. Corona, Calif., June 16, 1953; s. Frank R. and Mary A. (Cintas) M.; m. Jacqueline Fry, Dec. 28, 1975; children—David Frank, Kate Elise. A.B., U. Calif.-Berkeley, 1975; J.D., (Stone scholar), Columbia U., 1979. Bar: Ill. 1979. Assoc., Sonnenschein, Carlin, Nath & Rosenthal, Chgo., 1979-81; v.p., legal and corp. sec. The Westport Co. (Conn.), 1981-84; project exec. dir. 666 Assocs., Chgo., 1981-84; pres. First Columbia Corp., Chgo. and Miami, 1984-85; dir. Dade Savs. & Loan Assn., Miami, 1984, Greater N. Michigan Ave. Assn., Chgo. Mem. ABA, Ill. State Bar Assn., Chgo. Bar Assn. Home: 215 E Chestnut St Chicago IL 60611

MIRANDA, ROCKY V., linguistics educator; b. Mangalore, Karnataka, India, Sept. 19, 1937; came to U.S., 1964; s. Jacob F. and Veronica I. (Tauro) M.; m. Pushpa Devaki Bobde, June 20, 1983; 1 child, Elizabeth. B.A., Madras Christian Coll., India, 1957; M.A., Banaras Hindu U., India, 1960; Ph.D. in Linguistics, Cornell U., 1971. Lectr. in Hindi S.B. Coll., Karkala, India, 1960-62, Dhempe Coll., India, 1962-64; asst. prof. linguistics U. Minn., Mpls., 1971-77, assoc. prof., 1977—. Contbr. numerous articles to profl. jours. Am. Council of Learned Socs. grantee, 1965, 67, 77, Am. Inst. Indian Studies grantee, 1967, 77, 80, 82; numerous fellowships, grants, U. Minn. Mem. Linguistic Soc. Am., Linguistic Soc. India. Office: Dept Linguistics U Minn 320 16th Ave SE Minneapolis MN 55455

MIRKIN, L. DAVID, pathology educator; b. Buenos Aires, Argentina, Feb. 22, 1931; came to U.S., 1976; s. Moises and Celia (Wexman) M. M.D., Buenos Aires U., 1957. Diplomate Am. Bd. Pathology. Intern Children's Hosp., Buenos Aires, 1960-61, Children's Meml. Hosp., Chgo., 1962; vice head dept. pathology Children's Hosp., Buenos Aires, 1961-70; head dept. pathology R. Del Rio Hosp., Santiago, Chile, 1970-76; assoc. prof. pathology Riley Hosp. for Children, Indpls., 1978—, dir. pediatric pathology; cons. WHO, 1970. Contbr. articles to profl. jours. Mem. Internat. Soc. Pediatric Pathology, Internat. Acad. Pathology, Soc. Pediatric Pathology, Am. Assn. Pathologists, N.Y. Acad. Scis. Home: 5260 Woodbrook Dr Indianapolis IN 46254 Office: Riley Hosp for Children 236 702 Barnhill Dr Indianapolis IN 46223

MISCH, CARL ERWIN, implant dentist; b. Detroit, Nov. 17, 1947; s. Carl Otto and Mary Ann (Roman) M.; m. Lori Sally Walenga; children—Paula, Carl, Lara. B.S., Wayne State U., 1969; D.D.S., U. Detroit, 1973. Practice dentistry, specializing in implant dentistry, Dearborn, Mich.; asst. prof. Temple U. Dental Sch., 1983—; asst. chief implant dentistry Interfaith Hosp., Bklyn., 1984—; asst. prof. U. Pitts., 1984—; pres. Mich. Implant Dentistry, Dearborn, Mich., 1984—; pres. Quest Implants, Dallas, 1984. Author: Clinical Dentistry, 1983; editor: Implantologist, 1982—. Patentee mucosal insert, endodontic implant. Fellow Internat. Congress Oral Implant (sec. 1982—), Acad. Implant and Transplant (pres. 1983—) Royal Soc. Medicine, Am. Assn. Hosp. Dentistry, Acad. Gen. Dentistry, Acad. Implants (pres. 1983—). Republican. Roman Catholic. Club: Rotary. Home: 3668 Oakleaf St West Bloomfield MI 48033 Office: Mich Implant Dentistry 22691 Michigan Ave Dearborn MI 48124

MISEK, SHAMUS RORY, transportation executive; b. Cicero, Ill., Feb. 8, 1953; B.A. in History and Polit. Sci., Ill. Benedictine Coll., 1975; postgrad. U. Ill., 1978-80, Loyola U., Chgo., 1981—. Adminstr. Town of Cicero Pub. Works Dept., 1977-79, adminstrv. asst. to pres. 1979-80; coordinator Regional Transp. Authority, Chgo., 1980-82, mgr. paratransit dept., 1982—. Bd. dirs. Morton Twp. High Schs., 1976—, Cook County State's Atty Adv. Council, 1981—; bd. del. West Suburban Assn. Spl. Edn., 1977—; transp. chmn. Cicero Plan Commn., 1977—; vice chmn. Cicero Housing Authority, 1979-82; bd. dirs. Cicero-Berwyn YMCA, 1977-79. Mem. Assn. Supervision and Curriculum Devel., C. of C. Republican. Roman Catholic. Club: Odd Fellows. Home: 5831 W 26th St Cicero IL 60650 Office: Regional Transportation Authority 300 N State St Chicago IL 60610

MISENER, ANDREW GRANT, veterinarian, animal hospital administrator; b. Waterford, Ont., Can., July 1, 1912; came to U.S., 1938; s. Harvey G. and Elizabeth (Andrews) M.; m. Mildred Louise Taylor, Feb. 2, 1940; children—Robert Grant, Kenneth Taylor. B.S.A., Ont. Agrl. Coll., 1935; D.V.M., U. Toronto, 1938. Lic. veterinarian Ill. Gen. practice vet. medicine, Chgo., 1938—; owner, operator Misener Animal Hosp., 1938-77; sr. ptnr., adminstr. Misener Holley Animal Hosp., 1977—. Pres. Friends of U. Guelph Inc., 1977—; pres. Canadian Club Chgo., 1949. Recipient Disting. Alumnus award Ont. Vet. Coll. Alumni Assn., 1979; named hon. fellow U. Guelph, 1984. Mem. Chgo. Vet. Med. Assn. (pres. 1945, historian 1979—), Ill. State Vet. Med. Assn. (sec.-treas. 1949-54, pres. 1955, Outstanding Mem. award 1972), AVMA (Ill. ho. of dels. 1949-81, Disting. Mem. award 1976), Am. Animal Hosp. Assn., Rogers Park C. of C. (treas. 1968-72). Republican. Methodist. Lodges: Kiwanis of Rogers Park (pres. 1946), Elks (Chgo.). Editor Ill. State Vet. Med. Assn. Bull., 1949-54. Home: 8200 N Oketo Ave Niles IL 60648 Office: Misener Holley Animal Hosp 1545 W Devon Ave Chicago IL 60660

MISHRA, VISHWA MOHAN, educator; b. Hilsa, Patna, India, Nov. 12, 1937; s. Pandit Sheo Nath and Pandita Nitya (Rani) M.; came to U.S., 1956, naturalized, 1964; B.A. with honors, Patna U., 1954, M.A., 1956; M.A., U. Ga., 1958; Ph.D., U. Minn., 1968; m. Sally Schroeder, June 18, 1977; children—Aneil Kumar, Allan Kumar, Anand Kumar, Jennifer Kumari, Andrew Kumar. Staff reporter, Hindusthan Samachar, Ltd., Patna, India, 1950-56; exec. dir. India for Christ, Inc., Mpls., 1960-64; research fellow, instr. Sch. Journalism and Mass Communication, U. Minn., 1964-68; asst. prof. U. Okla., 1968-69; asso. prof. Mich. State U., East Lansing, 1969—; dir. market and communication research Panax Corp., East Lansing, 1975-76; adminstrv. asst., research cons. to pres. Lansing (Mich.) Community Coll., 1976—. Vice chmn. Eaton-Ingham Substance Abuse Commn. Recipient NSF award, 1969; Bihar Rastrabhasha Parishad Lit. award, 1st prize, 1954. Mem. Am. Mgmt. Assn., Am. Statis. Assn., Am. Pub. Opinion Research Council, Newspaper Research Council, Radio and TV News Dirs. Assn., Assn. Edn. in Journalism, Internat. Communication Assn., Am. Platform Assn., Smithsonian Instn. Assos., Kappa Tau Alpha, Sigma Delta Chi. Clubs: East Lansing Rotary, University. Author: Communication and Modernization in Urban Slums, 1972; The Basic News Media and Techniques, 1972; Law and Disorder; also monographs. Contbr. articles to scholastic jours. Home: 3911 Hemmingway Dr Okemos MI 48864 Office: Sch Journalism Mich State Univ East Lansing MI 48824

MISKUS, MICHAEL ANTHONY, electrical engineer, consultant; b. East Chicago, Ind., Dec. 10, 1950; s. Paul and Josephine M.; B.S., Purdue U., 1972; A.A.S. in Elec. Engring. Tech., Purdue U., Indpls., 1972; cert. mgmt. Ind. U., 1972, Ind. Central Coll., 1974; m. Jeannie Ellen Dolmanni, Nov. 4, 1972. Service engr. Reliance Electric & Engring. Co., Hammond, Ind., 1972-73; maintenance supr., maintenance mgr. Diamond Chain Co./AMSTED Industries, Indpls., 1973-76; primary and facilities elec. engr. Johnson & Johnson Baby Products Co., Park Forest South, Ill., 1976—; prin. Miskus Cons., indsl./comml. elec. cons., 1979—; plant and facilities engring. mgr. Sherwin Williams Co., Chgo. Emulsion Plant, Chgo., 1981-82, sr. facilities engr., 1982—; staff facilities engr. Bourns Inc., 1982—; instr., lectr. EET program Moraine Valley Community Coll., Palos Hills, Ill., 1979, Prairie State Coll., Chicago Heights, Ill., 1980—; mem. Elec. Industry Evaluation Panel. Mem. faculty adv. bd. Moraine Valley Community Coll., 1980—. Mem. IEEE, Assn. Energy Engrs., Illuminating Engring. Soc. N.Am., Internat. Platform Assn. Clubs: Purdue of Chgo., Purdue of Los Angeles. Home: 535 N Michigan Ave Suite 1415 Chicago IL 60611 Office: Miscon Assocs PO Box 55353 Riverside CA 92517

MISNER, JERRY BRIAN, advertising agency executive; b. Amarillo, Tex., Sept. 16, 1942; s. Dermont Sidney and Willie Pearl (Jordan) M.; m. Scottie Lou Bigge, Mar. 6, 1971; children—Jason, Kristen. B.A. in English, U. Wyo., 1966. Pub. relations assoc. Western Electric Co., Omaha, 1971-72; v.p., gen. mgr. KLNG Newsradio, Omaha, 1972-76; account supr. Frederickson/Hounshell Advt., Omaha, 1976-81; pres. Misner Advt., Omaha, 1981—. Served to capt. USMCR, 1966-70. Mem. Omaha Fedn. Advt. Republican. Episcopalian. Home: 144 Ginger Cove Rd Valley NE 68064 Office: 7171 Farnam St Omaha NE 68132

MISTRY, SORAB PIROZSHAH, biochemistry educator; b. Bombay, India, Dec. 18, 1920; s. Pirozshah Dorabji and Jerbai Pestonji (Patel) M.; m. Margrith Gertrude Buchi, May 7, 1953; children—Dinu, Darius. B.S., U. Bombay, 1942; M.S., Indian Inst. Sci., Bangalore, 1946; Ph.D., U. Cambridge, 1951. Postdoctoral fellow U. Cambridge, 1951-52, U. Ill., 1952-54; mem. faculty U. Ill., Urbana, 1954—, assoc. prof. biochemistry, 1961-66, prof., 1966—; cons.

nutrition surveys USDA, Orangeburg, S.C., 1972-75; prof. Swiss Fed. Inst. Tech., Zurich, 1979, 81, 83, 84, 85, Autonoma U., Madrid, Spain, 1971, 79, 84, U. Zurich, 1957, 63, U. Amsterdam, 1956, Indian Inst. Sci., Bangalore, 1970-71. Fellow NIH, 1963-64, Med. Research Council Eng., 1951, Sethna Found. India, 1947-50. Mem. Am. Soc. Biol. Chemists, Am. Inst. Nutrition, Brit. Biochem. Soc., Swiss Chem. Soc., Sigma Xi, Phi Kappa Phi. Democrat. Zoroastrian. Home: 1011 W Green St Champaign IL 61821 Office: Dept Animal Sci U Ill Urbana IL 61801

MITAL, ANIL, engineering educator; b. Barabanki, India, Nov. 13, 1951; came to U.S., 1975; s. Virendra Nath and Malti (Gupta) M.; m. Chetna Gupta, June 12, 1981; 1 son, Anubhav. B.E., Allahabad U., 1974; M.S., Kans. State U., 1976; Ph.D., Tex. Tech. U., 1980. Asst. prof. indsl. engring U. Wis.-Platteville, 1979-80; asst. prof. mech. and indsl. engring, 1981-84, assoc. prof., 1984—, human factors engring grad. coordinator U. Cin., Ohio, 1981—, dir. Ergonomics Research Lab., 1981—. Mem. Big Bros.-Big Sisters, Lubbock, Tex., 1977—. Nat. Inst. Occupational Safety and Health grantee, 1982-85; recipient Gold Medal for performance Allahabad U., 1974; Jr. Morrow Research Chair, 1982-83. Mem. Am. Indsl. Hygiene Assn. (chmn. nat. ergonomics com. 1984-85), Inst. Indsl. Engrs., Human Factors Soc. Am. (editorial bd., Outstanding Contbns. award Tri-State chpt. 1984), Human Factors Soc. Greater Cin. (pres., 1983-84), Inst. Indsl. Engrs. (treas. Cin. chpt. 1983-84), Soc. Automotive Engrs. (Ralph R. Tector award 1985), Pi Tau Sigma, Alpha Pi Mu, Tau Beta Pi (faculty adviser), Phi Kappa Phi, Omicron Delta Kappa, Delta Phi Epsilon, Sigma Xi (Disting. Research award 1984). Club: 100 Mile Joggers. Editor: Trends in Ergonomics/Human Factors I, 1984. Contbr. numerous articles to profl. jours. Home: 937 Gawain Circle West Carrollton OH 45449 Office: Dept Mech Engring ML 72 U Cincinnati Cincinnati OH 45221

MITBY, JOHN CHESTER, lawyer; b. Antigo, Wis., Jan. 7, 1944; s. Norman Peter and Luvern T. (Jensen) M.; m. Julie Kampen, June 10, 1972; 1 dau., Tana. B.S., U. Wis., 1966, LL.D., 1971. Bar: Wis. 1971. Ptnr. Brynelson, Herrick, Gehl & Bucida, Madison, Wis., 1973—; lectr. U. Wis. Law Sch. Served to capt. C.E., U.S. Army, 1966-68. Mem. ABA, Wis. State Bar Assn. (chmn.-elect litigation sect.), Dane County Bar Assn., Civil Trial Lawyers Wis. (bd. dirs.), Wis. Acad. Trial Lawyers, Assn. Trial Lawyers Am. Club: Nakoma Country (Madison). Home: 726 Oneida Pl Madison WI 53714 Office: Brynelson Herrick Gehl & Bucida 122 W Washington St Madison WI 53701

MITCH, PAUL STEVE, psychiatrist; b. Donora, Pa., Oct. 3, 1945; s. Steve Joseph and Rose Marie (Ferretti) M.; m. Sharon Dale Senger, June 13, 1970 (div. 1982); children—Jason, Nathan, Kristen. B.S., U. Dayton, 1967; M.D., Ohio State U., 1971. Diplomate Am. Bd. Psychiatry and Neurology, Biofeedback Cert. Inst. Am. Resident in psychiatry Med. Coll. Ohio, Toledo, 1971-74, clin. instr., 1974-76, asst. prof., 1976-77, clin. asst. prof., 1977—; med. dir. Community Mental Health Ctr.-West, Toledo, 1977—; pvt. practice medicine specializing in psychiatry, Toledo, 1977—; psychiat. cons. N.W. Ohio Devel. Ctr., Toledo, 1978—, Sunshine Children's Home, Maumee, Ohio, 1978—, Lott Group Home, Toledo, 1979—. Contbr. articles to profl. jours. Recipient Sandoz award Sandoz Pharms., 1972-73. Mem. Am. Psychiat. Assn., AMA (Physicians Recognition award 1984), Biofeedback Soc. Am., Wellness Assocs., N.W. Ohio Psychiat. Assn. (pres. 1979-80). Democrat. Roman Catholic. Avocations: Raising plants, especially cactus; music; motorcycling. Home: 12461 River Rd Grand Rapids OH 43522 Office: 3171 Republic Blvd North #101 Toledo OH 43615

MITCHELL, CYNTHIA, educator; b. Grindstone, Pa., Feb. 16, 1940; d. Murphy and Addie (Edwards) M.; m. George Robert Barnett, Apr. 18, 1960 (div.). B.S., Central State U., 1962; M.A., Mich. State U., 1968; M.A.T., Oakland U., 1974. Elem. tchr. Detroit Bd. Edn., 1962-74, middle sch. tchr., 1974-78, secondary tchr., 1978—, high sch. reading specialist, 1980—, mem. middle schs. textbook selection com. 1977. Program coordinator Kommunity Aides-United Community Services Summer Program, Inskter, Mich., 1982; active Friends Detroit Pub. Library, Afro-Am. Mus.; mem. St. Christine Parish Council; del. Detroit Archbishop's Pastoral Assembly. Mem. Internat. Reading Assn., Nat. Council Tchrs. English, Assn. Supervision and Curriculum Devel., LWV, Mich. Reading Assn., Mich. Secondary Reading Interest Council (treas.), Wayne County Reading Council, Mich. Council Tchrs. English, Amnesty Internat., NAACP, Nat. Council Negro Women, Alpha Kappa Alpha (chpt. pres.). Democrat. Roman Catholic.

MITCHELL, DWAIN JESSE, county official, civil engineer, land surveyor; b. Hettick, Ill., Aug. 9, 1922; s. Marvel Jesse and Eunice Edith (Joiner) M.; m. Ruth Elaine Whittaker, July 21, 1942; children—Carolyn Jean, Roger Michael. Student So. Ill. U., 1940-42, U. Md., 1943-44. Registered land surveyor, Ill. Engr., land surveyor Christian County Hwy. Dept., Taylorville, Ill., 1946—, asst. supt. hyws., 1965—; county plat rev. officer Christian County, 1964-74; liaison mem. Christian County Hwy. Commrs., 1975—. Leader Abraham Lincoln council Boy Scouts Am., 1956-68. Served to sgt. 1st class U.S. Army, 1943-46, ETO, 50-52. Fellow Am. Congress Surveying and Mapping; mem. Ill. Registered Land Surveyors Assn. (sec.-treas. 1970-74). Democrat. American Baptist. Lodge: Order of Arrow. Avocations: photography; camping; fishing; bowling. Home: 604 Taylorville Blvd Taylorville IL 62568 Office: Christian County Hwy Dept 1000 N Cheney St Taylorville IL 62568

MITCHELL, EUGENE R., insurance company executive; b. Detroit, Dec. 8, 1929; s. Max B. and Frances (Sklar) M.; m. Susan Carol, Dec. 19, 1954; children—Robert, Elizabeth, Stacey. B.A., Detroit Inst. Tech., 1957. Salesman E.R. Mitchell & Assocs., Detroit, 1960-68; pres. Profl. Life Underwriters Service, Inc., Troy, Mich., 1968—; M & G Market Services, Inc., Troy; mem. adv. bd. Life of Va., Am. Agy. Life, Midland Mut., 1982—. Past chmn. Alex Karras Charities; past mem. adv. bd. Profl. Golfers Assn. Mich.; mem. tournament com. Kaline-Gehringer Golf Tournament; mem. med. credentials com. St. Joseph Mercy Hosp., Pontiac, Mich. Named Agt. of Yr., Ins. Salesman mag., 5 times. Mem. Detroit Life Underwriters, Life Ins. Leaders of Mich. (life mem.; Humanitarian award 1984), Advance Assn. Life Underwriters. Clubs: Radrick Farms Golf, Katke-Couzens Golf, Danish, U. Mich. President's (life), Victor's (life), Oakland U. President's. Office: Profl Life Underwriters Service Inc 3001 W Big Beaver St Suite 100 Troy MI 48084

MITCHELL, GERALD B., mfg. co. exec.; b. 1927; married. With Dana Corp., Toledo, 1939—, v.p. mfg. Hayes Dana Ltd. subs., Thorold, Ont., Can., 1958-63, pres., 1963-67, pres. parent co., 1973—, now also chmn. bd., chief exec. officer, dir. Office: Dana Corp 4500 Dorr St Box 1000 Toledo OH 43697*

MITCHELL, JAMES HERBERT, JR., architect; b. Newport News, Va., Nov. 7, 1946; s. James Herbert and Norma Jean (Gardner) M.; m. Sharon E. LeDuc, Dec. 30, 1966; 1 child, Jennifer Lynn. Student Wright State U., 1964-67; B.S. in Architecture, Ohio State U., 1975. Draftsman, Elgar Brown, Cons. Engrs., Columbus, Ohio, 1974-75, Urban Calabretta Assocs., Columbus, 1975-78; architect John Ruetschle Assocs., Dayton, Ohio, 1978-84, Brightman & Mitchell, Architects, Dayton, 1984—. Served wtih USAF, 1968-72. Mem. AIA, Nat. Council Archtl. Registration Bds. Republican. Methodist. Avocations: bicycling, automobiles. Home: 5290 Beechview Dr Dayton OH 45424 Office: Brightman & Mitchell Architects Inc 13 E 4th St Dayton OH 45402

MITCHELL, JERALD FRANCIS, hospital executive; b. Marysville, Kans., Jan. 13, 1946; s. James Francis and Violet Amelia (Schwarz) M.; m. Pamela Bunting; children—Todd, Troy, Ashley. B.S. in Bus. Adminstrn., U. Nebr.-Omaha and Lincoln, 1973, M.B.A., 1980; M.H.A., U. Minn.-St. Paul, 1985. Acct., U. Nebr. Med. Ctr., Omaha, 1974-77; dir. budget and acctg. St. Joseph Hosp., Omaha, 1977-81, material services adminstr., 1981-82, fiscal dir. controls, 1982-84; dir. ancillary services Shands Hosp., U. Fla., Gainesville, 1984—; nominee Am. Coll. Hosp. Adminstrs., Chgo., 1981. Chmn. St. Margaret Mary Parish Bd. Edn., Omaha, 1982-84. Served with USNR, 1963-68. Mem. Assn. M.B.A. Execs., Health Care Fin. Mgmt. Assn. (dir. Ak-sar-ben chpt. 1981-83, newsletter editor 1979-81), Am. Hosp. Assn. Republican. Roman Catholic. Home: 2111 NW 20th St Gainesville FL 32605 Office: Shands Hosp U Fla Box J 326 Gainesville FL 32610

MITCHELL, JOHN F., electronics company executive; b. 1928; B.S., Ill. Inst. Tech., 1950; married. With Motorola, Inc., Schaumburg, Ill., 1953—, v.p., 1968-72, v.p. and gen. mgr. communications div., 1972-75, exec. v.p. and asst. chief operating officer, 1975-80, pres., asst. chief operating officer, 1980—, also dir. Served with USN, 1950-53. Office: Motorola Inc 1303 E Algonquin Rd Schaumburg IL 60196*

MITCHELL, MAURICE CLINTON, JR., educational technologist, college administrator; b. Erie, Pa., Aug. 13, 1940; s. Maurice Clinton and Alice Jane (Shimp) M.; m. M. Elizabeth Schipman, Feb. 5, 1966; children—Kathy, Laura. B.S.Ed., U. Ala., 1967, M.A., 1972; Ph.D., Fla. State U., 1978. Tchr., Hilton (N.Y.) Central Sch., 1967-70, Woodham High Sch., Pensacola, Fla., 1970-72; asst. dir. curriculum delivery system Project, Fla. State U., 1974-75; dir. instructional devel. Des Moines Area Community Coll., 1976-83, dir. Computer Literacy Inst., 1983—. Active Des Moines Ballet Assn. Served with USNR, 1960-62. Mem. Am. Vocat. Assn., Iowa Vocat. Assn. (dir. new and emerging), Assn. Devel. Computer-Based Instructional Systems. Democrat. Methodist. Contbr. numerous articles to profl. jours. Home: 1217 SW Lynn St Ankeny IA 50021 Office: 2006 S Ankeny Blvd Ankeny IA 50021

MITCHELL, MICHAEL JAMES, consulting company executive; b. Phila., June 21, 1945; s. Walter J. and Ruth (Hutchins) M. B.S., Nebr. Wesleyan, 1968; cert. in systems analysis design with distinction U. Minn., 1975. Cert. systems profl., cert. data processer. Systems analyst FBI, Washington, 1969-71, Norwest Computer Services, Mpls., 1971-75, Daytons, Mpls., 1975-78, Nat. Car Rental, Mpls., 1978-79; cons. Technalysis, Mpls., 1979—. Served to E-5 USN, 1968-69. Mem. Assn. Systems Mgmt., Data Processing Mgmt. Assn. Republican. Club: Lemans. Lodge: Masons. Avocations: skiing; sailing. Home: 5628 Logan Ave S Minneapolis MN 55419 Office: Technalysis Corp 6700 France Ave S Minneapolis MN 55435

MITCHELL, NED ELSWORTH, confectionery company executive; b. Chgo., Sept. 8, 1925; s. Charles Earling and Elsie Edna (Gliot) M.; m. Artemis Diane Safrithis, June 4, 1949; children—Charles John, Mark Dennis, Peter Ned. B.S.M.E., Northwestern U., 1947; M.B.A., U. Chgo., 1957. Factory mgr. E.J. Brach & Sons, Chgo., 1957-67, v.p., 1967-74, sr. v.p., 1974-76, exec. v.p., 1976-77, pres., 1977—. Editor: (with others) Flexography, 1969. Mem. bd. zoning appeals Village of Deerfield, Ill., 1960-61; mem. sch. bd. Sch. Dist. 110, Lake County, Ill., 1965-69; mem. planning commn. Village of Riverwoods, Ill., 1964; vice chmn. Evang. Health Found., Oakbrook, Ill., 1983-84. Served to 2d lt. U.S. Army, 1944-53. Mem. Am. Assn. Candy Technologists, Nat. Confectioners Assn. (sec., treas. 1982-85, v.p. 1985—), Chocolate Mfg. Assn. (bd. dirs. 1980-84, Candy Kettle award, 1984), Triangle Frat. (trustee). Clubs: Knollwood (Lake Forest); Exec. Program of U. Chgo., Economics (Chgo.). Avocations: golf, auto rebuilding, wood and metal working, flying. Home: 505 Thornmeadow Rd Riverwoods IL 60015 Office: E J Brach & Sons 4656 W Kinzie St Chicago IL 60015

MITCHELL, PHILIP JAMES, banker; b. Manchester, Eng., May 23, 1930; s. David Ernest and Marie (Dilbeck) M.; came to U.S., 1954, naturalized, 1965; grad. in controllership Sch. for Bank Adminstrn. U. Wis., 1973; m. Charlotte Studer, Aug. 10, 1957 (dec. Jan. 1979); 1 son, Mark Philip. Theatre mgr. J. Arthur Rank Orgn., London, 1952-54; chief accountant Whitehall Labs., Inc., Elkhart, Ind., 1955-66; asst. controller/cashier Midwest Commerce Banking Co. subs. Midwest Commerce Corp., Elkhart, 1966-83, asst. treas. parent corp., 1976-83, dir. employee benefits, 1983—. Bd. dirs., Elkhart County Mental Health Assn., 1967—, pres., 1973-75; bd. dirs. Mental Health Assn. Ind., 1975-77; treas. Elkhart Concert Club, Inc., 1973—. Served to sgt. Royal Corps Signals Brit. Army, 1948-52. Recipient awards for Service Elkhart County Mental Health Assn., 1975. Mem. Nat. Assn. Accountants, Bank Adminstrn. Inst. Episcopalian. Club: Lions (treas. local club 1970-76, charter Treas's. award 1970). Home: 54076 Bannock Circle Old Mill Estates Elkhart IN 46514 Office: 121 W Franklin St Elkhart IN 46516

MITCHELL, ROGER L., university administrator; b. Grinnell, Iowa, Sept. 13, 1932; m. Joyce Elaine Lindgren, June 26, 1955; children—Laura Grace, Susan Elaine, Sarah Elizabeth, Martha Cecille. B.S. in Agronomy, Iowa State U., 1954, Ph.D., 1961; M.S., Cornell U., 1958. Instr. agronomy Iowa State U., Ames, 1959-61, asst. prof., 1961-62, asst. prof. in charge Farm Operation Curriculum, 1962-63, assoc. prof. agronomy Farm Operation Curriculum, 1963-66, prof. agronomy, 1966-69; fellow in acad. adminstrn. Am. Council on Edn., U. Calif., Irvine, 1966-67; prof., chmn. dept. agronomy U. Mo., Columbia, 1969-72, dean extension div., 1972-75, chmn., prof. dept. agronomy, 1981-83; v.p. agr. Kans. State U., 1975-80; exec. dir. MidAm. Internat. Agrl. Consortium, 1981; dean Coll. Agr., dir. Agrl. Exptl. Sta., U. Mo., Columbia, 1983—, mem. dean's council, 1983—, cons. and lectr. in field. Contbr. articles to profl. jours. Named Prof. of Yr., Coll. Agr., Iowa State U., 1962; Danforth fellow, 1956-61. Fellow Am. Soc. Agronomy (pres. 1980-81, various coms.), AAAS; mem. Nat. Assn. State Univs. and Land-Grant Colls., Council Adminstrv. Heads Agr. (exec. com. 1984—), Nat. Acad. Scis., Nat. Research Council (bd. agr. 1982—, com. chmn. 1983—), Crop Sci. Soc. Am. (pres. 1976-77), Mid-Am. Agrl. Consortium (chmn. 1980, 1985—, bd. dirs. 1983—), Sigma Xi, Alpha Zeta, Gamma Sigma Delta, Phi Kappa Phi. Office: Coll Agr Agrl Exptl Sta U Mo Columbia 2-69 Agr Bldg Columbia MO 65211

MITCHELL, TERENCE EDWARD, metallurgist, materials scientist; b. Haywards Heath, Sussex, Eng., May 18, 1937; came to U.S., 1963; s. Thomas Frank and Dorothy Elizabeth (Perrin) M.; m. Marion Wyatt, Dec. 5, 1959; children—Robin Norman, Jeremy Neil. B.A., St. Catharine's Coll., Cambridge, Eng., 1958; M.A., Cambridge U., Eng., 1962, Ph.D. in Physics, 1962. Research fellow Cavendish Lab., Cambridge, 1962-63; asst. prof. metallurgy Case Inst. Tech., 1963-66, assoc. prof. metallurgy Case Western Res. U., 1966-75, prof. metallurgy, 1975—, chmn. dept., 1983—; vis. prof. Stanford U., 1975-76; cons. Contbr. numerous articles to profl. jours. Research fellow Electric Power Research Inst., Palo Alto, Calif., 1975-76; NSF grantee, 1966—, Dept. Energy grantee, 1970-83, NASA grantee, 1974—, U.S. Air Force Offices of Sci. Research grantee, 1964—. Mem. Cleve. Ethical Soc., Am. Ethical Union (past dir.), Electron Microscopy Soc. Am. (program chmn. 1981-82, dir. 1984—), Electron Microsopy Soc. N.E. Ohio (pres. 1983-84), Am. Ceramics Soc., Am. Soc. Metals, Metall. Soc. AIME, Materials Research Soc. Democrat. Avocations: mountain climbing; photography; skiing; soccer. Home: 3311 Avalon Rd Shaker Heights OH 44120 Office: Case Western Reserve Univ Dept Metallurgy and Materials Sci 10900 Euclid Ave Cleveland OH 44106

MITCHELL, THOMAS CLARK, university adminstrator, statistician; b. Horton, Kans., Nov. 24, 1939; s. Harry Laurence and Ida Mary (Forest) McConnell M.; m. Barbara Jean Spencer, July 4, 1964; children—Gregory Kent, Douglas Eugene. B.S., S.E. Mo. State U., 1966, M.A., 1969; Ed.D., Okla. State U., 1975. Prodn. supr. Pet Milk, Inc., Greeneville, Tenn., 1966-67; head resident S.E. Mo. State U., Cape Girardeau, 1967-69, dir. acad. advising, 1969-71; engring. counselor Okla. State U., Stillwater, 1971-75; dir. student affairs Ind. U. S.E., New Albany, 1975—; mem. adv. bd. So. Ind. Mental Health and Guidance Ctr., New Albany, 1980—; mem. adv. bd. Salvation Army, 1985—. Past pres. Incarnation Luth. Ch., Floyds Knobs, Ind. Served with USCG, 1959-60, USNR, 1962—. Named Outstanding Student Tchr., S.E. Mo. State U., 1966; Outstanding Adminstr., Ind. U. S.E., 1980; recipient Outstanding Service award Students Ind. U. S.E., 1979. Mem. Res. Officer's Assn., Naval Res. Assn., Navy League, Nat. Assn. Student Personnel Adminstrs., Floyd County C. of C. (bd. dirs. 1983—), Phi Eta Sigma, Phi Kappa Phi. Republican. Lutheran. Club: Rotary (past. pres.) (New Albany). Home: 1840 Ekin Ave New Albany IN 47150 Office: Ind U SE 4201 Grant Line Rd New Albany IN 47150

MITCHEM-DAVIS, ANNE, nursing educator; b. Boston, Dec. 17, 1929; d. Robert Thomas and Marian Carter (Franklin) Mitchem; divorced, 1960; 1 child, Leah Anne. B.S., Lincoln U., Jefferson City, Mo., 1959; diploma Ind. U., 1953; M.S., Simmons Coll., Boston, 1960; postgrad. Boston U., 1966. Nursing cons. Consultation and Edn. Program, Boston, 1970-71; nursing dir. out patient Boston City Hosp., 1971-73; asst. dean Coll. Nursing, Howard U., Washington, 1973-75; exec. dir. Alpha Kappa Alpha, Chgo., 1975-80; assoc. prof. nursing Chgo. State U., 1980—. Recipient Spl. Service award Ind. U. Sch. Nursing Alumni Assn., 1979. Mem. Am. Pub. Health Assn., Am. Nurses' Assn., Nat. League Nursing, Nat. Black Nurses Assn., Sigma Theta Tau, Alpha Kappa Alpha. Office: Chicago State U Coll Nursing 95th and King Dr Chicago IL 60628

MITCHEN, JOEL RAMON, medical technology company executive; b. Chgo., Mar. 25, 1942; s. Joseph Louis and Dorothy Loraine (Bradshaw) M.; m. Emiko Reuther; 1 child, Michael Joseph. B.A., Carthage Coll., 1964; M.S., Purdue U., 1969, Ph.D., 1971. With Roswell Park Meml. Inst., Buffalo, 1971-73, Life Scis., Inc., St. Petersburg, Fla., 1973-77, Argonne Nat. Labs., Ill., 1977-79, Abbott Labs., North Chicago, Ill., 1979-82; owner, sci. dir. Microtech Med. Co., Inc., Waukegan, Ill., 1982—. Contbr. sci. papers to profl. lit. Patentee in field med. diagnostics. Mem. Am. Soc. Microbiologists, Sigma Xi. Lutheran. Avocations: electronics; photography; skiing. Office: Microtech Med Co Inc 1701 Grand Ave Waukegan IL 60085

MITCHLER, JOHN DREW, geologist, cons; b. Aurora, Ill., Jan. 8, 1956; s. Robert W. and Helen L. (Drew) M.; B.S. in Geology, U. Ill., 1978. Senate page Ill. State Senate, Springfield, 1973-77; coal geologist William H. Smith & Assoc., Champaign, Ill., 1978-80; geologist Woodward-Clyde Cons., Mattoon, Ill., 1980-83; ind. oil and gas geologist, Champaign, 1983—. Ill. legis. scholar Ho. of Reps., 1974. Mem. Am. Assn. Petroleum Geologists, Ill. Geol. Soc., Assn. Engring. Geologists (assoc.), Ind. Geol. Soc., Ky. Geol. Soc., Prairie Gem and Geol. Soc. (editor 1981-85), Children Am. Revolution (pres. Ill. 1976). Republican. Methodist. Lodges: Moose, Masons. Avocations: camping, canoeing, reading. Home and Office: 2303 S 1st St Apt 302 Champaign IL 61820

MITROFANOV, NICHOLAS, nuclear physicist; b. Russia, Feb. 5, 1918; came to U.S., 1962, naturalized, 1970; s. Michael and Anastasia (Shirokov) M.; M.S., U. Moscow, 1940, Ph.D. in Physics, 1943; widower. Redactor jour. Columbus, Russian weekly in Austria, 1945-48; mem. faculty U. Chile, Santiago, 1950-62; research prof. U. Md., 1962-64; with Harshaw Chem. Co., Cleve., 1965—, sr. research scientist, 1962—; cons. in field. Author: Textbook of Physics, 1946; (poetry) Caravels, 1980; also articles. Patentee in field.

MITTELMAN, DAVID, pediatric ophthalmologist; b. Chgo., Apr. 18, 1945; s. Joseph and Pearl (Orlovsky) M.; m. Clarice Hollander, Sept. 8, 1968; children—Jillene, Bradley, Rebecca. B.S., U. of Ill.-Chgo. Circle, 1965, M.D., 1969. Diplomate Am. Bd. of Ophthalmology. Intern Cook County Hosp., Chgo., resident in ophthalmology U. of Ill. Chgo. Circle, 1970-73, fellow in pediatric ophthalmology, 1973-74, attending physician, 1974-78; chief pediatric ophthalmologist Cook County Hosp., Chgo., 1978-80; assoc. prof. ophthalmology, chief pediatric ophthalmologist Loyola U., Chgo., 1980—; cons. in ophthalmology Hines VA Hosp., Maywood, Ill., 1980—; cons. in vision Chgo. Bd. of Edn., 1982—. Contbr. articles to medical jours. on ophthalmology. Served to capt. USAR, 1970-76. Yarros scholar U. of Ill. Chgo. Circle, 1965. Fellow Am. Acad. Ophthalmology; mem. Am. Assn. for Pediatric Ophthalmology (membership chmn.), AMA, Ill. Med. Soc., Ill. Assn. of Ophthalmology, Chgo. Med. Soc., Chgo. Ophthalmological Soc. (mtg. chmn. 1983). Office: 1875 W Dempster St Suite 610 Park Ridge IL 60068

MITTELSTAEDT, JOAN NAOMI, educator, cons.; b. Fond du Lac, Wis., Feb. 9, 1950; d. H. Arthur and Naomi Genevieve (Maltby) Steiner; B.S. in Edn., U. Wis., Stevens Point, 1972, M.S. in Edn., 1978; 1 son, Robert John. Tchr., Menasha (Wis.) High Sch., 1972—, also owner Fox Valley Bus. Cons., Neenah, Wis., 1978—; tchr. English, facilitator Wis. Dept. Edn.; tchr. positive mental attitude classes for bus. people; leader sales tng. seminars; curriculum and sales tng. system developer; public speaker on free enterprise, entrepreneurship and assertiveness, 1978—. Cert. tchr. English and speech, Wis.; cert. Amway Gold Direct Distbr. Mem. Republican Presdl. Task Force, 1982. Mem. Nat. Council Tchrs. of English, Wis. Council Tchrs. of English, Wis. Regional Writers, Worldwide Diamond Assn., Nat. Assn. Female Execs. (network dir.), Am. Mgmt. Assn., Citizens Choice, Am. Fedn. Tchrs. (local sec. 1974-76), Assn. Supervision and Curriculum Devel., Internat. Platform Assn., Delta Zeta, Delta Kappa Gamma. Episcopalian. Research on imagists influence on contemporary poets. Home: 304 Quarry Ln Neenah WI 54956

MITTELSTAEDT, TYRONE PETER, educator, consultant; b. Detroit, Dec. 5, 1937; s. Henry Julius and Ethel Ruth (Eckhardt) M.; m. Mary Emmajean Smith; children—Amy Kathleen, Michael Damian. Student U. Detroit, 1955-57; B.S., Wayne State U., 1960, M.S., 1961, Ed.S., 1974. Cert. tchr., Mich. Tchr. educable mentally retarded Barbour Jr. High Sch., Detroit, 1961-64; tchr. educable mentally retarded workshop, Warren (Mich.) High Sch., 1964-67, developer program, 1967-68; work/study rehab. coordinator Warren Consol. Schs., 1968-71; tchr./cons. for learning disabled and emotionally impaired and vocat. rehab. services coordinator Sterling Heights (Mich.) High Sch., 1971—; instr. Wayne State U., Detroit, 1971-72; cons. spl. edn. vocat. edn. project Central Mich. U., 1971-73. Merit badge advisor Detroit Area council Boy Scouts Am., 1964-67; exec. producer, actor, Warren Consol. Schs. Player Group for Coll. Scholarships, 1965-67; mem. parent adv. com. Chippewa Valley Schs., Mt. Clemens, 1979—, fundraiser for preservation of gifted program, 1983; T-ball coach Clinton Valley Baseball Assn., Mt. Clemens, 1981; family learning team tchr. St. Michael's Catholic Community, Sterling Heights, 1980-81, minister of the word, 1982—. Recipient hon. mention Wayne State U. Art Show, 1959; Master Tchr. award Warren Consol. Schs., 1967-68. Mem. NEA, Mich. Edn. Assn., Warren Edn. Assn., State Council of Exceptional Children State Cons. (task force on mainstreaming), Nat. Honor Soc. Club: Optimist (hon. mem. Warren). Author: Curriculum Guide for Language Arts, Detroit Pub. Schs., 1962, curriculum, Warren Consol. Schs., 1971-73; co-author spl. edn. course study for Warren Consol. Schs., 1981-83. Home: 39214 Sunderland Dr Mount Clemens MI 48044 Office: 12901 Fifteen Mile Rd Sterling Heights MI 48077

MITTENTHAL, JAY EDWARD, biologist, educator; b. Boston, July 28, 1941; s. Hyman Samuel and Minnie (Feldman) M.; m. Suzanne Estelle Meyer, May 25, 1968; children—Laurel, Robin. B.A., Amherst Coll., 1960; Ph.D., Johns Hopkins U., 1970. Postdoctoral fellow Stanford U., Calif., 1970-73; asst. prof. Purdue U., West Lafayette, Ind., 1973-79; research assoc. U. Oreg., Eugene, 1979-82; asst. prof. U. Ill., Urbana, 1982—. Contbr. articles to profl. jours. Grantee NSF, USPHS, 1962—. Mem. Am. Soc. Zoologists, Soc. Developmental Biology, Am. Soc. Cell Biology. Democrat. Jewish. Office: Dept Anat Scis U Ill 506 S Mathews Ave Urbana IL 61806

MITZEL, DONALD H., savings and loan association executive. Pres., dir. First Federal of Mich., Detroit. Office: First Rederal of Mich 1001 Woodward Detroit MI 48226*

MITZEL, JAMES MICHAEL, owner specialty retail store; b. Bismarck, N.D., Jan. 28, 1945; s. Tony and Edna Mae (Larson) M.; m. Betty Lou Goetz, July 17, 1965; children—Matthew, Jason, Timothy. A.A., Bismarck Jr. Coll., 1965; B.A., Moorhead State U., Minn., 1967. Staff mem. Minn. League of Credit Unions, Mpls., 1970-73; realtor NHC Realty, Mpls., 1972-73; assoc. Zedlik & Harmala Architects, Mpls., 1973-74; pres. Community Credit Union, Bismarck, 1974-83; owner, mgr. The Rainbow Shop, Bismarck, 1983—. Co-author: Our Love Story, 1983. Bd. dirs. Kirkwood Mchts. Assn., 1984-85. Served with U.S. Army, 1968-69, Vietnam. Decorated Bronze Star; recipient Wall Street Jounalism award, 1963. Roman Catholic. Avocations: religious activities; Bible studies; fishing; golf. Home: 1807 N 22d St Bismarck ND 58501 Office: The Rainbow Shop Kirkwood Plaza Mall Bismarck ND 58501

MIX, JUDITH ANN, nursing education administrator; b. Casco, Wis., May 5, 1941; d. Edward Joseph and Ruby (DeChamps) Wendricks; m. Thomas Mix, Aug. 20, 1966. B. Nursing, U. Wis., 1967; M. Nursing, U. Cin., 1977, Ed.D., 1983. Nurse Holy Family Hosp., Manitowoc, Wis., 1962-65, St. Marys Hosp., Milw., 1965-67; instr. nursing St. Francis Hosp., Cin., 1967-72, nursing edn. adminstr., 1972-80; nursing educator adminstr. Great Oaks Joint Vocational Sch., Cin., 1980-82, Green Bay Tech. Inst., Wis., 1982—. Mem. Am. Nurses Assn., Am. Vocational Assn., Sigma Theta Tau. Office: Northeast Wis Tech Coordinator-Nursing 2740 W Mason St Green Bay WI 54303

MIYAMOTO, RICHARD TAKASHI, otolaryngologist; b. Zeeland, Mich., Feb. 2, 1944; s. Dave Norio and Haruko (Okano) M.; m. Cynthia Vander-Burgh, June 17, 1967; children—Richard Christopher, Geoffrey Takashi. B.S. cum laude, Wheaton Coll., 1966; M.D., U. Mich., 1970; M.S. in Otology, U.So. Calif., 1978. Diplomate Am. Bd. Otolaryngology. Intern Butterworth Hosp., Grand Rapids, Mich., 1970-71, resident in surgery, 1971-72; resident in otolaryngology Ind. U. Sch. Medicine, 1972-75; fellow in otology and neurotology St. Vincent Hosp. and Otologic Med. Group, Los Angeles, 1977-78; asst. prof. Ind. U. Sch. Medicine, Indpls., 1978-83, assoc. prof., 1983—. Served to maj. USAF, 1975-77. Named Arilla DeVault Disting. investigator Ind. U., 1983. Fellow Am. Acad. Otolaryngology (gov. 1982—), ACS, Am. Otological, Rhinological, and Laryngological Soc. (Thesis Disting. for Excellence award), Am. Neurotology Soc. Republican. Presbyterian. Avocation: tennis. Home: 7979 High Dr Indianapolis IN 46140 Office: Riley Hosp Suite A-56 702 Barnhill Dr Indianapolis IN 46223

MIZOTE, HISASHI EARL, optometrist; b. Oakland, Calif., Aug. 2, 1914; s. Sojuro and Shiu M.; m. Toye Uchiyama, Apr. 16, 1950; 1 child, Lisa. O.D.,

Chgo. Coll. Optometry, 1951; Ph.D., Kensington U., 1984. Police officer, Piedmont, Calif., 1934-38; practice optometry, Chgo., 1952—; adminstrv. to state rep. Ill., 1976; with U.S. Post Office, Chgo., 1951-72. Active Boy Scouts Am. Served with inf. U.S. Army, 1941-46, MTO. Named hon. Ky. Col., 1975; recipient commmendation Chgo. Police Dept., 1971. Mem. Ill. Sheriffs' Assn. Democrat. Avocations: research on Oriental history; mechanical experiments. Home: 1334 W Rosedale Ave Chicago IL 60660

MOAR, JAMES HOWARD, packaging equipment company executive; b. Chgo., Dec. 2, 1948; s. Glen Howard and Dorothy Ann (Zoller) M.; m. Sheila Joan Murphy, Sept. 11, 1971; 1 child, Amanda. B.S. in Engring., Princeton U., 1970; M.P.A., U.Calif.-Berkeley, 1971. Chief engring. City of New York, 1971-74; v.p. Citicorp., N.Y.C., 1975-78; div. gen. mgr. Internat. Paper Co., N.Y.C., 1979-82; pres. Liquipak Internat., Inc., St. Paul, 1983—. Bd. dirs. Ramsey Hill Assn., St. Paul, 1984. Avocations: reading; tennis; golf. Office: Liquipak Internat Inc 2285 University Ave Saint Paul MN 55114

MOATS, MICHAEL EMBRY, dentist; b. Akron, Ohio, Sept. 22, 1947; s. O. Embry and Helen Louise (Whitelaw) M.; m. Gloria Jean Vanderborg, Nov. 24, 1984. B.S., Davidson Coll., 1969; D.D.S., Loyola U., 1977. Lic. dentist, Ill. Sci. tchr. New Trier West High Sch., North Field, Ill., 1969-73; asst. clin. prof. Loyola U. Sch. Dentist, Maywood, Ill., 1977-78; gen. practice dentistry, Buffalo Grove, Ill., 1977—. Chmn., bd. dirs. Midwest Epilepsy Ctr., Lombard, Ill., 1983—; deacon Long Grove Community Ch., Ill., 1983—; bd. dirs. Am. Cancer Soc., Buffalo Grove, 1983-84; chmn. Family Life Conf. Chgo. II Conv., 1986. Mem. ADA, Ill. State Dental Soc., Chgo. Dental Soc., Soc. Occlusal Studies, Arlington Dental Study Club. Republican. Mem. Christian Ch. Lodge: Rotary (Pres. 1984-85). Avocations: jogging; scuba diving; model building. Office: 1401 W Dundee Rd Suite 212 Buffalo Grove IL 60089

MOBILE, DAVID CARMEN, aerospace company executive; b. Chgo., Nov. 10, 1946; s. Carmen Anthony and Irene Onolee (Kibort) M.; m. Sandra Simone Moore, Apr. 14, 1973; children—Shelly S., Deena M. B.S. in Mgmt. and Acctg. magna cum laude, St. Joseph's Coll., 1973; M.B.A. in Fin., Ind. U., 1977. Mgr. acctg., controller, corp. fin. mgr. LaSalle Steel Co., Hammond, Ind., 1976-81; asst. controller Midland-Ross Co., Columbus, Ohio, 1981-82, controller, 1982—; designer standard cost and fin. systems. Mem. Jaycees, 1976. Served with USCG, 1968-71. Mem. Nat. Assn. Accts., Am. Mgmt. Assn., Fin. Mgmt. Assn. Republican. Roman Catholic. Home: 8415 Netherlands Pl Worthington OH 43085 Office: Midland-Ross Corp 4200 Surface Rd Columbus OH 43228

MOCH, MARY INEZ, librarian; b. Chgo., Aug. 13, 1943; d. Charles Michael and Mary Anna (Howanic) M. A.A., Felician Coll., 1964; B.A., Mundelein Coll., 1968; M.A., No. Ill. U., 1976. Joined Felician Sisters, Roman Catholic Ch., 1961; tchr. St. Turibius Sch., Chgo., 1964-65; tchr. St. Damian Sch. Oak Forest, Ill., 1966-67, tchr./librarian, 1975-80; tchr./librarian St. Florian Sch., Hatley, Wis., 1968-72, Christ The King Sch., Lombard, Ill., 1972-75; librarian Providence High Sch., New Lenox, Ill., 1980-82; head librarian Felician Coll., Chgo., 1982—; cons. Felician Library Service, 1976—, sec., 1979-80. Mem. ALA, Cath. Library Assn., Ill. Online Computer Library Ctr. Users Group. Office: Felician Coll 3800 W Peterson Ave Chicago IL 60659

MOCK, JOHN DENNIS, medical billing service executive; b. Evanston, Ill., Sept. 10, 1940; s. John T. and Esther (Harloff) M.; m. Joann G. Watt, Dec. 23, 1961; children—Susan, Blake, Eric, Troy. B.A., Franklin Coll., 1962. Mgr., Med. Bus. Bur., Inc., Evanston, Ill., 1962-74; pres. John Mock & Assocs., Inc., Chgo., 1974—; del. govt. affairs com. Ill. Med. Soc., Chgo., 1983—, com. on econs. Ill. State State Soc. Anesthesiologist, Chgo., 1983—. Pres. North Suburban YMCA, Northbrook, Ill., 1985—; v.p. Arden Shore Home for Boys, Lake Bluff, Ill., 1983-84. Mem. Med.-Dental Hosp. Burs. Am., Inc. (Robert T. Hellrung award 1979, Stanley R. Mauck award 1979, cert. profl. bur. exec.), Ill. Collectors Assn., Chgo. Area Med. Group Adminstrs. (pres. 1985-86). Baptist. Club: No. Suburban Aquatic (Northbrook) (pres. 1978-79). Lodge: Rotary (pres. Evanston 1983-84). Office: John Mock & Assocs Inc 2301 W Howard St Chicago IL 60645

MOCKFORD, EDWARD LEE, educator biology; b. Indpls., June 16, 1930; s. Harry Grover and Helen (Lewis) M. A.B., Ind. U., 1952; M.S., U. Fla., 1954; Ph.D., U. Ill.-Urbana, 1960. Grad. asst. biology U. Fla., Gainesville, 1952-54; research asst. Ill. Natural Hist. Survey, Champaign, 1956-60; asst. prof. to prof. biol. scis. Ill. State U., Normal, 1960—; research assoc. Fla. Dept. Agr., Gainesville, 1959—; coop. scientist U.S. Dept. Agr., Washington, 1960—; vis. prof. Inst. Technologico, Monterrey, Mex., 1963-64. Contbr. articles to profl. jours. Served with U.S. Army, 1954-56. Am. Mus. Natural History Travel grantee, 1959; NSF Research grantee, 1961, 63, 65, 67, 83. Mem. Ill. Acad. Sci., Entomol. Soc. Am., Sociedad Mex. de Entomologia, Soc. Systematic Zoology, Soc. Tropical Biology. Democrat. Avocations: hiking; bird watching; swimming; fishing; fiction reading. Home: 511 Manchester Rd Normal IL 61761 Office: Ill State U Dept Biol Scis Normal IL 61761

MODELL, ARTHUR B., professional football team executive; b. Bklyn., June 23, 1925; m. Patricia Breslin, July 25, 1969; stepchildren—John, David. Owner, pres. Cleve. Browns football team, 1961—; pres. Nat. Football League, 1967-70. Office: Cleveland Stadium Cleveland OH 44114*

MODIC, JAMES PAUL, retail and rental company executive; b. Cleve., Nov. 9, 1936; s. James Vincent and Pauline Mary (Tabor) M.; ed. DePaul U., 1966-70, Am. Inst. Banking, 1967-70; m. Jeanette Marie Kraus, June 14, 1958; children—John Paul, Janis Pauline Modic Hodgdon, Jennifer Paula. Methods analyst Chgo. Police Dept., 1957-58, sr. methods analyst, 1959-61, prin. methods analyst, 1961-66; supr. methods div. Continental Ill. Bank, Chgo., 1966-70, mgr. trust dept., 1970-72; owner 6 stores Gingiss Formalwear Inc., Kansas City area, 1972—; regional adv., mem. chmns. club Gingiss Internat.; owner 3 retail food stores, Kansas City area; pres. J.J. Advt., Lenexa, Kans. Dir., Kansas City Chiefs Football Club, 1976—, 1st v.p., 1977-79, treas., 1980, mem. adv. bd., 1982—, mem. coach's club, 1980—, chmn. ticket drive, 1978, 79, 81. Mem. zone bd. Boy Scouts Am., Chgo., 1967-71; mem. Performing Arts Found. Served with USMC, 1954-57, Res., 1957-61. Recipient award for job placement program Kansas City (Kans.) Sch. System, 1978; award of excellence Gingiss Internat., 1979; cert. Distributive Edn. Clubs Am., 1982. Mem. Am. Mgmt. Assn. (lectr. 1967-69), Am. Formalwear Assn. (charter), Menswear Retailers Am., Overland Park C. of C. (planning commn. 1979), Kansas City C. of C., Nat. Alliance Businessmen (v.p. Chgo. chpt., cert. of merit), 1st Marine Div. Assn. Roman Catholic. Clubs: Improved Order Red Men Lenexa Tribe No. 5, Masons (32 deg.), Shriners, Red Coat (exec. com.), Porsche of Am., Com. 101. Home: 8426 Rosehill Rd Lenexa KS 66215 Office: 5809 Johnson Dr Mission KS 66202

MODICA, DOUGLAS GEORGE, systems analyst, consultant; b. Sioux Falls, S.D., July 1, 1948; s. Paul John and Ethel Evelyn (Hansen) M.; m. Mary Lois Opsata, June 6, 1970; B.S. in Math., Physics, Sioux Falls Coll., 1970; M.A. in Math., U. S.D., 1977. Math. tchr. Edison Jr. High, Sioux Falls, 1970-71, Wycliffe Bible, Peru, 1973-75; ops. researcher United Brands, Sioux Falls, 1977-79; systems analyst Automated Systems, Sioux Falls, 1979—; mem. sausage blending com. Blend Cons., Sioux Falls, 1979—. Author user documentation, 1984. Programmer software system, 11979. Served as FTM3 USN. 1970-73. Audio chmn. Central Baptist Ch., Sioux Falls, 1983. Mem. USS Halsey Sci. Fiction Club (v.p. 1983—). Republican. Avocations: play guitar, bass, sax, drums; sci. fiction; electronics. Home: 2708 W 29th St Sioux Falls SD 57105 Office: 3300 Madelyn Sioux Falls SD 57106

MOE, BARBARA ANN, counselor, educator; b. Grand Forks, N.D., June 24, 1955; d. Robert Alan and Ruth Ann (Wang) M. B.S. in Psychology, U. N.D., 1977, M.A. in Counseling and Guidance, 1979, B.S. in Elem. Edn., 1984. Cert. elem. tchr. and counselor, S.D., N.D. Sales clk. Vold Drug Store, Grand Forks, 1972-79; tchr. United Day Nursery, Grand Forks, 1977-78; social worker Cavalier County Social Services, Langdon, N.D., 1979-83; skin care cons. Jafra Cosmetics, Westlake Village, Calif., 1983—; elem. sch. counselor Douglas Sch. System, Ellsworth Air Force Base, S.D., 1984—. Vol. Big Sister Program, Grand Forks, 1978-84; leader Pine to Prairie Girl Scout Council, Langdon, N.D., 1980-82; tchrs. asst. Head Start Program, Grand Forks, 1979. Mem. Am. Assn. Counseling and Devel., NEA, AAUW (local branch newsletter editor 1980-81, branch sec. 1981-83), S.D. Edn. Assn., Am. Sch. Counselor Assn., S.D. Assn. Counseling and Devel., S.D. Sch. Counselor Assn., West River Personnel and Guidance Assn., Kappa Alpha Theta (newsletter, magazine article editor 1976-77). Club: Jaycettes (Langdon) (dir. 1982-83). Avocations: cooking; camping; curling; ceramics; creative writing. Home: 16 Signal Dr Rapid City SD 57701 Office: Francis Case School Ellsworth Air Force Base SD 57706

MOEBIUS, HOWARD EDWARD, printing company executive; b. Milw., Sept. 23, 1917; s. Carl William and Erna Agnes (Rudy) M.; m. Rosemary Babbs, Apr. 6, 1968; children—James, Dalana Schwitzer, Eric, Dallas Lillich, Jeffrey, Elisabeth. Student, Northwestern Mil. Acad., 1932-35. With Moebius Printing Co., Milw., 1935-42, 45—, pres., chmn. bd., 1977—. Bd. dirs. Milw. Symphony Orch., 1976—, Milw. Zool. Soc., 1976—. Served to 1st lt. USAAF, 1942-45. Decorated Air Medal, Purple Heart, D.F.C. Republican. Lutheran. Clubs: Town, University, Milwaukee. Lodge: Rotary. Home: 1800 E Fox Ln Milwaukee WI 53217 Office: 300 N Jefferson St Milwaukee WI 53202

MOEHLING, KARL AUGUST, merchant retail books, mental health educator; b. Rockford, Ill., Mar. 30, 1942; s. Arthur August and Alta Caroline (Morkal) M.; m. Kathryn Sue Thelen, June 3, 1967. B.A., Northern Ill. U., 1965, M.A., 1966, Ph.D., 1972. Part., Bookstall of Rockford, Ill., 1970—; educator mental health Singer Mental Health Ctr., Rockford, 1972—. Home: 800 E Riverside Blvd Loves Park IL 61111 Office: Bookstall of Rockford 606 Gregory St Rockford IL 61108

MOELLER, ROBERT RALPH, computer auditor, accountant; b. Mpls., Mar. 4, 1942; s. Ralph Henry and Clara Amelia (Gall) M.; m. Lois Patricia Hamblin, Sept. 9, 1969. B.Aero.Engring., U. Minn., 1968; M.B.A., U. Chgo., 1982. C.P.A., Ill. Systems analyst Sperry Corp., St. Paul, 1968-75, EDP audit mgr., 1975-78; internal audit mgr. Wickes Cos., Wheeling, Ill., 1978-81; internal audit dir. AM Internat., Chgo., 1981-82; nat. dir. computer audit Alexander Grant & Co., Chgo., 1982—. Assoc. editor Jour. Info. Systems and Computing Revs.; contbr. articles to profl. jours. Served with U.S. Army, 1965-67. Mem. Am. Inst. C.P.A.s, Chgo. Inst. Internal Auditors (v.p.), Inst. for Mgmt. Acctg. (regents adv. com.). Club: University. Avocations: skiing; sailing. Home: 1045 Ridge Ave Evanston IL 60202 Office: Alexander Grant & Co 600 Prudential Plaza Chicago IL 60601

MOEN, RODNEY CHARLES, state senator, communications company executive; b. Whitehall, Wis., July 26, 1937; s. Edwin O. and Tena A. (Gunderson) M.; m. Catherine Jean Wolfe, 1959; children—Scott A., Jon C., Rodd M., Catherine J., Daniel M. Student Syracuse U., 1964-65; B.A., U. So. Calif., 1972; postgrad. Ball State U., 1975-76. Contbg. editor Govt. Photography, 1970-74; gen. mgr. Western Wis. Communications Corp., Independence, Wis., 1976-83; mem. Wis. Senate, 1983—, chmn. agrl., health and human services com., 1983—. Served to lt. USN, 1955-76, Vietnam. Decorated Joint Services commendation medal. Recipient George Stoney award Nat. Fedn. Local Cable TV Programmers, 1980. Democrat. Lodge: Lions. Office: State Capitol PO Box 7882 Madison WI 53707

MOEN, RONALD DEAN, statistician; b. Osage, Iowa, Feb. 16, 1941; s. Lloyd Oscar and Molly Henrietta (Christiansen) M.; m. Bette Dean Davis, June 1, 1968; children—Evan Roger, Tracy Elizabeth. B.A. in Math., U. No. Iowa, 1963; M.S. in Teaching Math., U. Mo., 1966, M.A. in Stats., 1971. High sch. math. tchr., Greene, Iowa, 1963-64; teaching asst. U. Mo., Columbia, 1964-66, 69-71; math. instr. Murray State U., Ky., 1966-67, U. Wis.-Oshkosh, 1967-69; math. statistician U.S. Dept. Agr., Washington, 1971-76; dir. research applications Neotec Corp., Silver Spring, Md., 1976-82; dir. statis. methods Gen. Motors Corp., Pontiac, Mich., 1982—; instr. stats. U.S. Dept. Agr. Grad. Sch., Washington, 1973-76; instr. Deming Seminars George Washington U., Washington and Los Angeles, 1984-85. Contbg. author: (Ency. Brit. film) Road Map for Change: The Deming Approach, 1984 (Golden Eagle award 1985). Contbr. articles and papers to popular mags. and profl. publs. Active local Boy Scouts Am., 1982-84; mem. council Calvary Lutheran Ch., Clarkston, Mich., 1985—; bd. dirs. Cedar Crest Acad., Clarkston, 1984-85. NSF grantee summer insts. Rutgers U., 1967, U. Minn., 1968. Mem. Am. Soc. for Quality Control (asst. program chmn. automotive div. 1984-85), Am. Statis. Assn. (quality and productivity com. 1984-85), Am. Quality and Productivity Inst. (founding mem., awards chmn. 1983-85), Soc. Automotive Engrs. (organizer internat. congress quality and productivity session 1983-85). Avocations: tennis; swimming; skiing; hiking. Home: 7171 Deerhill Ct Clarkston MI 48016 Office: Pontiac Motor Div One Pontiac Plaza Pontiac MI 48053

MOERTEL, CHARLES GEORGE, physician, oncology educator, cancer center administrator; b. Milw., Oct. 17, 1927; s. Charles Henry and Alma Helen (Soffel) M.; m. Virginia Clair Sheridan, Mar. 22, 1952; children—Charles Steven, Christopher Lauren, Heather Lynn, David Matthew. B.S., M.D., U. Ill.-Chgo., 1953; M.S., U. Minn., 1957. Diplomate Am. Bd. Internal Medicine. Intern Los Angeles County Gen. Hosp., 1953-54; resident in internal medicine Mayo Found., Rochester, Minn., 1954-57; asst. to staff Mayo Clinic, Rochester, 1957-58, cons. oncology staff, 1958—; dir. Mayo Comprehensive Cancer Ctr., 1973; mem. oncology staff St. Mary's Meth. Hosps., Rochester, 1958—; Tabor prof. oncology Mayo Med. Sch., 1981—; chmn. gastrointestinal cancer com. Ea. Cooperative Oncology Group, 1972-74; co-chmn. gastrointestinal tumor study group Nat. Cancer Inst., 1973-79, mem. Phase I Study Group, 1973—, mem. com. on cancer immunotherapy, 1974-77, mem. bd. scientific counselors, 1980-83, chmn. com. Cancer Ctrs. and Community Activities, 1982-83; chmn. N. Cen. Cancer Treatment Group, 1983—; mem. oncologic drugs adv. com. FDA, 1984—. Assoc. editor: Cancer Yearbook, 1971-74, Cancer Medicine, 1976—; mem. editorial bd. Jour. Soviet Oncology, 1979—, Current Problems in Cancer, 1979—, Cancer Research, 1980-83, Internat. Jour. Radiation Oncology Biology & Physics, Jour. Ind. New Anticancer Agents, 1981—, Medical Pediatric Oncology, 1984—. Mem. Am. Coll. Physicians, Am. Gastroenterologic Assn., Am. Assn. Cancer Research, Am. Soc. Clin. Oncology, Soc. Surg. Oncology, Soc. Clin. Trials, Sigma Xi. Home: 1009 Skyline Ln Rochester MN 55902 Office: The Mayo Clinic 200 SW 1st St Rochester MN 55905

MOFFIT, WILLIAM C., musician, educator; b. New Philadelphia, Ohio; B.A. cum laude, Baldwin-Wallace Coll.; Masters Degree, U. Mich.; Mus.D. (hon.), Otterbein Coll. Tchr. pub. schs. in Mich. and Ohio, 10 years; mem. faculty Mich. State U., East Lansing; mem. faculty, dir. marching band U. Houston; now mem. faculty, dir. All-American marching band Purdue U. condr. Patterns of Motion Workshops at numerous colls. and univs.; adjudicator music festivals; guest condr. at major band events. Nat. Program Dir., Nat./Internat. Music Festivals. Recipient George Washington medal Freedoms Found. at Valley Forge, 1978; Distinguished Service to Music medal, Alumni Award Baldwin-Wallace Coll.; named Top Prof., U. Houston Mortar Board. Mem. Am., Tex. (pres., condr. Dirs. Band) bandmasters assns., Nat. Band Assn. (bd. dirs.), ASCAP, Kappa Kappa Psi (dist. gov.). Sponsor 12 ann. nat. band scholarship awards. Author: Patterns of Motion. Arranger: Soundpower Series; published works include numerous arrangements of patriotic music; first published version of all five U.S. Service Songs (Armed Forces Salute). Office: Hall of Music Purdue U West Lafayette IN 47907

MOGHISSI, KAMRAN S., physician, educator; b. Tehran, Iran, Sept. 11, 1925; came to U.S., 1959, naturalized, 1965; s. Ahmad and Monireh (Rohani) M.; m. Ida Laura Tedeschi, Jan. 2, 1952; children—Diana J., Soraya R. M.B., Ch.B., U. Geneva, Switzerland, 1952. Lic. physician Mich.; Cert. Am. Bd. Ob-Gyn. Intern, Univ. Hosp., Geneva, 1951-52, Horton Gen. Hosp., United Oxford Hosps., Banbury, Eng., 1952-53; resident in ob-gyn. Gloucestershire Royal Hosp., Eng., 1953-54, St. Helier Hosp., London, 1954-55, Leeds Regional Hosp. Bd., Yorkshire, Eng., 1955-56, Detroit Receiving Hosp., 1961, attending gynecologist, 1962; assoc. prof. ob-gyn. U. Shiraz Med. Sch., Iran, 1957-59; research assoc. ob-gyn. and physiol. chemistry, Wayne State U., Detroit, 1959-61, asst. prof., 1962-66, assoc. prof., 1966-70, prof., 1970—, dir. div. reproductive endocrinology and infertility, 1970—; sr. attending physician ob-gyn. Hutzel Hosp., Detroit, 1963, vice chief, 1978-82, chief, 1982-83; cons. and lectr. in field. Contbr. chpts. to books, articles to profl. jours. Developer exhibits in medicine, movies and teaching prodns.; mem. numerous editorial bds. in field. Fellow Am. Coll. Ob-Gyn. A.C.S., Am. Gynecol. Soc., Am. Assn. Ob-Gyn., Detroit Acad. Medicine; mem. Am. Fertility Soc., AMA, Soc. Study Reprodn., Assn. Profs. Ob-Gyn., AAAS, Assn. Planned Parenthood Physicians, Am. Soc. Andrology, Wayne County Med. Soc., Mich. State Med. Soc., Mich. State Med. Soc., Mich. Soc. Ob-Gyn, Central Assn. Ob-Gyn., N.y. Acad. Scis., Pacific Coast Fertility Soc., Detroit Acad. Medicine. Club: Lochmoor (Grosse Pointe). Home: 56 Moorland Dr Grosse Pointe Shores MI 48236 Office: 4727 St Antoine Suite 304 Detroit MI 48201

MOHAN, JOSEPH CHARLES, JR., chemical engineer; b. Phila., Nov. 2, 1921; s. Joseph C. and Margaret V. (McCarthy) M.; m. June I. Daniels, Nov. 29, 1947; children—Kyle S., Corey C. B.S. in Chem. Engring., Pa. State U., 1946. Chem. engr. Sinclair Co., Marcus Hook, Pa., 1947-48, Pennwalt Co., Whitemarsh, Pa., 1948-57; supr. research and devel. Am. Viscose/FMC, Fredericksburg, Va., 1957-69, Amoco Chems., Naperville, Ill., 1969—. Patentee in field. Served to lt. U.S. Merchant Marines, 1944-46. Mem. Am. Inst. Chem. Engrs. Avocations: golf; swimming; tennis; jogging; bicycling. Home: 1053 W Ogden Ave Apt 236 Naperville IL 60540 Office: Amoco Chems Corp PO Box 400 Naperville IL 60566

MOHLER, CHARLES WILLIAM, ophthalmologist; b. Balt., Nov. 24, 1944; s. Charles Whitaker and Dorothy Jane (Beckett) M.; m. Eileen Anne Rowan, Dec. 16, 1967; children—Amanda Eileen, Carolyn Jane. B.S. in Engring. Sci., Purdue U., 1966; Ph.D. in Biomed. Engring., Case Western Res. U., 1972, M.D., 1973. Diplomate Am. Bd. Ophthalmology. Resident Johns Hopkins Hosp., Balt., 1976-79; vitreoretinal fellow U. Iowa Hosp., 1980; vitreoretinal surgeon Ophthalmology, Ltd., Sioux Falls, S.D., 1980—; Served to lt. comdr. USPHS, 1972-76. Case Engring. fellow Ford Found., 1966, research fellow NIH, Bethesda, Md., 1972-76. Fellow Am. Acad. Ophthalmology; mem. S.D. Acad. Ophthalmology, S.D. Med. Soc., Sioux Falls C. of C. Republican. Methodist. Club: Westward Ho Country (Sioux Falls). Avocations: tennis, scuba diving. Home: 3605 Lewis Ct Sioux Falls SD 57103 Office: Ophthalmology Ltd 1200 S Euclid St Sioux Falls SD 57105

MOHLER, DELMAR RAY, institute director, accountant; b. Lafayette, Ind., Nov. 25, 1950; s. Martin T. and Donna Mae (Herrold) M.; m. Linda Ruth Mayo, May 10, 1974; children—Rachel Dawn, Elisabeth Ann, Grace Thalia. B.A., Cedarville Coll., 1979. C.P.A., Ill., Minn. Bus. mgr. New Life Media, Inc., Cedarville, Ohio, 1977-79; audit staff Benson Wells & Co., Mpls., 1979-80; audit mgr. W. Scott Wallace, C.P.A., St. Paul, 1980-84; dir. treasury ops. Moody Bible Inst., Chgo., 1984—. Elder, Trinity Ch., Mpls., 1982-84; mem. Keeneyville Bible Ch., Ill., 1984—. Served with USN, 1971-77. Recipient Wall St. Jour. award, 1979. Mem. Minn. Soc. C.P.A.s, Ill. Soc. C.P.A.s. Republican. Baptist. Avocations: golf; jogging; swimming. Home: 584A Rush St Roselle IL 60172 Office: 820 N LaSalle Dr Chicago IL 60610

MOHLER, TERENCE JOHN, psychologist; b. Toledo, July 8, 1929; s. Edward F. and Gertrude A. (Aylward) M.; m. Carol B. Kulczak, Oct. 1, 1955; children—Renee, John, Timothy. B.E., Toledo U., 1955, M.E., 1966, Ed.S. in Psychology and Counseling, 1975, postgrad., 1981-82; Ph.D., Walden U., 1979. Psychologist, Toledo Bd. Edn., 1969—; sr. partner Psychol. Assocs., Maumee, Ohio, 1970—; assoc. fellow Inst. for Advanced Study in Rational Psychotherapy, N.Y.C. Served with AUS, 1951-53; Korea. Lic. psychologist, Ohio. Mem. Am., Ohio, Northwestern Ohio, Maumee Valley psychol. assns., Soc. Behaviorists, Nat. Registry Mental Health Providers, Am. Personnel and Guidance Assn., Ohio Personnel and Guidance Assn., Council for Exceptional Children, Kappa Delta Phi. Lodge: Rotary. Home: 1113 Winghaven Rd Maumee OH 43537 Office: 5757 Monclova Rd Maumee OH 43537

MOHNS, BENJAMIN CHARLES, JR., construction company executive; b. Milw., Sept. 11, 1951; s. Benjamin Charles Mohns and Edith Lorraine (Tutsch) Nebel; m. Nancy Ann Weinitschka, June 26, 1976; children—Bradley, Benjamin III, Heather. Pres. Mohns Inc., Waukesha, Wis., to present. Mem. Nat. Assn. Remodeling Industry (Contractor of Yr. 1983, Nat. Contractor of yr. 1985, Regional Contractor of Yr. 1985). Lutheran. Club: Nat. Corvette Owners. Avocations: car restoration; bowling; racquetball; golf. Office: Mohns Inc 110 N 121st Wauwatosa WI 53226

MOHR, DONALD GEORGE, mapping company executive; b. Plymouth, Wis., Apr. 13, 1930; s. George and Meta Hanreatta (Kaufman) M.; m. Mark Harold, Ross Warren. Student, Oshkosh State U., 1947, Mission House Coll., 1948, U. Wis.-Madison, 1950-51. Surveyor, Foster Curtiss, Plymouth, 1951-58; cadastral surveyor U.S. Forest Service, Milw., 1958-59; survey chief Chgo. Aerial Survey, 1959-62, salesman, 1962-67, gen. mgr., 1967-69; pres., owner Aero-metric Engring., Sheboygan, Wis., 1969—. Participant ednl. tv program, 1968. Bd. dirs. First Interstate Bank, Sheboygan, Wis., 1983; bd. trustees Lakeland Coll., Sheboygan, 1984. Served with U.S. Army, 1948-49. Fellow Am. Congress Surveying and Mapping; mem. Am. Soc. Photogrammetry, Wis. Soc. Land Surveyors, Ill. Soc. Land Surveyors, Ill. Soc. Profl. Engrs. Republican. Club: Elkhart Lake Service (Wis.). Avocations: fishing; snowmobiling; boating. Home: 290 Crystal Lake Dr Plymouth WI 53703 Office: Aero-metric Engring 4708 N 40th St Sheboygan WI 53081

MOHR, RALPH EUGENE, city utilities official; b. Salem, Ohio, Nov. 24, 1941; s. Charles Auther and Olive Jane (Reed) M.; m. Alta Maxine Shipley, Aug. 20, 1960; children—Bryan Keith, Jennifer Jane. Grad. high sch. Cert. class III wastewater operator, class III waterworks operator Ohio EPA. Operator, lab. technician wastewater plant City of Salem, 1964-66, 69-71; chemist wastewater plant City of Canton, Ohio, 1966-68; dir. water and waste Village of Germantown, Ohio, 1968-69; chief operator water plant of Marietta, Ohio, 1971-75, utilities supt. 1975—. Mem. Am. Waterworks Assn., Water Pollution Control Conf. Club: Civitan (pres. Marietta 1984-85). Lodge: Moose. Avocations: coaching little league baseball, slow pitch softball. Home: 122 Riverview Dr Marietta OH 45740 Office: City of Marietta 304 Putnam St PO Box 836 Marietta OH 45740

MOHR, ROGER JOHN, advertising agency executive; b. Milw., Sept. 8, 1931; s. Reinhold and Clara (Meissner) M.; B.S. in Speech, Marquette U., 1953; postgrad. radio and TV, Northwestern U., 1955-56; m. Pauline Spicuzza, Oct. 18, 1958; children—Gregory, Mary Margaret, Kristin, Thomas, Kathleen. Staff announcer radio sta. WBKB, West Bend, Wis., 1952, WCAN, Milw., 1952-54; with Arthur Meyerhoff Assos., Inc., Chgo., 1956-80, pres., 1965-80; pres. BBDO, Chgo., 1980-82, chmn., 1983—. Chmn. Lake Bluff (Ill.) Plan Commn., 1972-75; bd. dirs. Chgo. City Ballet, 1982-84. Served with U.S. Army, 1954-55. Mem. Am. Assn. Advt. Agys. (chmn. Chgo. council 1966-67, sec.-treas. nat. bd. dirs. 1976-77), Evans Scholars Alumni Assn. (pres. 1964-65), Western Golf Assn. (dir. 1980—). Clubs: Knollwood (gov. 1980—) (Lake Forest, Ill.); Tavern (Chgo.); Off The Street (dir. 1976-78). Office: 410 N Michigan Ave Chicago IL 60611

MOLDANADO, SWARNALATHA ADUSUMILLI, nursing educator, researcher; b. Vijayawada, Andhra, India; came to U.S., 1977; d. Punnaih and Nagaratna (Chintapally) A.; m. Alexander Moldanado, Dec. 23, 1979; 1 child, Arjun. Registered nurse and midwife, Ill. Lectr. Postgrad. Inst. of Medical Edn. and Research, Chandigarh, India, 1971-77; research assoc., teaching asst. U. Ill. Coll. of Nursing, Chgo., 1977-81; tchr. practice Rush U. Coll of Nursing, Chgo., 1981-82; assoc. prof., chairman dept. nursing Rockford Coll., Ill., 1982—. Mem., vol. Hunger Watch Com. Am. Assn. Univ. Women, 1983-84. Mem. Am. Pub. Health Assn., Nat. League for Nursing, Ill. Sigma Xi Research Soc., Sigma Theta Tau. Avocations: music; gardening.

MOLER, DONALD LEWIS, educator; b. Wilsey, Kans., Jan. 12, 1918; s. Ralph Lee and Bessie Myrtle (Berry) M.; B.S., Kans. State Tchrs. Coll., Emporia, 1939; M.S., U. Kans., Lawrence, 1949, Ph.D., 1951; m. Alta Margaret Ansdell, Nov. 6, 1942; 1 son, Donald Lewis Jr. Tchr., Centralia (Kans.) High Sch., 1939-42, Carthage (Mo.) High Sch., 1946-48; asst. dir. Reading Clinic, U. Kans., 1948-51; dir. reading program Eastern Ill. U., 1951-70, prof. dept. ednl. psychology and guidance, 1963—, chmn. dept., 1963-84, dean Sch. Edn., 1980; vis. scholar U. Fla., 1965. Served with Signal Corps, U.S. Army, 1942-46. Recipient C.A. Michelman award, 1974; Disting Service award Ill. Assn. Counselor Educators, 1985. Mem. Ill. Guidance and Personnel Assn. (pres. 1968-69), Ill. Counselor Educators and Supvrs., Ill. Coll. Personnel Assn., Am. Personnel and Guidance Assn. (senator 1970-71), Assn. Counselor Edn. and Supervision, Assn. Humanistic Edn. and Devel., Phi Delta Kappa, Xi Phi, Pi Omega Pi, Pi Kappa Delta, Sigma Tau Gamma. Methodist. Asso. editor Ill. Guidance and Personnel Assn. Quar., 1970-84, mng. editor, 1984—. Home: 407 W Hayes St Charleston IL 61920 Office: Department of Ednl Psychology and Guidance Eastern Illinois University Charleston IL 61920

MOLINE, DONALD MARTIN, environmental administrator; b. Toledo, Feb. 13, 1947; s. Harry E. and Patricia A. (Reeves) M.; m. Martie Ann Horne, July 7, 1972; children—Kristen R., Tara K., Mary L., Phillip. B.S. in Chem. Engring., U. Toledo, 1973. Registered profl. engr., Ohio. Environmental engr. Environmental Services Agy., Toledo, 1974-79, chief engr., 1979-82, adminstr., 1982—. Served with U.S. Army, 1968-70. Mem. Air Pollution Control Ofcls. (dir. 1984—), Ohio Air Pollution Control Officers Assn. (vice chmn. 1984—), Water Pollution Control Fedn., Am. Insts. Chem. Engrs. Democrat. Roman

Catholic. Home: 4261 N Haven St Toledo OH 43612 Office: Environmental Services Agy 26 Main St Toledo OH 43605

MOLL, EDWIN ALLAN, business executive; b. Chgo., July 16, 1934; s. Maurice and Lillian (Lederman) M.; B.S., Loyola U., 1956; Ed.M., Northwestern U., 1960, Asso. in Police Sci., 1962; m. Natalie Kepner, Mar. 11, 1962; children—Kelli Lee, Dean Allan. Vice pres. Linnea Perfumes, Inc., 1950; owner, operator three restaurants, Chgo., 1952-56; producer, moderator radio shows This is Chgo., Grant Part Concert Rev., Fort Dearborn Concert, Chgo., 1957-65; bus. mgr. Chgo. Adler Planetarium, 1958-59; adminstrv. aide to mayor Chgo., 1959-63; pres. Edwin A. Moll Pub. Relations, Chgo., from 1963; pres. Profl. Adminstrv. Services Inc., 1975-78, Profl. Service System, Inc., 1975-78; chief ranger Cook County (Ill.) Forest Preserve, 1975-76; exec. Lee Optical Co., 1976-78; chmn. bd. Profl. Med. Guidance Corp.; dir. Glenwood State Bank; chmn. bd. Am. Travel Bur., Ltd., 1979, Edwin A. Moll and Assos.; pres. Riviera 400 Club; v.p. Outer Dr. E. Comml. Devel. Corp., 1983—; mgmt. cons. to professions; lectr. pub. relations and practice mgmt. Commr., Youth Welfare, Skokie, Ill., 1963-66. Exec. bd. mem. 40th ward Democratic Orgn., Chgo., 1948-68. Bd. dirs. Ill. Vision Services Corp., Nate Gross Found., Asthmacade. Recipient citation Red Cross, 1957. Mem. Am. Soc. Assn. Execs., Soc. Optometric Assn. Execs., Optometric Council for Polit. Edn. (exec. dir. 1968-69), Ill. Optometric Assn. (exec. sec. 1963-69, Optometric Layman of Year award 1967), Ill. Pub. Health Assn., Internat., Ill., West Suburban, South Suburban, North Suburban assns. chiefs of police, Ill. Police Assn., Internat. Platform Assn., Chgo. Forum Execs., Tau Delta Phi. Clubs: Illinois Athletic (Chgo.); President's (Washington). Author: Sell Yourself Big, 1966.

MOLLBERG, LONNIE W., oil company executive, geologist; b. Great Falls, Mont., Aug. 9, 1946; s. George C. and Delorus R. (Schultz) M.; m. Margaret Ruth Crowley, Oct. 6, 1969; children—Ramona Meghan, Michelle Lori, Sean George. B.A. in Geology, U. Mont., 1970, B.A. in Bus. Adminstrn., 1971; student Mont. Sch. Mines, 1964-69. Mining analyst McDermid, Miller, Calgary, Alberta, Can., 1971-75; mgr. planning and energy Burlington No., Billings Mont., 1975-78; pres., geologist GeoWest Geol., Billings, 1978-80, pres. GeoResources, Inc., Williston, N.D., 1980-83; corp. devel. Energy Resources, Williston, N.D., 1983-84; pres. R.M.S. Enterprises, Williston, N.D., 1983—; dir. Atlantic Pacific Gold Ltd., Calgary, 1983—. Mem. Yellowstone City Republican. Mem. Am. Assn. Petroleum Geologists, Soc. Petroleum Engrs., Can. Inst Mines. Roman Catholic. Club: Williston Country. Lodges: Elks, Rotary. Avocations: golf; hunting; fishing; skiing. Home: 409 22nd St East Williston ND 58801 Office: RMS Enterprises Inc PO Box 954 Williston ND 58801

MOLLET, CHRIS JOHN, lawyer; b. Bottineau, N.D., Jan. 31, 1954; s. Lyle F. and Aileen C. (Murdoch) M.; m. Lynne M. La Jone, Sept. 20, 1980. B.A. with distinction, U. Wis., 1976, J.D., 1979. Bar: Wis. 1979, Ill. 1980, U.S. Ct. Appeals (7th cir.) 1979. Staff counsel Michael Reese Hosp. and Med. Ctr., Chgo., 1980-82; assoc. Gardner, Carton & Douglas, Chgo., 1982—. Bd. dirs., v.p. Norwood Park Citizens Assn., Chgo., 1983-84. Mem. ABA, Wis. Bar Assn., Chgo. Bar Assn., Am. Acad. Hosp. Attys. Democrat. Office: 1 First Nat Plaza Chicago IL 60603

MOLLOY, MARY ALICE, architectural editor and writer; b. Detroit, Apr. 19, 1939; d. Brian Joseph and Therese M. (Mahoney) M. B.A., Newton (Mass.) Coll. Sacred Heart, 1961; postgrad. U. Mich., 1967—. Editorial asst. Detroit Free Press, 1962-65; publicist Wayne State U., Detroit, 1965-67; assoc. editor Ency. Brit., Chgo., 1967-74; freelance editor and writer, 1975—; editor: A Guide to Chicago's Public Sculpture (Ira J. Bach and Mary L. Gray), 1983; author: Glessner House Interiors: The Artists and Their Arts, 1983; Recent Chicago Architecture, 1984; docent Chgo. Architecture Found., 1976—, Docent of Yr. award, 1983. Mem. Soc. Archtl. Historians, Friends of Terra Cotta. Address: Chicago IL

MOLNAR, BELA, school administrator; b. Elyria, Ohio, May 12, 1951; s. Bela and Olga Margaret (Strong) M.; m. Nancy Lynn Campbell, Aug. 9, 1975; children—Eric Bela, Melinda Renee. B.A., Heidelberg Coll., 1973; M.Ed., Cleve. State U., 1977; postgrad., Kent State U., 1982-83, Akron U., 1983-84. Cert. secondary tchr., Ohio. Health, phys. edn. tchr. Ford Jr. High Sch., Brook Park, Ohio, 1973-79, athletic coach, 1973-79, health, physical edn. dept. chair, 1977-79; unit prin. Berea High Sch., Ohio, 1979-82; asst. prin. Copley High Sch., Ohio, 1982-83, prin. 1984—. Officer Copley High Sch. Parent-Tchr.-Student Assn., 1984—; mem. Arrowhead Primary Sch. PTA, Copley, 1984—. Mem. Nat. Assn. Secondary Sch. Prins., Ohio Assn. Secondary Sch. Adminstrs., Summit County Prins. Heidelberg Alumni Assn. Avocations: jogging; golf; tennis; registered Ohio High Sch. Athletic Assn. baseball, softball official. Home: 4320 Ridgewood Rd Copley OH 44321 Office: Copley High Sch 3807 Ridgewood Rd Copley OH 44321

MOLNAR-BONCELA, CATHERINE LEE, lawyer; b. Gary, Ind., Feb. 2, 1957; d. Robert Lee and Betty Lou (Murray) Molnar; m. Edward Carl Boncela, Sept. 24, 1982. B.A. magna cum laude in Communications, Valparaiso U., J.D., 1981; LL.M., DePaul U., 1983; postgrad. Ind. U.-Gary, 1983—. Bar: Ind. 1981. Research asst. Valparaiso (Ind.) U., 1980-81; law clk. Bankruptcy Ct., Gary, 1981-84; assoc. firm Goldsmith, Goodman, Ball & Van Bokkelen, Highland, Ind., 1984—; asst. Highland Forensics, Ind., 1980—; dir. ETX Systems, Inc., Griffith, Ind. Vol. ARC, 1976-81, various polit. campaigns, Lake County, Ind., 1984. Mem. Ind. State Bar Assn., ABA, Women Lawyers Assn., Moot Ct. Soc. Lutheran. Home: 1737 Selo Dr Schereville IN 46375 Office: Goldsmith Goodman Ball & Van Bokkelen 3737 45th St Highland IN 46332

MOLNIA, BRUCE FRANKLIN, geologist; b. N.Y.C., Oct. 17, 1945; s. David Sidney and Adella Edith (Weinstein) M.; m. Barbara Joyce Frank, June 25, 1967 (div. 1972); children—David, Meredith; m. Mary Antoinette Wiggers, Sept. 1, 1978; children—Michael, Bruce. B.A., Harpur Coll., 1967; M.A., Duke U., 1969; Ph.D., U. S.C., 1972. Cert. profl. geol. scientist. Sci. editor S.C. Ednl. TV Network, Columbia, 1971-72; asst. prof. Amherst Coll., Mass., 1972-73; geol. oceanographer U.S. Bur. Land Mgmt., Los Angeles, 1973-74; marine geologist U.S. Geol. Survey, Menlo Park, Calif., 1974-82; v.p. MESA2, Inc., Northridge, Calif., 1982-83; dep. chief Data Prodn. Distbn. br. EROS Data Ctr., Sioux Falls, S.D., 1983—; adj. prof. Calif. State U.-Northridge, 1982—; lectr., researcher Juneau Icefield Research Program, Alaska, 1975—. Author: Alaska's Glaciers, 1982. Editor: Glacial-Marine Sedimentation, 1983. Contbr. articles to profl. jours. Recipient Antarctic service medal U.S. Congress, 1968. Fellow Explorers Club, Geol. Soc. Am.; mem. Am. Assn. Petroleum Geologists, EROS Vanpooling Assn. (pres. 1984), Shelf Nearshore Dynamics Soc. (pres. 1979-80), Sigma Xi (life). Lodge: Elks. Avocations: photography, running. Home: 1909 Edgewood Rd Sioux Falls SD 57103 Office: US Geol Survey EROS Data Ctr Sioux Falls SD 57198

MOLTER, DONALD WILLIAM, counselor; b. Danville, Ill., May 15, 1958; s. Clifford William and Mary Louise (Sheppard) M. B.A. in Pub. Relations, Purdue U., 1980, M.S. in Counseling and Personnel Services, 1981. Counselor, Office of Dean of Students, Purdue U., West Lafayette, Ind., 1982—, dean students liaison Univ. Minister's Orgn., 1982—. Mem. Am. Assn. Counseling and Devel., Am. Coll. Personnel Assn., Assn. on Handicapped Student Service Programs in Post-Secondary Edn., Phi Eta Sigma. Democrat. Disciple of Christ. Club: Christian Concert Ministries (West Lafayette, Ind.) (adviser 1983—). Avocations: reading, water sports, backpacking, fishing, music. Home: 1200 Happy Hollow Rd Apt 707 West Lafayette IN 47906 Office: Hovde Hall Purdue U West Lafayette IN 47907

MOLUMBY, ROBERT EUGENE, architect, city planner; b. Willow Lake, S.D., May 22, 1936; s. Joseph A. and Irma Marian (Wilkinson) M.; B.Arch., U. Notre Dame, 1959; M.A. in City and Regional Planning, U. Calif., Berkeley, 1961; m. Edith Nina Taylor, Oct. 11, 1969; children—Katherine Hall, Nina Elizabeth. Architect-planner Perkins & Will Partnership, Chgo., 1965-71; sr. planner Village of Skokie, Ill., 1971-73, acting dir. planning, 1973, dir. planning, 1973—. Assoc. mem. Evanston (Ill.) Plan Commn., 1977-78, mem., 1978-84, vice chmn., 1982-84; mem. Evanston Zoning Bd. Appeals, 1985—; sr. warden St. Mark's Episcopal Ch., Evanston, 1980-82, vestryman, 1985—. Served as officer USN, 1961-65. Mem. Am. Planning Assn., Nat. Trust for Historic Preservation, Chgo. Archtl. Found., Chgo. Landmarks Preservation Council. Office: 5127 Oakton St Skokie IL 60077

MOMMSEN, JOHN WILLIAM, ranch owner; b. Rice Lake, Wis., Dec. 5, 1949; s. Myron F. and Evelyn M. (Rauchenstein) M.; m. Nancy Jean Olsen, Dec. 27, 1970; children—Elizabeth, Christina. Student U. Wis.-River Falls, 1967-70. Ptnr., Lazy A Ranch, Inc., Rice Lake, 1970-82, pres., 1982—; ptnr. Turtleback Golf and Country Club, Rice Lake, 1982—; dir. First Wis. Nat. Bank, Rice Lake. Mem. adv. council Wis. Indianhead Tech. Inst., 1980—; mem. U.S. Congressman Steve Gunderson Small Bus. Adv. Council, 1981—. Served with N.G., 1970-76. Named Outstanding Young Farmer, Rice Lake Area Jaycees, 1981, Wis. Outstanding Young Farmer, Wis. Jaycees, 1982, U.S. Outstanding Young Farmer U.S. Jaycees, 1983. Mem. Rice Lake Area C. of C., Wis. Potato Industry Bd. (sec. 1974, 75, 79, chmn. 1976-77), Nat. Potato Promotion Bd. (adminstrv. com. 1979-80), Nat. Potato Council (steering com. 1981-83). Lutheran. Clubs: Rice Lake Golf (dir. 1974-77), Elks. Office: Lazy A Ranch Inc Route 5 Rice Lake WI 54868

MONAGHAN, THOMAS S., professional baseball executive. Vice-chmn. Detroit Tigers. Office: Detroit Tigers Tiger Stadium Detroit MI 48216*

MONAHAN, JAMES EMMETT, physicist; b. Kansas City, Mo., Jan. 10, 1925; s. Leo and Helena (Schorgl) M.; m. Betty A. Connor, June 12, 1948. B.S., Rockhurst Coll., 1948; M.S., St. Louis U., 1950, Ph.D., 1952. Asst. physicist Argonne Nat. Lab., Ill., 1952-53, physicist, 1953-69, sr. physicist, 1967—. Contbr. articles to profl. jours. Served with U.S. Army, 1943-46. Recipient Alumni Merit award St. Louis U., 1961; Weisman fellow, 1967. Fellow Am. Phys. Soc. Home: 701 South Dr Burr Ridge IL 60521 Office: Argonne Nat Lab 9700 South Cass Ave Argonne IL 60439

MONAHAN, LEONARD FRANCIS, musician, singer, composer, publisher; b. Toledo, Aug. 19, 1948; s. Leonard Francis and Theresa Margaret (Geraldo) M.; m. Elaine Ann Welling, Oct. 14, 1978. B.S. in Psychology and Philosophy, U. Toledo, 1980. Musician, writer Len Monahan Prodns., Toledo, 1971-75; musician, composer, publisher World Airwave Music, Toledo, 1975—. Recipient Internat. Recognition of Christmas Music. Mem. Broadcast Music Inc., Internat. Platform Assn. Author: If You Were Big and I Were Small, 1971; The Land of Echoing Fountains, 1972; composer numerous songs. Office: 9967-US-A20 Delta OH 43515

MONASEE, CHARLES ARTHUR, corporate executive; b. Gary, Ind., Apr. 29, 1924; s. Sam Hasell and Phyllis (Kresham) M.; B.S., U. Chgo., 1944; m. Lyra Ann Halper, Jan. 28, 1950; children—Pam, Lisa. With Am. Community Stores, 1955-80, pres. Hinky Dinky div., 1968-71, pres. Am. Community Stores Corp., Omaha, 1971-80, exec. v.p. parent co. Cullum Companies, 1976-80; group pres. Riekes Group, ALCO Standard Corp., 1980-84; pres. Health Future found., 1984—; dir. Am. Charter Savs. and Loan Assn. Past pres., bd. dirs. United Way Midlands; bd. dirs. Omaha Symphony Assn.; past chmn. bd. Joslyn Museum; bd. dirs. Boys Town, 1973-79, Creighton U., Omaha; trustee Nebr. Meth. Hosp.; bd. govs. Boys Clubs Omaha; mem. adv. council Nebr. U. Med. Center; chmn. Omaha Jewish Community Center, 1972-75; nat. trustee NCCJ; councillor Ak Sar Ben. Served to lt. col. USAF, 1943-55. Decorated Bronze Star. Mem. Air Force Assn. Clubs: Highland Country, Omaha. Office: 9140 W Dodge Rd Omaha NE 68114

MONAT, WILLIAM ROBERT, university chancellor; b. Biwabik, Minn., Oct. 9, 1924; s. William Stephen and Milda Aleta (Sundby) M.; A.A., Virginia (Minn.) Jr. Coll., 1947; B.A. magna cum laude, U. Minn., 1949, Ph.D., 1956; postgrad. Wayne U., 1949-50; m. Josephine Ann Sclafani, Sept. 9, 1951; children—Lise Ann, Kathryn, Margaret, William Michael, Eric. Asst. prof. Wayne U., 1954-57; exec. asst. to Gov. Mich., 1957-60; assoc. prof. Pa. State U., 1960-65, prof. polit. sci., 1965-69, assoc. dir. Inst. Pub. Adminstrn., 1962-69; majority budget dir. Pa. Ho. of Reps., 1968-69; prof., chmn. dept. polit. sci. No. Ill. U., DeKalb, 1969-71, provost, 1976-78, pres., 1978-84, chancellor, bd. regents, 1984—; prof., dean faculties Baruch Coll., City U. N.Y., 1971-74, v.p. acad. affairs, 1974-76; cons. USPHS, 1956, Office of Sec. Dept. Labor, 1963-64, Bur. Labor Standards, 1966, Office of Gov. Pa., 1968; mem. Joint Council on Econ. Edn.; mem. Ill. Commn. Sci. and Tech. Served with AUS, 1943-46. Decorated Bronze Star medal; recipient Outstanding Achievement award U. Minn., 1982. Mem. Am. Polit. Sci. Assn., Am. Soc. Pub. Adminstrn., Phi Beta Kappa. Author: Labor Goes to War, 1965; The Public Library and its Community, 1967; Politics, Poverty and Education, 1968. Editor: Public Adminstration in Era of Change, 1962. Contbr. articles profl. jours. Home: 2106 Huntleigh Springfield IL 62704 Office: Bd Regents 616 Myers Bldg Springfield IL 62701

MONDELLO, MARY J., psychologist; b. Detroit, Nov. 12, 1927; d. Ralph and Josephine (Mudaro) Quasarano; m. Sam Serafino Mondello, Aug. 5, 1950 (dec. 1984); children—John, Judith, Joseph, Martha, Suzanne. B.A., Siena Heights Coll., 1949; M.A., Washington U.-St. Louis, 1971, Ph.D., 1982. Dir. student programs St. Louis U., 1969; counselor Blewett Jr. High Sch., St. Louis, 1970-71; dir. guidance St. Elizabeth Acad., St. Louis, 1971-74; assoc. prof., counselor St. Louis Community Coll. Meramec, St. Louis, 1975-82; psychologist Central Psychiat. Assn., St. Louis, 1982—; cons. depression El Centro Community Coll., Dallas, 1984, St. Louis Community Coll., 1984, Meramec, Florissant Valley, Forest Pk. Vol. Assn. Internat. Devel., Bogota, Columbia, 1961-66. Mem. Am. Psychol. Assn., Am. Counseling and Devel. (regional bd. mem. 1981-84), Am. Coll. Personnel Assn. (regional bd. mem. 1980-83), Mental Health Counselors (St. Louis task force 1985). Avocations: music; book discussion group. Office: Central Psychiat Assn 35 N Central Saint Louis MO 63105

MONDER, STEVEN I., orchestra executive. Gen. mgr. Cin. Symphony Orchestra. Office: Cincinnati Symphony Orchestra 1241 Elm St Cincinnati OH 45210*

MONDUL, DONALD DAVID, lawyer; b. Miami, Fla., Aug. 24, 1945; s. David Donald and Marian Wright (Heck) M.; m. Sharon Lynn Schramm, Apr. 25, 1971; children—Alison Marian, Ashley Megan. B.S., U.S. Naval Acad., 1967; M.B.A., Roosevelt U., 1976; J.D., John Marshall Law Sch., 1979. Bar: Ill. 1979, Fla. 1980, U.S. Patent Ct. 1980. Mktg. rep. Control Data Corp., Chgo., 1977-79; patent atty. Square D Co., Palatine, Ill., 1979-81, Ill. Tool Works, Chgo., 1981—; mem. adj. faculty W.R. Harper Coll., Palatine, Ill., 1979-83, Roosevelt U., Chgo., 1979-80. Served to lt. comdr. USN, 1967-77. Mem. ABA, Ill. Bar Assn., Fla. Bar, Chgo. Bar Assn., Patent Law Assn. Chgo. Presbyterian. Office: Ill Tool Works Inc 8501 W Higgins Rd Chicago IL 60631

MONE, PETER JOHN, lawyer; b. Brockton, Mass., Apr. 8, 1940; s. Edward Patrick and June E. (Kelliher) M.; m. Sharon Lee Bright, Oct. 9, 1965; children—Kathleen, Peter. A.B., Bowdoin Coll., 1962; J.D., U. Chgo., 1965. Ptnr., Baker & McKenzie, Chgo., 1968—. Mem. Winnetka Caucus, Ill., 1984—. Served to capt. U.S. Army, 1966-67; Vietnam. Decorated Purple Heart, Bronze Star, Air medal. Fellow Am. Coll. Trial Lawyers; mem. Soc. Trial Lawyers, Chgo. Trial Lawyers Club, Internat. Assn. Ins. Counsel. Democrat. Roman Catholic. Club: Skokie Country (Glencoe, Ill.). Avocations: photography; golf; paddle tennis; softball. Home: 1239 Scott Winnetka IL 60093 Office: Baker & McKenzie Prudential Plaza Chicago IL

MONG, ROBERT CLYDE, agricultural trailer company executive; b. Franklin, Pa., Aug. 4, 1930; s. Robert Ellsworth and Olive LaRue (Rowe) M.; m. Nadine Ruth Eske, June 9, 1956; children—Lisa, Lori. Student Anderson Coll., 1948-51, Wartburg Coll., 1953-54. Internat. ops. mgr. Hesston Corp., Kans., 1967-72, gen. mgr. Hesston Waste Equipment div., Elk Grove Village, Ill., 1972-75; pres., gen. mgr. Parker Industries Inc., Silver Lake, Ind., 1975-79, Hillsboro Industries Inc., Kans., 1979—. Served with US Army, 1951-53. Mem. Hillsboro C. of C. Republican. Lutheran. Home: 4 Ambleside Ln Newton KS 67114 Office: Hillsboro Industries Inc 220 Industrial Rd Hillsboro KS 67063

MONK, JAMES RUSSELL, lawyer, state senator; b. Sullivan, Ind., Oct. 5, 1947; s. Lyman Elihu and Charlotte May (Ellingsworth) M.; m. Sarah Jane Stewart, June 11, 1966; children—James Stewart, John Robert (dec.), Daniel Joshua. Student, Ind. State U., 1965-66; A.B., Ind. U., 1969; postgrad. U. Miami, 1974-75; J.D., U. Fla., 1977. Bar: Ind. 1978. Tchr. Plantation High Sch. (Fla.), 1969-71; tchr. South Plantation High Sch., 1971-76, dir. student activities, 1971-76; sole practice, Sullivan, 1978—; prosecutor Sullivan County, 1979-82, county atty., 1979-81; mem. Ind. State Senate, 1982—. Recipient Outstanding Freshman Legislator award Ind. Assn. Broadcasters, 1983. Mem. ABA, Ind. State Bar Assn., Sullivan County Bar Assn. Democrat. Roman Catholic. Lodges: Kiwanis (past pres.), Elks, K.C. (Sullivan). Home: Rural Route 1 Box 22 Sullivan IN 47882 Office: 110 S Main St Sullivan IN 47882

MONNIN, A. M., judge. Chief justice Ct. Appeal, Manitba, Can. Office: Ct Appeal Law Courts Bldg Winnipeg MB R3C OV8 Canada*

MONNINGER, ROBERT HAROLD GEORGE, ophthalmologist, educator; b. Chgo., Nov. 5, 1918; s. Louis Robert and Katherine (Lechner) M.; A.A., North Park Coll., 1939; B.S., Northwestern U., 1941, M.A., 1945; M.D., Loyola U., Chgo., 1953; Sc.D. (hon.), 1968; m. Anna Evelyn Turunen, Sept. 1, 1944; children—Carl John William, Peter Louis Philip. Intern St. Francis Hosp., Evanston, Ill., 1953-54; resident Presbyn.-St. Luke's, U. Ill. Research and Eye, VA hosps., 1954-57; mem. leadership council Ravenswood Hosp. Med. Center; instr. chemistry Lake Forest (Ill.) Coll., 1946-47; instr. biochemistry, physiology Loyola U. Dental Sch., 1948-49; clin. asso. prof. ophthalmology Stritch Sch. Medicine, Loyola U., Maywood, Ill., 1957-72; practice medicine specializing in ophthalmology, Lake Forest, 1957—; guest lectr. numerous univs. med. centers U.S., Can., Europe, Central and S.Am., Orient; resident lectr. Klinikum der Goethe-Universität, W. Ger., 1981; mem. panel Nat. Disease and Therapeutic Index; cons. Draize eye toxicity test revision HEW, cons. research pharm. cos. Nat. asso. Smithsonian Instn.; bd. dirs. Eye Rehab. and Research Found.; postgrad. faculty Internat. Glaucoma Congress; lectr. Hopital Dieu, Paris; lectr. postgrad. courses for developing nations physicians WHO; life mem. Postgrad. Sch. Medicine, U. Vienna; cons. Nat. Acad. Sci.; adv. bd. Madera Del Rio Found. Served with USMCR, 1941-44. Recipient citation Gov. Bahamas, 1960, Ophthalmic Found. award, 1963, Sci. Exhibit award Ill. State Med. Soc., 1966, Franco-Am. Meritorious citation, 1967, Paris Post No. 1 Am. Legion award, 1967, citation Pres. Mexico, 1968, Sightsaving award Bausch & Lomb, 1968, exhibit award Western Hemisphere Congress Internat. Surgeons, 1968, Research citation Japanese Soc. Opthalmology, 1969; Barraquer Gold Medallion; Physician's Recognition award AMA; Bicentennial citation Library of Congress Registration Book; meritorious citation Gov. of Ill.; citation and medal Lord Mayor of Rome, also Pres. of Italy, 1981; Civic Ctr. citation City of Evanston (Ill.), 1981; commendation and citation Ill. Gen. Assembly, 1982; cert. of accomplishment Loyola U. Alumni Assn., Chgo., 1983; Catherine White Scholarship fellow, 1945-46. Diplomate Am. Bd. Cosmetic Plastic Surgery. Fellow Internat. Coll. Surgeons (postgrad. faculty continuing edn.), Am. Coll. Angiology, Oxford Ophthal. Congress and Soc. (lectr. 1960-61), Royal Soc. Health, Internat. Acad. Cosmetic Surgery (editorial bd.), Sociedad Mexicana Ortopedia (hon.), C. Puestow Surg. Soc.; mem. AAAS, Internat. Soc. Geog. Ophthalmology (program course coordinator, lectr. ocular electrophysiology VI Internat. Congress, Rio de Janeiro), Pan Am. Assn. Ophthalmology, Assn. for Research Ophthalmology, Am. Assn. Ophthalmology, Am. Soc. Contemporary Ophthalmology, Internat. Glaucoma Soc., Ill. Soc. for Med. Research, Ill. Assn. Ophthalmology, Internat. Soc. Clin. Electrophysiology of Vision (hon., lectr. 1978), Brazilian Soc. Ophthalmology (hon. corr.), German Ophthal. Soc., Internat. Fedn. Clin. Chemists (lectr.), Primum Forum Ophthalmologicum (lectr.), European Ophthal. Soc. (lectr.), Internat. Congress Anatomists (lectr.), Association des Diabetologues Francaise (lectr.), German Soc. for Internal Medicine (lectr.), Met. Opera Guild, Fedn. Am. Scientists, N.Y., Ill. acads. sci., AAUP, Nat. Soc. Lit. and Arts, Nat. Hist. Soc., Rush Med. Sch.-Presbyn. St. Luke's Alumni Assn., Sociedad Poblana Oftalmologia (hon.; silver plaque, commemorative prestige lectr. 1982) (Mex.), Internat. Platform Assn., Cousteau Soc., Sigma Xi, Sigma Alpha Epsilon, Phi Beta Pi, Theta Kappa Psi. Cons. author Textbook of Endocrinology. Editorial bd. Clin. Medicine, 1958—, EENT Digest, 1958—, Internat. Surgery, 1972—, Internat. Bull., 1976—, Cosmetic Surgery, 1980—; contbr. articles to profl. jours.; spl. exhibit of works and writings held at Cudahy Meml. Library, Loyola U., Chgo., Oct. 1984. Home: 734 S Oak Knoll Dr Lake Forest IL 60045 Office: 320 E Vine St Lake Forest IL 60045

MONROE, WILLYS H(ERBERT), management consulting company executive; b. Pittsfield, Mass., Jan. 22, 1924; s. Willys Merritt and E. Marjorie (Bates) M.; B.A., Yale U., 1946; M.A., U. Mich., 1945; m. Virginia Church Gamwell, Jan. 7, 1945; children—Monroe Glasser, Willys G. Research asst., instr. Yale U., New Haven, 1946; indsl. psychologist Bigelow-Sanford Carpet Co., N.Y.C., 1946-51; cons. Psychol. Corp., N.Y.C., 1951-52; cons. to sr. v.p. Booz, Allen & Hamilton, N.Y.C. and Chgo., 1952-81, ret., 1981; pres. Willys H. Monroe, Cert. Mgmt. Cons., Inc., Chgo., 1981—; dir. Pillsbury Co., First Nat. Bank of Hinsdale (Ill.), St. Charles Mfg. Co. Served with M.I., 1943-46. Mem. Inst. Mgmt. Cons. Republican. Mem. United Ch. of Christ. Clubs: Hinsdale Golf, Univ. of Chgo., Mpls., Yale of Chgo. Home: 118 E Third St Hinsdale IL 60521 Office: 33 N LaSalle St Suite 2900 Chicago IL 60602

MONSON, CAROL LYNN, osteopathic physician, psychotherapist; b. Blue Island, Ill., Nov. 3, 1946; d. Marcus Edward and Margaret Bertha (Andres) M.; m. Frank E. Warden, Feb. 28, 1981. B.S., No. Ill. U., 1968, M.S., 1969; D.O., Mich State Coll. Osteo. Medicine, 1979. Lic. physician, Mich. Expeditor-psychotherapist H. Douglas Singer Zone Ctr., Rockford, Ill., 1969-71; psychotherapist Tri-County Mental Health, St. Johns, Mich., 1971-76; pvt. practice psychotherapy, East Lansing, Mich., 1976-80; intern Lansing Gen. Hosp., Mich., 1979-80; pvt. practice osteo. medicine, Lansing, 1980—; mem. staff Ingham Med. Hosp., Lansing Gen. Hosp.; field instr. Sch. Social Work, U. Mich., 1973-76; clin. instr. Central Mich. Dept. Psychology, 1974-75; clin. prof. Mich. State U., 1980—; mem. adv. bd. Substance Abuse Clearinghouse, Lansing, 1983-85, Kelly Health Care, Lansing, 1983-85, Americor Health Services, Lansing, 1984-85. Mem. Am. Osteo Assn., Internat. Transactional Analysis Assn., Mich. Assn. Physicians and Surgeons, Ingham County Osteo. Assn., Nat. Assn. Career Women (conv. com. 1984-85), Lansing Assn. Career Women. Lodge: Zonta (chmn. service com. Mid Mich. Capital Area chpt.). Avocations: gardening; orchid growing; antique collecting. Office: 3320 W Saginaw St Lansing MI 48917

MONSON, DIANNE LYNN, educator; b. Minot, N.D., Nov. 24, 1934; d. Albert Rachie and Iona Cordelia (Kirk) M. B.S., U. Minn., 1956, M.A., 1962, Ph.D., 1966. Tchr., Rochester Pub. Schs. (Minn.), 1966-59, U.S. Dept. Def., Schweinfurt, W.Ger., 1959-61, St. Louis Park Schs. (Minn.), 1961-62; instr. U. Minn., Mpls., 1962-66; prof. U. Wash., Seattle, 1966-82; prof. English edn. U. Minn., Mpls., 1982—. Co-author: New Horizons in the Language Arts, 1972; Children and Books, 6th edit., 1981; Experiencing Children's Literature, 1984; (monograph) Research in Children's Literature, 1976. Recipient Outstanding Educator award U. Minn. Alumni Assn., 1983. Fellow Nat. Conf. Research in English; mem. Nat. Council Tchrs. of English (exec. com. 1979-81), Internat. Reading Assn. (dir. 1980-83), ALA. Lutheran. Home: 740 River Dr Saint Paul MN 55116 Office: U Minn 350 Peik Hall Minneapolis MN 55455

MONTAYRE, MAXIMO ESCORIAL, accountant; b. Cebu City, Philippines, Nov. 18, 1936; s. Saturnino T. and Candelaria A. (Escorial) M.; B.S., U. San Carlos (Philippines), 1958; m. Concepcion Lamb Pacana, May 6, 1962; children—Arne, Joffre, Nelson, Bernard. Staff accountant Colgate-Palmolive Philippines, Inc., 1960-66, Gen. Motors Dealer, Philippines, 1967-69; cost accountant Stewart Warner Electronics, Chgo., 1969-70; corp. sr. tax acct. A.B. Dick Co., Niles, Ill., 1970-80, Am. Internat., Inc., 1981—; pres. M-R Realty, Inc. C.P.A., Philippines; lic. real estate broker, Ill. Mem. Bisaya Circle Am. (pres. 1979-80), Chgo. Philippine C.P.A. Assn. (chmn. reciprocity com. 1975-76), Chgo. Northside Real Estate Bd., Nat. Assn. Rev. Appraisers, Internat. Platform Assn. Roman Catholic. Clubs: Chgo. Tax, Toastmasters (pres. 1976-77). Home: 5519 N St Louis Ave Chicago IL 60625 Office: 2622 W Peterson Ave Chicago IL 60659

MONTEBELLO, ANTHONY R., management and human resource consultant, industrial psychologist; b. Springfield, Mo., Mar. 18, 1953; s. Andrew A. and Shigeno (Okino) M. B.A., St. Louis U., 1975, Ph.D., 1980; M.A., U. Ky., 1977. Personnel research psychologist City of St. Louis, 1976-77; vis. asst. prof., lectr. Bus. Sch., lectr. dept. psychology St. Louis U., 1979-81, assoc. dir., mgmt. cons. Ctr. for Application of Behavioral Sci., 1979-81; staff assoc. Colarelli Assocs., Inc., Clayton, Mo., 1981-83; mgr. orgn. and human resource devel. Farm Credit Banks; cons. to bus. and industry. Mem. Mo. Bot. Gardens, St. Louis. Recipient Leadership award Student Council, St. Louis U., 1975. Mem. Am. Psychol. Assn., Mo. Psychol. Assn., Soc. for Indsl. Organizational Psychology, Acad. of Mgmt. Roman Catholic. Contbr. articles to profl. jours. Home: 219 Jewel Saint Louis MO 63122 Office: 1415 Olive Saint Louis MO 63103

MONTEBURNO, MICHAEL VITO, communications company executive; b. N.Y.C., Dec. 1, 1938; s. Nicholas Paul and Rose (Sabatino) M.; m. Patricia Panos, Nov. 3, 1962; children—Lauren, Nicholas. B.S. in Elec. Engring., Polytech. Inst. Bklyn., 1960; M.S. in Elec. Engring., NYU, 1966. Project mgr. voice services Western Union Telegraph, Upper Saddle River, N.J., 1973-75, dir. quality service, 1975-77, mgr. planning, engring., N.Y.C., 1977-80, area mgr. network operations, Chgo., 1980-81, regional v.p. ops., 1981—; mem. adv. bd. Ill. Tech. Coll., Chgo., 1983—. Pres. Packanack Manor Homeowners Assn., Wayne, N.J., 1971. Avocations: tennis; running; traveling. Home: 161 Tanoak Ln Naperville IL 60540 Office: 427 S La Salle St Chicago IL 60605

MONTEIRO, MANUEL JAMES, manufacturing company executive; b. New Bedford, Mass., 1926; s. Joao and Beatrice (Oliveira) M.; m. Madelyn Wilcox, Dec. 15, 1946; children—Warren James, Mark Alan, Marguerite Ann Monteiro Cavett, Marilyn Jean Monteiro Allen, John Manuel, James Robert, Robert William. B.S. in Acctg. and Fin., Bryant Coll. With 3M Co., 1950—, cost analyst tape lab., St. Paul, 1950-54, various internat. positions in Colombia, Brazil, 1954-65, mng. dir. 3M Brazil, 1965-71, area dir. Latin Am. and Africa, 1971-73, div. v.p. Latin Am. and Africa, 1973-75, v.p. European ops., 1975-81, exec. v.p. internat. ops., 1981—. Served with U.S. Army, 1945-46. Recipient Disting. Alumni award Bryant Coll. Presbyterian. Office: 3M Co 3M Center 220-14E Saint Paul MN 55144-1000

MONTEIRO, MARILYN DONALDA SAUNDERS, educational administrator; b. Washington. B.A., U. Mass. 1970; Ed.M., Harvard U., 1973, Ed.D. in Ednl. Adminstrn., 1982. Tchr., tchr. trainer Delta Opportunities Corp., Greenville, Miss., 1970-71; program dir. Roxbury br. YWCA, Boston, 1973-74; dir. affirmative action Mass. Coll. Art, Boston, 1980-83; affirmative action officer U. No. Iowa, Cedar Falls, 1983—; instr. U. Mass.-Boston, 1974-80, Antioch U., 1980, Mass. Coll. Art., Boston, 1982-83; lectr. in field; cons. City Waterloo Civil Service Commn., Iowa, 1984, Parco Ltd., Cedar Falls, 1984; cons. evaluator Mass. Found. Humanities and Pub. Policy, 1980; program evaluator Am. Assn. Colls., N.Y.C., 1982-83. Mem. Cedar Falls Human Rights Commn. Harvard U. scholar, 1972-73; Ford Found. fellow, 1975-80. Mem. Nat. Assn. Women Deans, Adminstrs. and Counselors, NAACP, Trans-Africa, Am. Assn. Higher Edn., Assn. Study Negro Life and History, Am. Assn. Affirmative Action (regional dir.), Mid-Am. Assn. Ednl. Opportunity Program Personnel, Phi Delta Kappa. Home: 1716 Rainbow Dr Cedar Falls IA 50613 Office: U No Iowa Cedar Falls IA 50613

MONTESI, SUSAN JEAN, educational counselor, educator; b. Escanba, Mich., Jan. 15, 1945; d. Ernest J. and Jean R. (Bichler) Vanlerberghe; m. William A. Montesi, Apr. 16, 1966; children—Scott, Aimee. B.S., Ferris State Coll., 1966; M.A., Central Mich. U., 1970, M.S., 1976. Tchr. Morley Stanwood High Sch., Morley, Mich., 1966-68, Bay City Schs., Mich., 1968-70, Central Mich. U., Mt. Pleasant, Mich., 1972-75; counselor Delta Coll., University Center, Mich., 1970-74, chmn. counselor, 1974—, prof. evening coll., 1972—. Contbr. articles to profl. publs. Teen sponsor YWCA/YMCA, Bay City, 1968-72. Recipient Recognition award for Outstanding Service, AAUP, 1975. Mem. Am. Assn. Counseling and Devel., Am. Coll. Personnel Assn. (bd. dirs. Commn. XI 1975-78, 80-83, chmn. Commn. XI 1982—), Am. Assn. Women in Community and Jr. Colls., Nat. Council Student Devel., others. Avocation: Stained glass art. Home: 2080 Reppuhn Dr Bay City MI Office: Delta Coll K143 Counseling Ctr University Center MI 48710

MONTGOMERY, C. BARRY, lawyer. Ptnr., Jacobs, Williams and Montgomery Ltd., Chgo. Office: Jacobs Williams and Montgomery Ltd 20 N Wacker Dr Chicago IL 60606*

MONTGOMERY, JAMES W., clergyman. Bishop, Episcopal Ch., Chgo. Office: 65 E Huron St Chicago IL 60611*

MONTGOMERY, STEVEN RANDAL, lawyer; b. Dexter, Mo., July 24, 1952; s. Breman Lafayette and Carolyn Joan (Welborn) M.; m. Trudy Ann Krebsbach, Nov. 19, 1977; children—Alison Marie, Alexander, Breman. Student Southeastern Mo. State U., 1970-71; B.S. in Civil Engring., U.S. Mil. Acad., 1975; M.P.A., U. Okla., 1978, J.D., 1980; J.D., Oklahoma City U., 1979. Bar: Mo. 1981, U.S. Dist. Ct. (ea. dist.) Mo. 1981. Assoc. Powell and Ringer, Dexter, 1981; sole practice, Dexter, 1982—; apptd. interim prosecuting atty. Stoddard County, Mo., 1982-83. Bd. dirs. Southeastern Mo. U. Found., 1983. Named King of Beasts Corps of Cadets U.S. Mil. Acad., 1975, 4th regtl. comdr., 1974-75, Leadership award, 1975. Mem. Assn. Trial Lawyers Am., Dexter C. of C. (bd. dirs. 1983-84). Republican. Club: Optimist (founding pres. 1982-83). Office: 135 E Stoddard PO Box 188 Dexter MO 63841

MONTGOMERY, THEODORE VAN TIFFLIN (TODD), JR., investment executive; b. Milw., July 4, 1943; s. Theodore Van Tifflin and Marjorie (Schwab) M.; m. Mary Lou Mock, June 19, 1965 (div. Aug. 1981); children—Elizabeth, Theodore III; m. Susan Jane Crume, Apr. 10, 1982; children—Kristin, David. A.B. in Polit. Sci., Miami U., Oxford, Ohio, 1965; M.S. in Edn., U. Wis.-Milw., 1974, Ph.D. in Urban Edn., 1984. Tchr., coach Univ. Sch. Milw., 1968-73; curriculum developer Edn. Devel. Ctr., Cambridge, Mass., 1972-73; cons. urban planning Community Devel. Agy., Milw., 1975-76; instr. urban planning U. Wis., Milw., 1976-79, adj. prof., 1983—; exec. dir. Sci., Econs. and Tech. Ctr., Milw., 1978-79; investment officer Robert W. Baird & Co., Inc., Milw., 1979—; editor, writer, photographer Montgomery Media, Milw., 1984—. Editor, pub.; Now What Can I Do?, 1976; Now What Can I Do Now That I've Done That?, 1978. Exhibited photography, Milw. and Chgo., 1970-78; photographer for Milw. Pub. Mus. internat. expdn. to Nepal, 1974. Mem. planning and allocations com. United Way Greater Milw., 1978—; mem. Friends of Mus., Milw., 1984—; mem. Internat. Inst. of Milw. County, mem. lakefront planning com. Milw. Civic Alliance, 1982—; bd. dirs. Wis. Olympic Ice Rink Operating Corp., Milw., 1982—, pres., 1982-84. Served as lt. USNR, 1965-68, Vietnam. Mem. Nepal Studies Assn., U.S. Navy League, U. Wis.-Milw. Sch. Edn. Alumni Assn. (editorial adv. bd. Met. Edn. jour. 1985—). Club: Gyro Internat. (Milw.) (pres. 1985-86). Avocations: stamps; carpentry; gardening; photography. Office: Robert W Baird & Co Inc 777 E Wisconsin Ave Milwaukee WI 53202

MONTI, GREGORY L., marketing executive; b. Bklyn., Oct. 28, 1946; s. LeRoy John and Mary Alice (Foley) M.; B.S., St. Joseph's Coll., 1968; M.S., Roosevelt U., 1981. With Continental Ill. Nat. Bank, Chgo., 1970-71; with Monti & Assos., Inc., Arlington Heights, Ill., 1971—, v.p. sales and mktg., 1976—. Served with U.S. Army, 1968-70. Decorated Army Commendation medal. Mem. Air Conditioning and Refrigeration Wholesalers (asso.), Refrigeration Service Engrs. Soc., Refrigeration Machinery Assn. Home: 109 Horatio Blvd Buffalo Grove IL 60090 Office: 1050 E Addison Ct Arlington Heights IL 60005

MONTMINY, TRACY, artist; b. Boston, 1911; d. Edward and Ellen (Phalan) Tracy; m. Pierre Montminy, Jan. 25, 1941 (dec. 1973). B.A. in Fine Arts, Radcliffe Coll., 1933. Prof. art U. Mo., Columbia, 1948-63; vis. prof. Am. U. Beirut, 1963-64; prof. art U. Mo., Columbia, 1964-81. Prin. works include murals in pub. bldgs., Maine, Mass., Ill.; staircase murals biology bldg. U. Mo.; mural engring. bldg. U. Mo; mural Stephens Coll., Mo. Guggenheim fellow in painting, 1940-41. Mem. Nat. Soc. Mural Painters. Democrat. Home: 1506 Paris Rd Columbia MO 65201

MONZON, CARLOS MANUEL, physician; b. Guatemala, C.A., Dec. 16, 1949; came to U.S., 1977; s. Carlos Manuel and Amparo (Letona) M.; m. Evelyn David, Sept. 26, 1975; children—Carlos Rodolfo, Juan Pablo. M.D., U. San Carlos, Guatemala, 1976. Diplomate Am. Bd. Pediatrics, Am. Bd. Pediatric Hematology and Oncology. Resident in pediatrics U. San Carlos, Guatemala, 1976-77, U. Mo.-Columbia, 1977-80; fellow in pediatric hematology and oncology Mayo Grad. Sch. Medicine, Rochester, Minn., 1980-82; instr. pediatrics U. Mo.-Columbia, 1982-83, asst. prof. child health, 1983—. Contbr. articles to med. jours. Recipient Fritz Kenny Meml. award in pediatric research, Midwest Soc. Pediatric Research, 1981. Fellow Am. Acad. Pediatrics. Home: 4365 Santa Anna St Columbia MO 65201 Office: U Mo Health Scis Ctr Dept Child Health 1 Hospital Dr Columbia MO 65201

MOODY, JAMES I., judge. U.S. Dist. Judge Seventh Cir., No. Ind. Office: US Dist Ct 128 Federal Bldg Hammond IN 46320*

MOODY, JIM, congressman; b. Richlands, Va., Sept. 2, 1935. B.A., Haverford Coll., 1957; M.P.A., Harvard U., 1967; Ph.D. in Econs., U. Calif.-Berkeley, 1973. Served with CARE, Yugoslavia and Iran, 1958-60, Peace Corps, Bangladesh, Pakistan and Washington, 1961-64, AID, 1964-65, U.S. Dept. Transp., 1967, 69, World Bank, 1979; mem. 98th-99th Congresses from 5th Dist. Wis. Mem. Wis. State Assembly, 1977-78, Wis. State Senate, 1979-82. Democrat. Office: 1721 Longworth House Office Bldg Washington DC 20515

MOODY, ROBERT THOMAS, JR., public relations executive; b. Norton, Kans., Dec. 4, 1951; s. Robert Thomas and Helmi Elvira (Peckert) M.; m. Patricia Lynn Nelson, June 26, 1976; 1 child, Tristan Chamberlin. A.A., Colby Community Coll., 1971; B.S., U. Kans., 1977. Tech. writer Kans. State Econ. Opportunity Office, Topeka, 1978; informational writer Kans. State Dept. Health and Environment, Topeka, 1978-84, dir. pub. info., 1984—. Editor, contbg. author newsletter Kans. Environment, 1980-83. Mem. block grant adv. bd. Lawrence Community Devel. Agy., Kans., 1982—; v.p. North Lawrence Improvement Assn., Kans., 1981—. Recipient cert. of outstanding merit William Allen White Sch., U. Kans., 1977. Home: 539 Elm St Lawrence KS 66044 Office: Kans Dept Health and Environment Forbes Field Topeka KS 66620

MOON, BYONG HOON, pharmacology educator; b. Seoul, Korea, Jan. 15, 1926, came to U.S., 1955, naturalized, 1976; m. Chang Sook Kang, Apr. 16, 1957; children—Marjorie Mihi, Lillian Yunghee, Judieth Guihee, Daniel Sungpil. B.Sc., Seoul Nat. U., 1951; B.Sc., U. Nebr., 1960, M.Sc., 1964; Ph.D. in Pharmacology, Wash. State U., 1969. Registered pharmacist, Ill., Kans. Research assoc. in pharmacology U. Ill. Coll. Medicine, 1969; instr. pharmacogenetics Rush Med. Coll., Chgo., 1972, asst. prof. pharmacology, 1974-81, assoc. prof. pharmacology and internal medicine, 1981; assoc. prof. Grad. Coll., Rush U., 1981, course dir. nursing pharmacology Coll. Nursing, 1975—; course dir. med. pharmacology Rush Med. Coll., 1974—; sec., treas. Midwest Com. Drug Investigation, 1980-82. Mem. Am. Soc. Pharmacology and Exptl. Therapeutics, Rho Chi. Contbr. articles to profl. jours. Office: Dept of Pharmacology Rush Med Coll 1753 W Congress Pkwy Chicago IL 60612

MOON, JANINE ANNETTE, telephone company executive; b. Toledo, Nov. 2, 1948; d. Menard R. and Edith E. (David) Mossing; B.Sc., Bowling Green State U., 1970; M.A., Ohio State U., 1977; m. Burnell Thomas Moon, June 27, 1970; 1 child, Lara Nicholle. Instr., Bishop Luers High Sch., Ft. Wayne, Ind., 1970-72; instr. Mt. Mercy Acad., Grand Rapids, Mich., 1973; instr., drama-sports dir. Forest Hills No. High Sch., Grand Rapids, 1973-76; instr. N. Central Tech. Coll., Mansfield, Ohio, 1976-79; program dir. Ohio Program in Humanities, YWCA, Mansfield, 1977-78; devel. edn. coordinator N. Central Tech. Coll., Mansfield, 1978-79; curriculum specialist United Telephone Co. of Ohio, Mansfield, 1979-81, tng. and devel. cons., 1981-84, gen. adminstrn. mgr., liaison to Pub. Utilities Commn., 1984—; seminar, workshop leader mgmt. devel. tng. communications and women's concerns cons. Bd. dirs. YWCA, Mansfield, 1976-80, pres., 1979-80; coordinator/organizer, chmn. task force for women's resource center, Mansfield, 1978-79. Mem. Am. Soc. for Tng. and Devel. (region 3 coordinator Women's Network), Am. Soc. Profl. Cons., Nat. Assn. Female Execs., AAUW, LWV, NOW, Ohio State U. Alumni Assn. Office: 665 Lexington Ave PO Box 3555 Mansfield OH 44907

MOON, ROBERT ALLEN, dentist; b. Atlantic, Iowa, May 1, 1933; s. Clarence Allen and Effie (Berry) M.; B.S., Ind. U., 1955, D.D.S., 1958; m. Janice Lilian Hahn, Sept. 5, 1954, (div. May 1972); children—Robert, Mark, David, Kevin, Jeff, Gregory, Susan; m. 2d, Donna June Busse, Oct. 21, 1972. Practice dentistry, Hobart, Ind., 1961—; instr. Ind. U., 1975-80. Lake County dir. March of Dimes, 1971-72; mem. exec. bd. Ind. Bd. Health, 1984—, exec. dir., 1984, 85. Served with USAF, 1958-61. Recipient Sagamore of Wabash award, 1981. Mem. ADA (del. 1979, 80), Am. Coll. Dentists, N.W. Dist. Dental Soc. (pres. 1968-69, editor newsletter), Ind. Dental Assn. (trustee 1970-75, dir. ann. session programs 1976, 77, 78, pres. 1980-81), Internat. Coll. Dentists, Acad. Gen. Dentistry, Pierre Fauchard Acad., World Affairs Council N.W. Ind. (bd. dirs.), Phi Delta Kappa (pres. 1985), Delta Sigma Delta, Acacia. Methodist. Club: Rotary (pres. 1966-67). Home: 566 Harrison St Valparaiso IN 46383 Office: 904 W Ridge Rd Hobart IN 46342

MOONEY, ANDREW JAMES, business association executive; b. Evanston, Ill., Feb. 18, 1952; s. John and Anne (Meehan) M.; m. Kathleen M. Sloan, June 5, 1982. B.A. in Govt., U. Notre Dame, 1975; M.Div., U. Chgo., 1977. Dir., Office of Intergovtl. Affairs, Chgo., 1979-81; chmn., exec. dir. Chgo. Housing Authority, 1981-83; pres. Des Moines C. of C., 1983—; mem. bd. Nat. Housing Conf., 1982—. Danforth fellow. Mem. Phi Beta Kappa. Democrat. Clubs: Wakonda County, Des Moines (Des Moines). Avocations: flying; gardening; music. Office: 800 High St Des Moines IA 50307

MOONEY, EDWARD JOSEPH, JR., chemical company executive; b. Omar, W.Va., May 19, 1941; s. Edward Joseph Sr. and Johnny Mae (Kidd) M.; m. Mary Martha May, Aug. 22, 1964; children—Elizabeth Anne, Edward Joseph III. B.S. in Chemistry, U. Tex., 1964, J.D., 1967; Sr. Exec. Program, MIT, 1979. Bar: Tex. 1967, Ill. 1973. Corp. counsel Howe-Baker Corp., Tyler, Tex., 1969-70; gen. counsel Nalco Chem. Co., Oak Brook, Ill., 1970-80, group gen. mgr., 1980-82, v.p., 1982-84, sr. v.p., 1985—, div. pres., 1985—. Mem. Ill. Bar Assn., Am. Patent Law Assn.

MOONEY, JOHN ALLEN, business executive; b. Amery, Wis., May 17, 1918; s. Harry Edmon and Maybelle (Johnson) M.; student U. Wis., River Falls; m. Nettie O. Hayes, Aug. 29, 1940; children—John Allen, Suzanne, Jean, Nancy. Salesman, Reid Murdock & Co., Chgo., 1940-45, Consol. Foods Corp., Chgo., 1945-69; nat. sales mgr., v.p. M & R Sales Corp., Oak Park, Ill., 1969-78, pres., chief exec. officer, dir., 1978—; nat. sales mgr., v.p. Western Dressing, Inc., Oak Park, 1970-78, pres., chief exec. officer, dir., 1978—; dir. 1st Nat. Bank of LaGrange (Ill.), Waunakee Alloy Casting Corp. Bd. govs. Shrine Hosp. for Crippled Children, Chgo., Mpls., St. Paul; assoc. bd. govs. LaGrange Meml. Hosp.; chmn. Shrine Hosp. Day, Chgo., 1982; festmaster Oktoberfest U.S.A., LaCrosse, Wis., 1983; pres. Gundersen Med. Found., LaCrosse; bd. govs. Nat. Fishing Hall of Fame, Hayward, Wis.; treas. Shriners Hosp. Crippled Children, Chgo., 1983; mem. LaCrosse Luth. Hosp. Corp.; mem. exec. bd. Boy Scouts Am., Gateway Area council, also nat. rep., mem. nat. election council; mem. Rebild Nat. Park Soc., Aalborg, Denmark; hon. mem. LaCrosse Boychoir; mem. Heritage Club of LaCrosse Luth. Hosp. Named Man of Yr. LaCrosse C. of C., 1983; recipient Pope John XXIII award for Disting. Service, Viterbo Coll., LaCrosse, 1984, Community and Leadership award for Outstanding Community Leadership, LaCrosse Toastmasters, 1984; hon. Ky. Col.; awarded Order of Arrow, Boy Scouts Am. Clubs: La Crosse, LaCrosse Country, LaCrosse Plugs. Lodges: Masons (John Allen Mooney lodge named in his honor, Amery, Wis., potentate Zor Shrine Temple, Madison, Wis., hon. past potentate Medinah Shrine Temple, Chgo.), Sons of Norway, LaCrosse Elks, LaCrosse Moose. Office: 1515 N Harlem Ave Oak Park IL 60302

MOONEY, LAURA J., lawyer; b. Cleve., Feb. 2, 1954; d. Robert P. and Shirley A. (Meeker) M. B.A., Miami U., Oxford, Ohio, 1976; J.D., U. Dayton, 1979. Bar: Ohio 1979, U.S. dist. ct. (no. dist.) Ohio 1979. Sole practice, Cleve., 1979—; cons. Animation Plus, United Resources, Target Video, 1980—. Mem. Mus. Natural Sci., Ohio. Mem. Ohio Bar Assn., Greater Cleve. Bar Assn., Cleve. Women Lawyers Assn. Office: Suite 950 Standard Bldg Cleveland OH 44113

MOONEY, MARY PATRICIA, lawyer; b. Farmington, Minn., Sept. 30, 1951; d. Vincent Charles and Mavis Jeanne (Thompson) M.; m. John Howard Leber, Oct. 4, 1980. B.A. in Psychology, U. Minn.-Morris, 1976; J.D., Hamline U., 1979. Bar: Minn. 1979. Asst. county atty. Mille Lacs County, Minn., 1979-82; assoc. Kennedy Law Office, Mpls., 1983-84; sole practice, Mpls., 1984—; adv. atty. Chrysalis Resource Ctr., Mpls., 1983—. Bd. dirs. Dist. Dem.-Farmer-Labor Party, St. Paul, 1978-79; mem. adv. bd. Hamline Women's Resource Ctr., St. Paul, 1983-85; bd. dirs. Domestic Abuse Project, Mpls., 1984—. Mem. Minn. State Bar, Hennepin County Bar, Minn. Women Lawyers, Minn. Women's Network. Roman Catholic. Office: 3415 35th Ave S Minneapolis MN 55406

MOONEY, ROBERT JOHN, research administrator; b. St. Louis, Sept. 10, 1941; s. Harold John and Mary Jane (Farrell) M.; m. Susanne Wallace, Nov. 24, 1962; children—Robert John II., Kevin Michael. B.S., Tarkio Coll., 1980. Retail clk. Jansens IGA, 1970-78; retail telephone salesman Wetterau Inc., St. Louis, 1978-79, tng. mgr., 1979-80, dir. personnel, 1980-81, dir. retail tng., 1981-83, dir. research, 1983—, author and instr. tng. programs. Bd. mgrs. YMCA of Ozarks; bd. dirs. Wetterau Employee Credit Union; instr. Jr. Achievement Project Bus. Mem. Am. Soc. Tng. Dirs. Club: Dismas House (St. Louis) (supporting mem.). Lodge: Lions (chmn. constn. and by-law com.). Avocations: reading, fly-fishing, bow hunting, photography, power boating. Home: 225 Patterson Ln Florissant MO 63031 Office: Wetterau Inc 8920 Pershall Rd Hazelwood MO 63042

MOOR, DONALD R., office supply company executive; b. Cheyenne, Wyo., Dec. 30, 1939; s. Ross W. and Lois C. M.; m. Judy C. Chadwick, Apr. 6, 1963; children—Chad A., Kelly Jo, Jennifer L. Student Colo. State U., 1958-63. Mgr. Arabian horse farm, Rogers, Ark., 1963-64; mgr. feed mill, W.R. Grace Co., Ogallala, Nebr., 1964, rep. indsl. div., office mgr. indsl. div., adminstrv. asst. to dir. mktg. Walnut Grove Products Co., Atlantic, Iowa, 1965-69, div. mgr. for sales, St. Joseph, Mo., 1969-73; dist. mgr. Kemin Industries, Des Moines, 1973-82; pres. Midwest Office Supply, St. Jospeh, 1982—; farmer, breeder Australian shepherd dogs, Quarter horses, cattle. Recipient various sales awards Kemin Industries, 1973-82. Republican. Methodist. Avocations: rodeo; golf; fishing. Home: Route 1 Box 14 Easton MO 64443 Office: Midwest Office Supply 1501 S Belt Saint Joseph MO 64507

MOORE, ARTHUR WILLIAM, lawyer; b. Erie, Pa., Feb. 19, 1920; s. Arthur Gordon and Barbara P. (Dillon) M.; m. Geraldine Marie O'Brien, Apr. 5, 1943; children—Christopher A., Mary Judith Moore Salva. B.S.E., U. Pa., 1941; LL.B., Georgetown U., 1948. Bar: Ohio. Ptnr. Taggart Cox Moore & Hays, Wooster, Ohio, 1949-70; sole practice, Wooster, 1970-82; resident prin. lawyer Buckingham, Doolittle & Burroughs, LPA, Wooster, 1982—; dir. Wayne Steel, Inc., Wooster, Akron Rebar Co., Ohio; dir., sec. Wooster Products, Inc., 1954-82, Magni Power Co., Wooster, 1954-82, Magni-Fab Ga. Inc., Thomaston, Ga., 1978—. Bd. dirs., trustee Wooster YMCA, 1975-83; mem. Tax Appeals Bd., City of Wooster, 1983—; chmn. Wooster Chpt. ARC, 1984—. Served to maj. AUS, 1942-46, ETO. Decorated Bronze Star; recipient Pope John Benemerenti medal Cath. Ch., 1978. Mem. Wayne County Bar Assn. (pres. 1975), Ohio State Bar Assn., ABA. Roman Catholic. Lodge: Kiwanis (pres. 1956, lt. gov. 1958). Avocation: golf. Office: 201 E Liberty St Wooster OH 44691

MOORE, BENJAMIN LUTHER, psychology, educator, consultant; b. Atlanta, Jan. 19, 1940; s. Donald L. and Carolyn C. (Carson) M.; m. Mary Evelyn Ratteree, June 8, 1963; children—Donald Todd, Kevin Carson. B.A., Emory U., 1961, M.Div., 1969; M.S., Fla. State U., 1971, Ph.D., 1973. Registered psychologist, Ill.; cert. sch. psychologist, Ill. Asst. prof. dept. psychology Ill. State U., Normal, 1973-80, assoc. prof., 1980—; clin. dir. The Baby Fold, Normal, 1976—; vis. assoc. prof. dept. psychology Ill. Wesleyan U., Bloomington, 1980; adviser Gov.'s Commn. on Children's and Adolescent's Mental Health and Devel. Disabilities, 1979-80. Served to lt. USAF, 1962-66. Decorated Air Force Commendation medal with oak leaf cluster. H.B. Trimble fellow, 1968-69; USPHS fellow, 1970-72. Mem. Am. Psychol. Assn., Ill. Psychol. Assn., Assn. Behavior Analysis, Southeastern Psychol. Assn., Omicron Delta Kappa, Theta Phi. Democrat. Methodist. Office: 108 E Willow St Normal IL 61761

MOORE, CLIFFORD LEROY, pediatric psychologist; b. New Haven, June 7, 1945; s. Frederick Elvin and Helen Alberta (Morton) M. B.S., So. Conn. State Coll., 1967; M.S., U. Iowa, 1970, Ph.D., 1973. Asst. prof. pediatrics and child psychiatry Albany (N.Y.) Med. Coll., 1973-74; asst. prof. dept. pediatrics, dept. child psychiatry So. Ill. U. Med. Sch., Springfield, 1975-78; vis. assoc. prof. clin. psychology Pa. State U., State College, 1979-80; dir. Pediatric Psychology and Family Psychology Ctr., Mpls., 1980—; cons. Office of Dean, Pa. State U., 1979-80. Children's Bur. HEW fellow, 1968-70; Ford Found. dissertation fellow, 1972-73; U. Iowa scholar, 1972-73. Mem. Am. Psychol. Assn., Soc. Behavioral Medicine, Assn. Clin. Hypnosis, Minn. Psychol. Assn., Minn. Psychologists in Pvt. Practice, Am. Assn. Mental Deficiency, Assn. Care Children in Hosps. Contbr. articles to profl. jours. Office: Pediatric and Family Psychology Ctr 309 Park Ave Med Bldg 710 E 24th St Minneapolis MN 55404 also 310 Unity Profl Bldg 500 NE Osborne Rd Fridley MN 55432 also 307 Time Med Bldg 355 Sherman St Saint Paul MN 55102

MOORE, CURTIS HARRY, college administrator; b. Faribault, Minn., Mar. 22, 1914; s. Curtis Henry and Anna (Schumacher) M.; m. Helen Grace Hines, Oct. 25, 1942; children—Julie Ann, Paul Steven, Richard Eugene. A.B., Cornell Coll., 1936; M.A., Northwestern U., 1938; Ed.D., Columbia U., 1954; D.H.L. (hon.), Rockford Coll., 1979. Coordinator men's programs, dir. adult edn., Rockford Coll., Ill., 1954-55, dean of men, 1954-59, dean evening coll. and summer sessions, 1956-79, adminstrn. liaison officer, 1979-85; mem. pre-retirement planning staff Action Ind. Maturity, Rockford, 1979—; discussion leader Retirement Planning Seminar, Rockford, 1974—. Bd. dirs. Blackhawk Area council Boy Scouts Am., 1975—; pres. bd. Winnebago County Council on Aging, Rockford, 1980—; chmn. Lynn Martin's Adv. Council on Aging, 1982—. Recipient Bronze Leadership award Jr. Achievement, 1980, Service award Phi Delta Kappa, 1980, Beaver award Blackhawk Area council Boy Scouts Am., 1981—. Mem. Action for Ind. Maturity (cons. 1979—), Winnebago/Boone County Ret. Tchrs. Assn. (pres. bd. 1982—) Republican. Methodist. Lodge: Kiwanis (pres. 1967). Avocations: collecting owl figures; travel. Home: Wesley Willows Retirement Home 4042 Albright Ln Rockford IL 61103

MOORE, CYNTHIA MARIE, educator; b. Indpls., Dec. 23, 1954; d. James Cyrus and Jessie Mae (Brayton) Billheimer; m. Winford Ernest Moore, July 16, 1983. B.S. with distinction in Phys. Edn., Ind. U., 1978. Cert. athletic trainer. Tchr., athletic trainer Lake Station Community Schs. (Ind.), 1978—. Laity rep. Calumet dist. North Ind. Conf. Council Young Adult Ministries, United Methodist Ch., 1983-84; chairperson Council on Ministries, lay del. Portage First United Meth. Ch., 1984. Mem. Nat. Athlete Trainers Assn., Gt. Lakes Athletic Trainers Assn., Zeta Tau Alpha. Republican. Methodist. Club: Ind. U. Women's Track (pres. 1977). Home: 2389 Dombey Rd Portage IN 46368 Office: Lake Station Community Schs-Edison High Sch 3304 Parkside Ave Lake Station IN 46405

MOORE, DARRYL, publishing company executive, educator; b. Memphis, July 27, 1954; s. Joseph and Freddie (Moore) M. B.A., Ill. Wesleyan U., 1977; M.S. in Teaching Theory, U. Chgo., 1978. Tchr. U. Chgo. Lab. Sch., 1977-78, Glencoe Bd. Edn., Ill., 1978-80, Chgo. Bd. Edn., 1980-85; cons. James Lowry and Assocs., Chgo., 1982-84; adviser spl. accounts Open Ct. Pub. Co., LaSalle, Ill., 1984—. Active NAACP, Chgo., 1980—. Tchr. Social Action Network, Washington, 1981—, Chgo. Urban League, 1980—, Nat. Alliance Black Sch. Educators, Washington, 1980—, Lutheran Bd. Social Ministry, 1984—; hon. chmn. Provident Med. Ctr., Chgo., 1985. Democrat. Avocations: rare music collecting; travel; fine arts. Home: 8624 S King Dr Chicago IL 60619 Office: 53 W Jackson Blvd Suite 530 Chicago IL 60604

MOORE, DAVID EUGENE, English educator; b. Bloomdale, Ohio, Jan. 4, 1938; s. Edward G. and Marie R. (Brown) M. B.S., Bowling Green State U., 1960; M.Ed., Ohio State U., 1962. Tchr., English, Risingsun (Ohio) High Sch., 1960-61, Fairmont West High Sch., Kettering, Ohio, 1964-66; instr. English, Sinclair Community Coll., Dayton, Ohio, 1963-64, 66-68; asst. prof. English/speech Monroe County Community Coll., Monroe, Mich., 1968—. Elected Instr. of Year, Monroe County Community Coll., 1971, 80; Nat. Endowment for Humanities Fund humanist S.E. Mich. Consortium on Gerontology and Humanities, 1973-75. Mem. NEA, Mich. Edn. Assn., Nat. Council Tchrs. English, Midwest MLA, Sigma Tau Delta. Methodist. Co-editor: Reflections-Collection of Monroe County Sr. Citizens, 1974-75. Home: 7578 Ida East Rd Ida MI 48140 Office: Dept English Monroe County Community Coll 1555 S Rainsville Rd Monroe MI 48161

MOORE, DAVID SHELDON, statistics educator, researcher; b. Plattsburg, N.Y., Jan. 28, 1940; s. Donald Sheldon and Mildred (Roberts) M.; m. Nancy Kie Bok Hahn, June 20, 1964; children—Matthew, Deborah. A.B., Princeton U., 1962; Ph.D., Cornell U., 1967. Asst. to assoc. profl. stats. Purdue U., West Lafayette, Ind., 1967-76, prof. 1977—; program dir. NSF, Washington, 1980-82, cons. 1981—; cons. NRC, Washington, 1982—. Author: Statistics Concepts and Controversies, 1978, 2nd ed. 1985. Contbr. articles to profl. jours. Elder Presby. Ch. Danforth Found. Grad. fellow, 1962-67; research grantee NSF, 1978—. Fellow Am. Statis. Assn. (chmn. sect. educ. 1977-78), Inst. Math. Statis. (governing council 1984—); mem. Am. Soc. Quality Control, Mat. Assn. Am. Home: 4840 Jackson Hwy West Lafayette IN 47906 Office: Dept Stats Purdue Univ West Lafayette IN 47907

MOORE, DEBRA MAY, respiratory therapy educator; b. Newark, Ohio, Sept. 4, 1953; d. Walter Keith and Marian May (Stackhouse) M. B.A., Ohio State U., 1978; M.S., Ind. U., 1983. Cert. respiratory therapy technician, registered respiratory therapist Nat. Bd. Respiratory Care. Mem. staff Presbyn. Hosp. Ctr., Albuquerque, 1976-77, Licking Meml. Hosp., Newark, 1972-75, 77-79; clin. coordinator Ind. Vocat. Tech. Coll., Bloomington, Ind., 1979-84, mem. adv. com., 1979-84; adv. com. Muskingum (Ohio) Area Vocat. Sch.,

1977-79; grad. asst. Ind. U., 1985—. Mem. Am. Assn. Respiratory Therapy, Ind. Soc. Respiratory Therapy (bd. dirs. 1981-83, chmn. awards com. 1982-83), Am. Vocat. Assn., Ohio State Alumni Assn., Ind. Vocat. Assn., Council for Exceptional Children, Ind. U. Alumni Assn., Pi Lambda Theta, Eta Sigma Gamma. Republican. Methodist. Office: VES 840 State Rd 46 Bypass Room 111 Ind U Bloomington IN 47405

MOORE, GARY MITCHELL, lawyer; b. Oak Park, Ill., Dec. 28, 1952; s. Donald James and Mary Jane (Bouton) M.; m. Shireen Seif, Dec. 11, 1976. B.A., U. Ill., 1975, J.D., 1978. Assoc. G. William Richards, Aurora, Ill., 1978-81, Marvin Sacks, Ltd., Chgo., 1981-82, Overgaard & Davis, Chgo., 1982—. Treas., sec. Fairway of Country Lakes Townhouse Assn., Naperville, Ill., 1979-85. Mem. Naperville Jaycees (dir. 1984-85). Home: 1114 Langley Circle Naperville IL 60540 Office: Overgaard & Davis 535 S Washington St Naperville IL 60540

MOORE, GORDON PAUL, molecular biologist educator; b. New Brunswick, N.J., Aug. 7, 1950; s. Arnold Robert and Maxine (Stern) M.; m. Shelley Lyn Berger, Aug. 15, 1980. B.A., Brandeis U., 1972; Ph.D., Syracuse U., 1977. Postdoctoral fellow Calif. Inst. Tech., Pasadena, 1977-80; asst. prof. biology U. Mich., Ann Arbor, 1980—; group leader DuPont Co., Billerica, Mass., 1984—. Contbr. sci. research communications to profl. jours. NIH grantee, 1977—. Mem. Am. Acad. Sci. Avocations: chess; skiing; reading; music; bicycling. Home: 1207 Henry St Ann Arbor MI 48104 Office: U Mich Div Biology Ann Arbor MI 48109

MOORE, JACK FAY, labor union official; b. Springfield, Mo., Feb. 19, 1927; s. Elba Fay and Stella (Inmon) M.; student Drury Coll., 1959; m. Betty Lou Johnston, Dec. 29, 1950; children—Thomas Joseph, Deborah Moore Mills, Marilyn Faye Moore Simpson. Electrician, Aton-Luce Electric Co., Springfield, 1946-58; bus. mgr. Local 453 Internat. Brotherhood Elec. Workers, Springfield, 1958-76, mem. exec. council, 1966-76, internat. v.p., 1976—; labor mem. Mo. Bd. Mediation, 1971-75; pres. Springfield Labor Council, 1958-76. Mem. exec. bd. State Com. on Polit. Edn., 1964-76; Mem. Springfield Park Bd., 1962-68, Springfield Airport Bd., 1982—. Served with USNR, 1944-46, 50-51. Mem. Mo. Elec. Workers (pres. 1960-79). Democrat. Mem. Ch. of Christ. Home: 1300 Cozy St Springfield MO 65804 Office: 300 S Jefferson Ave Springfield MO 65806

MOORE, JAMES THOMAS, meteorology educator; b. Mineola, N.Y., Feb. 9, 1952; s. John Edward and Alice Elizabeth (Zeller) M.; m. Kathryn Esther Knenzin, Aug. 12, 1978. B.S. in Meterology, N.Y. U., 1974; M.S. in Atmospheric Sci., Cornell U., 1976, Ph.D., 1979. Asst. prof. meteorology State Univ. Coll. Oneonta, N.Y., 1978-80; mem. faculty St. Louis U., 1980—, asst. to assoc. prof. meteorology, 1985—. Contbr. articles to various publs. Postdoctoral fellow Nat. Aero. and Space Adminstrn., 1979, 80, Am. Soc. Engring. Edn., 1982; NSF grantee, 1983-85. Mem. Am. Meteorol. Soc., Nat. Weather Assn., Air Pollution Control Assn. Lutheran.

MOORE, KENNETH CAMERON, lawyer; b. Chgo., Oct. 25, 1947; s. Kenneth Edwards and Margaret Elizabeth (Cameron) M.; m. Karen M. Nelson, June 22, 1974; children—Roger Cameron, Kenneth Nelson. B.A. summa cum laude, Hiram Coll., 1969; J.D. cum laude, Harvard U., 1973. Bar: Ohio, 1973. Law clk. to judge U.S. Ct. Appeals, 4th Circuit, Balt., 1973-74; assoc. Squire, Sanders & Dempsey, Washington, 1974-75, Cleve., 1975-82, ptnr., 1982—. Chmn. Jimmy Carter Ohio Fin. Com., 1976; del. Democratic Nat. Conv., 1976; chief legal counsel Ohio Carter-Mondale Campaign, 1976; trustee, chmn. forum com. Cleve. Council World Affairs. Served with AUS, 1970-76. Mem. ABA, Ohio Bar Assn., Greater Cleve. Bar Assn. Club: Cleve. City. Home: 15602 Edgewater Dr Lakewood OH 44107 Office: 1800 Huntington Bldg Cleveland OH 44115

MOORE, KENNETH EDWIN, pharmacologist, researcher, educator; b. Edmonton, Alta., Can., Aug. 8, 1933; s. Jack and Emily Elizabeth (Tarbox) M.; m. Barbara Anne Stafford, Sept. 19, 1953; children—Grant Kenneth, Sandra Anne, Lynn Susan. B.Sc., U. Alta., 1955, M.Sc., 1957; Ph.D., U. Mich., 1960. Instr., asst. prof. Dartmouth Med. Sch., Hanover, N.H., 1960-66; from assoc. prof. to prof. pharmacology Mich. State U., East Lansing, 1966—; vis. scholar Cambridge U., Eng., 1974; cons. NIH, Washington, 1968—, various drug cos., 1974—. Author: Introduction to Psychopharmacology, 1971. Contbr. articles to profl. jours. Recipient Gold Medal award Alta. Pharmaceutical Assn., 1957. NIH grantee, 1962—. Fellow Am. Coll. Neuropsychopharmacology; mem. Am. Soc. Pharmacology and Experimental Therapeutics, Soc. Experimental Biol. Medicine, Soc. Neuroscience. Avocations: squash; golf. Home: 4790 Arapaho St Okemos MI 48864 Office: Mich State U Dept Pharmacology East Lansing MI 48824

MOORE, KURT RICHARD, anthropologist, art historian; b. Scott AFB, Ill., Oct. 9, 1955; s. Richard Vernal and Irmgard Ludwiga (Bennewitz) M. A.B., U. Ill., 1976, B.F.A., 1976; M.A., So. Ill. U., 1981, postgrad., 1981—. Grad. teaching asst. So. Ill. U. Field Sch. Archaeology, Carbondale, 1977, Center Continuing Edn., 1978, archaeol. field/lab. asst. Center Archaeol. Investigations, 1978-79, grad. research asst., 1979-80; archaeologist Ill. State Mus. Soc., Springfield, Ill., 1980-82; research archaeologist Am. Resources Group, Ltd., Carbondale, Ill., 1982—. Edmund J. James scholar U. Ill., Urbana, 1972-73, John T. Rusher Meml. scholar, 1975-76; So. Ill. U. scholar, 1981-84. Mem. African Studies Assn., Am. Anthrop. Assn., Am. Com. to Advance Study Petroglyphs and Pictographs, Artist Blacksmith Assn. N. Am., Assn. Field Archaeology, Current Anthropology (assoc.), Soc. Am. Archaeology, Soc. Archaeol. Scis., Vols. in Tech. Assistance, Central States Anthrop. Soc., Phi Kappa Phi. Author monographs; contbr. articles to profl. jours. and sci. meetings. Home: Box 523 Rural Route 1 Makanda IL 62958 Office: Am Resources Group Ltd 127 N Washington St Carbondale IL 62901

MOORE, LAWRENCE PETER, wine merchant, consultant; b. Fresno, Calif., June 21, 1944; s. Lawrence C. and Kathryn (Kalish) M.; m. Judith Light, Sept. 16, 1967; children—Jennifer Rae, Andrew Lawrence. B.A., Mich. State U., 1968, postgrad., 1968-70. Adminstrv. asst. Mich. Senate, Lansing, 1969-72; area dir. Am. Cancer Soc., Lansing, 1973-77; wine merchant, owner The Blue Goat, Traverse City, Mich., 1977—; wine instr. Northwestern Mich. Coll., Traverse City, 1978—; wine cons. to various restaurants, Traverse City, 1982—. Contbr. articles in field to mags. Ambassador, Nat. Cherry Festival, Traverse City, 1982—. Served as airman 2nd USAF, 1962-64. Ford Found. fellow, 1968-69. Mem. Soc. Wine Educators, Am. Wine Soc., Les Amis Du Vin (affiliate dir. 1978—), Delta Phi Epsilon. Republican. Episcopalian. Lodges: Lions, Rotary. Home: 154 Homestead Ln Traverse City MI 49684 Office: Blue Goat Inc 875 E Front St Traverse City MI 49684

MOORE, LYNN, business consultant; b. East Chicago Heights, Ill., Sept. 13, 1957; d. Clyde J. Moore and Irene S. (Dalian) Moore Kojder; student Corp. Edn. Ctr., Princeton U., 1977-78 postgrad. in bus. adminstrn. Loyola U. Office clk. Ralph M. Parsons Constrn., Lemont, Ill., 1975-76; project office mgr. Dart Industries, Joliet, Ill., 1976-77; mktg. orgn. Western Electric, Lisle, Ill., 1977-79; founder, pres., chief exec. officer Moore Efficiency Bus. Cons., Chgo., 1979—; v.p. Dombrowski and Holmes Inc., 1981—; speaker Nat. Conf. on Entrepreneurship; freelance singer, songwriter, 1971—; tchr. high sch., dir. musicals. Mem. staff Reagan for Pres. Campaign, 1976. Mem. Info. Mgmt. Assn. Chgo., Women's Enl. Services Assn. (founder, Ill. area dir. 1983—), AAUW, Nat. Assn. for Female Execs. Contbr. articles to various publs. Home and Office: 3804 N Washington St Westmont IL 60559

MOORE, MARY VIRGINIA, vocational educator, cosmetologist; b. Winston-Salem, N.C., Dec. 23, 1920; d. Odell James and Oreatha (Latimore) Moore; m. James Benson, Apr. 22, 1950 (div.). B.S., Edn., Wayne State U., 1972, M.A. in Indsl. Edn., 1974, Ed.D. in Vocat. Edn., 1977, Ed.M. in Ednl. Guidance and Counseling, 1980. Cert. vocat. educator, Mich. Pvt. practice as cosmetologist, Detroit, 1949—; dean Nat. Inst. Cosmetology, 1962—; tchr. Murray-Wright High Sch., Detroit, 1970—; mem. hostess com. Mich. March of Dimes. Recipient awards Vogue-Esquire, 1971, Theta Nu Sigma, 1975, Detroit Tchrs. Corp. master cons., 1979, Women's Conf. Concerns Achievement, 1980; cert. of merit State of Mich., 1980. Mem. NAACP, Wolverine State Cosmetology Assn. (past pres.), Am. Vocat. Assn., Nat. Beauty Culturists League, Mich. Council Cosmetology, Theta Nu Sigma, Phi Delta Kappa. Democrat. Lutheran. Clubs: Altar Guild, Ladies' Aid Soc. Author: Educational Modules for Cosmetology, 1976. Contbr. articles to jours.

MOORE, NORMAN WOLFF, accountant, farm management executive; b. Akron, Ind., Apr. 2, 1928; s. Norman Clair and Louise Josephine (Wolff) M.; m. Cornelia Sterk, Oct. 23, 1958; children—Ronald, Sheryl, Norman, Chris, Monique, Mark. B.S. in Gen. Agr., Purdue U., 1952. Profl. acct., notary public. Salesman Virginia-Carolina Fertilizer Co., Richmond, Va., 1954-59; Founder Moore Farm Mgmt. Service, Akron, Ind., 1959 (became C & N Moore Farm Mgmt. Service, Inc. 1976), sec., gen. mgr., 1976—. Mem. Republican Presdl. Task Force, 1980; mem. Rep. Nat. Com. Served with USNR, 1946-48, to sgt. U.S. Army, 1952-54. Decorated Korean Service medal, Mem. Legion of Honor, VFW, Nat. Assn. Pub. Accts., Ind. Assn. Pub. Accts., Am. Legion, DAV. Methodist. Lodges: Eastern Star, Masons, Moose, Shriners. Home: Route 2 Box 72 Akron IN 46910 Office: Route 2 Box 72 Akron IN 46910

MOORE, RALPH CORY, retired radiologist; b. Omaha, Nov. 23, 1911; s. John Clyde and Lura (Daggett) M.; B.Sc., U. Nebr., 1932, M.D., 1937; m. Dorothy Jean Keech, Apr. 13, 1946; children—Virginia, John, Barbara, David. House officer internal medicine Peter Bent Brigham Hosp., Boston, 1937-39, asst. resident radiology, 1940-41, resident, 1941-42; radiologist Nebr. Meth. Hosp., Omaha, 1946—, Childrens Meml. Hosp., Omaha, 1949—; prof. radiology U. Nebr. Coll. Medicine, 1957—. Served with AUS, 1941-46; PTO. Fellow Am. Coll. Radiology; mem. Radiol. Soc. N.Am., Am. Roentgen Ray Soc., AMA. Republican. Conglist. Contbr. articles on arteriography, decelleration trauma to profl. jours. Home: 1016 S 112 Plaza Omaha NE 68154

MOORE, RICHARD ALAN, marketing manager; b. Lebanon, Ind., Oct. 24, 1949; s. Max and Dorothy Jean Moore; B.S., Ind. U., 1977; diploma horology Bowmen Tech. Sch., 1970; postgrad. Butler U.; m. Mary B. Skroch, June 14, 1980. Retail cons. Wolfe's, Terre Haute, Ind., 1972-73; retail salesman F.R. Lazarus, Indpls., 1973, 74-75, L.S. Ayres, Indpls., 1976-77; mktg. research analyst Hyster Co., Danville, Ill., 1977-79; mgr.; market devel. Stewart-Warner Co., Indpls., 1979-83; product mgr. Kysor Indsl., Byron, Ill., 1983-84; mktg. mgr. Barrett Electronics Corp., Northbrook, Ill., 1984—. Mem. Am. Mgmt. Assn., Ind. Watchmakers Assn., Ind. U. Alumni Assn., Sigma Pi Alpha. Republican. Home: 103 Lindenwood Ct Vernon Hills IL 60061 Office: 630 Dundee Rd Northbrook IL 60062

MOORE, ROY FLINT, III, lawyer; b. Detroit, June 13, 1950; s. Roy Flint Jr. and Doris Ellen (Murphy) M. B.A. with distinction, Wayne State U., 1975, J.D., 1979. Bar: Mich. 1979, U.S. Dist. Ct. (ea. dist.) Mich. 1979. Mgmt. asst. Moore Signs, Inc., Detroit, 1968-77; freelance labor cons., Detroit, 1977-79; assoc. James A. Brescoll, P.C., Mt. Clemens, Mich., 1980-83, Wright & Goldstein, P.C., Birmingham, Mich., 1983—; sole practice, New Baltimore, Mich., 1983; tutor Psi Chi, Detroit, 1973; research asst. conflict resolution Wayne State U., Detroit, 1974; research asst. legal philosophy, 1977. Patron, Detroit Inst. Arts Founders Soc., 1983—. Mem. Mich. Bar Assn., ABA (comml., banking and fin. transactions litigation com. 1984—), Detroit Bar Assn., Macomb Bar Assn., Phi Beta Kappa. Lutheran. Office: Wright & Goldstein PC 255 E Brown St #430 Birmingham MI 48011

MOORE, THOMAS JAMES, III, hospital official; b. Detroit, Nov. 3, 1942; s. Thomas James and Marjorie Ruth (Kaiser) M. B.S. in Acctg., Wayne State U., 1964, M.B.A. in Adminstrv. Services, 1967. Mgmt. cons. Arthur Andersen & Co., Detroit, 1966-72; project leader J.L. Hudson Co., Detroit, 1972-74; project mgr. Nat. Bank Detroit, 1974-77, mgr. data security and privacy, 1977-79; mgr. computer systems Mich. Cancer Found., Detroit, 1979-81; mgr. data processing Harper-Grace Hosps., Detroit, 1981-82, mgr. systems devel. and computer services, 1982-83, dir. mgmt. info. services, 1983—. Active Founders Soc. of Detroit Inst. Arts. Mem. Wayne State U. Alumni Assn., Patrons of Wayne State U. Theaters, Detroit Econ. Club, Assn. Systems Mgmt., Data Processing Mgmt. Assn., Delta Sigma Pi, Omicron Delta Kappa. Home: 498 E Southlawn St Birmingham MI 48009 Office: Harper Grace Hosps 3990 John R Detroit MI 48201

MOORE, VERNON LEE, retired utility official; b. Kansas City, Kans., Mar. 26, 1923; s. Robert Sanford and Velma Margaret (Parker) M.; student Internat. Corr. Schs., 1963-65; m. Mary Bernice Janssens, Nov. 25, 1950; children—Russell Parker, Dana Margaret. With Kansas City Power & Light Co., Kansas City, Mo., 1948-85, tng. coordinator, 1979-85, ret., 1985, cons. tchr. Pin Oak Tng. Ctr., Kansas City, 1985—. Served with U.S. Navy, 1941-47. Mem. Am. Soc. Tng. and Devel. Presbyterian (elder). Club: Meadowbrook Golf and Country. Home: 5832 W 87th Terr Overland Park KS 66207 Office: Pin Oak Tng Ctr 5700 Eugene Field Rd Kansas City MO 64120

MOORE, WALTER EMIL, JR., rubber products manufacturing company executive; b. Pawtucket, R.I., May 26, 1925; s. Walter Emil and Gladys (Hobson) M.; m. Alta Tarbell Wilson, Sept. 15, 1948; children—Kathy Louise, Richard Emil, John Emil. B.S., MIT, 1948; M.S., Case Inst. Tech., 1960. With Firestone Tire & Rubber Co., Akron, Ohio, 1948—, mgr. pvt. brand tire devel., 1958-63, mgr. truck tire engring., 1964-66, mgr. race tire devel., tech. service, 1966-68, mgr. quality assurance, 1968-83, mgr. projects, 1983—. Served with AC, USNR, 1943-45. Sr. mem. Am. Soc. for Quality Control. Republican. Congregationalist. Avocations: flying; music; woodworking; personal computers. Home: 1330 Taft Ave Cuyahoga Falls OH 44223 Office: Firestone Tire & Rubber Co 1200 Firestone Pkwy Akron OH 44317

MOORE, WILLIAM SANBORN, electronics company executive; b. Cleve., Mar. 11, 1954; s. Jerald Powers Moore and Virginia (Gilkey) Herkes. B.S. in Journalism, Bowling Green State U., 1976. Sales rep. CAM/RPC Electronics, Cleve., 1976-77; sales mgr. Target Electronics, Solon, Ohio, 1977-79; mfrs. rep. KW Electronics, Shaker Heights, Ohio, 1979—; dir. Nightcoach (dance orch.), 1979—. Bd. dirs. Valley Arts Ctr., Chagrin Falls, Ohio, 1979-80. Named Best Sales Rep. Coil. Specialty Co., 1981-85. Avocations: boating; skiing; musician. Home: 7051 Pine St Chagrin Falls OH 44022 Office: KW Electronics 3645 Warr Ctr Rd Shaker Heights OH 44122

MOORE, WOODVALL RAY, librarian; b. Flatwoods, Ky., May 19, 1942; s. Clyde Raymond and Erma (Gallion) M.; A.A., So. Bible Coll., Houston, 1963, B.S., 1965; M.S. in L.S., U. Ky., 1972; m. Sarah Ellen Markham, Dec. 14, 1963; children—Tamra Sheri, Woodvall Allen. Dir. library So. Bible Coll., 1968-76; dir. library services Evangel Coll., Springfield, Mo., 1976—; ; bd. dirs. Mo. Library Network Corp.; pres. adv. council Southwestern Mo. Library Network; chmn. Mo. Data Base Com.; ordained Assemblies of God Ch., 1969. Precint chmn. Republican Party, Houston, 1972-76. Mem. ALA, Mo. Library Assn. (computer and info. tech. com.), Assn. Christian Librarians (dir. 1979—, v.p. 1982-83, pres. 1983-84), Springfield Librarians Assn. Republican. Office: 1111 N Glenstone St Springfield MO 65802

MOORHEAD, THOMAS EDWARD, lawyer; b. Owosso, Mich., Aug. 27, 1946; s. Kenneth Edward and Lillian Jane (Becker) M.; B.A. in Communication Arts, Mich. State U., 1970; J.D., Detroit Coll. Law, 1973; m. Marjorie E. Semans, Sept. 9, 1967; children—Robert Scott, Kristine Elizabeth. Admitted to Mich. bar, 1973; legal counsel Legis. Service Bur., State of Mich., Lansing, 1973-74; ptnr. firm Des Jardins & Moorhead, P.C., Owosso, 1974-85; sole practice, Owosso, 1985—. Pres., Bentley Sch. PTO, Owosso; mem. adminstrv. bd. 1st United Meth. Ch., Owosso; bd. dirs. Shiawassee Arts Council; treas. Cub Scout Pack 67 Boy Scouts Am.; mem. Shiawassee County Republican Exec. Com. Mem. Am. Bar Assn., Shiawassee County Bar Assn. (past pres.), State Bar of Mich., Owosso Jaycees (pres.; named Outstanding Local Pres. by state assn. 1977). Republican. Home: 1265 Ada St Owosso MI 48867 Office: 217 N Washington St Suites 105-107 Owosso MI 48867

MOORHEAD, WILLIAM RICHARD, JR., pharmacist; b. Pitts., July 27, 1953; s. William R. and Mary L. (Lelekacs) M.; m. Wendy Williams, June 28, 1980; 1 child, Dana Marie. B.S. in Pharmacy, Ohio No. U., 1976. Registered pharmacist, Ohio. Pharmacy intern Murrysville Pharmacy, Pa., 1971-76; pharmacist, asst. mgr. Cunningham Drugs, Mentor, Ohio, 1976-80; staff pharmacist Lake County Hosp., Painesville, Ohio, 1980—. Mem. Am. Soc. Hosp. Pharmacists, Ohio Pharm. Assn. Roman Catholic. Avocations: electronics; racquetball. Office: Lake County Meml Hosp East Liberty & High Sts Painesville OH 44060

MOORHOUSE, LINDA VIRGINIA, symphony administrator; b. Lancaster, Pa., June 26, 1945; d. William James and Mary Virginia (Wild) M. B.A., Pa. State U., 1967. With Brown Brothers Harriman & Co., N.Y.C., 1968-70; with San Antonio Symphony (Tex), 1970-76; gen. mgr. Canton Symphony Orch. (Ohio), 1977—. Mem. music panel Ohio Arts Council, 1980-82. Mem. Orgn. Ohio Orchs. (dir. 1982—, 1st v.p. 1984, pres. 1985), Met. Orch. Mgrs. Assn. (pres. 1983-85), Am. Symphony Orch. League (dir. 1983-84). Office: 1001 Market Ave N Canton OH 44702

MOORMAN, ROBERT CRAIN, equipment company executive, consultant; b. Cedar Rapids, Iowa, Dec. 22, 1933; s. Edwin Forlow and Clara Louise (Crain) M.; m. Susan Carol Rook, Jan. 7, 1956 (dec. 1968); children—Michelle, Deborah, Judith; m. Dianne Crew, Feb. 9, 1980 (dissolved 1985). B.A. in English Lit., State U. Iowa, 1958. With Moorman Equipment Co., Cedar Rapids, Iowa, 1955—, pres., chief exec. officer, 1965—; pres., chief exec. officer Am. Phys. Qualifications Testing Corp.; chmn. young execs. Associated Equipment Distbrs., Oak Brook, Ill., 1974. Mem. Ho. of Dels., Nat. Am. Cancer Soc., N.Y.C., 1975—, bd. dirs., 1979—, chmn. legacies and planned giving com., 1982—, mem. exec. com. bd. dirs., 1982—, vice chmn. crusade com., 1984—; pres. Iowa div. Am. Cancer Soc., Mason City, 1978-80, chmn. bd. dirs., 1984—; dir. YMCA, Cedar Rapids, 1980-83, Symphony Orch. Bd., Cedar Rapids, 1982-84; bd. dirs. Community Theatre, Cedar Rapids, 1974-77, 80-83, trustee, 1980—; commr. Linn County Regional Planning Commn., Cedar Rapids, 1965-77; chmn., treas. —Keep the Airport Commn. —, Cedar Rapids, 1984; mem. County Republican Central Com., Cedar Rapids, 1968-70. Presbyterian. Club: Country (Cedar Rapids) (dir. 1984—), Pickwick (Cedar Rapids) (pres. 1979-80). Lodge: Rotary (pres. 1969-70). Avocations: medicine; golf; ceramics; model boat building; travel; scuba; flying; racquetball; skiing; horses; lumberjacking. Office: Moorman Equipment Co 5950 6th St SW Cedar Rapids IA 52404

MOOSE, JAMES SAYLE, III, oil company executive; b. Teheran, Iran, Dec. 24, 1940 (parents Am. citizens); s. James Sayle and Eleanor D. (Wood) M. m. Claudia Stanley, Dec. 6, 1975; children—Emily, Katherine, Jamie; 1 stepdau., Kristin Ives. B.A., Harvard U., 1961; M.A., Oxford (Eng.) U., 1963; Ph.D., Harvard U., 1968. Chartered fin. analyst. Cons., Arthur D. Little Co., Cambridge, Mass., 1967-70; v.p., economist Loomis Sayles, Boston, 1970-79; dep. asst. sec. Dept. Energy, Washington, 1979-81; mgr. forecasting and analysis Sohio Oil Co., Cleve., 1981—. Reviewer Rev. Econs. and Stats., Energy Jour.; contbr. articles to profl. jours. Mem. New Eng. Capital and Labor Task Force, 1975, Regional Econs. Adv. Forum, Cleve., 1981—. Rhodes scholar, 1961-63; NSF scholar, 1964-67. Mem. Internat. Assn. Energy Economists, Soc. Chartered Fin. Analysts, Soc. of Cincinnati, Phi Beta Kappa. Episcopalian. Home: 32030 Woodsdale Ln Solon OH 44139 Office: Sohio Oil Co Midland Bldg Cleveland OH 44139

MORAGA, CHARMAINE LORAINE, marketing executive; b. Sheboygan, Wis., Aug. 2, 1955; d. Leslie Louis and Myrtle Anna (Lutze) Fischer; m. Roger Jason Moraga, July 31, 1976 (div. Aug. 1982). B.S., Carroll Coll., 1977. Personal banker United Banks Westgate, Madison, Wis., 1977; mgmt. trainee Valley Bank, Green Bay, Wis., 1978-80; v.p./corp. mktg. Valley Bancorp., Green Bay, 1980—. Bd. dirs. United Way, Brown County, Wis., 1983-85; mem. banking and fin. adv. com. Fox Valley Tech. Inst., Appleton, Wis., 1983—. Recipient Nat. awards Am. Advt. Fedn., Denver, 1983-84. Mem. Bank Adminstrn. Inst. (officer Fox Valley chpt. 1980—), Bank Mktg. Assn. (state conv. chairperson 1984), Wis. Bankers Assn. (dir. 1982—). Presbyterian. Avocations: downhill skiing; golfing; crafts. Home: 2630 Kenhill Dr Green Bay WI 54303 Office: Valley Bancorp 310 W Walnut St Green Bay WI 54306

MORAN, DANIEL E. (HENRY MORAN), VIII, executive arts administrator, producer, consultant; b. Dobbs Ferry, N.Y., Apr. 23, 1949; s. Daniel E. and Joan Linda (Greeff) Deschere; m. Melissa Matterson, June 29, 1974; children—Sally, Susannah; m. 2d, Madelyn Newcomer Voigts, Mar. 20, 1982; 1 dau., Sara. Student U. Tenn., 1967-69; B.F.A., Goodman Sch., Art Inst. Chgo., 1971; postgrad. in Bus. Mgmt. and Adminstrn., Wayne State U., Mich. State U., Wharton Sch.; M.B.A. candidate Rockhurst Coll. Project dir. Ill. Arts Council, Chgo., 1971-73; asst. dir. Mich. Council for Arts, Detroit, 1973-75; exec. dir. Mid-Am. Arts Alliance, Kansas City, Mo., 1975—, bd. dirs., 1977—; mem. adv. panel Nat. Endowment Arts; cons. Am. Urban Devel. Found. Bd. dirs. Folly Theatre; mem. Kansas City Jazz Commn. Recipient certs. merit Mich. State U., Smithsonian Inst. Episcopalian. Co-producer Five TV Programs Public Broadcasting Systems; composer/lyricist two children's musicals. Home: 6641 Linden Rd Kansas City MO 64113 Office: 20 W 9th St Suite 550 Kansas City MO 64105

MORAN, JAMES BYRON, judge; b. Evanston, Ill., June 20, 1930; s. James Edward and Kathryn (Horton) M.; A.B., U. Mich., 1952; LL.B. magna cum laude, Harvard U., 1957; m. Nancy; children—John, Jennifer, Sarah, Polly. Admitted to Ill. bar, 1958; law clk. to judge U.S. Ct. of Appeals, 2d Circuit, 1957-58; asso. Bell, Boyd, LLoyd, Haddad & Burns, from 1958, partner, 1966-79; judge U.S. Dist. Ct. No. Dist. Ill., Chgo., 1979—. Dir. Com. on Ill. Govt., 1960-78, chmn., 1968-70; vice chmn., sec. Ill. Dangerous Drug Adv. Counsel, 1967-74; chmn. sect. Gateway Houses Found., from 1969. Mem. Ill. Ho. of Reps., 1965-67; mem. Evanston City Council, 1971-75. Served with AUS, 1952-54. Mem. Ill., Chgo. bar assns., Chgo. Council Lawyers, Phi Beta Kappa. Clubs: Law, Legal, Chicago Yacht. Home: 1424 Judson Ave Evanston IL 60201 Office: US Courthouse 219 S Dearborn St Chicago IL 60604

MORAN, JOSEPH MICHAEL, earth science educator; b. Boston, Feb. 14, 1944; s. Joseph P. and Mary E. (Harkins) M.; m. Janet L. Lyle, June 2, 1971 (div. 1981). B.S. in Geology, Boston Coll., 1965, M.S. in Geophysics, 1967; Ph.D. in Meteorology, U. Wis.-Madison, 1972. Instr. earth sci. U. Wis.-Green Bay, 1969-72, asst. prof., 1972-74, assoc. prof., 1974-75, 76-80, prof., 1980—; vis. prof. U. Ill., Urbana, 1975-76, chmn. earth sci. dept., 1983—; cons. in field. Co-author: Introduction to Environmental Science, 1973, 80, 86; Introduction to Weather, 1986. Contbr. articles to profl. jours. Gov.'s appointee Wis. Air Pollution Control Council, Madison, 1980-82. Mem. Am. Meteorol. Soc., Assn. Am. Geographers, Nat. Assn. Geology Tchrs., Nat. Sci. Tchrs. assn., AAAS, Sigma Xi. Roman Catholic. Avocation: running. Home: 614 Harvest Rd Green Bay WI 54301 Office: U Wis SEC Green Bay WI 54301

MORAN, MICHAEL JOSEPH, business executive, accountant; b. Milan, Mo., July 18, 1949; s. Martin F. and Mary F. (Railing) M.; m. Cheryl J. Simmons, Mar. 9, 1974; children—Jason Michael, Christopher Cole. B.B.A., U. Mo., 1971. Acct., Fashion, Inc., Kansas City, Kans., 1971-74; staff acct. Guaranteed Foods, Inc., Lenexa, Kans., 1974-77; internal auditor R.H. Macy & Co., Inc., Kansas City, Mo., 1977-79; acctg. mgr. Quality Packaging Co., Iola, Kans., 1979-81; bus. mgr. Student Union Corp., Kansas City, 1981—, also dir. Coach Queen Holy Rosary Soccer Club, Overland Park, Kans., 1984, Johnson County Little League Softball, Overland Park, 1984. Mem. Nat. Assn. Accts., Nat. Assn. Coll. Stores, Nat. Assn. Coll. Aux. Services. Democrat. Roman Catholic. Avocations: golf, chess, billiards, soccer. Home: 6332 Goodman Dr Merriam KS 66202 Office: Student Union Corp Olathe and Rainbow Blvds Kansas City KS 66103

MORAN, THOMAS JOSEPH, state supreme court justice; b. Waukegan, Ill., July 17, 1920; s. Cornelius Patrick and Avis Rose (Tyrrell) M.; B.A., Lake Forest Coll., 1947, J.D. (hon.), 1977; J.D., Ill. Inst. Tech.-Chgo. Kent Law Sch., 1950; m. Mary Jane Wasniewski, Oct. 4, 1941; children—Avis Marie, Kathleen, Mary Jane, Thomas G. Admitted to Ill. bar; individual practice law, 1950-56; state's atty., Lake County, Ill., 1956-58; judge Probate Ct. 19th Circuit, 1961-64; judge Appellate Ct. 2d Dist., 1964-76; justice Ill. Supreme Ct., 1976—; mem. faculty Appellate Judges seminars N.Y. U., Continuing Legal Edn. seminars La. State U. Served with USCG. Mem. Inst. Jud. Adminstrn., Am. Judicature Soc., ABA, Ill. Bar Assn., Lake County Bar Assn. Office: 215 N Utica St Waukegan IL 60085*

MORAN-TOWNSEND, MARILYN, custom video productions company executive. B.A., Purdue U., 1976. Announcer Sta. WRFL, Purdue U., West Lafayette, Ind.; weeknight news anchor Purdue Radio Network; with Sta. WBAA, West Lafayette, 1973-76, Sta. KWSH, Wewoka, Okla., 1973, Sta. WLFI-TV, West Lafayette, 1973-76; producer/anchor weekend sports and weather Sta. WBBH-TV, Ft. Meyers, Fla., 1976-77; week night weather anchor Sta. WKJG-TV, Ft. Wayne, 1977; co-founder, chief exec. officer Custom Video Corp., Ft. Wayne, Ind., 1981—. Co-chmn. Greater Ft. Wayne Bus. Council, 1982—; bd. dirs. Pvt. Industry Council, 1983—; co-chmn. Ft. Wayne Fine Arts Found. Bus. and Industry div. fund drive, 1983-84, 85; bd. dirs. Better Bus. Bur. of No. Ind., 1985, Jr. Achievement, 1985, others. Winner nat. award for prodn. of best audio/visual campaign, Ft. Wayne Met. Human Relations Commn., 1983, for prodn. best pub. service announcement campaign, Ft. Wayne Community Schs., 1983; recipient AMA award for To Your Health series, 1978; Journalism award Ind. State Med. Assn., 1982, others. Mem. Ft. Wayne

C. of C. (dir.), Women Bus. Owners Assn. (founder, 1st steering com. co-chmn), Ft. Wayne Women in Communications (pres. 1980-81). Address: Custom Video Corp 1300 S Harrison St PO Box 11723 Fort Wayne IN 46860

MOREHEAD, PATRICIA S., state senator; b. Falls City, Nebr., July 21, 1936; d. Leo L. and Luella (Dowell) Stalder; m. Kenneth Edwin Morehead, 1967; Student MacMurray Coll., 1954-55; B.S., U. Nebr., 1958. Mem. Nebr. State Senate, 1983—. Mem. Gage County Democratic Women. Mem. PEO, Blue Valley Home Economists, Am. Trap Shooting Assn., Phi Upsilon Omicron, Chi Omega. Office: 2317 Elk St PO Box 369 Beatrice NE 68310

MORELAND, WILLIAM JOHN, real estate broker; b. Chgo., Feb. 21, 1916; s. James C. and Izora M. (McCabe) M.; A.B., U. Ill., 1938; student Northwestern U., 1937. With James C. Moreland & Son, Inc., real estate and home building, Chgo., 1938—, pres., 1952—; pres. Moreland Realty, Inc., Chgo., 1952-72. Builder, operator Howard Johnson Motor Lodge, Chgo., 1960-72. Helped develop model housing community, El Salvador, Central Am., 1960's. Presidential appointment to commerce com. for Alliance for Progress, 1962-64. Served to lt. USNR, 1941-46. Mem. Home Bldrs. Assn. Chicagoland (pres. 1961-62), Chgo. Assn. Commerce and Industry, Chgo., N.W. real estate bds., N.W. Bldrs. Assn., Nat. Assn. Home Bldrs. (hon. life dir. 1972—), Chi Psi. Republican. Roman Catholic. Office: 5717 Milwaukee Ave Chicago IL 60646

MORENO, FRANK, import/export company executive; b. Lima, Peru, Oct. 29, 1945, came to U.S., 1972, naturalized, 1985; s. Amador and Manuela (Vasquez) M.; children—Michael Amador, Vanessa Manuela. B.S., San Marcos U., Peru, 1967; student San Marcos Med. Sch., Peru, 1970. Asst. to surgeon Augustana Hosp., Chgo., 1972-75; physician assoc. Columbus Hosp., Chgo., 1975-76; pres. Moreno Enterprises, Chgo., 1977-82, Le Monde Enterprises, Hoffman Estates, Ill. 1983—; cons. Bensenville Clinic, Ill., 1981-85. Pres. Golden Group of Peru, Hanover Park, Ill., 1984-85; sec. Nicaraguan Social Ctr., Oak Park, Ill., 1983-84. Mem. Ill. Notary Assn. Democrat. Roman Catholic. Avocations: sailing; tennis; horseriding.

MORENO-MANKER, CRISTINA ALICIA, educational adminstrator; b. Alice, Tex., Apr. 28, 1928; d. Alberto and Maria de Jesus (Rodriguez) Moreno; m. Bernard E. Manker, Mar. 22, 1950; children—Hagen Bernhardt, Bernard E. III, Sally Jean. B.A., Central Mich. U., 1950; M.A., Ind. State U., 1970; Bilingual Endorsement, Grand Valley State Coll., 1977. Dir. bilingual and migrant edn. Holland Pub. Schs., Mich., 1975-84, dir. state and fed. programs, 1980-83, prin. elementary sch., 1982—. Mem. Latin Americans United for Progress, Holland, 1975-80; mem. affirmative action com. Hope Coll., Holland, 1978; mem. bilingual edn. adv. council, Lansing, Mich., 1976-79; mem. Migrant Edn. Adv. Com., Lansing, 1979-80. Named Hispanic Educator of Yr. Mich. Dept. of Edn., 1981. Mem. Nat. Assn. Elementary Sch. Prins., AAUW. Republican. Avocations: pilot; sailboarding; crafts; reading; traveling. Home: 266 E 11th St Holland MI 49423 Office: Lincoln Elementary Sch 257 Columbia Holland MI 49423

MORETTI, ROBERT JAMES, behavioral science educator; b. Chgo., Aug. 28, 1949; s. James John and Elva Eve (Bonini) M. B.S. in Psychology, Loyola U., Chgo., 1971, Ph.D. in Clin. Psychology, 1982; M.A. in Behavioral Sci., U. Chgo., 1976. Registered clin. psychologist, Ill.; listed Nat. Register Health Service Providers in Psychology. Research fellow Ill. State Psychiat. Inst., Chgo., 1974-76; clin. asst. prof. Loyola U. Sch. Dentistry, Chgo., 1976-81; asst. prof., chmn. behavioral scis. Northwestern U. Dental Sch., Chgo., 1981—, asst. prof. psychiatry Northwestern U. Med. Sch., 1983—; staff Charter Barclay Hosp., Chgo., Old Orchard Hosp., Skokie, Ill. Served with Ill. Army Nat. Guard, 1971-77. Kellogg fellow Am. Fund Dental Health, 1981. Mem. Am. Psychol. Assn., Ill. Psychol. Assn., Am. Soc. Clin. Hypnosis, Am. Assn. Dental Schs., Soc. Behavioral Medicine, Inst. Advancement Health. Contbr. articles to profl. jours. Home: 2620 W Balmoral Chicago IL 60625 Office: Northwestern U Dental Sch 311 Chicago Ave Chicago IL 60611

MOREY, LLOYD WILLIAM, JR., osteopathic physician, surgeon; b. Kirksville, Mo., Mar. 30, 1930; s. Lloyd W. and Lillian B. (Green) M.; m. Ruby C. McElhanry, June 20, 1952 (div. 1966); children—Robert, Richard, Ruth, Roger; m. Barbara J. Cooper, Dec. 30, 1967 (div. 1982); children—Billy, Barbie; m. Sally K. Olson, June 18, 1982. Cert. Gen. Practice, 1973; Manipulative Osteopathy, 1978. B.S., Northeast Mo. U., 1952; D.O., Kirksville Coll. Osteo. Medicine, 1956. Intern, Milw., 1957; pres., practicing medicine specializing in osteo. medicine, Family Med. Ctr., Wauwatosa, Wis., 1964—; pres. Family Clinics, Inc. Contbr. articles to profl. jours. Pres. Milw. Stake Sunday Sch., Ch. Jesus Christ of Latter Day Saints 1982. Fellow Am. Coll. Gen. Practitioners Osteo. Medicine and Surgery, 1967, Am. Acad. Osteo., 1971, recipient Honored Patron award Kirksville Coll. Osteo Medicine, named Wis. Gen. Practitioner of Yr., 1974. Bd. dirs. Northest Gen. Hosp.; mem. Am. Acad. Family Physicians, Am. Osteo. Assn., Wis. Assn. Osteo. Physicians and Surgeons, Milw. Dist. Soc. Osteo. Physicians and Surgeons, Am. Coll. Gen. Practitioners Osteo. Medicine and Surgery, Milw. County Med. Soc., Wis. Med. Soc., Ctr. for Chinese Medicine, Wis. Soc. Am. Coll. Gen. Practitioners in Osteo. Medicine and Surgery, Am. Acad. Osteopathy, Cranial Acad., North Am. Acad. Manipulative Medicine, Wisc. Acad. Family Physicians. Republican. Avocations: photography; hunting. Home: 4047 N 92nd St Wauwatosa WI 53222 Office: Family Med Ctr Ltd 4025 N 92nd St Wauwatosa WI 53222

MORFORD, WARREN NEWTON, JR., lawyer; b. Charleston, W.Va., Aug. 24, 1954; s. Warren Newton and Vivian Diane (Jones) M.; m. Kathy S. Baker, Oct. 9, 1982. B.A., Ohio State U., 1976; J.D., Thomas M. Cooley Law Sch., 1979. Bar: Ohio 1980, U.S. Dist. Ct. (so. dist.) Ohio 1980. Assoc. Burd & Morford, Chesapeake, Ohio, 1979-83; sole practice, Chesapeake, 1983—; referee Lawrence County Mcpl. Ct., Chesapeake, 1981-83; atty. Union Twp. Bd. Trustees, Chesapeake, 1984—; asst. pros. atty. Lawrence County, Ohio, 1985—. Mem. Ohio State Bar Assn., ABA, Lawrence County Bar Assn., Assn. Trial Lawyers Am. Republican. Home: 311 Orchard Dr South Point OH 45680 Office: 406-B 2d Ave PO Box 637 Chesapeake OH 45619

MORGAN, ANNE BRUCE, health care psychologist; b. Wilmington, Ohio, Sept. 20, 1950; d. Warren Brooke and Mary Bruce (Campbell) Morgan; m. Richard Lawrence Metzger, Dec. 18, 1971; m. 2d, Saul Julian Morse, Aug. 21, 1982; 1 child John Samuel Morgan. B.A., Muskingum Coll., New Concord, Ohio, 1971; M.A., U. N.D., 1975, Ph.D., 1978. Cert. psychologist, Ill. Psychology fellow specialist, div. health care psychology U. Minn. Hosps., 1977-78; lectr. psychology, clin. supr. Singamon State U., Springfield, Ill., 1979; instr. Lincoln Land Community Coll. Sch. Respiratory Therapy, Springfield, 1981; clin. psychologist-rehab. Meml. Med. Ctr., Springfield, 1979-82, dir. dept. health care psychology, 1982—. Mem. Am. Psychol. Assn., Midwestern Psychol. Assn., Ill. Psychol. Assn., Soc. Behavioral Medicine, Nat. Spinal Cord Injury Found., Nat. Head Injury Found., LWV. Jewish. Contbr. articles to profl. jours. Office: 800 N Rutledge Springfield IL 62781

MORGAN, BRADFORD ARTHUR, humanities educator, computer periodical editor; b. Bath, Maine, June 9, 1944; s. Harold Arthur and Agnes Kathleen (Long) M.; m. Barbara Elisa Trester, Mar. 4, 1967; children—Christian, Jessica. A.B., U. Calif., Berkeley, 1968; M.A., U. Denver, 1972, Ph.D., 1978. Asst. prof. Winona State U., Minn., 1977-79; dir. research and govt. relations St. Mary's Coll., Winona, Minn., 1976-80; asst. prof. U. Wis.-Eau Claire, 1979-81; assoc. prof. S.D. Sch. Mines and Tech., Rapid City, S.D., 1982—. Editor: English Notes, 1985. Contbr. articles to various monthly periodicals. City councilman City of Fountain City, Wis., 1981, mem. bd. rev., 1981; pres. West Blvd. Neighborhood Assn., Rapid City, S.D., 1985. Served with U.S. Army, 1968-70; ETO. Mem. Assn. Computers in Humanities, Modern Lang. Assn., Assn. Applied Linguistics, S.D. Soc. Profl. Engrs., Internat. Council Computers in Edn. (founding editor: Research in Word Processing Newsletter 1983—). Home: 1804 West Blvd Rapid City SD 57701 Office: Liberal Arts Dept SD Sch Mines and Tech Rapid City SD 57701

MORGAN, BRUCE BLAKE, banker, economist; b. Kansas City, Mo., Feb. 3, 1946; s. Everett Hilger and Dorothy Aletha (Blake) M.; m. Carol Berniese Tempel, Aug. 24, 1968 (div. 1983); children—Bruce Blake, Denise Dawn; m. Carol L. Lambert, June 9, 1984; B.S., Mo. Valley Coll., 1968; M.S., U. Mo.-Columbia, 1973; M.A., U. Mo.-Kansas City, 1977, Ph.D., 1979. Cert. profl. planner Am. Inst. Cert. Planners. Caseworker, counselor Mo. Dept. Social Services, Jefferson City, Mo., 1967-68; community devel. specialist U. Mo. Extension, Columbia, 1968-73; community devel. specialist Midwest Research Inst., Kansas City, Mo., 1973-83, also mgr. regional econs., assoc. dir., dir. econs. and social sci., sr. adv. for mgmt.; v.p. Bank of Kansas City, Mo., 1985—, Kansas City Bancshares, 1984—; dir. Westport Bank. Trustee, Jackson County Mental Health Levy Bd., Kansas City, 1982-83, Am. Humanics, 1982-85; chmn. bd. Kansas City CORO, 1982-83; bd. govs. Truman Med. Ctr., 1980-85. Mem. Am. Inst. Planners, Community Devel. Soc. Am. (dir. 1971-81), Am. Mktg. Assn. Office: Bank of Kansas City 1125 Grand Kansas City MO 64106

MORGAN, CLAUDE D'VAL, III, marketing firm executive; b. Carthage, Mo., Dec. 17, 1947; s. Claude D'Val and Margaret (Speer) M.; B.S. in Bus. Adminstrn., Mo. So. State U., 1970; m. Georgia E. Cook; children—Claude D'Val IV, Thomas Michael, Amelia Morrow; stepchildren—William, Markie and Deanie Cook. News dir. KDMO-AM, Carthage, 1965-67; news dir., regional sales mgr., gen. sales mgr., asst. sta. mgr. KTVJ-TV (CBS), Joplin, Mo., 1967-74; pres. Morgan & Assos., Inc., Joplin, 1974—. Bd. dirs. Mo-kan council Boy Scouts Am., 1979—, Spiva Art Center, 1979—; mem. Jasper County Republican Com., 1968—; mem. blue ribbon adv. council U. Mo. Sch. Journalism, 1975, Mo. Council for Higher Edn., 1978. Mem. Am. Assn. Advt. Agys., Public Utility Communicators Assn., Mo. Asso. Press Broadcasters Assn., Mo. Radio/TV News Dirs. Assn., Aircraft Pilots and Owners Assn., Joplin C. of C. (dir. 1978-80). Episcopalian. Office: Morgan & Assos Inc 3d and Main Sts Joplin MO 64801 also 4171 Crossover Rd Fayetteville AR 72701 Home: Loma Linda Estates Route 5 Box 1048 Joplin MO 64801

MORGAN, DON WESLEY, dentist, educator; b. Adrian, Tex., June 15, 1940; s. Donald Wilson and Lillian Alice (Ross) M.; m. Marianne Rae DeVries, Sept. 6, 1963; children—Jennifer, Jeffrey. A.A., Schreiner Coll., 1960; B.A., W. Tex. State U., 1962; D.D.S., Baylor U., 1966; M.A., Kans. U., 1978. Diplomate Am. Bd. Prosthodontics. Dental officer U.S. Army Dental Activity, Ft. Lewis, 1966-67, advanced through ranks to col., 1982; chief prosthodontic sect. 38th Med. Dental, Vietnam, 1967; dental surgeon 1st Infantry Div., Vietnam, 1968; officer-in-charge Dental Clinic 124 Med. Dental, Europe, 1968-71; chief resident prosthodontics Letterman Army Hosp., 1972-74; chief fixed prosthodontics U.S. Army Dental Activity, Ft. Leonardwood, Mo., 1974-76; dir. gen. practice residency, 1976; sect. leader Command and Gen. Staff Coll., Ft. Leavenworth, Kans., 1976-77; dir. dental hygiene program Acad. Health Scis., Ft. Sam Houston, 1978-80, chief dental lab. br., dir. dental lab. program, 1980-82; chief, mentor gen. practice residency fixed prosthodontic service, Ft. Riley Dental Activity, Kans., 1982—; cons. prosthodontics spl. Dental Design Support System, Manhattan, Kans., 1984—; lectr. Palo Duro Dental Study Group, Hereford, Tex., 1984. Contbr. articles to profl. jours. Post advisor Explorers Dental Post Boy Scouts Am., San Antonio, 1978-82; bd. dirs. Schreiner Coll. Former Students Assn., Kerrville, Tex., 1979-82; com. chmn. Boy Scouts Am., Manhattan, 1984—. Decorated Bronze Star (2), Meritorious Service medal (2), Army Commendation medal, Air medal, Vietnamese Cross of Gallantry, Combat Med. badge. Fellow Acad. Gen. Dentistry, Am. Coll. Prosthodontics; mem. ADA. Methodist. Avocations: jogging; racquetball; computer use; reading. Home: 3415 Dickens Manhattan KS 66502 Office: Dental Activity Ft Riley KS 66442 and Dental Design Support System 2314 Anderson Suite 207 Manhattan KS 66502

MORGAN, DONALD RALPH, fiberglass company executive; b. Richmond, Ind., Oct. 18, 1938; s. Ralph F. and Edna M. (Sharits) M.; m. Sahron Lynne Garrison, July 8, 1962; children—Eric, Heather. B.S., Purdue U., 1960. Cert. Meth. lay speaker. Work simplification coordinator Perfect Circle Corp., Hagerstown, Ind., 1960-69; sales promotion mgr. Dana World Trade Corp., Ft. Wayne, Ind., 1964-69, Majestic Co. Am. Standard, Huntington, Ind., 1969-71, Delta Faucet Co., Greensburg, Ind., 1971-75; acct. exec. Widerschein/Strandburg, Toledo, 1975-76; mktg. communications supr. Owens Corning Fiberglas, Toledo, 1976-80, mkt. devel. mgr., 1980—. Sunday sch. tchr. adults Edworth United Meth. Ch., Toledo. Mem. Ohio Speaker Forum, Nat. Speakers Assn., Alpha Sigma Phi (pres. nat.), Inst. Residential Mkgt. Republican. Avocations: handball; woodworking. Home: 3334 Gallatin Rd Toledo OH 43606 Office: Owens-Corning Fiberglas Fiberglas Tower Toledo OH 43656

MORGAN, FRANK J., food products company executive. Pres., chief operating officer, dir., Quaker Oats Co., Chgo. Office: Quaker Oats Co Merchandise Mart Plaza Chicago IL 60654*

MORGAN, FREDERIC LEE, allied health educator, curriculum consultant; b. Plymouth, Ind., Feb. 9, 1935; s. Charles Edward and Lura L. (Warner) M.; m. Joyce Ann Staldine, Sept. 4, 1955; children—Kimberle Lou, Michael Lee. B.S., Manchester Coll., North Manchester, Ind., 1957; M.A., Ball State U., Muncie, Ind., 1964, Ed.D., 1969. Sci. tchr., coach Richland Twp. Schs., Rochester, Ind., 1957-59; biology tchr., coach Argos Community Schs. (Ind.), 1959-66; doctoral fellow Ball State U., 1966-68; asst. prof. biology, 1968-69; chmn. biol. and health sci. Coll. Lake County, Grayslake, Ill., 1969-77; dir. allied health, assoc. prof. allied health careers and Sch. Medicine, So. Ill. U., Carbondale, 1977—; tchr. curriculum devel., adminstrn. in higher edn. Pres. Avon Schs. Sch. Bd., 1972-77; chair Lake Dist. camping Boy Scouts Am., 1972-77; mem. Comprehensive Health Planning in So. Ill., Inc., 1978—. HEW grantee, 1977-82, State of Ill. grantee, 1980—. Mem. NEA, Am. Soc. Allied Health Professions, Nat. Assn. Biology Tchrs., Ill. Community Coll. Biology Teaching Assn. Office: Sch of Tech Careers So Ill U Carbondale IL 62901

MORGAN, GARY KELLY, lawyer; b. Covington, Ky., Sept. 15, 1953; s. Albert Glenn and Carol Jean (Marz) M.; m. Katherine Ann Beck, Sept. 13, 1980. A.A., Thornton Community Coll., 1973; B.A. with honors, So. Ill. U., 1975; J.D., Washington U., St. Louis, 1980. Bar: Ill. 1980, U.S. Dist. Ct. (so. dist.) Ill. 1980, Mo. 1982, U.S. Dist. Ct. (ea. dist.) Mo. 1983. Assoc. Gundlach, Lee & Eggmann, Belleville, Ill., 1980-84, Lucas & Murphy, P.C., 1984—. Mem. staff Washington U. Urban Law Ann., 1978-80, primary editor, 1979-80. Mem. ABA, Bar Assn. Met. St. Louis, Ill. State Bar Assn., Mo. Bar Assn. St. Clair County Bar Assn., Southeastern Admiralty Law Inst., Phi Theta Kappa. Home: 217 Big Bend Blvd Belleville IL 62221 Office: Lucas & Murphy PC 818 Olive St Suite 440 Saint Louis MO 63101

MORGAN, GLEN BERNARD, judge; b. Cleve., June 25, 1928; s. William E. and Elsie E. (Haversaat) M.; m. Marianne Cavas, June 14, 1953; children—Craig, Martha. B.B.A., Case Western Res. U., 1951, J.D., 1954. Bar: Ohio 1954. Ptnr. Nahra & Morgan, Cleve., 1964-69, Zidar Morgan & Tobaro, Cleve., 1969-81; judge Ct. Common Pleas, Akron, Ohio, 1981—; law dir. and prosector City of Macedonia, Ohio, 1962-81; atty. North Hills Water Dist., Northfield Center, Ohio, 1965-78. Mem. ABA, Ohio Bar Assn., Akron Bar Assn., Cleve. Bar Assn. Republican. Episcopalian. Avocation: golf. Home: 8264 Shepard Rd Macedonia OH 44056 Office: Summit County Ct Common Pleas 209 S High St Akron OH 44308

MORGAN, JAMES NEWTON, economic behavior researcher, economics educator; b. Corydon, Ind., Mar. 1, 1918; s. John Jacob Brooke and Rose Ann (Davis) M.; m. Gladys Lucille Hassler, May 12, 1945; children—Kenneth, Timothy, John, Janet. B.A., Northwestern U., 1939; Ph.D., Harvard U., 1947. Asst. prof. econs. Brown U., Providence, 1947-49; Carnegie fellow Inst. Social Research U. Mich., Ann Arbor, 1949-51, study dir., 1951—, program dir., 1955—, prof. econs., 1958—; fellow Ctr. Advanced Study in the Bahavioral Scis., 1955-56, Wissenschaftskolleg Zu Berlin, 1963-64. Co-author: Income and Welfare in the United States, 1962; Productive Americans, 1966; Economic Behavior of the Affluent. Editor and co-author: Five Thousand American Families, 10 vols., 1974-83. Bd. dirs. Consumers Union, Mt. Vernon, N.Y., 1954—. Fellow Am Statis. Assn., AAAS, Am. Gerontol. Assn.; mem. Am. Econ. Assn., Nat. Acad. Scis. (com. sci. and pub. policy 1977-81), Nat. Research Council (chmn. behavioral sci. div. 1968-70, com. basic research in behavioral and social sci. 1983—). Home: 1217 Bydding Rd Ann Arbor MI 48103 Office: Inst Social Research Box 1248 Ann Arbor MI 48106

MORGAN, JAMES ROBERT, government researcher and consultant; b. Oshkosh, Wis., June 13, 1926; s. William Richard and Carrie (Vogtman) M.; m. Evonne Kellerman, Jan. 28, 1950 (dec. 1978); children—William, Jonathan, Carrie, James, Ann. B.S., U. Wis., 1950, LL.B., 1952, postgrad. in Pub. Adminstrn. Bar: Wis. 1952. Research atty. Wis. Taxpayers Alliance, Madison, 1953-64, pres., 1974—; sec. of revenue State of Wis., Madison, 1965-70; pres. Nat. Assn. Tax Adminstrn., 1969-70; chmn. Legis. Spl. Com. on County Home Rule, Madison, 1971-73; instr. local govt. Polit. Sci. Grad. Sch. U. Wis., Madison, 1970-72; chmn. Wis. Personnel Bd., 1977-78. Pres. Diocesan Council of Madison, 1970-72; mem. adv. bd. St. Mary's Med. Ctr., 1979-84; vice chmn. State of Wis. Ethics Bd., 1980—; mem. Wis. Strategic Devel. Commn., 1984—; sec. Univ. Research Park. Served with USAAF, 1944-46, Germany. Roman Catholic. Home: 216 Virginia Terr Madison WI 53705 Office: Wis Taxpayers Alliance 335 W Wilson St Madison WI 53703

MORGAN, JANE HALE, library administrator; b. Dines, Wyo., May 11, 1926; d. Arthur Hale and Billie (Wood) Hale; B.A., Howard U., 1947; M.A., U. Denver, 1954; m. Joseph Charles Morgan, Aug. 12, 1955; children—Joseph Hale, Jane Frances, Ann Michele. Mem. staff Detroit Public Library, 1954—, exec. asst. dir., 1973-75, dep. dir., 1975-78, dir., 1978—; mem. Mich. State Library Adv. Council, 1979-81; mem. Mich. Library Consortium Bd.; exec. bd. Southeastern Mich. Regional Film Library; mem. Mich. State Library Adv. Council. Trustee New Detroit, Inc.; v.p. United Found.; pres. Univ.-Cultural Center Assn.; bd. dirs. Rehab. Inst., YWCA, Met. Affairs Corp. Detroit and S.E. Mich., United Community Services Detroit. Recipient Anthony Wayne award Wayne State U., 1981; Detroit Howardite of Yr., 1983. Mem. ALA, Mich. Library Assn., Urban League, NAACP, Women's Econ. Club, Women's Nat. Book Assn., Assn. Mcpl. Profl. Women, LWV, Alpha Kappa Alpha. Democrat. Episcopalian. Home: 19358 Lauder St Detroit MI 48235 Office: Detroit Public Library 5201 Woodward Ave Detroit MI 48202

MORGAN, KAREN JOHNSON, nutritional assessment and food policy research educator, consultant; b. Watseka, Ill., Feb. 22, 1945; d. Howard Edgar and Margaret Lucille (Dilling) Johnson; m. Fred William Morgan, Jr., Aug. 26, 1967 (div. June 1974); 1 child, Todd Anthony; m. Rick Elam, Nov. 19, 1979; 1 stepchild, Paula Helene. B.S., Purdue U., 1967; M.S., Mich. State U., 1968; Ph.D., U. Mo., 1977. Instr. nutrition assessment and food policy research U. Mo., Columbia, 1973-74, grad. research asst., 1974-77, asst. prof., 1981-83, assoc. prof., 1983—; asst. prof. Mich. State U., East Lansing, 1977-81; cons. numerous food industries and pub. relation firms, 1979—. Author: Nutrients in Foods, 1983; computerized nutrient data bank at Mich. State U., 1979 (yearly updates). Editor Nutrition Data Bank Conf. Proc., 1980. Contbr. articles to profl. jours. Grantee USDA, HHS. Fellow Am. Coll. Nutrition; mem. Am. Inst. Nutrition, Nat. Acad. Scis. (com. foods additives survey data), Am. Agrl. Econs. Assn., Inst. Food Technologists, Am. Home Econs. Assn. Avocations: downhill skiing; reading. Office: Univ Mo Dept Human Nutrition 217 Gwynn Hall Columbia MO 65211

MORGAN, LAWRENCE ALLISON, educational administrator, educator; b. Norman, Okla., June 12, 1935; s. Lawrence Nelson and Catherine (Edwards) Morgan; m. Nancy Catherine Somogyi, July 3, 1960; children—Michael Lawrence, Katherine Elizabeth, Thomas Leverett. A.B., Harvard U., 1957; M.A., Washington U.-St. Louis, 1969, Webster U., 1977. Faculty, Thomas Jefferson Sch., St. Louis, 1957-66, trustee, 1959-66, dir. admissions, 1966-80, v.p., bd. trustees, 1966-80, headmaster, pres., 1980—. Candidate state rep. Democratic Party 43rd Dist., St. Louis County, 1970; bd. dirs. Jefferson Twp., Dem. Club, 1971-72. Episcopalian. Clubs: Harvard Club (St. Louis, Boston, N.Y.C.). Avocations: travel; photography; camping; cycling; hiking. Home: 9260 Robyn Rd Saint Louis MO 63127 Office: Thomas Jefferson Sch 4100 S Lindbergh Blvd Saint Louis MO 63127

MORGAN, LEE LAVERNE, tractor manufacturing company executive; b. Aledo, Ill., Jan. 4, 1920; s. L. Laverne and Gladys (Hamilton) M.; B.S., U. Ill., 1941; m. Mary Harrington, Feb. 14, 1942. With Caterpillar Tractor Co., Peoria, Ill., 1946—, mgr. sales devel., 1954-61, v.p. charge engine div., 1961-65, exec. v.p., 1965-72, pres., 1972-77, chmn. bd., chief exec. officer, 1977-85; dir. Carterpillar Tractor Co., Boeing Co., 3M Co., Comml. Nat. Bank, Midwest Fin. Group, Mobile Corp.; vice chmn. Adv. Council on Japan-U.S. Econ. Relations. Trustee Monmouth Coll., Proctor Community Hosp. Com. for Econ. Devel. Served to maj., AUS, 1941-46. Mem. Bus. Council, Soc. Automotive Engrs., Council Fgn. Relations. Presbyterian. Clubs: Peoria Country; Tucson Nat. Golf; Augusta Nat. Lodge: Masons. Office: Caterpillar Tractor Co 100 NE Adams St Peoria IL 61629

MORGAN, LEONARD EUGENE, medical and commercial illustration; b. Princeton, Ind., Dec. 12, 1948; s. Billy Gene and Ester June (Wright) M.; m. Frances Elizabeth Airdo, Jan. 31, 1970; children—Natalie Jean, Lindsay Ann. B.S. in Med. Art, U. Ill. Med. Ctr., 1974. Free-lance illustrator, serving numerous clients Naperville, Ill., 1976—; guest speaker U. Ill. Med. Ctr. Chgo., 1980—. Contbr. articles to profl. jour. Work appeared in Illustrators 27 Annual, 1985, Am. Illustration III Annual, 1985, Communication Arts Annual, 1985; recipient DESI award, 1985. Mem. Assn. Med. Illustrators, Midwest Med. Illustrators Assn. (publicity chmn.), Artists Guild Chgo. (silver medal 1984, council), Graphic Artists Guild N.Y. Avocations: Fishing, travel, family activities, air brush design innovations. Home: 131 Ridgewood Ct Bolingbrook IL 60439 Office: Leonard E Morgan Inc 1163 E Ogden Ave Ste 705 Rm 130 Naperville IL 60540

MORGAN, LEWIS V., JR., judge; b. Elmhurst, Ill., Dec. 17, 1929; s. Lewis V. and Meta (Schmidt) M.; B.A., DePauw U., 1951; J.D., U. Chgo., 1954; m. Marilyn F. Sherman, Nov. 17, 1950; children—Barbara Anne Oshlo, Lewis V. III, Diane Marie Rotunno; m. 2d, Alice E. Phillips, May 8, 1971; m. 3d, Linda L. Holmes, Mar. 31, 1978; 1 dau., Laura Lynne. Admitted to Ill. bar, 1954; mem. law firm Locke & Locke, Glen Ellyn, Ill., 1956-59; practice law, Wheaton, Ill., 1959-75; partner law firm Redmond, Morgan, Mraz & Bennorth, 1965-70, Morgan & Wilkinson, 1972-74, Morgan & Van Duzer, 1974-75; asso. circuit judge 18th dist., DuPage County, Ill., 1975-81, 82—, circuit judge, 1981-82; asst. state's atty., DuPage County, Ill., 1958-61; mem. Ill. Ho. Reps., 1963-71, chmn. elections com., 1967, 69, majority leader, 1969-71. Chmn. Milton Twp. Republican orgn., DuPage County, 1961; precinct committeeman Rep. party, 1957-66, 69-73. Chmn. Ill. Commn. on Atomic Energy, 1966-71; mem. County Bd. Sch. Trustees, DuPage County, 1973-75; trustee Wheaton Pub. Library, 1966-78; bd. dirs. DuPage County Family Service Assn., 1976-84. Served with AUS, 1954-56. Recipient Outstanding Legislator award Eagleton Inst. Politics, Rutgers U., 1965. Mem. Am. Acad. Matrimonial Lawyers (bd. dirs. 1978-82), Ill., DuPage County bar assns., Ill. Trial Lawyers Assn. (former dir.), Ill. Judges Assn. (dir. 1978-82), Sigma Nu. Methodist. Club: DuPage Writers. Contbg. author: DuPage Discovery, 1776-1976. Office: DuPage County Courthouse Wheaton IL 60187 Home: 325 W Park Ave Wheaton IL 60187

MORGAN, LOREN KEITH, electronics engineer; b. Portsmouth, Ohio, June 24, 1955; s. Charles Elias and Zelma Louise (Schomburg) M.; m. Sharon Ruth Neff, Aug. 25, 1978; children—Christopher Loren, Jessica Marie. A.A.S., Shawnee State Tech. Coll., 1975. Sales clk. Rinks Bargain City, Wheelersburg, Ohio, 1975-76; electronic assembly technician Thurman Scale Co., Columbus, Ohio, 1976-80, software trainee, 1979-80, system programmer, 1980-83, systems engr., 1983—; electronic hardware cons., Systems Datar, Columbus, 1985—; personal computer cons., 1983—. Republican. Mem. Ch. of Christ. Avocations: music; electronic gadgets; personal computing. Office: Thurman Scale Co 1939 Refugee Rd Columbus OH 43207

MORGAN, MARK PATRICK, lawyer, educator; b. Chicago Heights, Ill., Dec. 27, 1954; s. Gilbert Earl and Rosemary Catherine (Egan) M. B.A., DePaul U., 1976, J.D., 1979. Bar: Ill. 1979, U.S. Dist. Ct. (no. dist.) Ill. 1980. Ptnr. Miller and Morgan, Homewood, Ill., 1979-81; assoc. Don A. Moore & Assocs., Midlothian, Ill., 1981-82; ptnr., pres. Moore, Morgan and Vandenburg, P.C., Midlothian, 1982; sole practice, Midlothian, 1983—; corp. counsel Municipality of Bedford Park, Ill., 1981—; adminstr. Bedford-Summit Enterprise Zone, 1984—; spl. counsel Municipality of Posen, Ill., 1983—; pros. City of Oak Forest, Ill., 1985; dir. Camair Corp., Flossmoor, Ill., S.W. Econ. Devel. Corp., 1984—; mem. faculty Thornton Community Coll., South Holland, Ill. Author: A Corporate and Business Guide to Industrial Revenue Bonds, 1983. Active Homewood-Flossmoor Jaycees, 1980-83; mem. adv. com. Cook County Council Aging, 1984—; pres. Bremen Young Republicans, Oak Forest, 1980-84; treas. Bremen Twp. Rep. Orgn., Country Club Hills, Ill., 1981-82, bd. dirs., 1980—; chmn. leadership devel. Ill. Young Reps., Springfield, 1981-83; candidate for state rep. Ill. Reps., 1982; mem. Oak Forest Econ. Devel. Commn., 1985—. Mem. Ill. Bar Assn., Chgo. Bar Assn., South Suburban Bar Assn. Roman Catholic. Home: 7735 Foresthill Ln Oak Hills Country Club Palos Heights IL 60463 Office: 14730 S Kilbourn Midlothian IL 60445

MORGAN, MICHAEL FITZGERALD, dentist; b. Provo, Utah, Sept. 3, 1939; s. Ralph W. and Bessie Elizabeth (Fitzgerald) M.; m. Mary Lee Thatcher, Sept. 1, 1961; children—Michelle, Christine, Tamarah, Deborah, Michael, David, Victoria. B.S., Brigham Young U., 1961; D.D.S., Case Western Res. U., 1966. Pvt. practice dentistry, Zanesville, Ohio, 1966—. Dist. chmn. Boy Scouts Am., 1970—; bd. dirs. Am. Cancer Soc., 1968—. Recipient Silver Beaver award Boy Scouts Am., 1984. Mem. ADA, Ohio Dental Assn., Piere Fauchard Soc.

Republican. Mormon (bishop 1984). Club: Pendulum (pres.). Avocations: fishing; hunting; racquet ball; tennis. Office: 740 Princeton St Zanesville OH 43701

MORGAN, ROBERT EDWARD, state supreme court justice; b. Mitchell, S.D., Aug. 13, 1924; s. Chester Lawrence and Phyllis Mae (Saterlie) M.; student Creighton U., 1942, 46-47, 48; J.D., U. S.D., 1950; m. Mary Doyle, Oct. 28, 1950; children—Mary Alice, Michael Chester, Thomas Wayne, Margaret Jane; m. 2d, Mary Ann Ver Meulen, June 1, 1974; 1 son, Daniel James. Admitted to S.D. bar, 1950; mem. firm Mitchell & Chamberlain, S.D., 1950-76; assoc. justice S.D. Supreme Ct., Pierre, 1977—. Served with USAAF, 1943-45. Mem. ABA, S.D. Bar Assn. Club: Elks. Home: PO Box 412 Vermillion SD 57069 Office: care U SD Sch Law Vermillion SD 57069

MORGAN, RUTH MILDRED, medical technologist; b. Indpls., Mar. 8, 1917; d. James Franklin and Lula Floy (Heiny) M.; B.S. in Allied Health Edn., Ind. U.-Purdue U., Indpls., 1976; student Ind. U., 1954-57, 76-77, Butler U., 1958. Dental asst., med. asst. and med. technologist, Indpls., 1953—; tchr. hematology Med. Lab., 1970-79, supr. hematology, 1960-79, gen. supr., 1980—. Fin. chmn. 8th precinct 20th Ward of Indpls., 1977-79. Recipient citation Mayor Richard Lugar, 1976; registered med. technologist, lic. health facility adminstr. Mem. Am. Soc. Clin. Pathologists (affiliate), Am. Soc. Profl. and Exec. Women, Marion County Council Republican Women, Nat. Fedn. Republican Women, Am. Coll. Health Facility Adminstrs. (assoc., assoc. Ind. chpt.), Brown County Art Gallery Assn., Hoosiers for Econ. Devel. Club: Eastern Star (matron 1950). Inventor, patentee cabinets for indsl. use. Office: 5940 W Raymond St Indianapolis IN 46241

MORGAN, STANLEY LEINS, pharmaceutical company executive; b. Sandyville, Ohio, Jan. 28, 1918; s. Eben T. and Nora (Leins) M.; B.S. in Chem. Engring., Case Inst. Tech., 1939; m. Eloise Morkel, Feb. 22, 1941; children—Susan, Patricia, Ann. Chem. engr. Ben Venue Labs., Inc., Bedford, Ohio, 1940-42, mgr. blood plasma lab., 1942-44, gen. mgr., chief engr., 1944-61, v.p., 1961-63, exec. v.p., 1963—, also dir.; pres. Bon Vonne Generics Co.; dir. Medmarc. Registered profl. engr., Ohio. Fellow Am. Inst. Chemists; mem. Am. Chem. Soc., Health Industries Mfrs. Assn., Am. Inst. Chem. Engrs., N.Y. Acad. Sci., Cryobiology Soc., Parental Drug Assn., Cleve. Engring. Soc., Assn. Ofcl. Racing Chemist. Methodist. Clubs: Acacia Country (Cleve.). Home: 31051 Northwood Dr Pepper Pike OH 44124 Office: 270 Northfield Rd Bedford OH 44146

MORGEN, JOHN LEO, office furniture company executive; b. New Holstein, Wis., Dec. 1, 1932; s. Leo Henry and Rose Mary (Goebel) M.; m. Ellen Mary Shea, June 6, 1959; Kathleen, Eileen, Barbara, Jane. B.B.A., U. Wis.-Madison, 1957. Salesman, Remington Rand, Milw., 1957-61; sec., treas. M&M Office Furniture, Butler, Wis., 1961—. Mem. Wis. Rowing Assn. (bd. dirs. 1978—, Alumni Appreciation award 1984). Republican. Roman Catholic. Clubs: Eagles, Mendota, Nat. W (bd. dirs.). Avocations: golf; tennis; rowing; basketball; swimming. Home: 931 E Glenco Pl Bayside WI 53217 Office: M&M Office Furniture 12600 W Silver Spring Dr Butler WI 53007

MORGENS, KENNETH WADE, lawyer; b. Oklahoma City, Oct. 25, 1944; s. Alvin Gustav and Helen Alene (McFarland) M.; m. Rebecca Sue Klingele, Sept. 22, 1973; children—Meredith Elaine, Adam Christopher. B.S., U. Mo.-St. Louis, 1972; J.D., U. Mo.-Columbia, 1978; LL.M., U. Mo.-Kansas City, 1984. Bar: Mo. 1978, U.S. Dist. Ct. (we. dist.) Mo. 1978. Law clk. Jackson County Cir. Ct., Mo., 1978-79; asst. prosecutor Jackson County, 1979-85; sole practice, 1985—. Served with U.S. Army, 1967-70. Mem. Mo. Bar, Kansas City Met. Bar Assn., Bar Assn. of Met. St. Louis. Presbyterian. Office: Jones and Frankum PC 1125 Grand Suite 1616 Kansas City Mo 64106

MORGENSTERN, CONRAD JACK, lawyer; b. Cleve., Apr. 25, 1924; s. Irving and Estelle (Davidson) M.; m. Renee Saltzman, Nov. 4, 1951; children—Jonathan D., Margo Morgenstern Cohen, Richard L., Beth Ann. A.B., Adelbert Coll. of Western Res. U., 1948; J.D., Case Western Res. U., 1949. Bar: Ohio 1949. Pres. Morgenstern & Assocs., Cleve., 1949—; founder, sec., bd. dir., gen. legal counsel Midwestern Nat. Life Ins. Co., 1963-75. Mem. jud. scanning and selection com. Citizens League of Cleve., 1975—, moot ct. appellate trial judge Case Western Res. U. Sch. Law. Mem. Ohio Bar Assn., Greater Cleve. Bar Assn. (mem. unauthorized practice of law com., civil liberties com.), Cuyahoga County Bar Assn. (mem. profl. ethics com., grievance com., ins. com., judicial selection and scanning com., joint bar assn. judicial selection com.), Am. Arbitration Assn. Zionist Orgn. Am. (nat. v.p. 1970—). Avocations: tennis; world travel. Office: Morgenstern & Assocs 510 Leader Bldg Cleveland OH 44114

MORGENTHALER, DAVID TURNER, investment banker; b. Chester, S.C., Aug. 5, 1919; s. Henry W. and Elizabeth (Taylor) M.; B.S. in Mech. Engring., M.S., Mass. Inst. Tech., 1941; m. Lindsay Anne Jordan, May 17, 1945; children—David T., Gary J., Todd W., Gaye Elizabeth. Sales mgr. Ervite Corp., 1945-47; mech. engr. Copes Vulcan div. Blaw-Knox Co., 1947-50; v.p., dir. sales Delavan Mfg. Co., Des Moines, 1950-57; pres. Foseco, Inc., Cleve., 1957-68; chmn. bd. Foseco Technik Ltd., Birmingham, Eng., 1964-68; chmn. bd. API Instruments Co., 1968-70, dir., 1963-70; chmn. bd. Mfg. Data Systems, Inc., Ann Arbor, Mich., 1969—; chmn. exec. com., dir. LFE Corp., Waltham, Mass., 1970—; propr. Morgenthaler Assos.; dir. Access Corp., Cin., Fostoria Corp. (O.), E.F. Hauserman Co., Cleve., Space Comfort, Inc., Cleve., Ohio Industries, Inc., Cleve., Modular Computer Systems, Inc., Ft. Lauderdale, Fla. Trustee Lakewood Hosp., High Blood Pressure Research Council, Project Yardstick. Served to capt., AUS, 1941-45. Mem. Young Presidents Orgn. (past sr. v.p., dir.), Chief Execs. Forum, Mass. Inst. Tech. Alumni Assn. (past hon. sec.), Sigma Nu. Clubs: Westwood Country, Clevelander, Mid-Day. Home: 13904 Edgewater Dr Cleveland OH 44107 Office: PO Box 91052 Cleveland OH 44101

MORIARTY, C. MICHAEL, cell physiologist educator, college dean; b. Schenectady, N.Y., Apr. 12, 1941; s. Charles D. and Anne M. Moriarty; m. Donna R. Meirath, Sept. 5, 1975; children—Brent R., David E., Megan J. B.S., Carnegie-Mellon Coll., 1962; M.S., Cornell U., 1965; U. Rochester, 1969. Asst. prof. U. Nebr. Coll. Medicine, Omaha, 1970-74, assoc. prof., 1974-81, assoc. dean, 1981-83, prof. cell physiology, 1981—; cons. VA Hosps., Omaha, 1977—. Mem. AAAS, Am. Soc. Cell Biology, Am. Physiol. Soc. Office U Nebr Med Coll Dept Physiology Biophysics 42nd and Dewey Ave Omaha NE 68105

MORIARTY, JACK VAL, patent lawyer; b. Indpls., July 11, 1940; s. David J. and Agnes L. (Slick) M.; m. Martha Mary Dinn, Aug. 27, 1966; children—John, Robert, Greg, Anne. B.S. in Aero. Engring., U. Notre Dame, 1963; M.B.A., Ind. U., 1967, J.D., 1969. Bar: Ind.; registered profl. engr., Ind. Ptnr. firm Woodard, Welkart, Emhardt & Naughton, Indpls., 1969—. Mem. ABA, Ind. Bar Assn., Indpls. Bar Assn., Ind. Soc. Profl. Engrs. (pres. 1977). Democrat. Roman Catholic. Club: Indpls. Athletic (pres. 1981-83). Home: 8629 Seaward Ln Indianapolis IN 46256 Office: Woodard Welkart Emhardt & Naughton 1 Indiana Sq Indianapolis IN 46204

MORIN, ROBERT JAMES, retired railroad executive; b. Superior, Wis., Mar. 15, 1927; s. Peter Emil and Violet Alma (Saterstrom) M.; m. Muriel Joan Benson, June 17, 1950; 1 son, Robert Peck. Cert., Duluth (Minn.) Bus. U., 1948; cert. jr. bus. adminstrn. U. Minn.-Duluth, 1956. Stenographer, clk. Duluth Missabe & Iron Range Ry. Co., Duluth, 1948-50, sta. clk., 1952; trainmaster's clk. Gt. No. Ry. Co., Superior, Wis., 1952-58, sec. to v.p., gen. counsel, St. Paul, 1958-65, sec. to pres., 1965-70; with Burlington No. Inc., St. Paul, 1970-84, asst. corp. sec., 1980-84, asst. corp. sec. subs. Burlington No. R.R. Co., St. Paul, 1981-84, corp. sec. subs. Burlington No. Airmotive Inc., St. Paul, 1981-83; corp. sec. BN Fin. Services, Inc., St. Paul, 1983-84, Clarkland, Inc., St. Paul, 1982-84, Clarkland Royalty, Inc., St. Paul, 1982-84, 906 Olive Corp., St. Paul, 1982-84. Served with U.S. Army, 1946-48, 50-52. Republican. Lutheran. Club: Lost Spur Country (St. Paul). Lodges: Masons, Shriners. Home: 355 Millwood Ave W Roseville MN 55113

MORLANG, WILLIAM MACKAY, II, air force colonel, forensic dentist; b. Charleston, W.Va., Mar. 6, 1940; s. William MacKay and Louise Clair (Leesman) M.; m. Sarah Louis Sneed, Aug. 15, 1970; 1 child, Heather Mackay. A.A. in Biology, U. Fla., 1962; D.D.S., W.Va. U., 1966. Lic. dentist W.Va., 1966; cert. Am. Bd. Forensic Odontology, 1984. Commd. with U.S. Air Force, forensic dentist, 1970—, dental staff officer, 1972—, oral pathologist, 1973—, lectr. in forensic dentistry Armed Forces Inst. Pathology, Washington, 1977—, dir. Forensic Dentistry Lab., 1981—, command dental surgeon Hdqrs., Air Force Logistics Command, Wright-Patterson AFB, Ohio, 1983—, advanced through ranks to col.; lectr. forensic dentistry Northwestern U., Chgo., 1979, Wright State U., Dayton, Ohio, 1985; cons. in forensic dentistry to USAF Surgeon Gen., Armed Forces Inst. Pathology, 1979—. Co-author: Forensic Dentistry, 1982. Contbr. articles to profl. jours. Recipient numerous civilian awards and mil. decorations including: Legion of Merit with 1st Oak Leaf Cluster, Bronze Star. Fellow Am. Acad. Forensic Scis., Am. Coll. Dentists, Acad. Gen. Dentistry; mem. ADA, Acad. Dental Radiology, Am. Soc. Forensic Odontology, Am. Coll. Legal Medicine, Am. Bd. Forensic Odontology (bd. dirs. 1985), Fedn. Dentaire Internationale. Avocations: sailing; skiing; hunting; pistol shooting; rock climbing. Home: 3188 Southfield Dr Beavercreek OH 45385 Office: HQ AFLC/SGD Wright-Patterson AFB OH 45433

MORLEY, BRADFORD CHARLES, software company executive; b. Chgo., Dec. 13, 1946; s. Frederick Arthur and Elinor May (Smith) M.; m. Linda Jo Long, Sept. 14, 1968. B.S., Ohio State U., 1968. Div. controller Nat. Homes Co., Lafayette, Ind., 1972-73; corp. controller CINTAS, Cin., 1973-75; v.p. fin. and adminstrn. Structural Dynamics Research Corp., Cin., 1975-79; v.p., gen. mgr. computer-aided engring. Structural Dynamics Research Corp. div. Gen. Electric Co., San Diego, 1979-83, v.p. product mgmt., Cin., 1983—. Served with AUS, 1969-75. Republican. Home: 1600 Braintree Dr Cincinnati OH 45230 Office: SDRC 2000 Eastman Dr Milford OH 45150

MORLEY, HARRY THOMAS, real estate development corporation executive; b. St. Louis, Mo., Aug. 13, 1930; s. Harry Thomas and Celeste E. (Davies) M.; m. Nelda Lee Mulholland, Sept. 2, 1961; children—Lisa Dawn, Mark Thomas, Marci Lynn. B.S., U. Mo., 1955; M.A., U. Denver, 1959. Lic. real estate broker, Mo. Dir. student housing Iowa State Tchrs. Coll., Cedar Falls, 1955-57, U. Denver, 1957-60; psychol. cons. N.K. & Assocs., St. Louis, 1960-63; dir. adminstrn. St. Louis County, Clayton, Mo., 1963-70; asst. sec. HUD, Washington, 1970-73; pres. Regional Commerce and Growth Assn., St. Louis, 1973-78, also bd. dirs., 1950-53; pres. Taylor-Morley-Simon, Inc., St. Louis, 1978—; vice chmn. Mo. State Indsl. Devel. Bd., Jefferson City. Bd. dirs. St. Luke's Hosp., St. Louis, 1976-83; pres. exec. bd. Better Bus. Bur. Served with USN, 1949-53. Mem. Home Builders Assn. (bd. dirs.), Laclede's Landing (bd. dirs.). Republican. Episcopalian. Clubs: Mo. Athletic (St. Louis); St. Louis (Clayton). Home: 14238 Forest Crest Dr Chesterfield MO 63017 Office: Taylor-Morley-Simon Inc 12400 Olive Blvd Saint Louis MO 63141

MORLEY, JOHN C., electronic equipment manufacturing executive; b. 1931. B.A., Yale U., 1954; M.B.A., U. Mich., 1958. Mng. dir. Esso Pappas Chem. Ae., Greece, 1969-70; pres. Esso Eastern Chems. Inc., N.Y., 1970-71; exec. v.p. Enjay Chem. Co., 1971-74; pres. Exxon Chem. Co., U.S.A., 1974-78; sr. v.p. Exxon Co. U.S.A., Houston, 1978-80; pres. and chief exec. officer, dir. Reliance Electric Co., Cleve., 1980—. Served to lt. (j.g.) USNR, 1954-56. Office: Reliance Electric Co Inc 29325 Chagrin Blvd Cleveland OH 44122*

MORMAN, RONALD L(EE), manufacturing systems consultant; b. Independence, Mo., July 27, 1944; s. Virgil L. and Lola G. (Ertle) M.; m. Jane C. Bracht, Sept. 11, 1961; children—Russell, Deborah, Shawn. B.S. in Indsl. Mgmt. cum laude, Central Mo. State U., 1970. Computer operator Hallmark Cards, Kansas City, Mo., 1961-64; program supr. Thompson Hayward Chem. Co., Kansas City, Kans., 1964-66; data processing mgr. Butler Mfg. Co., Kansas City, Mo., 1966-82; pres. Morman & Assocs., Inc., Independence, 1982—; Mem. Am. Prodn. and Inventory Control Soc., Assn. Systems Mgmt. (cert. systems profl.), Independence C. of C. Democrat. Methodist. Home: 17704 Cheyenne Independence MO 64056 Office: 4205 S Hocker St Suite B Bldg 4 Independence MO 64055

MORRÉ, D. JAMES, research biochemist, educator, cancer center administrator; b. Drake, Mo., Oct. 20, 1935; m. Harvey Henry and Donnna Marie (Maurer) M.; m. Dorothy Marie Wibberg, Aug. 25, 1956; children—Constance, Jeffrey, Suzanne. B.S., U Mo-Columiba, 1957; M.S., Purdue U., 1959; Ph.D., Calif. Inst. Tech., 1963; D. h.c., U. Geneva, 1985. Asst. prof. Purdue U., West Lafayette, Ind., 1962-66, assoc. prof., 1966-71, prof. biochemistry, 1971—, dir. Purdue Cancer Ctr., 1977—; guest sr. scientist German Cancer Ctr., Heidelberg, 1976. Editor: Cancer-Cell Organelles, 1982; Membrane Receptors, 1984. Patentee in cancer detection. Served to 1st lt. USAR, 1958-65. Recipient Sr. Scientist award WHO, 1976, Cancer Research award Lions Club, 1978, Sr. U.S. Scientist award Alexander von Homboldt Found., 1984. Mem. Am. Assn. Cancer Research, Am. Soc. Biol. Chemists, Council Biology Editors, Am. Soc. Cell Biology, Am. Soc. Plant Physiologists, Am. Assn. Colls. Pharmacy. Avocations: traditional blacksmithing. Office: Purdue U Cancer Ctr West Lafayette IN 47907

MORREALE, ROLAND ANTHONY, college official; b. N.Y.C., Mar. 19, 1934; s. Peter and Martha (Moore) M.; B.A., U. Utah, 1955; M.S., Boston U., 1958; m. Janet L. McCroskey, July 6, 1963; 1 son, Craig. Asst. dir. Menorah Med. Center, Kansas City, Mo., 1960-65; mgmt. cons. Cresap, McCormack & Paget, N.Y.C., 1965-66; owner, cons. Roland A. Morreale & Assos., Overland Park, Kans., 1966-67; corp. tng. dir. Nat. Bellas Hess Co., Kansas City, Mo., 1967-69; asst. sales mgr. Funeral Security Plans Co., Kansas City, 1969-72; asst. dir. tng. Human Resources Corp., Kansas City, 1973; corp. dir. tng. Whitaker Cable Corp., North Kansas City, Mo., 1973-74; with Met. Community Colls., Kansas City, Mo., 1974—, placement counselor Project Outreach, Met. Inst., Community Services, 1974-75, program coordinator Pioneer Community Coll., 1975—; co-founder, Career Crossroads for Women, 1975—; creator Met. Computerized Vocat. Counseling Network, 1979; pres. O.G.A., Inc., 1980—. Founding bd. dirs. Kansas City chpt. Amigos de las Americas; co-chmn. auction com. Peter Marshall Golf Classic. Served with AUS, 1955-57. Mem. Personnel Mgmt. Assn. Greater Kansas City Mo. (Outstanding Achievement awards), Am. Soc. Tng. and Devel., Am. Soc. Personnel Adminstrn. Presbyterian. Club: Johnson County Leisure-Aires. Writer, producer Computerized Food Allergy Diet, 1983. Office: PO Box 4062 Overland Park KS 66204

MORRELL, GEORGE WALTER, business executive; b. Mineola, N.Y., Apr. 27, 1946; s. George Henry and Elizabeth Gladis (Pickering) M.; m. Ruth Ann Dougherty, Apr. 24, 1982. B.S., Ind. State U., 1969; M.B.A., Ind. U., 1976. Buyer William H. Block Co., Indpls., 1970-72, divisional sales mgr., 1973-76; area mgr. Thybony Inc., Indpls., 1977-84, Am. Textile Co., 1984-85, G. Morrell Assocs., Ltd., 1985—. Mem. adv. bd. Ind. State U., Terre Haute, 1982—; admissions counselor Mo. Mil. Acad. Mem. Am. Mktg. Assn., Profl. Ski Instrs. Am., Assn. Individual Investors, Ind. State U. Alumni Assn. (dir. 1981—), Indpls. Jaycees, Hon. Order Ky. Cols. Club: Indpls. Athletic. Home: 7010 Bloomfield Dr E Indianapolis IN 46259

MORRILL, THOMAS CLYDE, insurance company executive; b. Chgo., July 1, 1909; s. Walter and Lena Elpha (Haney) M.; student Central Coll. Arts and Scis., Chgo., 1928-29, Northwestern U., 1929-30; m. Hazel Janet Thompson, Oct. 18, 1930; children—Dorothy Mae (Mrs. Gerald L. Kelly), Charles T. With Alfred M. Best Co., Inc., 1929-45, asso. editor, 1940-45; with N.Y. State Ins. Dept., 1945-50, dep. supt. ins., 1947-50; with State Farm Mut. Automobile Ins. Co., Bloomington, Ill., 1950-77, v.p., 1952-77, chmn. bd. State Farm Fire and Casualty Co., 1970—; also dir., chmn. bd. State Farm Gen. Ins. Co., also dir.; dir. State Farm Life Ins. Co., State Farm Life and Accident Assurance Co. Chmn. exec. subcom. Nat. Hwy. Safety Adv. Com., 1971-73; chmn. tech. com. on transp. White House Conf. on Aging, 1971; mem. Pres.'s Task Force on Hwy. Safety. Clubs: Union League (Chgo.), Union Hills Country, Lakes (Sun City, Ariz.). Contbr. reports to N.Y. Ins. Dept. Office: One State Farm Plaza Bloomington IL 61701

MORRIS, BILL, state senator; b. Mar. 10, 1924; m. Dorothy Higgins, 1943. B.S., U. Tulsa, 1946. Mem. Kans. Ho. of Reps., 1972-76; mem. Kans. Senate, 1976—, asst. majority leader, 1980-84; exec. dir. Kans. Restaurant Assn. Republican. Office: 9822 Hardtner Wichita KS 67212

MORRIS, DONALD ARTHUR ADAMS, college president; b. Detroit, Aug. 31, 1934; s. Robert Park and Margaret Lymburn (Adams) M.; m. Zella Mae Stormer, June 21, 1958; children—Dwight Joseph, Julie Adams. B.A. Wayne State U., 1961; M.P.A., U. Mich., 1966; Ph.D., 1970. Copy boy Detroit Times, 1952-55, reporter, 1955-57, edn. writer, 1957-60; adminstrv. asst. Wayne State U., Detroit, 1960-62; mng. editor news service U. Mich., 1962-64, mgr. spl. programs, 1964-68; mgr. Met. Detroit Devel. Program, 1968-71; v.p. for devel. Hobart and William Smith Colls., Geneva, N.Y., 1971-76, exec. v.p., 1976-77; pres. Olivet Coll., Mich., 1977—, also prof. polit. sci., 1977—; chmn. Mich. Intercollegiate Athletic Assn., 1978-79, 85-86. Contbr. articles to profl. jours. Pres. Planned Parenthood of Finger Lakes, N.Y., 1975-77; bd. dirs. Genesee Regional Family Planning Program N.Y., 1975-77; trustee Olivet Coll., Mich. Colls. Found.; chmn. Assn. Ind. Colls. and Univs. of Mich., 1984-85; mem. exec. com., treas. Council Higher Edn. United Chs. of Christ. Mem. Am. Assn. Higher Edn., Acad. Polit. Sci., Olivet Alliance Com., Sigma Delta Chi, Alpha Lambda Epsilon, Kappa Sigma, Phi Mu Alpha Sinfonia. Congregationalist (deacon). Club: Detroit Athletic. Lodge: Rotary. Office: Office of Pres Olivet Coll Olivet MI 49076

MORRIS, GLENN JERAD, communications educator, consultant, psychological researcher; b. Oil City, Pa., July 15, 1944; s. Fredrick and Frances (McDaniel) M.; m. Martha B. Binford, Aug. 10, 1972 (div. 1979); m. 2d Linda Lee Phillips, Oct. 5, 1981; children—Shawn Homer, Terri Dawn. B.A., Pa. State U., 1968, M.A., 1973; Ph.D., Wayne State U., 1980. Announcer, Sta.-WCED, 1966; bartender The Phyrst Inc., 1967; adj. faculty Pa. State U.-Univ. Park, 1969; faculty (part-time) U. Windsor (Ont., Can.), 1972-74; adj. faculty Wayne State U., Detroit, 1972-75; dir. spl. projects Human Synergistics, Plymouth, Mich., 1975-80; asst. prof. Hillsdale (Mich.) Coll., 1980—, assoc. Dow Conf. Ctr., 1980—, exec. tng. cons. to Gen. Motors, 1985—; dir. cons. H.S.A. Inc., Ann Arbor, Mich. Mem. Republican Nat. Com. Served with U.S. Army, 1963-66. Cert. as black belt 1st degree Hoshinjutsu, Black Dragon Soc., 1965. Mem. AAUP, AAAS, ACLU, N.Y., Acad. Sci. Club: Elks (Hillsdale). Author: (with Clay Lafferty) The Grindtown Plant Project, 1976; (with Barbara Forisha-Kouach) The Personal Expectations Inventory (PXI), 1981, Organizational Synch., 1983; Managerial Attitude Perception and Stress Inventory, 1984. Home: 679 Langs Dr Jonesville MI 49250 Office: Dow Conf Ctr Hillsdale Coll Hillsdale MI 49242

MORRIS, JOHN CALVIN, manufacturing company executive; b. Kansas City, Mo., Oct. 8, 1921; s. Arthur Allen and Helen (Moore) M.; m. Mary Jane Anderson, June 12, 1943; children—John M., Kenneth A., Daniel G., Kevin P. Student Rockhurst Coll., 1946-47, U. San Francisco, 1951, Northwestern U., 1964-65. Asst. sales mgr. Maurer-Neuer Meat Packers, Kansas City, Kans., 1938-49; mgr. dist. mktg. Ekco Products Inc., Chgo., 1950-68, pres., 1973—; dir. mktg. Die Supply Corp., Cleve., 1968-70; v.p. mktg. Calar Industries, Wilmette, Ill., 1968-69; v.p. Chgo. Metallic Mfg. Co., Lake Zurich, Ill., 1970-71; pres. John C. Morris & Sons, Wilmette, 1971-73; exec. v.p. A&M Coatings, Arlington Heights, Ill., 1971-73, also dir.; guest lectr. Am. Inst. Baking, 1959-68, 73—, mem. ednl. adv. com., 1973—. Served to 1st lt. USAAF, 1942-45. Decorated Air medal with 4 oak leaf clusters. Mem. Bakers Club Chgo. (bd. dirs., pres.), Am. Soc. Bakery Engrs. (adv. bd.), Chgo. Bakery Products Men's Club, Allied Trades Baking Industry (bd. dirs.). Republican. Roman Catholic. Home: 918 Pontiac Rd Wilmette IL 60091 Office: 1949 N Cicero Ave Chicago IL 60639

MORRIS, KENTON, broadcast executive; b. Santa Monica, Calif. Apr. 20, 1947; s. Chester Brooks and Lili (Kenton) M.; m. Marguerite Marie Bauer, Dec. 13, 1970 (div. 1972); m. Cheryl A. Dorrier, Jan. 11, 1977. B.S., Northwestern U. Producer-dir. Sta. WGN-TV, Chgo., 1969-74; asst. programmer Sta. WGN Radio, Chgo., 1974-83, ops. mgr., 1983-85, dir. ops. and network services, 1986—Bd. dirs., past pres. Old Town Sch. Folk Music, Chgo., 1984. Avocations: travel; flying; guitar. Home: 5936 N Kenmore Chicago IL 60660 Office: WGN Radio 435 N Michigan Ave Chicago IL 60611

MORRIS, LUCIEN ELLIS, anesthesiologist, educator; b. Mattoon, Ill., Nov. 30, 1914; s. James Lucien and Pearl (Ellis) M.; m. Jean Pinder, June 27, 1942; children—James Lucien, Robert Pinder, Sara Jean, Donald Charles, Laura Lee. A.B., Oberlin Coll., 1936; M.D., Western Res. U., 1943. Diplomate Am. Bd. Anesthesiology. Resident in anesthesia U. Wis., Madison, 1946-48, instr., 1948-49; from asst. prof. to assoc. prof. anesthesiology U. Iowa, Iowa City, 1949-54; prof., head anesthesia U. Wash., Seattle, 1954-60, clin. prof., 1961-68; prof. dept. anaesthesia, faculty of medicine U. Toronto (Ont., Can.), 1967-70; chmn. dept. anesthesia Med. Coll. Ohio, Toledo, 1970-80, prof. anesthesiology, 1970—; vis. prof. London Hosp. Med. Coll., 1980-81; WHO travelling med. faculty to Israel and Iran, 1951; mem. com. on anesthetics NRC, 1956-61; ASA del. World Fedn. Socs. Anaesthesiology, 1960-64; dir. anesthesia research labs. Providence Hosp., Seattle, 1960-67; external examiner Coll. Medicine, U. Lagos (Nigeria), 1977. Served to capt. M.C., U.S. Army, 1944-46. Fellow Faculty Anaesthetists Royal Coll. Surgeons, Royal Soc. Medicine, Am. Coll. Clin. Pharmacology, Am. Coll. Anesthesiologists; mem. Anaesthetics Research Soc. Eng., Assn. Anaesthetists Gt. Britain and Ireland, Am. Soc. Regional Anesthesia, Assn. Univ. Anesthetists, Can. Anaesthetists Soc., Am. Soc. Anesthesiologists, Soc. for Exptl. Biology and Medicine, Internat. Anesthesia Research Soc., Am. Soc. Pharmacology, Internat. Assn. for Study of Pain, Australian Soc. Anaesthetists (hon.), Alpha Omega Alpha. Contbr. articles to profl. jours. Inventor of anaesthesia equipment, including copper kettle vaporizer. Home: 3425 Bentley Blvd Toledo OH 43606

MORRIS, M. DOUGLAS, real estate executive, consultant, syndicator; b. Balt., Sept. 10, 1951; s. Earl W. and Audrey Jane (Schrieber) M.; m. Jennifer J. Richardson, Feb. 20, 1984; children—Mac Allen, John Marshall. B.A., Ball State U., 1974. Examiner, Ind. Dept. Fin. Inst., Indpls., 1975-77; broker A. H.M. Graves, Indpls., 1977-82; owner, mgr. Multi Family Real Estate Co., Indpls., 1977—; pres. Property Services Co., Indpls., 1982—. Mem. Nat. Assn. Realtors, Indpls. Bd. Realtors, Lambda Chi Alpha (v.p. 1972-73). Republican. Presbyterian. Avocations: sports; foreclosures. Home: PO Box 20345 Indianapolis IN 46220 Office: Property Services Co 5388 Ralston Indianapolis IN 46220

MORRIS, RANDALL OTIS, retail sales executive; b. Red Oak, Iowa, Dec. 1, 1952; s. Jake David and Roberta Marie (Pendegraft) M.; m. Debra Lynn Householder, Dec. 31, 1982. B.S. in Edn., Northwest Mo. State U., Maryville, 1976; Emergency Med. Technician, Iowa Lakes Community Coll., Estherville, Iowa, 1983. Tchr., coach Sentral Community Sch., Fenton, Iowa, 1976-80; asst. mgr. Fleet of Algona, Iowa, 1980-84; buyer Fleet of Worthington, Minn., 1984—. Dir. pub. relations Algona Ambulance Service, 1984. Served to 1st lt. U.S. Army N.G., 1972-78. Recipient Danforth 4 Square award DAR, 1971; Jaycee of the Yr. award Region B Jaycees, 1983, Algona Jaycees, 1983. Avocations: softball.

MORRIS, RANDY CHARLES, lawyer, educator; b. Kansas City, Mo., Jan. 29, 1955; s. Harold Charles and Barbara Jean (Bouse) M.; m. Retha Ann Martin, July 4, 1975; children—Jason Charles, Jonathan Michael. B.A., U. Mo.-Kansas City, 1976, J.D., 1979. Bar: Mo. 1979, U.S. Dist. Ct. (we. dist.) Mo. 1979, U.S. Ct. Appeals (8th cir.) 1979, U.S. Ct. Mil. Appeals, 1981. Assoc. Donald L. Allen P.C., Lee's Summit, Mo., 1979-84; shareholder Allen & Morris, P.C., 1984—; part-time instr. Longview Community Coll., Lee's Summit, 1982—, Nat. Coll. Kansas City Extension, 1983—. Sr. staff mem. The Urban Lawyer jour., 1978. Treas. Lee's Summit Bicentennial Com., 1975-77; commr. Jackson County Redevel. Authority, Mo., 1984—; chmn. Citizens for Scoville, Kansas City, 1982—. Mem. Phi Kappa Phi, Pi Sigma Alpha, Phi Alpha Delta. Democrat. Baptist. Club: CCD, Inc. (Kansas City) (v.p. elections 1983—). Home: 611 SW 36th Terr Lee's Summit MO 64063 Office: 126 W 3d St Lee's Summit MO 64063

MORRIS, RICHARD MILTON, III, management and audit consultant; b. Circleville, Ohio, Sept. 2, 1944; s. Richard Milton, Jr. and Iva Jean (Packham) M.; m. Judy Lee Daniel, Aug. 21, 1982. B.S., Lewis and Clark Coll., 1967; M.B.A., Portland State U., 1978. Cert. internal auditor, chartered bank auditor. Asst. auditor Fed. Res. Bank San Francisco, Portland, Oreg., 1968-74, The Oreg. Bank, Portland, 1974-78; mgr. program devel. Inst. Internal Auditors, Altamonte Springs, Fla., 1978-80; dir. internal audit Wainoco Oil Corp., Houston, 1980-82; pres. R.M. Morris & Assocs., Inc., Atlanta, 1982-84, Spring Valley, Ohio, 1984—; instr. Portland State U., 1976-78, U. Houston, 1981-82; mem. adv. bd. Internal Audit Pilot Sch., La. State U., Baton Rouge, 1984—. Author: Developing a Charter for an Internal Audit Function, 1983; (with W. Blackstone) Bank Control and Audit, 1983. Editor: (with B. Williams) Readings in Internal Auditing, 1978. Contbr. to books and profl. jours. Mem. Engrs. Club Dayton, Inst. Internal Auditors, Inst. Indsl. Engrs. Office: RM Morris & Assoc Inc 10142 Mallet Dr Spring Valley OH 45370

MORRIS, SAMUEL SOLOMON, JR., bishop; b. Norfolk, Va., Nov. 1, 1916; s. Samuel Solomon and Mayme (Lawson) M.; m. Ermine Smith, Nov. 30, 1942; children—Joyce Green, Ermine, Samuel Solomon III. B.S., Wilberforce U., 1937; M.Div., Yale U., 1940; D.D. (hon.), Payne Sem., 1964; LL.D., Kittrell Coll., 1963. Ordained to ministry African Meth. Episcopal Ch., 1940. Pastor St. Luke A.M.E. Ch., Gallatin, Tenn. and St. John A.M.E. Ch.,

Springfield, Tenn., 1940-41, St. Paul A.M.E. Ch., Nashville, 1943-46, 1st A.M.E. Ch., Gary, Ind., 1949-56, Coppin A.M.E. Ch., Chgo., 1956-72; prof. Payne Sem. and Wilberforce U., 1941-43; pres. Shorter Coll., 1946-48, chmn. bd. trustees, 1972-76; bishop A.M.E. Ch., Little Rock, 1972-76, 11th dist., Jacksonville, Fla., after 1976. Pres. Chgo. br. NAACP, 1960-62; trustee Nat. Urban League. Recipient Silver Beaver award Boy Scouts Am., 1966. Mem. Alpha Phi Alpha. Address: 901 S Plymouth Ct Apt 1203 Chicago IL 60605

MORRISON, C.L., editor, author; b. Evanston, Ill., Jan. 14, 1956. B.A., Roosevelt U., 1976; postgrad. Chgo. Mus. Coll., 1981-83. Research editor Inst. Philos. Research, Chgo., 1975-77; Chgo. corr. Midwest Art Mag., Milw., 1976-80, Artforum Mag., N.Y.C., 1977-81; editor Format: Art & The World, Chgo., 1978—. Author: Defilement: A Story of the Art World, 1978; Cinderella and the Harmonious Instrument, 1984. Contbr. articles to profl. jours. Avocation: piano. Office: Care Format Mag 405 S 7th St St Charles IL 60174

MORRISON, DONALD THOMAS, lawyer; b. Chgo., Sept. 7, 1928; s. Donald T. and Stella (Brokamp) M.; B.S.L., Northwestern U., 1950, LL.B., 1955; m. Catherine E. Mariga, Aug. 18, 1956 (dec. July 1975); children—Joseph T., Sheila M., Mary E., Kathleen A., Eileen T., Margaret J., Frances C., Donald J. Admitted to Ill. bar, 1955; asso. firm Morgan, Halligan & Lanoff, Chgo., 1955-61; practice law, Highland Park, Ill., 1961-62, Waukegan, Ill., 1962-64; ptnr. firm Morrison & Nemanich, Waukegan, 1964-80; pres. Donald T. Morrison & Assocs P.C., 1980—; dir. Deerfield (Ill.) State Bank, 1970-73; spl. asst. atty. gen. Ill. for Condemnation, 1961-68. Comml. pilot, 1972—. Served with USNR, 1951-54. Fellow Am. Coll. Trial Lawyers, Am. Coll. Legal Medicine; mem. Am. (chmn. condemnation com. litigation sect.), Ill. (chmn. specialization com.), Lake County (pres. 1977-78), bar assns., Theta Xi, Phi Delta Phi. Democrat. Roman Catholic. Club: Bob-O-Link Country (Highland Park). Author: Condemnation Trial Technique, Illinois Eminent Domain Practice, 1971, 75, 79; Investigation and Development of the Product Liability Case, 1974. Home: 645 Westgate Deerfield IL 60015 Office: 32 N West St Waukegan IL 60085

MORRISON, GEORGE, artist, educator; b. Grand Marais, Minn., Sept. 30; s. James and Barbara (Mesaba) M.; m. Hazel Belvo, Dec. 13, 1960; 1 child, Briand Mesaba. Student Art Students League, 1946, U. Aix-Marseille, France, 1952; M.F.A., Mpls. Coll. Art and Design, 1969. Vis. artist Cornell U., Ithaca, N.Y., 1962, Pa. State U., State College, Pa., 1963; from asst. to assoc. prof. R.I. Sch. of Design, Providence, 1963-70; prof. art U. Minn., Mpls., 1970—. Represented in permanent collections Whitney Mus., Phila. Mus., Chgo. Art Inst., Mpls. Inst. of Arts. John Hay Whitney fellow, 1953; Vanderlip scholar, 1943; Fulbright scholar, 1952. Mem. Audubon Artists, Fedn. Modern Painters and Sculptors. Home: Box 376 Grand Portage MN 55605 Office: U Minn Art Dept Minneapolis MN 55455

MORRISON, HARRIET BARBARA, educator; b. Boston, Feb. 23, 1934; d. Harry and Harriet (Hanrahan) M. B.S., Mass. State Coll.-Boston, 1956, M.Ed., 1958; Ed.D., Boston U., 1967. Elem. tchr. Arlington (Mass.) Pub. Schs., 1956-67, U. Mass., summer 1967; asst. prof. No. Ill. U., Dekalb, 1967-71, assoc. prof. edn., 1971-85, prof. edn., 1985—. Mem. Am. Ednl. Studies Assn., Philosophy of Edn. Soc., Midwest Philosophy Edn. Soc., Assn. Supervision and Curriculum Devel., Ill. Assn. Supervision and Curriculum Devel., Assn. Tchr. Educators, Pi Lambda Theta. Home: 314 W Sunset Pl Dekalb IL 60115 Office: Coll Edn No Ill U Dekalb IL 60115

MORRISON, JAMES CLIFFORD, psychology educator; b. Salem, Oreg., June 16, 1939; s. John Charles and Blanche (Steele) M.; m. Sheila Lynn Martin, Aug. 25, 1962; children—Sharon, Anne, John. B.A., U. Oreg., 1961; M.A., U. Tenn., 1964; Ph.D., Mich. State U., 1970. Grad. asst. U. Tenn., Knoxville, 1961-64; teaching asst. Mich. State U., East Lansing, 1964-68; teaching fellow Albion Coll., Mich., 1968-69; successively asst. prof., assoc. prof., prof. Youngstown State U., Ohio, 1970—; chmn. dept. psychology, 1976—; cons. Youngstown Sheet and Tube, 1973-75. Pres., bd. dirs. Help Hot-Line, Inc., Youngstown, 1980—, Citizens League of Greater Youngstown, 1982—. Mem. Assn. Behavior Analysis, Midwest Psychol. Assn. Avocations: woodworking; computer programming, backpacking. Home: 44 S Shore Dr Youngstown OH 44512 Office: Dept Psychology Youngstown State U Youngstown OH 44555

MORRISON, JEAN ANN, human resources exec.; b. Cedar Falls, Iowa, Sept. 19, 1952; d. Dewey Raymond and Wava Helene (Trunnell) Breisch; certificat d'etudes (Rotary scholar) L'Institut de Touraine, Tours, France, 1970; B.A. summa cum laude, Concordia Coll., Moorhead, Minn., 1973; postgrad., U. Minn., 1977—; student Am. Inst. Banking, Mpls., 1974-78; m. John Edward Morrison, Dec. 15, 1973. Fgn. exchange asst. Northwestern Nat. Bank, Mpls., 1974-75, gen. devel. trainee, 1975-76, compensation specialist, 1976-77, ops. tng. and devel. coordinator, 1977-78; personnel dir. St. Joseph Bank, South Bend, Ind., 1978, Mich. Nat. Bank, Cassopolis, 1978-79; personnel mgr. Pillsbury Co., Mpls., 1979-80, personnel mgr. Green Giant Co. div., Chaska, Minn., 1980-81, dir. human resources research and devel., 1981—; tutor French, U. Minn. Coordinator, Jr. Achievement. Mem. Am. Soc. Tng. and Devel., Soc. Am. Mgmt., Twin Cities Personnel Assn., Am. Soc. Personnel Adminstrn., Am. Bus. Women's Assn., Inst. Food Technologists, YWCA, U. Minn. Alumni Assn., Rotex, LWV. Republican. Lutheran. Club: Jr. League (Mpls.). Home: 4524 Drexel Ave S Edina MN 55424 Office: Research and Devel Dept Pillsbury Co 311 2d St SE Minneapolis MN 55414

MORRISON, JOHN WASHBURN, banker; b. Mpls., June 1, 1922; s. Angus W. and Helen (Truesdale) M.; m. Charlotte Lewis, Dec. 28, 1942; children—John L., Helen. B.A., Yale U., 1944; M.B.A., Harvard U., 1948. With Honeywell Inc., Mpls., 1948-76, gen. mgr. marine systems div., Los Angeles, 1962-65, v.p. fin. and adminstrn. internat. ops., Mpls., 1965-68, treas., 1968, chief fin. officer, 1968-76, dir., 1970-76; chmn. bd., chief exec. officer Norwest Bank Mpls., N.A., 1976-80; vice chmn. Norwest Corp., Mpls., 1981, chmn., chief exec. officer, 1981-85, retired, chmn. bd., 1985; dir. Gen. Mills, Inc., Northwestern Nat. Life Ins. Co., PPG Industries, Inc. Trustee U. Minn. Sch. Mgmt.; Macalester Coll., Minn. Orchestral Assn., Metropolitan Econ. Devel. Assn. Served with USAF, 1943-45. Mem. Minn. Meeting, Conf. Bd. Club: Woodhill Country, Mpls. Office: Norwest Corp 2404 IPS Bldg Minneapolis MN 55479-0070

MORRISON, JOSEPH BENSON, city manager; b. Wheeling, W.Va., Oct. 8, 1925; s. Joseph Adams and Marjorie Amelia (Dennis) M.; m. Harriett Belle Howard, Feb. 24, 1953. Student, Bethany Coll., 1943-44, Franklin and Marshall Coll., 1944. Commd. ensign U.S. Navy, 1943, advanced through grades to comdr., 1962, ret., 1967; engring. rep. Travelers Ins. Co., Tampa, Fla., 1968-70; asst. to city mgr. City of Webster Groves, Mo., 1971-74, city mgr., 1974—. Mem. standing com. on fin. and taxation Mo. Mcpl. League, 1975-83. Mem. Internat. City Mgmt. Assn., Mo. City Mgmt. Assn., St. Louis County Mgmt. Assn., Ret. Officers Assn. Presbyterian. Clubs: Green Brier Hills Country, Army-Navy Country (Arlington, Va.). Home: 638 Lilac Ave Webster Groves MO 63119 Office: City Hall 4 E Lockwood Ave Webster Groves MO 63119

MORRISON, PATRICIA WRIGHT, communications company lawyer, educator; b. Cin., Apr. 15, 1941; d. Gregory Girard and Harriet Elsa (Wiggers) Wright; m. John Ainslie Morrison, Aug. 17, 1963; children—David Ainslie, Sarah Wright, Benjamin Heuck. B.A., Wellesley Coll., 1962; M.A.T., Harvard U., 1963; M.A., U. Cin., 1971, J.D., 1976. Bar: Ohio 1976, U.S. Dist. Ct. (so. dist.) Ohio 1977, U.S. Ct. Appeals (6th cir.) 1981. Tchr., Reading Meml. High Sch., Mass., 1963-65; adminstrv. specialist State of Ohio, 1972-73; asst. city solicitor City of Cin., 1976-81; div. counsel Warner Amex Cable Communications Co., Cin., 1981-83, v.p. legal affairs, 1983—; instr. U. Cin., 1984—. Founder New Sch., Cin., 1969-70; participant Am. Friends Service Com., Ibadan, Nigeria, 1969; mem. vestry Calvary Episcopal Ch., 1980; mem. Citizens Adv. Bd. Rollman's Psychiat. Inst., Cin., 1980; mem. Affirmative Action com. Community Chest, Cin., 1982—; trustee Diocese So. Ohio, 1983. Recipient Resolution of Commendation award Cin. Bd. Edn., 1978. Mem. ABA, Ohio Bar Assn., Cin. Bar Assn., Nat. Council Sch. Bd. Attys. (exec. com. 1980), Ohio Council Sch. Bd. Attys. (exec. bd. 1980). Club: Les Chaneaux Yacht (Cedarville, Mich.). Home: 3740 Clifton Ave Cincinnati OH 45220 Office: Warner Amex Cable Communications Co 11252 Cornell Park Dr Cincinnati OH 45246

MORRISON, ROBERT STIER, medical administrator, nephrologist; b. Kansas City, Mo., Aug. 3, 1922; s. Guy Thornton and Florida Elizabeth (Stier) M.; m. Marie Day Townsend, May 12, 1951; children—Robert T., Diane D., Nancy E., Ann R., Scott C. A.B., U. Mo., 1946; M.D., Harvard Med. Sch., 1950. Diplomate Am. Bd. Internal Medicine. Fellow in nephrology Peter Bent Brigham Hosp., Boston, 1953-55; chief nephrology Lemuel Shattuck Hosp., Boston, 1955-77, chief profl. services, 1972-77; chief medicine Kaiser Hosp., Honolulu, 1978-81; chief nephrology St. Louis U. Hosp., 1981-84; chief medicine VA Med. Ctr., Leavenworth, Kans., 1984—; assoc. prof. medicine Tufts Med. Sch., Boston, 1955-77; prof. medicine U. Hawaii, Honolulu, 1978-81; St. Louis Sch. Medicine, 1981-84. Contbr. chpts. to books, articles to profl. jours. Chmn. sci, adv. com. Mass. Kidney Found., 1974; sec. med. adv. com. Nat. Kidney Found., Boston, 1975; chmn. Bd. Health, Hingham, Mass., 1976; sci. adv. com. St. Louis Kidney Found., 1984. Recipient Teaching 25 Yrs. award Harvard U., 1977; Service to Commonwealth award Mass. Dept. Health, 1977; Dialysis Unit named in honor at Lemuel Shattuck Hosp., 1977; 11 Yrs. of Service award Hingham Bd. Health, 1977. Mem. Am. Soc. Nephrology, Am. Soc. Artificial Internal Organs, AMA, Mass. Med. Soc., Kansas City Geriatrics Soc. Democrat. Avocations: photography; camping; swimming. Home: VA Med Ctr Box 1782 Leavenworth KS 66048

MORRISON, SCOTT DAVID, telecommunications company engineer; b. Duluth, Minn., May 8, 1952; s. Robert Henry and Shirley Elaine (Tester) M.; m. Jana Louise Bergeron, May 29, 1976; children—Robert Scott, Matthew John. Cert. in welding Duluth Inst. Tech., 1971; student U. Wis.-Superior, 1976-77; Assoc. in Mfg. Mgmt., North Hennepin Community Coll., 1984. Lic. vocat. instr., Minn. Cert. welder, Litton Ship Systems, Pascagoula, Miss., 1971-72, Barko Hydraulics, Superior, Wis., 1972-76; cert. welder and non-destructive examination inspector Am. Hoist and Derrick Co., Mpls., 1978-80; quality supr. Colight Inc., Mpls., 1980, Tol-O-Matic, Inc., Mpls., 1980-82; design assurance engr. ADC Telecommunications, Mpls., 1982—. Judge, U.S. Amateur Boxing Fedn., Mpls., 1978—. Mem. Am. Soc. Quality Control (cert. quality engr.). Democrat. Roman Catholic. Avocations: oil painting; skiing; skydiving. Home: 4034 Regent Ave N Minneapolis MN 55422 Office: ADC Telecommunications 4900 W 78th St Minneapolis MN 55435

MORRISSON, NORMAN GARY, financial executive; b. Omaha, Dec. 12, 1945; s. Clifford H. and Dorothy Jane (McKenzie) M.; m. Linda Lee Rackow, Mar. 16, 1968; children—Amy, Scott. B.S., U. Minn., 1968. C.P.A., Minn., Mich. Supr. auditing Coopers and Lybrand, Detroit, 1970-75, mgr., Mpls., 1975-76; dir. auditing First Nat. Corp., Appleton, Wis., 1976-78; v.p., auditor F & M Savs. Bank, Mpls., 1978-82; v.p. audit dir. Twin Fed. Savs. and Loan, Mpls., 1982—; lectr. in field. Contbr. articles to profl. jours. Treas. United Methodist Ch., Golden Valley, Minn., 1983—. Served with U.S. Army, 1968-70. Mem. Am. Inst. C.P.A.s, Inst. Internal Auditors (internat vice chmn. 1983—, chmn. gen. conf., bd. dirs. 1979—), Minn. Soc. C.P.A.s, Mich. Assn. C.P.A.s. Republican. Club: Greenway Athletic (Mpls.). Avocations: personal computers, athletics. Office: Twin City Fed Savings and Loan 801 Marquette Ave Minneapolis MN 55402

MORROW, GEORGE LESTER, utility executive; b. New Haven, Apr. 27, 1922; s. Lester W.W. and Esther (Morrow) M.; B.S., Rutgers U., 1943; M.B.A., U. Chgo., 1954; m. Mary L. Evenburg, Dec. 27, 1946; children—Susan (Mrs. William Donaldson), William, John, Thomas. With Peoples Gas Light and Coke Co., Chgo., from 1947, v.p. operations, 1966-71, pres., 1971-77, also dir.; pres. Natural Gas Pipeline Co. Am., 1977-83; vice chair Midcon Corp., 1983—; pres. North Shore Gas Co. Trustee Ill. Inst. Tech., Chgo.; bd. govs. Chgo. Heart Assn. Served to capt. AUS, 1943-46. Registered profl. engr., Ill. Mem. Chgo. Assn. Commerce and Industry, Am. Gas Assn., So. Gas Assn. (dir.), Interstate Natural Gas Assn. (dir.), Ill. C. of C. (dir.), Delta Chi. Presbyterian (elder). Clubs: Econ., Execs., Chicago, Univ. (Chgo.). Office: 701 E 22d St Lombard IL*

MORROW, MARK ARTHUR, lawyer, lecturer; b. Detroit, Oct. 18, 1953; s. Arthur James and Pearl (Bolton) M.; m. Pamela Barey, Feb. 19, 1983 (div. June 1984). B.S., Eastern Mich. U., 1976; J.D., Thomas Cooley Law Sch., 1980. Bar: Mich. 1980, U.S. Dist. Ct. (ea. dist.) Mich. 1980. Benefit plans rep. Gen. Motors Corp./UAW, Livonia, Mich., 1972-76; Gen. Motors Acctg. Rep. Blue Cross/Blue Shield Ins., Detroit, 1976-77; judicial clk. Oakland County Probate Ct., Pontiac, Mich., 1978-80; ptnr. Otlewski & Morrow, P.C., Rochester, Mich., 1980—. Bd. dirs. Rochester Area Youth Guidance, Mich., 1981—. Mem. ABA, State Bar Mich., Am. Trial Lawyers Assn., Mich. Trial Lawyers Assn. Democrat. Roman Catholic. Home: 1190 Larch St Pontiac MI 48054 Office: Otlewski & Morrow PC 118 Walnut St Suite B Rochester MI 48063

MORROW, RICHARD M., oil company executive; b. Wheeling, W.Va., 1926; B.M.E., Ohio State U., 1948; married. With Standard Oil Co. (Ind.), Chgo., 1948—, exec. v.p. Amoco Internat. Oil Co., 1966-70, exec. v.p. Amoco Chem. Corp., 1970-74, pres., 1974-78, pres. parent co., 1978-83, chmn., chief exec. officer, 1983—; dir. First Chgo. Corp., First Nat. Bank Chgo. Trustee U. Chgo., Rush-Presbyn.-St. Luke's Med. Ctr., Am. U. in Cairo. Mem. Am. Petroleum Inst. (bd. dirs.), NAM (bd. dirs.) Office: Amoco Corp (Ind) 200 E Randolph Dr Box 5910 A Chicago IL 60680

MORTENSEN, ARVID LEGRANDE, insurance company executive; b. Bremerton, Wash., July 11, 1941; s. George Andrew and Mary Louise (Myers) M.; B.S. in English and Psychology, Brigham Young U., 1965, M.B.A. in Mktg. and Fin., 1967; diploma in life ins. mktg. Life Underwriters Tng. Council, 1974; J.D. cum laude, Ind. U., 1980; m. Elaine Marie Mains, Aug. 2, 1968; children—Marie Louise, Anne Catherine, Joseph Duncan. Bar: Ind. 1980, U.S. Supreme Ct. 1983, Mo. 1985, D.C. 1985. C.L.U. Agt., Connecticut Mut. Life Ins. Co., Salt Lake City, 1967-68, agt. and br. mgr., Idaho Falls, Idaho, 1968-74; with Research and Rev. Service Am., Inc./Newkirk Assos., Inc., Indpls., 1974-83, sr. editor, 1975-79, mgr. advanced products and seminars, 1979-80, dir. mktg., 1980-83; mem. sr. mgmt. com., v.p. Allied Fidelity Corp., 1983-85, Allied Fidelity Ins. Co., 1983-85, Tex. Fire and Casualty Ins. Co., 1983-85; v.p. Gen. Am. Life Ins. Co., St. Louis, 1985—; v.p., officer, dir. Gen. Am. Ins. Co., St. Louis, 1985—; also tchr., lectr. Missionary, Ch. Jesus Christ of Latter-day Saints, 1960-62, bishop, 11th ward, Idaho Falls, Idaho, 1969-74, mem. High Council, Indpls North Stake, 1975-82, first counselor Indpls. North Stake presidency, 1982-85. Recipient award for outstanding legal scholarship in ins. law Am. United Life, 1980, award for service to Ind. Law Rev., Am. Fletcher Nat. Bank, 1978, award for demonstrated legal excellence Lawyers Coop., 1978, 80. Mem. Assn. Advanced Life Underwriting, Estate Planning Council Indpls., ABA, Ind. Bar Assn., Indpls. Bar Assn., Am. Soc. C.L.U.s, Indpls. Soc. C.P.U.s, Nat. Assn. Life Underwriters, Ind. Assn. Life Underwriters, Indpls. Assn. Life Underwriters, Internat. Assn. Fin. planners. Author: Employee Stock Ownership Plans, 1975; Fundamentals of Corporate Qualified Retirement Plans, 1975, 78, 80; (with Norman H. Tarver) The IRA Manual, 1975, 76, 78, 79, 80, 81, 83, 84, 85 edits.; (with Norman H. Tarver) The Keogh Manual, 1975, 77, 78, 80 edits.; (with Norman H. Tarver) The Section 403 (b) Manual, 1975, 77, 78, 80, 84, 85 edits.; (with Leo C. Hodges) The Life Insurance Trust Handbook, 1980; contbr. articles to profl. jours., mags.; editor-in-chief Business Insurance Course, 1974-80, The Estate Protection Course, 1974-80, The Pensions and Profit-Sharing Course, 1974-80; Estate Planner's Service, 1979-80; In Sound, 1979-80; bd. editors Ind. Law Rev., 1977-78. Home: 480 Hunters Hill Dr Chesterfield MO 63017 Office: 700 Market St PO Box 396 Saint Louis Mo 63166

MORTIMER, DAVID ROBERT, advertising researcher; b Detroit, Oct. 14, 1946; s. Robert Maxwell and Elaine Elva (Haskell) M.; m. Karen Kay Larson, Nov. 26, 1971; 1 child, Jeffrey David. B.S., Mich. State U., 1968; M.A., U. Iowa, 1971. Research analyst Leo Burnett Inc., Chgo., 1972-74, research supr., 1974-77, assoc. research dir., 1977-79, v.p., ptnr., 1979-82, group research dir., 1982—; instr. mgmt. seminar Nestle Co., Vevey, Switzerland, 1979. Mem. Am. Mktg. Assn., Am. Psychol. Assn. Avocations: skiing; flying; tennis; fishing; jogging. Home: 1410 Douglas Flossmoor IL 60422 Office: Leo Burnett USA Prudential Plaza Chicago IL 60601

MORTIMER, JEYLAN TEKINER, sociologist, educator; b. Chgo., Aug. 12, 1943; d. Sami S. and Roselle (Martin) Tekiner; m. James A. Mortimer, Aug. 7, 1965; 1 child, Kent Douglas. B.A., Jackson Coll., 1965; M.A., U. Mich., 1967, Ph.D., 1972. Asst. prof. U. Md., College Park, 1971-73; prof. U. Minn., Mpls., 1974-84, assoc. chmn. dept. sociology, 1984—. Assoc. editor Am. Jour. Sociology, 1978-80. Author (with others) Work, Family, and Personality Transition to Adulthood, 1986. Contbr. articles to profl. jours. Woodrow Wilson Found. fellow, 1965-66; grantee NSF, 1976-78, NIMH, 1974-79, Nat. Inst. Aging, 1982-84. Mem. Am. Sociol. Assn. (mem. social psychology council 1984-85), AAAS. Unitarian. Office: Dept Sociology 1114 Social Sci Bldg U Minn Minneapolis MN 55455

MORTON, DAVID ALLEN, lawyer; b. Cleve., Feb. 18, 1950; s. Thomas Harold and Rosalie Mary (Tilton) M.; m. Nancy Clare Plesser, May 25, 1974; children—Matthew Paul, Benjamin Patrick, Jessica Kathleen. B.S. in Bus. Adminstrn., summa cum laude, Franklin U., 1977; J.D., U. Notre Dame, 1980. Bar: Ohio 1980, U.S. Dist. Ct. (so. dist.) Ohio 1981, U.S. Tax Ct. 1983. Assoc. Baker & Hostetler, Columbus, Ohio, 1980-81, Alexander, Ebinger, et al., Columbus, 1981-83, Shayne, Fein, & Vande Werken, Columbus, 1983; prin. Morton, Hessler & Derr, Columbus, 1983—. Author: Michigan Consumer Compliance Manual, 1978. Mem. March of Dimes Telethon Com., 1985—; vice chmn., bd. dirs. Gahanna Ohio Community Reinvestment Commn., 1984; trustee Gahanna Community Improvement Corp., 1984—; mem. St. Matthew Bd. Edn., Gahanna, 1984—; parish rep. Columbus Diocese Bd. Edn., 1984—. Mem. ABA, Federal Bar Assn., Ohio State Bar Assn., Columbus Bar Assn. (mem. common pleas, fin. instns. and municipal ct. coms.), Assn. Trial Lawyers Am., Ohio Acad. Trial Lawyers, Cleve. Bar Assn., Franklin U. Alumni Assn. (mem.-at-large, trustee, chmn. alumni clubs 1985—). Republican. Roman Catholic. Club: Notre Dame. Office: Morton Hessler & Derr Co LPA 85 East Gay St Ste 507 Columbus OH 43215

MORTON, RICHARD FRANCIS, merchandising executive; b. Seacucus, N.J., Sept. 30, 1952; s. Ernest L. and Genevieve F. (Konselor) M. B.S., U. Chgo., 1971; postgrad. Goethe Inst., U. Heidelberg (W.Ger.), 1968-69. Mgr. K-Mart Corp., Chgo., 1972-77; mgr. Charming Shoppe Corp., Mich., Ind., Ill., 1978-81, distbn. mgr., 1981-83; founder, chief exec. officer Rags to Riches, Ltd., Chgo., 1983-85; chief exec. officer Aerial Burial Corp., 1985—; mem. Urban Econ. Devel. Commn. Mem. C. of C. (Chgo. Lakeview group). Democrat. Developer theory of velocity mgmt. for use in retail merchandising with mainframe computers, point of sale terminals. Home: 6126 S Parkside Chicago IL 60638 Office: 3145 N Lincoln Ave Chicago IL 60657

MORTON, STEPHEN DANA, chemist; b. Madison, Wis., Sept. 7, 1932; s. Walter Albert and Rosalie (Amlie) M.; B.S., U. Wis., 1954, Ph.D., 1962. Asst. prof. chemistry Otterbein Coll., Westerville, Ohio, 1962-66; postdoctoral fellow water chemistry, pollution control U. Wis., Madison, 1966-67; water pollution research chemist WARF Inst., Madison, 1967-73; head environ. quality dept., 1973-76; mgr. quality assurance Raltech Sci. Services, 1977-82; pres. SDM Cons., 1982—. Served to 1st lt. Chem. Corps, AUS, 1954-56. Mem. Am. Chem. Soc., Am. Water Works Assn., Am. Soc. Limnology and Oceanography, Water Pollution Control Fedn., AAAS. Author: Water Pollution—Causes and Cures, 1976. Home: 1126 Sherman Ave Madison WI 53703 Office: 979 Jonathon Dr Madison WI 53713

MOSER, HARRY CRANE, machine tool company executive; b. Elizabeth, N.J., Feb. 3, 1944; s. Raymond Jacob and Nancy Lyon (Crane) M.; m. Barbara Tomkinson, Mar. 1967 (div. 1977); 1 child, Robert; m. Mary Jo Harris, Jan. 19, 1980. B.S., MIT, 1967, M.S., 1967; M.B.A., U. Chgo., 1980. Mfg. mgr. program Gen. Electric Co., Schenectady, San Jose, 1967-68; indsl. liaison officer MIT, Cambridge, 1968-71; dir. mktg. research Disamatic, Inc., Burr Ridge, Ill., 1971-77; mgr. bus. planning Acme-Cleve., Inc., 1977-81, mgr. aftermarket sales, 1981-83; pres., gen. mgr. Roto-Finish Co., Inc., Kalamazoo, 1983-85; pres., gen. mgr. Charmilles Techs. Corp., Mt. Prospect, Ill., 1985—. Mem. Shaker Heights Task Force, Ohio, 1980. Mem. Am. Soc. Mfg. Engrs., MIT Alumni (v.p. 1981-83), Sigma Xi, Pi Tau Sigma, Tau Beta Pi. Republican. Presbyterian. Avocations: running, politics, economics, investments, classical music. Home: 4 Kensington Dr Lincolnshire IL 60015 Office: Charmilles Techs Corp Mount Prospect IL 60056

MOSER, JOHN BENEDIKT, biological materials educator, dental materials and color science consultant; b. Salzburg, Austria, Oct. 17, 1923; came to U.S., 1951, naturalized, 1956; s. Berthold Benedikt and Halina (Witlin) M.; m. Hannah Schlesinger, Mar. 6, 1954; 1 child, Barbara. B.Sc., Sir George Williams U., Can., 1950; M.S., Northwestern U., 1958, Ph.D., 1961. Assoc. scientist Argonne Nat. Lab., Ill., 1962-70; postdoctoral fellow Northwestern U., Chgo., 1970-71, asst. prof., 1971-76, assoc. prof., 1976-81, prof., 1981—; cons. ADA, Chgo., 1980—, Greenmark Inc., Niles, Ill., 1980—. Contbr. articles to profl. jours. Fellow Acad. Dental Materials; mem. Internat. Assn. Dental Research, Sigma Xi, Omicron Kappa Upsilon. Home: 415 Audubon Rd Riverside IL 60546 Office: Northwestern U Dental Sch 311 E Chicago Ave Chicago IL 60611

MOSESON, DARRELL D., agricultural supply company executive; b. Howard, S.D., July 27, 1926; s. Gustav Leonard and Clara Amanda (Arneson) M.; children—Nancy, Joan. B.A. cum laude in Econs., Augustana Coll., 1950. With Cenex (Farmers Union Central Exchange), St. Paul, 1951—, credit mgr., 1957-62, asst. gen. mgr., 1962-71, sr. v.p. fin., 1971-81, pres., 1981—; chmn. Central Bank for Coops., Denver. Bd. dirs. Lutheran Social Service Minn. Club: Athletic (St. Paul). Office: Farmers Union Central Exchange 5500 Cenex Dr Inver Grove Heights MN 55075*

MOSHER, GREGORY DEAN, theatre director; b. N.Y.C., Jan. 15, 1949; s. Thomas Edward and Florence Christine M.; student Oberlin Coll., 1967-69; B.F.A., Ithaca Coll., 1971; postgrad. Juilliard Sch., 1971-74. Dir., Stage 2, Goodman Theatre, Chgo., 1974-77, artistic dir., 1978—; dir. Broadway prodn. Glengarry Glen Ross (David Mamet), 1984; producer new works by Tennessee Williams, Studs Terkel, David Mamet, Elaine May, Shel Silverstein, John Guare, Michael Weller, Wole Soyinka, Edward Albee, David Rabe; producer Samuel Beckett's first directing work in U.S., Krapp's Last Tape, 1979, Endgame, 1980. Office: Goodman Theatre Chicago IL 60603

MOSHER, KATHLEEN JOY, editor, author; b. Elgin, Ill., Sept. 10, 1943; d. Carlton Lee and Ruth Mildred (Hansen) Bolin; m. Harry D. Mosher, Aug. 7, 1965; children—Michael Scott, Melissa Sue. B.S., Ball State U., 1965, M.A. in Elem. Edn., 1975. Cert. elem. tchr., Ohio, Ind. Tchr. East Cleve. Pub. Sch., 1965-67, Washington Twp. Schs., Indpls., 1967-71, 77-78, Eagle-Union Schs., Zionsville, Ind., 1980-81; assoc. editor Humpty Dumpty, Jack & Jill, Child Life & Turtle Mags., Children's Better Health Inst., Indpls., 1981—, editor Children's Playmate Mag., Children's Digest Mag., 1983—; mem. adv. bd. Nat. Young Writer's Contest, Falls Church, Va., 1985—. Contbr. articles to children's mags. Dir. Children's Ch., Union Chapel United Meth. Ch., Indpls., 1974-82; mem. Indpls. Mus. Art. Mem. Ednl. Press Assn., Internat. Reading Assn., Ind. Tchrs. of Writing, NEA, Sigma Kappa Alumni Assn. Republican. Clubs: North Willow, Jaycee Wives. Avocations: arts and crafts; needlework; gardening; swimming. Home: 2031 Brewster Rd Indianapolis IN 46260 Office: Children's Playmate-Children's Digest Children's Better Health Inst 1100 Waterway Blvd PO Box 567 Indianapolis IN 46206

MOSIMANN, GARY FRED, educational administrator; b. Greenville, Ill., Aug. 31, 1938; s. Fred August and Ruth Caroline (Wade) M.; B.S., So. Ill. U., 1966, M.S. in Adminstrn., 1969, specialist ednl. adminstrn. cert., 1974, postgrad., 1979—; m. Joyce Ann Eaves, Dec. 17, 1960; children—Kimberly Ann, Laura Lynn. Tchr., Cahokia (Ill.) Unit Sch. 187, 1966-75, prin. Chenot Middle Sch., 1980-83, adminstrv. asst. to supt. 1984—; cons. Area Service Center, Lebanon, Ill., 1972-76; site coordinator Tchr. Corps, 1979, So. Ill. U., Edwardsville/Cahokia, 1979-80, also mem. adv. com. ednl. adminstrn. Supt. Sunday Sch., Bethany United Meth. Ch., Columia, Ill., 1981, lay leader, 1980. Served with M.I., AUS, 1962-65. Mem. Ill. Assn. Supervision and Curriculum Devel., Nat. Assn. Supervision and Curriculum Devel., Cahokia Admintrv. Assn. (pres.), So. Ill. U. Alumni Assn., Phi Delta Kappa. Club: Columbia Bath and Tennis. Home: PO Box 257 Columbia IL 62236 Office: 1700 Jerome Ln Cahokia IL 62206

MOSKOWITZ, LARRY NEIL, metallurgist; b. N.Y.C., Feb. 3, 1949; s. Carl Irving and Lillian Rose M.; m. Daria Julianne Rudziak, Aug. 6, 1978; children—David Michael, Robert Alan. B.S. in Materials Engring, Rensselaer Poly. Inst., Troy, N.Y., 1970; M.S. in Metallurgy, MIT, 1972. Coop engr., Wyman-Gordon Co., Worcester, Mass., 1967-70; materials engr. Pratt & Whitney Aircraft, East Hartford, Conn., 1972-75; sr. metallurgist SCM Corp., Cleveland, 1975-82; project engr. Imperial Clevite, Cleve., 1982-83; staff research engr. Standard Oil Co. (Ind.), Naperville, Ill., 1983—. Contbr. articles in field. Patentee in field. Recipient award for tech. excellence Chem. Div. SCM Corp., 1981. Mem. Am. Soc. Metals, Am. Welding Soc., Sigma Xi, Alpha Sigma Mu. Office: Standard Oil Co (Ind) PO Box 400 M/S F-8 Naperville IL 60566

MOSLEY, KATHRYN SHEFFER, educator; b. Cleve., Nov. 14, 1951; d. Bruce M. and Magdalene Mary (Hilber) Sheffer; m. Bruce Edward Bower, July 13, 1974; m. 2d, John Thomas Mosley, Sept. 30, 1978. B.A., Mich. State U.,

1973; M.A. in Edn., U. Mo.-Kansas City, 1978. Cert. tchr., Mich., Kans., Mo., Conn., Tex. Retail mgr. Sanger-Harris, Tex., 1973-75; Bergdorf Goodman, N.Y.C., 1978-79; tchr. English South Grand Prairie (Tex.) High Sch., 1975-76, Eastgate Jr. High Sch., Mo., 1976-78, Central Catholic High Sch., Norwalk, Conn., 1979-80; tchr. word processing Katherine Gibbs Sch., Norwalk, 1980; substitute tchr. Wichita (Kans.) Ind. Sch. Dist., 1982—; tutor English, Middle Sch. Planning Com., Dist. Lang. Arts Com.; performer USO European tour, 1973. Recipient Achievement award U. Mo. Sch. Edn., 1979. Mem. Nat. Cath. Edn. Assn., Nat. Council Tchrs. English. Republican. Roman Catholic. Club: Ninnescah Yacht (Wichita). Co-author, editor tchr. manual instructing adolescent lit. Home: 155 N Bluff St Wichita KS 67208 Office: 428 S Broadway St Wichita KS 67202

MOSS, GARY WILLIAM, wildlife artist; b. Mpls., Dec. 15, 1946; s. Elmer Frederick and Stella Marie (Zajak) M.; m. Linda Kendrick Brown; children—Marianna Lynn, Colin Frederick. B.F.A., Mpls. Coll. Art and Design, 1966. Photographer artist; Minnetonka, Minn., 1984. Shows: exhbns. include Nat. Gallery Fine Art; Carnegie Mus., Boston, Brit. Mus., London, Royal Acad. Art; Edinburgh, Am. Miniatures, Tucson Settlers West, 1984, 85, 86, Wildlife Sporting Heritage, Dallas, Leigh Yawkey Woodson Art Mus., Wausau, Wis., 1978, 79, 81-85. Served with USMC, 1968-70; Vietnam. Named Artist of Yr. Turn-in-Poachers Orgn., 1985, Pheasants Forever Orgn., 1984, Combat Artist of Yr. USMC Traveling Exhibit Smithsonian, 1970, Artist of Yr. Ruffled Grouse Soc., 1984, Bird Art Smithsonian Instn. Traveling Exhbn. award, 1981. Address: Route 2 PO Box 485 Cambridge MN 55008

MOSS, KIRBY G., lawyer; b. Elizabeth City, N.C., July 8, 1954; s. Lindy G. and Jeanne H. (Howie) M. B.S. in Acctg., Ind. U.-Bloomington, 1976; J.D., Ind. U.-Indpls., 1979. Bar: Ind. 1979, U.S. Dist. Ct. (no. and so. dists.) Ind. 1979, U.S. Supreme Ct. 1982. Assoc. Torborg, Miller, Moss, Harris & Yates and predecessors, Ft. Wayne, Ind., 1979-83, ptnr., 1984—. Bd. dirs. Harold W. McMillen Ctr. Health Edn., Ft. Wayne, 1980-84, chmn. nominating com., 1984, treas., 1984. Mem. Allen County Bar Assn. (trial lawyers and young lawyers div. 1979—, lawyer referral com. 1984), Ind. State Bar Assn. (young lawyers div. 1979—), Ind. Trial Lawyers Assn., ABA (family law div. 1983—, young lawyers div. 1979—, litigation sect., mem. trial practice com. 1980—), Assn. Trial Lawyers Am. Office: Torborg Miller Moss Harris & Yates 1800 Fort Wayne Bank Bldg PO Box 10839 Fort Wayne IN 46854

MOSS, MIRANDA, graphic designer; design consultant; b. Washington, Feb. 24, 1942; d. John Wilson and Mary Caroline (Moss) Umholtz; m. Peter Seitz, Aug. 24, 1963; children—Christopher, Bryan, Mandy. B.F.A. magna cum laude, Md. Inst. Art, 1964; postgrad. Am. U., U. Minn., St. Catherine's Coll. Fashion art dir. Dayton's Dept. Store, Mpls., 1965-67; art resource tchr. Mpls. pub. schs., 1965-68; freelance designer, illustrator children's books Lerner Publs., Meadowbrook Press, Guthrie Theatre, Minn. Zoo, Augsburg Press; instr. Mpls. Coll. Art and Design, 1976-79; co-founder, ptnr. Seitz Yamamoto Moss, Inc., Mpls., 1979—. Reicpient N.Y. Art Dirs. award, 1980, Soc. Typographic Art awards, 1982, 83, 84, 85, Desi award, 1980, 81, 82, Minn. Graphic Designers Assn. award, 1982, 83. Mem. Soc. Typographic Arts, Am. Inst. Graphic Artists, Minn. Graphic Designers Assn., LWV, Feminist Caucus, Mpls. C. of C., Downtown Council, Walker Art Center, Mpls. Soc. Fine Arts, Minn. Zool. Soc., Sci. Mus. Democrat. Lutheran. Publ. in Print, Graphis, Communication Arts, Trademarks and Symbols of the World, IDEA Mag. Tokyo. Home: 110 1st Ave NE Minneapolis MN 55413 Office: 252 1st Ave N Minneapolis MN 55401

MOSSBAUER, LOUIS, optometrist; b. Bavaria, Germany, Mar. 1, 1902; s. Karl and Margaret (Meister) Mossbauer; student Fortbildungsschule and Musikschule, Bavaria; postgrad. Hosp. and Med. Sch., Chgo., 1945; O.D., Monroe Coll. Optometry, 1946; m. Alice Harkness, Nov. 15, 1947; 1 son, Louis Carl. Came to U.S., 1927, naturalized, 1937. Dir. United Artists Conservatories Music, Balt., 1928-40; owner Berman Optical Co., Washington, 1940-47; practice optometry, Chgo. and Elmhurst, Ill., 1946—; pres. Midwestern Sch. Optics, 1946-52; pres. German-Am. Contact Lens Mfg. Co., Elmhurst; founder Internat. Contact Lens Specialists. Mem. Am. (hon. life mem.), Ill. (trustee 1959-61) optometric assns., N.E. Ill. Optometric Soc. (rec. sec. 1953-56, 59-63, pres. 1957-58, 64-65), Ednl. Council Optometry (past sec.), Am. Pub. Health Assn. (vision com.), Med. Research Assos. Adv. Panel, Ill. Soc. for Prevention Blindness, AAAS, Ill. Coll. Optometry Alumni Assn., Tomb and Key, Kappa Phi Delta. Rotarian (past dir. Elmhurst). Research in fitting and mfg. latest types corneal contact lenses. Home: Elmhurst IL 60126 Office: 191 Addison Ave Elmhurst IL 60126

MOTANKY, GUY URBAN, clinical psychologist; b. Chgo., Feb. 17, 1938; s. Robert R. and Julia M. (McGrath) M.; m. Linda A. Caiazzo, Oct. 8, 1971; children—Laura, Jason. B.Ed., Chgo. Tchrs. Coll., 1961, M.S., 1962, Ph.D., 1966. Registered psychologist, Ill. Asst. chief psychology VA Lakeside Hosp., Chgo., 1968-73; asst. prof. psychology Northwestern U. Med. Sch., Chgo., 1968-73; lectr. Northwestern U. Dental Sch., Chgo., 1969-79; pvt. practice psychotherapy, Chgo., 1966—; area mgr. Personal Performance Consultants Inc., 1983—; cons. for employee assistance programs in industry. USPHS pre doctoral fellow, 1962-66; recipient A.E. Bennett award Soc. Biol. Psychiatry, 1966. Mem. Am. Psychol. Assn., Am. Acad. Psychotherapy, Psi Chi, Sigma Xi. Contbr. articles to profl. jours. Home: 614 Ridge Rd Wilmette IL 60091 Office: 333 No Michigan Ave Suite 2121 Chicago IL 60601

MOTES, MARVIN EUGENE, cleaning co. exec.; b. Chillicothe, Ohio, Oct. 25, 1935; s. John Griffith and Lorraine Louise (Litter) M.; B.S. in Bus. Adminstrn., Ohio State U., 1961; m. Loretta Lee Maughmer, Feb. 2, 1957; children—Kelly Lee, Julia Ann, Lisa Joan. Office mgr. Research div. Mead Corp., Chillicothe, 1956-66; pres., gen. mgr. AA Cleaning Co., Inc., Chillicothe, 1963—, AA Cleaning Supply Co., Inc., Chillicothe, 1965—, Pickaway Indsl. Packaging Co., Inc., Circleville, Ohio, 1979—. Bd. dirs. Med. Center Hosp., Chillicothe, 1977-80, chmn. fin. com., 1979-80, treas., 1979-80; active Small Bus. Adminstrn. Mem. Bldg. Services Contractors Assn. Democrat. Methodist. Club: Elks. Home: 1 Applewood Dr Chillicothe OH 45601 Office: 28155 River Rd Circleville OH 43113

MOTT, ROBERT LEE, mechanical engineering technology educator, author; b. Urbana, Ohio, Sept. 4, 1940; s. William Bernard and Marcella Rose (McLaughlin) M.; m. Margaret Ann Blasy, Apr. 15, 1961; children—Lynne Sue, Robert Lee, Jr., Stephen Michael. B.S. in Mech. Engring., Gen. Motors Inst., Flint, Mich., 1963; M.S., Purdue U., 1965. Registered profl. engr., Ohio. Research engr. Frigidaire div. Gen. Motors Corp., Dayton, Ohio, 1958-66; prof. mech. engring. tech. U. Dayton, 1966—; engring. cons., Dayton, 1973—. Author: Applied Fluid Mechanics, 1972, revised, edit., 1979; Applied Strength of Materials, 1978; Machine Elements in Mechanical Design, 1985. Recipient Ralph R. Teetor award Soc. Automotive Engrs., 1968, Tchr. of Yr. award U. Dayton, 1981. Mem. ASME, Am. Soc. Engring. Edn., Computer and Automated Systems Assn., Soc. Mfg. Engrs., Assn. for Integrated Mfg. Technology. Pi Tau Sigma. Roman Catholic. Office: U Dayton 300 College Pk Dayton OH 45469

MOULTON, JOHN WESLEY, state official; b. Princeton, Ill., July 18, 1949; s. John Edward and LaWanda Rose (Miller) M.; m. Janet Lynn Drag, June 26, 1982. Student Ill. State U., 1972-75. Vet. service officer Ill. Dept. Vets. Affairs, Springfield, 1975-79, exec. II, mgr. ops. and grants, 1979—. Mem. standing com. Interagy. Com. on Handicapped Employees, 1980—; coordinator United Way Campaign, 1980—; active Citizens for Reagan. Served with USAF, 1967-71; Korea; to 1st lt. U.S. Army, 1981. Mem. Ill. Assn. for Advancement of Archaeology, N.G. Assn. Ill. and U.S., Amvets, VFW, Am. Legion, Officer Candidate Alumni Assn. (treas. Ill.). Lutheran (ch. council). Home: 29 Lambert Ln Springfield IL 62704 Office: 208 W Cook St Springfield IL 62704

MOULTRIE, JOHN WESLEY, JR., state official; b. Marion, S.C., May 23, 1904; s. John Wesley and Missouri (Crockett) M.; A.B., Allegheny Coll., Meadville, Pa., 1927; postgrad. Harvard Law Sch., 1927-28, U. Mich. Law Sch., 1929-30, U. Minn., 1935-36, 38-39; M.A., Roosevelt U., 1967; m. Alice Gibson, Oct. 1, 1939 (dec. Nov. 1962); children—John Wesley III, Stanton Randolph. Prin. rural sch., Jacksonville, Fla., 1932-33; editor-in-chief The Spotlight, Chgo., 1934-35; dir. Consumer Center, Phyllis Wheatley House, Mpls., 1941-42; interviewer, unit supr. Minn. State Employment Service, Mpls., 1942-54; interviewer, counselor Gen. Indsl. Office, Ill. State Employment Service, Chgo., 1959-65, counseling supr., 1965-69, program coordinator, 1969-81, asst. mgr. local office, 1981—; real estate broker, Chgo., 1955—, ins. broker, Chgo., 1956—. Mem. Internat. Assn. Personnel in Employment Security. Methodist (pres. ch. credit union). Home: 4354 S Martin Luther King Dr Chicago IL 60653 Office: Ill State Job Service 14829 S Dixie Hwy Harvey IL 60426

MOUNT, HOWARD CHARLES, investment executive; b. Henry County, Ill., Aug. 11, 1928; s. Claude Charles and Myrtle Irene (Thorp) M.; m. Jeannette Marie Benson, Sept. 3, 1948; children—Scott, Kristine, Jan; m. Donna Jean Petersen, Feb. 7, 1975. B.S., Aurora Coll., 1960; M.B.A., No. Ill. U., 1968. Chartered fin. analyst. Supr. rates No. Ill. Gas, Naperville, 1960-68; group v.p. Duff and Phelps, Inc., Chgo., 1968—. Trustee Village Bd., North Aurora, Ill., 1969-82. Served with USN, 1946-48. Mem. Fin. Analysts Fedn., Chgo. Investment Analysts Soc. Republican. Presbyterian. Club: Union League (Chgo.). Avocation: gardening. Office: Duff and Phelps Inc 55 E Monroe St Chicago IL 60603

MOUNTIN, THOMAS EDMUND, lawyer; b. Milw., Sept. 6, 1949; s. Walter Joseph and Elizabeth Mary (Carrigan) M.; m. Susan Marie Moser, Oct. 18, 1974; children—Matthew Emmet, Zachary Paul. B.A., St. Francis DeSales Coll., 1971; J.D., Loyola U., Chgo., 1978; LL.M., DePaul U., 1981. Bar: Wis. 1978, U.S. Tax Ct. 1979, U.S. Ct. Appeals (7th cir.) 1983. Assoc. Meldman, Case & Weine, Ltd., Milw., 1978-82, mem. firm, 1982—; instr. Sch. Bus. Adminstrn., U. Wis.-Milw., 1981-85. Author: (with Robert E. Meldman) Federal Taxation Practice and Procedure, 1983. Mem. Wis. Bar Assn., Milw. Bar Assn. Democrat. Roman Catholic. Home: 3408 N 47th Milwaukee WI 53216 Office: Meldman Case & Weine Ltd 788 N Jefferson Milwaukee WI 53202

MOWERY, JOHN HENRY, psychologist; b. Cin., Jan. 22, 1920; s. John Henry and Minna Henrietta (Hageman) M.; B.A., Bowling Green State U., 1950; M.A., Kent State U., 1951; m. Carolyn Rubel, June 4, 1960. Clin. psychologist Ind. Mental Health Div., Indpls., 1952; personnel psychologist Aero Mayflower Transit Co., Indpls., 1952-55; personnel adminstr. Am. Legion Nat. Hdqrs., Indpls., 1955-56; psychologist Am. Legion State Hdqrs., Indpls., 1956; asst. personnel dir. Hook Drugs Inc., Indpls., 1956-60; staff psychologist Psychol. Service Center, Toronto, Ont., Can., 1960-62; pvt. practice clin. psychologist, Mpls., 1963—; cons. psychologist Lutheran Social Service Minn., 1970—. Served with USAAF, 1942-46. Lic. and cert. psychologist, Minn., Ont. Mem. AAAS, N.Y. Acad. Scis., Am., Minn., Internat. psychol. assns., Nat. Register Health Services Providers in Psychology, Psi Chi, Theta Chi. Methodist. Clubs: Mason, Statesman's, Regency. Home: 3101 E Calhoun Pkwy Minneapolis MN 55408

MOWRY, JOHN L., lawyer; b. Baxter, Iowa, Dec. 15, 1905; s. William and Grace (Conn) M.; B.A., U. Iowa, 1929, J.D., 1930; student Ohio State U., 1926-27; m. Irene E. Lounsberry, June 7, 1941; 1 dau., Madelyn E. (Mrs. Stephen R. Irvine). Admitted to Ia. bar, 1930, N.Y. bar, 1945; spl. agt. F.B.I., 1930-34; mem. staff firm Thomas E. Dewey, N.Y.C., 1935-36; with U.S. Army Air Force, 1941-45; mem. exec. dept. N.Y. State, 1946; pvt. practice law, Marshalltown, Iowa, 1936-41, 47—; owner Evans Abstract Co., also G.M.K. Inc., Marshalltown, 1950—; county atty. Marshall County (Iowa), 1939-41; mayor City of Marshalltown, 1950-55. Mem. Iowa Ho. of Reps., 1956-68, majority floor leader, 1963-65; mem. Iowa Senate 1968-72; del. Republican Nat. Conv., Miami, Fla., 1972. Mem. Soc. Former Spl. Agts. FBI (nat. pres. 1945), Marshall County, Iowa bar assns., Iowa Pioneer Lawmakers Soc., Marshall County Hist. Soc., SAR. Republican. Presbyn. Mason (Shriner), Elk. Home: 503 W Main St Marshalltown IA 50158 Office: 25 N Center St Marshalltown IA 50158

MOYANO, MARCELO HERBERT, data processing executive; b. Cordoba, Argentina, July 18, 1945; came to U.S., 1980; s. Hector Marcelo and Stella Maris (Walker) M.; m. Maria Elisa Torti, Sept. 11, 1972; children—Diego Sebastian, Martin, Fernando Esteban. B.S.E.E., Nat. U. Cordoba, 1973. System operator City of Cordoba, 1973-76; system analyst Computacion Rio Tercero, Cordoba, 1977-78; data processing mgr. Mainero & Co., Cordoba, 1978-80; programmer Paxson Machine Co., Salem, Ohio, 1980-83; data processing mgr. Duracote Corp., Ravenna, Ohio, 1983—. Avocations: photography; carpentry; camping. Home: 891 Homewood Ave Salem OH 44460 Office: Duracote Corp 350 N Diamond St Ravenna OH 44266

MOYER, JOHN PETER, stockbroker; b. Youngstown, Ohio, July 2, 1936; s. Sidney S. and Helen W. M.; m. Sandra Louise Meyers, Oct. 26, 1940; children—Andrew Mark, Paul Howard, Karyn Elizabeth. B.A. in History, Washington and Lee U., 1958. Sec. Moyer Mfg. Co., Youngstown, 1958-66; stockbroker Singer Deane & Scribner (now Butcher & Singer, Inc.), Youngstown, 1966—. Active Mahoning Valley council Boy Scouts Am., 1963—; chmn. Jewish Community Relations Council, 1980-83. Recipient Silver Beaver award Boy Scouts Am., 1981. Club: Rotary. Address: 5701 Sampson Dr Girard OH 44420

MOYERS, CHESTER EUGENE, electrical engineer, lay minister; b. St. Louis, May 17, 1934; s. Earl P. and Hazel Christene (Ellison) M.; m. Janet Rose Schoech, May 29, 1955; children—Candace Lynne Moyers Wyne, Gail Ann Moyers McWilliams, Jon Mark. B.S.E.E., U. Mo., 1959. Registered profl. engr., Mo. Design engr. Sangamo Electric Co., Springfield, Ill., 1959-62; sr. engr. McDonnell Douglas, St. Louis, 1962-74; project engr. Marvel-Schebler Tillotson Div. Borg-Warner Corp., Decatur, Ill., 1974-79, sr. project engr., 1979-82, engring. mgr., 1982—; mem. Real-Time Gemini Spacecraft Analysis Team, Real-Time Skylab Spacecraft Analysis Team. Bd. dirs. Internat. Christian Embassy Jerusalem, Tampa, 1984—, Television Channel 23, Decatur, Ill., 1977-84; elder interdenominational Fellowship, St. Louis, Decatur. Served with USN, 1951-55, Korea. Decorated Korean Ribbon with 2 battle stars, UN Ribbon, Am. Defense Ribbon; Design awards George C. Marshall Space Flight Ctr., 1972, McDonnell Douglas Corp., 1973, NASA, 1974. Recipient plaque Inspirational Films, 1982, World Wide Pictures, 1982, Television Channel 23, 1983. Mem. Soc. Automotive Engrs. Republican. Avocation: camping. Home: 2049 Spring Lane Decatur IL 62521 Office: Marvel Schebler Tillotson Div Borg Warner Corp 707 Southside Dr Decatur IL 62525

MOYERS, SAM, rental company executive; b. Elmira, N.Y., June 11, 1939; s. Edward Badger and Kathryn (Farkas) M.; m. Mardelle Young, Dec. 22, 1962; children—Marjorie (Gigi), John, Kerin. B.B.A., So. Meth. U., 1961, M.B.A., 1962. Salesman, McCormick Shilling, Inc., Dallas, 1960-62; dir. mktg. Jim Dandy Co., Birmingham, Ala., 1965-72; v.p. mktg. Pizza Hut, Inc., Wichita, Kans., 1972-80, Rent-A-Center, Inc., Wichita, 1980—; pres. S.E. Moyers & Assocs., Inc., Wichita, 1980—; dir. Inst. of Logopedics, Wichita, 1984—. Bd. dirs. Wichita Youth Home, 1977-80. Served to lt. USNR, 1962-65. Republican. Presbyterian.

MUCCIOLI, ANNA-MARIA, artist, gallery owner; b. Detroit, Apr. 23, 1922; d. Anthony and Josephine (Coccardi) DiPascale; m. Joseph E. Muccioli, Dec. 26, 1942; children—Ronald, Nathan, Edward, James. Student, Soc. Arts and Crafts (now Ctr. for Creative Studies-Coll. Artland Design). Exhbns. include: Ford Motor Co. Art Exhbn. (17 award 1979), 1961-79, Scarab Club-Watercolor Exhbn. (3d prize 1971), 1965-81, Artists Market Drawing and Print Show, 1966, Ann Arbor St. Art Fair, 1966, 67, Lafayette Park Community Assn. (1st place in watercolor 1967), 1967-69, Detroit-Windsor Internat. Freedom Festival, Art Competition (2d place, honorable mention) 1967, 68, Mich. Watercolor Soc. Travelling Show (honorable mention), 1968-71, Mich. State Fair Art Exhibit, 1968-78, Butler Inst. Am. Art, Youngstown, Ohio, 1969, Am. Watercolor Soc., Nat. Acad. Galleries, N.Y.C., 1971, Nat. Art Club N.Y., 1971, Scarab Club Silver Medal Exhbn. (honorable mention in sculpture), 1971-79, Watercolor Soc. Ala., Birmingham Mus. Arts, 1974, Art Ctr. Fibers Exhbn., Mt. Clemens, Mich., 1977. Mem. Founders Soc. Detroit Inst. Arts, Friends Modern Art. Address: 511 Beaubien St Detroit MI 48266

MUCKALA, KENNETH ARTHUR, physician; b. New York Mills, Minn., Feb. 16, 1942; s. William Arthur and Beatrice (Tuuppukka) M.; m. Linda Joanne Galberg, July 13, 1963; children—David, Jill, Jane. Student St. Cloud State Coll. 1963; B.S. in Medicine, U. S.D., 1965; M.D., U. Minn., 1967. Diplomate Am. Bd. Family Practice. Intern Sioux Valley Hosp., Sioux Falls, S.D., 1967-68; gen. practice medicine Vermillion Med. Clinic, S.D., 1968-74; staff student health service U. S.D., 1968-74; staff Wadena Med. Ctr., Minn., 1974—; bd. dirs. Found. Health Care Evaluation, Mpls., 1982. Contbr. articles to profl. jours. Chmn. Wadena County Republican Party, 1982—. Fellow Am. Acad. Family Physicians; mem. Minn. Med. Assn. (chmn. hosp. med. staff 1983—). Lutheran. Home: 311 10th St SW Wadena MN 56482 Office: Wadena Med Ctr Ltd 4 NW Deerwood St Wadena MN 56482

MUCKERMAN, RICHARD IGNATIUS CHRISTOPHER, physician; b. St. Louis, Feb. 23, 1922; s. Richard Christopher and Rozalia Monica (Medler) M.; m. Barbara Lee Hagnaver, Jan. 8, 1949; children—Barbara, Richard C., Diane, Margo. Student, Georgetown U., 1939-42; M.D., St. Louis U., 1945. Diplomate Am. Bd. Ob-Gyn. Intern St. John's Hosp., St. Louis, 1945-46, resident in ob-gyn, 1948-50; chmn. dept. ob-gyn St. John's Mercy Med. Ctr., St. Louis, 1963-74, chief of staff, 1965—. Served to capt. M.C., U. S. Army, 1948-50. Fellow Am. Coll. Ob-Gyn, ACS, Central Assn. Ob-Gyn; mem. AMA. Republican. Roman Catholic. Home: 1314 Log Cabin Ln Saint Louis MO 63124 Office: Mercy Doctors Bldg 621 S New Ballas Saint Louis MO 63141

MUDGE, LEWIS SEYMOUR, theologian, educator, university dean; b. Phila., Oct. 22, 1929; s. Lewis Seymour and Anne Evelyn (Bolton) M.; m. Jean Bruce McClure, June 15, 1957; children—Robert Seymour, William McClure, Anne Evelyn. B.A., Princeton U., 1951, M.Div., 1955, Ph.D., 1961; B.A. with honors in Theology, Oxford U., 1954, M.A., 1958. Ordained to ministry Presbyterian Ch., 1955. Presbyn. univ. pastor Princeton U., N.J., 1955-56; sec. dept. theology World Alliance Ref. Chs., Geneva, 1957-62; minister to coll. Amherst Coll., Mass., 1962-68, asst. prof. philosophy and religion, 1962-64, assoc. prof., 1964-70, prof. philosophy and religion, 1970-76, chmn. dept. philosophy and religion, 1968-69, 75-76; dean faculty, prof. theology McCormick Theol. Sem., Chgo., 1976—; mem. Commn. on Faith and Order, Nat. Council Chs., 1965-71; sec. spl. com. on confession faith United Presbyn. Ch., 1965-67, chmn. spl. com. on theology of the call, 1968-72; chmn. Theol. Commn., U.S. Consultation on Ch. Union, 1977—; co-chmn. Internat. Ref.-Roman Cath. Dialogue Commn., 1983—. Author: One Church: Catholic and Reformed, 1963; Is God Alive?, 1963; Why Is the Church in the World?, 1967; The Crumbling Walls, 1970; also articles and revs. Editor: Essays on Biblical Interpretation (Paul Ricoeur), 1980. Pres. Westminster Found. in New Eng., 1963-67; chmn. bd. Nat. Vocation Agy., 1972-75. Mem. Phi Beta Kappa. Democrat. Home: 1218 E Madison Park Ave Chicago IL 60615 Office: McCormick Theol Sem 5555 S Woodlawn Ave Chicago IL 60637

MUEHLEIS, VICTOR EMANUEL, business executive; b. Schwaebisch Gmuend, W.Ger., May 12, 1926; came to U.S., 1957. s. Victor E. and Ernestine (Kleile) M.; m. Ilse Herta Benz; 1 son, Peter-Michael. B.S., Lakeland Coll., 1972; M.S. in Anatomy, Med. Coll. Wis., 1975; D.D.S., Marquette U., 1979. Ptnr., Benz & Co., Ulm, W.Ger., 1949-57; with W.W. Jung & Co., C.P.A.s, Sheboygan, Wis., 1957-67; v.p. fin. Sheboygan Paper Box Co., 1967-77, pres., 1977—, also dir.; v.p., dir. T & L Realty Corp.; v.p., chmn. exec. com. Chilton-Globe, Inc., Manitowoc, Wis.; dir. Rockline Inc., Sheboygan. Served with German Army, 1944-45. Mem. Nat. Assn. Accts. (pres. chpt., dir. 1974-75). Republican. Lutheran. Clubs: Pine Hills Country (Sheboygan); Kohler (Wis.) Sports Core. Office: Sheboygan Paper Box Co 716 Clara Ave Sheboygan WI 53081

MUEHRCKE, ROBERT CARL, medical educator; b. Cin., Aug. 4, 1921; s. Bernard and Otillia Muehrcke; m. JoAnn Medenwaldt; children—Robert, Allan, Conrad, Derek, Eric, Michael, John. B.S., U. Ill., 1947, M.S., 1952, M.D., 1952. Diplomate Am. Bd. Internal Medicine. Intern Cin. Gen. Hosp., 1952-53; resident U. Ill. Hosp., Chgo., 1953-55; fellow U. London Postgrad. Med. Sch., 1956-57; dir. West Suburban Kidney Ctr., Oak Park, Ill., 1968—, Nephrology Assocs. of No. Ill., Oak Park, 1968—; dir. med. edn. West Suburban Hosp. Med. Ctr., Oak Park, 1965—; prof. medicine Rush Med. Coll., Chgo., 1977—; sec. Muehrcke Family Found., Oak Brook, Ill; vis. prof. Taiwan U. Med. Sch., Republic of China. Served to lt. inf. U.S. Army, 1945. Decorated Purple Heart with 3 oak leaf clusters, Bronze Star with 2 oak leaf clusters, Combat Infantryman's badge; Ill. Kidney Found. grantee, Chgo., 1983. Fellow ACP; (gov. adviser 1971-83, gen. chmn. ann. session 1973); mem. Chgo. Soc. Internal Medicine (pres. 1978), Chgo. Med. Soc. (pres. Aux Plaines br. 1971), Heart Assn. of West Cook County (pres. 1971-73). Club: Mountain Oyster (Tucson). Avocation: collector of oriental art. Home: 9 Windsor Dr Oak Brook IL 60521

MUELLER, DON SHERIDAN, school administrator; b. Cleve., Nov. 4, 1927; s. Don P. and Selma Christina (Ungericht) M.; B.S., Mt. Union Coll., 1948; M.A., U. Mich., 1952; Ed.S., Mich. State U., 1968; Ph.D., Clayton U., 1977; m. Vivian Jean Santrock, Aug. 27, 1947; children—Carl Frederick, Cathy Ann. Tchr., Benton-Harbor Fair Plain (Mich.) Schs., 1947-52; dir. music edn. Okemos (Mich.) Pub. Schs., 1952-64; jr-sr. high prin. Dansville (Mich.) Schs., 1964-68; prin. DeWitt (Mich.) High Sch., 1968-73; supt. Carsonville-Port Sanilac Schs., Carsonville, Mich., 1973—. Recipient Community Leader of Am. award, 1968, 72, 73-74; Acad. Am. Educators award, 1973-74. Mem. Am., Mich. assns. sch. adminstrs., Mich. Assn. Sch. Bds., NEA, Assn. Supervision and Curriculum Devel., Clinton Prins. Assn. (pres. 1972-73), Ingham Prins. Assn. (pres. 1967-70), Mich. Sch. Band/Orch. Assn. (sec. 1962-63, pres. dist. 5 1958-60), Okemos Edn. Assn. (pres. 1962-63), River Area Supts. Assn. (pres. 1979-80). Home: 188 S High St Box 257 Carsonville MI 48419 Office: 100 N Goetze Carsonville MI 48419

MUELLER, JAMES STEPHEN, project engineer; b. Chgo., Sept. 9, 1951; s. Frank Joseph and Lorraine Eileen (Anderson) M. B.S. in Engring., U. Ill.-Chgo., 1973. Acct. Bell & Howell, Chgo., 1969-79; sr. project engr. Dynascan, Chgo., 1979—; cons. Dynaphonics, Northbrook, Ill., 1982—. Avocations: personal computing; tennis; golf; canoeing. Home: 9350 Hamilton Ct Dr Des Plaines IL 60016 Office: Dynascan Corp Telemotive Div 6460 W Cortland St Chicago IL 60635

MUELLER, JOHN EDWARD, educator; b. Wishek, N.D., Nov. 5, 1939; s. Walter and Hulda F. (Buchholz) M.; m. Donna Mae Miller, Aug. 19, 1962. B.S., U. N.D., 1961; M.S., St. Cloud State U., 1968. Cert. tchr., Minn.; cert. data educator. Tchr., Anoka-Hennepin Dist. II, Coon Rapids, Minn., 1961-67, 68—; faculty St. Cloud State U., Minn., 1967-68; demonstrator/developer In-Tech, Coon Rapids, 1983, 84; mem. com. software evaluation Minn. Dept. Edn., 1983, 84. Instr., CAP, 1965-71. Served with U.S. Army, 1958-65. Mem. Anoka-Hennepin Edn. Assn. (bldg. rep. 1982-84), Minn. Edn. Assn., NEA, Minn. Bus. Educators. Avocation: flying. Home: 14633 Bowers Dr Anoka MN 55303 Office: 11299 Hanson Blvd Coon Rapids MN 55433

MUELLER, ROLAND FREDERICK, surgeon; b. St. Joseph, Mo., Aug. 29, 1905; s. Charles Frederick and Elizabeth (Krebs) M.; A.A., Kansas City (Mo.) U., 1925; student Kans. U., 1926; M.D. cum laude, Washington U., 1929; m. Norma Grace Johnson, 1982; children by previous marriage—Nancy (Mrs. Robert H. Pecha), Judith (Mrs. Roger W. Hall), Kathryn Lucile (Mrs. Rex Logemann). Resident in surgery Barnes Hosp., St. Louis, 1929-33; instr. surgery Washington U., 1930-33; practice surgery, Canton, Mo., 1933-37; chief surgeon Two Harbors (Minn.) Hosp., 1937-46, also asso. chief surgeon Duluth, Mesabi & Iron Range R.R., 1937-46; practice surgery, Lincoln, Nebr., 1949—; attending surgeon St. Elizabeth's Hosp., Bryan Meml. Hosp.; prof. surgery Creighton U.; cons. VA Hosp., Lincoln; pres. Lincoln Community Blood Bank, 1976, 78, States Oil Royalty Co. U.S. del. 7th Inter-Am. Congress Surgery, Peru, 1950. Recipient 25 Year Faculty award Creighton U., Outstanding Prof. in Surgery award, 1978. Fellow A.C.S.; mem. Central Surg. Assn., Southwestern Surg. Congress, Internat. Soc. Surgery, Peruvian Acad. Surgery (hon.), Am. Thyroid Assn., AMA, Nebr. State, Lancaster County (pres. 1977) med. assns., Phi Beta Pi, Alpha Omega Alpha. Clubs: University (Lincoln); Washington University (St. Louis). Contbr. articles to profl jours. Home: 1000 Fall Creek Rd Lincoln NE 68510 Office: 1000 Fall Creek Rd Lincoln NE 68510

MUELLER, ROSE ANNA MARIA, language arts educator; b. Bisacquino, Italy, Dec. 24, 1948; came to U.S., 1954, naturalized, 1966; d. Vincenzo and Antonina (Adamo) Siino; m. Robert Raymond Mueller, June 21, 1971; children—Benjamin, Christopher. B.A., Hunter Coll., 1971; M.A., CCNY, 1977, Ph.D., 1977. Instr. lang. arts Am. U., Washington, 1977-79, Ill. Benedictine U., Lisle, 1979-81, Morton Coll., Cicero, Ill., 1982—. Author poetry; translator Italian Poetry Today (poetry), 1981. Nat. Endowment for the Humanities fellow, 1985; mem. MLA, Ill. Lang. Tchrs. Assn., Ill. Region Honors Council, Sigma Delta Pi. Home: 102 N Kensington LaGrange IL 60525 Office: Morton Coll 3801 S Central Cicero IL 60650

MUELLER, SHARRON ANN, insurance executive; b. Cleve., Mar. 12, 1941; d. Francis Joseph and Elizabeth Jane (Romp) O'Neill; m. Joseph B. McPhilliamy, June 29, 1963 (div. Mar. 1975); children—Raymond Joseph, Michael Shaun; m. Richard Mueller, Dec. 17, 1976; stepchildren—Richard D. Mueller, Rosalind D. Mueller Karshner. Student Capital U., 1959-61. Cert. profl. ins. woman. Personal lines mgr. Dawson Ins. Co., Rocky River, Ohio, 1971-75; account sect. Ins. Underwriters Co., Lakewood, Ohio, 1975-77,

Graydon Co., Parma, Ohio, 1977-78; officer mgr. Four Star Ins. Agy., Parma, 1978-82; asst. account exec. Republic Hogg, Robinson of Ohio, Inc., Cleve., 1982-85; sec. Project Invest, Cleve., 1979—; instr. Cleve. State U. Careers Day, 1982, Ins. Women of Cleve., 1981; speaker-instr. SBA, 1980—. Sec., Concordia Lutheran Ch. Bd., Independence, 1979-82; sec. and pres. Xenia Jaycee Wives (Ohio), 1966-69; petitioner Workers Compensation Issue, State of Ohio, 1981-82; sec. Congress Sq. II Homeowners Assn., Middleburg Heights, Ohio, 1973-76; mem. Mothers Against Drunk Drivers, 1982-83. Named Jaycee Wife of Year, 1969. Mem. Ins. Women of Cleve. (Ins. Woman of Yr. 1983, program chmn. 1982-83, edn. chmn. 1981-82, dir. 1980-83, 2d v.p. 1984-85), Ins. Bd. Cleve. (fellow), U.S. Power Squadron, Exec. Women's Roundtable. Republican. Clubs: Normandy Music, Normandy Sports (Parma). Office: Republic Hogg Robinson of Ohio Inc 3690 Orange Pl Beachwood OH 44122

MUELLER, TIMOTHY CRAIG, pharmacist, pharmacy executive; b. Jamestown, N.D., April 8, 1951; s. Theodore and Ruby Rose (Zottnick) M.; m. Betty Ann Luetticke, Oct. 25, 1975; children—Vanessa Elizabeth, Ryan Timothy. B.S., U. Minn., 1974. Registered pharmacist, Minn. Pharmacy intern Supplee's 7-Hi Enterprises, Minnetonka, Minn., 1973-75, staff pharmacist, 1975-77, asst. mgr., staff pharmacist, 1977-80, chief pharmacist, mgr., 1980—; preceptor, cons. U. Minn. Coll. Pharmacy, 1980—. Recipient Melendy award U. Minn., 1971. Mem. Nat. Assn. Retail Druggists, Minn. State Pharm. Assn., U. Minn. Alumni Assn., U. Minn. Alumni Club, Maple Plain Jaycees (advt. chmn. 1979), Rho Chi Soc. Republican. Lutheran. Club: Sunday Nite Caps (pres. 1984-85) (Long Lake, Minn.). Avocations: sports, fishing, wild life print collecting, coin collecting. Home: 1470 Rainbow Ave Maple Plain MN 55359

MUELLER, VAN DYCK, educational administration educator, consultant; b. Manistique, Mich., June 23, 1929; s. William Frederick and Alice Margaret (Van Dyck) M.; m. Mildred Irene Kerridge, Feb. 18, 1952; children—Vanessa, Kerry, Edith. B.S., Central Mich. U., 1951; M.A., U. Mich., 1958; Ed.D., Mich. State U., 1964. Tchr. Mt. Morris High Sch., Mich., 1954-57; high sch. prin. Ashley High Sch., Mich., 1957-59; supt. Ashley/Ithaca Schs., 1959-62; prof. dept. ednl. adminstrn. U. Minn., Mpls., 1964—; Minn. coordinator Edn. Policy Fellowship Program, Washington, 1978—; mem. adv. bd. Bush Pub. Sch. Execs., St. Paul, 1976—; cons. Univ. Research Consortium, Mpls., 1983—. Contbr. articles to profl. jours. Pres. Minn. PTA, St. Paul, 1977-80; v.p. Nat. PTA, Chgo., 1984—; commr. Edn. Commn. of States, Denver, 1978-82. Served to 1st lt. U.S. Army, 1951-54. Recipient Disting. Alumni award Dept. Adminstrn. and Higher Edn., Mich. State U., East Lansing, 1980. Mem. Am. Edn. Fin. Assn. (bd. dirs. 1984—, editor yearbook 1984, 85), Am. Assn. Sch. Adminstrs., Am. Ednl. Research Assn., Minn. Assn. Sch. Adminstrs., Phi Delta Kappa (disting. service award 1980). Mem. Democratic Farm Labor Party. Methodist. Home: 3609 Maplewood Dr Minneapolis MN 55418 Office: 224 Peik Hall U Minn 159 Pillsbury Dr SE Minneapolis MN 55455

MUELLER, VIOLET HUBBARD HOLSINGER, designer, educator; b. Belleville, Ill., Mar. 16, 1907; d. Jacob Wilson and Violet Eldro (Hubbard) Holsinger; m. Harry Edgar Mueller, Aug. 25, 1932. Student McKendree Coll., 1924-26, Parsons Sch. Design, 1926-28; B.S., U. Ill., 1937. Tchr., Granite City Schs., Ill., 1929-32, Salem Schs., Ill., 1941-42, 46-50; designer Stix Baer & Fullar, St. Louis, 1952-79; interior designer Cons. in Design and Color, Belleville, Ill., 1979—. Design works include: interior Grace United Methodist Ch., Salem, 1970. Republican. Methodist. Avocation: designing. Office: Cons in Design and Color 2920 W Main St Belleville IL 62221

MUELLER, WERNER DIEBOLT, lawyer; b. Cleve., Aug. 17, 1925; s. Omar Eugene and Elsa Louise (Weideman) M.; m. Margaret Crowl Reid, Sept. 6, 1952; children—Frederick R., John M., Lydia W., Felice C., Omar Eugene II. B.A. cum laude, Harvard U., 1949, J.D., 1954. Bar: Ohio 1954. Mgmt. trainee Central Nat. Bank, Cleve., 1954-57, trust officer, 1958-68, v.p., 1968-73; v.p., mgr. personal trust div., Union Commerce Bank, Cleve., 1973; ptnr. Nicola, Gudbranson, Mueller & Cooper, 1974—. Past treas., trustee Children's Aid Soc., Cleve.; trustee Standard Products Charitable Found., Cleve. Served with AUS, 1943-46, ETO. Mem. Ohio Bar Assn., Greater Cleve. Bar Assn. Republican. Presbyterian. Clubs: Union, Tavern (Cleve.); Kirtland Country (Willoughby, Ohio); Winous Point Shooting (Point Clinton, Ohio). Home: 8848 Music St Russell Twp PO Novelty OH 44072 Office: Nicola Gudbranson Mueller & Cooper 2750 Terminal Tower Cleveland OH 44113

MUELLER, WILLYS FRANCIS, JR., pathologist; b. Detroit, July 15, 1934; s. Willys Francis and Antoinette Frances (Stimac) M.; M.D., U. Mich., 1959; m. Dolores Mae Vella, Aug. 25, 1956; children—Renee Ann, Willys Francis, Paul E., Mark A., Maria D., Beth M., Matthew P. Intern, Providence Hosp., Detroit, 1959-60, resident, 1960-62; resident Wayne County Gen. Hosp., Eloise, Mich., 1962-64; asst. pathologist Grace Hosp., Detroit, 1964; asso. pathologist Hurley Hosp., Flint, Mich., 1964-66; asso. pathologist Hurley Med. Center, Flint, 1968—, dir. lab., 1981—; chief dep. med. examiner Genesee County, Mich., 1971—; pres. Pathology Assos. Inc.; assoc. clin. prof. Coll. Human Medicine, Mich. State U.; dir. blood services Wolverine region ARC, 1981—. Served with M.C., U.S. Army, 1966-68. Fellow Am. Soc. Clin. Pathologists, Coll. Am. Pathologists, Am. Acad. Forensic Scis.; mem. AMA (Physician's Recognition award 1974-77, 78-81, 81-84, 85-87), Genesee County, Mich. State med. socs., Mich. Soc. Pathologists (sec.-treas. 1981-83, pres. elect 1984, pres. 1985), Nat. Assn. Med. Examiners. Republican. Roman Catholic. Club: K.C. Editor: Bull. of Genesee County Med. Soc. Home: 13335 Pomona Dr Fenton MI 48430 Office: Dept Pathology Hurley Med Center Flint MI 48502

MUELLNER, JOHN PHILLIP, librarian, educator; b. Chgo., June 20, 1936; s. John William and Catherine (McMahon) M.; div.; children—April, Phillip, Erich, Owen. A.A., Wright Jr. Coll., 1957; B.E., Chgo. State U., 1960, M.E., 1963; postgrad. Loyola U., Chgo., 1964. Cert. librarian, high sch. English tchr., elem. tchr., Ill. Tchr.-librarian Chgo. pub. schs., 1958—; librarian Schiller Park Pub. Library (Ill.), 1964—. Home: 2602 N Racine Chicago IL 60614 Office: Schiller Park Pub Library 4200 Old River Rd Schiller Park IL 60176

MUGGLI, CLARA BARBARA, civic worker; b. Hebron, N.D., Nov. 10, 1927; d. Matt and Mary (Schneider) Maershbecker; student Dickinson State Coll.; m. Ewald Muggli, Sept. 27, 1948; children—Allen, Linda, Joyce, Carol, Gary, Holly. Tchr. rural schs., 1945-48; county chmn. establishment Bookmobile, 1960, bd. dirs., 1960—; bd. dirs., librarian Glen Ullin (N.D.) Public Library, 1956—; social services home health aide, 1972-76; co-owner, mgr. Rock Mus., Glen Ullin, 1970—, also instr. rocks and minerals, 1970—; sec. Glen Ullin Hist. Soc., 1978—; tchr. Sacred Heart Ch., 1969—, dir. religious edn., 1982—; weekly columnist Glen Ullin Times, 1977-84. Recipient State Homemakers award for Cultural Arts, 1975; K. C. Religious Edn. award, 1979; Best of Show award Dakota Gem and Mineral Show, 1979, 84. Mem. Morton County Hist. Soc., Central Dakota Gem and Mineral Assn., Badlands and Knife River Rock Clubs, Art Assn., Am. Legion Aux. Clubs: Homemakers. Co-author: Glen Ullin Yesteryears, 1983, A Century of Catholicism, 1984. Home: 701 Oak Ave Glen Ullin ND 58631

MUHAMMAD, FAQUIR, internist, family practitioner; b. Pali, Rajistan, India, Dec. 5, 1947; s. Allah Rakha and Aisha M.; m. Mariam Jamila, 1968; children—Abdul Malik, Abdul Khaliq, Sabina, Nila. Came to U.S., 1972, naturalized, 1983. H.S.C., Govt. Coll., Hyderabad, Pakistan, 1966; M.B., B.S., Liaquat Med. Coll., Sind U., Hyderabad, Pakistan, 1971. Diplomate Am. Bd. Internal Medicine. Intern, Kenmore Mercy Hosp., N.Y., 1973-74; med. resident Martland Hosp., Newark, 1974-77; emergency room physician Wilson Hosp., Johnson City, N.Y., 1977-78; pvt. practice medicine specializing in internal medicine and family practice, St. Louis, 1978—; mem. staff Christian Hosp., St. Louis, 1978—, De Paul Health Ctr., Bridgeton, Mo., 1979—. Mem. ACP, St. Louis Met. Med. Soc., Mo. State Med. Assn., So. Med. Assn. Islamic religion. Club: Vic Tanney Health (St. Louis). Office: 11155 Dunn Rd Suite 210E Saint Louis MO 63136 also 3394 McKelvey Rd Suite 106 Bridgeton MO 63044

MUHIC, ALLEN RAYMOND, environmental planner; b. Cleve., Aug. 7, 1952; s. Nick F. and Betty (Szoke) M. B.S.C.E., MIT, 1975, B.S. in Life Scis., 1975. Aquatic ecologist, planner Howard Needles Tammen & Bergendoff, Cleve., 1975-78; environ. project mgr. URS Dalton, Cleve., 1978—; cons. Recipient cert. of appreciation Internat. Joint Commn., 1978, Nat. Wildlife Fedn., 1982. Mem. Nat. Assn. Environ. Profls., Air Pollution Control Assn. Democrat. Home: 11406 Fowlers Mill Rd Chardon OH 44024 Office: 3605 Warrensville Center Rd Cleveland OH 44122

MUHLENBRUCH, CARL WILLIAM, mgmt. cons.; b. Decatur, Ill., Nov. 21, 1915; s. Carl W. and Clara Agnes (Theobald) M.; B.C.E., U. Ill., 1937, C.E., 1945; M.C.E., Carnegie Inst. Tech., 1943; m. Agnes M. Kringel, Nov. 22, 1939; children—Phyllis Elaine Muhlenbruch Wallace, Joan Carol Muhlenbruch Wenk. Research engr. Aluminum Research Labs., Pitts., 1937-39; cons. civil engr., 1939-50; mem. faculty Carnegie Inst. Tech., 1939-48; assoc. prof. civil engring. Northwestern U., 1948-54; pres. Tec-Search, Inc., Wilmette, Ill., 1954-67, chmn. bd. dirs., 1967—; pres. Profl. Centers Bldg. Corp., 1961-76. Bd. dirs. Aid Assn. for Lutherans, 1964-76; mem. Bd. Local Improvements Wilmette, 1972—. Registered profl. engr., Ill., Pa. Mem. Am. Indsl. Devel. Council, ASTM (Sanford Thompson award 1945), Am. Planning Assn., ASCE, Am. Soc. Engring. Edn., Nat. Soc. Profl. Engrs., Sigma Xi, Tau Beta Phi. Republican. Lutheran-Mo. Synod (dir., mem. exec. com., vice chmn. 1965-79). Club: Rotary Internat. (dist. gov. 1980-81). Author: Experimental Mechanics and Properties of Materials, 1955; contbr. articles to engring. jours. Home: 4071 Fairway Dr Wilmette IL 60091 Office: 1000 Skokie Blvd Wilmette IL 60091

MUIR, RUTH BROOKS, counselor, substance abuse service coordinator; b. Washington, Nov. 27, 1924; s. Charles and Adelaide Chenery (Masters) B.; m. Robert Mathew Muir, Nov. 26, 1947; children—Robert Brooks, Martha Louise, Heather Sue. B.A. in Art, Rollins Coll., Winter Park, Fla., 1947; M.A. in Rehab. Counseling, U. Iowa, 1979. Cert. substance abuse counselor, Iowa. Program advisor Iowa Meml. Union, Iowa City, 1959-66; counselor, coordinator Mid Eastern Council on Chem. Abuse, Iowa City, 1976-81; patient rep. Univ. Hosp., Iowa City, 1982-85; research project interviewer dept. psychiatry U. Iowa Coll. Medicine, 1985—. Treas. bd. dirs. Crisis Ctr., Iowa City, 1975-77; sec. council elders Sr. Citizens Ctr., Iowa City, 1980-82; pres. Unitarian-Universalist Women's Fedn., Iowa City. Mem. Nat. Soc. Patient Reps., Iowa Hosp. Assn., Substance Abuse Assn. Iowa. Unitarian. Home: 6 Glendale Ct Iowa City IA 52240 Office: 6 Glendale Ct Iowa City IA 52242

MUKALLA, CLAUDETTE JOAN, publisher; b. Detroit, June 14, 1946; d. Michael A. and Lily (Sayegh) M.; Grad. high sch., Detroit. Asst. dir. Librarie du Liban, Beirut, Lebanon, 1972-73; owner, operator Internat. Book Ctr., Troy, Mich., 1973—. Vol., Beaumont Hosp., Oak Park, Mich., 1975. Mem. Nat. Women's Book Assn., Arab Am. U. Grads., Mich. Assn. Ednl. Reps., Troy C. of C. Republican. Roman Catholic. Avocations: green belt karate, oil painting, yoga. Office: Internat Book Ctr PO Box 295 Troy MI 48099

MUKHERJEE, KALINATH, metallurgical engineering educator, researcher; b. Calcutta, India, Feb. 19, 1932; naturalized U.S. citizen, 1966; s. Ramkrisna and Saraju M.; m. Patricia Stapleton, Aug. 20, 1959; children—Joia S., Maia S., Janam S. B.E., Calcutta U., India, 1956; M.S., U. Ill.-Urbana, 1959; Ph.D., 1963. Metallurgist, Indian Iron and Steel Co., 1956-57; research asst. U. Ill.-Urbana, 1957-63, research assoc. and instr., 1963-64; asst. prof. SUNY-Stony Brook, 1964-67; assoc. prof. Poly. Inst. Bklyn., 1967-72, prof., 1972-80, dept. head metallurgy, Poly. Inst. N.Y., 1974-80; prof. Mich. State U., East Lansing, 1980—. Recipient Disting. Tchr. award Poly Inst. N.Y., 1971, Disting. Prof. award, 1979. Fellow Am. Soc. Metals, AAAS; mem. AIME, Am. Phys. Soc., Am. Soc. Engring. Edn., Sigma Xi, Alpha Sigma Mu. Democrat. Club: Metals Sci. of N.Y. Co-editor: Lasers in Metallurgy, 1982; sr. editor Met./Mat. Sci. Edn. Yearbook, 1974—; contbr. numerous articles to profl. jours. Office: Dept Metallurgy Mech and Material Sci Mich State U East Lansing MI 48824

MUKOYAMA, JAMES HIDEFUMI, JR., securities executive; b. Chgo., Aug. 3, 1944; s. Hidefumi James and Miye (Maruyama) M.; m. Kyung Ja Woo, June 20, 1971; children—Sumi Martha, Jae Thomas. B.A. in English, U. Ill., 1965, M.A. in Social Studies, 1966; honor grad. U.S. Army Inf. Sch., 1966; grad. U.S. Army Command and Gen. Staff Coll., 1979, U.S. Army War Coll., 1984. Registered prin., sr. registered options prin. Nat. Assn. Securities Dealers. Asst. dept. mgr. Mitsui & Co. (USA), Inc., Chgo., 1971-74; mem. Chgo. Bd. Options Exchange, 1974-75; v.p. 1st Omaha Securities, Chgo., 1975-76, Heartland Securities, Chgo., 1976—; allied mem. N.Y. Stock Exchange; v.p. Lefta Advt., Chgo., 1976—. Mem. exec. bd. Hillside Free Methodist Ch., Evanston, Ill., 1982—. Served with U.S. Army, 1965-70; col. Res., 1971—. Decorated Silver Star, Purple Heart, 3 Bronze Stars; Vietnamese Army Cross of Gallantry; Japanese Army Parachutist badge; recipient cert. of merit Korean Army, others. Mem. U. Ill. Alumni Assn. (life), Assn. U.S. Army, Mil. Order Purple Heart, Am. Legion, Res. Officers Assn. Home: 4009 Tracey Ct Glenview IL 60025 Office: Heartland Securities Inc 208 S LaSalle St Chicago IL 60604

MULARZ, EDWARD JULIUS, II, aerospace engineer; b. Lakewood, Ohio, Nov. 24, 1943; s. Edward J. and Loyola M. (Leonard) M.; m. Cecilia L. Lorenger, June 17, 1967; children—Edward Julius III, Caroline M. B. Mech. Engring., U. Detroit, 1966; Ph.D., Northwestern U., 1971. Aerospace engr. propulsion lab. U.S. Army Research Tech. Lab., Cleve., 1971-81, head combustion fundamentals sect., 1981-84, chief modeling and verification br., 1984—. Contbr. articles to profl. jours. Fellow AIAA (assoc.); mem. ASME, Combustion Inst., Train Collectors Assn. Roman Catholic. Avocations: toy trains; softball; racquetball. Home: 4066 Brewster Dr Westlake OH 44145 Office: US Army Research Tech Lab Propulsion Lab MS5-11 21000 Brook Park Rd Cleveland OH 44135

MULARZ, STANLEY LEON, credit information services executive; b. Chgo., Apr. 11, 1923; s. Stanley A. and Frances (Baycar) M.; A.B., St. Louis U., 1944; M.A., De Paul U., 1956; M.B.A., U. Chgo., 1960; Ph.D., Loyola U., Chgo., 1971; m. Lillian M. (dec.); children—James P., Thomas E., Geraldine E., Joanne F., John F., Paul S., Donna M. Tchr., Benedictine Jr. Coll., Savannah, Ga., 1945-46, Grant Community High Sch., Fox Lake, Ill., 1946-47; fgn. corr. Continental Ill. Nat. Bank, 1947-48; tchr., adminstr. Morgan Park Mil. Acad. and Jr. Coll., 1948-51; mgr. Spiegel, Inc., 1951-52; regional credit mgr. Aldens, Inc., Chgo., 1952-54, ops. mgr., 1954-67, mgr. indsl. relations, 1967-68, credit div. group mgr., 1968-69; pres. Credit Info. Corp., 1969-79, Trans Union Credit Info. Co., Chgo., 1979—; v.p. Trans Union Systems Corp., Chgo., 1972-79; mem. consumer adv. council Fed. Res. Bd., 1981-83; lectr., adv. consumer edn. Mem. Gov.'s Commn. Schs./Bus. Mgmt. Task Force; chmn. State Info. Systems Com., 1974-77. Trustee, Felician Coll., 1982—. Mem. Internat. Consumer Credit Assn. (pres. Dist. V 1975-77), Mchts. Research Council (dir., treas. 1975—), Associated Credit Burs. (dir. 1978—), Soc. Cert. Consumer Credit Execs. (pres. 1980-81), Am. Statis. Assn., U. Chgo. Exec. Program Club, Phi Delta Kappa (pres. chpt. 1970-71). Office: Trans Union Credit Info 111 W Jackson Blvd Chicago IL 60604

MULHALL, EVELYN STARR, insurance agency executive; b. Oak Park, Ill., May 9, 1947; d. Allan Baker and Charlotte Catherine (Link) Frost; student U. Ill., 1965-66; 1 dau., Valerie Lynn. Ins. dept. supr. Great Lakes Mortgage Corp., Chgo., 1966-70; account exec., v.p. Forest Agy., Inc., Oak Park, Ill., 1973-84 Bd. dirs. Hephzibah Children's Assn., Oak Park, Ill., 1980-84, corr. sec., 1982-84. C.P.C.U. Mem. Soc. Chartered Property and Casualty Underwriters, Nat. Assn. Ins. Women. Home: 533 S Clarence Oak Park IL 60304 Office: 150 S Wacker Chicago IL 60606

MULLALLY, PIERCE HARRY, steel company executive; b. Cleve., Oct. 6, 1918; s. Pierce Harry and Laura (Lynch) M.; student U. Western Ont., 1935; B.S., John Carroll U., 1939; M.D., St. Louis U., 1943; m. Mary Eileen Murphy, Feb. 22, 1943; children—Mary Kathleen, Pierce Harry. Intern, St. Vincent Charity Hosp., Cleve., 1943, resident in surgery, 1944, 47-50, staff surgeon, 1951-62, head peripheral vascular surgery, 1963-76, dir. med. edn., 1967-73, dir. dept. surgery, 1968-75, trustee, 1977—; plant physician Republic Steel Corp., Cleve., 1952-68, med. dir., 1968-76, corp. dir. occupational medicine, 1976-84; cons. LTV Steel Co., 1984—; med. dir., chmn. med. adv. bd. Ohio Health Choice Plan Inc. Vice-chmn. Cleve. Clinic-Charity Hosp. Com. Surg. Residency Tng., 1970-78; health com. Bituminous Coal Operators Assn.; bd. dirs. Phoenix Theatre Ensemble, 1982—. Served to capt. U.S. Army, 1944-46; PTO. Diplomate Am. Bd. Surgery. Fellow ACS, Am. Coll. Angiology; mem. Am. Iron and Steel Inst. (chmn. health com. 1977-79), Am. Acad. Occupational Medicine, Am., Ohio occupational med. assns., Acad. Medicine, Cleve. (dir. 1969-72), Cleve. Surg. Soc., Western Res. Med. Dirs., Soc. Clin. Vascular Surgery. Roman Catholic. Clubs: Cleve. Skating, Cleve. Playhouse, Serra. Home: 2285 Harcourt Dr Cleveland Heights OH 44106

MULLANE, ROBERT E., manufacturing company executive; b. Cin., May 27, 1932; s. Robert E. and Marie Mullane; grad. Georgetown U., 1954, Harvard Bus. Sch., 1956; children—Katherine, Constance, Margaret, Sarah. With Wilson and Co., Bache and Co., A.A.V. Co., now pres., chmn. bd., chief exec. officer Bally Mfg. Corp., Chgo.; dir. Bally's Park Place, Inc. Office: Bally Mfg Corp 8700 W Bryn Mawr Chicago IL 60631*

MULLEN, EDWARD JOHN, Spanish language educator; b. Hackensack, N.J., July 12, 1942; s. Edward John and Elsie (Powell) M.; m Helen Cloe Braley, Apr. 3, 1971; children—Kathleen Jean, Julie Ann. B.A., W.Va. Wesleyan U., 1964; M.A., Northwestern U., 1965, Ph.D., 1968. Asst. prof. Spanish, Purdue U., Lafayette, Ind., 1967-71; assoc. prof. Spanish, U. Mo.-Columbia, 1971-78, prof., 1978—. Author: Carlos Pellicer, 1977; Langston Hughes in the Hispanic World, 1977; El cuento hispánico, 1984; The Life and Poems of a Cuban Slave, 1982. Woodrow Wilson fellow, 1965; Am. Council Learned Socs. grantee, 1979; recipient diploma of honor Instituto de Cultura Hispánica, 1964. Mem. MLA, Am. Assn. Tchrs. of Spanish and Portuguese, Langston Hughes Soc., Coll. Lang. Assn. Home: 207 Edgewood Ave Columbia MO 65203 Office: U Mo Columbia MO 65211

MULLEN, JOSEPH ALAN, advertising executive; b. Dubuque, Iowa, Nov. 9, 1945; s. Ralph Louis and Ann Mary (Biever) M.; m. Mary Lou Mulert, June 17, 1968; 1 dau., Teri Ann. B.A., Loras Coll., 1967. Salesman, KDUB-TV, Dubuque, Iowa, 1971-73; sales mgr. WYXE Radio, Madison, Wis., 1973-75; v.p. client services Dave Carman & Assocs. Advt. Agy., Madison, Wis., 1975-79; dir. advt. Tracor No., Inc., Middleton, Wis., 1979—; seminar leader U. Wis., 1978—; cons. lectr. Madison Area Tech. Coll., 1980—; teaching assoc. Am. Assn. Retired Execs., 1978—. Mem. Madison Advt. Fedn. Roman Catholic. Home: 157 W Goodland St Sun Prairie WI 53590 Office: 2551 W Beltline Hwy Middleton WI 53562

MULLER, CLAUDYA BURKETT, state librarian; b. Furth, Bavaria, Germany, Sept. 14, 1946; came to U.S., 1952; d. Ralph Leon and Elfiede Katherine (Hilpert) Burkett; m. William Albert Muller III, Dec. 12, 1965; 1 child, Martha Genevieve. B.A., Ga. So. Coll., 1967; M.L.S., Emory U., 1968. Asst. to head circulation Ga. State U., 1968-69; asst. dir. War Women Regional Library, Ga., 1970-72; assoc. dir. Ottumwa Heights Coll. Library, Ia., 1973; bookmobile librarian Gallia County Dist. Library, Ohio, 1976; dir. Jackson County Pub. Library, W.Va., 1976-78; dir. Worcester County Library, Snow Hill, Md., 1978-83; state librarian State of Iowa, Des Moines, 1983—. Editor: University Press Books for Public Libraries, 1979, 80; also proceedings. Tommie Dora Barker fellow, 1967; recipient W.Va. Communicators' Laurete award for Writing for Print, 1978; Good Citizenship award Rotary, Snow Hill, 1983. Mem. ALA, Pub. Library Assn., Library Adminstrn. and Mgmt. Assn. Roman Catholic. Office: State Library of Iowa Historical Bldg Des Moines IA 50319

MULLER, RICHARD W. (WILHELM GUSTAV), importer architectural textiles, consultant on fabrics, designer, writer, former operatic baritone; b. Cologne, Germany, Aug. 15, 1909; came to U.S., 1926; s. Richard Otto Andreas and Magda Maria (Fassbinder) Muller; m. Marjorie Kathryn Alcorn, Aug. 15, 1936; children—Richard L., Marshall K. Tchr.'s cert. Am. Conservatory of Music, Chgo., 1929; B.A., Sherwood Music Sch., 1934; postgrad engring. and writing, Northwestern U., 1940. Sec. Sherwood Music Sch., Chgo., 1930-31; maintenance supr. Sinclair Refining Co., Chgo., 1931-40; spl. tng. apprentice Stroock's Woolen Mills, Newburgh, N.Y., 1926-27; test engr., asst. shift supt. Buick div. Gen. Motors, Melrose Park, Ill., 1940-45; pres., prin. Richard W. Muller & Assocs., Chgo., 1946—; witness com. on trade, Ways and Means Com., U.S. Ho. of Reps., 1981. Designer Lyric Opera entries Venetian Nights, 1982 (1st place award 1982, 83, 1st place overall 1983); asst. Frank Lloyd Wright, Keland Home, Racine, Wis., 1958; boy soprano Cologne Cathedral, 1918-19. Mem. German Am. Nat. Congress; sustaining mem. Republican Nat. Com., 1979—. Club: Chgo. Corinthian Yacht. Home: 2076 Greenleaf Ave Chicago IL 60645 Office: Richard W Muller & Assocs 162 W Hubbard St Chicago IL 60610

MULLIGAN, BARBARA E., university official; b. Grand Rapids, Mich., June 25, 1927; d. Raymond Christopher and Gertrude (Moran) Mulligan; B.A., Marquette U., 1962, M.A., 1964. Instr. polit. sci., asst. dir. continuing edn. Alverno Coll., Milw., 1966-68, dir. continuing edn., 1968-71, asst. dean, 1971-72, co-dir. Research Center on Women, 1970-72; asst. dir. div. continuing edn., Marquette U., 1972-74, asso. dir. div. continuing edn. and summer sessions, 1974—, acting dir., 1979. Mem. Gov.'s Commn. Status of Women, 1967-71; gov.'s appointee Wis. Ednl. Approval Bd., 1968-71. First vice chmn. Wis. Women's Republican Club, 1964-68. Bd. dirs. Greater Milw. chpt. ARC, 1973-74. Mem. Adult Edn. Assn. Wis. (dir. 1969-71, 75-77), Wis. Polit. Sci. Assn. (treas. 1970-72), Milw. Council Adult Learning, Wis. Soc. Health and Tng., Nat. Univ. Extension Assn., Marquette U. Alumni Assn., AAUW, Am. Assn. Univ. Adminstrs. (dir. Delta chpt. 1975-76), Council on Continuing Edn. Unit, Am. Assn. Higher Edn., Smithsonian Assos. Home: 2703 N Hackett Ave Milwaukee WI 53211

MULLIGAN, WILLIAM HENRY, JR., library administrator; b. Bklyn., Apr. 10, 1948; s. William Henry and Aileen Katherine (Colvin) M.; m. Alice Patricia Gallagher, June 14, 1969; children—William Henry III, Robert Gallagher. A.B., Assumption Coll., 1970; A.M., Clark U., 1973, Ph.D., 1982. Historian, Northborough Am. Revolution Bicentennial Commn., Mass., 1974-75; instr. history Worcester Poly. Inst., Mass., 1975-77; asst. to dir. Regional Econ. Hist. Research Ctr., Greenville, Del., 1977-82; asst. prof. history Central Mich. U., Mt. Pleasant, 1982-83, adj. prof. history, 1984—, dir. Clark Hist. Library, 1983—; vis. lectr. Assumption Coll., Worcester, 1976; lectr. history Widener U., Chester, Pa., 1979-82. Author: Northborough during the American Revolution, 1974, Northborough: The Town and Its People, 1985; also revs. and articles. Clark U. fellow, 1970-73; Early Am. Industries Assn. grantee, 1980. Roman Catholic. Club: Rotary. Lodge: K.C. Avocation: stamp collecting. Home: 219 N Lansing St Mount Pleasnt MI 48858 Office: Clarke Hist Library Central Mich U Mount Pleasant MI 48859

MULLINAX, ROBERT LEE, lawyer; b. Harrisburg, Pa., Jan. 8, 1946; s. Burgin Lee and Maude (Barnes) M.; m. Carol Wright, Dec. 19, 1970. B.S. in Bus. Adminstrn., U. N.C., 1967, J.D., 1973. Bar: N.C. 1973, Ohio 1974, U.S. Dist. Ct. (no. and so. dists.) Ohio 1974, U.S. Ct. Appeals (6th cir.) 1976. Atty., Ohio State Legal Services, Columbus, 1973-75; dir. Food Action and Edn., Program, Columbus, 1976-77; sr. atty. Ohio State Legal Services, Columbus, 1977-83; chief legal counsel, Ohio Dept. Human Services, Columbus, 1983—; cons. Nat. Legal Aid and Defender Assn., Washington, 1978-82, Legal Services Corp., Washington, 1978-83. Contbrng. author: Administrative Law-Human Services, 1983; Guide to Public Assistance, 1981. Reginald Heber Smith fellow, 1973-75; recipient Alvin J. Arnett award Nat. Clients Council, 1981. Democrat. Home: 377 Clinton Heights Ave Columbus OH 43202 Office: Ohio Dept Human Services 30 E Broad St 32d Floor Columbus OH 43215

MULLINS, BARBARA JEANNE, business executive; b. Day, Fla., Aug. 29, 1938; d. James Eli and Bessie Geraldine (Johnson) Grantham; cert. acctg. Longview Community Coll., Mo., 1977; A.S., Johnson County Community Coll., 1983; m. Mikel Burton Mullins, Dec. 20, 1956; children—Ronald Lee, Richard Bryan, Mikel Duane. Fin. asst. J. M. Fields, Melbourne, Fla., 1962-63; acctg. clk. Radiation, Inc., Melbourne, 1963-64; bookkeeper/sec. Sam Hammonds, C.P.A., Oklahoma City, 1964-65; with Bride Co., Leawood, Kans., 1970-82 bookkeeper, 1970-74, chief acct., 1974-75, controller, 1975-79, v.p. adminstrn., 1979-82, corp. sec., 1973-82, registered agt., 1973-80; corp. sec. Data Freight, Inc., 1980-82; pres. Mullins Inc., 1982—; dir. Randy Shepard Enterprises, 1982—, treas., 1983—. Recipient 1st Pl. award Distributive Edn. Clubs Am. Mo. Competition, 1976. Mem. Nat. Assn. Accts. (dir. Kansas City chpt. 1978-82, officer 1982—, treas. Heartland regional council 1981-82, sec. 1984-85, dir. 1985—). Democrat. Baptist. Home: 24303 W 86th Terr Olathe KS 66061

MULLINS, OBERA, microbiologist; b. Egypt, Miss., Feb. 15, 1927; d. Willie Ree and Maggie Sue (Orr) Gunn; B.S., Chgo. State U., 1974; M.S. in Health Sci. Edn., Governors State U., 1981; m. Charles Leroy Mullins, Nov. 2, 1952; children—Mary Artavia, Arthur Curtis, Charles Leroy, Charlester Teresa, William Hellman. Med. technician, microbiologist Chgo. Health Dept., Chgo., 1976—. Mem. AAUW, Am. Soc. Clin. Pathologists (cert. med. lab. technician). Roman Catholic. Home: 9325 S Marquette St Chicago IL 60617 Office: 3026 S California Ave Chicago IL 60623

MULLINS, RICHARD AUSTIN, chem. engr.; b. Seelyville, Ind., Apr. 22, 1918; s. Fred A. and Ethel (Zenor) M.; B.S. in Chem. Engring., Rose Poly. Inst., 1940; postgrad. Yale, 1942-43; m. Margaret Ann Dellacca, Nov. 27, 1946; children—Scott Alan, Mark Earl. Chemist, Ayrshire Collieries Corp., Brazil,

Ind., 1940-49; chief chemist Fairview Collieries Corp., Danville, Ill., 1949-54; preparations mgr. Enos Coal Mining Co., Oakland City, Ind., 1954-72, Enoco Collieries, Inc., Bruceville, Ind., 1954-62; mining engr. Kings Station Coal Corp.; mgr. analytical procedures Old Ben Coal Corp., 1973-84. Am. Mining Congress cons. to Am. Standards Assn. and Internat. Orgn. for Standards, 1960-74; mem. indsl. cons. com. Ind. Geol. Survey, 1958-72; mem. organizing com. 5th Internat. Coal Preparation Congress, Pittsburgh, 1966. Mem. exec. bd. Buffalo Trace council Boy Scouts Am., also mem. speakers bur. Bd. dirs. Princeton Boys Club. Served with AUS, 1942-46; ETO. Decorated Medaille de la France Liberee (France); recipient Eagle Scout award, Boy Scouts Am., 1935, Silver Beaver award, 1962, Wood Badge Beads award, 1960; Outstanding Community Service award Princeton Civitan Club, 1964; Engr. of Year award S.W. chpt. Ind. Soc. Profl. Engrs., 1965; Prince of Princeton award Princeton C. of C., 1981. Registered profl. engr., Ind., Ill. Mem. AIME, ASTM (sr. mem.), Am. Chem. Soc., Nat. Soc. Profl. Engrs. (life mem.), Ind., Ill. mining insts., Ind. Coal Soc. (pres. 1958-59), Am. Mining Congress (chmn. com. coal preparation 1964-68), Am. Legion, 40 and 8 (past comdr.), Ind. Soc. Profl. Land Surveyors, Rose Tech. Alumni Assn. (pres. 1976-77, Honor Alumnus 1980), Order of Ring, Sigma Nu. Methodist (lay speaker). Mason, Elk. Contbr. articles to profl. jours. Home: Rural Route 4 Box 159 Princeton IN 47670

MULVANEY, MARY JEAN, physical education and athletics educator; b. Omaha, Jan. 6, 1927; d. Marion Fowler and Blanche Gibons (McKee) M. B.S., U. Nebr.-Lincoln, 1948; M.S., Wellesley Coll., 1951. Instr. phys. edn. and athletics Kans. State U., 1948-50, U. Nebr.-Lincoln, 1951-57, asst. prof., 1957-62; asst. prof. phys. edn. and athletics U. Kans., Lawrence, 1962-66; assoc. prof. phys. edn. and athletics U. Chgo., 1966-76, prof., 1976—, chmn. dept. phys. edn. and athletics, 1976—. Mem. Nat. Collegiate Athletic Assn. (council 1983—), AAHPERD, Nat. Assn. Phys. Edn. in Higher Edn., Pi Lambda Theta. Methodist. Avocation: Camping. Home: 5825 S Dorchester Ave Chicago IL 60637 Office: U Chgo 5640 S University Ave Chicgo IL 60637

MUMA, RICHARD ALLEN, insurance agency manager; b. Warren, Mich., Dec. 29, 1940; s. Forest Amber and Elizabeth Maude (Troyer) M.; B.S. in Edn., No. Mich. U., 1972; m. Dagmar Ann Brock, June 12, 1965; children—Jeffrey Michael, Cheryl Lynn, David Richard. Dir. phys. edn. Pinconning (Mich.) Area Schs., 1972-73; with Schater Chevrolet, Pinconning, Mich., 1974-76; agt. Prudential Ins. Co., Grand Rapids, Mich., 1976-82, new manpower devel. mgr., 1977-82, agy. mgr. Mut. Security Life, 1982—. Served with USN, 1959-67. Recipient No. Star award, Prudential Ins. Co. Am., 1978, 79. Mem. Nat. Assn. Life Underwriters (life underwriters polit. action com.). Reformed Ch. of Am. Clubs: Ch. Golf League. Home: 7788 Emberly St Jenison MI 49428 Office: MSL Assocs 4246 Kalamazoo SE Grand Rapids MI 49508

MUMMERT, THOMAS ALLEN, manufacturing company executive; b. Toledo, Ohio, Dec. 24, 1946; s. James Allen and Betty Alice (Thomas) M.; student U. Toledo, 1965-66; m. Icia Linda Shearer, Dec. 17, 1966; children—Sherry Lynn, Robert Thomas, Michael Allen. Pres., Mummert Electric & Mfg. Co., Inc., Toledo, 1969-70; research engr. Am. Lincoln Corp., Bowling Green, Ohio, 1970-73; test engr. Dura div. Dura Corp., Toledo, 1973-74; research dept. head Jobst Inst., Inc., Toledo, 1975-84, mgr. med. equipment design, 1984—. Served with USN, 1968-69. Mem. AAAS, Laser Inst. Am., Biol. Engring. Soc., Ohio Acad. Sci., N.Y. Acad. Sci., Am. Soc. for Quality Control, Am. Soc. Engring. Edn., Nat. Mgmt. Assn., Assn. for Advancement of Med. Instrumentation, ASTM. Baptist. Inventor sequential dual window operating mechanism, 1974, therapeutic appliance for flexing joints, 1980, sequencing valve mechanism, 1981, electronic circuit for dynamic pressure wave pneumatic control system, 1981, artificial foot, 1981, and others; patentee in field. Home: 1448 Palmetto Ave Toledo OH 43606 Office: 653 Miami St Toledo OH 43694

MUNDA, RINO, surgeon, educator; b. Rome, Feb. 2, 1943; came to U.S., 1967, naturalized, 1983; s. Salvador and Marina (Tabusso) M.; m. Margarita Landra, Nov. 11, 1968; children—Sergio, Franco, Elisa. B.S., Universidad Nacional Mayor de San Marcos, Lima, Peru, 1960; M.D., Facultad de Medicina Cayetano Heredia, Lima, 1967. Diplomate Am. Bd. Surgery. Intern, Mt. Sinai Hosp., N.Y.C., 1967-68, resident, 1969-70; resident N.Y. Med. Coll., 1971-73, instr., 1972-73; asst. prof. research surgery U. Cin., 1974-75, asst. prof. surgery, 1975-79, assoc. prof., 1979—; mem. adv. com. Cin. Kidney Found., 1979—; cons. surgery Dialysis Clinics, Inc.; mem. med. rev. bd. Ohio Valley Renal Network, 1981-83. Am. Diabetes Assn. Cin. Affiliate grantee, 1981-82. Mem. Surg. Soc. N.Y. Med. Coll., Assn. Acad. Surgery, Am. Soc. Transplant Surgeons, Transplantation Soc., ACS, Surg. Infection Soc. Contbr. articles to profl. publs. Home: 315 Lafayette Ave Cincinnati OH 45220

MUNDELL, WILBUR LEWIS, corporation executive, playwright; b. Waltersburg, Pa., Mar. 12, 1928; s. Clyde Stirling and Mary Audrey (Boord) M.; m. Elva Jean Cannon, Aug. 25, 1948; children—Douglas Allen, Deborah Jean, Gregory Lee, Laura Susan. B.S. in edn., Waynesburg, Coll., 1953; M.A. in Edn., George Washington U., 1966. Cert. secondary sch. tchr., Pa. Adminstr., mem. faculty Ohio U., Chillicothe, 1966-70; exec. v.p. Scioto Soc., Inc., Chillicothe, 1970-73, pres. 1973—; exec. dir. Ross-Chillicothe Conv. and Visitors Bur., Ohio, 1983—; internat. cons. outdoor drama, Chillicothe, 1977—; writer Chillicothe, 1973—. Writer, TV series Mutual Omaha's Wild Kingdom, 1973; author (plays) Blue Jacket, 1980, Viking, 1982; (screenplay) This Sacred Ground, 1983. V.P. Chillicothe Bd. Edn., Ohio, 1970-71, pres. 1972-73; minister music Meth. Ch., Chillicothe, 1968-80; mem. Bicentennial com., Chillicothe, 1975-76. Served to capt. U.S. Army and USMC, 1946-66. Recipient Ohio Travel award Gov. Ohio, 1973, Statehood Day award Kiwanis, 1973. Avocations: nat. and Am. hist. Home: 88 Fruit Hill Dr Chillicothe OH 45601 Office: Scioto Soc Inc PO Box 73 Chillicothe OH 45601

MUNDER, TERRIE ROBERTA, personal and family counselor; b. Berwyn, Ill., Aug. 7, 1930; d. James Aloysius and Marie (Nohava) Hollowed; m. John E. Birch, Nov. 4, 1950 (div. Apr. 1969); children—John Edward, Christopher James, Terrie Johnice Birch Kallal, Laurence Patrick; m. 2d, Lee Munder, May 11, 1983. B.A. cum laude in Psychology, Rosary Coll., 1974; M.S. in Counseling Psychology, George Williams Coll., 1976. Sec.-treas. John Birch & Co., Lombard, Ill., 1953-66, prin. Terrie Birch & Co., Lombard, 1953-66, Alert Carpentry, Lombard, 1953-66, Durable Masonry, Inc., Lombard, 1953-66, Cherrywood Homes, Lombard, 1953-66; travel counselor, 1969-71; vocat. testing and counselor Women's Inc., Hinsdale, Ill., 1975-78, Office Manpower Planning, DuPage County (Ill.) Ctr., Wheaton, 1975-78; dir. vol. services Holy Family Hosp., Des Plaines, Ill., 1978-83, mem. aux.; mem. adv. com. Bensenville Home Soc. Ret. Sr. Vol. Program. Meml. and honor chmn., dir. Infant Welfare Soc., Chgo., 1963-65, pres. Western Springs Ctr., 1967; mem. career adv. council Wheeling (Ill.) High Sch. Mem. Ill. Soc. for Dirs. Vol. Services, Am. Soc. Dirs. Vol. Services, Chgo. Council Dirs. Vol. Services (edn. chmn.), U. Ill. Alumni Assn., AAUW, Drama League, Mensa, Pi Gamma Mu. Club: Oak Brook Women's. Home: 170 Briarwood N Oak Brook IL 60521

MUNDHENKE, STEPHANIE ANN, lawyer, banker; b. Mpls., Oct. 8, 1951; d. Alden Runge and Nina Lavina (Hanson) Chester; m. Gary Wayne Mundhenke, Sept. 12, 1981. B.A. magna cum laude, Augustana Coll., 1973; J.D., U. S.D., 1977; postgrad. C.F.S.C., ABA Nat. Grad. Trust Sch., Evanston, Ill., 1984. Bar: S.D. 1977, Minn. 1979. Asst. counselor Minnehaha County Juvenile Ct. Ctr., Sioux Falls, S.D., 1972-73; child care worker Project Threshold, Sioux Falls, 1973-74; legal intern Davenport, Evans, Hurwitz & Smith, Sioux Falls, 1976; law clk. S.D. Supreme Ct., Pierre, 1977-78; originations dept. buyer Dain Bosworth, Inc., Mpls., 1978-79; v.p., trust officer 1st Bank of S.D., N.A., Sioux Falls, 1979—; bd. dirs., mem. program com. Sioux Falls Estate Planning Council, 1983-85; Projects and research editor S.D. Law Rev., 1977; author law rev. comment. Mem. fund raising coms. S.D. Symphony, Sioux Falls Community Playhouse, Augustana Coll., 1982-83; mem. S.D. div. Nat. Women's Polit. Caucus; mem. events com. Augustana Coll. Fellows, Sioux Falls, 1984; bd. dirs. YWCA, Sioux Falls, 1984, Sioux Falls Arena/Coliseum, 1985; mem. Sioux Falls Jr. Service League, 1984. Augustana Coll. scholar, 1969-73; Augustana Coll. Bd. Regents scholar, 1973. Mem. S.D. Bar Assn., Minn. Bar Assn., ABA, 2d S.D. Jud. Circuit Bar Assn., Nat. Assn. Bank Women (state conv. com. 1983-85), Phi Delta Phi, Chi Epsilon. Republican. Lutheran. Clubs: Network, Portia (Sioux Falls). Office: 1st Bank of SD PO Box 1308 Sioux Falls SD 57117

MUNDSTOCK, AILEEN M., writer, technical information specialist; b. Milw., Oct. 16, 1926; d. John Theodore Henry and Helen Mary (Schauwitzer) Krueger; m. Kenneth Paul Mundstock, July 8, 1955 (dec. 1967); children—Patricia, Virginia, Robert, Marianne Mundstock Sawyer, John. B.A., Valparaiso U., 1950; M.A. in Library Sci., U. Wis.-Milw., 1976. Tchr., missionary Lutheran Synodical Conf. of St. Louis, Nigeria, West Africa, 1950-56; newspaper reporter Shinners Publs., Waukesha, Wis., 1970-71; sec., librarian Universal Foods Corp., Milw., 1971-76, tech. info. specialist, 1976—; del. Wis. Gov's Conf. on Library and Info. Sci., Madison, 1978. Contbr. articles to profl. jours. Mem. Friends of Wauwatosa Pub. Library, 1984—. Mem. Spl. Libraries Assn. (pres. Wis. chpt. 1983-84, membership chmn. 1978-79, treas. 1976-78, chmn. career guidance and affirmative action com. 1981-82, sec. food and nutrition div. 1980-81). Home: 12235 W Dearbourn Ave Wauwatosa WI 53226 Office: Universal Foods Corp 6143 N 60th St Milwaukee WI 53218

MUNKACHY, LOIS DEUTSCH, educator, hypnotherapist; b. Detroit, Sept. 16, 1929; d. Louis and Ethel (Nagy) D.; B.Music Edn., Baldwin Wallace Coll., 1951; M.A., U. Mich., 1969, Ph.D., 1974; m. Ernest Frederick Munkachy, Mar. 29, 1950; 1 son, Richard Lee David. Tchr. elem. music Dearborn (Mich.) public schs., 1952-54, high sch. tchr. English and music, Westwood, Mich., 1954-68; jr. high sch. tchr. English and social studies, Woodhaven, Mich., 1968-69; tchr. elem. music Romulus (Mich.) Community Schs., 1969-72; tchr. drama, English and choir Romulus High Sch., 1972-84; hypnotherapist Universal Self-Help Center, 1981—; pres. S'unlimited and Assocs., Inc., distbrs. Success Motivation Internat., Inc., 1984—. Mem. Assn. Supervision and Curriculum Devel., NEA, Mich. Edn. Assn., Nat. Writers Club, Assn. Advance Ethical Hypnosis, Internat. Platform Assn. (profl. speaker), Phi Delta Kappa. Clubs: Huron Valley Gun Collectors, Rosicrucians. Office: 51 E Huron River Dr Belleville MI 48111

MUÑOZ, MARIO ALEJANDRO, city official; b. Havana, Cuba, Feb. 27, 1928; s. Ramón and Concepción (Bermudo) M.; came to U.S., 1961, naturalized, 1968; M.Arch., U. Havana, 1954; postgrad. City Colls. Chgo., 1974; m. Julia Josephine Garrofe, Jan. 17, 1970. Owner, Muñoz Bermudo-Construcciones, Havana, 1954-61; designer various cos., Chgo., 1961-65; designer Chgo. Transit Authority, Mdse. Mart, Chgo., 1965-69; civil engr. Dept. Water and Sewers, City of Chgo., 1969-79, supervising engr. Dept. of Sewers, 1979-85, coordinating engr., 1985—; mem. central area subway system utilities com. City of Chgo., 1974—, mem. computer graphics com., 1977-78. Mem. Am. Pub. Works Assn., Western Soc. Engrs., Chgo. Architecture Found., Chgo. Council Fgn. Relations. Roman Catholic. Clubs: Ground Hog, Execs. (speaker's table com.) (Chgo.); Oak Brook Polo. Home: 5455 N Sheridan Rd Apt 1912 Chicago IL 60640 Office: 121 N LaSalle St Chicago IL 60602

MUNRO, RODERICK ANTHONY, quality engineer; b. Toronto, Ont., Can., Jan. 16, 1955; s. William George and Georgina Antoniette (Shembri) M.; came to U.S., 1956; m. Pamela Ruth Jones, Feb. 23, 1980. B.A., Adrian Coll., 1979, secondary provisional cert., 1981; M.S., Eastern Mich. U., 1984. Cert. quality engr. Production worker Kewaunee Sci., Adrian, Mich., summers 1973, 74, 79; tchr. Lincoln Park High Sch., Mich., 1980-82; prodn. worker Prodn. Finishing, Wyandotte, Mich., 1981-82; mgmt. trainee Fabricon Automotive, River Range, Mich., 1982-84; quality services coordinator ASC, Inc., Southgate, Mich., 1984—. Active Amazing Grace Evangel. Lutheran Ch., Taylor, Mich., 1980—. Served to sgt. USMCR, 1974-80. Mem. Aircraft Owners and Pilots Assn., Am. Soc. Quality Control (cert., asst. chmn. edn. Detroit chpt. 1985—), ASTM, Am. Statis. Assn., Am. Soc. Nondestructive Testing. Office: ASC Inc One Sunroof Ctr Southgate MI 48195

MUNSON, NORMA FRANCES, biologist, ecologist, educator; b. Stockport, Iowa, Sept. 22, 1923; d. Glenn Edwards and Frances Emma (Wilson) M.; B.A., Concordia Coll., 1946; M.A., U. Mo., 1955; Ph.D. (NSF fellow 1957-58, Chgo. Heart Assn. fellow 1959), Pa. State U., 1962; postgrad. Ind. U., 1957, Western Mich. U., 1967, Lake Forest Coll., 1971, 72, 78; student various fgn. univs., 1964-71. Tchr., Aitkin (Minn.) High Sch., 1946-48, Detroit Lakes (Minn.) High Sch., 1948-54, Libertyville (Ill.) High Sch., 1955-79; researcher in nutrition, Libertyville, 1965—. Ruling elder First Presbyn. Ch., Libertyville, 1971-77; pres. Lake County Audubon Soc., 1975-85, Libertyville Edn. Assn., 1964-67; active Rep. Party of Ill., Citizens to Save Butler Lake, Citizens Choice, The Defenders; mem. U.S. Congl. Adv. Bd., 1985—; bd. dirs. Holy Land Christian Mission Internat. Recipient Hilda Mahling award, 1967, C. of C. award, 1971, Ill. Best Teacher's award, 1974; Best Biology of Yr. award, 1971; NSF fellow, 1970-71. Mem. Nat. Biology Tchrs. Assn. (award 1971), AAAS, Am. Inst. Biol. Sci., Ill. Environ. Council, Ill. Audubon Council, Nat. Health Fedn., Internat. Platform Assn., Nat. Wildlife Fedn., N.Y. Acad. Scis., Parks and Conservation Assn., Delta Kappa Gamma. Contbr. research articles to publs. Home and Office: 206 W Maple Ave Libertyville IL 60048

MUNZINGER, JUDITH MONTGOMERY, educator; b. Dayton, Ohio, June 16, 1944; s. Russell Eric and Margaret Lois (Weltzheimer) Montgomery; m. John Stephen Munzinger, May 28, 1977; children—Laurie Anne, Lisa Michelle. B.S. in Edn., Ohio State U., 1966, M.A., 1979, cert. remedial reading, 1980. Cert. tchr., Iowa. Tchr. elem. sch., Lafayette, Ind., 1966-69, Hilliard, Ohio, 1976-79; remedial reading tchr. Sioux City, Iowa, 1979-82; instr., dir. early childhood devel. Briar Cliff Coll.; talented and gifted coordinator, Sioux City; rep. Piper, Jaffray and Hopwood, Sioux City, 1985—. Treas. Siouxlanders for Talented and Gifted; mem. Coalition for Children; judge for Iowa Future Problem Solving Bowl, 1982; active Jr. League; mem. vestry, clk. St. Thomas Episcopal Ch., 1982-84; mem. Children's Hosp. support group, Columbus, Ohio, 1972-79; active Women's Assn. for Columbus Zoo, 1973-76, PTA; asst. Girl Scouts U.S.A., 1980-82. Recipient Service commendation Girl Scouts U.S.A., 1980. Mem. Iowa Reading Assn., Internat. Reading Assn., Ohio State U. Alumni Assn., Delta Zeta. Republican. Home: 4521 Country Club Blvd Sioux City IA 51104 Office: Piper Jaffray and Hopwood 421 Nebraska St Sioux City IA 51101

MURDOCH, ARTHUR ROY, chemistry educator; b. Duboise, Nebr., Aug. 25, 1934; s. Albert Roy and Dorothy Enid (Johns) M.; m. Gail Reeves, July 28, 1957; children—Scott Kevin, Kristy Lynn. B.A., Westmar Coll., 1956; M.S., Yale U., 1958, Ph.D., 1964. Secondary teaching cert., Iowa. Asst. prof. chemistry Morningside Coll., Sioux City, Iowa, 1962-65, assoc. prof., 1965-68; assoc. prof. Mt. Union Coll., Alliance, Ohio, 1968-80, prof. chemistry, 1980—, chmn. chem. dept., 1968—. Mem. AAUP, (pres. Ohio 1977-78), Am. Chem. Soc., Fedn. Am. Scientists, Union Concerned Scientists. Presbyterian. Avocations: boating, camping, water skiing. Home: 1457 Robinwood Rd Alliance OH 44601 Office: Chemistry Dept Mt Union Coll Alliance OH 44601

MURDOCK, EUGENE CONVERSE, history educator; b. Lakewood, Ohio, Apr. 30, 1921; s. Stanley Howard and Elizabeth Kathryn (Carter) M.; m. Margaret Bowes McColl, Oct. 7, 1950; children—Gordon Graham, Kathryn Carter. Asst. prof. social sci. Rio Grande Coll., Ohio, 1952-56, asst. dean, 1953-56; faculty Marietta Coll., Ohio, 1956—, prof. history, 1963—, chmn. dept., 1972—; mem. adv. bd. historians Ohio Civil War Centennial Commn., 1960-65. Author: Ohio's Bounty System in the Civil War, 1963; Patriotism Limited, 1862-1865, 1967; One Million Men-The Civil War Draft in the North, 1971; (with William Heacock) Fenton Glass, 2 vols., 1978, 80; Ban Johnson-Czar of Baseball, 1982; Mighty Casey-All-American, 1984. Editorial bd. Ohio History, 1964-74; Pro Football Digest, 1967-69; Jour. Sport History, 1974-78. Contbr. to Ency. So. History, Insider Baseball, Dictionary Am. Sport. Contbr. articles and revs. to profl. jours. Served with AUS, 1943-46. Mem. Am. Hist. Assn., Orgn. Am. History, Ohio Acad. History (exec. council 1970-73, pres. 1984-85), Soc. Am. Baseball Research (pres. 1976-78). Avocations: music, racketball, compiling baseball scrapbooks. Home: 415 Columbia Ave Williamstown WV 26187 Office: Dept History Marietta Coll Marietta OH 26187

MURDOCK, NORMAN ANTHONY, lawyer; b. Cin., Nov. 6, 1931; s. Charles and Anna Murdock; m. Patricia Higgins, Feb. 16, 1957; children—Norman, Louis, Patrick, Suzanne, Michael, John. B.S., Xavier U., 1955; J.D., U. Cin., 1968. Bar: Ohio. Lic. pub. acct., Ohio. Dist. scout exec. Boy Scouts of Am., Dodge City, Kans., 1956-59; pub. acct., Cin., 1959—; ptnr. Ahlrichs & Murdock, Cin., 1968—; trustee Coll. Mt. St. Joseph, Cin., 1975-81. Clk., treas. Delhi Township, Cin., 1964-67; mem. Ohio Ho. of Reps., Cin., 1967-78; commr. Hamilton County, Cin., 1979—; vice chmn. Intergovtl. Adv. Council on Edn., Washington, 1982—. Served to 2d lt. U.S. Army, 1956. Recipient Disting. Service award Arthritis Found., 1978; named Legislator of Yr., Ohio Pharm. Assn., 1972, Legislator of Yr., Ohio Assn. Trial Lawyers, 1976, Man of Yr., Ohio Pub. Transit Assn., 1975. Mem. Cin. Bar Assn., Ohio Bar Assn., ABA. Republican. Roman Catholoc. Home: 628 Conina Dr Cincinnati OH 45238 Office: Ahlrichs & Murdock LPA 4037 Glenway Ave Cincinnati OH 45205

MURMAN, MICHAEL ELLIS, lawyer, prosecutor; b. Cleve., Aug. 14, 1946; s. Charles Edward and Agnes Z. (Zaytoun) M.; m. Drue Koran, Apr. 23, 1982; 1 child, Meryl Leslie. B.A., U. Dayton, 1968; J.D. magna cum laude, Cleve. State U., 1975. Bar: Ohio 1975, Fla. 1976. Tchr., Dayton Pub. Schs., Ohio, 1968-72; sole practice law, Lakewood, Ohio, 1975—; asst. pros. atty. Cuyahoga County, Cleve., 1976-79; pros. atty. City of Lakewood, 1979—. Trustee Lakewood Improvement Corp., 1978-81; pres. council St. Luke Ch., Lakewood, 1982-83. Mem. Ohio State Bar Assn., Fla. Bar Assn., Cuyahoga County Bar Assn., Cuyahoga County Law Dirs. Assn. Republican. Roman Catholic. Office: Michael E Murman Atty Law 14701 Detroit Ave Lakewood OH 44107

MURNIK, MARY RENGO, biology educator; b. Manistee, Mich., Aug. 30, 1942; d. John Everett and Lorraine P. (ReVolt) R.; m. James M. Murnik, July 30, 1970; 1 child, John. Student Marquette U., 1960-62; B.S., Mich. State U., 1964, Ph.D., 1969. Asst. prof. Fitchburg State Coll., Mass., 1968-70; from asst. prof. to prof. Western Ill. U., Macomb, 1970-80; prof., head biol. sci. dept. Ferris State Coll., Big Rapids, Mich., 1980—. Contbr. articles to profl. jours. Author two lab. manuals. NIH fellow HEW, Mich. State U., 1965-68; NIH grantee Western Ill. U., 1976; grantee Environ. Mutagen Soc., Edinburgh, Scotland, 1977, Western Ill. U., 1972-79. Mem. AAAS, Genetics Soc. Am., Behavior Genetics Soc. Roman Catholic. Home: 331 W Slosson St Reed City MI 49677 Office: Dept Biol Scis Ferris State Coll Big Rapids MI 49307

MURPHY, CHARLES ARNOLD, physician, surgeon, businessman; b. Detroit, Dec. 29, 1932; s. Charles L. and Hazel C. (Robinson) M.; m. Mary Lightford, Aug., 1955; m. 2d, Judith L. Dennis, Nov. 12, 1966; 1 son, Charles A. III; m. 3d, Sandra M. Walker, July 17, 1971. Student, Wayne State U., 1949-53; D.O., Coll. Osteo. Medicine and Surgery, Des Moines, 1957. Diplomate Am. Osteo. Bd. Gen. Practice. Intern, Flint Osteo. Hosp. (Mich.), 1957-58; gen. practice medicine, Detroit, 1958—; mem. staffs Kirwood Hosp., 1964-66, Martin Place Hosp., 1958-64; mem. staff Mich. Osteo. Med. Ctr., 1959—, past chief staff, now trustee, mem. fin. com.; osteo. physician City of Detroit, 1959-63; sr. police surgeon Detroit Police Dept., 1977-79; assoc. clin. prof. family medicine Coll. Osteo. Medicine, Mich. State U.; bd. dirs. and exec. com. Mich. HMO Plans; mem. central peer rev. adv. com. Mich. Dept. Health; mem. council med. dirs. Health Care Network. Fellow Am. Coll. Osteo. Gen. Practitioners, Am. Osteo. Assn. (ho. of dels. 1981-83), Greater Detroit Area Hosp. Council, Mich. Osteo. Assn. (ho. of dels. 1970—, trustee 1981—), NAACP (life), Wayne County Osteo. Assn. (pres. 1976, 77), Mich. Assn. Gen. Practitioners in Osteo. Medicine and Surgery, Coll. Osteo. Medicine and Surgery Alumni Assn., Atlas Club, Kappa Alpha Psi, Psi Sigma Alpha. Methodist. Club: Detroit Yacht. Office: 12634 E Jefferson Detroit MI 48215

MURPHY, DANIEL MERRITT, real estate developer, farm and ranch management company executive; b. Indpls., May 3, 1941; s. Merritt D. and Olive Elizabeth (Jessup) M.; m. Carolyn Del, Nov. 22, 1980. B.S. in Animal Sci., Iowa State U., 1963. Partner, mgr. Bic-Mur Agrl. Mgmt., Columbus, Nebr., 1979-82; v.p. mktg. Sand Livestock, Columbus, 1975-79; racecar driver Cicada Racing, Indpls., 1974-75; dir. tech. services Murphy Products Co., Burlington, Wis., 1967-74; sales rep. Elanco Products, Indpls., 1963-66; owner, chief exec. officer Murphy Ag Mgmt., Dalhart, Tex., 1982—; tchr. community class Platte Coll., Columbus, Nebr., 1982. Mem. Profl. Farmers Am. Republican. Clubs: British Auto Racing (Weyhill, Eng.); Sportcar of America (Denver). Lodge: Elks. Home: 46 Lakeshore Dr Columbus NE 68601 Office: PO Box 510 East Hwy 54 Dalhart TX 79022

MURPHY, DENNIS PERRY, broadcast executive; b. Sioux City, Iowa, Nov. 3, 1938; s. Ray Perry and Rosalia Bernadine (Simeon) M.; m. Sharon Rae DeWitt, May 24, 1959; children—Dennis Perry, Ray Perry. Grad. Elkins Electronic Sch., New Orleans, 1965, Lockmasters Safe Sch., Satellite Beach, Fla., 1979; student Edgewood Coll., Madison, Wis. Program dir. Sta. KUDL, Kansas City, Mo., 1962-65; program dir. Sta. WTIX, New Orleans, Sta. KOMA, Oklahoma City, 1969; program dir. Sta. WIFE, Indpls., 1969-71, Sta. KCBS-FM, San Francisco, 1971; cons. in broadcasting sales and programming, Madison, Wis., 1972-76; exec. v.p. Cummings Communications Corp./WNAM/WAHC, Neenah, Wis., 1976—; owner, sec./treas. Media Hitech Research, Inc., Neenah, Wis. Mem. Vols. in Probation, Outagamie County; vol. Huber Law Inmate Program, Outagamie County, Wis.; chmn. Fox Cities Small Bus. Com., 1985-86. Served with AUS, 1957-59. Aide de camp Gov. McKithen of La., 1965; named Program Dir. of Yr., Bill Gavin Poll, 1969. Mem. Fox Valley Broadcasters Assn., Fox Cities C. of C. (past chmn. awareness com.), Neenah Businessmans Adv. Group, Aero. Modelers Assn., Internat. Platform Assn., Nat. Assn. Broadcasters. Republican. Methodist. Lodges: Masons, Knights of Malta. Home: 306 S Schaefer St Appleton WI 54915 Office: Box 707 Neenah WI 54956

MURPHY, DIANA E., federal judge; b. Faribault, Minn., Jan. 4, 1934; d. Albert W. and Adleyne (Heiker) Kuske; B.A. magna cum laude, U. Minn., 1954, J.S. magna cum laude, 1974; postgrad. Johannes Gutenberg U., Mainz, Germany, 1954-55, U. Minn., 1955-58; m. Joseph E. Murphy, Jr., July 24, 1958; children—Michael, John E. Bar: Minn. 1974. Mem. Lindquist & Vennum, 1974-76; mcpl. judge Hennepin County, 1976-78, dist. judge, 1978-80; judge U.S. Dist. Ct. Minn., Mpls., 1980—; instr. Law Sch., U. Minn., 1977—, U.S. Dept. Justice Advocacy Inst., 1981—; bd. govs. Minn. State Bar, 1976-81. Bd. dirs. Spring Hill Conf. Center, 1978-84, Amicus, 1976-80, organizer, 1st chmn. adv. council; mem. Mpls. Charter Commn., 1973-76, chmn., 1974-76; bd. dirs. Ops. De Novo, 1971-76, chmn., 1974-75; mem. Minn. Constitutional Study Commn., chmn. bill of rights com. 1971-73; bd. regents St. Johns U., 1978—; bd. dirs. Bush Found. Fulbright scholar; recipient Amicus Founders' award; Outstanding Achievement award YWCA, U. Minn., 1983. Fellow Am. Bar Found.; mem. ABA (ethics and responsibility judges' adv. com. 1981—), Minn. Bar Assn., Hennepin County Bar Assn. (gov. council 1976-81), Hennepin County Bar Found. (bd. dirs., pres. 1983-84), Am. Judicature Soc. (bd. dirs. 1982—), Am. Law Inst., Fed. Judges Assn. (bd. dirs. 1982—), Nat. Assn. Women Judges, Minn. Women Lawyers, U. Minn. Alumni Assn. (bd. dirs. 1975-83, pres. 1981-82), Order of Coif, Phi Beta Kappa. Bd. editors U. Minn. Law Rev. Office: 609 US Courthouse Minneapolis MN 55401

MURPHY, DUDLEY C., art educator; b. Danville, Ky., April 16, 1940; s. Dudley C. and Gladys (Royce) M.; m. Martha Bradley, May 11, 1968; children—Michael Quinn, Jennifer Lynn. B.A., U. Tulsa, 1965, M.A., 1969; M.F.A., Okla. U., 1971. Free-lance graphic designer, Tulsa, 1965-68; supply instr. Southwestern Mo. State U., Springfield, 1969-70; curator of edn. Springfield Art Mus., Mo., 1971-78; assoc. prof. art Drury Coll., Springfield, 1978—; sculptor in wood, steel and impermanant materials. Author: Straw: A Portfolio of Straw Sculpture, 1971. Exhibited nat. and internat. one man shows, group shows, 1965—, Bd. dirs. Founders Mus. of Fishing History, Springfield, 1982—. Recipient of numerous art awards. Mem. Internat. Sculpture Ctr., Nat. Council for Edn. in Ceramic Arts, Springfield Ad Club (1st Place Print Div. award 1980, Honorable Mention award 1982). Baptist. Avocations: acoustic guitar music, antique fishing tackle collector, fishing, outdoor activities. Office: Drury Coll 900 Benton St Springfield MO 65802

MURPHY, EARL PAULUS, JR., English educator, writer, researcher; b. St. Louis, Dec. 2, 1944; s. Earl Paulus and LaVerne Roberta (Tentschert) M.; m. Janet Ellen Schey, Jan. 23, 1945 (div.); children—Heather, Vonya. B.A., Western Ky. U., 1967, M.A., 1971; Ph.D., St. Louis U., 1977; postdoctoral Columbia U., Washington U., Oxford U., Northwestern U. Tchr. English, Western Ky. U., Bowling Green, 1967-68, St. Louis U., 1973-77, Harris-Stowe State Coll., St. Louis, 1977—; tchr. U. Md., Taipei, Taiwan, Fla. Jr. Coll. Jacksonville, Forest Park Community Coll., St. Louis. Served with USAF, 1969-72. Inst. for Internat. Edn. fellow, summer 1974; NEH grantee, 1979, 80-81, 83. Mem. MLA, Popular Culture Assn. Lutheran. Contbr. articles to profl. jours. Home: 2 Grantview Ln Saint Louis MO 63123 Office: 3026 LaClede Ave Saint Louis MO 63103

MURPHY, ELISABETH ANNE, educator; b. Jacksonville, Ill., Dec. 23, 1950; d. Paul and Mary (Henderson) Hogan; B.A., MacMurray Coll., 1973; m. Donald Edward Murphy, Nov. 29, 1975; children—Megan Elisabeth, Matthew Edward. Instr. sign lang. John A. Logan Coll., Carterville, Ill., 1976-79; instr. sign lang. div. continuing edn. So. Ill. U., 1979—; tchr. high sch. deaf students Williamson County Spl. Edn. Coop., 1973—. Cert. Council Edn. Deaf, cert. tchr., Ill. Mem. Marion Edn. Assn., Ill. Edn. Assn., NEA, Ill. Tchrs. Hearing Impaired, Ill. Assn. Deaf, Telecommunictors of Central Ill., Telecommunications ofr Deaf So. Ill. Interpretors of Deaf, Little Egypt Assn. Deaf. Roman Catholic. Home: 1104 W White St Marion IL 62959 Office: 700 E Blvd Marion IL 62959

MURPHY, JAMES EDWARD, food co. exec.; b. East St. Louis, Ill., Sept. 6, 1936; s. John J. and Margaret V. (Powers) M.; B.J., U. Ill., 1958; m. Patricia M. Galus, Sept. 29, 1962; children—Jason, Sean, Courtney. Reporter, Buffalo Evening News, 1958-59; asst. dir. public relations Nat. Gypsum Co., Buffalo, 1959-62; mgr. public relations Owens-Corning-Fiberglas, Toledo, 1962-68, dir. public relations and merchandising, 1968-72, gen. mgr. decorative and home furnishings div., 1972-76, gen. mgr. Weaver Products div., 1976-78; v.p. public affairs Beatrice Foods Co., Chgo., 1978-80, sr. v.p., dir. corp. relations, 1980—. Former v.p., treas. Greater Toledo Public TV Found.; mem. bus. adv. com. U. Ill.; former trustee Maumee Valley Country Day Sch.; mem. Pres.'s Council, Nat. Coll. Edn.; mem. Chgo. adv. com. Local Initiative Support Group; trustee, treas. North Shore Country Day Sch. Served with C.I.C., AUS, 1959-61. Named Outstanding Young Man of Yr., Toledo, 1968. Mem. Public Relations Soc. Am. (accredited; 2 Silver Anvil awards, past pres. N.W. Ohio). Clubs: Union League (Chgo.); Atrium (N.Y.C.); Palmetto Golf (Aiken, S.C.). Office: 2 N LaSalle St Chicago IL 60602

MURPHY, JANET GORMAN, college president; b. Holyoke, Mass., Jan. 10, 1937; d. Edwin Daniel and Catherine (Hennessey) G. B.A., U. Mass., 1958, Ed.D., 1974; M.Ed., Boston U., 1961; LL.D. (hon.), U. Mass., Amherst, 1984. Tchr. jr. high sch., Holyoke, 1958-60, Springfield, Mass., 1961-63; dir. devel. Mass. State Coll. System, Boston, 1964-77, provost, 1975-76; pres. Lyndon State Coll., Lyndonville, Vt., 1977-83, Mo. Western Coll., St. Joseph, Mo., 1983—. Author: career guidance column Boston Record Am., 1967-69; Reorganization of Public Higher Education in Massachusetts, 1974. Bd. dirs. Leadership 58, St. Joseph, United Way St. Joseph. Recipient John Gunther Teaching award High Rds. Tchrs. Award Program, 1961; named Outstanding State Employee, State of Mass., 1975, Outstanding Alumnus, U. Mass., 1981. Mem. Am. Assn. State Colls. and Univs. (bd. dirs.), Vt. Bar Assn., AAUP. Democrat. Roman Catholic. Office: Mo Western State College 4525 Downs Dr Saint Joseph MO 64507

MURPHY, JEANETTE CAROL, education educator; b. Hot Springs, S.D., June 6, 1931; d. George W. and Jessie S. (Whetstone) M.; A.B., U. S.D., 1960; M.S. in Edn., Chadron State Coll., 1978, Ed.S., 1979. Mgr. central supply and operating rooms Luth. Hosp., Hot Springs, 1957-58, 60-61; tchr. Spanish and French, Sidney (Nebr.) High Sch., 1962-64; reservations clk. Peninsula Hosp., Burlingame, Calif., 1964-65; tchr. San Lorenzo Valley Unified Schs., Felton, Calif., 1965-67; propr. Masters Career Inst., Salinas, Calif., 1969-70; tchr. Oglala Community High Sch., Pine Ridge, S.D., 1970-72, Hot Springs High Sch., 1971-73; clk. Fall River County (S.D.) Treas.'s Office, 1973-74; Title I tchr. Loneman Day Sch., Ogala, S.D., 1974-75, adminstr., 1975-77; contract dir. and exec. officer bd. Unified Sch. Bd. Found., Inc., Pine Ridge, 1977-78; grad. asst. div. edn. and psychology Chadron (Nebr.) State Coll., 1978-79; supt. schs. Lyman (Nebr.) Pub. Schs., 1979-80, Kadoka (S.D.) Sch. Dist., 1981-83; registered rep. for IDS/Am. Express, 1983-84; grad. teaching asst. doctoral program in edn. adminstrn. with spl. emphasis in polit. sci. U. Mo., 1984—; asst. state dir. for Mo. North Central Assn., 1984—. Chairperson Heart Fund Drive, Hot Springs, 1974-76; Bible sch. tchr. United Presbyn. Women, 1976-77; mem. choir Presbyn. Ch., 1970-76. Served with WAC, 1954-57. Mem. Am. Assn. Sch. Adminstrs., Nebr. Council Sch. Adminstrs., Nebr. Assn. Women Adminstrs., S.D. Sch. Adminstrs. Assn., S.D. Sch. Supts. Assn., S.D. Assn. Sch. Bus. Ofcls., Assn. Sch. Bus. Ofcls., Assn. Sch. Curriculum Devel., Assn. Sch., Coll. and Univ. Staffing, Nebr. Coalition for Women, AAUW, Delta Kappa Gamma, Phi Delta Kappa. Democrat. Clubs: Order Eastern Star, Daus. of Nile. Home: 346 S 6th St Hot Springs SD 57747

MURPHY, JEROME V., physician, educator; b. N.Y.C., July 28, 1936; s. John R. Murphy; m. Rachel Morris; children—George, John, Katherine. A.B., Princeton U., 1958; M.D., Johns Hopkins U., 1962. Diplomate Am. Bd. Pediatrics. Intern, New Eng. Med. Ctr., Boston, 1962-63; resident in pediatrics Columbia-Presbyn. Med. Ctr., N.Y.C., 1963-65; fellow in neurology Mass. Gen. Hosp., 1967-70, Harvard U., Boston, 1967-70; asst. prof. U. Pitts. Sch. Medicine, 1970-75; assoc. prof. Med. Coll. Wis., Milw., 1975-81; prof. dept. neurology and pediatrics, 1981-82, clin. prof. dept. pediatrics, 1982—; mem. staff Children's Hosp. Pitts., 1970-75, chief dept. neurology Milw. Children's Hosp., 1975-81, Froedtert Meml. Lutheran Hosp., 1980—; courtesy staff St. Michael's Hosp., 1982— St. Joseph's Hosp., St. Francis Hosp., West Allis Hosp., St. Mary's Hosp.; cons. staff Milw. Psychiat. Hosp.; dir. So. Wis. Ctr. Epilepsy Clinic, Union Grove, 1977—; mem. Epilepsy Med. Rev. Bd., State of Wis., 1978—; mem. Devel. Disabilities Council State of Wis., 1979-82. Mem. community adv. bd. Willowglen Acad., 1977—; mem. Allegheny County chpt. Assn. Retarded Citizens, Wis., 1974-75. Recipient Tchr. of Yr. award Milw. Children's Hosp., 1982; grantee Med. Coll. Wis., NIH, Milw. Children's Hosp., Abbott Labs. Mem. Milw. Pediatric Neurology Soc. (pres. 1984—), Child Neurology Soc., (chmn. sci. selection com. 1976—), Am. Acad. Neurology, Wis. Neurol. Soc., Soc. Pediatric Research, Am. Epilepsy Soc., Milw. Acad. Medicine, Central Soc. Neurol. Research, Upper Midwest Child Neurology Soc. (program dir. 1977), Assn. Research Nervous and Mental Diseases, Soc. Study Inborn Errors of Metabolism, Am. Med. Joggers Assn. Home: 2018 E Lake Bluff Blvd Shorewood WI 53211

MURPHY, JOHN BERNARD, electrical manufacturers agency executive; b. Geddes, S.D., July 29, 1924; s. William J. and Helen Louise (McGinnis) M.; children—Michael, Brian, Patrick. Student Sch. Bus., U. Minn., 1948. With mktg. dept. Westinghouse & Gen. Cable Corp., Mpls., 1951-63; pres., founder J.B. Murphy Assocs., Inc., Mpls., 1964—. Served with U.S. Army, World War II. Mem. North Central Elec. League, Beta Theta Pi. Democrat. Roman Catholic. Club: DeCathlon Athletic. Home: 9600 Oxborough Rd Bloomington MN 55437 Office: JB Murphy Assocs Inc 2204 W 94th St Minneapolis MN 55431

MURPHY, JOHN THOMAS, insurance company executive; b. Detroit, Dec. 18, 1928; s. Herbert F. and Edna (Gallier) M. B.S. cum laude, U. Notre Dame, 1950; M.B.A., Harvard U., 1952. Services trainee Allstate Ins. Co., Chgo., 1954-55, office supr., Detroit, 1955-56, operation div. supt., 1956-57, pub. relations mgr., Milw., 1957-63, pub. affairs mgr., Skokie, Ill., 1963-71, state and community relations dir., Northbrook, Ill., 1971—, exec. dir. Allstate Found., 1971—. Chmn. Milw. County Heart Assn.; bd. dirs. Wis. Council Safety, Chgo. chpt. USO, Skokie Valley United Fund; bd. dirs., mem. fin. com. Nat. League Nursing, N.Y.C.; bd. dirs., treas. Donors Forum of Chgo., 1974-76. Served to 1st lt. USAF, 1952-54. Mem. Skokie C. of C. (pres.), Pub. Relations Soc. Am., Milw. Assn. Commerce. Clubs: Press (Milw.); Univ. (Milw. and Detroit); Chgo. Athletic Assn., Chgo. Press (Chgo.). Home: 111 E Chestnut Apt 41G Chicago IL 60611 Office: Allstate Plaza Northbrook IL 60062

MURPHY, KATHRYN LOUISE, librarian, educator; b. Beatrice, Nebr., Apr. 19, 1932; d. Edward Philip and Bess Bertha (Weingarten) Bachle; m. Roy Edward Murphy, June 18, 1950 (dec. Jan. 1965); children—Timothy Micheal, Daniel Lee, Holly Ann Murphy Barstow. Student Hastings Coll., 1949-50; B.S. in Edn., N.W. Mo. State U., 1970; M.A., U. Mo., 1980. Bookkeeper, typist Western Tablet and Stationery, St. Joseph, Mo., 1950-55; pvt. piano tchr., St. Joseph and Maryville, Mo., 1955-64; periodicals clk., browsing room librarian Wells Learning Resources Ctr., N.W. Mo. State U., Maryville, 1965-69, cataloger, 1970-76, head cataloger, 1976-81, asst. to dir., 1983-84, asst. dir., 1984, head circulation services, 1981-83, head circulation services Owens Library, 1983-85, temp. acting dir., 1981-84, head library automated services, 1985—. Trustee, First Presbyn. Ch., Maryville, 1978-81, bd. deacons, 1971-74, 82-84, mem. session, elder, 1985—. Mem. ALA, Mo. Library Assn. Presbyterian. Home: 110 S Buchanan St Maryville MO 64468 Office: NW Mo State U BD Owens Library Maryville MO 64468

MURPHY, MARY KATHLEEN, nurse; b. Cleve., Nov. 5, 1950; d. Pierce Harry and Mary Eileen (Murphy) Mullally; m. Raymond Michael Murphy, Aug. 28, 1976; children—John Brendan, Ellen Kathleen. Student St. Louis U., 1969-71; diploma St. Vincent Charity Hosp. Sch. Nursing, Cleve., 1974. Staff nurse George Washington U. Med. Ctr., Washington, 1974, Case Western Res. U. Med. Ctr., Cleve., 1974-76, ARC, Cleve., 1976-78, Case Western Res. U. Hosps., Cleve., 1980. Bd. dirs. Catherine Horstmann Home, 1984; chmn. ann. fund raiser Help Home for Retarded Children, 1978. Mem. Carmelite Guild (corr. sec. 1982-83, co-chmn. ann. fund raiser 1983). Roman Catholic. Home: 15121 N Deepwood Ln Chagrin Falls OH 44022

MURPHY, MARY KATHRYN, industrial hygienist; b. Kansas City, Mo., Apr. 16, 1941; d. Arthur Charles and Mary Agnes (Fitzgerald) Wahlstedt; B.A., Avila Coll., Kansas City, 1962; M.S., Central Mo. State U., 1975; m. Thomas E. Murphy, Jr., Aug. 26, 1963; children—Thomas E., III, David W. Indsl. hygienist Kansas City area office Occupational Safety and Health Adminstrn., 1975-78, regional indsl. hygienist, 1979—; asst. dir. safety office U. Kans. Med. Center, 1978-79. Summer talent fellow Kaw Valley Heart Assn., 1961; cert. in comprehensive practice of indsl. hygiene. Mem. Am. Indsl. Hygiene Assn. (sec.-treas. Mid-Am. sect. 1978-79, dir. 1981, mem. auditcom.), Am. Chem. Soc., Am. Conf. Govt. Indsl. Hygienists (mem. chem. agts. threshold limit value com.), Am. Acad. Indsl. Hygiene, N.Y. Acad. Scis., AAAS, Internat. Soc. Environ. Toxicology and Cancer, Am. Coll. Toxicology, Am. Conf. on Chem. Labeling. Home: 10616 W 123rd Street Overland Park KS 66213 Office: 911 Walnut St Suite 406 Kansas City MO 64106

MURPHY, MAX RAY, lawyer; b. Goshen, Ind., July 18, 1934; s. Loren A. and Lois (Mink) M.; B.A., DePauw U., 1956; J.D., Yale Law Sch., 1959; student Mich. State U., 1960; m. Ruth Leslie Henricson, June 10, 1978; children—Michael Lee, Chad Woodrow. Admitted to Mich. bar, 1960; legal asso. Glassen, Parr, Rhead & McLean, Lansing, Mich., 1960-67; instr. Lansing Bus. U., 1963-67; partner firm Dalman, Murphy, Bidol, & Bouwens, P.C., Holland, Mich., 1967—. Democratic candidate for Ingham County (Mich.) Pros. Atty., 1962, 1964; asst. pros. atty. Ottawa County, Mich., 1967-70. Mem. Ottawa County, Ingham County, Am. bar assns. Clubs: Holland Country, Michigan Jaycees. Home: 4941 Rosabelle Beach Holland MI 49423 Office: 272 E 8th St Holland MI 49423

MURPHY, PATRICK DENNIS, advertising executive, writer, designer; b. Saginaw, Mich., Mar. 22, 1947; s. Patrick Leo and Mildred Ann (Rork) M.; m. Pauline Sue Zlotnik, Aug. 26, 1967; children—Pamela Ann, Philip John. Student Mich. State U., 1965-66, Kendall Sch. Design, Grand Rapids, Mich., 1966-69. Artist, Aves Advt., Grand Rapids, 1966-67; layout artist Jaqua Advt., Grand Rapids, 1967-69; v.p., co-owner, creative dir. Bradford-LaRivere, Inc., Saginaw, Mich., 1969-74; pres., creative dir. P.D.M. Design Co., Saginaw, 1974—; pres. Concept to Reality, Saginaw, 1982—; tchr. layout and design Northwood Inst., Midland, Mich., 1977-82. Designer, cartoon characters, graphics and performance posters. Mem. membership com. Saginaw YMCA; mem. publicity com. Saginaw Community Found. Mem. Am. Advt. Fedn. Roman Catholic. Club: Saginaw. Office: 2702 McCarty Rd Saginaw MI 48603

MURPHY, RICHARD CARDEN, construction company executive; b. Berwyn, Ill., June 3, 1947; s. Carden R. and Marguerite (Skocovsky) M.; m. Merriellyn Kett, Jan. 7, 1984; 1 child, Kett Clare. A.B., Georgetown U., 1969; J.D., U. Paris, 1973. Treas. A.C.S. Industries, Inc., Chgo., 1974-75, pres., 1975-79, chmn., 1982—; chmn. Guardian Mech. Systems, Chgo., 1979-82; dir. Janata Mgmt. Co., Chgo., Willow Automotive, Inc., Chgo., M&M Supply Co., Berwyn, Chgo. Bldg Co. Author: Long Term Planning in Eurodollar Economics, 1971; Practical Sailing in French Polinisia, 1978; Building in the Third World, 1980. Bd. dirs. Kett/Murphy Found., Chgo., 1980—. Mem. several bar assns. and constrn. trade assns. Democrat. Roman Catholic. Clubs: Chgo. Yacht, Chgo. Athletic (bd. dirs. 1980-85, sec. 1985—); Bora-Bora Yacht (Tahiti); U.S. Yacht Racing Union. Office: ACS Industries Inc 1929 W Schiller St Chicago IL 60622

MURPHY, ROBERT, management consulting and auditing company executive; b. Davenport, Iowa, Aug. 25, 1941; s. James and Patricia (Cahill) M. B.S., U. Ill. Med. Ctr.-Chgo., 1963. Registered pharmacist, Ill. Dir. orgn. and human resource devel. Walgreen Co., Chgo., 1963-73; dir. exec. search Coopers & Lybrand, Chgo., 1973—. Contbr. articles to Venture mag., hosp. mgmt. jour. Mem. Am. Soc. Personnel Adminstrs., Young Execs. Club, Am. Pharm. Assn., Am. Personnel and Guidance Assn., Council on Hotel Restaurant and Instnl. Edn., Am. Mgmt. Assn. (co-author tng. program How to Improve Individual Management Performance). Club: River. Office: Coopers & Lybrand 222 S Riverside Plaza Chicago IL 60606

MURPHY, ROBERT FRANCIS, finance company executive; b. N.Y.C., Dec. 30, 1921; s. Frank J. and Mary (Neely) M.; m. Madeline L. Fleming, June 16, 1951; children—Marilyn C., R. Morgan, Philip M. B.S., Columbia U., 1949. With Gen. Motors Acceptance Corp., Detroit, 1949—, treas., 1960-67, v.p., 1967-78, exec. v.p., 1978-80, pres., 1980—, also chmn. exec. com., dir.; dir. Motors Ins. Corp., 1978—, chmn., 1980—; dir. GMAC Mortgage Corp.; trustee Mortgage and Realty Trust. Bd. dirs. Hwy. Users Fedn.; mem. consumer adv. council Fed. Res. Bd., 1984—. Served with AUS, 1943-46. Mem. Nat. Assn. Home Builders (mortgage roundtable 1985—). Clubs: Washington Golf and Country (Arlington, Va.); Detroit Recess. Office: Gen Motors Acceptance Corp 3044 W Grand Blvd Detroit MI 48202

MURPHY, ROBERT GRANT, forging company executive; b. Caracas, Venezuela, Aug. 13, 1952; s. Benton Franklin and Jane Olive (Billingsley) M.; m. Cartha Darlene DeCoster, Nov. 3, 1979; children—Angela Maria, Kristen Leigh. B.A., Ind. U., 1975; M.P.A., 1977. Coordinator Ind. U. Police Acad., Bloomington, 1972-76; investigator Inst. Research in Pub. Safety, Bloomington, 1976-77; patrolman Boulder Police Dept. (Colo.), 1977-79; v.p. Wodin Inc., Bedford Heights, Ohio, 1979—, also treas. Bd. dirs., corr. sec. Concern for Children, Shaker Heights, Ohio, 1983-85; head usher Fairmount Presbyn. Ch., Cleveland Heights, 1982-85. Mem. Am. Mgmt. Assn. Presbyterian. Home: 59 Trumbull St Hudson OH 44236 Office: Wodin Inc 5441 Perkins Rd Bedford Heights OH 44146

MURPHY, STEPHEN J(OSEPH), lawyer; b. St. Louis, Jan. 29, 1938; s. Stephen J. and Martha G. (Gorman) M.; m. Mary Beth Berra, Oct. 14, 1961; children—Stephen J., Christina M. B.S. in Commerce, St. Louis U., 1959, M.S. in Commerce, 1968, J.D., 1974. Bar: Mo. 1984, Asst. dir. personnel Rexall Drug Co., St. Louis, 1960-65; personnel mgr. Kroger Foods, St. Louis, 1965-66; mgr. indsl. relations Carling Brewing Co., Belleville, Ill., 1966-73; dir. indsl. relations St. Louis Ship, 1973-76; sole practice law, St. Louis, 1976—; mcpl. judge City of St. George, Mo., 1983—. Served with USAR, 1959-66. Mem. Assn. Trial Lawyers Am., Bar Assn. Met. St. Louis. Roman Catholic. Clubs: K.C., Concord Democratic (exec. v.p. 1982—, pres. 1985-86). Home: 7227 Briarview Dr Affton MO 63123 Office: 59 Grasso Plaza 112 Saint Louis MO 63123

MURPHY, STEVEN PATRICK, petroleum geologist, consultant; b. Hays, Kans., Dec. 30, 1952; s. John Patrick and Coralie Jennine (Niedens) M.; m. Patricia Anne Smith, Apr. 16, 1977; 1 child, Taylor Patrick. B.S. in Geology, Ft. Hays State U., 1982. Geologist, Green Oil Ops., Hays, 1980-82; sr. geologist Energy Exploration Inc., Wichita, Kans., 1982-84; cons. petroleum geologist, Wichita, 1984—. Served with USN, 1971-75. Mem. Am. Assn. Petroleum Geologists, Kans. Geol. Soc. Republican. Lutheran. Avocations: hunting, flying, skiing, fishing. Home: 2321 Inwood Circle Wichita KS 67226 Office: Murphy Petroleum Inc PO Box 3846 Wichita KS 67201

MURPHY, THOMAS, lawyer; b. Cin., Aug. 24, 1942; s. Edward Charles and Bianca (Terranova) M.; m. Virginia Stoll, July 16, 1965; children—Caroline, Jason. B.A. in Econs., U. Cin., 1964, J.D., 1967. Bar: Ohio 1967, U.S. Dist. Ct. (so. dist.) Ohio 1968, U.S. Ct. Appeals (6th cir.) 1971, U.S. Ct. Appeals (D.C. cir.) 1976. Assoc., White & Getgey, Cin., 1967-69; trial atty. U.S. Dept. Labor, Cin., 1969-70; prof. law, assoc. dean U. Cin., 1970-74; v.p., sr. counsel Kroger Co., Cin., 1974—; cons. in field. Contbr. articles to profl. jours. Mem. Cin. Leadership, 1983—; chmn. Am. Heart Assn., 1984—; Bd. dirs. Cin. Model Cities program, 1971, Legal Aid Soc., 1972-74, Chriss King Sch., 1980-83. Mem. Ohio State Bar Assn. (labor law sect.). Republican. Roman Catholic. Avocations: running; bicycling; fiction; writing. Office: Kroger Co 1014 Vine St Cincinnati OH 45202

MURPHY, TRAVIS LEE, accountant; b. Moline, Ill., June 12, 1956; s. James Noal and Margaret Francis (Glidewell) M.; m. Laurel Marie Holdorf, Oct. 10, 1980; B.S. in Acctg., U. Ill., 1979. C.P.A., Minn. Acct. Price Water House, Mpls., 1979-82; acctg. supr. Magnetic Controls, Mpls., 1982-83; controller Bio Medicus Inc., Eden Prairie, Minn., 1983—. Mem. Am. Inst. C.P.A.'s, Minn. Soc. C.P.A.'s, Nat. Assn. Accts. Republican. Lutheran. Avocations: golf; tennis; skiing; camping; reading. Office: Bio-Medicus Inc 9600 W 76th St Eden Prairie MN 55344

MURPHY, WALLACE HAYDEN, school administrator; b. Evansville, Ind., Mar. 29, 1937; s. Lloyd Jennings and Gertrude Clarkie (Hatcher) M.; m. Verlaine Van Zegeren, Aug. 9; children—James, Robert, Michael, David. B.A., Murray State U., 1958; M.A., Mich. State U., 1966, Western Mich. U., 1975. Cert. tchr. Ky., Mich., cert. adminstr., Mich. Tchr. Godwin Pub. Schs., Wyoming, Mich., 1958-73, asst. prin., 1973-76, prin., 1976—; middle sch. prin. Goodwin Pub. Schs., Wyoming, 1977—. Executed mural Ft. Buchanan, San Juan, P.R.; prin. works of sculpture include Ft. Buchanan, 1963. Vol. Com. to Establish Wyoming City Library, 1973-74. Served as sgt. U.S. Army, 1961-63. Mem. Mich. Assn. Secondary Sch. Prins., Nat. Acad. Sch. Execs., Nat. Assn. Secondary Sch. Prins. Democrat. Baptist. Home: 3662 Giddings SE Grand Rapids MI 49508 Office: Godwin Pub Schs 111 36th St SE Wyoming MI 49508

MURPHY, WILLIAM ALEXANDER, JR., diagnostic radiologist, educator; b. Pitts., Apr. 26, 1945; s. William Alexander and LaRue (Eshbaugh); m. Judy Marie Lang, June 8, 1977; children—Abigail Norris, William Lawrence, Joseph Ryan. B.S., U. Pitts., 1967; M.D., Pa. State U., 1971. Diplomate Am. Bd. Radiology. Medicine intern Barnes Hosp., St. Louis, 1971-72, staff radiologist, 1975—; radiology resident Washington U., St. Louis, 1972-75, prof. radiology, 1983—; sect. chief Mallinchrodt Inst. Radiology, St. Louis, 1975—; cons. Office Med. Examiner City and County St. Louis, 1977—. Contbr. numerous articles to profl. jours. and books. Fellow Am. Acad. Forensic Scis., Am. Coll. Radiology; mem. Radiol. Soc. N.Am., Am. Roentgen Ray Soc., Am. Soc. Bone and Mineral Research, Internat. Skeletal Soc., Assn. Univ. Radiologists. Methodist. Home: 60 Kingsbury Pl Saint Louis MO 63112 Office: Mallinckrodt Inst Radiology 510 S Kingshighway Blvd Saint Louis MO 63110

MURPHY, WILLIAM MARK HICKEY, educational administrator; b. Hartford, Conn., Dec. 7, 1944; s. William Mark Hickey II and Dorothy (MacVeagn) Hickey-Murphy; m. Grace Daniels, June 9, 1967; children—Christin, Jonathan, Kevin. B.A., Norwich U., 1967; M.A., U. Buffalo, 1969. History instr. Buffalo Sem., N.Y., 1969-72; investment officer Marine Midland Bank, Buffalo, 1972-76; asst. headmaster Park Sch. of Buffalo, 1976-79, headmaster, 1979-81, Keith Country Day Sch., Rockford, Ill., 1981—. Bd. dirs. Keith Country Day Sch., 1981. Mem. Greater Chgo. Assn. Independent Schs., Council for Advancement and Support of Edn., Nat. Assn. Independent Schs., Phi Alpha Theta. Lodge: Rotary. Avocations: golf, sailing, coaching ice hockey, skiing. Office: Keith Country Day Sch #1 Jacoby Pl Rockford IL 61107

MURRAY, ALAN EDWARD, radio broadcast engineer; b. Rice Lake, Wis., Oct. 27, 1946; s. Marcus S. and Verna M. (Gallenger) M.; m. Lois Ann Heil, Aug. 18, 1973. Student U. Wis., 1963, U. Wis.-River Falls, 1971-72, Wis. State Coll., 1964-67. FCC radio licenses 1960-62, 71, 82. Staff WJMC-FM, Rice Lake, 1962-63; dir. engring. sta. WRFW-FM, River Falls, 1971—; engr. sta. WHWC/W55AP TV, Wis. Pub. TV, 1981—. Served with radio corps USN, 1967-71. Recipient U. Wis. Outstanding Service award, 1982. Mem. Handi Ham System, Am. Radio Relay League, Soc. Broadcast Engrs. Club: Saint Croix Valley Repeaters. Office: Sta WRFW-FM 306 North Hall University of Wisconsin River Falls WI 54022

MURRAY, ARNETTE MARIE, educational administrator; b. Chgo., Dec. 17, 1934; d. Arnett Bedford Francis and Hazel Marie (Lumpkins) Murray; B.S., U. Ill., 1957; M.S., Coll. Racine, 1974; Ph.D., So. Ill. U., 1981; div.; children—Victor, Vincent, Victoria. Tchr., Holy Child High Sch., Waukegan, Ill., 1957-60; tchr. Zion (Ill.) Elem. Dist. No. 6, 1969-70, Title I dir., 1970-76; ednl. cons. reading, tchrs. centers, gifted edn., coordinator tchr. tng./staff devel. Ill. State Bd. Edn., Springfield, Ill., 1976—; cons. U.S. Dept. Edn., NEA. Vol. workshop leader Springfield Housing Authority, 1980; Right-to-Read dir. Zion-Benton Twp., 1974-76; mem. Zion Environ. Commn., 1974; chairperson Selective Service Civilian Rev. Bd., Springfield, Ill., 1984—. Mem. Am. Assn. Sch. Adminstrs., Assn. Tchr. Educators, Ill. Assn. Supervision and Curriculum Devel., Am. Assn. Supervision and Curriculum Devel. Home: 2908 Woodward Ave Springfield IL 62703 Office: 100 N 1st St Springfield IL 62777

MURRAY, BARBARA ANN, banker; b. Mitchell, S.D., Apr. 17, 1953; d. John Richard and Shirley Ann (Larson) McNary; m. Wayne Allan Murray, Jan. 25, 1975; children—Corissa Ann, Rebecca Lea, Jeffrey Wayne. B.S. in Edn., Dakota State Coll., 1975. Substitute tchr. Sioux Falls Pub. Schs., S.D., 1975; assoc. Murray Constrn., Sioux Falls, 1975-82; telephone rep. Citibank S.D. NA, Sioux Falls, 1982-83, sr. service rep., 1983-84, unit mgr. customer service, 1984—. Mem. Nat. Assn. Female Execs. Democrat. Lutheran. Clubs: Mothers (pres. 1977-78), Christian Women's (prayer adviser 1980-82). Lodge: Order Eastern Star. Avocations: sewing; camping; hiking; sports. Home: Route 2 Box 65 Country Villa Estates Hartford SD 57033

MURRAY, CALVIN JAMES, sales executive; b. Battle Creek, Mich., Feb. 17, 1924; s. George E. and Eden R. (Johnston), M.; children—Pamela, Daniel, Molly, Julie; m. Kathryn Day, Feb. 17, 1980. B.S.M.E., Notre Dame, 1950. Sales engr. Consumers Power, Jackson, Mich., 1950-54; contract supr. Davis Electric, Traverse City, Mich., 1954-56; service mgr. Gallmeyer & Livingston, Grand Rapids, Mich., 1956-68, sales mgr., 1968—. Served with USN, 1943-46. Club: Engineer (Grand Rapids) (pres. 1960-61). Avocations: golf; boating. Office: Gallmeyer & Livingston Co 336 Straight Ave SW Grand Rapids MI 49504

MURRAY, CHARLES ALBERT, dentist; b. Lansing, Mich., Aug. 15, 1929; s. Donald Albert and Ruth Arlene (Legge) M.; m. Margery Ann Boos, June 26, 1954; children—Barbara, Donald, Susan, Megan. B.S., U. Mich., 1951, D.D.S., 1955. Gen. practice dentistry, Birmingham, Mich., 1955—. Scoutmaster Detroit Area council Boy Scouts Am., 1969-71. Served to lt. USN, 1955-57. Fellow Internat. Coll. Dentistry, Pierre Fauchoud Acad.; mem. ADA, Mich. Dental Assn. (chmn. legis. com. 1979-80), Phi Kappa Phi, Omicron Kappa Upsilon, Phi Gamma Delta. Republican. Episcopalian. Club: Birmingham Athletic (pres. 1972-73). Avocations: fishing, hunting, squash, basketball. Home: 600 Waddington St Birmingham MI 48009 Office: 3684 W Maple St Birmingham MI 48010

MURRAY, GREGG ALLEN, lawyer; b. Mpls., Feb. 12, 1954; s. Michael William and Lorraine Mae (Rusch) M.; m. Constance Elizabeth Thomas, June 29, 1984; children—Jonathan Daniel, Michael Christopher. Linguist Def. Lang. Inst., 1976; B.A. magna cum laude, Hamline U., 1978; J.D., William Mitchell Coll. Law, 1982. Bar: Minn. 1982. Sole practice, Long Lake, Minn., 1982—; cons. Parents Without Ptnrs., Minn., 1984—. Editorial bd. William Mitchell Coll. Law Rev., 1980-82. Served to airman 1st class USAF, 1974-76. Mem. Minn. Bar Assn., ABA, Hennepin County Bar Assn., Ramsey County Bar Assn., Minn. World Trade Assn., Long Lake C. of C. (v.p. 1983-84), Delta Phi Alpha, Kappa Phi. Democrat. Roman Catholic. Home: 2717 Shannon Ln Mound MN 55364 Office: 1850 W Wayzata Blvd Long Lake MN 55356

MURRAY, JAMES ARTHUR, human services administrator; b. Winona, Minn., Feb. 14, 1948; s. Clifford A. and Muriel E. (Pike) M.; children—Megan, Matthew. B.A., Lawrence U., 1970; postgrad. U. Minn., 1975-76. Counselor Paul A. Dever Sch., Taunton, Mass., 1970-72, Main House, Winona, 1979-81; tchr. Faribault State Sch., Minn., 1972-74, 76-78; asst. U. Minn-Mpls., 1975-76; coordinator Winona Vol. Services, 1981—. Bd. dirs. Minn. Assn. Retarded Citizens, Mpls., 1975, Montessori Sch., Faribault, 1976-78; pres. Catter Sch.-Home Assn., Winona, 1983-84. Recipient Outstanding Project award Faribault State Sch., 1978. Mem. Minn. Assn. Vol. Dirs., Nat. Assn. Retarded Citizens, Am. Assn. Mental Deficiency. Roman Catholic. Avocations: music, cross country skiing, biking, reading. Home: 227 E 7th St Winona MN 55987

MURRAY, JAMES EDWARD, insurance company safety executive; b. Chgo., May 9, 1929; s. Edward Henry and Elizabeth (Cotter) M.; m. Marie J. Runzo, Apr. 14, 1973; children—Betty Anne, Valerie, Marie, Rhonda, David, Paul. Student Chgo. City Jr. Coll., 1953-54. Lic. pilot. Mapmaker, Sanborn Map Co., Pelham, N.Y., 1954-72; casualty loss control supr. Assn. Mill & Elevator Mut. Ins. Cos., Chgo., 1972—; lectr. in field. Served as sgt. USAF, 1947-53. Mem. Am. Soc. Safety Engrs., Nat. Safety Council (exec. com.), Nat. Fire Protection Assn., Ins. Loss Control Orgn., Am. Chem. Soc. (safety and health div.), Soc. Fire Prevention Engrs. Home: 539 Walker Dr Bolingbrook IL 60439 Office: The Mill Mutuals 2 North Riverside Plaza Chicago IL 60606

MURRAY, JOHN L., food processing company executive. Chmn., chief exec. officer Universal Foods Corp., Milw., also dir. Office: Universal Foods Corp 433 E Michigan St Milwaukee WI 53202*

MURRAY, JOHN PATRICK, psychologist, scientist; b. Cleve., Sept. 14, 1943; s. John Augustine and Helen Marie (Lynch) M.; m. Ann Coke Dennison, Apr. 17, 1971; children—Jonathan Coke, Ian Patrick. Ph.D., Cath. U. Am., 1970. Mem. Nat. Register of Health, D.C., Nebr., Mich. Research dir. Office of U.S. Surgeon Gen., NIMH, Bethesda, Md., 1969-72; asst., then assoc. prof. psychology Macquarie U., Sydney, Australia, 1973-76, assoc. prof., 1977-79; fellow pediatric psychology U. N.C. Med. Sch., 1972-73; assoc. prof. psychology U. Mich., Ann Arbor, 1979-80; dir. youth and family policy Boys Town Ctr., Boys Town, Nebr., 1980-85; prof., head dept. family devel. Kans. State U., 1985—. Mem. Nebr. Foster Care Rev. Bd., 1982-84; mem. Advocacy Office for Children and Youth, 1980—; mem. Nat. Council Children and TV, 1982—; mem. Crime Prevention Council, Nat. Sheriffs Assn., 1984—; mem adv. bd. Nat. Ctr. Abused Handicapped Children, 1984—; mem. research grants com. Meyer Children's Rehab. Inst., 1984—. Fellow Am. Psychol. Assn.; mem. Am. Sociol. Assn., Soc. Research in Child Devel. Clubs: Royal Commonwealth Soc. (London), Omaha Press. Author: (with E. A. Rubinstein, G.A. Comstock) Television and Social Behavior, 3 vols., 1972; Television and Youth: 25 Years of Research and Controversy, 1980; (with H. T. Rubin) Status Offenders: A Sourcebook, 1983; (with G. Solomon) The Future of Children's Television, 1984; contbr. numerous articles to profl. jours. Home: 1731 Humboldt St Manhattan KS 66502 Office: Dept Family and Child Devel Kans State U Manhattan KS 66506

MURRAY, JOHN RICHARD, consulting scientist; b. Chgo., Oct. 6, 1921; s. William G. and Olive M. (Kimmet) M.; B.S., U. Mich., 1947; J.D., DePaul U., 1950; m. Grace M. Gast, June 7, 1944; children—John Terrence, Mary Jill, Kathleen, Nancy, Carolyn, William G. Pres., cons. meteorologist Murray & Trettel, Northfield, Ill., 1947—; cons. in meteorology Commonwealth Edison Co., No. Ill. Gas Co., U.S. Steel Corp., Res. Mining Co., others; councilman City of Lake Forest (Ill.), 1965-67. Served with USAAF, 1943-46. Cert. cons. meteorologist. Fellow Am. Meteorol. Soc.; mem. AAAS, Am. Pub. Works Assn. (life). Roman Catholic. Club: Knollwood. Home: 240 Buckminster Ct Lake Bluff IL 60044 Office: 414 W Frontage Rd Northfield IL 60093

MURRAY, LAWRENCE LEO, JR., social agency executive; b. Pitts., Apr. 28, 1920; s. Lawrence L. and Julia F. (Ford) M.; m. Mary Louise Vath, Feb. 5, 1943; children—Lawrence L. III, Patrick J., Mary Anne, James J. B.A., Duquesne U., 1941. Sales mgr. U.S. Gypsum Co., Pitts., 1939-52; v.p. sales D.J. Kennedy Co., Pitts., 1952-56; v.p. sales mktg. Grand Rapids Gypsum Co., Mich., 1956-74; exec. dir. Area Agy. on Aging, Grand Rapids, 1974—; dir. Mich. Soc. Gerontology, Lansing, 1978—, Nat. Assn. Area Agencies on Aging, Washington, 1984—; natl. chmn. Soc. St. Vincent De Paul Aging Com., St. Louis, 1980—. Served with USAF, 1942-46, PTO. Democrat. Roman Catholic. Clubs: Press, Breakfast (Grand Rapids). Lodge: K.C. Avocations: walking, swimming, reading. Home: 482 Barkwood NW Grand Rapids MI 49504 Office: Area Agency on Aging of Western Mich 2 Fountain Pl Grand Rapids MI 49504

MURRAY, LEANNE MADELINE, educational administrator; b. Wichita, Kans., Feb. 13, 1949; d. Marvin Francis and Marjorie Pauline (Finkle) Daggett; m. George S. Murray III, Feb. 14, 1982; 1 child, Jessica Kyle. B.A., Wichita State U., 1971; M.A., U. Okla., 1975. Instr. Okla. State U., Oklahoma City, 1973-75; asst. dir. prison edn. St. Mary Coll., Leavenworth, Kans., 1976-81; dean gen. edn. DeVry Inst. Tech., Kansas City, Mo., 1981—. Mem. Nat. Council Tchrs. English, MLA, Am. Soc. Engring. Edn. Democrat. Presbyterian. Avocations: tennis; writing; cooking. Home: 5703 Locust St Kansas City MO 64110

MURRAY, MARY THERESE, communications and marketing executive; b. Chgo., Dec. 13, 1956; d. James William and Helen Therese (Nichin) Murray. B.A. in English and Communications, DePaul U., Chgo., 1978. Adminstrv. asst. advt. Frank J. Corbett, Inc. div. BBDO Internat., Inc., Chgo., 1978-80; asst. account exec. advt., mktg. and pub. relations Mallof, Abruzino & Nash Mktg., Lombard, Ill., 1980; asst. dir. alumni relations and devel. DePaul U., 1981-84; account coordinator Burke Promotional Mktg. div. Communication Industries, Inc., Chgo., 1984—. Mem. benefit planning com. Alliance Maison Francaise de Chgo., 1979-82; active Big Sisters Chgo., 1981—; adj. bd. dirs. Access Living affiliate Rehab. Inst. of Chgo., 1982—, also co-chmn. benefit com., 1984—; mem. Democratic Women's Council Cook County, Chgo. Mem. Women in Communications (chmn. ann. seminar publicity North Shore chpt. 1983, chmn. chpt. fundraising and devel. 1983-84, v.p. membership 1984-85), Delta Zeta. Home: 1118 N Columbian Oak Park IL 60302 Office: 1165 N Clark St Chicago IL 60610

MURRAY, MAURICE ALLEN, ceramic engineer, consultant; b. Augusta, Ga., Aug. 4, 1919; s. Allen Malone and Annie (Kelly) M.; m. Mildred Christine Lawrence, June 23, 1943; children—Teresa Allen, Judith Michelle, Norman Lawrence. B.S., Va. Poly. Inst., 1941. Registered profl. engr., Tenn. Ceramic engr. Am. Ceramic Corp., Chattanooga, 1941-53, Page-Maden Co., Mineola, N.Y., 1953-54, Isolanthe Mfg. Corp., Sterling, N.J., 1954-55, BG Corp., Ridgefield, N.J., 1955-58, Vernitron Corp., Bedford, Ohio, 1958-81; cons. engr., Stow, Ohio, 1980—. Patentee in field. Served to lt. col. AUS, 1941-46, PTO. Mem. Nat. Inst. Ceramic Engrs., Am. Ceramic Soc. (emeritus). Republican. Episcopalian. Club: HRRVC, Inc. (pres. Karon, Ohio 1983). Home and Office: PO Box 1521 Stow OH 44224

MURRAY, MERRILL R., college official; b. New Castle, Ind., Aug. 3, 1917; s. Arthur Gray and Mary (Dixon) M.; student Hanover Coll., 1935-36, Kent State U., 1943; B.S., Ball State U., 1949, M.S., 1951; Ed.D., Ind. U., 1960; m. Eva Jean Yergin, Mar. 30, 1940; 1 son, Michael Russell. Math. tchr. high sch., New Castle, Ind., 1949-51, 53-54; dir. USAF Dependents Schs., Burtonwood, Eng., 1952-53; prin. high sch., Ridgeville, Ind., 1954-56; research asso. Ind. U., Bloomington, 1956-58; dean of students Tri-State U., Angola, 1958-59; dean specialized edn. div. Ferris State Coll., Big Rapids, Mich., 1959-65, asst. dean Sch. Gen. Edn., 1965-69, asso. dean, 1969—, assoc. dean Coll. Optometry, 1977-82, assoc. dean emeritus, 1982—. Served with USAAF, 1943-47; col. USAF (ret.). Mem. Nat. U. Continuing Edn. Assn. (div. chmn.), Mich. Coordinating Council Continuing Higher Edn. (pres.), Am. Personnel and Guidance Assn., Am. Optometric Assn. (asso.), Mich. Optometric Assn. (asso.), Air Force Assn., Mich. Assn. Schs. and Colls., Res. Officers Assn., Am. Assn. Higher Edn., Ferris State Coll. Emeriti Assn. (pres.), Mil. Order World Wars. Phi Delta Kappa, Kappa Delta Phi, Sigma Mu Sigma. Presbyn. (elder). Lodges: Masons, Rotary (pres. 1964-65). Home: 14851 Chula Vista Dr Big Rapids MI 49307 Office: Ferris State Coll Optometry Big Rapids MI 49307

MURRAY, RICHARD BLAINE, lawyer; b. Coshocton, Ohio, May 19, 1936; s. Ross Wesley and Lynna Eleanor M.; m. Susan B. Wallace, Sept. 8, 1961; children—Robert B., Ross B. B.A., Ohio State U., 1959; J.D., Capitol U., 1977. Bar: Ohio 1977. With indsl. mgmt. Becton Dickinson, Coshocton, Ohio, 1960-63, 63-67, asst. to gen. mgr., Brussels, 1963, plant mgr., Mt. Vernon, 1967-77; individual practice law, Mt. Vernon, Ohio, 1977—. Served with U.S. Army, 1960-63. Mem. ABA, Ohio Bar Assn., Knox County Bar Assn. Lodge: Rotary. Avocations: golf; music. Office: Richard B Murray 110 E Gambier St Mount Vernon OH 43050

MURRAY, ROBERT EUGENE, coal company executive; b. Martins Ferry, Ohio, Jan. 13, 1940; s. Albert Edward and Mildred Etheline (Shepherd) M.; B.Engring., Ohio State U., 1962; postgrad. Case Western Res. U., 1968-70, Harvard U. Grad. Sch. Bus. Advanced Mgmt. Program, U. N.D., 1982-83; m. Brenda Lou Moore, Aug. 26, 1962; children—Sherri Sue (dec.), Robert Edward, Jonathan Robert, Ryan Michael. Asst. to mgr. indsl. engring. and coal preparation N.Am. Coal Corp., 1961-63, sect. foreman, plant foreman, gen. mine foreman, Ohio div., 1963-64, asst. supt., 1964-66, supt. 1966-68, asst. to pres., Cleve., 1968-69, v.p. operations, v.p. eastern div., 1969-74, pres. Western div., 1974-83; exec. v.p. and pres. coal ops. N.Am. Coal Corp., 1985—; pres. Coteau Properties Co., Falkirk Mining Co., Western Plains Mining Co., Mo. Valley Properties Co., Quarto Mining Co., 1983—, v.p., dir. Nacco Mining Co.; dir. Sabine Mining Co.; pres. mining engring. departmental asst. Ohio State U., 1960-62; past pres., chmn. bd. N.D. Lignite Council. Past mem. exec. bd., v.p. dist. ops. No. Lights council Boy Scouts Am.; past pres., bd. dirs. United Way of Bismarck; bd. regents Mary Coll. Registered profl. engr., Ohio. Mem. Am. Mining Congress, Mining Electro-Mech. Assn. (pres. Ohio Valley br. 1967-68), Pitts. Coal Mining Inst. Am., Soc. Mining Engrs. AIME (bd. dirs., exec. com., past chmn. coal div., exec. com. coal div.), Soc. Mining Engrs. (dir.), Rocky Mountain Coal Mining Inst. (past pres., program chmn.), Nat. Coal Assn. (dir.), Ohio (pres. east Ohio chpt. 1966-67), Nat. socs. profl. engrs., Ohio Engrs. in Industry (mem. bd. govs. 1966-67). Republican. Methodist (past trustee, mem. adminstrv. bd. 1968-69, lay speaker, tchr.). Mason (32 deg., Shriner). Home: 32 Cotswold Ln Moreland Hills Chagrin Falls OH 44022 Office: 12800 Shaker Blvd Cleveland OH 44120

MURRAY, ROBERT HALE, III, development corporation executive; b. Roanoke, Va., Sept. 24, 1953; s. Robert Hale and Martha Francis (Mitchell) Murray; m. Nancy Grace Hilchen, May 13, 1978; 1 child, Robert Hale IV. B.A., Coll. William and Mary, 1975; M.B.A., Va. Poly. Inst. and State U., 1979. Cert. property mgr. Retail dept. mgr. Best Products Co., Roanoke, Va., 1975-78; property mgr. Snyder Hunt Co., Blacksburg, Va., 1979-83; regional property mgr. Mid-Am. Corp., Fort Wayne, Ind., 1983, Northill Devel. Corp., 1984—. Author jour. of Property Mgmt., Fort Wayne Apt. Guide, Policy and Procedures Manual (1st place award 1985), Residential Tenant Manual (nat. award 1985). Bd. dirs. Muscular Dystrophy Found., 1984—. Mem. Am. Mgmt. Assn., Fort Wayne Apt. Assn. (bd. dirs. 1985—), Fort Wayne Bd. Realtors, Accredited Residential Mgrs. Assn., Residential Apt. Mgrs. Assn. Avocations: pilot; horseback riding; scuba diving; golf. Home: 2524-6 Abbey Dr Fort Wayne IN 46815 Office: Northill Devel Corp 2615 Abbey Dr Fort Wayne IN 46815

MURRAY, ROBERT KISTLER, management consultant; b. Tulsa, Jan. 31, 1938; s. Richard Cranston and Mildred (Kistler) M.; m. Carolyn Braun, Sept. 7, 1963; children—Robert K. II, William Mark. B.S., U. Kans., 1960. Cert. profl. bus. cons. Acctg. dept. supr. Allstate Ins. Co., Kansas City, Mo., 1963-64; mgmt. cons. Profl. Mgmt. Midwest, Waterloo, Iowa, 1964-67; pres. Profl. Cons. Services, Inc., Columbia, Mo., 1967—; editorial cons. Physicians Mgmt., Teaneck, N.J., 1970—; seminar cons. U. Mo. Sch. Medicine, Columbia, 1974—. Contbr. articles to profl. jours. Served to capt. USMC, 1960-63. Mem. Soc. Med. Dental Mgmt. Cons. (pres. 1969-70), Inst. Cert. Bus. Cons. Methodist. Avocations: Hunting; fishing. Home: 3716 W Rollins Rd Columbia MO 65203 Office: Profl Cons Services Inc 310 Tiger Ln Columbia MO 65203

MURRAY, THOMAS ARTHUR, medical device industry executive, consultant; b. Lima, Ohio, Aug. 24, 1928; s. Harry Edward and Mildred Agnes (Shillito) M.; m. Shirley Mae Hatmaker, Feb. 5, 1955; children—Michele Lynn, Victoria Louise, Jacqueline Kay. B.A. in Indsl. Psychology, Mich. State U., 1951; M.B.A., U. Chgo., 1968. Asst. personnel dir. Ethyl Corp. Research, Detroit, 1954-63; exec. com. benefits-Sales Chrysler Corp., Detroit, 1963-64; staff asst. to pres. Wis. Steel div. Internat. Harvester, Chgo., 1964-70; dir. human resources and community devel. Medtronic, Inc., Mpls., 1970-76; pres. Murray & Murray, Inc., Scottsdale, Ariz., 1976-77; ptnr. Ropes Assocs., Inc., Fort Lauderdale, Fla., 1977-79; v.p. operational devel. and planning Med. Inc., Inver Grove Heights, Minn., 1979—; bus. advisor Vine St. Florist, Hudson, Wis., 1981—; dir. Med-Lab Systems, Edina, Minn., 1984—. Served with U.S. Army, 1951-53. Republican. Avocation: career counselor. Home: 6101 W 101st St Bloomington MN 55438

MURRAY, THOMAS AZEL, housing and urban development executive; b. Chgo., Jan. 15, 1929; s. Arnette Bedford Francis and Hazel Marie (Lumpkins) M.; m. Gale Patricia Roberts, Aug. 22, 1983. Student Ohio State U., 1950-51; M.A. in Counseling, Sangamon State U., 1976, M.A. in Communication, 1977; Ph.D. in Edn., So. Ill. U., 1982. Equal opportunity specialist Ill. Nat. Guard, 1973-75; civil rights officer U.S. Fed. Hwy. Adminstrn., Springfield, Ill., 1975-78; affirmative action officer Ill. State Bd. Edn., 1978-84; dir. compliance HUD, Chgo., 1984—. Commr. Human Relations Commn., Springfield, 1979; bd. dirs. Chgo. Baptist Assn., 1971-72. Served with Air N.G., 1972-73. Mem. U.S. Army Ret. Res. Assn., Sangamon State U. Alumni Assn. (bd. dirs. 1979-85), Ill. Affirmative Action Officers Assn. (parliamentarian, exec. bd. 1979—), Phi Kappa Phi. Office: US Dept HUD Room 2110 300 S Wacker Dr Chicago IL 60606

MURRAY, THOMAS EDWIN, health care consultant; b. Chgo., Apr. 19, 1938; s. Edwin M. and Mary A. (Nelson) M.; m. Frances Sue Severtsen, Apr. 30, 1966; children—T. Patrick, Megan M., Erin K. B.S., Loyola U., Chgo., 1960, M.Ed., 1971, Ed.D., 1977. Cert. tchr., adminstr., Ill. Tchr., counselor St. Gregory High Sch., Chgo., 1962-67; mgmt. trainee Abbott Labs., North Chicago, Ill., 1967-68; univ. and healthcare adminstr. Loyola U., Chgo., 1968-78, also bd. commrs. corp v.p. Alexian Bros. Health System, Ill., 1978-84; pres. SMW Cons., Chgo., 1984—; trustee Missionary Sisters Health Corp., Waukegan, Ill., 1983—. Founder Cath. Health System Planners Group, 1984. Pres. Peterson Woods Community Orgn., Chgo., 1971-72, St. Hilary Parish Council, Chgo., 1973; trustee St. Xavier Coll., Chgo., 1977-78. Arthur J. Schmitt fellow, 1973. Mem. Am. Coll. Hosp. Adminstrs., Am. Hosp. Assn., World Futures Soc., Soc. for Hosp. Planning. Roman Catholic. Avocations: sailing, camping. Office: Severtsen Murray Wozniak Inc 5715 N Lincoln Ave Chicago IL 60659

MURRAY, WILLIAM ROBERT, dentist; b. Storm Lake, Iowa, Dec. 14, 1930; s. W.C. and Mary (Kestel) M.; m. Jane E. Murray, 1953; children—Jeff, Jim, Eugene, Timothy, Pete, Pat, Elizabeth, Eileen. B.A., St. Ambrose Coll., 1953; D.D.S., Iowa U., 1957. Lic. dentist, S.D. Gen. practice dentistry, Sioux Falls, S.D., 1960—. Chmn. dental div. Dept. of Health, Sioux Falls, 1980-83. Served to capt. USAF, 1957-60. Mem. Southeast Dist. Dental Assn. (pres.), S.D. Dental Assn. (pres. 1982-83). Roman Catholic. Lodges: Elks, K.C. Avocations: flying, fishing, golfing. Home: RFD 3 Box 32 Sioux Falls SD 57106 Office: 825 W 10th St Sioux Falls SD 57106

MURRELL, CASTELLA BURNLEY, educator, biology consultant; b. Nashville, Jan. 26, 1926; d. Stephen Alexander and Maynie (Young) Burnley; m. Irvin Maurcie Murrell (dec. 1975); children—Janis, Irvin, Bertrand, Audrey. B.S., U. Louisville, 1948; M.S., U. Ill., Urbana, 1950; postgrad. U. Chgo., summers 1960-65. Microbiologist Provident Hosp., Chgo., 1950-52; research asst. U. Ill.-Chgo., 1952-54; microbiologist U. Chgo., 1954-58; research asst. Armour Research, Chgo., 1959-60; tchr. biology Chgo. Bd. Edn., 1960—, biology cons., 1969-72. Contbr. articles to profl. jours. Recipient Sci. Fair awards Chgo. Area Sci. Tchrs. Assn., 1964, 65, 67, Ill. Outstanding Tchr. award Chgo. Bd. Edn., 1966, Fellowship Honor award, 1967, citation Chgo. Heart Assn., 1967, 68. Mem. Nat. Sci. Tchrs. Assn., Nat. Assn. Female Execs., Ill. Soc. Microbiologists, Ill. Sci. Tchrs. Assn., Chgo. Biology Roundtable, Christian Educators Assn., Alpha Kappa Alpha. Methodist. Avocations: photography; tennis. Home: 9730 S Green St Chicago IL 60643

MURRIN, LEONARD CHARLES, II, pharmacology educator, researcher; b. Iowa City, Oct. 9, 1943; s. Leonard Charles and Huberta Frances (Jones) M.; m. Kathryn Grace McDermott, Aug. 17, 1968; children—Leonard Charles, Rose Colleen, Clare Rita. B.A., St. John's Coll., 1965; student Kearney State Coll., 1967-69; Ph.D., Yale U., 1975. Postdoc. assoc. Yale U. Med. Sch., New Haven, 1975; postdoctoral fellow Johns Hopkins U. Med. Sch., Balt., 1975-78; asst. prof. U. Nebr. Med. Sch., Omaha, 1978-83, assoc. prof., 1983—. Contbr. articles to profl. jours. and chpts. to books. Adv. med. bd. Southeast Nebr. March of Dimes, Omaha, 1979—; treas. Boyd Sch. PTA, Omaha, 1979; pres. Keystone Community Task Force, Omaha, 1982; bd. dirs. 1980—. Fellow NIH, 1975-78; grantee Nat. Sci. Found., 1980—, March of Dimes Found., 1982—; recipient Basil O'Connor award March of Dimes Found., 1979. Mem. Am. Soc. Pharmacology Exptl. Therapeutics, Am. Soc. Neurochemistry, Soc. for Neurosci., Internat. Soc. Neurochemistry, Internat. Soc. Devel. Neurosci. Avocations: golf; wine tasting; reading. Home: 5204 N 86th St Omaha NE 68134 Office: Dept Pharmacology Univ Nebraska Med School 42nd & Dewey Ave Omaha NE 68105

MURRY, CHARLES EMERSON, state official; b. Hope, N.D., June 23, 1924; s. Raymond Henry and Estelle Margarete (Skeim) M.; m. Donna Deane Kleve, June 20, 1948; children—Barbara, Karla, Susan, Bruce, Charles; B.S., U. N.D., 1950, J.D., 1950. Admitted to N.D. bar, mem. firm Nelson & Heringer, Rugby, 1950-51; dir. N.D. Legis. Council, 1951-75; adj. gen. N.D., Bismarck, 1975-84; cons. Council State Govts.; mem. res. forces policy bd. for sec. def. Vice pres. Missouri Slope Lutheran Home, Bismarck. Mem. Am., N.D. bar assns., NG Assn., Nat. Legis. Conf. (past chmn.), Adjs. Gen. Assn. (sec.), Commrs. on Uniform State Laws. Clubs: Masons; Elks; Exchange of Bismarck (past pres.). Recipient Sioux award U. N.D., Gov.'s Nat. Leadership award. Contbr. articles to profl. jours. Home and office: Star Route 9 Box 246 Bismarck ND 58501

MUSCH, HERMAN PETER, pediatrician; b. Cochabamba, Bolivia, June 11, 1942; came to U.S., 1974; s. Peter Hermann and Julia Maria (Rocha) M.; m. Blanca Maria Canedo, May 6, 1972; children—Maria Ximena, Ines Erika, Herman Peter. M.D., Universidad Mayor de San Simon, Bolivia, 1969. Dir. Unidad Sanitaria Pocona, Bolivian Govt., 1969-71; staff Patino Hosp., Cochabamba, 1971-74; intern Mercy Hosp., Des Moines, 1974-75; resident in pediatrics Meth. Hosp., Des Moines, 1976-79; practice medicine specializing pediatrics, Baraboo, Wis., 1985—. Fellow Am. Acad. Pediatrics; mem. N.Y. Acad. Scis., AMA. Avocation: cross-country skiing.

MUSCHENHEIM, WILLIAM EMIL, architect, educator; b. N.Y.C., Nov. 7, 1902; s. Frederick Augustus and Elsa (Uncer) M.; m. Elizabeth Marie Bodanzky, Nov. 29, 1930 (dec. July 1967); children—Carl Arthur, Anna Elizabeth Muschenheim Arms. Student Williams Coll., 1919-21, MIT, 1921-24; M.Arch., Behrens Master Sch. of Architecture, Acad. Fine Arts, Vienna, 1929. Archtl. designer Joseph Urban, Architect, N.Y.C., 1929-33; prof. architecture U. Mich., Ann Arbor, 1950-72; pres. Muschenheim, Hammarskold & Arms, Architects, Ann Arbor, 1968-71; prin. William Muschenheim, Architects, N.Y.C. and Ann Arbor, 1984—. Author: Elements of Art of Architecture, 1964; Why Architecture?, 1980. Contbr. articles to profl. jours. Horace H. Rackman grantee, 1958, 64, 72; recipient Gold medal Mich. Soc. Architects, 1984; established Muschenheim fellow in architecture Coll. Architecture, U. Mich., 1984. Fellow AIA. Home: 1251 Heatherway Ann Arbor MI 48104

MUSE, D. J., accountant; b. Zanesville, Ohio, Oct. 11, 1955; s. Donald J. and Martha J. Muse; m. Lyndell Kaye Woodyard, June 14, 1980. B.A., Ohio No. U., 1976. C.P.A., Ohio. Staff acct. Kentner, Sellers, Clark, Hines & Steinke, C.P.A.s, Vandalia, Ohio, 1976-77; practice pub. acctg., McConnelsville, Ohio, 1977-83; with Rea & Assocs., Inc., C.P.A.s, Cambridge, Ohio, 1983—. Tchr., Washington Tech. Coll., Marietta, Ohio, 1977, 78, 79. Mem. Morgan County Regional Airport Authority, 1979-82; trustee Washington Tech. Coll., Marietta, Ohio, 1983—; bd. dirs. Guernsey County Jr. Achievement. Recipient Dist. award SBA, 1977. Mem. Am. Inst. C.P.A.s, Ohio Soc. C.P.A.s, Ohio C.P.A. Practitioners Conf., Morgan County C. of C. (pres. 1982), Malta-McConnelsville Jaycees (treas. 1979). Methodist. Lodges: Masons, Rotary (pres. 1981). Home: 8865 N Rokeby Circle NW McConnelsville OH 43756 Office: PO Box 807 Cambridge OH 43725

MUSE, NORMAN L., advertising company executive. Chmn. bd. Leo Burnett Co., Chgo. Office: Leo Burnett Co Inc Prudential Plaza Chicago IL 60601*

MUSHKAT, BARBARA SACKS, lawyer; b. Rochester, N.Y., Feb. 23, 1940; d. Herman W. and Lillian (Rappaport) Sacks; m. Jerome Mushkat, June 18, 1961; children—Linda, Steven. B.A., Syracuse U., 1961; J.D., U. Akron, 1970. Bar: Ohio 1970, U.S. Dist. Ct. (6th dist.) Ohio 1971. Sole practice, Akron, Ohio, 1970—; dir. Pacific Internat. Resorts Inc. Campaign chmn. Common Pleas Ct. judge, 1984; panel mem. Akron United Way, 1979; chmn. Profl. Women's div. Jewish Welfare Fund, 1981; trustee Ohio Ballet, 1982—; bd. dirs. Legal Aid Soc., 1976-78, Children's Services Bd., 1981—, Vis. Nurse Service, 1981—. Mem. Akron Bar Assn. (exec. com. 1980-83), Ohio Bar Assn., ABA, Ohio State Bar Assn. Club: Women's Network (founding mem.). Avocations: cooking; reading; traveling. Address: 411 Wolf Ledges #200 Akron OH 44311

MUSHRUSH, JANET LYNNE, library computer services executive; b. Columbus, Ohio, Feb. 7, 1951; d. Vaughn Faber and Margaret Loretta (Rees) M.; m. Barry E. Backner, June 30, 1972 (div. 1974). B.B.A., Capitol U., Columbus, 1979. Systems analyst Huntington Nat. Bank, Columbus, 1970-76; dir. client services U.S. Computer Corp., Chgo., 1976-78; cons. Nars and Newlyn, Inc., Paoli, Pa., 1978-80; mgr. tech. tng. Warner Amex Cable, Columbus, 1980-83; owner, mgr. Applied Bus. Concepts, Columbus, 1983—; acctg. mgr. Comtech Systems, Inc., Columbus, 1984-85; user tng. mgr. Online Computer Library Ctr., Dublin, Ohio, 1985—; dir. Mid-Ohio Tng. Consortium, Columbus, 1984—. Bus. adv. council mem. Central Ohio Rehab. Ctr., Columbus, 1984—; Mem. adv. bd. U.S. Entrepreneurship Inst., Columbus, 1984-85; div. chmn. United Way of Franklin County, Columbus, 1974; del. People to People Orgn., Republic of China, 1981. Mem. Assn. Systems Mgmt. (pres. elect 1984-85, bd. dirs. 1982—), Central Ohio Fedn. Info. Processing Socs. (rep. 1983—), Central Ohio Data Processing Educators (trustee 1981-83), Delta Theta Tau (v.p. 1980-81). Office: On Line Computer Library Ctr 6565 Frantz Rd Dublin OH 43017

MUSSELMAN, PETER ROGERS, university administrator; b. Balt., Mar. 29, 1928; s. J. Rogers and Paula (Wilson) M. B.A., Harvard U., 1969; J.D., Cleve. Marshall Law Sch., 1957. Chartered fin. analyst. Vice pres., sec. Union Commerce Bank, Cleve., 1949-69, sec.-treas., 1963-69; v.p. adminstrn., treas. Case Western Res. U., Cleve., 1969—, adminstrv. v.p., treas., 1970-72, univ. v.p., treas., 1972—; pres. Univ. Circle Research Corp., Cleve., 1973—; pres. Med. Ctr. Co., Cleve., 1985-86; v.p. Village, Inc.; pres. Lorain Dock Co., Ohio, 1981—. Trustee, chmn. investment com. YMCA, Cleve., 1984, mem. fin. com., 1984; trustee John Huntington Fund for Edn., Cleve., 1984; mem. fin. adv. com. Benjamin Rose Inst., Cleve., 1984; pres. bd. trustees Cleve. Internat. Film Festival. Served to maj. U.S. Army, 1950-52. Mem. Inst. Chartered Fin. Analysts, Cleve. Soc. Security Analysts, Cleve. Bar Assn. Club: Rowfant (Cleve.). Home: 2405 Overlook Rd Cleveland Heights OH 44106 Office: Case Western Res U 2040 Adelbert Rd Cleveland OH 44106

MUSSEY, ROBERT DELEVAN, physician, orthopedic surgeon; b. Rochester, Minn., Nov. 5, 1916; s. Robert Daniel and Madge (Ayres) M.; m. Jean Wiggers, Apr. 3, 1943; children—Carol, Ruth, Robert Jr., Ann, David. A.B. Dartmouth Coll., 1938; M.B., U. Minn., 1942, M.D., 1943; M.S. in Orthopedic Surgery, Mayo Clinic, 1940. Diplomate Am. Bd. Orthopedic Surgery. Orthopedic surgeon Carle Clinic, Urbana, Ill., 1949—; clin. assoc. U. Ill. Sch. Medicine, Urbana, 1972—. Served to lt. j.g. USNR, 1944-46. Fellow Am. Acad. Orthopedic Surgeons; mem. Mid Am. Orthopedic Assn. (founding mem.), Clin. Orthopedic Soc., Ill. Orthopedic Soc. (pres. 1973-74). Republican. Presbyterian. Home: 2 Persimmon Circle Urbana IL 61801 Office: Carle Clinic 602 W University Ave Urbana IL 61801

MUSTION, ALAN LEE, pharmacist; b. Oklahoma City, Feb. 6, 1947; s. Granville E. and Iris E. (Graham) M.; B.S. in Pharmacy, Southwestern Okla. State U., 1970; children—Jeffrey Alan, Jennifer Chere; m. Mary Jane Bozek, Dec. 4, 1982. Staff pharmacist VA Med. Center, Oklahoma City, 1970-74; dir. pharmacy VA Med. Center, Saginaw, Mich., 1974-76; asst. dir. pharmacy VA Med. Center, Richmond, Va., 1976-77; dir. pharmacy VA Med. Center, Iowa City, Iowa, 1977—; clin. instr. clin./hosp. div. U. Iowa, 1977—. Served to maj. USAR. Recipient VA Spl. Achievement awards, 1973, 77; VA Suggestion awards, 1979, 82, 83; research grantee Travenol Labs., 1980-84. Mem. Am. Soc. Hosp. Pharmacists, Iowa Soc. Hosp. Pharmacists, Assn. Mil. Surgeons of U.S., Am. Assn. Colls. Pharmacy, Res. Officers Assn., Kappa Psi. Methodist. Contbr. articles to profl. jours. Home: 821 Spencer Dr Iowa City IA 52240 Office: VA Med Center Hwy 6 West Iowa City IA 52240

MUSTOE, DAVID WINSTON, association executive; b. Bunceton, Mo., May 4, 1930; s. Harold Devon and Lea Alleine (Knowles) M.; m. Ruth Madelyn Waddle, Sept. 1, 1957; children—Steven, Chris, Daniel, Anne. B.S. in Edn., Northeast Mo. State U., Kirksville, 1957; M.Ed., Lincoln U., 1968; Ed.D., U. Mo., 1980. Cert. bus. edn. tchr., Mo., secondary sch. adminstrn., Mo. Chief acct. Pub. Sch. Retirement System of Mo., Jefferson City, 1957-68, asst. exec. sec., 1968-81, exec. sec., 1981—; mem. exec. com. Nat. Council on Tchr. Retirement, 1983—. Govt. Fin. Officers Assn. (com. on pub. employee retirement adminstrn. 1980—). Served to sgt. U.S. Army, 1952-54, Korea. Mem. Phi Delta Kappa. Lodges: Lions, Elks. Avocations: reading, fishing, hunting. Office: Pub Sch Retirement System of Mo PO Box 268 Jefferson City MO 65102

MUSUNGU, AYANNA-LINDA DIAN, community programs developer; b. Jeffersonville, Ind., Aug. 24, 1949; d. LaRue and Earline (Wright) G. B.S., Drake U., 1984. Program coordinator Young Women's Resource Ctr., Des Moines, Iowa, 1978—, Palladium-Item, Gannett Inc., Richmond, Ind., 1985—. Vol. tchr. Kenya, Nairobi, 1974-75; publicity mgr. Langston Hughes Co. Players, Des Moines, 1983-84. Author: (with others) August Candlelight, 1977. Contbr. articles to mags. Pluralism task force leader Girl Scouts Am., 1983—; bd. dirs. Iowa Coalition for Divestment, Des Moines, 1983; mem. imperative com. YMCA, Des Moines. Mem. NAACP, Pan-African Orgn. Avocation: writing.

MUTZ, JOHN MASSIE, lieutenant governor of Indiana; b. Indpls., Nov. 5, 1935; s. John Loughery and Mary Helen (Massie) M.; B.S. in Advt. and Bus. Mgmt., Northwestern U., 1957, M.S., 1958; m. Carolyn Hawthorne, June 21, 1958; children—Mark, Diana. Copy editor Indpls. News, summer 1953, 54; dir. public relations for residential bldg. products Aluminum Co. Am., Pitts., 1958-60; dir. advt. and public relations, sec., asst. to pres. Perine Devel. Corp., Indpls., 1960-61; instr. dept. public and environ. affairs Ind. U., Indpls.,

1976-79; v.p. Circle Fin. Corp., Indpls., 1962-79; v.p. Circle Leasing Corp., Indpls., 1962-79; v.p. Fast Food Mgmt. Corp., 1978-79; mem. Ind. Ho. of Reps., 1967-71, chmn. interim sch. fin. com., 1962-69, chmn. taxation subcom. of ways and means com., 1969-70; Republican candidate state treas. Ind., 1970; mem. Ind. State Senate, 1972-80, chmn. budget subcom. of fin. com., chmn. affairs of Marion County com., chmn. met. affairs com.; lt. gov. Ind., 1981—. Mem. Sch. Property Tax Control Bd. Indpls., 1975-76; bd. govs. United Way Indpls., 1978-79; mem. bd. missions United Meth. Ch., Indpls., 1976-78; bd. dirs. Suemma Coleman Agy., 1975-79, Community Services Council Indpls., 1976-77; trustee Christian Theol. Sem., 1976-79. Mem. Nat. Restaurant Assn. (dir. 1978-79), Ind. Restaurant Assn. (dir. 1977-79), Marion County Mental Health Assn., Northwestern U. Alumni Assn., Pi Alpha Mu, Deru (pres. 1956-57), Beta Theta Pi (v.p. 1956-57). Office: Office of Lt Gov 333 State House Indianapolis IN 46204*

MUZI, ANDREW, trading company executive; b. Sept. 29, 1953. G.E.D. diploma, 1971. Purchasing mgr. Yellow Jersey Ltd., Madison, Wis., 1975—, gen. mgr., 1978—, chief exec. officer, 1984—; founder, chief exec. officer Ariel Trading Co., 1981—. Office: Yellow Jersey Ltd 419 State St Madison WI 53703

MWAUNGULU, GEOFFREY SETA, physician; b. Karonga, Malawi, Dec. 31, 1944; s. Morrison Thomas and Mary Musoba (Msiska) M.; m. Flora Denise Cox, June 30, 1975; m. Mary Thelma Mondiwa, May 27, 1980; children—Tumpale, Wakisa, Geoffrey. B.A., Swarthmore Coll., 1968; M.D., Temple U., 1972. Diplomate Am. Bd. Internal Medicine. Intern, Henry Ford Hosp., Detroit, 1972-73, resident, 1973-76; physician specialist Southeast Comprehensive Health Ctr., Los Angeles, 1976-77; asst. prof. Charles R. Drew Postgrad. Med. Sch., Los Angeles, 1976-77; med. specialist Kamuzu Central Hosp., Lilongwe, Malawi, 1977-79; lectr. U. Nairobi Med. Sch., Kenya, 1979-83; sect. chief Osawatomie State Hosp., Kans., 1983—; cons. physician Kenyatta Nat. Hosp., Nairobi, 1979-83. Bd. dirs. Div. Vehicles, State of Kans., 1984. Contbr. articles to med. jours. Mem. N.Y. Acad. Sci., Avocations: Jogging; tennis. Home: 21248 Dartmouth Southfield MI 48076 Office: 19401 Hubbard Dr Dearborn MI 48126

MYBECK, JOHN WALTER, foundation administrator, consultant; b. Crown Point, Ind., Sept. 14, 1940; s. Walter Raymond and Genevieve Lucille (Carlsten) M.; m. Mary Louis Topercer, Aug. 14, 1965; children—John, Jeffrey, Kevin, Matthew. B.S., Purdue U., 1962, M.S., 1965; Ph.D., 1970. Asst. dean for evening adminstrn. Purdue U.-Calumet, Hammond, Ind., 1970-73, dean community services, 1973-77, dir. univ. relations, 1977-79, exec. asst. to chancellor, 1980-81; exec. v.p. Calumet Nat. Bank, Hammond, 1979-80; exec. dir. Constrn. Advancement Found., Griffith, Ind., 1981—; bd. dirs. Munster Med. Research Found., Ind., 1980—; exec. dir. Operation Keystone, Griffith, Ind., 1984—. Editor procs. Assn. of Continuing Higher Edn., 1971. Chmn. Lake County Community Devel. Com., Ind., 1981; pres. Northwest Ind. Symphony Soc., Gary, 1980; mem. town bd. Town of Munster, 1976-79; trustee Sch. Town of Munster, 1982—; pres. Babe Ruth League, Munster, 1985. Recipient Citizenship award Purdue U. Alumni Assn., 1983, Disting. Service award Purdue Calumet Alumni Assn., 1984, Testimonial of Appreciation Munster Democratic Precinct Orgn., 1979. Mem. Am. Soc. Assn. Execs., Nat. Sch. Bds. Assn., Ind. Sch. Bds. Assn. Methodist. Club: John Purdue (Lafayette, Ind.). Lodges: Elks (East Chicago, Ind.), Masons (Crown Point, Ind.). Avocations: golf, reading, boys' baseball. Home: 8152 Hawthorne Dr Munster IN 46321 Office: Constrn Advancement Found 200 W Ridge Rd Suite A Griffith IN 46319

MYDLER, PAUL THOMAS, state development agency executive; b. St. Louis, Oct. 11, 1935; s. Thomas Walter and Josephine M. (Ceglinski) M.; m. Vietta Anne Sutter, 1959; children—Thomas T., Vietta Mary, Venetia R. B.S. in Mech. Engring., Washington U., 1959; M.B.A., St. Louis U., 1965. Plant engr. Monsanto Silicon Plant, St. Peters, Mo., 1960-62; chief engr. Mo. Portland Cement, St. Louis, 1962-66; dep. commr. City St. Louis, 1966-76; v.p. M.D. Magary Constrn. Co., St. Louis, 1976-81; cir. spl. projects Bi-State Devel. Agy., St. Louis, 1981—; cert. smoke reader City, 1967. Author air pollution control ordinances, 1967. Appointee, Mayor's Urban Crisis Com., St. Louis, 1970; del. St. Louis Sister City-Suwa, Japan, 1971; mem. Landmarks Preservation Bd., 1981—, v.p. 1984. Served to 1st lt. armed forces, 1959-60. Mem. Conf. Mayors Assn., Air Pollution Control Assn. (bd. dirs. 1976-80, pres. 1980-81), Ducks Unltd. Roman Catholic. Clubs: Fathers (DeSmet High Sch.); Fathers (St. Joseph Acad. Girls). Lodge: Kiwanis. Office: Bi-State Devel Agy 707 N 1st Saint Louis MO 63101

MYEROWITZ, P. DAVID, cardiac surgeon; b. Balt., Jan. 18, 1947; s. Joseph Robert and Merry (Brown) M.; B.S., U. Md., 1966, M.D., 1970; M.S., U. Minn., 1977; m. Susan Karen Macks, June 18, 1967; children—Morris Brown, Elissa Suzanne, Ian Matthew. Intern in surgery U. Minn., Mpls., 1970-71, resident in surgery, 1971-72, 74-77; resident in cardiothoracic surgery U. Chgo., 1977-79; practice medicine, specializing in cardiovascular surgery, Madison, Wis., 1979—; asst. prof. thoracic and cardiovascular surgery U. Wis., Madison, 1979-85, assoc. prof., 1985—, chief sect. cardiac transplantation, 1984—. Served with USPHS, 1972-74. Mem. ACS, Am. Coll. Cardiology, Assn. for Acad. Surgery, Soc. Univ. Surgeons, Soc. Thoracic Surgery, Am. Coll. Chest Physicians, Am. Heart Assn., Internat. Soc. Heart Transplantation, Internat. Soc. Cardiovascular Surgery. Jewish. Contbr. articles to profl. jours. Office: 600 Highland Aye Madison WI 53792

MYERS, CAROLE ANN, artist, educator; b. Shawnee, Okla., Dec. 28, 1934; d. Daniel and Ardith Irene (Dawkins) Ash; m. Roy William Myers, Mar. 2, 1952; children—Randall Craig, Lisa Danelle Myers. Tchr. watercolor workshops Valles San Luis Potosi, Mexico, 1979-81, Oaxaca, Mexico, 1982, 84 Artists Coop. Workshops, Ft. Myers, Fla., 1984, Creative Workshops of Mich., Dearborn, 1984, Dillman's Sandlake Lodge, Lac du Flambeau, Wis., 1984. Exhibits include Nat. Acad. Galleries, N.Y.C., 1979, 26th ann. exhbn. Nat. Soc. Painters in Casein and Acrylics, Am. Acad. and Inst. Arts and Letters, 82, San Diego Watercolor Soc. Internat. Exhbn., 1983. Recipient more than 300 awards including First award Mo. State Fair, Sedalia, Mo., 1984, St. Louis Artist's Guild, 1983; Artists-in-Residence grantee Nat. Endowment for Arts, Stoddard County, Mo., 1972. Mem. Am. Watercolor Soc. (assoc.; awards), Nat. Soc. Painters in Casein and Acrylic, Nat. Assn. Women Artists, Acad. Profl. Artists, others.

MYERS, DAVID N., automobile dealership executive; b. Syracuse, N.Y., Oct. 4, 1942; s. Donald F. and Joyce R. (Richer) M.; m. Kathie Ann Denesha, Sept. 11, 1965; children—Deborah, Kimberley, Matthew. A.A.S., Auburn Community Coll., N.Y., 1962. Merchandising mgr. Gen. Motors, Cleve., 1964-78; pres. David Myers Chevrolet, Inc., North Jackson, Ohio, 1978—. Served with U.S. Army, 1962-66. Mem. Youngstown C. of C., Eastern Ohio Auto Dealers Assn. (chmn. bd. trustees 1984—). Republican. Roman Catholic. Club: Men's (Youngstown, Ohio) (pres. 1983-84). Lodge: Kiwanis (pres. 1983-84). Avocations: tennis; golf; fishing; softball. Home: 14861 Robinson Rd Newton Falls OH 44444 Office: David Myers Chevrolet 10535 Mahoning Ave North Jackson OH 44451

MYERS, FRED WILLIAM, advertising consultant; b. Indpls., Aug. 24, 1926; s. Fred W. Sr. and Irene H. (Hooper) M.; m. Mary Davis, Dec. 2, 1968; children—Hillary, Graham, Frederick III. B.S., Purdue U., 1950. Advt. mgr. Faultless Caster Corp., Evansville, Ind., 1952-57; owner, pres. Graphic Arts, Inc., Evansville, 1957-74; sales mgr. H-N Advt. & Display, Indpls., 1976-80; owner, mgr. F. Myers & Assocs., Indpls., 1976—. Served with U.S. Army, 1944-46. Office: Fred W Myers Assocs 5660 Caito Dr Suite 122 Indianapolis IN 46226

MYERS, JOHN THOMAS, congressman; b. Covington, Ind., Feb. 8, 1927; s. Warren E. and Myra (Wisher) M.; B.S., Ind. State U., 1951; m. Carol Carruthers, May 30, 1953; children—Carol Ann, Lori Jan. Farmer Covington, 1951—; with Fountain Trust Co., Covington, from 1952; mem. 90th-99th Congresses from Ind. 7th Dist. Served with AUS, 1944-46; ETO. Mem. Am. Legion, VFW, Wabash Valley Assn., Res. Officers Assn., Sigma Pi. Republican. Lodges: Masons, Elks, Lions. Office: 2372 Rayburn House Office Bldg Washington DC 20515*

MYERS, LANCE FLORIAN, telephone company executive; b. Goodland, Kans., Dec. 19, 1938; s. Lawrence Dave and Dorothy (Shultz) Myers Chaney; m. Rosalie Garrison; children—Sean Florian, Seth Garrison. Student in civil engring. U. Wichita, 1957-58; B.A. in Bus. Adminstrn., Bellevue Coll., 1983. Cert. data processor. Programmer, designer Cudahy Packing Co., Omaha, 1959-64; programmer/designer Northwestern Bell, Omaha, 1965-66, project mgr., 1966-68; programming dist. mgr., 1968-78, support dist. mgr., 1978—, data base adminstr., 1978—. Chmn. Republican Precinct Com., Malvern, Iowa, 1978-82. Mem. Assn. Systems Mgmt. (div. bd. dirs. 1980-81), Data Processing Mgmt. Assn. (v.p. 1973), Am. Arbitration Assn., Alpha Kappa Chi. Republican. Methodist. Avocations: genealogy, boating. Home: 106 S 37th St Suite 1 Omaha NE 68131 Office: Northwestern Bell Telephone Co 100 S 19th St Room 1170 Omaha NE 68102

MYERS, PATRICIA ANN, lawyer; b. Evanston, Ill., Aug. 25, 1955; d. Richard James and Mary (Tyrrell) M.; m. Thomas Edward Cloud, Aug. 14, 1982. B.A., Barat Coll., 1976; J.D., John Marshall Law Sch., 1980. Bar: Ill. 1981, U.S. Dist. Ct. (no. dist.) Ill. Mng. atty. claims Shand, Morahan & Co., Evanston, Ill., 1980—. Ill. State scholar, 1972. Mem. Ill. Bar Assn., ABA. Office: Shand Morahan & Co Inc Shand Morahan Plaza Evanston IL 60201

MYERS, R. FRASER, travel tour manager; b. Washington, Apr. 14, 1941; s. Gilbert Barlow and Janet Stirrat (Clark) M. B.A., Dartmouth Coll., 1962; M.A., Cath. U. Am., 1967. Tour mgr. Olson-Travelworld, Los Angeles, 1967—. Served to lt. comdr. USNR, 1962-84. NSF grantee summer Inst. Glaciol. Scis., Juneau Icefield Research Program, 1966; apptd. U.S. Fgn. Exchange rep. to Belgium-Netherlands Antarctic Expdn., 1966. Fellow Royal Geog. Soc. (London); mem. Explorers Club. Club: Travelers' Century (Los Angeles). Home: 14728 Clifton Blvd Lakewood OH 44107-2522

MYERS, THOMAS ANDREWS, college administrator; b. Latrobe, Pa., Mar. 24, 1949; s. Clarence Rolland and Mary Ruth Myers; m. Sherry K. Ransford, Dec. 11, 1982. B.A., Allegheny Coll., 1971; postgrad. Clarion State Coll. (Pa.), 1972. Asst. dir. Cable TV-13, Meadville, Pa., 1971-73; mgr. advt. and pub. relations Teledyne Vasco, Latrobe, 1973-83; advt. cons. Teledyne, Inc., Eastern Group, 1976-83; instr. continuing edn. St. Vincent Coll., Latrobe, 1981-83; dir. pub. relations Kalamazoo Coll. (Mich.), 1983—. Chmn. adv. com. coll. communications Seton Hill Coll., Greensburg, Pa., 1975-80; mem. exec. com. Alumni Congress, Allegheny Coll. (Blue Citation 1984), Meadville, 1978-84. chmn. communications com., 1978-82, v.p., 1982-84. Mem. Laurel Highlands Advt. Assn. (dir. 1975-79, pres. 1978-79). Office: Dept Pub Relations Kalamazoo Coll Kalamazoo MI 49007

MYERS, WILLIAM GEORGE, clergyman; b. Faulkton, S.D., Aug. 29, 1938; s. William Edwin and Harriett Constance (Kuhl) M.; B.S. in Edn., No. State Coll., Aberdeen, S.D., 1956-60; M.Div. in Theology, Garrett-Evang. Theol. Sem., Evanston, Ill., 1965; M.A. in Liturgy, U. Notre Dame, 1984. Ordained elder United Methodist Ch., 1966. Asst. pastor Ingleside-Whitfield United Meth. Parish, Chgo., 1962-65; pastor-dir. Christ the Carpenter Parish and Christian Ctr., Rockford, Ill., 1965-76; chaplain, instr. St. Mary's Acad., Nauvoo, Ill., 1976—; assoc. pastor Colusa/Dallas City/Nauvoo United Meth. Chs., Ill., 1976—; dir. Radio-TV Ministry, Rockford, 1967-71; sec. Midwest Religious Broadcasting Commn., 1967-71. Advisor southside youth council NAACP, 1962-64; bd. dirs. Central Day Care Ctr., Rockford, 1969-72, Protestant Welfare Services, Rockford, 1972-74; bd. dirs., pres. Family Consultation Services, Rockford, 1974-76; pres. Nauvoo Hist. Soc., 1979-84, dir. resource and research ctr., 1984—; treas. Hancock County Theatre for Performing Arts, Ill., 1979-84; mem. United Meth. Fellowship for Worship and Other Arts. Mem. Nat. Council Tchrs. English, Ill. Council Tchrs. English, Nat. Cath. Edn. Assn., Order of Saint Luke (sub-dean), Nauvoo Ministerial Assn., Sigma Tau Delta. Democrat. Home: 290 N Page St Nauvoo IL 62354 Office: Saint Mary's Acad Nauvoo IL 62354

MYLONAKIS, STAMATIOS GREGORY, research and development executive; b. Athens, Greece, Aug. 18, 1937; came to U.S., 1963; s. Gregory and Vassiliki (Charalampopoulos) M.; m. Pamela H. Morton, May 15, 1965 (dec. Mar. 1978); 1 son., Gregory John. B.S. in Chemistry, U. Athens, 1961; M.S. in Phys. Organic Chemistry, Ill. Inst. Tech., 1964; Ph.D. in Phys. Organic Chemistry, Mich. State U., 1971. Research scientist Brookhaven Nat. Lab., Upton, N.Y., 1965-68; instr. U. Calif.-Berkeley, 1971-73; group leader Rohm and Haas Co., Springhouse, Pa., 1973-76; supr. DeSoto Inc., Des Plaines, Ill., 1976-79; staff scientist Borg-Warner Chems., Inc. Des Plaines, 1979-81, research and devel. mgr., 1981—. Author numerous research papers; patentee in polymer synthesis and applications fields. Served as lt. arty., Greek Army, 1961-63. Ill. Inst. Tech. fellow, 1963-64; Mich. State U. fellow, 1968-71. Mem. Am. Chem. Soc., Sigma Xi. Office: Borg-Warner Chemicals Inc Wolf and Algonquin Rds Des Plaines IL 60018

MYSZEWSKI, ALAN NORBERT, public safety official; b. Milw., Mar. 19, 1944; s. Harry Leonard and Paula Herma (Gardocki) M.; m. Janice Lynn Delker, Apr. 25, 1970; 1 child, Adam Dean. A.A., Marquette U., 1976, B.S., 1979; cert. FBI Nat. Acad., 1981. Cert. law enforcement officer, Wis. patrol officer Whitefish Bay Police, Wis., 1969-76, investigator, 1976-79, detective, 1979-82, police and fire chief, dir. pub. safety 1982—. Recipient Safe Place to Live in 80's award Whitefish Bay Found., 1984. Mem. Milw. Met. Chiefs of Police Assn. (sec./treas. 1985—), Milw. Fire Chiefs' Assn. (chmn. legis. com. 1984—), Wis. Police Chiefs' Assn., Wis. Fire Chiefs' Assn., Internat. Assn. Chiefs' of Police, Internat. Fire Chiefs' Assn., Wis. Fire Chiefs' Edn. Assn., FBI Nat. Acad. Assocs. (nat. and Wis. chpt.). Avocations: collecting cartoon art, bicycling; cooking. Office: Whitefish Bay Police/Fire Depts 5300 N Marlborough Dr Whitefish Bay WI 53217

NAAS, SISTER M. JOLINDA, elementary school administrator; b. Haubstadt, Ind., May 14, 1937; d. Joseph P. and Elizabeth B. (Brenner) N. B.S., St. Benedict Coll., Ferdinand, Ind., 1967; M.A. in Elem. Edn., Ball State U., 1976, postgrad., 1978-83; Cert. elem. adminstrn. and supervision, Ind. Tchr. diocese Evansville, Ind., 1956-69, adminstr., 1972—; tchr. Archdioces of Los Angeles, 1969-70, adminstr., 1970-72. Mem. Assn. for Supervision and Curriculum Devel., Ind. Assn. for Supervision and Curriculum Devel., Nat. Assn. Elem. Sch. Prins., Ind. Assn. Elem. and Middle Sch. Prins. Club: Holy Family Athletic Booster. Home and office: 990 Church Ave Jasper IN 47546

NABER, BRIAN NIEL, chemical company sales representative, business executive; b. Teaneck, N.J., July 27, 1949; s. Walter Jerome and Sigrid Virginia (Bakke) N.; m. Elizabeth Jane Wills, May 25, 1974; children—Katherine Elizabeth, Christopher Nils. B.S., U. Mo., 1973. Sales rep. Am. Cyanamid Co., Springfield, Ill., 1973-77; regional sales mgr. Internat. Minerals & Chem. Corp., Ankeny, Iowa, 1977-79; sr. sales rep. Mobil Chem. Co. (now Rhone-Poulenc Inc.), Normal, Ill., 1979—, sales trainer, 1980-82. Mem. Citizens Utility Bd., Bloomington, Ill., 1985; usher First Assembly of God Ch., Normal, 1985. Recipient Golden Oval award Am. Cyanamid Co., 1976, Golden Pick award Am. Cyanamid Co., 1976, News Snapshot award Kodak Internat., 1984. Republican. Avocations: reading; negotiation; photography; video production; traveling. Home: 307 Garden Rd Normal IL 61761

NABER, RALPH NOLAN, city official; b. Humphrey, Nebr., Jan. 30, 1950; s. Walter G. and Arla Mae (Witt) N.; m. Diane Lynn Krause, Aug. 21, 1976; children—Chris, Jeff, Brian, Dan. B.A. in Edn., Wayne State Coll., 1972. Water commr. City Albion, Nebr., 1978—; v.p. Nebr. Rural Water Assn., 1983—. Mem. sch. bd. St. Michael's Sch., Albion, 1984. Recipient cert. of appreciation State Health Dept., Nebr., 1984; Efficiency in Performance Plaque award Nat. Rural Assn., 1984. Mem. Nebr. Rural Water Assn. (dir. 1983—, Scott Wilber award, 1978, 81, 82, 83), Water Pollution Control Assn., Am. Waterworks Assn. Democrat. Roman Catholic. Lodge: K.C. (grand knight 1983—). Home: 502 S 6th St Albion NE 68620 Office: City of Albion 420 W Market Albion NE 68620

NACHBAUER, LOUIS JOSEPH, educational administrator; b. Weil der Stadt, Germany, May 14, 1927; came to U.S., 1928, naturalized, 1935; s. Ludwig P. and Anna Klara (Essig) N.; m. Janice Mae Brotman, June 15, 1950; children—Rebecca Lu, Roberta Mae. A.B., Augustana Coll., Rock Island, Ill., 1952; M.Ed., U. Ill., 1960. Cert. edni. adminstr., Ill. Tchr., coach Calvin Coolidge Jr. High Sch., Moline, Ill., 1953-66, asst. prin., 1966-70; prin. John Deere Jr. High Sch., Moline, 1970—. Mem. Ill. Congress Parent and Tchrs., Moline, 1953—; mem. tchr. edn. adv. council Augustana Coll., 1975-78. Served with USAF, 1946-47. Named Tchr. of Yr., Am. Legion, 1969; recipient Cert. Appreciation, City of Moline, 1976, Book Recognition award Ill. Congress Parents and Tchrs., 1977. Mem. Ill. Prin.'s Assn. (charter mem.), Nat. Assn. Secondary Sch. Prins., Moline Adminstrs. Assn., Ill. Assn. Supervision and Curriculum Devel. Republican. Jewish. Avocations: golf; bridge; home repairs; furniture refinishing. Home: 4413 24th Ave Rock Island IL 61201 Office: John Deere Jr High Sch 2035 11th St Moline IL 61265

NADEAU, LIONEL CARL, French, English educator; b. Edmundston, N.B., Can., Apr. 24, 1934; came to U.S., 1956, naturalized, 1965; s. Sylvio C. and Jeannette (Dube) N. B.A., St. Louis Coll., Edmundston, 1953; M.A., St. Francis Coll., 1964; Ph.D., Ball State U., 1979. Assoc. prof. French, English, St. Francis Coll., Ft. Wayne, Ind., 1962—, grad. cons., 1975; doctoral fellow Ball State U., Muncie, Ind., 1973-74. Contbr. articles to newspapers, religious jours. Violinist ch., Coll. groups, 1983—; guest lectr. bus. groups. Mem. AAUP. Democrat. Roman Catholic. Avocations: violinist; cathedral tour guide; lectr. on world travels. Home: 425 E Wayne St Apt 38 Fort Wayne IN 46805 Office: Saint Francis Coll 2701 Spring St Fort Wayne IN 46808

NADLER, HENRY LOUIS, physician, university dean, researcher; b. N.Y.C., Apr. 15, 1936; s. Herbert H. and Mary (Kartiganer) N.; m. Benita Weinhard, June 15, 1957; children—Karen, Gary, Debbie, Amy. A.B., Colgate U., 1957; M.D., Northwestern U., 1961; M.S. in Med. Genetics, U. Wis., 1965. Diplomate Am. Bd. Pediatrics, Am. Bd. Med. Genetics. Intern, Bellevue Hosp., N.Y.C., 1961-62, resident, 1962-64; practice medicine specializing in pediatrics, Chgo., 1965-81; mem. staff Children's Meml. Hosp., head div. genetics, 1968-81, chief of staff, 1970-81; mem. affiliate staff Evanston Hosp., 1974-81; mem. vis. staff div. medicine Northwestern Meml. Hosp., 1972-81; practice medicine specializing in pediatrics, Detroit, 1981—, mem. staff Children's Hosp. Mich.; teaching asst. pediatrics NYU Sch. Medicine, 1962-63, clin. instr., 1963-64; clin. instr. pediatrics U. Wis. Sch. Medicine, 1964-65; assoc. pediatrics Northwestern U. Med. Sch., Chgo., 1965-66, asst. prof., 1966-68, assoc. prof., 1968-70, Irene Heinz Given and John LaPorte Given prof. pediatrics, chmn. dept., 1970-81, prof. Grad. Sch., 1971-81; prof. pediatrics, dean Wayne State U. Sch. Medicine, Detroit, 1981—, prof. obstetrics, 1984—. Mem. editorial bd. Pediatrics jours., 1972-82, Comprehensive Therapy jour., 1974-84, Pediatrics in Rev., 1980-83, Am. Jour. Diseases of Children, 1982—; chmn. editorial com. Pediatrics jour., 1977-80; assoc. editor Am. Jour. Human Genetics, 1979-82; contbr. editor Miami Children's Hosp. Internat. Jour., 1984—. Contbr. numerous articles to sci. publs. Bd. dirs. Children's Meml. Hosp., Chgo., 1970-81, McGraw Med. Ctr., Northwestern U., 1975-81, Detroit Med. Ctr., 1981—, Comprehensive Cancer Ctr., 1981—, Mich. Cancer Found., 1983—, Sci. and Engring. Fair Met. Detroit, Inc., 1983-84, Research Inst. William Beaumont Hosp., 1984—; trustee Marygrove Coll., 1983—, Harper Grace Hosp. Health Systems, 1984—; mem. health com. New Detroit, 1981—; mem. Detroit Health Care Coalition for Homeless, 1984—; mem. adv. expert panel on human genetics Internat. Pediatric Assn.; chmn. clin. research com. Nat. Found. March of Dimes; mem. Task Force on Medicaid Reimbursement, Task Force on Physician Manpower and Distbn. Recipient Outstanding Alumni award Northwestern U., 1978. Fellow Am. Acad. Pediatrics (E. Meade Johnson award 1973, genetics com., pediatric edn. study group), Am. Soc. Clin. Investigation, Am. Soc. Human Genetics, Am. Pediatric Soc., Soc. Pediatric Research, Midwest Soc. Pediatric Research, Pan Am. Med. Assn., Soc. for Exptl. Biology and Medicine, Soc. for Inherited Metabolic Diseases, Assn. Am. Med. Colls., Assn. Acad. Health Ctrs., Mich. State Med. Soc., Mich. Med. Schs. Council Deans (chmn. 1984—), Alpha Omega Alpha (hon.). Home: 4669 Maura Ln West Bloomfield MI 48033 Office: Wayne State U Sch Medicine Office of Dean 540 E Canfield Ave Detroit MI 48201

NADLER, KENNETH DAVID, plant physiology and genetics educator, researcher; b. Bronx, N.Y., Sept. 18, 1942; s. Herbert R. and Anne N.; m. Ronnie D. Rubin, Dec. 24, 1967; children—Samuel, Jessica. B.S. in Physics, Rensselaer Poly. Inst., 1963; Ph.D., Rockefeller Inst., 1968. USPHS postdoctoral fellow U. Calif.-San Diego, 1968-70, lectr., 1969; prof. plant physiology, genetics Mich. State U., East Lansing, 1970—; vis. assoc. prof. John Innes Inst., Norwich, Eng., 1979-80; vis. prof. McGill U., Montreal, Que., Can., 1983; Bd. dirs. Congregation Kehillat Israel, Lansing, Mich., 1983—. Mem. Am. Soc. Microbiology, Am. Soc. Plant Physiologists. Avocations: stamp collecting; gardening; swimming; cycling; hiking. Office: Botany Dept Mich State U East Lansing MI 48823

NAEVE, NANCY JAMMER, pharmacist; b. Gunnison, Colo., Feb. 14, 1931; d. Arthur John and Norma Naomi (Nichols) J.; m. Milo Merle, July 18, 1954. B.S. in Pharmacy, U. Colo., 1953, M.S. in Pharmacy, 1957. Registered pharmacist, Colo., Del., Va., Ill. Pharmacist Weldorado Drug Co., Greeley, Colo., 1953-54; instr. U. Colo., Boulder, 1955-57; pharmacist Cutsler Drug Co., Wilmington, Del., 1957-67, Berkeley Drug Co., Williamsburg, Va., 1967-71, Koehler Drug Co., Colorado Springs, Colo., 1971-74, Dinet & Delfosse Drug Co., Chgo., 1975—. Bd. dirs. Chapin Hall for Children, Chgo., 1975—, pres., 1979-81; bd. mgrs. Admiral Old People's Home of Chgo., 1976—; mem. vestry St. Chrystostom's Ch., Chgo., 1985—. Mem. Am. Pharm. Assn., AAUW, Am. Inst. of History of Pharmacy, Acad. Pharamcy Practice, Rho Chi, Sigma Xi, Kappa Epsilon (sec. Ill. 1976—). Episcopalian. Clubs: Contemporary (bd. dirs. 1982-84), Jr. League of Chgo. Home: 1240 N Lake Shore Dr Apt 3-A Chicago IL 60610 Office: Dinet and Delfosse Drug Co 30 N Michigan Ave Chicago IL 60602

NAGABHUSHAN, BELLUR LAKSHMINARAYANA, aerospace engineer; b. Tiptur, Karnataka, India, May 23, 1949; came to U.S., 1971; s. Bellur Achappa and Subbagowramma Lakshminarayana Swamy; m. Uma Rao, Apr 5, 1978. B.Tech. in Aero. Engring., Indian Inst. Tech., Madras, India, 1971; M.S. in Aerospace Engring., Va. Polytech. Inst., 1973, Ph.D. in Aerospace Engring., 1976. Researcher, instr. Va. Polytech. Inst. and State U., 1971-76; engring. specialist, project leader Goodyear Aerospace, Akron, Ohio, 1976—. Editor Jour. of Aircraft, 1985—. Contbr. articles to profl. jours. Inventor in field. Indian Inst. Tech. scholar, 1967. Fellow AIAA (mem. nat. tech. com., assoc.); mem. Aero. Soc. India. Avocations: music; traveling; sports. Home: 4526 Honeysuckle Dr North Canton OH 44720 Office: Goodyear Aerospace Corp 1210 Massillon Rd Akron OH 44315

NAGAN, MARK THOMAS, manufacturer's representative; b. Kaukauna, Wis., Sept. 19, 1941; s. Mark Alphonse and Marie Josephine (Schumann) N.; m. Catherine Anne McCoy, June 27, 1964; children—Catherine Marie, Mark McCoy. B.M.E., Marquette U., 1963. Sr. test engr. Gen. Dynamics, Groton, Conn., 1963-65; staff engr. Commonwealth Edison, Morris, Ill., 1965-66; field sales engr. Leeds & Northrup, Davenport, Iowa, 1966-71; mfr.'s rep. White Equipment, Bettendorf, Iowa, 1971-79; mfr.'s rep., pres. BSI Ltd., Betterdorf, 1979—. Mem. ASME, ASHRAE (chpt. historian 1983—), Instrument Soc. Am. Republican. Roman Catholic. Club: Davenport Country (Pleasant Valley, Iowa). Avocations: boating, tennis, family geneology. Office: BSI Ltd 1123 Grant St Bettendorf IA 52722

NAGEL, DAVID CHARLES, monk dietetic technician; b. Milw., Feb. 6, 1951; s. Harold Grover and Joyce Rita (Kaffka) N. A.A., Cardinal Stritch Coll., Milw., 1974. Cert. dietary mgr., dietetic technician. Joined Bros. in Sacred Heart Fathers and Bros., Roman Catholic Ch., 1969. Asst. food service mgr. Sacred Heart Monastery, Milw., 1971-74; dir. food service St. Joseph's Indian Sch., Chamberlain, S.C., 1974-82, dir. ops., 1982—; v.p. Dehon Industries, Chamberlain, 1982-85, Lakota Devel. Council, Chamberlain, 1982-85. State winner Nat. Chicken Council, 1979; winner recipe contest Food Mgmt. Mag., 1977. Mem. Am. Dietetic Assn., Am. Sch. Food Service Assn., Dietary Mgrs. Assn. (state pres. 1976, chpt. treas. 1984-85). Democrat. Avocations: computers; piano and organ. Home and Office: St Joseph's Indian Sch N Main St Chamberlain SD 57325

NAGEL, ROLAND FRANK, industrial educator; b. St. Charles County, Mo., Dec. 10, 1920; s. Arthur August and Dena (Neiweg) N.; m. Virginia Sue Warden, July 15, 1943; children—Susan Lynn, Lisa Marie. B.E., Northeast Mo. State U., 1943; M.Ed., U. Mo., 1950, Ed.D., 1952. Tchr. indsl. arts sr. high sch., Muscatine, Iowa, 1946-47, jr. high sch., Kirksville, Mo., 1947-49; assoc. prof. Northwestern State Coll., Natchitoches, La., 1952-56; prof. indsl. edn. Northeast Mo. State U., Kirksville, 1956-68, head div. practical arts, 1968-85. Editor in-house newsletter, 1958-78. Bd. dirs. ARC, Kirksville, 1960-63. Served with USAF, 1942-46, ETO. Recipient E.M. Carter award U. Mo., 1950, Good Neighbor award Alpha Gamma Rho, 1981. Mem. Am. Vocat. Assn., Nat. Assn. Indsl. Tchr. Educators, Am. Indsl. Arts Assn. (state rep. 1958-60), Mo. Vocat. Assn. (bd. dirs. 1965-68), Am. Council Indsl. Arts Tchr. Edn., Delta Tau Alpha (hon.). Baptist. Lodge: Lions (pres. 1965). Avocations: singing, travel, camping, gardening, woodworking. Home: 1716 S Downing St Kirksville MO 63501

NAGEL, SIDNEY ROBERT, physics educator; b. N.Y.C., Sept. 28, 1948; s. Ernes and Edith (Haggstrom) N. B.A., Columbia U., 1969; M.A., Princeton U., 1972, Ph.D., 1974. Research assoc. Brown U., Providence, R.I., 1974-76; asst. prof. physics U. Chgo., 1976-81, assoc. prof., 1981-84, prof., 1984—.

Contbr. articles to profl. jours. Alfred Sloan Found. fellow, 1978-82. Mem. Am. Phys. Soc., AAAS. Office: James Franck Inst U Chgo 5640 S Ellis Ave Chicago IL 60637

NAGI, MOSTAFA HELMEY, social scientist, educator; b. Samalig, Egypt, June 15, 1934; came to U.S., 1964, naturalized, 1975; s. Faried and Hamida (Shenishen) N.; m. Wiam Youssif Abdualahad, Aug. 15, 1977; 1 child, Suhair. B.Sc., Cairo U., 1958; M.A., Bowling Green State U., 1967; Ph.D., U. Conn., 1970. Specialist, Council Pub. Services and Ministry of Agr., Egypt and Syria, 1958-64; asst. prof. sociology Bowling Green (Ohio) State U., 1969-71, assoc. prof., 1972-80, prof., 1980—; sr. cons. Govt. of Iraq, Arab Project and Devel. Inst., Lebanon, 1974-75; vis. prof. Kuwait U., 1977-79, 84-86; referee NSF, profl. jours. and pub. cos. NSF grantee, 1979; NIH grantee, 1972. Mem. Am. Sociol. Assn., Population Assn. Am., Am. Gerontol. Soc., AAAS, Ohio Acad. Sci., North Central Sociol. Assn., Soc. for Sci. Study Religion, Acad. Polit. Sci., Internat. Platform Assn. Contbr. articles to profl. jours. Home: 1127 Clark St Bowling Green OH 43402 Office: Dept Sociology Bowling Green State U Bowling Green OH 43403

NAGIN, IRA, hospital management consultant; b. Los Angeles, Jan. 10, 1936; s. Eugene and Helen (Yohalem) N.; student Occidental Coll., 1954-56; B.S. in Mech. Engring., U. Calif., Berkeley, 1958; postgrad. M.I.T., 1963-64. Sr. engr. Aerojet-Gen. Corp., Sacramento, 1958-69; mgmt. engr. cons. staff Drake, Sheahan, Stewart, Dougall, N.Y.C., 1970; mgmt. engr. trainee Johns Hopkins Hosp., Balt., 1971; hosp. mgmt. engr. Mary Washington Hosp., Fredericksburg, Va., 1972-74, Potomac Hosp., Woodbridge, Va., 1974-76; hosp. indsl. engr. Walter Reed Army Med. Center, Washington, 1976-77; hosp. mgmt. engr. Cleve. Clinic Hosp., 1977-80; dir. mgmt. engring. St. Vincent Hosp., Green Bay, Wis., 1980-81; sr. mgmt. engr. St. Joseph Mercy Hosp., Ann Arbor, Mich., 1981-83; cons. Support Mgmt. Systems, Appleton, Wis., from 1983; cons. Sheraton-Fredericksburg Motor Inn, 1974-76. Served with USAF, 1958-62. Mem. Hosp. Mgmt. Systems Soc., Am. Inst. Indsl. Engrs., Soc. for Advancement of Mgmt., Am. Hosp. Assn., Am. Mgmt. Assn. Contbg. author: Am. Hosp. Assn. Guide to Selection and Employment of Management Counsultants for Health Care, 1978. Home and office: 2520 Bittersweet Ave Green Bay WI 54301

NAGODAWITHANA, TILAK W., research manager; b. Colombo, Sri Lanka. B.S., U. Ceylon, Colombo, 1962; M.S., U. Philippines, Manila, 1969; Ph.D., Cornell U., 1973. Mgr. distillery Sri Lanka Sugar Corp., Colombo, Sri Lanka, 1962-70; group leader Schlitz Brewing Co., Milw., 1973-77; mgr. research Anheuser Busch Inc., St. Louis, 1977-81; mgr. research Universal Foods Corp., Milw., 1981—. patentee in field. Contbr. articles to various publs. Mem. Inst. Food Technologists, Am. Soc. Microbiology. Office: 6143 N 60th St Universal Foods Corp Milwaukee WI 53218

NAGORI, J. F., project engineer, engineering manager; b. Sholapur, India, Dec. 27, 1937; came to U.S., 1959, naturalized, 1974; s. Fulchand G. and Sharyu F. (Soni) N.; m. Mary Ann Boldman, May 9, 1964; children—Anita, Aaron. B.Engring., Osmania U., 1958; M.S. in Mech. Engring., U. Kans., 1961. Registered profl. engr., Mo. Shift engr. Nat. Rayon Corp., Ltd., Bombay, India, 1958-59; mech. engr. Black & Veatch, Engrs.-Architects, Kansas City, Mo., 1961-73, project engr., 1974-81, comceptual design mgr., 1981-84, engring. mgr., 1984—, cons. engr., 1961—; dir., pres. TAJ Enterprises, Inc., Kansas City, 1973—; advisor Met. Energy Assembly, Kansas City, 1982-84. Advisor Jr. Achievement, Overland Park, Kans., 1966-67. Mem. ASME (chmn. Kansas City sect. 1978-79, sec. Region VII 1984—. Centennial Medallion 1980, Dedicated Service award 1984), Am. Nuclear Soc. (Mo.-Kans.), India Engrs. and Scientists of Greater Kansas City. Republican. Hindu. Club: India (Kansas City). Avocations: international travel; bowling; bridge; teaching. Home: 9820 Carter Dr Overland Park KS 66212 Office: Black & Veatch 1500 Meadow Lake Pkwy Kansas City MO 64114

NAGORKA, FRANK WALTER, lawyer; b. Cleve., Mar. 9, 1955; s. Frank and Anna Margaret (Petrocy) N. B.A. in Psychology, Northwestern U., 1976; J.D., Ohio State U., 1979. Bars: Ohio 1979, Ill. 1980, U.S. Ct. Appeals (7th cir.) 1981. Asst. corp. counsel City of Chgo., 1981—; advisor social security program Northwestern U., Chgo., 1982; advisor moot ct. Loyola U., Chgo., 1982. Rep. ARC, Chgo., 1979—; chmn. high adventure Chgo. council Boy Scouts Am., 1981—. Mem. ABA, Ill. State Bar Assn., Am. Trial Lawyers Assn. Democrat. Roman Catholic. Office: Dept Law City of Chicago 121 N LaSalle St #511 Chicago IL 60602

NAGY, BELA FERENC, biochemistry educator, researcher; b. Nagybanhegyes, Hungary, May 15, 1926; came to U.S., 1957, naturalized, 1961; s. Bela and Julianna (Fruehwirth) N.; m. Barbara Peyser, Jan. 19, 1958 (div. 1974); m. Henryka Ursula Bialkowska, Nov. 13, 1980; children—Andrew, Julianna. Diploma U. Budapest, Hungary, 1953; Ph.D., Brandeis U., 1964. Asst. prof. U. Budapest, 1953-57; research assoc. Rockefeller Inst., N.Y.C., 1957-58, NYU Med Sch., N.Y.C., 1959-60, Boston Biomed. Research Inst., 1964-78; spl. research fellow Brandeis U., Waltham, Mass., 1960-64; prin. assoc. Harvard U. Med. Sch., Boston, 1970-78; assoc. prof. neurology, pharmacology and cell biophysics U. Cin. Med. Coll., 1978—, research dir. neurology dept., 1978—. Contbr. research papers to profl. jours. and chpts. to scholarly texts. Recipient Career Devel. award NIH, 1967-72; fellow Nat. Acad. Sci., 1957-59, NIH, 1961-64; grantee NIH, NSF, Muscular Dystrophy Assn., 1973—. Mem. AAAS, Am. Chem. Soc., Biochem. Soc. of London, Biophys. Soc. Am., Soc. Biol. Chemists. Club: Soaring 7th Flying (pres. 1984-85). Avocation: private pilot. Home: 3580 Epworth Ave Cincinnati OH 45211 Office: U Cin Med Coll Dept Neurology 231 Bethesda Ave Cincinnati OH 45267

NAGY, DENES, consulting engineer; b. Budapest, Hungary, Oct. 19, 1929; s. Denes and Margit (Lukacs) N.; came to U.S., 1957, naturalized, 1962; student Hungarian Comml. Inst. Pest, 1950; B.A., Tech. U. Budapest, 1954, B.S. in Mech. Engring., 1954, M.S. in Mech. Engring., 1954; m. Margarita Penaherrera, Jan. 13, 1968. Design engr. Gebr. Van Swaay, Mij., engrs. and constructors, The Hague, Holland, 1956-57; project engr., design engr. Walter Scholer & Assocs., Inc., architects and engrs., Lafayette, Ind., 1957-65; project engr. Dalton-Dalton Assos., Inc., architects and engrs., Cleve., 1965-67; pres., dir., chief engr. Environ. Engring. Corp., Chgo., 1967-72; pres., dir. Martin-Nagy-Tonella Assos., Inc., cons. engrs., Chgo., 1972-76; partner, dir. MNT Internat., Quito, Ecuador, 1975—; owner, pres. Denes Nagy Assos., Ltd., Chgo. Registered profl. engr., Ind., Ill., Wash., Wis., Mass., N.Y., Calif., W.Va.; cert. energy mgr. Mem. ASME, ASHRAE, Internat. Dist. Heating Assn., Nat. Soc. Profl. Engrs., Ill. Soc. Profl. Engrs., Nat. Fire Protection Assn., Constrn. Specifications Inst., Air Pollution Control Assn., Automated Procedures for Engring. Cons. (trustee 1968-71), Soc. Am. Value Engrs., Am. Cons. Engrs. Council, Cons. Engrs. Council Ill., Ill. Architect-Engr. Council (pres. 1979, mem. exec. com.), U.S. Power Squadron, U.S. Coast Guard Aux., Internat. Visitors Center, Chgo. Council on Fgn. Relations. Home: 505 N Lake Shore Dr Apt 2604 Chicago IL 60611 Office: 65 W Division St Chicago IL 60610

NAGY, MARGARITA EUGENIA, nutritionist; b. Quito, Ecuador, Oct. 18, 1938; d. Gonzalo A. and Eugenia (Mateus) Penaherrera; came to U.S., 1958; B.S. in Home Econs. (Internat. scholar), Purdue U., 1962; M.S. in Nutrition, State U. Iowa, 1964; m. Denes Nagy, Jan. 13, 1968. Nutrition intern State U. Iowa Hosps., 1962-63, therapeutic dietitian, 1963; cons. to two Vozandes hosps. and to physicians in Ecuador, 1964-65; dietitian Maternidad Isidro AYORA, Quito, 1964; research asst. dept. foods and nutrition Purdue U., 1965-66; research nutritionist Highland View Hosp., Cleve., 1966-68; research asso. sect. food sci., dept. foods and nutrition AMA, Chgo., 1968-71, research asso. clin. nutrition, 1971-80, sec. nutrition adv. group, 1971-80; v.p., sec. Denes Nagy Assocs., Ltd., Chgo., 1977-81; coordinator sci. and tech. Stokely Van Camp, Inc., Indpls., 1981-83; v.p. nutritional products and orphan drugs Ascot Hosp. Pharms. Inc., Skokie, Ill., 1983—; participant nat. and internat. confs. on nutrition. Active, Internat. Visitors Center, Chgo. Council on Fgn. Relations, U.S. Power Squadron, U.S. Coast Guard Aux. Recipient Stanley Louise Latin Am. award Am. Home Econs. Assn., 1961. Mem. Am. Dietetic Assn., Am. Soc. for Parenteral and Enteral Nutrition (sec., mem. exec. council), Inst. Food Technologists, Critical Care Dietitians (chmn. nominating com.), Dietitians in Bus. and Industry, Gerontological Nutrition, Health Care Delivery Systems, Research Dietitians, others. Club: Toastmasters Internat. Author: (with C.J. Geiger and P.L. White) Nutritional Assessment of Hospitalized Patients, 1979; editor: (with P.L. White) Total Parenteral Nutrition, 1974; (with J.L. Breeling) Symposium on Newer Food Processing Technology: Safety and Quality Assurance, 1973; (with A.C. Bach and V.K. Babayan) Medium-Chain Triglycerides: An Update, 1982. Office: 7701 N Austin Ave Skokie IL 60077

NAGY, ROBERT ALEXANDER, lawyer; b. Toledo, Nov. 24, 1937; s. Alexander S. and Irene L. (Tarczali) N.; m. Ann Louise Mensendiek, Dec. 28, 1959 (div. 1979); children—Robert R. II, Elizabeth Ann, Christine Julia; m. Phyllis A. Pensak, Mar. 30, 1979. B.A., DePauw U., 1960; J.D., Duke U., 1963. Bar: Ohio 1963. Ptnr. Bogart & Nagy, Elyria, Ohio, 1976-80; ptnr. Jenson, Mackin & Nagy, Avon Lake, Ohio, 1966-76; chief asst. dist. atty. Lorain County, Elyria, 1969—; spl. counsel to atty. gen. State of Ohio, Columbus, 1971-79; prosecutor City of Amherst, Ohio, 1974-79; pres. Robert A. Nagy Co., Elyria, 1980—. Bd. dirs. Lorain County Crime Lab., 1980—. Served with USAF, 1963-66, lt. col. Res., 1969—. Mem. Assn. Trial Lawyers Am., Nat. Dist. Attys. Assn., Ohio Bar Assn., Ohio Assn. Trial Lawyers, Lorain County Bar Assn., Res. Officers Assn., Delta Theta Phi, Lambda Chi Alpha. Republican. Clubs: Nisi Prius, Elyria Country. Avocation: golf. Home: 231 Antioch Dr Elyria OH 44035 Office: 704 Lorain County Bank Bldg Elyria OH 44035

NAGY, WILLIAM, engineer; b. Richard Mine, N.J., Jan. 1, 1916; m. Lucie Rose Wachter, Sept. 15, 1955 (div.); children—Susan, William Warren. B.A. in Aero. Engring., Poly. Inst. N.Y., 1953; B.Sc., Fairleigh Dickinson U., 1953. Registered profl. engr., Wis., Ill., Wash. Asst. project engr. Douglas Aircraft, Inglewood, Calif., 1938-42; asst. mgr. prodn. control Hindustan Aircraft, Bangalore, India, 1942-45; asst. div. chief China Nat. Aviation, Calcutta, India, 1945-46; salesman aircraft, Calcutta, 1946-47; test engr. rockets Curtis Wright Corp., Caldwell, N.J., 1947-52; chief process engr. Fed. Telephone and Radio, Clifton, N.J., 1952-53; research engr. Bell Aircraft Corp., Niagara Falls, N.Y., 1953-55; project engr. Reaction Motors, Inc., Denville, N.J., 1955-57; engring. exec. Chrysler Corp., Warren, Mich., 1957-59; engring. supr. Boeing Co., Seattle, 1960-71, resident rep., Brigham City and Utah and Cin., 1979-85; salesman N.Y. Life Ins. Co., Seattle, 1971-72; supervising mech. engr. Met. Sanitary Dist., Chgo., 1972-76; supr. bldg. maintenance Maintenance Services Inc., Chgo., 1976-77; construction grants mgmr. staff U.S. EPA, Chgo., 1977-78; mem. mkt. devel. staff Art Anderson Assocs., Bremerton, Wash., 1978-79. Contbr. articles to profl. publs. Fellow AIAA (assoc.); mem. Soc. Allied Weight Engrs. Republican. Avocations: pilot; multi-engine instrument; military history. Home: 5959 Rhode Island Ave Cincinnati OH 45237

NAHAT, DENNIS F., ballet artistic director; b. Detroit, Feb. 20, 1946; s. Fred H. and Linda M. (Haddad) N. Student Juilliard Sch. Music, 1970. Dancer Joffrey Ballet, N.Y.C., 1966-68; prin. dancer Am. Ballet, N.Y.C., 1969-79; choreographer Jumpers and Two Gentlemen of Verona; singer, dancer Sweet Charity; artistic dir. Cleve. Ballet. Office: Cleveland Ballet 1375 Euclid Ave #330 Cleveland OH 44115

NAHRA, JOSEPH J., judge; b. Cleve., Mar. 20, 1927; s. Maflah J. and Ida (Abood) N.; m. Barbara Hall, July 13, 1961; children—Kirk, Paul, Carol, Joseph. B.A., Case Western Res. U., 1949; J.D., Harvard U., 1952. Bar: Ohio. Mem. firm Nahra & Morgan, Cleve., 1952-69; judge Ct. Common Pleas, Cleve., 1969-77, Probate Ct., Cleve., 1977-80; assoc. firm Kelly, McCann & Livingstone, Cleve., 1980-82; judge Ct. Appeals, Cleve., 1982—. Served with U.S. Army, 1945-46. Republican. Roman Catholic. Home: 2745 Derbyshire Rd Cleveland Heights OH 44106 Office: Ct Appeals 1 Lakeside Ave Cleveland OH 44113

NAHRWOLD, DAVID LANGE, surgeon, educator; b. St. Louis, Dec. 21, 1935; s. Elmer William and Magdalen Louise (Lange) N.; m. Carolyn Louise Hoffman, June 14, 1958; children—Stephen Michael, Susan Alane, Thomas James, Anne Elizabeth. A.B., Ind. U..-Bloomington, 1957, M.D., Ind. U.-Indpls., 1960. Diplomate Am. Bd. Surgery, Am. Bd. Thoracic Surgery. Intern, then resident Ind. U. Med. Ctr., 1960-65; postdoctoral scholar in gastrointestinal physiology VA Ctr., UCLA, 1965-66; asst. prof. surgery Ind. U. Sch. Medicine, 1968-70; from assoc. prof. to prof. surgery Pa. State U. Coll. Medicine, Hershey, 1970-82, vice chmn. dept. surgery, 1971-82, chief div. gen. surgery, 1974-82, assoc. dean patient care, 1978-80, assoc. provost, dean health affairs, 1981-82; Loyal and Edith Davis prof. surgery Northwestern U. Med. Sch., Chgo., 1982—, chmn. dept. surgery, 1982—; surgeon-in-chief Northwestern Meml. Hosp., Chgo., 1982—. Mem. editorial bd. Surgery, 1981—, Surgical Gastroen., 1982—, Archives of Surgery, 1983—. Contr. articles to profl. jours. and abstracts. Served to capt. U.S. Army, 1966-68, Vietman. Fellow ACS; mem. Am. Fedn. Clin. Research, AMA, Am. Physiol. Soc. (assoc.), Am. Surg. Assn., Chgo. Med. Soc., Chgo. Soc. Gastroen., Chgo. Surg. Soc., Collegium Internat. Chriurgia Digestivae, Ill. Med. Soc., Ill. Surg. Soc., Internat. Biliary Assn., Societe Internat. De Chirurgie, Soc. Clin. Surgery, Soc. Health and Human Values, Soc. Surgery of Alimentary Tract (chmn. admissions com. 1983—, trustee 1983—, sec. 1985—), Soc. Univ. Surgeons, Univ. Assn. Emergency Med. Services, Soc. Am. Gastrointestinal Endoscopic Surgeons, Western Surg. Assn. Clubs: Midwest Gut, Surg. Biology. Office: Dept Surgery Northwestern U Med Sch 250 E Superior St Chicago IL 60611

NAHRWOLD, MICHAEL LANGE, anesthesiologist; b. St. Louis, Nov. 23, 1943; s. Elmer William and Magdalen (Lange) N.; m. Janice Elaine Geitz; children—Stacey Marie, Marny Michelle, Daniel Alan. A.B., Ind. U., 1965, M.D., 1969. Diplomate Am. Bd. Anesthesiology. Asst. prof. Hershey Med. Ctr., Pa., 1975-77; assoc. prof. U. Mich., Ann Arbor, 1977-81, prof. anesthesiology, 1981—. Editor in chief Anesthesiology Rev., 1984. Served with USPHS, 1973-75. Mem. Am. Soc. Anesthesiologists, Internat. Anesthesia Research Soc., Am. Physiol. Soc., Am. Acad. Clin. Anesthesiologists (chmn. bd. educators, 1983—), AMA, Assn. Univ. Anaesthetists. Republican. Lutheran. Avocations: music; fitness. Home: 2292 Tessmer Rd Ann Arbor MI 48103 Office: Anesthesiology Dept U Mich Ann Arbor MI 48109

NAIDEN, JAMES, poet, literary critic, journalist; b. Sept. 24, 1943; grad. Seattle U.; postgrad. U. Iowa, U. Ark. Poet, critic lit. jour., 1968—; journalist newspapers, jours., U.S., Europe, 1968—; broadcast journalist KROS news, Clinton, Iowa, 1979-80; broadcast journalist, 1978—; author: Asphyxiations/1-40 (poetry), 1986; contbr. articles to lit. jours; editor The North Stone Rev., 1971—; poetry critic Mpls. Star and Tribune. Recipient Guillaume Apollinaire Prix, La Nuit Blanche, 1968. Mem. Com. Small Mags., Editors and Pubs., Poetry Soc. Am., Dramatists Guild. Address: D Station Box 14098 Minneapolis MN 55414

NAJARIAN, JOHN SARKIS, surgeon, educator; b. Oakland, Calif., Dec. 22, 1927; s. Garabed L. and Siranoush (Demirjian) N.; m. Arlys Viola Mignette Anderson, Apr. 27, 1952; children—Jon, David, Paul, Peter. A.B. with honors, U. Calif.-Berkeley, 1948; M.D., U. Calif.-San Francisco, 1952; D.Sc. (hon.) U. Athens, 1980, Gustavus Adolphus Coll., 1981. Diplomate Am. Bd. Surgery. Intern then resident U. Calif. Med. Sch., San Francisco, 1952-60; asst. prof. surgery, chief transplantation service, dir. surg. research labs. U. Calif.-San Francisco, 1963-66, prof., vice chmn. dept. surgery, 1966-67; prof., chmn. dept. surgery U. Minn., Mpls., 1967—; vis. prof. numerous hosps. and univs.; lectr. in field. Mem. numerous editorial bds. Markle scholar, 1964-69; recipient Calif. Trudeau Soc. award, 1962, Ann. Brotherhood award NCCJ, 1978, Disting. Achievement award. Modern Medicine, 1978, Internat. Great Am. award B'nai B'rith Found., 1982, Kabakjian award, 1983, Man of Yr. award Sta. WCCO, Mpls., 1983, Disting. Alumnus of Yr. award Oakland High Sch., 1984, Disting. Minnisotan award Bemidji State U., 1985. Fellow ACS; mem. AAAS, Am. Assn. Lab. Animal Sci., Am. Assn. Immunologists, Am. Diabetes Assn., Am. Heart Assn., AMA, Am. Soc. Exptl. Pathology, Am. Soc. Nephrology, Am. Soc. Transplant Surgeons (pres. 1977-78, chmn. edn. com. 1980-81), Am. Surg. Assn., Assn. Acad. Surgery, Central Surg. Assn., Hagfish Soc., Halsted Soc., Hennipen County Med. Soc., Internat. Soc. Surgery, Kansas City Surg. Soc., Mpls. Surg. Soc., Minn. Med. Assn., Minn. Surg. Soc., Soc. Exptl. Biology and Medicine, Soc. Clin. Surgery, Soc. Univ. Surgeons, Transplantation Soc., Golden Key Nat. Honor Soc., Alpha Omega Alpha, Sigma Xi. Home: 4345 E Lake Harriet Blvd Minneapolis MN 55409 Office: U Minn Hosps 516 Delaware St SE Minneapolis MN 55455

NALEFSKI, ANDREW THOMAS, lawyer; b. Decatur, Ill., June 27, 1952; s. Richard Anthony and Sandra (Leek) N. B.A., So. Ill. U., 1974, M.S. in Edn., 1975; J.D., U. Ark.-Fayetteville, 1980. Bar: Ill. 1980, U.S. Dist. Ct. (so. dist.) Ill. 1981. Atty./intern Madison County States Atty., Edwardsville, Ill., summer 1980; assoc. Lakin & Herndon, P.C., East Alton, Ill., 1980—. Mem. Ill. State Bar Assn., Ill. Trial Lawyers, Assn. Trial Lawyers Am., Madison County Bar Assn., Alton-Wood River Bar Assn. Home: 609 Beacon Alton IL 62002 Office: Lakin & Herndon PC 303 N Shamrock East Alton IL 62024

NALYWAJKO, EUGENE, business executive, production consultant; b. Zolotchiv, Ukraine, Aug. 8, 1926; s. John and Maria (Dudar) N.; m. Myroslawa Zalopany, May 12, 1951. B.S. in Tech., U. Mich., 1956; diploma engr. Tech. U., Regensburg, W.Ger., 1950. Plant mgr. Protexol Corp., Kenilworth, N.J., 1956-60; supr. quality control Plywood Fabricator Service, Denver, 1960-65, dir. quality control, Chgo., 1965-66; v.p. ops. Lester's of Minn., Inc., Lester, Prairie, 1966—, also dir. Mem. Forest Products Research Soc. Eastern Rights Catholic. Club: Toastmaster (Hutchinson, Minn.). Home: 230 Maple St N Lester Prairie MN 55354 Office: Lester's of Minnesota Inc Lester Prairie MN 55354

NAMDARI, BAHRAM, surgeon; b. Oct. 26, 1939; s. Rostam and Sarvar Namdari; M.D., 1966; m. Kathleen Diane Wilmore, Jan. 5, 1976; 3 children. Resident in gen. surgery St. John's Mercy Med. Ctr., St. Louis, 1969-73; fellow in cardiovascular surgery with Michael DeBakey, Baylor Coll. Medicine, Houston, 1974-75; practice medicine specializing in gen. and vascular surgery and surg. treatment of obesity, Milw., 1976—; mem. staff St. Mary's, St. Luke's, St. Michael, Mt. Sinai, Good Samaritan, Trinity Meml., St. Anthony, Family, St. Francis hosps. (all Milw.). Diplomate Am. Bd. Surgery. Fellow ACS, Internat. Coll. Surgeons; mem. Med. Soc. Milwaukee County, Milw. Acad. Surgery, Wis. Med. Soc., Wis. Surg. Soc., Royal Soc Medicine Eng. (affiliate), Am. Soc. for Bariatric Surgery, AMA, World Med. Assn., Internat. Acad. Bariatric Medicine (founding mem.), Michael DeBakey Internat. Cardiovascular Soc. Contbr. articles to med. jours.; patentee med. instruments and other devices. Office: Great Lakes Med and Surg Ctr SC 2315 N Lake Dr Milwaukee WI 53211 also 6000 S 27th St Milwaukee WI 53221

NANCE, DONALD SYLVESTER, lawyer; b. Cleve., Apr. 19, 1940; s. Sylvester and Mary (Latimer) N.; m. Deborah Jean Ethridge, Feb. 14, 1978 (div.); 1 child, Teresa Anne. B.A. with honors, U. Calif.-Santa Cruz, 1970; J.D., Cleve. State U., 1975; postgrad U. Calif.-Berkeley, 1970-71. Bar: Ohio, U.S. Dist. Ct. (no. dist.) Ohio Assoc. atty. San Francisco Neighborhood Legal Assistance Found., 1975-76; atty. San Francisco Pub. Defender, 1978-79; cons. Spectrum Norhtwest, San Francisco, 1976-78; ptnr. Jone & Nance, Medina, Ohio, 1979-80; sole practice, Cleve., 1980—; currently ptnr. Hardiman, Alexander, Buchanan, Pittman & Howland, L.P.A., Cleve. Founder Operation Greater Cleve. Big Vote, Cleve., 1980. Served with USAF, 1960-64. Mem. ABA, Ohio Bar Assn., Norman S. Minor Bar Assn. Office: Hardiman Alexander Buchanan Pittman & Howland Co LPA 1900 Euclid Ave Suite 800 Cleveland OH 44115

NANEY, ALVA PAUL, physician; b. St. Louis, Sept. 15, 1918; s. Alvah Paul and Dora Florence (Horn) N.; children—Alan Paul, Robert Hayes. M.D., Washington U., St. Louis, 1943. Diplomate Am. Bd. Internal Medicine. Intern, Presbyn. Hosp., Chgo., 1943; resident VA Hosp., McKinney, Tex., 1947-49; gen practice medicine, Flora, Ill., 1949-60; physician Flora Clinic Ltd., 1960—; dir. Ill. Heart Assn. (now Am. Heart Assn.), Springfield, Ill., 1951—, pres., 1960-61. Mem. bd. edn. Flora High Sch. Dist., 1961-63. Served to maj. AUS, 1943-46, ETO. Fellow ACP, Am. Coll. Cardiology, Am. Heart Assn. (council clin. cardiology); mem. Ill. State Med. Soc., AMA, Ill. Soc. Internal Medicine, Am. Soc. Internal Medicine. Lodge: Elks. Avocations: aircraft flying; scuba diving, photography. Home: 224 E 5th St Flora IL 62839 Office: Flora Clinic Ltd 433 E 7th St PO Box 40 Flora IL 62839

NANGLE, JOHN FRANCIS, judge; b. St. Louis, June 8, 1922; s. Sylvester Austin and Thelma (Bank) N.; A.A., Harris Tchrs. Coll., 1941; B.S., U. Mo., 1943; J.D., Washington U., St. Louis, 1948; 1 son, John Francis Jr. Admitted to Mo. bar, 1948; practiced in Clayton, 1948-73; judge U.S. Dist. Ct., St. Louis, 1973—, chief judge, 1983—. Mem. Mo. Republican. Com., 1958-73; mem. St. Louis County Rep. Central Com., 1958-73, chmn., 1960-61; pres. Mo. Assn. Reps., 1961, Reps. Vets. League, 1960; mem. Rep. Nat. Com., 1972—. Bd. dirs. Masonic Home Mo. Served with AUS, 1943-46. Named Mo. Republican of Year, John Marshall Club, 1970, Mo. Assn. Reps., 1971; recipient Most Disting. Alumnus award Harris-Stowe Coll. Mem. Am. Judicature Soc., Jud. Conf. U.S., Legion of Honor DeMolay, ABA, Mo., St. Louis, St. Louis County bar assns. Office: US Courthouse 1114 Market St Saint Louis MO 63101

NANNE, LOUIS VINCENT, hockey club executive; b. Sault Ste. Marie, Ont., Can., June 2, 1941; s. Michael and Evelyn N.; B.S. in Mktg., U. Minn., 1963; m. Francine Yvette Potvin, Aug. 22, 1962; children—Michelle, Michael, Marc, Marty. Player, Minn. North Stars, 1967-78, gen. mgr., 1978—. Roman Catholic. Office: 7901 Cedar Ave S Bloomington MN 55420*

NANTKES, RYLAND REED, printing company executive; b. Bellwood, Nebr., Feb. 25, 1923; s. Harry Andrew and Isabel (Selzer) N.; m. Patricia Ann Andrews, Feb. 27, 1942 (div. 1961); children—Andrew Reid, Karen Ann; m. 2d, Okla Viola Sandlin, July 12, 1969. Vice pres. mfg. Epsen Lithographing Co., Omaha, 1941-60, pres., 1972—; v.p. mfg. Paramount Paper Products, Omaha, 1960-71; pres. Ralph Printing, Omaha, 1971-72; pres. Hillmer Graphics Co., also dir.; dir. HG Profl. Forms, Omaha, HG Label Works, Inc., Omaha. Republican. Presbyterian. Clubs: Omaha Country, Omaha. Home: 601 Martin Dr N Bellevue NE 68005 Office: Epsen Lithographing Co 2000 California St Omaha NE 68102

NAPIER, JAMES LEWIS, life insurance company executive; b. Albia, Iowa, Jan. 30, 1925; s. Lewis O. and Madeline A. (Graw) N.; B.S., Marquette U., 1950, M.A., 1951; m. Irene M. Tuohy, Aug. 11, 1951; children—James L., Margaret, Robert. With Am. Life Ins. Co., Chgo., 1950—, chn. bd., 1975—, pres., 1982—; chmn. bd. Buckingham Life Ins. Co., Chgo., 1980—. County ofcl. McHenry County (Ill.), 1974; vice consul of Iceland, Chgo., 1975—. Served with U.S. Army, 1943-46. Decorated Bronze Star with oak leaf cluster. Mem. Nat. Assn. Health Underwriters (sec.-treas. 1977-78), Ill. Assn. Life Cos. (pres. 1975-76). Republican. Roman Catholic. Office: 221 N LaSalle St Chicago IL 60601

NAPIER, MARK WAYNE, lawyer, lecturer; b. Louisville, May 5, 1953; s. Gerald Edward and Martha Nell (Tatum) N.; m. Maureen Frances Moore, June 28, 1980. B.S. in Bus. Adminstrn., Ohio State U., 1975; J.D., Ohio No. U., 1978; cert. Nat. Coll. Advocacy, 1983. Bar: Ohio 1978, U.S. Dist. Ct. (so. dist.) Ohio 1983. Asst. prosecutor Franklin County, Ohio, Columbus, 1978-79; assoc. Baran & Baran Co., L.P.A., Mansfield and Lima, Ohio, 1979-81; sole practice, Columbus, 1981-83; assoc. Martin M. Young & Assocs. Co., L.P.A., Cin., 1983—; lectr. Am. Inst. Paralegal Studies, Columbus and Cin., 1982—. Mem. Assn. Trial Lawyers Am., Ohio State Bar Assn., Ohio Acad. Trial Lawyers, Cin. Bar Assn. Home: 3221 Lookout Dr Cincinnati OH 45208 Office: Martin M Young & Assocs Co LPA 130 E 6th St Cincinnati OH 45202

NAPOLI, DONALD J., library director; b. Somerville, Mass., Mar. 10, 1941; s. Pasquale and Lucy (DeDeominicis) N.; m. Carol M. Kirk, July 6, 1968; children—Lisa, Anne, Mary Elizabeth. A.B., Boston Coll., 1964; M.S.L.S., Cath. U. Am., 1969. Cert. librarian, Ind., Ohio. Trainee, Enoch Pratt Free Library, Balt., 1967-68; info. specialist Essex br., 1969-71, asst. br. librarian Loch Raven br., 1971-72, br. librarian II, Parville-Carney br., 1972-75, IV, 1975-77; dir. South Bend Pub. Library, Ind., 1977—; exec. dir. Cuyahoga County Library, Cleve., 1985. Served to capt. Ordnance Corps, U.S. Army, 1965-67. Ind. State Library grantee, 1984. Mem. ALA, Ind. Library Assn. (Outstanding Librarian of Yr. 1985), Ohio Library Assn., South Bend C. of C. Democrat. Roman Catholic. Lodge: Rotary (South Bend). Avocations: chess; music; woodworking. Home: 1841 N Adams St South Bend IN 46628 Office: 122 W Wayne St South Bend IN 46601

NAPOLI, LAWRENCE RANDOLPH, public relations and marketing consultant; b. Poughkeepsie, N.Y., July 11, 1950; s. Joseph Lenord and Lucy Ann N.; m. Marianne Gerilyn Watson, Aug. 20, 1976; 1 son, Ryan Michael. B.A., Syracuse U., 1972. Publs. editor Hartford Steam Boiler Ins. & Inspection Co., Hartford, Conn., 1972-74; account exec. Juhl Advt. Agy. Inc., Elkhart, Ind., 1974-75; pub. relations advisor, sr. writer Johnson & Dean, Inc., Grand Rapids, Mich., 1975-76; v.p. pub. relations Nordstrom-Cox Mktg. Inc., Grand Rapids, 1976-81; gen. mgr. Western Mich. dist. Anthony M. Franco, Inc., Lansing, Mich., 1981-82; dir. corp. mktg. and pub. relations The Hager Group Cos., Grand Rapids, 1982—; lectr. Mich. State U., Grand Valley State Coll., Acquinas Coll.; profl. adviser Grand Valley State Colls. Vice-chmn. pub. info. com. Mich. div. Am. Cancer Soc., 1981—. Mem. Pub. Relations Soc. Am., Counselors Acad., Western Mich. Pub. Relations Soc. Am. (pres. 1982, 83), Grand Rapids Area C. of C. (communications com. 1980—), Grand Rapids Press Club. Roman Catholic. Contbr. articles to trade mags.

NARA, HIROSHI, linguist; b. Maruko, Japan, June 10, 1951; came to U.S., 1979; s. Kansuke and Kesaji (Saitoh) N. B.F.A., U. de las Americas, Puebla, Mex., 1974, B.A. in Art History, 1975; M.A. in Linguistics, U. Kans., 1982, M.Phil., 1984, doctoral candidate, 1985. Chief English sect. BFA Co., Ltd., Tokyo, 1976-79; instr. linguistics U. Kans., Lawrence, 1983, instr. Japanese, 1980—; computational linguist Weidner Communications, Inc., Provo, Utah, 1983-84. Editor: Kansas Working Papers in Linguistics, 1980-81. Author: Introduction to English Grammar, 1979; also articles. U. Kans. grantee, 1984. Mem. Linguistics Soc. Am., N.Y. Acad. Scis., AAAS, Assn. Computational Linguistics, Phi Kappa Phi. Avocations: painting; composing music; flute. Home: 911 Sunset Dr Lawrence KS 66044 Office: U Kans 2118 Wescoe Lawrence KS 66045

NARAMORE, LLOYD STAN, physician, hospital administrator; b. Middletown, Conn., Mar. 2, 1945; s. Lloyd Stanley and Genevieve Eloise (Blood) N.; m. Pamela Sue Hilles, July 14, 1984. B.S., Albion Coll., 1972; D.O., Michigan State Univ., 1975. Diplomate Nat. Bds. Med. Examiners. Intern, Lansing Gen., Mich., 1976, resident; practice medicine specializing in emergency medicine; med. dir. Salem Hosp., Ohio, 1982—. Contbg. editor Jour Postgrad. Medicine, 1982-84. Served to staff sgt. USAF, 1965-69; Middle East, Southeast Asia. Mem. Am. Coll. Emergency Physicians, Aircraft Owners and Pilots Assn. Avocations: comml. pilot; computerophile. Home: 865 Superior St Salem OH 44460 Office: Salem Hospital Emergency Dept State St Salem OH 44460

NARDY, VINCE ANTHONY, accountant; b. Youngstown, Ohio, Aug. 6, 1958; s. Vincent L. and Nancy Nardy (Burns) N. B.S.B.A. in Acctg. and Fin., also M.B.A., Youngstown State U. Inventory analyst Republic Steel, Warren, Ohio, 1981-83; plant acctg. mgr. Avery Internat., Painsville, Ohio, 1983—. Mem. Youngstown Jaycees, Alpha Phi Delta. Democrat. Roman Catholic. Avocations: jogging, racquetball, skiing. Home: 3083 Athena Dr Bethlehem PA 18017 Office: 250 Chester St Painesville OH 44077

NARROW, NANCY HENTIG, lawyer; b. Chgo., May 16, 1954; d. William Hector and Geneva Jeanette (Hofer) H.; m. Steven Robert Narrow, Apr. 24, 1982; children—Megan Michelle, Timothy Charles. B.A., Salem Coll., 1974; J.D., Washington U., St. Louis, 1981. Bar: Mo. 1981. Asst. pub. defender State Mo., Jackson, 1981-82, pub. defender, Benton, Mo., 1983—. Bd. dirs., chmn. fundraising WISER Inc. Women's Ctr. and Safehouse, Cape Girardeau, 1982—. Mem. ABA, Mo. Bar Assn., Am. Trial Lawyers Assn., Mo. Assn. Criminal Def. Lawyers, Scott County Bar Assn., Cape Girardeau County Bar Assn. Phi Delta Phi. Lutheran. Club: Zonta. Home: 2215 Bainbridge Rd Jackson MO 63755 Office: Public Defender 33d Jud Circuit PO Box 429 Benton MO 63736

NARSCIUS, KAZYS, physician; b. Papile, Lithuania, Apr. 3, 1924; came to U.S., 1949, naturalized 1956; s. Jonas and MaryAnn (Jaugaite) N.; m. Caezilie Matilda Sauerborn, Dec. 8, 1962. B.S., U. Detroit, 1956; M.D., U. Bonn, Fed. Republic Germany, 1961. Diplomate Am. Bd. Family Practice. Intern McNeil Meml. Hosp., Berwyn, Ill., 1963, resident in surgery, 1963; practice medicine, Bethalto, Ill.; chief of staff St. Anthonys Hosp., Alton, Ill., 1983-85. Mem. Ill. State Med. Soc., AMA, Civil Aviation Med. Assn. Home: Fairmount Addition Alton IL 62002 Office: 117 S Prairie Bethalto IL 62010

NASBY, CHARLES LELAND, JR., construction supply company executive; b. Mpls., Dec. 11, 1928; s. Charles Leland and Esther (Fjeldstad) N.; m. Patricia Ann Ree, July 18, 1953; children—Gregory Charles, Timothy Arthur. B.A., St. Olaf Coll., Minn., 1951; postgrad. U. Minn., 1951-52. Cert. profl. engr., Minn. With Ceco Corp., Mpls., 1953-70, asst. mgr., 1965-70; pres., treas. dir. Charles Nasby Assocs., Inc., Mpls., 1970—, Span-Dock, Inc., Mpls., 1977—. Served with USNR, 1953-56. Vice chmn. bd. dirs. Ebenezer Soc., Mpls., 1968—; pres. Lutheran Ch. Good Shephard, 1982. Mem. Mpls. Builders Exchange (pres. 1981, bd. dirs. 1976—), ASCE, Minn. Soc. Profl. Engrs., Constrn. Specifications Inst. (sec. 1981), Comml. Constrn. Industries. Republican. Clubs: Edina Country, Torske Klubben, Rotary. Patentee in field. Home: 4624 Bruce Ave Minneapolis MN 55424 Office: 5300 Excelsior Blvd Minneapolis MN 55416

NASH, BRENDA JOYCE, librarian; b. Dyersburg, Tenn., Aug. 28, 1940; d. Edward Hamilton and Lula Arlene (Turner) Claiborne; m. Gary Alvin Nash; children—LaDonna, Timothy, Chad. B.A., Evangel Coll., Springfield, Mo., 1962; M.S., in Edn., Central Mo. State U., Warrensburg, 1966. Tchr. Green Forest Sch., Salem, Mo., 1962-63, Fort Osage Sch. Dist., Indpendence, Mo., 1963-66; tchr. Blue Springs (Mo.) Sch. Dist., 1966—, elem. library coordinator, 1968—; librarian Dist. Profl. and Resource Library, 1980—. Mem. Mo. Assn. Sch. Librarians, Mo. State Tchrs. Assn., Blue Springs Commmunity Educators Assn., Ednl. Media Services, Internat. Reading Assn. Mem. Assembly of God Ch. Home: 1200 Arawak Blue Springs MO 64105 Office: 16th and Vesper Blue Springs MO 64015

NASH, DANE PATTERSON, judge; b. Tipton, Ind., Mar. 7, 1941; s. Robert Lee and Sarah Josephine (Surratt) N.; m. Sidenia Maines; 1 son, Robert L.; m. Carol Ann Ross, 1975 (div. 1982); children—Jessica Rains, Sarah Elizabeth, Kathryn Taylor; m. Jane Ellen Foley, Sept. 14, 1983; stepchildren—Mary, Janet, Angela, Gregory. B.A., Purdue U., 1971; M.S., Butler U., 1973; J.D., Ind. U.-Indpls., 1982. Bar: Ind. 1983, U.S. Dist. Ct. (So. dist.) Ind. 1983. Dep. sheriff County of Tipton, 1974-76, probation officer, 1977-82; judge Tipton County Cir. Ct., 1983—; dir. East Central Legal Services, Inc., Anderson, Ind. Served as capt. U.S. Army, 1962-68; Vietnam. Decorated D.F.C., Bronze Star, Air medal with oak leaf cluster, Purple Heart. Fellow Phi Delta Phi; mem. ABA, Ind. Bar Assn., Am. Judicature Soc., Assn. Trial Lawyers Am., DAV, Am. Legion (judge adv.), Lodges: Rotary (bd. dirs. local club), Masons (jr. warden local lodge). Office: Circuit Ct Courthouse Tipton IN 46072

NASH, JEFFREY EUGENE, sociology educator; b. Tulsa, Dec. 11, 1942; s. Eugene James and Kathrine Jenney (Hathaway) N.; m. Anedith J. Bond, Jan. 24, 1964; children—Marcus J., Jason M. B.A., Baylor U., 1964; M.A., La. State U., 1965; Ph.D., Wash. State U., 1971. Asst. prof. Tulsa U., 1971-74; faculty Macalester Coll., St. Paul, 1974—, asst. prof., 1974-79, assoc. prof., 1979-85, prof., 1985—, chmn. sociology dept., 1982—. Author: Social Psychology: Society and Self, 1985; (with Anedith Nash) Deafness in Society, 1981. Editor: (with James P. Spradley) Descriptive Sociology, 1976. Contbr. articles to various publs. Served with U.S. Army, 1966-68. Mem. Am. Sociol. Assn., Midwest Sociol. Soc., Soc. Study Symbolic Interaction (midwest rep. 1983—). Democrat. Home: 669 S Howell St Saint Paul MN 55116 Office: Dept of Sociology Macalester Coll 1600 Grand Ave Saint Paul MN 55105

NASH, JOHN PRITCHARD, lawyer; b. Manitowoc, Wis., Dec. 29, 1908; s. Archie Lyman and Mary (Pritchard) N.; student Lake Forest Acad., 1925; grad. Lawrenceville Sch., 1927; B.A., Princeton, 1931; LL.B., Harvard, 1934; m. Ruth Chapelle, Nov. 3, 1951; children—Barbara Pritchard, James Lyman. Admitted to Wis. bar, 1934, Fed. Dist. Ct., Eastern Dist. Wis., Western Dist. Wis., 7th U.S. Ct. Appeals bar; practice law Manitowoc, 1934—, with Nash & Nash, 1934-36, partner Nash & Nash (now Nash, Spindler, Dean & Grimstad), 1936—; dir. The Manitowoc Co., Inc., Richter Vinegar Corp. Chmn. fund raising Manitowoc County unit Am. Cancer Soc., 1954-56; active Manitowoc Community Fund, 1940-60; mem. adv. council boy Scouts Am., 1972—. Chmn. Manitowoc County com. Higher Edn., 1960-64; chmn., Wis. Commn. Higher Ednl. Aids, 1967-69; mem. state adv. council Fed. Higher Edn. Act., 1965-79, vice chmn., 1966-68, chmn., 1968-79; mem. citizens adv. council U. Wis.-Green Bay, 1969—; mem. Gov.'s Commn. Edn., 1969-71. Bd. dirs. Holiday House, Rahr-West Fund Bd.; pres. Manitowoc Meml. Hosp., 1980-82; bd. dirs. Manitowoc Day Care Center, YMCA; bd. advisers Salvation Army. Served to major, AUS, 1942-46. Decorated Bronze Star medal. Recipient Certificate Merit Manitowoc, 1967, award of merit U. Wis., 1972. Mem. Am., Wis., Manitowoc County (pres. 1958-59) bar assns. Manitowoc C. of C. Presbyn. (trustee 1957-60, elder 1965-68; trustee Wis. Synod 1969-72). Rotarian (pres. 1959-60). Clubs: B and B, Branch River Country (Manitowoc); University (Milw.). Home: 819 N 14th St Manitowoc WI 54220 Office: 201 E Waldo Blvd Manitowoc WI 54220

NASSAR, RAJA, statistics educator, researcher, consultant; b. Lebanon, 1936; came to U.S., 1958, naturalized, 1971; m. Ita G. Schaeffer, 1965; 1 child, Mark. B.S., Am. U. Beirut, Lebanon, 1958; M.S., U. Idaho, 1960; Ph.D., U. Calif.-Davis, 1963. Research fellow U. Idaho, Moscow, 1958-60; research asst. U. Calif.-Davis, 1960-63, research assoc., 1963-64; mem. vis. faculty U. Minn., St. Paul, 1964-66; asst. prof. Kans. State U., Manhattan, 1966-68, assoc. prof., 1968-74, prof. stats., 1974—; vis. prof. Govt. Research Inst., Hamburg, Fed. Republic Germany, 1969-70, Nat. Research Inst., Toulouse, France, 1974-75, U. Kiel, Fed. Republic Germany, 1982-83. Contbr. articles to sci. jours. Alexander von Humboldt fellow, 1969, 82, French govt. fellow, 1974; NSF grantee, 1982—. Mem. Am. Statis. Assn., Biometric Soc., Sigma Xi, Pi Mu Epsilon. Greek Orthodox. Avocations: tennis, travel, piano, reading. Office: Dept Stats Kans State U Manhattan KS 66506

NASSAU, ROBERT HAMILL, manufacturing company executive; b. Plainfield, N.J., Nov. 30, 1941; s. Charles Francis and Helen (Hudson) N.; m. AnnRae Falicki, July 13, 1968; children—Aimee, Robbie, Rebecca. A.B., Dartmouth Coll., 1962; M.B.A., Amos Tuck Sch., 1963. Fin. analyst Ford Motor World Hdqrs., Dearborn, Mich., 1964-67; with Ford Tractor, Troy, Mich., 1967-72, mgr. market and product analysis, 1971-72; asst. controller N.Am. truck ops. Ford Motor Co., Dearborn, 1972-73; agrl. product planning mgr. Ford Tractor, Troy, 1973-76, gen. sales mgr. overseas direct markets, 1976-78, gen. mgr. intercontinental ops., 1979-80; sr. v.p. mktg. and corp. planning J.I. Case Co., Racine, Wis., 1980-82, exec. v.p. Worldwide agrl. ops., 1982; pres., chief operating officer Am. Hoist & Derrick Co., St. Paul, 1982-84, pres., chief exec. officer, 1984—; dir. First Bank St. Paul. Key firms chmn. United Way, St. Paul, 1983; bd. dirs. Minn. World Trade Ctr., St. Paul, 1983. Mem. Beavers, Republican. Congregationalist. Clubs: Minnesota, St. Paul Athletic, Mini Kahda Country. Home: 260 S Mississippi River Blvd Saint Paul MN 55105 Office: Am Hoist & Derrick Co 1800 Amhoist Tower Saint Paul MN 55102

NASSTROM, ROY RICHARD, educational administration educator; b. Oakland, Calif., Oct. 28, 1930; s. Roy Richard and Edith Dolores (Spilman) N., m. Sally Louise Shaw, Aug. 29, 1964; children—Karen, Eric. B.A., U. Calif.-Berkeley, 1956, M.A., 1964, Ph.D., 1971. Asst. to supt. Ravenswood Sch. Dist., East Palo Alto, Calif., 1964-65; acting instr. edn. U. Calif.-Berkeley, 1965-68; asst. prof. ednl. adminstrn. U. Ky., Lexington, 1969-70; asst. prof. edn. Purdue U., West Lafayette, Ind., 1971-76; asst. grad. dean Winona State U., Minn., 1976-77, prof., chmn. ednl. adminstrn. dept., 1976—; cons., speaker various orgns. and schs., 1969—. Mem. editorial bd. Ednl. Administrn. Abstracts, 1976-83; manuscript reviewer Edn. Researcher, 1983—. Contbr. articles to profl. jours. Served as cpl. U.S. Army, 1952-54. Recipient numerous grants, 1969-77. Mem. Midwest Council Ednl. Administrn., Am. Ednl. Research Assn., Nat. Conf. Profs. of Ednl. Administrn., Phi Delta Kappa, Pi Sigma Alpha. Avocations: photography, bicycling. Home: 1702 Edgewood Rd Winona MN 55987 Office: Winona State U Dept Ednl Adminstrn Winona MN

NATHAN, JOHN EDWARD, pediatric dentist, educator, researcher; b. Chgo., May 12, 1949; s. Irwin E. and Dorothy (Blonski) N.; m. Patricia C. Christian, Aug. 21, 1977; children—Jennifer Elizabeth, Elizabeth Anne. B.S., U. Ill., 1971; D.D.S., Northwestern U., 1975; M.Dental Sci., U. Conn., 1983, cert. in pediatric dentistry, 1979. Diplomate Am. Bd. Pedodontics. Asst. prof. dept. pediatric dentistry U. Ill.-Chgo., 1979—, dir. postgrad. program dept. pediatric dentistry, 1983—; vis. asst. prof. depts. pediatrics and surgery Rush Med. Coll., Chgo., 1980—; mem. hemophilia adv. com. Ill. Dept. Pub. Health, Chgo., 1981—; cons. Nat. Inst. Dental Research, Washington, 1982—. Contbr. articles to profl. jours. Fellow Am. Acad. Pediatric Dentistry; mem. Am. Soc. Dentistry for Children (pres. Ill. chpt. 1985—), Am. Assn. Dental Schs., Internat. Assn. Dental Research. Avocations: skiing, tennis, golf, basketball. Office: U Ill Dept Pediatric Dentistry 801 S Paulina St Chicago IL 60612

NATHANSON, SAUL DAVID, surgical oncologist, research immunologist; b. Johannesbury, Transvaal, South Africa, Dec. 12, 1943; came to U.S., 1975; s. Hyman Barnett and Freda Charlotte (Weinberg) N.; m. Maxine Elaine Zacks, Nov. 29, 1966 (div. 1978); children—Laurence Cecil, Joshua Russel; m. Jerrilyn Marie Burke, Feb. 18, 1979; children—Abigail Mary, Alison Megan. M.D., U. Witwatersrand, South Africa, 1966. Diplomate Am. Bd. Surgery. Intern U. Pretoria, South Africa, 1967; lectr. human anatomy U. Witwatersrand, 1968, resident in surgery, 1969-74; postdoctoral fellow in immunology UCLA, 1975-77, postdoctoral fellow in surgery, oncology, 1977-80; chief resident in surgery U. Calif.-Davis, Sacramento, 1980-82; dir. surg. research Henry Ford Hosp., Detroit, 1982—, surg. oncologist, 1982—; clin. assoc. prof. U. Mich., Herndon prof. investigative oncology, 1985—. Contbr. numerous articles to profl. jours. Named Outstanding Surg. Resident U. Calif.-Davis, 1982; Ford Found. grantee, 1982. Mem. Am. Soc. Clin. Oncology, Am. Assn. Cancer Research, Am. Assn. Acad. Surgeons, Mich. Soc. Med. Research (bd. dirs. 1984—), Detroit Surg. Assn., AAAS, Wayne County Med. Soc., Earl F. Wolfman, Jr. Surg. Soc., South West Oncology Group, Royal Coll. Surgeons of Edinburgh, N.Y. Acad. Scis., Med. Assn. S. Africa. Republican. Jewish. Avocations: photography, classical music. Office: 2799 W Grand Blvd Detroit MI 48202

NAUERT, ROGER CHARLES, management consultant; b. St. Louis, Jan. 6, 1943; s. Charles Henry and Vilma Amelia (Schneider) N.; B.S., Mich. State U., 1965; J.D., Northwestern U., 1969; M.B.A., U. Chgo., 1979; m. Elaine Louise Harrison, Feb. 18, 1967; children—Paul, Christina. Bar: Ill. 1969. Asst. atty. gen. State of Ill., 1969-71; chief counsel Ill. Legis. Investigating Commn., 1971-73; asst. state comptroller State of Ill., 1973-77; dir. adminstrn. and fin. Health and Hosps. Governing Commn. Cook County, Chgo., 1977-79; nat. dir. health care services Alexander Grant & Co., Chgo., 1979—; vis. lectr. health adminstrn. Vanderbilt U.; vis. lectr. econs., fin. and health U. Chgo., 1978—; preceptor Wharton Sch., U. Pa., cons. health care mktg. Am. Mktg. Assn., 1977—. Fin. commr. Village of Bloomingdale (Ill.). Ford Found. grantee, 1968-69. Mem. Am. Hosp. Assn., Am. Public Health Assn., Am. Coll. Hosp. Adminstrs., Am. Assn. Healthcare Cons., Nat. Health Lawyers Assn., State Bar Ill., Hosp. Fin. Mgmt. Assn. (faculty mem.), Alpha Phi Sigma, Phi Delta Phi, Delta Upsilon. Club: Plaza. Author: The Comptroller—Illinois' Chief Fiscal Control Officer, 1976; A Sociology of Health, 1977; The Demography of Illness, 1978; Proposal for a National Health Policy, 1979; Health Care Feasibility Studies, 1980; Health Care Planning Guide, 1981; Health Care Strategic Planning, 1982; Overcoming the Obstacles to Planning, 1983; Principles of Hospital Cash Management, 1984; Healthcare Networking Arrangements, 1985; Strategic Planning for Physicians, 1986. Home: 310 Hempstead Ln Bloomingdale IL 60108 Office: 6th Floor Prudential Plaza Chicago IL 60601

NAUGHTON, GARY GRANT, educator; b. Sedan, Kans., July 2, 1937; s. John Thomas and Opal Irene (Locke) N.; m. Mary Mae Smith, Aug. 10, 1958; children—Mark, David, Joseph, John. B.S. in Forestry, Utah State U., 1959; M.S. in Forestry, U. Mo.-Columbia, 1969; LL.B., LaSalle Extension U., 1972. Forester trainee Bur. Land Mgmt., U.S. Dept. Interior, Lakeview, Oreg., 1957-59, range conservationist, Vale, Oreg., 1961-65, forester, Boise, Idaho, 1965-66; extension forester Kans. State U., Manhattan, 1966-83, prof. forestry, 1983—; rep. for African affairs Mid-Am. Internat. Agr. Consortium, Columbia, Mo., 1983—; gen. mgr. Pawpaw Land and Timber Co., Manhattan, 1970-84. Contbr. articles to profl. jours. Active Boy Scouts Am., 1973-83; sec.-treas. Kans. Tree Farm Com., 1972-83. Served to 1st lt. U.S. Army, 1959-61. Named Forest Conservationist of Yr., Kans. Wildlife Fedn., 1973; recipient 25 Year Govt. Service award U.S. Dept. Agr., 1982. Mem. Soc. Am. Foresters, Walnut Council (chmn. 1980-81), Kans. Acad. Sci. Republican. Methodist. Club: Sigma Pi. Lodge: Rotary. Office: Dept Forestry 2610 Claflin Rd Manhattan KS 66502

NAULT, JAMES EDWARD, psychologist, educator; b. Milw., June 23, 1930; s. Howard J. and Lora L. (Rapp) N.; m. Christine Curro, June 8, 1968; children—Michael, Andrew, Matthew. B.S., U. Wis.-Milw., 1956; M.S., U. Wis.-Madison, 1958; Ph.D., Iowa State U., 1978. Lic. psychologist, Wis. Tchr. spl. edn. Milw. pub. schs., 1956-57; counselor Marquette U. Guidance Clinic, 1959-60; dir. guidance, sch. psychologist Franklin pub. schs., Milw., 1960-61; mgr. agy. and spl. services, psychologist, Milw. Area Tech. Coll., 1961—, admissions officer, 1985—; cons. in field; pvt. practice psychology. Active Milwaukee County council Boy Scouts Am., 1978—. Served with USAF, 1948-49, 50-51. Mem. Am. Psychol. Assn., Wis. Psychol. Assn., Amway Distbrs. Assn., Am. Legion. Club: St. Josephs Athletic. Office: 1015 N 6th St Milwaukee WI 53203

NAVIS, VIRGIL JAMES, educator; b. Sheboygan, Wis., May 6, 1942; s. Benjamin and Lelia (Prinsen) N.; m. Rhea Gail Baganz, Aug. 8, 1964; children—Bryon, Denise, Brent, Brett. B.S. in Edn., Marian Coll., Fond du Lac, Wis., 1965; M.Ed., Marquette U., 1982. Cert. tchr., Wis. Tchr. lang. arts Sheboygan Falls (Wis.) pub. schs., 1962-64, Cedar Grove (Wis.) pub. schs., 1964—. Elder, 1st Christian Ref. Ch. Mem. Assn. for Supervision and Curriculum Devel., United Teaching Profession, Sheboygan County Edn. Assn. (past pres.), Cedar Grove Edn. Assn. (past v.p.), Pine Haven Men's Chorus (past pres.). Author curriculum guides for the teaching of lit. units and creative writing. Home: Route 2 Box 572 Oostburg WI 53070

NAVRATIL, FRANK JOSEPH, III, university administrator; consultant; b. Omaha, Oct. 6, 1947; s. Frank Joseph and Frances (Pamedit) N.; m. Jean Ann Zamastil, Aug. 29, 1970; children—Lisa C., F. Joseph, Michael J. B.S., Iowa State U., 1969; M.A., U. Notre Dame, 1972, Ph.D., 1974. Asst. prof. John Carroll U., Cleve., 1973-78; fin. economist Nat. Credit Union Adminstrn., Washington, 1978-79; vis. scholar Fed. Home Loan Bank Bd., Washington, 1983-84; prof., chmn. econs. John Carroll U., Cleve., 1975-85, dean Sch. Bus., 1985—; cons. Cleve. Ctr. Office Econ. Edn., Cleve., 1974-83. Contbr. articles to profl. jours. Recipient Kazanjian award for Teaching Econs., Joint Council on Econs. Edn., N.Y.C., 1973. Mem. Am. Econ. Assn., So. Econ. Assn., Midwest Econ. Assn. Roman Catholic. Avocations: sports, gardening. Home: 2395 Loyola Rd University Heights OH 44118 Office: Sch Bus John Carroll U Cleveland OH 44118

NAWROCKI, JOHN EDWARD, retail corp. exec.; b. Chattanooga, Jan. 30, 1944; s. Felix Anthony and Mary June (Shelford) N.; student U. Cin., 1962-64; m. Sherry Lynn, July 31, 1976. Various positions R.L. Polk Co., Cin., 1966-74, Singer Bus. Machines, Utica, N.Y., 1974-77; mgr. retail data processing Federated Dept. Stores, Cin., 1977—; dir. Corp. Data Ctr. 1983; chief exec. officer Clipper Enterprises, Inc., 1983—; mem. adv. com. SE Ind. Vocat. Tng. Program, 1978—. Served with U.S. Army, 1968-69. Mem. Cin. Hist. Soc., College Hill Hist. Soc., Data Processing Mgmt. Assn. (student club coordinator 1978-82, v.p. edn. 1981-82). Contbr. papers to profl. lit. Home: 5434 Hamilton Ave Cincinnati OH 45224 Office: Federated Dept Stores 222 W 7th St Cincinnati OH 45202

NAYLOR, GEORGE LEROY, lawyer, railroad executive; b. Bountiful, Utah, May 11, 1915; s. Joseph Francis and Josephine Chase (Wood) N.; student U. Utah, 1934-36; student George Washington U., 1937; J.D. (Bancroft Whitney scholar), U. San Francisco, 1953; m. Maxine Elizabeth Lewis, Jan. 18, 1941; children—Georgia Naylor Price, RoseMaree Naylor Hammer, George LeRoy II. Admitted to Calif. bar, 1954, Ill. bar, 1968; v.p., sec., legis. rep. Internat. Union of Mine, Mill & Smelter Workers, CIO, Dist. Union 2, Utah-Nevada, 1942-44; examiner So. Pacific Co., San Francisco, 1949-54, chief examiner, 1955, asst. mgr., 1956-61; carrier mem. Nat. R.R. Adjustment Bd., Chgo., 1961-71, chmn., 1970-77; atty. Village of Fox River Valley Gardens, Ill., 1974-77; practice law, legal cons., Barrington, Ill., 1977—; gen. counsel for Can-Veyor, Inc., Mountain View, Calif., 1959-64; adj. instr. dept. mgmt. U. West Fla., 1981. Served with AUS, World War II. Mem. ABA, Ill. Bar Assn., Calif. Bar Assn., Chgo. Bar Assn., San Francisco Bar Assn. Mem. Ch. Jesus Christ of Latter-Day Saints. Author: Defending Carriers Before the NRAB and Public Law Boards, 1969, Choice Morsels in Tax and Property Law, 1966, Underground at Bingham Canyon, 1944; National Railroad Adjustment Board Practice Manual, 1978. Home: 515 S Prospect Ave Champaign IL 61820 Office: 128 Center St Barrington IL 60010

NAYLOR, GREG ALAN, lawyer, writer; b. Albert Lea, Minn., Jan. 2, 1953; s. Roger A. and Dorothy (Hunt) N.; m. Julianne Worcester, Aug. 24, 1974; children—Benjamin John, Mark Robert. B.A. in Polit. Sci., U. Iowa, 1975; J.D., Drake U., 1978. Bar: Iowa 1978, U.S. Dist. Ct. (so. and no. dists.) Iowa 1978, U.S. Ct. Appeals (8th cir.) 1978, Mich. 1981, U.S. Dist. Ct. (so. dist.) Mich. 1981, U.S. Ct. Appeals (6th cir.) 1981. Mem. firm Davis, Hockenberg, Wine, Brown & Koehn, Des Moines, 1978-81, The Fishman Group, Detroit, 1981-82, Nyemaster, Goode, McLaughlin, Emery, & O'Brien, Des Moines, 1982—. Author: Puggies Tell the Truth, 1984. Contbr. articles to profl. publs. Ptnr. YMCA Ptnr. with Youth, Des Moines, 1981—; mem. bldg. com. Clive City Council, Iowa, 1984—; mem. Republican Presdl. Task Force, Washington, 1984—. Mem. ABA (labor law sect.), Iowa State Bar Assn. (mem. com. on labor law 1982—; recipient Mason Ladd Legal Writing award 1983), Polk County Bar Assn., Iowa Def. Counsel Assn., Assn. Trial Lawyers Am., Des Moines C. of C. Presbyterian. Home: 1875 NW 80th Pl Clive IA 50322 Office: Nyemaster Goode McLaughlin Emery & O'Brien 10th Floor Hubbell Bldg Des Moines IA 50309

NAYLOR, ROBERT EARLE, lawyer; b. Conneaut, Ohio, Feb. 13, 1947; s. Robert Frank and Dorothy Leona (Barringer) N.; m. Christine Marie Thayer, July 11, 1970; children—Jonathan, Nancy, Tarry, Jill. B.A., Case Western Res. U., 1969, J.D., 1972. Bar: Ohio 1972, U.S. Dist. Ct. (no. dist.) Ohio 1973. Asst. pros. atty. Ashtabula County, Ohio, 1972; ptnr. Thayer & Naylor, 1972—; law dir. City of Conneaut, 1973-84; dir. Am. Turned Products; ptnr. Lake Erie Investors Co., 1976—. Fellow Ohio State Bar Found.; mem. Ohio Bar Assn., Ashtabula County Bar Assn., Sons of Legionaires, Jaycees. Democrat. Club: Exchange. Lodge: Elks. Home: 915 Lincoln Dr Conneaut OH 44030 Office: Thayer & Naylor 171 Broad St Conneaut OH 44030

NAYMIK, JAMES JOHN, process design engineer; b. Youngstown, Ohio, July 9, 1946; s. Joseph and Mary (Petrisin) N. B.S.M.T., Cleve. State U., 1974; M.B.A., Baldwin Wallace U., 1977. Project engr. Davy McKee Corp., Cleve., 1974-82; application engr. AGA Gas, Inc., Cleve., 1982-83; sr. process design engr. Imperial Clevite Inc.; cons. traffic accident reconstrn., Cleve., 1983—. Served to cpl. USMC, 1968-70. Mem. ASME, Soc. Automotive Engrs. Eastern Orthodox. Home and Office: 6614 Crossview Rd Cleveland OH 44131

NAZEM, FARAMARZ F., chemical engineer; b. Rasht, Gillan, Iran, Jan. 22, 1943; s. Hassan and Afsar (Hasarie) N.; m. Linda Jean Delfino, Sept. 6, 1969; children—Rika Denise, Dariush Justin. B.S.Ch.E., Ohio State U., 1968; M.S. in Chem. Engring., Washington U., St. Louis, 1971, Sc.D., 1973. Project assoc. U. Wis.-Madison, 1973-74, assoc. scientist, 1974-75; mgr. research and devel. Union Carbide Corp., Parma, Ohio, 1975—, mgr. electrode devel., 1983—. Patentee in field. Mem. Soc. Rheology, Am. Inst. Chem. Engrs. Avocations: sports, stamp collecting. Home: 10745 Waterfall Rd Strongsville OH 44136 Office: Union Carbide Corp PO Box 6116 Cleveland OH 44101

NAZEM, SUFI MUHAMMAD, decision science educator; b. Bohera, India, Jan. 4, 1937; came to U.S., Aug., 1973; s. Amir Ali and Afia (Khatoon) N.; m. Margaret Anne Holden, Aug. 1, 1973; children—Omar Asif, Samaira Asifa. B.S., Aligarh U., 1958, M.S., 1960; Ph.D., Manchester U., 1970. Lectr. U. Manchester, Eng., 1966-73; assoc. prof. U. Petroleum and Minerals, Dhahran, Saudi Arabia, 1975-76; assoc. prof. Creighton U., Omaha, 1976-77; cons. U. Guam, 1981; assoc. prof. U. Nebr., Omaha, 1977-81, prof. decision scis., 1981—; cons. Union Pacific R.R., Omaha, Farm Credit Banks, Omaha, Nat. Bd. Prices and Incomes, London. Mem. Am. Statis. Assn., Am. Inst. for Decision Scis., Inst. Mgmt. Scis., Internat. Inst. Forecasters. Avocations: bridge, hiking.

NAZOS, DEMETRI ELEFTHERIOS, obstetrician, gynecologist; b. Mykonos, Greece, July 20, 1949; came to U.S., 1967, naturalized, 1983; s. Eleftherios D. and Anousso (Grypari) N.; m. Dorothea A. Lazarides, Dec. 3, 1977; children—Anna D., Terry E. B.S., Loyola U., Chgo., 1971; M.D., U. Athens, 1976. Diplomate Am. Bd. Ob-Gyn. Intern U. Athens Hosps., 1975-76; resident Harper Grace Hosp., Wayne State U., Detroit, 1976-80; practice medicine specializing in ob-gyn., Livonia, Mich., 1980-81, Joliet, Ill., 1981—; mem. staff St. Joseph Med. Ctr., Silver Cross Hosp. Fellow Am. Coll. Ob-Gyn., Am. Fertility Soc., mem. Royal Soc. Medicine-Eng., AMA, Greek Med. Assn., Am. Assn. Laparoscopists, Ill. Med. Assn., Southeastern Surg. Soc. Mich., Will-Grundy County Med. Soc. Greek Orthodox. Lodge: Rotary. Avocations: photography; hunting; gun collecting. Home: 608 E Palladium Dr Joliet IL 60435 Office: 330 N Madison St Joliet IL 60435

NEABLING, SUSAN MARIE, office and school supply company executive, bookstore administrator; b. Milw., Apr. 5, 1947; d. William J. and Eleanor C. (Schmidt) Schlapman; m. Roland L. Neabling, July 19, 1969; children—Ryan Louis, Robyn Lynn. B.A., U. Wis.-Oshkosh, 1969. Research analyst U. Wis.-Oshkosh, 1969-70, supply mgr. Univ. Bookstore, 1970-77, dir., 1977—; pres., owner Atlas Office & Sch. Supply, Inc., Neenah, Wis., 1980—; retail cons., 1980—. Chmn. parish edn. com. Grace Lutheran Ch., Winchester, Wis., 1977-80; mem. adv. bd. Luth. Campus Ministry, 1980-82. Mem. Nat. Assn. Coll. Stores (various coms.), Wis. Assn. Coll. Stores (pres. 1975-78). Republican. Office: Univ Bookstore U Wis Oshkosh WI 54901

NEAGU, GEORGE VICTOR, mental health therapist, administrator; b. Gary, Ind., Aug. 21, 1928; s. John and Victoria N.; m. Marece Thacker, Feb.

13, 1951; children—Monica, Mara-Lisa, Martin; m. Jeanette D'Arcy, July 8, 1973; children—Eric, Nevin, Erin-Jean. B.A., Roosevelt U., 1954; M.A., U. Chgo., 1964. Caseworker Lake County Dept. Pub. Welfare, 1957-63; probation officer, head domestic relations unit Gary City Ct., Ind., 1962-63; community unit dir. So. Unit, Chgo. Commn. on Youth Welfare, 1964-66; assoc. instr. Ind. U., South Bend, 1966-67; exec. dir. South Bend Human Relations Commn., 1966-68; dist. exec. Mich. Civil Rights Commn., 1968-70; adminstrv. asst. Chgo. region Ill. Dept. Children and Family Services, 1970-79; sr. therapist, staff devel. coordinator Swanson Ctr., Michigan City, Ind., 1979—; specialist police-community relations Mich. State U. Contbr. articles to profl. jours. Bd. dirs. North River Mental Health Ctr., Chgo., 1978-79; trustee Found. for Freedom and Democracy in Community Life, Inc., 1969—; pres. Am. Fedn. of State, County and Mcpl. Employees Lake County, Ind. Welfare Worker's Union, 1960-61, 61-62, Ind. Citizens Fair Housing Com.; officer Lake County Com. on Alcoholism; neighborhood commr. Gary council Boy Scouts Am.; Gt. Books leader; mem. Mayor's adv. com., Gary; chmn. Combined Citizens Com. on Open Occupancy in Gary; mem. housing com. Ind. NAACP. Recipient Human Relations award Gary Civic Club, 1963, Ovington award Gary br. NAACP, 1963. Merit award United Citizens Com. for Freedom of Residence, 1964, Nat. Champion of Open Occupancy award Eureka Coll., 1965; NCCJ scholar, 1967. Mem. Mental Health Assn. Ind., Isaac Walton League Am. Home: 3739 Lexington Rd Michigan City IN 46360 Office: Marquette Mall Office Bldg 6th Floor US 20 and Franklin St Michigan City IN 46360

NEAL, CHARLOTTE ANNE, ednl. adminstr.; b. Hampton, Iowa, May 8, 1937; d. Sebo and Marion Bradford (Boutin-Clock) Reysack; B.A., U. No. Iowa, 1958; M.Ed., DePaul U. (Chgo.), 1966; postgrad. No. Ill. U.; m. Paul Gordon Neal, Mar. 29, 1969; children—Rachel Elizabeth, Kory Bradford. Tchr., 4th grade, Des Moines Ind. Sch. Dist., 1958-59; tchr., 3d grade Glenview (Ill.) Pub. Schs., 1959-61, tchr. 3d grade, psychol. ednl. diagnostic Schaumburg Dist. Schs., Hoffman Estates, Ill., 1961-69; supr. learning disabilities and behavior disorders Springfield (Ill.) Pub. Schs., 1969-73; psycho-ednl. diagnostician Barrington (Ill.) Sch. Dist. 220, 1973-77; ednl. strategist Area Edn. Agy. 7, Cedar Falls, Iowa, 1978—; ednl. cons. Spl. Edn. Dist. Lake County, Gurnee, Ill., summer, 1968. Certified K-14 teaching and supervising in guidance, counseling, elementary supervisory K-9, elementary K-9 teaching, spl. K-12 learning disabilities. Mem. NEA, Ill. Edn. Assn. Author: Handbook for Learning Disabilities Tchrs., 1971. Home: 1102 Sunset Dr Parkersburg IA 50665 Office: 3712 Cedar Hts Dr Cedar Falls IA 50613

NEAL, JUDSON SHELLY, hospital equipment company sales executive; b. Kansas City, June 5, 1947; s. John Roy and Jewell Bess (Cartland) N.; m. Stephanie Marie Neal, June 7, 1968 (div. Apr. 1978); 1 son, Scott Judson; m. Linda Kathleen Neal, Feb. 16, 1980. B.S. in Bus. Adminstrn., U. Mo., 1969; M.B.A., Rockhurst Coll., 1982. With Puritan Bennett Corp., Kansas City, Mo., 1973—, mgr. adminstrv. services, 1982-83, nat. sales mgr., 1983, div. mktg. mgr., 1983—. Mem. Bd. Edn. Holy Cross Lutheran Sch., Kansas City, 1982—. Mem. Delta Sigma Pi. Republican. Lutheran. Home: 11120 W 121st Terr Overland Park KS 66213 Office: Puritan Bennett Corp 10800 Pflumm Rd Lenexa KS 66215

NEAL, STERLING, city official; b. Cleve., Aug. 30; s. Thurman and Margaret Neal; m. Willie R. Ford, Aug. 7, 1982; children—Otis, Rickey, Cecilia, Wanda, Taunja, Youlanda. Police Tng. Course, Western Res. U., 1970; student in Comml. Law, Bus. and Ins., U. MEDC, 1976, also student in Bus. Procedure, Payroll and Taxes, 1977. Lic. Class A investigator, Ohio; FCC lic. Class C and D transmitters. Dir. security Cuyahoga Bur. Investigation Inc., Cleve., 1973-83, chief of police, 1983—; dir. nat. sales CBI Wholesalers & Distbrs., 1979-82, dir. adminstrn., 1981-83. Bd. dirs. Kinsman Opportunity Ctr., 1976, mem. adv. bd., adminstrn. dir., outreach chmn. Served with U.S. Army, 1960-62. Recipient awards Ohio Bur. Employment Services, 1979, 83. Mem. Nat. SBA, Internat. Police Congress (spl. agt. Washington). Lodge: Masons, Shriners. Home: 9203 Bessemer Ave Cleveland OH 44104 Office: 4900 Euclid Ave 206 Cleveland OH 44103

NEAL, WILLIAM JOSEPH, geology educator; b. Princeton, Ind., Nov. 19, 1939; s. Garland and Helen Marie (Read) N.; m. Mary Edith McKannan, Feb. 7, 1959; children—Jean Marie, Julie Anna, Heather Jo. B.S. in Geology, U. Notre Dame, 1961; M.A. in Geology, U. Mo., 1964, Ph.D. in Geology, 1968. Postdoctoral fellow McMaster U., Hamilton, Ont., Can., 1967-68; asst. prof. Ga. So. Coll., Statesboro, 1969-71; asst. prof. Grand Valley State Coll., Allendale, Mich., 1971-73, assoc. prof., 1973-79, prof. geology, 1979—; adj. prof., research assoc. Skidaway Inst. Oceanography, Savannah, Ga., 1969-71; sr. fellow Duke U., Durham, N.C., 1976-77, vis. scientist, 1980-81; chmn. dept. geology Grand Valley State Coll., 1975-79. Author: (with others) Coastal Design, 1983; Living with the Shore (series), 1983-87 (also co-editor). Contbr. articles to profl. jours. Research grantee Fed. Emergency Mgmt. Agy., also NOAA, 1979-84, short course NSF, 1980, assoc. investigator NSF, 1978-79; faculty fellow NSF, 1976-77. Mem. Am. Assn. Petroleum Geologists, Internat. Assn. Sedimentologists, Soc. Econ. Paleontologists and Mineralogists, Nat. Assn. Geology Tchrs. (sect. treas. 1982-85), Mich. Acad. Sci., Arts, Letters, Sigma Xi (sec. Grand Valley 1984-85). Roman Catholic. Avocations: stamp collecting, photography. Office: Grand Valley State Coll Dept Geology Allendale MI 49401

NEALER, JAMES KEIFER, educational adminstrator; b. Indiana, Pa., Nov. 4, 1928; s. Alphonse William and Margaret Louise (Moore) N.; m. Beulah Jane Gift, June 25, 1949; children—Judith, Michael, Stephen. B.A., SUNY-Fredonia, 1975; M.A., Beacon Coll., Washington, 1982. Mem. research engring. staff Allegheny Ludlum Steel Co., Brackenridge, Pa., 1947-66, prodn. mgr., Dunkirk, N.Y., 1966-78; counselor Appalachian Regional Commn., Cortland, N.Y., 1978-81; dir. career planning Earlham Coll., Richmond, Ind., 1981—; ptnr. Career and Life Planning Assn., Richmond, 1981—, Career and Life Planning Ctr., Syracuse, N.Y., 1980-81. Author: So You Want to Get A Job, 1982; (manual) Writing the Right Resume, 1981. Mem. Mid-West Coll. Placement Assn., Am. Coll. Personnel Assn., Am. Assn. Counseling and Devel., Gt. Lakes Coll. Assn. Roman Catholic. Avocations: jogging, skin diving, tinkering with cars. Home: 1007 S 21st St Richmond IN 47374 Office: Earlham Coll National Rd W Richmond IN

NEALIS, PAUL JAMES, lawyer; b. Evergreen Park, Ill., Feb. 16, 1946; s. George James and Catherine Mary (Loftus) N.; m. Jane Ann Meany, July 2, 1976; 1 child, Jinelle Ann. B.A., Chgo. State U., 1973; J.D., Lewis U., 1978. Bar: Ill. 1978, U.S. Dist. Ct. (no. dist.) Ill. 1978. Detective, sgt. homicide Chgo. Police Dept., 1967-79, law instr., 1978-79; felony trial lawyer Cook County State's Atty., Chgo., 1979-83; sr. ptnr. Nealis & Bradley, Chgo., 1983—. Served to sgt. USMC, 1964-67, Vietnam. Decorated Purple Heart, Navy Commendation. Mem. Ill. Bar Assn., Chgo. Bar Assn. Roman Catholic. Office: Nealis & Bradley 10325 S Western Ave Chicago IL 60643

NEARY, DENNIS PATRICK, state senator; b. La Porte, Ind., Feb. 11, 1944; s. Charles Joseph and Loretta (Vollrath) N.; B.S., Murray (Ky.) State Coll., 1967; M.A., Ind. U., 1973; m. Mary Beth Holloway, Nov. 29, 1969; children—Robert, Ryan, Abigail. Tchr., Michigan City (Ind.) schs., 1968—; mem. Ind. Senate from 8th Dist., 1976—, caucus chmn. Democratic precinctman, 1968—. Roman Catholic. Address: 2316 Hazeltine Dr Michigan City IN 46360

NEBEL, LARRY HARMAN, sales executive; b. Jefferson City, Mo., July 6, 1942; s. Emil Harman and Dixie Dean (Cutler) N.; B.S. in Elec. Engring., U. Mo., Columbia, 1965; m. Helen Noreen, June 6, 1964; children—Andrew Harman, Larra Noreen. Applications analyst Control Data Corp., Houston, 1965-66; mem. tech. staff Sci. Data Systems, Santa Monica, Calif., 1966-67; area mgr. Remote Computing Corp., Los Angeles, 1967-75; regional mgr. Tymnet, Inc., Houston, 1975-79; v.p. sales Uninet, Inc., Kansas City, Mo., 1979—. Chmn., Uninet United Way campaign, 1980; arbitrator Better Bus. Bur., 1980—; mem. Com. 88, Emmanuel Bapt. Ch., 1980, usher, 1980, usher chmn., 1981—, deacon, 1983—, benevolence chmn. deacons com., 1983—, audio-visual com., 1983—; mem. exec. bd. Nottingham Forest Homes Assn., 1981—, also chmn. security com., co-chmn. community relations com. Clubs: Memorial West Community (pres. 1979, dir.), Blue Valley Optimist. Home: 12002 Goddard St Overland Park KS 66213 Office: 9101 W 110th St Suite 224 Overland Park KS 66210

NEBENZAHL, KENNETH, rare book and map dealer; b. Far Rockaway, N.Y., Sept. 16, 1927; s. Meyer and Ethel (Levin) N.; student Columbia U., 1947-48; L.H.D., Coll. William and Mary, 1983; m. Jocelyn Hart Spitz, Feb. 7, 1953; children—Kenneth (dec.), Patricia Suzanne (Mrs. William J. Frish), Margaret Spitz (Mrs. Constantino Quintong, Jr.), Suzanne Spitz (Mrs. Walter David Nichol). Solicitor new bus. United Factors Corp., N.Y.C., 1947-50; sales rep. Fromm & Sichel, Inc., N.Y.C., 1949-53; v.p. Cricketeer, Inc., Chgo., 1953-57; pres. Kenneth Nebenzahl, Inc., Chgo., 1957—; mem. Lloyds of London, 1978—; dir. Imago Mundi, Ltd., London, 1976—. Sponsor, Kenneth Nebenzahl, Jr. Lectures history cartography Newberry Library, Chgo., 1965—; trustee Glencoe Public Library, 1963-69, pres., 1966-69; bd. govs. Antiquarian Bookseller Ctr., N.Y.C., 1966-69; bd. dirs. North Suburban Library System, 1966-69, Friends of U. Iowa Libraries, 1964-71 mem. Glencoe (Ill.) Village Planning Commn., 1968-69; mem. exec. com. Northwestern U. Library Council, 1973-75; assos. bd. govs. Newberry Library, 1965-78, chmn., 1976-78, trustee, 1978—; bd. govs. Newberry Library Assocs., 1965-78, chmn., 1976-78; mem. assos. council John Crerar Library, Chgo., 1972—, trustee, 1976—; bd. dirs. Beverly Farm Found., Godfrey, Ill., 1961-67; trustee Adler Planetarium, Chgo., 1969—, v.p., 1974-77, chmn., 1977-81; bd. dirs. Evanston Hosp. Corp., 1978-85, Nature Conservancy of Ill., 1980—; mem. vis. com. to library U. Chgo., 1978—, trustee, 1980—, mem. Am. Geog. Soc. Collection adv. com. U. Wis.-Milw., 1979—; mem. Friends U. Iowa Libraries, 1964-71. Served with USMCR, 1945-46. Fellow Royal Geog. Soc., Internat. Map Collectors Soc. London (Tooley award 1974), Am. Geog. Soc.; mem. Manuscript Soc. (dir. 1965-71), Am. Library Trustees Assn. (nat. chmn. com. intellectual freedom 1967-68), Antiquarian Booksellers Assn. Am. (bd. govs. 1965-67, v.p. 1978-79), Am. Antiquarian Soc. (bd. govs. 1980—), Soc. History of Discoveries (dir. 1974-76), Chgo. Map Soc. (dir. 1976—), Bibliog. Soc. Am., Hakluyt Soc. Clubs: Caxton (bd. govs. 1961-68, pres. 1964-66), Arts, Tavern (bd. govs. 1979—), Wayfarers' (pres. 1979-80) (Chgo.); Lake Shore Country (Glencoe, Ill.); Century, Grolier (N.Y.C.). Author: Atlas of the American Revolution, 1974; Bibliography of Printed Battle Plans of the American Revolution, 1975; contbr. articles to profl. jours. Home: 135 Crescent Dr Glencoe IL 60022 Office: 333 N Michigan Ave Chicago IL 60601

NEBERGALL, DONALD CHARLES, banker; b. Davenport, Iowa, Aug. 12, 1928; s. Ellis W. and Hilda (Bruhn) N.; B.S., Iowa State U., 1951; m. Shirley Elaine Williams, Apr. 12, 1952; children—Robert W., Nancy L. Nebergall Bosma. With Poweshiek County Nat. Bank, 1958-72, sr. v.p., to 1972; founding pres., dir. Brenton Bank and Trust Co., Cedar Rapids, Iowa, 1972-82, chmn. bd., 1982—, dir. Brenton Banks, Inc.; dir. Telephone & Data Systems, Inc.; bd. dirs. Iowa Automated Clearing House; vice-chmn. ITS, Inc. (both subs. Iowa Bankers Assn.). Vice-pres., dir. Iowa 4-H Found., 1972-76; div. campaign chmn. United Way; bd. dirs. ARC, Boy Scouts Am.; bd. dirs., treas. Meth-Wick Manor Retirement Home; founding trustee Cedar Rapids Community Sch. Dist. Found. Served with AUS, 1946-48. Recipient Ptnr. in 4-H award Iowa 4-H, 1983. Mem. Cedar Rapids Greater Downtown Assn. (pres., dir.), Alpha Zeta, Gamma Sigma Delta, Delta Upsilon. Republican. Methodist. Club: Rotary Internat. Office: Brenton Bank & Trust Co 150 1st Ave NE Cedar Rapids IA 52401

NECHEMIAS, STEPHEN MURRAY, lawyer; b. St. Louis, July 27, 1944; s. Herbert Bernard and Toby Helen (Wax) N.; m. Marcia Rosentein, June 19, 1966, (div. Dec. 1981); children—Daniel Jay, Scott Michael; m. Linda Adams, Aug. 20, 1983. B.S., Ohio State U., 1966; J.D., U. Cin., 1969. Bar: Ohio 1969. Ptnr., Taft, Stettinius & Hollister, Cin., 1969—. Tax comment author: Couse's Ohio Form Book, 6th edit., 1984; contbg. author Mathew Bender Ohio Taxes, 1984. Mem. Cin. Bar Assn. (chmn. taxation sect.). Democrat. Jewish. Home: 777 Cedar Point Dr Cincinnati OH 45230 Office: Taft Stettinius & Hollister 1800 First National Bank Center Cincinnati OH 45202

NEDRICH, JOHN LAWRENCE, transportation executive; b. Nanty-Glo, Pa., Mar. 16, 1940; s. John and Ann (Demchak) N.; B.B.A., Cleve. State U., 1970; M.B.A., Lehigh U., 1975; m. Elaine Ann Bell, Oct. 20, 1962; children—Christal Fern, Shawn Lawrence, Kelly Elaine. With, Air Products & Chems., Allentown, Pa., 1963-79, fleet mgr. AGA Burdox, Cleve., 1979-80; gen. mgr. Contract Transp. Systems subs. Sherwin Williams, Cleve., 1980-83; pres. Fleet Service Co., Cleve., 1983-85, Cloverdale Transp., Human Resource Mgmt. Co., Berea, Ohio, CKS Mgmt. Inc., 1985—. Scoutmaster, Boy Scouts Am., 1978-79. Served with USCG, 1959-61. Mem. Pvt. Carrier Conf. (dir.), Pa. Motor Truck Assn., Contract Carrier Assn., Am. Transp. Assn. (pvt. truck council), Inst. Traffic and Transp. (chief officer bd. 1984—), Nat. Council Phys. Distbn. Mgrs., Am. Soc. Traffic and Transp., ICC Practitioners Assn. (dist. v.p.). Roman Catholic. Office: Fleet Service Co PO Box 266 Cleveland OH 44107

NEDWEK, THOMAS WAYNE, association executive; b. Milw., Sept. 30, 1933; s. Thomas Anton and Josephine Ruth (Felski) N.; m. Charlotte A. Jager, June 16, 1956 (div. Jan. 1982); children—Thomas W. Jr., David J., Peter C., Annemarie R., Paul J. B.S. in Bus. Adminstrn., Marquette U., 1955; postgrad. San Diego State Coll., 1958, Marquette U., 1960-61. Tchr., English Cathedral High Sch., San Diego, 1958-60; radio announcer Sta. WISN, Milw., 1960-65; instr. English Milw. Sch. Engring., 1960-62, Messmer High Sch., Milw., 1962-65; mem. pub. relations staff AC Electronics div., Gen. Motors Corp., Milw., 1965-70; sr. reporter Sta. WISN-TV, Milw., 1970-72, dir. pub. relations, 1972-76; v.p. pub. relations Milw. Sch. Engring., 1976-80; exec. dir. Milw. Bar Assn., 1980—. Alderman, City of Glendale (Wis.), 1976—, plan commr., 1976-84; bd. dirs. St. Joseph's Hosp., 1980-85, Milw. Council on Alcoholism, 1980—, World Festivals, Inc., 1978—; sec. Milw. Bar Found., 1983—. Served to lt. (j.g.) USN, 1955-58. Mem. Pub. Relations Soc. Am. (past pres. Wis. chpt., assembly del.), Am. Soc. Assn. Execs., Nat. Assn. Bar Execs., Wis. Soc. Assn. Execs. Roman Catholic. Club: Milw. Press (sec. 1983-85). Home: 2620 W Custer Ave Glendale WI 53209 Office: 605 E Wisconsin Ave Milwaukee WI 53202

NEDZA, EDWARD A., state senator; b. Chgo., July 26, 1927; ed. U. Calif.; m. Tina Pretzer; children—James Edward, Kathleen Ann. Former resident engr. Chgo. Dept. Public Works; asst. commr. Dept. Water, Chgo.; now asst. commr. Dept. Streets and Sanitation, City of Chgo.; mem. Ill. Senate, 1978—. Comitteeman 31st Ward Democratic Party, 1976—. Served with USMC, World War II. Mem. Chgo. Assn. Commerce and Industry, Am. Soc. Cert. Engring. Technicians, Inst. Engring., Am. Pub. Works Assn., Inst. Transp., Inst. Adminstrv. Mgmt. Office: State Capitol Rm M103D Springfield IL 62706

NEE, JOHN GERALD, JR., mechanical engineering educator, consultant; b. Beloit, Wis., Mar. 28, 1939; s. John Gerald and Doris Anne (Hansberry) N.; m. Kathleen Mary Walsh, Feb. 4, 1967; children—Christine Ann, Lynn Marie. B.S., U. Wis.-Stout, Menomonie, 1966, M.S., 1967; Ed.D., U. Minn., 1972. Cert. mfg. engr. Designer Beloit Corp., 1960-64; cons. State of Minn., Mpls., 1969-71; instr. Lincoln Land Coll., Springfield, Ill., 1971-73; asst. dir. Richland Community Coll., Decatur, Ill., 1973-75; prof. Central Mich. U., Mt. Pleasant, 1975—; pres. Edutech Cons., Mt. Pleasant, 1982—; cons. Macmillan Pub. Co., N.Y.C., 1981—. Author: Jig and Fixture Design, 1979; Mechanism Design, 1980; Mechanical Engineering Technology, 1983; Engineering Graphics, 1985. Chmn. citizenship com. Central Mich. U., 1983-85, Grantee U.S. Dept. Energy, 1978, Macmillan Pub. Co., 1984. Mem. Soc. Mfg. Engrs. (grantee), Nat. Assn. Indsl. and Tech. Tchr. Edn. (sec.), Nat. Rifle Assn. Roman Catholic. Home: 1530 Briarwood Dr Mount Pleasant MI 48858 Office: Central Mich U Indsl Engring Dept 202 Wightman St Mount Pleasant MI 48859

NEEDLEMAN, SAUL B(EN), disposable medical devices company official, biochemical researcher; b. Chgo., Sept. 25, 1927; s. Jack L. and Celia (Magad) N.; m. Sondra Audrey Goldberg, June 13, 1954; children—Martin Craig, Arthur Alan, Beth Hali, Heidi Ruth. B.S. in Organic Chemistry, Ill. Inst. Tech., 1950, M.S. in Biochemistry, 1955; Ph.D. in Biochemistry and Medicine, Northwestern U., 1957. Assoc. prof. biochemistry and neurology Northwestern U., 1960-73; chief nuclear medicine VA Research Hosp., Chgo., 1965-73; chmn. dept. biochemistry Roosevelt U., Chgo., 1973-75; coordinator sci. affairs Abbott Labs., North Chicago, Ill., 1974-79; dir. clin. affairs Schering-Plough, Memphis, 1979-81; dir. med. affairs Hollister, Inc., Libertyville, Ill., 1981—; cons. U.S. Naval Dental Research Program. Gt. Lakes, Ill. Mem. Highland Park City Zoning Commn., Highland Park Sch. Bd.; precinct capt. Served with USNR, 1945-47. Recipient Presdl. award Abbott Labs., 1979; Toni Research fellow, 1954-55; Gillette Research fellow, 1953-54; recipient RESA Sci. Research award, 1960. Mem. Am. Soc. Biol. Chemistry, Am. Numis. Assn. (dist. rep.), Am. Numis. Soc., Am. Israel Numis. Assn. Author: Protein Sequence Determination, vol. 8A, 1970, 8B, 1975; Advanced Methods in Protein Sequence Determination, vol. 25, 1977; contbr. articles to tech. jours., articles on numis. history to periodicals; patentee in field. Office: PO Box 250 2000 Hollister Dr Libertyville IL 60048

NEEDLES, BELVERD EARL, JR., accounting educator; b. Lubbock, Tex., Sept. 16, 1942; s. Belverd Earl and Billie (Anderson) N.; B.B.A., Tex. Tech U., 1964, M.B.A., 1965; Ph.D., U. Ill., 1969; m. Marian Powers, May 23, 1976; children—Jennifer Helen, Jeffrey Scott. C.P.A., Ill.; cert. mgmt. acct. Asst. prof., assoc. prof. acctg. Tex. Tech U., Lubbock, 1968-72; dean Coll. Bus. and Adminstrn., Chgo. State U., 1972-76; prof. acctg. U. Ill., Urbana, 1976-78; dir. Sch. Accountancy, DePaul U., Chgo., 1978—. Treas., bd. dirs. C.P.A.s for Pub. Interest, 1978—. Gen. Electric fellow, 1965-66; Deloitte Haskins and Sells fellow, 1966-68. Fellow Am. Acctg. Assn. (sec. internat. sect. 1984-86); mem. Fedn. Schs. Accountancy (dir. 1980—, pres. 1986), Am. Inst. C.P.A.s, Acad. Internat. Bus., Ill. C.P.A. Soc., European Acctg. Assn., Fin. Execs. Inst., Nat. Assn. Accts., Phi Delta Kappa, Phi Kappa Phi, Beta Alpha Psi, Beta Gamma Sigma. Club: Chgo. Athletic. Author: Accounting and Organizational Control, 1973; Modern Business, 2d edit., 1977; Principles of Accounting, 1980, 2d edit., 1984; Financial Accounting, 1982; The CPA Examination: A Complete Review, 6th edit., 1985; Comparative International Auditing Standards, 1985; editor Accounting Instructor's Report, 1981—.

NEELY, DAVID EDMUND, college dean, law educator, lawyer; b. Chgo., Feb. 26, 1952; s. David L. and Lottie V. (Brown) N. B.A., Fayetteville State U., 1970-75, M.A., U. Idaho, 1978; J.D., U. Iowa, 1981. Bars: Ill. 1982, U.S. Dist. Ct. (central dist.) 1982. Dir. minority student programs U. Idaho, Moscow, 1976-77; assoc. in edn. Washington State U., Pullman, 1977-81; ombudsman U. Iowa, Iowa City, 1979-81; dir. affirmative action, assoc. prof. law Ill. State U., Normal, 1981-83; asst. dean John Marshall Law Sch., Chgo., 1983—; chmn. legal redress com. NAACP, Chgo. Contbr. articles to profl. jours. Legal counsel Ill. Com. on Black Concerns in High Edn., Ill. Affirmative Action Officers Assn., Ill. Mcpl. Human Relations Assn.; councilman First Congl. Dist. Edn. Legis. Adv. Council, Chgo. Grantee Law Sch. Admissions Council, 1984. Mem. Ill. State Bar Assn., ABA, Nat. Bar Assn. (regional dir.), Chgo. Bar Assn., Chgo. Council Lawyers, Cook County Bar Assn., Alpha Phi Alpha. Office: John Marshall Law Sch 315 S Plymouth Ct Chicago IL 60604

NEELY, JOANNE LUCINDA, school counselor; b. Pitts., July 3, 1942; d. John Miller and Gladys Elizabeth (Bartels) N. B.S., Indiana U. Pa., 1964; M.A., W.Va. U., 1967. Elem. tchr. West Jefferson Hills Sch. Dist., Clairton, Pa., 1964-67; tchr., instrnl. cons. Ritenour Sch. Dist., St. Louis, 1967—, sch. counselor, 1973—. Mem. Assn. Children with Learning Disabilities, Mo. Tchrs. Assn., Mo. Sch. Counselor Assn. Republican. Presbyterian. Lodge: Order Eastern Star (worthy matron 1977). Home: 8427 Lackland Rd Saint Louis MO 63114 Office: Ritenour Sch Dist 2420 Woodson Rd Saint Louis MO 63114

NEELY, RICHARD SAMUEL, osteopathic physician, anesthesiologist; b. Ann Arbor, Mich., Aug. 25, 1929; s. Hayden Elmo and Easter (Black) N.; m. Maureen Ann Mascott, Dec. 1, 1951; children—Susan Carol, Jo Ann, Mark Richard, Cynthia Lynn; m. 2d, Sandra Kay Radelt, June 22, 1969. Student Wayne U., Detroit, 1947-51, U. Detroit, 1953-56; D.O., Kansas City Coll. Health Scis., 1960. Intern, Clare (Mich.) Gen. Hosp., 1960-61; anesthesiologist Lapeer County (Mich.) Gen. Hosp., 1966—; chief anesthesia, 1972—, chief of staff, 1979-82. Mem. Lapeer County (Mich.) Republican Party; sustaining mem. Nat. Rep. Party. Mem. Am. Osteo. Assn., Mich. Assn. Osteo. Physicians, Lapeer County Osteo. Soc., Am. Soc. Anesthesiologists, Mich. Soc. Anesthesiologists, Am. Osteo. Soc. Anesthesiologists, Mich. Osteo. Soc. Anesthesiologists. Home: 1512 RuLane Dr Lapeer MI 48446 Office: PO Box 39 Lapeer MI 48446

NEETZEL, RAYMOND JOHN, transportation analyst; b. St. Paul, Apr. 2, 1937; s. John R. and Alyce I. (Berge) N.; m. Laurel A. Neetzel. B.A., U. Wis.-Green Bay, 1973; cert. urban transp. planning, 1976; postgrad. St. Thomas Coll., 1978. Free-lance photographer, St. Paul, 1955-72; planning cons. City of Green Bay (Wis.), 1972-73; transit analyst Met. Transit Commn., St. Paul, 1973-76, sr. transit analyst, 1977—, mgmt. trainer, 1979—; owner Neetzel's Wood Works, Inc., 1979—; lectr., U. Aston, Birmingham, Eng., 1972, U. Wis., Green Bay, 1973; panelist Nat. Transp. Research Bd., 1977, 83. Sec. Neenah (Wis.) Planning Commn., 1967-69. Mem. Nat. Inst. Transp. Engrs., Norwegian Am. Mus. (life), Boundary Waters Conservation Alliance, Nat. Forest Recreation Assn. (nat. bd. dirs.), Nat. Assn. Alpha Phi Omega. Author: Winter Survival Techniques, 1980; also research papers in field. Office: Metropolitan Transit Commission 560 6th Ave N Minneapolis MN 55411

NEFF, N. THOMAS, engineering company executive, consulting engineer; b. Pitts., Jan. 5, 1925; s. Richard and May (Thomas) N.; m. Anne Johnston, Jan. 10, 1948; children—Thomas M., William R., Gordon J. B.S. in Gen. Engring., U. Pitts., 1955. Registered profl. engr., Pa., Ohio, Calif., Wis., Ala., Maine. Mech. engr. Peter F. Loftus Corp., Pitts., 1951-59; spl. projects engr. H.H. Robertson, Inc., Ambridge, Pa., 1959-61; project mgr. Ehrhardt & Assocs., Los Angeles, 1965-68; v.p. Hoad Engrs., Inc., Ypsilanti, Mich., 1977-80; v.p. A.M. Kinney, Inc., Cin., 1961-65, 68-77, 80—. Author, co-author tech. articles and papers. Ch. sch. supt. Christ Ch. Glendale, Ohio, 1970-74; youth activities leader Boy Scouts Am., Glendale, Calif., 1966-68. Mem. ASME (assoc. editor Jour. Engring. for Power 1981-83, chmn. indsl. ops. 1981-83, Cin. sect. 1983-84, exec. com. power div. 1985—, Best Paper award Indsl. Ops. Com. 1983), TAPPI (sec. energy mgmt. com. engring. div. 1984—, steam and power com. 1980—), Phi Delta Theta. Republican. Episcopalian. Avocation: history. Home: 7612 Lakewater Dr Montgomery OH 45242 Office: A M Kinney Inc 2900 Vernon Pl Cincinnati OH 45219

NEFF, RAY ALLEN, emeritus health and safety educator; b. Bristow, Va., Jan. 23, 1924; s. Charles Edward and Mary Elizabeth (Runion) N.; B.A., Bridgewater Coll., 1950; postgrad. Med. Coll. Va., 1954; M.S., Jefferson Med. Coll., 1960; Ed.D., Ball State U., 1975; m. Augusta Mae Kossman, Dec. 19, 1948; children—Charles Frederick, Robert Allen. Food cons. Commonwealth Va. Dept. Health, Richmond, 1950-54; analyst FDA, HEW, 1955; sr. analyst Smith, Kline & French Labs., Phila., 1956-58; Walter G. Karr research fellow Jefferson Med. Coll., Phila., 1958-60; health officer Cape May County (N.J.) Dept. Health, 1960-67; asst. prof. dept. health and safety Ind. State U., Terre Haute, 1967-75, assoc. prof., 1975-84, emeritus, 1984—. Vice pres., dir. research and devel. Visu-Phonics, Inc., Terre Haute, 1968-79, also dir.; dir., chmn. bd., pres. Ray A. Neff Assocs., Inc., cons., Terre Haute, 1979—; cons. Sunn Classics Prodns., Salt Lake City, 1976-78. Served with USNR, 1944-45. Fellow Soc. Mil. Historians. Am. Pub. Health Assn.; mem. Ind. Pub. Health Assn., N.J. Health Officers Assn., Royal Soc. Health (Gt. Britain). Pub., Abraham Lincoln Lithographs, 1968; Pawn of Traitors, 1969. Patentee solvent extractor, aircraft proximity device. Home: 514 N 8th St Marshall IL 62441 Office: PO Box 2507 Terre Haute IN 47802

NEFF, ROBERT HUDSON, homesite developer; b. Canfield, Ohio, Jan. 24, 1916; s. Roy J. and Laura M. (Noll) N.; m. Maxine Dwiggins, Dec. 21, 1940; children—Jennifer Neff Thomas, Holly Neff Broom, Candace. B.S., Ohio State U., 1939. Territorial sales mgr. Sheaffer Pen Co., Columbus, Ohio, 1939-42, 46-50; pres., homesite developer Neff Land Co., Canfield, 1950—. Served to lt. (s.g.) USNR, 1942-45. Methodist. Clubs: Rotary, Salem (Ohio) Golf; Inner Circle (Delray Beach, Fla.); Elks.

NEFF, WALTER LOREN, insurance company executive; b. Dayton, Ohio, Apr. 27, 1940; s. Alfred A. and Ruth (Whittington) N.; m. Carol Townsend, Oct. 19, 1963; children—Karen, Scott, Julie. B.S., Ohio State U., 1962. Investment officer Winters Nat. Bank, Dayton, 1962-69; asst. v.p. Huntington Nat. Bank, Columbus, 1969-78; dir. investments Grange Mut. Cos., Columbus, 1978—. Pres. Family Counseling and Crittenton Services, Columbus, 1975-76. Fellow Fin. Analysts Fedn.; mem. Columbus Soc. Fin. Analysts (pres. 1974-75), Columbus Stock and Bond Club (pres. 1976-77), Ohio State U. Marching Band Alumni Club (treas. Columbus 1980—). Club: Worthington Hills Country (Ohio). Lodge: Masons. Avocations: golf. Office: Grange Mut Cos 650 S Front St Columbus OH 43216

NEFF, WILLIAM LLOYD, dentist; b. Detroit, Feb. 26, 1934; s. Lloyd R. and Helen (Downey) N.; m. Cecile A. Timmis, July 20, 1957; children—Julie, Bill Michael, Kelly, Susan. B.S., U. Detroit, 1958, D.D.S., 1962. Practice dentistry, West Bloomfield, Mich., 1962—. Served with U.S. Army, 1953-55. Mem. Oakland County Dental Soc., Detroit Dist. Dental Soc. (assoc.), Chgo. Dental Soc. (assoc.), Mich. Dental Golf Assn. (bd. dirs. 1975—). Republican. Roman Catholic. Club: Oakland Hills Country (asst. golf chmn. 1985) (Birmingham, Mich.). Avocations: golf, hockey, jogging, paddle tennis. Home: 5554 Normanhurst St West Bloomfield MI 48033 Office: 7499 Middle Belt West Bloomfield MI 48033

NEHAL, SYED M., engineer, consultant; b. Ranchi, India, Dec. 8, 1933; came to U.S., 1957, naturalized, 1964; s. Syed A. and Safia B. Zafar; m. Idella E. Norman, May 13, 1960; children—Yasmin, Jeffrey, Jason, Susan. B.S., Aligarh U. (India), 1955; B.S.E.E., Ind. Inst. Tech., 1959; M.S. in Engring., Akron U., 1966. Registered profl. engr., Ohio, Va., W.V., Ct.; cert. energy auditor and tech. analyst, Ohio. Home study dir. Air Conditioning Tng. Sch., Youngstown, Ohio, 1961-63; dir. profl. services Rohrer & Assocs. Cons. Engrs., Akron, Ohio, 1964-71; prin., pres. Nehal & Assocs., Inc., Akron, 1971—; expert witness Expert Adv. Service, 1981. Mem. council Bethel Luth. Ch., Bath-Richfield, 1980, 84; vol. Cuyahoga Falls Gen. Hosp., 1983. Mem. ASHRAE, ASME (local chpt. chmn. Engrs. Week, 1980), Nat. Soc. Profl. Engrs. (bd. dirs. local chpt. 1969), Nat. Soc. Fire Protection Engrs., Profl. Engrs. in Pvt. Practice, Profl. Engring. Soc. (pres. 1976). Lodge: Kiwanis (bd. dirs. 1979). Avocations: gardening; painting; drawing; dogs. Home: 2343 N Revere Rd Akron OH 44313 Office: Syed M Nehal & Assocs Inc 2117 Grant Ave Cuyahoga Falls OH 44223

NEHER, LESLIE IRWIN, engineer, former air force officer; b. Marion, Ind., Sept. 15, 1906; s. Irvin Warner and Lelia Myrtle (Irwin) N.; m. Lucy Marion Price; 1 son, David Price; m. Cecelia Marguerite Hayworth, June 14, 1956; B.S. in Elec. Engring., Purdue U., 1930. Registered profl. engr., Ind., N.Mex. Engr. high voltage research, 1930-32; engr. U.S. Army, Phila., 1933-37; heating engr. gas utility, 1937-40; commd. 2d lt. U.S. Army, 1929, advanced through grades to Col., 1947; dir. tng., Tng. Command, Heavy Bombardment, Amarillo AFB, Tex., 1942-44; dir. mgmt. tng., 15th AF, Colorado Springs, Colo., 1945-46; mgr. Korea Electric Power Co., Seoul, 1946-47, ret., 1960; engr. Neher Engring. Co., Gas City, Ind., 1960—. Chmn. Midwest Indsl. Gas Council, 1969. Named Outstanding Liaison Officer, Air Force Acad., 1959; Ambassador for Peace, Republic of Korea, 1977; recipient Republic of Korea Service medal, 1977. Mem. Ind. Soc. Profl. Engrs. (Outstanding Engr. 1982), Nat. Soc. Profl. Engrs., Midwest Indsl. Gas Assn. (chmn. 1969). Republican. Methodist. Lodge: Kiwanis (Disting. sect. 1979-85, lt. gov. 1964; Disting. Service award 1962).

NEIBEL, OLIVER JOSEPH, JR., med. services exec.; b. Kansas City, Mo., Apr. 17, 1927; s. Oliver Joseph and Eula Lee (Durham) N.; J.D., U. Va., 1952; B.S., U. Ariz., 1949; m. Patricia Helen O'Keefe, June 24, 1950 (div. 1971); children—Oliver Joseph III, Deborah Sue; m. 2d, Diane Bachus Nelson, Apr. 11, 1981. Instr., U. Washington, 1952-53; admitted to Wash. bar, 1952, Ill. bar, 1961, Nebr. bar, 1973; practiced in Seattle, 1953-57; asst. atty. gen. State of Wash., 1957-61; legislative atty. AMA, Chgo., 1961-63; exec. dir., gen. counsel Coll. Am. Pathologists, Chgo., 1963-72; v.p., gen. mgr. Physicians Lab., Omaha, 1973—. Justice of peace, Mountlake Terrace, Wash., 1955-57. Served with USNR, 1945. Mem. Am. Wash., Nebr., Ill. bar assns., Med. Group Mgmt. Assn., Phi Kappa Psi (chpt. pres. 1948-49), Delta Theta Phi, Alpha Kappa Psi, Delta Sigma Rho. Mason, Elk, Rotarian. Clubs: Wash. Athletic (Seattle); Tavern (Chgo.); Omaha Press, University (Nebr.). Home: 7918 Potter Plaza Omaha NE 68122 Office: 105 N 37th St Omaha NE 68131

NEIDERT, DAVID LYNN, educational administrator; b. Akron, Ohio, Nov. 4, 1954; s. Wiliam K. and Violet P. (Barker) N.; m. Rhonda Elaine Rider, June 25, 1977; children—Sarah, David Benjamin. B.A., Anderson Coll., Ind., 1973-77. Dir. personnel Anderson Coll., Ind., 1978-82, dir. support services, 1982—, asst. to curator, 1981—. Chmn. bd. dirs. North Anderson Ch. of God, Anderson, 1984. Mem. Nat. Assn. Ednl. Buyers (sec.-treas. Ind. chpt.). Democrat. Club: IMC Mgmt. (1st v.p. 1983-84, pres. 1984—) (Anderson). Avocations: antique car models, music, painting, photography, history. Office: Anderson Coll 1100 E 5th St Anderson IN 46012

NEIHEISEL, THOMAS HENRY, toy manufacturing company executive; b. Cin., Dec. 1, 1953; s. Vincent John and Mary Jane (Haverkos) N.; m. Cynthia Lynn Dirk, Aug. 5, 1977; children—Matthew Thomas and Andrew John (twins). B.B.A., U. Cin., 1977, M.B.A., 1981. Group project leader The Procter & Gamble Co., Cin., 1974-77; mgr. project services Burgoyne, Inc., Cin., 1977-81; dir. market research Kenner Products, Cin., 1982—. Alpha Kappa Psi scholar, 1977; John Burgoyne research scholar, 1976; U. Cin. Honor scholar, award, 1972; recipient Eagle Scout award Boy Scouts Am., 1968. Mem. Am. Mktg. Assn., Assn. M.B.A. Execs., Market Research Assn., Alpha Kappa Psi. Roman Catholic. Home: 10061 Cliffwood Ct Cincinnati OH 45241 Office: 1014 Vine St Cincinnati OH 45202

NEIL, GERARD DANIEL, lawyer; b. Grand Forks, N.D., Nov. 1, 1954; s. Kenneth H. and Elizabeth (Vasek) N.; m. Cynthia N. Wavra, Aug. 19, 1978; children—Erick D., Scott D. B.S. in Bus. Adminstrn., U. N.D., 1977, J.D., 1981. Bar: N.D. 1981, Minn. 1981, U.S. Dist. Ct. N.D., 1981. Ptnr. German & Neil, Ltd., East Grand Forks, Minn., 1979—; dir. Area Vocat. Tech. Inst., East Grand Forks, 1984—. Pres. Sacred Heart Parish Council, East Grand Forks, 1984; bd. dirs. United Way; exec. com. Potato Bowl. Recipient various grants. Mem. N.D. Bar Assn. (sec./treas. bus./corp. div. 1983—), Minn. Bar Assn., Assn. Trial Lawyers Am., Minn. Trial Lawyers Assn., 14th Dist. Bar Assn., Greater Grand Forks Bar Assn., Jaycees (bd. dirs. 1982—, v.p. 1983-84), East Grand Forks C. of C. (bd. dirs. 1984, v.p. 1985). Lodges: Elks, Optimists (v.p. 1983, pres. 1984). Home: 1110 21st St NW East Grand Forks MN 56721 Office: German and Neil Ltd 208 3d Ave NW East Grand Forks MN 56721

NEIMAN, ROBERT LEROY, management consultant; b. Chgo., Feb. 9, 1930; s. Maurice and Shirley (Albin) N.; B.S. in Communications with honors, U. Ill., 1951, M.A. in Social and Behavioral Scis., 1952; m. Marlene Kaufman (dec. Mar. 1972); m. Barbara Milkes (dec. Mar. 1983); 1 dau., Debra Bea. Asst. to pres. Utility Plastic Packaging Co., Chgo., 1953-54; from dept. mgr. to v.p. Castle and Assos., Chgo., 1954-73; v.p. Mendheim Co., Chgo., 1973-77, sr. v.p., 1977—; guest radio speaker on cancer research fund raising, 1984. Chmn. Marlene K. Neiman Meml. Found. of Am. Cancer Soc., 1972-75, chmn. Barbara J. Neiman Meml. Found. for Lung Cancer, 1983; bd. dirs. Morton Grove, Ill. unit Am. Cancer Soc. Served as 1st lt. USAF, 1951-53. Recipient Presdl. citation; Joggers award Lehmann Sports Club. Mem. Am. Personnel and Guidance Assn., Am. Inst. Indsl. Engrs., Soc. Mfg. Engrs., Am. Mgmt. Assn., Nat. Assn. Corp. and Profl. Recruiters, Air Force Assn., North Shore Assn. for Retarded, Sigma Delta Chi, Sigma Delta Pi. Club: Skokie Valley Kiwanis (program chmn.). Author articles in field. Home: 9401 Natchez Ave Morton Grove IL 60053 Office: 6055 N Lincoln Ave Chicago IL 60659

NEIMARK, PHILIP JOHN, financial consultant; editor; b. Chgo., Sept. 13, 1939; s. Mortimer William and Hortense Adrienne (Peters) N.; student U. Chgo., 1956-58, Northwestern U., 1958-59; D. Bus. Mgmt. (hon.), Ricker Coll., Houlton, Maine, 1976; m. Barbara Lynn; children—Tanya Lee, Joshua Daniel. Mem. Chgo. Mercantile Exchange, 1968-74; owner Josephson Neimark Trading Co., Chgo., 1972-73; partner Rosenthal & Co., Chgo., 1973-77; owner, prin. Philip J. Neimark Investments, Miami, Fla., 1977-79, Chgo., 1979—; pres. Neimark Fin. Pub. Co., 1985—; editor, pub. Philip J. Neimark Viewpoint, N.Y.C., 1976—, Low Priced Stock Edit., 1984—; fin. editor Money Maker mag., 1979-85; mem. Internat. Monetary Market, 1971-74, N.Y. Mercantile Exchange, 1973-74, Chgo. Bd. of Options Exchange, 1973-75; editor, pub. Low Priced Stock Edition, 1984—, Pro Trade, 1985—. Bd. dirs. Lutheran Gen. Med. Found. Mem. Fla. Exec. Planning Assn., South Fla. Fin. Planners Assn., Investment Co. Inst., Nat. Paso Fino Assn. (founder). Author: How to Be Lucky, 1975; contbg. editor Consumers Digest mag., 1977-85. Office: 1648 Mdse Mart Chicago IL 60654

NEINER, A. JOSEPH, controller; b. Ft. Scott, Kans., Feb. 15,1950; s. Andrew W. and Celeste H. (Beck) N.; m. Linda M. Koenig, Aug. 16, 1969; children—Carrie L., Christine M., Joseph M., Elizabeth A. B.S.B.A., U. Mo.-St. Louis, 1972; M.B.A., St. Louis U., 1976. Fin. analyst Chrysler Corp., St. Louis, 1972-75; fin. mgr. Gen. Cable Corp., St. Louis, 1975-79; controller Consol. Aluminum, St. Louis, 1979-80, group controller, 1980-83, ops. controller, 1983-85, corp. controller, 1985—; condr. fin. workshop Alusuisse Ltd., Zurich, Switzerland, 1985. instr. St. Louis Jr. Coll., 1978-80, U. Mo.-St. Louis, 1978. Mem. Am. Mgmt. Assns. Roman Catholic. Home: 15104 Appalachian Trail Chesterfield MO 63017 Office: Consol Aluminum 11960 Westline Industrial Dr Saint Louis MO 63146

NEINFELDT, GERALD OTTO, educational administrator; b. Janesville, Wis., Dec. 1, 1937; s. Otto E. and Freda C. (Gackstaetter) N.; B.E., U. Wis., Whitewater, 1959; M.S. in Bus. Edn., U. Wis., Madison, 1967; m. Judith A. Kehl, Nov. 8, 1958; children—Laurie, Timothy, Jennifer. Instr. bus. edn. Pittsville (Wis.) Pub. Schs., 1959-60, Wisconsin Rapids (Wis.) Vocat. Sch., 1959-60; instr. bus. edn. Elkhorn (Wis.) Sch. Dist., 1960-67, bus. mgr., 1967—; adult evening supr. Gateway Tech. Inst., Elkhorn, Wis., 1979-81. Registered sch. bus. adminstr.; cert. tchr., sch. bus. ofcl., Wis. Mem. Am. Assn. Sch. Adminstrs., Assn. Sch. Bus. Ofcls., Am. Mgmt. Assn., Wis. Assn. Sch. Bus. Ofcls. (dir. 1983-85), Delta Kappa, Phi Pi Epsilon. Lutheran. Home: 519 N Edgewood Ave Elkhorn WI 53121 Office: Adminstrv Service Center 1887 Bldg Elkhorn WI 53121

NELIDOW, IRINA, editor, writer; b. N.Y.C.; d. Alexander and Dorothy Gordon (King) N. A.B. magna cum laude, Bryn Mawr Coll., 1950, M.A., 1952. Research assoc. in chemistry MIT, Harvard U., 1951-54; market editor Aviation Week, N.Y.C., 1954-56; sci. editor McGraw-Hill Book Co., St. Louis, 1965-69; asst. dir. sci. program CEMREL, St. Louis, 1969-70; sr. editor World Book Ency., Chgo., 1971-72; cons. editor U. Chgo. Press, 1973-74; pres. Nelidow Communications, Chgo., 1975—; instr. photography Field Mus. Natural History, Chgo., 1982-83. Bd. dirs. Dance Concert Soc., St. Louis, 1967-71. Mem. Ind. Writers Chgo., Am. Med. Writers Assn., Chgo. Women in Pub., Common Cause, Sierra Club, Nature Conservancy, Sigma Xi. Contbr. book revs. to St. Louis Post-Dispatch.

NELIS, ROBERT LUKEN, village official; b. Jackson, Mich., June 16, 1947; s. William Michael and Rosemary Julia (Luken) N.; m. Sheila Rose Castillo, Mar. 8, 1975; children—Lisa Maria Sunshine Castillo, Robert Luken II, Kateri Joy Castillo. B.A., St. Marys Coll., 1969; M.S. in Urban Planning and Policy, U. Ill., 1975. Community devel. dir. Village of Woodridge, Ill., 1976-78; pres. Wicker Park Devel. Corp., Chgo., 1979-80; adminstrv. asst. Village of Oak Park, Ill., 1980-82, asst. to mgr., 1982-83, personnel dir., 1983—; adj. lectr. Elgin Community Coll., Ill., 1979—; cons. on zoning, 1979—. Served with U.S. Army, 1970-72. Mem. Am. Soc. Personnel Adminstrs., Internat. City Mgrs. Assn., Ill. Pub. Employer Labor Relations Assn. Roman Catholic. Office: Village of Oak Park One Village Hall Plaza Oak Park IL 60302

NELL, MARGARET KATHLEEN, home economics educator; b. McDonough County, Ill., Jan. 2, 1939; d. Henry Daniel and Bessie Mae (Weber) Block; m. Kenneth W. Nell, June 2, 1962; children—Kenneth Dale, Kathryn D. B.S.T. with honors in Home Econs. Edn., Western Ill. U., Macomb, 1979. Tchr. Astoria (Ill.) High Sch., 1979—; instr. part-time Spoon River Coll., Canton, Ill., 1980—. Mem. Am. Home Econs. Assn., Am. Vocat. Assn., Ill. Vocat. Home Econs. Tchrs. Assn., Ill. Consumer Edn. Assn., Phi Kappa Phi, Kappa Delta Pi. Home: Rural Route 1 Littleton IL 61452 Office: Astoria High Sch Astoria IL 61501

NELLEMANN, ROBERT JOHN, manufacturing executive; b. East Chicago, Ind., July 26, 1943; s. Oscar and Berniece (Urbelis) N.; m. Jo Ann Miner, Oct. 2, 1971; children—Christian, Jonathan. B.S. in Econs., Purdue U., 1966; M.Mgmt., Northwestern U., 1979. Product mgr. Motorola, Inc., Schaumburg, Ill., 1974-75; dir. mktg. Energy Absorption Systems, Inc., Chgo., 1975-82; v.p. mktg. Diebel Mfg. Co., Morton Grove, Ill., 1982—. Served to lt. USN, 1966-69, PTO. Mem. Midwest Planning Assn., Am. Metal Stamping Assn. (chmn. com. 1983—), Am. Mktg. Assn. Club: Midwest Sailing (cruise dir.) (Chgo.). Avocations: sailing, hunting, fishing, sports. Home: 1003 W Thomas St Arlington Heights IL 60004 Office: 6505 Oakton St Morton Grove IL 60053

NELSEN, LAUREL GAYE, pharmacist; b. Duluth, Minn., Oct. 1, 1958; d. Robert I. and Terry K. (Donnelly) N. B.S. in Pharmacy, U. Minn., 1981. Registered pharmacist, Minn. Pharmacy intern Minn. Dept. Pub. Welfare, St. Paul, 1979-81, Boyce Kenwood Pharmacy, Duluth, 1981; relief pharmacist Chicago Lakes Hosp., Chicago City, Minn., 1982-83; pharmacist Highland Drug Ctr., St. Paul, 1982-83, Duluth Clinic Ltd., 1983—; mem. Minn. Drug Utilization Rev., Duluth, 1984—. Speaker, panel mem. St. Mary's Hosp., Duluth, 1984. Mem. Minn. State Pharm. Assn., Duluth Area Pharmacists (pub. edn. com. 1984—), Am. Pharm. Assn., Rho Chi Mu, Phi Kappa Phi, Iota Sigma Pi. Methodist. Avocations: jazzercise; downhill skiing; calligraphy; cartooning. Office: Duluth Clinic Ltd Pharmacy 400 E 3rd St Duluth MN 55805

NELSON, ALBERT LEROY, teacher educator; b. Scandia, Kans., Feb. 19, 1921; s. Otto Clarence and Olive Hulda (Lundquist) N.; m. Elizabeth June Street, Aug. 20, 1947; children—James Randall, Julie Elaine. B.A., Kans. Wesleyan U., 1950, L.H.D., 1983; M.S. in Edn., U. Kans., 1955, Ed.D., 1965. High sch. tchr. Dist. R-4, Cawker City, Kans., 1950-53; dir. audio visual services U. Kans., Lawrence, 1953-56; dir. summer sch. Kans. Wesleyan U., Salina, 1981—, dir. tchr. edn., 1956—; manuscript editor Prentice-Hall, Inc., Englewood Cliffs, N.J., 1980—; pvt. coll. rep. Teaching Profl. Standards Bd., Kans., 1972-78. Contbr. articles to profl. jours. Pres. Salina South High Sch. PTA, 1976-77. Served to lt. (j.g.) USNR, 1942-46, PTO. Recipient Disting. Achievement award Kans. Wesleyan Alumni, 1981; Disting. Service award Kans. Wesleyan Alumni, 1979; fellow Tri-Univ. Project, 1968-69; Danforth Found., 1964. Mem. Nat. Council Social Studies, Assn. Tchr. Educators, NEA, Ret. Officers Assn., Phi Delta Kappa. Republican. Methodist. Avocations: Photography; woodworking; fishing; writing. Home: 1819 Gebhart St Salina KS 67401 Office: Kans Wesleyan Coll 100 E Claflin St Salina KS 67401

NELSON, AMERICA ELIZABETH, pediatrician; b. Chgo., Apr. 9, 1932; d. Lorenzo Raymond and Blanche Juanita (Crawford) Nelson; A.B. in English, U. Mich., Ann Arbor, 1952, M.S. in Zoology, 1954; postgrad. Tenn. State U., 1952-53, U. Chgo., 1955-56; M.D., Howard U., 1961; M.P.H., U. Ill., 1973. Intern, Hahnemann Med. Sch. and Hosps., Phila., 1961-62; resident pediatrics Michael Reese Hosp., Chgo., 1962-63, U. Mich., Ann Arbor, 1964; practice medicine specializing in pediatric cardiology, Detroit, 1963; with father, practice medicine specializing in pediatrics, Baldwin, Mich., 1964-71, 75—; pediatrician Tice Clinic, U. Ill., Cook County Hosp., 1965, 66; pediatrician Mile's Sq. Health Center, Chgo., 1967; pediatrician Infant Welfare Soc., Chgo., 1968; cons. pediatrician, child devel. Kalamazoo Child Guidance Clinic, 1969-70, coordinator drug abuse program, 1969-70; med. dir. Chgo. Residential Manpower Center, 1971-72; pediatrician, child devel. Dyslexia Meml. Inst., Chgo., 1972—; founder, project dir., med. dir. Deerwood Developmental Center, Inc., Cherry Valley Twp., Lake County, Mich.; lectr. U. Ill. at Chgo. Circle, 1972-73; clin. instr. U. Ill.-Presbyn.-St. Luke's Hosp.; asst. prof. Mental Retardation Inst., N.Y. Med. Coll., 1974; cons. in field. Mem. AAAS, Pi Lambda Theta. Contbr. articles to profl. jours. Home: PO Box 760 Baldwin MI 49304

NELSON, CHARLES ALEXANDER, III, psychology educator; b. Flushing, N.Y., Mar. 7, 1953; s. Charles Alexander and Pearl (Potash) N.; m. Gwen Ann Werner, June 13, 1981. B.A. with honors in Psychology, McGill U., 1975; M.S. in Ednl. Psychology, U. Wis., 1976, M.S. in Psychology, 1977; Ph.D. in Child Psychology, U. Kans., 1981. Project asst. U. Wis.-Madison, 1975-76, research asst., 1976-78; NIH pre-doctoral trainee U. Kans., Lawrence, 1978-81; NIH postdoctoral fellow U. Minn., Mpls., 1981-83, research assoc., 1983; asst. prof. Purdue U., West Lafayette, Ind., 1983—. Cons., lectr. in field. Recipient 2d prize Chester McNaghten Creative Writing Contest, McGill U., 1973. Mem. Am. Psychol. Assn., Soc. Research in Child Devel., Psychonomic Soc., AAAS, Sigma Xi. Contbr. numerous articles to profl. jours., chpts. to books. Office: Dept Psychol Sci Purdue U West Lafayette IN 47907

NELSON, DAVID ALDRICH, lawyer; b. Watertown, N.Y., Aug. 14, 1932; s. Carlton Low and Irene Demetria (Aldrich) N.; m. Mary E. Dickson, Aug. 25, 1956; children—Fred, Claudia, Caleb. A.B., Hamilton Coll., Clinton, N.Y., 1954; postgrad. Cambridge U., Eng., 1954-55; LL.B., Harvard U., 1958. Bar: Ohio 1958. Assoc. Squire Sanders & Dempsey, Cleve., 1958-67, ptnr., 1967-69, 72—; gen. counsel U.S. Post Office Dept., Washington, 1969-71; sr. asst. postmaster gen., gen. counsel U.S. Postal Service, Washington, 1971; dir. Blount, Inc., Montgomery, Ala. Trustee Hamilton Coll., 1984—. Served to 1st lt. USAF, 1959-62. Fulbright scholar Cambridge U., 1954-55. Fellow Am. Coll. Trial Lawyers; mem. ABA, Fed. Bar Assn., Ohio Bar Assn., Cleve. Bar Assn. Republican. Congregationalist. Clubs: Ct. of Nisi Prius, Union (Cleve.). Home: 2699 Wadsworth Rd Shaker Heights OH 44122 Office: Squire Sanders & Dempsey 1800 Huntington Bldg Cleveland OH 44115

NELSON, DAVID EARL, educational administrator, educator; b. Oak Park, Ill., June 4, 1942; s. Warren Earl and Evelyn Inez Nelson. B.A., No. Ill. U., 1964, M.S., 1967; M.A., DePaul U., 1970; Ph.D., Northwestern U., 1974. Assoc. prof. Lamar U., Beaumont, Tex., 1975-79; asst. supt. pub. schs., Houston, 1979-82; chair Sch. Edn., Washburn U., Topeka, Kans., 1982-85; disting. chair Sch. Edn. Pittsburg State U., Kans., 1985—. Kellogg Found. fellow, 1972. Mem. Internat. Reading Assn., Assn. Supervision and Curriculum Devel., Internat. Soc. Ednl. Planners, Nat. Orgn. Legal Problems in Edn., Am. Assn. Colls. Tchr. Edn., Phi Delta Kappa. Lodge: Kiwanis. Author: Teaching Elementary Language Arts, 1982; Activities to Enrich the Language Arts, 1982; The Secondary School Principal, 1983; The Principal as Instructional Leader, 1984; contbr. articles to profl. jours. Office: 1700 College St Topeka KS 66621

NELSON, DAVID LEONARD, process management company executive; b. Omaha, May 8, 1930; s. Leonard A. and Cecelia (Steinert) N.; B.S., Iowa State U., 1952; m. Jacqueline J. Zerbe, Dec. 26, 1952; 1 child, Nancy Jo. Marketing adminstr. Ingersoll Rand, Chgo., 1954-56; systems engr. Indsl. Accuray Corp., Columbus, Ohio, 1956-58, sales engr., 1958-61, area sales mgr., 1961-64, mgr. corp. planning and devel., 1964-65, mgr. new product devel. dept., 1965-66, v.p. ops., 1966, exec. v.p., gen. mgr., 1967, pres., 1967—, chief exec. officer, 1970—, also dir.; dir. Herman Miller, Inc., Cardinal Govt. Securities Trust. Bd. dirs. The Cardinal Fund, Inc., Cardinal Tax Exempt Money Trust. Served to capt. USMCR, 1952-54. Mem. IEEE, Instrument Soc. Am., Newcomen Soc. N.Am., Tau Beta Pi, Phi Kappa Phi, Phi Eta Sigma, Delta Upsilon. Patentee in field. Office: 1768 Millwood Dr Columbus OH 43221

NELSON, DONALD A., professional basketball coach; b. Muskegon, Mich., May 15, 1940; student U. Iowa. Player profl. basketball team, Chgo., 1962-63, Los Angeles Lakers, 1963-65; with Boston Celtics, 1965-76; head coach Milw. Bucks, 1976—. Address: Milw Bucks 901 N 4th St Milwaukee WI 53203*

NELSON, DONALD EDWARD, marketing executive; b. Rochester, Minn., Jan. 28, 1946; s. Donald Ivan and Lucille Nelson; m. Bonnie Nelson (div. 1974); 1 child, Kimberly; m. Pamela Marie Casperson, Oct. 27, 1976; children—Donald Edward, Nathan Joseph. Grad. high sch. Vice-pres. Sunstar Enterprises, Dubuque, Iowa, 1977-81; owner, pres. Nelson Mktg., Dubuque, 1981—; supr. Herbalife Internat., Los Angeles, 1984—. Inventor. Served with U.S. Army, 1964-66, Vietnam. Mem. Christian. Ch. Avocations: reading, weightlifting, gadgets. Office: Nelson Mktg 2606 University Ave Dubuque IA 52001

NELSON, EDWARD THEODORE, dentist; b. Kennedy, Minn., Oct. 30, 1928; s. Albin Morris and Lillie Eleanor (Johnson) N.; m. Helen Mae Johnson; children—Peter, Thomas, Kari, Lisa. B.S., U. Minn., 1957, D.D.S., 1959. Gen. practice dentistry, Thief River Falls, Minn., 1959—; dental examiner Central Regional Dental Testing Service, Topeka, Kans., 1979—; mem. Minn. Bd. Dentistry, 1979-82, pres., 1982. Pres. Thief River Falls Concert Assn., 1969; bd. dirs. Minn. Dental Polit. Action Com., 1973-75, Health Planning Council, Grand Forks, N.D., 1974-76, Minn. Easter Seal Soc., 1974-76, Northwest Regional Library Bd., 1977-79; chmn. Thief River Falls United Way, 1977; dir. First Fed. Savs. and Loan Assn., 1981—. Served to S/sgt. U.S. Army, 1950-53. Recipient Disting. Service award Minn. Bd. Dentistry, 1983. Fellow Am. Coll. Dentistry; mem. Pierre Fauchard Acad., ADA, Minn. Dental Assn., Northwest Dist. Dental Soc. (pres. 1969), U. Minn. Dental Alumni Soc. (dir. 1975-79), Thief River Falls C. of C. (dir. 1975-78), Am. Legion, Omicron Kappa Upsilon. Lodges: Elks, Rotary (pres. 1972-73). Avocations: sailing, photography, reading. Home: 1010 Oakland Park Thief River Falls MN 56701 Office: 321 N LaBree Thief River Falls MN 56701

NELSON, EDWIN C., college president; b. Dallas, S.D., Apr. 19, 1922; s. Clifford and Vera (Usher) N.; m. Avis Hedrix, Nov. 15, 1941; children—Judy Nelson Yost, Roger. B.A., Kearney State Coll., 1950; M.A., West Tex. State Coll., 1953; Ed.D., U. Nebr., 1959; postgrad. U. Minn., 1959. Math and sci. instr., Neponee Schs., Nebr., 1947-48; math, sci. and athletics instr. Riverdale Schs., Nebr., 1948-50; supt. schs., Huntley, Nebr., 1950-52; aircraft mechanics instr. Amarillo AFB, Tex., 1952-53; supt. schs., Wilcox, Nebr., 1953-56, Red Cloud, Nebr., 1956-59; assoc. prof. edn. Kearney State Coll., Nebr., 1959-61; dean Chadron State Coll., Nebr., 1961-67, pres., 1967-73, 75—, exec. officer bd. trustees, 1973-75. Contbr. articles to profl. jours. Bd. govs. Coop. Study in Colls. and Univs., 1977—; trustee Mid-continent Regional Ednl. Lab., 1960-73. Recipient Disting. Service award Kearney State Coll., 1968; named Boss of Yr., Chadron Jaycees, 1971. Mem. Nat. Council Accreditation of Tchrs. Edn. (visitation team 1970-76), North Central Assn. (subcom. on insts. for tchr. edn.), Am. Assn. Sch. Adminstrs., Am. Assn. State Colls. and Univs. (Nebr. rep. 1970—), Nebr. Council Econ. Edn. (trustee 1969-73), Edn. TV Commn., Nebraskans for Pub. TV (bd. dirs. 1970-76), Nebr. State Edn. Assn. (pres. 1967), Nebr. Ednl. TV Council for Higher Edn. (pres. 1967), Nebr. Council on Tchr. Edn. (exec. com. 1965-67, state accreditation com. 1958-72). Lodges: Kiwanis, Elks. Home: 809 East 5th St Chadron NE 69337 Office: Chadron State Coll 10th and Main Sts Chadron NE 69337

NELSON, FRANCES ANN, children's theater executive; b. Mpls., Nov. 5, 1948; d. Russell Julius and Frances Elizabeth (Sedgwick) N. B.A., Macalester Coll., 1970. Assoc. ptnr. Arts Devel. Assocs., Mpls., N.Y.C., 1974-76; mgr. Friends Gallery, Mpls. Inst. Arts, 1974-76; assoc. dir. devel. Children's Theatre, Mpls., 1976-79, dir. devel., dir. Children's Theatre Co. and Sch., 1979—. Contbr. bimonthly column Am. Kennel Club Gazette, 1980—. Bd. dirs. Minn. Citizens for Arts, 1980-81, Hennepin County Humane Soc., Mpls. Mem. English Springer Spaniel Field Trial Assn. Republican. Baptist. Clubs: Bloomington Obedience Tng. (pres. 1972-76); Mpls. Twin Cities Voyageur English Springer Spaniel Assn. (pres. 1980, 82). Avocation: breeding and exhibiting purebred English springer spaniels. Office: Children's Theatre Co and Sch 2400 3d Ave S Minneapolis MN 55404

NELSON, GARY LEE, cutlery manufacturing company executive; b. Cedar Falls, Iowa, May 20, 1959; s. Arthur N. and Yvonne M. (Chapman) N.; m. Cindy M. Rear, Aug. 9, 1980; 1 child, Daniel L. B.A. in Fin. and Mgmt., U. No. Iowa, 1981. Mgr. adminstrv. services Rada Mfg. Co., Waverly, Iowa, 1981-82, gen. mgr., 1982-83, v.p., 1984—. Mem. Iowa Mfrs. Assn., Iowa Small Bus. Employers. Avocations: golf, basketball, bowling, hunting, woodworking. Home: 301 9th St NE Waverly IA 50677 Office: Rada Mfg Co Rural Route 2 Box 838 Waverly IA 50677

NELSON, GLENN LAWRENCE, applied economics educator, consultant; b. Elbow Lake, Minn., Feb. 29, 1944; s. Elmer Lawrence and Viola Roxy (Ellison) N.; m. Margaret Elizabeth Dewar, June 18, 1983. B.S., U. Minn., 1965; M.A., Stanford U., 1966; Ph.D., Mich. State U., 1973. Economist Office of Econ. Opportunity, Washington, 1971-73; chief food analysis Cost of Living Council, Washington, 1973-74; asst. prof. Purdue U., West Lafayette, Inc., 1974-77; sr. staff economist Council of Econ. Advisers, Washington, 1982-83; prof. applied econs. U. Minn., St. Paul, 1977—; cons. NRC, Washington, 1979-81, Mich. Dept. Edn., Lansing, 1970-71; dir. econ. analysis Minn. Dept. Fin., St. Paul, 1985-86. Contbr. articles to profl. jours. Contbr. chpts. to Lessons of Wage and Price Controls, 1977. Co-editor: Rural American in Passage, 1981. Mem. Citizen's League, Mpls., 1977—. Resources for Future fellow, Washington, 1984-85. Mem. Am. Agrl. Econ. Assn., Am. Econs. Assn., Am. Statis. Assn., Econometrics Soc., Pub. Choice Soc. Mem. United Ch. Christ. Avocation: sailing. Home: 1538 Grantham St Saint Paul MN 55108 Office: Dept Agr and Applied Econs U Minn Saint Paul MN 55108

NELSON, J. DANIEL, ophthalmologist, dakryologist; b. Duluth, Minn., July 4, 1950; s. John A. and Virginia B. (Erickson) N.; m. Carol M. Kaldor, Aug. 11, 1973; children—Mark D., Peter D., Jessica J. B.S. magna cum laude, U. Minn.-Duluth, 1972; M.D., U. Minn.-Mpls., 1975. Diplomate Am. Bd. Ophthalmology. Intern, St. Paul Ramsey Med. Ctr., 1976-77; resident U. Minn., Mpls., 1978-81; staff physician St. Paul-Ramsey Med. Ctr., St. Paul, 1982—, interim dept. chmn., 1983-84, dept. chmn. ophthalmology, 1984—, dir. dry eye and tear research ctr., 1984—; asst prof. ophthalmology U. Minn., 1982—. Contbr. articles to profl. publs. Fellow Am. Acad. Ophthalmology; mem. AMA, Assn. Research in Vision and Ophthalmology, AAAS, St. Paul Ophthal. Soc. (sec.-treas.). Baptist. Avocations: Sports; guitar; banjo. Office: St Paul-Ramsey Med Ctr Dept Ophthalmology 640 Jackson St St Paul MN 55101

NELSON, JAMES, clergyman. Chairperson, judge Baha'i Faith Nat. Spiritual Assembly, Wilmette, Ill. Office: 536 Sheridan Rd Wilmette IL 60091*

NELSON, JAMES B., mechanical engineer; b. Lebanon, Inc., Mar. 8, 1935; s. Charles S. and Myra (Bartlett) N.; m. Janet L. Powell, Mar. 12, 1960; children—David, Julie, Mark, Michael. B.S. in Mech. Engring., Purdue U., 1958. Registered profl. engr., Ind. Engr. Lebanon Utilties, 1958-73, mgr., 1973—. Served with U.S. Army, 1958-59. Mem. Am. Water Works Assn., Ind. Mcpl. Elec. Assn. (Man of Yr. 1984, sec.-treas. 1973—), Ind. Mcpl. Power Agy. (treas. 1981, bd. dirs.). Mem. Christian Ch. (Disciples of Christ). Lodges: Kiwanis, Masons. Office: Lebanon Utilities 201 E Main St Lebanon IN 46052

NELSON, JANIE MAE, psychologist; b. Clarks, La., Nov. 23, 1935; d. Ermon and Helen (Stewart) N.; B.Ed., Chgo. Tchrs. Coll., 1956; M.A., Roosevelt U., 1968, 77; Ph.D., Kent State U., 1981. Tchr., elem. sch., psychologist Chgo. Public Schs., 1956—. Pres., v.p. Holy Angel's Blessed Sacrament Soc., 1975-77; bd. dirs. Nat. Alliance Black Feminists, 1979-81. Mem. Operation PUSH, Am. Psychol. Assn., Assn. Black Psychologists, Woman's Orgn. for Minority Affairs and Needs (co-founder, dir.), NOW, Phi Delta Kappa. Home: 7659 S Normal Blvd Chicago IL 60620

NELSON, JEANNE ALLENBACH, school administrator; b. Peoria, Ill., May 9, 1931. A.A., Mt. Vernon Jr. Coll., 1951; B.F.A., Bradley U., 1953, M.A., 1968. Dir., Title I ESEA, Peoria (Ill.), Pub. Schs., 1972-81, dir. chpt. 1, ECIA and summer program, 1981—. Mem. Assn. Supervision and Curriculum Devel., Internat. Reading Assn., Jr. League Peoria, Phi Delta Kappa. Office: 3202 N Wisconsin Peoria IL 61603

NELSON, JENNY STEWART, dietitian; b. Caney, Kans., July 6, 1949; d. James Harold and Frances Viola (Rekestraw) Stewart; m. Gary Leroy Nelson, Apr. 26, 1975 (div.). B.A., U. No. Colo., 1971; M.S., Oreg. State U., 1983. Dietetic intern U. Oreg. Med. Sch., Portland, 1971-72; adminstrv. dietitian Meth. Hosp., Indpls., 1972-73; food service supr. Portland State U., 1973; clin. dietitian St. Vincent Hosp., Portland, 1973; food service mgr. U. Oreg. Health Sci. Ctr., Portland, 1973-75; asst. dir. food service Dammasch State Hosp., Wilsonville, Oreg., 1975-83; asst. dir. food and nutrition service U. Chgo. Med. Ctr., 1983-84; asst. dir. food service St. Catherine Hosp., East Chicago, Ind., 1984; chief dietitian U.S. Med. Ctr. for Fed. Prisoners, 1984—; instr. diet tech. program Portland Community Coll., 1978-80, Head Start Program, Greeley, Colo., 1971. Author: Field Feeding for the U.S. Army Reserve, 1981. Active Republican Women's Orgn., 1980. Recipient scholarship for dietetic interns Colo. Dietetic Assn., 1971; Oreg. State U. grantee, 1982; Army commendation medal, 1980, 82; Oreg. Young Dietitian of Yr. award, 1980. Mem. Am. Dietetic Assn., Ill. Dietetic Assn., Am. Soc. Hosp. Food Service Adminstrs., Soc. Advancement Food Service Research, Am. Correctional Food Service Assn., Nat. Assn. Female Execs. Republican. Episcopalian. Home: 2015 S Ciccone Dr Springfield MO 65807 Office: US Med Ctr Fed Prisoners 1900 W Sunshine St Springfield MO 65802

NELSON, JOEL SIDNEY, pharmacist, educator, coach; b. Tioga, N.D., Nov. 3, 1918; s. John Samuel and Henrietta (Everson) N.; m. Bertha Catherine Danielson, Mar. 9, 1943; children—Joelanne Nelson Asp, Jon Samuel. B.S. in Edn., N.D. State U., 1941, B.S. in Pharmacy, 1949, M.S. in Hosp. Pharmacy, 1966. Registered pharmacist, N.D., Minn. Tchr., coach Tower City High Sch., N.D., 1941-42; pharmacist Nelson Drug Co., Grafton, N.D., 1949-54, owner, pharmacist, 1954-62; pharmacist Moorhead Drug Co., Minn., 1964-66, ptnr., pharmacist 1966-82, pharmacist, 1982-84. Served to lt. (s.g.) USN, 1943-45, PTO. Mem. N.D. Pharm. Assn. (pres. 1963-64), Northeast Counties Drug Assn. (pres. 1960-61). Republican. Lutheran. Lodge: Lions (pres. 1983-84). Avocation: flying. Home: 1802 27th Ave So Moorhead MN 56560

NELSON, JOHN CARL, statistician, consultant; b. Sterling, Ill., Feb. 11, 1958; s. Carl Harold and Esther Mae (Stern) N. B.S. in Math., Kans State U., 1980, M.S. in Stats., 1981; M. Engring. Mgmt., Northwestern U., 1985. Statistician, Travenol Labs., Inc., Morton Grove, Ill., 1981-83; cons. ZS Assocs., Evanston, Ill., 1984-85; founder, prin. Applied Research Co., Chgo., 1985—. Mem. Am. Statis. Assn., Inst. Mgmt. Sci., Pi Mu Epsilon. Club: U.S. Tennis Assn. Office: Applied Research Co 53 W Jackson Suite 720 Chicago IL 60604

NELSON, JOHN HOWARD, food products company executive; b. Bozeman, Mont., Feb. 5, 1926; s. John Albert and Lillian Mae Nelson; m. Marilyn Joan Carlson, June 28, 1952; children—John Victor, Janet Marilyn, Marjorie Ann. B.S., Mont. State U., 1950; M.S., U. Wis., 1951, Ph.D., 1954. Successively dir. research, v.p. research and devel., v.p. corp. devel. Dairyland Food Labs., 1954-77; mgr. regulatory compliance Kraft, Inc., Glenview, Ill., 1977-78, dir. quality assurance and regulatory compliance, 1979-81, v.p. quality assurance and regulatory compliance, 1981—; food adv. council Wis. Dept. Agr.; research com. Nat. Cheese Inst.; mem. U.S. nat. com. Internat. Dairy Fedn. Served with USNR, 1944-46. Mem. Am. Dairy Sci. Assn. (past dir.), Am. Chem. Soc., Inst. Food Technologists, Assn. Food and Drug Ofcls., AAAS, Sigma Xi, Alpha Zeta. Contbr. articles profl. jours.; patentee in field. Office: Kraft Ct Glenview IL 60025

NELSON, JOHN WILLIAM, JR., dentist; b. Marlborough, Mass., June 13, 1949; s. John William and Barbara Ann (Russell) N. B.A., Ottawa U., 1971; M.P.A., U. Mo., 1978, D.D.S., 1982. With Kansas City Police Dept., Mo., 1971-77, Supr., 1975-77; practice dentistry, Independence, Mo., 1982—; dir. Kansas City's Policemen's Credit Union, 1974-77. Vice pres. bd. dirs. Vaile Soc.-Mus., Independence, Mo., 1983-84. Recipient Meritorious Service award Kansas City Police, 1974, 1977; Bronze award, Met. Police Chiefs, 1974; Profl. Growth award Internat. Coll. Dentists, Chgo., 1982. Mem. Am. Soc. Dentistry for Children (award 1982), ADA, Acad. Gen. Dentistry, Greater Kansas City Dental Soc., Mo. Dental Assn., Am. Acad. Profl. Law Enforcement. Republican. Roman Catholic. Lodges: Masons (32d degree), Shriners. Avocations: stamp collecting, short wave radio. Home: 1242 Huntington Rd Kansas City MO 64113 Office: 300 S Liberty St Independence MO 64050

NELSON, JOHN WILTON, symphony conductor; b. San Jose, Costa Rica, Dec. 6, 1941; came to U.S., 1953; s. Wilton Mons and Thelma (Agnew) N.; B.Mus., Wheaton Coll., 1963; M.Mus. (teaching fellow), Julliard Sch., 1965, postgrad. diploma (teaching fellow), 1967; m. Anita Christine Johnson, Sept. 4, 1964; children—Kirsten, Kari. Music dir. Pro Arte Chorale, Ridgewood, N.J., 1965-74; condr. N.Y. Mozart Festival, 1967, Julliard Opera Theatre, N.Y.C., 1968; music dir. Greenwich Philharm. Orch., N.Y.C., 1966-74; condr. N.Y.C. Opera, 1973-75, Santa Fe Opera, 1973, Geneva (Switzerland) Grand Theatre, 1974, Met. Opera, N.Y.C., from 1974; condr., music dir. Indpls. Symphony Orch., 1977—; music adv. Nashville (Tenn.) Symphony Orch., Cin. Orch., London Royal Philharm., Swiss Romade and others; conducting faculty Julliard Sch., N.Y.C., 1968-72; dir. Aspen Choral Inst., 1968-73. Recipient Irving Berlin Conducting award, 1967. Office: care Indianapolis Symphony Orchestra PO Box 88207 Indianapolis IN 46208*

NELSON, JOSEPH DAVID, artistic director, writer; b. Cody, Wyo., Aug. 24, 1953; s. John Hollywood and Rose Mary (Rensch) N.; m. Jeanne Marie Zeck, July 26, 1982; 1 child, Kate Lisbeth. Co-author, performer Dakota Theatre Caravan, Midwest, 1981, artistic dir., Sioux Falls, S.D., 1983—; actor San Rio Films (Japan), Vermillion, S.D., 1982; performer Friends Mime Theatre, Milw., 1982-83; stage mgr. Milw. Chamber, 1982-83; organizer ACT, Aberdeen, S.D., fall 1980; cons. Dakota Musical Col., Wall, S.D., 1982, co. mgr., 1984. Playwright: (with others) Welcome Home, 1981, Prairie Tales, 1984. Author (songs) Last Cowboy, others. Mem. Sioux Falls Cultural Affairs Com., 1983-84; vol. Tom Daschel for Congress, Sioux Falls, 1984. Mem. Actors Equity Assn. Democrat. Avocations: playing guitar; horseback riding. Home: Box 1014 Spearfish SD 57783 Office: Dakota Theatre Caravan Box 1014 Spearfish SD 57783

NELSON, LARRY JAMES, insurance company executive; b. St. Cloud, Minn., Feb. 3, 1949; s. Harold Franklin and Luella A. (Dircks) N.; m. Barbara Gaye Mead, Aug. 21, 1971; children—Jacob Miles, Paul Harold. B.S. in Vocal Music Edn., St. Cloud State U., Minn., 1971. Music tchr. Pierz Pub. Sch. (Minn.), 1971-73; field rep. Horace Mann. Cos., Brainerd, Minn., 1973-76, agy. mgr., Roseville, Minn., 1977-83, asst. v.p., Springfield, Ill., 1984—, tng. officer, 1984—; mem. multi-state ins. liscensing program test devel. com. Ednl. Testing Service, Princeton, N.J., 1983—. Mem. Nat. Assn. Life Underwriters, Minn. Assn. Life Underwriters (edn. chmn. 1979-81), Am. Soc. C.L.U., Gen. Agts. and Mgrs. Assn. (sec./treas. 1984—), Paul Bunyan Life Underwriters Assn. (sec./treas. 1974-76). Roman Catholic. Club: St. Charles Ushers (Mpls.) (sec./treas. 1983). Office: Horace Mann Cos #1 Horace Mann Plaza Springfield IL 62715

NELSON, MICHAEL UNDERHILL, procedures analyst, association executive; b. Balt., May 5, 1932; s. Cyril Arthur and Elise Hastings (Macy) N.; m. Barbara Gail Hutchins, June 25, 1960; children—Kevin Underhill, Bronwyn Hastings, Gayle Hutchins, Corey Williams. A.B., Rutgers U., 1957, Ed.M., 1968. Salesman, J&N Distbg. Co., New Brunswick, N.J., 1957-59; extension assoc. Rutgers U., New Brunswick, 1959-61, asst. dir. summer session, 1961-68; asst. dean Sch. Continuing Edn., Washington U., St. Louis, 1969-75, dir. summer sch., 1969-81, dir. profl. and community programs, 1975-78; exec. sec. N.Am. Assn. summer sessions, St. Louis, 1978—; account rep. Trio Printing Co., St. Louis, 1982-84; sr. procedures analyst McDonnell Douglas Corp., St. Louis, 1984—. Served as sgt. USMC, 1951-54. Mem. Alpha Sigma Lamda, Phi Delta Kappa. Episcopalian. Avocations: carpentry, music, sports coaching. Home: 11728 Summerhaven Dr Creve Coeur MO 63146 Office: Dept H360 Hdqrs Bldg McDonnel Douglas Corp Saint Louis MO 63166

NELSON, OSCAR FRED, water utility executive, engineer; b. St. Louis, July 6, 1929; s. Oscar Fred and Lillie Rachel (Suter) N.; m. JoAnn Dick, Apr. 12, 1951; children—Boyd, Nancy, Carol, Diane, Keith, Gail. B.S. in Civil Engring, Washington U., St. Louis, 1955. Registered profl. engr., Mo., Wis. Asst. div. engr. St. Louis Water Div., 1955-60; gen. mgr. Kenosha Water Utility, Wis., 1960—. Contbr. articles to profl. jours. Mem. adv. commn. Southeast Wis. Regional Planning Commn., Waukesha, 1975—. Served with U.S. Army, 1947-49. Mem. Am. Water Works Assn. (state chmn. 1969-70, Fuller award 1971), ASCE, Water Pollution Control Fedn. (Bedell award 1981, nat. bd. dirs. 1980-83), Central States Water Pollution Control Assn. (pres. 1973-74). Lodge: Rotary (pres. 1971-72). Home: 2715 Buchanan Rd Kenosha WI 53140 Office: Kenosha Water Utility 812-56th St Kenosha WI 53140

NELSON, PETER ALAN, marketing executive; b. Oak Park, Ill., July 11, 1932; s. Theodore Martin and Katherine (Child) N.; m. Peggy A. Amaden, June 24, 1960; 1 son, Charles. A.B. in Econs., Monmouth Coll., 1954. With Needham, Harper & Steers, Inc., Chgo., 1956-84, pres., chief operating officer Needham, Harper & Steers/U.S.A. Inc., Chgo., 1983-84, dir., 1976-84; sr. v.p. mktg. McDonald's Corp., Oak Brook, Ill., 1984—; dir. Del E. Webb Corp. Served with U.S. Army, 1954-56. Republican. Methodist. Clubs: Barrington Hills Country, Tavern, Lake Zurich Golf. Office: McDonald's Corp McDonald's Plaza Oak Brook IL

NELSON, RALPH ALFRED, physician, medical educator; researcher; b. Mpls., June 19, 1927; s. Alfred Walter and Lydia (Johnson) N.; m. Rosemarie Pokela, Aug. 7, 1954; children—Edward, Audrey, Elizabeth, Andrew, Evan. B.A., U. Minn., 1949, M.D., 1953, Ph.D., 1961. Diplomate Am. Bd. Internal Medicine. Intern Cook County Hosp., Chgo., 1953-54; resident Mayo Found. and Clinic, Rochester, Minn., 1976-78; dir. George Scott Research Lab., Cleve., 1962-66; assoc. prof. Mayo Found., Rochester, Minn., 1967-78, U. S.D., Sioux Falls, 1978-79; dir. research Carle Found. Hosp., Urbana, Ill., 1980—; prof. medicine and nutrition U. Ill., Urbana, 1979—. Author: Mayo Clinic Renal Diet Cook Book, 1974. Contbr. articles on hibernation and clin. nutrition to profl. jours. Served as cpl. USAAF, 1944-47, ETO. Recipient Mayo Clinic Alumni award, 1959. Fellow ACP, Am. Coll. Nutrition; mem. Am. Physiol. Soc., Am. Soc. Clin. Nutrition, Am. Gastroent. Assn. Avocations: hiking, bicycling, canoeing. Home: 2 Illini Circle Urbana IL 61801 Office: Dept Med Research Carle Found Hosp 611 W Park St Urbana IL 61801

NELSON, R(ALPH) DAVID, audiologist, hearing aid dealer; b. Milford, Iowa, Sept. 21, 1940; s. Ralph Walter and Martha Margaret (Wilson) N.; m. Martha Jane West, June 20, 1965 (div. 1972); m. Julie Linda Bottlefeson, June 4, 1977; children—Judith Ann, Sarah Elizabeth, Catherine Carole, Paul David. B.A., Augustana Coll., 1962; M.A., U. Iowa, 1970. Tchr. Pub. Schs., Storm Lake, Iowa, 1962-65; instr. Kent State U., 1970-73; audiologist in pvt. practice, Canton, Ohio, 1973-75; salesman Knox Hearing Aid Service, Canton, 1975-76; audiologist, owner Nelson Hearing Aid Service, Spencer, Iowa, 1976—; pres. Hearing Aid Mgmt. Systems Inc., Spencer, 1984. Pres. Spencer Area Concert Assn., 1983—. Mem. Am. Speech, Hearing and Lang. Assn., Acoustical Soc. Am., Nat. Hearing Aid Soc., Iowa Hearing Aid Soc. (bd. dirs. 1983—). Democrat. Methodist. Lodges: Kiwanis (dir. 1980-82), Masons (Worshipful Master 1982). Avocations: singing; church choir; woodworking. Home: Box 255 Ruthven IA 51358 Office: Nelson Hearing Aid Service 513 1st Ave E Spencer IA 51301

NELSON, RICHARD ARTHUR, lawyer; b. Fosston, Minn., Apr. 8, 1947; s. Arthur Joseph and Thelma Lillian Nelson; m. Kathryn Louise Sims, Sept. 25, 1976; children—Jennifer Kathryn, Kristen Elizabeth. B.S. in Math., U. Minn., 1969, J.D., 1974. Bar: Minn. 1974. Law clk. U.S. Ct. Appeals, Washington, 1974-75; ptnr. Faegre and Benson, Mpls., 1975—. Note and articles editor Minn. Law Rev., 1973-74. Active Democratic-Farmer-Labor State Central Com., Minn., 1976—, del. dist. and local coms. and convs., 1970—; student rep. bd. regents U. Minn., Mpls., 1973-74; v.p. Minn. Student Assn., 1968-69. Served with U.S. Army, 1970-72. Mem. ABA, Minn. Bar Assn., Order of Coif, Tau Beta Pi. Lutheran. Office: Faegre and Benson 2300 Multifoods Tower Minneapolis MN 55402

NELSON, ROBERT EDDINGER, management and development consultant; b. Mentone, Ind., Mar. 2, 1928; s. Arthur Irven and Tural Cecile (Eddinger) N.; B.A., Northwestern U., 1949; L.H.D., Iowa Wesleyan Coll., 1969; m. Carol J., Nov. 24, 1951; children—Janet K. Nelson Callighan, Eric P. Asst. dir. alumni relations Northwestern U., Evanston, Ill., 1950-51, 54-55; v.p. and dir. pub. relations Iowa Wesleyan Coll., Mt. Pleasant, 1955-58; vice chancellor for devel. U. Kansas City, 1959-61; v.p. instl. devel. Ill. Inst. Tech., Chgo., 1961-68; pres. Robert Johnston Corp., Oak Brook, Ill., 1968-69, Robert E. Nelson Assocs., Inc., Elmhurst, Ill., 1969—; dir. Chautauqua Workshop in Fund Raising and Instl. Relations, 1970-74; dir. Continental Bank of OakBrook Terrace; nat. conf. chmn. and program dir. Am. Coll. Pub. Relations Assn., 1961; trustee, Iowa Wesleyan Coll., 1962-68; faculty mem. Ind. U. Workshops on Coll. and Univ. Devel., 1963-65, Loretto Heights Summer Inst. for Fund Raising and Pub. Relations, 1964-68; mem. Pub. Review Panel for Grants Programs, Lilly Endowment, Inc., 1975. Served with U.S. Army, 1951-54. Mem. Council on Fin. Aid to Edn. (bd. dirs. 1957-63), Public Relations Soc. Am., Nat. Soc. Fund Raisers, Nat. Small Bus. Assn., Chgo. Soc. Fund Raising Execs., Blue Key, Delta Tau Delta. Methodist. Clubs: Execs., Econ., Union League (Chgo.); Masons. Author chpt. in Handbook of Coll. and Univ. Adminstrn., 1970. Home: 5 Oak Brook Club Dr N101 Oak Brook IL 60521 Office: 180 W Park Suite 10 Elmhurst IL 60126

NELSON, RONALD ERWIN, educational administrator; b. Painesville, Ohio, Sept. 29, 1944; s. Everett Erwin and Betty Jane (Boehnke) N.; m. Paula Beth Manz, July 21, 1969; children—Jason, Kristin. B.S. in Edn., Concordia Coll., Seward, Nebr., 1968; M.Edn., Memphis State U., 1973. Prin. Holy Cross Lutheran Sch., Memphis, 1968-75, C.C. Hadden Sch., Painesville, Ohio, 1975-80; office mgr. Alperts Ohio, Inc., North Randall, Ohio, 1980-81; dir. pub. relations Concordia Sem., Fort Wayne, Ind., 1981—; cons. WLAB-FM Radio, Fort Wayne, 1984—. Author: (booklet) Planning School Buildings, 1974. Creator, host TV program, 1980. Editor newspaper Called to Serve, 1981—. Coordinator voters Sen. Howard Baker Campaign, 1972; corr. sec. Young Republicans Shelby County, Memphis, 1972-75; cons. direct mail Lutheran Ch.-Mo. Synod, St. Louis, 1982—. Mem. Fort Wayne C. of C. (pub. relations com. 1981—, conv. bur. 1983—), Internat. Assn. Bus. Communicators (chmn. edn. com., bd. dirs. 1984, Bronze Quill 1984), Auto License Plate Collectors Assn. (nat. recognition award 1979). Republican. Lutheran. Avocations: collecting license plates, photography, golf, swimming. Home: 6719 Kirkdale Dr Fort Wayne IN 46815 Office: Concordia Theol Sem 6600 N Clinton St Fort Wayne IN 46825

NELSON, RONALD HARVEY, animal science educator, consultant; b. Union Grove, Wis., Aug. 10, 1918; s. Harvey August and Myra Francis (Sheen) N.; m. Elizabeth Jane Lappley, Apr. 13, 1940; children—David Peter, Marjorie Jean, Linda Louise, Ronda Elizabeth. B.S., U. Wis.-Madison, 1939; M.S., Okla. State U., 1941; Ph.D., Iowa State U., 1943. Farmer, Union Grove, Wis., 1943-45; asst. prof. animal sci. Mich. State U., East Lansing, 1946-47, assoc. prof., 1947-49, prof., 1949-84, prof., chmn. animal sci. dept., 1950-84; cons. Am. Angus Assn., St. Joseph, Mo., 1956-62, Govt. Uruguay, Montevideo, 1978; chief of party Mich. State U.-Argentina, Balcarce, 1966-68. Contbr. (with others) articles to profl. jours. Fellow Am. Soc. Animal Sci. (Internat. Animal Agr. award 1978, Animal Industry award 1984), Sigma Xi (sec.-treas. 1960), Phi Kappa Phi (pres. 1962). Republican. Methodist. Lodge: Masons. Home: 1545 N Harrison East Lansing MI 48823 Office: Mich State U 102 Anthony East Lansing MI 48824

NELSON, VINCENT CARROLL, university official; b. Clarinda, Iowa, July 14, 1946; s. Carroll Vincent and Verna Beatrice (Schantz) N.; m. Pamela Jo Mulder, Aug. 3, 1968. B.M.E., Drake U., 1968, M.M.E., 1970, postgrad., 1981—. Dir. bands Dowling High Sch., West Des Moines, Iowa, 1968-75; asst. dir. bands Drake U., Des Moines, 1970-77, asst. dir. admissions, 1975-79, assoc. dir. alumni, 1977-79, dir. alumni relations, 1979—; choirmaster and dir. music St. Timothy's Episcopal Ch., West Des Moines, 1970—. Author: A Study of Selected Works Written for Winds, 1970; contbr. article to profl. jour. Recipient Gold medal for alumni programing and Silver medal for alumni scholarship program, 1985; Servant of Yr. award St. Timothy's Episcopal Ch., 1985. Mem. Council for Advancement and Support of Edn. (spl. merit awards 1981-83, citations for alumni programming 1982, exceptional achievement award 1983). Club: Des Moines. Home: 7204 Colby Ave Des Moines IA 50311 Office: Office of Alumni Relations Drake Univ 26th & University Des Moines IA 50311

NELSON, WARREN BRYANT, commodity brokerage executive; b. Manhattan, Kans., Sept. 29, 1922; s. Oscar William and Eda Caroline (Hokanson) N.; B.S. cum laude in Agrl. Econs., Kans. State U., 1942, postgrad., 1950; postgrad. Am. U., 1947; m. Betty Lou Wiley, Dec. 24, 1944; children—Barbara Ann, David William, Marcia Lynn, Robert Warren. Statistician agrl. div. Bur. Census, U.S. Dept. Commerce, Washington, 1945-48, Statis. Reporting Service, U.S. Dept. Agr., Topeka, 1948-50; price analyst Longstreet Abbott & Co., St. Louis, 1951-59, partner, 1959-69; sec. Clayton Brokerage Co., St. Louis, 1959-69, exec. v.p., 1969-72, pres., 1972-77, vice chmn. bd., 1977—. Served to lt. USAAF, 1942-45. Decorated D.F.C. with 2 oak leaf clusters, Air medal with 3 oak leaf clusters. Mem. Commodity Option Market, Index, Debt and Energy Market, Index and Option Market, Chgo. Bd. Trade, Chgo. Merc. Exchange, Internat. Monetary Market, N.Y. Cotton Exchange, Index and Option Market. Republican. Lutheran. Club: St. Louis. Home: 839 Elm Tree Ln Kirkwood MO 63122 Office: 7701 Forsyth Blvd Suite 300 Clayton MO 63105

NELSON, WILLIAM JOSEPH, educational adminstrator, educator; b. Brainerd, Minn., Feb. 24, 1951; s. Hilding Magnus and Rita Pauline (Rudolph) N.; m. Susan Denise Breeton, June 28, 1975; children—Anna Emily, Andrew. B.A. in Sociology and Polit. Sci., U. Minn.-Morris, 1973; M.A. in Adminstrn. of Community Edn., Coll. St. Thomas, St. Paul, 1975; M.S. in Studies of Future, U. Houston, Clear Lake City, Tex., 1978. Coordinator community edn. Mpls. Pub. Schs., 1973-77; research assoc. Future Systems, Inc., St. Paul, 1978-79; coordinator part time students U. Minn.-Waseca, 1979-83, div. dir., 1983—, speaker, 1979—. Contbr. articles to profl. jours. Mem. Waseca Community Edn. Adv. Council, 1980-84, chmn., 1983-84. Grantee M.S.I. Ins. and Coop. League, 1984, U. Minn., 1981-82. Mem. Assn. Coop. Educators, Minn. Assn. Coll. Tchrs. Agr., Nat. Assn. Coll. Tchrs. Agr., Southeast Minn. Bus. Educators, World Future Soc. Home: 304 7th Ave SE Waseca MN 56093 Office: U Minn Tech Coll Waseca MN 56093

NELTING, GEORGE, religious and charitable organization executive. Territorial comdr., commr. central ter. The Salvation Army, Chgo. Office: Salvation Army 860 N Dearborn St Chicago IL 60610*

NEMAZI, JOHN EVERETT, patent lawyer; b. Detroit, June 5, 1952; s. Mehdi and Mary T. (Jackson) N.; m. Lisa L. Smith, Dec. 13. 1975. B.M.E., Gen. Motors Inst., 1975; M.B.A., Wayne State U., 1976; J.D., Detroit Coll. Law, 1981. Bar: Mich. 1981, U.S. Dist. Ct. (ea. dist.) Mich. 1982, U.S. Patent Office, 1982, U.S. Ct. Appeals (D.C. cir.) 1983. Project engr. Gen. Motors Corp., Warren, Mich., 1975-82; assoc. Burton, Parker & Schramm, P.C., Mt. Clemens, Mich., 1982—; dir. GMI Engring. and Mgmt. Inst., Bus. and Industry Devel. Ctr. Patentee adjustable roof engine swirl inlet port, 1983. Mem., Oakland County Republican Com., Birmingham, Mich., 1983—; pres. Troy Republican Club, Mich., 1984. Mem. State Bar. Mich. (chmn. trademark trade secret com. 1983-85), U.S. Trademark Assn. (state trademark com. 1984-85), Mich. Patent Law Assn, Jaycees (bd. dirs. Troy chpt. 1984-85). Episcopalian. Lodge: Optomists (v.p. Mt. Clemens area chpt. 1984). Home: 3660 Carmel Troy MI 48084 Office: Burton Parker & Schramm P C 59 N Walnut Suite 301 Mount Clemens MI 48043

NEMEC, STANLEY S., physician; b. Yugoslavia, June 16, 1911; s. Adolf and Josefina (Koblizek) N.; M.D., St. Louis U., 1936; m. Katherine M. Vidakovich Barr, June 15, 1940; children—Edward S., Mary K., Charles S., Robert S., Louise K., Dorothy K., Barbara K. Gen. med. practice, 1936-43; radiologist, St. Louis City Hosp., 1943-46; practice medicine specializing in radiology, 1946—; cons. radiologist Wabash R.R. Woodland Hosp., Moberly, Mo.; radiologist St. Charles Clinic, Marian Hosp.; asst. in radiology St. Louis U. Sch. Medicine. Diplomate Am. Bd. Radiology, Nat. Bd. Med. Examiners, Fellow Am. Coll. Radiology; mem. Radiology Soc. N.A., A.M.A., So. Med. Assn., St. Louis Med. Soc., St. Louis Soc. Neurology and Psychiatry. Author: History of the Croatian Settlement in St. Louis, 1931; Yugoslav Sokol Almanac, 1933. Editor: Sokol Magazine, 1931-34, The Koch Messenger, 1939. Contbr. articles to profl. jours. Home: 2870 S Lindbergh Blvd Huntleigh Village St Louis County MO 63131 Office: Suite 1 6500 Chippewa St St Louis MO 63109

NEMITZ, NANCY LEE, bank exec.; b. Chamberlain, S.D., Nov. 1, 1949; d. Gerrit and Irene Theresa (Buettner) Brink; student Augustana Coll., 1968-70, Mankato State U., 1970-74, Coll. Gt. Falls, 1977-79, Mundelein Coll., 1981—; m. Floyd Brian Nemitz, Sept. 27, 1975; stepchildren—Todd, Robyn, Jeff, Chris, Rodney, Wendy; 1 fosterchild, Christine Russell. Aide firm Churchill, Sauer, Manolis & Hoyt, 1968; transit clk. First Nat. Bank, Sioux Falls, S.D., 1969-70; ops. staff First Nat. Bank, Owatonna, Minn., 1971-74; regional examiner First Bank System, Inc., Mpls., 1974-76, regional audit officer, 1976-77; auditor First Nat. Bank of Gt. Falls, Mont., 1977-78, ops. officer, 1978-79; corp. compliance officer First Bank System, Inc., Mpls., 79-80, asst. v.p. compliance, 1980-81, asst. v.p., dir. product mgmt., 1981-83, v.p., mgr. Bankcards, 1983—; lectr. on consumer laws in bank industry, mktg. and bank card mgmt.; condr. compliance seminars; instr. Am. Inst. Banking, Bank Adminstrn. Inst.; faculty Am. Bankers Assn. schs., Lobbyist for foster care reform, Mont., 1979; treas. Gt. Falls Foster Parent Assn., 1979. Named Outstanding Young Career Women, Mont. Bus. and Profl. Women, 1978. Mem. Am. Inst. Banking (bd. dirs.), Nat. Assn. Bank Women (nat. steering com., nat. by-laws chmn., Minn. state council, chmn. state conf., regional dir.). Home: 9601 Utica Rd Bloomington MN 55437 Office: PO Box 9487 Minneapolis MN 55479

NEPTUNE, TYLER GREGG, JR., lawyer; b. St. Paul, Dec. 22, 1948; s. Tyler Gregg and Clara Belle (Byus) N.; m. Maureen Ann Armstrong, Mar. 29, 1980; children—Kelly, Amy, Tyler III. B.A. in Psychology, Macalester Coll., 1971; J.D., John Marshall U., 1980. Bar: Ill. 1980, U.S. Dist. Ct. (no. dist.) Ill. 1980. Employment mgr. UARCO Inc., Barrington, Ill., 1974-80; assoc. Clancy, McGuirk & Hulce, St. Charles, Ill., 1980-83; sole practice, Geneva, Ill., 1983—. mem. oversight com. Kane County Ct., Geneva, 1982—. Served to 1st lt. U.S. Army, 1971-74. Mem. Kane County Bar Assn. (chmn. admissions com. 1984), Ill. State Bar Assn., ABA, Assn. Trial Lawyers Am. Republican. Club: Lions. Home: 2000 Normandy Ln Geneva IL 60134 Office: 128 James St PO Box 372 Geneva IL 60134

NERONI, PETER J., business executive; b. Cleve., Dec. 21, 1932; s. Decenzio and Maria (Casalena) N.; m. Barbara Baldwin, Sept. 7, 1960; children—Barbara, Michael, Mark, Timothy. B.S., John Carroll U. Regional mgr. Dayco Corp., Dayton, Ohio, 1960-71; sales mgr. Dayco Plastics Div., Dayton, 1971; v.p. Plastics Div., Dayton, 1971-73; exec. v.p. Dayflex Co., Dayton, 1973-74, pres., 1974-76; corp. group v.p., Dayco Corp., 1976-82, exec. v.p., 1982—. Office: Dayflex Co 333 W 1st St Dayton OH 45402

NERUD, ANTHONY FRANCIS, lawyer; b. Dodge Center, Minn., Sept. 10, 1951; s. Benjamin R. and Anna D. (Tupy) N.; m. Melanie R. Cear, Feb. 16, 1974 (div. Oct. 1979); children—Margaret Ann, Deborah Elizabeth; m. Kathleen D. Bruns, Oct. 4, 1980; 1 child, Amanda Kathleen. B.S., U. Minn., 1973; J.D., William Mitchell Coll., 1979. Bar: Minn. 1980. Asst. county atty. Sibley County Atty.'s Office, Gaylord, Minn., 1980-84; ptnr. McGarthy-Nerud, Winthrop, Minn., 1982-84; sole practice, Arlington, Minn., 1984—; asst. 1st dist. pub. defender, 1984—. Pres. Winthrop Community Theatre, 1984—; sec. Sibley County Democratic Farmer Labor Party, 1983-85 Mem. ABA, Minn. Trial Lawyers Assn. Office: 325 W Main Arlington MN 55307

NESBIT, ROBERT GLENN, industrial training consultant, writer; b. Chgo., Dec. 16, 1934; s. Harold Robison and Frances Harriet (Gray) N.; m. Janet Parker, Aug. 25, 1956; children—Robert P., Martha J., Kathryn A., James C., Susan T. B.S. in Journalism, U. Ill., 1957; M.B.A. in Mktg., U. Chgo., 1963. Salesman Pillsbury Co., Mpls., 1958-60; staff writer Pure Oil Co., Palatine, Ill., 1960-63; ednl. writer Psychotechnics, Inc., Glenview, Ill., 1963; indsl. designer Tng. Dynamics, Inc., Glen Ellyn, Ill., 1963-65; cons. Robert G. Nesbit, Ltd., Park Ridge, Ill., 1965-78; exec. v.p. Universal Tng. Systems Co., Northbrook, Ill., 1978-82; owner, pres. Robert G. Nesbit, Glenview, Ill., 1982—. Author:

How To Review and Evaluate Employee Performance, 1975. Pres. elem. sch. PTA, Park Ridge, 1973; dir. for tax levy Sch. Dist. 64, Park Ridge, 1974. Served to 2d lt. U.S. Army, 1957-78. Recipient 1st prize for tng. program design Ill. Tng. Dirs. Assn., 1973. Mem. Chgo. Sales Tng. Assn. Republican. Episcopalian. Club: Park Ridge Country. Home: 423 N Elmore St Park Ridge IL 60068 Office: 1900 Pickwick St Glenview IL 60025

NESPECHAL, ROBERT JOHN, engineering company executive; b. Chgo., Aug. 18, 1946; s. Robert John and Eleanor (Doornbos) N.; m. Susan Mary Browning, Dec. 30, 1971; children—Kristina Marie, Katherine Susan. B.S. in Engring. U. Ill.-Chgo., 1973; M.B.A., DePaul U., 1978. Registered profl. engr., Ill., Calif., Fla., Minn., Mich., Ind., Wis. Draftsman, Sargent & Lundy, Chgo., 1971-73, engring. analyst, 1973-75, mech. engr., 1975-77, project engr., 1977-79; engring. mgr. Voluud USA Ltd., Oak Brook, Ill., 1979-83, v.p. engring., 1983—. Served as sgt. USMC, 1968-70, Vietnam. Mem. ASME, Western Soc. Engrs., Soc. Am. Mil. Engrs., Nat. Soc. Profl. Engrs. Avocation: officer USNR. Home: 4458 Burgundy Pl Lisle IL 60532 Office: Voluud USA Ltd 900 Jorie Blvd Oak Brook IL 60521

NESS, GARY CLIFFORD, historical society administrator; b. Sioux City, Iowa, Apr. 8, 1940; s. Clifford S. and Elsie L. (Lindgren) N.; m. Heather Humphreys, Dec. 21, 1963; children—Andrew, Joshua, John. B.S., Iowa State U., 1963; M.A., Duke U., 1969, Ph.D., 1972. Fin. analyst Cummins Engine Co., Columbus, Ind., 1963-64; asst. prof. history U. Cin., 1970-77, asst. univ. dean grad. studies, 1977-80; dir. Ohio Hist. Soc., Columbus, 1980—; cons. in field. Served to 1st lt. U.S. Army, 1964-66. Woodrow Wilson Found. fellow, Duke U., 1969-70. Club: Rotary (Columbus). Home: 700 Gatehouse Ln Worthington OH 43085 Office: Ohio Hist Soc 1985 Velma Ave Columbus OH 43211

NESSE, RANDOLPH MARTIN, psychiatrist, researcher; b. Toledo, July 10, 1948; s. Arthur Christopher and Dorothy Inga (Rovelstad) N.; m. Margaret Bryce Howell, June 15, 1974; children—Erika, Laura. B.A. cum laude, Carleton Coll., 1970; M.D. cum laude, U. Mich., 1974. Diplomate Am. Bd. Psychiatry and Neurology. Intern Univ. Hosp., Ann Arbor, Mich., 1974-75, resident, 1975-77; instr dept psychiatry U. Mich. Med. Sch., Ann Arbor, 1977-79, asst. prof., 1979-85, assoc. prof., 1985—, dir. resident and fellow edn., 1981—. Contbr. articles to profl. jours. Laughlin fellow Am. Coll. Psychiatry, 1977. Mem. Am. Psychiat. Assn. Am. Psychosomatic Soc., Am. Assn. Dirs. Psychiatry Residency Tng., Animal Behavior Soc., Phobia Soc. Am., Internat. Soc. Human Ethology. Office: Univ Hosp PO Box 056 Ann Arbor MI 48109

NESTOR, LULA B., art educator, consultant, artist; b. Werton, W. Va., Jan. 23; d. Nick John and Athena Marie (Tsaroutis) N.; m. Steve Pete Christodoulou, Nov. 4, 1969; children—Eva, Charles. Student W.Va. U., 1955-56; B.A. in Edn., West Liberty State Coll., 1957; M.A. in Art, Eastern Mich. U., 1973, postgrad., 1973-77. Cert. tchr., Mich. Tchr. Richie Jr. High Sch., Wheeling, W.Va., 1957-58, Elida High Sch., Ohio, 1958-59, South Lima Jr. High Sch., Ohio, 1960-62; art instr., dir. art dept. Hartland High Sch., Mich., 1968-78; tchr. adult art classes; pres. Nestor & Assocs. Inc. (fine art cons.). one-woman shows include Holy Cross Greek Orthodox Ch., Mt. Lebanon, Pa., 1975, U. Mich. Commons Gallery, 1975, Bowling Green U., Ohio, 1984, Carole Hooberman Gallery, Birmingham, Mich., 1985; exhibited in group shows at Butler Inst. Art, 1973, 75, Calif. Nat. Watercolor Soc., 1974-83 (award), Carnegie Mus., 1975, Foothills Art Ctr., 1975, 76 (spl. award 1975), Nat. Gallery of Acad. N.Y., 1976, Habatat Gallery Exhbn., 1974, Michelson's Gallery, 1975, Cranbrook Acad. of Art Mus., 1976, Lansing Art Gallery Exhbn., 1976, Balt. Orthodox Cathedral Exhbn., 1977, Flint Mus., 1973, Mich. and Detroit Inst. Art, 1972-78; represented in permanent collections Holy Cross Greek Orthodox Ch., Pittsburgh Plate Glass Co., Balt. Ins. Co., Cathedral of Annunciation, U. W.Va., Mich. Edn. Assn., also pvt. collections. Bd. dirs. Hartland Regional Fine Arts Festival, 1968-78, Mich. Council for Arts, 1976, Livingston Art Assn. exhbn. First Fed. Savs. Bank, 1972. Mem. Mich. Watercolor Soc. (bd. dirs.), Ann Arbor Art Assn., Midwestern Watercolor Assn., Ann Arbor Women Painters, Livingston County Art Assn., Hartland Art Council (bd. dirs.), Mich. Art Edn. Assn., Mich. Edn. Assn., Nat. Watercolor Soc. of Am. Club: Scarab (Detroit). Home: 9865 Edwards Dr Brighton MI 48116 Office: Nestor & Assocs 9865 Edwards Dr Brighton MI 48116

NESTOR, ONTARIO HORIA, physicist; b. Youngstown, Ohio, Sept. 20, 1922; s. Constantin and Carolina (Bretza) N.; m. Ellen Adams Ingham, Sept. 4, 1943; children—Jon Ontario, David Alan. A.B. magna cum laude, Marietta Coll., 1943; M.S., U. Minn., 1949; Ph.D., U. Buffalo, 1960. Research assoc. Union Carbide Corp., Indpls., 1949-71; research dir. Crystal Optics, Ann Arbor, Mich., 1971-74; research mgr. Harshaw-Filtrol Partnership, Solon, Ohio, 1974—. Contbr. articles to profl. jours. Served with U.S. Army, 1944-46. Mem. Am. Phys. Soc., Am. Assn. Crystal Growth, Materials Research Soc., Phi Beta Kappa. Democrat. Presbyterian. Avocations: golf, literature, bridge.

NESVAN, GERALDINE ROOT, psychologist; b. Council Bluffs, Iowa, June 28, 1927; d. Fred E. and Mildred S. (Means) Root; m. Mirko Nesvan; children—Polly, Denis Ann, Debra, Jill. B.A., U. Omaha, 1959; M.A., U. Nebr., 1960, Specialist, 1970. Dir. psychol. services Omaha Pub. Schs., 1960-76; dir. psychol. services Children's Meml. Hosp., Omaha, 1978-84; cons. Nebr. Sch. for Deaf, 1976-82; cons. staff Omaha Children's Clinic, 1982-84, pvt. practice, 1982—; v.p. Cats Corp., 1985—. cons. Methodist Midtown Adolescent Chem. Dependency Unit, 1978-82. Pres. bd. dirs. scholarship bd. Edwards Found. Mem. Am. Psychol. Assn., Am. Assn. Mental Deficiency (past state and regional pres., chmn. Region 8), Nat. Assn. Sch. Psychologists (past state rep.), Nebr. Psychol. Assn., Nebr. Assn. Mental Deficiency. Eastern Orthodox. Club: Zonta (past local pres.). Home: 7040 Rainwood Rd Omaha NE 68152 Office: 12808 Augusta Ave Omaha NE 68144

NETHERS, CARL RAYMOND, animal feed company official; b. Coshocton, Ohio, Nov. 5, 1931; s. Samuel W. and Leila E. (Johnston) N.; m. Martha Louise Goetz, Sept. 20, 1953; children—Susan, Mark, Carolyn. B.S., Ohio State U., 1953. Dist. salesman Ralston Purina Co., Waverly, Ohio, 1956-63, regional product sales mgr., Mpls., 1963-65, div. sales mgr., Cedar Rapids, Iowa, 1965-66, nat. product mgr., St. Louis, 1966-68, dir. ops., Bloomington, Ill., 1968-77, Omaha, 1977-85, mktg. mgr., St. Louis, 1985—. Bd. dirs. Assn. Commerce and Industry, McLean County, Ill., 1975-77; Nebr. rep. Ralston Purina Com. for Good Govt., 1978—; 2d v.p. Fontenelle Hills Homeowners Assn., Bellevue, Nebr., 1984—. Served to 1st lt. U.S. Army, 1954-56. Mem. Greater Omaha C. of C. (exec. com. agrl. council 1982—), Nebr. Assn. Commerce and Industry, U.S. C. of C. Republican. Episcopalian. Avocations: golf; travel. Home: 16419 Farmers Mill Ln Chesterfield MO 63017 Office: Purina Mills Inc 800 Chouteau Ave Saint Louis MO 63164

NETSCH, DAWN CLARK, state senator; b. Cin., Sept. 16, 1926; B.A. with distinction, Northwestern U., 1948, J.D. magna cum laude, 1952; m. Walter A. Netsch. Admitted to Ill. bar; individual practice law, Washington, Chgo.; law clk. U.S. Dist. Ct. Chgo.; adminstrv. and legal aide Ill. Gov. Otto Kerner, 1961-65; prof. law Northwestern U., 1965—; mem. Ill. Senate. Del. Ill. Constl. Conv.; adv. bd. Nat. Program Ednl Leadership, LWV, Mus. Contemporary Art, Ill. Welfare Assn. Democrat. Author: (with Daniel Mandelker) State and Local Government in a Federal System; contbr. articles to legal jours. Office: State Capitol Springfield IL 62707*

NETZLER, BRUCE WILLIAM, geologist; b. Cin., July 16, 1955; s. Kenneth Clifford and Joyce (Bone) N.; m. Roxane Lee Marquis, Dec. 3, 1977; 1 child, Kate Marie. B.S., Miami U., Oxford, Ohio, 1977; M.S., U. Mo.-Rolla, 1981. Well logger Core Labs., Oklahoma City, 1977-78; research asst. Rock Mechanics and Explosives Research Ctr., Rolla, 1978-80; geologist Mo. Geol. Survey, Dept. Natural Resources Div. Geol. and Land Survey, Rolla, 1980—. Contbr. articles to profl. jours. Mem. Am. Assn. Petroleum Geologists, Soc. Econ. Paleontologists and Mineralogists. Democrat. Mem. Christian Ch. Avocations: fishing, photography, travel. Home: 599 S Rolla St Rolla MO 65401 Office: Mo Geological Survey Div Geological and Land Survey Dept Natural Resources PO Box 250 Rolla MO 65401

NEUBERT, GEORGE W., museum director, sculptor; b. Mpls., Oct. 24, 1942; s. George W. and Juanita Neubert; m. Eva Saenz, 1965; 1 child, Evangeline. B.S., Hardin-Simmons U., 1965; postgrad. spl. studies San Francisco Art Inst., 1967; M.F.A., Mills Coll., 1969. Trefethen fellow Mills Coll., Oakland, Calif., 1969; curator of art Oakland Mus., 1970-80; assoc. dir. San Francisco Mus. Modern Art, 1980-83; dir. Sheldon Meml. Art Gallery, Lincoln, Nebr., 1983—; mem. adv. bd. Archives of Am. Art, Smithsonian, 1972—. Co-author: Robert Graham Statues, 1981; Nathan Oliveira Survey, 1984; editor catalogues various exhbns., 1970-84. One-man show: Gallery Paule Anglim, San Francisco, 1971; Gallery 72, Omaha, 1984; group shows: Mus. Conceptual Art, San Francisco, 1981, Impressions Gallery, Boston, 1982, Sculpture, Traditions in Steel, N.Y.C., 1983. Mem. Project Sculpture/Public Site, San Francisco, 1980-83; mem. panel Art in Pub. Places, NEA, 1976-79, 1978; project dir. 4th Triennael New Delhi/USIA, 1977-78. NEA grantee, 1980; Ctr. for Great Plains Studies fellow, 1983—. Mem. Art Mus. Assn. Am. (bd. dirs.), Assn. Art Mus. Dirs. Office: Sheldon Meml Art Gallery U Nebraska Lincoln NE 68588

NEUEFEIND, WILHELM, educator; b. Viersen, Ger., Mar. 6, 1939; s. Wilhelm and Berta N.; m. Ingrid Leuchtenberg, Mar. 30, 1966; children—Nicole, Bettina. M.B.A., U. Cologne, 1962, M.A. in Math., 1969; Ph.D., U. Bonn, 1972. Lectr., U. Bonn, Germany, 1973-77; vis. scholar U. Calif., Berkeley, 1974-75; prof. econs. Washington U., St. Louis, 1977-83, chmn. dept. econs., 1983—. Mem. Econometric Soc., Am. Econ. Assn., Assn. for Advancement Econ. Theory. Office: Washington Univ Dept Econs Lindell and Skinker Campus Box 1208 Saint Louis MO 63130

NEUENS, COLETTA MARIE, nursing administrator; b. Chgo., Oct. 23, 1941; d. Michael Joseph and Margaret Elizabeth (Kenny) Burke; m. Edward J. Bankert, May 30, 1967 (dec.); children—Marianne, Sharon; m. 2d Michael T. Neuens; children—Michael, Gina, Jodi. Diploma, St. Bernard's Hosp. Sch. Nursing, Chgo., 1961; B.S., St. Francis Coll., 1971-74; prin. F.P. ... Charge nurse St. Bernard's Hosp., 1961; operating room nurse U. Ill.-Chgo., 1962-64, supr. out-patient clinics, 1964-66, clin. nursing cons., 1966-69; staff nurse obstetrics Christ Hosp., Oak Lawn, Ill., 1972-75, supr. nursing service, 1975-77, dir. nursing quality assurance dept., 1977-78, dir. nursing service, 1978-80, asst. adminstr. nursing service, 1980—; ednl. cons. Cross Roads Publs., N.Y.C. Mem. Am. Soc. Nursing Adminstrs., Bus. and Profl. Women's Orgn., Nat. League Nursing, Nat. Ill. Soc. Nursing Adminstrs., Forum for Adminstrs. of Nursing Service, Rush-Presbyn.-St. Luke's Combined Hosp. Network Council, Chgo. Met. Area Nursing Adminstrs. Home: 1633 Ridge Rd Homewood IL 60430 Office: Christ Hosp 4440 W 95th St Oak Lawn IL 60453

NEUENSCHWANDER, FREDERICK PHILLIP, bus. exec.; b. Akron, Ohio, Mar. 19, 1924; s. Willis Lee and Esther (Mayer) N.; student Franklin and Marshall Coll., 1942-43, U. Akron, 1946-48; m. Mary Jane Porter, Mar. 19, 1948; children—Carol, Frederick Philip, Lynn, Dean, Richard. Chief insp. Retail Credit Co., Akron, 1948-55; exec. v.p. Wadsworth (Ohio) C. of C., 1955-62, Wadsworth Devel. Corp., 1955-62, Wooster (Ohio) C. of C., 1962-63, Wooster Expansion, Inc., 1962-63; dir. devel. dept. State of Ohio, Columbus, 1963-71; exec. v.p. James A. Rhodes & Assos., Columbus, 1971-74; prin. F.P. Neuenschwander & Assos., Columbus, 1975—. Mem. adv. council Small Bus. Adminstrn. Exec. dir. Wadsworth United Fund, Inc., 1956-62; pres. Templed Hills, Inc.; pres. Central Ohio exec. bd. Boy Scouts Am.; vice-chmn. Ohio Water Commn., Ohio Expns. Commn.; chmn. Ohio Water and Sewer Rotary Fund Commn.; mem., past chmn. Midwest Gov.'s Adv. Council; sec. Ohio Devel. Council, Ohio Devel. Finance Commn. Adv. council Rio Grande Coll.; 1st chmn. bd. trustees Ohio Transp. Research Center; bd. dirs. League Against Child Abuse, United Ch. Bd. for World Ministries. Served with AUS, 1943-46. Named Outstanding Young Man of Year, Wadsworth Jr. C. of C., 1958; recipient SIR award for directing outstanding state indsl. devel. program N. Am., 1966, 68, Ohio Gov.'s award 1967. Mem. Am., Gt. Lakes indsl. devel. councils, C. of C. Execs. of Ohio, Huguenot Soc. Am., Am. Legion, Ohio Soc. N.Y. (res. v.p.). Mem. United Ch. of Christ (property mgmt. com. Ohio Conf.). Club: Worthington Hills Country. Home: 1155 Clubview S Worthington OH 43085 Office: 2066 Henderson Rd Worthington OH 43085

NEUENSCHWANDER, MARY IRENE, dental laboratory executive; b. Terre Haute, Ind., Sept. 3, 1954; d. Don Richard and Betty (Scheifler) N. B.S. in Bus. Adminstrn., Ind. State U., 1980. Sales dir. Radi Corp., Arecibo, P.R., 1977-82; mktg. coordinator Johns Dental, Terre Haute, 1982—; pres. Neuen Corp., Terre Haute, 1984-85; dir. Dental Lab. Conf.; asst. tchr. Dale Carnegie course, Cloverdale, Ind., 1985. Mem. Alpha Lambda Delta. Lutheran. Avocations: photography; scuba diving; music; conversational spanish. Office: Johns Dental PO Box 606 Terre Haute IN 47808

NEUGER, DEBRA ANN, psychotherapist; b. Mpls., Dec. 26, 1956; d. Edwin and Lorraine (Wallen) N. B.A., Gustavus Adolphus Coll., 1979; M.A., U. Minn., 1981. Lic. psychologist. Career counselor Macalester Coll., St. Paul, 1982; counselor Mpls. Coll. Art and Design, 1982-83, dir. counseling, 1983-85, dir. student services, 1985—. Vol. counselor Walk-In Counseling Ctr., Mpls., 1982-84; bd. dirs. Mpls. Crisis Nursery Assocs., 1984. Mem. Minn. Women Psychologists (social action com. 1984), Am. Psychol. Assn., Minn. Psychol. Assn., Minn. Assn. Field Experience Learning (bd. dirs. 1983-84). Office: Mpls Coll Art and Design 133 E 25th St Minneapolis MN 55404

NEUHAUS, OTTO WILHELM, biochemistry educator; b. Zweibrucken Germany, Nov. 18, 1922; came to U.S. 1927, naturalized 1944; s. Clemens Jakob and Johanna Amalie (Schnorr) N.; m. Dorothy Ellen Rehn, Aug. 30, 1947; children—Thomas William, Carol Alida, Joanne Marie. B.S., U. Wis., 1944; M.S., U. Mich., 1947, Ph.D., 1953. Research chemist Huron Milling Co., 1951-54; research assoc. Wayne State U., Detroit, 1954-58, asst. prof., 1958-65, assoc. prof., 1965-66; prof., chmn. dept. biochemistry U. S.D. Vermillion, 1966-75, chmn. div. biochemistry, pysiology and pharmacology, 1976-81, prof., chmn. biochemistry, 1982—. Contbr. articles to profl. jours. NATO research fellow, 1961-62. Fellow AAAS; mem. Am. Chem. Soc., Am. Soc. Biol. Chemists, Sigma Xi, Phi Sigma, Phi Lambda Upsilon. Democrat. Lutheran. Home: 1090 Valley View Dr Vermillion SD 57069 Office: U SD 144 Lee Med Bldg Vermillion SD 57069

NEUMAN, KERMIT, lawyer, accountant, educator; b. Blumberg, Germany, July 30, 1906; came to U.S., 1911; s. Rudolph Leo and Johanna (Falk) Neumann; B.B.A., Northwestern U., 1932; J.D., Ohio No. U., 1974; m. Newell A. Hahn, Aug. 19, 1939; children—Marilyn Joanne Neuman Reid, Kermit William. Pvt. practice acctg., Chgo., 1928-50, Coldwater, Ohio, 1950—; with Avco New Idea div. Avco Corp., Coldwater, 1950-71; admitted to Fla. bar, 1974, Ohio bar, 1974; individual practice Law, Coldwater, 1974—; tchr. acctg. Ohio No. U.; solicitor Village of Coldwater, 1976-79. Pres. Rockland Fire Dept., Lake Bluff, Ill., 1949. Served as comdr. USNR, 1941-46. C.P.A., Ill., Wash., Ohio. Mem. Am. Bar Assn., Ohio Bar Assn., Mercer County Bar Assn., Am. Inst. C.P.A.'s, Ill. Soc. Cert. Pub. Accountants, U.S. Naval Inst., Navy League, Res. Officers Assn., Ret. Officers Assn. Club: Elks. Home and Office: 214 N Cedar St Coldwater OH 45828

NEUMAN, PATRICIA ANN POWELL, university counselor, educator, consultant; b. Elgin, Ill., Nov. 22, 1947; d. Marshall Albert Jr. and Viola Lillie (Wassinger) P.; m. Paul Vincent Neuman, Feb. 3, 1968; 1 child, Rhett Paul. B.A. in Psychology, U. Minn., 1969; M.S.Ed. in Guidance and Counseling, Chgo. State U., 1972; Ed.S. in Counseling, U. Minn., 1981. Nat. cert. counselor. Counselor Moorhead State U., Minn., 1972—, tchr. counselor edn. program, 1972—, developer intervention and treatment for eating disorders Fargo, N.D., 1972-77, Moorhead, Minn., 1977; cons. in field. Sr. author: Anorexia Nervosa and Bulimia: A Handbook for Counselors And Therapists, 1983. Contbr. articles, papers to prof. lit. Foster parent, Clay County, Minn., 1977—; lector, eucharistic minister St. Joseph Catholic Church, Moorhead, 1980—. Recipient Disting. Leadership award Fargo, Moorhead and West Fargo Communities and YWCA, 1982, Univ. award, 1984. Mem. Am. Assn. Counseling and Devel., Minn. Assn. Counseling and Devel., Am. Coll. Personnel Assn., Minn. Coll. Personnel Assn. Avocations: tennis; travel; skiing; reading; volleyball. Office: Moorhead State U Counseling Ctr PO Box 147 Moorhead MN 56560

NEUMANN, FREDERICK LLOYD, plant breeder; b. Waterloo, Iowa, Apr. 9, 1949; s. Lloyd Frederick and Leita Evangeline (Otto) N.; B.S., Iowa State U., 1972, M.S., 1974; m. Diane Marie Brown, Aug. 18, 1973; children—Bradley, Brian. Research dir., plant breeder Ames Seed Farms Inc. (Iowa), producers hybrid popcorn seed, 1973-85; plant breeder Crow's Hybrid Corn Co., Milford, Ill., 1985—; mem. research com. Popcorn Inst., Chgo., 1976-85, mem. prodn. and seed research subcom., 1982-85. Treas., Laurel Tree Nursery Sch., Inc., 1981-83. Mem. Am. Soc. Agronomy, Iowa Crop Improvement Assn. (com. to recommend to bd. dirs. certification requirements for hybrid corn and hybrid sorghum 1979), Crop Sci. Soc. Am., Phi Kappa Phi, Gamma Sigma Delta. Republican. Episcopalian. Home: RR 3 Box 164 Watseka IL 60970 Office: Box 306 Milford IL 60953

NEUMANN, FREDERICK RICHARD, securities analyst; b. Ft. Lauderdale, Fla., Aug. 24, 1957; s. Frederick Leland and Dorothy Jeanne (Gusa) N. B.B.A., U. Mich., 1979; M.B.A., U. Chgo., 1981. Chartered fin. analyst. Investment analyst NBD Bancorp, Detroit, 1981-82, asst. investment officer, 1983, investment officer, 1984—. Mem. Fin. Analysts Soc. Detroit, Beta Gamma Sigma. Office: Nat Bank of Detroit 611 Woodward Ave Detroit MI 48226

NEUMANN, JEFFREY JAY, photographer; b. Cleve., Aug. 6, 1948; s. Fred and LaVerne (Vavra) N.; m. Charlene Rose Sparrow, Apr. 21, 1968 (dec.); children—Stephan, Corene, Lara; m. 2d, Carolyn Hannah, Nov. 4, 1972; 1 son, Jeffrey. Lithographer, camera operator Advertype, Inc., Cleve., 1972; lab. technician Vista Color Lab., Cleve., 1972-73; prodn. mgr. Mort Tucker Photography, Cleve., 1973-78; owner/photographer Photography by Jeffrey Neumann, Wadsworth, Ohio, 1978—; mem. Small Bus. Mgmt. Adv. Com., 1980-83. Mem. Internat. Platform Assn., Profl. Photographers Am. (awards), Wedding Photographers Internat. (awards), Profl. Photographers Ohio (awards), Akron Soc. Profl. Photographers. Jehovah's Witness. Club: Wadsworth (Ohio) Growth Assn. Home: 9960 Mount Eaton Rd Wadswoth OH 44281 Office: 191 College St Wadsworth OH 44281

NEUMEIER, THOMAS CHARLES, dentist, consultant; b. Menominee, Mich., Dec. 3, 1938; s. Charles Frank and Helen Violet (Hermanson) N.; m. Shirley Ann Endres, June 10, 1961; children—Charles, Jeffrey, Bruce. B.S., U. Mich., 1961, D.D.S., 1965. Instr. U. Mich., Ann Arbor, 1961-65; owner, pres. Neumeier Dental Lab., Ann Arbor, 1961-65; gen. practice dentistry, Menominee, Mich., 1968—; cons. Northern Chems., Menominee, 1969—. Co-author: (lab manual) Tissue Culture, 1964. Contbr. articles to sci. publs. Leader, com. mem. Bay Lakes council Boy Scouts Am., 1960—. Recipient Disting. award of Merit, Boy Scouts Am., 1981, Silver Beaver award, 1983, Golden Pelican award, 1984. Mem. Mich. Dental Assn., Am. Dental Assn., West German Armed Forces Dental Soc., Am. Legion. Lodges: Kiwanis, Elks. Avocations: art, camping, hunting, fishing, gardening. Home: 3508 17th St Menominee MI 49858 Office: 2101 23d Ave Menominee MI 49858

NEUSCHEL, ROBERT PERCY, management educator, administrator; b. Hamburg, N.Y., Mar. 13, 1919; s. Percy J. and Anna Martha (Becker) N.; m. Dorothy Virginia Maxwell, Oct. 20, 1944; children—Kerr Anne Zipríck, Carla Becker Wyckoff, Robert Friedrich. B.A., Denison U., 1941; M.B.A., Harvard U., 1947. Indsl. engr. Sylvania Elec. Products Co., Inc., N.Y.C., 1947-49; mgr. indsl. engring. McKinsey & Co., Inc., N.Y.C. and Chgo., 1950-67, sr. ptnr., dir., 1967-79; mng. dir. Transp. Ctr., Northwestern U., Evanston, Ill., 1979—, prof. corp. governance J.L. Kellogg Grad. Sch. Mgmt., 1979—; dir. Butler Mfg. Co., KME, Templeton, Kenly & Co. Mem. Reagan's Transp. Task Force, 1980-81; bd. dirs. Loyola U., Chgo.; pres. Lake Forest (Ill.) Bd. Edn., 1965-70; rep. Nat. council Boy Scouts Am., 1970; bd. chmn. Lake Forest Symphony, 1973. Served to capt. USAAF, 1946. Mem. McKinsey Found. Mgmt. Research Inc., Nat. Ctr. Vol. Action Inst. Mgmt. Cons., Internat. Council Edn. of Teaching, N.E. Exec. Council. Republican. Presbyterian. Clubs: Mid-Am. (Chgo.); Onwentsia (Lake Forest). Contbr. articles to profl. jours. Home: 890 Larchmont Ln Lake Forest IL 60045 Office: 1936 Sheridan Rd Evanston IL 60201

NEUSSENDORFER, JOSEPH FRANK, journalist; b. Lawrence, Kans., Aug. 13, 1943; s. Bernard Frank and Lenora Jane (Atkins) N. Constrn. journalist Detroit Builders Exchange, 1974—. Mem. U.S. Selective Service System Bd., City of Pontiac Zoning Bd. Served with USAF, 1961-64. Recipient Robert Boger award Constrn. Writers Assn., 1976; Gov. Mich. award, 1982; award Nat. Exchange Club, 1978. Mem. Nat. Assn. Bus. Economists, Am. Statis. Assn., Constrn. Writers Assn., Pub. Relations Soc. Am., Engring. Soc. Detroit, Detroit Press Club. Democrat. Roman Catholic. Home: 287 Voorheis Rd Pontiac MI 48053 Office: 1351 E Jefferson Ave Detroit MI 48053

NEVALAINEN, DAVID ERIC, medical technology researcher, hematologist, medical educator; b. Moose Lake, Minn., June 30, 1944; s. Eric Nevalainen and Anna Catherine (Keyport) Chernugal; m. Patricia Eileen Goodrich, Dec. 17, 1966; 1 child, Eric David. Student Coll. St. Thomas, 1962-64; B.S. in Med. Tech. with honors, U. Minn., 1966, Ph.D. in Hematology and Pathology, 1972. Lab. supr. Fairbanks Meml. Hosp., Alaska, 1972-73; asst. prof. Mich. Tech. U., Houghton, 1973-76, assoc. prof., 1976-79; assoc. prof. U. Wis.-Milw., 1979-81; clin. project mgr. Abbott Diagnostics div. Abbott Labs., North Chicago, Ill., 1981-83, project mgr. research and devel., 1983—; clin. assoc. prof. Rush Med. Coll., Chgo., 1984—. Co-author: Hematology: Laboratory Evaluation of Blood Cells, 1978. Contbr. articles to profl. jours. Mem. growth com. North Shore Congl. Ch., Fox Point, Wis., 1983-84, mem. stewardship com., 1980-83. Recipient Pres.'s award Abbott Labs., 1983. Mem. AAAS, Am. Soc. Clin. Pathologists (cert. med. technologist, splty. hematology, com. membership activities 1977—, chmn. product devel. sub-com. 1980-81, editorial adv. bd. Lab. Medicine jour. 1984—), Am. Assn. Blood Banks. Avocations: fishing, gardening, photography, canoeing. Home: 5011 N Berkeley Blvd Whitefish Bay WI 53217 Office: Abbott Labs North Chicago IL 60064

NEVEL, ETTA KATHRYN, obstetrician, gynecologist; b. Westchester, Pa., Nov. 20, 1951; d. Robert Leo and Ardath Anna (Anders) Coolidge; m. Thomas Paul Miller, Jan. 6, 1973 (div. 1978); m. Bernard Paul Nevel, Mar. 8, 1980; children—Maura, Adam. B.S., Earlham Coll., 1973; M.D., Ind. U., 1977. Diplomate Am. Bd. Ob-Gyn. Intern, St. Joseph Hosp., South Bend, Ind., 1977-78; resident Ill. Masonic Hosp. Chgo., 1978-81; practice medicine specializing in ob-gyn Houser-Norborg Med. Corp., South Bend, Ind., 1981—; mem. med. com. Planned Parenthood, South Bend, 1983—. Fellow Am. Coll. Obstetricians and Gynecologists; mem. AMA, Am. Med. Women's Assn., Am. Assn. Gynec. Laparoscopists, Phi Beta Kappa, Alpha Omega Alpha. Home: 1131 E Eckman St South Bend IN 46614 Office: Houser-Norborg Med Corp 515 N Lafayette St South Bend IN 46601

NEVELS, ZEBEDEE JAMES, physician, surgeon; b. Nowata, Okla., Nov. 13, 1926; s. Zebedee James and Mary Christine (Meigs) N.; m. Virginia Nell Glass, May 5, 1951; children—Karen Leslie, James Norman. B.A., U. Kans., 1950; M.D., Howard U., 1958. Diplomate Am. Bd. Surgery. Resident in surgery Mt. Sinai Hosp., Milw., 1960-62; staff VA Hosp., Wadsworth, Kans., 1962-65; chmn. dept. surgery St. Anthony Hosp., Milw., 1973-80; practice medicine and surgery, Milw., 1980—. Served with U.S. Army, 1945-46. Mem. County Med. Soc., State Med. Soc. Wis., Nat. Med. Assn., AMA, Cream City Med. Soc. (pres. 1978-79). Democrat. Baptist. Avocations: fishing; hunting; golf; gardening. Office: 2130 W Fon du Lac Ave Milwaukee WI 53206

NEVENHEIM, ARNOLD VINCENT, hospital manager; b. Rochester, Minn., Mar. 26, 1947; s. Hervey Richard and Mary Bernadine (Haushofer) N.; m. Susan Ann Nevenheim (div.); children—Andrew John, Amy Jean. Supr. Rochester Park and Recreation Dept., 1965-67; with Rochester Methodist Hosp., 1967—, asst. dir. central supply, 1976-81, mgr. central supply, 1981—; mem. adv. bd. Rochester Area Vocat. Tech. Inst. Chmn. United Way campaign at Rochester Meth. Hosp., 1981; chmn. hosp. div. United Way of Olmsted County (Minn.), 1983. Mem. Am. Soc. Hosp. Central Service Personnel, Internat. Soc. Hosp. Central Service Personnel. Roman Catholic. Home: 308 8th St NW Rochester MN 55901 Office: 201 W Center St Rochester MN 55901

NEVIN, JOHN J., tire and rubber company executive; b. Jersey City, Feb. 13, 1927; s. Edward Vincent and Anna (Burns) N.; B.S., U. Calif., 1950; M.B.A., Harvard U., 1952; m. Anne Filice, June 16, 1951; children—Stanley James, John Joseph, Richard Charles, Paul Edward, Gerald Patrick, Mary Anne. With Ford Motor Co., Dearborn, Mich., 1954-71, v.p. mktg., 1969-71; with Zenith Radio Corp., Chgo., 1971-79, pres., 1979, chmn., chief exec. officer, 1977-79; with Firestone Tire and Rubber Co., Akron, Ohio, 1979—, chmn. bd., pres., chief exec., 1980—; dir. First Chgo. Corp., First Nat. Bank Chgo., FMC Corp. Gen. chmn. Detroit United Found., 1970. Served with USNR, 1945-46. Office: Firestone Tire and Rubber Co 1200 Firestone Pkwy Akron OH 44317

NEWBERGER, SHEL, packaging executive; b. Chgo., Nov. 30, 1925; s. Oscar and Daisy N.; B.A., U. Chgo., 1944; m. Natalie Bernard, Oct. 22, 1946; children—Steven, Richard, David, Jill. Packaging salesman Cleary Box Co., Chgo., 1946-48, Chippewa Paper Products, Chgo., 1948-63, Lanzit Corrugated Box Co., Chgo., 1950-63, Consol. Packaging Corp., Chgo., 1960-63; pres., Apollo Containers, Inc., Evanston, Ill., 1963—, prin., pres., Boyer Corp., Evanston, 1976-84. Alderman, Evanston, 1967-71; officer Evanston Recreation Bd., 1971-85. Served with U.S. Army, 1944-46. Mem. Chgo. Assn. Commerce and Industry, Evanston C. of C. Home: 100 Dempster St Evanston IL 60202 Office: 2902 Central St Evanston IL 60201

NEWBLATT, STEWART ALBERT, U.S. district court judge; b. Detroit, Dec. 23, 1927; s. Robert Abraham and Fanny Ida (Grinberg) N.; B.A. with distinction, U. Mich., 1950, J.D. with distinction, 1952; m. Flora Irene Sandweiss, Mar. 5, 1965; children—David Jacob, Robert Abraham, Joshua Issac. Admitted to Mich. bar, 1953; partner firm White & Newblatt, Flint, Mich., 1953-62; judge 7th Jud. Circuit Mich., 1962-70; partner fir. Newblatt & Grossman, and predecessor, Flint, 1970-79; U.S. dist. judge Eastern Dist. Mich., Flint, 1979—; adj. instr. U. Mich.-Flint, 1977-78. Mem. Internat. Bridge Authority Mich., 1960-62. Served with AUS, 1946-47. Mem. Fed. Bar Assn., State Bar Mich., Dist. Judges Assn. 6th Circuit. Jewish. Office: Federal Bldg 600 Church St Flint MI 48503

NEWBROUGH, ARTHUR TRUETT, educational administrator; b. Connellsville, Pa., Dec. 15, 1946; s. Edgar Truett and Muriel Ethelyn (Amos) N.; m. Florence E. Ross, Jan. 27, 1968; children—Brett, Truett, Tiffany Diane. B.S. in Edn., Ill. State U., 1968, M.S. in Counseling, 1969; cert. advanced studies in ednl. adminstrn., No. Ill. U., 1980, Ed.D., 1985. Counselor Bloomington High Sch., Ill., 1968-70; counselor, cons., dir. Deerfield High Sch., Ill., 1970-81; ednl. cons. Ill. State Bd. Edn., Springfield, 1981-82; sch. adminstr. Highland Park High Sch., Ill., 1982—; v.p. Newbrough Resource Group, Cape Coral, Fla., 1982—. Author: Accessing the Community for Student Learning in Vocational Education, 1982; Rainbow Builders, 1983. Chief negotiator Sch. Bd. Dist. 15, McHenry, Ill., 1980—, v.p., 1983-84, pres., 1984—. Recipient Supt.'s Option award Twp. High Sch. Dist. 113, 1972-80. Mem. Nat. Experience Based Career Edn. Assn. (bd. dir., pres. 1983-84), Lake County Career Guidance Consortium (v.p. 1984-85, bd. dirs.). Avocations: tennis; racquetball; skiing; reading; writing. Home: 4910 W Pyndale Dr McHenry IL 60050 Office: Highland Park High Sch 433 Vine Ave Highland Park IL 60035

NEWBY, MELANY STINSON, lawyer, university official; b. Columbus, Ohio, Nov. 21, 1948; d. Byron Briggs and Eleanor Marie (Manly) Stinson; m. R. Dean Newby, June 11, 1983. B.A., Ohio State U., 1971; J.D., U. Cin., 1974, exec. program cert., 1982. Bar: Ohio 1974, U.S. Dist. Ct. Ohio, 1974, U.S. Supreme Ct. 1980. Asst. city solicitor civil div. City of Cin., 1974-78; dir. legal services U. Cin., 1978—; vol. Vol. Law Poor Found., Cin., 1983—. Trustee Travelers Aid Internat. Inst., Cin., 1979-84, Heart Assn., Cin., 1980—; mem. Leadership Cin., Greater Cin. C. of C., 1981-82; chmn. Bruggeman Scholarship Com., 1982—. Mem. Ohio Bar Assn., Cin. Bar Assn., Nat. Assn. Coll. and Univ. Attys. (arrangements chmn. 1984, membership co-chmn. 1982-84, bd. dirs. 84-87, mem. nominations com. 1984-85, co-chmn. publs. 1984-85), U. Cin. Alumni Assn. (bd. govs., sec. 1983—), Leadership Cin. Alumni Assn. (bd. dirs., sec. 1983—). Kappa Alpha Theta Alumnae (adv. bd. 1978-82). Club: Clifton Track (Cin.) (pres. 1979-81). Home: 2136-D Madison Rd Cincinnati OH 45208 Office: 300 Adminstrn Bldg U Cin Clifton Ave Cincinnati OH 45221

NEWBY, RICHARD PROUTY, clergyman; b. Des Moines, Apr. 13, 1923; s. James Moore and Bertha (Prouty) N.; B.A., William Penn Coll., 1945, D.D. (hon.), 1985; m. Doris Prignitz, June 1, 1945; children—Darlene Ann, James Richard, John Charles. Pastor Soc. of Friends Ch.; pastor, Pleasant Plain, Iowa, 1945-47, Mpls., 1947-58, Muncie (Ind.) Friends Ch., 1958-67, University Friends Ch., Wichita, Kans., 1967-73, College Ave. Friends Ch., Oskaloosa, Iowa, 1973-74, Friends Meml. Ch., Muncie, 1974-85; presiding clk. Iowa Yearly Meeting of Friends, 1955-58; asst. presiding clk. Ind. Yearly Meeting of Friends, 1978-82, presiding clk., 1982—; chmn. bd. on Christian edn. Friends United Meeting, 1955-66; pres. Delaware County Council Chs., 1965-66, Wichita Council Chs., 1970-71. Chmn. Muncie Mayor's Com. on Human Relations, 1962-63, Muncie Human Rights Commn., 1981-83; pres. Christian Ministries Delaware County (Ind.), 1983-84. Bd. dirs. Am. Friends Service Com., 1960-64; trustee William Penn Coll., 1955-58, Earlham Coll., 1962-67, 77-84, William Penn Coll., 1984—; Friends U., Wichita, 1970-74; bd. advisers Earlham Sch. Religion, 1976-84; chmn. Muncie Human Relations Com., 1982-83. Recipient award of merit William Penn Coll., 1957. Mem. Delaware County Ministerial Assn. (pres. 1961-62). Home and Office: PO Box 230 Muncie IN 47305

NEWCOMB, ROBERT DOUGLAS, optometrist, clinician, educator; b. Middletown, Ohio, Jan. 8, 1947; s. Huber Charles and Betty Marie (Martz) N.; m. Pamela Kristine Yerian, June 16, 1984. Student Ohio No. U., 1965-67; B.S. in Physiol. Optics, Ohio State U., 1970, O.D., 1971; M.P.H., U. Ala.-Birmingham, 1975. Diplomate Nat. Bd. Examiners Optometry; lic. optometrist Ohio, Fla. Chief optometry service VA Med. Ctr., Birmingham, Ala., 1976-80; chief optometry service VA Outpatient Clinic, Columbus, Ohio, 1980—; assoc. prof. optometry, U. Ala., Birmingham, 1976-80; asst. clin. prof. optometry, Ohio State U., Columbus, 1980—; cons. Nat. Bd. Examiners in Optometry, 1981—, Ohio State Bd. Optometry, Council on Optometric Edn., Council on Clin. Optometric Care; planning bd. VA Med. Dist. 13, 1982—; invited lectr. profl. orgns. in field; adv. com. Optometric Assisting Tech., Columbus Tech. Inst.; chmn. facility planning com. Columbus VA Outpatient Clinic. Co-editor textbook: Public Health and Community Optometry, 1980 (best project award Am. Pub. Health Assn. 1982); contbr. articles in field. Active Big Bros. Greater Jacksonville (Fla.), 1972-74; mem. United Methodist Ch., Franklin, Ohio, 1960—. Served as lt. USN, 1971-74. Robert Wood Johnson health policy fellow candidate, U. Ala.-Birmingham, 1977; recipient Spurgeon Eure best lecture award So. Congress Optometry, 1976; Delbert L. Pugh award nominee Ohio Hosp. Assn., 1984; Achievement award VA, 1983. Fellow Am. Acad. Optometry (program com. 1982—); mem. Am. Optometric Assn. (editorial bd. 1977-83, Optometric Recognition award 1980), Am. Pub. Health Assn. Nat. Assn. VA Optometrists (treas. 1976—, Pres. 1976-83), Ohio Optometric Assn. (treas. zone 12, 1984—), Assn. Mil. Surgeons U.S., Epsilon Psi Epsilon (trustee 1982—). Republican. Avocations: Tennis; music.

NEWELL, DAVID R., state legislator; b. Oakland, Calif., Oct. 14, 1946; A.A., Norfolk Jr. Coll., 1967; B.S., U. Nebr.-Omaha, 1971, postgrad.; m. Arlene Paider, Mar. 30, 1974; children—John, Sarah. Mem. Nebr. Legislature, 1976—, chmn. urban affairs; chmn. Nebr. State Dem. Party-Former state pres., past nat. committeeman Young Democrats; adminstrv. asst. to dir. adminstrv. services, state exec. and central coms. Democratic Party. Served with U.S. Army, 1967-69; Vietnam. Mem. Am. Legion, Phi Alpha Theta. Address: Room 1402 State Capitol Lincoln NE 68509

NEWELL, JUDITH MAY, medical laboratory administrator, educator; b. Princeton, Ill., July 16, 1944; d. LaRue Parker and Nell May (Prather) Stratton; m. Carlier J. Lauer, Oct. 15, 1962 (div. June 8, 1972); m. James W. Newell, Sept. 16, 1973; children—Carlier J. Lauer, Eric Andrew Lauer. B.S., No. Ill. U., 1972; cert. Med. Tech., Luth. Gen. Hosp., 1973; M.A., Central Mich. U., 1985. Cert. med. tech. Staff tech. Community Hosp., Munster, Ind., 1973-75, supr., 1975-76; sr. tech. St. Margaret Hosp., Hammond, Ind., 1976-80, supr., 1980-82; dir. med. lab. Ind. U., Gary, 1982—; cons., adj. instr. St. Margaret Hosp., Hammond, 1982—. Bd. dirs. Am. Cancer Soc., 1984. Named Outstanding Tchr. Ind. U. Alumni Assn., 1983, 84; nominated for Excellence in Tchg. Ind. U. faculty, 1984. Mem. Ind. Soc. Med. Techs. (pres. 1984—), Am. soc. Med. Techs., Omicron. Avocations: stitchery; gardening. Home: 7131 Stateline St Hammond IN 46324

NEWHOUSE, CAROLINE LEE, career services administrator; b. Evansville, Ind., May 31, 1957; d. Jerald Alan and Rosemarie (Wiseman) N. B.A. in Psychology, Ind. U., 1979, M.S. in Coll. Adminstrn., 1984. Divisional jr. buyer Macy's Corp., Kansas City, Mo., 1979-80; asst. coordinator residence life Ind. U., Bloomington, 1980-82, career counselor ednl. placement, 1983-84; dir. admissions Harlaxton Coll., Grantham, Eng., 1982-83; asst. dir. career services Beloit Coll., Wis., 1984—, adviser Beta Theta Pi frat. Recipient Asst. Buyer award Macy's, 1979. Mem. Midwest Coll. Placement Assn. (standing com.), Nat. Assn. Student Personnel Adminstrs., Am. Coll. Personnel Assn., Ind. U. Alumni Club. Avocations: traveling; reading; swimming. Office: Beloit Coll Box 185 Beloit WI 53511

NEWLON, CAROL SHAW, molecular genetics educator; b. Winter Haven, Fla., Nov. 28, 1944; d. Robert Leon and Edna Ruth (Peacock) Shaw; m. Michael C. Newlon, June 5, 1971. B.A., U. Fla., 1965; Ph.D., MIT, 1971. Postdoctoral fellow U. Wash., Seattle, 1972-73; asst. prof. molecular genetics U. Iowa, Iowa City, 1974-79, assoc. prof., 1979-85; assoc. prof. microbiology N.J. Med. Sch., Newark, 1985—; mem. study sect. NIH, 1980-84. Editorial bd. Jour. Yeast, 1984—. NIH grantee, 1974—. Mem. Genetics Soc. Am. (bd. dirs. 1986—), Am. Soc. Microbiology, AAAS. Democrat. Avocations: bird watching. Office: Dept Microbiology NJ Med Sch Newark NJ

NEWMAN, ANABEL POWELL, reading educator, educational administrator; b. Mabton, Wash., Mar. 9, 1930; d. Glen Rex and Iva D. (Williams) Powell; m. Philip Edward Newman, June 10, 1959. Student U. Wash., 1947-48; B.A., Principia Coll., 1951; student Sorbonne, 1957; M.A., U. Iowa, 1962; Ed.D., SUNY-Buffalo, 1971. Tchr., Cedar Rapids, Iowa, 1962; research assoc., instr., lectr. SUNY-Buffalo, 1966-71; asst. prof. reading edn. Ind. U., Bloomington, 1971-73, assoc. prof., 1973—, dir. Reading Practicum Ctr., 1974—; dir. literacy instr. tng., 1976—, asst. dean for adminstrn. Sch. Edn., 1982-84; cons. adult edn.; nat. cons. Coalition for Literacy. Faculty Research grantee, summer 1975; Spencer Found. grantee, 1976-77. Mem. Internat. Reading Assn. (runner-up Outstanding Dissertation award 1972), Nat. Reading Council, Nat. Assn. Adult Pub. Sch. Educators, Ind. Assn. Adult Pub. Sch. Educators, Ind. Reading Profs. Assn., AAUP, Pi Lambda Theta (Ella Victoria Dobbs Outstanding Research award 1973, Disting. Service award (1980-81), Delta Kappa Gamma. Author numerous ednl. studies, reports, manuals, student and tchr. guides; contbr. articles to profl. jours. Office: Edn 211 Ind U Bloomington IN 47405

NEWMAN, DAVID WILLIAM, plant physiology and biochemistry educator; b. Pleasant Grove, Utah, Oct. 26, 1933; s. Frank Byrd and Edna (Holdaway) N.; m. JoAnne Marie Slighting, May 16, 1956; 1 son, Steven D. B.S., U. Utah, 1955, M.S., 1957, Ph.D., 1960; postgrad. Oak Ridge Inst. Nuclear Studies. Research fellow U. Utah, 1956-59; asst. prof. Miami U., Oxford, Ohio, 1960-66, assoc. prof., 1966-74, prof. dept. botany, 1974—. Served with U.S. Army, 1957-62. NSF grantee; indsl. research grantee; finalist nat./internat. photog. contests. Fellow Ohio Acad. Scis.; Mem. AAAS, Am. Chem. Soc., Am. Soc. Plant Physiologists, Am. Oil Chemists Soc., Société Francaise de Physiologie Vegetaie, Friends of Photography, Calumet Photog. Soc. (charter), Internat. Platform Assn., Sierra Club, Phi Beta Kappa, Sigma Xi, Phi Kappa Phi, Phi Sigma. Editor: Instrumental Methods of Experimental Biology, 1964; contbr. articles to profl. jours. Home: 3713 Pamajera Dr Oxford OH 45056 Office: Botany Dept Miami U Oxford OH 45056

NEWMAN, JAMES EDWARD, meteorologist, climatologist, educator; b. Brown County, Ohio, Dec. 22, 1920; s. Roy Lee and Lola Rae (Schweickart) N.; m. Persis Haas, July 17, 1949; children—C. Shelley, Roy C., Arnold H. B.S., Ohio State U., 1947, M.S., 1949; postgrad. Purdue U., 1950-53; U. Wis., 1957-58; U.S. Weather Bur., 1959. Cert. profl. meteorologist. Asst. agronomist, Ohio Agrl. Experimental Station, 1947-49; asst. prof. agronomy Purdue U., West Lafayette, Ind., 1949-59, assoc. prof., 1960-67, prof. bioclimatology, 1968—; vis. prof. hort. scis. U. Calif., 1965-66; vis. scientist U. Alaska, 1970; editor-in-chief Agrl. Meteorology, 1973-76; vis. prof. Wye Coll. U. London, 1977. Served with Army Air Force, World War II, 1942-46. Decorated Meritorious Service citation. Fellow AAAS, Am. Soc. Agronomy (soils and crops award 1965), Ind. Acad. Sci.; mem. Internat. Soc. Biometeorology (pres. elect 1984-87, agrl. meteorology award 1976), Am. Meteorol. Soc., Sigma Xi. Methodist. Club: Optimist. Contbr. chpts. to textbooks, articles to profl. jours. Home: 1635 Potomac Ave Lafayette IN 47905 Office: Dept Agronomy Purdue U West Lafayette IN 47907

NEWMAN, JOHN KEVIN, classics educator; b. Bradford, England, Aug. 17, 1928; came to U.S., 1969, naturalized, 1984; s. Willie and Agnes (Shee) N.; m. Frances Marilyn Stickney, Sept. 8, 1970; children—Alexandra, John, Victoria. B.A. in Classics, Exeter Coll., Oxford U., 1946-50, B.A. in Russian, 1952, M.A., 1953; Ph.D., Bristol U., Eng., 1967. Classics master Downside Sch., Somerset, Eng., 1955-69; assoc. prof. classics U. Ill., Urbana, 1970-80, prof., 1980—, chmn. dept., 1981-85; mem. Sr. Common Room, Corpus Christi Coll., Oxford, 1985-86. Author: Augustus and the New Poetry, 1967; Latin Compositions, 1976; Pindar's Art, 1984; The Classical Epic Tradition, 1985. Editor Jour. Ill. Classical Studies, 1981—. Recipient Silver medal Vatican, 1960, 63, 66. Mem. Am. Philol. Assn. Roman Catholic. Home: 703 W Delaware St Urbana IL 61801 Office: Dept Classics U ILL 707 S Mathews St Urbana IL 61801

NEWMAN, LEONARD JAY, retail jewel merchant, gemologist; b. Milw., Oct. 25, 1927; s. David and Pia Goldie (Smith) N.; m. Louise Shainberg, Jan. 14, 1951; children—Shelley, Marty, Alan, Heidi, Dee. B.S., Purdue U.; postgrad. Washington U, St. Louis. Owner, mgr. Newman's Diamond Ctr., Jasper, Ind., 1951—; tchr. The Jasper Ctr., Ind., 1970-80. Bd. dirs. VUJC Found., State Bd. Health Systems Agy., sub area Health Systems Agy.; 1st v.p. Vincennes Univ. Found.; past pres. Jasper Community Arts Commn.; pres. Friends of Arts; commnr. Boy Scouts Am.; mem. Dubois County Mental Health Assn.; pres. Jasper Edn. Fund. Recipient Outstanding Citizenship award Purdue U. Alumni Assn., 1980. Mem. Nat. Assn. Jewelry Appraisers (sr.), Ind. Jewelers Orgn., Jasper C. of C., Jaycees (Rooster, past pres., past nat. bd. dirs., Disting. Service award 1957). Lodges: Lions, Masons, Shriners (past pres.). Home: 923 McArthur Jasper IN 47546 Office: Newman's Diamond Ctr 3D Plaza Jasper IN 47546

NEWMAN, PAUL, linguistics educator; b. Jacksonville, Fla., Mar. 7, 1937. B.A., U. Pa., 1958, M.A., 1961; Ph.D., UCLA, 1967. Asst. prof. linguistics, then assoc. prof. Yale U., New Haven, 1966-73; prof. Bayero U., Kano, Nigeria, 1972-75, U. Leiden, Netherlands, 1975-82, Ind. U., Bloomington, 1983—. Author: Tera Folktale Texts, 2 vols., 1968; A Grammar of Tera: Transformational Syntax and Texts, 1970; (with Anthony Kirk-Greene) West African Travels and Adventures: Two Autobiographical Narratives from Northern Nigeria, 1971; The Kanakuru Language, 1974; (with Roxana Ma Newman) Modern Hausa-English Dictionary, 1977; The Classification of Chadic within Afroasiatic, 1980. Editor spl. Chadic issue Jour. African Langs., 1971; (with Roxana Ma Newman) Papers in Chadic Linguistics, 1977. Contbr. articles to profl. publs. Named to Personal chair in African Linguisitcs, Juliana, Queen of the Netherlands, 1979. Office: Ind U Dept Linguistics Bloomington IN 47405

NEWMAN, PHILIP ROBERT, psychologist; b. Utica, N.Y., Dec. 17, 1942; s. Samuel M. and Sara Rose (Dumain) N.; A.B. with high distinction, U. Mich., 1964, Ph.D. (Woodrow Wilson fellow 1964, Univ. fellow 1964-66, Horace H. Rackham Research scholar 1969-71), 1971; m. Barbara Miller, June 12, 1966; children—Samuel Asher, Abraham Levy, Rachel Florence. Asst. prof. psychology U. Mich., Ann Arbor, 1971-72; asst. prof. psychology Union Coll., Schenectady, 1972-76; dir. human behavior curriculum project Am. Psychol. Assn., Washington, 1977-81; pvt. practice psychology, Columbus, Ohio, 1978—; cons. Agy. Instructional TV, 1979. Mem. Am. Psychol. Assn., Internat. Assn. Applied Psychology, Internat. Sociol. Assn., Soc. Psychol. Study Social Issues, Am. Sociol. Assn., Nat. Council Family Relations, Groves Conf. Marriage and Family, Eastern Psychol. Assn., Midwestern Psychol. Assn., Western Psychol. Assn., N.Y. Acad. Sci., Gerontol. Soc. Am., Am. Orthopsychiat. Assn., Phi Beta Kappa, Sigma Xi, Phi Kappa Phi. Author: (with B. Newman) Development through Life: A Psychosocial Approach, 1975, 2d edit., 1979, 3d edit., 1984; Infancy and Childhood Development and Its Contexts, 1978; An Introduction to the Psychology of Adolescence, 1979; Personality Development through the Life Span, 1980; Living: The Process of Adjustment, 1981; Understanding Adulthood, 1983; Principles of Psychology, 1983; Adolescent Developments, 1986; editor: (with B. Newman) Development Through Life: A Case Study Approach, 1976. Home and Office: 1969 Chatfield Rd Columbus OH 43221

NEWMAN, RICHARD LANCASTER, aviation consultant, educator; b. Oakland, Calif., Mar. 9, 1938; s. Richard Lancaster and Eleanor June (Wagstaff) N.; m. Marianne Mason Large, Mar. 21, 1964 (div. 1980); 1 child, James Lancaster; m. Angela Maria Henriques, Oct. 13, 1984. B.S., Rensselaer Poly. Inst., 1960; postgrad. Pa. State U., 1960-62; M.S., Purdue U., 1974. Engr. Douglas Aircraft, Santa Monica, Calif., 1962-66; pilot Northwest Airlines, St. Paul, 1966; sr. engr. Allison div. Gen. Meotors, Indpls., 1967-74; prin. Crew Systems, Yellow Springs, Ohio, 1974—; adj. asst. prof. Ohio State U., Columbus, 1982-85; adj. instr. U. Dayton, Ohio, 1975-79; adviser Internat. Civil Aviation Orgn., UN, Sao Jose dos Campos, Brazil, 1984. Co-patentee vibration damping coatings. Author research articles. Adviser Vol. Adv. Corps, Indpls., 1970-73; mem. Sugar Creek Ski Patrol, Bellbrook, Ohio, 1983-85. Named Flight Instr. of Yr., Central region, FAA, 1978. Fellow AIAA (assoc., sect. chmn. 1966-85), Can. Aero. and Space Inst. (assoc.), Soc. Exptl. Test Pilots (assoc.); mem. System Safety Soc. (sr.), Human Factors Soc. Avocations: Skiing; soaring. Office: Crew Systems Cons PO Box 481 Yellow Springs OH 45387

NEWMAN, ROBERT ALTON, real estate developer; b. Portsmouth, Ohio, Jan. 19, 1932; s. William Albert and Bethel (Holley) N.; m. Frances Carolyn Faine, Dec. 22, 1953. Student U. Cin., 1949-53. Constrn. mgr. William A. Newman Co., Portsmouth, 1955-62; owner, contractor Newman Constrn. Co., Portsmouth, 1962-67; owner, designer Bob Newman & Assocs., Portsmouth, 1967-77; exec. v.p. Scioto Econ. Devel. Corp., Portsmouth, 1977-83; mng. dir. Ohio Southland Devel. Group, New Boston, Ohio, 1983—; lectr. in field. Contbr. articles to profl. publs. Founding pres. Scioto Valley Festival Assn., Portsmouth, 1964-66; founding officer River Days Festival, Portsmouth, 1964; founding bd. dirs. Portsmouth Area Arts Council, 1965; pres. Portsmouth Sesquicentennial Celebration, 1965. Served with U.S. Army, 1953-55. Recipient Restaurant Design award Food Service Mag., 1968, Nat. Case Study award Nat. Assn. County Ofcls., 1979, 80, 81, 82, Nat. Excellence award HUD, 1982. Mem. Am. Inst. Building Design (Comml. Remodeling-Bank award 1970), Am. Soc. Landscape Architects, Am. Soc. Interior Designers, Urban Land Inst., Am. Econ. Devel. Council, Portsmouth Jaycees (pres. 1963). Baptist. Lodge: Rotary, Masons. Home: 4425 Hickory Ln Portsmouth OH 45662

NEWMAN, WARREN P., company executive; b. Harrisonburg, Va., Nov. 1, 1932; s. Joseph Armfield and Effie Ester (Nesselrodte) N.; m. Edith Vera Komatz, Oct. 20, 1951; children—Sherry Newman Spenzer, Connie Newman Litz, Wyatt, Roxanne. Pres. Newman Co., Avon Lake, Ohio, 1953—. Mem. Nat. Rifle Assn. Lodge: Masons (32d degree). Avocations: hunting; lapidary; gardening. Home and Office: 31793 Lake Rd Avon Lake OH 44012

NEWNUM, RAYMOND LAVERN, internist; b. Kingman, Ind., June 18, 1925; s. Robert P. and Sylvia Grace (Alward) N.; student Purdue U., 1943-44; B.S. in Anatomy and Physiology, Ind. U., Bloomington, 1948, M.D., 1951; M.Sc., U. Minn., 1958; m. Betty Lou Coffing, Dec. 20, 1944; children—Kathleen Sue Newnum Roetzer, Janice Marie Newnum Sbrocchi, Betsy Rae, Paul Douglas, Lisa Dawn Newnum Pfleger. Rotating intern Ind. U., 1951-52; gen. practice medicine, Hagerstown, Ind., 1952-55; resident in internal medicine Mayo Found., Rochester, Minn., 1955-58; cons. in internal medicine Carle Clinic, Urbana, Ill., 1958-61; practice medicine specializing in internal medicine, Evansville, Ind., 1961-80; asst. dean, dir. Evansville Center for Med. Edn., Ind. U. Sch. Medicine; pres. staff St. Mary's Hosp., 1970-71, chief of medicine, 1965-67, clin. instr. medicine, 1973-77, cons. internal medicine, 1961-77; asst. prof. medicine Ind. U. Served with USNR, 1943-47. Diplomate Am. Bd. Internal Medicine. Fellow A.C.P. (life); mem. AMA, Ind., Vanderburgh County med. socs., Evansville, Ind. Soc. Internal Medicine (bd. dirs.), Am. Soc. Internal Medicine. Mem. Ch. Christian Fellowship. Home: 6710 Washington Ave Evansville IN 47715 Office: PO Box 3287 Evansville IN 47732

NEWPHER, JAMES ALFRED, JR., management consultant; b. New Brighton, Pa., Nov. 14, 1930; s. James Alfred and Olive Myrtle (Houlette) N.; B.S., U. Pa., 1952; M.B.A., Wharton Sch. U. Pa., 1957; m. Mildred Taylor, Aug. 23, 1953. Indsl. engr., Corning Glass Works (N.Y.), 1957-58, plant supr., 1958-60, prodn. supt., 1960-61, plant mgr., 1961-63, dept. mgr. advance products, 1963-64; asso. Booz, Allen & Hamilton, Inc., Chgo., 1964-69; v.p., mng. officer Lamalie Assos., Chgo., 1969-73; pres., chief exec. officer Newpher & Co., Inc., Chgo., 1973—; dir. D.B. Corkey Co., Design Tech., Inc. Served with USN, 1951-56. Decorated Purple Heart. Mem. Naval Res. Assn., Inst. Mgmt. Cons., Res. Officers Assn. Presbyn. Club: Metropolitan Chgo. Home: 1655 We-Go Trail Deerfield IL 60015 Office: 2215 York Rd Suite 202 Oakbrook IL 60521

NEWREN, EDWARD FRANK, human resource development training educator; b. Chgo., May 13, 1933; s. Edward Frank and Margaret (Jones) N.; m. Mary Rita Connolly, Sept. 10, 1955; children—Edward David, Timothy Joseph, Catherine, David Gerard, Jon William, Rita Marie. Student St. Mary's Coll., 1952-54; B.A., DePaul U., 1957; M.Ed., Chgo. State U., 1963; Ed.D., Ind. U., 1975. Instr., program supr. Ind. U., Bloomington, 1966-69; asst. prof. U. Minn., Mpls., 1969-71, U. Mich., Ann Arbor, 1971-75; assoc. prof., chmn. dept. Miami U., Oxford, Ohio, 1975-79, prof. instructional tech. human resources devel. tng., chmn., 1979—. Author: Japanese Science Films, 1973. Contbr. articles to profl. jours. U.S. Office Edn. grantee U. Okla., 1969; Mt. Scholastica Coll. grantee, 1966; NDEA grantee Ind. U., 1965. Mem. Am. Soc. Tng. and Devel., Assn. Ednl. Communications and Tech. (pres. info. systems div. 1974, exec. bd. 1971-74), Ohio Ednl. Library and Media Assn. (chmn. higher edn. div. 1981-82) Roman Catholic. Home: 718 Melissa Dr Oxford OH 45056 Office: Dept Ednl Media Miami U Oxford OH 45056

NEWSOM, FRANCIS CARTER, physician; b. Union Point, Ga., May 14, 1918; s. Erle Thornton and Ethel (Perry) N.; m. Mary Elizabeth Varner, Mar. 20, 1943; children—Barbara Ann, Mary Carter. Student, U. Ga., 1935-37, Emory U., 1939-40; M.D., Med. Coll. Ga., 1943. Diplomate Am. Bd. Psychiatry and Neurology. Intern U.S. Naval Hosp., Portsmouth, Va., 1944; resident in psychiatry VA Hosp., Topeka, Kans., 1946-49; fellow Menninger Sch. Psychiatry, 1946-49; staff psychiatrist Topeka State Hosp., 1949-50; practice medicine specializing in psychiatry, Wichita, Kans., 1951—; clin. asst. prof. psychiatry U. Kans. Sch. Medicine, Wichita, 1974—; cons. VA Med. and Regional Office Ctr., 1951—; active med. staff St. Francis Regional Med. Ctr., 1951—; pres. med. staff St. Francis Hosp., 1968. Served to lt. (j.g.) USN, 1944-46, 50-51. Fellow Am. Psychiat. Assn.; mem. Kans. Psychiat. Soc., AMA, Kans. Med. Soc., Med. Soc. Sedgwick County (bd. dirs. 1970-73). Republican. Episcopalian. Avocations: spectator sports; music; dancing; theatre. Home: 3807 E Funston St Wichita KS 67218 Office: Morrow & Newsom 3310 E Douglas St Wichita KS 67208

NEWSOME, STEVEN CAMERON, librarian; b. Norfolk, Va., Sept. 11, 1952; s. Barbara Newsome; m. Jeanie Suarez, Aug. 26, 1972 (div.); 1 child, Sanya. B.A., Trinity Coll., 1974; M.Librarianship, Emory U., 1975. African-Am. studies reference librarian Northwestern U., Evanston, Ill., 1975-78; legal research asst. Keck, Mahin & Cate, Chgo., 1979; asst. librarian Nat. Clearinghouse for Legal Services, Chgo., 1979; asst. reference librarian U. Ill., Chgo., 1980-82, acting head reference dept., 1982-83; curator Vivian G. Harsh Collection of Afro-Am. History and Lit., Chgo. Pub. Library, Woodson Regional Library, 1983—; cons. Chgo. Reporter, 1977. Reviewer Choice mag., 1985—. Mem. Fleetwood Jourdain Community Theatre, Evanston, Ill., 1981-84; bd. dirs. Black Designers Forum, Chgo., 1985—. Mem. ALA, NAACP, Soc. Am. Archivists, African Am. Mus. Assn., Ill. Library Assn. Democrat. Baptist. Office: Vivian G Harsh Collection of Afro Am History and Lit Woodson Regional Library 9525 S Halsted Chicago IL 60628

NEWTON, ALAN KEITH, management consultant; b. Shelbyville, Ind., Dec. 6, 1957; s. Thomas Henry and Dorothy Lee (Turner) N.; m. Mary Kathryn Hopfinger, Oct. 1, 1983. B.S. in Physics, Ind. U., 1982. Cert. data processor; cert. systems profl. Programmer, Arthur Andersen & Co., Chgo., 1980-81; programmer/analyst SCM Corp., Marion, Ind., 1981-82; analyst State of Ind., Indpls., 1982; analyst Federated Investors, Inc., Pitts., 1982-83; cons. McGladrey Hendrickson & Pullen, Schaumburg, Ill., 1983—. Mem., Shelby County Young Republicans, 1976, Ind. U. Republicans, 1976. Named Life Scout, Boy Scouts Am., 1970. Mem. Data Processing Mgmt. Assn., Assn. Inst. Cert. of Computer Profls., Assn. Systems Mgmt. Republican. Club: Indiana University Tennis. Avocations: Music, basketball, running, tennis. Home: 3935 Nautilus Ln Hanover Park IL 60103 Office: McGladrey Hendrickson & Pullen 1699 E Woodfield Rd Suite 410 Schaumburg IL 60195

NEWTON, ROBERT DALE, counselor; b. Detroit, Apr. 20, 1946; s. Francis W. and Elizabeth J. (Huff) N.; m. Candy P. Fisher, June 8, 1974; children—Shaun, Stephen, Robert, Shayla. B.S. in Mktg., Ferris State Coll., 1974; M.A. in Counseling, Central Mich. U., 1982. Cert. career counselor, Mich., Wis. Social worker, Dept. Social Services, Detroit, 1975-78; tchr. spl. edn. Petoskey High Sch., Mich., 1978-79; dir. career ctr. N. Central Mich. Coll., Petoskey, 1979-84; mental health counselor Community Mental Health Ctr., Petoskey, 1984-85; career counselor Nicolet Coll., Rhinelander, Wis., 1985—. Author: Community Resources, 1982. Coach, Petoskey Youth Soccer Assn., 1984; coach, treas. No. Mich. Youth Soccer League, Petoskey, 1984; founder, pres. Northwoods Wis. Youth Soccer League. Served with U.S. Army, 1965-68; Ger. Mem. Bridge Area Counselors Assn., Am. Assn. Counseling and Devel., Mich. Personnel and Guidance Assn., Am. Bd. Vocat. Experts, Nat. Vocat. Guidance Assn. Methodist. Avocations: bicycling, backpacking, cross-country skiing, reading. Home: 1697 Lake Rd PO Box 144 Rhinelander WI 54501 Office: Nicolet Coll Brown St Rhinelander WI 54501

NEWYEAR, PATRICIA KATHARINE RIDDLE, home economist, food services executive; b. Cleve., Dec. 8, 1941; d. Wilbur David and Katharine

Addelle (Ellis) Riddle; m. Raymond Willis Newyear, June 25, 1966; children—Karl David, Douglas Charles. B.S. in Home Econs., U. Maine, 1963; postgrad. Lake Erie Coll., John Carroll U., Kent State U. Cert. tchr., Ohio. Supr., Hough Bakeries, Cleve., 1962; foods tchr. Willowick Jr. High Sch. (Ohio), 1963-67; foods service tchr. Auburn Career Ctr., Lake County Joint Vocat. Sch., Painesville, Ohio, 1979-84; adult regional cons. State of Ohio, 1980-84; substitute tchr., vocat. cons. Lake County Med. Health Services; food and beverage supr Centre One, Eastlake, Ohio, 1984—. Former sr. warden Grace Episcopal Ch. Mem. Nat. Restaurant Assn. (ednl. mem.), Am. Vocat. Assn., Ohio Vocat. Assn., Greater Cleve. Home Econs. Assn. Hotel, Restaurant and Instl. Edn. Assn. (council), AAUW, Delta Delta Delta. Home: 39058 Johnnycake Ridge Willoughby OH 44094

NEY, EDWARD PURDY, astronomy educator; b. Mpls., Oct. 28, 1920; s. Otto F. and Jessamine (Purdy) N.; m. June Felsing, June 20, 1942; children—John, Judith, Arthur, William. B.Sc., U. Minn., 1942; Ph.D., U. Va., 1946. Research assoc. U. Va., Charlottesville, 1943-46, asst. prof., 1947; asst. prof. astronomy U. Minn., Mpls., 1947-50, assoc. prof., 1950-55, prof., 1955-74, Regents prof., 1974—. Author: Electromagnetism and Relativity, 1962. Contbr. articles to profl. jours. Mem. Nat. Acad. Scis., Internat. Astron. Union, Am. Acad. Arts and Scis., Am. Astron. Soc., Am. Phys. Soc., Am. Geophys. Union. Lodge: Masons. Home: 1925 Penn Ave S Minneapolis MN 55405 Office: U Minn Astronomy Dept 116 Church St SE Minneapolis MN 55455

NEYER, JEROME CHARLES, consulting civil engineer; b. Cin., July 15, 1938; s. Urban Charles and Marie Helen (Hemsteger) N.; m. Judy Ann Drolet, June 17, 1961; children—Janet, Karen. B.C.E., U. Detroit, 1961; M.C.E., U. Wash., 1963. Registered profl. engr. 16 states. Facilities engr. Boeing Co., Seattle, 1961-62; found. engr. Metro Engrs., Seattle, 1962-65; project engr. Hugo N. Helpert Assocs., Detroit, 1965-70; pres. Neyer, Neyer, Tiseo & Hindo, Ltd., Farmington Hills, Mich., 1970—; adj. prof. U. Detroit, 1973-79. Contbr. articles to profl. jours. Chmn. bldg. appeals bd. City of Farmington Hills, 1983; mem. mineral well adv. bd., Lansing, Mich., 1975, mem. constrn. safety standards bd., 1982. Mem. ASCE (br. pres. 1973-74), Engrng. Soc. of Detroit, Cons. Engrs. of Mich. (pres. 1981), Mich. Soc. Profl. Engrs. (bd. dirs. 1980), ASTM. Roman Catholic. Avocations: golfing; tennis. Home: 37972 Tralee Trail Northville MI 48167 Office: Neyer Tiseo & Hindo Ltd 309999 Ten Mile Rd Farmington Hills MI 48024

NG, CHUNG-MAN, marketing executive; b. Canton, China, Aug. 3, 1953; s. Sik-Luen and Wan-Chun (Wong) N.; m. Theresa Kehaulani Looney, May 22, 1977. A.A. in Mech. Engrng., Glendale Community Coll., 1975; B.S. in Mgmt., Ariz. State U., 1978; M. Internat. Mgmt., Am. Grad. Sch. Internat. Mgmt., Glendale, Ariz., 1979. Internat. mktg. coordinator Far East, Hyster Co., Portland, Oreg., 1980-83; internat. mktg. mgr. Far East, AMF Paragon Co., Two Rivers, Wis., 1983—. Adviser Jr. Achievement, 1982. Mem. Soc. Advancement Mgmt., Manitowoc-Two Rivers C. of C., Northeast Wis. World Trade Assn. Home: 2911-I 40th St Two Rivers WI 54241 Office: AMF Paragon Electric Co 606 Parkway Blvd Two Rivers WI 54241

NG, SAMUEL YUWAI, geotechnical consultant; b. Hong Kong, Oct. 21, 1940; s. Fook-Man and Kwok-Ching (Chui) N.; came to U.S., 1963, naturalized, 1977; B.S., Hong Kong Bapt. Coll., 1962; M.S., U. Miss., 1965; Ph.D., Okla. State U., 1970; m. Virginia Thuc-Hoa, Dec. 26, 1970; children—Randy, Debbie. Teaching asst. Hong Kong Bapt. Coll., 1961-62, instr., 1962-63; research asst. U. Miss., 1963-65, research engr., 1965; research asst. dept. civil engring. Okla. State U., 1965-70; geotech. engr., sr. project engr. Soil Exploration Co., St. Paul, 1970-79, prin. engr., dir. research and devel., 1979—; adv. soil mechanics div. dept. civil and mineral engring. U. Minn., 1979-80; pres. Animascope, 1983—. Social activities chmn. Elim Youth Group T.S.T. Bapt. Ch., Hong Kong, 1960-61; deacon Chinese Christian Ch., St. Paul, 1971-77, 79-80, chmn. bd. deacons, 1981—, chmn. evangelism and missions com., 1977-80, adult Sunday Sch. tchr., 1978—. Christian Student scholar and distinction scholar Hong Kong Bapt. Coll., 1961, David J. Carver Jr. Meml. Fund scholar U. Richmond, 1964, U. Miss. fgn. student scholar, 1964; registered profl. engr., Minn., Iowa, Wis., Wyo., N.D., S.D. Mem. ASCE, Transp. Research Bd.-NRC, Internat. Soc. Soil Mechanics and Found. Engring., Engring. Inst. Can., Minn. Geotech. Soc., Sigma Xi, Phi Kappa Phi. Baptist.

NGUYEN, DUY DO, surgeon; b. Hanoi, Viet Nam, May 19, 1942; came to U.S., 1974, naturalized, 1982; s. Thu Van Nguyen and Duc Thi Do; m. Hue Kim Ly, Feb. 22, 1977. B.S., U. Saigon (Viet Nam), 1962, M.D., 1971. Diplomate Am. Bd. Surgery. Intern, Strong Meml. Hosp., Rochester, N.Y., 1974-76; resident Charleston Area Med. Ctr., Charleston, W.Va., 1976-78; instr. surgery U. Wis., Madison, 1978-79; asst. prof. U. Ill., Urbana-Champaign, 1979—; staff surgeon VA Hosp., Danville, Ill., 1979—; chief vascular surgery Vets. Hosp., Danville, 1983—. Fellow ACS; mem. Soc. Clin. Vascular Surgery. Buddhist. Avocations: camping; hunting; fishing. Home: 908 James St Danville IL 61832 Office: VA Hosp Surgery 1900 Main St Danville IL 61832

NICHIPORUK, WALTER, chemist; b. Poland, Sept. 5, 1919; came to U.S., 1946, naturalized, 1952; s. Alex Andrew and Anna Josephine (Radchuk) N.; student U. Warsaw, 1938-39; U. Munich, 1946; M.S., U. Chgo., 1950; m. Elizabeth Kellner, Aug. 14, 1958; 1 son, Brian. Technologist, Enrico Fermi Inst., U. Chgo., 1950-52; chemist Calif. Inst. Tech., Pasadena, 1952-68; research asso. Ariz. State U., Tempe, 1968-74; cons. chemist, Tempe, 1974-77; chemist U.S. Dept. Energy, Argonne, Ill., 1977—; mem. translation panel Plenum Publ. Corp., N.Y.C., 1967-77. Served with UNRRA, Germany, 1945-46. Fellow Meteoritical Soc.; mem. Am. Chem. Soc., Internat. Assn. Geochemistry and Cosmochemistry, Geochem. Soc., Sigma Xi. Asso. editor Bibliography of Meteorites, 1953; translator, reviser (V.V. Cherdyntsev) Raprostranennost' Khimicheskikh Elementov, 1961; contbr. articles to profl. jours. Home: 107 W 65th Lake Dr Westmont IL 60559 Office: US Dept Energy/New Brunswick Lab Argonne IL 60439

NICHOLAS, LEONARD STEPHEN, electrical contractor, county official, educator; b. Tarrytown, N.Y., May 15, 1942; s. Leonard Dominic and Helen Ceclia (Pesaric) N.; m. Beth Ann Ciancio, Mar. 23, 1984 (div. Oct. 1984). Student Akron U., 1963-68; cert. vocat. edn. Kent State U., 1982. Pres. D&L Electric & Heating, Akron, 1978—; tchr. Maplewood Joint Vocat. Sch., Ravenna, Ohio, 1981-83; plant engr. Cuyahoga Machine Co., Akron, 1981-83; electric insp. Summit County Dept. Bldg. Inspection, Akron, 1983—; instr. Akron U., 1983—. Author sr. electricity course, 1983. Served with USAF, 1960-62. Mem. Internat. Assn. Elec. Insps., Aircraft Owners and Pilots Assn. Republican. Club: Akron City. Avocations: motorcycle riding, restoring of cars. Home: 623 E Buchtel Ave Akron OH 44304

NICHOLAS, MICHAEL PATRICK, marketing executive; b. Chgo., May 31, 1947; s. Nicholas Nick and Mary Eileen (Doody) N.; m. Bonnie Francis Zigmont, Sept. 27, 1969; children—Christopher, Carrie. B.S. in Mech. Engring., Ill. Inst. Tech., 1969, M.S. in Indsl. Engring., 1972; M.B.A., U. Chgo., 1980. Gen. foreman Mcc Clayton Mark, Evanston, Ill., 1971-73, supt. prodn., 1973-75, v.p., gen. mgr. div. reconditioning, 1975-78; pres. Center Line, Tulsa, 1978-83; sr. v.p. marketing Mark Controls, Evanston, Ill., 1983—. Mem. Pi Tau Sigma. Republican. Roman Catholic. Avocations: tennis, reading, travel.

NICHOLAS, SUSAN KEHOE, communications and training company executive, consultant; b. Cleve., Dec. 5, 1947; d. John William and Mary Margaret (Swicia) Kehoe; m. Gerald Nicholas, May 15, 1970 (div.); children—Patricia, Mark. B.A., U. Detroit, 1970; M.A., Oakland U., 1980, Ph.D., 1983. Cert. secondary tchr., Mich. Trainer ESL Utica Community Schs., Mich., 1974-78; coordinator program Oakland Univ., Rochester, Mich., 1980-83; adj. prof. mktg. Wayne State Univ., Detroit, 1983-85, U. Mich., Ann Arbor, 1984-85; pres., owner Nicholas & Assocs., Inc., Birmingham, Mich., 1983—; trainer, program designer Gen. Motors, Detroit, 1984—; trainer, cons. Nat. Steel, Ecorse, Mich., 1984—; trainer, speech coach AM Gen., Livonia, Mich., 1984—; presenter Nat. Reading Conf., 1981, 83, Internat. Reading Assn., 1982, Am. Edn. Research Assn., 1982, Conf. on Coll. Composition, 1984. Mem. Am. Soc. for Tng. and Devel., Internat. Assn. Bus. Communicators, Internat. Reading Assn., Pub. Relations Soc. Am. Avocations: reading; travel; dancing. Home and Office: 3858 Lincoln West Birmingham MI 48010

NICHOLLS, MERVILLE LYNN, JR., business educator; b. Decatur, Ill., Mar. 30, 1943; s. Merville L. and Agnes Louise (Larrabee) N.; m. Marea Louise Jolley, Aug. 29, 1964; children—Lynn, Layne. B.S.I.E., Millikin U., 1969; M.R.E., Grace Theol. Sem., 1972; M.Div., 1976; M.S. in Bus. Adminstrn., Saint Francis Coll., Fort Wayne, Ind., 1981, M.B.A. in Fin., 1982. Instr., bookstore mgr. Calvary Bible Coll., Kansas City., Mo., 1972-75; salesman Leiter Real Estate Co., Warsaw, Ind., 1977-79; ins. counselor Wes Miller & Assoc., Warsaw, 1980—; vis. prof. Hong Kong Christian Coll., summer 1979; prof. Ind. Vocat. Tech. Coll., Warsaw, 1979-82; prof. Fort Wayne Bible Coll., Ind., 1982—. Bd. dirs. Child Evangelism Fellowship, Fort Wayne, 1982—, Liberty Hills Assn., Fort Wayne, 1983—; precinct inspector nat. election, Fort Wayne, 1984. Mem. Christian Ministries Mgmt. Assn., Internat. Council on Edn. for Teaching. Republican. Mem. Missionary Ch. Lodge: Kiwanis. Avocations: genealogy; antiques; growing cacti; instrumental and vocal music; French language. Home: 5120 Tall Timber Trail Fort Wayne IN 46804

NICHOLS, DENISE LYNN, nurse; b. St. Louis, Jan. 5, 1952; d. Leroy and Beatrice Vernita (Small) Nichols. B.A. in Liberal Arts, Howard U., 1974. R.N., Mo. Staff nurse Jewish Hosp., St. Louis, 1980—. Baptist. Home: 3007 Capehart Dr Saint Louis MO 63121

NICHOLS, JOHN D., manufacturing company executive; b. Shanghai, China, 1930. B.A., Harvard U., 1953, M.B.A., 1955. Various operating positions Ford Motor Co., 1958-68; dir. fin. controls ITT Corp., 1968-69; exec. v.p. and chief operating officer Aerojet-Gen. Corp., 1969-79; exec. v.p. Ill. Tool Works Inc., Chgo., 1980, pres., 1981—, chief operating officer, 1981-82, chief exec. officer, dir., 1982—. Served to lt. U.S. Army, 1955-58. Office: Ill Tool Works Inc 8501 W Higgins Rd Chicago IL 60631

NICHOLS, ROBERT HASTINGS, lawyer; b. Mpls., Aug. 12, 1941; s. James Hastings and Judith (Beach) N.; m. Jean Christy, Nov. 30, 1968; children—Marc O., Seth J., Ethan D., Rebecca J. A.B., Yale U., 1963; cert. in Pub. Affairs, CORO Found., 1964; J.D., U. Chgo., 1967. Bar: Ill. 1967, U.S. Dist Ct. (no. dist.) Ill. 1967, U.S. Dist. Ct. (ea. dist.) Wis. 1975; U.S. Ct. Appeals (7th cir.) 1972, U.S. Ct. Appeals (8th cir.) 1975, U.S. Ct. Appeals (D.C. cir.) 1976. Ptnr. Cotton, Watt, Jones & King, Chgo., 1967—; chmn. United Airlines Pilots' System Bd. of Adjustment, Elk Grove Village, Ill., 1970—; cons. Govt. of New Zealand, Auckland, 1980; mem. Lawyers Coordinating Com., AFL-CIO. Contbr. articles to legal publs. Mem. ABA, Ill. State Bar Assn., Chgo. Council Lawyers, Chgo. Bar Assn. Democrat. Presbyterian. Club: Columbia Yacht. Home: 1030 E 49th St Chicago IL 60615 Office: Cotton Watt Jones King One IBM Plaza Chicago IL 60611

NICHOLS, THEODORE GEORGE, hosp. engr.; b. Chgo., July 27, 1927; s. Michael Feodor and Sophia (Lewandowski) N.; Student Wright Jr. Coll., 1950-53, Ill. Inst. Tech., 1956-61: m. Barbara McKillip, Mar. 14, 1975; children by previous marriage—Michael J., Julie Ann, Theodore George. Supt., Paschen Contractors, Ill. and Ind., 1947-56; dir. phys. plant Ill. Inst. Tech. Research Inst., Chgo., 1956-69; dir. engring. Rush Presbyn. St. Luke's Med. Center, Chgo., 1969—. Deacon, sec. council St. Andrews Ch., 1966-68; com. chmn., instl. rep. Chgo. Area Council Boy Scouts Am., 1967-68. Mem. Am. Hosp. Assn., Inst. Plant Maintenance, Western Soc. Engrs., Chgo. Supts. Assn. Supervised constrn. 1st indsl. nuclear reactor, 1955. Home: 111 Fernwood Dr Glenview IL 60025 Office: 1753 W Congress Pkwy Chicago IL 60612

NICHOLS, VIRGINIA LLOYD, personnel exec.; b. Inverness, Fla., Feb. 6, 1921; d. Strauss L. and Ida Mae (Baker) Lloyd; B.S., Fla. State Coll. for Women, 1942; m. Ralph Charles Nichols, Dec. 31, 1947; 1 dau., Cheryl Nichols Campbell. Home economist Fla. Power Corp., St. Petersburg, 1942-47; state home economist Graybar Electric Co., Jacksonville, Fla., 1950-55; home economist Ind. and Mich. Electric Co., South Bend, Ind., 1956-58; with Snelling & Snelling, South Bend, 1970-78, asst. mgr., 1973-74, gen. mgr., 1974-75, v.p. ops., 1975-78; pres., gen. mgr. Nichols & Assos., Inc., d/b/a Snelling & Snelling, Merrillville, Ind., 1978—, Highland, Ind., 1981—, mem. nat. exec. council Snelling & Snelling, 1981-82, nat. exec. com., regional rep., 1981—. Bd. dirs. Family and Childrens Center, South Bend, 1962-70; bd. dirs. Better Bus. Bur. N.W. Ind., 1981—, exec. bd., treas., 1983—; chmn. Joan E. Snelling Meml. Com.; mem. adv. bd. Projects with Industry, Goodwill Industries Michiana, South Bend, 1975-78; mem. Republican Precinct Com., 1958-70; deacon Sunnyside Presbyterian Ch., 1962-66. Recipient nat. citation Goodwill Industries, 1976, numerous awards Snelling and Snelling. Mem. N.W. Ind. Personnel Assn. (v.p. 1980-82), Nat. Assn. Personnel Cons., Ind. Assn. Personnel Cons., Am. Soc. Personnel Adminstrn., Smithsonian Instn. Soc., Nat. Audubon Soc., Bus. and Profl. Womens Club. Clubs: Conservation of Kosciuosko County, Conservation of Ind. Author: Eating Right Can Be Fun, 1955. Office: 1000 E 80th Place Twin Towers Suite 302S Merrillville IN 46410

NICHOLSON, DAVID LEE, state senator; b. Richmond, Ind., Dec. 6, 1947; s. Elmer William and Velma Sturm (Robinson) N.; m. Charlene Lucille Cougill, Mar. 9, 1968; children—D. Larry, C. Angela, C. William. B.A., Ind. U.-East, Ind.U.-Purdue U.-Indpls., 1977; student Ball State U., 1983—. Mgr., Plaza Lane Restaurant, Connorsville, Ind., 1973-74; optician H&T Optical Co., Richmond, Ind., 1974; gen. laborer Manpower Inc., Richmond, Ind., 1977-78; group leader Champion Target Co., Richmond, Ind., 1978-83; mem. Ind. State Senate, 1982—. Democratic precinct committeeman, 1977—. Served with USMC, 1966-69, USMCR, 1969-74. Decorated Purple Heart. Democrat. Lutheran. Clubs: Marine Corps League, Internat. Order Odd Fellows. Office: Senate Statehouse Indianapolis IN 46204

NICHOLSON, DWIGHT ROY, physicist, educator; b. Racine, Wis., Oct. 3, 1947; s. Forrest Arlyn and Johanna Jacoba (Bergsma) N.; m. Jane Alice Mechling, June 14, 1969. B.S., U. Wis., 1969; Ph.D., U. Calif.-Berkeley, 1975. Research assoc. and lectr. U. Colo., Boulder, 1975-78, asst. prof., 1978; asst. prof. U. Iowa, Iowa City, 1978-81, assoc. prof. dept. physics and astronomy, 1981—; cons. Los Alamos Nat. Lab., 1977—, Sci. Applications, Inc., Boulder, 1976-78. Author: Introduction to Plasma Theory, 1983; author tech. articles. Johnson's Wax scholar, 1965-67; NSF trainee, 1969-72; univ. faculty scholar U. Iowa, 1983—. Mem. Am. Phys. Soc., AAAS, Union Radio Scientifique Internationale, Am. Geophys. Union. Home: 402 Kimball Rd Iowa City IA 52240 Office: Physics and Astronomy Dept Univ Iowa Iowa City IA 52242

NICHOLSON, EVELYN JUNE TANTYPE, academic counselor; b. East St. Louis, Ill., Aug. 27, 1933; d. Luther Tantype and Charlotte Ruth (King) Howard; m. Henry Nicholson, July 27, 1957; children—Scarlet June, Corwin Van, Octavia Claudette. B.S., So. Ill. U., 1966, M.S., 1969. X-ray technologist Jewish Hosp., St. Louis, 1954-58; tchr. Cahokia Sch. Dist. (Ill.), 1966-70, counselor, Centreville, Ill., 1969-70; coordinator counseling/advisement State Community Coll., East St. Louis, Ill., 1970—. Active voter registration drive, East St. Louis, 1982-83. Mem. Am. Assn. Counseling Devel., Am. Coll. Personnel Assn., Nat. Assn. Smithsonian Instn. Office: State Community Coll 601 Thompson Blvd East Saint Louis IL 62201

NICHOLSON, LAUREL ANNE, communication consultant; b. Chgo., June 6, 1950; d. Melvin J. and Rita Helen (Goldman) Stern; m. Donald D. Nicholson, Apr. 8, 1972; children—Emily, Ellen, Benjamin. B.S. in Journalism, Bowling Green State U., 1972. Editor and prodn. coordinator McDonald's Corp., Oak Brook, Ill., 1972-75; owner, pres. Nicholson Communications, Elmhurst, Ill., 1975-82; communication cons. The Wyatt Co., Chgo., 1982—. Recipient Photography award of merit Soc. Publ. Designers, N.Y.C., 1975. Mem. Internat. Assn. Bus. Communicators, Chgo. Women's Network (sec., editor 1984), Women's Am. Orgn. Rehab. Through Tng. (calendar chairperson 1982). Club: Met. (Chgo.). Home: Elmhurst IL Office: The Wyatt Co 233 S Wacker Dr Suite 5600 Chicago IL 60606

NICHOLSON, MARION CRAWFORD, mayor, mfrs. rep.; b. College Park, Ga., Jan. 31, 1917; s. William Malcolm and Marion Melissa (Neely) N.; certificate aero. engring. Ga. Inst. Tech., 1940; m. Catherine Vaughn Wise, Apr. 5, 1947; children—Catherine Marion, Barbara Ann. With Atlanta Constn. Pub. Co., 1937-40; sta. mgr. Eastern Air Lines, St. Louis, Memphis and Lake Charles, La., 1940-53; owner, operator M.C. Nicholson & Assocs., mfrs. sales rep., St. John, 1953—, Aetna Metal Products Co., St. John, 1973—; councilman, St. John, 1974, mayor, 1974-77, 83—. Pres. PTA concil Normandy Sch. System, 1966-67. Mem. Nat. Assn. Mfrs. Agts., St. Louis Bd. Elec. Trade. Democrat. Presbyterian. Address: 3901 Engler Ave St Louis MO 63114

NICHOLSON, STUART ADAMS, lawyer, ecologist/environmental scientist; b. Albany, N.Y., May 24, 1941; s. Kenneth Gerald and Gladyce (Wenz) N.; children—Laura Ellice, Paul Michael. B.S. in Biology, SUNY-Albany, 1964, M.S. in Biology, 1965; Ph.D. in Botany, U. Ga., 1970; J.D., U. N.D., 1983. Bar: N.D. 1983, Minn. 1984. Research assoc. atomospheric sci. SUNY-Albany, 1970-71; asst. prof. biology State U. Coll., Fredonia, N.Y., 1971-75; ecologist Environment Cons. Inc., Mayville, N.Y., 1975-76; lectr. biology U. So. Pacific, Suva, Fiji, 1976-78; sr. research analyst St. Lawrence-Eastern Ont. Commn., Watertown, N.Y., 1979-80; sr. research scientist U. N.D., Grand Forks, 1980-82, assoc. dir., 1982-83, program dir., 1983-84; atty. Jim Olds Ltd., Mpls., 1984—; cons. firms, corps., 1973-79; sr. practitioner Legal Aid Assn. N.D., Grand Forks, 1982-83; mem. Voluntary Income Tax Assistance, Grand Forks, 1981; tchr. U. Ga., State U. Coll., Fredonia, U. South Pacific, Empire State Coll., 1965-67, 71-79. Contbr. articles to profl. jours. Reviewer Bull. of Torrey Bot. Club, 1974, 83. Ecology resource advisor N.Y. State Dept. Environ. Conservation, Albany, 1973; bd. dirs. Chautauqua County Environ. Def. Council, Jamestown, 1973-75, Grand Forks Food Coop., Grand Forks, 1984; advisor govtl. orgns., 1972-84; organizer Biology Chautauqua Lake symposium, 1974. Grantee U. South Pacific, 1976, 77, 78, NSF, 1974; State U. Coll. fellow, 1972-75; N.D. Pub. Service Commn. research contract 1983, Office Surface Mining research contract, 1982. Mem. ABA, Ecol. Soc. Am., Brit. Ecol. Soc., Minn. State Bar Assn., State Bar Assn. N.D., Sigma Xi, Phi Sigma, Beta Beta Beta. Home: Box 201312 Bloomington MN 55420 Office: Jim Olds Ltd 10800 Lyndale Ave S Minneapolis MN 55420

NICHOLSON, THEODORE H., educational administrator; b. Chgo., July 27, 1929; B.S., Loyola U., Chgo., 1951; M.S. (State of Ill. Vets scholar), No. Ill. U., 1955; postgrad., Rockford Coll., 1955; Ph.D. (NDEA fellow, 1966-67), U. Wis.-Madison, 1967; children—Craig, Kimberlee, Christine, Rhonda, Katrina, Alexandra. Tchr., Morris Kennedy Sch., Winnebago County, Ill., 1951-53, Rockford (Ill.) Public Schs., 1953-55, evening sch., 1956-60; prin. Marsh Schs., Dist. 58, Winnebago County, 1955-59, supt., 1959-66; supt. Dearborn Twp. Sch. Dist. 8, Dearborn Heights, Mich., 1967-68, Wilmington (Ohio) City Sch., 1968-72; supr. schs., Wausau, Wis., 1972—; vis. prof. Central State U., Wilberforce, Ohio, 1969-70; teaching asst., research asst., lectr. U. Wis., summer 1976; lectr., cons. Univ. Council Ednl. Adminstrn.; mem. coordinating com. Partnership Schs.; v.p. N.C. Data Processing Center, 1974-81. Active Central Wausau Progress, 1973-82; mem. Pvt. Industry Council. Served with USN, 1943-46. Recipient Citizenship award City of Rockford, 1960, 64; Community Leader award Sta. WXCO, Wausau, 1974. Mem. Am. Assn. Sch. Adminstrs., Wis. Assn. Sch. Dist. Adminstrs. (state bd. dirs.), Am. Assn. Supervision and Curriculum Devel., C. of C. (bd. dirs., edn com.), Phi Delta Kappa. Clubs: Elks, Optimists. Contbr. articles in field to profl. publs. Office: Bd Edn Office 1018 S 12th Ave Wausau WI 54401

NICHOLSON, WILLIAM NOEL, clin. neuropsychologist; b. Detroit, Dec. 24, 1936; s. James Eardly and Hazel A. (Wagner) N.; A.B., Wittenberg U., 1959; M.Div., Luth. Theol. Sem., Phila., 1962; Ph.D. (HEW fellow), Mich. State U., 1972; m. Nancy Ann Marshall, June 15, 1957; children—Ann Marie, Kristin, Scott. Ordained to ministry Lutheran Ch., 1962; parish pastor Our Savior Luth. Ch., Saginaw, Mich., 1962-69; psychologist Ingham-Eaton-Clinton Mental Health Bd., 1971-72; psychologist Bay-Arenac Mental Health Bd., 1972-74; dir., psychologist Riverside Center, Bay City, Mich., 1974-75; pres. Bay Psychol. Assos., P.C., Bay City, 1975—; cons. Gov.'s Office of Drug Abuse, 1972-74. Cert., Nat. Register Health Care Providers in Psychology. Mem. Am. Psychol. Assn., Midwest Psychol. Assn., Mich. Psychol. Assn., Soc. Behavioral Medicine, Mental Health Assn. (pres. Bay-Arenac Chpt. 1981). Lutheran. Clubs: Bay City Yacht, Rotary. Author: A Guttman Facet Analysis of Attitude-Behaviors Toward Drug Users by Heroin Addicts and Mental Health Therapists, 1972; contbr. articles to profl. jours. Office: Allen Medical Bldg 200 S Wenona St Bay City MI 48706

NICKEL, JEAN RENEE, nurse, school nurse; b. Ft. Dodge, Iowa, Feb. 14, 1930; d. William Wesley and Lillian Beatrice (Poduska) Eral; m. Bernard Edward Nickel, Aug. 4, 1951; children—Timothy Jerome, Theresa Ann. R.N., St. Francis Sch. Nursing, Grand Island, Nebr., 1951; B.S. in Psychology, Kearney State Coll., 1981. Office nurse Brewster Clinic, Holdrege, Nebr., 1952-58; staff nurse Valley County Hosp., Ord, Nebr., 1962-71; sch. nurse Ednl. Service Unit 10, Kearney, Nebr., 1974-76; sch. nurse Loup City Sch. Dist. (Nebr.), 1974—. Mem. Central Nebr. Sch. Nurse Assn., Am. Legion Aux. Democrat. Roman Catholic. Home: 769 R St Loup City NE 68853 Office: Loup City Middle Sch 800 N 8th Loup City NE 68853

NICKEY, KARYL KRISTINE, accountant; b. Elmhurst, Ill., Oct. 1, 1950; d. Edward Albert and Verna Eulalia (Bergdahl) N.; student Western Ill. U., 1968-69; B.A. in Acctg. (Farmers Ins. Group scholar), B.A. in Psychology, North Central Coll., 1977. Billing and accounts payable clk. NBC, 1972-75; acct. Oak Brook Devel. Co., 1976-77; acctg. mgmt. trainee A.C. Nielsen Co., Northbrook Ill., 1977-78, supr. payroll and payroll taxation, 1978-80; corp. payroll mgr. Brunswick Corp., Skokie, Ill., 1980—. Tchr. swimming to handicapped ARC; founder, coach Villa Park Swim Team, 1967-69; asst. coach Oak Brook Bath and Tennis Club, 1969-71, swimming instr., 1968-73; asst. instr. Horseback Riding for the Handicapped, 1976-77; vol. Good Shepherd Hosp., Barrington, Ill., unit co-chmn. vols. for orthopedics and obstets., 1980-82; mem. Horsemasters Drill Team; appeared in film Managing Your Emotions. Mem. Nat. Assn. Accts. (asso. dir. meetings Chgo. chpt. 1979-80, dir. meetings 1980-81, program dir. 1981-82), Am. Payroll Assn. Mem. First Ch. of Oak Brook. Club: Riding (Barrington Hills, Ill.), Oak Brook Bath and Tennis. Office: 1 Brunswick Plaza Skokie IL 60077

NICOLANTI, DAVID RAYMOND, educational administrator; b. Cornellsville, Pa., July 24, 1947; s. Oberdan Louis and Mary Magdalin (Zimmerman) N.; m. Mary Anne Vrabel, May 17, 1969 (div. Oct. 1976); children—Loretta Anne, David Steven. B.S. in Bus. Adminstrn., John Carroll U., 1969; M.B.A., Case-Western Res. U., 1976. C.P.A., Ohio. Economist, statistician Nat. Screw Machinery Prodn. Assn., Cleve., 1973-74; exec. v.p. Ohio Coll. Podiatric Medicine, Cleve., 1977—. Trustee Alta House, Cleve., 1980—. Mem. Ohio Soc. C.P.A.s, Am. Soc. C.P.A.s, Am. Assn. Colls. Podiatric Medicine. Roman Catholic. Avocations: chess, computers, boating, fishing. Home: 12414 Calvin Dr Brecksville OH 44141 Office: Ohio Coll Podiatric Medicine 10515 Carnigie Ave Cleveland OH 44106

NICOSON, DAN J., university administrator, consultant; b. Beech Grove, Ind., May 30, 1946; s. Angus J. and Beautona Alice (Ford) N.; m. Linda Joyce Harkness, Jan. 28, 1966 (dec. 1982); children—Scott Bradley, Brent Joseph. B.S., Ind. Central U., 1968; M.S., Ind. State U., 1973. Tchr., coach Mt. Vernon Community Sch. Corp., Fortville, Ind., 1968-69, Sch. Dist. of Pike Twp., Indpls., 1969-73; dir. devel. Ind. Central U., Indpls., 1973—; pres., dir. Achievement Dynamics Inc., Beech Grove, Ind., 1984—; cons. various charitable orgns., Ind., 1978—. Contbr. articles to profl. jours. Mem. sch. bd. Beech Grove City Schs., 1983—; dirs. Beech Grove City Parks, 1978-83; bd. dirs., treas. Beech Grove Little League, 1982-85; mem. nominating com. mem. Girls Clubs of Greater Indpls., 1983-85. Mem. Ind. Council of Fund Raising Execs. (pres. 1980, bd. dirs. 1979-81), Nat. Soc. Fund Raising Execs. (cert. 1982, bd. dirs. 1982-84), Estate Planning Council Indpls. Republican. Methodist. Lodge: Kiwanis. Avocations: public speaking, sports officiating. Home: 1915 E Southern Ave Beech Grove IN 46107 Office: Ind Central Univ 1400 E Hanna Ave Indianapolis IN 46227

NIDELCHEFF, JOHN S., educational administrator; b. Jackson, Mich., July 25, 1928; s. Sam and Jannie (Vacheff) N.; m. Marjorie Anne Estes, Mar. 9, 1955; children—John S., Sheryl Anne. B.A., Albion Coll., 1952; M.A., Western Mich. U., 1954; postgrad. U. Mich., 1964-66, Mich. State U., 1964-66, Wayne State U., 1967-68. Tchr., Albion (Mich.) Pub. Schs., 1951-52, Jackson (Mich.) High Sch., 1952-63, Parkside High Sch., 1963-64; dir. vocat. edn. Jackson Pub. Schs., 1964-73, prin. Jackson Area Career Ctr., 1973-84. Bd. dirs., Jr. Achievement, 1971—; Mem. campaign com. United Way, 1970—. Served to 1st lt. U.S. Army, 1945-48, 50-51; Korea. Recipient Boss of Yr. award Am. Bus. Women's Assn., 1976. Mem. Nat. Secondary Sch. Prins. Assn., Mich. Secondary Sch. Prins. Assn., Am. Vocat. Assn., Mich. Assn. for Vocat. Adminstrs. Democrat. Club: Exchange. Contbr. articles to profl. jours. Home: 2405 Midday St Jackson MI 49203 Office: 6800 Browns Lake Rd PO Box 1160 Jackson MI 49204

NIDETZ, MYRON PHILIP, medical adminstrator, health delivery systems consultant; b. Chgo., Dec. 29, 1935; s. David J. and Rose Y. (Yudell) N.; B.S., U. Ill., 1958; M.B.C., Hamilton Inst., Phila., 1972; M.P.A., Roosevelt U., 1981; m. Linda Freeman, Dec. 18, 1960; children—Julia, Allison. Dir., Union Coop. Eye Care Center, Chgo., 1961-65; dir. med. adminstrv. services Michael Reese

Hosp. and Med. Center, Chgo., 1966-75; asso. dir. program to improve med. care and health services in correctional instns. AMA, 1975-79; exec. dir. N. Central Dialysis Centers, Chgo., 1979—. Adj. faculty U. Ill. Active Suburban Health Systems Agy., Oak Park, Ill., HCFA Network 15. Served with U.S. Army, 1959-60. Fellow Am. Acad. Med. Adminstrs., Am. Public Health Assn., Royal Soc. Health; mem. Assn. Hosp. Med. Edn., Am. Acad. Polit. and Social Sci., Am. Geriatrics Soc., Am. Hosp. Assn., AMA, Inst. of Soc., Ethics and Life Scis., Gerontol. Soc., Assn. Univ. Programs Health Adminstrn. Home: 14800 S Minerva Ave Dolton IL 60419 Office: 55 E Washington St Chicago IL 60602

NIEDLING, HOPE HOTCHKISS, dietitian; b. Meriden, Ill., Feb. 14, 1922; d. Bert and Myrle Glenn (Vaughn) Hotchkiss; student North Central Coll., 1939-40; B.S., U. Ill., 1943; M.S. in Food Sci. and Nutrition, U. Wis. 1974; m. Ivan Martin Niedling, June 26, 1948. Teaching dietitian U. Hosp., Balt., 1944; dietitian public sch. cafeterias, Balt., 1944-48; dir. admissions Thomas Sch. Retailing, Phila., 1954-55; instr. foods U. Wis., Stevens Point, 1967-68; food service supr. instr. Mid-State, N.Central and Fox Valley Tech. Insts., Wis., 1973-75; cons. dietitian nursing homes in Wis., 1973—. Chmn., Village of Plover Cancer Fund Drive, 1977-78; pres. Portage County Republican Women, 1969-74; chmn. 7th dist. Wis. Fedn. Rep. Women, 1969-74; advisor U. Wis.-Stout Alumni Assn., 1977—; sec.-treas. Joint Com. on Edn., Wis., 1978—; bd. dirs. Stout Found., U. Wis., 1977—, mem. exec. com., 1978—. Recipient Loyalty award U. Ill., 1978, award of merit U. Ill. Home Econs. Assn., 1979. Mem. Am. Dietetic Assn. (ho. of dels. 1974-77), Wis. Dietetic Assn., No. Wis. Dietetic Assn. (pres. 1971-73), Soc. for Nutrition Edn., Nutrition Today Soc., Nutritionists in Bus., DAR (sec. 1977-80, 1st vice regent 1980-83, nat. state vice regents club 1980—, Wis. regent 1983—, nat. officer's club), Nay-osh-ing chpt. DAR (organizing regent 1972-73, chpt. regent 1973-77, chpt. registrar 1977—, nat. bd. mgmt.), Colonia Dames XVII Century (2d v.p. 1979-81, 1st v.p. 1981-83, pres. 1983—), Daus. Am. Colonists, Nat. Soc. Women Descs. of Ancient and Hon. Arty. Co., Nat. Soc. Daus. of Founders and Patriots Am., Wis. Assn. Registered Parliamentarians (corr. sec. 1978-80), Nat. Assn. Registered Parliamentarians, Wis. Public Health Assn. (mem. aging com. 1974-78), Portage County Humane Soc. (sec. 1973—), Wis. Fedn. Women's Clubs (pres. 1980-82), Gen. Fedn. Women's Clubs (bd. dirs. 1980—, sec.-treas. Gt. Lakes Region 1982—, chmn. internat. aid div. 1982—), U. Ill. Alumni Assn. (dir. 1973-79), NCCJ (disting. merit citation 1976, vice chmn. Wis.), AAUW (pres. Stevens Point br. 1968-72, scholarship award 1970, state corr. sec. 1971-73), Gamma Sigma Delta, Epsilon Sigma Omicron. Methodist. Clubs: Order Eastern Star, Order of Amaranth (royal matron 1978-79, dist. dep. grand royal matron 1979-80, asst. grand lectr. 1980-81, grand rep. 198—), Order White Shrine of Jerusalem, Stevens Point Area Woman's (pres. 1970-74, 76-78), Stevens Point Women's (pres. 1970-72) Gen. Fedn. Women's (pres. Gt. Lakes region 1984—). Address: 1008 3rd St Stevens Point WI 54481

NIELSEN, BRUCE JOHN, engineering and construction firm executive, real estate developer; b. Racine, Wis., Feb. 18, 1948; s. Clayton H. and Irene G. (Chapas) N.; m. Sandra Kay Ridley, Sept. 13, 1975; children—Scott Clayton, Jennifer Lee. B.S. in Civil Engring., U. Wis.-Madison, 1972, M.S. in Constrn. Adminstrn., 1972. Registered profl. engr., Wis. Exec. v.p. Nielsen Iron Works, Inc., Racine, 1972-83; pres. Nielsen Bldg. Systems, Inc., Racine, 1983-84; owner, prin. Bruce Nielsen, P.E., Racine, 1972—; owner, prin. B.J. Nielsen Real Estate, Racine, 1976—. Bd. dirs. Racine YMCA, 1982, Community Action Program, 1977, Tri-County Contractors Assn., 1970-82; chmn. Caledonia Indsl. Devel. Com.; chmn. adv. bd. Gateway Tech. Inst. Mem. Racine Jaycees (pres. 1976), Racine Area Mfrs. and C. of C. Office: Nielsen Building Systems Inc 4820 Six Mile Rd Racine WI 53402

NIELSEN, BRUCE MONRAD MEILINGGAARD, health care executive; b. Greenwich, Conn., Mar. 20, 1947; s. Einar Monrad and Daphne Heyel (Archer) Meilinggaard; m. Kathleen Whalen, Aug. 2, 1969; children—William David Meilinggaard, Robert Michael Meilinggaard. B.Gen. Studies, U. Mich., 1971, M.H.A., 1979. Unit supr. Henry Ford Hosp., Detroit, 1971-72, supr. admitting and discharge, 1972-76, rep. of adminstrn. in evening adminstrn. office, 1974-76; successively adminstrv. asst., adminstr., v.p. gen. services Meml. Hosp. div. S.W. Mich. Health Care Assn., St. Joseph, 1976-79; asst. adminstr. East Liverpool (Ohio) City Hosp., 1979-80, acting adminstr., 1980, adminstr., 1980-81, pres., 1981—. Dir. Health Systems Agy. Eastern Ohio, 1980-82, v.p., 1984—; bd. dirs. Vol. Health Planning and Promotional Council Eastern Ohio, 1982-83, East Liverpool YMCA, 1980—, Berrien County ARC, 1977-79; mem. Columbiana County Overall Econ. Devel. Com., 1982—; adv. com. Columbiana County Pub. Health League, 1981—, Home Health Agy. of Columbiana County, 1982—. Nominee Am. Coll. Hosp. Adminstrs.; mem. Forum Health Services Adminstrs. Lodge: East Liverpool Rotary. Home: 49926 S Park Circle PO Box 2675 East Liverpool OH 43920 Office: East Liverpool City Hospital 425 W 5th St East Liverpool OH 43920

NIELSEN, HARALD CHRISTIAN, chemist; b. Chgo., Apr. 18, 1930; s. Svend Aage and Seena (Hansen) N.; m. Eloise Wilma Soule, Dec. 19, 1953; children—Brenda Mae, Paul Erick, Gloria Lynn. B.A., St. Olaf Coll., 1952; Ph.D., Mich. State U., 1957. Chemist, cereal grain proteins No. Regional Research Ctr., Dept. Agr., Peoria, Ill., 1957—. Pres. local 3247 Am. Fedn. of Govt. Employees, AFL-CIO, 1977—; mem. Peoria Area Combined Fed. Campaign Coordinating Com., 1980—. Recipient Dept. Agr. Group Superior Service award, 1964. Fellow AAAS; mem. Am. Chem.-Soc. (sec. Peoria sect. 1977), Am. Assn. Cereal Chemists, Sigma Xi. Democrat. Lutheran. Contbr. articles to profl. jours. Home: 2318 N Gale Ave Peoria IL 61604 Office: 1815 N University Ave Peoria IL 61604

NIELSEN, KENNETH A., petroleum products and agricultural supplies company executive. Pres., chief executive officer, dir. Farmland Industries Inc., Kansas City, Mo. Office: Farmland Industries Inc 3315 N Oak Trafficway Kansas City MO 64116*

NIELSEN, PAUL ERNESTO, health facility administrator; b. Rosario, Argentina, Apr. 14, 1950; came to U.S., 1951; s. Vernon K. and Olwyn L. (Watson) N.; m. Margaret A. Jarvis, July 24, 1971; children—Erik A., Emily A. B.A., Ohio State U., 1972; M.B.A., Baldwin Wallace Coll., 1982. Credit reporter Dun & Bradstreet, Cleve., 1972-73; adminstrv. services coordinator Cleve. Clinic, 1973-75, dept. head, adminstrv. services coordinator, 1975-82, adminstr. colorectal and gen. surgery depts., 1982—. Bd. mgrs. Euclid YMCA (Ohio), 1982—. Mem. Am. Hosp. Assn., Health Care Adminstrs. Assn. of N.E. Ohio. Office: Cleve Clinic 9500 Euclid Ave Cleveland OH 44106

NIELSEN, STEVEN JEROME, dentist; b. Amery, Wis., Apr. 21, 1947; s. Gordon P. and Betty Lu (Olson) N.; m. Joan E. Geiser, Jan. 30, 1971; children—Stephanie Rae, Lindsay Joan. Student Gustavus Adolphus Coll., 1965-67; B.S., D.D.S., U. Minn., 1971. Intern W.Va. U., 1971-72; practice dentistry, Golden Valley, Minn., 1972—; pres. Bassett Creek Dental, Golden Valley, 1980—; cons. nursing homes. Mem. ADA, Minn. Dental Assn., Mpls. Dist. Dental Soc., Am. Acad. Dental Group Practice, W.Va. Soc. Hosp. Dentists. Republican. Lutheran. Lodge: Lions (pres. 1980-81, 100% Pres.'s award 1981). Avocations: boating; sailboarding; skiing; racquetball. Home: 3300 Carman Rd Excelsior MN 55331 Office: 5851 Duluth St Golden Valley MN 55422

NIEMANN, BARRY RICHARD, personnel company executive; b. Warsaw, Ind., July 26, 1943; s. Erwin Herman and Evelyn Alma (Fritche) N.; m. Patricia Ann Ellis, Dec. 8, 1963; children—Barry, Angie, Derrick. Student Ind. U., 1962. Cert. personnel cons., Ind. Gen. mgr. Falcon Co., Pitts., 1968-72, v.p., 1972-75; chmn. bd. Tigre Systems, Carmel, Ind., 1975—, dir., Balt., 1977—; dir. Am. Tigre Inc., Indpls., 1975—, Calif., 1981—; dir. Niemann Inc., Pitts., 1976—; cons. and lectr. in field; testifier subcom. on employment productivity U.S. Senate, 1981. Contbr. article to profl. jour. sponsor, coach Carmel Dad's Club, 1983-84. Mem. Nat. Assn. Personnel Cons. (treas. 1984—), Ind. Assn. Personnel Cons. (pres. 1982-83) (presdl. award 1982), Central Ind. Assn. Personnel Cons. (pres. 1980-81) (presdl. award 1980), Republican. Lutheran. Office: Tigre Systems 11550 N Meridian Suite 430 Carmel IN 46032

NIEMANN, CHARLES MICHAEL, computer service company executive; b. Belleville, Ill., Oct. 20, 1938; s. Eugene H. and Marie Emily (Stewart) N.; A.A. Belleville Area Coll., 1965; B.S. Washington U., 1966, B.A., 1966; M.S.C., St. Louis U., 1970; m. Phyllis Jean Niemann; children—Karen Lynn, Steven Michael. Fin. Analyst Chrysler Corp., Detroit, 1966-67; budget dir. Cerro Corp., Sauget, Ill., 1968-70; corp. budget dir. Intertherm Inc., St. Louis, 1970-; gen. mgr. McDonnel Automation Co., Belleville, 1970—; mem. faculty (part-time) Belleville Area Coll., 1970—; dir. Belleville Indsl. Devel. Corp., 1976-77, Belleville New Industries, 1976—. Mem. adv. bd. Sch. Dist. 201 Co-op Edn., 1970—; mem. Sunset Legis. Adv. Commn., St. Clair County, 1976—; mem. bd. Mayor's Prayer Breakfast Com., Belleville, 1976—; adv. City and County Affairs Com., Belleville, 1972-73; chmn. adv. bd. Sch. Dist. 201 Coop. Edn., 1980-81. Served with U.S. Army, 1957-60. Mem. Belleville Area C. of C. (1st v.p. 1975-76, pres. 1976-77, treas. 1974-75), Metro East C. of C. Assn. (pres. 1976-77), Ill. Police Assn. Clubs: Elks, Optimist (bd. govs. 1975-76). Home: 4232 Oak Ln Belleville IL 62223 Office: 1704 N Belt W Belleville IL 62223

NIEMANN, SCOTT THOMAS, lawyer; b. Crookston, Minn., July 16, 1951; s. Donald Leon and Jean Carol (Stumbo) N.; m. Bonnie Lyn Carr, Nov. 23, 1978; children—Michelle, Carol. B.A., MacMurray Coll., 1973; J.D., Ind. U., 1980. Bars: Ind. 1980, U.S. Dist. Ct. (no. and so. dists.) Ind. 1980, U.S. Ct. Appeals (7th cir.) 1984. Social service rep. Ill. div. Vocat. Rehab., Belleville, Ill., 1973-74; field service rep. United Mine Workers Am. Health and Retirement Funds, Evansville, Ind., 1974-75, field service specialist, 1975-76, asst. regional administrator, midwest region, 1976-77; assoc. Rothberg, Gallmeyer, Fruechtenicht & Logan, Ft. Wayne, Ind., 1980-84, ptnr., 1985—. Author: (with others) Local Government Computer Acquisition: A User's Guide, 1979. Recipient Letter of Commendation, Nat. Merit Scholarship award, 1969. Mem. Ind. Trial Lawyers Assn., Allen County Bar Assn., Ind. State Bar Assn., ABA, Order of Coif. Democrat. Baptist. Home: 405 W Rudisill Blvd Fort Wayne IN 46807 Office: Rothberg Gallmeyer Fruechtenicht and Logan PO Box 11647 Fort Wayne IN 46859

NIEMI, PETER G., library administrator; b. Ironwood, Mich., July 24, 1937; s. William B. and Hazel M. (Walker) N.; m. Rochelle I. McCormick, Nov. 25, 1968; children—Rebecca, Tanya. B.S., U. Mich., 1963, M.L.S., 1969. Cert. library adminstr. grade I, Wis. Librarian, Flint Pub. Library, Mich., 1965-68; library dir. Fremont Pub. Library, Mich., 1968-70, Champaign Pub. Library, Ill., 1970-78, Kent County Pub. Library, Grand Rapids, Mich., 1978-83, Madison Pub. Library, Wis., 1983—. Mem. ALA, Wis. Library Assn., Am. Mgmt. Assn. Office: Madison Public Library 201 W Mifflin St Madison WI 53703

NIES WURSTER, LORIE, public relations executive, consultant; b. Chgo., Dec. 26, 1951; d. Albert B. and Geraldine C. Nies; m. Carl Freeman Wurster, May 30, 1981. B.A. in Communications, Marquette U., 1973; postgrad. Institut Catholique, Paris, 1977. Producer, dir. pub. relations Sta. WNUS, Chgo., 1973-75; dir. pub. relations Chgo. Bar Assn., 1975-77; co-host Careerscope, Sta. WCFC-TV, Chgo., 1978; dir. pub. relations Job Service, Ill. Dept. of Labor, Chgo., 1979-81; dir. pub. relations Nat. PTA, 1981—; mem. media adv. com. Operation ABLE, Chgo. Active Nancy Reagan's War on Drugs, Nat. Children in TV Week. Mem. Pub. Relations Soc. Am., Chgo. Press Club, Chgo. Publicity Club, Women in Mgmt. (Women in Achievement award 1981). Roman Catholic. Club: Carlton. Home: 215 E Chicago St Apt 2413 Chicago IL 60611 Office: Nat PTA 700 N Rush St Chicago IL 60611

NIESZ, GEORGE MELVIN, tool and die co. exec.; b. Norwood, Ohio, Aug. 6, 1926; s. George John and Anita Agnes Lucille (Chialastri) N.; student pub. schs., Norwood and Deer Park; m. Evelyn Catherine Rayburn, Oct. 18, 1946; children—Nancy L., George J., Jr. Profl. baseball player St. Louis Cardinals Orgn., 1944-45; tool and die maker Steelcraft Mfg. Co., Cin., 1946-51; supt., mgr. Abco Tool & Die Co., 1951-70; founder, pres. Niesz Tool & Die Co., Cin., 1970—. State dir., v.p. Sycamore-Deer Park Jr. C. of C., 1956-59. Ky. Col. Mem. Am. Soc. Metals, Soc. Mfg. Engring., Cin. C. of C., Anderson Twp. C. of C. Republican. Clubs: Masons (32 deg); Shriners. Patentee portable tool attachment; chess champion. Home: 4171 Winesap Ct Cincinnati OH 45236 Office: PO Box 44147 Cincinnati OH 45236

NIETZ, CONNIE COLLINS, pharmacist; b. Toledo, Nov. 3, 1956; d. Clifford Merchant and Martha Lee (Lawrence) Collins; m. Gerald George Nietz, Oct. 4, 1980; 1 child, James Collins. B.S. in Pharmacy, Ohio Northern U., 1979. Registered pharmicist, Ohio. Pharmacy intern Collins & Parker, Inc., Oregon, Ohio, 1976-79, Mem. Med. Coll. of Ohio, Toledo, 1978-79; registered pharmacist Collins & Parker, Inc., 1979—, Aller's Pharmacy, North Baltimore, Ohio, 1980—. Del., Wood County Republican Conv., Bowling Green, Ohio, 1984. Mem. Ohio State Pharm. Assn. Republican. Mem. United Brethren Ch. Club: Jr. Lit. and Lyric Circle (North Baltimore). Avocations: music (piano and voice), needlework, calligraphy. Home: 203 Southlawn Dr North Baltimore OH 45872 Office: Aller's Pharmacy 127 N Main St North Baltimore OH 45872 or Collins & Parker Inc 2513 Woodville Rd Oregon OH 43616

NIEUWSMA, MILTON JOHN, hospital executive; b. Sioux Falls, S.D., Sept. 5, 1941; s. John and Jean (Potter) N.; B.A., Hope Coll., Holland, Mich., 1963; postgrad. Wayne State U., 1963-65; M.A., Sangamon State U., 1978; m. Marilee Gordon, Feb. 1, 1964; children—Jonathan, Gregory, Elizabeth. Public info. officer Wayne State U., Detroit, 1963-69; public relations dir. Sinai Hosp., Detroit, 1969-72; dir. div. officer services Am. Hosp. Assn., Chgo., 1972-73; asst. prof. journalism Wayne State U., Detroit, 1974; dir. public relations and devel. Meml. Med. Center, Springfield, Ill., 1975-79; v.p. for public affairs Grant Hosp., Chgo., 1979—; governing mem. Chgo. Zool. Soc., 1981—. Bd. dirs. Springfield (Ill.) Boys Clubs, 1979-80, Sangamon County Heart Assn., 1978-80, Riverside Community Fund (Ill.), 1983—; pub. relations chmn. Sangamon County Heart Fund Campaign, 1978; pres. Ford Com., 1975-76; bd. dirs. United Meth. Housing Corp., Detroit, 1968-70; chmn. Sch. Dist. 205 Caucus, 1983—. Mem. Public Relations Soc. Am., Nat. Assn., Hosp. Devel., Acad. Hosp. Public Relations, Am. Hosp. Assn., Ill. Hosp. Assn., Lincoln Park C. of C. Republican. Presbyterian. Contbr. articles in field to profl. jours. Home: 322 Scottswood Rd Riverside IL 60546 Office: 550 W Webster Ave Chicago IL 60614

NIGHTINGALE, EDMUND ANTHONY, transportation economist, educator; b. St. Paul, July 17, 1903; s. Edmund Alexander and Katherine Ellen (Eagan) N.; B.B.A., U. Minn., 1933, M.A., 1936, Ph.D., 1944; m. Lauretta A. Horejs, June 5, 1937; children—Edmund Joseph, Paul Lawrence. With operating dept. various railroads, 1920-33; teaching asst. econs. U. Minn., 1933-36, instr. in econs., transp., 1936-44, asst. prof., 1944-47, assoc. prof., 1947-52, prof., 1952-72, prof. emeritus, 1972—, dir. insts. in rail transp., 1948-49. Cons. to Mpls. Mayor's Citizen Adv. Com. on streetcar and bus matters, 1952-54; cons. transp. economist. Editorial statistician Minn. State Planning Bd., 1936; prin. indsl. specialist, prin. transp. economist WPB, Washington, 1942-43; cons. transp. economist to Minn. Resources Commn., Minn. Iron Range Resources and Rehab. Commn., 1941-48; cons. to dir. mil. traffic service Office Sec. Def., Washington, 1950-53; cons. Minn. Legis. Interim Com. to Study R.R. and Warehouse Commn., 1956-57; mem. Transp. Research Adv. Com., U.S. Dept. Agr., 1960-63, mem. adv. com. mktg. research and service programs, 1963-66; mem. Gov.'s Transit Authority Study Com., 1964-69; research cons. Mid-Am. Gov.'s Transp. Council, 1965-72; cons. Minn. Pub. Service Commn., 1965-72, U.S. Dept. Transp., 1969-70. Mem. Gov's Transp. Adv. Com., 1968-72. Chmn. Highlands dist. Indianhead council Boy Scouts Am., 1955-58, mem.-at-large, exec. bd., 1958-74. Recipient diploma of honor internat. prize jury VIII Pan-Am. Congress, Washington, 1953; St. George award, Cath. Com. Scouting Archdioces St. Paul, 1960. Registered practitioner ICC. Mem. Am. Soc. Traffic and Transp., Transp. Club Mpls. and St. Paul, AAUP, Am. Econ. Assn., Am. Agr. Econ. Assn., Assn. Transp. Practitioners (pres. chpt. 1957-58; regional v.p. 1961-63, chmn. com. edn. for practice 1971-73), Internat. Assn. Assessing Officers, Nat. Tax Assn. (com. on taxation pub. utility and transp. 1971—), Midwest Econs. Assn., Royal Econ. Soc., Nat. Assn. Shippers Adv. Bds. (legis. com. 1969—), N.W. Shippers Adv. Bd. (mem. legislative com. 1952-69, chmn. 1960-67), Associated Traffic Clubs Am. (v.p. edn. and research 1958-62, v.p. W. N. Central States 1962-63; Distinguished Transp. Educator, 1966), Transp. Research Forum, Beta Gamma Sigma, Beta Alpha Psi, Alpha Kappa Psi. Clubs: Transp., Campus (Mpls.). Co-author: Aviation in Minnesota, 1952; Foreign Trade via the St. Lawrence Seaway, 1965; Transportation Problems and Policies in the Trans-Missouri West, 1967. Contbr. to Freight Traffic Management at Installations of the Military Depts., Dept. of Defense, rev. edit., 1952. Contbr. articles econs., taxation, transp. jours. Home: 2120 Niles Ave Saint Paul MN 55116 Office: Grad Sch Mgmt University of Minn Minneapolis MN 55455

NIGHTINGALE, EDMUND JOSEPH, clinical psychologist; b. St. Paul, Jan. 10, 1941; s. Edmund Anthony and Lauretta Alexandria (Horejs) N.; student Nazareth Hall Prep. Sem., 1959-61; A.B., St. Paul Sem., 1963; A.B. magna cum laude, Catholic U. of Louvain (Belgium), 1965, M.A., 1967, S.T.B. cum laude, 1967; postgrad. U. Minn., 1971; M.A., Loyola U., Chgo., 1973, Ph.D. in Clin. Psychology, 1975; m. Marie Arcara, Apr. 9, 1978; 1 son, Edmund Bernard. With Cath. Archdiocese of St. Paul and Mpls., 1967-73; intern in clin. psychology Michael Reese Hosp. and Med. Center, Chgo., 1973-74, W. Side VA Hosp., Chgo., 1974-75; staff psychologist, student counseling center, Loyola U., Chgo., 1975; staff psychologist and clin. coordinator of inpatient unit, drug dependency treatment center Hines (Ill.) VA Hosp., 1975-79, acting chief drug dependency treatment center, 1979-80; chief psychology VA Med. Center, Danville, Ill., 1980—; mem. personnel bd. Archdiocese of St. Paul and Mpls., 1968-70; lectr. psychology, Loyola U., Chgo., 1975; asst. professorial lectr. psychology, St. Xavier Coll., Chgo., 1975-78; adj. asst. prof. psychology in psychiatry, Abraham Lincoln Sch. Medicine, Med. Center U. Ill., Chgo., 1977-82; adj. prof. psychology Purdue U., 1981—; clin. asst. prof. U. Ill. Sch. Medicine, Urbana/Champaign, 1982—; mem. grad. faculty in counseling psychology Ind. State U., Terre Haute, 1983—. Bd. dirs. Inst. Postgrad. Studies, Ill. Psychol. Assn., Registered psychologist, Ill.; lic. cons. psychologist, Minn.; certified Nat. Registry of Health Service Providers in Psychology. Mem. Am. (clin. psychology, public service, psychoanalysis and psychotherapy divs.), Ill. (clin. psychology and acad. sects.; sec. 1982-83, pres.-elect 1983-84, pres. 1984-85) psychol. assns., AAAS, Assn. for Advancement of Psychology, Am. Group Psychotherapy Assn., Am. Soc. Clin. Hypnosis. Founding editor: Louvain Studies, 1966; editor: VA Directory of Psychology Staffing and Services, 1982, 83, 84, 85. Home: 92 Country Club Dr Danville IL 61832 Office: VA Med Center Danville IL 61832

NIGROVIC, VLADIMIR, anesthesiologist, pharmacologist, educator; b. Sarajevo, Yugoslavia, Mar. 3, 1934; came to U.S. 1966, naturalized 1972; s. Bela and Marica (Biljanic) N.; m. Elisabeth Johanna Ziegler, Dec. 27, 1963; children—Mario V., Peter A., Nina M. M.D., U. Heidelberg, Germany, 1962. Research assoc. Nuclear Research Ctr., Karlsruhe, W.Ger. 1961-66, U. Minn., Mpls., 1966-68; asst. prof. dept. pharmacology Med. Coll. Ohio, Toledo, 1968-73, assoc. prof., 1973—, resident in anesthesiology 1977-78, asst. prof. dept. anesthesia, 1979—, vice chmn. 1981—; intern Univ. Clinics, Gutenberg U., Mainz, W.Ger., 1975-76. Contbr. articles to profl. jours. German Acad. Exchange Service fellow Bonn, 1958-62. Mem. Am. Soc. Pharm. and Exptl. Therapeutics, Am. Soc. Anesthesiologists, German Soc. Anesthesiologists, Soc. Exptl. Biology and Medicine. Home: 2637 Letchworth St Toledo OH 43606 Office: Dept Anesthesiology Med Coll Ohio CS 10008 Toledo OH 43699

NIKISHIN, IGOR FEDOR, surgeon; b. Kharkov, Russia, Dec. 25, 1917; s. Fedor F. and Maria A. (Dikarev) N.; came to U.S., 1949, naturalized, 1954; A.B., French Lyceum Prague, Czechoslovakia, 1936; M.D., Charles U., Prague, 1941; children—Nina, Alexander, Michael, Igor. Intern, George August U. Med. Sch., Goettingen, Germany, 1941-42, resident, 1942-46; chief surgeon 326th Res. Detachment Mil. Govt. Hosp., Brit. Army of the Rhine, 1945-47, sr. med. officer hdqrs. 509, 1947-48; sr. med. officer 609 Hdqrs. Control Commn. Germany, 1948-49; chmn. dept. surgery, sr. attending surgeon Aultman Hosp., Canton, Ohio, 1970—; asst. prof. surgery George August U., Goettingen, Germany, 1943-47; sr. attending surgeon Timken Mercy Hosp., Canton, 1959-80; assoc. prof. dept. human anatomy NE Univs. Coll. Medicine. Pres., Canton Symphony Assn., 1964-68, East Central Heart Assn., 1965-67; bd. dirs. Am. Cancer Soc., 1976; bd. dirs. AmDoc., Santa Barbara, Calif., 1965-69. Diplomate Am. Bd. Surgeons, Am. Bd. Abdominal Surgeons. Mem. AMA, Am. Soc. Abdominal Surgeons, ACS, Am. Coll. Angiology, Am. Geriatrics Soc., Ohio State Med. Assn., Ohio State Surg. Assn., N.Y., Ohio acads. scis., Med. Educators Assn. N.E. Ohio, Stark County Med. Soc. Club: Canton. Contbr. articles to profl. jours. Home: 5646 Channel Dr NW Canton OH 44718 Office: 214 Dartmouth Ave SW Canton OH 44710

NIKOLICH, GOJAN, public relations agency executive, writer; b. Kirchen-Hausen, W.Ger., Mar. 26, 1949; s. Srecko and Erika (Hirter) N.; m. Leslie Ann Guenveur, May 10, 1975; 1 dau., Lauren Marie. B.A. in English, DePaul U., 1975, M.A. in English, 1977. Editor, Glenview (Ill.) Times, 1974-75; dir. mktg. Ill. Dept. Tourism, Chgo., 1975-81; pres. Dunham-Nikolich Communications, Inc., Hinsdale, Ill., 1981—; writer, broadcaster WGN Radio, Chgo., 1978—; exec. dir. No. Ill. Tourism Council, 1982—. Mem. adv. com. chmn. mktg. com. Chgo.-Ft. Dearborn Hist. Commn. Served with U.S. Army, 1970-73. Decorated Army Commendation medal with oak leaf cluster. Mem. Soc. Am. Travel Writers, Assn. Gt. Lakes Outdoor Writers. Author novels: The Killer Gave Flowers, 1984; newspaper travel columnist, 1976-81. Chmn. editorial com. Journey Mag. Home: 185 Walnut St Elmhurst IL 60126 Office: Dunham-Nikolich Communications Inc 15 Spinning Wheel Rd Suite 1403 Hinsdale IL 60521

NILLES, WILLIAM O., savings and loan association executive. Pres., dir. Metropolitan Federal Bank FSB, Fargo, N.D. Office: Metropolitan Federal Bank FSB 215 N Fifth St Fargo ND 58102*

NIMMO, HERBERT LEE, engineer; b. Kansas City, Kans., Oct. 8, 1934; s. Forrest Herbert and Velma Irene (Barker) N.; m. F. Elizabeth Turner, June 7, 1963; 1 child, Martha Ann. B.S. in Mech. Engring., Finlay Engring. Coll., 1959. Cert. mfg. engr.; registered profl. engr., Mo. Design engr. United Mfg. & Engring. Corp., Independence, Mo., 1960-61; sr. design engr. George W. Johnson Mfg., Kansas City, Mo., 1961-62; sr. process engr. Remington Arms Co., Inc., Lake City Plant, Independence, Mo., 1962-69, area process engr., 1969-83, chief supr. quality assurance, 1983-84, chief process engr., 1984—; co-chmn. tech. adv. bd. Central Mo. State U., Warrensburg, Mo., 1984—. Contbr. articles to profl. jours. Served with U.S. Army, 1954-57. Recipient Pub. Service award Am. Radio Relay League, Inc., 1977. Mem. Soc. Mfg. Engrs. (chpt. chmn. 1986-87, Achievement award 1982-83), Mo. Soc. Profl. Engrs. (chmn. profl. engrs. in industry), Am. Soc. Metals (chmn. pub. relations), Am. Soc. Quality Control, Soc. Am. Mil. Engrs., Am. Legion, Nat. Rifle Assn. Clubs: Independence FM Amateur Radio, Am. Radio Relay League. Avocations: amateur radio; personal computing. Home: Route 1 Box 121 Higginsville MO 64037 Office: Remington Arms Co Inc Lake City Plant Independence MO 64050

NIMS, CHARLES FRANCIS, clergyman, egyptologist; b. Norwalk, Ohio, Oct. 19, 1906; s. Joel Benjamin and Grace (Wildman) N.; student U. Toledo, 1924-25; A.B., Alma Coll., 1928; B.D., McCormick Theol. Sem., 1931; Ph.D., U. Chgo., 1937; m. Myrtle Eileen Keillor, Apr. 18, 1931. Ordained to ministry Presbyn. Ch., 1931; pastor, First Ch., Eldorado, Ill., 1940-43; research asst. Oriental Inst., 1934-40; staff Sakkarah Expdn., Egypt, 1934-36; staff Epigraphic Survey, 1937-39; egyptologist Epigraphic Survey, 1946-63, field dir., 1964-72; research asso. dept. Oriental lang. U. Chgo., 1948-67, faculty mem., 1960-61, assoc. prof., 1967-70, prof., 1970-72, emeritus, 1972—; staff mem. Chgo. Archeol. Expdn., Tolmeita, Libya, 1954, 56, 57, 58; lectr. adult edn. Field Mus. Natural History, 1976. Mem. Found. Egyptologique Reine Elizabeth, Egypt Exploration Soc., Soc. Bibl. Lit., Am. Oriental Soc., Am. Photog. Soc. Am Schs. Oriental Research, Mil. Chaplains Assn. U.S., AAUP, Am. Research Center in Egypt, L'Association Internationale pour l'Étude du Droit Pharaonique (hon. pres.); ordinary mem. Deutsches Archaologisches Instut; assoc. mem. L'Institut d' Egypte; mem. Phi Beta Kappa. Served as chaplain (capt.) U.S. Army, 1943-46. Author: (with H.H. Nelson et al) Medinet Habu IV, 1940; (with Prentice Duell) Mastaba of Mereruka, 1938; (with G.R. Hughes) Reliefs and Inscriptions in Karnak, III, 1954; Medinet Habu V-VIII (with G.R. Hughes), 1957-70; Thebes of the Pharoahs, 1965; (with E.F. Wente) The Tomb of Kheruef, 1980, The Temple of Khonsu, I, 1979; (with William Murnane) The Temple of Khonsu, II, 1981. Contbr. articles to profl. jours. Home: 5540 Blackstone Ave Chicago IL 60637 Office: Oriental Inst U Chgo Chicago IL 60637

NIMS, ROBERT WALTER, accountant; b. Jackson, Mich., Mar. 4, 1950; s. Wellington Dewitt and Doris Irene (Gramer) N.; m. Jennifer Christina King, Aug. 12, 1972; children—Robert W., Jonathan R., David D. M.B.A., Central Mich. U., 1974. C.P.A., Mich. Ptnr. Nims-Ogger C.P.A.s, Mt. Pleasant, Mich., 1983—. Patentee tape reroll apparatus. Commr. Mt. Pleasant Housing Bd. Appeals, 1979-81; mem. Mt. Pleasant Planning Commn., 1981-84 chmn., 1983. Lodge: Lions. Home: 600 W Hopkins Mount Pleasant MI 48858 Office: Nims-Ogger CPAs 433 S Mission Mount Pleasant MI 48858

NINKE, ARTHUR ALBERT, accountant, management consultant; b. Coloma, Mich., Aug. 20, 1909; s. Paul F. and Theresa Grace (Warskow) N.; student acctg. Internat. Bus. Coll., 1928; diploma commerce Northwestern U., 1932; m. Claudia Wagner, Sept. 13, 1930; children—Doris Ninke Hart, Donald, Marion, George, Arthur Albert, Thomas, Mark, Albert. Auditor, Arthur Andersen & Co., C.P.A.s, Chgo., 1929-36, St. Louis, 1950-55, Midwest

Stock Exchange, 1936-41, SEC, 1942-45; expense controller Butler Bros., Chgo., 1946-49; office mgr. Hargis Electronics, 1956-59; auditor HUD, Detroit, 1960-64; owner Urban Tech. Staff Assoc., cons. urban renewal projects and housing devel., Detroit, 1965-81; pres. Simplified Systems & Service, 1978—, Urban Computerized Services, Inc., 1984—, Computer Mgmt. Services, 1985—; Complete Bus. Service, Dallas, 1979-82, Loving Shepherd Nursing Home, Warren, Mich., 1981-85; sec. Gideons Detroit North Woodward, 1981-85. Controller, Lake Superior R&D Inst., Munising, Mich., 1973-76; pres. Luth. Friendship Homes, Inc., 1975—; treas. Luth. Ch., 1985—; mng. dir. Family Evangelism Found., 1977—; controller S.E. Mich. Billy Graham Crusade, 1976-77; pres. Project Compassion Met. Detroit, Inc., 1982—; bd. dirs. Lutheran Credit Union Greater Detroit, 1982—. Recipient tribute Mich. State Legislature, 1982. Mem. Nat. Soc. Pub. Accts., Nat. Assn. Housing and Redevel. Ofcls. (treas. Mich. 1973-75), Luth. Center Assn. (treas. 1975-81, dir. 1975-81), Internat. Luth. Laymen's League (treas. S.E. Mich. 1971-75, dir. 1976-81), Am. Mgmt. Assn. Author: Family Bible Studies; Computer Networking. Developer simulated machine bookkeeping system; trade mark holder Record-Checks-Systems, 1981—. Home: 22405 Riverdale Dr Southfield MI 48034 Office: 17600 Northland Park Ct Southfield MI 48075

NISBETT, SUSAN ISAACS, journalist, dance critic; b. Bklyn., Jan. 29, 1948; d. Melvin and Dorothy (Paisak) Isaacs; m. Richard Eugene Nisbett, June 29, 1969; children—Matthew, Sarah. B.A., Bklyn. Coll., 1968; M.Phil. in French Lit., Yale U., 1971. Foreign student advisor U. Mich., Ann Arbor, 1975-79; dance critic The Ann Arbor News, 1975-84, 85—, features stringer, 1980-85, asst. features editor, 1985—; dance critic Sta. WUOM/WVGR-FM, 1976-82, Detroit News, 1984-85; staff writer The Ann Arbor Observer, 1979-80. Lectr.; free-lance journalist. Trustee Papagena Opera Co., Ann Arbor. Nat. Endowment Arts fellow, 1976. Mem. Ann Arbor Profl. Women in Communication, Dance Critics Assn., Detroit Women Writers, Phi Beta Kappa. Jewish. Contbr. articles to newspapers, dance and other publs.; editor U. Mich. Law Sch. Alumni Mag., 1983-85. Home: 837 W Huron St Ann Arbor MI 48103 Office: U Mich Law Sch Ann Arbor MI 48109

NJUS, DAVID LARS, biophysicist; b. Honolulu, Oct. 17, 1948; s. Kasper M. and Alice M. Njus; m. Deborah Handrinos, Aug. 18, 1984; 1 child, Jessica. B.S., MIT, 1970; Ph.D., Harvard U., 1975. Vis. scientist U. Oxford, 1975-78; asst. prof. Wayne State U., Detroit, 1978-82, assoc. prof. biol. scis., 1982—. Contbr. articles to profl. jours. Mem. Common Cause, Founders Soc. Detroit Inst. Arts; mem. research rev. com. Am. Heart Assn. Mich., 1983-86. Recipient Nat. Research Service award NIH, 1976-78; NSF fellow, 1975. Fellow AAAS; mem. Am. Heart Assn., Am. Soc. Neurochemistry, Am. Soc. Biol. Chemists. Office: Wayne State U Dept Biol Sci Detroit MI 48202

NODDINGS, THOMAS CLAYTON, investment company executive; b. Perth Amboy, N.J., Dec. 30, 1933; s. William Clayton and Sarah Stevenson N.; B.S., Purdue U., 1955; M.B.A., Rutgers U., 1958; m. Edna Francene Christoph, Feb. 6, 1954; children—Douglas, Thomas, John. Product mgr. The Trane Co., LaCrosse, Wis., 1958-67; dir. engring. Crane Co., Chgo., 1967-71; stockbroker E. F. Hutton, Chgo., 1971-75; sr. v.p. Woolard & Co., Chgo., 1975-77; pres. Noddings, Calamos & Assocs., Chgo., 1977—. Author: The Dow Jones-Irwin Guide to Convertible Securities, 1973; Listed Call Options, 1975; How the Experts Beat the Market, 1976; Advanced Investment Strategies, 1978; The Investor's Guide to Convertible Bonds, 1982; Low Risk Strategies for the High Performance Investor, 1985; Super Hedging, 1986. Office: 2001 Spring Rd Oak Brook IL 60521

NOE, ELNORA (ELLIE), chemical company executive; b. Evansville, Ind., Aug. 23, 1928; d. Thomas Noe and Evelyn (West) Dieter; student Ind. U.-Purdue U., Indpls. Sec., Pitman Moore Co., Indpls., 1946; with Dow Chem. Co., Indpls., 1960—, public relations asst. then mgr. employee communications, 1970—. Past mem. public relations com. ARC, Indpls. Named Indpls. Profl. Woman of Yr., 1985. Mem. Am. Bus. Women Assn. (woman of yr. 1965; past pres.), Ind. Assn. Bus. Communicators, (communicator of yr. 1977), Women in Communications (Louise E. Kleinhenz award 1984), Nat. Fedn. Press Women, Women's Press Club Ind. (past v.p.), Learn About Bus. (steering com.), Corp. Community Affairs Discussion Group. Club: Zonta Internat. (dist. public relations chmn. 1978-80. area dir. 1980-82, pres. Indpls. 1977-79). Office: PO Box 68511 Indianapolis IN 46268

NOE, FRANCES ELSIE (MRS. ROBERT DAVIES), physician; b. Beacon Falls, Conn., May 23, 1923; d. Alfred and Edith (Carlson) Noe; B.A., Middlebury Coll., 1944; M.N., Yale, 1947; M.D., U. Vt., 1954; m. Robert Davies, June 16, 1956; children—Kenneth Roger, Ralph Eric. Intern, Mary Hitchcock Meml. Hosp., Hanover, N.H., 1954-55; fellow cardiovascular research Mich. Heart Assn., 1955-56; resident pulmonary div. Henry Ford Hosp., Detroit, 1956-57; fellow cardiopulmonary research Wayne State U. Coll. Medicine, 1957-58, instr. anesthesia dept., 1958-61, asst. clin. prof. anesthesia dept., 1961-65, 76—; asso. staff, div. research Sinai Hosp. of Detroit, 1965-70, chief pulmonary physiology sect., div. research, 1970—. Mem. Am. Soc. Anesthesiologists, Sigma Xi. Contbr. articles in field to profl. jours. Home: 1601 Kirkway Bloomfield Hills MI 48013 Office: Sinai Hosp Detroit MI 48235

NOEL, DOUGLAS ALLEN, accountant, educator; b. Detroit, May 3, 1950; s. Milton Ernest and Gerildene Marie Theresa (Knapp) N.; m. Marie Ann Feterrer, June 26, 1976; children—Michele, Jason. B.A., Concordia Coll., 1978; student U. Nebr., 1979-82. Cert. tchr., Ohio, Nebr. Owner, Doug's Snowclearing Service, River Forest, Ill., 1975-78; acct. Union Oil Co. of Calif., Schaumburg, Ill., 1978-82; prin., tchr. St. John Luth. Sch., Madison, Nebr., 1982-83; tchr., minister edn. Immanuel Luth. Ch. and Sch., Hamilton, Ohio, 1983—; owner, mgr. Noel Acctg. Services, Hamilton, 1983—. Mem. Republican Presdl. Task Force, 1982-83. Mem. Ohio Assn. Elem. Sch. Adminstrs., Nat. Assn. Elem. Sch. Prins., Luth. Edn. Assn. Office: Box 13264 Hamilton OH 45013

NOERENBERG, PAUL FREDERICK, computer operations administrator; b. Olney, Ill., May 17, 1949; s. Frederick Hugo and Betty Lou (Harms) N.; m. Beverly Kay Strawser, June 5, 1971; 1 child, Sandra Kay. B.S. in Edn., Eastern Ill. U., 1971, M.A., 1975; postgrad. Parkland Coll., 1981-82. Music dir. Milford High Sch., Ill., 1975-76; instrumental music dir. S.E. Parke Schs., Montezuma, Ind., 1976-77; cutter Collegiate Cap and Gown, Champaign, Ill., 1977-81; computer ops. mgr. Russell Stewart Oil Co., Urbana, Ill., 1982—. Adult choir dir. Tolono United Meth. Ch. (Ill.), 1978—. Republican. Methodist. Club: Lions (pres. 1982-83). Home: 313 Philip Dr Tolono IL 61880 Office: Russell Stewart Oil Co 1301 E Washington St Box 279 Urbana IL 61801

NOETH, CAROLYN FRANCES, speech-language pathologist; b. Cleve., July 21, 1924; d. Sam Falco and Barbara Serafina (Loparo) Armaro; A.B. magna cum laude (Univ. scholar), Western Res. U., 1963; M.Ed., U. Ill., 1972; postgrad. Nat. Coll. Edn., 1975—; m. Lawrence Andrew Noeth, June 29, 1946; children—Lawrence Andrew, Barbara Marie. Speech therapist Chgo. Public Schs., 1965; speech, lang. and hearing clinician J. Sterling Morton High Schs., Cicero-Berwyn, Ill., 1965-82, tchr. learning disabilities/behavior disorders, 1982, dist. ednl. diagnostician, 1982-84; Title I Project tchr., summers 1966-67, lang. disabilities cons., summers 1968-69, in-service tng. cons., summer 1970, dir. Title I Project, summers 1973-74, learning disabilities tchr. W. Campus of Morton, 1971-75, chmn. Educable-Mentally Handicapped-Opportunities Tchrs. Com., 1967-68, spl. edn. area and in-sch. tchrs. workshops, 1967—. Precinct elections judge, 1953-55; block capt. Mothers March of Dimes and Heart Fund, 1949-60; St. Agatha's rep. Nat. Catholic Women's League, 1952-53; collector for charities, 1967; mem. exec. bd. Morton Scholarship League, 1981-84, corr. sec., 1981-83; vol. Am. Cancer Soc., 1985—. First recipient Virda L. Stewart award for Speech, Western Res. U., 1963, recipient Outstanding Sr. award, 1963. Mem. Am. (certified), Ill. speech and hearing assns., Council Exceptional Children (div. for learning disabilities, chpt. spl. projects chmn., exec. bd. 1976-81, chpt. pres. 1979-80), Assn. Children with Learning Disabilities, Council for Learning Disabilities, Profls. in Learning Disabilities, Internat. Platform Assn., Kappa Delta Pi, Delta Kappa Gamma (chmn., co-chmn. chpt. music com. 1979—, mem. state program com. 1981-83, chpt. music rep. to state 1982—). Roman Catholic. Clubs: St. Norbert's Women's (Northbrook, Ill.), Case-Western Res. U., U. Ill. Alumni Assns., Lions (vol. Northbrook, 1966—). Chmn. in compiling and publishing Student Handbook, Cleve. Coll., 1962; contbr. lyric parodies and musical programs J. Sterling Morton High Sch. West Retirement Teas, 1972-83. Home and Office: 1849 Walnut Circle Northbrook IL 60062

NOGGLE, LAWRENCE WESLEY, mechanical engineer; b. Dayton, Ohio, Oct. 9, 1935; s. William Henry and Lula Evelyn (O'Dell) N.; B.M.E., Gen. Motors Inst., 1959; B.A., Simpson Coll., 1965; M.Sc., Ohio State U., 1972, Ph.D., 1973; postgrad. Indsl. Coll. of Armed Forces, 1980-81; m. Alwilda June Yount, Nov. 20, 1952; children—Lawrence Wesley, Yvonne, Grant, Matthew, Dorinda. Coop. student, jr. project engr. Gen. Motors Corp., Indpls. and Oak Ridge, 1954-61; aerospace engr. USAF, Wright-Patterson AFB, Ohio, 1961-62; computer room supr. Wells Fargo Bank, San Francisco, 1962-65; research engr. Boeing Co., Seattle, 1965-66; aerospace engr., sr. aerospace engr., study mgr. aero. systems div. Wright Patterson AFB, 1966-76, program mgr., mission area planner, 1976-80, chief tactical devel. planning, 1981-82, dep. dir. tactical programs/integration, 1982—; tchr. Simpson Coll., 1962-63. Active PTA, Little League, Brookville Band Boosters. Gen. Motors Corp. fellow, 1954-58, USAF fellow, 1970-71; recipient Outstanding Performance award USAF, 1968, 69, 73, 74, 80, 82, 83. Mem. AIAA (tech. com. air transp. systems 1978-80), Air Force Assn., Ohio State U. Alumni Assn., Gen. Motors Inst. Alumni Assn., Sigma Xi, Tau Beta Pi, Chi Alpha Omega. Mem. Christian and Missionary Alliance Ch. Contbr. articles to profl. jours. Home: 12257 Air Hill Rd Brookville OH 45309 Office: Aeronautical Systems Div Wright Patterson AFB OH 45433

NOHA, EDWARD J., insurance company executive; b. 1926; B.B.A., Pace Coll.; married. With Dept. Justice, 1944-52, Met. Life Ins. Co., 1952-55; exec. v.p. Allstate Ins. Co., 1955-74; chmn. bd., pres., chief exec. officer Continental Casualty Co.; chmn. bd., pres., chief exec. officer Continental Assurance Co., Chgo.; chmn. bd. Nat. Fire Ins. Co. of Hartford, Inc., Transcontinental Ins. Co. Office: Continental Casualty Co CNA Plaza Chicago IL 60685*

NOLAN, SANDRA JEAN, mgmt. cons.; b. Milw., May 26, 1947; d. Harry Ernest and Mary Patricia Polley; B.S., U. Wis., Milw., 1974; m. Timothy M. Nolan, July 29, 1967; children—Tracy, Stephanie, Alissa. Pres. Early Learners Child Devel. Centers, Inc., Milw., 1971—; v.p. Nolan Assocs., Inc., Milw., 1973-78, Innovative Tng. and Devel. Assocs., Inc., Milw., 1973-84; v.p. Innovative Outcomes, Inc., Milw., 1984—, The Entrepreneurial Group, Milw., 1984—; pres. Strategic Mktg. Assocs., Milw., 1984—. Editor: The Corporate Entrepreneur, 1985—. Co-author: Handbook for School Board Members, 1977; Achieving Excellence, 1985. Mem. Am. Mgmt. Assn., Am. Soc. Tng. and Devel. Office: 13202 W Cleveland St New Berlin WI 53151

NOLAND, JAMES ELLSWORTH, U.S. judge; b. LaGrange, Mo., Apr. 22, 1920; s. Otto Arthur and Elzena (Ellsworth) N.; A.B., Ind. U., 1942, LL.B., 1948; M.B.A., Harvard, 1943; m. Helen Warvel, Feb. 4, 1948; children—Kathleen Kimberly, James Ellsworth, Christopher Warvel. Admitted to Ind. State bar, 1948, since practiced in Bloomington; partner law firm of Hilgedag and Noland, Indpls., 1955-56, 1st asst. city atty., Indpls., 1956-57; dep. atty. gen., Ind., 1952; spl. asst. U.S. atty. gen., 1953; appointed Ind. State Election Commr., 1954; U.S. judge So. Dist. Ind., 1966—. Mem. com. on magistrates system Jud. Conf. U.S., 1973-81. Mem. 81st (1949-51) Congress, 7th Ind., Dist.; sec. Ind. Democratic Com., 1960-66. Chmn. bd. visitors Ind. Law Sch., Indpls., 1974-76. Served as capt., Transp. Corps., AUS, 1943-46. Mem. Am., Ind. bar assns., Ind. Assn. Trial Lawyers (pres. 1956), Nat. Conf. Fed. Trial Judges (chmn. 1981-82), Phi Delta Phi, Phi Kappa Psi. Mem. Moravian Ch. Home: 8979 Pickwick Dr Indianapolis IN 46260 Office: Federal Ct Bldg Indianapolis IN 46204

NOLD, EDWARD, director university pharmaceutical services, consultant, author, speaker; b. Detroit, Mar. 9, 1947; s. Edward A. and F. Marie (Graham) N.; m. Lucinda J. Heck, Mar. 27, 1976; children—Andrew, Lisa. B.Pharm., U. Mich., 1970; M.S., Ohio State U., 1973. Registered pharmacist, Ohio, Ill. Resident, Ohio State U. Hosps., Columbus, 1971-73, staff pharmacist, 1970-71, asst. dir. pharmacy, 1973-74, assoc. dir. pharmacy, 1974-78; dir. pharm. service U. Chgo. Med. Ctr., 1978—; pres. Pharm. Control, Inc., Hinsdale, Ill., 1983—. Designer computer systems for hosp. pharmacies, 1975, 83. Co-author: Managing Computer Systems, 1983. Author, editor series of articles: Fin. Mgmt. Hosp. Pharmacies, 1984. Contbr. 37 articles to profl. jours. Mem. Am. Soc. Hosp. Pharmacists (contbg. editor 1982—, Research Found. award 1984), Ill. Council Hosp. Pharmacists. Avocations: Tennis; running; reading. Office: Pharmaceutical Control Inc Box 392 Hinsdale IL 60522

NOLL, CHARLES GORDON, physicist; b. Sunbury, Pa., Dec. 2, 1948; s. J. Herman and Helen Elisabeth (Gelnett) N.; B.A., Bloomsburg (Pa.) State Coll., 1970; M.S., Ohio State U., Columbus, 1974, Ph.D., 1975; m. Alice Marie Walters, Dec. 20, 1971; children—Carlton Leigh, Benjamin Douglass, Jennifer Nicole. Lectr. physics Ohio State U., 1975-76; researcher research and devel. United McGill Corp., Columbus, 1976-78, corp. physicist, Groveport, Ohio, 1978-83, mgr. corp. research and devel., 1983—; cons. environ. problems. Mem. Am. Phys. Soc., IEEE, Electrostatics Soc. Am., Sigma Xi, Sigma Pi Sigma. Author: Ensemble Theory for Electrostatic Precipitation, 1980; Computer Aided Research Tools for Pilot Testing of Pollution Control Equipment, 1981. Home: 121 Academy Ct Gahanna OH 43230 Office: One Mission Park Groveport OH 43125

NOLL, KENNETH EUGENE, air resources engineering educator; b. Brantwood, Wis., Aug. 20, 1936; s. Virgil R. and Pearl (Copland) N; m. Patricia Urbanik, Nov. 28, 1959; children—Michael, Elizabeth. Registered profl. engr., Calif., Tenn., Ill. Sr. air resources engr. State of Calif., 1963-70; prof. air resources U. Tenn., 1970-75; prof. air resources engring. Ill. Inst. Tech., Chgo., 1975—; dir. Regional Air Pollution Tng. Ctr. U.S. EPA. Author: Recovery, Recycle and Reuse of Industrial Waste, 1984; Air Monitoring Survey Design, 1977. Chmn. Knox County Air Pollution Control Bd., 1972-75. Served to 1st lt. USAF, 1959-63, Korea. U.S. EPA research fellow, 1968-69. Mem. ASCE, Air Pollution Control Assn. Home: 569 Carlisle Ct Glen Ellyn IL 60137 Office: Dept Environ Engring Ill Inst Tech 3200 S State St Chicago IL 60616

NOLL, STEVEN HARRY, lawyer; b. Jackson, Tenn., June 15, 1952; s. Harry George and Ruth Jane (Armbruster) N. B.S. with honor, Mich. State U., 1974; J.D., Ohio State U., 1977. Bar: Ill. 1978, Ohio 1978, U.S. Patent and Trademark Office 1978, U.S. Dist. Ct. (no. dist.) Ill. 1979, U.S. Ct. Appeals (7th and 8th cirs.) 1979, U.S. Ct. Appeals (fed. cir.) 1980, U.S. Ct. Appeals (6th cir.) 1981, U.S. Supreme Ct. 1982. Elec. engr. Magnavox Co., Fort Wayne, Ind., 1974-75; ptnr. Hill, Van Santen, Steadman & Simpson, P.C., Chgo., 1978—. Mem. Patent Law Assn. Chgo., Am. Intellectual Property Law Assn., Chgo. Council of Lawyers, Assn. Trial Lawyers Am., Internat. Trade Commn., Nat. Lawyers Guild, IEEE, ACLU, NOW, Ohio State Alumni Assn., Mich. State Alumni Assn., Eta Kappa Nu. Club: East Bank (Chgo.). Home: 644 W Arlington Apt 5G Chicago IL 60614 Office: Hill Van Santen Steadman & Simpson PC Sears Tower 70th Floor Chicago IL 60606

NOLLAN, RICHARD CHARLES, religious printing and pub. co. exec.; b. Neenah, Wis., Oct. 29, 1935; s. Walter Theodore and Emily Anne (Vondrachek) N.; student Northwestern U., eves. 1958-62. Mgr. data processing Wine & Spirits Liquor Co., Chgo., 1957-67, Gold Seal Liquors Co., Chgo., 1967-72; dir. mgmt. info. services J.S. Paluch Co., Schiller Park, 1972-84, v.p. 1984—. Served with USMC, 1953-57; Korea. Mem. Data Processing Mgmt. Assn., Office: 3825 N Willow Rd Schiller Park IL 60176 Home: 5328 N Linder Ave Chicago IL 60630

NOONAN, ROBERTA LEE, college adminstrator; child care center owner; b. Pitts., May 1, 1933; d. Harry Sidney and Nellie Catherine (Johnston) Lamneck; m. Joseph George Noonan, Oct. 23, 1955; children—James, Kathleen, Michael, Patricia, Mary, Nora, Joe. B.A., St. Xavier U., 1970, M.A., 1973; Ed.D., Nova U., 1980. Asst. buyer Boggs & Buhl, Pitts., 1949-50; pub. relations Bell Telephone, Pitts., 1951-53; service rep. pub. relations Delta Airlines, Chgo., 1953-56; columnist South Town Economist, Chgo., 1959-61; owner, dir. Bobbie Noonan's Child Care, Worth, Ill., 1964-73; child care coordinator Moraine Valley Community Coll., Palos Hills, Ill., 1973—; cons. Riley pre-sch. project, East Chicago, Ind., 1973-74, Parent-Tchr. Groups and Industry, Ill., 1983—; workshop leader pub. and pvt. pre-schs. and day care ctrs., Ill., 1980—. Author: Bold Beginning, 1973; Finger Plays for Little Folks, 1984. Mem. Pre-Sch. Owners Assn., South Suburban Assn. for Edn. Young Children (bd. dirs., sec. 1984-85), Am. Bus. Women's Assn. Republican. Roman Catholic. Avocations: nutrition counseling; music; reading; swimming. Home: Ironwood Ct Frankfort IL 60423 Office: Moraine Valley Community Coll 10900 S 88th Ave Palos Hills IL 60465

NOONEY, GREGORY JOSEPH, retired real estate executive; b. St. Louis, Aug. 12, 1903; m. Anna M. Frein, June 24, 1930; children—Gregory J., Ann Marie, John J. B.C.S., St. Louis U., 1926. Pub. acct. Touche, Niven & Co., St. Louis, 1924-28; asst. sec.-treas. Stix, Baer & Fuller, St. Louis, 1928-33, treas., dir., 1949-50; sec.-treas., dir. Ky. Hotel Co., Louisville, 1928-33; sec.-treas., dir. Lesser Goldman Co., St. Louis, 1933-45; founder G.J. Nooney & Co., St. Louis County, Mo. and East St. Louis, Ill., 1945, chmn. bd., 1969-83, chmn. emeritus, 1983—. Former dir. Boatmen's Nat. Bank, Fed. Compress & Warehouse Co., Memphis, others. Mem. City Plan Commn. St. Louis, 1933-47, chmn., 1938-39; former mem. Mo. Mental Health Commn., St. Louis County Police Bd. Clubs: Old Warson Country (pres. 1960), Mo. Athletic (life; pres. 1948), St. Louis (pres. 1965-66); Ekwanok Country (Manchester, Vt.); Everglades (Palm Beach, Fla.); Ocean (Ocean Ridge, Fla.). Home: 900 S Hanley Rd Saint Louis MO 63105

NOPPER, RALPH JACOB, civil engr.; b. Toledo, July 5, 1916; s. Charles Joseph and Martha Elizabeth (Rippel) N.; B.Engring., U. Toledo, 1939; m. Roberta R. Newcomb, July 31, 1943; children—Linda E. (Mrs. Kenneth J. Keiser). Structural engr. A. Bentley & Sons Co., Toledo, 1937-38; constrn. engr. E.B. Badger & Sons Co., Boston, 1938-39; engr., H.C. Baker Co., Toledo, 1939-40; chief maintenance engr. Libbey-Owens-Ford Co., Toledo, 1940-81; self-employed as cons. engr., Toledo, 1940—. Registered profl. engr., Ohio. Mem. ASCE (pres. Toledo sect. 1954), Nat., Ohio, Toledo (pres. 1953) socs. profl. engrs., Toledo Tech. Council (pres. 1952-53). Home: 3710 Harley Rd Toledo OH 43613

NORD, DOUGLAS CHARLES, political science educator, researcher, foreign affairs consultant; b. Pasadena, Calif., Aug. 17, 1952; s. Charles Seward and Kathleen Mariane (Reid) N. A.B. summa cum laude, U. Redlands, 1974; M.A. in Polit. Sci., Duke U., 1976, Ph.D., 1979. Asst. dir. Can. Studies Program, Duke U., Durham, N.C., 1976-77, lectr. polit. sci. dept., 1978-79; guest scholar Brookings Instn., Washington, 1977-78; asst. prof. polit. sci. U. Minn.-Duluth, 1979-85, assoc. prof., 1985—, coordinator Internat. Studies Program. Bd. adv. Head of Lakes UN Assn.; mem. Minn. Fgn. Policy Assn. Recipient U. Minn.-Duluth Outstanding Faculty award, 1982, Internat. Faculty Devel. award, 1981. Mem. Am. Polit. Sci. Assn., Can. Polit. Sci. Assn., Internat. Studies Assn., Am. Assn. Can. Studies, Midwest Can. Studies Assn. (pres.). Contbr. writings to profl. publs.

NORDBERG, JOHN ALBERT, federal judge; b. Evanston, Ill., June 18, 1926; s. Carl Albert and Judith Ranghild (Carlson) N.; m. Jane Spaulding, June 18, 1947; children—Carol, Mary, Janet, John. B.A., Carleton Coll., 1947; J.D., U. Mich., 1950. Bar: Ill. 1950, U.S. Dist. Ct. (no. dist.) Ill. 1957, U.S. Ct. Appeals (7th cir.) 1961. Assoc., Pope & Ballard, Chgo., 1950-57, ptnr. Pope, Ballard, Shepard & Fowle, Chgo., 1957-76; judge Circuit Ct. Cook County, Ill., 1976-82; judge U.S. Dist. Court (no. dist.) Ill., Chgo., 1982—; magistrate circuit court, justice of the peace Ill., 1957-65; Editor-in-chief, mem. bd. editors: Chgo. Bar Record, 1966-74. Served with USN, 1944-46, PTO. Mem. ABA, Chgo. Bar Assn., Ill. State Bar Assn. (assembly rep. 1971-76), Am. Judicature Soc., Law Club Chgo., Legal Club Chgo., Order of Coif. Clubs: Univ., Union League (Chgo.) Lodge: Rotary. Office: US Dist Court 219 S Dearborn St Chicago IL 60604

NORDLAND, GERALD J(OHN), museum director; b. Los Angeles, July 10, 1927; s. Arthur Andre and Doris Monica (Johnston) N.; A.B., U. So. Calif., 1948, J.D., 1950; m. Mary Lou Lindstrom, 1948 (div. 1972); children—Brady Lynn, Todd Jefferson; m. Paula Giannini, 1981. Art critic various mags. and newspapers, 1955-64; dean Chouinard Art Inst., Los Angeles, 1960-64; dir. Washington Gallery Modern Art, D.C., 1964-66, San Francisco Mus. Art, 1966-72, Frederick S. Wight Art Gallery, UCLA, 1973-77; dir. Milw. Art Mus., 1977-84, holder Disting. Scholars chair, 1985. Commr. Calif. State Fair, 1974-76. Served with U.S. Army, 1953-55. Gaston Lachaise Found. grantee, 1973-74; John Simon Guggenheim Meml. Found. fellow, 1985-86. Mem. Assn. Art Museum Dirs. Author: Paul Jenkins, 1972; Gaston Lachaise—The Man and His Work, 1974.

NORDLING, BERNARD ERICK, lawyer; b. Nekoma, Kans., June 14, 1921; s. C.R. Ebben and Edith (Freeburg) N.; A.B., McPherson Coll., 1947; student George Washington U., 1941-43; LL.B., J.D., Kans. U., 1949; m. Barbara Ann Burkholder, Mar. 26, 1949; children—Karen, Kristine, Leslie, Erick, Julie. Clerical employee FBI, 1941-44; admitted to Kans. bar, 1949; practiced in Hugoton, Kans., 1949—; mem. firms Kramer & Nordling, 1950-65, Kramer, Nordling, Nordling & Tate, 1966—; city atty., Hugoton, 1951—; county atty. Stevens County (Kans.), 1957-63. Sec., Raycolor, Inc., Hugoton, 1968-81; exec. sec. S.W. Kans. Royalty Owners Assn., 1968—; Kans. mem. legal com. Interstate Oil Compact Commn., 1969—, mem. supply tech. adv. com. Nat. Gas Survey, FPC, 1975-77; mem. Kans. Energy Adv. Council, 1975-78, exec. com., 1976-78. Mem. Hugoton Sch. Bds., 1954-68, pres. grade sch. bd., 1961-66; pres. Stevens County Library Bd., 1957-63. Trustee McPherson Coll., 1971-81, mem. exec. com., 1975-81. Served with AUS, 1944-46. Mem. Nat. Honor Soc., Nat. Assn. Royalty Owners (bd. govs. 1980—), Order of Coif. Home: 218 N Jackson St Hugoton KS 67951 Office: 209 E 6th St Hugoton KS 67951

NORDLUND, DONALD E., executive, lawyer; b. Stromsburg, Nebr., Mar. 1, 1922; s. Elmer C. and Edith O. (Peterson) N.; B.A., Midland Coll., 1943, LL.D. (hon.), 1975; J.D., U. Mich., 1948; m. Jane Houston, June 5, 1948; children—Craig, William, Sally, Peter. Bar: Ill. 1949. Assoc. firm Stevenson, Conaghan, Velde & Hackbert, Chgo., 1948-56; counsel A.E. Staley Mfg. Co., Decatur, Ill., 1956-58, v.p. law and adminstrn., 1958-65, pres., 1965-80, chief exec. officer, 1973—, chmn., 1975—, also dir.; dir. Amsted Industries, Citizens Nat. Bank Decatur, Ill. Bell Telephone Co., Sentry Ins. Co., Mid-Con Corp., Sundstrand Corp., Midwest Fin. Group, Inc., Peoria, Ill. Trustee, Millikin U., 1960—, chmn. bd. trustees, 1979, 1984—; trustee Athens (Greece) Coll.; bd. dirs. Decatur Meml. Hosp., 1966-75, grad. dir. council; mem. Pres. Reagan's Adv. Council on Private Sector Initiatives; mem. Gov.'s Commn. Sci. and High Tech., Ill. Served with U.S. Army, 1943-46, 50-52; Korea. Mem. Am. Bar Assn., Chgo. Bar Assn., U.S. Corn Refiners Assn., Inc. (past chmn., hon. dir.). Clubs: Decatur, Country of Decatur, Tavern of Chgo. Office: 2200 Eldorado St Decatur IL 62525

NORFLEET, DAVID ALLEN, anesthesiologist; b. Higginsville, Mo., Mar. 16, 1949; s. Tandy Agee and Evelyn (Bales) N.; m. Candace Jean Clarke, Aug. 5, 1972; children—Ashley, Ryan. Student Central Mo. State U., 1967-68; B.S. in Pharmacy, U. Mo., 1972; D.O., U. Health Scis., Kansas City, 1976. Diplomate Nat. Bd. Osteo. Physician Examiners. Intern Osteo. Hosp. of Maine, Portland, 1976-77; resident Normandy Osteo. Hosp., St. Louis, 1977-79; anesthesiologist Community Anesthesiologists, Phoenix, 1979-80, St. Charles Anesthesia Group (Mo.), 1980—; Mem. St. Louis Soc. Osteo. Physicians, Mo. Assn. Osteo. Physicians, Am. Osteo. Assn., St. Louis Soc. Anesthesiologists, Mo. Soc. Anesthesiologists, Am. Soc. Anesthesiologists, Internat. Anesthesia Research Soc. Methodist.

NORGAARD, ORLAN WILLMAN, fire chief; b. Arlington, S.D., July 16, 1941; s. Willie and Elsie (Henrickson) N.; m. Gloria Jean Berg, Jan. 29, 1966; children—Brenda, Ryan. With Sioux Falls Fire Dept., S.D., 1964—, fire fighter, 1964-70, lt. II, 1970-75, capt., 1975-78, bn. chief, 1978-80, 1984—, chief, 1980-84; pres. Minnehaha County Fire Chiefs, Sioux Falls, 1984; pres. Internat. Fire Fighters Local 814, 1970-78; state v.p. Internat. Fire Chiefs, S.D., 1981-84. Served with U.S. Army, 1960-63. Named State Fire Fighter Yr., S.D. Fire Fighters Assn., 1974; Fire Fighter of Yr. K.C., Sioux Falls, 1978. Mem. S.D. Fire Fighters, S.D. Fire Chiefs, Internat. Assn. Fire Chiefs. Democrat. Lutheran.

NORMAN, JOHN WILLIAM, oil co. exec.; b. Harrisburg, Ill., Sept. 4, 1910; s. Walter Jacob and Clarissa May (Bush) N.; student pub. schs., Saline County, Ill.; m. Marcella Mary Souheaver, July 2, 1937. Dist. mgr. Martin Oil Co., 1936-54; with Am-Bulk Oil Co. (name changed to Norman Oil Co., 1960), Lisle, Ill., 1949—, pres., 1960—. Served with USNR, 1943-44. Mem. VFW, Am. Legion. Home: 4333 Main St Lisle IL 60532 Office: 1018 Ogden Ave Lisle IL 60532

NORMOYLE, JOHN LOUIS, writer, editor, syndicated columnist; b. Chgo., Mar. 27, 1922; s. John Joseph and Catherine Henrietta (Shrodi) N.; grad. Morton Jr. Coll., 1947; B.S., Northwestern U., 1952; m. June Rose Bastlin, Sept. 8, 1947 (div. Sept. 1969); children—Janice, Judy, Joyce, Jennifer. Asso. editor Brick and Clay Record mag., Chgo., 1950-53; publicity supr. Allstate Ins. Co., Skokie, Ill., 1953-60; account exec. Philip Lesly Co., Chgo., 1960-62; pub. relations dir. Alberto Culver Co., Chgo., 1963; exec. v.p. Compass 4 Pub.

Relations, Chgo., 1964-67; dir. press info. Bonsib Advt., Fort Wayne, Ind., 1968-69; mng. editor Lab. Medicine mag., Chgo., 1969-77; dir. public info. Am. Soc. Clin. Pathologists, Chgo., 1977-80; prin. Normoyle Writing/Editorial Services, Chgo., 1981—. Guest lectr. pub. relations and journalism Mich. State U., East Lansing, 1965-66, Columbia Coll., Chgo., 1961, YMCA Central Coll., Chgo., 1970-71, U. Ill., 1973, Chgo. Med. Coll., 1974-75, Northwestern U., 1976, Sangamon Coll., Springfield, Ill., 1977. Served with AUS, 1942-45. Decorated Bronze Star medal, Purple Heart with oak leaf cluster. Recipient Honor award for best feature writing, Publicity Club of Chgo., 1962, award for best continuing pub. relations campaign, 1964. Mem. Chgo. Press Club, Mensa, 82d Airborne Div. Assn. Author: The News Release Format, 1956. Contbr. articles to profl. jours.; column syndicated by Dickson-Bennett Features. Home and Office: 1630 W Farwell Ave Chicago IL 60626

NORRED, LARRY ROSS, music publishing company executive; b. Piggott, Ark., June 17, 1951; s. Kenneth Harris and Wanda Jean (Wiley) N.; m. Cathy Jane Jones, July 1, 1978; 1 son, Geoffrey Ross. B.Mus., Baylor U., 1973; B.Mus., U. Miami, 1975. Asst. music editor Hal Leonard Music Pub. Co., Winona, Minn., 1975-78; mng. editor Jenson Publs., New Berlin, Wis., 1978-80, prodn. mgr., 1980-83, prodn. ops. mgr., 1983-84, v.p. prodn., 1984—; music coordinator Kettle Moraine Bapt. Ch. Mem. ASCAP (recipient awards for new composers, 1979—). Republican. Baptist. Composer numerous arrangements, cantata: And His Name is Jesus, 1982; Toyland (musical). Home: 151 Lake St Mukwonago WI 53149 Office: 2770 S 171st St PO Box 248 New Berlin WI 53151

NORRIS, JOHN HART, lawyer; b. New Bedford, Mass., Aug. 4, 1942; s. Edwin Arter and Harriet Joan (Winter) N.; m. Anne Kiley Monaghan, June 10, 1967; children—Kiley Anne, Amy O'Shea. B.A., Ind. U., 1964; J.D., U. Mich., 1967. Bar: Mich. 1968, U.S. Ct. Mil. Appeals 1969, U.S. Supreme Ct. 1974, U.S. Ct. Claims 1975, U.S. Tax Ct. 1979. Assoc., then ptnr. Monaghan, Campbell, LoPrete, McDonald and Norris, 1970-83; ptnr. Dickinson, Wright, Moon, Van Dusen, & Freeman, 1984—; dir. Holly's Hotsock, Stark Hickey Ford, Inc., RTR Distbn., Prime Securities Corp., Ray M. Whyte Co., Ward-Williston Drilling Co. Mem. Republican State Fin. Com.; mem. fin. com. gubernatorial candidate for 1982; co-founder, co-chmn. Rep. majority club; bd. dirs. Boys and Girls Clubs of Met. Detroit, 1979—, Mercy Coll.; mem. Detroit Hist. Soc., 1984—; mem. nat. council Salk Inst. Served with M.I., U.S. Army, 1968-70. Recipient numerous civic and non-profit assn. awards; mem. Blue Key Nat. Honor frat. Fellow Mich. State Bar Found.; mem. ABA, Mich. Oil and Gas Assn. (legal and legis. com.), State Bar Mich. (chmn. environ. law sect.), Oakland County Bar Assn., Detroit Bar Assn., Detroit Zool. Soc., Sons of Whiskey Rebellion, Phi Delta Phi. Roman Catholic. Clubs: Bloomfield Hills Country; Thomas M. Cooley, Detroit Athletic, Hundred, Prismatic, Turtle Lake, Yondotega, Contbr. articles to profl jours. Home: 1325 Buckingham St Birmingham MI 48008 Office: 525 N Woodward Ave Bloomfield Hills MI 48013

NORRIS, WILLIAM C., data processing executive; b. Inavale, Nebr., July 14, 1911; s. William H. and Mildred A. (McCall) N.; B.S., U. Nebr., 1932; m. Jane Malley, Sept. 15, 1943; children—W. Charles, George, Daniel, Brian, Constance, Roger, Mary N., David. Sales engr. Westinghouse Electric Mfg. Co., Chgo., 1935-41; v.p., gen. mgr. Engring. Research Assocs., 1946-55; v.p., gen. mgr. Univac div. Sperry Rand Corp., 1955-57; pres. Control Data Corp., from 1957, now chmn. bd., chief exec. officer, chmn. policy com.; bd. dirs. N.W. Bank Corp., N.W. Growth Fund, Tronchemics, Inc. Trustee Hill Reference Library; adv. com. White House Conf. on Balanced Nat. Growth and Econ. Devel., from 1978. Served to comdr. USNR, 1941-46. Office: Control Data Corp 8100 34th Ave S Minneapolis MN 55440*

NORTH, KENNETH EARL, lawyer; b. Chgo., Nov. 18, 1945; s. Earl and Marion (Temple) N.; m. Susan C. Gutzmer, June 6, 1970; children—Krista Erin, Kari Elizabeth. A.A. with high honors, Coll. of DuPage, Glen Ellyn, Ill., 1970; B.A. with high honors, No. Ill. U., 1971; J.D., Duke U., 1974. Bar: Ill. 1974, Guam 1978. Ptnr. firm Chew, Yorke & North, Wheaton, Ill., 1975-76; div. chief DuPage County State's Attys. Office, Wheaton, 1976-78; spl. asst. U.S. atty. Terr. of Guam, Agana, 1978-79, atty. gen., 1979-80; ptnr. firm Solomon, Rosenfeld, Elliott, Stiefel & Glovka Ltd., Chgo., 1982—; adj. prof. law John Marshall Law Sch., Chgo., 1985—; cons. Terr. of Guam, 1980-81. Contbr. articles to legal publs. Vice pres. Glen Ellyn Manor Civic Assn., 1981—; police commr. Village of Glen Ellyn, 1982—. Mem. Assn. Trial Lawyers Am., ABA, Computer Law Assn., Ill. Bar Assn., Chgo. Bar Assn., Mensa. Republican. Pioneer use of computer in ct. Office: Solomon Rosenfeld Elliott Stiefel & Glovka Ltd 30 N LaSalle St Chicago IL 60602

NORTH, RALPH MASON, III, appraising company salesman; b. Glen Ridge, N.J., Aug. 15, 1930; s. Ralph Mason and Margaret (McManus) N.; children—Ralph Mason IV, Margaret North Schnabl, Lauren Adams. M.E., Stevens Inst. Tech., 1952. Registered profl. engr., Wis. Engr., Walter Kidde & Co., Belleville, N.J., 1952-53; real estate broker Donald C. North Co., Verona, N.J., 1955-61; appraiser, salesman Am. Appraisal Assocs. Inc., Milw., 1961—. Contbr. articles to profl. jours. Alderman, Waukesha City Council, Wis., 1969-83, pres., 1980; pres. Waukesha Civic Theater, 1980-83. Served with USCG, 1953-55. Mem. Am. Soc. Appraisers (sr.), Wis. Assn. Profl. Engrs. Republican. Roman Catholic. Avocations: sports, gardening, acting, numismatics, antique repair and restoration.

NORTH, WILLIAM DENSON, trade association lawyer, executive; b. Apr. 4, 1930; s. William Edward and Paula (Denson) N.; m. Carol Linden, Apr. 23, 1960; children—Anita, William Linden. B.S. in Commerce, U. Ill., 1952; J.D., Harvard U., 1959. Bar: Ill. 1959, U.S. Ct. Claims 1973, U.S. Supreme Ct. 1973. Assoc., Kirkland & Ellis, Chgo., 1959-65, ptnr., 1965-78; ptnr. Reuben & Proctor, Chgo., 1978-80; sr. v.p., gen. counsel Nat. Assn. Realtors, Chgo., 1980—; sec. Home Investors Fund, Washington, 1983—; mem. adv. bd. Am. Bd. Family Practice, Lexington, Ky., 1983—; pres. Freedom to Read Found., Chgo., 1981-84; dir. Intumescent Tech., Inc., Chgo., 1981—. Recipient Immroth award ALA, 1985. Mem. ABA, Ill. Bar Assn., Chgo. Bar Assn., Chgo. Estate Planning Council, Am. Soc. Assn. Execs., Legal Club of Chgo., Copyright Soc. of U.S.A., U. Ill. Alumni Assn. (dir. 1968-74), U. Ill. Found., Am. Legion, SAR, Republican. Unitarian. Clubs: Union League, Caxton (Chgo.), Harvard (N.Y.C.). Contbr. articles to profl. jours. Office: Nat Assn Realtors 430 N Michigan Ave Chicago IL 60611

NORTHRUP, ARTHUR HARRY, lawyer, economist; b. Indpls., June 3, 1920; s. Leonard Evart and Margaret (Couden) N.; B.A. in Econs. with honors, Harvard U., 1942, M.B.A., 1946; J.D., U. Mich., 1949; m. Anne Mary Holmes, July 31, 1948; children—Arthur Harry, Nancy Anne Northrup Eastman, m. 2d, Deborah Lee Norris, Sept. 19, 1969; children—Heather Lynn, Christopher A., Holly Margaret. Quality control engr. Wright Aero. Corp., 1943-44; admitted to Ind. bar, 1949; since practiced in Indpls.; mem. Gregg, Fillion, Hughes & Northrup, 1951-70, Martz, Beattey, Hinds & Wallace, 1970-78; sole practice, 1978—; lectr. econs. Earlham Coll., 1949, Butler U., 1950-57, 59-76; asst. city atty., Indpls., 1951-54, 68-76; mem. Ind. Ho. of Reps., 1969-70; gen. counsel Ind. Consumer Finance Assn., 1954-74, Ind. Restaurant Assn., 1951-56. Sec. Ind. Corps. Survey Commn., 1958-77, mem., 1978—. Pres. Washington Twp. Republican Club, 1966-68; sec. bd. dirs. Summer Mission for Sick Children; bd. dirs. West Dist. YMCA. Served with USNR, 1944-46. Mem. ABA, Seventh Circuit, Ind. (chmn. probate trust and real estate sect.), Indpls. bar assns., Am. Legion (past post comdr.), SAR (pres. Ind. 1956). Republican. Episcopalian. Clubs: Century (pres. 1960), Ind. Harvard (pres. 1954), Harvard Bus. Sch. (pres. 1955), U. Mich. (pres. Indpls. alumni 1975-77) (Indpls.), Meridian Hills Country, Contemporary. Editor: Forms for Indiana Corporations, 1966, 77. Contbr. articles on trusts, income tax and other tax laws to profl. jours. Home: Indianapolis IN Office: 130 E Washington St Indianapolis IN 46204

NORTHUP, WILLIAM CARLTON, acct.; b. Columbia, Mo., Dec. 1, 1930; s. Lansford Lionel and Elsie Rebecca (Eaton) N.; B.S. in Statistics, U. Mo., 1953, M.B.A., 1974; m. Sharon Joan Carlson, June 27, 1970; children—Richard Carlton, Karen Frances. Research asso. Mo. Crippled Children's Service, Columbia, 1968-69, asst. supt. research and records, 1969-70, supt., 1970-76; broker London Commodity House, Inc., Chgo., 1976-77; chief accountant Nat. Congress PTA, Chgo., 1977-78; mgmt. analyst fin. systems for health and hosps. Cook County Governing Commn., Chgo., 1978-79; acct. V Cook County Hosp., 1979—; controller, dir. pub. health statistics, coordinator automatic data processing, supt. ins. Mo. Crippled Children's Service; asst. prodn. mgr., chief estimator, account exec. Am. Press; spl. advisor to Gov. Mo. on printing and pub., 1965. Mem. Columbia Fin. Study Commn., 1974, steering com. Columbia Town Meeting, 1976; bd. dirs. Camp Wannanoya, 1976; mem. steering com. Teen Auto Club, 1972; vol. probation officer Boone County Juvenile Office, 1971-72. Mem. Am. Mgmt. Assn., Am. Statis. Assn., Mo. Pub. Health Assn., Assn. M.B.A. Execs., Hosp. Fin. Mgmt. Assn., Mensa, Delta Sigma Pi. Republican. Baptist. Club: Optimists. Home: 24 Williamsburg Terr Evanston IL 60203 Office: 1825 W Harrison St Chicago IL 60612

NORTHWAY, WILLIAM MARTIN, orthodontist, researcher, educator; b. Ann Arbor, Mich., July 26, 1945; s. Robert Orcutt and Georgia (Kasischke); m. Ellen Auwers, June 27, 1970; children—William Martin Jr., Tobin John. B.A., Kenyon Coll., 1968; D.D.S., U. Mich., 1972; Dip.Orth., U. Montreal, Que., Can., 1974, M.S., 1976. Practice dentistry specializing in orthodontics, St. Bruno, Que., 1974-80, Traverse City, Mich., 1980—; lectr., clin. instr. McGill U., Montreal, Que., 1974-80; vis. researcher Ctr. Human Growth and Devel., Ann Arbor, 1972—; vis. lectr. U. Detroit, 1981—, and others. Contbr. articles to profl. jours. Bd. dirs. YMCA, Traverse City, Mich., 1982—. Mem. Am. Assn. Orthodontists, ADA, Mich. Dental Assn., Mich. Soc. Orthodontists, Edward H. Angle Soc. Orthodontia. Avocations: sailing, skiing, camping, fishing.

NORTON, JOHN JEFFREY, dentist; b. St. Paul, May 28, 1948; s. John Charles and Margret (Jeffrey) N.; m. Catherine Ann Borbas, June 14, 1974 (div. 1979); m. Concetta Marie Serafina, Jan. 30, 1981; children—Cara Elizabeth, Kelsey Ann, John Matthew. Student Coll. St. Thomas, 1966-70, Coll. Osteo. Medicine of Pacific, 1981-83; D.D.S., Creighton Dental Sch., 1974. Gen. practice dentistry, Cottage Grove, Minn., 1974—; lectr. in field. Advisor State Ins. Commn. and Comml. Commn., St. Paul, 1984—. Mem. Mid-Am. Orthodontic Soc. (sec. 1976—), Minn. Acad. of Orthodontics for the Gen. Practitioner (bd. dirs. 1976—). Roman Catholic. Club: St. Croix Sailing. Avocations: sail boat racing; running; skiing; cross-country skiing. Office: 7501 80th St S Cottage Grove MN 55016

NORUM, ROBERT ANTHONY, physician, researcher; b. Ames, Iowa, July 3, 1943; m. Marjorie J. Taylor, July 3, 1970. B.A., N.D. State U., 1964; M.D., Johns Hopkins U., 1968. Diplomate Am. Bd. Internal Medicine, Am. Bd. Med. Genetics. Intern, Johns Hopkins Hosp., Balt., 1968-69, resident, 1969-70; asst. prof. Cornell U. Med. Coll., N.Y.C., 1975-78; dir. genetics research lab. Henry Ford Hosp., Detroit, 1978—; clin. asst. prof. medicine U. Mich., Ann Arbor, 1979—. Author jour. articles. Served to maj. U.S. Army, 1973-75. NIH research grantee, 1976, 81. Fellow ACP; mem. Central Soc. Clin. Research, Am. Fedn. Clin. Research, AAAS. Office: Henry Ford Hosp 2799 W Grand Blvd Detroit MI 48202

NORVICH, STEVEN N., data processing executive; b. Mpls., June 13, 1943; s. Samuel G. and Ethel (Bennesovitz) N.; married, July 30, 1970 (div. 1982). A.A., Harper Coll., 1984; M.B.A., U. Chgo., 1977; B.A., SUNY-Albany, 1985, B.S., 1985. Dir., Crane Co., Chgo., 1969-70; pres. Cyborg Internat., Chgo., 1970-77; gen. mgr. UOP Litigation Services, Des Plaines, Ill., 1977-84; dir. G C Services, Chgo., 1984—; cons. 1983-84. Contbr. articles to profl. jours. Republican. Avocations: golf; bridge; white water rafting; landscaping. Office: G C Services 2 N Riverside #400 Chicago IL 60606

NOTHERN, ELLA LOUISE, nurse; b. Salina, Kans., Jan. 30, 1931; d. Herman Herbert and Eva Alice (Beil) Will; m. M. Roland Nothern, Nov. 22, 1950; children—David Will, Matthew Roland, Nathan Jon. B.A., Kans. Wesleyan U., Salina, 1973; Assoc. degree in Nursing, Cloud County Community Coll., Concordia, Kans., 1981. R.N., Kans. Pre-sch. tchr., Glasco, Kans., 1974-75; tchr. Galsco High Sch., 1975-76; clk. bus. office Mitchell County Hosp., Beloit, Kans., 1976-77; activity dir. Nicol Home, Glasco, 1977-79; nurse psychol. unit St. Joseph's Hosp., Concordia, 1981-84; charge nurse Good Samaritan Ctr., Minneapolis, Kans., 1985—. Mem. exec. com. Central Kans. Library System, Great Bend, 1977-83; bd. dirs. Pawnee Mental Health Ctr., Manhattan, Kans., 1982-83; mem. ambulance crew Glasco Ambulance Service, 1979-82. Mem. ALA (co-chmn. publicity com. trustee div. 1983), Lutheran Missionary Soc. (pres. 1960-61), Epsilon Sigma Alpha (pres. 1964-65). Republican. Home: Route 1 Salina KS 67401 Office: Good Samaritan Ctr Minneapolis KS

NOTOWIDIGDO, MUSINGGIH HARTOKO, information systems executive; b. Indonesia, Dec. 9, 1938; s. Moekarto and Martaniah (Brodjonegoro) N.; B.M.E., George Washington U., 1961; M.Sc., N.Y. U., 1966, postgrad., 1970; m. Sihar P. Tambunan, Oct. 1, 1966 (dec. Nov. 1976); m. 2d, Joanne S. Gutter, June 3, 1979; children—Matthew Joseph, Jonathan Paul. Cons., Dollar Blitz & Assocs., Washington, 1962-64; ops. research analyst Am. Can Co., N.Y.C., 1966-69; prin. analyst Borden Inc., Columbus, Ohio, 1969-70, mgr. ops. research, 1970-71, mgr. ops. analysis and research, 1972-74, asst. gen. controller, officer, 1974-77, corp. dir. info. systems/econ. analysis, officer, 1977-83; v.p. info. systems Wendy's Internat., 1983—; adj. lectr. Grad. Sch. Adminstrn. Capital U. Mem. Fin Execs. Inst. (chmn. MIS com.), Ops. Research Soc., Inst. Mgmt. Sci., Am. Mgmt. Assn., Nat. Assn. Bus. Economists, Long Range Planning Soc., Am. Statis. Assn., AAAS, World Future Soc., Data Processing Mgmt. Assn., Soc. Info. Mgmt. Republican. Clubs: Capital, Racquet. Home: 1965 Brandywine Dr Upper Arlington OH 43220 Office: 4288 W Dublin-Granville Rd Dublin OH 43017

NOTTKE, WILLIAM HARRY, packaging company executive; b. Kankakee, Ill., Aug. 27, 1951; s. William Harry and Adeline Mae (Brinkman) N.; m. Lora Leigh Kronsbein, Apr. 3, 1980; children—Crystal, Ashley. Student Kankakee Community Coll., 1970-72, Western Ill U., 1969-70. Customer service supr. Baker & Taylor Co., Momence, Ill., 1971-73; sales/service corr. Kankakee Container Corp. (Ill.), 1973-76; sales/service mgr. Keystone Container Corp., St. Louis, 1976-79; owner, pres. Riverdale Packaging Corp., St. Louis, 1979—, also chmn. bd. Mem. Assn. Ind. Corrugated Converters (v.p. St. Louis chpt.). Methodist. Office: Riverdale Packaging Corp 4165 Duncan St St Louis MO 63110

NOVACK, RICHARD VICTOR, diamond and gem brokerage executive; b. Mpls., Aug. 8, 1945; s. Maurice and Alice (Offerman) N.; m. Bogumila Maria-Antonia Strutynska Berlicz-Sas, July 17, 1980; 1 child, Maurice Louis Strutynski Berlicz-Sas. Degree in International Relations, U. Minn., 1967. Pres. M.L. Novack Inc., Mpls., 1967-74, Midwest Diamond Exchange, Inc., Mpls., 1975—, Diamond Exchange Assocs., Inc., 1979—, Diamond Trading Corp., Mpls., 1979—. Author: Consumers Guide to Diamond Grading, 1975. Author/inventor Computerized Diamond Trading System, 1976. Address: Midwest Diamond Exchange IDS Crystal Ct Minneapolis MN 55402

NOVAK, JAMES ALAN, architect; b. Cedar Rapids, Iowa, Apr. 30, 1947; s. Elroy Henry and Arlene Jean (Dvorak) N.; m. Christina Kay Lottman, June 2, 1972; 1 son, Richard. B.A. in Architecture, Iowa State U., 1974, M.Arch., 1977. Cert. Nat. Council Archtl. Registration Bd.; registered architect, Iowa, Colo. Prin., project architect Olson, Popa, Novak, Architects P.C., Marion, Iowa, 1979—. Bd. dirs. Cedar Rapids-Marion Arts Council, ARC, Nat. Multiple Sclerosis Soc. Mem. AIA, Tau Sigma Delta. Clubs: East Cedar Rapids-Marion Rotary. Home: 136 Tomahawk Trail SE Cedar Rapids IA 52403 Office: 790 11th St Marion IA 52302

NOVAK, STEVE GLYNN, state senator, realtor; b. Mpls., May 26, 1949; s. Emil Steven and Glynndolyn (Jones) Novak Stokes; m. Julie Caroline, Oct. 5, 1951; children—Natalie, Jewel. B.A., U. Minn.-Duluth, 1971. Mem. Minn. Senate. Office: State Senate Minnesota Room 203 State Capitol Saint Paul MN 55155

NOVOTNEY, JOHN R., JR., engineer, land surveyor, ski instructor; b. Streator, Ill., Nov. 5, 1947; s. John R. and Marcella A. (Uhren) N.; m. Mary Jo Kinney, Aug. 22, 1981; children—Jesse M., Jayme A., Jon R. B.S. in Mech. Engring., U. Dayton, 1970; M. Engring. Adminstrn., Bradley U., 1976. Registered profl. engr., Ill. Registered land surveyor, Ill. Engr.-in-tng. Ill. Dept. Transp., Ottawa, 1968; enging. aide Renwick & Assocs., Ottawa, 1969, project mgr., 1970—, dir., 1978—. Mem. Overall Econ. Devel. Com. La Salle County, Ill., 1976-83. Mem. Ill. Soc. Profl. Engrs. (pres. Ill. Valley chpt. 1982-83), Nat. Soc. Profl. Engrs., Ill. Assn. Water Pollution Control Operators, Profl. Ski Instrs. Am. (registered). Roman Catholic. Club: Ottawa Ski Team (pres. 1981-84, treas. 1984—). Avocations: alpine skiing; water skiing; nordic skiing; softball. Home: 131 Riverview Dr Ottawa IL 61350 Office: Robert H Renwick & Assocs Inc 228 W Main St Ottawa IL 61350

NOVOTNY, THOMAS FRANCIS, lawyer; b. Chgo., May 23, 1948; s. Thomas James and Lillian (Zamiatala) N.; m. Mary Anita Point, Aug. 21, 1971; children—Thomas Francis Jr., Anne Marie. B.A., with high honors, Lewis Coll., 1970; J.D. with highest honors, Ill. Inst. Tech.-Chgo. Kent, 1981. Bars: Ill. 1981, U.S. Dist. Ct. (no. dist.) Ill. 1981, U.S. Ct. Appeals (7th cir.) 1982. Educator, St. Rita High Sch., Chgo., 1970-73; police officer Chgo. Police Dept., 1973-79, sgt., 1979-81; assoc. Seyfarth, Shaw, Fairweather, Geraldson, Chgo., 1981-84; sole practice, Chgo., 1984—; presenter, lectr. West Suburban Hosp., Oak Park, Ill., 1982—, Little Co. of Mary Hosp., Evergreen Park, Ill.; 1982—; cons. Families and Amputees in Motion, Inc., Chgo., 1984—, Morgan Park Beverly Hills Bus. Assn., Chgo., 1984—. Author various policies and procs. for Chgo. Police Dept. Mem. ABA, Ill. State Bar Assn., Chgo. Bar Assn., S.W. Bar Assn., Ill. Workers Comp Lawyers Assn. Roman Catholic. Home: 10207 S Washtenaw Chicago IL 60642 Office: 10046 S Western Ave Chicago IL 60643

NOWACZEK, FRANK HUXLEY, cable television executive; b. Bklyn., July 6, 1930; s. Frank Huxley and Louise (Blake) N.; m. Alice Elaine Novak, May 21, 1955; children—Richard Alan, Elaine. Student St. Lawrence U., 1948-50; B.S. in Hotel Adminstrn., Cornell U., 1952; postgrad. in polit. sci. and pub. relations George Washington U., 1954-58, Am. U., 1954-57. Spl. agt. spl. ops. br. security div. Nat. Security Agy., Def. Dept., 1954-59; asst. to pres., dir. research Nat. Cable TV Assn., Washington, 1959-64; asst. to pres. TeleSystems Corp., Glenside, Pa., 1964-66; v.p., part-owner Newport Cablevision (Vt.), 1966-68; v.p. Blackburn & Co., Inc., Washington, 1968-76; v.p. Mid Atlantic region Warner Amex Cable Communications, N.Y.C., 1976-80, sr. v.p. eastern div., Ft. Washington, Pa., 1980-82, sr. v.p. nat. div., Columbus, Ohio, 1982-83; owner Cable Media Co., Worthington, Ohio, 1983—; pres. Newcable TV Corp., 1985—; mng. gen. ptnr. Newcable TV Ptnrs. I, II, III and IV, 1985—; speaker various orgns. Served with CIC, U.S. Army, 1952-54. Mem. Soc. Relay Engrs. (Gt. Britain), Nat. Cable TV Pioneers Assn., Pa. Cable TV Assn. (pres., dir.), Pa. Cable TV Pioneers Assn., Phila. Cable TV Club (founder), Cornell Soc. Hotelmen, Am. Mgmt. Assn., Nat. Cable TV Assn. (sec. tech. standards com. 1961 chmn. membership com. 1965-66), IEEE, Cornell U. Alumni Club, Phi Delta Theta. Republican. Mem. Dutch Reformed Ch. Home and Office: 283 Meditation Ln Worthington OH 43085

NOWAK, CHESTER JOSEPH, optometrist; b. Chgo., Jan. 30, 1923; s. Peter Joseph and Josephine (Starsiak) N.; O.D., Ill. Coll. Optometry, 1945; m. Florence J. Wardach, Feb. 14, 1943; children—Sandra Jane, Susan Michaline, Sharlene Joyce, Pamela Jo, Robert Chester, Jerome Cyril. Pvt. practice optometry, Chgo., 1946-56, Niles, Ill., 1956—; sch. lectr. children's visual problems; mem. Optometric Extension Program Found., 1947-85. Mem. Am. Optometric Assn. (Optometric Recognition award 1981-85), Ill. Optometric Assn. Nat. Eye Research Found. (cert. in contact lenses), Better Vision Inst., Am. Pub. Health Assn., Ill. Pub. Health Assn., Coll. Optometrists in Vision Devel. (assoc.). Roman Catholic. Club: K.C. Author: What Parents Should Know About Their Children's Eye Vision, 1972; The Brain's Vision, 1981. Patentee devices for diagnosing and correcting eye abstract fusion and neuro-reflex, others. Office: 8150 N Milwaukee Ave Niles IL 60648

NOWAK, MARIE SHEERAN, educator; b. St. Louis, June 24, 1920; d. Frank Thomas and Marie Regina (Connors) Sheeran; m. Joseph Nowak, 1942; children—Pauline Hayes, James. B.A., Harris Tchrs. Coll., 1942; M.A., Washington U., St. Louis, 1956. Cert. tchr., Mo. Tchr., St. Louis pub. schs., 1949—, tchr. math. and social studies Lafayette Sch., 1949-51, Carondelet Sch., 1951-56, Werner Sch., 1956-80, tchr. math. and history Long Sch., 1980-83, curriculum coordinator Stevens Sch., 1983—. Pres. St. Louis Met. Womens Polit. Caucus, 1973-74, St. Louis New Dem. Coalition, 1979-81. Mem. Mo. State Tchrs. Assn. (state exec. com., pres. St. Louis Dist. 1981-82), Am. Bus. Women's Assn., Delta Kappa Gamma. Lodge: K.C. Aux. Home: 4333 Hanover Ct Saint Louis MO 63123 Office: Stevens Middle School 1033 N Whittier St Saint Louis MO 63113

NOYES, RICHARD FRANCIS, optometrist; b. Des Moines, May 8, 1952; s. Robert F. and Mary C. N.; children—Jennifer, Bethany. B.S. in Gen. Sci., U. Iowa, 1975; B.S. in Visual Sci., Ill. Coll. Optometry, 1976, O.D., 1978. Family practice optometry, Marion, Iowa, 1978—. Bd. dirs. Haiti Med. Mission, 1978—. Fellow Am. Coll. Optometric Physicians; mem. Iowa Optometric Assn. (legis. com. 1984), Am. Optometric Assn., Jaycees, Beta Sigma Kappa. Republican. Lutheran. Lodge: Lions (bd. dirs. 1979—, Disting. Service award 1983). Home: 1640 25th Ave Marion IA 52302 Office: 675 S 11th St Marion IA 52302

NUCCITELLI, SAUL ARNOLD, consulting civil engineer; b. Yonkers, N.Y., Apr. 25, 1928; s. Agostino and Antoinette (D'Amicis) N.; m. Concetta Orlandi, Dec. 23, 1969; 1 child, Saul A. B.S., NYU, 1949, M.C.E., 1954; D.C.E., MIT, 1960. Registered profl. engr., N.Y., Mo., Colo., Conn., Mass.; lic. land surveyor, Mo., Colo., Conn., Mass. Asst. civil engr. Westchester County Engrs., N.Y.C., 1949-51, 53-54; project engr. H.B. Bolas Enterprises, Denver, 1954-55; asst. prof., research engr., U. Denver, 1955-58; mem. staff MIT, 1958-60; asst. prof. engring. Cooper Union Coll., N.Y.C., 1960-62; pvt. practice cons. engring., Springfield, Mo., 1962—; organizer Met. Nat. Bank, Springfield; adviser, dir. Farm & Home Savs. and Loan Assn. Contbr. articles to profl. jours. Chmn. Bd. City Utilities, Springfield; mem. Adv. Council on Mo. Pub. Drinking Water; bd. dirs. Community Found. Greene County, Mus. of Ozarks. Served with C.E., U.S. Army, 1951-53. Recipient Cert. of Appreciation, Mo. Mcpl. League, 1981; named Mo. Cons. Engr. of Yr., 1973. Mem. Nat. Soc. Profl. Engrs., Mo. Soc. Profl. Engrs., ASCE, Boston Soc. Civil Engrs., Am. Concrete Inst., Am. Inst. Steel Constrn., Am. Welding Soc., ASTM, Am. Soc. Mil. Engrs., Springfield C. of C. (past v.p.). Home: 2919 Brentmoor Ave Springfield MO 65804 Office: 122 Park Central Sq Springfield MO 65806

NUGENT, DONALD CLARK, judge; b. Mpls., Mar. 7, 1948; s. Paul Donald and Kathleen June (Leasman) N. B.A., Xavier U., 1970, Loyola U.-Rome, Italy, 1969; J.D., Cleve. State U., 1974. Bar: Ohio 1974. Prodn. supr. C. Schmidt & Sons, Inc., Cleve., 1971-75; pros. atty. Cuyahoga County, Ohio, 1975-85; judge Common Pleas Ct. Cuyahoga County, 1985—. Mem. exec. com. Cuyahoga County Democratic Party, 1976—. Served with USMC, 1970-71. Mem. Nat. Dist. Attys. Assn., Ohio Bar Assn., Greater Cleve. Bar Assn., Cuyahoga County Bar Assn. Roman Catholic. Avocations: marathon running; classical guitar. Home: 328 Cornwall Rd Rocky River OH 44116 Office: Common Pleas Court Justice Ctr 1200 Ontario Ave Cleveland OH 44113

NUNEMAKER, WESLEY, grain and livestock rancher, utility assn. exec.; b. Langdon, Kan., July 9, 1919; s. Joseph J. and Gladys Mary (Kabler) N.; student Southwestern Coll., Winfield, Kans., 1937-38, Kan. State U., 1938-39; m. Twila Virl Reece, Aug. 22, 1937; children—Marcia (Mrs. Jack Castleberry), Wayne Wesley. Farm, ranch mgr., operator, Langdon, Kans., 1940—. Dir. Ark. Valley Electric Co-op. Assn., Inc., 1955-61, 73—, chmn., 1959-61. Dist. bd. chmn. Lerado Cemetery, 1952-58; mem. Reno County Extension Council, 1949-53, chmn., 1951-53; active United Fund and Christian Rural Overseas Program drives Bell Twp., 1959-62; twp. committeeman Agrl. Stablzn. and Conservation Service, 1960-66; mem. Reno County Spl. Edn. Bd. of Control, 1973. Bd. dirs. Local High Schs., 1952-73; trustee Hutchinson Community Jr. Coll., 1959—, chmn., 1959-60, 67-68, 73-74, 78-79; bd. dirs. Central Kans. Area Vocat. Tech. Sch., 1975—, pres. 1978-79; trustee Kans. Electric Power Coop., 1976—. Recipient Kans. Master Farmer award, 1973. Mem. Kans. Farm Bur., Kans. Wheat Growers Assn., Kans. Farm. Mgmt. Assn., Top Farmers Am. Assn., Reno County Bankers Soil Conservation (mem. awards selection com. 1953), Kans. Master Farmer Assn. (pres. 1976—). Mem. Christian Ch. (elder 1971—, Sunday sch. supt. 1941-46). Home: Langdon KS 67549

NUNEZ, YOLANDA RULL, accountant; b. Havanna, Cuba, Oct. 6, 1952; came to U.S., 1966, naturalized, 1976; d. Miguel Angel and Yolanda (Suarez) Gonzalez; m. Victor J. Nunez, June 26, 1976; 1 child, Sergio. B.S., U. Ill., 1979. Acct., O.M.A.R., Inc., Chgo., 1977—, full charge bookkeeper, 1971-77, office mgr. supr., 1982—, office mgr., 1981-82; acct. WBBS-TV Sta./Channel 60, Chgo., 1979-83, Hat-Co, Chgo., 1978—; keypuncher/data processing social sci. dept. Northwestern U., Evanston, Ill., 1969; research-field work supr. O.M.A.R., Inc., Chgo., 1968-69, audio technician, 1972-73; asst. radio producer Buenos Dias Chgo. Radio Program WEDC, Chgo., 1969-70; treas. Cuban Am. C. of C. Credit Union, Chgo., 1975-76. Mem. Ctr. for Research and Polit. Leadership, Chgo., 1967-82; mem., bookkeeper Cuban Intellectuals for the Liberty of Cuba, 1982-83. Recipient award H. Whitney MacMillan Co., Chgo., 1983. Roman Catholic. Home: 7657 Long St Skokie IL 60077 Office: OMAR Inc 5525 N Broadway Chicago IL 60640

NUNN, PHILIP CLARK, III, management scientist; b. Cin., Apr. 4, 1933; s. Philip Clark and Frances Kay (Patton) N.; student Kenyon Coll., 1951-53; B.A., Aquinas Coll., 1969; M.S., Western Mich. U., 1983; m. Hildegarde Loretta Bauer, Jan. 17, 1953; children—Annette, Catherine, Margaret, Christopher. Cert. Project Mgmt. Profl., 1984. With Lear Siegler, Inc., Grand Rapids, Mich., 1957-70, devel. project coordinator, 1962-70; mgr. environ. systems devel. Nat. Sanitation Found., Ann Arbor, Mich., 1970-74; dir. urban and environ. studies inst. Grand Valley State Colls., Allendale, Mich., 1974-80; internat. coordinator research and devel. Amway Corp., Ada, Mich., 1980—; engring. and research mgmt. cons., Comstock Park, Mich.; adj. prof. F.E. Seidman Grad. Coll. Bus. and Adminstrn., 1976-81. Health dir. Cin. area Boy Scout Camp, 1952; regular panel mem. Soundings weekly radio program WOOD-AM and FM, Grand Rapids, Mich., 1973-80; vice chmn. community health planning sect. W. Mich. Health Systems Agy., 1976-80; mem. central planning com. W. Mich. Comprehensive Health Planning Unit, 1973-76; chmn. environ. simulation sect. Summer Computer Simulation Conf., 1972; bd. dirs. Kent County Conservation League, 1964-65. Served with USAF, 1953-57. Kenyon Coll. scholar, 1951. Mem. Soc. Gen. Systems Research (chmn. orgn. and mgmt. studies 1970-74), Soc. Computer Simulation, Project Mgmt. Inst., Am. Mgmt. Assn., Alpha Delta Phi. Episcopalian. Contbr. articles to profl. jours. Home and office: 201 Netherfield St Comstock Park MI 49321

NUTTER, ORLA RICHARD, dentist; b. Richland Center, Wis., Jan. 19, 1928; s. Orla Ray and Hattie Catharine (Scholl) N.; m. Barbara Ruth Becker, June 9, 1951; children—Elizabeth, Thomas, Nancy, Ann Nutter Swenson. B.S., Wartburg Coll., 1950; D.D.S., Marquette U., 1957. Nat. and N.D. State Board Cert. D.D.S. Gen. practice dentistry, Rugby, N.D., 1957-59, Minot, N.D., 1959—. Pres. P.T.A., Minot, 1968. Served as tech. sgt. USAF, 1950-53. Fellow Am. Coll. Dentists, Pierre Fauchard Acad.; mem. ADA (state del. 1972—), N.D. Dental Assn. (pres. 1975), Am. Legion. Republican. Lutheran. Lodges: Elks, Eagles, Masons, Shriners, K.T. Avocations: hunting; fishing; boating; lake living; cross country skiing. Home: 2 Fair Way Minot ND 58701

NUZMAN, CARL EDWARD, hydrologist; b. Topeka, Aug. 5, 1930; s. Loren Manuel and Lorraine Lillian (Bowler) N.; B.S. in Agrl. Engring., Kans. State U., 1953; M.S. in Water Resources Engring., U. Kans., 1966; m. Janet Ruth Steck, Aug. 23, 1952. Engr. div. water resources Kans. Bd. Agr., Topeka, 1957-65; hydrologist Kans. Water Resources Bd., Topeka, 1965-66; hydrology supr., sales engr. Layne-Western Co., Inc., Shawnee Mission, Kans., from 1967, now mgr. hydrology div. Treas. local sch. bd., 1958-59. Served to 1st lt. USAF, 1953-56. Registered profl. engr., Kans., Mo. Mem. Am. Soc. Agrl. Engrs., ASCE, Am. Geophys. Union, Kans. Engring. Soc. (sec.-treas. 1965-68, Outstanding Young Engr. award Topeka chpt. 1965), Nat. Soc. Profl. Engrs., Alpha Kappa Lambda, Sigma Tau, Steel Ring. Elk. Contbr. articles to profl. jours.; author, inventor. Home: 3310-B NW Huxman Rd Silver Lake KS 66539 Office: 610 S 38th St Kansas City KS 66106

NWIDEEDUH, SAMUEL BARILEKAANA, university administrator, researcher; b. Kwawa, Rivers State, Nigeria; came to U.S., 1974; s. Nwideeduh and Tungloo N. Diploma Drama U. Ibadan, Nigeria, 1972; B.A. in Telecommunications, Ind. U., 1977, M.Ed., 1978; Ph.D., U. Minn., 1985. Cultural officer Rivers State Arts Council, Port Harcourt, Nigeria, 1972-74; instr. Opportunities Industrilization Ctr., Richmond, Ind., 1978; asst. registrar U. Port Harcourt, 1981; program coordinator mini courses U. Minn., Mpls., 1982—, dir. discussion group on Nigerian affairs U. Minn., chmn. newspaper publ. com., 1983-85, mem. ednl. affairs assembly com., 1984-85, mem. internat. students assembly com., 1984-85, chmn. tech. com. discussion group, 1984-85. Recipient President's award U. Minn., 1985, Plaque award Discussion Group of Nigerian Affairs, U. Minn., 1984. Mem. Phi Kappa Phi (Outstanding Acad. award 1984). Avocations: reading; traveling; story writing; film. Home: PO Box 13041 Minneapolis MN 55414

NWOKE, MARTINS NNADI, hospital administrator, import company executive; b. Umuahia, Nigeria, May 7, 1946; came to U.S., 1972, naturalized, 1983; s. Shedrach Irokwe and Bessie Ihiaku N.; m. Cecilia Ugomma, Aug. 13, 1972; children—Theodore Ulonnaya, Cynthia Uzoma. B.B.A., John F. Kennedy Coll., Wahoo, Nebr., 1974; M.B.A., U. Nebr., 1976. Bus. developer Mid-City Bus. and Profl. Assn., Omaha, 1974-77; bus. mgr. Eastern Nebr. Human Services Agy., Omaha, 1977-79; comptroller Douglas County Hosp., Omaha, 1979-80, dir. gen. services, comptroller, 1980-83; pres. Bus. Enterprises Internat., Inc., Omaha, 1983—. Cited for outstanding contbn. to Mid-City Bus., 1976. Mem. Health Care Fin. Mgmt. Assn., Am. Mgmt. Assn. Democrat. Methodist. Lodge: Prince Hall. Home: 5722 Manderson St Omaha NE 68104

NYGAARD, LANCE COREY, nurse, data processing consultant; b. Casper, Wyo., June 21, 1952; s. Miles Adolph and Jenile Hansine (Mosman) N.; m. Ruth Ann Soulek, Dec. 29, 1978; 1 child, Kari Melissa. A.A. in Nursing, U. S.D., 1980; B.S. in Chemistry, 1974; M.L.S., U. Ill., 1975. Registered emergency med. technician. Library asst. Brookings Pub. Library, S.D., 1971-75, asst. dir., 1975-77; emergency med. technician Brookings Hosp., 1976-78; sr. emergency med. technician Vermillion Ambulance, S.D., 1978-80; nurse McKennan Hosp., Sioux Falls, S.D., 1980—; owner operator Data Processing Services, Sioux Falls, 1983—; applications cons. Computer Dimensions, Sioux Falls, 1984-85. Mem. Am. Heart Assn. Republican. Lutheran. Club: Chemistry (Vermillion) (pres. 1973-74). Lodge: Sons of Norway (guard 1976-77). Avocations: World War II military history; rose gardening; photography; amateur radio. Home: 2305 Royal Ct Sioux Falls SD 57106 Office: McKennan Hosp 800 E 21st St Sioux Falls SD 57106

OAKAR, MARY ROSE, congresswoman; b. Cleve.; B.A., Ursuline Coll., Cleve., 1962, L.H.D. (hon.); M.A. in Fine Arts, John Carroll U., Cleve., 1966; postgrad. Columbia U., 1967—, London U.; LL.D. (hon.), Ashland Coll.; L.H.D. (hon.), Ursuline Coll. Clk., Higbee Co., 1956-58; long distance operator Ohio Bell Telephone Co., 1957-62; instr. English and drama Lourdes Acad., Cleve., 1963-70; asst. prof. English, speech and drama Cuyahoga Community Coll., 1968-75; mem. 95th-98th Congresses from 20th Ohio Dist., whip at large, mem. banking, fin. and urban affairs com., select com. on aging, post office and civil service com., com. on house adminstrn., also mem. numerous subcoms.; mem. Nat. Commn. on Unemployment Compensation; chmn. task force on employment and tng. N.E.-Midwest Coalition; mem. North Atlantic Assembly of NATO; treas. U.S. Congress to Interparliamentary Union; chmn. Task Force on Libraries and Memls. Ward leader Cuyahoga County Democratic Com., 1972-76; mem. Dem. Steering and Policy Com.; mem. Cleve. City Council, 1973-76; state central committeewoman 20th Congl. Dist., 1974-76; co-chmn. N.E. Ohio Congl. Del. trustee or mem. adv. bd. Fedn. for Community Planning, Health and Planning Commn., Community Info. Services, Cuyahoga Community Coll., Cleve. Ballet, Soc. for Crippled Children, YWCA; mem. adv. com. Pub. Services Occupational Group, Mothers Against Drunk Driving, Overseas Edn. Fund; mem. Sr. Citizens Resources, Inc. of Cleve. Recipient Outstanding Service award OEO, 1973-75, Community Service awards Am. Indian Center, 1973, Nationalities Service Center, 1974, Club San Lorenzo, 1976; named Cuyahoga County Dem. Woman of Yr., Alumna of Yr., Ursuline Coll., numerous other awards. Home: 1892 W 30th St Cleveland OH 44113 Office: 2436 Rayburn House Office Bldg Washington DC 20515 also 523 Fed Ct Bldg 215 Superior Ave Cleveland OH 44114

OAKES, ROBERT JAMES, physics educator; b. Mpls., Jan. 21, 1936; s. Sherman E. and Josephine J. (Olson) O.; m. Diane M. Swenson, June 11, 1955; children—Cindy L., Lisa A. B.S., U. Minn., 1957, M.S., 1959, Ph.D., 1962. NSF fellow Stanford U., Calif., 1962-64, asst. prof. physics, 1964-68; assoc. prof. physics Northwestern U., Evanston, Ill., 1968-70, prof. physics, 1970-76, prof. physics and astronomy, 1976; vis. staff mem. Los Alamos Sci. Lab., 1971—; vis. scientist Fermi Nat. Accelerator Lab., Batavia, Ill., 1975—; faculty assoc. Argonne Nat. Lab., Ill., 1982—. Fulbright-Hays Disting. prof. U. Sarajevo, Yugoslavia, 1979-80; A.P. Sloan fellow, 1965-68; Air Force Office Sci. Research grantee, 1969-71; NSF grantee, 1971—. Fellow Am. Phys. Soc.; mem. AAAS, N.Y. Acad. Sci., Ill. Acad. Sci., Sigma Xi, Tau Beta Pi. Club: Physics (Chgo.). Office: Dept Physics and Astronomy Northwestern U Evanston IL 60201

OAKLEY, JUDITH IVA, middle school administrator; b. Van Buren, Mo., March 3, 1942; d. James Gayle and Ancil Geneve (Cowin) Sanders; m. Wesley Eugene Oakley, Oct. 28, 1961; 1 child, Palma Suzanne. M.A., S.E. Mo. State U., 1972; B.A., 1966. Cert. Edn. Adminstrn., Mo. Tchr, various schs., Mo., 1974-77; middle sch. prin. Carter County Reorganized Sch. Dist., Van Buren, Mo., 1977—; reader-evaluator State Dept. Edn., 1982-83; chpt. coordinator Carter County Reorganized Sch. Dist., Van Buren, 1980-84. Named Outstanding Elem. Tchr. of Am., Washington, D.C., 1973. Mem. Mo. State Tchr's Assn., Secondary Prins. Assn., Community Tchrs. Assn., Mo. State Resource Conservation and Devel. (vice-chmn. 1984), Big Spring Resource Conservation and Devel. Council (sec.-treas. 1984, chmn. U. Mo. Extension Council 1982, 84). Lodge: Order Eastern Star. Home: PO Box 249 Van Buren MO 63965

OAKS, GILBERT EARL, JR., international financial consultant; b. Monterey, Calif., July 16, 1944; s. Gilbert E. and Wanda F. (Stevenson) O.; B.S. in Elec. Engring., Findlay Engring. Coll., 1966, B.S. in Mech. Engring.; M.B.A., Frostburg State Coll., 1974; Ph.D. in Internat. Fin., Am. Western U., Okla., 1981; m. Dana L. Crawford; 1 son. Engr., Panhandle Eastern Co., Kansas City, Mo., 1962-66, AEC, Kansas City, 1966-69, chief engr., 1969-70, fin. analyst, 1970-71, spl. asst. tech. affairs, Washington, 1971-74; pres. Oaks Mgmt. Associates Internat., Elm Grove, Wis., 1974-82; pres., chief exec. officer IMA-TEC Ltd., Muskego, Wis., 1982—. Dist. commr. Potawatomi council Boy Scouts Am., 1977-84. Mem. Internat. Assn. Fin. Planners, Internat. Soc. Financiers, Mortgage Bankers Assn. Am., Assn. M.B.A. Execs., Internat. Solar Energy Soc., Ind. Bus. Assn. Wis., Internat. Assn. Bus. and Fin. Cons., Am. Inst. Indsl. Engrs., Nat. Assn. Fin. Cons. Republican. Mem. Christian Ch. Pub. Internat. Financialist, 1980—. Home: 1422 E Racine Ave Waukesha WI 53186 Office: 581 W18878 Apollo Dr Muskego WI 53150

OATES, KATHLEEN MARIE, lawyer; b. Chgo., Dec. 2, 1955; d. William Robert, Jr., and Ethelyn Rose (Calhoun) O. Student l'Université de Clare-mont-Ferrand, France, 1976-77; B.A., Kalamazoo Coll., 1978; J.D., U. Wis., 1981. Bar: Wis. 1981, Minn. 1981, U.S. Dist. Ct. Minn. 1981, U.S. Dist. Ct. (ea. dist.) Wis. 1983. Assoc. Larkin, Hoffman, Daly & Lindgren, Ltd., Mpls., 1981—. Mem. Assn. Trial Lawyers Am., Minn. Bar Assn., Wis. Bar Assn., Hennepin County Bar Assn., Minn. Trial Lawyers Assn., Phi Beta Kappa, Alpha Lambda Delta, Phi Eta Sigma. Office: Larkin Hoffman Daly & Lindgren Ltd 7900 Xerxes Ave S Suite 1500 Minneapolis MN 55431

OATEY, JENNIFER SUE, university administrator; b. Rochester, Minn., Aug. 30, 1949; d. Elwyn Brown and Phyllis Eileen (Quammen) Larson; B.A., N. Mex. State U., 1971, M.A., 1973; Ph.D. in Edn., U. Minn., 1981. Asst. dir. recreational sports U. Mich., Ann Arbor, 1976-77; intramural supr. Stephen Austin State U., Nacogdoches, Tex., 1975-76; campus center coordinator Brainerd (Minn.) Community Coll., 1974-75; phys. edn. instr., asst. intramural dir. N.Mex. State U., Las Cruces, 1973-74; assoc. dir. recreational sports U. Minn., Mpls., 1977—. Bd. dirs. Univ. YWCA, 1981-83, Minn. Council on Health, 1983—; mem. Gov.'s Council on Health Promotion and Wellness, 1981-83. Mem. Nat. Intramural-Recreational Sports Assn. (dir. Minn. 1977-81, mem. editorial bd. Jour., 1981—), Can. Intramural Recreation Assn., Sons of Norway, U. Minn. Alumni Assn., Phi Theta Kappa. Lutheran. Home: 333 Oak Grove Apt 308 Minneapolis MN 55403 Office: 108 Cooke Hall U Minn Minneapolis MN 55455

OATIS, ROBERT, police captain, criminal justice educator; b. Marion, Ind., Feb. 18, 1945; s. Robert E. and Catherine N. (Zike) O.; m. LaDonna G. Fisher; children—Jennifer J., Sarah C. B.S., Marion Coll., 1978; diploma FBI Nat. Acad., 1979; postgrad. Ball State U., 1980—. Motorcycle officer Marion Police Dept., 1968-69, detective, 1970-74, patrol sgt., 1974-76, uniform capt., 1976-80, tng. capt., 1980-82, capt. detectives, 1982—; seminar presenter U. Tenn., Chattanooga, 1978; lectr. Ball State U., Muncie, Ind., 1983, 84. Adult Sunday sch. tchr. Lakeview Wesleyan Ch., Marion, 1978—, bd. dirs., 1980. Served to maj. U.S. Army, 1966—. Decorated Expert Infantryman's badge U.S. Army, 1984; recipient Police Officer of Yr. award Exchange Club of Marion. Fellow Nat. Acad. Crisis Interveners; mem. Am. Acad. Crisis Interveners, FBI Nat. Acad. Assn. Republican. Home: 1412 North Dr Marion IN 46952 Office: Marion Police Dept 301 S Branson Marion IN 46952

O'BANNON, FRANK LEWIS, lawyer, state senator; b. Louisville, Jan. 30, 1930; s. Robert Pressley and Rosella Faith (Dropsey) O'B.; A.B., Ind. U., 1952, J.D., 1957; m. Judith Mae Asmus, Aug. 18, 1957; children—Polly, Jennifer, Jonathan. Admitted to Ind. bar, 1957, since practiced in Corydon; partner firm Hays, O'Bannon & Funk, 1966-80, O'Bannon, Funk & Simpson, 1980—; mem. Ind. State Senate, 1970—, minority floor leader, 1979—, asst. minority floor leader, 1972-76; pres., dir. O'Bannon Pub. Co., Inc. Served with USAF, 1952-54. Mem. Ind. Dem. Editorial Assn. (pres. 1961), Am. Judicature Soc., Am. Bar Assn., Ind. Bar Assn. Democrat. Methodist. Office: 303 N Capitol St Corydon IN 47112

OBENBERGER, J(OSEPH) D(ENNIS), lawyer; b. Milw., May 21, 1954; s. Joseph Albert and Theresa Carol (Sottile) O.; m. Mary Ann Matejov, May 17, 1980. B.A. in Polit. Sci. and History, U. Wis., 1976, J.D., 1979; postgrad. DePaul U., 1976-77. Bar: Wis. 1979, U.S. Dist. Cts. (ea. and we. dists.) Wis. 1979, U.S. Dist. Ct. (no. dist.) Ill. 1984, U.S. Ct. Claims 1979, U.S. Ct. Mil. Appeals 1979, U.S. Ct. Appeals (7th cir.) 1979, U.S. Ct. Appeals (fed. cir.) 1984, Ill. 1983. Sole practice, Highland Park, Ill., 1983-84; assoc. Tyrrell & Flynn, Chgo., 1984—. Exec. dir. Wis. Federated Teenage Republicans, Madison, 1971; committeeman Rep. Party of Village of Fox Point, Wis., 1972; mem. city devel. com. City of Highwood, Ill., 1983, mem. city plan commn., 1984, mem. zoning bd. appeals, 1984. Served to capt. U.S. Army, 1979-83. Decorated Army Commendation medal; recipient Outstanding Achievement award Wis. Fedn. Young Reps., 1970; U.S. Army ROTC scholar, 1972. Mem. Wis. Bar Assn., Lake County Bar Assn., Chgo. Bar Assn. Roman Catholic. Home: 322 North Ave Highwood IL 60040 Office: Tyrrell & Flynn 200 W Madison St Suite 2020 Chicago IL 60606

OBERLANDER, R. ALLAN, architect; b. Sioux Falls, S.D., July 19, 1953; s. Richard Earl and Joann L. (Helder) O.; m. Thea Helene Lubbers, Aug. 26, 1978. Student S.D. State U., 1971-73; B.A. with distinction in Architecture, Iowa State U., 1975, M.Architecture, 1978. Registered architect, Iowa. With design and drafting dept. Foss Engelstad Heil Co., Sioux City, Iowa, 1976-77; teaching asst. dept. architecture Iowa State U., Ames, 1977; designer, project architect Bussard Dikis Assocs., Des Moines, 1979-81; assoc., designer, project architect, 1981—; com. chmn. sand castle competition for design profls., 1982, 83. Com. chmn. Community Rewards recognition pub. design contbns., Des Moines, 1981; mem. Des Moines Leadership Inst., 1983-84; bd. govs., 1984-85; bd. govs. Des Moines Leadership Alumni, 1985—. Recipient Premium of Acad. Excellence award Iowa State U., 1977, 78; Leo A. Daly award Iowa State U., 1977. Mem. AIA, Des Moines Architects Council (pres. 1982, exec. bd. 1980-83). Democrat. Roman Catholic. Clubs: Des Moines, Oakmoor. Home: 5010 Country Club Blvd Des Moines IA 50312 Office: Bussard Dikis Assocs 300 Homestead Bldg 303 Locust St Des Moines IA 50309

OBERLE, KEVIN RAY, mktg. communications specialist; b. Columbus, Ohio, Nov. 24, 1948; s. Raymond Zeigler and Kathern Viola (Hickerson) O.; B.S. in Communication (Zousmer Meml. award), Ohio U., 1971. Broadcast technician Sta. WLWC-TV, Columbus, 1971; prodn. asst. Sta. WSTV-TV, Steubenville, Ohio, 1972; dir. Sta. WTVN-TV, Columbus, 1972-74; broadcast technician Sta. WLWC-TV, Columbus, 1974; community relations dir. Goodwill Industries of Central Ohio, Inc., Columbus, 1974-77, pub. relations cons. Goodwill Industries Am., Inc., Washington, 1976-77; regional field rep. St. Jude Childrens Research Hosp., Memphis, 1977-78; mktg. communications specialist splty. materials dept. Gen. Electric Co., Worthington, Ohio, 1978—. Mem. spl. events com. United Way Franklin County. Served with Signal Corps, U.S. Army, 1971-72. Mem. Pub. Relations Soc. Am., Nat. Acad. TV Arts and Scis., Internat. TV Assn., Columbus Advt. Fedn. Club: Kiwanis. Home: 1150-A Fountain Ln Columbus OH 43213 Office: 6325 Huntley Rd Worthington OH 43085

OBERLEY, TERRY DEWAYNE, pathologist, educator; b. Effingham, Ill., Jan. 23, 1946; s. James Donald and Ruby Eloise (Moore) O.; m. Edith Marjorie Toole, June 20, 1968; children—Matthew James, Alexander John. B.S. in Biology, Northwestern U., 1968, Ph.D. in Microbiology, 1973, M.D., 1974. Diplomate Am. Bd. Pathology. Intern, then resident U. Wis., 1978; asst. prof. dept. pathology U. Wis., Madison, 1977-82, assoc. prof., 1983—; chief electron microscopy William S. Middleton VA Hosp., Madison, 1983—. Contbr. articles to profl. jours. Bd. dirs. Nat. Kidney Found., 1980—, chmn. research com., 1982-83. Am. Cancer Soc. fellow, 1977; grantee NIH, VA, Nat. Kidney Found., U. Wis. Med. Grad. Schs. Mem. Am. Soc. Cell Biology, Am. Assn. Pathologists, Am. Soc. Microbiology, Am. Soc. Nephrology, N.Y. Acad. Scis. Democrat. Unitarian. Avocation: science fiction. Home: 5418 S Hill Dr Madison WI 53705 Office: William S Middleton VA Hosp 2500 Overlook Terr Madison WI 53705

OBERLIN, DONALD JERRY, gen. contractor; b. Bryan, Ohio, June 8, 1947; s. Charles Franklin and Donna Vee (Shough) O.; B.S. in Edn., Bowling Green State U., 1969; m. Marsha Mae Gerencser, June 15, 1968; children—Gabriel, Benjamin, Matthew. Indsl. arts tchr. Perrysburgy (Ohio) High Sch., 1969-70, Hicksville, Ohio, 1970-73; gen. contractor Black Swamp Builders, Inc., Antwerp, Ohio, 1973—; gen. contractor/partner Tri-State Solarcrete Bldg. Systems, Antwerp, 1979—; solar energy instr. N.W. Tech. Coll., Archbold, Ohio, 1982—. Bd. dirs. Antwerp Community Improvement Corp., 1975—. Licensed constrn. supt., Allen County, Ind., Ft. Wayne, Ind. Mem. N.E. Ind. Solar Collective, Antwerp Jaycees (pres. 1977). Home: PO Box 43B Route 1 Antwerp OH 45813 Office: 319 S Main St Antwerp OH 45813

OBERLIN, RICHARD, arts administrator; b. Dayton, Ohio, Aug. 16, 1928; s. Robert C. and Lois R. (Young) O.; m. Shirley J. Cousins, May 28, 1966. B.A., Coll. Wooster, 1952; postgrad. U. Ind., 1952-54. Radio announcer, account exec. Sta. WCMW, Canton, Ohio, 1954-55; actor, stage dir. The Cleve. Play House, 1955-71, dir. theatre, 1971—; mem. part-time faculty Cleve. State U., 1969-71; adj. prof. Case Western Res. U., 1972—. Theatre panelist Ohio Arts Council, Columbus, 1971-76. Served as seaman 1st class USN, 1946-48. Recipient Gold Medal of Excellence, Amoco Co., 1977; OTA Lifelong Achievement award Ohio Theatre Alliance, 1980; Arts Prize Citation in theatre Women's City Club, Cleve., 1980; Arts Adminstr. award Ohio Arts Council, 1982. Mem. League Resident Theatres (exec. com.), Nat. Theatre Conf. (bd. trustees). Office: Cleve Play House 8500 Euclid Ave PO Box 1989 Cleveland OH 44106

OBERMAN, MOISHE DAVID, magazine publisher; b. Springfield, Ill., Mar. 3, 1914; s. Harry and Ida (Guralnik) O.; student St. Louis Coll. Pharmacy, 1931-33; m. Bobbye Friedman, Oct. 8, 1939; children—Michael Alan, Martin Jay, M.H. William, Marjorie Ann. Scrap metals broker, Springfield, 1937-41; founder Scrap Age Mag., 1944, Mill Trade Jour., 1963, Waste Age Mag., 1969, Encyclopedia of Scrap Recycling, 1976; pres., editor, pub. 3 Sons Pub. Co., Niles, Ill., 1944; pres. Emde Realty Devel. Corp., Springfield, 1957-63; exec. sec. Midwest Scrap Dealers Assn., 1941—; treas. North Shore Investments, Highland Park, Ill., 1968; exec. dir. Springfield Area Devel. and Tourist Commn., 1963-68; mem. Ill. Inst. Environ. Quality Solid Waste Task Force Com., 1971. Pres. Ill. Assn. Jewish Centers, 1934-40; editor congregation publs., treas. North Suburban Synagogue Beth El. Mem. War Production Bd., 1942-44. Recipient Meritorious Service award for outstanding contbns. to iron and steel industry St. Louis Steel Assn., 1961. Mem. Nat. Solid Waste Mgmt. Assn., Am. Pub. Works Assn. (solid waste mgmt. task force), Execs. Inc. (pres. 1963-67), Am. Soc. Assn. Execs., Internat. Platform Assn., Nat. Press Club, Springfield Jr. C. of C. (pres. 1946-47), Springfield Assn. Execs., Springfield Assn. Commerce and Industry. Jewish. Club: B'nai B'rith (sec. 1935-39, pres. 1942-45). Home: 857 Stonegate Dr Highland Park IL 60035 Office: 6311 Gross Point Rd Niles IL 60648

OBERRATH, KAREN LYNN, college administrator; b. Mansfield, Ohio, Mar. 10, 1954; d. Charles W. and Dorothy E. (Juergens) O. B. degree, Wittenberg U., 1976; M. degree, Ohio State U., 1979. Dir. residence hall Wittenberg U., Springfield, Ohio, 1976-77; sorority head resident Ohio State U., Columbus, 1977-78, asst. to assoc. athletic dir., 1978-79; area coordinator U. Detroit, 1979-80; asst. dir. acad. studies, Ohio State U.-Mansfield, 1980—; cons. Leadership Unltd., Mansfield C. of C., 1985-86; Discovery Sch., Mansfield, 1984, Richland County Found., Mansfield, 1983—. Contbr. articles to newsletters. Bd. dirs. YWCA, Mansfield, 1983—, grant writer, 1984—; vocat. asst. Altrusa, Mansfield, 1984-85. Mem. Nat. Assn. Women Deans (adminstr. counselors 1982-84, resolutions presenter), Ohio Assn. Women Deans (adminstr. counselors, co-chmn. program 1984-85), Am. Coll. Personnel Assn., Ohio Assn. Coll. Personnel, AAUW (program planner, legis. chmn.). Republican. Lutheran. Avocations: sports; classical piano and guitar; camping; outdoor landscaping. Home: 901 Brookfield Dr Apt 1 Mansfield OH 44907 Office: 1680 University Dr Ohio State U Mansfield OH 44906

OBERSTAR, JAMES L., congressman; b. Chisholm, Minn., Sept. 10, 1934; s. Louis and Mary (Grillo) C.; B.A. summa cum laude, St. Thomas Coll.; postgrad. in French, Laval U., Que., Can.; M.A. in Govt. (scholar), Coll. Europe, Bruges, Belgium; postgrad. in govt. Georgetown U.; m. Marilynn Jo Garlick, Oct. 12, 1963; children—Thomas Edward, Katherine Noelle, Ann-Therese, Monica Rose. Adminstrv. asst. to Congressman John A. Blatnik, 1963-74; adminstr. Pub. Works Com., U.S. Ho. of Reps., 1971-74; mem. 94th-99th Congresses from 8th Minn. Dist. Mem. Am. Polit. Sci. Assn. Democrat. Home: 317 NW 9th St Chisholm MN 55719 Office: 2351 Rayburn House Office Bldg Washington DC 20515

OBEY, DAVID ROSS, congressman; b. Okmulgee, Okla., Oct. 3, 1938; s. Orville John and Mary Jane (Chellis) O.; B.S. in Polit. Sci., U. Wis., 1960, M.A., 1962; m. Joan Therese Lepinski, June 9, 1962; children—Craig David, Douglas David. Mem. Wis. Assembly from Marathon County, 1963-69, asst. minority leader, 1967-69; mem. 91st-99th Congresses from 7th Dist. Wis., mem. Democratic steering com., vice chmn. house Dem. study group, mem. appropriations com., house budget com., subcoms. on labor, HEW and fgn. ops., chmn. commn. adminstrv. rev. Mem. adminstrv. com. Wis. Democratic Party, 1960-62. Named Edn. Legislator of Year rural div. NEA, 1968; recipient Legis. Leadership award Eagelton Inst. Politics, 1964. Office: 2217 Rayburn House Office Bldg Washington DC 20515*

OBLINGER, JOSEPHINE KNEIDL HARRINGTON (MRS. WALTER L. OBLINGER), state legislator; b. Chgo., Feb. 14, 1913; d. Thomas William and Margaret (Kneidl) Harrington; B.S., U. Ill., 1933; J.D., U. Detroit, 1968; L.H.D., Sioux Empire Coll., 1966; m. Walter L. Oblinger, Apr. 27, 1940; 1 son, Carl D. Tchr. Lanphier High Sch., Springfield, Ill., 1951-62; clk. Sangamon County, assessor Capital Twp., Springfield, 1962-69; asst. dir. Ill. Dept. Registration and Edn., Springfield, 1970—; exec. dir. Gov.'s Com. on Voluntary Action, 1970-73; asst. to pres. Lincoln Land Community Coll., 1973-77; dir. Ill. Dept. on Aging, 1977-78; mem. Ill. Ho. Reps., 1978—. Sec. Springfield and Sangamon County Community Action, 1965-70 pres., 1970-74; mem. finance com. Child and Family Service, Springfield, 1965-70; mem. Nat. Com. for Day Care of Children, 1960—; pres. Springfield Fedn. Tchrs. AFL-CIO, 1957-59, Ill. Fedn. Tchrs. AFL-CIO, 1959-63; mem. adv. com. to Gov.'s ACTION Office; mem. Planning Consortium for Services to Children in Ill., pres., 1978-79; chmn. mothers' march Sangamon County March of Dimes, 1980. Officer, Republican Women's Luncheon Club, 1959, pres., 1963-67; chmn. Sangamon County Rep. com., 1965—; past pres. Ill. Fedn. Rep. Women. Del. to White House Conf. on Children, 1960. Bd. dirs., pres. Sangamon-Menard County Council on Alcoholism and Drugs, Nat. Center Vol. Action; mem. bd. Sangamon County Salvation Army, Ret. Sr. Vol. Program. Mem. Ill. Assn. County Clks. and Recorders (past pres.), Am. Bus. Women's Assn., Am., Ill., Sangamon County bar assns., Am. Assn. Vol. Services Coordinators (dir., chmn. pub. policy com.), NAACP (exec. bd.), Urban League, Am. Arbitration Assn., U. Ill. Alumni Assn., Nat. Assn. Recorders and Clks., Sangamon County Hist. Soc., Ill. Council Continuing Edn. (exec. com.), P.E.O., Kappa Delta Pi, Sigma Delta Pi, Delta Delta Delta. Clubs: Springfield Women's; Altrusa (pres. 1968-70) (Springfield). Home: Auburn IL 62615 Office: Room E-1 Stratton Office Bldg Springfield IL 62706

OBORN, CHARLES STEPHEN, educational administrator; b. Mansfield, Ohio, Apr. 14, 1950; s. Charles William and Ruth Leonna (Starr) O.; m. Vicki Ann Cole, June 10, 1972; 1 child, Stephanie Starr. B.A., Capital U., Columbus, Ohio, 1972; M.A., Ohio State U., 1981, postgrad., 1981—. Cert. elem. sch. tchr., secondary sch. tchr., Ohio. Tchr., Marion City Schs. (Ohio), 1972-81; high sch. prin. Ridgedale Local Schs., Morral, Ohio, 1981-85; supt. Northmor Local Schs., Galion, Ohio, 1985—; cons. Hammond & Stephens, Freemont, Nebr., 1983—. Author newspaper column Chalk Talk, 1983—. Dep., ednl. cons. Marion County Sheriff's Office, 1973—; foster parent Marion County Children's Service, 1977-81; youth adviser Marion County Red Cross, 1981. Named to Star Spotlight, The Marion Star, 1982-84. Mem. Ohio Assn. Secondary Sch. Adminstrn., Nat. Assn. Secondary Sch. Adminstrn., Buckeye Assn. Sch. Adminstrn., Ohio Sch. Bds. Assn., Phi Delta Kappa, Pi Lambda Theta. Republican. Lutheran. Lodge: Lions. Avocations: Pilot: flight instructor in airplanes, gliders, instruments and balloons; swimming, scuba diving. Home: 460 Brightwood Dr Marion OH 43302 Office: Northmor Adminstrn Office 5353 County Rd Galion OH 44833

O'BRIEN, CHARLES RICHARD, counselor, educator, student personnel administrator; b. Boston, Nov. 10, 1934; s. Charles Richard and Dorothy Margaret (DeBesse) O'B. B.A., St. John's Coll., 1954; M.S., N.D. State U.,

1968; Ed.D., U. Wyo., 1972. Instr., dir. guidance Cardinal Muench Sch., Fargo, N.D., 1966-69; asst. prof. edn. N.D. State U., Fargo, 1969-73; vis. instr. Fitchburg State Coll., Mass., 1973-74; assoc. prof. counselor edn. and coll. student personnel Western Ill. U., Macomb, 1974-82, dir. Counseling Ctr., 1982—, dir. Univ. Advising Ctr., 1984—; cons. Ill. Office Edn., N.D. Office Employment Security, Newman Found. Mem. editorial bd. Counseling and Values, Wyo. Personnel and Guidance Jour. Contbr. articles to profl. jours., chpts. to books. Served with USNR, 1962-72. Recipient Cert. of Recognition, Ill. Guidance and Personnel Assn., 1976, Cert. of Appreciation, Am. Personnel and Guidance Assn., 1977, Presidential Merit award Western Ill. U., 1978. Mem. Am. Psychol. Assn., Am. Coll. Personnel Assn., Am. Mental Health Counselors Assn. Assn., Nat. Assn. Acad. Counselors.

O'BRIEN, DENNIS SEAN, lawyer; b. Springfield, Ill., June 19, 1953; s. Edward Patrick and Virginia (Davlin) O'B.; m. Laurie Lynne Barnes, Aug. 6, 1977; children—Sean Patrick, Kathleen Erin. A.A., Springfield Coll., Ill., 1973; B.A., Rosary Coll., 1975; J.D., Loyola U., Chgo., 1978. Bar: Ill. 1978, U.S. Dist. Ct. (no. dist.) Ill. 1978; U.S. Dist. Ct. (cen. dist.) Ill. 1980. Asst. states atty., felony div. Lake County States Atty's Office, Waukegan, Ill., 1978-80; ptnr. Livingstone, Mueller, Gunning, O'Brien and Davlin, Springfield, 1980—. Bd. dirs. Springfield Mcpl. Opera, 1971-75. Named to Outstanding Young Men Am., U.S. Jaycees, 1976. Mem. Sangamon County Bar Assn., Ill. Bar Assn., Phi Alpha Delta. Democrat. Roman Catholic. Home: 2037 S Walnut Springfield IL 62704 Office: Livingstone Mueller Gunning O'Brien and Davlin 620 E Edwards Springfield IL 62701

O'BRIEN, DONALD EUGENE, district judge; b. Marcus, Iowa, Sept. 30, 1923; s. Michael John and Myrtle A. (Toomey) O'B.; LL.B., Creighton U., 1948; m. Ruth Mahon, Apr. 15, 1950; children—Teresa, Brien, John, Shuivaun. Admitted to Iowa bar, 1948, U.S. Supreme Ct. bar, 1963; asst. city atty., Sioux City, Iowa, 1949-53; county atty., Woodbury County, Iowa, 1955-58; mcple. judge, Sioux City, Iowa, 1959-60; U.S. atty., No. Iowa, 1961-67; individual practice law, Sioux City, 1967-78; U.S. Dist. judge, Sioux City, 1978—. Served with USAAF, 1943-45. Decorated D.F.C., air medals. Mem. Woodbury County Bar Assn., Iowa State Bar Assn. Roman Catholic. Office: PO Box 3141 Sioux City IA 51101

O'BRIEN, ELMER JOHN, librarian; b. Kemmerer, Wyo., Apr. 8, 1932; s. Ernest and Emily Catherine (Reinhart) O.; m. Betty Alicee Peterson, July 2, 1966. B.A., Birmingham So. Coll., 1954; M.Th., Iliff Sch. Theology, 1957; M.A., U. Denver, 1961. Ordained minister United Methodist Ch., 1957. Pastor, Meth. Ch., Paposa Spring, Colo., 1957-60; circulation reference librarian Boston Sch. Theology, 1961-65; asst. librarian Garret Evang. Theol. Sem., Evanston, Ill., 1965-69; librarian, prof. United Theol. Sem., Dayton, 1969—. Editor: Bibliography of Festschriften in Religion, 1960, 1972; Religion Index Two: Festschriften, 1960-69, 1980. United Meth. Ch. faculty research grantee, 1985. Mem. ALA, Am. Theol. Library Assn. (pres. 1978-79). Democrat. Club: Dayton Torch (pres. 1982-83). Home: 7818 Lockport Blvd Dayton OH 45459 Office: United Theol Sem 1810 Harvard Blvd Dayton OH 45406

O'BRIEN, GEORGE MILLER, congressman; b. Chgo., June 17, 1917; s. Matthew J. and Isabel (Hyde) O'B.; A.B., Northwestern U., 1939; J.D., Yale U., 1947; m. Mary Lou Peyla, Sept. 6, 1947; children—Caryl Isabel O'Brien Bloch, Mary Deborah O'Brien Persby. Bar: Ill. 1947. Sr. partner O'Brien & Garrison, Joliet, 1966-78; mem. 93d-97th Congresses from 17th Dist. Ill., 98th-99th Congresses from 4th Dist. Ill., mem. appropriations com. Chmn., Will County chpt. ARC, 1957-58; pres. Joliet-Will County Community Chest Program; mem. Will County Bd. Suprs., 1956-64; mem. Legis. Adv. Com. to Northeastern Ill. Planning Commn., 1971-72; mem. Ill. Ho. of Reps., 1970-72, mem. exec. and judiciary II coms. Served to lt. col. USAAF, 1941-45. Recipient Disting. Service award Joliet Boys' Club. Mem. ABA, Ill., Chgo., Will County bar assns., Trial Lawyers Assn. Ill., Am. Legion, VFW, Phi Beta Kappa. Roman Catholic. Clubs: Elks, Rotary, Union League (Chgo.). Office: 2369 Rayburn House Office Bldg Washington DC 20515

O'BRIEN, JAMES ALOYSIUS, Japanese literature educator; b. Cin., Apr. 7, 1936; s. James Aloysius and Frieda (Schirmer) O'B.; m. Rumi Matsumoto, Aug. 26, 1961. B.A., St. Joseph's Coll., Rensselaer, Ind., 1958; M.A., U. Cin., 1960; Ph.D., Ind. U., 1969. Instr. English, St. Joseph's Coll., Rensselaer, 1960-62; asst. prof. Japanese lit. U. Wis.-Madison, 1968-74, assoc. prof., 1974-81, prof., 1981—. Author: Dazai Osamu, 1975. Translator: Dazai Osamu: Selected Stories and Sketches, 1983; Muro Saisei: Three Works, 1985. Fellow Japan Found, 1977-78, Social Sci. Council, 1973-74. Mem. Assn. Asian Studies, Assn. Tchrs. Japanese (pres. 1984—). Home: 2533 Branch St Middleton WI 53562 Office: East Asian Languages and Lit U Wis 1206 Van Hise Hall Madison WI 53706

O'BRIEN, JOHN EDWARD, retail executive; b. St. Louis, May 30, 1929; s. Edward Joseph and Norma Mary (Yaw) O'B.; m. Marilyn Jean, Aug. 15, 1953; children—Mary Pat, Cathryn Jean, Lynn Marie. A.B., N. Notre Dame, 1952. Assoc. advt. mgr. paper div. Procter & Gamble, 1954-67; v.p., dir. Campbell-Muthun Advt. Agy., Chgo., 1967-72; v.p. mktg., dir. Calgon Consumer Products, Pitts., 1972-77; pres. NoNonsense Fashions, Inc., Greensboro, N.C., 1977-82, Rexall Corp., St. Louis, 1982—. Served with USNR, 1952-54. Republican. Roman Catholic. Home: 304 Brentwood Blvd Clayton MO 63105 Office: 77 Westport Plaza St Louis MO 63141

O'BRIEN, MARIAN PISCOPO, health care executive; b. Chgo., Nov. 14, 1950; d. John Michael and Marjorie Maxine (Sadler) P.; student U. Ill., St. Xavier Coll.; m. Robert J. O'Brien, Jan. 8, 1982. Various secretarial positions, 1968-79; mgr. Women's Health Cons., S.C., Chgo., 1979—; system mgr. Health Computer Assos., Chgo., 1979—; guest lectr. Triton Coll., River Grove, Ill., 1981—. Mem. Nat. Assn. Female Execs., Group Practice Mgmt. Assn., MUMPS Users Group, COSTAR Users Group, Am. Horse Show Assn., U.S. Dressage Assn., U.S. Combined Tng. Assn., Ill. Dressage Assn. Republican. Roman Catholic. Author articles on dressage. Home: 7 Dan-Mar Trail Palos Park IL 60464 Office: 1725 W Harrison St Suite 450 Chicago IL 60612

O'BRIEN, MARK STEPHEN, physician; b. Ottumwa, Iowa, Jan. 1, 1954; s. Richard James and Kathleen (Pfeiffer) O.; m. Murline Yvonne Guffey, Apr. 26, 1974; children—Matthew David, Michelle Renee, Melody Faith. B.S., Northeast Mo. State U., 1979; D.O., Kirksville Coll. Osteo. Medicine, 1981. Intern, Kirksville Osteo. Health Ctr., Mo., 1981-82; physician Monroe Clinic, Unionville, Mo., 1982—; chief of staff Putnam County Meml. Hosp., Unionville, 1983-84. Active mem. Putnam County R-1 Sch. Bd. Mem. Am. Osteo. Assn., Mo. Soc. Gen. Practitioners, North Central Mo. Osteo. Assn., The Mo. Assn. Osteo. Physicians and Surgeons, Putnam County Jaycees. Lodge: Rotary. Home: Rt 3 Box 122 Unionville MO 63565 Office: Monroe Clinic 1615 Union Unionville MO 63565

O'BRIEN, MAURICE JAMES, business executive; b. Chgo., Aug. 30, 1925; m. Frances McDonald; children—Marynell, James M., Paula, Elizabeth, William, Martha, Timothy, John, Joe, Peter, Clare, Catherine, Jane. B.S., Northwestern U., 1947, J.D., 1949; LL.D., Coll. Great Falls, Mont., 1967. Asst. to pres. Robinson Bros. & Co., Chgo., 1950—; founder, pres. Chgo. Coke Co., (changed to Bulk Chems. Co., then Luria Bros., subs. Ogden & Co., N.Y.), 1951-61; v.p. sales Marblehead Lime Co., Chgo., subs. Gen. Dynamics Corp., St. Louis, 1961, pres., 1966, chmn. bd. subsidiaries Darlington Brick & Clay Products Co., Pa., Powell & Minnock Brick Works, Inc., Albany, N.Y.; dir. 1st Nat. Bank, Evanston, Advance Ross Corp., Chgo., Pepper Constrn. Co., Chgo., Laidlaw Industries, Hinsdale, Ill. Bd. dirs. former chmn. bd. St. Francis Hosp., Evanston. Served with U.S. Army, 1943-45. Recipient Merit award Northwestern U., 1968. Mem. Ill. Mfrs. Assn. (vice chmn.), NAM (former dir.), Nat. Lime Assn. (former chmn., merit award 1967). Clubs: John Henry Wigmore (former dir.) (Northwestern U. Sch. Law); Chgo., University (Chgo.); Econ., Bob O'Link Golf, Glen View. Home: 808 Hill Rd Winnetka IL 60093

O'BRIEN, STEPHEN GERARD, law enforcement educator; consultant; b. London, Sept. 12, 1923; s. Stephen Patrick and Alma Annie (Stephens) O'B.; came to U.S., 1975; m. Jean Winifred Boyle, Jan. 3, 1945; children—Josephine Anne, Frances Elizabeth, Sarah Jean. Cert. in Edn. with distinction, U. London, 1968; M.A., U. Detroit, 1979; grad. Nat. Police staff Coll. Bramshill, Eng., 1961. Chief supt. police Met. Police New Scotland Yard, London, 1947-75; prof. law enforcement Macomb Community Coll., Mt. Clemens, Mich., 1976—; adj. prof. criminal justice U. Detroit, 1976-78; ptnr. Security Tng. Systems, Sterling Heights, Mich., 1984—. Co-author: The Environment of the First Line Supervisor, 1980. Served with bomber command Royal Air Force, 1941-47; ETO. Awarded Air Crew Europe Star and Clasp, 1945; recipient Police Long Service medal H.M. Queen Elizabeth II, 1969. Mem. Internat. Assn. Chiefs of Police, Am. Acad. Criminal Justice Scis., Am. Soc. Indsl. Security, Royal Air Forces Assn. (life). Home: 43360 Saal Rd Sterling Heights MI 48078 Office: Macomb Community College 44575 Garfield St Mount Clemens MI 48044-3197

O'BRIEN, WILLIAM P., real estate development company executive; b. Dallas, Dec. 20, 1946; s. Robert David O'Brien and Frances (Buster) Gould. B.Arch., U. Tex.-Arlington, 1970; M.Arch., U. Pa., 1977, M. in City Planning, 1977. Dir. devel. Good Fin. Corp., Dallas, 1971-73; real estate cons., Dallas, 1974-75; sr. project mgr. Trammel Crow Co., Chgo., 1977-81; v.p., regional mgr. Coldwell Banker, Chgo., 1981-85; pres. Rescorp Devel. Co., Chgo., 1985—. Mem. Nat. Assn. Indsl. and Office Parks, Am. Planning Assn., Nat. Realty Com., Urban Land Inst., Alpha Rho Chi (Nat. Gold medal 1970). Office Rescorp Devel Co 7 S Dearborn St Chicago IL 60603

O'BRYAN, LONNIE IRVIN, police officer, retired army officer; b. Cantonment, Fla., Jan. 2, 1937; m. Jerita Horn, Apr. 30, 1956; children—Lonnie Jr., Tracy K., Kerry D. Student in criminal justice Garden City Community Coll., Kans., grad. Criminal Investigations Sch. U.S. Army Mil. Police Sch. Enlisted U.S. Army, 1954, advanced through grades to sgt. 1st class, 1974, investigator/supr. Mil. Police Corp. U.S. Army, Ft. Riley, Kans., 1976-79, ret., 1979; dep. sheriff Sheriffs Dept. Geary County, Junction City, Kans., 1979-80, under-sheriff Rush County, LaCrosse, Kans., 1981-82; patrolman LaCrosse Police Dept., Kans., 1981-82; master patrolman Ellsworth Police Dept., Kans., 1983, Hugoton, Kans., 1983—. Decorated Bronze Star, Vietnam Service medal, Armed Forces Expdn. medal, Meritorious Service medal. Mem. Kans. Police Officers Assn., Vietnam Vets. Assn. Democrat. Avocation: photography. Home: PO Box 363 Hugoton KS 67951 Office: Hugoton Police Dept 114 E 5th St Hugoton KS 67951

OCHILTREE, NED A., JR., metals manufacturing company executive; b. Omaha, Dec. 23, 1919; s. Ned A. and Garnett (Briggs) O.; B.S., Purdue U., 1942; m. Isabel Hayden, Oct. 25, 1946; 1 dau., Judith Ann Ochiltree Herseth. Research engr. Gen. Motors Research Labs., 1942-47; with Ceco Industries, Inc., Oakbrook, Ill. 1947—, exec. v.p. mfg., 1964-70, exec. v.p. sales and prodn., 1970-71, pres., 1971-80, chief exec. officer, 1976-84, chmn. bd., 1979—, also dir.; dir. Oak Park Trust & Savs. Bank (Ill.). Mem. Chgo. Crime Commn., 1966—. Presbyterian. Clubs: River Forest Tennis; Oak Park Country; University, Economic, Mid-Am., Exec. (Chgo.); Butler Nat. Office: 1400 Kensington Rd Oak Brook IL 60521

OCHS, SIDNEY, neurophysiology educator; b. Fall River, Mass., June 30, 1924; s. Nathan and Rose (Kniaz) O.; m. Bess Ratner; children—Rachel F., Raymond S., Susan B. Ph.D., U. Chgo., 1952. Research assoc. Ill. Neuropsychiat. Inst., Chgo., 1952-54; research fellow Calif. Inst. Tech., Pasadena, 1954-56; asst. prof. dept. physiology U. Tex. Med. Br., Galveston, 1956-58; assoc. prof. dept. physiology Ind. U., Indpls., 1958-61, prof., 1961—, chmn. biophysics program, 1968—. Served with U.S. Army, 1943-45. Mem. Internat. Brain Research Orgn., Am. Physiol. Soc., Soc. Neurosci., Am. Soc. Neuro-chemistry. Democrat. Jewish. Author: Elements of Neurophysiology, 1965; Axoplasmic Transport and Its Relation to Other Nerve Functions, 1982; editor-in-chief Jour. Neurobiology, 1969-76; assoc. editor Jour. Neurobiology, 1977—. Office: 635 Barnhill Dr Indianapolis IN 46223

OCHSNER, OTHON HENRY, II, importer, restaurant critic; b. Chgo., May 19, 1934; s. Othon Henry and Louise Catherine (Schlichenmaier) O. A.A., Chgo. City Coll., 1961. Pub. relations staff Walgreen Co., Chgo., 1961-65; sales mgr. Porsche Car Imports, Northbrook, Ill., 1966-67; nat. sales mgr. Pirelli Tire Corp., N.Y.C., 1968-73; pres., chief exec. officer Ochsner Internat., Chgo., 1974—; pres. Swiss-U.S.A. Racing Team, Chgo., 1976—. Author: Ochsner Pocket Guide to the Finest Restaurants in the World, 1984. Mem. Mus. Sci. and Industry Bus. Alliance, Chgo., 1984. Served with U.S. Army, 1957-59. Republican. Baptist. Avocation: visiting and reviewing world class French and Swiss restaurants worldwide. Home: 5885 N Forest Glen Ave Chicago IL 60646 Office: Ochsner Internat Inc 4341 W Peterson St Chicago IL 60646

O'CONNELL, AMY A., speech and language therapist, tutor; b. Oak Park, Ill., May 15, 1936; m. William J. O'Connell, Aug. 4, 1962 (div. July 1980); children—Amy Elizabeth, William Joseph, Barrett Thomas. B.S. in Edn., Eastern Ill. U., Charleston, 1958; cert. travel agt., Roberta Fisher Travel Sch., Arlington Heights, Ill., 1978; M.A. in Spl. Edn., Northeastern Ill. U., Chgo., 1983; doctoral candidate No. Ill. U., 1984—. Speech therapist pub. schs., Springfield, Ill., 1958-60; speech and hearing therapist Sch. Dist. 67, Morton Grove, Ill., 1960-63; co-author Speechmaster series Go-Mo Publications, Cedar Rapids, Iowa, 1965-80; travel agt. Robert Fisher Travel, 1977-78; speech and lang. therapist Sch. Dist. 15, Palatine, Ill., 1981—; travel agt. outside sales Cove Travel; 1983—. Bd. dirs. Prizel Academic Inst., Mount Prospect, 1983—. Mem. Am. Speech and Hearing Assn., Ill. Council on Understanding Learning Disabilities, Am. Council on Learning Disabilities, Northwest Speech Assn. Home: 708 E Lynden Ln Arlington Heights IL 60005

O'CONNELL, THOMAS PHILIP, medical radiography specialist; b. Chgo., Nov. 28, 1954; s. David Walter and Gertrude Ann (Schmidt) O'C.; m. Barbara Jane Lange, Aug. 21, 1976; 1 child, Meghan Ann. A.A.S. with high honors, Oakton Community Coll., 1974; B.S., U. Health Scis./Chgo. Med. Sch., 1976; student Dale Carnegie and Assocs., Chgo., 1982. Chief technologist Chgo. Osteo. Hosp., 1976-79, St. Joseph Hosp., Elgin, Ill., 1979-80, Copley Hosp., Aurora, Ill. 1980; tech. specialist Pyne Corp., Itasca, Ill., 1980-84, sr. tech. specialist, edn. coord., 1984—; lectr. various profl. meetings. Mem. Am. Registry Radiologic Technologists (cert. in med. radiography). Republican. Roman Catholic. Home: 1256 Robin Ln Elk Grove Village IL 60007 Office: Pyne Corp 1540 W Norwood Ave Itasca IL 60143

O'CONNOR, EARL EUGENE, judge; b. Paola, Kans., Oct. 6, 1922; s. Nelson and Mayme (Scheetz) O.; B.S., U. Kans., 1947, LL.B., 1950; m. Florence M. Landis, Nov. 3, 1951 (dec. May 1962); children—Nelson, Clayton; m. 2d, Jean A. Timmons, May 24, 1963; 1 dau., Gayle. Admitted to Kans. bar, 1950; practiced in Mission, Kans., 1950-51; asst. atty. Johnson County, Kans., 1951-53; probate and juvenile judge, 1953-55; dist. judge 10th Jud. Dist., Olathe, Kans., 1955-65; justice Kans. Supreme Ct., 1965-71; judge U.S. Dist. Ct., Dist. of Kans., Kansas City, 1971—, chief judge, 1981—. Served with AUS, World War II: ETO. Mem. ABA, Kans. Bar Assn., Nat. Conf. Fed. Trial Judges, Nat. Conf. State Trial Judges, Phi Alpha Delta. Lodges: Masons, Rotary. Office: US Courthouse Kansas City KS 66101

O'CONNOR, JAMES JOHN, utility executive; b. Chgo., Mar. 15, 1937; s. Fred James and Helen Elizabeth (Reilly) O'C.; B.S., Holy Cross Coll., 1958; M.B.A, Harvard U., 1960; J.D., Georgetown U., 1963; m. Ellen Louise Lawlor, Nov. 24, 1960; children—Fred, John, James, Helen Elizabeth. Admitted to Ill. bar, 1963; with Commonwealth Edison Co., Chgo., 1963—, asst. to chmn. exec. com., 1964-65, comml. mgr., 1966, asst. v.p., 1967-70, v.p., 1970-73, exec. v.p., 1973-77, pres., 1977—, chmn., 1980—; chmn. Inst. for Nuclear Power Ops.; dir. Borg-Warner Corp., Corning Glass Works, Talman Home Fed. Savs. & Loan Assn., Bell & Howell Co., Tribune Co., De Vry, Inc., United Air Lines; bd. dirs. Midwest Stock Exchange. Civilian aide to sec. Army for Ill., 1978-80; bd. dirs. Chgo. unit Am. Cancer Soc., chmn. bd., 1971-73; bd. dirs. Leadership Council for Met. Open Communities, v.p., 1976—; bd. dirs. Lyric Opera Chgo., Spl. Children's Charities, Cath. Charities Chgo., Reading is Fundamental; v.p., treas. Chgo. World's Fair 1992 Corp.; mem. citizens bd. U. Chgo. trustee Adler Planetarium, Michael Reese Med. Center, Northwestern U., Mus. Sci. and Industry, St. Xavier Coll.; chmn. bd. trustees Field Mus.; past chmn. bd. Chgo. Conv. and Tourism Bur.; past bd. dirs., past chmn. Chgo. Urban League; trustee Coll. Holy Cross; mem. exec. bd. Boy Scouts Am.; v.p. adv. bd. Mercy Hosp.; chmn. bd. Citizenship Council Met. Chgo.; mem. citizens bd. U. Chgo.; exec. v.p. Hundred Club Chgo. Served with USAF, 1960-63. Named One of Chgo.'s 10 Outstanding Young Men, Chgo. Jr. Assn. Commerce and Industry, 1970. Mem. Am., Ill., Chgo. bar assns., Chgo. Assn. Commerce and Industry (dir.), Assocs. Harvard U. Grad. Sch. Bus. Adminstrn. Roman Catholic. Clubs: Comml., Econ., Chgo., Chgo. Commonwealth, Met. (Chgo.). Home: 9549 Monticello Ave Evanston IL 60203 Office: PO Box 767 One First Nat Plaza Chicago IL 60690

O'CONNOR, JEROME ARMAND, village manager, management consultant; b. Hartford, Wis., July 14, 1934; s. George Howard and Dorothy Barbara (Lackas) O.; m. Virginia Mary Lenzner, Aug. 5, 1961 (div.); children—Edward Patrick, Kathleen Mary, Annette Marie, Michael John. M.Pub. Adminstrn., Nova U., 1978. Clk., treas., adminstr. City of Hartford (Wis.), 1968-74; dir. mgmt. services local govt. State of Wis., Germantown, 1977—; owner, mgmt. cons. community research and mgmt. The Madison Group, Germantown; exec. dir. Mid-Moraine Municipal Assn. Bd. mgrs. YMCA. Served with U.S. Army, 1952-61, Res. Mem. Internat. City Mgmt. Assn., Wis. City Mgmt. Assn. (exec. bd.) Germantown Area C. of C. Roman Catholic. Club: Lions. Author publs. in field. Home: N114W16955 Armada Dr PO Box 181 Germantown WI 53022 Office: N122W17177 Fond du Lac Ave Germantown WI 53022

O'CONNOR, ROBERT NIALL, charitable organization executive; b. Blackrock, County Dublin, Ireland, Nov. 24, 1939; came to U.S., 1964; s. Eugene and Nora (Wiseman) O'C.; m. Diane M. Baran, Sept. 2, 1967; children—Ailish, Rory, Ciara, Aidan. B.Sc., Trinity Coll., Dublin, 1963; postgrad. NYU Grad. Sch. Bus., 1965-69. Dir. product devel. FMC Corp., N.Y.C., 1970-74; corp. dir. mktg. Hysan Corp., Chgo., 1974-85; pres., founder Irish Children's Fund, Downers Grove, Ill., 1981—. Contbr. articles to mktg. jours. Mem. Calvary Temple, Naperville, Ill., Ill. Right to Life. Mem. Am. Mktg. Assn., Am. Mgmt. Assn., Ill. Council Ethnicity, Irish Am. Heritage Soc., N.Y. Irish Rugby Club (founder). Mem. Christian Ch. Avocations: marathon running; Bible study. Office: 5602 Hillcrest Rd Downers Grove IL 60516

O'CONNOR, THOMAS AUSTIN, foreign language and literature educator; b. N.Y.C., Aug. 19, 1943; s. James Francis and Catherine (Cribbin) O'C.; m. Rae Carolyn Schroeder, Dec. 31, 1969; children—Thomas Austin, Jr., Carolyn Ann. Spanish tchr. Bishop Gibbons High Sch., Schenectady, N.Y., 1965-67; cons. N.Y. State Edn. Dept., Albany, N.Y., 1969-71; asst. to assoc. prof. SUNY, Cortland, N.Y., 1971-76; assoc. to prof. Tex. A&M U., College Station, 1976-80; prof., dept. head modern langs. Kans. State U., Manhattan, 1980—. Contbr. articles to profl. jours. NDEA fellow SUNY-Albany, 1967-70, Am. Council Learned Societies fellow SUNY-Cortland, 1975. Mem. MLA, Am. Assn. Tchrs. Spanish and Portuguese, Internat. Assn. Hispanists, Cervantes Soc. Am. Democrat. Roman Catholic. Avocations: coin collecting, swimming. Home: RR#3 Eastern Hills Dr Manhattan KS 66502 Office: Dept Modern Languages Kansas State Univ Eisenhower Hall 104 Manhattan KS 66506

O'DANIEL, MAURY, automobile dealership executive; b. Evansville, Ind.; m. Gerry O'Daniel; 6 children. B.B.A., Gen. Motors Inst., 1954. With O'Daniel-Ranes Oldsmobile, Datsun, Evansville, 1958-78; pres. Maury O'Daniel Olds, AMC/Jeep/Renault, Fort Wayne, 1979—. Chmn. bd. dirs. Jr. Achievement of Northeastern Ind.; bd. dirs. Salvation Army, past chmn. adv. bd.; dir. exec. com. Summit Tech. and Research Transfer; bd. dirs. St. Joseph Hosp., Leadership Fort Wayne; 2nd v.p. United Way of Allen County; mem. sch. bd. Bishop Dwenger High Sch., Fort Wayne. Recipient Time Quality Dealer award, 1985. Mem. C. of C. (dir.), Ind. Auto. Dealers Assn. (pres.). Address: 1912 Bluffton Rd Fort Wayne IN 46809

O'DAY, RAYMOND BENEDICT, instrument company executive; b. Elizabeth, N.J., Sept. 1, 1935; s. Raymond Alouisious and Florence Rose (Williams) O'D; m. Delores Ann Myers, May 21, 1965; children—Carolyn Jean, Matthew Edward. B.S. in Biology, Rutgers U., 1957. Specialist sales Bioquest, Cockeysville, Md., 1967-73; mgr. sales Inolex, Chgo., 1973-76; sales mgr. Boehringer Mannhiem, Indpls., 1976-82; sr. product mgr. Inolex Packard Instrument Co., Downers Grove, Ill., 1982—. Served with USN, 1959-67. Mem. DAV (life), Soc. Cryobiology (charter), Nat. Rifle Assn. (life). Avocations; cabinet making; skiing; racquetball.

ODEGAARD, DANIEL OWEN, dentist, dental educator; b. Mpls., Jan. 22, 1949; s. Carroll O. and Gladys R. (Ihnot) O.; m. Mary Jo Zelenovich, June 3, 1978; children—Andrew, Paul, Kristin. B.S., U. Minn., 1970, D.D.S., 1972. Pvt. practice dentistry, Mpls., 1974—; clin. asst. prof. U. Minn., Mpls., 1974—. Served to capt. USAF, 1972-74. Mem. Am. Acad. Crown and Bridge, Minn. Acad. Restorative Dentistry, Minn. Prosthodontic soc., ADA, Minn. Dental Assn., Mpls. Dist. Dental Soc. Lutheran. Club: Campus (Mpls.). Avocation: Musician. Office: Daniel O Odegaard DDS 1001 Med Arts Bldg Minneapolis MN 55402

ODEGARD, LAWRENCE RAYMOND, social work educator; b. Oakland, Calif., Mar. 28, 1926; m. Laura Hebel, Apr. 11, 1947; 6 children. A.B., Calif. State U.-San Francisco, 1949; B.D., Am. Bapt. Sem. of West, 1952; M.S.W., U. Iowa, 1972. Ordained to ministry Am. Bapt. Ch., 1952. Pastor, Bapt. Chs., Calif., Nev. and S.D., 1952-68; social work supr. Alameda County Welfare Dept., Oakland, Calif., 1959-70; asst. prof. social work, chmn. div. edn. and social scis. U. Dubuque, Iowa, 1972—. Mem. Nat. Assn. Social Workers, Acad. Cert. Social Workers. Democrat. Presbyterian. Avocation: building model airplanes, boats and railroads. Office: U Dubuque 2000 U Dubuque IA 52001

ODEGARD, ROBERT JAMES, university vice president, owner private business; b. Princeton, Minn., Dec. 22, 1920; s. Odin James and Mabel Elizabeth (Borneke) O.; m. Barbara Perkins, Feb. 17, 1945; children—Stephen, Susan, Kevin, Nancy. B.B.A., U. Minn., 1942; student Northwestern U., 1966, Harvard U., 1979. Owner, operator Odegard Farms Co., Princeton, 1946-66, Odegard Garage Inc., 1946-66, Odegard Potato Co., 1946-66; registered rep. Dain, Bosworth, Mpls., 1966-70; assoc. v.p. U. Minn., Mpls., 1970-84; dir. Am. Home Mut. Ins. Co., Mpls., 1963—, Minn. Pub. TV, St. Paul, 1978—, Insight Bond Mgmt., Mpls., 1983—, Double Exempt Elex Fund, Mpls., 1983—. Rep. Minn. State Legis., 1961-62; congl. candidate Minn. Sixth Dist., 1962, 1964. Served to lt. (j.g.) USN, 1944-46, PTO. Named Profl. Fund Raiser of Yr., Nat. Soc. Fund Raisers, 1983. Mem. Gamma Sigma Delta. Republican. Congregationalist. Clubs: Minn. Alumni, Sky Light, Mpls., Grey Friars, Wayzata Country. Avocations: golf, hunting, fishing, bridge, politics. Home: 2245 Acorn Rd Saint Paul MN 55113 Office: 100 Church St 120 Morrill Hall U Minn Minneapolis MN 55113

ODELL, CLARENCE BURT, geographer, editor, lecturer, consultant; b. Normal, Ill., Sept. 3, 1907; s. William Henry and Ruby F. (Conklin) O.; m. Madelyn Chellnissa Adams, June 11, 1931; 1 child, Sarah Jane. B. Ed., Ill. State U., 1930; M.A., U. Ill. 1931; Ph.D., U. Chgo., 1937. Cartographer McKnight & McKnight Pubs., 1927-30; teaching fellow U. Nebr., 1931-32; cartographer U. Chgo., 1932-37, Grad. Library Sch., 1935-36, vis. assoc. prof. geography, summer 1948, lectr. geography Univ. Coll., 1948-49, 49-50; physiography cons. Tymstone Studios, Chgo., summer 1934; instr. geography and geology Oak Park Jr. Coll., Ill., 1936-37; instr. dept. geography Memphis State U., summer 1937; assoc. prof. geography Stephen F. Austin State U., Nacogdoches, Tex., 1937-39; instr. geography U. Mo., 1939-43, asst. prof., 1943-46; div. asst. Office of Geographer, Dept. State, Washington, 1942-43; chief population sect. div. geography and cartography (later div. functional and internat. intelligence), 1943-46; chief cartography dept. Ency. Brittanica, Chgo., 1946-50; lectr. geography Univ. Coll., Northwestern U., 1947; geog. editor Denoyer-Geppert Co., Chgo., 1950-51, mng. editor, 1951-70, v.p., 1964-73; editor The Geographer, 1970-73; ret., 1973; mem. faculty Sch. Edn., Northwestern U., summers 1961, 63, 65; part-time prof. Northeastern Ill. U., 1967-73; dir. Geog. Research Inst., Wilmette, Ill., 1973—. Fellow Am. Geog. Soc., AAAS, Am. Congress Surveying and Mapping (life), Nat. Council Geog. Edn., Geog. Soc. Chgo. (pres. 1957-59, life dir. 1985); mem. Assn. Am. Geographers, Sigma Xi. Congregationalist. Club: Acacia (life mem.). Lodges: Masons (50 yr. mem.), Rotary (treas. Chgo. 1974-75, v.p. div. 1 1976-77). Home: 2410 Greenwood Ave Wilmette IL 60091

O'DELL, LYNN MARIE LUEGGE (MRS. NORMAN D. O'DELL), librarian; b. Berwyn, Ill., Feb. 24, 1938; d. George Emil and Helen Marie (Pesek) Luegge; student Lyons Twp. Jr. Coll., La Grange, Ill., 1957; student No. Ill. U., Elgin Community Coll., U. Ill., Coll. of DuPage; m. Norman D. O'Dell, Dec. 14, 1957; children—Jeffrey, Jerry. Sec., Martin Co., Chgo., 1957-59; adminstrv. librarian Carol Stream (Ill.) Pub. Library, 1964—; chmn. automation governing com. DuPage Library System, v.p., 1982-85, pres. exec. com. adminstrv. librarians. Named Woman of Year, Wheaton Bus. and Profl. Woman's Club, 1968. Mem. ALA, Ill. Library Assn., Library Adminstrs. Conf. No. Ill. Lutheran (organist). Home: 182 Yuma Ln Carol Stream IL 60188 Office: 616 Hiawatha Dr Carol Stream IL 60188

O'DELL, MARGOT NUMAN, life insurance company executive; b. Green Bay, Wis., Feb. 26, 1942; d. Garno Orange and Geraldine Mae (Farrell) Numan; B.S. in Bus. Adminstrn., Franklin U., Columbus, Ohio, 1974; m. Willard Gerald Hill, II, Aug. 25, 1979; 1 child, Kathleen. Dept. mgr. Donaldson's Dept. Store, Mpls. and Rapid City, S.D., 1962-67, Lerner Shop, N.Y.C., 1967-68; buyer Hislop's Dept. Store, Auburn, N.Y., 1969-71; asst.

mgr. Gentlemen's Clothing, Columbus, Ohio, 1972-74; agt. Aetna Life Ins. Co., Columbus, 1974-78; brokerage supr., 1978-80; pres. O'Dell Ins. Agy., Inc., Gahanna, Ohio, 1980—. Named Bus. Woman of Year, Columbus Profl. and Bus. Women, 1979; mem. Women's Leaders Round Table, 1976-78, Leading Producers Round Table, 1974-82, C.L.U., 1979. Mem. Nat. Assn. Health Underwriters (nat. pres. trustees Leading Producers Round Table 1980), Nat. Assn. Life Underwriters, Am. Soc. C.L.U.s, Ohio Assn. Health Underwriters (pres. 1980, sec. 1984, 1st v.p. 1984, pres. 1985), Gahanna C. of C. (1st v.p. 1984). Republican. Episcopalian. Home: 5288 Wolf Run Dr Gahanna OH 43230 Office: 129 N Stigler Rd Gahanna OH 43230

ODELL, MARY JANE, state official; b. Algona, Iowa, July 28, 1923; d. Eugene and Madge (Lewis) Neville; B.A., U. Iowa, 1945; m. John Odell, Mar. 3, 1967; children—Brad Chinn, Chris Odell. Host public affairs TV programs, Des Moines and Chgo., 1955-79; with Iowa Public Broadcasting Network, 1975-79, host Assignment Iowa, 1975-78, Mary Jane Odell Program, 1975-79; sec. of state State of Iowa, 1979—; tchr. grad. classes in communications Roosevelt U., Chgo., Drake U., Des Moines. Chmn. for Iowa Easter Seals campaign, 1979-82; mem. Midwest Com. Future Options; bd. dirs. Iowa Shares. Recipient Emmy award, 1972, 75; George Washington Carver award, 1978; named to Iowa Women's Hall of Fame, 1979. Republican. Address: 725 Hickman Rd Des Moines IA 50314 Office: Office Sec State State House Des Moines IA 50319

ODER, DONALD RUDD, medical center executive, educator; b. Gibbon, Okla., Sept. 16, 1931; s. Lowell Burgess and Bessie Sarah (Rudd) O.; m. Roberta Pauline Sallee, Aug. 2, 1958; children—Joseph Rudd, Jennifer Susan, Karl Lyndon. B.S., Wichita State U., 1956; M.B.A., U. Chgo., 1980. C.P.A., Ill. Audit mgr. Arthur Andersen & Co., Chgo., 1956-66; v.p. fin. Rush-Presbyn.-St.Luke's Med. Center, Chgo., 1966-75, treas., 1970—, sr. v.p. and treas., 1975—, acting pres., 1983-84; asst. prof. health systems mgmt. Rush U. Coll. Health Scis., 1972-79, assoc. prof., 1979-85, prof., 1985—. Apptd. by gov. to Ill. Health Fin. Authority, 1979-82; bd. dirs. Better Bus. Bur., 1977—. Served with U.S. Army, 1950-53. Mem. Chgo. Assn. Commerce & Industry, Am. Coll. Hosp. Adminstrs., Am. Hosp. Assn. (regional adv. bd. 1981—), Am. Inst. C.P.A.s, Ill. C.P.A. Soc. (chmn. com. health care instns. 1975-76), Ill. Hosp. Assn. (chmn. bd. trustees 1982-83); fellow Healthcare Fin. Mgmt. Assn. (William G. Follmer award 1974, Robert H. Reeves award 1978, Alice V. Runyon award 1980), Inst. Medicine; mem. Alpha Kappa Psi. Home: 1280 Warwick Ct Deerfield IL 60015 Office: Rush-Presbyn-St Luke's Med Center 1725 W Harrison St Chicago IL 60612

O'DESKY, RICHARD NEIL, osteopathic occupational medicine physician, engineer; b. Toledo, Aug. 2, 1948; s. Louis Terril and Elizabeth Jane (Amdal) O'D. B.S. in Engring., U. Toledo, 1970; D.O., U. Health Scis., Kansas City, Mo., 1978; M.S., Inst. Environ. Health, U. Cin., 1983. Engr. Richards, Bauer & Morehead, Toledo, 1972; intern Brentwood Hosp., Cleve., 1978-79; chief med. officer Indian Health Service, Chippewa Health Ctr., USPHS, Lac Du Flambeau, Wis., 1979-81, med. dir., 1979-81; resident in occupational medicine U. Cin. Med. Ctr., 1981-83; sr. assoc. Chem. Info. Services Cin., 1983-84; mem. sci. adv. com. Am. Porphyria Found, 1982—; cons. occupational health systems delivery and devel. Nat. Occupational Med. Assocs., Cin., 1983—. Served to lt. comdr. UPSHS, 1979-81; mem. Res. Mem. AMA, Am. Osteo. Assn., Am. Coll. Gen. Practitioners, Am. Occupational Med. Assn., Am. Coll. Sports Medicine, Am. Indsl. Hygiene Assn., Nat. Soc. Profl. Engrs., Sigma Sigma Phi. Office: Nat Occupational Med Assocs 15th Floor Columbia Plaza 250 E 5th St Cincinnati OH 45202

O'DILLON, RICHARD HILL, physician; b. Watkinsville, Ga., Dec. 11, 1934; s. Herman Thomas and Elizabeth (Hill) O'D.; B.S., U. Ga., 1956; M.D., Med. Coll. Ga., 1960. Intern, Athens (Ga.) Gen. Hosp., 1960-61; resident Grady Meml. Hosp., Atlanta, 1963; practice medicine, specializing in clin. investigation, Rochester, N.Y., 1964—; asst. med. dir. Strasenburgh Labs., 1964-65, asso. med. dir., 1966; group dir. product devel., clin. research Merrell-Nat. Labs., Cin., 1966-75, group dir. gastrointestinal clin. research, 1975-78; dir. clin. research Duphar Labs., Inc., 1979—. Served as capt. USAF, 1961-62. Mem. AMA, So. Med. Assn., N.Y. Acad. Scis., Am. Acad. Dermatology, Ohio Med. Assn., Acad. Medicine Columbus and Franklin County, Am. Geriatrics Assn., AAAS, Gamma Sigma Epsilon, Phi Eta Sigma, Alpha Epsilon Delta, Delta Phi Alpha. Home: 728 Bluffview Dr Worthington OH 43085 Office: 200 Old Wilson Bridge Rd Worthington OH 43085

ODIOSO, RAYMOND C., company scientific executive; b. Pitts., Apr. 17, 1923; s. John A. and Michelina Odioso; m. Mary Lucas, May 23, 1953; children—Richard, Maureen, Patricia, Paul, Michael, Karen. B.S., Duquesne U., 1947; M.S., Carnegie-Mellon U., 1950, D.Sc., 1951. Research fellow Mellon Inst. Indsl. Research, Pitts., 1951-54; sect. mgr. Gulf Research and Devel. Co., Harmarville, Pa., 1954-61; assoc. dir. Colgate Palmolive Co., Piscataway, N.J., 1961-68; v.p. research and devel. The Drackett Co., Cin., 1968-83, v.p. sci. dir., 1983—; mem. phys. sci. adv. bd. No. Ky. U., Highland Heights, from 1972; mem. adv. council chemistry dept. Xavier U., Cin., 1980—. Served to 1st lt. U.S. Army, 1942-46, Philippines. Mem. Am. Chem. Soc., Am. Assn. Corrosion Engrs., Soc. for Advancement of Mgmt., Sigma Xi, Phi Kappa Phi. Republican. Roman Catholic. Clubs: Bankers (Cin.); Hidden Valley Golf (Aurora, Ind.). Avocations: Golf; reading; art; photography. Home: 1588 Beech Grove Dr Cincinnati OH 45238 Office: Drackett Research and Devel Lab 5020 Spring Grove Ave Cincinnati OH 45232

O'DONNELL, DAVID DANIEL, educational services company executive; b. Washington, Aug. 31, 1941; s. Ferd D. and Angelina O'Donnell; m. Carol Knackstеadt, June 14, 1965 (div. 1969); 1 son, David Sean; m. Kay Boughner, Oct. 27, 1970; children—Daniel Joseph, Richard Robert. Student East Carolina U., 1964, Am. U., 1965-66, LaSalle Extension U., Chgo., 1965-66. Ops. mgr. Record Sales, Washington, 1956-61; v.p. sales Capitol Sewing Machine Co., Washington, 1967-70; cons. Macro Systems, Silver Spring, Md., 1970-71; sales mgr. Control Data Corp., Miami, 1971-73; key accounts mgr. Sealy, Miami, 1973-75; dir. mktg. ITT-ITT Ednl. Services, Inc., Indpls., 1975—; gen. mgr., v.p. ITT Employment and Tng. Systems, Inc., Indpls., 1985—; guest speaker, lectr., cons. Served with USMCR, 1961-65. Mem. Am. Mgmt. Assn., Direct Mktg. Assn. Republican. Lodge: Eagles. Home: 9018 Ironwood Ct Indianapolis IN 46260 Office: 3500 DePauw Blvd Bldg 1 PO Box 68888 Indianapolis IN 46268

O'DONNELL, DAVID RICHARDSON, civil engr.; b. Bishop, Calif., June 2, 1937; s. Herbert Preston and Minerva Elizabeth (Richardson) O.; A.A., Am. River Community Coll., 1959; B.S., U. Idaho, 1961; children—Derek T., Irene Denise. Jr. civil engr. Calif. Dept. Water Resources, Sacramento, 1962-67; hydraulic engr. Pioneer Service & Engring. Co., Chgo., 1969-72; hydraulic structures engr. Harza Engring. Co., Chgo., 1973-75; chief engring. dept. Urban Planning Consultants, Inc., Chgo., 1975-77, Milw. Pollution Abatement Program; now sr. assoc. engr. City of Detroit. Served with U.S. Army, 1961-62. Registered profl. engr., Del., Pa., N.J., Ill., Ind., Iowa, Mich. Mem. ASCE, Am. Water Works Assn., Water Pollution Control. Fedn., Nat. Soc. Profl. Engrs. Republican. Home: 111 Cadillac Sq Apt 12 I Detroit MI 48226 Office: 735 Randolph St Detroit MI 48226

O'DONNELL, JAMES THOMAS, pharmacist, nutritionist, consultant; b. Chgo., Sept. 9, 1946; s. James John and Margaret Mary (Sullivan) O'D.; m. Sylvia Jean Gervasi, Sept. 20, 1969; children—Kimberly, James John III. B.S., U. Ill., 1969; D.Pharmacy, U. Mich., 1971; M.S. in Nutrition, Rush U., 1982. Asst. dir. pharmacy Cook County Hosp., Chgo., 1971-76, Rush Presbyn. St. Luke's Med. Ctr., Chgo., 1976—; pres. Assoc. Pharmacist Consultants; expert generic drug bd. Dept. Pub. Health, 1977—, Chgo. Bd. Health, 1983—. Mem. Am. Pharm. Assn., Am. Soc. Hosp. Pharmacists, Ill. Pharmacists Assn. (bd. dirs.). Author textbooks in pharmacology, nutrition and law; column editor Infusion, 1980—; contbr. articles to profl. jours. Home: 1792 Prestwick Dr Inverness IL 60067 Office: 1753 Congress St Chicago IL 60612

O'DONNELL, JOHN, real estate broker; b. Omaha, May 16, 1925; s. John Francis and Gertrude Edith (Alderman) O'Donnell. Officer Lincoln Fire Dept., Nebr., 1954-77; pres. Capitol Realty and Auction Co., Lincoln, 1972—. Served with USN, 1943-46. Republican. Roman Catholic. Lodge: VFW. Avocation: flying. Home: 1630 H St Unit B-1 Lincoln NE 68508 Office: Capitol Realty Co 2021 Garfield St Lincoln NE 68502

O'DONNELL, MICHAEL JAMES, computer science researcher and educator; b. Spartanburg, S.C., Apr. 4, 1952; s. William Joseph and Linnie Lucille (Hynds) O'D.; m. Julie Ann Nerini, Feb. 6, 1982; 1 child, Benjamin Michael. B.S., Purdue U., 1972; Ph.D., Cornell U., 1976. Research assoc. U. Toronto, 1976-77; asst. prof. Purdue U., West Lafayette, Ind., 1976-81, assoc. prof., 1981— vis. assoc. prof. Johns Hopkins U., Balt., 1983-84, assoc. prof. computer sci., 1984—; cons. AT&T Bell Labs., Murray Hill, N.J., 1984—. Author: Computing in Systems Described by Equations, 1976; A Programming Logic, 1977; Equational Logic as a Programming Language, 1985. Mem. Assn. Computing Machinery, Lafayette Folk Dance Club (pres. 1981-83), Phi Beta Kappa. Democrat. Home: 138 Regester Ave Baltimore MD 21212 Office: Dept Elec Engring and Computer Sci Johns Hopkins U 34th at Charles St Baltimore MD 21218

O'DONNELL, PRISCILLA SUE, judge, lawyer; b. Dayton, Ohio, Oct. 23, 1937; d. Kenneth R. and Mary Elizabeth (Bruce) Reed; m. Ronald W. O'Donnell, Aug. 1, 1959 (div. 1979); children—Jennifer, Kelly, Stacey. B.A., U. Cin., 1973; J.D., No. Ky. U., 1977. Bar: Ohio 1977, U.S. Dist. Ct. 1977. Asst. pub. defender Clermont County, Batavia, Ohio, 1978-82; sole practice, Batavia, 1978—; judge Clermont County, Batavia, 1983—. Bd. dirs. Community Chest, Batavia, 1983—, YWCA House of Peace, Batavia, 1983—, Juvenile Ct. Advisory, Batavia, 1983—. Recipient Woman of Yr. award Altrusa Club of Clermont County, 1983. Mem. Clermont County Bar Assn. (v.p. 1984-85), Ohio State Bar Assn., Mcpl.-County Ct. Judges Assn. (bd. dirs. 1985). Democrat. Club: Altrusa (pres. 1984). Avocations: scuba diving. Office: 202 Main St Batavia OH 45103

O'DONNELL, WILLIAM DAVID, construction firm executive; b. Brockton, Mass., Aug. 21, 1926; s. John Frank and Agnes Teresa (Flanagan) O'D.; m. Dixie Lou Anderson, Jan. 31, 1951; children—Craig Patrick, Ginger Lynn. B.S., U. N.Mex., 1953. Registered profl. engr., Ill., 1958. Engr., State of Ill., 1953-59; with Gregory-Anderson Co., Rockford, Ill., 1959—, gen. mgr., 1960-61, sec., 1961-81, pres., 1981—; dir. 1st Nat. Bank & Trust Co. of Rockford, 1st Community Bancorp, Inc., Growth Enterprise. Dir. St. Anthony Med. Ctr.; bd. dirs. Rockford YMCA, pres., 1984. Served with USN, 1943-47. Recipient Friend of the Boy award Optimist Club, 1966, Excalibur award for community service Rockford Register Star, 1971; named Titan of Yr., Boylan High Sch., 1974. Fellow ASCE, Nat. Soc. Profl. Engrs.; mem. No. Ill. Bldg. Contractors, Aircraft Owners and Pilots Assn., Balloon Fedn. Am., Sigma Tau, Chi Epsilon, Tau Beta Pi. Club: Forest Hills Country (Rockford); Adventurers (Chgo.). Lodges: Elks, Rockford Rotary (Service Above Self award 1972; v.p. 1983, pres. 1984). Home: 2004 Bradley Rd Rockford IL 61107 Office: 2525 Huffman Blvd Rockford IL 61103

O'DRISCOLL, THOMAS EDWARD, educational administrator; b. St. Louis, May 9, 1933; s. Thomas James and Margaret Ellen (Roberts) O'D.; m. Janet Claire Crescio, June 16, 1956; children—Thomas L., John P., Martha C. B.S., Quincy Coll. (Ill.), 1956; M.Ed., U. Ill., 1962; postgrad. U. Maine, 1968. Cert. tchr., guidance specialist, Ill. Tchr., coach Quincy Notre Dame High Sch., Quincy, 1956-59; counselor, coach Quincy Pub. Schs., 1959-62; dir. pupil, personnel service High Sch. Dist. 214, Mount Prospect, Ill., 1962-71, athletic dir., 1971-84; dist. dir. phys. edn., 1981-84; prin. John Hersey High Sch., Arlington Heights, Ill., 1984—. Mem. Nat. Assn. Secondary Prins., Ill. Prins. Assn., Dist. 214 Admistrn. Assn. (exec. bd. 1982-84). Lodge: Rotary (com. chmn. 1984)., Avocations: bridge, tennis. Home: 1040 Carpenter Palatine IL 60067 Office: John Hersey High Sch 1900 E Thomas St Arlington Heights IL 60004

OEST, JENNY ELIZABETH, electronic data systems specialist, computer consultant; b. Williamsburg, Va., Nov. 10, 1958; d. John Roger and Shirley Jane (Brigance) Oest. B.A., Earlham Coll., 1980. Programmer, Chemineer, Inc., Dayton, Ohio, 1980-82, programmer/analyst, 1982-85; cons. Computer Specialties, Dayton, 1984—; personal computer support co-ordinator Electronic Data Systems div. Gen. Motors, Dayton, 1985—. Mem. Miami Valley Mgmt. Assn., Assn. Systems Mgmt. Episcopalian. Avocations: volleyball; aerobics; dancing. Home: 4123 E Indian Runn Dayton OH 45415 Office: EDS-GM-Inland Mail Code 04-8 2701 Home Ave Dayton OH 45417

OESTERREICHER, PAUL EDWARD, lawyer; b. Knox, Ind., Nov. 28, 1954; s. Peter George and Walli (Brauer) O.; m. Karen Cole, June 3, 1980; children—Paul Elliot, Kimberlie Lynn. B.A. in Polit. Sci., SW Mo. State U., 1977; J.D., Washburn Law Sch., 1980. Bar: Mo. 1981. Asst. prosecutor Randolph County, Moberly, Mo., 1981-82, pros. atty., 1983—; sole practice, Moberly, 1981—. Treas., Randolph County Young Democrats, 1982—. Mem. ABA, Mo. Bar Assn., Randolph County Bar Assn. (pres. 1985). Mem. Ch. of Jesus Christ of Latter Day Saints. Club: Kiwanis. Home: 421 S 5th St Moberly MO 65270 Office: Pros Atty PO Box 482 223 N Williams Moberly MO 65270

OESTREICH, GEORGE LOUIS, pharmacist; b. Fulton, Mo., May 19, 1947; s. Miller Crews and Lucille Agnes (McCuine) O.; m. Barbara Lee Dunavant, Aug. 27, 1967 (div. 1979); m. Jana Lynn Davis, June 21, 1980; 1 son, Andrew Oliver. B.S., U. Mo., 1970, M.P.A., 1982. Pres., Comprehensive Pharm. Services, Inc., Fulton, Mo., 1972—, Advanced Apothecaries, Inc., 1981—; cons. nursing homes and hosps., 1974—. Mayor, City of Fulton, Mo., 1978—. Served with USPHS, 1970-72. Mem. Am. Pharm. Assn., Mo. Pharm. Assn., Nat. Assn. Retail Druggists, Am. Coll. Apothecaries, Am. Soc. Cons. Pharmacists, Phi Kappa Phi, Omicron Delta Kappa., Phi Alpha Alpha, Rho Chi. Democrat. Methodist. Club: Fulton Country. Home: 103 Collier Ln Fulton MO 65251 Office: Comprehensive Pharmaceutical Services Inc 600 Court St Fulton MO 65251

O'FALLON, NANCY MCCUMBER, university official; b. Jackson, Miss., Oct. 25, 1938; d. Murrell Chester and Louise Marie (Paquette) McCumber; m. John Robert O'Fallon, June 14, 1962; children—John Michael, Brian Douglas, Deborah Lynne. B.S. in E.E., St. Louis U., 1960; M.S. in Nuclear Engring., U. Ill.-Urbana, 1961, Ph.D. in Physics, 1966. Part-time asst. prof. U. Mo., St. Louis, 1967-72, vis. asst. prof. physics, 1972-74; asst. physicist Argonne Nat. Lab., Ill., 1974-76, physicist, 1976-83, program mgr. Inst. and Control for Fossil Energy, 1978-83; asst. v.p. research U. Chgo., 1983—. Contbr. articles to profl. jours. Recipient Leadership award in edn. YWCA Met. Chgo., 1984. Nat. Merit scholar, 1956-60. Mem. Am. Phys. Soc., AAAS, Assn. Women in Sci. (nat. councilor 1980-81; treas. 1984-85), Chgo. Network. Office: Univ of Chgo 9700 S Cass Ave Bldg 201 Argonne IL 60439

O'FLYNN, JAMES MAGUIRE, association executive; b. St. Louis, Mar. 4, 1933; s. John Stanley and Katherine Butler (Maguire) O'F.; m. Barbara Jeanne Wingbermuehle, Sept. 19, 1959; children—Bridget, Mary Margaret, Kathryn, James Maguire. B.A., St. Louis U., 1984. Vice pres. Bank of St. Louis, 1966-72, exec. v.p., 1974-76; v.p. Gen. Bancshares, St. Louis, 1972-74; chmn. bd., chief exec. officer Traders Nat. Bank, Kansas City, Mo., 1976-78; pres. St. Louis Regional Commerce and Growth Assn., 1978—. Bd. dirs. VP Fair, 1982—, Lindenwood Coll., 1983—; bd. dirs. The Backstoppers, 1979—, v.p., 1980, pres., 1981, membership chmn., 1982, treas., 1983; bd. dirs. Cath. Charities, 1982—, pres., 1983-84; trustee St. Louis Coll. Pharmacy, 1981—, mem. nominating com., 1982, mem. budget com., 1983; trustee Laclede Sch. Law, 1982—; trustee, chmn. pub. relations com., mem. devel. com. St. Louis Art Mus., 1983—; mem. Mo. State 4-H Youth Adv. Council, 1981—; chmn. Port of Met. St. Louis Promotion Com., 1978—. Served with U.S. Army, 1955-57. Roman Catholic. Clubs: Mo. Athletic, St. Louis, Old Warson Country. Home: 5597 Lindell Blvd Saint Louis MO 63112 Office: St Louis Regional Commerce and Growth Assn 10 Broadway Saint Louis MO 63102

O'GARA, MICHAEL J., equipment company executive; b. Chgo., May 13, 1955; s. Thomas Edward and Eileen (Lamb) O'G.; m. Susan Virginia Schulte, Aug. 19, 1978. B.S. in Econs., U. Ill., 1977. Mktg. trainee IBM, Rolling Meadows, Ill., 1977-78; assoc. mktg. rep., 1978, mktg. rep., 1978-82; dist. mgr. Itel Rail Corp., Chgo., 1982-83, regional mgr., 1983, dir. mktg., 1984—; v.p. First Bus. Schs. Inc., Evanston, Ill., 1982—. Roman Catholic. Club: Union League (Chgo.) Avocation: sports. Home: 2521 Maple Ave Northbrook IL 60062 Office: Itel Rail Corp 19 S La Salle Chicago IL 60603

OGBORN, LOREN ONIS, banker; b. Zionsville, Ind., Nov. 10, 1928; s. Loren E. and Carrie E. Ogborn; m. Dorothy L. Howard, June 11, 1949; children—Steven R., Sabrina R. Student Ind. Central Bus. Sch., 1946, La Salle Corr. Schs., 1946-48; Purdue U. Extension, 1960-63, Lake Forest Coll., 1968. With Hygrade Food Products Co., Indpls., 1949-59, asst. mgr. data processing; mgr. data processing Hammond Valve Corp. (Ind.), 1959-69; mgr. computer ops. Blue Cross-Blue Shield, Indpls., 1969-71; v.p., mgr. data processing Gainer Bank, Gary, Ind., 1971—. Mem. Data Processing Mgmt. Assn., Assn. for Systems Mgmt. Home: 982 W 73d Ave Merrillville IN 46410 Office: PO Box 209 Gary IN 46402

OGDEN, WILLIAM S., bank executive. Chmn., chief executive officer, dir. Continental Ill. Nat. Bank & Trust Co. of Chgo. Office: Continental Ill Nat Bank and Trust Co of Chgo 231 S LaSalle St Chicago IL 60697*

OGLE, RICHARD GAYUS, oral surgeon; b. Marshall, Minn., May 10, 1940; s. Russell G. and Ethel (Geer) O.; m. Patricia Ann Reese, June 21, 1961; children—Dana K., Michelle M., Sandra L., Thomas R. B.S., U. Minn., 1962; D.D.S., 1964, M.S., 1968, M.D., 1975. Diplomate Am. Bd. Oral and Maxillofacial Surgery, Nat. Bd. Med. Examiners. Pvt. practice oral and maxillofacial surgery, Mankato, Minn., 1968-71; assoc. prof. U. Minn., Mpls., 1971-77; pvt. practice oral and maxillofacial surgery, Owatonna, Minn., 1977—. Contbr. articles to sci. jours. Basketball coach Owatonna Park and Recreation Dist., 1980-82; leader 4-H, Lakeville, Minn., 1973-75; dep. Steele County Mounted Possee, Owatonna, 1978-83. Mem. Am. Bd. Oral and Maxillofacial Surgeons (exec. adv. bd.), ADA, AMA, Internat. Coll. Surgeons, Minn. Soc. Oral and Maxillofacial Surgery (pres.), Nat. Bd. Dental Examiners (test constructor advisor com. 1976-81). Avocation: horseback riding. Office: Ogle Amundson PA 605 Hillcrest St Owatonna MN 55060

OGLESBY, PAUL LEONARD, JR., lawyer; b. Decatur, Ill., Aug. 17, 1955; s. Paul Leonard and Dorothy E. (Yeoman) O. B.A., U. Ill., 1977; J.D., So. Ill. U., 1980. Bar: Ill. 1980. Asst. state's atty. Coles County, Charleston, Ill., 1981-83; assoc. Dilsaver, Nelson & Ryan, Mattoon, Ill., 1983—. Mem. ABA, Res. Officers Assn., Ill. State Bar Assn., Coles-Cumberland Bar Assn. Republican. Methodist. Home: 417 N Elm St Windsor IL 61957 Office: Dilsaver Nelson & Ryan 1632 Broadway Ave Mattoon IL 61938

O'GRADY, DONALD JOHN, clinical psychologist; b. Providence, R.I., Mar. 16, 1942; s. John Miles and Mary (Muldowney) O'G.; m. Dee Ann Hammond, June 19, 1965; children—Erin, Michael. B.A., U. Notre Dame, 1964; M.A., U. Toledo, 1965; Ph.D., U. Cin., 1968. Diplomate in Clin. Psychology. Staff psychologist Cin. Ctr. Devel., 1967-73; dir. psychology Children's Hosp., Cin., 1973—; prof. clin. pediatrics U. Cin. Coll. Medicine, 1984—. Editor: Child Health Psychology, 1982; contbr. articles to profl. jours. and book. Mem. Am. Psychol. Assn., Cin. Acad. Profl. Psychology (pres. 1985—). Office: Children's Hosp Med Ctr Elland and Bethesda Aves Cincinnati OH 45229

OGRODNICK, JOHN ALEXANDER, professional hockey player. Left wing Detroit Red Wings, NHL. Office: Red Wings 600 Civic Center Dr Detroit MI 48226*

O'HALLORAN, THOMAS ALPHONSUS, JR., physics educator; b. Bklyn., Apr. 13, 1931; s. Thomas Alphonsus and Nora (Sheehan) O'H.; m. Barbara Joyce Hug, June 9, 1954; children—Theresa Joyce, Maureen Ann, Kevin Thomas, Patrick Joseph. Student San Jose State Coll., 1948-50; B.S., Oreg. State Coll., 1953, M.S., 1954; Ph.D., U. Calif., Berkeley, 1963. Research assoc. Lawrence Berkeley Lab., (Calif., 1963-64; research fellow Harvard U., 1964-66; prof. physics U. Ill., Urbana, 1966—. Contbr. articles to profl. jours. Served to lt. USN, 1954-58. Guggenheim fellow, 1979-80. Fellow Am. Phys. Soc. Home: 706 W Iowa St Urbana IL 61801 Office: Dept Physics U Ill Urbana IL 61801

O'HARA, MICHAEL JAMES, law educator, researcher; b. Detroit, Feb. 4, 1953; s. Edward Richard and Eileen Mary (Friel) O.; m. Mary Catherine Cortese, June 1, 1981. B.A. in Sociology, U. Nebr., 1975, J.D., 1978, M.A. in Econs., 1979, Ph.D. in Econs., 1983. Bar: Nebr. 1978, U.S. Dist. Ct. Nebr. 1978. Research asst. S.E. Nebr. Health Systems Agy., Lincoln, 1979; legis. aide State of Nebr., Lincoln, 1979-81; instr. econs. U. Nebr., Omaha, 1981-82; asst. prof. law, 1982—. Contbr. articles to profl. jours. Econs. advisor 2nd Congl. Dist. Campaign, Omaha, 1984; mem. Nebr. Power Rev. Bd., 1985—. Mem. ABA (sect. on antitrust law, forum com. on franchise law), Am. Econs. Assn., Omicron Delta Epsilon. Home: 6005 Charles St Omaha NE 68132 Office: Univ Nebr at Omaha 60th and Dodge Sts Omaha NE 68182

O'HARA, PHYLLIS JEAN, association executive; b. Des Moines, May 2, 1945; d. Ronald Earl Slaymaker and Helen Agnes (Ware) Wetteland; m. James Michael Trombley, June 21, 1980; children—James Brian, Michael Patrick, Erica Megan. Student U. Nebr., 1971-74. Exec. dir. Nebr. Commn. on Status of Women, Lincoln, 1974—; organizational effectiveness trainer Nat. Assn. Commns. for Women, 1983. Co-author: Organizational Handbook for Commissions on Women, 1983. Bd. dirs. Lincoln Council on Alcoholism and Drugs, 1984—; com. chmn. Gov.'s Task Force on Sexual Assault, Lincoln, 1981—; mem. Nebr. Coalition for Women, 1980—; chmn. Older Women's League, Lincoln, 1981—; com. mem. Gov.'s Conf. on Women Bus. Owners, 1984—. Mem. Nat. Assn. Commns. for Women (v.p.), Nat. Com. on Pay Equity, Nat. Women's Polit. Caucus, Nebr. Task Force on Displaced Homemakers. Democrat. Unitarian. Home: 1217 N 38th St Lincoln NE 68503 Office: Nebr Commn on Status of Women 301 Centennial Mall South Lincoln NE 68509

O'HARE, J. MICHAEL, physicist, educator; b. Des Moines, Oct. 2, 1938; s. Larence and Eleanor Ann (McGillicuddy) O'H.; m. Patricia Ann Cronin, June 20, 1964; children—Maureen, Colleen, Erin, Jennifer. B.S., Loras Coll., 1960; M.S., Purdue U., 1962; Ph.D. in Physics, SUNY-Buffalo, 1966. Instr. physics SUNY-Buffalo, 1965-66; asst. prof. U. Dayton, Ohio, 1966-71, assoc. prof., 1971-77, prof. physics, 1977—, chmn. dept., 1983—; vis. scientist AF Materials Lab., 1977-78; sr. research physicist U. Dayton Research Inst., 1979-80. Contbr. articles to sci. jours. Mem. Am. Phys. Soc., Optical Soc. Am., Sigma Pi Sigma, Delta Epsilon Sigma. Avocations: piano; banjo; jogging. Home: 6179 Laurelhurst Ln Centerville OH 45459 Office: U Dayton Dayton OH 45469

O'HEARN, MARY, educational consultant; b. Detroit, Mar. 5, 1933; d. Maurice Michael and Genevieve (Clor) O'H. B.A., Siena Heights Coll., 1960; postgrad. Mich. State U., 1961, Wayne State U., 1963, 63, 65, 66, U. Detroit Law Sch., 1981—; M.A., Oakland U., 1977. Tchr. English, jr. high sch., Des Moines, 1952-55, Chgo., 1955-62, Warren, Mich., 1962-77; tchr. English, sr. high sch., Warren, 1977-79, lang. arts cons., 1979—; legal intern NLRB, Detroit, summer 1985. Mem. ABA, NEA, Mich. Edn. Assn., Warren Edn. Assn., Assn. Supervision and Curriculum Devel., Mich. Reading Assn., Mich. Mensa, Oakland U. Alumni Assn. Club: Mich. Masters Swimmers. Home: 300 Riverfront Park Apt 5A Detroit MI 48226 Office: 31300 Anita St Warren MI 48093

OHL, FERRIS ELWOOD, music educator, conductor; b. Crawford County, Ohio, Sept. 10, 1914; s. George M. and Josie E. (Solze) O; m. Dorothy Doolittle, May 24, 1942; children—Vicki Ohl Braley, Laura Ohl Ross. B.M., Heidelberg Coll., 1936; M.M., Cin. Conservatory, 1946; M.S., Columbia U., 1950, diploma, 1952, Ed.D., 1955, postgrad., 1964-65. Dir. vocal and instrumental music Pioneer (Ohio) Pub. Schs., 1936-41; asst. prof. voice and chorus Heidelberg Coll., Tiffin, Ohio, 1946-47, assoc. prof., 1949-52, prof., 1953-85, chmn. dept. music, prof., 1965-85; vis. prof. Columbia Tchrs. Coll., N.Y.C., 1964-65; condr. Heidelberg Concert Choir, 1946-82, Tiffinian Male Chorus Trinity UCC Choir, 1946-66; dir. ann. Messiah; guest condr. and clinician, Ohio. Programming cons. Tiffin Arts Council. Served to maj. AUS, 1941-46. Decorated Bronze Star (2). Recipient medal U. Heidelberg (W. Ger.), 1978. Fellow Internat. Inst. Art and Letters, Internat. Sci. Info. Service, Am. Inst. Arts and Letters; mem. Nat. Assn. Tchrs. Singing (past pres.), Am. Choral Dirs. (past lt. gov.), Ohio Music Educators Assn., Ohio Music Tchrs. Assn., Internat. Platform Assn. Arranger: Ferris Ohl Choral Series, 1961-65. Lodges: Elks, Tiffin Rotary. Home: 98 Woodmere Dr Tiffin OH 44883 Office: Heidelberg Coll East Perry St Tiffin OH 44883

OHL, GREGORY FRANCIS, principal; b. Oelwein, Iowa, Mar. 9, 1951; s. Donald Frederick and Mary Virginia (Barnes) O.; m. Chintana Nernurai, July 30, 1976; children—Anthony J., Alexander D., Angela C. B.S., Bemidji State U., 1976; M.S., 1981. Cert. in secondary adminstrn. and counseling, Minn. Tchr. Wells-Easton High Sch., Wells, Minn., 1977-79; adminstrv. asst. Redlake Sch. Dist., Minn., 1980-84; secondary prin. Willow River High Sch., Minn., 1984—; ednl. cons. Ministry Edn., Bangkok, Thailand, 1984—, Internat. Bus. Acad., Bangkok, 1984—. Served with U.S. Army, 1969-72, Vietnam. Mem. Nat. Assn. Secondary Sch. Prins., Minn. Assn. Secondary Sch. Prins., DAV, Shorinryu Karate Assn. (regional rep.). Democratic. Lodge: Masons (Bemidji, Minn.). Avocations: 6th degree Black Belt Okinawan Karate. Office: PO Box 66 Willow River High Sch Willow River MN 55795

OHLBAUM, MORTON KING, optometrist; b. Bklyn., July 30, 1929; s. Richard and Sadie (Weinstein) O.; m. Nov. 19, 1950; children—Karen Beth, Lori Ann. B.S., Ill. Coll. Optometry, 1953, O.D., 1954; M.S., Ind. U., 1968, Ph.D., 1973. Clin. practice optometry Waterbury, Conn., 1954-59; commd. lt. U.S. Air Force, 1959, advanced through grades to maj., 1979; clin. optometrist U.S. Air Force, Wright-Patterson Air Force Base, Ohio, 1959-66, research optometrist, 1966-78; clin. optometrist I.G. Loewit Assocs., Beavercreek, Ohio, 1979—. Contbr. articles to profl. jours. Fellow Am. Acad. Optometry. Jewish. Avocation: gun collector. Home: 286 Chatham Dr Fairborn OH 45324

OHMAN, RICHARD MICHAEL, artist, educator; b. Erie, Pa., May 8, 1946. B.A., Mercyhurst Coll., 1972; M.F.A., Ohio U., 1975. Instr. Ohio U., Chillicothe, 1974-80, asst. prof. art, 1980—. Exhibited in group shows at Butler Mus., Exhbn. of Contemporary Art Palm Beach, Am. Painters in Paris, others. Recipient Wagnalls Meml. award, 1978; Yassinnoff Meml. award, 1977, Ohio Arts Council grantee. Home: PO Box 9448 Cincinnati OH 45209

OJALA, RICHARD HENRY, hotelier; b. Ann Arbor, Mich., May 1, 1950; s. Reuben Henry Ojala and Donna (Yon) Roberts; m. Cynthia Marie Cryderman, Oct. 6, 1973; children—Richard Preston, Rachel Marie, Steven Eric. B.S. in Child Devel. cum laude, Lake Superior State Coll., 1979. Ptnr. Energy Enterprises, Sault Ste. Marie, Mich., 1981-83, owner, mgr., 1983—; gen. mgr. Doral Motel, Inc., Sault Ste. Marie, 1981—; owner Doral Motel/Friendship Inn, Sault Ste. Marie, 1985—. Founder, bd. dirs. Crisis Pregnancy Ctr., 1982—, Christian Action Council, 1980; bd. dirs. Child Evangelism Fellowship, 1980—, past pres. Served with U.S. Army, 1969-71. Mem. Sault Ste. Marie C. of C., Mich. Lodging Assn. Baptist. Avocations: fishing; hunting; tennis; golf. Home: 536 E Portage St Sault Ste Marie MI 49783 Office: Doral Motel/Friendship Inn 518 E Portage St Sault Ste Marie MI 49783

OKA, TAKESHI, chemistry and astronomy educator; b. Tokyo, June 10, 1932; came to U.S., 1981; s. Shumpei and Chiyoko Ozaki O.; m. Keiko Nukui, Oct. 24, 1960; children—Ritsuko, Noriko, Kentaro, Yujiro. B.S., U. Tokyo (Japan), 1955, Ph.D., 1960. Research physicist Nat. Research Council, Ottawa, Canada, 1963-80; prof. U. Chgo., 1981—. Fellow Am. Physical Soc., Royal Soc. Canada, Royal Soc. London. Home: 1463 E Park Pl Chicago IL 60637 Office: Dept Chemistry Univ Chicago 5735 S Ellis Ave Chicago IL 60637

O'KEEFE, FRANCIS RONALD, lawyer; b. Gt. Neck, N.Y., Oct. 7, 1950; s. Francis Joseph and Bridget Anne (Coady) O'K.; m. Pamelinda Lee, Aug. 18, 1979. A.B., Georgetown U., 1972; J.D., Cleve.-Marshall Coll., 1977. Bar: Ohio 1977, U.S. Dist. Ct. (no. dist.) Ohio 1978. Assoc. Csank & Csank Co., L.P.A., Cleve., 1977-79, ptnr., 1979—. Composer: Shoes of Truth, 1984. Recipient Sindell Tort Competition prize Cleve.-Marshall Law Sch., 1977. Mem. ABA, Ohio State Bar Assn., Greater Cleve. Bar Assn., Delta Theta Phi (Article Most Useful to Practicing Attys. award 1977). Avocations: musical compositions; art.

OKERHOLM, RICHARD ARTHUR, chemical company administrator; b. Woburn, Mass., Nov. 10, 1941; s. Theodore and Elizabeth Anne (Johnston) O.; m. Rita V. Hutchinson, June 26, 1965; children—Heidi Ann, Erik Paul. B.S. in Chemistry, Lowell Tech. Inst., 1964, postgrad. student in organic and organometallic chemistry, 1964-65; Ph.D. in Biochemistry, Boston U., 1970. Instr. quantitative analysis Lowell Tech. Inst., Mass., 1962-65; grad. teaching fellow in gen. chemistry Boston U. Sch. Medicine, 1964-65, grad. teaching fellow organic chemistry, 1965-66; research biochemist Parke-Davis & Co., Ann Arbor, Mich., 1970-73, sr. research biochemist, 1973-77; sect. head drug metabolism dept. Merrell Dow Pharms. Inc. subs. Dow Chemistry Co., Cin., 1977-79, head drug metabolism dept., 1979—. Author: Competitive Protein Binding, 1973; (with others) A Simplified Method for the Analysis of Perhexiline in Human Plasma, 1978; Photochemical Degradation of Dapsone, 1972. Contbr. articles to profl. jours. Treas., Fairfield Soccer Assn. Youth, Ohio, 1979-80. Predoctoral fellow NIH, 1966-69, postdoctoral fellow NIH, 1969-70. Mem. Am. Chem. Soc., Am. Soc. Clin. Pharmacology and Therapeutics, Am. Soc. Mass Spectrometry, Am. Soc. Pharmacology and Exptl. Therapeutics, Am. Pharm. Assn., N.Y. Acad. Scis., Soc. Exptl. Biology and Medicine, Sigma Xi (research award 1964). Lodge: Optimists (bd. dirs. 1980-82). Avocations: coaching youth soccer, tennis, gardening, fishing. Home: 5664 Williamsburg Way Fairfield OH 45014 Office: Merrell Dow Research Inst 2110 E Galbraith Rd Cincinnati OH 45215

OKRAGLEY, SUSAN JOYCE-HEATHER, nurse, mechanic; b. Lakewood, Ohio, July 11, 1945; d. Richard George Bersin, Sr. and Ireene R. (Brenner) Kinsner; m. Robert Joseph Okragley, Dec. 23, 1972; 1 child, Anna Claire. B.S.N., Kent State U., 1976. R.N., Ohio. Nurse, Deaconess Hosp. Cleve., 1976-80, St. Luke's Hosp., Cleve., 1980-81, St. John's Hosp. Cleve., 1981-84; vehicle technician Corvair Repair and Mobile Service and Demolition Co., Cleve., 1971—. Vol. ARC, Cleve., 1980-84; leader Lake Erie council Girl Scouts U.A., 1983—. Served with USN, 1963-66. Republican. Avocations: Building race cars and and airplanes, skydiving, skuba diving. Home and Office: 10609 St Mark Ave Cleveland OH 44111

OKUNIEFF, MICHAEL, physician; b. Wilno, Poland, Apr. 24, 1923; came to U.S., 1951; s. Pinchos and Paula (Deweltow) O.; m. Beverly Sue Kailes, Apr. 21, 1956; children—Paul G., Paula E., Rise J., Rhoda Lee. M.D., U. Munich, 1949. Diplomate Am. Bd. Family Practice. Intern, Beth David Hosp., N.Y.C., 1951-52; resident in internal medicine Morrisiana City Hosp., Bronx, N.Y., 1952-53, U. Ill. Research and Ednl. Hosps., Chgo., 1953-55; practice medicine specializing in family practice, Chgo., 1956—; mem. staffs Hyde Park Community Hosp., Chgo., South Shore Hosp., Chgo. Mem. Ill. Acad. Family Practice (del. 1980-83), AMA, Ill. Med. Soc., Chgo. Med. Soc., Am. Acad. Family Practice. Home: 116 Plum Tree Ln Wilmette IL 60091 Office: 7271 S Exchange Ave Chicago IL 60649

OLANOFF, LAWRENCE SHELDON, clinical research physician, scientist; b. N.Y.C., Jan. 31, 1952. B.S., Tufts U., 1974; M.S., Rutgers U., 1975; Ph.D., Case Western Res. U., 1980, M.D., 1981. Research fellow Case Western Res. U., Cleve., 1980-81, Med. U., S.C., Charleston, med. resident, 1981-82, clin. fellow pharmacology, 1982-84; physician investigator, scientist The Upjohn Co., Kalamazoo, 1984—. Contbr. articles to profl. jours. and book chpts. Drug Sci. Found. scholar. Mem. Am. Soc. Clin. Pharmacology Therapeutics, Controlled Release Soc., Am. Fed. Clin. Research, Am. Soc. Artificial Internal Organs, Biomaterial Soc. Office: Kalamazoo Clin Investigational Complex 526 Jasper St Kalamazoo MI 49007

O'LAUGHLIN, JOSEPH CHRISTOPHER, gastroenterologist, educator; b. Phila., Dec. 23, 1949; s. James Clare and Sarah Catherine (Bookford) O'L.; m. Deborah Caroline Ventrone, Dec. 27, 1975; 1 child, Matthew Christopher. B.S. in Biology, U. Scranton (Pa.), 1971; D.O., Phila. Coll. Osteo. Medicine, 1975. Diplomate Am. Bd. Internal Medicine. Intern, Detroit Osteo. Hosp., 1975-76, resident in internal medicine, 1976-78; sr. postdoctoral fellow in gastroenterology U. Mo. Sch. Medicine, Columbia, 1978-80; pvt. practice medicine specializing in gastroenterology, Warren, Mich., 1980—; mem. staff BiCounty Hosp., Warren, 1980—, Mt. Clemens (Mich.) Gen. Hosp., 1980—; clin. asst. prof. medicine Mich. State U., East Lansing, 1980—. Recipient Outstanding Contbrn. Med. Edn. award Mt. Clemens Gen. Hosp., 1982. Mem. Am. Gastroenterol. Assn., Am. Soc. Gastrointestinal Endoscopy, Detroit Gastroenterol. Soc. Contbr. chpts. to books, articles to profl. publs. Office: Tri-County Gastroenterology PC 13552 Martin St Suite A Warren MI 48093

OLD, HAROLD EVANS, JR., state official; b. Mansfield, Ohio, Sept. 11, 1939; s. Harold Evans and Pearl Edna (Beaschler) O.; m. Georgia A. Bernath, June 9, 1962 (div. July 1982); children—Eric K., Philip E. B.S., Marquette U., 1961; M.A., Western Mich. U., 1970; Ph.D., Mich. State U., 1973; postgrad. Naval War Coll., 1982-83. Grad. asst. Western Mich. U., Kalamazoo, also Mich. State U., East Lansing, 1967-72; instr. U. Conn., Storrs, 1972-73; exec. mgr. Ponderosa Systems, Lansing, Mich., 1973-74; adminstr. Mich. Dept. Pub. Health, Lansing, 1974-79, Mich. Dept. Labor, Lansing, 1979—; pres. Cedar Wood Homes, Inc., Schaumburg, Ill., 1983—. Served to lt. USNR, 1961-67; capt. Res. NROTC scholar, 1957. Mem. Am. Polit. Sci. Assn., Res. Officers Assn., Naval Inst., Am. Soc. Pub. Adminstrn. (pres. Lansing 1982-83), Naval Res. Assn. (pres. Lansing 1970-73, 75—), Navy League, Am. Def. Preparedness Assn., Blue Jackets Assn. Club: Mich. Comdrs.

OLDBERG, CARL MALCOLM, public relations executive; b. Kansas City, Mo., Nov. 4, 1947; s. Philip Perry and Muriel (Swanson) O.; m. Linda Jane Swendson, Nov. 25, 1972; 1 child, Elizabeth Ann. A.A., Met. Jr. Coll., 1967; B.A. in Journalism, U. Mo.-Columbia, 1970, M.B.A., 1972. With pub. relations dept. Motorola Inc., Schaumburg, Ill., 1972-77; sr. v.p. Ruder Finn & Rotman, Chgo., 1977—. Recipient Best Ideas award ITT, 1981, 82, 83. Mem. Am. Mktg. Assn., Pub. Relations Soc. (Silver Anvil award 1979), Publicity Club Chgo. (Golden Trumpet award, 1979, 82), Internat. Assn. Bus. Communicators (Silver Quill award 1984). Home: 1627 Portsmouth Ln Schaumburg IL 60194

OLDFORD, JOSEPH ROSS, urologist; b. Detroit, Dec. 2, 1931; s. Joseph and Jennie (Kahkola) O.; m. Mary Elaine NacKay, July 9, 1955; children—Joseph, Roberta, Gregory, Jeffrey. B.S., U. Detroit, 1952; M.D., St. Louis U., 1956. Diplomate Am. Bd. Urology. Intern, Mt. Carmel Hosp., Detroit, 1 year, resident in gen. surgery, 1 year; resident in urology Grace Hosp., Detroit, 3 years; practice medicine specializing in urology, Farmington Hills, Mich., 1963—; asst. clin. prof. Wayne State U., Detroit, 1976—; chief urology Harper-Grace Hosps., Detroit, 1978-84; vice-chief urology, 1984—. Jr. warden of vestry Ch. of Redeemer, Southfield, Mich., 1984, 85. Served to capt. USAF, 1961-63. Mem. Am. Urol. Assn. (pres. Mich. branch 1978), Am. Fertility Soc., ACS, Am. Assn. Clin. Urologists, Mich. State Med. Soc. (del. 1981-84), Wayne County Med. Soc. (del. 1981-84), Detroit Acad. Scis. Republican. Episcopalian. Avocations: tennis, golf. Office: 28501 Orchard Lake Rd Farmington Hills MI 48018

OLDHAM, DALE RALPH, life insurance company executive; actuary; b. Topeka, Kans., May 31, 1943; s. Ralph W. and Anna Marie (Minch) O.; m. Marilyn D. Morris, June 5, 1965; children—Kent D., Kevin L. B.S. magna cum laude, Washburn U., 1965; A.M., U. Mich., 1967. Asst. actuary Nat. Res. Life, Topeka, Kans., 1967-72, assoc. actuary, 1972-74, v.p., assoc. actuary, 1974-76, v.p., chief actuary, 1976-84; also dir.; sr. v.p. adminstrn. Security Benefit Group, Topeka, 1984—; pres. Kansas City Actuaries Club, 1980-81. Mem. adv. council Unified Sch. Dist., Topeka, 1981-84. Fellow Soc. Actuaries; mem. Am. Acad. Actuaries, Kansas City Actuaries Club, Adminstrv. Mgmt. Soc. (bd. dirs. 1975-82, pres. 1981-82, Merit award 1980), also several socs. Republican. Home: 6011 SW 26th St Topeka KS 66614 Office: Security Benefit Group Inc 700 Harrison Topeka KS 66636

OLDS, JERRY CLYDE, geologist; b. Bloomburg, Tex., July 31, 1935; s. Clyde Wilson and Pauline Helen (Bentley) O.; m. Contance J. Sperry, Aug. 28, 1955; children—Kelly B., Kimberly K. B.S. in geol. engring., Tex. A&M, 1957. Geologist Amoco Prodn. Co. Standard Ind., Lafayette, and New Orleans, La., 1957-64; cons. geologist in pvt. practice, Worthington, Ohio, 1964—; pres. and dir. Frontier Energy Inc., Newark, Ohio, Derrick Industries, Inc., Somerset, Ohio, Solid Rock Energy Inc., Worthington. Served to 1st lt. U.S. Army, 1958-59. Fellow Am. Assn. Petroleum Geologists (ho. dels. 1982—), Ohio Geol. Soc. (pres. 1979-80), Ohio Oil and Gas Assn. (trustee 1983—), Soc. Exploration Geophysicists, Soc. Petroleum Engrs. of AIME. Republican. Baptist. Office: 625 High St PO Box 556 Worthington OH 43085

OLDS, JOHN WARD, physician, educator; b. Canal Zone, Panama, Apr. 25, 1935 (parents U.S. citizens); s. Thayer Stevens and Dorris (Laventure) O.; m. Rosemary Burns, July 10, 1957; children—David, James, Betsey. B.S., Iowa State U., 1956; M.D., U. Tenn., 1967. Diplomate Am. Bd. Internal Medicine, Am. Bd. Infectious Diseases. Intern San Francisco Gen. Hosp., 1967-68; resident, fellow U. N.Mex., 1968-72; practice internal medicine, Des Moines, Iowa, 1972—; dir. continuing med. edn. Iowa Methodist Med. Ctr., 1983—, cons. infectious diseases, 1972—, attending physician, 1972—; asst. clin. prof. U. Iowa, Iowa City, 1978—. Contbr. articles to med. jours. Served to lt. USNR, 1956-61. Recipient Roche award U. Tenn., 1966. Fellow ACP; mem. AMA, Iowa Med. Soc. (councilor 1980-84), Iowa Found. Med. Care (dist. chmn. 1981-83, bd. dirs. 1985—). Democrat. Episcopalian. Club: Med. Library (pres. 1985-86). Avocation: playing squash. Office: Internal Med Clin 2932 Ingersoll St Des Moines IA 50312

O'LEARY, FRANCIS BERNARD, emeritus librarian; b. N.Y.C., Oct. 6, 1926; s. Bernard and Bridget (O'Sullivan) O'L.; B.S., Manhattan Coll., N.Y.C., 1949; M.S. L.S., Columbia U., 1952; m. Antoinette M. Walbroel, Sept. 26, 1964; 1 son, Paul. Zoology-botany librarian Columbia U., 1949-53, asst. librarian for natural scis., 1953-57; librarian Inst. Tech., U. Minn., 1957-60; librarian Med. Center, St. Louis U., 1960-84, emeritus, 1984; project dir. Med. Library Network Bistate Regional Med. Program, 1970-73. Mem. Grand Jury, Bronx County, N.Y., 1956-57; rep. Assn. Coll. and Reference Libraries to 4th Nat. Conf. on Health in Colls., N.Y.C., 1953. Mem. Spl. Libraries Assn. (pres. Greater St. Louis chpt. 1963-64), AAUP, Med. Library Assn. (chmn. med. schs. sect. 1968-69), AAAS. Club: Naval Records. Author articles in field. Editor: Science Reference Notes (Columbia), 1954-57. Home: 5865 Delor St Saint Louis MO 63109

O'LEARY, MARY MARGARET, nursing administrator; b. Chgo., Apr. 27, 1941; d. John Jeremiah and Ruth (Creek) O'L. B.S. in Nursing, Villanova U., 1963; postgrad. Nat. Coll. Edn., 1974-75; M.H.P.Ed., U. Ill., 1979. Staff nurse Presbyterian-St. Luke's Hosp., Chgo., 1963-64, coordinator in-patient child psychiatry, 1964-68; asst. head nurse Veterans Research Hosp., Chgo., 1968-70; instr. coop. health occupations assts. program Chgo. Bd. Edn., 1970-72, tchr.-nurse child parent ctr. program, 1972-75; clin. nursing cons. dept. nursing U. Ill. Hosp., Chgo., 1975-80; dir. nursing edn. eval. and research Michael Reese Hosp. and Med. Ctr., Chgo., 1980—. Contbr. articles to profl. jours. Vol., Sta. WITW, Chgo., 1980-85, Lyric Opera of Chgo., 1983-85. Mem. Am. Soc. Nursing Service Adminstrs., Chgo. Met. Area Nursing Adminstrs., Chgo. Nursing In-Service Orgn., Ill. Soc. Nursing Service Adminstrs., Midwest Nursing Research Soc., Nat. Intravenous Therapy Assn. (chairperson continuing edn. com. 1979-82). Roman Catholic. Office: Michael Reese Hosp & Med Ctr 31st St and Lake Shore Dr Chicago IL 60616

OLECKNO, WILLIAM ANTON, educator; b. St. Charles, Ill., Dec. 16, 1948; s. Adolph B. and Barbara (Walrod) O.; m. Karen Marie Guzauskas, Dec. 27, 1975. B.S., Ind. U.-Indpls., 1971; M.P.H., U. Pitts., 1973; H.S.D., Ind. U., 1980. Registered profl. sanitarian, Ind. Sanitarian, DuPage County Health Dept., Wheaton, Ill., 1970-71, Ill. Dept. Public Health, Aurora, Ill., 1972; research assoc. Consad Research Corp., Pitts., 1973; instr., coordinator environ. health scis. program Ind. U. Med. Sch., Indpls., 1973-76; asst. prof., coordinator environ. health scis., 1976-80; assoc. prof., dir. community health program No. Ill. U., DeKalb, 1980—; pub. health and safety cons. Nat. Automatic Merchandising Assn., Chgo., 1975-80; vis. lectr. Ind. U., Bloomington, 1977-78; mem. health manpower adv. council Ind. Health Careers, Inc., 1976-80; v.p. bd. dirs. Am. Heart Assn., DeKalb County, 1981-83; chmn. DeKalb County Health Planning com., 1982-83. Recipient A. Harry Bliss editorial award Jour. Environ. Health, 1984; Ill. State Merit scholar, 1967; USPHS traineeship, 1972; USPHS grantee, 1973-78; Regional Ind. Med. Program grantee, 1975-76; HHS grantee, 1981. Mem. Nat. Environ. Health Assn. (chmn. individual and community water supply com. 1983-85, chmn. publs. com. 1985-86, presdl. citation 1984), Am. Pub. Health Assn., Ill. Environ. Health Assn. (editorial bd. jour. 1985-86), Ill. Pub. Health Assn., Eta Sigma Gamma, Phi Delta Kappa. Author: Water Quality Parameters, 1982; Alternative Methods of Centralized Wastewater Treatment, 1982; mem. editorial bd Hoosier Sanitarian, 1977-78, editor, 1978-80; contbr. articles on environ. and pub. health to profl. jours.

OLINGER, EDWARD JAY, gastroenterologist, medical educator; b. Bklyn., Feb. 21, 1947; s. Leon and Stella (Rosenberg) O.; m. Barbara Joan Smith,, Aug. 8, 1971; children—Sarah, Andrea. A.B., U. Calif.-Berkeley, 1968; M.D., Yale U., 1972. Diplomate Am. Bd. Internal Medicine. Intern U. Chgo., 1972-73, resident in medicine, 1973-74; clin. assoc. NIH, Bethesda, Md., 1974-76; fellow in gastroenterology U. Pa., Phila., 1976-78; assoc. chief gastroenterology Northwestern U., Chgo., 1979-81, asst. prof. medicine, 1978—; cons. gastroenterology Lincoln Park Zoo, Chgo., 1981—. Contbr. articles to med. jours. Served to lt. comdr. USPHS, 1974-76. Recipient Research prize Chgo. Soc. Gastroenterology, 1981, Komarov Research award Phila. Soc. Gastroenterology, 1978; Coon fellow, 1978-80. Mem. Am. Gastroent. Assn., Am. Soc. Study Liver Diseases, Am. Fedn. Clin. Research, ACP. Club: Cliffdwellers (Chgo.). Office: 707 N Fairbanks Chicago IL 60611

OLINGER, GLENN SLOCUM, manufacturing executive; b. New Castle, Ind., May 3, 1929; s. Glenn Arthur and Eva Lucille (Slocum) O.; m. Diana Sue Hurst, Oct. 2, 1982; m. Phyllis Lucille Roper, July 6, 1949 (div. Oct. 1981); children—Deborah, Glenn Alan, Craig W., Gwen G. B.S., U. Chattanooga, 1952; M.B.A., Northwestern U., 1955. With Gen. Electric Co., Louisville, 1955-75, gen. mgr. mktg. home laundry div., 1971-73, gen. mgr. room air conditioner dept., 1973-75; pres. Speed Queen div. McGraw Edison, Ripon, Wis., 1975-79; gen. mgr. internat. Gen. Electric, Louisville, 1979-82; pres. KitchenAid div. Dart & Kraft, Troy, Ohio, 1982—. Served with USN, 1946-49, 52-53. Mem. Mensa. Republican. Presbyterian. Club: Dayton Country. Lodge: Masons. Office: KitchenAid Div Troy OH 45374

OLINS, GILLIAN MARY, research biochemist; b. White Plains, N.Y., Oct. 18, 1953; m. Peter Olafs Olins, May, 1978. B.S. with honors, Liverpool U., Eng., 1975, Ph.D., 1979. Research assoc. U. Wis., Madison, 1979-83; sr. research biochemist Monsanto Co., St. Louis, 1983—. Author: Peptides: Synthesis, Structure, Function, 1981. Mem. AAAS, Biochem. Soc. Office: Monsanto Co 700 Chesterfield Village Pkwy Saint Louis MO 63198

OLIVAS, ADOLF, lawyer, city official; b. Hamilton, Ohio, Jan. 31, 1956; s. Henry and Eloina (Lopez) O. B.A., U. Cin., 1978, J.D., 1981. Bar: Ohio 1981, U.S. Dist. Ct. (so. dist.) Ohio 1981. Law clk., U.S. Dist. Ct. Ea. Dist. Ky., Covington, 1981; assoc. Holbrock, Jonson, Bressler & Houser, Hamilton, Ohio, 1981-85; ptnr. Rogers & Olivas, 1985—. Mem. Hamilton City Council, 1983-85; mem. exec. com. Butler County Democratic Com., 1983—; bd. dirs. Open Door Food Pantry, Hamilton, 1982-85; county coordinator Ohio State Gov. Celeste, 1982—. Mem. Butler County Bar Assn., Cin. Bar Assn., ABA, Assn. Trial Lawyers Am., Ohio State Bar Coll., U.S. Jaycees. Roman Catholic. Home: 1385 Carriage Hill Ln #88 Hamilton OH 45013 Office: Rogers & Olivas 1037 High St PO Box 1240 Hamilton OH 45012

OLIVE, JOHN, playwright; b. Fukuoka, Japan, Dec. 12, 1949; s. John Thomas and Elizabeth (Brinkman) O. B.A. in Theatre Arts, U. Minn., 1973. Plays include Standing on My Knees, Manhattan Theatre Club, N.Y.C., Clara's Play, 1980, Careless Love, produced by Wisdom Bridge Theatre, Chgo.; playwright Circle Repertory Co.; author: Minnesota Moon in Best Short Plays of 1982. Minn. Arts Bd. grantee, 1978, 80; Nat. Endowment Arts grantee, 1982. Mem. Dramatists Guild, New Dramatists Co. Home: 1604 Mt Curve Ave Minneapolis MN 55403

OLIVER, ALAN MARK, osteopathic physician; b. Kansas City, Mo., Feb. 28, 1952; s. William and Freda Rose (Zackowitz) O.; m. Shirley Ann Owen, Aug. 7, 1980. D.O., U. Health Scis. Coll. Osteo. Medicine, Kansas City, Mo., 1979. Diplomate Am. Bd. Emergency Medicine. Flexible Intern Richmond Heights Gen. Hosp. (Ohio), 1979-80; resident in emergency medicine U. Ky. Med. Ctr., Lexington, 1980-82; spl. fellow critical care medicine Cleve. Clinic Found., 1981—; mem. staff St. Luke's Hosp., 1983—, chief surg. intensive care div., 1983—. NSF research grantee, 1972, 73. Mem. Soc. Critical Care Medicine, Am. Coll. Emergency Physicians, Am. Osteo. Assn., Psi Sigma Alpha. Home: 25000 S Woodland St Beachwood OH 44122 Office: 11311 Shaker Blvd Cleveland OH 44104

OLIVER, EDWARD CARL, investment executive; b. St. Paul, May 31, 1930; s. Charles Edmund and Esther Marie (Bjugstad) O.; m. Charlotte Severson, Sept. 15, 1956; children—Charles E., Andrew T., Peter A. B.A., U. Minn., 1955. Sales rep. Armstrong Cork Co., N.Y.C., 1955; registered rep. Piper, Jaffray & Hopwood, Mpls., 1958; mgr. Mut. Funds, Inc. subs. Dayton's, Mpls., 1964; mgr. NWNL Mgmt. Corp. subs. Northwestern Nat. Life Ins. Co., Mpls., 1968-72, v.p., 1972-81, pres., dir., 1981—; v.p. Select Cash Mgmt. Fund, Inc., Select Capital Growth Fund, Inc., Select High Yield Fund, Inc., Northwestern Cash Fund, Inc. Bd. dirs. Hennepin County United Way, 1963; mem. Minn. Republican Party State Central Com., 1972-75. Served to sgt. USAF, 1951-52. Mem. Life Ins. Mktg. and Research Assn. (fin. products mktg. com.), Internat. Assn. Fin. Planners (past pres. Twin City chpt., mem. nat. governing com.), Psi Upsilon. Presbyterian (elder). Club: Mpls. Athletic. Home: 3901 Hillcrest Rd Wayzata MN 55391 Office: 20 Washington Ave S Minneapolis MN 55440

OLIVER, JOHN EDWARD, geography educator; b. Dover, England, Oct. 21, 1933; came to U.S., 1967; s. Albert Edward and Florence (Allen) P.; m. Sylvia Margaret Oberholzer, Aug. 10,. 1957; children—Frances Janine, Andrea Leigh. B.Sc., London U., 1956; M.A., Columbia U., 1966, Ph.D., 1969. Geographer, Bermuda Govt., 1958-64; asst. prof. geography Columbia U., N.Y.C., 1969-72, assoc. prof., 1972-73; prof. Ind. State U., Terre Haute, 1973—, chmn. dept. geography and geology, 1984—; chmn. AAG Climate Specialty, Washington, 1984—. Author: Climate and Man's Environment, 1973; Physical Geography, 1978; Climatology: Application, 1981; Climatology, 1984. Editor: Encyclopedia of Climatology, 1985. Editor jour. Physical Geography, 1979. Mem. Am. Meteorol. Soc., Assn. Am. Geographers, Ind. Acad. Sci., Sigma Xi. Home: 8282 S 30th St Terre Haute IN 47802 Office: Ind State U Dept Geography and Geology Terre Haute IN 47809

OLIVER, LYDA MONTESDE OCA, research biochemist; b. Cali, Valle, Colombia, July 31, 1945; came to U.S., 1973; d. Ricardo Montes de Oca, and Aura Renteria; m. George Edward Oliver, Jan. 4, 1973. Med. technologist, Universidad del Valle, Cali, Colombia, 1967; postgrad. exec. master's program Northwestern U., 1983—. Med. technologist Pub. Health Dept., Cali, 1968-73; med. technologist Northwestern U., Chgo., 1974-75, research technologist, 1975-78, sr. research technologist, 1978—, mgr. urology lab., 1983—; founder Oliver Imports & Exports, Inc. Contbr. articles to sci. jours. Vol., 48th ward Republican orgn., 1982-83, elections judge, 1982—. Mem. Northwestern U. Profl. Women's Assn. Roman Catholic. Avocations: jogging; bicycling; reading. Home: 6033 N Sheridan Rd 29 E Chicago IL 60660 Office: Northwestern U 303 E Chicago Ave Chicago IL 60611

OLIVER, THORNAL GOODLOE, healthcare executive; b. Memphis, Aug. 26, 1934; s. John Oliver and Evelyn Doris (Goodloe) Mitchell; m. Pauline Reid, Oct. 1, 1959. B.S., Tenn. State U., Nashville, 1956; M.H.A., Washington U., St. Louis, 1973. Cert. nursing home adminstr., Mo. Asst. dir., King Meml. Hosp., Kansas City, Mo., 1973-75; evening mgr. Truman Med. Ctr., Kansas City, Mo., 1975-77; asst. adminstr. Mid-Am. Radiation Ctr. U. Kans. Coll. Health Sci., Kansas City, Kans., 1977-81; dir. CHS, Inc., Lenwood, Kans., 1981-82; adminstr. Poplar Bluff Hosp., Mo., 1982-83; adminstr. The Benjamin F. Lee Health Ctr., Wilberforce, Ohio, 1983—; cons. in field. Contbr. articles to profl. jours. Served with U.S. Army, 1957-59, USAR, 1957-63. Fellow Am. Coll. Hosp. Adminstrs.; mem. Am. Hosp. Assn., Nat. Assn. Health Services Execs., Am. Med. Record Assn., Mo. League of Nursing Home Adminstrs. Home: 10641 N Grand Ave Route 20 Kansas City MO 64155 Office: The Benjamin F Lee Health Ctr PO Box 201 Lackey-Lee Bldg Wilberforce OH 45384

OLIVERA, PASCUAL, JR., dancer; b. Canton, Ohio, July 15, 1944; s. Pascual and Remedios (Cabezas) O.; m. Angela Olivera, Feb. 20, 1976. Grad. high sch., Spain. First Dancer Jose Greco Ballet, N.Y.C., 1968-72; producer/dir. Pascual Olivera and Angela Del Moral Celebration of Spain, Chgo., 1976—. Served with U.S. Army, 1965-67; Ger. Recipient Gold medal for Culture, Soka Gakkai Inst., Tokyo, 1984. Ter. dir. Nichiren Shoshu Acad., Chgo., 1968—. Home: 4728 N Paulina Chicago IL 60640

OLIVIER, SOLANGES DESROCHES, nurse; b. Jeremie, Haiti, Feb. 18, 1933; came to U.S., 1956; d. Benoit and Aglaée (Vilvalex) Desroches; m. Oswald Olivier, June 20, 1959; children—Mildred, Ernst, Oswald. Grad. Sch. Nursing, Port-au-Prince, 1955; student Communicable Disease Nursing, Chgo., 1957; B.S. in Nursing, Coll. St. Francis-Joliet, 1979. Nurse, Mother Cabrini Hosp., Chgo., 1957-61, Norwegian Am. Hosp., Chgo., 1961-65; nurse in charge Ill. State Psychiat. Inst., 1960-63; supr. Orthodox Jewish Home for Aged, Jewish Gen. Hosp., Montreal, Que., Can., 1968-69; nurse N.W. Community Hosp., Arlington Heights, Ill., 1969—; sch. nurse Ill. Deaf and Blind Sch., Glen Ellyn, Ill., 1983—. Producer craftwork, dolls for Haitian orphans. Active Our Lady of the Wayside Women's Club, Arlington Heights, 1969—; mem. altar com. Our Lady of the Wayside, 1969—; mem. St. Viator fund-raiser com., 1969—; mem. Sacred Heart of Mary Mothers Club, 1974-78, Interracial Group, Arlington Heights, 1969—. Recipient cert. appreciation for aid to orphan children of Haiti, UNICEF, 1970-79. Mem. Haitian Nurses Assn., Can. Nurses Assn., Orthopedic Nurses Assn., R.N. Assn., Assn. St. Francis Alumnae. Roman Catholic. Home: 417 S Patton Arlington Heights IL 60005

OLIVIERI, HENRY JOHN, JR., lawyer, educator, real estate broker; b. Chgo., Aug. 1, 1951; s. Henry John and Ann Marie (Giannoni) O. B.S., U. Ill., 1973, M.S., 1974; J.D., St. Louis U., 1977. Bar: Ill. 1978, U.S. Dist. Ct. (no. dist.) Ill. 1979. Assoc. Kwiatt & Silverman, Ltd., Chgo., 1978-79; sole practice, Chgo., 1979—; counsel to majority leader Ill. Ho. of Reps., Springfield,

1981-83; mem. faculty Chgo. Kent Coll. Law, Ill. Inst. Tech., 1982—; real estate broker HJO Realty Chgo., 1972—; instr. Real Estate Edn. Co., Chgo., 1974—; instr. Ill. Inst. Continuing Legal Edn. 1979—; dir., bank counsel East Side Bank & Trust Co., Chgo. Author Ill. Inst. Continuing Legal Edn. Real Estate Brokers' Exam Rev. Materials, 1979-85. Editor, contbg. author: Case Studies and Instructors' Manual for Real Estate Investment Analysis, 1974. Mem. Chgo. Bar Assn., Ill. State Bar Assn., Ill. Trial Lawyers Assn., Justinian Soc. Lawyers, Lawyers for Creative Arts, Open Land Project/Friends of Chgo. River. Republican. Roman Catholic. Home: 1524 N Dearborn Pkwy Chicago IL 60610 Office: 35 E Wacker Dr Chicago IL 60601

OLMSTEAD, A(LLEN) DENNIS, optometrist; b. Detroit, June 11, 1953; s. George Melvin and Doris Teresa (Le Blanc) O.; m. Diane Grace Henderson, July 9, 1977; 1 child, Angela Diane. B.S., Mich. State U., 1975; O.D., Ferris State College, 1979. Diplomate Am. Bd. Optometry. Clin. assoc. Ferris State Coll., Big Rapids, Mich., 1979—; gen. practice optometry, Lansing, Mich., 1979—. Contbr. articles to profl. jours. Coach, Greater Lansing Amateur Hockey Assn., Mich., 1982—; asst. coach Ferris State Varsity Hockey Team, Big Rapids, 1977. Mem. Am. Optometry Assn., Mich. Optometric Assn. (co-chmn. edn. com. 1981—), Central Mich. Optometric Soc. (pres. 1982-83). Roman Catholic. Club: Mich. State Blue Line (v.p. 1982-83) (East Lansing). Avocations: sports; physical fitness. Home: 1155 Hillgate Way Lansing MI 48912 Office: 1515 W Mt Hope Lansing MI 48910

OLOFFSON, RICHARD WAYNE, lawyer; b. Princeton, Ill., Sept. 19, 1953; s. Richard B. and Lila J. (Roush) O.; m. Margaret Sue Miller, Aug. 16, 1975; 1 child, Richard Miller. B.A. cum laude, Western Ill. U., 1975; J.D. with honors, John Marshall Law Sch., 1978. Bars: Ill. 1978, U.S. Dist. Ct. (no. dist.) Ill. 1978. Assoc., Taylor, Miler, Sprowl, Hoffnagle & Merletti, Chgo., 1978—; legal counsel A. Montgomery Ward Found., Chgo., 1980—. Recipient Outstanding Sr. Law scholarship Phi Delta Phi, 1978. Mem. Chgo. Bar Assn. (chmn. case law subcom. insurance law com. 1984-85), Ill. Bar Assn., ABA. Home: 7530 Walnut Ave Woodridge IL 60517 Office: Taylor Miller Sprowl Hoffnagle & Merletti 120 S LaSalle St Chicago IL 60603

OLOFSON, TOM WILLIAM, business executive; b. Oak Park, Ill., Oct. 10, 1941; s. Ragnar V. and Ingrid E. O.; B.B.A., U. Pitts., 1963; m. Jeanne Hamilton, Aug. 20, 1960; children—Christopher, Scott. Various mgmt. positions Bell Telephone Co. of Pa., Pitts., 1963-67; sales mgr. Xerox Corp., Detroit, 1967-68, nat. account mgr., Rochester, N.Y., 1968, mgr. govt. planning, Rochester, 1969, mgr. Kansas City (Mo.) br., 1969-74; corp. v.p. health products group Marion Labs., Inc., Kansas City, Mo., 1974-78, sr. v.p., 1978-80; exec. v.p., dir. Electronic Realty Assns., Inc., 1980-83; chmn. bd., chief exec. officer ETL Corp., 1983—, Emblem Graphic Systems, Inc., 1983—. dir. Optico Industries, Kalo Labs., Am. Stair-Glide, Marion Health and Safety, Marion Sci., Marion Internat., Bank of Kansas City, Kansas City Bank & Trust Co., ASG Corp., ICP, Inc. Mem. Menninger Found.; trustee Barstow Sch.; chmn. bd. trustees Village United Presbyn. Ch.; bd. dirs. Kansas City Better Bus. Bur., Mid. Am. Immunotherapy and Surg. Research Found., Inc. Mem. Omicron Delta Kappa, Sigma Chi. Republican. Presbyterian. Club: Kansas City. Home: 4808 W 87th St Prairie Village KS 66207 Office: 501 Kansas Ave Kansas City KS 66105

OLOFSSON, DANIEL JOEL, lawyer; b. Chgo., Sept. 29, 1954; s. Joel Gustav and Patricia Marie (Casey) O.; m. Debra Lynn Dreyer, Sept. 11, 1982; 1 dau., Nicole Lynn. A.A., Thornton Community Coll., 1974; B.A., U. Ill., 1976; J.D. with honors, Chgo.-Kent Coll. Law, Ill. Inst. Tech., 1979. Bar: Ill. 1979, U.S. Dist. Ct. (no. dist.) Ill. 1979, U.S. Ct. Appeals (7th cir.) 1979, U.S. Tax Ct. 1980. Assoc. Jerry L. Lambert, Flossmoor, Ill., 1979-80, John P. Block, Chgo., 1980-82; sole practice, Dolton, Ill., 1982—. James scholar U. Ill., Champaign, 1976. Mem. Chgo. Bar Assn., South Suburban Bar Assn., Ill. State Bar Assn., ABA, Phi Theta Kappa. Democrat. Roman Catholic. Lodges: Rotary, Elks. Home: 14905 S Michigan Dolton IL 60419 Office: 14207 Chicago Rd Dolton IL 60419

OLORUNSOLA, VICTOR ADEOLA, political science educator; b. Nigeria, Mar. 23, 1939; m.; 3 children. B.A. with high honors, Friends U., 1963; M.A., Ind. U., 1964, Ph.D., 1967. Research asst. Ind. U., 1964-65; lectr. Peace Corps. tng. program Ind. U., 1964-65; asst. prof. Calif. State Coll., Long Beach, 1967; asst. prof. Iowa State U., Ames, 1967-70, assoc. prof., 1970-75, prof., coordinator grad. studies, 1975-77, prof., chmn. dept. polit. sci., 1977—; vis. assoc. prof. Ohio U., 1971; mem. NSF evaluation com. for fellowships in the social and behavioral scis., 1976-79, 82-83, mem. evaluation com. for minority fellowships, 1979-81, 82-83; bd. dirs. Partnership for Productivity; cons. Aspen Inst. Humanistic Studies, 1978, 79; cons. famine studies Nat. Ctr. Atmospheric Study, 1974-75. Author: The Politics of Cultural Sub-Nationalism in Africa, 1972; Societal Reconstruction in Two African States, 1977; Soldiers and Power, 1977; State Versus Ethnic Claims: An African Policy Dilemma, 1983. Mem. editorial bd. Jour. African Studies, Nigerian Behavioral Scis. Jour. Mem. Ames Sch. Bd. Com. on Multi-Cultural Non-Sexist Curriculum, 1977-82; mem. Ames Prins. Adv. Com., 1983—. Inst. Internat. Edn. scholar, 1961, Phelps Stokes scholar, 1963, Ford Found. grad. scholar, 1963-64, Ford Found. dissertation research grantee, 1965-66, Iowa State U. faculty research grantee, 1968, Iowa State U. small grantee, 1971, Internat. Devel. and Research Ctr. grantee, 1971-72, Social Sci. Research Council grantee, 1971-72, Ford Found. faculty research fellow, 1971-72, nat. fellow Hoover Instn. for Study of War, Revolution and Peace, 1974-75, Ford Found. research grantee, 1980, Rockefeller grantee, 1981, Rothchild Found. grantee, 1981, Inter-Univ. Seminar on Armed Forces and Soc. fellow, 1972-79. Mem. Assn. for Advancement Policy Research and Devel. (mem. bd. 1981), Am. Polit. Sci. Assn. (mem. the council), Nat. Conf. Black Polit. Scientists, Internat. Studies Assn., African Studies Assn. (mem. exec. com., bd. dirs. 1978-81), Royal African Soc. Eng., Midwest Polit. Sci. Assn. (chmn. nominations com. 1981), Internat. Personnel Mgmt. Assn. Home: 4021 Ross Rd Ames IA 50010 Office: Dept Polit Sci 509 Ross Hall Iowa State U Ames IA 50011

OLSCAMP, PAUL JAMES, university president, philosophy educator; b. Montreal, Que., Can., Aug. 29, 1937; s. James J. and Luella M. (Brush) O.; m. Ruth I. Pratt, Dec. 2, 1978; children—Rebecca Ann, Adam James. B.A., U. Western Ont., 1958, M.A., 1960; Ph.D., U. Rochester, 1962. Instr. Ohio State U., 1962-63, asst. prof., 1963-66, assoc. prof., 1966-69, assoc. dean, 1969-70; v.p. acad. affairs, dean of faculties, prof. philosophy Roosevelt U., 1970-72; prof. philosophy, exec. asst. to chancellor and pres. Syracuse U., 1972-73, prof. philosophy, vice chancellor student programs, 1973-75; prof. philosophy, pres. Western Wash. U., Bellingham, 1975-82, disting. service prof., 1982; prof. philosophy, pres. Bowling Green (Ohio) State U., 1982—; mem. bd. Culture and Performance, book series, London, Ont., Can., 1983—. Bd. govs. St. Joseph's Hosp., Bellingham, 1981-83; trustee Toledo Symphony Orch., 1982—. Recipient Alfred J. Wright award Ohio State U., 1970, Disting. Service award Syracuse U. Inter-Fraternity Council, 1975; named one of 100 leaders under 46 in Am. higher edn. Change Mag., 1978; grad. fellow U. Western Ont., 1959, U. Rochester, 1961-62; grad. studies fellow U. Rochester, 1960, U. Glastow, 1960; Danforth Found. assoc., 1966. Mem. Am. Philos. Assn. Author: Descartes: The Discourse, Optics, Geometry and Meterology, 1965; The Moral Philosophy of George Berkeley, 1970; Philosophy: An Introduction, 1971; Malebranche: The Search After Truth, 1980; contbr. revs. and articles to profl. jours., chpts. to books. Office: Presidents Office Bowling Green State University Bowling Green OH 43403*

OLSEN, DAGNE B., state legislator; b. Dalton, Minn., Mar. 19, 1933; d. Glenn F. and Esther J. (Stortroen) Borg; m. Duane D. Olsen, June 25, 1955; children—Deanna, Douglas, Dick. B.S. in Edn., U. N.D., 1955. Cert. life secondary sch. tchr., N.D. Tchr. Gilby High Sch., 1955-57, Midway High Sch., 1960-62; mem. N.D. Ho. of Reps., 1980—, mem. edn. com., social services com. Active Manvel Community Betterment Program, 1959—; vol. chmn., past pres. United Hosp. Aux., Grand Forks; leader 4-H Club; bd. dirs. Agassiz Enterprises Tng. Ctr., Grand Forks, pres., 1982; mem. governing bd. United Hosp.; mem. N.D. Gov.'s Adv. Council on Volunteerism, 1984—; mem. exec. com. N.D. Devel. Disabilities Council, 1982—, bd. dirs. Nat. Assn. Devel. Disabilities Councils, 1985—; pres. Grand Forks County Spl. Edn. Bd.; mem. com. of 100, U. N.D., 1980; treas. council Manvel Trinity Luth. Ch.; mem. Nat. Ch. Task Force, 1979-80; mem. Eastern N.D. Dist. Ch. in Soc., 1982—; bd. dirs. Assn. Retarded Citizens N.D., 1966—; precinct committeewoman, vice chmn. dist. 19 Republican Party, 1974-80; del. N.D. Rep. Conv., 1976, 78, 80, 82, 84, mem. platform com., 1980; co-chair N.D. Legislators for Reagan-Bush, 1984. Recipient Gov.'s Statewide Leadership award for community betterment program, 1964; Outstanding Vol. Service award Office N.D. Gov., 1979; Soil Conservation award N.D. Soil Conservation Dist., 1980; Outstanding Parent award Assn. for Retarded Citizens of N.D., 1977, Mem. of Yr. award 1981; North Central Region Mem. of Yr. award Assn. Retarded Citizens U.S., 1982; named Grand Forks Woman of Yr., 1978; Outstanding Employer of Handicapped, Grand Forks Mayor's Com., 1984; Outstanding Employer of Handicapped, Gov.'s Com. on Employment of Handicapped, 1985. Mem. Nat. Order. Women Legislators, Nat. Rep. Legislators Assn., Am. Legis. Exchange Council, Farm Bur., Am. Agri-Women, N.W. Farm Mgrs. Assn., Assn. Profl. Vols., Am. Legion Aux., Gen. Fedn. Woman's Clubs (past pres. Manvel, past state chmn.), Pi Lambda Theta, Delta Phi Delta, Delta Zeta. Home: Rural Route 1 Manvel ND 58256 Office: State Capitol Bldg Bismarck ND 58505

OLSEN, HAROLD LOUIS, mechanical engineer; b. Chgo., Dec. 31, 1925; s. Arthur L. and Louise E. Olsen; B.S., Cornell U., 1948; M.S., Purdue U., 1951; m. Marlene C. Lukitsch, July 2, 1951; children—Paul D., David A., Philip S., Janet G. Designer of aircraft heating and air conditioning Pacific Airline Equipment Co., Chgo., 1946-48; application engr. Allis Chalmers, Milw., 1948-51; designer heating, air conditioning and refrigeration systems Harry F. Wilson & Assos., Milw., 1951-52; designer of railway and bus air conditioning Waukesha (Wis.) Motor Co., 1952-53; designer Wis. State Bur. Engring., Madison, 1953-55; pres., chief mech. engr. Olsen & Evans, Madison, 1954-78; chief mech. engr. Donohue & Assos., Madison, 1978-81; mgr. mech. dept. Marshall Erdman & Assocs., Madison, 1981—. Served with USN, 1943-46. Registered profl. engr., Wis., Iowa, Mich., Minn., Ill. Fellow Constrn. Specifications Inst.; mem. ASHRAE. Lutheran. Home: 5713 Dorsett Dr Madison WI 53711 Office: Marshall Erdman & Assos 5117 University Ave Madison WI 53705

OLSEN, JANUS FREDERICK, III, library adminstr.; b. Portland, Oreg., Jan. 4, 1942; s. Janus Frederick and Edna Mae (Petersen) O.; B.F.A. in Art Edn., U. S.D., 1964; postgrad. Luther Theol. Sem., St. Paul, 1964-65; M.L.S., U. Western Ont. (Can.), 1971; m. Doris Marie Scheetz, Apr. 19, 1974. Successively reference librarian, head cataloging and tech. processing, field coordinator in-service tng. public and instl. librarians, cons. to tribal, public, organizational, sch. and govt. libraries, acting asst. dir., acting dir. S.D. State Library Commn., Pierre, 1971-73; dir. Mitchell (S.D.) Public Library, 1973-80; dir. Alexander Mitchell Public Library, Aberdeen, S.D., 1980—. S.D. Interium Documents Study Commn., 1972, Mitchell Prehistoric Indian Village Commn., 1974-75; chmn. Davison County Centennial Commn., 1975; cdn. chmn. Mitchell Bicentennial Commn., 1975-77; pres. Mitchell Area Arts Council, 1976. Served with arty. U.S. Army, 1965-67. Mem. Am. Library Assn., S.D. Library Assn. (pres. 1977, chmn. centennial com. 1981—, chmn. ad hoc com. on state union catalog of audio-visual materials), Mountain Plains Library Assn. (exec. bd. 1977), Can. Library Assn., Corn Palace Reading Council (pres. 1975), Mitchell Right-to-Read Comm., Aberdeen Assn. Adminstrs. (sec.), Oscar Howe Cultural Center, Mitchell C. of C., Internat. Soc. Artists. Lutheran. Club: Am. Legion. Contbr. articles in field to profl. jours. Home: 1619 12th Ave SE Aberdeen SD 57401 Office: 519 S Kline St Aberdeen SD 57401

OLSEN, LESLIE A., agricultural education educator; b. Hardy, Nebr., Apr. 13, 1935; s. Ezra P. and Inger M. (Andersen) O.; m. Corrine Louise Wright, July 17, 1960; children—Catherine, Carrie, Carla. B.S., Kans. State U., 1957, M.S. in Agrl. Edn., 1964. Vocat. agr. instr. Waterville High Sch., Kans., 1957-59, Riley County High Sch., Kans., 1959-63; agr. rep. Citizens State Bank, Waterville, 1963-65; vocat. agr. instr. Riley County High Sch., 1965-69, Clay Ctr. High Sch., Kans., 1969-72; ednl. program specialist in agrl. edn. Kans. State Dept. Edn., Topeka, 1972—; vice chmn. Nat. Council Vocat. and Tech. Edn. in Agr., 1985-86. Pres., First Luth. Ch., Topeka, 1979-80. Named Outstanding Young Farmer Advisor, Kans. Young Farmers, 1968; Hon. State Farmer, Kans. Future Farmers Am. Assn., 1971; Hon. Am. Farmer, Nat. Future Farmers Am., 1981. Mem. Kans. Vocat. Agr. Tchrs. Assn. (pres. 1970-71), Nat. Assn. Suprs. Agrl. Edn. (region v.p. 1980-82, nat. pres. 1982-83), Kans. Future Farmers Am. (state adv. 1976—). Avocations: hunting; fishing. Home: RR 1 Mayetta KS 66509 Office: Kans Dept Edn 120 E 10th St Topeka KS 66612

OLSEN, RICHARD GEORGE, virology educator, researcher; b. Independence, Mo., June 25, 1937; s. Ben Barth and Ruth Naome (Myrtle) O.; divorced; children—Cynthia Gail, David Glen, Susan Beth, John Daniel. B.A., U. Mo., 1959; M.S., Atlanta U., 1963; Ph.D., SUNY-Buffalo, 1969. Prof. Ohio State U., Columbus, 1969—. Author: Veterinary Immunology and Immunopathology, 1979. Contbr. articles to profl. jours. Developed feline leukemia vaccine, 1983. Recipient Dept. Defense contract Nat. Cancer Inst., Air Force Office Sci. Research, 1980; NIH grantee. Mem. Am. Soc. Microbiologists, Tissue Culture Assn., Am. Soc. Virology, Internat. Soc. Immunopharmacologists, Am. Assn. Cancer Research. Home: 2255 State Route 56 London OH 43140 Office: Ohio State Univ 1925 Coffey Rd Columbus OH 43210

OLSEN, SAMUEL RICHARD, JR., printing company executive; b. Hamilton, Ohio, May 1, 1938; s. Samuel Richard and Hazel Mildred (Berg) O.; Asso. Applied Sci., Rochester Inst. Tech., 1961; children—Kristin, Erika, Samuel Richard III; m. Roberta Apa, June 1, 1974; children—Lonnie, Erik. Vice-pres. mfg. Datagraphic N.Y., Inc., Rochester, N.Y., 1965-68; pres., chief exec. officer Form Service, Inc., Schiller Park, Ill., 1968—; pres., chief exec. officer Dealers Press, Inc., Rosemont, Ill., 1973—, also dir; v.p., dir. Form Service West, Inc., Camarillo, Calif.; founder, chief exec. officer Bus. Form Service East, Inc., Balt., 1980, Omega Mgmt. Ltd., 1983—, Computer Preferred, Inc., 1984—. Served with USMC, 1960-63. Recipient Voight award Graphic Arts Tech. Found., 1981. Mem. Nat. Bus. Forms Assn. (officer, dir.), Forms Mfg. Credit Interchange (chmn. 1973-74), Printing Industries Am., Internat. Bus. Forms Industries, Nat. Assn. Printers and Lithographers. Home: 772 Halbert Ln Barrington IL 60010 Office: 9500 Ainslie St Schiller Park IL 60176

OLSON, BETTYE VIRGINIA JOHNSON, artist, art educator; b. Mpls., Jan. 16, 1923; d. Emil A. and Irene W. (Wandtke) Johnson; m. Howard E. Olson, July 16, 1949; children—Martha, Jeff, Barbara, Virginia. B.S. in Art Edn., U. Minn., 1945, M.E. in Art, 1949. Cert. secondary tchr. Art instr. Summit Sch. for Girls, St. Paul, 1945-47, U. Minn., Mpls., 1947-49; art instr. painting and design Concordia Coll., St. Paul, 1975-76, 78-84; painting instr. Augsburg Coll., Mpls., 1983-84; founder, cooperator West Lake Gallery, Mpls., 1964-83; artist in residence Holden Village Retreat Ctr., Chelan, Wash., 1967, 68, 70, 79. One-woman shows include Lutheran Brotherhood Co., 1983, Smaland Mus., Vaxjo, Sweden, 1982, Am. Swedish Inst., 1982, Lake Harriet Meth. Ch., 1982, U. Minn. St. Paul Campus Gallery, 1981, U. Minn. Wilson Library, 1981, Luther Coll., Decorah, Iowa, 1980, Augsburg Coll., 1979, Jerome Gallery, Aspen, Colo., 1978, Plymouth Congl. Ch., Mpls., 1978, House of Hope Ch., St. Paul, 1978, Westlake Gallery, Mpls., 1964, 67, 71, 75, 78, 82, St. Olaf Coll., Northfield, Minn., 1977, Concordia Coll., St. Paul, 1975, 85, Met. Med. Ctr., Mpls., 1974; exhibited in group shows: Butler Inst. AM. Art, Youngstown, Ohio, 1977, Water Color U.S.A., Springfield, Mo., 1977, Boston U., 1981, Arboretum Invitational, 1983, Finland Kuopio Art Mus. 1982; represented in permanent collections: Augsburg Coll., Luth. Brotherhood Co., Luther Coll., Pillsbury World Hdqs., Cray Research, St. Paul Co., Met. Med. Ctr., Minn. Mining Co., Concordia Coll. Bd. dirs. LWV, St. Paul, 1967; mem. council Royal Redeemer Lutheran Ch., St. Paul, 1978-84, chmn., music, worship, art coms., 1983, 84; bd. dirs. Luth. Women's Caucus, Minn., 1982-84; past pres. Norwegian Chamber Congress Women, Mpls. Recipient Merit award St. Paul Gallery Art, 1961, Juried Exhibit, Biennial Mpls. Art Ins., 1947, Walker Art Ctr., 1947; Purchase award various corp. collections, Mpls., 1967-84. Mem. Minn. Artists Assn. (bd. dirs.), Artists Equity Inc. (bd. dirs.), Delta Phi Delta (pres. 1946). Clubs: New Century (St. Paul) (mem. bd.), AAUW (St. Paul) (mem. creative arts bd.). Home: 615 Maple Park Dr Saint Paul MN 55118

OLSON, CLITUS WILBUR, surgeon; b. Omaha, Oct. 20, 1916; s. Enock and Nellie (Rotsten) O.; m. Dorothy Mae Nord, Mar. 20, 1948; children—Paul, Eleanor, Barbara, Joan. B.A. with distinction, U. Nebr.-Omaha, 1939, M.D. with distinction, 1948. Diplomate Am. Bd. Surgery. Intern Jefferson Hillman Hosp., Birmingham, Ala., 1948-49; resident Mercy Hosp., Des Moines, 1949-50, Tropical Medicine, Inst. Medicine Tropicale, Antwerp, Belgium, 1951; resident in surgery U. Nebr.-Omaha, 1959-63; missionary physician Evang. Covenant Ch., Belgian Congo, Zaire, 1951-71; dean med. sch. U. Libre De Zaire, Kisangani, 1970-71; surgeon VA Ctr., Hot Springs S.D., 1971-73; practice medicine specializing in surgery Northwest Kans. Med. Ctr., Goodland, 1973—; Fellow A.C.S.; Mem. AMA, Kans. Med. Soc., Am. Assn. Gynecol. Laparoscopists, Alpha Omega Alpha. Lodge: Kiwanis. Avocations: music; photography; genealogy; reading. Home: 610 Harrison St Goodland KS 67735 Office: 520 Main St Goodland KS 67735

OLSON, DAVID DENNIS, district extension forester; b. Detroit, Dec. 8, 1928; s. Stanley G. and Elfrieda K. (Koll) O.; m. Emily L. Olah, July 14, 1951; children—David S., Gary S., Paul W. B.S. in Forestry, U. Mich., 1950; M.S. in Resource Devel., Mich. State U., 1970. Registered forester, Mich. Mgmt. forester U.S. Dept. Interior, Bur. Land Mgmt., Roseburg, Oreg., 1952-54, forest mgmt. div., Mich. Dept. Natural Resources, Lansing and various locations, 1954-64; forest land use agt. Mich. State U., Coop. Extension, 1964-76, dist. extension forester Upper Peninsula, Marquette, 1976—; tech. advisor Mich. Resources Inventory Program, 1979-84; apptd. state commr. Dept. Natural Resources, 1985; mem. various state planning coms. Author booklets: Forest Economics of Upper Peninsula, 1982; Timber Products Economy of Michigan, 1981. Pres. Gt. Lakes Forestry Expn., Mio, Mich., 1975, 76. Recipient Presdl. citation Mich. 4-H Assn., 1965, Mich. County Agts. Assn., 1968, Pub. Info. award Amchem. Products, 1974; Outstanding Service award Future Farmers Am., 1976. Fellow Soc. Am. Foresters (Continuing Edn. award 1982, Outstanding Service award 1981); mem. Mich. Forest Assn. (pres. 1972), Mich. Soc. Am. Foresters (state chmn. 1981. Lodge: Lions (pres. Mio 1972). Home: 609 Mountain Marquette MI 49855 Office: Upper Peninsula Extension Ctr Mich State U 1030 Wright Marquette MI 49855

OLSON, DONALD GEORGE, university computer services administrator; b. Minot, N.D., May 16, 1941; s. George James and Ellen (Ranta) O.; B.M.E., U. N.D., 1963; M.M.E., N.D. State U., 1968; 1 son, Todd B. Analyst, programmer Bur. Reclamation, Denver, 1963-66; asst. dir. computer center N.D. State U., Fargo, 1966-69; data processing mgr. U. Calif. Sci. Lab., Los Alamos, 1969-74; dir. data processing nat. assessment ednl. progress Edn. Commn. States, Denver, 1974-77; staff mgr. Mountain Bell, Denver, 1977-80; dir. computer services Mankato (Minn.) State U., 1980—; cons. in field. Mem. Mankato Area Execs. Assn. Registered profl. engr., certified data processor. Mem. AAAS, Assn. Computing Machinery, YMCA, Phi Delta Theta. Republican. Presbyterian. Club: Kiwanis. Home: 1336 N 4th St Mankato MN 56001 Office: Computer Services Box 45 Mankato State U Mankato MN 56001

OLSON, EARL B., poultry company executive. Chmn., Jennie-O Foods Inc., Willmar, Minn., also dir. Office: Jennie-O Foods Inc 2505 Willmar Ave SW Willmar MN 56201*

OLSON, EUGENE RUDOLPH, printing company executive; b. St. Paul, Apr. 9, 1926; s. Rudolph and Martha E. (Karlson) O.; m. Leona F. Solie, June 28, 1952; children—Kathleen, Wayne, Brian. With Deluxe Check Printers Inc., St. Paul, 1944—, mgr. related products div., 1964-70, nat. dir. market research, 1970-72, v.p., 1972-76, pres., 1976—, chief exec. officer, 1977—, also dir.; dir. Data Card Corp., First Trust Co., St. Paul; trustee Minn. Mut. Life Ins. Co. Bd. dirs. Bapt. Hosp. Fund. Mem. Bank Stationers Assn. (dir.). Baptist. Clubs: Minneapolis, Midland Hills Country. Home: 2024 Evergreen Ct Saint Paul MN 55113 Office: 1080 W County Rd F Saint Paul MN 55112

OLSON, GARY DUANE, college administrator, history educator; b. Spring Grove, Minn., July 30, 1939; s. Raymond G. and Ethel N. (Storlie) O.; m. Rosaaen Marie Skifton, Sept. 4, 1960; children—Erik Lee, Timothy Karl, Lars Christian. B.A., Luther Coll., 1961; M.A., U. Nebr., 1965, Ph.D., 1968. Social studies tchr. Kerkhoven Pub. Schs., Minn., 1961-63; asst. prof. history Augustana Coll., Sioux Falls, S.D., 1968-73, assoc prof., 1973-79, prof., 1979—, dean academic services, 1981—. Author: (with H. Krause) Prelude to Glory, 1974. Contbr. articles to profl. jours. Mem. Inst. Early Am. History, Orgn. Am. History, Am. Assn. Coll. Registrars and Admissions Officers. Lutheran. Avocation: woodworking. Home: 2505 S Main Ave Sioux Falls SD 57105 Office: Augustana Coll Sioux Falls SD 57197

OLSON, GORDON LAVERN, historian, consultant; b. Frederic, Wis., Apr. 5, 1943; s. Clifford Harold and Viola Muriel (Lindh) O.; m. Christine Ann Broniszewski, Oct. 6, 1968. B.S., Wis. State U., 1966, M.S., 1968; Ph.D. course work U. Wyo., 1969-72. Curator Wyo. State Mus., Cheyene, 1971-73; asst. dir. Grand Rapids Pub. Mus., Mich., 1973-79; city historian City Grand Rapid, Mich., 1979—; cons. Western Interp. Services, Sheridan, Wyo., 1971-73; pub. Grand River Valley Review, Grand Rapids, Mich., 1979—, history cons. various businesses and orgns., Grand Rapids, Mich., 1980—. Author: Calkins Law Office, 1976, History of Peninsular Club, 1982. Author (with others) Russel Kirkhof: Mech to Millionaire, 1983, History of Amway Corp., 1985. Contbr. articles to profl. jours. Bd. dirs. Citizens Bee Assn., Grand Rapids, Mich., 1981—, Grand Rapids Area Council for Humanities, Mich., 1976-83; co-founder Grand River Whaling Expdn., Grand Rapids, 1979—; pres. W. Mich. Telecommunications Found., Grand Rapids, 1981-83. Fellow U. S. Dept. HEW, 1966-68, Colonial Williamsburg, 1973, Am. Assn. State and Local History, Nashville, 1979, 80. Mem. Orgn. Am. Historians, Am. Assn. State and Local History (chmn. 1985), History Soc. Mich. (pres.), Nat. Council Pub. History, Soc. Am. Archivists. Avocations: Racquetball, softball. Home: 1911 Glendale NE Grand Rapids MI 49503 Office: City Historian Pub Library 60 Library Plaza NE Grand Rapids MI 49503

OLSON, JAMES ALEXANDER, industrial distribution executive; b. Sioux City, Iowa, June 12, 1930; s. Clifford Charles and Nina Mae (Coulson) O.; m. Mary Ellen Wetzler, Aug. 14, 1954; children—John Alexander, Thomas Charles. Student Morningside Coll., 1948-50, Iowa State U., 1950-52. Foreman service dept. Novelty Machine & Supply, Sioux City, 1951-55, sales, 1957-62, v.p., 1962-72, pres., 1972—; dir. Security Nat. Bank. Bd. dirs. St. Lukes Regional Med. Ctr., Sioux City, 1976—, chmn. fin., 1980—, vice chmn., 1983; bd. dirs. Siouxland Blood Bank, Sioux City, 1978—, Goodwill Industries, Sioux City, 1980—. Served with C.E., U.S. Army, 1955-57. Mem. Sioux City C. of C. Republican. Methodist. Lodge: Toastmaster (dist. gov. 1959-62), Kiwanis (dir. 1960-62), Masons. Home: 3832 Sylvian Way Sioux City IA 51104 Office: Novelty Machine & Supply Co 901 5th St Sioux City IA 51101

OLSON, JAMES BURTON, health care administrator; b. Fargo, N.D., Mar. 19, 1951; s. Clarence Calvin and Louise Marie (Godwin) O. B.A. in Psychology and Chemistry, St. Olaf Coll., 1973; M.A. in Health Services Adminstrn., U. Wis.-Madison, 1975. Dist. mgr. Wis. Profl. Rev. Orgn., Madison, Wis., 1975-76; asst. adminstr. St. Francis Med. Ctr., La Crosse, Wis., 1976-82; adminstr. St. Francis Home, LaCrosse, 1976-82; adminstr. Bethel Home, Viroqua, Wis., 1982—; mem. Vernon County Health Forum. Bd. dirs. Vernon County Community Options Program; pres. Viroqua Hockey Assn. Mem. Am. Coll. Hosp. Adminstrs., Health Care Fin. Mgmt. Assn., Am. Coll. Nursing Home Adminstrs., Blue Key. Republican. Lutheran. Lodge: Lions (Viroqua). Office: 614 S Rock St Viroqua WI 54665

OLSON, JAMES MARTIN, systems programmer, consultant; b. Blair, Nebr., July 1, 1947; s. Milton C. and Esther L. (Nelson) O.; m. Linda S. Plugge, March 21, 1970; children—Douglas J., Sonja M. B.S., Nebr. Wesleyan Coll., Lincoln Nebr., 1970. Application programmer Woodmen of The World Life Ins., Omaha, 1972-80; systems programmer Conagra Inc., Omaha, 1980-84; sr. systems support Sather's Inc., Round Lake, Minn., 1985—. Mem. Assn. Systems Mgmt. Republican. Methodist. Lodge: Woodmen of World (pres. Nebr. jurisdiction 1978-79, nat. rep. 1983-85). Developer computerized letter writing system, multi system interface. Avocations: antique cars; outdoor activities. Office: Sather's Inc 1 Sather's Plaza Round Lake MN 56167

OLSON, JANE CECILIA, residence hall director; b. Milw., Nov. 30, 1954; d. Robert Charles and Patricia Anne (Regan) O.; B.A., Marquette U., 1977; M.S., Shippensburg U., 1979. Residence dir. Ball State U., Muncie, Ind., 1979-81; area coordinator Appalachian State U., Boone, N.C., 1981-83, asst. dir. residence life, 1983-84; residence dir. Mich. State U., East Lansing, 1985—. Recipient award Southeastern Housing Officers, 1984. Mem. Am. Assn. Counseling and Devel., Am. Coll. Personnel Assn., Nat. Assn. Student Personnel Adminstrs., Assn. Coll. and Univ. Housing Officers. Avocations: catering; sewing; counted cross stitch; reading; travel. Home: 126 S Hubbard Hall Mich State U East Lansing MI 48825 Office: Univ Housing Programs Office 338 SSB Mich State U East Lansing MI 48823

OLSON, JOHN MICHAEL, lawyer, state senator; b. Grafton, N.D., Feb. 9, 1947; s. Clifford I. and Alice (Schwandt) O.; m. Carol Kay Green, June 22, 1968; children—Dana Michel, Kirsten Lee. B.A., Concordia Coll., 1969; J.D., U. N.D.-Grand Forks, 1972. Bar: N.D. 1972, U.S. Dist. Ct. N.D. 1972, U.S.

Ct. Appeals (8th cir.) 1975, U.S. Supreme Ct. 1979. Spl. asst. atty. gen., Bismarck, N.D., 1972-74; state's atty. Burleigh County, Bismarck, N.D., 1975-82; mem. N.D. State Senate, 1982—; sole practice law, Bismarck, N.D., 1983—. Mem. N.D. Bar Assn. Republican. Lutheran. Lodges: Masons, Elks. Office: 304 E Rosser Bismarck ND 58501

OLSON, JUDY MAE, geography, cartography educator, consultant; b. Waupaca, Wis., May 15, 1944; d. Leonard A. and Hilma R. (Johnson) O. B.S., Wis. State U., Stevens Point, 1966, M.S., U. Wis., Madison, 1968, Ph.D., 1970. Asst. prof. U. Ga., Athens, 1970-74; asso. prof. Boston U., 1974-83; mem. faculty Mich. State U., East Lansing, 1983—, prof. geography, 1983—; vis. asst. prof. U. Minn., Mpls., 1973, vis. assoc. prof., 1981; cons. U.S. Bur. Census, Washington, 1975, U.S. Army Engr. Topog. Labs., Washington, 1983, U.S. Dept. Transp., Boston, 1980. Editor: The Am. Cartographer, 1977-82. Contbr. articles to profl. jours. Recipient Presdl. citation Am. Congress Surveying and Mapping, 1979, 80, 84, 85. Fellow Am. Congress Surveying and Mapping (dir. 1976-79, 81-82), Am. Cartographic Assn. (pres. 1981-82), Assn. Am. Geographers. Office: Mich State Univ 315 Natural Sci Bldg East Lansing MI 48824

OLSON, KATHLEEN ROMANE, nurse; b. Blue Earth, Minn., Sept. 14, 1950; d. Walter Gust and Evelyn Winifred (Espeland) Belau; m. Steven Craig Olson, Aug. 24, 1979. B.S., Mankato State U., 1974; R.N., Lutheran Deaconess Hosp., 1978. Tchr. Sanborn Schs. (Minn.), 1974-75; nursing asst. St. Luke's Home, Blue Earth, 1975-76; tchr. Sacred Heart Sch., Uvalde, Tex., 1976-77; staff nurse critical care Fairview Hosp., Mpls., 1978-79; sch. nurse migrant sch., Blue Earth, 1979; charge nurse, asst. dir. nursing, infection control nurse St. Luke's Home, 1979-80; dir. nursing Bapt. Residence, Winnebago, Minn., 1981—. Mem. Gopher State Nurses Assn. (regional dir. nursing). Roman Catholic. Home: RR2 Blue Earth MN 56013 Office: Baptist Residence 211 6th St NW Winnebago MN 56098

OLSON, KATHY A(NN), lawyer; b. Columbus, Ohio, Jan. 16, 1952; d. Gordon L. and Mary (Griffith) O. B.A. in Theatre and Cinema, Denison U., 1974; J.D., Capital U., Columbus, 1977. Bar: Ohio 1977, U.S. Dist. Ct. (so. dist.) Ohio 1978. Atty. Battelle Meml. Inst., Columbus, 1978-83, sr. atty., 1984—. Active Columbus Area Leadership Program, 1981-82; bd. dirs. Seal of Ohio council Girl Scouts U.S., 1983—. Mem. Ohio Bar Assn., Columbus Bar Assn. Office: Battelle Meml Inst 505 King Ave Columbus OH 43201

OLSON, MARGARETTE ADELINE, clinical psychologist; b. Crosby, Minn.; d. D.V. Nystrom; m. Alfred O. Olson, Jan. 1, 1942; 1 son, Mark David. B.S., U. N.D., 1944, M.S., 1948, Ph.D., 1951; postdoctoral studies Columbia U., Southwest Okla. State U., U. Minn. Lic. psychologist, S.D.; lic. nursing home adminstr. Bus. tchr. Mary Hardin-Baylor Coll., Belton, Tex., 1944-45; field supt. Gulf Coast Bus. Schs., Bay City, Tex., 1945-47; asst. prof., dept. chmn. U. N.D., Grand Forks, 1947-56; prof., dept. chmn. State Coll., Mayville, N.D., 1956-62; dean women, assoc. dean students Nebr. State Coll., Chadron, 1962-65; resident clin. psychology Jamestown (N.D.) and Hastings (Nebr.) State Hosps., 1965-66; prof. psychology Southwest Okla. State U., Weatherford, 1966-71; cons. clin. psychologist Okla. Gen. Hosp., Clinton, 1967-71, Concho Indian Sch. and Clinton Indian Hosp. and Indian Pub. Health, 1968-71; clin. psychologist S.D. Human Services Ctr., Yankton, 1971-85; marriage counselor. Mem. Govs. Com. (children and youth, aging, and edn. for aging. Mem. AAUW (grantee 1966, pres. N.D. div. 1958-60), Am. Psychol. Assn., N.D. and S.D. Fedn. Women's Clubs, Bus. and Profl. Women's Club, Nat. Assn. Women Deans, Internat. Council Psychologists (N.D. and S.D. chairperson 1980-81), S.D. Psychol. Assn. (sec.-treas. 1978-80), Internat. Platform Assn., PTA, Pi Lambda Theta (nat. treas. 1958-60). Republican. Methodist. Home: 2307 Mulberry St Yankton SD 57078 Office: Box 778 Yankton SD 57078

OLSON, MARIAN EDNA, nurse, social pschologist; b. Newman Grove, Nebr., July 20, 1923; d. Edwrd and Ethel Thelma (Hougland) Olson; diploma U. Nebr., 1944, B.S.N., 1953; M.A., State U. Iowa, 1961, M.A. in Psychlogy, 1962; Ph.D. in Psychology, UCLA, 1966. Staff nurse, supr. U. Tex. Med. Br., Galveston, 1944-49; with U. Iowa, Iowa City, 1949-59, supr. 1953-55, asst. dir. 1955-59; asst. prof. nursing UCLA, 1965-67; prof. nursing U. Hawaii, 1967-70, 78-82; dir. nursing Wilcox Hosp. and Health Center, Lihue, 1970-77; chmn. Hawaii Bd. Nursing, 1974-80; prof. nursing No. Mich. U., 1984—. Mem. Am. Nurses Assn. (mem. nat. accreditation bd. continuing edn. 1975-78), Nat. League Nursing, Am. Hosp. Assn., Am. Public Health Assn., LWV. Democrat. Roman Catholic. Home and office: 6223 County 513T Rd Rapid River MI 49878

OLSON, MARLIN LEE, educator; b. Triumph, Minn., July 29, 1927; s. Carl Leonard and Inez Viola (Johnson) O.; m. Gunvor K. Olson, Sept. 5, 1952; children—Cheryl Lynn, Deborah Lee, Jerald Leonard, Marlei Louann. B.A. in Bus. Adminstrn. and Edn., Seattle Pacific U.; also M.E. in Adminstrn., Ed.S., doctoral candidate Mich. State U. Tchr. Shoreline pub. schs., Seattle, 1953-58; adminstr. Morrison Schs. Assn., San Francisco, 1958-71; dir. Christian edn. Berean Ch., Seattle, 1971-77; assoc. prof. Grace Bible Coll., Wyoming, Mich., 1977—, acad. dean, 1985—; cons. Internat. Ctr. for Learning, Ventura, Calif. Served with U.S. Navy, 1945-48. Mem. Nat. Assn. Elem. Sch. Prins., Assn. Supervision and Curriculum Devel., Phi Delta Kappa. Republican. Participating author: Internat. Center for Learning, 1971-77. Home: 3936 Honeybrook SW Grandville MI 49418 Office: 1011 Aldon SW Wyoming MI 49509

OLSON, NILS ARTHUR, osteopathic physician; b. St. Louis, Jan. 12, 1948; s. John C. and E. Hildegarde H. (Duever) O.; m. Shirley Rae Ledford, Oct. 15, 1977; children—Erik Arthur, Kirsten Rae. A.B., U. Mo., 1969; D.O., Kirksville Coll. Osteo. Medicine, 1973. Diplomate Am. Osteo. Bd. Gen. Practice. Gen. practice osteo. medicine, Mercer, Wis., 1974—; chmn. dept. family practice Howard Young Med. Ctr., Woodruff, Wis., 1985—. Mem. North Lakeland Elem. Sch. Bd. Edn., Manitowish Waters, Wis., 1977—, v.p., 1977-84, pres., 1984—; v.p. Vilas County Republican party, Eagle River, Wis., 1977-79. Mem. Am. Osteo. Assn. (alt. del. Ho. of Dels. 1982-84), Wis. Assn. Osteo. Physicians and Surgeons (pres. 1981-82), Mo. Assn. Osteo. Physicians and Surgeons, Am. Coll. Gen. Practitioners in Osteo. Medicine and Surgery (Wis. Gen. Practitioner of Yr. 1982). Lodges: Lions (dep. dist. gov. 1979-80, pres. 1976-77), Masons (master 1979-80). Home: S Turtle Rd Winchester WI 54567 Office: PO Box B Mercer WI 54547

OLSON, NORMA JEAN, educator; b. Des Moines, Dec. 3, 1930; s. Floyd Robert and Faye (Spears) Brown; B.S., U. Iowa, 1952; M.A., U. Minn., 1966, Ph.D., 1978; m. Alfred Barber Olson, July 21, 1950; children—Cheri Lynne, Alan Kent. Mem. faculty North Hennepin Community Coll., Mpls., 1966-67, 70—, prof. bus., 1970—; mem. faculty Arapahoe Community Coll., 1967-69, Normandale Community Coll., 1969-70; cons. St. Benedictine Coll., Gen. Mills, U. Iowa, State of Minn. Mem. NEA, Minn. Edn. Assn., Minn. Bus. Edn., North Central Bus. Educators, AAUW, Am. Soc. Tng. Dirs., Hennepin Community Coll. Faculty Assn. (pres. 1982-83), Delta Pi Epsilon. Democrat. Methodist. Home: 6890 Utica Terr Chanhassen MN 55317 Office: 7411 85th Ave N Minneapolis MN 55445

OLSON, O(SCAR) WILLIAM, lawyer, business executive; b. Oak Park, Ill., Feb. 1, 1927; s. Oscar William and Eudora (Landstrom) O.; A.B., DePauw U., 1949; J.D., John Marshall Law Sch., 1953; m. Margaret Greiner; children—Peter W., Stephen W., Martha L. Bar: Ill. 1953, U.S. Supreme Ct. Chmn. bd., pres., chief exec. officer Safeway Enterprises, Inc., Chgo., Intercontinental Sales, Ltd., Intercontinental Services, Ltd., Intercontinental Enterprises Ltd., Intercontinental Steel Corp., Dahltron Corp. Served with USAAF, 1944-46: ETO. Mem. ABA, Ill., Chgo. bar assns. Clubs: Monroe, Union League, Chgo. Athletic Assn., Execs.; Edgewood Valley Country (LaGrange, Ill.); Palm Aire Country (Pompano Beach, Fla.). Home: 19W201 Old Tavern Rd Oakbrook IL 60521 Office: 111 W Washington St Chicago IL 60602

OLSON, PAUL BUXTON, marketing educator; b. Waterloo, Iowa, Feb. 5, 1937; s. Ethan Sidney and Esther May Olson; m. Jean Elaine Rinehart, Aug. 18, 1962; children—Brent Sidney, Kimberly Jean, Julie Elaine. B.A. cum laude, Tarkio Coll., 1958; M.Ed., U. Mo., 1966; Ed.S., U. No. Iowa, 1975. Mgr., Schiff Shoes, Waterloo/Des Moines, Iowa, 1953-60; tchr. bus. edn. Riverton/Farragut Community Schs., 1962-68; mktg. and distributive edn. tchr. Mason City (Iowa) Community Schs., 1968—; night instr. mktg. No. Iowa Area Community Coll., Mason City, 1969—; salesman Sears Roebuck & Co., Mason City, 1968—. Active Jr. Achievement. Served with U.S. Army, 1960-62. Named Outstanding Distributive Edn. Tchr., Iowa Distributive Edn. Tchrs. Assn., 1978; Leadership award Jr. Achievement, 1977; Writer's award Interstate Distributive Edn. Curriculum Consortium, 1975; named to Mktg. Edn. Hall of Fame, 1985. Mem. NEA (life), Am. Vocat. Assn. (life), Nat. Bus. Edn. Assn., Mktg. Edn. Assn. (life), Distributive Edn. Clubs Am., Iowa State Edn. Assn., Iowa Mktg. Educators (rep.), Iowa Bus. Edn. Assn. (rep.), Iowa Vocat. Assn. (rep.), Mason City Edn. Assn. (past treas.)., Assn. Supervision and Curriculum Devel., Delta Pi Epsilon, Phi Delta Kappa (life). Republican. Methodist. Lodge: Sons of Norway. Home: 2731 1st St SW Mason City IA 50401 Office: 1700 4th St SW Mason City IA 50401

OLSON, RAMON LEONARD, aerospace engineering executive; b. Chgo., Jan. 3, 1926; s. Arthur H. and Catherine (Salem) O.; m. Doris A. E. Nelson, May 22, 1948; children—Linda, Elaine E., David R., Steven J., Mark R., Christine A. B.S. in M.E., Ill. Inst. Tech., 1946; M.S. in M.E., U. Mich., 1947. Supr. engrng. IIT Research Inst., Chgo., 1947-53; cons. Caywood-Schiller, Chgo., 1953-54; supr. engrng. AMF, Chgo., 1954-57; v.p. engrng. OEA, Inc., Des Plaines, Ill., 1957-76; pres. Scot, Inc., Downers Grove, Ill., 1976—. Instr. Ill. Inst. Tech., Chgo., 1949-52; dir. Scot, Inc., Chgo., 1976—. Active Boy Scouts Am., Deerfield, Ill., 1961-80. Served to ensign USNR, 1944-47. Mem. Am. Inst. Aero. and Astronautical Engrs., Survival and Flight Equipment Soc., Am. Def. Prepardness Soc., Tau Beta Pi. Home: 1780 Chris Ct Deerfield IL 60015 Office: Scot Inc 2525 Curtiss Downers Grove IL 60515

OLSON, ROBERT HOWARD, lawyer; b. Indpls., July 6, 1944; s. Robert Howard and Jacqueline (Wells) O.; m. Diane Carol Thorsen, Aug. 13, 1944; children—Jeffrey, Christopher. B.A. summa cum laude, Ind. U., 1966; J.D. cum laude, Harvard U., 1969. Bar: Ohio 1969, Fla. 1981, Ariz. 1985, U.S. Dist. Ct. (no. and so. dists.) Ohio 1971, U. S. Dist. Ct. (no. dist.) Ind. 1971, U.S. Supreme Ct. 1973. Law clk. U.S. Dist. Ct., Ft. Wayne, Ind., 1969-70; assoc. Squire, Sanders, Dempsey, Cleve., 1970-71, 1976-80, ptnr., 1981—; asst. atty. gen. State of Ohio, Columbus, 1971-72, chief civil rights sect., 1972-73, chief consumer frauds and crimes sect., 1973-75; chief counsel to atty. gen., 1975, first asst. to atty. gen., 1975-76; cons. Ohio Hosp. Assn., Columbus, 1982-85. Contbr. articles to profl. jours. Mem. Ariz. Bar Assn., Fla. Bar Assn., Ohio Bar Assn., Greater Cleve. Bar Assn. (sec. health law sect. 1984-85), Am. Acad. Hosp. Attys., Ohio Hosp. Assn. Democrat. Unitarian. Avocations: swimming; tennis.

OLSON, RONALD DALE, grain industry executive; b. Fort Dodge, Iowa, Oct. 22, 1947; s. Albert Dale and Gladys Marie (Peters) O.; m. Lynn Diane Rustwick, Nov. 22, 1969; children—Jenna, Jill. B.S., Iowa State U., 1969, M.S., 1971. Various merchandising positions Continental Grain, Portland, Oreg., 1971, San Francisco, 1972, Fairmont, Minn., 1973, Mpls., 1974-82, regional mgr., v.p., Mpls., 1982—; pres. Northwest Terminal Elevator Assn., Mpls., 1984—; chmn. bd. Mpls. Grain Exchange, 1984—. Mem. ch. council Mount Olivet Lutheran Ch., Mpls., 1983—. Avocations: Sports; music. Office: Continental Grain Co 815 Grain Exchange Minneapolis MN 55415

OLSON, ROY ARTHUR, government official; b. Ashland, Wis., Dec. 8, 1938; s. Elof Herman and Beatrice Lorraine (Dolezal) O.; m. Elisabeth Rigge Behrens, June 24, 1967; children—Heather Elisabeth, Peter Roy. B.S., Northwestern U., 1960. Lic. real estate salesman, Ill. Writer, editor Chgo. Am., 1956-68; pres. Roy Olson Pub. Relations Co., Oak Park, Ill., 1968-70; asst. regional adminstr. SBA, Chgo., 1970—; dir. Am.food industries, Chgo., Convenant Village Retirement Ctr., Northbrook, Ill., 1975-81, Brandel Care Ctr., Northbrook, 1975-81. Chmn. Northbrook Covenant Ch., 1980-81. Mem. Soc. Profl. Journalists, Art Inst. Chgo. Clubs: City (media com.), Executives, Chgo. Press, Chgo. Headline (past dir. 1964-66), Northwestern (Chgo.). Home: 2015 Prairie St Glenview IL 60025 Office: US Small Bus Adminstrn 230 S Dearborn St Chicago IL 60604

OLSON, RUE EILEEN, librarian; b. Chgo., Nov. 1, 1928; d. Paul H. and Martha M. (Fick) Meyers; student Herzl Coll., 1946-48, Northwestern U., 1948-50, Ill. State U., 1960-64; m. Richard L. Olson, July 18, 1964; children—Catherine, Karen. Accountant Ill. Farm Supply Co., Chgo., 1948-59; asst. librarian Ill. Agrl. Assn., Bloomington, 1960-66, librarian, 1966—. Mem. area Com. Nat. Library Week, 1971, area steering com., 1972; mem. adv. council of librarians Grad. Sch. Library Sci. U. Ill., 1976-79; mem. Ill. State Library Adv. Com. for Interlibrary Cooperation, 1979-80; del. Ill. White House Conf. on Library and Info. Services, 1978. Mem. Am., Ill., McLean County (pres. 1970-71) library assns., Spl. Libraries Assn. (pres. Ill. 1977-78), Internat. Assn. Agrl. Librarians and Documentalists, Am. Soc. Info. Sci., Am. Mgmt. Assn. Home: 103 Radliff Rd Bloomington IL 61701 Office: 1701 Towanda Ave Bloomington IL 61701

OLSON, VERNON ARTHUR, automotive educator; b. Mpls., Aug. 2, 1924; s. Reuben Arthur and Almeda Victotia (Carlson) O.; m. Mamie Ruth Stoker, Mar. 15, 1947; children—Judy Ann, Nancy Jo, Susan Louise, Steven Arthur. Student Northeast Mo. State U., U. Mo., Harris-Stowe U., 1979-83. Owner, Standard Oil sta., 1951-79; tchr. automobile servicing, 1979—. Author article in field. Active St. Louis council Boy Scouts Am., 1960-75; treas. Council Exceptional Children, St. Louis, 1985—. Served to sgt. USAF, 1943-46, PTO. Mem. Mo. Vocat. Spl. Needs Assn., Mo. Vocat. Assn. (cert. 1981, nominated Tchr. of Yr. 1985), NEA (Mo. chpt., mem. salary and welfare com., bldg. rep. for sch. dist.), Am. Legion. Republican. Lutheran. Lodges: Masons, Rotary (v.p.). Avocations: coin collections; computers. Home: 9409 White Ave Brentwood MO 63144

OLSSON, MILTON LEE, music educator; b. North Anderson, Ind., Sept. 21, 1940; s. Jonas Albin and Florence Rose (Wolf) O.; m. Trudy Kinzli, Dec. 12, 1959; children—David Carl, Stephan Bernie, Paul-Josef. B.A., Wayne State U., 1964, M.Mus., 1970; D.Mus. Arts, U. Colo., 1975. Fine arts instr. Detroit Inst. Tech., 1964-69; dir. mus. activities Detroit Parks and Recreation Dept., 1969-70; dir. talent devel. Met. Arts Complex, Detroit Model Cities Program, 1970-72; dir. choral and orchestral activities Mich. Tech. U., Houghton, 1976—, dir. arts, 1982—; adjudicator; cons. Mich. Council Arts. Mem. Am. Choral Dirs. Assn., Am. Symphony Orch. League, Coll. Music Soc., Mich. Choral Dirs. Assn., Mich. Orch. Assn., Mich. Sch. Vocal Assn., Nat. Assn. Jazz Educators. Club: Rotary (Houghton). Composer choral works, musicals, jazz arrangements. Office: Arts and Humanities Michigan Technical U Houghton MI 49931

OLTARZ-SCHWARTZ, SARA, lawyer; b. Ostrow, Poland, May 5, 1945; came to U.S., 1950, naturalized 1956; d. Simon and Mindy (Salzburg) Oltarz; m. Michael Alan Schwartz, Dec. 8, 1973; children—Carl, Justin. B.A., NYU, 1969, J.D., 1972. Bar: N.Y. 1973, Mich. 1980, U.S. Dist. Ct. (so. and ea. dists.) 1974, U.S. Ct. Appeals (2d cir.) 1975, U.S. Ct. Mil. Appeals 1976, U.S. Ct. Appeals (6th cir.) 1983, U.S. Supreme Ct. 1976. Asst. dist. atty. City of Bklyn., 1972-77; adj. prof. N.Y. Law Sch., 1978-79; of counsel David F. DuMouchel, P.C., Detroit, 1983—; sole practice, Detroit, 1983—. Recipient Am. Jurisprudence award for N.Y. practice Lawyers Coop. Pub. Co., 1972. Mem. ABA, State Bar Mich., Oakland County Bar Assn., Internat. Assn. Jewish Lawyers and Jurists. Office: 1954 Buhl Bldg Buhl Bldg Detroit MI 48226

OLTMAN, DWIGHT, orchestral conductor and educator; b. Imperial, Nebr., May 27, 1936; s. George and Lois (Wine) O.; m. Shirley Jean Studebaker, May 30, 1966; children—Michelle, Nicole. B.S., McPherson Coll., 1958, M.Mus., Wichita State U., 1963; postgrad. U. Cin., 1967-70; studied composition with Nadia Boulanger, Paris, 1960, conducting with Pierre Monteux, 1963. Orchestral condr. Manchester (Ind.) Coll., 1963-67; music dir. Bach Festival and symphony orch. Baldwin-Wallace Coll., Berea, Ohio, 1970—; music dir., condr. Ohio Chamber Orch., Cleve., 1972—; music dir., prin. condr. Cleve. Ballet, 1976—; guest condr. orchs. U.S., Can., Europe. Mem. Am. Symphony Orch. League, Condrs. Guild, Orgn. Ohio Orchs. (dir. 1982—), Am. Fedn. Musicians. Democrat. Protestant.

OLTROGGE, RALPH EDWIN, utility executive; b. Readlyn, Iowa, Dec. 11, 1930; s. Herman J. and Florence (Schuecknecht) O.; divorced; 1 child, Samuel. B.S. in Bus. Adminstrn., Wartburg Coll., 1953. Auditor, D.W. Baker, C.P.A., Waterloo, Iowa, 1955-57; assoc. Ill. Electric Coops., Springfield, 1957-61; auditor, br. mgr. ABCC div. Whirlpool Corp., Mich., 1961-66; staff mgr. Fla. Keys Electric Co., Tavernier, 1966-67; asst. mgr. Irwin Electric Co., Ocilla, Ga., 1967-73; gen. mgr. Oconto Electric Coop., Oconto Falls, Wis., 1973—; pres. Oconto Econ. Devel. Corp., 1983—, treas., 1978-83, dir. 1976-78. Mem. Oconto Falls Council Boy Scouts Am., 1975-79; mem. ch. council Grace Lutheran Ch., 1976-78; active campaign Toby Roth for Congress, Oconto Falls County, 1984. Mem. Oconto Falls C. of C., Wis. Elec. Coops. (com. mem.). Republican. Lutheran. Club: Electric Mgrs. (pres. 1980-82). Home: Route 1 Box 125 Oconto Falls WI 54154 Office: Oconto Electric Coop Hwy 22 E Oconto Falls WI 54154

OLYSAV, DAVID J., orthopedic surgeon; b. West Mifflin, Pa., Dec. 17, 1946; s. John F. and Mary L. (Horvat) O.; m. Jean Ann Elger, July 3, 1971; 1 child, Brian D. B.S., U. Wis. 1968, M.D., 1973. Diplomate Am. Bd. Orthopaedic Surgery Intern Saginaw Coop. Hosp., Mich., 1973-74; resident in orthopedics So. Ill. U. Sch. of Medicine, Springfield, 1976-80, Clin. Assoc., 1980—; practice medicine specializing in orthopedic surgery, Springfield, 1980—; dir. amputee clinic Meml. Med. Ctr., Springfield, 1983—. Served to lt. USN., 1974-76. Fellow Am. Acad. Orthopaedic Surgeons; mem. Internat., Soc. Prosthetics and Orthotics, AMA, Ill. State Med. Soc., Sangamon County Med. Soc. Methodist. Avocations: boating; fishing. Office: 901 W Jefferson St Springfield IL 62702

O'MALIA, DANIEL JOSEPH, retail grocery executive; b. Indpls., Sept. 22, 1947; s. George Joseph and Lois Evelyn (Walters) O.; m. Rita Kaye Doyle, June 28, 1969; children—Janet Lynn, Shannon Eileen, Colleen Danielle. B.S., Xavier U., 1969; M.A., Butler U., 1975. English tchr. St. Andrew Sch., Indpls., 1969-73, Cathedral High Sch., 1973-75; with O'Malia Food Markets, 1966—, exec. v.p., 1975—. Bd. dirs. Carmel-Clay Edn. Found., 1981—, Cathedral High Sch., Indpls.; mem. admissions com. United Way of Greater Indpls., 1982—. Mem. Am. Mgmt. Assn., Food Mktg. Inst., Ind. Retail Grocers Assn. (dir. 1981—). Roman Catholic. Club: Sertoma. Office: O'Malia Food Markets Inc 1555 Westfield Rd Noblesville IN 46060

OMANS, CLARENCE D., optometrist; b. Detroit Lakes, Minn., Dec. 25, 1914; s. Earl D. and Mary (Shasky) O.; m. June W. Shoup, Jan. 8, 1919; children—Patricia Ann Omans Harrison, Clara Lynn Sue Omans Dinning. O.D., Ill. Coll. Optometry, Chgo., 1940. Pres. Vision Services, P.C., Battle Creek, Mich., 1972—. Trustee, Battle Creek Adventist Hosp., 1960—. Named Hosp. Trustee of Yr., Mich. Hosp. Assn., 1984. Fellow Am. Acad. Optometry; mem. Mich. Optometric Assn., Am. Optometric Assn. Lodge: Lions. Home: 14 Highlander Ln Hendersonville NC 28739 Office: 32 W Van Buren Battle Creek MI 49017

O'MARA, MICHAEL MARTIN, chemical company executive; b. Lackawanna, N.Y., Jan. 24, 1942; s. Bernard R. and Catherine (Smith) O'M.; m. Carole Ann Brinkman, Dec. 11, 1965; 1 dau., Lauren Beth. B.S., Canisius Coll., 1964; Ph.D., U. Cin., 1968. Scientist research and devel. B.F. Goodrich Co., Cleve., 1968-76, mgr. research and devel., 1976-78, gen. mgr., 1978-81, v.p. research and devel., 1981—. Contbr. articles to tech. jours. Mem. Am. Chem. Soc., AAAS. Avocations: Stamp collecting; racquetball; competitive running. Home: 29017 Lincoln Rd Bay Village OH 44140 Office: 6100 Oak Tree St Cleveland OH 44131

OMOIELE, MARNA TAMBURA, sociologist, radio station moderator; b. Dayton, Ohio, May 6, 1948; d. Morgan and Mary Louise (Marshall) Revere; m. Robert Alexander Turner Jr., Apr. 30, 1983 (div. 1984); children—Nyota Binta Ain Omoiele, Robert Alexander Turner III, Christopher Turner, Yemane Turner. B.A. in Sociology, Wright State U., 1974, postgrad. in liberal arts, 1978-79; M.S. in Corrections, Xavier U., Cin., 1976. Cert. secondary edn. tchr., Ohio; lic. cosmetologist. Pre-sentence investigator Montgomery County Adult Probation Dept., Dayton, 1973-75; social counselor Hamilton County Adult Parole, Cin., 1975-77; tchr. Huber Heights Sch., Dayton, 1979; mem. exec. bd., treas. West Montgomery County Fed. Program, Dayton, 1979—. Chmn. internat. div. Nat. Council of Negro Women, N.Y., 1979—; mem. Dayton Urban League, 1982—. Recipient Employee of Yr. award City of Dayton 1981. Mem. Dayton and Montgomery County Black Mgr. Assn., Democratic Voters League, Nat. Black Ind. Polit. Party, Nat. Assn. Blacks in Criminal Justice (charter), Am. Soc. Criminology, Fedn. of Dayton/N.Y. Bus. and Profl. Women, Inc. (chmn. ways and means 1982-84). Baptist. Home: 332 Kenwood Ave Dayton OH 45405 Office: City of Dayton 702 Salem Ave Dayton OH 45406

ONDREJKA, RONALD, music conductor; b. N.Y.C., Oct. 12, 1932; s. Louis and Antonia (Scandurra) O.; B.M., Eastman Sch. Music, 1953, M.M., 1954; children—Paul Louis, Nicholas Anton. Asso. condr. Radio City Music Hall Orch., 1957-60, Monterey County (Calif.) Symphony, 1960-61, Buffalo Philharmonic Orch., 1961-63, Cin. Symphony, 1963-65, Pitts. Symphony, 1965-67; music dir. Santa Barbara (Calif.) Symphony, 1967-78, Fort Wayne (Ind.) Philharmonic, 1978—; faculty U. Calif., Santa Barbara, 1967-78. Served with U.S. Army, 1954-56. Address: Fort Wayne Philharmonic 1107 S Harrison St Fort Wayne IN 46802

O'NEAL, WINSTON JAMES, JR., magazine publisher and editor, record producer; b. Ft. Wayne, Ind., Nov. 25, 1948; s. Winston James and Mary Margaret (Burns) O'N.; m. Amelia van Singel, July 11, 1970. B.S. in Journalism, Northwestern U., 1970, M.S. in Journalism, 1974. Co-founder Living Blues mag., Chgo., 1970—, co-editor, 1970—; co-owner Rooster Blues Records, 1979—, Rooster Reggae Records, 1983; bd. advisors Ctr. for Study So. Culture, U. Miss., Blues Found., Delta Blues Mus., Nat. Acad. Blues; cons. for TV series ABC, NBC, CBS, PBS, Miss. ETV, Auburn TV, BBC, WDR (W.Ger.), Fuji Telecasting (Japan); mem. artist-in residence program Ill. Arts Council; mem. concert program Mus. Contemporary Art, Field Mus. Natural History; made Am. Blues Legends tour, Eng., Am. Living Blues tour, France, Blues Festivals tours, Mex.; with Berlin Jazz Festival; cons. Maxwell Street Blues film U. Ill.-Chgo., U. Chgo. Folk Festival, Chgo. Blues Festival/Mayor's Office Spl. Events, various programs Chgo. Hist. Soc., Chgo. Cultural Ctr., Smithsonian Inst., Memphis State U., Jazz Inst. Chgo., U. Liege, Belgium, also other instns., univs. and radio stas.; tchr. Loop Coll., Chgo., 1974. Served alt. service at Chgo.-Read Mental Health Ctr., 1971-73. Recipient W.C. Handy Blues award for best publ., 1980, Blues single of yr. award, 1981, 82, Blues album of yr. award, 1982, 83, Footprints in Sands of Time award for contbns. to Black Am., U.S. Grant Pub. Sch., 1982. Mem. Nat. Acad. Rec. Arts and Scis., Nat. Assn. Ind. Record Distbrs., Blues Found. (Classics of Blues Lit. award 1982), Nat. Acad. Blues (Best Blues Publ. award 1981), Broadcast Music Inc. Contbr. articles and photographs to publs. in U.S., Europe and Japan. Home and office: 2615 N Wilton Ave Chicago IL 60614

O'NEIL, MICHAEL GERALD, tire company executive; b. Akron, Ohio, Jan. 29, 1922; s. William Francis and Grace (Savage) O'N.; A.B., Coll. of Holy Cross, 1943; postgrad. Sch. Bus., Harvard U., 1948; LL.D., U. Akron, 1962, Ashland, Coll., 1967; m. Juliet P. Rudolph, Jan. 7, 1950 (dec. 1981); children—Michael, Gregory, Jeffrey, Shawn, Julie, Nancy, Susan; m. 2d, Jean Bowman, Oct. 2, 1981. With Gen. Tire Co., 1947—, staff inter-plant ops., Venezuela, 1947-48, dir., 1950—, exec. asst. to pres., 1951-60, pres., 1960-82, chmn. bd., 1981—, mem. exec., finance coms.; dir. 1st Nat. Bank of Akron. Served as lt. USAAF, 1944-45. Clubs: Portage Country, Akron City; Sharon Golf. Office: One General St Akron OH 44329

O'NEILL, PATRICK J., professional baseball executive. Chmn. bd. Cleve. Indians. Office: Cleve Indians Cleve Stadium Cleveland OH 44114*

ONG, JOHN DOYLE, rubber products company executive; b. Uhrichsville, Ohio, Sept. 29, 1933; s. Louis Brosee and Mary Ellen (Liggett) O.; B.A., Ohio State U., 1954, M.A., 1954; LL.B., Harvard U., 1957; L.H.D. (hon.), Kent State U., 1982; m. Mary Lee Schupp, July 20, 1957; children—John Francis Harlan, Richard Penn Blackburn, Mary Katherine Caine. Admitted to Ohio bar, 1958; asst. counsel B.F. Goodrich Co., Akron, Ohio, 1961-66, group v.p., 1972-73, dir., 1973—, exec. v.p., 1973-74, vice chmn. bd., 1974-75, pres., 1975-77, pres. and chief operating officer, 1978-79, pres., 1979-84, chmn. bd., chief exec. officer, 1979—; asst. to pres. Internat. B.F. Goodrich Co., Akron, 1966-69, v.p., 1969-70, pres., 1970-72; dir. Cooper Industries, Kroger Co., Ohio Bell Telephone Co., RNC Fin. Corp., Pitts. Nat. Bank, 1981—; bd. dirs. Nat. Alliance Bus., 1981—. Vice pres. exploring Gt. Trail council Boy Scouts Am., 1974-77; bus. adv. com. Transp. Center, Northwestern U., 1975-78. Trustee St. John's Home for Girls, Painesville, 1969-71, Kent State U. Found., 1974-76, Bexley Hall Sem., Rochester, N.Y., 1974-81; trustee Western Res. Acad., Hudson, Ohio, 1975—, pres. bd. trustees, 1977—; trustee Case Western Res. U., 1980—, Kenyon Coll., 1983—; nat. trustee Nat. Symphony Orch., 1975-83; pres. bd. trustees Akron Community Trusts; adv. bd. Blossom Music Center; bus. adv. council Carnegie Mellon U., 1978—. Served with Judge Adv. Gen.'s Corps, AUS, 1957-61. Mem. Ohio Bar Assn. (corp. counsel sect. bd. govs. 1962-73, chmn. 1970), Rubber Mfrs. Assn. (dir.), Chem. Mfrs. Assn. (dir.), Hudson Library and Hist. Soc. (pres. 1971-72, trustee), Conf. Bd., Phi Beta Kappa, Phi Alpha Theta. Episcopalian. Clubs: Akron City, Portage Country

(Akron); Links, Union League (N.Y.C.); Union (Cleve.); Rolling Rock (Ligonier, Pa.); Met. (Washington); Castalia (Ohio) Trout. Office: BF Goodrich Co 500 S Main St Akron OH 44318

ONODA, BRIGHT YASUNORI, physician; b. Cosmopolis, Wash., July 25, 1921; s. Sanjuru and Yaeko (Shingai) O.; B.S., Hillsdale (Mich.) Coll., 1948; M.D., U. Mich., 1952; m. Teresa Peters, Aug. 13, 1976; children—Carol, Paul. Intern, Harper Hosp., Detroit, 1952-53; resident U. Chgo. Clinics, 1956-57, St. Luke's Hosp., Chgo., 1957-58; dir. dept. anesthesiology Augustana Hosp., Chgo., 1973—, med. dir. respiratory care dept., 1968—, also mem. exec. com., treas. med. staff. Bd. dirs. Augustana Hosp., 1978—. Served in U.S. Army, 1945-48. Diplomate Am. Bd. Anesthesiology. Fellow Am. Coll. Anesthesiologists; mem. AMA, Chgo. Med. Soc., Am. Soc. Anesthesiologists, Ill. Soc. Anesthesiologists, Am. Legion. Home: 9023 Tamaroa Skokie IL 60076 Office: 411 W Dickens Chicago IL 60614

OOSTHUIZEN, ADRIAN J. R., computer company executive; b. Calitzdorp, South Africa, Dec. 3, 1935; s. Jan L. and Cornelia M. (Roux) O.; m. Antoinette Diana Pappas, Sept. 1959; children—Mark J., Adele M., Dione, Lael A. B.Comm., U. Pretoria, South Africa, 1955, C.T.A., 1956. Div. mgr. data processing NCR Corp., South Africa, 1972-73; mgr. data processing CI/MEG and fin. div., South Africa, 1974-75; vocat. dir. internat. mktg. services CI/MEG div. Dayton, Ohio, 1975-76, v.p. systems div., 1980—; v.p. NCR Can. CI/MEG div., Toronto, Ont., 1976-77; pres. NCR Can. Ltd., Toronto, 1978-80. Office: NCR Corp Ci/MEG Systems Div 1700 S Patterson Blvd Dayton OH 45479

OPENSHAW, CALVIN REYNOLDS, surgeon; b. Salt Lake City, Nov. 4, 1921; s. Clarence Roy and Elna Dehlin (Shipp) O.; B.S., U. Utah, 1942, M.D., 1944; M.S., U. Minn., 1953; m. Blanche Hiley, Dec. 11, 1948; children—Calvin Reynolds, Susan Beaver, Michael Browne; m. 2d, Evelyn Constance Miller, Dec. 19, 1973. Intern, Salt Lake County Gen. Hosp., 1944-45; resident, research fellow surgery U. Utah, Salt Lake City, 1946-47; fellow in surgery Mayo Found., 1948-51, fellow in thoracic surgery, 1951-53; chief thoracic surgery VA Hosp., Fort Douglas, Utah, 1955-56; practice medicine specializing in surgery, Hutchinson, Kans., 1957—; mng. ptnr. GGC Enterprises, 1980—; asst. clin. prof. surgery U. Utah, 1955-56; chief dept. surgery Hutchinson Hosp., 1977-81, 85-87. Bd. dirs. Hutchinson Hosp. Corp., 1979—. Served with USN, 1945-46, 53-54; PTO. Mem. AMA, A.C.S., Southwestern Surg. Congress, Internat. Soc. for Philos. Enquiry (assoc.), Prometheus Soc., Am. Legion. Republican. Congregationalist Club: Elks. Home: 1824 N Main St Hutchinson KS 67502 Office: 2020 N Waldron Hutchinson KS 67502

OPENSHAW, DALE KIM, educator, therapist; b. Salt Lake City, Mar. 10, 1950; s. Richard D. and Naoma Lillian (Tischner) O.; m. Anita B. Evans, Jan. 12, 1973; children—Damian, Cammarie, Derek, Jeffrey, Cody, Shandee. B.A., U. Utah, 1973, M.S.W., 1976; Ph.D., Brigham Young U., 1978. Prof. human devel. U. Wis.-Stout, 1978-79; child devel. and family life specialist U. Wis.-Madison, 1979-81; prof., dir. marriage and family therapy Utah State U., Logan, 1981—, adj. prof. adolescent devel. psychology. Active Optimist Internat. NIMH grantee U. Utah, 1974-76. Mem. Nat. Assn. Social Workers, Soc. Research Child Devel., Am. Assn. Marriage and Family Therapy, Nat. Marriage Consortium, Omicron Nu. Mem. Ch. of Jesus Christ of Latter-Day Saints. Presenter numerous workshops; contbr. articles to profl. jours.

OPPENHEIM, BERNARD EDWARD, nuclear physician; b. Chgo., July 5, 1937; s. Michael Robert and Mae (Greenwald) O.; m. Renee Lee Roth, June 9, 1963; children—Stephen Barry, David Jeffrey, Sharon Beth, Daniel Howard. B.S., U. Ariz., 1959; M.D., U. Chgo., 1963. Diplomate Am. Bd. Radiology, Am. Bd. Nuclear Medicine. Intern. Michael Reese Hosp., Chgo., 1963-64; resident in radiology U. Chgo., 1964-67, asst. prof. radiology, 1971-75, acting dir. nuclear medicine, 1974-76, assoc. prof. radiology, 1975-76; assoc. prof. radiology Ind. U., Indpls., 1976-81, prof. radiology, 1981—; cons. Nat. Cancer Inst., Bethesda, Md., 1974-79, Nat. Acad. Scis., Washington, 1977-78. Contbr. articles to profl. jours. Served to maj. U.S. Army, 1967-70. James Picker Found. scholar, 1972-74; Nat. Heart, Lung and Blood Inst. grantee, 1979-82. Mem. Soc. Nuclear Medicine, Radiol. Soc. N.Am., AMA, AAAS, Am. Coll Nuclear Physicians. Jewish. Lodge: B'nai Brith. Avocations: computer programming; music; history. Office: Dept Radiology Ind U Sch Medicine 926 W Michigan St Indianapolis IN 46223

OPPENHEIMER, CHARLES K(ENNETH), JR., financial executive, consultant; b. Hartford, Conn., Dec. 8, 1949; s. Charles Kenneth and Marjorie (Harlow) O.; m. Bonnie Ann Toriani, Jan. 22, 1972 (div. 1977). Student Hartford Inst. Acctg., 1977-79. Pres., C & M Oppenheimer Notepaper Co., (now Park Nat. Industries), 1961—; newspaper exec. Hartford Times, 1967-75; founder, pres. Circulation Systems, Inc. (now div. Pacific Crest Communications Corp.), 1971—; exec. v.p. Gt. Northern Trust, 1974-79, also dir.; founder, pres. Plant City Corp., 1976—; newspaper exec. Jour. Pub. Co., Manchester, Conn., 1978-79; newspaper fin. mgmt. exec. Kansas City (Mo.) Star Co., 1981-83; pres., chief exec. officer Paperchase Corp. (name changed to Armcrest Corp.), 1983—, Crane & Co. Inc., 1985—, exec. officer Park Nat. Corp., Plant City Corp., Herald Office Equipment Co. Inc., Transrail Corp., Pacific Crest Communications Corp.; Quill & Scroll Ltd.; mgmt. and pub. cons.; condr. seminars. Mem. Internat. Circulation Mgrs. Assn., Nat. Assn. Advt. Pubs., Inst. Newspaper Controllers and Fin. Officers, Printing Industries Am., Nat. Office Machine Dealers Assn., Nat. Office Products Assn., N.Y. Fin. Execs. Assn., Advt. Club Kansas City, Kans. Rail Passenger Coalition. Clubs: Western Mass. Appaloosa Assn. (pres. 1975-76, dir. 1976-79), Quinniapiac River Doberman Pinscher (treas. 1975-77). Author: Expense Code Numbering System, Central Purchasing Mgrs. Manual. Address: PO Box 23036 Kansas City MO 64141 also 300 W Maple St Independence MO 64050

OPPERMAN, DWIGHT DARWIN, publishing executive; b. Perry, Iowa, June 26, 1923; s. John H. and Zoa L. (Bickal) O.; m. Jeanice Wifvat, Apr. 22, 1942; children—Vance K., Fane W. J.D., Drake U., 1951. Bar: Iowa 1951. Editor/asst. editorial counsel West Pub. Co., St. Paul, 1951-64, Reporter and Digest dept. mgr., 1964-65, v.p., 1965-68, asst. to pres., 1967-68, pres., 1968—, chief exec. officer, 1978—. Trustee, United Way St. Paul, James J. Hill Reference Library, Drake U.; mem. nat. adv. com. Nat. Inst. Citizen Edn. in the Law. Served with U.S. Army, 1942-45. Recipient Disting. Service award Drake U. Nat. Alumni, 1974, Centennial award, 1981. Mem. Am. Judicature Soc. (bd. dirs., exec. com.; Herbert Harley award 1984), Supreme Ct. Hist. Soc. (trustee), Nat. Lawyers Club, ABA, Fed. Bar Assn., Drake U. Law Sch. Alumni Assn. Clubs: Minnesota (past pres.), Capitol Hill. Office: PO Box 64526 Saint Paul MN 55164

OPPERMANN, JAMES ALEX, research pharmacologist; b. Milw., Nov. 18, 1942; s. Alex Ervin and Evelyn S. (Marks) O.; m. Beth Ellen Schwantes, Oct. 9, 1965 (div. Nov. 1984); children—Dawn, Dean. B.S., U. Wis.-Madison, 1965, M.S., 1967, Ph.D., 1970. Research staff G.D. Searle & Co., Chgo., 1970-75, group leader, 1975-84, dir. drug metabolism dept., 1984—. Contbg. author: Aspartame, 1984. Mem. Am. Chem. Soc., Internat. Soc. Study of Xenobiotics, Sports Car Club Am. Lutheran. Avocation: professional auto racing. Office: GD Searle 4901 Searle Pkwy Skokie IL 60680

ORAVECZ, MICHAEL GEORGE, physicist, researcher; b. Akron, Ohio, Jan. 31, 1956; s. John and Miriam Jane (Partsch) O. B. in Physics, U. Chgo., 1978; M. in Physics, SUNY-Stony Brook, 1979. Jr. research asst. Cloud Physics La. Dept. Geophysics U. Chgo., 1975-76; Yerkes Obs., Williams Bay, Wis., 1977; teaching asst. physics SUNY-Stony Brook, 1978-79, research asst. quantum electronics group physics, 1979; project scientist Sonoscan, Inc., Bensenville, Ill., 1981—. Contbr. articles to profl. jours. Sustainer Inst. for Independent Social Journalism. Mem. Am. Ceramics Soc., Am. Soc. Metals, Am. Soc. Nondestructive Testing, Internat. Soc. Hybrid Microelectronics, Am. Soc. Mech. Engrs. (mem. tech. com. on biomed. uses of acoustics, 1984—), NOW. Club: Kaypro Users Group (Glenview, Ill.) (librarian 1983-84). Avocations: computers; classical music. Home: 1141 W Grace Apt 2N Chicago IL 60613-2847 Office: Sonoscan Inc 530 E Green St Bensenville IL 60106

ORDINACHEV, JOANN LEE, educator; b. Rogers, Ark., Mar. 17, 1936; d. Floyd Andrew and Irene Elnora Elizabeth (Johnson) Walkenbach; m. J. Dean Harter, Dec. 24, 1953 (div. 1977); m. 2d, Miles Donald Ordinachev, Mar. 11, 1978. B.S., U. Mo., 1971; M.A.T., Webster U., 1974; postgrad. St. Louis U., 1978—. Office mgr. Edwards Constrn. Co., Joplin, Mo., 1954-58; with Jasper Welfare Office, Joplin, 1958-61; tchr. St. Louis Archdiocean, 1963-68, 70-71; TV personality, tchr. Sta. KDMO Cablevision, Carthage, Mo., 1968-69; tech. reading and remedial math. specialist West County Tech. Sch., St. Louis, 1974—; owner Jody's Dyslexia Lab., Concord Village, Mo., 1982—. Mem. Am. Vocat. Assn., Mo. Vocat. Assn., Spl. Dist. Tchrs. Assn. (pres.), NEA (pres. 1980-81), Orton Dyslexia Soc., Sch. Psychologists Assn., Council Exceptional Children. Democrat. Eastern Orthodox.

ORDING, JEFFREY CHARLES, real estate executive; b. Chgo., Sept. 15, 1953; s. Charles Henry and Elizabeth Ann Ording; m. Connie Ording, May 7, 1983. Vice pres. Hemisphere Corp., Barrington, Ill., 1980-82; pres. Cable Comml. Brokerage, Inc., Northbrook, Ill., 1982—. Home: 2150 Hassell Rd Hoffman Estates IL 60195 Office: Cable Comml Brokerage Inc 3482 N Milwaukee Ave Northbrook IL 60062

ORDUZ, EFRAÍN, educational adminstrator; b. Boyacá, Colombia, S.Am., Sept. 29, 1944; came to U.S., 1969; s. Buenaventura and Ana Rosinda (Naranjo) O.; children—Karen Eugenia, David Alberto. B.A., Javeriana U., Bogotá, Colombia, 1969; M.Ed., Loyola U., Chgo., 1973, M.B.A., 1978; postgrad. U. Ill.-Chgo., 1969-75. Classroom tchr. Chgo. Pub. Schs., 1971-82, resource tchr., 1982-84, trainer, 1984, prin., 1984—. Mem. Am. Assn. Sch. Adminstrs., Chgo. Prins. Assn., Phi Kappa Phi, Phi Delta Kappa. Roman Catholic. Avocations: tennis; camping; soccer. Home: 5243 N Hoyne St Chicago IL 60625 Office: James Monroe Sch 3651 W Schubert St Chicago IL 60647

ORDWAY, ELLEN, biology educator, entomology researcher; b. N.Y.C., Nov. 8, 1927; d. Samuel Hanson and Anna (Wheatland) O. B.A., Wheaton Coll., Mass., 1950; M.S., Cornell U., 1955; Ph.D., U. Kans., 1965. Field asst. N.Y. Zool. Soc., N.Y.C., 1950-52; research asst. Am. Mus. Natural History, N.Y.C., 1955-57; teaching asst. U. Kans., Lawrence, 1957-61, research asst., 1959-65; asst. prof. U. Minn., Morris, 1965-70, assoc. prof. biology, 1970—; cooperator and cons. U.S. Dept. Agr. Bee Research Lab., Tucson, Ariz., 1971, 1983. Contbr. articles to sci. jours. Mgr. preserves Nature Conservancy, Mpls., 1975—; lectr. Morris area service clubs, 1972—. Mem. Ecol. Soc. Am., Entomol. Soc. Am., Soc. Systematic Zoology, Soc. Study Evolution, Kans. Entomol. Soc., Internat. Bee Research Assn., AAAS, AAVP (v.p. 1975-76, sec.-treas. 1971-73 Morris chpt.), Sigma Xi, Sigma Delta Epsilon. Episcopalian. Avocations: travel, photography, raquetball. Office: Div Sci Math U Minn Morris MN 56267

ORE, STANLEY HARRISON, JR., principal; b. Madison, Wis., Nov. 1, 1935; s. Stanley Harrison and Marian Elizabeth (Powell) O.; m. Nancy Lu Bauer, Apr. 18, 1958; children—Pam, Stephen, Julia, Gerard. B.E., Wis. State Coll., 1961; M.S., U. Wis., 1964, cert. edn. spl., 1965. Tchr. English, Burlington Union High Sch., Wis., 1961-63; NDEA fellow U. Wis., Madison, 1963-65; asst. prin. Appleton Sr. High Sch., Wis., 1965-67; prin. Appleton High Sch. East, 1967—; dir. North Central Assn. Schs. and Colls., Boulder, Colo., 1979-83; pres., exec. com. Sch. Evaluation Consortium, Madison, 1979-84. Served with USN, 1953-56, PTO. Mem. Assn. Wis. Sch. Adminstrs., Res. Officers Assn., Nat. Ret. Tchrs. Assn., Nat. Assn. Secondary Sch. Prins. Methodist. Lodge: Rotary (dir. 1972-76, 85—). Avocations: reading, jogging, movies. Home: Route 1 Box 219B Hortonville WI 54944 Office: Appleton High Sch E 2121 Emmers Dr Appleton WI 54915

OREFFICE, PAUL FAUSTO, chemical company executive; b. Venice, Italy, Nov. 29, 1927; s. Max and Elena (Friedenberg) O.; came to U.S., 1945, naturalized, 1951; B.S. in Chem. Engring., Purdue U., 1949; m. Franca Giuseppina Ruffini, May 26, 1956; children—Laura Emma, Andrew T. With Dow Chem. Co., 1953—, assigned to Switzerland, Italy, Brazil and Spain, to 1969, pres. Dow Chem. Latin Am., Coral Gables, Fla., 1969-70, corp. fin. v.p., Midland, Mich., 1970-75, pres. Dow Chem. U.S.A., 1975-78, pres., chief exec. officer Dow Chem. Co., 1978—; dir. Coca-Cola Co. CIGNA Corp., Dow Corning, No. Telecom. Mem. policy com. Bus. Roundtable; trustee Am. Enterprise Inst., Conf. Bd., Midland Community Ctr.; bd. govs. Purdue U. Found. Served with AUS, 1951-53. Decorated Encomienda del Merito Civil (Spain), 1966. Mem. Chem. Mfrs. Assn. Office: Dow Center 2030 Dow Ctr Midland MI 48674

O'REILLY, CHARLES TERRANCE, university administrator, educator; b. Chgo., May 30, 1921; s. William Patrick and Ann M. Elizabeth (Madden) O'R.; m. Rosella Catherine Neilland, June 4, 1955; children—Terrance, Gregory, Kevin, Joan Bridget, Kathleen Ann. B.A., Loyola U., Chgo., 1942, M.S.W., 1948; postgrad. Universita Cattolica, Milan, Italy, 1949-50; Ph.D., U. Notre Dame, 1954. Instr., DePaul U., Chgo., 1948-49; asst. in psychology U. Cattolica, 1940-50; case worker Catholic Charities, N.Y.C., 1953-54; exec. dir. Family Service, Long Branch, N.J., 1954-55; asst. prof. social work Loyola U., Chgo., 1955-59, dean Sch. Social Work, 1976—; vis. lectr. Ensiss Sch. Social Work, Milan, Italy, 1959-60; asst. prof. U. Wis., Milw., 1961-64, prof., assoc. dir., Madison, 1965-68; dean social welfare SUNY, Albany, 1968-76, also v.p. acad. affairs. Author: OAA Profile; 1961, People of Inner Core North, 1965; Men in Jail, 1968. Contbr. articles to profl. jours. Pres. Community Action Com., Dane County, Wis., 1967-68; bd. dirs. Council Community Services, Albany, Family and Children's Service, Albany. Served with AUS, 1942-46, 1951-52, USAR, 1953-78. Fulbright scholar, 1949-50, fellow, 1959. Mem. Nat. Assn. Social Workers, Council Social Work Edn. Roman Catholic. Home: 4073 Bunker Ln Wilmette IL 60091 Office: Loyola Univ Sch Social Work Chicago IL 60611

OREL, HAROLD, literary critic, educator; b. Boston, Mar. 31, 1926; s. Saul and Sarah (Wicker) O.; m. Charlyn Hawkins, May 25, 1951; children—Sara Elinor, Timothy Ralston. B.A. cum laude, U. N.H., 1948; M.A., U. Mich., 1949, Ph.D., 1952; postgrad. Harvard U., 1949. Teaching fellow dept. English, U. Mich., Ann Arbor, 1948-52; instr. dept. English, U. Md., College Park, 1952-54, 55-56, overseas program, Ger., Austria, Eng., 1954-55; tech. editor Applied Physics Lab., Johns Hopkins U., Balt., 1953-56; flight propulsion lab. dept. Gen. Electric Co., Cin., 1957; assoc. prof. English, U. Kans., Lawrence, 1957-63, prof., 1963-74, disting. prof., 1974—, asst. dean faculties and research adminstrn., 1964-67; evaluator English depts. numerous univs., 1970—; cons. univ. presses, scholarly jours. Served with USN, 1944-46. Am. Council Learned Socs. grantee, 1966; NEH grantee, 1975; Am. Philos. Soc. grantee, 1964, 80. Unitarian. Author: Thomas Hardy's Epic-Drama: A Study of The Dynasts, 1963; The Development of William Butler Yeats, 1885-1900, 1968; English Romantic Poets and the Enlightenment: Nine Essays on a Literary Relationship in Studies in Voltaire and the Eighteenth Century, vol. CIII, 1973; The Final Years of Thomas Hardy, 1912-1928, 1976; Victorian Literary Critics, 1984; The Literary Achievement of Rebecca West, 1985; contbg. author: Thomas Hardy and the Modern World, 1974; The Genius of Thomas Hardy, 1976; Budmouth Essays on Thomas Hardy, 1976; contbr. numerous articles on English lit. history and criticism to mags.; co-editor Thomas Hardy Rev., 1975—; editor: The World of Victorian Humor, 1961; Six Essays in Nineteenth-Century English Literature and Thought, 1962; Thomas Hardy's Personal Writings: Prefaces, Literary Opinions, Reminiscences, 1966; British Poetry 1880-1920: Edwardian Voices, 1969; The Nineteenth-Century Writer and his Audience, 1969; Irish History and Culture, 1976; The Dynasts (Thomas Hardy), 1978; The Scottish World, 1981; Rudyard Kipling: Interviews and Recollections, 2 vols., 1983; delivered oration at ceremony commemorating 50th year since Thomas Hardy's death, Westminster Abbey, 1978. Home: 713 Schwarz Rd Lawrence KS 66044 Office: English Dept U Kans Lawrence KS 66045-2115

ORENSTEIN, JEFFREY ROBERT, political science educator, consultant; b. Cleve., Mar. 21, 1944; c. Philip F. and Beatrice (Zalinsky) O.; m. Virginia Kay Waltz; children—Alison, Daniel. B.A., Ohio State U., 1966; M.A., U. Wis.-Madison, 1967, Ph.D., 1971. Instr. polit. sci. Cuyahoga County Coll., Cleve., 1969-70; asst. prof. Kent State U., Ohio, 1970-75, assoc. prof., 1975—; pres. Achievement Cons., Canton, Ohio, 1980—. Co-author, co-editor: Politics of Community, 1973. Co-author: Contemporary Issues in Political Theory, 1977, 85. Mem. exec. com. Stark County Democratic Party, 1980—; campaign mgr. U.S. Congl. Race, Canton, 1980; candidate U.S. Congress, Canton, 1982. Democrat. Avocations: photography, transportation history. Office: Kent State U 6000 Frank Ave NW North Canton OH 44720

ORGAN, ARNOLD THOMAS, fire protection company official; b. Mpls., July 19, 1938; s. George E. and Ferne C. (McCarty) O.; m. Norma Jean Bartz, May 19, 1962; children—Thomas Paul, Debra Marie, Robert Michael, Michelle Renee. B.B.A., U. Minn., 1958. With Lyon Aircraft Services, Burbank, Calif., 1959-60; freight rate analyst Soo Line R.R., Mpls., 1960-65; with Ansul Co., Marinette, Wis., 1965—, corp. dir. purchasing, 1980—. Mem. Nat. Assn. Purchasing Mgrs., Menominee C. of C. Roman Catholic. Lodge: KC. Home: 4709 13th St Menominee MI 49858 Office: Ansul Co 1 Stanton St Marinette WI 54143

ORLADY, ROGER MONROE, business executive; b. Chgo., Feb. 3, 1949; s. Harry Werle and Olga Ellen (Monroe) O.; B.S. in Acctg. (Nat. Merit scholar), U. So. Calif., 1971; m. Nancy Kay Jacobson, June 10, 1978. Staff acct. Peat Marwick Mitchell & Co., Los Angeles, 1971-72; controller Ralph Williams Leasing, Beverly Hills, Calif., 1972-73; sr. acct. Alfred V. Hill and Co., Marshfield, Wis., 1973-75, Robert W. Klinner and Assos., Medford, Wis., 1975-78; asst. chief fin. officer, MIS dir. Weather Shield Mfg., Inc., Medford, 1978-84; controller Valleycast Inc., Appleton, Wis., 1984—. Bd. dirs. Taylor County March of Dimes, 1977, pres., 1978. C.P.A. Mem. Am. Inst. C.P.A.s, Wis. Inst. C.P.A.s (state C.P.A.s in industry com.; chmn. chpt. C.P.A.s in industry com.), Data Processing Mgmt. Assn., U. So. Calif. Midwest Alumni Club (bd. dirs.). Club: Jaycees (v.p. Medford 1980, dir. 1982, outstanding project chmn. Region 12, 1980). Home: 1043 Kalfahs St Neenah WI 54956 Office: 908 N Lawe St Appleton WI 54911

ORLANDO, JOYCE RYAN, public relations director; b. Steubenville, Ohio, Aug. 9, 1942; d. Orel B. and Alice (Mountford) Ryan; m. Joseph M. Orlando, Sept. 1, 1962 (div. Feb. 1976); children—Suzanne Elizabeth, Melissa Ann. Student U. Steubenville, 1981—. Mktg. dir. Fort Steuben Mall, Steubenville, 1974-81; asst. dir. pub. relations U. Steubenville, 1981-83, dir. pub. relations, 1983—. Bd. dirs. Jeffco Workshop, Steubenville, 1982—; chmn. Jefferson County Leukemia Soc., 1980—; mem. Steubenville Fiesta Com., 1984; past bd. dirs. Nat. Found. Birth Defects, United Way. Author/editor: A Guide to Steubenville for the Handicapped, 1974. Democrat. Episcopalian. Avocations: skiing; racquetball. Home: 136 Meadow Rd Wintersville OH 43952 Office: U Steubenville Franciscan Way Steubenville OH 43952

ORLANDO, POMPEI LEONARD, JR., lawyer; b. Balt., Nov. 5, 1946; s. P. Leonard Sr. and Carmel Veronica (Corvaia) O.; m. Lucia Marie Hartman, Sept. 15, 1973; children—P. Leonard III, Christopher James. B.S. in Bus. Adminstrn., Lewis Coll., 1968; J.D., Lewis U., 1978. Bar: Ill. 1979. Negotiator U.S. Army Corps of Engrs., Chgo., 1971-73; constrn. mgr. U.S. Postal Service, Chgo., 1973-75; sole practice, Libertyville, Ill., 1979-80; ptnr., sec./treas. Smith & Orlando, P.C., Libertyville, 1980-84, Smith, Orlando & Mulroy, P.C., Libertyville, 1984—; instr. law Oakton Community Coll., Ill., 1979-84; dir. Mettawa Enterprises, Mundelein, Ill., U.S. Govt. Contractors, Wilmette, Ill., Arc Light, Inc., Libertyville. Bd. advisors Vietnam Vets. Leadership Program, Buffalo Grove, Ill., 1983, atty. pro bono, 1983—. Served to lt. USMC, 1968-72. Mem. Naval Res. Assn. (chmn. legis. com. Great Lakes chpt. 1984), Delta Theta Phi (Sir Edward Cooke Senate). Office: Smith Orlando & Mulroy PC 1590 S Milwaukee Ave Suite 305 Libertyville IL 60048

ORMSON, JAMES GABRIEL, insurance company executive; b. Mauston, Wis., Mar. 22, 1929; s. Gilbert G. and Minerva Fern (Northcott) O.; m. Laura Jean Loomis, June 21, 1952; children—James Loomis, Mark John, Eric Jeffrey, Nancy Jean. B.S., U. Wis., 1950. Vice pres. Richland County Bank, Richland Center, Wis., 1956-58; investment analyst Aid Assn. for Lutherans, Appleton, Wis., 1958-63, sr. investment analyst, 1963-65, securities mgr., 1965-67, dir. securities, 1967-72, asst. v.p., 1972-74, 2d v.p., 1974-77, v.p., dir. investments, 1978-83, v.p. investments, treas., 1983—. Mem. Fraternal Investment Assn. (pres. 1973), Milw. Investment Analysts of Fin. Analysts Fedn. Club: Riverview Country (Appleton, Wis.). Office: Aid Assn for Lutherans 4321 N Ballard Rd Appleton WI 54919

ORNEST, HARRY, professional hockey team executive. Chmn. bd., pres., gov. St. Louis Blues, NHL. Office: St Louis Blues 5700 Oakland Ave Saint Louis MO 63110*

OROSZ, CHARLES GEORGE, biomedical researcher, medical educator; b. Cleve., Jan. 9, 1949; s. George John and Mary Helen (Palmer) O.; m. Nancy Marie O'Linn, Aug. 23, 1974; children—Matthew Michael and Kathleen Elizabeth (twins), Molly Nielan. B.S., Cleve. State U., 1971, M.S., 1975, Ph.D., 1978. Postdoctoral fellow U. Wis., Madison, 1978-80; vis. research fellow U. Minn., Mpls., 1980-81, asst. prof. lab. medicine and pathology, 1981-83; asst. prof. surgery Ohio State U., Columbus, 1983—. Contbr. articles to sci. jours. Served with USNR, 1967-73. Recipient New Investigator award, NIH, 1982; Research awards Nat. Kidney Found., 1984, NIH, 1984. Mem. Am. Soc. Histocompatability and Immunology, Comprehensive Cancer Care Ctr., Transplantation Soc., Am. Assn. Immunologists, Inter-Am. Soc. for Chemotherapy, Leukemia Soc. Am. (bd. dirs. central Ohio chpt. 1984—, spl. fellow 1982). Roman Catholic. Avocations: woodworking; jogging; racquetball. Office: Dept Surgery Ohio State Univ Room 258 Means Hall 1655 Upham Dr Columbus OH 43210

OROSZ, RICHARD THOMAS, lawyer; b. Painesville, Ohio, Dec. 26, 1942; s. Gabriel John and Helen Anna (Black) O.; m. Elizabeth Ann Dempsey, June 28, 1969; Karen, Gregory, Megan. B.S., Lake Erie Coll., 1967; J.D., Cleve. State U., 1970. Bar: Ohio 1971, U.S. Dist. Ct. (no. dist.) Ohio 1976, U.S. Supreme Ct. 1977. Sole practice, Painesville, 1971—; acting judge Painesville Mcpl. Ct., 1977—; foreman Lake County Grand Jury, 1979. Trustee Morley Library Assn. Mem. ABA, Ohio State Bar Assn., Lake County Bar Assn., Lake County Law Library Assn. (sec. 1973—). Roman Catholic. Club: Exchange (pres. 1984) (Painesville). Lodge: Elks. Avocations: golf; jogging. Home: 261 Wickland St Painesville OH 44077 Office: Richard T Orosz 56 Liberty St Suite 207 Painesville OH 44077

O'ROURKE, JAMES SCOFIELD, IV, air force officer; b. Billings, Mont., July 25, 1946; s. James Scofield and Joan Louise (Boardman) O'R.; m. Pamela Jean Spencer, Aug. 24, 1968; children—Colleen Kerry-Ann, Molly Scofield, Kathleen Spencer-Boardman. B.B.A., U. Notre Dame, 1968; M.S., Temple U., 1970; M.A., U. N.Mex., 1973; Ph.D., Syracuse U., 1980. Prof. communication Communication Inst. Ireland, 1970; commd. 2d lt. U.S. Air Force, 1968, advanced through grades lt. col., pub. info. officer Kirtland AFB, N.Mex., 1970-73, comdr. Am. Forces Radio and TV Stas., Goose AB, Labrador, Can., 1973-75; asst. prof. aerospace studies Syracuse U., 1975-78; assoc. prof. English, U.S. Air Force Acad., 1978-83, dir. media instrn. and profl. services, 1982-83; prof. pub. affairs, chief policy and info. div. Def. Info. Sch., Ft. Benjamin Harrison, Ind., 1983—; sr. faculty adv. Rocky Mountain Collegiate Press Assn.; adj. assoc., prof. communications U. Colo.-Colorado Springs, 1981-83. Decorated Air Force Commendation medal, Meritorious Service medal. Harold B. Fellows Meml. scholar, Nat. Assn. Broadcasters, 1968-70. Mem. Soc. Profl. Journalists and Broadcasters, Sigma Delta Chi, Phi Delta Kappa. Roman Catholic. Clubs: Notre Dame of Colorado Springs (pres. 1982—). Author: (with J.J. Zigerell and T.W. Portre) Television in Community and Junior Colleges; An Overview and Guidelines, 1980; Reflections in the Dome, 1985. Mem. editorial rev. bd. Jour. Broadcasting, 1982—. Contbr. articles to profl. jours. Home: 1044 Selkirk Ln Indianapolis IN 46260 Office: Dept Pub Affairs Def Info Sch Fort Benjamin Harrison IN 46260

ORR, GREGORY JAMES, cable television executive; b. Norton, Va., Sept. 28, 1957; s. James Carrol Orr and Wilma Jean (Hubbard) Carter; m. Martha Melissa Sams, Oct. 2, 1981. B.A.A., U. Tenn., 1979. System mgr. Mountain Cable TV, Wise, Va., 1974-80, Century Communications Corp., Norton, Va., 1980-82, Continental Cablevision, Pekin, Ill., 1982—. Campaign worker Republican Party, Pekin, 1984. Mem. Ill.-Ind. Cable TV Assn. (bd. dirs. 1984—), Downtown Businessman's Assn. Mem. Ch. of God. Lodge: Rotary. Avocations: golf; bowling; softball; travel. Home: 2425 Lakeshore Dr Pekin IL 61554 Office: Continental Cablevision 341 Court St Pekin IL 61554

ORR, JIM TOLFREE, motel owner, operator; b. West Branch, Mich., Mar. 18, 1936; s. Melvin Edward and Joan Geraldine (Tolfree) O.; m. Mary Monica Tetu, July 25, 1964; children—Lynne, Julie, Kim, Robert. B.A., Alma Coll., 1958. Sales rep. Adler Co., Cin., 1960-65; motel owner, operator Tri Terrace Motel, West Branch, Mich., 1965—; dir. 1st of Am. Mid Mich., West Branch, 1982—. Mem. Am. Hotel and Motel Assn., Mich. Lodging Assn., 1982—, West Branch C. of C. Republican. Episcopalian. Club: Optimist. Lodges: Kiwanis (pres. 1969), Masons (25 year pin). Home: PO Box 246 West Branch MI 48661 Office: Tri Terrace Motel 2259 Bus I-75 West Branch MI 48661

ORR, KAY A., Nebraska state treasurer; b. Burlington, Iowa, Jan. 2, 1939; d. Ralph Robert and Sadie Lucille (Skoglund) Stark; m. William Dayton Orr, Sept. 26, 1957; children—John William, Suzanne. Student U. Iowa, 1956-57. Exec. asst. to Gov. Nebr., 1979-81; apptd. treas. State of Nebr., 1981-, elected state treas., 1982—. Co-chmn. Republican Nat. Platform Com., 1984; trustee, mem. pres.'s council Hastings Coll., Nebr., 1985—. Mem. Nat. Assn. State Treas. (v.p. 1984-85), Women Execs. in State Govt. (charter mem. 1984), Nat. Women's Coalition. Office: Room 2003 State Capitol Lincoln NE 68509

ORR, ROBERT DUNKERSON, governor of Indiana; b. Ann Arbor, Mich., Nov. 17, 1917; s. Samuel Lowry and Louise (Dunkerson) O.; B.A., Yale U., 1940; postgrad. Harvard Bus. Sch., 1940-42; hon. degrees Ind. State U., 1973, Hanover Coll., 1974, Butler U., 1977, Vincennes U., 1982, Ind. U., 1985; m. Joanne Wallace, Dec. 16, 1944; children—Robert Dunkerson, Susan Orr Jones, Marjorie R. Orr Hail. Officer, dir. Orr Iron Co., 1946-60, Sign Crafters, Inc., 1957-74, Hahn, Inc., 1957-69, Indian Industries, Inc., 1962-73; mem. Ind. Senate, 1968-72; lt. gov. Ind., 1973-81, gov., 1981—; chmn. Midwest Govs. Conf., 1984-85; dir. Amtrak, Dixson, Inc., Grand Junction, Colo. Leader Fgn. Ops. Adminstrn. evaluation team to Vietnam, 1954; pres. Buffalo Trace council Boy Scouts Am., 1957-58; v.p. Evansville's Future, Inc., 1958-62; chmn. Vanderburgh County Republican Com., 1965-71; alt. del. Rep. Nat. Conv., 1956, 76, del., 1984; trustee Hanover Coll., Willard Library, Evansville YMCA, 1950-70. Served to maj. AUS, 1942-46. Decorated Legion of Merit. Mem. Scroll and Key Soc., Delta Kappa Epsilon. Presbyterian (elder, trustee, deacon). Clubs: Oak Meadow Golf, Meridian Hills, Columbia; Rotary. Office: 206 State House Indianapolis IN 46204

ORRINGER, MARK BUNTON, surgeon; b. Pitts., Apr. 19, 1943; s. Harry B. and Alta M. (Moses) O.; m. Susan Michaels, June 20, 1964; children—Jeffrey Scott, Lisa Jill. B.A. magna cum laude, U. Pitts., 1963, M.D., 1967. Diplomate Am. Bd. Surgery, Am. Bd. Thoracic Surgery. Intern The Johns Hopkins Hosp., Balt., 1967-68, asst. resident in surgery, 1968-72, chief resident in surgery, 1972-73; registrar in Thoracic surgery Frenchay Hosp., Bristol, Eng., 1970; asst. prof. surgery, sect. thoracic surgery, U. Mich., Ann Arbor, 1973-76, assoc. prof., 1976-80, prof., 1980—, head of sect. thoracic surgery, 1985. Contbr. articles to surg. jours. Mem. editorial bd. Jour. Cirugia Espanola, 1983—. Author: (with others) Operative Surgery, 1983; Complications in Surgery and Trauma, 1984; Mastery of Surgery, 1984; Current Surgical Therapy, 1984. Served to capt. M.C., U.S. Army, 1974-76. Invited participant in multiple internat. symposia on esophageal disease, 1979-84; fellow Am. Cancer Soc.; grantee NIH, 1978-83. Fellow Am. Coll. Chest Physicians, ACS; mem. Soc. Thoracic Surgeons, Am. Assn. Thoracic Surgery, Soc. Univ. Surgeons, Central Surg. Assn. Am. Surg. Assn., Phi Beta Kappa, Phi Eta Sigma, Alpha Epsilon Delta, Alpha Omega Alpha, Phi Delta Epsilon. Office: Univ Hosp Section of Thoracic Surgery C-7079 Box 32 Ann Arbor MI 48109

ORSZULAK, RICHARD STEWART, accountant; b. Girard, Kans., Oct. 4, 1957; s. John Andrew and Cleo Nadine (Shaffer) O.; m. Tammy L. Orszulak. B.S. in Bus. Adminstrn., Pittsburg (Kans.) State U. 1979. Acct., Biron, Inc., Chanute, Kans., 1981-82, DFW Petroleum, Inc., Iola, Kans., 1982-83; chief acct., asst. to pres. Hagman Corp., Pittsburg, Kans., 1983-84; acct. Helio Aircraft, Inc., Pittsburg, 1984, controller, 1984—. Missions treas. Girard (Kans.) Bible Ch., 1979, ch. treas., 1980-83. Mem. Am. Econ. Assn., Nat. Assn. Accts., Eastern Kans. Oil and Gas Assn., Fin. Mgmt. Assn., Am. Fin. Assn., Am. Football Coaches Assn., Kans. Farm Bar., Pittsburg State U. Alumni Assn. Republican. Baptist. Home: 1207 S Elm PO Box 1795 Pittsburg KS 66762 Office: PO Box 604 Pittsburg KS 66762

ORT, DONALD RICHARD, biochemist, educator; b. Weymouth, Mass., Feb. 20, 1949; s. Eldon Lloyd and Margaret (Smith) O.; m. Sara Elizabeth Martin, July 17, 1971; children—Heather, Eldon. B.S., Wake Forest U., 1971; Ph.D., Mich. State U., 1974. Postdoctoral Purdue Univ., West LaFayette, Ind., 1974-76, U. Wash., Seattle, 1976-78; asst. prof. biochemistry U. Ill., Urbana, 1978-82, assoc. prof., 1982—; plant biochemist Dept. Agr., Urbana, 1978—. Mem. Biophys. Soc., Am. Soc. Plant Physiology (editorial bd. 1984—). Office: Univ Ill Dept Plant Biology 289 Morrill Hall 505 S Goodwin Ave Urbana IL 61801

ORTH, HARVEY CLINTON, JR., osteopathic physician; b. Lewistown, Pa., Feb. 22, 1926; s. Harvey Clinton and Mary Marjorie (Brindle) O.; m. Dolores Marie Thibault, Dec. 21, 1949; children—Mary Margaret, James Harvey, Mary Patrice, Jeffrey Clinton, Julie Marie. Student, Gettysburg Coll., Pa., 1943-44, U. So. Calif., 1944-45, Coll. Osteopathic Physicians and Surgeons, Los Angeles, 1944-46; D.O., Kirksville Coll. Osteopathy and Surgery, Mo., 1948. Diplomate Am. Osteopathic Bd. Ob-Gyn. Intern Detroit Osteo. Hosp., 1948-49, resident, 1949-51; resident Riverside Osteo. Hosp., Trenton, Mich., 1951-52; practice osteo. medicine specializing in ob-gyn, Trenton, 1953-83; assoc. prof. obstetrics and gynecology Ohio U. Coll. Osteo. Medicine, Athens, 1983—. Fellow Am. Coll. Osteo. Obstetricians and Gynecologists (pres. 1979-80). Republican. Lutheran. Clubs: Grosse Ile Golf and Country (Mich.); Athens Country. Avocations: Reading, golf. Home: 9-204 Monticello Village Athens OH 45701 Office: Ohio U Coll Osteopathic Medicine 328 Grosvenor Hall Athens OH 45701

ORTLOFF, SIG KURT, hotel executive; b. Mengen, Fed. Republic Germany, Dec. 27, 1946, came to U.S. in 1967; s. Siegfried M. and Paula Maria (Froese) O.; m. Debra K. Wood, Jan. 27, 1979; children—Eric, Kevin, Samantha. Student Hotel and Restaurant Sch., Bad Uberkingen, Fed. Republic Germany, 1961-63; cert. gen. mgr., Holiday Inn U., 1980. Exec. chef Hilton Hotels, Denver, 1974-76; food and beverage dir. Sheraton Hotels, Newport Beach, Calif., 1976-79; food and beverage dir. Holiday Inns Inc., Chgo., 1979-80, dist. mgr., St. Louis, 1980-81, gen. mgr., Columbus, Ohio, 1981—. Fellow Columbus Chef's Assn., Am. Culinary Fedn. (cert. exec. chef), Columbus Hotel Assn. (treas. 1983-85, 1st v.p. 1983-84). Club. Skal (treas. 1984-85). Avocations: skiing, World War II aircraft, racquetball. Office: Holiday Inn-Airport Hotel 750 Stelzer-James Rd Columbus OH 43219

ORTMAN, WILLIAM ANDREW, SR., lawyer, business executive; b. Detroit, Mar. 22, 1934; s. Frank J. and Marcella Pauline (Gfell) O.; B.A., Wayne State U., 1958; grad. Bus. Sch. U. Mich., 1960; J.D. (regional outstanding student 1962, scholarship cert. and key, jurisprudence awards), U. Detroit, 1963; m. Lavina Mae Ladson, June 29, 1957; children—William A., Nancy Lee, Merrie Jo, Kristy Ann, Keira Therese. Bar: Mich. 1963, Ohio 1963. Radio sta. mgr., 1953-56; para-legal Law Offices Frank J. Ortman, 1956-60, real estate broker, co-partner, 1956—; indsl. relations analyst FoMoCo, 1960-62; pub. info. specialist Dept. Def., Detroit, 1962-63; sr. atty. Ortman & Ortman, Detroit, 1964—; pres. ORT-FAM Inc., 1984—; co-ptnr. The Ortman Co., 1956—; investment counselor, fin. planner, mgmt. cons.; polit. campaign specialist, 1964—; real-estate, mortgage broker, 1956—; gen. counsel, mktg. mgr. Computers Tandem Assocs., CADO of Southeast Mich., Computer Alliance Corp., 1982-83; cons. pub. relations and advt., 1962—, computer systems, 1982—; lectr. St. Joseph Comml. Coll., 1961-62; del. China-U.S. Sci. Exchange, 1984. Bd. govs., past dean Detroit Metro. Alumni Senate; councilman, Farmington Hills area, 1968-75; nominee Mich. Supreme Ct., 1972. Served with U.S. Army, 1953-56. Mem. ABA, Mich., Oakland bar assns., Delta Theta Phi (dean Hosmer Senate 1961, 62), Alpha Kappa Delta. Clubs: Detroit Athletic, German-Am. Cultural Center, Elks. Contbr., author and editor nat., state and local legal jours. Home: 28010 S Harwich Dr Farmington Hills MI 48018 Office: PO Box 42 Franklin MI 48025

ORTQUIST, RICHARD THEODORE, history educator; b. Muskegon, Mich., Dec. 22, 1933; s. Richard Theodore, Sr. and Beatrice M. (Bushman) O.; married, 1985; children—Leslie Jean, Bruce Richard. A.B., Hope Coll., Holland, Mich., 1956; M.A., U. Mich., 1961, Ph.D., 1968. Tchr. Grandville High Sch. (Mich.), 1956-60; prof. history Wittenberg U., Springfield, Ohio, 1964—, chmn. history dept., 1980—. Author: Depression Politics in Michigan, 1982. Contbr. articles to profl. jours. Mem. Ohio Acad. History, Orgn. Am. Historians, Am. Hist. Assn. Democrat. Lutheran. Avocations: Golf, tennis, reading, music, movies. Home: 366 Northfield Blvd Springfield OH 45503 Office: Wittenberg U Dept History Box 720 Springfield OH 45501

ORTWERTH, JOHN GLENNON, physical education educator; b. St. Louis, Oct. 21, 1931; s. Hubert Conrad and Katherine Ann (Petschel) O.; m. Joanne Jean Schmitz, June 15, 1956; children—Shelly, John, Teresa, Katherine, Mary, Ann. M.S. in Edn., Ill. State U., 1957. Instr. Quincy Coll., Ill., 1957-60, basketball coach, athletic dir., 1960-74, chmn. physical edn. dept. 1974—; commr. Midlands Conf., Ill., Iowa, Wis., 1972-74. Contbr. articles to profl. jours. Pres. Exchange Club of Quincy, 1983-84, Community Youth Orgn., 1978; bd. dirs. Quincy Notre Dame High Sch., 1982—. Served to capt. U.S. Army, 1951-54. Recipient Ill. Coach of Yr. award Nat. Assn. Intercollegiate Athletics, 1963, 66, 67; Hall of Fame award Ill. State Univ. 1973, Hall of Fame award Quincy Coll., 1978. Mem. Quincy Dist. Ofcls. Assn. (pres. 1980—), Nat. Athletic Instrs. Assn. (Huck award 1972), Am. Assn. of Health, Physical Edn., Recreation, and Dance, Ill. Assn. of Health, Physical Edn., Recreation and Dance (bd. dirs.). Avocations: tennis; football, basketball, baseball official. Home: No 7 Springdale Ave Quincy IL 62301

ORWOLL, GREGG S. K., lawyer; b. Austin, Minn., Mar. 23, 1926; s. Gilbert M. and Kleonora (Kleven) O.; B.S., Northwestern U., 1950; J.D., U. Minn., 1953; m. Laverne M. Flentie, Sept. 15, 1951; children—Kimball G., Kent A., Vikki A., Tristen A., Erik G. Bar: Minn. 1953, U.S. Supreme Ct. 1973. Assoc. firm Dorsey, Owen, Marquart, Windhorst and West, Mpls., 1953-59, partner, 1959-60; assoc. counsel Mayo Clinic, Rochester, Minn., 1960-63, gen. counsel, 1963—; gen. counsel, dir. Rochester Airport Co., 1962-84, sec., 1962-81, v.p., 1981-84; gen. counsel Mayo Med. Services, Ltd., 1972—; sec., gen. counsel Mayo Med. Resources, 1984—; asst. sec. Mayo Found., Rochester, 1972-76, 82—, sec., 1976-82; dir. Travelure Motel Corp., 1968—, sec., 1972-83, v.p., 1983—; adj. prof. William Mitchell Coll. Law, St. Paul, 1978—. Trustee Minn. Council on Founds., 1977-82, Mayo Found., 1982—, William Mitchell Coll. Law, 1982—; pres. Rochester Council of Chs., 1968-69; mem. bd. advisors YWCA, Rochester, 1966-72; bd. dirs. Rochester Med. Center Ministry, Inc., 1975-81, Zumbro Luth. Ch., 1962-64, 77-79, pres., 1964-65; bd. dirs. Rochester YMCA, 1966-70; trustee Courage Found., 1974-80, YMCA-YWCA Bldg. Corp., 1966-73. Served with USAAF, 1944-45. Mem. Am. Soc. Hosp. Attys., Minn. Soc. Hosp. Attys. (bd. dirs. 1981—), Minn. State Bar Assn. (chmn. legal med. com. 1977-81), ABA, Olmsted County Bar Assn. (v.p. 1977-78 pres. 1978-79), U. Minn. Law Alumni Assn. (bd. dirs. 1984—), Rochester C. of C., Phi Delta Theta, Phi Delta Phi. Republican. Lutheran. Lecturer. Contbr. articles to legal and medico-legal publs.; bd. editors HealthScan 1984—; editorial bd. Minn. Law Rev., 1952-53. Office: Mayo Clinic 200 1st St SW Rochester MN 55905

ORYSHKEVICH, ROMAN SVIATOSLAV, physician, physiatrist, dentist, educator; b. Olesko, Ukraine, Aug. 5, 1928; s. Simeon and Caroline (Denesz-czuk) O.; came to U.S., 1955, naturalized, 1960; D.D.S., Ruperto-Carola U., Heidelberg, Germany, 1952, M.D., 1953; Ph.D. cum laude, Rupert-Charles U., Heidelberg, 1955; m. Oksana Lishchynsky, June 16, 1962; children—Marta, Mark, Alexandra. Research fellow in cancer Exptl. Cancer Inst., Rupert-Charles U., 1953-55; rotating intern Coney Island Hosp., Bklyn., 1955-56; resident in diagnostic radiology N.Y. U. Bellevue Med. Center and Univ. Hosp., 1956-57; resident, fellow in phys. medicine and rehab. Western Res. U. Highland View Hosp., Cleve., 1958-60, also orthopedic surgery Met. Gen. Hosp., Cleve., 1959; asst. chief rehab. medicine service VA West Side Med. Center, Chgo., 1961-74, acting chief, 1974-75, chief, 1975—; dir. edn. integrated residency tng. program U. Ill. Affliated Hosp., 1974—; clin. instr. U. Ill., 1962-65, asst. clin. prof., 1965-70, asst. prof., 1970-75, asso. clin. prof., 1975—. Founder, pres. Ukrainian World Med. Mus., Chgo., 1977; founder, 1st pres. Am. Mus. Phys. Medicine and Rehab., 1980—. Diplomate Am. Bd. Phys. Medicine and Rehab.; cert. electromyography and electrodiagnosis. Fellow Am. Acad. Phys. Medicine and Rehab., Am. Congress Rehab. Medicine, mem. Assn. Acad. Physiatrists, AAUP, Am. Assn. Electromyography and Electrodiagnosis, Ill. Soc. Phys. Medicine and Rehab. (pres., bd. dirs. 1979-80; Louis B. Newman Disting. Service award; established award in his honor 1980), Ukrainian Med. Assn. N.Am. (bd. dirs., pres. Ill. chpt. 1977-79, fin. mgr. 17th med. conv. and congress, Chgo. 1977, adminstr. and conv. chmn. 1979), World Fedn. Ukrainian Med. Assns. (co-founder 1977, 1st exec. sec. for research and sci. 1977-79), Internat. Rehab. Medicine Assn., Rehab. Internat. U.S.A., Nat. Assn. VA Physicians, AAAS, Assn. Med. Rehab. Dirs. and Coordinators, Nat. Rehab. Assn., Nat. Assn. Disability Examiners, Am. Acad. Manipulative Medicine, Am. Med. Writers Assn., Pan Am. Med. Assn., Biofeedback Research Soc. Am., Chgo. Soc. Phys. Medicine and Rehab. (pres., founder 1978-79), Ill. Rehab. Assn., Ukrainian Acad. Med. Scis. (founder, pres. 1979-80), Gerontol. Soc., Internat. Soc. Electrophysiol. Kinesiology, Internat. Soc. Prosthetics and Orthotics, Fedn. Am. Scientists, Internat. Platform Assn. Ukrainian Catholic. Author and editor: Who and What, 1978. Contbr. articles profl. jours.; splty. cons. in phys. medicine and rehab. to editorial bd. Chgo. Med. Jour., 1978—. Home: 1819 N 78th Ct Elmwood Park IL 60635 Office: 820 S Damen Ave Chicago IL 60612

OSBON, DONALD BRIAN, oral and maxillofacial surgery educator; b. Balt., Mar. 10, 1930; s. John W. and Alice E. (Hahn) O.; m. Joan E. Hart, Sept. 1, 1951; children—James, Janet. B.S., U. Pitts., 1952, D.D.S., 1954. Diplomate Am. Bd. Oral and Maxillofacial Surgery. Commd. 2d lt. Dental Corps, U.S. Army, 1953, advanced through grades to col.; ret., 1973; prof., chmn. div. oral surgery, dir. grad. oral surgery U. Iowa Hosps. and Clinics, 1973-79, prof., head dept. oral surgery, acting chmn. dept. dentistry, 1979-81, chmn. dept. dentistry, 1981—; prof., head dept. oral and maxillofacial surgery U. Iowa, 1981—; cons. Councils Dental Edn., Hosp. Dental Services and Commn. on Accreditation ADA, 1975—. Fellow Internat. Assn. Oral Surgeons, Am. Coll. Dentists, Am. Assn. Oral and Maxillofacial Surgeons, Am. Assn. Hosp. Dentists, Am. Dental Soc. Anesthesiology; mem. U. Pa. Grad. Sch. Medicine Oral Surgery, Assn. Mil. Surgeons U.S., Am. Assn. Dental Schs., Internat. Assn. Dental Research, Iowa Dental Assn., Univ. Dist. Dental Soc., Johnson County Dental Soc., Iowa Soc. Oral and Maxillofacial Surgeons, Midwestern Soc. Oral and Maxillofacial Surgeons, Am. Heart Assn., Iowa Heart Assn., Am. Coll. Sports Medicine. Republican. Methodist. Clubs: Nat. Sr. Sports Assn. (Washington); U. Iowa Athletic. Lodges: Elks, Rotary. Author surg. films; contbr. articles to profl. jours. Home: 4 Longview Knoll Iowa City IA 52240 Office: Dept Hosp Dentistry U Iowa Hosps and Clinics Iowa City IA 55242

OSBORN, GERALD GUY, psychiatrist, educator, consultant; b. Cin., Nov. 6, 1947; s. Guy Henry and Doris Irene (Taylor) O.; m. Sue Ellen Granger, July 9, 1983; children—Erica Tyrell, Eric Gerald. B.A., Wilmington Coll., 1969; student Schiller U., Klein-Ingersheim, Germany, 1968-69; D.O., Kirksville Coll. Osteo. Medicine, 1973; postgrad. in psychiatry U. Sheffield (Eng.), 1973. Diplomate Am. Osteo. Bd. Neurology and Psychiatry (bd. examiners 1982), Am. Bd. Psychiatry and Neurology. Rotating intern Lansing (Mich.) Gen. Hosp., 1973-74; resident, postdoctoral fellow dept. psychiatry Mich. State U., East Lansing, 1974-77, chief resident in psychiatry, 1976-77, instr. in psychiatry, 1974-77, asst. prof., 1977-82, assoc. prof., 1982—, dir. residency tng. osteo. div., 1979-81, assoc. dean for acad. affairs Coll. Osteo. Medicine, 1981—; cons. in field; psychiat. reviewer Mich. Dept. Social Services; chmn. Lansing Area Psychiatry Council, 1983. Med. dir. Catholic Social Services and Family and Child Services of Lansing; active Physicians for Social Responsibility, East Lansing. Recipient Med. Writing award Mich. Osteo. Coll. Found., 1976; teaching awards Mich. State U., 1979, 80, 82, Prof. of Yr. award, 1981; Kettering scholar, 1968. Mem. Am. Osteo. Assn. Mich. Assn. Osteo. Physicians and Surgeons, Ingham County Osteo. Soc., Am. Psychiat. Assn., Mich. Psychiat. Soc., Am. Coll. Neuropsychiatrists (sr.; bd. govs. 1982—), Mich. Osteo. Neuropsychiat. Soc., Osteo. Physicians and Surgeons Calif. (assoc.), Am. Assn. Dirs. Psychiat. Residency Tng., Aircraft Owners and Pilots Assn., U.S. Internat. Sailing Assn., Sigma Sigma Phi. Democrat. Quaker. Contbr. articles to profl. publs. Home: 1313 Basswood Circle East Lansing MI 48823 Office: Mich State U Acad Affairs A-329 E Fee Hall East Lansing MI 48824

OSBORN, KENNETH LOUIS, financial exec.; b. Belleville, Ill., Jan. 9, 1946; s. William Arthur and Louise Mary (Brueggemann) O.; B.B.A., U. N.Mex., 1968; m. Roberta Marie Vodicka, Oct. 23, 1971; 1 son, David Anthony. Auditor, Ernst & Ernst, Albuquerque, 1968; budge mgr. Rockwell Internat., Chgo., 1970-74; mgr. internat. acctg. Allied Van Lines, Chgo., 1974-76; fin. mgr. Sealy, Inc., Chgo., 1976-79; sr. fin. analyst Newark Electronics, Chgo., 1979-80, internat. dir. credit, 1980-82; bus. mgr. Prime Computer, 1982; fin. cons. Sealy, Inc. Served with AUS, 1968-70. Decorated Air medal. Roman Catholic. Office: 500 N Pulaski St Chicago IL 60624

OSBORN, KENT, insurance company executive; b. Stewartsville, Mo., June 10, 1940; s. Maro V. and Cleta M. O.; m. Dorcas Jean Vanderau, Apr. 10, 1960; 1 son, Bradley Craig. Acct., Cameron Mut. Ins. Co. (Mo.), 1958-61, mgr. data processing, 1961-75, acctg. mgr., 1975-77, v.p. acctg., 1977—, asst. treas., 1983—; owner Uptown Cleaners, Cameron, 1968-78. Treas., dir. Cameron Manor Nursing Home Dist., 1972-77; chmn. Cameron Chamber Indsl., 1971—; mem. Cameron Park Bd., 1969, 77; pres. Clinton County (Mo.) Indsl. Authority, 1980; deacon Baptist Ch. Named Cameron Citizen of Yr., Mcpl. League N.W. Mo., 1973. Mem. Cameron Jaycees (treas. 1960, pres. 1961, sec. 1962), Cameron C. of C. (dir.), Data Processing Mgmt. Assn. (Kansas City chpt. dir., v.p. 1976, exec. v.p. 1977, pres., 1978-79; recipient Internat. awards Bronze 1981, Silver 1981, Gold 1982), Ins. and Acctg. Statis. Assn. (v.p. property and liability Midwest chpt. 1977-78, pres. 1980-81). Office: 214 McElwain Dr Cameron MO 64429

OSBORN, ROBERT WILLIAM, fire department executive; b. Terre Haute, Ind., Aug. 16, 1923; s. William Russell and Esther Josephine (Smith) O.; m. Mildred Martha Marcinko, Nov. 16, 1940; children—Robert E., Nancy Jo, Donald P. Student pub. schs., Terre Haute, Ind. Chauffer engr. Terre Haute Fire Dept., 1957-72, mem. bomb disposal squad, 1962-68, chief inspector, 1972-80, fire chief, 1980—. Mem. Nat. Fire Prevention Assn., Ind. Fire Chiefs Assn., Internat. Fire Chiefs Assn. Democrat. Home: 1706 N 10th St Terre Haute IN 47804 Office: Terre Haute Fire Dept 1300 Fort Harrison Rd Terre Haute IN 47805

OSBORN, VERNON EUGENE, dentist; b. Fairbury, Nebr., July 18, 1932; s. Burton Walker and Sophia Creighton (Kirkland) O.; b. Sara Lee Hahn, Jan. 31, 1959; children—John Burton, David Eugene, Thomas Edward. B.A., U. Kans., 1959; D.D.S., U. Mo.-Kansas City, 1963; M.Rehab. Counseling, Emporia U., 1986. Diplomate Am. Nat. Bds. Dentistry. Practice dentistry, Salina, Kans., 1963—; mem. Kans. Golden Belt. dist. Dental Peer Rev. Com., 1971-72, 80-81, chmn., 1983, 84; mem. Kans. Bd. Welfare Dental Rev., 1973-74; chmn. dental staff St. John Hosp., Asbury Hosp., Salina, 1985—. Cubmaster, Cub Scout Pack, Salina, 1973-74; mem. United Sch. Dist. 305 Bd. Edn., Salina, 1979-83, pres., 1982-83; chmn. Kans. Large Dist. Edn. Forum, 1982-83, Episcopal Diocese Western Kans. Cursillo Movement, 1982-83, 84. Served with USMC, 1951-55. Recipient Nat. St. Francis Disting. Service to Youth award St. Francis Boys' Homes, 1971. Fellow Am. Coll. Dentistry, Acad. Gen. Dentistry; mem. Am. Soc. Dentistry for Children (pres. Kans. 1975-76, nat. v.p. 1975-80, chmn. profl. relations com. 1977-78, chmn. pub. relations com. 1978-80), ADA, Kans. Dental Soc., Salina Dental Soc. (pres. 1969-70, 74-75). Democrat. Lodges: Kiwanis (pres. Salina 1970), Masons, Shriners. Avocations: skiing; scuba diving; marathon swimming; hunting, motorcycling. Home: 2113 Northwood Ln Salina KS 67401 Office: 643 S Ohio St Salina KS 67401

OSBORNE, ARTHUR ELLSWORTH, JR., retail executive; b. Chgo., May 21, 1920; s. Arthur Ellsworth and Esther Irene (Harrison) O.; student, Grinnell (Iowa), 1942; m. Barbara Jane Rupp, May 21, 1943; children—Arthur Ellsworth, Richard Harrison, David Charles. Asst. to dir. personnel Marshall Field & Co., 1945-46, group mgr. fine jewelry, 1947-65, v.p. women's apparel, 1966-71, v.p., gen. mgr., 1972-75, sr. v.p., 1975-79, dir., 1976-81, pres. Chgo. div., 1977-79, corp. exec. v.p., 1979-85; dir. Winona Knitting Mills, Winona Sports Wear, Inc. Chmn. Chgo. crusade Am. Cancer Soc., 1975, vice chmn. Chgo. chpt., 1976-79, chmn., 1979-81; chmn. State St. Council 1972-77; bd. dirs. Evanston Hosp., 1974-82, Chgo. Hist. Soc., 1976-85, Chgo. Boys Clubs, 1978—, Chgo. Crime Commn., 1979—, Chgo. Conv. Tourism Bur. Served to capt. USAAF, 1942-45. Decorated D.F.C., Purple Heart, Air medal, Presdl. Citation. Mem. Nat. Retail Mchts. Assn. (exec. com. 1973), Chgo. Assn. Commerce and Industry (dir. 1979—). Episcopalian (vestry). Clubs: Chicago, Glen View, Mid-America, Carlton; Country of Fla., Ocean. Home: 1531 Palmgren Dr Glenview IL 60025 also 2075 S Ocean Blvd Del Ray Beach FL 33444 Office: 124 N Wabash Ave Chicago IL 60602

OSBORNE, OWEN DALE, electrical engineering educator; b. Versailles, Mo., May 9, 1943; s. William M. and Hazel R. (Owens) O.; m. Judith L. Holt, Oct. 13, 1961; children—Cathy L., Jennifer T. B.S., U. Mo., 1966; M.S., Okla. State U., 1967, Ph.D., 1972. From asst. to assoc. prof. elec. engring. Oreg. State U., 1971-82; assoc. prof. elec. engring. Iowa State U., Ames, 1982—, dir. engring. extension service, 1982—; cons. Nat. Environ. cons., Corvallis, Oreg., 1975—. Contbr. articles to profl. jours. NDEA fellow, 1966. Mem. Am. Soc. Engring. Edn., IEEE, Nat. Univ. Extension Assn., Am. Soc. Tng. and Devel., Iowa Assn. Lifelong Learning. Democrat. Office: Engring Extension Service Harber Rd Ames IA 50011

O'SHEA, PATRICK ANTHONY, natural gas researcher; b. Chicago, Sept. 27, 1947; s. John Joseph and Margaret Anne (Haugh) O'S.; m. Margaret Anne Flynn, Dec. 23, 1972 (div. Aug. 1984); 1 child, Patrick Joseph. B.S. in Geology summa cum laude, No. Ill. U., 1977, M.S. in Math., 1979. Golf profl., Chgo., 1970-75; exploration systems analyst Amoco Prodn. Co., Houston, 1978-80, petroleum geologist, Chgo., 1981; natural gas research mgr. Gas Research Inst., Chgo., 1981—. Contbr. articles to profl. jours. Editor in Focus - Tight Gas Sands, 1984—. Served with U.S. Army, 1966-68; Vietnam. Chevron Oil Co. grantee No. Ill. U., 1977. Mem. Am. Assn. Petroleum Geologists, Soc. Petroleum Engrs., Soc. Exploration Geophysicists. Republican. Roman Catholic. Avocations: golf, swimming, reading. Office: Gas Research Inst 8600 W Bryn Mawr Ave Chicago IL 60631

OSHER, FRANCIS MARIO, osteopathic physician, surgeon; b. Bklyn., June 27, 1937; s. Harry S. and Christina Maria (Porcaro) O.; m. Betty Lou Percy, Nov. 26, 1965; children—April Elizabeth, Michael David. B.S., St. John's U., 1959; D.O., Kirksville Coll. Osteopathic Medicine, 1964. Intern, Flint Gen. Hosp., Mich., 1964-65; resident Garden City Hosp., Mich., 1965-66; family practice osteo. medicine, Mount Morris, Mich., 1966—; health officer Thetford Twp., Genesee County, Mich., 1966—; dept. coroner Saginaw County Health Dept., Mich., 1970-81; wing med. officer CAP, Grosse Isle, Mich., 1972-77; med. examiner FAA, 1975-81. Served to maj. USAF, 1976-81. Mem. Am. Osteopathic Assn., Mich. Assn. Osteo. Physicians, Genesee County Osteo. Assn. Republican. Roman Catholic. Club: Order Scottish Clans. Lodge: Kiwanis. Avocations: amateur rodeo; flying; playing bagpipes; gunsmithing; fencing. Home: 4177 E Lake Rd Clio MI 48420 Office: 728 Genesse St Mount Morris MI 48458

OSINSKE, MARILOU ANNE, university administrator, counselor educator; b. Chgo., Apr. 18, 1931; d. Matthew and Lillian Ella (Ray) O. A.B., U. Ill., 1953; A.M., Ind. U., 1956; postgrad., U. Wis., 1955-56, U. Mich., 1965-66. Asst. dean of women U. Cin., 1958-72, assoc. dean student devel., 1972-78, dir. ednl. advising, adj. prof. edn., 1978—, budget chmn. Univ. Senate, 1974-75. Chmn. Pres'. Council on Women, Cin., 1984—. Mem. AAUW (corp. rep. 1984—), Am. Coll. Personnel Assn. (dir. 1983—, recipient service merit 1983), Nat. Assn. of Student Personnel Adminstrs., Nat. Assn. Women Deans, Adminstrs. and Counselors (placement chmn. 1975-76). Episcopalian. Club: Women's City (Cin.). Office: U Cin ML 90 Cincinnati OH 45221

OSKIN, ERNEST THOMAS, chemical engineer, plastics company executive; b. Chgo., Dec. 29, 1927; s. Benedict Cornelias and Mary Theresa (Kozlowski) O.; m. Barbara Ann Cremers, Mar. 21, 1958; children—John Bennett, Mary Catherine. B.Chem. Engring., U. Fla., 1949; M.Engring., Princeton U., 1956. Chem. engr. Mathieson Chem., Lake Charles, La., 1949-50; plastics engr. B.F. Goodrich, Marietta, Ohio, 1952-54; sales engr. DuPont Co., Wilmington, Del. and Detroit, 1956-63; pres., dir. Huron Plastics Inc., St. Clair, Mich., 1963—; dir. Croswell Plastics (Mich.), Scottsburg Plastics (Ind.), Huron Products Corp., Omega Plastics, Mt. Clemens, Mich., QCP, Inc., St. Clair D&A Industries, Croswell, Mich. Served with U.S. Army, 1954-56. Mem. Soc. Plastics Engrs., Soc. Automotive Engrs., Soc. of Plastic Industry. Clubs: St. Clair Golf St. Clair Investment, Otsikita Yacht. Lodge: Rotary (pres. St. Clair chpt. 1976-77). Author: Stress Relaxation and Dynamic Properties of Ethylene Polymers, 1956; contbr. tech. articles to profl. publs. Home: 982 N Riverside Dr Saint Clair MI 48079 Office: PO Box 195 Saint Clair MI 48079

OSSOFF, ROBERT HENRY, head and neck surgeon; b. Beverly, Mass., Mar. 25, 1947; s. Michael Max and Eve Joan (Kladky) O.; B.A., Bowdoin Coll., 1969; D.M.D., Tufts Dental Sch., 1973; M.D., Tufts Med. Sch., 1975; m. Lynn Spilman, 1984; 1 son by previous marriage, Jacob. Intern, Northwestern Meml. Hosp., Chgo., 1975-76; resident in otolaryngology Northwestern Med. Sch., Chgo., 1976-80, NIH Research fellow dept. otolaryngology, 1977-78, Am. Cancer Soc. clin. fellow, 1980-81, jr. faculty clin. fellow, 1981-84; practice medicine specializing in head and neck surgery and laryngology, Chgo., 1975—; mem. staff Children's Meml. Hosp., Chgo., 1980-81; chmn. div. otolaryngology Evanston (Ill.) Hosp., 1983; chief div. otolaryngology VA Lakeside Hosp., Chgo., 1982—; asst. prof. Northwestern Dental Sch., 1980—, asst. prof. Northwestern Med. Sch., 1980-85, assoc. prof., 1985—. Trustee, Ill. Biolaser Inst., Chgo., 1981—, Midwest Biolaser Inst., bd. dirs., Laser Inst. Am., 1984. Recipient Lederer-Pierce award, Chgo. Laryngol. Soc., 1978. Fellow ACS; mem. AMA, Am. Acad. Oral Medicine, Am. Council Otolaryngology, Am.

Acad. Oral Pathology, Am. Acad. Otolaryngology-Head and Neck Surgery (chmn. laser surgery com. 1983—), Am. Soc. Laser Medicine and Surgery (bd. dirs. 1985—), Soc. Head and Neck Surgeons, Am. Soc. Head and Neck Surgery Am. Broncho-esophagological Assn., Soc. Ear, Nose and Throat Advances in Children. Jewish. Mem. editorial rev. bd. Otolaryngology-Head and Neck Surgery. Contbr. chpts. to books, articles to profl. jours. Office: 2500 Ridge Ave Suite 302 Evanston IL 60201 also 303 E Chicago Ave Chicago IL 60611

OSTENSO, BRIAN TANG, electronics company executive; b. Baraboo, Wis., July 6, 1951; s. Richard S. and Victoria (Akit) O.; m. Jane McGlynn, Nov. 2, 1974; children—Anna, Lauren. B.B.A., U. Wis.-Eau Claire, 1974; M.B.A., Coll. St. Thomas, 1978. Mgr. internat. banking Medtronic Inc., Mpls., 1975-78; controller Northwest Microfilm Inc., Mpls., 1978-80; v.p. fin. Kalvar Corp., Mpls., 1980-82, pres., chief exec. officer, 1982—; dir. Slyvan Learning Ctrs., Inc., Edina, Minn., Bus. Planners Inc., Mpls.; lectr. Coll. St. Thomas, St. Paul, 1980—. Boy Scout master Chippewa Valley council, Eau Claire, 1972; coach little league, Eau Claire, 1973; advisor Jr. Achievement, Mpls., 1977. Home: 5420 3d Ave S Minneapolis MN 55419 Office: Kalvar Corp 15 S 9th St Minneapolis MN 55402

OSTER, ALLEN BURTON, dentist; b. Cleve., June 30, 1934; s. Robert Hyman and Lillian G. (Ginsburg) O.; m. Rosalyn B. Waxman, June 17, 1956 (div. Sept. 1974); children—Michael, Karen; m. Jane Elizabeth Dunlap, Aug. 10, 1975; 1 child, Robert. B.Sc., Ohio State U., 1956, D.D.S., 1961. Gen. practice dentistry, Cleve., 1961-74; assoc. Schermer & Assocs., Cleve., 1974-82; pres. Convenient Dental Convenient Mgmt., Cleve., 1982—. Mem. ADA, Ohio State Dental Soc., Cleve. Dental Soc., Am. Acad. Group Practice. Jewish. Lodge: K.P. (pres. 1976). Home: 4583 McFarland Rd South Euclid OH 44121 Office: Convenient Mgmt Service Inc 1496 Green Rd South Euclid OH 44121

OSTER, CLAUDE, osteopathic physician; b. Paris, July 9, 1936; s. Isidore and Jolana (Kreisman) Osztreicher; came to U.S., 1952; m. Terry Baren, July 3, 1958; children—Lisa, Allan, Scott. Student Wayne State U., 1954-58; D.O., Coll. Osteo. Medicine and Surgery, Des Moines, 1962. Cert. Am. Osteo. Bd. Rehab. Medicine. Intern, Detroit Osteo. Hosp., 1962-63; preceptorship in phys. medicine and rehab. Garden City (Mich.) Osteo. Hosp., 1968-71; practice osteo. medicine specializing in rehab. medicine, Detroit, 1971—; co-dir. Muscular Dystrophy Assn. Detroit Met. Clinic, 1970-77; exec. dir. Southfield (Mich.) Rehab. Ctr., 1981—; mem. staff Detroit Osteo. Hosp., Bi-County Hosp., Garden City Hosp.; prof. Mich. State U. Coll. Osteo. Medicine; mem. med. adv. com. Mutiple Sclerosis Assn. State of Mich.; mem. Workers Compensation Health Care Cost Containment Adv. Com.; Oakland County Dep. Med. Examiner; program chmn. Mich. State U. Pain Seminars, 1979-83; cons. in field. Mem. Acad. Applied Osteopathy, Am. Heart Assn. (stroke council), Am. Geriatrics Soc., Am. Osteo. Assn., Am. Osteo. Coll. Rehab. (trustee), Congress Rehab. Medicine, Am. Osteo. Coll. Rheumatology, Internat. Rehab. Medicine Assn., Internat. Assn. for Study of Pain, Am. Soc. for Study of Pain, Midwest Soc. for Study of Pain, Internat. Assn. Rehab. Facilities, Internat. Congress of Gerontology, Mich. Assn. Osteo. Physicians and Surgeons, Oakland County Assn. Osteo. Physicians and Surgeons, N.Am. Acad. Manipulative Medicine. Contbr. articles to profl. jours. Office: Southfield Rehab Ctr 22401 Foster Winter Dr Southfield MI 48075

OSTER, SUSAN MARY, educational association administrator; b. Des Moines, Oct. 2, 1953; d. Lewis H. and Mary L. (Mills) O. B.A., Purdue U., 1975; M.A., U. Iowa, 1980. Cert. counselor, 1983. Tchr., Palm Beach County Schs., West Palm Beach, Fla., 1975-77; dir. placement, instr. Coll. Lake County, Grayslake, Ill., 1980-83; central zone field services coordinator Coll. Placement Council, Inc., Bethlehem, Pa., 1983—; Bd. dirs. Connections crisis line, Libertyville, Ill., 1981-82; sec. St. Gilbert Ch. Parish Council, Grayslake, Ill. Mem. Women in Mgmt. (Woman of Achievement in Edn. award Lake Suburban chpt. 1984), Midwest Coll. Placement Assn. (chmn. 1982-83), Am. Assn. Counseling and Devel., Am. Coll. Personnel Assn., Am. Soc. Personnel Adminstrs. Club: Toastmasters (1st place award N. div. 1983). Roman Catholic. Avocations: travel; needlework; tennis; swimming; bridge. Office: Coll Placement Council PO Box 767 Grayslake IL 60030

OSTERBUHR, MICHAEL DENNIS, college administrator; b. Minden, Nebr., July 19, 1952; s. Dennis Thomas and Catherine Ann (Filbin) O.; m. Carol Lynne Frost, June 20, 1974 (div. Oct. 1975); m. Mary Monica Silver, Aug. 19, 1978. B.S. in Music Edn., Kearney State Coll., 1974; M.A. in Counseling Psychology, U. Nebr., 1983. Cert. tchr., Nebr. Tchr. music Ansley Pub. Schs., Nebr., 1975-77; dist. agt. Prudential Ins. Co., Lincoln, Nebr., 1978-80; craftsman Snyder Industries, Lincoln, 1980-82; tchr. music Rokeby Sch., Nebr., 1982-83; resident dir. U. Kans., Lawrence, 1983—, mem. staff selection com., 1983—, mem. leadership devel. com. 1983—. Contbr. to So. Poverty Law Ctr., Montgomery, Ala., 1976. Recipient Intern award Housing Office, U. Nebr., Lincoln, 1983. Mem. Am. Assn. Counseling and Devel., Am. Coll. and Univ. Housing Officers Internat. (research and info. com. 1984—), Kans. Personnel and Guidance Assn., Kans. Assn. for Counseling and Devel., Phi Mu Alpha Sinfonia. Democrat. Roman Catholic. Avocations: photography, downhill skiing, collecting cameras, singing. Home: 1515 Engel Rd Lawrence KS 66045

OSTERLE, DALE PERANER, artist; b. Boston, May 17, 1939; d. Charles and Ida (Walkenstein) Peraner; m. Heinz Dieter Osterle, Jan. 11, 1960; children—Eric, Bruce, Karen. B.F.A., R.I. Sch. Design, 1960; postgrad. art edn. So. Conn. State Coll., 1972. Free-lance fashion illustrator, designer, Washington, N.Y. and Conn., 1960-72; staff illustrator, Yale U., New Haven, Conn., 1969-72, etchings exhibited in galleries in N.Y.C., Chgo., Atlanta and Appleton, Wis. Mem. student adv. bd. Mus. Contemporary Art, Chgo., 1980—. Winner purchase prizes, DuPage County Library System, Geneva, Ill., Bradley Nat. Print Show, Peoria, Ill., 1981. Mem. LWV, Artists Guild Chgo., Chgo. Artists Coalition. Democrat. Jewish.

OSTERMEIER, TERRY HARLAN, communications educator; b. New London, Wis., Apr. 15, 1937; s. George Aubert and Virginia Ruth (Dexter) O.; m. Arlene Louise Bjorngaard, May 19, 1964; children—Marc Alan, Eric Jon. B.S., Wis. State U.-Oshkosh, 1959; M.A., Marquette U., 1961; Ph.D., Mich. State U., 1967. From instr. to asst. prof. SUNY, Buffalo, 1963-67; from assoc. prof. communications to prof. U. Wis., Whitewater, 1967—, dept. chmn. 1968—. Contbr. articles to profl. jours. Mem. Internat. Communication Assn., Speech Communication Assn., Internat. Listening Assn., Soc. Intercultural Edn., Tng. and Research, Assn. Communication Adminstrs., Pi Kappa Delta, Roman Catholic. Clubs: 4-H (Whitewater), Founders & Patriots (U. Wis.) (councillor 1984—). Avocations: antique radios, genealogy, hunting, gardening, traveling. Home: Route 1 Box 137 Whitewater WI 53190 Office: Dept Communication U Wisc-Whitewater Main Street Whitewater WI 53190

OSTLING, LAURENCE WILLIAM, employee benefit design company executive; b. Los Angeles, Mar. 9, 1923; s. Laurence William and Beatrice Mary (McIntyre) O.; m. Constance Annette Pruitt, Sept. 7, 1946; children—Kathy Anne, Laurence Donald, Thomas Michael, Linda Marie, James William. Student, Cornell U., 1941-43; B.S.B.A., Northwestern U., 1948, M.B.A., 1954. CLU, Am. Coll. Life Underwriters; MSPA, Am. Soc. Pension Actuaries. Regional group mgr. State Mut. Am., Chgo., 1955-73, regional sales v.p., 1973-81; exec. v.p., dir. Midwest Benefits Corp., Mt. Prospect, Ill., 1981—; lectr. sales mgmt. Harper Coll.; dir. FRLM, Inc., Southfield, Mich. Chmn., Mt. Prospect Police and Fire Commn., 1968-73. Served with AUS, 1943-46. Decorated Bronze battle stars. Mem. Am. Coll. Life Underwriters, Am. Soc. Pension Actuaries, Soc. Profl. Benefit Adminstrs., Sigma Chi, Beta Gamma Sigma, Delta Mu Delta. Republican. Roman Catholic. Club: Mt. Prospect Golf. Office: 800 W Central Rd Suite 103 Mount Prospect IL 60056

OSTREM, WALTER MARTIN, librarian, educator, consultant; b. Mpls., May 27, 1930; s. Oscar Martin and Helen Therese (Marcio) O.; m. Gertrud Franciska Tunkel, Aug. 6, 1956; children—Thomas, Paul, Francine. B.A., U. Minn., 1953, M.A., 1958; B.S., Mankato State U., 1962, M.S., 1964; postgrad. U. Mich., U. Iowa. Serials librarian Agr. Library U. Minn., 1958-59; acquisitions librarian Mankato State U., Minn., 1959-66, Eastern Mich. U., 1966-67; dir. media Iowa City Sch., 1967-69; librarian John F. Kennedy Sch., Berlin, W.Ger., 1969-73; dist. profl. librarian St. Paul Schs., 1973—; cons. in field. Served to 1st lt. U.S. Army, 1954-55. Recipient Ency. Brit. 1st place Sch. Library Media System award, 1969. Mem. Minn. Ednl. Media Orgn., Am. Fedn. Tchrs., M Club, Phi Delta Kappa. Contbr. articles in field. Home: 5536 Harriet Ave S Minneapolis MN 55419 Office: 360 Colborne St Saint Paul MN 55102

OSTROFSKY, BERNARD, nondestructive testing consultant; b. N.Y.C., Jan. 14, 1922; s. Charles and Anna (Klinman) O.; m. Florence Menov, July 4, 1945: children—Charles, Ellen. B.S., City Coll. N.Y., 1945; grad. Polytechnic Inst. Bklyn., 1945-49. Phys. chemist Manhattan Project Columbia U., N.Y.C., 1942-45; sr. physicist. Nat. Lead Co., Bklyn., 1945-1954; sr. research assoc. Standard Oil Co., Naperville, Ill., 1954-81; owner Bernard Ostrofsky Assoc. Inc., 1981—. Assoc. tech. editor Materials Evaluation, 1972—. Contbr. articles to profl. jours. Patentee in field. Bd. dirs. Community Radio Watch, Naperville, Recipient John C. Vaalor award Chem. Engring., 1968. Fellow Am. Soc. for Non-Destructive Testing (cert.); mem. Am. Chem. Soc. (emeritus), Am. Crystallographic Assn., Microbeam Analysis Soc., ASTM. Club: Am. Radio Relay League (Newington, Conn.). Lodge: Moose. Avocations: amateur radio, music, photography, computers. Office: Bernard Ostrofsky Assoc Inc PO Box C Naperville IL 60566

OSTROY, SANFORD EUGENE, biological sciences and biochemistry educator; b. Scranton, Pa., Dec. 28, 1939; s. Alexander and Ida (Kitoff) O.; m. Zipora Pomerantz, June 17, 1962; children—Allen and Paul. B.S., U. Scranton, 1961; postgrad. U. Mich., 1961-63; Ph.D., Case-Western Reserve, 1966. postdoctoral fellow Cornell U., 1966-68; asst. prof. biol. scis. and biochemistry Purdue U., W. Lafayette, Ind., 1968-73, assoc. prof. biol. scis. and biochemistry, 1973-80, prof. biol. scis. and biochemistry, 1980—; adj. asst. prof. physiology Ind. Univ. Sch. of Medicine, Indpls., 1972-81; hon. research assoc. in biology Harvard Univ., Cambridge, Mass., 1974-75; adj. prof. biology Brandeis Univ., Waltham, Mass., 1983-84. Editor: Molecular Processes in Vision, 1981. Contbr. articles to profl. jours. NIH grantee, 1971-76; recipient numerous grants for vision research, 1968—. Mem. Am. Chem. Soc., Am. Fedn. Biol. Chemists, Assn. for Research in Vision and Ophthalmology, Biophys. Soc., Soc. for Neurosci. Home: 226 E Sunset Ln West Lafayette IN 47906 Office: Dept Biol Scis Purdue Univ West Lafayette IN 47907

OSWALD, JAMES OLIVER, univ. adminstr.; b. Millersburg, Ohio, June 1, 1944; s. John A. and Ida (Lenhart) O.; B.A., Cedarville Coll., 1967; B.S., Central State U., 1967; M.A., U. Akron, 1980; m. Ruth Ann Mast, Nov. 23, 1962; children—Todd Anthony, Lori Anne. Tchr. coll. English and journalism, coach West Holmes High Sch., Millersburg, 1967-68; editor employee communications Rubbermaid, Inc., Wooster, Ohio, 1968-79; mgr. internat. communications United Telephone Co. Ohio, Mansfield, 1969-71; dir. dept. univ. publs. U. Akron, Ohio, 1971—. Mem. NEA, Internat. Assn. Bus. Communicators, AAUP, Am. Assn. Higher Edn., Ohio Edn. Assn., Univ. and Coll. Designers Assn., Council Advancement and Support of Edn., Pub. Relations Soc. Am. Republican. Mennonite. Clubs: Akron Press. Home: 306 Washington Blvd Orrville OH 44667 Office: University of Akron 225 S Forge St Akron OH 44325

OSWEILER, TIMOTHY JAMES, researcher; b. Marshalltown, Iowa, June 7, 1950; s. Cletus Howard and Donna Margaret (Calvin) O. B.S., U. Iowa, 1972, B.S. in Geology, 1983. Research asst. U. Iowa Hosp., Iowa City, 1974—. Served with U.S. Army, 1972-74. Mem. Am. Assn. Petroleum Geologists, Sigma Gamma Epsilon. Avocations: weightlifting, martial arts, fishing, bicycling, backpacking, photography. Office: Dept Pediatrics Room 219 ML U Hosp Iowa City IA 52242

OSWICK, LAWRENCE HENRY, dentist; b. Cleve., Feb. 22, 1947; s. Henry Paul and Evelyn (Goliat) O.; m. Barbara Reminger, Apr. 8, 1972; children—Amy C., L. Pierce, Erica L. B.A., Colgate U., 1969; D.D.S., Case Western Res. U., 1973. Gen. practice dentistry, Chagrin Falls, Ohio, 1975—; successively sec., treas., v.p., pres. Heights Dental Study, Cleve., 1975—; sec., treas. Cleve. Acad. Advanced Dental Edn., 1980—. Pres. Aurorafest, Aurora, Ohio, 1980. Served to lt. USN, 1973-75. Mem. Cleve. Dental Soc., Ohio Dental Assn., ADA, Acad. Gen. Dentistry, Psi Omega. Republican. Roman Catholic. Lodge: Kiwanis (Kiwanian of Yr. 1979-81). Avocations: skiing, sailing, swimming, snorkeling. Office: 8505 Tanglewood Square Chagrin Falls OH 44022

OTHMAN, TALAT MOHAMAD, financial consultant, investment banker; b. Betunia, Palestine, Apr. 27, 1936; came to U.S., 1947, naturalized, 1954; s. Mohamad Racheed and Damelizz (Ahmed) O.; m. Isabelle Irene Ross, Nov. 1957; children—Joseph, Suad, Jamil, Rashid. Student Northwestern U. With Harris Bank, Chgo., 1956-78, v.p., div. head, 1974-78; gen. mgr., chief exec. officer Al Saudi Bank Holdings, N.V., Paris, 1978-83; pres. Dearborn Financial, Inc., Chgo., 1983—; dir. Marine Corp., Milw. Contbr. chpts. to Technique of Foreign Exchange Trading, 1975; also articles and booklets. Fund raiser Republican candidates, Chgo., 1984; bd. dirs. United Holy Land Fund, Chgo., 1983—. Mem. Arab Bankers Assn. (pres. 1985—), Mid Am. Arab C. of C. (bd. dirs. 1974-78, 84—, founding pres. 1977), Forex Assn. N.Am. (founding pres. 1977). Moslem. Clubs: Chicago, Attic (Chgo.). Avocations: tennis, racquetball. Office: Dearborn Financial Inc 33 N Dearborn St Chicago IL 60602

OTHMER, EKKEHARD, psychiatrist, researcher, educator; b. Koenigsberg, Germany, Oct. 15, 1933; came to U.S. 1967; s. Hermann Philipp and Ella Elisabeth (Horn) O.; m. Sieglinde Charlotte Gierth, Apr. 10, 1964: children—Konstantin, Johann Philipp, Julia Christie. M.S. in Psychology, U. Hamburg, W. Ger., 1960, Ph.D. in Psychology, 1965, M.D., 1966. Diplomate Am. Bd. Psychiatry and Neurology. Research assoc. dept. medicine U. Hamburg, 1961-66; surg. intern Waldklinik Oerrel, W. Ger., 1967; asst. prof. psychology, dir. sleep lab., asst. prof. exptl. psychology Washington U., St. Louis, 1968-74; resident in psychiatry Washington U. M.S. Renard Hosp., St. Louis, 1971-74; assoc. prof. psychiatry U. Ky., Lexington, 1974-77; prof. psychiatry U. Kans., Kansas City, 1977—, dir. outpatient psychiatry clinic, 1977—. Author psychiat. test: The Psychiatric Diagnostic Interview, 1981; also numerous articles, chpts. Assoc. editor Jour. Clin. Psychiatry, 1980—. Reviewer Am. Jour. Psychiatry. Recipient Research award Stiftung Die Welt, Hamburg, 1958; Studienstiftung des Deutschen Volkes scholar, 1959-66. Fellow Am. Psychiat. Assn.; mem. AMA (Physician Recognition awards 1976—), Soc. Neurosci., Soc. Biol. Psychiatry, Psychiat. Research Soc. Lutheran. Avocations: skiing; scuba diving; sailboarding; bridge. Office: U Kans Med Ctr 39th St and Rainbow Kansas City KS 66103

OTIS, CAROL ANN, guidance counselor, educator; b. Poughkeepsie, N.Y., June 5, 1950; d. David William and Katherine L. (Van Tassel) Corwin; m. Dana Fredrick Otis, Feb. 27, 1970; children—Jackie Otis, Jaimee. Student William Woods Coll., Fulton, Mo., 1968-69; B.S., W.Va. Wesleyan Coll., Buckhannon, 1972; M.S., Dayton U., 1975, now postgrad. Cert. tchr., counselor, prin., Ohio. Tchr. phys. edn. Edison Local Schs., Hammondsville, Ohio, 1972-80, tchr. health, 1972-80, dir. girls athletics, 1975-80, guidance counselor, 1975—; counselor Camp Laurel, Maine, 1965-68. Dir. Town Recreation, New Paltz, N.Y., 1968-69; instr. swimming and first aid ARC, Steubenville, Ohio, 1972-85; advisor 4-H, Wintersville, Ohio, 1980-85; tchr. sunday Sch. United Methodist Ch., Wintersville, 1980-84. Mem. Ohio Edn. Assn., Ohio Guidance Counselors Assn., Assn. for the Gifted Children (Corresponding sec. 1983-84), Ohio Assn. Gifted Children, Delta Kappa Gamma.

OTLEWSKI, J(AMES) DOUGLAS, lawyer; b. Detroit, Mar. 1, 1953; s. James Wilbert and Patricia Jean (Morris) O.; m. Patricia Jean Watson, Oct. 23, 1982. B. Gen. Studies, U. Mich., 1975; J.D., U. Detroit, 1978. Bar: Mich. 1978. Law clk. Oakland County Probate Ct., Pontiac, Mich., 1978-79; ptnr. Simon & Otlewski, Detroit, 1979-80, Wick, Minnet & Otlewski, Rochester, Mich., 1980; mem., pres. Otlewski & Morrow, P.C., Rochester, 1980—. Mem. Oakland County Council for Children at Risk, Mich., 1981—; chmn. membership Rochester Area Youth Guidance, 1982—; big brother vol. Rochester Plus Program, 1982—; active Children's Charter of Mich., Lansing, 1983—. Recipient cert. of appreciation Oakland County Probate Ct., 1981, 82, 83, 84. Mem. Oakland County Bar Assn. (chmn. mental health com. 1982-83, seminar speaker, cert. appreciation 1981, Book award 1983), Mich. Bar Assn. (negligence law com. 1979—), Mich. Trial Lawyers Assn., Assn. Trial Lawyers Am. Office: Otlewski & Morrow PC 118 Walnut Suite B Rochester MI 48063

O'TOOLE, ROBERT FRANCIS, Biblical studies educator, Jesuit priest; b. St. Louis, June 20, 1936; s. William Francis and Anastasia (Earner) O'T. A.B., St. Louis U., 1960, M.A. and Ph.L., 1961, S.T.L., 1968; S.S.L., S.S.D., Pontifical Biblical Inst., 1970, 1975. Tchr., prefect of discipline St. John's Coll., Belize, Central Am., 1961-64; tchr. Regina Mundi, Rome, 1972-74; instr. to assoc. prof. St. Louis U., 1973-84, chairperson theol. studies, 1982—, prof., 1984—; trustee Rockhurst Coll., Kansas City, Mo., 1983—. Author; Acts 26: The Christological Climax of Paul's Defense, 1978; The Unity of Luke's Theology: An Analysis of Luke-Acts, 1984, also articles. Mem. Soc. Biblical Lit., Catholic Bibl. Assn., Inst. Theol. Encounter with Sci. and Tech., Am. Acad. Religion, Studiorum Novi Testamenti Societas. Avocations: hiking, swimming, gardening. Home: Bellarmine House of Studies 3700 W Pine Blvd Saint Louis MO 63108 Office: Chmn Dept Theological Studies St Louis Univ 3634 Lindell Blvd Saint Louis MO 63108

OTTE, CARL, state senator; b. Sheboygan, Wis., June 24, 1923; s. John and Magdalena (Verconteren) O.; m. Ethel Dorothy Braatz, Nov. 1, 1949; children—Allen Carl, Jane Karen, Julie Beth, Lynn Carol. Mem. Wis. State Assembly, 1967-82; mem. Wis. Senate from 9th Dist., 1983—. Mem. Sheboygan County Bd. Suprs., 1962-68; mem. Democratic Party of Wis.; mem. VFW. Served with U.S. Army, 1943-45. Mem. Am. Fedn. Musicians. Lutheran. Lodge: Am. Legion.

OTTE, NANCY ELLEN, optometrist; b. Seymour, Ind., June 10, 1954; d. John W. Otte and Janet C. (Mattox) Sullivan. B.S. in Optometry, Ind. U., 1976, O.D., 1978. Pvt. practice optometry, Jasper, Ind., 1978—. Pres., lay asst. Redeemer Luth. Ch. Council, Jasper, 1984. Mem. Better Vision Inst., Am. Optometric Assn., Ind. Optometric Assn., Ind. S.W. Optometric Soc., Jasper Bus. and Profl. Women. Avocations: camping; fishing; photography. Office: PO Box 726 609 Main St Jasper IN 47546

OTTEN, TERRY RALPH, English educator; b. Dayton, Ky., Apr. 15, 1938; s. Henry Howard and Alyce Lucille (Harris) O.; m. Jane Sharp, Aug. 20, 1960; children—Keith Andrew, Julie Anne. A.B. cum laude, Georgetown Coll., 1959; M.A., U.Ky., 1961; Ph.D., Ohio U., 1966. Instr. Western Ky. State U., Bowling Green, 1961-62, Ohio U., Athens, 1965-66; prof. English, Wittenberg U., Springfield, Ohio, 1966—, also chmn. dept. English; reader Advanced Placement Exam, Princeton, N.J., 1981—; reader, evaluator various jours. and univ. presses, 1975—. Author: The Deserted Stage, 1972; After Innocence, 1982. Contbr. articles to profl. jours., chpts. to books. Grantee Bd. Higher Edn., 1971, NEH, 1974; recipient Disting. Tchr. award Wittenberg U., 1975. Mem. Conf. Christianity and Lit. (midwest steering com. 1984—), MLA, Coll. English Assn., Midwest Modern Lang. Assn. Office: Wittenberg U PO Box 720 Springfield OH 45501

OTT-HANSEN, HENRY, investment corporation executive; b. New Haven, Conn., June 11, 1929; s. Christian Alexander and Florence (Onderdonk) Ott-Hansen; m. Anne Gaylord Buckley, June 16, 1956; 1 child, Sarah Anne Ott-Hansen Hirsch. B.A., Yale U., 1951; M.B.A., Case Western Reserve U., 1963. Vice pres., mgr. Drexel, Harriman, & Ripley, Cleve., 1970-73; v.p. Dean Witter Reynolds, Inc., Cleve., 1973—. Trustee, Diocese of Ohio, Cleve., 1979—; mem. Diocesian Council, Cleve., 1976-78; chmn. dept. fin. Diocese of Ohio, Cleve., 1976-78; sr. warden vestryman St. Paul's Episcopal Ch., Cleve. Heights, Ohio, 1974-78. Served to lt. USNR, 1951-55, Korea. Mem. Cleve. Soc. Security Analysts, Bond Club Cleve. Clubs: Union (Cleve.), Tavern (Cleve.), Kirtland Country (Cleve.). Home: 22275 Parnell Rd Shaker Heights OH 44122 Office: Dean Witter Reynolds Inc Suite 1014 Bond Ct Bldg 1300 E 9th St Cleveland OH 44114

OTTING, FREDERICK PAUL, manufacturing executive; b. Milw., Mar. 4, 1916; s. Fred E. and Hilda (Felber) O.; m. Juel Papenthien, June 18, 1938; m. 2d, Margaret Steffenhagen, Sept. 2, 1978; children—Robyn M., Derf N. Student Marquette U., U. Wis.-Milw. Plant supr. Western Leather Co., Milw., 1939-48; v.p. Racine Glove Co., Rio, Wis., 1948-79; pres. Gaskets Inc., Rio, 1961—. Mem. exec. com. Nat. Safety Council. Mem. Nat. Welding Supply Assn., Am. Welding Soc., Am. Soc. Safety Engrs., Internat. Platform Assn. Republican. Presbyterian. Clubs: Marco Island Country, Marco Island Yacht; Madison; Masons, Shriners. Office: Gaskets Inc 100 Hy 16 W Rio WI 53960

OTTMAR, TIMOTHY JON, lawyer, municipal judge; b. Grand Forks, N.D., Oct. 19, 1954; s. Clinton Ray and Grace Bertha (Gackle) O.; m. Joanne Harriet Hager, June 3, 1978; children—Steven Timothy, Jeffrey Clinton. B.A. in Bus. Adminstrn. summa cum laude with honors, Jamestown Coll., 1976; J.D., U. N.D., 1979. Bar: N.D. 1979, U.S. Dist. Ct. N.D. 1979. Ptnr. Ottmar & Ottmar, Jamestown, N.D., 1979—; asst. mcpl. judge City of Jamestown, 1980-82, mcpl. judge, 1982—; asst. mcpl. judge City of Valley City, N.D., 1981—. Bd. dirs. United Way, Jamestown, 1979-81. Named to Outstanding Young Men Am., 1981. Mem. ABA, Stutsman County Bar Assn. (pres. 1983-84). Republican. Methodist. Lodges: Rotary (asst. sec. local club 1982—), Elks. Home: 1023 James Ave NE Jamestown ND 58401 Office: Ottmar & Ottmar PO Box 1397 400 2d Ave SW Jamestown ND 58402-1397

OTTO, HERMAN LUTHER, JR., architect, educator, consultant; b. Bristol, Pa., Feb. 18, 1953; s. Herman Luther and Blodwen (Harris) O.; m. Wendy Marie LeBouton, Aug. 19, 1978. B.Arch., Pa. State U., 1976. Registered architect, Mich., Fla., Pa. Draftsperson, Bohlin & Powell Architects/Planners, Wilkes-Barre, Pa., 1975; designer Richard Merrill Sweitzer, Architect, Elmira, N.Y., 1976; job capt. The Warren Holmes-Kenneth Black Co., Lansing, Mich., 1977; architect Wakely Assocs., Mt. Pleasant, Inc., Mt. Pleasant, Mich., 1978-81; asst. prof. archtl. tech. Ferris State Coll., Big Rapids, Mich., 1981—, prin. Herman L. Otto, Jr., AIA, Mt. Pleasant, 1981—; chairperson Art Reach of Mid Mich., Inc., Mt. Pleasant, 1983—. Vice chairperson City Planning Commn. of Mt. Pleasant, 1983, chmn., 1984. Mem. Mich. Soc. Architects, Soc. Archtl. Historians, AIA (treas. Saginaw Valley chpt. 1982, v.p., 1983, pres. 1984), Environ. Design Research Assn., Pa. State Alumni Assn. Home: 310-B Oak St PO Box 284 Mount Pleasant MI 48858 Office: Swan 108 Ferris State College Big Rapids MI 49307

OUDMAN, BONNIE KAY, systems/program manager; b. McBain, Mich, May 29, 1956; d. William and Henrietta O. Assoc., Davenport Coll., 1976. Programmer Medcom Services, Grand Rapids, Mich., 1976-78; programming instr. Key-V Inst., Grand Rapids, 1978-79; programmer, analyst Mich. Bulb Co., Grand Rapids, 1979-82, systems/program mgr., 1982—.

OUGHTON, JAMES HENRY, JR., business executive, farmer; b. Chgo., May 14, 1913; s. James H. and Barbara (Corbett) O.; student Dartmouth Coll., 1931-35; m. Jane Boyce, Jan. 23, 1940; children—Diana (dec.), Carol Oughton Biondi, Pamela Oughton Armstrong, Deborah Oughton Callahan. Pres., dir. L.E. Keeley Co., Dwight, Ill., 1936—, Nev. Corp.; past adminstr. The Keeley Inst., Dwight, 1938—; dir 1st Nat. Bank of Dwight, Ill. Valley Investment Co.; farmer, farm mgr., livestock feeder, Ill.; sec., dir. Dwight Indsl. Assn.; past mem. Ill. Ho. of Reps. Co-chmn. 1st Indsl. Conf. on Alcoholism, 1948; chmn. Midwest Seminar on Alcoholism for Pastors, 1957, 58, 59, 60; chmn. adv. bd. Ill. Dept. Corrections; chmn. Gov.'s Task Force on Mental Health Adminstrn., 1971-72; mem. adv. bd. Ill. Dept. Mental Health; dir., mem. exec. bd. W.D. Boyce council Boy Scouts Am. Served as lt. (j.g.) USNR, 1944-46; PTO. Republican. Episcopalian. Clubs: Univ., Union League (Chgo.). Address: 103 W South St Dwight IL 60420

OUTCALT, JON HARRIS, financial executive; b. Cleve., June 11, 1936; s. Richard Franklin and Virginia (Harris) O.; m. Jane Quayle, Aug. 27, 1960; children—Jon H., Jr., David B., Kenneth W. B.A., Trinity Coll., 1959; M.B.A., U. Pa., 1961. Chartered fin. analyst. Securities analyst Van Cleef, Jordan & Wood., N.Y.C., 1961-63; v.p. Alexander, Van Cleef & Wood, Inc., Cleve., 1963-68, pres. owner, 1968-75; sr. v.p., dir. Alliance Capital Mgmt. Corp., Beachwood, Ohio, 1975—; pres. owner Fed. Process Co., Beachwood; dir. Ohio Savs. Fin., Cleve., Capitol Am. Fin., Cleve., Myers Industries, Inc., Akron, Ohio. Pres. Big Bros./Big Sisters, Greater Cleve., 1971-73, trustee, 1969—, Big Bros./Big Sisters Am., Phila., 1974-77, Playhouse Sq. Found., Cleve., 1983—. Mem. Cleve. Soc. Security Analysts (treas. 1970-71). Clubs: Union (Cleve.); Country, Cleve. Racquet (Pepper Pike). Avocations: art; athletics; travel. Home: 7 Brandywood Dr Pepper Pike OH 44124 Office: Alliance Capital Mgmt Corp 3737 Park East Suite 203 Beachwood OH 44122

OUTCALT, MERLIN BREWER, child care center administrator, consultant; b. Reedsburg, Wis., Aug. 26, 1982; s. Raymond Ansil and Ruby (Brewer) O.; m. Ruth Ann Auble, Sept. 22, 1950; children—Roger Lee, Dennis Alan, Steven Len. B.S., Ind. U., 1955, M.A. in Social Service, 1957; postgrad Ind. U. Cert. social worker. Probation officer Juvenile Court, Indpls., 1957-59; exec. dir. Travelers Aide Soc., Cin., 1959-65, Methodist Youth Service, Chgo., 1965-68; cons. United Meth. Ch., Evanston, Ill., 1968-74; exec. dir. Group Child Care Services, Chapel Hill, N.C., 1974-77, Webster-Cantrell Hall, Decatur, Ill., 1977—; Contbr. articles to profl. jours. and mags. Lay leader Decatur Dist. United Meth., Ill., 1980—; mem. Council Community Services, Decatur, 1980-84, United Meth. Global Ministries, N.Y.C., 1984-88. Served as cpl. U.S.

Army, 1950-52. Mem. Acad. Cert. Social Workers. Lodge: Rotary. Avocations: camping, traveling. Office: Webster-Cantrell Hall 1942 E Cantrell St Decatur IL 62521

OUTCALT, ROGER LEE, social worker; b. Indpls., Aug. 14, 1951; s. Merlin Brewer and Ruth Ann (Auble) O.; m. Roberta Sue Coombs, Aug. 27, 1972; children—Jared Michael, Cherrylynn Marie. B.A., M.S.W., Ind. Central U. Cert. social worker, Ill., Acad. Cert. Social Workers. Caseworker, Salvation Army, Indpls., 1974-76, casework supr., 1977-78, asst. dir., 1978-83; residential dir. Progress Resources Ctr., Decatur, Ill., 1983—. Bd. dirs., chmn. Gleaners FoodBank of Ind., Indpls., 1980-83, Central Ill. Foodbank, Springfield, 1984—. Named Outstanding Young Man of Am., Jr. C. of C., 1975. Mem. Nat. Assn. Social Workers, Acad. Cert. Social Workers. Methodist. Lodge: Kiwanis (Decatur). Avocations: Softball; bowling; camping; canoeing. Home: 210 N Dennis Decatur IL 62522 Office; Progress Resources Ctr 3475 N Maple Ave Decatur IL 62526

OUTHOUSE, JAMES BURTON, animal sciences educator, consultant; b. Canandaigua, N.Y., Sept. 20, 1916; s. Burton A. and Bessie (Brown) O.; m. E. Louise Reinohl, Mar. 21, 1940; children—Robert B., David S., Janet L. Outhouse Overton. B.S., Cornell U., 1938; M.S., U. Md., 1942; Ph.D., Purdue U., 1956. With U. Md., Coll. Park, 1938-52, assoc. prof. animal husbandry to 1952; instr., asst. prof., assoc. prof., then prof. animal scis., Purdue U., West Lafayette, Ind., 1952-83, emeritus, 1983—; vis. prof. animal prodn. U. Edinburgh, Scotland, 1970-71; short-term adviser Portugal-U.S. AID, Vila Real, 1982, Evora, 1984. Co-author: Handbook of Livestock Management Techniques, 1981. Author numerous research and extension publs. Served to lt. USNR, 1944-47, PTO. Recipient Outstanding Tchr. in Agr. award U. Md., 1950; Sr. Extension Specialist award Purdue U., 1981; co-recipient F.L. Hovde award, Purdue U., 1981; named Ky. Col., 1976, Sagamore of the Wabash, 1982. Fellow Am. Soc. Animal Sci. (hon.); mem. Am. Registry of Profl. Animal Scientists (animal prodn. and sheep sect.), Brit. Soc. Animal Prodn., Ind. Livestock Breeders Assn. (portrait in Hall of Fame), Nat. Block and Bridle Club (nat. pres. 1965-67), Sigma Xi, Gamma Sigma Delta, Alpha Gamma Rho. Republican. Presbyterian. Avocations: travel; photography. Address: 2643 Duncan Rd Lafayette IN 47904

OUTLAW, NORMA BRIAN, nurse; b. Indpls., Nov. 28, 1943; d. John Montgomery Brian and Agnes Brian Degischer; m. John Melvin Rader, Aug. 16, 1964; m. William Edgar Outlaw, Dec. 29, 1973. B.S.N., Ind. U., 1966, M.S.N., 1972. R.N., Ind., Ill. Staff nurse, asst. head nurse, head nurse, asst. to dir., chmn. med. nursing Ind. U. Med. Ctr., Indpls., 1966-73; clin. specialist, supr., U. Chgo. Med. Ctr., 1973-75; asst. nursing adminstr. Chgo. Osteo. Hosp., 1975-79; cons. Church Home, Chgo., 1977-79; dir. nursing MacNeal Meml. Hosp., Berwyn, Ill., 1979—. Bd. dirs. Am. Cancer Soc., 1982-83; Served as maj. USAR, 1979—. Mem. Am. Soc. for Nursing Service Adminstrs., Ill. Soc. for Nursing Service Adminstrs., Res. Officers Assn., Ind. U. Alumni Assn., MacNeal Meml. Hosp. Assn., MacNeal Meml. Hosp. Aux. Methodist. Home: 187C Kendall Ct Bloomingdale IL 60108 Office: MacNeal Mem Hosp 3249 S Oak Park Ave Berwyn IL 60402

OUTLAW, WILLIAM EDGAR, JR., pastoral psychotherapist, clinical pastoral education supervisor; b. Watson, Ark., June 5, 1936; s. William Edgar and Bonnie Lee (Gibson); m. Roxie Ann Outlaw, June 5, 1955 (div. 1972); children—William Edgar, III, Brian, April Rose; m. Norma Sue Brian, Dec. 29, 1973 (div. 1984); m. Kathleen A. Manuel, Aug. 31, 1985. B.A., U. Ark., 1957; B.Div., Vanderbilt U. Div. Sch., 1960; M.Ministry Christian Theol. Sem., 1973; D.Ministry, McCormick Theol. Sem., 1978. Ordained elder United Methodist Ch., 1960; cert. Coll. of Chaplains, Am. Prot. Hosp. Assn.; cert. clinical pastoral edn. supr. Assn. Clin. Pastoral Edn. Pastor Almyra Meth. Ch., Ark., 1960-61, Douglassville Meth. Ch., Little Rock, 1961-65, Carr Meml. Meth. Ch., Pine Bluff, Ark., 1965-69; chaplain U.S. Navy, 1969-72; minister of counseling and clin. pastoral edn. supr. The Chgo. Temple, First United Meth. Ch., 1974-77; clinical pastoral edn. supr. Alexian Brothers Med. Center, Elk Grove Village, Ill., 1977, counselor alcoholism treatment unit, therapist sexual dysfunctional clinic, 1978-81; pastoral counselor Grace Episcopal Ch., Chgo., 1977-80; clinical dir., clinical pastoral edn. supr. St. Matthew Pastoral Counseling Service, Inc., Itasca, 1981—. Pres., bd. dirs. Alcoholism Halfway House, Chgo., 1976. Lt. col. U.S. Army Res. Chaplain Corps. Decorated Navy Commendation medal, Army commendation medal. Mem. No. Ill. Conf. Meth. Ch., Res. Officers Assn., Aircraft Owners and Pilots Assn. Club: Neo Flytes Flying (Elmhurst, Ill.). Lodge: Masons.

OVENS, STEPHEN ALEXANDER, geologist, petroleum consultant; b. Dunedin, Otago, New Zealand, Oct. 29, 1950; came to U.S., 1977; s. Ian James and Lorna Margaret (Walesby) O.; m. Jill Annette Blance, Jan. 12, 1974; children—Nicholas, Simon, Dustin. B.S., U. Auckland, New Zealand, 1973, M.S., 1976. Geologist Earth Scientists Ltd., New Zealand, 1975-77, sr. geologist, Coffeyville, Kans., 1977-82; self employed geologist, Coffeyville, 1982—; pres. Cherokee Basin Perforators, Coffeyville, 1982—; v.p. High Cotton Gas Pipeline, Coffeyville, 1984—. Mem. Am. Inst. Profl. Geologists (cert., sec.-treas. Kans. sect. 1985—), Am. Assn. Petroleum Geologists, Geol. Soc. Am., Kans. Geol. Soc. Anglican. Avocations: flying; scuba diving; racquetball; mineral specimens; stamp collecting. Home: Route 1 2305 Timberlane Dr Coffeyville KS 67337 Office: 3804 W 8th St Coffeyville KS 67337

OVERMYER, EDWIN LEE, insurance agency executive; b. Ft. Wayne, Ind., June 10, 1939; m. Mary Jane Ross, Dec. 23, 1961; children—Greg, Shelly, Dan. B.S., Ohio State U., 1961. Sales rep. Central Mutual Ins. Co., Van Wert, Ohio, 1961-65; partner Jaeger Ins. Agy., Columbus, Ohio, 1965-73; pres., Berwanger Overmyer Assocs., Inc., Columbus, Ohio, 1973—. Bd. dirs. Upper Arlington Civic Assn., Central Ohio Chpt. Leukemia Soc., Columbus, Northwest Mental Health Services, Columbus. Mem. Soc. CPCUs, (cert., nat. dir.), Columbus Soc. CPCUs (pres. 1977-78), Ind. Ins. Agents Assn. Republican. Lutheran. Clubs: Arlington (gov. 1979-80), Scioto Country, Ohio State Univ. Presidents. Avocations: hunting; fishing; tennis. Home: 2480 Stonehaven Pl Columbus OH 43220 Office: Berwanger Overmyer Assocs Inc 3360 Tremont Rd Columbus OH 43221

OVERTON, GEORGE WASHINGTON, lawyer; b. Hinsdale, Ill., Jan. 25, 1918; s. George Washington and Florence Mary (Darlington) O.; A.B., Harvard U., 1940; J.D., U. Chgo., 1946; m. Jane Vincent Harper, Sept. 1, 1941; children—Samuel Harper, Peter Darlington, Ann Vincent. Admitted to Ill. bar, 1947; counsel Wildman, Harrold, Allen & Dixon, Chgo. Pres. Textile Soc., Art Inst. Chgo., 1982—. Mem. Am., Ill., Chgo. (bd. mgrs. 1981-83) bar assns., Assn. Bar City N.Y. Home: 5648 S Dorchester Ave Chicago IL 60637 Office: One IBM Plaza Chicago IL 60611

OVERTON, MICHAEL KEVIN, broadcasting sales and marketing consultant; b. Decatur, Ill., June 2, 1952; s. Charles William and Alice Lillian (Irons) O.; m. Lynn Ann Kindlesparger, Aug. 10, 1974; children—Darcy Lynn, Michelle Dawn. Student Milliken U., 1970-72; cert. radio mktg. cons. Radio Advt. Bur. Radio announcer, newsman stas. WDZ and WSOY, Decatur, 1968-72; asst. news dir. Sta. KSAL, Salina, Kans., 1972-75; sta. mgr. Sta. KYEZ-FM, Salina, 1975-76, gen. mgr., 1981-83; gen. mgr. Sta. KMNS/KSEZ, Sioux City, Iowa, 1976-77; v.p. MarketAide Inc., Salina, 1978-81; pres. Profl. Alarm Systems and Answering Service, Inc., Salina, 1983, Overton Assocs., Salina, 1984—; pres. PPA/USA, Inc., Eugene, Oreg. Bd. dirs. Decatur YMCA, 1970-71, Salina Child Care Assn., 1981-83. Mem. Salina Area C. of C. Republican. Lutheran.

OVERTURF, JUDITH ELEN, lawyer; b. St. Clair County, Ill., Aug. 30, 1945; d. Frederick Leroy and Imogene Elizabeth (Ernst) Madorin; m. Wayne Edward Overturf, July 26, 1969; children—Justine Elen, Whitney Eugene, Weston Erick. B.S., Purdue U., 1967; J.D., Ind. U.-Indpls., 1978. Bar: Ind. 1978, U.S. Dist. Ct. (so. dist.) Ind. 1978, U.S. Tax Ct. 1982. Atty. IRS, Indpls., 1978-82; dep. prosecutor, 19th Jud. Circuit, 1982-83; assoc. Harrison & Moberly, Indpls., 1983—. Active Fall Creek Valley Republican Club, Indpls., 1971—; mem. Equal Opportunity Adv. Bd., City of Indpls., 1979-85. Mem. Indpls. Bar Assn., Ind. State Bar Assn., Alpha Chi Omega (nat. property mgmt. team 1983-85). Lutheran. Home: 7002 Stewart Ct Indianapolis IN 46256 Office: Harrison & Moberly 777 C of C Bldg 320 N Meridian St Indianapolis IN 46204

OVERWEIN, JOSEPH H., automobile company executive, engineer; b. Covington, Ky., Dec. 13, 1921; s. Joseph M. and Minnie (Rehkamp) O.; m. Betty J. Mayl, Nov. 16, 1946 (dec.); 1 dau., Mari T.; m. 2d, Martha A. Bucher, Jan. 29, 1977. B.S. in Chem. Engring., U. Dayton, 1943. Registered profl. engr., Ohio Jr. engr. Inland div. Gen. Motors Corp., Dayton, Ohio, 1943-56, dir. labs., 1956-60, asst. chief engr., 1960-63, asst. factory mgr., 1963-67, asst. chief engr., 1967-72, dir. prodn. engring., 1972-74, dir. quality control, 1974—. Bd. dirs. Honor Seminar Met. Dayton. Served to 1st lt. U.S. Army, 1944-46. Mem. Soc. Automotive Engrs., Soc. Plastics Engrs., Am. Chem. Soc., Tau Beta Pi. Roman Catholic. Club: Dayton Racquet. Office: PO Box 1224 Dayton OH 45401

OVITT, RODNEY LUTHER, sales executive, interior designer; b. Detroit, Nov. 2, 1950; s. Jeremiah Edward and Alice (Smith) O.; m. Janice Ann Russell, Sept. 21, 1973; children—Philip Daniel, Paul Jeremiah. Student Lawrence Inst. Tech., Mich., 1969-71, Wayne State U., 1971-73. News dir. Sta. WTGN-AM, Lima, Ohio, 1972-75; dir. mktg. C.S.S. Publ. Co., Lima, 1975-77; gen. mgr. Design Tec div. Noonan Co., Lima, 1977-82; dir. sales and mktg. Productive Bus. Interiors, Fort Wayne, 1982—; facility use cons. Copeland Corp., Sidney, Ohio, 1982-83; cons. interior finished and colors SOHIO, Cleve., 1983. Mem. Adminstrv. Mgmt. Soc., Profl. Services Mgmt. Assn. Republican. Baptist. Home: 1913 Curdes Ave Fort Wayne IN 46805 Office: PBI 202 W Berry St Suite 120 Fort Wayne IN 46802

OWEN, ARCHIBALD ALEXANDER, mfg. co. exec.; b. Nashville, Oct. 4, 1932; s. Archibald Alexander and Elizabeth Fairchild (Spyker) O.; B.S., in Chem. Engring., Bucknell U., 1954; M.B.A., George Washington U., 1968; m. Glenn Allen Brown, Dec. 30, 1958; children—Archibald Alexander, Carter Brown, Henry Spyker. With Celanese Corp., 1959-71, prodn. mgr., Lanaken, Belgium, 1963-65, devel. supt., Rock Hill, S.C., 1966-71; mgr. mfg. Gen. Electric Co., Selkirk, N.Y., 1971-73, Pittsfield, Mass., 1973-74; mgr. mfg. FMC Corp., Parkersburg, W. Va., 1974-75, dir. mfg. film, Phila., 1975-78; plant mgr. Kurz-Hastings, 1979-80; mgr. energy utilization and maintenance services Anchor Hocking Corp., 1981-83, v.p. corp. energy mgmt., 1983—; instr. marine engring. U.S. Naval Acad., Annapolis, 1957-59. Served with USN, 1954-59. Mem. Am. Inst. Chem. Engring (sec. Carolinas sect. 1967-68), Toastmasters Internat. (pres. local chpt. 1969-70, regional gov., 1970-71, named Man of Year S.C., 1970), Bucknell Engring. Alumni Assn. (dir. 1971—, pres. 1977—). Republican. Presbyterian. Home: 15714 Ladino Run Cypress TX 77429 Office: 1749 W Fair Ave Lancaster OH 43130

OWEN, EMERIAL LEE, JR., educational administrator, psychology and education educator; b. Fairfield, Ill., Nov. 21, 1925; s. Emerial Lee, Sr. and Leona Virginia (Mason) O.; m. Stephanie Olive Hill, Aug. 9, 1963; 1 child, Elizabeth Lee. A.B. summa cum laude, McKendree Coll., 1951; Ed.M., St. Louis U., 1958, Ph.D., 1967. Tchr. Pearl High Sch., Ill., 1951-52; tchr., principal O'Fallon Twp. High, Ill., 1952-55; registrar McKendree Coll., Lebanon, Ill., 1955-65, v.p., acad. dean, 1967-76, prof., chair div. social sci. and edn., 1976—; registrar, acting Ohio Wesleyan U., Delaware, 1965-67; vis. prof. Chapman Coll., Orange, Calif., 1981; condr. psycho/socio training for hospice vols. Belleville Hospice, Inc., Ill., 1982—; condr. workshops in field. Pres., bd. dirs. Call for Help, Inc., Belleville, 1976—. Served to petty officer 2nd class USN, 1944-46. Recipient Assoc. award Danforth Found., 1978; postdoctoral Sangamon State U., Springfield, Ill., 1977-82, U. So. Calif., 1979-83. Recipient Grandy Faculty award McKendree Coll. Alumni Assn., 1984. Recipient numerous grants Dept. of Aging. Mem. Ill. Consortium in Gerontology, Ill. Guidance and Personnel Assn., Am. Assn. Higher Edn., Am. Assn. Ret. Persons, Alpha Phi Omega. Methodist. Clubs: Dickens Fellowship (pres. 1977-79), Honoral Order of Ky. Colonels. Avocation: collecting books. Home: 523 N Stanton Lebanon IL 62254 Office: McKendree Coll Lebanon IL 62254

OWEN, GEORGE EDWIN, JR., sound and communications mfg. co. exec.; b. Chgo., Mar. 26, 1926; s. George Edwin and Elizabeth Owen; B.E.E., Kans. State U., 1950; M.E.E., Northwestern U., 1962; M.B.A., U. Chgo., 1971; m. Josephine Frances DeRose, June 6, 1953; children—Mary Lynn, Frank Joseph, Edward George, Elizabeth Josephine, Anne Therese. Devel. engr. Motorola Inc., Chgo., 1950-57, project engr., 1957-66, chief engr., 1966-68, dir. audio product engring., 1968-74; product mgr. Quasar Electronics Corp., Franklin Park, Ill., 1974-76; group product mgr. Motorola Auto div., Shaumburg, Ill., 1976-79; v.p. engring. Rauland-Borg Corp., Chgo., 1979—. Served with USNR, 1944-46. Mem. Sigma Xi, Sigma Tau, Eta Kappa Nu. Patentee audio and radio tech. Home: 1316 N 12th Ave Melrose Park IL Office: Rauland Borg Corp 3535 W Addison St Chicago IL 60618

OWEN, LARRY MALCOLM, electric company executive; b. Lincoln, Nebr., Jan. 1, 1928; s. Leonard J. and Ruth L. (Anderson) O.; m. Marilyn Wilkens, Aug. 6, 1950; children—David L., Sue Ellen Owen Hook. B.S. in Bus. Adminstrn., U. Nebr., 1950; Dr. Bus. Adminstrn. (hon.), S.D. Sch. Mines and Tech., 1984. Mgmt. trainee J.C. Penney Co., Lincoln, 1950-52; with mgmt. Nebr. City C. of C., Nebr., 1952-55, Columbus C. of C., Nebr., 1955-57, Rapid City C. of C., Nebr., 1957-66; exec. v.p. Cedar Rapids C. of C., Iowa, 1967-70; chmn., pres., chief exec. officer Black Hills Power & Light Co., Rapid City, 1970—. Mem. exec. com. Nat. Coll., Rapid City, 1982-83; chmn. bd. trustees Rushmore Nat. Health, Rapid City, 1984-85. Served with USN, 1945-46. Mem. Edison Electric Inst. (dir. 1984-86), North Central Electric Assn. (pres. 1984), Rocky Mountain Electric League (dir. 1980—). Republican. Presbyterian. Home: 223 Berry Blvd Rapid City SD 57702 Office: Black Hills Power & Light Co PO Box 1400 Rapid City SD 57709

OWEN, STANLEY PAUL, biochemist, pharmaceutical company executive; b. Earlie, Alta., Can., Mar. 30, 1924; s. Paul and Mertha Margaret (Davidson) O.; m. D. Evelyn McCaig, July 5, 1946; children—Donna Marie, James Douglas. B.Sc. in Agr., U. Alta., Edmonton, 1950, M.Sc. in Biochemistry, 1952; Ph.D. in Biochemistry, U. Wis., 1955, postgrad., 1963. Scientist The Upjohn Co., Kalamazoo, Mich., 1955-62, research scientist, 1962-67, head, 1967-69, mgr., 1969-76, group mgr., 1976-81, dir., 1981-85, exec. dir., 1985—; mem. com. of revision U.S. Pharmacopiae, Rochville, Md., 1977-80, mem. exec. com. drug standards div., 1980-85, mem. gen. com. of revision, 1985—. Served with RCAF, 1942-45. U. Alta. research scholar, 1950-51; recipient Wis. Alumni Research Found. award, 1952-55. Mem. Internat. Assn. Biol. Standardization, Fedn. Internat. Pharmaceutique, Am. Soc. Microbiology, AAAS, Am. Pharm. Assn., Sigma Xi, Phi Lambda Upsilon. Presbyterian. Avocations: history of American Indians.

OWEN, SUZANNE, savings and loan executive; b. Lincoln, Nebr., Oct. 6, 1926; d. Arthur C. and Hazel E. (Edwards) O.; B.S. in Bus. Adminstrn., U. Nebr., Lincoln, 1948. With G.F. Lessenhop & Sons, Inc., Lincoln, 1948-57; with First Fed. Lincoln, 1963—; v.p., dir. personnel, 1975-81, 1st v.p., 1981—. Mem. Adminstrv. Mgmt. Soc. (past bd. dirs. local chpt.), Lincoln Personnel Mgmt. Assn., Phi Chi Theta. Republican. Christian Scientist. Clubs: Altrusa, Wooden Spoon Twig Daniels Network, Exec. Women's Breakfast Group, Pi Beta Phi Alumnae, Order of Eastern Star (Lincoln). Office: First Fed Lincoln 13th and N Sts Lincoln NE 68508

OWENS, JAMES HILLIARD, management consultant; b. Conyers, Ga., Mar. 7, 1920; s. Alfred Pink and Eula Leona (McLendon) O.; m. Lavonia McInnis, May 21, 1941; children—Bonnie Faye, Virginia Carol. Grad. exec. devel. program Stanford U., 1957. With Pillsbury Co., 1938-75, corp. v.p. mktg. until 1975; pres. James H. Owens Assocs. Inc., Mpls., 1983—. Served to 2d lt. inf. U.S. Army, World War II. Mem. Assn. Mgmt. Cons. Republican. Presbyterian. Clubs: Internat., (Chgo.); Pendennis (Louisville); Minn. Alumni (Mpls.); Jefferson (Louisville). Home: 310 Peavey Rd Wayzata MN 55391

OWENS, JANET KATHLEEN, pharmacist; b. Hastings, Nebr., Apr. 1, 1950; d. Chester Dale and Helen J. (Dominy) O. B.S., U. Nebr., 1973. Registered pharmacist, Nebr. Pharmacist, Bert's Rexall Drug, Hastings, 1973-74, Keith's Pharmacies, Hastings, 1974—; cons. Hastings Family Planning, 1975—. Active Hastings Community Theatre, 1980—. Named Best Supporting Actress, Hastings Community Theatre, 1984, recipient Behind-the-Scenes award, 1983. Mem. Nebr. Pharmacists Assn., S. Central Nebr. Pharmacists Assn., Xi Beta Theta (corr. sec. 1983-84, rec. sec. 1984—, v.p. 1985—), Alpha Pi (treas. 1978-79, sec. 1979-80, pres. 1980-81). Republican. Presbyterian. Avocations: counted cross stitch; community theatre; reading; sports. Home: 835 Williams Ave Hastings NE 68901 Office: Keith's Pharmacies 2115 N Kansas St Hastings NE 68901

OWENS, KEVIN F., restaurant owner; b. Three Rivers, Mich., Sept. 11, 1956; s. Charles Victor and Cheryl Mae (Kreighbaum) O.; m. Kristy Jann Kramer, Aug. 31, 1984; 1 child, Charles Francis. Student Purdue U., 1975-76, Ind. U., 1976-78. Floor constructor Parkwood, Elkhart, Ind., 1977-78; parts mgr. Georgie Bay Mfg., Elkhart, 1978; salesman Sam White Motor Home, Houston, 1978-79; prodn. planner Miles Labs., Elkhart, 1979-83; owner J & H Restaurant, Elkhart, 1985—. Republican. Roman Catholic. Lodge: Moose. Avocation: flying. Office: J & H Restaurant 1609 W Bristol St Elkhart IN 46514

OWENS, LEWIS FILLMORE, sports administrator, consultant, park planner; b. Lexington, Ky., Nov. 10, 1949; s. Fred Lewis and Helen Lorain (Sharpe) O.; m. Linda Sue Gress, Dec. 23, 1969; children—Forrest, Joy. B.S., Milligan Coll. (Tenn.), 1971; M.S., U. Ky., 1976. Lic. real estate agt.; lic. flight instr. Phys. dir. YMCA, Frankfort, Ky., 1971-72; tchr., coach Frankfort High Sch. (Ky.), 1972-73; coach, grad. asst. U. Ky., 1973-74; supt. E. P. Sawyer State Park, Louisville, Ky., 1974-80; nat. adminstr. AAU/U.S.A. Junior Olympic Program, 1980-85; exec. dir. AAU, 1985—; cons.; park planner; instr. for sports adminstrn. Mem. Nat. Parks and Recreation Soc., Nat. Council of Youth Sports Dirs., AAU (pres. Ky. Assn. 1980). Mem. Christian Ch. Contbr. articles to profl. jours.

OWENS, RICHARD GEORGE, mental health administrator; b. Clinton, Iowa, June 1, 1946; s. Murray Riley and Margaret McBain (Owens) O.; B.A., Hope Coll., 1968, tchr. cert., 1970; M.A., Mich. State U., 1979, postgrad., 1979; m. Susan Elizabeth Sentman, June 15, 1968; 1 son, Joshua Morgan. Designer, draftsman Stone Container Corp., Chgo., 1968-69; chmn. art dept. Covert (Mich.) public schs., 1970-73; staff writer, art cons. United Educators, Inc., Lake Bluff, Ill., 1972-74; client supr. work activity center Allegan County Com. Mental Health Services, Allegan, Mich., 1974-75, supr. sheltered workshop, 1975-76; prodn. supr. Celebration Candle, Hart, Mich., 1976-77; direct care worker Alternative Services, Inc., Royal Oak, Mich., 1978-79, home mgr., 1979-80, Lansing area adminstr., 1980-84, tng. dir., 1984—, chmn. ad hoc com. on staff tng. and devel., 1981—; bd. dirs. Life Ctr., Inc., 1984—; instr. adult edn. Pres., Saugatuck Renaissance Guild, 1974-75. Mem. Assn. Supervision and Curriculum Devel., State Wide Care Assn., East Lansing Arts Workshop. Presbyterian. Author: Ceramics As A Career, 1973; Kohoutek and the Queen, 1974. Home: 1203 B University Village East Lansing MI 48823 Office: 1606 Greencrest St East Lansing MI 48823

OXBORROW, GORDON SQUIRES, research microbiologist; b. Ely, Nev., Dec. 7, 1939; s. Joseph Bryant and Leah (Squires) O.; m. Dora Talbot, June 30, 1961; children—Rhonda, Glade, Ondrea, Tawnya, DeAnna. B.S. in Microbiology, Utah State U., 1964; M.P.H., U. Minn., 1968. Microbiologist, Ctr. Disease Control, Phoenix, 1965-67, Cape Canaveral, Fla., 1968-74; research microbiologist Jet Propulsion Lab., Pasadena, Calif., 1974-76, FDA, Mpls., 1976—; dir. Sterility Research Ctr., Mpls., 1981—. Recipient Apollo Service award NASA, 1969, FDA Award of Merit, 1979, Superior Service award, 1981, Commendable Service award, 1983. Mem. Assn., Official Analytical Chemists (gen. referee 1982—), Assn. Advancement Med. Instrumentation (com. mem. 1979—). Republican. Mormon. Avocations: golf, woodworking. Home: 14120 Fisher Ave NE Prior Lake MN 55372 Office: FDA 240 Hennepin Ave Minneapolis MN 55401

OXENDER, DALE LAVERN, biological chemistry educator, genetic engineering researcher; b. Constantine, Mich., Aug. 30, 1932; s. Harry Bryan and Myrtle Ruth (Sherck) O.; m. Nila Jean Johnson, June 5, 1955; children—Derrick Bryan, Theodore Lavern. A.B., Manchester Coll., 1954; M.S., Purdue U., 1956, Ph.D., 1959. Research assoc. U. Mich., Ann Arbor, 1959-63, asst. prof. biol. chemistry, 1963-68, assoc. prof., 1968-75, prof., 1975—; acting dir. Ctr. for Molecular Genetics, U. Mich., 1982—. Editor 3 sci. research books; mem. editorial bd. 5 sci. jours. Contbr. articles to profl. jours. Research grantee NIH, 1963—. Mem. Am. Chem. Soc., Am. Soc. Biol. Chemists, Am. Soc. Microbiology. Mem. Ch. of Brethren. Avocation: lapidary; camping. Office: Univ Mich Dept Biol Chemistry 5319 Med Sci I Ann Arbor MI 48109

OXHANDLER, RICHARD MALCOLM, psychologist; b. N.Y.C., Nov. 8, 1946; s. Norman and Cordelia (Thrasher) O.; m. Jerie Wood, Dec. 12, 1984. B.A. in Anthropology, SUNY-Binghamton, 1968; M.S. in Higher Edn., Syracuse U., 1970; Ed.D. in Counseling, Western Mich. U., 1975. Nat. cert. counselor. Asst. dean students Kalamazoo Coll., 1970-74; dir. career guidance program Kalamazoo Valley Community Coll., 1975-77; instr. counseling Western Mich. U., Kalamazoo, 1977-78, counseling psychologist, 1978—, co-dir. grad. tng. Counseling Ctr., 1980—; outdoor edn. instr. Pretty Lake Adventure Centre, Kalamazoo, 1978—, pres. bd. trustees, 1984-85; cons. Battle Creek Central High Sch., Mich., 1983-84. Served with U.S. Army, 1969-75. Recipient cert. Commr.'s Nat. Conf. on Career Edn., U.S. Office Edn., 1976; George H. Hilliard award Western Mich. U., 1977. Mem. Am. Assn. for Counseling and Devel., Assn. for Exptl. Edn., Am. Coll. Personnel Assn. (Innovations in Counseling award 1981), Mich. Personnel and Guidance Assn. (conf. registrar 1980-81), Kalamazoo County Personnel and Guidance Assn. (pres. 1978-79). Club: Gt. Lakes Adventure (Kalamazoo). Avocations: backpacking; canoeing; caving; travel. Home: 6571 Ravine Rd Kalamazoo MI 49009 Office: Counseling Center Western Mich Univ Kalamazoo MI 49008

OXLEY, LEO LIONEL, psychiatrist; b. Raleigh, N.C., July 9, 1934; children—Keith Oxley, Claire Oxley. M.D., Meharry Med. Coll., Nashville, 1959; postgrad U.S. Navy Sch. Aviation Medicine, 1963-64. Intern, William Beaumont Army Hosp., El Paso; resident Walter Reed Gen. Hosp., 1960-63; asst. supr. Western Mo. Mental Health Center, Kansas City, 1967-69; dir. Bklyn. S.I. Mental Health Service for Health Ins. Plan Greater N.Y., 1971-73; chief psychiatry VA Hosp., Newington, Conn., 1973-78; prof. psychiatry Emory U., Med. Sch., Atlanta, 1978-80, Med. Sch. Morehouse Coll., 1978-80; supt. Ga. Mental Health Inst., Atlanta, 1978-80; asst. prof. psychiatry U. Conn., 1974-78; mem. staff Inst. Living, Hartford; chief psychiatry VA Med. Ctr., Chillicothe, Ohio, 1982-85; chief Mental Hygiene Clinic VA Med. Ctr., Wade Park Cleve., 1985—; cons. in field. Served to maj. U.S. Army, 1958-67. Mem. Am. Psychiat. Assn., Black Psychiatrists Am., Alpha Phi Alpha, Alpha Omega Alpha. Democrat. Office: VA Med Center 10701 East Blvd Cleveland OH 44106

OXLEY, MICHAEL GARVER, congressman; b. Findlay, Ohio, Feb. 11, 1944; s. George Garver and Marilyn Maxine (Wolfe) O.; B.A., Miami U., Oxford, Ohio, 1966; J.D., Ohio State U., 1969; m. Patricia Ann Pluquez, Nov. 27, 1971; 1 son, Chadd. Admitted to Ohio bar; former FBI agt.; mem. Ohio Ho. of Reps., 1973-81; mem. 97th-99th Congresses, mem. energy and commerce com., subcom. on telecommunications, consumer protection and fin., subcom. on oversight and investigations, subcom. on energy conservation and power, subcom. on fossil and synthetic fuels. Mem. Am., Ohio, Findlay bar assns., Soc. Former Spl. Agts. FBI, Ohio State Assn. Twp. Trustees and Clks., Ohio Farm Bur., Findlay Area C. of C., Sigma Chi. Omicron Delta Kappa. Club: Rotary. Home: Findlay OH 45840 Office: 1108 Longworth House Office Bldg Washington DC 20515

OYLER, ROBERT LEON, personnel services exec.; b. Jackson, Miss., Feb. 17, 1944; s. John G. and Sara Catherine (Beckley) O.; B.A., Butler U., 1966; M.S., U. Wis., 1968; children—Kelly, Stephanie. Exec. dir. Wis. Council on Developmental Disabilities, 1969-73; pres., gen. mgr. Life Style Services, Inc., Madison, Wis., 1973—, chmn. bd. Mem. Adminstrv. Mgmt. Soc. (bd. dirs.), Am. Soc. Personnel Adminstrs., Nat. Assn. Personnel Cons., Wis. Assn. Personnel Cons., Inter-City Personnel Cons., Madison C. of C., Phi Eta Sigma, Sigma Chi. Club: Madison. Contbr. article to Am. Jour. Health. Home: W14202 Selwood Dr Rt 1 Lodi WI 53555 Office: 415 W Main Madison WI 53713

OZANNE, DOMINIC LAURANT, lawyer, construction company executive; b. Cleve., Apr. 10, 1953; s. Leroy and Betty Jean (Peyton) O. B.S./B.A., Boston U., 1975; J.D., Harvard U., 1978. Bar: Ohio 1979. Assoc. Thompson, Hine & Flory, Cleve., 1978-80; gen. counsel Ozanne Constrn. Co. Inc., Cleve. Trustee Ctr. for Venture Devel., Cleve., 1983—. Mem. Nat. Assn. Minority Contractors (sec. 1983). Roman Catholic. Office: Ozanne Constrn Co Inc 1635 E 25th St Cleveland OH

OZBIRN, WILLIE PAUL, electronics company executive; b. San Diego, Feb. 17, 1944; s. Howard Paul and Fannie Elizabeth (Kennedy) O.; m. Mailetta Kay Sullins, June 1, 1963 (div. June 1984); children—Emily Kay, Paula Sue. B.S. in Chemistry and Math., Central State U., Edmond, Okla., 1966; Ph.D. in Phys. Chemistry, Iowa State U., 1971; cert. in Mgmt. Arts, Aurora Coll., 1973. Prodn. engr. CTS Knights, Sandwich, Ill., 1971-74, v.p. mfg., 1974-76; Far East ops. mgr. CTS Taiwan, Kaashiung, 1976-80; pres., gen. mgr. CTS Bentonville,

Ark., 1980-81; mgr. tech. devel. CTS Corp., Elkhart, Ind., 1981-83, v.p. corp. research and devel., 1983—. Inventor watch crystal package. Mem. IEEE, Components Hybrids and Mfg. Tech., Kaoshiung C. of C. (pres. 1978). Mem. Christian Ch. (Disciples of Christ). Avocations: scuba diving; fishing; hunting; skiing; running. Home: 10774 E Jefferson Osceola IN 46561 Office: CTS Corp 905 N West Blvd Elkhart IN 46514

OZKAN, GUNER, physician, surgeon; b. Izmir, Turkey, Feb. 18, 1945; came to U.S., 1975; s. Ismail and Raziye (Tekin) O.; m. Gunay Karasu, Aug. 14, 1970; children—Ozgur Ismail, Zeynep Ozlem. M.D., Ege Universitesi, Izmir, 1968; specialist in physiology Ataturk U., Erzurum, Turkey, 1970. Diplomate Am. Bd. Surgery. Intern Washington Hosp. Ctr., 1975-76, resident, 1976-80; asst. prof. Ataturk U., 1968-73; staff surgeon VA Med. Ctr., Grand Island, Nebr., 1981—. Research grantee Turkish Sci. and Tech. Found., 1967-70; recipient Achievement award Upjohn Co., 1980. Islam. Avocation: swimming. Home: 1709 S Doreen St Grand Island NE 68801 Office: VA Med Ctr 2201 N Broadwell Grand Island NE 68801

OZMUN, KENT FREDERICK, lawyer; b. Akron, Ohio, Feb. 17, 1929; s. Sylvester P. and Elizabeth (Bedford) O.; m. Mary Louise Fox, Oct. 8, 1960; children—Janelle, Richard. B.A., Baldwin-Wallace Coll., 1951; J.D., Ohio State U., 1955. Bar: Ohio 1956. Assoc. Lane, Huggard & Alton, Columbus, Ohio, 1956-58; asst. atty. gen. State of Ohio, Columbus, 1958-59; adminstr. appraisal bur. State of Ohio, Columbus, 1959-63; mgr. Harrisburg Bank, Grove City, Ohio, 1963-65; sole practice Grove City, 1965—. Law dir. City of Grove City, 1966-70; lay leader Grove City United Methodist Ch., 1983-84. Served as cpl. U.S. Army, 1951-53. Mem. Columbus Bar Assn., Ohio State Bar Assn. Lodge: Kiwanis (pres. Grove City chpt. 1966-67). Home: 2167 Hillswood Dr Grove City OH 43123 Office: Law Offices 4178 Broadway St Grove City OH 43123

OZONOFF, IDA, artist, teacher; b. La Crosse, Wis., July 27, 1904; d. Meyer and Tillie (Selznik) Franklin; m. Jacob Ozonoff, July 25, 1926 (dec. 1957); children—Maer, Ethel Ozonoff Lieberthal, David. Grad. Milw. State Tchrs. Coll., 1924; student Milw. Downer Coll., 1958-59, U. Wis., Milw., 1960-64, 69, 70, Layton Sch. Art, Milw. Tchr. Milw. Pub. Schs., 1924-29, tchr. spl. edn., 1958-61; one woman show: Abilene Fine Arts Mus., Tex., 1971; group shows: Internat. Women's Art Festival, N.Y.C., 1976, St. Paul Library System, 1974 (purchase award), Rahr-West Mus., Manitowoc, Wis., 1980 (purchase award), Univ. Art Mus., Milw., 1985; represented in permanent collections: Milw. Jour., Smithsonian Instn., others. Recipient Benjamin Altman prize Nat. Acad. Design, N.Y.C., 1968; Meml. Art Ctr. award, Milw., 1962; featured in The Art of Collage by G.F. Brommer, 1978, Wis. Acad. Rev., 1983. Home: 500 W Bradley Rd Apt C 216 Milwaukee WI 53217

OZZELLO, LAWRENCE MURAL, professor of accountancy, consultant; b. Wis., Feb. 28, 1927; s. James Louis and Marie (Church) O.; m. Patricia E. Anderson, Nov. 4, 1950; children—Janice L., David C., Brian W., Lori J. B.S., No. Mich. U., 1949; M.A., U. Mich.--Ann Arbor, 1955; Ph.D., Mich. State U., 1967; postgrad. U. Chgo., U. Wis., U. Mont., 1949-69. Cert. mgmt. acct. Supr. fin. dept. Kaiser Mfg. Co., 1951-53; prin. Mesick Area Schs., Mich., 1953-55; asst. prof. bus. Ferris State U., Big Rapids, Mich., 1955-64; instr. Mich. State U., East Lansing, 1964-66; prof., div. chmn. bus. Lake Superior State Coll., Sault Ste. Marie, Mich., 1966-71; prof., chmn. dept. accountancy U. Wis., Eau Claire, 1971—; sales mgr. Aluminum Co. Am., New Kennington, Pa., 1956-64; cons. various U.S. and Can. Corps. Author: (with others) Principles of Accounting, 1985; NCSA-Ski Manual 1983. Served with USN, 1944-46; PTO. Recipient Pres's. award Nat. Coll. Ski Assn., 1984; Excellence in Teaching award U. Wis. Eau Claire, 1985. Mem. Am. Acctg. Assn., Inst. Indsl. Accts., Nat. Collegiate Ski Assn. (dir. 1972—), Beta Gamma Sigma, Beta Alpha Psi. Roman Catholic. Avocation: skiing.

PAARLBERG, NORMAN LOUIS, geologist; b. Harvey, Ill., Oct. 25, 1944; s. Harry John and Ruth E. (Kooy) P.; m. Roberta Ann Sass, June 24, 1967; children—Kimberly Ann, Robin Lynn. B.S., No. Ill. U., 1967, M.S., 1969. Mine geologist, St. Joe Minerals Corp., Viburnum, Mo., 1969-75, div. geologist, 1975—. Editor: Viburnum Trend Guide Book, 1979. Mem. Task Force for Definition Geology, State of Mo., 1983. Mem. Assn. Petroleum Geologists, Soc. Econ. Geologists, Soc. Econ. Paleontologists and Mineralogists, Assn. Mo. Geologists (pres. 1979). Republican. Methodist. Avocations: coin collecting; golf. Home: Box 415 Viburnum MO 65566 Office: St Joe Minerals Corp Box 500 Viburnum MO 65566

PAASWELL, ROBERT EMIL, civil engineer, educator; b. Red Wing, Minn., Jan. 15, 1937; s. George and Evelyn (Cohen) P.; m. Rosalind Snyder, May 31, 1958; children—Judith Marjorie, George Harold. B.A., Columbia U., 1956, B.S., 1957, M.S., 1961; Ph.D., Rutgers U., 1965. Field engring. asst. Spencer White & Prentis, Washington, 1954-56, engr., N.Y.C., 1957-59; research scientist Davidson Lab., N.J., 1964; research fellow Greater London Council, 1971-72; research and teaching asst. Columbia U., 1959-62; asst. prof. civil engring. SUNY-Buffalo, 1964-68; chmn. bd. govs. Urban Studies Coll., 1973-76, assoc. prof., 1968-76, prof. civil engring., 1976-82; dir. Ctr. for Transp. Studies and Research, 1979-82, chmn. dept. environ. design and planning, 1980-82; prof. transp. engring. U. Ill.-Chgo., 1982—; dir. Urban Transp. Ctr., 1982—; faculty-on-leave Dept. Transp., 1976-77, cons., 1981—; v.p. Faculty Tech. Cons., Inc., 1974-84, Midwest Systems Scis., Inc., 1982—; dir. Urban Mass Transp. Adminstrn. Summer Faculty Workshop, 1980-81; vis. lectr. Jilin U. Tech., Changchun, People's Republic China, 1985; cons. transp. planning energy and soil mechanics; spl. cons. to Congressman T. Dulski, 1973. Author: Problems of the Carless, 1977. Contbg. author: New Horizons in Travel Behavior Research, 1981; Decisions for the Great Lakes, 1982. Bd. editors: Jour. Environ. Systems, 1971—, Jour. Urban Systems, 1974—, Transp., 1978—. Contbr. articles to profl. jours. Mem. Buffalo Environ. Mgmt. Commn., 1972-74, Area Com. for Transit Mayor's Energy Adv. Bd., 1974, Block Grant Rev. Com., City of Buffalo, Gov.'s Task Force for Transp. for Handicapped, 1984—; chmn. com. on transp., mem. rev. adv. bd. Research and Planning Council Western N.Y.; mem. Chgo. Transit Authority Citizen's Adv. Bd., 1985—; mem. transp. com. Chgo. 1992 Worlds Fair; organizer Mayor's Conf. on Transp., 1983, Regional Transp. Authority Strategic Plan Conf., 1984. Recipient Dept. Transp. award, 1977; Ford Found. fellow, 1956; SUNY faculty fellow, 1965-66. Mem. ASCE (pres. Buffalo sect.), Transp. Research Bd. (chmn. com. on transp. disadvantaged), AAAS, Sigma Xi. Home: 167 W Goeth St Chicago IL 60610 Office: Urban Transp Ctr U Ill-Chgo Box 4349 Chicago IL 60680

PAAU, ALAN SHIUKEE, industrial microbiologist; b. Macau, Dec. 16, 1951; came to U.S., 1971, naturalized, 1985; s. Lokfu and Ping (Li) P. Ph.D., U. Houston, 1978. Teaching coordinator U. Houston, 1974-78; research assoc. U. Wis.-Madison, 1978-79, project scientist, 1979-81; scientist, project leader Cetus Madison Corp., Middleton, Wis., 1982-84; sr. scientist, project mgr. Agracetus Corp., Middleton, 1984—; cons. in field. Recipient Outstanding Grad. Student award, Am. Soc. Plant Physiologists, 1974. Sigma Xi grantee, 1980. Mem. Am. Soc. Microbiology, Am. Soc. Plant Physiologists, AAAS, Sigma Xi. Roman Catholic. Contbr. articles to profl. jours. Patentee. Home: 5405 Jonquil Ct Middleton WI 53562 Office: 8520 University Green Middleton WI 53562

PABST, ROBERT DEAN, audio products manufacturing company executive; b. Poynette, Wis., Apr. 11, 1936; s. Kenneth J. and Dorothy M. (Tomlinson) P.; m. Bobbie June Medders, Sept. 23, 1956; children—Laura K., Sandra D. B.S.E.E., N.Mex. State U., 1959; M.B.A., Golden Gate U., 1968. Vice pres. Transaction Systems, Inc., Palo Alto, Calif., 1971-72; v.p., gen. mgr. Twin City Tool Co., Olathe, Kans., 1972-76; pres. Electro-Voice, Inc. Buchanan, Mich., 1976—. Served to 1st lt. USAF, 1959-62. Republican. Methodist. Avocation: musician. Home: 17030 Barryknoll Way Granger IN 46530 Office: Electro-Voice Inc 600 Cecil St Buchanan MI 49107

PACE, HARLAN EDWARD, hospital administrator; b. Muscatine, Iowa, Mar. 6, 1935; s. Harold E. and Evelyn D. (Wagner) P. B.S. in Instn. Mgmt., Iowa State U., 1971. Registered dietitian. With Bishop's-Stoddard Cafeteria Co., Cedar Rapids, Iowa, 1961-62; supr. Iowa Methodist Hosp., Des Moines, 1963-64; restaurant mgr. Congress Inn Motal, Iowa City, 1964-65; asst. mgr. John R. Thompson Co., Inc., Chgo., 1965-69; dir. food service, acting adminstr. Lutheran Homes, Muscatine, 1971-76; asst. dir. dietary dept. Edgewater Hosp., Chgo., 1979—; mem. career edn. council Muscatine High Sch. Served with U.S. Army, 1958-59. Mem. Chgo. Nutrition Assn. (chmn. arrangements com. 1981-82), Am. Dietetic Assn., Chgo. Dietetic Assn., Inst Food Technologists, Am. Soc. Hosp. Food Adminstrs., Soc. Nutrition Edn. Republican. Methodist. Clubs: Iowa State U. (Chgo.), Masons. Home: 4735 N Magnolia St Chicago IL 60640 Office: Edgewater Hosp 5700 N Ashland Ave Chicago IL 60660

PACE, PAUL JOSEPH, public health administrator; b. Milw., Feb. 2, 1927; s. Paul Roman and Rose Angeline (Robakowski) P.; m. Alma Martha Bartholomew, Aug. 30, 1950; children—Paul Bartholomew, Peter Adam. A.B., Ripon Coll., 1950; postgrad. Iowa State U., 1950-51; U. Wis., Milw., 1955, Marquette U. Med. Sch., 1956-61; M.S., Marquette U., 1963, postgrad., 1963-67. Specialist in pub. health Nat. Registry of Microbiology. Expediter, Square D Co., Milw., 1951-52; bacteriological lab. technologist Milw. Health Dept., 1952-54, bacteriologist I, 1954-58, bacteriologist II, 1958-64, bacteriologist III, asst. chief bacteriologist, 1964-67, bacteriologist V, chief bacteriologist, 1967-82, adminstr. bur. community health services, 1982—; cons. Treas., dir. Norman B. Barr Camp, Inc., Williams Bay, Wis. Served with USNR, 1945-46; PTO. Mem. Am. Pub. Health Assn., Wis. Pub. Health Assn., AAAS, Wis. Acad. Arts Scis. and Letters, Am. Soc. for Microbiology, Wis. Assn. Milk and Food Sanitarians (Sanitarian of Yr. 1975), Internat. Assn. Mil, Food and Environ. Sanitarians (Disting. Service award 1981), Soc. Applied Bacteriology, Inst. Food Technologists, Conf. State and Territorial Pub. Health Lab. Dirs., Sigma Xi. Contbr. articles to profl. jours. Home: 5140 S 20th St Milwaukee WI 53221 Office: 841 N Broadway Milwaukee WI 53202

PACE, STANLEY CARTER, manufacturing company executive; b. Waterview, Ky., Sept. 14, 1921; s. Stanley Dan and Pearl (Carter) P.; B.S., U. Ky., 1940; postgrad. U.S. Military Acad., 1943; M.S. Calif. Inst. Tech., 1949; m. Elaine Cutchall, Aug. 21, 1945; children—Stanley, Lawrence, Richard. With TRW, Inc., 1954—, v.p., gen. mgr. Tapco group (now Aircraft Components Group, 1958-71, exec. v.p., 1965-77, head Automotive Worldwide, 1971-77, asst. to pres., 1976-77, pres., chief operating officer, 1977-84, vice chmn. bd., 1985—; also dir.; dir. Nat. City Bank, Consol. Natural Gas Co., Republic Steel. Mem. exec. bd. Greater Cleve. council Boy Scouts Am.; chmn. gen. campaign United Way; chmn. distbn. com. Cleve. Found.; chmn. Greater Cleve. Roundtable. Served with AC U.S. Army, 1943-47, USAF, 1947-54. Decorated Air medal with 2 Bronze Oak Leaf clusters, Purple Heart. Recipient Silver Antelope award, Boy Scout Am., 1976. Mem. Soc. Automotive Engrs., AIAA, Am. Inst. Mgmt., Nat. Aeros. Assn., NAM (chmn.). Clubs: Pepper Pike, Union (Cleve.). Office: 23555 Euclid Ave Cleveland OH 44117

PACK, GEORGE ROBERT, medical science educator; b. Bay Shore, N.Y., Sept. 29, 1946; s. George Scofield and Lydia Catherine (Foehrenback) P.; m. Yda O'Kurliand, Aug. 24, 1975; children—Sasha, David. B.S., Providence Coll., 1968; Ph.D., SUNY-Buffalo, 1973. Research assoc. U. Rochester, N.Y., 1973-74; postdoctoral fellow NYU, 1974-75; postdoctoral scholar Stanford U., Calif., 1975-78; asst. prof. U. Ill. Coll. of Medicine, Rockford, 1978-83, assoc. prof., 1983—. Contbr. articles to profl. jours. Recipient Nat. Research Service award Nat. Inst. Environ. Health Scis., 1974-75; Sci. Research grantee Nat. Inst. Gen. Med. Scis., 1981—. Mem. Am. Chem. Soc., AAAS. Office: U Ill Coll Medicine at Rockford 1601 Parkview Ave Rockford IL 61107

PACKARD, SANDRA PODOLIN, university provost, art educator, therapist; b. Buffalo, Sept. 13, 1942; d. Mathew and Ethel (Zolte) P.; m. Martin T. Packard, Aug. 2, 1964; children—Dawn, Shana. B.F.A., Syracuse U., 1964; M.Ed., Ind. U., 1966, Ed.D., 1973. Tchr. art pub. schs., N.Y. and Ind., 1964-68; asst. prof. art edn. Buffalo State Coll., 1972-74; assoc. prof. art edn. Miami U., Oxford, Ohio, 1974-80, spl. asst. to v.p., 1979-80, assoc. provost, 1980-81; dean edn. Bowling Green U., 1981-85; provost U. Tenn.-Chattanooga, 1985—; cons. Butler County Community Mental Health, Hamilton, Ohio, 1976-78; pvt. practice therapy cons., Oxford, Ohio, 1973-78; cons., lectr. Nobel Sch. for Retarded, Indpls., 1968. Editor: Studies in Art Education, 1977-81. Mem. Ohio Commn. on Excellence in Edn., 1983-84. Ohio Dept. Edn. grantee, 1982—. Mem. Nat. Art Edn. Assn. (dir. higher edn. div. 1983—), Am. Art Therapy Assn. (chmn. standards bd. 1980-81), Am. Council on Edn. (mem. nat. adv. council 1981-82), Tchr. Edn. Council State Colls. and Univs. (mem. exec. bd. 1983—). Avocations: sailing, traveling. Home: 1234 Mountain Brook Circle Signal Mountain TN 37377 Office: Office of Provost U Tenn Chattanooga TN 37403

PACYNIAK, THADDEUS ADAM, architect, consultant; b. Loches, France, May 3, 1946; s. Jan and Kathy (Wowczanczyn) P.; m. Teresa Jadwiga Grygo, Apr. 24, 1971. B.Arch., U. Ill.-Chgo., 1968; student Ecole Speciale D'Architecture, Paris, 1969. Registered architect, Ill., Wis., Mo. Sr. architect Skidmore, Owings & Merrill, 1969-76; corp. architect Walgreen Drug Co., 1976-78; chief architect Anvan Corp., 1978-80; owner, operator Pacyniak & Assocs., Libertyville, Ill., 1980—. Mem. appearance com. Village of Libertyville; pres. Chgo. Intercollegiate Council, 1973. Served with U.S. Army, 1975. Mem. AIA (dir. Northeast Ill. chpt.), Nat. Council Archtl. Registration Bds., Chgo. Soc. Roman Catholic.

PADBERG, HELEN SWAN, violinist; b. Shawnee, Okla., May 3, 1919; d. Frank Pusey and Birdie B. (Rudell) Swan; A.A., Stephens Coll., 1938; Mus.B., U. Okla., 1940; Mus.M., Northwestern U., 1941; student Jacques Gordon; m. Frank Padberg, Feb. 6, 1943; children—Frank, Kristen. Solo performances and concerts, 1932—; mem. faculty string quartet and symphony soloist Stephens Coll., 1937-38; violinist Oklahoma City Symphony Summer Concerts, 1940; soloist Northwestern U. Symphony, 1941; mem. and soloist USO Orch., 1941-44; violinist Nat. Orchestral Assn. and Am. Youth Orch., N.Y.C., 1944-46; tchr. strings Public Schs. Maywood (Ill.), 1946-47; asst. concertmaster West Suburban Symphony, Chgo., 1947-48; mem. Chgo. Women's Symphony, Chgo. Civic Orch. and chamber music groups, 1947-51; violinist Ark. String Trio, 1952-58; concertmaster Ark. Symphony and Little Rock Philharmonic, 1953-57, Marjorie Lawrence TV Series, Ark., 1953-54; pvt. tchr. violin, Little Rock, 1953-66; accompanist and performer on piano, harp. Pres., Ark. Med. Soc. Aux., 1962-63, historian, 1963—. Mem. Am. Harp Soc., Chgo. Harp Soc. (sec. 1979—), Am. Fedn. Musicians, Am. Opera Soc. (v.p. and program chmn. Chgo. chpt. 1981-82, pres. 1984—), Pi Kappa Lambda, Mu Phi Epsilon, Pi Beta Phi (pres. Little Rock Alumnae Club). Presbyterian. Clubs: Aesthetic (pres. Little Rock); Woman's Athletic of Chgo. Home: 175 E Delaware Pl Chicago IL 60611

PADDOCK, BENJAMIN HENRY, III, banker; b. Detroit, Feb. 8, 1928; s. Benjamin Henry and Mary (Bulkley) P.; m. Anne Sherer, Aug. 23, 1959; children—Benjamin Henry, Anthony, Matthew, Ann. B.A., Trinity Coll., 1950; M.B.A., U. Mich., 1952. Asst. v.p., loan officer Nat. Bank Detroit, 1956-65; exec. v.p. City Nat. Bank, Detroit, 1968-70, pres., chief exec. officer, 1970-77; pres. No. States Bancorp, Detroit, 1973-77; pres. B.H. Paddock & Assocs., Detroit, 1977-80; exec. v.p. AmeriTrust Co., N.A., Cleve., 1980-84, sr. exec. v.p., 1984—; pres./dir. Minbanc Capital Corp., 1976—; dir. Gt. Lakes Constrn. Co., 1985—. Bd. dirs. Soc. for Crippled Children, Cleve., 1983, Gt. Lakes Shakespeare Festival, Cleve., 1984; mem. steering com. YMCA, Cleve., 1984. Served to lt. USN, 1952-56. Mem. Assn. Res. City Bankers, Robert Morris Assocs., Am. Inst. Banking. Episcopalian. Clubs: Country, Yondotega (Detroit); Kirtland Country (Ohio); Union, Clevelander (Cleve.). Office: AmeriTrust Co NA 900 Euclid Ave Cleveland OH 44101

PADDOCK, ROBERT ALTON, environmental scientist; b. Port Washington, N.Y., Dec. 10, 1942; s. Cheston Howard and Mary Margaret (Bohn) P.; m. Connie Rae Smith, June 9, 1967; children—Tracy, Michael, Holly. B.S., Washington and Lee U., 1964; M.S., Mich. State U., 1966, Ph.D., 1969. Asst. prof. physics Ripon Coll. (Wis.), 1969-74; environ. scientist Argonne Nat. Lab (Ill.), 1975—. Author tech. reports, articles, presentations. Mem. Am. Phys. Soc., Phi Beta Kappa. Home: 2040 Templar Dr Naperville IL 60565 Office: EES Div Argonne Nat Lab Argonne IL 60439

PADEN, BETTY BURNS, educator; b. Evanston, Ill., July 9, 1937; d. Joseph Ferdinand and Estelle (Taggart) Burns; m. Alvin Robert Paden, Aug. 18, 1962; children—Renee Lynn, Tina Jo. A.A., Kendall Coll., 1958; B.A., Roosevelt U., 1961, M.A., 1963; Ed.D., Loyola U., Chgo., 1970; J.D., No. Ill. U., 1979. Bar: Ill. 1980. Tchr., Chgo. Pub. Schs., 1961-67; editor, writer Scott Foresman Pub. Co., Glenview, Ill., 1967-68; instr. Loyola U., Chgo., 1968-70; cons., author Addison-Wesley Pub. Co., Scott Foresman Pub. Co., Lyon and Carhahan Pub. Co., Tangley Oaks Pub. Co., Harper Row Pub. Co., 1967-82; cons. Chgo. Bd. Edn., State of Ill., Chgo. Consortium of Colls. and Univs., 1973-82; prof. elem. edn. Northeastern Ill. U., Chgo., 1970—, assoc. chairperson elem. edn. dept., 1972-77; practice law, Evanston, Ill., 1980—. Bd. dirs. Evanston Zoning Bd. Appeals, Evanston Community Devel. Corp. Named Woman of Yr., NAACP, 1983; Kalm scholar, 1957-58; Com. Organized Research, Northeastern Ill. U. grantee, 1974-75; UNI Found. fellow, 1984; UNI Kellogg fellow, 1984; UNI grantee, 1985-86. Mem. Ill. Bar Assn., Chgo. Bar Assn., Am. Bar Assn., Internat. Reading Assn., Assn. Supervision and Curriculum Devel., Assn. Tchr. Educators. Author, editor: More Power and Moving Ahead, Open Highways Series, 1968; What Are They Up To? and What Does It Take?, 1971; What a Week!, Carmen Takes a Bow, Jamila, The Young America Basic Reading Program, 1973; The Birthday Surprise, 1976; The Ruby Pin Mystery, 1976; Truth is Stranger than Fiction, 1981; What is Big? What is Small?, Ann's Surprise, Make a Clown, 1983. Office: 5500 N St Louis Ave Room 3019 Chicago IL 60625

PAGANESSI, ARTHUR BRIAN, financial planner; b. Chgo., Jan. 8, 1946; s. Arthur and Frances (Radzwonovicz) P.; m. Nancy G. Johnson, Jan. 21, 1967; children—Jennifer Lynn, Laura Ann, Peter Johnson. B.S. in Edn., No. Ill. U., 1968. C.L.U.; chartered fin. cons. Tchr., Batavia Pub. Schs., Ill., 1968-73; ins. agt. Larry Gordon Agy. Glenview, Ill., 1973-82; pres. Kane DuPage Fin. Planning & Service Group Ltd., Geneva, Ill., 1982—; cons. in field; dir. S & N Mfg., Geneva, 1984—. Mem. Million Dollar Round Table, Internat. Assn. Fin. Planners, Ill. West Suburban chpt. Am. Soc. C.L.U.s (v.p. 1984-85, pres. 1985-86). Avocations: Trout fishing; pheasant hunting; scuba diving. Office: Kane DuPage Fin Planning and Service Group Ltd PO Box 132 Geneva IL 60134

PAGANO, RONALD ANTHONY, lawyer; b. N.Y.C., Sept. 20, 1952; s. Salvatore and Gloria Theresa (Iandiorio) P.; m. Susan Hope Privin, June 17, 1979; 1 son, Matthew Wallach. B.S. in Criminal Justice, SUNY-Buffalo, 1977; J.D., Ohio No. U., 1980. Bar: Ohio 1980, U.S. Dist. Ct. (no. dist.) Ohio 1981. Sole practice, Lima, Ohio, 1980-82, Troy, Ohio, 1983—; assoc. Swinehart & Princi Co., L.P.A., Troy, 1982-83; trustee non-profit bd. Harco Industries, Inc., Kenton, Ohio, 1982-83. Mem. Pres. Com. on Employment Handicapped, Washington, 1974-77; solicitor Village of Pleasant Hill, Ohio, 1983—. Recipient cert. of merit IRS, Cleve., 1980. Mem. ABA, Assn. Trial Lawyers Am., Ohio Assn. Trial Lawyers, Comml. Law League. Democrat. Roman Catholic. Club: Gt. Miami Longrifles (counsel 1983-84) (Sidney, Ohio). Home: 354 Monroe Concord Rd Troy OH 45373 Office: 1304 W McKaig Ave Troy OH 45373

PAGE, DOZZIE LYONS, educator; b. Tiptonville, Tenn., Apr. 13, 1921; d. Lessie LeRoy and Carrie (Oldham) Lyons; B.S.Ed., Chgo. Tchrs. Coll., 1968; M.S.Ed., Chgo. State U., 1976; M.A. in Bus. Edn., Govs. State U., 1979; children—Rita, Gerald. Cashier receptionist Unity Mut. Life Ins. Co., Chgo., 1939-47; sec. United Transport Service Employees Union, Chgo., 1947-51; sec. to dir. YMCA West Side, Chgo., 1951-53; sec., office mgr. Joint Council Dining Car Employees AFL CIO, Chgo., 1957-59; sr. stenographer Chgo. Police Dept., 1962-65; tchr. office practice Manpower Devel. Tng. Act, Chgo. Bd. Edn., 1965-67; tchr., coordinator distributive edn. Dunbar Vocat. High Sch., Chgo., 1968—. Mem. Office Occupations Club, Distributive Edn. Assn., Chgo. Urban League, Chgo. Bus. Edn. Assn. (exec. bd. 1983—), Ill., Am. personnel and guidance assns., Am. Vocat. Assn., Nat., Ill. bus. edn. assns., Chgo. State U. Alumni Assn., Governor's State U. Alumni Assn., Phi Delta Kappa. Home: 6127 Justine St S Chicago IL 60636 Office: 3000 ML King Dr Chicago IL 60616

PAGE, JOHN GARDNER, research institute advisor, scientist; b. Milw., Sept. 14, 1940; s. Raymond G. and Leone B. (Churchill) P.; m. Joyce Ann Krueger, July 7, 1962; children—Teresa Ann, Kimberly Christine. B.S., U. Wis.-Madison, 1963, M.S., 1966, Ph.D., 1967. Diplomate Am. Bd. Toxicology. Sr. Scientist NIH, Bethesda, Md., 1967-69, Eli Lilly Co., Indpls., 1969-77; dir. toxicology and pathology Rhone Poulenc, Inc., Ashland, Ohio, 1977-79; dir. toxicology, Toxigenics, Inc., Decatur, Ill., 1979-83; sr. research advisor Battelle Meml. Inst., Columbus, Ohio, 1983—. Contbr. articles to profl. jours. Bd. dirs. Am. Cancer Soc., Greenfield, Ind., 1973-77. Recipient Rennebohm Outstanding Tchr's award U. Wis., 1964. Mem. AAAS, Fedn. Am. Socs. Exptl. Biology, Am. Soc. Pharm. Exptl. Therapeutics, Soc. Toxicology, Am. Coll. Toxicology, Internat. Soc. for Study Xenobiotics, Sigma Xi, Rho Chi. Avocations: photography; hiking, fishing. Home: 1269 Castleton Rd N Columbus OH 43220 Office: Battelle Meml Inst 505 King Ave Columbus OH 43201

PAGE, JOHN IRWIN, Bible college president; b. Ft. Scott, Kans., Oct. 2, 1930; s. John Ellis and Ava Leona (Brown) P.; m. Virginia Maxine Witt, Aug. 1, 1951; children—Brenda, Carma, Courtney, Jonathan. B.A., Kans. City Coll. and Bible Sch., 1952; M.S., Pitts. State U., 1955, Ed.S., 1969; Ph.D. candidate, Kans. State U., 1985—. Pastor Ch. of God (Holiness), Stockton, Mo., 1952-58, Ft. Scott, Kans., 1959-80; prin. Ft. Scott Christian Heights Sch., 1954-80; mgr. Ironquill Estates, Ft. Scott, 1975-80; pres. Kansas City Coll. and Bible Sch., Overland Park, 1980—; v.p. Witt Engring., Inc., ElDorado Springs, Mo., 1968-80, Plainview Farms, Inc., Ft. Scott, 1974—; pres. Bourbon County Police Chaplaincy, Ft. Scott, 1965-80. Pres. Multi-County 4-C, Ft. Scott, 1970; bd. dirs. Human Relations Com., Ft. Scott, 1971; precinct worker Republican Party, Bourbon County, 1963. Named Outstanding Alumnus, Ft. Scott Community Coll., 1980, Hon. Police Col. Bourbon County Police Chaplaincy, 1965. Mem. Phi Delta Kappa (Continuous Service award 1985), Overland Park C. of C. Avocations: hunting, golf, sports. Home: 5301 W 83d St Prairie Village KS 66208 Office: Kansas City Coll and Bible Sch 7401 Metcalf St Overland Park KS 66204

PAGE, LINDA KAY, state official; b. Wadsworth, Ohio, Oct. 4, 1943; s. Frederick Meredith and Martha Irene (Vance) P. Student Franklin U., 1970-75, Sch. Banking, Ohio U., 1976-77; cert. Nat. Personnel Sch., U. Md.-Am. Bankers Assn., 1981; grad. banking program U. Wis.-Madison, 1982-84. Asst. v.p., gen. mgr. Bancohio Corp., Columbus, Ohio, 1975-78, v.p., dist. mgr., 1979-80, v.p., mgr. employee relations, 1980-81, v.p., div. mgr., 1982-83; commr. of banks State of Ohio, Columbus, 1983—; guest speaker, lectr. various banking groups. Bd. dirs. Clark County Mental Health Bd., Springfield, Ohio, 1982-83, Springfield Met. Housing, 1982-83; bd. advisers Orgn. Indsl. Standards, Springfield, 1982-83. Recipient Leadership Columbus award Sta. WTVN and Columbus Leadership Program, 1975, 82, Outstanding Service award Clark County Mental Health Bd., 1983. Mem. Nat. Assn. Bank Women (pres. 1980-81), Bus. and Profl. Women's Club, LWV, Conf. State Bank Suprs. (bd. dirs. 1984-85), dist. chmn. 1984-85), Ohio Bankers Assn. (bd. dirs. 1982-83). Democrat. Lodge: Zonta. Avocations: tennis; animal protection; matchbook collecting. Home: 1330 Erickson Ave Columbus OH 43227 Office: Dept Commerce Div of Banks 2 Nationwide Plaza Columbus OH 43215

PAGE, RUTH, dancer; b. Indpls.; d. Lafayette and Marian (Heinly) Page; student Tudor Hall, Indpls., N.Y.C.; D.H.L. (hon.), DePaul U., 1980, Ind. U., 1982; hon. degree, Columbia Coll., Chgo.; m. Thomas Hart Fisher, Feb. 8, 1925 (dec.); m. Andre Delfau, May 16, 1983. Dancer with Pavlowa at age of 15; performed in leading role of J. Alden Carpenter's The Birthday of the Infanta, produced by Chgo. Opera Co., 1919, later in N.Y.C.; toured U.S. as prin. dancer with Adolph Bolm's Ballet, later appeared in London with Mr. Bolm; premiere danseuse 2d Music Box Revue, N.Y.C., 1921-23, Chgo. Allied Arts performances, 1924, 25, 26; studied under Enrico Cecchetti at Monte Carlo, 1925; premiere danseuse Mcpl. Opera Co., Buenos Aires, Ravinia Opera Co., 1926-31; guest soloist with Met. Opera Co., 1926-28; guest artist at enthronement ceremonies for Emperor Hirohito, Japan, 1928; performed series of Am. dances before Sophil Soc., Moscow, 1930; ballet dir. Chgo. Opera, 1934-37, 42-43, 45; dir. Fed. Theatre Dance Project, Chgo., 1938-39; S. Am. tour with first dance group as co-dir. Page-Stone Ballet, 1940; guest choreographer with Bentley Stone, dancer Frankie and Johnny for Ballet Russe de Monte Carlo, 1945; guest choreographer, dancer The Bells for Ballet Russe de Monte Carlo, 1946, Billy Sunday, 1948; Impromptu au Bois, and Revanche, Les Ballets des Champs-Elysees, 1951, Royal Festival Ballet, Vilia, 1953; co-dir. Les Ballets Americains, Theatre des Champs Elysees, Paris, 1950; ballet mistress Chgo. Lyric Opera, 1954-69; choreographer, dir. Ruth Page's Chgo. Opera Ballet, 1956-66, Ruth Page's Internat. Ballet, 1966-70; choreographer Merry Widow Ballet, 1956, Susanna and the Barber, 1957, Salome, 1957, Triumph of Chastity, 1958, El Amor Brujo, 1958, Camille, 1958, Carmen, 1959, Fledermaus, 1960, Concertino, 1961, Mefistofela, 1962, Bullets or Bon-Bons, 1965, Nutcracker, 1965—, Carmina Burana, 1966, Bolero, 1967, Dancer's Ritual, 1968, Alice in the Garden, 1970, also Alice in Wonderland and Alice Through the Looking Glass at Pitts. Ballet Theatre, 1971, Catulli Carmina, 1973, Chain of Fools, 1973, Alice in Wonderland ballet, 1978, Frankie and Johnny, produced by Dance Theater of Harlem, Covent Garden, London, 1981, N.Y.C., 1982; lectr. tour Ruth Page's Invitation to the Dance, 1971-72; pres., treas. Ruth Page Found. and Ballet Sch. Recipient award Adult Council Greater Chgo., 1963; citation outstanding service Ballet Guild Chgo. Mem. Chgo. Nat. Assn. Dance

Masters (hon.). Clubs: Arts, Friday, Racquet (Chgo.). Contbr. to mags. Address: Ruth Page Found Sch Dance 1016 N Dearborn St Chicago IL 60610

PAGE, SALLY JACQUELYN, university official; b. Saginaw, Mich., July 6853 1943; d. William Henry and Doris Effie (Knippel) P.; B.A., U. Iowa, 1965; M.B.A., So. Ill. U., 1973. Copy editor, C.V. Mosby Co., St. Louis, 1965-69; edit. cons. Edit. Assos., Edwardsville, Ill., 1969-70; research adminstr. So. Ill. U., 1970-74, asst. to pres., affirmative action officer, 1974-77; civil rights officer U. N.D., Grand Forks, 1977—, lectr. mgmt., 1978—; polit. comentator Sta. KFJM, Nat. Public Radio affiliate, 1981—. Contbr. to profl. jours. Pres., Pine to Prairie council Girl Scouts U.S.A., 1980—; mem. employment com. Ill. Commn. on Status of Women, 1976-77; mem. Bicentennial Com. Edwardsville, 1976, Bikeway Task Force Edwardsville, 1975-77; mem. Civil Service Rev. Task Force, Grand Forks, 1982, civil service commr., 83, chmn., 1984. Mem. AAUW (dir. Ill. 1975-77), Coll. and Univ. Personnel Assn. (research and publs. bd. 1982—) Am. Assn. Affirmative Action, Soc. Research Adminstrs., M.B.A. Assn. Republican. Presbyterian. Home: 3121 Cherry St Grand Forks ND 58201 Office: Univ ND Grand Forks ND 58202

PAGE, T. EDWARD, lawyer; b. Bad Cannstatt, Germany, Jan. 14, 1954; came to U.S., 1954; s. Charles Arthur and Jeanne (Brizius) P. B.A., U. Ill., 1975; J.D., Ind. U., 1978. Bar: Ind. 1978, U.S. Dist. Ct. (so. dist.) Ind. 1978, U.S. Ct. Appeals (7th cir.) 1980, U.S. Dist. Ct. (no. dist.) Ind. 1984. Intern pub. defender, Monroe County, Ind., Bloomington, 1977-78; law clk. Criminal Ct. Marion County, Ind., Indpls., 1978-79; dep. pros. atty. Lake County, Ind., Crown Point, 1979-84; commr. Superior Ct. of Lake County, Ind., 1984—. Parliamentarian, Lake County Republican Central Com., Crown Point, 1984; del. Rep. State Conv., 1984, Rep. Nat. Conv., 1984. Recipient Order of the Arrow, Boy Scouts Am., 1968, also Eagle Scout award. Mem. ABA, Ind. Bar Assn., Nat. Dist. Attys. Assn., Assn. Trial Lawyers Am., Am. Inst. Parliamentarians. Roman Catholic. Home: 8052 Matterhorn Ln Crown Point IN 46307 Office: Superior Ct Lake County 2293 N Main St Crown Point IN 46307

PAGELS, CHARLES FREDERICK, educational administrator; b. Chgo., June 19, 1946; s. Charles F. and Anna A. (Olson) P.; m. Jacque Stallings, Feb. 12, 1975; children—Lezah, Charles. B.S., Ill. State U., 1969, M.S., 1970; Ed.D., U. Va., 1973. Cert. supt., Ill. Asst. prof. Marquette U., Milw., 1973-74; asst. prin. John Yeates High Sch., Suffolk, Va., 1974-75; asst. supt. Porta Sch. Dist., Petersburg, Ill., 1975-78; asst. supt. Indian Prairie Sch. Dist., Naperville, Ill., 1978—. Republican precinct committeeman. Served with USMC, 1965-71. Mem. Dupage County County Curriculum Developers (bd. dirs.), Assn. Supervision and Curriculum Devel., Ill. Assn. Supervision and Curriculum Devel. (v.p. chpt.), Am. Assn. Sch. Adminstrs., Naperville C. of C. (edn. com.), Lodges: Rotary, Kiwanis. Contbr. articles to profl. jours. Home: 2230 W Illinois Ave Aurora IL 60506 Office: 30W026 Ogden Ave Naperville IL 60540

PAGLINO, VINCENT MICHAEL, manufacturing company executive; b. Queens County, N.Y., Sept. 7, 1941; s. Salvatore and Gaetana Anna (Russo) P.; m. Danna Usher Cobb, Oct. 24, 1964; children—Justin Cobb, Ethan James. B.Aero. Engring. (N.Y. State Sci. scholar 1959-63, Rensselaer scholar 1959-60), Rensselaer Poly. Inst., Troy, N.Y., 1963; M.S. in Aerospace (research asst.) 1963-64), W. Va. U., 1964; M.B.A. in Fin. summa cum laude (Guy Goetner award 1975), U. Bridgeport (Conn.), 1975. With Sikorsky Aircraft div. United Technologies Corp., Stratford, Conn., 1964-81, chief bus. planning systems, 1975-81; mgr. operational planning and bus. devel. Gen. Electric Co., Erie, Pa., 1981-82; corp. dir. strategic planning SENCORP, Cin., 1982—; instr. applied math. Bridgeport Engring. Inst., 1965-66. Mem. Am. Helicopter Soc., Planning Execs. Inst., Beta Gamma Sigma. Club: Queechee Lakes (Vt.) Country. Author papers in fields of bus. planning and aerodynamics. Inventor yawed blade element method for helicopter design. Home: 13068 Coopermeadow Ln Cincinnati OH 45242 Office: SENCORP 8485 Broadwell Rd Cincinnati OH 45244

PAHANISH, EDMUND, manufacturing company executive; b. Washington, Pa., Jan. 24, 1928; s. Michael and Anna Margaret (Graytok) P.; m. Delores Anita Pyle, Oct. 6, 1948; children—Richard Wayne, Brenda Faye, Deborah Kathleen. Student Kent State U., 1970. Machinist, Chester Hoist Co., Lisbon, Ohio, 1943-46; molder Eljer Co., Salem, Ohio, 1947-59; salesman Western & So. Life Ins. Co., 1959-62; welder Columbiana (Ohio) Boiler Co., 1962-65; welder-fitter Fordees Corp., Leetonia, Ohio, 1965-68; pres. Spl. Equipment Corp., Salem, 1968-78; plant mgr. JLG Industries, Bedford, Pa., 1978-82; Delta Fab Co., Salem, 1983—. Pres., Junction-Miller Rd-Inc., 1969—. Served with Signal Corps, U.S. Army, 1945-46. Named Personality of Week, Everett (Pa.) Newspaper, 1981. Mem. Am. Prodn. and Inventory Control Soc., So. Alleghenies Planning and Devel. Commn. Roman Catholic. Lodge: Rotary (Bedford, Pa.). Patentee gutter rake; inventor stenciling machine, digger, cable cutter. Home: 40090 Miller Rd Leetonia OH 44431

PAINTER, MARK PHILIP, judge; b. Cin., Apr. 6, 1947; s. John Philip and Marjorie (West) P. B.A., U. Cin., 1970; J.D., 1973. Bar: Ohio 1973, U.S. Dist. Ct. (so. dist.) Ohio 1973, U.S. Supreme Ct. 1980. Sole practice, Cin., 1973-82; judge Hamilton County Mcpl. Ct., Cin., 1982—. Contbr. articles to profl. jours. Bd. dirs. Citizens Sch. Com., Cin., 1974-76; trustee Freestore Foodbank, Cin., 1984—, Mary Jo Brueggeman Meml. Found., Cin., 1981—; mem. Republican Central Com., Cin., 1972-82. Recipient Superior Jud. Service award Ohio Supreme Ct., 1982. Mem. ABA, Ohio State Bar Assn., Cin. Bar Assn., Am. Judges Assn., Nat. Criminal Justice Assn. Club: Bankers (Cin.). Home: 2232 Wheeler St Cincinnati OH 45219 Office: Hamilton County Mcpl Ct 222 E Central Pkwy Cincinnati OH 45202

PAINTER, MILTON MCFARLAND, manufacturing company executive; b. Friars Point, Miss., Dec. 6, 1920; s. Milton McFarland and Ernestine (Cobb) P.; B.A., La. State U., 1942; m. Frances Elwanda Groves, Apr. 4, 1955; children—Michael Cobb, Cynthia Lee, Judy Frances. Creative dir., merchandising dept. Walgreen Drug Stores, Chgo., 1946-50; account exec. Chek-Chart Corp., 1950-53; asst. dir. advt. and sales promotion Ency. Brit., Inc., 1953-56; advt. supr., canned meat div. and frozen food div. Libby, McNeil & Libby, 1956-66; account exec. Young & Rubicam, Inc., 1966-68; advt. and sales promotion mgr. Westclox div. Gen. Time Corp., LaSalle, Ill., 1968-72; advt. and sales promotion mgr. Republic Molding Corp., Chgo., 1972—. Served to tech. sgt. USAAF, 1942-45; to lt. col. USAFR, 1946-80. Mem. Smithsonian Assocs., Res. Officers Assn., Ill. Sheriffs Assn., SAR, Sons of Confederate Vets., Art Inst. Chgo., La. State U. Alumni Fedn., Mil. Order Stars and Bars, Chgo. Council on Fgn. Relations, Air Force Assn., Daggers, Sigma Alpha Epsilon. Home: 881 Darlington Ln Crystal Lake IL 60014

PAINTER, THOMAS JAY, financial executive; b. Evanston, Ill., June 24, 1944; s. Richard Leland and Marge (Russell) P.; m. Barbara Frances Rochow, Jan. 28, 1967; children—Steven, David, Ryan. B.S. in Elec. Engring., U. Md., 1966; M.B.A., Harvard U., 1970. Systems analyst Gen. Electric Co., Roslyn, Va., 1967-68; fin. analyst Air Products & Chems., Allentown, Pa., 1970-73; v.p. fin. Arcair Corp., Lancaster, Ohio, 1973-76; controller ITT Phillips Drill, Michigan City, Ind., 1976-80; v.p. fin. ITT Lester Industries, Bedford Heights, Ohio, 1980—. Baseball coach Kiwanis Club, Hudson, Ohio, 1980-84; treas. Troop 321, Boy Scouts Am., Hudson, 1982-83. Mem. Nat. Assn. Accts., Am. Mgmt. Assn., Tau Beta Pi, Omicron Delta Kappa, Beta Kappa Nu. Republican. Club: Harvard Business (Cleve.). Avocations: skiing; golf. Home: 7713 Salem Dr Hudson OH 44236 Office: ITT Lester Industries Inc 25661 Cannon Rd Bedford Heights OH 44146

PAIRENT, FREDERICK WILLIAM, university dean, biochemistry educator; b. Phila., Jan. 18, 1932; s. Frederick Henry and Marie C. (Carney) P.; m. Constance Ferris, Sept. 13, 1958; 1 child, Denise H. B.S. in Chemistry, St. Joseph's U., 1953; M.S. in Biochemistry, Loyola U., 1959, Ph.D. in Biochemistry, 1961. Analytical chemist Smith, Kline & French Labs., Phila., 1956-57; instr. biochemistry Loyola U., Chgo., 1961-65; from instr. to asst. prof. Hahnemann Med. Coll., Phila., 1965-83, assoc. dean for med. edn., 1975-83; prof., dean Sch. Allied Health Professions U. Wis.-Milw., 1983—. Contbr. articles to profl. jours. and books; presenter papers to workshops. Served with U.S. Army, 1954-55, Germany. Recipient Disting. Teaching award C.R. and M.F. Lindback Found., 1973. Mem. Am. Assn. Med. Colls., Am. Soc. Allied Health Professions. Avocation: photography. Home: 744 Grand Ave Thiensville WI 53092 Office: Sch Allied Health Professions Univ Wis PO Box 413 Milwaukee WI 53201

PAJA, RONALD PHILIP, lawyer; b. Chgo., Aug. 8, 1952; s. Albert George and Irene Phylis (Waksmulski) P.; m. Mary Kay Collins, June 19, 1976; children—Megan Marie, Kevin Matthew. B.A., U. Notre Dame, 1974; J.D., No. Ill. U., 1979. Bar: Ill. 1979, U.S. Dist. Ct. (no. dist.) Ill. 1979. Maintenance adminstrn. Village of Deerfield, Ill., 1973-77; prin. Law Office of Ronald P. Paja, Chgo., 1979-82, Kearney & Phelan, Ltd., Barrington, Ill., 1982-85; ptnr. Cox & Paja, Attys., 1985—. Mem. Ill. State Bar Assn., Jo Daviess County Bar Assn. Office: Cox & Paja Attys 116 S Main St PO Box 124 Stockton IL 61085-0124

PAJIC, SVETOMIR, veterinarian; b. Obrenovac, Serbia, Yugoslavia, Nov. 24, 1932; came to U.S., 1963, naturalized, 1968; s. Ljubomir and Paulina (Vukajlovic) P.; m. Gerda Martha Hanschmann, July 24, 1960; 1 child, Renata. D.V.M., Vet. Med. U., Belgrad, Yugoslavia, 1957; D.V.M., Vet. Med. U., Hannover, Fed. Republic Germany, 1964, Ph.D. in Clin. Pathology and Bacteriology 1964. Gen. practice vet. medicine specializing in large animals, Obrenovac, 1957-58; cons. Animal Health Inst., Obrenovac, 1957-58, Hemmersam & Rasmussen, Luebeck, Fed. Republic Germany, 1959-60; insp. in charge Slavonia Packing House, Osijik, Yugoslavia, 1960-62; gen. practice vet. medicine specializing in large animals, Lensahm. Fed. Republic Germany, 1962-63; vet. med. officer U.S. Dept. Agr., Elburn, Ill., 1964-68, supr. vet. med. officer, 1968—. Mem. AVMA. Serbian Orthodox. Club: Chess (St. Charles, Ill.). Lodge: Lions. Home: 1702 Jay Ln Saint Charles IL 60174 Office: Grant St North Aurora IL 60542

PAK, KOON YAN, cancer researcher; b. Mui Yuan, Canton, Peoples Republic of China, Aug. 9, 1950; came to U.S., 1971, naturalized, 1985; s. Chi-Chung and So-Mui (Siu) P.; m. Siu-Chun Ng; children—Victoria Ming-Yan, Edward Sing-Yan. B.A., SUNY-Plattsburgh, 1974; M.S., U. Pitts., 1977; Ph.D., Memphis State U., 1981. Postdoctoral researcher Wistar Inst., Phila., 1981-83; researcher scientist Mallinckrodt Inc., St. Louis, 1983—. Mem. Hybridoma, AAAS. Home: 1242 Hyannis Dr Creve Coeur MO 63146 Office: Mallinckrodt Inc 675 McDonnell Blvd Hazelwood MO 63134

PAKER, PHILLIP ERROL, business executive; b. Chgo., July 8, 1945; s. Abraham Daniel and RoseJoy (Noren) P.; B.A. in Bus. Adminstrn., Bellevue (Nebr.) Coll., 1967; postgrad. DePaul U., 1978; m. Diane Marie Breon, July 12, 1966; children—Edward Phillip, Mathew Shane, Deborah Ann, Aaron David, Joshua Nathaniel. Systems rep., sr. programmer analyst Honeywell, 1969; cons. PEPI Consulting, Chgo., 1969—; data base analyst Continental Nat. Assurance, 1976-78; mgr. data base systems and adminstrn. consulting COMSI, Oak Brook; Ill., 1978-79; mgr. data base adminstrn. Target Stores, Fridley, Minn., 1979-82; mgr. mgmt. cons. services Coopers & Lybrand, Mpls., 1980-83; owner/cons. Problem Solvers, 1983—. Served with USAF, 1965-69. Mem. M.B.A. Assn., Nat. Rifle Assn. Home: 22603 Cedar Dr Bethel MN 55005

PAKIN, SHERWIN ELVIN, computer consulting company executive; b. Chgo., Jan. 3, 1938; s. Peter B. and Sylvia (Stoller) P.; m. Sandra Sue Preis, Dec. 18, 1960; children—Scott D., Stacy R. B.S., Ill. Inst. Tech., 1961, B.S., 1965; M.B.A., U. Chgo., 1969. Mem. mktg. dept. IBM Corp., Chgo., 1961-78; exec. v.p. SP & A, Inc., Chgo., 1978—. Contbr. articles to profl. jours. Sec. bd. dirs. Light Opera Works, Evanston, Ill., 1984—; mem. adv. council Ill. Inst. Tech., 1984—. Served to 1st lt. U.S. Army, 1961-67. Mem. Soc. for Tech. Communications, Ind. Computer Cons. Assn. (bd. dirs. 1981), Soc. for Info. Mgmt., Data Processing Mgmt. Assn., Assn. for Systems Mgmt. Home: 6007 N Sheridan Rd Chicago IL 60660 Office: SP & A Inc 6007 N Sheridan Rd Chicago IL 60660

PAKULIS, IVARS ERVINS, instrumentation company executive; b. Riga, Latvia, May 25, 1933; came to U.S., 1951; s. Martins and Lucija Anna (Lieknejs) P.; m. Linda Sue Dressler, Apr. 30, 1977. Student McCoy Coll., 1958-61. Research asst. Johns Hopkins U., Balt., 1958-62; sr. field engr. Bendix BFE, Columbia, Md., 1962-70; service mgr. Dann Co., Cleve., 1970-72; br. mgr. Bendix COMSCO, Chgo., 1972-74; sr. applications engr. Kay-Ray, Inc., Arlington Heights, Ill., 1974-81; v.p. R&D, Advanced Moisture Tech., Wauconda, Ill., 1981—. Contbr. articles to profl. jours. Served with U.S. Army, 1953-55. Mem. Assn. Advancement of Med. Instrumentation, Internat. Microwave Power Inst. Office: Advanced Moisture Tech Inc 219 S Main St Wauconda IL 60084

PAKYZ, LAWRENCE JOSEPH, dentist; b. Chgo., Feb. 9, 1943; s. Izydor J. and Dorothy I (Frederickson) P.; m. Carol Marie Potvin, June 24, 1965; children—Christopher, Troy. D.D.S., Marquette U., Milw., 1967. Pres. Sauk Prairie Dental Assocs., S.C., Prairie du Sac, Wis., 1968—; staff dentist Sauk Prairie Meml. Hosp., Prairie du Sac, 1968—, dental dir. Maplewood Nursing Home, Prairie du Sac, 1975—. Served to major USAR, 1969-76. Fellow Am. Endodontic Soc.; mem. ADA, Wis. State Dental Assn., Sauk Jr. Dental Soc. (pres. 1973-74). Roman Catholic. Club: Optimist (Sauk Prairie) (pres. 1969-70). Avocations: professional photography; hiking; camping. Home: Route 2 Box 282 Sauk City WI 53583 Office: Sauk Prairie Dental Assocs SC 335 Galena St Prairie Du Sac WI 53578

PALENCHAR, ROBERT EDWARD, diversified industry exec.; b. Detroit, Apr. 8, 1922; s. John Peter and Irene Ann (Repicky) P.; A.B. in Econs. and Personnel Adminstrn., U. Notre Dame, 1942; postgrad. U. Mich., 1943; m. Ethel Lindsay, Sept. 10, 1942; children—Patricia Ann (Mrs. Richard K. Atchinson), James Lindsay. With Ex-Cell-O Corp., Detroit, 1949-62, dir. indsl. relations, 1962; v.p. employee relations automotive div. Budd Co., Detroit, 1962-66; v.p., dir. employee relations Sunbeam Corp., Chgo., 1966-69; v.p. personnel and pub. relations Esmark, Inc., 1969-77, v.p. corp. affairs and personnel, 1977—, dir. subholding cos. Pres., Esmark, Inc. Found., 1971—. Served with U.S. Army, 1943. Mem. Chgo. Bd. Commerce, Bus. Roundtable (labor-mgmt. com.), Ill. C. of C., Notre Dame Alumni Assn., Am. Mgmt. Assn., Conf. Bd. Club: Mid-America (Chgo.). Home: 64 Joyce Ct Glen Ellyn IL 60137 Office: 55 E Monroe St Chicago IL 60603

PALERMO, EUGENE JAMES, chemist, marketing manager; b. Melrose Park, Ill., Jan. 2, 1946; s. Peter Paul and Concetta (D'Anza) P.; m. Marietta Nobile, May 1, 1976. B.S. in Chemistry, U. Ill.-Chgo., 1971; M.B.A., Loyola U., Chgo., 1977. Research chemist Richardson Co., Melrose Park, Ill., 1971-78; sales rep. Lydall, Inc., Chgo., 1978-79; research chemist Am. Can Co., Barrington, Ill., 1979-80; mktg. mgr. Lydall, Inc., Chgo., 1981-83, group mktg. mgr., 1984—. Served with U.S. Army, 1965-68; Vietnam. Mem. Am. Mgmt. Assn. Office: Lydall Inc 3010 Woodcreek Dr Downers Grove IL 60515

PALIA, CHARLES CANTARDO, ednl. adminstr.; b. Spring Valley, Ill., Sept. 5, 1923; s. Cantardo and Mary Lou (Barto) P.; B.S. in Zoology, So. Ill., 1950; M.S., No. Ill.U, 1960; m. Enise M. Nanni, Aug. 2, 1947; children—Charles, David Damian. Tchr. math. and sci. Spring Valley Elementary Schs., 1950-60; prin. Lincoln Sch., Spring Valley, 1960-64; supt. schs., Spring Valley, 1964—. Post adviser Explorer Scouts; active civil def., Salvation Army, A.R.C., Tri-County Humane Soc. Bd. dirs. Spring Valley Assn. City Library, 1965-71; pres. adult bd. Spring Valley Youth Center. Served with USNR, 1942-45. Recipient Silver Beaver award Boy Scouts Am., 1971. Mem. Ill. Assn. Mental Health, Ill. Assn. Sch. Adminstrs., Bur. County Adminstrs., Ill. Sch. Bd. Assn., Am. Legion, Bqr.-Marshal-Putnam Tri-County Spl. Ednl. Coop. (chmn. 1971—), Am. Sch. Food Service Assn. Clubs: K.C., Rotary (pres. Spring Valley 1974-75). Home: 325 W Minnesota St Spring Valley IL 61362 Office: 800 N Richard Ave Spring Valley IL 61362

PALLASCH, MAGDALENA HELENA (MRS. BERNHARD MICHAEL PALLASCH), artist; b. Chgo., Sept. 6, 1908; d. Frank and Anna (Meier) Fixari; student Chgo. Acad. Fine Arts, 1922-26, Am. Acad. Fine Arts, 1926-30, U. Chgo., 1960, Art Inst. Chgo.; pvt. study with Joseph Allworthy, 1935-38; m. Bernhard Pallasch, Nov. 26, 1931 (dec. Nov. 1977); children—Bernhard Michael, Diana Pallasch Miller. Contbr. two murals and ten life size figures for Century of Progress Exhbn., Chgo., 1933-34; free-lance portrait artist, subjects include Cardinal Cody, Chgo., 1958—; represented in permanent collections Loyola U., Chgo., Barat Coll., Lake Forest, Ill., Internat. Coll. Surgeons, Chgo., Med. Library, Columbus Hosp. Mem. Presentation Ball Aux.; mem. President's Club, Loyola U., also mem. women's bd. Recipient first award for still life Arts Club, N.Y.C., 1960; First award Nat. League Am. Pen Women, 1972; 1st place and best of show State Exhibit, Springfield, Ill., 1973; 1st award Chgo. Woman's Club, 1978; hon. mention for portrait Italian Cultural Ctr.; hon. alumna award Loyola U., Chgo. Mem. Nat. League Am. Pen Women (v.p. Chgo. br. 1966-68, art chmn. 1978-80, Margaret Dingle Meml. award 1979), Mcpl. Art League Chgo., Nat. Soc. Arts and Letters (art chmn. chgo. chpt. 1982—), Friends of Austria, Friends of D'Arcy Gallery of Medieval and Renaissance Art. Clubs: Ill. Cath. Women (gov. 1979—), Cuneo Meml. Hosp. Aux. (dir.), Fidelitas (dir.). Home and Home and Studio: 723 Junior Terr Chicago IL 60613

PALMATIER, ROBERT ALLEN, linguist, educator; b. Kalamazoo, Mich., July 22, 1926; s. Karl Ernest and Cecile C. (Chase) P.; m. Marion Dolores Babilla, Dec. 21, 1946; children—David Eugene, Denise Marie Palmatier Mulder. B.A. magna cum laude, Western Mich. U., 1950, M.A., 1955; Ph.D., U. Mich., 1965. Instr. English Western Mich. U., Kalamazoo, 1955-57, asst. prof. English, 1957-64, assoc. prof. English, 1964-67, prof. English, 1967-68, prof. linguistics, 1968—, dept. chmn., 1968—, dir. Latvian studies program, 1981—. Author: A Descriptive Syntax of the Ormulum, 1969; A Glossary for English Transformational Grammar, 1972; also articles. Served with U.S. Army, 1944-46. Mem. Linguistic Soc. Am., MLA, Mich. Linguistic Soc. (pres. 1973-74). Club: Beacon. Avocations: golf; yardwork; car repair. Home: 1326 Hardwick Ave Kalamazoo MI 49002 Office: Western Mich U Dept Langs and Linguistics Kalamazoo MI 49008

PALMER, EDWARD HENRY, consulting and development company executive; b. Chgo., Feb. 12, 1932; s. Brian Charles and Catherine Dorothy P.; m. Davalyn D. Nelson, June 4, 1982. B.A., Hanover Coll., 1955; S.T.M., Yale U., 1958; postgrad. Northwestern U., 1960-62. Asst. rector St. Pauls Ch., New Haven, 1958-60; with Chgo. Housing Authority, Chgo., 1960-62; with Hyde Park Kenwood Community Orgn., Chgo., 1962-64; chmn. Palmer France Assocs. Ltd., Chgo.; lectr. Ill. Inst.Tech., U. Ill.; speaker profl. orgns. Episcopalian. Clubs: Cliff Dwellers, Carlton, Quadrangle (Chgo.). Contbr. articles on housing to profl. jours. Home: 812 S Kensington LaGrange IL 60525 Office: Palmer France Assocs Ltd 1 N LaSalle Chicago IL 60602

PALMER, HEATHER, radiation therapy technologist, administrator; b. Erie, Pa., July 28, 1947; d. Robert E. and Iris J. (Harridine) Wheeler. Grad. Radiology Sch., Hamot Med. Ctr., Erie, Pa., 1965-67, grad. Radiation Therapy Sch., 1971-72; cert. in allied health/dosimetry U. Kans.-Kansas City, 1978-79; B.A. in Allied Health/Mgmt., Nat. Coll. Edn., 1984. Staff x-ray technologist Hamot Med. Ctr., 1967-69, staff radiation therapy technologist, 1969-74; asst. chief radiation therapy tech., instr. U. Kans., 1974-78; dosimetrist St. Joseph Hosp., Elgin, Ill., 1979-81, chief technologist, program dir. Radiation Therapy Sch., 1981—. Mem. adv. com. for Coll. Palmer House Crystal Lake (Ill.) City Council, 1980. Mem. Am. Assn. Med. Dosimetrists (charter), Am. Registry Radiologic Technologists, Am. Assn. Physicists in Medicine, Ill. Soc. Radiation Therapy Technologists. Author articles. Home: 820 Broadway Ave Crystal Lake IL 60014 Office: 77 N Airlite St Elgin IL 60120

PALMER, JERRY RICHARD, lawyer; b. Jefferson City, Mo., Aug. 22, 1940; s. Noble Edison and Harriet Jane (McCall) P.; m. Ann Leffler, Aug. 20, 1965; children—Christopher Paul, Andrea Leffler. B.A., U. Kans., 1962, J.D., 1966. Bar: Kans. 1966. Ptnr. Fisher, Patterson, Sayler & Smith, Topeka, 1966-70; assoc. Fisher & Benfer, 1971-74; sole practice, 1975-77; ptnr. Stumbo, Palmer et al., 1978-80; pres. Jerry R. Palmer P.A., 1980—. Mem. Assn. Trial Lawyers Am. (bd. govs. 1982-85), Kans. Trial Lawyers Assn. (pres. 1977), Nat. Bd. Trial Advocacy. Democrat. Episcopalian. Advocations: skiing; sailing; photography. Home: 305 Greenwood Topeka KS 66606 Office: Jerry R Palmer 112 SW 6th St Suite 102 Topeka KS 66603

PALMER, LYELLE LEE, teacher educator, instruction theorist, special education specialist; b. San Jose, Calif., Mar. 4, 1938; s. Lyelle Alonzo and Hope Olive (Hershberger) P.; m. Mary Frances Myers O'Connor, Aug. 27, 1962; 1 child, Madeline Myers. Mus.B. in Music Edn., So. Meth. U., 1962, Mus. M. in Music Lit. and History, 1963; Ph.D. in Secondary Edn. and Psychology, North Tex. State U., 1974. Dir. Reading and Ednl. Clinic, Dallas, 1968-75; asst. prof. edn. Iowa State U., Ames, 1975-77; prof. edn. Winona State U., Minn., 1977—; cons. Chgo. Pub. Schs., 1985—. Editorial bd. Jour. Accelerated Learning and Teaching, Ames, 1978—. Contbr. articles to profl. jours.; editor: Developmentalist, 1979-84. Bd. dirs. Winona County Devel. Achievement Ctr., 1982-84. Mem. Council Learning Disabilities (state pres. 1981-83), Council Exceptional Children Facility (advisor 1975—), AAAS, Minn. Edn. Assn., Phi Delta Kappa (local pres. 1983-84). Methodist. Club: Winona Sailing (v.p. 1978). Lodge: Kiwanis (v.p. 1985). Home: 1402-G McNally Dr Winona MN 55987 Office: Dept Edn Winona State U Winona MN 55987

PALMER, MARGARET LOUISE, speech and lang. pathologist; b. Flint, Mich., Sept. 18, 1935; d. Frederick William and Sylvia Elvira (Mattsen) P.; B.A., Mich. State U., 1959, M.A., 1967. Speech and lang. pathologist Ingham Intermediate Sch. Dist., Mason, Mich., 1959—; cons. Ednl. Consultation Center. Lic. pvt. pilot. Mem. Am. Speech and Hearing Assn. (certificate of clin. competence), Council of Exceptional Children, Mich. Speech and Hearing Assn., Aircraft Owners and Pilots Assn., Phi Kappa Phi. Home: 408 Durand St East Lansing MI 48823 Office: 2630 W Howell Rd Mason MI 48854

PALMER, MELVIN GERALD, gemologist, consultant; b. Springfield, Ill., May 9, 1937; s. Melvin G. and Helen C. (Bleser) P.; m. Linda Lee Ball, May 16, 1964; children—Tonya Lee, Shawn Ann. Watch commander (lt.) Police Dept., Springfield, 1961-83 (ret.); owner, chief exec. LubeMaster 10 min. Oil Change, Springfield, 1978—, J.& L. Palmer, Inc., Springfield, 1983—. Author Palmer's Diamond Buying Guide, 1984. Served with USN, 1954-58. Fellow Am. Assn. Criminology; mem. Gemological Inst. Am. Alumni Assn., Ill. Police Assn., Policeman's Benevolent and Protective Assn. Ill. (life), Greater Springfield C. of C., Better Bus. Bur. Clubs: Abe Lincoln Gun, Shuto Kan Karate. Lodge: K.C. Avocations: shooting; karate; painting; gemology. Office: J&L Palmer Inc Myers Bldg Suite 510 Springfield IL 62701

PALMER, PEGGY NESS, public relations executive; b. Clear Lake, S.D., Mar. 31, 1951; d. Oscar Percy and Karen Marie (Anderson) Ness; m. Anthony M. Palmer, July 9, 1977; 1 child, Melissa Heather. B.A., in Journalism, U. Minn., 1973; postgrad. U. Minn.-Morris, 1973—. Reporter Swift County Monitor, Benson, Minn., 1973; asst. dir. coll. relations Mt. Senario Coll., Ladysmith, Wis., 1973-74; acting dir. univ. relations, alumni affairs U. Minn.-Morris, 1979; editorial asst. 1974-79, pub. relations rep., 1979—; mem. steering com. Improve Understanding Liberal Learning, 1982-84. Bd. dirs. Morris Area Bus. Profl. Women, 1982-84, Country Day Nursery Sch., 1984—; co-chmn. Prairie Pioneer Festival, Morris, 1984—. Recipient Most Improved Publs. award Council for Advancement and Support Edn., 1979. Mem. Pub. Relations Soc. Am., Univ. Coll. Designers Assn., All Univ. Relations Group, All Univ. Editors Group, Rural Women Mean Bus., Morris Area C. of C. (bd. dirs. 1984-85). Avocations: local history and folklore; photography; writing; cross country skiing. Home: 100 E 8th St Morris MN 56267 Office: Univ Relations U Minn Morris MN 56267

PALMER, RAYMOND A., library association executive; b. Louisville, Ky., May 8, 1939. M.L.S., U. Ky., 1966; B.A. in Biology, U. Louisville, 1961. Mgmt. trainee Joseph E. Seagram & Sons, Louisville, 1961-64, supr. warehouse dept., 1964-65; grad. asst. U. Ky., Lexington, 1965-66; adminstrv. asst. to dir. Welch Med. Library, Balt., 1966-69; asst.librarian Francis J. Countway Library of Medicine, 1969-74; health scis. librarian, assoc. prof. library adminstrn. Wright State U., Dayton, Ohio, 1974-82; exec. dir. Med. Library Assn., Chgo., 1982—; vis. lectr. Library Sch., U. N.C., Chapel Hill, 1984. Mem. Am. Assn. Execs., Biomed. Communication Network, Chgo. Soc. Assn. Execs. Office: Med Library Assn 919 N Mich Ave Chicago IL 60611

PALMER, RICHARD EDWARD, philosophy and religion educator, author; b. Phoenix, Nov. 6, 1933; s. Edward Y. and Agnes Mae (Smith) P.; m. Bette Louise Wheaton, Sept. 15, 1956; children: Kay, Kent, Scott. A.A., Phoenix Coll., 1953; B.A. in music, U. Redlands, 1955, M.A. Comparative Lit., 1956, Ph.D. in Comparative Lit., 1959. Asst. prof. English, MacMurray Coll., Jacksonville, Ill., 1959-64, assoc. prof. humanities, 1964-69, dir. humanities core lit. program, 1962-74, full prof., 1969—, prof. philosophy, lit., 1972-80, prof. philosophy, 1980—, chmn. dept religion & philosophy, alternate yrs., 1980, 82, 84. Cons. to various publishers. Author: Hermeneutics, 1969. Contbr. articles to profl. jours. Translator book and several articles. Postdoctoral fellow Am. Council of Learned Societies, 1964-65, NEH, 1971-72. Mem. Soc. Phenomenology and Existential Philosophy, Heidegger Conf. of Scholars, MLA, Am. Comparative Lit. Assn. Democrat. Mem. Society of Friends. Avocations: working for world peace, playing piano, speaking Spanish and German, futurism, ecology. Home: 866 Grove Jacksonville IL 62650 Office: MacMurray Coll Jacksonville IL 62650

PALMER, ROBERT R., performing arts adminstr.; b. Chicago, Sept. 8, 1950; s. Marvin R. and Martha P. B.A. cum laude, Augustana Coll., Rock Island, Ill., 1973; M.A. in Arts Adminstrn., U. Wis.-Madison, 1975. Mgr., U. Wis.-Madison Symphony Orchs., 1974-75, Madison Civic Music Assn., 1975—; tchr. music appreciation U. Wis. Extension, Madison Area Tech. Coll. Treas., mem. exec. com. of bd. dirs. Dane County Arts Council, 1979-80; mem. Madison Com. for the Arts. Mem. Beta Gamma Sigma, Omicron Delta Kappa, Phi Mu Alpha, Alpha Phi Omega. Office: 211 N Carroll St Madison WI 53703

PALMER, ROBERT TOWNE, lawyer; b. Chgo., May 25, 1947; s. Adrian Bernhardt and Gladys (Towne) P.; B.A., Colgate U., 1969; J.D., U. Notre Dame, 1974; m. Ann Therese Darin, Nov. 9, 1974; children—Justin Darin, Christian Darin. Bar: Ill. 1974, D.C. 1978, U.S. Supreme Ct. 1978. Law clk. Hon. Walter V. Schaefer, Ill. Supreme Ct., 1974-75; assoc. McDermott, Will & Emery, Chgo., 1975-81, ptnr., 1982—; mem. adj. faculty Chgo-Kent Law Sch., 1975-77, Loyola U., 1976-78. Mem. ABA, Ill. State Bar Assn. (2d place Lincoln award 1983), Chgo. Bar Assn., D.C. Bar Assn., Orch. of Ill. Assn. (dir. 1981—, v.p. 1982-84), Mensa. Republican. Episcopalian. Clubs: Chgo., Univ. Chgo., Saddle & Cycle; Dairymen's. Contbr. articles to legal jours. and textbooks. Home: 5555 N Sheridan Rd Chicago IL 60640 Office: 111 W Monroe St Chicago IL 60603

PALMER, STEVEN NELSON, investment executive; b. Alliance, Nebr., Jan. 31, 1947; s. Vernon D. Palmer and Marie (Nelson) Fellers; m. Mary Ellen Beck, Mar. 20, 1976; children—AnnMarie, William Nelson. B.S. in Econs., Mo. Valley Coll., 1970; M.B.A. with distinction, Rockhurst Coll., 1984. Lic. pilot. Pilot (capt.) U.S. Air Force Res., Richards-Gebaur AFB, Grandview, Mo., 1970-78; sr. v.p. 1st Nat. Bank of Kansas City, Mo., 1970-85, mem. supervisory com. trust div. 1982-85; sr. v.p. CFW Mgmt. Co., Bd. dirs. St. Paul's Day Sch., Kansas City, Mo., 1984—; trustee endowment funds Diocese of West Mo., Episc. Ch., Kansas City, 1984—; treas., fin. chmn. Family and Children Services of Kansas City, 1983-84; mem. fin. com. St. Paul's Episc. Ch., 1984—. Mem. Fin. Analyst Soc. Club: Carriage (Kansas City). Avocations: tennis, golf. Office: CFW Mgmt Co One Ward Pkwy Suite 145 Kansas City MO 64112

PALMERSHEIM, THOMAS F., music educator, entertainer; b. St. Cloud, Minn., Jan. 7, 1932; s. William J. and Rosalie M. (Kuffel) P.; m. Peggy Joy Hendrickson, June 9, 1956 (dec. Oct. 3, 1981); children—Julie, Jill, Pamela, Mary, Katie. B.S., St. Cloud State U., 1953; M.A., Denver U., 1959. Music tchr. Three Forks High Sch., Mont., 1956-58, Williams Bay High Sch., Wis., 1959-64; music instr. Hibbing Community Coll., Minn., 1964—; summer entertainer Mars Resort, Lake Geneva, Wis., 1978—. Served to cpl. U.S. Army, 1953-55. Mem. Nat. Assn. Jazz Educators, Am. Fed. Musicians, ASCAP, Minn. Music Educators Assn. Avocations: biking; sailing; music composing; entertaining. Home: 2118 E 9th Ave Hibbing MN 55746 Office: Hibbing Community Coll Hibbing MN 55746

PALMIERI, VICTOR H., diversified holding company executive. Chmn., chief exec. officer, dir. Baldwin-United Corp., Cin. Office: Lee Enterprises Inc 130 E 2nd St Davenport IA 52801*

PALMORE, JULIAN IVANHOE, III, mathematics educator, aeronautical and astronautical engineering educator; b. Balt., Sept. 26, 1938; s. Julian Ivanhoe Palmore, Jr., and Josephine Keith (Shellman) Smith; m. Bland Hawkins, May 27, 1967; children—Andrew Hanson, Rebecca Keith. B. of Engring. Physics, Cornell U., 1961; M.A. in Math., U. Ala., 1964; M.S.E. in Aeros., Princeton U., 1965; M.S. in Astronomy, Yale U., 1966, Ph.D. in Astronomy, 1967; Cand. Phil. in Math., U. Calif.-Berkeley, 1971, Ph.D. in Math., 1973. Research assoc. U. Minn., Mpls., 1967-68; instr. MIT, Cambridge, 1973-75; vis. asst. prof. U. Mich., Ann Arbor, 1975-77; from asst. to full prof. math., U. Ill., Urbana, 1977—; vis. scientist Los Alamos Nat. Lab., 1980, 83, 84—; lectr. various univs. Contbr. articles to profl. jours. Served to lt. USN, 1961-64. Recipient Am. Rocket Soc. award, 1960; NSF grantee, 1974—. Fellow Royal Astron. Soc.; assoc. fellow AIAA; mem. Am. Math. Soc., Planetary Soc., Sigma Xi. Home: 402 W Vermont Urbana IL 61801 Office: U Ill Dept Math 1409 W Green St Urbana IL 61801

PALOMBO, PAUL MARTIN, university administrator, composer; b. Pitts., Sept. 10, 1937; s. Domenico and Sophia P.; m. Joyce Lee Fletcher, Aug. 21, 1965; 1 son, Paul Martin. B.S., Indiana (Pa.) State U., 1962; postgrad. Peabody Conservatory (Balt.), 1963-66, Johns Hopkins U., 1963, 65; Ph.D., Eastman Sch. Music, U. Rochester, 1969. Prof. composition, head elec. music lab, U. Cin., 1969-72, chmn. composition, theory, musicology dept., 1972-75, assoc. dean Acad. Affairs, 1975-78; dir. Sch. Music, composer-in-residence U. Wash., Seattle, 1978-82; dean. Coll. Fine Arts, U. Wis.-Stevens Point, 1982—. Pres., Central Wis. Symphony Bd.; bd. dirs. Stevens Point Arts Council, Inc. Served with USN, 1955-58. Recipient Rockefeller Selection award Balt. Symphony Orch., 1965, Howard Hanson prize Eastman Sch. Music, 1969, Composer of Yr. award Washington Music Tchrs. Assn., 1980. Mem. Broadcast Music Inc., Nat. Assn. Schs. Music, Internat. Conf. Fine Arts Deans. Roman Catholic. Lodge: Kiwanis. Works include: Proteus, Ballet in Two Acts, 1969, Ritratti Anticamente, 1974, Metatheses, 1970, Morphosis, 1970, Prisma, 1984, canto d'un' Altra Volta, 1985. Office: 202A Fine Arts Center U Wis-Stevens Point Stevens Point WI 54481

PANABAKER, J. H., insurance company executive. Chmn., chief exec. officer, dir. Mutual Life Assurance Co. of Can., Waterloo, Ont. Office: Mutual Life Assurance Co of Can 227 King St South Waterloo ON N2J 4C5 Canada*

PANCERO, JACK BLOCHER, restaurant exec.; b. Cin., Dec. 27, 1923; s. Howard and Hazel Mae (Blocher) P.; student, Ohio State U., 1941-44; m. Loraine Fielman, Aug. 4, 1944; children—Gregg Edward, Vicki Lee. Partner, Howard Pancero & Co., Cin., 1948-66; stockbroker Gradison & Co., Cin., 1966-70; real estate assoc. Parchman & Oyler, Cin., 1970-72; v.p. Gregg Pancero, Inc., Kings Mills, Ohio, 1972—. Methodist. Clubs: Western Hills Country, Cincinnati, Engrs. Table, Masons, Shrine; Bear's Paw Country (Naples, Fla.). Home: 5730 Pinehill Ln Cincinnati OH 45238 Office: Kings Island Columbia Rd Kings Mills OH 45034

PANCRAZIO, SALLY BULKLEY, educational researcher; b. Endicott, N.Y., Dec. 4, 1939; d. Edwin Randall and Elsie (Novak) Bulkley; m. James J. Pancrazio, May 20, 1961; children—Joseph Jewell, James Joseph. B.S., Ill. State U., 1960; M.S., Ind. State U., 1966; Ed.D., U. Ill., 1970. Tchr. bus. edn. Jamaica Consol. High Sch., Sidell, Ill., 1960-61; grad. asst. U. Ill., Urbana, 1967-70, instr., 1970-71; asst. prof. Ill. State U., Normal, 1971-72; researcher Ill. State Edn. Agy., Springfield, 1972-73; mgr. research and stats. Ill. State Bd. Edn., Springfield, 1973—; asst. prof. ednl. adminstrn. Ill. State U., Normal, 1980—; cons. Nat. Ctr. for Ednl. Stats., Washington, 1978—. Chair Springfield Women's Polit. Caucus, Ill., 1979-80; com. woman Sangamon County Democratic Com., precinct 42, Springfield, Ill.; mem. Central Ill. Dem. Women, Springfield. Mem. Am. Ednl. Research Assn. (chair spl. interest group state edn. agys. 1979-80), Ill. Ednl. Research Evaluation Assn., Phi Delta Kappa. Democrat. Roman Catholic. Avocations: reading; theatre. Home: 301 Astoria Rd Springfield IL 62704 Office: Ill State Bd Edn Research and Stats Sect 100 N 1st St Springfield IL 62777

PANDEY, RAMESH CHANDRA, chemist; b. Naugaon, India, Nov. 5, 1938; came to U.S., 1967; s. Gauri Dutt and Jivanti Pandey. B.Sc., U. Allahabad (India), 1958; M.Sc., U. Gorakhpur (India), 1960; Ph.D., U. Poona (India), 1965. Jr. research fellow C.S.I.R. Nat. Chem. Lab., Poona, India, 1960-64, research officer, 1965-67, scientist organic div., 1970-72; research assoc. dept. chemistry U. Ill., Urbana, 1967-70, vis. scientist, 1972-77; sr. scientist fermentation program Nat. Cancer Inst. Frederick (Md.) Cancer Research Facility, 1977-82, head chem. sect., 1982-83; sr. scientist Abbott Labs., North Chicago, Ill., 1983—; cons. Washington U. Sch. Medicine, St. Louis. Patentee graft thin layer chromatography. Mem. Am. Chem. Soc., Am. Soc. Microbiology, Am. Soc. Mass Spectrometry, Am. Soc. Pharmacognosy, Indian Sci. Congress Assn. Home: 1043 Rosewood Terr Libertyville IL 60048 Office: D-47S Abbott Laboratories Route 43 and 137 North Chicago IL 60064

PANDEYA, NIRMALENDU KUMAR, air force officer, osteopathic plastic surgeon; b. Bihar, India, Feb. 9, 1940; came to U.S., 1958, Naturalized, 1965; s. Balbhadra and Ramasawari (Tewari) P.; m. Rosadele Ruth Hahn, Dec. 1, 1961; m. Cygnet S. Schroeder, Sept. 20, 1978; children—Alok, Kiran. B.Sc., M.S., Coll., Bihar U.-Motihari, 1958; M.S., U. Nebr., 1962; postgrad. U. Minn., 1959, Ft. Hays State Coll., 1961, D.O., Coll. Osteo. Medicine and Surgery, Des Moines, 1969; grad. Sch. Aerospace Medicine, U.S. Air Force, 1979. Diplomate Nat. Bd. Osteo. Med. Examiners. USPHS fellow dept. ob-gyn Coll. Medicine, U. Nebr., Omaha, 1963-65; intern Doctors Hosp., Columbus, Ohio, 1969-70; resident in gen. surgery Des Moines Gen. Hosp., 1970-72, Richmond Heights Gen. Hosp. (Ohio), 1972-73; fellow in plastic surgery Umea U. Hosp. (Sweden), 1973, Karolinska Hosp., Stockholm, 1974-75; assoc. prof. clin. scis. Coll. Osteo. Medicine and Surgery, Des Moines, 1975-76, also adj. clin. prof. plastic and reconstructive surgery; practice osteo. medicine specializing in reconstructive and plastic surgery, Des Moines, 1975—; mem. staff Des Moines Gen. Hosp., Mercy Hosp. Med. Ctr., Charter Community Hosp., Iowa Luth. Hosp., Davenport Osteo. Hosp., Franklin Gen. Hosp., Ringgold County Hosp. Served to lt. col. M.C., USAF; flight Surgeon Iowa Air N.G. Regents fellow U. Nebr., Lincoln, 1961-62. Mem. Assn. Plastic Surgeons of India (life), Assn. Surgeons of India (life), Assn. Mil. Surgeons of U.S. (life), Assn. Mil. Plastic Surgeons, AMA, Am. Osteo. Assn., Polk County Med. Soc., Iowa Soc. Osteo. Physicians and Surgeons, Polk County Soc. Osteo. Physicians and Surgeons (pres. 1978), Soc. U.S. Air Force Clin. Surgeons, Aerospace Med. Assn., Air N.G. Alliance of Flight Surgeons, AAUP, Am. Coll. Osteo. Surgeons, Am. Acad. Osteo. Surgeons (cert.), Soc. U.S. Air Force Flight surgeons. Hindu. Club: Army Navy. Contbr. numerous articles to profl. jours. Home: 10208 SW 72d St Cumming IA 50061 Office: 1440 E Grand Ave Suite 2B Des Moines IA 50316

PANDOLFI, JAMES LAURENCE, accountant; b. Peekskill, N.Y., Nov. 20, 1945; s. Vincent C. and Alessandra (Musto) P.; m. Ellen Small, Aug. 20, 1967; children—James L., Jr., Kenneth J. B.S., St. Joseph's Coll., Rensselaer, Ind., 1967. C.P.A., N.Y., Ill. Staff acct., Price Waterhouse & Co., N.Y.C., 1967-70; group controller Helmsley-Spear & Co., N.Y.C., 1970-72; v.p. fin., controller Cine Magnetics Inc., Mamaroneck, N.Y., 1972-74; dep. dir. Dept. Registration and Edn. State of Ill., Springfield, 1974-76; ptnr. Pandolfi, Topolski, Weiss & Co., Chgo., 1976—. Treas., Italo Am. Nat. Union, Wheaton, Ill., 1983. Mem. Mcpl. Fin. Officers Assn. (mem. spl. rev. com. 1980—). Republican. Roman Catholic. Home: 561 Alchester Dr Wheaton IL 60187

PANDYA, NAVINCHANDRA NARMADASHANKER, engineer; b. Mangrol, India, Jan. 30, 1928; came to U.S., 1957, naturalized, 1970; s. Narmadashanker and Rambhaben B. (Joshi) P.; B.Civil Engring., Gujarat U., 1954; M.S. in Civil Engring., Wayne State U., 1959; doctoral candidate U. Mich.; m. Snehlata P. Joshi, Apr. 29, 1954; children—Sonal, Pranav, Prashant. Chief civil engr. Atul Products, India, 1954-57; instr. Wayne State U., Detroit, 1959-62; designer, project engr. Giffels Assos., Inc., Southfield, Mich., 1962-73, dir. computer applications, 1973-78, dir. advance techs., 1978; mng. partner Real Investment Co., Universal Investment Devel. Co.; pres. Prayag Assocs.; cons. in field; mem. various nat. coms. Pres. Cultural Soc. of India, 1975—; v.p. Bharatiya Temple, 1976. Registered profl. engr., Mich. Mem. AAAS, ASCE (pres. SE Br. Mich. Sect., 1975-76). Am. Concrete Inst., Soc. Computer Applications in Engring., Planning, Arch., Chi Epsilon. Club: Toastmasters Internat. (pres. 1978). Contbr. papers to confs., articles to profl. jour. Office: 25200 Telegraph Rd Southfield MI 48037 Home: 25788 Hunt Club Blvd Farmington Hills MI 48018

PANEK, ALLEN FRANK, utility executive; b. Chgo., Jan. 21, 1939; m. Marguerite Karen Swanson, Sept. 19, 1964; children—Brian, David. B.S., North Central Coll., Naperville, Ill., 1961. Cert. Class A water supply operator, Ill.; Class I wastewater treatment operator, Ill. Chemist Argonne Nat. Lab., Ill., 1961-76; supt. water supply and wastewater treatment City of Naperville, 1976—. instr. Coll. DuPage; 1971, 78-79. Author tech. publs. and conf. presentations. Named Water Supply Operator of Yr., Ill. EPA, 1981. Mem. Am. Water Works Assn. (chmn. Ill. sect. 1984-85), Water Pollution Control Fedn. Office: City of Naperville 175 W Jackson Ave Naperville IL 60566

PANERAL, KENNETH LAWRENCE, security analyst; b. Chgo., June 18, 1935; s. Albert James and Sophia (Toppen) P.; m. Gale Rossmann, July 6, 1957; children—Kimberly Diane, Stephen Lawrence, Robert Allen. B.S., DePaul U., 1959. Chartered fin. analyst. Sr. analyst Continental Bank, Chgo., 1962-67; v.p. A.G. Becker, Chgo., 1967-78; stockbroker William Blair & Co., Chgo., 1979; v.p. Blunt, Ellis & Loewi, Chgo., 1980-82, Rotan Mosle Inc., Chgo., 1982—; dir. Transp. Soc. Chgo., 1973, dir., 1973-75. Served with U.S. Army, 1954-56. Recipient Instl. Investor All Star Recognition award Instl. Investor Mag., 1976, 78. Mem. Fin. Analysts Fedn., Chgo. Analyst Soc. Republican. Roman Catholic. Avocations: golf; coin collecting; bridge. Address: 21 Park Ln Golf IL 60029

PANETTIERE, JOHN MICHAEL, construction machinery manufacturing company executive; b. Kansas City, Mo., July 25, 1937; s. Andrew H. and Helen B. (Ferril) P.; B.S., Westminster Coll., 1959; grad. Rockhurst Coll. Advanced Indsl. Mgmt., 1963; m. Wanda Ann Melching, Dec. 2, 1961; children—Andrew, Brian, Christopher. Warehouse ops. mgr. Ford Motor Co., 1959-63; nat. distbn. mgr. MoPar div. Chrysler Corp., 1966-68; gen. parts mgr. Kaiser Jeep Corp., 1968-70; dir. ops. parts div. Am. Motors Co., 1970-73, dir. sales and mktg., 1973-75; v.p., gen. mgr. parts div. Volvo of Am., 1975-77; v.p., gen. mgr. parts ops. Fiatallis N.Am., Deerfield, Ill., 1977-80, sr. v.p. ops., 1980-81, pres., chief operating officer, 1981—; dir. Fiatallis Singapore, Inc., Fiatallis D.S.C., Inc. Mem. U.S.-USSR Trade and Econ. Council. Served with USNG, 1959-60. Recipient Alumni of Yr. award Westminster Coll., 1982. Mem. Am. Mgmt. Assn., Constrn. Industry Mfrs. Assn., Alumni Assn. Westminster Coll., Phi Delta Theta. Clubs: Exmoor Country (Highland Park, Ill.); Richmond (Ill.) Hunting. Office: Fiatallis NAm Box F 106 Wilmot Rd Deerfield IL 60015

PANG, JOSHUA KEUN-UK, trade co. exec.; b. Chinnampo, Korea, Sept. 17, 1924; s. Ne-Too and Soon-Hei (Kim) P.; came to U.S., 1951, naturalized, 1968; B.S., Roosevelt U., 1959; m. He-Young Yoon, May 30, 1963; children—Ruth, Pauline, Grace. Chemist, Realemon Co. Am., Chgo., 1957-61; chief-chemist chem. div. Bell & Gossett Co., Chgo., 1961-63, Fatty Acid Inc., div. Ziegler Chem. & Mineral Corp., Chgo., 1963-64; sr. chemist-supr. Gen. Mills Chems. Inc., Kankakee, Ill., 1964-70; pres., owner UJU Industries Inc., Broadview, Ill., 1971—, also dir. Bd. dirs. Dist. 92, Lindop Sch., Broadview, 1976—; chmn. Proviso Area Sch. Bd. Assn., Proviso Twp., Cook County, Ill., 1976-77; bd. dirs. Korean Am. Community Services, Chgo., 1979-80; mem. governing bd. Proviso Area Exceptional Children, Spl. Edn. Joint Agreement, 1981-84; alumni bd. govs. Roosevelt U., 1983—. Mem. Am. Chem. Soc., Am. Inst. Parliamentarians (region 2 treas. 1979-81, region 2 gov. 1981-82), Internat. Platform Assn., Ill. Sch. Bd. Assn., Chgo. Area Parliamentarians, Parliamentary Leaders in Action (pres. 1980-81), Nat. Speakers Assn. (dir. Ill. chpt. 1981-82, nat. parliamentarian 1982-84, 2d v.p. chpt. 1983-84). Club: Toastmasters (dist. gov. 1970). Home: 2532 S 9th Ave Broadview IL 60153 Office: PO Box 351 Broadview IL 60153

PANIAGUAS, JOHN STEVEN, lawyer; b. Gary, Ind., Sept. 7, 1951; s. John and Anne (Mako) P.; m. Kathy Rae Taylor, Apr. 1, 1978; children—Nicole, Joshua. B.S.E., Purdue U., 1973; J.D., DePaul U., 1982. Bar: Ill. 1982, U.S. Dist. Ct. (no. dist.) Ill. 1982, U.S. Ct. Appeals (7th cir.) 1983, U.S. Patent and Trademark Office, 1983, U.S. Ct. Appeals (fed. cir.) 1984; registered profl. engr., Ind., Ill. Elec. engr. Sargent & Lundy, Chgo., 1973-76, 79-83, No. Ind. Pub. Service Co., Hammond, 1976-79; patent atty. McGraw Edison Co., Rolling Meadows, Ill., 1983—. Mem. St. Colette Sch. Bd., Rolling Meadows, 1984. Mem. Am. Intellecutal Property Law Assn., Patent Assn. Chgo., ABA, Ill. State Bar Assn., Chgo. Bar Assn., Am. Jurisprudence Lawyers Co-op, Tau Beta Pi. Roman Catholic. Office: McGraw Edison Co One Continental Tower 1701 Golf Rd Rolling Meadows IL 60008

PANICH, DANUTA BEMBENISTA, lawyer; b. East Chicago, Ind., Apr. 9, 1954; s. Fred and Ann Stephanie (Grabowski) B.; m. Nikola Panich, July 30, 1977; children—Jennifer Anne, Michael Alexei. A.B., Ind. U., 1975, J.D., 1978. Bar: Ill. 1978, U.S. Dist. Ct. (no. dist.) Ill. 1978. Assoc. Mayer Brown & Platt, Chgo., 1978—. Mem. Ill. State Bar Assn., ABA. Republican. Roman Catholic. Office: Mayer Brown & Platt 231 S LaSalle St Chicago IL 60604

PANICI, VIRGINIA KERASOTES, book store proprietor, educator, librarian; b. Springfield, Ill., Jan. 26, 1937; d. Louis George and Georgia Elizabeth (Allen) Kerasotes; m. Pat John Panici, Feb. 19, 1961; children—Georgia, Anthony. B.A., Milliken U., 1959. Tchr. history and math. Williamsville Elementary Sch., Ill., 1960-61; head librarian Alsip Sch. Dist., Ill., 1970-72; children's librarian Harvey Pub. Library, Ill., 1972-74; library media specialist, tchr. English, Glenwood Sch. for Boys, Ill., 1974-78; bookstore owner, mgr. Paperback Shop, Chicago Heights, Ill., 1978—. Sponsor, Little League Baseball, Chicago Heights, 1978—. Avocations: collecting cookbooks; golf; tennis; travel. Office: Paperback Shop 165 Olympia Plaza Chicago Heights IL 60411

PANKOW, J. STEPHEN (STEVE), university director; b. South Bend, Ind., May 31, 1958; s. James Henry and Margaret Virginia (Davis) P. B.S. in Bus., Ind. U., 1980, M.S. in Edn., 1982. Resident asst. Ind. U., Bloomington, 1980-82, asst. coordinator, 1981-82; dir. residence hall Western Ill. U., Macomb, 1982-84, dir. complex, 1984—, chmn. community devel. com. student residential programs, 1983—. Blood donor ARC, 1976—. Mem. Am. Coll. Personnel Adminstrs., Am. Assn. Counseling and Devel., Delta Upsilon (v.p. Bloomington chpt. 1978-79). Episcopalian. Avocations: golf; racquetball; self-hypnosis. Home: 1 Lincoln Hall Macomb IL 61455 Office: Student Residential Programs Western Ill U Seal Hall Macomb IL 61455

PANNABECKER, DAVID RAY, designer; b. Toronto, Ont., Can., Mar. 15, 1951; s. Earl Ray and Elizabeth Ruth (Hallman) P.; m. Lois Marie (Sousley), Sept. 7, 1974; children—Michelle Lynn, Andrew David. B.A., Bethel Coll., 1974, M.A., Wheaton Grad. Sch., 1981. Chmn. music dept. Friends Bible Coll., Haviland, Kans., 1976-79; audio visual technician Billy Graham Ctr. Mus., Wheaton, Ill., 1980-81; pres. Puppetoire, Inc., Carol Stream, Ill., 1981—; music dir. Lombard Baptist Ch. Mem. Puppeteers Am. United Missionary Church. Numerous puppet characters copyrighted; created mascot for Amway Corp., 1982; creative works include: Oh Brother (musical), 1982, various TV shows and commls. in U.S., Can., Netherlands. Home and Office: 799 Erie Ct Carol Stream IL 60188

PANSKY, MIROSLAV, music director, conductor; b. Prague, Czechoslovakia, Apr. 16, 1933; came to U.S., 1959, naturalized, 1974; s. Antonin and Marie P. Diploma, Conservatory of Music, Prague, 1953. Condr. opera, ballet, orchs., Europe, U.S.A.; music dir., condr. Green Bay (Wis.) Symphony Orch., 1972—; adj. prof. U. Wis.-Green Bay, 1982—.

PANTALONE, J. RICHARD, principal; b. Waterbury, Conn., Feb. 15, 1937; s. Alfred and Genevieve (DiSalvatore) P.; m. Joan Marie Zuber, June 25, 1977. B.S.E., Bowling Green State U., 1968; M.S.E., St. John Coll., Cleve., 1974; postgrad. Akron U., 1975-76. Tchr., Bellefontain (Ohio) City Schs., 1964-68, Elyria (Ohio) City Schs., 1968-73; asst. prin. Roosevelt Elem. Sch., Elyria, 1973-75; prin. Johnson Sch., Barberton, Ohio, 1975-78; vice prin. Vinton County High Sch., McArthur, Ohio, 1978-79; prin. Chester Elem. Sch., Wooster, Ohio, 1979—. Mem. tchr. devel. com. Wayne County, 1980. Served with U.S. Army, 1961-64. Mem. Assn. Supervision and Curriculum Devel., Phi Delta Kappa. Clubs: KC, Kiwanis, Eagles, Elks. Home: 6722 Towpath St Canal Fulton OH 44614 Office: 7509 W Smithville-Western Rd Wooster OH 44691

PANTAZIS, JOHN DIONYSIOS, engineer, executive; b. Volos, Thessale, Greece, Dec. 18, 1936; came to U.S., 1962; naturalized, 1968; s. Dionysios and Argyro (Kalae) P.; m. Helena John Mefsout, Dec. 26, 1968; children—Dennis, Argy. B.S.A.E., Chgo. Tech. Coll., 1968, B.S.E.E., 1965. Registered profl. engr., Ill., Wis., Ind. Engr., prin. engr. various cons. firms in Chgo. area, 1965-78; pres., chief exec. officer John D. Pantazis and Assocs. Ltd., Chgo., 1978—. Dir. Plato Sch. Bd., Greek Orthodox Ch. Assumption, Chgo., 1977-79. Served to staff sgt. Greek Army, 1959-60. Mem. ASHRAE, Nat. Soc. Profl. Engrs., Ill. Soc. Profl. Engrs., Assn. Energy Engrs. Avocations: golf; swimming; boating; bicycling. Home: 1309 Conway Rd Lake Forest IL 60045 Office: John D Pantazis & Assocs 222 W Adams St Chicago IL 60606

PANUSKA, HAROLD JOSEPH, oral maxillo-facial surgeon; b. St. Paul, Aug. 27, 1928; s. Wolfgang Frank and Anna (Savel) P.; m. Margaret Marry Judge, June 13, 1953; children—Robert, John, Steve. B.A., U. Minn.-Mpls., 1951, B.S., 1953, D.D.S., 1955, M.S.D., 1958. Clin. instr. U.Minn., Mpls., 1955-60, asst. prof., 1960-78, guest lectr., 1978-82; pvt. practice oral maxillo-facial surgery, Edina, Minn., 1958—; chmn. midwinter clinic Mpls. Dist. Dental Soc., 1983. Sec. gen. Internat. Health Service, Mpls., 1980; consul Republic of Honduras, Tegucigalpa, 1983. Served to cpl. USMC, 1946-48. Fellow Am. Dental Soc. Anesthesiology, Internat. Coll. Dentists; mem. Soc. Advancement of Anesthesia in Dentistry (hon.), ADA. Republican. Episcopalian. Club: Am. Wine Soc. Lodges: Masons, Shriners, Lions. Avocations: enology; cattle raising; pilot; ham radio. Home: 3140 Watertown Rd Long Lake MN 55356 Office: 66th and France Aves 670 Southdale Med Bldg Edina MN 55435

PAOLINI, ALFRED PAUL, mining equipment and engineering marketing manager; b. Pitts., June 21, 1929; s. Humbert A. and Dorothy E. (Cianelli) P.; married, Jan. 1, 1947; children—Susan L. Paolini Quinn, Barbara A. Paolini Circelli, Debra L. Paolini Sheely, Phillip A., Tony P., Jeffrey J. Student Ohio State U., 1946-48; cert. mech. engring., Internat. Corr. Sch., 1962; cert. Va. Poly. Inst., 1974. Designer Bonded Scale & Machinery Co., Columbus, Ohio, 1951-53, jr. sales engr., 1953-55; designer Jeffrey Mining Machinery Co., Columbus, 1955-63, supr. design engr., 1963-72, group mgr. engr., 1972-78, sr. product mgr., 1978—. Patentee in field. Baseball mgr. Franklin Post Am. Legion, Columbus, 1965, St. James the Less Ch., 1979. Republican. Roman Catholic. Lodge: Giulianova Teramo (pres. 1970-76). Avocations: boating; fishing; hunting. Home: 2906 Granada Hill Dr Columbus OH 43229 Office: Jeffrey Mining Machinery Co 274 E 1st Ave Columbus OH 43216

PAOLINO, ALBERT FRANCIS, clinical psychologist; b. Kearny, N.J., Dec. 14, 1921; s. Louis and Rose (Minelli) P.; m. Rosetta Bastulli, June 15, 1957; children—Albert Z., Renee L., Andrea R. B.S., Rutgers U., 1947; Ph.D., Western Res. U., 1956. Diplomate Am. Bd. Psychology. Chief psychologist Cleve. Boys Sch., 1950, Summit County Receiving Hosp., 1951-56, Cleve. Psychiat. Inst., 1956-63, 1973-82; research fellow surgery Western Res. U. Med. Sch., 1961-63; sr. research psychologist Brecksville VA Hosp., 1963-65; project/lab. dir. Lab. Psychosocial Research, Cleve. Psychiat. Inst., 1965-73; pvt. practice psychology, 1962—; cons. Cleve. Roman Catholic Diocese. Served with USAAF, 1942-46. Mem. Am. Psychol. Assn., Midwest Psychol. Assn., Cleve. Psychol. Assn., Cleve. Acad. Cons. Psychologists, AAAS, N.Y. Acad. Sci. Roman Catholic. Contbr. articles to profl. jours.

PAPACEK-SAGER, SALLY ANNE, lawyer; b. Laporte, Ind., Jan. 8, 1947; d. Roscoe J. and Phyllis (King) Markwith; m. John C. Papacek, June 17, 1967 (div. Oct. 22, 1984); children—Jeff Joseph, Nancy Anne; m. Frederick J. Sager, July 20, 1985. B.S. in English, Ind. U., 1969, M.S. in Elem. Edn., 1973, J.D., 1979. Bar: Ind. Research asst. Ind. Jud. Ctr., Indpls., 1978-79; assoc. Bolinger, Bolinger, Papacek & Welke, Kokomo, 1979-83; ptnr; Andrews & Sager, Kokomo, 1983—. Mem. Howard County United Way, Kokomo, 1983—, pres.-elect, 1985; bd. dirs. Howard County Migrant Council, 1980-83, pres. 1984—; bd. dirs. Northwestern Sch. Corp., Kokomo, 1982—, pres. 1985. Mem. Howard County Bar Assn. (sec., treas. 1979-80), Ind. State Bar Assn., ABA. Republican. Club: Extension Homemakers (Kokomo) (pres. 1983-84). Lodge: Altrusa. Avocations: skiing; jogging. Home: 1820 S Armstrong St Kokomo IN 46902 Office: Andrews & Sager 300 N Main St Kokomo IN 46901

PAPAIOANNOU, STAMATIOS E(VANGELOS), biochemical pharmacologist, researcher; b. Athens, Greece, Mar. 27, 1934; came to U.S., 1961, naturalized, 1972; s. Evangelos J. and Antigoni S. (Tzaneti) P.; m. Maria S. Karavida, 1968. B.S. in Chemistry, Nat. U. (Greece), 1957; M.S. in Food Sci., Oreg. State U., 1962, Ph.D. in Biochemistry, 1966. Vis. researcher Salk Inst., La Jolla, Calif., 1974—. Contbr. articles to profl. jours. Served to 2d lt. Greek Air Force, 1957-61. Greek Found. scholar, 1960. Mem. Endocrine Soc., Am. Chem. Soc., AAAS. Home: 7930 Luna St Morton Grove IL 60053 Office: GD Searle & Co 4901 Searle Pkwy Skokie IL 60077

PAPAVASILIOU, STATHIS SPYRO, molecular endocrinologist; b. Athens, Attica, Greece, May 1, 1950; arrived in U.S., 1974, s. Spyro and Maria Papavasiliou; m. Antigone Antonios Syrigou, Aug. 7, 1974; children—Spyro, Anthony. M.D., U. Athens, Greece, 1974, Didactoricon, 1977. Diplomate Am. Bd. Internal Medicine. Fellow U. Calif.-San Francisco, 1974-77; intern Henry Ford Hosp., Mich., 1977-78, resident in medicine, 1980-82; fellow in endocrinology U. Mich., Ann Arbor, 1982. Contbr. articles to med. books, jours. Bay Area Heart Research Com. fellow, 1976-77; recipient AMA Physicians Recognition award, 1982, Young Scientist award Mellon Found., 1984. Mem. ACP, AAAS, N.Y. Acad. Scis. Avocations: music, chess, athletics. Office: U Mich Dept Internal Medicine 48109

PAPE, BARBARA HARRIS, lawyer; b. Casper, Wyo., Aug. 12, 1936; d. Herbert Garfield and Leah Jean (Case) Harris; m. William Martin Pape, June 28, 1969; children—Kyri Dannan, Kirsten Tara. A.A. in Theatre, Stephens Coll., 1956; B.J., B.A., U. Mo., 1960, M.A., 1966, B.S. in Edn., 1968, Ph.D., J.D., 1980. Bar: Mo. 1981, U.S. Dist. Ct. (we. dist.) Mo. 1981. Mem. faculty U. Mo., Columbia, 1966-74; daily TV show hostess Triton Prodns., Inc., Columbia, 1973-76; realtor Tara Realty, Columbia, 1977-81; sole practice, Columbia, 1981-82; ptnr. Cronan, Robinson, Lampton & Pape, Columbia, 1982—. Assoc. editor Litigation mag., 1983—. Contbr. articles to mags. Bd. dirs. Columbia Resource Ctr., Inc., 1981—; pres. adv. bd. YWCA, YMCA, Columbia, 1977-78; trustee Coll. Arts and Scis., Stephens Coll., 1983—. Mem. ABA, Mo. Bar Assn., Boone County Bar Assn., Assn. Trial Lawyers Am., Mo. Assn. Trial Lawyers, Mo. Criminal Def. Lawyers, Kappa Tau Alpha, Delta Theta Phi. Democrat. Home: 3301 Westcreek Circle Columbia MO 65203 Office: Cronan Robinson et al 1200 Rogers Suite 200 Columbia MO 65201

PAPE, GLENN MICHAEL, lawyer; b. Evergreen Park, Ill., Aug. 20, 1954; s. Gilbert Thomas Pape and Janine Elizabeth (Beheyt) Pape Riveros; m. Nancy Ann Vaske, Apr. 7, 1979; 1 child, Katherine Jo. B.A. in Classics, U. Chgo., 1978, M.B.A., 1981; J.D., DePaul U., 1979. Cons. tax div. No. Trust Co., Chgo., 1980-81, fin. planner, 1981-82; fin. counselor Continental Ill. Nat. Bank, Chgo., 1982-84; tax mgr. Arthur Andersen & Co., Chgo., 1984—. Active Five Hosp. Homebound Elderly Program, Chgo., 1981; treas. Chamber Music Council Chgo., 1982. Mem. Chgo. Bar Assn. (fed. taxation com.), Ill. State Bar Assn., ABA, Internat. Assn. Fin. Planners (dir. Chgo. chpt.), U.S. Chess Fedn. Home: 2033 N Racine Ave Chicago IL 60614 Office: Arthur Andersen & Co 33 W Monroe St Chicago IL 60603

PAPERMAN, JACOB BERNARD, accountancy educator; b. Phila., May 6, 1925; s. Joseph B. and Esther K. (Rosenkrantz) P.; m. Vera O. Reisinger, Aug. 13, 1956; children—Eric B., Joseph B. B.S. in Commerce, Drexel U., 1951; M.B.A., Inst. Tech. (Ohio), 1960; Ph.D., U. Cin., 1976. Enlisted in U.S. Air Force, 1951, commd. officer and advanced through ranks to lt. col., 1968; retired, 1970; asst. prof. U. Dayton, Ohio, 1970-72; assoc. prof. Miami U., Oxford, Ohio, 1972-81; prof., chmn. accountancy Wright State U., Dayton, 1981—. Contbr. articles to profl. jours. Recipient Elijah Watt Sells cert. of hon. mention Am. Inst. C.P.A.s. Mem. Am. Acctg. Assn., Am. Inst. C.P.A.s, Ohio Soc. C.P.A.s (award 1971), Nat. Assn. Accts., Assn. Govt. Accts., Gamma Sigma, Phi Kappa Phi, Sigma Rho. Home: 2449 S Old Oaks Dr Beaver Creek OH 45431 Office: Wright State U 240 Rike Hall Dayton OH 45435

PAPP, GERARD MICHAEL, osteopathic orthopedic surgeon; b. Trenton, N.J., Aug. 2, 1944; s. John and Mary (Novak) P.; m. Kathleen Ann Magee, Aug. 9, 1969; children—Melissa, Jennifer, Susan, Elizabeth. B.A. in Biology, LaSalle Coll., 1967; D.O., Phila. Coll. Osteo. Medicine, 1971. Diplomate Am. Osteo. Acad. Orthopedics. Intern Drs. Hosp., Columbus, Ohio, 1971-72, resident in orthopedic surgery, 1972-76, program dir. dept. orthopedic surgery, 1983-84; fellow in pediatric orthopedics A. I. DuPont Inst., Wilmington, Del., 1975; fellow in hand surgery U. Pa., Phila., 1975; practice medicine specializing in osteo. orthopedic surgery Orthopedics, Inc.-Drs. West, Columbus, 1976—; mem. staff Drs. Hosp., Columbus, St. Ann's Hosp., Columbus, Union Meml. Hosp., Maryville, Ohio; mem. clin. faculty Coll. Osteo. Medicine, Ohio U., Columbus, 1977—; mem. Ohio Occupational Therapy and Phys. Therapy Bd., Columbus, 1984—. Regional editor Orthopod, 1982-85. Mem. St. Agatha Adult Choir, 1977-84. Mem. Am. Osteo. Assn., Ohio Osteo. Assn., Am. Osteo. Acad. Orthopedics (chmn. sci. display 1982—), Am. Coll. Osteo. Surgeons (Geigy award 1977, Best of Show and Best Orthopedic Sci. Display 1981, 83, 2d Place Orthopedic Sci. Display 1984), Ohio Postural Screening Com., Upper Arlington Civic Assn. (mgr. 1980). Roman Catholic. Home: 4271 Woodhall Rd Columbus OH 43220 Office: Work Fitness Clinic 1275 Olentangy River Rd Columbus OH 43212

PAPPAS, JOSEPH EDWARD, music educator; b. St. Louis, May 22, 1950; s. Harry Edward and Mary Lee (Campbell) P.; m. Barbara Eilers, June 12, 1976; 1 child, Darren. B. Music Edn., S.E. Mo. State U., Cape Girardeau, 1972, M.Music Edn., 1976; postgrad. N.E. Mo. State U., Kirksville, 1981, 83. Tchr. band and vocal music Bell City Schs., Mo., 1972-76; tchr. instrumental music Illmo-Scott City Sch., Scott City, Mo., 1976-79, Mexico Pub. Schs., Mo., 1979—; performer Cape Girardeau Band, 1969-79; profl. musician jazz and country bands, Mexico, 1980—. Composer: Plain Songs, 1975 (Rafferty award 1974-75), Rhythmic Dances I, 1975 (Rafferty award 1974-75). Recipient Disting. Service award Jaycees, Mexico, 1981. Mem. ASCAP, Mo. State Tchrs. Assn., Phi Beta Mu, Phi Mu Alpha. Democrat. Roman Catholic. Lodges: Optimists (pres. 1981-82), Rotary (pres. 1974-75). Avocations: taxidermy, hunting, fishing. Home: 810 Ringo St Mexico MO 65265 Office: 639 Wade St Mexico MO 65265

PAPPAS, LEONARD JOHN, lawyer; b. Cleve., Aug. 6, 1952; s. Leonard Gust and Effie (Vamis) P. B.A. cum laude, Cleve. State U., 1974; J.D., Case Western Res. U., 1983. Bar: Ohio 1984, U.S. Dist. Ct. (no. dist.) Ohio 1984. Mktg. sales exec. Bobbie Brooks, Inc., Cleve., 1975; gen. mgr. Agora Inc., Painesville, Ohio, 1977-81; bus. cons. Gatsby's Inc., Mentor, Ohio, 1983-84; sole practice, Shaker Heights, Ohio, 1984—. Mem. Assn. Trial Lawyers Am., Ohio Bar Assn., Bar Assn. Greater Cleve., Cuyahoga County Bar Assn., Am. Judicature Soc., Zeta Psi. Democrat. Greek Orthodox. Office: Ohio Savs Bldg 20133 Farnsleigh Rd Shaker Heights OH 44129

PAPPAS, RICHARD JAY, college dean; b. Midland, Mich., Sept. 20, 1951; s. Charles N. and Sydell (Sheinberg) P.; m. Pamela Lee Crowder, Aug. 21, 1976; children—Brian Andrew, Lisa Kimberly, Dana Jennifer. B.B.E., Eastern Mich. U., 1973; M.A., U. Mich., 1974, Ed.D., 1984. Instr. Snead St. Jr. Coll., Boaz, Ala., 1974-75; assoc. prof. Jackson Community Coll., Mich., 1975-79, dean of division, 1982—; agent Conn. Gen. Life Ins., Southfield, Mich., 1979-81; v.p. Pappas Enterprises, Birmingham, Flint, Mich., 1981-82; instr. Eastern Mich. U., Ypsilanti, 1976—. Trustee Oakland Community Coll., Bloomfield Hills, 1980-82; bd. dirs. Jackson Symphony Orchestra Assn., Jr. Achievement, Jackson, Am. Cancer Soc., Jackson, 1982-83; solicitor trainer United Way Jackson County, 1983-84. Recipient Honor Table Membership award Conn. Gen. Life, 1981, Pres. Club award, 1980, 81. Mem. Mich. Community Coll. Community Services Assn. (v.p.), Sales and Mktg. Execs. Assn. (Jackson chpt. bd. dirs.), Internat. Sales and Mktg. Execs. Assn. Democrat. Avocation: sports. Home: 6966 Paddock Ln Jackson MI 49201 Office: Jackson Community Coll 2111 Emmons Rd Jackson MI 49201

PAQUETTE, EDWARD JOSEPH, educational administrator; b. Superior, Wis., Feb. 16, 1947; s. Joseph Sidney and Patricia (Cotter) P.; m. Martha Jean Yates, June 15, 1968; children—Derek Yates, Patricia Walker. B.S. in Edn., Northwestern U., 1969; M.S. in Edn., Canisius Coll., 1974, M.S. in Counseling, 1975. Salesman A.B. Dick Co., Buffalo, 1969-70; educator, adminstr. Nichols Sch., Buffalo, 1970-77; headmaster Lake Forest Acad., Ill., 1978—. Pres. Parant-Parent-Infant Spl. Care, Evanston, Ill., 1984; dir., v.p. Parents of Premature and High Risk Infants, N.Y.C., 1984. Kranz scholar Northwestern U., Evanston, 1969. Mem. Nat. Assn. Ind. Schs., Ind. Schs. Assn. Central States, Nat. Assn. Coll. Admission Counselors, Council and Support Basic Edn. Republican. Roman Catholic. Clubs: Onwentsia (Lake Forest); University (Chgo.). Avocations: squash; golf; tennis; fishing. Home and Office: 1500 W Kennedy Rd Lake Forest IL 60045

PARAN, MARK LLOYD, lawyer; b. Cleve., Feb. 1, 1953; s. Edward Walter and Margaret Gertrude (Ebert) P. A.B. cum laude in Sociology, Harvard U., 1977, J.D., 1980. Bar: Ill. 1980. Assoc. Wilson & McIlvaine, Chgo., 1980-83, Lurie Sklar & Simon, Ltd., Chgo., 1983—. Mem. Chgo. Council of Lawyers, Chgo. Bar Assn., Ill. State Bar Assn., ABA. Home: 1030 N State St Apt 39F Chicago IL 60610 Office: Lurie Sklar & Simon Ltd 180 N Michigan Ave Suite 2000 Chicago IL 60601

PARASIUK, WILSON DWIGHT, Canadian government official; b. Stenen, Sask., Can., May 6, 1943; s. William and Lillian (Gogol) P.; m. Wilma Hewitson, Aug. 12, 1967; children—Michael William, Laurel Ann. B.A. with honors, U. Man., 1965, M.A., 1966; M.A., Oxford U., 1968. Socio-econ. devel. planner Govt. Can., Ottawa, Ont., 1968-69; pres. Leaf Rapids Devel. Corp., Winnipeg, Man., Can., 1972-77; asst. sec. Govt. Man., Winnipeg, 1970-73, sec. to cabinet com., 1973-77, mem. legis. assembly for Transcona, 1977—, minister energy and mines, 1981—. Rhodes scholar, 1966. Mem. New Democratic Party. Club: Oxford Heights Community (Winnipeg). Home: 900 Plessis Rd Winnipeg MB R2C 3C2 Canada Office: Ministry Energy and Mines 301 Legis Bldg Winnipeg MB R3C 0V8 Canada

PARCELLS, ALAN JEROME, research biochemist; b. Los Angeles, Jan. 29, 1929; s. George S. and Sudie K. (Ratliff) P.; m. Lynne Sprague Williams, July 2, 1960; children—Barbara Ann, Carolyn Joan. A.A., Pasadena City Coll., 1948; A.B., U. Calif.-Berkeley, 1954, Ph.D., 1958. Postdoctoral fellow U. Utah, Salt Lake City, 1958-59; research scientist Upjohn Co., Kalamazoo, 1959—. Patentee on bovine growth hormone. Author sci. articles. Served with U.S. Army, 1950-52; Korea. Mem. AAAS, Am. Chem. Soc. Unitarian. Avocations: model railroads; photography. Office: Upjohn Co 7000 Portage Rd Kalamazoo MI 49001

PARCELLS, CHARLES ABRAM, JR., investment company executive; b. Grosse Pointe, Mich., Feb. 17, 1920; s. Charles Abram Parcells and Carolyn (Hubbard) Lucas; m. Frances Heartt Hamilton, Feb. 14, 1948; children—Charles A. III, Frances A., Elizabeth H., Frederick L., Kathryn H., David H. B.A. in Math., Yale U., 1940; M.B.A., U. Mich., 1948. Pres. Charles A. Parcells & Co., Detroit, 1953—. Pres. William Lyon Phelps Found., Detroit, 1948—. Mem. Fin. Analysts Soc. Republican. Clubs: Detroit, Country of Detroit, Econ. of Detroit. Home: 178 Lothrop Grosse Pointe Farms MI 48236 Office: Charles A Parcells & Co 3560 Penobscot Bldg Detroit MI 48226

PARENTEAU, JAMES EDWARD, retired military communications officer; b. Superior, Wis., Nov. 4, 1921; s. Edward Peter and Clara Mary (Malchow) P.; m. Winifred Virginia McCairns, July 2, 1942; children—Bonnie Ann Parenteau Bruck, Frank Edward. Student U. Md., 1956-58. Served to chief warrant officer U.S. Air Force, 1941-62; communications radio operator Army Air Corps, 1941-45; communications clk. Western Union Telegraph Co., Newark, 1945-46; communicaitons relay ctr. supr. U.S. Air Force, 1946-57, communications officer automatic switching ctr., 1957-62; ops. mgr. automatic digital network Air Force Communications Service, Gentile AFB, Ohio, 1962-77, ret. Recipient Outstanding Unit award Def. Communication Agy., 1969; named Outstanding Automatic Electronic Switching Ctr., Def. Communication Agy., 1976. Republican. Methodist. Clubs: Officers (Wright Patterson AFB, Ohio); Square Dance (Fairborn, Ohio) (sec., sunshine chmn.) Avocations: artistic stained glass; square dancing; volunteer medical work. Home: 1840 Bordeaux Dr Fairborn OH 45324

PARFET, RAY T., JR., pharm. co. exec. Dir., Upjohn Co., 1958—, v.p., 1958-59, exec. v.p. charge research, legal, financial and personnel activities, 1960-62, pres., gen. mgr., 1962-69, chmn. bd., chief exec. officer, 1969—; dir. 1st Nat. Bank & Trust Co. Mich., Kalamazoo, The Aro Corp., Bryan, Ohio, Gilmore Bros. Dept. Store, Kalamazoo, Union Pump Co., Battle Creek, Mich. Bell, Detroit, 1st Am. Bank Corp., Kalamazoo. Trustee, Bronson Meth. Hosp., Kalamazoo, Nat. 4-H Council, Washington, Mem. Pharm. Mfrs. Assn. (past chmn., past dir.), Internat. Fedn. Pharm. Mfrs. Assns. (past dir.). Office: 7000 Portage Rd Kalamazoo MI 49001

PARFITT, ALWYN MICHAEL, physician; b. Nottingham, Eng., May 10, 1930; came to U.S., 1971; s. David Neil and Winifred (Childs) P.; B.A., Cambridge U., 1951, M.B., B.Ch., 1954; m. Elaine Evans, July 31, 1951; children—Caroline, Nigel, Jeremy. Intern St. James Hosp., London, 1955, St. Stephen's Hosp., London, 1956, Brook Hosp., Woolwich, Eng., 1956; resident Nat. Hosp. for Nervous Diseases, London, 1957, St. George's Hosp., London, 1957-58, Nat. Orthopaedic Hosp., London, 1958-60; research fellow Univ. Coll. Hosp., 1960-62; sr. lectr. U. Queensland, Australia, 1960-71; physician Royal Brisbane Hosp., Australia, 1962-71; vis. scientist Cedars-Sinai Med. Ctr., 1968-69; attending physician Henry Ford Hosp., Detroit, 1971—, dir. Bone and Mineral Research Lab., 1971—; clin. prof. medicine U. Mich., 1973—. Mem. editorial bds. Mineral and Electrolyte Metabolism, 1980, Metabolic Bone Disease and Related Research, 1978. Contbr. chpts. to med. textbooks. Mem. Gov. Milliken's Com. on Fluoridation, 1974-78. Fellow Royal Coll. Physicians (London), Royal Australasian Coll. Physicians, ACP; mem. Endocrine Soc., Am. Fedn. Clin. Research, Am. Soc. Bone and Mineral Research, Am. Soc. Nephrology, Physicians for Social Responsibility (mem. exec. com. Detroit chpt.), Central Soc. Clin. Research. Home: 693 N Glenhurst St Birmingham MI 48009 Office: Henry Ford Hosp 2799 W Grand Blvd Detroit MI 48202

PARINS, ROBERT JAMES, lawyer, professional football executive; b. Green Bay, Wis., Aug. 23, 1918; s. Frank and Nettie (Denissen) P.; m. Elizabeth L. Carroll, Feb. 8, 1941; children—Claire, Andrée, Richard, Teresa, Lu Ann. B.A., U. Wis.-Madison, 1940, LL.B., 1942. Bar: Wis. Supreme Ct. 1942. Sole practice law, Green Bay, 1942-68, dist. atty. Brown County, Wis., 1949-50, circuit judge Brown County, 1968-82, res. judge, 1982—; pres. Green Bay Packers, Inc., 1982—. Mem. Wis. State Bar Assn. Roman Catholic. Office: 1265 Lombardi Ave Green Bay WI 54303

PARISH, RICHARD MCKAY, educational administrator; b. Superior, Wis., Sept. 19, 1929; s. Vincent James and Elizabeth (McKay) P.; m. Janice Mae Drolson, June 2, 1951; children—Renee Louise, Pamela Jean. B.S., U. Wis.-Stout, 1958; M.S., U. Wis.-Superior, 1965. Cert. vocat. tech. and adult edn. adminstr., Wis. Locomotive fireman Great No. Ry., Superior, Wis., 1950-58; machinist Benson Electric Co., Superior, 1958-59; tchr. Superior Vocat. Sch., 1959-63; coordinator Superior Tech. Inst., 1963-65; asst. adminstr. Indianhead Tech., Superior, 1965-69, campus adminstr., 1969—. Pres. Breakfast Optimist, Superior, 1970; treas. YMCA, Superior, 1972-76; trustee Village of Lake Nebagamon, Wis., 1981-83. Served with USN, 1952-54, Japan. Mem. Superior C. of C. (bd. dirs. 1978-81). Republican. Presbyterian. Avocations: woodworking, snowmobiling, trapshooting. Home: Route 1 Box 186 Lake Nebagamon WI 54849 Office: Indianhead Tech Inst 600 N 21st St Superior WI 54880

PARISH, SHIRLEY RAE, nurse; b. Great Bend, Kans., Aug. 29, 1956; d. Lee Allen and Edna Mae (Nusser) Parish. A.S., Seward County Community Jr. Coll., 1976; B.S.N., West Tex. State U., 1978; M.N., Wichita State U., 1984. R.N., Tex., Kans. Staff nurse Tex. Tech U. Health Scis. Ctr., Lubbock, 1978-79; staff nurse St. Francis Hosp., Wichita, Kans., 1979-80; staff nurse Wesley Med. Ctr., Wichita, 1980—. Wesley Med. Ctr.-Wichita State U. fellow, 1983. Mem. Am. Nurse's Assn., Oncology Nursing Soc., Wichita Area Oncology Nursing Assn. (nominating com. 1982-84), Baptist. Office: Wesley Med Ctr 550 N Hillside Wichita KS 67214

PARK, JOHN RAYMOND, physician; b. Milw., Aug. 8, 1942; s. Casimir F. and Janet Pauline (Kaczmarowski) P.; m. Elizabeth M.; children—Karen, Adam. B.S. in Biology, 1964; M.D., George Washington U., 1968; M.S. in Otolaryngology, U. Minn., 1975. Diplomate Am. Bd. Otolaryngology. Intern Cleve. Met. Gen. Hosp., 1968-69; resident in otolaryngology U. Minn. Hosps., 1969-74; practice medicine specializing in otolaryngology, Holyoke, Mass., 1974-80, Milw., 1981-83, Brookfield, Wis., 1983—. Served to lt. comdr. M.C., USNR, 1969-75. Fellow ACS; mem. Wis. Otolaryngology Soc., Waukesha Med. Soc., Wis. State Med. Soc. Roman Catholic. Lodge: Rotary of Brookfield. Home: 19260 Tanala Dr Brookfield WI 53005 Office: 17050 North Ave Brookfield WI 53005

PARK, LEONE HOFFMAN, banker; b. Wichita, Kans., Aug. 29, 1919; d. Thad Leon and Amy Louise (Hene) Hoffman; m. John Edward Park, Dec. 21, 1941 (div. May 1975); children—John Edward, Daisy Park. B.A., Kans. U., 1940. With United Mo. Bank of Kansas City, N.A., 1968—, asst. v.p., 1969-70, v.p., 1970-77, sr. v.p., 1977-82, exec. v.p. personal fin. services div., head trust mktg. div., 1982—. Vice pres. Conv. and Visitors Bur., 1982, sec.-treas., 1983; pres. Univ. Assocs., 1983; bd. dirs. Child Advocacy Service Ctr., 1976—. Mem. Nat. Assn. Bank Women, Am. Bankers Assn., Bank Mktg. Assn., Mo. Bankers Assn., Am. Inst. Banking, C. of C., English-Speaking Union (pres. 1982). Republican. Episcopalian. Clubs: Women's City (3d v.p. fin. 1974-84), Jr. League (pres. 1958), Women's Central Exchange (Kansas City, Mo.); Mission Hills (Kans.) Country. Home: 1231 Arno Rd Kansas City MO 64113 Office: United Missouri Bank of Kansas City NA 10th St and Grand Ave Kansas City MO 64106

PARK, OK-CHOON, researcher, educator; b. South Korea, Dec. 30, 1944; came to U.S., 1974, naturalized, 1982; s. Dal-Moon and Eon-Nyun (Yook) P.; m. Young-soon Yang, Sept. 10, 1974; children—Michael Hun, Christine Jin. M.A., U. Minn., 1976, Ph.D., 1978. Research fellow Health Service Research Ctr., U. Minn., Mpls., 1978-79; asst. prof. SUNY-Albany, 1981—; prin. researcher/ednl. cons. Control Data Corp., Mpls., 1979—. SUNY research grantee, 1981-82. Mem. Am. Psychol. Assn., Am. Ednl. Research Assn., Assn. for Devel. of Computer-based Edn. Contbr. articles to profl. jours.; reviewer profl. jours. Office: 511 11th Ave S Minneapolis MN 55415

PARKE, WALTER SIMPSON, artist; educator; b. Little Rock, Ark., Dec. 30, 1909; s. Clyde Wise and Gilvia Maude (Eastman) P.; m. Kathryn Imogene Arendale, Mar. 21, 1941; children—Vicki Elizabeth, Rebecca Jo. Student Art Inst., Chgo., Am. Acad., Chgo., Wellington Reynolds Studio, Chgo. One man shows include Chgo. Galleries, Brooks Meml. Gallery, Memphis, Seabury Western Theol. Seminary, Nashville Mus. Art., Mint Mus. Art., Charlotte, N.C., Columbia Art Mus., S.C., J.B. Speed Mus. Art., Louisville, Hall Art Gallery, Greenville, S.C., Brown County Art Gallery, Nashville, Ind., Hartford Plaza, Chgo., exhibited in group shows at Union League Club, Chgo., Art Inst. Chgo., Denver Art Mus., Brooks Meml. Art Gallery, Ill. State Fair, Art Gallery Pompano Beach, Fla., Profl. League N.Y.C.; represented in permanent collections Du Page Library, U. Ill. Coll. Dentistry, and pvt. collections. Recipient numerous awards both in fine art and advertising. Mem. Municipal Art League, Union League Civic and Arts Found., Palette and Chisel Acad., Brown County Art Guild. Avocation: golf. Home and Office: 30 W 225 Argyle Naperville IL 60540

PARKER, DORIS SIMS, association executive; b. Marvel, Ark., Aug. 23, 1931; d. Percy L. and Earlie M. (Sims) Watson; children—Karen Stewart, Terri. B.A., Ind. Central U., 1959. Acctg. clk. U.S. Army Fin. Ctr., 1952-66; adjudicator VA Regional Office, Indpls., 1966-73; dir. recruiting, placement and regional relations Ind. Vocat. Tech. Coll., Indpls., 1973-82; exec. dir. YWCA, Indpls., 1982—; mem. State Adv. Council Vocat. Edn., 1978—; trainer Leadership Devel. for Pub. Service, 1968-76. Vice-chmn. human relations/human services Greater Indpls. Progress Com., 1979—; pres. Hoosier Capital council Girl Scouts U.S.A., 1979-82; mem., chmn. Nat. Com. Campaign for Human Devel., U.S. Catholic Conf., 1973-76; trustee St. Mary of the Woods Coll., Terre Haute, Ind., 1985—. Named B'nai B'rith Woman of Yr., 1968; recipient Brotherhood award NCCJ, 1975; Those Spl. People award Women in Communications, Inc., 1979. Mem. Am. Vocat. Assn., Am. Personnel and Guidance Assn., Mid-Am. Assn. Edn. Opportunity Program Personnel, Greater Indpls. Women's Polit. Caucus, Alpha Kappa Alpha. Democrat. Roman Catholic. Office: 4460 Guion Rd Indianapolis IN 46254

PARKER, EDWIN CHAMBERLIN, manufacturing company executive; b. St. Louis, Mar. 9, 1933; s. Josiah Atkins and Margaret Sinclaire (Chamberlin) P., VIII; m. Barbara Taylor, Dec. 21, 1955; children—Josiah Atkins IX, Edwin Chamberlin, Nathan Seth. B.B.A., U. Mich.-Ann Arbor, 1954, M.B.A., 1955. Lending officer Harris Bank, Chgo., 1959-65; treas. Marshall Field & Co., Chgo., 1965-71; sr. v.p., chief fin. officer Gould Inc., Rolling Meadows, Ill., 1971-80; chmn., dir. Dur-o-wal, Inc., 1981—; chmn. Bridge Products Inc., Chgo., 1983—, also dir.; dir. Banco Di Roma, Chgo., Bridge Port Brass S.P.A., Bergamo, Italy. Bd. dirs. USO, Chgo., 1974, Heart Assn., Chgo., 1979. Served to lt. (j.g.) USNR, 1955-58. Clubs: Chicago, Mid-Am.; Knollwood (Lake Forest, Ill.). Office: Bridge Products Inc 2215 Sandres Rd Northbrook IL 60062

PARKER, EUGENE NEWMAN, physics educator; b. Houghton, Mich., June 10, 1927; s. Glenn Hugh and Helen Dorland (MacNair) P. m. Niesje Meuter, Nov. 24, 1954; children—Joyce Marie, Eric Glenn. B.S., Mich. State U., 1948, D.Sc., 1975; Ph.D., Calif. Inst. Tech., 1951. Instr. math. U. Utah, Salt Lake City, 1951-53, asst. prof. physics, 1953-55; research assoc. Fermi Inst., U. Chgo., 1955-57, faculty, 1957—, prof., 1962—. Author: Interplanetary Dynamical Processes, 1963; Cosmical Magnetic Fields, 1979. Fellow Am. Phys. Soc.; mem. Nat. Acad. Scis., Am. Geophys. Union, Am. Astron. Soc.

PARKER, EVELYN CAMILLE HILL KILLIAN, physician, surgeon; b. Columbus, Ohio, June 28, 1918; d. John Vincent and Myrtle (Kagy) Hill; student U. Chgo., 1942-43; B.S., U. Ill., 1945, M.D., 1946; postgrad. in ophthalmology Northwestern U., 1947-48; m. E.W. Killian, Apr. 25, 1943 (dec.); children—Paul Wesley, Clyde Bernard; m. 2d, Francis W. Parker, Dec. 7, 1958. Intern, Wesley Meml. Hosp., Chgo., 1946-47; resident in ophthalmology Ill. Eye and Ear Infirmary, Chgo., 1949-51; practice medicine specializing in med. and surg. ophthalmology, Logansport, Ind., 1951—; sec. staff Meml. Hosp., Logansport, 1959; pres. med. staff St. Joseph Hosp., Logansport, 1965. Pres. Logansport Council for Public Schs., 1961-62; mem. Lake Maxinkuckee Mgmt. Com., Culver, Ind., 1981—; chmn. social concern Methodist Ch., 1963-65, ofcl. bd., 1961-65. Recipient Service award Culver Mil. Acad., 1969. Diplomate Am. Bd. Ophthalmology. Fellow Am. Acad. Ophthalmology and Otolaryngology; mem. Soc. Eye Surgeons (charter), AMA (physicians recognition award 1971, 75, 79, 82), Logansport C. of C., Cass County Med. Soc. (pres. 1971), Ind. State Med. Assn., Ind. Acad. Ophthalmology and Otolaryngology (pres. 1979-80). Republican. Clubs: Altrusa (v.p. 1967-69), Culver Mothers (pres. 1968-69). Home and Office: 2500 E Broadway Logansport IN 46947

PARKER, GEORGE, See *Who's Who in America,* 43rd edition.

PARKER, JEFFREY BERRYMAN, data processing specialist; b. Detroit, Jan. 6, 1950; s. Benjamin L. and Jean Hart (Woodard) P.; m. Charlotte J. King, May 24, 1980. B.Continuing Studies, U. Nebr.-Omaha, 1983. Cert. systems profl. Sr. programmer Foremost Ins. Co., Grand Rapids, Mich., 1978-81; project leader Mut. of Omaha, 1981-84; dept. mgr. ALR Systems & Software, Omaha, 1984—. Served with USAF, 1970-78. Fellow Life Office Mgmt. Assn.; mem. Assn. Systems Mgmt. (chpt. sec. 1983-85, spl. publs. chmn. 1985—). Republican. Mem. Christian Ch. Avocations: strategic simulations; cooking; wine making; stained glass; bookbinding. Office: ALR Systems 10334 Ellison Circle Omaha NE 68134

PARKER, LEONARD EMANUEL, physics educator; b. N.Y.C., May 13, 1938; s. Jack and Anna P.; m. Gloria Drucker, Aug. 13, 1961; children—David, Michael, Deborah. A.B., U. Rochester, 1960; A.M., Harvard U., 1962, Ph.D., 1967. Instr., U. N.C., Chapel Hill, 1966-68; mem. faculty U. Wis., Milw., 1968—, prof. physics, 1975—; vis. mem. Inst. Advanced Study, Princeton, 1973, 77 summers; vis. staff Princeton U., 1971-72. Contbr. articles to profl. jours. Recipient Gravity Research Found. award 1974, 80, 84. Fellow Am. Phys. Soc.; mem. AAAS, Am. Assn. Physics Tchrs., N.Y. Acad. Scis. Office: Dept Physics U Wis Milwaukee WI 53201

PARKER, MARGARET MARSH, patent agent; b. Kans. City, Mo., Jan. 8, 1922; d. John Davis and Nancy (McBride) Marsh; m. Norman William Parker, Mar. 15, 1947; children—Norman William, Margaret Parker Trentacosti. Student Ill. Benedictine Coll., 1972. Registered profl. engr., Ill. Technician, U.S. Signal Corps, Dayton, Ohio, 1942-43; engr. Gould Co., Cleve., 1943-48; instr. N.Y. Tech. Inst., Cin., 1948-50; editor Electronic Preview, Elmhurst, Ill., 1956-57; engr. Motorola, Inc., Chgo., 1951-53, 72-73, sr. patent agent, 1974—. Presbyterian. Home: 1302 N Scott St Wheaton IL 60187 Office: Motorola Inc 1303 E Algonquin Schaumburg IL 60196

PARKER, MARYLAND (MIKE), reporter, photographer; b. Oklahoma City, Feb. 5, 1926; d. Clarence N. and Minzola (Perkins) Davis; student U. Ark., Pine Bluff, 1970-71; student Marymount Coll., 1974-77; m. John Harrison Parker, Nov. 25, 1944 (dec.); children—Norma Jean Parker Brown, Janice Kay Parker Shelby, Joyce Lynn, John H. (dec.), Cherie D. Parker Hite, Patrick Scott, Charles Roger. Beautician, Maryland's Ho. of Beauty, Salina, Kans., 1964-69; youth adv. NAACP, Salina, 1970-72; newspaper reporter BACOS Newsletter, Salina, 1971-77; radio announcer Kina's BACOS Report, Salina, after 1973; reporter, photographer Kans. State Globe. Mem. Salina County Democratic Women, 1960—; part-time vol. Salvation Army, Salina, 1979—; bd. dirs. Salina Child Care Assn. Mem. NAACP (life), Nat. Fedn. Press Women, Kans. Press Women, Internat. Platform Assn., VFW Aux., Am. Legion Aux. Mormon. Home: 920 Birch Dr PO Box 2412 Salina KS 67401

PARKER, PATRICK STREETER, manufacturing executive; b. Cleve., 1929. B.A., Williams Coll., 1951; M.B.A., Harvard U., 1953. With Parker-Hannifin Corp. and predecessor, Cleve., 1953—, sales mgr. fittings div., 1957, mgr. aerospace products div., 1963, pres. Parker Seal Co. div., 1965, corp. v.p., 1967, pres., 1969, pres. and chief exec. officer, 1971, chmn. bd. and chief exec. officer, 1977-84, chmn. bd., 1984—, pres., 1982-84, also dir.; dir. Acme-Cleve. Corp., Sherwin-Williams Co., Soc. Corp., Reliance Electric Co.; Pres. and trustee Woodruff Hosp. of Cleve. Served with USN, 1954-57. Office: Parker-Hannifin Corp 17325 Euclid Ave Cleveland OH 44112*

PARKER, PAUL JULIAN, university administrator; b. Phoenix, Feb. 5, 1947; s. Marsena R. and Lillian R. (Kohler) P.; m. Patti Esta Ross, Aug. 17, 1970; children—Lara Marie, Jennifer Lynn. B.A., Loyola U., New Orleans, 1969; M.A., U. Mo.-Kansas City, 1973, Ph.D., 1976. Dir. student programs U. Mo.,

Kansas City, 1973-77, asst. dean students, student life, 1977-78, asst. dean students, health scis., 1978-79; dean of students Butler U., Indpls., 1979-82, v.p. student affairs, 1982—. Trustee Orchard Country Day Sch., Indpls., 1984—; bd. dirs. Childrens Bur. Indpls., 1982—, 1st v.p., 1985. Served with U.S. Army, 1969-71; Vietnam. Mem. Nat. Assn. Student Personnel Adminstrs. (named Outstanding New Profl. 1979), Am. Assn. Higher Edn., Ind. Coll. Personnel Assn., Phi Kappa Phi, Omicron Delta Kappa. Office: Butler U 4600 Sunset Ave Indianapolis IN 46208

PARKER, ROBBIE, former community school district administrator; b. Detroit, May 19, 1922; d. Johnnie and Estella (Woods) Hall; m. Howard Thompson, Apr. 23, 1949; 1 dau., Muriel Ward; m. 2d Bernard Parker, Nov. 23, 1958. B.A., W.Va. State U., 1943; M.A., U. Mich., 1957. Tchr., Clintondale Community Sch. Dist., Mt. Clemens, Mich., 1943-57, prin., 1957-71, dir. curriculum, 1971-77, asst. supt., 1977-79, dep. supt., 1979-83, acting supt., 1983-84. Robbie Hall Parker Elem. Sch. named in her honor Clintondale Community Sch. Dist. Mem. Detroit Hist. Soc., Assn. Supervision and Curriculum Devel., Mich. Negotiations Assn., Am. Assn. Sch. Adminstrs., Mich. Assn. Professions, Delta Sigma Theta. Congregationalist. Office: 35100 Little Mack St Mount Clemens MI 48043

PARKER, STANLEY EUGENE, electrical engineering supervisor; b. Walton, Ky., Oct. 9, 1942; s. Stanley Jewel and Frances Sue (Collins) P.; m. Betty Robinson, Sept. 10, 1967 (div. 1983); children—Stanley, Brian Keith. Ed., Chgo. Tech. Coll., Allen Hancock Coll., U. Cin. Elec. designer Lodge & Shipley, Cin., 1966-68; design engr. Gen. Electric, Cin., 1968-70; elec. design engr. Am. Tool, Cin., 1970-78; supr. elec. engring. WCI Machine Tools, Cin., 1978—; cons. Industry Research, Florence, Ky., 1981—. Music dir. New Banklick Bapt. Ch., Walton, Ky. Served with USAF, 1963-66. Mem. AIM, Parents Without Ptnrs. Republican. Baptist. Avocations: Car restoring; collecting Japanese art objects. Home: 219 Maher Rd Walton KY 41094 Office: WCI Machine Tools & Systems 720 E 2d St Cincinnati OH 45202

PARKER, WILLIAM LAWRENCE, JR., lawyer; b. Pratt, Kans., Feb. 27, 1931; s. William Lawrence and Mabel (Atkinson) P.; m. Donna Lee Smith, Dec. 31, 1981; children—William Lawrence, III, Karen Elaine. B.A., Washburn U., 1955, J.D., 1957. Bar: Kans. 1957, U.S. Supreme Ct. 1963. Ptnr. McCullough, Parker, Wareheim & LaBunker, Topeka, Kans., 1957-71; pres. W.L. Parker, Jr., Chartered, Topeka, 1972—; mgr., house counsel Kans. Constrn. Industry Fringe Benefit Funds, Topeka, 1972—. Editor-in-chief Washburn Law Rev., 1956-57. Trustee Kans. Pub. Employees Retirement System, Topeka, 1972-76; trustee, fin. chmn. Washburn Coll., Topeka, 1973—; tech. dir. Topeka Civic Theatre, Topeka, 1974-82; tech. designer Dance Arts Topeka, 1974-83; pres. Health Care Cost Containment Task Force, Mo. and Kans., 1984—; mem. Gov.'s Task Force on Health Care, 1984—. Recipient Spl. Service award Kans. Bldg. Trades Health and Welfare Fund, 1984. Fellow Fin. Analysts Fedn.; mem. ABA (co.-chmn. subcom. 1971—), Fringe Benefit Execs. Assn. (pres. 1974-81), Internat. Found. Employee Benefit Plans. Baptist. Lodge: Masons. Avocations: horses, farming, golf. Home: Rural Route 1 Box 154A White City KS 66872 Office: W L Parker Jr Chartered PO Box 5168 4101 Southgate Dr Topeka KS 66605

PARKISON, PAUL WILLIAM, accounting educator; b. Muncie, Ind., Dec. 2, 1936; s. Forrest Bernard and Jeanne Elizabeth (Goodwin) P.; m. Nancy Kay Ingle, Dec. 8, 1967; children—Dale Alan, Brian Paul. B.S., Ball State U., 1958, M.A., 1961; D.Bus. Adminstrn., Ind. U., 1967. C.P.A., Ind. Bus. tchr. Warren Central High Sch., Indpls., 1958-63; grad. teaching assoc. Ind. U., Bloomington, 1963-66; prof., head accounting dept. Ball State U., Muncie, 1966—; bd. mem. Ind. State Bd. Pub. Accountancy, Indpls., 1976-82. Contbr. articles to profl. jours. Bd. dirs. Jr. Achievement, Muncie, 1968-70. Named Prof. of Yr., Delta Sigma Pi, Ball State U., 1970, 72, Alumni Prof. of Yr. Coll. Bus. Alumni Assn., Ball State U., 1983. Mem. Am. Inst. C.P.A.s, Am. Acctg. Assn., Nat. Assn. Accts. (N. Central Ind. chpt. pres. 1970-71), Ind. C.P.A. Soc. (sec. 1972-74, bd. mem. 1974-77), Beta Gamma Sigma, Beta Alpha Psi. Republican. Methodist. Club: Exchange (pres. 1976-77). Avocations: Gardening; reading; fishing. Home: Rural Route 2 Box 483A Yorktown IN 47396 Office: Ball State U Dept Acctg Muncie IN 47306

PARKS, DOUGLAS RICHARD, linguist, bookseller; b. Long Beach, Calif., Aug. 28, 1942; s. Benjamin H. and Mary O. (Pemberton) P. A.B. in Anthropology, U. Calif.-Berkeley, 1964, Ph.D. in Linguistics, 1968. Asst. prof. anthropology Idaho State U., Pocatello, 1968-73; post-doctoral fellow Smithsonian Instn., Washington, 1973-74; dir. Indian langs. program Mary Coll., Bismarck, N.D., 1974-83; assoc. scholar Ind. U., Bloomington, 1983—; dir. Title VII bilingual program White Shield Sch., Roseglen, N.D., 1983—; propr. Dacotah Book Co., Bloomington, 1983—. Author: A Grammar of Pawnee, 1976; An Introduction to Arikara Language, 1979. Editor: Ceremonies of the Pawnee, 1982. Fellow Am. Council Learned Socs., 1982-83. Mem. Plains Anthrop. Assn. (pres. 1981-82), Am. Soc. for Ethnohistory, Am. Anthrop. Assn. Republican. Roman Catholic. Home: 8275 E State Rd 46 Bloomington IN 47401 Office: Dept of Anthropology Rawles Hall Ind U Bloomington IN 47405

PARKS, OATTIS ELWYN, geologist; b. Atlanta; s. James E. and Jennie O. Parks; B.A. in Geology, Emory U., 1947, M.A., Tex. Christian U., 1954; m. Loretta I. Latulippe, Jan. 5, 1959; children—Oattis Elwyn, Henry B., Camilla F., Michelle M., Richard Dumais. Mem. faculty Fla. State U., 1965-67; guest lectr. U. Mass., Fla. A&M U., 1964-67; v.p. exploration and devel. AMAX Coal Co., Indpls., 1967-72; v.p. AMAX Internat., Indpls., London, 1972-74; founder, pres. NEWCO Engring. & Coal Devel. Co., Inc., Indpls., 1975—; pres. NEWSEL, Inc., Indpls., 1977—. Served to col. USAF, 1940-64; ETO. Decorated Presdl. citation, Army Commendation medal, USAF Commendation medal with 2 oak leaf clusters, D.F.C., Silver Star, Air medal with 4 oak leaf clusters. Mem. Assn. Profl. Geol. Scientists, Geol. Soc. Am., Soc. Econ. Geologists, Ind. Acad. Sci. Presbyterian. Clubs: Indpls. Athletic, Masons. Author tech. papers in field. Office: 8060 Knue Rd Suite 132 Indianapolis IN 46250

PARKYN, JOHN DUWANE, nuclear engineer; b. La Crosse, Wis., Feb. 20, 1944; s. Lionel Eric and Florence Katrina (Klum) P.; student Wis. State U., 1962-64, U. N.Mex., 1968-69; B.S. in Nuclear Engring. and Physics, U. Wis., 1972; m. Betty Christine Tarnutzer, Aug. 13, 1966; children—Christine Peggy, Sarah Katherine, John Martin. Asst. plant engr. Ohio Med. Products Co., 1966-67; party chief U.S. Geol. Survey, Madison, Wis., 1971-72; asst. operations group Point Beach Nuclear Plant, Two Rivers, Wis., 1972-74; asst. supt. La Crosse Boiling Water Reactor, Genoa, Wis., 1974-82, supt., 1982—. Mem. Two Rivers City Council, 1974; mem. Vernon County Bd. Suprs., 1976—, now vice chmn., mem. fin. com., chmn. human services rev. bd., chmn. community options program; assessor Bergen Twp. (Wis.), 1976-77, Sterling Twp. (Wis.), 1977-79; chmn. Vernon County Library Com., 1976—; chmn. personnel com. Vernon County Bd. Equalized Values; chmn. Vernon County Com. for Programs of Aging; bd. dirs. Winding Rivers Library System; treas. Sch. Dist. of La Crosse; 1st v.p. Riverland council Girl Scouts U.S.A.; adv. Order of DeMolay. Served with U.S. Army, 1967-69. Cert. assessor, Wis.; registered profl. nuclear engr., Calif.; lic. sr. reactor operator. Mem. Am. Nuclear Soc. (chmn. Wis. sect.), Nat. Assn. of Former Youth Govs., Am. Legion Mem. United Ch. of Christ. Lodge: Masons. Home: Pleasant Valley Stoddard WI 54658 Office: La Crosse Boiling Water Reactor Route 1 Genoa WI 54658

PARMELEE, HAROLD JAMES (JIM), paper company technician; b. Marshfield, Wis., Nov. 18, 1930; s. Harold Fred and Lillian Myrtle (Coaty) P.; m. Shirley Ann Bumgarner, Sept. 5, 1953; children—Rose, Kathleen, Tammy, Linda, Nancy, Michelle. Owner, Jim Parmelee Apts., Marshfield, Wis., from 1964; paper tester tech. dept. Consol. Papers, Inc., Wisconsin Rapids, Wis. Republican. Lutheran. Clubs: Eagles (past pres.), United Commercial Travelers. Home and Office: 419 E Franklin St Marshfield WI 54449

PARMER, ANITA FLOY, nurse epidemiologist; b. Braymer, Mo., May 2, 1941; d. Floyd Earl and Leola Frances (Penny) Mason; m. Kenneth Dale Parmer, Sept. 6, 1964; children—Kenneth Dale, John Earl. Diploma Trinity Luth. Hosp. Sch. Nursing, Kansas City, 1962; student William Jewell Coll., Liberty, Mo., 1963; B.S. in Nursing, U. Mo., 1964. R.N., Mo. Staff nurse U. Mo. Med. Ctr., Columbia, 1962, Excelsior Springs (Mo.) Hosp., 1963; staff nurse Boone County Hosp. (name changed to Boone Hosp. Ctr.), Columbia, 1963, operating room staff nurse, supr., 1964-73, ednl. services instr., 1973-78, nurse epidemiologist, 1978—. Recipient Florence Nightingale award Trinity Luth. Hosp. Sch. Nursing, 1962. Mem. Am. Nurses Assn., Assn. for Practitioners in Infection Control. Republican. Methodist. Home: 35 Trails West Dr Route 5 Box 73 Columbia MO 65202 Office: Boone Hosp Ctr 1600 E Broadway Columbia MO 65201

PARMER, DAN GERALD, veterinarian; b. Wetumpka, Ala., July 3, 1926; s. James Lonnie and Virginia Gertrude (Guy) P.; student Los Angeles City Coll., 1945-46; D.V.M., Auburn U., 1950; m. Donna Louise Kesler, June 7, 1980; 1 son, Dan Gerald; 1 dau. by previous marriage, Linda Leigh. Gen. practice vet. medicine, Galveston, Tex., 1950-54, Chgo., 59—; veterinarian in charge Chgo. Commn. Animal Care and Control, 1974—; chmn. Ill. Impaired Veterinarians Com.; tchr. Highlands U., 1959. Served with USNR, 1943-45; PTO; served as staff veterinarian and 2d and 5th Air Force veterinarian chief USAF, 1954-59. Decorated 9 Battle Stars; recipient Veterinary Appreciation award U. Ill., 1971. Mem. Ill. (chmn. civil def. and package disaster hosps. 1968-71), Chgo. (bd. govs. 1969-72, 74—, now pres. 1982), South Chgo. (pres. 1965-66) veterinary med. assns., Am. Animal Hosp. Assn. (dir.), AVMA (nat. com. for impaired veterinarians), Ill. Acad. Vet. Practice, Nat. Assn. of Professions, Am. Assn. Zoo Veterinarians, Am. Assn. Zool. Parks and Aquariums, VFW. Democrat. Clubs: Masons, Shriners, Kiwanis, Midlothian Country, Valley Internat. Country. Discoverer Bartonellosis in cattle in N.Am. and Western Hemisphere, 1951; co-developer bite-size high altitude in-flight feeding program USAF, 1954-56. Address: 4350 W Ford City Dr Apt 402 Chicago IL 60652

PARRIS, EILEEN KAY, English educator; b. Cin., Dec. 4, 1935; d. Henry Kennedy and Mary (Wood) P. B.S. in Edn., U. Cin., 1958, B.A. in Classics, 1958, M.A. in Classics, 1959. Cert. tchr., Ohio. Tchr., Oak Hills High Sch., Cin., 1959-62; tchr. Norwood (Ohio) High Sch., 1962—, coordinator dept. English, 1976-84. Mem. NEA, Ohio Edn. Assn., Assn. Supervision and Curriculum Devel., Nat. Council Tchrs. English, Phi Beta Kappa. Home: 2145 Quatman Ave Norwood OH 45212 Office: 2020 Sherman Ave Norwood OH 45212

PARRISH, BARRY JAY, advertising executive; b. Chgo., Sept. 3, 1946; s. Hy J. and Shirley F. (Fimoff) Perelgut; B.A., Columbia Coll., 1968; M.B.A., U. Chgo., 1971; 1 son, Jeffrey Scott. Asst. advt. mgr. Libby McNeill & Libby, Chgo., 1965-67; advt. and promotion mgr. McGraw-Hill Publs. Co., Chgo., 1967-69; creative dir./account exec. Bozell & Jacobs, Chgo., 1969-72; account supr. Dailey & Assos., San Francisco, 1972-75; v.p./account supr. internat. Arthur E. Wilk Advt., Chgo., 1975-76; exec. v.p. Shaffer/MacGill & Assos., Chgo., 1976-81; v.p., dir. Grey II, Grey Advt., Chgo., 1981—. TV commls. judge CLIO awards, 1978, 79, U.S. Film Festival, 1980-81, 84. Served with USMC, to 1972. Recipient awards Houston Internat. Film Festival, Nat. Employment Assn., others. Mem. Am. Mgmt. Assn., Chgo. Council on Fgn. Relations, Art Inst. Chgo., Lincoln Park Zool. Soc. Club: Chgo. Advertising. Contbr. articles to profl. jours., newspapers, mags. Home: 10 E Ontario St Chicago IL 60611 Office: Grey-Chicago Inc 2200 Merchandise Mart Plaza Chicago IL 60654

PARRISH, FREDERICK CHARLES, animal science and food technology educator, researcher; b. Olney, Mo., July 18, 1933; s. Frederick Charles and Georgiana (Hammonds) P.; m. Fern Rose Westerman, June 7, 1953; children—Deborah June, Randall Douglas, Rhonda Lea, Richard Brent. B.S., U. Mo., 1959, M.S., 1960, Ph.D., 1965. Instr. U. Mo., Columbia, 1960-65; asst. prof. Iowa State U., Ames, 1965-69, assoc. prof., 1969-76; food scientist U.S. Dept. Agr. Washington, 1972-73, prof. animal sci., food tech., 1976—. Contbr. articles to profl. jours. Served with U.S. Army, 1953-55, Korea. Mem. Am. Meat Sci. Assn. (bd. dirs. 1972-74), Am. Soc. Animal Sci., Inst. Food Tech. Republican. Baptist. Lodge: Kiwanis (pres. 1984—). Home: 1225 Arizona Ave Ames IA 50010 Office: 150 Food Technology Lab Iowa State University Ames IA 50011

PARRISH, JOHN EDWARD, circuit judge; b. Lebanon, Mo., June 10, 1940; s. Folie and Thelma (Osborn) P.; m. Claudia Barbee, Sept. 1, 1962; children—Mark Everett, Michael Brett. B.B.A., U. Mo., 1962, J.D., 1965. Acct. Arthur Andersen & Co., St. Louis, 1965-66; ptnr. Phillips & Parrish, Camdenton, Mo., 1968-73; prosecuting atty. Camden County, Camdenton, 1969-73; circuit judge State of Mo., Camdenton, 1973—; mem. State Adv. Group on Juvenile Justice, Jefferson City, Mo., 1981—; vice chmn. Mo. Bd. Cert. Court Reporter Examiners, Jefferson City, 1974—. Pres. bd. dirs. Lake of the Ozarks Gen. Hosp., Osage Beach, Mo., 1983—. Served to capt. U.S. Army, 1966-68. Mem. Mo. Bar Assn., Mo. Council Juvenile Court Judges (pres. 1978-79), Mo. Judicial Conf. (exec. council 1980-84), Nat. Council Juvenile and Family Court Judges. Republican. Mem. Christian Ch. (Disciples of Christ). Lodge: Rotary (pres. 1977-78). Home: Route 2 Box 274 Camdenton MO 65020 Office: Circuit Court Camdenton MO 65020

PARRISH, NANCY ELAINE BUCHELE, educator, state senator; b. Cedar Vale, Kans., Nov. 9, 1948; d. Julian Milton and Vergie May (Bryant) Buchele; B.S. in Edn., Kans. State U., 1970; M.S. in Spl. Edn., U. Kans., 1974; J.D. magna cum laude, Washburn U., 1984; m. James Wesley Parrish, Jan. 31, 1970; children—Leslie Elgin, Tyler Jonathan. Tchr., Topeka Public Schs., 1970-75; spl. edn. tchr. Topeka State Hosp., 1975-81; mem. Kans. Senate, 1980—; mem. edn. task force Council of State Govts., 1981-84; mem. fiscal affairs task force Nat. Council State Legislatures, 1985—; policy chmn. Senate Minority Party, 1985—. Bd. dirs. Mental Health Assn., Topeka, Boys Club, Topeka, Jr. League, Kans. Action for Children; mem. East Topeka Council on Aging; bd. advisors Sch. of Future. Mem. LWV. Democrat. Club: Topeka Knife and Fork (bd. dirs. 1981—, pres.-elect 1985). Office: Room 403 State Capitol Bldg Topeka KS 66612

PARRISH, VIRGINIA, softball coach, educator; b. Salt Lake City, Feb. 17, 1952; d. LaMar Steed and Lona (Udy) Parrish. B.S., Weber State Coll., 1973; postgrad. U. B.C., 1973-74; M.S., U. Ariz., 1980. Softball coach, instr. U. Ariz., Tucson, 1977-79, U. Iowa, Iowa City, 1980—. Contbr. articles to profl. jours. Named Outstanding Female scholar, Weber State Coll., 1973; E.R. Moore scholar, 1969-73. Mem. Am. Assn. Health, Phys. Edn. and Recreation, Cardinal Key Honor Sorority, Phi Kappa Phi. Home: 705 Edgewater Dr Coralville IA 52241 Office: Univ Iowa Women's Athletics Carver Hawkeye Arena Iowa City IA 52242

PARROTT, LESLIE, clergyman, college b. Clarksville, Tenn., Apr. 2, 1923; s. Alonzo Leslie Parrott and Lucille Elliott; m. Lora Lee Montgomery, July 7, 1943; children—Richard, Roger, Leslie. A.B., Olivet Nazarene Coll., 1944; M.A., Willamette U., 1949; Ph.D., Mich. State U., 1959. Ordained to ministry Ch. of Nazarene 1944. Pastor, First Ch. Nazarene, Portland, Oreg., 1961-70; pres. Eastern Nazarene Coll., Quincy, Mass., 1970-75, Olivet Nazarene Coll., Kankakee, Ill., 1975—. Author: Sons of Africa, 1980. Home and Office: 240 E Marsile Bourbonnais IL 60914

PARROTT, RAY JENNINGS, Russian language and literature educator; b. Elmhurst, Ill., Feb. 11, 1937; s. Ray Jennings and Claire Louise (Schacht) P.; m. Mary Louise McKinley, June 14, 1963; children—Andrew, Barbara. B.A., Cornell Coll., Mt. Vernon, Iowa, 1963; M.A., U. Mich., 1967, Ph.D., 1974. Teaching fellow dept. Slavic langs. U. Mich., Ann Arbor, 1963-68, lectr., 1969-71; instr. dept. Russian, Iowa U., Iowa City, 1971-74, asst. prof., 1974-77, assoc. prof., 1977—, chair dept., 1975—. Translator: Arkhangelsky-Parodies, 1976; (with Weber) Lermontov, 1981. Editor-translator: Russian Prose, 1984. Contbr. articles to profl. jours. Served with U.S. Army, 1956-59. Rackham Grad. fellow U. Mich., 1968-69; NEH fellow. Mem. Am. Council Tchrs. of Russian (bd. dirs. 1982—), Am. Assn. Advancement of Slavic Studies, Am. Assn. Tchrs. of Slavic and East European Languages. Avocations: camping, woodworking, gardening. Office: Univ of Iowa Dept of Russian 230 Jessup Hall Iowa City IA 52242

PARSA, CYRUS, pathologist, educator; b. Tehran, Iran, July 13, 1943, came to U.S., 1958, naturalized 1970; s. Ahmad and Simin Parsa; m. Lila Parsa, July 31, 1976; children—Roxanne, Ranna. B.A., Calif. State U., 1966; D.O., Univ. Health Scis., Kans. City, Mo., 1970. Diplomate Am. Bd. Pathology, Am. Osteo. Bd. Pathology. Intern, then resident Lakeside and St. Lukes Hosps., Kansas City, Mo., 1971-75; fellow U. Kans. 1975-76; assoc. prof., dept. head pathology, U. Health Scis., Kansas City, Mo., 1976—. Contbr. articles to profl. jours. Fellow Am. Soc. Clin. Pathologists; mem. Am. Coll. Osteo. Pathologists, Kans. City Soc. Pathologists. Office: Univ Health Scis 2105 Independence Ave Kansas City MO 64124

PARSLEY, ANN(A) LOUISE, educational administrator; b. Jefferson Twp., Ind., May 28, 1926; d. Lloyd F. and Elizabeth E. (McDowell) Miller; m. Albert Parsley, July 14, 1948; children—Cheryl Ayn Parsley Hanning, Theresa Lynn Parsley Nelson. B.S., Ind. U., 1947, M.S., 1966, Adminstr.'s Lic., 1976; Elem. Edn. Lic., Valparaiso U., 1961; Counseling Lic., Purdue U., 1968. Service rep. Ind. Bell Telephone, 1947; elem. tchr. LaPorte (Ind.) Community Schs., 1959-68, elem. counselor, Kingsford Heights and Stillwell Schs., 1968-71, elem. tchr., 1972, home counselor for attendance, 1973-76; prin. Kingsford High Sch., 1976-82, Stillwell Sch., 1982—. Charter mem. LaPorte Hosp. Aux.; mem. Am. Legion Aux.; bd. dirs., past pres. LaPorte County Youth Service Bur.; past pres. LaPorte Community Pre-Sch. Bd., LaPorte Mental Health Assn. Mem. Nat. Elem. Prins. Assn., Ind. Elem. Prins. Assn., AAUW (past pres.), Ind. Assn. for Supervision and Curriculum Devel., Ind. Congress of Parent-Tchr. Assn., Delta Kappa Gamma (charter mem. Gamma Kappa chpt., pres. 1984—). Republican. Presbyterian. Clubs: Bridge, Elks Women. Home: 0694 S Mapleleaf Ln LaPorte IN 46350 Office: 0106 N State Rd 104 Stillwell IN 46351

PARSLEY, ROBERT MORRIS, banker, leasing corporation executive; b. Holden, W.Va., Nov. 8, 1938; s. Leland Morris and Ida Irene (Spaulding) P.; m. Ruth Ann Bostic, June 10, 1960; children—Robert Martin, Brian Leland, Lea Ann, Aimee Lynne. B.A., W.Va. Tech. U., 1961; M.B.A., Xavier U., Cin., 1975; banking cert., Rutger's U., 1972, U. Wis.-Madison, 1977. C.P.A., Ohio. Tchr. Logan County High Schs., W.Va., 1961-63; cashier Logan Bank & Trust Co., 1964-70, Peoples State Bank, Granville, Ohio, 1970; chief fin. officer Park Nat. Bank, Newark, Ohio, 1970—; sec., treas. Park Leasing Corp., Columbus, Ohio, 1975—. Mem. Nat. Assn. Accts., Am. Inst. Banking, Am. Inst. C.P.A.s, Ohio Soc. C.P.A.s. Republican. Baptist. Lodge: Masons. Avocations: photography; golf. Home: 414 E College St Granville OH 43023 Office: Park Nat Bank 21 S 1st St Newark OH 43055

PARSONS, DAVID GUY, media specialist, videographer; b. Mt. Morris, Ill., June 7, 1952; s. Rex and Violet (Marger) P.; m. Jeannie Belinda Bales, May 20, 1972 (div. Jan. 1979); children—Jaron Martin, Dylan James; m. Deborah Mary Uhlis, July 14, 1979. B.S. in Journalism/Mass Communication, B.S. cum laude in Social Sci., Kans. State U., 1974. News reporter Sta. KSAC, Manhattan, Kans., 1972-73; video field producer Sta. KSU-TV, Manhattan, Kans., 1973-74; program dir. Communications Services Inc., Junction City, Kans., 1974-77; media services supv. Mo. Dept. Edn., Jefferson City, 1978—; ptnr. Midwest Video Group, central Mo., 1979-82; freelance videographer, 1982—. Host, dir. TV series A Conversation With... (NCTA award of excellence), 1975; producer, dir. TV series People Helping People (NCTA award of excellence), 1976; co-producer, dir. TV program Education: A State Responsibility (NASEDIO award of distinction), 1982. Fund Drive com. United Way, Junction City, Kans., 1975-77. Recipient Outstanding Newcomer of the Yr. award Alpha Epsilon Rho, 1972, Outstanding Broadcaster in Radio and TV, 1972, 1973, also numerous community service awards local and state businesses, 1975—. Mem. Internat. TV Assn. (chpt. v.p. 1984—), Nat. Assn. State Edn. Media Profls., Alpha Epsilon Rho (v.p. 1973-74). Avocations: boating, racquetball, audiophile, water and snow skiing. Home: 1605 Westview Dr Jefferson City MO 65101 Office: Mo Dept Elem and Secondary Edn Box 480 Jefferson City MO 65102

PARSONS, GERALD ANTHONY, educator, counselor; b. Orlando, Fla., Oct. 29, 1939; s. Gerald Arthur and Edna (Franco) P.; m. Marcia Stine, Nov. 30, 1968; children—Stephen Curtis, Linda Beth. B.A., Monmouth Coll., 1961; M.A., Northwestern U., 1964. Cert. psychologist, Ill. Counselor, North Chicago High Sch., Ill., 1964-66; instr./coach North Park Coll., Chgo., 1966-68; dir. edn. North Shore Mental Hosp., Winnetka, Ill., 1968; tchr./coach New Trier West High Sch., Northfield, Ill., 1969-75; counselor/coach Glenbrook Souh High Sch., Glenview, Ill., 1975-79; counselor/tchr. Monticello High Sch., Ill., 1979-85; tchr., coach Univ. High Sch., Normal, Ind., 1985—; lectr. in psychology Kendall Coll., Evanston, Ill., 1965, 75; instr. Coll. Lake County, Grayslake, Ill., 1972-79; asst. prof. psychology Richland Community Coll., Decatur, Ill., 1980-84; Olympic track and field official, 1984. Mem. adv. bd. Human Behavior, 1983-84. Mem. Northfield Youth Commn., 1966-69, Evanston Jr. Coll. Planning Com., 1967-68, Diversified Occupations, Glenview, 1971-74. NSF summer scholar, 1973; Williams scholar, 1957. Mem. Am. Psychol. Assn., Fellowship of Christian Athletes, Am. Personnel and Guidance Assn., Ill. Assn. Coll. Admissions Counselors (downstate com. 1983-85), Ill. High Sch. Assn. (ofcl. 1979—), Sigma Phi Epsilon. Clubs: Glenview Road Runners (pres. 1975-78); Sage City Striders (pres. 1979-83) (Monticello, Ill.). Lodge: Lions (treas. 1971-77). Avocations: competitive running; baseball cards. Home: 1718 Braden Dr Normal IL 61761 Office: Univ High Sch 500 W Gregory St Normal IL 61761

PARSONS, JAMES BENTON, federal judge; b. Kansas City, Mo., Aug. 13, 1911; s. James Benton and Maggie (Virgia) P.; A.B., James Millikin U., 1934; M.A., U. Chgo., 1946, LL.D., 1949; also hon. degrees; m. Amy Maxwell, Dec. 24, 1952 (dec.); 1 son, Dieter K. Faculty, Lincoln U. Mo., 1934-40, asst. to dean of men, instr. polit. sci., acting head music dept., 1938-40; supr. pub. schs., Greensboro, N.C., 1940-42; faculty John Marshall Law Sch., Chgo.; asst. corp. counsel City of Chgo., 1949-51; asst. U.S. atty., Chgo., 1951-60; judge Superior Ct. of Cook County, Ill., 1960-61; judge U.S. Dist. Ct., No. Dist. of Ill., Chgo., 1961—, chief judge, 1975-81. Active Boy Scouts Am.; mem. nat. exec. bd., adv. council Reading Research Found.; mem. citizens com. U. Ill., Champaign; mem. pres.'s council St. Ignatius Coll. Prep. Sch., Chgo.; mem. centennial anniversary com. Loyola U., Chgo.; hon. chmn. Chgo. Conf. on Religion and Race and Tri-Faith Employment Ser.; exec. bd. Chgo. Community Music Found.; adv. bd. Ill. Masonic Hosp., Chgo. Trustee Millikin U., Decatur, Ill., Ada S. McKinley Community Sers.; bd. dirs. Harvard-St. George Sch., Chgo., Leukemia Research Found., Chgo., Mercy Halfway House Corp., Chgo.; nat. bd. trustees NCCJ. Office: US Dist Ct US Courthouse 219 S Dearborn St Chicago IL 60604*

PARSONS, JAMES EUGENE, microbiologist, educator, consultant; b. Lima, Ohio, Nov. 10, 1939; s. Virgil Lorain and Dorothy Mae P. B.Sc., Ohio State U., 1961, M.Sc., 1963, Ph.D., 1977; postgrad. U. Nebr., 1964-68, 70-71. Chief clin. microbiology service Akron (Ohio) Gen. Med. Ctr., 1977-81; chmn. bd. Animalcule Ltd., Akron, 1978—; asst. prof. biol. and allied health scis. Bloomsburg U. Pa., 1982—; asst. prof. clin. microbiology in pathology Coll. Medicine, Northeastern Ohio U., 1978-81; adj. prof. biology U. Akron, 1979-81, Inst. Bio-Med. Engring. Research, U. Akron, 1979-81; cons. Medina Community Hosp., 1978—. Pres., Council Grad. Students, Ohio State U., 1973; pres. Grad. Student-Faculty Assn., U. Nebr., 1965, Ohio Assn. Grad. Student Orgns., 1973, 74. Recipient Tchr. of Yr. award Sch. Med. Tech., Akron Gen. Med. Ctr., 1979; NASA trainee U. Nebr., 1965-67; Ohio State U. adminstrn. trainee, 1973. Mem. Am. Soc. Microbiology, Electron Microscopy Soc. Am., Med. Mycol. Soc. Ams., Nat. Registry Microbiologists, N.Y. Acad. Sci., Ohio Acad. Sci., South Central Assn. Clin. Microbiology, Am. Acad. Microbiology (cert.), Pa. Acad. Sci., Ohio State U. Alumni Assn., Sigma Xi, Phi Kappa Phi. Contbr. articles to profl. jours.

PARSONS, JOHN GORDON, dairy chemistry educator; b. Manitoba, Can., Dec. 3, 1939; s. Gordon P. and Thelma (Smith) P., m. Penelope Rae Dugdale, Aug. 8, 1963; children—Kevin, Nancy. B.S., U. Manitoba, 1961, M.S., 1963; Ph.D., Pa. State U., 1968. Grad. asst. U. Man., Winnipeg, 1961-63; research asst. Pa. State U., University Park, 1963-68; asst. prof. S.D. State U., Brookings, 1968-73, assoc. prof., 1973-78, assoc. prof., head dept. dairy sci., 1978-79, prof., 1979—. Contbr. articles to profl. jours. and popular mags. Lectr. nat. meetings. Mem. Am. Dairy Sci. Assn., Inst. Food Tech., Am. Cultured Dairy Products Inst., Council Agrl. Sci. and Tech., Sigma Xi (Brookings chpt. pres. 1978-79). Republican. Presbyterian. Lodge: Rotary. Home: 790 Main Ave Brookings SD 57006 Office: Dairy Sci Dept SD State Univ Brookings SD 57007-0647

PARSONS, ROBERT WILTON, physician; b. Los Angeles, Dec. 25, 1929; s. Harold Hunt and Ellen Grace (Henderson) P.; m. Elise Hampton, Dec. 12, 1953; children—Ann Elise, Keith Hampton, Kimberly Ellen, Susan Greer. Ph.B. U. Chgo., 1949; M.D., Washington U., 1954. Diplomate Am. Bd. Surgery, Am. Bd. Plastic Surgery. Asst. chief plastic surgery Walter Reed Army Hosp., Washington, 1962-66; chief plastic surgery Second Gen. Hosp., Landstuhl, W. Ger., 1966-69, Walter Reed Hosp., 1969-77; assoc. prof. Ind. U. Sch. Medicine, 1977-79; prof. in surgery U. Chgo., 1979—cons. to Surgeon Gen. U.S. Army, Washington, 1969-77. Contbr. articles to medical jours. Elder Presbyterian Ch.; bd. dirs. Assn. House of Chgo., 1984—. Served to col. M.C.,

U.S. Army, 1955-77. Decorated Legion of Merit. Mem. ACS, Am. Assn. Plastic Surgeons, Am. Soc. Plastic and Reconstructive Surgeons, Am. Soc. for Aesthetic Plastic Surgery, Am. Soc. Maxillofacial Surgeons, Am. Cleft Palate Assn. (v.p. 1984-85). Office: Univ Chgo Pritzker Sch Medicine 5841 S Maryland Ave Box 269 Chicago IL 60637

PARSONS, WILLIAM ANDREWS, environmental engineer; b. Cedar Rapids, Iowa, Nov. 11, 1923; s. Douglas Eugene and Olive Lyle (Chandler) P.; m. Amelia Skovenski, Jan. 12, 1953; children—Ted Richard, Nancy Ellen. B.S., U. Ill., 1949; Ph.D. in Environ. Sci., Rutgers U., 1954. Registered profl. engr., N.J., Va., N.C. Asst. research specialist Rutgers U., New Brunswick, N.J., 1953-56; prof. Va. Poly. Inst., Blacksburg, 1956-67; assoc. Quirk Lawler Matusky Engrs., N.Y.C., 1967-70; exec. engr. Davy McKee Co., Cleve., 1970-82; tech. dir. H.K. Ferguson Co., Cleve., 1983—. Author: Chemical Treatment of Wastes. Contbr. articles to profl. jours. Mem. ASCE, Am. Inst. Chem. Engrs., Water Pollution Control Fedn., Am. Water Works Assn., Sigma Xi. Home: 3412 Ridge Park Dr Cleveland OH 44147 Office: HK Ferguson Co 1 Erieview Plaza Cleveland OH 44114

PARTLAN, CHARLES, sheet metal company executive; b. Pontiac, Mich., Nov. 1, 1948; s. Robert L. and Natalie R. (Welch) P.; m. Sandra L. Chuk, Sept. 6, 1969; children—Eric William, Kristofer Charles. B.S., Mich. State U., 1970. Instr. Lake Huron Sailboats, Bay City, Mich., 1968; clk. Partlan-Labadie Sheet Metal Co., Troy, Mich., 1969, asst. sec., 1970-77, v.p., Oak Park, Mich., 1977—. Trustee Mariners Inn, Detroit, 1983-84. Roman Catholic. Avocations: computer programming; sailing. Home: 26250 Pembroke Huntington Woods MI 48080 Office: Partlan-Labadie Sheet Metal 21100 Fern Oak Park MI 48237

PARTLO, RICHARD BRUCE, farmer, portrait photographer; b. Bay City, Mich., Sept. 27, 1940; s. Raymond William and Beth D. (Tobias) P.; m. Sandra L. Whalen, June 24, 1961; children—Teri Lee, Kurt A., Lori S., Lisa K. B.S., Central Mich. U., 1962, M.A., 1969, 74. Tchr. Mayville High Sch., Mich., 1962-65, Caro High Sch., 1965-74; farmer Akron, Mich., 1974—; photographer, Akron, 1962—; sales distbr. S.M.C., S.M.I., Inc., Waco, Tex., 1980—. Vice pres. bd. dirs. Akron-Fairgrove Schs., Fairgrove, Mich., 1980-84, pres., 1984—; mem. membership drive com. Farm Bur. Bd., Caro, Mich., 1980-82; sec. Farmers Petro Co-Op Bd., Caro, 1980—; lay speaker Methodist Ch., 1980-84. Mem. NEA (life), Mich. Farm Bur., Mich. Sch. Bd. Assn. Republican. Lodge: Rotary (v.p. 1983-84). Avocations: snowmobiling, woodworking. Home and Office: 4560 Elmwood Rd Akron MI 48701

PARTRIDGE, MILTON ARTHUR, university adminstrator; b. Cin., May 13, 1924; s. John Arthur and Lillian Frances (Bender) P.; m. Estelle Marie Glucek; children—Mary, Carolyn, Thomas, John, Suzanne. Ph.B., Xavier U., 1949, M.A., 1951; Ed.D., U. Cin., 1964. Budget clk. U.S. Navy Dept., Washington, 1951-52; congl. sec. U.S. Ho. of Reps., Washington, 1952-53; tchr. Cin. Pub. Schs., 1953-64; prof. dept. edn. Marquette U., Milw. 1964-71; adminstr., prof. edn. Xavier U., Cin., 1971—. Contbr. articles to edn. jour. Mem. sch. bd. Archdiocese of Cin., 1970-76. Served with U.S. Army, 1943-45, ETO. Recipient Cert. of Merit, Xavier U. Alumni Assn., Cin., 1974. Mem. AAUP, Ohio Valley Philosophy of Edn. Soc. Democrat. Roman Catholic. Avocation: tennis. Home: 952 Spruceglen Dr Cincinnati OH 45224 Office: Xavier U 3800 Victory Pkwy Cincinnati OH 45207

PARUNAK, ANITA GENE, statistician; b. Washington, Apr. 13, 1946; d. Gene and Isabella (Winter) Nowlin; m. Henry Van Dyke Parunak, June 9, 1973; 1 child, Gene Philip. B.A. in Math., U. Pa., 1968, postgrad., 1969; Ph.D. in Statistics, Princeton U., 1973. Computer programmer Market Research Corp. Am., Princeton, N.J., 1966-69; teaching asst. Princeton U., N.J., 1969-73; research asst. statistics dept. Harvard U., Cambridge, Mass., 1975-79; asst. prof. biostatistics U. Mich., Ann Arbor, 1979-81; research scientist Transp. Research Inst., Ann Arbor, 1979-81; self-employed statistician, Ann Arbor, 1981—. Contbr. articles to profl. publs., chpt. to book. Mem. Am. Statis. Assn. Home and Office: 1027 Ferdon St Ann Arbor MI 48104

PASCAL, HAROLD SAUNDERS, health care exec.; b. Coffeyville, Kans., Mar. 16, 1934; s. Michael William and Jacqueline V. P.; B.S., So. Meth. U., 1956; M.B.A., Ga. So. U., 1973; m. Dinah L. Filkins, Aug. 13, 1955; children—Lee Ann, Tracey Michele. Commd. 2d lt. U.S. Army, 1957, advanced through grades to maj., 1967; served med. service dept.; asso. exec. dir. Gen. Hosp., Humana Inc., Ft. Walton Beach, Fla., 1974-75, adminstr. Sarasota (Fla.) Palms Hosp., 1975-76, exec. dir. Llano (N.Mex.) Estacado Med. Center, 1976-77; pres. Americana Hosp. Co. (Cenco Inc.), Monticello, Ill., 1977-80, Continental Health Care Ltd., 1980—. Pres. PTA, San Antonio, 1969-70; bd. dirs. NE Sch. Dist., San Antonio, 1968-69; dir. community blood drive, San Francisco, 1964-65. Decorated Bronze Star, Air Medal, Purple Heart, Cross of Gallantry, Combat Med. Badge. Fellow Am. Acad. Med. Adminstrs.; Am. Hosp. Assn., Am. Coll. Hosp. Adminstrs., Am. Soc. Hosp. Engrs., Ill. Hosp. Assn., Fla. Hosp. Assn., Fedn. Am. Hosps. (dir.), Psi Chi. Presbyterian. Clubs: Hunter Riding (pres., 1972-73), Rotary, Toastmasters. Author: Plight of the Migrant Worker, 1974; Installation Supply Procedures, 1968; programmed text on Supply Procedures, 1969; Dictionary of Supply Terms, 1969. Home: 10 S 321 Jaime Ln Hinsdale IL 60521 Office: 101 N Scoville Oak Park IL 60302

PASCHAL, WILLIAM BARRON, mechanical engineer; b. Chgo., Feb. 26, 1948; s. William Kiernan and Sophie Marie (Kaczmar) P.; B.S. in Mech. Engring., U. Ill., Chgo., 1971; m. Rosanne A. Pancerz, May 27, 1972. Project engr. Sherwin Stenn Engrs. Inc., Chgo., 1969-76; project supr. heating, ventilating and air conditioning Sargent and Lundy Engrs., Chgo., 1976—; cons. on bldg. design and constrn. to architects and owners. Registered profl. engr., Ill. Mem. ASME, Am. Soc. for Engring. Mgmt., Am. Soc. Profl. Engrs., ASHRAE, Am. Nuclear Soc., Ill. Soc. Radiologic Technologists. Roman Catholic. Home: 1725 Taylor St Downers Grove IL 60516 Office: 55 E Monroe St Chicago IL 60603

PASCHALL, HOMER DONALD, physiology educator; b. Clarksville, Tenn., Aug. 29, 1926; s. Homer Stoddard and Beulah Elma (Dawdy) P.; children—Donald Paul, Linda Gail, David Wayne, Brenda Kay. A.B., Trevacca Nazarene Coll., 1948; B.S., Austin Peay State U., 1950; M.A., George Peabody Coll. for Tchrs., 1950; Ph.D., Iowa State U., 1963. Sci. tchr. Greenbrier High Sch., Tenn., 1948-49; tchr. elem. sch., Fort Campbell, Ky., 1950-51; instr. Nazarene Coll., Bethany, Okla., 1951-55; prof. physiology and health sci. Ball State U., Muncie, Ind., 1955—. Pres. Muncie Tech. Soc., Ind., 1980; trustee Olivet Nazarene Coll., Kankakee, Ill., 1971-73. Served with USN, 1944-46. NSF fellow, 1960-61. Mem. Ind. Acad. Sci., Am. Sci. Affiliation, Sigma Xi, Phi Delta Lambda, Sigma Zeta. Republican. Mem. Ch. of Nazarene. Home: 3013 W Twickingham Dr Muncie IN 47304 Office: Ball State Univ Muncie IN 47306

PASCHKE, RICHARD EUGENE, educator; b. Chgo., Mar. 13, 1937; s. Edward and Waldrine (Mackiewicz) P.; m. Lynn Diane Russ, June 30, 1962; children—David Garrett, Elizabeth Ann. Ph.D., Purdue U., 1969. Lic. psychologist, Mich. Instr., U. Conn.-Storrs, 1970-71; assoc. prof. psychology Grand Valley State Coll., 1971—; adj. faculty Sch. Nursing, Grand Valley State Coll., 1974-75; clin. intern Mary Free Bed Hosp. and Rehab. Ctr., Grand Rapids, Mich., 1976-77; trainer, seminar leader, 1976—; adj. faculty Hope Coll., Holland, Mich., 1981; cons. neuropsychodiagnostics, 1976—; cons. in field. Bd. dirs. South Kent Community Mental Health, 1980-82. Served with U.S. Army, 1958-60. NIMH assistantship, 1964-65, fellow, 1965-71. Mem. Am. Psychol. Assn., Midwestern Psychol. Assn., Mich. Psychol. Assn., Grand Rapids Area Psychol. Assn., AAAS. Democrat. Contbr. articles to profl. jours. Office: Grand Valley State Coll Landing Allendale MI 49401

PASCOE, CHARLES MILTON, insurance agent; b. Sandusky, Ohio, May 30, 1936; s. Milton Charles and Marie (Maunus) P.; m. Caroline Joy Cummings, Feb. 2, 1962 (div. Nov. 23, 1984); children—Julie C., Kristen C. B.A., Hobart Coll., 1958. C.P.C.U. Agt., sec. Pascoe Agy., Inc., Sandusky, 1959-69, pres., treas., 1969—; dir. North Central TV, Sandusky, 1977-81. Bd. dirs. Sandusky YMCA, 1968, Erie County United Way, 1970. Served to 2d lt. U.S. Army, 1959-64. Mem. Sandusky Jaycees (internat. senator 1973; named Outstanding Young Man 1968). Republican. Lutheran. Club: Plum Brook Country (Sandusky). Lodge: Masons. Home: 3318 E Beverly Dr Sandusky OH 44870 Office: Box 415 610 W Washington St Sandusky OH 44870

PASEK, MICHAEL ANTHONY, computer technologist; b. Duluth, Minn., Sept. 5, 1951; s. Antone William and Helene (Tunsky) P.; ed. pub. schs., tech. schs. and colls. Operator, Bd. Pensions, Lutheran Ch. in Am., 1973-75; corp. mgr. Microtex Corp., Cloquet, Minn., 1975-79; v.p. internat. ops. Microtex Corp., Mpls., 1979-81, pres., 1981—; systems programmer NCR Comten, Inc., 1977-80, supr./sr. systems programmer, network software devel., 1980-83, chief software engr. switching software devel., 1984-85, lead software engr. switching software devel., 1985—; mem. Data Communications Adv. Panel. Mem. Am. Philatelic Soc. Home: 9741 Foley Blvd NW Coon Rapids MN 55433 Office: 2700 N Snelling Roseville MN 55113

PASKEY, RONALD CHRISTIAN, business educator; b. Detroit Lakes, Minn., June 28, 1935; s. Clarence Michael and May Ann (Schmidt) P.; m. Ruth Ann Gores, Dec. 30, 1968; children—Tracy, Nancy, Ann, Chris, Jana. B.S.B.A., U. N.D., 1957; B.S.B.E., Moorhead State U., 1968. Merchandiser, Universal Food Corp., Milw., 1959-64; salesman Elliot Packing Co., Fargo, N.D., 1964-65; faculty Detroit Lakes Area Vocat. Tech. Inst., Minn., 1968—, chmn. bus. dept., 1975—; owner, mgr. Lakecrest Resort, Detroit Lakes, 1958—. Served to 1st lt. U.S. Army, 1958-65. Mem. Am. Vocat. Assn., Minn. Bus. Educators. Roman Catholic. Lodges: Elks, Eagles. Avocations: fishing; hunting. Home: Route 1 Box E Detroit Lakes MN 56501 Office: Detroit Lakes Area Vocat Tech Inst Hwy 34 E Detroit Lakes MN 56501

PASS, RICHARD ALAN, architect; b. St. Louis, Aug. 12, 1947; s. Wendelin John and Helen Marie (Johnson) P.; m. Shari Lee Astey, Mar. 10, 1973; 1 son, Ryan Wendelin. B.Arch., U. Ill., 1970; diploma, Harrington Inst. Interior Design, 1975-77. Cert. Nat. Council of Archtl. Registrations Bds. Head, community design ctr. Architects Workshop, Phila., 1970-72; designer Lister, Drew & Assocs., Weybridge, Surrey, Eng., 1973-74; prin. architect, dir. SACI, Assoc., Ltd., Mt. Prospect, Ill., 1974-83; project architect Hansen Lind Meyer, P.C., Chgo., 1983—. Mem. AIA. Home: 311 S Can-Dota Ave Mount Prospect IL 60056 Office: Hansen Lind Meyer PC 123 W Madison Suite 1400 Chicago IL 60602

PASSANO, LEONARD MAGRUDER, zoologist, educator; b. N.Y.C., Dec. 16, 1924; s. Leonard Magruder Jr. and Grace (Dyer) P.; m. Kari Nordback, June 1956 (div. July 1981); 1 child, Elizabeth Anne; m. Elizabeth Atkinson Howe, July 29, 1981. A.B., Harvard U., 1948; Ph.D., Yale U., 1952. Instr. zoology U. Wash., Seattle, 1953-55; instr. Yale U., New Haven, 1955-57, asst. prof., 1957-64; assoc. prof. U. Wis., Madison, 1964-71, prof., 1971—. Editor: Behavioral Physiology of Coelenterates, 1965. Served to pfc. U.S. Army, 1943-46; ETO. Mem. Soc. Exptl. Biology, Am. Soc. Zoologists (sec. comparative physiology div. 1963-65), Marine Biol. Lab. Democrat. Club: Signet Soc. (Cambridge, Mass.). Avocation: pvt. pilot. Home: 2838 Regent St Madison WI 53705 Office: Univ Wis 426 Birge Hall 430 Lincoln Dr Madison WI 53706

PASSMORE, JOHN MURRAH, JR., physician; b. Columbus, Ga., June 2, 1947; s. John Murrah and June (Mabrey) P.; m. Donna Olney, June 21, 1969; children—Starr, Dawn, Skye, Grant. B.S., Davidson Coll., 1969; M.D., Vanderbilt U., 1973. Diplomate Am. Bd. Internal Medicine, Am. Bd. Emergency Medicine. Resident in internal medicine Ind. U. Med. Ctr., 1973-76, fellow in endocrinology, 1976-77; chief emergency services Decatur Hosp., Greensburg, Ind., 1977-81, chief intensive care, 1982-84; fellow in critical care U. Pitts., 1981-82; fellow in cardiology U. Tex., Houston, 1984—; pres. Questar, Inc., Indpls., 1976—, JPSA, Inc., Indpls., 1979—, Optima, Inc., Indpls., 1977—, Greensburg Med. Assocs. P.C., 1977—. Author: Endocrine Aspects of Critical Care, 1985; Cardiovascular Aspects of Critical Care, 1985. Contbr. articles to profl. jours. Fellow Am. Coll. Emergency Physicians; mem. Soc. Critical Care Medicine, Internat. Brotherhood of Magicians, Mensa. Methodist. Avocations: handball; racquetball tournaments; piano music composition; performing magic; writing science fiction novel. Home: 6015 Warm Springs St Houston TX 77035 Office: 712 N Lincoln Greensburg IN 47240

PASSOVOY, ROBERT DAVID, internist; b. Chgo., Dec. 26, 1946; s. Mitchell and Lorraine Martha (Lewis) P.; m. Ann Elizabeth Wickerham, Nov. 24, 1971; children—Robin Ellen, Gillian Marie, Robert Christopher Mitchell. B.S., U. Ill., 1968; M.D., U. Md., 1972. Intern, Rush Presbyn. St. Luke's Hosp., Chgo., 1972-73, resident, 1973-75, fellow in nephrology, 1975-76, asst. dir. emergency room, 1976-77; attending physician, ptnr. Health Specialists S.C., Chgo., 1977—; affiliate faculty Chgo. Heart Assn., 1984-85, cons. advanced cardiac life support programs Grant Hosp., Mt. Sinai Hosp., Rush-Presbyn.-St. Luke's Hosp., Chgo., McNeil Meml. Hosp., Berwyn, Ill., 1983-85. Mem. AMA, Ill. State Med. Soc., Chgo. Med. Soc., Dorsai Irregulars Ltd. (pres. 1980-85). Albigensian. Club: Ill. Sci. Fiction Convs. (bd. dirs. 1984—). Avocations: reading science fiction, art auctioneering, convention management, softball, model railroading. Home: PO Box 5093 Chicago IL 60680 Office: Family Health Specialists 8100 S Western Chicago IL 60620

PATCH, JOE HOWARD, lube oil marketing company executive; b. East St. Louis, Ill., Mar. 4, 1929; s. Howard Frank and Kate Knight (Boswell) P.; m. Virginia Marie Sloan, June 7, 1950; children—Howard R., Joe S., Patricia E. Sanford, Dan A., Scott J., Paul A. B.A., Cornell U., 1952. Chemist, Procter & Gamble, Cin., 1952-53; refinery chemist Shell Oil Co., Houston, 1953-56, indsl. mktg., 1956-82; pres. Spec Oils Inc., Indpls., 1982—. Mem. Alpha Chi Sigma. Republican. Christian. Lodge: Elks. Home: 4241 Melbourne Road E Dr Indianapolis IN 46208

PATCHEN, RICHARD VINCENT, lawyer; b. Steubenville, Ohio, Aug. 21, 1935; s. Joseph Anthony and Josephine Louise (Marook) P.; m. Ellin Lucille Teichert, July 30, 1960; children—Joseph, Sarah, Elizabeth. B.A., U. Steubenville, 1957; LL.B., Ohio State U., 1959. Bar: Ohio 1959. Asst. atty gen. State of Ohio, Columbus, 1959-61; assoc. Schwartz, Gurevitz & Schwartz, Columbus, 1961-63; ptnr. Carlile, Patchen, Murphy & Allison, Columbus, 1963—; dir. Franklin Bank, Columbus, 1982—. Mem. ABA, Ohio State Bar Assn., Columbus Bar Assn. Clubs: Univ., Brookside Country (Columbus). Home: 589 Tucker Dr Worthington OH 43085 Office: Carlile Patchen Murphy & Allison 100 E Broad St Columbus OH 43085

PATCHETT, KERMIT BOYD, airport operator; b. Martinsville, Ill., Oct. 27, 1915; s. Herman Glenn and Berniece Sybil (Spittler) P.; m. Eileen Patchett, Sept. 28, 1940; children—Linda Lou, Lawrence Kermit, Patricia Eileen. Grad. high sch., Martinsville. Cert. flight instr., multi engine rating, helo rating. Mechanic Sinclair Imperial, Martinsville, 1937-40; with Dilly Aircraft, Kansas City, Mo., 1940-41; final assembly insp. Piper Aircraft, Lock Haven, Pa., 1941-42; insp. Yellow Cab, Pontiac, Mich., 1942-43; airport operator Patchett Flying Service, Casey, Ill., 1946—; dir. Ill. Pub. Airport Assn., Ill. Airport Trades Assn. Named Fixed Base Operator of Yr., 1981. Served with USN, 1943-46. Lodges: Masons, Moose (local gov. 1946-50). Home: Rural Route 3 Casey IL 62420 Office: PO Box 416 Casey IL 62420

PATE, LARRY EUGENE, management educator, researcher, consultant; b. Dayton, Ohio, Jan. 27, 1945; s. Leslie Edgar and Mildred Georgia (Miller) P.; m. Pamela May Paton, Jan. 20, 1969; 1 son, Benjamin David; m. Kathryn Anne Clyde, July 9, 1979; children—Anna Kathryn, Lesley Elizabeth. B.A. summa cum laude (Honors scholar), U. Calif.-Irvine, 1971, M.S., 1973; Ph.D., U. Ill., 1979. Research asst. U. Calif. System, 1972-73; engr. schedules analyst McDonnell Douglas Astronautics, 1972-73; research/teaching asst. U. Ill., Urbana, 1973-75; vis. asst. prof. mgmt. U. Nebr., Lincoln, 1975-77, U. Wis., Madison, 1977-78; vis. assoc. prof. orgnl. behavior U. So. Calif., Los Angeles, summer 1981, vis. assoc. prof. Inst. Safety and Systems Mgmt., summer 1982; asst. prof. orgn. and adminstrn. Sch. Bus., U. Kans., Lawrence, 1978-81, assoc. prof. organizational behavior, 1981—. YMCA Soccer coach, Kansas City, 1981-82. Served to capt. U.S. Army, 1965-70; Vietnam. Decorated Bronze Star, Air medal, Purple Heart, Vietnamese Cross of Gallantry. Mem. Acad. Mgmt., Organizational Devel. Inst. (chmn. membership com. 1985—), AAAS, Am. Inst. Decision Sci., Am. Psychol. Assn., Brit. Psychol. Soc., Soc. Psychol. Study Social Issues, Internat. Assn. Applied Psychology. Contbr. articles to profl. jours.; mem. editorial bd. Jour. Mgmt., 1983-84; mem. editorial rev. bd. Roxbury Press, 1984—; bd. advisors Faculty Scholar, U. Kans., 1981-83. Home: 3217 Saddlehorn Dr Lawrence KS 66044 Office: 315 Summerfield Hall Univ Kan Lawrence KS 66045

PATEL, JASHU PURUSHOTTAM, library educator; b. Baroda, India, July 11, 1939; came to U.S., 1970; s. Purushottam H. and Suraj (Patel) P.; m. Georgianna R. Brethauer, July 20, 1973; 1 child, Joshua. B.A., U. Baroda, 1959; M.L.S., U. Pitts., 1973, Ph.D., 1977; postgrad. Northwestern Poly. Sch. Librarianship, London, 1966. Library asst. pub. library, Slough, Bucks, Eng., 1961-63; supr. reference reading room U. London Sch. Oriental and African Studies Library, 1963-70; instr. No. Ill. U., DeKalb, 1972-73; asst. prof. Eastern Ill. U., Charleston, 1977-79; asst. prof. library sci. Chgo. State U., 1979-82, assoc. prof., 1982—; vis. prof. Governors State U., Park Forest, Ill., summer 1980; mem. summer sch. faculty Rosary Coll. Grad. Sch. Library and Info. Sci., River Forest, Ill., 1983; panel chair, presenter papers Confs. on South Asia, U. Wis., 1981, 82, 84. Contbr. articles to library jours. Named Tchr. of Yr., Chgo. State U., 1981; grantee Chgo. State U. and Found., 1982, 83, 84, U. Ill. Pacific/Asian Am. Research Methods, 1983. Mem. ALA (session leader ann. conf. 1985), Assn. Library and Info. Sci. Edn. (conf. facilitator 1985), Assn. Am. Library Sch., Brit. Library Assn. Home: 65 W 146th St Riverdale IL 60627

PATEL, MULCHAND SHAMBHUBHAI, biochemist, researcher; b. Sipor, India, Sept. 9, 1939; came to U.S., 1965; s. Shambhubhai J. and Puriben (Patel) P.; m. Kankuben M. Patel; children—Sumitra, Yashomati, Mayank. B.S., Gujarat U., 1961; M.S., U. Baroda, 1964; Ph.D., U. Ill., 1968. Asst. prof. pediatric research Sch. Medicine Temple U., Phila., 1970-72, research asst. prof. medicine, 1972-75, research asst. prof. biochemistry, 1970-75, research assoc. prof. biochem. medicine, 1975-78; assoc. prof. biochemistry Case Western Res. U. Sch. Medicine, Cleve., 1978—. Author, co-author research articles. Recipient Gold Medal in Biochemistry, U. Baroda, 1973; prin. investigator, research grantee NIH. Mem. Am. Soc. Biol. Chemists, Am. Inst. Nutrition, Biochem. Soc. London, Am. Soc. Neurochemists, Internat. Soc. Neurochemistry. Office: Dept Biochemistry Sch Medicine Case Western Res U 2119 Abington Rd Cleveland OH 44106

PATERAKIS, ANGELA GREGORY, art educator, consultant, writer; b. Oak Park, Ill., June 1, 1932; d. Kostas and Sophia (Spiliotou) Gregory; m. George A. Paterakis, July 31, 1958. B.A.E., Sch. of Art Inst. Chgo., 1954; M.A., U. Ill., 1955; art therapy cert., 1985. Tchr. jr. high sch., Oak Park, Ill., 1955-60; prof. art edn. and art therapy Sch. of Art Inst. Chgo., 1961—; mem. arts advocacy groups, Ill. Author numerous articles, pamphlets on art edn. Recipient Service Recognition award Ill. Alliance for Arts Edn., 1985; U. Ill. fellow, 1954-55. Mem. Nat. Art Edn. Assn., Ill. Art Edn. Assn. (named Outstanding Art Educator 1981), NEA (life). Office: Sch of the Art Inst Chicago Columbus Dr and Jackson Blvd Chicago IL 60603

PATERSON, PHILIP Y., physician; b. Mpls., Feb. 6, 1925; s. Donald Gildersleeve and Margaret (Young) P.; B.S., U. Minn., 1946, M.B., 1947, M.D., 1948; m. Virginia Lee Bray, Mar. 22, 1947; children—Anne, Peter, Benjamin. Intern, Mpls. Gen. Hosp., 1948-49; research fellow div. infectious diseases Tulane U. Sch. Medicine, 1949-50, instr. medicine, Am. Heart Assn. research fellow, 1950-51; Am. Heart Assn. research fellow dept. microbiology U. Va. Sch. Medicine, 1953, asst. resident and co-resident in medicine univ. hosp., 1953-55, asst. prof. microbiology, instr. medicine, established investigator Am. Heart Assn., 1955-57; med. officer Lab. Immunology, Nat. Inst. Allergy and Infectious Diseases, NIH, Bethesda, Md., 1957-60; vis. asst. prof. microbiology N.Y. U., 1957-60, assoc. prof. medicine, 1960-65; asso. prof. medicine, dir. Samuel J. Sackett Research Labs. and chief sect. infectious diseases, dept. medicine Northwestern U., 1965-66, Samuel J. Sackett prof. medicine and chief infectious diseases, hypersensitivity sect., dept. medicine Northwestern U.-McGaw Med. Center, 1966-72, Samuel J. Sackett prof. medicine and microbiology, chief infectious diseases, hypersensitivity sect., 1972-75, prof. microbiology-immunology, chmn. dept. microbiology-immunology Northwestern U. Med. and Dental Schs., Chgo., 1975—, Guy and Anne Youmans prof. microbiology-immunology, 1982—; prof. neurobiology and physiology Northwestern U., Evanston, Ill., 1983—; Christine Larsen lectr. Sch. Medicine, Albuquerque, 1973; Disting. lectr. Ann. Meeting, Assn. Am. Physicians and Western sect. Am. Fedn. Clin. Research, Carmel, Calif., 1974; Grace Faillace Meml. lectr. Leo Goodwin Inst. Cancer Research, Nova U., 1978; Ernest Witebsky Meml. lectr. 6th Internat. Convocation on Immunology, Niagara Falls, N.Y., 1978; Joseph E. Smadel Meml. lectr. Ann. meeting, Infectious Diseases Soc. Am., Atlanta, 1978; mem. drug evaluation com. Nat. Multiple Sclerosis Soc., 1973—; mem. immunol.-microbiol. research study com. Am. Heart Assn., 1978-81; mem. internat. med. adv. bd. Internat. Fedn. Multiple Sclerosis Socs., 1973—; mem. adv. panel Am. Bd. Med. Lab. Immunology, 1978—; cons. Gt. Lakes Naval Base, Ill., 1967-74. Served to capt. M.C., USAR, 1951-53. Mem. Am. Fedn. Clin. Research, AAAS, Am. Soc. Microbiology. Am. Assn. Immunologists, Harvey Soc., Am. Soc. Clin. Investigation, Infectious Diseases Soc. Am. (Gold medal 1978), Central Soc. Clin. Research, Am. Rheumatism Assn., Assn. Am. Physicians, Am. Clin. and Climatol. Assn., Sigma Xi, Alpha Omega Alpha. Editor and contbg. author: (with others) The Biological and Clinical Basis of Infectious Diseases, 1975, 3d edit., 1985; contbr. numerous articles, chpts. and revs. on neuroimmunology, host-parasite interactions and infectious diseases to profl. jours.; mem. editorial bd. Procs. Soc. Exptl. Biology and Medicine, 1968-73, 1977-83, Cellular Immunology, 1969—, Infection and Immunity, 1970-81, Clin. and Exptl. Immunology, 1970—, Clin. Immunology and Immuno-pathology, 1978—, Jour. Clin. and Lab. Immunology, 1979—, Jour. Immunology, 1981-84; asso. editor Jour. Infectious Diseases, 1979-83. Office: 303 E Chicago Ave Chicago IL 60611

PATRICK, JANE AUSTIN, association executive; b. Memphis, May 27, 1930; d. Wilfred Jack and Evelyn Eudora (Branch) Austin; m. William Thomas Spencer, Sept. 11, 1952 (div. Apr. 1970); children—Anthony Duke, Tonilee Candice Spencer Hughes; m. 2d, George Milton Patrick, Oct. 1, 1971. Student Memphis State U., 1946-47; B.S.B.A., Ohio State U., 1979. Service rep. So. Bell Telegraph and Telephone, Memphis, 1947-52; placement dir. Mgmt. Personnel, Memphis, 1965-66; personnel asst. to exec. v.p. E & E Ins. Co., Columbus, Ohio, 1966-69; Ohio exec. dir. Nat. Soc. for Prevention of Blindness, Columbus, 1969-73; regional dir. Ohio and Ky. CARE and MEDICO, Columbus, 1979—; lectr., cons. in field. Mem. choir 1st Community Ch., Columbus; bd. dirs. Columbus Council on World Affairs, 1981—, sec., 1983—. Recipient commendations Nat. Soc. Prevention Blindness and Central Ohio Lions Eye Bank, 1973. Mem. Non-Profit Orgn. Mgmt. Inst. (pres.), Nat. Soc. Fund-Raising Execs. (cert., nat. dir.), Pub. Relations Soc. Am. (cert.), Ins. Inst. Am. (cert.), Mensa Internat., Columbus Dental Soc. Aux., Alpha Gamma Delta, Epsilon Sigma Alpha. Home: 2511 Onandaga Dr Columbus OH 43221 Office: 35 E Chestnut St Columbus OH 43215

PATRICK, ROY HENRY, law enforcement administrator, educator; b. Memphis, Oct. 15, 1938; s. Lillian (Casey) P.; m. Vivian Greene, June 6, 1970; children—Roy T., Royond M., Ronita D. B.S. in Psychology and Edn., Ill. Inst. Tech., 1969; M.S. in Guidance, DePaul U., 1972, M.S. in Sch. Adminstrn., 1976. Cert. tchr., Ill. Tchr., PACE Inst., Chgo., 1969-70, ednl. dir., 1970-75; part-time instr. City Colls., Chgo., 1983—; supt. Cook County Dept. Corrections, Chgo., 1978—; mem. Operation PUSH Prison Outpost Program, Chgo., 1981—. Mem. Beverly Human Relations Council, Chgo., 1983—; bd. dirs. Southwest YMCA, Chgo., 1984; chief advisor Operation Leadership Youth Orgn., Chgo., 1966. Recipient recognition award Chgo. Dept. Human Services, 1977; appreciation award Englewood Community Ctr., 1978, Substance Abuse Program, Cook County Jail, 1980; merit award, Am. Friendship Club, Chgo., 1969. Mem. Nat. Orgn. Black Law Enforcement Execs. (v.p. Chgo. 1982—), Ill. Acad. Criminology (exec. bd. dirs. 1983—), Nat. Jail Assn., Am. Corrections Assn., Manassas Alumni Assn. (pres. 1976-82). Democrat. Office: Cook County Dept Corrections 2700 S California Ave Chicago IL 60608

PATT, CAROL PRINS, consultant to non-profit organizations; b. N.Y.C., Aug. 23, 1940; d. J. Warner and Gertrude (Buttenwieser) Prins; m. Stephen L. Patt, Feb. 6, 1966; children—Jessica Eve, Audrey Elizabeth, Joseph Stephen. Student Vassar Coll., 1958-59, Barnard Coll., 1962, The Neighborhood Playhouse Sch. of Theatre, N.Y.C., 1962-64. Ptnr., Just Causes, Chgo., 1979—; cons. Music of the Baroque, Chgo., 1982—, DePaul Conservatory of Drama, Chgo., 1983—, Saralee Corp., Chgo. Bd. dirs. United Charities of Chgo.; women's bd. dirs. Am. Cancer Soc., Goodman Theatre, Chgo.; costume com. Chgo. Hist. Soc.; bd. dirs. North Dearborn Assn., Michael Reese Hosp. Research Council. Mem. Nat. Soc. Fund Raising Execs. (Chgo. chpt.), Publicity Club of Chgo. Jewish. Club: Art. Avocations: gardening, travel. Home: 1405 N Dearborn Pkwy Chicago IL 60610 Office: Just Causes 1405 N Dearborn Pkwy Chicago IL 60610

PATTERSON, CHARLES RICHARD, university counselor; b. Bellefontaine, Ohio, Dec. 8, 1952; s. Ralph Edward and Winnifred Martha (Vellenga) P.; m. Pamela Ann Evans, July 24, 1976; children—Michael, Jon. B.S., Bowling Green State U., 1975, M.Ed., 1978. Tchr. spl. edn. Napoleon High Sch., Ohio, 1975; skill evaluator 4-County Vocat. Sch., Fulton, Ohio, 1976; freshman adviser Miami U., Oxford, Ohio, 1978-80; athletic acad. counselor U. Mo., Columbia, 1980—. Mem. Am. Assn. Counseling and Devel., Am. Coll.

Personnel Assn., Nat. Assn. Acad. Advisors for Athletics, Nat. Acad. Adv. Assn. Presbyterian. Avocations: running, reading, golf, tennis. Home: 309 Phyllis St Columbia MO 65202 Office: U Mo Athletic Dept Box 677 Columbia MO 65205

PATTERSON, HARLAN RAY, finance educator; b. Camden, Ohio, June 27, 1931; s. Ernest Newton and Beulah Irene (Hedrick) P.; B.S., Miami U., 1953, M.B.A., 1959; Ph.D., Mich. State U., 1963; m. Carol Lee Reighard, Aug. 31, 1970; children—Kristan Lee, Elizabeth Jane (previous marriage), Leslie, Nolan Gene. Asst. prof. finance U. Ill. at Urbana, 1962-66; assoc. prof. finance Ohio U., Athens, 1966-77, prof., 1977—; fin. cons. Research projects for Bank of Am., Morgan Guaranty Trust, Am. Investment Corp., City Pub. Service Bd. of San Antonio. Chmn. Athens Adv. Bd., Ohio State scholarship com. of Rainbow for Girls. Served as officer USN, 1953-56. Stonier fellow, 1961; Found. Econ. Edn. fellow, 1965, 67, 69, 71; vis. prof., fellow Chgo. Merc. Exchange, 1971; Chgo. Bd. Trade summer intern fellow, 1983. Mem. Phi Beta Kappa, Beta Gamma Sigma, Phi Eta Sigma, Omicron Delta Epsilon, Pi Kappa Alpha, Alpha Kappa Psi. Republican. Mason (32 deg., Shriner). Contbr. articles in field to profl. and acad. jours.

PATTERSON, JOHN WILLIAM, JR., materials science and engineering educator; b. Cleve., Mar. 14, 1936; s. John William and Dawn Juanita (Oden) P.; m. Shirley Ann Finkel, Feb. 13, 1960; children—John Kenneth, Daniel Chad. B.S. in Mining Engring., Ohio State U., 1962, M.S. in Mining Engring., 1962; Ph.D. in Metall. Engring., 1966. Registered metall. engr., Iowa. Asst. prof. Iowa Stte U., Ames, 1966-71, assoc. prof., 1971-76, prof. materials sci. and engring., 1976—. Contbr. articles to profl. jours. Served with U.S. Army, 1955-57. Mem. U.S. Electrochem. Soc., Am. Soc. Metals, AAAS, Nat. Soc. Profl. Engrs., Iowa Acad. Sci. Avocations: conjuring; mathematics. Home: 3603 Woodland St Ames IA 50010 Office: Dept Materials Sci and Engring Room 110 Engring Annex Iowa State U Ames IA 50011

PATTERSON, RONALD MAURICE, optometrist; b. Richmond, Ind., Aug. 29, 1956; s. Maurice Clifford and Dorothy (Vaile) P. Student Miami U., Oxford, Ohio, 1974-76; B.S. in Psychology, Ind. U., 1978, O.D., 1981. Registered optometrist Ind., Ill., Fla., Calif. Gen. practice optometry, Merillville, Ind., 1981—. Co-author chpt. in Primary Care Optometry, 1981. Home: 5249 Cedar Point Dr Crown Point IN 46307

PATTON, CARL VERNON, dean; b. Coral Gables, Fla., Oct. 22, 1944; s. Carl V. and Helen Eleanor (Benkert) P.; m. Gretchen West, July 29, 1976. B.S. in Community Planning, U. Cin., 1967; M.S. in Urban Planning U. Ill.-Urbana, 1969, M.S. in Pub. Adminstrn., 1970; M.S. in Pub. Policy, U. Calif.-Berkeley, 1975, Ph.D. in Pub. Policy, 1976. Instr. to prof. U. Ill., 1968-83, dir. Bureau of Urban and Regional Planning Research, 1977-79, prof., chmn. dept., 1979-83; prof., dean Sch. Architecture and Urban Planning, U. Wis., Milw., 1983—. Author: Academia in Transition, 1979; (with others) The Metropolitan Midwest, 1985. Assoc. editor Jour. of Planning Edn. and Research, 1983—. Contbr. articles to profl. jours. Chmn. Community Devel. Commn., Urbana, 1978-82; com. mem. Civic Design Center, Milw., 1983—. Fellow NIMH, 1973-75, U. Ill. Center for Advanced Studies, 1973-74. Mem. Am. Planning Assn., Am. Int. Cert. Planners, Assn. Collegiate Schs of Planning (exec. com.). Avocations: racquetball, jogging, photography, travel. Home: 4477 N Prospect Shorewood WI Office: Sch Architecture and Urban Planning U Wis Milw PO Box 413 WI

PATTON, CONNIE GARCÍA, foreign language educator; b. Luarca, Spain, Nov. 7, 1941; d. Antonio García Mendez and Palmira García Lavin de Mendez; B.A., U. N.Mex., 1964, M.A., 1966, postgrad.; m. Michael G. Patton, July 5, 1970; children—Michael Anthony, Ryan Blake. Instr., Peace Corps, 1964-66; assoc. prof. fgn. lang. Emporia (Kans.) State U., 1966—; court translator Lyon County Courthouse, 1974—. Bd. dirs. Sexual Offense Services, 1974-78; v.p. Big Bro.-Sister, 1977-79. Ford Found. grad. fellow, 1963-66; Nat. Endowment for Humanities grantee, 1976, 78; named Outstanding Young Kansan, Jaycees, 1977. Mem. Am. Assn. Tchrs. Spanish and Portuguese, MLA, Rocky Mountain MLA, AAUP, Sigma Delta Pi. Author: Spanish Vocabulary Units, 1975. Home: 2919 Monterey Dr Emporia KS 66801 Office: 1200 Commerical St Emporia KS 66801

PATTON, JOHN BARRATT, geologist, educator; b. Marion, Ind., July 1, 1915; s. Barratt Marsh and Mary Frances (Kuntz) P.; m. Jean Glenn, July 28, 1941; children—Barratt Marsh II, Roger Craig, Frank Jamison Campbell, Ian Alastair. A.B. in Chemistry, Ind. U., 1938, A.M. in Geology, 1940, Ph.D. in Econ. Geology, 1954. Geologist Magnolia Petroleum Co., Tex. and Ill. Basin, 1940-47; head indsl. minerals sect. Ind. Geol. Survey, Bloomington, 1947-53, prin. geologist, 1951-59, state geologist, dir., 1959—; asst. prof. geology Ind. U., Bloomington, 1948-52, assoc. prof., 1952-55, prof. econ. geology, 1955—, chmn. dept. geology, 1959-71, assoc. dean for research and advanced studies, 1973-75; cons. on preservation of The Alamo, The Dabney Group, San Antonio, 1984—. Contbr. articles to profl. jours. Chmn. Environ. Quality and Conservation Commn., Bloomington, 1971-73; mem. Ind. Energy Devel. Bd., Indpls., 1980—; bd. dirs. The Old Library, Inc., Bloomington, 1977-80, 84—. Fellow Geol. Soc. Am., Ind. Acad. Sci. (pres. 1975); mem. Soc. Econ. Geologists (councilor 1968-71), Soc. Econ. Paleontologists and Mineralogists, Am. Assn. Petroleum Geologists (Pub. Service award 1983), The Ind. Acad., AIME, Assn. Am. State Geologists (pres. 1966), Interstate Oil Compact Commn., ASTM, Ind.-Ky. Geol. Soc. (hon.), Phi Beta Kappa, Sigma Xi. Avocation: historic preservation. Home: 809 Sheridan Rd Bloomington IN 47401 Office: Ind Geol Survey 611 N Walnut Grove Bloomington IN 47405

PATTON, MICHAEL QUINN, social scientist; b. Pewee Valley, Ky., Sept. 5, 1945; s. James Quinn and Eleanor (Powell) P. B.A., U. Cin., 1967; M.S., U. Wis.-Madison, 1970, Ph.D., 1973. Vol., Peace Corps, Fada N'Gourma, Upper Volta, 1967-69; mem. faculty U. Minn.-St. Paul, 1973—, program dir. Office of Internat. Agr., 1980—; dir. Minn. Ctr. for Social Research, Mpls., 1975-80, Action Research, St. Paul, 1977—. Author: Utilization-Focused Evaluation, 1978; Qualitative Evaluation, 1980; Creative Evaluation, 1981; Practical Evaluation, 1982. Editor: Culture and Evaluation, 1985. Named Outstanding Teacher of Year, U. Minn., 1976. Mem. Evaluation Research Soc. (recipient Myrdal award for Outstanding Contbns. to Use and Practice of Evaluation Research 1984), Am. Sociol. Assn., Phi Kappa Phi (named Emerging Scholar of Yr. 1984). Avocation: public speaking. Home: 2199 St Clair Ave Saint Paul MN 55105 Office: 64 COB Univ Minn 1420 Eckles Ave Saint Paul MN 55108

PATTON, RAY BAKER, urban planner, investment broker, economist; b. Enid, Okla., Jan. 24, 1932; s. Dwight Lyman Moody and Opal (Hembre) P.; B.A., U. Okla., 1955, M.R.C.P., 1960, M.A.P.A., 1969; designated profl. advisor; m. Gloria Ruth Chambers, June 6, 1954; children—David Baker, Dayna Erin. Asst. dir. planning San Joaquin, Calif., 1959-61; dir. planning City of Norman (Okla.) and planning cons. U. Okla., Norman, 1961-65; dir. planning Oklahoma City, 1965-67; dir. planning St. Louis County, Mo., 1967-71; pres. Creative Environments, Inc., Clayton, Mo., 1972-74; chmn. Creative Consultants, Inc., Clayton, 1972-75; v.p. Land Dynamics, Inc., 1973-74; pres. Patton Real Estate, Inc., Success Power, Inc., St. Louis; prin. Raymond B. Patton & Assocs., Ballwin, Mo., 1975-81; dir. pub. works and planning, health commr., zoning enforcement officer City of Des Peres, Mo., 1977-79; zone mgr. Investors Diversified Services, Chesterfield, Mo., 1980-81; investment broker, fin. planner A.G. Edwards & Sons, Inc., Clayton, 1981-83; fin. planning coordinator, dir. seminars E.F. Hutton & Co., Inc., St. Louis, 1983-84; registered securities prin. The Patton Fin. Group, Inc.; also motivational speaker; mem. faculty Nat. Inst. Farm and Land Brokers, 1971-76. Scoutmaster, St. Louis Area council Boy Scouts Am., 1976-80, vice chmn. adult tng., 1977-83; mem. Christian Bus. Men's Com., Chesterfield, Mo. Served with USMC, 1955-58. Named Outstanding Mcpl. Employee, State of Okla., 1963; recipient IOS Mercury award, 1980; A.G. Edwards & sons Crest award, 1982; Outstanding Exec. award E.F. Hutton, 1983, Blue Chip award, 1983. Mem. Am. Inst. Cert. Planners, Nat. Assn. Home Bldrs., Urban Land Inst., Internat. Platform Assn., Internat. Assn. Fin. Planners, Eagle Scout Assn. (life), Lambda Chi Alpha (pres. 1953-54). Methodist (minister of music, Ballwin 1979-83). Club: Kiwanis (Moberly, Mo.). Contbr. articles to profl. jours. Home: 610 Morewood Ct Saint Louis MO 63011 Office: Suite 130 755 S New Ballas Rd Saint Louis MO 63141

PATTULLO, DOUGLAS ERNEST, hospital administrator; b. Battle Creek, Mich., Nov. 25, 1947; s. Andrew and Jean (Fralick) P.; m. Leslie A. Weesner; children—Brad, Jamie. B.A. in Bus. Adminstrn., Western Mich. U., 1970; M.H.A., U. Mich., 1974. Indsl. engr. dept. sytems devel., Bronson Methodist Hosp., Kalamazoo, Mich., 1971-72; asst. dir. Central Maine Hosp., Lewiston, 1974-76; assoc. adminstr. Central Mich. Community Hosp., Mt. Pleasant, 1976-82; chief exec. officer Tolfree Meml. Hosp., West Branch, Mich., 1983—. Mem. hosp. ball com. Central Mich. Community Hosp. Aux., 1976-78, props chmn., 1978, hosp. follies com., 1976, 1978, 1980; pres. United Way of Isabella County, 1981, v.p., 1979-81, mem. exec. com., 1979-82; coach Ogemaw Swim Team, 1983—. Served with USAR, 1969-75. Mem. Am. Hosp. Assn., Hosp. Council of Eastern Central Mich., Mich. Hosp. Assn., Am. Coll. Hosp. Adminstrs., West Branch Area C. of C., Mt. Pleasant Area C. of C. Lodges: Optimists, Rotary. Avocations: outdoor sports, reading, antique collecting. Home: 227 N Third St West Branch MI 48661 Office: Tolfree Meml Hosp 335 E Houghton Ave West Branch MI 48661

PATWARDHAN, BHALCHANDRA HARI, scientist; b. Amraoti, Maharashtra, India, Dec. 25, 1947; s. Hari Waman and Kamala H. P.; m. Rehka B. Swar, May 6, 1975; 1 child, Vikram B.. B.Sc., Inst. Sci., Nagpur, India, 1967; M.Sc., Nagpur U., 1969, Ph.D., 1973. Reserch assoc. Inst. Organische Chemie, Bern, Switzerland, 1974; Heinemann postdoctoral fellow U. Catholique de Louvain, Louvain La Neuve, Belgium, 1975-76; research assoc. SUNY, Syracuse, 1979-81; research scientist Miles Labs., Elkhart, Ind., 1982-83, sr. research scientist, 1983-84, staff scientist, 1984—. Contbr. articles to profl. jours. Sr. research fellow Council Sci. and Indsl. Research, New Delhi, 1974. Mem. Royal Inst. Chemistry, Am. Chem. Soc., Sigma Xi. Office: Miles Labs Inc 1127 Myrtle St Elkhart IN 46514

PAUGH, WILLARD STANLEY, JR., printing company executive; b. Marinette, Wis., Aug. 8, 1930; s. Willard Stanley and Norma Minnie (Peth) P.; m. Delores Jean King, Sept. 5, 1953; children—Debra L. Paugh Glodowski, Robert S., Thomas W. Student U. Wash., 1949-50; B.S., U. Wis., 1956. With R. R. Donnelley & Sons Co., Crawfordsville, Ind., Chgo. and Willard, Ohio, 1956—, indsl. engr., supr., prodn. control mgr., mfg. supt., group supt., 1956-74, group research and devel. mgt., Crawfordsville, 1976—; cons. to Her Majesty's Bur., Teheran, Iran, 1974-75. Served with USN, 1948-52. Mem. Am. Mgmt. Assn., Am. Inst. Indsl. Engrs., Book Mfrs. Inst. Republican. Lutheran. Developer automated adhesive mfg. system for protein base and hydroexpansivity theory for cellulose fibre materials. Home: 17 Meahme Trail Crawfordsville IN 47933

PAUL, ARA GARO, dean professor of pharmacognosy; b. Mar. 1, 1929; s. John Hagop and Mary (Injejikian) P.; m. Shirley Elaine Waterman, Dec. 21, 1962; children—John Bartlett, Richard Goyan. B.S. in Pharmacy, Idaho State U., 1950; M.S. in Pharmacognosy, U. Conn.,-Storrs, 1953, Ph.D., 1956. Cons. plant physiology Argonne Nat. Lab., Ill., 1955; asst. prof. pharmacognosy Butler U., Indpls., 1956-57; from asst. prof. to assoc. prof. U. Mich., Ann Arbor, 1957-69, prof., 1969—, dean Coll. Pharmacy, 1975—; visiting prof. microbiology, Tokyo, 1965-66; visiting faculty chemistry U. Calif., Berkeley, 1972-73. Contbr. articles to profl. jours. Recipient Outstanding Teaching award U. Mich., 1969; Outstanding Alumnus award Idaho State U., 1976; fellow NIMH, 1972-73, G. Pfeiffer Meml. Am. Found. on Pharmacy Edn., 1965-66. Fellow AAAS; mem. Am. Pharmaceutical Assn., Am. Soc. Pharmacognosy, Am. Assn. Colls. Pharmacy, Mich. Pharm. Assn., Acad. Pharm. Sci., Am. Soc. Hosp. Pharmacists. Office: Coll Pharmacy U Mich 428 Church St Ann Arbor MI 48109-1065

PAUL, DONALD LEE, food company executive; b. Washington, Iowa, May 24, 1924; s. Donald Charles and Halle Darlene (Nichols) P.; m. Lois Evalyn Mace, June 18, 1947; children—Mark, Scott, Jill, Andrew. B.S. in Chemistry, Iowa State U., 1949, M.S. in Food Tech., 1951. With Oscar Mayer Foods Corp., 1951—, mng. dir. Prima Meat Packers, Tokyo, 1972-75, v.p., plant mgr. Oscar Mayer Foods Corp., Davenport, Iowa, 1975-77, v.p. quality assurance and regulatory affairs, Madison, Wis., 1977—. Mem. sci. affairs com. Am. Meat Inst.; dir. Promega-Biotec Corp. Bd. dirs. Friends of WHA-TV, Madison, 1982—. Served to 1st lt. AC, U.S. Army, 1943-46. Decorated Air medal with 2 oak leaf clusters. Mem. Inst. Food Technologists, Am. Soc. Quality Control, Assn. Food and Drug Ofcls., Am. Meat Sci. Assn. Clubs: Madison, Maple Bluff Country. Home: 933 Farwell Dr Madison WI 53704 Office: PO Box 7188 Madison WI 53707

PAUL, JUSTUS FREDRICK, history educator and administrator; b. Boonville, Mo., May 27, 1938; s. Firdel William and Emma Louise (Frankenfeld) P.; m. Barbara Jane Dotts, Sept. 10, 1960; children—Justus, Rebecca, Ellen. A.B., Doane Coll., 1959; M.A., U. Wis., 1960; Ph.D., U. Nebr., 1966. Tchr. Wausau High Sch., Wis., 1960-62; instr. history U. Nebr., Lincoln, 1963-66; asst. prof. to prof. history U. Wis., Stevens Point, 1966—, chmn. dept., 1969—, chmn. faculty senate, 1977-79, 83-85, faculty rep. 1977-79, 83-85. Author: Senator Hugh Butler and Nebraska Republicanism, 1976. Editor: Selected Writings of Rhys W. Hays, 1977; co-editor: The Badger State: A Documentary History of Wisconsin, 1979. Mem. Portage County Bd. Adjustment, Stevens Point, 1976—, chmn. 1982—. Grantee U. Wis., Am. Assn. State and Local History; recipient Univ. Service award U. Wis., 1984. Mem. Am. Hist. Assn., Orgn. Am. Historians, State Hist. Soc. Wis., Nebr. State Hist. Soc., Assn. U. Wis. Faculties. Mem. United Church of Christ. Avocations: tennis, softball, roller skating, singing. Home: 2001 Country Club Dr Stevens Point WI 54481 Office: Dept History Univ Wis Stevens Point WI 54481

PAUL, PROSPER FREDERICK, hotel-motel exec.; b. Mansfield, Mass., July 31, 1932; s. Alexander J. and Blanche (Dion) P.; B.S., U. Mont., 1954; m. Mary Ellen F. Truckner, Nov. 7, 1964; children—Kevin, Jeffrey Mark. Asst. mgr. Hotel Florence, Missoula, Mont., 1957-59, gen. mgr., 1959-63; gen. mgr. Abbey Resort, Lake Geneva, Wis., 1963-64, Holiday Inn, Jackson, Mich., 1964—. Served to 1st lt. AUS, 1955-57. Mem. Am. Hotel and Motel Assn. (dir. 1961-63), Mich. Hotel and Motor Hotel Assn. (treas. 1972-73, pres. 1974-75). Club: Rotary (pres. 1963-64) (Jackson). Home: 1951 Elmhurst Ln Jackson MI 49201 Office: 2000 Holiday Inn Dr Jackson MI 49202

PAUL, ROBERT MILTON, personnel executive; b. Richmond, Va., Aug. 1, 1942; s. Milton Alexander Paul and Ruth (Smith) Davis; m. Priscilla Cunningham, June 15, 1964 (dec. 1964); m. Anna Macklen, Oct. 2, 1965; children—Robert Anthony, Michele Kristine, Nicole Marie. Student Lees-McRae Jr. Coll., 1960; B.S., Va. Poly. Inst., 1964; M.S., U. So. Calif., 1971. Employment supr. Owens-Corning Fiberglas, Aiken, S.C., 1972-73, plant personnel mgr., Huntingdon, Pa., 1973-76, personnel mgr. textile and indsl. operating divs., Toledo, 1976-79, personnel mgr. roofing div., 1979-82, dir. compensation and benefits, 1982—; corp. program com. Internat. Found. Employee Benefit Plans, Wis., 1983—. Served to maj. USAFR, 1965—. Mem. Internat. Found. Employee Benefits, Council Employee Benefits, Am. Soc. Personnel Adminstrn., Am. Compensation Assn., Benefits Planning Council. Republican. Methodist. Lodge: Masons. Avocations: golf, tennis, hunting, woodworking. Office: Owens-Corning Fiberglas Corp Fiberglas Tower Toledo OH 43659

PAUL, THOMAS WILLIAM, healthcare center administrator; b. St. Paul, Mar. 30, 1946; s. Gilbert William and Genevieve Bell (Thomas) P.; m. Marie Kathleen Tennis, Dec. 11, 1965; children—Terra Michelle, Shantell Kathleen, Anissa Justine, Chaleece Marie. Cert. in comml. art Mpls. Vocat. Tech. Inst., 1965; diploma Chgo. Tech. Coll., 1971; credential advanced studies health service adminstrn. U. Minn., 1981. Lic. nursing home adminstr., Minn. Photo lab technician Headliners of Twin Cities, Mpls., 1965-67; asst. adminstr. Birchwood Health Care Facility, Forest Lake, Minn., 1967-71, Colonial Acres Health Ctr., Golden Valley, Minn., 1971-73; exec. dir. Crest View Luth. Home, Columbia Heights, Minn., 1973—. Chmn. nursing homes div. United Way of Mpls., 1976; bd. suprs. Forest Lake Town, 1977-82, chmn., 1979-82; basketball coach Forest Lake Community Edn., 1980, softball coach, 1982; active various election campaigns, 1978-82; bd. dirs. St. Paul Camp Fire, 1979-81, United Way of Forest Lake, 1981, Forest Lake Sch. Dist., 1983-86. Recipient Community Service award Anoka County Retarded Citizens Assn., 1981; Luth. Social Services grantee, 1979-80. Fellow Am. Coll. Health Care Adminstrs. (cert.); mem. Minn. Soc. Adminstrs. Nursing Care Facilities, Columbia Heights C. of C. (dir. 1982-85), Forest Lake Jaycees (life, outstanding young man 1976), U.S. Jaycee Pres.' Club. Republican. Lutheran. Contbr. articles to profl. jours. Office: Crest View Luth Home 4444 Reservoir Blvd NE Columbia Heights MN 55421

PAUL, WAYNE LUVERNE, dean, psychologist; b. Mason City, Iowa, Apr. 1, 1947; s. Loral L. and Wilma (Worden) P.; m. Neva Rita Wilson, Aug. 8, 1980; children—Mishelle, Robert, David. Ph.D., U. Mo.-Kansas City, 1979. Lic. psychologist, Mo. Program dir. student services Kansas City (Mo.) Regional Council for Higher Edn., 1974-78; head resident Rockhurst Coll., Kansas City, 1974-78; student activities coordinator Rockhurst Coll., 1978-81; dir. counseling Kansas City (Kans.) Community Coll., 1981-84; dean student life Dickinson State Coll., N.D., 1984-85; dean of students DeVry Inst. Tech., Kansas City, Mo., 1985—. Served with U.S. Army, 1969-70. Mem. Nat. Assn. Student Personnel Adminstrs., Am. Psychol. Assn., Am. Personnel and Guidance Assn., Phi Delta Kappa. Methodist. Contbr. articles to profl. jours. Home: 13210 Grand Ave Kansas City MO 64145 Office: 11224 Holmes Rd Kansas City MO 64131

PAULETT, HARRY KENNETH, packaging machinery manufacturing company sales and marketing executive; b. Cleve., May 4, 1924; s. Thomas A. and Johanna (Morrissey) P.; m. Margaret Mary Martin, June 18, 1949; children—John, Ken, Terence, Mary Jo, Ray, Margaret, Kathleen, Tom, Suzanne. Student bus. adminstrn. John Carroll U., 1946-49. Regional mgr. Permacel div. Johnson & Johnson, Cleve., 1960-65; product mgr. Orchard Corp., St. Louis, 1965-70; mktg. dir. Internat. Packaging & Machines, Naples, Fla. 1978—, sales mgr., 1983—; pres., chief operating officer Pace Mfg. Co., 1984—; seminar speaker in field. Served with Signal Corps, U.S. Army, 1942-46. Mem. Packaging Inst., Soc. Packaging and Handling Engineers. Democrat. Roman Catholic. Designer various packaging attachments and systems dealing with pallet wrapping. Home: 1560 Rydalmount Rd Cleveland Heights OH 44118 Office: 2909 E 79th St Cleveland OH

PAULETTE, ROBERT GRIEBIE, retired civil engineer, engineering firm executive; b. Halstead, Kans., Aug. 30, 1920; s. Robert Justice and Jessie Augusta (Griebie) P.; m. Roberta Hills Kingman, Dec. 22, 1941; children—Robert J., Nancy R., Marilyn M. B.S.C.E., Univ. Kans., Lawrence, 1941. Registered profl. engr. Pa., Ill., Ind., Kans., Ia., Ohio, Wis., Ga., Mo. Engr., Paulette & Wilson, Topeka, Kans., 1941-42; field engr. INFILCO, Inc., Chgo., Buffalo, Pitts., Joliet, Ill., 1946-55; project engr. Municipal Service Co., project mgr. J. F. Pritchard and Co., Kansas City, Mo., 1955-66; v.p., project mgr. Stanley Cons., Muscatine, Iowa, 1966-83; retired, 1983. Contbr. numerous articles on water supply and treatment, municipal and indsl. waste-water treatment and related subjects to profl. publs. Vice pres. Am. Cancer Soc., Muscatine, 1984-85; v.p. Muscatine County Arts Council, 1985. Served to capt. USAAF, 1943-46; ETO. Diplomate Am. Acad. Environ. Engrs., 1979—. Fellow ASCE (life mem.); mem. Am. Water Works Assn. (life), Water Pollution Control Fedn. (life), Soc. Am. Mil. Engrs. (pres. Rock Island, Ill. post, 1982-83); retired from others. Republican. Episcopalian. Clubs: Artists in Action, Muscatine. Lodge: Elks. Avocations: Watercolor and oil painting, woodwork, golf. Home: 1618 Mulberry Ave Muscatine IA 52761

PAULI, STANLEY JAY, information services manager; b. Monroe, Wis., Aug. 12, 1939; s. John Wilhelm and Sylvia (Klassey) P.; m. Nancy Seeley, Nov. 11, 1961 (div. 1972); children—Daniel John, Eric Jay; m. Lee Judith Johnson, June 10, 1978. B.S., U. Wis., 1962; M.S., Syracuse U., 1965. Tchr. Platteville High Sch., Wis., 1962-64; instr. math. U. Wis.-Wausau, 1965-67, U. Wis.-Waukesha, 1969-70; systems engr. IBM, Ann Arbor, Mich., 1968; info. systems mgr. Milw. Schs., 1970—. Served with U.S. Army, 1959-62. Mem. Data Processing Mgmt. Assn. Democrat. Congregationalist. Avocations: skiing; running; reading. Home: 9806 W Center St Milwaukee WI 53222 Office: Milw Pub Schs 5225 W Vliet St Milwaukee WI 53208

PAULISSEN, JAMES PETER, physician, county official; b. Chgo., Aug. 14, 1928; s. Joseph Edward and Louise Catherine (Muno) P.; m. Lorraine Antoinette Polly, Sept. 11, 1954; children—Linda, Steven, Mark, Daniel. Student Loyola U., 1946-49, M.D. cum laude, 1953; M.P.H., Johns Hopkins U., 1966. Diplomate Am. Bd. Pediatrics. Intern Milw. County Hosp., 1953-54; resident Milw. Children's Hosp., 1957-59; practice medicine specializing in pediatrics Wauwatosa Children's Clinic, Wis., 1959-65; chief Bur. Maternal and Child Health, Ill. Dept. Pub. Health, Springfield, 1966-70, chief Div. Family Health, 1970-76; exec. dir. DuPage County Health Dept., Wheaton, Ill., 1976—; bd. dirs., mem. exec. com. Suburban Cook-DuPage Health Systems Agy., Oak Park, Ill., 1976-82; bd. dirs., past pres. Comprehensive Health Council Met. Chgo., 1977—; dir. Sr. Home Sharing, Inc., Wheaton, 1981-83. Mem. Ill. Commn. on Children, 1971—, vice chmn., 1983—, chmn. Ill. Perinatal Adv. Com., 1981—; mem. Ill. Sch. Health Adv. Com., 1982—, Gov.'s Adv. Council on Devel. Disabilities, 1973-76; del. White House Conf. for Children, 1970. Served to capt. USAF, 1954-56. Fellow Am. Acad. Pediatrics, Am. Pub. Health Assn., Am. Coll. Preventive Medicine; mem. Am. Acad. Pediatrics (mem. exec. com. Ill. chpt. 1978-81), Ill. Pub. Health Assn. (pres. 1977-78; Disting. Service award 1983), Ill. Assn. Maternal and Child Health (pres. 1975-76). Avocation: model railroading. Home: 28W660 Hawthorne Ln West Chicago IL 60185 Office: DuPage County Health Dept 111 N County Farm Rd Wheaton IL 60187

PAULSEN, FAYETTA MAE, university official; b. Muskegon, Mich., Sept. 9, 1925; d. Alfred and Gladys May (Irish) P. B.S., Western Mich. U., 1947; M.S., MacMurray Coll., 1948; postgrad. U. Colo., 1950, Syracuse U., 1953-55, 56-61. Teaching fellow MacMurray Coll., 1948; asst prof. health and phys. edn. St. Olaf Coll., Northfield, Minn., 1948-52; chmn. health and phys. edn. for women Augustana Coll., Rock Island, Ill., 1952-53; dean women Luther Coll., Decorah, Iowa, 1955-63; asst. v.p. student affairs Bowling Green State U., Ohio, 1963—. Mem. Ohio Assn. Women Deans, Adminstrs., Counselors (pres. 1972-73), Nat. Assn. Women Deans, Adminstrs., Counselors (parliamentarian 1983-84), Ohio Coll. Personnel Assn. (pres. 1976-77), Am. Coll. Personnel Assn., Ohio Assn. Student Personnel Adminstrs. (pres. elect 1984-85), Am. Counseling Devel. Assn., AAUW (corp. del. 1963—). Methodist. Club: Bowling Green Country. Home: 1001 Boone Ct Bowling Green OH 43402 Office: 425 Student Services Bldg Bowling Green State U Bowling Green OH 43402

PAULSEN, JOHN KEVIN, surgeon; b. Woodstock, Ill., June 1, 1947; s. Lyle Francis and Mary Mercedes (Shields) P.; m. Pamela Gielincki, June 22, 1974; children—Amy, Amanda. B.S., U. Notre Dame, 1969; M.D., U. Ill., 1973. Diplomate Am. Bd. Surgery. Intern, Henry Ford Hosp., Detroit, 1973-74, resident in surgery St. Francis Hosp., Peoria, Ill., 1974-78; practice medicine specializing in surgery, Peoria, Ill., 1978—; mem. staff St. Francis Hosp., Meth. Hosp., Proctor Hosp. Fellow ACS; mem. Ill. Surg. Soc., Midwest Surg. Assn. Avocation: jogging. Office: 120 NE Glen Oak St Suite 208 Peoria IL 61603

PAULSEN, LESLIE JAMES, high technology company executive; b. Osceola, Wis., June 25, 1927; s. Nels Peter and Thora (Hansen) P.; m. Darlene Mae Bruce, May 2, 1953; children—Peter J., Bruce N. (dec.), Heather L. B. Mech. Engring., U. Minn., 1950. Sales engr. Honeywell, Inc., Omaha, 1951-59, br. mgr., Mpls., 1959-64, regional mgr., Chgo., 1964-70, nat. sales mgr., Mpls., 1970-72, regional dir., Phila., 1972-77, nat. service mgr., Mpls., 1977-79, v.p., field dir., Mpls., 1979—. Served with USN, 1945-46. Mem. ASHRAE. Republican. Lutheran. Lodge: Masons. Avocations: hunting; fishing; skiing. Home: 18112 Priory Ln Minnetonka MN 55345 Office: Honeywell Inc Honeywell Plaza MN274156 Minneapolis MN 55408

PAULSON, RICHARD CLARENCE, orthodontist; b. St. Cloud, Minn., June 18, 1934; s. Clarence Edwin and Olive Roberta (Livingstone) P.; m. Elizabeth Ann Price, Sept. 8, 1956 (div. June 1976); children—Anne E., Leslie R.; m. Marilee Fern Gordon, Aug. 11, 1982. B.S., U. Minn., 1956, D.D.S., 1958; M.S. in Dentistry, U. Nebr., 1962. Diplomate Am. Bd. Orthodontics. Assoc. clin. prof. Sch. Dentistry, U. Minn., Mpls., 1962-70; pvt. practice orthodontics, Golden Valley, Minn., 1962—. Mem. Golden Valley City Council, Minn., 1970-73. Served to capt. USAF, 1958-60. Nat. Inst. Dental Research postdoctoral fellow, 1961-62. Mem. Am. Assn. Orthodontists, ADA, Edward H. Angle Soc. Orthodontists, Minn. Dental Assn., Omicron Kappa Upsilon. Republican. Congregationalist. Club: Golden Valley Country. Avocations: golf; skiing. Home: 7128 Mark Terrace Dr Edina MN 55435 Office: 5851 Duluth St Golden Valley MN 55422

PAULSON, WILLIAM LEE, former state supreme court justice; b. Valley City, N.D., Sept. 3, 1913; s. A.P. and Inga G. Paulson; B.A., Valley City State Tchrs. Coll., 1935; J.D. U. N.D., 1937; m. Jane E. Graves, Sept. 8, 1938; children—John T., Mary (Mrs. Mikal Simonson). Bar: N.D. 1937. Practiced in Valley City, 1937-66; state's atty. Barnes County, 1941-50, 59-66; justice N.D. Supreme Ct., 1967-83; ret., 1983. Mem. N.D. Combined Law Enforcement Council, 1969; mem. nat. awards jury Freedoms Found., Valley Forge, Pa., 1969, 71, 77. Mem. alumni adv. bd. U. N.D., 1971-82. Recipient Disting. Alumni award U. N.D., 1972, Valley City State Coll. Alumni Assn., 1981. Mem. Am., N.D. (ex officio mem. com. unified court system) bar assns., N.D.

States Attys. Assn. (pres. 1964), Nat. Dist. Attys. Assn. (state dir. 1963-65), Valley City Jr. C. of C. (pres. 1943, Outstanding Jaycee award 1945, dist. v.p. 1945-46), Valley City C. of C. (dir. 1960, 61). Episcopalian (chancellor N.D. 1965-83). Lodges: Masons, Shriners, Elks, Eagles, K.P. Home: Box 444 Valley City ND 58072

PAULU, BURTON, retired media educator; b. Pewaukee, Wis., June 25, 1910; s. Emanuel Marion and Sarah Marie (Murphy) P.; m. Frances Tuttle Brown, June 29, 1942; children—Sarah Leith, Nancy Jean, Thomas Scott. B.A. cum laude, U. Minn., 1931, B.S., 1932, M.A., 1934, postgrad., 1934-38; Ph.D., NYU, 1949. Mgr. Sta. KUOM, U. Minn., Mpls., 1938-57, prof., dir. radio and TV, 1957-72, prof., dir. media resources, 1972-78, ret. lectr. Sch. Journalism and Dept. of Speech, 1951-78; vis. prof. U. So. Calif., 1958, Los Angeles State Coll., 1961; assoc. dir. study of new ednl. media in Kennedy Cultural Ctr., Washington, 1949-62; Fulbright lectr. faculty of journalism Moscow State U., USSR, 1980-81; lectr. U.S. Info. Agy., Spain and Fed. Republic Germany, 1983. Author: A Radio and Television Bibliography, 1952; Lincoln Lodge Seminar on Educational Television Proceedings, 1953; British Broadcasting: Radio and Television in the United Kingdom, 1956; British Broadcasting in Transition, 1961; Radio and Television Broadcasting on the European Continent, 1974; Radio and Television Broadcasting in Eastern Europe, 1974; Television and Radio Broadcasting in the United Kingdom, 1981. Served with U.S. Office of War Info., 1944-45. Grantee Rockefeller Found., 1942, Ford Found., 1958-59, 64-65, 70, 78, U. Minn., 1965-73; Fulbright scholar, 1953-54; recipient Citation of Radio and TV Broadcasting on European Continent, Nat. Journalism Soc., 1967, Pioneering award Internat. Broadcasting Soc. of Netherlands, 1968, Broadcast Preceptor award San Francisco State U., 1968, 82. Mem. Minn. Fulbright Alumni Assn. (bd. dirs. 1985), U. Minn. Retirees Assn. (bd. dirs, pres.), AAUP, Phi Beta Kappa, Phi Kappa Phi, Phi Delta Kappa, Kappa Delta Pi, Phi Alpha Theta, Sigma Delta Chi. Democrat. Congregationalist. Avocations: photography, travel; reading; music. Home: 5005 Wentworth Ave Minneapolis MN 55419

PAULU, FRANCES BROWN, organization executive; b. Hastings, Minn., June 22, 1920; d. Thomas Andrew and Florence Ida (Tuttle) Brown; B.A. magna cum laude, U. Minn., 1940, postgrad. Sch. Social Work, 1942-44; m. Burton Paulu, June 29, 1942; children—Sarah Leith Paulu-Boittin, Nancy Jean Paulu-Hyde, Thomas Scott. Case worker Family Welfare Assn. Mpls., 1943-45; interviewer Community Health and Welfare Council, Mpls., 1963; sch. social worker Project Head Start, Mpls., 1966; program dir. Minn. Internat. Center, Mpls., 1970-72, exec. dir., 1972-84; exec. dir. Minn. Internat. Ctr./World Affairs Ctr., 1984—. Pres. UN Rally, 1970-72; chmn. Mpls. Charter Commn., 1972-74; bd. dirs. Urban Coalition of Mpls., 1967-70, Minn. World Affairs Center, 1972—; mem. tourism adv. com. City of Mpls., 1976-83; dir. Minn. World Trade Week, 1977-81; mem. mgmt. team Minn. Awareness Project, 1982—; adv. council Minn. World Trade Ctr., 1984—. DeWitt Jennings Payne scholar, 1939-40. Mem. Nat. Council for Internat. Visitors (officer and/or exec. com. mem. 1975-81), Nat. Assn. for Fgn. Student Affairs, LWV (pres. Mpls. 1967-69), UN Assn. Minn. (adv. council 1979—), Mpls.-St. Paul Com. on Fgn. Relations, Phi Beta Kappa, Alpha Omicron Pi, Lambda Alpha Psi. Club: Faculty Women's U. Minn. (dir. profl. women's sect. 1981-83). Home: 5005 Wentworth Ave Minneapolis MN 55419 Office: Minn Internat Center 711 East River Rd Minneapolis MN 55455

PAULUS, STEPHEN HARRISON, composer; b. Summit, N.J., Aug. 24, 1949; s. Harrison C. and Patricia J. Paulus; m. Patricia Ann Stutzman, July 18, 1975; 1 child, Gregory. B.A. in Piano Performance, U. Minn., 1971, M.A. in Theory and Composition, 1974, Ph.D., 1978. Composer of orchestral, chamber and solo works and operas, 1973—; co-founder, mgr., v.p. Minn. Composers Forum, St. Paul, 1973-84; composer-in-residence Minn. Orch., 1983—; works include: Concerto for Orch.; The Postman Always Rings Twice (opera); Spectra for Small Orchestra; The Village Singer (opera), The Woodlanders (3-act opera), Ordway Overture, Reflections, Echoes between the Silent Peaks, So Hallow'd Is the Time, All My Pretty Ones, Art Sons, Seven Short Pieces, Translucent Landscapes, North Shore, Canticles, Music for Contrasts. State of Minn. Arts Bd. grantee, 1977; Nat. Endowment for Arts fellow, 1978; Guggenheim fellow, 1982-83. Home: 1710 Jefferson Ave Saint Paul MN 55105

PAULY, RICHARD JOHN, credit manager; b. Bloomington, Ill., Sept. 9, 1937; s. John Peter and Beulah Mary (Boland) P.; m. Sharon Ann Ryan, June 18, 1960; children—Laura L., Julia A., Richard R., Michelle M., John P. Grad. Loras Acad., Dubuque, Iowa, 1955; student Loras Coll., 1955-57; B.S., U. Iowa, 1960. Pharmacist, asst mgr. Hartig Drug Co., Dubuque, 1960-62; owner, mgr. pharmacist Pauly Rexall Drug, East Dubuque, 1963-68; pres., mgr., pharmacist Holscher's Apothecary, Inc., Dubuque, 1968-77; benefits adminstr. Dubuque Packing Co., 1978-82; regional credit mgr. FDL Foods, Inc., Dubuque, 1982—. Mem. Dubuque County Democratic Central Com., 1976. Scholar U. Iowa, 1959, Torbert Drug Co., 1959. Mem. Rho Chi Soc. Roman Catholic. Club: Snomad Ski (Dubuque) (treas.) Avocations: skiing, water skiing, boating, travel. Home: 1275 Loras Blvd Dubuque IA 52001 Office: FDL Foods Inc 2040 Kerper Blvd Dubuque IA 52001

PAUTSCH, THOMAS ROY, educational administrator; b. Milw., May 28, 1931; s. Roy Robert and Adele W. (Wichman) P.; m. Louise Sylvia Madritsch, Aug. 16, 1952; children—Laura, Suzan, Gregory, Bryan. B.S., Wis. State Coll., 1953; M.S., U. Wis.-Madison, 1962. Tchr., counselor Edison Jr. High Sch., Milw., 1957-61; asst. prin. Fulton Jr. High Sch., Milw., 1961-66, John Marshall Jr. High Sch., Milw., 1966-70, Cedarburg High Sch., Wis., 1970-71; prin. Webster Transitional Sch., Cedarburg, 1971—; cons. WRISE, Madison, Wis., 1981-84, Hobart Schs., Ind., 1983. Author: (with others) Three-year Progress Report, Webster Transitional School, 1977. Contbr. articles to profl. jours. Bd. dirs. Cedarburg Community Scholarship Fund; vol. Cedarburg Fire Dept.; coordinator March of Dimes, Cedarburg, Cedarburg Music Festival. Served to lt. USN, 1953-57, PTO. Recipient Excellence in Edn. award U.S. Dept. Edn., 1983. Mem. Nat. Middle Sch. Assn., Nat. Assn. Middle Sch. Adminstrs., Assn. Wis. Sch. Adminstrs., Phi Delta Kappa. Lutheran. Office: Webster Transitional Sch W75 N624 Wauwatosa Rd Cedarburg WI 53012

PAVARINI, PETER ALFRED, lawyer; b. N.Y.C., Feb. 21, 1952; s. Alfred S. and Anne M. (Pertusi) P.; m. Colleen A. Wulf, Apr. 12, 1980. B.A. summa cum laude, SUNY-Albany, 1973; J.D., Boston Coll., 1977. Bar: Mass. 1977, D.C. 1979 Ohio 1981. Aide, N.Y. State Office of Gen. Services, Albany, 1973-74; research asst. Boston Coll., 1975-76; intern Office of Mass. Atty. Gen., Boston, 1976-77; atty. HHS, Washington, 1977-81; assoc. Murphey Young & Smith, Columbus, Ohio, 1981—; adj. prof. Park Coll., Ft. Myer, Va., 1979-80. Contbr. articles to profl. jours. Trustee, Trinity Players, Washington, 1978-79. Recipient Congressman's medal of Merit, 1970; Gen. Counsel's award HEW, 1979. Fellow Am. Acad. Hosp. Attys.; mem. Nat. Health Lawyers Assn., ABA Health Law Forum, Columbus Bar Assn. (sec. hosp. law com. 1983-84), Ohio Bar Assn. (chmn. subcom. reimbursement 1984—). Lodge: Kiwanis (Columbus). Avocations: sailing; bicycling; skiing; geology. Office: Murphey Young & Smith 250 E Broad St Columbus OH 43215

PAVELKA, DEBORAH DIANNE, accountancy educator, consultant, researcher; b. Gary, Ind., Nov. 12, 1950; d. Paul L. and Louise Ann (Defenser) Pavelka; m. Robert James Fischer, Aug. 29, 1970 (div. Dec. 1983); children—Ian Alexander, Gina Renee. B.S., Western Ill. U., 1971, M.S., 1972, M.Acctg., 1980; Ph.D. in Accountancy U. Mo., 1985. C.P.A., Ill. Instr. in math. Western Ill. U., Macomb, 1974-76, 77-78, instr. accountancy, 1978-80, asst. prof. accountancy, 1982-85; asst. prof. accountancy U. Tex., El Paso, 1985—; teaching asst. in accountancy U. Mo., Columbia, 1980-81; cons. police. U. Mo. Coll. Bus. fellow, summer 1981, Sch. Accountancy fellow, fall 1981. Mem. Am. Inst. C.P.A.s, Am. Acctg. Assn., Nat. Assn. Accts. Clubs: Univ. Women. Home: 140 Shadow Mountain Dr Apt B-8 El Paso TX 79912 Office: 224 Business Adminstrn Bldg Univ Tex El Paso TX 79968

PAVELKA, ELAINE BLANCHE, mathematics educator; b. Chgo., Feb. 4; d. Frank Joseph and Mildred Bohumila (Seidl) P.; B.A., M.S., Northwestern U.; Ph.D., U. Ill. Mathematician, Northwestern U. Aerial Measurements Lab., Evanston, Ill.; instr. Leyden Community High Sch., Franklin Park, Ill.; now prof. math. Morton Coll., Cicero, Ill.; participant profl. confs.; presenter paper 3d Internat. Congress on Math. Edn., Karlsruhe, Fed. Republic Germany, 1976. Recipient Westinghouse Sci. Talent award. Mem. Am. Ednl. Research Assn., Am. Math. Assn. of Two-Year Colls., Am. Math. Soc., Mensa, Assn. Women in Math., Canadian Soc. History and Philosophy of Math., Ill. Council Tchrs. of Math., Ill. Math. Assn. for Community Colls., Intertel, Math. Assn. Am., Math. Action Group, Ga. Center for Study of Learning Teaching Mathematics, Nat. Council Tchrs. of Math., Sch. Sci. and Math. Assn., Spl. Interest Group Research in Math. Edn., Soc. Indsl. and Applied Math., Northwestern U., U. Ill. alumni assns., Pi Mu Epsilon, Sigma Delta Epsilon. Home: 1900 Euclid Ave Berwyn IL 60402 Office: Morton Coll 3801 S Central Ave Cicero IL 60650

PAVEY, ROBERT DAVIDSON, investment company executive; b. Dayton, Ohio, June 16, 1942; s. Paul Austin and Sara Josephine (Davidson) P.; m. Patricia Lucy Lee, June 19, 1965; children—Deborah, Susan. B.S. in Physics, Coll. William and Mary, 1964; M.S. in Metall. Engring., Columbia U., 1965; M.B.A., Harvard U., 1967. Product mgr. Foseco, Inc., Cleve., 1967-69; gen. ptnr. Morgenthaler Ventures, Cleve., 1969—; exec. v.p. Morgenthaler Mgmt. Corp., Cleve., 1981—; dir. Advanced Robotics Corp., Columbus, Ohio, Applied Intelligent Systems, Ann Arbor, Mich., Intelledex Corp., Corvallis, Oreg., United Agriseed, Champaign, Ill., Via Systems, Inc., North Billerica, Mass. Bd. trustees Children's Aid Soc., Cleve., 1979—; mem. adv. com. Econ. Edn. in Cleve. Pub. Schs., 1979—; chmn. Cleve. Ctr. Econ. Edn., University Heights, Ohio, 1980—. Mem. Nat. Venture Capital Assn. (bd. dirs. 1984—). Clubs: Harvard Bus. Sch. of Cleve. (bd. trustees), Union, Westwood Country. Home: 420 Parklawn Dr Rocky River OH 44116 Office: Morgenthaler Ventures 700 National City Bank Bldg Cleveland OH 44114

PAVIN, ALEX JOHN, purchasing agent; b. Chgo., Nov. 11, 1949; s. Alex J. and Inez M. (Detoni) P.; m. Barbara K. Newman, July 14, 1974 (div.). B.A., DePaul U.-Chgo., 1972. Buyer U.S. Gypsum, Chgo., 1974-77, asst. purchasing mgr., 1977-83; purchasing agt. L & W Supply Corp., Chgo., 1983—. Treas. Ill. Theatrical Co., Chgo., 1972-75; dep. chmn. Young Rep. Nat. Fedn., Washington, 1983—, auditor, 1981-83, rules com. chmn., 1979-81; asst. to chmn. Young Rep. Orgn. of Ill., Springfield, 1977-79; mem. selections com. U.S. Youth Council, 1984—. Named Man of Yr. Cook County Young Reps., Chgo., 1973. Mem. Blue Key. Roman Catholic.

PAVLATOS, STACEY ROBERT, lawyer; b. Springfield, Ohio, Oct. 15, 1951; s. Robert Basil and Evelyn Ingrid (Guether) P.; m. Jan Elaine Recknagel, Oct. 11, 1980. B.A. in Polit. Sci., Wittenburg U., 1973; student DePaul U., 1974; J.D., U. Dayton, 1977. Bar: Ohio 1977, U.S. Tax Ct. 1979. Ptnr. Pavlatos & Pavlatos, Springfield, 1977-80; pres. Pavlatos & Catanzaro, L.P.A., Springfield, 1980—. Chmn. com. South Fountain Preservation, Commn., Springfield, 1982-84; chmn. Springfield Hist. Landmarks commn., 1984—; vice chmn. Project Woman, Springfield, 1982-84; chmn. Springfield Bd. Bldg. Appeals, 1984—. Mem. Clark County Bar Assn. Republican. Greek Orthodox. Lodge: Kiwanis. Avocations: sports, building rehabilitation. Home: 724 S Fountain Ave Springfield OH 45506 Office: 700 E High St Springfield OH 45505

PAVONE, MICHAEL PHILLIP, music educator, organist, composer; b. Buffalo, Dec. 11, 1945; s. Anthony Benedict and Mary Grace (Muche) P.; m. Karen Ann Krahling, June 3, 1972. Mus.B., Westminster Choir Coll., 1968, Mus.M., 1976. Instr. music Abraham Clark Sch., Clark, N.J., 1969-72; chmn. music dept. Brooks Sch., North Andover, Mass., 1974-76, Tabor Acad., Marion, Mass., 1976-79; grad. teaching assoc. Ohio U., Athens, 1979-81; asst. prof. music, chmn. dept. Ohio Dominion Coll., Columbus, 1981—; guest organist, guest conductor various music festivals. Composer choral and handbell works. Founder, dir. Clarktown Boys Choir, 1969-72; active Merrimack Valley Arts and Humanities Council, Mass. and N.H., 1974-75; participant Hispanic Awareness Week, Columbus, 1983. 1st Baroque Acad.-/Aston Magna Found. fellow, 1977; choral scholar Classical Music Seminar, Austria, 1977; recipient commendation N.Y. State Senate, 1977, Bronze medal Internat. Choral Festival, Rome, 1975. Mem. Am. Guild Organists (sub-dean 1977-79), Am. Assn. Choral Dirs., Nat. Pastoral Musicians (program coordinator), Royal Sch. Ch. Music, Coll. Music Soc. Republican. Avocations: poetry; swimming; film; tennis. Home: 1173 Sunbury Rd Columbus OH 43219 Office: Ohio Dominion Coll 1216 Sunbury Rd Columbus OH 43219

PAWLEY, HOWARD RUSSELL, Canadian provincial minister; b. Brampton, Ont., Can., Nov. 21, 1934; s. Russell and Velma Leone (Madill) P.; m. Adele Schreyer, Nov. 26, 1960; children—Christopher Scott, Charysse. Ed. Man. Tchrs. Coll., United Coll., U. Winnipeg, Man. Law Sch. Called to bar. Mem. Man. (Ont., Can.) Legislature, 1969—; premier of Man., 1981—; minister pub. works, 1969-71, mcpl. affairs, 1969-76; atty. gen. and keeper of Gt. Seal, 1973; minister responsible for Liquor Control Act, 1976, Man. Pub. Ins. Corp. and Man. Housing and Renewal Corp.; leader Man. New Democratic Party (N.D.P.), 1979. Office: Office of Premier Legis Bldg Room 204 Winnipeg MN R3C OV8 Canada*

PAWLITSCHEK, DONALD PAUL, bus. cons.; b. Heron Lake, Minn., Aug. 5, 1941; s. Paul P. and Marion (Erickson) P.; student Southwest Tech. Inst., 1960, Mankato State Coll., 1965-66; m. Korrine Kunerth, Oct. 9, 1965; children—Andrew, Jennifer, Heidi, Sarah, Benjamin. Farmer, Heron Lake, 1967-73; pres. Dundee Steel Inc., 1973-75, Alpha Prime Inc., Heron Lake, 1975-80, Prime Ventures, Inc., 1980—; dir. Am. Search and Referral Co. Served with AUS, 1960. Mem. Nat. Assn. Fin. Cons., Am. Entrepreneurs Assn., Am. Legion. Conservative. Roman Catholic. Club: Elks. Patentee livestock flooring. Address: Rt 2 Heron Lake MN 56137

PAXTON, ALBERT ELWYN, chrome plating company executive; b. Chgo., May 19, 1902; s. Frederick H. and Harriet I. (Griffiths) P.; B.S., U. Ill., 1925; m. Edna Marjorie Rehm, July 11, 1930; children—Marilyn V., Nancy L. Editor, Mill Supplies, McGraw-Hill Publs., Chgo., 1926-34, mgr., N.Y.C., 1934-37; mgr. engring. News Record-Constrn. Methods, N.Y.C., 1938-45, pub., 1945-48; v.p. western region McGraw Hill Pub. Co., Chgo., 1945-67; pres. Nova Chrome, Inc., Franklin Park, Ill., 1967—. Clubs: Chgo., Univ., Westmoreland Country. Home: 667 Sheridan Rd Winnetka IL 60093

PAXTON, JACK DUNMIRE, plant pathologist, educator, researcher; b. Oakland, Calif., Feb. 17, 1936; s. Glenn Ernest and Frances Willa (Dunmire) P.; m. Sarah Elizabeth Clough, Sept. 4, 1960; children—Anne, Paul. Research assoc. U. Ill., Urbana, 1964-65, asst. prof., 1965-71, assoc. prof. plant pathology, 1971—. Contbr. articles to profl. jours. Patentee in field. Fulbright fellow, 1971. Mem. Am. Phytopathol. Soc. (membership chmn.), Plant Physiol. Soc. Am., Phytochem. Soc. N.Am., Sierra Club (group chmn. Urbana 1966-68), Avocations: skiing; hiking; photography; gardening; canoing. Home: 2603 Brownfield Rd Urbana IL 61801 Office: 1102 S Goodwin Urbana IL 61801

PAYNE, ALVIE ELLIS, retail store executive; b. Bertrand, Nebr., Sept. 23, 1912; s. John Ellis and Catherine Ann (Griffith) P.; m. Ruth Elizabeth Sherer, Aug. 6, 1939; children—John Warren, Charles Ellis, Ronald Keith. B.S., Kearney State Coll., 1939. Supt. Meadow Grove Pub. Schs., Nebr., 1939-42; owner, operator Payne Enterprises, Inc., Kearney, Nebr., 1945-83; dir. 1st Nat. Bank, Nebr. Pub. Power Dist., 1975-83; Nebr. diplomat Dept. State Econ. Devel. Bd. dirs. Kearney Civic Devel., 1970—, Central Platte Natural Resource Dist., Grand Island, Nebr., 1969-79; pres. Kearney State Coll. Found., 1982. Civilian adminstrv. asst. USAAF, 1942-45. Recipient Disting. Service award Kearney State Coll., 1982. Mem. Kearney Area C. of C. (pres. 1959, Life Mem. award 1983), Kearney State Coll. Alumni (pres. 1961). Lodges: Mason, Shriners, Elks. Avocations: flying; fishing; hunting; golf; copper enameling. Home: 3403 4th Ave Kearney NE 68847

PAYNE, ARTHUR EDDIE, III, (poetry), singer, songwriter; b. Kansas City, Kans., Mar. 9, 1955; s. Arthur Eddie and Marion Maxine (Metcalfe) P.; 1 dau., Araina Sheree Rachelle. Student Rockhurst Coll., 1973-74, Park Coll., 1975-77, Charles Parker Music Acad., 1978-79, U. Mo.-Kansas City, 1980-82, Am. Dance Acad., 1982. Cargo serviceman Braniff Internat., Kansas City, 1978; salesman Buie and Stark Clothing, Kansas City, Mo., 1978-79; custodian Park Place Meadows, Raytown, Mo., 1979-80; transfer agt. D.S.T. Inc., Kansas City, Mo., 1980—; cons. to music bus. Recipient Cert. Appreciation Boy's Club Movement, 1980. Mem. Broadcast Music Inc. Roman Catholic. Composer over 700 songs.

PAYNE, GORDON DOUGLAS, lawyer, researcher; b. Washington, Nov. 28, 1950; s. Gordon Ronald and Marrilee (Gibbs) P.; m. Janet Louise Lynch, June 23, 1984. A.B., Franklin and Marshall Coll., 1971; A.M., Rutgers U., 1973; J.D., Chgo. Kent Coll. Law, Ill. Inst Tech, 1979. Bar: Ill. 1979, U.S. Dist. Ct. (no. dist.) Ill. 1979, Wis. 1983, U.S. Dist. Ct. (we. dist.) Wis. 1983. Loan officer Cragin Fed. Savs. and Loan, Chgo., 1973-74, Skokie Trust and Savs. Bank, Ill., 1974-76; asst. v.p. Olympic Savs. and Loan, Berwyn, Ill., 1976-78; v.p. Gary-Wheaton Bank, Ill., 1978-80; mgr. product devel. div., atty. U.S. League Savs. Instn., Chgo., 1980-82; assoc. gen. counsel Credit Union Nat. Assn.-/CUNA Service Group, Madison, Wis., 1982—; dir. H.B., Inc., Milw. Treas., bd. dirs. Boys Club, Hoffman Estates, Ill., 1975-77; committeeman Republican Committeeman Orgn., Downers Grove, Ill., 1978-82, mem. exec. com., 1980-82. Recipient Lord Strathcona medal Govt. of Can. Mem. ABA, Wis. Bar Assn., Chgo. Bar Assn., Co. Mil. Historians. Baptist. Home: 7738 Ox Trail Way Verona WI 53593

PAYNE, GRAFTON SAMUEL, JR., county official; b. Charlottesville, Va., Apr. 1, 1931; s. Grafton S. and Stella (Roberts) P.; m. Bernice Davis, May 19, 1963; 1 child, Debroah Jo. B.S., N.C. Agrl. and Tech. U., 1952; M.S., Xavier U., 1974; cert. Inst. Ct. Mgmt., Denver, 1979; cert. Spl. Offenders, Youngstown U., 1969. Tchr. Charlottesville Pub. Schs., Va., 1955-57; clk. U.S. Post Office, Dayton, Ohio, 1957-68; probation officer Common Pleas Ct., Dayton, 1968-73, probation supr., 1973-81; asst. dir. Adult Probation Ct. Montgomery County, Dayton, 1981—; instr. sociology and corrections Sinclair Coll., Dayton, 1975—. Bd. dirs. Equal Opportunity Adv. Bd., Montgomery County, 1980, Human Rehab. Ctr., Dayton, 1983—. Served to cpl. U.S. Army, 1953-55. Recipient Meritorious Service award Ct. Common Pleas, Dayton, 1980; named Ct. Mgr. of Yr., 1985. Mem. Am. Correctional Assn., Ohio Correctional and Ct. Services Assn. Democrat. Club: Dayton Bridge (Ohio) (pres. 1982-83). Lodge: Masons (noble 1969—). Avocations: bridge; golf; gardening; sporting events. Home: 4018 Brynford Pl Dayton/Trotwood OH 45426 Office: Montgomery County Adult Probation 41 N Perry St Dayton OH 45422

PAYNE, KEITH LLOYD, insurance agency executive; b. Moline, Ill., May 16, 1943; s. Francis Lee and Vivian Ruth (Stevenson) P.; m. Susan Elizabeth Johnson, June 13, 1964; children—Michelle Leigh, Frances Lynn. B.S., Western Ill. U., Macomb, 1965. Owner, Payne Ins. Agy., Orion, Ill., 1965—. Clk., Village of Orion, 1969-79, mayor, 1979-81; sec. Crime Stoppers of Henry County, Inc., 1983—; pres. bd. dirs. Spoon River Mental Health Ctr., Galesburg, Ill. Mem. Henry County Ind. Ins. Agts. (sec.-treas. 1983-84, pres. 1985-86), Ind. Ins. Agts. of Ill., Ind. Ins. Agts. of Am. Democrat. Methodist (pres., trustee 1984—). Lodges: Lions, Masons. Home: 1120 4th St Orion IL 61273 Office: Payne Ins Agy 1000 3d St Orion IL 61273

PAYNE, MARGARET BERNETA, religious association executive, educator, consultant; b. Colville, Wash., Nov. 15, 1935; d. Daniel Grinim and Doris Evelyn (Thing) Knauss; m. Donald Lewis Payne, Oct. 30, 1959; children—Kathryn Doris, Diane Lynda. B.A. in Edn., Seattle Pacific U., 1957; postgrad. Eastern Wash. U., 1958-59, Seattle U., 1972-73, U. South Fla., 1965-66, Fla. State U., 1963-64. Tchr. elem. schs., Wash., 1957-60, Fla., 1962-70; tchr. Head Start of Stevens County, Chewelah, Wash., 1970-72, dir., 1972-74, dir. Home Start and Mobile Presch. Programs, 1973—; cons. Region X HEW, 1972-79; ednl. specialist Dist. 105 Yakima (Wash.) County, 1976-80; asst. dir. N.E. Wash. Rural Resource Devel. Assn., Colville, 1974-76; curriculum specialist, editor Free Methodist World Hdqrs., Winona Lake, Ind., 1980-81, dir. children's ministries, 1981—; part-time instr. Yakima (Wash.) Valley Coll., 1977-79; cons. in field. Mem. Wash. Futures, 1970-72; mem. Tri County State Planning Com., Wash. Dept. Social and Human Services, 1973-74; mem. Stevens County (Wash.) Planning Commn., 1974-76; mem. Stevens County Council for Children, 1974-76; bd. dirs. Neighborhood Forums, Stevens County, 1975-76; mem. Yakima Valley Coll. Services for Handicapped Com., 1978-79; dir. Christian edn. Yakima Free Meth. Ch. Mem. Exec. Women's Service Orgn., Lakeland Community Concert Assn. Republican. Author tng., instrnl. and curriculum guides for tchr. use. Home: Route 3 Box 151 Warsaw IN 46580 Office: Free Methodist World Hdqrs 901 College Ave Winona Lake IN 46590

PAYNE, RICHARD GREEN, aerospace company executive; b. Webster, Ky., Dec. 2, 1926; s. Chester and Flora (Osborn) P.; m. Jean Payne, Jan. 16, 1954; children—John R., Donald L., Mark. A. B.S. in Mech. Engring., Ohio State U., 1950. Supr., RCA, Indpls., 1950-52; asst. works mgr. Brown Brockmeyer, Dayton, 1952-53; mgr. Rockwell Internat., Columbus, 1953—. Mem. Salem Civic Assn., Columbus, 1980—. Served to staff sgt. U.S. Army, 1945-47. Mem. AIAA, Aircraft Owners and Pilots Assn. Republican. Lutheran. Avocations: flying; physical culture; golf. Home: 5750 Sinclair Rd Columbus OH 43229 Office: Rockwell Internat 4300 E 5th Ave Columbus OH 43216

PAYNE, TAP ROBIN, theatre arts educator; b. Carlsbad, N.Mex., Jan. 30, 1951; s. Arnold and Ladye Margarete (Stogner) P.; m. Margaret Love Pellegrini, Feb. 1, 1972; children—Justin St. Giles, Liliana Love Ostia. Tech. dir. Tap & Toad Enterprises, Portales, N.Mex., 1969-73; designer, tech. dir. Estern N.Mex. U., Portales, 1973; company lighting designer Carnival Theater, Eugene, Oreg., 1978-79; lighting designer, tech. dir. Lane Community Coll., Eugene, 1979; designer, tech. dir., assoc. prof. theatre arts U. Minn., Morris, 1979; theatre cons. Served to capt. USMC, 1973-77. Recipient Purchase award US. Inst. Theatre Tech., 1982. Mem. U.S. Inst. Theatre Tech., Am. Theatre Assn., Brit. Theatre Assn., Univ. Coll. and Theatre Assn. Republican. Roman Catholic. Home: 106 E 4th St Morris MN 56267 Office: Dept Theatre Univ Minn Morris MN 56267

PAYNE, V. MARLENE, antique dealer; consultant; b. Sesser, Ill., July 3, 1940; d. Wayne K. Cockrum and Martha Roberta (Sample) C.; m. Charles E. Payne, June 6, 1959; children—Kimberly Payne Lewis, Lori L. Gen. mgr. Stieferman Bros., St. Louis, 1972-79, Fry-Wagner Moving, Bridgeton, Mo., 1979-80; cons. interstate commerce, Bridgeton, 1980—; owner, mgr. French Towne Antiques, St. Charles, Mo., 1981—. Mem. Frenchtown Antique Dealers Assn. (treas. 1983-84). Republican. Baptist. Home: 3960 Havercliff Ln Bridgeton MO 63044 Office: French Towne Antiques 1215 N 2d St St Charles MO 63301

PAYNE, WILLIAM J., manufacturing company executive; b. Danville, Ill., June 28, 1940; s. Joseph C. and Nina C. (Faris) P.; m. Nan Elliott Kirby, Feb. 2, 1969; children—Nina Faris, Thomas Kirby. B.S., Trinity U., San Antonio, 1962. Gen. mgr., chief exec. officer Howell Playground Equipment Co., Danville, Ill., 1971—. Chmn. bd. dirs. Danville Area Community Coll., 1974-79; mem. Ill. Community Coll. Bd., 1979—; trustee Ill. State Univs. Retirement System, 1980-83. Served to lt. comdr. USN, 1966-71. Mem. Nat. Recreation and Park Assn., Nat. Sch. Supply and Equipment Assn. (treas. 1982—). Republican. Episcopalian. Club: Danville Country. Lodges: Rotary, Elks. Home: 44 Country Club Dr Danville IL 61832 Office: 1710 E Fairchild St Danville IL 61832

PAYTON, WALTER, See *Who's Who in America,* 43rd edition.

PAZDUR, RICHARD, physician, medical educator and administrator; b. Hammond, Ind., May 5, 1952; s. John Joseph and Joan Patricia (Hudzik) P.; m. Mary P. Bagby, Mar. 12, 1981. B.A., Northwestern U., 1973; M.D., Loyola Stritch Sch. Medicine, 1976. Diplomate Am. Bd. Internal Medicine. Intern Loyola U. Hosp., Maywood, Ill., 1976-77, resident internal medicine, 1977-79; fellow med. oncology RushLuke's Hosp., Chgo., 1979-81, U. Chgo., 1981-82; asst. prof. medicine Wayne State U., Detroit, 1982—, dir. oncology fellowship program, 1984—. Contbr. research papers to med. jours. Fellow Am. Cancer Soc. (registered clin.); mem. ACP, Am. Soc. Clin. Oncology, Am. Assn. Cancer Research. Roman Catholic. Home: 318 Moran Rd Grosse Pointe Farms MI 48236 Office: Div Med Oncology Wayne State U PO Box 02188 Detroit MI 48201

PAZIK, GEORGE JAMES, editor, pub.; b. Milw., Apr. 7, 1921; s. Richard Francis and Josephine (Bartos-Bucek) P.; B.S., U. Wis., 1944; m. Bernice Emily Thiele, June 19, 1943; children—Marjorie Anne, Carol Sue. Mgr., Pazik's Delicatessen, Milw., 1946-54; owner Kitchens by Pazik, Milw., 1952-59; exec. dir. Upper 3d St Comml. Assn., Milw., 1959-64; exec. v.p., founder Northtown Planning and Devel. Council, Milw., 1964-74; editor, pub. Fishing Facts mag., Menomonee Falls, Wis., 1970—. Chmn. Milwaukee County Expressway and Transp. Commn., 1971-74; chmn. Wis. state com. of U.S. Commn. on Civil Rights, 1970-72. Served with U.S. Army, 1944-46. Recipient Human Relations award Milw. Council B'nai B'rith, 1968. Mem. Outdoor Writers Assn. Am., AAAS, Sierra Club, Wilderness Soc. Lutheran. Home: 8549 N Servife Dr Unit 204 Milwaukee WI 53223 Office: N84 W13660 Leon Rd Menomonee Falls WI 53051

PEAK, WILBUR JAMES, cons. pub. relations; b. Quincy, Ill., Mar. 6, 1907; s. Roy Thomas and Violetta (Lay) P.; B.S., Knox Coll., 1928; m. Ruth Visny, Aug. 28, 1937; children—Kathy Ann Peak Miller, Thomas J. Accountant, Ill.

Bell Telephone Co., 1928, supr., 1936, supr. tng., 1938, employee info. supr., 1942, pub. relations and demonstrations supr., 1945, gen. info. mgr., 1949, asst. v.p., 1955-71; cons. pub. relations, 1971—; dir. State Bank of Geneva (Ill.). Recipient Achievement award Knox Coll., 1968. Mem. Telephone Pioneers Am., Chgo. Jr. C. of C. (life mem., pres. 1942-43), Chgo. Assn. Commerce and Industry, Pub. Relations Clinic, Pub. Relations Soc. Am. (pres. 1963). Methodist. Clubs: Masons, Press, Lake Shore (pres. 1963-64), Publicity (pres. 1955-56), Tavern, Headline, Econ., Knox Alumni (pres. 1950) (Chgo.), Lions. Home: 301 Charles St Geneva IL 60134

PEAKER, RONALD LINDSAY, automotive executive; b. Bridgeport, Conn., Apr. 16, 1936; s. Charles Ronald and Dorothy Alice (Van Horne) P.; m. Barbara Jean Anderson, Dec. 22, 1956; children—Deborah Lindsay Peaker Sells, Douglas Andrew. B.S., U. Vt., 1957; M.B.A., Tulane U., 1959; postgrad. Indsl. Coll. Armed Forces, 1962. With Ford Motor Co., 1963—, asst. dist. sales mgr. Autolite div., Des Moines, 1969-70, Boston, 1970-71, dist. mgr. customer service, Kansas City, Mo., 1971-72, mgr. service tech. communications, Detroit, 1972-77, dist. mgr. parts and service, Seattle, 1977-83, Milw., 1983—; instr. mktg. Rollins Coll., Winter Park, Fla., 1960-62, European div. U. Md., 1962-63, Henry Ford Community Coll., Dearborn, Mich., 1964-67. Bd. dirs. Better Bus. Bur., Seattle, 1983. Served as 1st lt. USAF, 1960-63. Republican. Episcopalian. Office: Ford Parts and Service Div Suite 350 16535 W Bluemound Rd Brookfield WI 53005

PEANASKY, ROBERT JOSEPH, biochemist, medical educator; b. Menominee, Mich., Oct. 19, 1927; s. Joseph John and Sophia E. (Simeth) P.; m. Elizabeth R. Bender, Sept. 12, 1953; children—Joseph F., Michael J., Paul J., Robert A., John S. B.S. cum laude, Marquette U., 1951, M.S., 1953; Ph.D., U. Wis.-Madison, 1957. NSF trainee Marquette U., Milw., 1957, 58, 60, Dartmouth U., Hanover, N.H., 1959; asst. prof. Marquette U. Med. Sch., Milw., 1960-65, assoc. prof., 1965-67; assoc. prof. U. S.D. Med. Sch., Vermillion, 1967-70, prof., 1970—; vis. scientist U. Ky. Med. Ctr., Lexington, 1965, U. Marseille-aix-en-Provence, 1966-67; vis. prof. Purdue U., West Lafayette, Ind., 1977; participant confs. in field; mem. Great Plains Regional Review and Research Adv. Com., 1969-72. Served to cpl. U.S. Army, 1946-47. USPHS fellow, 1960-62; recipient Career Devel. award USPHS, 1962-67; NIH grantee, 1961—. Mem. Am. Chem. Soc. (chmn. sect. 1972), Am. Soc. Biol. Chemists, Soc. Exptl. Biology and Medicine (referee editor proceedings 1969-78, mem. council 1976-79), S.D. Acad. Scis. (exec. com. 1983—), Sigma Xi (pres. local chpt. 1979-80). Democrat. Roman Catholic. Clubs: Coyote Coaches (Vermillion, S.D.), Quarterback. Home: 916 Jane St Vermillion SD 57069 Office: U SD Med Sch Dept Biochemistry Vermillion SD 57069

PEARL, WAYNE BLAIN, educational adminstrator; b. Shelbyville, Ind., Jan. 2, 1940; s. Lawrence W. and Ida Helen (Blain) P.; m. Glenda Maxine King, Jan. 31, 1959; children—Kenneth A., Lawrence J., Cheryl Lynn, Sharon Denise. B.A. in History, Tulane U., 1962; M.S., Purdue U., 1966, Ed.S., 1971. Prin. Union Sch. Corp., Modoc, Ind., 1971-72; tchr. social studies Rossville Sch. Corp., Ind., 1972-76; supt., prin. Kewanna Schs., Ind., 1977-79; prin. West Clark Community Sch., Sellersburg, Ind., 1979-84, North Daviess Sch., Elnora, Ind., 1984—. Mem. Nat. Assn. Secondary Sch. Prins., Ind. Secondary Sch. Adminstrs. Methodist. Avocations: fishing; golf. Home: Rural Route 1 Box 91 Odon IN 47562 Office: North Daviess Jr-Sr High Sch Rural Route 1 Elnora IN 47529

PEARLMAN, ALAN LEE, neurologist, neurobiologist; b. Des Moines, June 30, 1936. A.B., State U. Iowa, 1958; M.D., Washington U., 1961. Diplomate Am. Bd. Psychiatry and Neurology. Intern, Barnes Hosp., St. Louis, 1961-62; resident Mass. Gen. Hosp., Boston, 1964-67; asst. prof., then assoc. prof. Washington U. Sch. Medicine, St. Louis, 1969-78, prof. neurobiology and cell biology, 1979—; cons. NIH, Bethesda, Md., 1984—. Editor: (with R.C. Collins) Neurological Pathophysiology, 1984. Served as surgeon USPHS, 1962-64. Mem. Soc. Neurosci., Am. Acad. Neurology, Am. Neurol. Assn. Office: Washington U Sch Medicine 4566 Scott Ave Saint Louis MO 63110

PEARLMAN, JERRY KENT, electronics company executive. Chmn., pres., chief exec. officer Zenith Electronics corp., Glenview, Ill., also dir. Office: Zenith Electronics Corp 1000 N Milwaukee Ave Glenview IL 60025*

PEARSON, DENNIS RALPH, printing company executive; b. Hamilton, Ohio, Mar. 10, 1946; s. Ralph Leslie and Mildred Barbara (Schlenk) P.; m. Audrey Jane Swenson, Dec. 11, 1976; children—Dennis Ryan, David Lowe. B.S., Ohio U., 1968. Western dist. mgr. Harris Corp., Chgo., 1970-74; nat. sales mgr. Butler Automatic Inc., Canton, Mass., 1974-79; nat. sales and mktg. mgr. Bowers Printing Inks Coatings and Resins div. PPG Industries Inc., Chgo., 1979-85; v.p. sales and mktg. Metroweb Corp., 1985—. Deacon, Northminster Presbyn. Ch., 1983-86. Mem. Printing Industries Am. Republican. Office: PO Box 7073 Evanston IL 60204

PEARSON, JAMES EUGENE, art educator, artist; b. Woodstock, Ill., Dec. 12, 1939; s. John Clarence and Arline (Harrison) P. B.S. in Edn., No. Ill. U., 1961, M.S. in Edn., 1962, M.F.A., 1964. Tchr., Woodstock High Sch., 1961—; instr. art McHenry County Coll., Crystal Lake, Ill., 1970—; dir. art WIVS Radio, Crystal Lake, 1970—, WXRD radio, Woodstock, Ill., 1974—; editor art The Rectangle Jour., DeKalb, Ill., 1970—. One man shows include No. Ill. U., DeKalb, 1962, Elgin Acad., Ill., 1966; exhibited in group shows at Chgo. Artists Exhbn., 1958, U. Ill., Urbana, 1961, 69, Fine Arts Festival, Chgo., 1963, XXI Am. Drawing Biennial, Norfolk, Va., 1965, Miss. River Craft Show, Memphis, 1965, 18th, 20th N. Miss. Valley Artists exhbns., Springfield, Ill., 1965, 67, 1st, 2d ann. exhbns. Ricks Coll., Rexburg, Idaho, 1965, 67, 2d Salon Internat. de Charleroi, Palace Fine Arts, Charleroi, Belgium, 1969, 5th Internat. Grand Prize Painting and Etching, Monte Carlo, Monaco, 1969, 2d, 3d ann. McHenry County Coll. Art Fair, Crystal Lake, 1970, 71, 29th Ill. Invitational Exhbn., Springfield, 1971, others; represented in permanent collections No. Ill. U., DeKalb, Palais des Beuvx Arts, Charleroi, Belgium, pvt. collections. Mem. regional adv. com. Scholastic Art Award sect. Scholastic mag., 1964—. Recipient William Boyd Andrews best show award McHenry County Art Fair, 1961; 1st place Town and Country Art Exhibitors, 1961, 64; purchase award oil Waukegan News-Sun newspaper, 1969; Taft campus purchase prize No. Ill. U., 1969; 1st place sculpture award McHenry County Coll., 1970, 71; Outstanding Young Educator award Woodstock Jr. C. of C., 1968. Fellow Royal Soc. Arts, Mfgs. and Commerce (Eng.); mem. Centro Studl E Scambl Internezionall (Rome, Italy), Coll. Art Assn., Ill. Art Edn. Assn., Ill. Craftsmen's Council, Ill. Edn. Assn., Audubon Soc., Am. Fedn. Arts, SAR, Internat. Platform Assn., Kappa Pi, Phi Delta Kappa. Home: 5117 Barnard Mill Rd Ringwood IL 60072 Office: 501 W South St Woodstock IL 60098

PEARSON, JOHN EDGAR, insurance company executive; b. Mpls., Jan. 17, 1927; s. Edgar Clarence and Viola Esther (Quist) P.; m. Sharon M. Nessler, Nov., 1950; children—Cynthia Lynn, Thomas Calvin. Student Gustavus Adolphus Coll., St. Peter, Minn., 1944-45, Northwestern U., 1945-46; B.B.A., U. Minn., 1948. Salesman, 3M Co., Mpls., 1948-49, Marsh & McLennan, Seattle, 1951-53; salesman Northwestern Nat. Life Ins. Co., Mpls., 1953-62, v.p., 1962-73, pres., 1973-81, chmn., chief exec. officer, dir., 1981—; chmn. bd. dirs. N. Atlantic Life Ins., Jerico, N.Y., 1979—, Northern Life Ins. Co., Seattle, 1977—; dir. Norwest Bank, Mpls., Northern States Power Co., Mpls., Bd. dirs. Minn. Bus. Partnership, Mpls., 1977—, United Way Mpls. Area, 1979—, Mpls. Soc. Fine Arts, 1980—; bd. dirs. Greater Mpls. Met. Housing Corp., 1980—, pres., 1982-84. Mem. Health Ins. Assn. Am. (bd. dirs., chmn. 1983-84), Am. Council Life Ins. Ins. (bd. dirs.), Life and Health Ins. Med. Research Fund (bd. dirs., pres. 1983—), Inst. Fedn. Minn. (bd. dirs., chmn., 1981-83), Minn. Ins. Info. Ctr. (bd. dirs., vice chmn. 1981—). Clubs: Mpls. (pres. 1984—), Minikahda. Avocations: golf, skiing. Office: Northwestern Nat Life Ins Co 20 Washington Ave S Minneapolis MN 55440

PEARSON, JOHN KING, lawyer; b. St. Paul, Nov. 15, 1945; s. John S. Pearson and Jacqueline H. (Anderson) Pearson Purkey; m. Sue M. Stordahl, June 22, 1968; children—Linnea H., Kaaren M. B.A. in Germany and History, U. Wis., 1968; student Ludwig Albert U., Freiberg, Fed. Republic Germany, 1965-66; J.D., Hastings Coll. Law, 1973. Bar: Kans. 1974, Calif., 1974, U.S. Supreme Ct., 1980, U.S. Ct. Appeals (9th and 10th cirs.) 1974, U.S. Dist. Ct. (no. dist.) Calif. 1982, U.S. Dist. Ct. (cen. dist.) Calif. 1982, U.S. Dist. Ct. Kans. 1974. Asst. U.S. trustee Dept. Justice, Wichita, Kans., 1979-82; mng. atty. McDowell, Rice & Smith, Chartered, Wichita, 1982—; adj. prof. law Wichita State U., 1978-84. Author/editor: Kansas Bankruptcy Handbook, 1982; A Bank's Rights in Bankruptcy, 1982. Recipient Spl. Achievement award U.S. Dept. Justice, Wichita, 1980. Home: 355 N Quentin Wichita KS 67208 Office: McDowell Rice & Smith Chartered 221 N Main St PO Box 3446 Wichita KS 67201

PEARSON, LINLEY E., state attorney general; b. Long Beach, Calif., Apr. 18, 1946. B.A., The Citadel, 1966; M.B.A., Butler U., 1970; J.D., Ind. U., 1970. Bar: Ind. 1970, U.S. Dist. Ct. (so. dist.) Ind. 1970, U.S. Ct. Appeals (7th cir.) 1977. Law clk. judge Richard Givan Ind. Supreme Ct., 1969-70; pros. atty., Clinton County, 1971-81; atty. gen. State of Ind., Indpls., 1981—; ptnr. Campbell, Hardesty, Pearson & Douglas, Frankfort, Ind., 1971-81. Mem. Ind. Bar Assn., Clinton County Bar Assn. (pres. 1973). Office: Office Atty Gen 219 State House Indianapolis IN 46204*

PEARSON, LONNIE JAMES, personnel administrator; b. Shaw, Miss., June 16, 1947; s. Lonnie James and Alice Mae (Stanford) P.; m. Ra-Nelle Lynn Talley, Feb. 19, 1972; children—Rashad F., Alicia J. B.S.B.A. in Acctg., Roosevelt U., 1977. Reconciler, No. Trust Bank, Chgo., 1970-72, sr. reconciler, 1973-74, asst. supr., 1974-75, sect. mgr., 1975-78; personnel adminstr., affirmative action coordinator Lincoln Bank, Ft. Wayne, Ind., 1979—. Mem. adv. com. sr. citizens Ft. Wayne Urban League, 1982—; mem. Ft. Wayne Affirmative Action Assn., 1980—; mem. Ft. Wayne Handicapped Adv. Council, 1981—; lectr. Opportunities Industrialization Ctr., 1980—. Served to sgt. USMC, 1966-70. Recipient cert. appreciation Black Profl. Women's Club, 1981, 82, 83. Mem. Am. Soc. Personnel Adminstrn., Am. Mgmt. Assn., Am. Inst. Banking, Am. Bankers Assn., Ind. Bankers Assn., NAACP (life, Pres. award 1982, chmn. labor and industry sect. 1980—, 3d v.p. 1982-83, youth advisor 1982-83), Black Democratic Forum. Lutheran. Lodge: Masons. Office: 116 E Berry St Fort Wayne IN 46802

PEARSON, LOUISE MARY, manufacturing company executive; b. Inverness, Scotland, Dec. 14, 1919 (parents Am. citizens); d. Louis Houston and Jessie M. (McKenzie) Lenox; grad. high sch.; m. Nels Kenneth Pearson, June 28, 1941; children—Lorine Pearson Walters, Karla. Dir. Wauconda Tool & Engring. Co., Inc., Algonquin, Ill., 1950-80; reporter Oak Leaflet, Crystal Lake, Ill., 1944-47, Sidelights, Wilmette, Ill., 1969-72, 79-82. Active Girl Scouts U.S.A., 1955-65. Recipient award for appreciation work with Girl Scouts, 1965. Clubs: Antique Automobile of Am. (Hershey, Pa.); Veteran Motor Car (Boston); Classic Car of Am. (Madison, N.J.). Home: 125 Dole Ave Crystal Lake IL 60014

PEARSON, NELS KENNETH, manufacturing executive; b. Algonquin, Ill., May 2, 1918; s. Nels Pehr and Anna (Fyre) P.; student pub. schs.; m. Louise Mary Houston Lenox, June 28, 1941; children—Lorine Marie Pearson Walters, Karla Jean. Assembler, Oak Mfg. Co., Crystal Lake, Ill., 1936-38, machine operator, assembly line foreman, 1938-43, apprentice tool and die maker, 1946-50; co-founder, pres. Wauconda Tool & Engring. Co., Inc., Algonquin, 1950—; co-founder, treas. Kenmode Tool & Engring. Co., Inc., Algonquin, 1960-72. Mem. McHenry County Edn. and Tng. Com., 1961—, treas., 1961—. Served with AUS, 1943-46. Mem. Am. Soc. Tool and Mfg. Engrs. Clubs: Moose, Antique Auto, Classic Car, Vet. Motor Car, Horseless Carriage. Home: 125 Dole Ave Crystal Lake IL 60014 Office: Huntley Rd Algonquin IL 60102

PEARSON, NORMAN, town planning consultant, author; b. Stanley, County Durham, Eng., Oct. 24, 1928; s. Joseph and Mary (Pearson) P.; came to Can., 1954; B.A. with honors in Town and Country Planning, U. Durham (Eng.), 1951; Ph.D. in Land Economy, Internat. Inst. Advanced Studies, 1979; M.B.A., Pacific Western U., Colo., 1980, D.B.A., 1982; m. Gerda Maria Josefine Riedl, July 25, 1972. Cons. to Stanley Urban Dist. Council, U.K., 1946-47; planning asst. Accrington Town Plan and Bedford County Planning Survey, U. Durham Planning Team, 1947-49; planning asst. to Allen and Mattocks, cons. planners and landscape designers, Newcastle upon Tyne, U.K., 1949-51; adminstrv. asst. Scottish Div., Nat. Coal Bd., Scotland, 1951-52; planning asst. London County Council, U.K., 1953-54; planner Central Mortgage and Housing Corp., Ottawa, Ont., Can., 1954-55; planning analyst City of Toronto Planning Bd., 1955-56; dir. of planning Hamilton Wentworth Planning Area Bd., Hamilton, Ont., Can., 1956-59; dir. planning for Burlington (Ont.) and Suburban Area Planning Bd., 1959-62, also commr. planning, 1959-62; pres. Tanfield Enterprises Ltd., London, Ont., Can., 1962—, Norman Pearson & Assocs. Ltd., Can., 1962—; cons. in planning, 1962—; life mem. U.S. Com. for Monetary Research and Edn., 1976—; spl. lectr. in planning McMaster U., Hamilton, 1956-64, Waterloo (Ont.) Luth. U., 1961-63; asst. prof. geography and planning U. Waterloo (Ont.), 1963-67; assoc. prof. geography U. Guelph (Ont.), 1967-72; prof. polit. sci. U. Western Ont., London, 1972-77; mem. Social Scis., Econ. and Legal Aspects Com. of Research Adv. Bd. Internat. Joint Commn., 1972-76; cons. to City of Waterloo, 1973-76, Province of Ont., 1969-70; adviser to Georgian Bay Regional Devel. Council, 1968-72; real estate appraiser, province of Ont., 1976—; pres., chmn. bd. govs. Pacific Western U., Canada, 1983-84. Pres. Unitarian Ch. of Hamilton, 1960-61. Served with RAF, 1951-53. Knight of Grace, Sovereign Order St. John of Jerusalem. Fellow Royal Town Planning Inst. (Bronze medal award 1957), Royal Econ. Soc.; mem. Internat. Soc. City and Regional Planners, Am., Canadian insts. planners, Canadian Polit. Sci. Assn. L'Association Internationale des Ingenieurs et des Docteurs ès Sciences Appliquées à l'Industrie. Clubs: Masons, Empire; Ontario; University (London). Author: (with others) An Inventory of Joint Programmes and Agreements Affecting Canada's Renewable Resources, 1964. Editor, co-author (with others) Regional and Resource Planning in Canada, 1963, rev. edit., 1970; editor (with others) The Pollution Reader, 1968. Contbr. numerous articles on town planning to profl. jours. and chpts. in field to books. Office: PO Box 5362 Station A London ON N6A 4L6 Canada

PEARSON, PHILLIP THEODORE, veterinarian, educational administrator, orthopedic surgeon; b. Story County, Iowa, Nov. 21, 1932; s. Theodore B. and Hazel C. (Christenson) P.; m. Mary Jane Barlow, Aug. 28, 1954; children—Jane Catherine, Bryan Theodore, Todd Wallace, Julie Ann. D.V.M., Iowa State U., 1956, Ph.D., 1962. Diplomate Am. Coll. Vet. Surgeons. Intern, Angell Meml. Animal Hosp., Boston, 1956-57; instr. vet. medicine and surgery Iowa State U., Ames, 1957-60, asst. prof., 1960-63, assoc. prof., 1963-64, prof. vet. clin. scis. and biomed. engring., 1965-72, chmn. Small Animal Clinic, 1967-72, dean Coll. Vet. Medicine, dir. Vet. Med. Research Inst., prof. vet. clin. scis., 1972—; prof. vet. medicine and surgery, assoc. clin. dir. Sch. Vet. Medicine, U. Mo., Columbia, 1964-65; v.p. Iowa State U. Meml. Union, Ames, 1970-80; pres. council deans Assn. Am. Vet. Med. Colls., Washington, 1978-79; chmn. bd. regents Am. Coll. Vet. Surgeons, Chgo., 1978-79. Contbr. sci. papers to profl. jours. Bd. dirs. Lutheran Student Assn., Ames, 1968-70; mem. Mayor's Sr. Citizen's Com., Ames, 1974-78; pres. Community Ctr., Ames, 1977-79, Bethesda Lutheran Ch., Ames, 1982-83. Mem. AVMA, Iowa Vet. Med. Assn., Am. Assn. Vet. Clinicians, Phi Zeta (pres. 1960), Alpha Zeta, Gamma Sigma Delta, Phi Kappa Phi, Sigma Xi. Lodge: Ames Kiwanis (pres. 1970-71). Home: 1610 Maxwell Ave Ames IA 50010 Office: Iowa State U Coll Vet Medicine Ames IA 50011

PEARSON, SAMUEL CAMPBELL, university administrator; b. Dallas, Dec. 10, 1931; s. Samuel Campbell and George Edna (Fetters) P.; m. Mary Alice Clay, Oct. 15, 1955; children—William Clay, John Andrew. A.B., Tex. Christian U., 1951; D.B., U. Chgo., 1953, A.M., 1960, Ph.D., 1964. Adminstrv. asst. to dean Disciples Divinity House, U. Chgo., 1956-60; acting asst. prof. social scis. Lynchburg Coll., Va., 1961-62; assoc. prof. history St. Paul's Coll., Lawrenceville, Va., 1962-64; asst. prof. history So. Ill. U., Edwardsville, 1964-69, assoc. prof., 1969-74, prof. hist. studies, 1974—; chmn. dept. hist. studies, 1972-77, 1981-83, dean Sch. Social Scis., 1983—; vis. prof. history and theology Benedictine Coll., Atchison, Kans., 1968-69; lectr. to profl. confs. Contbr. articles to profl. jours. Pres. bd. dirs. Joint Community Ministries Inc., St. Louis, 1984-85. Served to lt. USNR, 1954-56. Post-doctoral research U. London, 1970-71; NEH grantee Yale U., 1976. Mem. Am. Hist. Assn., Am. Soc. Ch. History, Am. Acad. Religion, Orgn. Am. Historians. Mem. Disciples of Christ. Home: 443 Westgate Ave Saint Louis MO 63130 Office: Office of the Dean Sch of Social Scis So Ill U Edwardsville IL 62026

PEARSON, VERA MAE, business educator; b. McCune, Kans., Feb. 2, 1927; d. Charlie Lee and Mattie Mae (Guy) Westervelt; m. Richard V. Pearson, Oct. 30, 1948. Assoc. degree LaBette Community Coll., 1960; B.S. in Bus. Edn., Pittsburg State U., 1962, M.S. in Bus. Edn., 1964; postdoctoral Kansas State U. Sec. Bill Dearth, Inc., Parsons, Kans., 1958-61; tchr. High Sch., Parsons, 1962-64, Community Coll., Parsons, 1964—; mem. adv. council, Parsons, 1980—. Mem. Humane Soc., Parsons, 1980—. Mem. NEA, Kans. NEA, Kansas Bus. Edn. Assn., Nat. Bus. Edn. Assn., Kappa Delta Gamma. Methodist. Advocations: reading; collecting collectibles. Office: LaBette Community Coll 200 S 14th St Parsons KS 67357

PEASE, DONALD JAMES, congressman; b. Toledo, Sept. 26, 1931; s. Russell Everett and Helen Mary (Mullen) P.; B.S. in Journalism, Ohio U., Athens, 1953, M.A. in Govt., 1955; Fulbright scholar Kings Coll., U. Durham, (Eng.), 1954-55; m. Jeanne Camille Wendt, Aug. 29, 1953; 1 dau., Jennifer. Mem. Ohio Senate, 1965-66; mem. Ohio Ho. of Reps., 1969-74; mem. Ohio Senate, 1975-76; mem. 95th-97th Congresses from Ohio. Chmn., Oberlin Pub. Utilities Commn., 1960-61; mem. Oberlin City Council, 1961-63. Served with U.S. Army, 1955-57. Home: 140 Elm St Oberlin OH 44074

PEASE, EDWARD ALLAN, lawyer, state senator; b. Terre Haute, Ind., May 22, 1951; s. Robert Richard and Joanna Rose (Pilant) P.; A.B. with distinction (Wendell Willkie scholar), Ind. U., Bloomington, 1973, J.D. cum laude, Indpls., 1977; postgrad. Memphis State U., 1975-76, Ind. State U., 1978—. Gen. law clk. appellate and contracts div. Office Ind. Atty. Gen., Indpls., 1974-75; nat. dir. alumni affairs Pi Kappa Alpha Frat., Memphis, 1975-76; admitted to Ind. bar, 1977; partner firm Thomas, Thomas & Pease, Brazil, Ind., 1977-84; of counsel firm Thomas & Thomas, Brazil, 1984—; asst. to pres. for legal affairs Ind. State U., Terre Haute, 1984—; mem. Ind. Senate, 1980—, chmn. Judiciary Com.; mem. adv. bd. 1st Bank & Trust Co. Clay County. Bd. dirs. Brazil-Clay County YMCA, Ind. Asbury Towers, Greencastle; lay leader 1st United Meth. Ch., Brazil; mem. exec. bd. Wabash Valley council Boy Scouts Am., 1972—, v.p., 1977-84, pres., 1984—, mem. nat. Order of Arrow com., 1984—. Recipient Silver Beaver award Boy Scouts Am., 1975. Mem. Ind. Bar Assn., Phi Beta Kappa. Republican. Club: Columbia (Indpls.). Office: PO Box 194 Brazil IN 47834

PEAVY, HOMER LOUIS, JR., real estate executive, accountant; b. Okmulgee, Okla., Sept. 4, 1924; s. Homer Louis and Hattie Lee (Walker) P.; children—Homer Martin, Daryl Mark. Student Kent State U., 1944-49; grad. Hammel-Actual Coll., 1962. Sales supr. Kirby Sales, Akron, Ohio, 1948-49; sales mgr. Williams-Kirby Co., Detroit, 1949-50; area distributor Peavy-Kirby Co., Phila., 1953-54; salesman James L. Peavy Realty Co., Akron, 1954-65; owner Homer Louis Peavy, Jr., Real Estate Broker, Akron, 1965—; pvt. practice acctg., Akron, 1962—; fin. aid officer Buckeye Coll., Akron, 1982. Bd. dirs. Internat. Elvis Gold Soc., 1978—; charter mem. Statue of Liberty-Ellis Island Found., 1984. Recipient Am. Film Inst. Cert. Recognition, 1982, Award of Merit cert. World of Poetry 10th ann. contest, 1985, Golden Poet award World of Poetry, 1985. Mem. Ohioana Library Assn., Internat. Black Writers Conf., Acad. Am. Poets, Manuscript Club Akron, Kent State U. Alumni Assn. Democrat. Author: Watt Watts, 1969; poetry: Magic of the Muse, 1978, P.S. I Love You, 1982; contbr. poetry to Am. Poetry Anthology, 1983, New Worlds Unlimited, 1984, Treasures of the Precious Moments, 1985, Our World's Most Cherished Poems, 1985; songs: Sh..Sh, Sheree, Sheree, 1976, In Akron O, 1979; teleplay: Revenge, 1980. Home and Office: 1160 Cadillac Blvd Akron OH 44320

PECK, THERESA M., hospital administrator; b. Milw., Oct. 14, 1934. R.N., St. Mary's Hosp., Milw., 1955; B.S. in Nursing, Marillac Coll., 1959; M.B.A., George Washington U., 1969. Adminstr. Seton Home Health Services, London, Ky., 1971-73, St. Joseph Hosp., Alton, Ill., 1973, St. Mary's Med. Center, Evansville, Ind., 1974-78; pres. St. Vincent Hosp. and Health Care Center, Inc., Indpls., 1978—; dir. Alliance of Indpls. Hosps., Am. Fletcher Nat. Bank, Indpls., Am. Fletcher Corp., Indpls., St. Thomas Hosp., Nashville, St. Vincent Stress Center, Indpls., Meridian Insurance, Indpls., Daughters of Charity Hosp. Info. Systems, Evansville; pres. Ind. Cath. Hosps., Indpls., 1982—; charter mem. Major Catholic Teaching Hosps., Crestwood, Mo., 1983—. Author: Wellness: The Revolution in Health Care, 1983. Recipient Sagamore of the Wabash award Gov. Ind., 1981. Mem. Am. Coll. Hosp. Adminstrs., Assn. Univ. Programs in Health Adminstrn., George Washington U. Alumni Assn., Ind. State C. of C. Avocations: skiing; tennis; swimming; reading. Home: 2141 Dugan Dr Indianapolis IN 46240

PECK, WILLIAM HENRY, museum curator, art historian, archaeologist, author, lecturer; b. Savannah, Ga., Oct. 2, 1932; s. William Henry Peck and Mildred (Bass) Peck Tuten; m. Ann Amelia Keller, Feb. 2, 1957 (dec. 1965); children—Alice Ann, Sarah Louise; m. Elsie Holmes, July 7, 1967; 1 child, William Henry IV. Student Ohio State U., 1950-53; B.F.A., Wayne State U., 1960, M.A., 1961. Jr. curator Detroit Inst. Arts, 1960-62, asst. curator, 1962-64, assoc. curator, 1964-68, curator ancient art, 1968—, acting chief curator, 1984—; lectr. art history Cranbrook Acad. Art, Bloomfield Hills, Mich., 1963-65; vis. lectr. U. Mich., Ann Arbor, 1970; adj. prof. art history Wayne State U., Detroit, 1966—; excavations in Egypt, Mendes, 1964-66, Precinct of Mut, Karnak, 1978—. Author: Drawings from Ancient Egypt, 1978; co-author: Ancient Egypt: Discovering its Splendors, 1978; Mummies, Diseases and Ancient Cultures, 1980; also articles. Served with U.S. Army, 1953-55. Ford Motor Co. travel grantee, 1962; Am. Research Ctr. Egypt fellow, 1971; Smithsonian Instn. travel grantee, 1975. Mem. Archaeol. Inst. Am., Am. Research Ctr. Egypt, Internat. Assn. Egyptologists, Soc. Study Egyptian Antiquities, Am. Assn. Mus. Democrat. Episcopalian. Avocations: origami; performance of early music. Office: Detroit Inst Arts 5200 Woodward Ave Detroit MI 48202

PECKENPAUGH, ROBERT EARL, investment adviser; b. Potomac, Ill., July 17, 1926; s. Hilery and Zella (Stodgel) P.; m. Margaret J. Dixon, Sept. 21, 1945; children—Nancy Lynn, Carol Sue, David Robert, Daniel Mark, Jeanne Beth, Douglas John. Student, Ind. U., 1946-47; B.S., Northwestern U., 1949, M.B.A. with distinction, 1952. Chartered fin. analyst. with First Nat. Bank Chgo., 1949-52; pres. Security Suprs., Inc., Chgo., 1952-73; v.p. Chgo. Title & Trust Co., 1973-77; pres. Hotchkiss & Peckenpaugh, Inc., Chgo., 1977-84; investment mgr. Morgan Stanley Asset Mgmt. Inc., 1984—. Chmn., Evang. Covenant Ch. of Hinsdale, 1981-84. Served with USNR, 1944-46. Mem. Investment Analyst Soc. Chgo. (pres. 1963-64). Clubs: Chgo., Mid-Day, Chgo. Athletic, Econ., Hinsdale Golf. Home: 429 S County Line Rd Hinsdale IL 60521 Office: Morgan Stanley Asset Mgmt Inc 115 S LaSalle St Chicago IL 60603

PECKHAM, ROBERT WILSON, English educator; b. Detroit, Nov. 8, 1932; s. Joseph Leroy and Othello Josephine (King) P.; m. Dolores Mary Wierzbicki, June 27, 1969; 1 child, John. A.B., Sacred Heart Sem., 1954; M.A., U. Detroit, 1958; Ph.D., U. Notre Dame, 1965. Instr. Sacred Heart Sem., Detroit, 1963-66, asst. prof. 1966-75, assoc. prof. 1975-79, prof., 1979—. Mem. Nat. Council Tchrs. English, MLA. Roman Catholic. Avocation: choral music. Office: Sacred Heart Sem 2701 Chicago Blvd Detroit MI 48206

PECORARO, VINCENT LOUIS, chemistry educator; b. Freeport, N.Y., Aug. 31, 1956; s. Jerome Dominic and Gloria (Fragnito) P. B.S., UCLA, 1977; Ph.D., U. Calif.-Berkeley, 1981. Lab. technician UCLA, 1976-77; research asst. U. Calif.-Berkeley, 1977-81, teaching assoc., 1977-79; NIH fellow U. Wis.-Madison, 1981-84; asst. prof. chemistry U. Mich., Ann Arbor, 1984—. Horace Rackham fellow, 1985. Mem. AAAS, Am. Chem. Soc., N.Y. Acad. Scis., Am. Assn. Biol. Chemists, Am. Film Inst., Sigma Xi, Phi Eta Sigma. Roman Catholic. Contbr. articles to profl. jours. Home: 3625 Greenbrier Ave #161C Ann Arbor MI 48105 Office: U Mich Ann Arbor MI 48109

PECUCH, RAMON, investment company executive; b. Shoendorf, Germany, Jan. 24, 1946; came to U.S., 1950; s. Paul and Kataryna (Malecki) P.; m. Joanne Gangale, Aug. 16, 1969; 1 child, Alexsis. A.A., Cuyahoga Community Coll., 1968; B.A., Case Western Res. U., 1970; M.B.A., So. Ill. U., 1978. Chartered fin. analyst. Instr. St. Joseph High Sch., Cleve., 1970-71; trust officer Nat. City Bank, Cleve., 1977-80; v.p. Roulston & Co., Cleve., 1980—; dir. Cosmicoat, Wooster, Ohio. Pres. Millstone Home Assn., Munson, Ohio, 1982—; mem. Greater Cleve. Growth Assn., 1984—. Served to lt. comdr. USN, 1971-77. Mem. Inst. Chartered Fin. Analysts, Res. Officers Assn. Greek Catholic.

PEDDICORD, ROLAND DALE, lawyer; b. Van Meter, Iowa, Mar. 29, 1936; s. Clifford Elwood and Juanitas Irene (Brittain) P.; children—Erin Sue, Robert Sean. B.S. in Bus. Adminstrn., Drake U., 1961, J.D., 1962. Bar: Iowa 1962. Asst. atty. gen. State of Iowa, 1962-63; assoc. Steward, Crouch & Hopkins, Des Moines, 1962-65; ptnr. Peddicord & Wharton, Des Moines, 1965—; lectr. in law Drake U., 1962-78; lectr. law Coll. Osteo. Medicine, Des Moines, 1965-72. Nat. bd. dirs., mem. nat. council YMCAs of Am.; bd. dirs., chmn., mem. exec. com. Mid-West field com. YMCAs U.S.; bd. dirs. Greater Des Moines YMCA, 1968—, chmn. fin. devel. com. bd. dirs., 1976-85, vice chmn. bd., 1982—, chmn. strategic planning com., 1984—; mem. fin. com. nat. bd. YMCAs,

1982—, chmn. com. on membership standards, 1984— Served with USMC, 1954-57. Mem. ABA, Iowa State Bar Assn., Polk County Bar Assn., Assn. Trial Lawyers Am., Iowa Trial Lawyers Assn., Iowa Acad. Trial Lawyers, Iowa Workers' Compensation Attys., Iowa Def. Counsel Assn., Def. Research Inst., Lawyer and Pilots Bar Assn., Aircraft Owners and Pilots Assn., Order of Coif, Delta Sigma Chi, Omicron Delta Kappa, Beta Gamma Sigma. Republican. Methodist. Clubs: Embassy, Pioneer Gun, Chaine Des Rotisseurs (vice-chancelier Argentier du Bailliage De Des Moines); Bulldog (Drake U.) (chmn., mem. adv. bd. 1983—). Editor and chief Drake Law Rev., 1961-62. Office: 300 Fleming Bldg Des Moines IA 50309

PEDEAUX, WILLIAM WALLACE, air force officer, pilot; b. New Orleans, Nov. 26, 1953; s. Numa Louis and Barbara Beth (Smith) P.; m. Christine Marie Smith, July 2, 1982; 1 child, Christopher Brendan. B.S., La. State U., 1975; M.A. in Personnel Mgmt., Central Mich. U., 1983. Commd. 2d lt. U.S. Air Force, 1976, advanced through grades to capt., 1979; B-52 co-pilot, Minot AFB, 1977-81, comdr. 91st CSG Hdqrs. Squadron, 1979, B-52 aircraft comdr., 1981-84, B-52 instr. pilot, 1984, 5th bomb wing tactics officer, 1984—. Mem. Jr. Officers Council, 1977-84, v.p., 1979-80, pres., 1980-82; adviser Minot C. of C. Mil. Affairs Commn., 1979-83. Mem. Air Force Assn., Order Daedalians, Arnold Air Soc. (pres. 1974-75, alumni), Delta Tau Delta. Home: 520 5th Ave SW Minot ND 58701 Office: 5BMW/DONBT Minot AFB ND 58705

PEDERSEN, KEN, graphic arts company executive; b. Phelps, Wis., Aug. 15, 1911; s. Andrew and Marie (Olsen) P. Student U. Wis., 1929-30, Chgo. Acad. Art, 1936-37, Northwestern U., 1949-50. Salesman, Bielfeld Studio, Chgo., 1946-51; pres. Handelan & Pedersen, Chgo., 1968-83, chmn., 1983—. Served to sgt. USMC, 1942-45; PTO. Mem. Artists Guild Chgo. (treas. 1965-66). Clubs: Medinah Country, Tavern (Chgo.); Broken Sound Golf (Boca Raton, Fla.); Internat. Home: 260 E Chestnut St Chicago IL 60611 Office: Handelan & Pedersen 333 N Michigan Ave Suite 1005 Chicago IL 60601

PEDERSON, LEONARD SEVERIN, communications equipment manufacturing company official, accountant; b. Mpls., May 4, 1947; s. Bernt Severin and June Lenore (Hansen) P.; m. Emilie May Rumpf, Aug. 7, 1971; children—Leah June, Leonard Severin. B.S., Calif. Poly. State U., 1970; M.S.B.A., Boston U., 1976. C.P.A., Ill. Commd. 2d lt. U.S. Army, 1970, advanced through grades to capt., 1973; served in Vietnam 1971-72, Europe, 1973-76; resigned, 1977; supr. Kimble div. Owens-Ill. Corp., Chicago Heights, 1977-78; applications specialist GE Info. Systems Co., Oakbrook, Ill., 1978-79; mgr. GTE Communications Systems, Northlake, Ill., 1979—. Served to maj., insp. gen. USAR, 1977—. Leader, Elmhurst YMCA Youth Program, Ill., 1979—. Decorated Bronze Star. Mem. Am. Inst. C.P.A.s, Ill. Soc. C.P.A.s, Res. Officers Assn., Assn. U.S. Army, Mensa, Beta Gamma Sigma, Phi Theta Kappa. Republican. Lutheran. Avocations: racquetball; jogging; bridge; combat simulations. Home: 44 W LeMoyne Ave Lombard IL 60148 Office: GTE Communication Systems 400 N Wolf Rd Northlake IL 60164

PEDERSON, WAYNE DOUGLAS, college administrator; b. Kennedy, Minn., May 9, 1941; s. Harvey Norwood and Dorothy Marie (Turner) P.; m. Lynette Yvonne Prosser, Sept. 1, 1962; children—Tamra, Carey, Kristin. B.S., Concordia Coll., 1963. C.P.A., Minn. Tchr. Warren Pub. Schs., Minn., 1963-66; acct. Adrian Helgeson, Mpls., 1966-69; controller Augsburg Coll., Mpls., 1969-77, v.p. fin., 1977—. Mem. Am. Inst. C.P.A.s, Minn. Soc. C.P.A.s. Avocations: hunting; running; singing; old car restoration. Home: 9265 Annapolis Ln Maple Grove MN 55369 Office: Augsburg Coll 731 21st Ave S Minneapolis MN 55454

PEDICINI, LOUIS JAMES, manufacturing company executive; b. Detroit, June 29, 1926; s. Louis I. and Myra Ann (Bergan) P.; B.S.E.E., Wayne U., 1955; m. Ellen Sylvia Mulden, June 5, 1948; 1 son, Eric Louis. Dept. head Gen. Motors Corp., 1948-58; exec. v.p. Lester B. Knight & Assocs., Inc., Chgo., 1959-76; exec. v.p. ops. Pullman Trailmobile, Chgo., 1976-81; mng. dir. Ingersoll Engrs., Inc., Rockford, Ill., 1981-82; pres. George Fischer Foundry Systems, Inc., Holly, Mich., 1982—. Served with U.S. Army, 1944-46. Fellow Inst. Brit. Foundrymen; mem. Am. Foundrymen's Soc. (past dir.). Republican. Clubs: Skokie Country (Glencoe, Ill.); Plaza (Chgo.). Home: 405 Sheridan Rd Kenilworth IL 60043 Office: 407 Hadley St Holly MI 48442

PEDIGO, HOWARD KENNETH, engineer; b. Charleston, Ill., Aug. 5, 1931; s. Clarence and Cecil (Elliot) P.; B.S. in Civil Engring., Rose Poly. Inst., 1953; M.B.A., Ohio State U., 1963; m. Doris Dean Mullins, Mar. 21, 1954; children—Susan Kay, John Jay. Stress analyst Bendix Corp., South Bend, Ind., 1955-61; project engr. Wright Field, Dayton, Ohio, 1961-63; project mgr. TRW Corp., Cleve., 1963-64; exec. v.p. Universal Tank & Iron Co., Indpls., 1964-85; engr. Ind. Dept. Natural Resources, 1985—. Chmn., United Way Hendricks County (Ind.), 1973-75; bd. dirs. United Way Greater Indpls., 1975-77; bd. indsl. adviser Rose-Hulman Inst. Served to 1st lt. U.S. Army, 1953-55. Registered profl. engr., Ala., Ill., Ind., N.J., Ohio, Tenn., Wis. Mem. ASCE, Am. Water Works Assn. (steel tank com.), Steel Plate Fabricators Assn., Rose Tech. Alumni (class agt. 1971-73), Lambda Chi Alpha. Methodist. Lodge: Elks. Home: 633 Elm Dr Plainfield IN 46168 Office: 11221 Rockville Rd Indianapolis IN 46231

PEDOTO, GERALD JOSEPH, product acceptance specialist; b. Jersey City, Jan. 5, 1948; s. Salvatore Joseph and Rosalie (Benigno) P.; B.S., Bowling Green State U., 1970; M.B.A., U. Akron, 1976; m. Karen Sue Knutty, June 28, 1975; children—Deborah Louise, Donald Lee, Timothy Scott. Trainee indsl. engring. Timken Co., Canton, Ohio, 1970, asso. indsl. engr., 1972-73, supervisory candidate, 1973-74, foreman product inspection, 1974-75, supr. indirect labor, 1975-80, supr. heat treatment, 1980-82. Active United Way, YMCA fund drs. Served with U.S. Army, 1970-72; Korea. Decorated Army Commendation Medal; cert. mgr. Inst. Cert. Profl. Mgrs. Mem. Internat. Mgmt. Council, Nat. Mgmt. Assn., Assn. M.B.A. Execs., Am. Soc. for Quality Control, Alpha Tau Omega, Beta Gamma Sigma, Omicron Delta Kappa. Republican. Mem. United Ch. of Christ. Home: 3419 Cain St NW North Canton OH 44720 Office: Canton Gen Offices Timken Co 1835 Dueber Ave SW Canton OH 44706

PEDRO, JOAN DANIELS, educator, consultant, researcher; b. Green Bay, Wis., Oct. 18, 1935; d. Ray Leslie and Vivian Marion (Grandy) Daniels; m. David Kawiki Pedro, Dec. 27, 1957; children—David Kawiki, Danielle Joan. B.S., U. Wis.-Menomonie, 1957, M.S., 1959; M.S., U. Wis.-Madison, 1971; Ph.D., U. Iowa, 1978. Cert. counselor edn. Counselor Middleton High Sch., Wis., 1970-75; counselor, lectr. U. Iowa, Iowa City, 1975-78; researcher U. Wis.-Madison, 1978-80, prof., 1980-85; founder Nat. Forum for Women, Ill., 1980; adv. com. Sci. World, State of Wis., 1982—. Contbr. articles to profl. jours. Recipient Recogniton award Wis. Dept. Pub. Instrn., 1982. Mem. Am. Assn. Counseling and Devel., Am. Edn. Assn., Spl. Interest Group on Research on Women (paper reviewer 1983-84), Coll. Tchrs. of Retailing. Democrat. Unitarian. Avocation: gardening. Home: 5917 Old Middleton Rd Madison WI 53705

PEEBLES, HERBERT ELMER, science and mathematics educator; b. Buffalo, May 30, 1943; s. Elmer Alton and Gladys Mae (Murray) P.; m. Alice Goertz, Nov. 23, 1963; children—Brent H., Lisa Renee. B.S. in Math. and Edn., Goshen Coll., 1966; student Purdue U., 1967-68; M.A. in Math., U. Notre Dame, 1970; D.A. in Math., Idaho State U., 1973. Tchr. math. Goshen Community Schs., Ind., 1966-69; instr. math. U. Notre Dame, Ind., 1970-71; assoc. prof. math. St. Bonaventure U., N.Y., 1973-79; div. chairperson sci. and math. Lorain County Community Coll., Elyria, Ohio, 1979—; workshop leader Ctr. Occupational Research and Devel., Waco, Tex., 1983—; lectr., 1983—. Contbr. articles to profl. jours. Mem. Assn. Computing Machinery, Am. Mus. Natural Hist., Am. Math. Assn. Two Yr. Colls. Mennonite. Home: 33020 Leafy Mill Ln North Ridgeville OH 44039 Office: Lorain County Community Coll 1005 Abbe Rd Elyria OH 44036

PEECHATKA, WALTER NORMAN, conservation association executive; b. East Stroudsburg, Pa., Sept. 3, 1939; s. Walter Clinton and Lillian Mae (Post) P.; m. Bonnie L. Umholtz, Apr. 20, 1968; children—Troy, Trent. B.S., Pa. State U., 1961. Service forester Bur. Forestry, Prospect, Pa., 1964-67, asst. supr. coop. forest mgmt., 1967-69; program specialist Pa. State Conservation Commn., Harrisburg, 1969-71; dir. Bur. Soil and Water Conservation, Harrisburg, 1971-82; exec. v.p. Soil Conservation Soc. Am., Ankeny, Iowa, 1982—; pres. Assn. Soil Conservation Adminstrn. Officers, 1978; mem. exec. com. Nat. Conservation Tillage Info. Ctr., 1983-84. Served to capt. USAR, 1962-64. Mem. Soil Conservation Soc. Am. (presdl. citation 1983), Am. Soc. Assn. Execs. Lutheran. Office: Soil Conservation Soc Am 7515 NE Ankeny Rd Ankeny IA 50021

PEEK, TERRY JEAN, social worker; b. Alton, Ill., Nov. 29, 1948; s. Jean Eldon and Lorene Kathreen (Quirk) P.; m. Janet Louise Speer, June 27, 1970; children—Brian William, Tyler Joseph. B.A., So. Ill. U., 1971; M.S.W., St. Louis U., 1976. Cert. social worker. Program dir. Madison County Mental Health, Alton, Ill., 1976-81, coordinator services, 1981-82, exec. dir., 1982—; chief exec. officer Crisis Service Madison County, Alton, 1983—, Ednl. Therapy Ctr., East Alton, Ill., 1981—; adminstrv. cons. Mental Health Devel. Corp., Alton, 1981—. Mem. Exec. Roundtable, 1983. Mem. Nat. Assn. Social Workers, Assn. Labor Mgmt. Cons. on Alcoholism, Assn. Community Mental Health Agys. Roman Catholic. Club: Alton Woodriver Sportsmans (Godfrey). Lodge: K.C. Avocation: softball. Home: 5115 Williams Pl Godfrey IL 62035 Office: Madison County Mental Health Ctr Inc PO Box 1054 2615 Edwards Alton IL 62002

PEEL, GARY EVAN, lawyer; b. East St. Louis, Ill., Mar. 15, 1944; s. Stanley and Earlene (Starnes) P.; m. Deborah Jeanne Rodgers, June 2, 1967; children—David Stanley, Jennifer Elizabeth, Jeffrey Charles. B.A., So. Ill. U., 1966; J.D., U. Ark., 1968. Bar: Ill. 1968, U.S. Dist. Ct. (so. dist.) Ill. 1971, U.S. Ct. Appeals (7th cir.) 1974; U.S. Supreme Ct. 1975, Ariz. 1979, U.S. Ct. Appeals (11th cir.) 1980, Mo. 1981, U.S. Dist. Ct. (ea. dist.) Mo. 1982. Assoc., Reed, Armstrong, Gorman & Coffey, Edwardsville, Ill., 1969-74, Chapman & Chapman, Granite City, Ill., 1974-78, Lakin, Herndon & Peel, P.C., E. Alton, Ill., 1978-83; sole practice, Edwardsville, 1983—. Mem. ABA, Ill. State Bar Assn., Ariz. State Bar Assn., Mo. State Bar Assn., Madison County Bar Assn. (sec. 1972-73, v.p. 1982-83, pres. 1983-84), Ill. Trial Lawyers Assn., Assn. Trial Lawyers Am., Nat. Bd. Trial Advocacy (civil trial advocate). Club: Sunset Hills Country. Home: 532 Sunset St Edwardsville IL 62025 Office: 40 Edwardsville Profl Park Edwardsville IL 62025

PEELER, JED ALAN, research chemist, quality assurance manager; b. Chgo., Dec. 13, 1948; s. Harold Floyd and Magdalen Mary (Lutz) P. B.S. in Chemistry, U. Ill.-Chgo. Circle, 1971. Foreman, Daubert Chem. Co., Chgo., 1972-77; foreman prodn. dept. Teledyne Getz, Elk Grove Village, Ill., 1977-78, mgr. quality control, 1978-79, mgr. quality assurance, 1982-84; owner, mgr. Gen. Dental Products, Elk Grove Village, 1984—; cons. Teledyne Getz Co., 1984—. Fellow Acad. Dental Materials. Libertarian. Roman Catholic. Avocation: target shooting. Home: 316 N Elm St Mount Prospect IL 60056 Office: Gen Dental Products Inc 2281 Devon Ave Elk Grove Village IL 60007

PEELER, ROBERT REX, engineering company executive; b. Kokomo, Ind., Oct. 10, 1930; s. Floyd Allen and Zela (Fox) P.; m. Cynthia R. Reynolds, Aug. 20, 1950; children—Christopher, Bradley, Lisa, Susan. Student Ind. U.-Kokomo, 1948-50; DePauw U., 1950-51; B.S. in Civil Engring., Purdue U., 1953. Registered profl. engr., Ind., Fla. Engr., N.Y. Central R.R., Indpls., 1953; asst. plant engr. Haynes-Satellite, Kokomo, Ind., 1953-59; v.p. Illingworth Engring., Indpls., 1959-69, pres., 1969-84; pres. Peeler Engring., Indpls., 1984—; pres. Peeler Design & Engring, Tarpon Springs, Fla., 1984—. Mem. ASHRAE, Air Conditioning Contractors Am. (past v.p.), Assn. Energy Engrs. Republican. Lutheran. Clubs: Woodland Golf and Country, Optimist (past pres., dir. 1979—). Lodge: Masons. Avocations: Golf, tennis, swimming. Home: 3721 Bay Rd N Dr Indianapolis IN 46240 Office: Peeler Engring Inc 724 E Ohio St Indianapolis IN 46202

PEHLKE, ROBERT DONALD, metallurgical engineer, educator; b. Ferndale, Mich., Feb. 11, 1933; s. Robert William and Florence Jenny (McLaren), P.; m. Julie Anne Kehoe, June 2, 1956; children—Robert Donald, Elizabeth Anne, David Richard. B.S. in Engring., U. Mich., 1955; M.S., MIT, 1958, Sc.D. in Metallurgy, 1960; postgrad R.W. Tech. Inst., Aachen, Fed. Republic Germany, 1956-57. Asst. prof. metall. engring U. Mich., 1960-63, assoc. prof., 1963-68, prof., 1968—, chmn. dept., 1973-84. Author: Unit Processes of Extractive Metallurgy, 1973, (with others) Computer Simulation of Solidification, 1971. Editor BOF Steelmaking, 1975-76. Contbr. articles to profl. jours. Dir., pres. Amateur Hockey Assn., Ann Arbor, Mich., 1976-81. Fulbright fellow, 1956-57. Fellow Am. Soc. Metals (tech. bd. 1982-84), AIME (metall. soc., dir. iron and steel soc. 1976-79, Gold medal sci. 1976, Disting. life mem.); mem. Japan Soc. Iron and Steel, German Soc. Iron and Steel, Am. Foundrymen's Soc. Tau Beta Pi, Alpha Sigma Mu (internat. pres.) Clubs: Barton Hills, Golf and Outing. Avocations: ice hockey, golf, tennis, water skiing. Home: 9 Regent Dr Ann Arbor MI 48104 Office: U Mich Materials and Metall Engring 2300 Hayward St Room 2158 Dow Bldg Ann Arbor MI 48109

PEK, SUMER BELBEZ, medical educator; b. Ankara, Turkey, Aug. 17, 1933; came to U.S., 1960; s. Sevket and Mihrunnisa (Belbez) P. B.S., Am. Robert Coll., Istanbul, Turkey, 1953; M.D. magna cum laude, U. Munich, 1959. Diplomate Turkish Bd. Internal Medicine, Am. Bd. Internal Medicine, Am. Bd. Endocrinology. Intern, U. Munich Children's Hosp., 1960, Wayne County Gen. Hosp., Eloise, Mich., 1960-61; resident in internal medicine U. Mich. Hosp., Ann Arbor, 1961-64, USPHS fellow in endocrinology and metabolism, 1966-69; asst. prof. internal medicine U. Mich. Med. Sch., 1969-72, assoc. prof., 1973-79, prof., 1979—, mem. faculty cellular and molecular biology program, 1978—; assoc. prof. U. Ala. Sch. Medicine, Birmingham, 1972-73; hon. research fellow tumor immunology unit Imperial Cancer Research Fund, Univ. Coll. London, 1983; cons. VA Hosp., Ann Arbor, 1973—; mem. metabolism study sect. NIH, 1978, 81-82, 82—; mem. research com. Am. Diabetes Assn., 1984—. Mem. editorial bd. Diabetes, 1976-82; editor Endocrinology, 1979-82. Served to lt. M.C., Turkish Army, 1964-66. Recipient award Am. Diabetes Assn., 1969-70, 70-71. Fellow ACP; mem. Am. Fedn. Clin. Research (sect. council 1970-72, chpt. council 1970-72), Am. Diabetes Assn. (state bd. dirs. 1977-83, 84—), Endocrine Soc., Central Soc. Clin. Research. Home: 50 Dhu Varren Rd Ann Arbor MI 48105 Office: U Mich Med Ctr D4113 MPB Box 02 Ann Arbor MI 48109

PELANDA, RAYMOND VICTOR, college administrator; b. Alliance, Ohio, Feb. 25, 1928; s. Gaetano Mario and Adele (Perotti) P.; m. Katherine Rose, Apr. 25, 1953; children—Raymond Paul, Kevin Lee, Melanie Anne, Kenneth Blaine. B.S.Ed., Kent State U., 1952; M.B.A., 1962. High sch. tchr., Canton, Ohio, 1952-66; asst. dir. Trumbull campus Kent State U., Ohio, 1966-69, coordinator retail ops. regional campuses, 1969-70, coordinator bus. affairs regional campuses, 1970-75, bus. mgr. regional campuses, 1974-79; bus. and fin. officer, treas. Northeastern Ohio Univs. Coll. Medicine, Roostown, 1979—; asst. prof. acctg. Kent State U., 1967-79; discussion leader Inst. Civic Edn., Akron U., 1980-82. Mem. bd. edn. Cath. Diocese of Youngstown, Ohio, 1975-81, pres., 1979-81; mem. Ohio Bishops Adv. Com., 1981—. Served with USN, 1946-48. Mem. Phi Delta Kappa. Republican. Lodges: Rotary (treas. 1980-82) (Ravenna, Ohio); Elks. Avocations: outdoor sports; golf; swimming; jogging. Home: 915 24th St NE Canton OH 44714 Office: 4209 State Rt 44 Rootstown OH 44272

PELL, EDWARD WARDWELL, insurance company executive; b. N.Y.C., Oct. 31, 1938; s. Francis Livingston Jr. and Clarissa (Wardwell) P.; m. Pheruze Risilija, May 15, 1977; 1 son, Harry. B.A. summa cum laude, Princeton U., 1960; postgrad. in politics and econs. New Coll., Oxford U., 1960-62; J.D., NYU, 1973. Bar: N.Y. Polit. and security affairs adviser U.S. mission to UN, N.Y.C., 1962-70; law clk. Olshan, Grundman & Frome, N.Y.C., 1970-75; v.p., sec. Met. Property & Liability Ins. Co., Warwick, R.I., 1975-82; sr. v.p. personal lines Montgomery Ward Ins., Schaumburg, Ill., 1982—; adj. prof., lectr. in law and econs. Sch. Continuing Edn., NYU. Past mem. bd. dirs. New Eng. Polit. Action Com., Met. Polit. Action Com., R.I.; past founding bd. mem. West Greenwich Rescue Unit, R.I. Rhodes scholar Oxford U., Eng., 1960-62. Mem. ABA (adminstrv. law sect.), Am. Coll. Orgonomy (bd. dirs.), Phi Beta Kappa. Republican. Episcopalian. Office: Montgomery Ward Ins Co 200 N Martingale Rd Schaumburg IL 60194

PELL, MARY CHASE (CHASEY), civic worker; b. Binghamton, N.Y., May 23, 1915; d. Charles Orlando and Mary (Lane) Chase; m. Wilbur F. Pell, Jr., Sept. 14, 1940; children—Wilbur F., Charles Chase. B.A., Smith Coll., 1937. Case worker Binghamton State Hosp., 1937; sociology tchr. Charles W. Wilson Meml. Hosp., Johnson City, N.Y., 1938; commentator travel and industry, sta. WSVL, Shelbyville, Ind., 1962-67. Contbr. articles to pubs. Chmn. Ind. Fund Raising Com. for Smith Coll., Indpls., 1961; bd. dirs. Nat. Mental Health Assn., 1961-79, pres. 1976-77; pres. Ind. Mental Health Meml. Found., Indpls., 1964-65, Mental Health Assn. Ind., Indpls., 1962-63; commr. Ind. Mental Health Planning Commn., Indpls., 1964-65; mem. Central Ind. Task Force on Mental Health Planning, 1965-66; mem. Ind. Com. on Nursing, Indpls., 1965-66, Central Ind. Regional Mental Health Planning Com., 1968; chmn. Manpower Conf. on Mental Health, Washington, 1969; del. Ind. Republican Conv., 1951; vice chmn. Shelbyville Rep. Com., 1951; sec. Ind. Com. for Rockefeller, 1969-70; pres. Indpls. Smith Coll. Club, 1969-70; participant Nat. Health Forum of Nat. Health Council, N.Y.C., 1971; pres. Mental Health Assn. Ill., Springfield, 1975; mem. Gov.'s Commn. for Revision of Mental Health Code Ill., 1975-76; v.p. for N.Am., World Fedn. for Mental Health, 1977-79; bd. dirs. Vis. Nurse Assn. Evanston (Ill.), 1975, v.p. 1981-84, pres., 1984—; community mental health adviser Jr. League of Chgo., 1979-83; mem. Ill. Guardianship and Advocacy Commn., 1978—, chmn., 1981; mem. adv. com. to sect. on psychiatry and the law, Rush-Presbyn.-St. Luke's Med. Ctr., Chgo., 1978—; mem. home health adv. com. to Dept. Pub. Health, State of Ill., 1982—; pres. Mental Health Assn. Chgo., 1983-84; pres. Smith Coll. Alumnae of Chgo., 1984—; mem. Aux. of Evanston and Glenbrook Hosps.; pres. Ind. Lawyers' Wives, Indpls., 1959-60; treas. Nat. Lawyers' Wives, 1961-62. Recipient Outstanding Citizen award Shelby County C. of C., 1959-60, Outstanding Vol. of Yr. award Indpls. Jr. League, 1962, Leadership award Mental Health Assn. Ind., 1971, Arts and Humanities award, Shelbyville Rotary Club, 1981; named One of Ten Most Newsworthy Women In Ind., Indpls. News, 1962, Disting. Leader in Vol. Mental Health Movement, Ill. Ho. of Reps., 1976, One of Ten Top Vols. of Yr., North Shore Mag., 1984, Miss. Col., 1976, Hon. Lt. Gov. Ala., 1980. Presbyterian. Clubs: Fortnightly; Garden, Jr. League, University Guild (Evanston). Home: 1427 Hinman Ave Evanston IL 60201

PELL, ROBERT ALEX, lawyer; b. Brazil, Ind., Jan. 27, 1955; s. John Ruh and Evelyn Vivian (Alsip) P. A.B., Ind. U., 1977; J.D., Ind. U.-Indpls., 1980. Bar: Fla. 1980, Ind. 1981, U.S. Dist. Ct. (so. dist.) Ind. 1981. Atty. E. T. Hunter, P.A., Hollywood, Fla., 1980; bailiff, law clk. Dade County Fla. Cir. Ct., Miami, 1981-82; sole practice, Brazil, Ind., 1982—; chief dep. pros. atty. Clay County Prosecutor, Brazil, 1982—; atty. Town of Harmony, Ind., 1983—; atty. Harrison Twp., Clay City, Ind., 1983—. Mem. Ind. State Bar Assn., State Bar Fla. Republican. Presbyterian. Clubs: Jackson Twp. Community Band (Brazil, Ind.), Ducks Unltd. Lodge: Elks. Office: 13 W National Ave Brazil IN 47834

PELL, WILBUR FRANK, JR., U.S. circuit judge; b. Shelbyville, Ind., Dec. 6, 1915; s. Wilbur Frank and Nelle (Dickerson) P.; A.B., Ind. U., 1937, LL.D. (hon.), 1981; LL.B. cum laude, Harvard U., 1940; LL.D., Yonsei U., Seoul, Korea, 1972, John Marshall Sch. Law, 1973; m. Mary Lane Chase, Sept. 14, 1940; children—Wilbur Frank III, Charles Chase. Admitted to Ind. bar, 1940; practice law, Shelbyville, 1940-42, 45-70; spl. agt. FBI, 1942-45; sr. partner Pell & Good, 1949-56, Pell & Matchett, 1956-70; judge 7th Circuit, U.S. Ct. Appeals, 1970—, now sr. judge; dep. atty. gen. Ind., 1953-55; dir., chmn. Shelby Nat. Bank, 1947-70. Bd. dirs. Shelbyville Community Chest, 1947-49, Shelby County Fair Assn., 1951-53; dir. Shelby County Tb Assn., 1948-70, pres., 1965-66; dist. chmn. Boy Scouts Am., 1956-57; mem. pres.'s council Nat. Coll. Edn., 1972—; dir. Westminster Found., Ind. U.; hon. dir. Korean Legal Center. Fellow Am. Coll. Probate Counsel, Am. Bar Found.; mem. ABA (Judge Edward R. Finch Law Day U.S.A. Speech award 1973, ho. of dels. 1962-63), Ind. (pres. 1962-63, chmn. ho. of dels. 1968-69), Fed., Ill., Shelby County (pres. 1957-58), 7th Fed. Circuit bar assns., Am. Judicature Soc., Am. Coun. Assn., Shelby County C. of C. (dir. 1947-49), Nat. Conf. Bar Presidents, Riley Meml. Assn., Ind. Soc. Chgo. (pres. 1978-79), Sagamore of Wabash, Blue Key, Kappa Sigma, Alpha Phi Omega, Theta Alpha Phi, Tau Kappa Alpha, Phi Alpha Delta (hon.). Republican. Presbyterian. (elder, deacon). Clubs: Chicago Rotary (dist. gov. 1952-53, internat. dir. 1959-61), Union League, Legal (pres. 1976-77), Law (pres. 1984-85) (Chgo.). Office: 219 S Dearborn St Room 2746 Chicago IL 60604

PELLERITO, PETER MICHAEL, university administrator; b. Detroit, May 13, 1945; s. Sam Joseph and Rosalie Ann (Palazzola) P.; m. Lisa Ann Brock; children—Sam Brock, Billie Ann. B.S., Calif. State U.-Los Angeles; M.S., Mich. State U. Reporter, Los Angeles Times, 1968-69; asst. dean Northwestern Coll., Traverse City, Mich., 1970-75; broadcaster WZZM-TV, Grand Rapids, Mich., 1976-78; dir. community relations U. Mich., Ann Arbor, 1978—. Editor, writer Travel Mag., 1978-80. Pres., Am. Lung Assn. Mich., 1983-85; v.p. Ann Arbor C. of C., 1985. Recipient Exptl. Achievement award Council Advancement and Support Higher Edn., 1981; Silver Anvil award Pub. Relations Soc. Am., 1982. Mem. Council Advancement and Support Higher Edn. Office: U Mich 2040 Fleming Bldg Ann Arbor MI

PELOWSKI, JAMES FORNEY, college executive; b. Omaha, Oct. 14, 1942; s. Robert James and Alice (Forney) P.; m. Barbara Gould, Jan. 29, 1966; 1 dau., Elizabeth Clarke. B.A., U. Nebr.-Omaha, 1964; M.A., Syracuse U., 1966; Ph.D., Mich. State U., 1979. Cert. higher edn. adminstrn., Ohio. Instr. speech U. Cin., 1966-69; Kellogg intern Mich. State U., East Lansing, 1970-71; asst. to pres. Lake Erie Coll., Painesville, Ohio, 1971-79, v.p., 1975-77; v.p. for instl. advancement Findlay Coll. (Ohio), 1980-84; chief devel. officer Am. U. in Cairo (Egypt), 1984—. Bd. dirs. Greater Cleve. Riding Ctr. for Handicapped, Mentor, Ohio, 1973-76, Ohio Citizens Com. for Arts, Columbus, 1983-84; bd. dirs. Findlay Area Arts Council, 1980-84, v.p., 1983. Named an Outstanding Young Man Am., U.S. Jaycees, 1976. Mem. Am. Assn. Higher Edn., Council for Advancement and Support Higher Edn., Phi Delta Kappa. Episcopalian. Clubs: Findlay Country, Mentor Harbor Yacht. Home: PO Box 1605 Findlay OH 45840 Office: American U in Cairo Box 2511 113 Kasr El Aini St Cairo Egypt

PELOZA, STANLEY JOSEPH, hospital official; b. Vele Mune, Istria, Yugoslavia, May 16, 1919; s. John and Anna (Zadkovic) P.; came to U.S., 1928, naturalized, 1928; student St. Louis U., 1946-48, Duquesne U., Pitts., 1957-58, Ind. U., 1963-64; m. La Rita Inez Russell, Feb. 28, 1941; 1 dau., Stana Jo Peloza Bowman. Enlisted in USMC, 1937, advanced through ranks to sgt. maj., 1961; service in China, Hawaii and U.S., Philippines, Okinawa, South Vietnam; bn. sgt. maj., acting div. sgt. maj. 3d Marine Div., Fleet Marine Force Far East, 1964-65; 2d Force Service Regt., Camp Lejeune, N.C., 1966-67; ret., 1967; mem. mgmt. staff Wishard Meml. Hosp., Indpls., 1968—, supt. bldgs., 1968-78, mem. staff security dept., 1978—, asst. dir. hosp. security, mem. infection control and safety coms., 1969-77; bd. dirs. United Hosps. Service, Inc., Indpls., 1975-77, chmn. stadardization com., 1975-76. Mem. Naval Fleet Res. Assn., Marine Corps Assn., Croatian Fraternal Union, Ind. Sheriffs Assn. (asso.), Devon Civic League. Roman Catholic. Clubs: Elks, K.C. (4 deg.). Home: 4340 Ashbourne Ln Indianapolis IN 46226 Office: Wishard Meml Hosp 1001 W 10th St Indianapolis IN 46202

PELTIER, THOMAS JAMES, accountant, financial analyst; b. Detroit, June 29, 1956; s. James Roy and Virginia Marie (Kirchner) P. B.B.A., Western Mich. U., 1978. Jr. acct. Guardian Industries, Northville, Mich., 1978-80; sr. acct. White Motor Co., Farmington Hills, Mich., 1980-81, Fed. Mogul Co., Detroit, 1981-82; cost acct. Lear Siegler Co., Berkley, Mich., 1982-83; fin. analyst Comerica Inc., Detroit, 1983—. Registered stock broker. Clubs: Ski (Warren, Mich.); Tennis (Troy, Mich.). Home: 2060 Somerset #103 Troy MI 48084

PELZER, CHARLES FRANCIS, geneticist, biology educator, researcher; b. Detroit, June 5, 1935; s. Francis Joseph and Edna Dorothy (Ladach) P.; m. Veronica Ann Killeen, July 7, 1972; 1 child, Mary Elizabeth. B.S. in Biology, U. Detroit, 1957; Ph.D. in Human Genetics, U. Mich., 1965. Postdoctoral fellow Wabash Coll., Crawfordsville, Ind., 1965-66; instr. U. Detroit, 1966-68; asst. prof. Saginaw Valley State Coll., University Center, Mich., 1969-74, assoc. prof., 1974-79, prof., 1979—; research assoc. Mich. State U., East Lansing, 1976-77; research fellow Henry Ford Hosp., Detroit, 1982-83; v.p. Saginaw Valley Retinititis Pigmentosa Found., Mich., 1979-81; vis. scientist Am. Inst. Biol. Scis., Washington, 1975-78; grant reviewer U.S. Dept. Edn., Washington, 1984-85, Contbr. articles to profl. jours. Recipient Alumni award Saginaw Valley State Coll. Alumni Assn., 1971; grantee Ford Hosp. Found., 1983, Mich. State U., 1977, Saginaw Valley State Coll. Found., 1975-85. Fellow Human Biology Council; mem. Am. Soc. Human Genetics, Genetics Soc. Am., N.Y. Acad. Sci., Electrophorisis Soc., Nat. Assn. Biology Tchrs., others. Home: 4900 Schneider Saginaw Twp MI 48603 Office: Saginaw Valley State Coll 2250 Pierce Rd University Center MI 48710

PEMA, PETER JAMES, osteopathic physician, educator; b. Atlantic City, Sept. 11, 1934; s. Peter and Katherine (Kendro) P.; m. Diana M. Allegrini; children—Deborah, Peter, Robert, Lisa, Jennifer. Student Temple U., 1952-55; D.O., Phila. Coll. Osteo. Medicine, 1959. Intern, Garden City-Ridgewood Hosp., Garden City, Mich., 1959-60; resident in internal medicine Detroit Osteo. Hosp., 1966-69; practice medicine specializing in internal medicine; gen.

practice, Vandercook Lake, Mich., 1960-66; chief of staff Jackson (Mich.) Osteo. Hosp., 1965-66, chmn. bd. trustees, 1966; practice internal medicine, Columbus, Ohio, 1969—; chmn. dept. internal medicine Doctors Hosp., Columbus, 1975-76, vice-chmn., 1977-78; clin. assoc. prof. internal medicines Ohio U. Coll. Osteo. Medicine, Athens, 1978—; mem. City Hosp. Planning Council, Jackson, 1964-65; med. examiner Nat. osteo. Bd. Licensure, 1971—; founding mem. Med. Adv. Bd., Upper Arlington, Ohio, 1975—; hosp. insp. intern tng. Am. Osteo. Assn. Recipient Outstanding Teaching award Doctors Hosp., 1970, 71. Fellow Am. Coll. Osteo. Internists; mem. Am. Osteo. Assn., Ohio Osteo. Assn., Columbus Acad. Osteo. Medicine. Albanian Orthodox. Office: 94 W 3d Ave Columbus OH 43220

PEN, RUDOLPH THEODORE, artist, art educator; b. Chgo., Jan. 1, 1918; s. John and Agnes (Klemczak) P.; m. Yvonne Fillis, June 29, 1946; children—Ronald, Allen, Yvonne Pauline. B.F.A., Art Inst. Chgo., 1943. Mem. faculty Art Inst. Chgo., 1948-62; pres. Alumni Art Inst., Chgo., 1960; dir. Summer Sch. Painting, Saugatuck, Mich., 1964; dir. Rudolph Pen Painting Sch., Chgo., from 1963; mem. faculty North Shore Art League, Winnetka, Ill., 1946—. One-man shows include: Marshall Fields, Chgo., 1947, 53, 59, Frank Oehlschlaeger, Chgo., 1962, Vincent Price, Chgo., 1968, North Shore Art League, Winnetka, Ill., 1984, Univ. Club, Chgo., 1985; group shows include: Library of Congress, Washington; Washington and Lee Coll., Lexington, Va., Davenport Mus., Iowa. Joseph Ryerson Traveling fellowship, Art Inst. Chgo., 1943; Huntington Hartford grantee, 1958. Mem. Am. Watercolor Soc., Civic Arts Found. Clubs: Union League, Arts. Home: 55 W Schiller St Chicago IL 60610

PEÑA, RENE PROSIA, physician; b. Cebu, Phillipines, June 10, 1942; came to U.S., 1968; s. Jesus S. and Casilda (Prosia) P.; m. Lydia Tañedo, Apr. 14, 1968; children—Roehl, Anjanette, Brian. M.D., Cebu Inst. Medicine, 1965. Diplomate Am. Bd. Surgery. Intern Overlook Hosp., Summit, N.J., 1968-69; resident in gen. surgery Luth. Med. Ctr., Bklyn., 1970-74; mem. med. staff Mercy Ctr., Aurora, Ill., 1975—, Copley Meml. Hosp., Aurora, 1975—. Fellow ACS; mem. AMA. Roman Catholic. Office: 1240 N Highland Ave Aurora IL 60506

PENCAK, MARY AGNES, hospital nursing administrator; b. Chgo., Jan. 30, 1913; d. Julian and Angela (Mrozowski) P. Grad. St. Mary of Nazareth Sch. Nursing, Chgo., 1940; B.S.N. in Edn., DePaul U., 1950; M.S.N., Cath. U. Am., 1955. Joined Sisters of Holy Family of Nazareth, Roman Cath. Ch., 1933; staff nurse, med./surg. supr. St. Mary of Nazareth Hosp. Ctr., Chgo., 1940-43, operating room supr., 1947-48, asst. dir. nursing service, 1953-62, 64-65, dir. nursing service, 1965-77, asst. adminstr. nursing, 1977—, instr. med./surg. fundamentals Sch. Nursing, 1948-53, convent superior, 1977-83; med/surg. supr. Loretto Hosp., Dalhart, Tex., 1943-45, Holy Cross Hosp., Taos, N.Mex., 1945-47; dir. nursing service and Practical Sch. Nursing, Mother Frances Hosp., Tyler, Tex., 1962-64. Mem. Nat. League for Nursing, Am. Hosp. Nurse Adminstrs. Assn., Sigma Theta Tau. Home: 233 W Division St Chicago IL 60622

PENCE, NEIL ALAN, optometrist; b. Huntington, Ind., Feb. 24, 1952; s. Dale M. and Marjorie Ann (Williams) P.; m. Ann M. Pajakowski, Aug. 21, 1976; 1 child, Brian Andrew. B.S. in Physics, Purdue U., 1974; O.D., Ind. U., 1979. Practice optometry Columbus, Ind., 1979—; asst. prof. Ind. U. Sch. Optometry, Bloomington, 1979—, dir. continuing Edn., 1984—. Contbr. articles to profl. jours. Recipient Bausch & Lomb award; grantee Bausch & Lomb, Cooper Vision Care, CIBA Vision Care, Alcon, Ind. U. Contact Lens Research Clinic. Mem. Am. Acad. Optometry (John P. Davey Outstanding Lecture award 1979), Am. Optometric Assn. (Optometric Recognition award 1985), Assn. Optometric Contact Lens Educators, Stonebelt Optometric Soc., Ind. U. Optometry Alumni Assn. Roman Catholic. Club: Purdue Club of Bartholomew County (Columbus). Office: 1505 25th St Columbus IN 47201

PENCEK, TERRENCE LYLE, med. educator; b. Berwyn, Ill., Aug. 24, 1947; s. Robert Joseph and Lillian (Stefula) P.; B.S., Valparaiso U., 1969; Ph.D. (NSF trainee), Ill. Inst. Tech., 1975; M.D. (DuPage Med. Soc. scholar, Sandoz award), Rush Med. Coll., 1981; m. Pamela Fay Turner, Aug. 11, 1973. Asst. prof. dept. physiology and neurology Rush Med. Coll., Chgo., 1977-81, instr. dept. neurology, 1976; mem. Multiple Sclerosis Center, Rush-Presby.-St. Luke's Med. Center, Chgo., 1980—. Nat. Multiple Sclerosis Soc. grantee, 1976-78; NIH grantee, 1977. Mem. Am. Physiol. Soc., Biophys. Soc., AMA, N.Y. Acad. Sci., Soc. for Neurosci., Chgo. Med. Soc., Sigma Xi. Lutheran. Contbr. articles to profl. jours. Home: 919 Brookwood St Bensenville IL 60106 Office: 1725 W Harrison St Chicago IL 60612

PENDELL, DONALD EUGENE, direct mail and marketing executive, consultant; b. Columbus, Ohio, Aug. 9, 1943; s. Clyde Elmo and Elsie Myrtle (Schaefer) P.; m. Donna Sue Lepley, Feb. 8, 1969; 1 child, Donald Glen. Free-lance advt. writer, Dayton, Ohio, 1970-72; creative specialist E.F. MacDonald Incentive Co., Dayton, 1972-76; sr. creative writer Needham Harper & Steers Advt., Dayton, 1976-77; dir. sales and mktg. promotions Shopsmith, Inc., Dayton, 1978-85; ind. direct mail mktg. cons. Don Pendell & Assocs., Dayton, 1985—. Contbr. articles to profl. jours. Chmn. Tri-County United Appeal Kick-Off Meeting, Dayton, 1973; writer, developer advt. support materials Kettering Optimists Club Bike Safety Week, 1974, incentive plan Dayton Air Fair, 1976. Served with USN, 1962-66. Avocations: writing; woodworking. Address: 2622 Wayland Ave Dayton OH 45420

PENDLETON, JAMES RALPH, auto agency executive; b. St. Joseph, Mo., Nov. 7, 1917; s. James Ralph and Lillian Beatrice (Squires) P.; m. Geraldine LaFae Harrington, Dec. 8, 1941 (dec.); m. 2d Alice Corinne Harrison, Mar. 4, 1961; children—Kathryn, John, Rebecca, J. Allen, Kenneth, Margaret. Student Central Coll., 1936. Dist. mgr. Kaiser-Frazer Sales Corp.; with fin. div. Bank of St. Louis; with Ford Motor Credit Co., owner Dodge Agy., Springfield, Ill., from 1965; now owner, prin. Pendleton Motors Inc., Toyota Agy. Served with USN, 1942-46. Mem. Ill. New Car Dealers Assn. (dir.) Methodist. Clubs: Illini Country, Sangamo. Lodge: Elks. Home: 1615 Wiggins Springfield IL 62704 Office: 3009 Singer Springfield IL 62703

PENDLETON, MARY ENGSTROM, books and antiques executive; b. Winona, Minn., June 28, 1918; d. George Willard and Ada (McLeod) Engstrom; m. John Carlton Pendleton, May 5, 1945; children—John Christopher, David George. B.E., Winona State Tchrs. Coll., 1939; B.S., U. Minn., 1940. Mem. topographical survey party USDA, Beltsville, Md., 1942-43; reference librarian U. Richmond, Va., 1943-45; 1st asst. young peoples dept. Milw. Pub. Library, 1946-48; reference librarian Winona Pub. Library, Minn., 1962-69; owner Mary Twyce Antiques & Books, 1970—. Mem. Nat. Assn. Dealers in Antiques, Wenonahland Antiques Dealers Assn., P.E.O. Republican. Congregationalist. Club: Portia. Home: 161 W Wabasha St Winona MN 55987 Office: Mary Twyce Antiques & Books 601 E 5th St Winona MN 55987

PENDLETON, THELMA BROWN, physical therapist, health service administrator; b. Rome, Ga., Jan. 30, 1911; d. John O. and Alma (Ingram) Brown; diploma Provident Hosp. Sch. Nursing, 1931; certificate Loyola U., 1942, Northwestern U., 1946; m. George W. Pendleton, Mar. 2, 1946; 1 son, George William. Pediatric nurse Rosenwald Found., Chgo., 1931-32; staff nurse Vis. Nurse Assn., Chgo., 1932-45; chief phys. therapy Provident Hosp., Chgo., 1946-55; phys. therapy cons. Parents Assn., Inc., Chgo., 1956-60; cons. United Cerebral Palsy of Greater Chgo.'s Pipers Portal Schs., 1961-63, dir., 1963-64; dir. phys. therapy services LaRabida Children's Hosp. and Research Center, Chgo., 1964-75; mem. nat. com. Joint Orthopedic Nursing Adv. Services, 1947-55; clin. supr., instr. programs in phys. therapy Northwestern U. Med. Sch., Chgo., 1947-55, 64-75; cons. United Cerebral Palsy, 1970-75; lectr. Japanese service com. on Cerebral Palsy, 1970; mem. Ill. Phys. Therapy Exam. Com., 1952-62. Recipient certificate of Commendation CSC Cook County (Ill.), 1961, Citation of Merit, Wands Cerebral Palsy Unit, 1961. Mem. Am., Ill. phys. therapy assns., Provident Hosp. Nurses Alumni Assn. Democrat. Clubs: Washington Park Swimming, Tu-Fours Bolivia. Author: Low Budget Gournet, 1977; contbr. articles on phys. therapy to profl. jours. Address: 2631 S Indiana Ave Chicago IL 60616

PENG, CHAO-YING JOANNE, statistics educator; b. Taipei, Sept. 1, 1951; s. Shou-Chih and Whai-Jane (Chai) P. B.S., Nat. Taiwan U., 1973; M.S., U. Wis.-Platteville, 1974; M.S., U. Wis.-Madison, 1977; Ph.D., 1979. Statis. cons. U. Wis.-Madison, 1974-78; asst. prof. U. Iowa, Iowa City, 1978-81; vis. asst. prof. U. N.C., Chapel Hill, 1981-82; asst. prof. stats. Ind. U., Bloomington, 1982—; statis. cons. Eli Lilly Co., 1984—. Author: Learn Statistics by Computers, 1981; Analytical Approaches to Statistics, 1984; Statistical Design of Education Research- A Programmed Approach, 1984. Grantee Spencer Found., 1984, Profit Endowments, 1984, Ind. U., NIH, 1979-80; Old Gold summer fellow U. Iowa, 1980. Mem. Am. Ednl. Research Assn. (pres. SIG 1982-83), Psychometric Soc., Nat. Council Measurment in Edn., Am. Statis. Assn., SAS Users Group (coordinator 1984—). Avocations: sports. Office: Dept Counseling and Ednl Psychology Smith Research Ctr Bloomington IN 47405

PENN, DAVID C(LYDE), salesman, clergyman; b. Chgo., Jan. 23, 1953; s. Robert Worth and Edmonia Alice (Kennedy) P.; m. Brenda Joyce Martin, May 18, 1974; children—Dortricia Kenyatta, Danielle Edmonia. A.A., Mich. Christian Coll., 1972; B.S., Heed U., 1978; M.R.E., Internat. Sem., 1981. Ordained to ministry Ch. of Christ, 1978. Assoc. minister 79th St. Ch., Chgo., 1975-78, Sheldon Heights Ch., Chgo., 1978-81, 82—; resident minister Beecher St. Ch., Cin., 1981-82; salesperson Sheldon Heights/Jays Foods, Chgo., 1975—; counselor, Sheldon Heights Ch., 1978—; co-chairperson Tri-State Youth Conf., Ill., Ind., Wis., 1979-81. Recipient Police award Chgo. Patrolmen's Assn., 1974; Stewardship award Sheldon Heights Ch., 1981. Fellow Mich. Christian Alumni Assn. Democrat. Club: VIP (pres. 1970-71). Home: 432 W 102d St Chicago IL 60628 Office: 11325 S Halsted St Chicago IL 60628 also 1540 W 44th St Chicago IL 60637

PENNELL, DANNY JOE, social worker; b. Jacksonville, Ill., Aug. 31, 1945; s. Donald Louis and Lela Geneva (Murray) P.; m. Janis Evelyn Reynolds, Dec. 26, 1984; children—Joel, Jason, Jaime, Chad, Colter. B.A., U. Ill., 1970, M.S.W., 1972. Social worker Dept. Child and Family Services, Danville, Ill., 1971-72, social work supr., Rockford, Ill., 1972-74; instr. Rockford Coll., 1977-78; exec. dir. Goldie B. Floberg Ctr., Rockton, Ill., 1974—; bd. dirs. Winnebago County Child Protection Assn., Rockford, 1974-76, Child Care Assn. Ill., Springfield, Ill., 1980—; cons. in field. Grantee Ill. Dept. Children and Family Services, 1970-72. Mem. Nat. Soc. Fund Raising Execs. (bd. dirs., sec. 1984—), Am. Assn. Mental Deficiency, Nat. Assn. Retarded Citizens, Coordinating Council for Handicapped Children, Nat. Assn. Devel. Disabilities Mgrs. Home: 472 S Blackhawk St Janesville WI 53545 Office: Goldie B Floberg Ctr 58 W Rockton Rd Rockton IL 61072

PENNEQUIN, ALBERT ELIE, land surveying educator; b. Tournai, Belgium, Feb. 11, 1928; came to U.S. 1970; s. Edgar and Jeanne Selly (Polak) P; m. Marie-Louise Dandov, July 30, 1952 (dec. 1971); children—Didier F.E., Roland M.; m. Marguerite Marie Trottereau, June 22, 1974. Degree in Geometre, Inst. Royal for Geometres-Experts Immobilliers, Brussels, Belgium, 1953; postgrad. U. Wis.-Whitewater, 1975—. Registered profl. land surveyor, Wis. Land surveyor Belgian govt., 1949-58; educator, land surveyor Congo govt., Coquilhatville, Mbandaka, 1958-65; French instruction supr. Caterpillar Tractor Co., Belgium, 1965-70; fgn. lang. master Lake Forest Acad., Ill., 1970-73, land surveying instr., program chmn. Gateway Tech. Inst., Elkhorn, Wis., 1973—; land surveyor, Elkhorn, 1973—; land surveyor's cons., Belgium, 1953-58, 1965-70. Contbr. articles to profl. jours. Served with Belgium Army, 1946-49. Fellow Am. Congress on Surveying and Mapping (local student chpt. advisor 1975—), mem. Wis. Soc. Land Surveyors (edn. com.). Avocations: flying; sailing; astronomy; piano playing. Office: Gateway Tech Inst Hwy H and Centralia Ave Elkhorn WI 53121

PENNEY, WILLIAM HARRY, quality assurance manager, consultant; b. Rochester, Minn., June 16, 1929; s. William Halbert and Helen A. (Kerkow) P.; m. Mabel Yarkie, Aug. 4, 1955; children—Susan, Kathryn, Thomas, Ellen. Cert. petroleum refining engring., Colo. Sch. Mines, 1951; Ph.D., U. Minn., 1955. Chem. engr. 3-M Co., St. Paul, 1955-58, chem. process supr., 1958-63, tech. mgr., 1963-68, lab. mgr., 1968-83, quality assurance mgr., 1983—, cons. 3M Co., St. Paul, 1980—. Patentee in field. Recipient numerous industry awards. Mem. Sigma Xi. Republican. Episcopalian. Office: 3-M Co 3-M Center Bldg 236-1 Saint Paul MN 55118

PENNINGS, PAUL DAMON, sales executive; b. Iron Mountain, Mich., Mar. 7, 1954; s. Lawrence G. and Alice C. (Brey) P.; m. Deborah Beuder, Sept. 3, 1977. B.S., Western Ill. U., 1976; M.S., Roosevelt U., Chgo., 1984. Salesman, Nationwide Papers, Elk Grove Village, Ill., 1976-78; mktg. rep. Ludlow Corp., Chgo., 1978-81; cons. Tactics, Inc., Arlington Heights, Ill., 1981-84; sales exec. Videotex Am., Chgo., 1984—; instr. mktg. mgmt. Roosevelt U., Chgo. Mem. Am. Mktg. Assn. (chmn. chpt. 1981—). Republican. Roman Catholic. Avocations: cooking; rose breeding. Home: 512 W South St Arlington Heights IL 60005 Office: Videotex America 8410 W Bryn Mawr Chicago IL 60631

PENNINGTON, JOAN, patent lawyer; b. Beckley, W.Va., Oct. 19, 1951; d. Robert Lee and Dixie Lee (Lafferty) P.; 1 son by a previous marriage, Lee Pennington Marco. B.S. in Elec. Engring., W.Va. U., 1972; J.D., John Marshall Law Sch., Chgo., 1980. Bar: Ill. 1980, U.S. Patent and Trademark Office, 1982. Engr., EOS/Xerox subs., Pasadena, Calif., 1972-73; engr./supr. No. Ill. Gas Co., Aurora, 1973-75; engr. Internat. Harvester, Hinsdale, Ill., 1976-78, Ill. Bell Telephone, Chgo., 1978-80; patent atty. U.S. Dept. Energy, Argonne, Ill., 1980-81, Silverman, Cass & Singer, Ltd., Chgo., 1981-83, Motorola, Inc., Schaumburg, Ill., 1983-84; assoc. Mason Kolehmainen, Rathburn & Wyss, Chgo., 1984—. Mem. ABA, Ill. Bar Assn., Patent Law Assn., Chgo., IEEE. Home: 1665C Williamsburg Ct Wheaton IL 60187 Office: Mason Kolehmainen Rathburn & Wyss 20 N Wacker Dr Suite 4200 Chicago IL 60606

PENNISTON, JOHN THOMAS, research biochemist, educator; b. St. Louis, Sept. 10, 1935; s. Alonzo Schofield and Esther Rosella (Thomas) P.; m. Joyce Carolyn Kendall, June 11, 1960; children—Sarah Constance, Mary Grace. A.B. magna cum laude, Harvard U., 1957, A.M., 1959, Ph.D., 1962. Vis. asst. prof. chemistry Pomona Coll., Claremont, Calif., 1963-64; research fellow Enzyme Inst., U. Wis.-Madison, 1964-66, asst. prof. Enzyme Inst., 1966-71; assoc. prof. chemistry U. N.C., Chapel Hill, 1971-76; assoc. prof. biochemistry Mayo Clinic/Found., Rochester, Minn., 1976-79, prof. biochemistry, 1979—; mem. phys. biochemistry study sect. NIH, Bethesda, Md., 1982-86. Contbr. articles to profl. jours. Harvard Coll. scholar, 1953-57; NSF Predoctoral fellow, 1957-62; grantee NIH, NSF, 1972-88. Mem. Am. Soc. Biol. Chemists, Am. Chem. Soc., Fedn. Am. Scientists, AAAS. Democrat. Episcopalian. Avocations: computers; music. Home: 835 10 1/2 St SW Rochester MN 55902 Office: Mayo Clinic Biochemistry Sect 200 1st St SW Rochester MN 55905

PENNY, TIMOTHY JOSEPH, congressman; b. Albert Lea, Minn., Nov. 19, 1951; s. Jay C. and Donna (Haukoos) P.; m. Barbara J. Christianson, Oct. 18, 1975; children—Jamison, Joseph, Molly. B.A., Winona State U., 1974; postgrad., U. Minn., 1975. Mem. Minn. Senate from Dist. 30, 1977-82, 98th-99th Congresses from 1st Minn. Dist.; mem. agr. com., vets affairs com. 98th Congress from 1st Minn. Mem. Minn. State Univ. Bd., 1974-77. Recipient disting. service award U. Minn., 1982, Spark Plug award Communicating for Agr., 1980. Mem. New Richland (Minn.) Jaycees, Waseca Pals, Inc., Waseca and Freeborn County Assn. for Retarded Citizens. Democrat. Lutheran. Office: US Ho of Reps Room 501 Cannon House Office Bldg Washington DC 20515

PENROD, WALTER JAY, vocational education association administrator; b. Claypool, Ind., Aug. 11, 1928; s. Walter J. and Beulah M. (Cauffman) P.; m. Mary Jenet E. Elder, Nov. 10, 1950; children—Kathryn M., Sharon L., Susan D., Marilyn R., Walter J. Student Manchester Coll., 1947-49; B.S., Purdue U., 1951; M.S., Ball State U., 1964. Farmer, North Manchester, Ind., 1957; tchr. vocat. agr. Met. Sch. Wabash (Ind.), 1960-65; dir. Upper Wabash Vocat. Sch., 1965-67; asst. state dir. Dept. Pub. Instrn., Div. Vocat. Edn., Indpls., 1967-70, state dir., exec. officer Ind. Rehab. Services, Indpls., 1970-76; exec. dir. Ind. Adv. Council Vocat. Edn., Indpls., 1977—; mem. Ind. Congress on Edn., 1983-84; chmn. planning com. Joint Conf. Nat./State, Washington, 1982-83; sec. People in Am. for Vocat. Edn., Inc., Washington, 1983-84. Mem. Gov. Orr's Adv. Com., 1984, Hoosiers for Econ. Devel. Served to cpl. U.S. Army, 1951-53. Named Disting. Hoosier, Gov. Ind., 1971; recipient Ind. Rehab. Service award Indpls. Goodwill Industries, 1973; Cert. of Appreciation, Ind. Employment and Tng. Assn., 1982; Disting Service to his profession award, 1984. Mem. Nat. Assn. State Adv. Councils on Vocat. Edn. (dir., sec. 1983—), Assn. Exec. Dirs. State Adv. Councils Vocat. Edn. (regional v.p. 1982-83; Sire award 1982), Am. Vocat. Assn., Ind. Vocat. Assn. (Merit award 1967, 70, 83). Republican. Methodist. Home: 1023 Bristol Rd Indianapolis IN 46280 Office: Ind Council Vocational Edn 17 W Market St Indianapolis IN 46204

PENSLER, ALVIN VICTOR, dentist; b. Detroit, Jan. 17, 1928; s. Max E. Pensler and Irene (Eisenman) Kraft; m. Joanne Aran, Aug. 31, 1960 (div. 1978); children—Elizabeth, Karen, Catherine, Michele (dec.); m. Anita Louise Rosenblatt, Dec. 12, 1982; children—Wendy Loberstein, Lisa Hammond. B.A., Wayne U., 1949; D.D.S., U. Detroit, 1959. Lic. dentist, Mich. Dentist, Garden City Diagnostic Ctr., Garden City, Mich., 1959—; cons. in field. Contbr. articles to profl. jours. Advisor Southfield Bd. Edn. Served to capt. USAF, 1951-53. Fellow Royal Soc. Health, Acad. Gen. Dentistry; mem. ADA, Mich. State Dental Assn. (advisor), Detroit Dist. Dental Assn., Chgo. Dental Soc., Western Dental Soc., Royal Soc. Health. Jewish. Club: Photo Soc. Am. Lodge: K.P. Avocations: photography, camping. Home: 5172 Rock Run West Bloomfield MI 48033 Office: Garden City Diagnostic Ctr 6255 N Inkster Garden City MI 48135

PENSON, EDWARD MARTIN, university chancellor, educator; b. N.Y.C., Aug. 30, 1927; s. Michael and Cecile (Cohan) P.; m. Georgann Ellen McCune, June 25, 1975; children—Jeffery, Albert, Cynthia. B.A., U. Fla. 1950; M.A., Ohio U., Athens, 1951; Ph.D., U. Fla., 1955. Prof. communication Ohio U., 1955-75, dean, 1965-68, v.p., 1969-75; pres., prof. Salem (Mass.) State Coll., 1975-78; chancellor, prof. U. Wis.-Oshkosh, 1978—; cons. in field; mem. Ohio Student Loan Commn., Columbus, 1971-75. Bd. dirs. Assn. Retarded Citizens, Salem, 1975-78, Econ. Devel. Council, North Shore, Mass., 1976-78. Served with USN, 1945-46. Mem. Oshkosh C. of C. (dir. 1978—), Communication Assn. Am., Am. Speech Assn., Am. Assn. State and Land Grant Colls. and Univs., Nat. Assn. Student Personnel Adminstrs., Sigma Alpha Eta, Phi Kappa Phi, Alpha Lambda Delta. Lodge: Rotary. Contbr. chpts. to Fundamentals of Speech, 1975-78; assoc. editor Jour. of Communication, 1964-65; contbr. articles to profl. jours. Home: 842 Algoma Blvd Oshkosh WI 54901 Office: 800 Algoma Blvd Oshkosh WI 54901

PENTIUK, RANDALL ALAN, lawyer; b. Garden City, Mich., Mar. 15, 1955; s. Eugene Otto and Marjorie Bernice (Baynes) P.; m. Sheila Rene Hopper, Dec. 21, 1979; 1 child, Amanda Rene. B.S. in Bus. Adminstrn., Wayne State U., 1976; J.D. magna cum laude, Detroit Coll. Law, 1981. Bar: Mich. 1981, U.S. Dist. Ct. (ea. dist.) Mich. 1981, U.S. Ct. Appeals (6th cir.) 1984, U.S. Supreme Ct. 1984, D.C. 1985. Research atty. Mich. Ct. Appeals, Detroit, 1981; assoc. Logan, Huchla, Wycoff & Pentiuk and predecessor Logan, Huchla & Wycoff, P.C., Riverview, Mich., 1981-84, ptnr., 1984—. Chmn. Trenton Planning Commn., Mich., 1982—. Down River Republican Club, Trenton, 1983—; bd. dirs. Detroit City Rescue Mission, 1982—. Mich. Consol. Gas scholar Detroit Coll. Law, 1978, Burton scholar, 1979, Alumni scholar, 1980. Mem. State Bar Mich., ABA, Comml. Law League Am., Fed. Bar Assn., Christian Legal Soc. Baptist. Lodge: Kiwanis. Home: 1784 Grange Rd Trenton MI 48183 Office: Logan Huchla Wycoff & Pentiuk 13900 Sibley Rd Riverview MI 48192

PENWELL, MARVIN DEAN, osteopathic physician, educator; b. Decatur, Ill., May 18, 1930; s. Harry David and Mary Delema (Jackson) P.; m. Gloria Jean Liechty, June 28, 1952; children—Robert Todd, Polly Denise. B.A., Greenville Coll., 1952; D.O., Kansas City Coll. Osteopathy and Surgery, 1966. Diplomate Am. Osteo. Bd. Gen. Practice. Intern Flint Osteo. Hosp., Mich., 1966-67, mem. staff, 1967—, vice chief of staff, 1974; assoc. physician Swartz Creek Community Clinic, Mich, 1967-71; family physician Linden Med. Ctr., Mich., 1971—; cons. staff mem. Genesee Meml. Hosp., Flint; asst. clin. prof. Mich. State U., Lansing, 1978—; preceptor in edn. osteo. med. studies Phila. Coll. Osteo. Medicine, 1978-79; guest speaker Pfeizer Corp., arthritis awareness program Flint Osteo. Hosp. Mem. Mich. Assn. Osteo. Physicians and Surgeons, Am. Osteo. Assn., Am. Coll. Gen. Practitioners, Genesee County Osteo. Assn., Am. Guild Organists (Flint chpt.), Aircraft Owners and Pilots Assn. Republican. Lodge: Gideons. Avocations: aviation; boating; water skiing; fishing; snowmobiling. Office: Linden Med Ctr PC 319 S Bridge St Linden MI 48451

PENZEL, CARL GENE, construction company executive, civil engineer; b. Jackson, Mo., Jan. 10, 1934; s. Carl Linus and Mettie Jane (Killian) P.; m. Alice Sue Meier, June 19, 1960; children—Philip Carlyle, Christopher Noel. B.C.E.E., U. Mo.-Rolla, 1952. Registered profl. engr., Mo. Engr., Allis-Chalmers Co., West Allis, Wis., 1955; with Penzel Constrn. Co., Inc., Jackson, Mo., 1959—, v.p., 1959-80, pres., 1981—; dir. Jackson Exchange Bank. Alderman, City Council, Jackson, 1966; pres. Indsl. Devel. Co., Jackson, 1981. Served to lt. USNR, 1955-59. Named Young Engr. of Yr., Southeast Mo. sect. Mo. Soc. Profl. Engrs., 1966; Disting. Service award Jackson Jaycees, 1968. Mem. Nat. Soc. Profl. Engrs., Assn. Gen. Contractors Mo. (pres. 1980). Republican. Mem. United Ch. of Christ. Home: 1110 Jackson Trail Jackson MO 63755 Office: Penzel Constrn Co Inc Hwy 72 W Jackson MO 63755

PEOPLES, JAMES BLAIR, surgeon, educator; b. Altoona, Pa., Feb. 13, 1945; s. Don Miguel and Beverly Jan (Yingling) P.; m. Charlotte Virginia Fretz, May 27, 1967 (div. 1977); 1 child, Jessica Lynn; m. Kathleen Terry, Aug. 30, 1977. A.B., Franklin and Marshall Coll., Lancaster, Pa., 1967; M.D., NYU, 1971. Diplomate Am. Bd. Surgery. Intern, U. Pitts., 1971-72; resident in surgery, 1972-77; asst. prof. surgery Wright State U., Dayton, Ohio, 1979-85, assoc. prof., 1985—, dir. surg. techs. lab., 1980—; surg. cons. USAF Hosp., Dayton, 1980—; coordinator surg. edn. Good Samaritan Hosp., Dayton, 1983—. Contbr. articles to profl. jours. Recipient Resident's award Pitts. Surg. Soc., 1976, Southwest Pa. chpt. ACS, 1976. Fellow ACS; mem. Midwest Surg. Assn., Am. Assn. VA Surgeons, Assn. Acad. Surgery, Am. Pancreatic Assn., Phi Beta Kappa. Republican. Lutheran. Avocations: Model railroading, gardening, cooking. Home: 152 Patterson Rd Dayton OH 45419 Office: Good Samaritan Hosp 2200 Philadelphia Dr Dayton OH 45406

PEOPLES, JAMES YOUNG, high school administrator; b. Snowhill, Ala., June 1, 1932; s. James and Virginia (Davis) P.; m. Dorothy Sneed, June 22, 1963; 1 son, Cedric. B.S., Ky. State U., Frankfort, 1955; M.Ed., DePaul U., 1973; postgrad. Highland U., Tenn., 1977—. Tchr., coach football Marshall High Sch., Chgo., 1956-68; counselor, chmn. human relations com. Sch. Dist. 147 Harvey, Ill., 1968-73; assoc. prin. for instrn., dir. continuing edn. Hillcrest High Sch., Country Club Hills, Ill., 1973—. Bd. dirs., treas. Human Resources Devel. Inst., Inc.; trustee Ky. State U. Found., Inc.; bd. dirs. vice chmn. Midway Rehab. Services Inc. Treas., ruler elder Chatham-Bethlehem Presbyn. Ch. Served with U.S. Army N.G., 1948-51. Recipient Disting. Alumni award Ky. State U., 1965, named to Athletic Hall of Fame, 1975. Mem. Assn. Supervision and Curriculum Devel., Am. Personnel and Guidance Assn., South Suburban Curriculum Assn. (pres.), Ill. Personnel and Guidance Assn., Ky. State U. Alumni Assn. (pres. 1970-74), Delta Epsilon Sigma, Kappa Alpha Psi. Democrat. Lodge: Masons. Home: 7348 S Constance Ave Chicago IL 60649 Office: Hillcrest High Sch 175th and Pulsaski Rd Country Clus Hills IL 60648

PEOPLES, JOHN, JR., physicist; b. Staten Island, N.Y., Jan. 22, 1933; s. John and Annie Alice (Wall) P.; m. Brooke Detweiler, Dec. 16, 1955; children—Jennet, Vannessa. B.S., Carnegie Inst. Tech., 1955; M.A., Columbia U., 1961, Ph.D., 1966. Engr. Martin Co., Middle River, Md., 1955-60; asst. prof. physics Columbia U., N.Y.C., 1966-69; from asst. prof. to assoc. prof. Cornell U., Ithaca, N.Y., 1969-72; scientist Fermilab, Batavia, Ill., 1972—; mem. high energy physics adv. panel U.S. Dept. Energy, 1975-80. Contbr. articles to profl. jours. Alfred P. Sloan Found fellow 1972. Fellow Am. Phys. Soc. (exec. com. div. particles and fields 1983—, chmn. 1984). Home: 201 Ford St Geneva IL 60134 Office: Fermilab PO Box 500 MS 341 Batavia IL 60510

PEPER, CHRISTIAN BAIRD, lawyer; b. St. Louis, Dec. 5, 1910; s. Clarence F. and Christine (Baird) P.; A.B. cum laude, Harvard, 1932; LL.B., Washington U., 1935; LL.M. (Sterling fellow), Yale, 1937; m. Ethel C. Kingsland, June 5, 1935; children—Catherine K. (Mrs. Kenneth B. Larson), Anne C. (Mrs. John M. Perkins), Christian B. Admitted to Mo. bar, 1934, since practiced in St. Louis; partner Peper, Martin, Jensen, Maichel & Hetlage. Lectr. various subjects Washington U. Law Sch., St. Louis, 1943-61; partner A.G. Edwards & Sons, 1945-67; pres. St. Charles Gas Corp., 1953-72; chmn. St. Louis Steel Casting Inc., Hydraulic Press Brick Co. Mem. vis. com. Harvard Div. Sch., 1964-70. Trustee St. Louis Art Mus. Recipient Alumni citation Washington U. Law Sch., 1984. Mem. Am., Mo., St. Louis bar assns., Order of Coif, Phi Delta Phi. Roman Catholic. Clubs: Noonday, University, Harvard (St. Louis); East India, Devonshire (London). Contbr. articles to profl. jours. Home: 1454 Mason Rd Saint Louis MO 63131 Office: 720 Olive St Saint Louis MO 63101

PEPIN, ROBERT FRANCIS, environmental scientist; b. Buffalo, Apr. 11, 1958; s. Francis and Florence (Salmon) P. B.A., SUNY-Oswego, 1980; M.A., Ind. U., 1984, M.S. in Environ. Sci., 1983. Assoc. instr. dept. biology Ind. U., Bloomington, 1980-82; environ. scientist EPA, Chgo., 1982—. Recipient performance awards EPA, 1983. Mem. AAAS. Club: Sierra (Chgo.). Office: EPA 230 S Dearborn St Chicago IL 60604

PEPPER, JOYCE M., lawyer; b. Chgo., July 23, 1946; d. LaVerne E. and Marian (Hudek) P. B.S. in Journalism, Northwestern U., 1968; M.A. in Journalism, U. Wis., 1970; J.D., DePaul U., 1979. Bar: Ill. 1979, U.S. Dist. Ct. (no. dist.) Ill. 1979. Copywriter, pub. relations staff AT&T, Chgo., 1970-72; editor, speech writer, Sears Roebuck and Co., Chgo., 1973-80, atty., 1980—; asst. sec. Sears Polit. Action Com., Chgo. Mem. ABA, Ill. Bar Assn., Chgo. Bar Assn. Home: 2728 N Hampden Ct Chicago IL 60614 Office: Sears Roebuck and Co Sears Tower Chicago IL 60684

PEPPLER, ALICE STOLPER, publishing company marketing director; b. Saginaw, Mich., Mar. 14, 1934; d. Lothar E. and Hulda M. (Koenig) Stolper; B.S., Concordia Tchrs. Coll., River Forest, Ill., 1956; postgrad. U. Ill., 1966-67; children—Jeanne, Jon, Jan. Elem. sch. tchr., librarian, music dir. Bethany Luth. Sch., Chgo., 1956-63; editor lang. arts materials Scott, Foresman & Co., Chgo., 1963-71; sr. editor lang. arts materials Lyons & Carnahan, Chgo., 1972-74; mktg. dir. lang. arts, fgn. langs. and social studies Rand McNally & Co., Chgo., 1974-77; mktg. dir. lang. arts Scott, Foresman & Co., Chgo., 1977—; piano tchr., 1956-63. Organist, music dir. First Luth. Ch. of Trinity, 1967-76; organist, choir dir. Mt. Olive Luth. Ch., Chgo., 1976—; leader singles seminars and workshops, 1975—. Mem. Internat. Reading Assn., Nat. Council Tchrs. English, Nat., Luth. edn. assns., Evang. Luths. in Mission. Author: Bible Children I Know, 1971; God's Love for Everyone, 1971; Why Jesus Came, 1972; Divorced and Christian, 1974; Who Put the Finger on God?, 1975; Single Again—This Time with Children, 1982; also articles, poems, monograph; editor Luth. Edn. Assn. Yearbook, 1972-74. Home: 1815 Tangelwood Glenview IL 60025 Office: 1900 E Lake Ave Glenview IL 60025

PERALTA, MODESTO MANGASI, JR., cardiovascular and thoracic surgeon; b. Manila, Oct. 19, 1941; came to U.S., 1965; s. Modesto Ferrer and Jorgia (Mangasi) P.; m. Lita Racaza, May 9, 1965; children—Lorraine, Modesto III, Michelle, Nicole. B.S., Letran Coll., Manila, 1960; M.D., U. Santo Tomas, 1964. Diplomate Am. Bd. Surgery, Am. Bd. Thoracic and Cardiovascular Surgery. Instr. anatomy St. Rita Hosp., Manila, 1964-65; intern St. Joseph Hosp., Lorain, Ohio, 1965-66; resident in surgery Huron Rd. Hosp., Cleve., 1966-70; resident in thoracic surgery Hahnemann Med. Coll., Phila., 1970-72; practice medicine, specializing in thoracic and cardiovascular surgery, Cleve., 1972—; chief thoracic surgery Euclid Gen. Hosp.; chief thoracic and cardiovascular surgery Huron Rd. Hosp.; mem. staff Huron Rd. Hosp., Elyria Meml. Hosp., Lake County Meml. Hosp. Recipient Best Research Paper award Huron Rd. Hosp., 1969, Best Resident award, 1970; recipient Best Research paper award Ohio chpt. ACS, 1971. Mem. AMA, ACS, Am. Coll. Chest Physicians, Soc. Thoracic Surgeons, Ohio Med. Assn., Cleve. Vascular Soc., Cleve. Acad. Medicine, Cleve. Surg. Soc., Soc. Philippine Surgeons in Am., Philippine Am. Soc. Ohio (v.p. 1984-85), Assn. Philippine Physicians in Ohio (pres. 1984). Roman Catholic. Club: Mayfield Village (Ohio) Racket. Contbr. articles to med. jours. Home: 9766 Rollin Rd Waite Hill OH 44094 Office: 3070 Mayfield Rd Cleveland Heights OH 44118

PERCEFULL, ROBERT LEE, air force officer, computer systems consultant; b. Bearden, Ark., Aug. 15, 1942; s. Everett Deward and Irma Ruth (Matthews) P.; m. Patricia Alta Brown, Nov. 23, 1963 (div. 1972); children—Robert Lee, Jr., Ronald Lynn; m. Carol Diane Wills, Apr. 26, 1983. A.A., Henderson State U., 1962; student Fla. State U., 1966-67; B.S. in Computer Sci., U. Nebr.-Omaha, 1974. Cert. data processor. Enlisted U.S. Air Force, 1962, commd. 2d lt., 1975, advanced through grades to capt., 1979; electronics technician, N.Mex. and P.R., 1963-60; tech. mgr., Merced, Calif., 1970-72; computer ops. mgr., Omaha, 1972-75; data base mgr., Omaha, 1975-79; chief configuration mgmt., Dayton, Ohio, 1980-84; tech. services mgr., Dayton, 1984-85; pres. Robert Lee Percefull Assocs., Computer Systems Cons., Dayton, 1983—; mgr. Infotec Devel. Inc., Dayton, 1985—. Scoutmaster Mid-Am. Council Boy Scouts Am., 1974-79; commr. Mound Builders Area Council Boy Scouts Am., 1983—. Mem. Soc. for Advancement of Mgmt., Am. Mgmt. Assn., Am. Legion. Republican. Methodist. Avocations: hiking, swimming, canoeing, camping, auto restoration. Home: 110 Frazer Dr Middletown OH 45042

PERDUE, DON CLAYTON, pharmacist; b. Kenova, W.Va., Nov. 12, 1949; s. Wendell Clayton and Mary Magdalene (Buehler) P.; m. Mary Jo Dudek, Apr. 16, 1977; children—Erin Colleen, Sean Patrick. B.S. in Chemistry, Marshall U., 1972, B.S. in Philosophy, 1972; B.S. in Pharmacy, Ohio Northern U., 1974. Registered pharmacist, W.Va., Ohio, Ky. Employee pharmacist Stakers Drugs, West Portsmouth, Ohio, 1974-76, Flanagan Pharmacy, Kenova, W.Va., 1976-78, Plyburn's Pharmacy, Barboursville, W.Va., 1978; staff pharmacist Cabell-Huntington Hosp., W.Va., 1978-83; dir. pharmacy Bellefonte Hosp., Ashland, Ky., 1984—; cons. pharmacist Nursing Home service, Catlettsburg, Ky., 1983. Contbr. articles and short stories to periodical The Gamecock. Pollworker Lawrence County Citizens for Tb Levy, Ohio, 1984. Mem. Am. Soc. Cons. Pharmacists, So. W.Va. Pharmacists Assn. (v.p. 1977-79), Gamefowl Breeders Assn. (pres. Ohio chpt. 1983—, bd. dirs. exec. com. 1983—, editor Ohio Quart. 1982—). Democrat. Baptist. Lodges: Masons, Elks. Avocations: Golfing; breeding and rearing Am. game fowl; hunting; skiing. Home: Box 196 Route 3 Ironton OH 45638 Office: Our Lady of Bellefonte Hosp St Christopher Dr Ashland KY 41101

PEREZ, CARLOS JOE, actor; b. Iola, Kans., Apr. 6, 1956; s. Harry and and Virginia Maxine (Fritts) P.; m. Toni L. Snyder, Aug. 23, 1985. A.A. Johnson County Community Coll., 1976; B.A., Avila Coll., 1979. Dir. The C.A.S.T., Kansas City, Kans., 1981—; video cons. Austin House Video, Overland Park, Kans., 1981—; acctg. coordinator, Christenson, Barclay & Shaw, Kansas City, Mo., 1984—; tchr. Theatre for Young Ams., Overland Park, Kans., 1983—; dir. Independence City Theatre; actor 1984 World's Fair, New Orleans, summer 1984. Author: (children's plays) Berries, 1983, The Other Side, 1983, Teddy and Ralph the Dragoon, 1983; (children's story) The Boy Who Never Cried, 1981. Recipient theatre grantee, Avila Coll., Kansas City, Mo., 1977-79. Democrat. Baptist. Avocations: writing; directing; make-up design; tennis; fishing. Home: 11112 E 19th Independence MO 64052

PEREZ, JOHN MICHAEL, physician; b. Lafayette, Ind., Dec. 9, 1947; s. John Carlos and Martha (Gist) P.; m. Leslie Ann DeGroff, Nov. 1966 (div. 1977); children—Scott Michael, Jennifer Christine; m. Nancy Lynn Sanders, Apr. 28, 1979. A.B., Miami U., Oxford, Ohio, 1968; M.D., Ind. U., 1973. Diplomate Am. Bd. Urology. Intern, Community Hosp., Indpls., 1971-73; spl. resident in surgery, urology Ind. U., Indpls., 1973-78; urologist Arnett Clinic, Lafayette, Ind., 1978—, bd. dirs.; sec. surg. sect. St. Elizabeth Hosp., Lafayette, 1984—, sec. med. staff, 1985—. Fellow ACS (McCaskey award Ind. chpt. 1977), Am. Urologic Assn. (north central sect.), Chgo. Urological Soc., AMA (Physicians Recognition award 1983). Roman Catholic. Lodge: Elks. Avocations: fishing; golf; snow skiing; racquet ball; jogging; bowling. Home: 2000 Carlisle Rd West Lafayette IN 47906 Office: 2600 Greenbush Lafayette IN 47904

PEREZ, ROSANNE HARRIGAN, nursing educator, child development consultant; b. Miami, Fla., Feb. 24, 1945; d. John Henry and Rose (Hnatow) Harrigan; m. Helio C. Perez, May 29, 1965 (div. 1978); children—Dennis James, Michael Helio, John Henry. B.S., St. Xavier Coll. Chgo., 1965; M.S.N., Ind. U.-Indpls., 1974; Ed.D., Ind. U., Bloomington, 1979. Cert. pediatric nurse practitioner Nat. Bd. Pediatric Nurse Practitioners and Assocs. Staff nurse, evening charge nurse Mercy Hosp., Chgo., 1965-66; nursing educator Chgo. State Hosp., 1966-67; pediatric nurse practitioner Marion County Health and Hosp. Corp., Indpls., 1974-75; lectr. Ind. U.-Indpls., 1974-75, asst. prof. nursing, 1975-77, project dir. prenatal nursing program, 1978-85, assoc. prof., 1980-82, prof., chmn. dept. pediatrics, family and women's health Sch. Nursing, 1982-85, adj. prof. pediatrics Sch. Medicine, 1982-85; chief nursing sect. James Whitcomb Riley Hosp. Child Devel. Program, Indpls., 1982-85; Niehoff chair and prof. maternal child health Loyola U. Marcella Niehoff Sch. Nursing, 1985—; ednl. cons. Named Nurse of Yr., March of Dimes, 1978. Mem. Am. Nurses Assn., Ind. State Nurses Assn., Nurses Assn. of Am. Coll. Ob-Gyn. (pres. cert. corp.), Nat. Perinatal Assn. (bd. dirs.), Adult Edn. Assn. Am., Am. Nurses Found., Ind. U. Alumni Assn., AAAS, Sigma Xi, Pi Lambda Theta, Sigma Theta Tau. Republican. Roman Catholic. Club: Seroptomists. Author: Immunological Concepts Applied, 1978; Protocols for Perinatal Nursing Practice, 1981; contbr. articles to profl. jours. Office: 6525 N Sheridan Rd DH 411 Loyola U Chicago IL

PERINE, MAXINE HARRIET, educator; b. Worth County, Mo., May 11, 1918; d. Robert Rozwell and Della Dale (Martin) P.; B.S. in Edn., Central Mo. State U., 1944; M.A., Columbia U., 1954, profl. diploma, 1960, Ed.D., 1977, postdoctoral, 1979. Tchr., Worth County schs., 1935-44, Kansas City (Mo.) public schs., 1944-59; reading cons. Kansas City (Mo.) public schs., 1959-64; editor Holt, Rinehart, Winston, N.Y.C., 1964; mem. faculty U. Mich., Flint, 1964—, prof. specializing in reading, dept. edn., 1972—; editor Charles E. Merrill Pub. Co., 1984; vis. scholar Columbia U., 1978; speaker profl. confs. Mem. Internat. Reading Assn., AAUP, Kappa Delta Pi (chpt. founding counselor 1980—), Delta Kappa Gamma (named Women of Distinction 1972). Presbyterian. Author, editor in field. Home: 915 E Court St #400 Flint MI 48503 Office: U Mich 430 Classroom Office Bldg Flint MI 48503

PERISHO, CLARENCE ROBERT, retired chemistry educator; b. Newberg, Oreg., Apr. 29, 1917; s. Floyd Warder and Ethel (Lowe) P.; m. Margaret Eunice White, June 12, 1941; children—Robert C., Ethel Ruth, June Elizabeth. B.S., William Penn Coll., Oskaloosa, Iowa, 1938; M.A., Haverford Coll., Pa., 1939; Ph.D., NYU, 1963. Mem. faculty math. and sci., Friendsville Acad., Tenn., 1939-40, Nebr. Central Coll., Central City, 1940-44, McCook Jr. Coll., Nebr., 1944-47, Nebr. Wesleyan U., 1947-54; mem. faculty chemistry Mankato State U., Minn., 1954-82, prof., 1963-82, ret., 1982. Mem. AAAS, Math. Assn. (Eng.). Quaker. Home: 804 Belgrade Ave North Mankato MN 56001

PERKIN, THOMAS JOHN, college dean assistant, counselor; b. Flint, Mich., July 11, 1948; s. John Woolcock and Mary Annie (Jenkins) P.; m. Linda Ellen Putt, Jan. 9, 1971; children—Joel Thomas, Lindsey Marie. B.S. in Edn., Central Mich. U., 1971, M.A., 1983. Tchr. Morrice Area Schs., Mich., 1971-74; asst. gen. mgr. Standard Lumber Co., Owosso, Mich., 1976-80; asst. mgr. Pine Lumber Co., Owosso, 1981-84; asst. to dean Baker Jr. Coll., Owosso, 1984—. Chairperson citizens com. on vocat. edn. Corunna Schs., Mich., 1983—; mem. Council for Deaf, Owosso, 1984—; counselor Congregational Ch., Perry, Mich., 1983—. Mem. Am. Assn. Counseling and Devel., Am. Coll. Personnel Assn., Assn. Counselor Edn. and Supervision, Mich. Personnel Guidance Assn. Lodge: Kiwanis. Avocations: reading; skiing; swimming; fishing; camping. Office: Baker Jr College 1020 S Washington Owosso MI 48867

PERKINS, HOLLY ANN, physician, child psychiatrist; b. Greenville, Mich., May 20, 1955; d. Harry Leonard and Janice Louise (Schrader) P.; m. Fredric Norman Goldberg, June 13, 1981; 1 child, Brett Perkins Goldberg. B.S. in Zoology, U. Mich., 1976; M.D., Wayne State U., 1981. Intern, Butterworth Hosp., Grand Rapids, Mich., 1981-82; resident Mich. State U., Grand Rapids, 1982-84, fellow in child psyhciatry, 1982—. Mem. Urban Inst. Contemporary Arts, Grand Rapids, 1983, Nat. Republican Congl. Com., Washington, 1983. Mem. AMA, Am. Psychiat. Assn., DAR. Congregationalist.

PERKINS, JAMES HAROLD, data processing researcher, educator; b. Highland Park, Ill., Aug. 26, 1952; s. Robert James Perkins and Hildegarde Elizabeth (Skyrm) Perkins Matthews; m. Annette Marie Koch, Aug. 7, 1982. B.S., No. Ill. U., 1978, M.S., 1979. C.P.A.; cert. info. systems auditor; cert. internal auditor. Staff acct. Deloitte, Haskins & Sells, Chgo., 1980-81; EDP audit specialist Bank Adminstrn. Inst., Rolling Meadows, Ill., 1981—; computer cons. John Wiley & Sons, Inc., N.Y.C., 1982—; adj. prof. No. Ill. U., DeKalb, 1982—; mem. faculty U. Ill.-Chgo. Circle, DePaul U., Oakton Community Coll., 1980-82. Mem. Am. Inst. C.P.A.s, Ill. State Soc. C.P.A.s, Inst. Internal Auditors, Electronic Data Processing Auditors Assn. Served with USN, 1971-75. Republican. Roman Catholic. Home: 31 E Morningside St Lombard IL 60148 Office: Bank Adminstrn Inst 60 Gould Center Rolling Meadows IL 60008

PERKINS, JAMES PATRICK, âdvertising agency; b. Chgo., Dec. 6, 1939; s. John Alfred and Mary Grace (Quinlan) P.; student U. Ill., 1959-60, Western Ill. U., 1961; m. Sarah Reed Simkins, Sept. 13, 1975; children—Brian Patrick, Kevin Matthew, Quinn Cecile. Sales and mktg. exec. Glidden-Durkee, 1964-65; advt. mgr. Amvar Chem. Co., 1965-69; indsl. coatings rep. Benjamin Moore Co., 1969-71; account exec. JTC Advt., 1971-74; creative dir., pres. Laven, Fuller & Perkins Advt.-Mktg., Chgo., 1974—. Dir., Mem. adv. bd. Booth Meml. Hosp., Salvation Army, Chgo., 1978-81. Served with U.S. Army, 1961-62 Mem. Bank Mktg. Assn. Roman Catholic. Home: 1314 Scott Winnetka IL 60093 Office: 140 N Orlando Ave Winter Park FL 32789

PERKINS, JOANN M., hospice nurse; b. Swea City, Iowa, Dec. 24, 1936; d. Everett D. and Josephine Edna (Schmidt) Jensen; m. Harry Robert Perkins, Oct. 17, 1957; children—Daniel Lowell, Benjamin Edward, Jacqueline Marie, Billie Jo, Becky Anna, Kimberly Jean. R.N., St. Joseph's Mercy Hosp., 1957. Surg. nurse Holy Family Hosp., Estherville, Iowa, 1957-59, home health and hospice nurse, 1983—; head nurse Swift County Hosp., Benson, Minn., 1959-62; instr. Iowa Lakes Community Coll., Estherville, 1968-70. Mem. Iowa Hospice Orgn., Iowa Sch. Bd. Assn. Republican. Roman Catholic. Avocations: needle work; reading; boating. Home: Rural Route 2 Box 101 Estherville IA 51334 Office: Holy Family Hosp 826 N 8th St Estherville IA 51334

PERKINS, MARILYN JO, civic worker; b. Muscatine, Iowa, Aug. 11, 1944; d. John Bernard and Madge Mariam (Inglish) Vaira; m. Paul Dean Perkins, Mar. 18, 1961; children—Brian Dean, John Joseph. Grad. high sch., Centerville, Iowa. Sec. Bd. Health, Centerville, 1977—. Mem. care rev. com. Centerville Care Ctr., 1980-83; mem. Sch. Bd. Adv. Com., Centerville, 1982-83; bd. dirs. Centerville Sch. Bd., 1983—, Centerville/Appanoose Recreation Bd., 1985—. Mem. Bus. and Profl. Women U.S.A. (state corr. sec. 1983-84, local scholarship chmn. 1984-86), Centerville C. of C. Republican. Home: Rural Route 1 Box 71 Mystic IA 52574 Office: Appanoose County Bd Health Court House Centerville IA 52544

PERKINS, WILLIAM H., JR., financial company executive; b. Rushville, Ill., Aug. 4, 1921; s. William H. and Sarah Elizabeth (Logsdon) P.; ed. Ill. Coll.; m. Eileen Margaret Nelson, Jan. 14, 1949; 1 son, Gary Douglas. Legis. rep. CNA Fin. Corp., Chgo., 1949-79; pres. Howlett & Perkins Assos., Ltd., Chgo., 1979—. Mem. Nat. Armed Forces Mus. Adv. Bd. of Smithsonian Instn., 1964-83; mem. Ill. AEC, 1963—, sec., 1970—; mem. Ill. Traffic Safety Adv. Council; sgt.-at-arms Dem. Nat. Conv., 1952, 56, del.-at-large, 1964, 68, 72; spl. asst. to chmn. Dem. Nat. Com., 1960; mem. Presdl. Inaugural Com., 1961, 65, 69, 73. Served with AUS, 1944-46; aide to prime minister and Brit. ambassador at founding of UN, 1945. Mem. Ill. C. of C. (chmn. legis. com. 1971), Chgo. Assn. Commerce and Industry (legis com.), Health Ins. Assn. Am. Methodist. Clubs: Masons, Shriners; Sangamo (Springfield, Ill.); Riverside (Ill.); Fed. City (Washington). Home: 52 N Cowley Rd Riverside IL 60546 Office: 188 W Randolph St Suite 915 Chicago IL 60601

PERKINSON, DIANA ZOUZELKA, rug import company executive; b. Prostejov, Czechoslovakia, June 27, 1941; came to U.S., 1962, naturalized, 1965; d. John Charles and Agnes Diana (Sincl) Zouzelka; m. David Francis Perkinson, Mar. 6, 1965; children—Dana Leissa, David. B.A., U. Lausanne (Switzerland), 1960; M.A., U. Madrid, 1961; M.B.A., Case Western Res. U., 1963; cert. internat. mktg. Oxford (Eng.) U., 1962. Assoc. Allen Hartman & Schreiber, Cleve., 1963-64; interpreter Tower Internat. Inc., Cleve., 1964-66; pres. Oriental Rug Importers Ltd., Cleve., 1979—; pres. Oriental Rug Designers, Inc., Cleve., 1980—, Oriental Rug Cons., Inc., Cleve., 1980—; chmn. Foxworthy's Inc. subs. Oriental Rug Importers Ft. Myers, Naples, Sanibel, Fla.; dir. Beckwith & Assocs., Inc., Cleve., Dix-Bur Investments, Ltd. Trustee, Cleve. Ballet, 1979, exec. com., 1981; mem. Cleve. Mayor's Adv. Com.; chmn. grantsmanship Jr. League of Cleve., 1982; mem. Cleve. Found.-Women in Philanthropy, 1982. Mem. Women Bus. Owners Assn., Oriental Rug Retailers Am. (dir. 1983, pres.-elect). Republican. Roman Catholic. Clubs: Cleve. Racquet, Recreation League (Cleve.). Home: Ravencrest County Line Rd Cleveland OH 44022 also Stratford at Pelican Bay Crayton Rd Naples FL 33940 Office: Oriental Rug Importers Ltd Inc 23533 Mercantile Rd Beachwood OH 44122

PERKOVICH, ROBERT, lawyer; b. Chgo., Dec. 15, 1951; s. John George and Dora Catherine (Cappocci) P.; m. Debra Jo Johnson, May 28, 1971 (div. 1974); m. Debra Sue Benjamin, Aug. 11, 1979. B.A., Roosevelt U., 1976; J.D., John Marshall Law Sch., 1984. Bar: Ill. 1981, U.S. Dist. Ct. (no. dist.) Ill. 1981. Tax auditor IRS, Chgo., 1976-77; field examiner Nat. Labor Relations Bd., Chgo., 1977-81, field atty., 1981-84; exec. dir. Ill. Ednl. Labor Relations Bd., Chgo. and Springfield, 1984—. Active Chgo. Council Fgn. Relations, 1982, Art Inst. Chgo., Foster Parents Plan, Warwick, R.I., ACLU. Mem. ABA, Ill. State Bar Assn., Chgo. Bar Assn., Indsl. Relations Research Assn. (treas. 1985). Roman Catholic. Office: Ill Ednl Labor Relations Bd 188 W Randolph Chicago IL 60601 also 325 W Adams Springfield IL 62706

PERKOWITZ, MARC THOMAS, information systems manager; b. Evanston, Ill., Nov. 8, 1953; s. Robert Thomas and Jean Margret (Vogel) P.; m. Sally Lynn Shipman, Apr. 27, 1980. B.S., Ill. Inst. Tech., 1974, M.B.A., 1986. Cert. systems profl. Programmer, analyst MMS, Inc., Chgo., 1974-75, mgr. programming and devel., 1976; data base analyst McGraw-Edison Co., Arlington Heights, Ill., 1977-79; data base cons. Gould Inc., Rolling Meadows, Ill., 1980, mgr. tech. support, 1981, mgr. info. resource devel., 1982-83, mgr. ops. and tech. services. 1984, mgr. systems devel., 1985—. Treas. Lake-Cook chpt. Ill. Audubon Soc., Highland Park, Ill., 1984—; asst. scoutmaster N.W. Suburban Council Boy Scouts of Am., Prospect Heights, Ill., 1982—; acting mem. Moebius Theatre, Chgo. Avocations: birding, camping, photography. Office: Gould Inc 10 Gould Center Rolling Meadows IL 60008

PERNITZ, SCOTT GREGORY, lawyer; b. Milw., Jan. 28, 1953; s. William John and June Mary (Shaw) P.; m. Constance Denise Sheffer, Aug. 4, 1979; children—Justin William, Julia Dawn. B.A. cum laude in Polit. Sci., U. Wis.-Madison, 1975, J.D. cum laude, 1979. Bar: Wis. 1979, U.S. Dist. Ct. (we. dist.) Wis. 1979, U.S. Ct. Appeals (7th cir.) 1979. Assoc. Winner, McCallum, Hendee & Wixson, Madison, 1980-82; ptnr. Winner, McCallum, Wixson & Pernitz, Madison, 1983—. Mem. Wis. Acad. Trial Lawyers, ABA, Assn. Trial Lawyers Am., Dane County Bar Assn. Club: World Tae Kwon Do. Office: Winner McCallum Wixson & Pernitz 121 E Wilson Madison WI 53703

PEROTTI, ROSE NORMA, lawyer; b. St. Louis, Aug. 10, 1930; d. Joseph and Dorothy Mary (Roleski) Perotti. B.A., Fontbonne Coll., St. Louis, 1952; J.D., St. Louis U., 1957. Bar: Mo. 1958. Trademark atty. Sutherland, Polster & Taylor, St. Louis, 1958-63, Sutherland Law Office, 1964-70; trademark atty. Monsanto Co., St. Louis, 1971—. Mem. Honored with dedication of faculty office in her name, St. Louis U. Sch. Law, 1980. Mem. Mo. Bar Assn., Bar Assn. Met. St. Louis, ABA, Am. Judicature Soc., Smithsonian Assocs., Friends St. Louis Art Museum, Mo. Bot. Garden. Office: Monsanto Co 800 N Lindbergh Blvd Saint Louis MO 63167

PERPER, MICHAEL STEPHEN, pedodontist; b. Chgo., Jan. 22, 1948; s. Wallace and Rosalind (Garoon) P.; m. Gayle Susan Cohn, June 28, 1970; children—Daniel Aaron, Lindsey Michelle. B.S. U. Ill.-Chgo., 1968, D.D.S., 1972; clin. cert. Loyola U., Maywood, Ill., 1974. Practice dentistry specializing in pedodontics, Buffalo Grove, Ill., 1974—. Bd. dirs. Buffalo Grove Bd. Health, 1974-80. Avocations: sports. Office: 400 Dundee Rd Buffalo Grove IL 60090

PERPICH, RUDY GEORGE, governor; b. Carson Lake, Minn., June 27, 1928; s. Anton and Mary (Vukelich) P.; m. Delores Helen Simich, 1954; children—Rudy George, Mary Susan. A.A., Hibbing Jr. Coll., 1950; D.D.S., Marquette U., 1954. Mem. Hibbing (Minn.) Bd. Edn., 1956-62; mem. Minn. State Senate, 1962-70; lt. gov. Minn., 1970-76, gov., 1976-78, 82—; trade rep. Control Data Corp., Mpls., 1978-82. Served with U.S. Army, 1946-47. Mem. Nat. Govs. Assn. (chmn. com. on internat. trade and fgn. relations). Democrat. Address: Office of Governor 130 State Capitol Aurora Ave Saint Paul MN 55155

PERRET, MAURICE EDMOND, geography educator; b. La Chaux-de-Fonds, Switzerland, May 19, 1911; s. Jules Henri and Henriette Marie (Leuba) P.; Bac. es Lettres, U. Zurich (Switzerland), 1930; Licence es Lettres, U. Neuchatel (Switzerland), 1940; M.A. (Internat. House fellow 1940-42), U. Calif. at Berkeley, 1942; Doctorat es Lettres, U. Lausanne (Switzerland), 1950. Tchr., Petropolis and Lycee Francais, Rio de Janeiro, Brazil, 1935-37; asst. consulate Switzerland, San Francisco, 1942-43; del. internat. com. Red Cross, Washington, 1943-45; del. Aid to Arab Refugees, Palestine, 1949-51; asst. Internat. Telecommunication Union, Geneva, Switzerland, 1951-52; librarian La Chaux-de-Fonds, Switzerland, 1953-54; asst. Oltremare, Rome, Italy, 1955-56; prof. Avenches, Switzerland, 1957-63; prof. geography, map librarian U. Wis., Stevens Point, 1963-81, prof. emeritus, 1981—. Curator Roman Mus., Avenches, Switzerland, 1960-63. Mem. city council Avenches, Switzerland, 1961-63. Served with Swiss Army, 1939-40. Mem. Assn. Am. Geographers, Nat. Council Geog. Edn., Am. Geog. Soc., Wis. Acad. Scis., Arts and Letters, Société vaudoise de geographie (v.p. 1960-63), Fedn. Swiss Geog. Socs. (v.p. 1961-63). Club: Travelers Century. Editorial com. Atlas Switzerland, 1960-63. Contbr. articles to profl. jours. Office: Geography Dept U Wis Stevens Point WI 54481

PERRIN, EUGENE VICTOR DEBS KROPOTKIN, pathologist; b. Detroit, Mar. 7, 1927; s. Emanuel Anatol and Frances Theresa (Levin) Paperno; m. Jane Carol Schutter, Mar. 31, 1956; children—Daniel, Miriam, Adam, Joshua. Student Yale U., 1945-46; B.A., Wayne State U., 1948; postgrad. U. Chgo., 1948-49; M.D., U. Mich., 1953; D.D., Univ. Life Ch., 1980. Intern, Sinai Hosp., Detroit, 1953-54; resident Boston Children's Hosp., 1955-56, Lying-In Hosp., Boston, 1956-57, Lahey Clinic Hosps., Boston, 1957-58, Babies Hosp., N.Y.C., 1958-59; sr. research fellow, assoc. prof. pathology U. Cin., 1959-66; pathologist Cin. Children's Hosp., Hosp., Cin. Gen. and Booth Hosp., 1959-66; assoc. prof. pediatrics, pathology and reproductive biology Case Western Res. U., Cleve., 1966-74; prof. pathology Wayne State U., Detroit, 1974—, assoc. in pediatrics, obstetrics and anatomy, 1975—, adj. prof. anthropology, 1984—; mem. staffs Children's Hosp., Sinai Hosp., Hutzel Hosp., Receiving Hosp.; human health cons. Internat. Joint Com., Acquatic Ecosystems Objective, Com., Windsor, Ont., Can., 1979—. Editor: Pathobiology of Development, 1973; Moral Problems in Medicine, 1975; Pathology of Placenta, 1984. Contbr. articles to profl. jours. Bd. dirs. E. Mich. Environ. Action Council, 1975—, Nonviolent Action for Nat. Def. Inst., 1983—, Poetry Resource Ctr., Mich. chmn. med. adv. com. March of Dimes, 1983-85. Served with AUS, 1944-46. Mem. Internat. Assn. Great Lakes Research, Internat. Acad. Pathology; mem. Am. Soc. Cell Biology, Am. Assn. Pathologists, Am. Acad. Clin. Toxicology, Am. Coll. Toxicology, Am. Ornithol. Union, Teratology Soc., Pediatric Pathology Assn., Tissue Culture Assn., Physicians for Social Responsibility, Midwest Soc. Pediatric Research, Cooper Ornithol. Union. Hebrew. Avocations: poetry; gardening; cooking; back packing; choral singing. Home: 26318 Dundee St Huntington Woods MI 48070

PERRIZO, BARTON EUGENE, dentist; b. Pipestone, Minn., Sept. 19, 1925; s. Clarence Leo and Marie Olga (Ludtke) P.; m. Marian Patricia Larsen, Sept. 14, 1949 (dec. Apr. 1983); children—Michael, Janna, Patricia, Gregory, D.D.S., U. Minn., 1951, Pvt. practice dentistry, Jasper, Minn., 1951—; chmn. dental staff Pipestone County Med. Ctr., Minn., 1983-84. Instr. first aid ARC, Pipestone County, Minn., 1953-84; dir., chmn. Jasper Pub. Sch., Minn., 1960-84; chmn. bd. dirs. S.W. Minn. Telecommunications, Luverne, 1984. Mem. Minn. Dental Assn., So. Dist. Dental Soc. (pres. 1957-58), Am. Legion. Democrat. Roman Catholic. Club: Civic (pres. 1956-57) (Jasper, Minn.). Lodge: K.C. (treas. 1979-84). Avocations: golf; gardening; jogging; tennis. Home and Office: Box 158 Jasper MN 56144

PERRUCCI, CAROLYN CUMMINGS, sociology educator; b. Murfreesboro, Tenn., June 18, 1940; d. Clarence Land and Kathleen Geneva (McGraw) Cummings; m. Robert Perrucci, Aug. 4, 1965; children—Alissa C., Martin C. B.S., Middle Tenn. State U., 1961; M.S., Purdue U., 1963, Ph.D., 1965. Research assoc. Schs. Engring. Purdue U., 1964-66, asst. prof. sociology, 1966-70, assoc. prof., 1970—, chmn. women's studies, 1980; asst. equal opportunity employment officer, 1977-79; cons. in field. Author: Marriage and the Family, 1974, Women in Scientific and Engineering Professions, 1984. Contbr. articles in field. Recipient Schleman Gold Medallion award, 1981; NDEA fellow, 1961-64, Ford Found. fellow, 1973-74; grantee in field. Mem. Am. Sociol. Assn., Nat. Council Family Relations, N. Central Sociol. Assn. (chmn. 1985-86), Sociologists for Women in Soc., Soc. for Study Social Problems. Democrat. Office: Dept Sociology Purdue U West Lafayette IN 47907

PERRY, CHRISTOPHER JAMES, geologist; b. Cleve., Oct. 7, 1957; s. Norman Alexander and Laura Phyllis (McDonald) P. B.S. in Geol. Sci., Cleve. State U., 1980; M.S. in Engring. Geology, Purdue U., 1982. Cartographer, Madison & Madison, Internat., Cleve., 1979-80; research fellow Purdue U., West Lafayette, Ind., 1980-82; petroleum devel. geologist Unocal Corp. Olney, Ill., 1982—. Research fellow U.S. Dept. Edn., 1980-82. Mem. Am. Assn. Petroleum Geologists (jr. mem.), Ill. Geol. Soc. (sec.-treas. 1984-85, v.p. 1985—), Computer Oriented Geol. Soc., Cleve. State Geol. Assn. (pres. 1979-80). Avocations: study in geology and economics, classical music, hacking, outdoor sports. Home: 526 A S Wilson St Olney IL 62450 Office: Unocal Corp 801 S West St Olney IL 62450

PERRY, DALLIS KAY, psychology educator; b. Anacortes, Wash., Mar. 15, 1929; s. Wiley Fremont and Eunice May (Macomber) P.; m. Ellen Ann Corcoran, Dec. 27, 1952 (dec. Mar. 1980); children—Catherine Lebens, Brian Perry; m. Taeko Fujita, May 1, 1982. B.A., U. Wash., 1950; M.A., U. Minn., 1951, Ph.D., 1953. Lic. psychologist, Minn. Research analyst AFPTRC Maxwell AFB, 1954-55; research psychologist CIA, Washington, 1955-60; human factors scientist System Devel. Corp., Santa Monica, Calif., 1960-67; prof. psychology, asst. dir. U. Minn., Mpls., 1967—. Mem. Am. Edn. Research Assn., Am. Psychol. Assn., Assn. Counseling and Devel., Assn. Measurement and Evaluation in Counseling and Devel., Minn. Assn. Counseling and Devel. Office: Univ Counseling Services U Minnesota 192 Pillsbury Dr SE Minneapolis MN 55455

PERRY, DIANNE KAY, school guidance administrator, psychologist; b. Saginaw, Mich., Jan. 30, 1946; d. Merritt B. and Wanda Lois (Kimmel) Perry; m. Britau W. Twitty, 1984. B.A., Alma Coll., 1968; M.Ed., Wayne State U., 1972; Ph.D. in Edn., U. Mich., 1981. Cert. tchr., Mich.; lic. psychologist, Mich.; cert. hypnotherapist. Guidance adminstr. Detroit pub. schs., 1979—, cons., 1972—; part-time instr. Wayne County Community Coll., 1971-79; counselor, ednl. cons., human relations cons.; practice psychology, Detroit, 1982—; assoc. cons. New Perspectives on Race. Mem. Mich. Personnel and Guidance Assn. (pres.-elect 1983-84), Guidance Assn. Met. Detroit (pres. 1982-83, newsletter editor 1981-82). Methodist. Author: Classroom Techniques to Improve Self-Concept, 1972; Congruencies and Incongruencies in the Expectations and Perceptions of the Role of the Elementary School Counselor in Detroit Public Schools, 1981. Home: 25051 Sherwood Circle Southfield MI 48075 Office: 5057 Woodward Ave Suite 644 Schools Center Bldg Detroit MI 48202 also: Ten-Southfield Clinic 17603 W Ten Mile Rd Southfield MI 48075

PERRY, DONALD DEAN, art educator, artist; b. Hutchinson, Kans., Sept. 29, 1939; s. Theodore Earl and Alice Elizabeth (Collins) P.; m. Sharon Lynn Harz, Aug. 19, 1962; children—Brett Alan, Mark Evan. B.F.A., Pittsburg State U., Kans., 1962; M.S., Kans. State U., 1967; M.F.A., U. Wis., 1967. Art tchr. Salina Pub. Schs., Kans., 1962-66; tchr. extension div. art inst. Kans. State U., Manhattan, 1964-66; instr. art U. Wis., Marshfield, 1967-72; asst. prof. Emporia State U., Kans., 1972-77, assoc. prof., 1977-84, prof., 1984—; chmn. art dept., 1977-84, dir. Eppink Art Gallery, 1977—; studio art reader Ednl. Testing Service, Princeton, N.J., 1983—. One man exhbn., 1983. Bd. dirs. Emporia Arts Council, 1979. Research grantee U. Wis., Marshfield, 1968, research and creativity grantee Emporia State U., 1974, 75, 76; drawing exhbn. grantee Kans. Arts Commn., Topeka, 1982-85, presenter exchange grantee Mid-Am. Arts Alliance, Kansas City, Mo., 1983. Recipient various awards for artwork. Mem. Kansas City Artist Coalition. Home: 1908 Coronado Ave Emporia KS 66801 Office: Emporia State U Art Dept 1200 Commercial St Emporia KS 66801

PERRY, ELI, chemical engineer, consultant; b. Phila., Dec. 28, 1920; s. Louis and Fannie (Segal) P. B.S., U. Pa., 1942; S.M., MIT, 1947; tchr.'s diploma Gratz Coll., Phila., 1940. Registered profl. engr., Tex. Asst. dir. research Monsanto Co., Texas City, Tex., 1955-59, 61, research assoc., Zurich, Switzerland, 1960, Durham, N.C., 1962-67, St. Louis, 1968-79, sr. tech. assoc., 1980-82; prin. Eli Perry Assocs., St. Louis, 1983—. Editorial bd. Jour. Membrane Sci., 1979—. Contbr. articles to profl. jours. Patentee in field (45). Recipient Hugo Otto Wolf prize U. Pa., 1942. Fellow AAAS, Royal Soc. Chemistry; mem. Soc. Plastics Engrs., Am. Chem. Soc., Am. Inst. Chem. Engrs., Sigma Xi Tau Beta Pi. Avocations: reading; photography; volunteer work. Home: 1056 Willow Brook Dr Saint Louis MO 63146

PERRY, ESTON LEE, business executive; b. Martburg, Tenn., June 16, 1936; s. Eston Lee and Willimae (Heidle) P.; m. Alice Anne Schmit, Oct. 21, 1961; children—Julie Anne, Jeffrey John, Jennifer Lee. B.S., Ind. State U., 1961. With Oakley Corp., 1961—, treas., 1961-70, dir., 1965—, v.p., 1981—; corp. officer Ind. State Bank, Terre Haute, 1975-80; pres. One Twenty Four Madison Corp., Terre Haute, 1979—, chmn. bd., 1981—. Bd. dirs. Oakley Found., 1975—; bd. dirs. Aviation Commn., Terre Haute, pres., 1970; bd. dirs. Salvation Army, Terre Haute, 1975—, mem. exec. adv. bd., 1979—; bd. dirs. Vigo County Dept. Pub. Welfare, 1979-82, 124 Madison Corp., 1979—, Jr. Achievement Wabash Valley, 1980—, United Way of Wabash Valley, 1984—, United Way of Ind., 1984—, Terre Haute Symphony Orch., 1984—, Goodwill Industries of Terre Haute, 1984—, Leadership Terre Haute, 1984—; bd. dirs. Central Eastside Assocs., 1984—, pres., 1984-85; mem. President's Assocs., Ind. State U., adv. bd. Ctr. Econ. Devel., 1984—; bd. overseers Sheldon Swope Art Gallery of Terre Haute, 1984—; nat. mem. Council on Founds.; mem. adv. com. comml. air service study Ind. Dept. Commerce. Served with U.S. Army, 1955-57. Mem. Jaycees Terre Haute (v.p. 1967-69), C. of C. Terre Haute (bd. dirs. 1984—), Edgewood Grove Assn. (pres. 1982), Wabash Valley Pilots Assn., Aircraft Owners and Pilots Assn., Air Safety Found., Aviation Trades Assn., Lambda Chi Alpha. Clubs: Country of Terre Haute; Sycamore Varsity (Ind. State U.). Lodges: Lions (pres. Terre Haute 1983-84), Elks. Home: 124 Madison Blvd Terre Haute IN 47803 Office: 8 S 16th St Terre Haute IN 47807

PERRY, JEFFREY STEVEN, actor; b. Highland Park, Ill., Aug. 16, 1955; s. Harold Joseph and Eleanor Jane (Irving) P.; m. Laura Elizabeth Metcalf, Mar. 21, 1983; 1 child, Zoe Jane. Student Ill. State U. Founding mem. Steppenwolf Theatre Co., Highland Park, Ill., 1976, artistic dir., Chgo., 1983-85, also mem ensemble. Office: Steppenwolf Theatre Co 2851 N Halsted St Chicago IL 60657

PERRY, NANCY ESTELLE, psychologist, educator; b. Pitts., Oct. 30, 1934; d. Simon Warren and Estelle Ceclia (Zaluski) Reichard; m. Robert Joseph Perry, Dec. 17, 1955; m. 2d, John Otis Cleveland, Mar. 1, 1980; children—Scott, Elaine, Karen. B.S. in Nursing, Ohio State U., 1956, M.A. in Psychology, 1969, Ph.D. in Psychology, 1973. Lic. clin. psychologist, Ohio, Wis.; R.N., Ohio, Wis. Nurse, Mt. Carmel Hosp., Columbus, Ohio, 1956-57; psychologist Madison County (Ohio) Sch., 1971-73, project dir. Human Devel. Project, 1973-76; pvt. practice psychology, cons. psychology, Columbus, 1976-79; pvt. practice psychology, Milw., Wis., 1979—; asst. prof. psychology Sch. Nursing, U. Wis.-Milw., 1979—. Ednl. Profl. Devel. Act fellow, 1970-71. Mem. Am. Psychol. Assn., Wis. Psychol. Assn., Am. Nurses Assn., Am. Assn. Mariage and Family Therapists, Orgn. Devel. Network, Internat. Assn. Applied Social Scientists. Home: 2210 W Charter Mall Mequon WI 53092 Office: 1200 E Capital Dr Shorewood WI 53211

PERRY, RICHARD DOUGLAS, restaurateur; b. Chgo., Oct. 24, 1938; s. Ralph Marion and Nell Jane (Alexander) P. B.A., U. Ill., 1961. Expansion dir. Delta Sigma Phi, Denver, 1961-66; sales rep. McGraw hill Book Co., N.Y.C., 1966-71; propr. Richard Perry restaurant, St. Louis, 1971—. Mem. Inst. Am. Food and Wine (charter), Master Chef's Inst. (charter), St. Louis Vintner's Forum (founding), Am. Culinary Fedn., Nat. Restaurant Assn., Mo. Restaurant Assn., Nat. Inst. for Off Premise Catering (charter). Home and Office: 3265 S Jefferson Ave Saint Louis MO 63118

PERRY, ROBERT LEONARD, electronics company executive; b. Bklyn., Dec. 23, 1941; s. Charles and Bella (Opatowsky) P.; m. Linda Joyce Richman, Aug. 15, 1964; children—Michelle, Lisa. B.A., SUNY-Binghamton, 1963; M.S., Mich. State U., 1965; Ph.D., Rutgers U., 1970. Statis. cons. computer center Rutgers U., New Brunswick, N.J., 1969-71; group leader math. services dept. Procter & Gamble Co., Cin., 1971-83; dir. operational analysis McDonnell Douglas Electronics Co., St. Charles, Mo., 1984—; adj. assoc. prof. U. Mo., St. Louis, 1985—. Contbr. articles to profl. jours. Served with USPHS, 1967-69. Fellow Am. Soc. for Quality Control; mem. Am. Statis. Assn., Biometric Soc. Avocations: running; skiing; stamp collecting. Office: McDonnell Douglas Electronics Co PO Box 426 Saint Charles MO 63302

PERRY, WASH M., JR., photographic consultant; b. Chgo., Sept. 18, 1950; s. Wash M. and Mary O. (Gray) P.; m. Theresa Alexander, Mar. 4, 1972; children—Talae, Kiaya Student in engring. U. Ill.-Chgo., 1969-72; student in photography Columbia Coll., Chgo., 1982-84; student in bus. law Loop Jr. Coll., Chgo., 1982-84. Mgr. Helix Ltd., Chgo., 1976—. Mem. Midwest Indsl. Photographers Assn. Methodist. Avocations: archery; chess; computers; racquetball; scuba diving. Office: Helix Ltd 325 W Huron Chicago IL 60610

PERRY, WILLIAM HENRY, JR., manufacturing company executive; b. Webb City, Mo., Jan. 9, 1918; s. William H. and Tressa (Pepper) P.; m. Marion E. Barmore, Sept. 5, 1938; children—William III, David H., Rebecca J. Student Joplin Sch. Law and Commerce, Mo., 1934-36. Sales mgr. The Webb Corp., Webb City, Mo., 1936-57; with Cardinal Scale Mfg. Co., Webb City, Mo., 1950—, now pres. Councilman City Webb City, 1950-54; chmn. City Water Bd., Webb City, 1964-70; pres., mem. Webb City Sch. Bd., 1960-75. Mem. Nat. Assn. Scale Mfrs. Assn. (pres. 1980-83), Nat. Scale Mens Assn. (pres. 1963). Republican. Presbyterian. Club: Lion (pres. 1948-49. Home: 7 Colonial Dr Webb City MO 64870 Office: Cardinal Scale Mfg Co 203 E Daugherty St Webb City MO 64870

PERRY, WILLIAM WADE, music educator; b. Cameron, Tex., Apr. 1, 1931; s. Wilson Wade and Lorene Inola (Hillegeist) P.; m. Alice Louise Field, Dec. 22, 1953; children—Elizabeth, Margaret, Edwin. B.Music Edn., North Tex. State U., Denton, 1952, M.Music Edn., 1957, Ed.D., 1966. Dir. band and orch. pub. sch., Beaumont, Tex., 1952-58; prin. solo flutist Beaumont Symphony Orch., 1953-58; prin. flutist Wichita (Kans.) Music Theatre, 1971-83; piccoloist, flutist Wichita Symphony Orch., 1964-74; prof. music Friends U., Wichita, 1962—; musical dir., condr. Friends U.-Community Symphony Orch., 1962—, Camerata Musica Chamber Orch., Wichita, 1980-81. Bd. dirs. George B. Tack Flute Audition Com. Served with U.S. Army, 1953-55. Mem. AAUP, Kans. Music Educators Assn., Music Educators Nat. Conf., Phi Mu Alpha Sinfonia. Republican. Methodist. Author: The Flute, 1963. Office: 2100 University Ave Wichita KS 67213

PERSHING, ROBERT GEORGE, telecommunications company executive; b. Battle Creek, Mich., Aug. 10, 1941; s. James Arthur and Beulah Francis P.; B.S.E.E., Tri-State Coll., Angola, Inc., 1961; m. Diana Kay Prill, Sept. 16, 1961; children—Carolyn, Robert. Communications engr. Am. Elec. Power, Ind., N.Y. and Ohio, 1961-69; design supr. Wescom, Inc., Ill., 1969-74; dir. engring. Tellabs, Inc., Lisle, Ill., 1974-78; pres. Teltrend, Inc., St. Charles, Ill., 1979—, also dir.; engring. cons. Mem. IEEE. Office: 620 Stetson Saint Charles IL 60185

PERSKY, SEYMOUR HOWARD, lawyer; b. Chgo., May 22, 1922; s. Joseph E. and Bertha (Solomon) P.; A.A. magna cum laude, City Coll., Chgo., 1949; B.A., Roosevelt U., 1952; J.D., DePaul U., 1952; postgrad. Northwestern U., 1961-62; m. Beverly M. Lipsky, July 8, 1962; children—Jonathan E., Abbe Joan. Admitted to Ill. bar, 1952, U.S. Supreme Ct. bar, 1965; resident counsel Mid-West Loan Co., Chgo., 1953-58; sr. ptnr. firm Persky, Phillips & Berzock, Chgo., 1961-63; practiced in Chgo., 1963—; pub. defender Narcotics Ct., Municipal Ct. of Chgo., 1964—; lectr. Truman Jr. Coll.; mem. Internat. Options Market, Internat. Monetary Market (Chgo. Merc. Exchange). Vice pres. Peoples Rehab. Found.; Yiddish Theater Assn.; vice gen. chmn. bd. govs. Israel Bonds of Greater Chgo., chmn. young peoples div., 1970-72, chmn. lawyers div., 1973-74, pres. Prime Minister's Club; bd. govs. Ida Crown Jewish Acad.; bd. dirs. Hillel Torah North Suburban Day Sch., Skokie, Ill. 1973, Arie Crown Day Sch., 1977—, Skokie Valley Synagogue, 1977—, Anti-Defamation League B'nai B'rith, Jewish Nat. Fund, YIVO-Inst. for Jewish Research; commr. Highland Park Hist. Preservations Commn.; ptnr. DePaul U. Coll. Law; mem. endowment bd. DePaul U.; mem. Highland Park Historic Preservation Commn., Ill. Served with USAAF, 1941-44. Mem. ABA, Ill. Bar Assn. (chmn. subcom. unauthorized practice law com. 1962), Chgo. Bar Assn. (criminal law com., def. prisoners com.) , Ill. Acad. Criminology, Decalogue Soc., Def. Lawyers Assn., Am. Trial Lawyers Assn., Nat. Trust for Historic Preservation, Lex Legio DePaul U., Soc. Fellows DePaul U., DePaul U. Alumni Assn (chmn. alumni class 1952), Chgo. Assn. Commerce and Industry, Landmarks Preservation Council, Greater N.Mich. Ave. Assn., Mensa, Nu Beta Epsilon. Clubs: City, Covenant of Ill., Execs., Lincoln Park Builders (Chgo.); Quadrangle (dir.) (U. Chgo.). Home: 65 Prospect Ave Highland Park IL 60035 Office: 105 W Madison St Chicago IL 60602

PERSON, DAVID STEWART, project manager; b. Des Moines, Iowa, Aug. 27, 1945; s. Dean LaVerne and Phyllis Maxine (James) P.; m. Judy Kay Rinehart, Oct. 9, 1965; children—Jennifer Jill, Ryan David. A.A.S., Iowa State U., 1965. Estimator, Pitts.-Des Moines Steel Co., Des Moines, 1965-77; sales agt. Stanbrough Realtors, 1977-79, sales mgr. Mitchellville, Iowa, 1979-80; project. mgr. real estate and fin. Weitz Corp., Des Moines, 1980—. Town councilman Town of Runnells, Iowa, 1969-75; rep. Des Moines Met. Area Solid Waste Agy., 1970-75; elder Runnells Christian Ch., 1973—; bd. dirs. Southeast Polk Community Sch. Dist., 1976-85. Democrat. Lodge: Lions, Masons. Avocations: golf; fishing; bicycling. Home: Rural Route 2 Runnells IA 50237 Office: Weitz Corp 800 2d Ave Des Moines IA 50309

PERSON, JEAN KATHRYN, career counselor; b. Mpls., June 17, 1953; d. Willis Bagly and Loretta Fay (Ferren) P. B.A., Willamette U., 1975; M.S.Ed., So. Ill. U., 1981. Career counselor Ind. U., Bloomington, 1981—; workshop leader Job Hunters' Service Ctr., Bloomington, 1983. Co-author: Basic Career Planning, 1985. Treas., Bloomington Women's Network, 1983-84; mem. program com. Nat. Women's Music Festival, Bloomington, 1982-83; bd. dirs. Tri-County Displaced Homemakers, 1984—. Mem. Am. Soc. Tng. and Devel., Am. Assn. Counseling and Devel., Am. Vocat. Guidance Assn., Am. Coll. Personnel Assn., Nat. Assn. Student Personnel Adminstrs. Democrat. Avocations: sailing; writing poetry; reading; aerobics. Office: Ind U 625 N Jordan Bloomington IN 47405

PERSON, LUCY WU, software engineer; b. Shanghai, China, Nov. 7, 1934; came to U.S. 1958, naturalized 1964; d. Tsoo Wu and Wen (Yu) Wu; m. James C. Person, Jan. 30, 1960; children—Amy, Maria, Nancy. Chem. Engr., Nat. Taiwan U., China, 1950; engr. Nat. Tsnj Hu, China, 1956-58; Ph.D., U. Calif.-Berkeley, 1961; postgrad. U. Chgo., 1981. Software engr. AT&T Bell Labs., Naperville, Ill., 1981—; computer scientist Argonne Nat. Lab., Ill., 1963-81; lectr. Ill. Benedictine Coll., Lisle, 1965-66; research assoc. U. Calif.-Berkeley, 1961-63; invited panelist Internat. Computer Conf., Taiwan, 1982; guest lectr. Nat. Tsnj Hu U., China, 1975. Author: Introduction to Chinese, 1978. Founder Chinese Language Sch., 1971-73; vice pres. Orgn. Chinese Am., Chgo., 1977-78; corp. mem. Bd. United Ch. Homeland Ministry, 1982—; observer to World Council Chs. meeting MIT, Boston, 1979; Chinese ch. lay leader, 1965-78; observer, reporter United Ch. Christ Nat. Women Meeting, Ohio, 1979; seminar leader Ill. Ch. Women Conf., 1980. Named 1st in graduating class Nat. Taiwan U., 1956; fellow Tsnj Hu Found., 1958-60, Univ. fellow, 1960-61. Mem. Am. Nuclear Soc. (program com. 1978-81), IEEE (sr. mem.), Women in Sci., Sigma Xi. Clubs: Orgn. Chinese Am. (Chgo.) (v.p. 1978-80), Council for Fgn. Affairs (Chgo.). Home: 424-57th St Downers Gove IL 60516

PERSSON, ERLAND KARL, electrical engineer, electrical company executive; b. Soderala, Sweden, Oct. 9, 1923; came to U.S., 1949, naturalized, 1953; m. Elaine Darm; children—Ann Monn, Eric. B.S.E.E., U. Minn., 1955. Registered profl. engr., Minn. Prin. engr. Gen. Mills, Mpls., 1956-61; v.p. engring. Electro-Craft Corp., Hopkins, Minn., 1961-72, v.p. research and devel., 1972-83, sr. v.p., chief tech. officer, 1983—. Contbr. articles to profl. jours. Contbr. chpts. to books. Patentee in field. Mem. Mech. Engring. Adv. Com. U. Minn.; bd. dirs. Minn. High Tech. Council, 1984—. Fellow Audio Engring. Soc. (founder Midwest chpt. 1974); mem. Am. Electronics Assn., Electronic Motion Control Assn., Incremental Motion Control Soc., IEEE (mem. subcom. Single Phase & Fractional Horsepower, Indsl. Drives com.), Minn. Assn. Commerce and Industry, Robotics Internat. Soc. Mfg. Engrs., Eta Kappa Nu. Office: Electro-Craft Corp 1600 2d St South Hopkins MN 55343

PESARESI, DANIEL JOSEPH, manufacturing company executive; b. Logansport, Ind., July 17, 1939; s. Walter and Theresa Marie (DiGilio) P.; m. Vivian Ann Montz, Aug. 26, 1961; children—Annamaria, Daniel Joseph. B.S., St. Joseph Coll., 1961. With Winamac Coil Springs, Kewanna, Ind., 1961—, pres., 1961—. Pres. Winamac Council on Aging, 1982—; pres. Winamac Econ. Devel. Corp., 1978—. Mem. Farm Equipment Mfrs. Assn. Republican. Lodges: K.C., Moose, Eagles. Home: Rural Route 4 Box 56 Winamac IN 46996 Office: Winamac Coil Springs Box 278 Kewanna IN 46939

PESCHAU, DAVID FRED, television network executive; b. Mpls., Apr. 1, 1948; s. Kenneth E. and Jean H. Peschau; m. Helen Noble; children—Matthew, Christopher. B.A., Luther Coll., 1970. Account exec. sta. WAOW-TV Wausau, Wis., 1971-73, sta. WKOW-TV, Madison, Wis., 1973-74; gen. mgr. sta. WXOW-TV, La Crosse, Wis., 1974-76, v.p., 1976—; v.p. stas. WKOW-TV, WAOW-TV, WXOW-TV, WQOW-TV, Wis. TV Network, 1977—; chmn. ABC's VIE com. Bd. dirs. Am. Cancer Soc.; pres. Our Redeemer Luth. Ch. Served with U.S. Army N.G., 1969-75. Mem. Nat. Assn. Broadcasters, Wis. Broadcasters Assn. (pres.-elect), TV Bur. Advt., Downtown La Crosse Bus. Assn., La Crosse C. of C. (v.p.). Republican. Office: WXOW TV PO Box 128 La Crosse WI 54602

PESEK, BORIS PETER, economics educator; b. Most, Czechoslovakia, Sept. 21, 1926; came to U.S., 1950; s. Karel and Anna (Vondrakova) P.; m. Milena M. Lambertova, Oct. 28, 1948. B.A., Coe Coll., Cedar Rapids, Iowa, 1951; M.A., U. Chgo., 1953, Ph.D., 1956. Rockefeller Found. fellow Johns Hopkins U., Balt., 1956-57; prof. Mich. State U., East Lansing, 1957-67; prof. econs. U. Wis.-Milw., 1967—; vis. prof. U. Vienna, 1986; participant East European Nat. Income Project, Columbia U., 1957-63. Mem. Am. Econ. Assn. Roman Catholic. Co-author: Money, Wealth and Economic Theory, 1966; Foundations of Money and Banking, 1967. Home: 12928 N Colony Dr Mequon WI 53092 Office: U Wis-Milw Box 413 Milwaukee WI 53201

PESEK, CYRIL PAUL, JR., electronics executive; b. Mpls., Oct. 9, 1932; s. Cyril Paul and Muriel E. (Fossum) P.; m. Rae Huntington, Jan. 20, 1955; children—Kate, Julia, Elizabeth. B.S.E., Yale U., 1954; M.B.A., Harvard U., 1958. Exec. v.p. Colight, Inc., Mpls., 1962-67; pres., chief exec. officer Pesek Engring. and Mfg. Co., Mpls., 1967-76; mgr. OEM div. CPT Corp., Mpls., 1977-78; pres. Western Lithoplate, St. Louis, 1979-83; chmn. bd., chief exec. officer Moniterm Corp., Mpls., 1983—. Patentee etching machine. Chmn. Wayzata Planning Commn., Minn., 1966-69; vestryman St. Martin's Ch., Wayzata, 1977-79; mem. Orono City Council, Minn., 1977-79; commr., St. Louis Mus. Sci., 1981-84; bd. dirs. United Theol. Sem., 1985—. Served to 1st lt. U.S. Army, 1954-56. Mem. Am. Electronics Assn. Republican. Episcopalian. Club: St. Louis Racquet (bd. dirs. 1983-84). Avocations: tennis; cross-country skiing. Home: 1235 Lyman Ave Wayzata MN 55391 Office: Moniterm Corp 5740 Green Circle Dr Minnetonka MN 55343

PESEK, JAMES ROBERT, management consultant; b. Chgo., May 30, 1941; s. James F. and Elizabeth A. (Ord) P.; m. Bonnie L. Bowen, Nov. 1963; children—Becky, Shelly. B.S.M.E. with honors, U. Ill., 1964; M.B.A., U. Nebr., 1966. Cert. mgmt. cons. Adminstrv. services mgr. Cummins Engine Co., Columbus, Ind., 1966-68; cons. div. Arthur Andersen & Co., Milw., 1968-72; mgr. distbn. div. ADG, Indpls., 1972-74; mgr. Mgmt. Adv. Services Wolf & Co., Chgo., 1974-79; pres. Ind. Mgmt. Services, Hinsdale, Ill., 1979—; cons.; spkr., tchr. Mem. Am. Prodn. and Inventory Control Soc., Inst. Mgmt. Cons., Am. Arbitration Assn. Home: 6273 Fairmount Downers Grove IL 60516 Office: 201 E Ogden Ave Hinsdale IL 60521

PESHKIN, SAMUEL DAVID, lawyer; b. Des Moines, Oct. 6, 1925; s. Louis and Mary (Grund) P.; B.A., U. Iowa, 1948, J.D., 1951; m. Shirley Isenberg, Aug. 17, 1947; children—Lawrence Allen, Linda Ann. Admitted to Iowa bar, 1951, since practiced in Des Moines; partner Bridges & Peshkin, 1953-66, Peshkin and Robinson, 1966—; chmn. Iowa Bd. Law Examiners, 1970-76. Bd. dirs. Sch. Religion, U. Iowa, U. Iowa Old Gold Devel. Fund, 1955—, Iowa Meml. Union, 1957—, State U. Iowa Found., 1957—. Served with USNR, 1943-45. Fellow Am. Bar Found., Internat. Soc. Barristers; mem. Internat., Inter-Am., Am. (bd. govs. 1973—, ho. of dels. 1968—, chmn. standing com. on membership 1959—), Iowa State (pres. jr. bar sect. 1958-59, bd. govs. 1958-59, chmn. com. on ann. meeting 1953—, award of merit 1974), Polk County bar assns., Am. Law Inst., Am. Judicature Soc., State U. Iowa Alumni Assn. (pres. 1957—, dir., 1951—). Home: 3857 Woodland Ave Apt 6 West Des Moines IA 50265 Office: 1010 Fleming Bldg Des Moines IA 50309

PESOLA, WILLIAM ERNEST, cable television company executive; b. Marquette, Mich., May 2, 1945; s. Ernest Ensio and Janice Mary (LeDuc) P.; m. Kathleen Mary Deschaine, July 9, 1966; children—Christie Lynn, Laurie Anne. B.S., No. Mich. U., 1968, M.S., 1971. Route driver Coca Cola Co., Marquette, 1963-68; tchr. Gwinn (Mich.) Schs., 1968-78; pub. Sch. News, 1969; pres. Pesola Mgmt., Marquette, 1974—; pres. Humboldt Ridge, Marquette, 1977—; treas. Elite Bar, Inc., Marquette, 1978—; v.p. Marquette Cablevision, 1981—, also dir. Pres. Gwinn Edn. Assn., 1975-77; regional pres. Upper Peninsula Edn. Assn., 1977-78; mem. Marquette City Commn., 1977-81. Mem. NEA, Mich. Edn. Assn. Roman Catholic. Lodge: Rotary. Home: 1026 N Front St Marquette MI 49855

PESONEN, KENNETH PAUL, radio engineer; b. Detroit, May 25, 1957; s. Paul Benjamin and Jean Elvira (Tauriainen) P. A.A., Alpena Community Coll., 1977. Field engr. asst. Presque Isle Electric Coop., Onaway, Mich., 1977-78; announcer Sta. WHSB, Alpena, Mich., 1977-78, Sta. WATZ, 1979-81, WJML, Petoskey, Mich., 1981-82; engr., ops. mgr. Sta. WZXM, Gaylord, Mich., 1982—. Avocations: photography; music; boating; computers. Home: Route 3 Box 725 Avalon Dr Hillman MI 49746 Office: Sta WZXM-FM/AM 650 E Main St PO Box 159 Gaylord MI 49735

PESSES, PAUL, real estate and investment management company executive; b. Davenport, Iowa, Oct. 4, 1955; s. Marvin and Elaine (Katz) P.; m. Kim Meisel, Aug. 19, 1978. B.A. in Econs. summa cum laude, Ohio State U., 1977; M.B.A., Harvard U., 1980. Bus. analyst engineered products group Cabot Corp., Boston, 1979-80; v.p., treas., dir. Metcoa, Inc., Solon, Ohio, 1980-82, Columbia Alloys Co., Twinsburg, Ohio, 1980-82; adminstrv. mgr. splty. metals and alloys Ashland Chem. Co. div. Ashland Oil, Inc., Cleve., 1983; pres. Stonestreet Capital Mgmt. Corp., Shaker Heights, Ohio, 1983—, also dir. Trustee Cleve. com. UNICEF; vol. Cleve. Playhouse, Kidney Found. Ohio, United Way campaign; big bro., trustee Big Bros.; treas. Pesses Charitable Found. Mem. Phi Eta Sigma, Phi Kappa Phi. Clubs: Northeast Yacht., Harvard Bus. Sch. (officer) (Cleve.).

PESTER, JACK CLOYD, oil company executive; b. Seymour, Iowa, Mar. 12, 1935; s. Cloyd Russell Pester and Esther O. (Long) Marston; m. Patricia Joanne Shay, July 21, 1956 (div. 1979); m. Barbara Dee Brazil, Aug. 13, 1979. B.S. in Bus. Adminstrn., Drake U. Dealer Pester Corp., Grinnell, Iowa, pres., Corydon, Iowa, dir., Des Moines; dir. Stoner Broadcasting, Inc., Des Moines, Nat. By-Products, Inc., Des Moines, Am. Mutual Life Ins. Co., Des Moines. Commr. Iowa Devel. Commn., Des Moines; vice chmn. bd. trustees, exec. com. Drake U., Des Moines. Served with U.S. Army, 1957. Reciepient Disting. Alumni award Drake U., 1979, One in a Hundred Alumni award Drake U., 1981. Mem. Iowa Assn. Bus. and Industry. Republican. Roman Catholic. Clubs: Wakonda, Des Moines. Home: 3708 Southern Hills Dr Des Moines IA 50321 Office: Pester Corp 303 Keosauqua Way Des Moines IA 50309

PETEFISH, WILLIAM MARCELLUS, heavy equipment manufacturing company executive; b. Springfield, Ill., Mar. 7, 1937; s. William M. and Helen (Ainsworth) P.; m. Judith I. Withey, Aug. 11, 1961; children—William, Jeffrey, Heidi. B.S.E.E., U. Ill., 1959, M.B.A., 1965. Cert. data processing. With mgmt. tng. program Ill. Bell Telephone Co., Springfield, 1958; mem. tech. staff Hughes Aircraft Co., Bonn, Fed. Republic Germany, 1959-63; computer operator U. Ill., Champaign, 1964-65; ops. tech. support mgr. Caterpillar Tractor, Peoria, 1965—; instr. Bradley U., Peoria, 1983—. Scoutmaster Boy Scouts Am., 1973-77; pres., coach Pleasant Hill Little League, East Peoria, Ill., 1972-80; treas. East Peoria Community High Sch. Booster Club, 1983—. Mem. Data Processing Mgmt. Assn., U. Ill. M.B.A. Alumni Assn. (chmn. 1984—). Club: Am. Radio Relay League. Lodge: Masons. Avocation: Amateur Radio. Home: 108 Patricia East Peoria IL 61611 Office: Caterpillar Tractor Co 600 W Washington St East Peoria IL 61630

PETER, ROLLIE WAYNE, technology educator, consultant; b. Ellinwood, Kans., June 8, 1953; s. Lorin L. and Thelma Jean (Reed) P.; m. Denise L. Gerken, Sept. 27, 1980. B.S., Kans. State Coll.-Pittsburg, 1976; M.S., Pittsburg State U., 1978. Welder, Ruskin Mfg., Great Bend, Kans., 1972-73; carpenter Strobl & Yarmer Constrn., Ellinwood, Kans., 1974; ranch hand, operator Lorin L. Peter & Sons Farm and Ranch, Ellinwood, 1963-78; owner, operator Pete's Repair, Pittsburg, Kans., 1977—; instr. dept. tech. Pittsburg State U., 1978—; cons. agr., drafting, heavy equipment instrn. Mem. Am. Soc. Agrl. Engrs., Soc. Automotive Engrs. (chmn. membership and student activities Kansas City sect., sec. Kansas City sect., Outstanding Faculty 1981, Outstanding Younger mem. 1983, 84, 85), Heavy Equipment Maintenance Council, Fluid Power Soc., Am. Vocat. Assn., Kans. Vocat. Assn., Profl. Assn. Diving Instrs., Aircraft Owners and Pilots Assn., Pilot Internat. Assn., Epsilon Pi Tau, Omicron Delta Kappa, Tau Kappa Epsilon. Home: Rt 3 Box 88 Pittsburg KS 66762

PETERS, DAVID LOUIS, food company executive; b. Mt. Pleasant, Pa., Oct. 12, 1945; s. William O. and Mary (Macipa) P.; m. Barbara J. Kelanic, Oct. 18, 1968; children—Marian, Michael. B.A., California (Pa.) State U., 1971; M.A., Central Mich. U., 1977. Area mgr. Hormel Co., Austin, Minn., 1971-76; v.p. sales Holsum Co., Waukesha, Wis., 1976-80; v.p. sales and mktg. PVO Internat., St. Louis, 1981; mgr. Stoppenbach Co., Jefferson, Wis., 1982—. Pres. Time-Out, Inc. Served with USMC, 1963-67. Mem. Am. Mgmt. Assn., Internat. Platform Assn., Am. Legion. Republican. Mem. Brethern Ch. Home:

632 Wakefield Downs Wales WI 53183 Office: 1 Rock River Rd Jefferson WI 53549

PETERS, DIANNE KAY, property management company official; b. Plainwell, Mich., Nov. 26, 1953; d. Clarence J. and Evelyn Jean (Hadaway) Wesseling; m. David Richard Peters, Aug. 11, 1978; children—David M., Kelly Jean. Cosmetologist, State Coll. Beauty, 1972. Cosmetologist, Loraine's Beauty Shop, Plainwell, 1972-74; asst. adminstr. Monarch Mgmt. Co., Newport Beach, Calif., 1974-78; adminstr. Paul Ash Investment, Tucson, 1978-79, Summit Mgmt., Kalamazoo, 1979-81; adminstr. acctg. U. Tex. Med. Br., Galveston, 1981-82; adminstr. Con Am Mgmt. Corp., San Diego, 1982—. Active McCarthy Presdl. Campaign, Mich., 1971-72. Rotary Club scholar, 1971. Mem. Nat. Assn. Female Execs., Mus. Natural History, Smithsonian Inst. Republican. Mem. Ch. of God. Home: 331 12th St A-14 Plainwell MI 49080

PETERS, DOROTHY MARIE, program development consultant; b. Sutton, Nebr., Oct. 23, 1913; d. Sylvester and Anna (Olander) Peters; A.B. with high distinction, Nebr. Wesleyan U., 1941; M.A., Northwestern U., 1957; Ed.D., Ind. U., 1968. Tchr. Nebr. pub. schs., 1931-38; caseworker Douglas County Assistance Bur., Omaha, 1941; hosp. field dir., gen. field rep. ARC, 1941-50; social worker Urban League, Meth. Ch., Washington, 1951-53; asst. prin., dir. guidance, Manlius (Ill.) Community High Sch., 1953-58; dean of girls, guidance dir. Woodruff High Sch., Peoria, Ill., 1958-66; vis. prof. edn. Bradley U., Peoria, 1959-77; coordinator counseling and guidance programs Peoria Public Sch. System, 1966-68, dir. pupil services, 1968-72; dir. Title I Programs, 1972-73; vol. dir. youth service programs, vol. program cons. Central Ill. chpt. and Heart of Ill. div. ARC, Peoria, 1973-77; owner, operator Ability-Achievement Unlimited Cons. Services, Saratoga Springs, N.Y., 1978-81; spl. cons. Courage Center, Golden Valley, Minn., 1981—; coordinator spl. projects Sister Kenny Inst., Mpls. mem. sr. adv. bd. F&M Marquette Nat. Bank, 1981—. Bd. dirs., home service com. disaster com. Peoria chpt. ARC, 1958-73; pres., bd. dirs. Ct. Counselor Program; mem. Mayor's Human Resources Council, City of Peoria; chmn. met. adv. com. transp. for handicapped; ednl. dir., prin., bd. dirs. Catalyst High Sch., 1975-77; hon. life bd. mem. Am. Nat. Red Cross; mem. Saratoga Springs Hosp. Bldg. Rehab. Com.; founder, steering com. Open Sesame, Saratoga Springs, 1978-81; appointee N.Y. State Employment and Tng. Council, 1979-81, Saratoga County Employment and Tng. Com., 1979-81; bd. dirs. Unlimited Potential, 1979-81; mem. Metro Mobility Adv. Task Force, Mpls., 1981—; mem., chair Metro Mobility Mgmt. Policy Com., 1984—; mem. Minn. State Council on Devel. Disabilities, 1983—; mem. council on sr. ministries Hennepin Ave. United Meth. Ch., Mpls., 1985—. Mem. Peoria Edn. Assn. (v.p. 1962-64), Ill. Guidance and Personnel Assn. (v.p. Area 8, 1963-64), NEA, Ill. Edn. Assn. (del. 1962-64), Am. Personnel and Guidance Assn., Am. Sch. Counselors Assn., Nat. Assn. Women Deans and Counselors (K-12 task force chmn. 1974—, editorial bd. Jour.), Ill. Vocat. Guidance Assn. (dir.), Ill. Assn. Women Deans and Counselors, Phi Kappa Phi, Psi Chi, Pi Gamma Mu, Pi Lambda Theta, Delta Kappa Gamma, Alpha Gamma Delta. Home: 2523 Portland Ave S Apt 1501 Minneapolis MN 55404

PETERS, ELIZABETH ANNE, educator; b. Hebron, Ill., June 9, 1940; d. Tibbets E. and Ruby Marie (Giddens) Rolls; B.S., U. Ill., 1962, M.S., 1967; postgrad. U. Ill., 1970-74, Iowa State U., 1974, Northwestern U., 1980; div. Tchr., Bremen High Sch., Midlothian, Ill., 1962-65, Waller High Sch., Chgo., 1965-67, Evanston (Ill.) High Sch., 1967-70; instr., coordinator food service adminstrn. and hotel mgmt. Coll. DuPage, Glen Ellyn, Ill., 1970-75; clin. dietitian U. Chgo. Hosps. and Clinics, 1975; asst. restaurant mgr. Hyatt Regency, Chgo., summer 1980; prof., coordinator hospitality mgmt. program Chicago City-Wide Coll., 1976—; cons. bds. health, colls. Mem. adv. com. No. Ill. U.; judge various food contests; mem. Chgo. Council on Fgn. Relations; mem. Chgo. Lyric Opera Guild, v.p. Near North chpt.; mem. Alliance of Art Inst.; trustee Three Arts Club Chgo. Recipient Nat. Restaurant Assn. Fellowship award, 1980; Master Tchrs. Seminar Fellowship award, 1974; Nat. Leadership Devel. Fellowship award, 1975. Registered Dietitan. Mem. Nat. Restaurant Assn., Ill. Restaurant Assn., Chgo. Restaurant Assn., Am. Dietetic Assn. (com. dietetic technician edn. accreditation), Ill. Dietetic Assn., Chgo. Nutrition Assn., Ill. Nutrition Com., Chgo. Dietetic Assn. (dir.), Soc. Nutrition Edn., Inst. Food Technologists, Restaurant Women's Club Chgo. (dir.), Council on Hotel-Restaurant Edn. Clubs: Flossmoor Country, Lake Geneva Yacht, Canyon. Home: 215 E Chestnut St Chicago IL 60611 Office: 30 E Lake St Chicago IL 60601

PETERS, GALEN ROGER, mathematics educator, consultant; b. Eureka, Kans., Sept. 30, 1942; s. George C. and Sara Frieda (Regier) P.; m. Ella Brubaker Lefever, Aug. 13, 1965; children—Ann Elizabeth, Sara Ella, George Robert. B.A., Bethel Coll., 1964; Ph.D., Iowa State U., 1971. Tchr. math., sci. Twillingate Central High Sch., Nfld., Can., 1964-66; grad. asst. Iowa State U., Ames, 1966-69, instr., 1969-71; faculty Greenville Coll., Ill., 1971—, prof. math., 1976—, chmn. dept., 1974—; vis. research scientist McDonnell Douglas Research Labs., St. Louis, 1977-78, 84-85, cons., 1978—. Contbr. articles to profl. jours. Mem. Math. Assn. Am., Internat. Assn. Math. and Computers in Simulation, Phi Kappa Phi. Methodist. Club: Bond County Saddle (treas. 1982—). Avocations: horsemanship; farming; reading detective novels. Home: 804 Durley St Greenville IL 62246 Office: Dept Math Greenville Coll 315 E College St Greenville IL 62246

PETERS, HOWARD NEVIN, educational administrator; b. Hazleton, Pa., June 29, 1938; s. Howard Eugene and Verna Catherine (Miller) P.; m. Judith Anne Griessel, Aug. 24, 1963; children—Elisabeth Anne, Nevin Edward. B.A., Gettysburg Coll., 1960; Ph.D., U. Colo., 1965. Asst. prof. fgn. langs. Valparaiso U., Ind., 1965-69, assoc. prof., 1969-75, dir. grad div., 1967-70, acting dean, 1970-71, assoc. dean, 1971-74, dean, 1974-81, prof. fgn. langs, 1975—. NDEA fellow, 1960-63. Mem. Midwest MLA, Phi Beta Kappa, Sigma Delta Pi, Phi Sigma Iota. Lutheran. Home: 860 N County Rd 500 E Valparaiso IN 46383 Office: Meier Hall Room 110 Valparaiso Univ Valparaiso IN 46383

PETERS, JAMES B., law enforcement official, security company executive; b. Wichita, Kans., Jan. 16, 1947; s. Charles E. and Virginia H. Peters; m. Jan. R. Shelton, June 21, 1975; children—Steven A., Jason H. Degree in Adminstrn. of Justice, Wichita State U., 1973. With Sedgwick County Sheriff's Dept., Wichita, 1971—, sgt., 1973-75, lt., 1975—; founder, pres. Security Midwest, Inc., Wichita, 1976—; Recipient Bronze Medal Valor, Wichita Police Dept., 1977. Mem. Kans. Peace Officers Assn., Kans. Sheriff's Assn. Republican. Roman Catholic. Office: 525 N Main St Wichita KS 67202

PETERS, JAMES WILLIAM, lawyer; b. Zanesville, Ohio, Sept. 7, 1954; s. George Joseph and Mary Virginia (Stine) P.; m. Kay Frazier, July 8, 1978; children—James Leland, Kylie Kay. Student Ohio U., 1972-73; B.A., Ohio State U., 1976; J.D., Capital U., 1980. Bar: Ohio 1981, W.Va., 1983. Sole practice, Woodsfield, Ohio, 1981—; asst. prosecutor Wetzel County, W.Va., 1983—; spl. counsel to atty. gen. State of Ohio, 1983—. Pres. bd. dirs. Mental Health and Retardation Bd., Monroe County, Ohio, 1984—. Mem. Assn. Trial Lawyers Am., Ohio Acad. Trial Lawyers, W.Va. Trial Lawyers Assn., Ohio State Bar Assn., ABA, VFW. Democrat. Lodge: Moose. Home: RD1 Box 133B Woodsfield OH 43793 Office: PO Box 596 Woodsfield OH 43793

PETERS, JEROME CHARLES MILLER, physician; b. Washington, Mo., July 18, 1951; s. Edward George and Violet May (Miller) P.; m. Maureen Pamela Kubler, Nov. 17, 1982. B.A., Central Meth. Coll., Fayette, Mo., 1973; postgrad. U. Mo., 1973-74, St. Louis U., 1974-75; D.O., Kansas City Coll. Osteo. Medicine, 1980. Intern Normandy Hosps., St. Louis, 1980-81; family practice osteo. medicine, Hermann, Mo., 1981-83; gen. practice Hermann Med. Arts, Inc. Mem. Mo. Osteo. Assn., Mo. Soc. Gen. Practitioners, Am. Osteo. Assn., Osage Valley Assn., Hermann C. of C. Republican. Mem. United Ch. Christ. Club: Hermann Missouriana. Home: 212 Washington St Hermann MO 65041 Office: 134 W 6th St Hermann MO 65041

PETERS, JERRY LEON, vocational education educator; b. Union City, Ind., June 9, 1951; s. Keith L. and Martha B. (Tillson) P.; m. Susan Merrill, Dec. 30, 1972; children—Jennifer, Jason. B.S., Purdue U., 1973, M.S., 1974; Ph.D., Ohio State U., 1980. Research asst. Purdue U., West Lafayette, Ind., 1973-74; tchr. S. Henry Sch. Corp., 1974-77; teaching assoc. Ohio State U., Columbus, 1977-80; vis. prof. Purdue U., 1980-81, asst. prof. vocat. edn. sect., 1981-85, assoc. prof., 1985—; cons. in field. Internal Support Research grantee, 1981—; Agrl. Edn. Summer Apprentice program, State Bd. Vocat. Tech. Edn., 1981. Mem. Am. Ednl. Research Assn., Am. Vocat. Edn. Research Assn., Am. Assn. Tchr. Educators in Agr., Nat. Vocat. Agr. Tchrs. Assn., Ind. Vocat. Assn., Phi Delta Kappa, Purdue U. Alumni Assn. Democrat. Contbr. articles to profl. jours. Home: 3138 State Rd 26W West Lafayette IN 47906 Office: SCC F25 Vocational Edn Sect West Lafayette IN 47907

PETERS, KERRY MICHAEL, engineer; b. Taylorville, Ill., June 15, 1959; s. Jerry Fay and Ruth Marie (Jackson) P. B.S. in Engring., U. Ill., 1982. Coop. engr. Sundstrand, Rockford, Ill., 1979-81, project engr. I, 1982-84, II, 1984—. Designer (with others) Self Launching Sport Sailplane (honorable mention award AIAA 1982). Recipient Dale S. Margerum Meml. award U. Ill., 1982. Mem. No. Ill. Soaring Assn. (treas. 1984—). Republican. Club: Rockford Rugby. Avocations: soaring; rugby; hunting. Home: 8909 Yankee Clipper Cherry Valley IL 61016 Office: Sundstrand Energy Systems 4747 Harrison Ave Rockford IL 61125

PETERS, LARRY DEAN, artist, art gallery director; b. Manhattan, Kans., July 15; s. Ralph Eugene and Vera Adaline (Watkins) P.; m. Joyce L. Laton, Sept. 14, 1974 (div. Mar. 1984). B.F.A., Washburn U., 1962; M.F.A., So. Ill. U., 1965. Readers advisor fine arts dept. Topeka Pub. Library Gallery, Kans., 1965-72, gallery dir., 1972—; mem. adv. panel Kans. Arts Commn. Collage artist; represented by Jan Weiner Gallery, Topeka. Mem. Kans. Mus. Assn. (pres. 1982-83), Mountain Plains Mus. Assn. (Kans. state rep., pres. exhibits affinity group 1984-86), Kans. Artists Craftsman Assn. (pres. 1971-73), Topeka Art Guild (bd. dirs.), Topeka Arts Council. Democrat. Avocations: fishing; railroading. Office: Topeka Pub Library Gallery 1515 W 10th St Topeka KS 66604

PETERS, MICHAEL BARTLEY, editorial cartoonist; b. St. Louis, Oct. 9, 1943; s. William Ernst and Charlotte Burt (Wiedeman) P.; B.F.A., Washington U., St. Louis, 1965; m. Marian Connole, Sept. 11, 1965; children—Marci Michelle, Tracy Patricia, Molly Martha. Polit. cartoonist Chgo. Daily News, 1965-66, 68, Dayton (Ohio) Daily News, 1969—; syndicated with United Features Syndicate, 1971—; Mother Goose & Grimm Syndicated with Tribune Media Services, 1984—; author: The Nixon Chronicles, 1976; Clones You Idiot, I Said Clones, 1978; Win One for the Geezer, 1982; The World of Cartooning with Mike Peters: How Caricatures Develop, 1985; The Gang of Eight, 1985; inventor editorial animation features Motion Punctures, NBC Nightly News, PBS Series, The World of Cartooning with Mike Peters; lectr. Bd. dirs. Dayton Living Arts Center, from 1975. Served with AUS, 1966-68. Recipient Sigma Delta Chi award, 1975; Ohio Man of Yr., ACLU, 1980; Disting. Alumni award Washington U., 1981; Pulitzer prize, 1981; Headliners award, 1983; Rueban award Nat. Cartoonists Soc., 1983, 84, nominee for Cartoonist of Yr., 1985; Ohio Gov.'s award, 1985. Mem. Am. Assn. Editorial Cartoonists (dir. 1973—), Social Health Assn. (dir. 1970—), Civitan (dir. 1969-73), Sigma Chi. Office: 4th and Ludlow Sts Dayton OH 45401

PETERS, MICHAEL THOMAS, energy corporation executive, consultant; b. West Branch, Mich., Jan. 21, 1949; s. Raymond J. and Doris I. (Carrick) P.; m. Stephanie A. Mason, Aug. 26, 1972. B.S. in Geology, Mich. State U., 1974, B.S. in Zoology, 1978. Geologist, Energy Acquisition, Okemos, Mich., 1974, Don Yohe Drilling Co., Armada, Mich., 1974-77; exploration geologist Hunt Energy Corp., Dallas, 1978-81; sr. exploration geologist Mich. Oil Co., Jackson, 1981-84; pres., cons. geologist ORION Energy Corp., Lansing, Mich., 1984—. Mem. Am. Assn. Petroleum Geologists, Soc. Exploration Geophysicists, Mich. Basin Geol. Soc. (bus. mgr. 1981-82), Mich. Oil and Gas Assn., Rocky Mountain Assn. Geologists. Avocations: scuba diving, skiing, sailing, camping, tennis. Office: ORION Energy Corp PO Box 27068 940 Long Blvd Suite 4 Lansing MI 48910

PETERS, MILTON EUGENE, educational psychologist; b. Anderson, Ind., July 22, 1938; s. Olen A. and Dorothy LaVerne (Lambert) P.; m. Carol Ann Dudycha, Aug. 27, 1960. B.A., Wittenberg U., 1960; M. Div., Hamma Sch. Theology, 1963; M.A., Bowling Green State U., 1965; Ph.D., U. Toledo, 1975. Lic. psychologist, Ohio. Pastor Lutheran Ch. Am., 1966-69; instr. psychology Defiance (Ohio) Coll., 1969-70, Bluffton (Ohio) Coll., 1970-72; tchr., research asst. U. Toledo, 1973-75; vis. asst. prof., 1975-76; dir. instl. research, asst. prof. psychology Findlay (Ohio) Coll., 1976-85, assoc. prof. psychology, 1985—; cons., lectr. in field. Mem. long-range planning research and evaluation com. Findlay City Schs., 1982—. Mem. Am. Psychol. Assn., AAAS, Am. Ednl. Research Assn., Assn. Instl. Research, Midwestern Psychol. Assn., Ohio Assn. Instl. Research. Clubs: Findlay Torch, Fostoria Power Squadron. Contbr. articles to profl. and religious jours. Home: 614 Winterberry Dr Findlay OH 45850 Office: 1000 N Main St Findlay OH 45840

PETERS, RICHARD CRAIG, engineer; b. Circleville, Ohio, Mar. 4, 1956; s. Chester Cromley and Carolyn Asenith (Courtright) P.; m. Susan Gayle Glitt, Aug. 19, 1978; children—Matthew Richard, Nathan Andrew. B.S. in Mech. Engring., Ohio State U., 1978. Assoc. engr. Timken Co., Canton, Ohio, 1979-80, design engr., 1980-84, mfg. engr., 1984—. Chmn. Christian edn. Bethany United Meth. Ch., Canton, 1981—. Mem. Nat. Soc. Profl. Engrs., Soc. Mfg. Engrs. (chmn. 1984—), Canton Joint Engring. Council (chmn. tabloid dist. 1984—). Republican. Methodist. Lodges: Kiwanis, Masons, Shriners, K.P. Avocations: golf, racquetball, basketball, fishing. Home: 8075 Emerald Ave NE North Canton OH 44721 Office: Timken Co 1835 Dueber Ave SW Canton OH 44706

PETERS, RICHARD EUGENE, JR., delivery service official; b. Cleve., Feb. 1, 1948; s. Richard Eugene and Jean L. (Bowler) P.; m. Shirley Yvonne Kindred, Aug. 30, 1948; 1 dau., Angela Renee. A.A., Cuyahoga Community Coll., 1969; B.S., Lake Erie Coll., 1978; M.A., John Carroll U., 1983. Ops. Supr. United Parcel Service, Cleve., 1969—. Trustee Sanctuary Baptist Ch., Fedn. Catholic Charities, 1983; chmn. bd. Martin DePorres Ctr., 1980—; mem. Council Human Relations, 1980, Bus. Industry and Edn. Council, 1983. Served with U.S. Army, 1970-76. Mt. Olive Bapt. Ch. scholar, 1966-67. Mem. Am. Personnel and Guidance Assn. Democrat. Baptist. Office: 4300 E 68th St Cleveland OH 44105

PETERS, ROBERT PAUL, middle school principal; b. Elyria, Ohio, Dec. 28, 1925; s. Robert Frank and Mary Marthe (Lange) P.; m. Dorothea Louise Husemann, June 9, 1951; children—Robert William, Paul Edgar. A.B. in Math., Valparaiso U., 1950; M.Ed. in Guidance, Kent State U., 1954, M.Ed. in Ednl. Adminstrn., 1956. Cert. Ednl. adminstrn. and guidance, Ohio. Prin. Learwood Middle Sch. Choir dir. Faith Luth. Ch., Avon, Ohio, 1975-83. Served with U.S. Army, 1944-46, ETO. NSF fellow, 1955, Inst. of Life Ins. fellow, 1958. Mem. North Assn. Colls. and Schs., (commr. 1979—), Ohio Com. North Central Assn. Schs., Ohio Assn. Secondary Sch. Adminstrs. Republican. Avocations: model railroading.

PETERSEN, DEBORAH LYNN, commercial investment realtor; b. Chgo., Dec. 30, 1950; d. Robert A. and Betty Jean (Melvin) Easton; m. William Hugh Fitzsimmons, Feb. 14, 1981. Student U. Nev.-Reno, 1968-69, Ill. Realtors Inst., 1975-77; cert. in comml. investment Realtors Nat. Mktg. Inst., 1981; cert. fin. planner Coll. Fin. Planning, Denver, 1984. Real estate broker Mel Foster Co., Moline, Ill., 1974-77; realtor Comml.-Investment Div., Weiner & Assocs., Inc., Moline, 1977-79; project mgr. comml. investment div. Boeye Realtors, Inc., Rock Island, Ill., 1979—; mem. real estate adv. com. Black Hawk Coll., 1979—. Trustee Mississippi Valley Regional Blood Ctr., 1983. Named Realtor of Yr., Rock Island County Bd. Realtors, 1983, Arthur Bud Hill Award, 1978. Mem. Rock Island County Bd. Realtors (dir., past treas.), Nat. Assn. Realtors, Ill. Assn. Realtors, Inst. Cert. Fin. Planners, Nat. Assn. Female Execs., Upper County C. of C., Gamma Phi Beta. Club: Jr. Women's of East Moline (pres. 1977-78). Home: 2101 31st St Rock Island IL 61201 Office: 3900 18th Ave Rock Island IL 61201

PETERSEN, DONALD EUGENE, automobile company executive; b. Pipestone, Minn., Sept. 4, 1926; s. William L. and Mae (Pederson) P.; B.M.E., U. Wash., 1946; M.B.A., Stanford U., 1949; m. Jo Anne Leonard, Sept. 12, 1948; children—Leslie Carolyn, Donald Leonard. With Ford Motor Co., Dearborn, 1949—, asst. to v.p. N.Am. ops., 1965-66, car product planning mgr., 1966-69, exec. dir. adminstr. engring. and indsl. design, 1969, v.p. car planning and research, 1969-71, v.p. truck and recreation products ops., 1971-75, exec. v.p. diversified products ops., 1977—, exec. v.p. internat. automotive ops., 1977-80, pres., 1980-85, chmn., 1985—, dir., 1977—. Bd. trustees Cranbrook Ednl. Community, Bloomfield, Mich., 1973—. Served with USMCR, 1946-47, 51-52. Mem. Soc. Automotive Engrs., Engring. Soc. Detroit, Phi Beta Kappa, Sigma Xi, Tau Beta Pi. Episcopalian. Clubs: Renaissance, Detroit, Bloomfield Hills Country. Office: Ford Motor Co The American Rd Dearborn MI 48121*

PETERSEN, GERALD THORNTON, special machinery company executive; b. Chgo., Sept. 1, 1934; s. Waldemar R. and Marion (Thornton) P.; m. Carol Krametbauer, June 22, 1957; children—Charles, James. B.S. in Chem. Engring., Northwestern U., 1957, Advanced Mgmt. cert., 1974; M.S., MIT, 1958, Ph.D., 1960. Various positions Gen. Electric Co., 1960-68; dir. engring. A-C Advanced Electronic Chem. Products, Greendale, Wis., 1968-70; dir. adv. tech. ctr. Allis-Chalmers Corp., Milw., 1970-76; v.p. mktg. A-C Energy & Minerals Co., Milw., 1983-84; exec. v.p., gen. mgr. A-C Coal Gas Corp., Milw., 1980-83, 84—; corp. rep. World Energy Conf., Washington, 1970-74; corp. del. Nat. Council on Synfuels Prodn., Washington, 1983—; panelist 6 internat. confs. Contbr. papers to profl. lit. Patentee coal gasification process utilizing rotary kiln. Bd. dirs. Lakes Improvement Assn., Elkhorn, Wis., Chgo. Symphony Assn. Milw.; bd. dirs. adv. council Marquette U.; active adv. council U. Wis.-Milw., 1975-80. Mem. Am. Inst. Chem. Engrs., Wis. Profl. Engrs. Soc., Am. Mining Congress (energy com. Washington 1975-80), Sigma Xi, Tau Beta Pi, Pi Mu Epsilon, Phi Mu Epsilon. Republican. Congregationalist. Club: Westmoor Country (Brookfield, Wis.). Avocations: sailing; skiing; photography. Home: Lauderdale Lakes Apt 116 Route 1 Box 49D Elkhorn WI 53121 Office: A-C Coal Gas Corp Box 512 1126 S 70th St West Allis WI 53201

PETERSEN, JURGEN WILLIAM, information systems manager, sales and marketing manager; b. Clinton, Iowa, Aug. 4, 1933; s. William and Leona (Kroigaard) P.; m. Mary Kay Harmsen, July 3, 1966; children—Renee Mary, Eric Jurgen. A.A., Clinton Jr. Coll., 1953; B.B.A., Iowa State U., 1960. Owner, operator The Market Research Co., Mpls., 1960-62; nat. sales and mkgt. analyst 3M Co., St. Paul, 1962-73, sales adminstrn. supr., 1973-78, sales adminstr. mgr., 1978-82, mktg. info. systems mgr., 1982—. Republican. Lutheran. Home: 8735 Ivywood Ave South Cottage Grove MN 55016 Office: 3M Co 3M Ctr Saint Paul MN 55144

PETERSEN, RAYMOND HATTON, JR., technical sales representative; b. Syracuse, N.Y., Apr. 16, 1959; s. Raymond Hatton and Theodora (McGrath) P.; m. Erika Ann O'Brien, Aug. 5, 1978; 1 child, Jennifer Elizabeth. B.A. in Econs. and History, Lake Forest Coll., 1982. Coll. agent Northwestern Mutual Life Inst. Co., Lake Forest, Ill., 1980-82; mktg. mgr. Am. Sci. Products, McGaw Park, Ill., 1982, sales rep., Mpls., 1982-83; tech. sales rep. U.S. Surgical Corp., Eau Claire, Wis., 1983—. Home and Office: 3711 Golf Rd Eau Claire WI 54701

PETERSEN, RONALD LYNN, broadcasting executive; b. Goodland, Kans., Aug. 30, 1945; s. Peter Alvin and Ruth Irene (Weber) P.; m. Celia Louise Hitzman, Nov. 14, 1964; children—Ronald Lynn, Renee, Patty, Michael, Kathy. Student Central Tech. Inst., Kansas City, Mo., 1963-64. Salesman, Cutco div. Aluminum Co. Am., Kansas City, 1964-65; account exec. KDMO Radio, Carthage, Mo., 1965-68, sales mgr., 1968-73; gen. mgr. KDMO-KRGK, Carthage, 1973-83, v.p., 1983—; mktg. mgr. Cityvision Cable TV, 1983—; dir. Mo. NET, Brownfield Network, 1980—. Pres., Carthage Indsl. Devel. Authority, 1981-83, sec., 1983—; pub. info. officer Carthage Civil Def., 1979—; bd. citizens Adv. Bd. Probation and Parole, Carthage, 1981—, pres., 1981-84. Mem. Mo. Broadcasters Assn. (dir. 1983-84, sec.-treas. 1984-85), Carthage Area C. of C. (bd. dirs. 1985—). Roman Catholic. Club: Rotary (bd. dirs.). Home: 1020 S McGregor St Carthage MO 64836 Office: 231 E 4th St Carthage MO 64836

PETERSEN, WILLIAM JOHN, writer, educator; b. Dubuque, Iowa, Jan. 30, 1901; s. Charles Lewis and Bertha Louise (Helm) P.; B.A., U. Dubuque, 1926; M.A., U. Iowa, 1927, Ph.D., 1930; LL.D. (hon.), Iowa Wesleyan Coll., 1958; m. Bessie Josephine Rasmus, Sept. 25, 1937. Grad asst., fellow U. Iowa, 1926-30, instr. history, 1930-36, lectr. history, 1936—, asso. prof., 1948-69; research asso. State Hist. Soc. Iowa, 1930-47, supt., 1947-72; hist. lectr. Am. Sch. Wild Life, summers 1932, 36-40, Drake U. Tours, summers 1933, 34; prof. history Washington U., St. Louis, summers 1940, 41, 65, Iowa Wesleyan Coll., summers 1962, 63. Bd. dirs. Alvord Meml. Commn., 1940; mem. Iowa Centennial Com., 1946; chmn. Johnson County Red Cross War Fund, 1945. Recipient Iowa Library Assn. award for best contbn. to Am. lit. by an Iowan, 1937. Mem. Am., So., Miss. Valley (editorial bd. 1953-56) hist. assns., Soc. Am. Archivists, Am. Acad. Polit. and Social Sci., Minn., Kans. hist. socs., State Hist. Soc. Iowa, Phi Kappa Delta, Pi Gamma Mu, Zeta Sigma Pi, Delta Upsilon. Republican. Presbyterian. Clubs: Iowa Author (pres. 1940-42); Propeller (Quad City); Westerners, Cliff Dwellers, Caxton (Chgo.); Research (sec.-treas. 1944-46) Triangle, S.P.C.S. Rotary, C. of C. (Iowa City), Masons (32 deg.). Author: True Tales of Iowa (with Edith Rule), 1932; Two Hundred Topics in Iowa History, 1932; Steamboating on the Upper Mississippi, 1937, rev. edit., 1968; Iowa: The Rivers of Her Valleys, 1941; A Reference Guide to Iowa History, 1942; Iowa History Reference Guide, 1952; The Story of Iowa, 2 vols., 1952; Mississippi River Panorama: Henry Lewis Great National Work, 1979; Towboating on the Mississippi, 1979. Editor: (John Plumbe, Jr.) Sketches of Iowa and Wisconsin, 1948; (Isaac Galland) Galland's Iowa Emigrant, 1950; (John B. Newhall) A Glimpse of Iowa in 1846, 1957; author-editor: The Pageant of the Press, 1962; The Annals of Iowa-1863; Illustrated Historical Atlas of the State of Iowa in 1875 (A.T. Andreas), 1970; contbr. to profl. mags. Home: 329 Ellis Ave Iowa City IA 52240

PETERSILGE, ROBERT, lawyer; b. Cleve., Apr. 4, 1917; s. Arthur Ferdinard Moritz and Esther S., P.; m. Janet Robertson Macdiarmid, June 12, 1948; children—Janet E., Robert J., David A. A.B., Adelbert Coll., 1939; LL.B., Western Res. U., 1941. Staff atty. gen. counsel's office U.S. Treasury Dept., Washington, 1941-42; ptnr. Matz, Petersilge & Weimer, Akron, Ohio, 1946—. Mem. Silver Lake Village Council, Ohio, 1953; pres. Vis. Nurse Service Summit County Ohio, Akron, 1975. Served to lt. USCG, 1942-46. Mem. Akron Bar Assn., Ohio State Bar Assn. (mem. probate bd. govs.), ABA. Republican. Congregationalist. Lodge: Rotary, Masons. Avocations: tennis; skiing; playing organ. Home: 2912 Parkwood Dr Silver Lake Coyahoga Falls OH 44224 Office: Matz Petersilge & Weimer 411 Wolf Led Pkwy Akron OH 44311

PETERSON, ANN SULLIVAN, physician, association executive; b. Rhinebeck, N.Y., Oct. 11, 1928. A.B., Cornell U., 1950, M.D., 1954; M.S., MIT, 1980. Diplomate Am. Bd. Internal Medicine. Intern Bellevue Hosp., N.Y.C., 1954-55, resident, 1955-57; fellow in medicine and physiology Meml.-Sloan Kettering Cancer Inst., Cornell Med. Coll., N.Y.C., 1957-60; instr. medicine Georgetown U. Sch. Medicine, Washington, 1962-65, asst. prof., 1965-69, asst. dir. clin. research unit, 1962-69; assoc. prof. medicine U. Ill., Chgo., 1969-72, asst. dean, 1969-71, assoc. dean, 1971-72; assoc. prof. medicine, assoc. dean Coll. Physicians and Surgeons, Columbia U., N.Y.C., 1972-80; assoc. prof. medicine, assoc. dean Cornell U. Med. Coll., N.Y.C., 1980-83; assoc. dir. div. med. edn. AMA, Chgo., 1983—. Bd. regents Uniformed Services U. Health Scis., 1984—. John and Mary R. Markle scholar, 1965-70; Alfred P. Sloan fellow, 1979-80. Contbr. articles to med. jours. Fellow ACP; mem. AMA, Am. Fedn. Clin. Research, Mortar Board, Alpha Omega Alpha, Alpha Epsilon Delta. Office: AMA 535 N Dearborn St Chicago IL 60610

PETERSON, ARTHUR FERDINAND, investment management executive; b. Brainerd, Minn., Apr. 17, 1899; s. Toger and Pauline (Gulbrandsen) P.; m. Delma Drusella Coovert, Jan. 31, 1920 (dec. Dec. 1977); 1 child, Vivian Rozmund Peterson Wolter; m. Muriel Frances Herting Beisswanger, June 17, 1978. Ph.G., Valparaiso U., 1919, Ph.C., 1920. Alexander Hamilton Inst., 1925; B.S., U. Minn., 1927, postgrad. Pharmacist, G.H. Sohrbeck Co., Moline, Ill., 1920-21; salesman E.R. Squibb & Sons, Chgo., 1922-24; chemist Nat. Lead Battery Co., St. Paul, 1925; profl. service rep. William S. Merrell Co., Mpls., 1926; instr. chemistry U. Minn., Mpls., 1927-29; profl. service rep. to supr. E.R. Squibb & Sons, Chgo., 1929-38; mgr. profl. service to mgr. domestic sales div. Schering Corp., Bloomsfield, N.J., 1939-46; sales mgr. biologics div. Heyden Chem. Corp., N.Y.C., 1947-48; dir. mktg., mem. mgmt. com. Geigy Pharms., N.Y.C. and Ardsley, N.Y., 1949-64; pvt. practice investment mgmt., Elmhurst, Ill., 1965—. Author: Pharmaceutical Selling, Detailing and Sales Training, 1949, 2d edit., 1959; contbr. articles to profl. jours. Served with S.A.T.C., 1918. Mem. Am. Pharm. Assn., Am. Assn. Individual Investors, Midwest Pharm. Advt. Club, Am. Inst. History of Pharmacy, Am. Legion (comdr. Cedar Grove, N.J. 1953), Stockholders of Am. Inc., Tau Kappa Epsilon, Phi Delta Chi. Republican. Lutheran. Club: First Chicago Torch (Elmhurst). Lodges: Masons, Shriners. Avocation: writing. Home and Office: 110 W Butterfield Rd #201 Elmhurst IL 60126

PETERSON, C(ARL) DONALD, justice state supreme court; b. Mpls., Feb. 2, 1918; s. Karl Emil and Emma Marie (Sellin) P.; B.A. cum laude, U. Minn., 1939; J.D. with honors, U. Ill., 1941; m. Gretchen Elaine Palen, Dec. 6, 1952; children—Barbara Elaine, Peterson Burwell, Craig Donald, Mark Bradley,

Polly Suzanne, Todd Douglas, Scott Jeffrey. Bar: Minn. 1941, U.S. Supreme Ct. 1950. Ptnr. firm Howard, Peterson, LeFevere, Lefler, Hamilton & Pearson, 1941-66; assoc. justice Minn. Supreme Ct., St. Paul, 1967—; chmn. Minn. News Council, 1971-80; co-chmn. Nat. Task Force of 20th Century Fund.; mem. Minn. Ho. of Reps., 1959-63. Contbr. articles to legal jours. Republican candidate for lt. gov. State of Minn., 1962; elder, congregation pres. Christ Presbyterian Ch., Edina, Minn. Served with USAAF, 1942-45, with USAF, 1951-52. Decorated Bronze Star; named Outstanding Legislator; recipient Disting. Service to Journalism award Minn. Newspaper Assn., 1977, award of merit Sigma Delta Chi, 1979. Mem. Am., Minn. bar assns, Hennepin County Bar Assn., Inst. Jud. Adminstrn., Am. Law Inst., Am. Judicature Soc. Clubs: Minn., Torske Klubben. Office: 230 State Capitol Bldg Saint Paul MN 55155

PETERSON, CARL OSCAR, librarian, educator; b. Chgo., Oct. 20, 1921; s. Carl Oscar and Corine Marguerite (Pearson) P.; m. Marjorie Sylvia Demikis (dec. 1972); m. 2d, Shannon Mary Troy, Sept. 21, 1975; 1 son, Brian Carl. B.S. in Edn., Art Inst. Chgo., 1954, B.F.A., 1954; M.S. in Edn., Chgo. State Coll., 1970; Ed.D., Nova U., 1980. Designer, producer, purchaser printed and other forms of communications materials City of Chgo., 1955-57; with Argonne (Ill.) Nat. Lab., 1957-60; mem. staff U. Chgo., 1960-70; librarian, lectr. bus. info./communication Governors State U., Park Forest South, Ill., 1970—; vol. career counselor on careers in pub. and graphic arts in various high schs. Served with USN, 1942-46. Recipient Freedoms Found. group award, 1959. Mem. Internat. Graphic Arts Edn. Assn., Am. Vocat. Assn., Spl. Libraries Assn. Author: Business and Government Information Sources, 1972.

PETERSON, CAROL ANN, data processing supervisor; b. Cleve., Mar. 15, 1942; d. Anthony Roman and Angeline Eva Klaus; m. Charles Joseph Peterson, July 14, 1962; children—Jeffrey Allen, Ricky Charles, Sherry Lee. Grad. Washington High Sch., Two Rivers, Wis. Cert. NCR, 1968, IBM, 1976. Clk. I, City of Two Rivers, Wis., 1960-61, clk. II, 1962-68, programmer-processer, 1969-71, acctg. clk., 1972-78, data processing supr., 1979—; mem. credit com. City Employees, Two Rivers, 1974-76. Chmn. United Way, 1976, 1981, 1982-86, co-chmn., 1979-80; treas. Credit Union, Two Rivers, 1977-84. Snow Queen, Two Rivers Snow Festival, 1960. Mem. Lioness (treas. 1985-86) Womens Bowling Assn. (pres. 1970), Tri-Co MIS Users Group (treas. 1982—), Washington High Booster Club (sec. 1982-84). Roman Catholic. Avocations: bowling; boating; snowmobiling; crafts. Home: 3610 Lowell St Two Rivers WI 54241 Office: City of Two Rivers PO Box 87 Two Rivers WI 54241

PETERSON, CHERYL CELIA, jewelry consultant; b. Eau Claire, Wis., Feb. 4, 1959; d. Robert L. and Rose F. (Zurek) Fenner; m. Bradley A. Peterson, Oct. 24, 1981. A.A., Dist. I Tech. Inst., 1980; diploma Gemological Inst. Am., 1981. Jewelry sales (part-time) Consumer's Co-op. Jewelry Dept., Eau Claire, 1976-77; buyer, trainee for jewelry Phillips Catalogue Showroom, Eau Claire, 1980-81; diamond cons. Husar's House of Fine Diamonds, West Bend, Wis., 1981-83; diamond cons., asst. mgr. Armond's Jewelers, Milw., 1983; diamond cons. William's Keepsake Diamond Ctr., Eau Claire, 1984—. Mem. Gemological Inst. Am. Lutheran. Avocations: snow skiing; fishing; boating; camping; outdoor activies. Office: Williams Keepsake Diamond Ctr 2830 London Sq Eau Claire WI 54701

PETERSON, CLIFFORD BRENT, artist, futurist, entrepreneur; b. Longmont, Colo., May 22, 1947; s. Sigurd Gustav and Isabelle Clare (McCauley) P.; m. Lisa Lee, May 1, 1982; 1 child, Toby Wing-hei. A.B. in Visual and Environ. Studies, Harvard Coll., 1972; M.S. in Environ. Design., Notre Dame U., 1977. Marshall Fund in Demark fellow, Copenhagen, 1975-76; pres. Farmhouse Studio, Inc., LaPorte, Ind., 1977—; chmn. bd. Trillium Concepts Inc., LaPorte, 1984—; artist-in-residence Purdue North Central U., Westville, Ind., 1985—; bd. advs. Environic Found. Internat., Notre Dame, Ind., 1978—. One man shows include Purdue North Central, 1985, Indpls. Mus. of Art, 1975, Mus. of Decorative Art, Copenhagen, 1977, South Jutland Art Mus., 1977, Pan-Am. Soc. of Boston, 1973, MIT, 1971, Community Ctr. for the Arts, 1983. Illustrator, Heritage of 76, 1975. Mem. LaPorte County Leadership Program, LaPorte, 1984—, Agri-Business Study Com., LaPorte, 1985—. Mem. Screen Printing Assn. Internat., Area Artists Assn. Presbyterian. Club: Harvard (Chgo.). Avocations: reading; photography; poetry. Home: 2215 E 350 North LaPorte IN 46350 Office: Trillium Concepts Inc 2215 East 350 North LaPorte IN 46350

PETERSON, DAVID ALLAN, virologist; b. Hayward, Wis., Nov. 29, 1938; s. Allen H. and Faith I. (Olsen) P.; B.S., Wis. State U., Stevens Point, 1966; M.S., Ind. U., 1970, Ph.D., 1971; m. Bonnie J. Sablovitch, May 29, 1964; children—Frank A., Ruth A. Postdoctoral research fellow dept. microbiology Rush-Presbyn.-St. Luke's Med. Ctr., Chgo., 1970-71; asst. prof. dept. microbiology Rush U. Coll. Health Scis., Chgo., 1975-81, asst. prof. dept. microbiology Rush Med. Coll., 1971-81, safety and environ. control officer dept. microbiology, 1971-81; asst. scientist med. staff Rush-Presbyn.-St. Luke's Med. Ctr., 1971-81, chief diagnostic virology lab. dept. microbiology, 1971-81; lectr. Cook Coungy Grad. Sch. Medicine, 1975-81; clin. project mgr. Abbott Labs., North Chicago, 1981-82, sr. virologist, 1982—. Served with USAF, 1957-61. Mem. Am. Soc. Microbiology, AAAS, Soc. Exptl. Biology and Medicine, Tissue Culture Assn., Ill. Soc. Microbiology. Congregationalist. Contbr. articles to profl. jours. Home: 461 Edens Ln Northfield IL 60093

PETERSON, DAVID EUGENE, dentist, hospital administrator, clinical educator; b. Holdrege, Nebr., Apr. 9, 1947; s. Elvin Eugene and Patrica Phyllis (McGimsey) P.; m. Karleen Ann Lund, Aug. 15, 1970; children—Kwen Arik, Trond Trygve. Student Dana Coll., 1965-66; D.D.S., U. Nebr., 1972. Lic. dentist, Nebr., S.D., N.D., Wis. ADA rotating intern Fla. State Hosp., Chattahoochee, 1972-73; staff dentist Royal Dental Hosp., Melbourne, Australia, 1973-75; tutor and clin. demonstrator U. Melbourne, 1974-75; dental dir. Redfield State Hosp., S.D., 1976—; clin. instr. U. Nebr., Lincoln, 1977—; missionary dentist vol. Lutheran Sudan Mission Ngoundere, Cameroon, 1981-82; asst. clin. prof. U. S.D., Vermillion, 1977—; lectr.-preceptor Lake Area Vo-Tech Inst., Watertown, S.D., 1977—; clin. instr. Creighton U., Omaha, 1978-81; cons. dentist N.E. S.D. Head Start, Aberdeen, 1983—. Author: (with others) Nutrition for Handicapped, 1985. Editor: (booklet) A Referral Manual, 1977, 80; co-editor: Coll. U. Nebr. Dentistry Yearbook, 1972. Contbr. articles to profl. jours. Tchr. adult Bible class Our Savior's Lutheran Ch., Redfiled, S.D., 1976—, sr. hi youth group, 1976-80, congregation pres., 1984-85; council mem. World Mission Prayer League, Mpls., 1983-86. Mem. ADA (cert. of recognition, 1983), S.D. Dental Assn. (cert. of commendation, 1982-83, presidential award, 1983), No. Dist. Dental Soc. (del. 1979), Assn. Institutional Dentists (pres. 1983-84), Am. Cancer Soc. (outstanding Edn. Project S.D. div., 1978, Spink County bd. mem. 1976—), Wis. Dental Study Club, Uni-Hosp. Orthodontist Study Club, Uni-Hosp. Pedodontic Study Club. Avocations: jogging, bible study and teaching, reading, refinishing old furniture. Home: PO Box 410 NW 3d Ave Redfield SD 57469 Office: Dept of Dentistry Redfield State Hosp Redfield SD 57469

PETERSON, DONALD ALBERT, radio and publishing executive; b. Youngstown, Ohio, Sept. 18, 1917; s. Albert and Hattie M. (Anderson) P.; m. Josephine Phelps Hoiles, July 20, 1940; children—Donald A. Jr., Jill P. McCarty. Pres. Alliance (Ohio) Brick Corp., 1965-72; pub. Alliance Rev., 1962—; pres. Sta. WFAH/WDJQ, Alliance, 1967—; chmn. bd. Alliance Fed. Savs. and Loan; dir. Valley Forge Inc., Glamorgan Park Inc. Chmn. bd. Mt. Union Coll. Served to lt. (j.g.) USNR, 1944-46. Recipient United Way Award of Merit, 1956; Mt. Union Coll. Alumni Service award, 1981; named Alliance Boss of Yr., 1968. Mem. Ohio Broadcasters Assn., Am. Newspaper Pubs. Assn., Alliance Area C. of C. (bd. dirs.), Am. Legion. Sigma Delta Chi. Republican. Methodist. Clubs: Wranglers, Filibusters, Alliance Country. Lodges: Kiwanis, Elks (Alliance). Home: 1084 Glamorgan Alliance OH 44601 Office: 40 S Linden Alliance OH 44601

PETERSON, DORA ELVIRA, soft drink company executive; b. Ravenna, Mich.; d. Clarence and Bertha Patterson; diploma Muskegon (Mich.) Bus. Coll.; m. Paul Miller; children—Lois Miller Frausto, Donald; m. 2d, Gerald Peterson, Mar. 20, 1954. Asst. to service mgr. Sealed Power Corp., Muskegon, 1921-27; with Coca Cola Bottling Co. Muskegon, 1943—, pres., 1945—; dir. Muskegon Bank & Trust Co., 1975-80. Trustee Muskegon County Community Found. Named Bus. Woman of Year, 1972. Mem. Mich. Soft Drink Assn. (dir. 1975—, pres. 1980-81), Nat. Soft Drink Assn., Muskegon C. of C., Nat. C. of C., Mich. C. of C. Episcopalian. Club: Muskegon Zonta. Address: Coca Cola Bottling Co 1770 E Keating St Muskegon MI 49442

PETERSON, EVERNE HORACE, educator; b. Gary, Ind., Apr. 9, 1927; d. Thomas W. and Ardie Lue (Brown) Horace; m. Johnny James Peterson, Nov. 15, 1953; 1 dau., Valerie Kaye. B.S., Ind. State U., 1948; M.S., Nat. Coll. of Edn., 1982. Cert. elem. tchr. Tchr. elem. schs., Kansas City, Mo., 1948-52, Chgo., 1952-54; tchr. Gary Community Sch. Corp. High Sch. and Middle Sch., 1954—, chairperson speech dept. Recipient Outstanding Citizen of Northwest Ind. award in category of ednl. social events Info. Newspaper, 1980. Mem. NAACP, Nat. Council of Negro Women, Gary Hist. and Cultural Soc., Ind. Sheriff Assn., Gary Reading Council, English Council, Fedn. of Tchrs., AAUW, Phi Delta Kappa. Presbyterian. Clubs: Am. Woodmen. Home: 1736 Arthur St Gary IN 46404

PETERSON, GERALD LEONARD, psychology educator; b. Neenah, Wis., Aug. 22, 1945; s. Gerald F. and Mary E. (Letwon) P. B.S., U. Wis.-Oshkosh, 1968; M.A., U. Mo.-Kansas City, 1972; Ph.D., Kans. State U., 1975. Cert. psychologist, Pa. Asst prof. dept. psychology Duquesne U., Pitts., 1975-81; assoc. prof. dept. psychology Saginaw Valley State Coll., University City, Mich., 1981—. Served as sgt. U.S. Army, 1968-70. Mem. Am. Psychol. Assn., Midwestern Psychol. Assn., N.Y. Acad. Scis. Roman Catholic. Contbr. articles to profl. bulls., jours. Office: 2250 Pierce Rd 271 Wickes Hall Univ Center MI 48710

PETERSON, HARLAN FRANKLYN, radio sales manager; b. Beresford, S.D., Apr. 27, 1934; s. Franklyn Theodore and Alta Maxine (Fedderson) P.; m. Jeanine Carlson; children—Tracy, James, Randy Carlson. B.A. in Communications, U. S.D., 1956. News anchor Sta. KORN-TV, Mitchell, S.D., 1968-71, sales mgr. Sta. KORN, 1972-76; mgr. Sta. KCHF, Sioux Falls, S.D., 1976-78; sales mgr. Sta. KWSL, Sioux City, Iowa, 1978—. Mem. Beresford Centennial Com., 1983—. Served to maj. U.S. Army, 1956-68. Republican. Lutheran. Clubs: Sioux City Noon 1985 (pres.), Lions, Masons, Shriners. Home: 207 N 6th St Beresford SD Office: PO Box 3088 Sioux City IA 57102

PETERSON, JAMES R., writing implements manufacturing company executive. Pres., chief executive officer, dir. Parker Pen Co., Janesville, Wi. Office: Parker Pen Co One Parker Place Janesville WI 53545*

PETERSON, KARL LEWIS, insurance executive; b. Mojave, Calif., Oct. 27, 1943; s. Charles William and Thelma Ann (Bilski) P.; m. Nancy Marie Opalka, May 25, 1963; children—Karl Lewis, Joan Marie. B.A., Eastern Ill. U., 1963. Underwriter, Fed. Mut. Ins. Co., 1963-65, Charles L. Howard, Inc., Noblesville, Ind., 1965-66; treas. J.L. Hubbard Co., Decatur, Ill., 1966-76; ptnr., Overheul-Peterson Co., Decatur, 1980-83; pres. Creighton Jackson Co., Decatur, 1976—; mem. producer's lic. adv. com. Ill. Ins. Dept.; mem. agts. adv. bd. AI network Am. Internat. Group. Treas., Big Bros. Big Sisters, 1980-81; pres. Spring Creek Plaza low rent housing complex, 1981. Recipient Extra Spl. Person award Decatur Assn. Ins. Women, 1982. Mem. Am. Soc. C.P.C.U. (continuing profl. devel. designation), Ind. Ins. Agts. Ill. (dir. 1981—, edn. chmn.), Jonathan Trumbul Council Ins., Profl. Ins. Agts., Am. Bus. Club. Republican. Roman Catholic. Clubs: Kaskaskia Valley Bass (sec. treas. 1970-74, bd. dirs. 1976), Decatur Chess (founder, past pres.). Contbr. articles to ins. jours. Home: 44 Barnes Dr Decatur IL 62526 Office: 127 S 22d St Decatur IL 62521

PETERSON, KENNETH ALLEN, SR., superintendant of schools; b. Hammond, Ind., Jan. 20, 1939; s. Chester E. and Bertha (Hornby) P.; B.Ed. cum laude, Chgo. State U., 1963; M.S., Purdue U., 1970; NSF grantee U. Iowa, 1964-65; postgrad. U. Ill., 1977-81; m. Marilyn M. Musson, Jan. 3, 1961; children—Kimberly, Kari, Kenneth Allen. Tchr., Markham (Ill.) Sch. Dist. 144, 1961-67; prin. Brookwood Sch., Glenwood (Ill.) Sch. Dist. 1967, 1967-77, prin. Hickory Bend Sch., 1977-78, dir. spl. edn., 1978-80, asst. supt. schs., 1981-83, supt schs., 1983—; mem. No. Ill. Planning Commn. for Gifted Edn. Chmn. Steger (Ill.) Bicentennial Commn., 1976; vice chmn. Ashkum dist. Boy Scouts Am., 1981-83, lodge advisor, exec. bd. Order of Arrow Calumet council Boy Scouts Am.; program com. South Cook County council Girl Scouts U.S.A., 1971-73, 80-81, mem. fin. com., 1981—, also bd. dirs.; mem. Steger Community Devel. Commn. Recipient Order of Arrow Service award, Silver Beaver award, Dist. award of merit Boy Scouts Am. Mem. Council Exceptional Children, Assn. Supervision and Curriculum Devel., Nat. Assn. Elem. Sch. Prins., P.T.A. (life), Kappa Delta Pi. Republican. Lutheran. Home: 3208 Phillips Ave Steger IL 60475 Office: 201 Glenwood Dyer Rd Glenwood IL 60425

PETERSON, KIM DEL, telephone plant administrator, rancher; b. Mobridge, S.D., Sept. 24, 1954; s. Delbert Russell and Keloa Marie (Johnson) P.; m. Connie Means, Feb. 14, 1973 (div. Aug. 23, 1976); children—Tiffany, Delaine. Grad. high sch., Cheyenne-Eagle Butte, S.D. Telephone lineman C.R.S.T. Telephone Authority, Eagle Butte, 1975-78, plant foreman, 1978-80, plant supt., 1980-85, plant mgr., 1985—; also rancher. Mem. Parade Community Club, Eagle Butte. Democrat. Episcopalian. Avocations: fishing, hunting, softball. Home: Parade SD Office: CRST Telephone Authority Eagle Butte SD 57625

PETERSON, LARRY DOUGLAS, art educator, painter, gallery executive; b. Holdrege, Nebr., Jan. 1, 1935; s. Wallace L. and Gladyes (Anderson) P.; m. Sharon K. Hoback, Dec. 21, 1958; children—Penalton, Jane. B.A., Kearney State U., 1958; M.A., No. Colo. U., 1962; Ed.D., U. Kans., 1975. Tchr. art North Platte Coll., Nebr., 1958-66; prof. art Kearney State Coll., Nebr., 1966—; exhbns. include: Five State Art Exhibit, Scottsbluff, Nebr., 1963-68; Nebr. Gov.'s Art Exhibit, Omaha, 1961, 62, 63, 66; Fine Arts Festival, Chadron State Coll., 1963; Mid-Am. Art Fair, Topeka, 1970; 1st ann. Kans. U. Art Exhibit, 1971; 13th Midwest Biennial, Joslyn Art Mus., Omaha, 1974; One-Man Invitational Exhbn., Stuhr Mus., Grand Island, Nebr., 1972, 76-77; Ft. Hays State U., Kans., 1976; Midwest Landscape Exhbn., Elder Gallery, Nebr. Wesleyan U., Lincoln, 1977; Assn. Nebr. Art Clubs, 1965, 67, 79, 73-80, traveling exhbns., 1969-70, 73-74, 78-79; 5 State Exhbn., Sioux Falls, S.D., 1980; 5th Ann. Art Educators Exhibit, Elder Gallery, 1980; Nebr. State Office Bldg., 1983. Recipient Outstanding Educators Am. award, 1973; Internat. Dir. Arts award Cambridge, Eng., 1972-74; Assn. Nebr. Art Clubs award, 1980, Am.'s Artists of Renown award, 1980; Gov.'s Art award State of Nebr., 1981; Accademia Italia with gold medal, 1982; Kearney Community Service award, 1982; Roscoe Shields award Nebr. Art Tchrs. Assn., 1983, Deans award Kearney State Coll., 1984; and others. Mem. Nebr. Art Tchrs. Assn. (pres. 1966-84, award 1966), Nat. Art Assn. (advisor), Kearney State Coll. Edn. Assn. (past pres.), Assn. Nebr. Art Clubs (past pres.), Nebr. Art Collection (dir.), Nat. Art Edn. Assn., NEA, Nebr. State Edn. Assn., Kearney Artists Guild (bd. dirs. 1980-85). Democrat. Methodist. Club: Kearney Artists Guild (pres. 1983). Lodge: Elks (advisor). Avocations: collecting art; gardening. Home: 4 Seminole Ln Kearney NE 68847

PETERSON, MARGARET SCHAWDE, public relations executive, educator, writer; b. Dodgeville, Wis., May 29, 1927; d. Herman L. and Wilma L. (Murrish) Schawde; m. Joseph F. Peterson, June 22, 1948; children—Charles J., Alan A., Richard S. B.A. in Journalism, U. Wis., 1948. Faculty asst., librarian Sch. Journalism, U. Wis., Madison, 1948-49; freelance writer, 1949—; co-owner, operator Oak Grove Cheese, Muscoda, Wis., 1953-65; office supr. M.B. Victora Agy., Muscoda, 1962-65; pub. info. coordinator, continuing edn. agt. U. Wis. Ctr. Marshfield-Wood County and Univ. Extension, Marshfield, 1965-71; pub. info. specialist Mid-State Vocat., Tech., Adult Edn. Dist., Wisconsin Rapids, Wis., 1971-76; dir. pub. affairs St. Joseph's Hosp., Marshfield, 1976—. Past pres. Marshfield United Way; vice chmn. bd. dirs. Wis. div. Am. Cancer Soc.; past pres. Marshfield Art Com. Recipient Mehlberg award Wis. Hosp. Pub. Relations Council, 1979; writing awards Wis. Press Women, 1971-76, Nat. Honor Citation Am. Cancer Soc., 1981. Mem. Wis. Hosp. Pub. Relations Council, Am. Soc. Hosp. Pub. Relations, Central Wis. Pub. Relations Roundtable, Central and Western Wis. Press Clubs, Delta Kappa Gamma Internat. Methodist. Clubs: P.E.O., Bus. and Profl. Women (Marshfield). Contbr. articles to profl. jours. Home: 500 S Lincoln Ave Marshfield WI 54449 Office: St Joseph's Hospital 611 St Joseph Ave Marshfield WI 54449

PETERSON, NORMAN LEE, materials science researcher; b. Aurora, Ill., Jan. 16, 1935; s. Conrad Arnold and Mildred Sarah (Umbreit) P.; m. Mary Irene Lee, Oct. 12, 1963. B.S. in Metallurgy, MIT, 1957, M.S. in Metallurgy, 1959, Ph.D. in Metallurgy, 1961. Asst. metallurgist Argonne Nat. Lab., Argonne, Ill., 1961-64, assoc. metallurgist, 1964-70, group leader, 1966-68, assoc. dir., 1968-77, sr. metallurgist, 1970—, group leader, 1977—; mem. rev. com. Materials Research Lab. U. Ill., Urbana, 1981—. Editor: Radial Damage in Metals, 1976, Atomic Defects in Metals, 1978. Contbr. articles to profl. jours. Recipient Sr. Scientist award A. Von Humboldt Found., 1973; NSF fellow, 1964-65. Fellow Am. Soc. Metals (chmn. awards com.), Am. Ceramics Soc., Am. Phys. Soc.; mem. Metall. Soc. of AIME (chmn. awards com.). Office: Argonne Nat Lab 9700 S Cass Ave Argonne IL 60439

PETERSON, RICHARD ALLEN, furniture design and manufacturing company executive; b. Chgo., July 29, 1955; s. Lawrence William and Marian (Malmquist) P.; m. Patricia Anne McLaughlin, Dec. 21, 1980; 1 child, Christopher. B.A., So. Ill. U., 1980. Owner, mgr. Rick Peterson Design, Murphysboro, Ill., 1979-81; pres. Peterson Design Ltd., 1981—. Mem. Indsl. Designers of Am., Murphysboro C. of C. Republican. Methodist. Avocation: boating. Office: Peterson Design Ltd 430 S 19th St Murphysboro IL 62966

PETERSON, RICHARD CARSON, financial management company executive, healthcare consultant; b. Wilmington, N.C., Sept. 15, 1953; s. Graham Howard and Lillie Truman (Johnson) P.; m. Karen Zurn, Feb. 14, 1982. B.A. in Econs., Duke U., 1975, M.H.A. (Equitable Assurance Soc. U.S. Scholar), 1977. Adminstrv. resident The Duke Endowment, Charlotte, N.C., 1977; adminstrv. asst. N.C. Baptist Hosps., Inc., Winston-Salem, N.C., 1977-78; mgr. mgmt. info. cons. div. Arthur Andersen & Co., Chgo., 1978—. Mem. Am. Coll. Hosp. Adminstrs., Hosp. Fin. Mgmt. Assn., Hosp. Mgmt. System Soc., Duke U. Alumni Assn. Republican. Episcopalian. Home: 25W740 Wenona Ln Wheaton IL 60187 Office: Arthur Andersen & Co 33 W Monroe St Chgo IL 60603

PETERSON, RICHARD GUSTAF, literature educator, educational administrator; b. Chgo., Jan. 9, 1936; s. Stanley Gustaf and Mattie (DeHaan) P. B.A., U. Minn., 1956, Ph.D., 1963; M.A., Northwestern U., 1958. Instr. English, U. Minn., Mpls., 1960-62; asst. prof. English, St. Olaf Coll., Northfield, Minn., 1963-68, prof. English and classics, 1975—; exec. sec. Am. Soc. Eighteenth-Century Studies, Northfield, 1983—. Book rev. editor Eighteenth Century Studies, Davis, Calif., 1980-83. Contbr. numerous articles to profl. jours. Recipient William Riley Parker prize MLA, 1976; Am. Philos. Soc. research fellow, 1969-70. Mem. MLA, Am. Soc. for Eighteenth-Century Studies, AAUP, Classical Assn. of Midwest and South. Episcopalian. Avocations: cooking, photography, travel, woodworking. Office: Am Soc for Eighteenth-Century Studies St Olaf Coll Northfield MN 55057

PETERSON, RICHARD M., newspaper editor, publisher; b. Minot, N.D., Oct. 24, 1941; s. Hans G. and Emma M. (Heupel) P.; m. Hollys J. Narveson Howard, Feb. 14, 1978; stepchildren—Jay Howard, Danny Howard. A.A., Lake Region Jr. Coll., 1961; B.A., U. N.D., 1963. Editor, pub. Benson County Farmers Press, Minnewaukan, N.D., 1963-66, 1970—; pres. Prairie Press, Inc., New Rockford, N.D., 1980—, Consol. Newspapers, Inc., Minnewaukan, 1980—. Pres. Minnewaukan Comml. Club, 1981-83. Served to 1st lt. U.S. Army, 1967-70, Vietnam. Recipient award for best editorial (weekly) in state, 1971, 2nd best weekly editorial in state, 1982, best feature story in state, 1980. Mem. N.D. Newspaper Assn., Am. Legion, VFW, Sigma Delta Chi. Lodges: Elks, Masons. Office: Benson County Farmers Press 4318 B Ave Minnewaukan ND 58351

PETERSON, RICHARD MICHAEL, architect; b. Akron, Ohio, June 25, 1936; s. Pat P. and Elizabeth Jane (Eoveno) P.; m. Frances Therese Vorwerk, Nov. 8, 1958; children—Richard D., Mark M., Michael D. B.S. with honors in Architecture, Kent State U., 1958. Registered architect, Ohio; cert. Nat. Council Archtl. Registration Bd. Architect in tng. Keith Haag Assocs., Cuyahoga Falls, Ohio, 1956-62, assoc., 1962-72, v.p., 1972-75; pres. Peterson/-Raeder Inc., Architects, Akron, 1975—; guest design juror Kent State U. Sch. of Architecture. Served with USNR, 1954-62. Winner 2d place award Ohio Edison Illumination Design competition, 1957. Mem. AIA (pres. Akron Chpt. 1973), Architects Soc. Ohio (trustee 1973-75). Club: Optimist, Fairlawn (pres. 1981, award 1982). Republican. Roman Catholic. Home: 755 Sand Run Rd Akron OH 44313 Office: 2650 W Market St Akron OH 44313

PETERSON, ROBERT LLOYD, manufacturing company executive; b. Nebr., July 14, 1932; m. Oct. 4, 1952; children—Mark R., Susan P. Student cattle buyer Wilson & Co., 1951-52; cattle buyer Jim Boyle Order Buying, 1954-56, R & C Packing Co., 1956-61; cattle buyer plant mgr., v.p. carcass prodn. IBP, 1961-69; v.p. ops. Spencer Foods, 1969-71; pres. Madison Foods, Inc., 1971-76; pres. Iowa Beef Processors, Inc. (name now IBP, inc.) Dakota City, Nebr., 1976—, also chief exec. officer, chmn., dir.; exec. v.p. Occidental Petroleum Corp., also dir.; dir. Iowa Export-Import Trading Co. Bd. dirs. Greater Siouxland, Inc.; trustee U. Nebr. Found., also bd. counselors Med. Ctr. Served with U.S. Army, 1952-54. Mem. Newcomen. Soc. Club: Sioux City Country. Office: IBP inc Dakota City NE 68731

PETERSON, ROBERT MICHAEL, construction company official; b. Ada, Ohio, Nov. 30, 1943; s. Richard Earl and Sophia Viola (Novickas) P. Grad. U.S. Naval Communications Sch., 1962; student U. Wis., 1981—, Cuyahoga Community Coll., 1980—. Case worker IRS, Grand Rapids, Mich., 1972-75; preventive maintenance coordinator Morrison-Knudsen Co., Inc., Seabrook, N.H., 1977-80; equipment coordinator S&M Constructors, Inc., Solon, Ohio, 1980—, asst. claims adminstr., 1983—; asst. office mgr. Les Constrns. Scarmar Ltd., Prince George, B.C., Can., 1982-83. Served with U.S. Navy, 1961-64. Mem. Underground Space Assn. Club: City (Cleve.). Home: 32367 Hamilton Ct Apt 204 Solon OH 44139 Office: 29100 Hall St Solon OH 44139

PETERSON, SONJA, arts administrator, educator; b. Jamestown, N.D., July 18, 1938; d. Lawrence Theodore and Mabel Gertine (Gran) Ulsaker; m. Paul David Peterson, Dec. 16, 1961; children—Lisa, David, Katy. A.A. with honors, Stephens Coll., 1958; B.A., B.S. cum laude, U. Minn., 1961; Cert. tchr., Minn. English tchr., Kamehameha High Schs., Honolulu, Hawaii, 1961-63; freelance writer NEA, Washington, 1964; English tchr. Williamsburg Jr. High Sch., Arlington, Va., 1965-66; arts adminstr. West Central Regional Arts Council, Fergus Falls, Minn., 1984—; lit. arts rev. panel, Minn. State Arts Bd., Mpls., 1984; sec. Citizens United for Better Edn., West Central Minn., 1982-84. Author short stories, numerous poems. Chmn. Dist. 542 Sch. Bd., Battle Lake, Minn., 1974—; chmn. Joint Powers Bd. Interactive Edn. TV System, 1983—. Recipient Big Ten Pres. Council award, U. Minn., 1960; U. Minn. scholar, 1960-61. Mem. Minn. Sch. Bds. Assn., Phi Theta Kappa. Republican. Lutheran. Avocations: swimming; horseback riding; skiing. Office: West Central Regional Arts Council PO Box 661 Fergus Falls MN 56517

PETERSON, STEPHANIE CRAIG MCGINNIS, nurse, nursing educational administrator; b. Topeka, Dec. 30, 1945; d. Joseph Edward and Marjean Elaine (Meyer) McGinnis; m. Donald Stowe Peterson, Oct. 1, 1966 (div.). Diploma Stormont-Vail Sch. Nursing, 1966; B.S. in Health Arts, Coll. St. Francis, 1982. R.N., Kans., Mo. Instr. med. and surg. nursing Stormont Vail Sch. Nursing, Topeka, 1967-70; supr. surg. nursing Newman Meml. Hosp., Emporia, Kans., 1970-73; staff nurse Meml. Hosp., Topeka, 1966-67, inservice instr., 1976-77, spl. projects coordinator, 1977-78, asst. supt. nurses, 1973-75; asst. dir. edn. Spelman Meml. Hosp., Smithville, Mo., 1979, now staff nurse operating room; lectr., cons. in field. Mem. Am. Nurses Assn., Nat. League for Nursing, Am. Assn. Critical Care Nurses, Kans. State Nurses Assn., Am. Soc. Healthcare Educators and Trainers. Home: 7904 N Anita Kansas City MO 64151 Office: Spelman Meml Hosp PO Box 289 Smithville MO 64089

PETERSON, WALTER JOHN, manufacturing company executive, engineer; b. Sparta, Wis., Jan. 4, 1925; s. Walter Roy and Bertha Maude (McElwain) P.; m. Waverly Ruth Wendorf, Sept. 21, 1947; children—John, Jeffry, Jay, Ann. B.S. in Mech. Engring., U. Wis., 1948 . Asst. chief insp. Beloit Corp., Wis., 1948-61; v.p. engring. Felker Bros. Corp., Marshfield, Wis., 1961—. Pres. Marshfield Elec. and Water Commn., Marshfield, 1982. Served with USN, 1943-46. Recipient Service to Community award City of Marshfield, 1982. Mem. TAPPI (corrosion com.) Republican. Lutheran. Lodge: Rotary. Avocations: travel, fishing, skiing, hunting. Office: Felker Bros Corp PO Box 550 Marshfield WI 54449

PETHEO, BELA FRANCIS, art educator, painter and graphic artist; b. Budapest, Hungary; May 14, 1934; came to U.S., 1959, naturalized, 1965; s. Bela and Claire (Tauffer) P.; m. Kathleen Benko, June 28, 1970; children—Kristina, Elizabeth. M.A. in Art History, U. Budapest, 1956; Student Karl Lueger U., Vienna Austria, 1957-59; M.F.A. in Studio Art, U. Chgo., 1963. Instr. art U. No. Iowa, Cedar Falls, 1964-66; assoc. prof. art St. John's U., Collegeville, Minn., 1966—; freelance designer U. Chgo., 1960-62. Illustrator:

The Rise of the West, 1963. Subject of book: Bela Petheo: Painter of the Center in an Age of Extremes (J. Gray Sweeney), 1985. Mem. Los Angeles Printmaking Soc., AAUP. Avocations: swimming, travel. Home: 400 NE Riverside Ave St Cloud MN 56301 Office: St Johns Univ Collegeville MN 56321

PETIT, PATRICIA JEAN, religious ministry administrator; b. Pierre, S.D., Jan. 21, 1935; d. Benjamin Franklin and Betty Edna (Ward) Padilla; m. Irvin William Petit, Jr., June 4, 1955 (dec. June 1980); children—Theresa Marie (dec.), Michelle Jean Petit Porvasnik, Marcia Anne Petit Rank, Sharon Rose Petit Ames. Certificate, Nettleton Comml. Coll., Sioux Falls, S.D., 1955. Sec., Downtown Clinic, Pierre, S.D., 1953-54, John Morrell, Sioux Falls, 1954-55, Wilson Sch., Rapid City, S.D., 1966-68, S.D. Sch. Mines, Rapid City, 1968-73; sec., asst. editor West River Catholic paper, Rapid City, 1973-81; dir. Ministry to Separated, Divorced and Widowed Diocese of Rapid City, 1981—. Author newspaper column: Pat's Prayers for Peons, 1977-81. Democrat. Roman Catholic. Club: Catholic Daus. of the Am. (state and local officer 1958—). Office: Diocese of Rapid City PO Box 678 Rapid City SD 57709

PETO, JOAN BARBARA, swimming coach, educator; b. Bethlehem, Pa., Oct. 23, 1953; d. Julius John and Dorothea (Bunk) P. B.S., Pa. State U., 1975; M.Ed., Lehigh U., 1977. Cert. tchr., guidance counselor, Mich. Swimming coach Lehigh U., Bethlehem, Pa., 1975-77, No. Mich. U., Marquette, 1977—; chairperson Midwest com. Assn. Intercollegiate Athletics for Women, 1977-79, meet dir. 1981 Nat. Swimming and Diving Championships, Marquette, 1981. Founder and swim coach Watercat Aquatic Club, Marquette, 1978—. Mem. Am. Swim Coaches Assn. (dir. 1983—), Coll. Women's Swim Coaches Assn. (dir. 1981-83, Coach of Yr. 1982), Coll. Swim Coaches Assn. (dir. 1983—). Democrat. Presbyterian. Home: 1140 Northland Apt 11 Marquette MI 49855 Office: No Mich U Athletic Dept Marquette MI 49855

PETOSA, JASON JOSEPH, publisher; b. Des Moines, Apr. 26, 1939; s. Joseph John and Mildred Margaret (Cardamon) P.; m. Theodora Anne Doleski, Aug. 12, 1972; 1 child, Justin James. Dir. Alba House Communications, Canfield, Ohio, 1965-67; with office of radio and TV, Diocese of Youngstown, Ohio, 1969-71; dir. pub. relations, instr. Alice Lloyd Coll., Pippa Passes, Ky., 1971-76; freelance writer, cons., Bethesda, Md., 1976-79; pres. NCR Pub. Co., Inc., Kansas City, Mo., 1979—. Author newspaper column, 1983—. Chmn. Mayor's UN Day Com., Kansas City, 1984, shcolorship com. Kansas City Press Club, 1984, chmn. adv. bd. KCMW-FM, KMOS-TV, Warrensburg, Mo., 1984; bd. dirs., treas. Catholic Reading, Inc., 1984. Mem. Sigma Delta Chi. Office: Nat Catholic Reporter Pub Co Inc Box 281 Kansas City MO 64141

PETRACH, ROBERT VICTOR, tool manufacturing company executive; b. Racine, Wis., May 2, 1927; s. John Joseph and Marie (Mattal) P.; m. Marion Elaine Becker, Apr. 19, 1952; children—Robert Victor, S. Dawn, Lori E., Dianne E., John Joseph II. B.A., Mich. State U., 1950, M.A., 1955; J.D., John Marshall Law Sch., 1968. Bar: Ill. 1968, Ohio 1968. Instr. Milw. Sch. Engring., 1952-55; mgr. tng. and communications Warwick Electronics, Zion, Ill., 1955-61; v.p. indsl. relations Chgo. Hdwe Fdry Co., North Chicago, Ill., 1961-67; v.p. indsl. relations, dir. Ridge Tool Co., Elyria, Ohio, 1967—; dir., sec. Lorex Lorain County Export Co., 1982—; v.p., dir. Grafton Devel. Co., 1982—. Bd. dirs. Jr. Achievement of Lorain County, 1968—, Red Cross, 1969—; trustee Improvement Inst., 1981—, nat. pres., 1983, mem. adv. bd., 1984—. Mem. Ill. Bar Assn., Ohio Bar Assn., Lorain County Bar Assn., Lorain County Export Devel. Council (dir. 1981—), Phi Kappa Phi, Psi Chi. Methodist. Advocation: racquetball. Home: 14714 Cowley Rd Columbia Station OH 44028 Office: Ridge Tool Co 400 Clark St Elyria OH 44035

PETRAS, STEPHEN JOHN, JR., lawyer; b. Lakewood, Ohio, Feb. 28, 1954; s. Stephen John and Margaret (Nistor) P.; m. Mikaela Christina Soderstrom, May 27, 1978; children—Emily Kerstin, Stephen John III. B.A. in Physics, Wittenberg U., 1976; J.D., Case Western Res. U., 1979. Bar: Ohio 1979, U.S. Dist. Ct. (no. dist.) Ohio 1979. Sole practice, Cleve., 1979-82; assoc. Vorys, Sater, Seymour & Pease, Cleve., 1982—. Chmn. Metrowest Kiwanis Charitable Found., 1984. Mem. Bar Assn. Greater Cleve., Ohio State Bar Assn., Assn. Trial Lawyers Am., ABA (sci. and tech. sect. 1980—, internat. law sect. 1982—), Cleve. World Trade Assn. (chmn. law and tax workshop com. 1983—, sec. and dir. 1985—), Internat. Lawyers Group Cleve. Roman Catholic. Home: 26527 Normandy Rd Bay Village OH 44140 Office: Vorys Sater Seymour and Pease 2100 E Ohio Bldg Cleveland OH 44114

PETRETIC-JACKSON, PATRICIA, psychologist, educator; b. Youngstown, Ohio, Sept. 2, 1949; d. John Anthony and Mary Ann (Spak) Petretic; m. Thomas Larry Jackson, July 22, 1978. B.A., Youngstown State U., 1971; M.A., Bowling Green State U., 1975, Ph.D., 1981. Postdoctoral fellow U. S.D., Vermillion, 1978-81; asst. prof. psychology, 1981—; pvt. practice psychology, Vermillion, S.D., 1981—. Mem. exec. bd. Clay County Child Protection Team, East River Intra-agy. Child Abuse and Neglect Council, 1981—; sponsor Parents Anonymous, 1981—. Recipient C.M. Freeburne Teaching award Psychology Dept., Bowling Green State U., 1975; U.S. Gen. Research Fund grantee, 1982-84. Contbr. articles to profl. pubs. Mem. Am. Psychol. Assn. (mem. com. women in psychology, state rep.), Soc. Pediatric Psychology, S.D. Psychol. Assn., Gould Soc., Sigma Xi. Home: 14 Willow Vermillion SD 57069 Office: U SD Psychology Dept Room 107 Vermillion SD 57069

PETREY, KATHERINE GOSSICK, lawyer; b. Oak Ridge, July 27, 1948; d. Ben Roger and Jean Elizabeth (Koehler) Gossick; m. Kenneth Doyle Petrey, Jan. 6, 1973; 1 child, Samuel Harlan. B.A., U. Ky., 1970, J.D., 1974. Bar: Ohio. Assoc. Squire, Sanders & Dempsey, Cleve., 1974-84, ptnr., 1984—. Mem. Nat. Assn. Bond Lawyers, Ohio Bar Assn., Greater Cleve. Bar Assn., Legal Aid Soc. Cleve., Soc. Collectors. Democrat. Clubs: Womens City, Cleve. Rose Soc. Avocations: gardening; tennis. Office: Squire Sanders & Dempsey 1800 Huntington Bldg Cleveland OH 44115

PETRI, RONALD JOSEPH, engineer; b. Devils Lake, N.D., Jan. 24, 1958; s. William Joseph and Lucy Catherine (Rohde) P.; m. Camille Ann Wilhelmi, Jan. 2, 1982; 1 child, Michael William. B.M.E. cum laude, U. N.D., 1981. Registered engr. in tng., N.D., Order of Engr. Owner, mgr. Petri Fireworks, Nekoma, N.D., 1973-75; salesman Kinney Shoes, Grand Forks, N.D., 1975-76; equipment operator Petri Farm, Nekoma, 1972-78; research technician U. N.D., Grand Forks, 1979; engring. intern Clark Equipment Co., Gwinner, N.D., 1979-81; project engr. Rosemount, Inc., Burnsville, Minn., 1982—. Scholar No. States Power, 1976, Larimore-Mathews, 1976, Crouch, 1979, Francis R. O'Brien, 1981. Mem. Am. Inst. Aeronautics and Astronautics. Avocations: stained glass art; water and snow skiing. Home: 16264 Fishing Way Rosemount MN 55068 Office: Rosemount Inc 14300 Judicial Rd Burnsville MN 55337

PETRI, THOMAS EVERT, U.S. congressman; b. Marinette, Wis., May 28, 1940; s. Robert George and Marian Ingrid (Humleker) P.; m. Anne D. Neal. B.A., Harvard U., 1962, LL.B., 1965. Admitted to Wis. bar, 1965; with Peace Corps, Somalia, 1966-67; mem. Wis. Senate, 1973-79; mem. 96th-98th congresses from 6th Dist. Wis. candidate for U.S. Senate from Wis., 1974; Office: Room 1024 Longworth House Office Bldg Washington DC 20515

PETRIE, MICHAEL FRANCIS, banker; b. Logansport, Ind., Jan. 2, 1954; s. John Francis and Helen Louise (Hirsch) P.; m. Jody Jane Jones; 1 child, Emily JoAnn. Student U. Nev., 1972-76; B.S. in Bus. Adminstrn., Ind. U., 1979; M.B.A., 1983. Loan rev. analyst Mchts. Nat. Bank, Indpls., 1979-80, real estate investment officer, 1980-82, asst. v.p., 1982-84, v.p., 1984—; dir. Kenwood Place, Inc., Indpls., Near North Devel. Corp., Indpls.; treas. Multi-Family Property Mgmt., Inc., Indpls., 1984—. Pres. Central North Civic Assn., Indpls., 1983. Mem. Apt. Assn. Ind., Mortgage Bankers Assn., Penrod Soc., Indpls. Jaycees (v.p. 1983, v.p. charities 1984). Republican. Roman Catholic. Club: Highland Golf and Country. Lodge: Elks. Avocations: fishing; golf; skiing; basketball. Office: Merchants Mortgage Corp 1 N Capitol Suite 1000 Indianapolis IN 46255

PETRIE, THOMAS C., book and magazine publisher, horse breeder; b. Green Bay, Wis., Apr. 4, 1949; s. William Wallace and Margot Margo (Karlzen) P.; m. Patricia Ann-Marie Zierden, Sept. 9, 1975; children—Eric Anthony, Ruan Thomas, Jeremiah Benjamin. Editor, pub. Wis. Sportman, Inc., Oshkosh, 1972—; pres. Willow Creek Press, Oshkosh, 1975—; editorial dir. Mich. Sportsman, Oshkosh, 1976—; editorial dir. Minn. Sportsman, Oshkosh, 1977—; pres., pub. Great Lakes Sportsman Group and Willow Creek Press, 1977—. Avocations: hunting; fishing; sailing. Office: Great Lakes Sportsman Group 2663 Oregon St Oshkosh WI 54901

PETROFF, JOHN NICHOLS, executive consultant; b. Mpls., May 25, 1931; s. Nicholas P. and Athena (Bezat) P.; m. Joan Carol Worrall, Oct. 11, 1958; children—Dana Nicholas John, Phillip James Alexander. B.B.A., U.Minn., 1953; M.B.A., NYU, 1954. Dir. mgmt. info. services Hamm's Brewery, St. Paul, 1970-74; dir. materials Brown & Bigelow Co., St. Paul, 1974-77; gen. supr. Arabian Am. Oil Co., Dhahran, Saudi Arabia, 1977-79; dir. mfg. systems CPT Corp., Eden Prairie, Minn., 1979-81; exec. cons. Comserv Corp., Eagan, Minn., 1981—; dir. Corp. Travel Services, Inc., Mpls., 1971—. Contbr. articles to profl. pubs. Founder, past pres. Linden Hills Chamber Orch., Mpls., Mem. Am. Prodn. and Inventory Control Soc. (pres. 1983-84), Assn. Systems Mgmt., Assn. Inst. Certification Computer Profls. Home: 4000 Linden Hills Blvd Minneapolis MN 55410 Office: Comserv Corp 3400 Comserv Dr Eagan MN 55410

PETROSKI, RICHARD JAMES, bio-organic chemist, researcher; b. Jersey City, Apr. 26, 1948; s. Frank Henry and Paula (Toman) P.; m. Barbara J. Rosenberg, June 16, 1971. B.A. in Chemistry, U. Ct., 1970, Ph.D. in Pharmacognosy, 1978. Postdoc. fellow U. Ct. Health Ctr., Farmington, 1977-78; postdoctoral research assoc. U. Iowa Coll. Pharmacy, Iowa City, 1978-80; research chemist USDA Northern Regional Research Ctr., Peoria, Ill., 1980—. Contbr. articles to profl. jours. Recipient Bausch & Lomb Sci. medal 1966; grantee NIH 1977. Mem. Am. Chem. Soc., Am. Soc. Pharmacognosy, Am. Orchid Soc. Club: Peoria Checker (sec., treas. 1982—). Avocations: orchid hybridization; bridge; checkers; golf. Office: USDA Northern Regional Research Ctr 1815 N University St Peoria IL 61604

PETROSS, PRECIOUS DORIS, personnel administrator, lawyer; b. Chgo., d. Joseph and Olive (Williams) Johnson; B.A., U. Mich., Flint, 1967; M.A., Eastern Mich. U., 1974; J.D., Detroit Coll. Law, 1982; m. Robert G. Petross (div.); children—Charles Howard, Janice Elaine Petross Habashe, Michael Alan. Accredited exec. in personnel. Personnel technician City of Flint (Mich.), 1967-69, sr. personnel technician, 1969-72; asst. personnel dir. Hurley Med. Center, Flint, 1972-74, personnel dir., 1974-80, asst. med. center dir. for human resources, 1980-85; staff atty. UAW-GM Legal Services, Flint, 1985—; personnel cons.; participant oral appraisal bds. State of Mich. and City of Flint. Adv. bd. Mott Community Coll. Social Work Tech. Program, 1976—; bd. dirs. Fairwinds council Girl Scouts U.S.A., 1977-84, nat. bd. dirs., 1984—; bd. dirs. Flint YWCA; active LWV, Urban League of Flint. Recipient Human and Race Relations award St. James Meth. Episcopal Ch., 1977; Black Women's Polit. Leadership Caucus award, 1976; named Woman of Year, 1978; Nat. Civil Service League fellow, 1971. Mem. Internat. Personnel Mgmt. Assn., Am. Hosp. Assn., Mich. Hosp. Personnel Dirs. Assn., Am. Soc. Hosp. Personnel Adminstrn., Flint Personnel Assn., AAUW, Nat. Assn. Negro Bus. and Profl. Women's Clubs, U. Mich. Alumnae Assn., Zeta Phi Beta. Baptist. Clubs: Snow Birds Ski, Genesee Temple Elks. Office: Genesee Towers Flint MI 48502

PETROWSKY, DANA LEE, state official; b. Des Moines, Aug. 3, 1948; d. Duane D. and Dorothea M. (Heckle) Brown; m. Barry Michael Petrowsky, Oct. 12, 1974; children—Todd Joseph, Melissa Alexis. B.A., U. No. Iowa, 1970. Research asst. Nat. Council Crime and Delinquency, Davis, Calif., 1970-73; health planner Iowa Gov.'s Office Planning and Programming, Des Moines, 1973-75; chief div. health facilities Iowa State Dept. Health, Des Moines, 1973—; mem. com. nursing home regulation Inst. Medicine, Nat. Acad. Scis., 1983-85. Mem. Assn. Health Facility Licensure and Cert. Dirs. (sec., v.p and pres. 1981-83), Iowa Pub. Health Assn. Republican. Lutheran. Club: Des Moines Golf and Country (Waukee, Iowa). Avocations: swimming; golf; sewing. Home: 3207 Saundra Circle West Des Moines IA 52065 Office: Lucas Bldg Des Moines IA 50319

PETRUCCI, JUDITH B., lawyer; b. Chgo., Apr. 8, 1941; d. Robert Carl Bryan and Shirley (Kennedy) Bryan Moore; m. Fredric A. Petrucci, Oct. 26, 1963 (dec. July 1984), 1 child, Gina Lynn. A.B., Morton Coll., 1977; B.A., Lewis U., 1979; J.D., No. Ill. U., 1981. Bar: Ill. 1983, U.S. Dist. Ct. (no. dist.) Ill. 1983. Legal sec. Frank E. Mosetick, LaGrange, Ill., 1962-65, assoc., 1983-84; sole practice, Lyons, Ill., 1984—. Chmn. Lyons 4th of July Com., 1975, Crusade of Mercy, Lyons, 1975, Com. Against Home Rule, Lyons, 1978; leader West Cook Council Girl Scouts U.S., 1973-76; mgr. Lyons-McCook Little League, 1976-79; atty. No More Bars Com., Lyons, 1984. Mem. ABA, Ill. State Bar Assn., Chgo. Bar Assn., Du Page County Bar Assn., Ill. Trial Lawyers Assn. Roman Catholic. Club: St. Hugh Soc. Cath. Women. Home: 4521 S Cracow Lyons IL 60534 Office: 4344 S Lawndale Ave Lyons IL 60534

PETRY, NEIL ALLEN, nuclear pharmacist; b. Knox, Ind., Sept. 15, 1952; s. John W. and Lucille L. (Neil) P.; m. Joanna Ellen Gehris, Dec. 18, 1976; 1 child, Amelia Lynn. B.S., Purdue U., 1975, M.S. in Bionucleonics, 1977. Registered pharmacist, Ind., N.C., Mich.; cert. nuclear pharmacist. Pharmacist, Petry Drug Store, North Judson, Ind., 1975-76; nuclear pharmacist Nuclear Pharmacy, Inc., Milw., 1977-78, Duke U. Med. Ctr., Durham, N.C., 1978-83; dir. nuclear pharmacy U. Mich. Med. Ctr., Ann Arbor, 1983—; mem. content rev. com. Bd. Pharm. Spltys., Am. Pharm. Assn., 1985—. Contbg. author: Nuclear Radiology Syllabus, 1983. Mem. Am. Pharm. Assn., Am. Soc. Hosp. Pharmacists, Soc. Nuclear Medicine, Rho Chi. Lutheran. Avocations: nature photography; football; basketball; running; camping. Office: U Mich Med Ctr Box 021 1405 E Ann St Ann Arbor MI 48109

PETRY, THOMAS EDWIN, manufacturing company executive; b. Cin., Nov. 20, 1939; s. Edwin Nicholas and Leonora Amelia (Zimpelman) P.; m. Mary Helen Gardner, Aug. 25, 1962; children—Thomas Richard, Stephen Nicholas, Daniel Gardner, Michael David. B.S., U. Cin., 1962; M.B.A., Harvard U., 1964. Group v.p. Eagle-Picher Industries, Inc., Cin., 1968-81, pres., chief exec. officer, 1981—. Republican. Clubs: Queen City, Terrace Park Country, Cin. Country. Office: Eagle Picher Industries Inc 580 Walnut St Cincinnati OH 45202

PETTAPIECE, MERVYN ARTHUR (BOB), educator; b. Detroit, May 27, 1941; s. Alvy Merrill and Thelma Margaret (Mattson) P.; B.A., Mich. State U., 1963, 67; M.Ed., Wayne State U., 1971, ednl. specialist cert., 1973, Ed.D. (Univ. grad. prof. scholar), 1980; m. Sandra Marie Alber Howe, Aug. 26, 1977; 1 dau., Lori; stepchildren—Michelle Howe, Erin Howe. Tchr. math. Hutchins Jr. High Sch., Detroit, 1968-71; tchr. math. No. High Sch. Detroit, 1971-72, tchr. social studies, 1972-84; tchr. Community High Sch., Detroit, 1977—; part-time instr. Coll. Edn., Wayne State U.; computing cons. Detroit Ctr. for Profl. Growth and Devel. Mem. adv. bd. Met. Detroit Youth Found., 1977-80. Mem. Nat. Assn. Core Curriculum, Mich. Council for Social Studies, Mich. Assn. Core Curriculum (sec.-treas.), Internat. Council Computers in Edn., Mich. Assn. Computer Users in Edn., Mich. Atari Computer Enthusiasts, Phi Delta Kappa. Home: 14341 Artesian Detroit MI 48223 Office: 167 Old Main Wayne State U Detroit MI 48202

PETTERSON, JAN E., medical secretary supervisor; b. Whitewater, Wis., Oct. 11, 1936; d. Roy C. and Ethel H. (Matzke) Henning; m. J. Nels Petterson, Oct. 27, 1956; children—Jody Lynn, Randall Nels, Roy Scott. Grad. Mercy Hosp. Sch. Nursing, Janesville, Wis., 1956. Med. sec., Beloit, Wis., 1960-74; med. sec. Wausau Med. Ctr., Wis., 1974-75, adminstrv. asst., 1975-78, med. sec. supr., 1978—; mem. adv. com. North Central Tech. Inst., Wausau, 1980—. Democrat. Lutheran. Avocations: reading; knitting; crocheting; traveling. Office: Wausau Med Ctr 2727 Plaza Dr Wausau WI 54401

PETTIGREW, GARY EUGENE, artist, educator; b. Boulder, Colo., Dec. 30, 1935; s. Donald Wilson and Carolyn Ruth Pettigrew; m. Judith Ann Newlon, Sept. 10, 1960; 1 son, Robert Wilson. B.F.A., U. Colo., 1958; M.F.A., Ohio U., 1963. Mem. faculty Sch. Art Ohio U., Athens, 1962—, assoc. dir., 1976-79, prof., 1982—; guest artist, lectr. Western Mich. U., Kalamazoo, 1983, Cleve. Art Inst., 1982. Coll. William and Mary, Williamsburg, Va., 1980, Edinboro (Pa.) State Coll., 1973, 76; group shows include: More Than Land or Sky: Art From Appalachia, Nat. Mus. Am. Art, Smithsonian Instn., 1981-84; Soc. of Four Arts, Palm Beach, Fla., 1974, 79; Canton Art Inst. All-Ohio, 1979; Painting and Sculpture Biennial, Dayton Art Inst., Invitational, 1976; The Artist-Tchr. Today, SUNY-Oswego, 1968. Served with U.S. Air N.G., 1954-62; with USAF, 1961-62. Recipient Baker Fund award Ohio U., 1972, 83, research grantee, 1967; Logan award Chautauqua Art Assn., 1979; Art Assn. award, 1976; Strathmore award Butler Art Inst., Youngstown, Ohio, 1976, 75; award Dayton Art Inst., 1974, 66, Washington-Jefferson Coll., Washington, Pa., 1974; Best Painting award Springfield, (Ill.) Art Assn., 1974, Edinboro State Coll., 1972, others. Mem. Nat. Assn. Painters in Casein and Acrylic. Works represented in numerous collections. Home: 2 Forest St Athens OH 45701

PETTIJOHN, TERRY FRANK, psychologist; b. Wyandotte, Mich., June 7, 1948; s. Donald Everett and Ella Jean (Seavitte) P.; m. Bernadette Marguerite Ciemierek, Aug. 21, 1970; children—Terry Frank, Karen, Thomas. B.S., Mich. State U., 1970; M.A., Bowling Green State U., 1972, Ph.D., 1974. Psychologist, Ohio State U., Marion, 1974—. Author: Instructors' Manual, 1983; author research articles. Recipient teaching award, Ohio State U., 1980, teaching recognition Coll. Arts and Scis., Ohio State U., 1984. Mem. Am. Psychol. Assn. (teaching recognition award 1981), Psychonomic Soc., Animal Behavior Soc., Midwestern Psychol. Assn., Soc. for Computers in Psychology. Presbyterian. Avocations: Computer instruction; computer programming; reading; writing. Home: 508 Edgefield Dr Marion OH 43302 Office: Psychology Dept Ohio State U 1465 Mt Vernon Ave Marion OH 43302

PETTIT, KELLY BROOKS, metals recycling furnace manufacturing company executive; b. Wichita, Kans., Jan. 7, 1953; s. Donald Leroy and Bette Jean P.; student U. Kans., 1971-75. Aircraft salesman also commuter pilot Clopine Aircraft Co., Topeka and Lawrence Aviation (Kans.), 1970-75, part-time salesman, pilot United Corp., Topeka, 1970-75, sales mgr., 1975-78, pres., 1978—; chmn. bd., pres., chief exec. officer United Corp. Cert. airline transp. pilot. Mem. Topeka C. of C., Inst. Scrap Iron and Steel, Nat. Assn. Recycling Industries, Delta Upsilon. Republican. Episcopalian. Clubs: Topeka Country, Topeka Active 20-30's, Masons (32 deg.), Shriners. Home: 7630 Robin Ct Topeka KS 66604 Office: 1947 N Topeka Ave Topeka KS 66608

PETTY, HOWARD RAYMOND, cell biology educator; b. Toledo, Ohio, Aug. 1, 1954; s. Dale Eugene and Patricia Ann (Purvis) P.; m. Leslie Ellen Isler, June 8, 1980; 1 child, Aaron Raymond. B.S., Manchester Coll., 1976; Ph.D., Harvard U., 1979. Fellow Stanford U., Calif., 1979-81; asst. prof., Wayne State U., Detroit, 1981-84, assoc. prof., 1985—. Contbr. articles to profl. jours. Damon Runyon fellow Walter Winchell Fund, 1980-81; grantee NIH, 1982—, NSF, 1982—, Am. Heart Assn., 1983—. Mem. Biophys. Soc., Am. Assn. Immunologists, Am. Soc. Cell Biology, Reticuloendothelial Soc., Am. Soc. Microbiologists. Office: Wayne State U 410 W Warren Ave Detroit MI 48202

PETTY, PRISCILLA HAYES, writer, newspaper columnist, consultant; b. Nashville, Aug. 22, 1940; d. Anderson Boyd and Margaret Louise (Lauper) Hayes; m. Gene Paul Petty, Jan. 10, 1961; children—Eric, Damon, Boyd. B.A. in English, Vanderbilt U., 1962; student Russian Inst., Dartmouth Coll., 1965. Cert. tchr., Ohio. Tchr. English, Cin. Suburban Pub. Schs., 1962-65, head dept. English, tchr., 1971-79; newspaper columnist Cin. Enquirer, 1978—, also syndicated newspaper columnist Gannett News Service, Washngton, 1982—; cons. Arthur Andersen & Co., 1981-82; writer United Western Corp., 1982. Author: History of a Boardsman (oral history), 1979. Mem. Cin. Council World Affairs; chmn. Cin. Media-Bus. Exchange, 1983; pres. bd. trustees Cin. Oral History Found., 1984. Named Outstanding Tchr., Project Teach, Ohio Edn. Assn., 1978. Mem. Women in Communications (Outstanding Communicator of the Year 1985), Oral History Assn., Sigma Delta Chi. Club: Woman's City (Cin.). Home: 229 Oliver Rd Cincinnati OH 45215

PETTY, SUE WRIGHT, library director; b. Kenton, Ohio, May 17, 1953; d. Norman Wilbur and Cynthia Elizabeth (Sapp) W.; m. Raymond O. Petty, Apr. 23, 1983; 1 child, Jeremy Michael. B.A., Ohio No. U., 1975; M.L.S., Ind. U., 1977. Vol., VISTA, Iowa Falls, Iowa, 1975-76; tech. services librarian Bowling Green Pub. Library, Ky., 1978-82; library dir. Mary Lou Johnson-Hardin County Dist. Library, Kenton, Ohio, 1982—. Vice pres. adv. council WORLDS, Lima, Ohio, 1983. Mem. Ohio Library Assn., ALA. Democrat. Methodist. Clubs: Minerva, Newcomers (sec. 1983-84). Home: 416 N Market St Kenton OH 43326 Office: Hardin County Dist Library 325 E Columbus St Kenton OH 43326

PEUGEOT, GEORGE LEON, investment company executive; b. Augusta, Ga., Nov. 9, 1924; s. George Leon and Mae Elizabeth (Grimes) P.; 1 child. B.S., U. Mich., 1949; M.B.A., Ind. U., 1950. With orgn. planning dept. Ford Motor Co., Dearborn, Mich., 1950-68; v.p. orgn. planning and personnel G.D. Searle, Skokie, Ill., 1969-72; pres. S.P.A. Industries, Inc., Winnetka, Ill., 1972-85. Author: Better Idea Total Financial Planning, 1968. Mem. The Soc. of Analysts Chgo. Club: Bay Haven Yacht (Holland, Mich.). Avocations: skiing, skating, yachting. Office: SPA Industries Inc 799 Elm St #206 Winnetka IL 60093

PEVELER, KENNETH EDWARD, mechanical engineer; b. Bellflower, Mo., Sept. 19, 1956; s. William J. and Julia M. (Dungan) P.; m. Nancy Ann Futhey, July 5, 1980. B.S. in Mech. Engring., U. Mo.-Rolla, 1980. Engr. Iowa Electric Co., Cedar Rapids, 1980-82, shift tech. advisor, 1982-83, quality assurance engr., 1983—. Advisor Jr. Achievement, Cedar Rapids, 1984-85. Mem. Am. Nuclear Soc. Republican. Baptist. Avocations: bowling; softball; golf; basketball. Home: 5025 Twin Mound Dr NE Cedar Rapids IA 52402 Office: Iowa Electric Light and Power Co PO Box 351 Cedar Rapids IA 52406

PEZZUTO, JOHN MICHAEL, pharmacology educator; b. Hammonton, N.J., Aug. 29, 1950; s. Michael L. and Elizabeth (Brown) P.; m. Arlene A. Cannata, May 2, 1970 (div. Aug. 1984); 1 child, Jennifer Anne. A.B., Rutgers U., 1973; Ph.D., Coll. Medicine and Dentistry N.J., 1977. Postdoctoral assoc. MIT, Cambridge, 1977-79; instr. chemistry U. Va., Charlottesville, 1979-80; asst. prof. U. Ill.-Chgo., 1980-84, assoc. prof. Pharmacology, 1984—. Contbr. articles to sci. jours. NIH fellow, 1977-80; NIH Research Career Devel. awardee, 1984-89, grantee Nat. Cancer Inst., 1984-85, Nat. Inst. Dental Research, 1984-85. Mem. AAAS, Am. Chem. Soc., Am. Soc. Pharmacognosy, Am. Assn. Cancer Research. Home: 97 S Park Blvd Glen Ellyn IL 60137 Office: U Ill 833 S Wood St Chicago IL 60612

PFAFF, ARTHUR ANTHONY, educational adminstrator; b. Festus, Mo., Aug. 18, 1929; s. Anton Joseph and Philomena Elizabeth (Jokerst) P.; m. Barbara Lou Miller, July 26, 1958; children—Brad Anthony, Carrie Ann, Kristie Elizabeth. B.S. in Edn., Semo State U., Cape Girardeau, Mo., 1952; M.Ed., Mo. U., 1956. Tchr. North Kansas City High Sch. (Mo.), 1952-62; asst. prin. Maple Park Middle Sch., North Kansas City, 1963-65, Oak Park High Sch., North Kansas City, 1965-73; prin. New Mark Middle Sch., North Kansas City, 1973—. Contbr. articles to mags. Counselor Kansas City council Boy Scouts Am., 1965—; lay minister St. Charles Cath. Ch., Gladstone, Mo., 1974—. Served to sgt. U.S. Army, 1947-48. Mem. Mo. Middle Schs. Assn. (bd. dirs. 1976-78), Met. Jr. High Sch. Prins. Assn. (v.p. 1977-78), Nat. Middle Schs. Assn., Nat. Assn. Secondary Sch. Prins., Phi Delta Kappa. Roman Catholic. Avocations: Golf, reading, gardening. Home: 205 NW 59th St Gladstone MO 64118

PFAFF, JOHN WILLIAM, architect; b. St. Louis, Nov. 23, 1942; s. William Henry and Pearl Florence (Henckler) P.; m. Mary Margaret Liebmann, Nov. 28, 1970; children—Mark John, Mandy Christina. Student Southeast Mo. State U., 1960-62; B.A., Okla. State U., 1966. Registered architect, Mo. With Gornet & Shearman, St. Louis, 1968-69, Hoffman-Saur, 1970; v.p. Kromm, Rikimaru & Johansen, Inc., 1971—. Served with U.S. Army, 1966-68. Mem. AIA, Beta Sigma Psi. Home: 1295 Lombez Dr Manchester MO 63011 Office: Kromm Rikimaru & Johansen Inc 112 S Hanley Rd Clayton MO 63105

PFAHLERT, THOMAS HOPFNER, advertising and marketing communications agency executive, educator; b. Toledo, Mar. 23, 1938; s. Earl Joseph and Ellen Clarinda (Fettig) P.; m. Sandra Lee Kosuth, June 20, 1964; children—Mark Thomas, Matthew Joseph. Student in design Meinzinger Art Sch., Detroit, 1958-61. Art dir. Chiat/Day Advt., Los Angeles, 1965-69; sr. art dir. D'Arcy, McManus, Masius, Los Angeles, 1969-71; v.p., creative dir. Flournoy & Gibbs, Inc., Toledo, 1971-74; pres. Tom Pfahlert, Cons., Toledo, 1974-76, Mktg. Communications Group, Toledo, 1976—; assoc. prof. Bowling Green (Ohio) State U., 1980—. Served with U.S. Army, 1959-64. Recipient medal Art Dirs. Club N.Y., 1974-75, Art Dirs. Club Chgo., 1975, 76; nat. Addy awards, 1976, 77, 72. Mem. Art Dirs. Club Los Angeles (pres. 1970-71, gold medal 1970), Advt. Club Toledo (dir. 1972-75, gold medal 1972, 74, 75, 76), Toledo C. of C. Home: 2309 Garden Creek Dr Maumee OH 43537 Office: Mktg Communications Group Inc 900 Adams St Toledo OH 43624

PFALLER, MARK FRANK, II, architect; b. Milw., Apr. 23, 1948; s. Mark A. and Elizabeth Rae (Campbell) P. B.Arch., U. Notre Dame, 1973. Pvt. practice architecture, Milw., 1974-77; v.p. Mark F. Pfaller Assocs., Milw.,

1977-83, exec. v.p., 1978-83 (firm merged with Herbst Jacoby & Jacoby forming Pfaller Herbst Assocs., Inc. 1980); pres., owner Mark F. Pfaller, AIA, Architect/Constructor, 1984—; Bd. dirs. Pabst Theater, Milw., 1982—, Artist Series at the Pabst, 1983—. Recipient award Best Comml. Renovation Project, Builder's Choice Mag., 1982. Mem. AIA, Wis. Soc. Architects (Excellence in Architecture award 1977, 82, 83, 84, past v.p., co-chmn. pub. relations, chmn. Architecture Week Wis.), Nat. Trust for Hist. Preservation, League Hist. Am. Theaters. Clubs: Milw. Rugby Football, Milw. Rowing. Office: Milwaukee WI 53202

PFANNKUCHE, CHRISTOPHER EDWARD KOENIG, lawyer; b. Chgo., May 1, 1955; s. Edward Louis and Barbara (Koenig) P. B.A. in Polit. Sci., Loyola U., Chgo., 1977, B.S. in Edn., 1978, J.D., 1980. Bar: Ill. 1980, U.S. Dist. Ct. (no. dist.) Ill. 1980, U.S. Ct. Claims 1984, U.S. Ct. Internat. Trade 1984, U.S. Tax Ct. 1983, U.S. Ct. Mil. Appeals 1983, U.S. Ct. Appeals (7th cir.) 1983, U.S. Ct. Appeals (D.C. cir.) 1984, U.S. Supreme Ct. 1983. Asst. states atty. State's Atty.'s Office, Macon County, Decatur, Ill., 1981, Cook County, Skokie, Ill., 1981—. Author: Traffic Trial Procedure Handbook, 1981. Mem. Nat. Dist. Attys. Assn., ABA, Assn. Trial Lawyers Am., Am. Judicature Soc., Ill. Bar Assn., Ill. Trial Lawyers Assn., Chgo. Bar Assn., Decatur Bar Assn., N.W. Suburban Bar Assn. (membership chmn. 1982-83, law day chmn. 1982), Phi Alpha Delta. Roman Catholic. Home: 7220 W Greenleaf Ave Chicago IL 60631 Office: States Attys Office Cook County 5600 Old Orchard Rd Skokie IL 60077

PFEFFER, JOHN THOMAS, engineering educator, researcher; b. Ripley, Ohio, Oct. 2, 1935; s. William John and Lydia Marie (Thamert) P.; m. Marian Alice Turner, Aug. 30, 1958; children—Julie Leigh, Elizabeth Anne. B.S.C.E., U. Cin., 1958, M.S., 1959; Ph.D., U. Fla., 1962. Asst. prof. U. Kans., Lawrence, 1962-65, assoc. prof., 1965-67; assoc. prof. U. Ill., Urbana, 1967-69, prof. engring., 1969—; cons. UN, Nicosia, Cyprus, 1980, Waste Mgmt. Inc., Oak Brook, Ill., 1973—. Trustee Urbana and Champaign San. Dist., Urbana, 1975—. Mem. ASCE, Am. Soc. Microbiology, Water Pollution Control Fedn., Am. Soc. Engring. Edn. Democrat. Office: U Ill Dept Civil Engring 208 N Romine St Urbana IL 61801

PFEIFER, EUGENE, pharmacist; b. Melrose Park, Ill., Apr. 16, 1945; s. Eugene Paul and Leota Agnus (Dreher) P.; m. Susan Roberta Devine, Nov. 7, 1970; children—Teresa Marie, Jennifer Lynn. B.S. in Zoology, No. Ill. U., 1967; B.S. in Pharmacy, U. Ill.-Chgo., 1970; M.B.A., Keller Grad. Sch. Mgmt., 1983. Registered pharmacist, Ill., Va. Dir. pharmacy Westlake Community Hosp., Melrose Park, 1970-71; staff pharmacist Northwestern Meml. Hosp., Chgo., 1975-77; pharmacist in charge Whitehall Convalescent and Nursing Home, Chgo., 1975-76; asst. dir. pharmacy/metabolic support service St. Mary of Nazareth Hosp. Ctr., Chgo., 1977-85; pharmacy mgr./cons. pharmacist Conva-Care, Inc., Rolling Meadows, Ill., 1985—; off-site preceptor pharmacy residency program Rush Presbyn. St. Luke's Med. Ctr., Chgo., 1978-83. Served with USN, 1971-75. Mem. Ill. Council Hosp. Pharmacists, Am. Soc. Hosp. Pharmacists, Am. Soc. Parenteral and Enteral Nutrition, Am. Inst. Hist. Pharmacy, Kappa Psi. Roman Catholic. Contbr. articles to profl. jours. Home: 506 S Elmhurst Ave Mount Prospect IL 60056 Office: Conva-Care Inc 5420 Newport Dr Suite 57 Rolling Meadows IL 60008

PFEIFER, JOHN ROY, vascular surgeon; b. Morse, Sask., Can., Aug. 18, 1934; came to U.S., 1958; s. Charles O. and Eva Pfeifer; m. Jeanne Edith Pachal, June 22, 1957; children—Pamela, Jacqueline, Lauren, John. M.D., U. Sask., 1958. Intern, then resident in medicine Queen's Hosp., Honolulu, 1958-60; resident in surgery Henry Ford Hosp., Detroit, 1960-64; practice surgery Northland Vascular Clin., P.C., Southfield, Mich., 1967—; chmn. dept. surgery Providence Hosp., 1969—. Diplomate Am. Bd. Surgery. Fellow ACS; mem. Internat. Soc. Cardiovascular Surgery, Midwestern Vascular Surgery Soc. (founding sec.). Club: Rolls Royce Motor Region (bd. dirs. 1985—). Avocations: auto restoration; photography. Office: Northland Vascular Clin P C 22250 Providence Dr 700 Southfield MI 48075

PFEIFFER, DONALD GENE, wildlife biologist; b. Ft. Scott, Kans., June 13, 1947; s. Raymond Earl and Rachel Pauline (Johnston) P.; m. Cynthia A. Selzer, Sept. 29, 1973; children—Steven Shane, Nicholas Donald. B.S., Kans. State U., 1970; M.S., S.D. State U., 1972. Conservation aide Kans. State Fish and Game, Great Bend, 1969; research asst. S.D. Coop. Wildlife Unit, Brooking, 1970-72; wildlife biologist I, Iowa Conservation Commn., West Branch, 1972-77, wildlife biologist II, North Liberty, 1977-81, dist. wildlife supr., Brighton, 1981—. Mem. Iowa Wildlife Soc. (sec. 1979-83), Nat. Wildlife Fedn., Nat. Wild Turkey Fedn., Wildlife Soc. (cert. wildlife biologist), Izaac Walton League Am. Baptist. Clubs: Optimist (sec. 1978), Ducks Unlimited. Avocations: photography; hunting; public information. Office: Iowa Conservation Commn Rural Route 1 Dist Office Brighton IA 52540

PFENDER, EMIL, mechanical engineering educator; b. Stuttgart, West Germany, May 25, 1925; came to U.S., 1964, naturalized, 1969; s. Vinzenz and Anna Maria (Dreher) P.; m. Maria Katharina Staiger, Oct. 22, 1954; children—Roland, Norbert, Corinne. Student U. Tuebingen, 1947-49; Diploma in Physics, U. Stuttgart, 1953, D. Ing. in Elec. Engring., 1959. Assoc. prof. mech. engring. U. Minn., Mpls., 1964-67, prof., 1967—. Contbr. articles to profl. jours. Patentee in field. Fellow ASME; mem. Am. Phys. Soc., IEEE (assoc.). Home: 1947 Bidwell St West St Paul MN 55118 Office: U Minn 111 Church St SE Minneapolis MN 55455

PFINGSTEN, STEPHEN LLOYD, teacher educator; b. Oshkosh, Wis., Oct. 17, 1945; s. Lloyd Eugene Pfingsten and Dorothy Alberta Mae (Miller) Heindel; m. Patricia Margaret Nelson, Sept. 2, 1967; children—Jason, Jennifer, Matthew. B.S. in Bus. Adminstrn. and Econs., Carroll Coll., Waukesha, Wis., 1967; M.S. in Curriculum and Instrn., U. Wis.-Madison, 1969; Ph.D. in Curriculum and Instrn., Marquette U., 1983. Tchr. St. Cecelia Elem. Sch., Wisconsin Dells, 1969, Central High Sch., Duluth, Minn., 1969-78; instr. mgmt. dept. Coll. St. Scholastica, Duluth, 1978-80, 81-84, asst. prof., chmn. edn. dept., 1984—. Mem. Mayor's Edn. Task Force, Duluth, 1984—. Mem. Assn. Supervision and Curriculum Devel., Phi Delta Kappa, Pi Lambda Theta. Avocations: fishing; camping. Home: 1731 North Rd Duluth MN 55811 Office: Coll St Scholastica 1200 Kenwood Ave Duluth MN 55811

PFISTER, JAMES JOSEPH, publishing executive; b. N.Y.C.; Oct. 29, 1946; s. Stanley George and Rosemary Ann (Cullen) S.; m. Kendra Elaine Nelson, Mar. 23, 1974; 1 child, Charles Joseph. B.S., Northwestern U., 1970. Mktg. supr. Nat. Register Pub. Co., Wilmette, Ill., 1970-73, dist. sales mgr., 1973-76, nat. sales mgr., 1976-80, pub., 1980-85, pres., 1985—; pres. Marquis Who's Who, Inc., Chgo., 1985—. Sec. Libertyville Home Owners Assn., Ill., 1981-83, pres., 1983-85; mem. Com. to Re-elect Reagan, 1984. Served to sgt. U.S. Army, 1967-69, Vietnam. Decorated Bronze Star with oak leaf cluster, Air Medal, Purple Heart. Mem. Am. Assn. Museums, Chgo. Advt. Club. Republican. Avocations: model building; railroad equipment; running; water skiing. Home: 219 Pondridge Rd Libertyville IL 60048 Office: Nat Register Pub Co 3004 Glenview Rd Wilmette IL 60091

PFISTER, WILLIAM RICHARD, pharmaceutical research specialist, toxicologist; b. Paterson, N.J., Feb. 25, 1951; s. William Joseph and Dolores Francis (Tully) P.; m. Gail Marie Womer, May 24, 1975; children—William R. Jr., Nicole Ann. B.S. in Biochemistry, U. N.H., 1973; M.S. in Pharmacology/-Toxicology, Purdue U., 1976, Ph.D. in Pharmacology/Toxicology, 1978. Diplomate Am. Bd. Toxicology, Am. Coll. Toxicology. Sr. scientist Hoffmann-LaRoche, Nutley, N.J., 1978-80; sr. research investigator, toxicologist Am. Critical Care Corp., McGaw Pk., Ill., 1980-83; pharm. research specialist Dow Corning Corp., Midland, Mich., 1983—; cons. Pharmaco-Toxicodynamics, Park City, Ill., 1983. Author tech. papers. Active Gurnee Jaycees, Ill., 1983. Mem. Soc. Neurosci., N.Y. Acad. Scis., Am. Chem. Soc., Soc. Toxicology, Controlled Release Soc. Republican. Roman Catholic. Home: 505 W Midland Rd Bay City MI 48706 Office: Dow Corning Corp Midland MI 48640

PFLEGER, LAWRENCE RAYMOND, counselor, educator; b. Iowa City, Iowa, Aug. 13, 1944; s. Raymond and Virginal A. (Tracy) P.; m. Caroline R. Olig, Dec. 23, 1974. B.S., U. Wis.-Madison, 1967, M.A., 1969, Ph.D., 1977. Lic. cons. psychologist, Minn.; nat. cert. counselor; nat. cert. career counselor. Social studies tchr. Green Bay Pub. Schs., Wis., 1967-68; counselor Greendale Pub. Schs. (Wis.), 1970-74, asst. prin. jr. high, 1974-75; dir. freshman counseling Northeast Mo. State U., Kirksville, Mo., 1968-69; counselor, assoc. prof. counseling St. Cloud State U., Minn., 1979—. Contbr. articles to profl. publs., chpts. to books. Named outstanding Young Educator, Greendale Jaycees, 1973; recipient R. Wray Strong Meml. award Dept. Counseling and Guidance, 1977. Mem. Minn. Career Devel. Assn. (sec. 1984—), Am. Assn. Counseling and Devel., Nat. Vocat. Guidance Assn., Phi Kappa Phi, Phi Delta Kappa (v.p. 1982-83, pres. 1983-84, del. 1984—), St. Cloud Amateur Radio Club. Avocations: amateur radio operating, hobby computers. Office: St Cloud State U Counseling Ctr 118 Stewart Hall St Cloud MN 56301

PHAN, SEM HIN, pathologist, educator; b. Jakarta, Indonesia, Sept. 15, 1949; s. Joek Sioe and Hong Tek (Hauw) P.; came to U.S., 1967; m. Katherine Assimos, June 19, 1976; children—Nicholas, Louis. B.Sc., Ind. 1971, Ph.D., 1975; M.D., U. Ind.-Indpls., 1976. Diplomate Am. Bd. Pathology. Resident U. Conn. Health Ctr., Farmington, 1976-80; practice medicine specializing in pathology, Ann Arbor, Mich., 1980—; staff Univ. Hosp., U. Mich.; asst. prof. dept. pathology Sch. Medicine, U. Mich., Ann Arbor, 1980—; mem. pathology A study sect. NIH Pub. Health Service, Bethesda, Md., 1983-87. Contbr. articles to profl. jours. Grantee NIH, 1982—, Am. Heart Assn., 1984—; established investigatorship Am. Heart Assn., 1984—. Mem. Am. Assn. Pathologists, AAAS, Am. Thoracic Soc., N.Y. Acad. Scis., Am. Chem. Soc. Roman Catholic. Avocations: chess; philately; oenology; cooking. Office: U Mich Sch Medicine Dept Pathology MO45 Ann Arbor MI 48109

PHARES, JAMES SHERIDAN, industrial designer; b. Los Angeles, Mar. 29, 1941; s. Carl Frederick and Myrtle Elvene (Jensen) P.; m. Penelope Jane Wilson, June 10, 1967; 1 child, Heather Elizabeth. B. in Profl. Art with honors, Art Ctr. Coll. of Design, Pasadena, 1963. Designer corp. projects Ford Motor Co., Dearborn, Mich., 1963-66; designer Sandberg-Ferar, Southfield, Mich., 1966-67; designer, cons., pres. Phares Assocs., Birmingham, Mich., 1967-85, Farmington Hills, Mich., 1985—; vis. prof. indsl. design Ctr. for Creative Studies, Detroit, 1968—. Recipient HUD Design award, 1970, Volkswagen Design award, Parkhurst Pubs., 1971, Gov.'s Citation, Mich. Dept. Commerce, 1985. Mem. Indsl. Designers Soc. Am., Am. Soc. Interior Designers. Republican. Lodge: Lions. Avocations: golf; swimming; painting; photography; comparative political thought. Office: Phares Assocs Inc 37624 Hills Tech Dr Farmington Hills MI 48018-1221

PHELAN, JAMES BERNARD, insurance company executive; b. Akron, Ohio, Sept. 28, 1941; s. Bernard W. and Waneta (Magoteaux) P.; B.A., Kent State U., 1963; married; children—Todd W., Brent J. C.P.C.U.; C.L.U. Ins. agt. Phelan Ins. Agy., Inc., Versailles, Ohio, 1962-72; v.p. Midwestern Ins. Group, Cin., 1972-76; pres. Ins. Mktg. Assos., Versailles, 1976—; tchr. CLU program, Cin. Pres. Versailles Devel. Assn., 1969-70. Chmn. Versailles Poultry Days Festival, 1970, exec. dir., 1970, 71. Mem. Profl. Ins. Agts. of Ohio (dir. 1978-81; pres. 1984-85), Ind. Ins. Agts. Assn. of Ohio, Profl. Ins. Agts. of Am., Ind. Ins. Agts. Assn. Am., Western Ohio Trucking Assn., Soc. Chartered Life Underwriters, Soc. Chartered Property and Casualty Underwriters, So. Cert. Ins. Counselors, Nat. ARC/AMS Users Group (treas., pres. 1985-86, bd. dirs.). Republican. Roman Catholic. Clubs: Elks, K.C., Eagles, Rotary (pres. 1971-72). Home: 629 E Main St Versailles OH 45380 Office: 617 E Main St Versailles OH 45380

PHELPS, BERTHA BUTTERFIELD, historian, journalist; b. Mayville, Mich., July 17, 1909; d. Eri H. and Hildah Ann (Baxter) Butterfield; m. Willard S. Phelps, Feb. 16, 1931; children—Mary Ann, Joanna Murphy, Carole. B.A., Graceland Coll., 1974; M.A., Central Mich. U., 1980. Office mgr. No. Engravers, Saginaw, Mich., 1952-55; sec. to supt. schs. Marlette Schs., Mich., 1955-58; dir., curator Mayville Mus., Mich., 1971—. Author, compiler: History of Mayville and 4 Townships, 1979; Yesteryears of Juniata, 1983. Organizer Mayville Pub. Library, 1948; active Girl Scouts Am., 1950-72, former 2d v.p. Mem. Mich. Mus. Assn., Hist. Soc. Mich., Am. Assn. State and Local History. Mem. Reorganized Ch. of Jesus Christ of Latter-day Saints. Home: 2898 Saginaw Rd Mayville MI 48744 Office: Mayville Hist Mus 22 Turner St Mayville MI 48744

PHELPS, FREDERICK MARTIN, III, physicist, physics educator; b. Grand Rapids, Mich., June 11, 1933; s. Frederick Martin and Alics Elizabeth (Kellogg) P.; m. Marion Louise Riley, Mar. 2, 1957; children—Frederick IV, Dorothy, Richard. B.A. in Physics, Carleton Coll., 1955; M.S. in Physics, U. Mich., 1958; Ph.D. in Physics, U. Alta., Edmonton, 1963. Instr. Kalamazoo Coll., Mich., 1959-60; sessional instr. U. Alta., Edmonton, 1960-62; sessional lectr. U. Alta., Edmonton, 1962-64; research assoc. U. Mich., Ann Arbor, 1964-68; assoc. prof. Detroit Inst. Tech., 1967-69; head grating research Bausch and Lomb Optical Co., Rochester, N.Y., 1969-70; assoc. prof. Central Mich. U., Mt. Pleasant, 1970—. Author: MIT Wavelength Tables, Vol. 2, 1982. Contbr. articles to sci. jours. Assoc. editor Jour. Optical Soc. Am., 1965-77. Scoutmaster Boy Scouts Am., 1972—. Mem. Optical Soc. Am., Am. Assn. Physics Tchrs. Presbyterian. Home: 290 Cedar Dr Mount Pleasant MI 48858 Office: Physics Dept Central Mich U 221 Brooks Hall Mount Pleasant MI 48859

PHELPS, NANCY ANN, lawyer; b. Waukesha, Wis., July 26, 1941; d. Gilbert William and Ruth Ellen (Alldredge) Weideman; m. Richard E. Phelps, Aug. 3, 1963 (div. 1972); children—Lori, Libby, Melissa. B.S., Carroll Coll., 1963; J.D., Marquette U., 1972. Bar: Wis. 1972; registered med. technician, Wis.; real estate broker, Wis. With New Yorker Mag., 1963-64; with Andrews Advt., Milw., 1967-69; staff atty. Legal Aid Soc., Milw., 1972-73; sole practice law, Milw., 1973—; assessor Alverno Coll.; ptnr., sec., dir. Superior Ambulance Inc., Milw., 1979—; owner Marietta Imports, Nancy Phelps Realty. Bd. dirs. Clare Towers, Milw., 1983—; bd. dirs., 2 v.p. Multiple Sclerosis Soc. Milw., 1978—. Mem. Am. Jurisprudence award in domestic relations Marquette U., 1972. Mem. State Bar Wis., Milw. Bar Assn., Assn. Women Lawyers, Milw. Zool. So., Milw. Art Mus. Office: 731 N 16 St Milwaukee WI 53233

PHELPS, SHARON SCHMID, nurse; b. Milw., May 23, 1954; d. Merwin John and Doris Jean (Unke) Schmid; m. Roger William Phelps, Mar. 13, 1982. B.A.N., Coll. St. Catherines, 1976; postgrad. nursing Marquette U., 1976-79. Staff nurse Milw. Children's Hosp., 1976-77; public health nurse II, City Wauwatosa (Wis.) Health Dept., 1977-79; float staff nurse Milw. Children's Hosp., 1979-81; public health nurse II City Wauwatosa Health Dept., 1981—; real estate sales assoc. Schmid Realty Inc. Midwestern Ski queen U.S. Ski Assn., 1979. Republican. Roman Catholic. Clubs: Sitzmark Ski, Pewaukee Yacht, New Berlin Jr. Women's. Address: 3175 S Manor Dr New Berlin WI 53151

PHIBBS, CLIFFORD MATTHEW, surgeon, educator; b. Bemidji, Minn., Feb. 20, 1930; s. Clifford Matthew and Dorothy Jean (Wright) P.; B.S., Wash. State U., 1952; M.D., U. Wash., 1955; M.S., U. Minn., 1960; m. Patricia Jean Palmer, June 27, 1953; children—Wayne Robert, Marc Stuart, Nancy Louise. Intern, Ancker Hosp., St. Paul, 1955-56; resident in surgery U. Minn. Hosps., 1956-60; practice medicine specializing in surgery, Oxboro Clinic, Mpls., 1962—; mem. staff St. Barnabas Hosp., Children's Hosp. Ctr.; mem. staff Fairview-Southdale Hosp., 1965—, chief of surgery, 1970-71, sec.-treas., 1971-72, chmn. intensive care unit, 1973-76; clin. asst. prof. U. Minn., Mpls., 1975-78, clin. assoc. prof. Surgery, 1978—. Bd. dirs. Bloomington (Minn.) Bd. Edn., 1974—, treas., 1976, sec., 1977-78, chmn., 1981-83; mem. adv. com. for jr. coll. study City of Bloomington, 1964-66, mem. community facilities com., 1966-67, adv. youth study commn., 1966-68; vice chmn. bd. Hillcrest Meth. Ch., 1970-71; mem. Bloomington Adv. and Research Council, 1969-71; bd. dirs. Bloomington Symphony Orch., 1976—, Wash. State U. Found. dir. bd. mgmt. Minnesota Valley YMCA, 1970-75; bd. govs. Mpls. Met. YMCA, 1970—. Served to capt. M.C., U.S. Army, 1960-62. Diplomate Am. Bd. Surgery. Mem. AMA (Physician's Recognition awards 1969, 73-76, 76-79, 79-82, 83—), Assn. Surg. Edn., Royal Soc. Medicine, Minn. Med. Assn., Minn. Acad. Medicine, Minn., Mpls. surg. socs., Hennepin County Med. Soc., Pan-Pacific Surg. Assn., A.C.S., Bloomington C. of C. (bd. dirs. 1984—). Club: Jaycees. Contbr. articles to med jours. Home: 9613 Upton Rd S Minneapolis MN 55431 Office: 9820 Lyndale Ave S Minneapolis MN 55420

PHILLIP, JOSEPH, hospital supply company executive; b. Kottayam, Kerala, India, Apr. 14, 1928; came to U.S., 1960; s. Lukose and Mariam Joseph. B.A. with honors, U. Pa., 1956, M.A., 1958; M.B.A., U. Detroit, 1962; Ph.D., Wayne State U., 1968. Research dir. Blue Cross Assocs., Chgo., 1969-70; dir. Hosp. Research Ctr., Am. Hosp. Assn., Chgo., 1970-79; dir. corp. market research Am. Hosp. Supply Corp., Evanston, Ill., 1979—. Author: Factors Affecting Staffing Levels of Nurses, 1975; The Nature of Hospital Costs, 1976; Seasonal Patterns of Hospital Activity, 1979; Hospital Industry: A Time Series Analysis, 1982. Mem. Am. Statis. Assn., Am. Soc. Pub. Health. Home: 502 Dunsten St Northbrook IL 60062 Office: Am Hosp Supply Corp 1 American Plaza Evanston IL 60201

PHILLIPPI, ELMER JOSEPH, JR., data communications analyst; b. Canton, Ohio, May 31, 1944; s. Elmer Joseph and Rita M. (Tillitski) P.; m. Susan Mary Schrader, July 10, 1971. A.B., Cornell U., 1966; M.A., Rice U., 1970. Cert. energy auditor. Asst. prof. engring. tech. Muskingum Tech. Coll., Zanesville, Ohio, 1971-80; data communications analyst Chem. Abstracts Services, Columbus, Ohio, 1980—; part-time instr. physics Ohio U. NSF grantee, 1979. Mem. Assn. Computing Machinery (symposium com.), N.Y. Acad. Scis., Sigma Xi. Republican. Club: Cornell of Central Ohio. Home: 5557 Foster Ave Worthington OH 43085 Office: PO Box 3012 Columbus OH 43085

PHILLIPPI, JOHN CHARLES, regional planner; b. Canton, Ohio, July 23, 1950; s. Elmer J. and Rita M. (Tillitski) P.; 1 dau., Diana Lynne. Student Pahlavi U., Shiraz, Iran, 1971; B.A. in Social Scis., Kent State U., 1972. Cert. planner, Ohio. Assoc. planner Stark County Regional Planning Commn., 1972-74, chief regional planner, 1974-80, chief planner community devel., 1981—; lectr. in field.; mem. Stark County Community Housing Resource Bd., 1982, Ohio Conf. Community Devel. Mem. Am. Planning Assn., Am. Inst. Cert. Planners. Author numerous planning and community devel. related studies and reports. Office: Stark County Regional Planning Commn Canton OH 44702

PHILLIPS, ARLIE EMERSON, educator; b. Moorhead, Minn., Dec. 29, 1951; s. Cecil Donald and Dorothy Maxine (Kraig) P. Student U. N.D., 1968-71, postgrad. in econs., 1978-79; B.S. in Elem. Edn., Valley City State Coll., 1973. Cert. elem. tchr., S.D. Elem. tchr. Bur. Indian Affairs Low Mountain Boarding Sch., Chinle, Ariz., 1974, Eagle Butte Sch. Dist., S.D., 1975; securities trader, investor, Rutland, N.D., 1976-83; elem. and jr. high. sch. math tchr. Tiospa Zina Tribal Sch., Sisseton, S.D., 1983—. Mem. Nat. Council Tchrs. of Math., Internat. Council Computers in Edn. Avocations: reading, computers, stamp collecting, playing violin, golf. Home: Rural Route 1 Box 119 Summit SD 57266 Office: Tiospa Zina Tribal Sch Box 719 Sisseton SD 57262

PHILLIPS, CAROLE ANN, educator, photographer; b. Princeton, Ill., Nov. 1, 1936; d. Ward Elwood and Anna Victoria (West) Birkey; B.S., Ill. State U., 1961; M.Ed., Macalester Coll., 1970; M.S. of Ed., No. Ill. U., 1975; postgrad. Salzburg (Austria) Coll., 1978; nuclear physics program Fermi Lab., fall 1982; m. Bobby Elwood Phillips, Aug. 15, 1963; children—Keith Robert. Tchr., Walnut (Ill.) Pub. Schs., 1956-57, Wyanet (Ill.) Pub. Schs., 1958-60, Princeton (Ill.) Elementary Schs., 1960-63, Batavia (Ill.) Pub. Schs., 1963-71; with Hinsdale (Ill.) Health Mus. (now Robert Crown Center for Health Edn.), 1972-74; guidance counselor Aurora (Ill.) Central Cath. High Sch., 1974-81; tchr. math., physics and chemistry Valley Lutheran High Sch., St. Charles, Ill., 1981-84; photographer Fox Kane County Tourism Assn., Batavia, 1984—, Foxway mag., 1984—; cons. to Region V HEW, Chgo., 1972-74; lectr. in field. Exhibited in group shows Batavia Pub. Library, 1984, Community Hosp., Geneva, Ill., 1984. Contbr. to profl. pubs. Named Outstanding Phys. Sci. Tchr. of Chgo. Met. Region, Bell Labs., 1980; recipient grand champion award Kane County Fair, 1983; 2 best of show photograph awards Kane County Town and Country Art Show, 1984, No. Ill. Regional Show Town and Country Art, 1984. NSF grantee, 1969-70. Mem. NEA, Am. Guidance and Personnel Assn., Nat. Vocational Guidance Assn. Mem. United Ch. of Christ. Contbr. articles in field to profl. jours. Home: 1212 N Brandywine Circle Batavia IL 60510 Office: Kane County Office Tourism 719 Batavia Ave Geneva IL 60134 also Foxway Mag 127 State St Batavia IL 60510

PHILLIPS, DAVID JOSEPH, communications specialist; b. Battle Creek, Mich., Nov. 29, 1955; s. Dwight Donald and Dorothy A. (Miller P. B.S. in Bus. Adminstrn., Troy State U., Dothan, Ala., 1982; postgrad. Western Mich. U., Kalamazoo, 1983—. Airway facilities technician FAA, Dothan, 1978-82; electronic equipment specialist USAF Hdqrs. Logistics Command, Battle Creek, 1982-83; communications specialist Fed. Emergency Mgmt. Agy., Battle Creek, 1983—; tchr. electronics Battle Creek Central High Sch. Served with USAF, 1974-77. Mem. Non-Commd. Officers Assn. (Spl. Achievement award 1975, Minuteman citation 1975), Battle Creek Jaycees, Gamma Beta Phi. Home: 7983 Pennfield Rd Battle Creek MI 49017 Office: Federal Center Battle Creek MI 49016

PHILLIPS, DAVID NOLAN, optometrist; b. Evansville, Ind., Oct. 4, 1948; s. Nolan Jack and Mabel Lucille (Simpson) P.; m. Susanne Kay Sewell, June 27, 1970 (div. 1976); m. Lynn Marie Jourdan, Oct. 16, 1982; children—Melanie Lynn, Kasey Nolan, Jamie Lynn. Student Oakland City (Ind.) Coll., 1966-67; A.B. in Zoology, Ind. U., 1970, A.B. in Optometry, 1972, O.D., 1974; postgrad. Trinity Theol. Sem., Newburgh, Ind., 1984—. Cert. optometrist, Ind. Teaching asst. Ind. U., 1972-74; practice optometry, Newburgh, Ind., 1974-77, Evansville, 1977—; minister music Tennyson Baptist Ch., Tennyson, Ind., 1982—; cons. in field. Named Clinician of Yr. award Ind. U. Sch. Optometry, 1974. Mem. Southwestern Ind. Optometric Soc., Ind. Optometric Assn., Am. Optometric Assn. Republican. Lodges: Odd Fellow, Masons. Home: 5077 SR 161 Tennyson IN 47637 Office: 514 Main St Evansville IN 47708

PHILLIPS, DENNIS LESLIE, lawyer, army officer; b. Phila., Sept. 2, 1952; s. William Leslie and Margaret Katherine (Wenborne) P.; m. Linda Jane Pogue, June 23, 1974; children—Colleen, Michael, Brian. B.S., U.S. Mil. Acad., 1974; J.D. magna cum laude, Syracuse U., 1981. Bar: N.Y. 1982, U.S. Ct. Mil. Appeals 1982. Commd. 2d lt. U.S. Army, 1974, advanced through grades to capt., 1978; comdr. 284th M.P. Co., Frankfurt, 1977-78; trial def. counsel Trial Def. Service, Ft. Riley, Kans., 1981-83; dep. staff judge adv. U.S. Army Correctional Activity, Ft. Riley, 1983—. Instl. rep., com. chmn. Explorer Scouts, Boy Scouts Am., Frankfurt, 1977-78; merit badge counselor Hiawatha council Boy Scouts Am., 1979-81. Decorated Meritorious Service medal, Army Achievement medal. Mem. ABA, N.Y. State Bar Assn., Fed. Bar Assn., Assn. Trial Lawyers Am., Assn. U.S. Army, Nat. Eagle Scout Assn., Justinian Hon. Law Soc., Order of Coif. Republican. Episcopalian. Home: 3329 Trevelyan Ave Manhattan KS 66502 Office: Staff Judge Adv US Army Correctional Activity Fort Riley KS 66442

PHILLIPS, DONALD PAUL, tool company executive; b. Racine, Wis., May 19, 1935; s. Peter Woodrow and Josephine Rose (Falbo) P.; m. Judith Kay Sebastian, July 1, 1967; children—Laura C., Paul C., Melissa R. B.A. in Internat. Relations, U. Wis.-Milw., 1962. Mdse. control supr. Brunswick Internat. Corp., Chgo., 1963-65; asst. export mgr. Powers Regulator Co., Skokie, Ill., 1965-69; dir. of exports Ideal Industries, Inc., Sycamore, Ill., 1969-76; v.p. internat. Klein Tools, Inc., Chgo., 1976—. Served with U.S. Army, 1958-60. Mem. Internat. Bus. Council Mid-Am. (pres. 1967, dir. 1980-81). Republican. Roman Catholic. Avocations: golf; skiing; hiking. Home: 419 High Ridge Rd Barrington IL 60010 Office: Klein Tools Inc 7200 McCormick Rd Chicago IL 60645

PHILLIPS, ELWOOD HUDSON, bookstore executive, real estate executive; b. Ludlow, Ky., May 30, 1914; s. Clarence Bell and Hallie Josephine (Hudson) P.; m. Edna Mae Johnson, May 20, 1934; children—Janet Carolyn, Martha Lee. Student U. Cin., 1933, Anderson Coll., 1952-54. Foreman, supt. sales, service mgr., packaging engr. Container Corp. Am., Cin. and Rock Island, Ill., 1932-47; owner, mgr. Phillips Book Store, Springfield, Ohio, 1947—; mgr. bookstore Anderson Coll., Ind., 1950-68; owner, mgr. Phillips Real Estate, Anderson, 1956—. Mem. Nat. Bd. Realtors, Ind. Assn. Realtors, Am. Booksellers Assn., Anderson Bd. Realtors, Christian Booksellers Assn. Democrat. Mem. Ch. of God. Avocation: geneology. Home: 807 Nursery Rd Anderson IN 46012 Office: Phillips Book Store 16 N Limestone St Springfield OH 45502

PHILLIPS, FREDERICK FALLEY, architect; b. Evanston, Ill., June 18, 1946; s. David Cook and Katharine Edith (Falley) P.; m. Gay Fraker, Feb. 26, 1983. B.A., Lake Forest Coll., 1969; M.Arch., U. Pa., 1973. Registered architect, Ill., Wis. Draftsman, Harry Weese & Assocs., 1974, 75; pvt. practice architecture Frederick F. Phillips, Architect, Chgo., 1976-81; prin. Frederick Phillips and Assocs., Chgo., 1981—. Bd. dirs. Landmarks Preservation Council, 1981—; mem. aux. bd. Chgo. Architecture Found., 1975—. Recipient award Townhouse for Logan Square Competition, AIA and Econ. Redevel. Corp. Logan Square, 1980; Gold medal award Willow St. Houses, Ill. Ind. Masonry Council, 1982; Disting. Bldg. award for Willow St. Houses, Chgo. chpt., AIA, 1982 for Pinewood Farm, 1983. Mem. AIA, Chgo. Archtl. Club. Clubs: Racquet (bd. govs.), Arts, Cliff Dwellers (Chgo.). Office: 332 S Michigan Ave Chicago IL 60604

PHILLIPS, GARY STEVEN, environmental studies educator, consultant; b. Sioux City, Iowa, Jan. 19, 1950; s. Kirk E. and Marcella R. (La Plante) P.; m. Linda Jean Stratton, June 29, 1974. B.S., Iowa State U., 1972; M.A., U. No. Iowa, 1979, Ed.S., 1980. Cert. tchr., Iowa. Instr., U. No. Iowa, Cedar Falls, 1978-80, Iowa Lakes Community Coll., Estherville, 1982—; tchr. Laurens-Marathon High Sch., Iowa, 1980-82; cons. lake protective assns., city govt. Contbr. articles to profl. jours. Radiol. def. officer CD Emmet County, 1983, 84. Served with USN, 1972-76. Recipient Eagle Scout award Boy Scouts Am., 1967. Mem. Nat. Sci. Tchrs. Assn., Nat. Assn. Biology Tchrs., Iowa Acad. Sci., Nature Conservancy, VFW. Roman Catholic. Avocations: hunting; fishing; camping; jogging. Home: W 15 S 1st St Estherville IA 51334 Office: 300 S 18th St Estherville IA 51334

PHILLIPS, GREGORY SCOT, management consultant, manufacturing company executive; b. Chgo., May 24, 1952; s Morton Jeffrey and Alpha Mae (Hightower) P.; m. Marilyn Payne, May 24, 1974; children—Cassandra, Jennifer. B.S.E.E. magna cum laude, U. Ill.-Urbana, 1974; M. Mgmt., Northwestern U., 1978. Cert. info. systems auditor. Computer, market engr. Commonwealth Edison, Chgo., 1974-79; supr. Coopers & Lybrand, St. Louis, 1979-82; audit mgr. Chromalloy Am., Clayton, Mo., 1982—; speaker various assns., 1981—. Mem. EDP Auditors Assn. (instr. 1981-84, bd. dirs. 1981—, pres. 1985-86). Lodge: Kiwanis (v.p. 1985—). Avocations: chess; travel. Office: Chromalloy American 120 S Central Clayton MO 63005

PHILLIPS, JACK D., JR., management consultant; b. Chattanooga, Apr. 9, 1937; s. Jack D. and Verna Lee P.; B.A. in Psychology, Trevecca Coll., 1960; m. Janey Sue Little, June 19, 1959; 1 dau., Tandi Lee. Exec. dir. multinat. pub. enterprise, South Africa, 1965-71; dir. mktg. Design Group, Inc., 1972-79; v.p. mktg. The Bowman Group, 1979-81; pres. STRATAMARK, Inc., Columbus, Ohio, 1982—; pub. speaker; writer, cons. Recipient citation Gov. of Ky., 1977. Mem. Am. Mktg. Assn., Soc. Hosp. Planners, Soc. Mktg. Profl. Services. Clubs: Athletic of Columbus, Ohio State U. Faculty, Little Turtle Country. Author: Methods and Styles of Leadership, 1977; regular contbr. Columbus Bus. Jour. Home: 1823 Hightower Dr Worthington OH 43085 Office: 88 E Broad St Suite 1400 Columbus OH 43215

PHILLIPS, JAMES RICHARD, manufacturing company administrator, labor law specialist; b. Kenosha, Wis., Sept. 4, 1925; s. Lloyd James and Segna Agnes (Ledgerwood) P.; m. Joyce Elaine Huck, Aug. 15, 1944; children—Steven James, Mary Joyce. Student U. Wis.-Racine, 1945-47, SUNY-Catskill, 1970. Adminstrv. asst.-works mgr. Simmons Co., Kenosha, Wis., 1945-58; gen. mgr. L&B Products Corp., Stottville, N.Y., 1958-72; mfg. mgr. Vega Industries, Mt. Pleasant, Iowa, 1972-77; plant mgr. Preway, Inc., Wisconsin Rapids, Wis., 1977-81; div. mfg. mgr., Colt Industries, Necedah, Wis., 1981—; pres. Universal Tax Service, Kenosha, 1951-54. Served with USN, 1942-45, PTO. Mem. Wood County Indsl. Mgmt. Club (pres. 1980-81), Wood County C. of C. (bd. dirs. 1980-81). Republican. Roman Catholic. Club: Holy Name Soc. (Stottville) (pres. 1966-67). Lodges: Lions (tail-twister 1965), Elks (exalted ruler 1971-72). Home: 4010 Wedgewood Circle Wisconsin Rapids WI 54494

PHILLIPS, JOHN MILTON, lawyer; b. Kansas City, Mo., Dec. 16, 1915; s. John and Atha (Dennis) P.; A.B., U. Kans., 1937; J.D., Harvard, 1940; m. Mary Hamilton Bracken, Aug. 29, 1942; children—Mary Bracken, Patricia Ann, Jean Hamilton, John Milton, Daniel Dennis. Admitted to Mo. bar, 1940; asso. firm Stinson, Mag & Fizzell, 1940-46, partner, 1946—. Trustee Philharm. Assn. of Kansas City, pres., 1965-67; former v.p. dir. Am. Symphony Orch. League 1965-67; mem. adv. com., past pres. Citizens Assn. Kansas City; past bd. dirs. Kansas City chpt. ARC. Served from pvt. to capt. AUS, 1942-46. Mem. Kansas City Council on Edn. (past pres.), Am. Bar Assn., Mo. Bar Assn., Acad. Social and Polit. Sci., SR, Mil. Order of World Wars, Phi Gamma Delta, Delta Sigma Rho. Republican. Episcopalian. Clubs: Kansas City, Harvard. Home: 12704 Baltimore Ct Kansas City MO 64145 Office: 2100 Ten Main Center Kansas City MO 64105

PHILLIPS, JOSEPH WILLIAM, lawyer; b. Darby, Pa., Sept. 25, 1948; s. Joseph W. and Catherine S. (Quinn) P.; m. Margaret Elizabeth Meiran, May 17, 1982; children—Lara, Michael Anthony. B.A. in English Lit., Oakland U., 1970; J.D. in Law, Wayne State U., 1981. Bar: Mich. 1982, U.S. Dist. Ct. (ea. dist.) Mich. 1982. Pres. J. Phillips Leathercraft, Ann Arbor, Mich., 1971-80; assoc. Davis & Fajen P.C., Ann Arbor, 1981—; gen. counsel Mich. Atomic Vets., 1981-83. Fin. chmn. Com. to Elect John R. Minock, Ann Arbor, 1984. Mem. ABA, Assn. Trial Lawyers Am., Mich. State Bar, Mich. Trial Lawyers Assn., Washington County Bar Assn. Democrat. Office: Davis & Fajen PC 320 N Main St Suite 400 Ann Arbor MI 48104

PHILLIPS, JUDITH KAYE, nurse; b. Richmond, Ind., May 9, 1944; d. Dale Joseph and Ruth (Zook) Stoehr; m. Daniel David Semko, Nov. 15, 1970 (div. Feb. 1980); 1 child, Jena Semko; m. Richard Allen Phillips, June 25, 1983; 1 child, Marcie. Diploma Meth. Sch. Nursing, 1965; postgrad. DePauw U., Case Western Res. U., Ind. U. East-Richmond. R.N., Ind. Instr. Milw. County Gen. Hosp. Sch. Nursing, 1972-73; charge nurse Sage Nursing Home and Rehab. Ctr., Milw., 1973-76; dir. nursing Whitecliff Manor, Cleve., 1976-77; staff nurse VA Hosp., Cleve., 1977-78; head nurse Mt. Sinai Hosp., Cleve., 1978-80; staffing dir. Reid Meml. Hosp., Richmond, Ind., 1980—. Mem. Am. Nurses Assn., Ind. State Nurses Assn., Nat. Health Recruiters Assn. Baptist. Avocations: oil painting; writing poetry; needlepoint. Office: Reid Meml Hosp 1401 Chester Blvd Richmond IN 47374

PHILLIPS, KEVIN EMIL, lawyer; b. Cape Girardeau, Mo., May 3, 1955; s. Emil Christon William and Laverne Elizabeth (Smith) P. B.A., SE Mo. State U., 1977; J.D., U. Mo.-Kansas City, 1981. Bar: Mo. 1981, U.S. Dist. Ct. (ea. dist.) Mo. 1982. Ptnr. firm Lichtenegger Knowlan Phillips, Jackson, Mo., 1981—; asst. pros. atty. Cape Girardeau County, Mo., Jackson, 1981—. Chmn. 8th Congl. Dist. Republican Com., Mo., 1982—, Cape Girardeau County Rep. Com., 1982—; mem. Mo. Commn. on Human Rights, Jefferson City, 1982; bd. dirs. Jackson C. of C., 1985; mem. U. Mo. Cooperative Extension Council, 1985. Recipient Am. Juris. award Lawyers Coop. Pub., 1980. Lutheran. Home: Route 1 Box 229 Cape Girardeau MO 63701 Office: Lichtenegger Knowlan & Phillips PO Box 350 1210 Greenway Dr Jackson MO 63755

PHILLIPS, MELVIN ROMINE, minister, American Baptist Churches, U.S.A.; b. Parkersburg, W.Va., July 10, 1921; s. Chester Corliss and Julia Augusta (Romine) P.; m. Carolyn Beckner, Aug. 12, 1944; children—Ann Elizabeth, Ruth Elaine, Ralph, Beth Carol. B.A., Alderson-Broaddus Coll., 1944; B.D., Colgate Rochester Div. Sch., 1946; postgrad. Marshall U., 1949-50. Ordained to ministry, Am. Bapt. Ch., 1946. Pastor, Mumford, N.Y., 1944-46, Kingwood-Masontown Bapt. Parish, W.Va., 1946-49; univ. pastor Marshall U., Huntington, W.Va., 1949-50; pastor First Bapt. Ch., Shelbyville, Ind., 1950-57; Anderson, Ind., 1957-67, Jamestown, N.Y., 1967-73; exec. minister Assoc. Chs. of Fort Wayne and Allen County, Ind., 1973—. Bd. dirs. Mental Health Assn., 1976-77, Adler Inst., Samaritan Pastoral Counseling Ctr.; mem. 4th Dist. Adv. Council to Select Com. on Children, Youth and Families, U.S. Congress; bd. dirs. Ind. Council of Chs. Named Man of Year, Jaycees, 1954; recipient Ecumenical citations in Anderson and Jamestown. Mem. Ind. Council Chs. (recipient Ecumenical citation 1964, pres. 1962-64), Am. Bapt. Hist. Soc., Clergy United for Action, N.Am. Acad. Ecumenists, Nat. Assn. Ecumenical Staff, Bibl. Archaeology Soc., Amnesty Internat. Club: Rotary. Home: 4616 Tacoma Ave Fort Wayne IN 46807 Office: 227 E Washington St Fort Wayne IN 46802

PHILLIPS, MICHAEL JAMES, accountant; b. Cheboygan, Mich., May 18, 1949; s. James William and Therese Joanne (LaHaie) P.; m. Patricia Louise Kline, Aug. 16, 1969; children—Michael A., Holly J., Melissa L. B.B.A., Western Mich. U., 1971. Office mgr. B&C Supermarkets, Inc., Cheboygan, Mich., 1971-75, sec.-treas., 1975—. Mem. Cheboygan C. of C. (treas. 1980-83, dir.). Republican. Roman Catholic. Home: 520 Cleveland Ave Cheboygan MI 49721 Office: B&C Supermarkets Inc 992 S Main St Cheboygan MI 49721

PHILLIPS, NOEL, See *Who's Who in America,* 43rd edition.

PHILLIPS, NORMAN DAVID, photographer, lecturer; b. London, Oct. 30, 1931; came to U.S., 1980; s. Philip Schwartzberg and Edna (Rosenberg) Rose; m. Sadie Sandra Kurzfield, July 5, 1965; children—Ivan Cole, Leon Toby, Daniel Saul. Diploma in fashion design Fountayne Sch. Design, London, 1949; cert. comml. art Sir John Cass Tech. Inst., London, 1948; M.Photography, Master Photographers Assn., London, 1979. Gen. mgr. Eric Smale Studios, Kingston upon Thames, Eng., 1965-68; lectr. photography Inst. Inc. Photographers, Twickenham Coll. Tech. (Eng.), 1968-72; dir. ops. Capitol Color Labs., Ilford, Eng., 1972-73; dir. photography Wadham Artists Ltd., London, 1973-75; owner Town Square Studio, Southend on Sea, Eng., 1975-80, Norman Phillips of London, Highland Park, Ill., 1980—; lectr. P.P.A. Affiliates, Chgo. and Wis., 1983—; cons. Russell Color Labs., London, 1969-80, Kingston upon Thames Council, 1968-72. Contbr. articles to profl. jours.; author: Professional Photography (Merit award 1984, 85), 1983. Brit. del. World Assembly of Youth, Denmark, 1962; v.p. Nat. League Young Liberals, London, 1962; gen. sec. Homes for All Campaign, Eng., 1962-63; city councillor County Borough of West Ham, London, 1961-65; founder, pres. East London Young People's Debating Soc., 1962. Recipient Handelman award, 1984. Mem. Master Photographers Assn. U.K., Chicagoland Profl. Photographers Assn. (pres. 1984-85, Man of Yr. award 1985). Jewish. Office: Norman Phillips of London 458 Central Ave Highland Park IL 60035

PHILLIPS, PHILIP KAY, stained glass manufacturing and retail company executive; b. Kansas City, Mo., Jan. 3, 1933; s. Ernest Lloyd and Mildred Blanche (Moser) P.; B.A., Bob Jones U., Greenville, S.C., 1958; postgrad. Central Mo. State U., 1977-78, 81-83; m. Constance Diana Lucas, June 12, 1955; children—John Allen, David Lee, Stephen Philip, Daniel Paul, Joy Christine. Ordained minister Baptist Ch., 1959; pastor Mt. Moriah Baptist Ch., Clarksburg, Mo. 1958-59; security officer Mo. Dept. Corrections, Jefferson City, Mo., 1959-64; field mgr. office Darby Corp. and Piping Contractors Inc., Kansas City, Kans., 1965-72, safety and security dir. Darby Corp. and Leavenworth Steel Inc., Kansas City, 1972-84; with Stained Glass Creations, North Kansas City, Mo., 1984—. Mem. planning com. Kans. Gov.'s Indsl. Safety and Health Conf., 1977-78, chmn. mfg. sect., 1978. Mem. Nat. Safety Mgmt. Soc., Am. Soc. Safety Engrs. (chpt. exec. com. 1980-81, treas. chpt. 1981-82, sec. chpt. 1982-83, 2d v.p. chpt. 1983-84, 1st v.p. 1984-85, chpt. pres. 1985-86), Kans. Safety Assn. (v.p., mem. exec. com. 1979-80), Nat. Fire Protection Assn., Home: 3205 NE 66th St Gladstone MO 64119 Office: Stained Glass Creations 316 Armour Rd North Kansas City MO 64116

PHILLIPS, PHILIP SANFORD, lawyer; b. Kenton, Ohio, Sept. 27, 1948; s. Calvin L. and Gail M. (German) Phillips; m. Barbara J. Starrett, Jan. 24, 1969; children—Emily, Aaron. Student Cin. Bible Sem., 1966-68; A.B., Milligan Coll., 1970; postgrad., Emmanuel Sch. Religion, 1970-71; J.D., Ohio State U., 1975. Bar: Ohio 1975. Staff lawyer Allen County Legal Service, Lima, Ohio, 1975-77; mng. atty. Southeast Ohio Legal Services, Zanesville, 1977-82; sole practice law, Zanesville, 1982—; city law dir. Zanesville, 1984—. Trustee Area 9 Agy. on Aging, Cambridge, Ohio, 1983—, Big Brothers/Big Sisters of Zanesville, 1983—; v.p. Zanesville High Sch. Soccer Boosters Assn., 1982—. Mem. Ohio State Bar Assn., Muskingum County Bar Assn., Ohio Mcpl. Attys. Assn. Democrat. Office: 44 N 5th St Zanesville OH 43701

PHILLIPS, ROBERTA ANNE, nurse, nursing home adminstr.; b. Savannah, Ga., Aug. 11, 1943; d. Robert Nelson and Bertis Dorothy (Phillips) P.; R.N. diploma, Crawford W. Long Sch. Nursing, Emory U., 1965; B.A. in Psychology, Ga. State Coll., Atlanta, 1965; student rehab. nursing Chgo. Rehab. Inst., Northwestern U. Med. Center, 1979. Charge nurse ICU, Crawford Long Hosp., Atlanta, 1965-66; asst. head nurse ICU, Bapt. Meml. Hosp., Jacksonville, Fla., 1966-67; charge nurse cardiac ICU, Riverside Hosp., Jacksonville, 1967-69, evening supr., 1969-71; staff nurse surg. ICU Meml. Hosp., Jacksonville, 1971-72; supr. phlebotomy unit Ocean Plasma Corp., Jacksonville, 1972-75; staff nurse ICU, intravenous therapy Meth. Hosp., Jacksonville, Fla. 1976-77; dir. nursing Wincrest Nursing Home, Chgo., 1979-82; dir. nursing approved home, Chgo., 1982—; instr. CPR, Am. Heart Assn. Recipient Outstanding Service award Ocean Plasma Corp., 1974. Mem. Am. Nurses Assn. Home: 4607 N Sheridan Rd Apt 811 Chicago IL 60640 Office: 909 W Wilson Chicago IL 60640

PHILLIPS, SARAH VIRGINIA CYRUS, real estate executive, city official; b. Louisa, Ky.; d. W. Raymond and Isabelle Evelyn (Johnson) Cyrus; student pub. schs.; m. Donald Ray Phillips, Mar. 20, 1954; children—Donald Bruce, David Brian. Dep. circuit court clk. Lawrence County, Louisa, 1952-53; sec. Nationwide Ins. Co., Columbus, Ohio, 1953-56; jr. acountant Nationwide Mortgage Co., Columbus, 1957-63; gen. clk. Ohio State Life Ins. Co., Columbus, 1963-64; clk. council city clk., Whitehall, Ohio, 1964-71, city auditor, tax commr., 1981—; adminstrv. asst. City of Columbus, 1972-76; realtor assoc. Sparks Real Estate of Century 21, 1976-80; broker Nutrend Realty, 1980—, residential appraiser, 1976—. Publicity chmn. Whitehall Boys Baseball Assn., summers 1965-68; sec., publicity chmn. Whitehall Boys' Basketball; mem. Ohio Commn. on Status Women; pres. Downtown Women's Republican. Club, 1974-75; Whitehall Rep. Com., 1977; mem. Rep. Central Com., 1974—; mem. Whitehall City Council, 1977-81; trustee, sec.-treas. Whitehall Devel. Corp.; bd. dirs. Columbus Area Women's Polit. Caucus, 1977—. Mem. Central Ohio Mayors and Mcpl. Officers Council (exec. sec.-treas.), Ohio Municipal Clks. Assn. (trustee, v.p. 1971), Whitehall Civic Celebrations Assn. (sec., trustee 1968-71, v.p. 1978), Ohio Hist. Soc., LWV, Nat. Assn. Realtors, Whitehall Bus. Assn. (founding pres.), Central Ohio Fiscal Officers Network (founding chmn.). Internat. Toastmistress Club (Woman of Influence 1976, 77). Mem. Ch. of Christ (bd. dirs., treas., mem. youth com.). Home: 1010 S Yearling Rd Whitehall OH 43227 Office: 360 S Yearling Rd Whitehall OH 43213

PHILLIPS, TERRY LEMOINE, electrical engineer; b. Washington, July 27, 1938; s. Clifford LeMoin and Dorothy Louise (Schuman) P.; B.S., Purdue U., 1964, M.S., 1966; m. Lynne Ann Bruce, Aug. 12, 1962; children—Susan Rae, Stephen Kirk. Assoc. program leader, data processing Purdue U. Lab. Applications of Remote Sensing, West Lafayette, 1966-71, program leader, 1971-74, dep. dir., 1974—; cons. AID, Computer Scis. Corp. Scoutmaster, explorer adviser Boy Scouts Am., bd. dirs. Sagamore council; sports coordinator, youth sports, Battleground, Ind.; elder, deacon Presbyterian Ch. Served with USN, 1956-59. Mem. IEEE (sr.), Assn. Computing Machinery, Data Processing Mgmt. Assn. (internat. dir., co-founder, v.p., pres. Sagamore chpt.), Tau Beta Pi, Eta Kappa Nu. Club: Rotary (dir., treas.). Home: 1522 E 600 N West Lafayette IN 47906 Office: 1291 Cumberland Ave West Lafayette IN 47906

PHILLIPS, WAYNE WOODROW, II, lawyer; b. Norwalk, Ohio, Sept. 14, 1945; s. Wayne Woodrow and Iverna Martha (Sherman) P.; B.A., Ohio No. U., 1967, J.D., 1972; m. Patricia Smith, Jan. 10, 1981; twin daughters. Bar: Ohio 1972, Ind. 1973. Acct., Edward R. Moyer, C.P.A., Bellevue, Ohio, 1967-70; tax acct. Kern, Linnemeier & Co., C.P.A.s, Ft. Wayne, Ind., 1972-74; partner Stubbins, Phillips & Co., Zanesville, Ohio, 1974—; dir. Killbuck Inc., Buckeye Water Service, Buckeye Well Surveys, Inc. Chmn. bd. dirs. Zanesville Goodwill Industries, 1976—; treas. Friends of the Library, Zanesville, 1976-77. Named Zanesville Citizen of the Month, May, 1977. Mem. Am. Bar Assn., Ohio State Bar Assn., Ind. State Bar Assn., Muskingum County Bar Assn., Ohio Soc. C.P.A.s, Am. Inst. C.P.A.s, Am. Assn. Atty-C.P.A.s, Ohio Oil and Gas Assn, Zanesville Jaycees (treas. 1975-76, pres. 1976-77), Ohio Jaycees (asst. treas. 1977-78, treas. 1978-79; senator). Republican. Episcopalian. Club: Zanesville Quarterback (treas. 1978-81). Lodges: Rotary, Masons. Home: 260 Skyline Dr Zanesville OH 43701 Office: 925 Military Rd Zanesville OH 43701

PHILLIPS, WILLIAM GEORGE, business executive; b. Cleve., Mar. 3, 1920; s. Edward George and Ina Marie (Cottle) P.; A.B., Antioch Coll., 1942; m. Laverne Anne Evenden, Aug. 7, 1943; children—Karen Anne (Mrs. David F. Berry), Connie Allynette (Mrs. Richard Tressel), Scott William. Pub. accountant Price Waterhouse & Co., Cleve., 1945-48; tax accountant Glidden Co., Cleve., 1948-52, asst. treas., 1952, treas., dir., 1953-67, adminstrv. v.p., 1963-64, pres., 1964-67, chief exec. officer, 1967, pres. Glidden-Durkee div. SCM Corp., 1967-68; pres., chief exec. officer Internat. Multifoods Corp. (formerly Internat. Milling), Mpls., 1968-70, chmn. bd., 1970-85, now dir.; dep. chmn. Mpls. Fed. Res. Bank, 1979-82, chmn., 1982-85, also dir.; dir. Soo Line R.R. Co., Heileman Brewing, Firestone Tire & Rubber Co., No. States Power Co. Bd. overseers U. Minn. Coll. Bus. Adminstrn.; nat. corp. adv. bd. United Negro Coll. Fund; adv. bd. Nat. Alliance Businessmen; bd. dirs. Mpls. Downtown Devel. Corp.; mem. pres.'s adv. bd. Am. Diabetes Assn.; adv. bd. Inst. Internat. Edn.; trustee Hamline U., 1979—; bd. dirs. Nat. Jewish Hosp. at Denver. Am. Served to lt., inf. AUS, 1942-45. Mem. Conf. Bd., Ohio Soc. C.P.A.s, Conf. Bd. Mem. Community Ch. Clubs: Lafayette, Minneapolis (bd. govs.), Woodhill Country. Home: 6666 Smithtown Rd Victoria MN 55331 Office: 1200 Multifoods Bldg Minneapolis MN 55402

PHILLIPS, WINFRED MARSHALL, engineering educator, university administrator; b. Richmond, Va., Oct. 7, 1940; s. Claude Marshall and Gladys Marian (Barden) P.; children—Stephen, Sean. B.S.E.M., Va. Poly. Inst., 1963; M.A.E., U. Va., 1966, D.Sc., 1968. Mech. engr. U.S. Naval Weapons Lab., Dahlgren, Va., 1963; NSF trainee, teaching, research asst. dept. aerospace engring. U. Va., Charlottesville, 1963-67, research scientist, 1967-68; asst. prof. dept. aerospace engring. Pa. State U., University Park, 1968-74, assoc. to prof., 1974-80, assoc. dean research Coll. Engring., 1979-80; head Sch. Mech. Engring., Purdue U., West Lafayette, Ind., 1980—; vis. prof. U. Paris, 1976-77. Bd. dirs. Central Pa. Heart Assn., 1974-80; mem. Ind. State Boiler & Pressure Vessel Code Bd., 1981—. Fellow AAAS, AIAA (assoc.), ASME; mem. Am. Soc. Artificial Internal Organs (trustee 1982—), Nat. Assn. State Univs. and Land-Grant Colls. (com. quality of engring. edn.), Am. Phys. Soc., Am. Soc. Engring. Edn., Internat. Soc. Artificial Organs, Biomed. Engring. Soc., N.Y. Acad. Scis., Internat. Soc. Biorheology, Assn. Advancement of Med. Instrumentation, Sigma Xi, Pi Tau Sigma, Sigma Gamma Tau, Tau Beta Pi (eminent engr.). Clubs: Cosmos; Rotary. Contbr. articles to profl. jours., chpts. to books; assoc. editor ASME Jour. Biomech. Engring. Home: 300 Valley St Lafayette IN 47905 Office: Sch Mech Engring Purdue U West Lafayette IN 47907

PHIPPS, TERRY WAYNE, photographer, educator; b. Port Huron, Mich., June 2, 1946; s. George W. and Electrica (Smith) P. A.A., Port Huron Jr. Coll., 1966; B.S., Eastern Mich. U., 1968; M.A., U. Mich., 1975; cert. profl. photography, Famous Photographers, 1973. Cert. tchr., adminstr., Mich., Colo., Wash. Tchr. Davison Community Schs. (Mich.), 1968-85; owner, photographer The Abstraction, Davison, 1974-82; staff photographer Wheels, East Jordan, Mich., Racing News, Chesaning, Mich., Mich. Snowmoblier, East Jordan; owner Eaglenest, Traverse City, Mich.; freelance photographer various publs., lectr. Eastern Mich. U., Ypsilanti, 1977, WTRX Radio, Flint, Mich., 1977, WNEM, Saginaw, Mich., 1977, Cable 8, Port Huron, Mich., 1975. Author: Meadowlarks June Bugs and Dreams, 1976; The Queen of Almonds, 1985. Recipient Internat. Photography and Art Show awards, Eastman Kodak/Times Herald. Mem. Profl. Photographers Am., NEA, Mich. Edn. Assn., Davison Edn. Assn. (Edn. Service award 1983), Am. Soc. Mag. Photographers, Sierra Club. Avocations: Skiing, diving. Home: Box 3053 Traverse City MI 49685 Office: Eaglenest Box 3053 Traverse City MI 49685

PHUNG, THANH GIA, radiologist; b. Hanoi, Vietnam; came to U.S., 1975; s. Loc Tuan Phung and Chinh Thi Le; m. Thu-cuc Thi Tran; children—Angie, Charlie, Peter. B.S., Jean-Jacques-Rousseau Lyceum, 1965; diploma medicine, U. Saigon, Vietnam, 1973. Diplomate Am. Bd. Radiology. Resident in radiology Wayne State U., Detroit, 1977-81; radiologist Duy-Tan Mil. Hosp., Danang, Vietnam, 1973-75; X-ray technologist Riverton Hosp., Seattle, 1975-77; radiologist Plymouth Gen. Hosp., Detroit, 1977, Trail Clinics P.C., Detroit, 1977-83; fellow Oakwood Hosp., Dearborn, Mich., 1982-83; radiologist Harris-Birkhill-Wang-Songe, P.C., Dearborn, 1983—. Fellow Am. Coll. Radiology; mem. AMA. Avocations: electronics; tennis. Office: Oakwood Hosp Dept Radiology 18101 Oakwood Blvd Dearborn MI 48124

PHYE, GARY DEAN, psychology educator, consultant, researcher, author; b. Harper, Kans., Jan. 15, 1942; s. Jesse Evans and Marion Virginia (Mayberry) P.; m. Connie Jeanne Burns, June 2, 1962; 1 dau., Julie. B.A., Wichita State U., 1964; M.A., 1965; Ph.D., U. Mo., 1970. Instr. in psychology S.W. Mo. State U., Springfield, 1965-67; asst. prof. psychology and edn. Iowa State U., Ames, 1970-74, assoc. prof., 1975—. Grantee Iowa State U., 1975-76, Iowa State Research Inst. for Studies in Edn., 1977-78, Apple Edn. Found., 1982-83. Mem. Am. Psychol. Assn., Am. Ednl. Research Assn., Midwest Psychol. Assn. Roman Catholic. Author: (with others) Educational Psychology, 1983; editor: (with Reschly) School Psychology: Perspectives and Issues, 1979. Home: 2175 Ashmore Dr Ames IA 50010 Office: 112 W Quadrangle Iowa State U Ames IA 50011

PIACENTINI, VINCENT, theatre consultant; b. St. Louis, June 1, 1922; s. Vincent and Josephine (Davis) P. B.F.A., Washington U., 1945. Mng. dir. St. Louis Resident Theatre, 1947-50, stage, archtl. designer, 1945-55; stage, archtl. designer, Pitts., 1955, Ft. Wayne, Ind., 1955-60; mng. dir. Ft. Wayne (Ind.) Civic Theatre, 1960-61; designer Theatre Cons., N.Y.C., 1961, Washington, 1962-63, Atlanta, 1965-66; mng. dir., ptnr. The Prodn. Group, N.Y.C., 1964-67; sr. cons. Bolt Beranek & Newman, N.Y.C., 1967-71; prin. cons., dir. Piacentini/Auerbach Assocs., N.Y.C. and San Francisco, 1971-73; supervisory cons. Bolt Beranek & Newman, Boston, 1973-79; prin. cons., dir. V. Piacentini/P.A., St. Louis, 1979—; vis. designer, lectr. Pa. State U., 1966-67. Mem. Am. Soc. Theatre Cons., Archaeol. Inst. Am., Illuminating Engrs. Soc., Nat. Trust for Hist. Preservation, Soc. Stage Dirs. and Choreographers, United Scenic Artists.

PIACSEK, BELA EMERY, biology educator, researcher; b. Budapest, Hungary, Apr. 17, 1937; came to U.S., 1952, naturalized, 1958; s. Stephen Elek and Adriene Anna (Vasarhelyi) P.; m. Eniko Mary DePottyondy, June 9, 1962; children—Kristina Marie, Steven Bela, Kathleen Elizabeth, Thomas Charles. B.S., Notre Dame U., 1959, M.S., 1961; Ph.D., Mich. State U., 1966. Research fellow Harvard Sch. Medicine, Boston, 1966-68; asst. prof. Marquette U., Milw., 1968-73, assoc. prof., 1973-79, prof., 1979—. Contbr. chpts. to books, articles to profl. jours. Active St. Luke Choir, Brookfield, Wis., 1974—; v.p. New Berlin Citizens for Edn. (Wis.), 1984. Mem. Am. Physiol. Soc., Endocrine Soc., Soc. Study Reprodn. Roman Catholic. Avocations: distance running; tennis; gardening. Office: Marquette U Dept Biology 530 N 15th St Milwaukee WI 53233

PIATT, PHIL DELBERT, civil engineer; b. Hamilton, Kans., Nov. 5, 1932; s. Phil Delbert and Ruth Elizabeth (Milliken) P.; m. Virginia Claire Best, June 15, 1957; children—Stephen, Joseph, Sharon, Linda. B.S.C.E., U. Kans., 1955, M.P.A., 1984. Registered profl. engr., Kans. Engr., Finney & Turnipseed Cons. Engrs., Topeka, 1958-66, Van Doren, Hazard, Stallings, Schnacke Cons. Engrs., 1966-69; asst. city engr. City of Topeka, 1969-76; city engr. City of Overland Park, Kans., 1976—. Contbr. to profl. publs. Served to lt. (j.g.) USN, 1956-58. Mem. Am. Pub. Works Assn. (bridges com. 1974-75, chmn. 1976-77), ASCE, Nat. Soc. Profl. Engrs., Kans. Engring. Soc. Presbyterian. Home: 9221 Beverly St Overland Park KS 66207 Office: City of Overland Park 8500 Santa Fe St Overland Park KS 66212

PICARDI, GUY CARL, architect; b. St. Louis, Nov. 1, 1933; s. Guy Anthony and Elizabeth (Hall) P.; m. Mary Virginia Thompson, May 27, 1961; children—Steven Guy, Philip Vincent, Susan Dana. B.Arch., Washington U., 1955. Registered architect, Mo., Kans., Ind. Architect C.W. Lorenz, St. Louis, 1955-56; architect, v.p., exec. dir. St. Louis office Leo A. Daly Planners, Architects and Engrs., 1957—; profl. mem. St. Louis Regional Commerce and Growth Assn. Mem. fin. com. St. Richard's Parish, Creve Coeur, Mo., 1983—; mem. Hawthorn Found., St. Louis. Served to capt. U.S. Army, 1956-57, USAR, 1964. Mem. AIA, Constrn. Specifications Inst., Bldg. Ofcls. and Code Adminstrs., NCCJ, Sigma Nu. Republican. Roman Catholic. Clubs: St. Louis, Stadium (St. Louis). Avocation: jogging. Home: 11136 Bon Jour Ct Saint Louis MO 63146 Office: Leo A Daly Planners Architects Engrs 10114 Woodfield Ln Saint Louis MO 63132

PICCOLO, STEPHEN FOSTER, engineering and consulting company manager; b. Westerly, R.I., Nov. 1, 1954; s. Raymond Anthony and Juliette Katherine (Capalbo) P.; m. Mary Francesca Calabro; children—Sean, Lara. B.S. in Mech. Engring. and Applied Mechanics, U. R.I., 1976; postgrad. in L.S., Eastern Mich. U., 1984—. Engr.-in-tng., R.I. Plant engr. Ohio Edison, Akron, 1976-78; project coordinator Consumers Power Co., Jackson, Mich., 1978-79; outage mgr. Bechtel Power Corp., Cedar Rapids, Iowa, 1979-81, project engr., Monroe, Mich., 1981-83, supt. engring. service, Monroe, 1983—; maintenance analyst Detroit Edison, Monroe, 1984—; mem. speakers bur. Bechtel Power Corp., Ann Arbor, Mich., 1979—; mem. joint test group, cons. restart of Davis-Besse Nuclear Plant, 1985. Author writings in field of design and security. Stage mgr., bd. dirs. Saline Area Players, Mich., 1984; mem. Indsl. and Bus. Devel. Commn., Saline, 1984—. Mem. Am. Nuclear Soc. (pub. info. chmn. Mich. 1978-79), ASME, Project Mgmt. Inst. Club: Toastmasters. Avocations: Travel; building kit cars. Home: 989 Colony Ct Saline MI 48176 Office: Bechtel Power Corp 15740 Shady Grove Rd Gaithersburg MD 20877

PICHLER, JOSEPH A., See *Who's Who in America,* 43rd edition.

PICKEL, JOYCE KILEY, school psychologist; b. Boston, Dec. 20, 1939; d. James Joseph and Harriet Marie (Fougere) Kiley; B.S. in Edn., Boston State Coll., 1961; M.Ed., R.I. Coll., 1967; M.A., Mich. State U., 1969; postgrad. No.

Ill. U., 1979; m. Edward McDonald, Aug. 24, 1960 (div. Mar. 1977); children—Catherine, Maureen, Edward; m. Mark Pickel, Apr. 6, 1982. Tchr., Silver Lake Regional High Sch., Kingston, Mass., 1962; tchr. Easton (Mass.) Jr. High Sch., 1962-63, Meml. High Sch., Middleboro, Mass., 1963-64, Hope High Sch., Providence, 1965-66; guidance counselor Grand Ledge (Mich.) Jr. High Sch., 1977-79; psychometrist Hammond (Ind.) City Schs., 1969-70; diagnostician Eaton County Intermediate Sch. Dist., Charlotte, Mich., 1968-69; coordinator programs for emotionally disturbed and learning disabled, psychometrist N.W. Ind. Spl. Edn. Cooperative, Highland, 1970-72; instr. Ind. U., Northwest Campus, Gary, 1970-72; program dir. Trade Winds Rehab. Center for Children, Gary, 1972; supervising sch. psychologist Thornton Fractional Township High Sch., Calumet City, Ill., 1973—. Vice pres. Wilbur Wright Middle Sch. PTA, 1975-76; mem. planning bd. Lake Area United Way, 1973—; 1st v.p. Greater Hammond Community Council, 1976; mem. community adv. council Govs. State U. Recipient Hammond Community Council award, 1974-76; NDEA fellow, 1967-68. Mem. Nat. Assn. Sch. Psychologists, Council Exceptional Children, Am. Fedn. Tchrs., Ill. Psychol. Assn., Ill. Sch. Psychologists Assn. (pub. relations com.), S. Met. Assn. Sch. Psychologists (pres. 1982-83), Assn. Supervision and Curriculum Devel., Phi Delta Kappa. Unitarian. Home: 1419 Douglas Ln Crete IL 60417 Office: 1601 Wentworth Ave Calumet City IL 60409

PICKENS, CHARLES GLENN, mathematics educator; b. Clinton, Okla., Sept. 15, 1936; s. Kenneth and Lois C. (Dotson) P.; m. Beverly Jean Osborne, Jan. 11, 1958; children—Paula Jean, Jill Lynn, Janet Gail. B.S., Central State U., Okla., 1958; M.S., Okla. State U., 1960, Ed.D., 1967. Mem. faculty Kearney State Coll., Nebr., 1960—, prof., 1970—, chmn. dept., 1980—. Chmn., pres. United Way Kearney, 1974-76; mem. Kearney City Council, 1977—. Woodrow Wilson fellow, 1958-59; NSF sci. fellow, 1962, 64, 65-66. Mem. Nebr. Assn. Tchrs. Math., Nat. Council Tchrs. Math., Math. Assn. Am. Democrat. Presbyterian. Lodges: Kiwanis (lt. gov. 1976-77), Elks (Kearney). Avocation: football official. Home: 3310 10th Ave Kearney NE 68847 Office: Kearney State College Kearney NE 68849

PICKENS, RANKIN RAY, osteopathic physician; b. Clifton, W.Va., Apr. 2, 1924; s. Ray Wanday and Mary Helena (Natross) P.; m. Mary Georgina Hackett, Dec. 28, 1970; 1 son, Ray Rankin. Student Marshall Coll.-Huntington, W.Va., 1945; B.A., U. Minn., 1948; D.O., Kirksville Coll. Osteo., 1953. Cert. gen. practice, 1978. Intern, Grandview Hosp., Dayton, Ohio, 1953-54; physician Middleport (Ohio) Fire Dept., 1955; gen. practice osteo. medicine, Middleport, 1954—; chief of staff Veterans Meml. Hosp., Pomeroy, Ohio, 1964-75, vice chief of staff, 1975-78; coroner Meigs County, Ohio, 1969—; vol. clin. instr. dept. preventive medicine Ohio State U., Columbus, 1973—; vol. clin. faculty Ohio U. Coll. Osteo. Medicine, Athens, clin. assoc. prof. family medicine, 1976—. Served to lt. USN, 1942-45; USNR, 1945-66. Mem. Am. Osteo. Assn., Ohio Osteo. Assn., Ohio State Coroners Assn. Republican. Methodist. Lodges: Rotary (pres. 1982-83), Mason, Shriners. Home: 400 Riverview Dr Pomeroy OH 45769 Office: Jones Meml Clinic 509 S 3d Ave Middleport OH 45760

PICKERING, MARGARET ANN, business educator; b. Eureka, Kans., Nov. 10, 1946; d. Everett Clayton and Margaret Irene (Teeter) Parks; m. James William Pickering, Sept. 2, 1967. B.S. in Bus., Emporia State U (Kans.), 1967; M.S. in Bus. Edn., 1973. Sec.-bookkeeper Mr. T's Rental, Wichita, Kans., 1968-70; apt. mgr. Monterrey Apts., Emporia, 1970-72; grad. research asst. Emporia State U., 1972-73; legal sec. Wheeler & Wheeler, Marion Kans., 1973-76; instr. Hillsboro High Sch., Kans., 1976-77, Tabor Coll., Hillsboro, 1977—. Chmn. Pride, Marion, 1976—; mem. P.E.O., Marion, 1982—. Named Outstanding Young Woman Am., Marion C. of C., 1977. Mem. Nat. Bus. Edn. Assn., Mountain-Plains Bus. Edn. Assn., Kans. Bus. Edn. Assn. (treas. 1980-83, pres. 1984—), Assn. Info. Systems Profls., Delta Pi Epsilon (corr. sec. 1982—). Clubs: United Presbyterian Women (Marion) (pres. 1983—), So. Kans. Presbyterial, 20th Century. Avocations: snow skiing, reading, volunteer work.

PICKERT, JAMES, state education official. Chmn., State Bd. of Regents, State of Kans., Emporia. Office: State Bd Regents Emporia KS 66801*

PICKETT, ALBERT BERG, field quality engineer; b. Carmel, Ind., Feb. 22, 1918; s. Jasper E. and Christi Ann (Berg) P.; student pub. schs., Carmel; m. Phyllis Elaine Risinger, Aug. 1, 1941; children—Harriet Diane Pickett Stover, William Joe. Engaged in aerospace and electronics industry, 1951-71; with Indpls. Dept. Met. Devel., 1971-73; bldg. Commr., Carmel, 1973-76, mayor, 1976-82; field quality engr. FMC Ordnance Plant, San Jose, Calif., 1982—. Pres., Ind. Heartland Coordinating Commn.; vice chmn. policy com. Indpls. Regional Transp. Council. Mem. Ind. Assn. Cities and Towns (bd. dirs.), North Central Mayors Roundtable Assn. Republican. Quaker. Clubs: Rotary, Masons, Shriners, Kiwanis, U.S. Auto (tech. com.). Home: 901 S Main St Cicero IN 46034 Office: Twin Disc Inc 4600 21st St Racine WI 53405

PICKETT, MARY STEWART, computer scientist, researcher; b. Niagra Falls, N.Y., Dec. 19, 1946; d. Frederick Bruce and Mary Jean (Mundell) Pickett; m. Richard Earl Teets, Feb. 20, 1982. B.S. Iowa State U., 1968; M.S., Purdue U., 1970; M.B.A., U. Mich., 1984. With R.C.A., Camden, N.J., 1970-71; staff research scientist, group leader for CAD/CAM, Gen. Motors Research Labs., Warren, Mich. 1971—; co-chmn. Internat. Research Symposium on Solid Modeling, Warren, Mich., 1983. Editor: Solid Modeling by Computers: From Theory to Applications, 1984; contbr. articles to profl. jours. Mem. Assn. for Computing Machinery (pres. Detroit chpt. 1975-76) (treas. ann. conf. 1979), IEEE, Robotics Internat. Office: Gen Motors Research Labs Warren MI 48090

PICKUS, ALBERT PIERRE, lawyer; b. Sioux City, Iowa, Aug. 10, 1931; s. Sam G. and Mildred H. (Levy) P.; m. Nancy Ellen Silber, Dec. 17, 1958; children—Miriam I., Peter S., Matthew I. B.A., U. Mich., 1953; J.D., Case Western Res. U., 1958. Bar: Iowa 1958, Ohio 1958. Ptnr. Silber, Pickus & Williams and predecessors, Cleve., 1959-74; ptnr. Squire, Sanders & Dempsey, Cleve., 1974—. Mem. Bd. in Control of Intercollegiate Athletics, 1975-81, bd. dirs. Victors Club, Devel. Council, 1976-79, mem. vis. com. Med. Ctr. Alumni Soc., 1978-83, mem. exec. com. Pres.'s Club, 1978-81; mem. fin. com. Cleve. Mt. Sinai Med. Ctr., 1982-85. Mem. ABA, Iowa State Bar Assn., Ohio State Bar Assn., Bar Assn. Greater Cleve. (chmn. real estate law sect. 1983-84), Am. Land Title Assn., Lenders' Counsel Group (assoc.), Am. Coll. Real Estate Lawyers, U. Mich.-Ann Arbor Alumni Assn. (pres. 1973-75, dir. for life, Disting. Alumni Service award 1972), Greater Cleve. Growth Assn. Clubs: Commerce, Oakwood, Pine Lake Trout, Masons (32 degree), Shriners. Office: 1800 Huntington Bldg Cleveland OH 44115*

PIECEWICZ, WALTER MICHAEL, lawyer; b. Concord, Mass., Jan. 27, 1948; s. Benjamin Michael and Cecelia (Makuc) P.; A.B. magna cum laude, Colgate U., 1970; J.D., Columbia U., 1973; m. Anne T. Mikolajczyk, Oct. 28, 1978; children—Tiffany Anne, Stephanie Marie. Admitted to Ill. bar, 1973; mem. firm Levenfeld, Kanter, Baskes & Lippitz, Chgo., 1973-78, Boodell, Sears, Sugrue, Giambalvo & Crowley, Chgo., 1978—; dir. No. Data Systems, Inc. Mem. Am. Bar Assn., Ill. Bar Assn., Chgo. Bar Assn., Chgo. Estate Planning Council, Internat. Bus. Council, Phi Beta Kappa. Democrat. Roman Catholic. Home: 1103 N Lombard Ave Oak Park IL 60302 Office: Boodell Sears Sugrue Giambalvo & Crowley 69 W Washington St Chicago IL 60602

PIER, MICHAEL DUANE, optometrist; b. Belleville, Ill., Dec. 27, 1949; s. Duane E. and Regine (Mersinger) P.; m. Barbara Ann Wimberley, May 6, 1981; children—Laura, Nathan, Christopher, Benjamin. B.S., So. Coll. Optometry, 1975; O.D., 1976; student Memphis State U., 1972, So. Ill. U., 1968-72. Registered optometrist, Mo., Calif. Ptnr., Drs. Bradley & Pier, Warrensburg, Mo., 1979-83; owner Bradley Pier and Assocs., 1983—; clin. investigator Barnes-Hinds, Sunnyvale, Calif., 1984; dir. United Mo. Bank Warrensburg. Editor Jour. Mo. Optometric Assn., 1983-84. Served to lt. USNR, 1976-78. Mem. West Central Mo. Optometric Assn. (past pres.), Mo. Optometric Assn. (pres.-elect), Am. Optometric Assn. Republican. Roman Catholic. Club: Rotary. Lodge: Elks. Avocations: Aviation, golf. Office: Bradley Pier And Assocs 210 S Holden St Warrensburg MO 64093

PIERARD, CHARLENE BURDETT, librarian; b. Albuquerque, Jan. 31, 1938; d. Charles E. and Virginia (Rankin) Burdett; m. Richard V. Pierard, June 15, 1957; children—David, Cindy. B.A., U. Iowa, 1965; M.L.S., Ind. State U., 1974. Asst. br. librarian Vigo County Pub. Library, Terre Haute, Ind., 1974-80, br. librarian, 1980-85, supr. media-mobile services, 1985—; sec. long-range planning com. Vigo County Pub. Library, 1983—. Author: Supervision in the 1980s, 1981; editor Fellowship for Christian Librarians and Information Specialists newsletter, 1984—. Mem. ALA, Ind. Library Assn. Baptist. Home: 550 Gardendale Rd Terre Haute IN 47803 Office: Vigo County Pub Library 1 Library Square Terre Haute IN 47807

PIERCE, CARL WILLIAM, immunologist, pathologist, educator; b. Buffalo, Oct. 2, 1939; s. William Wright and Dorothea (Fuerch) P.; m. Judith Anne Kapp, Dec. 1, 1973. A.B., Colgate U., Hamilton, N.Y., 1962; M.D., U. Chgo., 1966, Ph.D., 1966. Intern, U. Colo. Hosps., Denver, 1966-67, asst. pathology, 1966-67; research assoc. NIH, Bethesda, Md., 1967-70, mem. immunobiology study sect., 1976-80; asst. prof. pathology Harvard Med Sch., Boston, 1970-73, assoc. prof. 1973-76; pathologist-in-chief Jewish Hosp., St. Louis, 1976—; prof. pathology and microbiology-immunology Washington U., St. Louis, 1976—. Contbr. articles to profl. jours. Served with USPHS, 1967-70. Recipient Parke Davis award, 1979. Mem. Am. Assn. Immunologists, Am. Assn. Pathologists, AAAS, Assn. Univ. Pathologists, N.Y. Acad. Scis. Home: 701 Dominion Dr St Louis MO 63131 Office: Jewish Hosp 216 S Kingshighway St Louis MO 63110

PIERCE, DELILA FRANCES, judge; b. St. Cloud, Minn., Jan. 21, 1934; d. Lawrence August and Alvina Elizabeth (Hechtel) Pierskalla. B.S., U. Minn.-Mpls., 1957, J.D. cum laude, 1958. Bar: Minn. 1958. Assoc. Robert L. Ehlers, St. Paul, Minn., 1958-59; ptnr. Mitchell & Pierce, Mpls., 1959-65; sole practice, Mpls., 1966-73; referee Family Ct., Dist. Ct., Hennepin County, Minn., Mpls., 1973-74; judge Hennepin County Mcpl. Ct., Mpls., 1974-83, Dist. Ct. Minn. (4th jud. dist.), 1983—; mem. adv. bd. Genesis II, Mpls., 1975-76. Fellow Am. Acad. Matrimonial Lawyers; mem. Am. Judges Assn., Nat. Assn. Women Judges, ABA, Am. Judicature Soc., Minn. State Bar Assn., Hennepin County Bar Assn., Minn. Dist. Judges Assn., Minnesota County Judges Assn., Hennepin Hist. Soc., Mpls. Soc. Fine Arts. Office: Dist Ct Minn 4th Jud Dist Hennepin County Govt Ctr Minneapolis MN 55487

PIERCE, DONALD FRED, law publishing executive; b. Granite City, Ill., Feb. 28, 1932; s. Fred Arthur and Agnes Ester (Shier) P.; student U. Ill., 1950-51; B.A. in Bus., Washington U., St. Louis, 1954; children—Donald Fred, Robert Craig. Mgr., Shier & Pierce Builders, Cahokia, Ill., 1954-58; salesman Oliver Parks Realty Co., Cahokia, 1958-60; pvt. practice real estate broker, Cahokia, 1960-61; pres. Graham-Pierce Legal Printers, Inc., Fairview Heights, Ill., 1961—. Served with U.S. Army, 1954. Republican. Presbyterian. Club: Exchange (Fairview Heights). Home: 214 Laurel Dr Fairview Heights IL 62208 Office: 2007 Highway 50 W Fairview Heights IL 62208

PIERCE, EDMOND SCOTT, manufacturing company executive, real estate broker; b. Montevideo, Minn., Feb. 4, 1927; s. Lessy Nathan and Ruby Ann (Waltz) P.; m. Ardys Marjorie Halldin, July 13, 1952; children—Thomas Dean, Mary Margaret. Student Macalester Coll., 1946-48; B.B.A., U. Minn., 1954. Unit mgr. First Nat. Bank, Mpls., 1957-62; treas. Pennock Oil Co., Minn., 1962-70; pres. Nelson Internat., Willmar, Minn., 1970-76; real estate broker Pierce and Assoc., Willmar, 1976-79; pres., chief exec. officer Am. Continental Co., Willmar, 1979—. Pres. Hwy. 12 Assoc. Minn., Willmar, 1967—; bd. dirs. Willmar Opportunities, Willmar, 19; elder Presbyn. Ch., Willmar, 1971-74. Served with USN, 1945-46, 51-52, PTO, Korea. Mem. Willmar C. of C. (pres. 1966), Am. Legion, VFW. Republican. Lodges: Elks (chmn. bd. 1976-81), Masons, Shriners. Avocations: flying, hunting, fishing, golf. Home: Country Club Terrace Willmar MN 56201 Office: Am Continental Products Inc South 71 Plaza Willmar MN 56201

PIERCE, GEORGE EDWARD, microbiologist; b. Meriden, Conn., June 6, 1947; s. George Howard and Jane Louise (Shumway) P.; m. Kathryn Elanor Fink, Aug. 23, 1969; 1 son, David Andrew. B.S., Rensselaer Poly. Inst., 1969, Ph.D., 1976. Postdoctoral fellow Rensselaer Poly. Inst., Troy, N.J., 1976-77; research scientist Battelle Meml. Inst., Columbus, Ohio, 1977-80, sr. research scientist, 1980-84, assoc. sect. mgr., 1984—. Editor Jour. Indsl. Microbiology, 1985. Contbr. articles to profl. jours. Served with U.S. Army, 1970-73. Mem. Soc. Indsl. Microbiology (dir. 1982—, chmn. publs. 1983-84), Internat. Union Microbiol. Soc. (del 1984—). Home: 6375 Hibiscus Ct Westerville OH 43081 Office: Battelle Meml Inst 505 King Ave Columbus OH 43201

PIERCE, JAMES KENNETH, chemical company executive; b. Kansas City, Mo., Aug. 31, 1944; s. Kenneth Lee and Elizabeth June (Moore) P.; m. Marcia Joy Love, June 3, 1966; children—Jeffrey Kenneth, Joseph Earl. A.B., William Jewell Coll., 1966; Ph.D. in Chemistry, U. Kans.-Lawrence, 1970. Sr. research chemist The Dow Chem. Co., Midland, Mich., 1970-75, group leader, 1975-80, safety engr., 1980-81, project mgr., 1981-84, sr. research mgr., 1984—. Contbr. articles to tech. jours. Patentee antimicrobial compounds. Mem. Am. Chem. Soc. (chmn. Midland sect. 1985—), Sigma Xi. Baptist (moderator 1982). Club: Kiwanis (pres. 1983). Avocations: travelling; skiing; golf. Home: 2516 Lambros Dr Midland MI 48640 Office: The Dow Chem Co 1604 Bldg Midland MI 48640

PIERCE, PHILLIP, financial planning company executive; b. Detroit, Nov. 15, 1951; s. Salather Lee and Ruth (Cooney) P.; m. Acquanetta Hurt, Sept. 4, 1982. B.B.A., Wayne State U., 1973. With auditing dept. Arthur Andersen & Co., Detroit, 1971-75; fin. mgmt. cons. Plante & Moran, Southfield, Mich., 1975-80; with internal auditing dept. Xerox Corp., Los Angeles, 1979-80; fin. mgmt. cons. Phil Pierce & Co., Detroit, 1980-83; pres. Pierce, Monroe & Assocs., Inc., Detroit, 1983—; cons. Emergency Loan Bd. State of Mich., Lansing, 1983—. Contbr. articles to profl. jours. Chmn. bd. dirs. Acctg. Aid Soc. Mich., Detroit, 1982—; treas. Mich. Minority Tech. Council, Lansing, 1984. Recipient Bus. Leadership award State of Mich., 1975; Business Leadership award City of Detroit, 1978. Mem. Nat. Assn. Black Accts. (nat. pres. 1982-83), Assn. Mgmt. Cons. Baptist. Club: Optimist. Office: Pierce Monroe & Assocs Inc One Kennedy Sq Suite 1230 Detroit MI 48226

PIERCE, RALPH, consulting engineer; b. Chgo., Apr. 14, 1926; s. Charles and Fay (Reznik) P.; B.E.E., Northwestern U., 1946; m. Adrian H. Rosengard, Sept. 3, 1978; children—Marc Fredrick, Deborah Ann, Elizabeth Allison. Test engr. Am. Elec. Heater Co., Detroit, 1946-47; sr. asso. engr. Detroit Edison Co., 1947-52; sec., chief utility engr. George Wagschal Assos., Detroit, 1952-58; sr. partner Pierce, Yee & Assos., Engrs., Detroit, 1958-73; mng. partner Harley Ellington Pierce Yee & Assos., 1973—; v.p. Mk/Hepy, Denver; mem. Dept. Commerce Mission to Yugoslavia. Served to ensign USNR, 1944-46; comdr. Res. ret. Registered profl. engr., Mich., Ind., Ill., Ohio, Ky., N.Y., Washington, Mo., Fla., Can., Calif., Colo. Mem. Nat. Council Engring. Examiners, Nat. Soc. Profl. Engrs., Engring. Soc. Detroit, IEEE, Soc. Coll. and Univ. Planners, Illuminating Engring. Soc., Mich. Soc. Architects (asso.). Home: 5531 Pebbleshire Rd Birmingham MI 48010 Office: 26111 Evergreen Rd Southfield MI 48076

PIERCE, RICHARD, search consultant executive; b. Chgo., Oct. 19, 1938; s. Ben L. and Carrah M. (Elam) P.; m. Susan Cox Kaspar, Sept. 2, 1961; children—Richard S., Edward M., Lauren S. B.S.B.A., U. Iowa, 1962. Research analyst CNA, Chgo., 1962-65; assoc. research dir. Kenyon & Eckhardt, Inc., Chgo., 1965-67; product mgr. First Nat. Bank of Chgo., 1967-74; mgr. mktg. Harris Bank, Chgo., 1974-76; exec. dir Russell Reynolds Assocs., Chgo. 1976—. Bd. dirs., Young Life, Hinsdale, Ill., 1982—; chmn. bd. trustees Hinsdale Bap. Ch., 1980-82. Mem. Kappa Sigma. Clubs: Hinsdale Golf (Ill.); Union League of Chgo. Office: Russell Reynolds Assocs Inc 200 S Wacker Dr Chicago IL 60606

PIERCE, ROBERT BENJAMIN, college dean; b. Salina, Kans., Nov. 16, 1930; s. William Otis and Margurite Harriet (Sherman) P.; m. Judy Jane Stinson, July 29, 1956; children—Robert Benjamin, Christopher Neil. B.A. in Bus. Adminstrn., Emporia State U., 1957, M.S., 1959; Ph.D. in Bus. Adminstrn., U. Iowa, 1968. Mgmt. trainee Sears Roebuck, Quincy, Ill., 1957-58; dir. Univ. Union Emporia State U., Kans., 1958-60; asst. prof. bus. adminstrn. Central Mo. State U., Warrensburg, 1960-69, dean Coll. Bus. and Econs., 1969—. Served with USAF, 1947-54. Home: Route 4 Box 886 Warrensburg MO 64093 Office: Dean Coll Bus and Econs Central Mo State Warrensburg MO 64093

PIERCE, SHELBY CRAWFORD, oil co. exec.; b. Port Arthur, Tex., May 26, 1932; s. William Shelby and Iris Mae (Smith) P.; B.S.E.E., Lamar State Coll. Tech., Beaumont, Tex., 1956; student M.I.T. Program for Sr. Execs., 1980; m. Marguerite Ann Grado, Apr. 2, 1954; children—Cynthia Dawn, Melissa Carol. With Amoco Oil Co., 1956—, zone supr., gen. foreman, maintenance, 1961-67, operating supt., 1967-69, coordinator results mgmt., Texas City (Tex.) refinery, 1969-72, dir. results mgmt., corp. hdqrs., Chgo., 1972-75, ops. mgr. refinery, Whiting, Ind., 1975-77, asst. refinery mgr., 1977-79, dir. crude replacement program, Chgo., 1979-81, mgr. refining and transp. engring., 1981—. Fin. chmn. Bay Area council Boy Scouts Am., 1974; dir. JETS (Jr. Engring. Tech. Soc.); chmn. bd., chmn. fin. com. Methodist Ch., 1967-72. Mem. Am. Inst. Chem. engrs. (dir. engring. constrn. contracting com.), Sigma Tau. Republican. Home: 18840 Loomis Ave Homewood IL 60430 Office: 200 E Randolph Dr Chicago IL 60601

PIERHAL, LEON MICHAEL, sales and marketing executive; b. Chgo., Nov. 10, 1946; s. Michael E. Pierhal and Elsie M (Gabor) Nowak; m. Janice Ellen Jankis, Aug. 25, 1968; children—Laura L., Jennifer L., Michele E. A.A. in Bus./Mktg., Wilbur Wright Coll., 1966. Regional v.p. SCS Corp., Chgo., 1968-73; asst. corp. sec. Computer Communications Inc., Torrance, Calif., 1973-76; regional dir. Anderson Jacobson Inc., Rosemont, Ill., 1976-79; dir. mktg. and sales Data Specialties Inc., Northbrook, Ill., 1979-81; chief exec. officer Applied Info. Systems, Chgo., 1981—; v.p. sales computer systems div. Amdahl Computer Corp., 1985—; chmn. bd. Internat. Tech., Inc., Chgo., 1984—; dir. Electronic Systems Accounting Controls Inc., Chgo. Author: Distribution-Alternative to Direct Sales, 1983. Pres. sch. bd. North Palos Sch. Dist. 117, Hickory, Palos Hills, Ill., 1976—; chmn. zoning bd. City of Palos Hills, 1979—. Served to cpl. USMC, 1966-68. Fellow Data Processing Mgmt. Assn., Am. Mgmt. Assn., Am. Legion. Roman Catholic. Lodge: Lions (charter). Avocations: sports; coaching of youth sports teams. Home: 9047 Oak Crest Lane Palos Hills IL 60465

PIERSON, DAVID LOWELL, orchestra manager; b. Hamilton, Ohio, Jan. 21, 1949; s. Raymond Charles and Irma Lucille (Vizedom) P.; B.Mus. Edn., Ind. U., 1972, M.A. in Arts Adminstrn., 1976; m. Deborah Pfleeger, June 11, 1977. Music tchr. Lurnea High Sch., Liverpool, N.S.W., Australia, 1972-73; asst. mgr. Dayton Philharm. Orch. Assn., Inc., 1976-77, gen. mgr., 1977—; cons. Ohio Arts Council. Adv. com. music program Career Acad, Dayton Public Schs., 1979-81. Ind. U. Arts Adminstrn. Program fellow, 1974-76. Mem. Orgn. Ohio Orchs. (dir. 1980, pres. 1983), Am. Symphony Orch. League, Ohio Citizens Com. for Arts, Pi Kappa Lambda. Club: Rotary. Home: 515 Southwood St Springfield OH 45504 Office: 125 E First St Dayton OH 45402

PIERSON, RUTH EDNA, manufacturing company executive; b. Rensselaer, Ind., Aug. 6, 1944; d. Bruce R. and Evelyn R. (Roush) P.; 1 child, Thomas Andrew. Grad high sch., Goodland, Ind. Purchasing mgr. Better Coil and Transformer, Goodland, Ind., 1983—. Mem. Nat. Assn. Purchasing Mgrs. Democrat. Baptist. Home: 110 S Benton St Goodland IN 47948 Office: Better Coil and Transformer Corp 90 E Union St Goodland IN 47948

PIETRI, CHARLES EDWARD, chemist, research administrator, consultant; b. N.Y.C., July 6, 1930; s. Charles Palmer and Marie Rosemond (Cropper) P.; m. Jeanne Gaub, May 25, 1951; children—Randolph, Dianna, Richard. B.A. in Chemistry, NYU, 1951; certs. Rutgers U., 1972-74. Chemist,E.I. DuPont de Nemours, Inc., Oak Ridge, Tenn. and Aiken, S.C., 1951-56; research chemist Curtiss-Wright Research Corp., Quehanna, Pa., 1956-58; chief plutonium chemistry U.S. AEC, New Brunswick, N.J., 1958-72; chief analytical chemistry, U.S. Dept. Energy, Argonne, Ill., 1972-76; asst. dir., 1976—; cons., dir. Planter Assocs., Chgo., 1981—. Contbr. articles to profl. jours. Patentee in field. Dist. chmn. Thomas A. Edison council Boy Scouts Am., New Brunswick, 1974-76; council commr. West Suburban council Boy Scouts Am., La Grange, Ill., 1978-81, council pres., 1982—. Recipient Silver Beaver award Boy Scouts Am., New Brunswick, 1974. Fellow Am. Inst. Chemists (cert.); mem. Am. Chem. Soc., Royal Soc. Chemistry, Inst. Nuclear Material Mgmt. (sr.), North Augusta U.S. Jr. C. of C. (v.p. 1953-56, S.C.), Sigma Xi. Episcopalian. Avocations: Boy Scouts, camping, stamp collecting, travel. Home: 8253 Lakeside Dr Downers Grove IL 60516 Office: US Dept Energy 9800 S Cass Ave Argonne IL 60439

PIETRINI, DENNIS ROY, dentist; b. Chgo., Nov. 2, 1945; s. Samuel and Millie (Cannova) P.; m. Elaine Bartley, Sept. 26, 1970; children—Jennifer Lynn, Deborah Sue. B.S. in Dentistry, U. Ill., 1968, D.D.S., 1970. Cert. dental surgeon, Ill. Pres., Franklin Park Dental Assocs., Ltd., Ill., 1976—; chmn. dental dept. Gottlieb Meml. Hosp., Melrose Park, Ill., 1979-81. Served to lt. USN, 1970-72. Mem. Am. Dental Assn., Ill. State Dental Soc., Chgo. Dental Soc., Acad. Gen. Dentistry. Republican. Avocations: golfing, tennis; skiing. Home: 33 Norfolk Ave Clarendon Hills IL 60514 Office: Franklin Park Dental Assocs Ltd 9767 W Franklin Ave Franklin Park IL 60131

PIETROFESA, JOHN JOSEPH, teacher educator; b. N.Y.C., Sept. 12, 1940; s. Louis John and Margaret (Proietti) P.; B.E. cum laude, U. Miami, 1961, M.Ed., 1963, Ed.D., 1967; lic. psychologist; lic. social worker; m. Cathy Marks, June 22, 1985; children—John, Paul. Counselor, Dade County (Fla.) pub. schs., 1965-67; prof. edn. Wayne State U., Detroit, 1967—, div. head theoretical and behavioral founds., 1977-83; cons. to various schs., hosps. and univs. Served to 1st lt. Mil. Police Corps, AUS, 1963-65. Mem. Am. Psychol. Assn., Am., Mich. personnel and guidance assns., Assn. Counselor Edn. and Supervision, Phi Delta Kappa. Author: The Authentic Counselor, 1971, 2d edit., 1980; School Counselor as Professional, 1971; Counseling and Guidance in the Twentieth Century, 1971; Elementary School Guidance and Counseling, 1973; Career Development, 1975; Career Education, 1976; College Student Development, 1977; Counseling: Theory Research and Practice, 1978; Guidance: An Introduction, 1980; Counseling: An Introduction, 1984; mem. editorial bd. Counseling and Values, 1972-75. Home: 481 Whippers Ln Bloomfield Hills MI 48013 Office: 321 Education Wayne State U Detroit MI 48202

PIETRZYK, DONALD JOHN, analytical chemistry educator; b. Detroit, Jan. 20, 1934. B.S., Wayne State U., 1956; Ph.D., Iowa State U., 1960. Asst. prof. U. Iowa, Iowa City, 1961-66, assoc. prof. 1966-71, prof. analytical chemistry, 1971—. Home: 2832 Brookside Dr Iowa City IA 52242 Office: U Iowa Dept Chemistry Iowa City IA 52242

PIGOTT, RICHARD J., See *Who's Who in America,* 43rd edition.

PIHERA, LAWRENCE JAMES, advertising agency executive; b. Cleve., Jan. 9, 1933; s. Charles and Dorothy P.; student U. Hawaii, Cooper Sch. Art, Cleve. Inst. Art; m. Patricia Dunn, Aug. 22, 1955; children—Lauren, Scott. Advt. mgr. Johnson Rubber Co. and subs., 1957-58; creative dir. Mansfield Advt. (Ohio), 1958-60, G. W. Young Public Relations, Dayton, 1960-70; pres. Phiera Advt. Assos., Inc., Centerville, Ohio, 1970—; pub. relations counsel City of Trotwood, 1982—, Madison Twp., 1984—; mktg. counsel Muir Pub., 1984—, Newport/Cocke County, Tenn., 1985—; publicity dir. Indpls. 500 Racing Team; lectr. in field; cons. environ. design. Bd. dirs. Centerville Fine Arts Commn. Served with USN. Recipient 1st Place Advt. Writing, 1970, 71, 74, 76, 77, 78. Mem. Soc. Bus. Cons., Art Center Dayton, Dayton Advt. Club, Centerville C. of C. (bd. (dirs.), Am. Bus. Club (dir.). Author: Making of a Winner, 1972; (juvenile Fiction) Wee Wams Wander, 1985; editor McCall Spirit, 1970, The Heritage Report, 1983—; architecture critic Instl. Mgmt. mag.; producer, writer (film) The Log Experience, 1985; contbr. articles to profl. jours.

PIKE, JOHN ROBERT, foundation executive; b. Madison, Wis., June 8, 1931; s. Robert Frederick and Helen Ann (Hartmeyer) P.; B.S. with honors in Econs., U. Wis., Madison, 1953, M.S., 1957, Ph.D., 1963; postgrad. London Sch. Econs., 1959; m. Ann H. Slichter, Dec. 27, 1958; children—Susanna, Elizabeth, Kathryn. Prof. fin. U. Ill., Urbana, 1963-68; exec. dir. Wis. Investment Bd., Madison, 1968-74; dep. dir. Wis. Alumni Research Found., Madison, 1974-76, mng. dir., 1976—; dir. Menasha Woodenware, Menasha Corp., 1977-82. Chmn. bus. and fin. com., bd. dirs. Madison Art Center, 1969-76; bd. dirs. Wis. chpt. Nature Conservancy, 1971-75; mem. fin. adv. bd. Wis. Bldg. Commn., 1975-81; bd. curators Wis. Hist. Soc., 1972-81; vice chmn. bd. Madison Gen. Hosp., 1975—; bd. dirs. John A. Johnson Found., 1977-84, chmn., 1984; bd. dirs. Madison Gen. Hosp., 1975-84, chmn., 1984—; trustee William A. Vilas Trust Estate, 1978—. Served with AUS, 1954-56; Korea. Mem. Am. Fin. Assn. Clubs: Madison Literary, Madison Literary. Contbr. articles to profl. jours. Home: 433 Woodward Dr Madison WI 53704 Office: 614 N Walnut St Madison WI 53705

PIKE, MARIAN SCHISSEL, state commissioner, poet; b. Gilmore City, Iowa, Jan. 12, 1913; d. Charles Henry and Mildred Isabel (Campbell) Schissel; m. Herbert Whittier Pike, Apr. 19, 1941; children—Julia Pike McCutcheon,

Charles Whittier. B.A., Grinnell Coll., 1934. Prin. Elvira Consol. Schs., Iowa, 1934-35; tchr. English and drama Webster City High Sch., Iowa, 1935-36; radio writer, actress Iowa Broadcasting Co., Des Moines, 1936-41; food editor Hoard's Dairyman, Ft. Atkinson, Wis., 1949-78; commr. State Conservation Commn., Des Moines, 1975—. Author: Whiting Centennial, 1973; Impressions of Mid-America, 1976. Mem. State Extension Adv. Council, Iowa, 1960s, Whiting Community Sch. Bd., 1962-75; area rep. Iowa Poetry Assn., 1970—. Recipient Rural Leadership award Omaha C. of C., 1961; Sioux-land Citizenship award SIMPCO, 1981; Friends of Extension award Iowa State Extension Service, Ames, 1983; Alumni award Grinnell Coll., 1984, also various poetry awards. Republican. Congregationalist. Home: Settlement Rd Whiting IA 51063

PIKE, WILLIAM BENEDICT, judge; b. Cleve., June 6, 1928; s. Benedict and Jennie Pike; m. Helen A., Nov. 24, 1960; children—Jay, Robert W. B.S., Kent State U., 1953; J.D., Cleve. Marshall Coll., 1958. Bar: U.S. Supreme Ct. 1972. Former law dir. City of Cuyahoga Falls, Ohio; chief referee domestic relations court Summit County; judge Cuyahoga Falls Mcpl. Ct. Served to sgt. U.S. Army, 1946-48. Mem. Akron Bar Assn., Ohio Bar Assn., Am. Judicature Soc., Ohio Judges Assn. Office: Cuyahoga Falls Mcpl Ct 2310 2nd St Cuyahoga Falls OH 44221

PILAR, NORBERTO ROMASANTA, hospital administrator; b. Manila, Dec. 13, 1948; came to U.S., 1971; s. Brigido Rey Pilar and Demetria (Paez) Romasanta; m. Cristina B. Oliveros, Sept. 17, 1983. Student marine engring. PMI Colls., Manila, 1965-69, Central YMCA Coll., Chgo., 1975-77; Rosary Coll., River Forest, Ill., 1984—. Lic. marine engr.; cert. respiratory therapy technician; registered respiratory therapist; lic. real estate salesman, Ill. Marine engr. Maritime Co. of the Philippines, Manila, 1969-71; critical care respiratory therapist Children's Meml. Hosp., Chgo., 1970-80; head respiratory care dept. Louise Burg Hosp., Chgo., 1980-81; dir. respiratory care and pulmonary services Hyde Park Community Hosp., Chgo., 1981—, also dir., 1981—. Mem. Ill. Soc. Respiratory Therapy, Am. Assn. Respiratory Therapy, Am. Soc. Respiratory Care Adminstrs., DuPage Bd. Realtors. Roman Catholic. Club: Marinduque (pres. 1985) (Chgo.). Avocations: tennis; camping; fishing; reading; playing musical instruments. Office: Hyde Park Community Hosp 5800 Stony Island Ave Chicago IL 60637

PILE, DONALD LEE ROY, chiropractor, researcher; b. Streator, Ill., Aug. 31, 1922; s. Frank S. and Ruby D. (Redman) P.; m. Doris Irene Johnson, Sept. 5, 1944; children—Forrest Lee, Diana Lorene. Student Eureka Coll., 1940-41; diploma Logan Basic Coll. Chiropractic, 1949. Gen. practice chiropractic medicine, Topeka, Kans., 1950—, researcher, 1960—. Served with AUS, 1942-45. Decorated Bronze Star. Mem. Am. Chiropractic Assn., Kans. Chiropractic Assn., Tau Kappa Epsilon. Lodge: Masons. Patentee in field.

PILLAERT, E(DNA) ELIZABETH, museum curator, consultant; b. Baytown, Tex., Nov. 19, 1931; d. Albert Jacob and Roseline Nettie (Kelley) P. B.A., U. St. Thomas, Houston, 1953; M.A., U. Okla., 1963; postgrad. U. Wis.-Madison, 1962-67, 70-73. Asst. curator archaeology Stovall Mus., Norman, Okla., 1959-60, ednl. liaison officer, 1960-62; research asst. U. Okla., Norman, 1962; research asst. U. Wis., Madison, 1962-65, curator of osteology, Zool. Mus., 1965—, chief curator, 1967—; cons. Archaeol. Faunal Analysis, 1965—. Active Madison Audubon Soc., Stoughton Hist. Soc., NOW, Lysistrata Feminist Coop., Athena. Mem. Soc. of Vertebrate Paleontology, Okla. Anthropol. Soc., Assn. Systematics Collections. Contbr. articles to profl. publs. including Wis. Archaeologist, Okla. Anthropological Soc. Home: 216 N Prairie St Stoughton WI 53589 Office: 434 Noland Bldg Zool Mus U Wis Madison WI 53706

PILLARD, HENRY PAUL, educational administrator; b. Anamosa, Iowa, Feb. 10, 1932; s. Emil Frederick and Thelma (Larson) P.; married, Oct. 17, 1953 (dec. Aug. 1982); 1 child, Deon K. B.S., U. Dubuque, 1957; M.S. Ind. U., 1961. Tchr. Eisenhower High Sch., Blue Island, Ill., 1957-65; tchr. Joliet Jr. Coll., Ill., 1965-67, adminstr. 1967—; wrestling coach Joliet Jr. Coll., Ill, 1965-84; recreation cons. Stateville Prison, Joliet, Ill., 1977-81. Patentee football tng. sled, totalizer-exercisor. Bd. dirs, George Werden Buck Boys Club, Joliet, Ill., 1971-81, Clean Communities, Joliet, 1985, World's Largest Internat. Wrestling Tournament, 1978-82; coach U.S.A.-NJCAA Wrestling, Iran, 1978; coach U.S.A. Jr. Pan Am. Wrestling, Mexico City, 1983. Served to cpl. U.S. Army, 1953-55. Recipient 25-Yr. award NCAA, East Rutherford, N.J., 1984; named to Hall of Fame NJCAA, Glen Ellyn, Ill., 1985; U.S.A. Congl. Record 97th Congress, Washington, 1981. Mem. Nat. Soc. Mfg. Engrs. (speakers bur.), Chicagoland Deans of Students Assn., Ill. C. of C. Student Activities Assn. Lodge: Masons (officer 1960-64). Home: Diamond K Ln Joliet IL 60433 Office: Joliet Jr Coll 1216 Houbolt Ave Joliet IL 60436

PILLAY, GERTRUD INGRID, product manager; b. Ojaby, Kronoberg, Sweden, Sept. 9, 1955; came to U.S., 1979; d. Inge Ruben and Ingrid Lovisa (Johansson) Magnusson; m. Suresh Pillay, July 23, 1982. M.A. in Internat. Mktg., U. Goteborg, Gothenburg, Sweden, 1979. Mktg. trainee Crane Packing Co., Morton Grove, Ill., 1979, exec. envoy AIESEC Internat., India, 1980; mktg. asst. Swedish Trade Office, Chgo., 1980-81, project mgr., 1981-82; market specialist Fasson RMD, Painesville, Ohio, 1983-84, product specialist, 1984-85, product mgr., 1985—. Mem. Cleve. Council on World Affairs, 1982—. Swedish-Am. scholar, 1974-75. Mem. Am. Mktg. Assn. Avocations: traveling, languages. Office: Fasson RMD Avery Internat 250 Chester St Painesville OH 44077

PILLSBURY, RONALD WHEELER, chewing gum company manager; b. Galesburg, Ill., May 2, 1957; s. Wilbur Fiske and Katherine Hildeguard (Wheeler) P.; m. Patricia Ann Hallahan, Dec. 1, 1984. B. Spl. Studies, Cornell Coll., Iowa, 1979; M.A. in Bus., U. Chgo., 1980. Sr. personnel counselor William Wrigley Jr. Co., Chgo., 1980, wage adminstr., 1980-82, personnel asst., 1982-83, mfg. supr., 1983-84, gen. mfg. prodn. mgr., 1984—; lectr. Cornell Coll., Mt. Vernon, Iowa, 1984—, Nathaniel Green Sch., Chgo., 1984. Recipient Lincoln-Douglas award Rotary Club. Mem. Am. Mgmt. Assn., Personnel Assn. of Chgo. Congregationalist. Avocations: hiking; downhill snow skiing; golf; tennis. Office: William Wrigley Jr Co 3535 S Ashland Ave Chicago IL 60629

PILZ, CLIFFORD GEORGE, physician, medical educator; b. Chgo., Apr. 20, 1921; s. Joseph Mathias and Theresa (Heiml) P.; m. Mechthilde Kempf, Feb. 27, 1957; 1 child, Theresa Marie. B.S., U. Ill., 1944, M.D., 1945. Intern, Cook County Hosp., Chgo., 1945-46, fellow in pathology, 1948, resident in medicine, 1949; resident in medicine Hines VA Hosp., Maywood, Ill., 1949-52; staff physician Iowa City VA Hosp., 1952-53; staff physician VA West Hosp., Chgo., 1953-58, asst. chief medicine, 1958-71, chief medicine, 1971—; faculty U. Ill., Chgo., 1968—, prof. medicine, 1968—. Recipient Alpha Omega Alpha Outstanding Teaching awards Chgo. Med. Sch., 1945-68, Outstanding Tchr. of Yr. award Phi Delta Epsilon, 1971, Golden Apple awards U. Ill., 1971-78, Attending Physician of Yr. award, 1978, Service to Practice of Medicine award, 1980, Lifetime of Caring award Chgo. Hosp. Council, 1984. Fellow ACP, Am. Coll. Cardiology; mem. Am. Fedn. Clin. Research, Am. Assn. for History of Medicine, Chgo. Soc. Internal Medicine.

PIMENTEL, JUAN RICARDO, engineering educator; b. La Libertad, Peru, Feb. 8, 1953; came to U.S., 1976; s. Ricardo and Consuelo Guilda (Flores) P.; m. Melissa Anne Beattie, Jan. 15, 1983. M.S. in E.E., U. Va., 1978, Ph.D., 1980. Instr. Universidad Nacional de Ingenieria, Lima, 1974-76; research asst. Nat. Radio Astronomy Obs., Charlottesville, Va., 1976-77; research asst. U. Va., Charlottesville, 1977-79; asst. prof. Gen. Motors Inst., Flint, Mich., 1979-83, assoc. prof., 1983—; cons. Indsl. Tech. Inst., Ann Arbor, Mich., Daviloti Ltd., Flint, Mich. Mem. IEEE, Sigma Xi, Eta Kappa Nu, Tau Beta Pi. Roman Catholic. Office: 1700 W 3d Ave Flint MI 48502

PINCUS, IRVING, research institute administrator; b. Bklyn., July 3, 1918; s. Louis and Mollie (Einbinder) P.; m. Faye Sager, May 23, 1943; children—Margaret, Roger, Daniel, Lynne. B.S., CCNY, 1938; M.S., George Washington U., 1947; M.S., Rensselaer Poly. Inst., 1960; Ph.D., Pa. State U., 1950. Sect. leader coal chems. Curtiss-Wright Corp., Quehanna, Pa., 1956-57; sr. devel. engr. Gen. Electric Co., Schenectady, 1957-60; product mgr., asst. research mgr. Raytheon Co., Waltham, Mass., 1960-63; chief materials engring. and devel. Martin Co., Balt., 1963-66; asst. to pres. IIT Research Inst., Chgo., 1966—; arbitrator Am. Arbitration Assn., 1984—; cons. Patentee in field. Contbr. articles to profl. jours. Served to 1st lt. USAF, 1943-45; ETO. Decorated D.F.C., Air medal with clusters, others. Fellow AIAA (assoc.); mem. Am. Chem. Soc., Licensing Execs. Soc., Transp. Research Bd., Am. Def. Preparedness Assn., Sigma Xi, Phi Lambda Upsilon. Jewish. Avocations: gardening; traveling; reading. Home: 1099 Linda Ln Glencoe IL 60022 Office: IIT Research Inst 10 W 35th St Chicago IL 60616

PINDERSKI, JEROME WILBERT, JR., lawyer; b. Chgo., Jan. 12, 1957; s. Jerome W. P.; m. Karen Marie Peterson, Oct. 1, 1983; children—Shaun, Heather. B.A. magna cum laude, Marquette U., 1978; J.D., Loyola U., Chgo., 1981. Bar: Ill. 1981, U.S. Dist. Ct. (no. dist.) Ill. 1981, U.S. Ct. Appeals (7th cir.) 1983. Ptnr., mng. dir. Pinderski & Pinderski Ltd., Palatine, Ill., 1981—; panel atty. Legal Assistance Found., Chgo., 1982—. Mem. ABA, Assn. Trial Lawyers Am., Ill. State Bar Assn., Ill. Trial Lawyers Assn., Chgo. Bar Assn., Palatine Jaycees (sec., legal counsel 1984). Palatine C. of C. and Industry (dir. 1982—, v.p. 1985—). Republican. Roman Catholic. Clubs: Meadows (Ill.); Plaza (Chgo.). Home: 1085 Meghan Ave Algonquin IL 60602 Office: Pinderski & Pinderski Ltd 115 W Colfax St Palatine IL 60067

PINE, MICHAEL BOEHMER, cardiologist, administrator, educator; b. N.Y.C., Feb. 15, 1942; s. Hugo and Esther (Meyerson) P.; m. Joan Louise Fenton, Aug. 1, 1970; children—Gregory John, Elizabeth Michele. B.A., Brandeis U., 1962; M.D., Harvard U., 1966. Diplomate Am. Bd. Internal Medicine, Am. Bd. Cardiology. Intern, resident in medicine Montefiore Hosp., Bronx, N.Y., 1966-68; fellow in cardiology, resident in medicine Columbia Presbyn. Med. Ctr., N.Y.C., 1970-73; fellow in cardiology U. Colo. Med. Sch., Denver, 1973-75; from instr. to asst. prof. medicine Harvard U. Med. Sch., Boston, 1975-79; cardiologist Long Beach VA Med. Ctr., Calif., 1979-81; chief cardiology Cin. VA Med. Ctr., 1981—; assoc. in medicine Beth Israel Hosp., Boston, 1975-79; asst. prof. medicine U. Calif., Irvine, 1979-81; assoc. prof. medicine U. Cin., 1981—. Contbr. articles to profl. jours. Served to lt. col. USPHS, 1968-70. Named mem. Exec. Medicine Program, VA, 1984—; spl. research fellow NIH, 1970-72. Fellow ACP, Am. Coll. Cardiology, Am. Heart Assn. (council on clin. cardiology); mem. Am. Fedn. Clin. Research, Am. Physiol. Soc., Phi Beta Kappa. Home: 520 Abilene Trail Wyoming OH 45215 Office: VA Med Ctr 3200 Vine St Cincinnati OH 45220

PINEAULT, JAMES JOSEPH, power company manager, consultant; b. Mpls., Nov. 22, 1932; s. Ferdinand Joseph and Regina (Lubinski) P.; m. Carol Elaine Petersen, Sept. 20, 1952; children—Susan Marie Pineault Fehr, Debra Carol Pineault Bauer, Verna Reinee. Student U. Minn., 1972-74, Mich. State U., 1968-69, Met. Coll., Mpls., 1970-73. Cert. safety profl. Operator No. States Power Co., Mpls., 1951-56; safety rep., supr. Continental Ins. Co., Mpls., 1956-74; loss control rep. CNA Ins. Co., Mpls., 1974-75; asst. dir. Occupational Safety and Health Adminstrn. State of Minn., St. Paul, 1975-79; mgr. occupational safety and health No. State Power Co., Mpls., 1979—; mem. faculty Inver Hills Community Coll.; cons. in safety field. Mem. Am. Soc. Safety Engrs. (pres. N.W. chpt. 1982-83, Safety Profl. of Yr. N.W. chpt. 1984), Edison Electric Inst. (safety, health com.), ASTM (F-18 com.). Democratic Farm Labor Party. Roman Catholic. Home: 5851 Central Ave NE Minneapolis MN 55432

PINHASIK, ANNETTE ESTHER, lawyer; b. Chgo.; d. Robert Louis and Fela (Schwarz) P. B.A., U. Ill.-Chgo., 1975; J.D., John Marshall Law Sch., 1978. Bar: Ill. 1978, U.S. Dist. Ct. (no. dist.) Ill. 1979. Multi-lingual interpreter City of Chgo., 1975-77; assoc. Parrillo, Bresler, Weiss & Moss, Ltd., Chgo., 1978-80, Harvey L. Walner, Ltd., Chgo., 1980—; trial instr. for fed. bar. Chgo. Bar Assn., 1983-84. Democratic asst. precinct capt., Chgo., 1977-78. Mem. ABA, Ill. Trial Lawyers Assn., Chgo. Bar Assn., Assn. Trial Lawyers Am. Office: Harvey L Walner & Assocs 230 W Monroe St Chicago IL 60606

PINKE, JUDITH ANN, state official; b. Ft. Snelling, Minn., Oct. 16, 1944; d. August Henry and Dorothy E. (Bartelt) Hinrichs; m. Kurt G.O. Pinke, June 29, 1974. B.A. cum laude, St. Olaf Coll., 1966; grad. Sr. Execs. Program, Kennedy Sch. Govt., Harvard U., 1980. Supr., tchr. Mpls. Pub. Schs., 1966-71; writer/editor U. Minn., Mpls., 1971-72; counselor Secretarial Placement, Edina, Minn., 1972-73; asst. to commr. Minn. Dept. Labor and Industry, St. Paul, 1973-76; mgr. info. resources Minn. Dept. Adminstrn., St. Paul, 1976-77; asst. commr. for fin. and adminstrn. Minn. Dept. Transp., St. Paul, 1977—; reader advanced placement exams. Ednl. Testing Service, Princeton, N.J., 1968-71; mem. steering com. Minn. Revenue Recapture Project, St. Paul, 1981. Producer televideo conf. presentation The Productive Office, 1984. Mem. Minn. User Council on Info. Mgmt., 1979—, chmn., 1982—; co-founder Women in State Employment, 1976—, exec. bd. chair, 1982—. Mem. Am. Soc. Pub. Adminstrn., Am. Mgmt. Assn., The Loft (founding), Women Execs. in State Govt., Horizon 100, LWV. Office: Minn Dept Transp 408 Transportation Bldg Saint Paul MN 55155

PINKERTON, ROBERT BRUCE, mfg. co. exec.; b. Detroit, Feb. 10, 1941; s. George Fulwell and Janet Lois (Hedke) P.; student M.I.T., 1959-61; B.S. in Mech. Engring., Detroit Inst. Tech., 1965; M.A.E., Chrysler Inst. Engring., 1967; J.D., Wayne State U., 1976; m. Barbara Ann Bandfield, Aug. 13, 1966; 1 son, Robert Brent. Various engring. positions Chrysler Engring. Office, Chrysler Corp., Highland Park, Mich., 1967-73, supr. body engring., 1973-76, sr. body engr., 1976-78, emissions and fuel economy planning specialist, 1978-80; dir. engring. Replacement div. TRW, Inc., Cleve., 1980-83, dir. engring. Automotive Aftermarket Group, 1983—; mem. Mich. Adv. Com. on Vehicle Inspection and Maintenance, 1979-80. Mem. exec. bd. Greater Cleve. council Boy Scouts Am.; trustee Nat. Automotive Tech. Edn. Found. Mem. Soc. Automotive Engrs. (chmn. parts div. nat. council on maintenance and repair), Automotive Tng. Mgrs. Council (bd. govs.), Cleve. Engring. Soc. Presbyterian. Club: Country of Hudson. Lodge: So. Hills Rotary (pres.). Home: 7337 Valerie Ln Hudson OH 44236 Office: 8001 E Pleasant Valley Rd Cleveland OH 44131

PINKHAM, JIMMY RANDOLPH, pediatric dentistry educator; b. Raleigh, N.C., Mar. 26, 1945; s. Jesse Randolph and Margaret Olivia (Strickland) P.; m. Alecia Smith Evanger, Aug. 10, 1971 (div. Apr. 26, 1977); m. Carol Lynn Sloniker, Oct. 27, 1979; children—Tylila Nicole and Beau James. B.S., U.N.C., 1967, D.D.S., 1970, M.S. 1972. Diplomate Am. Bd. Pedodontics, Asst. to assoc. prof. pedodontics U. Iowa, Iowa City, 1972-79, prof. and head pediatric dentistry, 1983—, dir. grad. pediatric dentistry, 1983—; chief of dentistry Kosa/Children's Hosp., Louisville, 1980-83, dir. grad. pediatric dentistry, 1980-83. Contbr. articles to profl. jours. and books. Recipient Award of Excellence Am. Acad. Oral Medicine, 1972; named Tchr. of Yr. U. Iowa Dental Coll., 1974. Fellow Am. Acad. Pediatric Dentistry (editorial cons. 1980—); mem. Am. Dental Assn., Am. Assn. Dental Schs. (chmn. sect. 1981-82), Internat. Assn. Dental Research, Am. Soc. Dentistry Children. Lodge: Rotary. Home: 2320 Cae Dr Iowa City IA 52240 Office: Dept Pediatric Dentistry Univ Iowa Iowa City IA 52242

PINKUS, CRAIG ELDON, lawyer; b. Indpls., Feb. 8, 1943; s. Seymour and Virginia M. (Schwartz) P.; A.B. magna cum laude, Butler U., 1965; J.D., Harvard U., 1968; m. Mary M. Mosby, Sept. 29, 1979; children—Aaron, Elizabeth, Sarah. Bar: Ind. 1968, U.S. Supreme Ct. 1971. Assoc. Barnes, Hickam, Pantzer & Boyd, 1968-69; exec. dir. Ind. Civil Liberties Union, Indpls., 1969-71; chief counsel Legal Services Orgn., Indpls. Inc., 1971-72; partner firm King, Pinkus & Beeler, Indpls., 1972-78, Mitchell, Yosha & Hurst, 1980-81, Mitchell Hurst, Pinkus, Jacobs & Dick, 1981—; host, writer program Family and Consumer Law, Ind. Higher Edn. TV Service, 1974; chief counsel Marion County (Ind.) Prosecutor, 1976-78; dir. Indy Runners, Inc., Village Records, Inc. Bd. dirs. Indpls. Corp. Challenge. Mem. ABA (Silver Gavel award 1975, Inst. on Computer in Litigation 1979, 80), Ind., Indpls. bar assns., Bar Assn. 7th Circuit. Democrat. Jewish. Contbr. article to profl. jour. Home: 7828 W 88th St Indianapolis IN 46278 Office: Stevens-Coffman Bldg 152 E Washington St Indianapolis IN 46204

PINNELL, RICHARD TILDEN, music educator, guitarist; b. Whittier, Calif., Jan. 9, 1942; s. George William Lewis and Helen (Whitaker) P.; m. Maria Piedad Yarza, June 10, 1966; children—Anny Claudine, Nicole, Catherine Helen. student, U. Utah; B.A., Brigham Young U., 1967, M.A., 1969; C.Phil., UCLA, 1973, Ph.D., 1976. Cert. community coll. tchr., Calif. Teaching fellow UCLA, 1970-75; instr. Santa Monica (Calif.) Coll., 1972-73, Los Angeles City Coll., 1972-77, Los Angeles Valley Coll., 1974-77, Mt. San Antonio Coll., Walnut, Calif., 1976-77; asst. prof. U. Wis.-Stevens Point, 1977-84, U. Wis.-La Crosse, 1984—. Performer, guest lectr., workshop participant. NDEA fellow UCLA; research grantee U. Wis.-Stevens Point, summers 1978, 79, 81; Univ. Scholar of the Yr., 1981. Mem. Am. Musicol. Soc., Am. Fedn. Musicians, Lute Soc. Am., Guitar Found. Am., U. Wis. Ctr. for Latin Am., Pi Kappa Lambda. Mormon. Author: Francesco Corbetta and the Baroque Guitar, 1980; contbr. articles to profl. jours. Home: 438 S 23rd St La Crosse WI 54601 Office: Dept Music University Wisconsin La Crosse WI 54601

PINNOW, ARNO LEE, quality assurance executive; b. Milw., July 21, 1941; s. Roy Lee and Lila Viola (Uphoff) P.; m. Leta Sheila Williams, Dec. 28, 1963; children—Christopher Gene, Marjorie Lee. B.S. in Chem. Engring., Ill. Inst. Tech., 1964. Registered profl. engr., Ill. Mgr. systems and tng. Amp-vial project Abbott Labs., North Chicago, Ill., 1971-72, mfg. quality mgr. Hosp. div., Rocky Mount, N.C., 1972-74, sect. mgr. quality audits, North Chicago, 1974-77, ops. mgr. quality evaluation, 1977-82; dir. quality assurance Hollister, Inc., Libertyville, Ill., 1981—; cons. in field, Gurnee, Ill., 1984—. Patentee in field. Judge Sci. Fair Gurnee Schs., 1968-70; leader Boy Scouts Am., 1959-77; mem. ch. council Lutheran Chs., Waukegan, Ill., 1971-73, Rocky Mount, 1971-73; mem. Citizens Adv. Bd. Warren Twp. High Sch., Gurnee, 1979-81. Mem. Nat. Soc. Profl. Engrs. Ill. Soc. Profl. Engrs., Am. Soc. Quality Control, Regulatory Affairs Profl. Soc., Am. Inst. Chem. Engrs., Marquetry Soc. Am., Woodworkers Assn. N.Am., Alpha Kappa Phi, Alpha Phi Omega. Lutheran. Avocations: wood working, stained glass, construction, landscaping. Home: 4170 Woodlawn Gurnee IL 60031

PINO, MARY CORNELIA, lawyer; b. Lansing, Mich., Sept. 25, 1955; d. James Oliver and Ruth Jeanette (Cook) P. B.A. with distinction, Wayne State U., 1976; J.D., Thomas Cooley Law Sch., 1980. Bar: Mich. 1980. Pvt. tchr. music, Laingsburg, Mich., 1977-85; law clk. Prosecutor's Office, St. Johns, Mich., 1979-80, asst. pros. atty., 1980—. Leader Girl Scouts Am., 1977; emergency med. technician Laingsburg Ambulance Service, 1979-85; merit counselor Boy Scouts Am., 1983-84. Mem. Mich. Bar Assn., Women Lawyer's Assn., Nat. Fedn. Bus. and Profl. Women. Democrat. Mem. Soc. of Friends. Home: 7891 Hollister Rd Laingsburg MI 48848 Office: Prosecutor's Office Courthouse Saint Johns MI 48879

PINTAR, ANTON JAMES, engineering educator, consultant; b. Painesdale, Mich., June 17, 1940; s. Anton Joseph and Evelyn Marie (Allen) P; m. Barbara Jane Kangas, Sept. 1, 1962 (div. April 1972); children—Anton John, Daniel James, Thomas Joseph, Sarah Jane, Edward Jonas; m. Shirley B. Pomeranz, Dec. 28, 1984. B.S. in Chem. Engring., Mich. Tech. U., 1962; PH.D. in Chem. Engring., IIT, 1968. Tech. asst. IIT Research Inst., Chgo., 1962-66; assoc. prof. Mich. Tech. U., Houghton, 1966—; cons. Cleve.-Cliffs Iron Co., Ishpeming, Mich., 1976-82; ednl. cons. Dow Corning Corp., Midland, Mich., 1981—. Chmn. Houghton County Democratic Party, Mich., 1969-72, 80-84; del., alt. del. Democratic Nat. Conv., 1976, 80, 84. ASEE Fellow NASA Lewis Research, Cleve., 1973, 74, indsl. fellow Catalytic, Inc., 1974-75. Mem. Mich. Environment Review Bd., Am. Inst. Chem. Engrs., Am. Chem. Soc. Roman Catholic. Avocations: politics; hockey; history. Home: Box 385 Hancock MI 49930 Office: Mich Tech Univ Houghton MI 49931

PINTER, WILLIAM DALE, health maintenance organization executive; b. Pinconning Mich., Feb. 18, 1943; s. Herman Gustav and Marie Emily (Fenwick) P.; m. Lynn Marie Stimac, Apr. 23, 1983; children—Bradford, Gregory, Jason. B.S. in Pharmacy, Ferris State Coll., 1965. Registered pharmacist, Ind., Mich. Pharmacist, Judd Drugs, Goshen, Ind., 1965-66; salesman Eli Lilley and Co., Detroit, 1966-67; owner, operator Nat. Pharm. Services, Inc., Detroit, 1968-84; v.p. pharmacy Independence Health Plans, Inc., Southfield, Mich., 1984—. Mem. Am. Pharm. Services, Nat. Assn. Retail Druggists, Mich. State Pharm. Assn., Health Maintenance Orgn. Pharmacists (Mich. sub-chpt.). Presbyterian. Office: Independence Health Plans 15565 Northland Dr Southfield MI 48075

PINTO, PATRICK RICHARD, industrial psychologist; b. Buffalo, June 21, 1945; s. Patrick R. and Rita (DeMeo) P.; B.S., Fordham U., 1966; M.S. in Indsl. Psychology, Purdue U., 1968; Ph.D., U. Ga., 1970; m. Eileen Ann Smyntek, Sept. 3, 1966; children—John P., David P., Susan K. Personnel research cons. Xerox Corp., Rochester, N.Y., 1966-69; asso. prof. indsl. relations and psychology U. Minn., Mpls., 1970—; pres. Performance Improvement Assos., St. Paul, Minn., 1973—; vis. prof. U. B.C., 1980-81. Lic. cons. psychologist; Mem. Am. Psychol. Assn., Human Resource Planning Soc., Acad. Mgmt., Am. Soc. Tng. and Devel., Am. Soc. Personnel Adminstrn., Phi Beta Kappa. Contbr. articles to profl. jours. Home: 2243 W Hoyt Ave Saint Paul MN 55108 Office: Univ Minn 271 19th Ave S Minneapolis MN 55455

PINZKE, HERBERT, designer, educator; b. Chgo., Jan. 3, 1917; s. William August and Ella (Kruse) P.; m. Nancy Lindberg, Dec. 13, 1980; children—Daniel, Nicholas; 1 child by previous marriage, Ilona. Student Art Inst. Chgo., 1935-39, Inst. Design Chgo., 1945-47. Freelance designer, 1933-47; asst. dir. design lab. Container Corp. Am., Chgo., 1947-53; designer, art dir. ency. Our Wonderful World, Grolier, Inc., Chgo., 1953-66; cons., trainer Franklin Book Program, 1964-66; prin. Herbert Pinzke Design, Inc., Chgo., 1957—; design cons. Highlights for Children mag., 1957-80; mem. faculty Columbia Coll., Chgo., 1964-73, head design dept., 1966-71; mem. faculty Inst. Design Chgo., 1949-52, 63-64 U. Chgo., 1956-62, 77-82, Mundelein Coll., 1963-64, Chgo. Sch. Profl. Art, 1963, Washington U., St. Louis, 1969-70, 72, Northeastern Ill. U., 1976-77, Roosevelt U., Chgo., 1976-77, 79; lectr.; show judge. Exhbns. include: Art Inst. Chgo., Soc. Typog. Arts, Art Dirs. Club Chgo., Am. Inst. Graphic Arts, N.Y.C., Chgo. Book Clinic, Chgo. Pub. Library, Visual Arts Ctr. Chgo.; exhibit designer. Mem. Chgo. Art Dirs. Club (pres. 1965, Spl. award 1967), Internat. Council Graphic Design Assns. (v.p. 1966-68), Internat. Design Conf. (v.p. 1954-57, 70-75, pres. 1958-59), Chgo. Soc. Communicating Arts, 27 Chgo. Designers, Airline Owners and Pilots Assn. Trustee Columbia Coll., 1970-71. Address: 1935 N Kenmore Chicago IL 60614

PIOTROWSKI, JOHN EUGENE, manufacturing company executive; b. Chgo., Aug. 1, 1952; s. Eugene John and Doris E. (Janus) P.; m. Elena Maria Rinaldi, July 20, 1974; children—Joseph Eugene, Joy Maria. Assoc. B.S., Triton Coll., 1976; B.A., Northeastern Ill. U., 1981; M.B.A., Rosary Coll., 1985. Cost estimator Elcen Metal Products, Franklin Park, Ill., 1972-75; custom fabric estimator, buyer A.M. Castle Metals, Inc., 1975-77; plant mgr. Triton Industries, Chgo., 1977-84; asst. plant mgr. Baron Blakeslee, Inc., Melrose Park, Ill., 1984—. Mem. Midwest Indsl. Mgmt. Assn. Lodge: Moose. Avocations: hunting; boating; fishing; photography; piano. Home: 7225 Kelly Pl Downers Grove IL 60516 Office: Baron Blakeslee Inc 2001 N Janice Ave Melrose Park IL 60160

PIPERNI, DEBORAH ANN, lawyer; b. Rochester, N.Y., June 29, 1955; d. Joseph J. and Josephine M. (Stewart) P. A.A.S., Monroe Community Coll., 1975; B.S., St. John Fisher Coll., 1977; J.D., U. Dayton, 1980. Bar: Ohio 1980, U.S. Dist. Ct. (no. and so. dists.) Ohio 1980, U.S. Ct. Appeals (6th cir.) 1981, U.S. Supreme Ct. 1983. Asst. atty. gen. Ohio Atty. Gen.'s Office, Columbus, 1980—. Mem. Ohio Assn. Attys. Gen., Ohio State Bar Assn., Columbus Bar Assn., ABA, Assn. Trial Lawyers Am., Ohio Young Democrats of Am., Franklin County Young Dems. Roman Catholic. Office: Ohio Atty Gen 30 E Broad St 26th Floor Columbus OH 43215

PIRKLE, JOSEPH WILLIAM, computer systems executive; b. Lawton, Okla., Oct. 1, 1950; s. William C. and Nola Gayle (Gaston) P.; m. Diana C. Smith, July 27, 1973; 1 child, Alexandra. A.S. in Data Processing Penn Valley Coll., 1982; student U. Mo.-Kansas City, 1983. Sales rep. H. D. Lee, Overland Park, Kans., 1974-78, Pitney Bowes, Kansas City, Mo., 1978-81; programmer-analyst P.D.A. Inc., Overland Park, 1981-82; asst. v.p. info. systems Kansas City Bd. Trade 1982—; instr. Penn Valley Coll., Kansas City, 1983—. Mem. IBM Computer Users Group, Computer Professionals Unltd. Avocation: golf Office: Kansas City Board of Trade 4800 Main Suite 303 Kansas City MO 64112

PIRMAN, JOSEPH JOHN, optometrist; b. Painesville, Ohio, Oct. 25, 1954; s. Joseph F. and Elizabeth (Zalar) P.; m. Cathy Lee Dougherty, Aug. 27, 1977; children—Lorie Lynn, Shaun Michael. B.S. in Biology, Bowling Green State U., 1977; B.S. in Visual Sci., Ill. Coll. Optometry, 1980, D. Optometry, 1982. Assoc. Drs. Miller, Sunkle & Assocs. Optometrists, Inc., Cleve., 1982. Mem. Council Smaller Enterprises, Cleve., West Side Community Council, Ohio City Redevel. Assn. Recipient Knight-Henry Meml. award Optometric Extension Program, 1982. James Blumenthal Functional Vision award Ill. Coll. Optometry, 1982. Mem. Am. Optometric Assn., Ohio Optometric Assn., Cleve. Optometric Assn. (bd. dirs. 1983—), Nat. Honor Soc., Tomb and Key Honor Fraternity, Beta Sigma Kappa. Democrat. Roman Catholic. Avocations: music; golf; tennis; bowling. Home: 6518 Sycamore Rd Mentor OH 44060

Office: Drs Miller Sunkle and Assocs Optometrists Inc 2620 Loraine Ave Cleveland OH 44113

PIROSCHAK, RICHARD STEPHEN, pharmacist; b. Pottstown, Pa., Jan. 20, 1956; s. Dolores Piroschak. B.A., Villanova U., 1977; B.S., Temple U. Pharmacy, 1982; postgrad., Seton Hall U., 1978. Registered pharmacist, Pa., Del., Kans., Mo. Pharmacist, Happy Harry's, Wilmington, Del., 1982-83; asst. mgr., pharmacist Revco DS, Inc., Claycomo, Mo., 1983—. Mem. Am. Pharm. Assn., Pa. Pharm. Assn., Nat. Pharm. Council (student mem.). Roman Catholic. Avocations: golf; tennis; travel. Home: 607 NE 115th Terr Kansas City MO 64155

PIRSCH, CAROL MCBRIDE, telephone company official, state senator; b. Omaha, Dec. 27, 1936; d. Lyle Erwin and Hilfrie Louise (Lebeck) McBride; student U. Miami, Oxford, Ohio, U. Nebr., Omaha; m. Allen I. Pirsch, Mar. 28, 1954; children—Pennie Elizabeth, Pamela Elaine, Patrice Eileen, Phyllis Erika, Peter Allen, Perry Andrew. Mem. data processing staff Omaha Public Schs.; with Western Electric Co., Omaha; legal sec., Omaha; office mgr. Pirsch Food Brokerage Co., Inc., Omaha; supr. community relations Northwestern Bell Telephone Co., Omaha; mem. Nebr. State Senate; justice of peace. Bd. dirs. Adams Sch. PTA and N.W. High Sch. PTSA, U. Nebr., Omaha Parents Assn.; Brownie leader Girl Scouts U.S.A.; mem. Mayor's Commn. Status of Women; del. White House Conf. of Families; mem. Republican County Central Com.; del. state and county Rep. convs.; deacon Benson Presbyterian Ch. Recipient Golden Elephant award; Outstanding Legis. Leadership award Nat. Orgn. Victim Assistance. Mem. Orgn. Women Legislators, Mgmt. Women's Assn., Nebr. Coalition for Victims of Crime (pres.), Tangier Women's Aux. Clubs: Pilot, Omaha Women's. Office: Dist 10 Room 1126 State Capitol Lincoln NE 68509

PISCIOTTA, ANTHONY VITO, medical educator; b. N.Y.C., Mar. 3, 1921; s. Andrew P.; m. Lorraine Gault, June 15, 1951; children—Robert Andrew, Nancy Marie, Anthony Vito. B.S., Fordham U., 1951; M.D., Marquette U., 1952, M.S., 1952. Intern, Internship Med. Ctr., Jersey City, 1944-45; resident pathology Fordham Hosp., N.Y.C., 1947-48; resident in internal medicine Milwaukee County Hosp., 1948-51. Diplomate Am. Bd. Internal Medicine. Instr. medicine Tufts U. Med. Sch., Boston, 1951-52; instr. medicine Marquette U. Sch. Medicine, Milw., 1952-54, asst. prof., 1954-57, assoc. prof., 1957-66, prof., 1966-70; prof. medicine Med. Coll. Wis., Milw., 1970—, Robert A. Uihlein Jr. prof. hematol. research, 1983—; vice-chmn. Radiation Effects Research Found., Nat. Acad. Scis., Hiroshima, Japan, 1981-83; dir. Blood Research Lab., Milw., 1952—; cons. hematology U.S. Naval Hosp., Gt. Lakes, Ill., 1960-75; research fellow hematology New Eng. Ctr. Hosp., Boston, 1951-52. Served to capt. U.S. Army, 1946-47. Recipient Encaenia award Fordham U., N.Y.C., 1956, Phi Chi Tchr. award Marquette U. Sch. Medicine, Milw., 1959, Alpha Kappa Kappa Teaching award Marquette U. Sch. Medicine, Milw., 1979, Alumnus of Yr. award Marquette U. Sch. Medicine, Milw., 1977, Disting. Service award Med. Coll. Wis., Milw., 1979. Fellow ACP; mem. Assn. Am. Physicians, AAAS, Am. Assn. Immunologists, AMA (fin. com. 1975-82), Am. Soc. Exptl. Pathology, Am. Soc. Hematology (fin. com.), Alpha Omega Alpha. Avocations: photography; music; fishing. Office: Milwaukee County Med Complex 8700 W Wisconsin Ave Milwaukee WI 53226

PISKOS, ROGER ALAN, information specialist; b. Cleve., Feb. 14, 1959; s. William Michael and Carol Ann (Meier) P. B.S., Baldwin-Wallace Coll., 1981; postgrad. Case Western Res. U. Jr. programmer Standard Oil Ohio, Cleve., 1981-82, programmer, 1982-83, programmer analyst, 1983-84, sr. programmer analyst, 1984-85. Adv., Jr. Achievement, Cleve., 1982-83. Recipient award Wall St. Jour., 1981; Milton C. Baldwin prize Baldwin-Wallace Coll., 1981; Eastman Kodak scholar, 1980. Mem. Assn. Individual Investors. Republican. Roman Catholic. Club: Sohio Rec (rep. 1981—) (Cleve.). Avocations: photography; skiing; racquetball; bowling. Home: 7390 Pine Ridge Ct Cleveland OH 44130 Office: 101 Prospect Ave 322 S Cleveland OH 44115

PISNEY, RAYMOND FRANK, museum director; b. Little Springs, Iowa, June 2, 1940; s. Frank A. and Cora H. Pisney; B.A., Loras Coll., 1963; postgrad. Cath. U. Am., 1963, St. Louis U., 1981—; M.A., U. Del., 1965. Asst. for adminstrn. and research, Mt. Vernon, Va., 1965-69; historic sites adminstr. N.C. Archives and Hist. Dept., Raleigh, 1969; asst. adminstr. div. historic sites and museums N.C. Dept. Art, Culture and History, Raleigh, 1969-72; exec. dir. Woodrow Wilson Birthplace Found., Staunton, Va., 1973-78; dir. Mo. Hist. Soc., St. Louis, 1978—; pres. Va. History and Museums Fedn., 1977-78; v.p. Mo. Museums Assos., 1979—. Hagley fellow U. Del., 1963-65; Seminar for Hist. Adminstrs. fellow, 1965. Mem. Am. Assn. Museums, Nat. Trust Historic Preservation U.S., Am. Assn. State and local History, Can. Museums Assn., Brit. Museums Assn., Internat. Council Monuments and Sites, Internat. Council Museums, Phi Alpha Theta. Roman Catholic. Author: Historical Markers: A Bibliography, 1977; Historic Markers: Planning Local Programs, 1978; A Preview to Historical Marking, 1976; Old Buildings: New Resources for Work and Play, 1976; editor: Virginians Remember Woodrow Wilson, 1978; Woodrow Wilson in Retrospect, 1978; Woodrow Wilson: Idealism and Realty, 1977; Historic Preservation and Public Policy in Virginia, 1978. Office: Jefferson Meml Bldg Forest Park Saint Louis MO 63112

PISONI, DONALD CHARLES, interior designer; b. Herrin, Ill., Sept. 22, 1929; s. Tony C. and Mary I. (Pessina) P.; m. Sheila R. Stelman, June 10, 1961; children—Maria L., Anne L. B.S., U. Ill., 1951; postgrad. Parson Sch. of Design, 1956-59. Dir. personnel Continental Baking, St. Louis, 1953-56; interior designer Lammert Furniture, St. Louis, 1959-61; pres., interior designer Don Pisoni Inc., St. Louis, 1961—. Served with U.S. Army, 1951-53. Mem. Am. Soc. Interior Designers (past bd. dirs. Mo. East chpt.). Office: 515 N Lindbergh St Saint Louis MO 63141

PITALIS, PAUL, insurance company executive, educator; b. Chgo., Nov. 11, 1934; s. Irving and Faye (Hellman) P.; m. Lois Ann Karno, Mar. 22, 1958; children—Lauren Beth, Rachael Joy. B.S., Ill. Inst. Tech., 1957. Vice pres. Ave. Ins. Service Chgo., 1960-70, Blvd. Ins. Services, Chgo., 1965-70, Instl. Ins. Co., Chgo., 1970-71; instr. Ins. Sch. Chgo., 1974—, Chgo. Bd. Underwriters, 1978-80; v.p. Merit Ins. Co., Chgo., 1971—; founder, dir. Acad. of Ins., Skokie, Ill., 1984—. Author: Insurance Principles and Practices, 1975; Insurance Company Operations, 1978; (test material, course) Casualty Insurance Course, 1978. Chmn. Niles Twp. Com. Spl. Edn., Ill., 1978-84; mem. Village of Skokie Traffic Commn., 1981—; chmn. Niles Twp. Council Sch. Bds.; pres. Sch. Bd. Skokie, Mem. Nat. Assn. Ind. Insurors (mem. spl. risks com. 1980—), C.L.U. Soc., Soc. C.P.C.U.s (treas. Chgo. chpt. 1978). Club: Old Orchard (Skokie) (pres. 1971). Lodges: B'nai B'rith, Masons. Home: 4516 Main St Skokie IL 60076 Office: Merit Ins Co 180 N La Salle Chicago IL 60601

PITCHER, GEORGIA ANN, psychologist, educator; b. Indpls., Feb. 22, 1927; d. Arling Edgar and Lyda Lucille (Doty) Pitcher; m. Donald Aubrey Baker, Aug. 21, 1948 (div.); children—Catherine Lucille, Martha Ann, Susan Jane, Daniel Pitcher. B.S., Butler U., 1948, M.S., 1951; Ph.D., Purdue U., 1969. Asst. prof. Butler U., Indpls., 1964-68; asst. prof. Purdue U., West Lafayette, Ind., 1969-74; dir. psychol. services St. Elizabeth Hosp., Lafayette, Ind., 1974-81; pvt. practice psychologist, Indpls., 1981—, assoc. faculty Ind. U.-Purdue U. at Indpls., 1985—. Bd. dirs. United Cerebral Palsy of Ind., 1981—; mem. protective services task force exec. com. State of Ind., 1976-77. Mem. Nat. Acad. Neuropsychology, Internat. Orgn. of Psychophysiology, Am. Psychol. Assn., Ind. Psychol. Assn., Am. Ednl. Research Assn., Kappa Kappa Gamma. Democrat. Presbyterian. Contbr. articles to profl. jours. Home: 3725 E Thompson Rd Indianapolis IN 46237 Office: 535 Turtle Creek South Dr Suite 7 Indianapolis IN 46227

PITKIN, EDWARD MEYER, chemical wholesale distributing executive; b. Martinsville, Ind., July 22, 1949; s. William VanArsdale and Joan (Cravens) P.; m. Judith Ann Hackman, July 8, 1972; children—Brian Edward, Michelle. B.A., Wabash Coll., 1971; Ind. Exec. Devel. Program, Ind. U., 1978. Trainee Dolly Madison Industries, Phila., 1969; trainee Ulrich Chem., Inc., Indpls., 1972, warehouse mgr., 1972-73, buyer, 1973-74, v.p. ops. and purchasing, 1974-76, exec. v.p., 1976-79, pres., 1979—. Mem. Nat. Assn. Chem. Distbrs. (region IV pres. 1983—, dir. 1983—), Am. Water Works Assn. (arrangements com. chmn. Ind. sect. 1978—), Ind. Mfrs. Assn., Purchasing Mgmt. Assn. Indpls., Indpls. C. of C., Chgo. Drug and Chem. Assn., Greater Wabash Found., Caleb Mills Soc., Stanley K. Lacy Exec. Leadership Series Alumni. Republican. Clubs: Ski, Columbia (Indpls.). Lodge: Rotary. Avocations: snow skiing; water skiing; jogging; scuba diving; wind surfing. Home: 10911 Brigantine Dr Indianapolis IN 46256 Office: Ulrich Chem Inc 3111 N Post Rd Indianapolis IN 46226

PITOT, HENRY CLEMENT, pathology educator; b. N.Y.C., May 12, 1930; s. Henry C. and Bertha (Lowe) P.; m. Julie Sybil Schutten, July 29, 1954; children—Bertha, Anita, Jeanne, Catherine, Henry, Michelle, Lisa, Patrica. B.S. in Chemistry, Va. Mil. Inst., 1951; M.D., Tulane U., 1955, Ph.D. in Biochemistry, 1959. Diplomate Am. Bd. Pathology. Instr. pathology Tulane U., New Orleans, 1955-59; asst. prof. oncology and pathology, U. Wis., Madison, 1960-63, assoc. prof., 1963-66, prof. oncology and pathology, 1966—, chmn. dept. pathology, 1968-71, dir. McArdle Lab. for Cancer Research, 1973—. Mem. Nat. Cancer Adv. Bd., 1976-82; bd. dirs. Damon Runyon-Walter Winchell Fund, 1976—; mem. bd. sci. counselors Nat. Toxicology Program, 1983—. Author: Fundamentals of Oncology, 1978, 2d edit., 1981, 3d edit., 1985; author jour. articles. Recipient Lederle Med. Faculty award, 1962-65; Parke-Davis award for meritorious research in exptl. pathology, 1968; Lucy-Wortham James Lab. Research award Soc. Surg. Oncology, 1981; Noble Found. Research Recognition award, 1983; Esther Langer award in cancer research. Fellow AAAS, N.Y. Acad. Scis.; mem. Am. Assn. Cancer Research (bd. dirs. 1969-72), Am. Assn. Pathologists (co-pres. 1976-77), Am. Soc. Biol. Chemists, Am. Soc. Cell Biology, Japanese Cancer Soc. (hon.). Democrat. Roman Catholic. Avocations: stamp collecting; fishing; bicycling. Office: McArdle Lab for Cancer Research Univ Wis 450 N Randall Ave Madison WI 53706

PITT, BERTRAM, cardiology educator; b. Kew Gardens, N.Y., Apr. 27, 1932; s. David and Shirley (Blum) P.; m. Elaine Liberstein, Aug. 10, 1962; children—Geoffrey, Jessica, Jillian. B.A., Cornell U., 1953; M.D., U. Basel, Switzerland, 1959. Diplomate Am. Bd. Internal Medicine, Am. Bd. Cardiology. Intern, Beth Israel Hosp., N.Y.C., 1959-60, resident, Boston, 1960-63; fellow in cardiology Johns Hopkins Hosp., Balt., 1966-67; from instr. to prof. Johns Hopkins U. Sch. Medicine, Balt., 1967-77; prof. medicine U. Mich., Ann Arbor, 1977—; pres. Cardiovascular Research Cons., Inc., Ann Arbor, 1980—. Author: Cardiovascular Nuclear Medicine, 1974; Atlas of Cardiovascular Nuclear Medicine, 1977. Served to capt. U.S. Army, 1963-65. Fellow Am. Coll. Cardiology; mem. Am. Soc. Clin. Investigation, Assn. Am. Physicians, Assn. Univ. Cardiologists, Am. Physiol Soc., Am. Heart Assn. Jewish. Office: 1405 E Ann St Ann Arbor MI 48109

PITT, GEORGE, lawyer; b. Chgo., July 21, 1938; s. Cornelius George and Anastasia (Geocaris) P.; B.A., Northwestern U., 1960, J.D., 1963; m. Barbara Lynn Goodrich, Dec. 21, 1963; children—Elizabeth Nanette, Margaret Leigh. Admitted to Ill. bar, 1963; assoc. firm Chapman and Cutler, Chgo., 1963-67; partner firm Borge and Pitt, and predecessor, 1968—. Served to 1st lt. AUS, 1964. Mem. Am., Ill., Chgo. bar assns., Phi Delta Phi, Phi Gamma Delta. Home: 872 Burr Ave Winnetka IL 60093 Office: 120 S LaSalle St Chicago IL 60603 also 20 Exchange Pl New York NY 10005

PITTARD, WILLIAM BULLOCK, III, pediatrician, neonatologist, educator; b. Little Rock, Oct. 24, 1946; s. William Bullock and Pen Lile (Compere) P.; m. Judith Ann Dowty, Aug. 21, 1971; children—William Bullock, Emily Lile, Andrew Gordon, Benjamin Wright. B.S. cum laude, Wake Forest U., 1968; M.D., U. Va., 1972. Diplomate Am. Bd. Pediatrics. Pediatric intern U. Va. Hosp., Charlottesville, 1972-73, resident in pediatrics, 1973-74; research fellow in neonatology, Rainbow Babies and Children's Hosp., Case Western Res. U., Cleve., 1974-76, sr. clin. instr. in pediatrics, 1976-77, asst. prof. pediatrics, Sch. Medicine Case Western Res. U., 1977-84, assoc. prof. pediatrics, 1984—, assoc. prof. Ob-Gyn, Reproductive Biology, 1984—, med. dir. McDonald House Nurseries, Univ. Hosps., 1980—, mem. McDonald House adv. com.; lectr. Gordon Research Conf., Colby Sawyer Coll., 1979, Fogarty Found, NIH, Bethesda, Md., 1979, People to People, Republic of China, 1983. Author writings in field. Project dir. USPHS tng. grant, 1977-84; participant NIH grant, 1983—, Ohio Dept. Health grant, 1983—; scholar Wake Forest U., 1964-65, Hankins upperclassman scholar, 1965-68; Norfolk Found. med. scholar, U. Va., 1968-72. Mem. Soc. Pediatric Research, Midwest Soc. Pediatric Research, No. Ohio Pediatric Soc., N.E. Ohio Pediatric Soc. (chmn. fetus and newborn com.), Ohio Perinatal Assn., Nat. Perinatal Assn., Phi Beta Kappa. Democrat. Methodist. Home: 1293 Ford Rd Lyndhurst OH 44124 Office: Rainbow Babies and Children's Hosp 2103 Adelbert Rd Cleveland OH 44106

PITTELKO, ROGER DEAN, clergyman; b. Elk Reno, Okla., Aug. 18, 1932; s. Elmer Henry and Lydia Caroline (Nieman) P.; A.A., Concordia Coll., 1952; B.A., Concordia Sem., St. Louis, 1954, M.Div., 1957, S.T.M., 1958; postgrad. Chgo. Luth. Theol. Sem., 1959-61; Th.D., Am. Div. Sch., Pineland, Fla., 1968, D.Div., 1977; D.Min., Faith Evang. Luth. Sem., Tacoma, 1983; m. Beverly A. Moellendorf, July 6, 1957; children—Dean, Susan. Ordained to ministry, Lutheran Ch.-Mo. Synod, 1958; vicar St. John Luth. Ch., S.I., N.Y., 1955-56; asst. pastor St. John Luth. Ch., New Orleans, 1958-59; pastor Concordia Luth. Ch., Berwyn, Ill., 1959-63; pastor Luth. Ch. of the Holy Spirit, Elk Grove Village, Ill., 1963—; chmn. Commn. on Worship, Luth. Ch.-Mo. Synod; asst. bishop Midwest region English dist., 1983. Mem. Luth. Acad. for Scholarship, Concordia Hist. Inst. Republican. Clubs: Maywood (Ill.) Sportsman; Itasca (Ill.) Country. Author: Guide to Introducing Lutheran Worship. Contbr. articles to jours. Home: 64 Grange Rd Elk Grove Village IL 60007 Office: 666 Elk Grove Blvd Elk Grove Village IL 60007

PITTNER, NICHOLAS ANDREW, lawyer; b. Ottoville, Ohio, Mar. 14, 1942; s. Andrew Martin and Catheryn (Boehmer) P.; m. Susan Eleanore Hess, June 19, 1965; children—Christina Marie, David Andrew, Victoria Susan. B.A., Ohio State U., 1964; J.D., Franklin Law Sch., Capital U., Columbus, 1970. Bar: Ohio 1970, U.S. Dist. Ct. (no. dist.) Ohio 1973, U.S. Dist. Ct. (so. dist.) Ohio 1971, U.S. Ct. Appeals (6th dir.) 1973. Computer systems analyst Anchor-Hocking Glass, Lancaster, Ohio, 1964-66, Reiland Page & Assocs., Columbus, Ohio, 1966-67; courtroom bailiff Franklin County Mcpl. Ct., Columbus, 1967-68; adminstrv. asst. Ohio Sec. State, Columbus, 1968-71; assoc. Means, Bichimer, Burkholder & Baker, Columbus, 1971—; presenter on field. Contbr. articles to profl. publs. Cons. Baker's Ohio Sch. Law, 1982—, Planning, Promoting and Passing School Tax Issues (booklet), 1983. Bd. dirs. Ohio Theatre for Youth, Columbus, 1984—, Upper Arlington Civic Assn., Ohio, 1985—. Mem. Columbus Bar Assn., Ohio State Bar Assn., ABA, Ohio Council Sch. Bd. Attys. (chmn. 1984), Nat. Council Sch. Attys., Columbus Amateur Radio Assn. (pres. 1980). Republican. Roman Catholic. Avocations: amateur radio, personal computing. Home: 1915 N Devon Rd Columbus OH 43212 Office: Means Bichimer Burkholder & Baker 14th Floor 42 E Gay St Columbus OH 43215

PITTS, ROBERT DUANE, religion educator, minister; b. Rockford, Mich., Feb. 16, 1932; s. Ralph Hays and Mildred (Jewell) Pitts; m. Marsha E. Weir, Aug. 15, 1952; children—Debra, Gregory, Sheila. Student Moody Bible Inst., 1950-52; A.B., Greenville Coll., 1955; M. Div., No. Bapt. Theol. Sem., 1958; M.A., U. Mich., 1964; D. Ed., Ind. U., 1969. Ordained to ministry Baptist Ch., 1958. asst. pastor Temple Bapt. Ch., St. Paul, 1959-61; asst. supt. Lydia Children's Home, Chgo., 1961-62; tchr. English, Greenville High Sch., Mich., 1962-63; dir. pub. relations and devel. Oakland City Coll., Ind., 1964-67; asst. dean, assoc. prof. Geneva Coll., Beaver Falls, Pa., 1969-73; prof. religion Taylor U., Upland, Ind., 1973—; v.p. acad. affairs, 1973-82; trustee AuSable Trails Inst. of Environ. Studies, Mancelona, Mich., 1973—. Contbr. articles to profl. jours. Mem. Evang. Mennonite Ch., Upland. Mem. Evang. Theol. Soc., Nat. Assn. Profs. Christian Edn., Am. Assn. Higher Edn., Bibl. Archaeology Soc. Republican. Baptist. Avocations: golf; hunting; photography. Home: 915 S Sechond St Upland IN 46989 Office: Dept Religion Taylor Univ Upland IN 46989

PITZ, JAMES MICHAEL, college administrator; b. Aurora, Ill., July 16, 1945; s. Wendell E. and Anne (Benson) P.; m. Jeanne Elizabeth Steytler, Dec. 29, 1970; children—Maureen Elizabeth, David Webster. B.S. in Bus. Adminstrn., Marquette U., 1967; M.B.A., U. Ill.-Urbana, 1973. Bus. mgr. Ricker Coll., Houlton, Maine, 1973-77; treas., bus. mgr. Clarke Coll., Dubuque, Iowa, 1977—. Served to capt. USAF, 1967-71. Mem. Nat. Assn. Coll. and Univ. Bus. Officers (fin. mgmt. com. 1984—). Avocations: gardening; cross-country skiing; sailing; camping; bicycling. Home: 125 S Dodge Galena IL 61036 Office: Clarke Coll 1550 Clarke Dr Dubuque IA 52001

PITZL, GERALD RUDOLPH, educator geography, researcher; b. St. Paul, Aug. 12, 1933. B.S., U. Minn., 1964, M.A., 1971, Ph.D., 1974. Tchr. Orono Jr./Sr. High Sch., Long Lake, Minn., 1964-65; instr. U. Minn., Mpls., 1965-68, 71-72; prof. Macalester Coll., St. Paul, 1972—; explorer Plaisted Polar Expeditions, 1967-68; mil. historian U.S. Marine Corps Hist. Ctr., Washington, 1981—. Contbr. articles to profl. jours. Communications adv. com. Met. Council, Minn., 1976-78, land use adv. com., 1980—. Served with USMC, 1952-59, 68-70. Mem. Assn. Am. Geographers, ACM, Minn. Council Geog. Edn. (pres. 1966-68), Pierce County Geog. Soc. (charter mem.), Marine Corps Officers Assn. Avocations: running; weight lifting; Brazilian music; reading. Home: 1412 Fairmount Ave St Paul MN 55105 Office: Macalester Coll 1600 Grand Ave St Paul MN 55105

PIVAN, DAVID BERNARD, management consultant; b. Chgo., June 30, 1921; s. Herman L. and Leona (Kirchner) P.; m. Rita Lois Birkner, July 26, 1942; children—Mark, Lynn, Janice. Student Case Sch. Applied Sci., 1942-43; B.S.E.E., Ill. Inst. Tech., 1948; postgrad. Sch. Bus. Northwestern U., 1950-52. Cert. profl. engr., Ill. Vice pres., chief engring Radio Sta. WMOR, 1948-50; pres., chmn. Pivan Engring. Co., 1954-75; exec. v.p., dir. Inmark, Inc., 1969-73, Hallmark, Inc., 1970-77, Comtel Corp., 1973-76; pres., owner Pivan Mgmt. Co., Skokie, Ill., 1976—; chmn., bd. dirs. Intermec Corp., Seattle, 1976—; dir. Corcom, Inc., Libertyville, Ill., Pakula & Co., Chgo., Providence, KNE Resources, Inc., Elk Grove Village, Ill., IQ Tech., Inc., Seattle. Bd. dirs. Northbrook Pub. Library, Ill., 1979-85. Served with U.S. Army, 1944-46, PTO. Mem. Electronic Reps. Assn., IEEE (sr.), Am. Radio Relay League, Airplane Owners and Pilots Assn. Club: Rainer (Seattle). Home: 1765 South Ln Northbrook IL 60062 Office: 7840 Lincoln Ave Skokie IL 60077

PIVARNIK, ALFRED J., See *Who's Who in America,* 43rd edition.

PIVARNIK, DAVID GEORGE, health and safety manager; b. Cleve., Aug. 10, 1952; s. George P. and Mary (Revilak) P.; m. Marguerite Monroe, June 25, 1977; 1 dau., Josie Monroe. B.S. in Indsl. Edn., U. Wis.-Stout, 1973, M.S. in Indsl. Safety, 1975. Cert. safety profl., Ohio. Safety rep. Liberty Mut. Ins. Co., Bala Cynwyd, Pa., 1975-76; safety supr. Olin Corp., Ashtabula, Ohio, 1976-77, mgr. health, safety, security and environ. affairs, 1978-79; mgr. health and safety Aircraft Components Group, TRW, Inc., Cleve., 1979—. Bd. dirs. Ashtabula County Cancer Soc. Mem. Am. Soc. Safety Engrs., Soc. Ohio Safety Engrs. Republican. Methodist. Contbr. articles to profl. jours. Home: 2528 Daniel Ave Ashtabula OH 44004 Office: 23555 Euclid Ave Cleveland OH 44117

PLAHN, DIANA LYNN, dentist, pharmacist; b. Kansas City, Mo., Nov. 25, 1956; d. Edgar Deatly and Pansy Louise (Axsom) Hodges; m. Craig Jay Plahn, July 18, 1981. B.S., U. Mo.-Kansas City, 1980, D.D.S., 1984. Practice dentistry, St. Louis, 1984—; pharmacist Walgreen's, St. Louis, 1984-85, Dolgin's, Kansas City and St. Louis, 1980-85, Skaggs, Kansas City, 1981-84. Mem. ADA, Rho Chi. Republican. Lutheran. Avocations: orchids; needlework; crafts. Home: 646 Nanceen Ct Ballwin MO 63021 Office: 1617 S Brentwood Blvd Suite 255 Saint Louis MO 63144

PLANEK, CHARLES WALTER, lawyer, pilot; b. Chgo., July 20, 1956; s. Charles Peter and Joanne Marie (Murphy) P.; m. Linda Bodo, April 13, 1985. B.A. with honors in Econs., DePaul U., 1978, J.D., 1981. Bar: Ill. 1981, U.S. Dist. Ct. (no. dist.) Ill. 1981, U.S. Ct. Appeals (7th cir.) 1981. Assoc. French & Rogers, P.C., Chgo., 1980-83, Johnson Cusack & Bell Ltd., Chgo., 1983—. Mem. ABA, Chgo. Bar Assn., Ill. State Bar Assn., Pi Gamma Mu. Roman Catholic. Home: 339 S Home Ave Oak Park IL 60302 Office: Johnson Cusack & Bell 211 W Wacker Chicago IL 60602

PLANK, ROBERT DAVID, engineer; b. Springfield, Mo., Jan. 1, 1936; s. Leslie Irl and Bessie Edith (Ingram) P.; m. T. Earline Moulder, Dec. 21, 1980; children—Ralph, Mark Stewart. B.A., Drury Coll., 1958, M.B.A., 1966; B.S., U. Mo.-Rolla, 1959; profl. degree civil engring. (hon.), U. Mo.-Rolla, 1975. Registered profl. engr., Mo.; registered land surveyor, Mo. Engr. water dept. City Utilities, Springfield, 1959-64, asst. mgr. water dept., 1964-67, mgr. water dept., 1967-76, mgr. engring. and planning, 1976—. Contbr. articles to profl. publs. Bd. dirs. Ozarks council Boy Scouts Am., 1975-80; pres. Springfield Community Ctr., 1985. Mem. Am. Water Works Asn. (Fuller award 1977, mem. plastic pipe com. chmn. Mo. sect. 1977). Club: University (v.p. 1985) (Springfield). Home: 3563 Linwood Dr Springfield MO 65804 Office: City Utilities 301 E Central Springfield MO 65802

PLANTS, HAROLD JAMES, fluid power company executive; b. Washington, Pa., Aug. 11, 1940; s. Harold James and Olive Frances (Black) P.; m. Judith Ann Barrett, May 6, 1961; children—James Gregory, Jacquie Renee. Student indsl. engring. Lakeland Coll., 1972-75. Laborer Universal Cyclops, Bridgeville, Pa., 1966-68; machinist Lincoln Elec. Co., Cleve., 1968-75; salesman Noll Equipment Co., Cleve., 1975-76; Pabco Fluid Power Co., Solon, Ohio, 1976-77; sr. ter. mgr. Miller Fluid Power Co., Bensenville, 1977—; assoc. prof. Lakeland Coll., Mentor, 1981-82. Served with USN, 1958-61, ETO. Republican. Lodge: Masons Home: 8 Meadowlawn 18 Mentor OH 44060 Office: Miller Fluid Power 7 No 15 York Rd Bensenville IL 60106

PLAPP, FREDERICK VAUGHN, physician, researcher; b. Kansas City, Mo., Jan. 27, 1949; s. Frederick Augustus and Betty Ruth (Plummer) P.; m. Beverly Jo Fox, July 5, 1974; children—Christopher Vaughn, Lauren Michelle. B.A. with distinction, U. Kans., 1971, Ph.D., 1974, M.D., 1975. Intern U. Chgo., 1975-76; resident in pathology Kans. U. Med. Ctr., Kansas City, 1976-78, asst. prof. pathology, 1977-82, assoc. prof., 1981-82, assoc. dean student affairs, 1981-82, dir. stats. lab., blood bank, 1979-82, dir. grad. studies in pathology, 1979-82; asst. med. dir. Community Blood Ctr., Kansas City, Mo., 1982—; dir. Heart of Am. Blood Bank Assn., Kans., Mo., 1981—. Contbr. articles to profl. jours. and med. books. Patentee Solid Phase Blood Groupings, 1983. Recipient Haden Medal, 1972, William H. Bailey Award, 1972, Walter Sutton prize, 1974, U. Kans. Med. Ctr. Mem. Am. Assn. Pathologists, Kans. City Soc. Pathologists, Am. Assn. Blood Banks, Sigma Xi, Phi Beta Kappa, Mem. St. Peter's Evang. and Reformed Ch. Home: 8319 Reeds Ln Overland Park KS 66207 Office: Community Blood Ctr 4040 Main St Kansas City MO 64111

PLATE, JANET MARGARET DIETERLE, scientist; b. Minot, N.D., Nov. 27, 1943; d. David and Bertha (Hoffer) Dieterle; m. Charles Alfred Plate, June 12, 1964; children—Jason, Stacey, Aileen. B.A., Jamestown Coll., 1964; Ph.D., Duke U., 1970. Am. Cancer Soc. postdoctoral fellow Mass. Gen. Hosp., Boston, 1970-72; research assoc. Harvard Univ.-Mass. Gen Hosp., Boston, 1972-78; asst. prof. Harvard Sch. Pub. Health, Boston, 1977-78; assoc. prof. Rush Med. Coll., Chgo., 1978—; sci. reviewer immunobiology study sect. NIH Bethesda, Md., 1979-83, Ill. div. Am. Cancer Soc., Chgo., 1979—; mem. sci. adv. bd. Nat. Cancer Cytology Ctr., N.Y. Ruling elder Community Presbyterian Ch., Clarendon Hills, Ill., 1980-83. Nat. Cancer Inst./NIH grantee, 1975, 78—. Mem. Am. Assn. Immunologists, Am. Soc. Histocompatibility and Immunogenetics, Transplantation Soc., Chgo. Assn. Immunologists (chmn. 1980-82). Office: Rush Presbyn St Luke's Med Ctr 1753 W Congress Pkwy Chicago IL 60612

PLATER, WILLIAM MARMADUKE, college dean, English educator; b. East St. Louis, Ill., July 26, 1945; s. Everett Marmaduke and Marguerite (McBride) P.; m. Gail Maxwell, Oct. 16, 1971; children—Elizabeth Rachel, David Matthew. B.A. in English, U. Ill., 1967, M.A., 1969, Ph.D., 1973; student Inst. for Ednl. Mgmt., Harvard U., summer 1978, Computer Sci. Workshop, U. Ill., 1981-83. Asst. dir. Unit One, U. Ill., Urbana, 1971-72, acting dir. Unit One, 1972-73, asst. dean coll. Liberal Arts and Sci., 1973-74, asst. dir. Sch. Humanities, 1974-77, assoc. dir. Sch. Humanities, 1977-83; dean liberal arts Ind. U., Indpls., 1983—; cons. numerous programs U. Ill.; cons. CEMREL, Inc., 1982-84; reader Ednl. Testing Service, winter 1982. Author: The Grim Phoenix: Reconstructing Thomas Pynchon, 1978; numerous poems, monographs, chpts. in books. Mem. editorial bd. Contbr. articles to profl. jours. Mem. adv. bd. Met. Interfaith Campus Ministries, Indpls., 1985—; bd. dirs. U. Ill. YMCA, 1982-83. U. Ill. Ctr. for Gerontology and Aging Studies, grantee, summer 1981; U. Ill. grantee, 1982; recipient prize Am. Acad. Ednl. Devel., 1982. Mem. MLA, Midwest MLA, Am. Studies Assn. (mem. fin. com. 1980-81). Democrat. Home: 5719 Winthrop Indianapolis IN 46220 Office: Indiana Univ 441 Cavanaugh Hall 425 Agnes Indianapolis IN 46202

PLATT, DWIGHT RICH, biology educator; b. Chgo., Aug. 4, 1931; s. Ferry Luther Platt and Selma Ione (Rich) Johnson; m. Edyth LaVonne Godwin, June 21, 1956; children—Kamala Joyce, Richard Dwight. B.S., Bethel Coll., 1952; M.A., U. Kans., 1954, Ph.D., 1966. Asst. instr. zoology U. Kans., Lawrence, 1952-54; edn. tech. Am. Friends Service Com., Barpali, Orissa, India, 1954-57;

prof. biology Bethel Coll., North Newton, Kans., 1957—; vis. prof. biology Sambalpur U., Orissa, India, 1970-71; bd. dirs. The Land Inst., Salina, Kans., 1980—; cons. Dyck Arboretum of the Plains, Hesston, Kans., 1982—. Contbr. articles on herpetology and prairie biology to profl. jours. Curator natural history Kauffman Mus., North Newton, Kans., 1982—. Mem. Kans. Nongame Wildlife Adv. Council to Kans. Fish and Game Commn., 1980—, chmn. 1982-84. Coop. grad. fellow NSF, 1960-62. Mem. Kans. Acad. Sci. (pres. 1985), Kans. Ornithological Soc. (pres. 1969-70, 72-74), Ecol. Soc. Am., Soc. Study Amphibians and Reptiles, Am. Ornithologists Union, Phi Beta Kappa. Avocations: birdwatching; gardening. Home: RFD 2 Box 209 Newton KS 67114 Office: Bethel Coll North Newton KS 67117

PLATT, GEORGE MILO, univ. adminstr.; b. Rapid City, S.D., Jan. 1, 1931; s. George Lee and Josephine M. (Paulson) P.; B.S., S.D. State U., 1953; M.A., Syracuse U., 1955, Ph.D., 1962. Asst. prof. U. S.D., 1962-65, U. Iowa, 1965-69; dir. planning and instl. research Wichita (Kans.) State U., 1969-79, asso. v.p., 1979—; Ford Found. adv. to secs. of local govt., East and West Pakistan, 1963, 65-66, 68. Served with AUS, 1955-57. Mem. Am. Soc. for Public Adminstrn., Am. Polit. Sci. Assn., Midwest Polit. Sci. Assn., Western History Assn., Soc. for Coll. and Univ. Planning. Author: (with Richard O. Niehoff) Local Government in East Pakistan, 1964; (with Alan L. Clem) A Bibliography of South Dakota Government and Politics, 1965, (with others) Administrative Problems in Pakistan, 1966. Home: 3527 E 15th St Wichita KS 67208 Office: Wichita State U Wichita KS 67208

PLATT, JENNIFER WOODARD, lawyer; b. Duluth, Minn., Mar. 20, 1954; d. Robert J. and Gretchen Joan (Brunt) W.; m. Michael Platt, Feb. 11, 1983; 1 dau., Rebecca Carrie. B.A., U. N.D., 1977; J.D., Northwestern U., 1980. Bar: Ill. 1981, U.S. Dist. Ct. (no. dist.) Ill. 1981. Assoc. Keck, Mahin & Cate, Chgo., 1980-81, Arvey, Hodes, Costello & Burman, Chgo., 1981-84, Friedman & Koven, Chgo., 1984—. Vol. atty. Lawyers for Creative Arts, Chgo., 1980—. Mem. Comml. Law League Am., ABA, Chgo. Bar Assn. Republican. Jewish. Club: East Bank (Chgo.). Office: Friedman & Koven 208 S LaSalle Chicago IL 60604

PLATT, JOE-ANN ELIZABETH, government official, clothing company executive; b. Moline, Ill., Sept. 27, 1933; d. Joe W. and Elizabeth Geraldine Sowder; m. John Bowman Platt, June 15, 1952; children—Judith, Jeb, Jo-Ellyn, Joe B. Corp. sec. Platt & Assocs., Davenport, Iowa, 1960-81, pres., 1981-83; founder, pres., chief ops. officer J.P.D., Inc. (The Home Place), Davenport, 1969—; exec. asst., regional rep. U.S. Dept. Labor, Kansas City, Mo. Nat. sec. Young Republican Nat. Fedn., 1968-71; Iowa del.-at-large Rep. Nat. Conv., 1968; mem. Iowa State Com. for Ronald Reagan, 1980. Mem. Nat. Assn. of Uniform Mfrs. and Distbrs. (dir. 1979-81, 82-84, first woman elected to orgn. in 50-yr. history). Episcopalian. Home: 103 W Bannister Rd Kansas City MO 64114 Office: J P D Inc 1114 W 51st St Davenport IA 52806

PLATT, JOHN EUGENE, JR., antiquarian bookdealer, book appraiser; b. Traverse City, Mich., Nov. 22, 1944; s. John Eugene and Dorothy Carolyn (Rodenbeck) P.; m. Marilyn Eadie Churchill, Nov. 4, 1979; children—John Jeremy Churchill, Owen Arthur Churchill. B.S.E. in Naval Architecture, U. Mich., 1968. Research asst. U. Mich., Ann Arbor, 1968-70; trade book mgr. Ned's Bookstore, Ypsilanti, Mich., 1971-74; antiquarian bookdealer West Side Book Shop, Ann Arbor, 1975—; lectr. book collecting, 1976—. Co-founder, mem. coordinating com. Ann Arbor Medieval Festival, 1969-78. Mem. Antiquarian Booksellers Assn. Am., Antarctican Soc., Am. Polar Soc., Ann Arbor Antiquarian Bookdealer Assn. (treas. 1976-82). Avocations: sailing; reading; woodworking. Home: 1128 W Washington St Ann Arbor MI 48103 Office: West Side Book Shop 113 W Liberty St Ann Arbor MI 48103

PLATTNER, STUART, anthropology educator; b. N.Y.C., Mar. 5, 1939; s. William and Ethel (Arfin) P.; m. Phyllis Baron, July 16, 1964; children—Daniel, Jessica. B.S., Columbia U., 1964; M.A., Stanford U., 1965, Ph.D., 1969. Asst. prof. anthropology U. Mo.-St. Louis, 1971-78, assoc. prof., 1978-85, prof., 1985—, chmn. dept. 1980-85. Editor: Formal Methods Economic Anthropology, 1975; Markets and Marketing, 1985. Com. mem. Cable TV, University City, Mo., 1982-85. Fellow Am. Anthrop. Assn.; mem. Am. Ethnol. Soc. (editor 1982-85), Soc. Econ. Anthropology (bd. dirs. 1980—). Office: Dept Anthropology U Mo Saint Louis MO 63121

PLATZ, HUBERTO RICARDO, utility company executive; b. C. Rivadavia, Argentina, Feb. 7, 1929; came to U.S., 1955, naturalized, 1961; s. Teodoro and Victoria Maria (Stadden) P.; m. Florence K. Kivlahan, Oct. 26, 1957; children—Victoria M., Elizabeth A., Cynthia L., Theodore W. Civil Engring., U. Buenos Aires (Argentina), 1954; postgrad. courses Pa. State U., 1960, U. Calif.-Berkeley, 1965, Ga. Inst. Tech., 1974, Edison Electric Inst., 1978. Registered profl. engr., Pa., Wis. Engring. intern Compañia Argentina de Electricidad, Buenos Aires, 1950-52; engring. trainee Allis Chalmers Mfg. Co., Milw., 1955, field supt., 1956-58; results engr. Duquesne Light Co., Pitts., 1958-60, sr. engr., 1960-61, mech. maintenance engr., 1962-64; project engr. Kaiser Engrs., Oakland, Calif., 1965-66; mgr. power plant engring. Wis. Electric Power Co., Milw., 1967-68, mgr. power plant dept., 1969-73, asst. v.p., 1974, v.p. power plants, 1975-76, v.p. engring., constrn., 1976—; adv. Advanced Systems Task Force, Electric Power Research Inst., Palo Alto, Calif., 1977-79, chmn. engring., econ. evaluations, 1980-82; mem. prime movers com. Edison Electric Inst., Washington, 1970-80, 83-84, mem. constrn. com., 1978-80. Fellow ASME (chmn. power div. 1979-80; James Landis medal 1982); mem. IEEE, Nat. Soc. Profl. Engrs., Wis. Soc. Profl. Engrs. Republican. Roman Catholic. Club: South Shore Yacht (Milw.). Lodge: Knights of Columbus. Avocations: sailing; ship modelmaking; photography. Home: 13330 Nicolet Ave Elm Grove WI 53122 Office: Wisconsin Electric Power Co 231 W Michigan Milwaukee WI 53201

PLEASANT, DEBORAH LEE, educator; b. Willard, Ohio, Feb. 25, 1951; d. Richard LeRoy and Martha Louise (Gill) Jacobs; m. James David Pleasant, Jr., May 22, 1971. Student Eastern Ky. U., 1969-70, Capital U., 1972-73; B.S. summa cum laude, Wright State U., 1977; postgrad. U. Dayton, 1981. Social studies tchr. Hamilton (Ohio) City Schs., Taft High Sch., 1977-79; social studies tchr., cheerleader coach Beavercreek (Ohio) Local Schs., 1979—, mem. curriculum improvement com., 1980-86, v.p., 1981-82, pres., 1982-83; advisor Am. Field Service, 1980—; mem. sr. social studies test devel. com. for Ohio Tests of Scholastic Achievement, Ohio Dept. Edn., 1985. Vol. voter registrar, 1980—. Mem. NEA, Nat. Council Social Studies, Nat. Hist. Soc., Assn. Supervision and Curriculum Devel., Ohio Edn. Assn., Ohio Council Social Studies, Ohio Hist. Soc., Ohio Acad. History, Western Ohio Edn. Assn., Internat. Platform Assn., Dayton Area Council Social Studies (sec.), Ohio Assn. Supervision and Curriculum Devel., Beavercreek Classroom Tchrs. Assn., Greene County Hist. Soc., Kappa Delta Pi, Phi Alpha Theta. Democrat. Clubs: Capital U. Alumni (Dayton, Ohio); Am. Field Service (Beavercreek, Ohio). Office: 2660 Dayton-Xenia Rd Beavercreek Schs Xenia OH 45385

PLEETS, WILBUR LAWRENCE, business development specialist, consultant; b. Standing Rock Sioux Indian Reservation, Ft. Yates, N.D., Oct. 15, 1937; s. Walter Frank and Agatha (Buffalo Boy) P.; m. Lois Ann Siegfried, Oct. 24, 1975; children—Lawrence, Laura, Lyndell. A.A., Haskell Indian Jr. Coll., Lawrence, Kans., 1959; student Black Hills State Coll., 1966-69; A.A., Standing Rock Community Coll., 1981; B.S. in Bus. Adminstrn., N.D. State U., 1982. Asst. community action program dir. Standing Rock Sioux Tribe, Ft. Yates, N.D., 1971-72, bus. mgr., 1972-75, project evaluation officer Indian Health Service, 1975-77, tribal health dir., 1977-80, researcher, 1981-82, bus. devel. specialist, 1982—; cons. health and human services, Ft. Yates, 1980-81; cons. Standing Rock Sioux Tribe Standing Rock Enterprises, Inc. Mem. Ft. Yates Planning Commn.; active Boy Scouts Am.; vol. Red Cross, Ft. Yates Fire Dept. and Ambulance Service; pres. local sch. dist. Title IV Cultural Program; pres. Headstart Parents Orgn., Ft. Yates Ednl. Task Force, Ft. Yates Comml. Devel. Corp.; vice chmn. Standing Rock Planning Commn. Served with USAF, 1957-63. Mem. Ft. Yates Alumni Assn., N.D. State U. Alumni Assn., N.D. Indian Edn. Assn., Ft. Yates Tenants Assn. (v.p.), Am. Legion (post adj.). Republican. Roman Catholic. Club: Ft. Yates Rodeo Club (pres.). Lodge: Lions. Author: Alternatives for the Establishment of an Indian Medical Referral Center, 1976-77; Health Status of the Standing Rock Sioux Indian People, 1977-78; Alcohol and the Standing Rock Tribe: A Twenty Year Follow Up Study, 1980. Home: PO Box 64 Fort Yates ND 58538 Office: PO Box D Fort Yates ND 58538

PLETCHER, PAT, mental health administrator; b. Rensselaer, Ind., May 11, 1948; d. Acy and Eva (May) McCarty; m. Mike Pletcher, Aug. 8, 1970; children—Troy, Kelli. B.A., Portsmouth Interstate Coll. Bus., 1967; postgrad. Ohio U., 1985—. Acct. Ohio U. Bookstores, Athens, 1967-71; teller People's Credit Union, Middletown, R.I., 1971-73; data control coordinator Boston U., 1973-74; adminstrv. asst. Southeastern Ohio Regional Council on Alcoholism, Athens, 1975-76, chmn., 1981, 82; dir. planning and fin. Athens Hocking Vinton Community Mental Health Bd., 1976—. Coordinator Chem. People, 1983; chmn. community issues com. Athens County, 1984, 85; chmn. Alexander Jr. High Sch. Bldg. Steering Com., Albany, Ohio, 1985. Recipient Elizabeth Mills Obleness award Ohio U., 1984. Mem. Assn. Mental Health Adminstrn., Ohio Budget Coalition. Democrat. Avocations: politics; reading; public education projects. Home: Route 1 Box 267A Albany OH 45710 Office: Athens Hocking Vinton Community Mental Health Bd PO Box 130 Athens OH 45701

PLEZBERT, MICHAEL JOSEPH, marriage and family counselor; b. Chgo., July 1, 1934, s. Michael and Regina (De Cristopher) P.; B.S., Evangel Coll., 1969; M.S. in Guidance and Counseling, Southwestern Mo. State U., 1972; postgrad. U. Calif., Santa Cruz, 1973-75, Heed U., Hollywood, Fla.; Ph.D. in Psychology, Columbia Pacific U., 1982; m. Janice Sherrill Pietrini, Feb. 13, 1965; 1 son, Michael Paul. Tchr. spl. edn. Spokane (Mo.) Sch. Dist., 1969-70; psychologist, counselor Family Service Assn., Watsonville, Calif., 1970-72; adult instr. hosp. adminstrn. and psychology Santa Cruz Dept. Edn., 1972-75; pres. Inst. Personal and Family Communications, Springfield, Mo., 1975—; dir. Alternatives Counseling Ctr., Springfield, Mo.; marriage, family and child guidance counselor and cons.; public speaker. Mem. Mo. Gov.'s Com. on Employment of Handicapped. Served with AUS, 1956-64. Mem. Greene County Mental Health Assn., Nat. Autistic Soc., Nat. Council Family Relations, Nat. Assn. Social Workers, Am. Personnel and Guidance Assn. Mem. Assemblies of God Ch. Club: Lions. Author: A Dynamic Approach to Counseling, 1983; The Courage to Love, 1984.

PLIER, ROBERT EDWIN, financial company executive; b. Port Washington, Wis., Apr. 8, 1947; s. Emil T. and Edna Plier; m. Carol L. Plier. B.B.A., U. Wis., Whitewater, 1969; postgrad. Bradley U., 1977, 78. Sr. staff accountant Clifton, Gunderson & Co., C.P.A.'s, Peoria, Ill., 1969-74; treas. Peoria Disposal Co., 1974-83; pres. Robert E. Plier & Assocs., Ltd., 1983—. Bd. dirs. Boys Club Peoria, 1977-78. Mem. Am. Mgmt. Assn., U.S. Jaycees (treas. 1978-79, senator 1981—), Ill. Jaycees (state chaplain 1975-76, dir. children's camp, 1977-79, ambassador, 1976—), Am. Inst. C.P.A.s, Nat. Assn. Accountants, Ill. Soc. C.P.A.s. Club: Kennel Lake Sportsmen's. Home: 1049 E Jefferson St Morton IL 61550 Office: 508 N Jefferson St Peoria IL 61603

PLISKA, ROBERT JAMES, real estate executive, accountant; b. Detroit, Oct. 4, 1947; s. Peter and Marcella (Cousino) P.; m. Kathleen Marie Drean, Oct. 8, 1946; children—Jennifer, Christine. B.S. cum laude, U. Detroit, 1969; M.B.A., Mich. State U., 1970. C.P.A., Mich.; lic. real estate broker, ins. agt. Mgr. Coopers & Lybrand, Detroit, 1970-80; v.p. Lambrecht Co., Detroit, 1980—. Mem. nat. alumni bd. U. Detroit, 1980-82. Mem. Am. Inst. C.P.A.s (profl. edn. instr., speakers bur.), Mich. Assn. C.P.A.s (profl. edn. instr., mem. speakers bur., chmn. pub. service com. 1981-85), Mortgage Bankers Assn. (chmn. income property com.), Nat. Assn. Realtors, Mich. Assn. Realtors, Detroit Bd. Realtors, Adminstrv. Mgmt. Soc., Beta Alpha Psi. Roman Catholic. Clubs: Economic of Detroit; Fairlane (gov. 1979-83) (Dearborn, Mich.); Renaissance (Detroit), Toastmasters (v.p., speakers bur., Competent Toastmaster award 1977). Home: 26011 Timber Trail Dearborn Heights MI 48127 Office: Lambrecht Co 3300 Penobscot Bldg Detroit MI 48226

PLOCHMANN, CAROLYN GASSAN, painter; b. Toledo, May 4, 1926; d. Edward Paul and Elizabeth Mildred Gassan; m. George Kimball Plochmann, Jan. 28, 1950; 1 child, Sarah Kimball. B.A., U. Toledo, 1947; M.F.A., State U. of Iowa, 1949. Art tchr., Toledo Mus. of Art Sch. of Design, 1943-47; art supr. So. Ill. U. Training Sch., Carbondale, 1949-50. One-man shows Evansville Mus. Arts and Sci., Ind., 1979, Kennedy Galleries, N.Y.C., 1983; exhibited in group shows: Minn. Mus Art, 1980, Kennedy Galleries, N.Y.C., 1983, Evansville Mus. of Arts and Sci., So. Ill. U. Sch. Medicine, Springfield. George W. Stevens fellow, Toledo Mus. of Art, State U. of Iowa, 1947-49, Tupperware Art Fund fellow Tupperware Corp., 1954; Recipient Emily Lowe award Emily Lowe Found., 1958, Phila. Watercolor Soc. award, 1968. Mem. Phila. Water Color Club, Woodstock Art Assn. Lutheran. Home: Box 104 Route 9 Carbondale IL 62901 Office: Kennedy Galleries 40 W 57th St New York NY 10019

PLOEGER, GARY WILLIAM, pharmacist; b. Tyler, Minn., Sept. 1, 1944; s. Vernon and Lorine (Pape) P.; m. Connie Jo Schmidtke, Oct. 11, 1964; children—Scott, Thomas, Stephanie. B.S., S.D. State U. Lic. pharmacist. Pharmacist, Thrifty Drug, Mpls., 1968-70; owner, pharmacist Rays drug, Brookings, S.D., 1971-74; mgr. Snyder Drug, Inc., Brookings, 1974-78, owner, pharmacist, Pipestone, 1979—. Trustee, St. Leo's Cath. Ch., Pipestone, 1983—. Mem. Minn. State Pharm. Assn. Republican. Lodge: Kiwanis. Avocations: travel Home: 902 6th Ave SE Pipestone MN 56164 Office: Snyder Drugs Hwy 30 & 8th Ave SE Pipestone MN 56164

PLOEN, DELBERT LEE, company executive; b. Green Island, Iowa, May 1, 1933; s. Albert P. and Juanita C. (Mielk) P., m. Peggy D. Addison, Dec. 27, 1958; children—Jeffrey Lee, Mark Steven, Kye Addison, Cory Scott. B.S. in Forestry, Iowa State Coll. Owner, operator restaurant, 1959; asst. mgr. Stabilized Vitamins, Clinton, Iowa, 1960-61; mgr., 1961-62; prodn. supr. Comml. Solvents, Peoria, Ill., 1962-63, Terre Haute, Ind., 1963-64, quality control dept., 1964-67; ptnr. min. golf course, 1966-67; ptnr. Quali-Tech Products, Inc., Hopkins, Minn., 1967-69, pres., chmn., Chaska, Minn., 1969—; chmn. Reedy Photoprocess, Mpls., 1983—. Served with USAF, 1955-58. Mem. Nat. Feed Ingredients Assn. (bd. dirs. 1978—). Club: Hazeltine Nat. Golf. Lodge: Rotary (Chaska). Avocations: hunting; fishing; handball; racquetball; golf. Office Quali-Tech Inc 318 Lake Hazeltine Dr Chaska MN 55318

PLOTKA, EDWARD DENNIS, reproductive endocrinologist; b. Utica, N.Y., Oct. 10, 1938; s. Maxim Jay and Marian Vivian (LaPoten) P.; m. Marie Christina Fischer, July 2, 1966. B.S., Del. Valley Coll., 1960; M.S., Oregon State U., 1963; Ph.D., Purdue U., 1966. Research asst. Oreg. State U., Corvallis, 1961-63, Purdue U., Lafayette, Ind., 1963-66; asst. prof. Purdue U., Lafayette, 1966-67; asst. research prof. U. Ga., Athens, Ga., 1967-69; reproductive endocrinologist Marshfield Med. Found., Wis., 1969—. Bd. dirs Wildwood Park Zool. Soc., Marshfield, Wis., 1976-83, North Wood County Humane Soc., Marshfield, 1976—. Research fellow Purdue U., 1963-66. Mem. Soc. Study Fertility, Soc. Exptl. Biology and Med., Soc. Study Reprodn. (chmn. membership com. 1975-77, chmn. publs. com., 1983-84), The Endocrine Soc., The Am. Fertility Soc. Lodge: Elks. Home: 11713 West Lane Marshfield WI 54449 Office: Marshfield Med Found 510 N St Joseph Ave Marshfield WI 54449

PLOTKIN, JACK, ophthalmologist; b. Columbus, Ohio, Dec. 15, 1935. B.S. cum laude, Ohio State U., 1958, M.D., 1962. Diplomate Am. Bd. Ophthalmology. Intern, then resident Mt. Sinai Hosp. Cleve., 1962-66; NIH research fellow Proctor Found. Univ. Calif.-San Francisco, 1968-69; gen. practice opthalmology Euclid Clin. Found., Cleve., 1971—; dir. eye pathology lab. Mt. Sinai Hosp. Cleve., 1970-73; asst. clin. prof. Case Western Res. U., 1980—. Contbr. articles to profl. jours. Served to capt. Med. Service Corps, U.S. Army, 1966-68. Mem. Am. Acad. Ophthalmology, Cleve. Ophthal. Soc., Phi Beta Kappa, Alpha Omega Alpha. Office: Euclid Clin 18599 Lake Shore Blvd Euclid OH 44119

PLOTSKY, NORMAN, communication service executive, engineer; b. N.Y.C., Oct. 4, 1930; s. Sam and Rose (Sher) P.; m. Charlotte Wilen, June 28, 1958; children—Melissa, Richard. B.S. in Chem. Engring., Pratt Inst., 1952; M.S. in Chem. Engring., NYU, 1955. Registered profl. engr., N.Y. Engr. Curtiss Wright Corp., Woodridge, N.J., 1956-59; project engr. Avco Corp., Stratford, Conn., 1959-64; sr. project engr. Curtiss Wright Corp., Woodridge, 1965-67, Sundstrand Aviation, Rockford, Ill., 1967-74; v.p., dir. Transceiver Midwest Inc., Dallas, 1980—; dir. Am. Facsimile Systems, Inc., Dallas, 1981-83. Patentee in field. Lodge: B'nai B'rith (pres. 1971-73). Avocations: athletics, boating. Home: 1069 Hohlfelder Rd Glencoe IL 60022 Office: Transceiver Midwest Inc Box 242 Glencoe IL 60022

PLOTZ, JUDITH LYNN, insurance broker; b. Cleve., Nov. 15, 1950; d. Charles D. and Pauline F. (McMillen) P.; 1 son, William Charles. Student Lakeland Coll., 1973-75, Scarritt Coll., 1975-76, Bankers Inst. Sch., 1977-79, Case Western Res. Law Sch. Buyer, Higbee Dept. Stores, Mentor, Ohio, 1968-71; dist. mgr. Res. Life Ins. Co., Panama City, Fla., 1975-79; sales mgr. Prudential Ins. Co., Tampa, 1979-82; account mgr. Rollins, Brudick Hunter, Cleve., 1982-83; asst. v.p. Frank B. Hall Cons. Co., Cleve., 1983—; pres. J.L. Plotz, Inc., 1984—; lectr. in field. Recipient award Marjory Wetzel Found., 1970; Nat. Quality award Nat. Assn. Life Underwriters, 1980-82. Mem. Life Underwriters Assn., Midwest Pension Orgn., Assn. Profl. Bus. Women (Top Achiever 1980). Office: J L Plotz & Co Inc One Erieview Plaza Suite 900 Cleveland OH 44114

PLUCKHAHN, J(OHN) BRUCE, sports museum executive; b. Milw., Oct. 10, 1924; s. William and Dorothea Johanna (Kolb) P.; m. Rose Mary Sattler, Feb. 14, 1946; children—Susan, John, William, Robert, Charles. B.S. in Journalism, U. Wis., 1949. Sports reporter Record Herald, Wausau, Wis., 1949-51, Daily News, Dayton, Ohio, 1951-54; pub. relations staff Am. Bowling Congress, Milw., 1954-77, mgr., 1957-77; project dir. Nat. Bowling Hall of Fame and Mus., Milw., 1977-80; curator Nat. Bowling Hall of Fame and Mus., St. Louis, 1980—. Co-author: Pins and Needlers, 1967; author sect. on bowling history Ency. Brit., 1974. Served with USAAF, 1943-45, PTO. Recipient Best Feature of Yr. award Bowling mag., 1954, Disting. Service award Fedn. Internat. des Quillers, European Zone, 1983. Disting. Service medal World Bowling Writers, 1984. Mem. Bowling Writers Assn. Am. (Meritorious Service award 1969, chmn. bd. dirs. 1970—), Assn. Sports Mus. and Halls of Fame (sec. 1975-79, 81—). Club: Press (St. Louis). Avocations: reading; travel; golf; jazz. Home: 6304 S Rosebury Clayton MO 63105 Office: National Bowling Hall of Fame and Museum 111 Stadium Plaza Saint Louis MO 63102

PLUMMER, KENNETH ALEXANDER, hospital administrator; b. Chgo., Mar. 24, 1928; s. Alexander Oliver and Estella Marie (Koziol) P.; student N. Central Coll., 1940-41, the Citadel, 1941-42, Far Eastern U. (Philippines), 1946-48; m. Marie M. Ricci, Oct. 10, 1943; children—Pamela, Diane, Kenneth, Stacy. Commd. 2d lt. U.S. Army, 1943, advanced through grades to col., 1966, ret., 1970; dir. Ancilla Domini Health Services, Inc., Des Plaines, Ill., 1970-82; dir. Oak Park Hosp. (Ill.), 1982—; cons. Cambodian Refugee Program for Cath. Relief Services; moderator, instr. Air War Coll. Non-Resident Program; installed med. relief teams in Cambodian refugee camps; dir. Cable Program Network, Chgo. Mem. govt. affairs com. Chgo. Assn. Commerce and Industry, 1976-79. Decorated Bronze Star, Meritorious Service medal, Army Commendation medal; recipient Assn. of U.S. Army citation, 1961; Res. Officers Assn. award, 1964; Cath. Relief Service award, 1980; Ancilla Domini Sisters award, 1980. Mem. Mil. Order World Wars (comdr. 1962-63), Hosp. Pub. Relations Soc., Chgo. Council on Fgn. Relations, Assn. U.S. Army, Ret. Officers Assn., Am. Hosp. Assn., Cath. Hosp. Assn. Roman Catholic. Club: Oak Park. Contbg. author Command Gen. Staff Review, 1961-64; editor Health Services Quarterly, 1974-79; contbr. Mgmt. Rev. Home: 415 N Elmwood St Oak Park IL 60302 Office: 520 S Maple Ave Oak Park IL 60304

PLUMMER, RICHARD DUANE, city manager; b. Emporia, Kans., Aug. 8, 1930; s. Robert Fleming and Roberta (Hamlin) P.; B.S., Kans. State Tchrs. Coll., Emporia, 1955, M.S., 1963; m. Audrey Myrtle Ogden, Dec. 19, 1954; children—Terri Lynne, Richard Duane II, Ross Delevan. Auditor, Kans. Power & Light Co., 1956-64; controller Kans. Transp. Dept., Commn., Topeka, 1964-77; asst. dir. Ariz. Dept. Econ. Security, 1977; controller Kans. Supreme Ct., 1978-80; bus. mgr. Marymount Coll., Salina, Kans., 1980; city adminstr. Horton, Kans., 1981, city mgr. Larned, Kans., 1982—. Mem. Seaman High Sch. Dist. 345 Sch. Bd., 1971-77, pres., 1971-75. Served with USAF, 1950-53. Mem. Internat. City Mgrs. Assn. Lodge: Rotary. Home: 923 E 3d St Larned KS 67550 Office: PO Box 70 Larned KS 67550

PLUNKETT, MELBA KATHLEEN, mfg. co. exec.; b. Marietta, Ill., Mar. 20, 1929; d. Lester George and Florence Marie (Hutchins) Bonnett; student public schs.; m. James P. Plunkett, Aug. 18, 1951; children—Julie Marie Plunkett Hayden, Gregory James. Co-founder, 1961, since sec.-treas., dir. Coils, Inc., Huntley, Ill. Mem. U.S. C. of C., Ill. Mfg. Assn., Ill. C. of C., Ill. Notary Assn. Roman Catholic. Home: Route 1 Sleepy Hollow Rd West Dundee IL 60118 Office: 11716 Algonquin Rd Huntley IL 60142

PLUNKETT, PAUL E., judge. U.S. Dist. judge Seventh Cir., No. Ill. Office: US Dist Courthouse 219 S Dearborn St Chicago IL 60604*

POAST, DAVID MICHAEL, lawyer; b. Middletown, Ohio, Oct. 4, 1939; s. John and Rachel (Metzger) P.; m. Rebecca Gusweiler, May 24, 1969; children—John G., F. Michael, Heather Rebecca. B.A., Denison U., 1961; LL.B., Harvard U., 1964; M.B.A., Xavier U., 1970. Bar: Ohio 1964. Assoc. Kyte, Conlan, Wulsin & Vogeler, Cin., 1964-78, Frost & Jacobs, Cin., 1978—. Trustee Legal Aid Soc., Cin., 1980—. Mem. ABA, Ohio State Bar Assn., Cin. Bar Assn., Cin. Assn. Clubs: University, Indian Hill (Cin.). Home: 7575 DeMar Rd Cincinnati OH 45243 Office: Frost & Jacobs 2600 Central Trust Ctr Cincinnati OH 45202

POCOCK, FREDERICK JAMES, scientist, water chemistry researcher, consultant; b. Canton, Ohio, May 28, 1923; s. Frederick Stanley and Mary Elizabeth (Tinker) P.; m. Lois Jean Rice, Jan. 12, 1952; children—Kathleen Jean, David Walter. B.S. in Chemistry, Mt. Union Coll., 1950. Registered profl. corrosion engr., Calif. With Republic Steel Corp., Berger div. Canton, Ohio, 1949-50; with Research and devel. div. Babcock & Wilcox, Alliance, Ohio, 1950—, sr. scientist A. McDermott Co., Research and Devel. div. Babcock & Wilcox, 1974—. Contbr. articles to profl. jours. Mem. ASME (chmn. research com. 1978-80, chmn. water tech. handbook steering com. 1981, exec. com. 1980, Prime Movers award 1962, Research Council award 1980), Nat. Assn. Corrosion Engrs. (past chmn. tech. unit, accredited mem.), Am. Chem. Soc. (Cert. of Merit 1967), ASTM. Republican. Avocation: travel. Home: 1718 Edmar St Louisville OH 44641 Office: Babcock & Wilcox Research and Devel Div 1562 Beeson St Alliance OH 44641

PODBOY, ALVIN MICHAEL, JR., lawyer, librarian; b. Cleve., Feb. 10, 1947; s. Alvin Michael and Josephine Esther (Nagode) P.; m. Mary Ann Gloria Esposito, Aug. 21, 1971; children—Allison Marie, Melissa Ann. A.B. cum laude, Ohio U., 1969; J.D., Case Western Res. U., 1972, M.S. L.S., 1977. Bar: Ohio 1972, U.S. Dist. Ct. (no. dist.) Ohio 1973. Assoc. Joseph T. Svete Co. L.P.A., Chardon, Ohio, 1972-76; dir. pub. services Case Western Res. Sch. Law Library, Cleve., 1974-77, assoc. law librarian, 1977-78; librarian Baker & Hostetler, Cleve., 1978—. Bd. overseers Case Western Res. U., 1981—, mem. vis. com. sch. library sci., 1980—; chmn. Case Western Res. Library Sch. Alumni Fund, 1979-80; Republican precinct committeeman Cuyahoga County, Cleve., 1981—, mem. exec. com., 1984—. Served to 1st lt. USAF, 1972. Mem. ABA, Ohio State Bar Assn., Bar Assn. Greater Cleve., Am. Assn. Law Libraries (cert.), Ohio Regional Assn. Law Libraries (pres. 1985), Case Western Res. U. Library Sch. Alumni Assn. (pres. 1981), Arnold Air Soc., Pi Gamma Mu, Phi Alpha Theta. Roman Catholic. Club: Citizens League (Cleve.). Lodge: K.C. Avocations: alpine skiing; boating. Home: 4637 Anderson Rd South Euclid OH 44121 Office: Baker & Hostetler 3200 National City Ctr Cleveland OH 44114

PODEWELL, KENNETH ROLAND, organization executive; b. Chgo., May 13, 1915; s. Edwin and Anna (Birkigt) P.; m. Dorothy Margaret Buehler, July 1, 1939; children—Roger, Nancy, Carol, Clifford. Chief ranger Ind. Order of Foresters, Blue Island, Ill., 1960-62, high chief ranger, Chgo., 1966-81, 1981—, supreme councillor Supreme Exec. Council, Toronto, Ont., Can., 1981—. Active Republican. Party campaign for presdl. campaign, 1980, 84. Recipient Grand Cross of Legion of Honor, Ind. Order Foresters, 1977. Mem. Traveler's Protective Assn. (pres. 1982-84), South Side Suburban Real Estate Bd. (pres. 1964), Mem. United Ch. of Christ. Home and Office: 2737 W 89th Pl Evergreen Park IL 60642

PODGORSKI, TERESA MARIE, college administrator; b. Hamburg, Ger., June 24, 1949; came to U.S., 1951, naturalized, 1970; d. Tadeusz John and Irene (Wojcik) P.; A.A.S., Essex County Coll., 1970; B.A., Montclair State Coll., 1972; Ed.M., U. Buffalo, 1977. Bookkeeper/sec. Archdiocese of Newark, 1966-73; instr. St. Thomas Aquinas High Sch., Edison, N.J., 1972-76; assoc. dean Bryant and Stratton Bus. Inst., Clarence, N.Y., 1976-80, acad. dean, 1980—; textbook reviewer/cons. Mem. Nat. Bus. Edn. Assn., Internat. Word Processing Assn., Ohio Bus. Tchrs. Assn., Ohio Word Processing Assn., Nat. Assn. Female Execs. Roman Catholic. Developer, writer curriculum for Cleve. br. Bryant and Stratton, 1980. Office: 26700 Brookpark Rd Extension North Olmsted OH 44070

PODOLIN, LEE JACOB, health planning executive; b. Buffalo, Oct. 23, 1930; s. David J. and Helen J. (Feldman) P.; B.A., U. Rochester, 1952; M.P.A., Syracuse U., 1953; M.P.H., Yale U., 1959, m. Catherine McIntosh, Nov. 22, 1956; 1 son, George Philip. Statis. analyst Eastman Kodak Co., Rochester, N.Y., 1956-57; asst. dir. Montefiore Hosp., N.Y.C., 1958-63; dir. facility planning Health & Hosp. Planning Corp., N.Y.C., 1963-68; exec. dir. Met. Health Planning Corp., Cleve., 1968-76; exec. dir. Milw. Regional Med. Center, 1976-83; cons. Glunz-Strathy Assocs., Milw., 1983-84; exec. dir. Univ. Physicians Milw. Clin. Campus Practice Plan, Inc., 1984—; clin. instr. U. Wis. Med. Sch., 1984—; asst. clin. prof. Med. Coll. Wis., Milw., 1976—; adj. asst. prof. Case Western Reserve U., Cleve., 1970-76; adj. instr. Ohio State U., Columbus, 1974-76; mem. med. assistance adv. council Dept. HEW, 1970-72. Trustee Village of Fox Point, 1980—, North Shore Library, 1980—; bd. dirs. Fox Point Found., 1980-81. Served with U.S. Army, 1953-56. Fellow Am. Pub. Health Assn.; mem. Am. Assn. for Comprehensive Health Planning (trustee 1973-76), Am. Hosp. Assn., Am. Coll. Hosp. Adminstrs. Club: Univ. (Mil.). Home: 7415 N Lombardy Rd Fox Point WI 53217 Office: 950 N 12th St PO Box 477 Milwaukee WI 53201

POE, EDWARD WILLIAM, JR., information systems executive; b. Chgo., Aug. 12, 1931; s. Edward William and Louise Clara (Heimlich) P.; m. June Ann Fredrickson, Dec. 27, 1953; children—Amy Dawn, Timothy Edward. B.A., Valparaiso U., 1953. Staff mgr. Ill. Bell Telephone Co., Chgo., 1955-70, dist. staff mgr., 1971-82; dist. mgr. info. systems AT&T Info. Systems, Morristown, N.J., 1983—. Commr. Village of Palos Park, Ill., 1979—; v.p. Family Care Services of Metro Chgo., 1970. Served to lt. j.g. USN, 1951-53. Mem. Data Processing Mgmt. Assn., Mcpl. Fin. Officer's Assn. Republican. Lutheran. Avocations: photography, music. Home: 9110 W 120th St Palos Park IL 60464 Office: AT&T Info Systems 155 N Wacker Dr Chicago IL 60606

POE, STEVEN DEE, physician; b. Newton, Iowa, Nov. 16, 1950; s. Donald Eugene and Doris (Berry) P. B.S. cum laude, Lincoln U., 1974; D.O., Kirksville Coll. Osteo. Medicine, 1979. Intern, Jacksonville Gen. Hosp., Fla., 1979-80; resident in emergency medicine U. Hosp. Jacksonville, 1980-82, chief resident, 1981-82; assoc. in emergency medicine Emergency Physicians, Inc., Jacksonville, 1982-83; dir. emergency medicine Normandy Hosp., St. Louis, 1983—; dir. Healthcare Place N.W. Plaza, St. Louis, 1984—; assoc. prof. emergency medicine Kirksville Coll. Osteo-Medicine, 1983—; assoc. lectr. St. Louis Community Coll., 1983—; resident liaison Jacksonville Bd. Fire Surgeons, 1981-82. Served with USMC, 1969-71. Mem. Am. Coll. Emergency Physicians (pub. relations com., govt. affairs com. Mo. chpt.), Am. Osteo. Assn., Mo. Emergency Physicians, Mo. Osteo. Assn., Am. Coll. Osteo. Emergency Physicians, St. Louis Osteo. Assn., Beta Kappa Chi. Republican. Methodist. Lodge: Elks. Avocations: flying; fishing; boating; snow skiing; hunting. Office: Normandy Osteopathic Hosp North and South 7840 Natural Bridge Saint Louis MO 63121

POE, WILLIAM JERALD, pharmacist; b. St. Louis, June 12, 1946; s. Isadore S. and Esther (Bluestein) P.; m. Renee Winter, Aug. 31, 1969; 1 dau., Stephanie Ruth. B.S., St. Louis Coll. Pharmacy, 1970. Registered pharmacist, Mo., Ill., Okla., Ariz. Pharmacist Walgreens, St. Louis, 1970-78, pharmacy supr., 1979—; pharmacy adv. com. Mo. Retailers Assn., Jefferson City, 1981—, Grace Hill Neighborhood Health Ctr., St. Louis, 1983—; med. adv. bd. Asthma and Allergy Found. Am., Washington, 1981—. Mem. adv. bd. St. Louis Coll. Health Careers, 1983, 84; notary pub., 1984—. Mem. Am. Pharm. Assn., Mo. Pharm. Assn., St. Louis Pharm. Assn., Okla. Pharm. Assn. Avocations: reading, tennis, golf, music. Office: Walgreen's Saint Louis Dist Office 440 N Hwy 67 Florissant MO 63031

POELKER, JOHN H., consultant; m. Ruth Gambron (dec. 1980); children—John S., Susan M., Kathy M. Student St. Louis U., 1934. With E.I. duPont Co., Nat. Ammonia div., St. Louis, 1930-42; spl. agt. FBI, various locations, 1942-53; assessor City of St. Louis, 1953-57, comptroller, 1957-73, mayor, 1973-77; v.p. J.S. Alberici Constrn. Co., Inc., St. Louis, 1977-79, Regional Commerce & Growth Assn., St. Louis, 1980-81; acting exec. dir. Bi-State Devel. Agy., 1981-82; cons. Regional Commerce & Growth Assn., St. Louis, 1982—. Bd. dirs. Boys Hope, Downtown St. Louis, Deaconess Hosp., St. Patrick's Ctr.; adv. bd. Boatmen's Nat. Bank; active various charitable orgns.; adv. bd. Victims of Crime; bd. dirs. Indsl. Devel. Authority, St. Louis Local Devel. Corp., St. Louis Ambassadors, others. Recipient Leadership award Nat. League Cities, 1977; Disting. Alumni award St. Louis U., 1977; Disting. Religious Leader, Conf. Christians and Jews, 1978; Levee Stone award Downtown St. Louis, 1980; St. Louis award, 1983; Human Relations award Am. Jewish Com., 1984. Address: 400 Mansion House 2402 Saint Louis MO 63102

POEPPEL, ROGER B., ceramist; b. S.I., N.Y., July 6, 1941; s. John and Elsie (Miller) P.; m. Sarah L. Goodwin, Mar. 25, 1967; children—Karen, Alan, Brian. B.Engring. Physics, Cornell U., 1964, Ph.D., 1969. Registered profl. engr., Ill. Ceramist, Argonne Nat. Lab., Ill., 1969—. Contbr. articles to profl. jours. Patentee in field. Mem. Am. Ceramic Soc. Avocation: sailing. Home: 67 Stephanie Ln Glen Ellyn IL 60137 Office: Argonne Nat Lab Bldg 212 Argonne IL 60439

POETKER, JOEL SMITH, educator; b. Jackson, Ohio, Oct. 1, 1934; s. Norman Oakly and Lola Wanda (Smith) P.; student Ohio Wesleyan U., 1952-54; A.B., Muskingum Coll., 1958; M.A., Miami U., Oxford, Ohio, 1961; Ph.D., Ohio State U., 1971; m. Mabel Marie Riegel, Sept. 12, 1954; children—Susan Johnson, Ann Poetker Hardin, Samuel. Tchr., Middletown (Ohio) Sr. High Sch., 1958-61, Bexley (Ohio) High Sch., 1961-68; teaching asso. edn. Ohio State U., Columbus, 1968-70; asso. v.p. academic affairs, prof. history and social studies edn. SUNY-Buffalo, 1970—, chmn. dept., 1972-76. Recreation dir. City of Bexley, 1965-67. Served with U.S. Army, 1954-56. John Hay Humanities fellow Williams Coll., 1963; Gen. Electric Econs. fellow Purdue U., 1964. Mem. Am. Hist. Assn., Nat. Council Social Studies, N.Y. State Council Social Studies, Can. Assn. Social Studies, Phi Delta Kappa, Phi Alpha Theta, Phi Gamma Delta. Presbyterian. Author: The Fourteen Points, 1969; The Monore Doctrine, 1968. Contbr. articles to profl. publs. Home: 98 N High St Jackson OH 45640 Office: 519 Grover Cleveland Hall SUNY Coll Elmwood Ave Buffalo NY 14222

POGUE, THOMAS FRANKLIN, economics educator, consultant; b. Roswell, N.Mex., Dec. 28, 1935; s. Talmadge Franklin and Lela (Cox) P.; m. Colette Marie LaFortune, June 3, 1961; children—Michael Frederick, Robert Franklin. B.S., N.Mex. State U., 1957; M.S., Okla. State U., 1962; Ph.D., Yale U., 1968. Asst. prof. econs. U. Iowa, Iowa City, 1965-69, assoc. prof., 1970-75, prof., 1975—, chmn. dept., 1983-84; vis. prof. Tex. Tech. U., Lubbock, 1975-76. Author: Government and Economic Choice, 1978. Contbr. articles to profl. jours. Author, researcher Gov.'s Tax Study, State of Iowa, Des Moines, 1967, Minn. Tax Study Commn., St. Paul, 1984. Served to capt. USAF, 1957-60. Grantee Nat. Inst. Justice, Washington, 1978-79, Consumers Research Group, Washington, 1970, HUD, 1970. Mem. Am. Econ. Assn., Nat. Tax Assn. Democrat. Presbyterian. Avocations: tennis; skiing. Home: 3 Wellesley Way Iowa City IA 52240 Office: Dept Econs U Iowa Phillips Hall Iowa City IA 52242

POGUE, WILLIAM ALEXANDER, steel products company executive; b. Birmingham, Ala., 1927. B.S., U.S. Mil. Acad., 1950; postgrad. So. Meth. U. With Chgo. Bridge and Iron Co., Oak Brook, Ill., 1954—, various depts. engring., mfg. and field constrn., 1954-56, sales N.Y. sales office, 1957, sales mgr., 1964, mgr. Houston ops., 1968, v.p. and mgr. so. area ops., 1971, sr. v.p. and mgr. ops., 1976, exec. v.p. and dir., 1979, sr. v.p. CBI Industries Inc., 1979, pres., 1981—, chmn. bd. and chief exec. officer, dir., 1982—; dir. No. Trust Co., Nalco Chem. Co. Served to capt. U.S. Army, 1943-54. Office: CBI Industries Inc 800 Jorie Blvd Oak Brook IL 60521*

POHL, KENNETH ROY, electronics company executive; b. Beloit, Wis., Nov. 11, 1941; s. Walter John and Ruth Margret (Wieck) P. Student Wis. State Coll., Whitewater, 1959-60, Milton Coll., 1963-66; A.A. in Liberal Arts. With Beloit Corp., 1960-63; mgr. trainee Faimly Fin. Corp., 1966; with Chrysler Corp., 1966-67; owner, operator bowling alley and lounge, 1967-68; with Automatic Electric Co., Genoa, Ill., 1968-69; buyer Fox Corp., Janesville, Wis., 1969-70; materials mgr. Clinton Electronic Corp., Loves Park, Ill., 1970-72, import-export mgr., supr. sales adminstrn., 1972-80, import-export mgr., corp. gen. traffic mgr., 1980—, distbn. mgr., 1981—; pres., chief exec. officer Tan Spa of Northgate Plaza Ltd., Beloit; dir. Air-Pack Enterprises Inc., Schaumburg, Ill. cons. internat. transp.; mem. Midwest Shippers Adv. Fed. Maritime Commn. Founder, exec. dir. Tri-State All Star Bowling Assn.; adv. Ladies Profl. Tournament Bowlers. Mem. Am. Prodn. and Inventory Control Soc., Ill. State C. of C. (internat. com. for trade and investments). Lutheran. Clubs: Lions, Rock River Valley Traffic; World Trade (charter mem.) (Northern, Ill.). Home: 134 Carry Dr PO Box L Clinton WI Office: 6701 Clinton Rd Box 2277 Loves Park IL 61131

POHLAD, CARL R., bottling company executive. Chmn., dir. MEI Corp., Mpls. Office: MEI Corp 90 South 6th St Minneapolis MN 55402*

POINDEXTER, MARK CAREY, educational broadcasting administrator, educator; b. St. Charles, Mo., Dec. 31, 1951; s. Russell L. and Jeanne Marie (Klinghammer) P.; 1 child, Claire Estelle. B.A., Lindenwood Coll., 1973; M.A., Central Mich. U., 1980; postgrad. U. Minn., 1983—. Mng. editor Lexington Advertiser-News, Mo., 1974-75; news dir. KCUR-FM, Kansas City, Mo., 1975-79; dir. broadcasting N.D. State U. KDSU-FM, Fargo, 1980—, instr. mass communication, 1980—. Producer radio documentaries, including Migrant Workers (RFK Jour. award 1980). Recipient award for Best Radio Documentary N.D. AP Broadcasters Assn., 1982, 1st place awards Mo. Broadcasters Assn., 1977-80. Mem. N.D. Pub. Radio Assn. (pres. 1982-83), Nat. Pub. Radio (rep.). Avocation: study of linguistics and anthropology. Office: ND State U Ceres Hall Fargo ND 58105

POINSETTE, DONALD EUGENE, business executive, value management consultant; b. Fort Wayne, Ind., Aug. 17, 1914; s. Eugene Joseph and Julia Anna (Wyss) P.; student Purdue U., 1934, Ind. U., 1935-37, 64; m. Anne Katherine Farrell, Apr. 15, 1939; children—Donald J., Eugene J., Leo J., Sharon Poinsette Smith, Irene Poinsette Snyder, Cynthia Poinsette West, Maryanne Poinsette Stohler, Philip J. With Gen. Electric Corp., RCA, Stewart Warner Corp., 1937-39; metall. research and field sales cons. P.R. Mallory Corp., 1939-49; dist. sales mgr. Derringer Metall. Corp., Chgo., 1949-50; plant engr. Cornell-Dubilier Electric Corp., Indpls., 1950-53; with Jenn-Air Corp., Indpls., 1953-74, purchasing dir., 1953-71, mgr. value engring. and quality control, 1969-74; bus. mgmt. cons. Mays and Assos., Indpls., 1974-76; Named to U.S. Finder's List, Nat. Engrs. Register, 1956. Pres., Marian Coll. Parents Club, Indpls., 1969-70; com. mem. Boy Scouts Am. Nat trustee Xavier U., 1972-73, Dad's Club, Cin. Mem. Nat. Assn. Purchasing Mgmt., Indpls. Purchasing Mgmt. Assn., Soc. Am. Value Engrs. (certified value specialist; sec.-treas. Central Ind. chpt. 1972-73), Soc. Ret. Execs. Indpls., Ind. U., Purdue U. alumni assns., Columbian (pres. 1972-73), Triad choral groups, Internat. Platform Assn., Tau Kappa Epsilon. Club: K.C. (4 deg.). Home: 5760 Susan Dr E Indianapolis IN 46250

POIRIER, JOHN ANTHONY, physics educator, researcher, consultant; b. Lewistown, Mont., May 15, 1932; s. Anton A. and Evelyn (Shannon) P.; m. M. Jule Griffin, Jan. 4, 1976; children—Michael, Steven, Gregory, Maureen, Laine. B.S., Notre Dame U., 1954; M.S., Stanford U., 1956, Ph.D., 1959. Lectr. U. Calif.-Berkeley, 1959-63; staff physicist Lawrence Berkeley Lab., Berkeley, 1959-63; NSF fellow European Orgn. Nuclear Research, Geneva, 1963-64; assoc. prof. physics Notre Dame U., Ind., 1964-69, prof., 1969—; program assoc. NSF, 1977-78. Contbr. articles to profl. jours. Grantee NSF. Mem. Am. Phys. Soc. (mem. div. particles and fields), Phi Beta Kappa, Sigma Xi. Office: Physics Dept U Notre Dame Notre Dame IN 46556

POISNER, ALAN MARK, pharmacologist; b. Kansas City, Mo., Oct. 15, 1934; s. Benjamin and Helen Sylvia (Ducov) P.; m. Roselle Burstein, July 15, 1962; children—David, Jonathan. B.S., Calif. Inst. Tech., 1956; M.D., U. Kans., 1960. Intern, U. Ill. Research Hosp., Chgo., 1960-61; USPHS postdoctoral fellow Albert Einstein Coll. Medicine, N.Y.C., 1961-64, asst. prof., 1964-68; assoc. prof. pharmacology U. Kans., Kansas City, 1968-73, prof., 1973—. Editor: The Secretory Process, 1983. Mem. Am. Soc. Pharmacology, Endocrine Soc. Avocation: tennis. Home: 8216 Beverly St Prairie Village KS 66208 Office: U Kans Med Ctr 39th and Rainbow Kansas City KS 66103

POKORNY, DANIEL HARRY, theology educator, sign language consultant; b. N.Y.C., Apr. 18, 1937; s. Harry and Anna (Kocsis) P.; m. Patricia Louise Florine, Apr. 25, 1964; children—James, Philip, David, Elizabeth. B.A., Concordia Sem., St. Louis, 1958, M.Div., 1961; M.S.W., Ind. U.-Indpls., 1967. Ordained to ministry Luthran Ch., 1961. Pastor Peace Luth. Ch., Indpls., 1961-67, Christ Luth. Ch., Washington, 1967-79; Luth. chaplain Galludet Coll., Washington, 1967-69; prof. practical theology Concordia Sem., St. Louis, 1979—, chmn. dept. practical theology, 1983-85, dir. continuing edn., 1985—; dir. Isaiah 29 Ctr., Washington, 1973-79. Editor: My Eyes Are My Ears, 1973; The Word In Signs and Wonders, 1976. Named Knight of Flying Fingers, Nat. Assn. of Deaf, 1975; recipient Algernon Sydney Sullivan award N.Y. So. Soc., 1974. Mem. Registry of Interpreters for Deaf (pres. St. Louis chpt. 1984—), Nat. Assn. of Social Workers. Lodge: Rotary (music chmn. 1983, 84). Office: Concordia Sem 801 DeMun Ave Saint Louis MO 63105

POLAKOSKI, KENNETH LEO, biochemist, andrologist; b. Fond du Lac, Wisc., Sept. 6, 1944; s. Clarence Sylvester and Amy (Dornstreich) P.; m. Bonita Sipple, Aug. 31, 1968 (div. Mar. 1977). B.S., U. Wis., 1966; M.S., U. Ga., 1971, Ph.D., 1972. Research assoc. U. Ga., Athens, 1972-73; research asst. prof. Washington U., St. Louis, 1973-77, from asst. prof. to assoc. prof. reproductive biology, 1977-84, prof., 1984—. Editor: Goals of Male Reproductive Biology, 1981. Contbr. articles to profl. jours. Recipient Research Devel. award NIH, 1979. Mem. Sos. Gynecol. Investigation, AAUP. Home: 509 Midvale Ave Saint Louis MO 63130 Office: Dept Ob-Gyn 4911 Barnes Hosp Saint Louis MO 63110

POLAREK, LOUISE, nurse; b. Chgo., July 19, 1927; d. Ernest William and Jonnie May (Hall) Bremer; m. Daniel Richard Hopkins, June 9, 1945 (div. 1965); children—Patricia Lynn, Daniel Mark; m. Robert Stanley Polarek, Aug. 6, 1966. Student portrait coloring, Chgo. Sch. Photography, 1946; student Selan's Beauty Sch., Chgo., 1971; diploma Chgo. Bd. Edn., 1981; diploma in Nursing, Triton Coll., 1981. Med. receptionist Rush Presbyn. St. Lukes Hosp., Chgo., 1964-66; med. sec. K.D. Kittleson, Chgo., 1971-73, Frederick J. Szymanski, Chgo., 1966-70, 1973-79; staff nurse MacNeal Meml. Hosp., Berwyn, Ill., 1981-82; charge nurse Pine Manor Nursing Center, Palos Hills, 1982-85; nurse West Side VA Hosp., Chgo., 1985—. Recipient Scholastic Honor award Chgo. Bd. Edn., 1981. Home: 3629 S Marshfield Ave Chicago IL 60609

POLASCIK, MARY ANN, ophthalmologist; b. Elkhorn, W.Va., Dec. 28, 1940; d. Michael and Elizabeth (Halko) P.; B.A., Rutgers U., 1967; M.D., Pritzker Sch. Medicine, 1971; m. Joseph Elie, Oct. 2, 1973; 1 dau., Laura Elizabeth Polascik. Jr. pharmacolgist Ciba Pharm. Co., Summit, N.J., 1961-67; intern Billings Hosp., Chgo., 1971-72; resident in ophthalmology U. Chgo. Hosp., 1972-75; practice medicine specializing in ophthalmology, Dixon, Ill., 1975—; pres. McNichols Clinic, Ltd.; cons. ophthalmology, Dixon Devel. Center; mem. staff Katherine Shaw Bethea Hosp., Dixon; cons. Dixon Devel. Center Hosp. Bd. dirs. Sinissippi Mental Health Center, 1975-81. Mem. AMA, Ill. State Med. Soc., Ill., Am. assns. ophthalmology, Am. Assn. Physicians and Surgeons, AAUW, Alpha Sigma Lambda. Roman Catholic. Clubs: Dixon Country, Galena Territory. Office: 120 S Hennepin Ave Dixon IL 61021

POLCZ, GYORGY GYULA, physician; b. Budapest, Hungary, June 16, 1943; came to U.S., 1963, naturalized, 1973; s. Gyula and Livia (Frisch) P.; m. Donna Marie Wetmore, July 6, 1974; children—Stephen, Susan, Rebecca. B.S., Ball State U., 1967, M.D., Ind. U., 1970. Intern, Ball Meml. Hosp., Muncie, Ind., 1970-71; v.p. Emergency Physicians Delaware County, Muncie, Ind., 1971—. Mem. Delaware-Blackford Med. Soc., Ind. State Med. Assn., Am. Radio Relay League, Acad. Model Aeronautics. Republican. Lutheran. Avocations: amateur radio; computers; electronics; model aviation. Home: 2800 W Berwyn Rd Muncie IN 47304 Office: 2809 Godman Ave Suite 7 Muncie IN 47304

POLETTE, PAUL LEROY, publishing company executive; b. Herculaneum, Mo., Jan. 15, 1928; s. Ferdinand and Fanny Marie (Justin) P.; m. Nancy Jane McCaleb, Dec. 23, 1950; children—Paula Jane, Keith Paul, Marsha Ellen. B.S. in Indsl. Mgmt., Washington U., St. Louis, 1969; M.B.A. in Mgmt., St. Louis U., 1974. Supr. McDonnell-Douglas Corp., St. Louis, 1952-82; pres. Book Lures, Inc., O'Fallon, Mo., 1979—; instr. bus. St. Mary's Coll., O'Fallon, 1970—. Photographer: Exploring Science Fiction, 1983, Supernatural, 1983, others. Mem. O'Fallon Planning Zoning Subcom., 1975, O'Fallon Bicentennial Com., 1976, St. Charles County Com. for Jr. Coll. Dist., 1984. Served as sgt. USAF, 1948-52. Mem. St. Charles City C. of C. Republican. Roman Catholic. Avocations: fishing, photography, travel.

POLIN, DONALD, animal science educator; b. Arlington, Mass., Dec. 7, 1925; s. Ralph and Bessie (Dickerman) P.; m. Ruth Meyer, Mar. 28, 1954; children—Barbara, Diane, Richard. B.S., U.S. Maritime Acad., 1950; B.S., Rutgers U., 1951, Ph.D., 1955. Research fellow Merck Inst. Therapeutic Research, Rahway, N.J., 1955-67; units leader Norwich Pharm. Co., N.Y., 1967-69; prof. dept. animal sci. Mich. State U., East Lansing, 1969—; cons. Am. Soybean Inst., 1982, Corn Products Internat., 1984-85, NIH, 1984. Contbr. articles to profl. jours. Judge U.S. Figure Skating Assn., 1979—. Travel grantee Am. Soybean Assn., 1982. Mem. Am. Inst. Nutrition, Soc. Exptl. Biology, Soc. Toxicology, Poultry Sci. Assn. (feed mfg. research award 1984), World's Poultry Sci. Assn. Jewish. Club: Skating (Lansing, Mich.) (v.p., bd. dirs. 1975-83). Avocations: music composition, ice dancing, farming, piano. Office: 132 ANH Dept Animal Sci Mich State U East Lansing MI 48824

POLITES, KONSTANTINE ELIAS, financial services executive, contract negotiator; b. Chgo., Sept. 20, 1955; s. Elias K. and Anastasia E. (Kollias) P. Grad. in internat. relations Northwestern U., 1974; postgrad. DePaul U. Law Sch. Regional mgr. Bus. and Profl. Cons., Skokie, Ill., 1978-79; cons. Petrolex Corp., Vaduz, Leichtenstein, 1979-80; cons. Banking Corp. Am., Washington, 1980-81, internat. bus. mgr., Washington, 1981-83, sr. v.p., 1983—, dir., 1981—; dir. Global Investment Assocs., Chgo., Eagle Petroleum, Athens, Greece, Premier Internat., Indpls. Exec. v.p. United Hellenic Voters Am., Chgo., 1981; mem. governing bd. Hellenic Am. High Sch., Chgo., 1984, Neon Kyma Messenias, Chgo., 1983; mem. AHIPAC, Washington, 1982. Recipient Disting. Service award United Hellenic Voters Am., 1982; Sports award Republic of China, 1981; del. spokesman U.S. Jr. Olympic B-Ball tour to USSR, 1979, Eastern Europe, 1982. Mem. Am. Arbitration Assn. (arbitrator), Ill. C. of C. Greek Orthodox. Home: 3366 Lake Knoll Dr Northbrook IL 60062 Office: Banking Corp Am 6200 N Hiawatha Suite 701 Chicago IL 60646

POLIVKA, CAROLYN JEAN, printing company executive, accountant; b. Chgo., Apr. 4, 1953; d. Edward Paul and Jean Louise (Pelton) P. A.A., Wright City Coll., Chgo., 1972; cert. in acctg. Oakton Community Coll., Des Plaines, Ill., 1982; postgrad. Roosevelt U., Chgo., 1983—. Head bookkeeper, supr. proof and transit First State Bank and Trust Co. of Park Ridge, Ill., 1972-76; fin. analyst-tech. Square D Co., Palatine, Ill., 1976—; treas. Advance Printing Service, Inc., Chgo., 1982—, also dir. Office: 1415 Roselle St Palatine IL 60067 also 5354 Northwest Hwy Chicago IL 60630

POLK, FRANKLIN ADELBERT, lawyer; b. Cleve., Apr. 26, 1911; m. Julia Gabriel, June 20, 1939; children—Franklin G., Loretta Polk Gainor. A.B. cum laude, John Carroll U., 1935; J.D., Cleve. State U., 1939. Bar: Ohio 1940. Sole practice, Cleve., 1940—. Officer Cleve. Bd. Edn., 1944-52; mem. Republican exec. com; Rep. candidate for mayor of Cleve., 1949; founder Broadway-55th Mchts. Assn., 1933, Broadway Devel. Corp., 1972; founder, trustee St. Michael's Sch. Endowment Trust Fund, 1980-84, lay minister, 1970-84. Recipient Pres.'s award Ripon Club, 1976; Herbert Harley award Am. Judicature Soc., 1984; Alumnus of Yr. award Cleve. State U., 1985. Fellow Ohio State Bar Found., Am. Judicature Soc., Am. Bar Found., ABA 2d Century Fund, Am. Bar Endowment, Roscoe Pound Found.; mem. Ohio State Bar Assn. (co-chmn. ann. meeting 1976, Assn. medal 1983, ho. of dels.), 6th Jud. ABA, Conf. (life mem.) Nat. Assn. Criminal Def. Lawyers (award of Merit 1978), Fed. Bar Assn. Cleve., Cuyahoga County Bar Found (pres. 1977-84), Cleve. Acad. Trial Lawyers (founder 1958, pres. 1975), Cuyahoga County Bar Assn. (pres. 1975), (pres. 1948), Ohio Trial Lawyers Assn., Assn. Trial Lawyers Am., Cleve. State U. Alumni Senate (dean 1951), Cleve. State Law Sch. Alumni Assn. (pres. 1947), John Carroll U. Nat. Alumni Assn. (pres. 1955, medal 1975). Lodge: K.C. (Cath. Man of Yr. award 1964, Citizen of Yr. award 1977). Home: 6504 Lafayette Blvd Independence OH 44131 Office: 5725 Broadway Cleveland OH 44127

POLK, JAMES ALEXANDER, veterans service officer; b. St. Louis, July 1, 1946; s. Tyndle Amos Polk and Juanita Paulina (Spray) Polk Worth; m. Phyllis Mary DeGeare, Mar. 6, 1971; children—Michelle R., Jamie L. B.A. in English and History, Mo. Baptist Coll., 1974. Vets. service officer Mo. Div. Vets. Affairs, Jefferson City, 1976—. Served with USN, 1967-71, Vietnam, Mem. Jefferson County Intervets (pres. 1983—), VFW (post 3777 commr. 1981-82, various state, dist. offices 1982—). Democrat. Baptist. Home: 1101 N Taylor Ave Crystal City MO 63019 Office: Mo Div Vets Affairs P O Drawer 147 Jefferson City MO 65102-0147

POLL, HEINZ, choreographer, artistic dir.; b. Oberhausen, West Germany, Mar. 18, 1926; s. Heinrich and Anna Margareta (Winkels) P.; came to U.S., 1965, naturalized, 1975. Dancer with Gottinge Mcpl. Theatre, 1946-48, Deutsches Theatre Konstanz, 1948-49, East Berlin State Opera, 1949-50, Nat. Ballet of Chile, 1951-62, Ballet d la Jeunesse Musicales de France, 1963-64; guest appearances with Nat. Ballet Chile, 1964, Am. Dance Festival, 1965; choreographer works for Nat. Ballet Chile, Paris Festival Ballet, Ballet de la Jeuness Musicales de France, Nat. Ballet Can., Pa. Ballet, Ohio Ballet co-founder, dir. The Dance Inst., U. Akron, 1967-77; founder, artistic dir., choreographer Ohio Ballet, Akron, 1968—; tchr. Chilean Instituto de Extension Musical, 1951-61, N.Y. Nat. Acad., 1965-66. Nat. Endowment for the Arts grantee, 1974-75; recipient Ohio Dance award, 1983. Office: 354 E Market Akron OH 44325

POLLACK, RHODA-GALE, theatre educator, director; b. Pitts., Dec. 30, 1937; d. Jacob Allen and Jessie (Sapolaky) Klein; m. Sanford S. Pollack, Dec. 25, 1957; 1 child, Jessica. B.F.A. in Drama, Carnegie Mellon U., 1958; M.A. in Drama, San Francisco State U., 1966; Ph.D. in Drama, Stanford U., 1971. Producer, dir. Ariz. Playmakers, Phoenix, 1959-61; freelance dir., 1959—; costume designer, 1960—; costumer U. Calif.-Berkeley, 1963-64; lectr. Mills Coll., Oakland, Calif., 1965-76; assoc. prof. theatre U. Wis.-Parkside, Kenosha, 1976—, chmn. fine arts div., 1980—; mem. adv. council Sta. WGTD-FM, Kenosha, 1980-84; mem. Racine Arts Council, 1983—; mem. dance and theatre panel Wis. Arts Bd., Madison, 1984. Dir. 30 prodns., costume designer 45 prodns. Contbr. articles to profl. jours. Active Heritage Bank Fin. Council, Racine, 1984—. Mem. Am. Theatre Assn., Wis. Theatre Assn., Internat. Council Fine Arts Deans. Avocations: flower gardening; cooking; moviegoing. Office: Fine Arts Div U Wis-Parkside Box 2000 Kenosha WI 53141

POLLAK, VICTOR EUGENE, physician, researcher; b. Johannesburg, S. Africa, Sept. 7, 1926; came to U.S., 1954, naturalized, 1962; s. Walter and Janie (London) P.; m. Natalie Ann Hall, July 7, 1956; children—Stephen, Elizabeth, Julian, Madeleine. B.A., U. Witwatersrand, S. Africa, 1944, M.B., B.Ch., 1950. From instr. to prof. medicine U. Ill., Chgo., 1956-70; dir. renal disease Michael Reese Hosp., Chgo., 1965-72; prof. medicine U. Chgo., 1970-72; prof. medicine, dir. nephrology U. Cin., 1973—; dir. Dialysis Clinic, Cin., 1977—; cons. NIH, 1964-68, 84—. Contbr. chpts. to books, articles to profl. jours. Recipient Established Investigator award Am. Heart Assn., 1959-64; Research Career Devel. award NIH, 1964-65. Fellow ACP, Royal Coll. Physicians (Scotland); mem. Am. Soc. Clin. Investigation, Central Soc. Clin. Research. Home: 400 Rawson Woods Ln Cincinnati OH 45220 Office: U Cin Med Ctr Div Nephrology 5363 MSB Cincinnati OH 45267

POLLARD, CHARLES WILLIAM, See *Who's Who in America*, 43rd edition.

POLLITT, GERTRUDE STEIN, clin. social worker, psychotherapist; b. Vienna, Austria; d. Julius and Sidoni (Brauch) Stein; came to U.S., 1949, naturalized, 1951; B.A., Roosevelt U., 1954; M.A., U. Chgo., 1956; certificate Chgo. Inst. Psychoanalysis, 1963; m. Erwin P. Pollitt, Jan. 13, 1951. Resident social worker Anna Freud, Essex, Eng., 1944-45; dep. dir. UN, U.S. Zone, Germany, 1945-48; psychiat. social worker Jewish Children's Bur., Chgo., 1955-63; pvt. practice as psychiat. and clin. social worker, Glencoe, Ill., 1961—; lecturer profl. devel. programs Chgo. Inst. for Psychoanalysis and U. Chgo., 1982; mem. faculty profl. devel. program U. Chgo. Sch. Social Service Adminstrn., 1984; condr. seminars; cons. Winnetka Community Nursery Sch., 1962-63, North Shore Congregation Nursery Sch., 1966-69, Oakwood Home for Aged, 1980. Bd. dirs. Glencoe Youth Service, Winnetka Orgn. for Rehab. and Tng. (Ill.); pres.-elect North Suburban Service Council, 1985-86. Fellow Am. Orthopsychiat. Assn., Ill. Soc. Clin. Social Work (dir., chmn. practice standards); mem. Nat. Registry Health Care Providers in Clin. Social Work, Acad. Certified Social Workers, Nat. Assn. Social Workers (chmn. pvt. practice com. 1967-70), Lic. Clin. Social Workers Calif., Menninger Found., Child Care Assn. Ill. Author articles in field. Home: 481 Oakdale Ave Glencoe IL 60022

POLLOCK, DAVIS ALLEN, insurance company executive; b. Douds, Iowa, Aug. 31, 1942; s. Davis Edwin and Bertha Dorothy (Barker) P.; B.S., Drake U., 1964; m. Marcia Tedrow, Jan. 1, 1965; children—Eric, Kirsten. With Central Life Ins., Des Moines, 1964—, v.p. corp. planning, 1979-82, sr. v.p.-group, 1982—. Fellow Soc. Actuaries; mem. Am. Acad. Actuaries, Des Moines Actuaries Club, Kappa Mu Epsilon, Omicron Delta Kappa. Republican. Methodist. Club: Mason. Office: 611 5th Ave Des Moines IA 50309

POLLS, IRWIN, aquatic biologist, water quality specialist; b. Thunder Bay, Ont., Can., Oct. 30, 1944; came to U.S., 1955, naturalized, 1963; s. Joseph and Fanny (Segal) P.; B.S., U. Ill., 1967; M.S. Oreg. State U., 1970; m. Jill Diane Lawrence, Apr. 11, 1981; 1 dau., Elissa Sara. Aquatic biologist research and devel. dept. Met. San. Dist. of Greater Chgo., 1971—. Served with U.S. Army, 1970-71. Decorated Bronze Star, Air medal. Mem. Internat. Assn. Water Pollution Research, Societas Internationalis Limnologiae, Am. Water Resources Assn., Water Pollution Control Fed., N.Am. Benthological Soc., Sigma Xi. Jewish. Contbr. articles on water quality to profl. jours. Office: 550 S Meacham Rd Schaumburg IL 60193

POLYDORIS, STEVEN NICHOLAS, communications engineer; b. Evanston, Ill., Sept. 12, 1954; s. Nicholas George and Gloria Anne (Lucas) P.; student Drake U., 1972-73; B.S.I.E., Northwestern U., 1983. With Wilder Engring. Co., 1978; pres. ENM Co., Chgo., 1979-83; pres. GN Communications, Ltd., Evanston, Ill., 1983—. Home: 128 16th St Wilmette IL 60092 Office: 1723 Howard St Evanston IL 60202

POMERANTZ, LOUIS, art conservator, educator; b. Bklyn., Sept. 26, 1919; s. Jacob and Gussie (Watnick) P.; m. Elisabeth Catherine Picard; children—Carrie Johanna Pomerantz Luke, Lonnie Roberta Pomerantz Schick. Student Art Students League, N.Y.C., 1938-40; student Academie Julian, Paris, 1949-50, Rijksmuseum, Amsterdam, Netherlands, 1950-51, Worcester Art Mus., Mass. and Clark U., 1951, Bklyn. Mus. and Columbia U., 1952-54, Central Lab. Belgium Mus., Brussels, 1956, Institut Royal du Patrimoine Artistique, Brussels, 1963. Ind. conservator, N.Y.C., 1952-56; part-time instr. and lab. asst. Bklyn. Mus., 1954-56; conservator dept. paintings and sculpture Art Inst. Chgo., 1956-61; ind. conservator, Spring Grove, Ill., 1961—; cons. Milw. Art Ctr., 1958—, Nat. Gallery Can., 1961, George F. Harding Mus., Chgo., 1965-68, UN Devel. Program in Israel/Israel Mus., Jerusalem, 1968; vol. Florence flood disaster, 1966; vis. cons. Can. Conservation Inst., Ottawa, 1975, Winterthur Mus./U. Del., 1977, Detroit Inst. Arts, 1977, Cooperstown Grad. Programs in Conservation, N.Y., 1977, Minn. Hist. Soc., 1976, Intermus. Conservation Assn., Oberlin, Ohio, 1977, Grad Sch. Fine Art, Rosary Coll., Florence, Italy, 1979; Field Mus. conservator Gamelan Restoration Project, 1976-77, Am. N.W. Coast Indian Totem Poles Project, 1978-80; founder Pomerantz Inst. for Advancement of Fine Arts Conservation, 1982; lectr. Author: Is Your Contemporary Painting More Temporary Than You Think?, 1962; (catalogue) Know What You See - The Examination of Paintings by Photo-Optical Techniques, 1970; also articles. Assoc. editor Am. Inst. Conservation Jour., 1983—. Bd. dirs. Urban Gateways, Chgo., 1965-70, Campbell Ctr. Hist. Preservation Studies, Mt. Carroll, Ill., 1983—; pres. Evanston Art Commn., Ill., 1975. Served with U.S. Army, 1941-45; NATOUSA, ETO. Fellow Internat. Inst. Conservation of Hist. and Artistic Works, Am. Inst. Conservation (past chmn. membership com., past chmn. ednl. affairs com., bd. dirs. 1979-82, designated hon. mem. 1985); mem. IIC-Am. Group (past pres.), Am. Assn. Mus., Internat. Com. Mus., Midwest Mus. Conf., U.K. Inst. Conservation of Hist. and Artistic Works, Mid-West Regional Conservation Guild, Chgo. Area Conservation Group (founding). Home: 6300 Johnsburg-Wilmot Rd Spring Grove IL 60081

POMERANZ, JOHN EDWARD, real estate systems developer; b. N.Y.C., March 25, 1944; s. Abner J. and V. S. (Weckstein) P.; m. K. Levi, Sept. 7, 1966 (div. 1982); children—Lisa Ellen, Benjamin Abner; m. Renee D. Stein, Nov. 23, 1984. A.B., U. Rochester, 1965; S.M., U. Chgo., 1972, Ph.D., 1972. prof. Purdue U., 1971-74; cons. A.T. Kearney, Chgo., 1974-78, Booz-Allen, Chgo., 1978-81; v.p. JMB Realty Corp., Chgo., 1981—; lectr. U. Chgo., 1976—. Assoc. editor Mgmt. Sci., 1976—. Contbr. articles to profl. jours., 1970-75. Bd. dirs. Urban Gateways, Chgo., 1976—. Mem. IEEE, Assn. Computing Machinery. Jewish. Home: 3270 Lake Shore Dr Chicago IL 60657 Office: JMB Realty Corp 875 Michigan Ave Chicago IL 60611

POMEROY, ELWAINE F(RANKLIN), lawyer; b. Topeka, June 4, 1933; s. Charles Franklin and Ada Frances (Owen) P.; A.B., Washburn U., 1955, J.D., 1957; m. Joanne Carolyn Bunge, Sept. 30, 1950; children—Janella Ruth, Duane Franklin, Carl Fredrick. Admitted to Kans. bar, 1957, since practiced in Topeka; sr. partner Pomeroy and Pomeroy, 1964—; pres. Topeka Escrow Service, Inc. Mem. Kans. State Senate, 1969-84; Republican precinct committeeman, 1961-80; mem. Kans. Jud. Council, 1977-84; chmn. Kans. Parole Bd., 1984—; commr. Nat. Conf. Commrs. on Uniform State Laws, 1979—. Mem. Am., Kans., Topeka bar assns. Mason, Eagle. Author: (with others) Principles of Accounting, 1957. Home: 1619 Jewell St Topeka KS 66604 Office: 1415 Topeka Ave Topeka KS 66612

POMEROY, G. MARK, electronics company official; b. Cin., Aug. 10, 1957; s. George W. and Geneva R. (Swafford) P.; m. Karen Louise Boettcher, June 19, 1982. B.M.E., Ga. Inst. Tech., 1980; M.S. in Mgmt., MIT, 1982. Student engr. Cin. Gas & Electric Co., 1975-77; utility relief operator Gen. Motors Corp., Atlanta, 1977-79; summer mgr. Procter & Gamble Co., Cin., 1980; mgmt. devel. trainee Gen. Electric Co., Arkansas City, Kans., 1982-84, program mgr., 1984—. Bd. dirs. Cherokee Strip Mus., Arkansas City, 1984—. Recipient Eagle Scout award Boy Scouts Am., 1974. Mem. Phi Eta Sigma, Tau Beta Pi, Pi Tau Sigma, Soc. Automotive Engrs. (chpt. pres. 1979-80), Grad. Mgmt. Soc. (officer 1980-82). Republican. Lodges: Eagles, Jaycees (treas. 1983-84, v.p. 1984-85, pres. 1985-86). Avocations: sports; woodworking; golf. Office: PO Box 797 Arkansas City KS 67005

POMINVILLE, JAMES ERNEST, automotive company executive; b. Detroit, Dec. 30, 1942; s. Ernest T. and Estelle M. (Badgley) P.; m. Antoinette T. Dumas, June 17, 1967; children—Michele, Jennifer. B.B.A., Pacific Western U., 1978. Supr. Detroit Diesel Allison div. Gen. Motors Corp., 1964-66, gen. supr., 1966-72, personnel supr., 1972-79, mgr. employment, 1979-85, dir. divisional employee devel., 1985—. Served with AUS, 1960-63. Mem. Am. Soc. Tng. and Devel., Vocat. Clubs Am. (state advisor 1980-85). Office: Detroit Diesel Allison div Gen Motors Corp Dept C-10 13400 W Outer Dr Detroit MI 48239-4001

PONDER, MARIAN RUTH, educator; b. Waterloo, Iowa, July 12, 1932; d. Lee Roland and Leone Hyacinth (Holdiman) Rigdon; B.A. (Purple and Gold math. scholar), U. No. Iowa, 1952; M.S.E., Drake U., 1960; postgrad. U. Wis., 1961-62, San Diego State U., 1980-81, Carleton Coll., 1980-81, U. No. Ia., 1961-66, Drake U., 1971-75; m. Joseph Glen Ponder, June 28, 1953; children—Dwight Lee, David Glen, Dean Joseph. Tchr. math., sci. Anamosa, Iowa, 1952-53, Monroe, Iowa, 1953-56, Newton, Iowa, 1956-64, 66—, head dept. math. Newton Schs., 1978—. Ch. treas. Community Heights Alliance Ch., 1980—, Sunday sch. secretariat, 1966-82. Maytag scholar, 1960; Maytag Corp. grantee, 1962; Delta Kappa Gamma scholar, 1960, 81. Mem. Nat. Council Tchrs. Math., NEA, Iowa Edn. Assn., Newton Community Edn. Assn., Iowa Council Tchrs. Math., Jasper County Hist. Soc., Delta Kappa Gamma (state treas. 1978—), Kappa Mu Epsilon, Kappa Delta Pi, Lambda Delta Lambda. Republican. Mem. Christian and Missionary Alliance Ch. Home: 620 E 17 St N Newton IA 50208 Office: E 4th St S Newton IA 50208

PONELEIT, SANDRA ANN, planning and consulting firm executive, consultant; b. Bridgeport, Conn., Nov, 29, 1953; d. Albert Eugene Poneleit and Ann Leontine (Winquist) Sayer. B.S. cum laude, Ohio State U., 1978; postgrad. U. Alta., 1978, Mich. State U., 1979-84. Research technician Ohio State U. Mus., Columbus, 1973-77; planning cons. Alta. Provincial Parks, Edmonton, Can., 1979; ptnr., mng. dir. Interpretive Assocs., Lansing, Mich., 1979-84, pres., planning and tng. dir., 1984—; asst. curator edn. and interpretation Mich. State U. Mus., East Lansing, 1980-84, humanist mus. edn. specialist East Lansing Pub. Schs., 1982-84; co-sponsor Mgmt. Encounters, TVA/Land Between the Lakes, Golden Pond, Ky., 1984-85; conf. co-dir. Mich. State U., 1980-83. Co-author tng. manual, systems plan, articles. Trustee, R.E. Olds Mus., Lansing, 1984-85, planning com., 1983-85, edn. and research com., 1984-85, co-chmn. exhibits com., 1985. Fellow in mus. edn. Kellogg Found./-Field Mus. Natural History Chgo., 1982; named Mich. State U. Woman Achiever Dept. Human Relations, 1982. Mem. Assn. Interpretive Naturalists (co-editor AINews 1982-85), Interpretation Canada, Western Interpreters Assn., Am. Assn. Zool. Parks and Aquariums, Am. Assn. Mus., Lansing Regional C. of C., Alpha Zeta, Gamma Sigma Delta. Republican. Lutheran. Clubs: Zonta, Ambassadors. Avocations: Weaving; photography; reading; stamp collecting; shell collecting. Home: 429 N Waverly Rd 213 Lansing MI 48917 Office: Interpretive Assocs PO Box 6095 East Lansing MI 48823-6095

PONKA, LAWRENCE JOHN, manufacturing analyst; b. Detroit, Sept. 1, 1949; s. Maximillian John and Leona May (Knobloch) P. A.A., Macomb County Community Coll., 1974; B.S. in Indsl. Mgmt., Lawrence Inst. Tech., 1978; M.A. in Indsl. Mgmt., Central Mich. U., 1983. Engr.'s asst. Army Tank Automotive Command, 1967-68; with Sperry & Hutchinson Co., Southfield, Mich., 1973, Chrysler Corp., Detroit, 1973; with Gen. Motors Corp., Warren, Mich., 1973-82, engring. systems coordinator engring. staff, 1976-82, current product engring. until 1982; mfg. engr. Buick-Oldsmobile-Cadillac Group, Gen. Motors Assembly Div.-Orion Pontiac, Mich., 1982-84, sr. analyst advanced vehicle engring. Chevrolet-Pontiac-Can. group Engring. Ctr., Warren, 1985—. Served with USAF, 1968-72; Vietnam. Decorated Air Force Commendation medal. Mem. Soc. Automotive Engrs., Engring. Soc. Detroit, Soc. Automotive Weight Engrs., Am. Legion, DAV. Roman Catholic. Home: 641 Highpoint Circle Rochester MI 48063 Office: Gen Motors Tech Center Warren MI 48092

PONKO, WILLIAM REUBEN, architect; b. Wausau, Wis., Apr. 4, 1948; s. Reuben Harrison and Ora Marie (Ranke) P.; m. Kathleen Ann Hilt, May 5, 1973; children—William Benjamin, Sarah Elizabeth. B.Arch. magna cum laude, U. Notre Dame, 1971. Cert. Nat. Council Archl. Registration Bds. Ptnr., architect, dir. ednl./instl. specialty LeRoy Troyer & Assocs., Mishawaka, Ind., 1971—; design instr. dept. architecture U. Notre Dame, 1976. Leonard M. Anson Meml. scholar, 1966-70. Mem. AIA (gold medal for excellence in archtl. edn. 1971), Ind. Soc. Architects (design excellence award 1978, chpt. pres. 1985). Prin. archtl. works include: St. Peter Luth. Ch., Mishawaka, Ind., 1979, 4 brs. for South Bend Pub. Library, 1983; Edward J. Funk & Sons office bldg., Kentland, Ind., 1976; Music Edn. bldg. Taylor U., Upland, Ind., 1982, Taylor U. Library, carillon tower, 1985. Office: 415 Lincolnway E Mishawaka IN 46544

PONOMARENKO, NICHOLAS, electrical engineer; b. Poltava, Russia, Feb. 19, 1949; came to U.S., 1976, naturalized, 1982; s. Michail Vasilievich and Katherina Prokhorovna (Olephirenko) P.; m. Ella Plotkin, Jan. 31, 1971; children—Vadim, Marian. M.S. in Elec. Engring., Kiev (Ukraine) Politech. Inst., 1972. Registered profl. engr., Mich. Elec. engr. Moscow Electrotech. Inst., Russia, 1972-75; designer Continental Connector Corp., N.Y.C., 1976-77; elec. engr. Treadwell Corp., N.Y.C., 1977-78, Commonwealth Corp., Jackson, Mich., 1978-79; sr. elec. engr. Bechtel Power Corp., Ann Arbor, Mich., 1979-84; staff elec. engr. Machine Vision Internat., Ann Arbor, 1983—. Mem. IEEE, Nat. Rifle Assn. Home: 3006 Lexington Dr Ann Arbor MI 48105 Office: 325 E Eisenhower Pkwy Ann Arbor MI 48104

PONTIKES, KENNETH NICHOLAS, computer leasing company executive. Chmn., pres. Comdisco Inc., Rosemont, Ill., also dir. Office: Comdisco Inc 6400 Shafer Ct Rosemont IL 60018*

PONTO, JAMES ALLEN, nuclear pharmacist; b. Charles City, Iowa, Oct. 29, 1953; s. Roger H. and Betty M. (Allen) P.; m. Laura L. Boles, June 4, 1977; children—Kevin, Erin. B.S. in Pharmacy, U. Iowa, 1977; M.S. in Radiopharmacy, U. So. Calif., 1978. Lic. pharmacist, Iowa; cert. nuclear pharmacy. Intern radiopharmacist Duke U., Durham, N.C., 1978; nuclear pharmacist, U. Iowa Hosps. and Clinics, Iowa City, 1978—; clin. assoc. prof. U. Iowa Coll. Pharmacy, 1978—, mem. various coms. on nuclear medicine tech.; cons. Iowa State Bd. Pharmacy, 1978—, Iowa Drug Info. Service, 1978—. Contbr. articles to profl. jours., chpts. to books in field. Reviewer Am. Jour. Hosp. Pharmacy, 1982—, U.S. Pharmacopeia Dispensing Info., 1983—. Iowa merit scholar, 1972; Am. Found. Pharm. Edn. scholar, 1976; grantee NIH, Iowa Heart Assn. Mem. Soc. Nuclear Medicine, Am. Soc. Hosp. Pharmacists (various coms.), Am. Pharm. Assn. (various coms.), Am. Coll. Nuclear Physicians, Rho Chi Delta. Methodist. Home: 430 E Davenport Iowa City IA 52240 Office: Div Nuclear Medicine U Iowa Hosps and Clinics Iowa City IA 52242

POORT, STEPHEN MILTON, college administrator; b. Topeka, Kans., Sept. 16, 1939; s. Milton C. and Edith Mae (Lyon) P.; m. Donna Marie Dunlap, Aug. 12, 1962; children—Kelly Lynn, Nikki Lynn. B.S., Kans. State U., 1961; M.S., U. Kans., 1965, Ed.D., 1968. Tchr. Washburn High Sch., Topeka, 1961-65; asst. supt. Ottawa Sch. Dist., Kans., 1966-68; dean acad. affairs State Fair Community Coll., Sedalia, Mo., 1968-72; v.p. instrn. Northampton Community Coll., Bethlehem, Pa., 1972-73, Indian Hills Community Coll., Ottumwa, Iowa, 1973—. Contbr. articles to profl. jours. Bd. dirs. Wapello County United Way, 1982—, Area 15 Regional Planning Commn., 1983—, Ottumwa Hosp., 1983—. Mem. Am. Vocat. Assn., Iowa Vocat. Assn., Iowa Assn. Deans Dirs., Iowa Curriculum Assistance System, Phi Delta Kappa. Republican. Methodist. Avocations: tennis; fishing. Office: Indian Hills Community Coll Grandview and Elm Ottumwa IA 52501

POPCHEFF, THOMAS MARK, state government official; b. Indpls., Apr. 5, 1951; s. George T. and Mary Hellen (Anton) P.; m. Lisa Miriam Roberts; children—Nikki, Alexa. Student in pub. affairs, U. Cin., 1969-71, in bus. adminstrn., Purdue U., 1971-73. Bailiff Marion County Cts., Indpls., 1973; exec. asst. Ind. Dept. Adminstrn., Indpls., 1974-81, dir. procurement, 1981-85, dep. commr., 1985—, chmn. facilities mgmt. com., 1984—. State dir. United Way Campaign State of Ind., 1976-77; adv. bd. Proud Hoosiers, Indpls., 1980-84; active Gov.'s Task Force on Directions in Mental Health, 1983. Mem. Council State Govts., Nat. Assn. State Purchasing Ofcls. Republican. Roman Catholic. Clubs: Columbia, State Capitol Optimist (bd. dirs.). Avocations: photography; woodworking; golf; tennis; total fitness. Office: Dept Adminstrn 100 N Senate Ave Indianapolis IN 46204

POPE, RHALL EDWARD, flight management systems executive; b. Pitts., July 19, 1945; s. Leo Norman and Catherine Marie (Rhall) P.; m. Kathleen Mary Kenny; children—Michaela Kathleen, Edward Rhall. B.S. in Physics, Duquesne U., 1967; M.S., Ph.D. in Aero. Engring., Purdue U., 1972. Engr. space shuttle design Honeywell Avionics, Downey, Calif., 1973-75, research engring. scientist Honeywell Systems & Research Ctr., Mpls., 1975-79, research mgr., sect. leader, 1979-83, bus. mgr. flight mgmt. systems Honeywell Avionics Div., Mpls., 1983—. Editor: AGARD Lecture Series Multivariable Analysis and Design Techniques, 1981. Mem. AIAA (mem. council 1983-84), Am. Helicopter Soc., Sigma Pi Sigma. Avocations: jogging; basketball; home restoration. Home: 124 Prospect Ave Minneapolis MN 55419 Office: Honeywell Avionics Div 5100 Gamble Dr Minneapolis MN 55416

POPEL, JUDITH JEPSEN, principal, educator; b. Kankakee, Ill., Sept. 3, 1940; d. Joseph Louis and Hilda Marie (Bourgeois) J.; m. Gary A. Popel, Sept. 2, 1961; children—Anne Popel Leonard, Therese Popel Wyman, Margaret. A.B. in Elem. Edn., Ga. State U., 1973; M.Ed., U. Ill., 1976. Advt. rep. Paxton Record, Ill., 1969-70; tchr. 1st grade Tolone Primary Sch., Ill., 1974-77; tchr. 4th grade St. Malachy Sch., Rantoul, Ill., 1977-79, tchr. 2d grade, 1979-81; chpt. 1 reading tchr. Ludlow Community Consol. Dist. 142, Ill., 1981—, prin., 1985—. Pres. Paxton Unit 2 Schs. Bd. Edn., 1979—; mem. zoning bd. City of Paxton, 1977-81; past pres., bd. dirs. Paxton Day Care Ctr., Paxton Hosp. Aux., 1965—, St.' Mary Council Cath. Women; founder, co-ordinator Paxton Meals on Wheels, 1981—. Named Woman of Yr., Council Cath. Women, 1967, Those Who Excel, Ill. State Bd. Edn., 1983. Mem. Ludlow Edn. Assn. (pres. 1981—), AAUW (legis. chair 1978—), Mortar Bd., Phi Delta Kappa, Kappa Delta Epsilon, Kappa Delta Pi, Delta Kappa Gamma, Beta Sigma Phi (officer 1962—). Club: Paxton Woman's (v.p. 1984—). Home: 358 W Pells St Paxton IL 60957 Office: PO Box 156 Ludlow IL 60949

POPLAWSKI, JOSEPH WALTER, glass mfg. co. exec.; b. Chgo., July 8, 1932; s. Joseph and Catherine P.; m. Geraldine Snell, May 24, 1952; children—Joseph, Thomas, Jerald, Julianne, Scott. With Phoenix Closures Co., Chgo., 1953-81, v.p. mfg., 1978-81; v.p., plant mgr. Kerr Glass Mfg. Co., Chgo., 1981—; dir. Loring Inc. Chmn. Mohawk council Boy Scouts Am., Chgo., 1963-65. Served with U.S. Army, 1949-52. Office: 2444 W 16th St Chicago IL 60608

POPMA, EUGENE JOHN, retired telephone company executive; b. Jackson, Mich., July 12, 1923; s. Nicholas John and Mary Agnes (Andrews) P.; m. Ann Connor, June 12, 1982; children—Jeffrey John, Valerie Marie. B.S. in Indsl. Mgmt., U. Detroit, 1948; M.S. in Indsl. Mgmt., MIT, 1958; postgrad. Dartmouth Coll., 1964. Acct., Pacific Tel. Co., Los Angeles, 1948-53; acct. AT&T, N.Y.C., 1953-55; asst. comptroller Ind. Bell Tel. Co., Indpls., 1955-61, gen. traffic mgr., 1961-73, asst. v.p. publ. relations, 1973-75, dir. adminstrv. services, 1975-83; owner Popma Enterprises, Inc., Naperville, 1983—; dir. Channel 20 Pub. Broadcasting Sta., Wesley-Otterbein Ins. Corp.; arbitrator Central Ind. Better Bus. Bur. Inc., Indpls. Mem. sch. bd. St. Luke Sch., Indpls., 1969-70; v.p. Boy Scouts Am., 1970-73; pres. Dad's Club and mem. Pres.'s Council Brebeuf Prep. Sch., Indpls. 1973; vice chmn., co-founder Life Today House for Drug Addicts, Indpls., 1971-73; bd. dirs. Martin Ctr. Inst. for Black Culture. Served with USNR, 1943-46. Sloan fellow, 1957-58. Mem. Ind. Assn. AAU (pres. 1974-75), AAU (exec. com. 1974), Devon Civic League (v.p. 1956-57), Antique Airplane Assn., Luscombe Assn., Exptl. Aircraft Assn., T-34 Assn., Pub. Relations Soc. Am. (accredited). Roman Catholic. Address: 9 S 215 Aero Dr Naperville IL 60565

POPP, FRANK DONALD, chemistry educator, researcher; b. N.Y.C., Dec. 25, 1932; s. Frank B. and Julia (Brown) P.; m. Barbara L. Freer, June 11, 1955 (div. 1975); children—Bruce D., James W.; m. Jane C. Cooksy, Apr. 30, 1977. B.S. in Chemistry, Rensselaer Poly. Tech. Inst., 1954; Ph.D., U. Kans., 1957. Asst. prof. U. Miami, Coral Gables, Fla., 1959-62; from asst. prof. to prof. chemistry Clarkson Coll. of Tech., Potsdam, N.Y., 1962-76; prof., chmn. dept. U. Mo., Kansas City, 1976—. Contbr. articles to profl. jours. Bd. dirs. Am. Cancer Soc., Jefferson City, Mo., 1984—, chmn., 1983; bd. dirs. Kansas City chpt. U. Kans. Alumni Assn., 1983—. Recipient Tchrs. award for research U. Mo., 1983. Fellow AAAS, Am. Assn. Cancer Research, N.Y. Acad. Sci., Royal Soc. Chemistry, Am. Inst. Chemists; mem. Am. Chem. Soc., Soc. Heterocyclic Chemistry. Avocations: travel, photography, sports, stamp collecting. Office: Chemistry Dept U Missouri Kansas City MO 64110

POPPE, WASSILY, chemist; b. Riga, Latvia, Nov. 10, 1918; s. Wilhelm and Barbara (Gogotoff) P.; student Kaiser Friedrich Wilhelm U., Berlin, 1936-39; cand. chem., U. Tubingen (Germany), 1947; dipl. chem. Inst. Tech. Stuttgart (Germany), 1949; Ph.D., U. Pitts., 1966; m. Larissa Heffner, Oct. 16, 1942; 1 dau., Katherine Poppe Zawadzkas. Came to U.S., 1959, naturalized, 1965. Chemist, Dr. Hans Kittel Chem. Lab., Germany, 1949-50; devel. chemist Karl Worwag Lack & Farbenfabrik, Germany, 1950-51, prodn. mgr. paint Pinturas Iris, Venezuela, 1951-53; lab. supr. Pinturas Tucan, Venezuela, 1953-54, tech. dir., 1954-57, plant mgr. paint prodn. 1957-59; chemist PPG Industries Springfield, Pa., 1959-64; research asst. phys. chemistry U. Pitts., 1964-66; group leader surface chemistry Avisun Corp., Marcus-Hook, Pa., 1966-68; research asso. Amoco Chems., Naperville, Ill., 1968—. Fellow Am. Inst. Chemists; mem. N.Y. Acad. Sci., Am. Chem. Soc., Sigma Xi. Home: 105 Main St Lombard IL 60148 Office: PO Box 400 Naperville IL 60540

POPPELE, RICHARD ELWOOD, neurophysiology educator; b. Irvington, N.J., Mar. 6, 1936; s. Richard C. and Emily M. (Feuerherm) P.; m. Meredith Blodgett, Feb. 7, 1959; children—Eric, Jessica, Kristen, Jonathan. B.S.E.E., Tufts U., 1958; Ph.D., U. Minn., 1965. Research assoc. U. Pisa, Italy, 1965-67; asst. prof. U. Minn., Mpls., 1967-70, assoc. prof., 1970-75, prof. neurophysiology, 1975—, dir., 1976—. Contbr. articles to sci. jours. Served to lt. USN, 1958-61. NIH fellow, 1965; named Tchr. of Yr. Minn. Med. Found., 1971. Mem. Am. Physiol. Soc., Soc. Neurosci., Biophys. Soc., N.Y. Acad. Scis., Internat. Brain Research Orgn., Tau Beta Pi. Democratic-Farmer-Labor. Office: 435 Delaware St SE Minneapolis MN 55455

POPRICK, MARY ANN, psychologist; b. Chgo., June 25, 1939; d. Michael and Mary (Mihalcik) P.; B.A., De Paul U., 1960, M.A., 1964; Ph.D., Loyola U., Chgo., 1968. Intern psychology Elgin (Ill.) State Hosp., 1961-62; staff psychologist, 1962; staff psychologist Ill. State Tng. Sch. for Girls, Geneva, 1962-63, Mt. Sinai Hosp., Chgo., 1963-64; lectr. psychology Loyola U. at Chgo,, 1964-67; asst. prof. Lewis U., Lockport, Ill., 1967-70, assoc. prof., 1970-75, chmn. dept. psychology, 1968-72; adj. asso. prof. South Chgo. Community Hosp. Sch. Nursing, Lewis U., 1975; postdoctoral intern clin. psychology Ill. State Psychiat. Inst., Chgo., 1972-73; pvt. clin. practice, assoc. with David Psychiat. Clinic Ltd., South Holland, Ill., 1973—; mem. assoc. sci. staff Riveredge Hosp., Forest Park, Ill., 1975, 76; sci. staff dept. psychiatry Christ Hosp., Oak Lawn, Ill., 1983—. Co-chmn. commn. on personal growth and devel. Congregation 3d Order St. Francis of Mary Immaculate, Joliet, Ill., 1970-71. Mem. Am., Midwestern, Calif., Ill. (sec.-treas. acad. sect. 1975-77, chairperson acad. sect. 1978-79, co-chmn. program com. 1984, sec. 1979-81, pres. 1982-83, rep. Am. Psycho. Assn. 1985—) psychol. assns., Assn. Advancement of Psychology, Chgo. Assn. for Psychoanalytic Psychology, AAAS, Kappa Gamma Pi, Psi Chi (sec. 1964-65, pres. 1965-66). Home: 547 Marquette Ave Calumet City IL 60409 Office: 645 E 170th St South Holland IL 60473

POREMBSKI, CHESTER PAUL, lawyer, pharmacist; b. Youngstown, Ohio, Apr. 5, 1957; s. Paul Kasimir and Eugenia (Fryda) P.; m. Louise Marie Flanagan, July 12, 1980. Student, Youngstown State U., Ohio, 1975-76; B.S. in Pharmacy, Ohio State U., 1980; J.D., Capital U. Law Sch., Columbus, 1984. Bar: Ohio 1984, U.S. Dist. Ct. (so. dist.) Ohio 1985; registered pharmacist, Ohio. Pharmacy supr. St. Anthony Med. Ctr., Columbus, 1980-85; dir. therapeutics DxRx, Inc., Columbus, Ohio, 1985—; staff atty. Comed Mgmt., Inc., 1985—. Mem. ABA, Ohio Bar Assn., Columbus Bar Assn., Central Ohio Soc. Hosp. Pharmacists, Assn. Trial Lawyers Am., Nat. Health Lawyers Assn. Roman Catholic. Avocations: golf; fishing; jogging; woodworking. Home: 605 Fawndale Pl Gahanna OH 43230

PORRECA, ANTHONY GABRIEL, educator; b. Providence, Apr. 8, 1941; s. Domenico Bliff and Mary Carmine (Scorpio) P.; B.A., Bryant Coll., 1963; M.A., Boston U., 1965, Ed.D., 1971. Asst. prof. Bryant Coll., Smithfield, R.I., 1966-71, Boston U., 1971-72; assoc. prof. U. Tenn., Knoxville, 1973-79; prof. bus. edn. Ohio State U., Columbus, 1979—; lectr. in field. Served with R.I. N.G., 1966-72. NSF grantee, 1966. Mem. Phi Kappa Phi, Omicron Tau Theta (founder), Delta Pi Epsilon (advisor). Author, pubs. editor; contbr. articles to profl. jours. Home: 4088 Mountview Rd Upper Arlington OH 43220 Office: 121 Ramseyer Hall Ohio State Univ Columbus OH 43210

PORRETTA, LOUIS PAUL, educator; b. Malvern, Ohio, Sept. 24, 1926; s. Peter A. and Rosa (Tersigne) P.; B.A., Eastern Mich. U., 1950; Ed.M., Wayne State U., 1959, Ed.D., 1967; m. Elizabeth M. Murphy, Oct. 13, 1951; children—Leslie Elizabeth, Paul Louis, Jeffrey Mark. Tchr. elem. sch. Mason Consol. Sch., Erie, Mich., 1952-53, tchr., prin., 1953-54; prin. Mason Jr. High Sch., Erie, Mich., 1954-59; asst. prof. edn. Eastern Mich. U., Ypsilanti, 1959-62, assoc. prof., 1962-66, prof. edn., 1967-71, prof. dept. curriculum and instruction, 1974-83, prof. emeritus, 1983—, dir. Office Internat. Projects, 1979-81; chief-of-party Nat. Tchr. Edn. Center, Somalia, 1967-70; mem. edn. survey team AID, Botswana, Lesotho and Swaziland, 1970, sr. adv. U. Botswana, Lesotho and Swaziland, 1972-74; campus coordinator Swaziland Primary Curriculum Devel. Project, AID, 1978; chief-of-party projects AID, Swaziland, 1975-78, Yemen, 1981-83. Chmn. March of Dimes, Westenaw County, Mich., 1956. Mem. Assn. Tchr. Educators, Inst. Internat. Edn., AAUP, Assn. for Supervision and Curriculum Devel., Phi Delta Kappa, Pi Gamma Mu. Club: Ypsilanti Rotary. Home: 719 Cornell St Ypsilanti MI 48197 Office: Eastern Mich Univ Ypsilanti MI 48197

PORTCH, STEPHEN RALPH, university administrator; b. Woolavington, Eng., Sept. 11, 1950; came to U.S., 1974; s. Graham George and Thelma Mary Jean (Morris) P.; m. Barbara Ann Barrows, June 18, 1974. B.A., U. Reading, 1973; M.A., Pa. State U., 1976, Ph.D., 1982. Master, St. Lawrence Coll., Ramsgate, Eng., 1973-74; asst. prof. English, U. Wis., Richland Center, 1976-81, campus dean, Wausau, 1981—. Cons., evaluator North Central Accreditation, Chgo., 1984—; examiner Internat. Baccalaureate, 1984—. Author: Literature's Silent Language, 1985. Contbr. articles to profl. jours. Bd. dirs. United Way of Marathon County, Wausau, Wis., 1983—, Wausau Conservatory of Music, 1984—, Wausau Area Vol. Exchange, 1984—. Mem. Wausau C. of C., Phi Kappa Phi. Club: Wausau. Avocations: riding; writing; fishing; golf. Home: 9104 Wesenick Dr Schofield WI 54476 Office: U Wis Marathon Ctr 518 S 7th Ave Wausau WI 54401

PORTER, DAVID STEWART, judge; b. Cin., Sept. 23, 1909; s. Charles Hamilton and Caroline (Pemberton) P.; m. Marjorie Bluett Ellis, July 26, 1956; children—Mary Stewart, Margaret Lee, Elizabeth Sue. A.B., U. Cin., 1932, J.D., 1934. Bar: Ohio 1934. Practice, Troy, Ohio, 1936-49; judge Common Pleas Ct., Miami County, Ohio, 1949-66; U.S. dist. judge So. Dist., Ohio, 1966-79; sr. dist. judge, 1979—; active Ohio Jud. Conf.; past pres. Ohio

Common Pleas Judges Assn.; faculty advisor Nat. Coll. State Trial Judges, 1964-65. Past bd. dirs. Ohio Blue Cross, Dettmer Hosp. Mem. ABA, Ohio Bar Assn., Cin. Bar Assn., Miami County Bar Assn., Federal Bar Assn., Am. Judicature Soc. Presbyterian. Office: 823 Post Office and Court House Cincinnati OH 45202

PORTER, DEAN ALLEN, art museum administrator, art historian, educator; b. Gouverneur, N.Y., June 13, 1939; s. Arnold W. and Gertrude V. Porter; B.A., Harpur Coll., 1961; M.A. in Art History, SUNY, Binghamton, 1966, Ph.D. in Art History, 1974; m. Carol DuBrava, July 27, 1963; children—Kellie Ann, Tracie Ann. Admissions counselor Harpur Coll., 1961-64; curator Art Gallery, U. Notre Dame, 1966-74, dir. Snite Mus. Art, 1974—, assoc. prof. art history, 1966—. Samuel H. Kress fellow. Mem. Coll. Art Assn. Am., Am. Assn. Mus. South Bend Art Center, Nat. Soc. Lit. and Arts, Michiana Arts and Scis. Council (dir.). Author exhbn. catalogues, the most recent being: Janos Scholz, Musician and Collector, 1980; A Guide to The Snite Museum of Art, 1980. Office: Snite Mus Art U Notre Dame Notre Dame IN 46556

PORTER, DONALD JAMES, U.S. district court judge; b. Madison, S.D., Mar. 24, 1921; s. Donald Irving and Lela Ann (Slack) P.; student Eastern Normal Coll., 1938-39; B.S., U. S.D., 1942, LL.B., 1943; m. Harriet J. Whitney, Aug. 22, 1948; children—Donald A., Mary Lela, William W., Carolyn S., Elizabeth C. Admitted to S.D. bar, 1943; individual practice law, Chamberlain, S.D., 1947-59; partner firm May, Porter, Adam, Gerdes & Thompson, and predecessor, Pierre, S.D., 1959-77; asso. justice S.D. Supreme Ct., Pierre, 1977-79; now U.S. dist. judge, S.D.; state atty., Brule County, S.D., 1948-52, 57-59; S.D. commr. to Nat. Conf. Commrs. on Uniform State Laws, 1973-76. Mem. S.D. Ho. of Reps., 1955-56. Served with U.S. Army, 1943-46; ETO. Mem. Am., S.D. bar assns., Am. Bd. Trial Advocates (charter mem. S.D. chpt.), Am. Judicature Soc. Roman Catholic. Office: US Dist Ct 413 Federal Bldg Pierre SD 57501*

PORTER, DONNA JUNE, interior designer; b. Alva, Okla., June 24, 1937; d. Floyd R. and Elsie Martha (Schick) Paris; B.S., Okla. State U., 1959, postgrad., 1960, 68, 69, Kansas City Art Inst., 1979; children—Terri Sue Walters, Bradford Paris Walters. Tchr. elem. schs., Lakewood, Colo., 1964-65; kindergarten tchr. Dist. 110 Schs., Overland Park, Kans., 1966-67; nat. rep. Chi Omega, 1972—; founder, owner, designer D.J. Interior Designer, Kansas City, 1972—; exec. bd. Gt. Am. Restaurant Co. Bd. dirs. Kansas City Conv. and Visitors Bur., 1975-78; trustee Country Club Meth. Ch., 1978—, also chmn. parsonage com. Recipient Alumnae Achievement award Chi Omega. Mem. Kansas City Panhellenic Assn., Historic Kansas City Soc., Kansas City Womens Philharmonic, PEO, Kansas City Alumnae Chi Omega (exec. bd.), Kansas City Arabian Horse Assn., Friends of Art, Internat. Arabian Horse Assn. Democrat. Interior designer Applewood's Restaurant, Oklahoma City, Old Washington St. Sta. and Village Green Restaurant of Kansas City, Muffin's Restaurant, Oklahoma City, Lt. Robert E. Lee Riverboat Restaurant, St. Louis, Blue Hills Country Club of Kansas City, Knickerbocker Restaurant, others. Address: 812 W 59th Terr Kansas City MO 64113

PORTER, FREDERIC EDWIN, research administrator, microbiologist, agronomist; b. Cleve., Dec. 9, 1922; s. Frank and Arabella (Chute) P.; children—Michael A., David A., Sarah. B.S., Ohio State U., 1948, M.S., 1950, Ph.D., 1952. Cert. profl. agronomist. Asst. instr. Ohio State U., Columbus, 1951-52; project leader Battelle Meml. Inst., Columbus, 1952-59; research microbiologist Northrup King Co., Mpls., from 1959, sucessively project mgr., dir. agronomic research, dir. research service, until 1984. Served with U.S. Army, 1942-46, 46-51. Republican. Presbyterian. Home: 9255 W 23d St Saint Louis Park MN 55426

PORTER, GEORGE DARWIN, manufacturing company executive; b. Dayton, Pa., July 25, 1937; s. Melvin Clair and Mary Gladys (Thomas) P.; diploma Robert Morris Sch., Pitts., 1957; m. Charlotte Louise Ferkan, June 8, 1963; children—George Darwin, II, Faye Ellen, Joseph Clair, David Eugene. Cert. systems profl. Mgr. data processing Magnetics, Inc., Butler, Pa., 1961-62, 63-67; computer operator Mellon Bank, Pitts., 1962-63; systems and procedures mgr. Dresser Industries Co., Bradford, Pa., 1967-68; info. systems mgr. Standard Transformer Co., Warren, Ohio, 1968-69; v.p. sales Pryor Corp., Chgo., 1969-83, pres., dir., 1983—; instr. data processing Pa. State U. Extension, Butler, 1966. Pres. North Rd. Elementary Sch. PTA, Warren, Ohio, 1974-75; lay pres. congregation St. Paul's Luth. Ch., Warren, 1974. Served with U.S. Army, 1958-61; ETO. Recipient numerous sales awards Pryor Corp., 1971-83. Mem. Data Processing Mgmt. Assn., Assn. Systems Mgmt. Republican. Clubs: Naperville Country, Brookdale Swim and Tennis. Lodge: Masons. Home: 1218 Langley Circle Naperville IL 60540 Office: 400 N Michigan Ave Chicago IL 60611

PORTER, JOHN EDWARD, congressman, lawyer; b. Evanston, Ill., June 1, 1935; s. Harry H. and Florence B. (Vahle) P.; student M.I.T., 1953-54; B.S. in Bus. Adminstrn., Northwestern U., 1957; J.D. with distinction, U. Mich., 1961; m. Kathryn Cameron Porter; children—John Clark, David Britton, Ann Lindsay. Bar: Ill. 1961, U.S. Supreme Ct. Atty. civil div., appellate sect. Dept. Justice, Washington, 1961-63; practice law, Evanston, 1963-80; mem. Ill. Ho. of Reps. from 1st Dist., 1973-79; mem. 96th-99th Congresses from Ill., mem. com. on appropriations, subcoms. on commerce, justice, state fed. judiciary, labor, health and human services, edn. and legis. Founder, co-chmn. Congl. Human Rights Caucus. Served with U.S. Army Res., 1958-64. Named Outstanding Legislator, Independent Voters Ill., 1974, League Conservation Voters, 1974, Chgo. Crime Commn., 1976. Mem. Am., Ill., Chgo., bar assns. Presbyterian. Asst. editor: Mich. Law Rev., 1960-61. Office: 104 Wilmot Rd Suite 410 Deerfield IL 60015 also 601 A County Bldg 18 N County St Waukegan IL 60085 also 1650 N Arlington Heights Rd Suite 104 Arlington Heights IL 60004

PORTER, JOSEPH THOMAS, JR., lawyer; b. St. Louis, Dec. 9, 1952; s. Joseph Thomas and Marie Mathilda (Tebeau) P.; m. Margaret Mary Dougherty, May 28, 1976; children—Elizabeth Anne, Joseph Thomas, III. B.S. cum laude, U. Mo.-St. Louis, 1976; J.D. cum laude, St. Louis U., 1979. Bar: Mo. 1979, U.S. Dist Ct. (ea. and we. dists.) Mo. 1979, U.S. Ct. Appeals (8th cir.) 1979, Ill. 1980. Assoc. Lewis & Rice, St. Louis, 1979-84, Beck, Tiemeyer & Zerr, St. Charles, Mo., 1985, Suelthaas, Kaplan, Cunningham, Yates, Fitzsimmons & Wright, P.C., Clayton, Mo., 1985—. Editor St. Louis U. Law Jour., 1978-79, The Young Lawyer, 1981-83. Mem. ABA, Mo. Bar (exec. com. young lawyer sect. 1982—, treas. 1984-85, young lawyer sect. Chmn. award 1982, 83, 84), Ill. State Bar Assn., Bar Assn. Met. St. Louis, St. Charles County Bar Assn., Phi Alpha Delta (justice St. Louis alumni chpt. 1981-82), Order of Woolsack, Beta Gamma Sigma, Alpha Sigma Nu. Democrat. Roman Catholic. Home: 429 Lemonwood Dr Saint Charles MO 63303 Office: 8000 Maryland Ave Clayton MO 63105

PORTER, PATRICIA JANE, computer company executive; b. Elmhurst, Ill., Aug. 7, 1954; d. Fred Thomas and Shirley Eleanore (Hamelink) P. Student No. Ill. U., 1972-73, Coll. DuPage, 1979-80. Supr. inventory control Chgo. Pneumatic Tool Co., Bensenville, Ill., 1973-76, supr. export, 1977-78; supr. data entry List Processing Co., Lombard, Ill., 1979-80, assembler programmer, 1980-81, mgr. data base, 1981-84, dir. tech. services, 1984—; small bus. cons. Sponsor Theosophical Order of Service, Wheaton, 1983—; active Lombard Hist. Soc., 1983—. Recipient First Ann. Mgr. of Yr. award List Processing Co., 1982. Mem. Women in Mgmt. Avocations: painting; jazz dance; yoga; metaphysical/theosophical studies. Home: 420 S Brewster Ave Lombard IL 60148

PORTER, ROSEMARY THERESE, nurse educator; b. LaCrosse, Wis., Feb. 3, 1944; d. Bernard P. and Marie C. (Mikshowsky) Hammes; m. Michael J. Porter, July 1, 1972; children—Benjamin Michael, Matthew Hammes. R.N., St. Mary's Sch. Nursing, 1965; B.S., U. Iowa, 1971, M.A., 1973; Ph.D., U. Mo., 1983. Staff nurse St. Mary's Hosp., Milw., 1965-66, St. Jude's Hosp., Fullerton, Calif., 1966-69; instr. U. Iowa, Iowa City, 1973-75; asst. prof. U. Tex., Houston, 1975-79; asst. prof. nursing U. Mo., Columbia, 1979—. Mem. Am. Nurses Assn., Nat. League Nursing, Phi Delta Kappa, Sigma Theta Tau, Pi Lambda Theta. Roman Catholic. Home: 1400 Truman St Columbia MO 65203 Office: U Mo Sch Nursing .Columbia MO 65211

PORTER, STUART WILLIAMS, investment company executive; b. Detroit, Jan. 11, 1937; s. Stuart Perlee and Alma Bernice (Williams) P.; B.S., U. Mich., 1960; M.B.A., U. Chgo. (Am. Accounting Assn. fellow), 1967, postgrad., 1967-68; m. Myrna Marlene Denham, June 27, 1964; children—Stuart, Randall. Investment mgr., partner Weiss Peck & Greer, 1978—. Chmn., Crusade of Mercy, 1973; chmn. investment com., v.p. bus. affairs com. Presbytery of Chgo. Served with USAF, 1961-62. Recipient award for excellence in bus. and accounting Fin. Exec. Inst., 1966. Mem. Midwest Pension Conf., Investment Analysts Soc. Chgo., Fin. Analysts Fedn., Investment Tech. Symposium N.Y., Beta Gamma Sigma. Presbyterian. Clubs: Renaissance (Detroit); Forest Grove Tennis (Palatine, Ill.); Turnberry Country (Crystal Lake, Ill.); Economic, Chgo. Athletic. Home: 130 Wyngate Dr Barrington IL 60010 Office: 30 N LaSalle St Chicago IL 60602

PORTER, TERENCE CLIFTON, lawyer; b. St. Joseph, Mo., Dec. 13, 1934; s. Ernest Clifton and Helen Francis (Denny) P.; B.S. in Agr., J.D., U. Mo., 1958; m. Joyce Newman, June 2, 1956; children—Katherine, Michael, David, Susan. Admitted to Mo. bar, 1958; with firm Clark & Becker, Columbia, Mo., 1958-60, Becker & Porter, 1960-61, Welliver, Porter & Cleveland, 1962-70, Porter, Sprick & Powell, 1970-78, Terence C. Porter, 1979—; pres., dir. Porter Investment Co., 1982—; sec., dir. Boone County Devel. Co., Hilton Inn of Columbia. Served to 1t. U.S. Army, 1958. Mem. Am., Mo. bar assns., Def. Research Inst. Democrat. Presbyterian. Club: Kansas City. Home: 1129 Danforth Circle Columbia MO 65201 Office: 10 N Garth Columbia MO 65201

PORTER, WALTER ARTHUR, judge; b. Dayton, Ohio, June 6, 1924; s. Claude and Estella Maie (Raymond) P.; m. Patricia Higdon, Dec. 3, 1947; children—Scott, David. B.S. in Gen. Engring., U. Cin., 1948, LL.B., 1949. Bar: Ohio 1949. Legal dep. Probate Ct., Dayton, 1949-51; asst. prosecutor Montgomery County, Dayton, 1951-56; assoc. Albert H. Scharrer, Dayton, 1956-62; ptnr. Smith & Schnacke, L.P.A., Dayton, 1962-85; judge Montgomery County Common Pleas Court, 1985—. Exec. com. Dayton Area Heart Assn., 1978—, Dayton Area Cancer Assn., 1982—; trustee Dayton Performing Arts Fund, 1980-85. Served with U.S. Army, 1943-45. Fellow Ohio State Bar Found. (pres. 1984), Am. Coll. Trial Lawyers, Am. Coll. Probate Counsel, Am. Bar Found.; mem. Ohio State Bar Assn. (pres. 1973-74). Democrat. Presbyterian. Clubs: Dayton Lawyers, Dayton Bicycle. Lodge: Masons. Home: 785 E Schantz Ave Dayton OH 45419 Office: 504 Montgomery County Courts Bldg 41 N Perry St Dayton OH 45422

PORTER, WILLIAM CARL, nuclear pharmacist; b. Chgo., Dec. 21, 1946; s. Hildred Lewis and Jennie (Narbone) P.; m. Suzanne DePalma, Dec. 13, 1969 (div. 1974); m. Susan Marie Sweet, Mar. 3, 1978; 1 child, Stacy Lynne. B.S., U. Ill., 1969; Pharm.D., U. Mich., 1974. Lic. pharmacist, Ill., Mich. Pharmacy intern Hillsdale Med. Arts Pharmacy, Chgo., 1966-69, E.L. Zegadio Pharmacy, Cicero, Ill., 1968-69; pharmacist Henry's Prescription Pharmacy, Ypsilanti, Mich., 1973-74; resident in pharmacy U. Mich. Hosp., Ann Arbor, 1972-74; nuclear pharmacist William Beaumont Hosp., Royal Oak, Mich., 1974—. Contbr. articles to profl. jours. Served to 1t. USPHS, 1969-72. Mem. Am. Soc. Hosp. Pharmacists, Am. Pharm. Assn., Soc. Nuclear Medicine. Republican. Avocations: camping; fishing; bridge. Office: William Beaumont Hosp Nuclear Medicine Dept 3601 W 13 Mile Rd Royal Oak MI 48072

PORTERFIELD, JOHN MCHANEY, research architect, energy consultant, educator; b. Davenport, Iowa, May 2, 1946; s. Reeder McHaney and Mary Elizabeth (Fox) P.; m. Marguerite McGee, June 2, 1968; 1 son, Alan Douglass. B.A. in Econs., U. Mo., 1968; B.Arch. U. Ill.-Chgo., 1976. Lectr., Coll. Architecture, U. Ill., Chgo., 1976-77, cons. Energy Resources Ctr., 1976—; founder, tech. dir. Potential Energy, Inc., 1979—; instr. Moraine Valley Community Coll., 1984—. Mem. Landmarks Preservation Commn., Chgo.; bd. dirs. Hyde Park-Kenwood Community Conf. Served with U.S. Army, 1969. Mem. AIA, Nat. Trust Hist. Preservation. Unitarian. Author: Guidelines for Energy Efficient Rehabilitation, 1980; Home Retrofiting for Energy Savings, 1981; How to House Doctor, 1983. Home: 1227 E 57th Chicago IL 60637 Office: U Illinois Energy Resources Ctr PO Box 4348 Chicago IL 60680

PORTHOUSE, J. DAVID, coatings company executive, fishing lure company executive; b. Ravenna, Ohio, Aug. 1, 1938; s. Cyril R. and Roberta (Diehl) P.; m. Jacqueline Spencer, June 15, 1963; children—David R., Diane D. B.S. in Chem. Engring., Purdue U., 1960; M.S. in Chem. Engring., Ohio State U., 1962, M.B.A. in Corp. Fin. and Mktg., 1963. Regional mgr. Carboline, St. Louis, 1972-74, sales mgr., 1974-79, v.p., 1979-81, chief operating officer, pres. 1981—, chief exec. officer, 1983—; pres. Porthouse Found., Akron, Ohio, 1981—; dir. Fred Arbogast Co., Akron, 1970—, Mark Twain Nat. Bank, St. Louis, 1983—. Mem. Am. Chem. Soc., Nat. Assn. Corrosion Engrs., Nat. Fedn. Ind. Bus., Nat. Paint and Coatings Assn. (dir., mem. fin. com. 1983—). Avocations: fishing; hunting; golf. Office: Carboline Co 1401 S Hanley Rd Saint Louis MO 63144

PORTWOOD, JOHN HARDING, lawyer; b. Port Huron, Mich., June 5, 1928; s. George Harding and Nina Louise (Powrie) P.; m. Anne Elizabeth Beck, Aug. 28, 1954; children—Elizabeth Anne Portwood Bieber, Steven Dana, Susan Eileen. B.A., Ohio State U., 1953, J.D., 1955. Bar: Ohio 1955. Atty. Toledo Scale Corp., 1955-63, atty., asst. sec., 1963-66, legal counsel, asst. sec., 1966-67; counsel, asst. sec. Reliance Electric Co., Cleveland, 1967-76, asst. gen. counsel, 1976-83, v.p., sec., gen. counsel, 1983—, dir., 1984—. Sustaining mem. Republican Nat. Com., Washington, 1984—. Served with U.S. Army, 1950-52. Mem. Ohio Bar Assn. Office: Reliance Electric Co 29325 Chagrin Blvd Cleveland OH 44122

POSCH, JOSEPH LOUIS, surgeon; b. St. Paul, Dec. 26, 1915; s. Louis Gustav and Frances Martha (Kurz) P.; B.S. cum laude, St. Thomas Coll., 1938; M.D., U. Minn., 1942; m. Martha Jane Stark, May 2, 1942 (dec. Nov. 1981); children—Mary Katherine Posch Gebeck, Joseph Louis; m. Gerri Fisher Jackson, Feb. 19, 1983. Intern, City of Detroit Receiving Hosp., 1942-43, fellow in surgery, 1943-44, resident in surgery, 1946-49, chief of staff, 1965; practice medicine specializing in surgery, Detroit; dir. hand surgery Hand Center, Harper-Grace Hosp., Detroit Med. Center, Wayne State U.; mem. staff Hutzel Hosp., Detroit Gen. Hosp., St. Joseph Mercy Hosp., Mt. Carmel Mercy Hosp., Children's Hosp. of Mich., St. John's Hosp., Sinai Hosp., Bon Secours Hosp., VA Hosp., USPHS Hosp.; clin. prof. surgery Coll. Medicine, Wayne State U., 1973, Rehab. Services Adminstrn.; HEW trainee in rehab. medicine (hand surgery), micro-surgery research lab. Wayne State U. Served with M.C., U.S. Army, 1944-46; ETO. Diplomate Am. Bd. Surgery. Mem. Am. Soc. for Surgery of the Hand, Am. Assn. for Surgery of Trauma, AMA, A.C.S., Indsl. Med. Assn., Detroit, Central, Western, Midwest surg. assns., Acad. Surgery of Detroit, Detroit Surg. Soc., Mich., Wayne County med. socs., Am. Soc. for Plastic and Reconstructive Surgery (asso.), Mich., Detroit, hist. socs., Detroit Inst. Arts Founders Soc., Anthony Wayne Soc., Grosse Pointe Power Squadron, Phi Chi. Roman Catholic. Clubs: Detroit Athletic, Grosse Pointe Yacht, K.C. Contbr. articles to profl. jours. Home: 73 Webber Pl Grosse Pointe Shores MI 48236 Office: 21331 Kelly Rd East Detroit MI 48021

POSEVITZ, LASZLO, osteopathic physician, surgeon, financial executive; b. Mohacs, Hungary, Oct. 2, 1941; came to U.S., 1957; s. Albert and Maria (Harczi) P.; m. Gabriella Szaszgaspar, June 24, 1972; children—Anthony, Gabriella, Christopher. B.S., U. Dayton, 1964; D.O., Chgo. Coll. Osteo. Medicine, 1968. Diplomate Am. Bd. Surgery. Intern, Grandview Hosp., Dayton, Ohio, 1968-69; resident in surgery, 1969-73; fellow in vascular surgery Seimelweiss U., Budapest (Hungary), 1971; fellow in thoracic and vascular surgery Jewish Hosp., Cin., 1973; Hosp. L'Aiguelongue, Service de Chirurgie Vasculaire, Montpellier, France, 1979; practice osteo. medicine specializing in thoracocardiovascular surgery, Dayton, 1974—; mem. staff Grandview Hosp., Ambulatory Care Ctr., Centerville, Ohio; chmn. dept. gen. surgery Grandview Hosp., 1980—; acting chmn. dept. thoracocardiovascular surgery, 1981—, dir. residency program, 1980—; assoc. clin. prof. peripheral vascular and thoracic surgery Ohio U. Sch. Medicine; clin. instr. dept. thoracic and cardiovascular surgery Wright State U., mem. exec. bd. Fla. Bank of Commerce Holding Co., Clearwater, Former bd. dirs. Dayton Opera. Mem. Am. Coll. Osteo. Surgeons, Dayton Surg. Soc., Am. Osteo. Assn., Ohio Osteo. Assn., Dayton Dist. Acad. Osteo. Medicine. Contbr. articles to profl. jours. Home: 7286 Mintwood St Dayton OH 45415 Office: 1217 Salem Ave Dayton OH 45406

POSEY, EDWIN DALFIELD, librarian; b. Dallas, Jan. 8, 1927; s. Jonathan R. and Illa I. (Golden) P.; m. Erica Grace Krumm, Apr. 9, 1962; children—Reba Alison, Michael John. B.A., U. Houston, 1967; M.S., Drexel U., 1969. Engr., Texteam Corp., Houston, 1960-68; librarian Princeton U., N.J., 1968-69, Purdue U., West Lafayette, Ind., 1969—. Author: Approval Plans, 1977; also articles. Served with USN, 1944-45. Mem. ALA, Am. Soc. Engring. Edn., Am. Soc. Info. Sci., Beta Phi Mu. Democrat. Avocations: book collecting; golf; auto racing. Home: 237 Schilling West Lafayette IN 47906 Office: Purdue U Libraries West Lafayette IN 47907

POSKO, THOMAS CHARLES, mech. engr.; b. Chgo., May 13, 1947; s. James L. and Marie F. (Mangan) P.; ward of Robert J. and Frances Murphy; A.S. in Archtl. Engring., Milw. Sch. Engring., 1968, B.S. in Archtl. Engring., 1973; student Loras Coll., 1965-67; m. Mary D. Marangelli, Sept. 4, 1971; children—Michael Edward, Andrew Robert. Coop. engr., jr. engr. Joseph P. Jansen Co., Milw., 1968-70; project engr., v.p. R.J. Miller Assos., Milw., 1973-80; pres. Posko Associates, Inc., Waukesha, Wis., 1980—; lectr. Milw. Sch. Engring., 1978-80. Active Chgo. council Boy Scouts Am., 1960-64; bd. dirs. Milw. Sch. Engring. Alumni Assn., 1978—. Served with USNR, 1969-72. Recipient Achievement award Milw. Sch. Engring., 1968; registered profl. engr., Wis., Mich., Ill. Mem. Constrn. Specifications Inst. (dir. 1977-79), ASHRAE, ASME, Scientists and Engrs. of Milw., Am. Inst. Plant Engrs., Wis. Paper Council. Republican. Roman Catholic. Club: Wisconsin. Home: Delafield WI 53018 Office: 20720 W Watertown Rd Waukesha WI 53186

POSNER, RICHARD ALLEN, See *Who's Who in America,* 43rd edition.

POSNICK, ADOLPH, chemical company executive; b. Yellow Creek, Sask., Can., May 3, 1926; s. Frank and Joanne (Shimko) P.; came to U.S., 1947; B.S. in Ceramic Engring., U. Sask., 1947; m. Sarah Anne Briggs, May 16, 1947; children—Joann Elizabeth, Barbara Ellen. Research engr. Ferro Corp., Cleve., 1947-50; tech. dir. Ferro Enamel-Brazil, Sao Paulo, 1950-56, mng. dir., 1956-65, v.p. internat. ops. Ferro Corp., Cleve., 1965-74, sr. v.p. ops., 1974-75, exec. v.p., 1975-76, pres., chief exec. officer, 1976—; dir. fgn. subsidiaries. Mem. Am., Brazilian ceramic socs., Cleve. World Trade. Clubs: Clevelander, Mid Day, Chagrin Valley Country, Union, Pepper Pike Country. Office: Ferro Corp 1 Erieview Plaza Cleveland OH 44114

POSSATI, MARCO, electronic measuring systems company executive; b. Bologna, Italy, Apr. 24, 1953; came to U.S., 1977; s. Mario and Gabriella (Manfredi) P.; m. Francesca Bortolotto, Feb. 11, 1979; 1 child, Alessandro Marco. EDP mgr. Marposs Corp., Troy, Mich., 1977-79, dist. mgr., Dallas, 1979-80, pres., Troy, Mich., 1980—. Mem. Am. Mgmt. Assn., Soc. Mfg. Engrs. Club: Bloomfield Open Hunt. Avocations: tennis; sailing. Office: Marposs Corp 2040 Austin Troy MI 48083

POST, MARGARET MOORE, journalist; b. Plainfield, Ind., Aug. 16, 1909; d. Robert Wans and Sara Virginia (Rupe) Stephenson; A.B., La. State U., 1930; L.H.D. (hon.), Franklin (Ind.) Coll., 1973; m. Everett L. Moore, Dec. 4, 1932 (dec. Mar. 1952); children—Jo Ann Moore Long, Sue Ellen Moore Walker; m. 2d. H. J. Post, 1970 (div. 1977). Reporter, then city editor Logansport (Ind.) Press, 1930-32; editor Mooresville (Ind.) Times, 1933-38; columnist Indpls. Star, 1932-42; head journalism dept. Franklin Coll., 1942-51; copy editor Indpls. News, 1952-53, with public relations dept. Indpls. Star, also Indpls. News, 1953-68, polit. and feature writer Indpls., News, 1968-83; tchr. journalism Ind. U., Indpls., also Def. Info. Center, Ft. Harrison, Indpls., 1954-56; mem. faculty Sch. Police Adminstrn., U. Louisville, 1973-75; editorial adv. bd. Franklin Coll. Mem. Ind. Criminal Justice Commn., 1969—, Ind. Juvenile Justice and Deliquency Adv. Bd., 1979—; mem. crime control panel U.S. C. of C., 1959-74; co-chmn. Ind. 1st Child Abuse Conf., 1977; coordinator Indpls. Anti-Crime Crusade, also Women Against Rape, 1962-75; mem. Presdl. Crime Prevention Commn., 1972; bd. dirs. United Cerebral Palsy Indpls.; founding mem. Ind. Assn. Prevention Blindness, Big Sisters Indpls. Recipient Nat. Recognition award Freedoms Found. at Valley Forge, 1968; 1st pl. award Gen. Fedn. Women's Club-Sears Roebuck Found., 1968; award Ind. Council Juvenile Judges, 1980; Casper Community Services award, 1956, 62, 65, 68, 72, 76, 76; name Sagamore of Wabash, 1970, 78, Ind. Mother of Yr., 1965. Mem. Women in Communications (nat. v.p. 1946-52; Headliner award 1968, Clarion award 1975, 75), Nat. Fedn. Press Women, Women's Press Club Ind., Ind. Acad. Gen. Fedn. Women's Clubs, AAUW, Am. Mothers' Com., Ind. Forum. Delta Gamma Mothers' Club. Republican. Quaker. Author: Wives of Indiana Governors, 1982; Plainfield, Indiana, A Pictorial History, 1985; co-author: The Lawbreakers, 1968. Home: 2805 Barbary Ln Apt E Indianapolis IN 46205 Office: 307 N Pennsylvania St Indianapolis IN 46206

POSTHUMA, ALBERT ELWOOD, surgeon; b. Grand Rapids, Mich., Apr. 25, 1919; s. Gerrit Pylman and Alice (Mandemaker) P.; A.B., Calvin Coll., 1940; M.D., U. Mich., 1943, M.S. 1949; m. Jean L. Swann, Aug. 17, 1974; children by previous marriage—Beth Alicia Posthuma Jenkins, Ann Maureen Posthuma Eizyk, Jane Marie, Sue Swann Frankforter. Intern, St. Mary's Hosp., Grand Rapids, 1943-44, resident, 1944-46, 48-50; practice medicine specializing in surgery, 1950—; cons. surgeon St. Mary's Hosp., 1972—, chief of staff, 1972-78; cons. surgeon Ferguson-Drost-Ferguson hosps. Pres., Kent County Med. Found., 1979. Served from 1st lt. to capt. AUS, 1946-48. Recipient citation U. Mich., 1949. Diplomate Am. Bd. Surgery. Fellow A.C.S.; mem. Pan-Pacific Surg. Assn., Kent County Med. Soc. (pres. 1978-79). Club: Blythefield Country. Home: 2117 Osceola Dr Grand Rapids MI 49506 Office: 153 Lafayette SE Grand Rapids MI 49503

POSTHUMUS, RICHARD EARL, state senator, farmer; b. Hastings, Mich., July 19, 1950; s. Earl Martin and Lola Marie (Wieland) P.; m. Pamela Ann Bartz, June 23, 1972; children—Krista, Lisa, Heather, Bryan. B.S. in Agrl. Econs. and Pub. Affairs Mgmt., Mich. State U., 1972. Exec. v.p. Farmers and Mfrs. Beet Sugar Assn., Saginaw, Mich., 1972-74, Mich. Beef Commn., Lansing, 1974-78; dir. constituent relations Republican Caucus, Mich. Ho. of Reps., 1979-82; self-employed farmer, 1974—. Third vice chmn. Mich. Republican Com., 1971-73. Mem. Alpha Gamma Rho. Home: 4102 Segwun Ave Lowell MI 49331

POSTMA, RICHARD, lawyer; b. Sheldon, Iowa, Jan. 3, 1951; s. Gerald J. and Jane Ann (London) P.; m. Helen Fredricks, June 1, 1972; children—Rebecca, Lisa, Catherine, Susan. B.A., Calvin Coll., 1973; J.D., U. Mich., 1975. Bar: Mich. 1975. Ptnr. Freihofer, Oosterhouse & DeBoer, Grand Rapids, Mich., 1978-83, Miller, Johnson, Snell & Cummiskey, Grand Rapids, 1983—; dir. Bergsma Furniture Co., Grand Rapids. Trustee Calvin Coll., Grand Rapids, Pine Rest Hosp., Grand Rapids. Mem. Grand Rapids Bar Assn., ABA, Fed. Bar Assn., Assn. Trial Lawyers Am. Republican. Christian Reformed Church. Club: Kent Country. Lodge: Kiwanis (pres. 1979). Office: Miller Johnson Snell & Cummiskey 800 Calder Plaza Bldg Grand Rapids MI 49503

POSTON, FREDDIE LEE, entomologist; b. Jacksonville, Fla., Nov. 19, 1946; m. Charlotte Eller, Mar. 17, 1967; children—Erin E., Lindsay. B.S. in Biology, W. Tex. State U., 1971; M.S. in Entomology, Iowa State U., 1973, Ph.D., 1975. Research assoc. Iowa State U., Ames, 1973-75; asst. prof. Kans. State U., Manhattan, 1975-80, assoc. prof., 1980-84, prof., 1985—, assoc. dir. extension, 1984—; entomologist Coop. State Research Service, USDA, Washington, 1980-81. Contbr. articles to profl. jours. Grantee in field. Mem. Entomol. Soc. Am., Central States Entomol. Soc. (pres. 1979). Avocation: flying. Office: Kans State U Umberger Hall Manhattan KS 66506

POSTON, LAWRENCE SANFORD, III, English educator; b. Louisville, Oct. 29, 1938; s. Lawrence Sanford Jr. and Nancy Wyatt (Greene) P.; m. Carol Anne Hoaglan, Nov. 25, 1966; children—Anne Wyatt, Andrew Sanford (dec.), Rachel Berkeley. B.A., U. Okla., 1960; M.A., Princeton U., 1962, Ph.D., 1963. From instr. to prof. U. Nebr., Lincoln, 1963-76; vis. prof. U. Tulsa, Okla., 1975-76; prof. English, U. Ill., Chgo., 1976—, chmn. dept., 1980-84, assoc. vice chancellor acad. affairs, 1984—. Author: Loss and Gain: An Essay on Browning's Dramatis Personae, 1974. Contbr. articles to profl. jours. Mem. MLA, Midwest Victorian Studies Assn. (exec. sec. 1977-80), AAUP (assoc. sec. 1969-71, editor Bull. 1970-75). Democrat. Episcopalian. Home: 528 Cuyler Ave Oak Park IL 60302 Office: Office Acad Affairs U Ill Box 4348 Chicago IL 60680

POTARACKE, ROCHELLE MARY, educator; b. La Crosse, Wis., Mar. 27, 1935; s. John and Theadora Sibylla (Kreibich) P. B.S., Viterbo Coll., 1964; M.A., Cath. U., 1969. Tchr. Sacred Heart Sch., Eau Claire, Wis., 1956-68; tchr. Our Lady Fatima, Spokane, Wash., 1958-60; tchr. Cathedral Sch., La Crosse, 1960-76; instr. Viterbo Coll., La Crosse, 1976-81, asst. prof., 1981—, Mem. Nat. Assn. Edn. Young Child, Great Rivers Assn. Edn. Young Child, Wis. Assn. Tchr. Edn., Am. Assn. Colls. for Tchr. Edn. Roman Catholic.

POTCHEN, E. JAMES, radiology educator; b. Queens County, N.Y., Dec. 12, 1932; s. Joseph Anton and Eleanore Joyce P.; children—Michelle,

Kathleen, Michael, Joseph. B.S., Mich. State U., East Lansing, 1954; M.D., Wayne State U., 1958; M.S., MIT, 1973; J.D. U. Mich., 1984. Diplomate Am. Bd. Nuclear Medicine, Am. Bd. Radiology (examiner 1968-78). Intern Butterworth Hosp., Grand Rapids, Mich., 1958-59; resident Peter Bent Brigham Hosp., Boston, 1961-64; gen. practice medicine, Grand Rapids, 1959-61; chief resident radiologist Peter Bent Brigham Hosp., Children's Hosp., Pondville State Cancer Hosp., 1964; jr. assoc. radiology Peter Bent Brigham Hosp., 1965; dir. div. Nuclear Medicine, Harvard Med. Sch., dept. radiology, Peter Bent Brigham Hosp., 1965-66; dir. nuclear medicine div. Mallinckrodt Inst. Radiology, Washington U. Sch. Medicine, 1966-73, chief diagnostic radiology, 1971-72; asst. prof. radiology Washington U., St. Louis, 1966, assoc. prof. radiology, 1967-70, prof. radiology, 1970-73; prof. radiology, dean mgmt. resources Johns Hopkins U., Balt., 1973-75; mem. faculty Mich. State U., East Lansing, 1975—, prof. radiology Coll. Human Medicine, prof. mgmt. Coll. Bus., prof. Lymann Briggs Coll., dir. Med. Service Plan, 1977—; chmn. Liaison Com. Med. Edn., 1982—; mem. Bur. Radiologic Health-Med. Radiation Adv. Com. FDA, 1982-85; mem. med. necessity in diagnostic imaging adv. com. Nat. Blue Cross/Blue Shield, 1981. Assoc. editor Investigative Radiology, 1968-72, Jour. Nuclear Medicine, 1969-74, Jour. Microvascular Research, 1970-78, Radiology, 1972—, Internat. Jour. Radiation Oncology, Biology and Physics, Continuing Edn. Radiology; mem. editorial bd. Radiology, 1970-71. Contbr. articles to various publs. Recipient awards including Dist. Alumni award Wayne State U., 1970; Scholar in Radiologic Research James Picker Found., 1967-68; Advanced fellow Academic Radiology, James Picker Found., Nat. Acad. Scis.-NRC, 1965-66; John J. Larkin award for basic med. research, 1963. Fellow ACP, Am. Coll. Chest Physicians; mem. Acad. Mgmt. (div. sec. 1977-78), Am. Cancer Soc. (div. bd. trustees 1977-78), AMA (council med. edn. 1979—), ABA Am. Physiologic Soc., Am. Radium Soc., Am. Roentgen Ray Soc., Am. Soc. Clin. Investigation, Assn. Am. Med. Colls., Assn. U. Radiologists (mem. exec. com. 1970-72; mem. com. 1971-72), Central Soc. Clin. Research, Fleischner Soc., Interam. Coll. Radiology, Ingham County Med. Soc. (mem. com. 1977—), Mich. State Med. Soc. (mem. adv. com. med. edn. 1980—), Nat. Inst. Health Found. Advanced Edn. Scis., Radiologic Soc. N.Am., Soc. Chmn. of Acad. Radiology Depts. (mem. exec. com.), Soc. Nuclear Medicine (nat. pres. 1975-76), Soc. Health and Human Values, Soc. Med. Decision Making (founding mem. 1979), Soc. Thoracic Radiology (founding mem., 1982—), Sigma Xi, Alpha Omega Alpha. Office: Mich State U Dept Radiology B-220 Clin Center East Lansing MI 48824

POTENTE, EUGENE, JR., interior designer; b. Kenosha. Wis., July 24, 1921; s. Eugene and Suzanne Marie (Schmit) P.; Ph.B., Marquette U., 1943; postgrad. Stanford U., 1943, N.Y. Sch. Interior Design, 1947; m. Joan Cioffe Potente, Jan. 29, 1946; children—Eugene J., Peter Michael, John Francis, Suzanne Marie. Founder, pres. Studios of Potente, Inc., Kenosha, Wis., 1949—; pres., founder Archtl. Services Assos., Kenosha, 1978—, Bus. Leasing Services of Wis. Inc., 1978—; past nat. pres. Inter-Faith Forum on Religion, Art and Architecture; vice chmn. State Capitol and Exec. Residence Bd., 1981-83. Sec., Kenosha Symphony Assn., 1968-74. Served with AUS, 1943-46; bd. dirs. Ctr. for Religion and the Arts, Wesley Theol. Sem., Washington, 1983-84 Mem. Am. Soc. Interior Designers (treas., pres. Wis. 1985—), Inst. Bus. Designers, Sigma Delta Chi. Roman Catholic. Club: Kenosha Towne. Lodge: Elks. Home: 1515 16th St Kenosha WI 53140 Office: 914 60th St Kenosha WI 53140

POTH, JAMES EDWARD, physics educator; b. Galion, Ohio, May 19, 1933; s. Ralph Edward and Laura Elizabeth (Wirick) P.; m. Alice Etheridge, June 25, 1960; children—Michael Edward, Elizabeth Ann, Amy Etheridge. B.S., Miami U., Oxford, Ohio, 1955, M.A., 1960; M.S., Yale U., 1962, Ph.D., 1966. Research physicist Yale U., New Haven, Conn., 1966; from asst. prof. to prof. physics Miami U., Oxford, 1966—; vis. research physicist Yale U., New Haven, 1974. Author: Study Guide for University Physics, 1984. Contbr. articles to profl. jours. Served to lt. USN, 1955-58, Fellow NASA, 1967. Mem. Am. Assn. Physics Tchrs., Am. Phys. Soc., Sigma Xi. Lutheran. Home: 410 Maxine Dr Oxford OH 45056 Office: Miami U Dept Physics Oxford OH 45056

POTHAST, HENRY LYNN, school social worker; b. Marshalltown, Iowa, Apr. 2, 1952; s. Lester Raymond and Annie (Dunham) P.; student Marshalltown Community Coll., 1970-71; B.A., U. Iowa, 1974, M.S.W., 1981; postgrad. U. No. Iowa, 1977-78, Iowa State U., 1983-85; m. June Dubberke, Feb. 14, 1976; children—Emily Ann, Laurel Rachael. Youth services worker Iowa Tng. Sch. for Boys, Eldora, 1974-75, youth counselor I, 1975-78, youth counselor II, 1978-79, instr. high sch. equivalency, 1975-77; social worker Area Edn. Agy. 6, Eldora, 1981—. Mem. Nat. Assn. Social Workers, Acad. Cert. Social Workers, Iowa Sch. Social Workers' Assn., Phi Beta Kappa. Club: DeMolay (orator 1969-70). Home: Route 1 Box 512 Hubbard IA 50122 Office: Area Edn Agy 6 Eldora IA 50627

POTKIN, NATHAN NORMAN, dentist; b. Chgo., Nov. 5, 1914; s. Max and Bessie (Gross) P.; B.S., U. Ill. Sch. Pharmacy, 1933; D.D.S., U. Ill., 1944, M. Bacteriology, 1935; m. Evelyn Goldman, June 3, 1940; children—Steven, Ralph, Jeffrey, Ben. Faculty, researcher U. Ill. Coll. Dentistry, 1944-53; practice dentistry, Chgo., 1944-53, 55—; chief dental staff Northeast Hosp., Chgo.; chief staff Forkosh Hosp. Mem. Hosp., also chmn. dental com. Active Cub Scouts Am., 1955-57. Served with AUS, 1953-55. Mem. Endodontic Soc., Internat. Dental Research Assn., Ill., Chgo. dental socs. Mason (Shriner). Contbr. to profl. publs. in field. Home: 6950 N Kenneth Ave Lincolnwood IL 60646 Office: 7001 N Clark St Chicago IL 60626

POTTER, CORINNE JEAN, librarian; b. Edmonton, Alta., Can., Feb. 2, 1930; d. Vernon Harcourt and Beatrice A. (Demaray) MacNeill; m. William B. Potter, Aug. 11, 1951 (div. Jan. 1978); children—Caroline, Melanie, Theodore, William, Ellen. B.A., Augustana Coll., 1952; M.S., U. Ill., 1976. Br. librarian Rock Island (Ill.) Pub. Library, 1967-73, children's work supr., 1973-74; dir. St. Ambrose Coll. Library, Davenport, Iowa, 1978—. Mem. ALA, Assn. Coll. and Research Libraries (sec., v.p., pres. Iowa chpt. 1979-82), Iowa Library Assn. (com. chmn. 1983-84). Office: McMullen Library St Ambrose Coll 518 W Locust St Davenport IA 52803

POTTER, DAVID GURNEY, government official; b. Vicksburg, Mich., Nov. 16, 1946; s. Francis Harold and June Magdaline (Gurney) P.; m. Kirsten Elizabeth Taylor, June 13, 1970; children—Rebecca, Matthew, Amanda. Student Whitworth Coll., 1964-65; B.S. in Wildlife Biology with distinction, Wash. State U., Pullman, 1968. Asst. refuge mgr., U.S. Fish and Wildlife Service, Las Vegas, summer, 1968, Tulelake, Calif., 1971-73, Jefferson, Oreg., 1973-77, Quincy, Ill., 1977-79, refuge mgr., Cayuga, N.D., 1979—. Contbr. articles to various newspaper, profl. jours. Pres. elect Salem Audubon Soc., Oreg., 1977; sec. edn. com. Oreg. chpt. The Wildlife Soc., Salem, 1977. Served with USCG, 1968-71. Recipient Suggestion award U.S. Fish and Wildlife Service, Portland, Oreg., 1975, Denver, 1983; Conservation award, Salem Audubon Soc., 1977. Mem. Wildlife Soc., Baptist. Am. Legion (comdr.). Mem. Quincy Audubon Soc. (newsletter editor 1978-79). Clubs: Kiwanis (Tulelake, Calif.); Toastmaster (Quincy, Ill.). Home: Rural Route 1 Box 74 Cayuga ND 58013 Office: Tewaukon Nat Wildlife Refuge Rural Route 1 Box 75 Cayuga ND 58013

POTTER, DONALD ALBERT, manufacturing company executive; b. Indpls., May 9, 1922; s. Donald Holmes and Gertrude Antoinette (Sullivan) P.; m. Marian Helen Loughery, Feb. 6, 1943; children—Donald V., Mary J., Richard J., Ann T., Robert A., William M., James P. B.S., Notre Dame U., 1942. Chief engr. Universal Castings Corp., Chgo., 1946-47; various positions Stewart-Warner Corp., Chgo., 1947—, v.p., 1960—, gen. mgr., 1959—; v.p., dir. Datafax Corp., Chgo.; pres., dir. Stewart-Warner Microcircuts, Sunnyvale, Calif.; v.p., dir. Stewart-Warner Display Systems, Chgo. Patentee electronic controls and heat transfer. Mem. Chgo. Research and Devel. Council; mem. Loyola U. Devel. Council, Chgo.; chmn. Citizens Bd. Loyola U., Chgo. Served to ensign USNR, 1943-45. Recipient Hon. Alumnus award Loyola U., Chgo., 1978. Mem. Am. Def. Preparedness Soc. (dir.), Automotive Engrs. (pres. 1977), Armed Forces Communications and Electronics Assn. (dir. 1963-67), ASME, Ill. C. of C. Clubs: Chgo. Athletic, Econ. Avocations: microcomputers; running; tennis; reading. Home: 250 Franklin Rd Glencoe IL 60022 Office: Stewart-Warner Electronics 1300 N Kostner Ave Chicago IL 60022

POTTER, JAMES DEAN, accountant; b. Milw., Jan. 14, 1941; s. Dean Lincoln and Geraldine (Fitzgerald) P.; m. Sharon Grace Waldron, June 30, 1962; children—Jayne, Carole. B.B.A., U. Wis.-Milw., 1964. C.P.A., Wis. Staff auditor Arthur Andersen & Co., Milw., 1966-70; controller Brake & Equipment Co., Milw., 1970-72; mgr. Wolf & Co., Milw., 1972-78, Broesch Jannsen & Co., C.P.A.s, Milw., 1978-80; ptnr. Potthoff & Co., C.P.A.s, Racine, Wis., 1980-85, James D. Potter, S.C., 1985—. Chmn., South Shore br. YMCA, Cudahy, Wis., 1983—; sec. Oak Creek Assembly of God Ch., Wis., 1977—; chmn. Oak Creek Civil Service Commn., 1982. Served to capt. U.S. Army, 1964-66. Mem. Wis. Soc. C.P.A.s, Am. Inst. C.P.A.s. Lodge: Kiwanis (past pres.). Avocations: jogging; cross country skiing; woodworking. Address: 10656 S Howell Ave Oak Creek WI 53154

POTTER, JANICE BABER, school superintendent, educator; b. Roann, Ind., May 15, 1938; d. Matthew and Emma E. (Shillinger) Baber; m. Marcus L. Potter III, Aug. 17, 1957; children—Susan, Julie. M.S., No. Ill. U., 1972, C.A.S., 1976, Ed.D. in Ednl. Adminstrn., 1979. Cert. spl. edn. tchr., chief sch. bus. ofcl., supt., Ill. Tchr. Winfield (Ill.) Pub. Schs., 1969-76; owner, operator Formative Yrs. presch., Wheaton, Ill., 1976-79; supr. Bloomingdale (Ill.) Pub. Schs., 1979-81; asst. dir./bus. mgr. So. Met. Assn., Harvey, Ill., 1981-84; supt. Lisbon Grade Sch., 1984—; mem. faculty Nat. Coll. Edn., 1970-82. Mem. Am. Assn. Sch. Adminstrs., Assn. Supervision and Curriculum Devel., Ill. Assn. Sch. Bus. officers, Assn. Children Learning Disabilities, Ill. Women Adminstrs. Presbyterian. Home: 28 W 070 Mack Rd Wheaton IL 60187 Office: Rural Route 1 Box 62 Newark IL 60541

POTTER, JOHN EDWARD, radio executive; b. Columbus, Ohio, Nov. 27, 1949; s. Edward John and Alverna E. (Sorg) P.; m. Kathleen Ann Heringer, Jan. 31, 1949; children—Nathan John, Sara Ann, Benjamin John. B.A., Ohio State U., 1972. Announcer Sta. WCOL, Columbus, 1969-70, Sta. WMNI, Columbus, 1970-72; announcer Sta. WTVN, Columbus, 1972-75, program dir. 1975-80, account exec. 1980-84, local sales mgr., 1984—. Bd. dirs. Franklin County Heart br., 1978-80; mem. exec. com. Multiple Sclerosis Soc., 1976-80; trustee Columbus U.S.A. Assn., 1977-80; trustee Secret Santa, 1975-80; active Boy Scouts of Am., 1968—; chmn. bd. trustees Rally in the Alley, Inc., 1977-81. Recipient Ten Outstanding Young Citizens award, Columbus Jaycee's, 1978, Chuck E. Selby award, 1979; Quarter Million Dollar Club award Taft Broadcasting, 1980-81, V.I.P. Sales Club award, 1981-82; Disting. Sales award Sales Exec. Club, 1981. Mem. Columbus Area C. of C., Radio Advt. Bur., Ohio Assn. Broadcasters. Roman Catholic. Clubs: Downtown Sertoma (bd. dirs.), YMCA Businessmen's, Catholic Businessmen's Luncheon. Mem. editorial bd. WTVN, 1975-80. Office: 42 E Gay St Suite 1500 Columbus OH 43215

POTTER, JOHN WILLIAM, judge; b. Toledo, Ohio, Oct. 25, 1918; s. Charles and Mary Elizabeth (Baker) P.; m. Phyllis May Bihn, Apr. 14, 1944; children—John William, Carolyn Diane Hoyt, Kathryn Susan Heintschel. Ph.B., U. Toledo, 1940; J.D., U. Mich., 1946. Bar: Ohio 1947, U.S. Dist. ct. (no. dist.) Ohio 1950. Assoc. Zachman, Boxell, Schroeder & Torbet, Toledo, Ohio, 1946-51; ptnr. Boxell, Bebout, Torbet & Potter, Toledo, 1951-69; asst. atty. gen. State Ohio, 1968-69; judge Ct. Appeals 6th Appellate Dist., State Ohio, 1969-82; U.S. dist. judge No. Dist. Ohio, Western div., Toledo, 1982—. Mayor, City of Toledo, 1961-67; pres. Ohio Mcpl. League, 1965; past assoc. mem. Toledo Labor-Mgmt. Commn.; past pres., past. bd. dirs. Com. on Relations with Spain; past bd. dirs. Cummings Sch., Toledo; hon. bd. dirs. Toledo Opera Assn.; past trustee Epworth United Methodist Ch., Toledo; bd. dirs. Conlon Ctr. Served to capt. U.S. Army, 1942-46, ETO. Recipient Leadership award Toledo Bldg. Congress, 1965, award of merit Toledo Bd. Realtors, 1966,67; named Hon. Chmn., Toledo Festival Arts, 1980. Mem. ABA, Am. Judicature Soc., Fed. Judges Assn., Ohio State Bar Assn., Lucas County Bar Assn., Toledo Bar Assn., 6th Jud. Cir. Dist. Judges Assn., Toledo Area C. of C. Clubs: Old Newsboys; Good Fellow Assn. (Toledo). Lodge: Kiwanis. Office: US Dist Ct 215 US Courthouse Toledo OH 43624

POTTER, NOEL MARSHALL, research chemist; b. Machias, Maine, May 11, 1945; s. W. Edwin and Charlotte Z. (White) P.; m. Gail B. Aganier, Aug. 9, 1969; children—Jennifer L., Jason E. B.S., Worcester Poly Tech. Inst., 1967; M.S., Cornell U., 1969, Ph.D., 1971. Sr. staff research scientist Gen. Motors Research Labs., Warren, Mich., 1971—. Contbr. articles to profl. jours. Mem. Am. Chem. Soc., Assn. Analytical Chemists, ASTM. Home: 7007 Grenadier Ct Utica MI 48087 Office: Gen Motors Research Labs Gen Motors Tech Ctr Warren MI 48090

POTTER, RICHARD CLIFFORD, lawyer; b. Providence, Nov. 25, 1946; s. Peter Rex Potter and Helen Louise (McDevitt) Potter St. Onge; m. Anne Algie, Mar. 22, 1975; children—Catherine Anne, David Henry. B.A., U. N.C., 1968; J.D. cum laude, Ind. U., 1973. Bar: Ill. 1973, U.S. Dist. Ct. (no. dist.) Ill. 1973, U.S. Ct. Appeals (8th cir.) 1975, U.S. Ct. Appeals (3d cir.) 1978, U.S. Ct. Appeals (4th and 5th cirs.) 1979, U.S. Ct. Appeals (9th cir.) 1980, U.S. Supreme Ct. 1979. research asst. Ind. U., Bloomington, 1971-73; assoc. Kirkland & Ellis, Chgo., 1973-75; assoc. Bell, Boyd & Lloyd, Chgo., 1975— lobbyist Boise Cascade Corp., Washington, 1981-84. Assoc. editor, exec. officer Ind. Law Jour., 1972-73. Bd. dirs. Northbrook Park Dist., Ill., 1982. Mem. ABA, Internat. Bar Assn., Fed. Bar Assn., Legal Club Chgo. Club: University (Chg.). Home: 2134 Butternut Ln Northbrook IL 60062 Office: Bell Boyd & Lloyd 70 W Madison Chicago IL 60602

POTTER, ROSARIO H., scientist, dentistry educator; b. Manila, Philippines, Aug. 21, 1928; came to U.S., 1959, naturalized, 1970; d. Thomas E.C. and Sun-Tee (Ho) Yap; m. Norman E. Potter, July 17, 1964; 1 child, Brent E. D.M.D. summa cum laude, U. of the East Coll. Dentistry, Manila, 1952; M.S.D., U. Oreg., 1961-63; M.S., Ind. U. Sch. Medicine, 1967. Research asst. Eastman Dental Ctr., Rochester, N.Y., 1960-61; research assoc. U. Oreg. Dental Sch., 1961-63, Ind. U. Sch. Medicine, 1963-67, from asst. prof. to prof. dentistry, 1967—, also dir. biostats. grant site visitor NIH Spl. Study Sect., 1983. Contbr. articles, abstracts to profl jours. and chpts. to books. Recipient 1st place award Philippine Nat. Dental Bds., 1955, Gold medal U. of East, 1955; Eastman Dental Ctr. fellow, 1959; USPHS trainee, 1966; grantee Ind. U., 1979—, NIH, 1981—, Am. Fund for Dental Health, 1982-84; invited lectr. WHO, 1983. Mem. Internat. Assn. Dental Research, Am. Assn. Dental Research, Am. Soc. Human Genetics, Am. Assn. Dental Schs., Sigma Xi. Mem. Christian Ch. Office: Ind Univ Sch Dentistry 1121 W Michigan St Indianapolis IN 46202

POTTER, STEVEN EARL, aeronautical engineer; b. Wichita, Kans., Feb. 19, 1945; s. Hershel Otto and Ruth Ida (McHenry) P.; m. Lana June Strait, Apr. 6, 1968; children—Stephaine Colleen, Kent Marion. B.S. in Aero. Engring., Wichita State U., 1971, M.S. in Engring. Mechanics. Design engr. Gates Lear Jet Corp., Wichita, 1967-68; structures engr. Beech Aircraft Corp., Wichita, 1968-74; sr. specialist engr. Boeing Co., Wichita, 1974—. Patentee in field. Deacon, Baptist Ch., Conway Springs, Kans., 1982—; scoutmaster Troop 809 Boy Scouts Am. Mem. AIAA. Republican. Club: Kans. Bassmasters (Wichita) (v.p. 1977). Lodge: Masons. Home: 214 S Cranmer Conway Springs KS 67031

POTTS, BARBARA JOYCE, mayor, radiology technician; b. Los Angeles, Feb. 18, 1932; d. Theodore Thomas and Helen Mae (Kelley) Elledge; m. Donald A. Potts, Dec. 27, 1953; children—Tedd, Douglas, Dwight, Laura Potts Ahrenholtz. A.A., Graceland Coll., 1951; R.T., Radiol. Tech. Sch., 1953. Radiol. technician Independence Sanitarium and Hosp., Mo., 1953, 58-59, St. Mary's Hosp., Balt., 1954-55; mem.-at-large City Council, Independence, 1978-82, mayor, 1982—; dir. Mo. Mcpl. League, Jefferson City, 1982—; chmn. Mid-Am. Regional Council, Kansas City, Mo., 1984, 85. Pres., Child Placement Services, Independence, 1972—; mem. Mo. Gov.'s Conf. on Edn., 1976; mem. Independence Charter Rev. Bd., 1977; bd. dirs. Hope House, Shelter for Abused Women, Independence, 1982—; trustee Independence Sanitarium and Hosp., 1982—; chmn. Mo. Commn. on Local Govt. Cooperation, 1985-88. Recipient Women of Achievement award Mid-Continent council of Girl Scouts, 1983; Jane Adams award Hope House, Shelter for Battered Women and Children, 1984; Community Leadership award Comprehensive Mental Health Services, Inc., 1984. Mem. Nat. Women's Polit. Caucus, LWV. Mem. Reorganized Ch. of Jesus Christ of Latter-day Saints. Home: 18508 E 30th Terr Independence MO 64057 Office: City of Independence City Hall 111 E Maple St Independence MO 64050

POULOS, JAMES THOMAS, endocrinologist, educator; b. Lynn, Mass., Apr. 11, 1938; s. Thomas Dimitrios and Christine Julia (Zorzy) P.; m. Mary Margaret White, June 22, 1963; 1 son, Christopher Kreag. B.S., Tufts U., 1959, M.D., 1963. Diplomate Am. Bd. Internal Medicine, Am. Bd. Endocrinology and Metabolism. Intern, New Eng. Med. Ctr., Boston, 1963-64, resident 1964-65; resident and fellow in endocrinology U. Chgo., 1967-70; practice medicine specializing in endocrinology Arnett Clinic, Lafayette, Ind., 1970—, v.p., bd. dirs., 1979—; adj. prof. clin. pharmacology Purdue U., West Lafayette, Ind., 1976—; clin. faculty Ind. U. Sch. Medicine; bd. dirs. Lafayette Home Hosp., 1980—, pres. med. staff, 1978-79; Active Nat. Republican Senatorial Com., Natl. Rep. Congl. Com. Served with M.C., U.S. Army, 1965-67. Mem. AMA, Am. Diabetes Assn. (dir. Ind. chpt. 1980—, pres.-elect 1985), Am. Lung Assn. (pres. West Central Ind. 1982-83), Lafayette C. of C. Co-author: The Metabolic Influence of Progestins Advances in Metabolic Disorders, 1971; contbr. articles to profl. publs. Home: 1000 Windwood Ln West Lafayette IN 47906 Office: 2600 Greenbush St Lafayette IN 47904

POUNIAN, ALBERT KACHOUNI, art curator; b. Chgo., Mar. 7, 1924; s. James Kazar and Dorothy (Garabedian) P.; m. Lois Elaine Morin, Aug. 5, 1950; children—Barbara, James, Susan. B.F.A., Sch. of the Art Inst. of Chgo., 1948, M.F.A., 1949. Instr. Sch. of the Art Inst., Chgo., 1948-56; prof. art Barat Coll., Lake Forest, Ill., 1949-79; corp. art curator Continental Bank, Chgo., 1979—; cons. OEO, Washington, 1965-67. Author: (with others) Encyclopedia. Exhibited in numerous shows. Mem. Com. on candidates Lake Forest Caucus, Ill., 1980-83; cons. South Loop Planning Bd., Chgo., 1982-85. Served to 2d lt. U.S. Army, 1942-46, ETO. Decorated Bronze Star. Fulbright-Hays Exchange scholar Belfast, N. Ireland, 1977-78. Mem. Assn. Corp. Art Curators (founding chmn., chmn., 1981-83). Democrat. Avocations: photography, tennis. Office: Continental Bank 231 S La Salle St Chicago IL 60697

POWDRILL, GARY LEO, plant engineering manager; b. Butte, Mont., Nov. 26, 1945; s. Harold Holmes and Genevieve Marie (Tansey) P.; B.S., Gonzaga U., 1969; M.B.A., U. Detroit, 1973; M.P.A. in Environ. Policy, Ind. U., 1984; m. Marsha A. McKeon, Oct. 6, 1979; 1 dau., Amy Marie. Plant design engr. Ford Motor Co., Sterling Heights, Mich., 1969-73, div. plant engr. Chassis div., 1973-74, supr. plant engring. sect., Indpls. plant, 1974-78, mgr. plant engring., 1978-80, mgr. engring. and facilities, 1980—. Mem. Indpls. Mayor's Tech. Adv. Com., 1975—. Lic. profl. engr., Ind.; cert. plant engr. Mem. Ind. Soc. Profl. Engrs. Roman Catholic. Elk. Home: Rural Route 1 Box SC8 New Palestine IN 46163 Office: 6900 English Ave Indianapolis IN 46206

POWE, JOSEPH W., county official, tax accountant, consultant; b. Greenville, Miss.; s. Collins Orange and Janie (McCall) P.; m. Dorothy N. Crittendton; 1 child, Terry Collins. B.B.A., Saginaw Valley Coll., 1975; M.B.A., Central Mich. U., 1977. Supr. Saginaw Steering Gear, Mich., 1962-73; instr. Delta Coll., Saginaw, 1978-82; acct., cons., Saginaw, 1975—; fin. mgr. Saginaw County Road Commn., 1980—, Pres. Buena Vista Bd. Edn., Mich., 1982. Mem. County Assn. Sch. Bds., v.p. Saginaw County, 1985, Nat. Assn. Black Sch. Bd. Mems. (bd. dirs. 1984). Mem. Am. Mgmt. Assn., County Road Assn. Mich., Nat. Assn. Sch. Bds., Mich. Assn. Sch. Bds. Club: Frontier Internt. (Saginaw), Lodge: Lions. Avocations: golf; tennis; fishing. Home: 322 S 30th Saginaw MI 48601 Office: Saginaw County Rd Commission 3020 Sheridan Saginaw MI 48601

POWELL, DORIS B., sales representative; b. Aberdeen, Miss., Oct. 15, 1951; d. Titus Theopolis and Josephine (Cockerham) P. B.S., So. Ill. U. Tchr. Chgo. Bd. Edn., 1975-80; health claims adjuster Kemper Ins., Long Grove, Ill., 1980-82; sales cons. ITT Edn. Services, Chgo., 1982—. Voters registration vol. Chgo., 1984; coordinator Walk Am. Am. Cancer Soc., Chgo. and DuPage County, 1982, 83; bike rider Sickle Cell Anemia Midwest Assn., Chgo., 1977, 81, 83; community action vol. PanHellenic Community Action Council, Chgo., 1983. Named Employee of Month ITT Edn. Services, Mem. Nat. Assn. Female Execs., Toastmasters (parliamentarian 1985—, Best Speaker award 1985). Democrat. Presbyterian. Avocations: gourmet cooking; reading; swimming; traveling.

POWELL, DYER JAMES, construction financing company executive; b. Miami, Ariz., July 4, 1938; s. James Orlando and Rachel Nadien Powell; B.S. in Bus., San Jose State Coll., 1962; m. Rita Marie, Oct. 6, 1967; children—Michael, Patrick. Vice pres. sales Miller & Schroeder, Inc., Mpls., 1968-79; chief exec. officer, chmn. Keenan & Clary, Inc., Mpls., 1979—. Bd. dirs. Elder Friends; ind. Republican del. state conv., 1982; bd. dirs. Minn. Epilepsy League. Served with U.S. Army, 1958-62. Teaching cert. securities and fin. Hennepin County Sch. Dist. Mem. Am. Mgmt. Assn. Roman Catholic. Club: Serra. Home: 5224 Richwood Dr Edina MN 55436 Office: 1200 2d Ave S Minneapolis MN 55403

POWELL, GEORGE EVERETT, JR., motor freight company executive; b. Kansas City, Mo., June 12, 1926; s. George Everett and Hilda (Brown) P.; student Northwestern U.; m. Mary Catherine Kuehn, Aug. 26, 1947; children—George Everett III, Nicholas K., Richardson K., Peter E. With Riss & Co., Inc., Kansas City, Mo., 1947-52, treas., 1950-52; with Yellow Freight System, Inc., Overland Park, Kans., 1952—, pres., 1957-68, chmn. bd., 1968—; dir. 1st Nat. Charter Corp., Butler Mfg. Co. Trustee, mem. exec. com. Mid-West Research Inst., Kansas City, Mo., 1961—, chmn. bd. trustees, 1969—; bd. govs. Kansas City Art Inst., 1964—, chmn. bd. trustees, 1973-75. Served with USNR, 1944-46. Mem. Kansas City C. of C. (bd. dirs. 1964-68). Office: Yellow Freight System Inc 10990 Roe Ave Box 7270 Overland Park KS 66207*

POWELL, HARRIET JEAN, wholesale executive, income tax preparer; b. Mentor, Ohio, Dec. 1, 1947; d. Nelson Burton and Harriet Hazel (Hale) Chase; m. Mitchell Elliot Bennett, Apr. 4, 1974 (div. 1979); 1 child, Russell; m. Warren Dean Powell, Dec. 18, 1982 (div. July 1985); 1 child, Sarah. B.S. in Theology, North East Bible Coll., Valley Forge, Pa., 1969. Caseworker Cuyahoga County Dept. Welfare, Cleve., 1970-73; real estate agt. Realty World-Eging Realty, Chardon, Ohio, 1976-81; computer cable sales rep. Innovative Digital Equipment, Bedford, Ohio, 1980-81; with sales payroll service Paychex, Solon, Ohio, 1981-82; sales rep. pagers, beepers Metro-Page, Ashtabula, Ohio, 1982-84; income tax preparer Bennetts Tax Service, Burton, Ohio, 1973—; owner, originator Garage Sale Store, Mentor, Ohio, 1982—. Office: Garage Sale Store 8655 Mentor Ave Mentor OH 44060

POWELL, JON TUDOR, communication educator; b. Ealing, Eng., Mar. 9, 1934. B.A. magna cum laude, St. Martin's Coll., 1954; M.S., U. Oreg., 1956, Ph.D., 1963. Grad. asst. U. Oreg., Eugene, 1954-56, instr. speech fundamentals, pub. speaking, 1960-63; asst. prof., dir. radio-TV So. Oreg. Coll., Ashland, 1963-64; assoc. prof. undergrad., co-ordinator sch. of radio-TV Ohio U., Athens, 1966-69; assoc. prof., then prof., coordinator radio-TV-film No. Ill. U., DeKalb, 1969-78, prof. communication studies, instructional tech., chmn. dept. communication studies, 1978—. Contbr. articles to profl. jours. Served with USAF, 1956-60. Mem. Am. Assn. Sch. Adminstrs., Assn. Communication Adminstrn., Broadcast Edn. Assn., Central States Speech Assn., Ill. Broadcasters Assn. (bd. dirs.), Ill. Speech and Theatre Assn., Internat. Inst. Communications, Internat. Radio and TV Soc., Nat. Acad. TV Arts and Scis., Speech Communication Assn. Office: No Ill U Dept Communications DeKalb IL 60115*

POWELL, VANCE DALY, JR., obstetrician-gynecologist, surgeon; b. N.Y.C., Apr. 10, 1945; s. Vance Daly and Josina (Benton) P.; m. Elaine Heinrich Olson, Apr. 4, 1968; m. 2d Laurel Ann Siegfried, May 10, 1981; children—Vance Daly III, Shannon Elaine. B.A., Va. Mil. Inst., 1967; D.O., Phila. Coll. Osteo. Medicine, 1975. Intern, Botsford Gen. Hosp., Farmington Hills, Mich., 1975-76, resident in ob-gyn and surgery, 1976-81; practice osteo. medicine specializing in ob-gyn. and gynecol. surgery, Farmington Hills, 1981—; dir. med. edn., acting med. dir. Botsford Gen. Hosp., 1981—, sec. dept. obstets/gynecology, 1981—; mem. staff N.W. Gen. Hosp., Detroit; asst. clin. prof. ob-gyn Mich. State U. Coll. Osteo. Medicine, 1983—; bd. dirs. Acad. Osteo. Dirs. Med. Edn. Mem. Clarenceville Sch. Bd., Livonia, Mich. Served as capt. U.S. Army, 1967-69; Vietnam. Decorated Bronze Star, Disting. Air Service. Mem. Am. Coll. Ob-Gyn, Mich. Assn. Osteo. Dirs. Med. Edn., Am. Osteo. Dirs. Med. Edn., Am. Osteo. Assn. Republican. Lutheran. Office: 28080 Grand River Suite 209 Farmington Hills MI 48024

POWELL-BROWN, ANN, publicist, educator; b. Boonville, Mo., Mar. 19, 1947; d. Edward Marsh and Ethel M. (Benton) Powell; B.S., Central Mo. State U., 1969, M.S.E., 1975; postgrad. U. Mo., Kansas City; m. Richard Lee Brown, Dec. 29, 1978. Tchr., Gulfport and Biloxi (Miss.) Schs., 1969-70; mem. adj. staff Providence Coll., Taichung, Taiwan, 1971-72; mem. reading and learning disabilities staff, Kansas City (Mo.) Bd. Edn., 1973-78, mem. learning disabilities identification team, 1978-79, mem. spl. edn. placement com., 1979-83; co-owner Am. Media Escorts, 1983—; learning disabilities cons., 1984—; v.p., bd. dirs. Nat. Tutoring Inst., 1976; adj. faculty Ottawa Coll., 1980, instr. English as 2d lang., 1976-77; adj. faculty U. Mo., Kansas City, 1981; speaker various orgns. Mem. public affairs com. Jewish Community Center, 1978; v.p. Com. for Indochinese Devel., 1977; mem. edn. council

Episcopal Diocese Western Mo., 1977; founder, bd. dirs. Friends of St. Mary's; mem. profl. adv. bd. Oak Park Home Health Care, 1983; mem. Kansas City Jazz Festival Com., 1983. Mem. Council Exceptional Children, Assn. Children with Learning Disabilities, Internat. Reading Assn. (state publicity com. 1983), Am. Booksellers Assn., Pubs. Publicity Assn., Nat. Orgn. Women Bus. Owners, Nat. Reading Council, Quality Edn. Coalition, Doctoral Student Spl. Interest Group, AAUW, Gt. Alkali Plainsmen, St. David's Welsh Soc., Phi Delta Kappa. Democrat. Episcopalian. Clubs: Challinor Guild, Eggs and Issues Breakfast. Home: 501 Knickerbocker Pl Kansas City MO 64111 Office: Am Media Escorts 501 Knickerbocker Pl Kansas City MO 64111

POWER, JOSEPH EDWARD, lawyer; b. Peoria, Ill., Dec. 2, 1938; s. Joseph Edward and Margaret Elizabeth (Birkett) P.; m. Camille June Repass, Aug. 1, 1964; children—Joseph Edward, David William, James Repass. Student Knox Coll., Galesburg, Ill., 1956-58; B.A., U. Iowa, 1960, J.D., 1964. Bar: Iowa 1964. Law clk. to judge U.S. Dist. Ct., 1964-65; mem. firm Bradshaw, Fowler, Proctor & Fairgrave, Des Moines, 1965—. Bd. dirs. Moingona council Girl Scouts U.S.A., 1968-77, pres., 1971-74; mem. Des Moines CSC, 1971-73; bd. dirs. Des Moines United Way, 1976-82, v.p., 1979-81; mem. Des Moines Civil War Roundtable. Served to comdr. USNR, 1965-81. Fellow Am. Coll. Probate Counsel, Am. Coll. Real Estate Lawyers; mem. ABA, Iowa Bar Assn. (chmn. probate, property and trust law com. 1983—), Polk County Bar Assn., Des Moines Estate Planners Forum (pres. 1982-83). Republican. Mem. United Ch. of Christ. Club: Des Moines. Home: 4244 Foster Dr Des Moines IA 50312 Office: 1100 Des Moines Bldg Des Moines IA 50307

POWERS, KATHRYN DOLORES, social services administrator; b. Chgo., Dec. 17, 1929; B.A., Colgate-Rochester U., 1951; M.S.W., Smith Coll., 1964. Child welfare worker, supr. Cook County Dept. Public Aid Children's Div., Chgo., 1953-68; dir. program Central Bapt. Children's Home/Family Services, Lake Villa, Ill., 1968-82, asst. exec. dir., 1983—; pres. bd. dirs. Community Residential Network, Inc., 1978-79; instr. field work U. Wis., 1975-76; mem. habilitation/rehab. task force Health Systems Agency, Kane, Lake and McHenry counties, Ill., 1979. Recipient Spl. Merit citation Am. Bapt. Homes and Hosps. Assn., 1979. Mem. Nat. Assn. Social Workers, Acad. Cert. Social Workers, Am. Orthopsychiat. Assn. Home: 309 Milwaukee St Lake Villa IL 60046 Office: Box 218 Lake Villa IL 60046

POWERS, MARK LYMAN, lawyer; b. Toledo, Jan. 31, 1955; s. Lyman Alfred and Martha Ann (Holman) P. B.A., Ohio No. U., 1977, J.D., 1980. Bar: Ohio 1980, U.S. Dist. Ct. (no. dist.) Ohio 1981. Legal intern Defiance County Prosecutor, Ohio, 1979-80; assoc. Saxer and Powers, Wauseon, Ohio, 1980—. Mem. Wauseon Homecoming Com., 1983; treas. Fulton County Mental Health Assn., Wauseon, 1983; mem. Wauseon Sch. Bd., 1984—; bd. dirs. Fulton County Red Cross, Ohio, 1980, Wauseon Community Chest, 1984—. Mem. Fulton County Bar Assn., Ohio State Bar Assn., N.W. Ohio Bar Assn., Wauseon Jaycees. Republican. Mem. Christian Ch. (Disciples of Christ). Lodge: Elks. Office: Saxer and Powers 114 N Fulton St PO Box 393 Wauseon OH 43567

POWERS, ROBERT M., manufacturing company executive; b. 1931; B.S., Emory U., 1952, M.S., 1953, Ph.D., 1958. Research chemist A.E. Staley Mfg. Co., Decatur, Ill., 1958-61, lab. head, 1961-62, group leader, 1962-67, dir. UBS div., 1967, dir. spl. product devel., 1968-69, dir. indsl. products research and devel., 1969-70, dir. research and devel., 1970-71, v.p. research and devel., 1971-75, v.p. agrl. products group, 1975-79, exec. v.p., 1979-80, pres., 1980—, also dir., chief operating officer. Served with U.S. Army, 1954-55. Office: AE Staley Mfg Co 2200 Eldorado St Box 151 Decatur IL 62525*

POWERS, WILLIAM FRANCIS, automobile manufacturing company executive; b. Phila., Dec. 11, 1940; s. Francis Simpson and Kathryn Emily (Thoroughgood) P.; m. Linda Nell Shelton, Sept.7, 1963; children—Stephen, Leigh. B.S. in Aerospace Engring., U. Fla., 1963; M.S., U. Tex., 1966, Ph.D., 1968. Aerospace engr. NASA Marshall Space Flight Ctr., Huntsville, Ala., 1960-65; faculty mem. U. Mich., Ann Arbor, 1968-79, prof. aerospace engring., 1976-79; mgr. Ford Motor Co., Dearborn, Mich., 1979—; cons. NASA Johnson Space Ctr., Houston, 1971-79, other cos., 1968-79. Contbr. articles to profl. jours. Editor: Astrodynamics, 1975, Jour. Astron. Scis., 1977-80. USSR research exchange scientist U.S. Nat. Acad. Scis., 1976. Assoc. fellow AIAA; mem. ASME, IEEE, Soc. Automotive Engrs. Home: 2032 Greenview St Ann Arbor MI 48103 Office: Ford Motor Co PO Box 2053 Dearborn MI 48121

POYNTON, JOSEPH PATRICK, aerospace engineer; b. Chgo., Aug. 28, 1934; s. Joseph P. and Marvel E. (Gaffney) P.; B.S. Aero. Engring., U. Notre Dame, 1956, M.S. Aero. Engring., 1958; m. Betty Jeanne Gorman, Oct. 1, 1971; 1 dau., Jeanne Louise. Teaching fellow U. Notre Dame, 1956, research asst., 1957; aerodynamics engr. Nike Zeus, Douglas Missiles Co., Santa Monica, Calif., 1958-59; sr. aerodynamic engr. SR. 71 and Apollo, Honeywell Inc., Mpls., 1959-64, sr. design engr. Fgn. Technology div., Dayton, Ohio, 1964; sr. aerospace engr. Polaris, Lockheed Space & Missiles Co., Sunnyvale, Calif., 1965-66; supervisory aerospace engr. U.S. Army-Dept. Def. Army Aviation Systems Command, St. Louis, 1966—, program decision rev. chmn. for aircraft survivability equipment, also supr. chem. and biol. protection, specialist in low speed aerodynamics Mem. AIAA, Am. Helicopter Soc., Sigma Xi. Roman Catholic. Author tech. papers. Home: 9624 Yorkshire Estates Crestwood MO 63126 Office: PO Box 209 Saint Louis MO 63166

POZORSKI, JOSEPH MICHAEL, JR., lawyer; b. Manitowoc, Wis., Aug. 10, 1957; s. Joseph A. and Alice (Lambert) F.; m. Lynn Marie Komorosky, Aug. 28, 1982; 1 child, Joseph, III. B.S., Marquette U., 1979; J.D., John Marshall Law Sch., 1982. Bar: Wis. 1982, U.S. Dist. Ct. (ea. dist.) Wis. 1982. Assoc. Kaminski & Rusboldt, Manitowoc, 1982—. Bd. dirs. Marco Manor, Manitowoc, 1984—. Club: Eagles (Manitowoc) (chmn. bd. 1984—). Home: 717 E Cedar Ave Manitowoc WI 54220 Office: Kaminski & Rusboldt 1020 S 9th St Manitowoc WI 54220

POZULP, NAPOLEON CHARLES, II, psychologist; b. Chgo., Nov. 1, 1947; s. Harry Lawrence and Bernice Pozulp; student U.S. Mcht. Marine Acad., 1965-68; B.A., Ind. U., 1970; M.A., No. Ill. U., 1973, Ph.D., 1976. Clin. therapist Rush-Presbyn.-St. Lukes Med. Center, Chgo., 1976-77; sr. therapist Tri-City Mental Health Center, East Chicago, Ind., 1977-79; dir. Asso. Cert. Psychologists, Chgo., 1979—; cons. in field. Mem. Am. Psychol. Assn., Ill. Psychol. Assn. Contbr. articles to profl. jours.; editor Psychology News, 1980—. Home: 12500 S 91st Ave Palos Park IL 60464 Office: 625 N Michigan Ave Suite 500 Chicago IL 60611

PRAEGER, HERMAN ALBERT, JR., research agronomist; b. Claflin, Kans., Jan. 2, 1920; s. Herman Albert and Gertrude Edna (Grizzell) P.; B.S., Kans. State U., 1941, M.S., 1947, Ph.D., 1977; 1 dau., Gwenneth Irene. Commd. lt., U.S. Army, 1941, advanced through grades to lt. col., 1973; mem. faculty Command and Gen. Staff Coll., 1963-67; comdg. officer U.S. Army Support Group, Joint Security Area, Korea, ret., 1973; research agronomist Kans. State U., Manhattan, 1978—; adminstr. improvement of pearl millet program AID, 1978—. Decorated Legion of Merit, Bronze Star with 3 oak leaf clusters, Medal for Merit, Joint Services Commendation medal, Army Commendation medal with oak leaf cluster, Purple Heart. Mem. Assn. U.S. Army, Am. Soc. Agronomy, AAAS, Crop Sci. Soc. Am., V.F.W. Republican. Episcopalian. Club: Elks. Home: 3008 Gary Ave Manhattan KS 66502 Office: Throckmorton Hall Kans State U Manhattan KS 66506

PRAGER, DAVID, justice Kans. Supreme Ct.; b. Fort Scott, Kans., Oct. 30, 1918; s. Walter and Helen (Kishler) P.; A.B., U. Kans., 1939, LL.B., 1942; m. Dorothy Schroeter, Sept. 8, 1945; children—Diane, David III. Admitted to Kans. bar, 1942; practiced in Topeka, 1946-59; dist. judge, Topeka, 1959-71; asso. justice Supreme Ct. Kans., 1971—; lectr. law Washburn Law Sch., 1948-68. Served to lt. USNR, 1943-46. Mem. Am., Kans., Topeka bar assns., Order of Coif, Phi Beta Kappa, Phi Delta Theta, Phi Delta Phi. Home: 5130 SW 53d St Topeka KS 66610 Office: Kans Jud Center Topeka KS 66612

PRALL, ELMER CLARENCE, dentist; b. Lamoni, Iowa, Mar. 9, 1902; s. Oscar Edward and Eleanor Margaret (Gibbons) P.; A.A., Graceland Coll., 1923, U. Iowa, summers, 1920-22, 24, 26; D.D.S., U. Iowa, 1930; m. Irma Caroline Reihman, June 25, 1927; 1 dau., Paula Prall White. Tchr., athletic coach Iowa High Schs., 1920-22, 23-24, 26-27; gen. practice dentistry, Mount Vernon, Iowa, 1930—. Pres., Mount Vernon chpt. ARC, 1947, v.p., water safety chmn., 1948-76. Mem. Mount Vernon City Council, 1934-76; mem. tax com. Iowa League Municipalities, 1936. Served to 1st lt. Dental Corps, U.S. Army, 1935-40. Fellow Am. Coll. Dentists (pres. Iowa sect. 1980); mem. Am. Soc. Dentistry for Children (unit pres. 1955), Am. (life), Iowa (supt. clinics. 1950, chmn. ins. council 1956-64) dental assns., University Dist. (pres. 1950, sec. 1945-50, 68-82), Cedar Rapids (pres. 1944-45) dental socs., Pierre Fauchard Acad., Alumni Assn. Dental Coll. U. Iowa (pres. 1957, treas. 1958-65), Mount Vernon C. of C. (pres. 1933). Methodist (trustee 1971-74). Lion (pres. 1937). Home: 419 S 2d St Mount Vernon IA 52314 Office: 125 1st St W Mount Vernon IA 52314

PRANGE, NEIL EDWARD, environmental engineer; b. St. Louis, Oct. 31, 1945; s. Orville Henry and Marie Henrietta (Selle) P.; m. Patricia Ann Beseau, June 25, 1971; children—Christine, Matthew, Mark. B.S. in Chem. Engring., U. Mo., 1968; M.S. in Civil Engring., U. Mo.-Rolla, 1975, M.S., 1981. Registered profl. engr., Mo. Product devel. engr. Olin Corp., East Alton, Ill., 1968-73; sr. engr. Monsanto Enviro-Chem, St. Louis, 1973-77; engring. specialist corp. engring. dept. Monsanto, St. Louis, 1977-80, environ. protection specialist Monsanto J. F. Queeny Plant, St. Louis, 1980-81, environ. protection supr., 1981-85, sr. environ. specialist Monsanto World Hdqrs., 1985—; St. Louis, v.p. Indsl. Waste Control Council, St. Louis, 1983—. Patentee in field. Treas. cub scout troop St. Louis Area council Boy Scouts Am., 1983—. Served with U.S. Army, 1969-71, Vietnam. Mem. Am. Inst. Chem. Engrs., Air Pollution Control Assn. Lutheran. Avocations: Hunting; fishing; boating; automobile repair; major appliance repair. Office: Monsanto 800 N Lindbergh Blvd Saint Louis MO 63167

PRANICA, ALAN JOHN, chemical company manager; b. Green Bay, Wis., Sept. 6, 1941; s. John Peter and Chesterine Helen (Warshall) P.; m. Valerie Annett Vaux, July 22, 1967; children—Alissa Eve, Eve Louise. B.S.Chem.E., U. Wis.-Madison, 1964; M.B.A., Governors State U., 1976. Plant engr. Mobil Chem. Co., High Point, N.C., 1968-70; plant engr. Gen. Mills Co., Ossining, N.Y., 1970-73, quality control mgr., Kankakee, Ill., 1973-75, prodn. mgr., 1975-80; mfg. mgr. Henkel Corp., Kankakee, 1980-82, plant mgr., Kankakee, Ill., 1982—. Bd. dirs. YMCA, Kankakee, Ill., 1984—; bd. dirs. St. Marys Hosp., 1984—; pres. Briarcliff Community Assn., Bourbonnais, Ill., 1984-85. Recipient Mfg. award Gen. Mills Co., 1976. Mem. Kankakee Indsl. devel. Assn. (treas. 1984), Mpls. Jr. C. of C. (Merit award 1966), Kankakee Area C. of C. (bd. dirs. 1985—), Kankakee Area Bus. and Edn. Council. Republican. Roman Catholic. Home: 1371 Westminster Ln Bourbonnais IL 60914 Office: Henkel Corp Kensington Rd Kankakee IL 60901

PRATHER, THOMAS PIERSON, hospital pharmacist, educator, consultant; b. Kansas City, Mo., Dec. 19, 1948; B.S. in Pharmacy, U. Mo.-Kansas City, 1972. Registered pharmacist, Mo. Hosp. pharmacist Menorah Med. Ctr., Kansas City, 1972-77; assoc. pharmacist Dolgin's Apothecary, North Kansas City, 1975—; medication cons. Myers Nursing Home, Kansas City, 1983-85; sr. hosp. pharmacist Truman Med. Ctr. West, Kansas City, 1977—; adj. prof. Sch. Pharmacy, U. Mo.-Kansas City, 1982—. Co-author: Hyperalimentation: A Workbook for Pharmacists, 1976. Instr. CPR Now, Kansas City, 1983; basic cardiac life support instr. Am. Heart Assn., 1982—, advanced cardiac life support provider, 1984—. Roman Catholic. Avocations: scientific reading, electronics, scuba diving, teaching, real estate investing. Office: Truman Med Ctr West 2301 Holmes Kansas City MO 64108

PRATSCH, LEONARD ROEMER, optometrist; b. Lorain, Ohio, Sept. 28, 1910; s. Louis John and Lydia Christine (Roemer) P.; m. Irene Adaline Weiler, May 28, 1940; children—Jane, Lew, Mary Lynn. B.S. in Applied Optics, Ohio State Univ., Columbus, 1934. Pvt. practice optometry, Cleve., 1938-60, Lorain, Ohio, 1935—; cons. Lions Club, Lorain, 1965-79. Developer rotating oscillating projector for visual tng., compound roll-along hand magnifier, others in field. Committeeman, Republican Party, Lorain, 1974, councilman candidate Rep. Party, Lorain, 1976; mem. Black River Hist. Soc., Lorain, 1984-85. Recipient Golden Circle Cert. Ohio State Alumni Assn., 1984. Mem. Ohio Optometric Assn. (life 1979), Am. Optometric Assn. (life 1979), Lorain County Optometric Soc. (sec., treas., pres. 1957-60). Mem. United Ch. of Christ. Club: Central Bus. Mens (Lorain, Ohio). Lodges: Lions, KP. Avocations: Woodworking, gardening, boating, fishing, bowling and golf. Home: 2401 W 40th St Lorain OH 44053

PRATT, DALE LEE, city official; b. Millett, Mich., Dec. 30, 1935; s. Romine Efrich and Lucille (Martin) P.; m. Camilla Joan Van Goethem, Sept. 16, 1961; children—Daniel Dale, Timothy John. Cert. Ferris State Coll., Big Rapids, Mich., 1967, Calif. State Univ., Sacramento, 1974. Burner service technician Community Oil Co., Charlotte, Mich., 1958-66, plant operator waste water treatment City of Charlotte, 1966—. Scoutmaster Chief Okemos Council, Boy Scouts Am., 1974-83, dist. advancement chmn., 1980-83, chmn. council nominating com., 1981-83; pres. Charlotte Pony Football League, Mich., 1973-77; v.p. Band Booster, Charlotte, 1979; v.p. St. Mary's Ch. Men's Club, 1975; bd. dirs. United Way, Charlotte, 1981-83; pres. Camp Frances, Charlotte, 1982. Recipient Scouters Key, Boy Scouts Am., 1976, Scouters Tng. award, 1978, Dist. award Merit, 1981, Silver Beaver, 1982; St. George Emblem Catholic Com. Scouting, 1980; Disting. Service award Charlotte Pony Football League, 1980; Outstanding Citizenship award State of Mich., 1980. Mem. Charlotte Jaycees (Outstanding Jaycee, Charlotte 1979, external v.p. 1970). Roman Catholic. Lodge: Rotary. Avocations: Camping; hiking; hunting; fitness. Home: 121 W Seminary Charlotte MI 48813

PRATT, GEORGE BYINGTON, III, pediatric radiologist; b. Goshen, Ind., Sept. 6, 1936; s. George Byington and Estelle (Hudson) P.; m. Patricia Mae Hammer, June 22, 1957 (div. 1970); children—George B. IV, Pamela; m. Susan Pettijohn, June 23, 1972; 1 child, Lisa Susan. B.A., DePauw U., 1958; M.D., Northwestern U., 1962; J.D., Ind. U., 1978. Diplomate Am. Bd. Radiology. Pediatric radiologist Radiologic Specialists of Ind., Indpls., 1968—. Contbr. articles to profl. jours. Pres. Marion City Child Abuse and Neglect Council, Indpls., 1984—; bd. dirs. Family Support Ctr., Indpls., 1984—; v.p. Zionsville Park and Recreation Bd., Ind., 1978—. Served to capt. USAF, 1963-65. Fellow Am. Coll. Legal Medicine, mem. AMA, Ind. State Med. Assn. (3d place award Med. Exhibit 1970). Lodges: Masons, Rotary. Avocations: snow and water skiing; sailing.

PRATT, PHILIP, fed. judge; b. Pontiac, Mich., July 14, 1924; s. Peter and Helen (Stathis) P.; student U. Chgo., 1943-44; LL.B., U. Mich., 1950; m. Mary Charlotte Hill, July 26, 1952; children—Peter, Laura, Kathleen. Admitted to Mich. bar, 1951; asst. pros. atty., Oakland County, Mich., 1952; practice law in Pontiac, 1953-63; circuit judge 6th Jud. Circuit Mich., 1963-70; judge U.S. Dist. Ct., Eastern Dist. Mich., Detroit, 1970—. Served with OSS, AUS, 1943-46. Decorated Bronze Star medal. Mem. Am., Mich., Oakland County (pres. 1959-60) bar assns., Am. Judicature Soc. Office: US Courthouse Detroit MI 48226

PRATT, SAMUEL MAXON, English and humanities educator; b. North Adams, Mass., May 10, 1919; s. Harry Edward and Ethel Mae (Davis) P.; widowed; 1 child, Samuel Henry. A.B., Dartmouth Col., 1941; Ph.D., Cornell U., 1951. Tchr., Greer Sch., Hope Farm, N.Y., 1941-42, Cornell U., Ithaca, N.Y., 1946-52; prof. English and humanities Ohio Wesleyan U., Delaware, 1952-84; ret., 1984; reader Ednl. Testing Service, Princeton, N.J., 1956-83. Contbr. articles to scholarly publs. Active, Episcopal Church. Served with U.S. Army, 1942-45, ETO. Mem. AAUP (pres. local chpt. 1955-56, state chmn. 1959-60). Democrat. Avocations: golf, water skiing, maintenance of property. Home: 34 Westgate Dr Delaware OH 43015 Office: Dept English Ohio Wesleyan U Delaware OH 43015

PRAUER, JEFFREY ERIC, symphony orchestra administrator, musician; b. Chgo., Nov. 5, 1950; s. Herbert H. and Charlotte J. Prauer. B.Music Edn., Northwestern U., 1972. Asst. mgr., 2d trombone Fla. Gulf Coast Symphony, Tampa-St. Petersburg, 1972-77; gen. mgr. Pasadena Symphony Orch., 1977-79; ops. mgr. Minn. Orch., Mpls.-St. Paul, 1979-82; gen. mgr. Duluth-Superior Symphony Orch., Duluth, Minn., 1982—; freelance musician. Phi Mu Alpha scholar, 1972. Mem. Am. Symphony Orch. League, Am. Fedn. Musicians, U.S. Inst. Theater Technology, Phi Mu Alpha. Office: 506 W Michigan St Duluth MN 55802

PRAY, WARREN CHARLES, publications art director; b. Onaga, Kans., Apr. 16, 1947; s. George Wayne and Dorothy Marie (Hollenbeck) P.; m. Nancy Bea Bryan, Aug. 11, 1968. B.A. in Art Edn., U. Kans., 1972; M.S., Kans. State U., 1977. Retail mgr. Berkowitz Investment, Kansas City, Mo., 1968-71; art tchr. Shawnee Mission Schs., Kans., 1971-72; designer Expt. Sta., Manhattan, Kans., 1972-81; art dir. extension service Kans. State U., 1981—. Univ. drive chmn. United Way Riley County, Manhattan, 1983; bd. dirs. United Way, 1985—. HEW grantee, 1971. Mem. Univ. and Coll. Designers Assn. (designer, pres. 1984, chmn. bd. dirs. 1985—, excellence award 1976, 77), Council Advancement and Support Edn. (designer, excellent achievement award 1976, 78, 82), Agrl. Coll. Editors (designer, superior award 1974-84). Republican. Avocations: golf, gardening. Home: 2832 Illinois Ln Manhattan KS 66502 Office: Extension Service Kans State U Umberger Hall Manhattan KS 66506

PREHN, DONALD FREDERICK, dentist; b. Wausau, Wis., June 19, 1927; s. Delos Carl and Anita Ida (Mueller) P.; m. Patricia Booth, Aug. 9, 1953; children—Ronald, Constance, Frederick, Robert. B.S., U. Wis.-Madison, 1949; D.D.S., Marquette U., 1953. Pvt. practice dentistry, Wausau, 1953—; mem., past chmn. Wausau Hosps. Dental Staff, Wis., 1953—. Mem., pres. Wausau Dist. Bd. Edn., 1966-78; pres., mem. exec. bd. Samoset council Boy Scouts Am., 1973—; sr. warden, vestryman St. John the Bapt. Episcopal Ch., Wausau, 1978-85; mem. exec. bd., fin. com. Episcopal Diocese Fond du Lac, Wis., 1976—; mem. Birch Trails council Girl Scouts U.S.A., 1972—. Recipient Dist. award of merit Rib Mountain dist. Samoset council Boy Scouts Am., 1975, Silver Beaver award, 1976. Served to 2d lt. U.S. Army, 1946-47. Mem. Wausau Area C. of C. Republican. Episcopalian. Club: Wausau. Avocations: skiing; boating; camping; hunting; fishing. Home: 1010 Adams St Wausau WI 54401 Office: Prehn Dental Office 413 Jefferson St Wausau WI 54401

PREKOP, MARTIN D., art educator, artist; b. Toledo, July 2, 1940; s. Martin W. and Laurel (Rohr) P.; m. Martha McIntosh, Oct. 4, 1963; children—Sam, John, Zachary. Student Cleve. Inst. of Art, 1958-60; B.F.A., Cranbrook Acad. Art, 1962; M.F.A., R.I. Sch. Design, 1964; postgrad. Slade Sch Art. London, 1964-65. Chmn. freshman found. Sch. Art Inst. of Chgo., 1968-72, chmn. dept. painting, 1977-80, grad. div., 1972-76, prof., chmn. undergrad. div., 1981—; vis. prof. Newcastle Poly., Newcastle-upon-Tyne, Eng., 1980-81. Exhibited at group shows San Cicero Gallery, 1975—. Fulbright Found. fellow, 1964. Home: 4050 W Cortland Chicago IL 60639 Office: Sch Art Inst of Chicago Jackson Blvd and Columbus Dr Chicago IL 60603

PRENDERGAST, TERRY NEILL, lawyer; b. Sioux Falls, S.D., May 25, 1953; s. Harry Neill and Dorothy Gretchen (Angerhofer) P.; m. Susan Jane Larson, Aug. 2, 1980; 1 child, Christopher Neill. B.A. cum laude, Augustana Coll., 1975; M.B.A., U. S.D., 1978, J.D. magna cum laude, 1978. Bar: S.D. 1978, U.S. Dist. Ct. S.D. 1978, U.S. Tax Ct. 1981, U.S. Ct. Appeals (8th cir.) 1981. Law clk. U.S. Dist. Ct., Sioux Falls, 1978-79; ptnr. Boyce, Murphy, McDowell & Greenfield, Sioux Falls, 1979—; chmn. continuing legal edn. com. State Bar S.D., Pierre, 1984—; city atty. Lennox, S.D., 1980-82. Mem. ABA (coms. on corp., banking and bus. law, sci. and tech.), Assn. Trial Lawyers Am., S.D. Trial Lawyers Assn., Comml. Law League Am. Democrat. Methodist. Lodges: Kiwanis (bd. dirs. 1981-83), Elks. Home: 2904 S 1st Ave Sioux Falls SD 57105 Office: Boyce Murphy McDowell & Greenfield 505 Norwest Bank Bldg Sioux Falls SD 57105

PRENTICE, DIXON WRIGHT, justice Ind. Supreme Ct.; b. Sellersburg, Ind., June 3, 1919; s. Walter E. and Maude (Wilson) P.; LL.B., Ind. U., 1942; m. Phyllis Catherine Ropa, Dec. 20, 1941; children—Penelope Prentice Rauzi, Peter K., William W. Admitted to Ind. bar; ptnr. firm Prentice & Prentice, Lawyers, Jeffersonville, Ind., 1946-71; partner Green Tree Assos., Jeffersonville, 1968-73; assoc. justice Ind. Supreme Ct., Indpls., 1971—; mem. Nat. Commn. Uniform State Laws, 1979—. Served with U.S. Navy, 1942-46; lt. comdr. USNR Ret. Mem. ABA, Ind. Bar Assn. (ho. of dels. 1954-56, bd. mgrs. 1964-66), Clark County Bar Assn. (pres. 1953), Indpls. Bar Assn., Am. Judicature Soc., Ind. Judges Assn. Clubs: Meridian Hills Country; Kingsway Country (Charlotte Harbor, Fla.). Lodge: Elks. Office: 306 State House Indianapolis IN 46204

PRENTICE, NEVILLE, chemist; b. Newcastle, Northumberland, Eng., Feb. 10, 1920; came to U.S., 1923; naturalized, 1934; s. Edmund Eugene and Annie (Medd) P.; m. Valdine Sigvaldason, Sept. 5, 1949; children—Margaret Anne, Carol Kristine. B.Sc. with honors, U. Man. Can., Winnipeg, 1950; M.S., U. Minn., 1955, Ph.D., 1956. Research chemist U.S. Dept. Agrl. Cereal Crops Research div., Madison, Wis., 1956—; instr. U.S. Brewers Assn., Madison, 1970—. Contbr. articles to profl. jours. Served to cpl. Royal Canadian AF, 1941-45. Mem. Am. Assn. Cereal Chemists (assoc. editor 1973-75), Am. Soc. Brewing Chemists (mem. editorial bd. 1980—) Lutheran. Avocation: running. Home: 1118 University Bay Dr Madison WI 53705 Office: US Dept Agrl Cereal Crops Research Unit 501 N Walnut St Madison WI 53705

PREPOLEC, JOHN IVAN, tool and die company executive; b. Croatia, Yugoslavia, Dec. 8, 1921; s. Joseph and Slavica (Solgat) P.; came to U.S., 1936, naturalized, 1944; m. Lucille Drazick, June 8, 1946; children—Linda, Karen, John. B.S., Wayne State U., 1948, M.S., 1952. With Northeastern Tool & Die Corp., Warren, Mich., 1946-81, exec. v.p., 1967-78, sec., pres. and chief exec. officer, 1978-81; chmn., chief exec. officer Prepolec Industries, West Bloomfield, Mich., 1981—. Bd. dirs. Detroit Symphony Orch., Detroit Grand Opera Assn. Served with USNR, 1944-46. Mem. Engring. Soc., Detroit Croatian Bd. Trade (charter), Oakland Univ. Pres.' Club (life mem.). Roman Catholic. Clubs: Detroit Athletic, Detroit Economic, U. Mich. Pres.', Anthony Wayne. Lodge: K.C. Home: 855 Harsdale Rd Bloomfield Hills MI 48013 Office: 3360 S Ocean Blvd Palm Beach FL 33480

PRESBERRY, RICHARD LEE, state official; b. Caruthersville, Mo., Dec. 23, 1948; s. Sylvester and Ethel P.; m. Iva Viola Walker, Apr. 23, 1949; children—Andrea LaShay, Richard L. B.S., Lincoln U., Mo., 1971; M.A., St. Louis U., 1975, postgrad., 1980—. With dept. elem. and secondary edn. Vocat. Rehab. div. Mo., Maplewood, 1972—, asst. dist. supr., 1976-79, dist. supr., 1979—. Mem. Nat. Rehab. Assn., Am. Personnel and Guidance Assn., Nat. Rehab. Adminstrs. Assn. (sec. treas.), Pi Lambda Theta, NAACP. Baptist. Home: 6426 Evergreen St Berkeley MO 63134 Office: 7355 Manchester St Maplewood MO 63143

PRESCOTT, LANSING MASON, biology educator, microbiologist; b. Tulsa, Sept. 29, 1941; s. B. Osborne and Margreta G. (Gunderson) P.; m. Linda Louise Ulbrich, June 13, 1964; children—Paul Anthony, Peter Alan. B.A., Rice U., 1963, M.A., 1964; Ph.D., Brandeis U., 1969. Asst. prof. biology Augustana Coll., Sioux Falls, S.D., 1969-74, assoc. prof., 1974-82, prof., 1982—, chmn. dept., 1972-75, 85—. Contbr. articles to profl. jours. NSF grad. fellow, 1963-67, NSF grantee, 1979, 80, 82. Mem. Am. Soc. Microbiologists, Electron Microscopy Soc. Am., S.D. Acad. Sci., Am. Chem. Soc. (div. biol. chemistry), Sigma Xi. Lutheran. Avocations: music; reading; chess. Home: 2113 S Lake Ave Sioux Falls SD 57105 Office: Biology Dept Augustana Coll Sioux Falls SD 57197

PRESKORN, SHELDON HARRISON, psychiatrist, educator, medical scientist; b. Wichita, Kans., May 3, 1948; s. Harrison H. and Marie E. (Distel) P.; m. Belinda G. Smith, June 13, 1970; 1 child, Erika Dianne. B.S., Wichita State U., 1970; M.D., U. Kans., 1974. Diplomate Am. Bd. Psychiatry and Neurology. Resident in pathology U. Kans. Med. Ctr., Kansas City, 1973-75, rotating intern, 1975-76; resident in psychiatry Washington U. Sch. Medicine, St. Louis, 1976-78, asst. instr. psychiatry, 1976-78, prof. psychiatry and pharmacology, 1984—; asst. prof. psychiatry and pharmacology, toxicology and therapeutics U. Kans. Sch. Medicine, Kansas City, 1978-81, assoc. prof., 1981-84, prof., 1984. Author: (with others) Tardive Dyskinesia, 1980. Assoc. editor Jour. Clin. Psychiatry. Contbr. numerous articles to profl. jours., chpts. to books. Reviewer jours. Recipient Chester M. Goodwin award, 1971, Kans. U. Med. Ctr. Pathology Housestaff award, 1975, Psychiatry Housestaff award, 1976, Walter C. Menninger Neuropsychiatry award, 1978, Mead-Johnson award, 1978, Roche Lab. award for Neurosci., 1978, A.E. Bennett Neuropsychiat. Research Found. award, 1978, Am. Acad. Clin. Psychiatry Ann. research award, 1982, NIMH Research Scientist Devel. award, 1980—; fellow Wichita State U. Honors, 1969-70, U. Kans. research, 1971, Maurice Falk Found., 1975-78. Mem. AMA, Am. Psychiat. Assn. (program com. 1978-82, chmn. subcom. on new research 1980-82, Council on Research and Devel. 1976-78, task force on tardive dyskinesia 1976-79), Am. Soc. Clin. Pharmacology and Therapeutics (sci. program com. 1983—), Soc. Biol. Psychiatry, Kans. Psychiat. Soc. (continuing edn. com. 1980-82), Alpha Omega Alpha, Phi Kappa Phi, Omicron Delta Kappa (pres. 1969). Office: Dept Psychiatry Washington U Med Ctr 4940 Audubon Ave Saint Louis MO 63110

PRESS, MICHAEL FREDRICK, pathologist; b. St. Louis, May 11, 1948; s. Oliver Herbert and Martha Elfriede (Weidenbach) P.; m. Sarah Elizabeth Pizzo,

Nov. 26, 1977; children—Oliver Anthony, Lara Catherine, Eric William, David Johann. B.A., Washington U., 1970; Ph.D., U. Chgo., 1975, M.D., 1977. Diplomate Am. Bd. Pathology. Resident physician U. Chgo., 1977-81, chief resident, 1979-81, asst. prof. dept. pathology, 1981—. Jr. faculty clin. fellow Am. Cancer Soc., 1982-85; Amoco Found. scholar, 1984-85. Mem. Internat. Acad. Pathology, Internat. Soc. Gynecol. Pathologists, Am. Assn. Pathologists. Office: Dept Pathology U Chgo 5841 S Maryland Ave Chicago IL 60637

PRESS, NEWTOL, biological sciences educator, researcher; b. N.Y.C., Nov. 27, 1930; s. Morris and Sylvia (Finkelstein) P.; m. E. Francine Greenfield, Dec. 23, 1951; children—Betty, David, Michael. B.A., NYU, 1951; M.S., U. Iowa, 1955, Ph.D., 1956. Research assoc. U. Iowa, Iowa City, 1952-56; instr. U. Wis.-Milw., 1956-58, asst. prof., 1958-64, assoc. prof., 1964-77, prof. biol. scis., 1977—. Contbr. articles to profl. jours. Pres. Maple Dale-Indian Hill Sch. Bd., Milw., 1972-79, Soc. Moral and Ethical Value Judgments in Medicine and Biology, Milw., 1980—. Mem. AAUP. Jewish. Home: 1055 W Ravine Ln Milwaukee WI 53217 Office: U Wis Dept Biol Scis PO Box 413 Milwaukee WI 53201

PRESSER, STANLEY, sociologist; b. Bklyn., Feb. 18, 1950; s. Sidney and Sydonia (Cohen) P. A.B., Brown U., 1971; Ph.D., U. Mich. 1977. Research investigator Survey Research Ctr. U. Mich., Ann Arbor, 1977-78, head of field office, 1981-83; research assoc. Inst. Research Social Sci.; U. N.C., 1978-81; dir. Detroit Area Study U. Mich., 1983—; bd. overseers Nat. Opinion Research Ctr. Gen. Social Survey, 1984—. Co-author: Questions and Answers in Attitude Surveys, 1981; co-editor: Sourcebook of Harris National Surveys, 1981. Mem. editorial bd. Pub. Opinion Quar., 1983—, Sociol. Methods and Research, 1980-83, Social Psychology Quar., 1979-82. Contbr. articles to profl. jours. and books. Home: 803 Edgewood Pl Ann Arbor MI 48103 Office: Detroit Area Study U Mich 3528 LS&A Ann Arbor MI 48109

PRESSLER, LARRY, U.S. senator; b. Humboldt, S.D., Mar. 29, 1942; s. Antone Lewis and Lorretta (Claussen) P.; m. Harriet Pressler. B.A., U. S.D., 1964; diploma in Econs. (Rhodes scholar), Oxford (Eng.) U., 1966; M.A., Harvard U., 1971, J.D., 1971; 2 hon. degrees. Mem. 94th-95th Congresses from 1st Dist. S.D.; mem. U.S. Senate from S.D., 1979—; mem. commerce, fgn. relations, small bus. coms., spl. com. on aging. All-Am. del. 4-H Agrl. Fair, Cairo, 1961. Served to 1st lt. AUS, 1966-68; Vietnam. Recipient Nat. 4-H Citizenship award, 1962, Report to Pres. 4-H award, 1962. Mem. AMA, D.C. Bar Assn., Am. Assn. Rhodes Scholars, VFW, DAV, Am. Legion, Phi Beta Kappa. Club: Lions. Home: 700 New Hampshire Ave NW Washington DC 20037 Office: 407A Russell Senate Office Bldg Washington DC 20510

PRESSLY, LAURENCE LEE, association executive; b. Lee's Summit, Mo., June 2, 1931; s. John L. and Katherine L. (Lienweber) P.; m. Janet Sue Wilson, June 14, 1959; 1 dau., Laurie Marie. B.S. in Agr., U. Mo., 1953. County agt. U. Mo. Extension Service, Independence, 1956-72; agribus. mgr. Greater Kansas City (Mo.) C. of C., 1973-74; assoc. gen. mgr. Am. Royal Assn., Kansas City, 1975-76, exec. v.p., gen. mgr. 1977—; adv. dir. Charter Bank, Lee's Summit. Mem. Lee's Summit City Council, 1969-73; bd. dirs., v.p. Westminster Gerontology Found., 1964-73; co-chmn. Show Me Vienna Com.; mem. Lee's Summit Planning and Zoning Commn., 1964-68; mem. Bd. Zoning and Adjustment, 1976—; mem. Indsl. Devel. Authority, 1978—; bd. dirs., v.p. Lee's Summit Hosp. Assn. Recipient Disting. award Lee's Summit Jaycees, 1956; Disting. Service award Mo. Holstein Assn., 1980; hon. Am. Farmer degree Future Farmers Am., 1974. Mem. Internat. Assn. Fairs and Expositions, Livestock and Rodeo Mgrs. Assn., Internat. Agribus. Club. Clubs: Optimist (pres., charter mem., 1968), Saddle and Sirloin, Rotary, Kansas City, Hillcrest Country. Presbyterian. Home: 209 Oxford St Lee's Summit MO 64063 Office: American Royal Association 1701 American Royal Ct Kansas City MO 64102

PRESSON, ELLIS WYNN, health services executive; b. Electra, Tex., Mar. 28, 1940; s. Ellis Wilbur and Juanita M. (Morgan) P.; B.B.A., U. Tex., 1963; M.H.A., Washington U., St. Louis, 1965; m. Andrea L., July 5, 1969; children—Eric, Garett, Amber. Adminstrv. asst. Methodist Hosp. of Dallas, 1964-66; asst. adminstr. Dallas County Hosp., 1966-70; pres. Swedish Am. Hosp., Rockford, Ill., 1970-77, Research Med. Center, Kansas City, Mo., 1977-80, Research Health Services, Kansas City, 1980—. Pres., Comprehensive Mental Health and Retardation, 1972-74; treas. bd. Rockford Med. Edn. Found., 1972-75; preceptor for adminstrn. extern U. Wis., 1975-76; search com. Rockford Sch. Medicine, U. Ill., 1975-76; regional com. mem. Hosp. Adminstrv. Surveillance Program, 1973-76; bd. dirs. Ill. Hosp. and Health Service, 1972-77; mem. Health Planning NW Ill., 1973-77; licensing bd. mem. Ill. State Ambulatory Surgery Treatment Center, 1974-76. Mem. Am. Hosp. Assn., Mo. Hosp. Assn. chmn. bd., del. to Am. Hosp. Assn., mem. labor relations com.), Kansas City Area Hosp. Assn. (chmn. fin. council, dir.). Clubs: Rotary, Indian Hills Country. Home: 15613 Overbrook Ln Stanley KS 66224 Office: 6400 Prospect Kansas City MO 64132

PRESTANSKI, HARRY THOMAS, public relations executive; b. Zanesville, Ohio, Aug. 31, 1947; s. Joseph Raymond and Della Theresa (Butryn) P.; m. Jeanene LaRee Versaw, Sept. 19, 1970; children—Lisa Jodene, Shari LaRee, Amy Elizabeth. B.S. in Journalism, Ohio U., 1972; postgrad. U. Dayton, 1973-74. Publs. editor Hobart Brothers, Troy, Ohio, 1972-75; v.p., account supr. Josephson, Cuffari & Co., Montclair, N.J., 1975-78; publicity mgr. Winnebago Industries, Forest City, Iowa, 1978-80; v.p., account group mgr. Creswell, Munsell, Fultz & Zirbel, Cedar Rapids, Iowa, 1980—. Served to cpl. USMC, 1966-69. Mem. Pub. Relations Soc. Am., Am. Med. Writers Assn., Republican. Roman Catholic. Contbr. articles to profl. jours. Home: 3419 Sue Ln NW Cedar Rapids IA 52405 Office: 4211 Signal Ridge Rd NE Cedar Rapids IA 52406

PRESTON, DENNIS RICHARD, linguist; b. Harrisburg, Ill., Feb. 10, 1940; s. Andrew and Mattie Rowena (Dennis) P.; m. Carol Ann Guagliardo, Jan. 10, 1974; children by previous marriage—Stephan McGhee (dec.), Ellen Blair. B.A., U. Louisville, 1962; Ph.D., U. Wis., 1965. Teaching asst. U. Louisville, 1962-63, U. Wis.-Madison, 1963-65; instr. U. Wis.-Milw., 1965-67; asst. prof. Ohio State U., Columbus, 1967-72; prof. SUNY-Fredonia, 1972-82; prof. linguistics Eastern Mich. U., Ypsilanti, 1982—; Fulbright lectr. U.S. Fulbright-Poznan, Poland, 1972-74; vis. prof. U. Hawaii, Manoa, 1980-81; Fulbright lectr. Porto Alegre, Brazil, 1981. Editor: Varieties of American English, 1979. Author: Bituminous Coal Mining Vocabulary of the Eastern United States, 1973, others. editor Hawaii Working Papers in Linguistics, 1982. U.S. Office Edn. grantee, 1979; SUNY grantee, 1978; NSF grantee, 1985. Mem. Linguistic Soc. Am., Am. Dialect Soc., Am. Name Soc., Dictionary Soc. N.Am., Tchrs. English to Speakers of Other Langs. Democrat. Avocations: Cooking, fishing, racquetball. Home: 2184 Georgetown Blvd Ann Arbor MI 48105 Office: Dept English Lang and Lit Eastern Mich U Ypsilanti MI 48197

PRESTON, ROBERT BRUCE, lawyer; b. Cleve., Feb. 24, 1926; s. Robert Bruce and Erma May (Hunter) P.; m. Agnes E. Stanley, Jan. 29, 1949; children—Robert B., Patricia, Judith H. A.B., Western Res. U., 1950; LL.B., 1952. Bar: Ohio 1952, U.S. Dist. Ct. (no. dist.) Ohio 1953, U.S. Ct. Appeals (6th cir.) 1959, U.S. Supreme Ct. 1964. Assoc. Arter & Hadden, Cleve., 1952-63, ptnr., 1964—; dir. Bettcher Mfg. Corp., Brookpark, Ohio, Service Stampings, Inc., Willoughby, Ohio. Trustee Womens Philanthropic Union, Cleve., 1978—; chmn. Charter Rev. Commn., Cleveland Heights, Ohio 1972; mem. legal com., Gates Mills, Ohio, 1981—; v.p. Citizens League, Cleve., 1967. Mem. Greater Cleve. Bar Assn., Ohio State Bar Assn., ABA, Maritime Law Assn. of U.S. Republican. Presbyterian. Clubs: City (Cleve.), Mid Day. Avocations: tennis; fishing; travel. Home: Chagrin River Rd Gates Mills OH 44040 Office: Arter & Hadden 1100 Huntington Bldg Cleve OH 44115

PRETLOW, THOMAS GARRETT, physician, pathology educator, researcher; b. Warrenton, Va., Dec. 11, 1939; s. William Ribble and May (Tiffany) P.; m. Theresa Pace, June 29, 1963; children—James Michael, Joseph Peter, David Mark. A.B., Oberlin Coll., 1960; M.D., U. Rochester, 1965. Intern, Univ. Hosps., Madison, Wis., 1965-66, fellow McArdle Lab., 1966-67; research assoc. Nat. Cancer Inst., Bethesda, Md., 1967-69; asst. prof. pathology Rutgers Med. Sch., Piscataway, N.J., 1969-70; assoc. prof. pathology, U. Ala., Birmingham, 1971-73, prof. pathology, 1974-83, prof. biochemistry, 1982-83; vis. prof. pathology Harvard Med. Sch., Boston, 1983-84; prof. pathology Case Western Res. U., Cleve., 1983—; cons. NIH, Bethesda, 1976-84; mem. editorial bd. Cell Biophysics, Cambridge, Mass., 1978-82. Editor: Cell Separation: Methods and Selected Applications, 3 vols., 1982, 83, 84. Mem. exec. bd. Birmingham council Boy Scouts Am., 1979-83, Greater Cleve. council Boy Scouts Am., 1984—. Served to lt. comdr. USPHS, 1967-69. Recipient Research Career Devel. award Nat. Cancer Inst., 1973-78; grantee for cancer research. Mem. Am. Assn. Pathologists, Am. Assn. Immunologists, Internat. Acad. Pathology, Am. Soc. Clin. Oncology, Am. Assn. Cancer Research. Club: Serra (pres. Birmingham chpt. 1982-83). Avocations: camping, fishing, Boy Scouts, classical music, biking. Home: 3061 Chadbourne Rd Shaker Heights OH 44120 Office: Inst of Pathology Case Western Reserve U Cleveland OH 44106

PREUS, DAVID WALTER, clergyman; b. Madison, Wis., May 28, 1922; s. Ove Jacob Hjort and Magdalene (Forde) P.; m. Ann Madsen, June 26, 1951; children—Martha, David, Stephen, Louise, Laura. B.A., Luther Coll., 1943, D.D., 1969; B.Th., Luther Sem., 1950; postgrad. U. Minn., 1946-47, Union Sem., 1951, Edinburgh U., 1951-52; LL.D., Wagner Coll., 1973, Gettysburg Coll.; D.D., Luther Coll., 1969, Pacific Luth. Coll., 1974, St. Olaf Coll., 1974; L.H.D., Macalester Coll. Ordained to ministry, 1950; asst. pastor First Luth. Ch., Brookings, S.D., 1950-51; pastor Trinity Luth Ch., Vermillion, S.D., 1952-57; campus pastor U. Minn.-Mpls., 1957-58; pastor Univ. Luth. Ch. of Hope, Mpls., 1958-73; v.p. Am. Luth. Ch., 1968-73, pres., 1973—; Luccock vis. pastor Yale Div. Sch., 1969; chmn. youth activity Am. Luth. Ch., 1960-68; mem. exec. council Luth. Council U.S.A., Luth. World Fedn.; mem. central com. World Council Chs., 1973-75; Luth. del. White House Conf. on Equal Opportunity; chmn. Greater Mpls. Fair Housing Com., Mpls. Council Chs., 1960-64. Active Mpls. Planning Commn., 1965-67; mem. Mpls. Sch. Bd., 1965-74, chmn., 1967-69; mem. Mpls. Bd. Estimate and Taxation, 1968-73, Mpls. Urban Coalition; bd. dirs. Mpls. Inst. Art, Walker Art Ctr., Hennepin County United Fund, Ams. for Children's Relief, Luth. Student Fedn., Research Council of Gt. City Schs., Urban League, NAACP; bd. regents Augsburg Coll., Mpls. Decorated comdr.'s cross Royal Norwegian Order St. Olav; recipient Regents medal Augustana Coll., Sioux Falls, S.D., 1973; Torch of Liberty award Anti-Defamation League, 1973. Office: 422 S 5th St Minneapolis MN 55415*

PREUS, ROBERT DAVID, educational administrator, minister; b. St. Paul, Oct. 16, 1924; s. Jacob A.O. and Idella (Haugen) P.; m. Donna Mae Rockman, May 29, 1948; children—Daniel, Klemet, Katherine, Rolf, Peter, Solveig, Christian, Karen, Ruth, Erik. B.A., Luther Coll., Decorah, Iowa, 1944; B.D., Bethany Luth. Sem., Mankato, Minn., 1947; Ph.D., Edinburgh U. (Scotland), 1952; D.Theol., Strasbourg U. (France), 1969. Pastor, First Am. Luth. Ch., Mayville, N.D., Bygland Luth. Ch., Fisher, Minn., 1947-49, Harvard St. Luth. Ch., Cambridge, Mass., 1952-55, Mt. Olive Luth. Ch., Cross Lake Luth. Ch., Clearwater Luth. Ch., Trail, Minn., 1955-57; prof. systematic theology Concordia Sem., St. Louis, 1957-74; pres., prof. Concordia Theol. Sem., Springfield, Ill. and Ft. Wayne, Ind., 1974—. Author: The Inspiration of Scripture, 1955; The Theology of Post-Reformation Lutheranism, vol. 1, 1970, vol. 2, 1972; Getting Into the Theology of Concord, 1977. Republican. Avocation: Cross country skiing. Home: 2829 Fox Chase Run Fort Wayne IN 46825 Office: Concordia Theol Sem 6600 N Clinton St Fort Wayne IN 46825

PREUSS, ROGER E(MIL), artist; b. Waterville, Minn., Jan. 29, 1922; s. Emil W. and Edna (Rosenau) P.; student Mankato Comml. Coll., Mpls. Sch. Art; m. MarDee Ann Germundson, Dec. 31, 1954 (dec. Mar. 1981). Painter of nature art; one man shows St. Paul Fine Art Galleries, 1959, Albert Lea Art Center, 1963, Hist. Soc. Mont., Helena, 1964, LeSueur County Hist. Soc. Mus., 1976; exhbns. include Midwest Wildlife Conf. Exhbn., Kerr's, Beverly Hills, Calif., 1947, Joslyn Meml. Mus., Omaha, 1948, Minn. Centennial, 1949, Federated Chaparral Authors, 1951, Nat. Wildlife Art, 1951, 52, N.Am. Wildlife Art, 1952, Ducks Unltd. Waterfowl exhibit, 1953, 54, St. Paul Winter Carnival, 1954, St. Paul Gallery Art Mart, 1954, Salmagundi Club, 1968, Grand Central Art Galleries, N.Y.C., 1971, Faribault Art Center, 1981, Wildlife Artists of World, Bend, Oreg., 1984, Holy Land Conservation Fund Exhbn., Tel Aviv, La Galerie Mouffe, Paris, Merrill's Gallery Fine Art, Taos, N.Mex.; represented in permanent collections Demarest Meml. Mus., Hackensack, N.J., Smithsonian Hall of Philately, N.Y. Jour. Commerce, Mont. Hist. Soc., Voyageurs Nat. Park Interpretative Center, Inland Bird Banding Assn., Minn. Capitol Bldg., Mont. State U., Wildlife Am. Collection, LeSueur Hist. Soc., Lucky'leven, VFW, Mpls., Nat. Wildlife Fedn. Collection, Stark Mus., Orange, Tex., Minn. Ceremonial House, Harris Fine Arts Center of Brigham Young U., U.S. Wildlife Service Fed. Bldg., Ft. Snelling, Minn., VA Hosp., Mpls., Luxton Collection, Banff, Alta., Can., Inst. Contemporary Arts, London, Mont. Capitol Bldg., Goldblatt Collection, Lyons, Ill., Minn. Dept. Econ. Devel., St. Paul, numerous galleries and pvt. collections; designer Fed. Duck Stamp, U.S. Dept. Interior, 1949, Commemorative Centennial Pheasant Stamp, 1981, Gold Waterfowl medallion Franklin Mint, 1983, Gold and Silver Stamp medallions Wildlife Mint Inc., 1983. Former judge ann. Goodyear Nat. Conservation Awards Program. Del. Nat. Wildlife Conf.; bd. dirs. Voyageurs Nat. Park Assn., Deep-Portage Conservation Found., Wetlands for Wildlife U.S.A., Wildlife Am.; dir. Minn. Conservation Fedn., 1952-54; panelist Sportsman's Roundtable, WTCN-TV, Mpls., 1953—; trustee Liberty Bell Edn. Found.; seminar instr. Minn. Coll. Art and Design. Served in USNR, World War II. Recipient Silver medal for wildfowl sculpture Nat. Sportsmans Show, 1951; Minn. Outdoor award, 1956; Patron of Conservation award, 1956; Minn. Sports Champion award, 1958; 1st award Am. Indsl. Devel. Council; citation of merit V.F.W.; award of merit Mil. Order Cootie, 1963; Nat. Art Print of Year award, 1973; merit award Minn. Waterfowl Assn., 1976; Mark Twain knighthood Mark Twain Soc., 1978; Silver medal Nat. Soc. SAR, 1978; honor degree U.S. Vets. Venison Program, 1980; Service to Arts and Environ. award Faribault Art Center, 1981; named Wildlife Conservationist of Year, Sears Found.-Nat. Wildlife Fedn. Program, 1966, Am. Bicentennial Wildlife Artist, 1976; named to Water, Woods and Wildlife Hall of Fame, 1977; hon. Ky. Col.; hon. mem. Ont. Chippewa Nation of Can., 1957, named Dean of Wildfowl Painters, 1981; featured artist Art West, 1980, 82, 84. Fellow Internat. Inst. Arts (life), Soc. Animal Artists N. Am. Mycol. Assn.; mem. Internat. Sci. Info. Service, Nat. Wildlife Fedn. (nat. wildlife week chmn. Minn.), Minn. Ducks Unltd. (dir.), Minn. Artists Assn. (past v.p., dir.), Wildlife Artists of World (charter), Outdoor Writers Am., Am. Artists Profl. League, Mpls. Soc. Fine Arts, Wildlife Soc., Zool. Soc., Minn. Mycol. Soc. (pres. emeritus, hon. life), Minn. Conservation Fedn. (hon. life), Deep Portage Conservation Found. (dir.), Le Sueur Hist. Soc. (hon.), Faribault Art Center (hon. life), Pheasants Inc. (hon.), Waseca Arts Council (hon. life). Clubs: Beaverbrook (hon. life), Minn. Press; Explorers (N.Y.C.). Author: Where Wildlife Meets the World of Real Art, 1984. Contbr. to Christmas Echos, 1955, Wing Shooting, Trap & Skeet, 1955; Along the Trout Stream, 1979; also illustrations and articles in periodicals. Asso. editor: Sports and Recreation mag., Out-of-Doors mag. Compiler and artist; Outdoor Horizons, 1957; Twilight over the Wilderness, 1972; featured artist Art West, 1980; ltd. edit. prints of wildfowl, 1981; appeared in film Your BFA - Care & Maintenance; contbr. Educators Guide to Science Materials; paintings and text Minnesota Today. Creator Preuss Wildlife Calendar; inventor Wildlife Am. Calendar. Studio: 2224 Grand Ave Minneapolis MN 55405

PREUSZ, GERALD CLYDE, higher education educator; b. Loogootee, Ind., Feb. 6, 1938; s. Victor Alvin and Mildred Beatrice (Jackman) P.; m. Janet Hayes McGeorge, Sept. 12, 1959; children—Pamela, Keith (dec.), Joseph, Patricia. B.S., Ind. U., 1960, M.S., 1966, Ed.D., 1970. Cert. secondary tchr., Ind. Tchr. Lake Forest Elem. Sch., Hobart, Ind., 1960-61; high sch. tchr. George Rogers Clark Sch., Hammond, Ind., 1961-66; coordinator students Ind. U., Gary, 1966-69; asst. dean students Ind. U.-Purdue, Indpls., 1970-73, dean student affairs, 1973-77, assoc. prof. higher edn., 1978—; cons. Ind. U. Dental Sch., Indpls., 1979-84; Ind. U. Northwest, Gary, 1983, North Central Assn., Bloomington, Ind., 1984. Contbr. articles to profl. jours. Troop chmn. Crossroads of Am. council Boy Scouts Am., Indpls., 1974-77, scoutmaster Troop 282, Indpls., 1977-79; active in Work Release Ctr. Prisoners, Indpls., 1972-75; scholarship selector Inland Container Corp., Indpls., 1975-77. Recipient Edward C. Moore teaching award Faculty Ind. U.-Purdue U., 1984, Outstanding Contbns. award Black Student Union 1975. Mem. Ind. Coll. Personnel Adminstrs. (sec., treas 1983-84), Am. Assn. Higher Edn., Nat. Assn. Student Personnel Adminstrs., Am. Coll. Personnel Adminstrs., Am. Assn. Counseling and Devel. Mem. Disciples of Christ Ch. Avocations: reading; camping; fishing; boating. Home: 118 Tulip Tree Ind U Bloomington IN 47405 Office: ES Bldg 902 W New York St Ind U-Purdue U Indianapolis IN 46223

PREVITS, GARY JOHN, accountancy educator, consultant; b. Cleve., Oct. 23, 1942; s. J.A. and L.M. (Guta) P.; m. F.A. Porubsky, Oct. 3, 1964; children—Robert, Susan, Joanne, Matthew. B.S.B.A. John Carroll U., 1963; M.Acctg., Ohio State U., 1964; Ph.D., U. Fla., 1972. C.P.A., Ohio, Ala. Staff Deloitte, Haskins & Sells, Cleve., 1963-68; asst. prof. Augusta Coll., Ga., 1968-70; instr. U. Fla., Gainesville, 1970-72; asst. prof. U. Ala, Tuscaloosa, 1973-79; prof. Case Western Res. U., Cleve., 1979—; vis. assoc. prof., Northwestern U., 1977; cons. in field. Author: (with others) A History of Accounting in America, 1979. Editor Accounting Historians Jour., 1977-80, Ohio C.P.A. Jour., 1982-85. Coach, Rocky River Baseball Recreation, Ohio, 1980-81. Served to 1st lt. U.S. Army, 1965-67. Named Beaudry Man of Yr., John Carroll U., 1963. Mem. Am. Inst. C.P.A.s, Acad. Acct. Historians (pres. 1974-76; Hourglass award 1980), Am. Acctg. Assn (Ohio region v.p. 1983-84), Ohio Soc C.P.A.s. Roman Catholic. Club: Playhouse. Avocation: reading biography. Home: 3420 Bradfords Gate Rocky River OH 44116 Office: Weatherhead Sch Mgmt Case Western Res U Cleveland OH 44106

PREWITT, MICHAEL WESLEY, respiratory therapist; b. Denver, July 11, 1950; s. William W. and Clara J. (Wilson) P.; m. Carolyn K. Frevert, July 22, 1972; children—Zachary M., Michelle K., Ashley N. B.S., U. Mo.-Columbia, 1976, M.Ed., 1978, Ph.D. in Edn., 1982. Registered respiratory therapist, Mo. Staff respiratory therapist Univ. Hosp., Columbia, 1972-76; instr. U. Mo., Columbia, 196-79, asst. prof., dir. respiratory therapist program, 1979—; area coordinator Cystic Fibrosis Found., 1979; cons. Ellis Fischell State Cancer Hosp., Columbia, 1977-78. Author: Respiratory Therapy Aide, 1984; also articles. Sec., Front Door Youth/Counseling Agy., Columbia, 1983—. Mem. Am. Assn. Respiratory Care (chmn. edn. com. 1984-86, sect. chmn.-elect 1985—), Am. Assn. Respiratory Therapy (chmn. edn. com. 1984-85, mem. long-range planning com. 1984), Am. Soc. Allied Health Professions, Alpha Eta, Pi Delta Kappa. Republican. Avocations: photography; jogging; racquetball. Home: 4038 Sonora Ct Columbia MO 65201 Office: U Mo 203 Clark Hall Columbia MO 65211

PREWITT, SALLY JOHNSON, airport executive; b. Springfield, Ill., Dec. 22, 1939; d. Francis Leonard and Allene (McClelland) Johnson; m. John David Jagitsch, May 12, 1958 (div. Aug. 1974); children—John David, Mark Wesley, Matthew Troy; m. Willard Rik Prewitt, July 13, 1979. Enumerator, R.L. Polk & Co., Springfield, 1969-73; sec.-bookkeeper Jacksonville Air Service, Ill., 1974-78, Starchief Aviation, Jacksonville, 1978-79; airport mgr. Jacksonville Airport, 1979—. Mem. Ill. Pub. Airport Assn. (pres. 1984—), Ill. Aviation Forum (vice-chmn. 1985—), Ill. Aviation Trades Assn. Republican. Avocations: floriculture; bowling; ballooning; painting. Home and Office: Rural Route 1 Box 259 Jacksonville IL 62650

PREYSZ, LOUIS ROBERT FONSS, JR., business consultant; b. Elkins, W. Va., July 15, 1916; s. Louis Robert Fonss and Lucile (Falardeau) P.; student U. Ky., 1946-47; m. Lucille Parks, Oct. 17, 1941 (dec. May 1981); children—Louis Robert Fonss III, Carole Preysz Carmichael, Marsha, James Jay, Lorentz Dreyer; m. June Boucher, 1981. Asst. to pres. North Star Corp., Indian Head Mining Co., Hazard, Ky., 1948-51; controller Meadow River Lumber Co., Rainelle, W.Va., 1951-55; agt. insp. Internal Revenue Service, Cin., 1955; controller Creamery Package Mfg. Co. (merged into St. Regis Paper Co.), Chgo., 1956-64, sec., Toronto, Ont., Can., 1956-64; v.p., treas. Gisholt Machine Co. (merged into Giddings & Lewis Inc.), Madison, Wis., 1964-66, dir. Gisholt Gt. Britain, London, Gisholt-Italia, Milan, 1964-70, exec. v.p., 1966-70, v.p. Giddings & Lewis, Inc. (parent co.), Fond du Lac, Wis., 1967-70; corp. cons., 1970—; chmn. exec. com., dir. T and T Tech., Inc., Madison, 1972, chmn. bd., chief exec. officer, 1972-73; fin. cons. to bd. dirs. Meadow River Lumber Co., Rainelle (co. merged into Ga. Pacific Corp.), 1970-72; dir. Norland Corp., Ft. Atkinson, Wis., Preysz Precision Instruments, Inc., Madison; cons. Cordis Corp., Miami, Fla., 1972-82. Bd. dirs. Madison YMCA, 1967-70. Served to capt. USMC, 1936-46. selected All-Am., Rd. Runner's Club Am. and Running Times mag., 1981; C.P.A., Ill., W.Va. Mem. Am. Inst. C.P.A.s, W.Va. Soc. C.P.A.s, Athletic Congress of U.S.A., Berea Coll. Alumni Assn., Ret. Marine Officers Assn. Episcopalian. Club: Milw. Athletic. Address: 2905 Post Rd Madison WI 53713

PRICE, BUDDY ALAN, podiatrist; b. Miami, Fla., Feb. 1, 1953; s. Grover Eugene and Beatrice (Shapiro) P.; student Rollins Coll., 1970-73; B.A. in Chemistry, U. South Fla., 1974; B.S. in Podiatric Medicine, Ill. Coll. Podiatric Medicine, 1979, D.P.M. cum laude, 1979. Diplomate Am. Bd. Podiatric surgery. Extern U. of Chgo. hosps., 1978; resident in podiatric medicine Northlake Community Hosp., Ill., 1979-80; rotating resident in podiatry Children's Meml. Hosp. and Schriner's Children's Meml. Hosp., both Chgo., 1979-80; practice gen. podiatry Lake Shore Foot and Ankle Ctrs., Chgo., 1980—, Munster, Ind.; adj. surg. faculty William Scholl Coll. Podiatric Medicine, Thorek Community Hosp., Chgo. Ctr. Hosp.; surg. staff Gary (Ind.) Meth. Hosp., Calumet Surg. Ctr., Munster, Broadway Community Hosp., Merrillville, Ind. Active, Big Bros. Am., Orlando, Fla., 1972-73. Cert. to CPR, Am. Heart Assn.; registered podiatrist, Ind., Ill., Fla. Mem. Ill. Podiatric Med. Assn., Am. Podiatric Med. Assn. Democrat. Jewish. Contbr. articles to profl. jours. Office: 16 W Erie St Chicago IL 60616 also 7550 Hohman Ave Suite 300 Munster IN 46321 also 10327 S Western Ave Chicago IL 60643 also 3017 Lake Ave Wilmette IL

PRICE, CALVIN ULYSSES, physician; b. Little Rock, May 14, 1924; s. Richard Meadows and Ozelma Baughnight; m. Dorothy (div.); 1 child, Cheryl Price. B.S., Detroit Inst. Tech., 1948; D.O., Chgo. Coll. Osteo. Medicine, 1959. Intern, Flint Gen. Hosp., Mich., 1959-60. Cert. Am. Bd. Gen. Practice. Practice osteo. medicine, Flint, 1960—; assoc. prof. clin. medicine Mich. State U., East Lansing, 1974—; med. examiner Genesee County, Mich., 1969—; mem. staff Flint Osteo., Genesee Meml. hosps., Hurley Med. Ctr.; chief of staff Flint Gen. Hosp., 1969—; lectr.; mem. Cardiac Task Force Genesee, Lapeer and Shiawassee counties. Mem. Am. Coll. Rehab. Medicine, Genesee County Osteo. Assn. (past pres.), Mich. Assn. Osteo. Physicians (state del.). Lodges: Shriners, Masons (33 deg.; past master). Address: 2740 Flushing Rd Flint MI 48504

PRICE, CAROL-ANN, data processing center executive; b. West Orange, N.J., Apr. 10, 1936; d. Clifford Harold and Helen Anna (Hollum) Minier; m. Thomas J. Price, Sr., Apr. 17, 1955; children—Thomas J. Jr., Robert Alan. B.A. in Bus. Adminstrn., Bellevue Coll., 1975; postgrad. in bus. Creighton U., 1982-83. Cert. Nat. Assn. Coll. and Univ. Bus. Officers. Bus. mgr. Nebr. Coll. Bus., Omaha, 1975-79; controller Bellevue Coll., Nebr., 1979-80, bus. mgr., 1980-81, seminar speaker, panelist, 1982—; mgr. adminstrv. services Land Bank Nat. Data Processing Ctr., Omaha, 1981-84, dir. mgmt. services, 1984—. Coordinator USAF Family Services Orgn., Madrid, Spain, 1958-63; bd. dirs. Am. Kindergarten, Madrid, 1963; team leader United Way Midlands, Omaha, 1973, 74, Bellevue Coll. alumni fund raiser, 1982-85; chmn. bd. dirs. San. Improvement Dist. #5, 1985. Mem. Adminstrv. Mgmt. Soc. Internat. (local pres. 1980-81, area asst. dir. 1982-83, internat. bd. dirs. 1983-85, internat. v.p. 1985—, Merit Scroll award 1982, Diamond Merit award 1984). Republican. Episcopalian. Club: Bay Hills Golf (bd. dirs. 1985—) (Plattsmouth, Nebr.). Avocations: opera; symphony; theatre; travel; golf. Home: Rural Route 2 Buccaneer Bay Plattsmouth NE 68048 Office: Land Bank Nat Data Processing Ctr 7300 Woolworth Ave Omaha NE 68124

PRICE, DEBRA C., lawyer, consultant, researcher; b. Chgo., Feb. 17, 1956; d. William F. and Holly (Chones) P.; B.A., U. Wis., 1976; M.S., Purdue U., 1978, Ph.D., 1980; J.D., John Marshall Law Sch., 1983. Bar: Ill. 1983, Fla. 1984, U.S. Dist. Ct. (no. dist.) Ill. 1983, U.S. Tax Ct. 1984. Mgr., Purdue U., West Lafayette, Ind., 1977-80, mgmt. cons. Supervisory devel. Inst., 1979-80; legal researcher Fred Lane & Munday, Chgo., 1983; prof. mgmt. dept. Roosevelt U., Chgo., 1983; assoc. Carrane, Freifeld & Uruba, Chgo., 1984—; graphoanalyst, Chgo., 1979—. ABA, Chgo. Bar Assn., Ill. State Bar Assn., Women's Bar Assn., Phi Delta Phi. Home: 5802 N Talman St Chicago IL 60659

PRICE, FAYE HUGHES, mental health administrator; b. Indpls.; d. Twidell W. and Lillian Gladys (Hazlewood) Hughes; A.B. with honors (scholar 1939-43), W.Va. State Coll., 1943; postgrad. social work (scholar) Ind. U., 1943-44; M.S.W., Jane Addams Sch., U. Ill., 1951; student summer insts. U. Chgo., 1960-65; m. Frank Price, Jr., June 16, 1945; 1 dau., Faye Michele. Supr. youth activities Flanner House, Indpls., 1945-47; program dir. Parkway Community House, Chgo., 1947-56, dir., 1957-58; dir. social services Chgo. Dept. Health, 1958-61, dir. community services, 1961-65, assoc. dir. planning and devel., 1965-69, regional program dir., 1969-75, asst. dir. mental health, 1975, acting dir., 1976, acting adminstrv. dir., 1976—; cons. various health, welfare and youth agencies; instr. U. Ill., U. Chgo., Atlanta U., George Williams U.; lectr. Chgo. State U., U. Ill., other profl. workshops, seminars and confs. Active mem. Art Inst. Chgo., Bravo chpt. Chgo. Lyric Opera, Chgo. Urban League, Southside Community Art Center, Chgo., Chgo. YWCA, 9897 Parnell Ave. Block Club, Chgo., DuSable Mus., Chgo. Recipient scholarship Mt. Zion Baptist Ch., 1938-39, Fisk U., 1943; Mother-of-Year award Chgo. State Women's Club, 1975. Mem. Nat. Assn. Social Work, Acad. cert. Social

Workers, Ill. Welfare Assn., Ill. Group Psychotherapy Soc., Nat. Conf. on Social Welfare, Council on Social Work Edn., Center for Continuing Edn. of Ill. Mental Health Insts., Am. Group Psychotherapy Assn., Am. Public Health Assn., Ill. Public Health Assn., Nat. Assn. Parliamentarians, Zonta Internat. (Chi South Side chpt.), Alpha Gamma Phi, Alpha Kappa Alpha, NAACP, U. Ill. Alumni Assn., Nat. Council Negro Women, Municipal Employees Soc. Chgo. Episcopalian. Clubs: Jack and Jill of Am. (asso.), Links Inc. (Chgo. chpt., nat. exec. council), Chums Inc. (Chi chpt.), Les Cameos Social. Office: Richard J Daley Center Chgo Dept Health Bur Mental Health Room 2853 Chicago IL

PRICE, JOHN MICHAEL, photographer; b. Indpls., Oct. 10, 1936; s. Chester Morris and Sarah Elizabeth (Ferguson) P.; grad. high sch.; m. Madalene Wing, May 8, 1956; children—Teresa Kay, Michael Chester. Farmer; owner, photographer Price Portrait Studio, Lizton, Ind., 1967—; owner Agri-Photo Belt Buckles. Cons., judge photography 4-H workshops, state and county fairs (Ind.), high schs., 1967—. Supt. agrl. displays 4-H fairs, Ind., 1966—; mem. youth adv. council Hendricks County (Ind.), 1970-71; pres. band boosters New Salem (Ind.) High Sch., 1970; instr. leather craft local orgns. Recipient honors 4-H Club Continued Service, 1971, 73. Mem. profl. photographers Am., Ind. Patentee in field. Address: Box 159 Rd 900 N Lizton IN 46149

PRICE, JOHN WESLEY, pharmaceutical manufacturing executive; b. Seattle, July 9, 1943; s. Frank Wesley and Ruth Elvira (Jerbert) P.; m. Faye Martin Rawes, Aug. 9, 1981. B.A., U. Wash., 1966; M.B.A., Calif. Coast U., 1979. Mgr. employee relations PACCAR, Inc., Bellevue, Wash., 1969-78; dir. human resources Physio-Control Corp., Redmond, Wash., 1978-81; dir. personnel Eli Lilly and Co., Indpls., 1981-83, dir. indsl. relations Eli Lilly Italia, Florence, Italy, 1983—; dir. Verchim Asterias S.p.A., Bologna, Italy. Labor relations advisor Mayor's Council, Sesto Fiorentino, Italy, 1984; bd. dirs. Am. Sch., Florence, 1985. Served to comdr. USNR, 1966—, Vietnam. Mem. Pacific N.W. Personnel Mgrs. Assn. (pres. 1980-81, Superior Merit award 1980), Am. Electronics Assn. (bd. dirs. 1978-81). Republican. Presbyterian. Avocations: skiing, fishing. Home: via Francesco Poeti 21/A 50014 Fiesole Florence Italy Office: Eli Lilly and Co 307 E McCarty St Indianapolis IN 46285

PRICE, JOSEPH B., data processing executive; b. Chgo., Apr. 19, 1935; s. Clayton C. and Alice (McNabb) P.; children—Clifford Hugh, Lauren D. Assoc. in Design, DeForest Coll., 1952; B.S., Columbia Coll., San Francisco, 1981; M.B.A., Nat. Coll., Evanston, Ill., 1984. Dept. mgr. Chgo. Addressing Co., Chgo., 1952; field mgr. IBM, Chgo., 1959, program mgr., White Plains, N.Y., 1964, br. mgr., Chgo., 1966, area ops. mgr., 1968, regional mgr., Australia, 1968-71, regional personnel mgr., Chgo., 1971, regional ops. mgr., 1972, dir. inventory and distbn., Mechanicsburg, Pa., 1971-74, dir. personnel, White Plains, 1976-78, regional mgr. field engring., Chgo., 1978—, region mgr. nat. service div., 1985; mem. European dist. council IBM World Trade, Paris, 1975; mem. nat. product council Com. Govt. Australia, Cambera, 1971; exec. com. Chgo. council Boy Scouts Am., 1983-84, also Bd. dirs and v.p. adminstrn. Active United Way, Chgo., 1983-84; metro chmn. Nat. Alliance of Businessmen, Harrisburg, Pa., 1974-75. Mem. Nat. Inventory and Distbn. Dirs. Assn., Am. Mgmt. Assn. Club: Adventures. Office: IBM One IBM Plaza Chicago IL 60611

PRICE, L. PARVIN, lawyer; b. Tell City, Ind., Feb. 1, 1952; s. Lester P. and Emma Jane (Schurter) P.; m. June 8, 1974. B.A. cum laude, U. Evansville, 1974; J.D., U. Louisville, 1976. Bar: Ind. 1977. Dep. atty. gen. State of Ind., Indpls., 1977-81; consumer counselor State of Ind., Indpls., 1981-85; gen. counsel Mcpl. Cons., Inc., Indpls., 1985—. Mem. Ind. State Bar Assn., Ind. Mcpl. Lawyers Assn., Sagamore of the Wabash, Blue Key Honor Soc., Phi Alpha Delta. Republican. Methodist. Home: 7704 Shady Hills Dr Indianapolis IN 46278 Office: Mcpl Cons Inc 1251 S Tower One Merchants Plaza Indianapolis IN 46204

PRICE, LUCILE BRICKNER BROWN, former personnel adminstr.; b. Decorah, Iowa, May 31, 1902; d. Sidney Eugene and Cora (Drake) Brickner; B.S., Iowa State U., 1925; M.A., Northwestern U., 1940; m. Maynard Wilson Brown, July 2, 1928 (dec. 1937); m. 2d, Charles Edward Price, Jan. 14, 1961 (dec. 1983). Asst. dean of women Kans. State U., Manhattan, 1925-28; mem. bd. student personnel adminstrn. Northwestern U., Evanston, Ill., 1937-41; with personnel research dept. Sears, Roebuck & Co., Chgo., 1941-42; overseas club dir. ARC, Eng., 1942-43, Africa, 1943, Italy, 1944-45; dir. Child Edn. Found., N.Y.C., 1946-56; del. Mid-Century White House Conf. Children and Youth, 1950; mem. Iowa State Extension Adv. Com., 1973-75, Winneshiek County (Iowa) CSC, 1978—. Bd. dirs. N.E. Iowa Mental Health Center, pres., 1960-61; trustee Porter House Mus., 1966-78, emeritus trustee, 1982—; mem. Winneshiek County Courthouse Clock Com., 1983. Recipient Alumni Merit award Iowa State U., 1975. Mem. Am. Coll. Personnel Assn. (life), AAUW (named gift award 1977; dir. Decorah br. 1965-75; life), Norwegian-Am. Museum (life, Vesterheim fellow), Winneshiek County Hist. Soc. (life; cert. of appreciation 1984), DAR, Am. Overseas Assn. (life; nat. bd. 1960-79), Pi Lambda Theta, Chi Omega. Instrumental in building of house designed specifically for retirement living and subject of TV show on aging; active on Historic Preservation com. of AAUW which secured grants from Nat. Endowment for Humanities, Nat. Endowment for Arts, also listing of dist. in Decorah on Nat. Register Historic Places. Address: 508 W Broadway Decorah IA 52101

PRICE, MELVIN, congressman; b. East St. Louis, Ill., Jan. 1, 1905; s. Lawrence Wood and Margaret Elizabeth (Connolly) P.; ed. parochial schs., East St. Louis; grad. St. Louis U. High Sch.; student St. Louis U., 1923-25; m. Garaldine Freelin, July 7, 1952; 1 son, William Melvin. Sports writer East St. Louis News-Rev., 1925-27; corr. East St. Louis Jour., 1927-33, St. Louis Globe-Democrat, 1943; sec. to Congressman Edwin M. Schaefer, 1933-43; mem. 79th and 80th Congresses (1945-49) from 22d Ill. Dist. 81st to 82d Congresses from 25th Ill. Dist., 83-92d Congresses from 24th Ill. Dist., 93d-97th Congresses from 23d Ill. Dist., mem. 98th-99th Congresses from 21st Ill. Dist., chmn. house armed service com. mem. commn. adminstrv. rev. Mem. St. Clair County Bd. Suprs., 1929-31. Served with AUS, 1943-44. Mem. Am. Legion, Amvets. Democrat. Roman Catholic. Clubs: KC, Moose, Eagle, Elk, Ancient Hibernians; Nat. Press (Washington). Home: 426 N 8th St E St Louis IL 62201 Office: 2110 Rayburn House Office Bldg Washington DC 20515

PRICE, MICHAEL BENJAMIN, sculptor, art educator; b. Chgo., Oct. 21, 1940; s. Louis and Florence (Raemer) P.; m. Susan Davis, Sept. 4, 1971; children—Peter, Daniel. A.B. in Math., U. Ill., 1963, M.A., 1964; M.F.A., in Sculpture, Tulane U., 1968. Instr. art U. Ala.-Huntsville, 1966; instr. asst. art Tulane U., New Orleans, 1966-67, instr. math., 1967-69; prof. art Hamline U., St. Paul, 1970—, chmn. dept. art, 1980—. One-man shows include Vincent Price Galleries, Chgo., 1969, Krasner Gallery, N.Y.C., 1973, 74, 77, 80; exhibited in group shows at Minn. Mus., St. Paul, 1971, Kohn Gallery, St. Paul, 1974, Mus. Art, Pa. State U., 1974, Maison Bernard, Caracas, Venezuela, 1975, Friends' Gallery, Mpls. Inst. Art, 1979, C.G. Rein Galleries, Mpls., 1982; represented in pvt. collections. Served with U.S. Army, 1964-66. Hamline U. grantee, 1984-85. Jewish. Avocations: trumpet, skiing, swimming. Home: 1954 Laurel Ave Saint Paul MN 55104

PRICE, PETER WILLIAM, savings and loan executive; b. Albany, N.Y., May 26, 1943; s. Philip M. and Dorothy Ethel (Brown) P.; m. Constance Ellen McKnight, Aug. 28, 1965 (dec. 1973); 1 child, Kristin; m. Denise Lynn Ballard, Sept 18, 1976; children—Leah, Seth, Nathan. B.B.A., Ohio U., 1965. Computer programmer Nat. Cash Register, Dayton, Ohio, 1965-66, 1969-72; systems analyst Burroughs Corp., Detroit, 1972-75, project mgr. 1976-77; asst. data processing mgr. Great Lakes Fed. Savings and Loan, Ann Arbor, Mich., 1975-76, sr. v.p., mgmt. info. systems, 1977—. Served to 1st lt. U.S. Army, 1966-69, Vietnam. Jehovah's Witness. Office: Great Lakes Fed Savings 401 E Liberty Ann Arbor MI 48104

PRICE, RAWSON STEELE, financial executive; b. Berkeley, Calif., Jan. 4, 1935; s. Jay Hamilton and Eunice (Steele) P.; m. Mary Elizabeth Lenz, Feb. 1, 1958; children—Thomas, Shelly. B.B.A., U. Wis., 1957; grad. Sch. Banking, 1970. Trainee First Nat. Bank, Mpls., 1958-62; asst. v.p. lending Univ. Nat. Bank, Mpls., 1962-66; asst. v.p. Citizens Bank, Sheboygan, Wis., 1966-74, v.p., 1974-82; sr. v.p. mktg. First Interstate Corp., Sheboygan, 1982-84; exec. v.p. First Interstate Bank, Gillett, Wis., 1984—. Chmn. fin. com. Sheboygan Area Sch. Bd., 1973-79; bd. dirs., treas. Sheboygan Family Service Assn., 1976-83. Republican. Presbyterian. Lodges: Elks, Kiwanis (dir. 1972-79). Home: 5609 Finnegan Lake Rd Gillett WI 54124 Office: First Interstate Bank Wis PO Box 158 Gillett WI 54124

PRICE, ROBERT DIDDAMS, JR., community planner, paramedic; b. Chgo., Apr. 18, 1943; s. Robert Diddams and Adelheid Marie (Haugan) P.; m. Susan Kay Mundhenk, Dec. 18, 1965; children—Jennifer, Robert III. B.S. in Community Planning, U. Cin., 1966, M.A. in Community Planning, 1968, M.A. in Geography, 1968. Cert. Am. Inst. Cert. Planners; cert. paramedic, Ohio. Sr. planner City-County Planning Commn., Rockford, Ill., 1968-70; chief research Central N.Y. Regional Planning and Devel. Bd., Syracuse, 1970-72; exec. dir. Warren County Regional Planning Commn., Lebanon, Ohio, 1972—; mem. exec. com. Ohio Ky.-Ind. Regional Council Govts., 1973—; bd. dirs., treas. Warren County Rehab., Inc., 1977—. Mem. Warren County Health Planning Com., 1978—; mem. Warren County Litter Adv. Bd., 1985—; chmn. Warren County New Horizons Fair Housing Task Force, 1980—; bd. dirs. Cert. Devel. Corp. of Warren County, 1981—. Sec., treas. Warren County Conv. and Visitors Bur., 1980—; mem. Clearcreek Twp. Life Squad, 1975—, first lt., 1977, chief, 1978-82; bd. dirs. Western Ohio Emergency Med. Services Council, 1978—, sec. 1980-84, sec.-treas., 1984—; chmn. Warren County Emergency Med. Services Council, 1981-82; county employee coordinator Warren County United Way, 1980; mem. council St. Paul Lutheran Ch., 1976-78, sec., 1976-77; merit badge counselor Boy Scouts Am., 1982—; mem. Camp Stoneybrook Bldg. Com., Girl Scouts U.S.A., 1981-82; CPR instr. ARC, 1978—; radiol. def. instr. Def. Civil Preparedness Agy., 1978—; mem., sec. Warren County Classification and Compensation Adv. Bd., 1984—. Recipient Community Service award Springboro-Clearcreek Twp. Jaycees, 1977; Chmn. award Ohio Jaycees, 1978 Ky. Col. award Commonwealth of Ky., 1978. Mem. Am. Planning Assn., Ohio Planning Conf. (bd. dirs. 1978—, v.p. 1979-80, pres. 1980-82), Warren County Emergency Med. Services Assn., Nat. Trust Hist. Preservation, Ohio Twp. Assn. (hon.), Ohio County Planning Dirs. Assn. (exec. com. 1982—, sec. treas. 1985—), County Commrs. Assn. Ohio (assoc.), Springboro Band Boosters (pres. 1985—). Lutheran. Clubs: Internat. Assn. Torch, Inc., Mountain Dulcimer Soc. Home: 205 Pinecone Ln Springboro OH 45066 Office: 320 E Silver St Lebanon OH 45036

PRICE, ROBERT M., computer company executive; b. 1930. B.S., Duke U., 1952, Ga. Inst. Tech., 1958. Research engr. Convair div. Gen. Dynamics Corp., 1954-56; research mathematician Ga. Inst. Tech., 1956-58; mathematician Standard Oil Calif., 1958-61; with Control Data Corp., Mpls., 1961—, gen. sales mgr. internat. ops., then EDP sales, 1966, v.p. sales, 1967, v.p. systems and data services mktg., 1969, v.p., group exec. services, 1970, sr. v.p., group exec. services, 1972, pres. systems and services, 1973, systems services and mktg., 1975, pres., Computer Co., 1977, pres., chief operating officer parent co., 1980—. Office: 8100 34th Ave S Minneapolis MN 55420*

PRICE, RUTH ELLEN, medical technologist, laboratory administrator; b. Chgo., May 19, 1931; d. Stanley and Kathryn Ellen (Carpenter) P.; B.A. in Biology, Willamette U., 1953; cert. in med. tech. Northwestern, 1954; M.A. in Mgmt., Central Mich. U., 1977. Med. technologist St. Catherine's Hosp., Kenosha, Wis., 1955—, clin. lab. supr., 1966—; product evaluator E. I. DuPont de Nemours, Wilmington, Del. Active Friends of the Museum, Kenosha. Mem. Am. Mgmt. Assn., Am. Soc. Clin. Pathology (assoc. mem., cert. med. technologist), Nature Conservancy, Am. Soc. Med. Tech., AAUW, Clin. Lab. Mgmt. Assn., Chi Omega. Episcopalian. Club: PEO. Home: 4510 18th St Kenosha WI 53142 Office: St Catherine's Hosp 3556 7th Ave Kenosha WI 53140

PRICE, STEPHEN CHARLES, business official; b. Highland Park, Ill., Dec. 27, 1950; s. Sterling Blackman and Catherine (Keefe) P.; m. Julia Deonne Dannenberg, Sept. 20, 1980; stepchildren—Kevin M. Morgester, Kurt R. Morgester. Assoc. degree Robert Morris Jr. Coll., Carthage, Ill., 1971; B.S., Carroll Coll., Waukesha, Wis., 1974. Sales rep. Wilson-Jones Co., Chgo., 1974—. Chmn. com. Midwest Travelers Club, St. Louis, 1977—. Recipient salesman award Wilson Jones Co., 1983, sales award, 1984. Home: 7067 Broken Oak Dr Saint Louis MO 63129 Office: Wilson Jones Co 6150 Touhy Ave Chicago IL 60648

PRICE, THELMA THOMAS, lawyer; b. Summerfield, La., Nov. 24, 1952; d. Robert Charles and Elsie Mae (Trimble) Thomas; m. Lowellton Price, Nov. 29, 1980. B.A., Grambling State U., 1973; J.D., Ohio State U., 1976. Bar: Ohio Supreme Ct. 1976. Tax atty. SCOA Industries, Inc., Columbus, Ohio, 1976-80, mgr. tax research, 1980—. Recipient Community Service award Nat. Black Am. Law Students Assn., 1977. Mem. ABA, Ohio State Bar Assn., Columbus Bar Assn. Franklin County Women Lawyers Assn., Nat. Retail Mchts. Assn. (tax com. 1979—), Am. Retail Fedn. (tax. com. 1980—), Tax Execs. Inst., Delta Sigma Theta. Democrat. Baptist. Home: 2656 Mitzi Dr Columbus OH 43209 Office: SCOA Industries Inc 33 N High St Columbus OH 43215

PRICE, THOMAS EMILE, export sales, investment, financial executive; b. Cin., Nov. 4, 1921; s. Edwin Charles and Lillian Elizabeth (Werk) P.; B.B.A., U. Tex., 1943; postgrad. Harvard U., 1944; m. Lois Margaret Gahr Matthews, Dec. 21, 1970; 1 dau. by previous marriage, Dorothy Elizabeth Wood Price; stepchildren—Bruce Albert, Mark Frederic, Scott Herbert, Eric William Matthews. Co-founder Price Y Cia, Inc., Cin., 1946—, sec., 1946-75, treas., 1946—, pres., 1975—, also dir.; co-founder Price Paper Products Corp., Cin., 1956, treas., 1956—, pres., 1975—, sec., 1956-75, also dir.; mem. Cin. Regional Export Expansion Com., 1961-63; dir. Central Acceptance Corp., 1954-55; founding mem. and dir. Cin. Royals Basketball Club Co., 1959-73. Referee Tri-State Tennis Championships, 1963-68, Western Tennis Championships, 1969-70, Nat. Father-Son Clay Court Championships, 1974—, Tennis Grand Masters Championships, 1975-77, 80; vol. coach Walnut Hills High Sch. Boys Team, Cin., 1970-81; chmn. and coach Greater Cin. Jr. Davis Cup, 1968-78; co-founder Tennis Patrons of Cin., Inc., 1951, trustee, 1951—, pres., 1958-63, 68; co-founder Greater Cin. Tennis Assn., 1979. Participant in fund raising drives Cin. Boys Amateur Baseball Fund; chmn. Greater Cin. YMCA World Service Fund Drive, 1962-64; trustee Cin. World Affairs Inst., 1957-60, gen. chmn., 1959. Served to 1st lt. USAAF, 1943-46; ETO. Elected to Western Hills High Sch. Sport Hall of Honor; named hon. Almaden Grand Master, 1980. Mem. Cin. World Trade Club (pres. 1959), U.S. Trotting Assn., Cin. Hist. Soc., U.S. Lawn Tennis Assn. (trustee 1959-60, 62-64, chmn. Jr. Davis Cup com. 1960-62, founder of Col. James H. Bishop award 1962), Ohio Valley (trustee 1948—, Gillespie award 1957, Dredge award 1973, pres. 1952-53), Western (trustee 1951—, mem. championships adv. com. 1969-78, pres. 1959-60, Melvin R. Bergman Disting. Service award 1979) tennis assns., Assn. Tennis Profls. (nat. championship adv. 1979—), Phi Gamma Delta. Republican. Presbyterian. Clubs: Cin. Country, Univ., Cin. Tennis (pres. 1957-58, adv. com. 1959—), Indoor Tennis, Eastern Hills Indoor Tennis. Lodge: Cin. Rotary.). Nationally ranked boys 15, 1936, jr. tennis player, 1939. History columnist Tennis Talk Greater Cin., 1978-80. Home: 504 Williamsburg Rd Cincinnati OH 45215 Office: Suite 925 Dixie Terminal Bldg Cincinnati OH 45202

PRIMAK, WILLIAM L., chemist, scientific consultant; b. N.Y.C., June 4, 1917; s. Nathan and Elizabeth (Kaimowitz) P.; m. Dorothy M. Newfang, Oct. 24, 1953 (dec. 1973); children—John Jefferson, Margaret Kay, Robert Carl. B.S., CCNY, 1937; M.S., Poly. Inst. Bklyn., 1943, Ph.D., 1946. Sr. chemist Argonne Nat. Lab., 1946-84; cons. Wolfe Loeb and Co., Hinsdale, Ill., 1984—. Contbr. articles to profl. jours. Patentee in field. Mem. Am. Chem. Soc., Am. Phys. Soc., Sigma Xi, Phi Lambda Upsilon. Mem. United Ch. Christ. Clubs: Chgo. Mountaineering; Alpine (Can.). Avocation: ballroom dancing. Office: Wolfe Loeb & Co 735 S Quincy St Hinsdale IL 60521

PRIMM, TERI MARSHA, distributing company executive; b. Mpls., Aug. 18, 1960; d. Ralph Casabyanica and Fannie (Marshall) P. B.S. in Bus., U. Minn., 1982. Auditor, Touche Ross and Co., Mpls., 1981-84, mem. broker/dealer/mktg. group, 1984; spl. projects and research acct. IDS/Am. Express, Mpls., 1984-85; exec. v.p. Vanguard Distributors, Savannah, Ga., 1985—. Recipient Outstanding Achievement award Bus. Assn. of Minorities, 1982. Am. Inst. C.P.A.s scholar, 1980-81, Minn. Soc. C.P.A.s scholar, 1980-82. Mem. Nat. Assn. Black Accts. (scholarship chmn 1981-82, 83-84, vice chmn. nat. election procedures com. 1983—). Baptist. Office: Vanguard Distributors Inc PO Box 493 Savannah GA 31402

PRIMOSCH, EDWARD GERARD, management consultant; b. Cleve., Oct. 7, 1950; s. Edward Joseph and Rose Marie (Potochar) P.; m. Margaret Ruth Piar, May 3, 1975; children—Michelle Therese, Jessica Marie. B.S., U. Dayton, 1972; M.B.A., Baldwin-Wallace Coll., 1980. Cert. in data processing. Mktg. officer Nat. City Bank, Cleve., 1972-80; sr. mgr. Peat Marwick, Cleve., 1980—. Mem. Assn. Systems Mgmt. (v.p. 1981-82), Assn. Inst. for Certification of Computer Profls. Roman Catholic. Avocations: golf, physical fitness training. Home: 10059 Glenhollow Ct Brecksville OH 44141 Office: Peat Marwick 1600 Nat City Ctr Cleveland OH 44114

PRIMUS, MARY JANE DAVIS, social worker, author; b. Marion, Iowa, May 31, 1924; d. Lawrence Henry and Verna Leona (Suman) Davis; B.S., Iowa State U., 1950; m. Paul C. Primus, Aug. 23, 1955; children—Kenneth Roy, Donald Karl. Asst. cashier First State Bank, Greene, Iowa, 1942-46; tchr. Oskaloosa (Iowa) pub. schs., 1950-52; extension home economist Iowa State U., Oskaloosa-Eldora, 1952-57; homemaker, dist. supr. Iowa Dept. Social Service, Webster City, 1970-77. Substitute tchr. Eldora Pub. Schs., 1966-68; homemaker health aide supr. Mid-Iowa Community Action OEO, Iowa Dept. Social Service, 1968-69; Author: Through the Window, 1973; Through the Window Twice, 1974; Tracery Windows, 1975; Shuttered Windows, 1977; Wings, 1979; Wings II, 1980; area news corr., 4 newspapers; columnist Iowa Wildlife Fedn.; contbr. poems to various publs. Den mother Boy Scouts Am., Steamboat Rock, Iowa, 1966-71; leader Girl Scouts Am., Steamboat Rock, 1969-72; mem. Iowa State U. Extension Family Living Council, Hardin County, 1961-65, 82-84; outreach chmn. Iowa Family and Children Services, 1966-72; field days women's program chmn. Iowa Soil Conservation, 1968. Mem. Am. Home Econs. Assn., Nat. Council Homemaker-Home Health Aide Services, Nat. League Am. Pen Women, Nat. Soc. Lit. and the Arts, Soil Conservation Soc. Am., Am. Legion, Internat. Platform Assn., P.E.O. Mem. Ch. of Christ (pres. 1963-65). Mem. Order Eastern Star. Club: Federated Women's (Steamboat Rock). Office: Steamboat Rock IA 50672

PRINCE, STEPHEN MICHAEL, optometrist; b. Libertyville, Ill., Apr. 29, 1951; s. Clyde Clinton and Faynetta (Loesch) P.; m. Judith Lynn Dunn, Dec. 12, 1970; children—Michelle, Michael. B.A., Oakland U., 1974; O.D., Pacific U., 1979. Lic. optometrist, Mich., Oreg. Gen. practice optometry, Harrison, Mich., 1979—. Trustee Budd Lake Area Assn., 1983—. Served to sgt. Mich. Air N.G., 1970-75. Mem. Am. Optometric Assn., Mich. Optometric Assn. Baptist. Avocations: sailing; alpine and cross-country skiing; photography; woodworking; audio art. Home: 1234 Hillcrest St Harrison MI 48625 Office: PO Box 280 444 S 1st St Harrison MI 48625

PRINCE, THOMAS RICHARD, educator; b. New Albany, Miss., Dec. 7, 1934; s. James Thompson and C. Florence (Howell) P.; B.S., Miss. State U., 1956, M.S., 1957; Ph.D. in Accountancy, U. Ill., 1962; m. Eleanor Carol Polkoff, July 14, 1962; children—Thomas Andrew, John Michael, Adrienne Carol. Instr., U. Ill., 1960-62; mem. faculty Northwestern U., 1962—, prof. acctg. and info. systems, 1969—, chmn. dept. accounting and info. systems Grad. Sch. Mgmt., 1968-75; cons. in field; dir. Applied Research Systems, Inc. Served to 1st lt. AUS, 1957-60. C.P.A., Ill. Mem. Am. Accounting Assn., Am. Inst. C.P.A.'s, Am. Econ. Assn., Inst. Mgmt. Scis., Fin. Execs. Inst., AAAS, Ill. Soc. C.P.A.'s, Nat. Assn. Accts., Alpha Tau Omega, Phi Kappa Phi, Omicron Delta Kappa, Delta Sigma Pi, Beta Alpha Psi. Congregationalist. Author: Extension of the Boundaries of Accounting Theory, 1962; Information Systems for Management Planning and Control, 3d edit., 1975. Home: 303 Richmond Rd Kenilworth IL 60043 Office: Leverone Hall Northwestern U Evanston IL 60201

PRINCEVAC, SINISA MOMIR, medical facility administrator; b. Croatia, May 12, 1941; came to U.S., 1971, naturalized, 1976; s. Momir Marko and Zlata Josip (Hopental) P.; m. Spasena D. Andelkovich, July 29, 1968; children—Boby, Otmar. M.D., Med. Facility Belgrade, Yugoslavia, 1966. Diplomate Am. Bd. Family Practice. Resident in internal medicine Columbus Hosp., Chgo., 1972-74; mgr. Health Care and Assoc. Med. Services Ltd., Chgo., 1977—. Active Republican Party Task Force, 1982-83. Served to lt. Yugoslav Army, 1967-68. Mem. Chgo. Med. Soc., Ill. Med. Soc., AMA, Am. Mgmt. Assn., Internat. Assn. Physicians, Chinese Medicine Assn. Serbian Orthodox. Office: 5011 N Lincoln Ave Chicago IL 60625

PRINDLE, LORI MAY, manufacturing company executive; b. Rockford, Ill., Aug. 20, 1952; d. William Gustav and LaVada Maxine (Kirkendall) Johnson; m. Michel Prindle, Mar. 12, 1977 (div. May 1984). B.S., Western Ill. U., 1975. Tchr., counsel, Bd. Edn., Rockford, Ill., 1979-80, spl. project adminstr., 1980-81; control asst. Sundstrand Corp., Rockford, 1982, supr. info. processing, 1982-84, mgr. concepts and devel., spl. events, 1984—. Mem. Soc. Tech. Communications, Internat. Exhibitors Assn., Kappa Delta Pi, Beta Sigma Phi. Methodist. Avocations: skiing, reading. Office: Sundstrand Corp 2430 S Alpine Rd Rockford IL 61108

PRINDLE, WILLIAM JAMES, educator; b. Chgo., Mar. 3, 1949; s. Donald Verne and Margaret Mary (Behan) P.; m. Gail Ivis Snyder, Aug. 21, 1971; children—Wendy, Holly. B.A., U. Ill.-Chgo., 1971, M.A., U. Wash., 1972; C.A.S., No. Ill. U., 1979. Cert. tchr., adminstr., Ill. Tchr., Butler Sch., Oak Brook, Ill., 1973, Oak Forest High Sch., Ill., 1973-80; asst. prin. Central Jr. High, Tinley Park, Ill., 1980-82, prin., 1982-85; dir. social studies, fine arts, Learning Materials Ctr., Niles North High Sch., Skokie, Ill., 1985—. Res. officer Tinley Park Police Dept., 1977—. Serving with USNR, 1982—. Recipient Disting. Service award Jaycees 1983. Mem. So. Suburban Police Pistol League (sec., treas. 1982—), Nat. Rifle Assn., U.S. Naval Inst., Nat. Orgn. on Legal Problems in Edn., Phi Delta Kappa, Kappa Delta Pi. Roman Catholic. Avocations: shooting sports, hunting, coin collecting. Office: Central Jr High Sch 17248 S 67th Ave Tinley Park IL 60477

PRINEAS, RONALD JAMES, epidemiologist, public health educator; b. Junee, New South Wales, Australia, Sept. 19, 1937; came to U.S., 1973; s. Peter John and Nancy (MacDonald) P.; m. Julienne Swynny, Apr. 21, 1961; children—Matthew Leigh, Anna Mary, John Paul, Miranda Jane. M.B.B.S., U. Sydney, Australia, 1960; Ph.D., U. London, 1969. Med. house officer Prince Henry Hosp., Sydney, 1961; sr. med. house officer Royal Perth Hosp., Australia, 1962; registrar in medicine Royal Glasgow Infirmary, Scotland, 1963-64; research fellow London Sch. Hygiene and Tropical Medicine, 1964-67, lectr., 1967-68; asst. in medicine U. Melbourne, Australia, 1968-72; prof. epidemiology U. Minn., Mpls., 1973—, prof. medicine, 1974—; cons. WHO, Geneva, 1976—, Nat. Heart Lung and Blood Inst., 1976—; prin. investigator hypertension detection and follow-up program Nat. Health Lung and Blood Inst., 1973-80. Author books, including; Blood Pressure Sounds; Their Measurement and Meaning, 1978; The Minnesota Code Manual of Electrocardiographic Findings, 1982; also numerous articles. Mem. Minn. affiliate Am. Heart Assn., Mpls., 1973—, chmn. adv. groups, 1975—; mem. Minn. Health Dept., Mpls., 1973—, chmn. adv. groups, 1978—. Nat. Heart Lung and Blood Inst. grantee, 1973—. Fellow Royal Coll. Physicians Edinburgh, Am. Coll. Cardiology, Am. Pub. Health Assn., Soc. Epidemiologic Research, Am. Heart Assn. Council on Epidemiology, Internat. Soc. Hypertension, Council on Human Biology, Internat. Soc. Cardiology, Soc. Controlled Clin. Trials; mem. Royal Coll. Physicians London. Avocations: reading; raising a family. Office: U Minnesota 611 Beacon St SE Minneapolis MN 55455

PRINS, ROBERT JACK, college administrator; b. Grand Rapids, Mich., Oct. 12, 1932; s. Jacob and Marie (Vanden Brink) P.; m. Ruth Ellen John, Oct. 10, 1950; children—Linda, Douglas, Debra, Nancy, Eric, Sarah. B.A., Hope Coll., 1954; D.B.A., Coll. Emporia, 1974. With Mich. Bell Telephone Co., Detroit area, 1954-66; dir. devel. Bethesda Hosp., Denver, 1966-68; v.p. planning and devel. Park Coll., Parkville, Mo., 1969-70; chief adminstrv. officer Coll. of Emporia, Kans., 1970-75; dir. fin. and devel. The Abbey Sch., Canon City, Colo., 1975-79; dir. devel. Kirksville Coll. Osteo. Medicine, Mo., 1979-84; v.p. devel. McKendree Coll., Lebanon, Ill., 1984—. Mem. Council for Advancement and Support of Edn., Lebanon C. of C. Republican. Office: McKendree Coll Office of Devel 701 College Rd Lebanon IL 62254

PRITCHARD, JAMES ROBERT, internist, coroner; b. Cleve., May 24, 1947; s. Donald William and Lucille Pritchard. B.S., Ohio State U., 1969; D.O., Phila. Coll. Osteo. Medicine, 1973. Diplomate Am. Bd. Internal Medicine. Intern, Cleve. Clinic, 1973-74, resident in internal medicine, 1974-76; internist Stark Med. Specialties, Massillon, Ohio, 1976—; staff physician, cons. Doctors Hosp., Massillon, 1976—; coroner, Stark County, Canton, Ohio, 1981—; clin. assoc. prof. medicine Ohio U., Athens, 1983—; lectr. forensic medicine Kent State U., Canton, 1981—; lectr., clin. tchr. internal medicine, cons. Ohio U. Coll. Osteo. Medicine, 1981—, Doctors Hosp. Stark County, 1976—; lectr. in forensic medicine, death investigation Canton Police Tng. Acad., 1981—, Stark County Sheriff's Tng. Acad., 1981—. Mem. Stark County Police Chiefs Assn., 1984—. Recipient spl. cert. merit Fraternal Order of Police, 1982; Cleve. Clinic Edn. Found. med. fellow, 1972. Mem. Nat. Assn. Med. Examiners, AMA, Am.

Osteo. Assn., Ohio State Med. Assn., Am. Coll. Osteo. Internists, Sigma Sigmi Phi, Sigma Nu. Democrat. Methodist. Avocation: photography. Office: Stark County Coroner 400 Austin Ave NW Massillon OH 44646

PRITCHARD, JOHN T., newspaper publisher; b. Galesburg, Ill., Dec. 11, 1955; s. William Custer and Barbara (Bauer) P.; m. Jane Ann Johnson, June 1, 1957; children—Sarah, John. Student Knox Coll., Galesburg, 1974-77. Treas., Galesburg Printing & Pub. Co., 1975—, pub., 1977—, sec., 1976—; dir. First Galesburg Nat. Bank and Trust Co., Galesburg Broadcasting Co.; officer Northwest Ill. Cable Corp. Treas., Knox County United Way, Inc., 1981, v.p., 1982, pres., 1983; mem. Knox County Econ. Devel. Council, 1982—. Mem. Am. Newspaper Pubs. Assn., So. Newspaper Pubs. Assn., Inland Daily Press Assn. Lutheran. Office: 140 S Prairie St Galesburg IL 61401

PRITIKIN, ROLAND I., ophthalmologist; b. Chgo., Jan. 9, 1906; s. Edward Jefferson and Bluma (Saval) P.; m. Jeanne DuPre Moore, May 25, 1940; children—Gloria Anne, Karin Eugenia Pritikin Heiser. B.S., Loyola U., Chgo., 1928, M.D., 1930. Diplomate Am. Bd. Ophthalmology. Intern, St. Mary of Nazareth Hosp., Chgo., 1929-30; resident U. Ill. Eye and Ear Infirmary, Chgo., 1936-38; mem. faculty Stritch Sch. Medicine, Loyola U., 1930-48; mem. attending staff Ill. Eye and Ear Infirmary, 1939-48; mem. faculty dept. ophthalmology Rockford Sch. Medicine, U. Ill., 1970-85, prof. emeritus, 1985—; cons. ophthalmology, lectr. ophthalmology Fifth U.S. Army and U.S. Army Health Services Command, Ft. Sheridan, Ill., 1968—, Mass. Eye Surgery, Henry Holland Eye Hosps., India and West Pakistan, Shikarpur, 1939, 57, 60, 66, 71, Quetta, 1963. Author: Essentials of Ophthalmology, 1950, 3d edit., 1978; World War Three is Inevitable, 1976. Contbr. articles to profl. jours. Bd. dirs. ARC, Winnebgo County, Ill., 1953-59. Served with U.S. Army, 1941-46. Recipient First award U.S. Com., World Med. Assn., 1964; Bronze plaque Am. Security Council, 1967. Fellow Soc. Mil. Ophthalmologists, Weizmann Inst. Sci. (life), Instituto Barraquer, Barcelona, Royal Soc. Medicine, Am. Coll. Nuclear Medicine, ACS, Internat. Coll. Surgeons; mem. N.G. Assn., Ret. Officers Assn. (pres. No. Ill. chpt. 1969), Res. Officers Assn., Internat. Assn. Secs. Ophthalmol. and Otolaryngol. Socs. (bd. dirs.), Soc. Med. Cons. Armed Forces, Internat. Agy. for Prevention Blindness, Pan Am. Soc. Ophthalmic Microsurgery, Ophthalmol. Soc. Canary Islands (hon.), Internat. Assn. History Medicine, Rock River Valley Ophthalmology Assn. (sec. 1978—), U. Ill. Alumni Assn. (life). Home: 3505 High Crest Rd Rockford IL 61107 Office: 1211 Talcott Bldg Rockford IL 61101

PRITZ, BENJAMIN LIONEL, consumer products company executive; b. Cin., Dec. 20, 1920; s. Walter Heineman Pritz and Dorothy Stix (Lowman) Pritz Steiner; m. Louise Clarisse Aggiman, Nov. 10, 1948; children—Neil Aggiman, Alan Lowman. Vice pres. Grandpa Brands Co., Cin., 1948-80, pres., 1980—. Served with USAAF, 1942-46. Mem. Graphic Arts Soc., Asian Soc. Jewish. Clubs: Fencers (chmn. bd. 1970-83), Pan American, Bankers. Office: Benjamin Pritz Grandpa Brands Inc 317 E 8th St Cincinnati OH 45202

PRITZKER, JAY ARTHUR, lawyer; b. Chgo., Aug. 26, 1922; s. Abraham Nicholas and Fanny (Doppelt) P.; B.Sc., Northwestern U., 1941, J.D., 1947; m. Marian Friend, Aug. 31, 1947; children—Nancy (dec.), Thomas, John, Daniel, Jean. Asst. custodian Alien Property Adminstrn., 1947; admitted to Ill. bar, 1947, since practiced in Chgo.; ptnr. firm Pritzker & Pritzker, 1948—; chmn. bd. Hyatt Corp., Marmon Group, Inc. Braniff Inc.; dir. Elsinore Corp., Midland Ross; ptnr. Chgo. Mill & Lumber Co., Mich.-Calif. Lumber Co. Trustee, U. Chgo. Served as aviator USNR, World War II. Mem. Am., Chgo. bar assns. Clubs: Standard, Comml., Lake Shore, Mid-Day, Arts, Vince (Chgo.). Office: 2 First Nat Plaza Chicago IL 60603

PRITZKER, ROBERT ALAN, manufacturing executive; b. Chgo., June 30, 1926; s. Abram Nicholas and Fanny (Doppelt) P.; B.S. in Indsl. Engring., Ill. Inst. Tech., 1946; postgrad. in bus. adminstrn. U. Ill.; m. Irene Dryburgh; children—James, Linda, Karen, Matthew, Liesel. Engaged in mfg., 1946—; chief exec. officer, pres., dir. The Marmon Group Inc., Marmon Indsl. Corp.; pres., dir. The Colson Group, Inc., Marmon Holdings, Inc., Gt. Lakes Holdings, Inc., Marmon Industries, Inc., Rego Group, Inc., Union Tank Car Co., Chgo.; dir. Hyatt Corp., Peoples Energy Corp., Dalfort Corp., Hyatt Internat. Corp. Vice pres., bd. dirs. Pritzker Found., Chgo.; trustee, vice chmn., Ill. Inst. Tech. Office: 39 S LaSalle St Chicago IL 60603

PRITZLAFF, KIM HOWARD, land surveyor; b. Milw., May 10, 1948; s. Fred Carl and Dorothy Lucy (Wilke) P.; m. Ellen Marie Grever, Nov. 17, 1973; children—Amy Lynn, Aaron Benjamin. Student, U.Wis.-Stevens Point, 1966-69, U. Wis.-Sheboygan, 1969-70; A.A. in Land Surveying, Madison Area Tech. Coll., 1973. Registered profl. land surveyor, Wis., Ill.; cert. soil tester, Wis. Survey crew chief H.A. Sime & Assocs., Tomah, Wis., 1975-77; survey chief P. Epping & Assocs., Oconto, Wis., 1976-77; survey dept. head Robert E. Lee & Assocs., Green Bay, Wis., 1977-79; pres., owner Aaron Assocs., Oconto Falls, Wis., 1979—. Republican county surveyor, Oconto, 1979—; mem. PTO, Oconto Falls. Forest service cadastral survey contractee U.S. Dept. Agr., 1981-82, 84-85. Mem. Wis. Soc. Land Surveyors, Ill. Soc. Land Surveyors, Am. Congress on Surveying and Mapping, Wis. County Surveyors Assn. Lutheran. Home: 342 S Washington St Oconto Falls WI 54154

PRIVRATSKY, RICHARD ARNOLD, optometrist; b. Dickinson, N.D., Dec. 17, 1939; s. Peter and Rose (Kudrna) P.; m. Bernadette Wanner, Aug. 28, 1962; children—Cheryl, Ryan. B.S., Pacific U., 1965, D.O., 1966. Lic. optometrist, N.D. Pvt. practice optometry, Dickinson, 1966—. Served with U.S. Army, 1958-60. Mem. N.D. Optometric Assn. (pres. 1985—), Am. Optometric Assn., Dickinson C. of C. Roman Catholic. Club: Toastmasters Internat. (1st v.p. 1984—). Lodges: Elks, K.C. Avocations: Skiing; volleyball; golf. Home: 657 Hillside Dr Dickinson ND 58601 Office: 446 3d Ave W Dickinson ND 58601

PROBALA, ANDREW EUGENE, designer, artist; b. Cleve., Nov. 16, 1908; s. Andras and Anna (Visoky) P.; m. Ruth J. Kulish, Nov. 24, 1934; 1 child, Paul A. Student Cleve. Sch. Art, 1922-30, John Huntington Poly. Cleve., 1927-29. Draftsman, designer Rorimer-Brooks Studio, Cleve., 1927-37; designer Irvin & Gormley, Inc., Cleve., 1937-40, Fisher Air Craft, Cleve., 1941, A.E. Probala, Designer, Cleve., 1941-65, 77—, Irvin & Co., Cleve., 1965-77. Mem. Cleve. Soc. Artists (pres. 1969-72). Republican. Avocations: designing; painting; building. Address: Andrew E Probala Designer 630 Osborn Bldg Cleveland OH 44115

PROBER, RICHARD, environmental engineer, educator; b. Chgo., May 30, 1937; s. Gabriel and Rose (Fox) P.; m. Joanne Shapiro, Aug. 30, 1959; children—Benjamin Steven, Daniel Lewis, Joshua Lee. B.S. in Chem. Engring., Ill. Inst. Tech., 1957; M.S., U. Wis., 1958, Ph.D., 1962. Registered profl. engr., Ohio. Engr. Shell Devel. Co., Emeryville, Calif., 1962-65; research engr. Permutit Research and Devel. Ctr., Princeton, N.J., 1965-69; assoc. prof. chem. engring. Case Western Res. U., Cleve., 1970-77, adj. prof., 1977—; sr. engr. GMP Assoc., Cleve., 1977-81; environ. engr. Havens & Emerson, Cleve., 1981-84; sr. engr. Engring.-Sci. Ltd., Cleve., 1984—. Contbr. articles to profl. jours. Patentee in field. Recipient McCormack award Am. Inst. Chem. Engrs., 1956; Electric Power Research Inst. award Internat. Ozone Inst., 1977. Mem. Am. Inst. Chem. Engrs. (sec. treas. 1983—), Water Pollution Control Fedn. Avocations: Civil War history, opera, jogging. Office: Engineering Sci Ltd 19101 Villageview Rd Cleveland OH 44119

PROCHNOW, HERBERT VICTOR, banker; b. Wilton, Wis., May 19, 1897; s. Adolph and Alvina (Liefke) P.; B.A., U. Wis.-Madison, 1921, M.A., 1922, LL.D. (hon.), 1956; Ph.D., Northwestern U., 1947; Litt.D. (hon.), Millikin U., 1952; LL.D. (hon.), Ripon Coll., 1950, Northwestern U., 1963, Lake Forest Coll., 1964; D.H.L. (hon.), Thiel Coll., 1965, Monmouth Coll., 1965, U. N.D., 1966; m. Laura Virginia Stinson, June 12, 1928 (dec. Aug. 1977); 1 son, Herbert Victor. Prin., Kendall (Wis.) High Sch.; asst. prof. bus. adminstrn. Ind. U.; advt. mgr. Union Trust Co., Chgo.; with First Nat. Bank Chgo., 1933-73, pres., dir., 1962-68, hon. dir., 1968-73; dir. Banco di Roma, Chgo.; sec. Fed. Res. Adv. Council, 1945—; spl. cons. sec. state, 1955, 57; dep. under sec. state econ. affairs, 1955-56; alt. gov. Internat. Bank and IMF, 1955-56. Chmn., U.S. del. GATT, Geneva, 1956; mem. U.S. del. Colombo Conf., Singapore, 1955, OECD, Paris, 1956; pres. Internat. Monetary Conf., 1968, now cons., hon. mem.; lectr. Loyola U., Northwestern U., dir. summer Grad. Sch. Banking, U. Wis., 1945-81, now lectr.; fin. columnist Chgo. Tribune, 1968-70. Treas., Nat. 4-H Clubs, 1962-69; former trustee McCormick Theol. Sem., Evanston Hosp. Served with AEF. Decorated comdr. Order of Vasa (Sweden); comdr.'s cross Order of Merit (W.Ger.); recipient award Harvard Bus. Sch. Assn., 1965, Ayres Leadership award Stonier Grad. Sch. Banking, Rutgers U., 1966, Silver Plaque award NCCJ, 1967. Mem. Am. Econ. Assn., Chgo. Assn. Commerce and Industry (pres. 1964-65), Chgo. Council Fgn. Relations (pres. 1966-67), Nat. Assn. Bus. Economists, Fgn. Policy Officers Assn., Am. Finance Assn., Beta Gamma Sigma (nat. honoree). Clubs: Chicago Sunday Evening (trustee), Univ., Chgo., Comml., Mid-Day, Rotary, Union League (Chgo.); Bankers, Executives, Glen View. Author: Great Stories from Great Lives (an anthology), 1944; Meditations on the Ten Commandments, 1946; The Toastmaster's Handbook, 1949; Term Loans and Theories of Bank Liquidity, 1949; Successful Speakers Handbook, 1951; 1001 Ways to Improve Your Conversations and Speeches, 1952; Meditations on the Beatitudes, 1952; The Speaker's Treasury of Stories for All Occasions, 1953; The Toastmaster's and Speaker's Handbook, 1955; The Speaker's Handbook of Epigrams and Witticisms, 1955; Speaker's Treasury for Sunday School Teachers, 1955; The New Guide for Toastmasters, 1956; A Treasury of Stories, Illustrations, Epigrams and Quotations for Ministers and Teachers, 1957; The New Speaker's Treasury of Wit and Wisdom, 1958; A Family Treasury of Inspiration and Faith, 1958; Meditations on the Lord's Prayer, 1957; The Complete Toastmaster, 1960; Speaker's Book of Illustrations, 1960; Effective Public Speaking, 1960; 1000 Tips and Quips for Speakers and Toastmasters, 1962; 1400 Ideas for Speakers and Toastmasters, 1964; Tree of Life, 1972; Speaker's Source Book, 1969; A Speaker's Treasury for Educators, Convocation Speakers, 1973; The Speaker's and Toastmaster's Handbook, 1973; co-author: The Next Century is America's, 1938; Practical Bank Credit, 1939, rev. edit., 1963; The Public Speaker's Treasure Chest, 1942, rev. edit., 1964, 77, 85; A Dictionary of Wit, Wisdom and Satire, 1962; The Successful Toastmaster, 1966; A Treasury of Humorous Quotations, 1969; Quotation Finder, 1971; The Changing World of Banking, 1974; The Toastmaster's Treasure Chest, 1979; A Treasure Chest of Quotations for All Occasions, 1983; editor: American Financial Institutions, 1951; Determining the Business Outlook, 1954; Federal Reserve System, 1960; World Economic Policies and Problems, 1965; The Five-Year Outlook for Interest Rates, 1968; The One-Bank Holding Company, 1969; The Eurodollar, 1970; The Five-Year Outlook for Interest Rates in the United States and Abroad, 1972; Dilemmas Facing the Nation, 1979; Bank Credit, 1981. Home: 2950 Harrison St Evanston IL 60201 Office: 1 First Nat Plaza Chicago IL 60670

PROCHNOW, HERBERT VICTOR, JR., banker, lawyer; b. Evanston, Ill., May 26, 1931; s. Herbert V. and Laura (Stinson) P.; A.B., Harvard U., 1953, J.D., 1956; A.M., U. Chgo., 1958; m. Lucia Boyden, Aug. 6, 1966; children—Thomas Herbert, Laura. Admitted to Ill. bar, 1957; with 1st Nat. Bank Chgo., 1958—, atty., 1961-70, sr. atty., 1971-73, counsel, 1973—, adminstrv. asst. to chmn. bd., 1978-81. Mem. Am., Ill., Chgo. (chmn. com. internat. law 1970-71) bar assns., Am. Soc. Internat. Law, Phi Beta Kappa. Clubs: Chicago; Harvard (N.Y.C.); Legal, Law, Onwentsia, Economic, Executives, University (Chgo.). Author: (with Herbert V. Prochnow) The Public Speaker's Treasure Chest, 1985; The Toastmaster's Treasure Chest, 1979; The Changing World of Banking, 1973; also articles in legal publs. Home: 949 Woodbine Pl Lake Forest IL 60045 Office: 1 First Nat Plaza Chicago IL 60670

PROCK, MICHAEL JOSEPH, SR., funeral director; b. Merrill, Wis., Nov. 25, 1925; s. Martin John and Catherine Ann (Hubley) P.; m. Lorraine E. Knutson, Jan. 16, 1947; children—John M., Michael Joseph, Steven J., Patrick T., David A., James O., Jeffrey L. Student Marquette U., 1943-45. Cert. funeral dir. and embalmer, 1947. Owner, operator Prock Funeral Home, Gold Cross Ambulance Service and Gold Cross Van & Courier Service, Eau Claire, Wis., 1964—. City dir. March of Dimes, 1949-53, county treas., 1953-59; commr. Boy Scouts Am., 1956-57, Order of Arrow, 1953; pres. Elk Lake Improvement Assn., 1957-58; pub. relations dir. Eau Claire Drum and Bugle Corps, 1959-64; mem. parish council Immaculate Conception Catholic Ch., 1968-72, Eau Claire County Health Adv. Forum Bd., 1969; v.p. Chippewa-Eau Claire Deanery, 1970-76; v.p. pastoral council Diocese of La Crosse, 1976-78, pres. fin. and adminstrn. commn., 1980-85; chmn. EMS adv. bd. Dist. 1 Tech. Inst., 1979; pres. Triniteam Bd. Dirs., 1981-83; dir. Eau Claire County EMS Council, 1982—; pres. Regis Found., 1984—; Recipient Service to Mankind award Sertoma, 1979. Mem. Nat. Funeral Dirs. Assn., Wis. Funeral Dirs. Assn. Club: Chippewa Valley Field Trial (pres. 1953-54); Lodge: Lions (1st v.p. 1982), K.C. (4 degree). Home: 906 Zephyr Hill Ave Eau Claire WI 54701 Office: 405 N Hastings Pl Eau Claire WI 54701

PROCTOR, JAMES PATTERSON, lawyer; b. Dayton, Ohio, Apr. 30, 1952; s. James Luke and Bernice Marie (Wallace) P., m. Ann Louise Bundy, July 5, 1975; children—Brian Patrick, Jennifer Ann. B.S., Ohio State U., 1974; J.D., U. Akron, 1980. Bar: Ohio 1980, U.S. Dist. Ct. (no. dist.) Ohio 1980. Assoc. Sani & Barnhouse Co. L.P.A., New Philadelphia, Ohio, 1980-83, R.E. Goforth Co., L.P.A., New Philadelphia, 1983—. Mem. Ohio State Bar Assn., Tuscarawas County Bar Assn. Republican. Methodist. Home: 1049 5th SW New Philadelphia OH 44663 Office: RE Goforth Co LPA 219 W High New Philadelphia OH 44663

PRONKO, PETER PAUL, physicist; b. Peckville, Pa., Mar. 29, 1938; s. Stephen and Mary (Mizerak) P.; m. Diana M. Dumas, Mar. 27, 1967; children—Andrea, Jocelyn. B.S., U. Scranton (Pa.), 1960; M.S., U. Pitts., 1962; Ph.D., U. Alta., Edmonton, Can., 1966. Asst. prof. U. Scranton, 1966-68; research assoc. McMaster U., Hamilton, Ont., Can., 1968-72; physicist Argonne Nat. Lab. (Ill.), 1972-80; chief scientist Universal Energy Systems, Dayton, Ohio, 1980—. Contbr. articles to profl. jours. Mem. Am. Phys. Soc., Materials Research Soc., Am. Soc. Metals, IEEE. Home: 3219 Bellflower St Kettering OH 45409 Office: Universal Energy Systems 4401 Dayton-Xenia Rd Dayton OH 45432

PROOST, ROBERT LAWRENCE, hospital construction director; b. St. Louis, Mar. 26, 1944; s. George Lawrence and Dorothy Ann (Saterfield) P.; m. Christy Wider, June 9, 1967; children—Merridee, Bob Jr., Chris, Carrie. Student Regis Coll., 1962-65, Washington U., St. Louis, 1965-67. Br. mgr. Ahart & Assoc., St. Louis, 1970; pres. CPM, Inc., St. Louis, 1972-75; project mgr. Hercules Constrn. Co., St. Louis, 1975-82; dir. constrn. and phys. facilities Sisters of St. Mary Health Care System, St. Louis, 1982—. Pres., founder Soccer Club for Youth, 1978—; pres. St. Louis Youth Soccer Assn., 1985—. Mem. Am. Hosp. Assn., Mo. Hosp. Assn., Am. Soc. for Hosp. Engrs. Republican. Roman Catholic. Office: Sister of Saint Mary Saint Louis MO 63117

PROSSER, DANIEL LEE, insurance company executive; b. Dallas, Dec. 28, 1951; s. Austin Peayand Francis Ruth (Richardson) P.; m. Nicolette Susan Indelicato, July 31, 1976; children—Zachary Lance, Christian Chase. B.S., U. Mo., 1974, M.Ed., 1981. C.L.U.; lic. secondary tchr., Mo. Tchr. pub. schs., Salem, Mo., 1974-76, Carl Junction, Mo., 1976-77; dist. sales mgr. J.I. Case Co., Racine, Wis., 1977-80, sales tng. supr., 1980-81; sales mgmt. trainee Prudential Ins. Co. Am., Newark, 1981-82, devel. mgr., St.Louis, 1982—. Named Outstanding Sales Mgr., J.I. Case Co., 1978; recipient Pres.'s Citation, Purdential Ins. Co. Am., Newark, 1984, V.P.'s trophy Prudential Ins. Co. Am., Houston, 1984. Mem. Nat. Assn. Life Underwriters, Gen. Agts. and Mgrs. Assn., Creve Coeur C. of C. Republican. Roman Catholic. Avocations: classic cars; golf. Home: 503 Falaise Dr Saint Louis MO 63141 Office: Prudential Ins Co of Am 9666 Olive Blvd Suite 700 Saint Louis MO 63132

PROSSER, FRANCIS WARE, JR., physics educator; b. Wichita, Kans., June 30, 1927; s. Francis Ware and Harriet (Corinne (Osborne) P.; m. Nancy Lou Baugh, Aug. 10, 1952; children—David Francis, Rebecca Ann, Martha Lou. B.S., U. Kans., 1950, M.S., 1954, Ph.D., 1955. Research assoc. Rice U., Houston, 1955-57; asst. prof. U. Kans., Lawrence, 1957-62, assoc. prof., 1962-67, prof. physics, 1967—; sr. postdoctoral assoc. Aerospace Research Lab., Dayton, Ohio, 1969-70; vis. scientist Argonne Nat. Lab., Chgo., 1975-76. Contbr. articles to profl. jours. Served with USNR, 1945-46. Fellow Am. Phys. Soc.; mem. Kans. Acad. Sci., N.Y. Acad. Scis., Am. Assn. Physics Tchrs., Sigma Xi, Sigma Pi Sigma. Home: 1622 Cambridge Rd Lawrence KS 66044 Office: Dept Physics and Astronomy Univ Kansas Lawrence KS 66045

PROSSER, HAROLD LEE, writer, sociology educator; b. Springfield, Mo., Dec. 31, 1944; steps. Frank L. nd Marjorie (Firestone) Hart; m. Grace Eileen Wright, Nov. 4, 1971; children—Rachael Maranda, Rebecca Dawn. A.A., Santa Monica Coll., 1968; student Calif. State U.-Northridge, 1968-69; B.S. in Sociology, So. Mo. State U., 1974, M.S.Ed., 1982. Instr. sociology Drury Coll., Springfield, 1982—. Author: Dandelion Seeds: Eighteen Stories, 1974; Goodbye, Lon Chaney, Jr., Goodbye, 1979; (non-fiction) Robert Bloch, 1985. Fellow Sci. Fiction Research Assn.; mem. Capricorn Seven Research Soc. (founder). Baptist. Avocations: book collecting; restoration of Victorian artifacts; fishing; traveling; hiking. Home: 1313 S Jefferson Ave Springfield MO 65807

PROUTY, CHILTON EATON, geology educator, consultant; b. Tuscaloosa, Ala., Sept. 8, 1914; s. William Frederick and Lucille (Thorington) P.; m. Norma Victoria Fruvog, Sept. 3, 1942; children—William Eaton, John Fruvog. B.S. in Geology, U. N.C., 1936; M.S., Mo. Sch. Mines, Rolla, 1938; Ph.D., Columbia U., 1944. Field geologist U.S. Geol. Survey, Washington, 1944-46; cooperating summer field geologist Pa. Geol. Survey, 1946-58; prof. geology U. Pitts., 1946-57, head dept., 1951-57; prof. geol. scis. Mich. State U., East Lansing, 1957—, chmn. dept., 1957-69; gen. geol. cons., Pa., Ohio, W.Va., Mich., 1946—; cons., examiner North Central Assn. Coll. and Secondary Schs., 1957-70; dir. Geo-Dynamics, Inc. Contbr. articles to profl. jours. Fellow Geol. Soc. Am.; mem. Assn. Geology Tchrs. (pres. Eastern sect. 1952, nat. pres. 1958), Paleontol. Soc. Am., Soc. Econ. Paleontologists and Mineralogists (pres. Gt. Lakes sect. 1979), Am. Inst. Profl. Geologists (editor, 1977-78), Sigma Xi. Methodist. Home: 4690 Kingswood Dr Okemos MI 48864 Office: Mich State Univ Dept Geol Scis East Lansing MI 48824

PROUTY, GARRY FRANKLYN, psychologist; b. Syracuse, N.Y., Aug. 21, 1936; s. Cyrus and Rita (McFall) P.; student Buffalo State Tchrs. Coll., 1954-57; B.A., U. Buffalo, 1959; postgrad. (LaVerne Noyes scholar) U. Chgo., 1966; 1 dau., Gwen Allison. Teaching fellow dept. sociology U. Buffalo, 1961-62; chief psychologist Kennedy Job Tng. Center, Palos Park, Ill., 1966-70; dir. mental health program Prairie State Coll., Chicago Heights, Ill., 1970-74; pvt. practice as psychologist, Park Forest, Ill., 1968-72; psychologist Southwell Inst., Olympia Fields, Ill., 1972—; founder, dir. pre-therapy research and treatment project Elizabeth Ludemann Ctr., Park Forest, 1981—; adj. prof. Union Grad. Sch., Yellow Springs, Ohio, 1972-74; mem. adv. bd. South Suburban Council on Alcoholism, 1978; psychol. cons. Found. I Drug Abuse. Fellow Chgo. Psychotherapy Center, 1975-77. Fellow Am. Orthopsychiat. Assn.; mem. Am. Psychol. Assn. (asso.), Am. Sociol. Assn., Internat. Soc. for Study of Symbols. Editorial bd. Psychotherapy Theory, Research and Practice, 1970—, Jour. Mental Imagery, 1977—. Office: Southwell Institute 2601 Lincoln Olympia Fields IL 60461

PROVANZANA, JOHN HARMS, electrical engineer; b. Bklyn., Dec. 27, 1941; s. Edward Joseph and Cecilia Sophia (Harms) P.; m. Marie I. Anderson, Sept. 2, 1967; children—Kathleen Michelle, Beth Marie, Suzanne Marie. B.E.E., Manhattan Coll., 1967; M.E.E., Rensselaer Poly. Inst., 1968; postgrad. NYU, 1973-74; A.E.P., U. Mich. Sch. Bus. Adminstrn., 1980. With Am. Electric Power Service Corp., 1967—, staff engr., 1977, sect. head, 1978, mgr. maj. elec. equipment sect., Columbus, Ohio, 1981—, mgr. maj. transmission equipment sect., 1984—. Served with USCG, 1959-63. Sr. mem. IEEE (Bendix award 1967); mem. Eta Kappa Nu. Republican. Roman Catholic. Contbr. articles to profl. jours. Home: 304 Delegate Dr Worthington OH 43085 Office: 1 Riverside Plaza Columbus OH 43216

PROVIS, DOROTHY LOUISE, artist, sculptor; b. Chgo., Apr. 26, 1926; d. George Kenneth Smith and Ann Hart (Day) Guest; m. William H. Provis, Sr., July 28, 1945; children—Timothy A., William H., Jr. Student Sch. Art Inst., Chgo., 1953-56, U. Wis.-Milw., 1967-68, 69-70. Sculptor, Port Washington, Wis., 1963—; pres. bd. dirs. West Bend Gallery of Fine Arts, Wis., 1984—, also dir.; speaker in field. Author, lobbyist Wis. Consignment Bill, Madison, 1979; panelist Women's Caucus for Art Conf., Phila., 1983. Wis. Arts Bd. designer-craftsmen grantee, NEA, 1981. Mem. Coalition of Women's Art Orgns. (del. to continuing com. Nat. Women's Conf. 1979, panelist conf. 1981, pres. 1982-84), Wis. Painters and Sculptors (editor newsletter 1982-85), Wis. Women in Arts (legis. liaison 1978-80). Artists for Ednl. Action (corr. 1979—). Home and Studio: 123 E Beutel Rd Port Washington WI 53074

PROXMIRE, WILLIAM, U.S. senator; b. Lake Forest, Ill., Nov. 11, 1915; s. Theodore Stanley and Adele (Flanigan) P.; A.B., Yale U., 1938; M.B.A., Harvard U., 1940, M.A. in Pub. Adminstrn., 1948; m. Ellen Hodges; children—Theodore Stanley, Elsie Stillman, Douglas Clark. Pres. Artcraft Press, Waterloo, Wis., 1953-57; U.S. senator from Wis., 1957—. Nominee for gov. Wis., 1952, 54, 56; assemblyman Wis. legislature, 1951. Democrat. Office: SD-530 Dirksen Office Bldg Washington DC 20510

PRUITT, RUSSELL CLYDE, industrial and interment foundries executive; b. Damascus, Va., Aug. 31, 1927; s. R. Martin and Pearl K. (Osborne) P.; B.A., Fenn Coll., 1954; postgrad. Western Res. U., 1957-62; m. Clarice Furchess, Apr. 5, 1947; children—Phyllis (Mrs. Dwain Parks), Russell C., Mark, Daniel. Auditor, Standard Oil Co., Cleve., 1948-53; controller Nelson Worldwide div. TRW, Lorain, Ohio, 1953-83; pres., treas., dir. Oreg. Brass Works, Portland, 1983—; dir. Sheidow Bronze Co., Williamsburg Bronze Co. Notary pub., Lorain County, 1958—; cons. income tax and investment. Mem. Sheffield Lake (Ohio) Charter Commn., 1960-62; chmn. finance com. Sheffield Lake City Council, 1964-66; pres. bd. edn. Black River, Medina County, Ohio, 1973—. Bd. dirs., treas. Lorain YMCA. Served with USNR, 1944-46, 50-51; PTO, Korea. Mem. U.S. Judo Fedn., Smithsonian Inst., Ohio Sch. Bds. Assn., Nat. Assn. Accountants, Am. Inst. Corp. Controllers, Am. Accounting Assn., Am. Quarter Horse Assn., Appaloosa Horse Club. Eagle. Home: Route 58 Wellington OH 44090

PRUSA, ANTHONY ALPHONSE, physical therapist, athletic trainer; b. Hoisington, Kans., Aug. 17, 1954; s. Alphonse Daniel and Lorena (Mater) P.; m. Jane Ann Rogers, Aug. 13, 1977; 1 child, Brandon Rogers. B.S. in Phys. Therapy, Kans. U., 1977. Staff phys. therapist Restorative Services, Inc., Hobart, Ind., 1978-79, chief phys. therapist, 1979-83, supr. phys. therapy, 1983—; chief instr. Save A Back, Hobart, Ind., 1984—; cons. for athletic tng. 10 area high schs., 1 univ., 1978—; pres. Ind. Back Sch., Inc., 1985—. Mem. Am. Phys. Therapy Assn. (cert.), Nat. Athletic Trainers Assn. (cert.). Democrat. Roman Catholic. Avocations: running, exercising. Office: 6335 Roosevelt Pl Merrillville IN 46410

PRUSOK, RUDI ALBIN, foreign language educator; b. East Orange, N.J., Dec. 26, 1934; s. Ernst Karl and Anna Elise (Kuntze) P.; m. Lois May Braroe, Sept. 19, 1964; children—Ellen K., Amy I. A.B., Lafayette Coll., 1957; M.S., U. Iowa, 1961; M.A., Washington U., St. Louis, 1965, Ph.D., 1967. Prof. German, No. Mich. U., Marquette, 1967—, head fgn. lang. dept., 1975—. Contbr. articles to profl. jours. Fulbright fellow, summer 1979. Mem. MLA, Am. Single Shot Rifle Assn. (editor 1980—), Am. Assn. Tchrs. German, Mich. Foreign Language Assn., Soc. for German-Am. Studies. Avocations: competitive shooting; canoeing. Home: 625 Pine St Marquette MI 49855 Office: Northern Michigan U Dept Fgn Langs Marquette MI 49855

PRUSSING, JOHN EDWARD, aeronautical engineer, educator, researcher; b. Oak Park, Ill., Aug. 19, 1940; s. Milton Carl and Elizabeth (Thompson) P.; m. Laurel Victoria Lunt, May 29, 1965; children—Heidi, Erica, Victoria. B.S., MIT, 1962, M.S., 1963, Sc.D., 1967. Lectr. U. Calif.-San Diego, 1967-69; asst. prof. aero. and astronautical engring. U. Ill., Urbana, 1969-72, assoc. prof., 1972-81, prof., 1981—; researcher U.S. Army Research Office, Durham, N.C., 1981-84. Fellow AIAA (assoc.; mem. astrodynamics tech. com. 1981-83); mem. Am. Astronautical Soc., Am. Soc. Engring Edn. Office: U Ill 104 S Mathews 101 TB Urbana IL 61801

PRUZAN, IRA, consumer products company executive; b. Chgo., Dec. 6, 1940; s. Alfred A. and Sally (Goldman) P.; m. Ina Pass, June 27, 1965; children—Brian Mark, Michael Jay. B.S., U. Ill., 1962, M.B.A., 1964. Fin. analyst Gen. Foods Corp., White Plains, N.Y., 1964-66; br. mgr. Quaker Oats Co., Chgo., 1966-71; v.p. Needham, Harper & Steers, Chgo., 1971-77; v.p. mktg. Associated Mills Inc./Pollenex, Chgo., 1977—. Patentee in field. Mem. Assn. Home Appliance Mfrs. (portable appliance exec. bd.). Clubs: Merchandising Execs. (dir. 1974-77), Northshore Toastmasters (pres. 1974-75; Disting. Service award 1974). Home: 53 Fernwood Dr Glenview IL 60025 Office: Associated Mills Inc/Pollenex 111 N Canal St Chicago IL 60606

PRYATEL, AUGUST, judge; b. Cleve. Sept. 20, 1913; m. Elaine M. Turk. B.A., Hiram Coll., 1936; LL.B., Cleve. Law Sch., 1942. Bar: Ohio, 1942. Asst. police prosecutor City of Cleve., 1944-49; dep. supt. ins. State of Ohio, 1949-55, supt. ins., 1955-57; judge Cleve. Municipal Ct., 1957-60, chief justice, 1960-65; judge Ct. Common Pleas, Cleve., 1965-77, Ct. Appeals 8th Dist, 1977—. Bd. dirs. Ohio Motorists Assn.-AAA, Cleve., 1962-84; trustee Suburban Community Hosp. Warrensville Heights, Ohio, 1965-83; pres. Greater Cleve. Safety Council, 1968-71, 1980-81; chmn. bd. trustees Rose-Mary Home, Cleve.,

1971-72, Suburban Community Hosp., 1980-82. Recipient Pub. Service medal Griffith Found., 1956; Disting. Service award Hiram Coll. Alumni Assn., 1967; Disting. Service aware Delta Theta Phi, 1972; Superior Jud. Service honor Supreme Ct. Ohio, 1975; Outstanding Alumnus award Cleve. Marshall Coll., 1984; Disting. Service award Blue Cross Ohio, 1984. Mem. Ohio Cts. Appeals Assn., Ohio Bar Assn., Bar Assn. Greater Cleve., Cuyahoga County Bar Assn., Am. Judicature Soc. Home: 37615 Fox Run Dr Solon OH 44139 Office: Ct Appeals Ohio 8th Appellate Dist 1 Lakeside Ave Cleveland OH 44113

PRYOR, BARBARA WRIGHT, educator, contralto; b. Stamps, Ark.; d. Joseph Dudley and Bernyce Eleanor (Hayes) Wright; B.E., Chgo. State U., 1961; M.A., Roosevelt U., 1978; M.Ed., Chgo. Conservatory Music, 1967; m. Harry Leonard Pryor, Jr.; 1 son, Harry Leonard III. Tchr. Am. history and govt. Wendell Phillips Upper Grade Center, Chgo., 1961-63; 8th grade tchr. George T. Donoghue Sch., Chgo., 1963-78; contralto soloist, dir. music St. James United Meth. Ch., Chgo., 1966-74; chorale dir. Duke Ellington, 1968; soloist Quinn Chapel A.M.E. Ch., Chgo., 1978-81; guidance counselor George T. Donoghue Sch., Chgo. Public Sch. System, System, 1979—. Bd. dirs. Soc. Black Cultural Arts, Inc., 1978—, chmn. artist selection com., 1978—; active Chgo. Lyric Opera Guild. Recipient Outstanding Tchr. of Year award Chgo. Public Schs., 1977; Key to City, Little Rock, 1982. Nat. cert. counselor. Mem. Chgo. State U. Alumni Assn., Am. Sch. Counselor Assn., Am. Assn. Counseling and Devel., AAUW, Nat. Assn. Negro Musicians, Ill. Assn. Supervision and Curriculum Devel., Chgo. Music Assn., Roosevelt U. Alumni Assn., Phi Delta Kappa. United Methodist. Author: Autism; Main-Streaming: Providing the Least Restrictive Environment for Handicapped Children, 1982. Composer: Hear Us, We Beseech Thee, 1968. Home: 8258 Morgan St Chicago IL 60620 Office: 707 E 37th St Chicago IL 60653

PRYOR, RICHARD SIMS, banker; b. Liberty, Mo., Dec. 20, 1935; s. Ted R. and Ruby Sims (Williams) P.; m. Linda Fitzgerald, July 10, 1960; children—Kelley Denise, Richard Alexander. A.A., Longview Coll., 1975; B.A., Columbia Coll., 1977 (Mo.); grad. Am. Inst. Banking, 1962, 66, 80; grad. Grad. Sch. Banking, U. Wis., 1969. Asst. cashier 1st Nat. Bank Liberty (Mo.), 1955-61; v.p. Nat. Bank North Kansas City, 1961-69; pres., chief exec. officer Thornton Nat. Bank, Nevada, Mo. 1969-73; pres., chief exec. officer Bank Jacomo, Blue Springs, Mo., 1973—; chmn. Ray County Bank, Richmond, Mo., 1978—; dir. Ind. Assurance Co. Kansas City. Councilman, mayor pro tem Liberty City Council, 1967-69; mem. Nevada Public Sch. Bd. (Mo.), 1972-73; charter mem. Clay County Indsl. Commn., 1968-69; chmn. Nevada City Library Bd., 1970-73; mem. Nevada Indsl. Devel. Corp., 1970-73; chmn. bd. Cottey Coll., Nevada, Mo., 1973-80; bus. chmn. Cancer Crusade, Blue Springs, 1981-83; chmn. bd. St. Mary's Hosp. Bd. Assocs., 1981; bd. dirs. Mid Continent Public Library, 1979—; pres. Performing Arts Council Blue Springs, 1980-81; mem. Mo. Agr. and Small Bus. Devel. Commn., 1981—. Served with AUS, 1957-59. Recipient Disting. Service award North Kansas City Jaycees, 1967, Mo. Jaycees, 1967, 4-H Outstanding Alum award, Vernon County, Mo., 1972; named Citizen of Yr., Blue Springs, Mo., 1980. Mem. Mo. Bankers Assn. (state conv. chmn. 1984), Bank Adminstrn. Inst. (community bank council 1983—), Am. Bankers Inst. (community bank council 1984), Clay County Bankers Assn. (pres. 1967). Republican. Methodist. Lodge: Rotary (pres., dist. treas.). Home: 707 N 16th St Blue Springs MO 64015 Office: Bank Jacomo 909 S 7 Hwy Blue Springs MO 64015

PUCHALSKI, CATHY ANN, association administrator; b. Chgo., May 10, 1957; d. John Aloysius and Eleanore Marie (Brzoska) Puchalski. B.S., Western Ill. U., 1978; postgrad. Roosevelt U. Recreation supr. Glenview Park Dist. (Ill.), 1978-81; adminstrv. coordinator No. Suburban Spl. Recreation Assn., Highland Park, Ill., 1981—; lectr. in field. Vol., Spl. Olympics, Highland Park, 1982. Mem. Nat. Park and Recreation Assn., Ill. Recreation and Park Assn. Roman Catholic. Office: No Suburban Spl Recreation Assn 636 Ridge Rd Highland Park IL 60035

PUCHTA-BROWN, KRISTINE MARIE, osteopathic physician; b. Fort Belvoir, Va., Feb. 12, 1952; d. Randolph Everett and Eunice Marie (Rohlfing) Puchta; m. Floyd William Brown, July 5, 1951; children—Sarah Courtney, Aaron Jamison, Wayne Karlton. B.A. in Biology, U. Mo., 1975; D.O., Kansas City Coll. Osteo. Medicine, 1979. Gen. practice osteo. medicine, Troy, Mo., 1979—; mem. staff Lincoln County Meml. Hosp., chief-of-staff, 1983, 84. Fellow Internat. Coll. Gen. Practice; mem. Mo. Assn. Osteo. Physicians and Surgeons, Central Mo. Assn. Osteo. Physicians and Surgeons, Troy Bus. and Profl. Women's Orgn., NOW. Mem. United Ch. of Christ. Office: Troy Surg Clinic 900 E Cherry St Troy MO 63379

PUCKETT, HELEN LOUISE, tax consulting company executive; b. Ripley, Ohio, Oct. 29, 1934; d. Joseph and Gladys Muriel (Madden) Haney; student Columbus Bus. U., 1971; m. Marvin R. Puckett, May 29, 1953 (dec.); children—Steven W., Thomas J. Office mgr. Al-Win Tng., Inc., West Jefferson, Ohio, 1971—, sec.-treas., 1971—, agt., 1977-79; owner, operator HLP Bus. Enterprises, bookkeeping and tax service; notary public, 1975—. Sunday Sch. tchr. London (Ohio) Ch. of Christ, 1975—, pres. Women's Fellowship, 1979-81. Mem. London Bus. and Profl. Women. Home: 130 Columbia Ave London OH 43140 Office: 485 Glade Run Rd West Jefferson OH 43162

PUCKETT, ROBERT HUGH, political science educator, consultant; b. Kansas City, Mo., July 16, 1935; s. John William and Marjorie (Shirlaw) P.; m. Barbara Chandley, Dec. 23, 1964; 1 child, Sarah Anne. B.A., DePauw U., 1957; M.A., U. Chgo., 1958, Ph.D., 1961. Asst. prof. Mary Washington Coll., Fredericksburg, Va., 1961-63; vis. scholar MIT, Cambridge, Mass., 1963-64; asst. prof. U. Va., Charlottesville, 1964-66, Mich. State U., East Lansing, 1966-68; prof. polit. sci. Ind. State U., Terre Haute, 1968—; cons. Ctr. for Polit. Research, Riverside, Calif., 1984-85. Author: America Faces the World, 1972. Contbr. chpt. to book, articles to profl. jours. Mem. adv. com. U.S. Commn. Civil Rights (Ind.), 1984-85; pres. Vol. Action Ctr., Terre Haute, 1984-85; bd. dirs. South Ind. Health Systems Agency, Bedford, 1978-83, South Ind. Health Found., Bedford, 1982-83. Recipient Blue Key awards, 1979, 84. Mem. Am. Polit. Sci. Assn., Internat. Studies Assn. (bd. dirs. Midwest 1982—), Indpls. Com. Fgn. Relations, Ind. Council World Affairs, Ind. Consortium for Security Studies, Inter-Univ. Seminar Armed Forces and Soc., Phi Beta Kappa, Phi Eta Sigma, Pi Sigma Alpha. Methodist. Lodge: Kiwanis. Home: 122 Marigold Dr Terre Haute IN 47803 Office: Ind State U Dept Polit Sci Terre Haute IN 47809

PUETZ, BOBBIE SHARON, physical education instructor; b. New Boston, Tex., Apr. 23, 1936; d. William Clifford and Bobbie Lela (Pierce) Shelton; m. Sylvester Joseph Puetz, Aug. 28, 1954; children—Gary Wayne, Cheryl Anne. B.A.E., Wichita State U., 1972. Phys. edn. instr. Bishop Carroll High Sch., Wichita, 1972—, dept. chmn., 1981—, asst. to A.D., 1982—. Named All-City Coach, Eagle Beacon Newspaper, Wichita, 1977-82. Mem. AAHPER, Kans. Health, Phys. Edn. Recreation Assn., Kans. Cath. Tchrs. Assn., Kans. Coaches Assn. (chmn. softball Kans. 1978-82; State Coach of Yr. 1979-80), Nat. High Sch. Coaches Assn. (co-chmn. softball 1979—; Nat. Dist. Coach 1980). Democrat. Roman Catholic.

PUGH, CHARLES STUART GREDELL, pharmaceutical company manager; b. Sioux City, Ia., Aug. 25, 1949; s. Philip F.H. and Elizabeth L. (Ramsdell) P.; m. Patricia Jean Carney, June 4, 1977; children—Alisa C. B.S. in Biochemistry, Ia. State U., 1973; Ph.D. with honors in Biochemistry, U. Kans., 1979. Salesman, Am. Sci Products, Charlotte, N.C., 1973-74; postdoctoral research fellow L. Weiner Neurology, U. So. Calif., Los Angeles, 1979-80, J. Adler Biochemistry, U. Wis., Madison, 1980-81; head R&D sect. diagnostics Abbott Labs, North Chicago, Ill., 1981—. Contbr. articles to Biochemistry, Jour. Virology, Jour. Biol. Chemistry. Recipient Nat. Research Service award NIH, 1981, Presdl. award Abbott Labs, 1983. Office: Abbott Labs Diagnostic Div D9ZR AP10 North Chicago IL 60064

PUGH, DAVID MILTON, physician, medical educator; b. Phila., July 13, 1929; s. Edward J. and Pauline S. (Stroedtman) P.; m. Virginia Wightman, June 25, 1955; children—Laurie, Catherine, Daniel. A.D., U. Rochester, 1951; M.D., Yale U., 1958. Intern, U.S. Naval Hosp., Bethesda, Md., 1958-59; resident in medicine U. Wash. Hosp., Seattle, 1959-61, fellow in cardiology, 1961-64; asst. prof. cardiology, U. Kans. Med. Ctr., Kansas City, 1965-70, assoc. prof., 1970-76, prof., 1970—. Served to lt. comdr. USNR, 1951-54, Korea, 1958-59. Fellow Am. Heart Assn. (council clin. cardiology 1970—), Am. Coll. Cardiology (pres. Kans. affiliate 1981-82), ACP, Am. Coll. Chest Physicians; mem. Wyandotte County Med. Soc. (pres. 1982). Office: Cardiovascular Sect U Kans Sch Medicine 39th and Rainbow Kansas City KS 66103 also 6445 Nall Dr Shawnee Mission KS 66202

PUGH, ELLEN ANN, pharmacist; b. Bklyn., Sept. 11, 1956; d. Alfred J. and Geraldine A. (Spizuco) Pawlowski; m. Stanley Charles Pugh, June 11, 1981. B.S. in Pharmacy, Auburn U., 1981. Registered pharmacist, Mo. Pharmacist, Lake of the Ozarks Gen. Hosp., Osage Beach, Mo., 1981-84, Glaize Drugs, Inc., Osage Beach, 1984—. Chmn. Camden County Am. Cancer Soc., Osage Beach, 1982, co-worker, 1983-84. Mem. Am. Soc. Hosp. Pharmacists, Am. Pharm. Assn., Mo. Pharm. Assn. Roman Catholic. Avocations: painting. Home: Route 1 Box 190-49 Osage Beach MO 65065

PUGH, J. THOMAS, journalism educator; b. Peoria, Ill., Apr. 26, 1930; s. Allie Allandia and Esther Caroline (Hartzell) P.; m. Margaret Jeanne Cornet, Apr. 5, 1952; children—Martha Jane Bergien, David Michael. B.S., Bradley U., 1952, M.A., 1955. Reporter, Peoria Jour. Star, 1947-62, assoc. editor, 1963-82; vis. lectr. U. Ill., Urbana, 1982—; lectr. Bradley U., Peoria, 1952-82, Ill. State U., Normal, 1973. Contbr. articles to profl. jours. Chmn. Ill. adv. com. U.S. Commn. on Civil Rights, 1982—. Served with U.S. Army, 1952-54. Recipient Illinois Valley Press Club awards, 1960, 65, 75; Meritorious Community Service award Peoria Heights Community, 1963-64. Mem. Am. Newspaper Guild (pres. local chpt. 86, 1960), Sigma Delta Chi (pres. Illinois Valley chpt. 1955-57). Methodist. Home: 500 W Melbourne Peoria IL 61604

PUGH, SANDRA (SASS) KAY, construction company executive; b. Aberdeen, S.D., June 3, 1950; d. John D. and Ellabeth A. (DeYoung) Pugh. Student Black Hills State Coll., 1968-72. Cert. electrician, S.D. Apprentice electrician Pugh Elec. Construction, Miller, S.D., 1974-81, mgr., journeyman electrician, 1981-83, owner, 1984—. Chmn., Hand County Teen Crippled Children, 1967-68; mem. Miller Civic and Commerce, 1983-85, Central Plains Arts Council, 1984-85. Recipient Govs. award in Photography S.D. State Fair, 1970. Club: Jobs Daughters (state office 1965). Contbr. poetry to West River Verses volume. Home: 620 1/2 W 4th St Miller SD 57362 Office: 616 W 4th St Miller SD 57362

PUGLISE, JOSEPH FRANCIS, planning executive; b. Washington, Apr. 4, 1935; s. Dominic J. and Mary (Presutti) P.; m. Roberta Ruder, May 19, 1959; children—Mark, Pamela, Christine, Virginia, Vicky, Michael. B.S., U. Md., 1957; M.B.A., Pepperdine U., 1982. Indsl. engr. Continental Can Co., N.Y.C., 1960-69; planning exec., 1969-77; indsl. engr. Crown Zellerbach, San Francisco, 1977-81; planning exec. Stone Container, Chgo., 1981-82, Griffith Labs., Alsip, Ill., 1982—. Mem. N.Am. Assn. Corp. Planners, Planning Execs. Inst., Am. Inst. Indsl. Engrs. Republican. Roman Catholic. Avocations: Golfing, racquetball. Home: 1717 Shire Ct Wheaton IL 60187 Office: Griffith Labs 12200 S Central Ave Chicago IL 60658

PUKACH, JOSEPH RUDOLPH, educational administrator, consultant; b. Wheeling, W.Va., Nov. 21, 1924; s. Michael Anthony and Anna (Jurik) P.; m. Wilma Lee Stites, Aug. 21, 1948. B.A., Shurtleff Coll., 1951; M.A., Washington U., St. Louis, 1955; E.D., U. Sarasota, 1976. Cert. tchr., adminstr., Ill., Fla. Dir. guidance, counseling and testing State of Ill., Springfield, 1962-64; dir. urban and community edn. U.S. Office Edn., Washington, 1963-65; adminstrv. asst. supt. Pinellas pub. schs., Clearwater, Fla., 1969-72; dir. Diagnostic Ctr., Belleville pub. schs., Ill., 1972-75; dean devel. Lewis and Clark Community Coll., Godfrey, Ill., 1975—; fed. procurement dir. Community Coll. and Dept. Commerce and Community Affairs, Godfrey and Springfield, 1984—; mem. com. Pvt. Iniative Com./Job Tng. Partnership Act, State of Ill., Springfield, 1984—. Chmn. bd. dirs. Econ. Opportunity Commn., Madison County, Ill., 1978-81, Madison County Manpower Council, 1979-82; exec. dir. Lewis and Clark Found., Godfrey, 1977-84; mem. council Pvt. Industry Council, Edwardsville, Ill., 1983—. Served with USMC, 1942-46; PTO. Harvard U. fellow, 1961; Paul Harris Found. fellow, 1984. Mem. Ill. Employment and Tng. Assn., NEA, Phi Delta Kappa. Republican. Episcopalian. Lodge: Rotary (bd. dirs. 1981-83). Avocations: golf; oil/water color painting; gardening; travel. Home: PO Box 593 Godfrey IL 62035 Office: Lewis and Clark Community Coll Godfrey Rd Godfrey IL 62035

PULFORD, ROBERT JESSE (BOB), professional hockey team manager; b. Newton Robinson, Ont., Can., Mar. 31, 1936. Formerly center Toronto Maple Leafs; past center, capt. Los Angeles Kings, also formerly coach; was coach, now gen. mgr. Chgo. Black Hawks. Office: care Chgo Black Hawks 1800 W Madison St Chicago IL 60612*

PULITZER, JOSEPH, JR., newspaper editor and publisher; b. St. Louis, May 13, 1913; s. Joseph and Elinor (Wickham) P.; student St. Mark's Sch., Southborough, Mass.; A.B., Harvard, 1936; m. Louise Vauclain, June 2, 1939 (dec. Dec. 1968); 1 son, Joseph IV; m. 2d, Emily S. Rauh, June 30, 1973. Reporter, San Francisco News, 1935; mem. staff St. Louis Post-Dispatch, 1936-48, asso. editor, 1948-55, editor and pub., 1955—. Served from ensign to lt. USNR, 1942-45. Office: St Louis Post Dispatch Saint Louis MO 63101*

PULITZER, MICHAEL EDGAR, newspaper editor; b. St. Louis, Feb. 23, 1930; s. Joseph and Elizabeth (Edgar) P.; grad. St. Mark's Sch., Southborough, Mass., 1947; A.B., Harvard, 1951, LL.B., 1954; m. Cecille Stell Eisenbeis, Apr. 28, 1970; children—Michael Edgar, Elizabeth E., Robert S., Frederick D., Catherine D. Hanson, Christina H. Eisenbeis, Mark C. Eisenbeis, William H. Eisenbeis. Admitted to Mass. bar, 1954; asso. firm Warner, Stackpole, Stetson & Bradlee, Boston, 1954-56; reporter Louisville Courier Jour., 1956-60; reporter, news editor, asst. mng. editor St. Louis Post-Dispatch, 1960-71, asso. editor, 1978—; editor, pub. Ariz. Daily Star, Tucson, 1971—; vice chmn. Pulitzer Pub. Co. and subs., 1984—. Bd. dirs. Pulitzer Pub. Co. Found. Clubs: St. Louis Country; Mountain Oyster (Tucson). Office: 900 N Tucker Blvd Saint Louis MO 63101

PULLIAM, CHARLES RICHARD, principal; b. Winchester, Ill., Oct. 9, 1929; s. Curtis Edward and Fern Hazel (Stierwalt) P.; m. Martha Elizabeth Wood, May 23, 1954; children—Paula, Curtis, George. B.S., Eastern Ill. U., 1957, M.S. in Edn., 1961. Tchr. pub. high schs., Ill., 1957-62; prin. Farmington East High Sch., Ill., 1962—; dir. Fulton County Sch., Masters, Ill., 1978—. Served to sgt. USAF, 1950-54, Korea. Named Prin. of Yr., Ill. Assn. Guidance Counselors, 1980. Mem. Ill. Prins. Assn., Am. Legion, Phi Delta Kappa. Republican. Baptist. Lodge: Masons. Avocations: photography, jeweler. Home: Box 263 Farmington IL 61531 Office: Farmington East High Sch 568 E Vernon Farmington IL 61531

PULLIAM, EUGENE SMITH, publisher; b. Kans., 1914; s. Eugene C. and Myrta (Smith) P.; A.B., DePauw U., 1935, LL.D., 1973; m. Jane Bleecker, 1943; children—Myrta, Russell, Deborah. Reporter, United Press, Chgo., Detroit and Buffalo burs., 1935-36; news editor radio sta. WIRE, Indpls., 1936-41; city editor Indpls. Star, 1947-48; mng. editor Indpls. News, 1948-62; now pub. Indpls. Star and Indpls. News; exec. v.p. Central Newspapers, Inc.; pres. Phoenix Newspapers Inc. Past vice pres. U.S. Golf Assn. Co-founder St. Richard's Sch. Served as lt. USNR, 1942-46. Mem. Am. Soc. Newspaper Editors, Am. Press Inst. (dir.), Am. Newspaper Pubs. Assn. (past pres. found.), Hoosier State Press Assn. (treas.), Ind. Acad., Delta Kappa Epsilon, Sigma Delta Chi. Episcopalian. Rotarian. Clubs: University (Indpls.); Crooked Stick (Carmel, Ind.); Woodstock; Links (N.Y.C.); Pine Valley Golf; Royal and Ancient Golf. Co-author textbook. Home: 8445 Olde Mill Circle W Indianapolis IN 46260 Office: Indianapolis News Indianapolis IN 46206

PULLIAM, FREDERICK CAMERON, educational administrator; b. Mesa, Ariz., Jan. 5, 1936; s. Fredrick Posy and Nathana Laura (Cameron) P.; AA., Hannibal LaGrange Coll., 1955; A.B., Grand Canyon Coll., 1958; M.Ed., U. Mo., Columbia, 1966, Ed.S., 1976, Ed.D., 1981; m. Deborah Jean Botts, June 1, 1979; children by previous marriage—Cameron Dale, Joy Renee. Tchr., Centerview (Mo.) Public Schs., 1958-59; ordained to ministry So. Baptist Conv., 1955; minister Bethel Bapt. Ch., Kansas City, Mo., 1959-61; adminstr. Fiti'uta, Manu'a sch., Am. Samoa, 1966-69; cons. in fin. Mo. State Tchrs. Assn., Columbia, 1969-79; supt. schs. Midway Heights C-VII, Columbia, 1979-83; dir. elem. edn. Brentwood Pub. Schs. (Mo.), 1983—; founder, coordinator Mo. Computer-Using Educators Conf., 1982—; cons. sch. fin., curriculum improvement. Mem. Columbia Am. Revolution Bicentennial Commn. Inst. Devel. Ednl. Activity fellow, 1969, 80-83. Mem. Mo. Assn. Sch. Adminstrs., Mo. Assn. Supervision and Curriculum Devel. (exec. sec.), Nat. Assn. Supervision and Curriculum Devel., Mo. Assn. Elem. Sch. Prins., Nat. Assn. Elem. Sch. Prins., Phi Delta Kappa (chpt. pres.). Republican. Clubs: Kiwanis, Masons, Shriners. Contbr. articles to profl. jours. Home: 1081-H Green Arbor Dr Saint Louis MO 63026 Office: Mark Twain Sch 8636 Litzsinger Rd Brentwood MO 63144

PULSIFER, THOMAS RICHARD, association executive; b. Winchester, Mass., Aug. 2, 1943; s. Frank and Janice (Goldsmith) P.; m. Eloise Ann Jones, Dec. 3, 1966; children—Bethany Lynne. A.B., Wilmington Coll., 1965; M.S.M., Wittenberg U., 1967. Tchr., Xenia City Schs. (Ohio), 1967-80; pres. Ohio Assn. R.R. Passengers, Xenia, 1976—; exec. dir. Ziebart Dealers Assn., Dayton, 1983—; mgr. advt. and spl. projects Dave Marshall, Inc., Dayton, 1980—. Ofcl., del. Midwest High Speed Rail Compact, Columbus, 1980-83, vice chmn., 1982; bd. dirs. Ohio Rail Transp. Authority, 1976-83, chmn., 1980. Organist, composer choral music; editor the 6:53 jour., 1973—. Bd. dirs. Community Concerts Assn., 1967-69; vice chmn. council Faith Lutheran Ch., 1980-81. Mem. High Speed Rail Assn., Assn. Ry. Editors, Nat. Assn. R.R. Passengers, Press Club Ohio. Lutheran. Office: Ohio Assn RR Passengers PO Box 653 Xenia OH 45385

PULSIPHER, DEE WAYNE, dentist, dental educator; b. Brigham City, Utah, July 23, 1937; s. Orsen Wayne and Leah Mae (Carlson) P.; m. Grace Neolia, Aug. 5, 1960; children—Brit Dee, Temia Lyn, Dyan Neolia. B.S., Idaho State U., 1962; D.D.S., Washington U., 1966. Diplomate Am. Bd. of Dental Medicine. Assoc. prof. Washington U. Dental Sch., St. Louis, 1966—; gen. practice dentistry, Kirkwood, Mo., 1966—; pediatric cons. VA Hosp., St. Louis, 1968—; dental cons. Shriners Hosp., St. Louis, 1966-75; chmn. Council of Profl. Affairs, St. Louis, 1973-78. Asst. scoutmaster St. Louis Area council Boy Scouts Am., Des Peres, Mo., 1977-82; pres. Parent, Tchrs. Orgn., Kirkwood, Mo., 1978; mem. Kirkwood C. of C., 1981—. Served with U.S. Army, 1955-58. Mem. Am. Assn. Dental Schs., Am. Soc. Dentistry for Children, Am. Dental Assn., Greater St. Louis Dental Soc. (chmn. 1982-83, bd. dirs. 1974-77), West Dist. Dental Soc. (pres. 1975-77), Washington U. Dental Alumni Assn. (pres. 1984—). Club: Lake St. Louis Sailing (1972-79). Lodge: Masons (1969—). Avocations: sailing; pingpong; antique radios; computers; lapidary. Office: 9929 Manchester Rd Kirkwood MO 63122-1985

PUMMILL, CAROL SUE, business official, author; b. Springfield, Ohio, Feb. 25, 1950; d. Earl Virgil and Jacqueline Ann (Thurman) P. B.S. in Bus., Wright State U., 1975, M.B.A., 1978. Mgr. Kroger Co., Troy, Ohio, 1976-77; mktg. analyst NCR Corp., Dayton, Ohio, 1978-81, cons. relations specialist, 1981, product mgr., 1981—; career bd. rep. Mademoiselle mag., N.Y.C., 1980—. Author essays, poems, newspaper articles. Active Young Democrats, Springfield, Ohio, 1984; canvasser Democratic Party, 1976. Recipient Grad. assistantship Wright State U., 1977. Mem. Recognition Techs. Users Assn., Am. Mktg. Assn., Nat. Assn. Female Execs., Assn. M.B.A. Execs. Roman Catholic. Office: NCR Corp 1700 S Patterson Blvd Dayton OH 45479

PUNDSACK, VERN ALFRED, management and computer consultant; b. Albany, Minn., Nov. 18, 1941; s. Raymond William and Alma (Sand) P.; m. Donna Lillian Wiederin, June 15, 1968; children—Stephanie, Jonathan. B.A., St. John's U., Collegeville, Minn., 1964; M.Hosp. and Health Care Adminstrn., U. Minn., 1979. Staff assoc. Minn. Hosp. Assn., Mpls., 1966-67; adminstrv. resident Robert Packer Hosp., Sayre, Pa., 1967-69; asst. adminstr. St. Vincent Hosp., Worcester, Mass., 1969-71; dir. adminstrv. services and planning Iowa Hosp. Assn., Des Moines, 1971-74; dir. planning, v.p. Iowa Meth. Med. Ctr., Des Moines, 1974-77; v.p. St. Mary's Hosp., Rhinelander, Wis., 1977-78; adminstr. Northwood Med. Assocs., S.C., Rhinelander, 1978-85; pres. Pundsack and Assocs., Rhinelander, Wis., 1985—. Mem. Iowa Gov.'s Emergency Med. Services Adv. Council, 1972-73, Invitational Nat. Health Planning Forum, 1974-77; mem. task force on cert. of need Iowa Legislature, 1976-77; mem. task forces on orgn., open heart surgery, data collection Des Moines Hosp. Consortium, 1975-77; co-chmn. Northwoods Community United Way Campaign, 1979; pres. St. Mary of Nazareth Parish Men's Club, Des Moines, 1976-77; mem., chmn. fin. com. St. Joseph's Parish, Rhinelander, 1978—; mem. adv. bd. Northwoods Health Careers Consortium, 1982—; mem. Wis. adv. council Mgmt. Systems of Wausau, Inc., 1982—. Served with USAR, 1958-65. Mem. Wis. Clinic Mgrs. Assn. (edn. com. 1982—), Med. Group Mgmt. Assn., Am. Coll. Med. Group Adminstrs., Am. Coll. Hosp. Adminstrs., Am. Hosp. Assn. Roman Catholic. Club: Kiwanis.

PUNT, LEONARD CORNELIS, educational services company executive; b. Bongondza, Zaire, Nov. 16, 1940; came to U.S., 1954, naturalized, 1960; s. Harry Marius and Clara (VandeGevel) P.; m. Sarah Elizabeth Walton, Dec. 18, 1966; children—John, Amy, Brian. B.A., Wheaton Coll., 1964, M.A., 1967; M.Ed., Loyola U., 1981. Owner, dir. The Reading Tree, Downers Grove, Ill., 1976—, pres. Am. Bus. Communications, Downers Grove, 1978—, Blue Chip Office Automation, Inc., 1983—. Mem. Downers Grove C. of C. (ambassador 1979-83). Presbyterian. Club: Oak Brook Exec. Breakfast. Lodge: Rotary. Office: Am Bus Communications 5006 Washington Downers Grove IL 60515

PUNWAR, ALICE JOHNSON, occupational therapy educator; b. Perry Twp., Wis., Sept. 9, 1932; d. Alfred S. and Ella (Ranum) Johnson; m. Jalamsinh K. Punwar, Jan. 15, 1955; children—Jay Singh, Kiran Kumar. B.S., U. Wis., 1954, M.S., 1969. Registered occupational therapist. Staff therapist Mendota State Hosp., Madison, Wis., 1957-59; part-time tchr. state and local Schs., Wis., 1965-69; asst. prof. U. Wis., Madison, 1969-73, assoc. prof., 1973-79, prof., chmn. occupational therapy programs, 1980—. Contbr. articles to profl. jours. Producer ednl. video tapes, 1980-81. Sec. Dane County Hist. Soc., Wis., 1984—. Fellow Am. Occupational therapy Assn. (roster of expert advisors 1975); mem. World Fedn. Occupational Therapists, Am. Assn. Mental Deficiency, Pi Lambda Theta. Avocations: music, travel, needlework, writing. Home: 614 Orchard Dr Madison WI 53711 Office: U Wis 1300 University Ave Madison WI 53706

PURCELL, TERRY ALLAN, retail executive; b. Paducah, Ky., Sept. 20, 1948; s. Allan Edward and Ruth Lorene P.; B.S., Murray State U., 1972; m. Marilyn Jean Robbearts, Dec. 1, 1973; children—Danielle, Gavin. With CMC Corp., various locations, 1976-83, v.p., regional sales mgr., Atlanta, 1979, St. Louis, 1979-80, v.p. sales, St. Louis, 1980—; with Intran, 1983—. Served with USAR, 1968-76. Named Store Mgr. of Yr., Montgomery Ward Co., 1973. Mem. Am. Mgmt. Assn. Republican. Lutheran. Club: Masons. Home: 549 Timberridge St Saint Charles MO 63301 Office: 12115 Lackland Rd Suite 150 Saint Louis MO 63141

PURDON, JAMES HERMAN, sheriff; b. Long Beach, Calif., Jan. 13, 1938; m. Judith Ann Gunn, May 6, 1960; children—Janene, James H. A.A.S., Lincoln Land Community Coll., 1972, B.A., Sangamon State U., 1982. mgr. sales Ill. Bell Telephone, Springfield, Ill., 1960-68; owner, mgr. Mid-Am. Cons., Springfield, 1968-69; dep. sheriff then sheriff Sangamon County, Springfield, 1969—; cons. U. Ill., also various tech. schs. Contbr. articles to profl. jours. Mem. Am. Legion, Amvets. Served with U.S. Army, 1956-59. Mem. Am. Bus. Club, Internat. Polit. Assn., FBI Nat. Acad. Assn., State Assn. Chiefs of Police, Nat. Assn. Chiefs of Police, Fraternal Order of Police, Internat. Acad. Criminology, Internat. Narcotic Officers Assn. Republican. Methodist. Lodges: Elks, Masons, Shriners. Avocations: boating; camping. Home: RR 1 Box 63 Pawnee IL 62558 Office: Sangamon County Sheriffs Dept Room 209 County Bldg Springfield IL 62701

PURDY, DORRIT WERNER, lawyer; b. Teplice, Czechoslovakia, Nov. 24, 1935; d. Martin Werner and Alice (Reethof) Werner Geiringer; m. John E. Purdy Jr., Dec. 10, 1955 (dec. Oct. 1973); children—John Christopher, Wynne Crossley. B.A., Mt. Holyoke Coll., 1955; J.D., Cleve. Marshall Law Sch., 1978. Bar: Ohio 1978, U.S. Dist. Ct. (no. dist.) Ohio 1978, U.S. Dist. Ct. (central dist.) Ill. 1981. Assoc. Robert E. Sweeney, Cleve., 1978-82; lead litigation atty. Sherwin Williams Co., Cleve., 1982—. Mem. nat. campaign staff Humphrey for Pres. Com., Oakland, Calif., 1972. Mem. Assn. Trial Lawyers Am., ABA, Ohio Bar Assn., Ohio Trial Lawyers Assn. Club: Cleve. Racquet. Office: Sherwin Williams Co 101 Prospect St NW Cleveland OH 44115

PURGA, ADELBERT JOHN, college dean; b. Wellsville, Y.Y., Sept. 25, 1949; s. Adelbert and Susan (Vena) P.; m. Margaret Sageman, Dec. 27, 1975. B.S., Ithaca Coll., 1971; M.B.A., U. Scranton, 1972; Ph.D., U. Fla., 1979. Chmn. bus. div. North Country Community Coll., Saranac Lake, N.Y., 1972-77; research assoc. U. Fla., Gainesville, 1979-80; dir. edn. services EICCD, Davenport, Iowa, 1980-82, assoc. vice chancellor edn., 1982—; dean acad. affairs Scott Community Coll., Bettendorf, Iowa, 1983—; project assoc. Associated Cons. Edn., Tallahassee, 1979; cons. U. Labs, Inc., Gainesville, Fla., 1979—; evaluator North Central Assn. Colls. and Schs., Chgo., 1984—. KAuthor: University Press, 1980. Contbr. chpts. to books, articles to profl. jours. Bd. dirs Iowa Council Staff and Orgn. Devel., 1980-81; pres. Nat. Council for Research and Planning, 1984—. Recipient Trustees Merit award North Country Community Coll., 1977; Disting. Service award Nat. Council for Research and Planning, 1982. Mem. Phi Kappa Phi, Phi Delta Kappa. Avocations: music, sailing, tennis, golf, skiing. Office: Scott Community Coll Belmont Rd Bettendorf IA 52722

PURI, MADAN LAL, mathematics educator; b. Sialkot, Punjab, India, Feb. 20, 1929; came to U.S., 1957; s. G.D. and S.V. (Wadhera) P.; m. Uma S. Kapur, Aug. 1962; children—Sandeep, Pradeep, Purnima. B.A., Punjab U., 1948; M.A., 1950, D.Sc., 1975; Ph.D., U. Calif.-Berkeley, 1962. Asst. prof. math. Coruant Inst., N.Y.C., 1962-65, assoc. prof., 1965-68; prof. Ind. U., Bloomington, 1968—; vis. prof. U. Dortmund, 1972-73, Technische Hochschule Aachen, W.Ger., 1973, U. Goteborg, 1976, Chalmers U. Tech., Sweden, 1976, U. Auckland, 1977, U. Wash., Seattle, 1978-79, U. Calif.-Irvine, 1978, U. Bern, Switzerland, 1982; Alexander von Humboldt prof. U. Gottingen, W.Ger., 1974-75. Co-author: Non Parametric Methods in Multivariate Analysis, 1971, Non Parametric Methods in General Linear Models, 1985; Editor: Non Parametric Techniques in Statistical Inference, 1970; Statistical Inference and Related Topics, 1975—; Stochastic Processes and Related Topics, 1975; co-editor: Non Parametric Statistical Inference, I, II, 1982. Contbr. articles to profl. jours. Recipient Sr. U.S. Scientist award Alexander Von Humbold Found., 1974, 84; NSF grantee. Fellow Inst. Math. Stats., Royal Statis. Soc., Am. Statis. Assn.; mem. Internat. Statis. Inst., Math. Assn. Am. Office: Ind U Dept Math Bloomington IN 47405

PURKERSON, MABEL LOUISE, physician, educator; b. Goldville, S.C., Apr. 3, 1931; d. James Clifton and Louise (Smith) P. A.B., Erskine Coll., 1951; M.D., U. S.C., Charleston, 1956. Diplomate Am. Bd. Pediatrics. Instr. pediatrics Washington U. Sch. Med., St. Louis, 1961-67, instr. medicine, 1966-67, asst. prof. pediatrics, 1967—, asst. prof. medicine, 1967-76, assoc. prof. medicine, 1976—, assoc. dean curriculum, 1976—; cons. in field. Editorial bd. Jour. Am. Kidney Diseases, 1981—; contbr. articles to profl. jours. USPHS spl. fellow, 1971-72. Bd. counselors Erskine Coll., 1971—. Mem. Am. Heart Assn. (exec. com.), Am. Physiol. Soc., Am. Soc. Nephrology, Internat. Soc. Nephrology, Central Soc. Clin. Research, Am. Soc. Renal Biochemistry and Metabolism, Sigma Xi (chpt. sec. 1974-76). Avocations: traveling; gardening; photography. Home: 20 Haven View St Louis MO 63141 Office: Renal Div Dept Medicine Box 8126 Washington Univ Sch Medicine 660 S Euclid Ave St Louis MO 63110

PURKEY, DONALD CHARLES, construction consultant; b. Salina, Utah, Sept. 16, 1941; s. John Raymond and Ada (Coleman) P.; m. Sylvia June Sorensen, Mar. 22, 1963; children—John Arthur, Nancy Jane, William Franklin. Student Wahoo Jr. Coll., 1959-60. Pres., Capp Distbg. Co., Fremont, Nebr., 1968-74; v.p. P & S Mfg. Co., Fremont, 1970-72; owner, pres. Purkey Constrn. Co., Fremont, 1968-83; constrn. cons. Purkey Constrn. Co., Brianhead, Utah, 1983—. Pres. Young Republicans, Dodge County, Nebr., 1964; Rep. del., Dodge County, 1970-72, 74-76; pres. Engring. Co. Fremont Vol. Fire Dept., 1980; active jails com., Dodge County, 1983. Recipient Pres.'s award Internat. Cosmopolitan Club, Saskatoon, Sask., Can., 1982, Cosmopolitan of Yr. award Pathfinder Cosmopolitan Club, 1981. Mem. Internat. Conf. of Building Ofcls. Baptist. Clubs: Pathfinder Cosmopolitan (pres. 1981-82), Cornbelt Cosmopolitan (west region gov. 1979-80). Lodge: Elks (Tyler). Avocations: hunting; fishing; golfing. Home: 10400 N Council St Oklahoma City OK 73132 also 250 W 100 S Parowan UT 84781 Office: Purkey Constrn Co Brianhead UT 84719

PURKHISER, E. DALE, swine specialist, educator; b. Reynolds, Ind., Aug. 8, 1931; s. Charles E. nd Bertha (James) P.; m. Vivian E. Snyder, Aug. 21, 1960; children—Karen Lynn, Lance Alan, Ty Brent. B.S., Purdue U., 1957, Ph.D., 1962; M.S., Mich. State U., 1958. Cert. animal scientist. Asst. prof. Rutgers U., New Brunswick, N.J., 1961-63; swine specialist, assoc. prof. U. Ky., Lexington, 1963-67; swine specialist, adj. assoc. prof. Mich. State U., Cassopolis, 1967—; cons. Nat. Pork Producers Council, 1967—. Author: Pork Industry Handbook, 1983, 84. Kellogg fellow, 1971-73. Recipient Service awards U.S. Dept. Agr., 1974, 84. Mem. Mich. Pork Council (exec. bd. 1976-85), Mich. Pork Producers Assn. (exec. bd. 1983-84), Am. Soc. Animal Sci., Am. Registry Cert. Animal Scientists. Presbyterian. Avocation: youth livestock shows. Home: 20024 Allegheny St Cassopolis MI 49031 Office: 24010 Hospital St Cassopolis MI 49031

PURSELL, CARL DUANE, Congressman; b. Plymouth, Mich., Dec. 19, 1932; B.A., Eastern Mich. U., 1957, M.A., 1962; LL.D. (hon.), Madonna Coll.; m. Peggy Jean Brown, 1956; children—Philip, Mark, Kathleen. Educator, small bus. owner; mem. Mich. Senate, 1971-76, mem. appropriations com.; mem. 95th and 99th Congresses from 2d Mich. Dist., mem. Edn. and Labor Com., Sci. and Tech. Com.; past mem. Mich. Crime Commn. Mem. Wayne County Bd. Commrs., 1960-70. Named Outstanding Young Man of Year Jr. C. of C., 1965; recipient Outstanding Environ. Legislator in Mich. award Fed. Environ. Protection Agy., 1976. Served as officer, inf., U.S. Army, 1957-59. Republican. Office: 1414 Longworth House Office Bldg Washington DC 20515*

PUSATERI, LAWRENCE XAVIER, lawyer; b. Oak Park, Ill., May 25, 1931; s. Lawrence E. and Josephine (Romano) P.; m. Eve M., July 9, 1956; children—Joanne, Lawrence F., Paul L., Mary Ann, Eva. J.D. summa cum laude, DePaul U., 1953. Bar: Ill. 1953. Asst. state's atty. Cook County, 1957-59; ptnr. Newton, Wilhelm, Pusateri & Naborowski, Chgo., 1959-77; justice Ill. appellate ct., Chgo., 1977-78; ptnr. Peterson, Ross, Schloerb & Seidel, Chgo., 1978—; mem. Ill. Supreme Ct. Com. on Pattern Jury Instrns., 1981—; mem. merit Selection Panel for U.S. Magistrate; lectr. law DePaul U., Chgo., 1962, Columbia U., N.Y.C., 1965, Marquette U., Milw., 1962-82, Northwestern U. Law Sch., Def. Counsel Inst., 1969-70, others. Contbr. articles to profl. jours. Chmn. Ill. Crime Investigating Commn. 1967-68, Ill. Parole and Pardon Bd., 1969-70; bd. dirs. Ill. Law Enforcement Commn., 1970-72; chmn. Com. on Correctional Facilities and Services. Served to capt. JAGC, AUS, 1955-58. Named One of Ten Outstanding Young Men in Chgo., Chgo. Jr. Assn. Commerce and Industry, 1960, 65; Outstanding Legislator Ill. Gen. Assembly, 1966. Mem. ABA (del. 1975-77), Ill. State Bar Assn. (pres. 1975-76, com. on fed. jud. and related appointments; Abraham Lincoln Legal Writing award 1959), Chgo. Bar Assn. (bd. mgrs. 1965-66). Republican. Roman Catholic. Clubs: Plaza, Elmhurst Country.

PUSEY, DANIEL IRVIN, civil engineer, land surveyor; b. Logansport, Ind., Aug. 5, 1947; s. Lloyd Wendell and Jane Louise (Seward) P.; m. Donna Darnell Bush, Aug. 12, 1972; children—William Lloyd, Dena Danielle, Anna Darnell, Kara Jane. A.A. in Gen. Edn., Middle Ga. Coll., 1971; B.S. in Civil Engring., Purdue U., 1974, B.S. in Land Surveying, 1977. Register profl. engr., land surveyor, Ind. Civil engr., land surveyor Phys. Plant/Engring. Services, Purdue U., West Lafayette, Ind., 1974—. Served with USAF, 1967-71. Fellow Am. Congress on Surveying and Mapping, mem. ASCE (pres. Central Ind. bd. 1984—), Ind. Soc. Profl. Land Surveyors (pres. Tecumseh chpt. 1982-84, dir., 1985—), Am. Legion. Republican. Methodist. Lodge: Masons. Avocations: photography; stamp collecting; history. Home: 1738 Klondike Rd West Lafayette IN 47906 Office: Purdue U Freehafer Hall 401 S Grant St West Lafayette IN 47907

PUSKARICH, MICHAEL, coal company executive; b. Hopedale, Ohio, Mar. 25, 1929; s. Frank Puskarich; m. Mary B. Holliday, June 29, 1957. Grad. Wayne High Sch., Bloomingdale, Ohio. With Polen Coal Co., 1948-49, Latrobe Constrn. Co., 1949-51; co-owner, sec., gen. mgr. Cravat Coal Co., Cadiz, Ohio, 1951—. Bd. dirs. Mining and Reclamation Council, Washington. Mem. Soc. Mining Engrs. Presbyterian. Club: Republican Senatorial Inner Circle. Lodges: Masons, Shriner. Home: 35500 Cadiz Piedmont Rd Cadiz OH 43907 Office: 48500 Cadiz Piedmont Rd Cadiz OH 43907

PUTNAM, ABBOTT ALLEN, research engineer; b. Wellsboro, Pa., Nov. 24, 1920; s. Allen Jerome and Kathryn Margaret (Abbott) P.; m. Anna Miriam Boyden, Dec. 25, 1942; children—Dianne C., Susan A. B.M.E., Cornell U., 1942. Registered profl. engr., Ohio, N.Y.; chartered engr., Gt. Britain. Jr. engr. Dravo Corp., Pitts., 1942-43; instr. mech. engring. Cornell U., Ithaca, N.Y., 1943-44; research engr. Nat. Adv. Com. for Astronautics, Hampton, Va., 1944-46; various positions to sr. research engr. Battelle Columbus Lab., Ohio, 1946—, co. rep. Am. Flame Research Com., also sec. Author: Combustion-Driven Oscillations in Industry, 1971, also papers in field. Editor: Injection and Combustion of Liquid Fuels, 1957. Patentee combustion apparatus. Fellow Inst. of Energy, ASME, AIAA (assoc.); mem. Combustion Inst., Sigma Xi. Republican. Baptist. Lodges: Masons (32 degree), Blue Lodge. Home: 471 Village Dr Columbus OH 43214 Office: Battelle Columbus Labs 505 King Ave Columbus OH 43201

PUTNAM, BRYAN FERRELL, systems programmer; b. West Lafayette, Ind., June 30, 1953; s. Calvin Richard and Emogene Mae (Ferrell) P.; m. Anne Sarchet Long, Oct. 13, 1982; 1 child, Valerie Anne. B.S., Purdue U., 1975; M.S., 1977, Ph.D., 1981. Grad. teaching asst., dept. physics Purdue U., West Lafayette, 1978-79, grad. research asst., 1977-81, research assoc., 1981-83; systems programmer Purdue Computing Ctr., West Lafayette, 1983—. Contbr. articles to profl. jours. Mem. Am. Phys. Soc., Sigma Xi, Sigma Pi Sigma.

PUTNAM, DALE C., bakery products holding company executive. Pres., chief exec. officer, dir. Interstate Bakeries Corp, Kansas City. Office: Interstate Bakeries Corp PO Box 1627 Kansas City MO 64141*

PUTNAM, PAUL ADIN, government agency official; b. Springfield, Vt., July 12, 1930; s. Horace Adin and Beatrice Nellie (Baldwin) P.; m. Elsie Mae (Ramseyer) June 12, 1956; children—Pamela Ann, Penelope Jayne, Adin Tyler II, Paula Anna. B.S., U. Vt., 1952; M.S., Wash. State U., 1954; Ph.D., Cornell U., 1957. Research animal scientist Agrl. Research Service, U.S. Dept. Agr., Beltsville, Md., 1957-66, investigation leader beef cattle nutrition, 1966-68, chief beef cattle research br., 1968-72, asst. dir. Beltsville Agrl. Research Ctr., 1972-80, dir.; 1980-84, dir. Central Plains Area, Ames, Iowa, 1984—. Contbr. articles to profl. jours. Recipient Kidder medal U. Vt.; Outstanding Performance award U.S. Dept. Agr., also cert. merit; Danforth fellow; Borden fellow; Purina Research fellow. Fellow AAAS (rep. sect. O); mem. Am. Soc. Animal Sci. (pres. North Atlantic sect., chmn. various coms.; N.E. sect. Disting. Service award), Am. Dairy Sci. Assn., Orgn. Profl. Employees U.S. Dept. Agr. (pres. Beltsville chpt.), Council for Agrl. Sci. and Tech.. Home: 3D Schilletter Village Ames IA 50010 Office: Central Plains Area USDA Dayton Ave Ames IA 50010

PUTTERMAN, ALLEN MICHAEL, oculoplastic surgeon, opthalmologist; b. Beloit, Wis., May 19, 1938; s. Mayer Leon and Mollie (Tankel) P.; m. Jacqueline Orner, Dec. 23, 1962 (div. 1978); 1 dau., Jill Tracy; m. 2d Lynett Solomon, Sept. 24, 1983. B.S., U. Wis., 1960, M.D. 1963. Intern, Cook County Hosp., Chgo., 1963-64; resident ophthalmology Michael Reese Hosp., Chgo., 1966-69; oculoplastic surgery fellow Manhattan Eye, Ear, Throat Hosp., N.Y.C., 1969-70; pvt. practice oculoplastic surgery, Chgo., 1970—; prof. clin. ophthalmology, chief oculoplastic surgery U. Ill. Eye and Ear Infirmary, Chgo., 1970—; sr. attending physician, dir. oculoplastic surgery Michael Reese Hosp., 1970—. Editor: Cosmetic Oculoplastic Surgery, 1983. Contbr. articles to profl. jours., chpts. to textbooks. Served to capt. USAF, 1964-66. Fellow ACS, Am. Soc. Ophthalmic Plastic and Reconstructive Surgery (Wendell Hughes lectr. 1984), Am. Acad. Ophthalmology. Republican. Avocations: Jogging, aerobic exercise, skiing, tennis. Home: 260 E Chestnut St Apt 3902 Chicago IL 60611 Office: 111 N Wabash St Suite 1722 Chicago IL 60602

PUTZ, LOUIS GEORGE, osteopathic physician; b. Detroit, Aug. 7, 1944; s. Jacob John and Mary Elizabeth (Thieman) P.; m. Marilynn Jean Bolf, June 4, 1972; 1 son, Jeffrey. B.S., U. Detroit, 1967; student Sacred Heart Sem., 1962-64; D.O., Coll. Osteo. Medicine and Surgery, Des Moines, 1972. Intern, Detroit Osteo. Hosp. Corp., 1972-73, resident in radiology, 1973-76; staff radiologist Bi-County Community Hosp., Warren, Mich., 1976-83; assoc. prof. Mich. State U., East Lansing, 1976-83. Mem. Radiologic Soc. N.Am., Mich. Osteo. Coll. Radiology, Mich. Assn. Osteo. Physicians and Surgeons, Am. Osteo. Assn., Am. Osteo. Coll. Radiology. Republican. Roman Catholic.

PYKE, THOMAS RICHARD, biochemist, researcher; b. Center, Ind., Jan. 8, 1932; s. Jesse Earl and Dorothy Lucille (Phillips) P.; m. Roberta Lou Warnock, Jan. 28, 1951 (div. 1982); children—Neil Richard, Lynn Marie, Ann Elizabeth. B.S., Purdue U., 1954, M.S., 1958, Ph.D., 1961. Sr. research microbiologist E.R. Squibb and Co., New Brunswick, N.J., 1960-62; sr. research scientist Upjohn Co., Kalamazoo, 1962-70, mgr. microbiology research, 1970-72, sr. research scientist fermentation research and devel., 1972-74, research mgr. biochem. process research and applied microbial genetics, 1974-82, research mgr. biochem. process research and preparations, 1982-85, assoc. dir. fermentation research and devel., 1985—. Patentee in field. Served to 1st lt. U.S. Army, 1954-56. Mem. AAAS, Am. Soc. Microbiology. Home: 7169 Hazelwood St Richland MI 49083 Office: Fermentation Research and Devel The Upjohn Co 7171 Portage Rd Portage MI 49002

PYLE, BEATRICE ALZIRA, educator; b. West Chester, Pa., May 21, 1922; d. Norman James and Audrey (Dilks) Pyle; B.S., Gettysburg Coll., 1944; M.S. in Hygiene and Phys. Edn., Wellesley Coll., 1946; certificate U. Oslo, 1960. Instr. Gettysburg Coll., 1938-40, Vassar Coll., 1946-52; tchr. pub. schs., Winnetka, Ill., 1952-57; asso. prof. phys. and health edn. Miami U., Oxford, Ohio, 1957—. Mem. Am. Pub. Health Assn., Royal Soc. Health Can. and Eng., Nat., Ohio edn. assns., AAHPER (coordinator aquatic insts. for aquatic council), Ohio Coll. Assn., Am. Camping Assn., AAUW, Ohio, Midwest assns. health, phys. edn. and recreation. Author: Small Craft: An Instructional Textbook for Teachers; Anatomy Handbook; Kinesiology Laboratory Manual. Home: 119 N Campus Ave Oxford OH 45056

PYLE, DONALD ALAN, music educator, tenor; b. Ridgewood, N.J., Jan. 12, 1933; s. Aime A. and Muriel Ann (Barbour) P.; m. Barbara Jean Sly, July 6, 1961 (dec.); m. 2d, Virginia R. Tinker, June 4, 1968. Student Juilliard Sch. Music, 1956-59; B.A. in Vocal Performance, U. So. Fla., 1969; Mus. M., Mus. D., Fla. State U., 1972. Mem. company South Shore Music Circus, Cohassett, Mass., 1958-59; tenor soloist John Harms Chorus, St. Michael's Episcopal Ch., Juilliard Opera Theatre, N.Y.C., Temple Bethel, Englewood, N.J., St. Leo Coll., Dade City, Fla., 1956-61; teaching asst. Fla. State U., Tallahassee, 1969-71, adj. faculty, 1971-72; instr. U. Mo.-Columbia, 1972-76, acting dean, Swinney Conservatory Music, Central Meth. Coll., Fayette, Mo., 1976-77, dean, prof. voice, 1977—; tenor soloist numerous U.S. colls. and univs.; tenor soloist world premiers Songs from the Ark, The Labyrinth, Of Mice and Men; performances include: Verdi Requiem, Rossini's Stabat Mater, Bach's St. Matthew's Passion, Mendelsohn's The Elijah and Les Troyens (under Sir Thomas Beecham). Served to sgt. USMC, 1951-54. U. So. Fla. scholar, 1966. Mem. Nat. Assn. Tchrs. Singing, Nat. Assn. Schs. Music, Blue Key, Gold Key, Phi Delta Kappa, Omicron Delta Kappa, Phi Mu Alpha, Pi Kappa Lambda. Roman Catholic.

PYNCKEL, GARY LEE, osteopathic physician; b. Moline, Ill., Nov. 22, 1952; s. Gerard A. and Margaret F. (Wisely) P. B.A., Monmouth Coll., 1974; postgrad. U. Ill., 1976; D.O., Chgo. Coll. Osteo. Medicine, 1980. Environ. biologist U.S. Corps of Engrs., 1974-76; intern Davenport (Iowa) Osteo. Hosp.; pvt. practice gen. osteo. medicine, Bettendorf, Iowa, 1981—. Served with USMC, 1971-74. Vol. physician Arrowhead Ranch Boys Home, 1981—; mem. prins. com. Osteo. Hosp. Davenport, 1982—. Mem. Am. Osteo. Assn., Iowa Soc. Physicians and Surgeons, Scott County Soc. Osteo. Physicians and Surgeons, Am. Acad. Osteopathy. Home: 1515 Fairland Dr Bettendorf IA 52722 Office: 1980 Spruce Hills Dr Suite 2 Bettendorf IA 52722

QADIR, GHULAM, psychiatrist; b. Jahania, Pakistan, Aug. 18, 1947; s. Mohammad Yar and Karam Khatoon; m. Shirin Akbar, Jan. 4, 1979; children—Nida, Rehmat, Rabah. M.B.B.S., Nishtar Med. Coll., Pakistan, 1971. Diplomate Am. Bd. Psychiatry. Resident in psychiatry Norwich Hosp., Conn., 1975-76, Maimonides Med. Ctr., Bklyn., 1976-78; physician Health Ministry Iran, Tehran, 1974-75; staff psychiatrist VA Med. Ctr., Allen Park, Mich., 1978-81; chief psychiatry Oakwood Hosp., Dearborn, Mich., 1983—; cons. psychiatrist Seaway Hosp., Trenton, Mich., 1979—, Riverside Hosp., Trenton, 1981—; attending psychiatrist Heritage Hosp., Taylor, Mich., 1981—. Contbr. articles to profl. jours. Served to capt. Pakistan Army, 1971-74. Mem. Am. Psychiat. Assn., Am. Acad. Clin. Psychiatrists. Acad. Psychosomatic Medicine, Am. Assn. Psychiat. Adminstrs., Assn. Pakistani Physicians. Office: Oakwood Med Bldg 18181 Oakwood Blvd Suite 305 Dearborn MI 48124

QUALEY, CARLTON CHESTER, historian, editor; b. Spring Grove, Minn., Dec. 17, 1904; s. Ole O. and Clara (Knatterud) Q.; m. Elizabeth Cummings, Apr. 29, 1933 (dec.); children—John, Mary. B.A., St. Olaf Coll., 1929; M.A., U. Minn., 1932; Ph.D., Colubmia U., 1938. From asst. prof. to assoc. prof. Bard Coll., Columbia U., 1936-44; assoc. prof. history Swarthmore Coll., Pa., 1944-45; assoc. prof. Grad. Sch., Columbia U., N.Y.C., 1945-46, assoc. prof. summer sessions, 1938-46; prof. history Carleton Coll., Northfield, Minn., 1946-70; dir. Minn. Hist. Soc., St. Paul, part-time, 1947-48; cons., lectr. in field. Author: Norwegian Settlement in the U.S., 1938, 3d edit. 1981. Editor: Thorstein Veblen, 1968; dir. research They Chose Manhattan, 1973-81. Contbr. articles to profl. jours. U. Minn. Shevlin fellow, 1929-32; Columbia U. fellow, 1932-33; Hill Found. grantee, 1954-55; NEH grantee, 1973-78. Mem. Am. Hist. Assn., Orgn. Am. Historians, Norwegian Am. Hist. Assn. (bd. editors), Minn. Hist. Soc. (dir. 1947-48), Upper Midwest Hist. Assn. (editor, pres. 1947-51, 81), Immigration History Soc. (editor, treas. 1973—). Democrat. Unitarian. Avocations: Skiing, sailing. Home: 2110 Carter Ave Saint Paul MN 55108 Office: Immigration History Soc Minn Hist Soc 690 Cedar St Saint Paul MN 55101

QUANEY, FRANK E., wholesale grocery company executive. Pres., chief exec. officer Associated Wholesale Grocers Inc., Kansas City, Kans., also dir. Office: Associated Wholesale Grocers Inc 5000 Kansas Ave Kansas City KS 66106*

QUARTON, JEAN ELSA RULF, psychologist; b. Hartford, Conn., Mar. 29, 1942; d. Walter Otto and Elsa Margareta (Blume) Rulf; m. David T. Quarton, Aug. 25, 1973 (div.); m. Conrad L. Bergendoff, Feb. 9, 1980. B.F.A., R.I. Sch. Design, 1964; M.A. in Home Econs., U. Iowa, 1968, Ph.D., 1974. Lic. psychologist, Ill. Staff psychologist Riverside Retreat, 1974-76; pvt. practice clin. psychology, Rock Island, Ill., 1976-81; clin. cons. to Quad-cities Indsl. Employee Assistance Programs, Internat. Harvester, 3M, John Deere, J.I. Case, Rock Island arsenal, Army C.E., 1977-81; pvt. practice clin. psychology, LaGrange Park, Ill., 1981-84; cons. Quad-Cities Alcoholism Info. Ctrs., 1977-80, Davenport (Iowa) Sch. System, 1977-78; staff psychologist ACP, Chgo., 1982-84; pres. Accredited Affiliated Psychologists, P.C.; clin. cons. Gen. Motors, Reuben Donnelley; adj. prof. psychology Augustana Coll., Rock Island, 1977. Mem. Quad-cities Career Women's Network, 1978-81, keynote speaker, 1978; lectr. in field. Spl. Research asst. U. Iowa, 1970-73. Mem. Rock Island Psychol. Assn. (sec. 1980-81), Chgo. Psychol. Assn. (chmn. newsletter com. 1982-83, editor newsletter 1982-83, pres. elect, chmn. program com. 1985-86), NOW, Bus. Networking Soc. (bd. dirs. Chgo. 1983—). Lutheran. Club: Bus. and Profl. Women's (chmn. pub. relations 1983—, named Woman of Achievement 1983). Contbr. articles to profl. jours. Home and Office: 9523 Jefferson Ave Brookfield IL 60513

QUATROCHI, NICHOLAS JOSEPH, data processing executive; b. Kansas City, Mo., Feb. 14, 1956; s. Michael and Ida Marie (Synder) Q. B.S.B.A., U. Mo., 1978, M.B.A., 1984. Inventory analyst Farmland Inds., Kansas City, 1978-79; service cons. Honeywell, Kansas City, 1979-80, edn. rep., 1980-83; data processing mgr. George K. Baum & Co., Kansas City, 1983—; cons. Kansas City, 1983—. Author: Fortran 77 Specifics, 1980. Mem. Am. Soc. Traffic and Transp. (cert.).

QUAY, JOHN FERGUSON, pharmacokinetic researcher; b. Galion, Ohio, Feb. 29, 1932; s. Paul Blair and Annabelle (Ferguson) Q.; m. Jean Marie Stebbins; children—Nana M., Katherine A., Paul D. B.Sc., Ohio State U., 1957, M.Sc. in Chemistry, 1958; Ph.D. in Physiology, Ind. U., 1968. Phys. chemist Eli Lilly and Co., Indpls., 1959-65, sr. phys. chemist, 1968-75, research scientist, 1976-83, research assoc., 1984—. Contbr. articles to profl. publs. Sr. warden Ch. of the Nativity, Indpls., 1984. Served with U.S. Army, 1953-55. Mem. Biophys. Soc., Soc. Study of Xenobiotics, Am. Phys. Soc., Am. Chem. Soc., Am. Soc. Study Microbiology. Republican. Episcopalian. Avocations: tennis, fishing, bridge. Home: 8950 Carriage Ln Indianapolis IN 46256 Office: MC 906 Lilly Corp Ctr Indianapolis IN 46285

QUAY, PAUL MICHAEL, priest, philosophy educator; b. Chgo., Aug. 24, 1924; s. Eugene and Effie (Alley) Q. A.B. in Classics, Loyola U., Chgo., 1950; Ph.L., West Baden Coll., Loyola U., Ind., 1952; B.S., MIT, 1955, Ph.D. in Physics, 1958; S.T.L., West Baden Coll., 1962. Joined Soc. of Jesus, 1946, ordained priest Roman Catholic Catholic Ch., 1961. Research assoc. physics Case Inst. Tech., Cleve., 1962-63; vis. prof. physics Loyola U., Chgo., 1965-67; asst. prof. physics St. Louis U., 1967-70, assoc. prof. physics-theology, 1970-83; research prof. philosophy Loyola U., Chgo., 1981—; external reader dept. physics Birla Inst. Tech., Mesra, Ranchi, India, 1971-81; cons. physics Nat. Bur. Standards, Boulder, Colo., summers 1966, 67. Contbr. articles to profl. jours. Served with Signal Corps, U.S. Army, 1942-46, PTO. NSF fellow, 1956-58. Mem. Am. Phys. Soc., Inst. for Theol. Encounter with Sci. and Tech., Philosophy of Sci. Assn., Fellowship of Cath. Scholars (bd. dirs. 1977-79), Soc. Christian Culture, Sigma Xi. Roman Catholic. Home: Jesuit Residence Loyola U 6525 N Sheridan Rd Chicago IL 60626 Office: Dept Philosophy Loyola U 6525 N Sheridan Rd Chicago IL 60626

QUAYLE, DAN, Senator; b. Indpls., Feb. 4, 1947; s. James C. and Corinne (Pulliam) Q.; B.A. in Polit. Sci., DePauw U., Greencastle, Ind., 1969; J.D., Ind. U., 1974; 1970-74. m. Marilyn Tucker, Nov. 18, 1972; children—Tucker Danforth, Benjamin Eugene, Mary Corinne. Admitted to Ind. bar, 1974. Ct. reporter, pressman Huntington (Ind.) Herald-Press, 1965-69, asso. pub., gen. mgr., 1974-76; mem. consumer protection div. Atty. Gen.'s Office, State of Ind., 1970-71; adminstrv. asst. to Ind. Gov. Edgar Whitcomb, 1971-73; dir. Ind. Inheritance Tax Div., 1973-74; mem. 95th-97th Congresses from 4th Ind. Dist.; tchr. bus. law Huntington Coll., 1975. Mem. Huntington Bar Assn., Hoosier State Press Assn., Huntington C. of C. Club: Rotary. Home: 7 N Jefferson St Huntington IN 46750 Office: 524 Hart Senate Office Bldg Washington DC 20510

QUEENER, SHERRY FREAM, pharmacology educator, researcher; b. Muskogee, Okla., July 8, 1943; d. Howard H. and Irene M. (Couri) Fream; m. Stephen W. Queener, Aug. 19, 1967; children—Wyatt Howard, Kelly Irene. B.S. with honors, Okla. Bapt. U., 1965; M.S., U. Ill., 1968, Ph.D., 1970. Instr. pharmacology Ind. U. Sch. Medicine, Indpls., 1971-73, asst. prof., 1973-78, assoc. prof., 1978-84, prof., 1984—. Author: Pharmacological Basis of Nursing Practice, 1982; also articles. Woodrow Wilson fellow, 1965. Mem. Am. Soc. Biol. Chemists, Am. Chem. Soc., Sigma Xi. Office: Ind U Sch Medicine Dept Pharmacology 635 Barnhill Dr Indianapolis IN 46202

QUERESHI, MOHAMMED YOUNUS, psychology educator, consultant; b. Haripur Hazara, Pakistan, Dec. 12, 1929; came to U.S., 1953; s. Mohammed Noor and Meryam Khatoon Q.; m. Nora Jane Knapp, May 27, 1958 (div. Nov. 1979); children—Ahmed, Amna Shukria, Shawn; m. Farzana Kaukab, May 17, 1980; children—Ajmel, Sabeeha, Azem. Ph.D., U. Ill., 1958. Lic. psychologist, Wis. Asst. prof. psychology U. Minn., Duluth, 1960-62, U. N.D., Grand Forks, 1962-64; assoc. prof. psychology Marquette U., Milw., 1964-70, prof., 1970—, chmn. dept. psychology, 1971-77; cons. psychologist. Pres. 81st Street Sch. PTA, 1968-70; merit badge counselor Milw. County council Boy Scouts Am., 1973—; pres. Islamic Assn. Greater Milw., 1978-83. NIH grantee, 1962-69; Office of Edn. grantee, 1970-71; TOPS Club grantee, 1969-76. Mem. Am. Psychol. Assn., Psychometric Soc., Am. Statis. Assn., AAAS, Sigma Xi. Author: Statistics and Behavior: An Introduction, 1980; contbr. articles to sci. and profl. jours. Home: 2759 N 68th St Milwaukee WI 53210 Office: 497 Schroeder Health Sciences and Education Complex Marquette U Milwaukee WI 53233

QUEZADA-DIAMONDSTEIN, MARIA DEL SOCORRO, political scientist; b. Loma Linda, Calif., Sept. 16, 1949; d. Jose Ramiro Quezada M. and Margarita Medrano de Quezada; teaching degree Instituto Pedagogico de Chihuahua (Mex.), 1967; B.A., U. Tex., Austin, 1970; postgrad. Sorbonne, Paris, 1971, Sophia U., Tokyo, 1973; M.A. in Polit. Sci., U. Tex., El Paso, 1977; postgrad. U. Chgo., 1979—; m. Bert M. Diamondstein, Aug. 11, 1978; 1 dau., Socorro Mayuko. Coordinator, lectr. workshops in social scis. and humanities Centro de Estudios Generales, Chihuahua, 1971-72; import-export supr. Admiral Corp. Am., Ciudad Juarez, Mex., 1974-75; instr. polit. sci. U. Tex., El Paso, 1975-78, El Paso Community Coll., 1978; asst. survey dir. III, Nat. Opinion Research Center, U. Chgo., 1979-82; producer/account exec. Ted Hearne Assocs., 1982-83; v.p. mktg. and communications Americas, Inc., 1983—; condr. workshops; asst. to pres. U. Autonoma de Chihuahua, 1971-72; prodn.-mktg. researcher Duraplay de Parral, 1973-74; mem. nat. Chicano research network Inst. Social Research, U. Mich., 1980—. Mem. Chgo. Council Fine Arts. Recipient prize for oil painting Banco Comercial Mexicano Ann. Art Exhbn., 1968; U. Calif., San Diego grantee, 1978. Mem. Latin Am. Studies Assn., Pi Sigma Alpha. Roman Catholic. Office: 612 N Michigan Ave Suite 817 Chicago IL 60611

QUICK, RICHARD CLEON, museum director; b. Chgo., Apr. 4, 1952; s. Frank Charles and Pauline Romaine (Zarris) Q. Student U. Wis.-Manitowoc, 1972; grad. Mus. Mgmt. Inst., Berkeley, Calif., 1983. Sec., Rahr-West Mus.,

Manitowoc, 1972-79, asst. dir., 1979-81, dir., 1981—. Mem. Am. Assn. Museums. Lodge: Rotary (dir. 1984). Avocations: reading, singing, travel. Office: Rahr-West Museum Park St at N 8th Manitowoc WI 54220

QUIGG, RICHARD JOHN, metallurgist, lawyer; b. Bethlehem Pa., Nov. 12, 1930; s. John Paul and Frances (Gruver) Q.; m. Joan Clampett, Apr. 6, 1956 (div. 1981); children—Richard, Jr., Daniel, Laura. B.S. in Metall. Engring., Va. Tech., Blacksburg, 1952; M.S. in Metall. Engring., Lehigh U., 1954; Ph.D., Case Western Res. U., 1959; J.D. Cleve. State U., 1966. Bar: Ohio 1966, Fla. 1972, N.J. 1975; registered profl. engr., Ohio. Mgr. materials and processing TRW Inc., Cleve., 1959-67; mgr. research and devel. TRW Metals div., Minerva, Ohio, 1967-70; pres. Jetshapes, Inc., Rockleigh, N.J., 1970-78; sr. materials engr. Pratt and Whitney, Hartford, Conn., 1978-80; v.p. mktg. Cannon Muskegon Corp., Muskegon, Mich., 1980—. Contbr. articles to profl. jours. Patentee in field. Recipient W.A. Tarr award Sigma Gamma Epsilon, 1952. Mem. AIME, ASTM, Am. Soc. for Metals. Club: West Shore Tennis (Muskegon). Home: 2270 Norcrest Dr Norton Shores MI 49441 Office: Cannon-Muskegon Corp Muskegon MI 49443

QUIGLEY, HERBERT JOSEPH, JR., pathologist, educator; b. Phila., Mar. 6, 1937; s. Herbert Joseph and Mary Kathleen (Carney) Q.; m. Jacqueline Jean Stocksdale, Nov. 28, 1965 (div. 1974); 1 child, Amelia Anne. B.S. in Chemistry, Franklin and Marshall Coll., 1958; M.D., U. Pa., 1962. Diplomate Am. Bd. Pathology. Chief pathology U.S. Naval Hosp., Key West, Fla., 1966-68, Monroe County Hosp., Key West, 1966-68; from asst. prof. to assoc. prof. pathology Creighton U., Omaha, 1968-72; chief pathology service VA Med. Ctr., Omaha, 1968—; prof. pathology Creighton U., 1972—; dir. Triton-Chito Inc., Omaha. Contbr. articles to profl. jours. Patentee in field. Bd. dirs., chmn. Parents without Ptnrs., Omaha, 1972—. Served to lt. comdr. USNR, 1966-68. Recipient Career Devel. award NIH, 1962-66; Borden prize med. research Borden Co., Inc., 1962; fellow NIH, Nat. Cancer Inst., 1958-62. Fellow Coll Am. Pathologists, Am. Soc. Clin. Pathologists, Am. Inst. Chemists; mem. Nebr. Assn. Pathologists, N.Y. Acad. Scis. Republican. Roman Catholic. Avocations: paleontology, geology. Home: 9511 Mockingbird Dr Omaha NE 68127 Office: VA Med Center 4101 Woolworth Ave Omaha NE 68105

QUIGLEY, MARK ALAN, pharmacist; b. Kansas City, Mo., Aug. 4, 1952; s. Gerald Leslie and Helen Lucile (McCullick) Q.; m. Julia Lynne McCrary, Aug. 10, 1974; 1 child, Laura Diane. B.S. in Pharmacy, U. Mo., 1976, M.S., 1979, postgrad., 1981—. Registered pharmacist, Mo. Sr. hosp. pharmacist Truman Med. Ctr., Kansas Cty, Mo., 1976-80; sr. clin. researcher Marion Labs., Inc., Kansas City, 1980-82, sr. scientist, 1982-84, mgr. med. dept. drug experience sect., 1984—; pharmacy preceptor U. Mo. Sch. Pharmacy, Kansas City, 1978-80; v.p. UniVial, Inc., Kansas City, 1983—. Contbr. articles to profl. jours. Mem. Mo. Pharmacy Polit. Action Com., Jefferson City, 1979. Mem. Am. Pub. Health Assn., Kansas City Soc. Hosp. Pharmacists (chmn. Poison Prevention Week 1979, chmn. Hypertension Week 1979, chmn. pub. relations 1980), Soc. Clin. Trials, Mo. Pharm. Assn., Drug Info. Assn., Phi Delta Chi, Rho Chi. Methodist. Avocations: Competitive shooting, hunting, scuba diving. Home: 5809 N Cypress Ave Kansas City MO 64119 Office: Marion Labs Inc 10236 Bunker Ridge Rd Kansas City MO 64137

QUIGLEY, MARTIN MARK, obstetrician, gynecologist; b. N.Y.C., Apr. 18, 1947; s. Martin Scofield and Katherine Julia (Dunphy) Q.; m. Jane Maureen Marrion, June 28, 1969; children—Martin Timothy, Patrick Griffin, Brendan Andrew, Jonathan Mark. B.S., Georgetown U., 1967, M.D., 1971. Diplomate Am. Bd. Ob-Gyn. Rotating intern Naval Hosp., Nat. Naval Med. Ctr., Bethesda, Md., 1971-72, resident, 1972-75; fellow in reproductive endocrinology and infertility Duke U. Med. Ctr., Durham, N.C., 1978-80, asst. prof. dept. ob-gyn, 1979-80; asst. prof., dir. div. reproductive endocrinology and infertility, dept. ob-gyn U. Tex. Health Sci. Ctr., Houston, 1981-84; dir. div. reproductive endocrinology and infertility Cleve. Clinic Found., 1984—. Contbr. articles to profl. jours. Served with M.C., USNR, 1970-78. Recipient Physician Recognition awards AMA, 1973—; Merck Manual award, 1971; Research award N.C. United Way Fund, 1979-80. Fellow Am. Coll. Obstetricians and Gynecologists; mem. Am. Fertility Soc., F. Bayard Carter Soc. Obstetricians and Gynecologists, Endocrine Soc., Soc. Study Reprodn. Republican. Roman Catholic. Office: Dept Gynecology Cleveland Clinic Found 9500 Euclid Ave Cleveland OH 44106

QUIGLEY, ROBERT LOUIS, messenger service executive; b. N.Y.C., Jan. 28, 1955. B.B.A., U. Notre Dame, 1977. Cost acct. Assoc. Mills, Inc., Chgo., 1977-78; inventory acct. Standard Brands, 1978-79; controller Deadline Express, 1979-83, owner, pres., 1983—. Avocations: camping; skiing; motorcycling.

QUIKO, EDUARD, political science educator, consultant; b. Jakarta, Indonesia, Sept. 15, 1941; s. Jozef and Juliana (Tjiong) Q.; m. Lily Santo, June 21, 1976; children—Albin, Anjelica. B.A., Bethel Coll., 1965; M.S., Fort Hays State U., 1967; Ph.D., So. Ill. U., 1970. Asst. prof. Sch. of the Ozarks, Point Lookout, Mo., 1970-72, assoc. prof., 1972-75; vis. assoc. prof. World Campus Afloat, Orange, Calif., 1975; prof. dept. polit. sci. Sch. of the Ozarks, Point Lookout, Mo., 1975—. Washington field trip program dir., 1972—, small city/county mgmt. dir., 1975-76; cons., pres. Am. Bus. Edn. Service, Inc., Springfield, Mo., 1983—. Author: The ABC's of State and Local Government in America, 1981. Editor: Firman Hidup, 1981. Contbr. articles to profl. jours. Title I grantee HEW and Mo. Dept. Community Affairs, Jefferson City, 1975-76. Mem. Am. Soc. Internat. Law, Mo. Polit. Sci. Assn. Avocation: Sports. Office: The Sch of the Ozarks Point Lookout MO 65726

QUINCY, RONALD LEE, government official; b. Detroit, Sept. 8, 1950; s. James Peter and Dorothy Ellen (Crawford) Q.; B.A., U. Detroit, 1971, M.A., 1973; Ph.D., Mich. State U., 1981; postgrad. John F. Kennedy Sch. Govt., Harvard U., 1984. Teaching asst. Mich. State U., East Lansing, 1974-76, co-research project dir., 1975-77; research assoc. Sch. Criminal Justice, Mich. State U., 1975; dir. Mich. Office Human Resource Policy and Spl. Projects; exec. dir. Mich. Equal Employment and Opportunity Council, 1978-82; spl. asst. to gov. State of Mich., Lansing, 1977-82; dir. Mich. Dept. Civil Rights, Lansing, 1982—; program dir. Cath. Youth Orgn., Detroit, 1973-74; instr. adult edn. Detroit Pub. Schs., 1971-72; cons. Nat. Conf. Equal Employment Opportunity/Affirmative Action Mgrs., Detroit, 1981. Active Mayor's Summer Youth Planning and Coordination Com., Detroit, 1974, Resolutions and Policy Com. Mich. NAACP Brs., 1978; statutory mem. Mich. Criminal Justice Commn.; mem. Mich. Equal Employment and Bus. Opportunity Council; co-chmn. State of Mich. U.S. Census Com. U.S. Dept. Justice grantee; Mich. State U. Human Rights grantee; White House fellow, 1985-86. Avocations: tennis; jogging; reading. Home: 1477 Balmoral Detroit MI 48203 Office: Mich Dept Civil Rights 303 W Kalamazoo St Lansing MI 48913

QUINLAN, MICHAEL R., fast food chain executive. Pres., chief exec. officer, dir. McDonald's Corp., Oak Brook, Ill. Office: McDonald's Corp One McDonald Plaza Oak Brook IL 60521*

QUINN, HERBERT, microbiologist, consultant; b. N.Y.C., Mar. 23, 1917; s. David Harris and Esther (Jacobson) Q.; m. Selma Marucs, Nov. 6, 1938; 1 dau., Marcia Louise Quinn Kadetz. B.A., Ohio State U., 1940; M.S. in Environ. Scis., U. Cin., 1976. Cert. microbiologist Nat. Registry Microbiologists. Lab. technician USPHS, 1940; microbiologist Seagrams, 1940-42; research microbiologist Kroger Food Found., 1942-43, Wyeth, Inc., 1943-44, Ben Venue Labs., 1944-45; microbiologist U. Tex. Med. Sch., 1945-46; research microbiologist Procter & Gamble, Cin., 1946-66; research microbiologist Andrew Jergens, Cin., 1967-78; owner, microbiologist Q Labs., Inc., Cin., 1966—; also cons.; v.p. Agatha, Inc. Mem. Am. Soc. Microbiology, Sigma Xi. Republican. Jewish. Patentee in field. Home and Office: 1034 Fuhrman Rd Reading Cincinnati OH 45215

QUINN, JAMES LEONARD, museum exec.; b. Chgo., Mar. 14, 1928; s. James Patrick and Elinor Minnie (Bartos) Q.; B.A., State U. Iowa, 1952; m. Daphne Phoebe Tobit, Sept. 27, 1975; children by previous marriage—Gary James, Terri Louise, Shawn Michael, Patrick Carleton. Asst. dir. Charlotte (N.C.) Nature Mus., 1952-53; asst. dir.-curator exhibits Neville Public Mus., Green Bay, Wis., 1953-58, dir. mus., 1958-85; dir. Historic Hazelwood owned by Neville Public Mus., Green Bay, 1964-85; pres. Seaway Underwater Divers, Inc., Green Bay, 1965-72, Seaway Underwater Research Forum, Inc., Green Bay, 1972-75; prin. underwater archeologist in raising of hist. sailing vessel Alvin Clark from Green Bay waters, 1968-69; collaborator underwater archaeology Dept. Interior Nat. Park Service, 1973-78. Pres. Wis. Izaak Walton League, 1960; mem. Brown County Wis. Conservation Alliance; chmn. Adult Edn. Council, Green Bay; v.p. Children's Theater, Green Bay, Brown County Visitor Service Bur.; com. mem. YMCA Summer Camp, Green Bay, Brown County Resources Study Com.; mem. vis. com. U. Wis., Green Bay, 1972-78, chmn., 1974, also mem. adv. com. Coll. Human Biology; cons. Northeastern Wis. Sch. Dist. Served with USN, 1946-47. Mem. Am. Assn. Museums, Internat. Council Museums, Midwest Museums Conf. (pres. 1970, chmn. nominating com. 1970, 82, 83, 84, chmn. sites com. 1970, mem. adv. bd. 1959-80 chmn. local arrangements 1984), Wis. Fedn. Museums (founder and 1st chmn. 1961, mem. adv. bd. 1961-85, Am. Assn. State and Local History (mus. cons.), Can. Museums Assn., Assn. Sci. Mus. Dirs. (charter), Soc. Underwater Archaeologists. Club: Green Bay Yachting. Contbr. articles to profl. jours. Office: 1985 Dir Nat Firearms Mus 1600 Rhode Island Ave NW Washington DC 20036

QUINN, JOHN STEVEN, counseling psychologist; b. Lynn, Mass., Apr. 4, 1947; s. Neal Albert and Alice Caroline (White) Q. A.A., Monterey Peninsula Coll., 1967; B.A., U. Tenn., 1970; M.S., U. N.D., 1975; Ed.S., U. Toledo, 1976; M. Rehab. Counseling, Bowling Green State U., 1977; Ph.D., Kent State U., 1981. Lic. psychologist, cert. rehab. counselor; cert. alcoholism counselor, clin. mental health counselor. Cons. Midwest Exec. Search, Toledo, 1976-77; rehab. counselor Ohio Bur. Vocat. Rehab., Oregon, Ohio, 1977; grad. research asst. Kent State U., 1978-80; predoctoral psychology trainee Massillon (Ohio) State Hosp., 1980-81; instr. Pyramid Career Services, Canton, Ohio, 1981-82; alcoholism counselor Interval Brotherhood Home, Akron, Ohio, 1982-85; grad. instr. Walsh Coll., Canton, Ohio, 1982-83; instr. Cuyahoga Community Coll., Cleve., 1984; pvt. practice, 1983—. Mem. Greater Canton C. of C. Served to capt. USAF, 1970-75; capt. Ohio Air N.G., 1976-80. Mem. Am. Psychol. Assn., Am. Assn. Counseling and Devel., Phi Kappa Phi, Kappa Delta Phi, Phi Delta Kappa.

QUINTANILLA, ANTONIO PAULET, physician, educator; b. Peru, Feb. 8, 1927; s. Leandro Marino and Edel Paulet Q.; came to U.S., 1963, naturalized, 1974; Ph.D., San Marcos U., 1948, M.D., 1957; m. Mary Parker Rodriguez, May 2, 1958; children—Antonio Paulet, Angela, Francis, Cecilia, John. Asso. prof. physiology U. Arequipa, Peru, 1960-63; asso. in physiology Cornell U., N.Y., 1963-64; prof. physiology U. Arequipa, 1964-68; asso. prof. medicine Northwestern U., 1969-80, prof., 1980—; chief renal sect. VA Lakeside Hosp., 1976—; lectr.; mem. adv. bd. Kidney Found. Ill., Am. Fedn. Clin. Research. Fellow A.C.P.; mem. Chgo. Heart Assn. (hypertension council), Central Soc. Clin. Research, Am. Soc. Clin. Pharmacology and Therapeutics, Am., Internat. socs. nephrology, Chgo. Soc. Internal Medicine, Am. Physiol. Soc. Contbr. articles on renal disease to med. jours.; author books. Home: 500 Ridge Ave Evanston IL 60202 Office: 333 E Huron St Chicago IL 60611

QUINTON, GRANVILLE LEWIS, aircraft company official; b. Magazine, Ark., Nov. 23, 1941; s. William Lewis and Nancy Lucille (Holt) Q.; m. Rebecca Lee Griffith, Nov. 18, 1966; children—Brant Lewis, Misty Renea. B.S. in Acctg., Central State U., Edmond, Okla. Cert. auditor and info. systems auditor. Joint venture auditor Champlin Petroleum, Enid, Okla., 1970-72; corp. systems mgr. TG4Y Stores Co., Oklahoma City, 1972-77; EDP and operational audit mgr. Pizza Hut, Inc., Wichita, Kans., 1977-78; dir. audit Cessna Aircraft Co., Wichita, 1978—. Author seminar in field. Served with USAF, 1960-64. Mem. Inst. Internal Auditors (pres. 1977-78, dir. Wichita 1978—, chmn. CIA exam. Wichita 1979—, CIA rev. chmn. 1979—), EDP Auditors Assn. Lodge: Masons. Home: 16110 Manor Rd Wichita KS 67230 Office: Cessna Aircraft Co 5800 E Pawnee Wichita KS 67201

QUIRK, JOHN EDWARD, personnel analyst; b. Chgo., Oct. 24, 1935; s. Maurice John and Mary Ella (Halpin) Q.; m. Hedy Amedo Castro, June 5, 1967; children—Michele Marie, Heather Noele. B.A., Coker Coll., 1975; M.S., Nat. Coll. Edn., 1982. With U.S. Army, 1954-75; personnel mgr. USS Lead Refinery, Inc., East Chicago, Ind., 1975-77; personnel dir. Quam-Nichols Co., Chgo., 1977; sr. personnel analyst Met. San. Dist., Chgo., 1977—, employee assistance program adminstr., 1983—; adj. faculty Nat. Coll. Edn. Mem. referral agt. program com. United Way of Chgo., 1984. Decorated Bronze Star, Combat Infantryman's Badge; Cross of Gallantry (Viet Nam). Independent. Roman Catholic. Avocations: reading, writing, acting. Home: 19247 Ada St Lansing IL 60438 Office: Met San Dist Greater Chgo 100 E Erie St Chicago IL 606ll

QUOCK, RAYMOND MARK, pharmacologist, researcher; b. San Francisco, June 9, 1948; s. Dick Gar and Madge (Mak) Q.; m. Lina Yen Chiu, Jan. 25, 1975; 1 child, Lauren Rae. B.S., U. San Francisco, 1970; Ph.D., U. Wash., 1974. Research lab. asst. U. Calif., San Francisco, 1964-70; USPHS predoctoral fellow U. Wash., Seattle, 1970-74, instr., 1974-75; asst. prof. U. Pacific, Stockton, Calif., 1975-79; asst. prof. Marquette U., Milw., 1979-82, assoc. prof., 1982—; cons. Calif. State Bd. Pharmacy, San Francisco, 1976-79; research assoc. in toxicology VA Med. Ctr., Wood, Wis., 1981—, cons. dentistry, 1982—. Contbr. articles to profl. jours. Exec. v.p. Wis. chpt. Orgn. Chinese-Ams., Milw., 1982-83; mem. research com. Am. Heart Assn. Wis., Milw., 1984—; bd. dirs. Asian Community Health Clinic, Seattle, 1971-75. Recipient Dr. Elwood Molseed award U. San Francisco, 1970, Dr. Leo Pinsky award Marquette U., 1983; named One of Outstanding Young Men of Am., U.S. Jaycees, 1978. Mem. Western Pharmacology Soc., Am. Soc. Pharmacology and Exptl. Therapeutics, Soc. Neurosci., (councillor Greater Milw. chpt. 1985—), N.Y. Acad. Sci., Internat. Brain Research Orgn., World Fedn. Neurosci. Office: Div Pharmacology Marquette U Sch Dentistry 604 N 16th St Milwaukee WI 53233

RAAB, RAYMOND MARK, automotive educator, consultant, writer; b. Mpls., Jan. 2, 1928; s. Frank Xavier and Estelle Agnes (Raymond) R.; m. Marian Nathalie Whitney, Jan. 22, 1948; children—Mark, Neil, Adrienne, Holly. B.S., U. Minn., 1950, postgrad. in philosophy and psychology, 1950-53. Automotive instr. Machinist Hubbard Mfg. Co., Mpls., 1953-54; case worker Child Service div. Hennepin County Welfare Dept. (Minn.), 1954-72; self-employed automotive ignition and carburation specialist, Mpls., 1972—; instr. Vo Tech Inst., White Bear Lake, Minn., 1972—; tng. dir. Auto Tech., 1977-79; automotive racer. Served with USAF, 1945-48. Recipient prizes and trophies for automotive racing. Mem. Automotive Technicians Minn. (bd. dirs., past pres.), Minn. Trades and Indsl. Assn., Minn. Vocat. Assn., Am. Vocat. Assn. Democrat. Author: (with P. Beck) Convert Your Car to Run on Alcohol, 1980; contbr. articles to profl. jours. Home: 4418 Nawadaha Blvd Minneapolis MN 55406 Office: 916 Vo Tech White Bear Lake MN 55110

RAABE, JANIS ASAD, educational writer and consultant; b. Lakewood, Ohio, Apr. 28, 1949; d. Theodore Charles and Jenifer Irene (Snitko) Asad; student St. John Coll. of Cleve., 1967-69; B.S. in Edn., Bowling Green State U., 1971, M.Ed. in Reading, 1972; m. Richard A. Raabe, Aug. 11, 1972; children—Jason Richard, Mark Richard. Grad. asst. Bowling Green State U., 1971-72; reading tchr. and cons. Mentor-Ridge Jr. High Sch., Mentor, Ohio, 1972-75; writer ednl. materials Modern Curriculum Press, Cleve., 1972—; freelance editorial cons. Ohio Dept. Edn., 1975-77; ednl. cons. Coronet Instructional Media, Chgo., 1976-79. Named one of Outstanding Young Women of Am., 1978. Mem. Internat. Reading Assn., Ohio Reading Assn., Kappa Delta Pi. Author: MCP Phonetic Primary Readers, sets 1-4, 1974-82, ednl. cons. Read-Along Beginning Phonics, sets 1 and 2, 1978. Home: 5901 Kerry Circle NW Canton OH 44718

RAAF, DONNA DELONG, hotel executive; b. Connelsville, Pa., Aug. 24, 1941; d. Jay Fred and Juanita Rose (King) Severt Kidwell; m. Robert Allen DeLong, Dec. 14, 1957 (div. Mar. 1970); children—Victoria Lynne, Robert Allen II, Deborah Rose; m. Joseph John Raaf, Sept. 17, 1983; cert. in hotel adminstrn., Am. Hotel & Motel Assn. Ednl. Inst., 1985. Desk clk. Howard Johnson, Zanesville, Ohio, 1969-71, mgr., 1971-72, Columbus, Ohio, 1972-74, area mgr., Newark, Ohio, 1974-77, St. Paul, 1977-83, gen. mgr., 1983—. Mem. Govt. Council on Emergency Housing, St. Paul, 1983; mem. Tourism Promotion Council, Minn., 1984—; chmn. Washington County Pvt. Industry Council, 1985; vice chmn. East Met. Pvt. Industry Council, Twin Cities, Minn., 1985. Mem. Am. Hotel and Motel Assn., Meeting Planner Internat., Upper Midwest Hosp. Assn. (bd. dirs. 1984—), Minn. Hotel Assn. (pres. 1984), St. Paul Hotel Assn. (pres. 1980-82), Suburban C. of C. Republican. Methodist. Clubs: Maplewood Singers (Minn.); Zonta Internat. (bd. dirs. 1984—); Eastwind Toastmasters Internat. (sec. 1980, pres. 1985). Avocations: singing; reading; macrame; fishing. Office: Howard Johnsons 6003 Hudson Rd Saint Paul MN 55125

RABB, GEORGE B., zoologist; b. Charleston, S.C., Jan. 2, 1930; s. Joseph A. and Teresa C. (Redmond) R.; B.S., Coll. Charleston, 1951; M.A., U. Mich., 1952, Ph.D., 1957; m. Mary Sughrue, June 10, 1953. Teaching fellow zoology U. Mich., 1954-56; curator, coordinator research Chgo. Zool. Park, Brookfield, Ill., 1956-64, asso. dir. research and edn., 1964-75, dep. dir., 1969-75, dir., 1976—; pres. Chgo. Zool. Soc., 1976—; research assoc. Field Mus. Natural History, 1965—; lectr. dept. zoology U. Chgo., 1965—, mem. Com. on Evolution Biology, 1969—; chmn. policy adv. group Internat. Species Inventory System, 1982—. Fellow AAAS; mem. Am. Soc. Ichthyologists and Herpetologists (pres. 1978), Herpetologists League, Soc. Systematic Zoology, Soc. Mammalogists. Soc. Study Evolution, Ecol. Soc. Am., Am. Soc. Zoologists, Soc. Study Animal Behavior, Am. Assn. Museums, Am. Soc. Naturalists, Am. Assn. Zool. Parks and Aquariums (dir. 1979-80), Am. Com. Internat. Conservation, Internat. Union Dirs. Zool. Gardens, Internat. Union Conservation of Nature (steering com. species survival commn. 1983—), Sigma Xi. Office: Chgo Zool Park Brookfield IL 60513

RABE, RICHARD FRANK, dentist, lawyer; b. Crystal Lake, Iowa, May 19, 1919; s. Otto Henry and Agnes Marie (Juhl) R.; m. Barbara Jean McNeal, Mar. 15, 1946; children—Richard Frank, Mary Elizabeth, Kathleen Ann, Michelle. A.A., Waldorf Coll., 1938; D.D.S., U. Iowa, 1942; J.D., Drake U., 1952. Bar: Iowa 1952. Practice dentistry, Des Moines, 1946—; sole practice law, Des Moines, 1952—; cons. M.F. Patterson Dental Supply Co., 1956-61, Nat. Bd. Dental Examiners, 1955-60; chmn. Iowa Bd. Dental Examiners, 1962-63, Iowa Bd. Nursing Home Examiners, 1980-84; lectr. dental assns. throughout U.S., Contbr. articles to profl. jours. Fellow Am. Coll. Dentists; mem. ADA (Vice chmn. council on legis. 1977-78), Am. Acad. Dental Practice Adminstrn., Iowa Dental Study Club (past pres.), Iowa Dental Assn. (pres. 1972, trustee 1960-71), ABA, Iowa Bar Assn., Des Moines Dist. Dental Soc. (past pres.), Milw. Dental Research Group, Central Regional Dental Testing Agy., Am. Inst. Parliamentarians., Psi Omega, Delta Theta Phi. Episcopalian. Clubs: Des Moines Golf and Country. Lodge: Masons, Shriners. Avocations: sailing; flying. Home: 5709 N Waterbury Rd Des Moines IA 50312 Office: 5731 Urbandale Ave Des Moines IA 50310

RABEDEAUX, RICHARD WAYNE, dentist, educator; b. Des Moines, Jan. 25, 1930; s. Burnell C. and Amanda (Miller) R.; m. Joyce Frauenholz, June 16, 1953; children—Steven Grant, Jolie. B.S., U. Iowa, 1951, D.D.S., 1955. Ptnr. The Dental Practice, Newton, Iowa, 1957—; adj. faculty U. Iowa, 1965—. Inventor stadium jak, solar collector (Presdl. award 1980). Founder Jasper County Retarded Children, Newton, 1960. Served to maj. USAF, 1955-57, Korea. Named Outstanding Young Republican, Des Moines, 1962; guest appearance TV show What's My Line?, 1962. Fellow Acad. Gen. Dentistry (pres. Region X 1973-75, pres. Iowa sect. 1973-75, Disting. Service award 1974); mem. ADA, Iowa Dental Assn. (honors clinic 1980), Des Moines Dist. Dental Assn. (pres. 1982), Isaac Walton League. Episcopalian. Clubs: Newton Country (bd. dirs. 1972-75), University Athletic. Lodges: Masons, Elks. Avocations: gardening; skiing; swimming; sports. Home: 2020 W 15th St S Newton IA 50208 Office: The Dental Practice 104 N 2d Ave E PO Box 276 Newton IA 50208

RABURN, LOUIS EARL, electronic engineer; b. Manhattan, Kans., June 4, 1919; s. George Ellsworth and Jessie (Lindsay) R.; m. Joan Murphy, Sept. 8, 1941; children—Elizabeth, Patricia, John, Julie, Amy. B.S. in E. E., Kans. State U., 1941; postgrad. Harvard U., 1943-44. Registered profl. engr., Pa. Research assoc. Harvard U., 1942-45; supr. Electronics Research, Evansville, Ind., 1946-51; sect. mgr. McDonnell Douglas, St. Louis, 1963-85; owner, mgr. Microray Co., St. Louis, 1970—. Served with USNR, 1940-41. Mem. Creve Coeur C. of C. Republican. Roman Catholic. Clubs: St. Louis Area Computer, Harvard Alumni. Lodge: Elks. Home and office: 1107 Woodlake Village Saint Louis MO 63141

RACHLIS, ARNOLD ISRAEL, rabbi, religion educator; b. Phila., Apr. 25, 1949; s. Burech and Pauline (Glanzberg) R.; m. Robin Claire Goldberg, July 4, 1974; 1 child, Adam. B.A., U. Pa.; 1970; M.A., Temple U., 1972; postgrad. Reconstructionist Rabbinical Coll., 1970-75; B.A. (hon.) Central High Sch., Phila., 1966. Ordained rabbi, 1975. Asst. dir. Hillel Found., Temple U., Phila., 1972-74; with Temple U., 1974-76; mem. faculty Spertus Coll., Chgo., 1976—; rabbi Jewish Reconstructionist Cong., Evanston, Ill., 1976—; host Hayom (Today) Syndicated Cable TV Show Sta. WJUF-TV, Chgo., 1982—; host Of Cabbages and Kings Program ABC-TV, Chgo., 1982—. Contbr. articles to profl. jours. Recipient Leadership Citation Jewish Reconstructionist Found., 1980. Mem. Reconstructionist Rabbinical Assn. (pres. 1977-79); Chgo. Bd. Rabbis (v.p. 1982—), Chgo. Action for Soviet Jewry (adv. council), Chevra. Avocations: theater; writing; hiking; foreign travel. Home: 1204 Madison Evanston IL 60202 Office: Jewish Reconstructionist Congregation 303 Dodge St Evanston IL 60602

RACHWALSKI, FRANK JOSEPH, JR., financial executive; b. Chgo., Mar. 26, 1945; s. Frank Joseph and Julia Alice (Cwikowski) R.; m. Judith Clair Ferrick, May 18, 1972; children—Mark, Karla, Brian. B.B.A., Loyola U., Chgo., 1967, M.B.A., 1969. Chartered fin. analyst. Systems analyst N. Am. Life/U.S. Life, Chgo., 1963-73; portfolio mgr. Kemper Fin., Chgo., 1973—; v.p. Kemper Fin. Services Inc., Chgo., 1979—; v.p. Kemper Investors Life Ins. Co., Chgo., and subs. cos., Cash Equivalent Fund Inc., Chgo. Mem. Investment Analyst Soc. Chgo. Roman Catholic. Club: Elmhurst Tennis (treas. 1979-81) (Ill.). Avocations: tennis, exercise. Home: 453 Parkview Elmhurst IL 60126 Office: Kemper Fin Services Inc 120 S LaSalle St Chicago IL 61026

RACIAK, RITA ROBERTA, communications company official; b. Chgo., Dec. 7, 1946; d. Stanley Joseph and Jeanne (Tokarz) R.; m. John Lasky, May 21, 1983. B.A. in Mktg., Mundelein Coll., 1980. With Sears, Roebuck and Co., Chgo., 1964-72; office mgr. Diaz & Co. Real Estate, 1972-73, Midwest Montessori Tchr. Tng. Ctr., 1973-74, Ben Friend Real Estate, 1974-75, By Jove Inc. Real Estate, Chgo., 1975-76; sec. to chmn. bd. Burke Communication Industries, Inc., Chgo., 1976-79, estimating service coordinator, 1979-80, dir. advt., 1980—; lectr. Oakton Community Coll., 1981. Clubs: Chgo. Advt., Women's Advt. of Chgo. Composer: Waves of the North Atlantic, 1982; Barbara's Waltz, 1982. Home: 6025 W Montrose Chicago IL 60634 Office: Burke Communication Industries Inc 1165 N Clark St Chicago IL 60610

RACKIS, JOSEPH JOHN, research biochemist, consultant; b. Somersville, Conn., July 29, 1922; s. Joseph Walter and Josephine (Winsoanitis) R.; m. Eugenia Evelyn Mihalopoulos, Dec. 31, 1953; children—Rebecca Ann, Steven Joseph. B.S. in Chemistry, U. Conn. 1950; Ph.D. in Biochemistry, U. Iowa, 1955. Chemist, U.S. Dept. Agr., North Regional Research Ctr., Peoria, Ill., 1955-84; pvt. practice cons., Peoria, 1984—. Contbr. articles to profl. jours. Served with USAAF, 1943-45, ETO. Recipient Merit award U.S. Dept. Agr., 1983. Mem. Am. Chem. Soc. (editorial bd. 1975-80). Am. Soc. Biol. Chemists, Am. Assn. Cereal Chemists (oilseed div. 1965-70), Inst. Food Technologists, Am. Oil Chemists Soc. (Bond award 1974), Phi Tau Sigma. Democrat. Roman Catholic. Club: Bergen Boosters Alumni (Peoria) (chmn. 1975-79). Avocation: gardening. Home: 3411 N Elmcroft Terr Peoria IL 61604

RACLIN, ERNESTINE MORRIS, banker; b. South Bend, Ind., 1927. Ed. Briarcliff Coll., St. Mary's Coll.; LH.D. (hon.), Converse Coll., 1974; LL.D. (hon.), Notre Dame U., 1978, Ind. State U., 1981. Chmn. bd. dirs. 1st Source Corp. and 1st Source Bank, South Bend, and 1st Source Bank, Marshall County; dir. First Chgo. Corp., First Nat. Bank Chgo., MidCon Corp., Chgo., No. Ind. Pub. Service Co., Hammond, Michiana Pub. Broadcasting Corp. Former mem. Gov.'s Commn. Directions in Mental Health; former chmn. Gov.'s Citizens Adv. Com. Title XX; co-chmn. YMCA Capital Campaign, Notre Dame U. fund drive; mem. Ind. Growth Opportunity Council, fin. com. to Re-elect Reagan, State of Ind.; mem. Early Birds for Qualye Com.; bd. dirs. United Way Internat., United Way of Ind., Ivy Tech. Found.; dir., past pres. Jr. Achievement South Bend, Inc.; dir., sec. bd. govs. United Way of Am.; trustee Housing Allowance Office, Project Future, First Presbyterian Ch., Notre Dame U., Stanley Clark Sch. (South Bend), Converse Coll., Recipient E.M. Morris award Ind. U., South Bend, St. Mary's Coll. Community Service award, Ivy Tech's Excellence in Edn. award. Mem. Associated Colls. Ind., Ind. State C. of C. (dir., chmn. edn. task force), South Bend-Mishawaka Area C. of C. (dir.), Ind. Acad., Beta Sigma Gamma. Address: 100 N Esther St South Bend IN 46617

RADABAUGH, DENNIS CHARLES, zoology educator; b. Detroit, Sept. 27, 1942; s. Door O. and Evelyn May (Gaberdiel) R.; m. Joan Dayle Maxwell, Mar. 19, 1967; children—John Maxwell, Carrie Lynn. B.A., Albion Coll., 1960-64;

M.S., Ohio State U., 1964-67, Ph.D., 1970. Teaching asst. Ohio State U., Columbus, 1965-67, teaching assoc., 1967-70; zoology faculty Ohio Wesleyan U., Delaware, 1970—. Contbr. articles on behavioral ecology and parasitology of fishes to profl. jours. Mem. AAAS, Animal Behavior Soc., Ohio Acad. Sci., Sigma Xi. Methodist. Avocation: photography. Office: Dept Zoology Ohio Wesleyan U Delaware OH

RADANDT, GEORGE JOHN, JR., excavation and block manufacturing company executive; b. Manitowoc, Wis., Dec. 7, 1944; s. George Earl and Marcella Barbara (Dubey) R.; m. Laura Lynn Jost, June 5, 1971; children—Jason, Brooke, Hilde, Leslie. Grad. Lakeshore Tech. Inst., Manitowoc, 1966. Laborer Fred Radandt Sons Inc., Manitowoc, summers, 1960-66, front end loader operator, 1970-74, dispatcher, 1974-78, salesman, 1978-82, gen. mgr., 1982—. Chmn. Manitowoc Safety Patrol, 1974—. Served with U.S. Army, 1966-69; Vietnam. Mem. Wis. Concrete Products (bd. dirs. 1981-83), Manitowoc Master Bldrs. (bd. dirs. 1981-83, pres. 1984-85), Jaycees (dir. 1970-71). Lutheran. Lodges: Elks, Eagles. Avocations: fishing, boating, skiing, camping. Home: 11701 Radandt Ln Manitowoc WI 54220 Office: Fred Radandt Sons Inc 1800 Johnston Dr Manitowoc WI 54220

RADCLIFF, WILLIAM FRANKLIN, lawyer; b. Fredericksburg, Ind., May 21, 1922; s. Samuel Pearl and Hester Susan (Sherwood) R.; B.A., Yale U., 1948; J.D., Ind. U., 1951; m. Elizabeth Louise Doeller Haines, May 15, 1982; children—Forrest Lee, Stephanie Anne; foster children—Cheryl Lynn, Sandra Lee, Richard Alan, Lezlie Laverne; stepchildren—Mark David, Laura Louise, Pamela Lynn, Veronica Lee. Bar: Ind. 1951. With firm DeFur, Voran, Hanley, Radcliff & Reed, and predecessors, Muncie, Ind., 1951—, ptnr., 1954—; dir., mem. exec. com. Am. Nat. Bank and Trust Co. Muncie; dir. Ben Zeigler Co., Inc., Muncie; dir., sec. Muncie Tennis and Country Club. Pres., Delaware County Mental Health Assocs., 1962-63; a founder Ind. Mental Health Meml. Found., 1962, sec., 1962—; bd. dirs. Delaware County Cancer Soc.; trustee Acad. Community Leadership. Served with AUS, 1940-46; PTO; lt. col. Res., ret. Mem. ABA, Ind. Bar Assn., Muncie Bar Assn., Muncie-Delaware County C. of C. (pres. 1972-73). Clubs: Masons, Exchange (pres. 1962); Delaware Country (pres. 1974), Muncie (Muncie). Home: 1809 N Winthrop Rd Muncie IN 47304 Office: 201 E Jackson St Muncie IN 47305

RADCLIFFE, GERALD EUGENE, judge, lawyer; b. Chillicothe, Ohio, Feb. 19, 1923; s. Maurice Gerald and Mary Ellen (Wills) R.; m. Edythe Kennedy, Aug. 11, 1947; children—Jerilynn K. Radcliffe Ross, Pamela J. Radcliffe Dunn. B.A., Ohio U., 1948; J.D., U. Cin., 1950. Bar: Ohio 1950, U.S. Dist. Ct. 1951, U.S. Supreme Ct. 1957. Sole practice, Chillicothe, 1950-66; asst. pros. atty. Ross County, Ohio, 1966-70; acting mcpl. judge Chillicothe Mcpl. Ct., 1970-72; judge probate, juvenile divs. Ross County Ct., Chillicothe, 1973—; mem. rules adv. com. Ohio Supreme Ct., 1984; mem. Ohio Legis. Oversite com., 1974-81; trustee Ohio Jud. Coll., 1979. Editor Cin. Law Rev., 1949-50. Co-author: Constitutional Law, 1979. Contbr. articles to profl. jours. Project dir. South Central Ohio Regional Juvenile Detention Ctr., 1971-72; co-chmn. Chillicothe United Way Fund Campaign, 1972; mem. Youth Services Adv. Council, 1984. Recipient Outstanding Citizen of Yr. award, Jr. C. of C., 1972, Superior Jud. award Ohio Supreme Ct., 1976-82, Meritorious Service award Probate Ct. Judges Ohio, 1984, Dirs. award Ohio Dept. Youth Services, 1984. Mem. Ohio Juvenile Judges Assn., (pres. 1983-84), Nat. Council Juvenile and Family Ct. Judges (trustee 1982-84), Ohio Jud. Conf. Democrat. Lodges: Kiwanis (lt. gov. 1983-84, Ohio Statehood Achievement award 1979), Masons. Avocation: golf. Home: 5 Edgewood Ct Chillicothe OH 45601 Office: Ross County Juvenile and Probate Ct Corner Paint and Main Sts Chillicothe OH 45601

RADEL, CURTIS VERNON, nurse anesthetist; b. Springfield, Minn., Jan. 27, 1944; s. Raymond A. and Dolores M. (Steinhaus) R.; m. Mary A. Lockart, Sept. 26, 1970; children—Kathryn, Sarah, Emily, Paul. B.A., Ottawa U., 1980; M.S., U. N.D., 1983. Anesthetist, dir. respiratory therapy Daviess County Hosp., Washington, Ind., 1971-73; chief anesthetist, dir. respiratory therapy Perry Meml. Hosp., Princeton, Ill., 1973-80; program dir. Grand Forks Sch. Anesthesia, United Hosp., N.D., 1980—; cons. U. N.D., 1982—. Mem. Nat. Bd. for Respiratory Therapy, Am. Assn. Nurse Anesthetists, N.D. Bd. Nursing, N.D. Assn. Nurse Anesthetists, Am. Assn. for Respiratory Therapy, Am. Registry Radiologic Technologists. Lutheran. Lodge: Elks. Avocations: hunting; fishing; music; racquetball; bowling. Home: 1311 Noble Cove Grand Forks ND 58201

RADEL, DENNIS WAYNE, systems and programming executive; b. Muskegon, Mich., July 19, 1947; s. George Washington and Grace Olien (Frazier) R.; m. Dianna Lynn Beachum, Aug. 26, 1972; children—Eric Jon, David Wayne, Bradley Alan. A.A., Muskegon Community Coll., 1967; B.S., Mich. State U., 1969. Programmer, analyst Misco div. Howmet Corp., Whitehall, Mich., 1970-72; systems analyst Muskegon Piston Ring, 1972-75; systems analyst, sect. head Instrument div. Lear Siegler, Grand Rapids, Mich., 1975-77; systems and programming supr. Gen. Products div. Teledyne Continental Motors, Muskegon, 1977—. Co-chmn. solicitations Sta. 35-TV, Grand Valley State Coll., 1984-85; chief Young Family Christian Assn. Indian Guides, Muskegon, 1984-85; dir. Reeths Puffer Summer Baseball League, 1984—. Mem. Assn. Systems Mgmt., Nat. Mgmt. Assn. (dir. 1983—, Disting. Service award 1984). Avocations: youth baseball, golfing, bowling. Home: 467 Westwind Dr North Muskegon MI 49445 Office: Gen Products Div Teledyne Continental Motors 76 Getty St Muskegon MI 49442

RADEMACHER, RICHARD JOSEPH, librarian; b. Kaukauna, Wis., Aug. 20, 1937; s. Joseph Benjamin and Anna (Wyuts) R.; A.B., Ripon Coll., 1959. M.S., Library Sch. U. Wis., 1961; m. Mary Jane Liethen, Feb. 12, 1966; children—Alicia Mary, Ann Marie, Amy Rose. Dir. Kaukauna Public Library, 1964-66, Eau Claire (Wis.) Public Library, 1966-69; librarian Salt Lake City Public Library, 1969-76; dir. Wichita (Kans.) Public Library, 1976—. Bd. dirs. Salt Lake Art Center, Reading Room for the Blind. Served with AUS, 1962-64. Mem. ALA, Mountain Plains Library Assn., Wichita Library Assn. Office: 223 S Main St Wichita KS 67202*

RADEN, LOUIS, tape and label corporation executive; b. Detroit, June 17, 1929; s. Harry M. and Joan (Morris) R.; B.A., Trinity Coll., 1951; postgrad. N.Y. U., 1952; m. Mary K. Knowlton, June 18, 1949; children—Louis III, Pamela, Jacqueline. With Time, Inc., 1951-52; with Quaker Chem. Corp., 1952-63, sales mgr., 1957-63; exec. v.p. Gen. Tape & Supply, Inc., Detroit, 1963-68, pres., chmn. bd., 1969—; pres. Mich. Gun Clubs, 1973-77. Fifth reunion chmn. Trinity Coll., 1956, pres. Mich. alumni, 1965-72, sec. Class of 1951, 1981—; trustee, Mich. Diocese Episcopal Ch., chmn. urban affairs com., 1977-79, v.p., 1980-82; vice chmn. bd. dirs. Robert H. Whitaker Sch. Theology, 1983-85. Mem. Nat. Rifle Assn. (life), Nat. Skeet Shooting Assn. (life, nat. dir. 1977-79), Greater Detroit Bd. Commerce, Automotive Industry Action Group, Mich. C. of C., C. of C. U.S., Greater Hartford Jaycees (exec. v.p. 1955-57, Key Man award 1957), Theta Xi (life; Disting. Service award 1957, alumni pres. 1952-57, regional dir. 1954-57). Republican. Clubs: Detroit Golf, Detroit Gun, Katke-Cousins Golf, Black Hawk Indians. Home: 1133 Ivyglen Circle Bloomfield Hills MI 48013 Office: 7451 W Eight Mile Rd Detroit MI 48221

RADER, CHARLES MAYER, clinical psychologist, research consultant; b. Bklyn., Aug. 22, 1950; s. Milton Joseph and Edna (Saperstein) R. B.A., Hamilton Coll., 1972; Ph.D., U. Minn., 1979. Lic. cons. psychologist, Minn. Psychol. assoc. Hennepin County Mental Health Ctr., Mpls., 1976-78; cons. Woodview Detention Home, St. Paul, 1976-77; cons. Youth Employment Programs, Mpls., 1978-79; clin. psychologist Vinson Mental Health Clinic, St. Paul, 1980-83; sr. clin. psychologist Ramsey County Mental Health Clinic, St. Paul, 1983—; guest lectr., cons. to treatment programs, group homes. Bd. dirs. Alpha House, Mpls., 1975—, v.p., 1979-81, pres., 1981-83; mem. adv. bd. Guild Hall, St. Paul, 1981—; precinct del. Dem. Farmer Labor Party, 1976—, chmn., 1978-81; counselor Walk In Counseling Ctr., 1979-80, Neighborhood Involvement Program, 1979-80; mem. utilization rev. bd. Norhaven and Sur la Rue, 1983—; mem. planning com. Minn. Network for Disaster Stress Intervention, 1985—. Mem. Am. Psychol. Assn., Minn. Psychol. Assn., Am. Soc. for Study Mental Imagery, Phi Beta Kappa, Sigma Xi. Jewish. Contbr. articles to profl. jours., chpt. to book. Home: 5817 Creek Valley Rd Edina MN 55435 Office: Ramsey County Mental Health Clinic 529 Jackson St Saint Paul MN 55101

RADKE, MERLE LOUIS, educator; b. Aurelia, Iowa, Feb. 25, 1922; s. Frederick Daniel and Marie (Winterhof) R.; m. Marjorie Ruth Huebuer, Aug. 3, 1944; children—Charlyne Berens, Jeaninne Meyer. B.S.Ed., Concordia Coll., 1948; M.A., Wayne State U., 1953; Ph.D., Northwestern U., 1965; Litt.D. (hon.), Concordia Coll., 1975. Prin., tchr. Luth. elem. schs., Mich., Idaho, 1943-57; instr. English, Concordia Coll., River Forest, Ill., 1957-58, asst. prof., 1958-60, assoc. prof., 1960-65, prof. English, 1965—. Editor Luth. Edn., Concordia Coll., 1965—. Assoc. editor Jour. Geography, 1965-70. Lutheran. Office: Concordia Coll 7400 Augusta River Forest IL 60305

RADKE, RODNEY OWEN, agricultural research executive, research biologist; b. Ripon, Wis., Feb. 5, 1942; s. Edward Ludwig and Vera Ione (Phillips) R.; m. Jean Marie Rutsch, Sept. 1, 1963; children—Cheryl Lynn, Lisa Diane, Daniel E. B.S., U. Wis., 1963, M.S., 1965, Ph.D., 1967. Research sci. Monsanto Agrl. Products Co., St. Louis, 1969-75, sr. research group leader, 1975-79, research mgr. 1979-81, mgr. research, 1981—. Contbr. articles to profl. jours. Served to capt. U.S. Army, 1967-69. Mem. Weed Sci. Soc. Am., Am. Soc. Agronomy. Lutheran. Club: First Capitol Soccer (coach 1981—) (St. Charles). Avocations: power boating; soccer; racquetball. Home: 1119 Grand Prix Dr Saint Charles MO 63303 Office: Monsanto 800 N Lindbergh Blvd Saint Louis MO 63167

RADMACHER, CAMILLE J., retired librarian; b. Monmouth, Ill., Apr. 14, 1917; d. Harry M. and Esther (Greenleaf) R.; student Monmouth Coll., 1935-37. With adult dept. Warren County Library, Monmouth, 1937-48, head county librarian, 1948-85, exec. dir. Western Ill. Library System, 1965-82; exec. dir. Nat. Library Week in State of Ill., 1959. Mem. Monmouth Coll. Community Concert Lecture Bd., 1967-72; mem. adv. com. Ill. State Library, 1962-72. Mem. Ill. Library Assn. (Ill. Librarian Citation award 1967), Women's Nat. Book Assn., DAR. Methodist. Clubs: Order Eastern Star, Altrusa (treas. 1968-69). Home: 424 Melrose St Chicago IL 60657

RADMER, MICHAEL JOHN, lawyer; b. Wisconsin Rapids, Wis., Apr. 28, 1945; s. Donald Richard and Thelma Loretta (Donahue) R.; B.S., Northwestern U., 1967; J.D., Harvard U., 1970; m. Laurie Jean Anshus, Dec. 22, 1983; children—Christina Nicole, Ryan Michael, Michael John. Admitted to Minn. bar, 1970; assoc. firm Dorsey & Whitney, Mpls., 1970-76, ptnr., 1976—; sec. or gen. counsel rep. for 26 investment cos., including St. Paul Securities, Inc.; instr. Hamline U. Sch. Law. Mem. ABA, Minn. Bar Assn., Hennepin County Bar Assn. Club: Mpls. Athletic. Contbr. articles to profl. jours. Home: 4329 E Lake Harriet Pkwy Minneapolis MN 55409 Office: Dorsey & Whitney 2200 1st Bank Pl E Minneapolis MN 55402

RADNOR, ALAN T., lawyer; b. Cleve., Mar. 10, 1946; s. Robert Clark and Rose (Chester) R.; m. Carol Sue Hirsch, June 22, 1969; children—Melanie, Joshua, Joanna. B.A., Kenyon Coll., 1967; M.S. in Anatomy, Ohio State U., 1969, J.D., 1972. Bar: Ohio 1972. Ptnr., Vorys, Sater, Seymour & Pease, Columbus, Ohio, 1972—; adj. prof. law Ohio State U., Columbus, 1979—. Contbr. articles to profl. jours. Bd. dirs., trustee Congregation Tifereth Israel, Columbus, 1975—, 1st v.p., 1983-85, pres., 1985—. Named Boss of Yr., Columbus Assn. Legal Secs., 1983. Mem. ABA, Ohio State Bar Assn., Columbus Bar Assn. (chmn. dr.-lawyer com. 1979-80), Columbus Def. Assn. (pres. 1980-81), Def. Research Inst., Internat. Assn. Ins. Counsel, Ohio Hosp. Assn. Democrat. Jewish. Avocations: reading; sculpture. Home: 400 S Columbia St Bexley OH 43209 Office: Vorys Sater Seymour & Pease 52 E Gay St PO Box 1008 Columbus OH 43216

RAFFEL, ALVIN ROBERT, art educator, lithographer; b. Dayton, Ohio, Dec. 25, 1905; s. Herman John and Pauline Louise (Kromann) R.; m. Mildred G. Rosenberger, Oct. 5, 1940. B.A., Art Inst. Chgo., 1933. Lithographer, Gartner & Bender, Chgo., 1925-36, Reynolds & Reynolds, Dayton, Ohio, 1939-42; instr. drawing and painting Sch. of Dayton Art Inst., 1946-73, part-time tchr., 1979—; instr. watercolor painting Centerville High Sch., Ohio; represented in permanent collections: Dayton Art Inst.; art jurist, Dayton, Cin., Columbus, Indpls. Served with AUS, 1943-44. Mem. AAUP, Dayton Soc. Painters and Sculptors. Home: 6720 Mad River Rd Dayton OH 45459

RAFFEL, JAMES NORMAN, social service executive; b. Milw., June 7, 1954; s. Norman Thomas and Betty Louise (Semrad) R.; m. Gail Ann Justin, Sept. 1, 1979. B.A., U. Wis.-Eau Claire, 1976. Guidance and edn. dir. Milw. Boys Club, 1976-78, teen ctr. dir., 1978-79, assoc. exec. dir., 1979-85, asst. exec. dir., 1985—. Mem. Nat. Soc. Fund Raising Execs. Presbyterian. Office: Milwaukee Boys and Girls Club 1437 N Prospect Ave Milwaukee WI 53202

RAFFEL, LOUIS BENJAMIN, food association executive; b. Chgo., Mar. 17, 1933; s. Martin G. and Donnette (Rogers) R.; m. Trudi Weiner, Sept. 11, 1955; childlren—Lawrence, Sharon, Mark. B.S., U. Ill., 1955. Account exec. Glassner & Assocs., Chgo., 1957-60, Buchen Pub. Relations, Chgo., 1960-62; asst. pub. relations dir. Am. Meat Inst., Chgo., 1962-68; pub. relations dir. Nat. Dairy Council, Chgo., 1968-70, Armour & Co., Chgo., 1970-72; v.p. pub. relations and advt. Greyhound Corp., Phoenix, 1972-76; pres. Am. Egg Bd., Chgo., 1976—. Mem. pub. relations com. Chgo. Crusade of Mercy, 1978—. Served with U.S. Army, 1955-57. Mem. Am. Soc. Assn. Execs. (cert.), Pub. Relations Soc. Am. (accredited, chpt. pres. 1975), Publicity Club Chgo. (pres. 1966-67, Pub-Clubber award 1964), Chgo. Soc. Assn. Execs. (bd. dirs. 1985—). Home: 5245 Wright Terr Skokie IL 60077 Office: 1460 Renaissance Dr Park Ridge IL 60068

RAFFERTY, MILTON DALE, geoscientist, educator; b. Jewell County, Kans., Nov. 24, 1932; s. Peter James and Martha Grace (Clemens-Marshall) R.; m. Emma Jean Frink, July 28, 1956; children—Dale Jean, Ronald Patrick. B.A. in Geography, Kans. State U., 1959, B.S., 1960; M.S. in Sci. Edn., U. Utah, 1965; Ph.D. in Geography, U. Nebr.-Lincoln, 1970. Cert. tchr., Mo. Tchr., Peabody (Kans.) High Sch., 1960-61, Salina (Kans.) High Sch., 1961-64; prof. geoscis. S.W. Mo. State U., 1966-71, head dept. geoscis., 1972—, dir. Ctr. Resource Planning and Mgmt., 1984—. Author: The Ozarks: Land and Life, 1980; Historical Atlas of Missouri, 1982, Missouri: A Geography, 1983; The Ozarks Outdoors, 1985. Mem. Springfield (Mo.) Planning and Zoning Commn., 1980-83. Served with AUS, 1953-55. Mem. Assn. Am. Geographers, Nat. Council Geog. Edn., Mo. Council Geog. Edn. (past pres.), Sigma Xi, Gamma Theta Upsilon. Avocations: Canoeing; tennis. Home: 1351 E Rosebrier St Springfield MO 65804 Office: Dept Geoscis SW Mo State U 901 S National St Springfield MO 65804-0089

RAGHEB, MAGDI, engineering educator, researcher; b. Nov. 25, 1946; m. Barbara Rose Wesolek, Feb. 16, 1980. M.S., U. Wis., 1976, Ph.D., 1979. Vis. research scientist Brookhaven Nat. Lab., Upton, N.Y., summers 1975, 81; research assoc. Oak Ridge Nat. Lab., summer 1978; research asst. U. Wis.-Madison, 1973-78, postdoctoral assoc., 1979; asst. prof. nuclear engring. U. Ill., Urbana, 1979—. Engring. Distinction fellow, 1965-70. Mem. Am. Nuclear Soc., AAAS, Sci. Research Soc., N.Y. Acad. Scis., AAUP, Sigma Xi. Contbr. articles on engring. to profl. jours. Home: 401 Edgebrook Dr Champaign IL 61820 Office: 223 Nuclear Engring Lab U Ill Urbana IL 61801

RAGLE, RONALD ALAN, insurance agency executive; b. Kansas City, Mo., Jan. 5, 1957; s. John W. and Lenora Irene (Gilgour) R.; m. Pamela S. Dammon, Apr. 4, 1980. Pres. Ragle Ins. Inc., Kearney, Mo., 1982—. Mem. fin. bd. No. Hills Baptist Ch., 1984—. Mem. Kearney C. of C. (bd. dirs. 1984-85). Avocations: raising and showing registered quarter horses. Home: Box 562 Kearney MO 64060 Office: Ragle Ins Box 557 115 Washington Kearney MO 64060

RAGONE, DAVID VINCENT, university president; b. N.Y.C., May 16, 1930; s. Armando Frederick and Mary (Napier) R.; m. Katherine H. Spaulding, Dec. 18, 1954; children—Christine M., Peter V. S.B., MIT, 1951, S.M., 1952, Sc.D., 1953. Asst. prof. chem. and metall. engring. U. Mich., 1953-57, assoc. prof., 1957-61, prof., 1961-62, dean Coll. Engring., 1972-80; with Gen. Atomic div. Gen. Dynamics, 1962-67; Alcoa prof. metallurgy Carnegie-Mellon U., 1967-69, prof. engr., 1969-70, assoc. dean Sch. Urban and Pub. Affairs, 1969-70; dean Thayer Sch. Engring., Dartmouth Coll., 1970-72; pres. Case Western Res. U., Cleve., 1980—; dir. Cleve.-Cliffs Iron Co., Nat. City Corp., Augat Inc., B.F. Goodrich Co., SIFCO Industries Inc.; trustee Mitre Corp. Trustee Greater Cleve. Roundtable, Henry Luce Found. Named Outstanding Young Engr. Engring. Soc. Detroit, 1957. Mem. AAAS, Nat. Soc. Profl. Engrs., AIME, Am. Soc. for Metals, Am. Chem. Soc. Clubs: Cosmos (Washington); Union (Cleve.). Contbr. articles to profl. jours.; patentee in field. Office: Case Western Res Univ 2040 Adelbert Rd Cleveland OH 44106

RAGOTZKIE, ROBERT AUSTIN, oceanography educator, research administrator; b. Albany, N.Y., Sept. 13, 1924; s. Robert William and Edith Nina (VanWormer) R.; m. Elizabeth Margaret Post, Sept. 27, 1949; children—Peter, Kim, Susan. B.S. in Biology, Rutgers U., 1948, M.S. in Sanitation, 1950; Ph.D. in Meteorology-Zoology, U. Wis., 1953. From asst. prof. to assoc. prof. biology U. Ga., Sapelo Island, 1954-59; from asst. prof. to prof. meteorology U. Wis., Madison, 1959—, dir. Sea Grant Inst., 1968—. Editor: Man and the Marine Environment, 1983. Served to 2d lt. USAF, 1943-45, PTO. Fellow AAAS; mem. Am. Meteorol. Soc., Am. Geophys. Union, Am. Soc. Limnology and Oceanography, Informational Assn. Great Lakes Research (past pres.), Sigma Xi. Office: Sea Grant Inst U Wis 1800 University Ave Madison WI 53705

RAHIMAN, RAHIM ABDUL, auditor; b. India, Oct. 19, 1938; s. Masthanrowther Abdul and Sarah Ammah (Muhagamadu) R.; came to U.S., 1964, naturalized, 1973; B.C.S., U. Madras, India, 1964; M.B.A., U. Detroit, 1966; m. Victoria Ancog, Dec. 18, 1965; 1 son, Jacob Sr. computer auditor Bank of the Commonwealth, Detroit, 1966-68; mgr. internal audit Blue Cross-Blue Shield of Mich., Detroit, 1970-74; gen. auditor, bank officer First Nat. Bank of St. Paul, 1975-84; v.p. First Bank System, Mpls., 1983-85; internal auditor Met. Waste Control Commn., Minn., 1985—. Chmn. United Way, 1974-75. Certified internal auditor. Mem. Inst. of Internal Auditors (sec. Detroit chpt. 1972-74, v.p. 1974-75, bd. govs. Twin Cities chpt. 1975—), Bank Adminstrn. Inst., Met. Econ. Devel. Assn. (dir. 1979—, treas. 1980—). Home: 1330 W Skillman St Roseville MN 55113 Office: 332 Minnesota St St Paul MN 55101

RAI, AMARENDRA KUMAR, electron microscopist, researcher; b. Varanasi, India, Oct. 20, 1952; came to U.S., 1979; naturalized, 1982; s. Dina Nath and Asharfi R.; m. Urmila, June 29, 1971. I.Sc., Queens Coll., Varanasi, India, 1968; B.Sc., Gorakhpur U., Varanasi, 1970; M.Sc., Banaras Hindu U., Varanasi, 1972, Ph.D., 1977. Jr. research fellow Council Sci and Indsl. Research, Varanasi, 1972-79, sr. fellow, 1974-78; research assoc. N.C. State U., Raleigh, 1979-81; scientist Universal Energy Systems, Dayton, Ohio, 1981-83, sr. scientist, 1983—. Contbr. articles to profl. jours. Mem. Am. Phys. Soc. Avocations: outdoor activities, tennis, swimming, jogging. Office: Universal Energy Systems Inc 4401 Dayton Xenia Rd Dayton OH 45432

RAIFSNIDER, LAURETTA JANE, library administrator and consultant; b. Detroit, Aug. 30, 1947; d. Jack Wilfred and Margaret Pearl (Shannon) Eakin; m. Ronald Dean Raifsnider, June 28, 1968; children—Geoffrey Alan, Kristina Michelle. B.A., Ind. U., 1976, M.S. in Library and Info. Sci., 1981. Reference librarian Area 3 Area Library Services Authority, Ft. Wayne, Ind., 1980-82, adminstr., 1982—. Author: Louis Fortriede Shoes: A Century of Shoemaking in Fort Wayne, 1980; editor Tri-ALSA Newsletter, 1982—. Mem. ALA, Assn. Specialized and Coop. Library Agys., Ind. Library Assn. (cons. intellectual freedom com. 1982—), Phi Beta Mu. Home: 801 Maxine Dr Fort Wayne IN 46807 Office: Tri-ALSA 900 Webster St PO Box 2270 Fort Wayne IN 46801

RAIFSNIDER, RHONDA SENA, technical writer, consultant; b. Fremont, Ohio, Aug. 4, 1954; d. Harold Dale and Ruth Elanore (Thoma) R. B.A., Bowling Green State U., 1976, M.Rehab. Counseling, 1977, M.A., 1982. Rehab. counselor Betty Jane Rehab. Center, Tiffin, Ohio, 1977-78; instr. English composition Bowling Green (Ohio) State U., 1978-80, documentation specialist, systems dept., 1982-83; research assoc. Med. Coll. Ohio, Toledo, 1980-82; tech. writer M & M Prodns., Bowling Green, 1983—; cons. med. and tech. writing. Bd. dirs. Easter Seal Soc. Sandusky County, 1973—. Mem. N.W. Ohio Electron Microscopy Soc. (Outstanding Student Poster Presentation award 1980), Electron Microscopy Soc. Am., Soc. for Tech. Communication (cert. of merit Dayton-Miami Valley chpt. 1979), Sigma Xi (cert. of recognition Ohio Med.-Toledo Chpt. 1981). Contbr. articles to profl. jours. Home: 1335 Gordon Pl Fremont OH 43420

RAIMONDI, NICHOLAS, land surveying company executive, civil engineer; b. Triggiano, Bari, Italy, Sept. 15, 1926; came to U.S., 1949, naturalized, 1955; s. Michael and Domenica (Carbonara) R.; m. Estelle C. Raimonde, Sept. 8, 1951; children—Michael, Michelle, Robert. B.S. in C.E., Ill. Inst. Tech., 1955. Land surveyor Nat. Survey Service Inc. Chgo., 1954—, pres., 1970—. Contbr. articles to profl. jours. Bd. dirs. Village of Broadview Library, Ill., 1968; bd. dirs. Village of Bannockburn, Ill., 1984. Named Man of Yr., Italian C. of C., 1981. Fellow Congress on Surveying and Mapping, Ill. Regional Land Survey Assn. (pres. 1965, Life Mem. prize 1984), Chgo. Profl. Land Surveyors (registered land surveyor Ill., Wis., Iowa, Mich., Ind.), ASCE, Am. Right of Way Assn., Columbian Club (pres. 1978). Avocations: Photography; classical guitar. Home: 1850 Meadow Ln Bannockburn IL 60015 Office: Nat Survey Service Inc 126 W Grand Ave Chicago IL 60610

RAINEY, JOHN MARION, JR., medical educator; b. Atlanta, June 20, 1942; s. John Marion and Margaret (Ulrich) R.; m. Sarah Stroud, June 14, 1969; children—Michael Edward, Margaret Emily. B.A., Vanderbilt U., 1963, M.D., 1969, Ph.D., 1972. Intern, Vanderbilt Hosp., Nashville, 1970-71, resident, 1971-74; asst. prof. Wayne State U. Med. Sch., Detroit, 1974—; acting dir. research adminstrn. Lafayette Clinic, Detroit, 1975-80, dir. research adminstrn.,1980—, co-dir. anxiety disorders research program and anxiety disorders clinic, 1982—; lectr. pharm. cos. Editor: Anxiety Disorders, 1984; Pharmacological Models of Anxiety in Man, 1985. Recipient W.C. Menninger award Central Neuropsychiat. Assn., 1974. Mem. Am. Psychiat. Assn., Soc. Biol. Psychiatry, AMA, AAAS, Sigma Xi. Club: Grosse Pointe Hunt (Mich.). Home: 766 Balfour Grosse Pointe Park MI 48230 Office: Lafayette Clinic 951 E Lafayette Detroit MI 48207

RAINS, MERRITT NEAL, lawyer; b. Burlington, Iowa, July 26, 1943; s. Merritt and Esther Lucille (Lepper) R.; m. Jean Baldwin, July 26, 1980; 1 child, Robert Baldwin. B.A., U. Iowa, 1965; J.D., Northwestern U., 1968. Bar: Ohio 1968, U.S. Supreme Ct. 1979. Assoc. Arter & Hadden, Cleve., 1968-76, ptnr., 1976—. Contbr. to books. Trustee Cleve. Play House, 1981—, Legal Aid Soc. Cleve., 1981-84, Citizens League Greater Cleve., 1983—. Served with U.S. Army, 1968-70. Mem. Def. Research Inst., Ohio Assn. Civil Trial Attys., ABA, Bar Assn. Greater Cleve. (chmn. young lawyers sect. 1975-76, chmn. continuing legal edn. com. 1974-75, cert. of merit 1975), Phi Beta Kappa, Omicron Delta Kappa, Phi Delta Phi. Democrat. Clubs: Cleve. Skating, Cleve. Play House, City. Office: Arter & Hadden 1100 Huntington Bldg Cleveland OH 44115

RAIS, KATHLEEN, entrepreneur; b. Huntington, N.Y., Aug. 24, 1955; d. Edward and Dorothy Anne (Filomena) R. B.A., Ind. U., 1978, M.L.S., 1982. Owner/mgr. K. Rais-Books, Phila., 1978—; founding ptnr. Wolk & Rais, Inc., Phila. and N.Y.C., 1980—; asst. dir. Arts Adminstrn., Bloomington, Ind., 1982-84; cons. Terhune Mus., Wayne, N.J., 1978—. Author: Albert Payson Terhune (bibliography), 1984; also articles. Mem. Dog Writers Assn. Am., Dog Mus. Am., Friends of Lilly Library, Bloomington Kennel Club, Greater Phila. Dog Fanciers, N.Y. Hist. Soc., Hist. Soc. Pa., Collie Club Am., Keeshond Club Am. Democrat. Avocations: writing and hist. research; dog breeding and showing; sailing; antiques; trains; tennis.

RAITHEL, FREDERICK J., information system specialist; b. Jefferson City, Mo., Nov. 20, 1949; s. Herbert C. and Mildred (Kemper) R. B.A. in Philosophy, Lincoln U., 1972; M.A. in Library Info. Sci., U. Mo., 1973. Asst. reference librarian Mo. State Library, Jefferson City, 1974; reference librarian Daniel Boone Regional Library, Columbia, Mo., 1974-78; network coordinator Mid-Mo. Library Network, Columbia, 1978-81; head access services U. Mo. Libraries, Columbia, 1981-84; info. system research analyst, dept. agrl. econs. U. Mo., 1984—; dir. Mid-Mo. Library Network, Columbia, 1984—; chmn. Automation Tech. Com. of Mo. Libraries Network Bd., 1983-86; pres. U. Mo. Sch. Library Info Sci Alumni Assn., 1977-79; cons. Mem. ALA, Mo. Library Assn. (founder/organizer computer info. tech. com.). Contbr. articles to profl. jours. Home: 501H Columbia Dr Columbia MO 65201 Office: Mid-Mo Library Network 100 W Broadway Columbia MO 65201

RAITT, JILL, educator; b. Los Angeles, May 1, 1931; d. Arthur Taylor and Lorna Genevieve (Atherton) R.; B.A., in Philosophy, San Francisco Coll. Women, 1953, M.A. in English, 1964; M.A. in Theology, Marquette U., 1967; M.A., U. Chgo, 1967, Ph.D., 1970. Instr., then asst. prof. theology San Francisco Coll. Women, 1963-64, Immaculate Heart Coll., Hollywood, Calif., 1967-68, St. Xavier Coll., Chgo., 1966-68; asst. prof. program religious studies U. Calif.-Riverside, 1969-73; assoc. prof. history theology Duke Div. Sch., 1973-81; prof., chmn. dept. religious studies U. Mo., Columbia, 1981—; Alexander Robertson lectr. U. Glasgow, Scotland, 1985. Contbr. articles and revs. to profl. religious jours. Faculty fellow U. Calif.-Riverside, 1970; NEH fellow, 1975-76; Radcliffe Inst. fellow, 1975-76; Duke Research Council fellow, 1975; U. Chgo. fellow, 1968-69; Humanities Inst. grantee, 1972-73. Mem. Am. Acad. Religion (sec. Western region, 1972-73, nat. sec., 1972-75, nat. pres. 1980-81, assoc. dir. 1981-83), Friends of Reformation Research (sec.). Roman Catholic. Office: Dept Religious Studies 416 GCB U Mo Columbia MO 65211

RAJAGOPAL, ADIKKAN OANTHAN, anesthesiologist; b. Trichy, Madras, India, Mar. 27, 1941; came to U.S., June, 1972; s. Lakshmanan, Adikkan (Patchaiammal) O.; m. Vasantha Bai, Nov. 7, 1965; children—Ravi, Suresh. M.B.B.S., U. Madras, 1962. Diplomate Am. Bd. Anesthesiology. Practice medicine specializing in anesthesiology, Coimbatore Med. Coll. Hosp., Madras, India, 1967-72; intern Altoona Hosp., Pa., 1972-73; resident in anesthesia, U. Ill., Chgo., 1973-75; attending in anesthesia Met. Gen. Hosp., Cleve., 1975-76; practice medicine specializing in anesthesia St. Lukes Hosp., Saginaw, Mich., 1976—, chmn. dept. anesthesia, 1983—. Century mem. Lake Huron Area council Boy Scouts Am., 1981. Mem. Am. Soc. Anesthesiologists, Mich. Soc. Anesthesiologists, Internat. Anesthesia Research Soc., Mich. State Med. Soc., Saginaw County Med. Soc. Hindu. Club: Germania. Avocations: gardening; swimming; fishing; tennis. Home: 5482 Overhill Dr Saginaw MI 48603

RAJCHEL, JAMES MICHAEL, educational administrator; b. East Chicago, Ind., June 7, 1946; s. Joseph Aloysius and Lottie Harriet (Wajda) R.; B.Music Edn., VanderCook Coll. Music, Chgo., 1968; M.Ed., Loyola U., Chgo., 1973; Ed.S., Purdue U., 1982; postgrad. Northern Ill. U.; m. Kathleen Marie Kogut, Aug. 3, 1968; children—Bonnie Marie, Deborah Ann. Dir. bands Sch. Dist. #155, Calumet City, Ill., 1968-78; prin. Woodrow Wilson Elem. Sch. and dist. spl. edn. coordinator, 1978—, now spl. edn. and gifted edn. coordinator Dist. 155. Supt., Sch. of Christian Living, St. Michael The Archangel Polish Nat. Cath. Ch., East Chicago, 1969-78, chmn. parish com., 1981-82; trustee VanderCook Coll. Music. Recipient grad. scholarship Kappa Delta Pi, 1985. Mem. Ill. Prins. Assn., Ill. Assn. Supervision and Curriculum Devel., Assn. Supervision and Curriculum Devel., Am. Fedn. Musicians, VanderCook Coll. Music Alumni Assn. (pres. 1982-84), Phi Delta Kappa, Kappa Delta Pi (v.p. Northern Ill. U. chpt. 1985-86). Home: 4814 Baring Ave East Chicago IN 46312 Office: Woodrow Wilson Sch Wentworth Ave and Memorial Dr Calumet City IN 60409

RAJENDRAN, NARAYANAN, engineer, researcher; b. Nachiapuram, India, June 27, 1948; came to U.S., 1972; s. Karuppiah Narayanan and Nachammai (Nachiappan) R.; m. Thillai Sithambaram, Aug. 21, 1975; children—Saravan, Karthik. B.Engring., U. Madras, 1969; M.S., SUNY-Buffalo, 1974, Ph.D., 1977. Engr. Ill. Inst. Tech. Research Inst., Chgo., 1978—. Inventor grease filter. Contbr. tech. articles to publs. Hindu. Advocations: tennis; chess; reading. Home: 6611 Maxwell Dr Woodridge IL 60517 Office: ITT Research Inst 10 W 35th St Chicago IL 60616

RAJU, NIRANJANA, physician; b. Davangere, Karnataka, India, Aug. 27, 1952; came to U.S., 1976; d. Malalkere and Parwathamma Ramappa; m. Rekha Raju, July 28, 1980. M.D., JJM Med. Coll., Davanegere, 1974; postgrad. internal medicine St. Vincent/Yale Affiliate, Bridgeport, Conn., 1977-80. Diplomate Am. Bd. Internal Medicine. Intern, Bowring Hosp., Bangalore, India, 1974-75, resident in medicine, 1975-76; resident in pathology St. Raphael Hosp., New Haven, Conn., 1976-77; resident in medicine St. Vincent/Yale Affiliate, Bridgeport, Conn., 1977-80; pvt. practice medicine, Ste. Genevieve, Mo., 1980—; cons. internal medicine and cardiology Ste. Genevieve County Meml. Hosp., 1980—. Mem. Ste. Genevieve-Perry County Med. Soc. (sec. 1984), AMA, Mo. State Med. Soc., Ste. Genevieve Med. Soc. Clubs: Rotary, Ste. Genevieve Golf. Avocations: Golfing, fishing. Home: Rural Route 2 Box 136 Lake Forest Estates Saint Genevieve MO 63670 Office: 990 Park Dr Saint Genevieve MO 63670

RAJU, PUTHANKURISSI SANKARANARAYAN, marketing educator; b. Kerala State, India, Sept. 14, 1950; came to U.S., 1971; s. Puthankurissi Appuier and Rajam Sankaranarayan; B.Tech., Indian Inst. Tech., 1971; M.S. (univ. fellow), U. Ill., Champaign-Urbana, 1976, Ph.D., 1977; m. Revathy Athmaraman, July 9, 1978. Mem. faculty Pa. State U., 1975-80, asst. prof. mktg., 1976-80; asst. prof. mktg. U. Ill., Chgo., 1980—. Ford Found. fellow, 1977. Mem. Am. Mktg. Assn., Product Devel. and Mgmt. Assn., Assn. Consumer Research. Address: Dept Mktg Box 4348 U Ill Chicago IL 60680

RAJURKAR, KAMLAKAR PURUSHOTTAM, mechanical engineering educator; b. India, Jan. 6, 1942; came to U.S., 1975; s. Purushottam S. and Indira P. Rajurkar; m. Sanjivani K. Natu, Feb. 3, 1972; children—Piyush, Suneela. B.Sc., Vikram U., India, 1962, B.Engring. with honors, 1966; M.S., Mich. Tech. U., 1978, Ph.D., 1981. Lectr. mech. engring. Govt. Poly., Bhopal, India, 1966-75; grad. teaching and research asst. Mich. Tech. U., Houghton, 1975-81, asst. prof., 1981-83; assoc. prof. U. Nebr., Lincoln, 1983—. Contbr. articles to profl. jours. Mem. ASME, Soc. Mfg. Engrs., Soc. Exptl. Stress Analysis, Sigma Xi, Tau Beta Pi. Home: 1101 Driftwood Dr Lincoln NE 68510 Office: U Nebr 175 NH Lincoln NE 68588

RAKES, GANAS KAYE, finance and banking educator; b. Floyd, Va., May 2, 1938; s. Samuel D. and Ocie J. (Peters) R.; m. Mary Ann Simmons, Oct. 1, 1961; 1 child, Sabrina Darrow. B.S., Va. Tech. Inst., 1960, M.S., 1964; D.B.A., Washington U., St. Louis, 1971. Assoc. prof. commerce U. Va., Charlottesville, 1968-80; O'Bleness prof. fin. and banking Ohio U., Athens, 1980—. Contbr. articles to profl. publs. Bd. dirs. Athens Small Bus. Ctr., 1984—. Served to 1st lt. U.S. Army, 1961-63. Mem. Fin. Mgmt. Assn., Midwestern Bus. Adminstrs. Assn., Eastern Fin. Assn., Southeastern Cultural Arts Assn. (bd. dirs. 1982—). Republican. Episcopalian. Club: Farmington Country (Charlottesville). Lodge: Rotary. Avocation: sailing. Office: Ohio U Copeland Hall Athens OH 45701

RALSTON, LAWRENCE ROBERT, educator; b. Chgo., Dec. 3, 1930; s. Lloyd Frederick and Mary Margaret (Hunt) R.; m. Edna May LeBeda, Sept. 5, 1953; children—Jean Marie Ralston Wojtyla, Carol Ann. B.S., DePaul U., 1952; M.A., Govs. State U., 1976. Phys. edn. instr. Chgo. Park Dist., 1952-55; with Chgo. Bd. Edn., 1955—, recreation dir. Hanson Park 1982—, stadium dir., 1984—; cons. Pres.'s Commn. on Olympic Sports, 1975-76. Named to Speedskating Hall of Fame, 1984. Mem. Nat. Assn. Sports Ofcls., U.S. Internat. Speedskating Assn., Amateur Skating Union of the U.S. (exec. sec. 1972-84, program dir. 1984—), Amateur Skating Assn. Ill. Roman Catholic. Club: Forester. Author: Beginning Speedskating, 1981; feature writer Recreational Ice Skating Mag., 1978—, Racing Blade, 1972—.

RAMALEY, ROBERT FOLK, biochemistry educator; b. Colorado Springs, Colo., Dec. 15, 1935; s. Edward Jackson and Pauline (Folk) R.; m. Judith Aitken, Apr., 1966 (div. 1976); children—Alan, Andy. B.S., Ohio State U., 1959, M.S., 1962; Ph.D., U. Minn., 1964. Postdoctoral fellow dept. chemistry UCLA, 1964-66; asst. prof. microbiology Ind. U., Bloomington, 1966-72; assoc. prof. biochemistry U. Nebr. Med. Sch., Omaha, 1972-78, prof., 1978—. Contbr. articles to profl. jours., chpts. to books. Chmn. Blue River Quarter social concerns com. Soc. of Friends, 1970. Mem. Am. Soc. Microbiology (pres. state chpt. 1971-72, nat. lectr. 1979), Am. Soc. Biol. Chemists. Home: 1517 N Happy Hollow Blvd Omaha NE 68104 Office Dept Biochemistry U Nebr Med Sch 42d and Dewey Omaha NE 68105

RAMAMURTI, KRISHNAMURTI, research chemist, state government official; b. Erthangal, India, Nov. 11, 1919, came to U.S., 1954, naturalized, 1971; s. S.V. Krishnamurti and Kamakshi Ammal; m. Rajalakshmi Ammal, May 23, 1945; children—Chandramouli, Sridar, Suresh, Lila. B.Sc. with 1st class honors, Madras U., 1937; M.A. with 1st class honors, Annamalai U., India, 1940; M.S. in Nutrition, Columbia U., 1955; D.Ed. in Nutrition Edn. Columbia U., 1956; M.Sc.Tech. in Indsl. Biochemistry, Manchester (Eng.) U., 1960; Ph.D. in Foods and Nutrition, Kans. State U., 1975. Asst. prof. chemistry Birla Coll., Pilani, India, 1948-50, assoc. prof. chemistry, 1950-52, prof., 1952-54; teaching asst. chemistry Columbia U., 1954-55, research assoc. AEC Research team, 1955-56; lectr. organic chemistry Coll. Sci. and Tech., Manchester U., 1957, sr. research fellow in biochemistry, 1957-60; sci. officer Central Food Technological Research Inst., Mysore, India, 1961-63; prof. chemistry, chmn. dept. Faculty of Sci., U. Libya, Tripoli, 1963-71; lectr. in nutrition Bklyn. Coll., CUNY and Kings County Med. Ctr., 1971-72; grad. research asst. dept. foods and nutrition Kans. State U., 1972-75; research chemist, head chem. research unit Bur. Materials and Research, Kans. Dept. Transp., Topeka, 1976—, project leader federally coordinated research program, 1983—. Gold medalist Madras U., 1937; Seagram's Inc. Internat. fellow, 1950; Pres.'s scholar Columbia U., 1956. Fellow Royal Soc. Chemistry, Am. Inst. Chemists; hon. corr. mem. Royal Soc. Arts (London); mem. Nutrition Soc. London, Inst. Biology London, India Assn. Topeka, Phi Upsilon Omicron. Contbr. articles to sci. jours. Home: 3101F Randolph Ave Topeka KS 66611 Office: Kansas Dept Transp 2300 Van Buren St Topeka KS 66611

RAMASWAMI, DEVABHAKTUNI, chemical engineer; b. Pedapudi, India, Apr. 4, 1933; came to U.S., 1958, s. Veeriah and Rangamma Devabhaktuni; m. Vijayalakshmi, June 30, 1967; 1 child, Srikrishna. B.Sc., Andhra U., 1953, M.Sc., 1954, D.Sc., 1958; Ph.D., U. Wis., 1961. Research scholar Andhra U., Waltair, India, 1954-56, Indian Inst. Tech., Kharagpur, 1956-57; asst. prof. Benaras Hindu U., Varanasi, India, 1957-58; research asst. U. Wis., Madison, 1958-61; research engr. IBM Corp., San Jose, Calif., 1961-62; chem. engr. Argonne Nat. Lab., Ill., 1962—. Contbr. numerous articles to profl. jours. Patentee in field. Am. Chem. Soc. Disting. and Promising Asian in U.S. award Asia Found., 1960. Fellow Am. Inst. Chem. Engrs. Avocation: photography. Home: 826 Columbia Ln Darien IL 60559 Office: Engring Div Argonne National Lab 9700 S Cass St Argonne IL 60439

RAMELLO, RICHARD J., lawyer; b. Oak Park, Ill., June 23, 1954; s. Elmo Joseph and Alfreda (Morez) R.; m. Kimberly Anne Scoville, May 17, 1980; children—Natalie Anne, Christine Scoville. B.S., Bradley U., 1976; J.D., DePaul U., 1979. Bar: Ill. 1979, U.S. Dist. Ct. (no. dist.) Ill. 1979, U.S. Ct. Appeals (7th cir.) 1979. Ptnr. LaSusa & Storino, Ltd., Des Plaines, Ill., 1979—; asst. prosecutor Village of Rosemont, Ill., 1979—; prosecutor Village of Glendale Heights, Ill., 1980—. Mem. Assn. Trail Lawyers Am., Ill. Trial Lawyers Assn., Ill. State Bar Assn., N.W. Suburban Bar Assn. Office: LaSusa & Storino Ltd 2340 Des Plaines Ave Des Plaines IL 60018

RAMER, JAMES LEROY, civil engineer; b. Marshalltown, Iowa, Dec. 7, 1935; s. LeRoy Frederick and Irene (Wengert) R.; student U. Iowa, 1953-57; M.S. in Civil Engring., Washington U., St. Louis, 1976, M.A. in Polit. Sci., 1978; postgrad. U. Mo., Columbia, 1984—; m. Jacqueline L. Orr, Dec. 15, 1957; children—Sarah T., Robert H., Eric A., Susan L. Civil engr. U.S. State Dept., Del Rio, Tex., 1964; project engr. H. B. Zachry Co., San Antonio, 1965-66; civil and constrn. engr. U.S. Army C.E., St. Louis, 1967-76, tech. advisor for planning and nat. hydropower coordinator, 1976-78, project mgr. for EPA constrn. grants, Milw., 1978-80; chief architecture and engring. HUD, Indpls., 1980-81; pvt. practice civil engring., 1981—; civil design and pavements engr. Whiteman AFB, Mo., 1982—, tech. adv. C.E., 1982—; cattle and grain farmer, 1982—; expert witness; adj. faculty civil engring. Washington U., 1968-78, U. Wis., Milw., 1978-80. Ga. Mil. Coll., Whiteman AFB.; adj. research engr. U. Mo., Columbia, 1985—. Mem. ASCE, Nat. Soc. Profl. Engrs., Soc. Am. Mil. Engrs., AAUP. Lutheran. Club: Optimists Internat. Home: Route 1 Box 51 Fortuna MO 65034 Office: Route 1 Box 50AA Fortuna MO 65081

RAMEY, DON THOMAS, college administrator; b. Covington, Ky., Mar. 23, 1949; s. Walter Thomas and Nellie (Adams) R.; m. Lora L. Billups, Dec. 28, 1974; 1 son, Evan Joseph. B.A., Eastern Ky. U., 1972, M.A., 1974; Ed.D., Ind. U., 1981. Adminstr., counselor Eastern Ky. U., Richmond, 1974-75, asst. dir. student activities, 1975-78; administrv. asst. Ind. U., Bloomington, 1978-80; assoc. dir. residential life U. Mo., Columbia, 1980-84; v.p. student services Franklin Coll., Ind., 1984—; editor, bd. dirs. Ctr. Study Coll. Fraternity, Bloomington, 1983—. Edn. chmn. Teke Ednl. Found., Indpls., 1984, 85; advisor Jr. Achievement, Franklin, 1984. Mem. Am. Assn. Counseling and Devel., Am. Coll. Personnel Assn. (directorate commn. IV 1980-84), Nat. Assn. Student Personnel Adminstrs., Am. Soc. Tng. and Devel. Republican. Lutheran. Avocations: golf; woodworking; spectator sports; piano. Office: Franklin Coll Ind Franklin IN 46131

RAMEY, ROY RICHARD, ceramic engineer; b. Kansas City, Mo., July 11, 1947; s. Richard Basil and Sarah Elise (Atkins) R.; m. Nancy Irene Wiggins, Jan. 24, 1970; children—Jennifer Lea, Michael Richard Thomas. B.S. in Ceramic Engring., U. Mo.-Rolla, 1970, M.S., 1972, Ph.D., 1974. Research engr. Inland Steel Co., East Chicago, Ind., 1974-79; sr. research mgr. A.P. Green Refractories Co., Mexico, Mo., 1979—. Mem. Am. Ceramic Soc., ASTM, Nat. Inst. Ceramic Engrs., Ceramic Edntl. Council. Avocation: family genealogy. Home: 1909 Osage Ave Mexico MO 65265 Office: AP Green Refractories Co Green Blvd Mexico MO 65265

RAMICK, CHARLES CONRAD, computer scientist; b. St. Louis, Nov. 5, 1946; s. Conrad Coburn and Marie Terese (Lodewyck) R.; m. Katherine Jameson, Oct. 1, 1983; children—Charles Coburn, Allison Lee; stepchildren—Jeffery Jameson, Nancy Jameson. A.A., Prairie State Coll., 1970, B.A., Governors State U., 1979; M.S., Nat. Coll. Edn., 1984. Mgr. mgmt. info. systems Brummer div. Borg-Warner Corp., Frankfort, Ill., 1973-77; mgr. prodn. control Folger Adam Co. Joliet, Ill., 1977-79; rep. communications systems Ill. Bell Co., Hinsdale, Ill., 1979-83; tech. cons. AT&T Info. Systems, Inc., Chgo., 1983—. Pres., Dist. 161 Bd. Edn., 1977-82; mem. Ill. State Bd. Edn. evaluation team, 1982; treas. HFHS Found., 1985. Mem. Data Processing Mgmt. Assn., Ill. Assn. Supervision and Curriculum Devel., IEEE. Republican. Office: 8398 Mississippi St Merrillville IN 46410

RAMMOHAN, MEENAKSHI, dietitian; b. Madras, India, May 14, 1943; came to U.S., 1965; d. Kumarappan and Lakshmi (Venkatachalam) Nagappan; m. Alagappa Rammohan Aug. 18, 1962; children—Parvathi, Chidambaram. B.S., U. Madras, 1961, M.S., 1963. Adminstrv. and therapeutic dietitian Bethany Methodist Hosp., Chgo., 1966-68; therapeutic dietitian Passavant Meml. Hosp., Chgo., 1968-72, research dietitian, 1972-73; clin. dietitian Northwestern Meml. Hosp., Chgo., 1973-81, research and renal dietitian, 1981—; cons. dietitian, nursing homes, Chgo., 1968-77; adj. faculty No. Ill. U., DeKalb, 1972—. Mem. Am. Dietetic Assn., Ill. Dietetic Assn., Chgo. Dietetic Assn., Ill. Council Renal Nutrition, Nat. Assn. Research Nurses and Dietitians. Mem. Vivekanandha Vedantha Soc. Author: Vegetarian Wheel, 1979; (with Stone) Fat Chance, 1980. Home: 1316 W Fargo St Apt 310 Chicago IL 60626 Office: 303 E Superior St Passavant Pavillion Room 470 Chicago IL 60611

RAMPERSAD, OLIVER RONALD, microbiologist, educator; b. Trinidad, W.I., Jan. 27, 1921; s. Soan Gocool and Roopnarinesingh; came to U.S., 1944; m. Peggy Ann Snellings, Mar. 19, 1955; 1 child, Gita. Oxford & Cambridge Higher Cert., St. Mary's Coll., Trinidad, 1936; Ph.B., U. Chgo., 1946; M.S., 1954, Ph.D., 1961. Teaching asst. in microbiology U. Chgo., 1954-61, research assoc. physiology and immunology, 1961-73, sr. technologist dept. pathology-clin. chemistry, 1973—. Bd. dirs. Friends of Internat. House, Chgo., Youth Council, Trinidad; mem. Ind. Voters Ill. Mem. Fedn. Am. Socs. for Exptl. Biology, AAAS, Am. Soc. Microbiologists, Sigma Xi. Hindu. Contbr. articles to profl. jours. Home: 5531 S Kenwood Ave Chicago IL 60637 Office: 950 E 59th St Chicago IL 60637

RAMSAY, CLAUDIA GRACE, lawyer; b. Albany, Ga., June 9, 1938; d. Frank Otis and Fannie Magdaline (Gillespie) R.; 1 child, Carey Ramsay Mumaw. B.Gen. Edn., U. Nebr., 1966; M.A., U. Ga., 1972; J.D., Washburn U., 1982. Bar: Kans. 1982, U.S. Dist. Ct. Kans. 1982. Enlisted U.S. Army, 1958, advanced through grades to lt. col., ret., 1978; spokeswoman U.S. Army, Pentagon, Washington, 1972-75; mem. grad. faculty U.S. Army Command and Gen Staff Coll., Fort Leavenworth, Kans., 1976-78; student tax and estate planning So. Meth. U., Dallas, 1982-83; dep. county atty., Cowley County, Winfield, Kans., 1983—; mil. advisor Sec. of Army's Fed. Women's Program Steering Group, Pentagon, 1975-78; retiree mobilization designee U.S. Army, 1978—. Author: Army Women, 1976-77. Decorated Legion of Merit, Meritorious Service medal with oak leaf cluster; recipient Am. Jurisprudence award Lawyers Coop Pub. Co., Bancroft-Whitney Co., 1981. Mem. ABA, Soc. Profl. Journalists, Am. Soc. Profl. Adminstrn., Women's Equity Action League, Assn. U.S. Army (sec. Southside Va. chpt. 1969-70, cert. of appreciation 1965), DAR (chmn. good citizen com. 1977), Nat. Soc. Dames of Ct. of Honor, Am. Legion. Republican. Methodist. Home: 2800 E 12th St Apt El Winfield KS 67156 Office: Dep County Atty Courthouse Winfield KS 67156

RAMSELL, RODNEY EUGENE, fisheries biologist, editor; b. Eldora, Iowa, May 29, 1953; s. Truman John and Wilma Mae (Reisinger) R.; m. Roberta Carol Ackland, Aug. 30, 1975. B.S., U. Minn., 1984. Editor mag. Muskie, Muskies Inc., St. Paul, 1977—; nat. dir. tagging Muskies Inc., contbng. author articles, 1977—. Recipient Service Recognition award Muskies Inc., 1981, Commendation award, 1976, Research Sponsership award, 1979. Mem. Am. Fisheries Soc., Outdoor Writers Assn. Am., World Profl. Muskie Assn., Muskies Inc. Club: Fishing Hall of Fame. Avocations: muskellunge fishing, golf, baseball, pencil sketching, outdoor photography. Office: Muskies Inc PO Box 65731 St Paul MN 55165

RAMSEY, DAVID SELMER, hospital executive; b. Mpls., Feb. 19, 1931; s. Selmer A. and Esther D. (Dahl) R.; m. Elinor Corfield, Aug. 15, 1953; children—Scott, Stewart, Thomas. B.S., U. Mich., 1953, M.S. in Microbiology, 1954, M.H.A., 1962. Research asst. Detroit Inst. Cancer Research, 1954-60; asst. adminstr. Harper Hosp., Detroit, 1962-68, assoc. adminstr., 1968-72; exec. v.p. Iowa Meth. Med. Ctr., Des Moines, 1972-83, pres., 1983—; chmn. bd. Des Moines Pastoral Counseling, 1981-84. Bd. dirs. Arts and Recreation Council Des Moines, 1983—; group chair United Way, 1984. Fellow Am. Coll. Hosp. Adminstrs.; mem. Iowa Hosp. Assn. (dir. 1974—), Am. Hosp. Assn. (del. 1982—). Republican. Presbyterian. Clubs: Des Moines, Wkonda (Des Moines). Lodge: Rotary. Avocations: golf; tennis; photography. Home: 2825 Caulder Des Moines IA 50321 Office: Iowa Meth Med Ctr 1200 Pleasant St Des Moines IA 50308

RAMSEY, F. W., bank executive; Exec. v.p. Ameritrust Co., Cleve., Office: Ameritrust Co 900 Euclid Ave Cleveland OH 44101*

RAMSEY, GREGORY JAY, electronics company executive; b. Chgo., Oct. 1, 1953; s. Roy Holt and Gladys Catherine (Shipman) R.; m. Janet Jean Huston, Oct. 23, 1976; children—Nathaniel, Justin. B.S., Iowa State U., 1976. Elec. engr. Motorola, Inc., Schaumburg, Ill., 1976-79, staff engr., 1979-80, sect. mgr., 1980-81, engring. mgr., 1981-84, chief engr, 1984-85; v.p., dir. engring. Digital Appliance Controls, Inc., Schaumburg, 1985—. Patentee in field. Del., Republican Party conv., Des Moines, 1972; mem. social action com. Congl. Ch., Arlington Heights, Ill., 1982. Mem. IEEE, Chgo., Jr. Assn. Commerce (sec. 1978-79), Am. Radio Relay League. Office: Digital Appliance Controls Inc 2401 Hassell Rd Hoffman Estates IL 60195

RAMSEY, LELAND KEITH, petroleum engineer; b. Topeka, May 31, 1952; s. Keith G. and Darlene (Berndt) R.; m. Kimberly M. Milner, Mar. 31, 1979; 1 child, Jessica Ray. B.S., Kans. State U., 1974. Field engr. Dowell div. Dow Chem. Corp., Rock Springs, Wyo., 1975-78, dist. engr., Williston, N.D., 1978-80, sr. dist. engr., 1980-81; dist. sales supr. Dowell/Schlumberger Inc., Williston, 1981—. Mem. Soc. Petroleum Engrs. (chpt. membership chmn. 1982-83, sec.-treas. 1983-84, vice-chmn., 1984-85), Sooner Oilmen's Club, Am. Assn. Petroleum Geologists, Am. Petroleum Inst. Republican. Baptist. Lodge: Elks. Avocations: golf; racquetball. Home: 618 15th Ave W Williston ND 58801 Office: PO Box 879 Williston ND 58801

RAMSEY, RANDALL SCOTT, optometrist; b. Long Beach, Calif., Apr. 3; s. Carl O. Ramsey and Mary Elena (Caldwell) Hotvedt. B.S., Wichita State U., 1971; O.D., So. Coll. Optometry, 1975. Lic. optometrist, Kans. Optometrist, Eye Clinic of Wichita, Kans., 1975-82; owner, ptnr. Blackman, Ramsey & Lentz O.D., P.A., Wichita, 1982—. Mem. Am. Optometric Assn., Kans. Optometric Assn., Am. Optometric Found., Better Vision Inst., Heart of Am. Contact Lens Soc. Methodist. Avocation: golfing. Office: 5900 E Central St Wichita KS 67208

RAMSEY, ROBERT BRUCE, plans and development manager; b. Moline, Ill., Jan. 4, 1944; s. Ralph Samuel and Florence Isabelle (Adams) R.; m. Penny Tina Germain, June 10, 1967; children—Anne Michelle, Sarah Elizabeth. B.A., Augustana Coll., 1966; Ph.D., St. Louis U., 1971; postdoctoral tng. U. London, 1971-73; M.B.A., St. Louis U., 1984. Asst. prof. St. Louis U., 1972-77, assoc. prof. neurology, 1977-79; mktg. specialist, mgr. clin. investigations Lancer div. Sherwood Med. Corp., St. Louis, 1979-81, product mgmt., 1981-83, product mgr. Argyle div., 1983-84, new bus. devel. mgr., 1984-85; mgr. plans and devel. McDonnell-Douglas Health Systems Co., St. Louis, 1985—. Contbr. articles to sci. publs. Mem. Am. Soc. Biol. Chemists, Biochem. Soc. (Eng.), Am. Chem. Soc., Am. Soc. Neurosci., N.Y. Acad. Sci. Republican. Presbyterian. Home: 415 N Price Olivette MO 63132 Office: McDonnell-Douglas Health Systems 600 McDonnell Blvd Hazelwood MO 63042

RAMSEY, STEVEN BARRY, developer, builder; b. Shelby, N.C., Sept. 1, 1940; s. Arcey and Edna (McFarland) R.; m. Oct. 2, 1960; children—Alan T., Christopher B., John Barton. Student, Lenoir Rhine Coll., 1961, Chgo. Tech. Coll., 1965. With A.A. Ramsey & Son, Shelby, N.C., 1954-59; engring. clk. Daniels Constrn., Greenville, S.C., 1959-61; pres. Ramsey Constrn. Co., Shelby, N.C., 1961-62; salesman Liberty Life Ins. Co., Greenville, S.C., 1962-64; estimator F.N. Thompson, Co., Charlotte, N.C., 1965-69; project mgr. Ervin Co., Charlotte, N.C., 1969-74; project mgr. Krause Anderson Inc., Mpls., 1974-79; pres., treas. Haven Enterprises, Inc., Minnetonka, Minn., 1979—. Mem. Gen. Constrn. of Am., Assoc. Gen. Contractors of Am. Republican. Baptist. Club: Mpls. Country. Lodge: Lions (pres. 1984). Office: Haven Enterprises Inc 14442 Excelsior Blvd Minnetonka MN 55345

RAMSEY, WILLIAM CRITES, JR., lawyer; b. Omaha, July 31, 1912; s. William Crites and Mary Elizabeth (Cook) R.; m. Mary Jane Kopperud, Mar. 24, 1942; children—Mary Laura Ramsey Foster, Barbara Lee, Carol Elizabeth, Julie Andrea Ramsey Cutright. A.B., Dartmouth Coll., 1934; LL.B., Harvard U., 1938. Bar: Nebr. 1938. Assoc. Spier, Ramsey, Ellick, Omaha, 1940-48; v.p., sec. Am. Rd. Equipment Co., Omaha, 1948-55; v.p. N.P. Dodge Co., Omaha, 1955-60; pres. Am. Savings Co., Omaha, 1960-75; ptnr. Fellman, Ramsey, Epstein, Omaha, 1975-85, Mitchell and Demerath, Omaha, 1985—. Dep. county atty. Douglas County, 1947; pres. Family Service Omaha, 1951-53, Urban League, Omaha, 1954-55, Nebr. State Bd. Edn., Lincoln, 1978-86; dir. Nat. Assn. State Bds. Edn., Alexandria, Va., 1985. Mem. Nebr. Bar Assn., Omaha Bar Assn., Nebr. Assn. Indsl. Loan Cos. (pres. 1960), Am. Assn. Indsl. Banks (dir. 1962-64). Democrat. Congregationalist. Lodge: Masons (master 1950-51). Avocations: tennis; squash; reading. Home: 6481 Cuming St Omaha NE 68132 Office: 440 Regency Pkwy Suite 150 Omaha NE 68114

RAMSTAD, JAMES M., state senator, lawyer; b. Jamestown, N.D., May 6, 1946; s. Marvin Joseph and Della Mae (Fode) R.; B.A., U. Minn., 1968; J.D. with honors, George Washington U., 1973. Adminstrv. asst. to speaker Minn. Ho. Reps., 1969; spl. asst. to Congressman Tom Kleppe, 1970; admitted to N.D. bar, D.C. bar, 1973, U.S. Supreme Ct. bar, 1976, Minn. bar, 1979; practiced in Jamestown, 1973, Washington, 1974-1978, Mpls., 1979—; mem. Minn. Senate, 1980—, asst. minority leader, 1983—; instr. Am. govt. Montgomery (Md.) Coll., 1974; adj. prof. Am. U., Washington, 1975-78. Bd. dirs. Children's Heart Fund, Northwest YMCA, Big Bros. of Mpls.; mem. Wayzata Area Chem. Health Commn. Served as 1st lt. U.S. Army Res., 1968-73. Mem. ABA Fed., Minn., Hennepin County, D.C., N.D. bar assns., George Washington Law Assn., U. Minn. Alumni Assn. (nat. dir.), Am. Legion, Plymouth Civic League, Twin West C. of C. (dir.), Phi Beta Kappa, Phi Delta Theta. Republican. Clubs: Mpls. Athletic, Lafayette, U. Minn. Alumni (past pres. Washington). Lodge: Lions. Home: 2618 Crosby Rd Wayzata MN 55391 Office: 123 State Office Bldg Saint Paul MN 55155

RAMSUE-SINGLETON, JOYCE ADALEEN, optometrist; b. Mocksville, N.C., June 17, 1956; d. Dave and Nellie Ruth (Holman) R.; m. Calvin Monroe Singleton, Jr., Apr. 10, 1982. Student U. N.C., 1974-77; B.S. in Visual Sci., Ill. Coll. Optometry, 1979, O.D., 1981. Cert. optometrist, N.C., Ohio, Ill. Optometrist, Kaiser Permanente Med. Ctr., Cleve., 1981—. Big sister Project Friendship, Cleve., 1984—; vol. Coventry Youth Ctr., Cleveland Heights, 1984—. Recipient Service award in vision care Chgo. Central City Optometric Soc., 1981; Advancement of Diagnostic Technique in optometry award Ohio Optometric Assn., 1984. Mem. Nat. Optometric Assn., Am. Optometric Assn. Democrat. Mem. Ch. of Christ. Avocations: racquetball; bike riding; traveling. Home: 3266 E Fairfax Rd Cleveland Heights OH 44118 Office: 19999 Rockside Rd Kaiser Med Offices Bedford OH 44146

RAMUNNO, LOUIS ANTHONY, educational administrator; b. Aliquippa, Pa., July 15, 1948; s. Salvatore and Mary Elizabeth (Bologna) R.; m. Kerry Lee Kowalski, June 5, 1971; children—Ross Edward, Mark Alan. B.S., Geneva Coll., 1970, M.Ed. Adminstrn., Westminster Coll., 1975. Instr. Washingtonville Elem. Sch., Leetonia, Ohio, 1970-71, Salem Jr. High Sch., Ohio, 1971-75; prin. McKinley Elem. Sch., Salem, 1975-77; adminstrv. dir. athletics Salem Schs. K-12, 1977-78; prin. Salem Jr. High Sch., 1978—; city superintendancy Youngstown State U., Ohio, 1983. Instr. St. Paul's Ch., Salem, 1972—; mem. adv. bd. Salvation Army, Salem, 1983—. Recipient Outstanding Young Educator award Jaycees, Salem, 1977. Mem. Ohio Assn. Secondary Sch. Adminstrs., Ohio Middle Sch. Educators Assn., Columbiana County Prins. Assn. Roman Catholic. Lodges: Kiwanis (2d v.p. 1984—), Elks (youth activities chmn. 1972—), K.C. Avocations: jogging; golf; gardening. Office: Salem Jr High Sch 230 N Lincoln Ave Salem OH 44460

RANCOUR, JOANN SUE, registered nurse; b. Elyria, Ohio, Nov. 10, 1939; d. Joseph and Ann (Donich) Sokol; diploma M.B. Johnson Sch. Nursing, 1960; B.S. in Profl. Arts, St. Josephs Coll., N. Windham, Maine, 1981; student in psychology Alfred Adler Inst., Chgo., 1976—, Lorain County Community Coll., 1973-75, Ursuline Coll., Cleve., 1976, Baldwin Wallace Coll., 1982; m. Richard Lee Rancour, July 29, 1961; children—Kathleen Ann, Donna Marie. Staff nurse Elyria Meml. Hosp., 1960-62, 72-75, head nurse psychiat. unit, 1975-79; sec-treas. Alfred Adler Inst. Cleve., 1978-79; detention home nurse Domestic Relations Ct. Lorain County, Elyria, Ohio, 1980; staff nurse VA Med. Center, Breckville, Ohio, 1981—. Active PTA, yearbook com., 1969-70, co-chmn. ways and means, 1971; Dem. poll worker, 1971-72; sec. St. Mary's Confrat. Christian Doctrine Program, 1970-71. Mem. Am. Nurses Assn. (cert. generalist practitioner psychiat. and mental health nursing practice), Ohio Nurses Assn., Am. Nurses Found., Alfred Adler Inst. Cleve., N.Am. Soc. Adlerian Psychology. Roman Catholic. Home: 205 Denison Ave Elyria OH 44035

RANCOURT, JOHN HERBERT, pharmaceutical company executive; b. Troy, N.Y., Aug. 10, 1946; s. Charles Dennis and Helen Mary (Keadin) R.; B.S. in Mgmt., Rensselaer Poly. Inst., 1968, M.S. in Mgmt., 1972, M.B.A., 1981; m. Susan Jane Koneski, Feb. 14, 1970; children—Karen Mary, John Herbert, Alison Jane, Elizabeth Anne, Maureen Ellen. Asst. to dir. research Rensselaer Poly. Inst., 1968-69; mgmt. trainee, buyer/purchasing agt., controller research div. Huyck Corp., Rensselaer, N.Y., 1969-74, corp. internat. project mgr., Wake Forest, N.C., 1974-76, adminstrv. service mgr. Formex div., 1976-77; sr. fin. analyst Abbott Labs., North Chicago, Ill., 1977-79, sect. mgr. sales acctg., 1979-80, mgr. fin. analysis, materials mgmt. div., 1980-82, mgr. fin. planning and analysis, pharm. products div., 1982-84; controller TAP Pharms subs. Abbott Labs., North Chicago, Ill., 1984—; instr. acctg. Coll. of Lake County, Grayslake, Ill., part-time, 1981—. Indian princess tribal leader YMCA, 1980—; solicitor United Way, 1981, 83. C.P.A., Ill.; cert. mgmt. acct. Mem. Nat. Assn. Accts., Am. Acctg. Assn., Am. Inst. C.P.A.s, Ill. C.P.A. Soc. Roman Catholic. Club: Liberty Road and Track. Home: 826 Furlong Dr Libertyville IL 60048 Office: Abbott Labs 14th and Sheridan Rd North Chicago IL 60064

RAND, PETER ANDERS, architect, association executive; b. Hibbing, Minn., Jan. 8, 1944; s. Sidney Anders and Dorothy Alice (Holm) R.; m. Nancy Ann Straus, Oct. 21, 1967; children—Amy, Dorothy. B.A., St. Olaf Coll., 1966; cert. Oslo Internat. Summer Sch., Norway, 1964; student U. Minn. Sch. Architecture, 1969-72. Registered architect, Minn. Designer, architect, dir. pub. relations Setter, Leach & Lindstrom, Inc., Mpls., 1972-78; dir. bus. devel. and head Eden Prairie Office, Archtl. Design Group, Inc., Minn., 1979-80; dir. mktg. and publs. Mpls. Soc. AIA, 1981-82, exec. dir., 1982—; pub. Architecture Minn. mag.; cons., archtl. designer. Chmn. bd. Project for Pride Living, 1980—; trustee Bethlehem Luth. Ch., 1980—, chmn. bd. trustees, 1985; mem. Minn. Ch. Ctr. Commn., 1981—, chmn., 1985; bd. dirs. Minn. Council of Chs., 1985—, Greater Mpls. Council of Chs., 1985—. Served with U.S. Army, 1966-69. Recipient honor award AIA Jour., 1981. Mem. AIA, Minn. Soc. AIA, Nat. Trust Hist. Preservation. Home: 1728 Humboldt Ave S Minneapolis MN 55403 Office: 314 Clifton Ave Minneapolis MN 55403

RANDALL, DICK, advertising and public relations company owner; b. Port Chester, N.Y., Nov. 12, 1945; s. Gene and Frances (Grandazzo) Cicatelli; B.A., Marquette U., 1967; m. Maureen Russell, Aug. 17, 1966; children—Gregory, Katharine. Writer, news reporter Sta. WISN-TV, Milw., 1966-67; news reporter, anchorman Sta. WEMP, Milw., 1967-70; consumer reporter, anchorman Sta. WISN-TV, Milw., 1970-77; pres. Aquarius Prodns., Inc., Waukesha, Wis., 1977—; adj. instr. Marquette U., 1973-78. Vice pres. parish council. St. Anthony on the Lake, Pewaukee, Wis. Served with USNR, 1968—. Mem. Am. Fedn. TV and Radio Artists, Milw. Advt. Club, Better Bus. Bur. Milw., Variety Club of Wis., Met. Milw. Assn. Commerce, Sigma Delta Chi, Roman Catholic. Home: W278 N2968 Rocky Point Rd Pewaukee WI 53072 Office: 280 Regency Ct Suite 200 Waukesha WI 53186

RANDALL, JAMES R., food products company executive; b. 1924; B.S. in Chem. Engring., U. Wis., 1948; married. Tech. dir. Cargill Inc., 1948-68; v.p. prodn. and engring. Archer-Daniels-Midland Co., Decatur, Ill., 1968-69, exec. v.p., 1969-75, pres., dir., 1975—. Served in U.S. Army, 1943-46. Office: Archer-Daniels-Midland Co 4666 Faries Pkwy Box 1470 Decatur IL 62525*

RANDALL, JOHN CARL, hospital official; b. Camden, N.J., July 12, 1949; s. Carl Eugene and Mary Elizabeth (Finck) R.; m. Barbara Jean Price, Oct. 30, 1971; children—Jonathan Edward, Shane William, Adam Gregory, Andrea Michal, Daniel Alan (dec.), Faith Ellen. Student Phila. Coll. Bible, 1968-71; cert. Nat. Exec. Housekeepers Assn., Akron U., 1982. Driver, salesman, Dy-Dee Services, Inc., Westmont, N.J., 1971-73; housekeeping-laundry mgr. Servicemasters Industries, Inc., Downers Grove, Ill., 1973-77; sta. mgr. Kirschner Bros. Oil Co., Inc., Haverford, Pa., 1977-78; unit mgr. ARA Services, Inc., Phila., 1978-80; dir. housekeeping and laundry Ashtabula (Ohio) Gen. Hosp., 1980-83; dir. housekeeping Lake County Hosps., Painesville and Willoughby, Ohio, 1983—; cons. Wooster Community Hosp. (Ohio); began housekeeping depts. Baptist East Hosp., Louisville, N.J. Rehab. Hosp., East Orange, Downstate Med. Ctr., Bklyn., Meml. Hosp. Roxborough, Pa., Burke Rehab. Ctr., White Plains, N.Y.; dir. housekeeping depts. Frankford Hosp., Phila., Burke Rehab. Ctr., Erie County Geriatric Ctr., Girard, Pa.; asst. dir. housekeeping Hopkins County Hosp., Madisonville, Ky., St. Christopher's Hosp. for Children, Phila. Named Resident Mgr. of Yr., Environ. Services Healthcare div. ARA Services, Inc., 1979. Mem. Nat. Exec. Housekeepers Assn. Office: Lake County Meml Hosps Painesville/Willoughby OH

RANDALL, SUSAN MANSAGER, sociology educator; b. Dell Rapids, S.D., June 22, 1948; d. Leland LeRoy and Vivian Geneva (Mansager) R.; m. Mark Dale Sanderson, Mar. 19, 1978; children—Randall, Alice. B.A., Augustana Coll., 1970; M.A., Boston Coll., 1974; Ph.D., Boston U., 1982. Tchr. English and speech Centerville High Sch., S.D., 1970-72; instr. sociology Middlesex Community Coll., Lexington, Mass., 1973-74, Garland Jr. Coll., Boston, 1973-75; legis. researcher Mass. Gen. Ct., Boston, 1975-77; asst. prof. sociology Augustana Coll., Sioux Falls, S.D., 1977—. Pres. bd. dirs. Family Service, Sioux Falls, 1980-85, Unitarian Universalist Fellowship, Sioux Falls, 1984—; mem. Bd. Adjustments, Sioux Falls, 1985; mem. edn. task force White House Conf. on Youth, Washington, 1970-71. Mem. Am. Sociol. Assn., Midwest Sociol. Soc., Rural Sociol. Soc., Nat. Women's Polit. Caucus, LWV, Dem. Forum. Democrat. Unitarian. Avocations: swimming, bicycling, interior design. Office: Dept Sociology Augustana Coll 29th and Summit Sioux Falls SD 57197

RANDALL, WILLIAM SEYMOUR, electric motor distribution company executive; b. Champaign, Ill., July 5, 1933; s. Glenn Seymour and Audrey (Honnold) R.; B.S., Ind. State U., 1959; m. Carol Mischler, Aug. 23, 1958; children—Steve, Cathy, Mike, Jennifer. Plant controller Scott Paper Co., Hoboken, N.J., 1963-64; div. controller Sheller Globe Corp., Montpelier, Ind., 1964-67; controller Amana Refrigeration Co. (Iowa), 1967-70; div. controller Trane Co., Clarksville, Tenn., 1970-74, corp. controller, LaCrosse, Wis., 1974-79; v.p., chief fin. officer, sec. Sta-Rite Industries, Milw., 1979-82; pres. Kurz Electric Service Corp., Appleton, Wis. Bd. dirs. Jr. Achievement, 1972-74, DePaul Hosp., Milw. Served with U.S. Army, 1954-55. Mem. Fin. Execs. Inst. Republican. Clubs: University, Butte Des Morts. Lodge: Rotary. Home: 6 Wagon Wheel Dr Appleton WI 54915 Office: PO Box 1697 Appleton WI 54913

RANDLES, BRUNO WILBER, musician, artist; b. Hutchinson, Kans., Jan. 17, 1928; s. Roy Sylvester and Helen May (Clark) R.; m. Mary Suzanne Orth, Jan. 3, 1950 (dec.); children—Racheal Hromadka, David, Vincent, Joseph, Mark, Peter, William, Paul, John, Julia. Grad. Hutchinson (Kans.) High Sch., 1945; student various pvt. insts. music and art, 1945-76. Player of trumpet, trombone, piano, organ with dance bands of all types, show bands, Dixieland bands, operating and recording as The Bruno Randles and The Jolly Brewers, 1951-58; played and recorded with 6 Fat Dutchmen, 1958-59; performer featured on Leo Greco TV show, Cedar Rapids, Iowa, 1959, 1969; painter landscapes, portraits, western paintings, 1950—; exhbns. include: Salone Contemporain, Paris, 1983; musician, painter, tchr. drawing Kirkwood Coll., Cedar Rapids, 1979—. Mem. Broadcast Music Inc. Republican. Roman Catholic. Composer various polkas and waltzes. Recs. for RCA Victor, Dot, Polkland, Columbia, Random. Home and office: 68 Devonwood Ave SW Cedar Rapids IA 52404

RANDOLPH, DANIEL PARKER, lawyer; b. Cin., Sept. 13, 1946; s. Charles H. and Ruth (Westerkamp) R.; m. Irene Rebecca Chestnut, Sept. 24, 1967; children—Benjamin Aaron, Marc Ari. B.S., Xavier U., 1969; M.S., Troy State U., 1972; J.D., Salmon P. Chase Sch. Law, 1977. Bar: Ohio 1977. Trust assoc. First Nat. Bank Cin., 1972-77; ptnr. Higgs Ritter & Armstrong, Cin., 1977-81, Ritter & Randolph, Cin., 1981—; law dir. City of Madeira, Ohio; adj. prof. law Salmon P. Chase Sch. Law, Highland Heights, Ky., 1978—; trustee Madeira Community Improvement Corp., 1982—; lectr. estate planning. Trustee Temple Sholom, 1981-82; mem. Madeira Planning Commn., 1979-81. Served to 1st lt. U.S. Army, 1969-72. Mem. Internat. Assn. Fin. Planners (trustee 1981-82), ABA, Ohio Bar Assn., Cin. Estate Planning Council, Nat. Inst. Mcpl. Law Officers, Ohio Assn. Trial Attys., Madeira Jaycees (trustee 1976-77). Lodge: B'nai B'rith (pres. 1983, trustee 1982-83). Home: 8133 Maxfield Ln Madeira OH 45243 Office: 105 E 4th St Suite 1100 Cincinnati OH 45202

RANDOLPH, DONALD APPLEBY, building materials mfg. co. exec.; b. Biscoe, Ark., May 3, 1939; s. Almarine Leon and Bennie Lee (Appleby) R.; B.S. in Chemistry, Ark. A.M.&N. Coll., Pine Bluff, 1960; M.A. in Chemistry, Fisk U., 1962; postgrad. U. Chgo., 1971-73; m. Edna Ruth Watkins, Sept. 30, 1962; children—Donald Appleby, Daron Anthony. Analytical chemist Am. Can Co., Maywood, Ill., 1962-66; advanced analytical chemist U.S. Gypsum Co., Des Plaines, Ill., 1966-68, group leader, 1968-71, analytical testing mgr., 1971-74, research mgr., 1974-84, mgr. tech. transfer, 1984—; cons. in field. Coach Briarcliffe Community Youth Baseball & Basketball, Wheaton, Ill., 1977-84; treas. Pack 382, Dupage Area council Boy Scouts Am., Wheaton, 1977-82. Recipient Cert. of Appreciation, U.S. Gypsum Co., 1976. Mem. Am. Chem. Soc., Soc. Applied Spectroscopy, Chgo. Gas Chromatography Discussion Group, Am. Mgmt. Assn., Kappa Alpha Psi (dir. Youth Guidance Found., Maywood-Wheaton chpt.). Methodist. Author chpt. Ency. of Indsl. Chem. Analysis, 1971; founder, editor U.S. Gypsum Co. Research Center news mag., 1968-70. Home: 1605 S Prospect St Wheaton IL 60187 Office: 101 S Wacker Dr Chicago IL 60606

RANDOLPH, TERRANCE LEE, public relations consultant; b. Mpls., Mar. 30, 1947; s. Robert Lee and Vivian Esther (Olson) R.; m. Judy Anne Smith, June 25, 1966 (div.); children—Bret Spencer, Tara Marie; m. Patricia Marie Reeve, May 5, 1979; 1 son: Blake Lawrence. A.A., Normandale Community Coll., Bloomington, Minn., 1972; B.A. in Journalism, U. Minn., 1974. Newsroom dispatcher, writer, reporter Sta. WCCO-TV, 1973-74; program dir. World Press Inst., St. Paul, 1974-76; account exec., pub. relations exec. Campbell-Mithun Inc., Mpls., 1976-80; pub. relations counselor Kerker & Assocs., Bloomington, Minn., 1980-83; pres. Randolph Ltd., Bloomington, 1983—; spkr., cons. in field. Pub. Info. vol. Minn. Cancer Soc., 1983; pub. relations officer Youth Futures Inc., 1983. Served with USAF, 1965-69. Recipient Best Single Pub. Relations awards Nat. Agri-Mktg. Assn., 1979-80; Barbara Flanagan award Com. Urban Environ., 1981, 83; CUE award, 1983. Mem. Pub. Relations Soc. Am., Minn. Press Club. Author: From Talking Machines to Milking Machines, a History of Babson Bros. Company, 1982; 50th Birthday of Foshay Tower, 1979. Home: 5601 Chowen Ave S Edina MN 55410

RANKIN, ALFRED MARSHALL, JR., business executive; b. Cleve., Oct. 8, 1941; s. Alfred Marshall and Clara Louise (Taplin) R.; m. Victoire Conley Griffin, June 3, 1967; children—Helen P., Clara T. B.A. in Econs. magna cum laude, Yale U., 1963, LL.B., 1966. Bar: Ohio 1967. Mgmt. cons. McKinsey & Co., Cleve., 1970-73; asst. to pres. Eaton Corp., Cleve., 1974, mgr. mktg.-truck group, 1974-75, ops. mgr. axle div., 1976-77, v.p. mktg. devel., 1978-80, v.p. materials handling group, 1980-81, pres. materials handling group, 1981-83, pres. indsl. group, 1984—; dir. N.Am. Coal Corp., Cleve. Mem. vis. com. Weatherhead Sch. Bus., Case Western Res. U., Cleve.; trustee Holden Arboretum, Mentor, Ohio, Mus. Arts Assn., Cleve., Hathaway Brown Sch., Shaker Heights, Ohio, Oberlin Coll. Served to 2d lt. USAF, 1966-68. Mem. Ohio State Bar Assn. Republican. Clubs: Chagrin Valley Hunt (Gates Mills, Ohio); Kirtland Country (Willoughby); Tavern, Union (Cleve.); Rolling Rock (Ligonier, Pa.). Home: Old Mill Rd Gates Mills OH 44040 Office: Eaton Corp Eaton Ctr Cleveland OH 44144

RANKIN, DONALD JOE, airport executive; b. Bedford, Iowa, Nov. 26, 1932; s. Carl and Louise (Masters) R.; m. Jo Earlene Peery, Nov. 26, 1950; children—Marcha Rankin Anderson, Kevin, Jay. Student Northwestern Mo. State U., 1956-58. Cert. flight and mech. insp., pilot examiner. Spray pilot, 1960-64; operator Maryville Mcpl. Airport, Mo., 1964-72; owner, mgr. Rankin Airport, Maryville, 1972—. Served with USAF, 1951-53. Mem. Airplane Insp. Authorization Assn., N.G. Assn., Porterfield Airplane Club.

RANKIN, JAMES ASBURY, electronics company executive; b. Covington, Ky., July 25, 1928; s. Grover C. and Alice Mae (Townsend) R.; m. Jane Butsch, July 26, 1952; children—Nancy, Peggy. B.S., Eastern Ky. U., 1950; postgrad. U. Cin., 1952-53, U. Ky., 1955-57, Stanford U., 1984. With NuTone div. Hamilton Beach/Scovill, Cin., 1955—, v.p., gen. mgr., 1970-75, group v.p., 1975-79, exec. v.p., 1979—. Served with U.S. Army, 1946-48. Office: NuTone Div Scovill Inc Madison and Red Bank Rds Cincinnati OH 45227

RANKIN, JOHN CARTER, consulting chemist; b. Knoxville, Tenn., Dec. 21, 1919; s. Nelson Henry and Rosine Bonna (Carter) R.; m. Ruth Elizabeth Kirk, Aug. 8, 1943; children—Christine, Mark, Ellen. B.S., Bradley U., 1942, M.S., 1955. Project leader derivatives and polymers, exploration research cereal products No. Regional Research Center, U.S. Dept. Agr., Peoria, Ill., 1946-79; cons. in starch chemistry, 1980—. Served with U.S. Army, 1944-46. Recipient Disting. Service award U.S. Dept. Agr., 1955, 64; Fed. Inventors award U.S. Dept. Commerce, 1980. Mem. Am. Chem. Soc., Am. Assn. Cereal Chemists, TAPPI, AAAS, Sigma Xi. Republican. Contbr. chpts. to sci. textbooks, numerous articles to profl. jours.; patentee. Home: 1734 E Maple Ridge Dr Peoria IL 61614

RANNEY, JAMES LARRY, school administrator, city official; b. East Peoria, Ill., Oct. 19, 1938; s. James Emerson and Helen Mae (Sperry) R.; m. Sandra Ruth Pfeiffer, Dec. 29, 1963; children—Christine Lynn, James Allen. B.S., Eureka Coll., 1962; M.A., Bradley U., 1965; Ph.D., So. Ill. U., 1970. Cert. tchr., counselor, adminstr., Ill. Tchr. Ashton (Ill.) Jr. High Sch., 1962; counselor Woodruff High Sch., Peoria, Ill., 1964-66; adminstr. Peoria Adult Edn. Ctr., 1966-67; instr. So. Ill. U., Carbondale, 1967-69; asst. dir. Dept. Research Ill. Dept. Edn., Springfield, 1970-71; asst. supt. Troy Elem. Dist., Joliet, Ill., 1971-73; dir. elem. curriculum Peoria Pub. Schs., 1973—. Mayor, East Peoria, Ill., 1979—, commr. pub. property, 1975-78; mem. East Peoria Bicentennial commn., Tri-County Planning Commn. NDEA grantee Ind. U., 1965; Raymond Foster meml. scholar So. Ill. U., 1969. Mem. Assn. Supervision and Curriculum Devel., Phi Delta Kappa, Sigma Zeta. Congregationalist. Club: Kiwanis. Office: 3202 N Wisconsin Ave Peoria IL 61603

RANSIER, FREDERICK LANGDON, III, lawyer; b. N.Y.C., Dec. 3, 1949; s. Frederick Langdon and Doris (Atwell) R., Jr.; m. Kathleen Hayes, Nov. 16, 1973; children—Bradley, Charles, Frederick, IV. B.A., Central State U., Wilberforce, Ohio, 1971; J.D., Ohio State U., 1974. Bar: Ohio 1974. Asst. atty. gen. State of Ohio, Columbus, 1974-75; ptnr. Johnson & Ransier, Columbus, 1976-79, Ransier & Ransier, Columbus, 1979—; law dir. Village Urbancrest, Columbus, 1978—. Trustee, sec.-treas. Legal Aid Soc. Columbus, 1984; trustees Marburn Acad., Columbus, 1984. Office: Ransier & Ransier 66 Thurman Ave Columbus OH 43206

RANSIER, KATHLEEN HAYES, lawyer; b. Huntington, W.Va., Oct. 20, 1947; d. Charles Richard and Catherine (Brown) Hayes; m. Frederick L. Ransier, III, Nov. 16, 1973; children—Bradley, Charles, Frederick, IV. B.A., Western Coll., Oxford, Ohio, 1969; J.D., Ohio State U., 1974. Bar: Ohio 1974. Assoc. systems engr. INCO, Huntington, W.Va., 1969-71; atty. insp. Ohio Dept. Commerce, Columbus, 1974-76; ptnr. Ransier & Ransier, Columbus, 1976—. Trustees Central Community House, Columbus, 1984, Children's Mental Health Ctr., Columbus, 1984, St. Vincent's Children's Ctr., Columbus, 1984, Alternative Choices, Columbus, 1984. Recipient Constance Baker Motley award NAACP, 1974. Home: 1801 E Long St Columbus OH 43206 Office: Ransier and Ransier 66 Thurman Ave Columbus OH 43203

RANSOM, DAVID DUANE, insurance company executive; b. Boscobel, Wis., Dec. 19, 1935; s. Ronald Edgar and Wilma Ann (Stuckey) R.; m. Margaret Ann Palmquist, July 20, 1960; 1 child, D. Burke. B.Edn., U. Wis.-Whitewater, 1957; M.A., Bowling Green State U., 1963. Instr. math. Lake Forest High Sch., Ill., 1957-67; systems analyst Continental Bank, Chgo., 1967-69; system analyst ASC, Lake Bluff, Ill., 1969-70; ptnr. Mel Jacobs & Assocs., Skokie, Ill., 1970-72; mgr. Blue Cross & Blue Shield Assn., Chgo., 1972—. Mem. Libertyville Bd. Edn., 1972-75, 78—; chmn. Ill. Sch. Dist. Liquid Asset Fund, Springfield, Ill., 1984-85. NSF scholar, 1961-63. Mem. Ill. Assn. Sch. Bds. (bd. dirs. 1978—). Avocations: reading, cooking. Home: 1037 Mayfair Dr Libertyville IL 60048 Office: Blue Cross & Blue Shield Assn 676 St Clair St Chicago IL 60611

RANSOM, WILLARD BLYSTONE, lawyer; b. Indpls., May 17, 1916; s. Freeman Briley and Nettie Lillian (Cox) R.; m. Gladys Lucille Miller, July 11, 1947; children—Philip Freeman, Judith Ellen. B.A. summa cum laude, Talladega (Ala.) Coll., 1936; LL.B., Harvard U., 1939. Bar: Ind. 1939. Dep. atty. gen. State of Ind., 1939-41; practice law, Indpls., 1939—; assoc. Bamberger & Feibleman, Indpls., 1971-83, of counsel, 1983—; gen. mgr. Madame C.J. Walker Mfg. Co., Indpls., 1954-71; dir. Mchts. Nat. Bank & Trust Co., Indpls. Bd. dirs. Legal Services Orgn.; mem. com., bd. dirs. Indpls. br. NAACP, former state pres. Served to capt. JAGC, U.S. Army, 1941-46; ETO. Recipient Disting. Alumnus award Talladega Coll., 1964; Traylor award Legal Services for the Poor, 1975. Mem. Ind. Bar Assn., Marion County Bar Assn., Indpls. Bar Assn., Omega Psi Phi. Democrat.

RANUM, JANE BARNHARDT, lawyer; b. Charlotte, N.C., Aug. 21, 1947; d. John Robert and Gladys Rose (Swift) B.; m. James Harry Ranum, Mar. 29, 1972; 1 child, Elizabeth McBride. B.S., East Carolina U., 1969; J.D., Hamline U., 1979. Bar: Minn. 1979, U.S. Dist. Ct. Minn. 1979. Tchr. elem. sch. Durham County, Durham, N.C., 1969-70; tchr. Dept. Def., Baumholder, W.Ger., 1970-72, Dist. 196, Rosemount, Minn., 1972-76; law clk. Hennepin County Dist. Ct., Mpls., 1982; asst. county atty. Hennepin County, Mpls., 1982—. Mem. exec. com., lobbying coordinator DFL Feminist Caucus, St. Paul, 1980-84; bd. dirs. Project 13 for Reproductive Rights, Mpls., 1981-82; state del. Minn. Democratic Farmer Labor Party Conv., 1982, 84, precinct del., 1974—. Mem. Minn. Women's Lawyers, Minn. Family Support and Recovery Council, Hennepin County Bar Assn., Minn. Bar Assn. Democrat. Home: 5030 Emerson Ave S Minneapolis MN 58419 Office: A-2000 Hennepin County Govt Center Minneapolis MN 55487

RAO, DEBEERU C., statistical geneticist, bio-statistician; b. Santhabommali, India, Apr. 6, 1946; came to U.S., 1972; s. Ramarao Patnaik and Venkataratnam (Raghupatruni) R.; m. Sarada Patnaik, 1974; children—Ravi, Lakshmi. B.S. in Stats., Indian Statis. Inst., Calcutta, 1967, M.S., 1968, Ph.D., 1971. Research fellow U. Sheffield, Eng., 1971-72; asst. prof., geneticist U. Hawaii, Honolulu, 1972-78, assoc. prof.-geneticist, 1978-80; assoc. prof., dir. div. biostats. Washington U. Med. Sch., St. Louis, 1980-82, prof. depts. biostats., psychiatry and genetics, 1982—, adj. prof. math., 1982—, dir. div. biostats., 1980—. Author: A Source Book for Linkage in Man, 1979; Methods in Genetic Epidemiology, 1983; Genetic Epidemiology of Coronary Heart Disease, 1984. Contbr. articles to profl. jours. NIMH research grantee, 1980—; MacArthur Found. grantee, 1983—, NIGMS grantee, 1980—. Mem. Am. Statis. Assn., Am. Soc. Human Genetics, Behavior Genetics Assn., Am. Epidemiol. Soc. Office: Div Biostatistics Washington U Sch Medicine 660 S Euclid Ave Box 8067 Saint Louis MO 63110

RAO, GUNDU H. R., pathologist, researcher, educator; b. Tumkur, India, Apr. 17, 1938; came to U.S., 1965, naturalized 1982; s. Rama H.V. and Annapoorna T.S. Rao; m. Yashoda T. Rao, June 11, 1965; children—Anupama T., Prashanth T. B.S., U. Mysore, India, 1957; B.S. with honors, 1958, M.S., 1959; Ph.D., Kans. State U., 1968. USPHS research fellow in pharmacology U. Minn., 1970-72, asst. scientist, 1972-73, scientist, 1973-75, asst. prof., 1975-81, assoc. prof., 1981—. Contbr. articles to sci. jours. Founding mem. Sch. Indian Lang. and Culture. Friends of Vellore fellow Christian Med. Coll., India; jr. fellow Council of Sci. Indsl. Research, India, 1961-62, sr. fellow, 1962-65. Mem. Am. Assoc. Clin. Chemists, Am. Assn. Pathologists, Internat. Soc. Thrombosis and Haemostasis, Nat. Thrombosis Council. Democrat. Hindu. Club: India (bd. dirs.) (Mpls.). Avocation: photography. Office: U Minn Box 198 Mayo Meml Bldg 420 Delaware St SE Minneapolis MN 55455

RAO, SERIN RANGENENI, environmental engineer; b. Hyderabad, India, Jan. 28, 1946; came to U.S., 1969, naturalized, 1983; s. Saraswathi Rao; m. Aban Jokhy, Aug. 26, 1977; children—Nadia, Shawn, Justin. B.S. Osmania U., Hyderabad, 1968; M.S., So. Ill. U., 1971; M.B.A., U. Ill., 1981. Registered profl. engr., Ill. Environ. engr. Ill. Dept. Pub. Health, Peoria, 1971-73, supervising environ. engr., 1973-76, asst. regional environ. engr., 1976—; environ. cons. Am. Environ. Cons. Inc., Chgo., 1971, Internat. Inst. for Environ. and Devel., 1984; faculty Ill. Central Coll., East Peoria, 1981—. Contbr. articles to profl. jours. Mem. Am. Acad. Environ. Engrs., Am. Pub. Health Assn., Nat. Environ. Health Assn., Ill. Environ. Health Assn., Ill. Pub. Health Assn., U. Ill. Alumni Assn. (life). Avocations: mini/micro computer systems, flying, tennis. Home: 6706 N Foxpoint Ct Peoria IL 61614 Office: Ill Dept Pub Health 5415 N University Ave Peoria IL 61614

RAO, TADIKONDA LAKSHMI KANTHA, anesthesiologist; b. Rajampet, India, Nov. 23, 1946; s. Atchuta T. and Lakshmi Rao; B.Sc., Govt. Arts Coll., 1963; M.D., Pondicherry Med. Coll., 1971; m. Vyjayanthi Rao, Oct. 9, 1971; children—Usha, Vijay, Madhavi. came to U.S., 1972, naturalized, 1976. Registrar, dept. anesthesiology Pondicherry Med. Coll., India, 1970-72; intern, resident Cook County Hosp., Chgo., 1972-74, assoc. chmn. clin. anesthesia, 1975-77; practice medicine specializing anesthesology, Chgo., 1976-81; assoc. prof. Loyola U. Med. Ctr., Maywood, Ill., 1978, chmn. dept. anesthesiology. Mem. AMA, Internat. Anesthesia Research Soc., Ill. Med. Assn., Chgo. Med. Soc., Am. Soc. Anesthesiologists, Am. Soc. Regional Anesthesia, Chgo. Soc. Anesthesiologists, Soc. Cardiovascular Anesthesiologists, Ill. Soc. Anesthesiologists Assn. Univ. Anesthetists. Contbr. articles to profl. jours. Home: 135E 20th St Lombard IL 60148 Office: 2160 S 1st Ave Maywood IL 60153

RAPOPORT, DAVID E., lawyer; b. Chgo., May 27, 1956; s. Morris H. and Ruth (Tecktiel) R.; m. Andrea Gail Albun; 1 child, Alyson Faith. B.S. in Fin., No. Ill. U., 1978; J.D. with high honors, Ill. Inst. Tech., 1981; cert. in trial work Lawyers Postgrad. Inst., Chgo., 1984. Bar: Ill. 1981, U.S. Dist. Ct. (no. dist.) Ill. 1981, U.S. Ct. Appeals (7th cir.) 1984. Litigation clk. Steinberg, Polacek & Goodman, Chgo., 1979-81; assoc. Katz, Friedman, Schur and Eagle, Chgo., 1981—; instr. legal writing Ill. Inst. Tech.-Kent Coll. Law, Chgo., 1981. Mem. Am. Trial Lawyers Assn., ABA, Ill. Bar Assn., Ill. Trial Lawyers Assn., Chgo. Bar Assn. (mem. workers compensation com. 1981—, tort litigation com. 1982—). Office: Katz Friedman Schur and Eagle 7 S Dearborn St Suite 1734 Chicago IL 60603

RAPP, GERALD DUANE, SR., lawyer, manufacturing company executive; b. Berwyn, Nebr., July 19, 1933; s. Kenneth P. and Mildred (Price) R.; m. Jane Carol Thomas, Aug. 14, 1954; children—Gerald Duane, Jr., Gregory T., Amy Frances. B.S., U. Mo., 1955; J.D., U. Mich., 1958. Bar: Ohio 1959, U.S. Dist. Ct. (so. dist.) Ohio 1960. Atty., sole practice, Dayton, 1960—; ptnr. Smith & Schnacke, 1963-70; asst. gen. counsel Mead Corp., 1970, v.p. human resources and legal affairs, 1973, v.p., corp. sec., 1975, v.p., gen. counsel, corp. sec., 1976, v.p., gen. counsel, 1979, sr. v.p., gen. counsel, 1981—. Past chmn. Oakwood Youth Commn.; past v.p., bd. dirs. Big Bros. Greater Dayton; mem. pres.'s visitors com. Univ. Mich. Law Sch.; trustee Ctr. Internat. Mgmt. Studies, Internat. YMCA, N.Y.C., 1975, Ohio Ctr. Leadership Studies, Ctr. for Applied Studies, Cambridge, Mass. Served to 1st lt. U.S. Army, 1958-60. Mem. ABA, Ohio Bar Assn., Dayton Bar Assn., Phi Kappa Psi, Phi Delta Phi, Beta Gamma Sigma. Presbyterian. Clubs: Rod and Reel, Moraine Country, Dayton Racquet, Dayton Bicycle; Metropolitan (Washington). Office: Courthouse Plaza NE Dayton OH 45463

RAPP, WILLIAM F., zoologist, entomologist; b. Newark, Mar. 24, 1918; s. William F. and Elizabeth (Kuebler) R.; m. Janet L. Cooper, Sept. 30, 1944; children—Patricia L., Susan K. B.Sc., Rutgers U., 1944; M.Sc., U. Ill., 1945. Registered profl. entomologist, Nebr. Teaching asst. U. Ill., Urbana, 1944-47; asst. prof. Doane Coll., Crete, Nebr., 1947-51; entomologist Nebr. State Health Dept., Lincoln, 1952-83. Author: (with S.K. Beranek) Industrial Archeaology of Nebraska, 1984. Contbr. articles to profl. publs. Mem. Nebr. Natural Resources Commn., Lincoln, 1968-83. Recipient Arthur Sidney Bedell award Fedn. Sewage and Indsl. Wastes Assn., 1955; Service award Nebr. Mosquito and Vector Control Assn., 1980. Mem. Am. Mosquito Control Assn. (bd. dirs. 1982-84), Entomol. Soc. Am., Am. Arachnology Soc., Brit. Arachnology Soc. Republican. Lodge: Eagles (v.p. 1984-85). Avocations: philately, railroad history. Home: 430 Ivy Ave Crete NE 68333

RAPPAPORT, CYRIL M., personnel administrator; b. N.Y.C., July 12, 1921; s. David M. and Saide (Newmark) R.; B.S., CCNY, 1942; M.A., Columbia U., 1943; postgrad. N.Y. U., 1943-44; m. Dorothy Pevsner, June 19, 1957 (dec. 1966); children—Stuart N., David M. Personnel cons., The Psychol. Corp., N.Y.C., 1943-44; indsl. relations asst. Emerson Radio Corp., N.Y.C., 1944-45; adminstrv. asst. A. Hollander & Son, Long Branch, N.J., 1946-52; prin. C.M. Rappaport, retailer, Hackensack, N.J., 1952-54; mem. exec. staff Martin E. Segal & Co., N.Y.C., 1954-56, Chgo., 1956-57; sec. Midcontinent Tube Service, Evanston, Ill., 1957-58; distbr. Investor's Diversified Services, Chgo., 1959-60; systems analyst Goldblatt Bros. Store, Chgo., 1960-64; personnel officer Ill. State Dept. Mental Health, 1964-69; dir. personnel Children's Meml. Hosp., Chgo., 1969-74, St. Joseph's Hosp., 1974-75, Edgewater Hosp., Chgo., 1975-76; dir. mgmt. and personnel services Jewish Vocat. Service, Chgo., 1976—; dir. Paket, Inc., 1960-61. Bd. dirs. Bernard Horwich Community Center, 1971-73; mem. personnel planning and cons. com. United Way, 1978-79; mem. Age Discrimination Sub. Com. Mayor's Coordinating Com. Old Age, 1979—; mem. rehab. com. Chgo. Hosp. Council, 1979—. Mem. Am. Public Health Assn., Am. Soc. Hosp. Personnel Adminstrn. (dir. 1971-72), Am. Soc. Mental Hosp. Bus. Adminstrn., Assn. of Mental Health Adminstrn., Am. Acad. Health Adminstrs., Indsl. Relations Research Assn., Chgo. Hosp. Personnel Mgmt. Assn., Chgo. Assn. Commerce and Industry (manpower devel. and tng. com.). Home: 4939 Coyle St Skokie IL 60077 Office: 1 S Franklin St Chicago IL 60606

RAPPLEYE, RICHARD KENT, financial executive, consultant, educator; b. Oswego, N.Y., Aug. 10, 1940; s. Robert Edward and Evelyn Margaret (Hammond) R.; m. Karen Tobe Greenberg, Sept. 7, 1963; children—Matthew Walker, Elizabeth Marion. A.B., Miami U., Oxford, Ohio, 1962; postgrad. Boston U. Sch. Theology, 1962-63; M.B.A., Wharton Grad. Sch., U. Pa., 1964; postgrad. DePaul U. Law Sch., 1965-66. C.P.A. Auditor, DeLoitte Haskins & Sells, Chgo., 1962-67, mgmt. cons., 1967-71; controller, United Dairy Industry Assn., Rosemont, Ill., 1971, dir. fin. and adminstrn., 1971-73, exec. v.p., 1973-74; asst. to exec. v.p. Florists' Transworld Delivery, Southfield, Mich., 1974-75, group dir. fin. and adminstrn., 1975-80; asst. treas. Erb Lumber Co., Birmingham, Mich., 1980, v.p. fin., chief fin. officer, 1981-83; sec.-treas. C.S. Mott Found., Flint, Mich., 1983—; cons.; instr. Oakland U., Rochester, Mich., 1981-83. Bd. dirs. Al Kaline Baseball, Birmingham YMCA. Mem. Fin. Execs. Inst., Am. Inst. C.P.A.s, Southeast Mich. Miami U. Alumni Assn. (pres.). Unitarian. Home: 503 Arlington Rd Birmingham MI 48009 Office: 503 S Saginaw Flint MI 48502

RARDIN, JOHN ARTHUR, publishing company executive; b. Charleston, Ill., Apr. 29, 1930; s. John Briggs and Margaret Fayette (Hopper) R.; B.S., Eastern Ill. U., 1954; M.S., U. Ill., 1961; m. Rosemary Boyd, Jan. 17, 1952; children—Byron, Erin, Jerrine, John A. Newspaper editor Eastern Ill. U., Charleston, 1951; editor, Charleston Daily News, 1952, 1955-57; financial editor Champaign-Urbana (Ill.) Courier, 1959-62; research asst. Ill. Bus. Review, Champaign-Urbana, 1956-59; tchr., Rockford and Des Plaines, Ill., 1963-66; owner Rardin Graphics, Charleston, 1966—; pres., Graphic Creations, Inc., Charleston, 1970—; v.p. G.I.R.E. Internat. Inc., Charleston, 1980—. Served with AUS, 1952-54. Mem. Nat. Assn. Printers and Lithographers, Aircraft Owners and Pilots Assn., Ill. Press Assn., Ill. Pilots Assn., Charleston C. of C., Am. Inst. Parliamentarians, Pi Delta Kappa. Clubs: Rotary, Toastmasters (area gov. 1981-82, No. Ill. div. lt. gov. 1982-84, Mo.-Ill. dist. gov. 1984-85). Home: 2606 Salem Rd Charleston IL 61920 Office: 617 18th St Charleston IL 61920

RASCHE, JOHN FREDERICK, process engineering administrator; b. Bonne Terre, Mo., Apr. 14, 1936; s. Benjamin F. and Margaret (Johnson) R.; m. Judith Ann Rodgers, June 6, 1958; children—Jeffrey Alan, Kay Ellen, David William. B.S. in Chem. Engring., U. Mo.-Rolla, 1958. Research devel. engr. A.E. Staley Mfg. Co., Decatur, Ill., 1958-75, research group leader, 1975-79; process engring. mgr., 1979—. Patentee in corn syrup area. Past treas., pres. Decatur Area Arts Council, 1977-84, treas., 1984. Served as 2d lt. U.S. Army, 1958-59. Recipient Research and Devel. Achievement award A.E. Staley Mfg. Co., 1980, Extraordinary Achievement award, 1985. Mem. Am. Inst. Chem. Engring. Methodist. Avocations: photography, electronics, music, genealogy. Home: 1821 Burning Tree Dr Decatur IL 62521 Office: AE Staley Mfg Co 22d and Eldorado Sts Decatur IL 62521

RASKAS, HESCHEL JOSHUA, food company executive, educator; b. St. Louis, June 11, 1941; s. Ralph and Annette (Geffen) R.; m. Adinah Waltuch, Sept. 2, 1962; children—Jonathan, Daniel, Aviva, Ruth, Mordechai. B.S., MIT, 1962; Ph.D., Harvard U., 1967. Dir. ctr. basic cancer research Washington U. Med. Ctr., St. Louis, 1977-80, assoc. prof. pathology and microbiology, 1973-77, prof., 1971—; pres. Raskas Foods, St. Louis, 1982—; mem. adv. com. microbiology and virology Am. Cancer Soc., N.Y.C., 1978-82. Assoc. editor Virology, 1975-78, 1983—. Contbr. articles to profl. jours. Mem. council Harvard Grad. Soc., 1984—. Mem. Am. Soc. Microbiology, AAAS, Food Tech. Assocs. Clubs: Harvard, MIT. Office: Raskas Foods Inc 25 N Brentwood Saint Louis MO 63130

RASMUS, ROBERT NELSON, bldg. materials mfg. co. exec.; b. Chgo., Sept. 17, 1925; s. Walter E. and Edith C. (Nelson) R.; B.S. in Gen. Engring., U. Ill., 1948; M.M.E., Cornell U., 1949; m. Annette E. Avery, Dec. 28, 1951; children—John, Richard. Vice pres. mfg. Masonite Corp. (since 1984 subs. U.S. Gypsum) Chgo., 1965-70, v.p., gen. mgr. Bldg. Products div., 1970-71, group v.p. board products group, 1971-74, exec. v.p., 1975-76, pres., 1976—, chief exec. officer, 1977—, chmn. bd., 1981—; dir. Brunswick Corp., U.S. Gypsum Co., Employers Ins. of Wausau. Served with AUS, 1943-46. Decorated Bronze Star with oak leaf cluster. Congregationalist. Clubs: Econ., Tower, Chicago (Chgo.); Skokie Country (Glencoe, Ill.). Office: 29 N Wacker Dr Chicago IL 60606

RASMUSSEN, DAVID LEE, manufacturing company executive, hydraulic engineer, consultant; b. Two Rivers, Wis., Dec. 28, 1947; s. Harry and Ruth Margaret (Darrow) R.; m. Carol Jean Krejcarek, Nov. 11, 1966 (div. Nov. 1977); 1 son, Brian Lee. Student pub. schs., Manitowoc, Wis. Product engr. Imperial Eastman Corp., Manitowoc, 1968-76, engring. mgr., Imperial Eastman UK-LTD., St. Neots, England, 1976-78; product devel. engr. Gates Rubber Co., Rockford, Ill., 1978-79; tech. mgr. Menominee Rubber Co., Milw., 1979-80; prin., v.p. Larkin Indsl. Products, Milw., 1980—; cons. product liability suits. Served with USNR, 1964-74. Mem. ASTM. Democrat. Roman Catholic. Author publs. in field. Office: Larkin Indsl Products 700 W Michigan St Milwaukee WI 53233

RASMUSSEN, JERRY LEE, biologist; b. Harlan, Iowa, Mar. 14, 1946; s. Raymond Christian and Fern Alfreda (Petersen) R.; m. Carole Rose Hodapp, Aug. 24, 1968 (div. Nov. 1981); children—Jennifer Linne, Aaron Cole. B.S., Iowa State U., 1968; M.S., Colo. State U., 1971. Registered entomologist, Mo. Dist. fisheries biologist Tenn. Game and Fish Com., Johnson City, 1971-72, Mo. Dept. Conservation, St. Joseph, 1972-74, U.S. Bur. Land Mgmt., Craig, Colo., 1976; assoc. aquatic biologist Midwest Research Inst., Kansas City, Mo., 1974-76; coordinator Upper Miss. River Conservation Com., U.S. Fish and Wildlife Service, Rock Island, Ill. 1976—. Author, editor: Upper Mississippi River Conservation Committee Fisheries Compendium, 1979; Upper Mississippi River Conservation Committee Newsletter, 1976—; Upper Mississippi River Conservation Committee Symposium on UMR Bivalve Mollusks, 1980. Served with USNG, 1969-75. Recipient Quality Performance award U.S. Fish and Wildlife Service, 1981, Letter of Commendation, 1982, Upper Miss. River Conservation Com. Outstanding Performance Award, 1982. Mem. Midwest Angler's Assn. (hon.), Am. Fisheries Soc. (cert. fisheries scientist), Am. Inst. Fishery Research Biologists, Upper Miss. Research Consortium. Lutheran. Club: Sitzmachers Ski (Moline, Ill.). Avocations: snow skiing; water skiing; little league baseball and football; camping; hiking. Home: 11608 W 27th St Milan IL 61264 Office: Upper Miss River Conservation Com 1830 2d Ave Rock Island IL 61201

RASMUSSEN, ROBERT MITCHELL, construction company executive; b. Fenwick, Mich., Apr. 1, 1921; s. William G. and Florence C. (Deja) R.; m. Lucille E. Griffith, Apr. 26, 1941; children—Douglas L., William P. Student schs. Sheridan, Mich. Salesman, P. Lorillard Tobacco Co., Amana Co., 1948-51; founder Rasmussem Siding & Roofing Co., Inc., Grand Rapids, Mich., 1952—, chmn. bd., 1979—. Active Grand Rapids Tourist Bur., 400 Club of Republican Party; bd. dirs. Better Bus. Bur., 1968-74. Served with U.S. Army. Recipient Presdl. Citation award Nat. Assn. Remodeling Industry, 1978, 80, 82; Hometown Hero award Grand Rapids Conv. Bur., 1982; Mich. Conf. on Small Bus. award Gov. of Mich., 1981. Mem. Nat. Assn. Remodeling Industry (nat. pres.), Grand Rapids C. of C. Club: Green Ridge Country. Lodges: Optimists, Elks, Danish Brotherhood. Editorial adv. bd. Home Improvement Contractor Mag. Office: 1803 Plainfield NE Grand Rapids MI 49505

RASOVSKY, YURI, radio drama producer-director, writer, actor, consultant, teacher; b. Chgo., July 29, 1944; s. Samuel Nathan and Clarice Norma (Diamond) Rasof; 1 child, Yuri Piotr Riidl; m. Ginny Boyle, Nov. 5, 1981 (annulled 1982). Mail boy Sta. WBKB-TV, Chgo., 1963-64; drama instr. Chgo. Park Dist., 1968-70; freelance editor, writer, cartoonist, actor, dir., 1969—; founding producer, dir. Nat. Radio Theatre, Chgo., 1973—; panelist Nat. Endowment Arts, Washington, 1976, Ill. Arts. Council, Chgo., 1983, Chgo. Office Fine Arts, 1984—, NEH, 1985; cons. Can. Broadcasting Corp., Toronto. Author radio prodns. including The Amorous Adventures of Don Juan, The Courier, Dracula, An Enemy of The People, Frankenstein, The Odyssey of Homer, A Tale of Two Cities, Three Tales of Edgar Allan Poe, The World of F. Scott Fitzgerald, numerous others. Author: The Publicity Survival Manual for Small Performing Arts Organizations, 1977. Producer, actor in Magic Circle prodn. Green Julia, 1976 (3 Joseph Jefferson Citations). Contbr. articles and revs. to Chicago Mag., Stagebill Mag., Chicago Sun-Times, other publs. Served with U.S. Army, 1964-67. Recipient Major Armstrong award, 1975, 76, 79, Ohio State award, 1975, 77, 80, 83, 85, George Foster Peabody Broadcasting award, 1978, 81, Nat. Fedn. Community Broadcasters Program award, 1981, San Francisco State Broadcast Media award, 1982, 85, Grabriel award, 1983, Corp. Pub. Broadcasting Program award, 1983, 85. Mem. Am. Inds. in Radio, Audio Inds. Inc. (founder, bd. dirs. 1979-81). Office: Nat Radio Theatre of Chgo 600 N McClurg Ct Chicago IL 60611

RATAI, WALTER ROBERT, mechanical engineering consulting firm executive; b. Milw., Aug. 4, 1929; s. Walter John and Inez (Nienen) R.; m. Carol Marie Grasse, June 1954 (div. 1970); m. Darlene Joy Aland, June 25, 1971. B.S.M.E., Marquette U., 1957. Registered profl. engr., Wis., other states. Design engr. Lofte & Frederickson, Milw., 1953-58, Marks & Ratai, Milw., 1959-63; pres., Walter R. Ratai, Inc., Milw., 1963—; chmn. State of Wis. Energy Conservation Code Com., Milw., 1975—. Cons. editor Specifying Engr., Chgo., 1977—. Mem. indsl. adv. bd. Milw. Sch. Engring., 1978—, Marquette U., Milw., 1984. Fellow ASHRAE (bd. dirs. 1973-75; Energy Conservation award 1981), Engrs. and Scientists of Milw. (bd. dirs. 1975-78). Republican. Lutheran. Avocations: tennis; golf; cross-country skiing; scuba diving. Home: 12932 N Colony Dr 23 W Mequon WI 53092 Office: Walter R Ratai Inc 6659 N Sidney Pl Milwaukee WI 53209

RATAJCZAK, HELEN VOSSKUHLER, research immunologist; b. Tucson, Ariz., Apr. 9, 1938; d. Maximillian Philip and Marion Harriet (Messer) Vosskuhler; m. Edward Francis Ratajczak, June 1, 1959 (div. 1968); children—Lorraine, Eric, Peter, Eileen. B.S., U. Ariz., 1959, M.S., 1970; Ph.D., 1976. Asst. research scientist U. Iowa Coll. Medicine, Iowa City, 1976-78; instr. U. Pitts., 1978-80; research assoc., 1980-81; asst. prof. Loyola U. Coll. Medicine, Maywood, Ill., 1981-83; research immunologist Ill. Inst. Tech., Research Inst., Chgo., 1983—. Fellow Am. Thoracic Soc., 1974-76, NIH, 1978; grantee Loyola U., 1981. Mem. Am. Thoracic Soc., Am. Assn. Immunologists, Chgo. Assn. Immunologists, N.Y. Acad. Scis., AAAS, Soc. Toxicology, Daus. Am. Colonists, Sigma Xi, Kappa Kappa Gamma. Republican. Roman Catholic. Avocations: Piano playing; sewing; baking. Office: Ill Inst Tech Research Inst 10 W 35th St Chicago IL 60616

RATH, GERALD ARTHUR, engineering educator, educator; b. Sioux City, Iowa, Jan. 22, 1933; s. Gus A. and Hulda A. (Kiepke) R.; m. Lois Ann Remde, June 16, 1956; children—Lawrence, Robin, Karen. B.S.E.E., Iowa State U., 1955; M.S.E., Purdue U., 1963. Registered profl. engr., Ind., Kans., Ill. Engr., Delco-Remy Div., Anderson, Ind., 1955-66; asst. prof. Purdue U., West Lafayette, Ind., 1966-76; assoc. prof. Wichita State U., Kans., 1976-85; prof. engring., chmn. dept. Rockford Coll., Ill., 1985—; cons. Great Plains Industries, Wichita, 1984, Barber-Colman Co., Rockford, Quality Engring. Assocs., Indpls., 1973-75, Pub. Service Co. Ind., Plainfield, 1971-73. Editor Engring. Tech. series, Marcel-Dekker, Inc. Served to 1st lt. USAF, 1955-57. Mem. IEEE (sr.; sect. chmn. 1981-82), Am. Soc. Engring. Educ. (div. chmn. 1981-83), Nat. Soc. Profl. Engrs. (state dir. 1979-81), Soc. Mfg. Engrs. (sr.). Republican. Lutheran. Avocations: snow skiing, camping. Home: 5922 Allerton Dr Rockford IL 61111 Office: Rockford Coll 5050 E State St Rockford IL 61108

RATH, PATRICIA MINK, author, educator; b. Chgo.; d. Dwight L. and Margaret (Strom) Mink; A.B., Oberlin Coll.; M.S. in Merchandising, Simmons Coll.; postgrad. U. Ill., Northwestern U.; 1 son, Eric Clemence. Instr. fashion merchandising Internat. Acad. Merchandising and Design, Ltd., Chgo., 1982—; lecturer fashion merchandising, Chgo. city-wide colls. Bd. dirs. Ill. Found. for Distbv. Edn., Inc. Mem. Am. Mktg. Assn., LWV, Am. Vocat. Assn., Chgo. Council Fgn. Relations. Author: (with Ralph E. Mason) Marketing and Distribution, 1968, 74; (with Mason and Herbert L. Ross) Marketing Practices and Principles, 3d edit., 1980. Address: 1037 Cherry St Winnetka IL 60093

RATHKE, JEROME WILLIAM, chemist; b. Humboldt, Iowa, July 10, 1947; s. Albert William and Josephine Elizabeth (Speltz) R.; m. Barbara Joanne Andrews, Aug. 31, 1968; children—Benjamin, Joseph. B.S., Iowa State U., 1969; Ph.D. Ind. U., 1973; postdoctoral appointment, Cornell U., 1973-75. Asst. chemist Argonne Nat. Lab., Ill. 1975-80, chemist, 1980—, group leader, 1981—. Recipient Performance award U. Chgo., 1979. Mem. Am. Chem. Soc., AAAS; Sigma Xi. Home: 581 Buckingham Bolingbrook IL 60439

RATHZ, DAVID VICTOR, school principal; b. Indpls., May 13, 1947; s. Edward Victor and Frances (Fowley) R.; m. Patricia Marie Ollom, Dec. 27, 1969; children—Kathleen, Deborah, Maureen. B.S. in Edn., U. Dayton, 1969; M.Ed., Cleve. State U., 1974, postgrad., 1976. Cert. secondary adminstrn., Ohio. Tchr. English, Valley Forge High Sch., Parma, Ohio, 1969-71; tchr., head dept. English, Greenbriar Jr. High Sch., 1971-76; sch. facilitator Schaaf Jr. High Sch., 1976-77; asst. prin. Chardon Middle Sch., Ohio, 1977-79; prin. Harmon Middle Sch., Aurora, Ohio, 1979-81; prin. Aurora High Sch., 1981—; cons. Cleve. State U. Sch. Edn. Contbr. articles to profl. jours. Sch. liaison person City of Aurora. Recipient Adminstrv. Leadership award Martha Holden Jennings Found., 1981; Jennings scholar, 1976. Mem. NEA, Ohio Assn. Secondary Sch. Adminstrs., Phi Delta Kappa. Democrat. Roman Catholic. Clubs: Holden Arboretum, Legacy. Lodge: K.C. Avocations: racquetball; tennis; reading; gardening; spectator sports. Home: 11741 Christian Ave Concord Township OH 44077

RATLIFF, MATTIE (MARTY) LULA, sales executive; b. Sylvester, Ga., Oct. 16, 1918; d. Smith and Netter Mae (Hawkins) Mathis; m. Olden W. Franklin; children—Joyce Ann, Olden Wesley, Gail Grace (dec.); m. Paul Ratliff; 1 child, Mark (dec.). Student Franklin U., 1952, 75, Ohio State U., 1975-76. Mem. staff Def. Constrn. Supply Ctr., Columbus, Ohio, 1951-65, Def. Personnel Support Ctr., Phila., 1965-73; sales person Horizons Land Cooperation Real Estate, Columbus, 1973-74, ITT Palm, Coast Real Estate, Columbus, 1974-75; mem. Coop. Extension Service 4-H for Ohio State U., 1976-81; mem. dept. mental retardaton Capital U., Columbus, 1974-75; sales person Fashion Two Twenty, Columbus, 1967-76, Aubrey Creations, 1981, dir., 1985—. Vice pres. Nat. Council of Negro Women, Columbus, 1979—; pres. Organized Martha Circle for Tabernacle Ch., 1982; mem. choir Trinity Ch.; pres. Eleanora Roosevelt Democratic Club and Parliamentarian of Franklin County, Columbus, 1981—; vol. court watcher Ch. Women United, Nat. Immunization Program. Recipient Cert. of Service, Mayor of Columbus, 1980. Clubs: Internat. Toastmistress (Columbus) (pres. 1974-75), Bus. and Profl. (Columbus) (v.p. 1981); Bexley Toastmistress (organizer, pres. 1979, 82-83); Internat. Tng. in Communications (Livingston) (organizer); Twin Rivers Bus. and Profl. (v.p. 1981). Avocations: sewing; reading; tennis; traveling. Home and Office: 5040 Chatterton Rd Apt 7 Columbus OH 43232

RATLIFF, PRISCILLA NEWCOMER, chemical company executive, information specialist; b. Uniontown, Pa., Dec. 26, 1940; d. John Kepple and Ruth (Johnson) Newcomer; m. Wendell Lee Ratliff, July 18, 1969; 1 child, Jason Kelse. Student Am. U. Beirut, 1960-61; B.S., Maryville Coll., Tenn., 1962; M.S., Vanderbilt U., 1964. Registered U.S. patent agt. Asst. editor Chem. Abstracts, Columbus, Ohio, 1964-67; info. scientist Battelle-Columbus Labs., 1967-73; tech. writer Warren-Teed Pharm. Co., Columbus, 1973-76; research chemist Ashland Chem. Co., Columbus, 1976-78, tech. info. supr., 1978—. Bd. dirs. Friends of the Libraries, Ohio State U., Columbus, 1982—. Recipient Chemistry award Maryville Coll., 1958. Mem. Am. Chem. Soc., Am. Soc. Info. Sci., Spl. Libraries Assn., Dublin Women in Bus. and Professions (mem. steering com., chmn. career day). Home: 1965 Glenn Ave Columbus OH 43212 Office: Ashland Chemical Co 5200 Blazer Pkwy Dublin OH 43017

RATNER, MARK ALAN, educator; b. Cleve., Dec. 8, 1942; s. Max and Betty (Wohlvert) R.; B.A., Harvard U., 1964; Ph.D., Northwestern U., 1969; m. Nancy Ball, June 16, 1969; children—Stacy, Daniel. Amanuensis, Aarhus U., Denmark, 1969-70; asst. prof. chemistry N.Y. U., 1970-74, asso. prof., 1974-75; asso. prof. Northwestern U., Evanston, Ill., 1975-79, prof., 1980—, asso. dean Coll. Arts and Scis., 1980—. Mem. Jewish United Front Bd. of Chgo., 1984—. Sloan fellow, 1974-76. Fellow Am. Phys. Soc.; mem. AAAS, Am. Chem. Soc., Chem. Soc., Sigma Xi. Jewish. Contbr. articles to profl. jours. Home: 25 Locust Rd Winnetka IL 60093 Office: Dept Chemistry Northwestern Univ Evanston IL 60201

RATTANANONT, PRASOP, surgeon; b. Ranong, Thailand, May 23, 1949; came to U.S., 1971, naturalized, 1975; m. Pimjai Sukunta; children—Piyaluck, Piyaporn. M.D., Chaingmai U., Thailand, 1969. Gen. prac. medicine specializing in surgery, emergency medicine, Aledo, Ill., 1978—; mem. active staff Mercer County Hosp., Aledo, 1978—; cons. Monmouth Community Hosp., Ill., 1979—. Fellow ACS; mem. Am. Coll. Emergency Room Physicians. Home: 406 NE 12th St Aledo IL 61231 Office: 301 NW 2nd St Aledo IL 61231

RATTER, MIKE JEROME, sport fishing council executive, writer; b. Chgo., Sept. 24, 1947; s. Ernest H. and Helen M. (Falkowski) R.; m. Shirley A. Kompir, May 16, 1970; 1 child, Jennifer M. Dir. pub. relations Salmon Unlimited, Dyer, Ind., 1977—, bd. dirs., 1977—, editor, 1977—; mem. factory research and promotional staff Luhr Jensen & Sons, Hood River, Oreg., Berkley Corp., Spirit Lake, Iowa. Fishing editor Hoosier Outdoors, Chesterton, Ind., 1978-80, Mid-West Outdoors Mag., Hinsdale, Ill., 1982—, Woods 'n Waters Mag. Recipient numerous awards and trophies. Mem. Lake County Fish and Game Protective Assn., Trollers Unlimited, Assn. Great Lakes Outdoor Writers. Clubs: Ind. Harbor Boat (East Chicago, Ind.), Hoosier Coho (Mich. City, Ind.). Home: 1554 Shirley Dr Calumet City IL 60409

RATTS, MARVIN L., petroleum geologist, consultant; b. Atlanta, Kans., May 31, 1924; s. Lawrence N. and Mary (Williams) R.; m. Dorothy Virginia Keen, June 6, 1950; children—Glennis, Patricia. B.S., Kans. State U., 1950. Service engr. Dowell Inc., Tulsa, 1950-56; co. geologist Shields Oil Producers, Russell, Kans., 1956—. Served with U.S. Army, 1943-46, ETO. Republican. Mem. Am. Assn. Petroleum Geologists (cert.), VFW. Lodge: Masons. Avocations: hunting; fishing; travel. Home: 944 E 2nd St Russell KS 67665 Office: Shields Oil Producers Inc Shields Bldg Russell KS 67665

RATTUNDE, JAMES KEITH, insurance agent; b. Mauston, Wis., Dec. 20, 1953; s. Marland John and Bonnie Jean (Oakes) R.; m. Ramona Lee Polze, Aug. 28, 1976; children—Rebecca L. and Ryan J. (twins). Asst. chief of police Necedah Police Dept., Wis., 1973-74; sargeant Juneau County Sheriff's Dept., Mauston, Wis., 1974-81; ins. agt. Rattunde Ins. Agy., Necedah, 1979—. Fireman, mem. ambulance/rescue squad Necedah Vol. Fire Dept., 1975—, capt., 1983—; mem. Necedah Area Sch. Bd., 1977—; bd. dirs. Mile Bluff Med. Ctr., Mauston, 1983; mem. CESA 12 Bd. Control, Portage, Wis. Mem. Necedah C. of C., Profl. Ins. Agts., Homeco Life Leader's Forum, Ins. Econs. Soc. Am. Roman Catholic. Avocations: Woodworking, building, piano playing. Home: Route 1 Box 572 Necedah WI 54646 Office: Rattunde Ins Agy 605 N Main PO Box 9 Necedah WI 54646

RAU, SCOTT ANDREW, systems analyst, software and systems consultant; b. Elgin, Ill., Sept. 27, 1963; s. Kurt John Rau. Systems analyst Automatic Data Processing, Schaumburg, Ill., 1983-85; programmer analyst Systems Mgmt., Rosemont, Ill., 1985; system, prodn. analyst United Air Lines EXO, Elk Grove, Ill., 1985—; cons. Ballas Engring., Schaumburg, 1984-85. Mem. Tau Kappa Epsilon. Republican. Roman Catholic. Home: 600 Salem Dr Suite 118 Hoffman Estates IL 60194 Office: United Air Lines EXOKD-INET PO Box 66100 Chicago IL 60666

RAUBOLT, RICHARD RALEIGH, clinical psychologist; b. Detroit, Nov. 13, 1948; s. Raleigh Richard and Esther L. (Petrie) R.; m. Linda Helen Sabo, May 7, 1971; children—Garrett, Jordan. B.A. (Waldo Sadgren scholar), Western Mich. U., 1971; M.A., Columbia U., 1972; Ph.D. Fielding Inst., 1979. Lic. psychologist, Mich. Psychologist, cons. Edgemont High Sch., Scarsdale N.Y., 1976-78; cons. Goodwill Industries, Grand Rapids, Mich., 1979-83; adj. prof. dept. psychiatry Mich. State U., Grand Rapids, 1978—; pvt. practice counseling psychology, Grand Rapids; supervising psychologist Pine Rest Christian Hosp., Grand Rapids; instr. dept. counseling psychology Western Mich. U. Mem. Am. Group Psychotherapy Assn., Am. Psychol. Assn. Am. Orthopsychiat. Assn., Mich. Soc. Lic. Psychologists, Phi Eta Sigma. Contbr. numerous articles to profl. jours. Home: 2352 Woodlawn SE Grand Rapids MI 49506

RAUENHORST, GERALD, design/build company executive; b. Mpls., Dec. 8, 1927; s. Henry and Margaret (Keltgen) R.; m. Henrietta Schmoll, Sept. 2, 1950; children—Judith, Mark, Neil, Joseph, Michael, Susan, Amy. B.A., Coll. St. Thomas, 1948, Dr. Laws (hon.), 1971; B.S.C.E., Marquette U., 1951. Engr., Peter Rasmussen & Son, Oshkosh, Wis., 1950, Viking Constrn., Mpls., 1951-52; pres., founder. Rauenhorst Corp., Mpls., 1953-82; chmn. bd., chief exec. officer Opus Corp., Mpls., 1982—; dir. Norwest Corp., Norwest-Bloomington, N.W. Bell Telephone Co., ConAgra. Mem. World Bus. Council, Mpls.; mem. exec. bd. Viking council Boy Scouts Am. Named Alumnus of Yr., Marquette U., 1969; Exec. of Yr., Corp. Report Mag., 1983. Mem. Minn. Soc. Profl. Engrs., ASCE. Roman Catholic. Clubs: Mpls., Minn., Interlachen. Avocations: fishing, golf, pottery. Office: Opus Corp PO Box 150 Minneapolis MN 55440

RAUN, EARLE SPANGLER, entomologist, researcher, business executive; b. Sioux City, Iowa, Aug. 28, 1924; s. Harold Everett and Beatrice Genevieve (Spangler) R.; m. Georgia Ann Hart, Aug. 28, 1946; children—Michele Arline, Nancy Lee, Patricia Ann. B.S., Iowa State U., 1946, M.S., 1950, Ph.D., 1954. Assoc. prof. entomology Iowa State U., Ames, 1956-60; entomologist U.S. Dept. Agr. Corn Borer Lab., Ankeny, Iowa, 1960-66; chmn. dept. entomology U. Nebr., Lincoln, 1966-71, assoc. dir. coop. extension, 1971-74; pres., entomologist Pest Mgmt. Cons., Inc., Lincoln, 1974-83, Pest Mgmt. Co., Lincoln, 1983—; mem. pesticide users adv. com. EPA, 1982—. Contbr. articles to profl. jours. Comdr. CAP, Lincoln, 1985—; chmn. Crestwood Christian Ch., Lincoln, 1979-81. Served with U.S. Army, 1944-45. Named Outstanding Entomologist in Agr., Registry of Profl. Entomologists, 1978. Mem. Entomol. Soc. Am. (pres. North Central br. 1983-84), Nat. Alliance Ind. Crop Cons. (pres. 1978-80), Nebr. Ind. Crop Cons. Assn. (pres. 1983), Avocations: flying, fishing, reading. Home: 3036 Prairie Rd Lincoln NE 68506 Office: Pest Mgmt Co 3036 Prairie Rd Lincoln NE 68506

RAUSCH, STEVEN KIRK, biochemist; b. Aurora, Ill., Nov. 17, 1955; s. Ralph Walter and Jo Ann (Young) R. B.S. in Chemistry, Purdue U., 1977; Ph.D., U. Ill., 1983. Research asst. Tex. Agrl. Exptl. Sta., College Station, 1981-82; research biochemist IMC Corp., Terre Haute, Ind., 1982—. Co-contbr. articles to Biochemistry. Mem. Community Theater of Terre Haute, 1983. U. Ill. fellow, 1977; USPHS grantee, 1978. Mem. Am. Chem. Soc., AAAS, Am. Soc. Biol. Chemists (assoc.), Sigma Xi. Avocations: theater; flute; broadcasting; science fiction; model rocketry. Home: 591 E 43 1/2 Dr Apt 3 Terre Haute IN 47802 Office: IMC Corp PO Box 207 Terre Haute IN 47808

RAUSCHENBERGER, JOHN MICHAEL, industrial psychologist; b. Jackson, Mich., Dec. 21, 1950; s. Richard Dale and Anastasia Theresa (Lapinski) R. Ph.D., Mich. State U., East Lansing, 1978. Personnel rep. Armco, Inc., Middletown, Ohio, 1978-80, sr. personnel rep., 1980-81, supr. personnel research, 1981-85; personnel research analyst Ford Motor co., Dearborn, Mich., 1985—. Mem. Acad. Mgmt., Am. Psychol. Assn. Roman Catholic. Office: Ford Motor Co Room 431-WHQ The American Rd Dearborn MI 48121-1899

RAUSCHENBERGER, SHARON ANN, researcher; b. Milw., Oct. 12, 1946; d. Richard Walter Gniot and Adele (Kurek) Gniot Graves; m. Gerald Arnold Dwyer, Jan. 22, 1966 (div. Apr. 1973); children—Guy Anthony, Jinny Ann; m. Charles Louis Rauschenberger, III, May 25, 1974; children—Denyse, Dikka, Charles Louis IV. Student U. Wis.-Madison, 1982. Mcpl. judge, Belleville, Wis., 1981—. Mem. Mcpl. Judges Manual Com., Madison, 1982—. Mcpl. Judges Program Com., Madison, 1982—, Drug and Alcohol Abuse Com., Belleville, 1984. Home: 20 W Pearl St Belleville WI 53508 Office: Village of Belleville 130 S Vine St Belleville WI 53508

RAVEN, JONATHAN EZRA, lawyer, optical chain executive; b. Chgo., Jan. 13, 1951; s. Seymour S. and Norma (Blackman) R.; m. Leslie Michelle Shapiro, Dec. 29, 1973; children—Jane Lara, David Louis. B.A. cum laude, Western Mich. U. 1972; J.D., U. Mich., 1975. Bar: Mich. 1975. Assoc., then ptnr., dir. firm Foster, Swift, Collins & Coey, P.C., Lansing, Mich., 1975-81; v.p., gen. counsel, sec., dir. NuVision, Inc., Flint, Mich., 1981—, also dir.; v.p., dir. Bell Optical Inc., Flint. Pres., dir. Stonelake Condominium Assn., East Lansing, Mich., 1978-81; mem. franchise working group Gov.'s Cabinet Council on Jobs and Econ. Devel., Lansing, 1983. Mem. ABA, State Bar Mich., Ingham County Bar Assn., Internat. Franchise Assn. (legis. com.), Am. Arbitration Assn. (panel arbitrators 1980—), Omicron Delta Kappa. Jewish. Office: NuVision Inc PO Box 2600 2284 S Ballenger Hwy Flint MI 48501

RAVEN, PETER HAMILTON, botanist, botanical garden administrator; b. Shanghai, China, June 13, 1936; s. Walter Francis and Isabelle Marion (Breen) R.; A.B., U. Calif., Berkeley, 1957; Ph.D., UCLA, 1960; m. Tamra Engelhorn, Nov. 29, 1968; children—Alice Catherine, Elizabeth Marie, Francis Clark, Kathryn Amelia. NSF postdoctoral fellow Brit. Mus., London, 1960-61; taxonomist Rancho Santa Ana Botanic Garden, Claremont, Calif., 1961-62; asst., assoc. prof. biol. scis. Stanford U., 1962-71; dir. Mo. Bot. Garden, Engelmann prof. botany Washington U., St. Louis, 1971—; chmn. Nat. Mus. Services Bd., 1984-87. Commr., Tower Grove Park, St. Louis, 1971—. Recipient Disting. Service award Am. Inst. Biol. Scis., 1981; Internat. Environ. Leadership medal UN Environ. Program, 1982; NSF grantee; John D. and Catherine T. MacArthur Found. Fellow AAAS, Calif. Acad. Scis., Am. Acad. Arts and Scis. Royal Soc. N.Z. (hon.); mem. Nat. Acad. Scis., (com. on human rights 1984—), Royal Danish Acad. Arts and Scis. (fgn. mem.), Linnaean Soc. London, Nat. Geog. Soc. (com. on research and exploration), World Wildlife Fund-U.S. (bd. dirs.), Orgn. Trop. Wildlife Studies. (pres. 1985-86), Am. Inst. Biol. Scis. (Disting. service award, 1981, pres. 1983-84), Phi Beta Kappa, Sigma Xi, others. Clubs: Univ., Cosmos. Author: Biology of Plants, 1971, 4th edit., 1985; Princip of Tzeltal Plant Classification, 1974, Biology, 1985; editor various sci. books papers, and conf. procs.; contbr. numerous articles to profl. jours. Office: Mo Bot Garden PO Box 299 Saint Louis MO 63166

RAWLINGS, THOMAS EDWARD, lawyer, accountant; b. Cumberland, engineer; Md., Feb. 23, 1952; s. Oberland and Dorothy (Lemmert) R.; m. Beverly Heath. B.S., Akron U., 1974, J.D., 1977. Registered profl. engr. Ohio; C.P.A., Ohio; bar: Ohio 1977. Assoc. Dinsmore & Shohl, Cin.; tax specialist Coopers & Lybrand, Akron, Ohio; v.p. Metrotec & Metrotel, 1979—; ptnr. Brouse & McDowell, 1980—. Author: Ohio Divorce Taxation, 1984; Federal Capital Gains Tax, 1985. Mem. ABA, Ohio Bar Assn., Akron Bar Assn. Club: Cascade. Lodge: Kiwanis. Avocations: swimming, reading. Home: 790 Kirkwall Dr Copley OH 44321 Office: Brouse & McDowell 500 First Nat Tower Akron OH 44308

RAWLS, CATHERINE POTEMPA, commodity futures executive, financial futures analyst; b. Chgo., Mar. 19, 1953; d. Stanley Louis and Mary Ann (Kuczmarski) Potempa; m. Stephen Franklin Rawls, July 30, 1983. B.A., Marquette U., 1975. Mem. Chgo. Bd. Trade, 1977-79, 83—; fin. futures analyst Geldermann Inc., Chgo., 1979-82, dir. research, 1982—; mem. Chgo. Merc. Exchange, 1982. Editor Fax & Figures newsletter, 1983, Geldermann-Peavey newsletter, 1983—. Recipient award Marquette U. chpt. Women in Communications, 1975. Mem. Futures Industry Assn. Roman Catholic. Home: 421-C Sandhurst Circle Glen Ellyn IL 60137 Office: Geldermann Inc One Financial Pl 20th Floor Chicago IL 60605

RAWLS, LARRY, record company executive; b. Mansfield, Ohio, Nov. 7, 1954; s. Martin and Vera (Easley) R. 1984. A.A., North Central Tech. Coll., Ohio, 1976; B.S., Urbana Coll., Ohio, With Gen. Motors Corp., Mansfield, 1979—; pres. Fun City Record Co., Mansfield, 1979—. Mem. Am. Soc. Tng. and Devel. Office: 291 5th Ave Mansfield OH 44905

RAWN, EDWIN LEROY, educational administrator, consultant; b. Alma, Mich., July 6, 1938; s. William Edwin and Dortha (Belle) Cloke R. B.M.E., Alma Coll., 1961; M.A., Central Mich. U., 1968; Ed.S., Central Mo. State U., 1974; Ed.D., U. Mo., 1979. Educator, Mich., N.Y., Mo., 1961-74; supt. schs. Sheridan Sch. Dist., Mo., 1974-76, North Andrew Sch. Dist., Rosendale, Mo., 1976-77; asst. state chmn. Mo./N.Central Assn., Columbia, 1977-79; research assoc. U. Mo., Columbia, 1980-83; secondary sch. prin. New Bloomfield Sch. Dist., Mo., 1983—; doctoral cons. Dept. ednl. adminstrn. U. Mo., Columbia, 1980—. Mem. aux. police New Bloomfield Police Dept., Mo., 1984; active Boy Scouts Am. Mem. Nat. Assn. Secondary Sch. Prins., Mo. Assn. Secondary Sch. Prins., Phi Delta Kappa, Phi Kappa Phi. Mem. Reorganized Ch. of Jesus Ch. of Latter-day Saints. Avocations: swimming; camping; cooking; reading. Home: Route 2 Box 140B New Bloomfield MO 65063 Office: New Bloomfield High Sch PO Box 188 New Bloomfield MO 65063

RAWSON, MERLE R., appliance manufacturing company executive; b. Chgo., June 9, 1924; s. Richard W. and Flora R.; student U. Ill., 1946-48; B.S. in Accounting, Northwestern U., 1949; m. Jane Armstrong, July 5, 1947; children—David M., Jeffrey M., Laurel J. Asst. to plant controller John Wood Co., 1949-58; asst. controller Easy Laudry Appliances, 1958-61; controller O'Bryan Bros., 1961; with Hoover Co., North Canton, Ohio, 1961—, controller, 1962-64, v.p., treas., 1964-69, sr. v.p., treas., 1969-75, chmn. bd., chief exec. officer, 1975—, pres., 1982, also dir.; exec. v.p. Hoover Worldwide Corp., 1971-75, chmn. bd., chief exec. officer, 1975—, also dir.; chmn., dir. Hoover plc (U.K.), 1978—; dir. Hoover Can. Inc., Hoover Mexicana, Hoover Holland, S.A. Hoover (France), Soc. Corp., Cleve., Hoover Industrial y Comercial S.A. (Colombia), Hoover Export Corp., Society Bank of Eastern Ohio. Trustee, Ohio Found. Ind. Colls.; mem. adv. council Pace U.; mem. Aultman Hosp. Assn., Aultman Hosp. Devel. Found. Served with F.A., AUS, 1943-46. Decorated chevalier Order of Leopold (Belgium); recipient Medal of the City of Paris, 1983. Mem. Council Fgn. Relations, Greater Canton C. of C., Stark County Bluecoats. Clubs: Rotary; Capitol Hill; Congress Lake Country; Canton. Office: 101 E Maple St North Canton OH 44720

RAY, CHARLES JOSEPH, dentist; b. South Sioux City, Nebr., June 4, 1911; s. Charles Joseph and Katherine Frances (Bridgeford) R.; m. Cecilia Estelle Radlinger, Nov. 22, 1933; children—Carole, Margie, Kathy, Jeane, Rita, Charles, Chrystal. E.E., S.D. Sch. of Mines, 1932; D.D.S., U. Minn., 1936; postgrad. Forsythe Dental Infirmary, Boston, 1936-37, Eastman Dental Dispensary, 1937-38. Pvt. practice dentistry, 1938—, with Ray Dental Group, Rapid City, S.D., 1953—; mem. S.D. Med. Adv. Bd., 1958-65. Active USO, 1959, pres. Rapid City chpt. 1952-60; pres. S.D. Crippled Children's Assn. Mem. Am. Dental Assn. (life), S.D. Dental Assn. (Gold Tooth award 1980, pres. 1964), Am. Prosthodontic Soc. (pres. 1980-81, exec. council 1981-82), Fedn. Prosthodontic Orgn. (sec. 1976-80), Am. Assn. Hosp. Dentists, Am. Soc. Psychosomatic Dentistry and Medicine, Pierre-Fauchard Acad. (award 1980), Am. Acad. Periodontology, Acad. Internat. Dentistry and Medicine, Am. Acad. Practice Adminstrn., Am. Acad. Gen. Dentistry, Am. Acad. Dental Group Practice, Colo. Prosthodontic Soc., Rapid City Dental Soc., Black Hills Dist. Dental Soc., Dental Group Mgmt. Assn., Chgo. Dental Soc. (assoc.), Rapid City C. of C., Omicron Kappa Upsilon. Roman Catholic. Clubs: Internateonal Cosmopolitan (pres. 1972), Rapid City Cosmopolitan (pres. 1962; Disting. Service award 1977), Sioux Land Study. Lodges: K.C., Elks. Home: Rural Route 1 Box 1040 Rapid City SD 57702 Office: Ray Dental Group PO Box 899 Rapid City SD 57709

RAY, FRANK ALLEN, lawyer; b. Lafayette, Ind., Jan. 30, 1949; s. Dale Allen and Merry Ann (Fleming) R.; m. Carol Ann Olmutz, Oct. 1, 1982; children—Erica Fleming, Robert Allen. B.A., Ohio State U., 1970, J.D., 1973. Bar: Ohio 1973, U.S. Dist. Ct. (so. dist.) Ohio 1975, U.S. Supreme Ct. 1976, U.S. Tax Ct. 1977, U.S. Ct. Appeals (6th cir.) 1977, U.S. Dist Ct. (no. dist.) Ohio 1980, Pa. 1983, U.S. Dist. Ct. (ea. dist.) Mich. 1983; cert. civil trial adv. Nat. Bd. Trial Advocacy. Asst. pros. atty. Franklin County, Ohio, 1973-75, chief civil counsel, 1976-78; dir. econ. crime project Nat. Dist. Attys. Assn., Washington, 1975-76; assoc. Brownfield, Kosydar, Bowen, Bally & Sturtz, Columbus, Ohio, 1978, Michael F. Colley Co., L.P.A., Columbus, 1979-83; sole practice, Columbus, 1983—; mem. seminar faculty Nat. Coll. Dist. Attys., Houston, 1975-77; mem. nat. conf. faculty Fed. Jud. Ctr., Washington, 1976-77. Editor: Economic Crime Digest, 1975-76. Mem. fin. com. Franklin County Republican Orgn., Columbus, 1979-84. Served to 1st lt. inf. U.S. Army, 1973. Named to Ten Outstanding Young Citizens of Columbus, Columbus Jaycees, 1976; recipient Nat. award of Distinctive Service, Nat. Dist. Attys. Assn., 1977. Mem. Columbus Bar Assn., Ohio State Bar Assn., ABA, Assn. Trial Lawyers Am., Ohio Acad. Trial Lawyers (trustee 1984—), Franklin County Trial Lawyers Assn. (treas. 1983—, chmn. com. negligence law 1983—). Presbyterian. Home: 5800 Olentangy Blvd Worthington OH 43085 Office: 330 S High St Columbus OH 43215

RAY, FRANK DAVID, government agency official; b. Mt. Vernon, Ohio, Dec. 1, 1940; s. John Paul and Lola Mae (Miller) R.; B.S. in Edn., Ohio State U., 1964, J.D., 1967; m. Julia Anne Sachs, June 11, 1976. Bar: Ohio 1967, U.S. Dist. Ct. 1969, U.S. Cir. Ct. Appeals (6th cir.) 1970, U.S. Supreme Ct. 1971. Legal aide to atty. gen. Ohio, 1965-66; bailiff probate ct., Franklin County, Ohio, 1966-67, gen. referee, 1967-68; with firm Stouffer, Wait and Ashbrook, Columbus, Ohio, 1967-71; jour. clk. Ohio Ho. of Reps., 1969-71; dist. dir. SBA, 1971—; mem. Ohio Pub. Defender Commn., 1983—; mem. Columbus Mayor's Econ. Devel. Council, 1983-84; mem. Small Bus. and High Tech. adv. com. Ohio Div. Securities, 1983-84; mem. tech. alliance Central Ohio Adv. Bd., 1983—. Mem. Upper Arlington (Ohio) Bd. Health, 1970-75; pres. Buckeye Republican Club, 1970, Franklin County Forum, 1970; chmn. Central Ohio chpt. Nat. Found.-March of Dimes, 1974-77; trustee Columbus Acad. Contemporary Art, 1976. Recipient Service award Nat. Found.-March of Dimes, 1974, 75, 76, 77; Am. Jurisprudence award for Excellence; named Ohio Commodore, 1973. Mem. Delta Upsilon, Alpha Epsilon Delta. Clubs: Ohio Press, Ohio State U. Pres., Shrine. Home: 4200 Dublin Rd Columbus OH 43220

RAY, HOPE WALKER, retired educator; b. McConnelsville, Ohio, Oct. 11, 1906; d. S. Carlton and Grace (Wells) Walker; student Malta Normal Sch., 1924-25, Ohio U., 1940-41; B.A. in Edn., George Washington U., 1958; m. Kenneth C. Ray, June 24, 1931; children—John Walker, Beverly Ann Ray Klincko. Tchr., Morgan County (Ohio) Schs., 1925-31. Mem. DAR (past regent), Daus. Colonial Wars, Columbian Women George Washington U., Pi Lambda Theta. Republican. Methodist. Lodge: Order Eastern Star. Author: (elementary grade workbooks) Number Trails, 1938. Address: 1135H Brandywine Blvd The Plains Zanesville OH 43701

RAY, JAMES ALLEN, consultant; b. Lexington, Ky., Feb. 21, 1931; s. Allen Brice and Elizabeth Logan (Simpson) R.; B.S. in Geology, U. N.C., 1958; M.S., N.C. State Coll., 1962; m. Mary Ruth Johnston, June 8, 1958; children—James Edward, Allen Bruce, John David. Chief petrographic research Master Builders div. Martin Marietta Corp., Cleve., 1959-73, asst. dir. research, 1973-77, dir. research, 1977-78, v.p. research, 1979-80, v.p. creative research, 1980-82; cons., 1982—. Served with USAF, 1951-55. Recipient Jefferson Cup, Martin Marietta Corp., 1977. Mem. Mineral. Soc. Am., Mineral. Soc. Can., Am. Concrete Inst., ASTM, Res. Officers Assn. (life), Nat. Rifle Assn. (life), Washington Legal Found. (life), Am. Security Council. Republican. Patentee in field. Address: 9891 Stamm Rd Mantua OH 44255

RAY, JOHN WALKER, physician; b. Columbus, Ohio, Jan. 12, 1936; s. Kenneth Clark and Hope (Walker) Ray; A.B. magna cum laude, Marietta Coll., 1956; M.D. cum laude, Ohio State U., 1960; postgrad. Temple U., 1964, Mt. Sinai Hosp. and Columbia U., 1964, 66, Northwestern U., 1967, 71, U. Ill., 1968, U. Ind., 1969, Tulane U., 1969; m. Susanne Gettings, July 15, 1961; children—Nancy Ann, Susan Christy. Intern, Ohio State U. Hosps., Columbus, 1960-61, clin. research trainee NIH, 1963-65, resident dept. otolaryngology, 1963-65, 1966-67, resident dept. surgery 1965-66, instr. dept. otolaryngology, 1966-67, 70-75, clin. asst. prof., 1975-82, clin. assoc. prof., 1982—; active staff, past chief of staff Bethesda Hosp.; active staff, chief of staff Good Samaritan Hosp., Zanesville, Ohio, 1967—, chief of staff, 1986—; courtesy staff Ohio State U. Hosps., Columbus, 1970—; radio-TV health commentator, 1982—. Past pres. Muskingum chpt. Am. Cancer Soc.; trustee Care One Health Systems, Ohio Med. Polit. Action Com. Served to capt. USAF, 1961-63. Recipient Barraquer Meml. award, 1965; named Ky. col., 1966. Diplomate Am. Bd. Otolaryngology. Fellow A.C.S., Am. Soc. Otolaryn. Allergy, Am. Acad. Otolaryngology (gov.), Am. Acad. Facial Plastic and Reconstructive Surgery; mem. Muskingum County Acad. Medicine, AMA (del. hosp. med. Staff sect.), Ohio Med. Assn. (del.), Columbus Ophthalmol. and Otolaryngol. Soc. (past pres.), Ohio Soc. Otolaryngology (past pres.), Pan-Am. Assn. Otolaryngology and Bronchoesophagology, Pan-Am. Allergy Soc., Am. Council Otolaryngology, Am. Auditory Soc., Am. Soc. Contemporary Medicine and Surgery, Phi Beta Kappa, Alpha Tau Omega, Alpha Kappa Kappa, Alpha Omega Alpha, Beta Beta Beta. Republican. Presbyterian. Contbr. articles to sci., med. jours. Collaborator, surg. motion picture Laryngectomy and Neck Dissection, 1964. Office: 2825 Maple Ave Zanesville OH 43701

RAY, PAUL ARTHUR, aerospace company executive; b. Rolla, Mo., Dec. 21, 1941; s. Clark Arthur and Ora Catheran (Gahr) R.; m. Patricia Jean Strothkamp, Aug. 24, 1963; children—Patrick, Paula. B.S.E.E., U. Mo.-Rolla, 1963, M.S.E.E., 1965, E.E. (hon.), 1984; M.B.A., Wichita State U., 1973. Engr. Boeing Mil. Airplane Co., Wichita, Kans., 1967-73, engring. mgr., 1973-77, new bus. mgr., 1977-83, program mgr., 1983—. Served to 1st lt. U.S. Army, 1965-67, Vietnam. Mem. Armed Forces Communications and Electronics Assn., Assn. Old Crows, Inst. Aeros. and Astronautics, Wichita Area C. of C. Home: 1001 Morrison Ct Derby KS 67037 Office: Boeing Mil Airplane Co 3801 S Oliver St Wichita KS 67210

RAY, PAUL DEAN, biochemistry educator; b. Monmouth, Ill., Dec. 7, 1934; s. Elmer Jefferson and Dorothy Evelyn (Larimer) R.; m. Annette May Thrift, June 15, 1957; children—Debra Ann, Kenneth Alan, Michael Edward, Linda Maureen. B.A., Monmouth Coll., 1956; Ph.D., St. Louis U., 1962. Postdoctoral fellow Enzyme Inst. U. Wis., 1967; asst. prof. U. N.D., Grand Forks, 1967-68, assoc. prof., 1968-74, prof. dept. biochemistry, Sch. Medicine, 1974—; mem. arthritis and metabolism study sect. NIH, 1968-72; mem. Gt. Plains Research Com., Am. Heart Assn., 1974-78. Author, co-author book chpts. and jour. articles. Am. Cancer Soc. postdoctoral fellow, 1962-65; established investigator Am. Heart Assn., 1967-72; various research grants including NIH and N.D. affiliate Am. Diabetes Assn. Mem. Am. Soc. Biol. Chemists, Am. Chem. Soc., Sigma Xi. Methodist. Avocations: hunting; fishing; reading; gardening. Home: 527 Schroeder Dr Grand Forks ND 58201 Office: U ND Sch Medicine Dept Biochemistry Grand Forks ND 58202

RAY, THOMAS K., clergyman. Bishop No. Mich. region Episcopal Ch. Office: 131 E Ridge St Marquette MI 49855*

RAY, THOMAS LEE, dermatologist; b. Portland, Oreg., June 2, 1946; s. Leon Frank and Barbara Jean (Reed) R.; m. Ingrid Clare Wehrle, June 11, 1972; children—Byron, Brynje. B.A., Williams Coll., 1968; M.D., U. Oreg., 1972. Diplomate Am. Bd. Dermatology, Nat. Bd. Med. Examiners. Intern Hennepin County Gen. Hosp., Mpls., 1972-73; resident U. Oreg., Portland, 1973-77; fellow U. Conn. Health Ctr., Farmington, 1977-79; instr., 1977-79; asst. prof. U. Iowa, Iowa City, 1979-83, assoc. prof., 1983—; cons. VA Hosp., Iowa City, 1979—. Contbr. articles to profl. jours. Contng. chpts. in books in field. Contbg. editor Internat. Jour. Dermatology, 1977—. Fellow Am. Acad. Dermatology; mem. Soc. Investigative Dermatology, Am. Fedn. Clin. Research, Am. Soc. Microbiology, Iowa Dermatol. Soc. (sec. treas. 1980-83, pres. 1984-85), Pacific Dermatol. Assn. (Nelson Paul Anderson award 1975), Lodge: Rotary. Office: Dept Dermatology U Iowa Coll Medicine Iowa City IA 52242

RAY, VERNON OLIVER, JR., speech communication educator, minister; b. St. Louis, Feb. 7, 1954; s. Vernon Oliver and Bettye Lou (Cole) R.; m. Kathie Searcy, Aug. 10, 1973; children—Joshua Vernon West, Jonathan David, Jessica Ann-Marie. B.A., Harding U., 1975, M.A., 1978; Ph.D. La. State U., 1985. Ordained to ministry Ch. of Christ, 1972. Minister Wilmette Ch. of Christ, Ill., 1976-77, Druid Hills Ch. of Christ, Atlanta, 1978, South Baton Rouge Ch. of Christ, 1979-82; instr. La. State U., Baton Rouge, 1981-82; chmn., asst. prof. York Coll., Nebr., 1982-85; v.p. Spectra Communication Assocs., New Orleans, 1984—; guest lectr., evangelist Chs. of Christ throughout U.S. and Europe, 1982—. Author: Without A Parable: The Art of Illustration, 1983. Contbr. articles to profl. jours. Recipient Outstanding Young Men of Am. award Am. Jaycees, 1979. Mem. Speech Communication Assn., Religious Speech Communication Assn., Internat. Communication Assn., Internat. Listening Assn., Soc. Bibl. Lit. Republican. Avocations: reading, writing, woodworking, raquetball, basketball, water skiing. Home: 521 Iowa Ave York NE 68467 Office: Spectra Communication Assoc Box 5031 Contract Station 20 New Orleans LA 70118

RAYBURN, TURNITTA FAYE, educator, educational administrator; b. Gary, Ind., Sept. 1, 1947; d. Turner and Esther E. (Houston) Patterson; m. Robert Louis Rayburn, May 20, 1967; children—Antoinette, Cameron. B.S. in Sociology, Central State U., Wilberforce, Ohio, 1971; M.S. in Ednl. Adminstrn., Purdue U., 1981. Cert. tchr., supr., adminstr., Ill. Sec. dept. sociology Central State U., Wilberforce, 1966-71; tchr. Gary Community Schs., 1971-79; tchr. Park Forest Pub. Schs., Ill., 1979-83; asst. prin. Deer Creek Jr. High Sch., University Park, Ill., 1983—. Recipient Merit award Ind. Dept. Pub. Instrn. Mem. Assn. for Supervision and Curriculum Devel. Home: 11 Westwood Ct Park Forest IL 60466 Office: Deer Creek Jr High Sch 635 Olmsted Rd University Park IL 60466

RAYBURN, WILLIAM B., manufacturing executive. Chmn., pres., chief exec. officer, dir. Snap-On Tools. Office: Snap-On Tools Corp 2801 80th St Kenosha WI 53140*

RAYL, LEO S., JR., industrial engineering educator, labor-management arbitrator; b. Kokomo, Ind., Feb. 22, 1923; s. Leo S. and Ruth (Martin) R.; m. Olivia Caroline Grisham, Jan. 14, 1945. B.S.M.E., Purdue U., 1948; M.S.I.M., Krannert Sch., West Lafayette, Ind., 1959; M.P.A., Western Mich. U., 1975; Ed.D., Pacific States U., Los Angeles, 1977. Indsl. engr. ALCOA, Alcoa, Tenn., 1948-52; indsl. engr. Johnson Wax Co., Racine, Wis., 1952-54, sr. project engr., 1954-58; asst. to v.p. Steel Industries, Crawfordsville, Ind., 1959-60; prodn. supt. Gen. Foods Corp., Battle Creek, Mich., 1960-62, mgr. indsl. engring., 1962-64; from asst. prof. to prof. indsl. engring. Western Mich. U., Kalamazoo, 1965-78, prof., 1978—; labor-mgmt. arbitrator. Author arbitration awards pub. by Bur. Nat. Affairs and Am. Arbitration Assn., 1973—. Adviser Jr. Achievement, Battle Creek, 1960. Served to maj. U.S. Army, 1943-46, PTO. Named hon. Ky. col., 1977, hon. navy recruiter Navy Recruitment Command, Mich., 1983. Mem. Am. Soc. Engring. Edn., Soc. Profls. in Dispute Resolution (charter), Indsl. Relations Research Assn. (charter, pres. Southwestern Mich. chpt. 1971-72, adv. bd. 1971—), Nat. Acad. Conciliators (profl.), Am. Arbitration Assn. Methodist. Clubs: Gull Lake Country (Richland, Mich.); Beacon (Kalamazoo). Lodge: Masons. Office: Western Mich U Dept Indsl Engring Kalamazoo MI 49008

RAYMOND, JOHN MORGAN, systems analyst; b. Detroit, July 24, 1942; s. Harold Francis and Margaret (Carter) R.; m. Laurel Joyce Schaftenaar, June 28, 1975. B.B.A. in Fin., Western Mich. U., 1965; M.B.A., Mich. State U., 1967. Systems analyst Burroughs Corp., Detroit, 1970-75; pres. Raymond Ford, Inc., Adrian, Mich., 1976-80; sr. systems analyst Sheller-Globe Corp., Toledo, 1981—. Served with U.S. Army, 1967-69. Mem. Assn. Systems Mgmt. Home: 3112 Norwood Dr Adrian MI 49221 Office: Sheller-Globe Corp 1505 Jefferson Ave Toledo OH 43697

RAYMOND, LOREN ANDREW, dentist; b. Barberton, Ohio, Sept. 2, 1940; s. Loraine William and Nelle Josephine (Marshall) R.; m. Gretchen Elizabeth Mueller, Aug. 10, 1962; children—Katherine, Kelly J. B.A. in English, U. Rochester, 1961; D.M.D., Tufts U., 1965. Gen. practice dentistry, Norton, Ohio. Mem. Norton Bd. Edn., 1972-80, v.p., pres., 1979-80; mem. Norton City Council, 1982-83, pres., 1983; founder, pres. Citizens Opposed to the Destruction of the Environment, 1981—. Served to capt. USAF, 1965-67. Recipient Outstanding Achievement award Internat. Coll. Dentists, 1965. Mem. Akron Dental Assn., Ohio Dental Assn., ADA. Democrat. Home: 4373 Shuttle Dr Norton OH 44203 Office: 4322 S Cleveland-Massachusetts Rd Norton OH 44203

RAYMOND, RITA, adult education educator; b. Indpls., Feb. 24, 1940; d. William Henry and Mary Marie (Kegrice) Sutt; m. David Adamson Raymond, June 26, 1971. B.A., Manhattan Bible Coll., 1961; M.Div., Christian Theol. Sem., 1964; M.Ed., Ind. U., 1984. Ordained to ministry Christian Ch. (Disciples of Christ), 1966; cert. secondary tchr., Ind. Pastor Christian Ch., Kans., 1959-61; staff Ind. Migrant Ministry, 1961-66; counselor-minister edn. Salvation Army Men's Social Service Ctr., Indpls., 1966-67; Community Action Against Poverty, U.S. Govt., Indpls., 1967-68; soc. service dir., chaplain Park Dept. Turtle Creek, Indpls., 1968-71; tchr. weekday religious edn., Indpls., 1971-75; minister to aging, shut-ins Westminster Presbyterian Ch., Indpls., 1975-80; tchr. adult edn. Indpls. Pub. Schs., 1980—; del. Ind. Literacy, Indpls., 1983-84. Contbg. author: Bright Ideals, 1983; Branching Out, 1984. Chaplain Civil Air Patrol, Indpls., 1971. Recipient Cert. of Appreciation Adult Edn. Indpls., 1984. Mem. Am. Assn. Adult Edn., Ind. Assn. Adult Edn., Disciples Chaplain Assn. CAP (disting. service plaque 1972), Disciples Congress, Internat. Assn. Women Ministers, Christian Theol. Sem. Alumni Assn., Ind. U. Alumni Assn. Republican. Lodge: Woodmen of World. Home: 4643 San Diego Dr Indianapolis IN 46241 Office: Adult Edn Indpls 120 East Walnut St #601 Indianapolis IN 46241

RAYNOR, REV JOHN PATRICK, university president; b. Omaha, Oct. 1, 1923; s. Walter V. and Mary Clare (May) R.; A.B., St. Louis U., 1947, M.A., 1948 L.Ph., 1949, S.T.L., 1956; Ph.D., U. Chgo., 1959. Joined Soc. of Jesus, 1941, ordained priest Roman Cath. Ch., 1954; tchr. St. Louis U. High Sch., 1948-51, asst. prin., 1951; instr. dept. edn., asst. to dean Coll. Liberal Arts, Marquette U., Milw., 1960, asst. to v.p. acad. affairs, 1960-62, v.p. acad. affairs, 1962-65, pres., 1965—; dir. Kimberly-Clark Corp.; mem. North Central Assn. Colls. and Secondary Schs., also cons., examiner; sponsor United Negro Coll. Fund; mem. Wis. Higher Ednl. Aids Bd. Corp. mem. United Community Services of Greater Milw.; mem. Froedtert Luth. Meml. Hosp. Corp.; bd. dirs. Am. Lung Assn. Wis.; hon. bd. dirs. Goethe House, Milw.; past pres. Wis. region NCCJ. Recipient Distinguished Service award Edn. Commn. of the States, 1977. Mem. Met. Milw. Assn. Commerce, Citizens Govtl. Research Bur., Wis. Found. Ind. Colls. (past pres.), Greater Milw. Com., Internat. Fedn. Cath. Colls. and Univs., Nat. Cath. Edn. Assn., Community Issues Forum, Am. Council Edn., Wis. Assn. Ind. Colls. and Univs. (past pres.), Assn. Jesuit Colls. and Univs. (dir., exec. com.), Phi Beta Kappa, Phi Delta Kappa, Alpha Sigma Nu. Home: 615 N 11th St Milwaukee WI 52233 Office: Marquette U Milwaukee WI

RAYSHICH, DANIEL, vocational teacher; b. Springfield Twp., LaPorte County, Ind., Nov. 7, 1922; s. Marko and Mildred Rayshich. B.S., Purdue U., 1962, M.S., 1964; postgrad. No. Ill. U., 1966, Ind. U., 1971, Ind. State U., 1966-75. Cert. tchr., Ind. Staff Pullman Car Mfg. Co., Michigan City, Ind., 1940, Weil McClain Boiler Co., 1940; toolmaker Gary-Pitts. Corp., Gary Ind., 1940-58; tchr. Horace Mann High Sch., Gary, 1962-64, John H. Hinds Area Vocat. Sch., Elwood (Ind.) Sch. Corp., 1964—. Pres. Elwood Devel. Commn., pres. Elwood Housing Authority. Named Ind. Tchrs. of Yr., Am. Vocat. Assn., 1980; recipient Citizen of Yr. award, Elwood, 1980; Gov. Otis Bowen award Council of the Sagamores, 1980. Mem. Vocat. Indsl. Clubs Am., Am. Indsl. Arts Assn., Nat. Assn. Indsl. Trade Edn. Democrat. Greek Orthodox. Author: Modern Mathematics in Machine Trades, 1973; Machine Trades Blueprint Reading, 1983. Home: 717 1/2 South A St Elwood IN 46036 Office: John H Hinds Area Vocational School Rural Route 4 North 19th Elwood IN 46036

RAZI, KATHLEEN ANN, human resources specialist; b. Schenectady, Jan. 12, 1950; d. Francis William and Mary Margaret (Strong) Schickel; m. Ahmad Razi, Aug. 26, 1972; 1 child, Marisa. B.A., Russell Sage Coll., 1972; M.S. in Social Adminstrn., Case Western Res. U., 1974. Social worker Cleve. VA Hosp., 1972-73, Fairhill Mental Health Ctr., Cleve., 1973-74; social worker, adminstr. Far West Ctr., North Olmsted, Ohio, 1976-79; adminstr. coop. edn. Baldwin-Wallace Coll., Berea, Ohio, 1979-80, adminstr. acad. advising, 1980-85; human resource devel. specialist Univ. Hosps. of Cleve., 1985—. Developer Project Tng. Manual, 1979. Mem. Nat. Assn. Advisers, Nat. Assn. Social Workers (cert.), Am. Assn. Counseling and Devel., Cleve. Assn. Jr. League. Roman Catholic. Avocations: volunteer projects. Home: 21736 Aberdeen St Rocky River OH 44116

READ, THOMAS, association executive; b. Boston, Aug. 15, 1928; s. Richard Welch and Clara (Enesbuske) R.; m. Joan Amy May Cooke, Mar. 24, 1951; children—Ellen, David Richard, Timothy. A.B., Harvard U., 1949, C.A.S., 1975; M.A., U. Toledo, 1961. Tchr. math. and sci. St. John's Sch. and Peddie Sch., 1950-61; head dept. sci. Maumee Valley Country Day Sch., 1956-61;

headmaster Hampton Roads Acad., Newport News, Va., 1961-67, St. Paul Acad. and Summit Sch., 1967-74, St. John's Sch., Houston, 1976-81; exec. dir. Tex. Assn. Non-Pub. Schs., Houston, 1981-82; pres. Ind. Schs. Assn. of Central States, Downers Grove, Ill., 1982—; cons. Nat. Assn. Ind. Schs.; trustee Minn. Outward Bound, 1970-75, pres., 1972-73; bd. govs. SW Outward Bound Sch., 1976—, vice chmn., 1980-81; chmn. Minn. Project Differentiated Staffing, 1969-74. Trustee, Dodge Found., 1970-72, James Jerome Hill Reference Library, 1972-76, Ind. Ednl. Services, 1983—; mem. exec. com. midwest region Coll. Bd., 1983—. Bush Found. Leadership fellow, 1974-75. Mem. Headmasters Assn., Country Day Sch. Headmasters Assn., Episcopalian. Clubs: Harvard Faculty, Harvard (Chgo.). Contbr. articles to ind. sch. bulls. Home: 5426 Brookbank St Downers Grove IL 60615 Office: 1400 W Maple Ave Downers Grove IL 60515

READEY, DENNIS WILLIAM, ceramic engineering educator, administrator; b. Aurora, Ill., Aug. 6, 1937; s. William George and Leona Katherine (Kopp) R.; m. Suzann Dalton, May 31, 1958; children—Michael, Kevin. B.S. in Metallurgy U. Notre Dame, 1959; Sc.D. in Ceramics, MIT, 1962. Group leader Argonne Nat. Labs., Ill., 1964-67; lab. mgr. Raytheon Co., Waltham, Mass., 1967-74; program mgr. U.S. ERDA, Washington, 1974-77; from assoc. prof. to prof., chmn. Ohio State U., Columbus, 1977—; mem. Nat. Materials Adv. Bd., Washington, 1984—; cons. to govt. and industry. Contbr. articles to profl. jours. Trustee Orton Found., Westerville, Ohio, 1982—; Served to capt. U.S. Army, 1962-64. Grantee NSF, Office Naval Research, Army Research Office. Fellow Am. Ceramic Soc. (chmn. basic sci. 1982, Ross Coffin Purdy award 1971); mem. AAAS. Roman Catholic. Avocations: jogging, woodcarving, model railroads. Home: 2315 Severhill Dr Dublin OH 43017 Office: Ohio State U 2041 College Rd Columbus OH 43210

READNOWER, JEFFREY ALLAN, carpentry company executive builder, developer; b. Dayton, Ohio, Jan. 27, 1951; s. Thomas Eugene and Marcella Katherine (Weaver) R.; m. Joyce Alma Hahn, Feb. 12, 1973 (div. 1975); 1 child, James Thomas. Student U. Cin., 1969-72. Janitor Chemcare Corp., Cin., 1972-73; laborer G. Geisen Co., Cin., 1973; apprentice carpenter County Constrn. Co., Loveland, Ohio, 1973-74, carpenter foreman, 1974-77; owner Quality Carpentry Co., Cin., 1977—. Recipient Standard Breaker 181 award Kettering YMCA, 1971, Standard Breaker 165, 1970, 3d So. Ohio Championship, AAU, 1970, 1st place U. Cin. Open Competition, 1972. Republican. Club: Kettering Barbell. Avocations: creative writing, competative weighlifting, music, literature, military history. Home: 2 Laurelwood Dr Milford OH 45150

READO, GERALDINE GLOVER, chemist; b. Houston, Dec. 14, 1948; d. Willard Eugene and Annie Lee (Warren) Glover. B.A. in Chemistry, Dillard U., 1970. Chemist B.F. Goodrich Co., Port Neches, Tex., 1970-74; sr. research chemist Dow Chem. U.S.A., Midland, Mich., 1974-79, devel. supr., 1979-80, product sales mgr., 1980-84, research leader, 1984—. Pres. Career Women in Industry, 1977-78. Recipient cert. of appreciation Dale Carnegie Assn., 1979, Outstanding Grad. Asst. award, 1979. Mem. Nat. Assn. Female Execs., Alpha Kappa Alpha (v.p. Mu Alpha Omega chpt. 1984-86, grad. advisor 1983—, Service award 1982). Baptist. Avocations: owl collector; golfing; dancing; traveling.

REAGAN, CHARLES ELLIS, philosophy educator; b. N.Y.C., Oct. 24, 1942; s. Lewis Martin and Gabrielle (Delores) Perreault; m. Sharon Elaine Stephan, Aug. 9, 1969; children—Lewis Matthew, Noah Paul, Laura Suzanne. A.B., Holy Cross Coll., Worcester, Mass., 1964; M.A. U. Kans., 1966, Ph.D., 1967. Asst., then assoc. prof. dept. philosophy Kans. State U., Manhattan, 1967-79, prof., chmn. dept., 1980—; Fulbright vis. prof. Universite de Toulouse, France, 1976-77. Author: Ethics for Scientific Researchers, 1971. Editor: Studies in the Philosophy of Paul Ricoeur, 1979; (with others) Readings for an Introduction to Philosophy, 1976; The Philosophy of Paul Ricoeur, 1978. Am. Philos. Soc. research grantee, 1982. Mem. Am. Philos. Assn., Southwestern Philos. Assn., AAUP (pres. Kans. conf. 1982-83). Club: K-State Flying. (safety office 1979—). Avocation: flying. Home: 2110 Timber Creek Manhattan KS 66502 Office: Dept Philosophy 216 Eisenhower Hall Manhattan KS 66506

REAGAN, MICHAEL TERENCE, lawyer; b. Charleston, W.Va., July 22, 1947; s. William J. and Helen G. (Kirk) R.; m. Deborah Bowe, Mar. 17, 1973; children—Terence, Daniel. B.S.M.E., Purdue U., 1969; J.D., Georgetown U., 1972. Bar: Ill. 1973, U.S. Dist. Ct. (no. dist.) Ill. 1981. Ptnr. Herbolsheimer, Lannon, Henson, Duncan & Reagan, Ottawa, Ill., 1981—; mem. Ill. Supreme Ct. Com. on Pattern Jury Instrns., 1985—; mem. product liability com. Def. Research Inst., Chgo., 1980—. Chmn. Ottawa Planning Com., 1973-76, Ottawa Zoning Bd., 1973-76; v.p. Reddick's Mansion Assn. Mem. Ill. State Bar Assn. Republican. Roman Catholic. Club: Chgo. Yacht. Home: 325 Pearl St Ottawa IL 61350 Office: Herbolsheimer Lannon Henson Duncan & Reagan 633 LaSalle St Ottawa IL 61350

REAMS, BERNARD DINSMORE, JR., lawyer, educator; b. Lynchburg, Va., Aug. 17, 1943; s. Bernard Dinsmore and Martha Eloise (Hickman) R.; B.A., Lynchburg Coll., 1965; M.S., Drexel U., 1966; J.D., U. Kans., 1972; Ph.D., St. Louis U., 1984; m. Rosemarie Bridget Boyle, Oct. 26, 1968; children—Andrew Dennet, Adriane Bevin. Instr., asst. librarian Rutgers U., Camden, N.J., 1966-69; admitted to Kans. bar, 1973; asst. prof. law and librarian U. Kans., Lawrence, 1969-74; asst. prof. law and librarian Washington U., St. Louis, 1974-76, assoc. prof., 1976, prof., 1976—. Mem. Am., Spl. library assns., Am. Assn. Law Libraries, ABA, Phi Beta Kappa, Beta Phi Mu, Phi Delta Phi, Order of Coif. Author: Law for the Businessman, 1974; (with Wilson) Segregation and the Fourteenth Amendment in the States, 1975; (with Kettler) Historic Preservation Law: An Annotated Bibliography, 1976; Reader in Law Librarianship, 1976; (with Haworth) Congress and the Courts: A Legislative History 1787-1977, 1978; (with Ferguson) Federal Consumer Protection: Laws, Rules and Regulations, 1979; The Internal Revenue Acts of the United States 1909-1950, 1979; Federal Price and Wage Control Programs 1917-1979: Legislative Histories, 1980; Human Experimentation: Federal Law's, Legislative Histories, Regulations and Related Documents, 1985. Adv. editor Historical Writings in Law and Jurisprudence, 1980. Office: Washington U Sch Law Box 1120 Saint Louis MO 63130

REARDON, B. SCOTT, III, distribution company executive; b. Sioux Falls, S.D., Sept. 10, 1948; s. B. Scott, II and Margaret (O'Connor) R.; m. Rosemarie A. Sorrentino, Apr. 12, 1975; children—Scott, John, Courtney. A.B. in Econs., Georgetown U., 1970; M.S. in Bus., Am. U., 1974. Fin. analyst Pinewood Devel. Corp., Mount Vernon, Va., 1971-72, B.F. Saul Real Estate Investment Trust, Chevy Chase, Md., 1972-74; mgr. DaKON, Inc., Sioux Falls, 1974—, pres., 1983—; pres., owner Sedgwick Broadcasting Corp., 1984—. Bd. dirs. Sioux council Boy Scouts Am., 1980—. Roman Catholic. Lodge: Rotary. Office: DaKON Inc 1100 W Delaware Box 909 Sioux Falls SD 57101

REARDON, JOHN EDWARD, mayor; b. Kansas City, Kans., Aug. 23, 1943; s. Joseph and Helen (Cahill) R.; m. Helen Marie Kasick, June 18, 1966; children—Joseph, Kathleen. A.A., Donnelly Coll., 1963; B.A., Rockhurst Coll., 1965. Registrar deeds Wyandotte County (Kans.), 1972-75; mayor City of Kansas City (Kans.), 1975—; tchr., dept. head Arrowhead Jr. High Sch., Kansas City, Kans., 1966-72. Recipient Community Service award Urban League, Kansas City, 1981; named Outstanding Young Kansan, Kansas Jr. C. of C., 1978. Mem. U.S. Conf. Mayors, Kans. League Municipalities, Kansas City C. of C. Club: Optimists. Roman Catholic. Address: One Civic Ctr Plaza Kansas City KS 66101

REARDON, TIMOTHY JOSEPH, lawyer; b. Detroit, Aug. 18, 1935; s. Timothy Joseph and Louise (Whelan) R.; m. Joan Maureen Coburn, Aug. 7, 1958; children—Thomas, Michael, Brian, Kathleen. B.B.A., U. Mich., 1957, M.B.A., 1958; J.D., Detroit Coll. Law, 1965. Bar: Mich. 1966, Ill. 1974. Personnel asst. Kroger Co., Ft. Wayne, Ind., 1958-60; mgr. labor relations Allied Products Corp., Detroit, 1960-64; asst. sec., ho. counsel Whitehead & Kales Co., River Rouge, Mich., 1964-69; sole practice law, Muskegon, Mich., 1969-74, Springfield, Ill., 1976—; chief legal counsel Ill. Dept. Personnel, Springfield, 1974-76. Recipient prize for Excellence in Labor Law, Bancroft-Whitney Pub. Co., 1965. Mem. Ill. State Bar Assn. (sec. labor law sect. council 1984—), ABA, Sangamon County Bar Assn. Roman Catholic. Clubs: Lions, Rotary. Home: 178 Golf Rd Springfield IL 62704 Office: 2020 Timberbrook Dr Springfield IL 62702

REAVIS, MARSHALL WILSON, III, insurance educator; b. Anderson, Ind., Feb. 19, 1933; s. Marshall Wilson, Jr. and Ruby Louise (Beaman) R.; m. Marjorie Arlene Varady; children—Carrie Jo, Marshall Wilson, Amy Michelle. A.B. in Govt., Ind. U., 1957, M.B.A. in Ins., 1958; Ph.D. in Bus. Adminstrn., U. Ga., 1975. C.P.C.U., C.L.U. Dist. mgr. Kemper Ins., 1958-61; v.p. G. Shannon Grover & Co., 1962-63; regional mgr. Consol. Underwriters, 1963-65; corp. ins. mgr. Wurlitzer Co., 1965-68; mgr. corp. ins. Baxter Labs., 1968-70; teaching asst. U. Ga., Athens, 1970-72; prof. bus. adminstrn. Gov's. State U., Park Forest South, Ill., 1972-76; assoc. prof. fin. Roosevelt U., Chgo., 1976-82; dean Ins. Sch. Chgo., 1975-79; assoc. prof. fin. DePaul U., Chgo., 1982—; chmn. bd., publisher Ins. Edn. Specialists, Ltd., 1976—. Trustee, Village of Clarendon Hills (Ill.), 1974-78. Served to comdr. USNR, 1955-57; now Res. John M. Breen fellow Kemper Ins. Found., 1970-72. Mem. Am. Risk and Ins. Assn., Western Risk and Ins. Assn., Soc. C.P.C.U.s, Midwest Bus. Adminstrn. Assn., Ins. Co. Edn. Dirs. Soc., Navy League of U.S. (pres. Chgo. council 1973-74, mem. exec. com. 1975—). Republican. Presbyterian. Club: Union League (Chgo.). Author: Handbook of Insurance Terms and Concepts, 1981; Essentials of Property and Casualty Insurance, 1983; Essentials of Life and Health Insurance, 1983; Illinois Insurance Law, 1983; contbr. articles to profl. jours. Home: 43 Norfolk Ave Clarendon Hills IL 60514 Office: 25 E Jackson Blvd Chicago IL 60604

REBBECK, LESTER JAMES, JR., artist; b. Chgo., June 25, 1929; s. Lester J. and Marie L. (Runkle) R.; B.A.E., Art Inst. Chgo., 1953, M.A.E., Art Inst. Chgo. and U. Chgo., 1959; m. Paula B. Phillips, July 7, 1951; 1 son, Lester J. Asst. prof. art William Rainey Harper Coll., Pallatine, Ill., 1967-72; dir. Countryside Art Gallery (Ill.), 1967-73; gallery dir. Chgo. Soc. Artists, 1967-68; now artist, tchr.; one man exhbns. include Harper Jr. Coll.; group exhbns. include Univ. Club, Chgo., 1980, Art Inst., Chgo., 1953. Served with U.S. Army, 1951-52. Mem. NEA, Ill. Edn. Assn., Ill. Art Educators Assn., Chgo. Soc. Artists, Coll. Art Assn., Art Inst. Chgo. Alumni Assn. Republican. Presbyterian. Home: 2041 Vermont St Rolling Meadows IL 60008

REBEC, GEORGE VINCENT, biopsychology educator, administrator; b. Harrisburg, Pa. Apr. 6, 1949; s. George Martin and Nadine (Bosko) R. A.B., Villanova U., 1971; M.A., U. Colo., 1974, Ph.D., 1975. Postdoctoral fellow U. Calif.-San Diego, 1975-77; asst. prof. Ind. U., Bloomington, 1977-81, assoc. prof., 1981-85, prof. psychology, 1985—, acting dir. program in neural sci., 1984—. Contbr. articles to profl. jours. Recipient Eli Lilly Teaching award, 1978; grantee NIDA, 1979—, NSF, 1985—. Mem. AAAS, Soc. for Neurosci. (chmn. Ind. U. chpt.). Roman Catholic. Avocation: sports. Home: 300 Gilbert Ave Bloomington IN 47401 Office: Ind U Dept Psychology Bloomington IN 47405

REBENNACK, JACK GEORGE, pharmacist; b. Cin., Dec. 28, 1952; s. Jack Carl and Laverne (Miller) R.; m. Mary Beth Gausman, Mar. 10, 1984; 1 child, Joel David. B.S., U. Cin., 1975; M.B.A., Xavier U., 1977. Registered pharmacist, Ohio, Colo. Pharmacist Schmidt Pharmacy, Cin., 1975-76, People's Pharmacy, Denver, 1976-79; pharmacist, head buyer Shillito Rikes, Cin., 1979-80; pharmacist Becker Drugs, 1980-83; dir. pharmacy ops. Kroger Co., 1983—. Author: Pharmakokinetics, 1975. Mem. Am. Pharm. Assn., Ohio State Pharm. Assn. Republican. Lodge: Rotary. Avocations: golf, racquetball. Home: 2677-23 Montana Ave Cincinnati OH 45211

REBER, DENNIS GENE, pharmacist; b. Rockford, Ill., May 31, 1958; s. Gene Edward and Constance Lee (King) R. B.S. in Pharmacy, Drake U., 1981. Registered pharmacist, Mich., Ill., Iowa. Asst. mgr. Osco Drug, Kankakee, Ill., 1981-82, Cedar Rapids, Iowa, 1982-83, Battle Creek, Mich., 1983-84, Portage, Mich., 1984, pharmacist, Chgo., 1984—. Mem. Am. Pharm. Assn., Ill. Pharm. Assn. Avocations: flying, reading, swimming, bicycling. Home: 3430 N Lake Shore Dr Chicago IL 60657 Office: Osco Drug 2940 Ashland Ave Chicago IL 60657

REBERS, PAUL ARMAND, chemist; b. Mpls., Jan. 24, 1923; s. Ernest Edward and Verna (Rand) R.; m. E. Louise Burrell, Dec. 14, 1952; children—Michael, John, Joseph. B.S. in Chem. Engring., U. Minn., 1944, M.S. in Chem. Engring., 1946, Ph.D. in Agrl. Biochemistry, 1953. Plant devel. chemist Rohm & Haas, Phila., 1946-48; research chemist Holly Sugar Co., Colorado Springs, Colo., 1953-55; asst. prof. Rutgers U., New Brunswick, N.J., 1955-61; research chemist USDA, Ames, Iowa, 1961—; cons. Continental Baking, Rye, N.Y., 1957-60. Contbr. numerous articles to profl. jours. Patentee mech. hand. Mem. Am. Assn. Immunologists, Am. Chem. Soc., Am. Soc. Microbiologists, Sigma Xi, Phi Kappa Phi, Phi Zeta. Republican. Methodist. Clubs: Toastmasters (Ames, Iowa) (pres. 1985). Lodges: Masons (worshipful master 1974-75), Order Eastern Star (worthy patron 1974—). Home: 627 14th St Place Nevada IA 50201 Office: USDA Nat Animal Disease Ctr Dayton Rd Ames IA 50010

REBOUCHE, CHARLES JOSEPH, biochemist, educator; b. New Orleans, Dec. 27, 1948. B.S., Tulane U., 1970; Ph.D., Vanderbilt U., 1974. Research assoc. U. Tex., 1974-75; fellow Mayo Found., Rochester, Minn., 1975-80, assoc. cons., 1980-84; asst. prof. U. Iowa, Iowa City, 1984—. Contbr. articles to profl. jours. Grantee NIH, 1980—, Muscular Dystrophy Assn., 1982-84. Mem. Am. Inst. Nutrition, Am. Chem. Soc. (div. biol. chemistry), Tissue Culture Assn. Office: Dept Pediatrics U Iowa Hosps Iowa City IA 52242

RECHENBERG, BASIL WILLIAM, priest, psychologist, educator; b. Memphis, June 27, 1928; s. Harry William and Clothilde Louise (Meacham) R.; B.A., So. Meth. U., 1948; L.Th., Seabury-Western Theol. Sem., 1952, B.D., 1953; M.A., Immaculate Conception Sem., 1967; postgrad. U. Chgo., 1948-49, 57-60. Joined Order St. Benedict; ordained priest Roman Cath. Ch., 1968; lic. psychologist, Mo. Psychologist Iowa State Penitentiary, Ft. Madison, 1953-57, psychologist Des Moines Child Guidance Ctr., 1960-63, Conception Sem. Coll., Mo., 1965—, dir. psychol. services, 1972—; prof. psychology and Latin, 1970—; cons. Benedictine Counseling and Cons. Inst., Maryville, Mo., 1979—. Contbr. articles to profl. jours. Fellow Am. Orthopsychiat. Assn.; mem. Am. Classical League, Am. Psychol. Assn. (assoc.), Classical Assn. Middle West and South, Soc. Personality Assessment (assoc.), Mo. Classics Assn. Republican. Home: Conception Abbey Conception MO 64433 Office: Conception Sem Coll Conception MO 64433

RECHTIN, MICHAEL DAVID, lawyer, engineering consultant, expert witness; b. Fort Smith, Ark., Feb. 1, 1944; s. George Lester and Catherine (Holmes) R.; m. Elisabeth Ann Lloyd, Aug. 20, 1966; children—Michael David Jr., Thomas P., Matthew S. B.S., U. Ill., 1966; Ph.D., MIT, 1970; J.D., Ill. Inst. Tech.-Chgo. Kent, 1981. Bars: U.S. Patent Office, 1980, Ill. 1982, U.S. Dist. Ct. (no. dist.) Ill. 1982, U.S. Ct. Appeals (7th cir.) 1982. NSF fellow, 1968; IBM fellow, instr. materials sci. MIT, Cambridge, 1970-73; research scientist Tex. Instruments Corp., Dallas, 1973-75; scientist, patent agent, Argonne Lab. and Dept. Energy, Ill., 1975-81; counsel, patent agent Standard Oil Co. (Ind.), Chgo., 1981-83; assoc. Welsh and Katz, Ltd., Chgo., 1983—; mem. exec. com., chmn. new bus. com. MIT Enterprise Forum, Chgo., 1983—; dir. Virtual Network Services Corp., Oak Brook, Ill. Contbr. articles to profl. jours. Chmn. ednl. council MIT, Chgo., 1978—. Academic scholar, 1979. Mem. ABA, Patent Law Assn. Chgo. (com. on tax), Chgo. Bar Assn. (computer law, fin., new bus., and patent coms.). Republican. Presbyterian. Club: MIT (bd. dirs. 1982—). Home: 2002 Coach Dr Naperville IL 60565 Office: Welsh and Katz Ltd 135 S LaSalle St Suite 1625 Chicago IL 60603

RECHTSCHAFFEN, ALLAN, sleep researcher, psychology educator; b. N.Y.C., Dec. 8, 1927; s. Philip and Sylvia (Yaeger) R.; m. Karen Ann Wold, Mar. 16, 1979; children—Laura, Katherine, Amy. B.S., CCNY, 1949, M.A., 1951; Ph.D., Northwestern U., 1956. Psychologist Fergus Falls State Hosp., Minn., 1951-53; lectr. Northwestern U., Chgo., 1956-57; research psychologist VA, Chgo., 1956-57; prof. U. Chgo., 1957—, dir. Sleep Research Lab., 1958—. Contbr. articles to profl. jours. Recipient Research Scientist award NIMH, 1977—, Nathanial Kleitman award Assn. Sleep Disorders Ctrs., 1985. Mem. Sleep Research Soc. (pres. 1978-82). Avocations: photography, shopwork. Office: Sleep Research Lab 5743 S Drexel Ave Chicago IL 60637

RECK, W(ALDO) EMERSON, public relations specialist, writer, university administrator emeritus; b. Gettysburg, Ohio, Dec. 28, 1903; s. Samuel Harvey and Effie D. (Arnett) R.; A.B., Wittenberg U., 1926; A.M., U. Iowa, 1946; LL.D., Midland Coll., 1949; m. Hazel Winifred January, Sept. 7, 1926; children—Phyllis Jean Reck Welch, Elizabeth Ann Reck Lada. Reporter, Springfield (Ohio) News, 1922-26; publicity dir. Midland Coll., Fremont, Nebr., 1926-28, dir. pub. relations, prof. journalism, 1928-40; dir. pub. relations Colgate U., 1940-48; v.p. Wittenberg U., Springfield, Ohio, 1948-70, v.p. emeritus, 1970—; pub. relations specialist Cumerford Corp., Ft. Lauderdale, Fla., 1970-78; hist. columnist Springfield (Ohio) Sun, 1973-81; spl. corr. AP, 1928-38; mng. editor Fremont Morning Guide, 1939; vis. lectr. pub. relations State U. Iowa, summers 1941, 42, U. Wyo., summer 1948; co-dir. Seminar on Pub. Relations for High Edn., Syracuse U., summers 1944, 45, 46. Recipient award Am. Coll. Pub. Relations Assn. for Distinguished Service, 1942, for Outstanding Achievement in Interpretation of Higher Edn., 1944, 47; award Council for Advancement and Support of Edn., 1977; medal of honor Wittenberg U., 1982. Mem. Am. Coll. Pub. Relations Assn. (v.p. in charge research 1936-38, editor assn. mag. 1938-40, pres. 1940-41, chmn. plans and policies com. 1944-50, dir. 1956, historian 1967-76), Luth. Coll. Pub. Relations Assn. (pres. 1951-53), Pub. Relations Soc. Am. (nat. jud. council 1952), Assn. Am. Colls. (com. on pub. relations 1945-48), AAUP, Springfield C. of C. (dir. 1958-60), Council for Advancement and Support Edn., Nat. Luth. Ednl. Conf. (chmn. com. pub. relations 1949-50), Ohio Coll. Pub. Relations Officers (pres. 1954-55), Archives Assos., Nat. Hist. Soc., Abraham Lincoln Assn., Ohio Hist. Soc., Smithsonian Assos., Nat. Trust Historic Preservation, Omicron Delta Kappa, Sigma Delta Chi, Pi Delta Epsilon, Delta Sigma Phi, Blue Key, Elbeetian Legion. Author: Public Relations: a Program for Colleges and Universities, 1946; (with others) The American College, 1949; contbr.: Public Relations Handbook, 1950, 60, 67; The Changing World of College Relations, 1976; Father Can't Forget, 1982; Abraham Lincoln's Last 24 Hours, 1986; editor: Publicity Problems, 1939; College Publicity Manual, 1948; contbr. to ednl., profl. and hist. publs. Mem. commn. on ch. papers, 1951-62, cons. com. dept. of press, radio and TV United Luth. Ch., 1955-60; mem. commn. on ch. papers Luth. Ch. in Am., 1962-64, 70-72, mem. exec. com., also chmn. com. periodicals of bd. publ., 1962-72, mem. mgmt. com. Office of Communications, 1972-76; chmn. pub. relations com. Council Protestant Colls. and Univs., 1961-65. Home: 3148 Argonne Ln North Springfield OH 45503

RECKARD, CRAIG REGINALD, physician; b. Phila., Dec. 21, 1940; s. C. John and Mary E. (Craig) R.; m. Jean M. Santoro, Nov. 9, 1968 (div. Dec. 1983); children—Jonathan, Justin. B.S., Ursinus Coll., 1962; M.D., U. Pa., 1967. Diplomate Am. Bd. Surgeons. Intern U. Pa., Phila., 1967-68, resident in surgery, 1968-74, transplantation fellow, 1970-72; assoc. prof. surgery U. Chgo., 1976-83; prof. surgery Loyola U., Maywood, Ill., 1983—. Served to maj. U.S. Army, 1974-76. Recipient Clin. Investigator award NIH 1977. Fellow ACS; mem. Am. Soc. Transplant Surgeons, Internat. Transplantation Soc., Chgo. Surg. Soc. Avocations: photography, skiing, tennis, racquetball. Office: Loyola U Med Ctr 2160 S 1st Ave Maywood IL 60153

RECORDS, RAYMOND EDWIN, opthalmologist, medical educator; b. Ft. Morgan, Colo., May 30, 1930; s. George Harvey and Sara Barbara (Louden) R.; 1 child, Lisa Rae. B.S. in Chemistry, U. Denver, 1956; M.D., St. Louis U., 1961. Diplomate Am. Bd. Ophthalmology. Intern St. Louis U. Hosp. Group, 1961-62; resident in ophthalmology U. Colo. Med. Ctr., Denver, 1962-65; instr. ophthalmology, 1965-67, asst. prof., 1967-70; prof. ophthalmology U. Nebr. Coll. Medicine, Omaha, 1970—, dept. chmn., 1970—. Author: Physiology of Human Eye (Med. Writers award 1980), 1979. Author, editor: Biomedical Foundations of Ophthalmology, 1982. Med. dir. Nebr. Lions Eye Bank, 1970-81. Fellow Am. Acad. of Ophthalmology (outstanding contbn. award 1978); mem. Nebr. Med. Assn., Omaha-Douglas County Med. Soc., Omaha Ophthal. Soc. (pres. 1981-82), Assn. Research in Vision and Ophthalmology. Home: 9916 Devonshire Dr Omaha NE 68114 Office: U Nebr Med Ctr Suite 25 Omaha NE 68105

RECTENWALD, GARY MICHAEL, marketing manager; b. Toledo, Dec. 31, 1949; s. Edgar E. and Dorothy C. (Antieau) R.; B.S. (cum laude), Ohio State U., 1971, M.S. in Computer Sci., 1972, M.B.A., 1978. Programmer trainee Ohio State U., 1970-71, grad. research asso., 1971-72; application systems programmer, 1972-77, mgr. application systems programming, 1977-78; mem. Instrn. and Research Computer Center; systems engr. IBM, Columbus, 1978-81, mktg. rep., 1982, large systems mktg. cons., 1983, mktg. mgr., 1984—. Served with Air N.G., 1970-76. Mem. Ohio State U. Marching Band, 1967-75 (most inspirational bandsman 1973), Phi Beta Kappa, Beta Gamma Sigma, Kappa Gamma Sigma, Pi Mu Epsilon, Kappa Kappa Psi. Roman Catholic. Home: 1164 Bryant St East Lansing MI 48823 Office: IBM 1 Michigan Ave Lansing MI 48909

RECTOR, GEORGE WILLIAM, optometrist; b. New Castle, Ind., July 16, 1947; s. Paul F. and Bernice L. (Ellis) R.; m. Sandra K. Burch, June 19, 1971; 1 child, Clifford P. B.S., Ind. U., 1969, O.D., 1971. Gen. practice optometry, New Castle, Ind., 1971—; cons. Community Care Center New Castle, Ind., 1973—; pres. Whitewater Valley Optometric Soc., Ind., 1975-77. Mem. Am. Optometric Found., Optometric Extension Program. Ind. U. Optometry Alumni, Ind. U. Alumni Assn. (life), Woodburn Guild. Mem. Christian Ch. Clubs: First Nighters Civic Theatre, Westwood Country (New Castle); Hoosier Hundred (Bloomington). Avocations: photography, theatre. Home: 3800 S Main St New Castle IN 47362 Office: 1500 Washington St PO Box 645 New Castle IN 47362

REDDEN, JAMES ERSKINE, linguistics educator; b. Louisville, Dec. 28, 1928; s. James Clyde and Leora Mae (Kerr) R.; m. Patricia Jane Stone, Apr. 7, 1950 (div. July 1984); children—Deborah, Virginia, Barry, David, Nathan, Alexander; m. Dorothy Louise Eggers Lyons, Aug. 5, 1984. B.A. in German, U. Louisville, 1950; Ph.D. in Linguistics, Ind. U., 1965. Sci. linguist Fgn. Service Inst., Dept. State, Washington, 1961-65; assoc. prof. linguistics Am. U. Beirut, Lebanon, 1965-67; prof. linguistics So. Ill. U., Carbondale, 1967—; sr. research fellow Fulbright Found., Fed. Republic U. Hamburg, Germany, 1973-74; U.S. Office Edn. researcher U. Yaoundeá, Cameroon, 1971; cons. Ford Found. Dakar, Senegal, Abidjan, Ivory Coast and Lagos, Nigeria, 1968-71, U.S. AID various Middle Eastern countries, 1965-71. Author: Descriptive Grammer of Ewondo, 1979; Twi Basic Course, 1963; Lingla Basic Course, 1963; MoreáBasic Course, 1966; Descriptive Grammar of Hualapai, 1986. Editor Ann. Procs. Hokan-Yuman Langs. Workshop. NDEA U.S. Office Edn. fellow Ind. U., 1960-61; Am. Council Learned Socs. grantee, 1963, 67; NSF grantee, 1979-80; Wenner-Gren grantee, 1981. Fellow Am. Anthropol. Assn.; mem. Linguistic Soc. Am., West African Linguistics Assn., Internat. Linguistics Assn., Societas Linguistica Europaea, Australian Linguistic Soc., Tchrs. English to Speakers Other Langs., Linguistic Assn. Gt. Britain, Can. Linguistic Assn. Mem. Christian Ch. Lodge: Lions (1st v.p. 1984-85, pres. 1985-86). Avocations: bridge, model trains. Home: 1908 Spruce St Murphysboro IL 62966 Office: So Ill U Dept Linguistics Carbondale IL 62901

REDDICK, BRYAN DEWITT, English educator, educational administrator; b. Austin, Tex., Feb. 4, 1942; s. DeWitt Carter and Marjorie Alice (Bryan) R.; m. Sheila Ann Farrell, Oct. 3, 1970; children—Bridget Louise, George William. B.A., U. Iowa, 1964; M.A., Syracuse U., 1966; Ph.D., U. Calif.-Davis, 1969. Fulbright teaching fellow U. Lyon, France, 1969-70; Maitre de Confs. U. Grenoble, France, 1970-71; asst. prof. English, Am. U., Washington, 1971-75; assoc. prof. Olivet Coll., Mich., 1975-80, prof., 1980—, assoc. dean, 1981-82, acad. v.p., 1982—. Author: Student Journalist and Effective Writing Style, 1976. Editor: Mass Media and the School, 1984. Contbr. articles to profl. jours. Chmn. Olivet Planning Commn., Mich., 1978. Recipient Faculty Research award Olivet Coll., 1979; NDEA fellow, 1966-69. Mem. Mich. Coll. English Assn., Phi Beta Kappa, Phi Mu Alpha, Omicron Delta Kappa. Lodge: Lions (sec. 1979-82, dir. 1982—). Home: 621 Washington Ave Olivet MI 49076 Office: Olivet Coll Olivet MI 49076

REDDING, GEORGE HYDE, JR., chemical company executive; b. Chgo., Nov. 21, 1921; s. George Hyde and Gladys Louise (Arlington) R.; m. Patricia Gwynn Garrison, Sept. 6, 1948 (div. 1966); children—George Hyde, William M., David G.; m. 2d Margaret LeMoyne Whiting, Dec. 30, 1966; 1 son, Graham W. A.B., Washington and Jefferson Coll., 1943; J.D., Northwestern U., 1948. Bar: Ill. 1949; ptnr. law firm Norman, Englehardt & Zimmerman, Attys., Chgo., 1953-67; exec. v.p. N. Marshall Seeburg & Sons, Inc., Chgo., 1967-79; pres. Great Lakes Chemical, Melrose Park, Ill., 1979—; dir. Pettibone Chgo. Inc. Village atty., Wilmette, Ill., 1955-65; trustee Village of Winnetka (Ill.), 1983—. Trustee, Washington and Jefferson Coll. Served to lt. comdr. USNR, 1943-46, 51-53. Mem. Chgo. Bar Assn. Republican. Congregationalist. Clubs: Union League, Tavern. Office: 1985 N Anson Dr Melrose Park IL 60160

REDDY, NALLAPU NARAYAN, economics educator; b. Nagaram, India, June 22, 1939; came to U.S., 1958; s. Narasimha N. and Shantha N. Reddy; m. Saroja N. Malladi, June 1, 1957; children—Lata, Mala. B.S., Mich. Technol. U., 1961; M.S., U. Mo., 1963; Ph.D., Pa. State U., 1967; M.A., U. Notre Dame, 1973. Asst. prof. Clarkson U., Potsdam, N.Y., 1967-72, assoc. prof., 1972-74; assoc. prof. econs. U. Mich.-Flint, 1974-79, prof., 1979—, chmn. dept., 1981-84; vis. prof. London Sch. Econs., 1981. Editor: Empirical Studies in

Microeconomics, 1985. Contbr. articles to profl. jours. Mem. Am. Econ. Assn., Eastern Econ. Assn., So. Econ. Assn., Western Econ. Assn., Phi Kappa Phi, Omicron Delta Epsilon. Home: 6250 Kings Shire Rd Grand Blanc MI 48439 Office: Dept Econs U Mich Flint MI 48502

REDDY, NARENDER PABBATHI, biomedical engineering educator; b. Karimnagar, India, May 5, 1947; came to U.S., 1969; s. Lakshma Pabbathi and Rathnamma (Annam) R.; m. Swarna Latha, Feb. 20, 1976; children—Hari-Charan, Vishnu-Krupa. B.E., Osmama U., 1969; M.S., U. Miss., 1971; Ph.D., Tex. A&M U., 1974. Research asst. Tex. A&M U., College Station, 1971-74, research assoc., 1974-75; research assoc. Baylor Coll. Medicine, Houston, 1975-77; postgrad. research physiologist U. Calif. Sch. Medicine, San Francisco, 1977-78; sr. research scientist Helen Hayes Hosp., West Haverstraw, N.Y., 1978-81; assoc. prof. U. Akron, Ohio, 1981—; adj. assoc. prof. Rensselaer Poly. Inst., Troy, N.Y., 1978-80; adj. staff mem. Edwin Shaw Hosp., Akron, 1984—. Contbr. articles to profl. jours., papers to internat. sci. meetings. Mem. Biomed. Engring. Soc. (sr.), ASME, Rehab. Engring. Soc. N.Am., Am. Soc. Engring. Edn. Hindu. Avocation: meditation. Home: 1231 Millhaven St Akron OH 44321

REDEBAUGH-LEVI, CAROLINE LOUISE, senior action center coordinator, registered nurse; b. Dixon, Ill., May 23, 1910; d. Charles R. and May Caroline (Barnes) Kreger; m. Richard E. Belcher, Nov. 24, 1934 (dec. 1964); children—Richard Charles, Mary; m. Charles H. Redebaugh, Dec. 3, 1966 (dec. 1979); m. Paul Levi, July 20, 1985. R.N., Katherine Shaw Bethea Sch. Nursing, 1930. Nurse, various hosps., 1930-49; adminstr. Mansion Nursing Home, Dixon, Ill., 1949-77; coordinator Sr. Action Ctr., Springfield, Ill., 1977—; mem. various adv. coms. advocating for srs. Contbr. articles to profl. jours. Mem. nat. adv. com., del. White House Conf. on Aging, 1981; v.p. Ill. Joint Council to Improve Health Care for Aged, 1953, pres., 1954. Mem. Capitol City Republican Women (v.p. 1983-84), State Council on Aging, Am. Coll. Nursing Home Adminstrs. (charter, edn. com., pres.), Am. Nursing Home Assn. (v.p. 1953), Ill. Nurses Assn. (bd. dirs.). Home: 1420 Eustace Dr Dixon IL 61021 Office: Sr Action Ctr 3 W Old Town Mall Springfield IL 62701

REDEKER, JERRALD H(ALE), banker; b. Waupun, Wis., Oct. 5, 1934; s. Samuel and Laura A. (Schinzel) R.; m. Elsie Delaine Vande Zande, June 22, 1957; children—Lisa, Joel, Cara, Allyson. B.A. in Bus. Adminstrn., Hope Coll., 1956; grad. cert. Am. Inst. Banking, 1964. Mgr., Old Kent Bank and Trust Co., Grand Rapids, Mich., 1962-65; v.p. Met. Nat. Bank of Farmington (Mich.), 1965-67; v.p. First State Bank of Charlevoix (Mich.), 1967-68, exec. v.p., 1968-69, pres., 1969-72; agt. Farm Bur. Mut. Ins. Co., Charlevoix, 1972-74; chmn. bd., pres., chief exec. officer Old Kent Bank of Holland (Mich.), 1974—; dir., vice chmn. Lakeshore Health Maintenance Orgn., Holland, 1985—. Bd. dirs. Holland Econ. devel. Corp., 1974—; bd. dirs. Holland Community Hosp., 1974—, chmn. bd., 1979-81; bd. dirs. bd. theol edn. Ref. Ch. in Am., 1978-84, bd. dirs. gen. synod exec. com., 1984—, chmn. bd. direction, 1985—. Served with U.S. Army, 1957-59; Germany. Named to Outstanding Young Men Am., U.S. Jaycees, 1970. Mem. Mich. Bankers Assn., Robert Morris Assocs., Bank Adminstrn. Inst., Holland Area C. of C. (bd. dirs. 1975-84, chmn. bd. 1981-82). Republican. Mem. Reformed Ch. in Am. Lodge: Rotary (dir. 1980—) (pres. 1985-86) (Holland).

REDFORD, GERALD ALAN, college administrator; b. Balt., Oct. 1, 1931; s. Percy Stewart and Louise Catherine (Favatt) R.; m. Barbara Lee Jettinghoff, June 19, 1954; children—Douglas, David, Christine, Carol, Sarah. B.A., Ohio State U., 1953; M.A., Sangamon State U., 1975. Reporter, photographer Crescent-News, Defiance, Ohio, 1955-58; with pub. relations dept. Ripon Coll., Wis., 1958-61; with pub. relations dept. Millikin U., Decatur, Ill., 1961-68, asst. to pres., 1968-80, acting dean, 1979-80, dean, 1980—. Served with U.S. Army, 1953-55. Mem. Phi Delta Kappa (pres. 1985—), Phi Kappa Phi, Omicron Delta Kappa. Home: 1553 W Main St Decatur IL 62522 Office: Millikin U Coll Arts and Scis Decatur IL 62522

REDMAN, GEORGE LOWELL, teacher educator, writer, consultant; b. Waseca, Minn., May 27, 1941; s. Otto E. and Adeline (Koechel) R.; m. Sharon Ruth Denesen, Oct. 31, 1971; children—Ryan Lowell, Angela Ruth. B.A., Hamline U., 1963; M.A., U. Minn., 1965, Ph.D., 1975. Cert. tchr., Calif., Minn. Sci. tchr. La Habra High Sch., Calif., 1965-69; instr. edn. U. Minn., Mpls., 1969-75, assoc. prof., 1975-76; chmn. edn. dept. Hamline U., St. Paul, 1976—, evaluation coordinator faculty devel. project, 1981-85, cons. Parenting for Self-esteem, Eden Prairie, Minn., 1984—. Author: Self-Esteem for Tots to Teens, 1984. Contbr. articles to profl. jours. Recipient nat. outstanding research award Assn. Tchr. Educators, 1976-77. Mem. Minn. Assn. Colls. Tchr. Edn. (outstanding research award 1977, 80), Minn. Assn. Tchr. Educators, Theta Chi. Republican. Avocations: reading, skiing, tennis, writing, traveling. Home: 6916 Rosemary Rd Eden Prairie MN 55344 Office: Hamline U Edn Dept St Paul MN 55104

REDMAN, MICHAEL WAYNE, retailer, editor, writer; b. Indpls., Oct. 2, 1950; s. Kenneth Wayne and Betty (Haus) R.; m. Sheryl Darlene Hull, June 21, 1975; children—Miranda Darlene, Andrew Wayne. B.S., Ind. U., 1973. Tchr. alternative edn. Alternative High Sch., Bloomington, Ind., 1975-79; editor Primo newspaper, Bloomington, 1975-79; pub. Real Times, Bloomington, 1979-83; owner, mgr. 25th Century Five & Dime store, Bloomington, 1984—; pres. Futura Communications, Inc., 1978-79. Contbr. articles and movie revs. to news publs. Avocations: photography, golf. Office: 25th Century Five & Dime 106 E Kirkwood St PO Box 7 Bloomington IN 47402

REDMOND, WALTER T., food products company executive; b. 1923; student Mich. State U. With Kellogg Co., Battle Creek, Mich., 1948—, controller, 1961-67, v.p., controller, 1967-75, exec. v.p., 1975-81, pres., 1981-85, chief adminstrv. officer, 1981—, vice chmn., 1985—, also dir. Office: Kellogg Co 235 Porter St Box 3423 Battle Creek MI 49016*

REDSTONE, DANIEL AARON, architect; b. Detroit, Apr. 24, 1942; s. Louis Gordon and Ruth Roslyn (Rosenbaum) R.; m. Barbara Osten, June 29, 1980; children—Adam, Carly. B.S., U. Mich., 1965, M.B.A., 1967. Registered architect, Mich. Architect., Louis G. Redstone Assocs., Inc., Detroit, 1967-70, Livonia, Mich., 1972—, v.p., treas., 1979—; pres. Air Michigan, Inc., Kalamazoo, 1970-72. Mem. allocation com. United Fund, Detroit, 1981-85; mem. West Bloomfield Residential Rev. Bd., 1984-85. Mem. AIA (pres. 1984-85), Livonia C. of C. (v.p., bd. dirs. 1981-85). Jewish. Avocations: numismatics, squash. Home: 3347 Bloomfield Shore Dr West Bloomfield MI 48033 Office: 28425 W Eight Mile Rd Livonia MI 48152

REDSTONE, LOUIS GORDON, architect; b. Poland, Mar. 16, 1930; came to U.S., 1923, naturalized, 1928; s. Abraham Aaron and Anna (Gordon) Routenstein; m. Ruth R. Rosenbaum, June 25, 1939; children—Daniel Aaron, Eliel Gordon. B.S. in Architecture, U. Mich., 1929; M.Arch., Cranbrook Acad. Arts, 1948. Engaged in practice architecture, Israel, 1933-37; founder firm Louis G. Redstone Assocs. Inc., architects/engrs./planners, Detroit, 1938, pres., 1945-79, chmn., 1979—; del. internat. congresses, Caracas, Venezuela, Tokyo, Moscow, Buenos Aires; exec. com. Pan Am. Fedn. Architects, 1955-70; juror archtl. and artists exhbns.; profl. adviser archtl. competitions sponsored by Dow Chem. Co., 1965; mem. Mich. Commn. on Art in State Bldgs., 1975-79, trustee, 1979—. Author: Art in Architecture, 1968; New Dimensions in Shopping Centers and Stores, 1973; The New Downtowns-Rebuilding Business Districts, 1976; Hospitals and Health Care Facilities, 1978; Institutional Buildings, 1980; Public Art-New Directions, 1981; Masonry in Architecture, 1983. Contbr. articles to profl. mags. and newspapers. Recipient Patron award Mich. Found. for Arts, 1977. Fellow AIA (pres. Detroit chpt. 1965, Gold medal outstanding contbn. to profession), Mich. Soc. Architects, Engring. Soc. Detroit, Royal Acad. Fine Arts Netherlands (hon.), Royal Acad. Fine Arts of San Fernando, Spain (corr. academician). Home: 19303 Appoline St Detroit MI 48235 Office: 28425 W Eight Mile Rd Livonia MI 48152

REECE, JAMES STEPHEN, business educator; b. Payson, Utah, June 5, 1942; s. James Sterling and Nelda (Snelson) R.; m. Bonnie Marie Bucks, June 10, 1967; children—Charles Sterling, Chloe Suzanne. A.B., Yale U., 1964, M.B.A., 1968; D.B.A., Harvard Bus. Sch., 1970. From asst. prof. to assoc. prof. Harvard Bus. Sch., Boston, 1970-75; assoc. prof. U. Mich. Grad. Sch. Bus. Adminstrn., Ann Arbor, 1975-77, prof., 1977—; dir. U. Cellar, Inc., Ann Arbor, Armour & Cape, Inc., Atlanta, Teng & Assoc., Inc., Chgo. Author: Accounting Principles, 1983; Accounting: Text and Cases, 1983; Fundamentals of Management Accounting, 1984. Editor: Controllers Handbook, 1978. Mem. Am. Acctg. Assn., Acad. Mgmt., Inst. Mgmt. Acctg. (disting. performance cert. 1974). Home: 339 Rock Creek Ct Ann Arbor MI 48104 Office: U Mich Grad Sch Bus Adminstrn Ann Arbor MI 48109-1234

REED, ALBERT PAUL, research microbiologist; b. St. Marys, Pa., July 4, 1954; s. Albert Paul and Veronica C. (Delullo) R.; m. Cynthia Lou Zerbe, July 1, 1978; children—Brandon Charles, Sarah Katherine. B.S., U. Pitts., 1976; M.S., Clarion State U., 1980. Research supr. Genex Corp., Gaithersburg, Md., 1981-83; assoc. sr. research investigator Norden Labs., Lincoln, Nebr., 1983—. Mem. Am. Soc. Microbiology. Republican. Roman Catholic. Avocations: shooting, hunting, outdoor sports. Home: 230 Redwood Ln Lincoln NE 68510 Office: Norden Labs 601 W Cornhusker Lincoln NE 68521

REED, DAVID KENT, research entomologist; b. Wichita Falls, Tex., Mar. 6, 1932; s. Claude A. and Vera E. (Hunn) R.; m. Shirley DeElla Smith, Sept. 1, 1957; children—Kelly Don, Kyle Lynn, Marla DeElla. B.S., Purdue U., 1956; M.S., Tex. A&M U., 1960; Ph.D., U. Calif.-Riverside, 1971. Sales rep. agrl. chemistry dept. Swift & Co., Harlingen, Tex., 1960-61; research entomologist Citrus Lab, Agrl. Research Service, Orlando, Fla., 1961-66, Weslaco, Tex., 1966-68, research entomologist, project leader, Riverside, Calif., 1968-76, research and location leader vegetable lab., Vincennes, Ind., 1976—; instr. Vincennes U., 1976—; asst. prof. Purdue U., West Lafayette, Ind., 1976-81, assoc. prof., 1981—. Contbr. articles to profl. jours., also chpts. to books. Served to 1st lt. U.S. Army, 1956-58. Recipient Outstanding Performance award USDA, 1964. Mem. Entomol. Soc. Am., Soc. Invertebrate Pathology, Ind. Acad. Sci., Internat. Soc. Chem. Ecology, Sigma Xi. Republican. Mem. Ch. of Christ. Lodge: Rotary (v.p. 1984-85). Avocation: golf. Home: 308 Whitson Dr Vincennes IN 47591 Office: USDA Agrl Research Service 1118 Chestnut St Box 944 Vincennes IN 47591

REED, ELINOR USHER, motel executive; b. St. Louis, June 8, 1908; d. Robert Thomas and Josephine L. T. (Boenecke) Usher; m. Clement A. Reed, Jr.; children—Robert T., Josephine, Edward. Student pub. schs., St. Louis. Owner, operator comml. dock., Kimberling City, Mo., to 1978; former owner Arrowhead Motel, Columbia Mo.; now owner, operator Lake Hills Motel & Restaurant, also recreational vehicle and mobile home park, Warsaw, Mo., 1978—. Mem. Hotel 7 Motel Assn. Lutheran. Office: Lakes Hills Motel Old Hwy 65 & 7 White Branch Exit S Warsaw MO 65355

REED, JAMES EDWARD, metal fabrication company executive; b. Chisholm, Maine, May 26, 1933; s. James Kenneth and Grace Rose (Berube) R.; m. Nancy Ann Decilles, Sept. 7, 1959; children—Danielle, James, Robert, Michelle. B.A., Norwich U., 1954; postgrad. U. Maine, 1956-57. Gen. foreman Continental Device Corp., Hawthorne, Calif., 1960-63; prodn. mgr. Fairchild Semiconductor, San Rafael, Calif., 1963-69; mfg. mgr. Gen. Electric Co., Gainesville, Fla., 1969-77; v.p. ops. Crown div. Allen Group, Inc., Wooster, Ohio, 1977—. Mem. Dalton Village Council, 1979-82; mem. exec. com. Wayne County Republican party, 1982—. Served to 1st lt. Signal Corps, U.S. Army, 1954-56. Mem. Am. Legion, VFW. Republican. Roman Catholic. Club: Elks. Home: 125 Briarwood Dr Dalton OH 44618 Office: Crown Div Allen Group Inc 315 Gasche St Wooster OH 44691

REED, LEROY WILLIAM, educational administrator; b. Marietta, Ohio, Feb. 24, 1944; s. Harold Leroy and Zena Lucille (Harper) R.; m. Janice Lynn Dahlke, Dec. 21, 1978; children—Angela Lynne, Alicia Nicole. B.S., Ohio State U., 1966, M.A., 1969. High sch. tchr. Licking Valley Schs., Newark, Ohio, 1966-69, elem. sch. prin., 1969-70; high sch. prin. Upper Scioto Valley Schs., McGuffey, Ohio, 1970-71; elem. sch. prin. Columbus Grove Schs., Ohio, 1971-77, Bath Local Schs., Lima, Ohio, 1977—. Mem. Columbus Grove Sch. Bd. Edn., 1982—, pres., 1984—; legis. liaison mem. Apollo Joint Vocat. Sch. Bd. Edn., Lima, 1984—. Mem. Ohio Assn. Elem. Sch. Adminstrs., Ohio Sch. Bds. Assn. Republican. Lodge: Lions (pres. 1977-78, dist. sec. 1978-79, dist. chmn. 1979—). Avocations: reading, fishing, boating. Home: 308 Birch Ave Columbus Grove OH 45830 Office: Bath Elem Sch 2501 Slabtown Rd Lima OH 45830

REED, MICHAEL GEORGE, lawyer; b. Columbus, Ohio, Aug. 8, 1956; s. Thomas W. and Lora G. (Gold) R.; m. Barbara Dee White, Aug. 5, 1979; 1 child, Benjamin David. B.S. in Bus. Adminstrn., Miami U., Oxford, Ohio, 1978; J.D., U. Cin., 1981. Bar: Ohio 1981, U.S. Dist. Ct. (so. dist.) Ohio 1981, U.S. Ct. Appeals (6th cir.) 1981. Atty. Reichert, Strauss & Reed, Cin., 1981—; panelist Am. Arbitration Assn., Cin., 1983—, Hamilton County Arbitration Assn., Cin., 1982—. Contbr. articles to profl. jours. Trustee, sec., Judah Touro Cemetary Assn., Cin., 1982—, Dance Cin., 1983—. Mem. Ohio State Bar Assn., Cin. Bar Assn. Jewish. Club: Crest Hills Country (Cin.) (trustee, parliamentarian 1982—). Home: 6500 Ridge Rd Cincinnati OH 45213 Office: Reichert Strauss & Reed 2510 Carew Tower 441 Vine St Cincinnati OH 45202

REED, QUENTIN HARRY, surgeon, consulting urologist; b. St. Louis, May 26, 1921; s. George Leslie and Elsie (Moore) R.; m. Imogene Moake, Sept. 23, 1945; children—John L., James A., Thomas M. B.Edn., So. Ill. U., 1942; M.D., U. Ill. Chgo., 1945. Diplomate Am. Bd. Urology. Urologist Carbondale Clinic, Ill., 1957-84, ret., 1984; cons. urologist VA Hosp., Marion, Ill., 1957-62, St. Joseph Hosp., Murphysboro, Ill., 1957—. Served to capt. U.S. Army, 1946-48. Fellow ACS; mem. Am. Urol. Assn. (nat. conf.), AMA, Ill. State Med. Soc., Ill. Urol. Soc. Republican. Avocations: photography, travel. Home: 902 Briarwood Dr Carbondale IL 62901

REED, RALPH CHARLES, land surveyor, genealogist; b. Dayton, Ohio, Aug. 3, 1930; s. Alonzo Newton and Mary Cecilia (Nameth) R.; m. Marjorie Ruth Hiller, Feb. 5, 1972. Registered land surveyor, Ohio. Rodman, City of Dayton, 1951-56; transit and level man Dayton Power & Light, 1956-62; engring. aide and surveyor, Miamisburg, Ohio, 1962-70; surveyor, owner RCR Land Surveying Co., Dayton, 1970—. Discoverer, Campobello Island, Great Miami River, Dayton, 1973. Served with USNR, 1965—. Mem. Ohio Soc. Profl. Engrs., Profl. Land Surveyors Ohio, Hist. Soc. Montgomery and Warren Counties, Am. Congress on Surveying and Mapping, Dayton C. of C., Naval Enlisted Res. Assn., Ohio Geneal. Soc., First Families Ohio, Am. Coll. Genealogy, SAR, Am. Legion. Republican. Roman Catholic. Lodge: K.C. Avocation: model railroading. Home: 127 Ventura Ave Dayton OH 45417 Office: Ralph C Reed Land Survey Co 127 Ventura Ave Dayton OH 45417

REED, ROBERT C., lawyer; b. Cleve., Feb. 27, 1949; s. Robert C. and Helen (Gerber) R. B.A., John Carroll U., 1972; J.D., Case Western Res. U., 1975. Bar: Ohio 1975, U.S. Dist. Ct. Ohio 1975. Assoc. Hyland & Hyland, Cleve., 1975-79, Carney & Broadbent, Cleve., 1979—; dir. Space Cable Inc., Cleve.; v.p. RMG, Inc., Olmsted Cable Corp., Cable Broadcasting Inc., Abbe Rood Assocs., Cleve., 1983—. Mem. Cuyahoga County Bar Assn., Greater Cleve. Bar Assn., Ohio Bar Assn. Avocations: skiing, sailing, tennis, photography. Office: Carney & Broadbent 1710 Ohio Savings Plaza Cleveland OH 44114

REED, ROBERT ERVIN, banker; b. Dayton, Ohio, Jan. 16, 1948; s. Harry E. and Mary (Gibson) R.; m. Linda Kay Whitley, June 20, 1970; 1 child, David Alan. B.S., Wright State U., 1970, M.B.A., 1973. Fin. analyst NCR Corp., Dayton, 1970-73; asst. v.p. 1st Nat. Bank, Dayton, 1973-79; sr. v.p./city exec. Huntington Nat. Bank, Cin., 1979-84; pres., chief exec. officer Miamibank, N.A., Fairborn, Ohio, 1984—. Contbr. articles to profl. jours. Chmn., Cin. Community Chest, 1983; chmn. edn. com. Hamilton County chpt. Am. Cancer Soc., 1982. Mem. Am. Inst. Banking, Cin. C. of C., Fairborn C. of C. (bd. dirs. 1985). Republican. Clubs: Rotary (Fairborn); Kenwood Country (Cin.); Dayton Country. Office: Miamibank 1 W Main St Fairborn OH 45324

REED, SELINA MAE, telephone company executive; b. Youngstown, Ohio, Dec. 16, 1946; d. Dorris Hightower; m. Charles Pickard, Oct. 16, 1965 (div. 1970); m. John Andrew Reed, Feb. 28, 1975; children—Latya Nicole, Jada Kawren. Operator, Ohio Bell Co., Youngstown, 1964-67, supr., 1967-69, service observer, 1969-71, asst. mgr., 1971-72, group chief operator, 1972-79, mktg. dir., 1972-82, asst. mgr., 1982—; dir., credit chmn. Saints Savs. & Trust. Fin. chmn. Republican Women, Youngstown, 1985—. Mem. Assn. Female Execs., Am. Film Inst., Nat. Trust for Hist. Preservation, Am. Entrepreneurs Assn. Mem. Apostolic Pentecostal Ch. Avocations: collecting brass figures, bells, crystal figurines, Goebel statues. Home and Office: 1149 Timbercrest Dr Youngstown OH 44505

REED, WILLIAM JOSEPH, systems analyst; b. Lafayette, Ala., June 10, 1948; s. William J. and Mary (Bowen) R.; m. Tresa Kathleen Frank, Aug. 6, 1977; children—Lisa, Barbra, Jason, Kristin, William. Student Auburn U., 1977-80. Parts salesman Burford Equipment Co., Montgomery, Ala., 1968-70; research analyst U.S. Marine Corps, 1970-73; programmer Burford Equipment Co., 1974-80; asst. data processing mgr. Covert Marine Co., Kansas City, Mo., 1981-82; sr. systems analyst Intercollegiate Press, Shawnee Mission, Kans., 1982-83; systems analyst Harlan Corp., Kansas City, Kans., 1983—. Served with USMC, 1970-73. Home: 508 S Harrison St Raymore MO 64083 Office: Harlan Corp Chrysler and Stanley Rds Kansas City KS 66115

REEDER, ARTHETTA CAROLYN, nurse educator; b. Cairo, Ill., July 19, 1947; d. Charles Edward Cook and Bernadine (McNeal) Cook Hudson; m. Harold Reeder, Aug. 29, 1970; children—Sharon, Harold (dec.), Gregory. Diploma South Chgo. Hosp. Sch. Nursing, 1968; B.S., U. Ill., 1972; M.A., St. Xavier Coll., 1981. R.N. Staff nurse Will County Health Dept., Joliet, Ill., 1968-74, Four-Season Nursing Ctr., Joliet, 1980; instr. Joilet Twp. Sch. Practical Nursing, 1974-76, dir. nursing, 1978—; cons. Community Home Health, Joliet, 1978-80; editorial reviewer W.B. Saunders, Phila., 1982; mem. adv. bd. Joliet Jr. Coll., 1978—. Instr. ARC, Joliet, 1980—. Mem. Ill. Council Lic. Practical Nurse Dirs., Sigma Theta Tau. Democrat. Baptist. Avocations: reading, music, crafts. Home: 100 Brookshore Dr Shorewood IL 60435 Office: Joliet Twp High Sch Adult Div Sch Practical Nursing 201 E Jefferson St Joliet IL 60432

REEDER, JAMES MARTIN, piano technician, restorer, pianist; b. Charlotte, Mich., Oct. 21, 1937; s. Elmer M. and Lora R.; m. Martha Silvia Covarrubias, July 18, 1965; children—Cindy, James, Christopher, Cheri. Student Andrews U., 1959-60, Columbian Union Coll., 1966. Owner, operator store specializing in restoring pianos, 1968—; pianist, accompanist; condr. tech. workshops; piano cons. Mem. Piano Tech. Guild. Adventist. Office: 602 S Clinton Grand Ledge MI 48837

REES, ANTHONY WARBURTON, financial executive; b. D.C., Aug. 2, 1946; s. Elias Davis and Mary Louise (Warburton) R.; m. Heide Annamaria (Weinmann); children—William Scott, Karly Annamaria. B.S., in Math., Carnegie Mellon U., 1968; M.B.A., U. Mich., 1973. Rep. marketing Westinghouse Electric Corp., Balt., 1968-71; mgr. fin. analysis Rockwell Internat., Alcester, Eng., Troy, Mich., 1973-77; dir. internat. planning, Medtronic Inc., Mpls., 1977-84; treas., chief fin. officer, Angiomedics Inc., Mpls., 1984—. Mem. Nat. Assn. Accts., Inst. Mgmt. Acctg.; Beta Gamma Sigma (hon.). Club: YMCA. Avocations: philately; traveling; reading; athletics. Office: Angiomedics Inc 2905 Northwest Blvd Minneapolis MN 55441

REES, JACK MADISON, interior designer; b. Stanton, Iowa, May 30, 1921; s. Ross Basil and Georgene (Madison) R.; m. Joan Martz, June 19, 1949; children—John Martz, Michael Stroud. Student Iowa State U., 1940-42; B.A. cum laude, Pratt Inst., Bklyn., 1947. Interior designer William Pahlman, Assocs., N.Y.C., 1947-48; interior designer, store lectr. L. Bamberger, Newark, 1948-50, W. & J. Sloane, N.Y.C., 1950-51; pres. Jack Rees Interiors, Kansas City, Mo., 1952—, Designers Prototype, Kansas City, 1978—. Editor: Decorating with Color, 1975. Founding mem. Bacchus Ball Charity Benefit, Kansas City, 1957; bd. dirs. Kansas City Lyric Opera. Served to 2d lt. USAF, 1942-46, PTO. Named Designer of Yr., Enterprise-Kansas City Art Inst., 1975. Mem. Am. Inst. Interior Design (pres. 1981), Am. Soc. Interior Design (pres. 1981-83, founder Home of Yr. program 1982), SAR. Republican. Episcopalian. Club: Carriage (Kansas City). Home: 5508 Central St Kansas City MO 64113 Office: Jack Rees Interiors Inc 4501 Belleview St Kansas City MO 64111

REES, LARRY LEE, educator, coach; b. Foster, Ky., Feb. 21, 1944; s. Maxine M. R. B.S., Eastern Ky. U., 1966, M.A.Ed., 1981. Tchr. vocat. bus. Greeneview Local Schs., Jamestown, Ohio, 1966—; cheerleading coach Wright State U., 1979—; commr. Kenton Trace Athletic Conf., 1978—; speaker, cons. for various cheerleading clinics and seminars. Treas. Jamestown-Area Bicentennial Com. Mem. Ohio Bus. Tchrs. Assn. (exec. com. 1978-79), Am. Vocat. Assn., Nat. Bus. Edn. Assn., NEA, Office Edn. Assn. (Recognition award 1979), Ohio Office Edn. Assn. (Ohio adv. com. 1976, adv. Region 3 1976, Recognition award 1982), Nat. Cheerleaders Assn., Ohio Vocat. Assn., Western Ohio Bus. Tchrs. Assn. (chmn. 1978), Phi Delta Kappa. Republican. Mem. Chs. of Christ. Home: 14 N Church St Jamestown OH 45335

REESE, MARTHA GRACE, lawyer; b. Newark, Ohio, Feb. 27, 1953; d. John Gilbert and Louella Catherine (Hodges) R.; m. William Pulliam Harman, June 10, 1983; children—Benjamin Victor Harman, Elizabeth Lang Harman, B.A., DePauw U., 1975; J.D., Ind. U., 1980. Bar: Ind. 1980, U.S. Dist. Ct. (so. dist.) Ind. 1980, U.S. Ct. Appeals (7th cir.) 1981. Law clk. U.S. Dist. Ct. (so. dist.) Ind., 1980-82; assoc. Baker & Daniels, Indpls., 1982-83; ptnr. Wilson, Hutchens & Reese, Greencastle, Ind., 1984—. Steering com. Ind. Leadership Celebration, 1983-85. Mem. ABA, Ind. State Bar Assn., Indpls. Bar Assn., Putnam County Bar Assn., Phi Beta Kappa. Home: 1006 S College Ave Greencastle IN 46135 Office: Wilson Hutchens & Reese 16 S Jackson St Greencastle IN 46135

REESE, RICHARD THOMAS, lawyer; b. Lima, Ohio, Sept. 13, 1956; s. Ronald Albert and Barbara Ann (Truesdale) R.; m. Cheryl Ann Skinner, Aug. 5, 1978. B.A., Ohio No. U., 1978, J.D., 1981. Bar: Ohio 1981, U.S. Dist. Ct. (no. dist.) Ohio 1982. Assoc. Joseph C. DaPore & Assocs. Co., L.P.A., Lima, 1981—. Mem. Delta Theta Phi. Republican. Methodist. Home: 109 Brandi Pl Ada OH 45810 Office: DaPore & Assocs Co LPA 130 W North St PO Box 1509 Lima OH 45802

REEVE, JACQUELINE ANNE, nurse; b. Warren, Ohio, Apr. 10, 1951; d. James Arnold and Thelma Joyce (Trask) R.; A.A. in Nursing, Kent State U., Ashtabula, 1971. Student Cleve. State U. Nursing supr. Char-Lotte Nursing Home, Inc., Rock Creek, Ohio, 1971-79; team leader Northeastern Ohio Gen. Hosp., North Madison, 1979-80; dir. nursing Con-Lea Nursing Home, Geneva, Ohio, 1980-81, Good Samaritan Nursing Home Corp., East Peoria, Ill., 1982; dir. nursing service Wickliffe (Ohio) Country Pl., 1982—; pvt. practice cons. for nursing homes; profl. reviewer med. records: mem. Ohio Health Care Assn. peer rev. survey team, 1981-82. Active ACLU, Cleve.; mem. Jefferson Vol. Fire Dept. Rescue Squad, 1978—, Lake County Council on Aging Mem. Nat. League Nursing, Cleve. Area Citizens League for Nursing, Cleve. Area Citizens League for Nursing Dirs., Greater Cleve. Hosp. Assn. (med. recs. and nursing coms Ctr. Health Affairs), Nat. Assn. for Female Execs., N.Y. Acad. Scis., Nat. Honor Soc., Quill and Scroll. Organizer, condr. inservice courses in field. Home: PO Box 93 Jefferson OH 44047 also 141 Steele Ave Apt 203 Painesville OH 44077

REEVES, ANGELA MARIE, college administrator; b. Indpls., Feb. 23, 1949; d. Ervin V. and Mary M. Holland; m. Dale Edward Reeves, Sept. 3, 1977; children—Samuel E., Rachel A. Student C.S. Mott Community Coll., 1967-68; B.S., Central Mich. U., 1971; M.A., Mich. State U., 1975. Cert. social worker, Mich. Jr. therapist Rubicon House, Flint, Mich., 1971; alcoholism therapist Hurley Med. Ctr., Flint, 1972-78; advisor C.S. Mott Community Coll., Flint, 1978-83, dir. admissions, 1983—. Recipient Cert. of Recognition, Gov. Blanchard, 1985; named one of Outstanding Young Women Am., 1983, Counselor of Yr., Mott Community Coll. Afro Am. Assn. 1980-81, Hon. Navy Recruiter, U.S. Navy, 1984. Mem. Mich. Personnel and Guidance Assn., Mich. Assn. Admissions Counselors, Genesee Area Personnel and Guidance Assn., Mich. Women's Studies Assn., Nat. Assn. Coll. Admissions, Nat. Assn. Negro Bus. and Profl. Women's Clubs Inc. (3rd v.p. 1982-83). Home: 5418 Marja St Flint MI 48505 Office: CS Mott Community Coll 1401 E Court St Flint MI 48502

REEVES, BETTY JENE, editor; b. Great Bend, Kans., Dec. 2, 1924; d. George Whitney and Alma Myrtle (Fesser) Bell; student Phillips U., 1943-44. Wichita Bus. Coll., 1944; m. Licurgous F. Reeves, Oct. 21, 1961; 1 stepson, Michael F. Floral designer, Bells Flower & Gift Shop, Great Bend, Kans., 1944-49; owner, operator City Floral, McPherson, 1951-53; owner, operator Betty's Flowers, Salina, 1953-55; designer Hutchinson Floral, (Kans.), 1955-61; lifestyle editor, feature writer Newton (Kans.) Kansan, 1968—. Named hon. Jaycee Jayne, 1974; recipient award Girl Scouts. Mem. Kans. Press Assn., Am. Legion Aux., Epsilon Sigma Alpha. Republican. Mem. Disciples of Christ Ch. Clubs: Soroptimists, Eagles Aux. (past pres.), Ladies Elks (pres.), Axtell Christian Hosp. Aux., VFW Aux. Pochontas (past state pres.). Home: 1206 N Duncan St Newton KS 67114 Office: 121 W 6th St PO Box 268 Newton KS 67114

REEVES, EARL JAMES, JR., college educator; b. Muskogee, Okla., Mar. 16, 1933; s. Earl James and Berneice Elizabeth (Jordan) R.; m. Wilma Gail Reece, Aug. 30, 1950; children—Barbara Gail, Gregory Alan, Carolyn Elaine. Student Kans. State U., 1950-51, Friends U., 1951-52; B.A., Wichita State U., 1954, M.A., 1959; Ph.D., U. Kans., 1962. Faculty U. Kan., Lawrence, 1961-62, U. Omaha, 1962-64, U. Mo., St. Louis, 1964-70, U. Tulsa, 1970-83; dir. urban studies program U. Tulsa, 1970-83, prof., 1971-83; pres. Mo. Valley Coll., Marshall, 1983—; cons. Central Midwestern Regional Edn. Lab., 1966-68, Tulsa C. of C., Leadership 1973-76, Tulsa Area Agy. on Aging, 1973-76. Bd. dirs. Kansas City Regional Council on Higher Edn.; v.p. city council, Berkeley, Mo., 1966-70; mem. Tulsa Community Relations Commn., 1971-76, chmn., 1975; mem. Met. Tulsa Growth Strategy Com., 1975-76; bd. dirs. Indian Nations Council Govts., 1977-83; chmn. Sales Tax Overview Com., City of Tulsa, 1980-83; mem. mission direction and priorities com. United Presbyn. Ch. U.S.A., 1977-81, candidate for moderator Gen. Assembly, 1982; pres. bd. Eastern Okla. Housing Corp. Author: Approaches to the Study of Urbanization, 1963, The Cross and the Flag: Evangelical Christianity and Contemporary Politics, 1972, Protest and Politics: Christianity and Contemporary Affairs, 1968, Back Talk: Press Councils in America, 1972, Urban Community, 1978. Research editor, pres. editorial bd. Midwest Rev. of Pub. Adminstrn., 1974-76, mem. editorial bd. Jour. Urban Affairs, 1982—. Contbr. articles to profl. jours. Served with USAF, 1954-58. Mem. Am. Soc. Pub. Adminstrn. Presbyterian (chmn. planning com. 1974-75, mem. met. ministries bd. 1970-76). Lodge: Rotary. Home: 404 E Mission St Marshall MO 65340 Office: Missouri Valley Coll 500 E College St Marshall MO 65340

REEVES, GENE, theological school dean, clergyman; b. Franklin, N.H., Apr. 2, 1933; s. Eugene Victor and Parmelie Beatrice (Twombly) R.; m. Joan Delice Shaw, Sept. 11, 1957; children—Eva Shaw, Anna Marie. B.A., U. N.H., 1956; S.T.B., Boston U., 1959; Ph.D., Emory U., 1963. Ordained to ministry Unitarian Universalist Assocs., 1960. Faculty Tufts U., Medford, Mass., 1962-67; faculty Wilberforce U., Ohio, 1967-79, prof. Philosophy, 1967-72, chmn. humanities dept., 1971-72, assoc. acad. dean, 1972-76, asst. to pres., 1976-79; dean, chief exec. Meadville/Lombard Theol. Sch., Chgo., 1979—; minister First Unitarian Ch., Dayton, Ohio, 1969-79. Editor: Process Philosophy and Christian Faith, 1971, Crane Rev., 1964-67; editorial bd. Am. Jour. Philosophy and Theology, 1982—, Jour. Religion, 1983—. Contbr. essays to profl. lit. Nat. bd. People for Am. Way, 1981—, ZeroPopulation Growth, 1969-73; ofcl. observer World Council Chs., 1983; mem. state bd. Ind. Voters Ill., 1984—. Served as lt. USAR, 1956-65. Cogswell Found. scholar, 1951; Robinson fellow Boston U., 1959; Emory U. fellow, 1960; James Luther Adams lectr. J.L. Adams Found., Columbus, Ohio, 1983. Mem. Am. Philos. Assn., Am. Acad. Religion, Ctr. for Process Studies, Collegium, Soc. for Coll. and Univ. Planning. Democrat. Home: 5309 S Greenwood Ave Chicago IL 60615 Office: Meadville/Lombard Theol Sch 5701 S Woodlawn Ave Chicago IL 60637

REEVES, MICHAEL STANLEY, public utility executive; b. Memphis, Oct. 2, 1935; m. Patricia Ann Board, June 27, 1959; children—Michael, Michelle. Student Iowa State U., 1954-56; B.A., Roosevelt U., 1964; M.B.A., Northwestern U., 1972. With People Gas Co., Chgo., 1956—, supr., 1967-69, asst. supt., 1969-72, supt., 1972-75, gen. supt., 1975-77, v.p. mktg. and customer relations, 1977—. Bd. dirs. Chgo. Commons Assn., St. Bernard Hosp., Better Bus. Bur. Served with U.S. Army. Mem. Chgo. Assn. Commerce and Industry, Am. Gas Assn., Am. Assn. Blacks in Energy, Chgo. Econ. Club. Club: University (Chgo.). Home: Chicago IL Office: 122 S Michigan Ave Suite 1525 Chicago IL 60603

REFETOFF, SAMUEL, physician, scientist; b. Roussee, Bulgaria, July 11, 1937; came to U.S., 1964; s. Isidore and Rennée (Panijel) R. B.S. with honors, U. Montreal, Que., Can., 1959; M.D., C.M., McGill U., Montreal, 1963. Intern Notre Dame Hosp., Montreal, 1963-64; resident Hosp. of Good Samaritan, Los Angeles, 1964-65, Lakey Clinic, Boston, 1965-65; fellow Peter Bent Brigham Hosp., Boston, 1966-68; instr. medicine Harvard Med. Sch., Boston, 1968-69; asst. prof. U. Chgo., 1969-73; assoc. prof., 1973-77; prof., 1977—, prof. pediatrics, 1983—; vis. prof. medicine and phamacology Free U. Brussels, Belgium, 1974-75, 82-83; dir. Thyroid Function Lab. U. Chgo., 1969—. Author med. textbooks. Contbr. articles to prof. jours. Mem. NIH (mem. endocrinology study sect div. of research grants, 1984—), Am. Fedn. Clin. Research, Am. Thyroid Assn., Endocrine Soc., Am. Soc. Clin. Investigation, European Thyroid Assn. Home: 4801 S Kimbark Chicago IL 60615 Office: U Chgo 5841 South Maryland Chicago IL 60637

REGAN, THOMAS EUGENE, broadcasting executive; b. Beloit, Wis., Aug. 26, 1950; s. Thomas Bernard and Anna Jane (Lynch) R.; m. Patricia Ellen Craig, June 3, 1980; 1 child, Marlowe Ann. B.A., U. Wis.-Milw., 1973, M.A., 1975. Program dir. Sta. WMRA-FM, Harrisonburg, Va., 1975-78; TV producer Milw. Humanities Program, Milw., 1978-80; freelance writer, Milw., 1980-81; music dir. Prairie Pub. Broadcasting, Bismarck, N.D., 1981-85, sta. mgr., 1985—. Pres. Bismarck Humane Soc., 1983-84; bd. dors. Bismarck-Mandan Orchestral Assn., 1983—. Office: Prairie Pub Broadcasting 1814 N 15th St Bismarck ND 58501

REGER, RICHARD PAUL, leasing company executive; b. Toledo, July 5, 1951; s. Joseph Paul and Eva Marie (Frick) R. B.B.A., U. Toledo, 1973; M.B.A., Xavier U., Cin., 1981. C.P.A., Ohio. Controller Sandusky County Savs. and Loan, Fremont, Ohio, 1973-74; zone controller Hertz Corp., Cin., 1974-78; asst. controller The Ltd., Inc., Columbus, Ohio, 1978-82; v.p., controller Truckway Leasing, Inc., Cin., 1982—. Mem. Mensa. Home: 2660 Lehman Rd Suite 808 Cincinnati OH 45204 Office: Truckway Leasing Inc 1200 Gest St Cincinnati OH 45203-1116

REGHANTI, THOMAS J., trucking company executive; b. Milw., 1925. B.S., U. Wis., 1950. With Fruehauf Corp., Detroit, 1950—, salesman, used trailer mgr. Fruehauf div., 1950, v.p. used trailers, 1966, v.p. and gen. sales mgr., 1968, v.p. sales and mktg., 1969, corp. v.p. and gen. mgr. Fruehauf div., 1970, pres., dir., 1980—, also chief operating officer; dir. Fruehauf Can. Inc. Served with USAAF, 1942-46. Office: Fruehauf Corp 10900 Harper Ave PO Box 238 Detroit MI 48232*

REGIER, BETTY LYNETTE, insurance claim representative; b. Newton, Kans., July 6, 1956; d. Gus Henry and Edna Helen (Claassen) R. Student Tabor Coll., Hillsboro, Kans., 1974-75, Ins. Inst. Am., 1979-80, Wichita State U., 1981—. Cert. profl. ins. woman Nat. Assn. Ins. Women. Claim clk. Comml. Union Co., Wichita, Kans., 1976-78; claim rep. Ins. Mgmt. Assocs., Wichita, 1978—. Mem. planning Occupational Health Seminar St. Francis Regional Med. Ctr., Wichita, 1982—. Mem. Ins. Women Wichita, Nat. Assn. Ins. Women, Wichita Claims Assn., Wichita Jaycees. Democrat. Office: Ins Mgmt Assocs Inc 600 IMA Plaza Wichita KS 67202

REGULA, RALPH, lawyer, congressman; b. Beach City, Ohio, Dec. 3, 1924; s. O.F. and Orpha (Walter) R.; B.A., Mt. Union Coll., 1948; LL.B., William McKinley Sch. Law, 1952; m. Mary Rogusky, Aug. 5, 1950; children—Martha, David, Richard. Sch. adminstr. Stark County Bd. Edn., 1948-55; admitted to Ohio bar, 1952; practiced law, Navarre; mem. Ohio Ho. of Reps., 1965-66, Ohio Senate, 1967-72; mem. 93d-98th congresses from 16th Dist. Ohio; partner Regula Bros. Mem. Pres.'s Commn. Fin. Structures and Regulation, 1970-71; mem. Ohio Bd. Edn., 1960-65; mem. adv. bd. Walsh Coll., Canton, Ohio. Trustee Mt. Union Coll., Alliance, Ohio, Stark County Hist. Soc., Stark County Wilderness Soc. Served with USNR, 1944-46. Recipient Community Service award Navarre Kiwanis Club, 1963; Meritorious Service in Conservation award Canton Audubon Soc., 1965; Ohio Conservation award Gov. James Rhodes, 1969; named Outstanding Young Man of Year, Canton Jaycees, 1957; Legislative Conservationist of Year, Ohio League Sportsman, 1969. Mem. ABA, Ohio, Stark County bar assns. Republican. Episcopalian. Office: 2209 Rayburn House Office Bldg Washington DC 20515*

REH, THOMAS EDWARD, radiologist, educator; b. St. Louis, Sept. 12, 1943; s. Edward Paul and Ceil Anne (Golden) R.; m. Benedette Texada, June 22, 1968; children—Matthew J., Benedette T., Elizabeth W. B.A., St. Louis U., 1965, M.D., 1969. Diplomate Am. Bd. Radiology, Nat. Bd. Med. Examiners. Intern St. John's Mercy Med. Ctr., St. Louis, 1969-70; resident St. Louis VA Hosp., 1970-73; fellow in vascular radiology Beth Israel Hosp., Boston, 1973-74; radiologist St. Mary's Health Ctr., St. Louis, 1974—; clin. asst. prof. radiology St. Louis U. Sch. Medicine, 1978—. Mem. Am. Coll. Radiology, AMA, Radiol. Soc. N.Am., St. Louis Met. Med. Soc., Alpha Omega Alpha, Alpha Sigma Nu, Delta Sigma Phi. Republican. Roman Catholic. Home: 9850 Waterbury Dr Saint Louis MO 63124 Office: St Marys Health Center 6420 Clayton Rd St Louis MO 63117

REHA, ROSE KRIVISKY, business educator; b. N.Y.C., Dec. 17, 1920; d. Boris and Freda (Stein) Krivisky; m. Rudolph John Reha, Apr. 11, 1941; children—Irene Gale, Phyllis. B.S., Ind. State U., 1965; M.A., U. Minn., 1967, Ph.D., 1971. With U.S. and State Civil Service, 1941-63; tchr. pub. schs., Minn., 1965-66; teaching assoc., part-time instr. U. Minn., Mpls., 1966-68; prof. Coll. Bus., St. Cloud (Minn.) State U., 1968—, chmn. bus. edn. and office adminstrn. dept., 1982-83; cons., lectr. in field. Camp dir. Girl Scouts U.S.A., 1960-62; active various community fund drives; sec., mem. relicensure rev. Com. Minn. Bd. Teaching Continuing Edn., 1984—. Recipient Achievement award St. Cloud State U., 1985; St. Cloud State U. Research and Faculty Improvement grantee, 1973, 78, 83. Mem. Am. Vocat. Assn., Minn. Econ. Assn., Minn. Women of Higher Edn., NEA, Minn. Edn. Assn. (pres. women's caucus 1981-83, award for outstanding contbns. 1983), Minn. Bus. Edn., Inc., St. Cloud U. Faculty Assembly (pres. 1975-76), St. Cloud State U. Grad. Council (chmn. 1983-84) Pi Omega Pi (sponsor St. Cloud State U. chpt. 1982—), Phi Chi Theta, Delta Pi Epsilon, Delta Kappa Gamma. Jewish. Contbr. articles to profl. jours. Home: 1725 13 Ave SE Saint Cloud MN 56301 Office: Coll of Bus Saint Cloud State U Saint Cloud MN 56301

REHFIELD, PATRICIA LYNN, osteopathic physician; b. Phila., Oct. 28, 1954; d. Lawrence and June A. (Grunhut) R.; m. David C. Tattan, Sept. 2, 1978; children—Timothy Daniel, Anna Emily. B.A., Johns Hopkins U., 1976; D.O., Mich. State U., 1979. Research asst. U.S. Dept. Agr., Beltsville, Md., 1972-74, NIH Gerontology Research Ctr., Balt., 1974-76; emergency physician Allegan Gen. Hosp., Mich., 1980-82; practice gen. osteo. medicine, Jamestown, Mich., 1982—; assoc. prof. Coll. Osteo. Medicine, Mich. State U., East Lansing, 1983—; sec. med. staff Zeeland Community Hosp., Mich., 1985. Mem. Am. Osteo. Assn., Am. Coll. Gen. Practice. Avocations: reading, jogging, swimming, gardening, travel. Office: 3165 24th Ave Jamestown MI 49427

REHM, FRED ROBERT, chemical engineer, air pollution consultant; b. Milw., May 18, 1921; s. Fred Andrew and Dorothy Alma (Schuler) R.; m. Rosemary Ann Heckel, May 11, 1946; children—Rick Michael, James Robert, Jayne Mary Rehm Lambrecht, Mary Kay Rehm Motl. B.S. in Chem. Engring. cum laude, U. Wis.-Madison, 1943; postgrad. Princeton U., 1944, MIT, 1944-45. Registered profl. engr., Wis. Research and devel. engr. Dow Chem. Co., Midland, Wis., 1946-48; dep. dir. air pollution control Milw. County, 1948-68, dir. air pollution control, 1968-75, dir. environ. services, 1975-81, dir. engring. energy and environ. services, 1981-85, ret., 1985; pres., cons. Wis. Chem. and Testing Co., Milw., 1954—. Contbr. articles to profl. jours. Pres. Nat. W Club, Madison, 1965-66; Wis. Alumni Club of Milw., 1966-67; active U. Wis. Athletic Bd., 1970-73; profl. basketball player Oshkosh All-Stars, 1943, 45-46, 48; gubernatorial appointee Wis. Air Pollution Adv. Council, 1967-73. Served to lt. (j.g.) USNR, 1943-46. Recipient Western Conf. medal U. Wis., 1943, Pub. Service award Fed. Civil Def. Adminstrn., 1955; Disting. Service award Wis. Alumni Club of Milw., 1975; Disting. Service award Wis. Alumni Assn., 1985. Mem. ASME (chmn. air pollution div. 1971-72, cert. of appreciation 1984), Am. Chem. Soc., Air Pollution Control Assn., Am. Pub. Works Assn., Am. Nat. Standards Inst. Roman Catholic. Avocations: recreational sports, do-it-yourselfer. Home: 2721 N 97th St Milwaukee WI 53222 Office: Wis Chem and Testing Co 2721 N 97th St Milwaukee WI 53222

REHM, RONALD L(EE), lawyer; b. Wooster, Ohio, Jan. 15, 1950; s. Lester L. and June H. (Stanley) R.; m. Kathy A. Fromant, Jan. 6, 1979; 1 child, Heather. A.B., Cornell U., 1972; J.D., Case Western Res. U., 1979. Bar: Ohio 1979, U.S. Dist. Ct. (no. dist.) Ohio 1980. Sole practice, Wooster, 1979-81; asst. pros. atty. Wayne County, Ohio, Wooster, 1981—. Pres., trustee Wayne-Holmes Mental Health Ctr., Inc., Wooster, 1983-85. Served to 1st lt. U.S. Army, 1973-76. Mem. Ohio Bar Assn., Wayne County Bar Assn., Republican. Lutheran. Lodge: Kiwanis. Home: 561 Catalina St Wooster OH 44691 Office: Prosecutors Office 538 N Market St Wooster OH 44691

REHMER, RICHARD JOHN, university adminstrator; b. Appleton, Wis., June 6, 1932; s. Elmer George and Gertrude Agnes (Kettenhofen) R.; m. Mary Jo Gilberto, Aug. 27, 1960; children—M. Cleo, Anthony W., Joseph A., Paula A. B.S., Marquette U., 1957; postgrad. U. Nebr., 1961-62. Indsl. relations rep. Ford Motor Co., Chgo., 1963-68; indsl. relations mgr. Glass Containers Corp., College Park, Ill., 1968-69; corp. dir. labor relations Consol. Aluminum Corp., Jackson, Tenn., 1969-70; personnel dir. Thatcher Glass Mfg. Co., Lawrenceburg, Ind., 1970-72; dist. dir. employee and labor relations U.S. Postal Service, Toledo, Ohio, 1972-76; dir. personnel services Bowling Green State U., Ohio, 1976—; trustee Pub. Employees Retirement System Ohio, Columbus, 1982—; chair bd. trustees Pub. Employees Deferred Compensation Bd., Columbus, 1982—; cons. Coll. and Univ. Cons. Acad., Washington, 1981, R.J. Rehmer, Inc., Bowling Green, Ohio, 1979. Athletic dir. St. Aloysius Parish, Bowling Green, Ohio, 1975; mem. Parks and Recreation Bd., Bowling Green, 1976; coach, commr. Little League, Bowling Green, 1977-78; impartial discipline adminstr. Wood County, Bowling Green, 1982. Grantee State of Ohio, Bowling Green State U., 1979, 80. Mem. Am. Soc. Personnel Adminstrs., Interuniv. Council Personnel Officers (chair 1984-85), Ohio Pub. Labor Relations Assn., Job Service Employers Commn. Wood County. Democrat. Roman Catholic. Avocations: skiing, golf, tennis, curling. Home: 620 Pasteur St Bowling Green OH 43402 Office: Bowling Green State U Shatzel Hall Bowling Green OH 43403

REHMUS, TERRELL WILLIAM, research pharmacist; b. East St. Louis, Ill., Dec. 28, 1956; s. Galvester and Lillian Mae (Schuchert) R. A.S., Belleville Area Coll., 1976; B.S. in Pharmacy, St. Louis Coll., 1979; M.A. in Mgmt., Webster U., 1985. Research pharmacist Norcliff Thayer, Inc., St. Louis, 1979—; staff pharmacist St. Mary's Health Ctr., Clayton, Mo., 1983—. Mem. St. Louis Soc. Pharmacists in Industry (pres. 1982, treas. 1981), Am. Pharm. Assn., Rho Chi (pres. 1978-79). Lutheran. Club: St Louis Ambassadors. Avocations: racquetball, movies, music, antique collecting. Home: 5432-A Lisette Saint Louis MO 63109

REIBMAN, PAUL JEROME, occupational consultant, educator; b. Chgo., Nov. 23, 1937; s. Abraham A. and Frieda (Liner) R.; m. Susan Jane Jones, Aug. 4, 1962; children—Elizabeth, Allen. B.S.C. in Mktg., DePaul U., 1962; M.S. in Edn., No. Ill. U., 1972. Vocat. coordinator Chgo. Bd. Edn., 1962—; instr. in bus. edn. and adminstrv. services Grad. Sch., No. Ill. U., 1973—; sr. cons. Occupational Cons., Glenview, Ill., 1978—; bd. dirs. Ill. Found. Mktg. and Distributive Edn.; pres. Ill. Adv. Com. on Distributive Edn., 1970-72. Served with U.S. Army, 1960. Named Ky. col., 1975; Chgo. Ambassador, Richard J. Daley, 1976; Distributive Edn. Man of Yr., Distributive Edn. Clubs Ill., 1977; recipient Mktg. award Sears Roebuck & Co., 1977; Ill. Service award Ill. Secondary Mktg. and Distributive Edn. Assn., 1980. Mem. Am. Personnel and Guidance Assn., Nat. Vocat. Guidance Assn. (cert. profl.), Am. Vocat. Assn., Ill. Vocat. Assn., Ill. Bus. Edn. Assn. Club: Kiwanis (chmn. career guidance 1975-80, Career award 1982). Cons. numerous career guides for State Ill. Office: 1030 Indian Rd Glenview IL 60025

REICH, JACK EGAN, See *Who's Who in America,* 43rd edition.

REICHARD, RONALD ELSWORTH, lawyer; b. Hazard, Ky., Feb. 10, 1947; s. Henry Isaac and Arlie Jeanette (Adams) R.; m. Susan Elizabeth Miller, Apr. 6, 1968 (div. 1984); children—Elizabeth, Michael, Deborah, Stephen; m. Debora Faith Teeters, Aug. 24, 1984; 1 stepdaughter, Dawn. B.S., U. Dayton, 1969; J.D., No. Ky. State U., 1974. Bar: Ohio 1974. Tchr. Mad River Twp. Sch. Dist., Dayton, Ohio, 1969-73; law clk. Montgomery County Common Pleas Court, 1973-74; mem. firm Pickrel, Schaeffer & Ebeling, 1974-85, Murphy & Mayl, 1985—. Mem. ABA, Ohio Bar Assn., Dayton Bar Assn., Miami County Bar Assn. Republican. Presbyterian. Lodge: Optimist. Avocations: reading; coins; stamps; chess. Home: 2265 Woodstock Court Troy OH 45373 Office: Murphy & Mayl 1400 3d Nat Bldg Dayton OH 45402

REICHEL, FRED EUGENE, lawyer; b. Chgo., Apr. 6, 1920; s. Fred Maxmilian and Ruth Florence (Oyen) R.; m. Ione Marie Hopfensperger, Feb. 22, 1946 (div. 1982); children—Michael Eugene, Thomas Arthur, Robert Patrick; m. Catherine Lucy Lipinski, Aug. 21, 1983; 1 stepchild—Gerald Sioen. B.A., U. Mich.-Ann Arbor, 1947; J.D., U. Detroit, 1951. Bar: Mich. 1951. Atty.-advisor Dept. Army, Detroit, 1951-55; sole practice law, Detroit, 1955-62; sr. atty. advisor Dept. Army, Warren, Mich., 1962-85. Served with USAAF, 1940-46. Mem. Delta Theta Phi, U. Detroit Law Alumni Assn., U. Detroit Law Sch. Alumni Assn. Democrat. Roman Catholic. Club: Elks. Avocations: golf; swimming. Home: 31306 Schoenherr St Warren MI 48093

REICHELT, FERDINAND HERBERT, insurance and real estate corporation executive; b. Chgo., Jan. 26, 1941; s. Ferdinand W. and Justine E. (Schuetpelz) R.; m. Diane Bethel Peters, Nov. 14, 1964; children—Christine, Brian. B.S., U. Ill., 1963; postgrad. Loyola U., Chgo., 1964. C.P.A., Ill. Supr., mgr. Peat Marwick & Mitchell, Chgo., 1963-70; actuary, 1966-68, mgr., Omaha, 1970-72; chief fin. officer CMI Investment Corp. and subs., Madison, Wis., 1972-78; exec. v.p. Verex Corp. and subs., Madison, 1978—, chief operating officer, 1983—, dir., 1980—. Treas. Madison Civic Ctr. Found., 1981—; bd. dirs. Festival of Lakes; chmn. Friends of WHA-TV, Inc., 1983; trustee Edgewood Coll.; mem. bd. advisors Clin. Cancer Ctr., U. Wis. Served with USAF, 1963-69. Mem. Nat. Assn. Accts., Nat. Investor Relations Inst., Wis. Inst. C.P.A.s, Ill. Inst. C.P.A.s, Nebr. Inst. C.P.A.s, Nat. Assn. Ind. Insurers, Fin. Execs. Inst. Lutheran. Clubs: PGA Nat. Golf (Palm Beach Gardens, Fla.); Nakoma Golf, Madison (Madison). Editor: Secondary Mortgage Market Handbook; guest columnist Barrons; contbr. to profl. publs. Office: Verex Corp PO Box 7066 Madison WI 53707

REICHGOTT, EMBER DARLENE, lawyer, state senator; b. Detroit, Aug. 22, 1953; d. Norbert Arnold and Diane (Pincich) R. B.A. summa cum laude, St. Olaf Coll., Minn., 1974; J.D., Duke U., 1977. Bar: Minn. 1977, D.C. 1978. Assoc., Larkin, Hoffman, Daly & Lindgren, Bloomington, Minn., 1977-84; of counsel Control Data Corp., Bloomington, Minn., 1984—; legal cons. Home Free Battered Women's Shelter, Plymouth, Minn., 1978—; mem. Minn. State Senate, 1983—. Trustee, N.W. YMCA, New Hope, Minn., 1983—. Youngest woman ever elected to Minn. State Senate, 1983; recipient Woman of Yr. award North Hennepin Bus. and Prof. Women, 1983; Award for Contbn. to Human Services, Minn. Social Services Assn., 1983; Disting. Service award Mpls. Jr. C. of C., 1984; named One of Ten Outstanding Young Minnesotans, Minn. Jr. C. of C., 1984. Mem. Minn. Bar Assn., Hennepin County Bar Assn. Mem. Minn. Democratic Farmer-Labor Party (del. nat. Dem. conv. 1984, state exec. com. 1980-82). Home: 7701 48th Ave N New Hope MN 55428 Office: Minn State Senate 27 State Capitol St Paul MN 55155

REICHLE, JAMES ELMER, developer, gen. contractor; b. LeMars, Iowa, Sept. 27, 1946; s. John Frank and Mathilda Ann (Christiansen) R.; m. Connie Jo Foster, Dec. 28, 1968; children—Jamie Jo, John Keenan, Brenna Elizabeth, Luke Jordan. Student pub. schs., Princeton, Minn. Mem. survey crew Minn. Hwy. Dept., Mpls., 1965; technician, ramp service United Airlines, Mpls., 1969-70; gen. contract Jim Reichle Constrn., Princeton, 1970—; owner Rike-Lee Elctric Co., Princeton, 1980—; sec.-treas. TFR Corp., Princeton, 1982—; pres. F&R Devel., Princeton, 1983—. Author Alt. Source Energy, 1980. Served to cpl. USMC, 1965-68; Vietnam. Mem. Nat. Assn. Home Builders, Princeton C. of C. Republican. Roman Catholic. Lodges: Lions, Am. Legion (Princeton). Office: Jim Reichle Constrn Route 4 Box 274A Princeton MN 55371

REID, GERRI WOLD (GERRI REID SKJERVOLD), artist; b. Portland, Oreg., Apr. 11, 1944; d. Alden Elroy and Verna (Kocinski) Wold; B.A. in Fine Art, Calif. State U., Sacramento, 1972, M.F.A., 1975; postgrad. Ind. U.-Purdue U. Instr. dental aux. edn. U. Minn., 1966-70; anthrop. research asst., 1975-76; asst. prof. dental aux. edn. Ind. U.-Purdue U., 1976-78; mng. editor Nat. Arts Guide, Chgo., 1978-80; freelance artist, Chgo., 1981—; pres. Chgo. Art Emerging Inc., 1983—; graphic artist Reid Communications, Chgo., 1981—; dir. show coordination Circle Fine Art, Chgo., 1981; seminar lectr., 1977; one-woman shows include Artists' Coop. Gallery, Santa Fe, 1976, Artlink, Ft. Wayne, Ind., 1979, D.E.O. Fine Arts, Inc., Chgo., 1982-83; group exhbns. include Crocker Art Mus., Sacramento, 1975, Ft. Wayne Mus. Art, 1978, Artists Guild Chgo., 1981, Charles A. Wustum Mus., Racine, Wis., 1983. Mem. Artists Guild Chgo., Chgo. Artists' Coalition.

REID, JARVE GARY, engineering analysis executive, educator; b. Newark, Nov. 12, 1945; s. Edwin B. and Karleen B. (Bennett) R.; m. Wendee V. Davenport, Aug. 26, 1967 (div. 1985); children—Jennifer G., Gregory B. B.S., U.S. Air Force Acad., 1967; S.M., MIT, 1968; Ph.D., Air Force Inst. Tech., 1975; postgrad. Indsl. Coll. Armed Forces, 1970, Wright State U., 1979. Commd. 2d lt. U.S. Air Force, 1967, advanced through grades to maj., 1980, ret., 1980; project officer Minuteman Guidance and Targeting Bd., San Bernrdino, Calif., 1968-71; group chief air Analysis Group, Air Force Avionics Lab., Wright-Patterson AFB, Ohio, 1973-75, chief engr. Fire Control Tech. Group, 1975-77; assoc. prof. elec. engring. dept. Air Force Inst. Tech., Wright-Patterson AFB, 1977-80; sr. engring. specialist Lear-Siegler Inc., Dayton, Ohio, 1980-83; program mgr. Systems Control Tech., Dayton, 1983-84; mgr. Dayton office Sci. Systems Inc., Dayton, 1984-85; sr. research engr. Sci. Systems Inc., Cambridge, Mass., 1985—. Author: Linear System Fundamentals: Continuous and Discrete, Classic and Modern, 1983. Contbr. articles to profl. publs. Daedalian fellow, 1967. Mem. IEEE (chmn. Dayton sect. 1978), AIAA, Full Gospel Bus. Men's Fellowship Internat. Mem. Assembly of God Ch. Home and Office: 5675 Chimney Circle Apt 1-B Kettering OH 45440

REID, LORINE MAY, lawyer; b. Toledo, Ohio, Apr. 29, 1932; d. Edwin McKechnie and Eleanora Mary (DeMars) R. B.A. in Speech, Wayne State U., 1958; M. Social Work, U. Mich., 1965; J.D., U. Toledo, 1969. Bar: Ohio 1973. Exec. dir. Mental Health Bd., 1970-72; planning dir. Pilot Cities Project, Dayton, Ohio, 1972-75; sole practice, Dayton, 1974—; legal dir. Childrens Service Bd., 1977-81; tchr. U. Dayton, 1977-80. Citizens adv. bd. Dayton Mental Health Ctr., 1978-85. Recipient Mental Health Service award Gov. of Ohio, 1984. Mem. Dayton Women Voters League, ABA, Ohio State Bar Assn., Dayton Bar Assn., Nat. Assn. Women Lawyers. Democrat. Club: Altrusa Internat. (pres. 1985—). Avocation: community theatre. Office: 5518 N Main St Dayton OH 45415

REID, MARGARET BACHMAN, librarian; b. Phila., June 15, 1945; d. Roy Bleim and Maybelle Marian (Lowe) Bachman; m. William F. Reid, Aug. 24, 1968; 1 child, Nathan Jeremy. B.A., Geneva Coll., Beaver Falls, Pa., 1967; postgrad. Villanova U., 1967-68; M.Ln., Emory U., 1972. Children's librarian Landsdowne Pub. Library, Pa., 1967-68, Richland County Pub. Library, Columbia, S.C., 1968-69, Sheppard Meml. Pub. Library, Greenville, N.C., 1969-71; asst. librarian Scott Chandler Br. Library, Decatur, Ga., 1973; head children's dept. Lynchburg Pub. Library, Va., 1974-81; librarian Ohio U. So. Campus, Ironton, 1981—; del. Govs. Conf. on Libraries, Va., 1979; mem. rev. team North Central Assn. of Colls. and Schs., Ohio, 1984. Reviewer, columnist: Greenville Reflector, 1970-71, Checklist, 1982—. Organizer Internat. Year of Child Com., Lynchburg, Va., 1979. Va. State Library grantee, 1977, 78, 80. Mem. ALA, Ohio Library Assn., Assn. Coll. and Research Libraries, Pub. Library Assn., Assn. Library Service to Children, Beta Phi Mu. Lawrence County, Nat. Assn. Preservation and Perpetuation of Storytelling, Beekeepers Assn. Story League Mennonite. Home: Route 1 Box 100 Willow Wood OH 45695 Office: Ohio U So Campus 1701 S 7th St Ironton OH 45638

REID, PAUL CAREY, dentist; b. Louisville, Ky., Sept. 4, 1924; s. Isaac Errett and Margaret Bright (Lawrence) R.; m. Kathryn Marie Lambrechts, June 8, 1946; children—Paul C., Jr., Julia W. Reid Galosy, Steven D., Susan E. Reid Cejka, Daniel J., Amy J. Reid Garvin. D.M.D., U. Louisville, 1947; M.P.H., Loma Linda U., 1970. Commd. dental officer USPHS, 1943, advanced through grades to dental surgeon, 1952, served as clin. dentist, Washington, St. Louis, Chgo., 1948-52; gen. practice dentistry, St. Louis, 1952-69; dep. dir. Regional Med. Programs, Loma Linda U. Med. Sch., Calif., 1970-72; chief pub. health dental officer Govt. of Guam, 1973-76; dir. dental health Mo. Div. Health, Jefferson City, 1976—. WHO fellow, 1974, 1976. Fellow Am. Coll. Dentists; mem. Mo. Dental Assn. (councils on legis. dental health, dentistry for handicapped and aged), Assn. State and Territorial Dental Dirs. (pres. 1984—), Am. Assn. Pub. Health Dentists, ADA, Am. Pub. Health Assn. Roman Catholic. Lodge: Elks. Avocations: golf; gardening; spectator sports. Home: 513 Maplewood Dr Columbia MO 65203 Office: Mo Div Health PO Box 570 Jefferson City MO 65102

REID, SHERRI JO, tax preparation company executive; b. Maquoketa, Iowa, June 22, 1941; d. William Earle and Luella Augusta (Teters) Wells; m. Gary Harrison Hicks, July 2, 1958 (dec. Apr. 1973); children—Bryon Keith, Scott Allen; m. 2d, Ronald Dwight Reid, July 21, 1977; stepchildren—Mark Douglas, Dwight David, Curtis Duane. Grad. pub. schs., Maquoketa, Iowa. Enrolled to practice before IRS. Proof operator Jackson (Iowa) State Bank, 1959-60; co-owner, mgr. Hicks TV & Appliances, Maquoketa, 1961-72; owner, tax cons. Sherri's Tax Service, Onslow, Iowa, 1975—. Mem. Nat. Assn. Tax Practitioners, Nat. Fedn. Ind. Bus. Republican. Methodist. Home: RR1 Onslow IA 52321 Office: Sherri's Tax Service RR1 Onslow IA 52331

REID, WANDA CATHERINE, bookstore manager; b. Oilfield, Ill., Mar. 2, 1933; d. Francis and Effie Elizabeth (Cox) Sandy m. Everett Alvernon, Sept. 23, 1956 (dec.); 1 child, Rudi Patrick. B.S., Eastern Ill. U. Commissary clk. Brown Shoe Co., Charleston, Ill., 1951-69; acctg. clk. Eastern Ill. U., Charleston, 1969-74, supr., 1974-77, chief clk., 1977-82, bookstore mgr., 1982—. Precinct committeeman Democratic Orgn., Charleston, 1984. Mem. Nat. Assn. Coll. Stores, Ill. Assn. Coll. Stores, Bus. and Profl. Women's Club. Democrat. Methodist. Club: Ducks Unltd. (Chgo.). Home: 515 Tyler St Charleston IL 61920 Office: Eastern Ill U Charleston IL 61920

REID, WILLIAM HOWARD, psychiatrist; b. Dallas, Apr. 10, 1945; s. Howard Clinton and Lucile (Brock) R. B.A., U. Minn., 1966, M.D., 1970; M.P.H., U. Calif., Berkeley, 1975. Diplomate Am. Bd. Psychiatry and Neurology, Am. Bd. Forensic Psychiatry. Intern, U. Calif., Davis, 1970-71, resident in psychiatry, 1973-75; clin., research and forensic psychiatrist, assoc. prof., vice chief of staff Nebr. Psychiat. Inst., Omaha, 1977-83; now prof. psychiatry, med. jurisprudence and humanities U. Nebr. Coll. Medicine; lectr. in psychiatry Northwestern U., vis. assoc. prof. and forensic cons. Rush Med. Coll., 1978-81; chair research sect. Cross Keys Internat. Conf. Psychiat. Aspects of Terrorism; U.S. del. Ver Heydn de Lancey Conf., Cambridge, Eng. Served with M.C., AUS, 1971-73. Mem. Am. Psychiat. Assn., Nebr. Psychiat. Soc. AMA, AAAS, Am. Acad. Psychiatry and the Law, Internat. Platform Assn. Author: The Psychopath: A Comprehensive Study of Antisocial Disorders and Behaviors, 1978; Psychiatry for the House Officer, 1979; Basic Intensive Psychotherapy, 1980; The Treatment of Antisocial Syndromes, 1981; Terrorism: Interdisciplinary Perspectives, 1983; Assaults within Psychiatric Facilities, 1983; Treatment of Psychiatric Disorders, 1983; Unmasking the Psychopath, 1986; contbr. over 70 articles to sci. jours. Composer 15 mus. compositions. Office: Nebraska Psychiatric Institute 602 S 45th St Omaha NE 68106

REIDER, JAMES WILLIAM, advertising and marketing consultant, health and safety professional; b. Mpls., June 25, 1952; s. William H. and Marilyn M. (Fish) R.; student Defiance Coll., 1970-72, U. Denver, 1972-74 B.A., U. Minn., 1983; m. Mary K. Johnson, July 10, 1976; children—Christina Marie, Jessica Anne. Safety and security mgr. K-Mart Corp., Mpls., 1974-76; ops. and safety mgr. Park Detective Agy., Inc., Mpls., 1976-77; ops. mgr. Twin City Security, 1977; security and safety officer Hennepin County Med. Center, Mpls., 1977-78, safety officer, 1978-81; corp. dir. security Abbott-Northwestern Hosp., Mpls., 1981; dir. tech. services Fred S. James & Co., 1982-84; pres. Write/Comm Inc., 1984—; account exec. M.R. Bolin Advt., 1984-85; cons. tech. writing, loss control. Active CAP, 1962-80, capt., 1978-80; mem. com. to draft city fire regulations ordinances for health care facilities Mpls. Fire Dept., 1980-81. Cert. protection profl.; cert. health care safety profl. Mem. Am. Soc. Safety Engrs., Nat. Safety Mgmt. Soc., Am. Soc. Indsl. Security, Sigma Phi Epsilon. Office: 9925 Lyndale Ave S Minneapolis MN 55420

REIF, WILLIAM BRUCE, lawyer; b. Elmhurst, Ill., May 27, 1953; s. Donald J. and Mariam M. (Sonenberg) R. A.A., Coll. DuPage, 1972; B.A., Ill. Benedictine Coll., 1976; J.D., U. Ill., 1979. Bar: Ill. 1980. Tech. advisor Ill. Dept. Ins., Springfield, 1980; sole practice, Springfield, 1980-83; asst. atty. gen. Consumer Protection div. State of Ill., Springfield, 1983—. Vice pres. Nat. Fedn. Blind, Springfield, 1984. Home: 428 1/2 W Edwards St Springfield IL 62704 Office: Atty Gen Hartigan 500 S 2nd St Springfield IL 62706

REIFENSTAHL, DEAN CLAY, JR., dentist; b. Cedar Rapids, Iowa, Aug. 12, 1948; s. Dean Clay and Ruth Louise (Klepach) R.; m. Frances Marie Arey, Aug. 14, 1971; children—Erik, Heidi. B.S. with distinction, U. Iowa Coll. Liberal Arts, 1970; D.D.S., U. Iowa Coll. Dentistry, 1973. Gen. practice dentistry resident Nat. Naval Med. Ctr., 1973-74; gen. practice dentistry, Cedar Rapids, Iowa, 1979—; staff St. Luke's Hosp., Cedar Rapids. Cub scout leader Boy Scouts Am., Cedar Rapids, 1982—, chmn. fund-raising chmn. Hawkeye Area council, 1984—, com. chmn., 1985—; fundraiser Mt. Mercy Coll., 1984; vol. dentist St. Lukes Dental Health Ctr., 1980-83; fund raiser United Way, 1981. Served to lt. comdr. USN, 1973-79, comdr. Res. Decorated Nat. Def. Service medal. Fellow Acad. Gen. Dentistry; mem. ADA, Iowa Dental Assn., Univ. Dist. Dental Soc., Linn County Dental Soc., Chgo. Dental Soc., U.S. Naval Inst., Psi Omega. Roman Catholic. Club: Optimist (com. mem.). Avocations: model shipbuilding; physical fitness; history; golfing; carpentry. Home: 5905 Underwood Ave SW Cedar Rapids IA 52404 Office: 211 Professional Park 119 3d St NE Cedar Rapids IA 52401

REIFF, JAMES STANLEY, addictions physician, osteopathic physician, surgeon; b. Chgo., Mar. 17, 1935; s. Nathan Edgar and Freda Matilda (Imhoff) R.; m. Sharon Ann Kraybill, June 9, 1956 (div. Apr. 1970); children—Gregory James, James Stanley II, Cynthia Diane, Jeffery Cameron. B.A. in Chemistry, Goshen Coll., 1957; D.O., Chgo. Coll. Osteo. Medicine, 1961. Biochemist Miles/Ames Pharm. Co., Elkhart, Ind., 1955-57; gen. practice medicine, Michigan City, Ind., 1962-69; addictions physician Oaklawn Psychiat. Ctr., Elkhart, Ind. 1974-84; clin. team leader, addictions team Oaklawn Ctr., Elkhart, 1980-83. Bd. dirs. Home for Runaway Kids - Victory House, Elkhart, Ind., 1974-76, 12 Step House Meth. Ch.-Halfway House, Elkhart, 1974-77; bd. dirs., treas. Caldwell Home Corp.-Social Rehab. Ctr. for Alcoholism, Elkhart, 1984. Mem. Am. Med. Soc. on Alcoholism, Ind. State Med. Assn. Avocations: organ and piano playing. Home: 501 Virginia Ave Elkhart IN 46516

REIGEL, DON, former business executive; b. Deer River, Minn., Sept. 4, 1914; s. Jake and Marion (Shabel) R.; B.A., cum laude, Carleton Coll., 1936; postgrad. Minn. Sch. Bus., 1942; grad. Command and General Staff Coll., Fort Leavenworth, Kans., 1963; postgrad. in polit. sci. Mankato (Minn.) State Coll.; m. Mary Jane Scott, Oct. 24, 1942; children—Marc, Kent. Auditor, Stearns Lumber Co., Hutchinson, Minn., 1936-42; advt. mgr. U.S. Check Book Co., Omaha, 1946-50, Journ.-Chronicle Co., Owatonna, Minn., 1950-56; pub., owner Photo News, Owatonna, 1956-73; pres. Reigel Corp., 1973-79; info. officer vocat. rehab./econ. devel. State of Minn., 1974-84. Tchr. U. Omaha and Van Sant Sch. of Bus., Omaha, 1946-50, Mankato State Coll., 1972-73, Rasmussen Sch. Bus., 1978-79, Globe Bus. Coll., 1981-84. Pres. Owatonna Community Chest, 1954; dist. chmn. Wasioja dist. Boy Scouts of Am., 1955-56; chmn. long range planning and research com. Minn. United Meth. Conf. Mem. Minn. Ho. of Reps. from Steele County, 1968-70. Bd. dirs. Paul Watkins Home, Winona, 1966-72. Served to capt. AUS, 1942-46; to lt. col. Res. Mem. Minn. Newspaper Assn. (chmn. advt. com. 1962-63), Nat. Editorial Assn. Club: Sr. Active. Lodges: Rotary (sec. 1955-76), Masons. Home: 558 E South St Owatonna MN 55060

REILLY, EDWARD FRANCIS, JR., state senator; b. Leavenworth, Kans., Mar. 24, 1937; s. Edward F. and Marian C. (Sullivan) R.; B.A., U. Kans., 1961. Vice pres. Ed Reilly & Sons, Inc., Leavenworth, 1967—; pres. Westside Village, Inc., Leavenworth, 1968-79, Yllier Lake Estates, Inc., Easton, Kans., 1965-79; v.p. First State Bank of Lansing, 1979—; mem. Kans. Ho. of Reps., 1963-64; mem. Kans. State Senate, 1964—, asst. majority leader, 1977—, vice-chmn. govtl. orgn., chmn. ins. subcom., chmn. fed. and state affairs com. Mem. Nat. Commn. on Accreditation of Law Enforcement Agys.; cultural chmn. Christian Youth Orgn.; del. to Republican Nat. Conv., Miami Beach, Fla., 1968; chmn. Leavenworth County Radio Free Europe Fund, 1972; bd. dirs. Kaw Valley Heart Assn., 1971-77, St. John's Hosp., Leavenworth, 1970-79, sec.; bd. dirs. Leavenworth Assn. for Handicapped, 1968-69, ARC, Leavenworth chpt., Kans. Blue Cross/Blue Shield, 1969-72. Mem. Leavenworth C. of C. (hon. dir. 1970-73), Assn. U.S. Army (Henry Leavenworth award 1960), Kansas City (Kans.) C. of C., Leavenworth Hist. Soc. (dir. 1968-73), Ancient Order of Hibernians. Republican. Roman Catholic. Clubs: Kiwanis (dir. 1969-70), K.C., Elks. Home: 430 Delaware Leavenworth KS 66048

REILLY, FRANCIS EUGENE, stockbroker; b. N.Y.C., May 1, 1910; s. Joseph Anthony and Ellen (Jones) R.; m. Antoinette Egan, 1936; children—Francis Eugene, Dennis, Antoinette, Robert R. B.S., U. Pa., 1932. Vice-pres., dir. Electrographic Corp., Chgo., 1933-82, chmn., dir., chief exec. officer, 1958-80, chmn. Electrographic Holding Corp., 1980-82; pres. Oxy Dry Corp., Chgo.-Elk Grove Village, Ill., 1946-58, chmn., chief exec. officer, 1958-80, chmn. Oxy Dry Corp., CMBH, Frankfort, W.Ger., 1967-80, Oxy Dry Corp. Ltd., Shannon, Ireland, 1962-80; pres. Ramdel Realty Corp., Chgo., 1960-80; ltd. ptnr. McMahon, Bronfmann and Morgan, N.Y.C., 1980—; leader minority group stockholders Oxy Dry Corp., 1980—. Bd. dirs. Marillac Settlement House, Chgo., 1946-54; sec., bd. dirs. Am. Irish Found., San Francisco, 1981—; mem. Pres.' Adv. Council, Heritage Found., 1981—; mem. Ill. Thoroughbred Racing Adv. Panel, 1982—. Clubs: Exmoor Country, Turf and Field, Post and Paddock, Internat., Shoreacres. Address: 210 S Ridge Rd Lake Forest IL 60045

REILLY, PETER C., chemical company executive; b. Indpls., Jan. 19, 1907; s. Peter C. and Ineva (Gash) R.; A.B., U. Colo., 1929; M.B.A., Harvard U., 1931; m. Jeanette Parker, Sept. 15, 1932; children—Marie (Mrs. Jack H. Heed), Sara Jean (Mrs. Clarke Wilhelm), Patricia Ann (Mrs. Michael Davis). With accounting dept. Republic Creosoting Co., Indpls., 1931-32; sales dept. Reilly Tar & Chem. Corp., N.Y.C., 1932-36, v.p., Eastern mgr., 1936-52; v.p. sales, treas. both cos., Indpls., 1952-59, pres., 1959-73, chmn. bd., 1973-75, vice chmn., 1975-82, chmn., 1982—; dir. Environ. Quality Control Inc.; past dir. Ind. Nat. Corp., Ind. Nat. Bank. Past bd. dirs. United Fund Greater Indpls., Indpls. Symphony Orch.; bd. govs. Jr. Achievement Indpls. Mem. adv. council U. Notre Dame Sch. Commerce, 1947—; mem. adv. council Winona Meml. Hosp. Mem. Chem. Spltys. Mfg. Assn. (life; treas. 1950-60, past dir.), Mfg. Chemists Assn. (past dir.), Am. Chem. Soc., Soc. Chem. Industry (past dir. Am. sect. 1979—). Clubs: Union League, Harvard, Chemist (N.Y.C.); Larchmont (N.Y.) Yacht; Indianapolis Athletic, Pine Valley Golf (N.J.), Meridian Hills Country, Columbia (Indpls.); Rotary, One Hundred (past dir.); Crooked Stick Golf. Home: 3777 Bay Rd North Dr Indianapolis IN 46240 Office: 1510 Market Square Center 151 N Delaware St Indianapolis IN 46204

REILLY, PETER JOHN, chemical engineering educator, researcher; b. Newark, Dec. 26, 1938; s. Edward Thomas and Anita (Galdieri) R.; m. Rae Georgine Messer, July 3, 1976; children: Diane Joyce, Karen Elizabeth. A.B., Princeton U., 1960; Ph.D., U. Pa., 1964. Research engr. E.I. Dupont & Co., Deepwater, N.J., 1964-68; asst. prof. U. Nebr., Lincoln, 1968-74; assoc. prof. Iowa State U., Ames, 1974-79, prof., 1979—; prof. invitéEcole Poly. Federale de Lausanne, Switzerland, 1983-84. Contbr. chpts. to books, articles to profl. jours. Mem. Am. Chem. Soc., Am. Inst. Chem. Engrs., AAUP, Sigma Xi, Phi Kappa Phi. Home: 1807 Wilson Ave Ames IA 50010 Office: Iowa State U 231 Sweeney Hall Ames IA 50011

REIMENSCHNEIDER, HERBERT WILLIAM, physician; b. Cleve., Sept. 2, 1939; B.A., Ohio State U., 1961, M.D., 1965. Diplomate Am. Bd. Med. Examiners. Intern, Ohio State U. Hosp., Columbus, 1965-66, resident, 1966-67; resident in urology Ind. U. Med. Ctr., 1967-70; practice medicine specializing in urology, Columbus, Ohio, 1972-82; physician pres. Riverside Urology, Columbus, 1982—; mem. staff Riverside Meth. Hosp., Children's Hosp., Grant Hosp., St. Ann's Hosp., 1981—; dir. urol. edn. Riverside Hosp. Contbr. articles to profl. jours. Chmn. med. adv. bd. Kidney Found., 1974-78. Fellow ACS; mem. Ohio State Med. Assn., Central Ohio Urol. Soc., Am. Bd. Urology, North Central Sect. Am. Urol. Assn. Office: 3545 Olentangy River Rd Columbus OH 43214

REIMER, RICHARD DALE, economics educator; b. Marion County, Kans., Oct. 6, 1931; s. David U. and Carolina (Voth) R.; m. Lois Mary Unruh, Sept. 10, 1958; children—David, Paul, Susan. B.A., Bethel Coll., 1957; M.S., Kans. State U., 1958; Ph.D., Mich. State U., 1962. Prof. Coll. Wooster, Ohio, 1962—; vis. research assoc. Inst. Devel. Studies, Nairobi, Kenya, 1969-70, research assoc. Addis Ababa, Ethiopia, 1974-75. Contbr. articles to profl. jours. Chmn., Ohio Economists for McGovern, 1972; pres. Wayne County Democratic Club, 1977-78. NSF faculty research grantee NSF, 1966, grantee NSF, 1966-68, Am. Philol. Soc., 1969-70. Mem. Am. Econ. Assn., Midwest Econ. Assn. (nominating com. 1968). Lodge: Lions (pres. 1971-72). Home: 5760 Fox Lake Rd Smithville OH 44677 Office: The College of Wooster Wooster OH 44691

REINEKE, JOHN LARRY, farmer; b. Smithville, Mo., Jan. 25, 1942; s. John Marion and Jean Janece (Brink) R.; m. Patricia Joyce Lyon, June 5, 1965; children—Brendon Keith, Whitney Paige. B.S. in Secondary Edn., Northwest Mo. State U., Maryville, 1967. Cert. secondary tchr., Mo. Tchr. West Platte R-II Sch., Weston, Mo., 1967-69; mktg. rep. Sun Oil Co., Chgo., 1969-71; owner, prin. Double L Western Store, Platte City, Mo., 1972-78; farmer, Kansas City, Mo., 1978—. Bus. coordinator Am. Cancer Soc., Kansas City, 1974-75, Platte County R-III Bd. Edn., Platte City, 1977—; chmn. Adminstrv. Council, Methodist Ch. Platte City., 1977-83; bd. dirs. Platte County Fair Assn., 1980-83. Democrat. Lodge: Rotary (treas. 1976-78). Avocations: camping, boating, collecting antiques, calligraphy. Home: Route 3 518 Thomas Dr Platte City MO 64079

REINERT, JAMES HENRY, manufacturing and productivity consultant; b. St. Jospeh, Mo., Oct. 16, 1946; s. Henry H. and Mary E. (Schmidt) R.; m. Connie L. Taff, Dec. 16, 1977 (div. 1984). B.S. in Mgmt., Mo. Western State Coll., 1973, B.S. in Mktg., 1974. Indsl. engr. U.S. Divers, St. Joseph, 1973-76; mining cons. Midwest Research Inst., Kansas City, Mo., 1976-78; indsl. engr. Rockwell Internat., Kearney, Nebr., 1978-79; prin., indsl. engring. cons. Arthur Young & Co., Kansas City, 1979—; peer rev. group team facilitator SBA, Kansas City, 1984—. Editor newsletter Indsl. Mgmt. in Perspective, 1984—. Team leader Am. Cancer Soc., Kansas City, 1979-84. Served as spl. agt. U.S. Army, 1968-71, Vietnam. Decorated Bronze Star; recipient Up-the-Corp.-Ladder award Kansas City Star, 1984. Mem. Inst. Indsl. Engrs. (conf. chmn. 1983-84, chmn. membership com. 1984-85, v.p. 1985—), Am. Mgmt. Assn., Phi Sigma Epsilon (v.p. 1972-73). Republican. Lutheran. Club: Midwest Social (pres. 1973-74) (St. Joseph). Home: 7819 N Garfield St Kansas City MO 64118 Office: Arthur Young & Co 920 Main Charter Bank Ctr Kansas City MO 64105

REINHEIMER, JOHN DAVID, chemistry educator; b. Springfield, Ohio, Dec. 23, 1920; s. Joseph P. and Dorothy A. (Nunlist) R.; m. Phyllis Ann Nelson, June 18, 1944; children—M. Susan Judd, Ruthann Pederson, Joseph P., Sarah Hofstetter, Dorothy A. B.A., Kenyon Coll., 1942; M.A., Johns Hopkins U., 1944, Ph.D., 1949. With chemistry dept. Coll. Wooster, Ohio, 1948—, prof. chemistry, 1958-85; dir. NSF programs. Contbr. articles to profl. jours. Served to lt. (j.g.) USN, 1944-46. Grantee NSF, Petroleum Research Fund, Office of Ordinance Research; Alexander Von Humboldt fellow, 1953. Mem. Am. Chem. Soc., Ohio Acad. Scis., Sigma Xi, Phi Beta Kappa. Lutheran. Home: 2244 Eddy Rd Wooster OH 44691 Office: College Wooster Dept Chemistry Wooster OH 44691

REINSDORF, JERRY MICHAEL, lawyer, executive; b. Bklyn., Feb. 25, 1936; s. Max and Marion (Smith) R.; B.A., The George Washington U., 1957; J.D., Northwestern U., 1960; m. Martyl F. Rifkin, Dec. 29, 1956; children—David Jason, Susan Janeen, Michael Andrew, Jonathan Milton. Admitted to D.C., Ill. bars, 1960; atty. staff regional counsel IRS, Chgo., 1960-64; asso. law firm Chapman & Cutler, 1964-68; partner law firm Altman, Kurlander & Weiss, 1968-74; of counsel firm Katten, Muchin, Zavis, Pearl & Galler, 1974-80; gen. partner Carlyle Real Estate Ltd. Partnerships, 1971-72; chmn. bd. The Balcor Co., Skokie, Ill., 1973-82, Balcor Co. (an Am. Express affiliate), 1982—; mng. partner TBC Films, 1975—; chmn. bd. Chgo. White Sox, 1981—, Chgo. Bulls, 1985—; dir. Shearson/Am. Express, 1982-85, Shearson/Am. Express Mortgage Corp., 1982-84, Shearson Lehman Bros. Inc., 1985—, Convenient Food Mart, Inc., Cole-Taylor Fin. Group, Inc.; lectr. John Marshall Law Sch., 1966-68; dir. Real Estate Securities and Syndication Inst., 1972-76. Bd. dirs. Chgo. Gastro-Intestinal Research Found., John Howard Assn., Ednl. Tape Rec. for Blind. Co-chmn., Ill. Profls. for Sen. Ralph Smith, 1970. C.P.A., Ill.; cert. specialist in real estate securities. Mem. Am., Ill., Chgo., Fed. bar assns., Nat. Assn. Rev. Appraisers and Mortgage Underwriters C.R.A., Alumni Assn. of Northwestern Law Sch. (dir.), Order of Coif, Omega Tau Rho. Author: (with L. Herbert Schneider) Uses of Life Insurance in Qualified Employee Benefit Plans, 1970. Office: 4849 Golf Rd Skokie IL 60077

REISCH, JOHN ALFRED, educator; b. Ponca City, Okla., Sept. 11, 1932; s. Warren A. and Hilda P. (Miller) R.; m. Donna J. Pratt, Apr. 29, 1961; children—Karla, Mark, Kristi, Troy. B.A., Wichita (Kans.) State U., 1970; M.Ed., 1974; Ph.D., 1983. Cert. tchr., Kans. Aux. operator Kans. Gas and Electric, Wichita, 1962-66; assembler Cessna Aircraft Co., Wichita, 1967-70; indsl. edn. tchr. Oxford (Kans.) High Sch., 1970-76, Goddard (Kans.) Jr. High Sch., 1976—; cons. Wichita State U., 1972, 1974, Wichita pub. schs., 1974; power and energy cons. Competency Project, Dept. Edn., 1976. Polit. action chmn. Goddard schs., 1981-82. Served with AUS, 1951-53. Recipient Outstanding Sr. award in Indsl. Edn., Wichita State U., 1970; Master Tchr. award Goddard Edn. Assn., 1980-81. Mem. NEA, Goddard Edn. Assn., Am. Vocat. Assn., Kans. Vocat. Assn., Kans. Indsl. Edn. Assn. Democrat. Baptist. Author hydraulics sect. in curriculum guide for power and energy Kans. State Dept. Edn., 1972. Home: 820 E 58th St S Wichita KS 67216 Office: 301 N Walnut Goddard KS 67052

REISERT, JOHN EDWARD, dean, consultant; b. Corydon, Ind., Mar. 16, 1930; s. Glenn Arthur and Laura Mae (Bulleit) R.; m. Carolyn Jane Herbstreit, Aug. 4, 1950; children—Rebecca S., John M., Jane E. B.S. in Edn., Ind. U.-Bloomington, 1951, M.S. in Edn., 1953; student No. Mich. U., 1960; Ed.D., Ind. U., 1965. Elem. prin. New Albany-Floyd County Schs., Ind., 1950-60; dir. tchr. edn. and cert. State of Ind., Indpls., 1960-64; assoc. prof. Ind. U., 1965-78; chmn. edn. div. Ind. U. Southeast, New Albany, 1969-78, dean, 1978—; cons. Marshall U., Huntington, W.Va., 1979-80, Valley City State Coll., N.D., 1979-81; lectr. ARAMCO, Dhahran, Saudi Arabia, 1982. Author: Encyclopedia of Education, 1971. Editor: The Role of the Principal, 1967. Contbr. articles to profl. jours. Exec. sec. Ind. Tchr. Training and Licensing Commn., 1960-64; pres. New Albany Plan Commn., 1976, New Albany Park Commn., 1977, New Albany Police Commn., 1978-85. Recipient Outstanding Young Man award Jr. C. of C. New Albany, 1960, Alpha award Phi Delta Kappa, 1965. Alice Blaylock Lectr. award Grambling Coll., 1969, Outstanding Hoosier Educator award Phi Delta Kappa, 1981. Mem. Ind. Assoc. Colls. for Tchr. Edn. (pres. 1975-76), Ind. Assoc. of Grad. Schs. (pres. 1981-82), Ind. Assn. Supervision and Curriculum Devel. (pres. 1972-73), Leadership Louisville (alumni). Democrat. Mem. Christian Ch. Club: University (Bloomington). Avocations: gardening; travel. Home: 13 Trimingham Rd New Albany IN 47150 Office: Ind U Southeast 4201 Grant Line Rd New Albany IN 47150

REISMAN, MICHAEL ALAN, ophthalmologist; b. Wichita, Kans., Sept. 8, 1950; s. Robert Daniel and Roslyn (Pollatschek) R.; m. Elizabeth Alice Hansen, May 24, 1980. B.A. in Biology, Wichita State U., 1972; M.D., Baylor Coll. Medicine, 1975. Diplomate Am. Bd. Ophthalmology. Intern Wesley Med. Ctr., Wichita, 1975-76; resident U. Tex., Dallas, 1976-79; clin. assoc. prof. U. Kans. Sch. Medicine, Wichita, 1981—; chmn. dept. ophthalmology Wesley Med. Ctr., Wichita, 1983—. Contbr. articles to profl. jours. Recipient Physicians Recognition awards AMA, 1980, 81, 84. Mem. Am. Acad. Ophthalmology, Sedgwick County Med. Soc., Kans. Med. Soc., Am. Intra-Ocular Implant Soc., Phi Kappa Phi. Republican. Lodges: Masons (32 degree), Moose. Office: 3243 E Murdock Suite 600 Wichita KS 67208

REISS, MARY LORANGER, educational administrator; b. Superior, Wis., Feb. 19, 1934; d. Egbert Fletcher and Mary J. Loranger; B.S., Wayne State U., 1955; M.A., U. Mich., 1965, Ph.D., 1971; children—Eric, Merritt. Health and sci. cons. Oak Park (Mich.) schs., 1961-63, sch.-community coordinator, 1963-65; edn. cons. Wayne County (Mich.) Intermediate Schs., 1965-70; cons. Mich. Dept. Edn., 1970-73, dir. adult extended learning service area, Lansing, 1978-83; assoc. dir. Higher Edn. Mgmt. Services, Lansing, 1983—; dir. allied health occupations Washtenaw Community Coll., 1973-74; dir. div. continuing edn. N.Y. State Edn. Dept. Albany, 1974-78; asso. prof. sociology Oakland Community Coll., 1967-69; guest lectr. various univs., colls., including Tchrs. Coll., Columbia U., CCNY; N.Y. State Dept. Edn. rep. Public Exec. Project, 1978; mem. Mich. Gov.'s Cons. Task Force on Volunteerism, 1979—; mem. Mich. Dept. Labor Task Force on Policy Analysis, 1979—; mem. Task Force on Implementation of State of Mich. Full Employment Act, 1979—. Recipient State award Mich. Welfare League, 1965. Mem. Nat. Assn. Public Continuing Adult Edn., Mich. Community Edn. Assn., Nat. Council State Dirs. Adult Edn., Nat. Teleconf. on Productivity in the Work Force. Research in field. Office: Ottawa St Bldg Lansing MI 48909

REISTER, RAYMOND ALEX, lawyer; b. Sioux City, Iowa, Dec. 22, 1929; s. Harold William and Anna (Eberhardt) R.; A.B., Harvard U., 1952, LL.B., 1955; m. Ruth Elizabeth Alkema, Oct. 7, 1967. Bar: N.Y. 1956, Minn. 1960. Assoc. Paul, Weiss, Rifkind, Wharton & Garrison, N.Y.C., 1955-56; assoc. Dorsey & Whitney, and predecessor, Mpls., 1959-63, partner, 1964—; instr. law U. Minn. Extension Div., 1964-66. Served to 1st lt. AUS, 1956-59. Mem. Am. Coll. Probate Counsel, Am. Law Inst., ABA, Minn., Hennepin County bar assns., Internat. Acad. Estate and Trust Law, Mpls. Soc. Fine Arts (trustee), Minn. Hist. Soc. (dir.). Clubs: Minneapolis, Harvard of Minn. (pres. 1969-70). Editor (with Larry W. Johnson) Minnesota Probate Administration, 1968. Home: 93 Groveland Terr Minneapolis MN 55403 Office: 2200 First Bank Pl Minneapolis MN 55402

REITZ, WILLIAM, construction company executive, mechanical engineer; b. Toluca, Ill., June 16, 1923; s. George William and Winifred Allison (Donnelly) R.; m. Ruth M. Maus, Oct. 9, 1951; 1 dau., Mary Allison. B.S.M.E., U. Ark., 1950. Registered profl. engr., Tex. Mech. engr. Jewel Mining Co., Paris, Ark., 1950, Silas Mason Co., Amarillo, Tex., 1951, F.H. McGraw & Co., Hartford, Conn., 1951-62; sr. v.p. Edward Gray Corp., Chgo., 1962—. Bd. dirs., treas. Morgan Park Improvement Assn., Chgo. Served with U.S. Army, 1942-46. Mem. ASME, Am. Nuclear Soc., Soc. Am. Mil. Engrs., ASTM, Am. Concrete Inst.

REKLAITIS, GINTAVAS VICTOR, chemical engineering educator, researcher, consultant; b. Posnan, Poland, Oct. 20, 1942; came to U.S., 1952, naturalized, 1957; s. Mechislav Martin and Halina (Lorenz) R.; m. Janine Konauka, Aug. 20, 1966; children—Victor, George. B.S. in Chem. Engring. Ill. Inst. Tech., 1965; M.S. in Chem. Engring., Stanford U., 1969, Ph.D. in Chem. Engring., 1969. Research asst. Stanford U., Calif., 1965-69; postdoctoral fellow Inst. for Ops. Research, Zurich, Switzerland, 1969-70; asst. prof. Purdue U., West Lafayette, Ind., 1970-80, assoc. prof., 1976-80, prof., 1980—, asst. dean engring. research, 1985—; sr. Fulbright lectr. Lithuanian Acad. Sci., Vilnius, 1980. Author: Introduction to Material Energy Balances, 1983; co-editor: Computer Applications to Chemical Engineering, 1980; Selected Topics on Computer Aided Process Design and Analysis, 1982; co-author: Engineering Optimization, 1983. NSF Postdoctoral fellow, 1969; grantee NSF, DOE, and indsl. founds. Mem. Am. Inst. Chem. Engrs. (Computing Chem. Engring. award 1984), Am. Chem. Soc., Ops. Soc. Am., Math. Progress Soc. Roman Catholic. Avocations: sailing; skiing; tennis; opera. Office: Purdue U Sch Chem Engring West Lafayette IN 47907

RELLE, FERENC MATYAS, chemist; b. Gyor, Hungary, June 13, 1922; came to U.S., 1951, naturalized, 1956; s. Ferenc and Elizabeth (Netratics) R.; B.S. in Chem. Engring., Jozsef Nador Poly. U., Budapest, 1944, M.S., 1944; m. Gertrud B. Tubach, Oct. 9, 1946; children—Ferenc, Ava, Attila. Lab. mgr. Karl Kohn Ltd. Co., Landshut, W.Ger., 1947-48; resettlement officer IRO, Munich, 1948-51; chemist Farm Bur. Coop. Assn., Columbus, Ohio, 1951-56; indsl. engr. N.Am. Aviation, Inc., Columbus, 1956-57; research chemist Keever Starch Co., Columbus, 1957-65; research chemist Ross Labs. div. Abbott Labs., Columbus, 1965-70, research scientist, 1970—; cons. in field. Chmn. Columbus and Central Ohio UN Week, 1963; pres. Berwick Manor Civic Assn., 1968; trustee Stelios Stelson Found., 1968-69. Mem. Am. Chem. Soc. (alt. councilor 1973, chmn. long range planning com. Columbus sect. 1972-76, 78-80), Am. Assn. Cereal Chemists (chmn. Cin. sect. 1974-75), Ohio Acad. Sci., Internat. Tech. Inst. (adv. dir. 1977-82), Nat. Intercollegiate Soccer Ofcls. Assn., Am. Hungarian Assn., Hungarian Cultural Assn. (pres. 1978-81), Ohio Soccer Ofcls. Assn., Ohio High Sch. Athletic Assn., Germania Singing and Sport Soc. Presbyterian. Club: Civitan (gov. Ohio dist. 1970-71, dist. treas. 1982-83, pres. Eastern Columbus 1962-64, 72-73; internat. gov. of yr. 1971, various awards). Home: 3487 Roswell Dr Columbus OH 43227 Office: 625 Cleveland Ave Columbus OH 43216

REMACK, ANDREW EDWARD, accountant; b. Springfield, Ill., May 19, 1951; s. Edward Fredrick and Josephine Pauline (Susinskas) R.; children—Della Marie, Jennifer Joanne. B.S. in Acctg., U. Ill., 1973, M.S. in Acctg., 1974. C.P.A., Ill. Tax ptnr. Kerber, Eck & Braeckel, Springfield, 1975—; Contbr. articles to newsletter; Tax Advisor. Chmn. Citizens for Edgar Tennis Fundraiser, Springfield, 1984, 85; mem. Citizens for Percy, Springfield, 1984; lay adv. bd., treas. St. Joseph Ch., 1981—; audit chmn. Springfield United Way, 1977-81; treas. Springfield Area Parents Anonymous, 1981-83, Jr. Achievement, 1983—; mem. citizens adv. bd. Jr. League of Springfield, 1983-84; bd. dirs. Rail Charity Golf Classic, 1984—. Mem. Am. Inst. C.P.A.s, Ill. C.P.A. Soc. (chmn. tax conf. 1981—), Sangamon Valley Estate Planning Council. Republican. Roman Catholic. Clubs: Am. Business, Exchange (Exchangite of Yr. 1981), Inter Civic Club Council (pres. 1983—) (Springfield). Home: 513 E Monroe Apt E Springfield IL 62701 Office: Kerber Eck & Braeckel 1000 Myers Bldg Springfield IL 62701

REMER, RICHARD POST, insurance executive; b. Paterson, N.J., Oct. 15, 1939; s. Richard F. and Carolyn B. (Post) R.; m. Adrienne A. Kriss, Nov. 18, 1961; 1 child, Richard F. B.S. in Indsl. Mgmt., Carnegie Inst. Tech., 1964.

C.P.C.U.; cert. EDP. Analyst, mgr. Gimbel Brothers, Pitts., 1962-66; sr. cons. Touche, Ross & Co., Chgo., 1967-69; mgr. fin. control Allstate Ins. Co., Northbrook, Ill., 1969-72, mgr. claims res., 1972—. Chmn. planning commn. Village of Cary, Ill., 1976, trustee, 1978, bd. dirs., 1982. Republican. Home: 407 Parkway Dr Cary IL 60013 Office: Allstate Ins Co Allstate Plaza A8 Northbrook IL 60062

REMINE, WILLIAM HERVEY, JR., surgeon; b. Richmond Va., Oct. 11, 1918; s. William Hervey and Mabel Inez (Walthall) ReM.; m. Doris Irene Grumbacher, June 9, 1943; children—William Hervey III, Stephen Gordon, Walter James, Gary Craig. B.S., U. Richmond, 1940; M.D., Med. Coll. Va., 1943; M.S. in Surgery, U. Minn., 1952; D.Sc. (hon.), U. Richmond, 1965. Diplomate Am. Bd. Surgery. Intern, Doctors Hosp., Washington, 1944; resident in surgery, fellow Mayo Found., Rochester, Minn., 1944-45, 47-50, asst. to surg. staff, 1950-52, cons. in surgery, Mayo Clinic, 1953—, also cons. in surgery, prof. surgery Mayo Grad. Sch. of Mayo Found., 1973—; vis. prof. various univs. and hosps., 1968-79; guest lectr. profl. socs. Served to capt. M.C., U.S. Army, 1945-47. Recipient St. Francis Surg. award St. Francis Gen. Hosp., Pitts., 1976, Disting. Service award Nat. Alumni Council of U. Richmond, 1976. Fellow ACS (Commn. on Cancer); mem. AAAS, Am. Assn. History of Medicine, AMA, Am. Med. Writers Assn., Am. Soc. Colon and Rectal Surgeons, Am. Surg. Assn., Assn. Mil. Surgeons U.S., Central Assn. Physicians and Dentists (pres. 1971-72), Central Surg. Assn., Digestive Disease Found., Internat. Soc. Surgery, Minn. Med. Assn., Minn. Surg. Soc. (pres. 1966-67), Soc. Surgery of Alimentary Tract (v.p., 1983-84), Priestley Soc. (pres. 1968-69), Soc. Med. Cons. to Armed Forces, Soc. Head and Neck Surgeons, Soc. Surg. Oncology, So. Surg. Assn., Western Surg. Assn. (pres. 1979-80), Zumbro Valley Med. Soc., Sigma Xi; hon. mem. numerous fgn. and Am. surg. socs. Editorial bd. Jour. Lancet, Rev. of Surgery; contbr. articles to profl. jours., chpts. to books. Office: Mayo Foundation Rochester MN 55905

REMINGER, RICHARD THOMAS, lawyer; b. Cleve., Apr. 3, 1931; s. Edwin Carl and Theresa Henrietta (Bookmyer) R.; A.B., Case-Western Res. U., 1953; J.D., Cleve.-Marshall Law Sch., 1957; m. Billie Carmen Greer, June 26, 1954; children—Susan Greer, Patricia Allison, Richard Thomas, Jr. Bar: Ohio 1957, Pa. 1978, U.S. Supreme Ct. 1961. Personnel and safety dir. Motor Express, Inc., Cleve., 1954-58; mng. ptnr. Reminger & Reminger Co., L.P.A., Cleve., 1958—; dir. U.S. Truck Lines, Inc. Del., Cardinal Casualty Co.; mem. nat. claims council adv. bd. Comml. Union Assurance Co., 1980—; lectr. transp. law Fenn Coll., 1960-62, bus. law Case-Western Res. U., 1962-64. Mem. joint com. Cleve. Acad. Medicine and Greater Cleve. Bar Assn. Trustee Cleve. Zool. Soc., Andrew Sch., Huron Road Hosp., Cleve.; bd. dirs. United Cerebral Palsy Assn., Inc. Served with AC, USNR, 1950-58. Mem. Fedn. Ins. Counsel, Trial Attys. Am. (mem. sect. litigation, also tort and ins. practice, trial technique com., medicine and law com., profl. liability com.), Fed., Am. (com. on law and medicine, profl. responsibility com. 1977—), Internat., Ohio, Ohio (sect. on litigation 1985—), Cleve. (chmn. med. legal com. 1978-79, profl. liability com. 1977—) bar assns., Cleve. Assn. Civil Trial Attys., Am. Soc. Hosp. Attys., Transp. Lawyers Assn., Soc. Ohio Hosp. Attys., Ohio Assn. Civil Trial Attys., Am. Judicature Soc., Def. Research Inst. (com. on med.-legal 1984—), Maritime Law Assn. U.S., Am. Coll. Law and Medicine, Nat. Health Lawyers Assn. Clubs: Mayfield Country (dir. 1972-82, pres. 1980-82), Union, Cleve. Playhouse, Hermit (pres. 1973-75) (Cleve.); Lost Tree (Fla.). Home: 34000 Hackney Rd Hunting Valley OH 44022 Office: Leader Bldg Cleveland OH 44114

REMLEY, AUDREY WRIGHT, educational administrator, psychologist; b. Warrenton, Mo., Dec. 26, 1931; d. Leslie Frank and Irene Lesetta (Graue) Wright; m. Alvin Remley, Mar. 25, 1951; children—Steven Leslie, David Mark. A.A., Hannibal-LaGrange Coll., 1951; B.S. in Edn. cum laude, U. Mo., 1963, M.A., 1969, Ph.D., 1974. Asst. prof. psychology Westminster Coll., Fulton, Mo., 1969-74, chmn. dept. psychology, 1975-78, dir. counseling services, 1975-79, dir. student devel., 1979-80, dir. acad. advising and counseling services, 1980—; cons. Serve, Inc., Fulton, 1980—, Family Service Div., 1983—. Recipient Outstanding Young Woman of Am. award Jaycettes, 1965; NDEA fellow, 1968. Mem. Am. Assn. Counseling and Devel., Am. Coll. Personnel Assn. (exec. council 1982-85, co-editor ACPA Developments, Outstanding State Div. Leader 1982), Mo. Coll. Personnel Assn. (pres. 1981-82), Am. Psychol. Assn., Mo. Psychol. Assn. (lic.). Presbyterian. Avocations: singing; antique collecting; knitting. Office: Westminster Coll Fulton MO 65251

REMMERS, EDWARD HENRY, business executive; b. Tomahawk, Wis., Dec. 5, 1936; s. Henry Albert and Marie Adelgunde (Bongers) R. Grad. high sch. Joined U.S. Navy, 1954, advanced through grades to lt. comdr., 1973, ret., 1975; field service rep. Transamerica Delaval, Inc., Trenton, N.J., 1977—. Decorated Bronze Star, Navy Commendation medal. Lutheran. Home: PO Box 331 Tomahawk WI 54487

REMMERT, MARK ALLEN, chemical company representative; b., Kansas City, Mo., Sept. 6, 1958; s. Rolland Robert and Norma Arlene (Macklin) R.; m. Judith Ann Cannehl, May 31, 1980. B.S., U. Wyo., 1980. Dist. engr. Dowell, Mt. Carmel, Ill., 1980-84; dist. sales engr. Dowell Schlumberger, Mt. Carmel, 1984; Service specialist Dow Chem. Co., Haubstadt, Ind., 1984—. Contbr. articles to profl. jours. Inventor crosslinked polymer application. Recipient Spl. Service award Ill. Oil and Gas Assn., 1982. Mem. Am. Assn. Petroleum Geologists, Soc. Petroleum Engrs., Soc. Mining Engrs. Lodge: Elks. Avocations: woodworking; backpacking. Home: RR 1 PO Box 549 Haubstadt IN 47639

REMSBERG, COLLEEN EVANS, real estate broker; b. Princeton, Ill., Oct. 20, 1940; d. James W. and Catherine M. (Spohn) Evans; m. Thomas A. Thompson, June 8, 1963 (div. Sept. 1973); children—Amy, John; m. Charles Remsberg, Feb. 25, 1984. Student pub. schs., Ohio and Ill. Lic. real estate broker, Ill. Stewardess, Am. Airlines, 1961-63; asst. ops. mgr. sch. dept. Rand McNally, 1974-76; broker, sales assoc. Century 21/Mitchell Bros., Evanston, Ill., 1976—; instr. North Shore Bd. Realtors. Bd. dir. young woman's aux. Woman's Club Evanston, 1968-74; bd. dirs. Child Care Ctr. aux. Family Counseling Service Evanston and Skokie Valley. Mem. Nat. Assn. Realtors, North Side Real Estate Bd., North Shore Bd. Realtors. Clubs: Kiwis. Home: 2114 Lincolnwood Dr Evanston IL 60201 Office: 2528 Green Bay Rd Evanston IL 60201

REMY, DAVID LEWIS, lawyer; b. Mansfield, Ohio, Sept. 6, 1949; s. Lewis Frank and Janice Beverly (McCollough) R. B.S. in Polit. Sci., Ohio No. U., 1972, J.D., 1975. Bar: Ohio 1975. Referee, Richland City Juvenile Ct., Mansfield, Ohio, 1975-77, Mansfield Mcpl. Ct., 1978-81; sole practice, Mansfield, 1975—; asst. law dir. City of Mansfield, 1984—, Pres., Pediatric Devel. Ctr. Inc., Mansfield, 1981—. Mem. Ohio State Bar Assn., Richland County Bar Assn. Republican. Lutheran. Club: Sertoma (Mansfield). Lodge: Kiwanis. Avocation: woodworking. Office: David L Remy Atty at Law 51 W First St Mansfield OH 44902

RENARD, BERNARD JAMES, pharmacist, drug store administrator; b. Toledo, June 13, 1955; s. Bernard George and Anna Mae (Zitzleberger) R.; m. Kim Frances Derlatka, June 21, 1975; children—Nicholas, Adam. B.S. pharmacy, Ohio State U., 1978. Staff pharmacist Lane Drug, Toledo, 1978, asst. mgr. pharmacy, 1978-79, mgr., 1979-84, dist. mgr., 1984—; preceptor Toledo U., 1982-84; tng. mgr. Lane Drug, Toledo, 1981-84; Co-chmn. United Way Drive Lane Drug, 1982-84, chmn. mgr's adv. com., Lane Drug, 1981-84. Mem. Ohio State Pharm. Assn. (pub. relations com. 1983-84), Toledo Acad. Pharmacy. Republican. Roman Catholic. Club: Adams Conservation. Avocations: bow hunting; fishing. Home: 2645 Castleton Toledo OH 43613

RENDA, BEN ANDREW, accountant; b. Chgo., June 26, 1950; s. S. and V. (Vitacca) R. B.S. in Acctg., Bradley U., 1972; M.B.A. in Internat. Bus., DePaul U., 1981. C.P.A., Ill. With Continental Group, Northbrook, Ill., 1972—, dir. fin. White Cap div., 1981—. Mem. Am. Inst. C.P.A.s, Ill. Soc. C.P.A.s, Nat. Assn. Accts., Beta Gamma Sigma, Delta Mu Delta, Beta Alpha Psi. Home: 8558 W Catherine Ave Chicago IL 60656 Office: Continental White Cap 2215 Sanders Rd Northbrook IL 60062

RENDINA, GEORGE, chemistry educator; b. N.Y.C., July 1, 1923; s. Gaetano and Giovannina (Barbero) R.; m. Irma Civia Esner, Sept. 28, 1948; children—Alan Ralph, Steven Jeremy, David Nathan, Frederick Thomas. A.B., NYU, 1949; M.A., Kans. U., 1953, Ph.D., 1955. Postdoctoral fellow U. Mich., Ann Arbor, 1955-57, Henry Ford Hosp., Detroit, 1958; instr. Johns Hopkins Med. Sch., Batl., 1959-61; chief biochem. research Tng. Sch., Vineland, N.J., 1961-65, Mendota State Sch., Madison, Wis., 1966; prof. chemistry Bowling Green State U., Ohio, 1967—. Office: Bowling Green State U Dept Chemistry Bowling Green OH 43402

RENDLEN, ALBERT LEWIS, state supreme court justice; b. Hannibal, Mo., Apr. 7, 1922; s. Charles E. and Norma (Lewis) R.; B.A., U. Ill., 1943; J.D., U. Mich., 1948; m. Dona Meeker; children—Albert Lewis, Susan Virginia. Admitted to Mo. bar, 1948; practice in Hannibal 1948-74; U.S. commnr. Eastern Dist. Mo., 1953-55; judge St. Louis dist. Mo. Ct. Appeals, 1974-77; justice div. 1, Mo. Supreme Ct., 1977—. Chmn. Mo. Republican Com., 1973-74; bd. regents N.E. Mo. State Coll., 1973-75; mem. nat., dist. adv. council SBA, 1970 bd. dirs. United Fund, 1970; mem. Marion County Family Planning Council, 1965, Marion County Welfare Commn., 1964; pres., 1948, Dist. council Boy Scouts Am., 1949. Served with AUS, 1943-46; to comdr. USCGR, 1951-70. Mem. ABA, Mo. Bar Assn., Hannibal C. of C., VFW, Am. Legion, Navy League, Res. Officers Assn. (past chpt. pres.). Address: Supreme Ct Bldg Jefferson City MO 65101*

RENEHAN, JULIE ANN, pharmacist, administrator; b. Colorado Springs, Colo., July 30, 1959; d. Donald Walter and Laura Mae (Meyer) Mason; m. Jeffrey Neil Renehan, Aug. 7, 1982. B.S. with honors in Pharmacy, Univ. Colo., Boulder, 1982. Pharmacist, Mills Drugs, Rapid City, S.D., 1982-84, Boyds Drug Mart, Rapid City, 1984; head pharmacist, mgr. Boyds Pharmacy, Rapid City, 1984—; cons. Black Hills Workshop, 1985—. Recipient Profl. Achievement award Univ. Colo. Sch. Pharmacy, 1982. Mem. Am. Pharm. Assn., Rapid City Pharm. Assn. (sec. 1982-83), Kappa Epsilon (v.p. Univ. Colo. 1980-81), Kappa Epsilon Nat. Assn., Rho Chi (Alpha Theta chpt. 1981), Republican. Methodist. Avocations: Sewing/crafts; skiing; bowling; cooking; candy-making. Office: Boyds Pharmacy 2929 S 5th St Suite 140 Rapid City SD 57701

RENFRO, AUTHORINE JEANETTE, home economics teacher; b. Blue, Okla., July 2, 1929; d. William Marvin and Viola (Rose) Lindley, m. Albert T. Renfro, May 4, 1927. B.S. in Edn., Southeastern State U., Durant, Okla., 1950; M.S. in Edn., Kans. State U., 1980. Home econs. tchr. Monroe (Okla.) High Sch., 1952, Satanta (Kans.) High Sch., 1953-57, Hugoton (Kans.) High Sch., 1958-62; head home econs. dept. Liberal (Kans.) High Sch., 1963—. Class tchr. First So. Bapt. Ch. Mem. Kans. Vocat. Home Econs. Assn., Delta Kappa Gamma. Democrat. Office: 6th and Lincoln Liberal KS 67901

RENGACHARY, SETTI SUBBIYER, neurosurgeon, educator; b. Palamcottah, India, July 15, 1936; came to U.S., 1963, naturalized, 1976; s. Setti and Lakshmiammal Subbiyer; m. Dhanalakshmi Nagaswamy, July 3, 1963; children: Usha, Dave Anand. M.D., Madras U., India, 1960. Diplomate Am. Bd. Neurol. Surgery. Resident in neurosurgery Kans. U. Med. Ctr., 1966-70; instr. Kans. U. Med. Ctr., Kansas City, 1971-75, asst. prof., 1975-77, assoc. prof., 1977-82, prof. neurosurgery, 1982—. Editor: Neurosurgery, 1985. Mem. Am. Assn. Neurol. Surgeons, Congress Neurol. Surgeons, N.Y. Acad. Scis., Rocky Mountain Neurol. Soc., So. Neurosurg. Soc. Avocations: photography; history of medicine; genetic engring. Office: Kansas City VA Med Ctr 4801 Linwood Blvd Kansas City MO 64128

RENNA, THOMAS JULIUS, history educator; b. Scranton, Pa., Aug. 18, 1937; s. Anthony T. and Alberta (Cesare) R.; m. Pamela Stacey; 3 children. B.A. in History and Philosophy magna cum laude, U. Scranton, 1965; M.A. in History, U. Nebr., 1967; Ph.D. in Medieval History, Brown U., 1970; postgrad. Université de Laval, Université de Dijon. Vice pres. Sacred Heart Ch. Parish Council, Saginaw, Mich., 1975-77; prof. history Saginaw Valley State Coll., University Ctr., Mich., 1970—. Author: Church and State in Medieval Europe, 1974; The West in the Early Middle Ages, 1977. Contbr. 30 articles to profl. jours. Fellow NDEA, 1968-70, Brown U., 1968; grantee NEH, 1973, Am. Philos. Soc., 1974, 83; recipient Mich. Acad. Arts, Sci. and Letters award, 1983; Mich. Assn. Governing Bds. award, 1984; F. Landee award for excellence in teaching Saginaw Valley State Coll., 1984. Mem. Am. Hist. Assn., Catholic History Assn., Medieval Acad. Am., Am. Soc. Ch. History, Mich. Acad., Mich. Ednl. Assn., Pax Christi, Phi Beta Kappa. Democrat. Roman Catholic. Home: 3269 Meyer Pl Saginaw MI 48603 Office: Saginaw Valley State Coll University Center MI 48710

RENNEKAMP, HERBERT ALPHONSE, information systems manager, educator; b. Cin., Dec. 11, 1946; s. William Lawrence and Velma Rose (Erhart) R.; m. Deborah Ann Rice, Jan. 31, 1970; children—Deana, Troy, Keith, Nathan. Computer programmer City of Cin., 1970-73; systems analyst Regional Computer Ctr., Cin., 1974-77, project mgr., 1977-79, mgr. info. systems, 1980—; instr. info. systems U. Cin. Evening Coll., 1980—; advisor on data processing curriculum Great Oaks Career Devel. Sch. System, Cin., 1981—. Soccer coach Monfort Heights Athletic Assn., 1980—; baseball coach St. Ignatius Athletic Assn., Cin., 1982—. Mem. Assn. Systems Mgmt., Delta Sigma Pi. Home: 4366 Runningfawn Dr Cincinnati OH 45247 Office: Regional Computer Ctr 138 E Court St Cincinnati OH 45202

RENNER, SISTER EMMANUEL, college president; b. Nevis, Minn. Sept. 2, 1926; d. Henry John and Beatrice (Fuller) R. B.A., Coll. St. Benedict, 1949; M.A., U. Minn., 1955; Ph.D., Catholic U., 1959. Chmn. integrative studies Coll. St. Benedict, St. Joseph, Minn., 1971-74, dean continuing edn., 1974-77, dir. planning, 1978-79, pres., 1979—; dir. First Am. Nat. Bank, St. Cloud, Minn. Bd. dirs. Neylan Commn., Washington, 1984—, United Way, St. Cloud, 1982—. Mem. Assn. Cath. Colls. and Univs. (bd. dirs.), AAUW, Minn. Hist. Soc., Delta Epsilon Sigma. Home: St Benedicts Convent St Joseph MN 56374 Office: Coll St Benedict St Joseph MN 56374

RENNER, RICHARD RANDOLPH, lawyer; b. Ann Arbor, Mich., July 24, 1958; s. Daniel S. and Carol (Barr) R.; m. Laura R. Yeomans, Aug. 21, 1982. S.B., MIT, 1978; J.D., NYU, 1981. Bar: Ohio 1981, U.S. Dist. Ct. (no. and so. dists.) Ohio 1981. Staff atty. S.E. Ohio Legal Services, Zanesville, 1981-82; research dir. Ohio Pub. Interest Campaign, Athens, 1983; staff rep. Am. Fedn. State County and Mcpl. Employees, AFL-CIO, Ohio Council 8, Athens, 1983-84; coordinator Central Am. Refugee Assistance Com., 1984—; mem. adv. bd. Appalachian Ohio Pub. Interest Campaign, Athens, 1982—. Editor Toxic Watch newsletter, 1983. Contbr. photographs to Freeze Focus, 1983. Mem. Lawyers Alliance for Nuclear Arms Control, Nat. Lawyers Guild, Clergy and Laity Concerned. Mem. Society of Friends. Home: 107 Elmwood Pl Athens OH 45701 Office: 50 S Court St 3d Floor PO Box 2629 Athens OH 45701

RENNER, ROBERT GEORGE, judge; b. Nevis, Minn., Apr. 2, 1923; s. Henry J. and Beatrice M. (Fuller) R.; B.A., St. John's U., Collegeville, Minn., 1947; J.D., Georgetown U., 1949; m. Catherine L. Clark, Nov. 12, 1949; children—Robert, Anne, Richard, David. Admitted to Minn. bar, 1949; pvt. practice, Walker, 1949-69; U.S. atty. Dist. Minn., 1969-77, U.S. magistrate, 1977-80, U.S. dist. judge, 1980—. Mem. Minn. Ho. of Reps., 1957-69. Served with AUS, 1943-46. Mem. Fed. Bar Assn., Minn. Bar Assn. Roman Catholic. Address: 738 US Courthouse Saint Paul MN 55101*

RENNICKE, JAMES JAY, lawyer; b. Des Moines, Aug. 18, 1957; s. John William and Carla (Gretchen) R. A. Liberal Arts, U. Minn., 1978; B.A., U. Minn., 1979; J.D., Hamline U., 1982. Bar: Minn. 1982, U.S. Dist. Ct. Minn. 1982, U.S. Ct. Appeals (8th cir.) 1985. Assoc. Paul A. Kyyhkynen Law Firm, Princeton, Minn., 1982-83; ptnr. firm Kyyhkynen & Rennicke, Princeton, 1983-84; assoc. Magsam, Harwig & Jude, Osseo, Minn., 1984—. Del. Democratic Farm Labor of Minn., Plymouth, 1984. Recipient Am. Jurisprudence award, 1981. Mem. ABA, Assn. Trial Lawyers Am., Minn. State Bar Assn., Minn. Trial Lawyers Assn., Phi Delta Theta. Methodist. Club: Toastmasters (Osseo, Minn.); St. Paul YMCA Judo (Minn.). Home: 10750 Rockford Rd Apt 115 Plymouth MN 55441 Office: Magsam Harwig & Jude 33 4th St NW Osseo MN 55369

RENO, OTTIE WAYNE, former judge; b. Pike County, Ohio, Apr. 7, 1929; s. Eli Enos and Arbannah Belle (Jones) R.; Asso. in Bus. Adminstrn., Franklin U., 1949; LL.B., Franklin Law Sch., 1953; J.D., Capitol U., 1966; grad. Coll. Juvenile Justice, U. Nev., 1973; m. Janet Gay McCann, May 22, 1947; children—Ottie Wayne II, Jennifer Lynn, Lorna Victoria. Admitted to Ohio bar, 1953; practiced in Pike County; recorder Pike County, 1957-73; common pleas judge Probate and Juvenile divs. Pike County, 1973-79. Mem. adv. bd. Ohio Youth Services, 1972-74. Mem. Democratic Central Com. Camp Creek precinct, 1956-72, 83—; sec. Pike County Central Com., 1960-70; chmn. Pike County Democratic Exec. Com., 1971-72; del. Dem. Nat. Conv., 1972; mem. Ohio Dem. Central Com., 1969-70; Dem. candidate 6th Ohio dist. U.S. Ho. of Reps., 1966; pres. Scioto Valley Local Sch. Dist., 1962-66. Recipient Distinguished Service award Ohio Youth Commn., 1974; 6 Outstanding Jud. Service awards Ohio Supreme Ct.; 15 times Ala. horseshoe pitching champion; named to Nat. Horseshoe Pitchers Hall of Fame, 1978; mem. internat. sports exchange, U.S. and Republic South Africa, 1972, 80, 82. Mem. Ohio, Pike County (pres. 1964) bar assns., Nat. Council Juvenile Ct. Judges, Am. Legion. Mem. Ch. of Christ. Author: Story of Horseshoes, 1963; Pitching Championship Horseshoes, 1971, 2d rev. edit., 1975; Who's Who in Horseshoe Pitching, 1983. Home: 148 Reno Rd Lucasville OH 45648

RENSING, SUE GILLETTE, nurse, educator; b. Grand Rapids, Mich., Apr. 15, 1949; d. Charles Woodrow and Dorothy May (Sharp) Gillette; m. James Paul Rensing, July 12, 1975. B.S. in Nursing, Mich. State U., 1971; M.S. in Nursing, Wayne State U., 1974. Cert. nursing adminstr., Am. Nursing Assn. Part-time staff nurse and supr. Kingswood Hosp., Detroit, 1973-74; dir. edn. and tng. N.Y. State Psychiat. Inst., N.Y.C., 1975-76; assoc. dir. nursing Westchester County Med. Ctr., Valhalla, N.Y., 1976-78; adminstrv. asst. nursing Edward W. Sparrow Hosp., Lansing, Mich., 1978-84, v.p. nursing, 1984—; mem. adj. faculty Mich. State U. Coll. Nursing. Recipient Recognition and Appreciation award Med. Edn. Dept., Sparrow Hosp., 1980. Mem. Am. Nurses Assn., Mich. Nurses Assn., Capitol Area Dist. Nurses Assn., Am. Soc. Nursing Service Adminstrs., Mich. Soc. Hosp. Nursing Adminstrs. (Appreciation award 1982, 83, 84), Midwest Alliance Nursing, Am. Nurses Found., Assn. Career Women, Sigma Theta Tau. Home: 1250 Dexter Trail Dansville MI 48819 Office: Edward W Sparrow Hosp 1215 E Michigan Ave Lansing MI 48909

RENTER, LOIS IRENE HUTSON, librarian; b. Lowden, Iowa, Oct. 23, 1929; d. Thomas E. and Lulu Mae (Barlean) Hutson; B.A. cum laude, Cornell Coll., Iowa, 1965; M.A., U. Iowa, 1968; m. Karl A. Renter, Jan. 3, 1948; children—Susan Elizabeth, Rebecca Jean, Karl Geoffrey. Tchr. Spanish, Mt. Vernon (Iowa) High Sch., 1965-67; head librarian Am. Coll. Testing Program, Iowa City, Iowa, 1968—; vis. instr. U. Iowa Sch. Library Sci., 1972—. Mem. Am. Soc. Info. Sci., ALA, Spl. Libraries Assn., Phi Beta Kappa. Methodist. Home: 1125 29th St Marion IA 52302 Office: Box 168 Iowa City IA 52243

RENTFRO, RICCI A., insurance company executive; b. Battle Creek, Mich., Sept. 16, 1952; s. Glenn and Janithe (Acker) R. A.Applied Arts, Kellogg Community Coll., 1976; postgrad., Nazareth Coll., 1983—. C.L.U.; chartered fin. cons. Mktg. service asst. Federal Home Life Ins. Co., Battle Creek, 1975-78, asst. tng. dir., 1978-79, gen. agy. asst., 1980-82, advanced sales specialist, 1983—. Fund raiser United Arts Council United Way, Battle Creek, 1982; co-chmn. Internat. Balloon Championships, Battle Creek, 1985; mem. Internat. Relations Com., Battle Creek, 1985; bd. dirs. Battle Creek C. of C., 1979-80. Mem. Battle Creek Assn. Life Underwriters, Am. Soc. C.L.U.s, Fed. Home Employee Orgn. (pres. 1982-83), Jaycees (pres. 1979-80, J.C.I. senatorship 1984, keyman 1979). Lodge: Optimists. Avocations: golf; softball; bowling; volleyball; fishing. Home: 117 Sherwood Dr Battle Creek MI 49017 Office: Federal Home Life Ins Co 78 West Michigan Mall Battle Creek MI 49017

RENTSCHLER, ALVIN EUGENE, mechanical engineer; b. Havre, Mont., Oct. 24, 1940; s. Alvin Joseph and Pauline Elizabeth (Browning) R.; B.S., Mont. State U., 1964; m. Marilyn Joan Bostrom, Dec. 7, 1974; children—Elizabeth Louise, Richard Eugene, Alison Lynn. Sci. and math. instr. Helena Pub. Schs., Mont., 1964-66; dist. mgr. Woodmen Accident and Life Co., Helena, 1966-69; profl. med. rep. Abbott Labs., Great Falls, Mont., 1969-72; sales engr. Agribest, Inc., Great Falls, 1973; design engr. Anaconda Co., Mont., 1974-77; ops. and maintenance engr. Rochester Meth. Hosp., Minn., 1977—; mem. engring. coordinating com. Franklin Heating Sta., 1977—. Bd. dirs. Mont. affiliate Am. Diabetes Assn., 1975-78, pres. Butte-Anaconda chpt., 1974-77; mem. citizens adv. com. Rochester Area Vocat.-Tech. Inst., 1978—, sec., 1982-84. Recipient Greatest Achievement award Combined Tng., Inc., 1977, Pres.' Club award Woodmen Accident & Life Co., 1968. Mem. ASME, Hosp. Engrs. of Am. Hosp. Assn., Internat. Congress Hosp. Engring., Am. Soc. for Hosp. Engrs. Mem. Covenant Ch. Office: 201 W Center St Rochester MN 55901

RENTZ, LOUIS EDWARD, osteopathic physician; b. Detroit, Mar. 15, 1934; s. Louis Edward and Mary (Fogarty) R.; m. Lorraine M. Rentz, Feb. 10, 1962; children—Danielle, Heather, Kristen. B.S., U. Detroit, 1956; D.O., Chgo. Coll. Osteo. Medicine, 1960. Intern, Chgo. Osteo. Hosp., 1960-61; fellow in neurology U. Ill. Neuropsychiat. Inst. and Chgo. Coll. Osteo. Medicine, 1961-64; practice osteo. medicine specializing in neurology, 1965—; pres. Glendale Neurol. Assocs., P.C., Birmingham, Mich., 1969—; mem. staff Oakland Gen. Hosp., Botsford Gen. Hosp., Garden City Hosp. (Osteo.), Pontiac Osteo. Hosp., Mich. Osteo. Med. Ctr.; clin. prof. neurology Mich. State U. Coll. Osteo. Medicine, 1970—; clin. asst. prof. Wayne State U. Coll. Medicine, 1972—; clin. assoc. prof. neurology Mercy Coll., Detroit, 1975—; adj. prof. neurology W.Va. Coll. Osteo. Medicine, 1977—. Fellow Am. Coll. Neuropsychiatrists; mem. Am. Bd. EEG (cert.), Am. Osteo. Assn., Mich. Assn. Osteo. Physicians and Surgeons, Oakland County Osteo Assn., Am. Coll. Neuropsychiatrists (pres. 1968-69), Central Assn. Electroencephalographers, Am. Acad. Neurology (sr.), Mich. Heart Assn. (pres. 1976-77), Epilepsy Ctr. Mich. (pres. 1972-73, dir. 1966—), Am. Epilepsy Soc., Mich. Neurol. Assn., Am. Soc. Neuroimaging, Mich. Osteo. Neuropsychiat. Soc., Central Neuropsychiat. Assn. Contbr. articles to med. jours. Office: 30400 Telegraph Rd Suite 133 Birmingham MI 48010

REPP, SUSAN ELAINE, educational administrator; b. Croswell, Mich.; d. Lawrence and Elizabeth (Quitter) Clarkson; m. Thomas John Repp, July 29, 1967; 1 child, Amy Sue. B.A., Central Mich. U., Mt. Pleasant, 1967, M.A., 1970; Ph.D., Mich. State U., 1980. Residence hall dir. Central Mich. U., 1967-72, asst. dir. housing, 1972-78, doctoral intern, adminstrv. asst. aux. services, 1979-80, dir. acad. assistance, 1980-82, asst. to v.p. student affairs, 1982-84, asst. v.p. student affairs, 1984—. Editor: Perspectives on Resident Assistant Training: A Source Book, 1981. Mem. Am. Assn. for Counseling and Devel., Am. Coll. Personnel Assn., Nat. Assn. Student Personnel Adminstrs. Office: Central Mich Univ 150 Foust Hall Mount Pleasant MI 48859

RESCIGNO, JOSEPH THOMAS, conductor; b. N.Y.C., Oct. 8, 1945; s. Joseph and Leona (Llewellyn) R.; m. Jeanne Marie Lo Pinto, Aug. 9, 1971. B.A., Fordham U., 1967; M.Mus., Manhattan Sch. Music, 1969. Conducting staff Manhattan Sch. Music, N.Y.C., 1969-76; assoc. condr. Concert Orch., L.I., N.Y., 1972-79; staff condr. Dallas Opera, 1976-82; artistic dir. Artists Internat., Providence, 1979-81; artistic advisor Florentine Opera, Milw., 1981—; guest condr. Washington Opera, 1979, 84, 85, Pitts. Opera, 1983, 84, St. Louis Opera, 1984, 85, N.Y.C. Opera, 1985. Recipient 2d prize Mozarteum, Salsburg, Austria, 1969; day of honor declared in his name Gov. R.I., 1981. Roman Catholic. Home: 711 West End Ave New York NY 10025 Office: Florentine Opera 750 N Lincoln Meml Dr Milwaukee WI 53202

RESEK, ROBERT WILLIAM, economist, educator; b. Berwyn, Ill., July 2, 1935; s. Ephraim Frederick and Ruth Elizabeth (Rummele) R.; m. Lois Doll, July 9, 1960; 1 son, Richard Alden. B.S., U. Ill.-Urbana, 1957; M.A., Harvard U., 1960, Ph.D., 1961. Asst. prof. U. Ill.-Urbana, 1961-65, assoc. prof., 1965-70, prof. econs., 1970—, dir. Bur. Econ. and Bus. Research, 1977—; vis. scholar MIT, 1964, 67-69; vis. prof. U. Colo.-Boulder, 1967, 74, 75, 76, 82, Kyoto (Japan) U., 1976; cons. Joint Econ. Com., U.S. Congress, Washington, 1978-79, ABA, Chgo., 1980-82. Editor: Illinois Economic Outlook, 1982, 83, 84, 85, Frontiers of Business and Economic Research Management, 1983; co-editor: The Midwest Economy: Issues and Problems, 1983. Mem. Assn. Bus. and Econ. Research (past v.p., pres.), Econometric Soc., Am. Econ. Assn., Am. Statis. Assn. Presbyterian. Home: 201 Holmes St Urbana IL 61801 Office: U Ill 1206 S 6th St Champaign IL 61820

RESEK, ROGER VERNE, corporate information systems planning manager; b. Milw., July 7, 1936; s. J. Verne and Johanna (Danziger) R.; m. Donna Lee Shapiro, Dec. 26, 1959; children—Jonathan, Lisa. B.S.M.E., Purdue U., 1958; M.B.A., Marquette U., 1962. Registered profl. engr., Wis. Indsl. engr. Johnson Controls Inc., Milw., 1958-61, systems analyst, 1961-64, systems mgr., 1964-71, mgr. systems, data processing, 1971-80, corp. mgr. info. systems planning, 1980—; chmn. Burroughs Users Group, 1978-80; pres. Matarah Industries, 1985—. Bd. dirs., treas. Jewish Vocat. Service, Milw., 1978—; adv. bd. St. Joseph's Hosp., Milw., 1978—; adv. com. City of Milw. Data Services, 1980. Mem. Assn. Systems Mgmt., Soc. Mgmt. Info. Systems. Avocations:

reading; tennis. Home: 4531 N Ardmore Ave Milwaukee WI 53211 Office: Johnson Controls Inc PO Box 591 Milwaukee WI 53201

RESLOCK, MARY HALE, information scientist; b. Hancock, Mich., Mar. 6, 1914; d. William T. and Mary F. (Ryan) Hale; m. E. James Reslock, June 19, 1943 (dec. May 1964); children—Mary J., Martha Reiff, Sophia Konecny, Ellen Blauer, James M. B.S. in Chemistry, Mich. Tech. U., 1938; M.S. in L.S., U. Mich., 1968. With Dow Chem. Co., 1940-79, sr. logician computations research lab., 1964-70, mgr. tech. info. service, 1971-79; with Mich. Molecular Inst., Midland, 1979-82; cons. in field. Past mem. adv. bd. G.H. Dow Library, Midland; mem. aux. bd. Midland Hosp. Mem. Am. Chem. Soc., Spl. Library Assn., Chem. Notation Assn. (award 1983), Sigma Xi. Roman Catholic. Clubs: Zonta, Brownson. Editor: (with others) Wiswesser Line Formula Chemical Notation, 2d edit., 1968; contbr. articles to profl. jours. Home: 530 N Saginaw Rd Midland MI 48640

RESNICK, MARK JEFFREY, school psychologist; b. Balt., Mar. 3, 1955; s. Martin Ronald and Thalia Ann (Dragon) R.; B.A., Oglethorpe U., 1977; M.A., Loyola Coll., Balt., 1980; postgrad. U. Kans., 1980—. Staff psychologist Glover-Tillman Learning Ctr. and Glover-Tillman Child Mental Health Service, Balt., 1979-80; psychologist Shawnee Mission (Kans.) Pub. Schs., 1980-84, Gardner-Edgerton-Antioch Unified Sch. Dist. 231, 1984-85; instr. psychology Penn Valley Community Coll., Kansas City, 1982-85; behavioral cons. Responsive Mgmt. Clinic, Overland Park, Kans., 1982-84; bus. and corp. cons. Koch, Resnick and Assocs., Kansas City, 1983-85; sch. psychologist Carroll County Pub. Schs., Westminster, Md., 1985—. Mem. Am. Psychol. Assn. (assoc.). Democrat. Jewish.

RESNIK, FRANK HASKELL, hospital supply company executive; b. Bridgeport, Conn., Apr. 16, 1942; s. Harry and Sadie Ruth (Landes) R.; m. Susan Leblang, Apr. 28, 1973. B.S., Antioch Coll., 1963; M.B.A., U. Chgo., 1964. C.P.A. Dir. market and fin. analysis Capitol Records, Hollywood, Calif., 1965-67; asst. dir. systems and procedures, Cook County, Chgo., 1967-69; dir. gen. services State of Ill., Springfield, 1969-73; asst. to asst. adminstr. GSA, Washington, 1973-74, regional adminstr., Chgo., 1974-77; v.p. Medline Industries, Mundelein, Ill., 1977—. Mem. Ill. C.P.A. Soc. Club: Union League (Chgo.). Home: 175 E Delaware St Chicago IL 60611 Office: Medline Industries 1 Medline Pl Mundelein IL 60060

RESSEGER, CHARLES SIDNEY, physician; b. Willard, Ohio, Feb. 1, 1945; s. Charles William and Esther Luella (Fritz) R.; m. Charlene Diane Arnold, June 14, 1969; children—Stacy Ann, Adam Ryan. Student, Kent State U., 1966; D.O., Coll. Osteopathic Med. and Surgery, Des Moines, Iowa, 1970. Intern Doctors Hosp., Columbus, Ohio, 1970-71; gen. practice medicine and allergy, Norwalk, Ohio, 1973—; chief of staff Fisher-Titus Hosp., Norwalk, 1983. Speaker, Christian Women's Club, Ohio and Mich., Christian Bus. Men's Club, Served to capt. USAF, 1971-73. Mem. Ohio Osteo. Assn. (pres. dist. V 1977-78, del. 1974), Am. Osteo. Assn. Republican. Avocations: raising and showing American saddlebred horses; tennis. Home: 141 W Main St Norwalk OH 44857 Office: 835 S Norwalk Rd W RFD #4 Norwalk OH 44857

RESSLER, ROBERT C., manufacturing company executive; b. Lancaster, Pa., 1923. Student Drexel Inst. Tech. Plant mgr. Bearing Corp. Am. div. Fed. Mogul Bower Bearing Inc., 1946-56; v.p. ball & bearing div. Hoover Universal Inc., Ann Arbor, Mich., 1956, group v.p., 1968, v.p. ops., 1969, sr. v.p., 1981, pres. and chief operating officer, 1982—, also dir.; dir. Gt. Lakes Fed. Savs. and Loan. Office: Hoover Universal Inc 825 Victors Way PO Box 1003 Ann Arbor MI 48106*

RESTIVO, RAYMOND M., health association executive, public health consultant; b. Chgo., Aug. 19, 1934; s. Frank M. and Angeline (Franzone) R.; B.S.A., Loyola U., Chgo., 1956; certificate pub. health adminstrn. U. Ill., 1968; C.A.E., 1978; children—Laura, Maria, Mark, Susan, Steven, John, Tony, Matthew. Adminstrv. asst. to pres. of S.K. Culver Co., Chgo., 1954-59; projects coordinator Chgo. Heart Assn., 1959-66, exec. dir., 1973—; pub. health adminstr. Chgo. Bd. Health, 1966-73, mem. adv. com., 1967-73, mem. editorial rev. com. for newsletter, 1968-73; cons. community health to various pub., vol. and ofcl. health agys., 1962—; del. to Pub. Service Inst. of City of Chgo., 1973; notary pub., Cook County (Ill.), 1971—; mem. oral bd. examiners for cardiovascular technologist, City of Chgo. Civil Service Commn., 1971-73. Sec., Morris Fishbein, Jr. Meml. Fund, 1973—; mem. Zoning Bd. Appeals, Forest Park, Ill., 1964-68; mem. Health Services Task Force, Oak Park, Ill., 1974-75; bd. dirs. Chgo. Health Research Found., 1976—; mem. Planning Com. 4th Nat. Congress Quality of Life AMA, 1977-78. Recipient Meritorious Service award Village of Oak Park, 1975; Recognition award Chgo. Pub. Schs., 1982. Mem. Ill. Pub. Health Assn. (mem. policy com. 1971-73, mem. health issues com. 1972-73), Am. Pub. Health Assn., Am. Heart Assn. Profl. Staff Soc., Am. Soc. Assn. Execs., Chgo. Soc. Assn. Execs., Am. Mgmt. Assn., Nat. Assn. of Emergency Care Technicians, Epidemiology Club of Chgo., City of Chgo. Exec. Devel., Loyola U. alumni assns. Clubs: Tower, University. Contbr. articles on heart disease to profl. publs. Office: 20 N Wacker Dr Chicago IL 60606

RETTENMAIER, MARVIN JOSEPH, manufacturing company official, mosaicist; b. Carroll, Iowa, Mar. 23, 1924; s. Edward E. and Bernadine (Bernholtz) R. Student Mpls. Inst. Art, 1945-46, U. Minn., 1947-48, Milw. Sch. Engring., 1966. Aircraft mechanic Northwest Orient Airlines, St. Paul, 1942-45; master stencil artist Photoplating Co., Mpls., 1945-49; 3d officer, purser North Central Airlines, Mpls., 1953; chief insp. W.H. Brady Co., Milw., 1953—; exhbn. micro mosaics include: Putnam Mus., Davenport, Iowa, Milwaukee County Pub. Mus., Morristown (N.J.) Coll., Cath. U. Library, Washington, First Wis. Ctr., Milw. represented in permanent collections: Alcoa Co., Pitts., Oberlin Coll., Wildwood Mus., Cape May, N.J., Ripley Internat., Toronto. Served with AUS, 1949-53. Mem. Am. Soc. Quality Control, (charter mem. insp. div.). Roman Catholic. Lodge: Eagles. Office: 2221 W Camden Rd PO Box 2131 Milwaukee WI 53201

REUM, ROBERT CHARLES, manufacturing company executive; b. Rockford, Ill., Nov. 19, 1933; s. Edward Frederick and Elsie Marie Reum; m. Joan Gail Keyes, July 27, 1954; children—Pamela Ruth, Mark Edward. Student Lutheran Bible Inst., 1951-52, Augustana Coll., 1952-53. Dir. purchasing Belvedere Products, Belvedere, Ill., 1975-81; purchasing agt. Motion Control, Rockford, 1981-83; purchasing mgr. Bedard & Morency, Elgin, Ill., 1983-85; v.p. adminstrn. Valley Countertop Co., Rockford, Ill., 1985—. Served with USN, 1953-57. Decorated UN medal. Mem. Am. Mgmt. Assn., Purchasing Mgmt. Assn. Clubs: LLL (Rockford); Anvil (Dundee, Ill.); Star of the East, Mason, Shriner, Elks. Office: Valley Countertop Co 6067 11th St Rockford IL 61109

REUSS, ROBERT P., telecommunication and water service company executive. Chmn., chief exec. officer, dir. Centel Corp., Chgo. Office: Centel Corp 5725 NE River Rd Chicago IL 60631

REUTER, JAMES WILLIAM, lawyer; b. Bemidji, Minn., Sept. 30, 1948; s. John Renee and Monica (Dugas) R.; m. Patricia Carol Creelman, Mar. 30, 1968; children—Kristine, Suzanne, Natalee. B.A., St. John's U., 1970; J.D., William Mitchell Coll. of Law, 1974. Bar: Minn. 1974, U.S. Dist. Ct. Minn. 1975. Editor, West Pub. Co., St. Paul, 1970-73; assoc. Terpstra & Merrill, Mpls., 1974-77; ptnr. Barna, Guzy, Merrill, Hynes & Giancola, Ltd., Mpls., 1977—. Recipient Cert. award Nat. Inst. Trial Advocacy, 1978. Mem. ABA (antitrust and civil litigation com.), Assn. Trial Lawyers Am., Minn. Trial Lawyers Assn. (comml. litigation com.), Minn. Bar Assn. (civil litigation and computer sects.), Hennepin County Bar Assn. (ethics com.), Anoka County Bar Assn. (pres. 1981-82, chmn. jud. selection com. 1982—). Lodge: Kiwanis (Columbia Heights-Fridley) (pres. 1978-79). Avocations: skiing; golf; camping; reading. Office: Barna Guzy Merrill Hynes & Giancola Ltd 701 Fourth Ave South Suite 500 Minneapolis MN 55415

REUTZEL, ROBERT JEROME, pharmacist, pharmacology educator; b. Swea City, Iowa, Sept. 29, 1934; s. Henry John and Anna Veronica (Matheis) R.; m. Renee Marcella Neubert, May 11, 1963; children—Jerome, Thomas, Jane. B.S., S.D. State U., 1961. Registered pharmacist, Minn., S.D. Pharmacist, Paulson's Pharmacy, Fairmont, Minn., 1961-62, Thro Drug Stores, Mankato, Minn., 1962-71; owner, mgr. Mankato Clinic Pharmacy, 1971-76, Prescription Care Center, Mankato, 1976—; instr. pharmacology of emergency drugs Mankato State U., 1975—; cons. Mankato Robert E. Miller Home Inc., 1976—. Republican precinct and county del. Mankato, 1962—. Mem. Nat. Assn. Retail Druggists, Am. Acad. Pharmacy Practice, Am. Pharm. Assn., Minn. State Pharm. Assn. (bd. dirs. 1961—), Mankato Area Pharmacist Soc., Mankato Area C. of C., Rho Chi. Republican. Roman Catholic. Lodges: Hilltop Kiwanis (bd. dirs. 1964-76), K.C. Avocation: music. Home: 208 Capital Dr Mankato MN 56001 Office: Prescription Care Ctr 1057 Madison Ave Mankato MN 56001

REY, CARMEN ROSELLO, researcher, food scientist; b. Santiago, Cuba, Feb. 14, 1923; came to U.S., 1961, naturalized, 1968; m. Alfredo Rey, May 16, 1948 (div. Dec. 1969); children—Lauri, Roberto. B.A. in Agrl. Engring. Havana U., 1945, B.S. in Sugar Chemistry, 1946; M.S., Iowa State U., 1968, Ph.D., 1975. Head quality control Alto Songo Sugar Co., Cuba, 1947-60; lab. technician dept. food sci. Iowa State U., Ames, 1963-65, research grad. asst., 1965-68, research assoc., 1968-70, assoc., 1970-75; chem. engr. Stokely-Van Camp, Inc., Indpls., 1975-76, sr. microbiologist, 1976-79, supr. microbiology labs., 1979-81, mgr. microbiology lab. services, 1981-83, mgr. research and devel., 1983; scientist John Stuart Research Ctr., Quaker Oats Co., Barrington, Ill., 1984, research scientist, 1985—. Past bd. v.p., mem. at large bd. dirs. Hispano Am. Multi Service Ctr.; bd. dirs., personnel com. Indpls. Settlements, Inc.; past sec. Indpls. Employment and Tng. Adv. Council. Recipient Profl. Achievement award Ctr. for Leadership and Devel., Inc., 1983. Mem. Inst. Food Technologists (mem. at large exec. com. microbiology div. 1979-81, chmn. nominating com. microbiology div. 1981), Am. Frozen Food Inst. (mem. microbiology and food safety com.), Nat. Assn. Agronomic and Sugar Engrs. of Cuba in Exile, Inc., Cuban Assn. Ind., Sigma Xi, Phi Kappa Phi, Gamma Sigma Delta. Club: Toastmasters (chpt. pres.). Contbr. articles to profl. jours. Office: 617 W Main Barrington IL 60010

REYES, EPIFANIO, chemical engineer; b. San Juan, Puerto Rico, June 20, 1952; s. Epifanio and Carmen M. (Ruiz) R.; m. Josefa Lenalda Silva, Jan. 30, 1982; children—Nathan, Anthony. B.S. in Chem. Engring., U. Fla., 1974, M.S. in Chem. Engring., 1976. Devel. engr. UOP Inc., Des Plaines, Ill., from 1975, tech. services engr., mktg. tech. adv., tech. sales rep., product engr. Avocations: travel; languages. Home: 1405 E Central Rd Arlington Heights IL 60005 Office: Box 5017 Plaza Des Plaines IL 60017-5017

REYES, HERNAN MACABALLUG, pediatric surgeon; b. Isabela, Philippines, Apr. 5, 1933; came to U.S., 1958; s. Leonor Bulcan and Anacleta (Macaballuf) R.; m. Dolores C. Cruz, Feb. 27, 1960; children—Cynthia, Michael, Maria, Patricia, Catherine. Student, U. Philippines, 1949-51; A.A.; M.D., U. Santo Tomas Sch. Medicine, Manila, 1957. Diplomate Am. Bd. Surgery. Intern, Cook County Hosp., Chgo., 1958-59, resident, 1959-64; clin. asst. dept. surgery Stritch Sch. Medicine, Loyola U., Maywood, Ill., 1964-65, 68, clin. assoc., 1969; instr. surgery, chief sect. pediatric surgery U. Santo Tomas Faculty Medicine and Surgery, Manila, 1966-67; asst. prof. dept. surgery Pritzker Sch. Medicine, U. Chgo., 1969-73, assoc. prof., 1973-76, acting chief sect. pediatric surgery, 1973-74; profl. dept. surgery, chief div. pediatric surgery U. Ill. Coll. Medicine, Chgo., 1976—, prof. clin. pediatrics, 1982—; acting pediatric surgeon Cook County Children's Hosp., Chgo., 1965, surgeon-in-chief, chmn. div. pediatric surgery, 1976—; attending surgeon, chief pediatric surgery U. Santo Tomas Hosp., Manila, 1966-67; cons. pediatric surgery Mercy Hosp. and Med. Ctr., Chgo., Mile Square Health Ctr., Chgo., Christ Hosp., Oak Lawn, Ill., Shriners Hosp. Crippled Children, Chgo.; attending surgeon Wyler Children's Hosp., U. Chgo., 1969-76, dir. emergency surg. services, 1973-74; attending surgeon Little Company of Mary Hosp., Evergreen Park, Ill., 1968—, dir. surgical edn. program, 1968-73; chief div. pediatric surgery U. Ill. Hosp., Chgo., 1976—. Contbr. articles to profl. publs., chpts. to books. Recipient Tchr. of Yr. award Little Company Mary Hosp., 1969, Disting. Physician award Philippine Med. Assn. Chgo., 1972, Recognition by Class, Pritzker Sch. Medicine, 1974, 75, Leadership award Soc. Philippine Surgeons, 1976, Cert. of Appreciation, Philippine Med. Assn., 1977. Mem. ACS (Chgo. com. on trauma), Am. Acad. Pediatrics, Am. Assn. Surgery Trauma, AAUP, AMA, Am. Pediatric Surg. Assn., Assn. Acad. Surgery, Central Surg. Assn., Chgo. Med. Soc. (councilor 1975-76), Chgo. Soc. Gastro, Chgo. Surg. Soc., Ill. Pediatric Surg. Assn. (sec.-treas 1976-77, pres. 1978-79), Ill. State Med. Soc., Ill. Surg. Soc., Inst. Medicine Chgo., N.Y. Acad. Scis., Soc. Philippine Surgeons Am. (founding pres.), Western Surg. Assn., AAAS, Am. Trauma Soc., Sigma Xi. Avocation: tennis. Office: Cook County Children's Hosp 700 S Wood St Room B-40 Chicago IL 60612

REYES, RUDY SAN PEDRO, import company executive; b. Manila, Nov. 27, 1941; s. Benito and Avelina (San Pedro) R.; Cecilia S.P. Suarez, Dec. 8, 1961; children—Ferdinand, Rudolf, Vanessa, Regina, Ronald. A.B. cum laude in Polit. Sci., Far Eastern U., Manila, 1965; M.B.A., U. Philippines, 1965. Exec. asst. to exec. v.p. Air Manila, Inc., 1969, gen. mgr. traffic and sales dept., 1970; honesty checker parking ops., Edison Parking Corp. (EPC), Newark, 1970-71; supr. Newark ops., Manhattan, N.Y.C. ops., 1972-73, gen. mgr. div. B, 1976; asst. to v.p. Denison Parking, Inc., Indpls., 1977; pres. and gen. mgr. Pacific Industries, Inc., Indpls., 1978—; pres. Econo Car Rent-a-Car of Indpls., owner A-1 Car Center of Indpls., chmn. bd. Pacific Imports Co., Inc., 1982—; chmn. bd. 220 Ave. Corp., Indpls., 1983—. Bd. dirs. Indpls. Zool. Soc., 1982—; bd. nat. govs. Philippine Heritage Endowment Found. at Ind. U.; liaison officer T. Sunggani dist. Boy Scouts Am., Indpls.; mem. Riley Area Revitalization Program; mem. Internat. Ctr. Indpls. Mem. Parking Assn. Indpls., Nat. Parking Assn. Club: Barangay Philipino-Am. (Indpls.) (pres. 1982-83). Lodges: Kiwanis (dir. 1982-84), Optimists (dir. 1980-84; Community Leadership award 1980-81) (Indpls.). Roman Catholic. Home: 8104 Teel Way Indianapolis IN 46256 Office: Pacific Group Industries 134 S Delaware St Indianapolis IN 46104

REYNARD, JACK POWELL, JR., lawyer; b. Springfield, Ohio, Aug. 9, 1939; s. Jack Powell and Elizabeth (Maurer) R.; m. Diane Larkin, May 25, 1968 (div. Jan. 1983); children—Stephen Michael, Deborah Ann. B.A., Wittenberg U., 1961; J.D., Ohio No. U., 1964. Bar: Ohio 1964, U.S. Dist. Ct. (so. dist.) Ohio, 1972. Juvenile officer Clark County, Springfield, 1964-65; judge adv. USAF, 1965-68; advisor Springfield Police Dept., 1972-74; sole practice, Springfield, 1968—. Bd. dirs. Oesterlin Services Youth, Springfield, 1974-82. Served to capt. USAF, 1965-68. Key scholar Delta Theta Phi, 1964. Mem. Springfield Bar Assn. Republican. Lutheran. Avocation: swimming; boating; sailing; reading. Lodge: Elks. Home: 108 E Harding Rd Springfield OH 45504

REYNES, WENDY WARNER, publisher's representative; b. Boston, Sept. 29, 1944; d. Philip Russell and Elizabeth (Patton) Warner; A.A., Conn. Coll., 1966; m. Jose (Tony) Antonio Reynes, III, Apr. 26, 1969; children—Jose (Tad) Antonio, Gabrielle Elizabeth. With Foote, Cone & Belding, N.Y.C., 1966-68; advt. sales rep. Cosmopolitan Mag., N.Y.C., 1968-69, Co-Ed Mag., N.Y.C., 1969-70; asst. product mgr. Avon Products, N.Y.C., 1970; advt. sales rep., Magazine Networks, N.Y.C. and Chgo., 1970-72; midwest mgr. advt. sales, Girl Talk Mag., Chgo., 1972-75; div. mgr. advt. sales, Pattis Group, Chgo., 1975-79; pres. Reynes & Assocs., Chgo., 1979—, Bd. dirs. Multiple Sclerosis, 1974—, St. Joseph's Sch. PTA, 1979-80, Marriage Encounter, 1976—; active Jr. League Greenwich, Conn., 1965-67, Jr. League N.Y.C., 1967-75. Mem. City Regional Mag. Assn. (bd. dirs.), Advt. Assn., Assn. Area Bus. Publs. Clubs: Agate (pres.), Women's Advt. Club Chgo. (chmn. Ad Women of Yr. 1980-82), Wilmette Tennis, East Bank. Home: 460 Ash Winnetka IL 60093 Office: Reynes & Assocs Inc 2 N Riverside Plaza Chicago IL 60606

REYNOLDS, BRADLEY WAYNE, meteorologist, consultant; b. Lincoln, Nebr., Jan. 20, 1952; s. Warren Leo and Pauline Rita (Brusseau) R.; m. Susan Kay Yaussi, Sept. 14, 1974 (div. Oct. 1979). B.A. in Chemistry, U. Nebr., 1970-74; M.S. in Atmospheric Scis., Oreg. State U., 1978. Bus. mgr., acct., sales mgr. Hillcrest Country Club Golf Shop, Lincoln, 1965-74; grad. research asst. dept. atmospheric scis. Oreg. State U., Corvallis, 1974-76, research asst. Air Resources Ctr., 1976-78; air pollution meteorologist Mo. Dept. Natural Resources, Jefferson City, 1979—; cons., lectr. in field. Contbr. articles to profl. jours. EPA fellow, 1974-77. Mem. Air Pollution Control Assn. tech. program and edn. coms., St. Louis Conf. 1981, panel Conf. on Dispersion Modeling of Complex Sources 1981, fugitive emissions steering com., St. Louis and Midwest sects., Am. Meteorol. Soc. Democrat. Roman Catholic. Club: Ozark BMW (sec.-treas.). Lodge: Elks. Avocations: athletics; automobiles (driving and repairing); music (guitar/vocalist); reading. Home: 304 Berry St Jefferson City MO 65101-1309 Office: Mo Dept Natural Resources PO Box 1368 Jefferson City MO 65102-1368

REYNOLDS, GARY NOLAND, railcar repair executive; b. Mt. Vernon, Ill., Nov. 27, 1940; s. Gilbert Noland and Opal (Ackley) R.; m. Dartera Lee Lyle, Jan. 15, 1966; children—Timothy, Robert. Student in Bus. Adminstrn., Northwestern U., 1976-77. Dir. plant ops. N.Am. Car Corp., Chgo., 1977-80, v.p. sales and mktg., 1980-81, v.p., gen. mgr. car repair, 1981-82, v.p. ops., 1982-83; pres. Quality Service Railcar Repair, Chgo., 1983—. Served with U.S. Army, 1962-65, Korea. Mem. Rail Car Repair Assn., Western Rwy. Club (bd. dirs. Chgo. 1981-84). Democrat. Home: 1021 Purdue Ln Matteson IL 60443 Office: Gen Electric Railcar Service Corp 33 W Monroe Chicago IL 60603

REYNOLDS, HAROLD IRWIN, materials scientist; b. Mpls., May 19, 1921; s. Zane Leroy and Ruby Lillian (Quant) R.; m. Delois Ruth Kipp, June 12, 1942; children—Linda, Diane, Pamela, Nancy. B.Chemistry, U. Minn., 1950. Materials engr. Honeywell Aero., Mpls. and Boeing Co., Seattle; chem. research engr. Moore Corp. Ltd., Grand Island, N.Y.; sr. prin. chemist NCR, Dayton, Ohio, 1969—; instr. U. Dayton, 1970-72. Served with USN, 1942-45. Recipient 1st place 12th Ann. Materials Engring. award Reinhold Pub. Co., 1968. Mem. Am. Chem. Soc., Sigma Xi. Author tech. reports; contbr. articles to profl. jours. Patentee in field U.S. and France. Office: NCR 9095 Washington Church Rd Miamisburg OH 45342

REYNOLDS, JOHN W., judge; Green Bay, Wis., Apr. 4, 1921; s. John W. and Madge (Flatley) R.; Ph.B., U. Wis., 1946, LL.B., 1949; m. Patricia Ann Brody, May 26, 1947 (dec. Dec. 1967); children—Kate M. Reynolds Lindquist, Molly A. Reynolds Jassoy, James B.; m. Jane Conway, July 31, 1971; children—Jacob F., Thomas J., Frances P., John W. III. Bar: Wis. 1949. Practiced in Green Bay, from 1949; dist. dir. Office Price Stblzn., 1951-53, U.S. commr., 1953-58; atty. gen. State of Wis., 1958-62; gov. State of Wis., 1963-65; judge U.S. Dist. Ct. Eastern Dist. Wis., 1965-71, chief judge, 1971—. Mem. ABA, State Bar Wis, Am. Law Inst., Brown County Bar Assn., Am. Law Inst. Democrat. Office: Room 471 US Courthouse 517 E Wisconsin Ave Milwaukee WI 53202

REYNOLDS, MURPHY LASTER, energy management company executive; b. Bridgeton, N.J., Dec. 2, 1941; s. Joseph Laster and Catherine Reynolds; m. Nanette Lee Smith, Aug. 26, 1972; children—Malika, Michon. B.S., N.C. Central U., 1965; M. City Planning, Harvard U., 1972. Peace Corps vol., Afghanstan, 1967-70; lectr. Brown U., Providence, 1972-75; asst. dean U.R.I., Kingston, 1975-76; cons. Urban League, Providence, 1977-78; dir. career service dept. Detroit Urban League, 1978-80; mng. dir. Reynolds Group, East Lansing, Mich., 1980—. Mem. Am. Assn. Higher Edn., Am. Soc. Planning Ofcls., Am. Inst. Planners. Avocations: fishing; reading; jogging. Home: 1126 Sunset Lane East Lansing MI 44823

REYNOLDS, PAMELA KAY, pharmacist, pharmacy executive; b. St. Louis, Jan. 1, 1948; d. Audrey and Dorothy Katherine (Durner) Freeze; m. Gary Keith Reynolds, May 13, 1972; children—Garth Kyle, Glenna Katrina. B.S. in Pharmacy, St. Louis Coll. Pharmacy, 1972. Registered pharmacist Ill., Mo. Mgr., pharmacist Ross Drug, Mt. Vernon, Ill., 1972-74; staff pharmacist Pine Street Pharmacy, Eldorado, Ill., 1974-75; relief pharmacist So. Ill. area, 1975-79; co-owner, operator, Reynolds Value-Rite Pharmacy, McLeansboro, Ill., 1973—; cons. Oak View Nursing Home, McLeansboro, 1975—, Life Care Ctr. of McLeansboro, 1984—. Com. mem. Cub Scout Park 30, Boy Scouts Am., McLeansboro, 1984-86, den leader, 1985-86. Mem. Am. Pharm. Assn., Ill. Pharmacist Assn., So. Ill. Pharmacist Assn. (Ho. of Dels. 1978-83), Hamilton County Pharmacist Assn. (treas. 1984—), Beta Sigma Phi (v.p. McLeansboro chpt. 1976-78, chmn. ways and means com. St. Louis chpt. 1971-72). Baptist. Avocations: Swimming; rose garden research; reading; sewing. Home: Route 3 McLeansboro IL 62859 Office: Reynolds Valu-Rite Pharmacy 107 North Jackson McLeansboro IL 62859

REYNOLDS, ROBERT WAYNE, national park administrator; b. Jackson, Wyo., June 25, 1945; s. Harvey Blair and Lois Elsie (Drewett) R.; m. Barbara Brooks Potter, Feb. 3, 1967; children—Kristina Jo, David Scott. B.S. in Zoology, U. Nebr., 1971. With Nat. Park Service, 1971—; ecologist Eastern Service Ctr., Washington, 1971; park ranger Pacific NW Regional Office, Seattle, 1972-73, Craters of the Moon Nat. Monument, Arco, Idaho, 1973-76; chief naturalist Capital Reef Nat. Park, Torrey, Utah, 1976-79, supt., 1985—; supt. Great Sands Dunes Nat. Monument, Mosca, Colo., 1979-82, Mt. Rushmore Nat. Meml., Keystone, S.D., 1982-85. Bd. dirs. Rapid City Conv. and Visitors Bur., S.D., 1984—, Story Brook Island Found., Rapid City, 1984—. Served with U.S. Army, 1965-69. Mem. S.D. Park and Recreation Assn., Assn. Nat. Park Rangers. Lodge: Rotary (bd. dirs.). Avocations: photography, reading, yard and garden.

REYNOLDS, THOMAS ELLIOTT, college administrator; b. New Orleans, Jan. 11, 1953; s. Jack Maurice and Mary Jean (Keith) R.; m. Deborah Kay Hart, May 1, 1976; children—Heather Elizabeth, Elisabeth Anne. Student Mich. State U., 1971-72; A.B. cum laude, U. Detroit, 1975. Staff writer, feature writer New Orleans Daily Record, 1974-75; freelance writer, public relations cons., Detroit and New Orleans, 1975-76; assoc. dir. instl. advancement Detroit Coll. Law, 1977—. Mem. Internat. Assn. Bus. Communicators, Pub. Relations Soc. Am., Sigma Delta Chi. Author: Renaissance Center-The Symbol of a Great City's Rebirth, 1980; The Detroit College of Law Student Guide, 1980.

REYNOLDS, THOMAS GEORGE, process industries consulting engineer; b. Kalamazoo, Apr. 9, 1906; s. Henry Tinch and Katharine (Jirsa) R.; B.S. in Civil Engring., U. Ill., 1928; M.S. in Chem. Engring., Columbia U., 1942; postgrad. NYU, 1941-42; m. Edith B. Pillatt, Aug. 23, 1928; children—Thomas Gordon, Barbara Ann Reynolds Barney, Katharine Sylvia, Nancy Edith Reynolds Bartlit, Cynthia Rose Reynolds, Susan Victoria Reynolds Lister; m. Jannetje de Otter, Feb. 13, 1965. Design engr. Engring. Service Co., Aurora, Ill., 1928-29, Standard Oil Co. Ind., Whiting, 1929-32; asst. constrn. supt., constrn. engr. M.W. Kellogg Co., N.Y.C., 1932-34; asst. resident engr. Continental Oil Co., Ponca City, Okla., 1934-36; resident engr., Balt., 1936-37; sr. project and process engr. Kellex Corp., 1943-45; chief engr. J.D. Pritchard & Co., Kansas City, Mo., 1945-47, Universal Engring. Co., Kansas City, Mo., 1947-48; chem. process engr. Research and Engring. div. Pitts. Consol. Coal Co., 1947; sr. chem. process engr. United Engrs. & Constructors, Inc., 1948-51; exec. engr. Catalytic Inc., 1951-56; pres., cons. engr. Reynolds-Bohna & Co., Inc., Phila., 1956-60; project mgr. SunOlin Chem. Co., 1960-61; mgr. indsl. process div. Thatcher & Patient, Clayton, Mo., 1961-62; project mgr. Badger Co., 1962-64; project mgr. Arthur G. McKee & Co., Cleve., 1964-67; cons. in process industries engring., 1964—. Fellow ASCE (life); mem. Am. Inst. Chem. Engrs., Am. Chem. Soc., AAAS, Fedn. Am. Scientists, N.Y. Acad. Scis., Phi Lambda Upsilon, Tau Kappa Epsilon. Patentee in chem. engring. Home: 11930 Marcy Rd W Canal-Winchester OH 43110

REYNOLDS, TIMOTHY RANDOLPH, lawyer; b. Toledo, Nov. 24, 1949; s. Ralph T. and Alvina E. (Glowczewski) R.; children—Wendi, Randy. B.S., Mich. State U., 1971; J.D., U. Toledo, 1978. Bar: Ohio 1979, U.S. Dist. Ct. (no. dist.) Ohio 1980, Mich. 1981, U.S. Dist. Ct. (ea. dist.) Mich. 1983. Ptnr. Sherman & Reynolds, Oregon, Ohio, 1979-81, Reynolds & Reed Co., Toledo, 1981-84; sole practice, Toledo, 1984—. Mem. State Bar Mich., Toledo Bar Assn., Lucas County Bar Assn., Phi Kappa Phi. Democrat. Lodge: Civitan (treas. local club 1983). Office: 1018 Adams St Toledo OH 43624

REYNOLDSON, WALTER WARD, chief justice Iowa Supreme Court; b. St. Edward, Nebr., May 17, 1920; s. Walter Scorer and Mabel Matilda (Sallach) R.; B.A., State Tchrs. Coll., 1942; J.D., U. Iowa, 1948; LL.D. (hon.), Simpson Coll., 1983; m. Janet Aline Mills, Dec. 24, 1942; children—Vicki (Mrs. Gary Kimes), Robert. Admitted to Iowa bar, 1948; practice in Osceola, 1948-71; justice Iowa Supreme Ct., 1971-78, chief justice, 1978—; lectr. seminar Sch. Law, Drake U., 1968; county atty. Clarke County (Iowa), 1953-57; pres. Nat. Ctr. State Cts., 1984-85. Trustee, Clarke County Community Hosp., Osceola; pres. bd. dirs. Osceola Ind. Sch. Dist. Served with USNR, 1942-46. Recipient Osceola Community Service award, 1968. Mem. Iowa Bar Assn. (chmn. com. on legal edn. and admission to bar 1964-71), ABA, Iowa Acad. Trial Lawyers, Am. Coll. Trial Lawyers, Am. Judicature Soc. (bd. dirs. 1983—), Conf. Chief Justices (pres. 1984-85). Contbg. author: Trial Handbook, 1969. Home: Rural Route 2 Osceola IA 50213 Office: State Capitol Bldg Des Moines IA 50319

REZABEK, PAUL FRANK, electromagnetic compatibility engineer, lighting protection engineer; b. Collinsville, Ill., Oct. 13, 1928; s. Paul Frank and Agnes Cecelia (Kanturek) R.; m. Josefina Garcia, June 17, 1950; children—Gail, Suzanne, Brenda, Richard. B.S. E.E., Washington U., St. Louis, 1961.

Communication engr. McDonnell-Douglas Corp., St. Louis, 1961-66, electro-magnetic compatibility engr. missiles, 1966-69, airplanes, 1969-84; contract engr. electromagnetic compatibility, Yoh Co., St. Louis, 1985—, sr. electronic specialist, 1985—. Co-patentee cabinet enclosure system. Author reports in field. Served with USAF, 1951-55. Republican. Roman Catholic. Club: MDC Bridge. Home: 28 Flamingo Dr Hazelwood MO 63042 Office: Yoh Co Suite 205 2222 Schuetz Rd Saint Louis MO 63146

REZNICEK, BERNARD WILLIAM, power company executive; b. Dodge, Nebr., Dec. 7, 1936; s. William Bernard and Elizabeth (Svoboda) R.; m. Mary Leona Gallagher; children—Stephen B., Michael J., Charles W., Mary E., Bernard J., James G. B.S.B.A., Creighton U., 1958; M.B.A., U. Nebr., 1979. With Omaha Public Power Dist., pres., chief exec. officer, 1981—; exec. Sierra Pacific Power, Reno, 1979-80; dir. Inst. Nuclear Power Ops., Atlanta, Atomic Indsl. Forum, D.C. Bd. dirs. Lutheran Med. Hosp., Omaha, 1982; trustee Father Flanagans Boys' Home, 1984. Mem. C. of C. (bd. dirs. 1981), Beta Gamma Sigma. Republican. Roman Catholic. Club: Oak Hills Country (sec. 1985). Lodge: Rotary (bd. dirs. 1984-85). Office: Omaha Public Power Dist 1623 Harney St Omaha NE 68102-2247

REZNICK, BRUCE ARIE, mathematician; b. N.Y.C., Feb. 3, 1953; s. Sidney and Sima (Goldberg) R. B.S., Calif. Inst. Tech., 1973; Ph.D., Stanford U., 1976. Asst. prof. Duke U., Durham, N.C., 1976-78; NSF postdoctoral fellow U. Calif.-Berkeley, 1978-79; asst. prof. U. Ill., Urbana, 1979-83, assoc. prof. math. dept., 1983—; problem composer William Lowell Putnam Math. Competition, 1982-85. Author: Chalking It Up, 1985. Bd. dirs. Champaign County ACLU, Urbana, 1984. NSF grad. fellow, Stanford U., 1973-76, Danforth grad. fellow, Stanford U., 1973-76, Nat. needs postdoctoral fellow NSF, U. Calif.-Berkeley, 1978-79, Sloan Found. fellow, 1983—, Beckman fellow U. Ill.-Urbana Ctr. for Advanced Study, 1984. Mem. Math. Assn. Am., Am. Math. Soc., Assn. Women in Math. Democrat. Avocations: baseball; pinball; humor. Home: 410 Brookens Dr Urbana IL 61801 Office: U Ill 1409 W Green St Urbana IL 61801

RHAME, FRANK SCORGIE, physician, educator; b. Pitts., Sept. 11, 1942; s. William Thomas and Thelma Grace (Scorgie) R.; m. Betsey Clark Ingraham, May 30, 1966; children—Lara, Caroline. B.S., Calif. Inst. Tech., 1964; M.D., Columbia U., 1968. Diplomate Am. Bd. Internal Medicine, Am. Bd. Infectious Diseases. Staff physician Palo Alto VA Med. Ctr., Calif., 1975-78; asst. prof. U. Minn., Mpls., 1979—. Served as asst. surgeon USPHS, 1970-72. Recipient Alex Langmuir award Epidemic Intelligence Service, 1972. Fellow Am. Coll. Epidemiologists; mem. Soc. Hosp. Epidemiologists Am. (treas. 1982—), Am. Soc. Microbiology, Am. Soc. Internal Medicine. Mem. Democratic Farm Labor Party. Avocation: running. Home: 29 Barton Ave SE Minneapolis MN 55414 Office: Box 421 Mayo Bldg U Minn Hosp Minneapolis MN 55455

RHATIGAN, MARILYN HALL, pharmacist; b. Des Moines, Iowa, Jan. 10, 1935; d. Francis V. and Helen Margaret (Struthers) Hall; m. Jack K. Rhatigan, Aug. 23, 1959; children—Shawn Dewey, Craig Francis, Shannon Kristal. B.S. in Pharmacy, Drake U., 1956; B.S. in Edn., Bemidji State Coll., 1959. Registered pharmacist, Iowa, Minn. Staff pharmacist Iowa Meth. Hosp., Des Moines, 1956-58, St. John's Hosp., St. Paul, 1959-61, 1965-68, Mounds Park Hosp., St. Paul, 1969-71; co-owner, opr. The Drug Shop, Iowa City, 1962-64; part-time staff pharmacist Bethesda Luth. Med. Ctr., St. Paul, 1972—; vol. speaker Cottage Grove, Minn. sch. dist., 1982—. Moderator Community United Ch. Christ, St. Paul Park, 1982-84; vol. United Way, St. Paul, 1975-82. Iowa Pharmacy Assn. scholar, 1952. Mem. Profl. Employed Pharmacists of Minn. (bd. dirs. 1972-74, negotiator 1974), Alpha Lambda Delta, Rho Chi, Lambda Kappa Sigma, Delta Zeta. Club: Pine Ridge Garden. Lodge: Ankeny Order Eastern Star. Avocations: gardening; bridge. Home: 8185 83d St S Cottage Grove MN 55016 Office: Bethesda Luth Med Ctr 559 Capitol Blvd St Paul MN 55103

RHEAD, WILLIAM JAMES, biochemical geneticist; b. Paris, Feb. 20, 1946; came to U.S., 1946; s. Wallace Max and Marie Jeanne (Muller) R.; m. Deborah Elizabeth Sheppard, July 15, 1972; children—Paul Joseph, Evan James. B.A. with highest honors, U. Calif.-San Diego, 1968; M.Ph., Yale U., 1969; M.D., U. Calif.-San Diego, 1974, Ph.D., 1975. Diplomate Am. Bd. Human Genetics, Am. Bd. Pediatrics. Intern and resident in pediatrics U. N.C.-Chapel Hill, 1975-77; fellow in human genetics and pediatrics Yale U. Sch. Medicine, 1977-79; asst. prof. pediatrics U. Iowa Coll. Medicine, 1979-84, assoc. prof. pediatrics, 1984—. Bd. dirs. Assn. for Glycogen Storage Disease, 1984—. Recipient Noel Raine award, Soc. Study of Inborn Errors of Metabolism, 1983. Fellow Am. Acad. Pediatrics; mem. Am. Soc. Human Genetics, Soc. Inherited Metabolic Disease, AAAS, Soc. Pediatric Research, Soc. Study Inborn Errors of Metabolism. Democrat. Avocations: Bicycling, tropical fish, travel, gardening. Home: 21 Highland Dr Iowa City IA 52240 Office: Dept Pediatrics Coll Medicine U Iowa Hosps and Clinics Iowa City IA 52242

RHIND, THOMAS ALEXANDER, police chief; b. Hammond, Ind., Nov. 8, 1937; s. Alexander William and Ella M. (Bussel) R.; m. Barbara Anne Stanners, June 1, 1957; children—Thomas Allen, Alexander William II, Robert Stanners. Drug enforcement, U.S. Dept. Justice, 1971; Criminal Justice, St. Joseph's Coll., 1974. Patrolman Munster Police Dept., Ind., 1963-69, sgt., 1969-73, lt., 1973-82, chief of police, 1983—. Counselor Calumet council Boy Scouts Am., 1974; mem. adv. bd. Salvation Army, Gary, Hammond, Munster, Ind., 1983, Ind. U., Gary, 1983; active in Drug Abuse Council, Munster, 1973, Ind. Regional Addiction Authority, Ind., 1976. Recipient Firearms Proficiency award Munster Police Dept. 1963-83; Firearms Proficiency award State of Ind. 1967-84; named Officer of Yr., Munster Rotary Club, 1975. Mem. Munster C. of C., Lake County Law Enforcement Council (v.p. 1984—, sec., treas. 1983-84), Fraternal Order Police (pres. Munster 1967), Internat. Assn. Chiefs Police (del. 1983), Ind. Assn. Chiefs Police (del. 1983, 84, 85). Presbyterian. Clubs: Football 100 (Evansville, Ind.), Huskie (U. No. Ill.). Lodges: Masons, Shriners. Avocations: hunting; fishing; camping; boating. Home: 8801 Meadow Ln Munster IN 46321 Office: Munster Police Dept 1001 Ridge Rd Munster IN 46321

RHINE, SAMUEL ALLEN, geneticist, educator; b. Burlington, Ind., Aug. 15, 1946; s. Cecil S. and Kathryn E. (Spann) R.; m. Pamela Lu Yoder, Nov. 27, 1968; children—Andrew Allen, Amy Nanette. A.B. in Zoology, Ind. U., 1968, M.A. in Genetics, 1972; postgrad. Harvard U., 1976-78. Geneticist, Noble Devel. Ctrs., Marion County (Ind.) Assn. for Retarded Citizens; counselor; lectr. on causes, prevention mental retardation at high schools throughout the country. Recipient CASPER award for outstanding community service Indpls. Community Service Council, 1982; NIH fellow Ind. U.; Lalor Found. fellow, March of Dimes Research fellow Harvard U. Mem. Am. Soc. Human Genetics, AAAS, Am. Assn. Mental Deficiency, Sigma Xi. Mem. Faith Missionary Ch. Patentee Antenatal Cell Extractor for 1st trimester prenatal diagnosis; contbr. articles to publs. Home: 13305 LaCanada Blvd Noblesville IN 46060 Office: 2400 N Tibbs Indianapolis IN 46222

RHOADES, RODNEY ALLEN, physiologist, educator; b. Greenville, Ohio, Jan. 5, 1939; s. John H. and Floris L. Rhoades; m. Judith Ann Brown, Aug. 16, 1961; children—Annelisa, Kirsten. B.S., Miami U., 1961, M.S., 1963; Ph.D., Ohio State U., 1966. Asst. prof. Pa. State U., State College, 1966-72, assoc. prof., 1972-75; research scientist NIH, Bethesda, Md., 1975-76; prof. Ind. U. Sch. Medicine, Indpls., 1976-81, prof., chmn., 1981—. Author: Physiology, 1984; also articles. Recipient NASA fellow, 1964-66; Research Career Devel. award NIH, 1975-80. Mem. Am. Physiol. Soc., Am. Heart Assn., Am. Thoracic Soc., Sigma Xi. Home: 7525 N Audubon Indianapolis IN 46250 Office: Ind U Sch Medicine 635 Barnhill Dr Indianapolis IN 46223

RHODES, ANNE-MARIE ELIZABETH, lawyer, educator; b. Rochester, N.Y., Nov. 14, 1951; d. Robert A. and Anne Marie (Ward) R.; m. David W. Hepplewhite, Nov. 23, 1984. B.A., Albertus Magnus Coll., New Haven, 1973; J.D., Harvard U., 1976. Bar: Ill. 1976. Assoc., Schiff Hardin & Waite, Chgo. and Washington, 1976-79; prof. law Loyola U., Chgo., 1980—; of counsel Sachnoff Weaver & Rubenstein, Ltd., Chgo., 1981—. Contbr. articles to legal jours. Mem. steering com. of tax planning adv. com. Loyola U., 1982. State of Conn. grantee, 1972. Mem. Am. Assn. Law Schs., Chgo. Estate Planning Council, Chgo. Bar Assn., Harvard Law Soc. Ill. (dir. 1977—).

RHODES, CHARLES KIRKHAM, physics educator; b. Mineola, N.Y., June 30, 1939; s. Walter Cortlyn and Evelyn Kirkham Rhodes; m. Barbara Dowe, Aug. 28, 1964 (div.); children—Lisa Porterfield, Gregory Cortlyn; m. Mary Cannon, Oct. 23, 1976; children—Edward Kirkham, Elizabeth Mayhew. B.E.E., Cornell U., Ithaca, N.Y., 1963; M.E.E., MIT, 1965, Ph.D. in Physics, 1969. Physicist, head gas laser group Lawrence Livermore Lab., U. Calif., 1970-75; lectr. dept. applied sci. U. Calif.-David, Livermore Extension, 1971-75; program mgr. molecular physics lab. SRI Internat., Menlo Park, Calif., 1975-78; cons. prof. Stanford U. (Calif.), 1975-78; prof. physics U. Ill.-Chgo., 1978-82, research prof., 1982—; cons. in field. Contbr. articles to profl. jours. Patentee in field. Fellow Am. Phys. Soc., Optical Soc. Am.; mem. IEEE (sr. mem.), Quantum Electronics and Applications Soc., European Phys. Soc. Office: U Ill Dept Physics PO Box 4348 Chicago IL 60680

RHODES, DAVID JOHN, printing company executive; b. Iron Mountain, Mich., Sept. 12, 1959; s. John Benjamin and Lorraine Beatrice (Schaffer) R. Assoc. in Mktg. Communications, Northeast Wis. Tech. Inst., 1980. Advt. mgr. Kramer Machinery Co., Green Bay, Wis., 1980-81; sales mgr. Ind. Printing Co., Depere, Wis., 1981—. Mem. Ad Fedn. Green Bay. Office: Ind Printing Co 549 Main Ave Depere WI 54115

RHODES, GEORGE HARRY, aviation consultant and broadcaster; b. East Cleveland, Ohio, Jan. 4, 1925; s. Henry George and Agnes Marie (Lancefield) R.; m. Leora Ann Agnew, May 16, 1964; children—Matthew George, Jennifer Grace. Student Hope Coll., 1943-44, San Francisco State Coll., 1949-50, U. Calif.-Berkeley, 1953-54. Cert. airline transport pilot, flight instr. Commd. 2d lt. U.S. Army, 1945, advanced through grades to capt., 1953; served Japan, Pacific, Okinawa, Korea, ret. 1953; sales rep. IBM, Pitts., 1954-58; prin. Dictation Assocs., Pitts., 1959-61; dist. mgr. MacMillan Ring-Free Oil Co., N.Y.C., 1962-65; bus. planning staffer Booz-Allen & Hamilton, Cleve., 1966-67; founder, owner, pres. Aviation Tng. Seminars, Cleve., 1967—; vol. accident prevention counselor U.S. Dept. Transp., FAA, Cleve., 1969—; author, host NBC 10-part TV series: Discover Flying: Just Like a Bird, 1969-81 (Earl D. Osborn Writing award 1970); producer, author, host weekly radio show Sta. WKYC: Discover Flight with George Rhodes, 1972-74 (Midwestern Conf. News Media award 1972); author, lectr. color slide presentation: A Private Pilot Ground School, 1967-69 (AFA Aerospace Award 1969). Named FAA Gold Seal Instr. Mem. Aviation/Space Writers Assn. (v.p. 1974-78), Aircraft Owners and Pilots Assn. (hon.), Internat. Soc. Air Safety Investigators. Republican. Presbyterian. Club: Willoughby Flying (pres. 1966-67). Lodges: Masons, Shrine. Avocations: military history; racquetball; old cars. Home: 6596 Maplewood Dr Cleveland OH 44124 Office: Aviation Training Seminars 6596 Maplewood Dr Cleveland OH 44124

RHODES, JACQUELINE YVONNE, marketing executive; b. Fairfield, Ala., Mar. 3, 1949; d. Lee Oliver and Jimmye Lucille (Warren) R.; m. Gerald Allen Turner, Feb. 14, 1981 (dec. 1984). Student pub. schs., Cleve. Bus. services rep. Ohio Bell Telephone Co., Cleve., 1969-82, bus. officer instr., 1973-74, spl. communications cons., 1974-76, account exec. II, 1976-80, personnel mgr., 1980-82; account exec. American Bell, Cleve., 1983; dir. sales and mktg. Psychassess, Inc., Cleve., 1983-85; telecommunication analyst Cleve. Clinic Found., 1985—; sec. Turner & Knight, Inc., Cleve., 1981-85. Vice pres. Harambee: Services to Black Families, Cleve. Mem. Nat. Assn. Female Execs., Urban League, Women's City Club. Baptist. Home: 17722 Tarkington Ave Cleveland OH 44128

RHODES, JAMES ARTHUR, political science educator; b. Bluffton, Ind., Jan. 23, 1939; s. Estel John and Margaret Wallbank (Palmer) R.; m. Barbara Ann Uhrick, Aug. 20, 1961; children—Charles Edmund, David Arthur, Matthew Aaron, Mark Andrew. B.A., Beloit Coll., 1960; M.A. in English, U. Ark., 1962; M.A. in Polit. Sch., U. Mich., 1964, Ph.D., 1973. Faculty, Luther Coll., Decorah, Iowa, 1968—, prof. polit. sci. Recipient Faculty Enrichment award Can. Embassy, 1983; Hoover fellow Hoover Presdl. Library Assn., 1984. Mem. Am. Polit. Sci. Assn., Midwest Polit. Sci. Assn., Iowa Conf. Polit. Scientists (pres. 1984). Democrat. Methodist. Home: 604 Plum St Decorah IA 52101 Office: Dept Polit Sci Luther College 126 Larsen Hall Decorah IA 52101

RHODES, JAMES BENJAMIN, medical educator, researcher; b. Kansas City, Mo., July 22, 1928; s. B.B. and Helen Elizabeth (Davis) R.; m. Betty Louise Alfini, Mar. 17, 1960; children—Benjamin Cave, Joan Elizabeth, Stephen Conway. B.A., U. Kans.-Lawrence, 1954; M.D., U. Kans.-Kansas City, 1958. Intern, resident, gastrointestinal fellow, U. Chgo., 1958-64, fellow in biochemistry, 1959-60; research assoc. Chgo. Med. Sch., 1964-66; asst. prof. medicine and physiology, Med. Ctr. U. Kans., Kansas City, 1966-70, assoc. prof., 1970-79, prof. medicine, 1979—, chmn. med. faculty steering com., 1972, advisor exec. vice chancellor, 1974; cons. Kansas City VA Hosp., 1966—. Contbr. writings to publs. in field. Served with USN, 1946-49, Pacific. Recipient Basic Sci. Teaching award, 1969; Disting. Med. Teaching award Kans. U. Alumni, 1972. Fellow ACP; mem. Am. Gastroenterology Assn., Am. Physiology Soc., Am. Soc. GI Endoscopists, Alpha Omega Alpha. Avocation: Photography. Home: 4701 Mullen Rd Shawnee KS 66216 Office: Dept Medicine U Kans Med Ctr 39th and Rainbow Blvd Kansas City KS 66103

RHODES, RICHARD DAVID, osteopathic physician, emergency care center executive; b. East Liverpool, Ohio, Nov. 2, 1935; s. Earl E. and Gladys (Robinson) R.; m. Mary Jo Marquette, Aug. 6, 1960; children—Mary Lorraine, Wendy Lynn, Kristen Leigh. Student Kent State U., 1954-57; D.O., Iowa Coll. of Osteo. Medicine and Surgery, 1961. Intern, Warren (Ohio) Gen. Hosp., 1961-62; pres. Emergency Physicians, Inc., Orwell, Ohio, 1972—; staff mem. Warren Gen. Hosp., chmn. dept. family practice, 1965; chief of staff, 1972; chmn. dept. emergency medicine Joint Twp. Hosp., St. Mary's, Ohio, 1972—; staff mem. St. Mary's (Ohio) Hosp., 1977—; pres. Rinn Lease Inc., 1976—, Medi Kwik. Mem. Am. Coll. Osteo. Emergency Medicine, Am. Coll. Emergency Medicine, Ohio Osteo. Assn., Am. Osteo. Assn., Sigma Sigma Phi.

RHOTEN, JESSIE FERNE, educator; b. Sterling, Nebr., Feb. 29, 1928; d. Ira Sherman and Clara Phoebe (Parker) Rhoten. B.A., Peru State Tchrs. Coll., 1949; M.S., U. Omaha, 1963; postgrad. various colls., 1970-76. English tchr., Murdock, Nebr., 1949-50, Dunbar, Nebr., 1950-53, Unadilla, Nebr., 1953-55; English tchr. ISC #2 Omaha Pub. Schs., 1955—. Mem. Omaha Edn. Assn., Nebr. Edn. Assn., Nebr. Council English Tchrs., Nat. Council English Tchrs., Greater Omaha English Tchrs., DAR, Kappa Kappa Iota, Phi Delta Gamma. Democrat. Mem. Ch. of Christ. Clubs: Order of Eastern Star, Willard Assn., Rhoten Assn. Author: History of Unadilla Nebraska, 1982. Home: 3918 Castelar Omaha NE 68105

RHOTEN, JULIANA THERESA, educational administrator; b. N.Y.C., June 28; d. Julius Joseph and Gladys Maude (Grant) Bastian; B.A., Hunter Coll., 1954; M.S., 1956; Ed.S., U. Wis., Milw., 1977; m. Marion Rhoten, Aug. 7, 1956; 1 son, Don Carlos. Tchr. elem. schs., Milw., 1957-65, reading specialist, 1965-71, adminstr., 1971-80; prin. Ninth St. Sch., Milw., 1980-83, Parkview Sch., Milw., 1983—. Mem. Assn. Supervision and Curriculum Devel., Internat. Reading Assn., Nat. Council Tchrs. English, Adminstrs. and Suprs. Council, Phi Delta Kappa, Alpha Kappa Alpha. Home: 7222 N 99th St Milwaukee WI 53224 Office: 10825 W Villard Ave Milwaukee WI 53225

RHUDY, WILLIAM PORTER, III, college dean; b. Penn Yan, N.Y., Dec. 31, 1955; s. William Porter and Betty Jean (Andrews) R. B.A., Syracuse U., 1978, M.S., 1981; doctoral candidate U. Iowa, 1982—. Counselor, Syracuse U., N.Y., 1977-78, asst. hall dir., 1978-79, hall dir., 1979-80; dean students St. Ambrose Coll., Davenport, Iowa, 1980—, alcohol task force coordinator, 1984—. Mem. com. Operation Clean Davenport, 1981—; active Boy Scouts Am.; coach Women's Golf team. Mem. Nat. Assn. Student Personnel, Am. Coll. Personnel Assn., Alcohol and Drug Problems Asn. Am., Iowa Student Personnel Assn., Alpha Phi Omega, Sigma Chi. Republican. Roman Catholic. Lodge: KC (membership dir. 1983-85) (Davenport). Avocations: ice hockey; jogging; golf. Home: 2205 N Gaines St Davenport IA 52804 Office: 518 W Locust St Davenport IA 52803

RHUTASEL, LARRY JOHN, environmental engineer; b. Mason City, Iowa, Aug. 18, 1940; s. August J. and Marjorie E. (Schlosser) R.; m. Marjorie Mae Slemmons, Sept. 4, 1961; children—Lance, Chad. B.S. in Civil Engring., U. Iowa, 1963; M.S. in Environ. Engring., U. Ill., 1973. Registered profl. engr., Ill., Mo., Iowa, Minn., Sanitary engr. Ill. Dept. Pub. Health, Springfield, 1963-69; pres. Rhutasel Assocs., Inc., Freeburg, Ill., 1969—. Pres. St. Paul's United Ch. of Christ, Freeburg, 1980. Mem. Ill. Soc. Profl. Engrs. (chpt. pres. 1975-76), Constrn. Engrs. Council Ill. (bd. dirs. 1982-85, sec.-treas. 1985-86), ASCE, Am. Acad. Environ. Engrs., Water Pollution Control Fedn., Freeburg Jaycees (pres. 1969-70). Lodge: Rotary (pres. 1984-85). Avocations: tennis, fishing, hunting. Home: Rural Route 2 Freeburg IL 62243 Office: Rhutasel and Assocs Inc 1 Sunset Dr Freeburg IL 62243

RIBELIN, ROSEMARY BINGHAM, college bookstore and campus center administrator; b. Indpls., Ind., Aug. 8, 1933; d. Remester Alexander and Joy Dorothy (Reed) Bingham; m. Richard Grant Ribelin, Aug. 16, 1957; children—Pamela Joy, Karen Sue. Student Indpls. schs. Sec. to mgr. Phoenix Mut. Life Ins., Indpls., 1952-61, office supr., 1971-76; sec. to pres. Franklin Coll., Ind., 1976-79, bookstore/campus ctr. dir., 1979—. Leader Hoosier Capital council Girl Scouts U.S.A., 1965-75; canvasser Multiple Sclerosis Soc., Am. Cancer Soc., Am. Heart Assn., 1965-77; canvasser Channel 20 Pub. Broadcasting Service, Indpls., 1968; active com. mem. J. K. Lilly School PTA, Indpls., 1965-75, pres., 1972; canvasser United Fund, Indpls., 1968-75, pres., 1971. Moneyraiser, poll worker Republican Party, Indpls. Deacon, Sunday Sch. tchr. First Presbyn. Ch. of Franklin. Mem. Philanthropic Nat. Soc. (pres. 1983-85), Delta Theta Tau (treas. Lambda Eta chpt. 1981-82). Lodges: Daus. of Nile, Order Eastern Star, Oriental Shrine. Avocations: Hooking rugs, reading, crocheting, playing cards, embroidery. Home: RR Box 151C Franklin IN 46131 Office: Franklin Coll Bookstore Campus Ctr Franklin IN 46131

RICE, CARL VENTON, lawyer, business; b. Lovilla, Iowa, Mar. 27, 1898; s. Walter Scott and Ida Isabelle (Chamberlain) R.; LL.B., U. Kans., 1918; m. Ruth Burton, Nov. 13, 1919 (dec. 1968); children—Ruth Isabelle Rice Mitchell, Carlene V. Rice Lind, Mary E. Rice Wells, Grace L. Rice Muder; m. 2d, Virginia Docking, 1978. Admitted to Kans. bar, 1918, U.S. Supreme Ct. bar, 1933; practiced in Kansas City, Kans., 1919-85; chmn. bd., pres. Pierce Industries, Inc., Andersen, Ind., 1954-64; now v.p. Rodar Leasing Corp., Kansas City, Kans. and Tampa, Fla., Fairfax Spltys., Kansas City, Kans., Graham Tubular Specialties, 3654 Cypress Corp., Tampa, Mission Groves, Inc., Ft. Pierce, Fla.; Hwy. commr. State of Kans., 1931-33; regional counsel RFC, 1933-38, CCC, 1934-50, Def. Plant Corp., 1941-50; counsel Kans. Banking Dept., 1937-39. Mem. exec. com. Democratic Nat. Com., 1948-52. Served with F.A., U.S. Army, World War I. Named to Kans. U. Athletic Hall of Fame. Mem. Am. Bar Assn., Kans. State Bar Assn., Delta Theta Phi. Clubs: Kansas City, Indian Hills Country (Kansas City, Kans.); Pelican Yacht (Ft. Pierce). Home: 2108 Washington Blvd Kansas City KS 66102 Office: 600 Security Nat Bank Bldg Kansas City KS 66101

RICE, DAVID LEE, university president; b. New Market, Ind., Apr. 1, 1929; s. Elmer J. and Katie B. (Tate) R.; m. Betty Jane Fordice, Sept. 10, 1950; children—Patricia Denise Rice Dawson, Michael Alan. B.S., Purdue U., 1951, M.S., 1956, Ph.D., 1958. Prof., dir. research Ball State U., Muncie, Ind., 1958-66; v.p. Coop. Edn. Research Lab., Indpls., 1966; research coordinator Bur. Research Office Edn., Washington, 1965; dean Ind. State U., Evansville, 1967-71, pres., 1971—, v.p. Terre Haute, 1976—; dir. Midwest Fed. Savs., 1979—; adminstrv. asst. Gov.'s Com. on Post-High Sch. Orgn. for Vo-cat.-Tech. Edn., 1964-65; mem. research staff Ind. Post-High Sch. Study Commn., 1961-62. Contbr. articles to profl. jours; author publs. in field. Chmn. subcom. Met. Evansville Progress Com.; mem. United Way Exec. Bd., Ind. Office Social Services; pres. WNIN Pub. TV Sta., Evansville. Served to sgt., inf. U.S. Army, 1951-53; Korea. Decorated Combat Infantry badge; recipient Citizen of Yr. award Westside Civitan Club, 1972; Service to Others award Salvation Army, 1974; Boss of Yr. award Am. Bus. Women's Assn., 1976. Mem. Am. Assn. for Higher Edn., Am. Ednl. Research Assn., Nat. Soc. for Study of Edn., Am. Assn. for State Colls. and Univs., Met. Evansville C. of C. United Methodist. Club: Leadership (Evansville). Lodge: Rotary. Avocations: camping, gardening, woodworking. Office: U Southern Indiana 8600 University Blvd Evansville IN 47712

RICE, DENNIS CARROLL, electro-mechanical manufacturing company executive; b. Carthage, Mo., June 25, 1954; s. Charles Eugene and Lillian Helen (Murphy) R.; m. Cynthia Lou Roper, Sept. 2, 1978; 1 child, Aaron Joseph. B.B.A., Mo. So. State U., 1976; M.B.A., Southwest Mo. State U., 1984. Indsl. engr. Leggett & Platt, Inc., Carthage, Mo., 1975-80, Motorola, Joplin, Mo., 1980-84; prodn. and indsl. engr. mgr. Birdview Satellite Commn., Chanute, Kans., 1984—. Mem. Inst. Indsl. Engrs., Am. Prodn. and Inventory Control Soc. Republican. Baptist. Avocations: reading; hunting. Home: Route 2 Box 321 Chanute KS 66720 Office: Birdview Satellite Communications Inc 908 W Chestnut Chanute KS 66720

RICE, ELIZABETH JANE, lawyer; b. Ottawa, Ill., Oct. 5, 1949; d. John Evans and Mabel Jane (Peck) Jackson; m. Charles R. Rice, Dec. 12, 1979; 1 dau., Amy Elizabeth. B.A., Ill. Wesleyan U., 1971; J.D., Chgo. Kent Coll. Law, Ill. Inst. Tech., 1980. Bar: Ill. 1980, U.S. Dist. Ct. (no. dist.) Ill. 1980. Pub. aid caseworker Ill. Dept. Pub. Aid, Ottawa, Ill., 1974-78, casework supr., 1978-83; asst. state's atty. LaSalle County, Ill., 1983—. Class of 1971 agt. Ill. Wesleyan Alumni Fund, Bloomington, 1978-83; mem. exec. bd. parent Tchr. Orgn., Jefferson Sch., Ottawa, 1983-84; mem. exec. bd. Ottawa chpt. ARC, 1983-84. Mem. LaSalle County Bar Assn., Ill. State Bar Assn., ABA. Presbyterian. Club: Roaming Wheeles Touring (bd. dirs. 1980-84) (Streator, Ill.). Lodge: Women of Moose. Home: 148 E Fremont St Ottawa IL 61350 Office: LaSalle County State's Atty's Office 707 Etna Rd PO Box 369 Ottawa IL 61350

RICE, FRED, superintendent police; b. Chgo., Dec. 24, 1926; m. Thelma Martin; children—Lyle, Judith. B.S., Roosevelt U., 1970, M.S. in Pub. Adminstrn., 1977. Mem. Chgo. Police Dept., 1955—, promoted to sgt., 1961, lt., 1968, capt., 1973, dist. comdr., 1970-78, dep. chief patrol, Area Four, 1978-79, chief patrol div., 1979-83, supt. police, 1983—. Served with U.S. Army, 1950-52; Korea. Recipient numerous awards for contbns. to community. Office: Chgo Police Dept 1121 S State St Chicago IL 60605

RICE, JEFFREY DALE, optometrist; b. Zanesville, Ohio, Feb. 24, 1955; s. Dale Eugene and Maxine F. (LeFeven) R.; m. Deborah Lynn Mell, Mar. 13, 1982; children—Shawn Lee, Jamie Marie. O.D., Ohio State U., 1980. Gen. practice optometry, Zanesville, 1980—. Vice pres. Am. Cancer Soc., Muskingam County Unit, 1983-84. Mem. Am. Optometric Assn., Ohio Optometric Assn., Mid-Eastern Ohio Optometric Assn. Republican. Lodge: Kiwanis (bd. dirs. 1984—). Avocations: sports, jogging, physical fitness. Home: 750 Fairmont Ave Zanesville OH 43701 Office: 740 Princeton Ave Zanesville OH 43701

RICE, JOHN RAY, social worker; b. Covington, Tenn., Jan. 3, 1949; s. Luttrell and Mary Alma (Walker) R. A.B.S., George Williams Coll., 1971, M.S.W., 1977. Lic. therapist, Ill. Psychiat. social worker Kane/Kendall County Mental Health Ctr., Ill., 1971-74; young adult coordinator Thresholds, Chgo., 1974-77; pvt. practice therapy, Chgo., 1977—; camp dir. Unions for Youth, Nat. Football League Players Assn., Elmhurst, Ill., 1979, Winchendon, Mass. social worker, instr. Behavior Sci.-Family Practice Residency Tng. Program, Ill. Masonic Ctr., Chgo., 1980; child-family therapist Habilitative Systems, Inc., Chgo., 1985—; field instr. George Williams Coll. Sch. Social Work Edn. Author: Thank You for Loving Me. Mem. coms. Ill. Commn. on Children. Mem. Nat. Assn. Social Workers, Nat. Assn. Black Social Workers, Acad. Cert. Social Workers. Baptist. Home: 1129 W Oakdale Chicago IL 60657 Office: PO Box 14556 Chicago IL 60614

RICE, JOY KATHARINE, clinical psychologist; b. Oak Park, Ill., Mar. 26, 1939; s. Joseph Theodore and Margaret Sophia (Bednarik) Straka; m. David Gordon, Sept. 1, 1962; children—Scott Alan, Andrew David. Student, Rosary Coll., 1956-57; B.F.A. with high honors, U. Ill., 1960; M.S., U. Wis., 1962, M.S., 1964, Ph.D., 1967. USPHS predoctoral fellow dept. psychiatry U. Wis. Med. Sch., Madison, 1964-65, asst. dir. Counseling Ctr., 1966-74, dir. Office Continuing Edn. Services, 1972-78, prof. ednl. policy studies and women's studies, 1974—; pvt. practice psychology, Madison, 1967—. Mem. State of Wis. Ednl. Approval Bd., 1972-73; mem. U.S. Office Career Edn. Adult Edn. Commn., 1978. Knapp fellow U. Wis., 1960-62; U. Wis. teaching fellow, 1962-63, Title I, Office Edn., HEW, Wis. post-secondary instl. grantee, 1974-77; Meritorious Service award Adult Edn. Asns. Am., 1978, 79, 80, 82. Mem. Am. Psychol. Assn., Am. Ednl. Research Assn., Internat. Council Psychologists, Am. Assn. Continuing and Adult Edn., Wis. Psychol. Assn. Unitarian. Mem. editorial bd. Lifelong Learning, 1979—, Jour. Nat. Assn. Women Deans, Counselors and Adminstrs. Contbr. articles to profl. jours. Author: Living through Divorce: A Developmental Approach to Divorce Therapy, 1985. Home: 4230 Waban Hill Madison WI 53711 Office: 243 Edn U Wis Madison WI 53706

RICE, MILTON LEROY, fire chief; b. Pritchett, Colo., Dec. 1, 1930; s. Albert M. and Ada A. (Eckel) R.; m. Eileen Ruth Parks, Dec. 22, 1951; children—Letitia Lou, Guy Roy, Lawilda Lee Hogan. Grad. high sch., Santa Ana, Calif. Fire fighter Fullerton Fire Dept., Calif., 1957-60, fire engr., 1960-69; fire insp. Liberal Fire Dept., Kans., 1969-72, fire chief, 1972—. Contbr. articles to newspapers. Treas., past pres. Seward County Safety Council, Liberal, 1975-84; chmn. City Safety Com., Liberal, 1972-84; treas., past pres. Liberal Ministerial Alliance, Kans., 1977-84; dist. pres. Reorganized Ch. of Jesus Christ of Latterday Saints, Western, Kans., 1983—. Served with U.S. Army, 1951-53. Mem. Kans. State Fire Chief Assn. (bd. dirs. 1982-84), Kans. State Fire Fighters Assn. (bd. dirs. 1975-80). Rebublican. Lodge: Kiwanis (pres. 1981-82, treas. 1984—). Avocation: helping people. Home: 1101 S Clay St PO Box 638 Liberal KS 67901 Office: Liberal Fire Dept 15th & Kansas Sts PO Box 830 Liberal KS 67901

RICE, OTIS LAVERNE, nursing home builder and developer; b. Emerson, Iowa, June 24, 1922; s. William Reuben and Bonnie Elizabeth (Cary) R.; m. Ferill Jeane Dalton, Mar. 7, 1946; children—LeVeria June McMichael, Larry Lee. Student Fox Valley Tech. Sch., 1971-72. Lic. electrician and contractor. With Tumpane Electric, Omaha, 1949-53; owner, pres. Rice & Rice, Inc., Kaukauna, Wis., 1953—. Served with U.S. Army, 1942-46. Decorated Bronze Stars. Mem. Associated Builders and Contractors, Fenton Art Glass Collectors of Am. Inc. (founder), Internat. Carnival Glass Collectors, Am. Carnival Glass Collectors, Heisey Collectors of Am. Republican. Clubs: Masons, Shriners, Eastern Star.

RICE, PAUL FREDERICK, structural engr.; b. Mandan, N.D., Dec. 8, 1921; s. Paul Frederick and Claire Olive (Des Jardins) R.; B.S., N.D. State Coll., 1941; postgrad. Ill. Inst. Tech., 1942; M.S., MIT, 1947; postgrad. U. Mich., 1953-57; m. Joan Carol Cannon, June 22, 1946; children—Paul Frederick, Clair Patrick, John Cassius, Richard Clay. Structural design engr. Cunningham-Limp Co., Detroit, 1947-49; structural field engr. Mich., Portland Cement Assn., Chgo., 1949-54; tech. dir. Am. Concrete Inst., Detroit, 1954-58; v.p. engring. Concrete Reinforcing Steel Inst., Chgo., 1958—; chmn. Concrete Improvement Bd. Detroit, 1955-56; vice chmn. Reinforced Concrete Research Council, ASCE, 1974-76. Served with C.E., AUS, 1942-46; ETO. Registered profl. engr., Mich.; registered structural engr., Ill. Fellow ASCE, Am. Concrete Inst. (Lindau award 1981); mem. Am. Welding Soc., ASTM, Structural Engs. Assn. Ill., Reinforced Concrete Research Council (Arthur J. Boase award 1985). Editor, author: Concrete Reinforcing Steel Institute (CRSI) Handbook, 1968, 71, 75, 78, 80, 82, 85; co-author: Structural Design Guide to ACI Building Code, Structural Design Guide to AISI Specifications. Home: 2033 Sherman Ave Evanston IL 60201 Office: 933 N Plum Grove Rd Schaumburg IL 60195

RICE, RICHARD CAMPBELL, state official, retired army officer; b. Atchison, Kans., Dec. 11, 1933; s. Olive Campbell and Ruby Thelma (Rose) R.; m. Donna Marie Lincoln, Aug. 4, 1956; children—Robert Alden, Holly Elizabeth. B.A. in History, Kans. State U., 1955; M.A. in Social Studies, Eastern Mich. U., 1965; grad. U.S. Army Command and Gen. Staff Coll., 1968, U.S. Army War Coll., 1977. Commd. 2d lt. U.S. Army, 1955; advanced through grades to col., 1976; with Joint Chiefs of Staff, Washington, 1975-76; faculty U.S. Army War Coll., Carlisle Barracks, Pa., 1977-79; chief staff Hdqrs. 3d ROTC Region, Ft. Riley, Kans., 1982-83; ret. 1983; dir. Mo. State Emergency Mgmt. Agy., Jefferson City, 1983-85, dir. Mo. Dept. Pub. Safety, Jefferson City, 1985—. Decorated Legion of Merit, Bronze Star (3), Meritorious Service medal (4), Air medal (2), Joint Service Commendation medal, Army Commendation medal (2); Republic of Vietnam Cross of Gallantry with Silver Star. Mem. Nat. Eagle Scout Assn., Assn. U.S. Army, Soc. First Div., Theta Xi. Republican. Lodges: Rotary. Avocation: sailing. Office: Mo Dept Public Safety Truman State Office Bldg Jefferson City MO 65102-0749

RICE, ROGER KARL, accelerator physicist; b. Talcottville, N.Y., Nov. 1, 1953; s. Chester Slye and Priscilla Jane (Edick) R. B.A., State U. N.Y., 1975; M.S., North Tex. State U., 1979, Ph.D., 1981. Accelerator physicist Fermi Nat. Accelerator Lab., Batavia, Ill., 1979—. Office: Fermi Nat Accelerator Lab PO Box 500 Batavia IL 60510

RICE, WALTER HERBERT, U.S. judge; b. Pitts., May 27, 1937; s. Harry D. and Elizabeth L. (Braemer) R.; B.A., Northwestern U., 1958; J.D., M.B.A., Columbia U., 1962; m. Bonnie Beaman; children—Michael, Hilary, Harry. Admitted to Ohio bar, 1963; asst. county prosecutor Montgomery County (Ohio), 1964-66; asso. firm Gallon & Miller, Dayton, Ohio, 1966-69; 1st asst. Montgomery County Prosecutor's Office, 1969; judge Dayton Mcpl. Ct., 1970-71, Montgomery County Ct. Common Pleas, 1971-80, U.S. Dist. Ct. So. Dist. Ohio, 1980—; adj. prof. U. Dayton Law Sch., 1976—, bd. visitors, 1976—; chmn. Montgomery County Supervisory Council on Crime and Delinquency, 1972-74; vice chmn. bd. dirs. Pretrial Release, Inc., 1975-79. Pres. Dayton Area Council Alcoholism on and Drug Abuse, 1971-73; chmn. trustees Stillwater Health Center, Dayton, 1976-79. Recipient Excellent Jud. Service award Ohio Supreme Ct., 1976, 77, Outstanding Jud. Service award, 1973, 74, 76; Man of Yr. award Disting. Service Awards Council, Dayton, 1977. Mem. Am. Jud. Soc., Ohio Bar Assn., Dayton Bar Assn. Author papers in field. Office: 200 W 2d St Dayton OH 45402

RICH, KENNETH LOUIS, management science educator, consultant; b. N.Y.C., Mar. 6, 1937; s. Leo Herbert and Margaret (Rice) R.; m. Deborah Jean Palmer, Mar. 29, 1980; children—Andrew P., Stephanie P. B.S., Purdue U., 1959; M.B.A., Harvard U., 1961; Ph.D., U. Pa., 1969. Cert. mgmt. acctg. Mgmt. cons. Rich & Assocs., Mpls., 1972-78; asst. prof. George Mason U., Fairfax, Va., 1977-78; market research mgr. Cardiac Pacemakers, Inc., St. Paul, 1978-79; pres. Rich & Assocs., Inc., Mpls., 1979—; 3M prof. mgmt. Coll. St. Catherine, St. Paul, 1981—; tech. cons. Consumer Research Corp., Mpls., 1975—. Author computer programs; also articles in mgmt. sci. Officer, del. Republican Party, Mpls., 1973-84; bd. dirs. Lowry Hill Assn., Mpls., 1984—. Mem. Inst. Mgmt. Sci., Am. Inst. Decision Scis., Inst. Mgmt. Acctg., Tau Beta Pi, Eta Kappa Nu, Tau Kappa Epsilon. Universalist. Club: Purdue of Minn. (pres. 1979—). Avocations: bridge; micro-computers. Home and Office: 1787 Colfax Ave S Minneapolis MN 55403 Office: Dept Mgmt College of Saint Catherine 2004 Randolph Ave Saint Paul MN 55105

RICH, ROBERT JOHN, JR., computer company executive; b. Sacramento, June 4, 1943; s. Robert John and Elizabeth Jane (McDonald) R.; m. Kristine L. Hanson; children—Robert John, III, Christopher Wetherby. B.A., U. Minn.-Duluth, 1965. Mgr. comml. loan dept. Northwestern Bank, Hopkins, Minn., 1973-78; pres. Computer Maintenance and Leasing Corp., Mpls., 1978-83; pres. Use 'R Computers, Inc., Mpls., 1983—. Served to capt. USAF, 1966-72. Mem. Am. Soc. Field Service Mgmt., Am. Soc. Sales and Mktg. Execs., Greater Mpls. C. of C., Twin West C. of C. Republican. Club: Calhoun Beach. Home: 14060 Stonegate Ln Minnetonka MN 55345 Office: Use 'R Computers Inc 12800 Industrial Park Blvd Minneapolis MN 55441

RICHARD, DOUGLAS WAYNE, lawyer; b. Harvey, Ill., Jan. 13, 1955; s. Lloyd N. and Myrtle (Rost) R. B.S. in Ops. Mgmt., No. Ill. U., 1977; J.D., John Marshall Law Sch., 1980. Bar: Ill. 1980, U.S. Dist. Ct. (no. dist.) Ill. 1980, U.S. Dist. Ct. (cen. dist.) Ill. 1984. Assoc. Tate & Assocs., Chgo., 1980-81; asst. state's atty. Vermilion County State's Atty.'s Office, Danville, Ill., 1981-84; assoc. Satter, Ewing & Beyer, Pontiac, Ill., 1985—. Mem. Ill. State Bar Assn., ABA. Republican. Methodist. Home: 1200 N Main Apt 3A Pontiac IL 61764 Office: Satter Ewing & Beyer 402 N Plum PO Box 440 Pontiac IL 61764

RICHARD, JOE E., police officer; b. McClure, Ohio, Mar. 25, 1941; s. Albert R. and Mildred (Orthwein) R.; children—Terri S., Melissa D. Student, Ohio State Patrol Acad., 1960-61. Police officer Ohio State Patrol, Hamilton, 1961-69, Office of Sheriff, Butler County, Ohio, 1969-70, Trenton Police Dept., Ohio, 1970—. Mem. Internat. Assn. Police Chiefs, Ohio Police Chiefs. Lodges: Kiwanis, Masons. Home: Box 94 Trenton OH 45067 Office: 11e State St Trenton OH 45607

RICHARD, WILLIAM RALPH, research chemist; b. Bklyn., Oct. 13, 1922; s. William Ralph and Helen (Brodie) R.; m. Joan Coombs, Aug. 23, 1947; children—Carol Lucile, Suzanne Louise, Janet Elizabeth. A.B. in Chemistry, Amherst Coll., 1943; M.S. in Chemistry, U. Mich., 1947, Ph.D. in Chemistry, 1950. Research chemist Monsanto Chem. Co., Springfield, Mass., 1943-46; DuPont fellow U. Mich., Ann Arbor, 1948-50; group leader research engring. div. Monsanto, Dayton, Ohio, 1950-63, mgr. research and devel. organic div., St. Louis, 1963-74; dir. research and devel. Monsanto Indsl. Co., St. Louis, 1974—, dir. research and devel. splty. chems., 1985—; mem. environ. risk com. Chem. Mfgrs. Assn., Washington, 1980-83. Contbr. articles to profl. jours. Patentee in field. Bd. dirs. Dayton Civic Ballet, 1959-61. Mem. Am. Chem. Soc., AAAS, Soc. Risk Analysis, Nat. Conf. Advancement of Research (bd. dirs. 1982—), Soc. Research Adminstrs. (indsl. div. pres. 1982, Hartford-Nicholson award 1981). Presbyterian. Avocations: tennis; sailing. Home: 729 Delchester Ln Kirkwood MO 63122 Office: Monsanto Co 800 N Lindbergh Blvd Saint Louis MO 63167

RICHARDS, HILDA, college dean; b. St. Joseph, Mo., Feb. 2, 1936; d. Togar and Rose Avalynne (Williams) Young Ballard. B.S. cum laude, CUNY, 1961; diploma nursing St. John's Sch. Nursing, St. Louis, 1956; M.Ed., Columbia U., 1965, Ed.D., 1976; M.P.A., NYU, 1971. Dep. chief dept. psychiatry Harlem Rehab. Ctr., N.Y.C., 1969-71; prof., dir. nursing Medgar Evers Coll., CUNY, N.Y.C., 1971-76, prof., assoc. dean, 1976-79; dean Coll. Health and Human Service, Ohio U., Athens, 1979—; mem. Gov.'s Council on Disabled Persons, Columbus, Ohio, 1982-84; mem. Gov.'s State Social Service Adv. Com., Columbus, 1982—; mem. Ohio Planning Com., Am. Council Edn., 1981—. Author: (with others) Curriculum Development and People of Color: Strategies and Change, 1983. Mem., chmn. Athens, Hocking, Vinton Community Health Bd., 1980—; mem. Community Relations Com., Athens, Ohio, 1984—; mem. Fair Housing Task Force, Athens County, Ohio, 1984—; mem. exec. com., bd. dirs. Consortium for Health Edn. in Appalachia Ohio, Inc., Athens, 1982—. Recipient Rockefeller Found. award Am. Council Edn., Washington, 1976-77; USPHS trainee, NIMH, Columbia U., N.Y.C., 1963-65, Martin Luther King grantee NYU, N.Y.C., 1969-70, Gunt Found. grantee Harvard Inst. Ednl. Mgmt., Cambridge, Mass., 1981. Mem. Nat. Black Nurses Assn. (bd. dirs., 1st v.p. 1984-86), Nat. Assn. Women Deans, Admissions and Counselors, Am. Soc. Allied Health Professions (chmn. equal representation in allied health), Am. Council Edn. (mem. exec. com. council fellows), Ohio Nurses Assn. (human rights com. and psychiat. mental health practice assembly). Democrat. Avocations: needlepoint; travel. Home: 31 Grosvenor St Athens OH 45701 Office: Ohio U 011 Grosvenor Hall Athens OH 45701

RICHARDS, HOWARD DEEN, banker; b. Hancock, Mich., Sept. 5, 1950; s. George Howard and Margaret Louise (Fien) R. B.B.A., U. Mich., 1972; M.B.A., U. Colo., 1973. Asst. examiner Fed. Res. Bank, Mpls., 1974-76; corr. services officer First Bank of Mpls., 1976-79, pricing adminstr., 1979-81, exec. banking officer, 1981-85; v.p. United Fed. Savs. Bank, Roseville, Minn., 1985—; dir. First Edition Restaurants. Mem. Am. Inst. Banking, Mpls. Jaycees (fin. v.p. 1981—). Republican. Methodist. Advocations: skiing; carpentry; classic automobiles. Home: 2016 Jerrold Ave Aroen Hills MN 55112 Office: United Fed Savs Bank 1711 West County Rd B Roseville MN 55113

RICHARDS, JOHN FLEMING, investment analyst; b. Washington, Sept. 28, 1947; s. George and Ann Marie (Fleming) R.; B.A., U. Va., 1969; postgrad. Wesleyan U., 1969-70; M.B.A., U. Chgo., 1972; m. Marilyn Murray, July 22, 1972; children—Matthew J., Andrew J., Scott M. Investment analyst William Blair & Co., Chgo., 1972-81, partner investment research, 1981—. C.P.A., Ill.; chartered fin. analyst. Mem. Investment Analysts Soc. Chgo. (pres. 1983-84, dir. 1984), Am. Inst. C.P.A.s, Ill. C.P.A. Soc., Inst. Chartered Fin. Analysts (candidate curriculum com., council examiners 1984—), Am. Math. Soc. Office: 135 S LaSalle St Chicago IL 60603

RICHARDS, L. DAN, JR., college adminstrator; b. East Liverpool, Ohio, July 22, 1942; s. L. Dan and Helen E. (Gamble) R.; m. Mary Lou Curren, Aug. 19, 1967; children—Holly C., L. Daniel III. B.A., Muskingum Coll., 1964; M.A., U. Akron, 1971. Tchr., Akron Pub. Schs., Ohio, 1964-69; teaching asst., lectr. U. Akron, 1969-71; assoc. prof. North Central Tech. Coll., Mansfield, Ohio, 1971-80, dir. gen. studies, 1980-84, v.p. acad. affairs, 1984—. Contbr. articles to profl. jours. Mem. Ohio Community and Tech. Colls. Orgn. for Instructional Officers, Ohio Bd. Regents Program Rev. Subcom. Episcopalian. Office: North Central Tech Coll PO Box 698 Mansfield OH 44901

RICHARDS, LACLAIRE LISSETTA JONES (MRS. GEORGE A. RICHARDS), social worker; b. Pine Bluff, Ark.; d. Artie William and Geraldine (Adams) Jones; B.A., Nat. Coll. Christian Workers, 1953; M.S.W., U. Kans., 1956; postgrad. Columbia U., 1960; m. George Alvarez Richards, July 26, 1958; children—Leslie Rosario, Lia Mercedes, Jorge Ferguson. Psychiat. supervisory, teaching, community orgn., adminstrv. and consultative duties Hastings Regional Center, Ingleside, Nebr., 1956-60; supervisory, consultative and adminstrv. responsibilities for psychiat. and geriatric patients VA Hosp., Knoxville, Iowa, 1960-70, 71-74, Fed. women's program coordinator, 1972-74, equal employment counselor, 1969-74; chief social worker, adult female service Mental Health Inst., Cherokee, Iowa, 1974-77; outpatient social worker VA Center, Sioux Falls, S.D., 1978—, also EEO counselor; field instr. for grad. students from U. Mo., 1966-67, also equal employment opportunity counselor, 1969-70, 71-74, com. chmn., 1969-70; field instr. Drake U., 1969-70, 73, also U. Iowa, U. No. Iowa, Morningside Coll., Buena Vista Coll., Westmar Coll., Hastings Coll., Wm. Penn Coll., Central Coll.; mem. adj. asst. prof. dept. social behavior U. S.D.; instr. minority studies Augustana Coll.; mem. civil rights com. Mental Health Inst. Mem. Knoxville Juvenile Adv. Com., 1963-65, 68-70, sec., 1965-66, chmn., 1966-68; sec. Urban Renewal Citizens' Adv. Com., Knoxville, 1966-68; canvasser community fund drives, Knoxville; bd. dirs., sec., exec. com., personnel com. Vis. Nurse Assn., 1979-82; bd. dirs. Ret. Sr. Vol. Program, 1983—; mem. edn. com. 1st United Meth. Ch., Sioux Falls; bd. dirs., mem. membership devel., pub. relations and program devel. coms. YWCA, 1984—; chmn. edn. com. Nat. Assn. Colored People, 1983—. Mem. Nat. Assn. Social Workers (co-chmn. Nebr. chpt. profl. standards com. 1958-59, chmn. minority affairs com. 1979-80, 82-84, pres. S.D. chpt. 1980-82, exec. com. 1982-84, social policy and action com. 1982-84, S.D. Social Worker of Yr. 1983), Acad. Cert. Social Workers, AAUW (sec. Hastings chpt. 1958-60), S.D. AMA Aux., 7th Dist. Med. Aux. United Methodist (past Sunday sch. tchr. adult div.; mem. commn. on edn. and missions 1968-74, chmn. health and welfare commn. 1973-74, mem. edn. com. 1979—, mem. task force experimental styles ministry and leadership 1972-73, mem. adult choir, ch. and soc. com., past sr. vol. program bd. mem.). Home: 1701 Ponderosa Dr Sioux Falls SD 57103

RICHARDS, NOEL J., university official. Chancellor, U. of Wis.-LaCrosse. Office: U Wis Office of the Chancellor LaCrosse WI 54601*

RICHARDS, R. RONALD, chemistry educator; b. Wenatchee, Wash., Nov. 22, 1937; s. Ralph Riley and Matilda J. (Reichelt) R.; m. Marilyn Joan Clark; children—Rhonda, Tamara, Rodney. B.S., Seattle Pacific U., 1959; Ph.D., U. Wash., 1964. Prof. Greenville Coll., Ill., 1964—. Contbr. articles to profl. publs. Patentee method of detecting pollutants. Mem. Am. Chem. Soc. Methodist. Avocation: photography. Home: 619 E College Ave Greenville IL 62246 Office: Greenville Coll 315 College Ave Greenville IL 62246

RICHARDS, RILEY HARRY, insurance company executive; b. North Judson, Ind., Oct. 6, 1912; s. Harry J. and Kjerstie (Johnson) R.; m. Eloise Quinn Smith, May 4, 1940; children—Roy, Lynne Richards Beck. A.B., U. Calif.-Berkeley, 1934; M.B.A., Harvard U., 1937. Chartered fin. analyst. Fin. analyst Savs. Banks Trust Co., N.Y.C., 1937-40; analyst SEC, Washington, 1940-45; acct. U.S. Steel Corp., Pitts., 1945-47; sr. v.p., treas. Equitable Life Ins. Co. Iowa, Des Moines, 1945-77; dir. F.M. Hubbell Son & Co.; trustee F.M. Hubbell Estate, 1977-84, Thompson Trust, 1976—; chmn. fin. sect. Am. Life Conv., Chgo., 1970-71. Chmn. investment com. Bd. Pensions United Presbyterian Ch., Phila., 1960-72; chmn. United Presbyn. Found., N.Y.C., 1979—; chmn. Des Moines Planning and Zoning Commn., 1968-70. Mem. Des Moines Soc. Fin. Analysts (pres. 1965-66). Republican. Presbyterian. Clubs: Des Moines (dir., treas. 1969-70), Golf and Country. Lodges: Rotary, Shriners. Home: 2880 Grand Ave Des Moines IA 50312 Office: Equitable of Iowa Cos 604 Locust St Des Moines IA 50309

RICHARDS, THOMAS JEFFREY, physicist; b. Berwyn, Ill., Feb. 28, 1944; s. James Henry and Caroline Emily (Patha) R.; B.A., Lake Forest Coll., 1966; M.A., Wake Forest U., 1968; Ph.D., St. Louis U., 1972. Sr. research engr. Caterpillar Tractor Co., Peoria, Ill., 1973-76, project engr., 1976-81, staff engr., 1981—. Mem. Am. Phys. Soc., AAAS. Patentee in field. Office: Research Dept TC-E Caterpillar Tractor Co Peoria Il 61629

RICHARDS, WARREN, wholesale tobacco distribution company executive; b. Harrison County, Ind., Feb. 16, 1943; s. Virgil Denton and Luella Wilhelmina (Schoen) R.; m. Julia Ann Boone Richards, Aug. 31, 1963; children—Sara Colleen, Anne Catherine. B.S. in Pharmacy, Butler U., 1966, M.B.A., 1975. Registered pharmacist, Ind. Chief pharmacy U.S. Air Force, Beale AFB, Calif., 1967-71; staff pharmacist Haag Drug Store, Kokomo, Ind., 1971-72, store mgr., Shelbyville, Ind., 1972-74, buyer/merchandiser, 1974-79; buyer/merchandiser People's Drug, Indpls., 1979-81; gen. mgr. Wiemuth & Son Co., Terre Haute, Ind., 1981—. Mem. capt.'s com. Terre Haute Ch. Softball, 1982-83; elder, mem. mission bd. Immanuel Lutheran Ch., Terre Haute, 1983-84; v.p. br. 407, Aid Assn. for Lutherans, Terre Haute, 1983-84; mem. solicitation com. for small bus. United Way, Terre Haute, 1983; mem. Leadership Terre Haute, 1983-84. Mem. Am. Pharm. Assn., Ind. Pharmacists Assn., Ind. Candy/Tobacco Wholesaler Assn. Lodges: Rotary (Terre Haute), Elks. Home: 70 Deming Ln Terre Haute IN 47803 Office: Wiemuth & Son Co Inc 1500 Wabash Ave Terre Haute IN 47807

RICHARDS, WILLIAM EARL, retired state social services official; b. N.Y.C., Oct. 19, 1921; s. John Earl and Camily Pauline (Deravaine) R.; m. Ollum Elizabeth Sadler, Sept. 16, 1949; 1 son, William Earl. B.A. in Econ., Washburn U., 1972. Enlisted in U.S. Army, commd. and advanced through grades to lt. col., 1970; served in Asiatic-Pacific Theatre, World War II, 1943-46; supervised Am. engrs. and technicians in Philippine Islands, and Saipan, the Marianas Islands, 1946-49; test and evaluation officer, 1951; asst. maintenance officer and ammunition insp., Korea, 1951-52; ammunition storage officer, Nara, Japan, 1952-54; chief inspection div., Phila., 1954-58; ops. and storage officer, Pirmasens, W.Ger., 1958-61; tng. officer, Ft. Hamilton, Bklyn., 1961-62; contracting officer, Saigon, South Vietnam, 1962-63; asst. commr. and contracting officer's rep., Joliet, Ill., 1963-67; deputy dir. procurement, Worms, W.Ger., 1967-70; ret., 1970; staff dir. and legis. agt. NAACP, Topeka Kans., 1972; asst. dir. Kans. Commn. Alcoholism, Topeka, 1972-73, dir. Div. Social Services, Dept. Social and Rehab. Services, 1973-80, commr. income maintenance and med. services, 1980-83. Adv. com. Kans. div. Services to Children and Youth, Dept. Agr. Com. on Equal Opportunity; bd. dirs. United Way of Greater Topeka. Decorated Legion of Merit. Mem. NAACP (life), Am. Pub. Welfare Assn., Nat. Council Pub. Welfare Adminstrs. (exec. com. 1982), Kans. Conf. Social Welfare, Ret. Officers Assn., Am. Def. Preparedness Assn., Assn. U.S. Army, Washburn Alumni Assn., Alpha Phi Alpha. Clubs: Shriners, K.T.

RICHARDSON, DEAN EUGENE, See *Who's Who in America,* 43rd edition.

RICHARDSON, DEJURAN, biostatistician, educator; b. Chgo., Dec. 18, 1958; s. Susie Richardson. B.A. in Math., Northwestern U., 1981, M.S. in Stats., 1983. Math. statistician Dept. of Navy, San Diego, 1981; ops. research analyst Standard Oil of Ind., Chgo., 1982; statistician G.D. Searle Co., Skokie, Ill., 1983-84; instr. math. Northwestern U., Evanston, Ill., 1984—. Fellow NSF, 1981, CIC, 1981. Mem. Am. Statis. Assn., Math. Assn. Am. Avocations: music; piano. Office: Dept Math Northwestern U Lunt Hall Evanston IL 60201

RICHARDSON, DONALD ALAN, lawyer, consultant; b. Pitts. July 13, 1941; s. William F. Richardson and Mildred (Benton) Loughman; m. Judith Ann Regester, (dec. Oct., 1980); children—Suzanne C., Amanda G. B.B.A., U. Pitts., 1962; L.L.B., J.D., Ohio State U., 1966. Bar: Ohio 1967, U.S. Dist. Ct. Ohio 1968, U.S. Ct. Appeals 1968. Mgmt. trainee J. C. Penney Co., Columbus, Ohio, 1964-66; assoc. McLeskey & McLeskey, Columbus, 1966-69; ptnr. Taylor & Richardson, Columbus, 1969-74; atty. City of Dublin, Ohio, 1974-78, sole practice, Dublin, 1978—. Contbr. articles to profl. jour. Candidate City Council, Dublin, Ohio, 1979. chmn. City Columbus Sign Com. 1972-74, Service Station Standards Com. 1970-72, Bd. Housing Appeals, 1972-75; pres. Northwest Sertoma Club, 1970-71, trustee Dublin Community Ch., 1979-81. Served to 1st lt. USAF, 1962-66. Recipient Gold Coat Club membership Sertoma Internat., Columbus, 1970-71. Freedom medal Daus. Am. Revolution, Pitts., 1962; Citizenship medal VFW, 1962; Cert. of Appreciation, Arthritis Found. Am., 1974. Mem. ABA, Ohio State Bar Assn. Columbus Bar Assn. (chmn. mem. com. 1969, mcpl. ct. com. 1970), Ohio Peace Officers Tng. Council, Dublin Safety Town (founder, trustee 1979-81), DAV, Ret. Officers Assn. Republican. Congregationalist. Club: Sertoma Internat. Avocations: international travel; studying city structure and planning in foreign countries; fishing; reading; writing. Home: 4510 Barton Dr Sarasota FL 33582

RICHARDSON, DONALD LEE, environmental engineer; b. Mt. Vernon, Ill., Aug. 26, 1954; s. Owen Lee and Shirley Jean (King) R.; m. Susan Joan Bryden, May 16, 1980; children—Lori A., Richard D., Jill R. B.S., So. Ill. U., 1977, M.S., 1981. Registered profl. engr., Ill. Engr. Ill. EPA, Springfield, 1977-81; engr. water quality Central Ill. Pub. Service, Springfield, 1981—. Adv. Jr. Achievement, 1984. Ill. State Commn. scholar, 1972. Mem. Water Polution Control Fedn., Ill. Groundwater Assn. Avocations: stereo, home remodeling. Home: 1728 S Park Springfield IL 62704 Office: Central Ill Pub Service Co 607 E Adams Springfield IL 62701

RICHARDSON, HOWARD DEE, health and physical education and recreation educator, educational administrator; b. Salt Lake City, June 21, 1926; s. William Wilshire and Mary Emaline (Dobson) R.; m. Lorna Ann Gleave, Nov. 28, 1951; children—Wendy, Ron Howard, Mark Reed, Shelly. B.A., Westminster Coll., 1950; M.S., U. Utah, 1962, D.Ed., 1967. Life teaching cert., Utah. Instr. Salt Lake City Sch. Corp., 1951-53; assoc. prof. Westminster Coll., Salt Lake City, 1953-66; dir. athletics, phys. edn. instr. U. Utah, Salt Lake City, 1966-67; prof., dir. athletics and phys. edn. Eastern Oreg. State Coll., LaGrand, 1967-71; dean Sch. Health, Phys. Edn. and Recreation, prof., Ind. State U., Terre Haute, 1971—; editorial cons. William C. Brown Inc., Prentice Hall Inc. Author articles in field. Chmn. Ind. Gov.'s Council for Phys. Fitness, Sports Medicine, 1980—; chmn. YMCA Bldg. Fund, Salt Lake City, 1963. Served with U.S. Army, 1943-46; PTO. Honored Coll. and Univ. Adminstrs. Council, 1980; named Basketball Coach of Yr., NAIA Dist. 7, 1961, 63, 65. Mem. AAHPERD, Assn. Adminstrn. Research Profl. Council and Socs. (pres. 1981, past pres. award 1982), Nat. Assn. for Phys. Edn. in Higher Edn. (western exec. com. 1959), Phi Delta Kappa. Republican. Avocations: Writing; golf; tennis. Home: Rural Route 21 Box 422 Terre Haute IN 47802 Office: Sch Health Phys Edn and Recreation Ind State Univ Terre Haute IN 47809

RICHARDSON, JOHN AIDAN, state board administrator; b. Fargo, N.D., July 2, 1939; s. John and Norah (Jordan) R.; m. Kristin Carol Earhart, Jan. 25, 1964; children—Mark Aidan, John Joseph. B.S., U. Oreg., 1961, M.S., 1965; Ph.D., Stanford U., 1975. Counseling asst., Wash. State U., 1965-66; research asst. Stanford U. Ctr. for Research and Devel. in Teaching, 1968-69; adminstrv. intern Oreg. State System of Higher Edn., 1970-71, asst. to chancellor, 1971-75, asst. chancellor, 1975-79; commr. higher edn. Mont. U. System, Helena, 1979-81; commr. State Bd. Higher Edn. State of N.D., Bismarck, 1981—; adj. asst. prof. edn. U. Oreg., 1975-78; vis. scholar Nat. Ctr. Higher Edn. Mgmt. Systems, Boulder, Colo., 1978-79; pres. Mont. Higher Edn. Student Assistance Corp., 1980-81. Trustee, Oreg. Episcopal Sch., Portland, 1975-78; bd. dirs. Greater Mont. Found., 1979-81; commr. Western Interstate Commn. for Higher Edn., 1979-81. Served with USNR, 1961-64. Kellogg fellow, 1967-68. Mem. Am. Assn. Higher Edn., Phi Delta Theta. Office: State Bd Higher Edn State Capitol Bismarck ND 58505-0154

RICHARDSON, JOHN THOMAS, clergyman, university president; b. Dallas, Dec. 20, 1923; s. Patrick and Mary (Walsh) R.; B.A., St. Mary's Sem., Perryville, Mo., 1946; S.T.D., Angelicum U., Rome, Italy, 1951; M.A., St. Louis U., 1954. Prof. theology, dean studies Kenrick Sem., St. Louis, 1951-54; lectr. Webster Coll., 1954; dean Grad. Sch. DePaul U., Chgo., 1954-60, exec. v.p., dean faculties, 1960-81, pres., 1981—, also lectr. Coll. Law and trustee, 1955—. Home: 2233 N Kenmore Ave Chicago IL 60614 Office: 25 E Jackson Chicago IL 60604

RICHARDSON, JOSEPH DOWNS, family physician; b. Rochester, Ind., June 23, 1935; s. Charles Lester and Ruth (Downs) R.; m. Ina Marie Knight, June 23, 1976; children—Constance, Cynthia, Julia; children by previous marriage—Kimberley, Charles, Edward. A.B., Ind. U., 1957; M.D., Ind. U.-Indpls., 1960. Diplomate Am. Bd. Family Practice. Rotating intern Meml. Hosp., South Bend, Ind., 1960-61; practice medicine specializing in family medicine, Rochester, 1961—; commr. Fulton County Health, Rochester, 1974—; dir. Canterbury Manor Nursing Home, Rochester, Rochester Nursing Home. Vice committeeman 7th precinct, Rochester, 1984—; alt. del. Republican Nat. Conv., Kansas City, Mo., 1976. Served to capt. U.S. Army, 1962-63. Fellow Am. Acad. Family Physicians. Lodges: Masons, Elks, Moose. Avocations: boating, travel. Office: 115 E 11th St Rochester IN 46975

RICHARDSON, JOSEPH HILL, physician; b. Rensselaer, Ind., June 16, 1928; s. William Clark and Vera (Hill) R.; M.S. in Medicine, Northwestern U., 1950, M.D., 1953; m. Joan Grace Meininger, July 8, 1950; children—Lois N., Ellen M., James K. Intern, U.S. Naval Hosp., Great Lakes, Ill., 1953-54; fellow in medicine Cleve. Clinic, 1956-59; individual practice medicine specializing in internal medicine and hematology, Marion, Ind., 1959-67, Ft. Wayne, Ind.,

1967—. Served to lt. MC USNR, 1954-56. Diplomate Am. Bd. Internal Medicine. Fellow ACP, AAAS; mem. Am. Fedn. for Clin. Research, Am. Med. Writers Assn., AMA. Mason. Contbr. articles to med. jours. Home: 8726 Fortuna Way Fort Wayne IN 46815 Office: 3010 E State Blvd Fort Wayne IN 46805

RICHARDSON, KEITH ERWIN, biochemistry educator, consultant; b. Tucson, Apr. 22, 1928; s. Edmund Arthur and Ivie (Romney) R.; m. Dorthene Beck, June 5, 1952; children—DeeAnn, Jay Scott, Kerri Lee, Steven Grant, Mark, Stacy. B.S., Brigham Young U., 1952, M.S., 1955; Ph.D., Purdue U., 1958. Post doctoral fellow Mich. State U., East Lansing, 1958-60; prof. Ohio State U., 1960—; cons. Ohio State Dept. Health, Columbus, 1979—. Contbr. articles to profl. jours. Patentee in field. Served to cpl. U.S. Army, 1952-54; NIH grantee, 1960-82. Mem. Am. Inst. Nutrition, Am. Soc. Biol. Chemists, Am. Soc. Plant Physiology, AAAS, Sigma Xi. Republican. Mormon. Office: Ohio State Univ 1645 Neil Ave Columbus OH 43210

RICHARDSON, LARRY JACK, geologist; b. Kansas City, Mo., Feb. 16, 1946; s. Donald Eugene and Hilda Elizabeth (Smith) R.; m. Linda Ruth Colgin, Jan. 17, 1965; children—Bradford, Jennifer. B.A., Wichita State U., 1971, M.S., 1977. Field geologist Hydrocarbon Survey, Inc., Wichita, Kans., 1972-74; petroleum geologist Texaco Inc., Tulsa, 1974-76, Tex. Oil & Gas Corp., Wichita, 1976-79; Pickrell Drilling Co., Wichita, 1979—. Contbr. articles to profl. jours. Chmn. United Way, Derby, Kans., 1979; chmn. Kans. Leadership Seminar, 1983, 85, program chmn., 1982, 84; chmn. celebration July 4th, Derby, 1982—. Mem. Am. Assn. Petroleum Geologists (com. rules and procedures, chmn. conv. 1983, treas. mid-continent sect.), Kans. Geol. Soc. (sec. treas. 1984, dir. 1985—), Jaycees (award 1979, 81, Starks K. Vincent award 1980, James O. Blass award 1981, Senatorship award 1984). Club: Derby Running (pres. 1983—). Avocations: running, working with home computer. Office: Pickrell Drilling Co 205 Litwin Bldg 110 N Market Wichita KS 67202

RICHARDSON, MICHAEL EDWARD, city official; b. Mpls., July 21, 1942; s. Vincent Frederick and Libby M. (Key) R.; m. Mary Ann DeMark, Aug. 29, 1964; children—Sarah, David. B.S., U. Wis.-Whitewater, 1964; M.A. (grad. asst.), Eastern Mich. U., 1967; M.P.A., No. Ill. U., 1980. Sr. planner Bi-State Plan Commn., Rock Island, Ill., 1965-67; chief planner N.E. Wis. Plan Commn., Appleton, 1971-72; dir. dept. planning City of Des Plaines (Ill.), 1972-82, dir. dept. mcpl. devel., 1982-85; dir. Dept. Community Devel., Hanover Park, Ill., 1985—. Pres., bd. dirs. N.W. Mcpl. Fed. Credit Union; lectr. Eastern Mich. U., U. Alaska. Mem. N.E. Ill. Plan Commn. Task Force; team mgr. Hoffman Estates (Ill.) Baseball Assn.; mem. planning/bldg. edn. com. Harper Coll., 1983—. Served with Intelligence, USAF, 1967-71. Decorated Bronze Star, USAF commendation medal; recipient Outstanding Grad. award USAF Officer Tng. Sch., 1967, recognition award Nat. Assn. Women in Constrn., 1985. Mem. Internat. City Mgmt. Assn., Am. Inst. Cert. Planners (charter), Am. Planning Assn., N.W. Bldg. Ofcls. and Code Adminstrs. Roman Catholic. Author: Flood Information Handbook, 1973; contbr. articles to profl. jours. Office: Dept Econ Devel 2121 W Lake St Hanover Park IL 60103

RICHARDSON, MYRTLE, retired abstracter, former judge; b. Jefferson County, Ohio, July 2, 1907; d. Thomas and Blanche (Whitecotton) Heinselman; student Kansas State Tchrs. Coll., 1926; A.A., Dodge City Community Coll., 1978; m. Harold Richardson, Mar. 4, 1929 (div.); 1 dau., Nancy Lee Richardson Ridgway. Tchr. pub. schs. Edwards County, Kans., 1924-28; reporter, advertiser Kinsley Graphic, Kinsley, Kans., 1928-35; editor, advt. mgr. S. Standard, McMinnville, Tenn., 1935-36; mgr. Kinsley Graphic, 1937-41; abstracter H.F. Thompson, Kinsley, 1943-54; editor Kinsley Mercury, 1954-57; abstracter, Kinsley, 1957-84; owner, mgr. Richardson Abstract Co.; probate judge, Kinsley, 1958-68; police judge, City of Kinsley, 1958-68. Bd. dirs. United Drive, 1947-57; bd. dirs. Edwards County chpt. ARC, 1940-50; community and project leader 4-H Club, 1943-52, Edwards County 4-H Who's Who Club, 1943-52; pres. PTA, 1940-44; vice chmn. Edwards County Dem. Central Com., 1956-81, chmn., 1981-84; charter mem. Edwards County Dem. Women's Federated Club, pres., 1970-84, dist. dir., 1981-82. Mem. C. of C. (Sec.-mgr. 1947-54), Edwards County Hist. Soc. (historian 1950-65), Nat. Council Juvenile Ct. Judges, Internat. Platform Assn., S. Central Kans. Probate Judges Assn. (pres. 1966). Author: Oft' Told Tales, a history of Edwards County, Kansas, to 1900, 1976; The Great Next Year Country, 1983. Home: 120 N 2d St Kinsley KS 67547

RICHARDSON, PHILIP EDWIN, real estate development and construction company executive; b. Logansport, Ind., July 1, 1953; s. Omer E. and Arlette (G.) R.; m. Katherine Reishus, June 29, 1974; children—Jennifer, Kristin. Student U. Wis.-Superior, 1971-72; B.S. in Bus. and Econ., Gustavus Adolphus Coll., 1975. Exec. v.p. Richardson Assocs., Inc., Wheaton, Ill., 1975—. Small bus. adv. bd. U.S. Rep. Thomas Corcoran, Aurora, Ill., 1983-84; pres. ch. council Geneva Lutheran Ch., 1984—. Nominated for First Decade award Gustavus Adolphus Coll., 1985. Mem. Nat. Assn. Home Builders (bd. dirs. 1984—), Home Builders Assn. Ill., (area v.p. 1985, bd. dirs. 1983-84), No. Ill. Home Builders Assn. (pres. 1984). Home: 734 Nordic Ct Batavia IL 60510 Office: Richardson Assocs Inc 330 Naperville Rd Wheaton IL 60187

RICHARDSON, ROBERT OWEN, lawyer; b. Gallatin, Mo., Sept. 7, 1922; s. Denver Oscar and Opal (Wellman) R.; m. Carroll Sparks, July 7, 1951 (div.); children—Robert Steven, Linda Colleen; m. 2d, Viola Kapantais Wempe, Dec. 22, 1977. B.S. in Physics, Drury Coll., 1946; LL.B., George Washington U., 1954, J.D., 1968; M.S., Fla. Inst. Tech., 1977. Bar: U.S. Dist. Ct. (D.C.) 1954, U.S. Patent Office 1954, U.S. Ct. Customs and Patent Appeals 1958, Calif. 1958, N.H. 1961, Iowa 1976, U.S. Supreme Ct. 1961, Can. Patent Office, 1962, U.S. Ct. Appeals (fed. cir.) 1982. Patent examiner U.S. Patent Office, Washington, 1949-54; patent atty. Navy Electronics Lab., San Diego, 1954-56, Gen. Dynamics, San Diego, 1956-60; chief patent counsel Sanders Assoc., Nashua, N.H., 1960-62; patent atty. TRW, Canoga Park, Calif., 1963-64, McDonnell Douglas, Santa Monica, Calif., 1964-75; patent counsel U.S. Army Armament Munitions Chem. Command, Rock Island, Ill., 1975-85; patent arbitrator Am. Arbitration Assn., 1984—; judge pro tem Los Angeles Mcpl. Ct., 1967-68. Author: How To Get Your Own Patent, 1981. Democratic nominee for Congress from Mo. 6th Dist., 1951. Served to lt. comdr. USNR, 1942-73. Mem. Govt. Patent Lawyer's Assn., Am. Patent Law Assn., Patent Law Assn. San Diego, Patent Law Assn. Los Angeles, Patent Law Assn. Boston, Patent Law Assn. Iowa. Lodges: Masons, Shriners.

RICHARDSON, ROY JOHN, social services administrator, therapist; b. St. Paul, Sept. 14, 1938; s. Charles J. and Grace E. (Sandbrink) R.; m. Bonnie Merida Sigstad, Oct. 15, 1960 (div. Feb. 1972); children—Glen, Joanne, Elizabeth, Mark, Tracy, Jon. B.A., Met. State U., St. Paul, 1981; M.S., Calif. Coast U., Santa Ana, 1985, postgrad., 1985—. Cert. chem. dependency practitioner. Acct., 1960-75; addictions therapist, St. Paul, 1976-81; dir. Dakota County Mental Health, South St. Paul, Minn., 1980-81, Parkview Chem. Dependency Program, Pueblo, Colo., 1981-83; exec. dir. Fountain Ctrs., Minn., Iowa, Ind., Sweden, 1983—. Author/researcher: Adult Chemical Dependency Diagnosis, 1980; Adolescent Chemical Dependency Diagnosis, 1981. State of Minn. grantee, 1984-85. Mem. Minn. Assn. Treatment Programs (bd. dirs. 1983—, mem. exec. com. 1985—), Minn. Chem. Dependency Assn. (bd. dirs. 1984-85), Am. Coll. Addiction Treatment Adminstrs., Nat. Assn. Alcoholism Treatment Programs, Mensa. Avocations: travel; languages; weaving. Home: 909 Janson Albert Lea MN 56007 Office: 408 Fountain St Albert Lea MN 56007

RICHARDSON, TERRY LEE, industrial technology educator; b. Cambridge, Nebr., Feb. 16, 1939; s. Lee Willard and Marjorie Deloris (Fabian) R.; m. Lynda Fern Payne, Nov. 25, 1960; children—Bradley Todd, Eric Lee. B.A., Kearney State Coll., 1962, M.S., 1966; Ed.S., Kans. State Coll., 1971, Ph.D., 1976. Cert. tchr., S.D. Instr., prin. Shickley Schs., Nebr., 1962-65; grad. asst. Kearney State Coll., Nebr., 1965-66; lectr. Indsl. Arts Curriculum Project workshop Kans. State Coll., Pittsburg, 1971; instr. indsl. edn. No. State Coll., Aberdeen, S.D., 1966-78, head dept. indsl. tech., 1979—; cons. Midwest Extruders, Webster, S.D., Viking, Rubber Co., Mpls., Cardinal Tool Co., Aberdeen, Dept. Elem. and Secondary Edn. S.D. Author: Modern Industrial Plastics, 1974; A Guide to Metrics, 1978; Modern Industrial Plastics, 1979; Plastics, 1983. Editor (newsletter) Disseminator. Mem. New Tech. Com., Aberdeen. Mem. Am. Vocat. Assn. (life), Am. Indsl. Arts Assn. (life), Am. Council Indsl. Arts Tchr. Edn., Epsilon Pi Tau (laureate citation), Phi Delta Kappa (pres. 1978). Republican. Methodist. Lodges: Elks, Kiwanis. Avocations: cabinet making; gunsmithing. Home: 1540 S Lloyd Aberdeen SD 57401 Office: Northern State College Aberdeen SD 57401

RICHARDSON, WILLIAM HENRY, consultant civil engineer; b. Oak Park, Ill., June 10, 1929; s. Andrew William and Jean (Robinson) R.; m. Marie Therese Pembroke, July 11, 1953; children—Kevin William, Andrew William, Timothy John. Student, Wright Jr. Coll., 1947-48; B.S.C.E., U. Ill., 1952; postgrad. student U. Louisville, 1954-57. Registered profl. engr., Ill., Ind., Ky., Mich., Wis., Ariz., Ohio, N.J. Civil engr. Alvord, Burdick & Howson, Chgo., 1952-65, ptnr., 1965—; preparer valuation studies; testified before state comms. for United Utilities Co., Ariz., Gary-Hobart Water Corp., Ind., Kokomo, Ind., Louisville Water Co., Farmers Br., Grand Prairie, Tex., Chgo., Peoria, Ill., Alton, Ill., Marion, Ohio; engr. water supply, Monrovia, Liberia, various locations through U.S.; engr. water pollution control facilities, Monrovia, various locations throughout U.S.; preparer water supply reports La Paz, Bolivia, Lagos, Nigeria, Istanbul, Turkey; preparer water rate studies Gary-Hobart Water Corp., Louisville Water Co., Tarrant County Improvement Dist. No. 1, Tex., Monrovia, various towns in Ill. Contbr. articles to profl. jours. Recipient Disting. Alumni award U. Ill. Civil Engring. Alumni Assn., 1984. Fellow ASCE (bd. dirs. Ill. sect. 1977); mem. Am. Water Works Assn. (pres. 1984-85, Fuller award 1984), Western Soc. Engrs. (pres. 1982-83, Octave Chanute medal 1981), Am. Acad. Environ. Engrs. (diplomate), Water Pollution Control Fedn., Nat. Soc. Profl. Engrs., Internat. Water Supply Assn. Clubs: Union League (Chgo.). Elgin Country. Lodge: Elks. Avocations: golf, sports, travel, reading. Home: 965 Webster Ln Des Plaines IL 60016 Office: Alvord Burdick & Howson 20 N Wacker Dr Chicago IL 60606

RICHEY, ROBERT WAYNE, educational administrator; b. Bradley, Ill., July 6, 1928; s. Robert Walter and Ina Lee (Thompson) R.; B.A. with honors, So. Ill. U., 1954, M.A., 1958; m. Anita Joann Sweeney, Jan. 7, 1950; children—Robert Bruce, Rebecca Lynn, Pamela Ann, Mary Beth (dec.). Budget officer State of Kans., Topeka, 1956-66; exec. sec. Iowa Bd. Regents, Des Moines, 1966—. Mem. Iowa Coordinating Council for Post High Sch. Edn., 1969—; mem. Iowa Planning Council on Developmental Disabilities, 1974—; mem. nat. adv. council Nat. Center for Higher Edn., 1974—; mem. Iowa Higher Edn. Facilities Commn., 1967-71; mem. adv. com. to Nat. Commn. on Correctional Edn., 1974-76, Iowa Coll. Aid Commn., 1981 and various others. Served with U.S. Army, 1946-47. Mem. State Higher Edn. Exec. Officers, commn., 1981 and various others. Office: Grimes State Office Bldg Des Moines IA 50319

RICHIE, ERNEST CARL, mfg. co. exec.; b. Mannheim, Germany, Aug. 25, 1912; s. Carl and Maria (Aberle) R.; came to U.S., 1954, naturalized, 1959; M.S. in Electronics, Tech. U. Berlin, 1936; m. Gertrude E. Heyartz, Apr. 22, 1948; children—Peter Carl, Patricia Monica, Raymond Ronald. Mgr. electronics factory Gen. Electric Co., Buenos Aires, 1938-54, dir., 1952-54; works mgr. tuner div. Sarkes Tarzian, Inc., Bloomington, Ind., 1954-77; pres. Tuner Service Corp., Bloomington, 1965—; gen. mgr. Sarkes Tarzian Mexicana, 1967-77; exec. v.p. Eastern Electronic Co., Taipei, 1970-77; pres. Cableconverter Service Corp., Bloomington, 1977-78; cons. Tonfunk, Karlsruhe, Germany, 1961, Dean Bros., Indpls., 1961-65. Author: Appliances, 1945; Radio Equipment for FM, 1945; contbr. articles to profl. jours. Home: 316 Lakewood Dr Bloomington IN 47401 Office: Tuner Service Corp 537 S Walnut St Bloomington IN 47401

RICHIE, WINSTON HENRY, dentist; b. Jersey City, Sept. 18, 1925; s. William Frederick and Celeste (Strode) R.; m. Beatrice, Sept. 5, 1953; children—Winston, Jr., Beth, Laurel, Anne. B.S., Western Res. U., 1948, D.D.S., 1952. Gen. practice dentistry, Shaker Heights, Ohio, 1953—. Councilman, City of Shaker Heights, 1970-82; exec. dir. East Suburban Council for Open Communities, 1984—. Served with USN, 1944-46. Mem. ADA, Ohio Dental Assn., Cleve. Dental Soc. Democrat. Home: 2741 Green Rd Shaker Heights OH 44122 Office: 16611 Chagrin Blvd Shaker Heights OH 44120

RICHMAN, DAVID PAUL, neurologist, researcher; b. Boston, June 9, 1943; s. Harry S. and Anne (Goodkin) R.; m. Carol Mae von Bastian, Aug. 31, 1969; children—Sarah Ann, Jacob Charles. A.B., Princeton U., 1965; M.D., Johns Hopkins U., 1969. Diplomate Am. Bd. Psychiatry and Neurology. Intern, asst. resident in medicine Albert Einstein Coll. Medicine, N.Y.C., 1969-71; resident in neurology Mass. Gen. Hosp., Boston, 1971-73, chief resident in neurology, 1973-74; instr. neurology Harvard Med. Sch., Boston, 1975-76; asst. prof. neurology U. Chgo., 1976-80, assoc. prof. dept. neurology and com. on immunology, 1981-85, prof. dept. neurology and com. on immunology, 1985—; mem. com. Nat. Inst. Aging, NIH, 1984—. Mem. AAAS, Am. Assn. Immunologists, Am. Acad. Neurology, Phi Beta Kappa, Sigma Xi. Office: Dept Neurology U Chgo 5841 S Maryland Ave Chicago IL 60637

RICHMOND, JAYNE ELISE, counseling educator; b. Hanover, N.H., May 24, 1956; d. Warren and Doris (Samuels) R.; m. Joseph Trava Pittle, Dec. 14, 1980. B.A., U. Fla., 1978, M.A., 1980, postgrad., 1980, Ph.D., 1982. Asst. prof. counseling and student personnel Kans. State U., Manhattan, 1982—. Contbr. articles to profl. jours. Bd. dirs. Riley County Mental Health Assn., 1983—. Price scholar, 1982. Mem. Am. Assn. Counseling and Devel. (research grantee 1984), Am. Coll. Personnel Assn. (research grantee 1984), Nat. Assn. Women Deans, Adminstrs., and Counselors (pres. 1983—, research grantee 1984), Kans. Coll. Personnel Assn. (pres. 1984—), Nat. Student Personnel Adminstrs. (coordinator women's network Region IV West 1983—). Democrat. Avocations: weaving; reading; theatre. Home: 726 Ridgewood Dr Manhattan KS 66502 Office: Kans State U 329 Bluemont Hall Manhattan KS 66506

RICHTER, ROBERTA BRANDENBURG (MRS. J. PAUL RICHTER), educator; b. Osborn, Ohio, Dec. 29; d. Warren F. and Mary M. (Davis) Brandenburg; student Miami-Jacobs Coll., 1930, Wittenberg U., 1930-31, Coll. Music, U. Cin., 1931-32, U. Dayton, 1954, 64; B.S., Miami U., Oxford, Ohio, 1958, M.Ed., 1959; postgrad. Wright State U., 1966-70, Ohio State U., 1969; m. Jean Paul Richter, Oct. 6, 1934; 1 son, James Paul. Bus. mgr. T.D. Peffley, Inc., 1929-32; sec., prodn. mgr. Delco Products div. Gen. Motors, 1932-34; exec. sec. LWV, 1935-38, Elder & Johnston Dept. Store, 1938-40; cts. and conv. reporter Montgomery County, 1940-46; adminstrv. asst. Ch. Fedn. Greater Dayton (Ohio), 1946-50; audio-visual cons. schs., chs. Twyman Films, 1950-53; legal asst. Nadlin Law Offices, 1953-58; instr. stenotype, office practice Miami-Jacobs Coll., Dayton, 1952-59; tchr. stenotype and bus. edn., guidance counselor Stebbins High Sch., Dayton, 1958-81; vocat. guidance coordinator Mad River Planning Dist., Montgomery County, Ohio, 1968-74; test coordinator Miami U. dist. Ohio Achievement Tests, State Bd. Edn.; adviser Nat. Honor Soc.; lectr. in field; prof. cellist; instr. workshops in stenotype (machine shorthand) and ct. reporting, prof. Wright State U., Dayton, 1970—; owner Dayton Stenographic Studio. Supt., tchr., adviser youth div. Grace United Meth. Ch., Dayton, 1942-72, sec. adminstrv. bd., 1940—, past pres. Ex-cel Club, mem. council on ministries, 1970-73, work area, Christian social concerns, Christian Edn. Commn., Christian Missions, Women's Soc. Christian Service; counselor Camp Miniwanca, Am. Youth Found., 1953-68; circle leader United Meth. Women, 1976—. Mem. Am., Ohio, Miami Valley personnel and guidance assns., Nat. Bus. Tchrs. Assn., Ohio Bus. Tchrs. Assn., Am., Ohio sch. counselor assns., Nat. Shorthand Reporters Assn., Nat., Ohio edn. assns., Nat. Vocat. Guidance Assn., Ohio Assn. Counselors, Deans and Adminstrs., Dayton Bus. Soc. (v.p. 1969-79), Internat. Platform Assn., AAUW, Pub. Speaker Bur., Council World Affairs, Delphian (past pres.), League Women Voters (past pres., dir., treas.), World Trade Club, Greater Dayton C. of C., Bus. and Profl. Women, Progressive Mother's Club Alumni, Pi Omega Pi. Clubs: Order Eastern Star, Progressive Mothers (chmn. program Dayton 1969-70), World Traveler. Author numerous ednl. handbooks, pamphlets. Contbr. articles to profl. jours. Home: 3865 Seiber Ave Dayton OH 45405

RICHTER, ROY, research scientist; b. Bklyn., Aug. 25, 1956; s. Sol and Hannah (Bean) R.; m. Anne Eisen; children—Stefan Eisen, Dana Eisen. B.S. in Math., Rensselaer Poly. Inst., 1975, B.S. in Physics, 1975; M.S. in Physics, Cornell U., 1979, Ph.D. in Physics, 1982. Postdoctoral fellow physics dept. Mont. State U., Bozeman, 1981-82; postdoctoral fellow physics dept. GM Research Labs., Warren, Mich., 1982, sr. research scientist, 1982-85, staff research scientist, 1985—. Mem. Am. Phys. Soc., Am. Vacuum Soc. Home: 603 Spring St Ann Arbor MI 48103 Office: GM Research Labs Physics Dept Warren MI 48090

RICK, FRANKLIN RICHARD, health care company executive; b. Midlothian, Ill., June 3, 1945; s. Jess Wilbur and Virginia Maryann (Rolston) R.; m. Carolyn Yvonne Carstens, Aug. 14, 1965; children—Barbara Susan, Jennifer Louise. B.A. in Acctg. and Econs., Luther Coll., Decorah, Iowa, 1967; postgrad. Claremont Grad. Sch., 1984. C.P.A., Minn. Audit mgr. Touche Ross, Mpls., 1967-79; dir. audit Medtronic, Inc., Mpls., 1979-81, dir. acctg., 1981-83, corp. controller, 1983—; dir. Medtronic Found., Mpls., 1984—. Coordinator Minnetonka 4-H Club, Minn., 1978—; fin. adviser Dakota County Vo-Tech Inst., St. Paul, 1978-80, City of Minnetonka, 1980-82; pres. Minnetonka Luth. Ch., 1983—. Mem. Am. Inst. C.P.A.s, Nat. Assn. Accts. (nat. dir. 1982-83, Mem. of Yr. 1969-70), Minn. Soc. C.P.A.s, Richfield Jaycees (bd. dirs. 1974-77). Republican. Lutheran. Clubs: Mpls. Athletic, Northwest Tennis. Avocations: cross country skiing, bowling, tennis, crafts, reading. Home: 15879 Tonkawood Dr Minnetonka MN 55345 Office: Medtronic Inc PO Box 1453 3055 Old Hwy 8 Minneapolis MN 55440

RICK, GREGORY GEORGE PHILIP, JR., gastroenterologist; b. Kansas City, Mo., Feb. 11, 1940; s. Gregory George Philip and Ruth (Weideman) R.; m. Phyllis Ann Hall, Aug. 11, 1962; children—Gregory G. III, John Philip, Brooke Elizabeth. A.B., Harvard U., 1962; M.D., Kansas U., 1966. Diplomate Am. Bd. Internal Medicine. Resident in internal medicine and gastroenterology Mayo Clinic, Rochester, Minn., 1967-71; practice medicine specializing in gastroenterology Gastrointestinal Assocs., Kansas City, Kans., and Kansas City, Mo., 1973—; pres. med. staff Shawnee Mission Med. Ctr., Kans., 1979. Served to maj. USAF, 1971-73. Mem. AMA, ACP, Kansas City Southwest Clin. Soc., Midwest Soc. Gastrointestinal Endocrinology (pres. 1980-82). Club: Milburn Country (Overland Park, Kans.). Avocations: golf; photography; fishing. Home: 17951 Berryhill Dr Stillwell KS 66085 Office: 8901 W 74th St Suite 372 Shawnee Mission KS 66204

RICKARDS, COLIN WILLIAM, journalist, author, broadcaster, business consultant; b. Purley, Surrey, Eng., Dec. 15, 1937; s. Arthur Leon and Helga Roer (Beck) R.; m. Ida Crosby, June 1, 1974; 1 son, Damian Colin. Student pub. schs. Jr. reporter Beaverbrook Newspapers, London, 1954-56, sr. reporter, 1958-65; with Internat. Pub. Co., London, 1965-66; fgn. corr. Daily Telegraph, The Times, Daily Express and Fin. Times, BBC, 1966-69; editor Caribbean Yr. Book, 1975-80; mng. editor Caribbean Bus. News, Toronto, Can., 1970—; bus. editor Radio Can. Internat., 1982—; pres. Caribbean Consultancy Services; mem. central council Brit. Caribbean Assn., London, 1960-69. Served with RAF, 1956-58. Mem. English Westerners' Soc. (exec. com. 1959-64), Co. of Mil. Historians, Nat. Assn. and Centre for Outlaw and Lawman History (dir. 1979-80), Order of Indian Wars. Presbyterian. Author: Caribbean Power, 1963; Buckskin Frank Leslie, 1964; Bowler Hats and Stetsons, 1966; Mysterious Dave Mather, 1967; The Man from Devil's Island, 1968; Charles Littlepage Ballard, 1968; How Pat Garrett Died, 1970; The Gunfight at Blazer's Mill, 1974. Office: 111 Queen St E Suite 332 Toronto ON M5C 1S2 Canada

RICKBEIL, CLARA EVELYN SHELLMAN (MRS. RAYMOND E. RICKBEIL), club woman; b. Gibson City, Ill.; d. Kilian and Anna Marie (Johnson) Shellman; grad. Brown's Bus. Coll., Champaign, Ill., 1922; student U. Ill., 1927-28; m. Raymond Earl Rickbeil, May 8, 1930. Office sec. Ford County Farm Bur., Gibson City, Ill., 1922-26; secretarial position Raymond E. Rickbeil, C.P.A., Springfield, Ill., 1928-61, Ernst & Ernst, Springfield, 1961-65. Program chmn. 21st dist. Ill. Fedn. Women's Clubs, 1968-69, corr. sec., 1969-71, dir., 1971-73; mem. nat. adv. bd. Am. Security Council; mem. Republican Women's Club Sangamon County, Nat. Fedn. Rep. Women Mem. Sangamon County Farm Bur., Child and Family Service Sangamon County; mem. Abraham Lincoln Meml. Garden Fund, Inc.; bd. dirs. Carrie Post King's Daus. Home for Women, 1967-69, also mem. Willing Circle. Recipient award for work pub. accounting legislation Ill. Soc. C.P.A.'s, 1956. Mem. U. Ill. Alumni Assn., Am. Legion Aux., YWCA, Sangamon County Hist. Soc., Meml. Hosp. Aux., Abraham Lincoln Assn., Am. Assn. Ret. Persons. Republican. Presbyterian. Mem. Order Eastern Star. Clubs: Springfield Woman's (reception com. 1962-63, social com. 1963-64, corr. sec. 1972-74), Mariama (chpt. chmn., mem. bd. 1969-71), Amateur Musical, Zonta (treas. 1954-57, finance chmn. 1957, 63, 66, service chmn. and mem. service com. 1953-62, mem. fin. com. 1967-83), Sangamo, U. Ill. Presidents; Three Hills Extension Homemakers (reporter 1982) (Kerrville, Tex.). Home: 937 Feldkamp Ave Springfield IL 62704

RICKE, DENNIS FRANK, media educator, consultant; b. Elmhurst, Ill., July 12, 1948; s. Cyril Timothy and Helen Jane (Glancey) R.; m. Linda Ellen Schultz, Mar. 20, 1971; children—Kimberly Ann, Matthew Steven. B.A., So. Ill. U., 1970, M.A., 1972; postgrad. No. Ill. U., U. Ill. Mem. media staff Sch. Dist. 108, Roselle, Ill., 1972-73, history instr. 1973-74; media specialist Sch. Dist. 303, St. Charles, Ill., 1974—; media cons. Singer Vocat. Edn., Chgo., 1982—; curriculum developer St. Charles Sch. Dist., 1983—. Author: Struggle for Equality: Illinois Blacks through the Civil War, 1974 (Leah M. Reef award 1974). Dep. registrar Kane County Clks., Geneva, Ill., 1976—. Reef scholar So. Ill. U., 1972; Title IV Fed. grantee; mem. Gifted Council State Ill., 1975-78. Mem. Ill. State Hist. Soc. (life), NEA, Ill. Edn. Assn., St. Charles Edn. Assn. (v.p., negotiator, rep. assembly 1978). Avocations: computer science; photography. Home: 1810 Walden Circle Aurora IL 60506 Office: Dist 303 9th and Oak St St Charles IL 60174

RICKENBACH, FRANCINE WOLF, association executive; b. Pitts., June 13, 1950; d. Edward and Sylvia (Harton) Wolf; m. Bruce Rickenbach, Mar. 25, 1972. B.A., Antioch Coll., 1972. Librarian, Green County Dist. Library, Yellow Springs, Ohio, 1973-77; coordinator activities Courthouse Sq., Dayton, Ohio, 1977-78; mgmt. exec. Bell PubliCom, Dayton, 1978-84; pres. Mgmt. Excellence Inc., Dayton, 1984—; exec. dir. North Am. Soc. Corp. Planning, Dayton, 1978-85, Titanium Devel. Assn., Dayton, 1983—. Mem. Am. Soc. Assn. Execs. Office: Mgmt Excellence Inc 11 W Monument Ave Suite 510 PO Box 2307 Dayton OH 45401

RICKERT, ROBERT CHARLES, chemist; b. Chgo., Dec. 3, 1948; s. William Herman and Sylvia (Simon) R.; m. Valerie Maria De Los Rios, June 11, 1978. B.S., Ill. Inst. Tech., 1970, Ph.D., 1976. Paint formulator Martin-Senour Paint Co., Chgo., 1968; chemist Nalco Chem. Co., Chgo., 1969-70; water treatment chemist First Chgo. Bldg. Corp., 1974-75; postdoctoral researcher U. Chgo., 1975-76, Ill. Inst. Tech., Chgo., 1976-76; teaching postdoctoral Marquette U., Milw., 1976-77; lectr. Loyola U., Chgo., 1977; chmn. dept. chemistry Mundelein Coll., Chgo., 1977-80; lab. mgr. Custom Organics, Chgo., 1980—. Contbr. articles to profl. jours. Indsl. rep. CIC High Sch. Career Conf., 1982-84. NSF grantee, 1978. Mem. Am. Chem. Soc., AAAS, Smithsonian Inst., Nat. Geog. Soc., Phi Lambda Upsilon. Christian Church. Avocations: shooting, archery, scuba; clarinet. Office: Custom Organics Inc 1445 W 42d St Chicago IL 60609

RICKERT, SHIRLEY ROSE, educator; b. Huntington County, Ind., Apr. 19, 1936; d. Paul H. and Marguerite P. (Brown) Gressley; m. Garl E. Miles, Jan. 21, 1956 (div. 1969); m. Roger Mark Rickert, June 24, 1976; children by previous marriage—Terrance Wayne, Timothy Garl, Tamarah Lynne. A.A.S., Purdue U., 1969, B.S., 1973; M.A., Western Mich. U., 1974; Ed.D., Ball State U., 1977. Cert. tchr., Ind. Mobility specialist, dir. edn. blind Anthony Wayne Rehab. Ctr., Ft. Wayne, Ind., 1969-77; itinerant tchr. visually handicapped Ft. Wayne Community Schs., 1977-79; prof. dept. supervision Purdue U., Ft. Wayne, 1979—; condr. workshops in field. Mem. Mayor's Commn. on Archtl. Barriers, Ft. Wayne, 1972-78, Ft. Wayne Women's Bur., 1980—. Mem. Am. Soc. Tng. and Devel. (chpt. sec.), AAUW, Am. Assn. Workers for Blind. Lodge: Order Eastern Star. Office: Purdue U at Fort Wayne N288 2101 Coliseum Blvd E Fort Wayne IN 46805

RICKETTS, GARY EUGENE, animal scientist; b. Willard, Ohio, Aug. 2, 1935; s. Franklin Edward and Berthalda Maria (Albright) R.; m. Audrey May Wheeler, Sept. 14, 1958; children—Dawn, John, Mark. B.S., Ohio State U., 1957, M.S., 1960, Ph.D., 1963. Registered profl. animal scientist. Livestock extension specialist U. Ill.-Urbana, 1964—; lctrs. in field; judge state and nat. shows. Contbr. articles to profl. and livestock jours. Coach, Little League, Urbana, 1972-75, 1980-83; leader 4-H Club, Urbana; active various coms. United Meth. Ch. Recipient G.R. Carlisle Extension award Dept. Animal Sci., 1979; Spl. Leadership award Ill. Sheep Industry, 1984; Sustained Excellence award Ill. Coop. Extension Service, 1984. Mem. Am. Soc. Animal Sci. (Extension award 1984, Young Scientist award in extension Midwest sect. 1971), Ill. Red Angus Assn. (Beef Booster award 1971); Epsilon Sigma Phi (Continuous Extension Leadership award 1984). Republican. Avocations: fishing, cards, reading. Home: 2506 S Cottage Grove Urbana IL 61801 Office: Dept Animal Sci 326 Mumford Hall 1301 W Gregory Dr Urbana IL 61801

RICKSECKER, RALPH EDWARD, metallurgical consultant; b. Cleve., Sept. 9, 1912; s. George Adulphus and Margaret (Tobold) R.; m. Ruth Arlene Iliff, Aug. 24, 1939; children—Ralph Edward, Ruth Ann. B.S., Case Western Res. U., 1944, M.S., 1950. Successively chem. analyst, chief chem. process metallurgist, chief metallurgist, dir. corp. metallurgy Chase Brass & Copper

Co., Cleve., 1930-77; metall. cons., Cleve., 1978—. Contbr. articles on copper and copper alloys to profl. jours. Republican. Mem. Disciples of Christ. Avocations: growing plants from seed; wine making; wood working; reading. Home and Office: 130 E 196th St Euclid OH 44119

RIDDLE, JAMES CONNER, genetic toxicologist; b. Cleve., Dec. 30, 1948; s. James Samson and Marjory Jane (Sinclair) R.; m. Robin Suzanne Center, Dec. 17, 1978; 1 child, Erin Suzanne. B.S. in Biology, Denison U., 1971; Ph.D. in Biomed. Scis., U. Tenn., 1979. Adv. research and devel. scientist B.F. Goodrich, Brecksville, Ohio, 1979-81, sr. research and devel. scientist, 1981-84, research and devel. assoc., supr. 1984—; cons. Chem. Mfrs. Assn., Washington, 1979—, ASTM, Phil., 1984—. Contbr. tech. articles to sci. jours. Nat. Inst. Gen. Med. Scis. fellow, 1972-78. Mem. AAAS, ASTM, Environ. Mutagen Soc., Tissue Culture Assn., Genetic Toxicology Assn., Ohio Acad. Scis., Sigma Alpha Epsilon (sec. bd. trustees Ohio Mu chpt.). Avocations: reading; drawing; painting; cycling; photography. Office: BF Goodrich R&D Ctr 9921 Brecksville Rd Brecksville OH 44141

RIDDLE, MAXWELL, newspaper columnist; b. Ravenna, Ohio, July 29, 1907; s. Henry Warner and Mary E. (Fitz-Gerald) R.; B.A., U. Ariz., 1929; m. Martha A. Hurd, Mar. 31, 1933 (dec. 1982); children—Betsy Riddle Whitmore, Henry W. III. Turf editor, columnist NEA Service, 1930, 39; kennel editor, columnist, pets columnist Cleve. Press, 1938-69; columnist Columbia Features, Inc., 1959-66; columnist Ledger Syndicate, 1966-73, Scott Editor Service, 1973—, Allied Feature Syndicate, 1975—; all breed dog judge, fgn. countries, 1955. U.S., 1960—. Recipient Cruikshank medal, 1941; Dog Writer of Year, 1949, 61, 83; Dogdom's Man of the Year, 1968, Dog. Journalist of Year, 1970, 72. Mem. Ohio Dog Owners Assn., Dog Writers Assn. (past pres.), Sigma Delta Chi, Delta Upsilon. Clubs: Western Reserve Kennel, Ravenna Kennel. Author: The Springer Spaniel, 1939; The Lovable Mongrel, 1954; This Is the Chihuahua, 1959; The Complete Book of Puppy Training and Care, 1962; Dog People are Crazy, 1966; Your Show Dog, 1968; A Quick Guide to the Standards of Show Dogs, 1972; (with Mrs. M.B. Seeley) The Complete Alaskan Malamute, 1976. The Complete Brittany Spaniel, 1974; The New Shetland Sheepdog, 1974; The Wild Dogs in Life and Legend, 1979; Your Family Dog, 1981; also articles; contbr. Hunters Ency., 1948, New Dog Ency., 1967, Internat. Dog Ency., 1972, World Book Ency.; assoc. editor Dog World Mag., 1961—. Home: PO Box 286 Ravenna OH 44266

RIDDLE, RAYMOND ERWIN, library administrator; b. Orlando, Fla., Nov. 9, 1947; s. Theadore Leslie and Margie (Jordan) R.; m. Cecelia Yvonne Reeder, Aug. 31, 1974. B.A., St. Andrews Coll., 1969; M.L.S., U. Miss., 1975. Dir. Humphreys County Library, Belzoni, Miss., 1975-78, Cass County Pub. Library, Harrisonville, Mo., 1978-85, Kansas City Pub. Library, Kans., 1985—; mem. Mo. Library Network Bd., 1981-85, pres. 1983-85; mem. Kansas City Met. Library Network Council, Independence, Mo., 1979—, pres., 1981-83; bd. dirs. Blue River-Kansas City Bapt. Assn., Lee's Summit, Mo., 1980-84; bd. govs. Mo. Eye Research Found., Columbia, 1980-85; mem. appellate bd. Western Mo. SSS, 1981—. Author: From Greasy Row to Catfish Capital, 1978; numerous short stories for children, 1974-78; also numerous profl. articles. Mem. ALA, Kans. Library Assn., Mo. Library Assn. (v.p. 1984-85), Assn. for Info. and Image Mgmt., Kansas City Area Wide Orgn. Librarians, Phi Delta Kappa. Republican. Baptist. Lodges: Lions (dist. gov. 1982-83). Home: 7708 New Jersey Kansas City KS 66112 Office: Kansas City Pub Library 625 Minnesota Ave Kansas City KS 66101

RIDENS, DANIEL JAY, production scheduler; b. South Bend, Ind., Nov. 10, 1960; s. Jack Lee and Marie Delores (Bierwagen) R. Drafting and Design Tech., Tri-State U., 1981. Design engr. Wheelabrator-Frye, Inc., Mishawaka, Ind., 1981-82; design engr. Owens Classic, Inc., Sturgis, Mich., 1982-84, prodn. scheduler, 1984—. Recipient Cert. Appreciation Jr. Achievement Am., 1982. Mem. Am. Mgmt. Assn. (cert. completion 1984), Am. Prodn. and Inventory Control Soc. Clubs: Michiana Corvairs (Elkhart, Ind.) (treas. 1980-82); Corvair Soc. Am. (Pensacola, Fla.). Avocations: golf, Corvairs, coin collecting. Office: Owens Classic Inc PO Box 628 Sturgis MI 49091

RIDGE, RICHARD, business economist; b. Wilkes-Barre, Pa., Aug. 26, 1946; s. Richard Peter and Kathryn Ann (Connelly) R.; m. Maureen Kennedy (div.); children—Daniel, Jennifer, Edward. B.S., Drexel U., 1969, M.S., 1970. Bus. planner Indsl. Valley Bank, Phila., 1968-70; sr. econ. analyst Gen. Electric Co., Phila., 1970-77, mgr. bus. research, Cin., 1980—; economist U.S. Dept. Commerce, Washington, 1977-80; cons. NSF. Presbyterian. Office: 1 Neumann Way J165 Cincinnati OH 45215

RIDGEWAY, B(ARBARA) LUANN, lawyer; b. Moberly, Mo., May 19, 1956; d. Donald William and Barbara Monique (Harris) Ridgeway; m. Richard D. Ridgeway, Apr. 7, 1984. B.A., William Woods Westminster Colls., 1978; cert. of completion Oxford U., 1978; J.D., U. Mo., 1981. Bar: Mo. 1981, U.S. Dist. Ct. (we. dist.) Mo. 1982, U.S. Ct. Appeals (5th, 8th and 10th cirs.) 1983, U.S. Ct. Appeals (D.C. cir.) 1984. Legis. aide to U.S. rep. H. L. Volkmer, Washington, 1977; intern-consumer protection Mo. Atty. Gen., Jefferson City, 1978; staff counsel Gulf & Gt. Plains Legal Found., Kansas City, Mo., 1981-85; mem. firm Wilkins & Millin, P.C., 1985—. Active Citizens Assn., Kansas City, 1983-84; treas. Country Club Christian Ch. Choir, Kansas City, 1983-84. Mem. Kansas City Lawyers Assn. (bd. govs. young lawyers sect. 1983-84), Kansas City Bar Assn., Assn. Trial Lawyers Am. Office: 1102 Mercantile Tower 1101 Walnut Kansas City MO 64106

RIDGWAY, JOHN EDWARD, pharmacist, consultant; b. Aberdeen, S.D., Oct. 1, 1948; s. Edward Willard and Shirley Jane (Smith) R.; m. Linda Lee Stansbury, May 2, 1970; children—Melissa, Allison. B.S. in Pharmacy, U. Nebr., 1971. Registered pharmacist, Ind., Nebr. Head pharmacist Osco Drugs, Terre Haute, Ind., 1971-73, Turn Style, Omaha, 1973-77; pharmacist Apothecary Assocs., Omaha, 1977-83, owner, head pharmacist, 1984—; pharmacy cons. Skyline Nursing Home, Omaha, 1977—; vol. faculty instr. Coll. Pharmacy, U. Nebr. Med. Ctr., Omaha, 1978—; cons. Bristol Myers, N.Y.C., Nebr. Dept. Social Services, Lincoln. Mem. steering com. Chem. People, Omaha, 1983-84; advisor Pride, Inc.-Omaha, 1983-85; advisor to Senator Jerry Chizek, Lincoln, Nebr., 1984—; chmn. Poison Prevention Week, Omaha, 1983-84. Named Preceptor of Yr., Nebr. Med. Ctr. Coll. Pharmacy, 1981. Mem. Nat. Assn. Retail Druggists (Pharmacy Leadership award 1981), Greater Omaha Pharmacists Assn. (pres. 1983), Nebr. Pharmacists Assn. (bd. dirs. 1982-85, Pub. Relations award 1984), Coll. Pharmacy Alumni Assn. (exec. com. 1984—). Republican. Methodist. Club: Cosmopolitan. Avocations: gardening; fishing; reading. Home: 14918 Jefferson Circle Omaha NE 68137 Office: Apothecary Assocs 8300 Dodge St Omaha NE 68114

RIDHA, RAOUF ABDUL, civil engineer; b. Karbala, Iraq, Aug. 25, 1937; came to U.S., 1962, naturalized 1971; s. Abdul and Zahra (Ibrahim) R.; m. Dalal Al-Sheibani, Nov. 7, 1973; children—Susan, Jennifer, Jeffrey. B.S., U. Baghdad, Iraq, 1959; M.S., U. Ill., 1963; M.B.A., Kent State U., 1978; Ph.D., U. Ill., 1966. Analytical specialist Bendix Corp., South Bend, Ind., 1966-73; research assoc. Firestone Tire & Rubber Co., Akron, Ohio, 1973-78; sect. head, physics and engrng. mechanic Gen. Corp. Inc., Akron, 1978-83; mgr. tire physics and math. Goodyear Tire & Rubber Co., Akron, 1983—. Author: (with others) Mechanics of Pneumatic Tires, 1981. Editor jour. Tire Sci. & Tech., 1984—. Contbr. articles to profl. jours. Mem. Zoning Appeals Bd., Sharon Twp., Ohio, 1979—. Fellow Am. Inst. of Aeros. and Astrophys. (assoc.); mem. Tire Soc., Soc. Exptl. Mechanics. Home: 6216 Ridge Rd Box 277 Sharon Center OH 44274-0277 Office: Goodyear Tire & Rubber Co Tech Ctr D/410C Akron OH 44316-0001

RIDLEN, JULIAN LEON, state official; b. Macon County, Ill., Feb. 4, 1940; s. Charles F. and Doris O. (Franklin) R.; B.A., Anderson (Ind.) Coll., 1963; J.D., George Washington U., 1967; m. Susanne Lee Smith, June 1, 1963. Tchr., Emerson Inst., also Washington Hall Jr. Coll., Washington, 1966-68; legal researcher, writer NEA, Washington, 1967-68; admitted to Ind. bar, 1967; mem. firm Smith & Ridlen, Logansport, 1968—; judge Logansport City Ct., 1969-78; treas. State of Ind., 1979—. Chmn. Cass County (Ind.) Bicentennial Com., 1974-76; pres. Cass County Youth Services Bur., 1971, Cass County chpt. ARC, 1971-73; v.p., bd. dirs. Logansport United Fund, 1972; v.p. Cass County Mental Health Assn., 1971-74; mem. Cass County Bd. Election Commrs., 1970; mem. staff Republican. Nat. Com., 1963-64; elder Calvary Presbyn. Ch., Logansport, 1971—. Recipient Disting. Service award Logansport Jaycees, 1971, Boss of Year award Logansport chpt. Nat. Secretaries Assn., 1976, Golden Deeds award Logansport Exchange Club, 1976, 78. Mem. Nat. Assn. State Treasurers (pres. 1984), Nat. Assn. State Auditors (exec. com. 1984), Comptrollers and Treasurers, ABA, Ind. Bar Assn., Cass County Bar Assn., Cass County Hist. Soc. (pres. 1974-78), Phi Alpha Delta. Clubs: Kiwanis, Elks (treas. state 1979—). Office: 242 State House Indianapolis IN 46204

RIECKER, JOHN E(RNEST), lawyer, banker; b. Ann Arbor, Mich., Nov. 25, 1930; s. Herman H. and Elizabeth (Wertz) R.; A.B. with distinction, U. Mich., 1952, J.D. with distinction, 1954; m. Margaret Ann Towsley, July 30, 1955; children—John Towsley, Margaret Elizabeth. Admitted to Mich. bar, 1954, Calif. bar, 1955, bar U.S. Tax Ct., U.S. Supreme Ct. Bar, U.S. Treasury Bar; asso. law firm Bonisteel & Bonisteel, Ann Arbor, 1954-55; partner firm Francis, Wetmore & Riecker. Midland, Mich., 1958-65; partner firm Gillespie Riecker & George, Midland, 1966-78; pres. Riecker, George, Hartley & Van Dam and Camp, P.C., 1978—; chmn. bd., dir. First Midland Bank & Trust Co., 1970-78; dir. Comerica Bank-Midland; sec., dir. numerous Mich. corps. Mem. NAM trade mission to EEC, 1964. Trustee, treas. Delta Coll., 1965-68; mem. bd. mgrs. United Fund Midland 1960-64, chmn., 1980—; sec. Midland City Charter Rev. Com., 1964, mem. Spl. Charter Commn., 1972; bd. dirs. Midland Found., 1974; mem. Bd. Ethics State of Mich., 1976—; sec. Mich. Molecular Inst., Dow Found., Towsley Found. Ann Arbor; mem. exec. com. Mich. United Fund, 1970-72; bd. govs. Northwood Inst., 1969-71; benefactor U. Mich.; vice chmn. bd. dirs. U. Mich. Devel. Council, 1982—; chmn. bd. dirs. Central Mich. U. Devel. Council, 1983—; bd. govs. Cranbrook Acad. Art, 1980-84; chmn. Matrix: Midland, 1981-83; bd. dirs. steering com. U. Mich. Grad. Sch. Bus., 1982—; mem. com. visitors U. Mich. Law Sch., 1981—; vice chmn. Campaign for Mich., 1984. Served as 1st lt., Judge Adv. Gens. Corps, AUS, 1955-58; now capt. Res. Recipient U. Mich. Outstanding Alumni award, 1984. Mem. Midland County (pres. 1962-63), Am., Calif., Mich. (tax council) bar assns., Midland C. of C. (pres. 1971), Phi Beta Kappa, Phi Kappa Phi, Phi Eta Sigma, Sigma Iota Epsilon, Alpha Delta Phi, Phi Delta Phi. Republican. Episcopalian. Clubs: Benmark, Midland Country, Saginaw, Saginaw Valley Torch; Detroit Athletic, Renaissance; Travis Pointe Country (Ann Arbor); President's, Benefactors (U. Mich). Mem. bd. editors Mich. Law Rev., 1953-54. Contbr. articles to profl. jours. Home: 3211 Valley Dr Midland MI 48640 Office: 414 Townsend St Midland MI 48640

RIEDEL, ROBERT GEORGE, psychologist, educator; b. Mar. 7, 1936; m. Theadora Ann Riedel; children—Elizabeth, Jennifer, Robert, Jonathan. B.S., Loyola U., Chgo., 1962, M.A., 1963, Ph.D., 1967. Lic. psychologist, Minn. Teaching asst., sr. fellow, lectr. Loyola U., Chgo., 1963-68; instr. Mundelein Coll., Chgo., 1963-64; asst. prof. dept. psychology Barat Coll., Chgo., 1964-67, assoc. prof., chmn. dept. psychology, 1967-68; assoc. prof. psychology Clarkson Coll., 1968-70; assoc. prof., chmn. psychology Southwest State U., Marshall, Minn., 1970-72, prof., chmn., 1972-76, prof., 1976—; lectr. U. Wash., Seattle, 1976-77; mem. staff Am. Lake VA Hosp., Tacoma, Wash., 1976-77; sole practice psychology, Marshall, Minn., 1978—; cons. and lectr. in field. Author: The Teacher Advisor System, 1972; Le Viellissement, 1983 (Spanish transl. 1984); Aging, 1984. Contbr. chpts. to books, articles to profl. jours. Mem. numerous editorial bds. in field. Chmn. adv. com. Com. for New Tomorrow, Gov.'s Crime Commn., Minn.; chmn. bd. dirs. Lyon County Daytime Activity Ctr.; mem. Marshall C. of C. Housing Com., Minn. Bd. on Aging, mem. tech. rev. com., state planning com.; bd. dirs. REAL: Housing for Handicapped, Prairie Home Hospice. Grantee in field from numerous profl. orgns. Recipient numerous awards for profl. excellence. Mem. Am. Psychol Assn., Gerontol. Soc., Assn. Rural Mental Health, Forum Death Edn., Coalition Terminal Care, Midwestern Psychol. Assn., Minn. Psychol. Assn., Minn. Gerontol. Soc. Address: Southwest State U Dept Psychology Marshall MN 56258

RIEDY, JAMES LAWRENCE, humanities educator, photographer; b. Milw., Dec. 27, 1943; s. Peter Paul and Martha (Langdon) R. B.A., U. Wis.-Madison, 1964, M.A., 1966; postgrad. Am. Conservatory of Music, Chgo., 1966-68, U. Chgo., 1968-70, Columbia Coll., Chgo., 1972-74. Assoc. prof. humanities Truman Coll. City Coll. Chgo., 1966—; specialist in sculpture photography. Exhibited in local shows. Pub. in local and nat. mags. Author: Chicago Sculpture, 1981. Mem. Internat. Sculpture Ctr.

RIEGEL, MARILYN RUTH, management consultant; b. Chgo., Oct. 13, 1944; d. Sam and Reva (Singer) Levine. B.A. in Secondary Edn., Northeastern Ill. U., 1969; Ed.M. in Spl. Edn., U. Ill.-Chgo., 1977; postgrad. Northwestern U., 1977-79. Dir. reading lab. Chgo. Pub. Schs., 1970-77; teaching asst. Northwestern U., 1977-79; dir. staffing and employee relations Urban Investment and Devel. Co., 1977-84; v.p. James H. Lowry & Assocs., Chgo., 1984—. State of Ill. fellow in spl. edn., 1978. Mem. Affirmative Action Assn. (pres. 1984—), Employment Mgmt. Assn., Am. Soc. Tng. and Devel., OD Network, Internatl. Assn. Personnel Women. Avocations: backpacking; running; fishing. Office: James H Lowry & Assocs 303 E Wacker Dr 1340 Chicago IL 60601

RIEGER, MITCHELL SHERIDAN, lawyer; b. Chgo., Sept. 5, 1922; s. Louis and Evelyn (Sampson) R.; A.B., Northwestern U., 1944; J.D., Harvard, 1949; 1 dau., Karen Gross Cooper; step-children by previous marriage—Jill Felsenthal Levi, Susan Felsenthal, Linda Felsenthal Hanan, James Geoffrey Felsenthal; m. Pearl Handelsman, June 10, 1973; stepchildren—Steven B. Newman, Mary Ann Malarkey, Nancy L. Newman. Admitted to Ill. bar, 1950; asso. firm Rieger & Rieger, Chgo., 1950-54; asst. U.S. atty. No. Dist. of Ill., 1954-60, chief tax div., 1954-55, chief criminal div., 1955-58, first asst. 1958-60; asso. gen. counsel SEC, Washington, 1960-61; partner firm Schiff Hardin & Waite and predecessor, Chgo., 1961—; instr. law John Marshall Law Sch., Chgo., 1952-54. Past pres., dir. Park View Home. Mem. Chgo. Crime Commn. Served to lt. (j.g.) USNR, 1943-46; comdr. Res. (ret.). Fellow Am. Coll. Trial Lawyers; mem. Am., 7th Circuit, Ill., Chgo., Fed. (pres. Chgo. chpt. 1959-60, nat. v.p. 7th dist. 1960-61) bar assns., Am. Judicature Soc., Phi Beta Kappa. Clubs: Metropolitan, Law, The Standard (Chgo.), Lake Shore Country (Glencoe). Contbr. articles to profl. jours. Home: 4950 Chicago Beach Dr Chicago IL 60615 Office: 7200 Sears Tower 233 S Wacker Dr Chicago IL 60606

RIEGLE, DONALD WAYNE, JR., Senator; b. Flint, Mich., Feb. 4, 1938; s. Donald Wayne and Dorothy (Fitchett) R.; B.A. in Bus. Adminstrn. and Econs., U. Mich.; M.B.A., Mich. State U., 1961; postgrad. Harvard Bus. Sch., 1964-66; m. Lori Hansen; children—Catherine Anne, Laurie Elizabeth, Donald Wayne III. Faculty Mich. State U., 1960-61; sr. pricing analyst IBM, 1961-64; cons. Harvard-Mass. Inst. Tech. Joint Center on Urban Studies; mem. 90th-94th Congresses Mich. 7th Dist.; mem. U.S. Senate from Mich., 1976—, mem. budget com., com. on banking, housing and urban affairs, com. on labor and human resources, com. on commerce, sci. and transp.; fellow-in-residence John Kennedy Inst. for Politics, Harvard, 1971. Recipient Distinguished Alumni award U. Mich. Bus. Adminstrn. Soc., 1967; named one of 10 Outstanding Young Men in Am., U.S. Jaycees, 1967; one of 200 Nat. Leaders Under Age 45, Time mag., 1974. Mem. Beta Gamma Sigma. Democrat. Author: O Congress, 1972. Office: Dirksen Senate Office Bldg Washington DC 20510

RIEGLE, GAIL DANIEL, physiology educator, university dean; b. DeSoto, Iowa, Feb. 19, 1935; s. James Floyd and Alice Gail (McDonald) R.; m. Barbara Jean Welch, Mar. 19, 1960; children—Gregory Allen, Kristen Marie. B.S., Iowa State U., 1957; M.S., Mich. State U., 1960, Ph.D., 1963. Asst. prof. Mich. State U., East Lansing, 1964-70, assoc. prof., 1970-76, prof. physiology, 1976—, asst. dean curriculum, 1980—. Contbr. chpts. to books, articles to profl. jours. Fellow Gerontol. Soc. Am., Am. Physiol. Soc., Soc. Exptl. Biology and Medicine, Sigma Xi. Lutheran. Home: 4875 County Dr Okemos MI 48864 Office: Mich State U Dept Physiology East Lansing MI 48824

RIEHL, RICHARD EUGENE, osteopathic physician, medical services executive; b. Portsmouth, Ohio, July 13, 1927; s. George Herman and Charlotte Bea (MacNeal) R. B.S., Ohio U., 1949; D.O., Kirksville Coll. Osteo. Medicine, 1954. Dir. Med. services U.S. Air Force Clinic, Newark, Ohio, 1976—. Mem. Am. Osteo. Assn., Am. Occupational Med. Assn., Am. Osteo. Occupational Med. Assn. Home: 1199 Briar Hills Heath OH 43056 Office: SGPOO Newark Air Force Sta Newark OH 43057-5000

RIEKE, REUBEN DENNIS, chemistry educator, researcher; b. Lucan, Minn., Mar. 7, 1939; s. Reuben Jacob and Caroline (Bahr) R.; m. Loretta Irene Hoffeld, Aug. 13, 1962; children—R. Dennis, Elizabeth Ann. B.S. in Chemistry, U. Minn., 1961; Ph.D., U. Wis., 1966. Postdoctoral fellow UCLA, 1965-66; asst. prof. chemistry U. N.C., Chapel Hill, 1966-71, assoc. prof., 1971-75, prof., 1975-76; prof. chemistry N.D. State U., Fargo, 1976-77, U. Nebr., Lincoln, 1977—, chmn. dept. chemistry, 1981—. Contbr. articles to chem. jours. Fellow Alfred P. Sloan Found., 1973-75, NATO, 1973-74, Alexander von Humboldt Found., Fed. Republic Germany, 1973-74; NSF grantee, 2 yr. extension for sci. creativity, 1981-83. Mem. Am. Chem. Soc., Sigma Xi, Phi Lambda Upsilon. Home: 6133 Heide Ln Lincoln NE 68512 Office: U Nebr Dept Chemistry Lincoln NE 68588

RIEMEN, DAVID CLARENCE, chief of police; b. Ft. Wayne, Ind., Mar. 8, 1944; s. Albert Joseph and Beulah Mary (Patterson) R.; m. Diane Mae Gebhard, July 11, 1964; children—David, Michael, Jennifer, Sara. A.S., Ind. U., 1981. With Ft. Wayne (Ind.) Police Dept., 1967—, chief of police, 1981—; tng. instr. Police Sch. Liaison Officers Clinic, Flint, Mich., Internat. Assn. Chiefs of Police Developing Computer Capabilities, Nashville. Mem. adv. bd. Ft. Wayne Women's Shelter. Mem. Internat. Assn. Chiefs of Police. Roman Catholic. Club: Toastmasters. Office: 1 Main St Room 280 Fort Wayne IN 46802

RIESS, FRANK GERALD, advertising executive; b. Detroit, Apr. 2, 1953; s. Frank Edwin and Geraldine Marie (Weber) R.; m. Susan Marie Miceli, Aug. 3, 1974 (div. Nov. 1977); 1 son, Robert Frank; m. Sharon Patricia Nowicki, Feb. 18, 1984. A.A. cum laude, Oakland Coll., 1973; B.S. cum laude in Mktg., Central Mich. U., 1975. Field dir. Hi-Scope Research Co., Southfield, Mich., 1975-76; analyst Market Opinion Research Co., Detroit, 1976-78, Can. Opinion Research Co., Toronto, Ont., 1976-78; advt. dir. Ziebart Corp., Troy, Mich., 1978—. Contbr. articles on mktg. to profl. jours. Named Eagle Scout Boy Scouts Am., 1968. Mem. Am. Mktg. Assn., Mktg. Research Assn., Am. Assn. Pub. Opinion Research, Adcraft Club of Detroit, Founders' Soc. of Detroit Inst. Arts. Democrat. Roman Catholic. Home: 6914 Tappon Ct Clarkston MI 48016

RIESS, JONATHAN BENJAMIN, art history educator, researcher; b. N.Y.C., Aug. 3, 1947; s. Chester Louis and Marion (Glazer) R.; m. Michele Morgan, June 15, 1980; 1 child, Christopher. B.A., Amherst Coll., 1968; M.A., Columbia U., 1970, M. in Philosophy, 1973, Ph.D., 1977. Preceptor, Columbia U., N.Y.C., 1971-73; asst. prof. U. Cin., 1976-81, assoc. prof., 1981—, chmn. dept. art history, 1981-84. Editor Midwest Art History Soc. Newsletter, 1982-83. Author: Political Ideals in Medieval Italian Art, 1981; contbr. articles to profl. jours. Kress Found., fellow, 1970, 72; Fulbright fellow, 1973; Woodbridge fellow Columbia U., 1973; Whiting fellow Columbia U., 1974; Harvard U. fellow Villa I Tatti, Florence, Italy, 1974; Am. Philos. Soc. grantee. Mem. Midwest Art History Soc. (adv. bd. 1983-84), Coll. Art Assn., Renaissance Soc. Am. Democrat. Jewish. Avocations: hiking; tennis. Home: 965 Avondale Ave Cincinnati OH 45229 Office: Dept Art History Cincinnati Cincinnati OH 45221

RIESS, PHYLLIS EVANS, social worker; b. Evansville, Ind., Aug. 28, 1941; d. Paul Franklin and Lucille Kathryn (Kuehn) Evans; m. John David Riess, Nov. 26, 1963 (div. 1985); children—John Howard, Jana Kathryn. Student U. Exeter-Eng., 1961-62; B.A., Hanover Coll., 1963; M.A., So. Ill. U., 1965. Registered social worker, Ill. Instr., So. Ill. U., Carterville, 1966-67; part-time instr. Carl Sandburg Coll., Galesburg, Ill., 1967-84; psychiatric social worker Dept. Mental Health, Galesburg, 1980—. Newspaper columnist Register-Mail, 1982—. Charter dir. Knox County Legal Aid Soc., Galesburg, 1975-77; chmn. City Plan Comm., Galesburg, 1979-80, 82-83, commr., 1974—. Zinc scholar, 1959-63; So. Ill. U. fellow, 1963-64. Mem. LWV (pres. Galesburg chpt. 1975-78, nominating com. Chgo. chpt. 1979-80). Avocations: photography; computing; painting.

RIFE, HARRY PETTUS, lawyer; b. Greenfield, Ohio, Dec. 13, 1937; s. Harry Clyburn and Doris Carmen (Mankin) R.; m. Marilyn Gene Dwight, Dec. 27, 1966 (div. 1983); children—Alan Stuart, Craig Edward. B.A., Ohio State U., 1959; J.D., 1962. Bar: Ohio 1962. Ptnr. Horn and Rife, Dayton, Ohio, 1967—; gen. counsel Digital Controls, Inc., Dayton, 1976-81; dir. Megacity, Inc., Dayton, RETS Tech. Ctr., Inc.; pres. Med. Ctr. Assocs., Kettering, Ohio, 1981; mem. Nat. Moot Ct. Team, Ohio State U., 1962. Served to capt. U.S. Army, 1963-67. Mem. Dayton Bar Assn. (judiciary com.), Ohio State Bar Assn., Kettering C. of C. (pres.-elect 1985). Republican. Methodist. Lodges: Kiwanis (pres. 1975), Rotary. Avocations: Jogging; tennis; skiing. Home: 1862 Brattleboro Ct Dayton OH 45440 Office: Horn and Rife 2185 S Dixie Ave Dayton OH 45409

RIGAZIO, MARK WILLIAM, lawyer; b. Spring Valley, Ill., Sept. 25, 1955; s. Anthony Wayne and Gretchen Kay (Raley) R.; m. Cindy Lou Tonioni; children—Mark Anthony, Joseph Michael. B.S., So. Ill. U., 1978; J.D., No. Ill. U., 1981. Bar: Ill. 1981. Asst. states atty. intern Putnam County, Hennepin, Ill., 1980; asst. states atty. LaSalle County, Ottawa, Ill., 1981-83; 1st asst. states atty. Grundy County, Morris, Ill., 1983—; corp. counsel Worldtronics, Inc., Oglesby, Ill., 1984—. Village trustee Village of Standard, Ill., 1982—; bd. dirs. Nutrition for Older Americans, Standard, 1982—; state del. Republican Party, Putnam County, Ill., 1984. Mem. ABA, Ill. State Bar Assn., Grundy County Bar Assn., LaSalle County Bar Assn. Clubs: Jaycees (Granville, Ill.) (sec. 1983—), Sacred Heart Men's Soc. (Granville, Ill.). Home: Box 89 Standard IL 61363 Office: Grundy County States Attys Office 111 E Washington St Morris IL 60450

RIGDON, RONALD MILTON, mgmt. cons.; b. Balt., Jan. 15, 1937; s. Leland Sanford and Betty Berniece (Roe) R.; student Kansas City (Mo.) Art Inst., 1958-60, William Jewell Coll., Liberty, Mo., 1955-58, 62-63; m. Arlene June Eddington, May 26, 1962; children—Ryan Todd, Rebecca Erin. Field adjuster CNA Ins. Corp., Kansas City, Mo., 1962-63; asst. mgr. Anchor Fin. Corp. Ins. Agy., Overland Park, Kans., 1963-64; mgr. First Mortgage Investment Co. Ins. Agy., Kansas City, Mo., 1964-67; pres. Programming Inst., Mission, Kans., 1967-70, RMR & Assos., Inc., Overland Park, 1970—; dir. Assn. Cons., Inc., Scheduling Systems, Inc. First v.p. Johnson County Mental Health Assn., 1968-70, Kans. Mental Health Assn., 1969-70. Mem. Mgmt. Cons. Inst., Profl. Ins. Mass-Mktg. Assn., Am. Mgmt. Assn., Assn. Chief Exec. Officers, Am. Profl. Assn. Group Ins. Adminstrs., U.S. Dressage Fedn., Kansas City Dressage Soc. Republican. Baptist. Author: Work Flow-Cost Reduction a Management Control System, 1978. Home: 12200 Big Bone Trail Olathe KS 66061 Office: 10875 Benson Dr Suite 103 Overland Park KS 66210

RIGDON, STEVEN EARL, statistician; b. St. Louis, July 31, 1955; s. Earl Everett and Clara Marie (Engel) R.; m. Mary Patricia Dummerth, Aug. 20, 1982; 1 child, Christopher. B.A. in Math., U. Mo.-St. Louis, 1977, M.A. in Math., 1980; M.A. in Stats., U. Mo.-Columbia, 1983. Teaching asst. U. Mo.-Columbia, 1979-80, research asst., 1980-82; math. statistician Monsanto Research Corp., Miamisburg, Ohio, 1982—; lectr. Sinclair Coll., Dayton, Ohio, 1983-84. Mem. Am. Stats. Assn., Am. Soc. Quality Control, Inst. Math. Stats., Psychometric Soc. Roman Catholic. Avocations: tennis; photography. Home: 2105 Sidney Wood Rd Apt D West Carrollton OH 45449 Office: Monsanto Research Corp PO Box 32 Miamisburg OH 45342

RIGGIN, RALPH MEREDITH, research scientist; b. Emporia, Kans., July 17, 1951; s. Harlan W. and Betty F. (Ravone) R.; m. Alice Rau, May 24, 1975; children—Esther Tonia, Daniel Evan. B.S. in Chemistry, Kans. State Coll., 1972; Ph.D. in Chemistry, Purdue U., 1976. Research scientist Battelle Meml. Inst., Columbus, Ohio, 1977-85, Eli Lilly Research Ctr., Indpls., 1985—; expert cons. Electric Power Research Inst., Palo Alto, Calif., 1982; peer rev. panelist EPA, Research Triangle Park, N.C., 1983—. Contbr. articles to various jours. Longhouse chief YMCA Indian Guides, Columbus, 1984. Mem. Am. Chem. Soc., Air Pollution Control Assn., AAAS, Ohio Acad. Sci., ASTM (task group chmn. 1978-83). Home: 8810 Staghorn Rd Indianapolis IN 46260 Office: Eli Lilly Research Ctr Indianapolis IN

RIGGS, JEANETTE TEMPLETON, civic worker; b. Little Rock, Mar. 13, 1933; d. Donald M. and Fay (Templeton) Brewer; student Little Rock U., 1950-51, Tex. Coll. for Women, 1951-52; B.S., U. Ark., 1955; m. Byron Lawrence Riggs, June 1955; children—Byron Kent, Ann Templeton. Founder, Rochester (Minn.) Ballet Guild, 1970, pres., 1974; mem. establishing bd., exec. bd. Rochester Arts Council, 1972, producer, dir. T.S. Elliot's The Rock, 1970; founder, performer So. Minn. Ballet Co., 1974; sponsor Nat. Ballet Cos., Rochester, 1970-75; exec. bd. for restoration 1875 Pattern Book House, Rochester Heritage Assn., 1975-77; exec. bd. Savino Ballet Nat., 1975-78; founder, exec. bd. Citizens Action Com., 1977-79; asso., commentator Women, Cable TV Program for Women, Rochester, 1979; mem. Mayor's Com. on Drug Abuse, 1979-80; mem. Olmsted County Steering Com. for George Bush, 1979-80, a founder, mem. exec. bd. Olmsted County Republican Women's

Orgn., 1979—, mem. Olmsted County Rep. Central Com., 1979—, exec. bd. issues com., 1979-80. Home: 432 SW 10th Ave Rochester MN 55901

RIGHTER, WALTER CAMERON, clergyman; b. Phila., Oct. 23, 1923; s. Richard and Dorothy Mae (Bottomley) R.; B.A., U. Pitts., 1948; M.Div., Berkeley Div. Sch., 1951, D.D., 1972; D.L., Iowa Wesleyan Coll., 1983; D.D., Seabury Western Sem., 1985; m. Marguerite Jeanne Burroughs, Jan. 26, 1946; children—Richard Stanton, Rebecca Jean. Ordained to ministry Episcopal Ch., 1951; vicar All Saints Ch., Aliquippa, Pa., 1951-54; rector Ch. of Good Shepherd, Nashua, N.H., 1954-71; consecrated bishop, 1972; bishop diocese of Iowa, Des Moines, 1972—; mem. exec. council Protestant Episcopal Ch., U.S.A., 1979-85, mem. Domestic and Fgn. Missionary Soc., 1979-85; mem. com. on health and human affairs Gen. Conv. Episcopal Ch., 1982-85. Bd. dirs. Orchard Place Home for Children, Des Iowa, 1975-81, Door of Faith Mission, Des Moines; past bd. dirs. Protestant Home for Children, Nashua, 1954-70, Morris Fund, 1978—; trustee Nashua Public Library, 1968-71. Served with AUS, 1943-45; ETO. Fellow Coll. Preachers Washington Cathedral; mem. Newcomen Soc. Clubs: Masons, Rotary (dir.). Contbr. articles to religious publs. Address: 225 37th St Des Moines IA 50312

RIGNEY, DAVID ARTHUR, metallurgical engineering educator; b. Waterbury, Conn., Aug. 8, 1938; s. John W. and Anne L. (Norling) R.; m. Ann F. Fairbairn, June 25, 1965; children—Mark D., Heather A. A.B., Harvard U., 1960, S.M., 1962; Ph.D., Cornell U., 1965. Postdoctoral research fellow U. Ill., Urbana, 1965-67; mem. faculty to prof. dept. metall. engring. Ohio State U., Columbus, 1967—. Editor: Fundamentals of Friction and Wear of Materials, 1981; Sourcebook on Wear Control Technology, 1978. Dep. editor Scripta Metallurgica, 1975—. Mem. Ohio Council on Natural Areas, 1970-75, chmn. 1972-74. Recipient research award Ohio State U. Coll. Engr., 1982, teaching award, 1983. Fellow Am. Soc. for Metals; mem. Metall. Soc. of AIME, Sierra, Ohio Environ. Council, Sigma Xi. Avocations: music; nature. Home: 747 Carruthers Dr Worthington OH 43085 Office: Ohio State U 116 W 19th Ave Columbus OH 43210

RIGSBY, HOWARD JOHN, lawyer; b. N.Y.C., Dec. 11, 1949; s. Douglas Stephan and Elaine (Schmidt) R.; m. Mary Therese McAuley, June 16, 1973; children—Megan, Molly Anne. B.A., George Mason U., 1977; J.D., John Marshall Law Sch., 1980. Bar: Ill. 1980, Pa. 1982, U.S. Dist. Ct. (no. dist.) Ill. 1982. Staff atty. Brodie & Reynolds, Chgo., 1980-84; assoc. Berman, Fagel, Haber, Maragos and Abrams, Chgo., 1984—. Served with USAF, 1968-72. Mem. Ill. State Bar Assn. (tort law, ins. law and civil practice coms.). Office: Berman Fagel Haber Maragos and Abrams 140 S Dearborn 14th Floor Chicago IL 60603

RIKIMARU, YUKI, archtl. designer, planner; b. Sacramento, Oct. 7, 1927; s. Joseph Iwasuke and Kiyono (Aramaki) R.; A.B. in Architecture, San Mateo City Coll., 1949; B.A. in Architecture Washington U., St. Louis, 1953; m. Kaoru Goto, Nov. 8, 1958; children—Raymond Kenji, Loryn Tamiko. Archtl. draftsman William B. Ittner, St. Louis, 1953-55; archtl. designer Russell, Mulgardt Schwarz, Van Hoeflin, St. Louis, 1956—; archtl. partner W.B. Kromm Asso., St. Louis, 1957—; prin. Kromm Rikimaru & Johansen Inc., architects, St. Louis, 1960—; v.p. Kromm, Rikimaru, Johansen & Aach Inc., architects, engrs. and planners, St. Louis, 1972, Archtl. Mgmt. Group Inc. Served with AUS, 1946-47. Mem. AIA, Nat. Council Archtl. Registration Bds., Mo. Council Architects. Prin. archtl. works include: Maplewood Municipal Bldg., St. Louis, 1961; Mineral Area Coll., Flat River, Mo., 1966; Fulton (Mo.) Juvenile Center, 1967; Delmar Gardens Nursing Home, St. Louis, 1968; Columbia (Mo.) Regional Hosp., 1972. Office: 112 S Hanley Rd St Louis MO 63105

RILES, GRANT CLAIR, agriculturist, educator; b. Clarion, Iowa, Jan. 10, 1955; s. Clifford Aldo and June E. (Kreitlow) R.; m. Melinda Jean Archdekin, June 26, 1981; 1 child, Tyler Grant. B.S., Iowa State U., 1977; postgrad. Northwest Mo. State U., 1980-81, Central Mich. U., 1984. Trainee, Fed. Intermediate Credit Bank, Omaha, 1977; agrl. loan officer Lincoln Prodn. Credit Assn., Syracuse, Nebr., 1977-79; chmn., instr. Jerry Litton Agri-Mgmt. Div., Platt Coll., St. Joseph, Mo., 1980-81; adj. faculty Park Coll., Parkville, Mo., 1981—; tng. specialist Farmland Industries, Inc., Kansas City, Mo., 1981-84, coordinator mid-mgmt. tng., 1985—. Author: Archdekins of Missouri, 1985. Mem. Assn. Coop. Educators, Am. Soc. Tng. and Devel., Nat. Soc. Accts. for Coops., Mensa, Iowa State U. Alumni Assn., Syracuse C. of C. (bd. dirs. 1978-79), Syracuse Jaycees (bd. dirs. 1978-79, sec. 1979). Lutheran. Avocations: genealogy; tennis; travel. Home: 3002 NE 68th Terr Gladstone MO 64119 Office: Farmland Industries PO Box 7305 Dept 23 Kansas City MO 64116

RILEY, BRADEN CRAGG, osteopathic physician; b. Kirksville, Mo., Nov. 25, 1953; s. Loyd Hart and Beverly Nann (Cragg) R.; m. Kimberly Jo Doyle, Nov. 7, 1982; 1 son, Matthew. B.A., Ind. U., 1975; D.O., Kansas City Coll. Osteo. Medicine, 1979. Intern, South Bend Osteo. Hosp., Ind., 1979-80, emergency room physician, 1980-85; practice osteo. medicine specializing in family practice, Granger, Ind., 1982—; team physician Schmucker Jr. High football team, Granger, 1982—. Mem. Am. Osteo. Assn., Ind. Assn. Osteo. Physicians and Surgeons. Republican. Avocations: golf; skiing; raquetball. Home: 50755 Tumbleweed Dr Granger IN 46530 Office: 12551 State Rd 23 Granger IN 46530

RILEY, DAVID EDWARD, lawyer; b. Ann Arbor, Mich., July 7, 1953; s. Edward Joseph and Mary Jane (Hunt) R.; m. Janine Lynn Rodman, July 30, 1982. B.A. in Econs., Wayne State U., 1976, J.D., 1979; LL.M. in Corp. Law, NYU, 1985. Bar: Mich. 1979, U.S. Dist. Ct. (ea. dist.) Mich. 1979, U.S. Ct. Appeals (6th cir.) 1984. Assoc. Martin S. Baum, PC, Detroit, 1979-82, Miller, Cohen, Martens & Ice, PC, Detroit, 1982—. Recipient Moot Ct. Achievement award Wayne State U., 1979. Mem. Detroit Bar Assn., Young Lawyers Assn., Order of Barrister, Am. Mensa Soc. (Southeast Mich. chpt.). Roman Catholic. Home: 915 Beaconsfield Grosse Point Park MI 48230 Office: 2400 1st Nat Bldg Detroit MI 48226

RILEY, DENNIS PATRICK, chemist; b. Tiffin, Ohio, Jan. 22, 1947; s. George William and Lillian Jeanette (Ballreich) R.; m. Carole Ann Clark, Sept. 1, 1973; 1 child, Eric William. B.S. in Chemistry and Math., Heidelberg Coll., 1969; Ph.D. in Chemistry, Ohio State U., 1975. Chem. indexer Chem. Abstracts, Columbus, Ohio, 1969-71; postdoctoral fellow U. Chgo., 1975-76; staff scientist Procter & Gamble, Cin., 1976-83, sect. head, 1983-84; sr. group leader Monsanto Co., St. Louis, 1984—. Patentee in field. Mem. Am. Chem. Soc., AAAS, Sigma Xi. Club: Sierra. Avocation: astronomy. Office: Monsanto Co 800 N Lindbergh Blvd Saint Louis MO 63167

RILEY, DOROTHY COMSTOCK, state supreme court justice; b. Detroit, Dec. 6, 1924; d. Charles Austin and Josephine (Grima) Comstock; m. Wallace Don Riley, Sept. 13, 1963; 1 child, Peter Comstock Riley. B.A. in Polit. Sci., Wayne State U., 1946, LL.B., 1949. Bar: Mich. 1950, U.S. Dist. Ct. (ea. dist.) Mich. 1950, U.S. Supreme Ct. 1957. Atty., Wayne County Friends of the Court, Detroit, 1956-68; ptnr. Riley & Roumell, Detroit, 1968-72; judge Wayne County Cir. Ct., Detroit, 1972, Mich. Ct. Appeals, Detroit, 1976-82; justice Mich. State Supreme Ct., Detroit, 1982-83, 1985—. Co-author law manual. Contbr. articles to profl. jours. Recipient Disting. Alumni award Wayne U. Law Sch., 1977; Headliner award Women of Wayne, 1977. Fellow Am. Bar Found.; mem. ABA (numerous sects.), Am. Judicature Soc., U.S. Jud. Conf. Commn. on State-Fed. Ct. Relations, Nat. Women Judges Assn., Nat. Women Lawyers Assn., Women's Econ. Club, Mich. Bar Assn. (family law sect. 1966—), Detroit Bar Assn. (past mem. numerous coms.), Karyatides, Pi Sigma Alpha. Republican. Roman Catholic. Avocations: Reading; gardening. Office: Mich Supreme Ct 1425 Lafayette Bldg Detroit MI 48226

RILEY, JAMES ASHTON, physics educator; b. Mpls., May 26, 1937; s. Charles Oscar and Evelyn Katherine (Johnson) R.; m. Eleanor Irma Riley, June 30, 1962; children—Megan Elizabeth, Patrick Charles. B.S., U. Minn., 1960, Ph.D., 1969; M.A., Temple U., 1964. Tchr. physics Cherry Hill Sch. Dist., Inkster, Mich., 1960-61, Wyandotte Sch. Dist., Mich., 1961-63; instr. physics Mankato State Coll., Minn., 1964-65; faculty Drury Coll., Springfield, Mo., 1969—, now prof. physics; cons., 1975—. NSF fellow, 1965-69. Mem. Am. Assn. Physics Tchrs., AAUP. Avocations: music; cross country skiing; canoeing. Home: 1147 E Walnut St Springfield MO 65806 Office: Drury Coll Springfield MO 65802

RILEY, JAMES JOSEPH, union exec.; b. Cleve., Nov. 12, 1919; s. Frank James and Mary Jane (Connor) R.; B.S., Western Res. U., 1940; m. Ruth Marie Pearce, Apr. 10, 1939; children—Janet M., Nancy C., Catherine A., James F., Thomas M., Dennis J., Ruth E., Mary H., John R. Mem. Cleve. Motion Picture Operators Union, Local 160, 1941—; partner Electric Speed Indicator Co., weather instrument maker, Cleve., 1965-67; bus. agt. Internat. Alliance of Theatrical Stage Employees and Moving Picture Operators of U.S. and Can., Cleve., 1967-78, internat. gen.-sec. treas., N.Y.C., 1978—, internat. trustee, 1969-78; v.p. Union Label dept. AFL-CIO, 1980—. Served to lt. USNR, 1943-46; PTO. Roman Catholic. Editor Bull., Internat. Alliance Quar., 1978—. Home: 15801 Edgecliff Rd Cleveland OH 44111 Office: Suite 601 1515 Broadway New York NY 10036

RILEY, T. A., wholesale and retail food company executive. Chmn., dir. Nash-Finch Co., Mpls. Office: Nash-Finch Co 3381 Gorham Ave Minneapolis MN 55426*

RILEY, WILLIAM E(DGAR), JR., technology development company marketing executive; b. Youngstown, Ohio, Feb. 2, 1930; s. William E. and Anne (Lynch) R.; m. Mary Curran Bringardner, June 27, 1953; children—Mary Lynn, Ann, Jean, Patrick, Michael. B.Sc., Ohio State U., 1952. Research engr. Battelle Meml. Inst., Columbus, Ohio, 1953-60; dir. project devel. systems and electronics dept. Battelle's Columbus Labs., 1960-70; mktg. coordinator Battelle Devel. Corp., Columbus, 1970-72, dir. mktg., 1972-84, gen. mgr. Lic. Devel. Ctr., 1984—. Mem. adv. com. internat. investment, tech. and devel. U.S. Dept. State. Served to ensign USN, 1952-53. Mem. IEEE, Am. Soc. Metals, Licensing Execs. Soc. U.S.A./Can. (trustee 1978-80, pres. 1980-81, internat. del. 1980—), Sigma Xi. Roman Catholic. Club: Ohio State Faculty (Columbus). Office: Battelle Devel Corp 505 King Ave Columbus OH 43201

RILEY-DAVIS, SHIRLEY MERLE, advertising agency executive, writer; b. Pitts., Feb. 4, 1935; d. William Riley and Beatrice Estelle (Whittaker) Byrd; m. Louis Davis; 1 child, Terri Judith. Student U. Pitts., 1952. Copywriter, Pitts. Mercantile Co., 1954-60; exec. sec. U. Mich., Ann Arbor, 1962-67; copy supr. N.W. Ayer, N.Y.C., 1968-76, assoc. creative dir., Chgo., 1977-81; copy supr. Leo Burnett, Chgo., 1981—; Writer of print, radio, and TV commercials. Bd. dirs. Epilepsy Services Chgo. Recipient Grand and First prize N.Y. Film Festival, 1974, Gold and Silver medal Atlanta Film Festival, 1973, Gold medal V.I. Film Festival, 1974, 50 Best Creatives award Am. Inst. Graphic Arts, 1972, Clio award, 1973, 74, 75, Andy Award of Merit, 1981, Silver medal Internat. Film Festival, 1982; Senatorial scholar. Mem. Women in Film, Facets Multimedia Film Theatre Orgn. (bd. dirs.), Nat. Assn. Female Execs. Democrat. Roman Catholic. Avocations: dance; poetry; design. Office: Leo Burnett USA Prudential Plaza Chicago IL 60601

RILLEMA, JAMES ALAN, endocrinology educator; b. Hudsonville, Mich., Nov. 6, 1942; s. Albert Rillema and Gertrude (Zylstra) De Young; m. Carol L. Blades, Aug. 10, 1968; children—Kurt A., Bradley J., Marc J. B.S., Calvin Coll., 1964; M.S., Mich. State U., 1966, Ph.D., 1968. Postdoctoral fellow in endocrinology Emory U. Sch. Medicine, Atlanta, 1968-70, research assoc., 1970-71; asst. prof. Wayne State U. Med. Sch., Detroit, 1971-75, assoc. prof., 1975-79, prof. endocrinology, 1979—. Contbr. articles to profl. jours. Grantee NIH, 1971—, Am. Cancer Soc., 1979—; Fogarty sr. internat. fellow Netherlands Cancer Inst., Amsterdam, 1980-81. Mem. Endocrine Soc., Am. Physiol. Soc. Detroit Physiol. Soc. Methodist. Home: 4619 Hedgewood St Birmingham MI 48010 Office: Dept Physiology Wayne State U Sch Medicine 540 Canfield Detroit MI 48201

RIMPILA, JULIAN JOHN, gastroenterologist; b. Chgo., Apr. 19, 1940; s. Charles Einar and Verna Catherine (Swanson) R.; B.A., Knox Coll., 1962; M.S., U. Chgo., 1966, M.D., 1966; m. Beverly Rose Dahlen, Apr. 30, 1966; children—John-Eric, Carl, Kari, Siiri, Heidi. Intern in medicine Northwestern U.-Evanston Hosp., 1966-67, resident in internal medicine, 1967-70; fellow in gastroenterology U. Chgo., 1973-76; practice medicine specializing in gastroenterology, Chgo., 1976—; chmn. dept. med. Henrotin Hosp., Chgo., 1984—; mem. med. staff Grant Hosp., Henrotin Hosp., Gottlieb Hosp.; mem. cons. staff Christ Hosp. Asst. scoutmaster Boy Scouts Am., Westchester, Ill., 1980—; councillor U. Chgo. Alumni Council, 1976-80. Served with M.C., U.S. Army, 1970-73. Recipient Leadership and Service award Boy Scouts Am., 1978, 79, 80. Mem. ACP, AMA, Am. Soc. Gastrointestinal Endoscopy, Chgo. Med. Soc., Assn. U.S. Army, Res. Officers Assn. U.S., Am. Scandinavian Found., Phi Beta Kappa, Tau Kappa Epsilon (Delta award Delta chpt. 1985). Sigma Xi. Republican. Lutheran. Mem. editorial bd. Medicine on the Midway, 1980—. Home: 11049 Windsor Dr Westchester IL 60153 Office: Suite 406 505 N Lake Shore Dr Chicago IL 60611

RINDOKS, ROLAND RAYNARD, steel company executive; b. East Chicago, Ind., June 16. 1925; s. Peter Stanley and Anna (Simon) R.; student Fenn Coll., 1944, Purdue U. Extension, 1946-47; m. Lillian Stone, Aug. 19, 1950; children—Roland Raynard, Bruce, Kurt, Brian. With M.W. Kellogg Constrn. Co., East Chicago, 1947-48; mech. designer Design Service, Inc., Chgo., 1948-49, Sumner S. Sollitt Constrn. Co., 1949-50; co-owner, mgr. Boulevard Pharmacy, East Chicago, 1950-53; mech. designer Petroleum Piping Contractors, Hammond, Ind., 1953-54; asst. plant engr. Gen. Am. Transp. Corp., East Chicago, 1954-62; project engr. Jones & Laughlin Steel Co. and precessor co., East Chicago, 1962—. Served with USAAC, 1943-46. Roman Catholic. Home: 7013 Ridgeland Ave Hammond IN 46324 Office: 3001 Dickey Rd East Chicago IN 46312

RINEBOLT, RICHARD J., judge; b. Bradner, Ohio, Sept. 14, 1922; s. Charles B. and Anna E. Rinebolt; m. Ruth C. Murphy, Oct. 1, 1955; children—David C., Ann L., Thomas H. Student, Northwestern U., 1940-42, Northwestern State Tchrs. Coll., 1943; J.D., Ohio No. U., 1948. Bar: Ohio 1948, U.S. Supreme Ct. 1966. Prosecutor, Findlay Mcpl. Ct., Ohio, 1956-63; asst. prosecuting atty. Hancock County, Ohio, 1958-64, prosecuting atty., 1965-72; mem. Hancock County Bd. Elections, 1973; judge Findlay Mcpl. Ct., 1977-78, Hancock County Common Pleas Ct., 1979—. Mem. Friends of Findlay Coll. Served to lt. col. USAF, 1942-45. Recipient Outstanding Jud. Service award, 1977, Superior Jud. Service award Supreme Ct. Ohio, 1978, Excellent Jud. Service award Supreme Ct. Ohio, 1980, 81, 82, 83, 84. Mem. ABA, Ohio Bar Assn., Northwestern Ohio Bar Assn., Findlay/Hancock County Bar Assn. (pres. 1958-59), Ohio Jud. Conf., Ohio Common Pleas Judges Assn., Am. Judges Assn., Am. Legion, Amvets (life), Aircraft Owners and Pilots Assn., Air Force Assn., Assn. Fourth Fighter Group, Delta Theta Phi (life). Club: Findlay Country. Lodge: Elks.

RINEHART, DANA GILLMAN, mayor, lawyer; b. Parkersburg, W.Va., Feb. 24, 1946; s. Paul George and Kathleen (Gillman) R.; m. Nancy Carol Grant, Nov. 28, 1968; children—Dana Gillman, Jr., Jenna Michelle, Jonathan Grant. B.A., J.D., Ohio State U. Bar: Ohio. Campaign aide Roger Cloud for Gov., Columbus, Ohio, 1970; assoc. Tyack, Scott & Colley, Columbus, 1970-72; ptnr. Matan, Rinehart, Smith, Columbus, 1972-84; treas. Franklin County, Columbus, 1977-84; mayor City of Columbus, 1984—. Co-author: Ohio in the 21st Century, 1981. Mem. Como Ave. Residents Assn., Columbus; ex officio mem. Franklin County Republican Orgn., Columbus, 1969—. Served with USN, 1984—. Recipient award Fin. Reporting Achievement, Nat. Mcpl. Fin., 1983, County Achievement award Nat. Assn. County Ofcls., 1979. Mem. U.S. Marine League, Amvets, Fraternal Order of Police and Assocs., Navy League (bd. dirs. 1982—). Methodist. Avocations: camping; fishing; boating; reading. Office: Office of Mayor City Hall 90 W Broad St Columbus OH 43215

RINEHART, JAMES RAYMOND, equipment parts manufacturing company executive; b. Hackensack, N.J., 1930; ed. Yale U., Harvard U. Chmn., chief exec. officer, pres. Clark Equipment Co., South Bend, Ind., Office: Clark Equipment Co 100 N Michigan St PO Box 7008 South Bend IN 46634

RINER, JAMES WILLIAM, lawyer; b. Jefferson City, Mo., Dec. 25, 1936; s. John Woodrow and Virginia Loraine (Jackson) R.; m. Carolyn Ruth Hicke, May 14, 1976; children—Alicia Gayle, Angela Gayle, Amity Gayle. B.A., U. Mo., 1957, LL.B., 1960. Bar: Mo. 1960, U.S. Dist. Ct. (we. dist.) Mo. 1982. Asst. atty. gen. Atty. Gen.'s Office Mo., Jefferson City, 1960; commd. 1st lt. U.S. Air Force, 1960, advanced through grades to lt. col., 1974; ret., 1981; ptnr. Inglish & Riner, P.C. and predecessor Inglish, Kay, Cartwright & Riner, P.C., Jefferson City, 1982—; city atty. Jefferson City, 1984—. Decorated Bronze Star, Meritorious service medal. Mem. Assn. Trial Lawyers Am., Mo. Assn. Trial Attys., Nat. Assn. Social Security Claimants Reps., Mo. Bar Assn., Cole County Bar Assn. Democrat. Lodge: Masons. Home: 601 Mesa Jefferson City MO 65101 Office: Inglish & Riner PC 222 Monroe Jefferson City MO 65101

RINER, RONALD NATHAN, cardiologist, consultant; b. Hot Springs, S.D., Mar. 7, 1949. A.B., Princeton, 1970; M.D., Cornell U., N.Y.C., 1974. Diplomate Am. Bd. Internal Medicine, Am. Bd. Cardiovascular Disease. Resident in internal medicine N.Y. Hosp., Meml. Sloan-Kettering, Hosp. for Spl. Surgery, 1974-79; resident in cardiology Mayo Grad. Sch. Medicine, Rochester, Minn., 1976-79; chmn. dept. internal medicine, St. Mary's Health Ctr., St. Louis, 1980-83, program dir. internal medicine, 1980-83; pvt. practice cardiology, St. Louis, 1983—; med. dir. BioMed. Systems, St. Louis, 1984—; asst. prof. medicine, Washington U. Med. Ctr., 1985—. Fellow N.Am. Coll. Cardiology; mem. N.Y. Acad. Scis., Mo. Soc. Internal Medicine (council), Mayo Alumni Assns., Cornell U. Alumni Assn., Princeton Alumni Assn. Club: Princeton U. Office: Univ Club Tower 1034 S Brentwood Blvd Suite 854 Saint Louis MO 63117

RING, ALVIN MANUEL, pathologist, hospital laboratory administrator; b. Detroit, Mar. 17, 1933; s. Julius and Helen (Krolik) R.; m. Cynthia Joan Jacobson, Sept. 29, 1963; children—Jeffrey, Melinda, Heather. B.S., Wayne State U., 1954; M.D., U. Mich., Ann Arbor, 1958. Intern, Mt. Carmel Hosp., Detroit, 1958-59; resident in pathology Michael Reese Hosp., Chgo., 1960-62; asst. pathologist King's County Hosp., Bklyn., 1962-63; assoc. pathologist El Camino Hosp., Mountain View, Calif., 1963-65; chief pathologist, dir. labs. St. Elizabeth's Hosp., Chgo., 1965-72; chief pathologist, dir. labs. Holy Cross Hosp., Chgo., 1972—; instr. SUNY, 1962-63, Stanford U., 1963-65; asst. prof. pathology U. Ill., Chgo., 1966-69, assoc. prof., 1969-78, prof., 1978—; adj. clin. prof. No. Ill. U., 1981—; chmn. histotech. Nat. Accrediting Agy. for Clin. Lab. Scis., 1977-81; inspector Coll. Am. Pathology, 1973—; spl. adv. com. Health Manpower, 1966-71; pres. Spear Computer Users Group, 1981-82; pres. Pathol. & Lab. Cons.; alt. councilor Chgo. Med. Soc., 1980-83, also mem. adv. com. on health care delivery; mem. adv. com. Mid-Am. chpt. ARC, 1979—; censor Chgo. Pathol. Soc., 1980-82, exec. com., 1984—. Fellow Coll. Am. Pathology; Am. Soc. Clin. Pathology; mem. AMA, Ill. Med. Soc., Chgo. Med. Soc., Ill. Pathol. Soc., Chgo. Pathol. Soc. (exec. com.), Am. Assn. Blood Banks, Phi Lambda Kappa. Author: Laboratory Correlation Manual, 1968, 74, 85; Laboratory Assistant Examination Review Book, 1971; Review Book in Pathology, Anatomic, 1985, Review Book in Pathology, Clinical, 1985; contbr. articles to med. jours; mem. editorial bd. Laboratory Medicine, 1975—. Home: 6843 N Lamon St Lincolnwood IL 60646 Office: 2701 W 68th St Chicago IL 60629

RING, LEONARD M., lawyer; b. Tauragena, Lithuania, May 11, 1923; s. Abe and Rose (Kahn) R.; brought to U.S., 1930, naturalized, 1930; student N.Mex. Sch. Mines, 1943-44; LL.B., DePaul U., 1949, J.D., 1971; m. Donna R. Cecrle, June 29, 1959; children—Robert Steven, Susan Ruth. Admitted to Ill. bar, 1949; since practiced in Chgo.; spl. asst. atty. gen. State Ill., 1967-72; spl. atty. Ill. Dept. Ins., 1967-73; spl. trial atty. Met. San. Dist. Greater Chgo., 1967-77; lectr. civil trial, appellate practice, tort law Nat. Coll. Advocacy, San Francisco, 1971, 72; guest lectr. civil trial practice U. Chgo. Law Sch., 1973; mem. com. jury instrns. Ill. Supreme Ct., 1967-71, 73—; nat. chmn. Attys. Congl. Campaign Trust, Washington, 1975-79. Trustee Roscoe Pound-Am. Trial Lawyers Found., Washington, 1974-80; chmn. bd. trustees Avery Coonley Sch., Downers Grove, Ill., 1974-75. Served with USA, 1943-46. Decorated Purple Heart. Fellow Am. Coll. Trial Lawyers, Internat. Acad. Trial Lawyers, Internat. Soc. Barristers; mem. Soc. Trial Lawyers, Appellate Lawyers Assn. (pres. 1974-75), Assn. Trial Lawyers Am. (nat. pres. 1973-74), Ill. Trial Lawyers Assn. (pres. 1966-68), Coll. of Advocacy Ill. Wesleyan Univ., Bloomington (asst. dir. 1983-85), Chgo. Bar Assn. (bd. mgrs. 1971-73), Am., Ill. bar assns., Lex Legio (pres. 1976-78). Club: Oak Brook Polo (Ill.).; Metropolitan, Monroe (Chgo.). Author: (with Harold A. Baker) Jury Instructions and Forms of Verdict, 1972; contbr. chpts. to books, articles to profl. jours. Home: 6 Royal Vale Dr Oakbrook IL 60521 Office: 111 W Washington St Chicago IL 60602

RING, PETER SMITH, management educator, researcher, lawyer; b. Norwich, Conn., Mar. 11, 1941; s. George Francis Jr. and Ellen (Donohue) R.; m. Jinx Anne Hack, Aug. 5, 1967; 1 dau., Kristin Anne. B.A. cum laude, St. Anselm's Coll., 1963; LL.B., Georgetown U., 1966; postgrad. Law Sch., Northwestern U., 1966-68; M.P.A., Harvard U., 1970; Ph.D., U. Calif.-Irvine, 1985. Bar: Conn. 1967. Legal adviser San Jose Police Dept., Calif., 1967-69; lead program planner N.Y.C. Office Mgmt. and Budget, 1970-72; asst. dir. personnel N.Y.C. Police Dept., 1972-75; dep. dir. budget Criminal Justice Coordinating Council, N.Y.C., 1975; assoc. prof. Justice Ctr., U. Alaska-Anchorage, 1975-79; assoc. prof. strategic mgmt. and orgn. Sch. Mgmt., U. Minn., Mpls., 1984—; research assoc. Pub. Policy Research Orgn., Irvine, 1980-82, Inst. Transp. Studies, Irvine, 1982-84; cons. LSA, Inc., Newport Beach, Calif., 1984. Contbr. articles to profl. jours., 1968—. Democrat. Roman Catholic. Home: 4761 Spring Circle Minnetonka MN 55345 Office: U Minn Sch Mgmt Dept Strategic Mgmt and Orgn 271 19th Ave S Minneapolis MN 55455

RINGE, MARION KAY, non-profit organization development executive; b. Detroit, Apr. 23, 1946; d. Norman Fred and Gladys Leona (Gohlke) R. B.A., Wayne State U., 1970, M.A., 1977. Asst. to v.p. advancement Merrill-Palmer Inst., Detroit, 1971-78; asst. dir. devel. Detroit Inst. Arts, 1978-80; asst. dir. devel. Harper-Grace Hosps., Detroit, 1980-85, dir. ann. support, 1985—. Mem. Nat. Assn. Hosp. Devel., Mich. Assn. Hosp. Devel., Nat. Soc. Fund Raising Execs. Republican. Lutheran. Home: 15405 Piedmont Ave Detroit MI 48223 Office: Harper-Grace Hosps 3990 John R Street Detroit MI 48201

RINGEL, HARVEY NORMAN, music educator; b. Peoria, Ill., Mar. 25, 1903; s. William Frederick and Mathilda Catherine (Wiesehan) R.; m. Marian E. Edwards, Aug. 30, 1931 (dec.); 1 dau., Marilyn; m. 2d, Lucile H. Hertel, Sept. 1, 1945. Mus.B., U. Ill., 1927; M.A., Columbia U., 1934; D.F.A., Chgo. Musical Coll., 1954; Mus.D. (hon.), U. Mo.-Kansas City, 1949. Tchr. singing Mercersburg Acad. (Pa.), 1927-29; instr. singing Wesley Coll., U. N.D., Grand Forks, 1929-31, dir. conservatory, assoc. prof. voice, 1931-35; pvt. voice instr., Chgo., 1935-46; adminstr., instr. Chgo. Mus. Coll., 1946-54; assoc. prof. voice Chgo. Music Coll., Roosevelt U., 1954-68, prof. voice, 1968-77, prof. emeritus, 1977—, dir. summer session, 1968; tchr. singing Am. Conservatory, Chgo., 1977—; cons. and lectr. in field. Fellow Nat. Assn. Tchrs. Singing (charter, editor bull. 1955-80, historian); mem. Soc. Am. Musicians (pres. 1976-78), Chgo. Singing Tchrs. Guild (pres. 1976-78), Am. Acad. Tchrs. Singing, Phi Mu Alpha, Sigma Phi Epsilon. Club: Cliff Dwellers. Author: The History of the National Association of Teachers of Singing, 1944-84, 1984. Condr. Midwest premiere The Redeemer (Martin Shaw), 1946. Home: 1139 Leavitt Ave Apt 203 Flossmoor IL 60422 Office: Am Conservatory of Music 116 S Michigan Ave Chicago IL 60603

RINGER, ROBERT KOSEL, avian physiologist, toxicologist, educator; b. Ringoes, N.J., Feb. 21, 1929; s. Louis and Louise Eleanor (Kosel) R.; m. Joan Lois Harwick, Aug. 18, 1951; 1 child, Kevin James. B.S., Rutgers U., 1950, M.S., 1952, Ph.D., 1955. Asst. prof. toxicology Rutgers U., New Brunswick, N.J., 1955-57; asst. prof. Mich. State U., East Lansing, 1957-61, assoc. prof., 1961-63, prof., 1963—; animal physiologist Unilever Labs., Sharnbrook, Eng., 1966; vis. scientist Corvallis Environ. Research Lab., EPA, Corvallis, Oreg., 1984-85; trustee Am. Assn. Accreditation Lab. Animal Care, 1969-81. Contbr. articles to profl. jours., chpts. to books. Pres. YMCA, Lansing, 1982. Fellow Poultry Sci. Assn.; mem. Am. Physiol. Soc., Am. Assn. Avian Pathologists, World's Poultry Sci. Assn., Soc. Environ. Toxicology and Chemistry, Sigma Xi, Alpha Zeta. Presbyterian. Home: 2607 Rockwood Dr East Lansing MI 48823 Office: Mich State U East Lansing MI 48824

RINGLAND, JAMES M., retail executive; b. Mpls. Student Trinity Coll., Hartford, Conn. With Sears, Roebuck & Co., gen. mgr. retail ops., St. Louis. Bd. dirs. Jr. Achievement, St. Louis; mem. arts and edn. council, Depaul Hosp. lay bd.; bd. dirs. United Way, St. Louis, Better Bus. Bur. Greater St. Louis. Lodge: Rotary. Address: 490 Northwest Plaza Saint Ann MO 63074

RINGLAND, ROBERT PAUL, judge; b. Cin., Oct. 6, 1945; s. James Wilson and Dorothy (Sandel) R.; 1 child, Adam Lyle. B.A., Ohio State U., 1963; J.D., U. Cin., 1970. Bar: Ohio 1971, U.S. Dist. Ct. (so. dist.) Ohio 1971. Atty. John Gehrig & Co., Cin., 1971-73; asst. pros. atty. Clermont County, Batavia, Ohio, 1973-77; sole practice, Batavia, 1973-83; judge Clermont County Ct., Batavia, 1977-83; judge Common Pleas Ct., Batavia, 1983—. Atty. Legal Aid Soc., Batavia, 1969-70. Served to 1st lt. U.S. Army, 1970-71. Recipient Superior Jud.

Service award Supreme Ct., Ohio, 1977-83, Dist. Award of Merit, Boy Scouts Am., Cin., 1984. Mem. 648 Bd. (chmn. 1973-74). Methodist. Lodges: Rotary (bd. dirs. 1979-80), Masons. Avocations: golf; fishing; racquetball; paleontology. Office: Common Pleas Ct 270 Main St Batavia OH 45103

RINGNESS, RONALD CHRISTIAN, marketing executive; b. Tampa, Fla., Oct. 17, 1949; s. Curtis Woodrow and Ruth Ann (Hargis) R.; m. Margaret Ann Trebilcock, Aug. 12, 1972; children—Julie, Jeffrey, Caitlin. B.S. in Bus. Adminstrn., Oral Roberts U., 1971; postgrad. S.W. Mo. State U., 1971-72. Exec. mgmt. trainee Ednl. Devel. Corp., Tulsa, 1972; mktg. mgr. Liberty Industries, Girard, Ohio, 1972-77, v.p. mktg., 1977-81, exec. v.p., 1981—, exec. v.p., ptnr., 1983—; ptnr. Charles Christian & Assocs., Advt., Girard, 1980—; dir. Liberty Industries, Girard, Kassko Enterprises, Youngstown, Ohio. Republican. Club: Youngstown Country. Avocations: jogging; golfing; tennis; skiing; reading. Home: 3735 Sampson Rd Youngstown OH 44505 Office: Liberty Industries Inc 555 Tibbetts Wick Rd Girard OH 44420

RINGOEN, RICHARD MILLER, manufacturing executive; b. Ridgeway, Iowa, May 15, 1926; s. Elmer and Evelyn Louise (Miller) R.; student U. Dubuque (Iowa), 1944-45, Marquette U., Milw., 1945-46; B.S. in Elec. Engring., U. Iowa, 1947, M.S., 1948; m. Joan Marie Brandt, June 7, 1953; children—David, John, Daniel. Vice pres. Collins Radio, Cedar Rapids, Iowa, 1948-59; dir. spl. projects Martin-Marietta Co., Denver, 1959-70; v.p., gen. mgr. Ball Brothers Research Corp., Boulder, Colo., 1970-74; corp. v.p. ops. Ball Corp., Muncie, Ind., 1974-78, pres., chief operating officer, 1978-80, pres., chief exec. officer, 1981—, also dir.; dir. Am. Nat. Bank & Trust Co., CTS Corp., Arvin Industries, Inc., Dorsey Corp.; chief exec. officer, dir. Tally Corp., 1973-78. Pres., Arapohoe County (Colo.) Sch. Bd., 1963-70; div. chmn. United Way, 1977-78; trustee Purdue U., Hudson Inst., Ind. State C. of C., Muncie Symphony Orch. Served with USN, 1944-46. Mem. Glass Packaging Inst., Can Mfrs. Inst., Ind. C. of C. (bd. dirs.), Muncie C. of C. Methodist. Club: Rotary Internat. Patentee in communications, navigation and electronics circuitry. Office: Ball Corp 345 S High St Muncie IN 47302

RINKEL, GENE KEITH, librarian, clergyman; b. Fayette County, Ill., Feb. 27, 1929; s. Walter M. and Jane E. (Dixon) R.; m. Margaret E. Causey, Aug. 4, 1950; children—Stephen D., Karen Rinkel Smith. A.B. in Philosophy and Religion, Greenville Coll., 1950; B.D., Asbury Theol. Sem., 1958; M.S. in L.S., U. Ill., 1967. Ordained to ministry Methodist Ch., 1950; minister, Free Meth. Ch., Athens, Ga., 1950-52, Davenport, Iowa, 1956-58, Aurora, Ill., 1958-63; librarian U. Ill., Urbana-Champaign, 1967—. Author, editor bibliographies, 1973; contbr. articles to profl. publs. Pres. and dir. Mahomet (Ill.) Pub. Library Bd., 1975—. Mem. ALA (coms. 1975—), Assn. Coll. and Research Libraries, Library Adminstrn. and Mgmt. Assn. Lutheran. Home: 404 N Weathering Dr Mahomet IL 61853 Office: Univ Ill 346-F Rare Book Room 1408 W Gregory Dr Urbana IL 61801

RINKEL, VERNON JOHN, electronics educator, consultant; b. Morrison County, Minn., Dec. 26, 1940; s. George and Mercedes (Beumer) R.; m. Mary Scully, July 13, 1963; children—Jeffry, Michaela, John, Andrea. Installer, Western Union Co., Omaha, 1960-63, ops. tech., 1965-70, city ops. mgr., 1965-70, city mgr., 1970-72; supr. engring. services Western Union Hawaii, Honolulu, 1972-74; instr. electronics tech. Wadena (Minn.) Area Vocat. Tech. Inst., 1974—, dept. head, 1980—; cons. electronics and mgmt.; lectr. in field. Mem. Am. Vocat. Assn., Minn. Vocat. Assn., Wadena Vocat. Assn., Am. Fedn. Tchrs., Minn. Fedn. Tchrs., Wadena Fedn. Tchrs., Nat. Inst. Cert. Engring. Technologies, Minn. Trade and Industry Assn. Mem. Democratic Farm Labor Party. Roman Catholic. Office: Wadena Area Vocat Tech Inst 405 SW Colfax St Wadena MN 56482

RION, JOHN HAYES, lawyer; b. Dayton, Ohio, Aug. 4, 1943; s. Paul West and Vera E. (Spitler) R.; m. Barbara Smith, July 31, 1965; children—Stacey, Jennifer, Jon Paul. B.A., Ohio State U., 1965; J.D., U. Toledo, 1969. Bar: Ohio 1970, U.S. Dist. Ct. (so. dist.) Ohio 1970, U.S. Ct. Appeals (6th cir.) 1983, U.S. Supreme Ct. 1977. Ptnr., Rion, Rion & Rion, Dayton, Ohio, 1970-78; v.p. Rion, Rion & Rion, L.P.A., 1978—; lectr. in field. Contbr. articles to profl. jours. Mem. jud. selection com. Republican Com., 1974. Mem. Ohio State Bar Assn. (faculty 1983), Nat. Assn. Criminal Def. Lawyers, ABA, Dayton Bar Assn. (Outstanding Service award 1977, 80, chmn. bar briefs 1975). Republican. Methodist (pres. Grace United Ch. Ushers Club 1982—). Clubs: Dayton Racquet, Comos (pres. 1982—). Lodges: Masons (32 degree), Shriners. Avocations: fly fishing; tennis. Office: Rion Rion & Rion Suite 1630 1 First Nat Plaza PO Box 1262 Dayton OH 45402

RIORDAN, RAY JOSEPH, telephone company exec.; b. Green Bay, Wis., Jan. 27, 1916; s. Daniel E. and Florence E. (Brooks) R.; student St. Norbert Coll., 1933-35; B.S., Marquette U., 1937; m. Eileen Kelly, June 25, 1941; children—Mary Eileen (Mrs. Richard Harper), Ray Joseph, Patrick D., Robert H. Editor, pub. Tri County News, Pulaski, Wis., 1938-41; salesman Yellow Pages, Mich., Wis. and Ind., 1941-42; telephone engr. Hercules Powder Co., Wilmington, Del., 1942-43; comml. mgr. Gen. Telephone Co., Wausau and Madison, Wis., 1943-46; comml. mgr. 6 state area Central Telephone Co., LaCrosse, Wis., 1946-52; exec. v.p. Wis. State Telephone Assn., Madison, 1952-81; pres. Shamrock Affiliates, Madison, 1959—; sec.-treas. Wis. State Telephone Found., Madison, 1965-81, trustee, 1981—; sec.-treas. N.E. Telephone Co., Pulaski, 1950—; mem. Wis. Emergency Number Systems Bd., 1981-82. Named to State Telephone Industry Hall of Fame. Mem. Council Telephone Execs. (pres. 1962, 70), Ind. Telephone Pioneers (pres. Badger chpt. 1954-55), Telephone Pioneers Am. (life). Clubs: Elks, Madison, Black Hawk Country. Home: 6711 N Dunlap Hollow Rd Mazomanie WI 53560 Office: 617 N Segoe Rd Suite 202 Madison WI 53705

RIORDAN, ROBERT VINCENT, archaeologist, anthropology educator; b. Newark, Sept. 19, 1946; s. Vincent John and Alice Elizabeth (Kindmark) R.; m. Sandra Elaine Neifert, Aug. 26, 1973; 1 son, Corey James. B.A., Colgate U., 1968; Ph.D., So. Ill. U., 1975. Archaeologist Md. Hist. Trust, Annapolis, 1975-76; asst. prof. anthropology Wright State U., Dayton, Ohio, 1976-82, assoc. prof. anthropology, chmn. dept. sociology and anthropology, 1982—; cons. archaeologist, Xenia, Ohio, 1976—. Author jour. articles and contracted reports. Recipient Liberal Arts Merit Teaching award Wright State U., 1981. Mem. Soc. Am. Archaeology, Soc. for Hist. Archaeology, Ohio Archeol. Council (trustee 1984—), Central States Anthrop. Soc., Sigma Xi. Avocations: collector of juvenile series books; tennis; swimming. Home: 1354 Old Springfield Pike Xenia OH 45385 Office: Dept Sociology and Anthropology Wright State U Dayton OH 45435

RIPLEY, RANDALL BUTLER, political science educator; b. Des Moines, Jan. 24, 1938; s. Henry Dayton and Aletha Fay (Butler) R.; m. Vivian R. Usher, June 17, 1961; children—Frederick Joseph, Vanessa Gail; m. 2d, Grace A. Franklin, Oct. 15, 1974. B.A., DePauw U., 1959; M.A., Harvard U., 1961, Ph.D., 1963. Intern., Office Dem. Whip, U.S. Ho. of Reps., 1963; research fellow, research staff Brookings Instn., 1963-67; assoc. prof. Ohio State U., 1967-69, prof., chmn. dept. polit. sci., 1969—. Trustee Opera Columbus (Ohio), 1981-84. Woodrow Wilson fellow, 1959-60; Danforth fellow, 1959-63. Mem. Am. Polit. Sci. Assn., Midwest Polit. Sci. Assn., Policy Studies Orgn., Phi Beta Kappa. Democrat. Author: Party Leaders in the House of Representatives, 1967; Majority Party Leadership in Congress, 1969; Power in the Senate, 1969; The Politics of Economic and Human Resource Development, 1972; American National Government and Public Policy, 1974; Congress: Process and Policy, 3d edit., 1983; co-author: Policy-Making in the Federal Executive Branch, 1975; Congress, the Bureaucracy, and Public Policy, 3d edit., 1984; A More Perfect Union, 3d edit., 1985; CETA Politics and Policy, 1973-82, 84; Policy Analysis in Political Science, 1985; Policy Implementation and Bureaucracy, 1986, editor several books; contbr. articles to profl. jours. Home: 2685 Berwyn Rd Columbus OH 43221 Office: Dept Political Science Ohio State U Columbus OH 43210

RIPPERT, ERIC THEODORE, oral and maxillofacial surgeon; b. Ft. Devens, Mas., Feb. 22, 1942; s. Jacob Kopf and Kathleen (Faugnan) R.; m. Mary Ellen Dormer, Nov. 25, 1965; children—Thomas Ashton, Kathleen Marie. A.B., Holy Cross Coll., 1960-64; D.M.D., U. Pa., 1968. Diplomate Am. Bd. Oral and Maxillofacial Surgery. Intern, Phila. Gen. Hosp., 1968-69, resident, 1973-76; commd. ensign Dental Corps, U.S. Navy, 1964, advanced through grades to capt., 1984; fellow in oral surgery Marine Corps Recruit Depot, San Diego, 1972-73; oral and maxillofacial surgeon U.S. Naval Hosp., Great Lakes, Ill., 1981—, Quantico, Va., 1979-81, USS Dwight D. Eisenhower, 1977-79; asst. clin. prof. oral surgery Med. Coll. Va., Richmond, 1979-81; assoc. prof. oral and maxillofacial surgery Temple U., Phila., 1984—; cons. Loyola U. Sch. Dentistry, Chgo., 1984—. Instr., Confraternity of Christian Doctrine; referee Am. Youth Soccer Orgn.; active Boy Scouts Am. Recipient Upjohn award Phila. Gen. Hosp., 1969. Fellow Am. Soc. Oral and Maxillofacial Surgeons; mem. Great Lakes Dental Soc. Republican. Roman Catholic. Club: Varsity. Office: Naval Hosp Great Lakes IL 60088

RIPPY, FRANCES MARGUERITE MAYHEW, educator, editor; b. Ft. Worth, Sept. 16, 1929; d. Henry Grady and Marguerite Christine (O'Neill) Mayhew; B.A., Tex. Christian U., 1949; M.A., Vanderbilt U., 1951, Ph.D. (fellow), 1957; postgrad. Birkbeck Coll. U. London (Eng.), 1952-53; m. N. Merrill Rippy, Aug. 29, 1955 (dec. Sept. 1980); children—Felix O'Neill, Conrad Mayhew, Marguerite Hailey. Teaching fellow Vanderbilt U., Nashville, 1951-52; instr. Tex. Christian U., 1953-55; instr. to asst. prof. Lamar State U., 1955-59; successively asst., assoc., prof. dept. English, Ball State U., Muncie, Ind., 1959—; assoc. prof., 1964-68, prof., 1968—; dir. English Ph.D. studies, 1966—, vis. prof. U. Puerto Rico, summers 1959, 60, 61, Sam Houston State U., summer, 1957; cons., evaluator North Central Assn. Colls. and Schs., 1973—, New Eng. Assn. Schs. and Colls., 1983—. Treas., Friends of Muncie Pub. Library, 1976-78. Named Danforth Asso., 1965—; Danforth summer grantee, 1962; MacClintock research scholar, 1965; Lilly Library grantee, 1979. Mem. MLA, Am. Soc. 18th Century Studies (charter), Johnson Soc. Central Region (sec. 1961-62), Coll. English Assn., Nat. Council Tchr. English, AAUP, Ind. Coll. English Assn. (sec.-treas. 1982-83, v.p. 1983-84, pres. 1984-85), Ind. Council Tchrs. English. Editor Ball State U. Forum. Author articles in profl. jours. Home: 4709 W Jackson St Muncie IN 47304

RISCH, RICHARD WILLIAM, horticultural manager; b. Milw., Jan. 8, 1941; s. Frederick William and Sophia (Banker) R. B.S., U. Wis.-Milw., 1965. Asst. floriculturist Mitchell Park Conservatory, Milw., 1968-72, asst. hort. dir., 1972-81, hort. mgr., 1981—. Editor, photographer: Mitchell Park Conservatory Souvenir Booklet, 1975, 81. Mem. Am. Assn. Bot. Gardens and Arborea (chmn. conservatory com. 1984—), Milw. Bonsai Soc. (June Kelley award 1982). Office: Mitchell Park Conservatory 524 S Layton Blvd Milwaukee WI 53220

RISCH, THOMAS JOSEPH, college administrator; b. St. Louis, Mar. 1, 1939; s. Arthur Frederick and Edna Marie (Reilly) R.; m. Constance Mae Townsend, July 4, 1964; children—Michael, Laura. B.S., Quincy Coll., 1961; M.S., Ill. State U., 1963; Ph.D., Ind. State U., 1969. Resident hall dir. Ind. State U., Terre Haute, 1964-67, doctoral fellow, 1967-69; dean men Bucknell U., Lewisburg, Pa., 1969-73; dean students Allegheny Coll., Meadville, Pa., 1973-78; dean student services Southeast Mo. State U., Cape Girardeau, 1978-83, v.p. student services, 1983—. Bd. dirs. St. Francis Mental Health Ctr., Cape Girardeau, 1984—; membership v.p. Boy Scouts Am., Cape Girardeau, 1983-85; coordinator Nat. Games U.S. Assn. Blind Athletes, Cape Girardeau, 1981; active in Gov.'s Task Force Ridesharing. Mem. Am. Assn. Higher Edn., Nat. Assn. Student Personnel Adminstrs., Am. Coll. Personnel Assn., Mo. Coll. Personnel Assn. Lodge: Lions. Avocations: little league coach; tennis. Home: 2748 Oakshire Circle Cape Girardeau MO 63701 Office: Southeast Mo State U 900 Normal Ave Cape Girardeau MO 63701

RISIK, ROBERT ALAN, government executive; b. Libertyville, Ill., Sept. 15, 1949; s. Albert Joseph and Viola Lorraine (Losey) R.; m. Joan Marie Dorfler, Nov. 27, 1971; children—Michael, Elizabeth. B.A. in Social Sci., U. Ill., 1971; M.S. in Urban Affairs, U. Wis.-Milw., 1974. Tchr., coach High Sch. Dist. 227, Park Forest, Ill., 1971-72; adminstrv. intern Village of Brown Deer (Wis.), 1974; asst. city mgr., Marquette, Mich., 1974-76; city mgr., Manistique, Mich., 1976-79; exec. dir. Mich. Base Conversion Authority, Kincheloe, Mich., 1979-82; regional dir. Mich. Upper Great Lakes Region Office, Sault Ste. Marie, 1982-83; pres. Lakeshore Enterprises, Inc., Sault Ste. Marie, 1983—; adj. instr. Lake Superior State Coll., Sault Sainte Marie, 1980-81; guest lectr. Northern Mich. U., Marquette, 1975-76; spl. community devel. cons. HUD, Internat. City Mgmt. Assn., 1980; spl. asst. Gov.'s Task Force, Hamtramck, 1980, Luce County, 1982. Recipient Mgmt. Innovation award Internat. City Mgmt. Assn., 1981; Urban Affairs Cudahy Found. grantee, 1974. Mem. Internat. City Mgmt. Assn., Am. Soc. Pub. Adminstrn.

RISLER, RICHARD ANTHONY, sheriff; b. Mondovi, Wis., Apr. 25, 1949; s. Henry and Matilda Anne (Bauer) R.; m. Kathleen Louise Butler, Feb. 1, 1969; 1 child, Rebecca K. Diploma Northwestern U., Evanston, Ill., 1976, diploma in Principles Police Mgmt., 1978. Recruiting, retention officer U.S. Army Res., Eau Claire, Wis., 1967-77; asst. chief of police Menomonie, Wis., 1970-81; sheriff Dunn County, Menomonie, 1981—. Sec. Dunn County Republicans, Menominie, 1982-84. Recipient Soldier of Yr. award Milw. Jour., 1969. Mem. Badger Sheriff Assn., Wis. Sheriff and Dep. Sheriffs Assn., Nat. Sheriffs Assn., Western Wis. Law Enforcement Info. Assn., Nat. Rifle Assn. Lodges: Moose; Kiwanis. Avocations: hunting, fishing, reading. Home: Route 4 PO Box 156 Valley View Rd Menominie WI 54751 Office: 714 17th St Menomonie WI 54751

RISMAN, WILLIAM BURTON, real estate developer, builder, lawyer; b. Cleve., Aug. 29, 1926; s. Joseph and Anna (Reisman) R.; m. Marion Carol Weinberg, Sept. 23, 1951; children—Wayne R., Robert Grant. J.D., U. Miami, 1950. Bar: Fla. 1951. Chmn. bd. Realtek Industries, Inc., constrn. co., Cleve., Consol. Mgmt., Inc., real estate mgmt. for Realtek Industries, Cleve.; mem. adv. bd. dirs. BancOhio, Columbus; dir. BancOhio Nat. Bank; founder, trustee State Bank & Trust Co., Mentor, Ohio; trustee U.S. Realty Investments, Cleve.; dir. European Homes, Paris. Trustee, Kent (Ohio) State U.; co-chmn., trustee Mt. Sinai Med. Ctr., Cleve.; mem. endowment investment com. St. Andrew Abbey, Benedictine Order, Cleve.; mem. nat. fin. com. John Glenn for Pres., Served with U.S. Army, 1944-46.

RISSLER, HERBERT J., history educator; b. Brazil, Ind., July 24, 1932; s. Herbert E. and Sarah (Burdon) R.; m. Carolyn Jane Smith, Dec. 16, 1966; children—Leslie Jane, Lisa Rose. B.S., Ind. State U., 1953; M.A., Ind. U., 1956, Ph.D., 1961. Resident lectr. Ind. U., South Bend, 1959-62; asst. prof. Ind. State U., Terre Haute, 1962-66, assoc. prof., 1966-70, prof. history, chmn. dept., 1970—; cons. Wabash Valley Supplementary Edn. Ctr., Terre Haute, 1966-70; chmn. Ind. State U. Archives Com., 1978—. Contbr. articles to profl. jours. Served with AUS, 1954-56. Recipient Research awards Ind. State U., 1967, 70. Mem. Am. Hist. Assn., Orgn. Am. Historians, Assn. Ind. Historians, Phi Alpha Theta, Pi Gamma Mu, Phi Delta Kappa, Pi Omega Pi, Blue Key. Democrat. Methodist. Lodge: Masons. Avocations: swimming; reading; travel. Home: Rural Route 15 Brazil IN 47834 Office: Dept History Ind State U Terre Haute IN 47809

RISTOW, GEORGE EDWARD, neurologist, educator; b. Albion, Mich., Dec. 15, 1943; s. George Julius and Margaret (Beattie) R.; 1 child, George Andrew Martin. B.A., Albion Coll., 1965; D.O., Coll. Osteo. Medicine and Surgery, Des Moines, 1969. Diplomate Am. Bd. Psychiatry and Neurology. Intern, Garden City Hosp., 1969-70; resident Wayne State U., 1970-74; fellow U. Newcastle Upon Tyne, 1974-75; asst. prof. dept. neurology Wayne State U., Detroit, 1975-77; assoc. prof. Mich. State U., East Lansing, Mich., 1977-83, prof., 1983-84, prof., chmn., 1984—. Fellow Am. Acad. Neurology; mem. AMA, Am. Osteo. Assn., Pan Am. Med. Assn., Am. Coll. Neuropsychiatrists (sr.). Home: 2576 Woodhill Okemos MI 48864 Office: Coll Osteo Medicine Dept Internal Medicine Mich St U B-305 West Fee Hall East Lansing MI 48824

RISTUBEN, PETER JOHN, college president; b. Black River Falls, Wis., Oct. 4, 1933; s. Oliver T. and Aleda (Johnson) R.; m. Nina Christine Olson, June 9, 1956; children—Ann Marit, Peter Jr., Erik P. A.A., Centralia Coll., 1953; B.A., Concordia Coll., 1955; M.A., U. S.D., 1957; Ph.D., U. Okla., 1964. Assoc. prof. history Pacific Luth. U., Tacoma, 1960-70; assoc. dir. overseas program SUNY-Albany, 1970-71; dean acad. affairs Wagner Coll., S.I., N.Y., 1971-73; v.p., dean Calif. Luth. Coll., Thousand Oaks, 1973-77; dean SUNY-Empire State Coll., Buffalo, 1977-83; pres. Bethany Coll., Lindsborg, Kans., 1983—; edn. advisor U.S. Peace Corps No. Nigeria, 1966-68; cons. Luth. Ch. Am., 1977, Qatar Gen. Petroleum Corp., Doha, 1983, U.S. Dept. Agr., 1983. Author: (with T. Lehmann) Colleges in Partnership, 1982. Contbr. articles to profl. jours. Mem. adv. bd. Community Service Soc. N.Y.C., 1973; mem. Thousand Oaks Planning Commn., Calif., 1976-77; bd. dirs. Ctr. Theol. Studies, Calif., 1973-77, Swedish Council Am., 1983—; chmn. gov. bd. Buffalo Gen. Hosp. Community Mental Health Ctr., 1981-83. Fellow Soc. Values in Higher Edn.; mem. Pacific N.W. Council Regional Research, (chmn. 1964-66), Kans. Ind. Coll. Assn. (treas. 1985), Nat. Conf. Luth. Coll. Deans (Chmn. 1975), Soc. Internat. Devel., Orgn. Am. Historians, Am. Assn. Higher Edn., Pi Gamma Mu, Phi Alpha Theta. Lodge: Rotary. Home: 604 N 3d Lindsborg KS 67456 Office: Bethany Coll Lindsborg KS 67456

RITCHEL, LILLIAN WILLENE, retail store executive, educator; d. Oscar Alford and Ruth (Provert) Baker; m. Russell Holmes Ritchel, Oct. 18, 1945; children—Russell, Jr., Jill Ellen, Keith Allen. Student U. Ill., 1944-45, Aurora Coll., 1960-65; B.S. in Edn., No. Ill. U., 1970. Nursery sch. tchr. New Engl. Ch., Aurora, Ill., 1959-62; dir. Christian edn. First Presbyn. Ch., Aurora, 1963-66; tchr. St. Joseph Sch., Aurora, 1968-73; owner, mgr. Cross Reference Bookstore, Aurora, 1973—. Contbr. articles to bookstore jours. Dir. sch. bd. Aurora Christian Sch.; mem. candidate com. Blackhawk Presbytery, Oregon, Ill.; area leader War on Proverty, Chgo., 1986. Mem. Christian Booksellers Assn. (area rep. 1980-84, exec. sec. bd. dirs. 1985—). Republican. Avocations: speaking; travel. Home: 1110 N Farnsworth #313 Aurora IL 60605 Office: Cross Reference Bookstore 630 N Lake St Aurora IL 60506

RITCHEY, KENNETH WILLIAM, special education administrator; b. Washington, June 7, 1947; s. Conrad Monroe and Katherine Costance (Sheris) R.; m. Nancy Jayne Kirk, Aug. 22, 1970; children—Kirk Damon, Erin Kathryn. B.S. in Edn., Shippensburg U., 1969; M.Ed., in Spl. Edn., U. Va., 1972; M.S. in Ednl. Adminstrn., U. Dayton, 1980. Spl. edn. tchr. Shippensburg (Pa.) Area Sch. Dist., 1969-71; head cross country coach Shippensburg U., 1970-74; master tchr., coordinator work experience program Lincoln Intermediate Unit, New Oxford, Pa., 1971-76; adult edn. tchr. Franklin County Prison, Chambersburg, Pa., 1972-76; asst. supt. mgmt. services Montgomery County Bd. Mental Retardation and Devel. Disabilities, Dayton, Ohio, 1977-83, supt. bd., 1983—; mem. part-time faculty spl. edn. dept. U. Dayton, 1983—. Vol. health div. II, United Way. HEW fellow U. Va., 1970. Mem. Am. Assn. Mental Deficiency, Assn. Supervision and Curriculum Devel., Am. Assn. Sch. Adminstrs., Profl. Assn. Retardation, Ohio Assn. Supts. County Bds. Mental Retardation, Council Ednl. Facility, Phi Delta Kappa. Democrat. Methodist. Former editor statewide newsletter for tchrs. and profls. in Work Experience. Home: 454 W Hudson Ave Dayton OH 45406 Office: 8114 N Main St Dayton OH 45415

RITENOUR, MICHAEL DAVID, lawyer; b. Detroit, Feb. 1, 1955; s. Edward Albert and Yvonne Kathleen (Sellers) R.; m. Susan Louise Carey, Aug. 4, 1979. B.A. with honors, U. Mich., 1977; J.D., Wayne State U., 1980. Bar: Mich. 1981, U.S. Dist. Ct. (ea. dist.) Mich. 1981, U.S. Ct. Appeals (6th cir.) 1982. Assoc., Gregory R. Kelly, P.C., Birmingham, Mich., 1980-81, Wallace & Ritenour, Bloomfield Hills, Mich., 1982-83; sole practice, Farmington Hills, Mich., 1983-84; pub. liability atty. Kmart Corp., Troy, Mich., 1984—. Editor: Handbook for Court Monitors, 1982; Republican Voters Guide, 1982. Treas., Southfield Republican Club, Mich., 1980-81; treas., lectr. Mothers Against Drunk Drivers, Oakland County chpt., Mich., 1982-83; bd. dirs. Oakland Citizens League, 1983—. Nat. Merit scholar, 1973; Mich. Competitive scholar State of Mich., 1973; Detroit News scholar, 1973. Mem. Assn. Trial Lawyers Am., ABA, Mich. Trial Lawyers Assn., Oakland County Bar Assn., U. Mich. Alumni Assn., Delta Theta Phi (dean 1979-80). Office: Law Offices of Michael D Ritenour 32969 Hamilton Ct Suite 101 Farmington Hills MI 48018

RITSEMA, DOUGLAS JAMES, lawyer, state legislator; b. Holland, Mich., Dec. 28, 1952; s. Herbert and Jeanne Elaine (VerBeek) R. B.A. in Math., Northwestern Coll., Orange City, Iowa, 1975; J.D., U. Iowa-Iowa City, 1978. Bar: Iowa 1979. Mem. Iowa Ho. of Reps., 1979-82; mem. Iowa Senate, 1983—. Mem. Iowa State Bar Assn. Republican. Mem. Reformed Ch.

RITSON, SCOTT CAMPBELL, construction management consultant, real estate management and development consultant; b. New London, Conn., July 20, 1945; s. Ian Douglas and Ann Breyer (Maxwell) R.; m. Diane Kischitz, May 16, 1966 (div. Oct. 1977); children—Mark Douglas (dec.), Carrie Stewart; m. 2d, Donna Diane Nietschmann, Feb. 25, 1978. Student U. Vt., 1963-65. Field engrs. asst. Gilbane Bldg. Co., Providence, 1966-67; project control engr. Olin Corp., Stamford, Conn., 1967-73; v.p. Reed Corp., Roxbury, Conn., 1973-76; pres., propr. Ritson & Assocs., Vernon Hills, Ill., 1976—; pres. Axeman Island, Ltd., Gananoque, Ont., Can., 1978-79, v.p., 1979—, dir., 1981—; pres. Ritson, Ryan Inc., Gurnee, Ill., 1983—. Charter mem. Congl. Adv. Com., Washington, 1982. Can. nat. sailfish champion, 1961. Mem. Internat. Assn. Profl. Planners and Schedulers (charter mem.). Clubs: Chgo. Yacht; Clayton (N.Y.) Yacht; Trident Yacht (Gananoque, Ont., Can.). Home: 131 Windsor Dr Vernon Hills IL 60061

RITT, ROBERT KING, mathematics educator, researcher; b. N.Y.C., Dec. 30, 1924; s. Oscar L. and Anna Ritt; m. Helen L. Grossfeld, Nov. 26, 1950; children—Franklin, Alexander, Michael, Adam. A.B., Columbia Coll., 1944, Ph.D., 1953. Asst. prof. math. U. Mich., Ann Arbor, 1953-58, assoc. prof. math., 1958-62; sr. research mathematician Conductron Corp., Ann Arbor, 1962-63, div. mgr., 1963-68; pres. Ritt Labs., Ann Arbor, 1968-71; chmn. dept. math., prof. math. Ill. State U., Normal, 1971—. Author: Fourier Series, 1971; also articles. Bd. dirs. Peoria Civic Opera, Ill., 1984—. Served to lt. (j.g.) USN, 1944-46. Pulitzer scholar, 1941. Mem. Union Radio Sci. Internat., Phi Beta Kappa, Sigma Xi. Home: 1017 Porter Ln Normal IL 61761 Office: Ill State U Dept Math Normal IL 61761

RITTENBERG, KURT GEORGE, hospital financial administrator; b. Dubuque, Iowa, Aug. 5, 1951; s. Everett Charles and Angeline (Arvanitas) R.; m. Carol Irene Naumes, Oct. 12, 1974; children—Christina, Kathryn. B.A., George Washington U., 1973. Adminstrv. asst. Evanston Hosp. (Ill.), 1974-76; budget dir. St. Joseph Hosp., Chgo., 1976-82, dir. patient accounts, 1982—. Mem. St. Mathias Sch. Bd., 1983—. Mem. Hosp. Fin. Mgmt. Assn. Roman Catholic. Home: 2208 W Leland Ave Chicago IL 60625 Office: St Joseph Hosp 2900 Lake Shore Dr Chicago IL 60657

RITTER, EDWARD MICHAEL, JR., educational administrator; b. Gary, Ind., June 23, 1948; s. Edward Michael and Mary (Churchia) R.; m. Barbara Lynn Williams, Mar. 30, 1979; 2 children—Amanda Lynn, Katherine Johanna. B.A. in English, Valparaiso U., 1970; M.S. in Edn., Ind. State U., 1975, Ed.S., 1979. Tchr. English, Hobart Jr. High Sch., Ind., 1970-74; asst. prin. Concord Jr. High Sch., Elkhart, Ind., 1974-77; prin. Brighton Sch., Ind., 1977-79, Lakeland Jr. High Sch., LaGrange, Ind., 1979—; chmn. N.E. Ind. Prins. Study Council, 1980-81. Served with USAR, 1970-78. Mem. N.E. Ind. Prins. Assn., Assn. Sch. Curriculum Devel., Nat. Middle Sch. Assn., Nat. Assn. Middle Sch. Prins. Republican. Lutheran. Club: Lions (chmn. 1982—). Avocations: traveling, camping, sports, reading. Home: 338 W Central St LaGrange IN 46761 Office: Lakeland Jr High Sch Rural Route 5 LaGrange IN 46761

RITTER, GEORGE, cardiologist, internist; b. Detroit, Nov. 22, 1921; s. Frank Alexander and Gisela (Gottlieb) R.; m. Mary J. Coracy, Dec. 23, 1944; children—James, John, William, George Thomas, Robert. B.S., Wayne State U., 1942, M.D., 1945. Diplomate Am. Bd. Internal Medicine. Intern Detroit Gen. Hosp., 1945-46, resident Fitzsimons Gen. Hosp., Denver, 1947-48, VA Hosp., Allen Park, Mich., 1948-51; practice medicine specializing in cardiology, 1951—; mem. staff Mt. Carmel Hosp., Detroit, 1951—; mem. staff Providence Hosp., Southfield, Mich., chief, div. medicine, 1966-69, assoc. chief, div. medicine, 1969-71, chief, sect. cardiology, 1972-84, mem. exec. com., 1978-83; clin. instr. Wayne State U. Sch. Medicine, Detroit, 1956-76, clin. asst. prof., 1977—; head, sect. cardiology Providence Hosp., 1969-83, pres. Med. Staff, 1981. Contbr. articles on cardiology to med. jours. Adv. mem. Oakland County Emergency Med. System, Mich., 1975-80. Served to capt. AUS, 1941-48. Fellow ACP (councilor 1984—), Am. Coll. Cardiology, Am. Heart Assn. Mich. (pres. 1981); mem. Detroit Heart Club (pres. 1967), Detroit Med. Club. Roman Catholic. Avocations: photography; travel. Home: 28420 Sunset Blvd W Lathrup Village MI 48076 Office: George Ritter MD 28245 Southfield Rd Lathrup Village MI 48076

RITZINGER, MARK LOUIS, optometrist, computer software consultant; New Richmond, Wis., May 6, 1952; s. Richard C. and Norma A. (Moen) R.; m. Jean A. Langholff, Sept. 1, 1973; children—Justin R., Bridget E. B.S., Ill. Coll. Optometry, 1974, O.D., 1976. Optometrist Ritzinger Optometric Clinic, River Falls Wis., 1976—; cons. River Falls Pub. Schs., 1977—, P.D.M.S., Edina, Minn., 1982—, Ellsworth Pub. Schs., Wis., 1983—. Co-chmn. River Falls Days, 1984-85. Recipient Lawrence P. Feigenbaum Clin. Optometry award Ill. Coll. Optometry, 1976, OEPF Devel. Optometry award Optometric Extension Program, 1976, Silver medal Beta Sigma Kappa, 1976. Mem. Indian Head Optometric Soc., Wis. Optometric Assn., Am. Optometric Assn., River Falls C. of C., Beta Sigma Kappa. Republican. Roman Catholic. Lodge: Lions.

Avocations: fishing, golf. Home: 1630 Southridge Ct River Falls WI 54022 Office: Ritzinger Optometric Clinic 711 N Main St River Falls WI 54022

RITZLIN, GEORGE, rare book and map dealer; b. Chgo., May 21, 1942; s. Philip and Pauline (Moskowitz) R.; m. Mary Eileen McMichael, Jan. 6, 1979; 1 child, David Michael. B.S.M.E., Ill. Inst. Tech., 1964; M.B.A., Ind. U., 1966. C.P.A., Ill. Asst. to v.p. fin. Chgo and North Western Ry. Co., Chgo., 1969-70; fin. analyst TransUnion Corp., Chgo., 1971; Adcock-Ingram Ltd., Johannesburg, South Africa, 1971-72; mgr. fin. analysis Blue Cross Assn., Chgo., 1973-77; controller G. W. Hoffman and Co., Chgo., 1978-79; pvt. practice C.P.A., Chgo., 1979-83, rare book and map dealer, Chgo., 1977—. Editor: Directory of Dealers in Antiquarian Maps, 1980. Contbr. articles to profl. jours. Mem. Newberry Library Assocs., Chgo., 1980—; treas. Sheffield Neighborhood Assn., Chgo., 1981-82; pres. 43d Ward Young Republicans, Chgo., 1969-70; arbitrator Better Bus. Bur., Chgo., 1978—. Served with U.S. Army, 1967-69. Mem. Ill. C.P.A. Soc. (Elijah Watts Sells hon. mention award 1973), Chgo. Map Soc., (pres., co-founder 1976-78, bd. dirs. 1976-83), Antiquarian Booksellers Assn. Am.,

RIVENBARK, JAN MEREDITH, corporate executive; b. Spartanburg, S.C., Feb. 22, 1950; s. George Meredith and Audrey Isabel (Frady) R.; m. Barbara N. Newton, Sept. 25, 1976; children—Abigail, Justin, Patrick. B.S. in Math., Duke U., 1972; postgrad., Ga. State U., 1980. Mgmt. trainee Citizens & So. Nat. Bank, Atlanta, 1972, br. mgr., 1974, employee relations mgr., 1975-77, v.p. compensation, benefits, payroll and data mgmt., 1977-80; mgr. personnel First Tenn. Bank, Memphis, 1980-81; dir. compensation and benefits Hanes Group, Consol. Foods Corp., Winston-Salem, N.C., 1981-83, exec. dir. compensation and benefits, Chgo., 1983-85—; exec. dir. internat. staff Sara Lee Corp., 1985—; dir. Health Point Preferred, Inc. Fund raiser United Way, Atlanta, 1973, Winston Salem, 1983; active polit. campaigns 1978, 80. Mem. Am. Compensation Assn., (cert. compensation profl.), Am. Mgmt. Assn., Alpha Tau Omega (chpt. pres. 1971-72). Republican. Home: 739 Foxdale Ave Winnetka IL 60093 Office: Sara Lee Corp Three First Natl Plaza Chicago IL 60602

RIZOWY, CARLOS GUILLERMO, lawyer, educator; b. Sarandi Grande, Uruguay, Mar. 5, 1949; came to U.S., 1973, naturalized, 1981; s. Gerszon and Eva (Visnia) R.; m. Charlotte Gordon, Mar. 14, 1976; 1 son, Brian Isaac. B.A., Hebrew U., Jerusalem, 1971; M.A., U. Chgo., 1975, Ph.D., 1981; J.D., Chgo. Kent Coll. Law, Ill. Inst. Tech., 1983. Bar: Ill. 1983, U.S. Dist. Ct. (no. dist.) Ill. 1983, U.S. Ct. Appeals (7th cir.) 1983. Asst. prof. polit. sci. Roosevelt U., Chgo., 1982—, chmn. dept. polit. sci., 1983—; ptnr. Ray, Rizowy, & Ross, Chgo., 1983—; adj. assoc. prof. Spertus Coll. Judaica, Chgo., 1984—. Vice pres. Orgn. Children of Holocaust Survivors, Chgo., 1982; mem. community relations com. Jewish Fedn. Met. Chgo., 1983-84; mem. adv. bd. Am. Jewish Congress, Chgo., 1983-85, Chgo. Action for Soviety Jewry, 1983-85; bd. dirs. Am. Friends of Hebrew U., Chgo., 1984—. Scholar Hebrew U., 1967-72, U. Chgo., 1972-78, Hillman Found., 1978, Peter Volid Found., 1980. Mem. ABA, Ill. State Bar Assn., Chgo. Bar Assn., Assn. Trial Lawyers Am., Am. Immigration Lawyers Assn., Am. Polit. Sci. Assn., Am. Judicature Soc. Lodge: Masons. Home: 561 W Cornelia Ave Chicago IL 60657 Office: Ray Rizowy & Ross 100 N LaSalle St Chicago IL 60602

RIZZI, JOSEPH VITO, banker; b. Berwyn, Ill., Dec. 5, 1949; s. Joseph and Mary Catherine (Mancini) R.; B.S. in Commerce summa cum laude, DePaul U., 1971; M.B.A., U. Chgo., 1973; J.D. magna cum laude, U. Notre Dame, 1976; m. Candace Kunz, June 24, 1972; children—Jennifer, Joseph. Admitted to Ill. bar, 1976; law clk. to judge U.S. Dist. Ct. No. Dist. Ill., 1976-77; exec. v.p. T.B.R. Enterprises, Inc., Downers Grove, Ill., 1977-83; asst. v.p. ABN/LaSalle Nat. Bank, Chgo., 1983—. Mem. Nat. Retail Merchants Assn., ABA, Ill. Bar Assn., Delta Epsilon Sigma. Roman Catholic. Club: Union League of Chgo. Assoc. editor Notre Dame Lawyer, 1975-76; contbr. articles to profl. publs. Home: 287 Bartram Rd Riverside IL 60546 Office: 7323 Lemont Rd Downers Grove IL 60515

ROACH, DONALD HARVEY, manufacturing company executive, entrepreneur; b. Fort Worth, Aug. 26, 1942; s. William H. and Goldie (Maquirk) R.; m. Lavena Taylor, Jan. 17, 1959; children—Staci Roach Chandler, Lori. Grad. Carter High Sch., 1959. Sales mgr. A&B Equipment Co., Fort Worth, 1964-68; dist. mgr. Melroe div. Clark Co., Gwinner, N.D., 1968-74; v.p. sales Thomas Southwest Co., Richardson, Tex., 1974-77, Snorkel div. Figgie Internat. Co., St. Joseph, Mo., 1977—. Republican. Methodist. Clubs: Royal Order Jesters, Moila Cyclist (treas. 1981-82). Lodges: Masons, Shriners. Home: 5002 Mockingbird Ln Saint Joseph MO 64506 Office: Snorkel Div Figgie Internat Co PO Box 65 Stockyards Station Saint Joseph MO 64504

ROACH, EUGENE GAYLE, psychiatrist, author, educator; b. Louisville, Jan. 12, 1932; s. Charles Herndon Roach and Mary (Conn) Gaines; m. Mildred Moorhouse, 1951; children—Charles, Glenna. B.S., U. Louisville, 1955, M.A., 1957; Ph.D., Purdue U., 1962; M.D., Ind. U., 1972. Diplomate Am. Bd. Psychiatry and Neurology. Resident in psychiatry Jackson Meml. Hosp., Miami, Fla., Ind. U. Med. Ctr., Indpls.; assoc. prof. Ind. U., Indpls., 1962-68, 76-80; dir. clin. psychiatry St. Francis Hosp. Ctr., Beech Grove, Ind., 1980—; cons. to minister of Social Affairs Cairo, Egypt, 1966-67. Author: Purdue Perceptual Motor Survey, 1967. Bd. dirs. Am. Cancer Soc., 1980—. Fulbright scholar, 1966-67. Mem. AMA, Ind. State Med. Assn. (legis. commr. 1983—), Marion County Med. Soc., Am. Psychiat. Assn. Republican. Presbyterian. Clubs: Columbia Skyline (Indpls.). Avocations: photography, art collecting. Office: Suite 907 1500 Albany Beech Grove IN 46107

ROACH, PETER JOHN, bichemist; b. Rangeworthy near Bristol, Eng., June 8, 1948; came to U.S., 1972; s. Albert George and Madge Irene R.; m. Anna Antonia DePaoli, Nov. 22, 1975. B.Sc., U. Glasgow, Scotland, 1969, Ph.D., 1972. Postdoctoral fellow in chemistry UCLA, 1972-74, postdoctoral fellow in pharmacology U. Va., Charlottesville, 1974-75; fellow Scuola Normale Superiore, Pisa, Italy, 1975-77; instr. pharmacology U. Va., Charlottesville, 1977-79; asst. prof. biochemistry Ind. U. Sch. Medicine, Indpls., 1979-83, assoc. prof., 1983—. Contbr. articles to profl. jours. NIH grantee, 1979—; Am. Diabetes Assn. grantee, 1979-81; Juvenile Diabetes Found. grantee, 1984—; Research Career Devel. award, NIH, 1982—. Mem. Am. Soc. Biol. Chemists. Office: Dept Biochemistry Ind U Sch Medicine 635 Barnhill Dr Indianapolis IN 46223

ROACH, THOMAS LEO, oil company engineer; b. Logansport, Ind., Feb. 26, 1950; s. Herbert Ralph and Lena (Hilbert) R.; m. Sheila Ann Govert, May 1, 1976. B.S., Purdue U., 1973. Engr. Atlantic Richfield Co., Harvey, Ill., 1973—. Contbr. articles to profl. jours.; patentee in field. Mem. Soc. Automotive Engrs. Avocations: reading; shooting sports. Home: 616 Cottonwood Dr Dyer IN 46311 Office: Atlantic Richfield 400 E Sibley Blvd Harvey IL 60426

ROALES, ROBERT R., natural science educator; b. N.Y.C., July 17, 1944; s. John and Gertrude (Buxo) R.; m. Francoise A. Galland, Nov. 29, 1969; 1 child, Nicole. B.S., Iona Coll., 1966; M.S., NYU, 1969, Ph.D., 1973. Asst. prof. Ind. U.-Kokomo, 1974-79, assoc. prof., 1979—, coordinator natural sci., 1981—. Contbr. articles to profl. jours. Mem. AAAS, Am. Fisheries Soc., Am. Inst. Biol. Sci., Am. Soc. Ichthyologists and Herpetologists, N.Y. Acad. Scis., Sigma Xi. Avocations: photography; gardening. Home: 1001 N Hickory Ln Kokomo IN 46901 Office: Ind U 2300 S Washington St Kokomo IN 46902

ROARK, DALLAS MORGAN, philosophy educator; b. Birchwood, Tenn., Dec. 15, 1931; s. Franklin A. and Mattie (White) R.; m. Elaine Joyce Musial, Mar. 19, 1955; children—Lyman, Dalaine. Th.B., No. Bapt. Coll., Chgo., 1954; M.A., U. Iowa, 1958, Ph.D., 1963. Assoc. prof. religion Wayland Coll., Plainview, Tex., 1960-66; prof. philosophy Emporia State U., Kans., 1966—, chmn. div. soc. scis., 1978—. Author: Dietrich Bonhoeffer, 1978; The Christian Faith, 1980; Introduction to Philosophy, 1982. Mem. Southwestern Philosophy Soc., Faith and History Assn., Assn. Bapt. Tchrs. of Religion. Baptist. Home: 1813 Calle de Loma Emporia KS 66801 Office: Emporia State U 1200 Commercial St Emporia KS 66801

ROAT, GARY WAYNE, neurologist; b. Flint, Mich., Jan. 1, 1937; s. Doyle Wayne and Margaret Rose (Deitering) R.; m. Dolores Mary Wascha, Dec. 26, 1959; children—Randy J., Susan T., Dennis W., Lauree L. A.Bus., Mott Community Coll., 1956; B.A., U. Mich., 1958; D.O., Kirksville Coll. Osteo. Medicine, 1963. Diplomate Am. Osteo. Bd. Neurology and Psychiatry; cert. Am. Soc. Neuroimaging and Computerized Tomography; lic. osteo. physician, Mich., Fla., Mo. Rotating intern Flint Oste. Hosp., Mich., 1963-64; gen. practice osteo. medicine, Flint, 1964-69; resident in internal medicine Flint Osteo. Hosp., 1969-71; resident in neurology St. Louis U. Med. Sch., 1971-74; practice osteo. medicine specializing in neurology, Flint, 1974—; mem. staff Flint Osteo. Hosp., lab. dir. Scanner Diagnostic Assocs., 1983-85; mem. staff Genesee Meml. Hosp., Hurley Med. Ctr.; asst. clin. prof. Mich. State U. Med. Sch., East Lansing, 1975—; chmn. bd. Smoke Rise Vacation Resort, Davison, Mich., 1982-84; owner Flint Neurosci. Ctr., 1983—; reviewer Health Care Analysis, Inc., Med. Quality Found.; dir. Health Plus of Mich., 1981—, mem. fin. com., 1984—; mem. care/quality/cost com. Genesee Health Care, 1984—, treas., 1984—. Contbr. articles to profl. jours. Bd. dirs. Genesee Health Found.; donor St. Francis Prayer Ctr., Flint, 1980-84. Recipient award Optimist Club, 1954. Mem. Am. Neurol. Assn., Am. Acad. Neurology, Am. Osteo. Assn., Am. Coll. Osteo. Neuropsychiatry, Mich. Osteo. Soc. Physicians and Surgeons, Genesee County Osteo. Assn., Flint Neurosci. Assn., Mich. Neurol. Assn., Am. Soc. Neuropsychiatrists, Am. Soc. Neuroimaging. Roman Catholic. Avocations: flying; photography; computers; karate. Office: G3239 Beecher Rd Flint MI 48504

ROBB, ANITA PORTE, lawyer, author; b. Kansas City, Mo., Dec. 30, 1958; d. Sanford and Marilyn (Miller) Porte; m. Gary Charles Robb, Apr. 30, 1983. B.A. with distinction, U. Mo., 1979; J.D. cum laude, U. Mich., 1982. Bar: Mo., U.S. Dist. Ct. (we. dist.) Mo., U.S. Ct. Appeals (8th cir.). Law clk. U.S. Ct. Appeals, Kansas City, Mo., 1982-83; v.p., chief legal counsel Midwest Ednl. and Pub. Assn., Kansas City, 1983-84; ptnr. Robb & Robb, Kansas City, 1984—; lectr. U. Mo. Sch. Law, Kansas City. Note editor U. Mich. Jour. Law Reform. Bd. editors Med. Malpractice Law and Strategy Newsletter; author articles. Corps de Ballet Kansas City Ballet, 1975-78; chmn. univ. scholars com. U. Mo. Alumni Assn. Roach fellow U. Mo., 1979. Mem. Assn. Trial Lawyers Am., Am. Soc. Law and Medicine, ABA, Mo. Assn. Trial Attys., Am. Bus. Women's Assn., Kansas City Bar Assn., Phi Kappa Phi, Pi Sigma Alpha. Republican. Clubs: Kansas City, Kansas City Athletic. Office: Robb & Robb Mark Twain Tower Suite 1500 106 W 11th St Kansas City MO 64105

ROBB, GARY CHARLES, lawyer; b. Kansas City, Mo., May 17, 1955; s. George Albert and Gabriela (Kleotzel) R.; m. Anita Candace Porte, Apr. 30, 1983. B.A. with distinction in Polit. Sci. and Communications, U. Mo.-Kansas City, 1977, M.A. in Econs., 1978; J.D. cum laude, U. Mich., 1981. Bars: Ill. 1981, U.S. Dist. Ct. (no. dist.) Ill. 1981, Mo. 1982, U.S. Dist. Ct. (we. dist.) Mo. 1982, U.S. Ct. Appeals (8th cir.) 1982. Assoc. Mayer, Brown & Platt, Chgo., 1981-82, Shughart, Thomson & Kilroy, Kansas City, Mo., 1982-84; ptnr. Robb & Robb, Kansas City, Mo., 1984—; adj. prof. law U. Mo., Kansas City; lectr., program chmn. Nat. Conf. on Products Liability Law, Chgo., 1983, lectr., 1984. Contbg. author: Tort Law, Missouri Bar Handbook, 1982; Products Liability, 1984. Exec. articles editor U. Mich. Jour. Law Reform, 1980-81; contbg. editor Products Liability, 1983; mem. bd. editors Products Liability Newsletter, 1982—; mem. bd. experts Lawyers Alert Newsmag. Contbr. articles to profl. jours. Mem. ABA (chmn. future programs and projects subcom., trial evidence com., sect. litigation, mem. products liability and consumer law com., tort and ins. practice sect.), Kansas City Bar Assn., Mo. Bar Assn. (fed. practice com.), Lawyers Assn. Kansas City, Assn. Trial Lawyers Am. (tort and aviation sects.), Mo. Assn. Trial Attys., Univ. Mo.-Kansas City Alumni Assn. (chmn. career planning com.), Phi Kappa Phi, Omicron Delta Epsilon, Pi Sigma Alpha (pres.), Pi Kappa Delta. Republican. Club: Kansas City. Office: Robb & Robb Mark Twain Tower Suite 1500 11th and Baltimore Sts Kansas City MO 64105

ROBBINS, ANDREW FERDINAND, JR., ophthalmologist; b. Bklyn., Dec. 28, 1947; s. Andrew F. and Fortune S. (Savarese) R.; m. Lauren Lahmann, May 22, 1976. B.S. in Natural Scis., Xavier U., Cin., 1969; M.D., U. Cin., 1973. Diplomate Am. Bd. Ophthalmology. Intern, Good Samaritan Hosp., Cin., 1973-74; resident U. Cin. Hosp., 1974-77; ptnr. Hyde Park Eye Physicians and Surgeons, Cin., 1977—; chmn. dept. ophthalmology Good Samaritan Hosp., Cin., 1983—; instr. dept. family practice U. Cin., 1983—; dir. internat. and regional seminars in field. Contbr. articles to profl. publs. Fellow Am. Acad. Ophthalmology, Internat. Coll. Surgeons, ACS; mem. Am. Intraocular Implant Soc., Ohio State Med. Soc., Cin. Acad. Medicine (jud. com. 1984—), Alpha Sigma Nu. Republican. Roman Catholic. Club: Hon. Order Ky. Cols. Avocation: Dale Carnegie Motivation Course. Office: Hyde Park Eye Physicians and Surgeons Inc 3710 Paxton Ave Cincinnati OH 45209

ROBBINS, FREDERICK CHAPMAN, physician; b. Auburn, Ala., Aug. 25, 1916; s. William J. and Christine (Chapman) R.; A.B., U. Mo., 1936, B.S., 1938; M.D., Harvard, 1940; D.Sc. (hon.), John Carroll U., 1955, U. Mo., 1958; LL.D., U. N.Mex., 1968; m. Alice Havemeyer Northrop, June 19, 1948; children—Alice, Louise. Sr. fellow virus disease NRC, 1948-50; staff research div. infectious diseases Children's Hosp., Boston, 1948-50, assoc. physician, assoc. dir. isolation service, assoc. research div. infectious diseases, 1950-52; instr., assoc. in pediatrics Harvard Med. Sch., 1950-52; dir. dept. pediatrics and contagious diseases Cleve. Met. Gen. Hosp., 1952-66; assoc. pediatrician U. Hosps., Cleve., from 1952; prof. pediatrics Case-Western Res. U., from 1952, dean Sch. Medicine, from 1966; vis. scientist Donner Lab., U. Calif., 1963-64. Served as maj. AUS, 1942-46; chief virus and rickettsial disease sect. 15th Med. Gen. Lab.; investigations infectious hepatitis, typhus fever and Q fever. Decorated Bronze Star, 1945; received 1st Mead Johnson prize application tissue culture methods to study of viral infections, 1953; co-recipient Nobel prize in physiology and medicine, 1954; Med. Mut. Honor Award for 1969. Diplomate Am. Bd. Pediatrics. Mem. Am. Epidemiol. Soc., Am. Acad. Arts and Scis., Am. Soc. Clin. Investigation (emeritus mem.), Am. Assn. Immunologists, Soc. Exptl. Biol. and Medicine, Am. Pediatric Soc., Nat. Acad. Scis., Nat. Inst. Medicine, Am. Philos. Soc., Phi Beta Kappa, Sigma Xi, Phi Gamma Delta. Office: 2119 Abington St Cleveland OH 44106

ROBBINS, GERALD HENRY, radio broadcast executive, consultant; b. Mpls., Feb. 24, 1931; s. Arthur E. and Anna M. (Noden) R.; m. Jane Eileen Carlson, Nov. 3, 1956. Student Brown Inst. Broadcasting and Electronics, 1952-53. Radio announcer Sta. KRBA, Lufkin, Tex., (internat. dir. Sta. KTRF, Thief River Falls, Minns., 1954-56; sales rep. Sta. KTOE, Mankato, Minn., 1956-59; sales mgr. Sta. KAGE, Winona, Minn., 1959-60; gen. mgr. Sta. KXGN TV/Radio, Glendive, Mont., 1960-67; pres., gen. mgr. WCMP Broadcasting Co., Pine City, Minn., 1967—; owner Profit Builder, pub. speaking/seminar co.; broadcasting cons. Served with U.S. Army, 1951-53; Korea. Decorated Purple Heart; recipient Ambassador of Good Will award Lions Internat., 1977; Internat. Pres. awards, 1974-81; named Lions Citizen of Yr., Pine City C. of C., 1977. Mem. Nat. Speakers Assn., Internat. Platform Assn., Nat. Radio Broadcasters Assn. (Minn. dir.), Minn. Broadcasters Assn. (dir.), Minn. United Press Broadcasters (v.p.). Republican. Lutheran. Club: Lions (internat. dir. 1975-77). Office: Rural Route 2 Pine City MN 55063

ROBBINS, JANE LOUISA, educator; b. Bangor, Maine, Dec. 25, 1944; d. Howard Allen and Rebekah May (Gross) Gray; B.S., Wright State U., 1975; M.B.A., 1981; m. Derek Robbins, Dec. 26, 1963; children—D. Christopher. Mgmt. asst., aero. systems div. Wright Patterson AFB, Ohio, 1971-73; instr. bus. edn., public schs., Bucksport, Maine, 1952-64; fin. specialist, aero. systems div. Wright Patterson AFB, 1977-79, cost analyst, 1979-81, asst. prof. quantitative contract price analysis Air Force Inst. Tech., Sch. Systems and Logistics, 1982—; nat. dir. Inst. Cost Analysis. Mem. drug intervention adv. group Beavercreek High Sch. Mem. Nat. Estimating Soc., Internat. Soc. Parametric Analysis, Nat. Assn. Female Exec., Kappa Delta Pi. Episcopalian. Office: Air Force Inst Tech Sch Systems and Logistics Wright Patterson AFB OH 45431

ROBBINS, KENNETH CHARLES, health care executive, lawyer; b. Boston, Oct. 26, 1942; s. Charles F. and Dorothy Rae (Gillis) R.; m. Marjorie Helen Dumas, June 25, 1965; children—Kimberly, Kerri, Susan. A.B., U. Mass., 1965; J.D., Suffolk U., 1973. Bar: Mass. 1973, Ill. 1976. Research dir. Com. Govt. Regulations Mass. Legislature, 1972-73, legal counsel, staff dir., 1973-76; ptnr. Pearlman & Robbins, 1974-76; dir. med.-legal affairs Ill. Hosp. Assn., Naperville, 1976-79, v.p., asst. gen. counsel, 1979-82, pres., 1983—; exec. dir. Ill. State Cost Containment Com., 1978, lectr. health care law Northwestern U. Served to capt. USAF, 1965-70; lt. col. Ill. Air N.G., 1976—. Mem. ABA, Ill. State Bar Assn., Am. Soc. Hosp. Attys., Nat. Health Care Lawyers Assn., N.G. Assn. U.S., N.G. Assn. Ill. Roman Catholic. Office: Ill Hospital Assn 1151 E Warrenville Rd Naperville IL 60566

ROBBINS, MARTHA FLOBERG, health care administrator; b. Evanston, Ill., June 23, 1955; d. Frederic O. and Ruth (Clohisy) Floberg; m. Morley M. deLashmutt-Robbins, Oct. 8, 1983. A.B. in History, Vassar Coll., 1977; M.H.A., U. Mich., 1981. Adminstrv. intern U. Mich. Hosps., Ann Arbor, 1980; research asst. Ebenezer Ctr. for Aging, Mpls., 1981-82; assoc. dir. Am. Hosp. Assn. Soc. for Hosp. Planning and Mktg., Chgo., 1982-85. Mem. Physicians for Social Responsibility, Cambridge, Ma., 1982-85, Chgo. Health Execs. Forum, 1982-85. Avocations: ski racing; organic gardening.

ROBBINS, WAYNE HAROLD, medical equipment company executive; b. Bedford, Ind., Aug. 16, 1918; s. Charles Omer and Mamie Ethyl Robbins; m. Mary Frances Granato, Feb. 14, 1942; children—Michael Anthony, Patrick Wayne. Student Ind. U., 1948; B.S., Butler U., 1952. Owner Robbins Concrete Co., Bedford, Ind., 1945-48; pharmacist Smallwoods Drugs, Oolitic, Ind., 1952-57; owner, pharmacist Profl. Pharmacy, Bedford, 1957-70; pres. Conva-Care Services, Inc., 1970-85, chmn. bd., 1985—. Served to maj. USAAF, 1941-45. Named Bus. Man of Yr. for Ind., 1978. Mem. Nat. Assn. Durable Med. Equipment, Nat. Retail Druggists, Assn., Am. Pharm. Assn., Ind. Pharm. Assn. Democrat. Roman Catholic. Home: 407 Lafayette St Oolitic IN 47451 Office: Conva-Care Services Inc 1201 5th St Bedford IN 47421

ROBE, EDWARD SCOTT, lawyer; b. Cumberland, Ohio, July 9, 1936; s. Thurlow Scott and Mary Alice (McKibben) R.; m. Sally Ann Allen, June 19, 1960; children—Lisa Kathleen Robe Clay, Scott McKibben, Jennifer Allen. A.B., Ohio U., 1959; J.D., Duke U., 1963. Bar: Ohio 1963, U.S. Supreme Ct. 1968. Ptnr., Bridgewater, Robe, Brooks & Keifer, Athens, Ohio, 1963—; pres. Law Abstract Pub. Co., 1973-74; bd. commrs. grievances and discipline Ohio Supreme Ct., Columbus, 1973-80. Chmn. bd. trustees Sheltering Arms Found., 1979; chmn. Athens County Bd. Elections, 1980-81; chmn. Athens County Republican Exec. Com., 1970-72. Served to capt. USNG, 1965-70. Fellow Ohio State Bar Found.; mem. Ohio State Bar Assn. (exec. com. 1971-74), Ohio Acad. Trial Lawyers, Athens County Bar Assn. (pres. 1969-70), Am. Judicature Soc. Methodist. Club: Symposiarchs. Lodge: Rotary (pres. 1981-82). Avocation: traveling. Home: 19 Roosevelt Dr Athens OH 45701 Office: Bridgewater Robe Brooks & Keifer 14 W Washington St Athens OH 45701

ROBENALT, JAMES DAVID, lawyer; b. Lima, Ohio, July 11, 1956; s. John Alton and Margaret Morgan (Durbin) R.; m. Elizabeth Ann Welch; children—James Leonard, Margaret Francis. A.B., Miami U., Oxford, Ohio, 1978; J.D., Ohio State U., 1981. Bar: Ohio 1981, U.S. Dist. Ct. (no. dist.) Ohio 1981, U.S. Ct. Appeals (6th cir.) 1981; diplomate Ct. Practice Inst. Assoc. Thompson, Hine and Flory, Cleve., 1981—. Loan exec. United Way Services, Cleve., 1982. Mem. Ohio State Bar Assn., Cleve. Bar Assn., Order of Coif, Phi Beta Kappa. Democrat. Roman Catholic. Home: 3592 Ingleside Shaker Heights OH 44122 Office: Thompson Hine and Flory 1100 Nat City Bank Bldg Cleveland OH 44114

ROBERSON, CAROLYN A., educator; b. McComb, Miss., Jan. 12, 1950; d. Vernon and Christine (Alexander) Williams; m. Sylvester Roberson, June 17, 1975; 1 dau., Carol Syleste. B.S., Abilene Christian U., 1972; M.S., Chgo. State U., 1978. Cert. spl. educator, bus. educator, phys. edn. instr. Tchr. phys. edn. and health Waukegan (Ill.) Sch. Dist., 1972-75; phys. edn. coordinator, asst. activities dir. Hamlin Ho., Chgo., 1975-76; mental health therapist Ridgeway Hosp., Chgo., 1976-77; adaptive phys. tchr. phys. therapy dept. Spalding High Sch., Chgo., 1977-78; tchr. emotionally and mentally handicapped Blue Island (Ill.) Sch. Dist., 1978-79; tchr. emotionally disturbed Ray Graham Assn., Desplaines, Ill., 1980; tchr. EMH, TMH, phys. edn., health Spalding High Sch., Chgo., 1980—, acting asst. prin. in charge of discipline, 1983-84, discipline counselor, 1984-85. Recipient Inst. Psychoanalysis Scholarship award, 1982-83, 83-84. Mem. Assn. Supervision and Curriculum Devel., Council of Basic Edn., Council of Exceptional Children, Ill. Assn. Health, Phys. Edn. and Recreation, NAACP. Mem. Ch. of Christ. Home: 10216 S LaFayette St Chicago IL 60628 Office: 1628 W Washington St Chicago IL 60612

ROBERT, ANDRE, research scientist; b. Montreal, Que., Can., Oct. 6, 1926; came to U.S., 1955, naturalized, 1983; s. Aristide and Eva (Paiement) R.; m. Rose Greenman, Dec. 8, 1984; children—Danielle, Jean-Baptiste, Pierre-Louis, Marie. B.A., Stanislas Coll., Montreal, 1944; M.D., U. Montreal, 1950; Ph.D., Inst. Exptl. Med. Surgery, U. Montreal, 1957. Asst. prof. endocrinology U. Montreal Med. Sch., 1952-55; vis. scientist NIH, Bethesda, Md., 1960-61, Ctr. for Ulcer Research and Edn., Los Angeles, 1980-81; sr. scientist The UpJohn Co., Kalamazoo, Mich., 1955—. Mem. AMA, Am. Gastroent. Assn., Am. Physiol. Soc., Soc. Exptl. Biol. Medicine, Corp. Physicians and Surgeons Quebec. Unitarian. Office: Diabetes and GI Research The Upjohn Co Kalamazoo MI 49001

ROBERT, HENRY FLOOD, JR., museum official; b. El Dorado, Ark., Feb. 26, 1943; s. Henry Flood and Margery (Hay) R.; m. Mary Beth Parkey, Apr. 20, 1968; children—Spencer Flood, Erika Ashley. B.F.A., Ariz. State U., 1970, M.F.A., 1973; diploma Inst. Arts Adminstrn., Harvard U., 1977. Dir. Meml. Union Gallery, Ariz. State U., 1969-70, asst. dir. Univ. Art Mus., 1970-72; asst. dir. Loch Haven Art Center, Orlando, Fla., 1973-74; dir. Montgomery (Ala.) Mus. Fine Arts, 1974-79, Joslyn Art Mus., Omaha, 1979—; guest curator Soleri Exhbn., Whitney Mus. Am., Art Corcoran Gallery Art, Mus. Contemporary Art; exhbn. dir. Art Inc. Author: Paolo Soleri: Arcology and the Future of Man, 1975; Venetian Drawings from the Collection of Janos Scholz, 1976; Corporate Collections in Montgomery, 1976; American Paintings: 190--1939, 1976; The George Verdak Collection: Eras of the Dance, 1976; Anne Goldthwaite, 1869-1944, 1977. Walter Gaudnek Retrospective, 1978. Mem. Internat. Council Mus., Am. Assn. Mus. (visitation com. for accreditation), Assn. Art Mus. Dirs. Episcopalian. Office: 2200 Dodge St Omaha NE 68102*

ROBERTS, ALBERT GEORGE, school administrator; b. Jersey City, Dec. 2, 1947; s. Albert F. and Helen M. (Matteucci) R.; m. Arlene Joan Kausch, Mar. 7, 1970; 1 dau., Karen. B.A., Jersey City State Coll., 1969; M.S., Fordham U., 1973; Ed.M., Columbia U., 1976, Ed.D., 1979. Cert. prin., tchr. Ohio, N.J., supr. N.J. Tchr. Teaneck (N.J.) schs., 1970-79; prin. Emerson sch., Teaneck, 1979-81, Lomond Sch., Shaker Heights, Ohio, 1981—; cons. N.J. Dept. Edn., 1978; dir. children's programming cable TV, 1978-79. Dir. recreation Summer Outreach, 1977-78. Mem. Am. Assn. Sch. Adminstrs., Assn. Supervision and Curriculum Devel., Nat. Sci. Tchrs. Assn., Ohio Assn. Elem. Sch. Adminstrs., Nat. Assn. Elem. Sch. Prins., Phi Delta Kappa. Author numerous curriculum guides in math., reading, sci. Office: 17917 Lomond Blvd Shaker Heights OH 44122

ROBERTS, ALLEN NATHAN, immunohematologist; b. Chgo., Sept. 26, 1946; s. Jack and Goldie (Solomon) R.; m. Sandra D. Rosenblatt (div. 1979); m. Carolyn K. Marcus, Oct. 11, 1981. B.S., U. Ill.-Chgo., 1969; M.S., Central Mich. U., 1979. Lab. mgr., blood bank supr. Edgewater Hosp., Chgo., 1972-75; adminstrv., tech. dir. blood bank Grant Hosp., Chgo., 1975—. Democratic pollwatcher, Highland Park, Ill., 1984. Served with U.S. Army, 1970-72. Mem. Am. Assn. Blood Banks (cons., inspector, 1975—), Am. Soc. Clin. Pathologists, Am. Soc. Med. Technologists, Ill. Soc. Med. Technologists, Chgo. Soc. Med. Technologists. Avocations: public speaking; reading; swimming. Office: Grant Hosp 550 W Webster Chicago IL 60614

ROBERTS, ARTHUR STANLEY, JR., systems company executive, dentist; b. Indpls., Jan. 21, 1946; s. Arthur Stanley and Rosemary Jane (Morris) R.; m. Karen Sue Strawn, Aug. 17, 1968; children—Meredith Holly, Arthur Stanley. Student Earlham Coll., 1964-65, Ind. U., 1965-67, postgrad., 1978-80; D.D.S., Ind. U.-Indpls., 1971. Intern William Beaumont Gen. Hosp., Ft. Bliss, Tex., 1971-72; staff dental officer USARSUPTHAI, Bangkok, Thailand, 1972-73; gen. practice dentistry, Rushville, Ind., 1973-81; pres. Geneva Cons., Shelbyville, Ind., 1981-83; chmn., founder, chief exec. officer Alpha Systems Resource Co., Shelbyville, 1983—; research assoc. oral facial genetics Ind. U. Med. Ctr., Indpls., 1981-83; faculty extramural Ind. U. Med. Ctr., Indpls., 1979—. Co-inventor pill mill. Acad. Gen. Dentistry fellow, 1980. Fellow Royal Soc. Health, Info. Industry Assn., Acad. Gen. Dentistry Clubs: Ind. Rugby, Columbia (Indpls.) Avocations: skiing; anthropology; sailing. Home: 203 W Washington St Shelbyville IN 46176 Office: Alpha Systems Resource Mausoleum Rd PO Box 688 Shelbyville IN

ROBERTS, BARBARA ANN, telephone company official; b. Milw., Feb. 21, 1929; d. Andrew Max and Ersilia (Celia) Gertrude (Comparoni) Maglio; student Milw. public schs.; m. Albert Lloyd Roberts, Sept. 3, 1949; children—Marybeth, Bradley J., David L. With Wis. Bell, Milw., 1961—, now group mgr. operator services. Mem. Bus. and Profl. Women Milw. (pres. 1979-81), Wis. Bus. and Profl. Women (dist. dir. Eastern Dist. 8 1981-82). Home: 8411 W Cheyenne St Milwaukee WI 53224 Office: 2140 Davidson Rd Waukesha WI 53186

ROBERTS, BURNELL RICHARD, forest products company executive; b. Lafayette County, Wis., May 6, 1927; s. Roy C. and Ann Mae R.; m. Karen Ragatz, Aug. 8, 1953; children—Evan, Kari, Paul, Nancy. B.B.A., U. Wis., 1950; M.B.A., Harvard U., 1957. Corp. controller Mead Corp., Dayton, Ohio, 1967-69, v.p. fin., 1969, group v.p. and pres. Mead Merchants, 1971-74, group v.p., pres. Mead Paper Group, 1974-79, sr. group v.p. pulp and forest products, 1979-80, exec. v.p. forest products and fin., 1980, pres., 1982, chmn. and chief exec. officer, 1982—; dir. Uniroyal, Inc., Middlebury, Conn., Nat. City Corp., Cleve., Ayco Fund, Albany, N.Y.; dir., mem. exec. com. Am. Paper Inst., N.Y.C.; chmn. Miami Valley Health Care Coalition, Dayton, Ohio; mem. operating bd. Am. Forest Inst., Washington; dir. Armco Corp., Middletown, Ohio; trustee Aspen Inst. Served with USNR, 1944-46. Home: 127 Lookout Dr Dayton OH 45409 Office: Mead Corp Courthouse Plaza NE Dayton OH 45463

ROBERTS, EDNA PEARL, retired legal secretary; b. Johnston City, Ill., Aug. 26, 1910; d. John Renison and AnnaBelle (Chenoweth) R. Student U. Wis., 1931-32, So. Ill. U., 1961-62. Legal sec., ct. reporter, Williamson County, Ill., 1954-77; clk. Williamson County Jury Commn., 1967-72, jury commr., 1967-85. Author: Glimpses of the Past, 1977. Contbr. articles on Williamson County history to mags. Mem. Johnston City Pub. Library Bd., 1943-65, 81—, pres., 1982—. Named Woman of Yr., Carbondale chpt. Nat. Secs. Assn., 1962, Williamson County chpt. Nat. Legal Secs. Assn., 1969, Career Woman of Yr., dist. 16 Ill. Fedn. Bus. and Profl. Women, 1969. Mem. Johnston City Bus. and Profl. Women's Club (pres. 1949, 56, 66), Nat. Secs. Assn. (pres. Carbondale chpt. 1960-61), Nat. Legal Secs. Assn. (pres. Jackson-Williamson County chpt. 1967), Williamson County Hist. Soc. (pres. 1978-82). Republican. Baptist. Avocations: genealogy; reading; cooking; local history. Address: 401 E 5th St Johnston City IL 62951

ROBERTS, ELIZABETH ANN, speech and theatre educator; b. Denver, July 1, 1944; d. Harold M. and Dorothy M. (Black) R. B.A. in History, Adams State Coll., 1967, M.A. in Speech/Theatre, 1968; postgrad. Purdue U., 1971-72; Ph.D., Ohio U., 1984. Instr. speech and oral interpretation, asst. dir. theatre Coll. Wooster, Ohio, 1968-70; instr. speech and theatre, dir. individual events and readers theatre Ohio No. U., Ada, 1973-77; dir. communication skills program, asst. prof. speech/theatre, 1977-85, assoc. prof., 1985—, parliamentarian Coll. Arts and Scis., 1973-80; teaching assoc. Sch. Interpersonal Communication, Ohio U., Athens, 1980-83; oral communications cons. Mem. Speech Communication Assn., Central States Speech Assn., Speech Communications Assn. Ohio, AAUW, Mortar Bd., Pi Kappa Delta, Theta Alpha Phi, Alpha Psi Omega, Alpha Omicron Pi, Phi Kappa Phi. Office: Dept Speech Ohio No U Ada OH 45810

ROBERTS, FRED CLARK, educational administrator; b. Freeport, Ill., Aug. 24, 1943; s. Russell Arnold and Marjorie May (Kleckner) R.; m. Melissa Jane Woods, Aug. 7, 1967 (div. Oct. 1978); children—Mike, Lisa; m. Diane Marie Starkey Bennett, May 25, 1980; children—Derek Bennett, Stefanie Bennett, Travis Bennett, Julie. B.A., No. Ill. U., 1971, M.S. in Edn., 1975. Skilled machinest Barber Colman, Rockford, Ill., 1967-68; asst. foreman DelMonte Corp., DeKalb, Ill., 1968-71; tchr., counselor Atkinson Schs., Ill., 1971-75; chmn. gen. studies Morrison Inst. Tech., Ill., 1975-77; exec. dir. Henry County Youth Services, Kewanee, Ill., 1977-82; high sch. prin. Brimfield Schs., Ill., 1982—. Author: First Things First, 1976. Mem. planning com. Pvt. Industry Council, Peoria, Ill., 1982-84; trustee Cornwall Twp. Bd., Atkinson, Ill., 1981-82, Atkinson Twp. Library, Ill., 1975-81. Served with spl. forces Green Berets, U.S. Army, 1961-64. Service provider grantee Dept. Labor, Henry/Mercer Counties, 1977-81. Mem. Ill. Athletic Dir. Assn. Club: Brimfield Area Men's (sec. 1983-84). Lodge: Masons (master 1979-80). Avocations: watching basketball; travel; reading; observing people. Home: Box 193 Brimfield IL 61517 Office: East Clinton St Brimfield IL 61517

ROBERTS, HELEN WYVONE, city official; b. Kirksville, Mo., Jan. 9, 1934; d. William Lawrence and Lectie Beryl (Boley) Chitwood; m. Philip C. Roberts, Jan. 9, 1952 (div. 1976); children—Christy, Cheryl, Gayla. Secretarial degree Chillicothe Bus. Sch., 1951; B.S., Lindenwood Coll., 1983. Exec. sec. McDonnel-Douglas Aircraft, St. Louis, 1962-65, Transit Homes, Inc., Greenville, S.C., 1970-76; exec. sec. City of St. Peters, Mo., 1976-79, asst. planning and devel. coordinator, 1979-81, adminstrv. asst. to city adminstr., 1981-84, purchasing agt., 1984—. Mem. Nat. Assn. Female Execs., Internat. Cities Mgmt. Assn., Am. Pub. Works Assn., Am. Mgmt. Assn., Am. Bus. Women's Assn., Mo. Indsl. Devel. Council, Alpha Sigma Tau. Baptist. Avocations: horseback riding; sports; reading. Home: 329 Karen St St Charles MO 63301 Office: City of St Peters PO Box 9 St Peters MO 63376

ROBERTS, JAMES OWEN, financial planning executive, consultant; b. Madison, Wis., Aug. 19, 1930; s. John William and Sada (Buckmaster) R.; m. Georgianna Timmons, Jan. 30, 1954; children—Stephen, Susan, Ellen, Timmons. B.S., Ohio State U., 1952; M.B.A., Case Western Res. U., 1970. Sales trainee Owens-Ill., Inc., Toledo, 1952, 54-55, salesman, Atlanta, 1955-58, N.Y.C., 1958-62, br. mgr., N.Y.C. and Cleve., 1963-71; mgr. corp. fin. Stone & Webster Securities Co., Cleve., 1971-74; regional dir. Mgmt. Planning, Inc., Cleve., 1976-80, v.p., 1980—; lectr. in field. Contbr. articles to profl. jours. Chmn. bd. trustees Fairmount Presbyn. Ch., Cleve., 1984; trustee Soc. for the Blind, Cleve., 1983—, Ohio Motorists Assn.; v.p. Children's Services, 1985—. Named Gem of a Clevelander, Cleve. Press, 1981. Mem. Fin. Analysts Fedn., Cleve. Soc. Security Analysts. Republican. Club: Cleve. Skating. Lodge: Rotary of Cleve. (pres. 1982-83, Paul Harris fellow 1982). Avocations: sailing; skiing; hiking; photography. Home: 2323 Stillman Rd Cleveland Heights OH 44118 Office: Mgmt Planning Inc 1520 Investment Plaza Cleveland OH 44114

ROBERTS, KAREN LOUISE, educator; b. Minco, Okla., Nov. 28, 1948; d. Hugh Jenkins and Alene Berniece (Anthony) McDaniel; m. Thomas Carrol Roberts, Dec. 21, 1968; children—Gregory Charles, Chad Daniel. B.S., Kans. State U., Manhattan, 1970, M.S., 1977, postgrad., 1981-83; postgrad. Emporia State U., 1980-83. Home economist Harper's Fabrics, Prairie Village, Kans., 1975-78; home economist, microwave tchr. Zenith Distbg. Corp., Lenexa, Kans., 1975-77; tchr. home econs. Paola High sch. (Kans.), 1979-82; instr. home econs. Mid-America Nazarene Coll., Olathe, Kans., 1982—. Den mother, Cub Scouts, 1982; chmn. Spl. Edn. Parent Adv. Council, 1981—; coordinator com. First United Methodist Concerns, 1981—. Mem. Am. Home Econs. Assn., Kans. Assn. Vocat. Home Econs. Tchrs., Greater Kansas City Home Econs. Assn., Council for Exceptional Children, Phi Upsilon Omicron. Republican. Home: 18235 Wildcat Rd Olathe KS 66062 Office: USD 230 Spring Hill KS 66083

ROBERTS, LEO JAMES, ophthalmologist; b. Chgo., Sept. 1, 1933; s. Leo Joseph and Marjorie Elizabeth (Palmer) R.; m. Joyce Ann Woods, May 24, 1969; children—Mary, Elizabeth, Jennifer, Catherine, Leo, Jessica. B.S., Loyola U., Chgo., 1956, M.D. cum laude, 1958. Diplomate Am. Bd. Ophthalmology. Intern Cook County Hosp., Chgo., 1958-59; resident in medicine VA Hosp., Westside, Chgo., 1959-60; resident in ophthalmology U. Ill. Hosp., Chgo., 1962-65; fellow UCLA Med. Ctr., Los Angeles, 1965; practice medicine specializing in ophthalmology, Hinsdale, Ill., 1966—; instr. ophthalmology U. Ill. Med. Sch., Chgo., 1966-70; clin. assoc. prof. ophthalmology Loyola Med. Sch., Maywood, Ill., 1970—. Served to capt. USAF, 1960-62. Fellow Am. Acad. Ophthalmology, ACS, Am. Intraocular Implant Soc.; mem. AMA, DuPage County Med. Soc. (bd. dirs. 1979). Republican. Roman Catholic. Club: Hinsdale Golf. Avocations: golf, tennis. Office: Leo J Roberts MD SC 40 S Clay St Hinsdale IL 60521

ROBERTS, MARIANNE, real estate saleswoman; b. Columbus, Ohio, May 27, 1930; d. George W. and Alice L. (Scott) Hunt; m. L.R. Foreman, Sept. 19, 1948 (dec. Aug. 1957); children—Georgia Foreman Masselli, L. Scott, Jeffrey W., Alyce Foreman Heminger; m. Knute Roberts, Apr. 5, 1962; children—Ruthie Roberts McCloud, L. Charlie L. Student Ohio State U., 1980-82. Lic. real estate saleswoman, Ohio; Grad. Realtors Inst., Ohio. Saleswoman, sec. Hunt Milling Co., Richwood, Ohio, 1947-64; reporter, feature writer Marion Star, Ohio and Marysville Jour., Ohio, 1974-80; saleswoman, appraiser Nelson Blue Agy., Richwood, 1972—. Pres., North Union Local Sch. Bd., Richwood, 1984-85; treas. First Baptist Ch., Richwood, 1979—; coordinator Fed./State Relations Network, Washington, 1983—; dir. Richwood Showboat Serenaders, 1980-82; sec. Union County Bd. Mental Retardation, 1971-79; emeritus bd. dirs. Lewis Sch. for Retarded, Marysville, 1983. Recipient numerous civic awards. Mem. Ohio Sch. Bds. Assn. (exec. com. 1983-84, pres.-elect 1985—). Republican. Clubs: Carpe Diem (sec. and v.p. 1982-84), Mother's Study (Richwood) (pres. 1952-54). Lodge: Order Eastern Star. Avocations: music; reading; embroidery; writing. Home: 28 George St Richwood OH 43344 Office: Blue Agy E Blagrove St Richwood OH 43344

ROBERTS, MERLE E., business executive; b. New Kensington, Pa., June 8, 1928; s. Merle B. and Marie E. Roberts; B.S., U. Pitts., 1949; M.B.A., Case-Western Res. U., 1952; m. Dorothy Bougher, July 1, 1950; children—Cynthia Grace, Lisa Bogumill, Keith, Courtney. Pres., owner Roberts Assocs., Inc., Columbus, Ohio, 1964—; pres. Food Group, Inc., Columbus, 1975-81; pres., dir. Luna Caster & Truck Corp., Phoenix dir. Nat. Packaging, Colamco Inc.; pres. Chrysalis Corp., Family Security Agy., Roberts Group Inc. and subs. F.O. Schoedinger Co., Columbus, L.H. Marshall Co., Columbus, Wescon Materials Inc., Beaverton, Oreg., Pleko Southeast Corp., Lakeland, Fla., Fosco Bldg. Products, Lakeland, Pleko Products, Inc., Tacoma, Wash.; mem. faculty Case-Western Res. U., 1953-55, Cleveland State Coll., 1954-56, Capital U., 1962-64, Ohio State U., 1964-68. Mem. U.S. Senatorial Adv. Bd., 1980-81. Republican. Presbyn. (elder, dir.). Address: 2646 Alliston Ct Columbus OH 43220

ROBERTS, PAT, congressman; b. Topeka, Apr. 20, 1936; B.A. in Journalism, Kans. State U., 1958; teaching cert. Ariz. State U., 1964; married. News dir. Sta. KWBY; editor, pub. Westsider News, Avondale, Ariz.; adminstrv. asst. to Senator Frank Carlson of Kans., 1967-69, to Rep. Keith G. Sebelius of Kans., 1969-80; mem. 97th-99th Congresses from 1st Kans. Dist. Served with USMC, 1958-62. Republican. Methodist. Mem. Sigma Delta Chi, Phi Kappa Alpha. Office: 1314 Longworth House Office Bldg Washington DC 20515*

ROBERTS, RICHARD OWEN, clergyman, theological publisher, library consultant; b. Schenectady, Sept. 9, 1931; s. John Earl and Mildred Hazel (Barden) R.; m. Margaret Ann Jameson, Sept. 8, 1962; children—Robert Owen, Gwynne Margaret. Student Gordon Coll., 1949-50; B.A., Whitworth Coll., 1955; postgrad. Fuller Theol. Sem., 1955-57. Ordained to ministry Congregational Ch. Pastor, evangelist University Park Congl. Ch., Portland, Oreg., 1957-61; minister-at-large Conservative Congl. Conf., Scotia, N.Y., 1961-65; pastor Evang. Community Ch., Fresno, Calif., 1965-75; dir. library Billy Graham Ctr., Wheaton, Ill., 1975-80; internat. evangelist, 1980—; owner Richard Owen Roberts, Pubs., Booksellers, 1961—. Author: Revival, 1982; Revival Literature, 1985; Whitefield in Print: A Preliminary Bibliography, 1985. Home and Office: 5 N 740 Dunham Rd Wayne IL 60184

ROBERTS, STEPHEN CRAWFORD, systems consultant; b. Nashville, July 25, 1955; s. Clarence Zebedee and Carolyn (Crawford) R. B.S., Vanderbilt U., 1977; M.B.A., U. Ala.-Tuscaloosa, 1980. Systems analyst McDonnell Douglas, St. Louis, 1980-81, sr. systems analyst, 1982; client cons. Maritz Motivation Co., Inc., St. Louis, 1982-84, sr. client cons., 1984—. Mem. Assn. for Systems Mgmt. Avocations: personal computers; raquetball; golf. Office: Maritz Motivation Co Inc 1375 N Highway Dr Fenton MO 63026

ROBERTS, THOMAS CHARLES, food association executive, agronomist; b. Burrton, Kans., Sept. 22, 1926; s. Ernest Eugene and Mildred Lorraine (Miller) Abston R.; m. Dixie Darlene Werner, Jan. 1, 1947; children—Thomas Carroll, Bradford Charles. B.S. in Agrl. Edn., Kans. State U., 1950. Vo-ag tchr. Lebanon High Sch., Kans., 1950-53, Lyndon High Sch., Kans., 1953-56; asst. sec. Kans. Crop Improvement, Manhattan, 1956-61; gen. mgr. Frontier Hybrids, Inc., Scott City, Kans., 1961-66; exec. v.p. Wheat Quality Council, Manhattan, Kans., 1966—. Mem., chmn. Park Bd. City of Manhattan, 1969-80; pres. Friends of Sunset Zoo, Manhattan, 1979-84. Served with USAF, 1945-46. Named Friend of County Agts., Kans. County Agt. Assn., 1974. Mem. Am. Assn. Cereal Chemists, Am. Soc. Agronomy. Republican. Methodist. Lodges: Lions (pres. 1978-79, dist. gov. 1981-82), Masons. Avocation: dancing instructor. Home: 2041 Arthur Dr Manhattan KS 66502 Office: Wheat Quality Council 404 Humboldt St Suite G Manhattan KS 66502

ROBERTS, THOMAS H., JR., agricultural products company executive. Chmn., pres., chief exec. officer, dir. DeKalb Agresearch, Inc., DeKalb, Ill. Office: DeKalb Agresearch Inc Sycamore Rd DeKalb IL 60115*

ROBERTSEN, JOHN ALAN, management services corporation executive, consultant; b. Kenosha, Wis., June 21, 1926; s. Tony and Alta Emma (Jensen) R.; m. Ann Coffeen Holton, Oct. 26, 1957; children—Christine Marie, Steven Anthony. B.S., U. Wis., 1952, M.S., 1956, Ph.D., 1958. Chief microbiology sect. Leprosy Study Ctr., USPHS, 1958-62; leader infectious disease research group Dow Chem. Co., Dow Research Ctr., Zionsville, Ind., 1962-65, co-founder biohazards dept., 1965-70; sr. ptnr. Robertsen and Assocs., Minnetonka, Minn., 1960—; v.p., chief operating officer Extensor Corp., Minnetonka, 1973—; chief cons. mktg., Sedna Corp., St. Paul, 1982—; cons. product planning Zinpro Corp., Chaska, Minn., 1983—. Patentee (9). Inventor internat. biohazard symbol. Contbr. articles on work measurement at mgmt. level to profl. publs. Mem. editorial bd. Topics in Hosp. Pharmacy Mgmt., 1983—. Former contbg. editor Internat. Jour. of Leprosy. Past mem. State of Minn. Comprehensive Health Planning Adv. Bd.; sci. curriculum adviser Minnetonka Sch. Dist. Served as sgt. Inf., U.S. Army, 1944-47, PTO. Recipient Meritorious Service award USPHS, 1961. Mem. Am. Acad. Microbiology (cert. in pathogenic microbiology), Am. Soc. Performance Improvement, Am. Radio Relay League, Am. Soc. Microbiology, Sales and Mktg. Execs. Internat., Twin Cities Productivity Forum, Indpls. Literary Club (past v.p.), U. Wis. Alumni Assn. (bd. dirs. Ind. chpt.), Friends of Hennepin County Park Res. Dist. (pres.). Avocations: bird watching; nature study; camping; canoeing; amateur radio communications. Office: Extensor Corp 17273 Hampton Ct Minnetonka MN 55345-2517

ROBERTSON, A. JOHN, JR., acctg. cons. and tax co. exec.; b. Mpls., Dec. 25, 1937; s. Alvin J. and Ruth (Whalen) R.; B.S. cum laude, Coll. Holy Cross, Worcester, Mass., 1958; m. Joan Davies Morahan, June 22, 1963 (div. 1982); 1 dau., Ellen Meredith. With Peat, Marwick, Mitchell & Co., 1960-65, 68—, partner, 1968—, mng. partner, Rome, 1968-72, partner-in-charge of European tng., Paris, 1972-73, sr. regional partner France, Spain and N. Africa, Paris La Defense, France, 1973-79, mng. partner, St. Louis, 1979—; asst. corp. controller Otis Elevator Co., 1965-68. Bd. dirs. St. Louis Symphony, Repetory Theatre St. Louis, Downtown St. Louis, Inc.; chmn. Dance St. Louis; trustee St. Louis Art Mus. Mem. Fin. Execs. Inst., Am. Inst. C.P.A's., N.Y. Soc. C.P.A's., Mo. Soc. C.P.A.'s, Ill. Soc. C.P.A.'s, Nat. Assn. Accts., St. Louis Regional Commerce and Growth Assn. (vice chmn. for econ. devel., mem. exec. com., dir.). Clubs: Am. (pres. 1978-79), Polo de Paris, Maxim's Bus. (Paris); Dance St. Louis (pres. 1980—, dir.), Old Warson Country, St. Louis, Racquet, Noonday (St. Louis). Home: 230 S Brentwood Blvd Apt 16C Saint Louis MO 63105 Office: 1010 Market St Saint Louis MO 63101

ROBERTSON, CHARLES EDWIN, geologist; b. Roanoke, Mo.; s. John Wesley and Alda Ruth (Wickes) R.; m. Esther Ellen Key, June 6, 1959; children—Charles Edwin Jr., Cindra Ellen, Joseph David. Diploma Moberly Jr. Coll., 1952; B.A., U. Mo., 1959, M.A., 1960. Geologist Mo. Geol. Survey, Rolla, 1960—. Served with U.S. Army, 1954-57, Korea. Mem. Am. Assn. Petroleum Geologists, AIME, VFW. Lutheran. Lodge: Optomists. Home: 1100 W 11th St Rolla MO 65401 Office: Mo Geol Survey PO Box 250 Rolla MO 65401

ROBERTSON, DAVID HASWELL, JR., lawyer; b. Evanston, Ill., Sept. 30, 1952; s. David Haswell and Barbara Ann (Hinners) R. A.B., Dartmouth Coll., 1971; J.D., Ill. Inst. Tech./Chgo.-Kent Coll., 1981. Bar: Ill. 1981, U.S. Dist. Ct. (no. dist.) Ill. 1981. Assoc. Leavitt & Schneider, Chgo., 1981-82; A.P. Herman & Assocs., Chgo., 1983—. Mem. Chgo. Bar Assn., Ill. State Bar Assn., ABA, Assn. Trial Lawyers Am. Congregationalist. Clubs: University, Lincoln Park Lacrosse (pres. 1982—). Home: 6807 N Lakewood #25 Chicago IL 60626 Office: AP Herman & Assocs 134 N LaSalle St Suite 415 Chicago IL 60602

ROBERTSON, DONALD CLAUS, microbiology educator; b. Rockford, Ill., Mar. 5, 1940; s. Fredrick Martin and Marion Lucille (Scott) R.; m. Ronna Marie Schwartz, Oct. 28, 1962; children—Sonja Marie, Mary Louise. B.S., U. Dubuque, 1962; Ph.D., Iowa State U., 1967. Research chemist U.S. Dept. Agr., Ames, Iowa, 1962-67; postdoctoral fellow Mich. State U., East Lansing, 1967-70; asst. prof. U. Kans., Lawrence, 1970-75, assoc. prof., 1975-80, prof. microbiology, 1980—; mem. bacteriology and mycology study sect. NIH, 1978-83. Contbr. articles to profl. jours. Honor lectr. Mid-Am. State Univs. Assn., 1981-82. Mem. Am. Soc. for Microbiology, AAUP, AAAS, Am. Soc. Biol. Chemists, Am. Acad. Microbiology, Sigma Xi. Avocations: golf; fishing; hiking; camping. Home: 201 Arizona Lawrence KS 66044 Office: Dept Microbiology U Kans Lawrence KS 66045

ROBERTSON, DONELSON ANTHONY, oil company executive; b. Salina, Kans., Sept. 26, 1924; s. Donelson Caffrey Jenkins Robertson and Maudie Etholwyn (Bates) Fuhrman; m. Joan Dolores Lingo, Aug. 2, 1947; children—Bruce F. (dec.), Brian B., Bonnie A. B.S., Centenary Coll., 1949; M.S., U. Ill., 1951. Registered profl. engr., Pa. Dist. geologist Shell Oil Co., Denver, Billings, Mont., Baton Rouge and Pitts., 1951-66; v.p. ops. N.E. div. Martin Marietta Corp., N.Y.C., 1966-76; exec. v.p. P.R. Berger & Assocs., Pitts., 1976-80; div. mgr. Patrick Petroleum Co., Pitts., 1980-82, v.p., Jackson, Mich., 1982-84; v.p., regional mgr. Ladd Petroleum Corp., Jackson, 1984—. Patentee external friction coupling, 1975. Served with U.S. Army, 1943-45, ETO. Recipient Silver Cup Honors Night award Martin Marietta Corp., 1974. Mem. Am. Assn. Petroleum Geologists, Am. Inst. Profl. Geologists (cert., charter), Petroleum Engrs. Soc. AIME, Assn. Engring. Geologists. Home: 2640 Walden Woods Blvd Jackson MI 49201 Office: Ladd Petroleum Corp 744 W Michigan Ave Jackson MI 49204

ROBERTSON, ELAINE BOSCO, nursing administrator; b. Lowell, Mass., May 4, 1945; d. Joseph and Emma (Pacillo) Bosco; m. Brian James Robertson, May 24, 1980; 1 child, Gina Elaina. B.S. in Nursing, Boston U., 1967, M.S. in Nursing, 1977. R.N., Ill., Mass., Colo. Staff nurse ICU, Univ. Hosp., Boston, 1967-68; staff and asst. head nurse nursery Malden (Mass.) Hosp., 1968-70; clinic nurse neurology/neurosurgery clinics Children's Hosp., Boston, 1971-76; pediatric practitioner-tchr. Rush U., Chgo., 1976-77; neurosurgery clin. specialist Children's Meml. Hosp., Chgo., 1978-80, clin. nurse educator, 1980-81, evening nursing adminstrv. coordinator, 1983—, cons., instr. pediatric intravenous insertion. Served to capt., Nurse Corps, U.S. Army Res., 1978-79. Nursing fellow, 1976-78. Mem. Neurosurg. Nurses Assn., Assn. Care of Children in Health Care Settings (dir. 1979-81), Sigma Theta Tau. Democrat. Roman Catholic. Home: 4425 N Sacramento St Chicago IL 60625 Office: 2300 Children's Plaza Chicago IL 60614

ROBERTSON, FLORENCE WINKLER, public relations specialist; b. Hampton, Va., Sept. 11, 1945; s. Fred and Florence Bernice (Shamo) Felty; m. John Park Winkler, June 24, 1967 (div. 1977); m. James Milton Robertson, Oct. 21, 1982. A.A., Palm Beach Jr. Coll., 1965; B.A., U. South Fla., 1967. Reporter, Lexington (Ky.) Leader, 1967-70; freelance writer, 1971-76; TV and radio news reporter Sta. KCRG, Cedar Rapids, Iowa, 1972-73; asst. dir. pub. relations Coe Coll., Cedar Rapids, 1973-78; info. specialist Cedar Rapids (Iowa) Pub. Schs., 1979-83; pub. relations specialist Nat. Promotions Network, Cedar Rapids, 1983—. Chmn. pub. relations com., mem. exec. com., bd. dirs. Grat Wood Area chpt. ARC. Recipient Regional award Council Advancement and Support Edn., 1975, 77, 78, nat. award CASE, 1977; Pub. Service awards Nat. Police Officers Assn., City of Shively (Ky.) and Am. Legion, 1970; Nat. award Nat. Sch. Pub. Relations Assn., 1981, 83. Mem. Pub. Relations Soc. Am., Nat. Sch. Pub. Relations Assn., Iowa Sch. Pub. Relations Assn. Home: 901 Staub Ct NE Cedar Rapids IA 52402 Office: Nat Promotions Network 213 1st Ave SE Cedar Rapids IA 52403

ROBERTSON, GEORGE JAMES, educational administrator; b. Freemont, Nebr., Feb. 16, 1947; s. Raliegh R. and Bernice M. (Vopalensky) R.; m. Karen M. Faist, June 7, 1969; children—Heather CheRee, Lindsay Layne. B.A. in Edn., Wayne State Coll. 1969; M.Ed., U. Nebr.-Lincoln, 1973, postgrad., 1979. Tchr. math. jr. high sch. Plattsmouth Community Schs., Nebr., 1969-80; prin. secondary sch. Newman Grove Pub. Schs., Nebr., 1980-85, West Point Pub. Schs., Nebr., 1985— sec.-treas. Nebr. State Secondary Prins. Region III, 1983-84. Developer computer billing system. Mem. Nat. Assn. Secondary Sch. Prins., Assn. Supervision and Curriculum Devel., Phi Delta Kappa. Democrat. Avocations: model trains, woodworking, country western singing. Home: 780 E Sheridan West Point NE 68788 Office: West Point Jr-Sr High Sch Box 188 West Point NE 68788

ROBERTSON, JOHN BERNARD, lawyer; b. Cleve., Dec. 22, 1936; s. John and Clara (Fairley) R.; m. Marlene Joann Skerl, July 26, 1958; children—Kevin, Suzanne, Eric, Renee. B.S. magna cum laude in Social Sci., John Carroll U., 1958; LL.B. summa cum laude, U. Detroit, 1961. Bar: Ohio 1961, Mich. 1962. Assoc. Gallagher, Sharp, Fulton & Norman, Cleve., 1964-73, ptnr., 1973—. Trustee Citizens League of Greater Cleve., 1982-84. Served to capt. U.S. Army, 1962-63. Mem. Cleve. Assn. Civil Trial Attys. (presdl. award 1984), Ohio Assn. Civil Trial Attys. (treas. 1984—), Ohio State Bar Assn. (council dels. 1985—), ABA, Cleve. Bar Assn. (trustee 1984—), Internat. Assn. Ins. Counsel, Def. Research Inst. Democrat. Roman Catholic. Home: 52 County Line Rd Gates Mills OH 44040 Office: Gallagher Sharp Fulton & Norman 6th Floor Bulkley Bldg Cleveland OH 44115

ROBERTSON, JOSEPH EDMOND, industrial grain processing company executive; b. Brownstown, Ind., Feb. 16, 1918; s. Roscoe Melvin and Edith Penina (Shields) R.; B.S., Kans. State U., 1940, postgrad., 1940; m. Virginia Faye Baxter, Nov. 23, 1941; 1 son, Joseph Edmond. Cereal chemist Ewing Mill Co., 1940-43, flour milling engr., 1946-50, feed nutritionist, 1951-59; v.p., sec. Robertson Corp., Brownstown, Ind., 1960-80, pres., 1980—. Pres. Jackson County (Ind.) Welfare Bd., 1948-52. Served with USAAF, 1943-45. Mem. Hardwood Plywood Mfrs. Assn. (v.p. affiliate div. 1971-73), Am. Assn. Cereal Chemists, Assn. Operative Millers, Am. Legion, Brownstown C. of C. (dir. All Am. city program 1955), Kans. State U. Alumni Assn. (life), Blue Key, Phi Delta Theta, Phi Kappa Phi, Alpha Mu. Presbyn. (elder 1954-69). Elk. Clubs: Country (Seymour, Ind.); Hickory Hills Country (Brownstown, Ind.). Home: Route 2 Lake and Forest Club Box A Brownstown IN 47220 Office: 200 Front St Brownstown IN 47220

ROBERTSON, LEON H., trucking company executive; b. Atlanta, Jan. 25, 1934; s. Grady Joseph and Pearline (Chandler) R.; m. S. Ann Parker, Aug. 27, 1971; children—Sharon, Michael. B.S., Ga. Inst. Tech., 1957, M.S., 1959; postgrad. student U. Okla., 1958, U. Mich., 1961; Ph.D., Ga. State U., 1968. Mgr. mgmt. info. div. Arthur Andersen & Co., Atlanta, 1960-65; prof. bus. adminstrn. Ga. State U., 1965-75; v.p. Tex. Gas Resources Corp., Owensboro, Ky., 1975-78, sr. v.p., 1982-83; chmn., chief exec. officer Am. Carriers Inc., Shawnee Mission, Kans., 1978—. Mem. Am. Trucking Assn. (v.p.-at-large, mem. exec. com.), Cen. and So. Motor Freight Tariff Assn. (dir.). Office: Am Carriers Inc 9393 W 110th St Overland Park KS 66210

ROBERTSON, TIMOTHY JOEL, statistics educator, researcher; b. Denver, Oct. 4, 1937; s. Flavel P. and Helen Claire (Oliver) Girdner; m. Joan K. Slater, Aug. 18, 1959; children—Kelly, Jana, Doug, Michael. B.A. in Math., U. Mo., 1959, M.S. in Math., 1961, Ph.D. in Math., 1966. Asst. prof. Cornell Coll., Mt. Vernon, Iowa, 1961-63; vis. prof. U. N.C., Chapel Hill, 1974-75, U. Calif.-Davis, 1983-84; prof. dept. stats. and actuarial sci. U. Iowa, Iowa City, 1965—. Contbr. articles to profl. jours. Fellow Am. Statis. Assn. (dist. rep. 1974-75), Inst. Math. Stats.; mem. Math. Assn. Am. (assoc. editor 1977-81, gov.-at-large 1978-81), Internat. Statis. Inst., Sigma Xi, Pi Mu Epsilon. Democrat. Avocations: camping; canoeing, bicycling; jogging. Home: 1811 Kathlin Dr Iowa City IA 52240 Office: U Iowa Iowa City IA 52242

ROBEY, LARRY WAYNE, information processing executive; b. Clayton, Wis., Sept. 23, 1939; s. Ferris M. and Josephine (Heider) R.; m. Alice J. Boomsma, June 9, 1962; children—Camille Ann, Thomas Charles. B.B.A., Northwestern U., 1971. Cert. data processing. Acct., J. I. Case Co., Racine, Wis., 1963-65; systems analyst Gen. Binding Corp., Northbrook, Ill., 1965-70; project mgr. Standard Oil Co. (Ind.), Chgo., 1970-81; dir. mgmt. info. systems U.S. Shoe Corp., Beloit, Wis., 1981—; part-time instr. Blackhawk Tech. Inst. Mem. Data Processing Mgmt. Assn., Soc. Info. Mgmt. Republican. Baptist. Home: 4043 Wilshire Ln Janesville WI 53545 Office: One Freeman Ln Beloit WI 53511

ROBEY, SUSANNA HORTON, mental health counselor, educator; b. Springfield, Mo., Oct. 2, 1937; d. George Vaughan and Dorothy Dickerson (Durst) H.; m. George Earl Robey, June 18, 1960; children—Susan Marie, Margaret Eve, Cynthia Dorita. B.A., Drury Coll., 1959; M.S. in Edn., U. Wis.-Platteville, 1982. Cert. tchr., Iowa. Tchr. jr. high sch. Kansas City Community Sch. Dist., Kans., 1959-60; tchr. Dubuque Community Schs., Iowa, 1967-76; supervising counselor Substance Abuse Services, Dubuque, 1982-83; career counselor Northeast Iowa Tech. Inst., Peosta, 1983-84; family therapist Mercy Hosp., Dubuque, 1984-85; mental health counselor Jane Addams Family Counseling and Mental Health Ctr., Galena, Ill., 1985—; founding sec., Montessori Adv. Group, Dubuque, 1969-70. Founding pres.

Suzuki Sch. Music, Dubuque, 1978-80; bd. dirs. Dubuque Community Schs., 1977—, Symphony Orchestra Aux., 1976-80; troop leader Little Cloud council Girl Scouts U.S.A., 1968-78; pres. council Dubuque PTA, 1974-76. Mem. Am. Assn. Counseling Devel., Am. Mental Health Counselors Assn., DAR (regent 1980-81), Kappa Delta Pi. Presbyterian. Clubs: Debonaires Dance (founding pres. 1964-66), PEO (v.p. 1980-81). Avocations: reading; golfing; singing; dancing. Home: 1130 S Grandview St Dubuque IA 52001 Office: Jane Addams Family Counseling and Community Mental Health Ctr 300 Summit St Galena IL 61036

ROBINS, DANIEL FREDERICK, consulting engineer; b. Highland Park, Mich., Dec. 19, 1932; s. Daniel Maurice and Eileen Georgiana (Kinney) R.; m. Joanne Alberta Tatrow, Sept. 22, 1961; children—Scott Kinney, Timothy Daniel, Amy Lynne. B.S. in Mech. Engring., Mich. State U., 1954, postgrad., 1959. Registered profl. engr., Ind., Mich., Ohio. Chief engr. Alma Trailer Co., Mich., 1959-60; engr. Chrysler Corp., Chelsea, Mich., 1962; sr. project engr. Owens-Ill., Inc., Toledo, 1962-76; asst. chief mech. engr. Hoad Engrs., Inc., Ypsilanti, Mich., 1976-79; prin. Robins Engineering, Toledo, 1979—. Parliamentarian, Maumee Parent Teachers Orgn., Ohio, 1982-83; v.p., 1984. Served to 1st lt. USAF, 1955-58, Korea. Mem. Am. Soc. Mech. Engrs. (mem. Northwest Ohio sect., treas. 1982-83, sec. 1983-84, chmn. 1984-85), Toledo Assn. Cons. Engrs. (v.p. 1984-85, pres. 1985—). Republican. Lodge: Moose (jr. gov. 1977-78). Avocations: sailing; photography; computer programming. Home: 4014 Greenbrook Ct Toledo OH 43614 Office: Robins Engring 4400 Heatherdowns Blvd Toledo OH 43614

ROBINS, ELI, psychiatrist, neurochemist, educator; b. Houston, Feb. 22, 1921; s. Abe and Ida (Schaffer) R.; B.A., Rice U., 1940; M.D., Harvard, 1943; D.Sc. (hon.) Washington U., St. Louis, 1984; m. Lee Nelken, Feb. 22, 1946; children—Paul, James, Thomas, Nicholas. Asst. in psychiatry Harvard, 1944-45; Boston U., 1948; intern Mt. Sinai Hosp., N.Y.C., 1944; resident Mass. Gen. Hosp., Boston, 1944-45, McLean Hosp., Waverly, Mass., 1945-46, Pratt Diagnostic Hosp., Boston, 1948-49; instr. neuropsychiatry Washington U., St. Louis, 1951-52, asst. prof. psychiatry, 1953-56, assoc. prof., 1956-58, prof., 1958-66, head dept. psychiatry, 1963-75, Wallace Renard prof., 1966—. Served to capt. U.S. Army, 1946-48. Recipient career research award USPHS, 1961-63; gold medal Soc. Biol. Psychiatry, 1974; Paul H. Hoch award Am. Psychopath. Assn., 1977; Award of Merit, St. Louis Med. Soc., 1978, hon. mem. award 1984, Cert. of honor membership, 1984; Salmon Medalist, New York Academy of Med., 1981; Disting. Service award Nat. Alliance for Mentally Ill., 1983. Diplomate Am. Bd. Am. Bd. Psychiatry and Neurology. Fellow Am. Psychiat. Assn. (Found. prize for research 1982), Royal Coll. Psychiatrists, Am. Coll. Neuropsychopharmacology (hon.); mem. Am. Soc. Clin. Investigation, Am. Soc. Biol. Chemists, Soc. Biol. Psychiatry, Psychiatric Research Soc., Am. Psychopath. Assn. Internat. Soc. Neurochemistry, Assn. for Research in Nervous and Mental Disease (v.p. 1960), Soc. Neurosci., St. Louis Med. Soc. (hon. mem.), Contbr. articles to med. jours. Office: 4940 Audubon Saint Louis MO 63110

ROBINS, GARY BRUCE, beverage company executive; b. Columbus, Ohio, June 6, 1946; s. Louis and Sara (Kahn) R.; student Ohio State U., 1964-66; m. Constance Kiefer, Aug. 11, 1967; children—Dean, Chad, Bret, Zach. Salesman, Excello Wine Co., Columbus, 1967-70, v.p., 1971—; pres. Hi-State Beverage Co., Columbus, 1977—, also dir.; v.p. The Robins Beverage Group, 1980—; sec.-treas. ACA of Columbus, Inc., 1984—. Active United Jewish Fund, 1970—; bd. dirs. Jewish Family Service, 1975; mem. Columbus Conv. and Visitors Bur.; mem. Columbus Quincentennial Exposition 1992; bd. dirs. Am. ORT Fedn., 1981—; bd. dirs. Columbus Jewish Fedn., 1981—, sec., 1985—; chmn. campaign United Jewish Appeal of Columbus, 1985. Mem. Wholesale Beer Assn. Ohio, Nat., Beer Wholesalers Assn., Wine and Spirits Wholesalers Am., Ohio Wholesale Wine Dealers Assn., Columbus Mfrs. Reps. Assn., Columbus C. of C., Ohio C. of C. Clubs: B'nai B'rith, Winding Hollow Country (bd. dirs. 1983—), Columbus Men's ORT (vice chmn. 1983—). Home: 435 S Columbia Ave Columbus OH 43209 Office: 871 Michigan Ave Columbus OH 43215

ROBINS, GREGG BRYAN, beverage distributing company executive; b. Columbus, Ohio, June 6, 1946; s. Louis and Sara (Kahn) R.; m. Bette Carol Weiss, May 23, 1970 (div. Oct. 1979); children—Adam Marc, Jeffrey Alan; m. Barbara Gaston, July 4, 1982. Student Ohio State U., 1964-67. Salesman, Excello Wine Co., Columbus, 1967-70, sec., treas., 1970—; exec. v.p. Hi-State Beverage Co., Columbus, 1977—; pres. Globe Wine & Spirits Co., Columbus, 1977—; sec., treas., dir. Robins Beverage Group, Columbus, 1980—; pres. ACA JOE of Columbus Inc., 1985—. Bd. dirs. Columbus Jewish Fedn., 1984—, Hillel Found., Ohio State U., Columbus, 1984—, Columbus Men's ORT, 1979—; mem. Wine and Spirits Wholesalers of Am., Ohio Beer and Wine Assn., Nat. Beer Wholesalers Assn. Jewish. Club: Winding Hollow Country (Columbus). Lodge: B'nai B'rith. Avocations: jogging; weight lifting. Home: 1391 Windrush Circle Blacklich OH 43004 Office: Robins Beverage Group 877 Ingleside Ave Columbus OH 43215

ROBINS, MARJORIE MCCARTHY (MRS. GEORGE KENNETH ROBINS), civic worker; b. St. Louis, Oct. 4, 1914; d. Eugene Ross and Louise (Roblee) McCarthy; A.B., Vassar Coll., 1936; diploma St. Louis Sch. Occupational Therapy, 1940; m. George Kenneth Robins, Nov. 9, 1940; children—Carol Robins Von Arx, G. Stephen, Barbara A. Foorman. Mem. Mo. Library Commn., 1937-38; mem. bd. St. Louis Jr. League, 1945, 46; mem. bd. Occupational Therapy Workshop of St. Louis, 1941-46, pres., 1945, 46; mem. bd. Ladue Chapel Nursery Sch., 1957-60, 61-64, pres. bd., 1963, 64; past regional chmn. United Fund; past mem. St. Louis Met. Youth Commn., St. Louis Health and Welfare Council; bd. dirs. Internat. Inst. of St. Louis, 1966-72, 76-82, 83—, sec., 1968, 2d v.p., 1969, 70, v.p., 1981; bd. dirs. Mental Health Assn. St. Louis, 1963-70, Washington U. Child Guidance and Evaluation Clinic, 1968-78; bd. dirs. Central Inst. for Deaf, 1970—, v.p., 1975-76, pres., 1976-78; bd. dirs. Met. St. Louis YWCA, 1954-63, 64-70, pres. bd., 1960-63, trustee, 1977—; mem. nat. bd. YWCA, 1967-79, nat. v.p., 1973-76; vol. tchr. remedial reading clinic St. Louis City Schs., 1968-71; trustee John Burroughs Sch., 1960-63, John Burroughs Found., 1965-80, Roblee Found., 1972—, Nat. YWCA Retirement Fund, 1979—; bd. dirs. Gambrill Gardens United Meth. Retirement Home, 1979-85, Thompson Retreat Center, 1981—; v.p. bd. dirs. Springboard to Learning Inc., 1980—. Clubs: Vassar (sec. and pres. 1939-40), Wednesday (dir. 1968-70, 77-79, 80-82) (St. Louis). Home: 45 Loren Woods Saint Louis MO 63124

ROBINS, NORMAN ALAN, steel company executive; b. Chgo., Nov. 19, 1934; s. Irving and Sylvia (Robbin) Robins; m. Sandra Ross, June 10, 1956; children—Lawrence Richard, Sherry Lynn. B.S. in Chem. Engring., MIT, 1955, M.S. in Chem. Engring., 1956; Ph.D. in Math., Ill. Inst. Tech., 1972. Asst. mgr. process systems and controls Inland Steel Co., East Chicago, Ind., 1962-67, assoc. mgr. process systems and controls, 1967-72, dir. process research, 1972-77, v.p. research, 1977-84, v.p. technol. assessment, 1984—. Mem. bd. edn. Homewood-Flossmoor High Sch., Ill., 1974-77. Mem. AIME (Nat. Open Hearth Conf. award 1972), Am. Inst. Chem. Engrs., Am. Iron and Steel Inst. (regional tech. meeting award 1967, 72), Indsl. Research Inst., Math. Assn. Am. Home: 2052 Collett Ln Flossmoor IL 60422 Office: Inland Steel Co 3210 Watling St East Chicago IN 46312

ROBINSON, DAVID JOSEPH, electronic technology educator, lawyer, consultant; b. Akron, Ohio, Nov. 11, 1937; s. George Howard and Martha Pauline (Howard) R.; m. Laura Lee Croskey, Nov. 26, 1960; children—Nancy Lynn, Judith Lee. B.E.E., U. Akron, 1963; M.S. in Engring., Case Western Res. U., 1967; J.D., U. Akron. Registered profl. engr., Ohio Bar: Ohio Aerospace engr. NASA, Cleve., 1963-70; prof. electronic tech. Akron U., 1970—; engring. cons., 1967—; sole practice, Akron, 1975—. Active Copley Twp. Bd. Zoning Appeals, 1984. Mem. Am. Soc. Engring. Educators, Akron Bar Assn., Ohio Bar Assn. Lodge: Copley Lions (pres. 1978-79). Avocations: golf; photography; college sports. Home: 1615 Centerview Dr Copley OH 44321 Office: U Akron Dept Engring and Sci Tech Akron OH 44325

ROBINSON, JACK F(AY), clergyman; b. Wilmington, Mass., Mar. 7, 1914; s. Thomas P. and Ethel Lincoln (Fay) R.; A.B., Mont. State U., 1936; D.B., Crozer Theol. Sem., 1939; A.M., U. Chgo., 1949, postgrad., 1950-52; m. Eleanor Jean Smith, Sept. 1, 1937 (dec. 1966); 1 dau., Alice Virginia Dungey; m. Lois Henze, July 16, 1968. Ordained to ministry Baptist Church, 1939; minister Bethany Ch., American Falls, Idaho, 1939-41, 1st Ch., Council Grove, Kans., 1944-49; ordained (transfer) to ministry Congregational Ch., 1945; minister United Ch., Chebanse, Ill., 1949-52, 1st Ch., Argo, Ill., 1954-58, Congl. Ch., St. Charles, Ill., 1958-64; assoc. minister Plymouth Congregational Ch., Lansing, Mich., 1964-66; tchr. Chgo. Pub. Schs., 1966-68; minister Waveland Ave. Congl. Ch., Chgo., 1967-79, First Congl. Ch., Des Plaines, Ill., 1979, Bethany Congl. Ch., Chgo., 1980, Eden United Ch. of Christ, Chgo., 1983—; hist. cons. Bell & Howell Co., Chgo., 1981-82. Assoc. Hyde Park dept. Chgo. YMCA, 1942-44. U. Chgo. Library 1952-54; chmn. com. evangelism Kans. Congl. Christian Conf., 1947-48; city chmn. Layman's Missionary Movement, 1946-51; trustee Congl. and Christian Conf. Ill., v.p., 1963-64; mem. exec. council Chgo. Met. Assn. United Ch. of Christ, 1968-70, sec. ch. and ministry com., 1982—; mem. gen. bd. Ch. Fedn. Greater Chgo., 1969-71; mem. Library Bd. Council Grove, 1945-49; city chmn. NCCJ, 1945-49; dean Northside Mission Council United Ch. of Christ, 1975-77. Mem. Am. Soc. Ch. History, Am. Acad. Polit. Sci., Am. Hist. Assn., C. of C. (past dir.), Internat. Platform Assn. Author: The Growth of the Bible, 1969; From A Mission to a Church, 1976; Bell & Howell Company: A 75 Year History, 1982. Home: 2614 Lincolnwood Dr Evanston IL 60201 Office: PO Box 4578 Chicago IL 60680

ROBINSON, JAMES LAWRENCE, biochemistry educator, researcher; b. Boston, Feb. 23, 1942; s. Lawrence Hanny and Carolyn Ruth (Conklin) R.; m. Janet Lynn Thorpe, Feb. 23, 1963; Mark, Marjorie, Glen. B.S. in Chemistry, U. Redlands, 1960-64; Ph.D. in Biochemistry, UCLA, 1968. Postdoctoral researcher Inst. Cancer Research, Phila., 1968-70; asst. prof. Univ. Ill., Urbana, 1970-76, asoc. prof., 1976-85, prof., 1985—; vis. scientist Inst. Nat. Recherche Agrom, Jouy-en Josas, France, 1978-79. Contbr. articles to prof. jours. Mem. Am. Soc. Biol. Chemists, Am. Dairy Sci. Assn., Am. Inst. of Nutrition. Democrat. Methodist. Avocations: camping; hiking; bicycling; tennis; gardening. Home: 902 Mumford Dr Urbana IL 61801 Office: U Ill Dept Animal Sci 1207 W Gregory Dr Urbana IL 61801

ROBINSON, JAMES ROSS, dentist, consultant; b. Chgo., Dec. 17, 1946; s. James Ross and Nina Cardine (Olson) R.; m. Kathleen Ellen Schoesrow, Dec. 17, 1972; children—Kristin, Brian, Kathryn, Jeffrey. B.S. U. Wis.-Eau Claire, 1969; D.D.S., Marquette U., 1973. Licensed dentist, Wis. Asst. tchr. U. Wis.-Eau Claire, 1967-69; orthodontic asst. Marquette U., 1971-73; dentist, Marshfield Dental Clinic, Wis., 1973-74; gen. practice dentistry, Waupaca, Wis., 1974—; cons. St. Josephs Hosp., Marshfield, 1973-74, Riverside Community Mem. Hosp., Waupaca, 1974—, Wis. Dental Exam. Bd., 1975-79. Mem. Waupaca C. of C. (bd. dirs. 1975-76), ADA, Waupaca County Dental Soc. (pres. 1981-82), Fox River Valley Dental Soc. (sec. 1984), Wis. Dental Assn. (del. 1977), Aircraft Owner Pilots Assn. Republican. Lutheran. Club Waupaca Conservation. Avocations: flying; fishing; hunting; skiing; hockey coaching. Home: Rt 1 Box 426B Waupaca WI 54981 Office: Riverhill Dental Bldg Assoc 701 Riverside Dr Waupaca WI 54981

ROBINSON, JERRY ALLEN, scientist gerontology program administrator; b. Danville, Ill., Dec. 18, 1939; s. Melvin Barto and Elizabeth Jane (Olson) R.; m. Sharon Annette Meismer, Aug. 30, 1969; children—Carrie Jayne, Kevin Troy. B.A., Wabash Coll., 1963; M.S., U. Cin., 1966, Ph.D., 1970. Grad. asst. U. Cin., 1968-70; postdoctoral trainee U. Cin., 1963-70, U. Wis., Madison, 1970-72; project assoc. U. Wis. Regional Primate Ctr., Madison, 1972, asst. scientist, 1972-78, assoc. scientist, 1978—; asst. dir. U. Wis. Inst. on Aging, Madison, 1982-85. Contbr. articles and abstracts on reproductive physiology to profl. jours. Asst. editor Biology of Reproduction, 1986—. Grantee Nat. Inst. Child Health Human Devel., 1977, Nat. Inst. on Aging, 1979. Mem. Soc. Study Reproduction, Endocrine Soc., Am. Soc. Primatologists, Am. Soc. Andrology, Sigma Xi. Office: Wis Regional Primate Research Ctr 1223 Capitol Ct Madison WI 53715

ROBINSON, JOHN MURRELL, physics educator; b. Lecompte, La., Mar. 26, 1945; s. Horace Chester and Lillian (Malone) R. B.S. in Physics, La. State U., 1967; M.S. in Physics, Fla. State U., 1970, Ph.D. in Physics, 1972. Tech. asst. U. Munich, Fed. Republic Germany, 1970-71; research assoc. Fla. State U., Tallahassee, 1972-73; assoc. prof. physics, dept. chmn. Ind.-Purdue U., Fort Wayne, 1973—. Author: (with P. Erdos) The Physics of Actinide Compounds, 1983. Contbr. articles to profl. jours. Grantee Research Corp., 1978, Ind.-Purdue U., 1975, Purdue U., 1974. Mem. Am. Phys. Soc., Am. Assn. Physics Tchrs., Sigma Pi Sigma. Avocations: tennis and racquetball; volleyball; cross-country skiing; ping-pong; jogging. Office: Ind-Purdue U Fort Wayne IN 46805

ROBINSON, LOIS HART, public relations executive; b. Freeport, Ill., Aug. 9, 1927; d. Seril N. and Cora (Stabenow) Hart; m. Noel M. Henze, Nov. 15, 1947 (div. 1964); m. Jack Fay Robinson, July 16, 1968; children—Susan Henze Bentley, Cynthia Henze Berkeley, Charles Henze. Student Oakton Community Coll., 1976-77, Northwestern U., 1977-81. Med. sec. Freeport Meml. Hosp., 1945-47; sec. No. Ill. Corp., 1947-49; adminstrv. asst. to supt. schs. Community Sch. Dist. 303, St. Charles, Ill., 1962-68; exec. sec. Bell & Howell Co., Chgo., 1969-73, supr. corp. relations, 1973-79, mgr. corp. communications, 1979—; pres., dir. Bell & Howell Found. Recipient Effie award Am. Mktg. Assn., 1983. Mem. Internat. Assn. Bus. Communications. Congregationalist. Home: 2614 Lincolnwood Dr Evanston IL 60201 Office: 5215 Old Orchard Rd Skokie IL 60077

ROBINSON, MARK ARTHUR, lawyer; b. Bryan, Ohio, Oct. 10, 1950; s. Richard Burton and Marian E. (Bruot) R.; B.S., Kent State U., 1972; M.A., Ohio State U., 1976; J.D., U. Toledo, 1979. Bar: Ohio 1979, U.S. Dist. Ct. (no. dist.) Ohio 1980, U.S. Ct. Appeals (6th cir.) 1982. Assoc. Rodney M. Arthur Co., L.P.A., Defiance, Ohio, 1979-81, Joseph W. Westmeyer Jr. Co. L.P.A., Toledo, Ohio, 1981—; instr. Am. Inst. Paralegals, Columbus, Ohio, 1983-84. Mem. Assn. Trial Lawyers Am., Ohio State Bar Assn., Ohio Acad. Trial Lawyers, Lucas County Bar Assn. (exec. com. 1983-86), Toledo Bar Assn. (grievance com. 1981—). Republican. Lutheran. Home: 1005 Village Trail Maumee OH 43537 Office: Joseph W Westmeyer Jr Co LPA 421 N Michigan St Toledo OH 43624

ROBINSON, ORLO JOHN, JR., physician; b. Ypsilanti, Mich., Aug. 15, 1921; s. Orlo John and Helen Louise (McBain) R.; m. Naomi Ann Jacka, Aug. 18, 1945 (dec. 1972); children—Christine A., Ralph S., Amy L., Elizabeth A.; m. Joan Louise Sutinen, Nov. 22, 1973; children—Debra S., Robert W., Patricia J. B.S., Eastern Mich. U., 1942; M.D., Wayne U., 1946. Intern, Women's and Children's Receiving Hosp., Detroit, 1946-47; practice medicine specializing in family medicine, Northville, Mich., 1948-84; med. dir. Chrysler Corp., Detroit, 1984—; mem. Orgn. Resource Councilors, Washington, 1984, Sloan-Kettering Inst., N.Y.C., 1984—. Mem., Northville Bd. Edn., 1968-76. Served to capt. USAF, 1947-49. Fellow Am. Acad. Family Physicians; mem. AMA, Wayne County Med. Soc., Mich. State Med. Soc., Am. Occupational Med. Assn. Republican. Presbyterian. Avocations: golfing; boating; hunting. Home: 778 Springfield Dr Northville MI 48167 Office: Chrysler Corp Highland Park PO Box 1919 Detroit MI 48288

ROBINSON, RALPH MYER, chemical engineer, pharmaceutical manufacturing company executive; b. Terre Haute, Ind., Aug. 17, 1926; s. Louis Henry and Rose (Schultz) R.; m. Georgia Levin, Apr. 15, 1956; children—Aron, Stephen. B.S. in Chem. Engring., U. Ill., 1949; M.S. in Chem. Engring., U. Mich., 1950. Devel. engr. Argonne Nat. Lab., Lemont, Ill. 1951-53, Abbott Labs., North Chicago, Ill., 1953-56, group leader high pressure lab., 1956-60, mgr. devel. engring., 1960-68, ops mgr., 1968—. Patentee in field. Co-pres. AAUW Nursery Sch., Waukegan, 1961; mem. Citizens Adv. Group Regional Transp. Authority, Lake County, 1968. Fellow Am. Inst. Chem. Engrs.; mem. Am. Chem. Soc. Lodge: B'nai B'rith (pres. 1968). Avocations: tennis, bridge. Home: 705 Colville Pl Waukegan IL 60087 Office: Abbott Labs 14th and Sheridan Rd North Chicago IL 60064

ROBINSON, RICHARD D., financial executive; b. Gary, Ind., Sept. 6, 1936; s. Clayton LaVerne and Edith Virginia (Ables) R.; m. Jan. 30, 1960. B.A., DePauw U., 1959. Area cost analyst U.S. Steel Co., Gary, Ind., 1959-62; cost acctg. mgr. Marsh Instrument Co., Skokie, Ill., 1962-74, Gen. Binding Corp., Northbrook, Ill., 1974-75; div. controller Intercraft Industries Corp., Chgo., 1975-80; dir. cost acctg. Switchcraft Inc., Chgo., 1980—. Author, originator of computer cost system. Served with USAF, 1954-62. Republican. Office: Switchcraft Inc 5555 N Elston Ave Chicago IL 60630

ROBINSON, ROBERT GEORGE, chemical engineer; b. Beacon, N.Y., Aug. 13, 1937; s. George Albert and Gladys B. (Hammond) R.; m. Rita Mary Fobare, June 25, 1960; children—Patrick T., Rachel A., Robert F. B. in Chem. Engring., Clarkson Coll., 1958, M. in Chem. Engring., 1960; Ph.D., Pa. State U., 1964. Research scientist Upjohn Co., Kalamazoo, 1964-77, sr. scientist, 1977-82, research mgr., 1982—. Contbr. articles to profl. jours. Pres., bd. dirs. Long Lake, Inc., Kalamazoo, 1975-82; coach Kalamazoo Optimist Hockey Assn., 1965-77; 4-H leader, 1977-83. Served to capt. U.S. Army, 1958-60. Mem. Am. Inst. Chem. Engrs. (bd. dirs. div. 1980-83, vice-chmn. div. 1984—), Am. Chem. Soc., AAAS. Avocations: tennis; backpacking; skiing; aviation history. Home: 8056 Greenfield Shores Scotts MI 49088 Office: Upjohn Co 7171 Portage Rd Kalamazoo MI 49002

ROBINSON, VIVIAN MARIE, electrical distributor executive; b. Los Angeles, Oct. 15, 1944; d. Bertrand Olander White and Myrtle Louise Lucas; m. Ray Robinson, June 26, 1979 (div. 1980). B.A. in Urban Tchr. Edn., Governor State U., 1976, M.A. in Human Relation Services, 1979, postgrad. in media communications, 1980—. Tchr. City Colls. of Chgo., 1978-82; mktg. and sales rep. Satellite Communications, Chgo., 1982-83; mktg. cons. Sonicraft, Chgo., 1983-84; pres., chmn. bd. dirs. Midwest Communications Supply Co., Chgo., 1984—. Mem. adv. bd. Olive Harvey Coll., Chgo., 1984—. Mem. Soc. Cable TV Engrs., Chgo. Minority Assn. Cable Contractors, Betty Winfield Baldwin Fedn. Women's Clubs, Chatham Bus. Assn., Phi Theta Kappa. Home: 5471 Hyde Park Blvd Chicago IL 60615 Office: Midwest Communications Supply Co 7205 S Chicago Ave Chicago IL 60619

ROBINSON, WAYNE ANTHONY, electric service owner; b. Gallipolis, Ohio, Feb. 21, 1957; s. James William and Lydia Elizabeth (Borden) R. B.A., Morehouse Coll., Atlanta, 1980. Mgmt. trainee Gallipolis Electric Service, Ohio, 1980-82, pres., 1982—. Co-founder, bd. dirs., treas. Ohio Valley Minority Bus. Assocs., Inc.; minority rep. Ohio Valley Regional Devel. Commn., 1981; mem. Gallipolis City Planning Commn., 1983. Recipient E.B. Williams award Morehouse Coll., 1979. Mem. Elec. Apparatus Service Assn., Am. Mgmt. Assn. Democrat. Baptist. Office: Gallipolis Electric Service 57 Pine St Gallipolis OH 45631

ROBINSON-BRUNS, SUSAN (LYNN), marketing professional; b. Sarnia, Ont., Can., Feb. 5, 1954; d. Martin C. and Patricia F. (Moran) Beebe; m. Harold Douglas Robinson, Apr. 19, 1975 (div. May 1980); 1 child, Patricia Ann Robinson; m. Thomas Walter Bruns, Feb. 4, 1982. Student Sinclair Coll., 1977-80, Capitol U., 1982-84. Lic. Realtor, Mich., Ohio. Programmer/operator Dayton Bag & Burlap Co., Ohio, 1978-79; mgr. EDP, Miami Valley Health Systems Agy., Dayton, 1979-80; analyst/programmer Outdoor Sports Hdqrs., Dayton, 1980-81; EDP specialist Robert Half of Dayton, 1981-82; mktg. rep. Computer Task Group, Dayton and Buffalo, 1982—; cons., 1979-82. Mem. Assn. Systems Mgmt. (chpt. sec. 1983-84, chpt. v.p. 1984-85, pres.-elect 1985-86), Data Processing Mgmt. Assn., Nat. Assn. Female Execs., Am. Bus. Women's Assn., Greater Dayton Corvette Club (sec. 1980-82). Republican. Roman Catholic. Avocations: racquetball; skiing; sailing; historic home restoration. Office: PO Box 786 Dayton OH 45402

ROBIRDS, SCOTT ROLAND, optometrist, clinical investigator; b. Luling, La., Sept. 21, 1955; s. William Roland and Joan (Wingfield) R.; m. Sheila Diane Watson, Aug. 8, 1976. Student U. Mo., 1973-76; B.S., Ind. U., 1976-78, O.D., 1976-80. Lic. optometrist, Ga., Mo., Tex. Staff optometrist and contact lens specialist N. Rex Ghormley, Inc., St. Louis, 1983—; clin. investigator Cooper Vision Optics, San Jose, Calif., 1983—, Wesley-Jessen, Chgo., 1983—, Ciba-Geigy, Atlanta, 1983—. Served to capt. U.S. Army, 1980-83. Recipient Bausch & Lomb award, Bloomington, Ind., 1980. Mem. Am. Optometric Assn., Am. Optometric Found. (award 1980), Am. Acad. of Optometry, Mo. Optometric Assn., St. Louis Optometric Assn. Republican. Methodist. Club: YMCA. Avocations: tennis; golf; outdoor activities. Home: 1493 Sandpointe Ct Ballwin MO 63011 Office: N Rex Ghormley Inc 10103 Concord School Rd Saint Louis MO 63128

ROBISON, EDWARD CORBIN, dentist; b. Hoisington Kans., July 29, 1941; s. Corbin Ellis and Kathryn J. (Atkin) R.; m. Marie Matilda Birzer, July 28, 1962; children—Kelda, Renee Elizabeth, Edward. B.A., U. Kans., 1964; D.D.S., U. Mo.-Kansas City, 1969. Gen. practice dentistry, Warrensburg, Mo., 1971—. Chmn. fin. comm. Sacred Heart Cath. Ch., Warrensburg, 1979-80; bd. dirs. Johnson County Extension Council, Warrensburg, 1982—. Served to capt. U.S. Army, 1969-71. Fellow Acad. Gen. Dentistry, 1984. Mem. Greater Kansas City Dental Soc. (bd. dirs. 1985—), Acad. Gen. Dentistry, ADA, Warrensburg C. of C. (bd. dirs. 1983—), Omicron Kappa Upsilon. Republican. Lodges: Elks, Rotary (Paul Harris Fellow). Avocations: hunting, fishing, travel, model rocketry. Home: Route 3 Box 80 Warrensburg MO 64093 Office: 215 1/2 E Gay St Warrensburg MO 64093

ROBLIN, JOHN MACKAY, steel company executive; b. Sagada, P.I., Feb. 20, 1931; s. John Hopper and Sarah Harriet (Mackay) R.; m. Vivian Corking, Feb. 21, 1964; children—Christopher, Keith, Maria. B.S. in Chem. Engring., Princeton U., 1953; M.S., MIT, 1955; Ph.D., Case Inst. Tech., 1962. Research supr. Republic Steel Corp., Cleve., 1956-68, head new products div., 1968-75, dir. process and materials planning, 1975-78, dir. research adminstrn. and devel., 1978-81, dir. corp. planning, 1981-84; dir. strategic planning LTV Steel Co., Cleve., 1984—. Contbr. articles to tech. jours. Chmn. bd. trustees Grantwood Recreation Park, Solon, Ohio, 1970-76; chmn. Solon Charter Rev. Commn., 1972, 74; pres. Solon Citizens League, 1970. Mem. Am. Iron and Steel Inst., North Am. Soc. Corp. Planners, Assn. Corp. Growth, Sigma Xi, Tau Beta Pi. Republican. Episcopalian. Clubs: Mayfield Country, Union. Home: 37275 Windy Hill Ln Solon OH 44139 Office: LTV Steel Co PO Box 6778 Cleveland OH 44101

ROBSON, MARTIN C., plastic and reconstructive surgeon, educator; b. Lancaster, Ohio, Mar. 8, 1939; s. Martin Cecil and Agnes Jean (Spears) R.; div.; children—Karen, Douglas, Martin III; m. Leslie Einfeldt, Oct. 1, 1983. Student Northwestern U., 1957-59; B.A., Johns Hopkins U., 1961, M.D., 1964. Diplomate Am. Bd. Surgery, Am. Bd. Plastic Surgery. Intern U. Chgo. Hosps. and Clinics, 1964-65; fellow dept. surgery Johns Hopkins U., Balt., 1965-67; chief resident gen. surgery Brooke Army Med. Ctr., San Antonio, Tex., 1968-69; chief resident plastic surgery Yale U., New Haven, Conn., 1971-73, assoc. prof., 1973-74; prof., chief plastic reconstructive surgery U. Chgo., 1974-84, prof., chmn. div. plastic and reconstructive surgery, Detroit, 1984—; chmn. Plastic Surgery Research Council, 1983-84; pres. Chgo. Soc. Plastic Surgery, 1980-81. Author: Comprehensive Care of the Burned Person, 1984. Contbr. articles to profl. jours. and books. Served as maj. U.S. Army, 1967-71. Am. Geriatrics Soc. fellow, 1968-69; Henry Strong Denison scholar, 1963-64; recipient Gerard B. Lambert award, 1973, Am. Med. Tech. Writing award, 1979-82, Resident award in Research Category Ednl. Founds. Chief Residents Conf., 1973, Mead Johnson Excellence Research award, 1972, Raymond Franklin Metcalfe award for surg. research, 1968. Fellow ACS (com. trauma), Am. Acad. Microbiology; mem. Am. Surg. Assn., Am. Assn. Plastic Surgeons (nominating com.), Soc. Univ. Surgeons, Assn. Acad. Surgery, Central Surg. Assn., Western Surg. Assn., Am. Trauma Soc., Am. Soc. Plastic and Reconstructive Surgeons (Basic Sci. award ednl. found. 1978, coordinating council for acad. policies), Soc. Head and Neck Surgeons, Am. Burn Assn. (pres. 1985—, Carl A. Moyer award 1972), Internat. Soc. Burn Injuries, Am. Assn. Surgery of Trauma, Am. Soc. Maxillofacial Surgeons, Am. Soc. Surgery of Hand (research com.), Am. Assn. Hand Surgery, Am. Soc. Microbiology, Midwestern Assn. Plastic Surgeons, Am. Cleft Palate Assn., Am. Soc. Artificial Internal Organs, Am. Soc. Aesthetic Plastic Surgery, AMA (ref. panel diagnostic and therapeutic tech. assessment), Am. Assn. Automotive Medicine, Societe Internationale De Chirurgie, Pan Am. Med. Assn., Sigma Xi, Alpha Omega Alpha, Beta Beta Beta, Phi Eta Sigma. Avocations: marathon running; skiing; boating. Office: 6-D Univ Health Ctr 4201 St Antoine St Detroit MI 48201

ROCCHI, JEANINE LEONE, educator; b. Chgo., June 25, 1952; d. Carl William and Leona Martha (Macey) Carlson; m. Michael Bernard Rocchi, Aug. 4, 1973; children—Stephen, Melissa. B.S., DePaul U., 1974, M.S., 1976. Research asst. DePaul U., Chgo., 1971-75, teaching asst., 1973-75; research asst. Rush Presbyterian Med. Ctr., Chgo., 1975-77; chemistry tchr. Notre Dame Middle Sch., Chgo., 1977-78; chemistry instr. Triton Coll., River Grove, Ill., 1980-84; tchr. sci. St. Celestine Jr. High Sch., Elmwood Park, Ill., 1983—. State of Ill. Edn. Improvement grantee, 1984-85. Mem. Am. Chem. Soc., Nat. Sci. Tchrs. Assn. Roman Catholic. Club: Micropartners (Elmwood Park). Home: 3044 N Octavia St Chicago IL 60635 Office: St Celestine Sch Elmwood Park IL 60635

ROCCHINI, ALBERT P., pediatric cardiologist, educator; b. Pitts., Dec. 18, 1946; s. Albert G. and Norma R. (Squitieri) R.; m. Arlene D. Garvey, Aug.

16, 1969; children—Albert J., Michael E. B.S. in Chem. Engring., U. Pitts., 1968, M.D., 1972. Intern, U. Minn., Mpls., 1972-73, resident in pediatrics, 1973-74; resident in pediatric cardiology Harvard Med. Sch., Boston, 1974-77; asst. prof. pediatrics U. Mich., Ann Arbor, 1979-82, assoc. prof. pediatrics, 1982—. Contbr. articles to profl. jours. Served as maj. M.C., U.S. Army, 1977-79. Recipient Young Investigators award Am. Coll. Cardiology, 1975, award Soc. Pediat. Research, 1983. Mem. Am. Heart Assn., Mich. Heart Assn., Am. Acad. Pediatrics. Roman Catholic. Home: 2240 Tilsby Ct Ann Arbor MI 48103 Office: U Mich Med Ctr Box 66 F1115 Ann Arbor MI 48109

ROCHE, ALEXANDER FRANCIS, obstetrics/gynecology educator, physician; b. Melbourne, Victoria, Australia, Oct. 17, 1921; s. Edward Francis and Myrtle Doris (Constantine) R.; m. Eileen Mary French, Jan. 11, 1945; children—Peter John, Stephen John, Margaret Anne. M.B., B.S., U. Melbourne, 1946, Ph.D., 1954, D.Sc., 1966, M.D., 1968. Dir. child growth study Melbourne U., 1954-68, reader dept. anatomy, 1962-68; prof. anthropology Antioch Coll., Yellow Springs, Ohio, 1968—; chief sect. on growth and genetics Fels Research Inst., Yellow Springs, 1968—, Fels prof. pediatrics, ob-gyn Wright State U. Sch. Medicine, Yellow Springs, 1977—; lectr., dir. U. Melbourne, 1951-68. Recipient Outstanding Profl. Achievement award Affiliated Socs. Council Engring. and Sci. Found., Dayton, Ohio, 1978, Research Writing award AAHPERD, 1984. Fellow Am. Dermatoglyphics Assn. (charter), Human Biology Council (charter); mem. Am. Assn. Phys. Anthropologists, Internat. Assn. Human Biologists (charter), Soc. Mexicana de Anatomia (hon. life). Home: PO Box 707 Yellow Springs OH 45387-0707 Office: Dept Pediatrics Div Human Biology Wright State U Sch Medicine 1005 Xenia Ave Yellow Springs OH 45387-1695

ROCHE, E. JAMES, investment counselor; b. Cin., Nov. 1, 1931; s. Edward J. and Helen (Delaney) R.; m. Hedy Heidacher, Sept. 15, 1955 (div. Feb. 1985); children—Sharon Roche Curran, Kerry Roche Kunkemoeller, Kelly, Brian, Molly. A.B., St. Michael's Coll., 1953; M.B.A., Xavier U., 1962. Chartered fin. analyst, investment counselor. Investment analyst Western So. Life Ins. Co., Cin., 1953-58; asst. v.p. investment Union Central Life Ins. Co., Cin., 1958-71; v.p. Lionel D. Edie & Co., Cin., 1971-76; v.p. investments, prin. Scudder, Stevens & Clark, Ltd., Cin., 1976—. Treas. Southwestern Ohio chpt. Am. Heart Assn., Cin., 1975—; pres. Friendly Sons of St. Patrick, Cin., 1985—. Mem. Inst. Chartered Fin. Analysts, Cin. Soc. Fin. Analysts (pres. 1974-75), Internat. Found. Employee Benefit Plans. Roman Catholic. Office: Scudder Stevens & Clark Ltd 540 Carew Tower Cincinnati OH 45230

ROCHE, GEORGE CHARLES, III, college president; b. Denver, May 16, 1935; s. George Charles and Margaret (Stewart) R.; m. June Frances Bernard, Feb. 11, 1955; children—George Charles, Muriel Eileen, Margaret Clare, Jacob Stewart B.S., Regis Coll., 1956; M.A., U. Colo., 1961, Ph.D., 1965; Dr. Pub. Service (hon.), Regis Coll., 1978; Dr. Social Sci., Universidad Francisco Marroquín, 1980. Mem. faculty U. Colo., Boulder, 1963-64, Colo. Sch. Mines, Golden, 1964-66; dir. seminars Found. for Econ. Edn., N.Y.C., 1966-71; pres. Hillsdale (Mich.) Coll., 1971—. Chmn. Nat. Council on Edn. Research, 1982-85. Served to 1st lt. USMC, 1956-58. Recipient Freedoms Found. award, 1972. Mem. Am. Assn. Presidents of Ind. Colls. and Univs., Phila. Soc., Mont Pelerin Soc., Young Presidents Orgn., Council for Nat. Policy (bd. govs.). Author: Power, 1967; American Federalism, 1967; Education in America, 1969; Legacy of Freedom, 1969; Frederic Bastiat: A Man Alone, 1971; The Bewildered Society, 1972; The Balancing Act: Quota Hiring in Higher Education, 1974; America by the Throat: The Stranglehold of Federal Bureaucracy, 1983; contbr. articles to profl. jours. Office: Hillsdale College 33 E College St Hillsdale MI 49242

ROCHE, JOSEPH EMMETT, hospital official; b. Ottawa, Ont., Can., Apr. 19, 1956; came to U.S., 1957; s. Emmett Francis and Mary Helen (Larter) R.; m. Laura Ruth Zella, Aug. 26, 1978; children—Matthew, Brian. B.S., Wayne State U., 1978; M.S.W., U. Mich., 1979; M.B.A., Oakland U., 1983. Clin. worker St. Vincent Ctr., Farmington Hills, Mich., 1979-80; psychiat. social worker Henry Ford Hosp., Detroit, 1980-81, emergency supr., 1981-83, mgr. out-patient substance abuse services, 1983—. Mem. Nat. Assn. Social Workers, Assn. M.B.A. Execs., Acad. Cert. Social Workers. Home: 23128 Dale Allen Mount Clemens MI 48043 Office: Henry Ford Hosp 2849 Cattermole Troy MI 48084

ROCHE, PATRICK ANTHONY, college president; b. Vellore, India, Apr. 13, 1937; came to U.S., 1969; s. Joseph Cyril and Geeta (Davis) R.; m. Florence Kokila Arul, May 8, 1969; children—Gitanjali, Patrick, Nirmala. M.A., Papal Atheneum, Poona, India, 1969, St. John's U., 1970, U. Chgo., 1972; Ph.D., U. Minn., 1977. Prin. St. Xavier's Sch., Chaibasa, India, 1962-64; dir. of edn. Archdiocese of Mpls., Minn., 1969-73; instr. U. Chgo., 1974-75; dir. undergrad. studies U. Sch. Mgmt., Mpls., 1975-80; assoc. dean instrn. Lakewood Community Coll., White Bear Lake, Minn., 1981-84; pres. Inver Hills Community Coll., Inver Grove Heights, Minn., 1984—. Author: Encyclopedia of Asian History, 1984, Social History of the Paravas, 1983, Contact, 1972. Sr. research fellow Smithsonian Inst., 1980, Am. Philos. Soc., 1980, Am. Inst. Indian Studies, 1972, Ford Found., 1972, McMillan Found., 1973. Mem. Am. Assn. Jr. Colls., Am. Assn. of Asian Studies, Am. Hist. Assn., Inver Grove Heights C. of C. Roman Catholic. Lodge: Rotary. Avocations: tennis; music; ethnic foods. Home: 2436 Sheridan Ave South Minneapolis MN 55405 Office: Inver Hill Community Coll 8445 Coll Trail Inver Grove Heights MN 55075

ROCHE-DELLARIO, LYNNE MARIE, marketing professional; b. Louisville, Nov. 4, 1958; d. Alfred Joseph and Sallie Margaret (Lechtenberg) Roche; m. Michael David Dellario, June 30, 1984. B.A., St. Louis U., 1981. Account exec. I.Q. & Assoc., St. Louis, 1981-83; mktg. rep. Busch Creative Services Corp., St. Louis, 1983—. Mem. Women in Bus. Network, Advt. Club of Greater St. Louis. Avocations: snow skiing; racquetball; travel. Home: 1554 Beacon Wood Manchester MO 63021 Office: Busch Creative Services Corp 5240 Oakland St Louis MO 63110

ROCHEN, DONALD MICHAEL, physician; b. Buffalo, Apr. 15, 1943; s. Leo Kent and Phoebe (Elkan) R.; m. Phyllis Helene Been, Aug. 15, 1971; children—Steven, Douglas, Deborah, Andrew. B.A., Northwestern U., 1964; D.O., Coll. Osteo. Medicine and Surgery, Des Moines, 1968. Intern, Detroit Osteo./Bi County Community Hosps., 1968-69, resident in otorhinolaryngology, 1969-73; practice otorhinolaryngology and oro-facial plastic surgery, Detroit, Warren and Mt. Clemens, Mich., 1973—; chmn. dept. otolaryngology and orofacial plastic surgery Detroit Osteo. Hosp., Highland Park, Bi County Community Hosp., Warren, Mich.; mem. staff Mt. Clemens Gen. Hosp. (Mich.); assoc. prof. Mich. State U. Coll. Osteo. Medicine and Surgery, 1975—; adj. prof. Coll. Osteo. Medicine and Surgery, Des Moines, 1981—. Fellow Osteo. Coll. Ophthalmology and Otorhinolaryngology (diplomate), Am. Acad. Otolaryngology, Head and Neck Surgery; mem. Am. Osteo. Assn., Mich. Assn. Osteo. Physicians and Surgeons, Wayne County Osteo. Assn., Macomb County Osteo. Assn. Jewish. Home: 4808 Tyndale Ct West Bloomfield MI 48033 Office: 211 Glendale Ave Highland Park MI 48203 also 30521 Schoenherr Ave Warren MI 48093

ROCHESTER, GREGG STEVEN, psychologist; b. Rapid City, S.D., Mar. 6, 1950; s. Lowell Leroy and Jacqueline B. (Smith) R.; m. Mary Ann, Sept. 26, 1970; children—Gabrielle, Luther, Adrienne. B.S., Dakota Wesleyan U., 1972; M.S., Ind. State U., 1977. Psychologist, human resource center Central Mesubi Med. Center, Hibbing, Minn., 1977-81; pvt. practice clin. psychology, Hibbing, 1981—. Mem. adv. council Minn. Child Devel. and Child Care, 1980—. Mem. Am. Psychol. Assn., Minn. Psychol. Assn. Home: 305 NW 3d Ave Chisholm MN 55719 Office: 116 1/2 E Howard St Hibbing MN 55746

ROCHETTO, EVELYN MARIE, educator; b. Chgo.; d. Lucius J. and Clara M. (Jung) Young; Ph.B., Northwestern U., 1952; m. Paul A. Rochetto, June 9, 1937. Profl. musician, 1930-50; membership sec. Internat. Soc. for Gen. Semantics, 1950-55, exec. sec., 1955-68, dir., 1952-68; tchr. Aurora Coll., 1968—; counselor State of Ill., 1970—. Pres., Chgo. Story League. Dir. Pan Am. Bd. Edn. Mem. AAUW (pres. Chgo. br. 1956—, mem. bd. 1953—), Am. Legion Auxiliary (mem. bd.), Alpha Sigma Lambda (dir.). Club: Woman's University (pres. 1966—). Home: 5240 Sheridan Rd Chicago IL 60640

ROCHMAN, KENNETH, businessman; b. Chgo., Sept. 5, 1948; s. Lou Rochman; divorced; children—Monica, Kiernan. Student mgmt. and bus. seminars Harvard U.; grad. Columbia Coll., 1967; Ph.D., U. Ill., 1970. Pres., owner Rochman Orgn., Chgo., 1980—; cons. Rochman Co., Ltd., Chgo. Avocations: scripophily; photography; philately. Home: Box 1604 Melrose Park IL 60160

ROCK, THEODORE FREDRICK, banker; b. Alton, Ill., Sept. 21, 1940; s. Theodore Adolph and Jewell (Cheatham) R.; m. Carolyn J. Klasing, Feb. 21, 1963 (div. June 1984); children—Vincent James, Theodore Michael, Kevin Walter; m. Valerie M. Allen, Sept. 7, 1985. B.S., U. Wyo., 1970; M.B.A., Loyola U.-Chgo., 1976. Programmer, analyst Western Electric, Warrenville, Ill., 1970-73; systems mgr. Ofcl. Airline Guide, Oakbrook, Ill., 1973-80; sr. cons. Am. Mgmt. Systems, Chgo., 1980-81; software mgr. Harris Bank, Chgo., 1981—; dir. Midwest Data Base/Data Communications User Group, Chgo., 1981—. Stewardship chmn. Chgo. Met. Assn., United Church of Christ, Chgo., 1984—; lay moderator First Congregational Ch., Downers Grove, Ill., 1983-84. Served with USN, 1959-68. Mem. Phi Kappa Phi. Club: Toastmasters Internat. (pres. 1985—). Avocations: playing English handbells; racquetball; jogging. Home: 5439 Carpenter Downers Grove IL 60515 Office: Harris Bank PO Box 755 Chicago IL 60690

ROCKE, RANDALL RICHARD, television producer, director; b. Bloomington, Ill., May 16, 1949; s. Norman Joseph and Audrey Mae (Hodel) R.; m. Betty Lou Troyer, Aug. 13, 1977. Student music edn. Ill. Wesleyan U., 1967-71; student music performance Ill. State U., 1976. Music dir. Euriskon, Inc., West Chicago, Ill., 1973-75; asst. mgr. Lowell's Distbr., Bloomington, Ill., 1976-78; photographer, salesman Salem & Click Camera, Dayton, Ohio, 1978-80; TV dir. Shiloh Ch., Dayton, 1980-84; media dir. First Community Ch., Columbus, Ohio, 1984—; mem. field faculty Capital U., Dayton, 1983-84; adviser bd. homeland ministries United Ch. of Christ, N.Y.C., 1984—. Recipient Cert. of Appreciation, Building Bridges, Inc., 1983, Wilbur award nomination Religious Pub. Relations Council, 1983. Mem. Nat. Acad. TV Arts and Scis. Avocations: photography; flying; singing; instrumental performance. Office: First Community Ch 1320 Cambridge Blvd Columbus OH 43212

ROCKER, MANUEL M., retired judge; b. Cleve., Nov. 8, 1908; s. Henry Alfred and Sadie (Hollander) R.; m. Harriet S. Sherman, Feb. 16, 1936; children—Jonathan S., Linda Rocker Sogg, Andrew D. Student in pre-law Ohio State U., 1927; LL.B., John Marshall Coll., 1933. Bar: Ohio 1934. Sole practice, Cleve., 1935-36; asst. police prosecutor City of Cleve., 1936-42; sole practice, Cleve., 1942-68; judge Shaker Heights Mcpl. Ct., Ohio, 1968-81. Author: Officer on the Stand, 1979, 82; co-author: Ohio Standard Jury Instructions, 1983. Recipient Superior Jud. Service award Supreme Ct. Ohio, 1975, 76, 77, 78, 79, 80, 81. Mem. Ohio State Bar Assn. (life), Cleve. Bar Assn. (life), Cuyhoga County Bar Assn. (life), Am. Judicature Soc., Ohio Mcpl. Judges Assn. (pres. 1974-76). Republican. Jewish. Lodge: Kiwanis (pres. 1965). Avocations: amateur radio operator; golf. Home: 27050 Cedar Rd Apt PH-1 Beachwood OH 44122

ROCKNAGE, STEPHEN GEORGE, psychology educator, therapist; b. Hamilton, Ont., Can., June 21, 1953; came to U.S., 1956, naturalized, 1969; s. George Jack and Mika (Reznicak) R.; m. JoAnn Dragelevich, June 25, 1977; children—Christopher Stephen, Mileva Katherine. B.A. in Psychology, Steubenville Coll., 1975; M.S. in Edn. and Counseling, Dayton U., 1977. Counselor youth programs CETA, Steubenville, Ohio, 1978-79; asst. dir. Jefferson County CETA Programs, Steubenville, 1979, dir., 1979-81; therapist Jefferson County Mental Health, 1979; asst. dir. counseling and career planning Steubenville U., 1981-82, dir., asst. prof., 1982—. Tchr. ch. sch. Holy Ressurection Serbian Eastern Orthodox Ch., Steubenville, 1974-75; asst. dir. Petar Krstich Ch. Choir, 1977—, treas., 1978-79. Mem. Diocesan Council Religious Edn., Am. Counselors Mental Health Assn., Am. Coll. Profl. Assn., Phi Delta Kappa. Democrat. Avocations: reading; singing.

ROCKSVOLD, PHYLLIS JEAN, computer company executive; b. Postville, Iowa, Sept. 16, 1947; d. Donald Virgil and Joyce Evelyn (Hinman) Montour; m. Thomas Dervin Rocksvold, Jan. 30, 1966 (div. 1974); children—Tiffany Ann, Erik Thomas. Student Kirkwood Coll., 1976. Legal sec. C.F. Neyland, Elkander, Iowa, 1966; dir. med. records Central Community Hosp., Elkander, 1974-76; product mgr. comml. and installment loans Fin. Info. Trust, Des Moines, 1977—. Mem. Assn. Systems Mgmt. Methodist. Avocation: photography. Home: 911 High Rd Norwalk IA 50211 Office: Fin Info Trust 907 Walnut Des Moines IA 50309

RODABAUGH, GARY LEE, environmental specialist; b. Flint, Mich., Oct. 20, 1951; s. Clarence Lee Rodabaugh and Nathalie Pearl (Kelly) Kranz; m. Debra Lyn Manning, Aug. 11, 1973; children—Eric Lee, Shawna Rae. A.S., C.S. Mott Coll., Flint, 1975; B.A., U. Mich.-Flint, 1976; M.S., Eastern Mich. U., 1981; postgrad. Mich. State U. Child care supr. Brookview, Inc., Fenton, Mich., 1972-74; teaching asst. U. Mich.-Flint, 1974-76; instr. C.S. Mott Coll., 1976-78, dir. intramural sports, 1977-78; instr. Eastern Mich. U., Ypsilanti, 1979-81; environ. specialist Gen. Motors Corp., Flint, 1981—; environ. cons. GLR Cons., Byron, Mich., 1981—; guest lectr. Byron Sch. System, 1980—. Emergency med. tech. Byron Vol. Ambulance, 1981—. Recipient capt.'s cert. of meritorious service S.D. State Police, 1981; Gen Motors fellow, 1983. Mem. Mich. Assn. Environ. Profls. Democrat. Home: 550 N Church St Byron MI 48418 Office: Chevrolet Mfg Gen Motors Corp 300 N Chevrolet Ave Flint MI 48555

RODANSKY, BASIL, physician; b. Kiev, Ukraine, Aug. 27, 1930; came to U.S., 1957, naturalized, 1963; s. Volodymyr and Tetiana (Foursenko) Roshdestvensky; m. Anna Karabin, June 25, 1971; children—Eva, Mark. M.D., Johannes Gutenberg U., Mainz, Fed. Republic Germany, 1960. Diplomate Am. Bd. Family Practice. Cert. advanced cardiac life support sci., advanced trauma life support sci. Intern and resident Augustana Hosp., Chgo., 1962-64; staff Woodlawn Hosp., Chgo., 1964-67; asst. clin. physician U. Chgo. Hosp., 1967-70; staff Ida Mae Scott Hosp., Chgo., 1970-72, Mary Thompson Hosp., Chgo., 1972-75, Edward Hosp., Naperville, Ill., 1975-80, First Care, Kokomo, Ind., 1980—. Served to maj. USAF, 1980-84. Fellow Am. Acad. Family Physicians; mem. Assn. Mil. Surgeons of U.S. Republican. Roman Catholic. Avocations: marathon swimmer; lifeguard; foreign languages; international affairs; italic handwriting.

RODDA, RICHARD EARL, writer, musician, educator; b. Bloomingdale, N.J., June 26, 1945; s. Richard and Mabel (Marion) R.; m. Donna Lee Slater, Sept. 7, 1968. B. Music Edn., Baldwin-Wallace Coll., 1967; postgrad. Yale U., 1967-68; M.A., Case Western Res. U., 1970, Ph.D., 1978. Tchr. Cleve. pub. schs., 1968-73; instr. U. Akron, 1976-77, Cuyahoga (Ohio) Community Coll., 1979; program annotator Dallas Symphony Orch., also orchs. of Richmond, Oklahoma City, Akron, Cedar Rapids, Austin, Springfield (Mass.); asst. program editor Cleve. Orch.; instr. Case Western Res. U.; Borromeo Coll. of Ohio; lectr. Blossom Music Ctr., Akron Symphony Orch.; trombonist; mem. Cleve. Fedn. Musicians. Yale U. grantee, 1967-68; Case Western Res. U. grantee, 1973-78; Omicron Delta Kappa scholar, 1966-67. Mem. Am. Musicol. Assn., Internat. Trombone Soc. Contbr. Stagebill mag. Address: 3983 Rosemond Rd Cleveland Heights OH 44121

RODDAN, RAY GENE, chiropractor; b. Springfield, S.D., Dec. 9, 1947; s. Glendon William and Marvel Grace (Brown) R.; m. Sheleth Lee, June 1, 1969; children—Erik, Kelene, Daniel. Student Oholone Coll., 1968-71, U. S.D., 1966-68; Dr. Chiropractic Medicine, Palmer Coll. of Chiropractic, 1978. Material control mgr. Guardian Packaging Corp., Newark, Calif., 1968-75; mid-states sales mgr. Agridustrial Electronic Co., Davenport, Iowa, 1975-78; gen. practice chiropractic medicine, Green Bay, Wis., 1978—; pres., clinic dir. J.&R. Chiropractic Office, S.C., Green Bay, 1980—; indsl. cons. Mem. Profl. Chiropractic Soc. Am. (named Chiropractor of Yr. 1983), Am. Chiropractic Assn., Wis. Chiropractic Assn., Christian Athletes Outreach, Pi Tau Delta. Republican. Mem. Assemblies of God. Ch. Clubs: Businessmen's (Green Bay) (v.p. 1979-80). Home: 1445 Avondale Dr Green Bay WI 54303 Office: J&R Chiropractic Office SC 1075 Brookwood Dr Green Bay WI 54304

RODDY, JOHN THOMAS, fitting manufacturing company executive; b. Cleve., Dec. 31, 1941; s. John James and Ann (Gallagher) R.; m. Andrea Paulette Scerba, Dec. 12, 1964; children—John J., William P., Julie A., Bradley J. B.B.A. in Mktg., Cleve. State U., 1973; M.B.A. in Systems Mgmt., Baldwin Wallace Coll., Berea, Ohio, 1984. Sales service coordinator Acme Cleve. Corp., Cleve., 1976-80, mgr. sales service, 1980-81, mgr. customer services, 1981-82, mktg. ops. analyst, 1982-83; mgmt. cons., Cleve., 1983-84; mgr. sales systems Crawford Fitting Co., Solon, Ohio, 1984—. Served with U.S. Army, 1964-66. Mem. Am. Mktg. Assn., Assn. Systems Mgmt., Data Processing Mgmt. Assn., Alpha Chi, Delta Mu Delta. Roman Catholic. Avocations: jogging, golf, bowling. Office: Crawford Fitting Co PO Box 39007 29500 Solon Rd Solon OH 44139

RODE, DANIEL FRANK, hospital administrator; b. Pitts., Oct. 18, 1946; s. Frank Charles and Magdalena Catherine (Keating) R.; m. M. Therese Butler, Oct. 1, 1977; children—Catherine Rene Rudy, Robert Frederick, Kenneth John Rudy, Margaret Danielle. B.S., Pa. State U., 1968; M.B.A., U. Minn., 1985. Bus. office mgr. U. Utah Med. Ctr., Salt Lake City, 1969-74, asst. patient acctg. mgr., 1974-75; asst. fiscal service dir. U. Minn. Hosps., Mpls., 1975-77, asst. controller, 1977-81, assoc. dir., 1981—. Editor profl. newsletter Vikingland Viewpoint, 1980-81. Field adv. Archdiocese of St. Paul and Mpls., 1980—; chmn. Troop 106 Indianhead council Boy Scouts Am., 1983—; chmn. bd. Catholic Ctr. for Separated and Divorced, St. Paul, 1981, U. Minn. Newman Ctr., 1979. Mem. Healthcare Fin. Mgmt. Assn. (treas. 1981-82, sec. 1982-84, pres.-elect 1983-84, chpt. pres. 1984-85, regional chpt. liaison and nat. matrix mem. 1985—, William G. Follmer award 1982, Robert H. Reeves award 1985), Alpha Phi Omega (life). Club: Toastmasters Internat. (parliamentarian 1983—); Penn State (Mpls.). Avocations: sailing; skiing; camping. Home: 1520 20th Ave NW New Brighton MN 55112 Office: U Minn Hosp and Clinics 420 Delaware St SE Minneapolis MN 55455

RODE, JAMES DEAN, See *Who's Who in America,* 43rd edition.

RODENBERG, ALBERT JOHN, JR., lawyer; b. Cin., Nov. 1, 1948; s. Albert John and Anne Xonia (Miskerik) R.; m. Kathleen Mary McPhillips, Mar. 23, 1979; children—Nicholas Carl, Bradley Jan. A.S. in Police Sci., U. Cin., 1970, B.S. in Criminal Justice, 1978, J.D., 1981. Bar: Ohio 1981, U.S. Dist. Ct. (so. dist.) Ohio 1981. Police cadet Cin. Police Dept., 1967-70; asst. prof. criminal justice U. Cin., 1979-85; ptnr. Rodenberg and Rodenberg, Cin., 1981—; dir. Shades, Inc., Cin., West Land, Inc., Cin. Active Hamilton County Republican Club, Ohio, 1980—, 26th Ward Rep. Club, Cin., 1980—. Served as capt. USMC, 1971-75. Mem. Assn. Trial Lawyers Am., ABA, Cin. Bar Assn., Ohio Acad. Trial Lawyers. Lodge: Lions. Home: 3584 Janlin Ct Cincinnati OH 45211 Office: Rodenberg and Rodenberg 3706 Cheviot Ave Cincinnati OH 45211

RODERICK, BARBARA HOLROYD, social worker; b. Kirin, Manchuria, China, Dec. 2, 1924 (parents Am. citizens); d. A. Waldie and Rose (Garrett) Holroyd; m. Glenn Edward Roderick, June 10, 1948; children—Carolyn, Lois. A.B., Hiram Coll., 1947; M.S.S.A., Western Res. U., 1950. Caseworker, Family Service Assn., Miami, Fla., 1950-53, Cleve., 1953-57; interim dir. Interfaith Housing Corp., Cleve., 1967-68; workshop dir. Heights Citizens for Human Rights, Cleve., 1969; housing coordinator, assoc. city planner, commr. real estate programs City of Cleveland Heights, Ohio, 1970-79; assoc. dir. Human Affairs, Inc., 1979—. Mem. bd. operation equality Urban League, 1967-74; chmn. Heights Christian Ch., 1981-83; bd. dirs. Heights Community Congress, 1972-73, Greater Cleve. Interch. Council, 1982—. Mem. Acad. Cert. Social Workers, Nat. Assn. Social Workers. Democrat. Mem. Christian Ch. (Disciples of Christ). Home: 3610 Cummings Rd Cleveland Heights OH 44118 Office: 5 Severance Circle Room 509 Cleveland Heights OH 44118

RODEWALD, JAMES MICHAEL, real estate company executive, real estate syndicator; b. Waco, Tex., Apr. 20, 1942; s. Howard Fred and Dorothy Mae (Faust) R.; m. Evelynn Brown, Dec. 19, 1965; children—Kara Lynn, Kevin James. B.A., William Jewell Coll., 1964; M.A., U. Wis., 1967; postgrad. Central Mo. U., 1970. Lic. real estate broker, Mo., Kans. Vol., Peace Corps, Malawi, Central Africa, 1967-68; property mgr. William C. Haas Co., Kansas City, Mo., 1970-72; exec. v.p., co-owner Roger L. Cohen Co., Kansas, City, 1972-81; pres. James M. Rodewald Co., Kansas City, 1981—; pres. Investment Realty Advisors, Inc.; cons. to regional stock house for real estate acquisitions. Mem. Nat. Republican Com.; mem. pres.'s adv. council William Jewell Coll.; bd. dirs. Downtown Inc., Kansas City. Served with U.S. Army, 1968-70; Vietnam. Gen. Motors scholar, 1960-64; Phi Gamma Delta scholar, 1965. Mem. Kansas City Real Estate Bd. (Comml. Realtor Assoc. of Yr.), Urban Land Inst., Nat. Assn. Office and Indsl. Parks, Real Estate Syndication Inst., Nat. Assn. Realtors, Mo. Assn. Realtors. Republican. Presbyterian. Club: Carriage. Home: 651 W 57th St Kansas City MO 64113 Office: 3217 Broadway Suite 306 Kansas City MO 64111

RODGERS, DENNIS BRUCE, lawyer; b. Decatur, Ill., Oct. 16, 1940; s. Richard Wilbur and Eleanor Frances (Cobb) R.; B.S., Trinity Coll., Hartford, Conn., 1962; J.D., Georgetown U., 1966; m. Marilynne Linda Wilson, Nov. 30, 1974; children—John, Andrew, Alainna, Aaron. Tchr., Bloomfield (Conn.) pub. schs., 1962-63; admitted to Ill. bar, 1966, since practiced in Decatur; mem. firm Denz, Lowe, Moore, Rodgers & See, 1966-77; legal planner Macon County Regional Plan Commn., 1970-76; part time prof. Richland Community Coll., 1976-79. Crusade chmn. Macon County unit Am. Cancer Soc., 1971-72, bd. dirs., 1972-77, chmn. bd., 1974-75; mem. Now and Tomorrow Council of Decatur Meml. Hosp., 1971-77; bd. dirs. Council Community Services, 1970-77, pres., 1975-77; pres. Sangamon Valley Assn., 1972-76; mem. Macon County Health Bd., 1981—; mem. Scholarships for Ill. Residents, 1970—; adminstrv. v.p. Decatur Jaycees, 1969-70; pres. Young Republican Orgn. Macon County, 1967-68; chmn. Lake Decatur Sedimentation Control Com., 1984—. Recipient Disting. Service award Decatur Jaycees, 1971; named to Outstanding Young Men of Am., 1969-72. Mem. Ill., Decatur bar assns., Metro-Decatur C. of C. (chmn. transp. com. 1977—, dir. 1980-83, 84—; Disting. Vol. award 1983), Alpha Chi Rho, Phi Alpha Delta (cert. disting. service 1966). Kiwanian (bd. dirs. Decatur 1970-72). Co-author: Oakley Reservoir and Water Development for Central Illinois, 1968. Home: 90 John Dr Mount Zion IL 62549 Office: Suite 352 Millikin Ct 132 S Water St Decatur IL 62523

RODGERS, JAMES ARTHUR, political science educator; b. Sallisaw, Okla., June 6, 1953; s. Stanley Bill and Violet Inez (Jackson) R.; m. Stephanie Martin, Sept. 28, 1984. B.A., Northwestern Okla. State U., 1975; M.A., Idaho State U., 1979, D.Arts, 1981. Environ. technician J.R. Simplot Co., Pocatello, Idaho, 1976-78; asst. prof. St. Mary's Coll., Winona, Minn., 1981—, chmn. dept. polit. sci., 1983—. Periodic cons. Minn. Small Bus. Devel. Ctr., St. Paul, 1982—. Questionnaire cons. City of Pocatello, 1980, Minn. Small Bus. Assn., 1982. Grad. fellow Idaho State U., 1979-81. Mem. Am. Polit. Sci. Assn., Social Sci. History Assn., Minn. Polit. Sci. Assn., Pi Gamma Mu, Pi Sigma Alpha. Mem. Ch. of Christ. Home: 105 N Baker St Winona MN 55987 Office: Dept of Polit Sci St Mary's Coll Winona MN 55987

RODGERS, LOUIS DEAN, surgeon; b. Centerville, Iowa, Nov. 24, 1930; s. John James and Anna Alice (Spraguer) R.; m. Gretchen Lynn Hendershot, Feb. 19, 1954; children—Cynthia Ann, Elizabeth Dee. M.D., U. Iowa, 1960. Diplomate Am. Bd. Surgery. Intern, Broadlawns Hosp., Iowa, 1960-61; resident Meth-Hosp., Des Moines, 1961-65; practice medicine specializing in gen. surgery, Des Moines, 1965—; chmn. dept. surgery Iowa Methodist Ctr., Des Moines, 1980-84, chief gen surgery, 1982—; clin. assoc. prof. surgery U. Iowa, Iowa City, 1983—. Mem. steering com. Gov.'s Campaign, Republican Party, Iowa, 1982; bd. dirs. Iowa Meth. Med. Found., Des Moines, 1983, Des Moines Symphony, 1984—. Served to staff sgt. U.S. Army, 1951-54. Named Surg. Tchr. of Yr., Iowa Meth. Med. Ctr. Dept. Surgery, 1978, 84. Fellow ACS (liaison to cancer com. 1973); mem. Western Surg. Assn. (mem. Iowa trauma com. 1983), Iowa Acad. Surgery (pres. 1982-83). Republican. Club: Des Moines Golf and Country. Home: 715 53d St Des Moines IA 50312 Office: Surgery PC 1212 Pleasant St #211 Des Moines IA 50309

RODGERS, TOMMIE JEAN, power company executive; b. Joplin, Mo., June 6, 1928; s. Onis Eugene and Laura Inez (Sester) R.; m. Joanne Delores King, May 28, 1955; children—Vicci, David, Lisa, Danon, Amy. B.S. in Chem. Engring., U. Mo., 1950; M.B.A., U. Pitts., 1961. Registered profl. engr., Wis. Quality assurance engr. Bettis Atomic Power Lab., Idaho, 1957-63, ops. supr., 1963-67; ops. supt. Wis. Electric Power Co., Point Beach Nuclear Plant, 1967-72, project aminstr., Milw., 1973-75, constrn. mgr., 1976-78, asst. to mgr., 1979-83, mgr., 1983—. Served to capt. USNR, 1946-82. Mem. Assn. Mech. Engrs., Am. Inst. Chem. Engrs. Republican. Baptist. Avocation: hunting. Home: 35317 Genesee Lake Rd Oconomowoc WI 53066 Office: Wis Electric Power Co 231 W Michigan St Milwaukee WI 53203

RODKEY, ROBERT FREDRICK, educator, coach; b. Kokomo, Ind., July 14, 1954; s. Robert Dean and Florence H. (Pachmayer) R.; m. Sheryl L. Bray, Aug. 11, 1979; 1 child, Elizabeth Christine. B.A., Ozark Bible Coll., 1976; M.A., Cin. Theol. Sem., 1984. Mem. faculty, coach St. Louis Christian Coll.,

Florissant, Mo., 1977—. Author: Reaching Higher, 1984. Ozark Bible Coll. scholar, 1976. Office: 1360 Grandview Dr Florissant MO 63033

RODKIN, DONALD T., computer consultant; b. Chgo., Apr. 15, 1939; s. Sidney and LaVerne (Hollison) R.; m. Dean S. Yellen, Aug. 6, 1961; children—Susan J., Gary A. B.S., Northwestern U., 1960; M.P.A., Ind. U., 1962. Programmer, No. Ind. Pub. Service Co., Hammond, Ind., 1961-66; ops. supr. Commonwealth Edison, Chgo., 1966-69; cons. Leasco Systems, Oak Brook, Ill., 1970-73; project dir. Tres Systems, Dallas, 1973-76; pres., cons. Mgmt. Systems Assocs., Oak Brook, Ill., 1976—. Republican. Home: 10 S 236 Birnam Trail Hinsdale IL 60521 Office: Mgmt Systems Assocs PO Box 911 Oak Brook IL 60522

RODNE, KJELL JOHN, city official; b. Haugesund, Norway, July 6, 1948; came to U.S., 1959; s. Johannes and Margit (Gautun) R.; m. Kathleen Anne Gordon, Sept. 21, 1966; children—Jay Robert, Lee Eric. B.S., U. Minn.-Duluth, 1971, M.S.W., 1985. Asst. youth dir. YMCA, Duluth, 1967-68; counselor Northwood, Duluth, 1968-71, team leader, 1971-76, social worker, 1976-77, program dir., 1977-85; personnel dir. City of Duluth, 1985—; bd. dirs. Minn. Council Residential Treatment Ctrs., St. Paul, 1977—. Mem. Duluth City Council, 1978—, pres., 1981; bd. dirs. United Devel. Achievement Ctr., Duluth, 1978—, Arrowhead Regional Devel. Commn., Duluth, 1981—, United Way of Duluth, 1981—. Mem. Nat. Assn. Homes for Children (accredited reviewer), Minn. Assn. Social Service Agys., Minn. Assn. Vol. Social Service Agys. (dir. 1977—). Democrat. Lutheran. Home: 129 N 28th Ave W Duluth MN 55806 Office: City of Duluth 313 City Hall Duluth MN 55802

RODOS, JOSEPH JERRY, osteopathic physician, educator; b. Phila., July 7, 1933; s. Harry and Lisa (Perlman) R.; m. Bobbi Golden, Apr. 6, 1957; (div. 1974); m. Joyce I. Pennington, Sept. 26, 1981; 1 child, Adam Justin. B.S., Franklin & Marshall Coll., 1955; D.O., Kirksville Coll. Medicine, Mo., 1959. Diplomate Am. Bd. Family Medicine, Am. Osteo. Bd. Pub. Health and Preventive Medicine. Intern; Grandview Hosp., Dayton, Ohio, 1959-60; gen. practice medicine, Cranston, R.I., 1960-78; exec. sec. R.I. Soc. Osteo. P/S, Cranston, 1978-79; dean New Eng. Coll. Osteo. Medicine, Biddleford, Maine, 1979-82; assoc. dean Chgo. Coll. Osteo. Medicine, 1982—; clin. dir. Dept. Mental Health, Providence, R.I., 1973-78; med. dir. Dept. Corrections, Providence, 1976-78; sr. cons. medicine Pub. Sector Cons., Lansing, Mich., 1980—; lectr. in field. Editor, Jour. Osteo. Annals, 1982. Bd. dirs. Cranston Red Cross, R.I. Camps, Inc., Dial Dictation, Inc., Cranston Mental Health Clinic; mem. Internat. Platform Assn., ACLU; lectr. Premarital Confs., Catholic Diocese Providence. Fellow Am. Coll. Gen. Practice, Acad. Psychosomatic Medicine; mem. Am. Coll. Osteo. and Obstetrics and Gynecology, Acad. Clin. and Exptl. Hypnosis. Avocations: breeding, showing Saint Bernards and Scottish Terriers. Home: 5204 S Lawn Ave Western Springs IL 60558 Office: Chgo Coll Osteopathic Medicine 5200 S Ellis St Chicago IL 60615

RODRIGUEZ-SIERRA, JORGE FERNANDO, anatomy educator, reseacher; b. Havana, Cuba, Sept. 18, 1945; came to U.S., 1962, naturalized, 1980; s. Fernando F. and Odilia (Ors) R.-S.; m. Maryjanet McNamara, Dec. 13, 1967 (div. 1973); 1 child, Marina. A.A., Pasadena City Coll., 1968; B.A., Calif. State U.-Los Angeles, 1970, M.A., 1972; Ph.D., Rutgers U., 1976. Research fellow Wis. Regional Primate Ctr., Madison, 1976-78; research fellow U. Nebr. Med. Ctr., Omaha, 1978, asst. prof., 1978-82, assoc. prof., 1982—; adj. assoc. prof. psychology U. Nebr., 1980—. Contbr. articles to profl. jours. and chpts. in books. Mem. patient edn. com. Planned Parenthood, Omaha, 1981; mem. com. affimative action EEO, Boston U., 1982; chmn. com. minority concerns, U. Nebr., 1982. Recipient Margaret Sanger award Planned Parenthood, Omaha, 1982. Mem. Endocrine Soc., Soc. Neurosci. (pres. Midland chpt. 1980—), Soc. Study Reproduction, Internat. Soc. Neuroendocrinology, Electron Microscopic Soc. Am. Clubs: Park Ave. Health, Omaha Sports. Office: Dept Anatomy Nebr Med Ctr 42d and Dewey Ave Omaha NE 68105

ROE, BRUCE ALLAN, chemistry educator; b. N.Y.C., Jan. 1, 1942; s. Sanford and Ann (LaMarca) R.; m. Judith Pessek, June 7, 1963; children—Nathan, Caroline. B.A., Hope Coll., 1963; M.A., Western Mich. U., 1967, Ph.D., 1970. Asst. prof. Kent State U., Ohio, 1973-77, assoc. prof., 1977-81, prof. chemistry U. Okla., 1981—; adj. prof. biochemistry Okla. U. Health Scis. Ctr., 1981—. Contbr. articles to various publs. Mem. Gov.'s Council Sci. and Tech., 1984. Postdoctoral research fellow NIH, SUNY-Stony Brook, 1970; recipient Research Career Devel. award Kent State U., 1976-81, Regents' award for research U. Okla., 1984; grantee NIH, 1973—, Am. Cancer Soc., 1977-79. Mem. Am. Soc. Biol. Chemists, AAAS, N.Y. Acad. Sci., Okla. Acad. Sci. Democrat. Presbyterian.

ROE, C(LARENCE) DENNIS, engineer; b. Granville, Ohio, Jan. 13, 1927; s. Clarence O. and Estelle L. (Adams) R.; m. Sally A. Hunt, Mar. 19, 1948; children—Linda, Denise, David. Student Ohio State U. Sch. Engring., 1947-52. With Sta. WBNS radio and TV, Columbus, Ohio, 1953-55; with CRISE controls ACRO Div. Robertshaw Fulton, 1955-60; with AT&T Bell Labs., Columbus, 1960—, mem. connector tech. group, 1973—; instr. basic electronics night sch. Franklin U., 1965-69. Vice pres. John D. Burlie Chpt. Telephone Pioneers; co-founder electronics curriculum Fairfield Sch. for Boys, Ohio Youth Commn., 1971. Served with Signal Corps U.S. Army, 1945-47. Fellow Coll. of Relay Engrs. Nat. Assn. Relay Mfrs. Methodist. Lodge: Masons. Co-author article to mag. in field; contbr. papers to profl. confs.; patentee. Home: 2936 Johnstown Rd Columbus OH 43219 Office: 6200 E Broad St Columbus OH 43213

ROE, DAVID GORDON, surgeon; b. Birmingham, Ala., June 11, 1944; s. Kermit Odley and Margaret (Teague) R.; m. Nanceylon Faith Swanquist, June 27, 1970; children—Bradley David, Erik Wallace, Virginia Faith. B.S., U. Ill.-Urbana, 1966, M.S., 1968; M.D., U. Ill.-Chgo., 1972. Diplomate Am. Bd. Surgery. Intern U. Ill. Research and Edn. Hosps., Chgo., 1972-73, resident, 1973-77; practice medicine specializing in surgery, Marion, Ind., 1977—; v.p. Surgeons, Inc., Marion, 1979—; chief surgery Marion Gen. Hosp., 1984-85, med. dir. intensive care unit, 1985—, co-dir. vascular lab., 1982—. Exec. dir. Citizens for Decency through Law, Marion, 1984-85; bd. dirs. Lakeview Life Ctr., Marion, 1982—. Fellow ACS; mem. Warren N. Cole Soc. Republican. Avocations: hunting; fishing; woodworking. Office: Surgeons Inc 500 Wabash Ave Suite 109 Marion IN 46952

ROEBUCK, JOSEPH CHESTER, leasing company executive; b. Detroit, Feb. 6, 1946; s. Joseph Leonard and Stella (Grochocki) R.; m. Susan A. Hatala, Mar. 26, 1977; children—Christopher, Jennifer. A.A., Northwood Inst., 1966; B.S. in Bus., Central Mich. U., 1968. Sales IBM Corp., Southfield, Mich., 1968-70; prin. Roebuck, Schaden & Assoc., Detroit, 1970-73; Salesman U.S. Leasing, Birmingham, Mich., 1973-76; sales mgr. Federated Fin., Southfield, Mich., 1976-77; v.p. Corp. Funding, Inc., Birmingham, 1977-84; pres. Corp. Resources, Inc., Birmingham, 1984—; lease cons., 1984—. Mem. Am. Assn. Individual Investors. Republican. Roman Catholic. Club: Detroit Golf. Avocations: Golf, flying, travel, racquetball.

ROEBUCK-HOARD, MARCIA VERONICA, magazine editor; b. Colon, Panama, Jan. 18, 1950; came to U.S., 1964; d. Ainsford Llewelyn and Daisy Viola (Briggs) Rowe; B.A. with honors, Nat. Coll. Edn., 1975, postgrad. 1975; 1 child, Turia Pilar. Textbook editor Scott, Foresman & Co., Glenview, Ill., 1976-79, quality control mgr., 1979-80; mng. editor Ebony Jr., Chgo., 1980—; lectr. in field. Exec. council Sta. WTTW-TV, Chgo., 1979—; bd. dirs. Chgo. UNICEF, 1980—, Literacy Vols. of Chgo., 1982—. Ill. State scholar, 1975; Nat. Endowment for Arts fellow, 1977. Mem. Minorities in Cable and New Techs., Ill. Black Writers Conf., Chgo. Assn. Black Journalists, Black Child Devel. Inst., Alpha Kappa Alpha. Roman Catholic. Office: 820 S Michigan Ave Chicago IL 60605

ROECK, MARY MARGARET (MEG), banker; b. New Holstein, Wis., May 12, 1948; d. Herbert John and Rita Rose (Groh) Roeck. Statis. clk. traffic Wis. Telephone Co., 1966-69; securities clk. trust dept. Marine Bank, Milw., 1969-71, systems analyst trust dept., 1971-73, purchasing-buyer, forms designer, 1973-78, adminstrv. systems forms analyst, 1978-80; jr. systems analyst, conversion mgmt., forms mgmt. Marine Bank Services Corp., Milw., 1980-82, systems analyst conversion mgmt. data processing, 1982—, data processing officer, 1983—; speaker on forms design Bus. Forms Mgmt. Assn., Milw., Madison and Racine, Wis., Mpls., Portland, Oreg., Pitts., Cleve.; speaker on purchasing/forms Am. Mgmt. Assn., Chgo., Atlanta, and Bank Adminstrn. Inst., Chgo. Recipient 1st Place Reprographics award Modern Office Procedures mag., 1975. Mem. Bus. Forms Mgmt. Assn. (recipient Meritorius award Milw. chpt. 1977-78, 78-79). Roman Catholic. Office: 1000 N Market St PO Box 2071 Milwaukee WI 53201

ROEHL, JANET, university official; b. Albuquerque, Mar. 25, 1953; d. A.F. and Frances H. (Mahan) Roehl. B.S. in Journalism, No. Ariz. U., 1975; M.A. in Journalism, Ariz. State U., 1976, Ph.D., 1981. Publs. coordinator Ariz. State U., Tempe, 1980-81; program specialist U. Wis.-Stout, 1981-82, assoc. dir. Office Continuing Edn., 1982—; presenter at confs. and symposia. Author: Computers for the Disabled, 1984; Teaching and Learning Basic Skills, 1984; contbr. articles to profl. jours. Bd. dirs. Menomonie Theater Guild; mem. Dunn County Sexual Assault Task Force; bd. dirs. Wis. Adult Edn. Lyceum Bd. Mem. Wis. Assn. Adult and Continuing Edn., Am. Assn. Adult and Continuing Edn., Am. Ednl. Research Assn. Home: 1002 Ingalls Menomonie WI 54751 Office: Administration Bldg University Wisconsin-Stout Menomonie WI 54751

ROEHM, MARYANNE EVANS, university dean; b. Vigo County, Ind., Nov. 29, 1925; d. Herbert and Fern Evans; m. Joseph L. Roehm, Aug. 10, 1947. B.S., Ind. State U.-Terre Haute, 1953, M.S., 1957; M.S. in Nursing, Ind. U.-Bloomington, 1965, Ed.D., 1966. Instr. nursing, asst. dir. Sch. Nursing, Union Hosp., Terre Haute, 1946-55; assoc. dir. edn. Sch. Nursing, St. Anthony Hosp., Terre Haute, 1957-64; asst. and assoc. prof. nursing Ind. State U., 1966-70, dir. continuing edn., 1970-78, dean Sch. Nursing, 1978—; mem. Ind. State Bd. Nursing Registration and Nursing Edn., 1978-81, pres., 1980-81; mem. adv. com. hypertension project Vigo County Health Dept., 1981; mem. health occupations adv. com. Ind. Vocat. Tech. Coll., 1970—. Mem. Vigo County Home Citizens Com., Ind., 1970—; mem. Vigo County Blood Donor Council, 1980; vice precinct committeeman Vigo County. Recipient Outstanding Leadership award Ind. div. Am. Cancer Soc., 1982. Mem. Ind. State Nurses Assn. (Cert. of Recognition 1978, named Outstanding Nurse Educator 1959). Home: Route 22 Box 561 Terre Haute IN 47802

ROEHRICH, ROBERT RONALD, educational adminstrator; b. Passaic, N.J., Jan. 26, 1947; s. Otto Francis and Helen Marie (Stendell) R.; m. Barbara Catsos, June 8, 1969; 1 dau., Sarah Lindsey. B.A. magna cum laude, Montclair State Coll., 1973; M.S., SUNY, 1974; Ph.D., Ohio State U., 1979. Customer service rep. United Parcel Service, N.Y.C., 1968-70; credit analyst Broadway Bank and Trust Co., Paterson, N.J., 1970-73; research assoc. Nat. Ctr. for Research in Vocat. Edn., 1978-79, research specialist, 1979-81; dean computer sci. for bus. program DeVry Inst. Tech., Columbus, Ohio, 1981-83; v.p. accreditation Bell & Howell Edn. group, Evanston, Ill., 1983; v.p. acad. affairs DeVry Inc., Evanston, 1983—; cons. Anchorage, Phila., Dallas, Milw. and Chgo. sch. dists. Edn. Professions Devel Act fellow, 1976-78. Mem. Am. Mgmt. Assn., Data Processing Mgmt. Assn., Am. Soc. for Tng. and Devel., Am. Vocat. Assn., Kappa Delta Pi, Phi Delta Kappa, Epsilon Pi Tau, Phi Kappa Phi. Roman Catholic. Author: The Criteria for Determining Technical Updating Needs in Two Year Technical Colleges as Perceived by Technical Instructors and Administrators, 1979. Home: 1047 Shambliss Ct Buffalo Grove IL 60089 Office: 2201 W Howard St Evanston IL 60202

ROEHRIG, KARLA LOUISE, food science and nutrition educator, consultant; b. Sycamore, Ill., Aug. 18, 1946; s. James H. and Louise (King) Reed; m. Frederick K. Roehrig, Aug. 19, 1967. B.S., U. Ill.-Urbana, 1967; Ph.D., Ohio State U., 1977; postgrad. Ind. U. Sch. Medicine-Indpls., 1978. Research asst. Ohio State U., Columbus, 1967-75, research assoc., 1975-77, asst. prof., 1978-83, assoc. prof. dept. food sci. and nutrition, 1983—; Showalter P.D. fellow Ind. U. Sch. Medicine, Indpls., 1977-78; mem. research adv. council Columbus Zoo, 1984—. Author: Carbohydrate, Biochemistry and Metabolism, 1984. Trustee Columbus Zoo, 1984—; troop leader Seal of Ohio council Girl Scouts U.S.A., 1968-72; neighborhood vol. March of Dimes, Columbus, 1982, 83. Burroughs Wellcome, grantee, Scotland, 1981; grantee NIH, USPHS. Mem. Biochem. Soc., Am. Diabetes Assn., N.Y. Acad. Scis., Sigma Xi, Gamma Sigma Delta. Presbyterian. Club: Jr. Open Ct. (sec. 1983-84). Avocations: computer architecture; gourmet cooking. Office: Dept Food Sci and Nutrition 122 Vivian 2121 Fyffe Rd Columbus OH 43210

ROEMBKE, JAMES EDWARD, college administrator, engineer; b. Hillsboro, Ind., Dec. 20, 1918; s. Edward Frederick and Lizzie Catherine (Williams) R.; m. Anita June Bilsland, Oct. 15, 1943; children—Lianne, Donna Joyce, Barbara Sue, James Edward, Jr. B.C.E., Purdue U., 1941. Registered profl. engr., Ind. Project engr. Ind. State Hwy. Dept., 1941-42; project engr. Link Belt Co. Indpls., 1946-50; dir. pub. works engrs. U.S. Navy, Hawthorne, Nev. and Guantanamo Bay, Cuba, 1950-56; project engr. research Fed. CD Adminstrn., Battle Creek, Mich., 1956-61; dir. architecture and engring. devel. div. Office Sec. Army, Sec. Def., Washington, 1961-72; dep. asst. dir. research and engring. Def. Civil Preparedness Agy., Washington, 1972-77; v.p. bus. and fin. Calvary Bible Coll., Kansas City, Mo., 1977—; mem. Nat. Acad. Sci., 1968-76; Nat. Sci. Found., 1968-76. Teaching fellow (hon.) Fed. CD Coll., Washington, 1961-72. Served to lt. comdr. USN, 1942-46. Fellow ASCE; mem. Am. Strategic Def. Assn. Republican. Club: Gideons Internat. (Va. state rep. 1975-76). Avocation: stamp collecting. Office: Calvary Bible College Kansas City MO 64147

ROEMEN, JAMES WILLIAM, pharmacist; b. Larchwood, Iowa, July 5, 1934; s. William J. and Magdelen (Neu) R. B.S., S.D. State U., 1959. Registered pharmacist, Iowa. Pharmacist, owner Corner Drugs, Rock Rapids, Iowa, 1962—; cons. pharmacist MPC Hosp., Rock Rapids, Rock Rapids Health Ctr. Served with U.S. Army, 1959-62. Roman Catholic. Home: 510 S Carroll Rock Rapids IA 51246 Office: 220 1st Ave Rock Rapids IA 51246

ROEMER, ARTHUR CHARLES, state official; b. Wabasha, Minn., Nov. 8, 1923; s. Charles E. and Anna M. (Schmidt) R.; m. Joan Marie Reding, June 11, 1966; children—John, Suzanne, Daniel. B.Sci.-Law, U. Minn., 1948, J.D., 1950. Asst. atty. gen. Minn. Atty. Gen. Office, St. Paul, 1955-60; dep. commr. revenue Minn. Dept. Revenue, St. Paul, 1960-71, 79-83, commr. revenue, 1971-79, 1983—; cons. Pub. Adminstrn. Service, Chgo., 1965-66. Contbr. articles to profl. jours. Served to lt. Q.M.C., U.S. Army, 1943-46, ETO. Mem. Nat. Assn. Tax Adminstrs. (bd. dirs. 1971—, pres. 1980-81), Nat. Tax Assn. (bd. dirs.), Tax Inst. Am. (bd. dirs. 1983—), Midwestern States Assn. Tax Adminstrs. (pres. 1971-72). Roman Catholic. Home: 2139 Sioux Blvd New Brighton MN 55112 Office: Minn Dept Revenue 201 Centennial Office Bldg Saint Paul MN 55145

ROEMER, JAMES ANTHONY, university director; b. South Bend, Ind., Jan. 15, 1930; s. William F. and Carmelita (Luther) R.; m. Mary Ann Earle, Jan. 31, 1953; children—Michael, Timothy, Daniel, Patrick, Kathryn. B.A., Notre Dame, 1951, J.D., 1955. Bar: Ind., 1955. Contracts mgr. Curtis Wright Aircraft, South Bend, 1955-59; subcontracts mgr. Lockheed Aircraft, Sunnyvale, Calif., 1959-69; ptnr. Roemer, Sweeney & Roemer, South Bend, 1969-73; city atty. City of South Bend, 1973-76; univ. atty. Notre Dame, South Bend, 1973-76, dean of students, 1976-84, dir. community relations, 1984—, adj. prof. Law Sch., 1975, adj. prof. Bus. Sch., 1983. Bd. dirs. Neighborhood Study Help, Inc., Holy Cross Assocs., Neighborhood Housing Services, Friends of the Unemployed; com. mem. United Religious Community, Shelter for Street People, Snite Mus.; chmn. United Way, Notre Dame. Recipient (with wife) Granville Clark award for social justice Notre Dame, Outstanding Community Relations Idea award Notre Dame. Mem. Ind. Bar Assn., South Bend/Mishawaka C. of C. (bd. dirs.). Democrat. Roman Catholic. Home: 54610 Whispering Oak Dr Mishawaka IN 46545 Office: 310-A Adminstrn Bldg Notre Dame IN 46556

ROENSCH, RONALD JOHN, lawyer, engineering and reconstruction consultant; b. Milw., Aug. 1, 1957; s. Donald A. and Dolores M. (Gutsmeidel) R.; m. Debbie A. Renner, Apr. 3, 1982. B.S.C.E., U. Wis.-Madison, 1979; J.D., Marquette U., 1983. Bar: Wis. 1983. Civil engr. City of West Bend, Wis., 1979-81; sole practice, West Bend, 1983—; cons. Reconstrn. Assocs., West Bend, 1984—. Mem. adv. bd. Friends for Battered Women, West Bend, 1984—; bd. dirs. Lakehaven Property Owners Assn., West Bend, 1984—. Mem. Assn. Trial Lawyers Am., Wis. Acad. Trial Lawyers. Roman Catholic. Office: 17 E Washington St West Bend WI 53095

ROERTY, GERARD JOSEPH, financial analyst; b. Jersey City, June 2, 1943; s. Joseph Gerard and Cecelia Jeanette (Wisniewski) R.; m. Mary Tecla, Sept. 4, 1965; children—Gerard J., Michelle Anne. B.S., St. Peter's Coll., Jersey City, 1965; M.B.A., Xavier U., Cin., 1973; Cert. Inst. Exec. Leadership, Southwestern U., Memphis, 1979. Staff auditor Arthur Andersen & Co., Newark, 1965-66; with Procter & Gamble, Cin., 1968—, mgr. fin. analysis dept. cellulose and specialties div., Memphis, 1976-78, mgr. plant acctg. dept., 1978-80, mgr. fin. analysis dept. packaged soap and detergent div., Cin., 1980-83, mgr. internat. paper fin. analysis div., 1983-85, spl. assignment Comptroller's Div., 1985—; pres. RoeGer Ops. Inc., tax and investments cons.; cons. in field. Author of numerous tax advice papers. Instr. Project Bus. Program, Jr. Achievement, Memphis, 1977-78, Cin., 1984; mem. Future Forest Hills Com., Forest Hills Sch. Bd., Cin., 1983. Served to capt. U.S. Army, 1966-68. Mem. Assn. M.B.A. Execs., Property Owners Assn. Republican. Roman Catholic Clubs: Beechmont Racquet (Cin.); Turpin Swim & Racquet. Home: 7114 Royalgreen Dr Cincinnati OH 45244 Office: Comptrollers Div Procter & Gamble Co 2 Procter & Gamble Plaza Cincinnati OH 45202

ROESCH, ROBERT EUGENE, dentist; b. Falls City, Nebr., July 10, 1951; s. Wilber H. and Vivian (Reese) R.; m. Susan M. Tuttle, Aug. 25, 1973. B.A., Midland Lutheran Coll., 1973; D.D.S., U. Nebr., 1976. Practice dentistry, Fremont, Nebr., 1979—; pub. info. officer Nebr. Acad. Gen. Dentistry, 1983—. Mem. exec. bd. Dodge County Republicans, Fremont, 1982—; bd. dirs., past pres. Midland Luth. Coll. Alumni Bd., Fremont, 1981—; mem. council, past pres. Sinai Luth. Ch., Fremont, 1981-83; bd. dirs. Dodge County Am. Cancer Soc., Fremont, 1984—. Served to capt. USAF, 1976-79. Mem. Am. Dental Assn., Am. Orthodontic Soc., Acad. Gen. Dentistry, Nebr. Dental Assn. (Dodge County dental health cons. 1981—), Tri-Valley Dental Soc. (v.p. 1984-85, pres. 1985-86), Omaha Dist. Dental Soc., Fremont C. of C. (diplomat). Republican. Lodge: Optimists (Fremont) (bd. dirs. 1982-83, 85—). Avocations: tennis; racquetball. Home: 750 N Clarkson St Fremont NE 68025 Office: 140 E 22d St Fremont NE 68025

ROESS, THOMAS JAMES, cardiologist; b. Lima, Ohio, Oct. 7, 1927; s. Otto Theodore and Martha Luella (Short) R.; m. Louise Ruth Dunn, June 25, 1976; children—Steven T., William J., Jane Roess Isley. B.A., Ohio State U., 1949; M.D., Western Res. U., 1953. Diplomate Am. Bd. Internal Medicine, Cardiovascular Disease. Intern Univ. Hosps. of Cleve., 1953-54, resident, 1954-56, teaching fellow in cardiology, 1976-77; practice medicine specializing in cardiology, Lima, Ohio, 1958—; mem. staff Lima Meml. Hosp.; asst. prof. medicine Med. Coll. Ohio, Toledo, 1983—; dir. cardiac rehab. services Lima Meml. Hosp., 1985. Served to capt. USAF, 1956-58. Fellow ACP, Am. Coll. Chest Physicians, Am. Coll. Cardiology; mem. Am. Soc. Echocardiology, Central Ohio Heart Assn. (trustee 1981-85). Home: 2210 Oakland Pkwy Lima OH 45805 Office: Lima Meml Hosp 1001 Belle Fontaine Ave Lima OH 45804

ROESSLER, DAVID MARTYN, physics researcher; b. London, Apr. 29, 1940; came to U.S., 1966, naturalized, 1984; s. Alfred Ernest Roessler and Elizabeth Minnie (Cornish) Roessler Collison; m. Linda Jean Beare, May 19, 1983; children—Elizabeth Ruth, Sarah Lindsay. B.Sc., U. London, 1961, Ph.D., 1966. Postdoctoral fellow U. Calif.-Santa Barbara, 1966-68; vis. mem. tech. staff Bell Telephone Labs., Murray Hill, N.J., 1968-70; staff research scientist Gen. Motors Research Labs., Warren, Mich., 1970—. Contbr. articles to profl. jours. Mem. U.K. Inst. Physics, Am. Phys. Soc., Optical Soc. Am., Am. Solar Energy Soc., Laser Inst. Am., Sigma Xi. Home: 22610 Oak Ct Hazel Park MI 48030 Office: Gen Motors Research Labs Physics Dept Warren MI 48090

ROGAN, ELEANOR GROENIGER, cancer researcher, educator; b. Cin., Nov. 25, 1942; d. Louis Martin and Esther (Levinson) G.; m. William John Robert Rogan, June 12, 1965 (div. 1970); 1 dau., Elizabeth. A.B., Mt. Holyoke Coll., 1963; Ph.D., Johns Hopkins, 1968. Lectr. Goucher Coll., Towson, Md., 1968-69; research assoc. U. Tenn., Knoxville, 1969-73; research assoc. U. Neb. Med. Ctr., Omaha, 1973-76, asst. prof., 1976-80, assoc. prof. Eppley Inst., 1980—. Contbr. articles to profl. jours. Activist, Common Cause, Omaha, 1974—. Predoctoral fellow USPHS, Johns Hopkins U., 1965-68. Mem. Am. Assn. Cancer Research, AAAS. Democrat. Roman Catholic. Home: 8210 Bowie Dr Omaha NE 68114 Office: Eppley Inst U Neb Med Ctr 42nd and Dewey Ave Omaha NE 68105

ROGERS, A. ROBERT, college dean; b. Moncton, N.B., Can., Sept. 9, 1927; came to U.S., 1956, naturalized, 1965; s. Amos Rollen and Ethel Lena (Lutes) R.; m. Rhoda Mae Page, Dec. 18, 1960; 1 child, Mark Alan. B.A., U. N.B., Can., 1948; M.A., U. Toronto, Ont., Can., 1950; postgrad. U. London, 1953; Ph.D., U. Mich., 1964. Asst., then head librarian U. N.B., Fredericton, 1951-56; adult asst. Detroit Pub. Library, 1957-59; asst., then acting dir., and dir. Bowling Green U. Library, Ohio, 1959-69; prof. library Sci. Kent State U., Ohio, 1969-76, dean Sch. Library Sci., 1978—; vis. prof. Pahlavi U., Shiraz, Iran, 1976-77; cons. Murray State U., Ky., 1968; tech. cons. Touche Ross Co., Cleve., 1982-83. Author: The Humanities, 2d edit., 1979, The Library in Society, 1984. Vice chmn. Pub. Library Financing and Support Com., Columbus, Ohio, 1983—. Mem. ALA (council 1972-76), Ohio Library Assn. (Librarian of the Yr. award 1976, pres. 1979-80), Library Assn. U.K., Bibliog. Soc. Can. Democrat. Methodist. Home: 1965 Pine View Dr Kent OH 44240 Office: Sch Library Sci Kent State U Kent OH 44242

ROGERS, BRYAN ALLEN, hosp. adminstr.; b. Akron, Ohio, Aug. 2, 1925; s. Jesse I. and Helen O. (Baker) R.; B.A., U. Akron, 1949; M.H.A., Washington U., St. Louis, 1954; m. Jean E. Hoffman, Dec. 29, 1950; children—Mark, Amy. Adminstrv. asst. Methodist Hosp., Indpls., 1954-57, asst. supt., 1957-60, asso. dir. 1960-66, asso. exec. dir., adminstr., 1966-71, exec. v.p., adminstr., 1971-72; adminstr. Toledo Hosp., 1972-77, pres., 1977—; dir. Toledo Trust Co.; charter mem. bus. adv. council U. Toledo Coll. Bus. Adminstrn.; adj. instr. health care adminstrn. Washington U., U. Toledo. Pub. Health Council, Ohio Dept. Health, 1978—, chmn., 1984-85; chmn. Task Force on Cost Effectiveness-Blue Cross, 1978—. Served with AUS, 1943-46. Fellow Am. Coll. Hosp. Adminstrs.; mem. Am. Hosp. Assn., Ohio Hosp. Assn. (chmn. 1984-85), Hosp. Council N.W. Ohio (chmn. 1985), Am. Pub. Health Assn., Toledo Area C. of C. (trustee). Presbyterian. Club: Rotary (Toledo). Home: 4626 Corey Rd Toledo OH 43623 Office: 2142 N Cove Blvd Toledo OH 43606

ROGERS, CAROL JEAN, computer systems consultant; b. St. Paul, Oct. 3, 1940; d. John Edward and Luella Grace (Holland) Christensen; grad. Estelle Compton Inst., Mpls., 1964, also specialized courses; m. Donald Dee Rogers, Jan. 23, 1971; children—Sue Ann Okun, Roxanne Leigh Okun, Wade Williams. Data entry specialist Hennepin County Dept. Ct. Services, Mpls., 1959-63; scheduling coordinator Sta. WTCN-TV, Mpls., 1963-65; coordinator for Minn., Miss Am. Teenager, St. Paul, 1967-69; upper Midwest coordinator Miss Universe, St. Paul, 1967-69; dir., instr. Mary Lowe Modeling Sch., Mpls., 1969-70; mktg. services coordinator Naidas Girl's Modeling Agy., Mpls., 1970-72; system flow tech. analyst Super Valu Stores, Inc., Hopkins, Minn., 1974-78, systems cons., 1980—; ind. systems cons., Wayzata, Minn., 1979—; adv. council Sawyer Sch. Bus., Mpls.; inst. Minn. public schs. Sunday sch. tchr. Grace Lutheran Ch., Deephaven, 1980-84. Mem. Nat. Assn. Female Execs., Am. Bus. Women's Assn. (past pres. chpt., Woman of Yr. 1985), Internat. Platform Assn. Home: 3305 Shores Blvd Wayzata MN 55391 Office: 18326 Minnetonka Blvd Wayzata MN 55391

ROGERS, DARRYL, professional football coach. Head coach Detroit Lions, NFL. Office: Detroit Lions 1200 Featherstone Rd PO Box 4200 Pontiac MI 48057*

ROGERS, DAVID ANTHONY, electrical engineer, educator, researcher; b. San Francisco, Dec. 21, 1939; s. Justin Anthony and Alice Jane (Vessey) R.; m. Darlene Olive Hicks, Feb. 20, 1965; 1 son, Stephen Arthur. B.S.E.E. cum laude, U. Wash., 1961, Ph.D. in Elec. Engring., 1971; M.S.E.E., Ill. Inst. Tech., 1964; M.Div. cum laude, Trinity Evangelical Div. Sch., Deerfield, Ill., 1966. Registered profl. engr., Wash., Sao Paulo, Brazil. Assoc. engr. Ford Aero., Newport Beach, Calif., 1961; tech. asst. IIT Research Inst., Chgo., 1963; predoctoral lectr. U. Wash., Seattle, 1964-71, acting asst. prof., 1971-72; asst. prof. State U. of Campinas, Brazil, 1972-77, assoc. prof., 1977-80; assoc. prof. elec. engring. N.D. State U., Fargo, 1980—; researcher microwaves, fiber optics, telecommunications. Served as 2d lt. Signal Corps, U.S. Army, 1961-62. Ill. Inst. Tech. research fellow, 1963-64; NSF Summer fellow, 1965; grantee Ford Found., 1969-70, TELEBRÁS (Brazil), 1973-80, N.D. State U.-Bush Found., 1981—. Mem. IEEE, Am. Soc. Engring. Edn. (grantee summer 1984), Nat. Soc. Profl. Engrs., N.D. Acad. Sci., Am. Sci. Affiliation, Am. Radio Relay League (life), Order of Engr., Sigma Xi, Tau Beta Pi. Evangelical. Co-author: Fiber Optics, 1984. Contbr. articles to profl. publs. Office: Elec Engring Dept North Dakota State Univ Fargo ND 58105

ROGERS, ERVIN RICHARD, chemical marketing company executive; b. Detroit, Dec. 1, 1940; s. Ervin John and Eugenia Kathryn (Kudla) R.;

B.S.M.E., Detroit Inst. Tech., 1962; postgrad. U. Nebr., 1967-69; m. Connie Jo Britton, Feb. 12, 1965; children—Richard, Robert. Pres., Rog-Bar Enterprises, Omaha, 1966-69; pres. Rogers Sales Co., Omaha, 1969-72; pres. Rogers & Sons Sales, Inc., Houston, Omaha and Kansas City, 1972—, chmn. bd., 1972—; pres. Rog-Fuss Oil Internat., Orange, Calif., 1983—; mktg. cons. Birkett Chem. Co., Inc. Served with USAF, 1962-66. Mem. ASME, ASHRAE, Am. Chem. Soc., Am. Welding Soc., Mfg. and Tool Engrs. Soc., Locomotive Maintenance Officers Assn. Republican. Roman Catholic. Office: 1521 N 11th St Omaha NE 68110

ROGERS, JOHN WILLARD, construction company executive; b. Oak Park, Ill., Dec. 20, 1908; s. Walter Alexander and Julia Margaret (Cushing) R.; student U. Wis., 1926-29; m. Ruth Woods Stiles, Apr. 16, 1933; 1 dau., Diane Rogers Carroll. With Bates & Rogers Constrn. Corp., 1929—; crane fireman, operator, carpenter, Ohio, 1929-31, civil engr., W.Va., 1931-32, foreman, Azusa, Calif., 1933-36, master mechanic, Dover, Ohio, 1936-37, supt., Villa Park, Ill., 1937-38, estimator, Chgo., 1939, tunnel supt., Chambersburg, Pa., 1939-40, div. supt. Kingsbury (Ind.) Ordinance Plant, 1940-41, project supt., Joliet, Ill., Duluth, Minn., 1941-42, Vicksburg, Miss., 1942, gen. supt. Alcan Hwy., Whitehorse, Yukon Ter., Alaska, 1943-45, dir., 1944—, sec., treas., Chgo., 1946-47, v.p., treas., 1948-61, exec. v.p., treas., 1961-67, pres., treas., 1968-79, chmn., chief exec. officer, 1979—, also dir. Bates & Rogers Found. Pres., trustee Glen Ellyn (Ill.) YMCA, 1937-58; mem. Glen Ellyn Sch. Bd., 1950-53; trustee, sec. bd. George Williams Coll., 1956—; bd. dirs., vice chmn. Jr. Achievement Chgo.; mem. adv. bd. B.R. Ryall YMCA; mem. indsl. liaison council U. Wis. Dept. Engring. Mem. ASCE, Western Soc. Engrs., Am. Inst. Constructors, Cons. Constructors Council (chmn.), Ohio Contractors Assn. (Hall of Fame), Associated Gen. Contractors Am. (dir., exec. com.), Associated Gen. Contractors Ill. (dir.), Builders Assn. Chgo. (past dir.), Ill. Legis. Network (chmn.), Nat. Assn. Gen. Contractors (regional chmn. legis. network, pub. relations and membership adminstrv. coms.), Bascom Hill Soc. of U. Wis., George Williams Coll. Soc. (chmn., spl. recognition medal), Beavers (founding mem.). Republican. Congregationalist. Clubs: Union League Chgo. (active Civic and Arts Found.), Execs., Econ.; Glen Oak Country (Glen Ellyn); Capitol Hill (Washington); Surf (Surfside, Fla.). Office: 600 W Jackson Blvd Chicago IL 60606

ROGERS, JUDY ANN, accountant; b. Pontiac, Mich., May 25, 1948; d. Charles Michael and Virginia (Perna) Crickon; drug sci. scholar, U. Mich., 1965; B.A. summa cum laude, Oakland U., Rochester, Mich., 1978; postgrad. Wayne State U. Law Sch., 1978-79; m. Ronald Richard Rogers, Aug. 30, 1967; 1 dau., Anne Michelle. Office mgr. Holforty Assos. Inc., Rochester, 1970-76; adminstr. asst. to controller Perry Drug Stores, Inc., Pontiac, 1976-78; office mgr. Artcraft Blueprint Co., Pontiac, 1978-81; plant acct. Gates Rubber Co., Pontiac, 1981-83; mgr. VR Bus. Brokers, Troy, 1983-85; owner, operator Fantastic Sam's (2 locations); instr. Oxford Sch. of Bus. Mem. Orion Twp. Environ. Task Force; treas. Friends of the Library; active local Republican Party. Walter Reuther Meml. Fund scholar, 1978. Mem. Nat. Assn. Exec. Females (v.p. programs univs. women 1981), Women's Comml. Real Estate Assn., Nat. Assn. Accts., Am. Bus. Women, Mich. Profl. Women's Network. Club: Deer Lake Racquet. Contbr. to The Poet, Our Twentieth Century's Greatest Poems, Today's Greatest Poems; columnist Women's Network. Home: 4383 Morgan Rd Pontiac MI 48055 Office: 1106 E Big Beaver Troy MI 48083

ROGERS, JUSTIN TOWNER, JR., utility company executive; b. Sandusky, O., Aug. 4, 1929; s. Justin Towner and Barbara Eloise (Larkin) R.; A.B. cum laude, Princeton, 1951; J.D., U. Mich., 1954; m. Virginia Logan Luscombe, May 6, 1955; children—Sarah Luscombe, Anne Larkin, Justin Towner, III. Admitted to Ohio bar, 1954; atty. Wright, Harlor, Purpus, Morris & Arnold, Columbus, O., 1956-58; atty. Ohio Edison CO., Akron, 1958-61, gen. coordinator personnel relations, 1961-67, div. mgr. Springfield. (O.) div., 1967-70. v.p., 1970-78, exec. v.p., 1978-79, pres., 1980—, also dir.; chmn. bd., dir. Pa. Power Co., New Castle; dir. 1st Nat. Bank Akron, First Bancorp. of Ohio. Past pres. and trustee Akron Child Guidance Center, Akron Community Trusts; past chmn. Akron Associated Health Agys.; trustee Akron Regional Devel. Bd.; vice chmn., trustee Akron Gen. Med. Center; mem. adv. com. Coll. Arts and Scis., U. Akron; past chmn. U. Akron Assos.; dir. Akron Devel. Corp., Akron Priority Corp. Served with AUS, 1954-56. Mem. Ohio Electric Utility Inst. (dir.), Edison Electric Inst. (bd. dirs.), Phi Delta Phi, Beta Gamma Sigma (hon.). Clubs: Akron City, Portage Country, Mayflower (Akron); Princeton (N.Y.C.); Capitol Hill (Washington). Office: 76 S Main St Akron OH 44308

ROGERS, KENNETH, realtor; b. Detroit, May 5, 1939; s. Joseph and Florence (Perna) R.; m. Jane Elizabeth Webster, Nov. 20, 1966; children—Daniel, Lisa, John, Laura. Grad. Central Mich. U., 1983. Advt. salesman Mich. Bell Co., Detroit, 1962-73; ptnr. realtor L.H.R. Evans & Assocs., Inc., Drayton Plains, Mich., 1973— Contbr. articles to newspapers. Mem. adv. council Waterford Sch. Dist., Mich., 1978; bd. dirs. North Oakland Bd. Realtors, 1977-81; mem. adv. bd. Pontiac Osteo. Hosp., Mich., 1980; bd. dirs., chmn. fundraising Pontiac-North Oakland United Way, Mich., 1982—; del. Gov.'s Conf. on Small Bus., Lansing, Mich., 1981; chmn. Mich. Gov.'s Republican Primary, 1982. Recipient Realtor Citizenship award Mich. Assn. Realtors, 1983, Resolution of Honor, Mich. State Senate, 1983, commendation recognition Oakland City Bd. Commrs., 1980. Mem. Oakland County C. of C. (pres. 1979), Mich. Assn. Realtors. Roman Catholic. Avocations: golf; travel; public speaking. Home: 6395 Waterford Hill Terr Waterford MI 48095 Office: L H R Evans & Assocs Inc 3756 Sashabaw St Drayton Plains MI 48020

ROGERS, MICHAEL K., state senator, public relations executive; b. Winchester, Ind., June 14, 1941; s. Robert E. and Margaret Pauline M. (Kennedy) R. B.S. in Radio and TV, Ind. U., 1964; M.A. in Journalism, Ball State U., 1970. News dir. Sta. WCTW, New Castle, Ind., 1964-67; asst. dir. radio and TV Ball State U., Muncie, Ind., 1967-71; v.p. Howard S. Wilcox, Inc., Indpls., 1971-75; dir. communications AMAX Coal Co., Indpls., 1975-84; pres. Rogers Communications, Inc., 1982—; rep. Ind. Legislature, 1966-72; mem. Ind. State Senate, 1981—. Sec. New Castle Mayor's Human Rights Commn., 1964-66; chmn. Wilbur Wright State Birthplace Commn., 1970-73; bd. dirs. Winona Meml. Found., Indpls., 1983—. Recipient Journalism award Ball State U., 1971; named Sagamore of the Wabash, 1974, 84, Ky. col., 1977. Mem. Sigma Delta Chi. Republican. Quaker. Clubs: Elks (New Castle); Skyline (Indpls.). Author: Indiana Legislative Process, 1985. Contbr. articles on legis. secrecy to periodicals. Office: Rogers Communications Inc PO Box 2720 Indianapolis IN 46206

ROGERS, MILLARD FOSTER, JR., art museum director; b. Texarkana, Tex., Aug. 27, 1932; s. Millard Foster and Jessie Bell (Hubbell) R.; B.A. with honors, Mich. State U., 1954; M.A., U. Mich., 1958; studied with John Pope-Hennessy; m. Nina Olds, Aug. 3, 1963; 1 son, Seth Olds. Gosline fellow Victoria and Albert Mus., London, Eng., 1959; curator Am. art Toledo Mus. Art, 1959-67; coordinator Ford Found. intern program; dir. Elvehjem Art Center, prof. art history U. Wis.-Madison, 1967-74; dir. Cin. Art Mus., 1974—; organizer Treasures from Tower of London exhbn., 1982. Pres. Mariemont Preservation Found., 1983—. Served with AUS, 1954-56. Recipient Sachs award, 1983. Mem. Assn. Art Mus. Dirs., Am. Assn. Mus., Phi Beta Kappa. Author: Randolph Rogers, American Sculptor in Rome, 1971; Spanish Paintings in the Cincinnati Art Museum, 1978; Favorite Paintings from The Cincinnati Art Museum, 1980. Address: care Cincinnati Art Museum Cincinnati OH 45202

ROGERS, RICHARD DALE, state official; b. Decatur, Ill., July 15, 1938; s. Lewie Delmer and Dora (Byrnes) R.; m. Sharon Ann Mahoney, Oct. 11, 1969; children—Michele, Angela, Alicia. B.S., Millikin U., 1964. Underwriter, Fed. Kemper, Decatur, Ill., 1965-71; chmn. Multi State Ins. Licensing Program, Princeton, Ill., 1980-81; chmn. credit property task force Nat. Assn. Ins. Commrs. Kansas City, Mo., 1981-82; dep. dir. Ill. Dept. Ins., Springfield, 1971—. Contbr. articles to profl. jours. Served with USAF, 1956-60. Mem. Charter Property and Casualty Underwriters. Roman Catholic. Club: Anchor Boat (Springfield). Lodge: K.C. Avocations: golf; jogging. Home: Rural Route 2 Box 24 Ashland IL 62612 Office: Ill Dept Ins 320 W Washington Springfield IL 62767

ROGERS, RICHARD DEAN, judge; b. Oberlin, Kans., Dec. 29, 1921; s. William Clark and Evelyn May (Christian) R.; B.S., Kans. State U., 1943; J.D., Kans. U., 1947; m. Helen Elizabeth Stewart, June 6, 1947; children—Letitia Ann, Cappi Christian, Richard Kurt. Admitted to Kans. bar, 1947; partner firm Springer and Rogers, Attys., Manhattan, Kans., 1947-58; instr. bus. law Kans. State U., 1948-52; partner firm Rogers, Stites & Hill, Manhattan, 1959-75; gen. counsel Kans. Farm Bur. & Service Cos., Manhattan, 1960-75; judge U.S. Dist. Ct., Topeka, Kans., 1975—. City commnr., Manhattan, 1950-52, 60-64; mayor Manhattan, 1952, 64; county atty., Riley County, Kans., 1954-58; state rep., 1964-68; state senator, 1968-75, pres. Kans. Senate, 1975. Served with USAAF, 1943-45. Decorated Air medal, Dfc. Mem. Kans., Am. bar assns., Beta Theta Pi. Republican. Presbyterian. Club: Masons. Office: 410 Federal Bldg 444 S E Quincy St Topeka KS 66683

ROGERS, RICHARD MICHAEL, judge; b. Lorain, Ohio, Dec. 8, 1944; s. Paul M. and Lillie R. (Morris) R.; m. Sophia Lydia Wagner, Dec. 23, 1967; children—L. Danielle, David K., Marisa D., Matthew D. B.A., Ohio No. U., 1966, J.D., 1972. Bar: Ohio 1972, U.S. Dist. Ct. (no. dist.) Ohio 1972. Assoc. Martin, Hall & Rogers, Marion, Ohio, 1972-76; ptnr. Rogers & Rogers, Marion, 1976-81; asst. solicitor, police prosecutor City of Marion, 1973-74, pub. defender, 1975; asst. county prosecutor Marion County, 1976-81; judge Marion Mcpl. Ct., 1982—. Mem. Marion Active 20/40 Service Club, 1973—, treas., 1976-80, bd. dirs., 1976—, pres., 1980-81; chmn. bd. dirs., pres. Marion Area Driver Re-edn. Project, 1974-81; v.p. Big Bros./Big Sisters Marion County, 1985—; mem. sch. bd. St. Mary's Elem. Sch., 1985—. Served with U.S. Army, 1968-69. Recipient Superior Jud. Service award Ohio Supreme Ct., 1982, 83. Mem. Ohio State Bar Assn. (jud. adminstrn. and legal reform com., modern cts. com.), Marion County Bar Assn. (pres. 1985—), Mcpl. Judges Assn. (jury instrn. com., legis. com.), Ohio Jud. Conf. (gen. adminstrn. legal reform com.), Ohio Bar Coll., Delta Theta Phi, Sigma Pi. Republican. Methodist. Avocations: golf; scuba diving. Home: 310 Edgefield Blvd Marion OH 43302 Office: Marion Mcpl Ct 233 W Center St Marion OH 43302

ROGERS, ROBERT LEE, novelist, educator; b. Chgo., July 26, 1933; s. Charles and Lydia Anna (Zimmerman) R.; m. Laura Lee Scrimpsher, July 25, 1965. B.S. in History, No. Ill. U., 1955, M.Ed., 1974. Elem. tchr. pub. schs., 1955. Author: All These Splendid Sins, 1979; Fire Bird, 1985.

ROGERS, RUSSELL REX, psychologist, educator; b. Orange, N.J., Apr. 22, 1953; s. Paul S. and Gwynne E. (Ihlenburg) R.; m. Jill K. Kresge, Jan. 24, 1981. B.A., Wheaton Coll., 1975; M.A., Western Ky. U., 1976; M. Human Resource Devel., U. Assocs., San Diego, 1983; Ph.D., Mich. State U., 1984. Assoc. dean Fort Wayne Coll., Ind., 1976-79; resident counselor Calvin Coll., Grand Rapids, Mich., 1979-80; research specialist Mich. State U., East Lansing, 1982-83, asst. prof., 1983—; sr. cons., InterAct Assocs., Lansing, Mich., 1981—. Contbr. articles to profl. jours. Adv. task force Gov's. Commn. Higher Edn., 1984. Recipient Dissertation Research award Sage Found., 1983. Mem. Am. Assn. Counseling and Devel., Am. Coll. Personnel Assn. (Annuit Coeptis award), Nat. Assn. Student Personnel Adminstrn., Am. Soc. Tng. and Devel., Phi Kappa Phi (life). Presbyterian. Avocations: reading; music; building friendships; personal growth; jogging. Home: 900 Long Blvd #816 Lansing MI 48910 Office: InterAct Assocs 900 Long Blvd Suite 816 Lansing MI 48910

ROGERS, VAN RENSSELAER, adminstrv. and sales cons.; b. nr. Lexington, Ky., Jan. 9, 1914; s. Edgar Alfred and Nellie Estella (Burton) R.; grad. Cleve. Inst. Art, 1937; m. Ruth Charlotte Reichelt, Aug. 3, 1941; 1 son, Peter Van. Commd. sculptor Walt Disney Enterprises, Hollywood, Calif., 1937-38; co-founder Rogers Bennett Studios, Cleve., 1938; pres., owner Rogers Display Studios div. NESCO, Inc. (now Rogers Displays Inc.), Cleve., 1959—; founder Van R. Rogers Prodns., Inc., 1983—; profl. sculptor, artist, designer, painter. Asst. registrar John Huntington Poly. Inst., Cleve., 1938-41. Chmn. Zoning Commn., Russell Twp., Geauga County, Ohio, 1974. Served to lt. comdr. USNR, 1942-46. Mem. Exhibit Designers and Producers Assn., Nat. Trade Show Exhibitor Assn. (founder, citation as Godfather of orgn. 1977), Archaeol. Soc. Ohio, Dunham Tavern Soc. Collectors, Ohio Hist. Soc., Geauga County Hist. Soc., Russell Twp. Hist. Soc., Nat. Trust Hist. Preservation, Found. Ill. Archeology, North and South Skirmish Assn., Nat. Muzzle Loading Rifle Assn., Greater Cleve. Growth Assn., Western Reserve Hist. Soc., Northwestern Archaeol. Soc., Genuine Indian Relic Soc., Nat. Hist. Soc., Ohio Acad. History, Archaeology Inst. Am., Imperial German Mil. Collectors Assn., Great Lakes Hist. Soc. Clubs: Hon. Order Ky. Cols.; Masons (32 deg.), K.T.; Advt. (Cleve.). Office: Rogers Displays Inc 26470 Lakeland Blvd Cleveland OH 44132

ROGERS, WILLIAM ARTHUR, journalist, photojournalist; b. Chgo., Apr. 12, 1920; s. Edwin Arthur and Astrid (Swensen) R.; m. Pauline Elizabeth King, Apr. 6, 1945; 1 dau., Pamela Kay Rogers Jannece. Student U. Dubuque, 1937-38, also various univ. and coll. seminars, 1966-76. Reporter, newscaster, news dir. Stas.-WSAI/WCKY, Cin., 1947-48; sales promotion mgr. Frederic W. Ziv Co., Cin., 1949-52; prin. Bill Rogers, Profitable Publicity, Chgo., 1953-58; reporter, photographer Southtown Economist, Chgo., 1959-60; prin. Bill Arthur Rogers & Intermedia Picture Service, Oak Park, Ill., 1960—; instr. Triton Coll., River Grove, Ill., 1971-75, U. Ill.-Chgo. Med. Ctr., 1972-73, Coll. DuPage, Glen Ellyn, Ill., 1980-81; chmn., coordinator Chgo. 74, 1974. Exhibited in one-man shows: Chgo. Pub. Library, 1970; travelling show Am. Soc. Mag. Photographers 25th Anniversary Show, 1969-70; photog. contbns. to (books) Hemingway, 1966; Rights in Conflict, 1968; Black Americans, 1969; Sweet Medicine, 1969; Dynamics of Health Care, 1974; also miscellaneous textbooks. Vestryman, editor and bishop's penceman St. Christopher's Ch., Oak Park, 1966—, mem. Diocesan Stewardship Commn., 1969-70; mem. Oak Park Cable TV Commn., 1982—; bd. dirs., chmn. income devel. Oak Park-River Forest chpt. Am. Cancer Soc., 1983—. Served with USMCR, 1941-45; Solomons, Bismarck Archipelago. Mem. Ind. Writers Chgo., Am. Soc. Mag. Photographers (pres. chpt. 1970-77, service award 1983), Artists Guild Chgo. (council 1973-78, Service award 1978), Indsl. Editors Chgo. (treas. 67), Nat. Writers Club, DAV. Episcopalian. Office: 846 Wesley Ave Oak Park IL 60304

ROGGE, DWAINE WILLIAM, investment company executive; b. Auburn, Nebr., Apr. 5, 1938; s. Elmer John and Gertrude Luella (Gerdes) R.; m. Wanda Lucille Teten, Aug. 17, 1958; children—D. Scott, Shari Louise, Paul Alan. B.Sc. in Civil Engring., U. Nebr., 1960; M.B.A., Harvard U., 1962. Mgmt. trainee Archer Daniels Midland, Mpls., 1962-64; exec. v.p. First MidAm., Lincoln, Nebr., 1964-74; pres. Commerce Capital, Inc., Lincoln, 1975—; dir. Commerce Investment Mgmt., Inc., Lincoln, Commerce Properties, Inc., Lincoln. Mem. Adv. bd. State Republican Fin. Chmn., Nebr., 1982. Served to 2d lt. U.S. Army, 1960. Mem. Omaha-Lincoln Soc. Security Analysts (treas. 1983-84), Family Service Assn. Lincoln (pres. 1974-75). Republican. Lutheran. Avocations: hunting; traveling. Home: 1835 Monterey Dr Lincoln NE 68506 Office: Commerce Capital Inc 646 NBC Ctr Lincoln NE 68508

ROGLER, JOHN CHARLES, animal science educator; b. Providence, Sept. 21, 1927; s. Frederick and Anne (Howarth) R.; m. Margaret E. Tamke, June 23, 1951; children—John F., Richard K. B.S., U. R.I., 1951; M.S., Purdue U., 1953, Ph.D., 1958. Asst. prof. Purdue U., West Lafayette, Ind., 1957-61, assoc. prof., 1961-66, prof. animal nutrition, 1966—. Contbr. articles to sci. jours. Served to cpl. U.S. Army, 1953-55. Fellow AAAS; mem. Am. Inst. Nutrition, Poultry Sci. Assn., Soc. for Exptl. Biology and Medicine, Sigma Xi. Home: 195 Blueberry Ln West Lafayette IN 47906 Office: Dept Animal Sci Purdue U West Lafayette IN 47907

ROGNAN, LLOYD NORMAN, artist, illustrator; b. Chgo., June 14, 1923; s. John and Gertrude Sophia (Hagen) R.; student Am. Acad. Art, 1941, 50, 51; diploma Acad. de la grande Chamiere, 1949; m. Sylvia Marcella Erickson, July 18, 1953; children—Bruce Byron, Cindy Lou. Cover artist French edit. Ellery Queen, Paris, 1947-49; religious film strip artist Concordia Pubs., St. Louis, 1950-53; art dir. Jahn & Ollier Engraving Co., 1954—; sci. fiction cover artist Greenleaf Publs., Evanston, Ill., 1956-58; with Meyer and Booth Studio, Chgo., 1958-61; biol. artist Golden Books Press, N.Y.C., 1961-63; cartoonist United Card Co., Rolling Meadows, Ill., 1966-71; art dir. Gallant Greetings, Chgo., 1972; artist, advt. posters (silk screen), Chgo., 1973-75; calendar artist Brown & Bigelow, St. Paul, 1976-79, Baumgarth, Brown & Bigelow, 1976-84, with Saga, Inc., ltd. edits. Western prints Albuquerque, 1977—; ltd. edit. plates Picard, Inc., Antioch, Ill., 1983-84; art dir., creative editor United Card Co., Arlington Hts., Ill., 1978—; represented in permanent collection Vesterheim Mus., Decorah, Iowa. Art counsellor Boy Scouts Am. Served with U.S. Army, 1943-46; ETO. Decorated Purple Heart. Home and studio: 3620 Linneman St Glenview IL 60025

ROGOVE, HERBERT JAY, osteopathic physician; b. Phila., May 8, 1947; s. Irving S. and Adele (Flashner) R.; m. Carolyn Marie Fix, July 28, 1984; children—Jordan, Gregory B.S., Albright Coll., 1969; D.O., Phila. Coll. Osteo. Medicine, 1973. Diplomate Am. Bd. Internal Medicine. Co-dir. critical care Mercy Hospital, Pitts., 1978-81, chmn. emergency medicine, 1978-81; dir. critical care services Riverside Methodist Hosp., Columbus, Ohio, 1981—. Contbr. articles to med. jours. Fellow ACP, 1984. Mem. Soc. Critical Care Medicine (sec. internal medicine sect. 1985-86), Ohio Soc. Critical Care Medicine (pres. 1984-85), Club of Mainz Internat. Home: 139 Glen Circle Worthington OH 43085 Office: Riverside Meth Hosp 3535 Olentangy River Rd Columbus OH 43214

ROGOVIN, RICHARD DAVID, lawyer; b. Cleve., June 4, 1939; s. Herman and Eva (Kraus) R.; m. Linda Diane Rocker, Dec. 25, 1961; children—Leslie, Catherine, Daniel. B.A., Cornell U., 1962; J.D., U. Pa., 1965. Bar: Pa. 1966, Ohio 1968, U.S. Dist. Ct. (so. dist.) Ohio 1975, U.S. Supreme Ct. 1980. Ptnr. Feibel, Feibel, et al, Columbus, Ohio, 1968-80, Guren, Merritt, Feibel, Sogg & Cohen, Columbus, 1980-84, Bricker & Eckler, Columbus, 1984—. Chmn. Columbus Pub. Rev. Commn., 1975-76; vice chmn. Ohio Elected Ofcl. and Jud. Compensation Rev. Commn., 1977; mem. Ohio Consumer Counsel Governing Bd., 1980-81; trustee Central Ohio Lung Assn., Columbus, 1984, Jefferson Acad. Music, Columbus, 1984. Mem. ABA, Ohio Bar Assn., Phila. Bar Assn., Columbus Bar Assn. Clubs: Capitol, University (Columbus). Avocations: tennis; sailing. Home: 5730 Concord Hill Dr Columbus OH 43213 Office: Bricker & Eckler 100 E Broad St Columbus OH 43214

ROHATGI, VIJAY KUMAR, mathematics educator; b. Delhi, India, Feb. 1, 1939; came to U.S., 1964, naturalized, 1974; s. Behari L. and Motal (Motal) R.; m. Bina G. Parab, Dec. 15, 1971; 1 child, Sameer. B.Sc., Delhi U. (India), 1958, M.A., 1960; M.S., U. Alta., Edmonton, Can., 1964; Ph.D., Mich. State U., 1967. Asst. prof. math. Catholic U., Washington, 1967-69, assoc. prof., 1969-72; assoc. prof. Bowling Green State U., Ohio, 1972-74, prof., 1974—, chmn. dept., 1983—; statis. officer Mcpl. Corp., Delhi, 1961-62. Author: Probability and Mathematical Statistics, 1976; (with others) Probability Theory, 1979; Statistical Inference, 1984. Editor: Contributions to Probability, 1981; Analytic Probability, 1981. Mem. Internat. Statis. Inst., Inst. Math. Statistics, Am. Statis. Assn., Am. Math. Soc. Club: Bowling Green Swim (dir.-at-large 1984—). Home: 408 Madison Ct Bowling Green OH 43402 Office: Math and Statistics Dept Bowling Green State U Bowling Green OH 43403

ROHRICH, JACOB HENRY, municipal official; b. Chester, Ill., July 25, 1950; s. Jake and Mildred (Lovin) R.; m. Charlotte Ann Hughes, Aug. 2, 1970; children—Jacob, Joshua. A.A.S., Crowder Coll., Neosho, Mo.; diploma Water and Waste Water Sch., Neosha. Supt. waste water City Works, Carterville, Ill., 1973-74, Village of Morton, Ill., 1974—; part time tchr. Carl Sandburg Coll., Galesburg, Ill., 1980-82, Ill. Central Coll., East Peoria, 1982—; adviser environ. classes, Ill. Central Coll., 1982—. Asst. cub master W.D. Boyce council Boy Scouts Am., 1981—. Served with U.S. Army, 1971-73. Mem. Ill. Soc. Water Pollution Control Operators (v.p. 1977-78, pres. 1978-79, Clarence Classen award 1981), Water Pollution Control Fedn. Avocation: Camping. Home: 118 Hemlock Dr Morton IL 61550 Office: Village Morton Pub Works 120 N Main Morton IL 61550

ROHRMAN, DOUGLASS FREDERICK, lawyer; b. Chgo., Aug. 10, 1941; s. Frederick Alvin and Velma Elizabeth (Birdwell) R.; m. Susan Vitullo; children—Kathryn Anne, Elizabeth Clelia. A.B., Duke U., 1963; J.D., Northwestern U., 1966. Bar: Ill. 1966. Legal coordinator Nat. Communicable Disease Center, Atlanta, 1966-68; assoc. Keck, Mahin & Cate, Chgo., 1968-73, ptnr., 1973—; exec. v.p., dir. Kerogen Oil Co., 1967—. Vice chmn., commr. Ill. Food and Drug Commn., 1970-72. Served as lt. USPHS, 1966-68. Mem. Am., Chgo. (chmn. com. on food and drug law 1972-73), 7th Circuit bar assns., Am. Soc. Law and Medicine, Selden Soc. Democrat. Episcopalian. Clubs: Legal, Metropolitan, Union League (Chgo.); River; Wigmore; Washington Duke. Co-author: Commercial Liability Risk Management and Insurance, 2 vols., 1978. Contbr. articles on law to various profl. jours. Home: 520 Brier St Kenilworth IL 60043 Office: 8300 Sears Tower Chicago IL 60606

ROL, PIETER KLAAS, materials science educator; b. Graft, The Netherlands, Nov. 22, 1927; came to U.S., 1966; s. Pieter and Neeltje (Bus) R.; m. Greta Rijkes, Mar. 29, 1952; children—Alida N., Neeltje M., Pieter J. Doctorandus, U. Amsterdam, Netherlands, 1953, Ph.D., 1960. Staff scientist Fundamentul Orderzoek der Materie, Amsterdam, 1953-60, research leader, 1962-66; vis. scientist G.D. Convair, San Diego, 1960-62; staff scientist G.D. Convair, San Diego, 1966-69; prof. materials sci., Wayne State U., Detroit, 1969—, dir. research, 1974-76, assoc. dean engring., 1976-78, assoc. provost, 1978-81, interim dean engring., 1985—. Author: Introduction in Vacuum Technology, 1967. Served to 1st lt. Dutch Army, 1949-50. Mem. Am. Phys. Soc., Am. Vacuum Soc. (chmn. local chpt. 1977-78), AAAS, Engring. Soc. Detroit, Sigma Xi. Presbyterian. Home: 22011 Ivanhoe Ln Southfield MI 48034 Office: Wayne State U Coll Engring Detroit MI 48202

ROLES, RICHARD CROSS, metal company executive; b. Cottage Grove, Oreg., June 5, 1948; s. Fred A. and Mary (Steele) R.; m. Grace Lanelle, Nov. 28, 1980; children—Stacey, Princess, Sean, Sherrey. B.S. in Bus. Adminstrn., Auburn U., 1968. Jr. auditor, U.S. Steel Co., Phila., 1968-69; sr. auditor, purchasing agt. Gould Inc., Phila., 1969-73; chmn. bd. MRI Corp., Phila., 1978-80; v.p. Fed. Alloys Corp., Detroit, 1973-80; pres. Resources Alloys & Metals, Farmington Hills, Mich., 1980—. Mem. Christian Fin. Concepts (bd. dirs. 1979—), Nat. Assn. Recycling (exec. com. 1976-84). Home: 7458 Pebble Ln West Bloomfield MI 48033 Office: Resources Alloys & Metals 24277 Indoplex Circle Farmington Hills MI 48018

ROLFE, GARY LAVELLE, forestry educator; b. Paducah, Ky., Sept. 5, 1946; s. George Washington and Inez (Holt) R.; m. Judy A. Moeller, June 22, 1968 (div. 1982); children—Terry Edwards, Coy Rolfe. B.S., U. Ill., 1968, M.S., 1969, Ph.D., 1972. Research asst. dept. forestry U. Ill.-Urbana, 1968-70, instr., 1971, research assoc., 1971-72, assoc. dir., prin. investigator, 1972-73, asst. prof., 1972-75, dir., prin. investigator, 1973-77, assoc. prof., 1975-80, asst. dir. Ill. Agr. Experiment Sta., 1977-81, prof. dept. forestry and inst. forestry, 1980—, head dept. forestry, 1981-85; chmn. Ill. Commn. Forestry Devel., 1985—; cons. Soil and Land Use Tech. Inc., 1980—, EPA-Research Triangle Park-Lead in the Environment, 1981-82, numerous others. Author: Integrating Ecology Education in Elementary Curricula, 1978; Field Activities in Ecology Education, 1981. Cons. in forestry City of Villa Grove, Ill. Named Outstanding Young Educator, Jr. C. of C., 1978. Mem. Ecol. Soc. Am., Am. Soc. Agronomy, Assn. Watershed Scientists, Soc. Am. Foresters, Gamma Sigma Delta, Xi Sigma Pi, Sigma Pi. Office: Dept Forestry 110 Mumford Hall 1301 W Gregory Dr Urbana IL 61801

ROLFE, MICHAEL N., management consultant; b. Chgo., Sept. 9, 1937; s. Mark Alexander and Antoinette (Wittgenstein) R.; A.B., U. Mich., 1959; postgrad. Grad. Sch. Bus., U. Chgo., 1962-64; m. Judith Mary Lewis, June 16, 1959; children—Andrew Jay, Lisa Kay, James Lewis. With Brunswick Corp., Chgo., 1962-68, mgr. systems and programming, 1966-68; with A.T. Kearney, Chgo., 1968-81, v.p., 1979-81; v.p., prin. in charge mgmt. cons., Peat Marwick Mitchell & Co., 1981—. Mem. Sch. Dist. No. 113 Bd. Edn., Highland Park-Deerfield, Ill., 1977-83, pres., 1979-81. Served with USNR, 1959-61. Mem. Soc. Mgmt. Info. Systems, Common Computer Users Group (dir.). Clubs: Northmoor Country, Standard (Chgo.). Home: 1730 Overland Trail Deerfield IL 60015 Office: 303 E Wacker Dr Chicago IL 60601

ROLFES, JAMES WALTER, SR., lawyer; b. Providence, May 21, 1942; s. George Henry and Mary Helen (Clark) R.; m. Dorothy Patricia Robison, Sept. 10, 1966; children—John George, James Walter, Jr. B.S., U. Cin., 1971; J.D., No. Ky. State Coll. (Salmon P. Chase Coll. Law), 1975. Bar: Ohio 1975, U.S. Dist. Ct. (so. dist.) Ohio 1975, U.S. Supreme Ct. 1985. Asst. sec. Eagle Savings and Loan, Cin., 1967-70; acct. Kings Island, Kings Mill, Ohio, 1970-73, Bode-Finn, Cin., 1973-76; asst. prosecutor Madison County, London, Ohio, 1976-79, mcpl. ct. judge, 1982—; sole practice, London, 1975—; tchr. Madison County Alcohol Diversion Program, London, 1982—, Ohio Peace Officers Tng. Acad., London, 1976-79. Chmn. Madison County Heart Assn., London, 1977, Madison County Mental Health Adv. Bd., London, 1980-84; pres. Fairfield Youth Assn. Recipient Millard W. Mack Scholarship U. Cin., 1970. Mem. Ohio Bar Assn., Madison County Bar Assn., Cin. Bar Assn., ABA, London Merchants Assn., Inc. (chmn. 1983—), Republican. Roman Catholic. Lodge: K.C. (grand Knight 1985—). Office: 17 S Main St London OH 43140

ROLL, DELIGHT ADREAN, nurse; b. Kalamazoo, Oct. 8, 1939; d. Harold George and Bessie Pearl (Flegal) Derksen; m. Harold Wilmont Frye, Nov. 16, 1968 (div. 1971); m. 2d, Mathew B. Roll, Oct. 6, 1972. Grad., Kalamazoo Practical Nursing Sch., 1960; A.S. in Nursing, Southwestern Mich. Coll., 1979; B.S. in Nursing, U. Mich., 1982; postgrad. Western Mich. U. Indsl. nurse Electronic Supply Corp., Kalamazoo, 1964-68; staff nurse Pipp Community Hosp., Plainwell, Mich., 1967-73; charge nurse Cunningham Nursing Home, Plainwell, 1974-78; agy. nurse Quality Care, Kalamazoo, 1978-81; charge nurse Provincial House Inc., Kalamazoo, 1981-83, Ridgeview Manor, Kalamazoo, 1983—. Contbr. article to profl. jour. Mem. Kalamazoo Practical Nurses Assn. (pres. 1967-69). Baptist. Home: 10811 Boniface Point Dr Plainwell MI 49080

ROLLAND, IAN MCKENZIE, ins. co. exec.; b. Fort Wayne, Ind., June 3, 1933; s. David and Florence (Hunter) R.; B.A., DePauw U., 1955; M.A., U. Mich., 1956; m. Miriam Vee Flickinger, July 3, 1955; children—Cheri Lynn, Lawrence David, Robert Arthur, Carol Ann, Sara Kay. With Lincoln Nat. Life Ins. Co., Fort Wayne, 1956—, sr. v.p., 1973-77, pres., chief exec. officer, 1977—, also chmn.; pres., chief exec. officer Lincoln Nat. Corp., 1975—, dir. affiliate cos.; dir. Central Soya Co., No. Ind. Public Service Co., Gen. Telephone of Ind., Lincoln Fin. Corp. Chmn. citizens bd. St. Francis Coll.; bd. dirs. United Way, Neighborhood Care, Inc., Parkview Meml. Hosp., YMCA, Met. Bd. Mem. Am. Acad. Actuaries, Health Inst. Assn. Am. (dir.), Am. Council Life Ins. (dir.). Methodist. Office: Lincoln Nat Corp 1300 S Clinton Fort Wayne IN 46801*

ROLLER, MARK CAMERON, insurance company executive; b. Springfield, Ohio, May 22, 1950; s. Cletus J. and Betty Jane (Caylor) R.; m. Karen Durica, Jan. 9, 1976; 1 child, Peter Elliott. B.A., Anderson Coll., 1972; M.B.A., Ball State U., 1980. Coll. rep. Anderson Coll., Ind., 1972-74, dir. admissions, 1974-79, prof. mgmt. mktg., 1980-84; mktg. mgr. Blue/Cross/Blue Shield, Indpls., 1985—; cons. Mgmt. Cons. and Research Services, Anderson, 1982—; seminar speaker, 1984—. Mem. personnel com. Park Palce Ch. of God, Anderson, 1980-82, Sunday sch. tchr., 1982-83; bd. dirs. Youth for Christ, Anderson, 1981-82. Mem. Am. Mktg. Assn., Midwest Bus. Adminstrn. Assn., Delta Mu Delta, Beta Gamma Sigma. Republican. Avocations: golf, computers, reading. Home: 4111 Northwood Ln Anderson IN 46011 Office: Blue Cross/Blue Shield Inc 120 W Market St Indianapolis IN 46204

ROLLINGER, KENNETH JOHN, machinist, manufacturing company executive; b. Chgo., May 20, 1947; s. Florian Frank and Dorothy (Zdrojewski) R.; m. Myong Cha, Sept. 16, 1969; children—Kimberly, Glen. Student Triton Coll., 1973-77. Repair machinist Stanadyne Co., Bellwood, Ill., 1973—; automotive machinist Triangle Engine Rebuilders, Chgo., 1969-73; cons. V & F Engring., Itasca, Ill., 1981—; owner Impossible Engring. and Mfg. Co., 1983—. Served with U.S. Army, 1966-69; Korea. Mem. ASME. Roman Catholic. Club: Salmon Unltd. (Chgo.). Modifier antique airplane brake systems. Home: 635 Gladys St Elmhurst IL 60126

ROLLINS, ARLEN JEFFERY, osteopathic physician; b. Cleve., June 30, 1946; s. Lee Roy and Celia (Madorsky) R.; m. Deborah Joyce Gross, Dec. 18, 1971; children—Aaron Jason, Howard Philip, Lee Craig. A.B., Miami U., Oxford, Ohio, 1968; D.O., Chgo. Coll. Osteo. Medicine, 1973; M.S. in Occupational Medicine, Environ. Health, U. Cin., 1984. Diplomate Am. Bd. Preventive Medicine. Intern, Phoenix Gen. Hosp., 1973-74; resident in environ. health/occupational medicine Cin. Gen. Hosp.-U. Cin., 1974-77; plant physician Ford Motor Co., Cin., 1974-77; assoc. med. dir. East Side Occupational Health Ctr., Cleve., 1977-79; med. dir. Ferro Corp., Cleve., 1979—, S.K. Wellman Corp., Cleve., 1979—, Piezoelectric div. Vernitron, Cleve., 1979—; pres. Occupational Health Mgmt. Cons.; cons. occupational health Ohio Bell Telephone Co., Cleve., 1981—; cons. Occupational Health Ctr., Univ. Hosps. of Cleve. Fellow Am. Acad. Occupational Medicine, Am. Occupational Med. Assn., Am. Coll. Preventive Medicine; mem. Ohio State Med. Assn., Cleve. Acad. Medicine (pub. health and immunization com., med.-legal com.), Western Res. Med. Dirs. Assn., Am. Osteo. Assn., Am. Osteo. Acad. Pub. Health and Preventive Medicine (dir.).

ROLLISON, STEPHEN FRANK, broadcast co. exec.; b. Atlanta, July 19, 1948; s. Ellie Frank and Ruth (Brogden) R.; B.A., U. Ga., 1973; M.Ed., Columbus Coll., 1975; postgrad. Auburn U., 1976-77. Broadcast journalist, anchorman Sta. WTVM-TV, Inc., Columbus, Ga., 1973-75; anchorman, reporter, producer Sta. WRBL-TV. Columbus, 1977-78; sales exec. community relations and estate planning depts. Prudential Ins. Co. Am., Albany, Ga., 1978; distributorship operator Atlanta Jour., 1978-79; assignment editor Sta. WQAD-TV, Moline, Ill., 1979-81; news dir. Sta. KAAL-TV, Austin, Minn., 1981—. Served with U.S. Army, 1968-71; to capt. Res., 1971-77. Decorated Bronze Star; Cross of Gallantry with bronze star, Cross of Gallantry with silver star (Republic of Vietnam). Mem. Radio and Television News Dirs. Assn., Am. Hist. Assn., Res. Officers Assn., U. Ga. Alumni Soc., Columbus Coll. Alumni Assn., Auburn U. Alumni Assn., Northwest Broadcast News Assn., Sigma Delta Chi, Phi Alpha Theta. Republican. Roman Catholic. Home: 5070 River Glen Dr Apt 411 Las Vegas NV 89103 Office: KAAL-TV PO Box 577 Austin MN 55912

ROMAN, STEPHEN BOLESLAV, mining co. exec.; b. Slovakia, Apr. 17, 1921; s. George and Helen Roman; student Agrl. Coll.; m. Betty Gardon, Oct. 20, 1945; 4 sons, 3 daus. Chmn. bd., chief exec. officer, dir. Denison Mines Ltd., Toronto, Ont., Can., chmn. bd., dir. Roman Corp., Ltd., Standard Trust Co.; dir. Pacific Tin Consol. Corp., Seagull Petroleum Ltd. Hon. bd. dirs. Royal Agrl. Winter Fair Assn. Can.; bd. dirs. John C. Diefenbaker Meml. Found., Inc., Father John Kelly, c.s.b. Found. Served with Canadian Army, World War II. Mem. Canadian Slovak League, Bd. Trade of Met. Toronto, Royal Can. Mil. Inst. (hon.). Roman Catholic. Clubs: Engineers, Capitol Hill, Lyford Cay. Office: PO Box 40 Royal Bank Plaza Toronto ON M5J 2K2 Canada

ROMAN, SUSAN, librarian; b. St. Louis, June 4, 1939; d. Frank M. and Beatrice (Weisman) Shucart; m. Richard A. Roman, Jan. 29, 1961; children—Jody, Beth, Shelly, David. A.B., Washington U., 1961; M.A.L.S., Rosary Coll., 1976; postgrad. U. Chgo., 1981—. Head children's services Deerfield Pub. Library, Ill., 1971-78; head youth services Northbrook Pub. Library, Ill., 1978-82; dir. reference services library and info. mgmt. AMA, 1985—. Author: Sequences: An Annotated Guide to Children's Fiction in Series, 1985. Editor book revs., 1981—. Contbr. articles to profl. jours. Bd. dirs. PTO, Deerfield, Ill., 1970-72; vol. pool mem., Northbrook, 1978—; leader Girl Scouts U.S.A., Deerfield, 1975-78; badge cons. Boy Scouts Am., Northbrook, 1980—. Mo. State scholar, 1957; U. Chgo. scholar, 1981—. Mem. ALA (dir. on bd. Assoc. for Library Services to Children, mem. com. young adult services), Ill. Library Assn. (children's section pres. 1983), Library Adminstrs. Council No. Ill., N. Surburban Library System. Office: AMA 535 N Dearborn Chicago IL 60610

ROMANOFF, MARJORIE REINWALD, educator; b. Chgo., Sept. 29, 1923; d. David Edward and Gertrude (Rosenfield) Reinwald; student Northwestern U., 1941-42, 43-45; B.Ed., U. Toledo, 1947, M.Ed., 1968, Ed.D., 1976; m. Milford M. Romanoff, Nov. 1, 1945; children—Bennett Sanford, Lawrence Michael, Janet Beth (dec.). Tchr., Old Orchard Elem. Sch., Toledo, 1946-47, McKinley Sch., Toledo, 1964-65; substitute tchr., Toledo, 1964-68; instr. Mary Manse Coll., Toledo, 1974; instr. children's lit. Sylvania (Ohio) Bd. Edn., 1977; supr. student tchrs. U. Toledo, 1968-73, 85-86, researcher, 1973-74, instr. Am. Lang. Inst., 1978—; adj. asst. prof. elem. edn. Bowling Green (Ohio) State U., 1978—. Trustee Children's Services Bd., 1974-76; pres. bd. Cummings Treatment Center for Adolescents, 1978-80; mem. Crosby Gardens Adv. Bd., 1976-82, Community Planning Council, 1980—, Citizens Rev. Bd. of Juvenile Ct., 1979—; mem. allocations com. Mental Health and Retardation Bd., 1980-81; mem. Bd. Jewish Edn., 1976—, pres., 1982-84; mem. Jewish Family Service, 1978-85, v.p., 1980-85; bd. dirs. Family Life Edn. Council, 1984—. Mem. Tchrs. English to Speakers Other Langs., Am. Assn. Supervision and Curriculum Devel., Am. Edn. Research Assn., Nat. Soc. for Study Edn., Am. Assn. Colls. Tchr. Edn., Toledo Assn. Children's Lit., Nat. Council Jewish Women, Orgn. Rehab. and Tng., Hadassah (chpt. pres. regional bd. 1961-64), Northwestern U. Alumni Assn., Phi Kappa Phi, Phi Delta Kappa, Kappa Delta Pi (pres./faculty adv. 1971-75), Pi Lambda Theta (chpt. pres. 1978-80, nat. com. 1979-84). Democrat. Home: 2514 Bexford Pl Toledo OH 43606 Office: U Toledo CEC 1006 Toledo OH 43606 also Coll Edn Bowling Green State U Bowling Green OH 43402

ROMANOFF, MILFORD MARTIN, building contractor, architectural designer; b. Cleve., Aug. 21, 1921; s. Barney Sanford and Edythe Stolpher (Bort) R.; student Coll. Arch., U. Mich., 1939-42; B.B.A., U. Toledo, 1943; m. Marjorie Reinwald, Nov. 6, 1945; children—Bennett S., Lawrence M., Janet Beth (dec.). Pres., Glass City Constrn. Co., Toledo, 1951-55, Milford Romanoff Inc., Toledo, 1956—. Co-founder, Neighborhood Improvement Found. Toledo, 1960; mem. Lucas County Econ. Devel. Com., 1979—; mem. citizens adv. bd. Recreation Commn. Toledo, 1973—; mem. campus adv. com. Med. Coll. Ohio, 1980—; trustee Cummings Treatment Center for Adolescents, 1981—; mem. Children's Services Bd. Lucas County, 1981—; pres. Ohio B'nai B'rith, 1959-60; bd. dirs. Anti-Defamtion League, 1955-60, Ohio Hillel Orgns.; chmn. Toledo Amateur Baseball and Softball Com., 1979-81; mem. Democratic Precinct Com., 1975-78; trustee Temple Brotherhood, 1956-58, 79—, bd. dirs., 1981—; pres. Cherry Hill Nursing Home, 1964-85; cons. U.S. Care Corp., 1985—; mem. Crosby Gardens Adv. Bd.; bd. govs. Toledo Housing for Elderly, 1982-85; mem. adv. bd. Salvation Army, 1984-87, Mental Health Bd., 1983—. Mem. U. Toledo Alumni Assn., Toledo Mus. Art (asso.), U. Mich. Alumni Assn., Toledo Zool. Soc., Zeta Beta Tau. Clubs: Masons; B'nai B'rith (pres. Toledo lodge 1958-59), Hadassah (assoc. Toledo chpt.). Address: 2514 Bexford Pl Toledo OH 43606

ROMANS, ROBERT CHARLES, biological sciences educator; b. Hawthorne, Wis., Oct. 12, 1937; s. James Harlan and Jeannette Caroline (Johnson) R.; m. Jean Marie Law, Jan. 4, 1983; 1 son, Bradley Keith. B.S., U. Wis.-Superior, 1965, M.S.T., 1966; Ph.D., Ariz. State U., 1969. Teaching asst. U. Wis.-Superior, 1965-66; research fellow Ariz. State U., Tempe, 1966-69; asst. prof. biol. sci. Bowling Green State U., Ohio, 1969-75, assoc. prof., 1975—. Editor: Geobotany, 1972; Geobotany II, 1976. Precinct committeeman Republican party, Foxboro, Wis., 1961; deacon Plain Congl. Ch., Bowling Green, Ohio, 1978-82. Recipient Disting. Teaching award Bowling Green State U. Alumni Assn., 1973, Faculty of Yr. award Alpha Lambda Delta, 1977, Faculty Excellence award Bowling Green State U. Student Govt. Assn., 1980. Mem. Internat. Orgn. Paleobotany, Bot. Soc. Am., Ohio Acad. Sci. (sec. 1983-84), Omicron Delta Kappa. Home: 940 Ferndale Ct Bowling Green OH 43402 Office: Biol Scis Bowling Green State U Bowling Green OH 43403

ROMBS, VINCENT JOSEPH, accountant, lawyer; b. Newport, Ky., Mar. 8, 1918; s. John Thomas and Mathilda (Fromhold) R.; student Xavier U., 1936-37; B.S. with honors, Southeastern U., 1941; J.D., Loyola U., Chgo., 1952; m. Ruth Burns, Aug. 15, 1942; 1 dau., Ellen (Mrs. James P. Herman). Bar: Ill. 1952. Tax ptnr. with local and nat. pub. acctg. firms, Chgo., 1952—; with firm Laventhol & Horwath, Chgo., 1970-75; of counsel Edelman & Rappaport, Chartered, 1975—, Ostrow Reisin Berk & Abrams, Ltd., 1977—. Bd. dirs. Miller Found. Served to lt. comdr., USNR, 1941-46. Recipient Scholarship Key award Delta Theta Phi, 1953. C.P.A., Ill. Mem. Am. Inst. C.P.A.s, Ill. Soc. C.P.A.s, Ill. Bar Assn. Home: 714 E Algonquin Rd #201 Arlington Heights IL 60005 Office: 1 N LaSalle St Suite 1714 Chicago IL 60602 also 676 St Clair St Suite 2100 Chicago IL 60611

ROMER, CARL WILLIAM, clergyman, goat farmer; b. nr. Bushong, Kans., July 28, 1904; s. C.H. William and Mary M. (Yount) R.; m. Violet Daisie Maxwell, June 1, 1930; children—Carl Louis, Francis William. Student Kans. State Coll., 1922-25; B.S., State U. Iowa, 1928; LL.B., Am. Extension U., 1929. Ordained to minisry Grace Christian Assemblies Ch., 1931. Instr. corr. study dept. math. Kans. State Coll., 1923-25; adminstr. pub. schs., Kans., 1925-27; head dept. engring. Rochester Jr. Coll., Minn., 1927-29; acting head dept. engring. Baker U., Baldwin, Kans., 1929-30, Ripon Coll., Wis., 1930-31; acct., adminstr. U.S. Post Office, Admire, Kans., 1935—; pastor Gospel Story Hour radio ministry, Emporia, Kans., 1944—; justice of peace, Admire, 1951—; lectr. Editor, pub.: Dairy Goat Year Book, 1942-68, Bible Expository volumes Founder, Grace Bible Research Ctr., Kansas City, Mo., 1978, tchr. and course designer; evangelist. Mem. Nat. Soc. Live Stock Record Assns. (hon.), Kans. Dairy Goat Soc. (co-organizer, pres.), Am. Goat Soc. (pres., bd. dirs.), French Alpine Breeders Assn. Am. (bd. dirs.), Nat. Alpine Breed Promotion Club (co-organizer, pres., nat. bd. dirs.). Home: Ivy Twp Admire KS 66830 Office: 7900 E 66th St Kansas City MO 64133

ROMERO, RAYMOND GILBERT, lawyer; b. Albuquerque, Jan. 17, 1954; s. Jose Miguel and Celia (Griego) R.; m. Rosa Isela Fonseca, Aug. 11, 1979; 1 child, Bianca. B.A., Oberlin Coll., 1976; J.D., Northwestern U., 1979. Bar: Ill. 1980, U.S. Dist. Ct. (no. dist.) Ill. 1980, U.S. Ct. Appeals (7th and 9th cirs.) 1981. Staff atty. Legal Assistance Found., Chgo., 1979-80; staff atty. Mexican Am. Legal Def. and Ednl. Fund, Inc., Chgo., 1980-82, assoc. counsel, 1982—, also bd. dirs. Deacon, Chgo. United Ch., 1983—; bd. dirs. ACLU, Chgo., 1980—, Friends of Chgo. Pub. Library, 1981-83, Casa Aztlan, Chgo., 1981-83. Named Outstanding Young Man Am., U.S. Jaycees, 1982; recipient Community Service award Latin Am. Police Assn., Chgo., 1984; named Atty. of Year, DePaul Latino Law Student Assn., 1985. Office: Mexican Am Legal Def and Ednl Fund Inc 343 S Dearborn Suite 910 Chicago IL 60604

ROMICK, JEROME MICHAEL, health care company executive; b. Houston, May 7, 1943; s. Arthur and Lillian Y. (Smolensky) R.; B.B.A., U. Tex., 1967; m. Ina Sue Hirsch, Aug. 8, 1971; 1 dau., Stephanie Alisha. With Procter & Gamble, Corpus Christi, 1967-68; self-employed, Victoria, Tex., 1968-69; with Drustar, Inc., Grove City, Ohio, 1969-72; pres. Artromick Internat., Inc., Columbus, Ohio, 1972—. Trustee, Citizens Research, Inc., Columbus, 1978-79. Served with U.S. Army, 1964-69. Recipient Small Bus. Person of Yr. award SBA, 1977. Mem. Am. Soc. Cons. Pharmacists (asso.), Am. Soc. Hosp. Pharmacists. Jewish. Patentee on unit dose medication handling system, 1974, visible file card system, 1977, others. Home: 170 N Drexel St Bexley OH 43209 Office: 2008 Zettler Rd Columbus OH 43227

ROMKEMA, ROBERT JOHN, business financing executive; b. Grand Rapids, Mich., Dec. 17, 1930; s. Joe and Violet E., (Anderson) R.; m. Elizabeth J. Musser, June 23, 1952; children—Linda, Sandra, Joe, Todd. B.S., Mich. State U., 1952. Registered profl. engr., Mich. Phys. plant supr. Grand Valley Coll., Mich., 1963-75; v.p. bus. fin. Eastern Mich. U., 1975—. Home: 1257 Island Dr 204 Ann Arbor MI 48105 Office: Eastern Mich Univ Room 137 Pierce Hall Ypsilanti MI 48197

ROMNESS, SHARON LEE, psychiat. nurse, counselor; b. Chgo., Feb. 6, 1945; d. Naurice Orville and Helen Francis (Olsen) R.; B.S.N., St. Olaf Coll., 1967; M.N., U. Wash., 1970; M.A., Roosevelt U., 1978; postgrad. Northwestern U., 1979—. Instr. psychiat. nursing U. Wis., Eau Claire, 1970-72; psychiat. clin. nurse specialist Lutheran Gen. Hosp., Park Ridge, 1972-73, program coordinator in patient psychiatry, 1973-77, developer Human Resource Center, 1979-80, coordinator employee assistance program Employee Health Center, 1980-83, staff asso. to v.p. human relations, 1977-79; psychotherapist to patients with chronic diseases, 1972—. NIMH stipend, 1968-69. Mem. Am. Diabetes Assn., Am. Nurses Assn., Ill. Psychol. Assn. (asso.), Am. Psychol. Assn. (asso.), Sigma Theta Tau, Phi Kappa Delta. Lutheran. Office: 1775 Dempster St Park Ridge IL 60068

ROMOSER, WILLIAM SHERBURNE, zoology educator; b. Columbus, Ohio, Oct. 18, 1940; s. William Karl and Clara Frances (Sherburne) R.; 1 child, Anne Elizabeth; m. Margaret Ann Meeker, Oct. 20, 1973; children—Regan Eileen, Kelley Irene. B.S., Ohio State U., 1962, Ph.D., 1964. Asst., then assoc. prof. zoology, Ohio U., Athens, 1965-75, prof., 1976—; entomologist Fla. Med. Entomology Lab., Vero Beach, summers 1971, 73, 74; NRC sr. research assoc. dept. entomology, U.S. Army Med. Research Inst. for Infectious Diseases, Ft. Detrick, Frederick, Md., 1984-85. Author: The Science of Entomology, 1973, 2d edit., 1981. Contbr. articles to profl. jours. Mem. AAAS, Entomol. Soc. Am., Am. Mosquito Control Assn., Am. Soc. Tropical Medicine and Hygiene. Avocations: canoeing; reading; racquet ball, camping; bowling. Office: Dept Zoological and Biomed Sci Ohio U Athens OH 45701

ROMP, WALTER GARY, osteopath; b. Urbana, Ill., Oct. 12, 1944; s. Arthur J. and Florence Mary (Massey) R.; m. Carole Knutson, June 10, 1967; children—Chip, Cindy, Curt. B.A. in Chemistry, Duke U., 1966; D.O., Des Moines Coll. Osteo. Medicine and Surgery, 1971. Intern, Cleve. Clinic Found., 1971-72; gen. practice osteo. medicine, Sandusky, Ohio, 1972—; team physician Sandusky High Sch. varsity football team. Pres., Sandusky Bd. Edn. Recipient Golden Medalion award Squibb Co., 1977; named Outstanding Young Man of Yr., Sandusky Jaycees, 1977. Mem. Am. Osteo. Assn., Ohio Osteo. Assn. Republican. Episcopalian. Clubs: Rotary (dist. gov. 1982-83), Masons. Office: 1313 W Bogart Rd Sandusky OH 44870

RONGSTAD, ORRIN JAMES, wildlife ecology educator; b. Northfield, Wis., Apr. 22, 1931; s. Johnny Chester and Cora (Larson) R.; m. Bernice Dorthea Satter, June 30, 1962; children—Kurt Marshall, Neil James, Amy Lynn. B.S., U. Minn., 1959; M.S., U. Wis., 1963, Ph.D., 1965. Research fellow U. Minn.-Mpls., 1965-67; faculty U. Wis.-Madison, 1967—, now prof. dept. wildlife ecology. Contbr. articles to profl. jours. Served to 1st lt. USAF, 1952-57. Mem. Am. Soc. Mammalogists, Wildlife Soc., Audubon Soc. Lutheran. Avocations: hunting; fishing. Home: 1527 Middleton St Middleton WI 53562 Office: U Wis Dept Wildlife Ecology Madison WI 53706

RONINGEN, JEWEL EDGAR, stockyards exec.; b. Pelican Rapids, Minn., Jan. 15, 1922; s. James Marion and Effie Amanda (Holt) R.; B.S., N.D. State U., 1943; m. Grace Marlyn Carlen, Jan. 16, 1943; 1 son, Bruce Jewel. Instr. vocat. agr., Pelican Rapids, 1944-45; county extension agt., McIntosh, Minn., 1945-47; dist. supt. U.S. Dept. Agr., Packers & Stockyards Adminstrn., Sioux City, Iowa, 1948-58; pres., gen. mgr. Sioux Falls (S.D.) Stockyards Co., 1958-67; pres., gen. mgr. Union Stockyards Co. of Fargo, West Fargo, N.D., 1967—, also dir.; mem. N.D. Beef Commn., 1979-82. Served with USMCR, 1943-44. Recipient Pilot Study Grant, EPA, 1970, Gamma Sigma Delta award, 1966. Mem. Fargo (chmn. N.D. hwy. users conf. 1973-77, chmn. N.D. Hwy. Hall of Honor com. 1974-77), West Fargo chambers commerce. Lutheran (mem. stewardship com. 1968—). Mason (Shriner), Elk, Rotarian. Home: 213 21st Ave N Fargo ND 58102 Office: Livestock Exchange Bldg West Fargo ND 58078

ROOK, TIMOTHY E., English and communication educator; b. Mansfield, Ohio, Nov. 26, 1949; s. William E. and Joan M. (Guthrie) R.; m. Sheryl A. McQuown, Dec. 22, 1971 (div. 1984); 1 child, Heather Ann. B.A., Heidelberg Coll., Tiffin, Ohio, 1973; M.A., Bowling Green State U., Ohio, 1978, Ph.D., 1982. Vocat. counselor Bur. Vocat. Rehab., Tiffin, 1974-77; facility adminstr. Seneca County Youth Ctr., Tiffin, 1979-82; chmn. dept. English and communication arts Tiffin U., 1982—; speaker in field. Producer, dir., editor films. Mem. Speech Communication Assn., Ohio Forensic Assn., Alpha Psi Omega, Pi Kappa Delta. Democrat. Lutheran. Avocations: Writing, restoration of automatic musical instruments, photography. Office: Tiffin U 155 Miami St Tiffin OH 44883

ROONEY, NORMA G., college dean; b. Harvey, Ill.; d. John and Marie Rooney. B.A., DePaul U., 1959, M.A., 1961; Ph.D., Loyola U., 1970. Tchr. Bremen High Sch., Midlothian, Ill., 1961-66; asst. prof. Purdue U., Hammond, Ind., 1966-69; dean career edn. Thornton Community Coll., South Holland, Ill., 1969—; examiner Ill. State Bd. Edn., Springfield, 1977—; cons. North Central Assn., Chgo., 1975—. Bd. dirs. Pvt. Industry Council, Chgo., 1982; mem. Regional Econ. Devel. Council, Chicago Heights, Ill., 1984. Mem. Am. Vocat. Assn., Ill. Vocat. Assn., Articualtion Round Table, South Suburban Work Edn. Council (v.p., bd. dirs. 1982-84, cert. appreciation, 1984). Roman Catholic. Club: Network Women Mgrs. (Harvey). Avocations: opera, ballet, travel.

ROONEY, RICHARD JOSEPH, pharmacist; b. Sioux City, Iowa, May 5, 1951; s. Thomas Benedict and Margaret Eileen (Hogan) R.; m. Mary Ann Elizabeth Maixner, Aug. 31, 1974; children—Kathleen Marie, Elizabeth Ann, Megan Rose. B.S. in Pharmacy, U. Nebr.-Omaha, 1974, Pharm.D., 1984. Registered pharmacist. Pharmacist Jame's Drug, South Sioux City, Nebr., 1974-78; staff pharmacist VA, Beckley, W.Va., 1978-80, Omaha, 1980-84, pharmacy mgmt. trainee, Iowa City, 1984-85; asst. dir. Pharmacy service VA Med. Ctr., Shreveport, La., 1985—. Recipient Dorsey award U. Nebr.-Omaha, 1974, Bristol award, 1974; Regents scholar, U. Nebr.-Omaha, 1973; Health Profession grantee, 1973. Mem. Am. Soc. Hosp. Pharmacists, Nebr. Soc. Hosp. Pharmacists, Rho Chi. Democrat. Roman Catholic. Lodge: K.C. Avocations: hunting; fishing; gardening flowers, fruits, vegatables; bridge. Home: 15420 Farnam Circle Omaha NE 68154 Office: VA Med Ctr 510 E Stoner Shreveport LA 71130

ROOSA, JAN BERTOROTTA, clinical psychologist; b. Champaign, Ill., Apr. 19, 1927; s. Walter Laidlaw and Giannina (Bertorotta) R.; m. Joan Herr, Apr. 14, 1982. B.S., U. Ill., 1950; M.A., U. Denver, 1951, Ph.D., 1957. Coordinator, clin. psychologist Child Research Council, Kansas City, Mo., 1954-57; supr., psychologist State Hosp. Number 1, Fulton, Mo., 1957-59; chief of psychotherapy VA Hosp., Kansas City, 1959-63; clinical psychologist in pvt. practice, Kansas City area, 1963-69; dir., co-founder Learning Resource Ctr., Kansas City, 1969-79; dir. Gestalt, Social Competence Inst., Kansas City, 1969—. Active Conflict Resolution of Met. Kansas City. Served with USNR, 1945-47, 1951-52. Mem. Greater Kansas City Psychol. Assn., Mo. Psychol. Assn., Kansas Assn. Profl. Psychologists, Am. Psychol. Assn. Author: Situation-Options-Consequences-Simulation: A Technique for Teaching Social Skills, 1973; Psychological and Social Competence Model and Skills, 1975. Office: 400 E Red Bridge Rd 337 Kansas City MO 64131

ROOSE, PAUL EUGENE, osteopathic physician, orthopedic surgeon; b. Hart, Mich., Aug. 22, 1947; s. Walter Leon and Genevieve Avon (Watters) R. B.S., Wayne State U., 1969; D.O., Kirksville Coll. Osteo. Medicine, 1973. Cert. orthopedic surgery Am. Osteo. Acad. Orthopedic Surgery. Intern, Mt. Clemens (Mich.) Hosp., 1973-74; resident in orthopedic surgery Doctor's Hosp., Massillon, Ohio, 1974-78, orthopedic surgeon, 1978-79; orthopedic surgeon Mercy Hosp., Cadillac, Mich., 1979—; cons. orthopedic surgeon Reed City Hosp., Mercy Hosp. Grayling, Clare Osteo. Hosp. Recipient Geigy award, 1978. Mem. Am. Osteo. Assn., Am. Coll. Osteo. Surgeons, Am. Osteo. Acad. Orthopedic Surgeons, Wexford County Med. Soc. Contbr. articles to profl. jours.

ROOT, ANNE, nurse; b. Champaign, Ill., Apr. 6, 1943; d. Wallace Clark and Linda (Fitz-Gerald) Root. B.A., George Williams Coll., 1969; A.D.N. Prarie State Coll., 1981. R.N., Ill. Surg. technician Central DuPage Hosp., Winfield, Ill., 1973-79; staff nurse surg. intensive care St. Anthony Med. Ctr., Crown Point, Ind., 1983, St. Joseph Hosp., Joliet, Ill., 1983-84; operating room staff Olympia Fields Osteo. Hosp., Ill., 1984; Gary Meth. Hosp., Ind., 1985—. Mem. Am. Assn. Critical Care Nurses, Assn. Operating Room Nurses, Cert. Surg. Technicians, Internat. Arabian Horse Assn., Mid-Am. Arabian Horse Assn. (pres. 1979—), Abu Arabian Horse Club (bd. dirs. 1984-85), Arabian Horse Registry, Am. Horse Shows Assn., DAR, P.E.O. Republican. Methodist. Home: 3040 Alexander Crescent Flossmoor IL 60422

ROOT, ELEANOR, sculptress; b. Chgo., Mar. 4, 1910; d. Michael and Catherine (Bas) Muszynski; student public schs., Chgo.; m. Herman Root, Sept. 29, 1934; children—Joan Root Ericksen, Randy. Bookkeeper, sec. Mut. Benefit Health & Accident Co., Chgo., 1925-30, Pon & Co., Chgo., 1930-34, Root Bros., Chgo., 1934-44, part-time 1944—; sculptress numerous busts of pub. figures, 1965—; works include Mayor Daley in bronze for Chgo. Heart Assn., Mayor and Mrs. Daley for Chgo. Hist. Soc., Pres. and Mrs. Kennedy, 1965, Pres. and Mrs. Johnson, 1966, John Wayne, Pope John Paul II, John Cardinal Cody, Pres. Jimmy Carter. Pres., Bus. and Profl. Women's Club of Roseland, Chgo., 1971-74; v.p. Merchants of C. of C. in Roseland; hon. bd. dirs Heart Assn. of South Cook County. Recipient hons. as publicity chmn. District II, Bus. and Profl. Women's Clubs of Ill., 1972-75. Mem. Chgo. Heart Assn., Sun Found., Gastrointestinal Research Found., Am. Legion Aux. Democrat. Roman Catholic. Office: 10324 S Prairie Ave Chicago IL 60628

ROOT, SAMUEL I., geologist, educator; b. Winnipeg, Man., Can., Mar. 1, 1930; came to U.S., 1963, naturalized, 1969; s. Shep and Rose (Olasker) R.; m. Esther Saltzman, Nov. 16, 1952; children—Sharon, Malcolm, Joel. B.Sc., U. Man., 1952, M.Sc., 1956; Ph.D., Ohio State U., 1958. Exploration geologist Exxon Corp., Colombia, Peru, 1958-63, Brazil, 1978-83; chief mapping Pa. Geol. Survey, Harrisburg, 1963-78; prof. Coll. Wooster, Ohio, 1983—; cons. World Bank, 1983. Contbr. articles to profl. jours. Fellow Geol. Soc. Am.; mem. Am. Inst. Profl. Geologists (cert.), Am. Assn. Petroleum Geologists, Soc. Econ. Geologists. Office: Dept Geology Coll Wooster Wooster OH 44691

ROOT, THOMAS WOODROW, biology educator; b. Beloit, Wis., Nov. 6, 1939; s. Fay Howe and Vera Maude (Sakemiller) R.; m. Mary Francis Hutchinson, Dec. 11, 1965; children—Lisa Ann, Katherine Marie. B.S., U. Ill., 1964, M.S. in Forestry, 1966; M.S. in Botany, Western Ill. U., 1973. Mem. faculty Black Hawk Coll., Moline, Ill., 1966—, now prof. biology. Com. mem. Ambient Air Quality Coordinating Com., Rock Island, Ill., 1975—; sec., treas. Coop. Extension Council, Rock Island, 1979-85. Mem. Ill. Assn Community Coll. Biologists (regional rep. to exec. com. 1980-81, sec.-treas. 1982, pres. 1984). Home: 1701 35th St Moline IL 61265 Office: Dept Biology Black Hawk Coll 6600 34th Ave Moline IL 61265

ROOTS, JOHN MCCOOK, author, lecturer, foreign correspondent; b. Hankow, China (parents Am. citizens) Oct. 27, 1903; s. Logan Herbert and Eliza Lydia (McCook) R. B.A. cum laude, Harvard Coll., 1925. Contbr. New York Times, Herald Tribune, Atlantic Monthly, Asia, Pace, Look, Reader's Digest, Time, Saturday Rev., others, 1927—; traveling rep., dir. Moral Re-Armament teams, S. Africa, 1929-31, U.S., 1932, Great Britain, France, Switzerland, The Netherlands, Germany, Italy, Can. Belgium, East Africa, Greece, Middle East 1932-68; lectr. U.S. and Can., 1964-81; fgn. corr. various publs., numerous countries including China, Egypt, Israel, Jordan, Lebanon, Syria, Saudi Arabia, Indonesia, Iran, 1927-80; assoc. Up With People orgn., 1968—; author: Chou: a Biography of China's Legendary Chou En-lai, 1978. Recipient Washburn Prize for History, Harvard Coll., 1925. Clubs: Harvard (N.Y.C.), Army and Navy (Washington) Home and Office: Mackinac Island MI 49757

ROOZEN, MARY LOUISE, bank holding company executive; b. Milw., Mar. 31, 1921; d. Edward E. and Margaret (May) Silverman; m. Edwin Cramer Roozen, Sept. 18, 1943; children—Mary Katrina Roozen Hass, Joanna Roozen Satorius, Margaret Anne. B.A. in Speech, U. Wis., 1942. With Met. Milw. Assn. Commerce, 1942-43; adminstrv. asst. Curative Workshop of Milw., 1968-69; adminstrv. asst. mktg. Marine Corp., Milw., 1969-70, mktg. officer, 1970-73, asst. v.p., 1973-76, v.p. pub. relations, 1976-84, v.p. pvt. banking, 1984—; v.p. Marine Bank, N.A., Milw., 1977—; dir. Germantown Marine Bank, 1976-83; v.p. Marine Found., Plaza Bldg. Mgmt. Bd. dirs. Neighborhood House, Milw., 1963-78, Curative Workshop, Milw., 1970-78, Wis. Humane Soc., 1976-85, Friends of Art, Milw., 1980-84, Ozaukee Humane Soc., 1983—; bd. dirs. Met. Milw. Assn. Commerce, chmn. promotions com. 1979-80; co-chmn. capital fund drive Neighborhood House, Milw., 1984. Recipient Recognition award Nat. Ctr. for Voluntary Action, 1977. Mem. Pub. Relations Soc. Am. (chmn. fin. insts. sect. 1983-85, exec. com. 1980—), Wis. Sr. Pub. Relations Forum, Nat. Assn. Bank Women (chmn. Milw. group 1976-77), Women's Club of Wis. (mem. fin. com. 1983-85). Episcopalian. Club: River Tennis (Milw.). Home: 9111 W Hawthorne Rd Mequon WI 53092 Office: Marine Bank NA 111 E Wisconsin Ave PO Box 2033 Milwaukee WI 53201

ROPER, WILLIAM ALFORD, JR., financial executive; b. Birmingham, Ala., Mar. 14, 1946; s. William Alford and Mildred Marguerite (McCorstin) R.; m. Melanie Anthony, May 26, 1984. B.A., U. Miss., 1968; degree in maths, Southwestern Grad. Sch. Banking, So. Meth. U., 1974. Br. mgr. Deposit Guaranty, Jackson, Miss., 1968-74; exec. v.p. Dobbs Industries, Atlanta, 1974-75; v.p., gen. mgr. Martin Sch. Equipment Co., Jackson, 1975-81, now dir.; treas. Bell & Howell Co., Chgo., 1981—; dir. Bell & Howell Acceptance Corp., Chgo., Allendale Ins., Chgo., Chgo. Community Ventures, Inc., SBIC. Republican. Baptist. Avocations: tennis; antiques; automobiles; travel. Home: 576 Sheridan Sq Evanston IL 60202 Office: Bell & Howell Co 5215 Old Orchard Rd Skokie IL 60077-1076

RORABACHER, DAVID BRUCE, chemistry educator, researcher, administrator; b. Ypsilanti, Mich., June 8, 1935; s. Bruce Turner and Grace Bridgman (Renwick) R.; m. Beverly Joan Brown, Mar. 8, 1958; children—Karin, John, Karl, Joanne. B.S. in Chemistry, U. Mich., 1957; Ph.D. in Chemistry, Purdue U., 1963. Research engr. Ford Motor Co., Dearborn, Mich., 1957-59; grad. asst. Purdue U., West Lafayette, Ind., 1959-63; mem. faculty Wayne State U., 1963—, assoc. dean, 1984—; research assoc. Max-Planck-Inst., Gottingen, West Germany, 1964-65. Co-editor: Mechanistic Aspects of Inorganic Reactions, 1982. Contbr. articles to profl. jours. Ford Motor Co. scholar, 1953-57; NSF Coop. Grad. fellow, 1961-63; NIH postdoctoral fellow, 1964-65; recipient Wayne State U. Faculty Recognition award, 1983. Mem. Am. Chem. Soc., Assn. Analytical Chemists Detroit, Sigma Xi, Phi Lambda Upsilon. Methodist. Home: 32131 Woody Rd Fraser MI 48026 Office: Wayne State U 175 Chemistry Detroit MI 48202

RORER, LEONARD GEORGE, psychology educator; b. Dixon, Ill., Dec. 24, 1932; s. Leonard Gleason and Marion Emma (Geyer) R.; B.A., Swarthmore (Pa.) Coll., 1954; Ph.D., U. Minn., 1963; m. Gail Evans, Apr. 30, 1958; children—Liat, Eric Evans; m. 2d, Nancy McKimens, Jan. 9, 1969; 1 dau., Mya Noelani. Research asso., then asso. dir. Oreg. Research Inst., Eugene, 1963-75; prof. psychology Miami U., Oxford, Ohio, 1975—, dir. clin. psychology tng. program, 1976—; pres. Oreg. Psychol. Assn., 1973-75. NIMH spl. research fellow, 1967-68; fellow Netherlands Inst. Advanced Study, 1971-72; postdoctoral fellow Inst. for Rational-Emotive Therapy, 1982-83. Mem. Am. Psychol. Assn. (council reps. 1968-72), Ohio Psychol. Assn., Midwestern Psychol. Assn., Assn. Advancement Behavior Therapy, Soc. Multivariate Exptl. Psychology. Author articles in field, mem. editorial bds. profl. jours. Home: 327 W Sycamore St Oxford OH 45056 Office: Psychology Dept Miami U Oxford OH 45056

ROSA, BRUNO ANGELO, automotive engineer, lawyer; b. Frisanco, Italy, May 12, 1940; came to U.S., 1946; s. Felix and Filomena (Dozzo) R.; m. Suzanne Marie Joyce, Apr. 30, 1966; children—Beth, Constance, Ann. B.S. in Mech. Engring., U. Toledo, 1962, J.D., 1971; M.S. in Nuclear Engring., Carnegie Mellon U., 1964. Registered profl. engr., Ohio. Bar: Ohio 1972. Aerospace engr. NASA, Cleve., 1962; research engr. TRW, Inc., 1966-67; with AP Parts Co., Toledo, 1967—, v.p. engring., 1975—. Bd. dirs., vice chmn. Automotive Exhaust Systems Mfg. Council, Teaneck, N.J., 1970—. Served to 1st lt. U.S. Army, 1963-65. Mem. Soc. Automotive Engrs., U. Toledo Alumni Assn. Office: AP Parts Co PO Box 965 Toledo OH 43696

ROSATI, DAVID ARTHUR (MASON), radio program director, announcer; b. Rochester, N.Y., Dec. 20, 1947; s. George Louis Rosati and Dorothy Rhea (Henderson) Du Breck; m. Margaret Alma Mattson, May 5, 1973 (div. 1978). Announcer, Sta. WSAY, Rochester, 1966-67; announcer, newsman Sta. WLEA, Hornell, N.Y., 1967-68, Sta. WENE, Endicott, N.Y., 1968-73; program dir. Sta. WBBF, Rochester, 1975-81, Sta. WGR, Buffalo, 1981-1983, Sta. WKRC, Cin., 1983—; pub. address announcer Rochester Amerks Hockey, 1980, Rochester Red Wings Baseball, 1981, Buffalo Sabers Hockey, 1984. Served with U.S. Army, 1968-71; Vietnam. Mem. AFTRA. Home: 1986 Robinway Dr Cincinnati OH 45230 Office: WKRC Radio 1906 Highland Ave Cincinnati OH 45219

ROSDAHL, CAROLINE BUNKER, nurse, educator author; b. Sauk Centre, Minn., May 15, 1937; d. Frank Everett and Pearl Louella (Gaalaas) Bunker; m. Ronald LeRoy Christensen, Dec. 19, 1981; 1 son by previous marriage, Keith Bunker Rosdahl. Assoc. in Liberal Arts, U. Minn., 1957, B.S. in Nursing, 1960, M.A. in Counseling and Guidance, 1968, also postgrad. R.N., Minn.; cert. tchr., adminstr., tchr. educator, vocat. edn. dir. Dir., Wright County Pub. Health Service, Buffalo, Minn., 1960-62; sch. nurse, counselor Hopkins (Minn.) Ind. Sch. Dist. 274, 1962-66; gen. staff nurse Hennepin County Med. Center, Mpls., 1964-66; instr. Northwestern Hosp. Sch. Nursing, Mpls., 1966-67; gen. staff nurse Med. Personnel Pool, Mpls., 1975—; instr. U. Minn., Mpls., 1971—; asst. dir. Anoka Area Vocat.-Tech. Inst., Minn., 1967—; site visitor Nat. League for Nursing, N.Y., 1982—; cons. McGraw-Hill, 1970-80; mem. nat. adv. com. in high sch. health careers Nat. Health Council, N.Y., 1970-73; mem. curriculum adv. com. Dist. 877, Buffalo, Minn., 1972-76; mem. U. Minn. Alumni Band, 1970—; ednl. cons. Gen. Coll. U. Minn., 1975-76. Named Woman of Distinction, 1982; EPDA fellow, 1975-76; Vocat. Rehab. trainee, 1966-67; Delta Kappa Gamma scholar, 1975-76. Mem. Minn. Vocat. Assn. (named Outstanding Vocat. Educator 1976), Am. Vocat. Assn., Nat. League for Nursing, Minn. Vocat. Asst. Dirs. Assn., Am. Nurses Assn., Minn. Nurses Assn., U. Minn. Alumni Assn., Mensa, Delta Kappa Gamma, Phi Mu. Lodge: Order Eastern Star. Author: (with E. Thompson) Textbook of Basic Nursing, 2d edit., 1973, sole author 3d edit., 1981, 4th edit., 1985; editor and cons. Nursing and Allied Health Series, 1976-80; contbr. articles on nursing edn. to profl. jours. Home: PO Box 95 Anoka MN 55305 Office: Anoka AVTI 1355 W Main St Anoka MN 55303

ROSE, CLIFFORD CHAUNCEY, electronics company executive; b. Huntington, W.Va., Feb. 16, 1930; s. Clifford and Vivian (Williams) R.; m. Helen Pace, Feb. 13, 1955; children—Vivian, Karen. Student Ohio State U., 1953-58. Instrumentation specialist Westinghouse Electric, Columbus, Ohio, 1954-69, facilities engr., 1953-76; founder, chief exec. officer, pres. Contronics, Columbus, 1965—; cons. in field. Asst. gen. exec. YMCA, Columbus, 1975-78. Served as electronics specialist USAF, 1950-53. Named Outstanding Black Entrepreneur, Ohio State U., 1978. Mem. Instrument Soc. Am., Aircraft Owners and Pilots Assn., Ohio State U. Alumni Assn. Clubs: Ohio State U. Pres., Ohio State U. Buckeye. Avocations: boating; fishing; model railroad building. Home: 183 Melyers Ct Worthington OH 43085 Office: Contronics 3021 E Dublin Granville Rd Columbus OH 43229

ROSE, DAVID E., lawyer; b. Columbus, Ohio, Feb. 21, 1944; s. Harvey S. and Florence (McCoy) R.; m. Virginia Lorenzen, June 3, 1967; 1 child, Suzanne. B.S., Ohio State U., 1966; J.D. Capital U., 1977. Bar: Ohio 1978, U.S. Dist. Ct. (no. dist.) Ohio 1982, U.S. Dist. Ct. (no. dist.) Tex. 1983, U.S. Supreme Ct. 1984, U.S. Ct. Appeals (5th, 6th, 7th, 8th cirs.) 1984, U.S. Dist. Ct. Nebr. 1984, U.S. Dist. Ct. (ea. and we. dists.) Wis. 1984. Mgr. prospecting O.M. Scott & Sons, Marysville, Ohio, 1967, regional sales mgr., 1969-71, mgr. retailer services, 1971-79; corp. atty. Na-Churs Plant Food Co., Marion, Ohio, 1979—. Served to 1st lt. U.S. Army, 1967-69. Mem. ABA, Ohio State Bar Assn., Marion County Bar Assn., Assn. Trial Lawyers Am. Home: 2125 Olde Sawmill Blvd Dublin OH 43017 Office: Na-Churs Plant Food Co 421 Leader St Marion OH 43302

ROSE, ERNST, dentist; b. Oldenburg, Germany, July 22, 1932; s. William and Elsie (Lowenbach) R.; came to U.S., 1940, naturalized, 1946; B.S., Georgetown U., 1955; D.D.S., Western Res. U., 1963; m. Shirley Mae Glassman, Dec. 24, 1960; children—Ruth Ellen, Michele Ann, Daniel Scot, Seth Joseph. Intern, Waterbury (Conn.) Hosp., 1964; pvt. practice dentistry, Hubbard, Ohio, 1964—; pres., treas. Dr. Ernst Rose, Inc. Lab. instr. Ohio State U., Columbus, 1956-57; dental adviser Asso. Neighborhood Center. Mem. Liberty Twp. Zoning Commn., 1967-74; chmn., 1970-74; chmn. Hubbard (Ohio) Urban Renewal Com., 1968-74. Served with AUS, 1957-59. Fellow Royal Soc. Health; mem. Chgo. Dental Soc., Am., Ohio dental assns., Corydon Palmer Dental Soc. (mem. council 1983—), Warren Dental Soc., Hubbard C. of C. (dir. 1973—), Jewish Chatauqua Soc. (life), Alpha Omega (council mem. 1968—, sec. 1970-71, v.p. 1971-72, pres. 1972-73). Jewish (mem. brotherhood bd. 1967—, treas. 1971-73, pres. 1975-77, temple bd. dirs. 1975-84). Mem. B'nai B'rith (pres. 1970-71, trustee 1971—), Rotarian (vice chmn. Kashrut com. 1983-85, chmn. Mikvah com. 1983—). Home: 418 Arbor Circle Youngstown OH 44505 Office: 30 N Main St Hubbard OH 44425

ROSE, GLADYS DORTCH, cytotechnologist; b. Memphis, Sept. 6, 1939; d. William Tell and Lillie (Thompson) Dortch; B.S., LeMoyne Coll., 1959; cert. in cytotech. U. Tenn., 1961; M.S. in Organizational Psychology, So. Ill. U., Edwardsville, 1978; m. Lucius Victor Rose, June 17, 1967; 1 dau., Gladys Ann. Substitute tchr. Memphis Public Schs., 1959, 61; supr. cytology Western Bapt. Hosp., Paduchah, Ky., 1961-67; part-time cytotechnologist Cardinal Glennon Hosp., St. Louis, 1979-82; ednl. coordinator profl. edn. in cytology St. Louis U. Sch. Medicine, 1980-81; supr. cytology lab. St. Luke's Hosp., St. Louis, 1967—; cons. in field. Recipient various service awards. Mem. Am. Soc. Clin. Pathology, Am. Cytology Soc., St. Louis Cytology Soc., St. Louis Med. Tech. Soc., Am. Public Health Assn., LWV, Nat. Assn. Univ. Women, Sigma Gamma Rho. Mem. A.M.E. Ch. Club: Order Calanthe. Author articles in field. Home: 7006 Stanford St St Louis MO 63130 Office: 5535 Delmar St St Louis MO 63112

ROSE, IRWIN WILLIAM, optometrist; b. Chgo., May 9, 1926; s. Jacob Joseph and Dora (Eisenberg) Rosenstein; m. Estelle Klein, June 29, 1952; children—Karen, Steven, Lawrence, Beth. O.D., Monroe Coll., 1946; postgrad. Chgo. Coll. Optometry, 1949-52. Gen. practice optometry, Watseka, Ill., 1960—. Pres. bd. dirs. Iroquois Mental Health Ctr., 1979-85. Served to cpl. U.S. Army, 1946-47, 1953-54. Mem. Am. Optometric Assn., Ill. Optometric Assn. (exec. bd. 1966-67), Corn Belt Optical Soc., Optometric Extension Program. Hebrew. Lodges: Lions, Elks, Odd Fellows (noble grand 1964-65). Office: 223 E Mulberry St Watseka IL 60970

ROSE, JOSHUA S., publisher; b. Kansas City, Mo., Nov. 5, 1947; s. Stephen F. and Carol S. (Brady) R.; m. Melissa Shawn Mallin, May 30, 1970; 1 child, Rebecca. B. Journalism, U. Mo., 1969, M.B.A., 1973. Account exec. Bernstein & Rein, Kansas City, Mo., 1974-76; advt. dir. Sun Publs., Overland Park, Kans., 1976-79, co-pub., 1979—; dir. Metcalf State Bank, Overland Park, 1984—, Humana Hosp. of Overland Park, 1980-83, Suburban Newspapers of Am., Chgo., 1980—. Pres. County Mental Health Bd., 1980-83. Named Outstanding Young Man, Met. Jaycees, 1982. Mem. Overland Park C. of C. (v.p.), Sigma Delta Chi. Club: Kansas City Press. Jewish.

ROSE, KAY ELLEN, insurance company official; b. Bay City, Mich., July 23, 1942; d. Frederick John and Margery Ellen (Palmer) Jankens; m. William Wallace Auger, July 23, 1960 (div. Mar. 1975); children—William Bruce, Sue Ellen; m. 2d, Robert James Rose, July 16, 1976. Diploma in gen. ins. Delta Coll., University Center, Mich., 1979. Cert. profl. ins. woman. Sec., Palmer Oil Co., Bay City, 1958-59; receptionist Drs. Wright and Chapin, Bay City, 1959-60; sec., bookkeeper Franklin Life Ins. Co., Bay City, 1973-75; agt. Shaw Ins. Agy., Inc., Bay City, 1975—, office mgr., 1977—, personal line coordinator, 1983—. Active United Fund, Bay County, Mich., 1982-83; mem. Am. Bus. Women-Penta Star, Bay City, 1983. Mem. Ins. Women of Saginaw Valley (sec. 1979-81, v.p. 1981-82, pres. 1982—, State Ins. Woman of Yr. award 1983), Ind. Ins. Agts. Bay County (sec.-treas. 1980—), Profl. Ins. Agts. Mich., Nat. Assn. Ins. Women (co-chmn. Mich. council 1983-84). Democrat. Methodist. Home: 207 N Kiesel St Bay City MI 48706 Office: Shaw Agy Inc 114 Washington Ave Bay City MI 48706

ROSE, KENNETH DWIGHT, physician; b. Hastings, Nebr., Sept. 8, 1912; s. Ralph A. and Iva (Snyder) R.; B.A., U. Nebr., 1941, M.A., 1943, M.D., 1947; m. Margaret Ellen McMaster, June 13, 1943; children—Beth Marie (Mrs. Robert Dwyer), Susan Kay (Mrs. Victor Kuklin), Douglas Kenneth, Priscilla Margaret (Mrs. Barry Cross), James Allen, John Steven, Mary Elizabeth (Mrs. Douglas Unger). Instr. bacteriology U. Nebr., Lincoln, 1943, research asst. Coll. Medicine, 1943-47, clinician, dir. div. med. research Health Service, 1959-73, dir. Phys. Fitness Research Lab., 1970-73, cons. physician, 1973—; intern Cin. Gen. Hosp., 1947-48; gen. practice medicine, Lincoln, 1948-59; mem. attending staff Bryan Meml. Hosp., staff physician emergency medicine, from 1973, now emeritus; emeritus staff Lincoln Gen. Hosp.; cons. physician to athletic dept. U. Nebr., Harris Labs., Eastmont Retirement Ctr. Served with M.C., AUS, 1943-46; to capt., M.C., AUS, 1954-56. Recipient Service citation USMC, Quantico, Va., 1969, Phys. Fitness Leadership award Nat. Jr. C. of C., 1971, Tuth Boynton award, 1974. Fellow Am. Coll. Sports Medicine (recipient Distinguished Service citation 1967, trustee 1969-73); mem. AMA (com. on med. aspects of sports 1965-73, com. exercise and phys. fitness 1965-72), Am. Acad. Family Practice, Nebr. Med. Soc., Nebr. Heart Assn., Nat. Athletic Trainers Assn. (hon.), Am. Orthopedic Soc. for Sports Medicine (hon.), Phi Beta Kappa, Sigma Xi, Phi Lambda Upsilon, Alpha Omega Alpha. Author: (with Jack Dies Martin) The Lazy Man's Guide to Physical Fitness, 1974; The Pioneer Rose Family of Adams County, Nebraska, 1983; Thoughts to Ponder While Waiting for the Doctor, 1983; A Search for Understanding—Memoirs of a Common Man, 1985. Emeritus mem. editorial bd. The Physician and Sports Medicine. Contbr. articles to med. jours. Home and office: Kilravock Farm RFD 8 Lincoln NE 68506

ROSE, PATRICIA ANN SHULTZ, pharmacist; b. St. Louis, July 4, 1958; d. Charles E. and Clotilda A. (Beffa) Shultz; m. Douglas Scott Rose, June 8, 1979; 1 child, Paul Scott. B.S. in Pharmacy, St. Louis Coll., 1982. Registered pharmacist, Mo., Ill. Hosp. student pharmacist Barnes Hosp., St. Louis, 1977-79; retail student pharmacist Walgreen's Drug Stores, St. Louis, 1979-80; hosp. student pharmacist St. Mary's Health Ctr., St. Louis, 1980-82; research grad. pharmacist Norcliff-Thayer Inc., St. Louis, 1982; IV additive/staff pharmacist Barnes Hosp., 1982-84; retail pharmacist Kare Drug Store, St. Louis, 1984—. Mem. St. Louis Soc. Hosp. Pharmacists, Rho Chi. Roman Catholic. Avocations: Needlecrafts; volleyball; baking; travel. Office: Kare Drug Store 5433 Southwest Saint Louis MO 63139

ROSE, PETER EDWARD, baseball player; b. Cin., Apr. 14, 1942; s. Harry R.; m. Karolyn Ann Englehardt (div.); children—Fawn, Peter.; m. Carol Woliung, Apr. 1984. With Cin. Reds, 1963-78, Phila. Phillies, 1979-83, Montreal Expos, 1984; player, mgr. Cin. Reds, 1984—; mem. Nat. League All-Star Team, 1965, 67-71, 73-79, 80-81. Author: (with Bob Hertzel) Charlie Hustle, 1975, Winning Baseball, 1976; (with Peter Golenback) Pete Rose on Hitting. Named Nat. League Rookie of Year, 1963; Most Valuable Player, 1973, World Series, 1975; Nat. League Player of Year The Sporting News, 1968; Ball Player of Decade, 1979. Second player in baseball history to exceed 4,000 hits. Office: Cin Reds 100 Riverfront Stadium Cincinnati OH 45202*

ROSE, RICHARD JOSEPH, psychology educator; b. Fairmont, Minn., Mar. 19, 1935; s. August Joseph and Catherine (Newville) R.; m. Virginia H. Leet, Sept. 15, 1956; children—Victoria, David, Kathryn, Daniel. B.A., U. Minn., 1957, Ph.D., 1964. Postdoctoral NSF research fellow, McGill U., Montreal, Que., 1964-65, asst. prof. U. Ill.-Urbana, 1965-69; assoc. prof. Ind. U., Bloomington, 1969-75, prof. psychology, med. genetics, 1975—; chmn. NIH Human Devel. Study Sect., Bethesda, Md., 1980-84. Author: Principles of Personality, 1976, Psychology of Personality, 1970. Cons. editor Jour. Abnormal Psychology, Am. Psychol. Assn., 1979—. Recipient James Shields Mem. award Behavior Genetics Assn., 1982; Internat. research program fellow NATO, Oslo, Norway, 1979; fellow John Fogarty Found., NIH, Helsinki, Finland, 1985. Mem. Soc. Behavior Medicine, Behavior Genetics Assn. (exec. bd. 1982), Sec. Epidemiology Am. Heart Assn., Research Soc. Alcoholism. Home: 1227 Southdowns Dr Bloomington IN 47401 Office: Dept Psychology Ind U Bloomington IN 47405

ROSE, ROBERT RICHARD, metal company executive; b. Chgo., Apr. 3, 1957; s. Robert K. and Dorothy T. (Syslo) R. A.A. in Electronics, Wright Coll., 1980. Dairy worker Kraml Dairy, Chgo., 1978-79; supr. Goldblatts Dept. Store, Chgo., 1979-80; plant mgr. James Metal, Chgo., 1980—; real estate salesman Abby Realty, Chgo., 1985—. Republican. Roman Catholic. Avocation: swimming. Home: 5843 N Oconto Chicago IL 60631 Office: James Metal 2929 N Oakley Chicago IL 60618

ROSE, ROSEMARY CATHERINE (S.), business official; b. Antigo, Wis., Jan. 2, 1931; d. Ernest J. and Rose F. Slizewski; secretarial cert. Bryant-Stratton Sch., Milw., 1953; real estate course Spencerian Sch., Milw., 1964-65; Am. Inst. Paralegal Studies, 1985-86; 1 child, Ted R. Lic. real estate broker, Wis. Adminstrv. asst. H. R. Salen, Waukesha, Wis., 1951-55; owner, operator motel, Brookfield, Wis., 1955-65, restaurant and dry cleaning plant, Lannon, Wis., 1960-65; exec. sec. E.P. Hoyer, New Berlin, Wis., 1967-70; owner, operator Sanitation Service Inc., Menomonee Falls, Wis., 1970-75, North Twin Supper Club, Phelps, Wis., 1975-79; v.p. systems O.L. Schilffarth Co. div. Crown Industries, Milw., 1979-82; adminstr. food service Meurer Bakeries of Milw., 1984; owner, operator R-Service Co., Germantown, Wis., 1980—; with Park East Hotel, Milw., 1984-85; office mgr. Cedar Disposal, Inc., Menomonee Falls, 1985—; gen. mgr. Hotel Rogers, Beaver Dam, Wis., 1982-83; broker, prin Alrose Realty Co. Mem. Nat. C. of C. for Women, Internat. Platform Assn., Nat. Assn. Female Execs. Home: N105 W15750 Hamilton Ct Germantown WI 53022 Office: N60 W16280 Kohler Ln Menomonee Falls WI 53051

ROSE, STANLEY JAY, newspaper executive; b. Kansas City, Mo., June 3, 1918; s. Joseph and Mae (Lund) R.; A.A., Los Angeles City Coll., 1939; B.J., U. Mo., 1941; m. Shirley Mallin, Oct. 7, 1942; children—Roberta Susan Rose Small, Stephen F. Chmn. bd., pub. Sun Publs., Inc., Overland Park, Kans., 1950—; pub. Kansas City (Mo.) Jewish Chronicle, Inc., 1964—, College Blvd. News, 1984—. Bd. dirs. Kaw Valley Heart Assn., Heart of Am. council Boy Scouts Am.; past chmn. bd. trustees Suburban Med Ctr.; trustee William Allen White Found.; mem. adv. council U. Kans. Med. Center. Served to lt. (j.g.) USNR, World War II; PTO. Recipient Sweepstakes, 1st place awards Kans. Better Newspaper Contest, 1968, 69, 70, 72, 73, William Allen White News Enterprise award, 1975; Bea Johnson award Am. Cancer Soc.; 1st place winner for gen. excellence Suburban Newspapers Am., 1983-84; honoree Matrix Table, 1980; named hon. col. Kans. Cav. Mem. Overland Park C. of C. (dir.), Kans. Assn. Commerce and Industry (dir.), Sigma Delta Chi. Mason (Shriner), Rotarian (Paul Harris fellow 1985). Club: Kansas City (Mo.) Press. Home: 8600 Mission Rd Prairie Village KS 66207 Office: Sun Publs Bldg Overland Park KS 66212

ROSELLE, WILLIAM CHARLES, librarian, educator; b. Vandergrift, Pa., June 30, 1936; s. William John and Suzanne Esther (Clever) R.; B.A., Thiel Coll., 1958; M.L.S., U. Pitts., 1963; m. Marsha Louise Lucas, Aug. 2, 1959; 1 son, Paul Lucas. Tchr., Milton Hershey Sch., Hershey, Pa., 1960-62; trainee Pa. State Library, 1962-63; asst. catalog librarian Pa. State U., 1963-65; engring., math. librarian U. Iowa, 1965-66, library adminstrv. asst., 1966-69, asst. dir. of libraries, 1969-71; prof., dir. library U. Wis.-Milw., 1971—, chmn. Morris Fromkin Meml. Lectr. com., 1972— chmn. planning task force on computing U. Wis. System, 1973-74, mem. library planning study com., 1978-79; chmn. computing mgmt. rev. team U. Wis.-Stout, 1976; chmn. Council U. Wis. Libraries, 1981-82; co-chmn. library automation task force, 1983-85; mem. bldg. com. Ctr. for Research Libraries, 1980-82. Served with U.S. Army, 1958-60. Fellow Am. Geog. Soc. (hon.); mem. ALA (life), Spl. Libraries Assn., Iowa Library Assn. (chmn. audit com. 1968-70, chmn. intellectual freedom com. 1969-70), Wis. Library Assn., Midwest Acad. Librarians Conf. (chmn. 1969-71), Council Wis. Librarians (chmn. 1973-74), AAUP (treas. U. Iowa chpt. 1969-70), Phi Kappa Phi, Beta Beta Beta, Beta Phi Mu, Phi Alpha Theta, Phi Delta Kappa. Lutheran. Contbr. articles to profl. jours. Editorial cons. Current Geog. Publs., 1978—, The Quest for Social Justice, 1983. Home: 324 Sunny Ln Thiensville WI 53092 Office: Univ of Wis-Milw Golda Meir Library PO Box 604 Milwaukee WI 53201

ROSEN, ARTHUR LEONARD, physiologist, educator; b. Chgo., Apr. 30, 1934; s. Victor and Edith (Gold) R.; m. Arlene Silver, Aug. 26, 1956; children—David, Laura. B.S., Roosevelt U., Chgo., 1957; M.S., U. Chgo., 1964, Ph.D., 1971. Physiologist, Michael Reese Hosp., Chgo., 1960-64, 77—, Hektoen Inst., Chgo., 1964-77; asst. prof. U. Ill.-Chgo., 1964-77, U. Chgo., 1981—. Contbr. articles to profl. jours. and chpts. to books. Served to Sp/4 Chem. Corps U.S. Army, 1958-60. Mem. Am. Physiol. Soc., IEEE, Shock Soc. Jewish. Avocation: chamber music. Home: 2323 Schiller St Wilmette IL 60091 Office: Dept Surgery Michael Reese Hosp 2900 S Ellis St Chicago IL 60616

ROSEN, BARRY HOWARD, museum director; b. Phila., June 26, 1942; s. Robert and Sylvia (Chanin) R.; m. Ann Adair Gould, Feb. 14, 1970; 1 son, David Joshua. B.S., Temple U., 1963, M.A., 1966; Ph.D., U. S.C., 1974. Asst. to provost U. S.C.-Columbia, 1973-74, asst. to pres., 1974-77; dir. museums, univ. archivist, dir. mus. mgmt. program, 1975-82; exec. dir. Kansas City Mus. (Mo.), 1982—; field reader Inst. Mus. Services, Washington, 1981—. Chmn. planning commn. Heritage League Kansas City, 1983—; mem. Kansas City Ctr. Mgmt. Assistance Task Force, 1983—; mem. spl. events com. Conv. and Visitors Bur., 1983—; mem. Kansas City Consensus-Task Force on Met. Funding, 1984, Mayors Task Force on Jazz Film Preservation, 1984. Mem. Am. Assn. State and Local History, Am. Assn. Museums (mem. accrediting com. 1982—), Midwest Mus. Conf., Mo. Mus. Assn. (dir. 1983), Heritage League Kansas City, Kansas City Arts Council. Jewish. Lodge: Rotary. Office: 3218 Gladstone Blvd Kansas City MO 64123

ROSEN, EDWARD MARSHALL, chemical engineer; b. Chgo., Jan. 28, 1930; s. Benjamin Gerson and Frances (Sokoloff) R.; m. Harriet Elaine Feinberg, Jan. 3, 1965; children—Howard, Sheila. B.S. Chem. Engring., Ill. Inst. Tech., 1951, M.S., 1953; Ph.D., U. Ill., 1959; postdoctoral Stanford U., 1962-63. Chem. engr., sr. fellow Monsanto Co., St. Louis, 1959—; sec. CACHE Corp., Austin, Tex., 1984—. Co-author: Material and Energy Computations, 1969. Contbr. articles to profl. jours. Served to cpl. U.S. Army, 1953-55. Mem. Am. Inst. Chem. Engring. (chmn. cast div. 1985). Home: 13022 Musket Ct Saint Louis MO 63146 Office: Monsanto Co CS7C 800 N Lindbergh Saint Louis MO 63167

ROSEN, MATTHEW STEPHEN, botanist, consultant; b. N.Y.C., Oct. 7, 1943; s. Norman and Lucille (Cass) R.; m. Deborah Louise Mackay, June 16, 1974 (div. Feb. 1983); children—Gabriel Mackay, Rebecca Mackay. M.F.Sc., Yale U., 1972; B.S., Cornell U., 1967. Instr. ornamental horticulture SUNY-Farmingdale, 1968-69; landscape designer Manhattan Gardener, N.Y.C., 1969-70; instr. ornamental horticulture McHenry County Coll., Crystal Lake, Ill., 1972-74; coordinator agrl. studies, asst. prof. biology, chemistry Mercer County Community Coll., West Windsor, N.J., 1974-79; botanical coordinator Des Moines Botanical Ctr., 1979—; cons. in field. Contbr. articles to profl. jours. Com. chmn. United Way Central Iowa, 1982, div. chmn. 1983-85; chmn. arts adv. com., bd. dirs. Arts and Recreation Council. Mem. Am. Assn. Botanical Gardens and Arboreta (edn. com.), Greater Des Moines C. of C. (team leader), Phi Kappa Phi, Pi Alpha Xi. Democrat. Jewish. Avocations: photography; reading; model trains; collecting old books; writing. Home: 1042 22d St West Des Moines IA 50265 Office: Des Moines Botanical Ctr 909 E River Dr Des Moines IA 50316

ROSEN, NORMAN ROBERT, engineering company executive, consultant; b. N.Y.C., Jan. 23, 1925; s. Samuel and Lydia (Marcus) R.; m. Beverly Ruth Rozansky, Feb. 15, 1953; children—Jacqueline Joyce, Max Steven, Miriam Rebecca. B.S., U.S. Mil. Acad., 1947; M.S.C.E., MIT, 1954; postgrad. U.S. Army War Coll., 1966. Registered profl. engr., Tex. D.C. Project mgr. Bechtel Inc., Washington, 1972, San Francisco, 1978; dir. spl. projects City and County of San Francisco, 1979-82; v.p. A. Epstein and Sons, Inc., Chgo., 1982-83, pres., 1983—. Served as col. U.S. Army, 1943-72; Korea, Vietnam. Home: 3100 N Sheridan Rd Chicago IL 60657 Office: A Epstein and Sons Inc 600 W Fulton St Chicago IL 60606

ROSEN, STEPHEN LOUIS, chemical engineering educator, educational administrator; b. N.Y.C., Nov. 25, 1937; s. Bernard J. and Jeannette (Schinasi) R.; B.S. in Chem. Engring., Cornell U., 1960, Ph.D., 1964; M.S., Princeton U., 1961. Asst. prof. Carnegie-Mellon U., Pitts., 1964-69, assoc. prof., 1969-75, prof., 1975-81; prof., chmn. dept. chem. engring. U. Toledo, Ohio, 1981—. Author: Fundamental Principles of Polymeric Materials, 1982. Contbr. articles to Encyclopedia Americana on Plastics, 1976. Contbr. articles to tech. jours. Mem. Am. Chem. Soc., Am. Inst. Chem. Engrs., Soc. Plastic Engrs., Sigma Xi, Phi Kappa Phi, Tau Beta Pi. Home: 2425 Bexford Pl Toledo OH 43606 Office: U Toledo 2801 W Bancroft St Toledo OH 43606

ROSENAUER, RONALD JAMES, organization executive, real estate broker; b. St. Joseph, Mo., Dec. 4, 1953; s. Carl James and Marilyn (McCabe) R. B.S. in History, Mo. Western State Coll., 1979, B.S. in Psychology, 1979, B.S. in Secondary Edn., 1979. Lic. real estate broker, Mo. Instr., pub. relations dir. Job Corps, St. Joseph, 1979-81; dir. recruitment for Job Corps Northwest Mo., Joint Action in Community Service, St. Joseph, 1981-82; dir. program devel. Econ. Opportunity Corp., St. Joseph, 1982—; real estate broker, salesman Century 21/Vineyard Realty, also Pasek Realty, St. Joseph, 1978. Columnist, Sights and Sounds of St. Joseph mag. Notary pub., Mo. exec. dir. Apple Blossom Festival Assn., 1979—; chmn. Mayor's Com. on Community Beautification, 1979; chmn. Pony Express Festival Parade, St Joseph, 1979, Jesse James Festival Parade, 1982; pres. Com. for Good Govt.; mem. City Charter Commn., St. Joseph, 1980; v.p. St. Joseph Amateur Athletic Assn., 1981; chmn. Buchanan County Planning and Recreation Commn., 1983-84; 8th ward committeeman Democratic party; chmn. Mo. 8th legis. dist. com.; chmn. Mo. 34th senatorial dist. com. Mem. St. Joseph Jaycees (Jaycee of Yr. 1980, pres. 1980-81, chmn. bd. 1981-82), St. Joseph Area C. of C. (Diplomats Club, urban devel., convs. and tourism, awareness coms.), Downtown St. Joseph Inc., Mo. Assn. for Community Action (legis. and edn. com., pub. informational functional group), Mo. Assn. Realtors (publicity and pub. relations com.), St. Joseph Bd. Realtors (chmn. neighborhood revitalization com. 1980, chmn. pub. relations com. 1982, edn. com.), Am. Mgmt. Assn., Mo. Tchrs. Assn., Mental Health Assn. St. Joseph, St. Joseph Assn. Realtors, Nat. Assn. Realtors, Mo. Western State Coll. Alumni Assn. Roman Catholic. Lodges: Eagles, Shriners, Lions, Optimists, Toastmasters. Avocations: tennis; bowling; bicycling; golf; fishing. Home: 1329 S 22d St Saint Joseph MO 64507 Office: Econ Opportunity Corp 113 7th St Saint Joseph MO 64501

ROSENBAUM, FRANK ALFRED, accountant; b. Chgo., July 21, 1945; s. Harold E. and Rosetta V. (McKeown) R.; m. Jill C. Cunningham, Sept. 26, 1970; children—Daryl, Julie, Bryan. B.S., So. Ill. U., 1969; M.B.A., U. Mich., 1975. C.P.A., Mich. Fin. analyst Ford Motor Co., Dearborn, Mich., 1969-76; supr. Peat Marwick Mitchell & Co., Detroit, 1976-79; prin. Frank A. Rosenbaum, P.C., West Bloomfield, Mich., 1979—. Bd. dirs. Mich. Assn. for Elderly, Deaf and Hearing Impaired, Royal Oak, Mich., 1982—. Mem. Am. Inst. C.P.A.s, Mich. Assn. C.P.A.s., U. Mich. Alumni Assn. Home: 5535 Beauchamp Pl Dr West Bloomfield MI 48033 Office: 5600 Maple St Suite 202 West Bloomfield MI 48033

ROSENBAUM, RANDALL, chamber orchestra manager; b. Phila., Dec. 29, 1954; s. Israel J. and Berta (Lesla) R.; m. Claire Marie Hennessy, Oct. 23, 1954; children—Jane Marie, Hannah Margaret. B.Mus.Ed., Temple U., 1976. Gen. mgr. Asheville (N.C.) Symphony, 1979-81; gen. mgr. Rome (Ga.) Symphony Orch., 1980; asst. to mgr. Jacksonville Symphony (Fla.), 1979; intern Am. Symphony Orch. League, Washington, 1979; gen. mgr. Ohio Chamber Orch., Cleve., 1981—. Mem. Am. Symphony Orchestra League, Orgn. Ohio Orchestras. Democrat. Jewish. Club: City of Cleveland. Office: 11125 Magnolia Dr Cleveland OH 44106

ROSENBERG, ABRAHAM, biochemistry educator; b. N.Y.C., Aug. 12, 1924; s. Isaac Joseph and Helen (Bohrer) R.; m. Estelle Rumanek, June 20, 1948; children—Ruth Ann, Jonathan. B.Sc., U. Ill., 1947; M.Sc., Poly. Inst. Bklyn., 1952; Ph.D., Columbia U., 1957. Research assoc. biochemistry Columbia U., N.Y.C., 1957-60, N.Y. Heart Assn. sr. postdoctoral fellow, 1960, asst. prof. biochemistry Coll. Physicians and Surgeons, 1961-67; U. Gothenburg guest prof., 1967; assoc. prof. M.S. Hershey Med. Ctr., Pa., 1968-71, prof. biochemistry, 1971-79; prof., chmn. dept. biochemistry and biophysics Loyola U. Stritch Sch. Medicine, Maywood, Ill., 1979-84, dir. div. developmental path. neurochemistry, 1984—; mem. mental retardation research com. Nat. Inst. Child Health and Human Devel., Washington, 1974-82; mem. med. adv. bd. Leukemia Research Found., Chgo., 1983—. Author: Biological Roles of Sialic Acid, 1967. Contbr. articles to profl. jours. Served with AUS, 1942-46, ETO. NIH research grantee, 1961—; Fulbright fellow U. Strasbourg, 1974. Fellow Am. Inst. Chemists; mem. Am. Soc. Biol. Chemists, Sigma Xi. Democrat. Jewish. Home: 325 N Oak Park Ave Oak Park IL 60302 Office: Stritch Sch Medicine Loyola U 2160 S 1st Ave Maywood IL 60302

ROSENBERG, CHARLES MARTIN, lawyer; b. Cleve., Nov. 8, 1942; s. Bernard Leonard and Helene (Rose) R.; m. Gayle T. Sernaker, June 22, 1969; children—Deborah Leigh, Alec Paul. B.A., Washington and Jefferson Coll., 1965; J.D., George Washington U., 1968. Bar: Ohio 1960, D.C. 1969, Fla. 1977. Trial atty. U.S. Dept. Justice, Washington, 1968-69; ptnr. Guren, Merritt, Feibel, Sogg & Cohen, Cleve., 1977-84, Benesch, Friedlander, Coplan & Aronoff, Cleve., 1984—. Trustee, Shaker Heights Library Bd., 1983-85. Served to capt. U.S. Army, 1969-73. Recipient Man of Yr. award Cleve. Jaycees, 1978. Mem. Ohio State Bar Assn., Fla. Bar Assn., D.C. Bar Assn. Jewish. Home: 21261 Almar Dr Shaker Heights OH 44122 Office: 850 Euclid Ave #1100 Cleveland OH 44114

ROSENBERG, DALE NORMAN, educator; b. St. Ansgar, Iowa, Dec. 12, 1928; s. Eddie Herman and Ella (Kirchgatter) R.; B.S., Mankato State Coll., 1956; M.Ed., U. S.D., 1959; postgrad. Ball State Tchrs. Coll., 1962, U. Nebr., 1961, Colo. State Coll., 1963-67; D.Arts, U. Central Ariz., 1978; m. Delrose Ann Hermanson, Sept. 10, 1950; children—Jean Marie, James Norman, Julie Ann, Lisa Jo. Tchr. public schs., Holstein, Iowa, 1956-60; prin., guidance dir., Crystal Lake, Iowa, 1960-62; prin. Grafton (Iowa) Jr. High Sch., 1962-66; psychol. tester Dept. Rehab., State of Iowa, 1960-66; prof. psychology North Iowa Area Community Coll., Mason City, 1966—; vis. lectr. Buena Vista Coll., Storm Lake, Iowa, 1984; invited speaker Inst. Advanced Philosophic Research, 1984-85. Served with USAF, 1949-53. Mem. NEA, Iowa Edn. Assn., Kappa Delta Pi, Phi Delta Kappa. Lutheran. Author multi-media curriculum for teaching disadvantaged introductory welding; author textbook-workbook, 1985. Home: Rural Route 3 Mason City IA 50401 Office: North Iowa Area Community Coll Mason City IA 50401

ROSENBERG, JAY ARTHUR, lawyer; b. Phila., Oct. 23, 1939; s. Sidney and Beatrice (Silon) R.; m. Rachelle Roth, June 20, 1962; children—Elizabeth, Ross. B.S. in Econs., U. Pa., 1961; J.D. with distinction, U. Mich., 1965. Bar: Ohio 1966, U.S. Tax Ct. 1966, U.S. Dist. Ct. (so. dist.) Ohio 1966, U.S. Dist. Ct. (ea. dist.) Ky. 1980. Assoc., then ptnr. Strauss, Troy & Ruehcumann Co., Cin., 1966-83; ptnr. Porter, Wright & Morris, Cin., 1983—. Served with U.S. Army, 1961-62. Mem. ABA, Cin. Bar Assn., Ohio Land Title Assn. (trustee 1979-83, pres. 1983-84). Jewish. Office: 201 E 4th St Cincinnati OH 45202

ROSENBERG, SAMUEL NATHAN, French educator; b. N.Y.C., Jan. 19, 1936; s. Israel and Etta (Friedland) R. A.B., Columbia Coll., 1957; Ph.D. in Romance Langs., Johns Hopkins U., 1965. Instr. in French, Columbia U., N.Y.C., 1961-62; lectr. dept. French and Italian, Ind. U., Bloomington, 1962-65, asst. prof., 1965-69, assoc. prof., 1969-81, prof., 1981—. Author: Modern French 'Ce', 1970; (with others) Harper's Grammar of French, 1983; transl. (with others) Ami and Amile, 1981. Editor: Chanter M'Estuet: Songs of the Trouveres, 1981; The Lyrics and Melodies of Gace Brulé, 1985; (with others) French Secular Compositions of the Fourteenth Century, 1970-72. Contbr. articles to profl. jours. Pres. Mid-Am. Festival of Arts, Bloomington, 1984—. Woodrow Wilson Found. fellow, 1958-60; Fulbright Found. grantee, 1960-61. Mem. MLA, Medieval Acad. Am., Am. Assn. Tchrs. French, Internat. Courtly Lit. Soc., Am. Lit. Translators Assn., Phi Beta Kappa. Home: PO Box 1164 Bloomington IN 47402 Office: Dept French and Italian Ind U Bloomington IN 47405

ROSENBLATT, JUSTIN LEE, clothing manufacturer; b. Mpls., Feb. 26, 1915; s. David B. and Flora (Lewis) R.; m. Phyllis Banks, May 14, 1941; children—David, Justin, Debra. B.S. in Econs., U. Pa., 1937. Exec. trainee Macy's, N.Y.C., 1937-39; treas. D.B. Rosenblatt, Inc., Mpls., 1939-58, pres., 1958-79, chmn. bd., 1979—, also dir.; dir First Midwest Corp., Mpls. Mem. Minn. Apparel Assn. (pres. 1956). Republican. Jewish. Clubs: Minneapolis, Oak Ridge Country (pres. 1984-85) (Mpls.); Boca Raton (Fla.). Home: 4000 W 25th St Saint Louis Park MN 55416 Office: 912 Currie Ave Minneapolis MN 55403

ROSENBLOOM, JUDY REITER, public relations/marketing consulting executive; b. Chgo., Jan. 18, 1944; d. Delbert J. and Harriet (Green) Reiter; m. Jack Alan Rosenbloom, Apr. 25, 1965; children—Douglas, Gregory, Mary. B.A., Roosevelt U., Chgo., 1974, M.S. in Market Communications, 1978. Publicity asst. Braniff Internat., Chgo., 1962-69; asst. account exec. Janet Diederichs & Assocs., Inc., Chgo., 1971-75, account exec., 1975-79, account supr., 1979-81, v.p., 1981—; cons. to White House (press advance for Rosalyn Carter), 1979-80; lectr. in field. Publicity coordinator Connection Telephone Counseling and Referral Service, Libertyville, Ill., 1983. Mem. Exec. Club Chgo., Pub. Relations Soc. Am., Publicity Club Chgo. Democrat. Jewish. Club: Hadassah. Office: 333 N Michigan Ave Suite 1205 Chicago IL 60601

ROSENBLUM, KENNETH IRA, stock exchange executive, lawyer; b. Bklyn., Apr. 27, 1941; s. Max and Gertrude (Cohen) R.; m. Barbara Menschel, July 31, 1966; children—Joelle, Gregg. B.B.A., CCNY, 1962; J.D., St. John's Law Sch., 1965. With criminal div. Dept. Justice, 1965-68; br. chief SEC, 1968-72; gen. counsel Midwest Stock Exchange, Chgo., 1972-79, sr. v.p., 1979-80, exec. v.p., 1980-83, pres., 1983—. Bd. dirs. Chgo. Boys Club, 1981-83. Clubs: Bond, Execs. (dir. 1985—), Monroe, LaSalle. Avocations: golf; tennis; jogging. Office: Midwest Stock Exchange Inc 440 S LaSalle St Chicago IL 60605

ROSENDAHL, JOHN MARTIN, automotive company executive; b. Lansing, Mich., Mar. 11, 1946; s. Elmer George and Alma Hermine (Schmidt) R.; m. Bonne Sue Hale, Oct. 5, 1967 (div. 1978); 1 child, John Martin; m. Brenda Sue Bishop, Aug. 2, 1981. Bus. Mgmt. cum laude, Lansing Community Coll., 1975, Labor Relations, 1976. Inspector quality control Gen. Motors Corp., Lansing, Mich., 1965-73, supr. mfg., 1973-81, labor relations analyst, 1981-82, quality of work life coordinator, 1982-83, organizational devel. cons., 1983—. Bd. dirs. joint labor mgmt. com. Lansing Area Joint Labor Mgmt. Com., Inc., 1982—. Republican. Lutheran. Avocations: golf; racquetball; bicycling. Home: 6064 Carriage Hills East Lansing MI 48823 Office: BOC Lansing Car Assembly Body Plant 401 Verlinden St Lansing MI 48901

ROSENDALE, GEORGE WILLIAM, aircraft company executive; b. Keenan, Okla., Nov. 4, 1933; s. John Webster and Laura Lee (Schawo) R.; student Okla. Baptist U., 1957-58, U. Wichita, 1959-63; B.A. in English, Wichita State U., 1969, M.S. in Adminstrn., 1971; m. Penney Sue Tillotson, Dec. 27, 1964; children—James Christopher, Kathleen Marie, John Charles. Diplomate Personnel Accreditation Inst., 1977-83. Engring. draftsman Skyline Corp., Wichita, Kans., 1952, Boeing Aircraft Co., Wichita, Kans., 1953, O.A. Sutton Corp., Wichita, 1956, engring. checker, 1956-57; dept. clk. Cessna Aircraft Co., Wichita, 1958-59, bench hand, 1959-61, scheduling clk., 1961-62, mfg. scheduler, 1962-67, personnel rep., 1967-69, tng. supr., 1969-73, mgr. employee tng. and devel., 1973-84, mgr. personnel projects, 1984-85, mgr. mgmt. resource devel., 1985—; vocat. instr. evening sch. Wichita pub. schs., 1963; personnel adviser Wichita Police Res., 1969-73; treas. Haysville Police Res., 1975—. Area comdr. United Fund, Wichita, 1971; sec., Haysville Jr. Football League, Haysville, Kans., 1973-75; study com. chmn. Wichita Community Planning Council, 1972-73; mem. Haysville Planning Commn., 1976—, chmn., 1977-79, 80-84; exec. com. Kans. State Employment and Tng. Council, 1979-82, chmn. employment and tng. services com., 1981-82; mem. Kans. 107 Planning Com. for Vocat. Edn., 1981-84, chmn., 1983-84; mem. Kans. High Tech. Task Force for Vocat. Edn., 1983-84; mem. tng. adv. com. div. vocat. and continuing edn. Wichita Pub. Schs., 1974; Sunday sch. tchr. Olivet Bapt. Ch., Wichita, 1951-53; children's choir dir. 2d Gen. Hosp. Chapel, Ger., 1955-56; music dir. Southside Bapt. Ch., Wichita, 1956-57; minister music Bapt. Ch., Hominy, Okla., 1957-60, youth dir., 1958-60; dir. tng. First Bapt. Ch., Mulvane, Kans., 1981-82; numerous other ch. positions; bd. dirs. Christian Braile Found., 1971-74; bd. dirs. Amigos de SER, Wichita, 1975-77. 81—, vice chmn., 1983, chmn., 1984; bd. dirs. Kans. SER, Inc., 1981—, treas., 1983-84; bd. dirs. Am. Cancer Soc., Sedgwick County (Kans.) unit, 1977—, Ark-Valley Jr. Football League, 1974-75. Served with U.S. Army, 1953-56. Recipient Campaign award United Fund of Wichita, 1969, 70, 71, Outstanding Service plaque award Am. Cancer Soc., 1978, 79, 81, 82; SER Individual Support award, 1979, others. Mem. Am. Mgmt. Assn., Am. Soc. Personnel Adminstrn. (pres. Wichita chpt. 1973-74, past president's plaque award 1975, chmn. nat. tng. and devel. com. 1979), Psi Chi. Republican. Club: Optimist (chmn. community service 1985—) (Haysville). Home: 424 Hollywood Dr Wichita KS 67217 Office: Cessna Aircraft Div PO Box 7704 Wichita KS 67277

ROSENFELD, JOEL CHARLES, librarian; b. Bklyn., June 16, 1939. B.A., U. Mich., 1961, A.M. in L.S., 1964. Br. librarian Flint Pub. (Mich.) Library, 1962-66; adult services cons. Lincoln Trail Libraries, Champaign, Ill., 1967-68; dir. Urbana (Ill.) Free Library, 1968-74; exec. dir. Met. Library Service Agy., St. Paul, 1974-79; exec. dir. Rockford (Ill.) Pub. Library 1980—. Mem. ALA, Ill. Library Assn., Pub. Library Assn. (dir.-at-large 1980-81, pres. met. library sect. 1979-80). Office: Rockford Public Library 215 N Wyman St Rockford IL 61101

ROSENFELD, MARTIN JEROME, legal executive; b. Flint, Mich., Oct. 3, 1944; s. Israel Edward and Lillian Edith (Natchez) R.; B.A. (named Outstanding Sr. 1966), Mich. State U., 1968; 1981-84). honors, Ind. No. U., (com. chmn. 1979; 1 son, Joshua. Adminstr., Care Corp., Grand Rapids, Mich., 1969-70, Chandler Convalescent Center, Detroit, 1970-71, Grand Community Hosp., Detroit, 1971-73; exec. v.p., chief exec. officer Msgr. Clement Kern Hosp. Spl. Surgery, Warren, Mich., 1973-84; pres. M.J. Rosenfeld Assocs., 1984-85; chief operating officer Dickinson, Wright, Moon, Van Dusen and Freeman, 1985—; instr. Marygrove Coll., 1975—; assoc. prof. Mercy Coll., Detroit, 1978—. Vice pres. Detroit chpt. Jewish Nat. Fund, 1978—; pres. Cranbrook Village Homeowners Assn., 1977; chmn. Community Hosps. of Southeastern Mich.; mem. tech. work group Comprehensive Health Planning Council of Southeastern Mich.; mem. fin. mgmt. com., mem. hosp. affairs bd. Greater Detroit Area Hosp. Council; bd. dirs. Detroit Symphony Orch., 1984—; bd. dirs., mem. fund raising com. Detroit Met. Orch., 1984—. Mem. Am. Assn. Health care Cons., Royal Soc. Health, Am. Podiatry Assn. (com. hosps. 1981-84). Warren C. of C. (com. chmn. 1975). Author papers in field. Mem. editorial bd. The Human-Size Hosp.; mem. panel of experts The Health Care News. Office: 800 First Nat Bldg Detroit MI 48226

ROSENFELD, ROBERT THOMAS, lawyer; b. Cleve., July 2, 1933; s. William Henry and Rose B. (Gold) R.; m. Patricia A. Smith, Mar. 21, 1959 (div. 1975); children—Alison B., Abby S.; m. Vivian L. Smith, Apr. 6, 1975. A.B., Brown U., 1954; LL.B., Case Western Res. U., 1958. Bar: Ohio 1958, U.S. Supreme Ct. 1966. Field atty. Nat. Labor Relations Bd., Seattle and Cleve., 1958-62; ptnr. Rosenfeld & Palay, Cleve., 1962-70; sole practice, Cleve., 1970-72; ptnr. Rosenfeld & Gross, Cleve., 1972-83, Walter, Haverfield, Buescher & Chockley, Cleve., 1983—. Bd. dirs. Friends of Crawford Mus., Cleve., 1983-84. Served to comdr. USCGR, 1956-57. Mem. ABA (labor law sect.), Ohio Bar Assn., Cleve. Bar Assn. Republican. Jewish. Club: Classic Car Rolls Royce Owners. Avocation: car collecting. Home: 2675 Fairmount Blvd Cleveland Heights OH 44106 Office: Walter Hayerfield Buescher & Chockley 1215 Terminal Tower Cleveland OH 44113

ROSENFIELD, ALAN ROBERT, metallurgist; b. Chelsea, Mass., Sept. 7, 1931; s. Samuel Walter and Gertrude Florence (Lavetts) R.; m. Margaret Ann Young, May 15, 1960; children—Ann Baker, Joel William. B.S., MIT, 1953, M.S., 1955, Sc.D., 1959. Research assoc. MIT, Cambridge, 1959-61; research fellow Liverpool U., (U.K.), 1961-62; research leader Battelle Meml. Inst., Columbus, Ohio, 1962—; cons. Open U., Milton Keynes, U.K., 1974. Author: (with others) Materials Under Stress, Learning from Materials Failure. Editor: Dislocation Dynamics, Inelastic Behavior of Solids, What Does The Charpy Test Really Tell Us. Contbr. articles to profl. jours. Grantee various U.S. Govt. agencies. Mem. Am. Soc. Metals, AIME, ASTM, Am. Ceramic Soc., Japan Iron and Steel Inst. Avocations: reading, travel. Office: Battelle Columbus 505 King Ave Columbus OH 43201

ROSENFIELD, ROBERT LEE, pediatric endocrinologist, educator; b. Robinson, Ill., Dec. 16, 1934; s. Irving and Sadie (Osipe) R.; m. Sandra L. McVicker, Apr. 1, 1973. B.S., Northwestern U., 1956, M.D., 1960. Diplomate Am. Bd. Pediatric Endocrinology. Intern, Phila. Gen. Hosp. and Children's Hosp., Phila., 1960-63, 65-68; practice medicine specializing in pediatric endocrinology; prof. pediatrics, medicine U. Chgo., 1968—. Contbr. research articles to profl. jours. Served to capt. USMC, 1963-65. Fogarty Sr. Internat. fellow, USPHS, Weizmann Inst., Israel, 1977-78. Mem. Am. Pediatric Soc., Lawson Wilkins Pediatric Endocrinology Soc., Endocrine Soc., Chgo. Pediatric Soc. (pres. 1981). Democrat. Jewish. Avocation: photography. Home: 5474 S Greenwood Chicago IL 60615 Office: U Chgo Med Ctr 5825 S Maryland Chicago IL 60637

ROSENKRANZ, HERBERT S., environmental toxicology educator, cancer researcher; b. Vienna, Sept. 27, 1933; came to U.S., 1948; s. Samuel and Lea Rose (Marilles) R.; m. Deanna Eloise Green, Jan. 27, 1959; children—Pnina Gail, Eli Joshua, Marguerite E., Dara V., Jeremy Emil, Sara C., Naomi, Cynthia. B.S., CCNY, 1954; Ph.D., Cornell U., 1959. Research assoc. biochemistry U. Pa., Phila., 1960-61; asst. prof. microbiology Columbia U., N.Y.C., 1961-65, assoc. prof., 1965-69, prof., 1969-76; prof., chmn. microbiology dept. N.Y. Med. Coll., Valhalla, 1976-81; prof. Case Western Res. U., Cleve., 1981—, dir Ctr. Environ. Health Sci., 1981-84, chmn. dept. environ. health sci., 1985—. Lalor Found. awardee, 1963; Nat. Cancer Inst. Research Career Devel. awardee, 1965-75. Mem. Am. Assn. Cancer Research, Am. Soc. Biol. Chemists, Environ. Mutagen Soc., AAAS. Jewish. Office: Case Western Res U Med Sch Cleveland OH 44106

ROSENSTON, ALLEN MICHAEL, engineer; b. Chgo., Mar. 22, 1940; s. David and Lillian (Perlis) R.; m. Karey Phillips, Feb. 2, 1963; children—Gary Lee, Bradley Scott. B.S. in Indsl. Engring., U. Ill., 1963; M.B.A., Xavier U., Cin., 1975. Registered profl. engr., Ohio, Ill. Sr. prodn. engr. Westvaco, Meriden, Conn., 1963-66; sr. indsl. engr. Armstrong Rubber Co., Des Moines, Iowa, 1966-68, Tee Pak Inc., Danville, Ill., 1968-71; mgr. indls. engring. Abbott Labs., Columbus, Ohio, 1971-80, North Chicago, Ill., 1980—. Author: The Labor Productivity Index, 1975. Cub master White Oaks council Boy Scouts Am., 1975-78; trustee Columbus Hebrew Sch., 1977-80. Mem. Inst. Indsl. Engrs. (pres. 1975-77, Achievement award 1975-79, 82-83, chmn. devel. com. 1983—, sr. mem.). Lodge: B'nai B'rith (pres. 1982-84). Avocations: reading, bicycling, bowling, wood working. Home: 28 Somerset Ln Buffalo Grove IL 60090 Office: Abbott Labs 14th and Sheridan Rds North Chicago IL 60064

ROSENTHAL, ETHEL, statistician; b. N.Y.C., June 17, 1921; d. Samuel and Pauline (Herzstein) Gaines; m. Ira M. Rosenthal, Oct. 17, 1943; children—Anne M., Judith L. A.B., Barnard Coll., 1941; M.S., U. Chgo., 1962. Statistician/programmer U. Chgo., 1964-67, 68-74; statis. cons., Chgo., 1975—. Bd. dirs. Health Scis. Aux., U. Ill.-Chgo., 1974—. Mem. Am. Statis. Assn. Democrat. Jewish. Home and Office: 5490 South Shore Dr Chicago IL 60615

ROSENTHAL, LEIGHTON ARYA, clothing company executive; b. Buffalo, Jan. 27, 1915; s. Samuel and Sadie (Dosberg) R.; m. Honey R. Rousuck, June 30, 1940; children—Jane Rosenthal Horvitz, Cynthia Rosenthal Boardman. B.S., U. Pa., 1936; postgrad. Phila. Textile Sch., 1936. Pres., Cleve. Overall Co., 1956-61, Work Wear Corp., Inc., Cleve., 1961—; dir. Cleve. Bd. of Huntington Nat. Bank. Bd. dirs. Greater Cleve. Growth Assn., Ohio Motorists Assn., Vocat. Guidance and Rehab. Services; trustee Jewish Community Redn. Cleve., Mt. Sinai Hosp. Cleve.; mem.-at-large, bd. overseers Jewish Theol. Sem. Am.; trustee Samuel Rosenthal Found. Fellow Am. Assn. Jewish Edn. Clubs: 50 of Cleve, Oakwood, Clevelander, Commerce, Univ.; Poinciana (Palm Beach, Fla.); Marks, Anabels (London). Avocations: tennis, travel. Office: Work Wear Corp Inc 1768 E 25th St Cleveland OH 44114

ROSENTHAL, RICHARD, publishing and printing executive; b. Montreal, Que., Can., Mar. 14, 1942; m. Laura Fisher, 1962; children—Mark, Mike and Jeff (twins). Grad. exec. devel. program Western Res. U., 1966; cert. in gen. mgmt. Ont. Dept. Edn. Mgmt. Devel. Bus. Sch., 1969; B.A., U. Windsor (Ont., Can.), 1971. With Sumner Press, Windsor, 1960—, pres., 1978—; pres. Teleprint, Inc., Windsor, 1978—, Sumner Printing & Pub. Co. Ltd., 1974—; dir. Controlled Publs. Chmn. Windsor Town Hall Meetings, 1982-83; pres. Hospice of Windsor; bd. govs., mem. senate, mem. exec. com., chmn. external relations com. U. Windsor; cabinet mem. 1983-85 United Way campaign, Windsor; v.p. Windsor Jewish Community Council; pres. Congregation Beth El, Windsor, 1974-76, trustee, 1965—; chmn. corp. donations Team Can.; mem. nat. exec. United Isreal Appeal Can.; sec., bd. dirs. Windsor Symphony Soc. Named Citizen of Week, Sta.-CKWW, 1970, Outstanding Young Citizen, Windsor Jaycees, 1981; recipient Outstanding Young Can. award of Recognition, Can. Jaycees, 1978. Mem. Windsor C. of C. (treas.), U. Windsor Alumni Assn. (life; pres. Windsor chpt. 1979-80), Graphic Arts Industries Assn. Can., Printing Industries Am., Graphic Communications Computer Soc., Nat. Composition Assn., Pacesetter Users Group (pres. 1976-77), Assn. Systems Mgmt. (profl.), Can. Fedn. Ind. Bus., DECUS. Lodges: B'nai B'rith (past pres. Windsor lodge 1011, v.p. Can.), Rotary. Office: 680 E C Row Ave Windsor ON N9A 6P8 Canada

ROSEVEAR, JOHN, orthodontist; b. Hammond, Ind., July 26, 1948; s. Henry J. and Helen Rae (Elledge) R.; m. Cheryl L. Swanson, Apr. 28, 1984; children—Joseph Ray, William Matthew. Student Hanover Coll., 1966-69; D.D.S., Ind. U., 1973; M.S., Northwestern U., 1976. Practice dentistry specializing in orthodontics, Lansing, Ill., 1976—; guest lectr. Northwestern U., Chgo., 1984; world lectr. on lingual orthodontic technique, 1981—. Mem. Am. Dental Assn., Am. Assn. Orthodontists (membership com. 1982—), Ill. Soc. Orthodontists (v.p. 1984—), Ill. Soc. Orthodontics (v.p.). Lodge: Rotary. Office: 18333 Burnham Ave Lansing IL 60438

ROSHAK, MICHAEL STEPHEN, optometrist; b. Stevens Point, Wis., Apr. 4, 1919; s. Michael Anton and Mary (Borchardt) R.; m. Carolyn Pronz, June 2, 1945; children—Alan B., Bruce B. Pre-Optometry, U. Wis., 1952; D.O., Chgo. Coll. Optometry, 1955. Supr., Freeman Contact Lens Co., Chgo., 1947-48; gen. practice optometry, Milw., 1955—. Mem. Adv. Council to Mayor, Milw., 1960-61; chmn. Nat. Ave. Advancement Assn., Milw., 1963-65; del. Council Advancement Assn., Milw., 1964-67. Served with USAAF, 1940-45, PTO. Decorated Bronze Star; recipient Cert. Appreciation, U.S. Fish and Wildlife Service, 1977. Mem. Optometric Edn. Extension Program, Metroptic Assn., Southside Civic Assn., Omega Epsilon Phi (vice chancellor 1954). Lodges: Moose, Eagles. Avocations: hunting, fishing, photography. Home: 1122 S Layton Blvd Milwaukee WI 53215 Office: 3208 W National Ave Milwaukee WI 53215

ROSHEL, JOHN ALBERT, JR., orthodontist; b. Terre Haute, Ind., Apr. 7, 1941; s. John Albert and Mary M. (Griglione) R.; B.S., Ind. State U., 1963; D.D.S., Ind. U., 1966; M.S., U. Mich., 1968; m. Kathy Roshel; children—John Albert III, James Livingston, Angela Kay. Individual practice dentistry, specializing in orthodontics Terre Haute, 1968—. Mem. ADA, Am. Assn. Orthodontists, Terre Haute C. of C., Lambda Chi Alpha, Delta Sigma Delta, Omicron Kappa Upsilon. Clubs: Terre Haute Country, Lions, Elks, K.C. Roman Catholic. Home: 1305 Royce Ave Terre Haute IN 47802 Office: 4241 S 7th St Terre Haute IN 47802

ROSICH, RONALD ALLEN, pharmacist; b. Gary, Ind., Apr. 28, 1958; s. George and Paula Ann (Pickford) R.; m. April Heather Carden, Sept. 1, 1984. B.S. in Pharmacy, Purdue U., 1981; M.S. in Bus. Adminstrn., Ind. U., Gary, 1985. Registered pharmacist, Ind. Asst. mgr., pharmacist Hooks Drugs Inc., Hobart, Ind., 1981-82, Winamac, Ind., 1982-85, mgr., pharmacist, 1985—. Recipient Silver Knight award Hooks Drugs Inc., Indpls., 1982, 83, Gold Knight award, 1984. Mem. Ind. Pharmacist Assn., Aircraft Owners and Pilots Assn. Kappa Psi. Republican. Methodist. Club: Mentone Flying (Rochester, Ind.). Lodges: Masons, Shriners, Lions (v.p. 1984-85). Avocations: pilot; antique cars. Home: Four Seasons Estates 71 Rochester IN 46975 Office: Hooks Drugs 174 850 N Plymouth Rd Winamac IN 46996

ROSOV, ROBERT JOHN, biomedical engineer, administrator; b. N.Y.C., Jan. 18, 1936; m. Jeanne L. Gaylets; 4 children—S.B., MIT, 1957; M.S.E.E., Poly Inst., Bklyn., 1964. Cert. clin. engr., Internat. Cert. Commn. for Clin. Engring. and Biomed. Tech. Med. engr., cons. Culter-Hammer, Inc., Deer Park, N.Y., 1963-69; research assoc. Oreg. Research Inst., Eugene, 1969-74; dir. med. engring. Izaak Walton Killam Children's Hosp., Halifax, N.S., Can., 1974-78; dir. biomed. engring Health Central, Inc., Brooklyn Ctr., Minn.,

1978-79; adj. asst. prof. pediatrics U. Miami, Fla., 1979-81; dir. biomed. engring. research div. Inst. Logopedics, Wichita, Kans., 1981—. Contbr. articles to profl. jours. Patentee spoken questionnaire method and apparatus, 1973, automatic bacterial specimen streaker, 1973. Recipient contract award U.S. Dept. Edn., 1983-85; grantee Deafness Research Found., 1983, 84. Mem. IEEE, Assn. Profl. Engrs. N.S. (cert.). Office: Inst Logopedics 2400 Jardine Dr Wichita KS 67219

ROSS, ALAN STUART, newspaper copy editor; b. Chgo., Aug. 20, 1932; s. Charles K. and Eleanor Merle (Neville) R.; m. Marie Esther Sassower Kish, Feb. 15, 1970; stepchildren—Betty Jo, Bobbie Jo, Patricia Ann. Student U. Ill.-Chgo., 1950-53, U. Mo., 1953-55; B.A., Columbia Coll., 1959. Reporter, copy boy City News Bur., News 1957-58; city editor Centralia Sentinel, Ill., 1959-60; sports editor Seymour Tribune, Ind., 1960-63; night news editor Frankfort Times, Ind., 1963-65; copy editor Indpls Star 1965—. Author articles on jazz and boating. Served with U.S. Army, 1955-57. Mem Indpls. Newspaper Guild, Sigma Delta Chi. Democrat. Unitarian. Clubs: Toastmasters, Optimists, Riviera, Eagle Creek Sailing. Avocations: sailing; trumpet; jazz; tennis; golf. Office: Indianapolis Star 307 N Pennsylvania St Indianapolis IN 46206

ROSS, CHARLES AUGUSTUS, physician, hospital administrator, educator, surgeon; b. Pittsburg, Pa., Apr. 4, 1922; m. Janet McIntyre, Aug. 31, 1966. B.S., Oberlin Coll., 1943; M.D., Columbia U., 1946. Diplomate Am. Bd. Surgery, Am. Bd. Thoracic Surgery. Surg. intern Barnes Hosp., St. Louis, 1946-47; resident fellow in surgery Washington U., Barnes Hosp., St. Louis, 1947-48, asst. resident in surgery Barnes Hosp., 1950-51, sr. resident in thoracic surgery VA Hosp., Jefferson Barracks, Mo., 1951-53, asst. chief surgery, 1953; practice medicine specializing in thoracic surgery, 1953—; instr. thoracic surgery, Washington, 1953-54; thoracic surgeon Barnes Hosp., St. Louis, 1953-54; princ. thoracic surgeon J.N. Adam Meml. Hosp., Perrysburg, N.Y., 1954-56; cons. Gowanda State Homeopathic Hosp., 1954-56, Tri-County Meml. Hosp., N.Y., 1954-56; chstr. surgery U. Buffalo Sch. Medicine, 1954-58; chief thoracic surgery Roswell Park Meml. Inst., Buffalo, 1957-58; asst. clin. prof. surgery SUNY Sch. Medicine, Buffalo, 1958-68; dir. med. edn. Perth Amboy Gen. Hosp., N.J., 1968-70, Iowa Meth. Med. Ctr., Des Moines, 1970-73; med. cons. Iowa Disability Determination Services, Des Moines, 1974—. Contbr. chpts. in books, articles to Gastroenterology, Archives of Surgery, Jour. Thoracic Surgery, others. Served as chief surgeon U.S. Army, 1948-50; Austria. Mem. Am. Assn. Cancer Research, Polk County Med. Soc., Alpha Omega Alpha. Home: 7940 NW 63rd Ct Johnston IA 50131 Office: Iowa Disability Determination Services 510 E 12th St Des Moines IA 50319

ROSS, CHESTER WHEELER, clergyman; b. Evansville, Ind., Nov. 3, 1922; s. Mylo Wheeler and Irma (Berning) R.; A.B. cum laude, Kans. Wesleyan U., 1952; M.Div., Garrett Theol. Sem., 1954; D. Ministry, St. Paul Sch. Theology, 1979; m. Ruth Eulaine Briney, Aug. 30, 1949; children—James W., Deborah R., Judith K., Martha S., John W. Ordained to ministry United Meth. Ch., 1953; enlisted pvt. USAAF, 1942, advanced through grades to lt. col., 1968; chaplain, Africa, Europe, Alaska, Greenland, Taiwan; installation chaplain, Columbus AFB, Miss., 1972-75; ret., 1975; pastor Unity Parish, Iuka, Kans., 1975-80, Ness City (Kans.) United Meth. Ch., 1980. Instr. Parent Effectiveness Tng., 1st aid ARC; cubmaster, scoutmaster, dist. chmn. Boy Scouts Am., recipient Silver Beaver award, 1975; vol. parolee counselor; mem. USD 303 Sch. Bd. Decorated Air medal (2), Meritorious Service medal (2). Mem. Ness City Ministers Assn., Conf. Council on Fin. and Adminstrn., Mil. Chaplains Assn., Acad. Parish Clergy, Ret. Officers Assn., Res. Officers Assn., Air Force Aid, Air Force Assn., Nat. Hist. Soc., Appalachian Trail Conf., Menninger Found., Kans. Sheriffs Assn. Assn. Ret. Persons, Order Ky. Col., Am. Legion, VFW. Lodges: Rotary Internat. Platform Assn. Address: 417 N School Ness City KS 67560

ROSS, DALE GARAND, substance abuse therapist, programming consultant; b. Detroit, May 31, 1948; s. Stanley Anthony and Kathleen Mary (Moore) Jamros. B.S. in Psychology, Mich. State U., 1970; M.S.W., Wayne State U., 1980. Cert. Nat. Acad. Cert. Social Workers. Ptnr. Unicorns, Detroit, 1970-76; pres. Realities, Ltd., Birmingham, Mich., 1976-78; counselor I univ. counseling Wayne State U., Detroit, 1980-82, counselor II ednl. resources/disabilities, 1982-84, counselor II, univ. counseling, 1984-85; therapist Substance Abuse Ctr., Warren, Mich., 1985—; founding mem. Wellness Networks, Inc., Detroit, 1983-84; cons. in field; pvt. practice Oakland Inst., Royal Oak, Mich., 1983—; presenter programs. Contbr. articles to profl. jours. Program chmn. Motor City Bus. Forum, 1983-84, chmn. community ctr. com., 1982-83. Recipient Am. Legion award, 1966, Library Key award Hazel Park Pub. Schs., 1966; Mich. Bd. Govs. grantee, 1978-79, 79-80. Mem. Nat. Assn. Social Workers, Am Coll. Personnel Assn., (men's task force), Nat. Orgn. for Changing Men (mental health task group, co-chmn. job-work satisfaction task group), Mich. Personnel and Guidance Assn., Mich. Assn. for Specialists in Group Work, Mich. Mental Health and Agy. Counselors Assn., Mich. Alcohol and Addiction Assn., Am. Assn. Counseling Devel. Avocations: antiques; ceramics. Home: 24818 Rensselaer Oak Park MI 48237

ROSS, DANNA LOUISE, pharmacist; b. Kansas City, Mo., Aug. 3, 1956; d. Louis A. Derringer and Shirley Jean (Case) Sousley; m. Michael Albert Ross, Feb. 27, 1981. A.S., Southwest Bapt. Coll., 1976; B.S. in Pharmacy, U. Mo.-Kansas City, 1979. Registered pharmacist, Mo., Kans. Staff pharmacist Truman Med. Ctr., Kansas City, Mo., 1979-80; mgr. Revco Drug Store, Belton, Mo., 1980—. Barrett S. Hedden fellow, 1978, scholar, 1979; recipient Achievement award Am. Coll. Apothecaries, 1979; Rexall award U. Mo., 1979. Mem. Am. Pharm. Assn., Rho Chi. Avocations: racquetball; bicycling. Home: 2704 Cinnabar Raymore MO 64083 Office: Revco Drugs 1827 E North Ave Belton MO 64012

ROSS, DONA RUTH, speech and hearing specialist; b. Hot Springs, S.D., June 17, 1930; d. Gordon Richard and Margaret Elizabeth (Emery) Bartell; student Aims Jr. Coll., 1968-69; B.A. (state scholar), U. No. Colo., 1972, M.A., 1973; postgrad. U. S.D., 1975—, Black Hills State Coll., 1974-75, No. State Coll., 1981, U. Eastern N.Mex., 1973; children—Judy, Barbara, Dale, Peggy, Randall. Speech pathologist Shannon County Schs., Pine Ridge Indian Reservation, Batesland, S.D., 1973-76, Yankton (S.D.) Schs., 1976-77; prin. New Underwood (S.D.) Schs., 1977-80, Pierre (S.D.) Indian Learning Center, 1980-81; speech pathologist Office Indian Edn. Programs, Bur. Indian Affairs Schs., Pine Ridge (S.D.) Indian Reservation, 1981-83; supr. speech/hearing programs Aberdeen Area Coop. Service Unit, Pierre (S.D.) Indian Learning Ctr., 1983—; cons. Oglala Sioux Tribe Early Childhood Programs, 1973-80. Sec. Shannon County Democratic Party, 1975-76. Mem. Am. Speech, Lang. and Hearing Assn., Council for Exceptional Children. Democrat. Congregationalist. Home: 3902 W Saint Louis St Rapid City SD 57702 Office: Aberdeen Area Coop Service Unit Rt 3 Pierre SD 57501

ROSS, DONALD ROE, judge; b. Orleans, Nebr., June 8, 1922; s. Roe M. and Leila H. (Reed) R.; LL.B., U. Nebr., 1948; m. Janice S. Cook, Aug. 29, 1943; children—Susan Jane, Sharon Kay, Rebecca Lynn, Joan Christine, Donald Dean. Admitted to Nebr. bar, 1948; practice law, Lexington, Nebr., 1948-53; mem. firm Swarr, May, Royce, Smith, Andersen & Ross, 1956-70; U.S. atty. Dist. Nebr., 1953-56; gen. counsel Republican party Nebr., 1956-58; mem. Rep. Exec. Com. for Nebr., 1952-53, nat. com. mem. Nebr., 1958-70; vice chmn. Republican Nat. Com., 1965-70; U.S. circuit judge 8th Circuit. U.S. Ct. Appeals, 1971—. Mayor City of Lexington, 1953. Office: Federal Bldg Omaha NE 68101

ROSS, DOUGLAS ALLEN, art educator; b. Los Angeles, Jan. 23, 1937; s. John Leroy and Maxine Edith (Parker) R.; m. Suzanne Olson, June 10, 1960 (div. 1973); children—Jennifer, Charles; m. Anita Lavaughn Murphy, June 28, 1975; children—Michael Harms, Nick Harms, Mark Harms. B.A., Carleton Coll., 1959; M.F.A., U. Minn., 1965. Instr. art U. Nebr.-Lincoln, 1966-68, asst. prof., 1969-72, assoc. prof., 1972-77, prof., 1979—; lectr. grade II Manchester Coll. Art and Design, Eng., 1969-70. Sculptures represented in U. Tex., Tyler, Joslyn Art Mus., Omaha, Muscatine Art Ctr., Iowa. Democrat. Home: 1933 B St Lincoln NE 68502 Office: U Nebr 207 New Bldg City Campus Lincoln NE 68588

ROSS, E. EARL, juvenile worker; b. St. Louis, July 3, 1942; s. Edward Earl and Ruth Randles (Loewen) R.; B.A. in Psychology, Central Mo. State U., 1965; M.A. in Corrections, Webster Coll., Webster Groves, Mo., 1976; m. Mary Donna Moore, May 31, 1964; 1 son, Damon Moore. Reporter, Warrensburg (Mo.) Daily Star-Jour., 1965; social worker St. Louis County Welfare Div., Maplewood, Mo., 1966-68; asso. dist. scout exec. Boy Scouts Am., St. Louis, 1968; dep. juvenile officer St. Louis County Juvenile Ct., Clayton, Mo., 1969-72; program dir. St. Louis County Detention Center, Clayton, 1972—; asst. supt. St. Louis County Detention Center, Clayton, 1978—; trainer statewide detention staffs. Recipient Outstanding Detention Program award Nat. Council Juvenile and Family Ct. Judges, 1982. Mem. St. Louis County Juvenile Justice Assn., Am. Corrections Assn., Mo. Juvenile Justice Assn., Am. Mgmt. Assn. Home: 15333 Appalachian Trail Chesterfield MO 63017 Office: 501 S Brentwood Blvd Clayton MO 63105

ROSS, EDWARD, physician; b. Fairfield, Ala., Oct. 10, 1937; s. Horace and Carrie Lee (Griggs) R.; B.S., Clark Coll., 1959; M.D., Ind. U., 1963; m. Catherine I. Webster, Jan. 19, 1974; children—Edward, Ronald, Cheryl, Anthony. Intern, Marion County Gen. Hosp., Indpls., 1963; resident in internal medicine Ind. U., 1964-66, 68, cardiology research fellowship, 1968-70, clin. asst. prof. medicine, 1970; cardiologist Capitol Med. Assn., Indpls., 1970-74; pvt. practice medicine, specializing in cardiology, Indpls., 1974—; staff cardiologist Winona Meml. Hosp., Indpls.; Methodist Hosp., Indpls. Mem. Central Ind. Health Planning Council, 1972-73; dir. Ind. chpt. Am. Heart Assn., 1973-74; dir. multiphasic screening East Side Clinic, Flanner Ho. of Indpls., 1968-71; med. dir. Nat. Center for Health Service Research and Devel., HEW, 1970; dir. hyptertensive screening State of Ind., 1974. Served to capt., MC, USAF, 1966-68. Woodrow Wilson fellow, 1959; Nat. Found. Health scholar, 1955; Gorgas Found. scholar, 1955. Diplomate Am. Bd. Internal Medicine. Fellow Royal Soc. Promotion of Health (Eng.), Am. Coll. Angiology (v.p. fgn. affairs), Am. Coll. Cardiology; mem. AMA, Am. Soc. Contemporary Medicine and Surgery, Nat. Med. Assn. (council sci. assembly 1983-87), Ind. Med. Soc., Marion County Med. Soc., Am. Soc. Internal Medicine, Am. Heart Assn., Ind. Soc. Internal Medicine (pres. 1986), Aesculapean Med. Soc., Hoosier State Med. Assn. (pres. 1980-85), NAACP, Urban League, Alpha Omega Alpha, Alpha Kappa Mu, Beta Kappa Chi, Omega Psi Phi. Baptist. Sr. editor Jour. Vascular Medicine, 1983—. Office: 3171 N Meridian St Suite 201 Indianapolis IN 46208

ROSS, EDWIN FRANCIS, former hosp. adminstr., health care consultant; b. Struthers, Ohio, June 19, 1917; s. Edwin Francis and Ehtel Marie (Wymer) R.; B.S., Mt. Union Coll., 1939; M.H.A., Washington U., St. Louis, 1949; m. Virginia Kerr, Apr. 26, 1941; children—Richard, David. Tchr., Public Schs. Struthers, 1940-42; adminstrv. resident Huron Rd. Hosp., East Cleveland, 1948-49; adminstr. Doctor's Hosp., Cleveland Heights, 1949-53; asst. dir. Univ. Hosp., Cleve., 1953-62; adminstr. Univ. Hosp., Omaha, 1962-66; pres., chief exec. officer Fairview Gen. Hosp., Cleve., 1966-82; health care cons., Cleve., 1983—; mem. faculty Coll. Medicine, U. Nebr., 1962-66; pres. Cleve. Area League Nursing, 1956. Mem. Greater Cleve. Hosp. Assn. (pres. 1972-74, chmn. exec. council 1974-75), Ohio Hosp. Assn., Am. Hosp. Assn., Am. Coll. Hosp. Adminstrs. Republican. Presbyterian. Clubs: Masons, Kiwanis. Office: 18101 Lorain Ave Cleveland OH 44111

ROSS, ESTHER, nurse, educator; b. East Chicago, Ind., Feb. 10, 1935; d. Solomon anbd Mattie Louise (Harris) R.; children—Michael and Michele Evans (twins). Diploma, St. Margaret Hosp. Sch. Nursing, 1959; B.S., Coll. St. Francis, 1979. Surgery nurse aide St. Margaret Hosp., Hammond, Ind., 1952-53, operating room technician, 1953-56, operating room staff nurse, clin. instr., 1960-65; staff nurse operating room Meth. Hosp., Gary, Ind., 1966-67; operating room head nurse, operating room supr., asst. dir. nursing services St. Catherine Hosp., East Chicago, Ind., 1968-71; dir. nursing services Gary Family Health Ctr., 1971; health occupations instr. Gary Area Career Center, 1971—. Bd. dirs. Gary Hist. and Cultural Soc.; del. Ind. State Dem. Conv., 1976, 78, 82; mem. Gary Civic Chorale. Recipient Humanitarian award Women's Community Federated Club. Mem. AAHPER, Ind. Vocational Assn., NAACP, Ind. Health Occupations Assn., Gary Bus. and Profl. Women, St. Margaret Hosp. Alumnae. Democrat. Methodist.

ROSS, FRANK HOWARD, III, management consultant; b. Charlotte, N.C., Aug. 28, 1946; s. Frank Howard and Alma (Richardson) R.; B.S. in Engring., N.C. State U., 1968; m. Beverly Hazel Ross, June 30, 1973; children—Martha McCausland, Frank Howard IV. Cons., Fails & Assocs., Inc., Raleigh, N.C., 1968-73; ptnr. Ross-Payne & Assocs., Inc., Arlington Heights, Ill., 1973—; dir. Gilldorn Savs. Assn., Brickman Cos. Mem. Inst. Mgmt. Cons. Club: Barrington Hills Country. Author: More $ Through $ Management, 1975; MIS and You, 1978; Planning and Budgeting, 1979; Profit by Design, 1981; Pricing for Profit, 1983; Wealthbuilding, 1984. Home: 536 Eton Dr Barrington IL 60010 Office: 1114 N Arlington Heights Rd Arlington Heights IL 60004

ROSS, HAROLD ANTHONY, lawyer; b. Kent, Ohio, June 2, 1931; s. Jules and Helen Assumpta (Ferrara) R.; m. Elaine Louise Hunt, July 1, 1961; children—Leslie Ann, Gregory Edward, Jonathan Harold. B.A. magna cum laude, Case Western Res. U., 1953; J.D., Harvard U., 1956. Bar: Ohio 1956. Assoc. Marshman, Hornbeck, Hollington, Steadman & McLaughlin, Cleve., 1961-64; pres. Ross & Kraushaar Co., Cleve., 1964—; gen. counsel Brotherhood of Locomotive Engrs., Cleve., 1966—. Trustee Citizens League Greater Cleve., 1969-75, 76-82, pres., 1981-82; active Charter Rev. Com. North Olmsted, 1970, 75. Served with AUS, 1956-58. Mem. ABA (co-chair rwy. and airline labor law sect. 1976-78), Ohio State Bar Assn., Cleve. Bar Assn., Phi Beta Kappa, Delta Sigma Rho, Omicron Delta Kappa. Roman Catholic. Office: 1548 Standard Bldg 1370 Ontario St Cleveland OH 44113

ROSS, HENRY A., horticultural park administrator; b. Cleve., Dec. 7, 1926; s. John and Frances (Dobin) R. B.S. in Hort., Ohio State U., 1949. Dir., founder Gardenview Hort. Park, Strongsville, OH 1949—. Patentee flowering crabapples; various other hybrid originations. Served to cpl. U.S. Army, 1945-46. Recipient Conservation Achievement award Ohio Dept. Natural Resources, 1975; Pres.'s award Internat. Lilac Soc., 1980, Profl. Citation Am. Hort. Soc., 1981. Fellow Royal Hort. Soc.; mem. Am. Hort. Soc., Am. Hosta Soc., Am. Azalea Soc., Am. Magnolia Soc. Avocations: photography; breeding, collecting and introducing suprerior new ornamental plants. Home and Office: Gardenview Hort Park 16711 Pearl Rd Strongsville OH 44136

ROSS, LOIS M., interior designer; b. Detroit, July 16, 1933; d. Jack H. and Eve Ketai; student Wayne State U., 1952-53; m. Shelly Ross, June 13, 1953; children—Sheri Ross-Rabins, Jay. Freelance interior designer, Southfield, Mich., 1964-66; owner, designer Room at Bottom Design Studio, Southfield, 1966—; lectr. in field. Mem. Am. Soc. Interior Designers (certified profl.), Nat. Home Fashions League (certified interior designer; exec. v.p.-treas. 1978-80), Hadassah. Office: 26555 Evergreen Rd Southfield MI 48034

ROSS, MONTE, electrical engineer; b. Chgo., May 26, 1932; s. Jacob Henry and Mildred Amelia (Feller) R.; B.S. in Elec. Engring., U. Ill., 1953; M.S., Northwestern U., 1962; m. Harriet Jean Katz, Feb. 10, 1957; children—Karyn, Dianne, Ethan. Devel. engr. Chance Vought, Dallas, 1953-54; sr. electronics engr. Motorola, Chgo., 1955-56, project engr., 1957-59; asso. dir. research, 1960-63; dir. research Hallicrafters Co., Chgo., 1964-65; mgr. laser tech. McDonnell Douglas Astronautics Co., St. Louis, 1966-70, now dir. laser communications; program mgr. Laser Space Communications, 1971-82. Guest lectr. various univs.; cons. NSF. Mem. alumni bd. elec. engring. and computer engring. dept. U. Ill. Fellow IEEE; mem. Sigma Xi. Author: Laser Receivers, 1966; tech. editor Laser Application Series, vol. 1, 1971, vol. 2, 1974, vol. 3, 1977, vol. 4, 1980. Patentee in field. Home: 19 Beaver Dr Saint Louis MO 63141 Office: PO Box 516 McDonnell Douglas Saint Louis MO 63166

ROSS, NEIL L., eye surgeon; b. Chgo., Dec. 5, 1948; s. John Gunther and Doris (Serrins) R.; B.S.E.E., B.S., MIT, 1971; M.D., Northwestern U., 1975; m. Lynn Elizabeth Hauser, June 20, 1975. Resident in ophthalmology Northwestern U. Med. Sch., 1975-79, fellow in retina, 1979-80; practice medicine specializing in cataract surgery, DeKalb, Ill., 1980—; mem. staff Kishwaukee Community Hosp., DeKalb, Sycamore Mcpl. Hosp.; instr. dept. ophthalmology Northwestern U. Med. Sch., 1980—; clin. asst. prof. Ophthalmology U. Ill., 1982—; lectr. Northwestern U., 1982—; project ophthalmologist early treatment diabetic retinopathy study Nat. Eye Inst. Diplomate Am. Bd. Ophthalmology. Fellow ACS; mem. DeKalb County Med. Soc., Ill. State Med. Soc., AMA, Am. Acad. Ophthalmology, Chgo. Ophthal. Soc., Sigma Xi. Club: Rotary. Office: 8 Health Services Dr Suite 2 DeKalb IL 60115

ROSS, NORMAN ALEXANDER, banker; b. Miami, Fla., Jan. 30, 1922; s. Norman DeMille and Beatrice (Dowsett) R.; children—Isabel, Susan, Diani, A.B., Stanford U., 1946; postgrad. Trinity Coll. (Oxford, Eng.), 1953; D.H.L., Lincoln Coll., 1959, Fisk U., 1978, Roosevelt U., 1979; Litt. D., Lake Forest Coll., 1967. Airport mgr. Pan Am. Airways, 1943; asst. to producer Metro-Goldwyn-Mayer, 1943-44; ptnr. Norman Ross & Co., 1947-50; owner Norman Ross Record Club, 1951-52; radio-TV commentator NBC, ABC, Chgo., 1953-64, ABC, WGN and WBKB, Chgo., 1964-68; v.p. pub. affairs First Nat. Bank Chgo., 1968—; sr. v.p. communications dept., 1979-83, sr. v.p. community affairs, 1983—; pres. Ross-McElroy Prodns., Inc., 1962-68; forner columnist Chgo. Daily News. Served with AUS, World War II. Decorated cavaliere Dell Ordine Repubblica Italiana; U.S. Army Outstanding Civilian Service medal; officier and cross of chevalier Legion of Honor (France); recipient Peabody award for TV program Off the Cuff, 1964. Mem. Phi Gamma Delta. Clubs: Raquet, Oxford, Mid Day, Econ. (Chgo.); Wayfarers. Home: 1366 N Dearborn Chicago IL 60610 Office: 1 First Nat Plaza Chicago IL 60670

ROSS, PHILIP E., aerospace company official; b. Springfield, Ill., June 12, 1947; s. Robert Penn and Beverly (Ellinwood) R.; m. Phyllis Louise Ross, Nov. 19, 1965; children—Jaime Ellen, Mellissa Louise, Adam Christopher. A.S., Rock Valley Coll., 1968; B.S., No. Ill. U., 1973. With Sundstrand Aviation Corp., Rockford, Ill., 1968—, pricing group supr., 1976-79, sect. mgr. pricing advanced tech. group, 1979—. Mem. Nat. Contract Mgmt. Assn. Republican. Lutheran. Office: Sundstrand Advanced Tech Group 4747 Harrison Ave Rockford IL 61103

ROSS, RICHARD LEE, lawyer; b. Columbus, Ohio, Sept. 23, 1951; s. Richard Earl and Dorothy Mae (Fitch) R.; m. Diana E. Gifford, Aug. 17, 1974; chidlren—Rebecca, Jeremiah. B.S., Centre Coll., 1973; J.D., Capitol U., 1976. Bar: Ohio. Law librarian Morgan County, McConnelsville, Ohio, 1977-80; solicitor Stockport, Ohio, 1977-80; pros. atty. Morgan County, 1981—. Chmn. various Republican coms. Mem. Ohio Pros. Attys. Assn., Morgan County Bar Assn., Nat. Dist. Attys. Assn., Nat. Sch. Attys. Assn. Mem. Ch. of Christ. Lodge: Kiwanis (sec. 1977-79). Avocations: golf, reading. Home: 1800 Pleasant Valley Rd Malta OH 43748 Office: 6 W Main St McConnelsville OH 43756

ROSS, ROBERT E, optometrist; b. Tiffin, Ohio, Dec. 3, 1931; s. George Eldrige and Evelyn D. (Roper) R.; m. Shirley Ann Cole, Dec. 18, 1955; children—Dianna Lynn, Janet Kay, Jane Ellen, Judy Ann, Dean Edward. B.S. in Optometry, Ohio State U., 1957. Diplomate State Bd. Optometry, Ohio. Gen. practice optometry, Tiffin, Ohio, 1957—. Served with USAF, 1949-53. Mem. Ohio Optometric Assn. (zone gov. 1959), Am. Optometric Assn. (25 year award). Republican. Mem. United Ch. Christ. Lodges: Rotary (bd. dirs.), Elks, Moose, VFW. Avocations: golfing, swimming, skiing. Home: 345 Coe St Tiffin OH 44883 Office: 34 W Market St Box 430 Tiffin OH 44883

ROSS, STEVEN CHARLES, business administration educator, consultant; b. Salem, Oreg., Jan. 14, 1947; s. Charles Reed and Edythe Marie (Calvin) R.; m. Meredith Lynn Buholts, June 15, 1969; children—Kelly Lynn, Shannon Marie. B.S., Oreg. State U., 1969; M.S., U. Utah, 1976, Ph.D., 1980. Cons., IRS Tng. Staff, Ogden, Utah, 1977-80; asst. prof. Marquette U., Milw., 1980—; govt. and industry cons. Mem. adv. com. Milwaukee County Mgmt., 1981-85. Served to capt. U.S. Army, 1969-75. Recipient research fellowship, U. Utah, 1977-79, Marquette U., 1981-84. Mem. Acad. Mgmt., Am. Psychol. Assn., Am. Inst. Decision Scis., Assn. for Computing Machinery, Mensa. Home: 5000 N Larkin St Whitefish Bay WI 53217 Office: Coll Bus Adminstrn Marquette U Milwaukee WI 53233

ROSS, SUZANNE IRIS, fund raising executive; b. Chgo., Feb. 2, 1948; d. Irving and Rose (Stein) R. B.A. in Secondary Edn., Western Mich. U., 1971. Dir. youth employment Ill. Youth Services Bur., Maywood, Ill., 1978-79; exec. dir. Edn. Resource Ctr., Chgo., 1979-82; asst. dir. devel. Art Inst. Chgo., 1982-83, mgr. govt. affairs, 1983-84, dir. govt. affairs, 1984-85; v.p. devel. Spertus Coll. Judaica, Chgo., 1985—; lectr. Sch. Art Inst., Chgo., 1982-85, Ill. Fire Inspectors Assn., Mt. Prospect, Ill., 1982-84, Episcopalian Archdiocese, Chgo., 1984; instr. Columbia Coll., Chgo., 1980—. Mem. adv. council Citizens Com. on Media, Chgo., 1978-80; adv. panelist Chgo. Office Fine Arts, 1981-82; mem. adv. council Greater Chgo. Food Depository, 1984-85; exec. com. Chgo. Coalition Arts in Edn., 1981-82. Mem. Nat. Soc. Fund Raising Execs., Am. Assn. Mus., Am. Council Arts, Ill. Arts Alliance. Democrat. Jewish. Avocation: Attending cultural events. Home: 3709 N Janssen #2RB Chicago IL 60613 Office: Spertus Coll Judaica 618 S Michigan Ave Chicago IL 60605

ROSSA, JOSEPH JOHN, dentist; b. New Chicago, Ind., Feb. 5, 1912; s. Joseph and Anna (Kozlowski) R.; m. Elizabeth J. Seidel, Sept. 29, 1940; children—Joseph W., Gail E., Robert G. D.D.S., Loyola U., 1939. Pvt. practice dentistry, Chgo., 1939—. Chmn. bd. St. Andrew Home, Niles, Ill., 1983—; active student asst. fund Loyola Dental, Maywood, Ill., 1982-85. Served to 1st lt. U.S. Army, 1943-45. Mem. Dental Arts, ADA, Fedn. Dentaire Internat., Internat. Acad. Gen. Dentistry, Ill. Dental Assn., Chgo. Dental Assn., St. Hedwig's Alumni Assn. (bd. dirs. 1984—), Am. Legion. Roman Catholic. Club: Itasca Country (Ill.). Avocations: golf; fishing.

ROSSEEL-JONES, MARY LOUISE, lawyer, educator; b. Detroit, Apr. 19, 1951; d. Rene Octavius and Marie Anne (Metcko) Rosseel; m. Mark Christopher Jones, Mar. 16, 1984. B.A., U. Mich., 1973, M.A., 1976; J.D., U. Detroit, 1981. Bar: Mich. 1982, U.S. Dist. Ct. (ea. dist.) Mich. 1982, U.S. Dist. Ct. (we. dist.) Mich. 1983, U.S. Ct. Appeals (6th cir.) 1983. Clk., Hinks, Knight et al, Detroit, 1979-80, Johnson, Auld et al, Detroit, 1980-81; fgn. lectr. law U. Clermont, France, 1981-82; assoc., of counsel Monaghan, Campbell et al, Bloomfield Hills, Mich., 1982-83; assoc. staff atty. Mich. Nat. Corp., Clawson, 1983-85; litigation atty. Am. Motors Corp., 1985—. Teaching fellow Wayne State U., 1973-74; Julia Emmanuel scholarship Henderson House Alumni Assn., 1974-75; teaching fellow U. Mich., 1974-76. Mem. Women Lawyers Assn. Mich., U. Detroit Fgn. Assts. Alumni Assn., U. Mich. Alumni Assn., State Bar Mich., ABA. Democrat. Roman Catholic. Office: Am Motors Corp 23800 Northwestern Hwy Southfield MI 48034

ROSSER, RICHARD FRANKLIN, univ. pres.; b. Arcanum, Ohio, July 16, 1929; s. Harold Arm and Margaret (Whitacre) R.; m. Donna Eyssen., Mar. 21, 1951; children—Eric, Carl, Edward. B.A., Ohio Wesleyan U., 1951; M.P.A., Syracuse U., 1952, Ph.D., 1961. Joined U.S. Air Force, 1952, advanced through grades to col., 1968; prof. polit. sci. U.S. Air Force Acad., Colorado Springs, Colo., 1959-73, head dept., 1967-73, ret., 1973; prof. polit. sci., dean Albion (Mich.) Coll., 1973-77; pres. DePauw U., Greencastle, Ind., 1977—. Author: An Introduction to Soviet Foreign Policy, 1969; Contbr. articles to profl. jours. Decorated Legion of Merit with oak leaf cluster. Mem. Am. Polit. Sci. Assn., Internat. Studies Assn., Internat. Inst. Strategic Studies, AAUP, Am. Assn. Advancement Slavic Studies, Phi Beta Kappa, Omicron Delta Kappa. Methodist. Office: DePauw University Greencastle IN 46135

ROSSI, ANTHONY GERALD, lawyer; b. Warren, Ohio, July 20, 1935; s. Anthony G. and Lena M. (Guarnieri) R.; m. Marilyn J. Fuller, June 22, 1957; children—Diana L., Maribeth T., Anthony G. B.S., John Carroll U., 1957; J.D., Catholic U., 1961. Assoc., Guarnieri & Seerest, Warren, 1961—; acting judge Warren Municipal Ct., 1973—. Trustee, Trumbull Art Guild, Warren, Warren Civic Music Assn. Served to capt. U.S. Army, 1958. Mem. Trumbull County Bar Assn. (pres. 1976-77), Ohio State Bar Assn., ABA, Am. Hosp. Assn., Ohio Acad. Trial Lawyers, Soc. Ohio Hosp. Attys., Mahoning-Shenango Estate Planning Council (sec.), Am. Arbitration Assn. Democrat. Roman Catholic. Club: Warren Olympic (pres.). Lodge: K.C. Avocations: gardening; sports. Home: 2500 Hidden Lakes NE Warren OH 44484 Office: Guarnieri & Secrest 151 E Market St Warren OH 44481

ROSSI, EUGENE ENRICO, insurance agent; b. Warren, Ohio, May 12, 1926; s. Anthony G. and Lena Marie (Guarnieri) R.; m. Virginia L. Porter, Sept. 18, 1948; children—Michael D., E. Jeffrey, Dennis A., Gregory L. Degree in Bus. Adminstrn., Youngstown Coll., 1953. Ins. agt. Rossi Ins. Agy., Warren, Ohio, 1951—. Treas., St. Joseph Hosp. Found., Warren, 1970—, Youngstown State Alumni Assn., 1981—; trustee YMCA of Trumbull County, 1978—. Served with U.S. Army, 1944-45. Mem. Nat. Assn. Profl. Ins. Agts., Trumbull County Assn. Life Underwriters (pres. 1956), Ind. Ins. Agts. Trumbull County (pres. 1959), Ind. Ins. Agts. Ohio (trustee 1974-77), Warren Area C. of C. (v.p.), Am. Legion, V.F.W. Democrat. Roman Catholic. Clubs: Trumbull Country (trustee), Oblate Sister (trustee). Lodges: K.C. (Grand Knight 1955), Elks. Avocations: travel; golf. Home: 621 Country Club Dr Warren OH 44484 Office: Rossi Ins Agy 420 High St PO Box 630 Warren OH 44482

ROSSING, DAVID ROBERT, internist; b. Detroit, Jan. 8, 1949; s. Robert Grangaard and Dolores (Christenson) R.; m. Ann Marie Tkacz, July 30, 1977; children—Brian, Philip. B.A., St. Olaf Coll., 1971; M.D., U. Tex., 1975.

Diplomate Am. Bd. Internal Medicine (Pulmonary Disease). Intern, Emory U. Affiliated Hosps., Atlanta, 1975-76, resident, 1976-78; fellow in pulmonary diseases U. Tex., 1978-80; practice medicine specializing in pulmonary medicine, Sioux Falls, S.D., 1980—; mem. staff McKennan Hosp., Sioux Valley Hosp., Royal C Johnson VA Hosp.; asst. prof. U. S.D., Sioux Falls, 1980—; assoc. med. dir. DaKota State Coll. Sch. Respiratory Therapy, Madison, 1980—. Fellow ACP, Am. Coll. Chest Physicians; mem. AMA, Am. Thoracic Soc., Phi Beta Kappa. Lutheran. Home: 7205 Pine Lake Dr Sioux Falls SD 57103 Office: Central Plains Clinic 2727 S Kiwanis Sioux Falls SD 57105

ROSSMANN, MICHAEL GEORGE, biological science scientist; b. Frankfurt, Ger., July 30, 1930; came to U.S., 1964; s. Alexander and Nelly (Schwabacher) R.; m. Audrey Pearson, July 24, 1954; children—Martin, Alice, Heather. B.S. in Math., Physics, U. London, Eng., 1950, B.Sc. in Physics, 1951, M.Sc. in Physics, 1953; Ph.D., U. Glasgow, Scotland, 1956; Dr. h.c., U. Uppsala, Sweden, 1983, U. Strasbourg, France, 1984. Postdoctoral fellow U. Minn.-Mpls., 1956-58; research scientist MRC Lab. of Molecular Biology, Cambridge, Eng., 1958-64; assoc. prof. biol. sci. Purdue U., 1964-67, prof., 1967-78, Hanley prof. biol. sci., 1978—. Fellow Am. Acad. Arts and Scis.; mem. Nat. Acad. Scis., Soc. Biol. Chemists, Am. Soc. Virology, AAAS, Fedn. Am. Socs. Exptl. Biology, Am. Crystallographic Assn., Biophys. Soc., Brit. Crystallographic Assn. Home: 1208 Wiley Dr West Lafayette IN 47906 Office: Purdue U Dept Biol Scis West Lafayette IN 47907

ROSSMILLER, RICHARD ALLEN, educational administration educator, consultant; b. Burlington, Wis., May 25, 1928; s. Harold Curtis and Lydia Sophia (Keller) R.; m. Lois Catherine Koch, July 5, 1952; children—Daniel, Stuart, David. B.S., U. Wis.-Madison, 1950, M.S., 1958, Ph.D., 1960. Supt. Racine County Agrl. Sch., Rochester, Wis., 1954-57; prin. Evanston Twp. High Sch., Ill., 1960-61; supt. Muskego-Norway Schs., Wis., 1961-62; prof. ednl. adminstrn. U. Wis.-Madison, 1962—; vis. prof. U. Fla., Gainesville, 1967-68, Pontificial Cath. U., Rio de Janeiro, Brazil, 1977; cons. RAND Corp., Santa Monica, Calif., 1977-81, CAPES Ministry of Edn. and Culture, Brasilia, Brazil, 1975, OECD. Author: Opportunities Unlimited, 1959, 1983. Co-author: The Law and Public School Operation, 1969, 1978; Individual Guided Education, 1977; Dimensions of Educational Need, 1969. Dir. State Supts. Task Force on Teaching, Madison, 1983; pub. mem. Wis. Legis. Council, Madison, 1975, 1978. Recipient Benjamin Constant medal Inst. of Edn. of Rio de Janeiro, 1980. Mem. Am. Edn. and Fin. Assn. (pres. 1981), Univ. Council Ednl. Adminstrn. (pres. 1984—), Am. Ednl. Research Assn., Council for Ednl. Devel. and Research (pres. 1975-76), Nat. Orgn. Legal Problems of Edn. Democrat. Lodge: Rotary (dir. 1982-83). Avocation: photography. Home: 5806 Cable Ave Madison WI 53705 Office: Dept Ednl Adminstrn 1025 W Johnson St Madison WI 53706

ROSSOW, LAWRENCE FRANCIS, educational law educator; b. Chgo., Mar. 21, 1947; s. Lawrence Vernon Rossow and Marie Antonia (Martino) Kuncl; m. Nancy Dort, Apr. 10, 1976. B.A., DePaul U., 1969; M.Ed., Loyola U., Chgo., 1971, Ed.D., 1983. Prin., St. Victor Sch., Monroe, Wis., 1973-75, Maternity B.V.M. Sch., Chgo., 1975-77; headmaster Hardey Prep Sch., Chgo., 1977-79; supt. schs. Creston Sch. Dist., Ill., 1979-80; dist. dir. curriculum Chicago Ridge Pub. Sch., Ill., 1980-84; assoc. prof. edn., adminstr., adj. assoc. prof. law Washburn U., Topeka, 1984—. Contbr. articles to profl. jours. Served to capt. U.S. Army, 1969. Mem. Nat. Orgn. Legal Problems in Edn. (membership chmn. 1984—), NEA. Roman Catholic. Home: 2040 Westwood Dr Topeka KS 66604 Office: Washburn U 1700 College Dr Topeka KS 66621

ROSTENKOWSKI, DAN, congressman; b. Chgo., Jan. 2, 1928; s. Joseph P. and Priscilla (Dombroski) R.; student St. John's Mil. Acad., 1942-46, Loyola U., 1948-51; m. LaVerne Pirkins, May 12, 1951; children—Dawn P., Kristie M., Gayle A., Stacy L. Mem. Ill. Gen. Assembly, 1952, Senate, 1954, 56; mem. 86th-97th Congresses, 8th Dist. Ill., chmn. ways and means com., chmn. joint com. on taxation; chmn. Democratic Caucus 90th, 91st Congresses; chief dep. majority whip 95th and 96th Congresses. Home: 1372 W Evergreen St Chicago IL 60622 Office: House Office Bldg Washington DC 20515

ROSTOKER, WILLIAM, metallurgy educator, consultant; b. Hamilton, Ont., Can., June 21, 1924; came to U.S., 1950, naturalized, 1955; s. Louis and Fanny (Silbert) R.; m. Fay Margaret Tippett, Sept. 2, 1949; children—Gareth, Alan, Glyn, Wendy. B.A. Sc., U. Toronto (Can.), 1945, M.A. Sc., 1946; Ph.D., Lehigh U., 1948. Lectr., U. Birmingham, Eng., 1948-50; asst. prof. Ill. Inst. Tech., Chgo., 1950-51; sr. sci. advisor Armour Research Found., Chgo., 1951-65; prof. metallurgy U. Ill.-Chgo., 1965—; research assoc. Field Mus., Chgo., 1984—; mem. sci. adv. bd. U.S. Army, Washington, 1975-78; mem. Nat. Materials Adv. Bd., Washington, 1966-70. Author: Metallurgy of Vanadium, 1958; Embrittlement by Liquid Metals, 1960; Interpretation of Metallographic Structures, 1965, 75. Recipient Pub. Service award NASA, 1981. Fellow Am. Soc. Metals. Home: 2052 W 108th Pl Chicago IL 60643 Office: U Ill Dept Civil Engring Mechanics and Metallurgy Box 4348 Chicago IL 60680

ROSTORFER, ALVIN VERNON, waste plant supervisor; b. Lakeview, Ohio, Mar. 4, 1921; s. William Forest and Cleo Ivierene (Wierman) R.; m. Dorothy Irene Rostorfer, Feb. 21, 1947; children—Addie Ruth, Alvin Eugene, Fredrick Allen; Grad. high sch., Jackson Ctr., Ohio. Sewage plant operator, Village of Jackson Ctr., 1960-67; sewage plant operator City of New Carlisle, Ohio, 1967-75, supr., 1975—. Served to sgt. Air Force, 1942-45, ETO. Mem. Ohio Water Polution Control (hon. mem.; Safety Program award, 1982-83). Republican. Home: 331 Fenwick Dr New Carlisle OH 45344 Office: City New Carlisle 432 N Main New Carlisle OH 45344

ROSZKOWSKI, STANLEY JULIAN, See *Who's Who in America,* 43rd edition.

ROTH, M. AUGUSTINE, nun, educator; b. Mpls., Jan. 16, 1926; d. J.A., and Anne A. (Boies) R. B.A., U. Minn., 1947, M.A., 1948; Ph.D., Cath. U. Am., 1961. Joined Sisters of Mercy, Roman Catholic Ch., 1949. Faculty Mt. Mercy Coll., Cedar Rapids, Iowa, 1948-79, 80—, now prof. dept. English and pub. relations; dir. dept. edn. Mercy Hosp., 1979-80, sec. bd. dirs. Mercy Hosp. Endowment Found., 1979—, trustee of hosp., 1972—. Author: Written in His Hands, 1976; With Mercy Toward All, 1979; Courage and Change, 1980. Home: 1330 Elmhurst Dr NE Cedar Rapids IA 52402

ROTH, MICHAEL JOSEPH, lawyer, anesthetist; b. Dayton, Ohio, Feb. 24, 1951; s. Jerome C. and Helen E. R.; m. Donna M. Brandstetter, Aug. 25, 1973; children—Christopher, Matthew, Kimberly. B.S. in Health Sci., Anesthesiology, Case Western Res. U., 1973, J.D., 1978. Bar: Ohio 1978, U.S. Patent and Trademark Office 1979, U.S. Ct. Customs and Patent Appeals 1979, U.S. Ct. Appeals (fed. cir.) 1982. Anesthesiologist's asst. Cleve. Metropolitan Gen. Hosp., 1976-78; patent atty. Procter & Gamble, Cin., 1978-84; patent and trademark atty. Abbott Labs., Abbott Park, Ill., 1984—; instr. Met. Anesthesia Instrumentation Course, Cleve., 1977-78. Author copyrighted med. software for evaluation of cardiac function, 1977. Parish council rep. St. Bartholomew Ch., Cin., 1982-84; Deanery rep. Archdiocese of Cin., 1982-84. Nat. Merit Scholar 1969-73. Mem. Cin. Bar Assn. (mem. com. on admissions), Cin. Patent Law Assn., Phi Delta Phi (magister 1976-77, vice magister 1977-78; Officer's cert. of merit 1977, 78). Democrat. Roman Catholic. Home: 9 Altoona Ct Vernon Hills IL 60611 Office: Abbott Labs D-377 AP6C Abbott Park IL 60064

ROTH, NEIL J., lawyer; b. Rochester, N.Y., May 14, 1955; s. George and Ann R. R. B.A., Colgate U., 1977; J.D., U. Ky., 1983. Bar: Ky. 1983, U.S. Dist. Ct. (ea. dist.) Ky. 1983, Ohio 1984. Claim rep. Aetna Casualty & Surety, Hartford, Conn., 1978-80; assoc. Waite, Schneider, Bayless & Chesley, Cin., 1983-84, Benjamin Faulkner Tepe & Sack, Cin., 1984—. Mem. ABA, Ohio Bar Assn., Ky. Bar Assn., Cin. Bar Assn., Assn. Trial Lawyers Am. Home: 880 Rue de la Paix Apt T-12 Cincinnati OH 45220 Office: Benjamin Faulkner Tepe & Sack 1500 Central Trust Tower 5 W 4th St Cincinnati OH 45202

ROTH, ROBERT EARL, environmental educator; b. Archbold, Ohio, Mar. 30, 1937; s. Earl Jonas and Florence Lena (Mahler) R.; m. Carol Sue Yackee, Aug. 8, 1959; children—Robin Earl, Bruce Robert. B.Sc., Ohio State U.-Columbus, 1959, B.Sc. in Secondary Sci. Edn., 1961, M.Sc. in Conservation Edn., 1960; Ph.D. in Environ. Edn., U. Wis.-Madison, 1969. Supr. conservation edn. Ethical Culture Schs., N.Y.C., 1961-63; naturalist, sci. tchr. Edwin Gould Found., Spring Valley, N.Y., 1963-65; instr. No. Ill. U.-Oregon, 1965-67; asst. prof. Ohio State U., Columbus, 1969-73, assoc. prof., 1973-78, prof. environ. edn., 1978—, chmn. div., 1978-85, coordinator Office of Internat. Affairs, 1985—. Exec. editor: Jour. Environ. Edn., 1975—. Mem., Old Worthington Assn., 1977—; committeeman Boy Scouts Am., 1983—; mem. Ctr. Sci. and Industry, Columbus, 1971—. Mem. N. Am. Assn. Environ. Edn. (past pres.), Nat. Sci. Tchrs. Assn., AAAS, Caribbean Conservation Assn., Ohio Alliance for Environ. Edn., Ohio Hist. Soc. Lutheran. Club: Cen. Ohio Anglers and Hunters. Avocations: Sailing, canoeing, camping, bicycling, fishing, archery. Home: 570 Morning St Worthington OH 43085 Office: Div Environ Edn Sch Natural Resources Ohio State Univ 2021 Coffey Rd Columbus OH 43210

ROTH, ROBERT PAUL, seminary educator, writer; b. Milw., Dec. 8, 1919; s. Paul Wagner and Rose Marie (Schulzke) R.; m. Margaret Agnes Beckstrand, June 17, 1943; children—Erik, Maren, Maarja, John, Sonja. B.A., Carthage Coll., 1941; M.A., U. Ill., 1942; M.Div., Northwestern Lutheran Sem., 1945; Ph.D., U. Chgo., 1947; D.D. (hon.), Roanoke Coll., 1958. Ordained to ministry Luth. Ch. in Am. Prof. Luthergiri Sem., Rajahmundry, India, 1946-48; pastor St. Paul Ch., Red Wing, Minn., 1949-53; prof. Luth. So. Sem., Columbia, S.C., 1953-61; dean Northwestern Luth. Sem., Mpls., 1968-76; dir. grad. studies Luther Northwestern Sem., St. Paul, 1976-83, prof., 1983—; pres. Minn. Consortium Sems. Minn., 1976-78; chmn. com. on worship Luth. Ch. Am., 1970-78, mem. Bd. Publ., Phila., 1978—. Author: Meaning and Practice of the Lord's Supper, 1961; Story and Reality, 1973; The Theater of God, 1985; editor: New International Bible, 1978. Research fellow: Am. Assn. Theol. Schs., 1966, Aid Assn. for Lutherans, 1976, 78, Luth. Brotherhood, 1983, Luth. Ch. Am. Div. for Profl. Leadership, 1983, Div. for Global Missions, 1983. Mem. Am. Acad. Religion. Avocations: Painting watercolors; poetry; sailing. Home: 4194 Hillcrest Ln Wayzata MN 55391 Office: Luther Northwestern Sem 2481 Como Ave Saint Paul MN 55108

ROTH, TOBY, Congressman; b. Oct. 10, 1938; B.A., Marquette U., 1961; m. Barbara Fischer, 1964; children—Toby, Vicky, Barbie. Realtor; mem. Wis. Ho. of Reps., 1972-78; mem. 96th to 99th Congresses from 8th Dist. Wis., mem. Fgn. Affairs Com., Banking, Fin. and Urban Affairs Com. Named Wis. Legislator of Yr., 1978. Mem. Am. Legion (hon.). Republican. Office: 215 Cannon House Office Bldg Washington DC 20515

ROTH, WILLIAM GEORGE, manufacturing executive; b. Lamberton, Minn., 1938. B.S. in Mech. Engring., U. Notre Dame, 1960; M.S. in Indsl. Mgmt., Purdue U., 1961. With Trane Co., La Crosse, Wis., 1961—, sales engr. CenTraVac and UniTrane sales depts., 1961-63, mgr. various sales depts., 1963-70, mgr. dealer distbn., 1971, sales and mktg. mgr. consumer products div., 1973-77, dep. chmn., 1977, chmn. and chief exec. officer, dir., 1978—; dir. Norwest Corp., G. Heilman Brewing Co. Mem. NAM (dir.). Office: Trane Co Inc 3600 Pammel Creek Rd La Crosse WI 54601

ROTHBARD, DAVID ROD, geologist; b. N.Y.C., Jan. 24, 1953. B.S. in Earth and Space Sci., SUNY-Stony Brook, 1974; A.M. in Geol. Sci., Harvard U., 1975; Ph.D. in Geology, U. Mo.-Columbia, 1982. Research technician Harvard U. Med. Sch., Boston, 1976-77; research assoc. U. Mo.-Columbia, 1977-82; sr. research geologist Sohio Petroleum Co., Cleve., 1982—. Contbr. articles to profl. jours. Mem. Am. Assn. Petroleum Geologists, Soc. Econ. Paleontologists Mineralogists, Geochem. Soc. Office: Sohio Petroleum Co Production Research Lab 4440 Warrensville Ctr Rd Cleveland OH 44128

ROTHE, CARL FREDERICK, physiologist, educator; b. Lima, Ohio, Feb. 6, 1929; s. Calvin H. and Katharine C. (Boegel) R.; m. Mary Louise Hawk, Aug. 16, 1952; children—Sarah Katharine Lee, Thomas Herbert. B.S., Ohio State U., 1951, M.S., 1952, Ph.D., 1955. Sr. asst. scientist USPHS, Savannah, Ga., 1955-58; instr. Ind. U. Sch. Medicine, Indpls., 1958-59, asst. prof., 1960-63, assoc. prof., 1963-70, prof. physiology and biophysics, 1970—; mem. cardiovascular study sect. NIH, 1971-75. Mem. gen. bd. Nat. Council Chs., 1963-68. Served with USPHS, 1955-58. Mem. Biomed. Engring. Soc. (bd. dirs. 1982-85), Am. Physiol. Soc., Am. Heart Assn. Mem. United Ch. of Christ. Home: 4649 Boulevard Pl Indianapolis IN 46208 Office: Ind U Med Ctr Dept Physiology and Biophysics 635 Barnhill Dr Indianapolis IN 46223

ROTHENBERG, ELLIOT CALVIN, lawyer; b. Mpls., Nov. 12, 1939; s. Sam S. and Claire Sylvia (Feller) R.; m. Sally Smayling; 1 child, Margaret. B.A. summa cum laude, U. Minn., 1961; J.D., Harvard U. (Fulbright fellow), 1964. Assoc. project dir. Brookings Inst., Washington, 1966-67; fgn. service officer, legal advisor U.S. Dept. State, Washington, 1968-73; nat. law dir. Anti-Defamation League, N.Y.C., 1973-74; legal dir. Minn. Public Interest Research Group, Mpls., 1974-77; admitted to Minn. bar, 1966; pvt. practice law, Mpls., 1977—; adj. prof. William Mitchell Coll. Law, St. Paul, 1983—. State bd. dirs. YMCA Youth in Govt. Program, 1981—; v.p. Twin Cities chpt. Am. Jewish Com., 1980—; mem. Minn. House of Reps., 1978-82, asst. floor leader (whip), 1981-82; pres., dir. North Star Legal Found., 1983—; mem. citizens adv. com. Voyageurs Nat. Park, 1979-81. Recipient Legis. Evaluation Assembly Legis. Excellence award, 1980; North Star award, U. Minn., 1961. Mem. Am. Bar Assn., Harvard Law Sch. Assn., Izaak Walton League, Minn. Bar Assn., Am. Legion, Mensa, Minn. Distance Runners Assn., Phi Beta Kappa. Republican. Jewish. Clubs: Rotary, B'nai B'rith. Contbr. articles to profl. and scholarly jours., newspapers; author: (with Zelman Cowen) Sir John Latham and Other Papers, 1965. Home: 3901 W 25th St Saint Louis Park MN 55416 Office: 500 Plymouth Bldg Minneapolis MN 55402

ROTHMAN, MICHAEL DAVID, communications executive; b. Chgo., Feb. 26, 1942; s. Lewis and Ann Doris (Glotzer) R.; m. Jacqueline Alice Harlow, July 16, 1967. Student U. Tulsa, Roosevelt U. Founder, pres. L&M Sales Co., Chgo., 1965—; asst. to pres., purchasing agt. Shear-Prinz Assocs. Inc., Chgo., 1967-68; asst. to pres. Weil Service Products Corp., Chgo., 1968-70; v.p. PriTec, Chgo. Republican nominee Ill. Senate, 1976; trustee Regional Bd. Sch. Trustees, Cook County, Ill., pres., 1976, 84; Republican committeeman 50th ward City of Chgo., 1984—. Jewish. Club: Rotary (Chgo.). Lodges: Masons, B'nai B'rith (pres. 1975-76). Home: 1402 W Busse Ave Mount Prospect IL 60056 Office: PriTec 5800 N Lincoln Ave Chicago IL 60659

ROTHMAN, RICHARD R., insurance company official; b. Wausau, Wis., Dec. 3, 1955; s. Roland Louis and Beth Lois (Hughs) R. B.S., U. Wis.-River Falls, 1978; M.P.A., U. Kans., 1980. Adminstrv. asst. to Glencoe (Ill.) village mgr., 1979-81; loss prevention rep. Gallagher Bassett Ins. Service, Rolling Meadows, Ill., 1981—. Kenneth White scholar, 1978. Mem. Am. Pub. Works Assn., Am. Soc. Safety Engrs., Ill. City Mgrs. Assn. Republican. Methodist. Home: 715 Grove Dr Apt 208 Buffalo Grove IL 60090 Office: 60 Gould Ctr Rolling Meadows IL 60008

ROTHMEIER, STEVEN GEORGE, airlines executive; b. Mankato, Minn., Oct. 4, 1946; s. Edwin George and Alice Joan (Johnson) R. B.B.A., Univ. of Notre Dame, 1968; M.B.A., U. Chgo., 1972. With Northwest Airlines, Inc., St. Paul, 1973—, corp. fin. analyst, 1973, mgr. econ. analysis, 1973-78, dir. econ. planning, 1978, v.p. fin., treas., 1978-82, exec. v.p., treas., 1982-83, exec. v.p. fin. and adminstrn., treas., 1983, pres. chief operating officer, 1983-85, pres. chief exec. officer, 1985—, also dir.; dir. First Nat. Bank St. Paul, First Bank System, Inc., Tomisato Shoji, Gatwick Handling Ltd., Honeywell Inc., Minn. Mut. Life Ins. Served to 1st lt. U.S. Army, 1968-71; Vietnam. Decorated Bronze Star, Army Commendation medal. Republican. Minneapolis Catholic. Clubs: Minneapolis (St. Paul); Mpls. Office: Northwest Airlines Inc Mpls/St Paul Internat Airport Saint Paul MN 55111

ROTH-ROFFY, JAMES KENNETH, pharmaceutical sales representative; b. St. Louis, Dec. 2, 1950; s. Kenneth Norbert and Nancy Theresa (Bultas) R-R.; m. Madeleine Cecelia Pettey, June 30, 1978; children—Margaret Emily, Anne Cecelia. B.S. in Pharmacy, St. Louis Coll. of Pharmacy, 1974. Registered pharmacist, Mo., Ill. Pharmacy mgr. Medicare/Glaser Co., St. Louis, 1974-78, Dolgins Pharmacy, St. Louis, 1978-80; profl. rep. Merck, Sharp & Dohme, West Point, Pa., 1980—. Mem. Ill. Soc. Hosp. Pharmacists, Kappa Psi. Roman Catholic. Club: Toastmasters. Avocations: softball; soccer; photography; sailing; classical guitar. Home and Office: 43 Chafford Woods St Louis MO 63144

ROTHSCHILD, BRUCE MAX, physician, medical educator; b. N.Y.C., Nov. 13, 1947; s. Melville Albert and Barbara Thelma (Sichel) R.; m. Carolyn Marton, June 13, 1978; children—Jeremiah Marton, Jessica Ilana. B.S., Seton Hall U., 1969; M.D., N.J. Coll. Medicine, 1973. Instr. medicine U. Tenn., Memphis, 1976-78; chief rheumatology sect. VA Med. Ctr., North Chicago, Ill., 1978-83, dir. div. rheumatology Chgo. Med. Sch., 1978-83; dir. med. edn. Menorah Med. Ctr., Kansas City, Mo., 1983—; assoc. prof. U. Kans., U. Mo., Cook County Postgrad. Sch.; chmn. Lake County (Ill.) Med. Services Adv. Bd., 1981-83; mem. exhibits com. Arthritis Found., 1982-84, Mus. Sci. and Industry of Chgo., 1982-83. NSF grantee. Fellow ACP, Chgo. Soc. Internal Medicine; mem. AMA, Am. Rheumatism Assn., Am. Fedn. Clin. Research, Am. Soc. Clin. Pharmacology and Therapeutics, Am. Becet's Club, N.Y. Acad. Sci., Am. Geriatric Soc., Am. Aging Assn., Chgo. Assn. Immunologists, Sigma Xi, Alpha Epsilon Delta, Phi Delta Epsilon. Author: Rheumatology: A Primary Care Approach, 1982; Rheumatology: Roentgenographic Evaluation, 1984. Contbr. numerous articles to med., profl. jours. Office: Menorah Med Ctr Kansas City MO

ROTTMAN, KENNETH PAUL, dentist, research technician; b. Chgo., Mar. 22, 1936; s. Morris Maxwell and Marion Esther (Marcus) R.; m. Patricia Blossom Gordon, Mar. 21, 1961 (div. 1977); children—Alan Gordon, Matthew Eric, Laura Francine. B.S., Tulane U., 1958; B.S., U. Ill.-Chgo., 1962, D.D.S., 1964. Pvt. practice dentistry, Chgo., 1964—; designer Gordon San. Systems, Chgo., 1964-65; technician Blood Bank, U. Ill. Hosp., Chgo., 1962-64, med. research technician, 1958-62; dir. dentistry Union Health Service Dental Ctr., Chgo., 1970-76. Contbr. to Quintessence Internat. Jour. Served with USAR, 1959-61. Fellow Acad. Gen. Dentistry, Acad. Dentistry Internat.; mem. Soc. Baromedicine and Dentistry (Founder, pres. 1980—), Chgo. Acad. Gen. Dentistry (pres. 1984), Chgo. Dental Soc. (sec. N. Side br. 1984), Ill. Acad. Gen. Dentistry (pub. info. officer 1984), Am. Equilibration Soc., Internat. Congress Oral Implantologists, Am. Acad. Functional Orthodontists. Jewish. Clubs: Sea Lancers, League Underwater Photographers. Avocations: photography, underwater photography, scuba diving, woodworking. Office: Water Tower Dental Assocs 535 N Michigan Ave Chicago IL 60611

ROUNER, EVELYN IRENE, human growth and development educator, home economics curriculum consultant; b. Iowa City; d. Jacob Frank and Emma Mae (Reber) R. B.A., U. Iowa, 1945; M.S., U. Ill., 1950, Ed.D., 1959. Tchr., prin. Amana High Sch., Middle Amana, Iowa, 1945-50; tchr. Hesston (Kans.) Coll., 1950-56; instr. nursery sch. U. Ill., 1957-59; prof., chmn. dept. home econs., family life Central Mich. U., 1959-81; prof., chmn. dept. home econs. Goshen Coll., 1981-82, dir. continuing edn., 1982-83. Chmn., Isabella County Social Service Bd., 1974-75, Isabella Child Devel. Bd., 1970-81; dir. sr. ctr., ednl. coordinator Greencroft Retirement Community, Goshen, Ind., 1984—; curriculum cons. early childhood edn. Bd. dirs. Ojibwa Lake Assn. Mem. Mich. Council on Family Relations (past pres.), Mich. Home Econs. Assn. (past pres.), Mich. Child Study Clubs, Nat. Council Family Relations, Mich. Council Family Relations, Am. Home Econs. Assn., Am. Vocat. Assn. Mennonite. Home: 1513 Dogwood Ct Goshen IN 46526

ROURK, JAMES ROBERT, EDP auditor; b. Gary, S.D., Sept. 7, 1948; s. Robert N. and Dorothy Marie (Dinger) R.; m. Darcy Lyn Wilbur, Aug. 17, 1972; children—Winona Kathleen, Kelsey Rebecca, Claire Colleen. B.S. in Music Edn., Dakota State Coll., 1970; M.B.A., Kans. State U., 1982. Condr., dir. North Queensland Youth Orch., Innisfail, Australia, 1974-76; mgr. bus. Susan Warden Dancers, Manhattan, Kans., 1979; researcher, instr. Kans. State U., Manhattan, 1980-82; pres. Rourk Entertainment Corp., Manhattan, 1980—; programmer, analyst Kans. Farm Bur., Manhattan, 1982—. Bd. dirs. McCain Auditorium, Kans. State U. Author: Computing for Elementary School Students, 1982. Composer: Wider Horizons, 1978. Contbr. artilces to profl. jours. Deacon, First Christian Ch., Manhattan, 1982—, dir. brass choir, 1982—; vol. United Way, 1984—; chmn. voter registration Dem. Party, 1982. Served to sgt. U.S. Army, 1970-73. Yamaha Internat. scholar, 1972. Mem. Winjammers Internat., Nat. Assn. Jazz Educators, Performing Arts Council, C. of C., Phi Mu Alpha. Club: Music Fedn. (pres. 1984) (Manhattan). Avocations: gardening, carpentry, composing. Home: 2100 Goodnow Circle Manhattan KS 66502 Office: Kansas Farm Bur Services 2321 Anderson Manhattan KS 66502

ROURKE, HAROLD JAMES, management executive; b. Bklyn., Aug. 31, 1928; s. Harold James and Grace Elizabeth (Desmond) R.; m. Mary Lorraine Jones, Aug. 20, 1955; children—Gregory, Therese, Amy. B.S., Fordham U., 1952. Jr. positions in data processing, Chgo., 1952-67; sr. systems assurance rep. IBM, Chgo., 1972-79, Washington 1967-71; v.p., treas. Bieniek & Rourke, Ltd., Chgo., 1979—. Bd. dirs. Montgomery County Assn. for Retarded Citizens, Wheaton, Ill., 1968-71, Ray Graham Assn. for the Handicapped, Addison, Ill., 1974-76. Served with U.S. Army, 1952. Republican. Roman Catholic. Avocations: fishing; hunting. Office: Bieniek & Rourke Ltd 449 Taft Ave Suite 300 Glen Ellyn IL 60137

ROUSE, JOHN RATCLIFFE, fine art consultant, former art museum dir., curator; b. Cunningham, Kans., Aug. 27, 1917; s. John R. and Edith Belle (Cole) R. B.A., Bethel Coll., Newton, Kans., 1939. With Fourth Nat. Bank & Trust Co., Wichita, Kans., 1940-46; asst. and mgr. Commodore Hotel, Wichita, 1946-56; art and antique cons., 1955—; dir., curator Wichita Art Assn. Galleries and Sch. Art 1972-83; ret. 1983. Mem. Wichita Hist. Mus. Assn. (trustee 1972-78), Wichita Art Assn. (pres. bd. 1973-75), Wichita Art Mus. Mems. Found., Fine Arts Council, Am. Assn. Mus., Mountain Plains Mus. Conf., Kans. Mus. Assn., Am. Crafts Council, Midwest Enamelist Guild, Newton Art Assn., Nat. Assn. Cert. Antique and Art Appraisers. Republican. Christian Scientist. Home: 115 S Rutan St Wichita KS 67218

ROUSE, LAWRENCE JOHN, management consultant; b. Milw., Nov. 26, 1946; s. William Hayden and Jean Laverne (Cook) R. B.A. in Psychology, Elmhurst Coll., 1976, B.B.A., 1976. Exec. supr. George S. May Internat., Park Ridge, Ill., 1976-78; gen. mgr. Solar Textiles, Skokie, Ill., 1974-76; pres. Associated Enterprises, Ltd., Downers Grove, Ill., 1978—; v.p. Mainstream Media, Downers Grove, 1981—; regional dir. fin. services Valtec Assocs., Arlington Heights, Ill., 1982-84; pres. Valuation Strategies, Downers Grove, 1984—; staff M.B.A. seminars Lewis U., Romeoville, Ill., 1984-85, staff S.B.A. student projects, 1984-85. Served with USMC, 1966-69. Mem. Am. Soc. Appraisers. Home: 440 Perrie Rd Apt 302 Elk Grove Village IL 60007 Office: Associated Enterprises Ltd 5627 Dunham Rd Downers Grove IL 60519

ROUSHAR, JOHN EDWARD, pharmacist; b. Belle Plaine, Iowa, Nov. 3, 1931; s. John J. and Jeanette (Nichols) R.; m. Bernadine Caroline McDonald, Aug. 12, 1953; 1 child, Brenda Roushar Cooney. B.S., U. Iowa, 1954. Owner, pharmacist Roushar Rexall Drugs, Victor, Iowa, 1955-60; mgr., pharmacist Paramount Pharmacy, Cedar Rapids, Iowa, 1960-70; owner, pharmacist Roushar Pharmacy, 1970—. Mem. Nat. Assn. Ind. Businessmen, Am. Pharmacists Assn., Iowa Pharmacists Assn., Linn County Pharmacists Assn. Democrat. Roman Catholic. Club: Elmcrest Golf and Country. Avocations: golf. Office: Roushar Pharmacy 811 5th Ave SE Cedar Rapids IA 52403

ROUSSEAU, MARK OWEN, sociologist; b. Ft. Wayne, Ind., Apr. 5, 1940; s. Richard Jackson and Wilma (Combs) R.; B.A., Ind. U., 1962, M.A., 1966; Ph.D., U. N.C., Chapel Hill, 1971; cert. III Degré, Alliance Francaise, Paris, 1972; m. Marion Frances Pruss, Aug. 18, 1973; 1 son, Mark Owen. Asst. instr. U. N.C., 1966-68; mem. faculty U. Nebr., Omaha, 1968—, asst. prof. sociology, 1971-82, assoc. prof., 1982—, sabbatical research leave, 1985; Nat. Endowment Humanities fellow, summer 1979; funded research, Paris, 1982. Mem. Am. Sociol. Assn., AAUP, Inst. Icarian Investigations (pres. 1976-83), Midwest Sociol. Soc., Am. Assn. Tchrs. French, Conf. Group on French Politics and Soc., La Société Tocqueville, Ind. U. Alumni Assn., Alpha Kappa Delta. Contbr. articles to profl. jours. Home: 5001 Izard St Omaha NE 68132 Office: Dept Sociology Univ Nebr Omaha NE 68182

ROVIARO, SUSAN ELIZABETH, clinical psychologist; b. Pittsfield, Mass., Sept. 10, 1949; d. Louis Peter and Elizabeth (Angelini) R.; m. Robert Paul Wisdom, June 18, 1983. B.A., U. Mass., 1971; M.A., U. Kans., 1977, Ph.D., 1981. Lic. psychologist. Grad. research and teaching asst. dept. psychology U. Kans., Lawrence, 1974-77; psychologist in tng. VA Med. Center, Topeka, 1975-77, research asst. depts. neuropsychology and medicine, 1977-79; predoctoral fellow dept. psychiatry Mount Zion Hosp. and Med. Center, San Francisco, 1979-80; clin. dir. Pawnee Mental Health Services, Manhattan, Kans., 1980—; health profl. affiliate Meml. and St. Mary's hosps., Manhattan. Mem. Am. Psychol. Assn., Kans. Psychol. Assn. (bd. govs.), Phi Beta Kappa. Home: 812 Colorado St Manhattan KS 66502 Office: 2001 Claflin Rd Manhattan KS 66502

ROWAN, ROBERT DALE, See *Who's Who in America,* 43rd edition.

ROWE, FRANK JOSEPH, pathologist; b. Newark, Aug. 14, 1923; s. Frank Joseph and Celia (Rusnak) R.; m. Barbara Hope Conway, June 27, 1952; children—Frank Joseph Jr., Diana Hope. M.D., George Washington U., 1952. Diplomate Am. Bd. Pathology. Intern, Queen Gen. Hosp., N.Y.C., 1952-53; resident in clin. and anatomical pathology Mallory Inst. Pathology, Boston City Hosp., 1953-57; instr. Harvard U., Cambridge, Mass., 1956-58, Boston U., 1956-58, Tufts U., Medford, Mass, 1956-58, Jefferson Med. Sch., Phila., 1957-63; asst. pathologist Boston Free Women's Hosp., 1957-58; assoc. pathologist Chestnut Hill (Pa.) Hosp., 1958-63, St. Michaels Med. Center, Newark, 1967-75; dir. labs. Goddard Meml. Hosp., Stoughton, Mass., 1963-67; prof. pathology N.J. Med. Sch., Newark, 1967-75; med. dir. Consol. Biomed. Labs., Columbus, Ohio, 1975-78; ptnr. Davidson Pathology Assocs., Columbus, 1978—. Served with USN, 1943-46. Am. Cancer Soc. grantee, 1957-58. Mem. N.J. State Med. Soc., Pa. State Med. Soc., AMA, Ohio State Med. Soc., Mass. State Med. Soc., George Washington U. Alumni Assn., Coll. Am. Pathologists, Am. Soc. Clin. Pathologists, Ohio Pathology Soc. Republican. Episcopalian. Contbr. articles to profl. publs. Home: 325 Blandford Dr Worthington OH 43085 Office: 267 E Broad St Columbus OH 43215

ROWE, HARVEY JOHN, building materials company executive; b. Oshkosh, Wis., Jan. 29, 1936; s. Harvey Jackson and Grace Linnea (Anderson) R.; B.A., U. Mo., 1959; m. Marjorie Susan Beckman, Feb. 28, 1959; children—Richard Edward, Renee Suzanne, Risa Lee. Mgmt. trainee, advt. merchandiser Walgreen Co., Chgo., 1954-63; buyer, asst. purchasing mgr. U.S. Gypsum Co., Chgo., 1963-72, mktg. mgr. chems. div., 1972-79, group dir. mktg. services, 1982-84, gen. mgr. metals div. USG Industries Inc., 1984—; gen. mgr. Arrowhead Drywall Supplies, Olathe, Kans., 1979-82. Trustee Village of Deer Park, Ill., 1975-79; pres., co-founder Barrington (Ill.) Area Hockey League, 1973-74; pres. Kansas City Amateur Hockey League, 1981-82. Served as ensign USN, 1958. Mem. Steel Service Center Inst., Sigma Phi Epsilon. Republican. Christian Scientist. Home: 25876 Tara Dr Barrington IL 60010 Office: US Gypsum Co 101 S Wacker Dr Chicago IL 60010

ROWE, JOHN WESTEL, organic chemist; b. Forest Hills, N.Y., Sept. 3, 1924; s. John Edward and Laura Robinson (Willoughby) R.; m. Mary Dorothey Lowens, June 26, 1949; children—Peter Willoughby, William Westel, Michael Delano. B.S., MIT, 1948; M.S., U. Colo., 1952; Sc.D., Swiss Fed. Inst. Tech., Zurich, 1956. With Forest Products Lab., Forest Service U.S. Dept. Agr., 1957—, project leader, Madison, Wis., 1966—, also supervisory research chemist; lectr. U. Wis. Active Boy Scouts Am., 1962-74. Served with USN, 1942-44. Recipient Wood Salutes award Wood & Wood Products, 1975. Fellow Internat. Acad. Wood Sci., AAAS, Am. Inst. Chemists; mem. Soc. Econ. Botany, Phytochem. Assn. N.Am., Am. Chem. Soc. (chmn. Wis. sect. 1968, 69, alt. counselor 1976-78), Am. Soc. Pharmacology, Forest Products Research Soc., Internat. Assn. for Biomass Utilization, TAPPI. Republican. Unitarian. Contbr. articles on wood and natural products chemistry to profl. jours. Home: 1001 Tumalo Trail Madison WI 53711 Office: US Forest Products Lab PO Box 5130 Madison WI 53705

ROWE, JOYCE MORGAN, health care consultant; b. Floral Park, N.Y., June 17, 1937; d. F. Howard and Else Helene (Rietheimer) Morgan; m. Allen Martin Rowe, Dec. 26, 1959; children—Amy, Jeffrey, Jon, Carrie Beth. B.S. in Edn., SUNY-Oneonta, 1959; 5th yr. health info. services cert. U. Seattle, 1978. Accredited record technician, registered record adminstr. Tchr., St. Paul's Sch., Norwich, N.Y., 1967-71; quality assurance coordinator St. Joseph's Hosp. and Health Ctr., Syracuse, N.Y., 1975-78; quality assurance specialist U. Ill. Med. Ctr., Chgo., 1979-82; mgr. med. records South Suburban Hosp., Hazel Crest, Ill., 1982-83; founder, pres. JR Assocs., Oaklawn, Ill., 1983—. Instr., Chgo. State U., 1979-83. Mem. adv. com. Morraine Valley (Ill.) Community Coll., 1982-83. Mem. Am. Med. Record Assn., Ill. Med. Record Assn., Chgo. Vicinity Med. Record Assn. (pub. relations com. 1983), Soc. Computer Sci., Fedn. Internat. Health Instrs., Bus. and Profl. Women (pres. chpt. 1977), Am. Legion Aux. (pres. chpt. 1966-67, treas. chpt. 1966-67), Theta Phi Epsilon. Contbr. articles to profl. jours.; author: Medical Record Maintenance: A Costing and Personnel Assessment. Home: 517 Barnsdale Rd Lagrange Park IL 60525

ROWE, NATHANIEL HAWTHORNE, dentist, pathology educator; b. Hibbing, Minn., May 26, 1931; s. Nathaniel Hawthorne and Edna (Bockler) R.; D.D.S., B.S., U. Minn., 1955, M.S.D., 1958; div.; children—Bradford Scott, Nathaniel Edwin, Lorna Michelle, Jonathan Alan. Teaching asst. dept. oral pathology Sch. Dentistry, U. Minn., 1955-56, research fellow, 1956-58, clin. instr., 1958-59; asst. prof. pathology Washington U. Sch. Dentistry, St. Louis, 1959-65, assoc. prof., 1965-69, prof. Grad. Sch. Arts and Scis., 1966-69, vis. prof. pathology Sch. Dentistry, 1969-71, chmn. dept. gen. and oral pathology, 1959-68, coordinator oral cancer teaching, 1959-68; assoc. research scientist Cancer Research Ctr., Columbia, Mo., 1967-71; assoc. prof. pathology Sch. Medicine, U. Mich., Ann Arbor, 1969-76, prof. pathology, 1976—, prof. dentistry Sch. Dentistry, 1968—, assoc. dir. Dental Research Inst., 1970—, sr. research scientist Virus Research Group, 1977—; cons. staff Jewish Hosp., St. Louis, 1960-68; cons. Ellis Fischel State Cancer Hosp., Columbia, 1967—, sci. adv. bd. Cancer Research Center, 1975-78; cons. oral pathology U.S. VA Hosps., St. Louis, 1965-68, Ann Arbor, 1969—, Mo. Dental Assn., St. Louis, 1967-69; civilian profl. cons. Office of Surgeon, 5th U.S. Army, 1967-83; cons. Bur. Medicine Adv. Panel System, HEW, dental agts. adv. com. FDA, 1968-70; mem. profl. adv. council on cancer Mich. Assn. Regional Med. Programs, 1969-73; mem. policy council Met. Detroit Cancer Control Program, 1976-82; Recipient D.E. Listiac award, faculty U. Minn. Sch. Dentistry, 1955; award Mich. div. Am. Cancer Soc., 1979, Tiffany nat. divisional award, 1979; Outstanding Civilian Service medal Dept. Army, 1979; named Hon. Alumnus Washington U. Sch. Dentistry, 1966. Diplomate Am. Bd. Oral Pathology. Fellow Am. Acad. Oral Pathology (councillor 1971-74, v.p. 1975-76, pres.-elect 1976-77, pres. 1977-78), Am. Coll. Dentists, Internat. Coll. Dentists; mem. AAAS, N.Y. Acad. Scis., Am. Assn. Cancer Research, ADA (cons. Council on Dental Edn. 1971-72, 75-83, mem. commn. on accreditation 1976-80, cons. com. on hosp. and instl. dental service 1979-81), Mich. Dental Soc. (cons. com. cancer control 1971-78, chmn. com. cancer control and hosp. dentistry 1978—), Dist. Dental Soc., Mich. Soc. Pathologists, Internat. Assn. Dental Research, Royal Soc. Health (Eng.), Fedn. Dentaire Internationale, Internat. Acad. Pathology, Am. Cancer Soc. (dir. St. Louis City and County unit 1964-68, chmn. profl. edn. com. 1967-68, v.p., 1967-68, dir. Mo. div. 1965-68, dir., mem. exec. com. Mich. div. 1970—, chmn. profl. edn. com. 1973-76, v.p. unit 1975-76, pres. 1976-77, pres. elect Mich. div. 1977-78, pres. 1978-79), Sigma Xi, Xi Psi Phi, Omicron Kappa Upsilon. Editor Proc. of Symposium: Salivary Glands and Their Secretion, 1973; Proc. of Symposium: Dental Plaque: Interfaces, 1974; Proc. of Symposium: Oral and Perioral Ulcerations: Cause and Control, Emphasis on Herpes Simplex Virus, 1975; Proc. of Symposium: Occlusion: Research in Form and Function, 1976; Proc. of Symposium: The Sci. Basis for Evaluation of Periodontal Therapy, 1977; Proc. of Symposium: Incipient Caries of Enamel, 1978; Proc. of Symposium: Diet, Nutrition and Dental Caries, 1979; Proc. of Symposium: Trends in the Prevention and Treatment of Periodontal Disease, 1983; Proc. of Symposium: Dental Pulp: Reactions to Restorative Materials in the Presence or Absence of Infection, 1982; Proc. of Symposium: Herpes, Hepatitis and AIDS: Current Concerns of the Health Practitioner, 1983; manuscript reviewer Cancer, 1967—, Jour. ADA, 1982—; mem. editorial bd. Jour. Mo. Dental Soc., 1963-69, Bull. Greater St. Louis Dental Soc., 1964-68, Cancer, 1967—, Oral Research Abstracts, 1967-78, Jour. Dental Research, 1971-73, Jour. Oral Pathology, 1973—, Jour. AMA, 1983—; contbr. articles to profl. jours.; also chpts. to books. Home: 1042 Greenhills Dr Ann Arbor MI 48105

ROWLAND, LANDON H., diversified company executive. Pres., chief exec. officer, dir. Kansas City So. Industries, Inc., Kansas City, Mo. Office: Kansas City So Industries Inc 114 W 11th St Kansas City MO 64105*

ROWLAND, ROBERT JOSEPH, JR., classics educator, association executive; b. Shenandoah, Pa., Mar. 27, 1938; s. Robert Joseph and Catherine (Brennan) R.; m. Carole S. Ricords, Aug. 16, 1960; children—Robert Joseph III, Francine Marie, Patrick Brennan, Maria Danielle. B.A., La Salle Coll., 1959; M.A., U. Pa., 1961, Ph.D., 1964. Instr. La Salle Coll., 1959-65; instr., then asst. prof. classics Villanova (Pa.) U., 1961-67, dir. Honors Coll., 1965-67; assoc. prof. classics U. Mo., Columbia, 1967-71, assoc. prof. history, 1971-73, prof., 1973-84; prof., chmn. dept. classics U. Md., College Park, 1984—; exec. sec. Vergilian Soc. Am. Past trustee Columbia Regional Library, Daniel Boone Regional Library, Columbia. Bennett fellow, 1961; Am. Philos. Soc. grantee, 1972, 84; Am. Council Learned Socs. grantee, 1974, 76, 81; NEH grantee, 1984. Mem. Am. Philol. Assn., Classical Assn. Midwest and South (pres. So. sect. 1982-84), Vergilian Soc. Am., Soc. Promotion Roman Studies (Eng.), Cambridge (Eng.) Philol. Assn., Association pour l'Etude de Civilisation Romaine, Am. Assn. Ancient Historians, Friends of Ancient History (sec. 1983, pres. 1983-84), Archeol. Inst. Am., Alpha Epsilon. Democrat. Roman Catholic. Author: I Ritrovamenti Romani in Sardegna, 1981; (with M. S. Balmuth) Studies in Sardinian Archaeology, 1984; contbr. numerous articles on ancient and medieval civilization and culture to profl. jours.

ROWLES, DONALD ROBERT, veterinarian; b. Canton, Ohio, Apr. 14, 1945; s. Robert David Tyson and Violet Kathleen (Walters) R.; m. Marcia Jean Fox, Mar. 15, 1969; children—Krista Lea, Kelly Elizabeth. D.V.M., Ohio State U., 1970. Chief surgery and radiology Amherst Animal Hosp., 1972-78; owner Landings Animal Hosp., Avon Lake, Ohio, 1978—, pres., 1980—; pres. Rowles and Assocs., Avon Lake, 1980—. Served to capt. USAF, 1970-72. Mem. Am. Animal Hosp. Assn., Am. Vet. Med. Assn., Ohio Vet. Med. Assn., Lorain County Vet. Med. Assn. (past pres.), Cleve. Acad. Vet. Medicine, Avon Lake Businessmen's Assn., Ohio State Alumni Assn., Stadium Dorm Alumni, Ohio Vet. Alumni Assn., Omega Tau Sigma. Republican. Mem. Assembly of God Ch. Clubs: Masons (Columbus, Ohio); Rotary (Avon Lake); Amherst Noonday (pres.).

ROWND, ROBERT HARVEY, biochemistry and molecular biology educator; b. Chgo., July 4, 1937; s. Walter Lemuel and Marie Francis (Joyce) R.; m. Rosalie Anne Lowery, June 13, 1959; children—Jennifer Rose, Robert Harvey, David Matthew. B.S. in Chemistry, St. Louis U., 1959; M.A. in Med. Scis., Harvard U., 1961; Ph.D. in Biophysics, 1963. Postdoctoral fellow Med. Research Council, NIH, Cambridge, Eng., 1963-65; postdoctoral fellow Nat. Acad. Scis.-NRC, Institut Pasteur, Paris, 1965-66; prof., chmn. molecular biology and biochemistry U. Wis.-Madison, 1966-81; John G. Searle prof., chmn. molecular biology and biochemistry Med. and Dental Schs., Northwestern U., Chgo., 1981—; cons. NIH, NSF, Nat. Acad. Scis.-NRC. Series editor: Advances in Plasmid Molecular Biology, 1984—. Assoc. editor Plasmid, 1977—. Mem. editorial bd. Jour. Bacteriology, 1975-81, editor, 1981—. Contbr. articles to profl. jours. Mem. troop com. treas. Four Lakes council Boy Scouts Am., 1973-77; mem. People to People Program del. of microbiologists to China, 1983; vice chmn. Gordon Conf. on Extrachromosomal Elements, 1984. Fellow NSF, NIH, 1959-66; research grantee, 1966—; tng. grantee, 1970-79, 82—; recipient Alumni Merit award and vis. prof. St. Louis U., 1984, USPHS Research Career Devel. award 1968-73. Mem. Am. Soc. Microbiology, Assn. Harvard Chemists, Am. Soc. Biol. Chemists, Am. Acad. Microbiology, N.Y. Acad. Scis. Home: 506 Lake Ave Wilmette IL 60091 Office: Northwestern U Med and Dental Schs 303 E Chicago Ave Chicago IL 60611

ROY, PATRICIA JANE, osteopathic physician; b. Muskegon, Mich., Feb. 27, 1956; d. Frank J. and Mary Jo (Gores) Stariha; m. Paul E. Roy, Jr., July 2, 1977; 1 dau., Jennifer Jo. Student U. Mich., 1974-75; B.S. magna cum laude, Aquinas Coll., 1978; D.O., Mich. State U., 1981. Intern, Muskegon (Mich.) Gen. Hosp., 1981-82; practice family medicine and obstetrics, Muskegon, 1982—; mem. staff Muskegon Gen. Hosp., Muskegon Hackley Hosp. Mem. med. adv. panel Hospice, Inc.; mem. med. adv. bd. Muskegon Area Planned Parenthood Assn.; med. dir. Lung Care, Inc.; mem. profl. edn. com. Muskegon County unit Am. Cancer Soc.; bd. dirs. West Mich. Health Care Network; chmn. com. on reproductive health Muskegon Pub. Schs.; del. City of Muskegon precinct, 1979-81. Named One of 5 Outstanding Young Women, Mich. Jaycees, 1984. Mem. Am. Osteo. Assn., West Mich. Osteo. Assn. (dir.), Fedn. Bus. and Profl. Women, Muskegon Quadrangle Club, Mich. Fedn. Bus. and Profl. Women (Young Career Woman Yr. 1983-84). Club: Century of Mich. (bd. govs.). Office: 1864 Lakeshore Dr Muskegon MI 49441

ROY, WILFRED ELMER (WILL), educator; b. Van Buren, Maine, Aug. 7, 1935; s. Leo and Isabel (Boudreau) R.; A.B. in English, Boston U., 1961; Ed.M., Salem State Coll., 1966; Ph.D. in Urban Edn., U. Wis., Milw., 1974; m. Michaeleen Kowalkowski; children—Denise, Patrice. Tchr., Amesbury (Mass.) High Sch., 1962-64, North Reading (Mass.) High Sch., 1964-67; asst. supt. schs., Windsor, Vt., 1967-69; Edn. Profl. Devel. Act fellow So. Ill. U., Edwardsville, 1969-70; assoc. prof. curriculum and instrn. dept. U. Wis., Milw., 1972—; cons. Nat. Center for Gifted, 1978-81, Am. Inst. for Human Interaction, 1978-81, Good Apple Inc., 1979—; speaker at convs. and confs. Served with USAF, 1953-57. NDEA fellow, 1967; fellow Robert A. Taft Inst. Practical Politics, 1967. Mem. Am. Humanist Assn., Assn. for Tchrs. Edn., N.Am. Soc. Adlerian Psychologists, World Congress of Logotherapy, Nat. Staff Devel. Council, Assn. Sch. Curriculum Devel., ACLU, Wis. Council for Gifted and Talented. Democrat. Roman Catholic. Author: Creative Coping: Ending the War with Yourself and Kids, 1980, 81; Using Language Arts to Motivate and Teach Communication Skills, 1982; Motivation and Communication, 1983, numerous others; contbr. articles to profl. publs. Home: 706 W Rock Pl Milwaukee WI 53209 Office: PO Box 413 Dept Curriculum & Instrn Sch Edn U Wis Milwaukee WI 53201

ROYKO, MIKE, newspaper columnist; b. Chgo., Sept. 19, 1932; s. Michael and Helen (Zak) R.; student Wright Jr. Coll., 1951-52; m. Carol Joyce Duckman, Nov. 7, 1954 (dec. 1979); children—M. David, Robert F. Reporter, Chgo. North Side Newspapers, 1956; reporter, asst. city editor Chgo. City News Bur., 1956-59; reporter, columnist Chgo. Daily News, 1959-78, Chgo. Sun Times, 1978-84, Chgo. Tribune, 1984—. Served with USAF, 1952-56. Recipient Heywood Brown award, 1968, Pulitzer prize for commentary, 1972. Mem. Chgo. Newspaper Reporters Assn. Club: LaSalle St. Rod and Gun. Author: Up Against It, 1967; I May Be Wrong but I Doubt It, 1968; Boss—Richard J. Daley of Chicago, 1971; Slats Grobnik and Some Other Friends, 1973; Sez Who? Sez Me, 1982. Office: Chgo Tribune 435 N Michigan Ave Chicago IL 60611*

ROYLE, RICHARD DWIGHT, instrument company executive; b. Mpls., Aug. 15, 1937; m. Donna Jean Opsal, Jan. 10, 1959; children—Craig, Jill. B.Mech.Engring., U. Minn., 1960. Engr., supr. Rosemount, Inc., Mpls., 1960-64, dept. mgr., 1964-67, br. sales mgr., San Francisco and Houston, 1967-74, dir. internat. ops., Mpls., 1974-77, sr. v.p., 1977—; dir. First Bank of Burnsville, Minn. Mem. Instrument Soc. Am. (sr.), Burnsville C. of C. (dir. 1983—). Avocations: micro-computers; automobile repair; reading. Office: Rosemount Inc 12001 W 78th St Eden Prairie MN 55344

ROZANSKI, EDWARD C(ASIMIR), editor, manager newspapers; b. Chgo., Mar. 7, 1915; s. Casimir Joseph and Bess (Kilinski) R.; m. Leocadia Procanin, Aug. 24, 1940. O.D., Ill. Coll. Optometry, 1948. Photographer, Washington Photo Studio, Chgo., 1931-39; photographer-reporter Zgoda, Polish daily, Chgo., 1939-42, 45-50, gen. mgr., editor, 1975—; shift supr. wet plate process chart and map reprodn. for U.S. Navy, U.S. Army, and U.S. Army Air Force with U.S. Coast and Geodetic Survey, USN, Washington, 1942-45; color specialist, gravure Cuneo Press, Chgo., 1950-75; gen. mgr. Dziennik Zwiazkowy, Polish daily, Chgo., 1975-85; mem. adv. bd. Chgo. Cath., 1983. Bd. dirs. Chgo. Access Corp.; mem. sch. bd., deacon St. Hyacinth Ch., Chgo.; mem. Ill. Hist. Records Adv. Bd.; active Polish Nat. Alliance, 1932—; v.p. PNA Youth Home Corp., 1975—; sec. Dist. XIII Polish Nat. Alliance, 1979—. Decorated chevalier Ordre Souverain Et Militaire du Temple de Jerusalem (France); Order Polonia Restituta, Gold Cross Legion of Honor, Gold Cross of Merit, Gen. Haller's Swords, Krzyz Zaslugi Cross of Merit (Poland); comdr. Order St. Lazarus of Jerusalem (Malta); Order Lafayette (U.S.); recipient citation Polish Legion Am. Vets, 1962, 63; citation Polish Combatans World War II, (4), Silver Emblem, 1968, Gold emblem, 1983; citation Polish Welfare Council Schenectady, 1964, Polonus Philatelic Soc., 1964; Lincoln plaquette Sta. WGN-Radio-TV, 1965, Silver medal Nat. Library Poland, 1980, Bronze medal Gen. Pulaski Museum, Warka, Poland, 1981, Legion of Honor medal Polish Falcons Am., 1982. Mem. Profl. Photographers Am., Photog. Soc. Am. (cornerstone mem.), Winona Sch. Profl. Photography (cornerstone mem.), Orchard Lake Schs. Alumni Assn. (hon.), Ill. Hist. Soc. (life), Societe Historique et Litteraire Polonaise (Paris life), Polish Mus. Am. (life), Polish Am. Congress (pres. Ill. div. 1966-70, 78-79, Heritage award 1983). Democrat. Lodges: KC, Giller Zann Soc., Polish Roman Cath. Union, others. Publisher: 100 Years of Polish Press in America, 1963; The Battle That Changed The Destiny of Europe, 1982; King John Sobieski, 1983; Life of Teofila Samolinska, 1980; Memoirs of General Kriz—Krzyzanowski Civil War General, 1963; editor PNA Almanac, 1977-84, Zgoda, 1982—. Home: 2650 N Monitor Ave Chicago IL 60639 Office: 6100 N Cicero Ave Chicago IL 60646

ROZELLE, LEE THEODORE, physical chemist; b. Rhinelander, Wis., Mar. 9, 1933; s. Theodore and Alice (Omholt) R.; B.S., U. Wis., 1955, Ph.D. (NIH fellow, 1958-60), 1960; m. Barbara J. Ingli, June 21, 1955; children—David, Steven, Carolyn, Ann, Kenneth. Research chemist DuPont Corp., Circleville, Ohio, 1960-63; prin. scientist-tech. coordinator Honeywell, Mpls., 1963-67; dir. chemistry div. North Star Research Inst., Mpls., 1967-74; v.p. research and devel. USCI div. C.R. Bard, Billerica, Mass., 1974-77; dir. engring. tech. div. Mellon Inst., Pitts., 1977-78; dir. research and devel. Permutit Co., Monmouth Junction, N.J., 1978-80; v.p. research and devel. Gelman Scis., Inc., Ann Arbor, Mich., 1980-82; v.p. sci. and tech. Culligan Internat. Co., Northbrook, Ill., 1982—; cons. Bd. dirs. Unitarian Ch., Andover, Mass., 1974-77. Fellow Am. Inst. Chemists; mem. Am. Chem. Soc., Am. Soc. Artificial Internal Organs, Health Industry Mfrs. Assn. (chmn. spl. activities com.), Water Pollution Control Fedn., Water Quality Assn. (chmn. sci. adv. com.), Am. Water Works Assn., AAAS, Filtration Soc., Am. Soc. Agrl. Engring., Sigma Xi, Eta Phi Alpha, Phi Lambda Upsilon. Contbr. chpts. to books, numerous articles to profl. jours. Home: 853 Sanborn Dr Palatine IL 60067 Office: One Culligan Pkwy Northbrook IL 60062

ROZRAN, JACK LOUIS, lawyer, courier service executive; b. Chgo., Mar. 4, 1939; s. Philip Reuben and Rose (Rosenberg) R.; m. Andrea Dale Rice, Sept. 6, 1965 (div.). B.A., Northwestern U., 1960; J.D., Harvard U., 1963. Bar: Ill. 1963. Law clk. to judge U.S. Dist. Ct. Ill., 1963-64; v.p. Cannonball, Inc., Chgo., 1964-66, pres., 1966—. Bd. dirs. Hull House Assn., 1972-78, 80—; sec. Erickson Inst., 1982. Mem. Messenger Service Assn. Ill. (pres. 1971—), Air Courier Conf. Am. (treas. 1980-82, pres. 1982-84), ABA, Chgo. Bar Assn., Beta Alpha Psi. Home: 2650 N Lakeview Ave Chicago IL 60614 Office: Cannonball Inc 400 N Orleans St Chicago IL 60610

RUBENS, SIDNEY MICHEL, technical advisor; b. Spokane, Wash., Mar. 21, 1910; s. Max Zvoln and Jennie Golda (Rubinovich) R.; B.S., U. Wash., 1934, Ph.D., 1939; m. Julienne Rose Fridner, May 11, 1944; 1 dau., Deborah Janet. Instr. U. So. Calif., 1939-40; research asso. U. Calif. at Los Angeles, 1940-41; physicist Naval Ordnance Lab., Washington, 1941-46; physicist Engring. Research Assos., St. Paul, 1946-52; mgr. physics Univac div. Sperry Rand, St. Paul, 1958-61, dir. research, 1961-66, staff scientist, 1969-71, dir. spl. projects, 1971-75; cons., 1975-81; technical adv. Vertimag Systems Corp., 1981—; lectr. U. Pa., 1960-61; mem. adv. subcom. on instrumentation and data processing NASA, 1967-69, panel on computer tech. Nat. Acad. Sci., 1969. Hon. fellow U. Minn., 1977—. Fellow IEEE; mem. Am. Phys. Soc., Am. Geophys. Union, AAAS, Acad. Applied Sci., Minn. Acad. Sci., Am. Optical Soc., Phi Beta Kappa, Sigma Xi, Pi Mu Epsilon. Patentee in magnetic material and devices. Author: Amplifier and Memory Devices, 1965. Contbr. articles to profl. jours. Home: 1077 Sibley Hwy Apt 506 St Paul MN 55118 Office: Vertimag Systems Corp 814 14th Ave SE Minneapolis MN 55414

RUBENSTEIN, ALBERT IRWIN, real estate developer, lawyer; b. Chgo., Mar. 28, 1927; s. William D. and Regina (Ribaysen) R.; student Herzl City Coll., 1944-46, Roosevelt Coll., 1946-48; LL.B., J.D., John Marshall Law Sch., 1951; m. Joyce Shirley Leeman, June 12, 1954; children—Jeffrey, Lauren, Jan. Bar: Ill. 1951. Sole practice law, Chgo., 1951-64; pres., chief exec. officer Fleetwood Realty Corp., Chgo., 1969—, also dir.; sr. partner Fleetwood Realty Co., Chgo., 1969-83; pres. Fleetwood Devel. Corp., 1983—; dir. Exec. Bus. Center, Inc., Fleetwood Industries; lectr. corp. real estate fin. and devel. Bd. dirs. Feinberg Charitable Found., 1969—, Hebrew Theol. Coll., 1975—; mem. Highland Park (Ill.) Planning Commn., 1980—, Highland Park Econ. Devel. Com., 1984; spl. real estate negotiator by mayoral appointment, Highland Park, 1980. Recipient Outstanding Alumnus award John Marshall Law Sch., 1982; named 1 of top 10 real estate developers Chicago mag., 1981. Mem. ABA, Ill. Bar Assn., Chgo. Bar Assn., Am. Trial Lawyers Assn., Chgo. Assn. Commerce and Industry, Nat. Real Estate Bd., Chgo. Real Estate Bd. (dir. 1980-82), Decalogue Soc. Lawyers, Nat. Realty Com., Inc., Am. Arbitration Soc. Clubs: Covenant, Execs. (Chgo.). Lodge: B'nai B'rith. Contbr. articles in field to profl. jours. Office: 200 W Jackson Blvd Chicago IL 60606

RUBENSTEIN, DAVID A., city official; b. Fresno, Calif., July 8, 1946; s. Ned H. Rubenstein and Edwina A. Atherton; m. Linda Rubenstein, May 11, 1967; children—Ned, Deborah. B.S., U. Wis-Superior, 1968; M.P.A., U. S.C., 1973. City supt. City of Zeeland (Mich.), 1973-77; city mgr. City of Englewood (Ohio), 1977-79, City of Walker (Mich.), 1981—; dep. county adminstr. Montgomery County, Ohio, 1979-81; lectr. Sinclair Community Coll., Dayton, Ohio, 1979-82, Aquinas Coll., Grand Rapids, Mich., 1984. Bd. dirs. Temple Emanuel, Grand Rapids, 1983—, 3d v.p., 1985-87; chmn. recreation bd., Walker; Vice-chmn. Policy and Research Com. GGREAT, Grand Rapids; mem. Labor Relations Adv. Com., Mich. Mcpl. League. Served to capt. USAF, 1968-73. Recipient Civic Service award City of Zeeland, 1976, Englewood City Council, 1979. Mem. Internat. City Mgmt. Assn. (data and info. services adv. council 1984-85), Montgomery City Mayors and Mgrs. Assn. (sec.-treas. 1979), West Mich. City Mgrs. Assn. (pres. 1985), Am. Soc. Pub. Adminstrs. Jewish. Avocations: astronomy, running, reading, chess. Office: City of Walker 4243 Remembrance Rd NW Walker MI 49504

RUBIN, CARL BERNARD, judge; b. Cin., Mar. 27, 1920; s. John I. and Ethel (Friedman) R.; B.A., U. Cin., 1942, J.D., 1944; m. Gloria Weiland, Sept. 23, 1945; children—Marc W., C. Barry, Pam G., Robert S. Bar: Ohio 1944. Practiced in Cin., 1944-71; asst. pros. atty. Hamilton County (Ohio), Cin., 1950-60; judge U.S. Dist. Ct. So. Dist. Ohio, 1971—, chief judge, 1979—; instr. criminal law Chase Coll. Law, Cin., 1965-67; mem. com. on ct. adminstrn. fed. cts. U.S. Jud. Conf., 1975-83; adj. prof. law U. Dayton Coll. Law, 1976. Mem. Cin. CSC, 1960-66, chmn., 1965-66; pres. S.W. Ohio Regional Transit Authority, 1971. Mem. Am. Contract Bridge League (dir. 1966-73, pres. 1970-71). Office: US Courthouse 5th and Walnut Sts Cincinnati OH 45202

RUBIN, LOUIS SELIK, historian, writer, poet; b. Vilno, Russia, Aug. 7, 1911; s. Sol and Nadia (Tsirulnicoff) R. Ed. Leningrad Cinema Inst., Herzen U., Detroit Cass Tech. Inst., Balt. John's Hopkins U., Western Res. U. Tchr. Russian lang.-history Ohio Sch. Social Scis.; transl. Russian poetry into English, English poetry into Russian; author poems on chess and designated poet laureate of chess; author: We Went to Vietnam; Digest of the Red Archives; interviewer late Israeli Minister Moshe Dayan, Israeli Supreme Ct. Justice Gabriel Bach. Address: 12819 Park Knoll Dr Cleveland OH 44125

RUBINGER, MARC DAVID, hospital and healthcare consultant, planner, business advisor; b. N.Y.C., Apr. 27, 1949; s. Louis S. and Beatrice R. (Sklar) R.; m. Carol Sevush, Dec. 26, 1971; children—Lauren, Rachel, Benjamin. B.A. in Biology, SUNY-Binghamton, 1971; M.H.A., George Washington U., 1973. Healthcare cons. MDC Systems, Inc., Washington, 1971-72; hosp. and facility planner Manor Care, Inc., Silver Spring, Md., 1972-77; hosp. cons. Ernst & Whinney, Washington, 1977-79, Cleve., 1979—, prin., healthcare cons., 1983—. Mem. Am. Coll. Hosp. Adminstrs. (nominee), Am. Hosp. Assn. Office: 2000 National City Center Cleveland OH 44114

RUBINS, IRA MARC, ednl. adminstr.; b. Cleve., Nov. 4, 1947; s. Alex and Betty (Buller) R.; B.A., Miami U., Ohio, 1969, M.A., 1971; postgrad. Kent State U.; m. Sherry Ruth Weintraub, Aug. 24, 1969; children—Jennifer Sarah, Dana Reed; m. Cathie Snyder, May 8, 1985; 1 child, Maxwell Hoffman. Producer of Radio Talk Music Show, Sta. WIXY, Cleve., 1970-71; chmn. broadcast mgmt. dept. Jones Coll., Jacksonville, Fla., 1971-72; announcer Sta. WKTZ, Jacksonville, Fla., 1971-72; faculty coordinator WIXY Sch. Broadcast Technique, Cleve., 1973-75; dir. edn. Ohio Sch. Broadcast Technique, Cleve., 1975-82; v.p. Ednl. Broadcast Services, Inc., Cleve., 1975-82; v.p. Nashville Sch. Broadcasting Technique, 1980-82; ctr. dir. Airco Tech. Inst., Cleve., 1982-84; sch. dir. PSI Inst., Cleve., 1984—; dir. auctions Renaissance Fine Arts Gallery, Cleve., 1974-82. Mem. Nat. Assn. of Trade and Tech. Schs. (public relations com. 1976-79, chmn. 1979-80), Nat. Assn. Ednl. Broadcasters (mem. broadcast edn. com. 1975-77), Radio TV Council Greater Cleve., Northeastern Ohio Chpt. Proprietary Schs. (sec. 1977-79, pres. 1979-80), Ohio Council Pvt. Colls. and Schs. (sec. 1977-80, dir. 1977-83). Jewish. Home: 3721 Gridley Rd Shaker Heights OH 44122 Office: 1858 Euclid Ave Cleveland OH 44115

RUBINSTEIN, ROY, physicist; b. Darlington, Eng., Sept. 12, 1936; came to U.S., 1962; s. Solly and Miriam (Hyams) R.; m. Nora Dodokin, Oct. 5, 1968; children—Alexander, Anita. B.A., U. Cambridge, Eng., 1958; Ph.D., U. Birmingham, Eng., 1961. Research fellow U. Birmingham, 1961-62; research assoc., acting asst. prof. Cornell U., Ithaca, N.Y., 1962-66; scientist Brookhaven Nat. Lab., Upton N.Y., 1966-73, scientist Fermi Nat. Accelerator Lab. Batavia, Ill., 1973—, asst. dir. 1983—. Contbr. articles to profl. jours. grantee NATO, 1984. Mem. Am. Phys. Soc. Home: 21 W 454 Fairway St Glen Ellyn IL 60137 Office: Fermi Nat Accelerator Lab PO Box 500 Batavia IL 60510

RUBLE, BERNARD ROY, consultant, educator; b. Greensburg, Ind., Apr. 4, 1923; s. Jesse Emory and Marietta (Ward) R.; B.S., Ind. U., Bloomington, 1949; postgrad. transactional analysis Midwest Inst. Human Understanding, 1972-75; m. Mary Helen Rullman, Dec. 22, 1946; children—Barry Reece, Blane Rodney. Asst. mgr. Morris 5 and 10 Stores, Greensburg, 1941; store keeper Public Service Co. Ind., Greensburg, 1941-43; asst. mgr. personnel Kroger Co., Cin., 1949-51, mgr., personnel, Madison, Wis., 1951-56, Ft. Wayne, Ind., 1956-58, Cleve., 1958-73, mgr. labor relations Erie Mktg. Area, Solon, Ohio, 1973-84; faculty Kroger Edn. Center, Cin., 1978-82; Indsl. Relations Ctr. Cleve. State U., 1985—; ; trustee Meat Cutters Health and Welfare Fund, 1971-79, Retail Clks. Union Health and Welfare Fund, Akron, 1970—, No. Ohio Hospice Council, 1981-84. Active United Appeal Greater Cleve., Community Chest Greater Cleve., Met. Health Planning Corp.; v.p., trustee Urban League Greater Cleve., 1968-75; adv. com. Family Health Care, Washington, 1977-78; trustee Community Health Found.; team rep. B.R. Ruble Racing, Chesterland, Ohio. Served with USAAF, 1943-45. Mem. Internat. Transactional Analysis Assn. (cert. clin), Ohio Transactional Analysis Assn. (trustee), Photog. Soc. Am., Soc. for Advancement Mgmt. (trustee Madison chpt. 1952-55), Am. Soc. Personnel Adminstrn., Cleve. Personnel Assn., Indsl. Relations Research Assn. (pres.). Clubs: Masons, Sertoma (trustee Madison 1952-58) (charter). Lic. minister Disciples Christ, 1975. Home and Office: 8644 Ranch Dr Chesterland OH 44026

RUBLOFF, BURTON, real estate broker, appraiser; b. Chisholm, Minn., June 1, 1912; s. Solomon W. and Mary R.; grad. Northwestern U., 1940; m. Patricia F. Williams, July 17, 1943; 1 dau., Jenifer. Entire business career with Arthur Rubloff & Co., Chgo. (now Rubloff Inc.), 1930—, v.p., 1947-76, sr. v.p., 1976—. Bd. dirs. Municipal Art League Chgo., Served as sgt. AUS, 36th Div., ETO, 1943-46. Mem. Am. Inst. Real Estate Appraisers (life), Nat., Ill., Chgo. (hon. life) assns. real estate bds., Bldg. Mgrs. Assn. Chgo., Greater State Street Council (real estate com.), Chgo. Real Estate Bd. (ethics com.), Lambda Alpha. Clubs: City (gov.); The John Evans (Northwestern U.), Plaza, Northwestern of Chgo. Home: 633 N Waukegan Rd Lake Forest IL 60045 Office: 69 W Washington St Chicago IL 60602

RUCKER, WILLIAM HALL, hazardous and nuclear materials transportation executive; b. Joplin, Mo., Sept. 5, 1945; s. Booker Hall and Louise Norwood (McConathy) R.; m. Glenda Marie Riley, Aug. 7, 1971; children—Jacqueline, Marie, Monica Nicole. B.S., Mo. So. State Coll., 1972, A.S., 1977. Operator Security Unltd., Joplin, 1970-71; customer relations rep. Tri State Motor, Joplin, 1972—. Chmn. Webb City United Way, Mo.; mem. Webb City Council, 1982; bd. dirs. Sr. Citizen Adv. Council, Webb City Park Bd. Served with U.S. Army, 1966-70; Vietnam. Decorated Bronze Star; recipient Cert. Merit, Mo. Betterment Com.; named Eagle Scout, Boy Scouts Am. Democrat. Presbyterian. Clubs: Soccer Assn. (treas. 1983—), Girls Softball (bd. dirs. 1983) (Webb City). Avocations: racquetball, golf, hunting, fishing, reading, refinishing furniture. Home: 303 Golf Rd Webb City MO 64870 Office: Tri State Motor Transit PO Box 113 Joplin MO 64801

RUCKERT, ROGER GARMS, medical electronics company executive, musician; b. Glen Ridge, N.J., Sept. 27, 1955; s. Ernest Herman and Virginia Viola (Fischbeck) R.; m. Kristine Irene Schroeder, Dec. 20, 1980; children—Claire Elizabeth, Paul Roger. B.A., Princeton U. 1977; M.F.A., U. Minn., 1979, D.Musical Arts, 1981, M.S. in Computer Sci., 1983. Sales rep. Hartz Mountain Corp., Bloomington, Minn., 1979-80; applications programmer U. Minn., Mpls., 1980-82; programmer/analyst Medtronic, Inc., Mpls., 1982-84, systems programmer, 1985—. Composer string quartet, 1980, 2 short pieces for piano, 1982. Mem. Assn. Computing Machinery. Lutheran. Avocations: chess; canoeing; camping. Office: Medtronic Inc 6970 Old Central Ave Minneapolis MN 55432

RUDD, AMANDA SULLIVAN, library ofcl.; b. Greenville, S.C., Apr. 9, 1923; d. Wesley and Delarion Sullivan; B.S., Fla. A&M U., 1955; M.L.S., Western Res. U., 1962. Tchr., librarian schs., S.C., Alaska, Fla. and Ohio; asst. supr. sch. libraries, Cleve. Public Schs., 1965-70; cons. ednl. services dept. Field Enterprises Ednl. Corp., Chgo., 1970-75; asst. chief librarian community relations and spl. program of service Chgo. Public Library, 1975, dept. commr., 1975-81, commr., 1981—. Bd. overseers Sch. Library Sci. Case Western Res. U.; mem. Chgo. dist. bd. ARC; mem. adv. council Chgo. Urban Skills Inst.; mem. adv. com. Ill. State Library. Mem. ALA, Public Library Assn., Ill. Library Assn., Case Western Res. U. Alumni Assn. Home: 601 E 32d St Chicago IL 60616 Office: 425 N Michigan Ave Chicago IL 60611*

RUDD, BERNARD J., ins. co. ofcl.; b. Louisville, Oct. 2, 1938; s. Leon and Effie R.; student public schs., Jeffersonville, Ind.; m. Linda Wolfe, Feb. 14, 1964; 1 son, Jason. With Prudential Ins. Co., 1961—, agt., New Albany, Ind., 1961-64, sales mgr., 1964-69, sales mgr., South Bend, Ind., 1969-71, agt., Lafayette, Ind., 1971, sales mgr., 1971-73, gen. mgr., Evansville, Ind., 1973—. Served with USAF, 1956-60. Recipient various sales awards. Mem. Nat. Assn. C.L.U .'s (dir.), Nat. Assn. Accts., Gen. Agts. and Mgrs. Assn. Methodist. Clubs: Old Time Car (v.p.), Optimists (pres.), Jaycees. Home: 300 Kingsvalley Rd Evansville IN 47711 Office: PO Box 888 Evansville IN 47706

RUDEN, VIOLET HOWARD (MRS. CHARLES VAN KIRK RUDEN), Christian Sci. tchr., practitioner; b. Dallas; d. Millard Fillmore and Henrietta Frederika (Kurth) Howard; B.J., U. Tex., 1931; C.S.B., Mass. Metaphys. Coll., 1946; m. Charles Van Kirk Ruden, Nov. 24, 1932. Radio continuity writer Home Mgmt. Club broadcast Sta. WHO, Des Moines, 1934; joined First Ch. of Christ Scientist, Boston, 1929; C.S. practitioner, Des Moines, 1934—; C.S. minister WAC, Ft. Des Moines, 1942-45; 1st reader 2d Ch. of Christ Scientist, Des Moines, 1952, Sunday sch. tchr., 1934—; instr. primary class in Christian Sci., 1947—. Trustee Asher Student Found. Drake U., Des Moines, 1973. Mem. Women in Communications, Mortar Bd., Orchesis, Cap and Gown. Republican. Club: Des Moines Women's. Home: 5808 Walnut Hill Dr Des Moines IA 50312 Office: 206 Kresge Bldg Des Moines IA 50309

RUDICK, MILTON MARTIN, civil engineer, contractor; b. Youngstown, Ohio, July 11, 1920; s. Ben and Dina (Greenblatt) R.; B.S., Carnegie Mellon U., 1946; m. Marie Taussig, June 28, 1945; children—Jerald David, Leonard Taussig, Lois. Engr., Truscon Steel Co., Youngstown, 1946-48; asst. chief engr. Ring Constrn. Co., Albany, N.Y., 1948-49; exec. v.p. Ben Rudick & Son, Inc., Youngstown, 1949-74, pres., 1974—; pres. Nat. Fire Repair, Inc., 1976—; bldg. damage cons., 1965—. Bd. dirs., pres. Rodef Sholom Temple. Served to 2d lt. C.E., AUS, 1943-45. Mem. ASCE (fire protection subcom.), Nat. Soc. Profl. Engrs., Builders Assn. Eastern Ohio and Western Pa. Clubs: Rotary, B'nai B'rith, Squaw Creek Country, Youngstown. Home: 579 Tod Ln Youngstown OH 44504 Office: 855 Tod Ave Youngstown OH 44502

RUDISILL, JOHN RICHARD, clinical psychologist, educator; b. Tulia, Tex., Jan. 2, 1947; s. Ray Burnley and Ruth Arlene (Blackburn) R.; m. Marla Elifritz, Aug. 30, 1969; children—John Stephen, Matthew James, Alisha Dawn. B.A. in Psychology, Denison U., 1969; Ph.D., Ind. U., 1974. Lic. psychologist, Ohio. Chief psychologist, program dir. Dayton (Ohio) Mental Health Ctr., 1977-79; dir. med. student edn. dept. psychiatry Wright State U. Sch. Medicine, Dayton, 1979—, coordinator behavioral sci. of family practice, 1979—; pvt. psychology, Dayton, 1977—; cons. Job Corp. Dartmouth Hosp., Dayton, 1977—; cons. Dayton VA Ctr., 1983—; cons. Wright AFB Med. Ctr., Dayton, 1982—, IAMS Co., Lewisburg, Ohio; mem. Montgomery County Mental Health Bd., vice-chair, 1984; mem. Juvenile Court Citizen Review Bd. Served to capt. USAF, 1973-77. Denison U. Founders' scholar, 1965-69; NIMH fellow, 1971, grantee, 1972-73; named Tchr. of Yr., Wright State U. Sch. Medicine, 1981-82; recipient Wright State's Chmn. award psychiatry, 1982. Mem. Am. Psychol. Assn., Ohio Psychol. Assn., Miami Valley Psychol. Assn. (past pres.), Mental Health Assn., Am. Orthopsychiat. Assn., Assn. Behavioral Scis. in Med. Edn., Assn. Advancement Psychology, Acad. of Marital and Family Sex Therapy. Methodist. Clubs: Ind. Alumni, Denison Alumni, D-Man. Contbr. articles in field to profl. jours. Home: 113 Herr St Englewood OH 45322

RUDMAN, EDITH GREENBERG, art gallery director; b. Cedar Rapids, Iowa, Dec. 11, 1941; d. Morris and Lillian (Bunes) Greenberg; m. Burton Lester Rudman, Apr. 6, 1969; 1 son, Arye David. B.A., State U. Iowa, 1964; postgrad. Roosevelt U., Chgo., 1965-67. Editorial asst. Scott, Foresman and Co., Chgo., 1964-65; English tchr. Hadassah Coll., Jerusalem, 1970-71; freelance writer and editor of ednl. filmstrips and materials, Chgo., 1972-73; English tchr. Iran-Am. Soc., Tehran, 1974, Lang. House, Tehran, 1974; documentation specialist Computer Scis. Corp., Tehran, 1975; dir. Gallery Lainzberg Specialists in Animation Art, Cedar Rapids, Iowa, 1976—; cons. Time-Life, 1978—. Mem. Internat. Animated Film Soc., Profl. Picture Framers' Assn. Jewish. Office: Corner of 3d Ave and 3d St 417 Guaranty Bldg Cedar Rapids IA 52401

RUDNIK, SISTER MARY CHRYSANTHA, college administrator; b. Winona, Minn., Dec. 2, 1929; d. Basil John and Sarah (Knopick) Rudnik; student Loyola U., 1951-52, Felician Coll., 1952-54, Cardinal Stritch Coll., 1954-57, Coll. St. Francis, 1957; Ph.B., DePaul U., 1958; postgrad. Mundelein Coll., 1959-60, Northeastern Ill. State U., 1964; M.A., Rosary Coll., 1962. Joined Congregation of Sisters of St. Felix of Cantalice, Roman Cath. Ch., 1948; cert. fund raising exec. Nat. Soc. Fund Raising Execs. Page, clk. Hill Reference Library, St. Paul, 1946-48; tchr. Holy Innocents Sch., Chgo., 1948-49, 50-54, St. Bruno Sch., Chgo., 1954-55, Holy Family Sch., Cudahy, Wis., 1955-57, Good Counsel High Sch., Chgo., 1958-67; instr. Felician Coll., Chgo., 1963—, head librarian, 1957-82, dir. devel. and public relations, 1975—. Organizer, coordinator Felician Library Service, 1966-74, Arts and Crafts Festival, 1972—; coordinator instl. self-study for accreditation North Central Assn.; mem. task force for study of instl. research for Ill. Assn. Community and Jr. Colls., 1968; library cons. St. Clement Sch., 1969. Rev. Andrew Bowhuis meml. scholar Cath. Library Assn., 1960. Cert. fund raising exec. Nat. Soc. Fund Raising Execs. Mem. Nat. Soc. Fund Raising Execs., Council for Advancement and Support of Edn., Cath. Library Assn. (life, chmn. No. Ill. unit 1968-69, exec. bd. 1981—), Council Support and Advancement Edn., Art Inst. Chgo. (life), Council on Library Tech. (v.p. 1970, pres. 1971). Address: 3800 Peterson Ave Chicago IL 60659

RUDY, DAVID ROBERT, physician; b. Columbus, Ohio, Oct. 19, 1934; s. Robert Sale and Lois May (Arthur) R.; B.Sc., Ohio State U.,1956, M.D., 1960; m. Rose Mary Sims; children by previous marriage—Douglas D., Steven W., Katharine L. Intern, Northwestern Meml. Hosp., Chgo., 1960-61; resident in internal medicine Ohio State U. Hosp., 1963-64; resident in pediatrics Children's Hosp., Columbus, Ohio, 1964; practice medicine specializing in family practice, Columbus, 1964-75; dir. Family Practice Center and residency program Riverside Meth. Hosp., Columbus, 1975-85; dir. Family Practice Ctr. and residency Monsour Med. Ctr., Jeannette, Pa., 1985—; clin. assoc. prof. Ohio State U. Served as capt., Flight surgeon, M.C., USAF, 1961-63. Diplomate Am. Bd. Family Practice (charter). Fellow Am. Acad. Family Physicians; mem. AMA, Ohio Med. Assn., Central Ohio Acad. Family Practice (pres. 1979), Pa. Acad. Family Physicians (bd. dirs. 1985—), Columbus Maennerchor, Columbus Med. Symposium (pres. 1981), Mensa. Republican. Contbr. articles to profl. jours. Home: 1633 Timberlake Dr Delaware OH 43015 also 432 Slate Run Rd Greensburg PA 15601 Office: 70 Lincoln Way E Jeannette PA 15644

RUEGSEGGER, DONALD RAY, JR., radiol. physicist, educator; b. Detroit, May 29, 1942; s. Donald Ray and Margaret Arlene (Elliot) R.; B.S., Wheaton Coll., 1964; M.S., Ariz. State U., 1966, Ph.D. (NDEA fellow), 1969; m. Judith Ann Merrill, Aug. 20, 1965; children—Steven, Susan, Mark, Ann. Radiol. physicist Miami Valley Hosp., Dayton, Ohio, 1969—, chief med. physics sect., 1983—; physics cons. X-ray dept. VA Hosp., Dayton, 1970—; adj. asst. prof. physics Wright State U., Fairborn, Ohio, 1973—, clin. asst. prof. radiology, 1976-81, clin. assoc. prof. radiology, 1981—, group leader in med. physics, dept. radiol. scis. Med. Sch., 1978—. Diplomate Am. Bd. Radiology. Mem. Am. Assn. Physicists in Medicine (pres.-elect chpt. 1981-82), Am. Coll. Radiology, Am. Coll. Med. Physics (founding chancellor), Am. Phys. Soc., AAAS, Ohio Radiol. Soc., Health Physics Soc. Baptist. Home: 2018 Washington Creek Ln Centerville OH 45459 Office: Radiation Therapy Miami Valley Hospital 1 Wyoming St Dayton OH 45409

RUESCHHOFF, NORLIN GERHARD, accounting educator; b. Howells, Nebr.; m. Ottilie Seifert, Dec. 29, 1958; 1 dau. B.S., Creighton U., 1955; M.A., U. Nebr., 1965, Ph.D., 1968. C.P.A., Nebr. Acct. J.L. Tucker Co., Omaha, 1952-55, controller, 1956-57; pvt. practice acctg., Omaha, 1955-69; internal auditor-internat. Stars and Stripes, Europe, 1958-61, chief acct., 1961-63; instr. acctg. U. Nebr., Lincoln, 1966-68, asst. prof., U. Notre Dame, Ind., 1969-72, assoc. prof., 1972—, dept. chmn., 1979-83; dir. F.I.R.E., Inc., South Bend, 1971—. Author: International Accounting and Financial Reporting, 1976; (with Adolf Enthoven) Accounting Education and the Third World, 1978; contbr. articles to profl. jours.; co-editor Internat. Acctg. Forum, 1983—. Mem. Am. Acctg. Assn., Internat. Assn. for Acctg. Edn. and Research, Nat. Soc. Accts. for Coops., Interamerican Acctg. Assn., Am. Inst. C.P.A.s, Acad. Internat. Bus., Inst. Internal Auditors, Nebr. Soc. C.P.A.s, Ind. C.P.A. Soc., European Acctg. Assn., Beta Alpha Psi, Beta Gamma Sigma. Home: 18553 S Cypress Circle South Bend IN 46637 Office: U Notre Dame Dept Acctg Notre Dame IN 46556

RUFF, CRAIG, consultant; b. Saginaw, Mich., Mar. 27, 1949; s. Marwood and Emma R.; m. Janice Felder, May 6, 1973. A.B., U. Mich., 1971, M.P.P., 1973. Spl. asst. to Gov. Milliken, Lansing, Mich., 1972-79; exec. asst. to Lt. Gov. Brickley, Lansing, 1979-83; v.p. Pub. Sector Cons., Inc., Lansing, 1983—. Address: Public Sector Consultants Inc 300 S Washington Sq Lansing MI 48933

RUFF, JULIUS RALPH, historian, educator; b. Staten Island, N.Y., Aug. 28, 1946; s. Julius Lincoln and Ruth Brownell (Wilbur) R.; m. Laura Ann Blair, Aug. 12, 1972; 1 child, Julia Blair. A.B. in History, Guilford Coll., 1968; M.A. in History Lehigh U., 1970; Ph.D. in History, U. N.C., 1979. Instr. history Lees-McRae Coll., Banner Elk, N.C., 1976-77; asst. prof. Averett Coll., Danville, Va., 1977-80, Marquette U., Milw., 1980-85, assoc. prof., 1985—; cons. Houghton-Mifflin Pub. Co., Boston, 1984. Author: Crime, Justice and Public Order in Old Regime France, 1984. Contbr. articles and book chpt. to profl. publs. George Lurcy fellow U. N.C., 1974-75; Mellon grantee Marquette U., 1983-85. Mem. Am. Hist. Assn., Am. Soc. Legal History, Soc. French Hist. Studies, Council European Studies, Soc. Sci. History Assn. Office: Marquette U History Dept Charles L Coughlin Hall Milwaukee WI 53233

RUFF, ROBERT LOUIS, neurologist, physiology researcher; b. Bklyn., Dec. 16, 1950; s. John Joseph and Rhoda (Alpert) R.; m. Louise Seymour Acheson, Apr. 26, 1980. B.S. with highest honors, Cooper Union, 1971; M.D. with highest honors in Medicine, U. Wash., 1976. Diplomate Am. Bd. Neurology and Psychiatry. Asst. neurologist N.Y. Hosp., Cornell Med. Sch., N.Y.C., 1977-80; asst. prof. physiology and medicine U. Wash., Seattle, 1980-84; assoc. prof. neurology Case Western Res. Med. Sch., Cleve., 1984; chief dept. neurology Cleve. VA Med. Ctr., 1984—; adv. Child Devel. and Mental Retardation Ctr., Seattle, 1980—, Burien Devel. Disability Ctr., Wash., 1982-84; mem. med. adv. bd. Muscular Dystrophy Assn., Seattle, 1984. Contbr. articles to profl. jours. and chpts. to books. NSF Fellow, 1971; grantee NIH, Muscular Dystrophy Assn.; N.Y. State Regents med. scholar, 1971, Tchr. Investigator awardee NIH. Fellow Am. Heart Assn. (stroke council); mem. Am. Physics Soc., Am. Acad. Neurology, AMA, Neurosci., Biophys. Soc., N.Y. Acad. Sci., Am. Geriatrics Soc., Sigma Pi Sigma (v.p. 1970-71), Alpha Omega Alpha (v.p. 1975-76). Democrat. Home: 2572 Stratford Rd Cleveland Heights OH 44110 Office: VA Med Ctr 127 W 10701 East Blvd Cleveland OH 44106

RUFFIN, RICHARD D(AVID), urologist; b. Cairo, Ill., July 7, 1924; s. Edward David and Alpha Mae (Curtis) R.; m. Yvonne White, May 14, 1953; children—Richard David, Patti Yvonne, Kenneth George. Student NO. Ill. U., 1940-41; student Ill. State U., 1941-43, U. Ill., 1946-47; M.D., Meharry Med. Coll., 1953. Intern Homer G. Phillips Hosp., St. Louis, 1953-54, resident in surgery, 1954-55, resident in urology, 1955-58; practice medicine specializing in urology, Columbus, Ohio, 1958—; mem. staff St. Anthony Hosp., Grant Hosp., Children's Hosp., St. Ann's Hosp.; cons. urology Ohio Dept. Rehab. and Correction, 1975-78. Served to cpl. U.S. Army, 1943-45; ETO. Recipient citation of citizenship Columbus Div. Police, 1971; Pres.'s award for 25 yrs. service Meharry Med. Coll., 1978; award for 25 yrs. Service Children's Hosp., 1984, Grant Hosp., 1984. Mem. Columbus Acad. Medicine, Ohio State Med. Assn., AMA, Central Ohio Urol. Soc. (sec.-treas. 1964-65, pres. 1967-68), Am. Urol. Assn., Columbus Assn. Physicians and Dentists. Home: 3236 E Livingston Ave Columbus OH 43227 Office: Franklin Park Med Ctr 1829 E Long St Columbus OH 43203

RUGER, ANTHONY TODD, theological seminary official; b. Huntington, N.Y., May 5, 1948; s. Henry William and Dorothy Rosa (Jennemann) R.; m. Deborah Jane Kapp, Jan. 17, 1976. B.A., Johns Hopkins U., 1970; M.Div., Union Theol. Sem., 1973; M.S. in Indsl. Adminstrn., Carnegie Mellon U., 1980. Mgr. Budget Union Theol. Sem., N.Y.C., 1973-75; dir. devel., sec. alumni, 1975-77; bus. mgr. McCormick Theol. Sem., Chgo., 1980-83, v.p. bus. affairs, 1983—; cons. United Theol. Sem., New Brighton, Minn., 1979-81, Robert Nelson Assocs., Chgo., 1982-83, Ghost Ranch, N.Mex., 1983, Auburn Theol. Sem., N.Y.C., 1984. Author: (with Badgett Dillard) Changes in Financial Support of Protestant Theological Education, 1971-1981, 1983. Treas. film prodn. Edgar Allan Poe project, 1983-84. Mem. Nat. Assn. Coll. and Univ. Bus. Officers. Avocation: golf. Home: 1528 E 59th St Chicago IL 60637 Office: 5555 S Woodlawn Chicago IL 60637

RUGGLES, MICHAEL LEE, insurance company executive; b. Danville, Ill., Dec. 30, 1938; s. Fred William and Mary Kathryn (Waltzer) R.; m. Adrienne May Spencer, Jan. 8, 1965; children—James, Gregory, David, Adrienne Michele. B.S. in Indsl. Tech., Ill. State U., 1963; postgrad. Internat. Safety Acad., 1972; cert. safety profl., 1976. Engr., Am. Mutual Liability Ins. Co., Louisville, 1964, sr. engr., 1966; safety rep. Ins. Co. of N. Am., Louisville, 1967, supr., 1972, mgr., 1974-76; malpractice loss control specialist, 1976, regional dir. loss control, Omaha, 1978, dir. home office, Phila., 1980; dir. safety mgmt. services AID Ins. Services, Des Moines, 1981—, asst. v.p. safety mgmt. service, 1982—; hosp. malpractice loss control cons. Ill. State scholar; recipient Good Samaritan award, 1972. Mem. Nat. Safety Mgmt. Soc., Am. Soc. Safety Engrs., Nat. Fire Protection Assn., Am. Contract Bridge League. Author: Principle of Half Tone Photography, 1963; Loss Control Techniques-A Success Story, 1973. Office: 701 5th Ave Des Moines IA 50304

RUHLMAN, RICHARD MORGAN, advertising agency executive; b. Cleve., Sept. 24, 1938; s. Randall Morris and Rose (Griffiths) R.; m. Carole Sue Spamer, July 14, 1962; 1 son, Michael Carl. B.A., Williams Coll., 1960; M.S., Northwestern U., 1962. New product mktg. Preformed Line Products, Cleve., 1962-63; copywriter Lang Fisher & Stashower, Cleve., 1963-67, assoc. creative dir., 1968-71, v.p., 1972-78, sr. v.p., creative dir., 1978—. Trustee, Big Bros. of Greater Cleve., 1968-73, Soc. Crippled Children, Cleve., 1983—. Mem. Cleve. Soc. Communicating Arts (pres. 1971-72). Home: 3384 Norwood Rd Shaker Heights OH 44122 Office: Lang Fisher & Stashower Advt 1010 Euclid Ave Cleveland OH 44115

RUIZ, CARLOS CARIBE, association executive; b. Cabo Rojo, P.R., May 8, 1926; s. Angel Ruis and Andrea (Caribe) R.; m. Edith, Aug. 9, 1947; children—Joe, Nilda, Judith, Richard, Sandra. Student Catherine Dunham Sch. Music, 1945-47, Ornato Sch. Modern Theatre, 1947-49; A.A., Wright Jr. Coll., 1953; grad. Julliard Sch. Music, 1969. Profl. entertainer, dancer, 1945-51; active in various Puerto Rican orgns., Chgo.; now exec. dir. P.R. Congress of Chgo.; founder P.R. Conservatory Music and Art, Chgo., 1966. Served with inf. U.S. Army, 1940-45. Decorated Purple Heart; recipient awards for youth work; Disting. Service award in music and humanities in P.R.; Man of Yr. award Chgo. Hispanic Community, 1985. Mem. Nat. Civil Rights Orgn., Ill. Spanish Speaking Commn. Democrat.

RULAU, RUSSELL, numismatic consultant; b. Chgo., Sept. 21, 1926; s. Alphonse and Ruth (Thorsen) R.; student U. Wis., 1946-48; m. Hazel Darlene Grizzell, Feb. 1, 1968; children by previous marriage—Lance Eric, Russell A.W., Marcia June, Scott Quentin, Roberta Ann, Kyle Christopher; 1 step-dau., Sharon Maria Kenowski. Entered U.S. Army, 1944-1950, served to master sgt. USAF, 1950-62; resigned active duty, 1962; asst. editor Coin World newspaper, Sidney, Ohio, 1962-74, editor World Coins mag., 1964-74, Numis. Scrapbook mag., 1968-74; editorial coordinator How to Order Fgn. Coins guidebook, 1966-74; editor in chief World Coin News newspaper, 1974-84, Bank Note Reporter, 1983-84; fgn. editor Numis. News newspaper, 1974-77; cons. editor Standard Catalog of World Paper Money, 1975-83; contbg. editor Standard Catalog of World Coins, 1974-81; pres. House of Rulau, 1984—; v.p. Keogh-Rulau Galleries, 1984—. Mem. U.S. Assay Commn., 1973. Sec., Numismatic Terms Standardization Com., 1966-74; vice-chmn. Waupaca County Republican party, 1977-79, chmn., 1979-82; chmn. county chairmen, 3d vice chmn. Wis. Rep. Party, 1981-83; del. Rep. Nat. Conv., 1980; exec. com. 6th Wis. Dist. Rep. Com., 1984—. Fellow Royal Numis. Soc., Am. Numis. Soc. (asso.); mem. Token and Medal Soc. (editor 1962-63), Am. Numis. Assn., Canadian, S. African numis. assns., Mont. Hist. Soc., Am. Vecturist Assn., Numis. Lit. Guild (dir. 1974-78, editor 1984—), VFW. Lutheran. Author: (with George Fuld) Spiel Marken, 1962-65, American Game Counters, 1972: World Mint Marks, 1966; Modern World Mint Marks, 1970; (with J. U. Rixen and Frovin Sieg) Seddelkatalog Slesvig Plebiscit Zone I og II, 1970; Numismatics of Old Alabama, 1971-73; Hard Times Tokens, 1980; Early American Tokens, 1981; U.S. Merchant Tokens 1845-1860, 1982; U.S. Trade Tokens 1866-1889, 1983; (with George Fuld) Medallic Portraits of Washington, 1985. Contbr. numis. articles to profl. jours. Home: Route 2 Box 11 Iola WI 54945 Office: Keogh-Rulau Galleries PO Box 12688 Dallas TX 75225

RULIFSON, DENNIS GRANT, real estate, commodity broker; b. Carroll, Iowa; Mar. 25, 1937; s. Ralph E and Leona E. R.; m. Rosalyn Kay Haugen, Aug. 4, 1962; children—David S., Brian C. B.A. in Psychology, U. Iowa, 1961; M.S. in Guidance, Northeast Mo. U., 1971. Peronnel mgr. Hawkeye Castings Co., Manchester, Iowa, 1961-63; tchr. social studies W. Delaware High Sch., Manchester, Ia., 1964-74; owner, broker Gibson Ptnrs., Realtors, Manchester, Iowa, 1974—; broker Farmers Grain, Livestock Co., Manchester, 1982—. Served with U.S. Army, 1956-58. Decorated Good Conduct medal. Recipient Silver award Boy Scouts Am., 1955. Mem. Nat. Assn. Realtors, Iowa Assn. Realtors, Backbone Bd. Realtors (dir.), NEA (life), Manchester C. of C. Republican. Club: Million Dollar. Lodge: Lions. Home: 104 Stearns Dr Manchester IA 52057 Office: 413 E Main Manchester IA 52057

RULON, GEORGE WILLIAM, sports association executive; b. Jamestown, N.D., May 9, 1921; s. George William and Kathryn (Mutz) R.; m. Corene Alys Billings, June 26, 1948; children—Jane Marie, Elizabeth Ann Rulon Kehlbeck. B.S., N.D. State U., 1946. Dept. service officer The Am. Legion, Fargo, N.D., 1946-57, dir. membership, Indpls., 1958-61; program coordinator Am. Legion Baseball, Indpls., 1961—; dir. U.S. Baseball Fedn., Hamilton Square, N.J., 1962—. Served to 1st lt inf. U.S. Army, 1943-45; ETO. Mem. Am. Baseball Coaches Assn. (exec. com. 1985—), Nat. Council Youth Sports Dirs. Republican. Roman Catholic. Lodge: Elks. Office: Am Legion Baseball 700 N Pennsylvania St Indianapolis IN 46204

RUMELY, EMMET SCOTT, ret. automobile co. exec., banker; b. N.Y.C., Feb. 15, 1918; s. Edward A. and Fanny (Scott) R.; grad. Phillips Exeter Acad., 1935; B.S., Yale, 1939; postgrad. U. Mich., 1940-41; m. Elizabeth Hodges, July 5, 1947; children—Virginia H., Elizabeth Scott Visser, Scott Hodges. Mgr., Marenisco Farms, La Porte County, Ind., 1939-73; dir. La Porte Hotel Co., Inc., 1938-70, pres., 1965-70; pres., dir. Rumely Corp., 1970—; product planning mgr. tractor ops. Ford Motor Co., Birmingham, Mich., 1961-70, asst. to v.p., gen. mgr., 1970-75; dir., mem. exec. com. 1st Nat. Bank & Trust Co., La Porte. Mem. Detroit Inst. Arts Founders Soc., Am. Soc. Agrl. Engrs., Soc. Automotive Engrs., Am. Mktg. Assn. Clubs: Orchard Lake (Mich.) Country; Huron Mountain (Big Bay, Mich.); Yale (Detroit). Home: 207 Abbey Rd Birmingham MI 48008 Office: 800 Jefferson Ave La Porte IN 46350

RUND, DOUGLAS ANDREW, physician; b. Columbus, Ohio, July 20, 1945; s. Carl Andrew and Caroline Amelia (Row) R.; B.A., Yale U., 1967; M.D., Stanford U., 1971. Intern in medicine U. Calif., San Francisco-Moffett Hosp., 1971-72; resident in gen. surgery Stanford U., 1972-74; Robert Wood Johnson Found. clin. scholar in medicine Stanford U., 1974-76; med. dir. Mid-Peninsula Health Service, Palo Alto, Calif., 1975-76; clin. instr. dept. medicine and preventive medicine Stanford U. Med. Sch., 1975-76, asst. dir. early clin. experience in family medicine program, 1975-76; asst. prof., dir. div. emergency medicine Ohio State Coll. Medicine, 1977-80; dir. emergency med. services Ohio State U. Hosps., 1977-80, dir. emergency medicine residency program, assoc. prof. dept. family medicine, 1976-80, assoc. prof. dept. preventive medicine; attending staff Ohio State U. Hosps., 1976-80; med. dir. CTI, Emergency Med. Services Dept.; pres. Internat. Research Inst. Emergency Medicine; examiner Am. Bd. Emergency Medicine. Bd. dirs. Big Bros. Assn., Columbus, Ohio 1978-80. Lic. physician, Ohio, Calif.; diplomate Nat. Bd. Med. Examiners, Am. Bd. Family Practice, Am. Bd. Emergency Medicine. Fellow Am. Coll. Emergency Physicians; mem. Soc. Tchrs. Emergency Medicine. Soc. for Health and Human Values, Univ. Assn. for Emergency Medicine, Alpha Omega Alpha. Author: Triage, 1981; Essentials of Emergency Medicine, 1982; Emergency Radiology, 1982; Emergency Psychiatry, 1983; Environmental Emergencies, 1985; editor: Emergency Medicine Ann., 1983, 84; Emergency Medicine Survey, Annals of Emergency Medicine; editor-in-chief Ohio State Series on Emergency Medicine, contbr. chpt. to Family Medicine Principles and

Practice, 1978, 2d edit., 1978; contbr. articles to profl. jours. Office: 450 W 10th Ave Columbus OH 43210

RUNGE, DONALD EDWARD, food wholesaleing company executive; b. Milw., Mar. 20, 1938; s. Adam and Helen Teresa (Voss) R.; children—Roland, Richard, Lori. Grad. Spencerian Coll., Milw., 1960. Fin. v.p. Milw. Cheese Co., Waukesha, Wis., 1962-69; pres., dir. Farm House Foods Corp., Milw., 1969—, Inland Merc. Corp., Milw., 1971—; pres. Gen. Industries, Inc., Milw., 1966—. Seventh-day Adventist. Office: Farm House Foods 777 E Wisconsin Milwaukee WI 53202

RUPERT, JOHN EDWARD, savings and loan executive; b. Cleve., Oct. 19, 1927; s. Edward J. and Emma (Levegood) R.; B.A., Cornell U., 1949, LL.B., 1951; cert. Grad. Sch. Savs. and Loan, Ind. U., 1958; m. Virginia Carlson, Oct. 27, 1951; children—Kristen, Karen, David. With Broadview Savs. & Loan Co., Cleve., 1953—, exec. v.p., 1964-74, mng. officer, 1965—, pres., chief exec. officer, 1974—, chmn., 1979—, also dir.; mem. Cleve. Real Estate Bd., 1955—. Mem. Lakewood (Ohio) Bd. Edn., 1971-77, pres., 1975—; trustee Lakewood Hosp., 1966-71, Cleve. Orch., WVIZ Ednl. TV, Cleve. Zool. Soc., Greater Cleve. Growth Assn., Ohio Motorists Assn., Neighborhood Housing Services; bd. dirs. West Side YMCA; mem. Lakewood Hosp. Found.; mem. Cornell U. Council, 1970-79, nat. chmn., 1977-79; pres. Cleve. Interfaith Housing Corp., 1972—), chmn. No. Ohio Research Info. Ctr., 1976-80. Served with USAF, 1951-53. Mem. Inst. Fin. Edn. (pres. 1970), ABA, Cleve. Bar Assn., Bluecoats, Inc., Delta Kappa Epsilon, Phi Delta Phi, Sphinx Head Soc. Clubs: Westwood Country; Union; Midday, Cleve. Yachting, Cornell (trustee) (Cleve.). Home: 18129 W Clifton Rd Lakewood OH 44107 Office: 6000 Rockside Woods Blvd Cleveland OH 44131

RUPORT, SCOTT HENDRICKS, lawyer; b. Paterson, N.J., Nov. 22, 1949; s. Fred Hendricks and Juyne (Kennedy) R.; m. Linda Darlene Smith, Sept. 12, 1970; children—Brittany Lyle, Courtney Kennedy. B.S. in Bus. Adminstrn., Bowling Green State U., 1971; J.D., U. Akron, 1974. Bar: Ohio 1974, Pa. 1984, U.S. Dist. Ct. for no. dist. Ohio 1974, U.S. Ct. Appeals for 6th circuit, 1975, U.S. Supreme Ct. 1978. Assoc. firm Schwab, Sager, Grosenbaugh, Rothal, Fort, Skidmore & Nukes Co., L.P.A., Akron, Ohio, 1974-76, Skidmore & George Co., L.P.A., Akron, 1976-79, Skidmore, Ruport & Haskings, Akron, 1979-83; ptnr. firm Roderick, Myers & Linton, Akron, 1983—; instr. real estate law U. Akron, 1976-77, adj. asst. prof. constrn. tech. Coll. Engring., 1983—. Served as capt., Fin. Corps, USAR, 1971-79. Mem. ABA, Akron Bar Assn., Ohio Bar Assn., Ohio Acad. Trial Lawyers, Assn. Trial Lawyers Am., Beta Gamma Sigma, Sigma Chi. Republican. Presbyterian. Home: 138 Overwood Rd Akron OH 44313 Office: 300 Centran Bldg Akron OH 44308

RUPPEL, HOWARD JAMES, JR., sociologist, sexologist, educator; b. Orange, N.J., July 22, 1941; s. Howard J. and Lillian M. (Wordley) R.; B.A., St. Joseph's Coll., Ind., 1963; M.A., No. Ill. U., 1968; postgrad. U. Iowa, 1968—; m. Barbara Margaret Wiedemann, June 3, 1967. Instr. social sci. St. Francis High Sch., Wheaton, Ill., 1963-65, debate coach, 1963-65; instr. sociology St. Dominic Coll., St. Charles, Ill., 1966-67; instr. sociology Cornell Coll., Mt. Vernon, Iowa, 1969-70, asst. prof., 1970-72, lectr., 1972-73; research dir. Social Sci. Research Assos., Cedar Rapids, Iowa, 1973-80; founder, co-dir. Center for Sexual Growth and Devel., Mt. Vernon, 1980—; instr. Sch. Social Work, U. Iowa, 1976-78, adj. asst. prof., 1979-81, adj. assoc. prof., 1981—; cons. Iowa Dept. Social Services, Mankato (Minn.) State Coll., Cath. U., Nijmegen, Holland, Sch. Social Work, U. Iowa, Kirkwood Community Coll., Cedar Rapids, Families Inc., West Branch, Iowa Hosp. Assn., Linn County (Iowa) Juvenile Probation Office, Mississippi Valley council Girl Scouts U.S.A., Rock Island, Ill. NSF fellow, 1968. Cert. sexologist Am. Coll. Sexologists. Mem. Am. Sociol. Assn., Harry Benjamin Internat. Gender Dysphoria Assn., Midwest Sociol. Soc., Nat., Iowa (sec. 1983-84, treas. 1985) councils family relations, Changing Family Conf. (bd. dirs. 1983—), Soc. Sci. Study of Religion, Soc. Study of Social Problems, Soc. Sci. Study of Sex Inc. (bd. dirs. 1983—, pres. Midcontinent Region, 1984-85, treas. 1986 chmn. membership com. 1983-85, chmn. exhibits com. 1983-85, treas. and ann. meeting chmn. 1986), Assn. Sexologists, Am. Assn. Sex Educators, Counselors and Therapists (cert. sex educator), Sex Info. and Edn. Council U.S. (assoc.), Soc. Sex Therapy and Research (research mem.), Harry Benjamin Internat. Gender Dysphoria Assn., Nat. Forensic League, No. Ill. U. Alumni Assn., Alpha Kappa Delta. Democrat. Co-editor: Sexuality and the Family Life Span, 1983; contbr. articles on complex orgns., marriage and the family, sexual attitudes and behavior, childhood and preadolescent sexuality, methodology and child care theory to profl. pubs. Home: 608 5th Ave N Mount Vernon IA 52314 Office: Sch Social Work North Hall U Iowa Iowa City IA 52242

RUPPELLI, TODD PHILLIP, aerosol manufacturing company executive; b. Devon, Pa., May 1, 1927; s. Luigi and Genivieve (Mastrilli) R.; m. Judy de Greck, Nov. 22, 1961; children—Todd J., Tim G., Thomas J., Tina M. Student St. Joseph's U., Phila., 1946-47. Salesman, Addressograph-Multigraph, Phila and Cleve., 1947-67; mgr. Rotanium div. Premier Indsl., Cleve., 1967-70; mgr. consumer products Sprayon Products, Bedford, Ohio, 1970-73; v.p. Plasti-Kote, Medina, Ohio, 1973—; dir. Automotive Systems, Hudson, Ohio. Co-chmn. Route 18 By-Pass Com., Medina, 1979. Served with U.S. Navy, 1945-46. Named Man of the Yr. Automotive Merchandising News, 1981. Mem. 500 Club Automotive Aftermarket Execs., Mfrs. of Original Equipment Maintenance Assn., Automotive Parts Assn. Am. (dir. 1981—). Republican. Roman Catholic. Home: 4240 Bagdad Rd Medina OH 44256 Office: Plasti-Kote 1000 Lake Rd Medina OH 44256

RUPPERT, RUPERT EARL, lawyer; b. Middletown, Ohio, Nov. 22, 1943; s. Paul Edward and Sarah Elizabeth (Morgan) R.; B.A., Ohio State U., 1968; J.D., Capital U., 1976; m. Candace E. Sheward, June 7, 1969; children—Jason, Ryan, Bradley, Matthew. Admitted to Ohio bar, 1976; asst. to gov. state of Ohio, Columbus, 1971-74, to atty. gen., 1974-77, spl. counsel to atty. gen. and to asst. atty. gen., 1977—; partner firm Ruppert, Bronson & Chicarelli, Franklin, Ohio, 1977—, also firm Riley & Ruppert, Franklin; pres., dir., atty. Miami Valley Bldg. & Loan Assn., Franklin, 1979—, also dir. Mem. Warren County Democratic Central Com., 1977—; chmn. Warren County Dem. Com., 1978-80; chmn. Warren County Brown for Atty. Gen., 1978; dep. campaign mgr. William J. Brown for Gov. Ohio, 1982; mem. Franklin City Charter Commn., 1978, Franklin CSC, 1978-79; v.p. Franklin City Schs. Bd. Edn., 1978-79, pres., 1979—. Served with AUS, 1968-70; Vietnam. Decorated Bronze Star, Combat Infantryman Badge; recipient Presdl. award for outstanding civic achievement among Viet Nam vets, 1979. Mem. Am. Bar Assn., Ohio Bar Assn., Warren County Bar Assn., Ohio Trial Lawyers Assn., Nat. Rifle Assn., Am. Legion, VFW. Home: PO Box 70 Franklin OH 45005 Office: 313 S Main St Franklin OH 45005

RUS, VLADIMIR JOSEPH, educational administrator; b. Rijeka, Yugoslavia, Feb. 12, 1925; came to U.S., 1951; s. Frank and Maria (Jordan) R.; m. Jovanka J. Kuznecow, Nov. 6, 1954; children—Vladimir Michael, Elizabeth Marie. D.Polit. Sci., U. Trieste (Italy), 1949; M.A. in Polit. Sci., Western Res. U., 1962; M.A. in Slavic Langs., U. Mich., 1965, postgrad., 1966. Asst. prof. Case Western Res. U., Cleve., 1966-72; dir. manpower planning City of Cleve., 1972-74, dir. human resources and econ. devel., 1974-77; dir. planning United Labor Agy., Cleve., 1978-79, exec. dir. (acting), 1980-81; dean Cuyahoga Community Coll., Cleve., 1979—. Trustee Fedn. for Community Planning, Cleve., 1976-82; pres. Slovenian-Am. Heritage Found., Cleve., 1983. Mem. Ohio Manpower Assn., Soc. Slovene Studies, Ohio Ethnic Studies Council, New Careers for Older Americans Council, Indsl. Relations Research Assn., Cleve. Machine Trades Assn. (trustee 1979—). Republican. Roman Catholic. Home: 2604 Ashurst Rd Cleveland OH 44118

RUSCH, HAROLD PAUL, oncologist, emeritus educator; b. Merrill, Wis., July 15, 1908; s. Henry Albert and Olga (Brandenburg) R.; m. Lenore Robinson, Aug. 6, 1940 (dec. 1978); children—Carolyn Elizabeth, Judith Ann (dec. 1976); m. Louise Van Wart, Oct. 20, 1979. B.A., U. Wis.-Madison, 1931; M.D., 1933. Intern, Wis. Gen. Hosp., Madison, 1933-34; instr. dept. physiology U. Wis.-Madison, 1934-35, asst. prof. oncology, 1941-43, assoc. prof., 1943-45, prof., 1945-79, prof. emeritus, 1979—, head dept. cancer research, 1940-46, dir. McArdle Lab. for Cancer Research, 1946-72, Wis. Clin. Cancer Ctr., 1972-78; mem. nat. cancer com. NRC, 1954-58, com. on growth, 1949-53; research adv. council Am. Cancer Soc., 1962-65, bd. dirs., 1965—, exec. com., 1970-74, nat. award, 1972, hon. life mem., 1974; mem. Nat. Adv. Cancer Council, 1954-58, Nat. Cancer Adv. Bd., 1972-74; mem. Commn. on Cancer Research, Internat. Union Against Cancer, 1954-58; mem. Pres.'s Com. on Heart Disease and Cancer, 1961, U.S. Senate Com. Cons. on Cancer, 1970. Author sci. articles. Editor-in-chief Cancer Research Jour., 1950-65; editorial bd. Perspectives in Biology and Medicine, 1959-73. Bowman Cancer fellow, research assoc. in medicine, vis. Am. and European cancer labs., 1935-39. Fellow Am. Acad. Arts and Scis.; mem. Am. Assn. Cancer Research (pres. 1953-54), Assn. Am. Cancer Insts. (pres. 1972-74), AAAS, Am. Soc. Exptl. Pathology, Soc. Exptl. Biology and Medicine, Madison Geol. Soc. (pres. 1946-47), Sigma Xi, Alpha Omega Alpha, Phi Kappa Phi. Home: 3511 Sunset Dr Madison WI 53705

RUSH, DAVID RAY, pharmacy and medicine educator, consultant; b. Celina, Ohio, Dec. 14, 1946; s. Raymond Harry and Helen Catherine Burmeister) R. B.S. in Pharmacy, Ohio No. U., 1969; Pharm.D., U. Ky., 1975. Pharmacist Davis Pharmacy, Lima, Ohio, 1969-72; resident in pharmacy U. Ky., Lexington, 1972-75; prof. medicine and clin. pharmacy U. Mo., Kansas City, 1975—; chmn. bd. Dr. of Pharmacy Cons., Inc., Kansas City, 1983—. Author: Endocrine and Metabolic Emergencies, 1984. Contbr. articles to profl. jours. Recipient numerous clin. pharmacology research grants, Achievement in Profl. Practice and Hosp. Pharmacy award, 1976, Tchr. of Yr. award Goppert Family Care Ctr., Bapt. Med. Ctr., 1985. Mem. Am. Coll. Clin. Pharmacy, Am. Soc. Hosp. Pharmacy, Am. Assn. Colls. Pharmacy, Am. Pharm. Assn., Am. Inst. History Pharmacy. Avocations: backpacking; fishing; wilderness conservation. Office: Dept Family Medicine Truman Med Ctr E U Mo 7900 Lee's Summit Rd Kansas City MO 64139

RUSH, GERALD ELMER, food service company executive; b. New Orleans, Aug. 5, 1930; s. Elmer H. and Alta (Billig) R.; B.S., Western Mich. U., 1953; M.S., U. Calif., San Fernando Valley, 1965; children—Diane E., Gerald E., Heidi E., David E. Designer, prodn. and executor nat. network TV shows for ABC, NBC, CBS, and ind. studios, including Dean Martin Show, Jack Benny Spl., Bob Hope Spls., Danny Thomas Spl., Laugh In, Bill Cosby Spl., Jonathon Winters Show, Let's Make a Deal, Hollywood, Calif., 1963-67; tchr. TV prodn. and stagecraft Pasadena Playhouse, Hollywood, Los Angeles, 1963-67; dir. tng. and personnel McDonald Corp., Los Angeles, 1967-73, Ky. Fried Chicken, Louisville and San Diego, 1973-77; dir. tng. Jonoth's, San Antonio, 1977-78, Interstate United Corp., Chgo., 1978-82, Hickory Farms of Ohio, Maumee, 1982-84; pres. GR Prodns., Toledo, Ohio, 1984—. Served with U.S. Army, 1953-63. Mem. Am. Soc. Tng. Dirs., Conf. Hotel and Restaurant Trainers, Nat. Restaurant Assn., Employment Mgmt. Assn., Nat. Audio-Visual Assn., Vietnam Vets. Assn., U.S. Parachute Assn. Home: 1251 S Reynolds Rd Apt 189 Toledo OH 43615

RUSH, ISABEL ENDSLEY, educator; b. Cuyahoga Falls, Ohio, Sept. 7, 1914; d. Hugh Harper and Caroline M. Endsley; B.A., U. Akron, 1975, M.S., 1979, Ed.D., 1983; m. George Arthur Rush, Sept. 12, 1936; 1 son, David Lee (dec.). Cafeteria mgr. Cuyahoga Falls Bd. Edn., 1947-71; foods instr. Cuyahoga Valley Joint Vocat. Sch., Brecksville, Ohio, 1971-75, Cuyahoga Community Coll., Cleve., 1975-80, U. Akron (Ohio), 1980—. Named Food Service Employee of Year, N.E. Ohio Assn. Public Sch. Employees, 1971. Mem. Am. Vocational Assn., Am. Home Econs. Assn., Postsecondary and Adult Vocat. Assn., Am. Sch. Food Service Assn., Ohio Home Econs. Assn., Ohio Vocat. Assn., Ohio Council Hotel, Restaurant and Instl. Educators, Pi Lambda Theta, Phi Delta Kappa. Mem. United Ch. of Christ. Clubs: Women's City, College, University (Akron); Order Eastern Star (Cuyahoga Falls); Order of Amaranth (Kent, Ohio). Home: 230 Wadsworth Ave Cuyahoga Falls OH 44221 Office: 102 New South Hall U Akron Akron OH 44304

RUSH, JAMES EUGENE, cattleman, art collector; b. Emerson, Nebr., Oct. 1, 1931; s. Leo J. and Evelyn H. (Daley) R.; m. Marilyn Jean Conley, Nov. 29, 1956; children—Patric C., Michael L., Kevin P. B.S., St. Edward's Coll., Tex., 1959. Officer, Rush Grain Co., Nebr., 1959-62; owner Rush Cattle, Sioux City, Iowa, 1964-74, Art Collection, Sioux City, 1970—. Active local Republican campaigns. Served with USN, 1952-54. Mem. DAV, Am. Legion. Republican. Roman Catholic. Home: 4701 Chatham Ln Sioux City IA 51104

RUSH, JAMES RAYMOND, state executive; b. Chgo., Sept. 18, 1944; s. Clyde G. and Winifred M. (Campbell) R.; student So. Ill. U., Carbondale, 1965-68; m. Linda Boeser, Dec. 30, 1973; 1 dau., Amanda. With Greater Egypt Regional planning and Devel. Commn., Carbondale, Ill., 1967-84, dir. spl. programs, 1978-84; exec. Ill. Dept. Law Enforcement, 1984—. writer, lectr. in field. Mem. Am. Planning Assn. (dir. 1981-82), Nat. Criminal Justice Planners Assn., Ill. Criminal Justice Planners Assn. (pres. 1974-77), Nat. Council Crime and Delinquency. Presbyterian.

RUSH, JON NEIL, sculptor, art educator; b. Atlanta, Sept. 24, 1935; s. Francis and Annabelle (Skuller) R.; m. Mary Jane Beattie, Dec. 21, 1957; children—Daniel, David. B.F.A., Cranbrook Art Acad., Bloomfield Hills, Mich., 1958, M.F.A., 1959. Instr. Columbus Coll. Art and Design, Ohio, 1959-62; prof. art U. Mich., Ann Arbor, 1962—. Prin. works include commd. pieces for Briarwood, Ann Arbor, 1980, Southwestern Mich. Coll., Dowagiac, 1984, U. Mich., 1965. Trustee Village of Dexter, Mich., 1981-85. Home: 7930 5th St Dexter MI 48130 Office: 7965 5th St Dexter MI 48130

RUSH, SHARON ELIZABETH, law educator; b. Jasper, Ind., Dec. 22, 1951; d. William Porter and Betty Iveline (Wright) R. B.A., Cornell U., 1974, J.D. cum laude, 1980. Bar: D.C. 1980. Assoc. Cadwalader, Wickersham & Taft, Washington, D.C., 1980-82; asst. prof. DePaul U. Law Sch., Chgo., 1982-85, assoc. prof., 1985—, mem. exec. bd. Ctr. for Ch./State Studies, 1983—; vis. assoc. prof. U. Fla., Gainesville. Contbr. articles and revs. to profl. jours. Recipient Outstanding Teaching award De Paul Coll. Law, 1983-84; summer research grantee De Paul Coll. Law, 1984. Mem. Cornell Law Assn., ABA, D.C. Bar Assn. Home: 2909 N Sheridan Rd #707 Chicago IL 60657 Office: De Paul Coll Law 25 E Jackson Blvd Chicago IL 60604

RUSH, WILLIAM JOHN, newspaper executive; b. Alliance, Ohio, Nov. 11, 1936; s. Serle Emmons and Doris Esther (Crider) R.; B.J., Ohio State U., 1958; m. Ruth Ann Lee, Feb. 29, 1972; children—Kayci, Wendy, Nathan, Jenny, Molly. Mgr., The Madison Press, London, Ohio, 1960-62; adv. mgr. Times Pub. Co., New Milford, Conn., 1962-65; asst. to pub. N.Adams (Mass.) Transcript, 1965-69; asst. to pub. Horvitz Newspapers, 1969-70; gen. mgr. Willoughby (Ohio) News-Herald, 1970-72; v.p./gen. mgr. Times Record, Troy, N.Y., 1972-82; assoc. pub., v.p. ops. Times Record and News Jour., Mansfield, Ohio, 1982—. Bd. dirs. Samaritan Hosp., United Fund. Mem. Greater Troy C. of C. (v.p., dir.), Nat. Co. Mil. Historians, Associated Pubs. N.Y. State (pres.), Theta Chi. Episcopalian. Clubs: Albany Univ.; Westbrook Country, Mansfield, Masons, Shriners, Elks. Home: 2210 Camden Ct Mansfield OH 44904 Office: News Jour 70 W 4th St Mansfield OH 44902

RUSHING, RICHARD LEE, railroad marketing executive; b. Simpson, Ill., Oct. 4, 1935; s. Lantha Lee and Eithel Rushing; m. Margaret Ann McKinney, June 24, 1956; children—Michael Lee, Jeffrey Brent. B.S. in Fin., So. Ill. U., 1956. With ICG R.R., Chgo., 1956—, regional sales mgr., 1968-75, gen. mgr. automotive, 1975-76, v.p. sales, 1976—. Bd. dirs. Ill. Central Gulf Hosp. Assn. Served to sgt. USAR, 1958-64. Mem. Sales and Mktg. Execs. Internat., Nat. Def. Transp. Assn., Nat. Freight Transp. Assn., Traffic Club Chgo. (bd. dirs.). Republican. Baptist. Home: 2907 Kathleen St Flossmoor IL 60422 Office: 233 N Michigan Ave Chicago IL 60601

RUSHKA, ROY JOHN, Canadian diplomat, engineer; b. Esterhazy, Sask., Can., Aug. 1, 1924; came to U.S., 1969; s. Jake Edward and Mary (Hruska) R.; m. Marjorie Estelle Trainor, Aug. 5, 1950; chidlren—Brian, Diana, Brenda, Robert. B.Sc. in Engring., U. Sask., Saskatoon, 1949. Registered profl. engr. Ont. Engring. supr. Comstock, Toronto, Windsor, Ont., Can., 1949-56; project engr. Westinghouse, Hamilton, Ont. and Toronto, 1956-62; mgr. engring. Electronic Materials, Ottawa, Can., 1962-66; fgn. service officer Can. Govt., Phila., Dallas, Brussels and Dayton, Ohio, 1966—. Author, producer family history books and presentation. Mem. Profl. Engrs. Ont., Profl. Assn. Fgn. Service. Avocation: geneology research. Home: 1732 E Alex-Bell Rd Dayton OH 45459 Office: Can Govt Office MCLDDP Wright Patterson AFB OH 45433

RUSK, THOMAS JOSEPH, anesthesiologist; b. Cleve., Nov. 27, 1933; s. Martin Stanley and Mary Elizabeth (Czech) Rusnaczyk; B.S. in Natural Sci., John Carroll U., 1955; postgrad. Case-Western Res. U., 1956-57; D.O., Chgo. Coll. Osteo. Medicine, 1961; m. Patricia Ann Creed, May 27, 1967; children—Mary Elizabeth, Pamela Kathleen, Barbara Rebecca, Thomas Baird. Intern, then resident to chief resident in anesthesiology Detroit Osteo. Hosp., 1961-64; practice medicine specializing in anesthesiology, 1964—; with Ucchino & Rusk Anesthesia Assos., 1964-71; v.p., sec. Warren (Ohio) Anesthesia, Inc., 1971—; courtesy staff Youngstown, Sharon (Pa.) hosps; chief of staff Warren Gen. Hosp.; asst. clin. instr. Coll. Osteo. Medicine, Ohio U., W.Va. Coll. Osteo. Medicine; clin. asst. prof. anesthesiology Osteo. Med. Ctr. of Phila., 1982—. Trustee, NE Ohio Health Planning Commn., Mahoning Valley Health Planning Bd., 1974-76; mem. Trumbull County Joint Hosp. Purchasing Com. Served to 1st lt. M.S.C., USAR, 1955-67. Diplomate Am. Osteo. Bd. Anesthesiology. Mem. Ohio, N.E. Ohio (trustee), Trumbull County (pres. 1978, 79) heart assns., Am. Osteo. Assn. (hosp. and physician inspection and exam. team 1972, 73), Ohio Osteo. Assn., 14 and 12 Dist. Acad. Osteo. Medicine (pres. 1974), Am. Osteo. Coll. Anesthesiology, Ohio (sec.-treas. 1971-75, pres. 1975—), Mich. socs. osteo. anesthesiology, Am. Coll. Osteo. Anesthesiologists (diplomate), Internat. Anesthesia Research Soc., Am. Soc. Regional Anesthesia, Ohio Prevention of Blindness Assn., Am. Thoracis Soc., Ohio Thoracic Soc., Ohio Med. Soc., Trumbull County Med Soc., N.Y. Acad. Scis. Republican. Roman Catholic. Home: 182 Marwood Dr Warren OH 44484 Office: 2838 Howland Wilson Rd Cortland OH 44410

RUSS, MARILYNN LOUISE, school psychologist; b. Spokane, Wash., Apr. 27, 1949; d. Herbert Carl and Lois Margaret (Benner) Kummer; m. Roger Allen Russ, July 21, 1973; 1 dau., Alissa Lynn. B.A., Whitworth Coll., 1971; M.S., Eastern Wash. U., 1973; postgrad. N.E. Mo. State U., 1979. Cert. sch. psychologist, Iowa, Wash. Instr. Vennard Coll., University Park, Iowa, 1973-75; client service coordinator Tenco Workshop, Ottumwa, Iowa, 1975-77; sch. psychologist So. Prairie Area Edn. Agy., Ottumwa, 1979—; cons. in field. Deacon, mem. personnel com., tchr. First Presbyn. Ch., 1975—. Recipient Cert. of Appreciation, Nat. Assn. Retarded Citizens, 1977. Mem. Am. Psychol. Assn., Nat. Assn. Sch. Psychologists, Iowa Sch. Psychologists Assn., Phi Alpha. Republican. Clubs: Lake Thunderhead (Unionville, Mo.); Spoke Folk (Ottumwa).

RUSSELL, BRIAN EARL, amusement company executive; b. Schenectady, Sept. 17, 1957; s. Robert R. and Ruth Elizabeth (Hoskins) R.; m. Elizabeth Hoyt, Apr. 19, 1980; 1 son, Kellen Hoyt. A.A.S., SUNY-Morrisville, 1977; B.S./B.A., Syracuse U., 1979. Spl. events mgr. Fun Services, Albany, N.Y., 1979; dir. pub. relations Fun Service Inc., Chgo., 1979-81, gen. mgr., 1981-82; asst. gen. mgr. Fun Service/Ace Novelty Corp., Chgo., 1982—; cons. in field. Mem. Nat. Employee Service and Recreation Assn., Pub. Relations Soc. Am., Internat. Fund Raising Assn., Nat. PTA, Chgo. Policeman Assn. Club: Chgo. Sport. Contbr. articles to profl. jours. Office: 221 E Cullerton St Chicago IL 60616

RUSSELL, DAVID WILLIAMS, lawyer; b. Lockport, N.Y., Apr. 5, 1945; s. David Lawson and Jean Graves (Williams) R.; A.B. (Army ROTC scholar, Daniel Webster scholar), Dartmouth Coll., 1967, M.B.A., 1969; J.D. cum laude, Northwestern U., 1976; m. Frances Yung Chung Chen, May 23, 1970; children—Bayard Chen, Ming Rennick. English tchr. Talledega (Ala.) Coll., summer 1967; math. tchr. Lyndon Inst., Lyndonville, Vt., 1967-68; instr. econs. Royalton Coll., South Royalton, Vt., part-time 1968-69; asst. to pres. for planning Tougaloo (Miss.) Coll., 1969-71, bus. mgr., 1971-73; mgr. will and trust rev. project Continental Ill. Nat. Bank & Trust Co. Chgo., summer 1974; law clk. Montgomery, McCracken, Walker & Rhoads, Phila., summer 1975; admitted to Ill. bar, 1976, Ind. bar, 1983; Winston & Strawn, Chgo., 1976-83; ptnr. Klineman, Rose, Wolf & Wallack, Indpls., 1983—; cons. Alfred P. Sloan Found., 1972-73; dir. Forum for Internat. Profl. Services, 1985—. Mem. nat. selection com. Woodrow Wilson Found. Adminstrv. Fellowship Program, 1973-76; vol. Lawyers for Creative Arts, Chgo., 1977-83. Woodrow Wilson Found. adminstrv. fellow, 1969-72. Mem. Am., Ill., Ind., Indpls., bar assns., Dartmouth Lawyers Assn., ACLU, Chinese Music Soc., Zeta Psi. Presbyterian. Home: 10926 Lakeview Dr Carmel IN 46032 Office: Suite 2130 Indiana Nat Bank Tower One Indiana Sq Indianapolis IN 46204

RUSSELL, ELWOOD MICHEL (WOODY), editor publisher; b. Stillwater, Ky., Dec. 21, 1919; s. William Edward and Grace Eula (Linkous) R.; m. Alice Marie Lintz, Jan. 2, 1946 (div. 1972); children—Douglas Alan, Karen Sue Russell Risher, Jill Lynn Russell Martinelli; m. 2d, Jessie Carol Summers, Aug. 5, 1977. Student schs. Russellville, Ky. With U.S. Post Office Dept., 1946-72; state news editor Ohio VFW News, 1965-70; editor, pub. Nat. Opportunities Classified, New Philadelphia, Ohio, 1969—, Nat. Hobby News, 1980-82; propr. mail order bus.; speaker in field. Band mgr., dist. program chmn. Boy Scouts Am., 1960-70. Served with U.S. Army, 1941-45, 50-51. Decorated Bronze Star. Named Ky. Col.; winner first place. nat. newspaper award Nat. VFW, 1969, 25 first place awards for Dist. VFW pub. contest Ohio, 1952-82; named outstanding dist. comdr. VFW of Yr., 1959. Mem. VFW (dist. comdr. 1958-59). Home: 125 3d St NW New Philadelphia OH 44663 Office: PO Box 612 New Philadelphia OH 44663

RUSSELL, GREGORY DAVID, city administrator, lawyer; b. Alliance, Ohio, Feb. 16, 1949; s. John L. and Mary Ellen (Bennion) R.; m. Linda Sue Moorehead, Dec. 14, 1975; 1 child, Frederick David. Student Case Western Res. U., 1967-68; B.A. in Polit. Sci., Philosophy, Mt. Union Coll., 1971; J.D., U. Akron, 1974, postgrad., 1982—. Bar: Ohio 1974, U.S. Dist. Ct. (no. dist.) Ohio 1975. Counselor, office mgr. County Action Council, Youngstown, Ohio, 1971; dist. staff coordinator McGovern for Pres., Canton, Ohio. 1972; ptnr. Russell and Marini, Alliance, 1974-84; sole practice, Alliance, 1984—; city law dir., Alliance, 1984—; grad. asst. dept. polit. sci. U. Akron, Ohio, 1982-83; bd. counsel Stark Community Action Agy., Canton, Ohio, 1982-84; legis. liaison State Rep. R. Gerberry, 1982—; Bd. dirs. Greater Alliance Devel. Corp., 1984—; v.p., pres. Alliance Area Democratic Club, 1972-77; counsel, pres., v.p. Alliance Vis. Nurses Assn., 1980-84, mem. Vestry Trinity Episcopal Ch., Alliance, 1984. Mem. Ohio State Bar Assn., ABA, Ohio Mcpl. Atty's Assn., Am. Polit. Sci. Assn., Alliance Area C. of C., Alliance Jaycees (legal counsel, v.p. 1976-80), Bracton's Inn, Pi Sigma Alpha. Democrat. Episcopalian. Clubs: Am. Contract Bridge League (Memphis); 64th Regiment of Foot, Brigade of Am. Revolution (legal counsel 1982—). Avocations: public opinion survey analysis, re-enacting revolutionary battles, restoring houses and furniture, softball, collecting antiques. Home: 419 S Union Ave Alliance OH 44601 Office: City Hall 470 E Market St Alliance OH 44601

RUSSELL, HENRY GEORGE, structural engineer; b. Tewkesbury, Eng., June 12, 1941; came to U.S., 1968. B.E., Sheffield U., Eng., 1962, Ph.D., 1965. Registered structural engr., Ill.; registered profl. engr., Wash. Research fellow Bldg. Research Co., Eng., 1965-68; structural engr. Portland Cement Assn., Skokie, Ill., 1968-74, mgr., 1974-79, dir., 1979—. Contbr. articles on reinforced and prestressed concrete to profl. jours. Fellow Am. Concrete Inst.; mem. Prestressed Concrete Inst. (Martin P. Korn award 1980). Office: Portland Cement Assn 5420 Old Orchard Rd Skokie IL 60077

RUSSELL, JOHN THOMAS, sales executive; b. Brainard, Minn., Dec. 5, 1933; s. Francis Newell and Ruth (Gleason) R.; m. Jana Marie Slunecko, Aug. 21, 1970; children—Kevin, Christopher. Owner, pres. Wig Warehouse, Chgo., 1961-71; mil. sales mgr. Ency. Britannica, Chgo., 1971-73, sales mgr., Milw., 1973-77, eastern exhibit dir., 1977-80, nat. dir. exhibits, 1980-82, Chgo. div. sales mgr., 1982—. Mem. Joint Council Med. Confs., Eastern Fair Assn., Internat. Assn. Fairs. Republican. Roman Catholic. Home: 9 Timberline Riverwoods IL 60015 Office: Ency Britannica 4747 W Peterson Chicago IL 60646

RUSSELL, KEITH CUSHMAN, investment banker, conservationist; b. Andover, Ohio, Apr. 30, 1920; s. Ford Bliss and Ruth Evelyn (Satterlee) R.; m. Marjorie Miriam Wilkins, Nov. 28, 1941; 1 child, Jacqueline Sue. B.A., Ohio Wesleyan U., 1941. Exec. v.p. Hayden, Miller & Co., Cleve., 1946-69; ptnr. McDonald & Co., Cleve., 1969-81; v.p. McDonald & Co., Securities, Cleve., 1981—; gov. Midwest Stock Exchange, Chgo., 1968-71; dir. Mobel Energy and Mining Co., Cin. Author, editor: The Duck-Huntingest Gentlemen, 1979; For Whom the Ducks Toll, 1984. Trustee Better Bus. Bur., Cleve., 1968-74. Served to lt. (j.g.) USNR, 1942-46, PTO. Named Man of Yr., Woods and Waters Club, Cleve., 1983. Mem. Ohio C. of C. (bd. dirs. 1980—), African Wildlife Found. (trustee 1979—), Am. Mus. Fly Fishing (bd. dirs. 1984—), Ducks Unltd. (sr. v.p. 1978-80), Trout Unltd. (nat. dir. 1981—), Canvasback Soc. (nat. pres. 1978—). Republican. Presbyterian. Clubs: Union (Cleve.); Rolling Rock (Ligonier, Pa.). Avocations: fly fishing, waterfowl and upland bird hunting, conservation. Office: McDonald & Co Securities 2100 Central Nat Bank Bldg Cleveland OH 44114

RUSSELL, MAURICE ROBERT, farm credit association executive; b. Cedar Rapids, Iowa, Dec. 19, 1948; s. Richard C. and Mary A (Pospisil) R.; m. Mardene R. Kramer, Oct. 5, 1974; children—Jared Russell, Tana Russell. B.S., Iowa State U., 1971. Area credit supr. FICB of Omaha, Ames, Iowa, 1974-78, v.p., Mitchell, S.D., 1978-84; pres. Central Iowa Prodn. Credit Assn., Newton, Iowa, 1984-85; pres. Farm Credit Region, Newton, 1985—. Pres. YMCA, Mitchell, 1982-84; bd. dirs. St. Joseph's Hosp., Mitchell, 1983-84. Served to sgt. Army N.G., 1969-75. Republican. Roman Catholic. Club: Mitchell Exchange (pres. 1983-84). Avocations: running; reading; management studies; gardening; wine making. Home: 120 Pioneer Lambs Grove Newton IA 50208 Office: Farm Credit Region Box 887 Newton IA 50208

RUSSELL, ROBERT EMERSON, JR., management, marketing and fund raising services executive, consultant; b. Indpls., Aug. 1, 1937; s. Robert E. and Nancy Schwenk (Kalleen) R.; B.A., Wabash Coll., 1959; postgrad. Nat. Indsl. Conf. Bd., 1965; m. Ruth Ellen Drake, May 26, 1967; children—Kristen Kalleen, Robert Emerson Russell, III. Writer, editor advt. and pub. relations, asst. mgr. employment Armstrong Cork Co., Lancaster, Pa., 1963-67; dir. placement and alumni fund Wabash Coll., Crawfordsville, Ind., 1967-68, dir. devel. and alumni affairs, 1968-71; div. devel. Rosary Coll., River Forest, Ill., 1971-72; dir. devel. and pub. affairs Rehab. Inst. of Chgo., 1972-76, assoc., 1976—; pres. Robert Russell & Assocs., Inc., Chgo. and Hillsdale, Mich., 1976—; v.p. mktg. Hillsdale Coll., 1983—. Mem. task force Chgo. Community Trust Edn. Network, 1977; chmn. conf. Nat. Assn. Hosp. Devel., 1975; pres., bd. dirs. operation ABLE Chgo., 1977-80; vestryman St. Mark's Episcopal Ch., Geneva, Ill., 1977-80; pres. Wabash Club of Chgo., 1974-78. Served with U.S. Army, 1960-63. Recipient Capital Funds award Nat. Assn. Hosp. Devel., 1975; Golden Trumpet award Chgo. Pub. Assn., 1974. named Outstanding Young Man of Mem. Nat. Soc. Fund Raising Execs., Nat. Assn. Hosp. Devel., Council Advancement and Support of Edn., Am. Mktg. Assn., Midwest and Midatlantic Coll. Placement Assn., SAR, Nat. Assn. Wabash Men (dir.), Blue Key, Sigma Chi, Alpha Psi Omega. Republican. Episcopalian. Club: University (Chgo). Office: 1717 N Naper Blvd Naperville IL 60540 also Hillsdale College Hillsdale MI 49242

RUSSELL, THOMAS FRANK, manufacturing company executive; b. Detroit, Apr. 7, 1924; s. Frank W. and Agnes V. (Kuhn) R.; student engring. Rutgers U., 1943; B.S. in Accounting, U. Detroit, 1948; m. Ruth H. Costello, June 25, 1949; children—R. Brandon, Scott K. With Fed.-Mogul Corp., Detroit, 1942—, controller, 1959-64, v.p. finance, 1964, v.p., group mgr., pres., 1972-75, chmn. bd., chief exec. officer, 1975—. Served with AUS, 1943-45; ETO. Home: 51 Clairview Rd Grosse Pointe Shores MI 48236 Office: Fed-Mogul Corp PO Box 1966 Detroit MI 48235

RUSSELL, VERNER STERN, educational administrator; b. Pitts., Dec. 14, 1941; s. Howard A. and Edith (Stern) R.; m. Carolyn L. Woods, Nov. 2, 1966 (dec. Nov. 1976); 1 child, Jason V.; m. Jacquelyn Banning, July 11, 1981; 1 child, Erica A. B.S., Lioncoln U., Mo., 1968, M.Ed., 1970; vocat. guidance cert. Kent State U., 1972; adminstrv. cert. Akron U., 1975. Vocat. guidance counselor Ravenna City Schs., Ohio, 1971-74; asst. prin. Canton City Schs., Ohio, 1974-79; prin., 1979—. Mem. Canton Citizens Rev. Bd., 1982. Served with U.S. Army, 1966-68. Jennings Found. scholar, 1980-8o. Mem. Ohio Assn. Secondary Sch. Adminstrs., Omega Psi Phi, Phi Delta Kappa. Methodist. Home: 1167 Sprucewood SE North Canton OH 44720 Office: 1824 3d St SE Canton OH 44707

RUSSELL-THOMAS, STEVEN GARDNER, educational adminstrator; b. Grand Junction, Colo., Aug. 11, 1943; s. Guy and Thelda (Gardner) Russell. A.M., Creighton U., 1968. Chmn. dept. English, Mt. St. Clare Coll., Clinton, Iowa, 1968-71; therapist Inst. Human Relations, Chgo., 1972-75; instr. humanities Columbia Coll., Chgo., 1975-77, asst. acad. dean, 1978—. Mem. N. Am. Patristics Soc., Lambda Iota Tau. Democrat. Roman Catholic. Author: Victims of Holiness, 1975; Me and the Drifter, 1976. Home: 2023 N Albany St Chicago IL 60647 Office: 600 S Michigan Ave Chicago IL 60605

RUSSO, JOSE, pathologist, educator; b. Mendoza, Argentina, Mar. 24, 1942; came to U.S., 1971; s. Felipe and Teresa (Pagano) R.; B.S., Agustin Alvarez Nat. Coll., 1959; M.D., U. Nat. Cuyo, 1967; m. Irma Haydee, Feb. 8, 1969; 1 child, Patricia Alexandra. Instr., Inst. Gen. and Exptl. Pathology, Med. Sch., Mendoza, 1961-66, asst. prof. Inst. Histology and Embryology, 1967-71; Rockefeller Found. postdoctoral fellow Inst. Molecular and Cellular Evolution, U. Miami, 1971-73; chief exptl. pathology lab. Mich. Cancer Found., Detroit, 1973-81; assoc. clin. prof. pathology Wayne State U., Detroit, 1979—, chmn. dept. pathology, 1981—, dir. pathology reference lab., 1983—; mem. Mich. Cancer Found., 1983—. USPHS grantee, 1978, 79; USHS grantee, 1984; Am. Cancer Soc. grantee, 1982; NRC Argentina fellow, 1967-71. Mem. Am. Assn. Cancer Research, Am. Soc. Cell Biology, Soc. Exptl. Biology and Medicine, Tissue Culture Assn., Am. Soc. Clin. Pathology Internat. Acad. Pathology, Am. Coll. Pathology, Internat. Acad. Pathology, Am. Coll. Pathologists, Sigma Xi. Roman Catholic. Author articles; editor books; research on breast cancer. Office: 110 E Warren Ave Detroit MI 48201

RUSSO, MARTY, congressman; b. Chgo., Jan. 23, 1944; s. Anthony and Lucille R.; B.A., DePaul U., 1965, J.D., 1967; m. Karen Jorgensen; children—Tony, Dan. Admitted to Ill. bar, 1967, U.S. Supreme Ct. bar, 1974, D.C. bar, 1977; law clk. Judge John V. McCormack, Ill. Appellate Ct., 1967-68; asst. state's atty. Cook County (Ill.), 1971-73; practice in Chgo., 1973—; mem. 94th-98th congresses from 3d Dist. Ill., mem. com. On ways and means, budget com., mem. Dem. steering and policy com.; dep. Whip Dem. House Leadership; mem. Congl. Steel Caucus, Dem. Study Group.; mem. steering com. of Congl. Travel and Tourism Caucus. Bd. dirs. St. Xavier Coll., Chgo.; mem. Joint Civic Com. of Italian-Ams.; mem. citizens bd. Ill. Masonic Med. Center. Recipient Disting. Service award Pinta Neri K.C., Ind. Bakers Assn., 1978; Man of Yr., Chgo. W. Suburban chpt. United Neighbors of Italy Community Orgns., 1975, Justinian Soc. Lawyers, 1976, Chgo. chpt. Magen David Adom, 1977; Outstanding Legis. Leader, Soc. Little Flower, 1975; One of Ten Outstanding Young People, Harvey (Ill.) Jaycees, 1977; Disting. Alumnus award De Paul U., 1981; others. Mem. Am., Fed., Ill., D.C., S. Suburban bar assns., Justinian Soc. Lawyers (named Man of Yr. 1976), Alpha Phi Delta Alumni Assn. Roman Catholic. Clubs: K.C., Elks, Order Sons of Italy. Office: 2233 Rayburn House Office Bldg Washington DC 20515

RUSSO, ROBERT RITTER, electronics company executive; b. N.Y.C., Aug. 19, 1926; s. Anthony and Dorothy (Ritter) R.; m. Dorothy Foster; children—Thomas, Steven, Judith. B.N.S., Tufts U., 1946, B.S. in Mech. Engring., 1948. Mgr. devel. engring. RCA Corp., Indpls., 1950-61, mgr. process devel., 1964—. Patentee in field. Served with USN, 1944-47. Methodist. Avocations: old and rare book collecting. Home: 3820 E 61 St Indianapolis IN 46220 Office: RCA Corp 600 N Sherman Dr Indianapolis IN 46201

RUSTEN, ELMER MATHEW, dermatologist; b. Pigeon Falls, Wis., Oct. 5, 1902; s. Ener E. and Clara L. (Benrud) R.; B.A., St. Olaf Coll., 1925; B.S., U. Minn., 1928, B.M., 1928, M.D., 1929, postgrad., 1929-31, U. Vienna, 1932; m. Helen Marthine Steidl, July 19, 1930; 1 son, Elmer Michael. Intern, Mpls. Gen. Hosp., 1929, resident, 1929-31; practice medicine specializing in dermatology, Mpls., 1933-82; instr. dermatology U. Minn., Mpls., 1934-38, clin. instr., 1938-42, clin. asst. prof., 1942-71; mem. cons. staff Mpls. Gen. Hosp., 1933-40, 51-60, Glen Lake Sanatorium, Oak Terrace, Minn., 1936-60; mem. attending staff Methodist Hosp., St. Louis Park, Minn., 1959-77, Abbott Hosp., Mpls., Minn., 1935—, Asbury Hosp., Mpls., 1934-50. Del. to 14th Internat. Tb Conf., New Delhi, India, 1957. Mem. Minn. Citizens Council, 1963-66; bd. dirs. Correctional Service of Minn., pres., 1963-67; bd. dirs. Minn. Dermatol. Found., 1950-54, Central Luth. Found., 1952-84. Diplomate Am. Bd. Dermatology. Mem. Am., Minn. med. assns., Mpls. Acad. Medicine (past pres.), Am. Acad. Dermatology, Soc. for Investigative Dermatology, Minn. (pres.), Chgo. dermatol. socs., Internat. Soc. Tropical Dermatology, Am. Acad. Allergy, Internat. Corrs. Soc. of Allergists, Hennepin County Med. Soc., Alaska Territorial Assn. (hon.), Phi Beta Pi (past pres. North Central chpt.). Republican. Lutheran. Clubs: Rotary (pres. 1961, Paul Harris fellow 1983), Boone and Crockett (hon. life mem., chmn. Big Game Competition 1961, 64, v.p. 1965-74), Big Game (pres. 1940, dir. Spl. Projects Found. 1970—). Author: Wheat, Egg and Milk-Free Diets, 1932; contbr. to Ofcl. Scoring System for N. Am. Big Game, 1971. Home: 18420 D 8th Ave N Plymouth MN 55447 Office: 816 Medical Arts Bldg Minneapolis MN 55402

RUSYNYK, DENNIS JOHN, former industrial executive; b. Cleve., May 6, 1948; s. Sam and Victoria (Gluszik) R.; B.B.A., Ohio U., 1970. Laborer, Union Carbide Corp., Cleve., summers 1966-70; press operator Airco Welding Products, Cleve., 1971-73; indsl. engr. Lamson & Sessions Co., Cleve., 1973-75; supr. Gen. Industries, Elyria, Ohio, 1975-81, plant mgr., 1981-84; supr. Premier Mfgr., Cleve., 1985—. Treas. Little League North, Elyria, 1977-78; advisor Jr. Achievement Assn., Cleve., 1974-75. Greek Catholic. Developer one resin formulations in bulk molding compounds. Home: 327 Canterbury Ct Elyria OH 44035

RUTAN, CHARLES ALAN, banker; b. Charleston, Ill., June 13, 1953; s. Charles F. and Susan R. (Decker) R.; m. Judith Ann Good, Aug. 20, 1974; children—Jeffrey Alan, Jonathon Matthew. B.S. in Bus. with honors, Eastern Ill. U. C.P.A., Ill. Mem. audit staff McGladry Hendrickson, Springfield, Ill., 1975-76; asst. auditor Champaign Nat. Bank, Ill., 1976-78, auditor, 1978-79, v.p., chief fin. officer, 1979—; instr. banking Parkland Community Coll., Champaign, 1979-80. Treas. Champaign County chpt. ARC, 1982—, Champaign-Urbana Little League, 1982—; sect. leader Am. Cancer Soc., 1982. Recipient Accountancy award McGladrey Hendrickson, 1975, Outstanding Vol. Service award ARC, 1984, Outstanding Vol. Service award United Way of Champaign County, 1984. Mem. Am. Inst. C.P.A.s (Eastern chpt.), Ill. Soc. C.P.A.s. Baptist. Avocations: softball, basketball, youth soccer coaching, baseball. Home: 1211 Foothill Ave Champaign IL 61821 Office: Champaign Nat Bank PO Box 250 Champaign IL 61820

RUTENBERG-ROSENBERG, SHARON LESLIE, journalist; b. Chgo., May 23, 1951; d. Arthur and Bernice (Berman) Rutenberg; student Harvard U. Summer Sch., 1972; B.A., Northwestern U., 1973, M.S.J., Medill Grad. Sch. Journalism, 1975; m. Michael J. Rosenberg, Feb. 3, 1980; children—David Kaifel, Jonathan Reuben (twins). Bus. mgr. Northwestern U. Yearbook, 1971-72; reporter-photographer Lerner Home Newspapers, Chgo., 1973-74; corr. Medill News Service, Washington, 1975; reporter-newsperson UPI, Chgo., 1975—; mem. exec. bd. Northwestern U. Student Adv. Council, 1972-73. Vol. worker Chgo.-Read Mental Health Center. Recipient Peter Lisagor award exemplary journalism in print feature category, 1980, 81; Golden Key award Nat. Adv. Bd. to Children's Oncology Services, Inc., 1981; Chgo. Hosp. Pub. Relations Soc. awards for news story and feature story, 1983, 84; cert. student pilot, cert. scuba diver. Mem. Hadassah, Hon. Order Ky. Cols., Sigma Delta Chi, Sigma Delta Tau. Covered Pres. of U.S., the Pope, prime minister of Israel. Home: 745 Marion Ave Highland Park IL 60035 Office: 360 N Michigan Ave Chicago IL 60601

RUTH, JOHN HOMER, farm equipment company executive; b. Scottdale, Pa., Mar. 2, 1936; s. John H. and Ruby H. (Bailey) R.; m. Martha Lee Rhodes, June 4, 1959; children—Melissa, Amy, John H. B.S., U.S. Mil. Acad., 1959. Gen. mgr. John Deere Thailand, Bangkok, 1969-72, gen. sales mgr., Nottingham, Eng., 1972-73, mng. dir. John Deere Sweden, Malmo, 1973-76; dir. European sales brs. Deere & Co., Mannheim, Germany, 1976-79; v.p. mktg. Massey Ferguson Ltd., Toronto, Ont., Can., 1979-81, pres. Massey Ferguson Inc., Des Moines, 1981—, also chief exec. officer; mem. exec. com. Farm and Indsl. Equipment Inst., Chgo., 1982—. Mem. Des Moines C. of C. (dir. 1982-83). Served with AUS 1959-62. Lodge: Rotary Internat. Home: 200 Foster Dr Des Moines IA 50312 Office: Massey Ferguson Inc 1901 Bell Ave Des Moines IA 50315

RUTHERFORD, JACK DOW, farm machinery manufacturing company executive. Vice chmn. Internat. Harvester, Chgo., also dir. Office: Internat Harvester 401 N Michigan Ave Chicago IL 60611*

RUTHMAN, THOMAS R., manufacturing company executive; b. Cin., May 24, 1933; s. Alois H. and Catherine (Gies) R.; grad. LaSalle U., 1970; m. Audrey J. Schumaker, Mar. 17, 1979; children—Thomas G., Julia C., Theresa K. With Ruthman Machinery Co., Cin., 1953—, gen. mgr., 1964-70, v.p., 1970-74, pres., 1974—, pres., owner Ruthman Corp., 1981—, Ruthman Machinery Co., Gusher Pumps, Inc., Fulflo Spltys. Co., Ruthman Pump Co. of New Castle, Gusher Pumps of Calif. Served with U.S. Army, 1953-55. Mem. Cin. Council World Affairs, Navy League U.S. Club: Rotary. Home: 6858 Dimmick Rd West Chester OH 45069 Office: 1212 Streng St Cincinnati OH 45223

RUTLEDGE, CHARLES OZWIN, pharmacology educator; b. Topeka, Oct. 1, 1937; s. Charles Ozwin and Alta (Seaman) R.; m. Jane Ellen Crow, Aug. 13, 1961; children—David Ozwin, Susan Harriett, Elizabeth Jane, Karen Ann. B.S., U. Kans., 1959, M.S., 1961; Ph.D., Harvard U., 1966. NATO postdoctoral fellow Gothenburg U., Sweden, 1966-67; asst. prof. U. Colo. Med. Ctr., Denver, 1967-74, assoc. prof., 1974-75; prof., chmn. dept. pharmacology U. Kans., Lawrence, 1975—; mem. med. adv. bd. Dysautonomia Found., N.Y.C., 1980—; mem. rev. com. NIMH, Bethesda, Md., 1982—. Editor pharm. exam. Pharmat Inc., Lawrence, 1977—. Contbr. articles on neuropharmacology to profl. jours. Grantee: NIH, 1970, Kans. Heart Assn., 1978. Mem. Am. Soc. Pharmacology and Exptl. Therapeutics (councillor 1982-84), Am. Assn. Coll. Pharmacy (chmn. biol. scis. sect. 1983-84), Soc. for Neurosci., Am. Pharm. Assn. AAAS. Democrat. Mem. United Ch. of Christ. Avocations: gardening; skiing. Home: 2620 Stratford St Lawrence KS 66044 Office: Dept Pharmacology and Toxicology Sch Pharmacy U Kans Lawrence KS 66045

RUTLEDGE, HARRY ROBERT, architect; b. Topeka, Mar. 24, 1941; s. Charles Ozwin and Alta Caroline (Seaman) R.; m. Elizabeth Ann Galloway, Aug. 2, 1969; children—Tavia Ann, Paula Helen. B.Arch., U. Kans., 1964; M.Sc. in Rural Planning, Aberdeen (Scotland) U., 1974. Registered architect, Mo., Kans., Okla., Colo., U.K. Sr. asst. architect Leeds Regional Hosp. Bd., Harrogate, Eng., 1966-67; assoc. ptnr. Derek Lovejoy Partnership, Freeport-/Nassau Bahamas, 1967-72; architect Baxter Clark & Paul, Aberdeen, 1973-74; prin. Mann & Co., P.A., Hutchinson, Kans., 1974—. Trustee, mem. exec. bd. KPTS-Public TV, 1978-84, 85—; mem. exec. bd. Health Systems Agy. S.E. Kans., 1976-78. Recipient 1st prize Presbyn. Ch. Complex, Freeport Bahamas, 1970; 2d prize Nat. Winton Heights House Competition, Bahamas, 1972. Mem. Kans. Soc. Architects, AIA (exec. com. 1978-84, pres. 1983), Am. Inst. Architects (regional council 1982-83), Am. Arbitration Assn., Royal Inst. Brit. Architects. Presbyterian. Office: 335 N Washington Hutchinson KS 67501

RUTTENBERG, HARVEY NOLAN, marketing executive; b. Chgo., May 8, 1942; s. Simon and Tillie (Trembot) R.; m. Phyllis Rubin, Jan. 5, 1964 (div. July 1981); children—Melissa Dawn, Gina Nicole; m. Leah Joanne Adelman, Apr. 25, 1982. B.A., U. Ill., 1964. Sales mgr. Mfr. Rep. Agy., Chgo., 1964-71; nat. acctg. mgr. Dow Chem. Co., Midland, Mich., 1971-74; v.p. mktg. Style Wood Co., Arlington Heights, Ill., 1974-79; mktg. mgr. Ekco Houseware Co., Franklin Park, Ill., 1979-82, Safety Kleen Co., Elgin, Ill., 1982—; design cons. in field. Mem. Automotive Service Ind. (officer 1980-84), Automotive Chem. Mfrs. Council (steering com. 1985, chmn. environ. interest com. 1985). Design Cons. (officer 1976-82), Nat. Retailer Assn. (officer 1980-82). Jewish. Avocations: design; mktg. lectr.; editorial contrb. Home: 1281 Bristol Ln Buffalo Grove IL 60089 Office: Safety Kleen Co Elgin IL

RUTZ, DUANE PHILIP, optometrist; b. Little Falls, Minn., Oct. 31, 1952; s. Leonard Philip and Betty Marie (Fedor) R.; m. Linda Lee Kohl, Sept. 1, 1973; children—Jennifer Lea, Miranda Renee. B.S. in Chemistry, St. Cloud State U., 1976; O.D., Ill. Coll. Optometry, 1981. Chemist H.B. Fuller Co., St. Paul, 1976-77; optometrist McAllen-Rutz Eye Clinic, Hallock, Minn., 1981—. Mem. Am. Optometric Assn., Minn. Optometric Assn., Hallock C. of C. (v.p. 1983), Tomb and Key; Beta Sigma Kappa. Lodge: Lions. Avocations: golf, fishing, hunting. Home: 341 E Broadway Hallock MN 56728 Office: 118 S 2d St Hallock MN 56728

RUVELSON, ALAN KENNETH, investment company executive; b. St. Paul, Sept. 5, 1915; s. Philip Godfrey and Eva (Lumpkin) R.; m. Ethel Newberg, 1938 (dec. 1965); children—Judith, Alan, Jr., Mary Ellen, Richard; m. Louise Loidolt, Dec. 26, 1966. Student Coll. St. Thomas., St. Paul, 1932-34; B.B.A., U. Minn., 1936. Diamond importer and wholesale jewelry salesman Phil G. Ruvelson Inc., Mpls., 1936-66; pres. First Midwest Corp., Mpls., 1959—; dir. Comserv Corp., Mpls., Dicomed Corp., Mpls., HEI, Inc., Victoria, Minn., Nutrition World, Inc., Mpls. Mem. exec. com. Regional Export Expansion Council, 1964-67; trustee St. Thomas Mil. Acad. Alumni Assn., 1965-68; founding mem. Gov. John Sargent Pillsbury Fellowship, U. Minn., 1966; mem. Gov.'s Adv. Commn. on Econ. Devel. for State of Minn.; trustee Coll. St. Benedict, St. Joseph, Minn., 1967-71, St. Thomas Acad., 1976-82, Convent of Visitation Sch., 1976-78, St. Catherine's Coll., 1980-83; chmn. adv. council Nat. Small Bus. Investment Co., 1969-70; chmn. lay adv. bd. St. Mary's Hosp., Mpls., 1970-71; mem. exec. com. Lawyers Profl. Responsibility Bd., 1978-81; bd. dirs. Found. Minn. Progress, 1978-79; mem. adv. council Coll. St. Thomas Small Bus. Devel. Ctr., 1979—; mem. all univ. honors com. U. Minn., 1980—; mem. exec. com. Bus.-Industry Polit. Action Com. Minn., 1980-81. Recipient Hames Meml. Alumni award St. Thomas Acad., 1979, Cross of Merit with Silver Star of Holy Sepulchre Jerusalem, 1983, SBA Silver Anniversary award, 1983; named to Minn. Bus. Hall of Fame, 1980. Mem. Nat. Assn. Small Bus. Investment Cos. (pres. 1961-62), Minn. Assn. Commerce and Industry (pres. 1973-74), U. Minn. Alumni Assn. (nat. pres., bd. dirs. 1978-79), Am. Arbitration Assn. (bd. dirs. Minn. chpt. 1975-78, vice chmn. 1981—), Minn. State Bar Assn. (com. on task force on principles of professionalism 1984—), Midwest Regional Assn. Small Bus. Investment Cos. (pres. 1964-65). Clubs: Minneapolis, Minn. (St. Paul), Town and Country; U. of Minn. Alumni (Mpls.). Home: 1293 Pinehurst Ave Saint Paul MN 55116 Office: First Midwest Corp 1010 Plymouth Bldg 12 S 6th St Minneapolis MN 55402

RUYLE, ELIZABETH SMITH (BETH), association executive; b. Atlanta, Oct. 26, 1946; d. Daniel Lester and Mae (Coley) Smith; B.A., U. Fla., 1968; M.P.A., U. Ga., 1975; 1 dau., Leigh Ann. Health planner Met. Council for Health, Atlanta, 1970-72; govtl. services coordinator Atlanta Regional Commn., 1972-75, govtl. relations coordinator, 1975-78; exec. dir. South Suburban Mayors' and Mgrs. Assn., Oak Forest, Ill., 1978—; exec. dir. South Towns Agy. Risk Mgmt., 1980—, South Towns Area Benefits Coop., 1983—, South Towns Bus. Growth Corp., 1983—; dir. South Suburban Cable Council, 78-85. Bd. dirs., mem. Work Edn. Council for South Suburbs; sec., bd. dirs. FOCUS Council on South Suburbs; mem. World's Fair Adv. Com., Met. Planning Council; mem. Cook County Housing Adv. Com. Mem. Internat. City Mgmt. Assn., Ill. City Mgmt. Assn., Met. Mgrs. Assn., Ill. Public Employer Labor Relations Assn., Public Risk and Ins. Mgmt. Assn., South Suburban Chiefs of Police Assn., Chgo. Assn. Commerce and Industry. Contbr. articles to profl. and devel. mags. Office: South Suburban Mayors and Mgrs Assn 15440 S Central Ave Oak Forest IL 60452

RUZICKA, VICKI PATRICIA, marketing executive; b. Chgo., Apr. 30, 1945; s. Victor Hugo and Ellyn Marie (Doyle) Reid R. B.S., Northeastern Ill. U., Chgo., 1976. Prodn. mgr. Signature Direct Response Mktg., Evanston, Ill., 1981-82, purchasing mgr., 1983-84; credit promotions media mgr. Montgomery Ward, Chgo., 1982-83; fulfillment purchasing mgr. The Signature Group, Schaumburg, Ill., 1984—. Author: Trips: Head, Bod and Side, 1968, Poetry Magazine, 1970. Served with USAF, 1979-83. Mem. Nat. Assn. Purchasing Mgrs., Direct Mail Mktg. Assn., Printing Inst. Ill., Chgo. Assn. Direct Mktg. Roman Catholic. Avocations: sailing; golf; classical piano; baseball. Office: The Signature Group 200 N Martingale Rd Schaumburg IL 60194

RYALL, JO-ELLYN M., psychiatrist; b. Newark, May 25, 1949; d. Joseph P. and Tekla (Paraszczuk) R.; B.A. in Chemistry with gen. honors, Douglass Coll., Rutgers U., 1971; M.D., Washington U., St. Louis, 1975. Resident in psychiatry Washington U., 1975-78, psychiatrist Student Health, 1980-84, clin. instr. psychiatry, 1978-83, clin. asst. prof. psychiatry, 1983—; inpatient supr. Malcolm Bliss Mental Health Center, St. Louis, 1978-80, psychiatrist outpatient clinic, 1980-82; pvt. practice medicine specializing in psychiatry, St. Louis, 1980—. Bd. dirs. Women's Self Help Center, St. Louis, 1980-83. Diplomate Am. Bd. Psychiatry and Neurology. Mem. Am. Psychiat. Soc. (pres. Eastern Mo. Dist. Br. 1983-85), Am. Med. Women's Assn. (pres. St. Louis Dist. br. 1981-82), AMA, St. Louis Met. Med. Soc. (del. to state conv. 1981—councilor 1985—), Manic Depressive Assn. St. Louis (bd. dirs.). Club: Washington U. Faculty. Office: 9216 Clayton Rd Saint Louis MO 63124

RYAN, DONALD PATRICK, contractor; b. Janesville, Wis., July 13, 1930; s. William H. and Myrtle (Westrick) R.; B.S. in Civil Engring., U. Wis., 1953, B.S. in Naval Sci., 1953; m. Diana Houser, July 17, 1954; children—Patrick, Susannah, Nancy, David, Josephine, Rebecca, Polly, Adam. Partner, Ryan Bros. Co., Janesville, Wis., 1949—; dir. Ryan, Inc., Janesville; pres. Engring. Service Corp., Janesville, 1959—; pres. P. W. Ryan Sons, Inc., Janesville; dir. Bank of Wis., Janesville, Bankwis Corp. Bd. dirs. U. Wis. Found. Served with USNR, 1953-55. Registered profl. engr., Wis., Ill. Mem. Nat. Soc. Profl. Engrs., Wis. Meml. Union Bldg. Assn. (trustee), U. Wis. Alumni Assn., Chi Epsilon, Phi Delta Theta. Home: 703 St Lawrence Ave Janesville WI 53545 Office: PO Box 1079 Janesville WI 53545

RYAN, GEORGE, lieutenant governor; b. Maquoketa, Iowa, Feb. 24, 1934; s. Thomas J. and Jeanette (Bowman) R.; B.S. in Pharmacy, Ferris State Coll., Big Rapids, Mich.; m. Lura Lynn Lowe, June 10, 1956; children—Nancy, Lynda, Julie, JoAnne, Jeanette, George. Vice-pres., Ryan Pharmacies, Kankakee, Ill.; mem. Ill. Ho. of Reps., 1972-82, minority leader, 1977-81, speaker, 1981-82; lt. gov. State of Ill., 1982—. Mem. Kankakee County Bd., 1966-70, chmn. 1971-72; hon. chmn. Ill. Easter Seal Kickoff, UN Internat. Year of Disabled Persons, 1981. Served with U.S. Army. Recipient Humphrey award Am. Pharm. Assn., 1980; Israel Peace medal, 1984; named 1 of 10 Outstanding Legislators, Nat. Republican Legislators Assn., 1981. Mem. Am. Pharm. Assn. (Hubert Humphrey award 1980), Ill. Pharm Assn. Republican. Methodist. Club: One Hundred. Lodges: Elks, Moose, Shriners. Office: 214 State Capitol Bldg Springfield IL 62706

RYAN, HOWARD CHRIS, chief justice Ill. Supreme Court; b. Tonica, Ill., June 17, 1916; s. John F. and Sarah (Egger) R.; B.A., U. Ill., 1940, LL.B., J.D., 1942; LL.D. (hon.), John Marshall Law Sch., 1978; m. Helen Cizek, Oct. 16, 1943; children—John F., Elizabeth Ellen, Howard Chris. Admitted to Ill. bar, 1942; practice in Decatur, 1946-47, Peru, 1947-57; asst. state's atty. LaSalle County, 1952-54; county judge LaSalle County, 1954-57, circuit judge, 1957-68, chief judge, 1964-68; judge Appellate Ct. 3d Jud. Dist. Ill., 1968-70; justice Ill. Supreme Ct., 1970—, chief justice, 1982-84. Served with USAAF, 1942-45. Mem. Am., Ill., LaSalle County bar assns., Am. Judicature Soc., Am. Legion, Phi Alpha Delta. Republican. Methodist. Mason (33 deg.), Elk, Odd Fellow. Home: Box 397 Tonica IL 61370 Office: 111 E Jefferson St Ottawa IL 61350

RYAN, JAMES EDWIN, plastics company executive, real estate company executive; b. San Antonio, June 23, 1943; s. Edwin F. and Margaret L (Hale) R.; m. Connie S. Roseberry, Nov. 30, 1966; children—Rebecca Morrow, Rachel Morgan. B.A. in Psychology, Ohio State U., 1965. Registered profl. engr., Ohio. Br. mgr. Dayton Plastics, Ohio, 1965-71, sec.-treas., 1971-85, pres., 1985—; pres. Metro Properties, Dayton, 1977—; dir. Ohio Products, Inc., Dayton. Editor: Handbook of Plastics, 1973. Bd. dirs. Soccer Internat., Dayton, 1979—. Mem. Soc. Plastics Engrs., Soc. Plastics Industry, Nat. Assn. Plastics, Nat. Assn. Land Developers, Young Pres. Am. Avocations: tournament tennis playing. Office: Metro Properties 860 W Centerville Rd Dayton OH 45459

RYAN, JAMES JOSEPH, lawyer; b. Cin., June 17, 1929; s. Robert J. and Marian (Hoffman) R.; m. Mary A. Noonan, Nov. 25, 1954; children—Kevin, Timothy, Nora, Daniel. A.B., Xavier U., 1951, J.D., U. Cin., 1954. Bar: Ohio 1954. Teaching assoc. Northwestern U., Chgo., 1954-55; ptnr. Dolle, O'Donnell & Cash, Cin., 1958-71, Taft, Stettinius & Hollister, Cin., 1971—; lectr. Coll. Law, U. Cin., 1960-65. Chmn. Health Planning Assn. Ohio River Valley, Cin., 1978—; bd. dirs. Hamilton County Bd. of Mental Retarded, 1968-80; trustee Resident Home for Mental Retarded, 1980—. Mem. ABA, Ohio Bar Assn., Cin. Bar Assn., Republican. Roman Catholic. Clubs: Queen City, Western Hill. Avocations: reading; sports. Home: 1386 Wynnburne Dr Cincinnati OH 45238 Office: Taft Stettinius & Hollister 1800 1st Nat Bank Ctr Cincinnati OH 45202

RYAN, JAMES LEO, See *Who's Who in America,* 43rd edition.

RYAN, LAWRENCE MATTHEW, internist, educator; b. Evergreen Park, Ill., Nov. 27, 1946; s. Matthew L. and Genevieve M. (Reynolds) R.; m. Polly A. Fish, Sept. 27, 1969; children—Meghan, Clare, Aileen, Martin. Student Loyola U., 1967; M.D. cum laude, Stritch Sch. Medicine, 1971. Diplomate Am. Bd. Internal Medicine. Intern, Milwaukee County Gen. Hosp., 1971-72; resident Med. Coll. Wis., Milw., 1971-74, chief resident, 1974-75, fellow in rheumatolgy, 1975-77, asst. prof., 1977-82, assoc. prof., 1982—, chmn. com. Human Research Rev., 1982-84; postdoctoral fellow Nat. Arthritis Found., Atlanta, 1978-81; investigator NIH, Bethesda, Md., 1982—. Contbg. author books in field. Editorial bd. jour. Arthritis and Rheumatism, 1984—. Contbr. articles to profl. jours. Served to capt. M.C. USAR, 1972-78. Fellow ACP; Mem. Central Soc. Clin. Research (councillor 1984—), Am. Rheumatism Assn., Soc. Exptl. Biology, Am. Fedn. Clin. Research. Roman Catholic. Home:

6428 W Betsy Ross Pl Wauwatosa WI 53213 Office: Med Coll Wis 8700 W Wis Ave Milwaukee WI 53226

RYAN, SISTER MARY ANNE, nun, criminal justice educator; b. Rochester, N.Y., Nov. 20, 1942; d. Wendell F. and Frances M. (Lester) R. B.A., Nazareth Coll. of Rochester, 1964; M.A., Cath. U. Am., 1970; M.S., U. Wis., 1977. Tchr. jr. high sch. St. Mary's Sch., Winona, Minn., 1966-67, Cathedral Sch., Winona, 1967-68, Sacred Heart Sch., Waseca, Minn., 1968; tchr. Pacelli High Sch., Austin, Minn., 1970-75, chmn. social sci. dept., 1971-75; fellow in Asian studies U. S.D., Yankton, 1973; instr. U. Wis.-Madison, 1977-80; asst. prof. dept. behavioral sci. Coll. St. Teresa, Winona, 1980—, chmn. behavioral scis., 1982-84. Recipient Teaching award U. Wis.-Madison, 1979; fellow Mount Marty Coll., Yankton, S.D., 1973. Mem. Am. Soc. Criminology, Acad. Criminal Justice Scis., Criminal Justice Club of Coll. St. Teresa (adviser 1980-85), Pi Gamma Mu. Roman Catholic. Avocations: travel; reading, knitting. Office: Coll St Teresa Box 460 Winona MN 55987

RYAN, MARY ELLEN, advertising materials distributing business official; b. Chgo., Oct. 24, 1951; d. Albert John and Helen Mary (Heinlein) Gubricky; m. Patrick M. Ryan. Cert. Arts, Richard J. Daley Jr. Coll., Chgo., 1972; B.S.Ed., No. Ill. U., 1974; M.A. in Curriculum Devel., U. Conn., 1977, postgrad., 1980-84. With Ill. Bell Telephone Co., Chgo., 1969-71; internat. acct. Mex. br. Ency. Brit. Ednl. Corp., Chgo., 1974-76; advt. cons. Buzz Barton & Assos., Inc., Chgo., 1977-78; varied advt. positions Dimensional Mktg. Inc., Chgo., 1978; tchr. Nativity of Our Lord Sch., Chgo., 1979; tchr. Mother McAuley High Sch., Chgo., 1979-82; substitute tchr. Oak Lawn and Evergreen Park, Ill., 1983-84; tchr. Montessori Elem. Sch., Blue Island, Ill., 1984; customer service rep. Martin Brower (M-B Sales), Chgo., 1985—.

RYAN, MARY REGINA, association executive; b. Madison, Wis., Sept. 26, 1941; d. Louis August and Marian Jane (O'Connell) Maier; A.B., Marquette U., 1963; M.S.W., (U.S. Children's Bur. scholar), St. Louis U., 1965; children by previous marriage—Christopher John Matek, Monica Marie Matek, Maria Regina Matek. Med. social worker Milwaukee County Gen. Hosp., 1965-67; cons. dept. sociology Marquette U., 1969-71; research asst. Mental Health Planning Com. Milwaukee County, 1971-73; field rep. Nat. Found. March of Dimes, 1976-77; dir. community services Orange County Health Planning Council, Tustin, Calif., 1977-82; mgmt. cons. Ryan Assocs., Milwaukee, 1982-85; dir. profl. affairs N.Y. State Podiatric Med. Assn., 1985—; cons. Western Ctr. Health Planning, San Francisco, 1978-83. Chmn., Tustin Traffic Commn., 1976-77; del. Wis. Democratic Conf., 1971; mem. citizens adv. com. Sta. KOCE-TV, mem. adv. com. Calif. Health Tng. Ctr., Family Service Assn. Orange County, United Cerebral Palsy Assn.; mem. coms. United Way, Orange County unit Am. Cancer Soc., 1978-83, Vol. Action Ctr., 1981-83; host, interviewer KOCM Community Forum Program, 1979-83. Mem. Am. Pub. Health Assn. (gov. council 1981-83), Am. Health Planning Assn., Jr. League. Roman Catholic.

RYAN, PATRICK G., insurance holding company executive. Pres., chief exec. officer, dir. Combined Internat. Corp., Northbrook, Ill. Office: Combined Internat Corp 707 Combined Circle Northbrook IL 60062*

RYAN, RAYMOND RICHARD, JR., optometrist; b. Anchorage, Alaska, July 13, 1954; s. Raymond Richard and Carol Rose (Cummings) R.; m. Marcia Leslie Pogue, June 30, 1979; children—Erin Kathleen, Kelly Rae, Brianna Jean. B.S. in Psychology, Pacific U., Forest Grove, Oreg., 1976. O.D., 1979; M.S.Ed., U. Wis.-Oshkosh, 1985. Staff optometrist Shopko Stores, Inc., Kimberly, Wis., 1979-85; pvt. practice, 1985—; guest lectr. U. Wis-Oshkosh, 1980—; presenter in field. Vice pres. bd. dirs. Kinderhaus Day Care Ctr., Kaukauna, 1980-84; bd. dirs. Kaukauna Assembly of God, 1980-83, Kaukauna Bowling Assn., 1984-85; fund raiser Cerebral Palsy, Kimberly, 1983-85. Recipient appreciation award Amigos de las Americas, 1978; named Outstanding Jaycee of Quarter, 1980. Mem. Kaukauna Jaycees (v.p., pres. 1979-81), Antigo Optimists. Lodge: Elks. Avocations: fishing, bowling, reading. Home: W8964 Hwy 64 Antigo WI 54409 Office: The Vision Ctr 810 5th Ave Antigo WI 54409

RYAN, RICHARD PATRICK, patent agent; b. Decatur, Ill., May 4, 1938; s. Richard Patrick and Ruby Naomi (Nowlin) R.; JoAnne Rizzuti, Aug. 6, 1960 (div. June 1975); m. Elaine Lindsey, Oct. 15, 1976; children—Randall K., Timothy J., Annette M. B.A., Milikin U., 1960; Ph.D., U. Ky. 1968. Bar: U.S. Patent and Trademark Office 1981. Sr. scientist Mead Johnson & Co., Evansville, Ind., 1968-71, group leader chem. research, 1971-75, clin. research assoc., 1975-77, sr. clin. research assoc., 1977-80; patent coordinator Bristol Myers, Evansville, 1981-82, patent agt., 1982-85, sr. patent agt., 1985—; instr. chemistry U. Evansville, 1969-72. Patentee in medicinal chemistry; contbr. articles to profl. jours. Fencing instr. Evansville Dept. Parks and Recreation, 1978-80; asst. coach Reitz High Sch. Boys Soccer, 1983. Paul J. Murrill fellow, 1965-66, 66-67. Fellow Am. Geriatrics Soc.; mem. Am. Chem. Soc., AAAS, Sigma Xi. Clubs: MeJo Tennis (pres. 1983-84), Tri State Ski (capt. 1980—). Home: 9300 Farmington Dr Evansville IN 47712 Office: Mead Johnson & Co 2404 Pennsylvania Ave Evansville IN 47721

RYAN, ROBERT COLLINS, lawyer; b. Evanston, Ill., Sept. 15, 1953; s. Donald Thomas and Patricia J. (Collins) R.; m. Joanne Kay Holata, Nov. 5, 1983. B.A. in Econs., B.S.I.E. with high honors, U. Ill., 1976; J.D., Northwestern U., 1979. Bar: Ill. 1979, U.S. Dist. Ct. (no. dist.) Ill. 1980, U.S. Ct. Appeals (Fed. cir.) 1982. Assoc., Allegretti, Newitt, Witcoff & McAndrews, Ltd., Chgo., 1979-83, ptnr. 1983—; lectr. engring. law Northwestern U. Tech. Inst., Evanston, Ill., 1981-85, adj. prof. engring. law, 1985—. Exec. editor Northwestern Jour. Internat. Law & Bus., 1978-79. Contbr. articles to profl. jours. James scholar U. Ill., 1976. Mem. ABA, Ill. State Bar Assn., Intellectual Property Law Assn. Chgo., Tau Beta Pi, Alpha Pi Mu, Phi Kappa Phi. Home: 2650 N Lakeview #3501 Chicago IL 60614 Office: Allegretti Newitt Witcoff & McAndrews Ltd 125 S Wacker Dr Chicago IL 60606

RYAN, ROBERT JOHN, endocrinology educator, researcher; b. Cin., July 18, 1927; s. Robert M. and Marian J. (Hoffman) R.; m. Elizabeth E. Kennedy, Apr. 18, 1954 (div. Jan. 1980); children—Kathleen, Michael, Robert, Thomas, James, Barbara; m. Gloria A. Patton, May 15, 1981. Student Xavier U., 1945, 47-48; M.D., U. Cin., 1952. Resident, U. Ill.-Chgo., 1953-57, asst. prof., 1959-63, assoc. prof., 1963-67; research fellow Tufts U., Boston, 1957-59; assoc. prof. Mayo Clinic, Rochester, Minn., 1967-71; prof. medicine Mayo Med. Sch., Rochester, 1971-81, prof. cell biology, 1981—. Contbr. articles to profl. jours. Mem. study sect. NIH, 1970-73, chmn., 1972-73; mem. population ctrs. com. NICHD, 1974-78, 81-85, chmn., 1982-85. Served with U.S. Army, 1945-46. Bartells prof., 1983; grantee NIH, 1960—. Mem. Endocrine Soc. (council 1974-77, v.p. 1977-78; Robert H. Williams award 1984), Soc. Study of Reprodn., Am. Soc. Biol. Chemistry, N.Y. Acad. Sci., AAAS, Am. Soc. Clin. Investigation. Republican. Avocation: stamp collecting. Office: Mayo Med Sch Rochester MN 55905

RYAN, WILLIAM FRANK, management consultant, insurance and risk consultant; b. Inkster, Mich., May 6, 1924; s. William Henry and Gertrude Mary (Kling) R.; m. Loke Waiau Akoni, Oct. 5, 1963; children—Ilima, Lokelani, Eugene. Student Georgetown U., 1948-49, Columbia U., 1951-52, U. Padua (Italy), 1950-51; B.A., U. Mich., 1948. Diplomatic assignments in Russia, Italy and Japan, 1949-53; investment broker N.Y.C., Detroit and Honolulu, 1953-63; mgmt. cons. Bus. Mgmt. Internat., Honolulu, 1963-68; officer, dir. numerous corps.; ins. and risk mgr. U. Mich., Ann Arbor, 1969—; mem. Nat. Univ. Property Pool Ins. Study Group, 1969-70; chmn. ins. com. Mich. Council State Coll. Pres., 1971-73; mem. Nat. Task Force on Instl. Liability, 1974-76; cons. Assn. Univs. for Research in Astronomy, 1984—; exec. cons. William Ryan Risk Mgmt. Assocs., 1984—; chmn. adv. com. Assoc. Degree program in health care risk mgmt. Oakland Community Coll., 1984—. Trustee Assn. Ind. Colls. and Univs. Mich. Workers Compensation Self-Ins. Fund. Served to lt. (j.g.) USN, 1943-46. Recipient Instl. Risk Mgr. of Yr. award Bus. Ins. mag., 1981. Mem. Am. Soc. Hosp. Risk Mgmt. (bd. dirs. 1981-84, pres. 1983), Univ. Risk Mgmt. and Ins. Assn. (dir.), Mich. Coll. and Univ. Risk Mgmt. Officers Assn. (chmn. 1973-75), Midwest Univ. Risk and Ins. Mgmt. Assn. (chmn. 1977-78). Democrat. Roman Catholic. Home: 801 Center Dr Ann Arbor MI 48103 Office: 326 E Hoover St Ann Arbor MI 48109

RYBERG, ERICK LEONARD, clinical social worker; b. Detroit, Feb. 16, 1947; s. Leonard Erick and Sophie Mary R.; B.A., U. Mich., 1969, M.S.W., 1972; m. Amy Beth Fox, Dec. 23, 1969; 1 child, Benjamin Charles. Clin. social worker Downriver Guidance Clinic, Lincoln Park, Mich., 1972-74, dir. emergency psychiat. services, 1974-76; dir. social services Cottage Hosp., Grosse Pointe, Mich., 1976-79; pvt. practice psychotherapy Eastpoint Mental Health Center, P.C., Harper Woods, Mich., 1978—; clin. field instr. U. Mich. Grad. Sch. Social Work, 1974-79. Fellow Am. Orthopsychiat. Assn.; mem. Nat. Assn. Social Workers, Acad. Cert. Social Workers, Mich. Soc. Clin. Social Work (treas. 1980-84, pres.-elect 1984-86), Acad. Psychosomatic Medicine, Social Workers' Task Force Mich. (charter dir., legis. chmn.), Nat Registry Health Care Providers in Clin. Social Work. Home: 30247 Overdale Ct Farmington Hills MI 48018 Office: 19959 Vernier Rd Harper Woods MI 48225

RYDBERG, ROGER ALLEN, diversified company executive; b. Mpls., Apr. 28, 1938; s. Walter Raymond and Clevia (Wills) R.; m. Carol Elizabeth Eliason, Nov. 22, 1958 (div.); children—Michael, Susan, David, John, Thomas; m. Carole Ann Covell, July 26, 1974; children—Martin, Susan, Andrea, Steven. B.S. in Bus., U. Minn., 1960. EDP audit mgr. Gen. Mills Co., Mpls., 1981-82, tech. planner, 1982-83, performance planner, 1983—. Mem. Assn. Computing Machinery (pres. Twin Cities 1978), Spl. Interest Group Data Processing (chmn. 1983, 84). Mem. Democratic Farm Labor Party. Unitarian. Avocations: sailing; jogging; home computers. Home: 3225 Wellington Ln Plymouth MN 55441 Office: Gen Mills Co 9200 Wayzata Blvd Minneapolis MN 55440

RYDER, EDWARD MICHAEL, JR., lawyer; b. Cleve., May 4, 1948; s. Edward Michael and Elizabeth Ann (Freeman) R.; m. Diane Jane Cuffman, June 12, 1971; children—Megan Elizabeth, Kathleen Nellie. B.A. in Polit. Sci., Cleve. State U., 1970; J.D., Cleve.-Marshall Coll. Law, 1977. Bar: Ohio 1971. Sr. claims atty. Progressive Ins. Co., Cleve., 1978-84; assoc. Kolt, Mazanec & Raskin Co., L.P.A., Solon, Ohio, 1984—. Mem. Ohio Ho. of Reps., 1971-72; clk. city council City of Euclid, 1978-79; mem. zoning commn. Newbury Twp., Ohio, 1984. Mem. Ohio State Bar Assn., Geauga Bar Assn. Republican. Home: 11590 Bell Rd Newbury OH 44065 Office: Kolt Mazanec & Raskin Co LPA 33325 Bainbridge Rd Solon OH 44139

RYDHOLM, RALPH WILLIAMS, advertising executive; b. Chgo., June 1, 1937; s. Thor Gabriel and Vivian Constance (Williams) R.; m. Jo Anne Beechler, Oct. 5, 1963; children—Kristin, Erik, Julia. B.A., Northwestern U., 1958, postgrad. Bus. Sch., 1958-59; A.M.P., Harvard U., 1982. Account trainee, copywriter Young and Rubicam Advt., Chgo., 1960-63; copywriter Post Keyes Gardner Advt., Chgo., 1963; copywriter E.H. Weiss Advt., Chgo., 1963-65; copy group head BBDO Advt., Chgo., 1965-66; copy group head J. Walter Thompson Advt., Chgo., 1966-69, creative dir., 1969-76, exec. creative dir., 1976—, sr. v.p., 1972—, exec. v.p., 1980—, dir., 1980—, chmn. worldwide creative dirs., 1983—; speaker in field. Mem. nominating bd. WTTW-Channel II Pub. Broadcasting, Chgo., 1980. Served with USAF, 1959-65. Recipient award Cannes Film Festival, 1973, Clio award, 1973, 85; IBA award Hollywood Radio and TV, 1977; Addy award, 1979. Mem. Chgo. Advt. Club, Chgo. Soc. Comml. Artists, ASCAP. Clubs: Econ. of Chgo., Saddle and Cycle (Chgo.). Office: J Walter Thompson 875 N Michigan Ave Chicago IL 60611

RYKER, GARY EDWARD, conglomerate executive; b. Camden, Ark., Aug. 8, 1949; s. Mose Andrew and Norma (Harrison) R.; m. Marsha Lynn Castagnoli, Apr. 17, 1976; 1 child, Angela Marie. B.S. in Mech. Engring., U. Ark., 1971; M.B.A., U. Utah, 1979. Advanced tech. cons. Rockwell Internat., Cedar Rapids, Iowa, 1979-80, mgr. flight instruments, 1980-81, mgr. advanced planning, 1981-82, mgr. bus. devel., 1982-84, mgr. mktg. and support, 1984—. Served with USAF, 1972-79. Mem. Am. Inst. Indsl. Engrs., ASME, Beta Gamma Sigma, Phi Kappa Phi. Mem. Christian Ch. (Disciples of Christ). Avocations: flying, flight instruction, teaching, stock market, cooking. Home: 416 Stonehaven Ln NE Cedar Rapids IA 52402 Office: Mail Sta 108 157 400 Collins Rd NE Cedar Rapids IA 52498

RYMAN, TERRI L., cattle feeding equipment manufacturing company financial executive; b. Newton, Kans., Feb. 25, 1954; d. Merle Duane and Elda May (Witt) Pulaski; m. Jerry Jay Ryman, Mar. 21, 1975. B.A. in Bus. Adminstrn. cum laude, Southwestern Coll., Winfield, Kans., 1976; M.B.A. in Mgmt., Rockhurst Coll., 1983. Clk., No. Natural Gas, Holcomb, Kans., 1976-78; with Butler Mfg. Co., 1978-80, budget analyst, Kansas City, Mo., 1980-81, div. acctg. supr., 1981-82, controller, Garden City, Kans., 1982—. Mem. Nat. Accts. Assn. Republican. Methodist. Home: 1718 Pawnee Garden City KS 67846 Office: Butler Mfg Co N Hwy 83 Garden City KS 67846

RYMAR, JULIAN W., manufacturing company executive; b. Grand Rapids, Mich., June 29, 1919; student Grand Rapids Jr. Coll., 1937-39, U. Mich., 1939-41, Am. Sch. Dramatic Arts, 1946-47, Wayne U., 1948-52, Rockhurst Coll., 1952-53; Naval War Coll., 1954-58; m. Margaret Macon Van Brunt, Dec. 11, 1954; children—Margaret Gibson, Gracen Macon, Ann Mackall. Entered USN as aviation cadet, 1942, advanced through grades to capt., 1964; chmn. bd., chief exec. officer, dir. Grace Co., Belton, Mo., 1955—; chmn. bd. dirs. Shock & Vibration Research, Inc., 1956-66; chmn. bd., chief exec. officer Bedtime Story Fashions; dir. Am. Bank & Trust; comdg. officer Naval Air Res. Squadron, 1957-60, staff air bn. comdr., 1960-64. Bd. dirs. Bros. of Mercy, St. Lukes Hosp.; adv. bd. dirs. St. Joseph Hosp.; trustee Missouri Valley Coll., 1969-74; pres. Rymar Found. Mem. Mil. Order World Wars, Navy League U.S. (pres. 1959-60, dir. 1960-70), Rockhill Homes Assn. (v.p.) Friends of Art (pres., chmn. bd. govs. 1969-70, exec. bd. 1971-74), Soc. of Fellows of Nelson Gallery Found. (exec. bd. 1972-77), Sigma Delta Chi. Episcopalian (dir., lay reader, lay chalice, vestryman, sr. warden, diocesan fin. bd., parish investment bd.). Clubs: Press, University of Mich. (Kansas City); Arts (Washington). Home: 1228 W 56th St Kansas City MO 64113 Office: Mill St Belton MO 64012 also 614 W Mill St Belton MO 64012

RYMER, TERRIE ADRIENNE, lawyer; b. Chgo., May 23, 1946; d. David Maurice and Myrna (Zaremsky) Rymer; m. Frank R. Vozak. B.A. with distinction, U. Mich., 1968; J.D., Northwestern U., 1981. Bar: Ill. 1981, U.S. Dist. Ct. (no. dist.) Ill. 1981. Social services worker various locations, Chgo. and N.Y.C., 1968-78; tutor Stanley Kaplan Ednl. Ctr., Chgo., 1978-79; assoc. Fischel & Kahn, Chgo., 1981-83; staff atty. AMA, Chgo., 1983—. Author: Physician-Hospital Contracts, 1983; also chpts. to books, articles. Bd. dirs. Ill. Human Rights Authority, Chgo., 1982—. Mem. ABA (mem. sect. individual rights and responsibilities 1981—, health law forum 1983—), Ill. State Bar Assn., Chgo. Bar Assn. (hosp. and health law com. 1983—). Jewish Office: Office of Gen Counsel AMA 535 N Dearborn St Chicago IL 60610

RYNO, JOSEPH JAMES, III, emergency medicine physician; b. Trenton, N.J., Oct. 15, 1946; s. Joseph James and Jessie E. (Ross) R.; m. Sue C. Szychowski, Dec. 27, 1977. B.S. in Zoology, Ariz. State U., 1970; M.S., Miami U., 1973; D.O., Des Moines Coll. Osteo. Medicine and Surgery, 1976. Lic. osteopath, Ohio, Ind. Intern, Parkview Hosp., Toledo, 1977; student health physician Purdue U. (Ind.), 1977; emergency medicine physician Joint Twp. Dist. Meml. Hosp., St. Mary's, Ohio, 1977-80; gen. practice medicine Bluffton Physicians Inc. (Ohio), 1980-81; emergency medicine physician Hardin Meml. Hosp., Kenton, Ohio, 1981—; med. advisor Hardin County Emergency Med. System Assn. Mem. Am. Osteo. Assn., Am. Coll. Emergency Medicine. Home: 10363 Grove Rd Bluffton OH 45817

RYSER, CAROL ANN, physician, director mental health organization; b. Kansas City, Mo., Apr. 24, 1937; d. Leland Farley and Mary Francis (Roberts) Carter; m. A. Thomen Reece, June 17, 1963; Stephanie, Andrea; m. 2d, Michael E. Ryser, Apr. 25, 1980. A.B. in Chemistry, William Jewell Coll., Liberty, Mo., 1959; M.D., U. Kans., 1963. Intern, U. Kans., Kansas City, 1963-64, resident in pediatrics, 1964-65, 67-68; asst. prof. Children's Rehab. Unit, U. Kans., 1967-76; pediatric cons. USAF, 1965-67; mem. staff Research Hosp., Gardner Med. Ctr.; pres., exec. dir. Matrix, Kansas City, Mo., 1977—. Named Outstanding Alumnus, William Jewell Coll. Fellow Am. Acad. Pediatrics; mem. AMA, Johnson County Med. Soc., Jackson County Med. Soc., Internat. Transactional Analysis Assn. (provisional teaching mem.). Republican. Baptist. Office: Matrix 7447 Holmes Suite 1 Kansas City MO 64131

RYTTING, JOSEPH HOWARD, pharmacy educator, editor; b. Rexburg, Idaho, June 12, 1942; s. George and Maxine (Bitter) R.; m. Barbara Kay Smith, Apr. 9, 1965; children—Barbara, Michael, Janae, Kiersten, Rebecca, Melinda, Heather, Erik, Cheryl, Nathan, Megan. B.A., Brigham Young U., 1966, Ph.D., 1969. Asst. prof. U. Kans., Lawrence, 1969-75, assoc. prof., 1975-80, prof. pharmacy, 1980—. Assoc. editor-in-chief Internat. Jour. Pharmaceutics, Amsterdam, 1984—. Contbr. articles to profl. jours. Patentee in field. Instl. rep., mem. com. Heart of Am. council Boy Scouts Am., 1972—; chmn. curriculum adv. com. PTA, Lawrence Sch. Dist., 1977-78; chpt. chmn. Am. Diabetes Assn., Lawrence, 1981-85, bd. dirs., Wichita, Kans., 1982—. Recipient Tensiochem. Internat. prize Italian Oil Chemists Soc., Milan, 1974, Lederle Pharm. faculty award, 1977. Mem. Am. Chem. Soc. (chmn. 1979), Am. Pharm. Assn., Acad. Pharm. Sci., Sigma Xi, Rho Chi. Republican. Mormon. Avocations: music; sports. Home: 3009 Topeka Ln Lawrence KS 66046 Office: U Kans Pharm Chem Dept Lawrence KS 66045

RYU, CHUNG KOUL, surgeon; b. Pusan, Korea, Oct. 29, 1939; came to U.S., 1964, naturalized, 1980; s. Ki Sun and Wha Sun (Park) R.; m. Sonia Choi, Mar. 30, 1963; children—Grace, Linda, Daniel, Jeannette, Richard. B.S., Yon Sei U., 1959; M.D., Korea U., 1963. Diplomate Am. Bd. Surgery. Intern, Nassau Hosp., Mineola, N.Y., 1964-65; resident in surgery Timken Mercy Hosp., Canton, Ohio, 1965-67, Huron Rd. Hosp., Cleve., 1967-69; resident in thoracic surgery L.I. Jewish Med. Ctr., Jamaica, N.Y., 1969-71; practice medicine specializing in surgery, Hillsboro, Ohio, 1972—; mem. staff Highland Dist. Hosp. Fellow Internat. Coll. Surgeons, Am. Soc. Abdominal Surgeons. Presbyterian. Home: 8764 State Rt 124 Hillsboro OH 45133

SAARI, DONALD GENE, mathematics educator; b. Ironwood, Mich., Mar. 9, 1940; s. Gene August and Martha Mary (Jackson) S.; m. Lillian Joy Kalinen, June 11, 1966; children—Katri Karin, Anneli Liisa. B.S., Mich. Technol. U., 1962; M.S., Purdue U., 1964, Ph.D., 1967. Research astronomer Yale U., New Haven, Conn., 1967-68; asst. prof. math. Northwestern U., Evanston, Ill., 1968-70, assoc. prof., 1970-74, prof., 1974—; adj. prof. Mich. Technol. U., Houghton, 1982—; cons. Nat. Bur. Standards, Gaithersburg, Md., 1979—. Contbr. articles to profl. jours. Editor Soc. Applied and Indsl. Math. Jour., 1980—. Mem. Am. Math. Soc., Math. Assn. Am., Econometric Soc., Am. Astron. Soc. (dynamical astronomy sect.), Soc. Applied and Indsl. Math. Avocation: sports. Office: Northwestern U Math Dept Evanston IL 60201

SABATINI, NORMA JEAN, banker; b. Connersville, Ind., Mar. 9, 1927; d. Rex E. and Goldie (Johnson) Murray; m. Pat J. Sabatini, Sept. 13, 1952; children—Robert A., Mary K. B.A., Ind. U., 1948; grad. Sch. Bank Mktg., U. Colo., 1982. Society editor Pharos-Tribune, Logansport, Ind., 1949-52; legal sec., Logansport, 1965-69; co-owner Sabatini Printing Co., Logansport, 1969-78; adminstrv. asst. 1st Nat. Bank, Logansport, 1978-81, mktg. officer, 1981—. Vice-pres., Cass County Council on Aging, 1984-86, sec., 1982. Mem. Am. Bankers Assn., Bank Adminstrn. Inst. (bd. dirs. Tippecanoe chpt. 1985—), Bank Mktg. Assn., Ind. Bank Mktg. Assn., Kappa Kappa Kappa (corr. sec. 1963-65), Theta Sigma Phi. Democrat. Roman Catholic. Club: Logansport Country Women's Golf (treas. 1977). Avocations: golf, bridge. Home: 3129 Summit Ave Logansport IN 46947 Office: 1st Nat Bank One First Nat Plaza Logansport IN 46947

SABAU, CARMEN SYBILE, chemist; b. Cluj, Romania, Apr. 24, 1933; naturalized U.S. citizen; d. George and Antoinette Marie (Chiriac) Grigorescu; m. Mircea Nicolae Sabau, July 11, 1956; 1 dau., Isabelle Carmen. M.S. in Inorganic and Analytical Chemistry, U. C.I. Parhon, Bucharest, Romania, 1955; Ph.D. in Radiochemistry, U. Fridericiana, Karlsruhe, W.Ger., 1972. Chemist, Argonne (Ill.) Nat. Lab., 1976—. Internat. Atomic Energy Agy. fellow, 1967-68; Humboldt fellow, 1970-72. Mem. Am. Chem. Soc., Am. Nuclear Soc., Am. Romanian Acad. Arts and Sci., Assn. for Women in Sci., N.Y. Acad. Sci., Sigma Xi. Author: Ion-exchange Theory and Applications in Analytical Chemistry, 1967; contbr. articles to profl. jours. Home: 6902 Martin Dr Woodridge IL 60517 Office: Argonne Nat Lab 9700 S Cass Ave Bldg 205 Argonne IL 60439

SABELLI, HECTOR CARLOS, psychiatrist, neuropharmacologist, educator; b. Buenos Aires, Argentina, July 25, 1937; came to U.S., 1966, naturalized, 1975; s. Antonio and Elena (DiBenedetto) S.; m. Nora Hajvat, Dec. 22, 1960 (div.); children—Martin, Guido; m. Linnea Carlson, Jan. 18, 1980. B.S., Colegio Mariano Moreno, Argentina, 1953; M.D., U. Buenos Aires, 1959, Ph.D., 1961. Diplomate Am. Bd. Psychiatry and Neurology. Intern P.V. de Cordero Hosp., Argentina; research fellow dept. pharmacology Argentine Council for Research, Chgo. Med. Sch., 1960-61; asst. prof. dept. pharmacology Chgo. Med. Sch. 1962-64, vis. prof., 1966-67, prof., 1967-79, chmn. dept. pharmacology, 1970-75; prof., chmn. inst. pharmacology U. Litoral, Rosario, Argentina, 1965-66; resident in psychiatry Rush-Presbyn.-St. Luke's Med. Ctr., Mt. Sinai Hosp. Med. Ctr., Chgo., 1976-79; asst. prof. dept. psychiatry Rush-Presbyn.-St. Luke's Med. Ctr., 1979-84, prof. dept. pharmacology, assoc. prof. dept. psychiatry, 1984, adj. attending, 1979-81, asst. attending, 1981—, dir. psychobiology lab., 1979—; psychiatrist, neuropsychiatric hosp., career investigator Argentine Council for Research, Buenos Aires, 1964-65. Editor: Chemical Modulation of Brain Function, 1973. Contbr. articles to profl jours. Recipient Bennett award Soc. Biol. Psychiatry, 1963, Sci. Research award Interstate Postgrad. Med. Assn. N.Am.; Best Tchr. Yr. award Chgo. Med. Sch., 1975; named runner-up 1984 Clin. Research award Am. Acad. Clin. Psychiatrists; research fellow Argentine Council for Research; grantee Retirement Research Found, Office Consol. Lab. Services, Roger McCormick Found. Mem. Am. Psychiat. Assn., Am. Soc. Pharmacology and Exptl. Therapeutics, Soc. Exact Philosophy (founding). Club: Philosophy (founding). Office: Midwest Neuropsychiatric Assocs Ltd 1725 W Harrison St Suite 1074 Chicago IL 60612

SABHARWAL, KULBIR, food scientist; b. Punjab, India, Jan. 5, 1943; s. Faqir Chand and Kesar (Devi) S.; m. Karuna Puri, Dec. 12, 1976; 2 children. B.S., Punjab Agrl. U., Ludhiana, India, 1964, M.S., 1966; M.S., Ohio State U., 1969, Ph.D., 1972. Research asst. Ohio State U., Columbus, 1967-69, research assoc., 1969-72; research asst. Punjab Agrl. U., 1966-67; dir. of research and devel. Fisher Cheese Co., Wapakoneta, Ohio, 1972—. Merit scholar Punjab Agrl. U., 1960-64, also Merit fellow, 1964-66. Mem. Inst. Food Technologists, Am. Dairy Sci. Assn., Am. Chem. Soc., Am. Oil Chemists' Soc., Gamma Sigma Delta. Hindu. Avocations: golf, racquetball, tennis. Home: 3366 Muirfield Pl Lima OH 45805 Office: Box 409 Wapakoneta OH 45895

SABLE, MORRIS HERBERT, obstetrician-gynecologist; b. Pitts., Nov. 6, 1930; s. Louis David and Sarah (Glantz) S.; m. Barbara Sue Glazer, July 3, 1955; children—Jeffrey Howard, Pamela Joy. B.A., W.Va. U., 1952, B.S., 1953; M.D., Chgo. Med. Sch., 1957. Diplomate Am. Bd. Ob-Gyn. Intern Mt. Sinai Hosp., Cleve., 1957-58, resident, 1958-61; assoc. chmn. dept. ob-gyn Mt. Sinai Med. Ctr., Milw., 1977-81, vice chief med. staff, 1981-83, chief med. staff, 1983—; assoc. clin. prof. ob-gyn U. Wis. Med. Sch., Madison and Milw., 1977—. Served to lt. comdr. USN, 1961-63. Fellow ACS, Am. Coll. Ob-Gyn. Democrat. Jewish. Office: 788 N Jefferson St Milwaukee WI 53202

SABO, JOHN BENJAMIN, pharmacist; b. Herminie, Pa., Nov. 11, 1927; s. Julius Louis and Lottie Belle (Eckenrod) S.; B.S. in Pharmacy, Purdue U., 1950; m. Helen Marie Calhoun, June 30, 1951; children—Cynthia Jean, Michael John. Mgr., Hook's Drugs, Gary, Ind., 1950-53; pharmacist Black Oak Pharmacy, Gary, 1953-58; owner Park Plaza Pharmacy, Merrillville, Ind., 1958-62; mem. staff Methodist Hosp., Gary, 1962-81, chief pharmacist, 1968-69, dir. pharmacy, 1969-75, dir. pharmacy services, 1975-81; dir. pharmacy services Broadway Meth. Hosp., Merrillville, 1975-81; pharmacy staff Our Lady of Mercy Hosp., Dyer, Ind., 1981—; cons. Norwich Lab., Eaton Lab.; clin. instr. Purdue U. Sch. Pharmacy. Served with USNR, 1945-46. Recipient service and recognition awards. Mem. Am. Soc. Hosp. Pharmacists, Ind. Soc. Hosp. Pharmacists (pres. 1968-69). Methodist. Home: 1830 Dale Dr Merrillville IN 46410

SABO, MARTIN OLAV, Congressman; b. Crosby, N.D., Feb. 28, 1938; s. Bjorn O. and Klara (Haga) S.; m. Sylvia Ann Lee, 1963; children—Karin Margaret, Julie Ann. B.A. cum laude, Augsburg Coll., 1959. Mem. Minn. Ho. of Reps., 1961-78, minority leader, 1969-73; Speaker of House, 1973-79; mem. 96th-99th Congress from 5th Dist., Minn., 1978—. Participant Eagleton Inst. for Young Legislators, 1972; former regent Augsburg Coll., Mpls. Named Man of Year, Mpls. Jr. C. of C., 1973-74, One of Ten Outstanding Young Men of Year, 1974; One of 200 Rising Young Leaders Am., Time Mag., 1974. Lutheran. Office: 436 Cannon House Office Bldg Washington DC 20515

SABO, ROGER L., lawyer; b. Newark, Ohio, June 16, 1943; s. Frank T. and Mary Ann (Yonker) S.; m. Sue Ann White, Aug. 20, 1966 (div. May 1978); children—Eric D., Karen M. B.A., Ohio State U., 1965; J.D., Georgetown Law Ctr., 1968. Atty. appellate enforcement NLRB, Washington, 1968-71; ptnr. Knepper, White, Arter & Hadden, Columbus, Ohio, 1971—, speaker at seminars. Author: Construction Law, 1983; Law in Ohio: History of Public Employee Collective Bargaining Act, 1983. Steering com. Devel. Com. Greater Columbus, 1978—. Mem. ABA (labor law sect., occupational safety and health com. 1985—, NLRB practice and procedure com. 1985—), Ohio State Bar

Assn. (chmn. 1983—), Columbus Bar Assn. (labor law sect. 1981—), Indsl. Relations Research Assn., Ohio State U. Alumni Assn. (pres. Franklin County 1978, bd. dirs. 1975-83). Club: Capital (Columbus). Avocations: photography, sailing. Home: 3855 Norbrook Columbus OH 43220 Office: Knepper White Arter & Hadden 180 E Broad St Columbus OH 43215

SABOURIN, THOMAS DONALD, comparative toxicologist; b. Bay City, Mich., May 31, 1951; s. Donald Joseph and Genevieve (Paradowski) S.; m. Josanne Marie Rizzo, Aug. 10, 1974. B.A., U. Mich., 1973; M.A., Hayward State U., 1977; Ph.D., La. State U., 1981. Analytical chemist Sel-Rex div. Occidental Petroleum Co., Chatsworth, Calif., 1973-74; teaching asst. Hayward State U., Calif., 1976, La. State U., Baton Rouge, 1977, 79, 80; predoctoral research fellow Nat. Marine Fisheries Service, Auke Bay, Alaska, 1978, Petroleum Refiners Environ. Council of La., La. State U., 1977, 79, 80, Robert A. Lefleur fellow, 1980-81; postdoctoral research fellow Nat. Inst. Environ. Health Scis., Oreg. State U., Newport, 1981-82; prin. research scientist environ. and health scis. Battelle Columbus Labs., Ohio, 1982—. Contbr. articles to profl. jours. Lerner Fund for Marine Research grantee Am. Mus. Natural History, 1980-81. Mem. AAAS, Am. Soc. Zoologists, Soc. Toxicology, Western Soc. Naturalists, Sigma Xi (grantee 1980-81). Office: Battelle Columbus Labs 505 King Ave Columbus OH 43201

SABSAY, BORIS IOSEPH, physician, medical researcher; b. Moscow, Nov. 9, 1932; came to U.S., 1979; s. Ioseph Israel and Gitel (Israelson) S.; m. Julia M. Mirkin, Mar. 24, 1962; 1 son, Vitaly. M.D., 1st Moscow Med. Sch., 1957; Ph.D., Inst. Normal and Path. Physiology, Acad. Med. Scis., 1963. Intern, Clinics and Hosps. 1st Moscow Med. Sch., 1956-57; resident Central City Hosp., Moscow, 1957-57; fellow in gastroenterology Clinic for Med. Nutrition, Inst. Nutrition, Acad. Med. Scis., Moscow, 1961-64; practice medicine specializing in surgery/oncology, Moscow, 1957-59; research assoc. Inst. Physiology, Acad. Med. Scis., Moscow, 1959-66; sr. cons. gastroenterology, City Hosp., 1966-78; sr. research assoc. Northwestern U. Dental Sch., Chgo., 1979—. Mem. Sigma Xi. Contbr. numerous articles to sci. publs. Office: Northwestern U Dental Sch 303 E Chicago St Ward 13-049 Chicago IL 60611

SACCO, GEORGE JOSEPH, JR., rubber company executive; b. Pitts., July 20, 1942; s. George Joseph and Thelma Virginia (Cannistra) S.; m. Madeleine Gail Curry, June 5, 1965; children—Kimberly Ann, Anthony Brennan. B.S. in Personnel Mgmt., U. Dayton, 1964. With Goodyear Tire & Rubber Co., 1967—, employment mgr., North Chicago, Ill., 1969-73, mgr. personnel and purchasing, San Angelo, Tex., 1973-76, personnel mgr., Sun Prairie, Wis., 1976-77, mgr. research and devel. for personnel devel., Akron, Ohio, 1978-80, research adminstr., Akron, 1980—; guest lectr. colls. and univs. Jr. Achievement coordinator, Rotary Club, North Chicago, 1969-73; corp. solicitor United Way, 1970-73; pres. PTA Holy Angels Sch., San Angelo, 1974-75; trustee Towpath Homeowners' Assn., Akron, 1982-84. Served to capt. U.S. Army, 1965-67. Named Bus. Assoc. of Yr., Beacon chpt. Am. Bus. Women's Assn., 1983. Mem. Am. Soc. Personnel Adminstrn., Personnel Mgrs. Assn., Goodyear Mgmt. Club (sec.-treas. 1980-81, pres. 1981-82), Soc. for Research Adminstrs. Clubs: Goodyear Racquet (pres. 1981). Contbr. articles to profl. jours. Home: 2426 Laurel Valley Dr Akron OH 44313 Office: 142 Goodyear Blvd Akron OH 44316

SACHA, ROBERT FRANK, osteopathic physician, allergist; b. East Chicago, Ind., Dec. 29, 1946; b. S. Frank John and Ann Theresa Sacha; m. Carolyn Sue Levon, June 21, 1969; children—Joshua Jude, Josiah Gerard, Anastasia Levon, Jonah Bradley. B.S., Purdue U., 1969; D.O., Chgo. Coll. Osteo. Medicine, 1975. Diplomate Am. Bd. Pediatrics, Am. Bd. Allergy and Immunology. Pharmacist, asst. mgr. Walgreens Drug Store East Chicago, Ind., 1969-75; intern David Grant Med. Ctr., San Francisco, 1975-76, resident in pediatrics, 1976-78; fellow in allergy and immunology Wilford Hall Med. Ctr., 1978-80; staff pediatrician, allergist Scott AFB (Ill.), 1980-83; practice medicine specializing in allergy and immunology Cape Girardau, Mo., 1983—; assoc. clin. instr. St. Louis U., 1980—; clin. instr. Purdue U., 1971-72, Pepperdine U., 1975-76, U. Tex.-San Antonio, 1978-80. Pres., Parent Tchrs. League. Served to maj. M.C., USAF, 1975-83. Fellow Am. Coll. Allergy, Am. Coll. Chest Physicians; mem. AMA, Am. Acad. Pediatrics, Am. Coll. Allergy, Am. Acad. Allergy, Assn. Mil. Allergists, ACP, Am. Coll. Emergency Physicians, Mil. Surgeons and Physicians. Republican. Roman Catholic.

SACHS, SAMUEL, II, museum director; b. N.Y.C., Nov. 30, 1935; s. James Henry and Margery (Fay) S.; m. Susan McAllen, Aug. 17, 1957 (div. 1968); children—Katherine, Eleanor; m. Jerre S. Hollander, Nov. 8, 1969 (div. 1983); 1 son, Alexander. B.A. cum laude, Harvard U., 1957; M.A., NYU, 1962. Asst. in charge prints and drawings Mpls. Inst. Arts, 1958-60; asst. dir. U. Mich. Mus. of Art, Ann Arbor, 1963-64; chief curator Mpls. Inst. Arts, 1964-73, dir., 1973-85; dir. Detroit Inst. Arts, 1985—. Trustee Middlesex Sch. Decorated knight 1st class order North Star, Sweden, order of Dannebrog, Denmark. Mem. Am. Fedn. Arts, Coll. Art Assn., Am. Assn. Museums, Harvard Alumni Assn. Clubs: 555, Skylight, Century Assn., Harvard. Office: Detroit Inst Arts 5200 Woodward Ave Detroit MI 48202

SACHTLEBEN, BETTY JUNE, social worker; b. Centralia, Ill., Oct. 29, 1929; d. William Charles and Nellie Josephine (Winstead) Sissom; B.S., Washington U., 1962, M.S.W., 1966; m. Roland Sachtleben, Feb. 9, 1951; children—Stewart Gary, Cynthia Barbara, Sherwood Roland, Sanford Stanley, Kristin Charles. Psychiat. social worker Malcolm Bliss Mental Health Center, St. Louis, 1966-67; with div. pupil personnel St. Louis Public Schs., 1967-68; supr. social service dept. Parkway Sch. Dist., Chesterfield, Mo., 1969-72; social worker Family and Childrens Service, St. Louis, 1972-73; pvt. practice psychiat. social work, St. Louis, 1973-75; exec. dir. Mo. Counseling Service, Bridgeton, Mo., 1975-81; dir. coordinator social service dept. Phelps County Regional Med. Ctr., Rolla, Mo., 1982—; adj. asst. prof. St. Louis U.; instr. Washington U. Bd. dirs. New Hope Found. for Retarded Children, 1972-73; dir., sec. Sunshine Found., 1973—; dir. Parents Without Partners, 1975—. Mem. Nat. Assn. Social Workers, Am. Assn. Marriage and Family Therapists. Lutheran. Home: 1001 W 12th St Rolla MO 65401

SACHTLER, JOHANN WOLFGANG ADRIAAN, chemist; b. Heemstede, Netherlands, Oct. 18, 1954; came to U.S., 1978; s. Wolfgang Max Hugo and Luise Anne-Lore (Adrian) S. M.S., State U. Leiden, Netherlands, 1978, Ph.D., 1982. Postdoctoral researcher U. Calif.-Berkeley, 1978-81; sr. research chemist, Signal Research Ctr. Inc., Des Plaines, Ill., 1982—. Contbr. articles to profl. publs. Mem. Am. Chem. Soc. (div. petroleum chemistry, div. colloid and surface chemistry), Chgo. Catalyst Club. Home: 1366 Van Buren Ave Des Plaines IL 60018 Office: Signal Research Ctr Inc 50 E Algonquin Rd Box 5016 Des Plaines IL 60017-5016

SADEK, SALAH ELDINE, consulting pathologist; b. Cairo, Egypt, June 9, 1920; s. Ahmad A. and Zienab (Zahran) S.; D.V.M., U. Cairo, 1945; M.R.C.V.S., U. Edinburgh, 1948; M.S., Mich. State U., 1950; Ph.D., U. Ill., 1956; m. Helen Ann Phoenix, Apr. 12, 1952; children—Craig, Ramsay, Mark. Asst. prof. U. Cairo, 1945-48; asst. U. Ill., Urbana, 1953-55; pathologist Dow Chem. Co., Midland, Mich., 1956-67; head of pathology Hoffmann La Roche, Nutley, N.J., 1967-85, also asst. dir.; clin. prof. pathology N.J. Coll. Medicine and Dentistry, Newark; cons. in exptl. pathology and toxicology. Pres., Midland County Humane Soc., 1965-67. Diplomate Am. Bd. Indsl. Hygiene. Mem. Am. Vet. Med. Assn., N.Y. Acad. Sci., British Vet. Assn., Royal Coll. Veterinary Surgeons, Mich. Soc. Pathologists, N.Y. Pathol. Soc., Soc. Toxicology, Soc. Toxicologic Pathologists, Internat. Acad. Pathology, AAAS, Am. Acad. Indsl. Hygiene. Club: Midland Country. Home and Office: 3910 Valley Dr Midland MI 48640

SADJADI, FIROOZ AHMADI, electrical engineer, consultant, researcher; b. Tehran, Iran, Mar. 18, 1949; came to U.S., 1968; s. Akbar Ahmadi and Fakhri (Mohsen) S.; m. Carolyn JoAnne Elkins; 1 child, Farzad. B.S.E.E., Purdue U., 1972, M.S.E.E., 1974; E.E.E., U. So. Calif., 1976; postgrad. U. Tenn., Knoxville, 1983. Research asst. Image Processing Inst., U. So. Calif., Los Angeles, 1974-76; cons. Oak Ridge Lab., Knoxville, 1980; researcher dept. elec. engring. U. Tenn., 1977-83; research scientist Honeywell Systems and Research Ctr., 1983—. Mem. IEEE, Soc. Photo-Optical Instrumentation Engrs., Sigma Xi. Contbg. author numerous profl. publs. Office: Honeywell Systems and Research Ctr 2600 Ridgeway Pkwy MN17-2357 Minneapolis MN 55440

SADLER, JAMES BERTRAM, psychologist, clergyman; b. Albuquerque, Mar. 29, 1911; s. James Monroe and Mary Agnes (English) S.; m. Vera Ellen Ahrendt, Apr. 10, 1938. A.B., U. N.Mex., 1938; B.D., Crozer Theol. Sem., 1941, Th.M., 1948; M.A., U. Pa., 1941, Ed.D., 1959. Cert. psychologist, S.D. Ordained to ministry Baptist Ch., 1941; pastor First Bapt. Ch., Mt. Union, Pa., 1941-42; chaplain USAF, 1943-48; pastor Hatboro (Pa.) Bapt. Ch., 1948-61; chmn. dept. psychology Sioux Falls (S.D.) Coll., 1961-75; pvt. practice psychology, Sioux Falls, 1975—; cons. in psychology and religion. Mem. ministers council Am. Bapt. Conv. Mem. Am. Psychol. Assn., Am. Assn. Counseling and Devel., Soc. for Sci. Study Religion. Clubs: Mason, Rotary (pres. 1960). Contbr. articles to profl. jours. Home: 4312 Glenview Rd Sioux Falls SD 57103

SADOVE, ALAN MICHAEL, physician; b. Chgo., Oct. 8, 1948; s. Max Samuel and Ethel (Segall) S.; m. Armin Altshuler, June 1, 1974; 1 son, Scott Lawrence. A.B., Washington U., 1970; M.D., Loyola U., Maywood, Ill., 1974; M.S., U. Ill.-Chgo., 1977. Intern, Presbyn.-St. Luke's Hosp., Chgo., 1974-75, resident in gen. surgery, 1975-79; resident in plastic surgery U. Va., Charlottesville, 1979-81; fellow in plastic surgery NYU-Inst. Reconstructive Plastic Surgery, N.Y.C., 1981-82; asst. prof. surgery Ind. U. Sch. Medicine, 1982—; chief plastic surgery service James Whitcomb Riley Hosp. for Children, Ind. U. Med. Ctr., 1982—, med. dir. Burn Ctr., 1982—, dir. Oral-Facial Clinic, 1983—, med. dir. Craniofacial Anomalies team, 1982—; cons. VA Med. Ctr., Indpls.; mem. attending staff Wishard Meml. Hosp., Indpls. Mem. Chgo. Med. Soc., Ill. Med. Soc., AMA, ACS, Am. Soc. Plastic and Reconstructive Surgeons, Am. Cleft Palate Assn., Am. Burn Assn., Assn. Acad. Surgery, Am. Soc. Maxillofacial Surgeons, Marion County Med. Soc., Ind. State Med. Soc., Ohio Valley Soc. Plastic and Reconstructive Surgery, Sigma Xi. Office: Sect Plastic Surgery Ind U Med Ctr 702 Barnhill Dr Riley Hosp Room 1172 Indianapolis IN 46223

SAEGER, ARTHUR WILLIAM, real estate appraiser; b. St. Louis, Nov. 4, 1943; s. Kenneth Lloyd and Ethel Catherine (Donnelley) S.; B.S. in Bus. Adminstrn., Ind. U., 1972; m. Kathleen Anne Mathis, Aug. 17, 1968; children—Ashlie Anne, Heather Anne. Dir. adminstrn. mktg. dept. State Life Ins. Co., Indpls., 1968-71; with Fletcher Savs. and Loan Assn., Indpls., 1972-79, corp. officer, head mortgage loan ops., 1976-79; pvt. practice real estate appraising, Indpls., 1979—. Mem. Soc. Real Estate Appraisers, Am. Right of Way, Indpls. Met. Bd. Realtors, Ind. Bd. Realtors, Nat. Bd. Realtors. Republican. Roman Catholic. Clubs: Indpls. Sailing, Internat. Yacht Racing Union. Home: 8470 North Park Ave Indianapolis IN 46240 Office: 921 E 86th St Suite 107 Indianapolis IN 46240

SAEKS, KEITH ALLEN, lawyer; b. Dayton, Ohio, Aug. 2, 1935; s. Abraham Benjamin and Josephine (Segal) S.; m. Beverly Arnovitz, July 7, 1957 (div. Nov. 1980); children—Jennifer Saeks Schoenfeld, Sumner, Carrie; m. Stephanie Roe Jocobson, Dec. 26, 1980. J.D., Ohio No. U., 1960. Bar: Ohio 1961, U.S. Dist. Ct. (so. dist.) Ohio, U.S. Ct. Appeals (5th cir.). Assoc., Goldman, Bogan & Fox, Dayton, 1960-62; pros. atty. Montgomery County, Ohio, 1961-63; ptnr. Abrahamson, Arnovitz & Saeks, 1963-67, Arnovitz & Saeks, 1967-73, Holden & Saeks, Dayton, 1981—; chief referee, dir. Montgomery County Juvenile Ct., 1973-79. Founder Hillel Acad. Parochial Day Sch., 1961. Republican. Jewish. Avocations: official amatuer boxing; official professional boxing; jogging; tutoring. Office: Holden & Saeks 345 W 2d St 310 Mumma Bldg Dayton OH 45402

SAENT-JOHNS, GERALDINE MCCORMICK, painter, miniaturist, sculptor; b. Montreal, Que., Can., Sept. 12, 1930; d. Alexander Gerald and Anne (Lubkowski) McCormick; came to U.S., 1952, naturalized, 1965; student McGill U. Freelance artist, 1969—; owner, operator Eden Mood Studios 1973—; lectr. animals in art; miniature painting on gemstone rep. in collection of 8th Duke of Wellington, Pres. and Mrs. Gerald Ford. Mem. East African Wild Life Soc. (pres. Ohio area chpt.), Nat. Wildlife Fedn., Aircraft Owners and Pilots Assn., Canadian Nature Fedn. Republican. Home: 4800 Lander Rd Chagrin Falls OH 44022

SAEWERT, GEORGE CHARLES, fraternal organization officer; b. Park Ridge, Ill., June 22, 1922; s. Charles W. and Dorothy H. (Pagel) S.; m. Lillian Marie Curtin, Feb. 9, 1946; children—Sandra Lee, Saewert Thorne, Scott George Saewert. Various positions including supr., sales engr., regional mgr. Contour Saws, Inc. & DoAll Co., Des Plaines, Ill., 1941-84. Served to sgt. U.S. Army, 1942-45, PTO. Mem. VFW (commdr. Des Plaines Post 2992 1980-82, pres. meml. corps Ill. 1984-85). Avocations: golf; gardening. Home: 2721 Oakton St Park Ridge IL 60068

SAFFELS, DALE EMERSON, federal judge; b. Moline, Kans., Aug. 13, 1921; s. Edwin Clayton and Lillian May (Cook) S.; A.B., Emporia State U., 1947; LL.B., J.D. cum laude, Washburn U., 1949; m. Margaret Elaine Nieman, Apr. 2, 1976; children by previous marriage—Suzanne Saffels Gravitt, Deborah Saffels Knorr, James B.; stepchildren—Lynda Cowger Harris, Christopher Cowger. Admitted to Kans. bar, 1949; individual practice law, Garden City, Kans., 1949-71, Topeka, 1971-75, Wichita, Kans., 1975-79; U.S. dist. judge, Dist. of Kans., Kansas City, 1979—; chmn. bd. Fed. Home Loan Bank of Topeka, 1978-79. Bd. govs. Sch. Law Washburn U.; pres. Kans. Dem. Club, 1957; Dem. nominee Gov. of Kans., 1962; county atty. Finney County, Kans., 1951-55; mem. Kans. Ho. of Reps., 1955-63, minority leader, 1961-63, mem. Kans. Corp. Commn., 1967-75, chmn., 1968-75, mem. Kans. Legis. Council, 1957-63; Kans. rep. Interstate Oil Compact Commn., 1967-75, 1st vice chmn., 1971-72; pres. Midwest Assn. Regulatory Commn., 1972-73; pres. Midwest Assn. R.R. and Utilities Commrs., 1972-73; bd. dirs. Nat. Assn. Regulatory Utility Commrs., 1972-75. Served to maj. Signal Corps, U.S. Army, 1942-46. Recipient Disting. Alumnus award Emporia State U., 1974; Alumnus of Yr., Washburn U. Sch. Law, 1983. Mem. Am. Bar Assn., Kans. Bar Assn., Sedgwick County Bar Assn., Am. Judicature Soc. Lutheran. Home: 8901 Maple Dr Overland Park KS 66207 Office: 118 US Courthouse PO Box 1278 Kansas City KS 66117

SAFFIOTI, CAROL LEE ANN, humanities educator; b. Paterson, N.J., Nov. 24, 1949; d. Joseph Francis and Dorothy Grace (Porter) Saffioti. B.A. in English magna cum laude, U. N.C., 1971; M.A., Princeton U., 1973, Ph.D., 1975. Instr. communication skills, Princeton U., 1974-75; vis. asst. prof. U. Victoria, B.C., Can., 1976; asst. prof. humanities div., U. Wis.-Parkside, Kenosha, 1976-82, assoc. prof., 1983—. Grantee Danforth Found., 1975, NEH, 1978; Danforth Found. fellow, 1971-75. Mem. Soc. Tech. Communications Nat. Council Tchrs. English, Wis. Council Tchrs. English, Gt. Lakes Rhetoric Assn., U. N.C. Golden Chain Honor Soc., Phi Beta Kappa. Mem. Unity Ch. Contbr. articles, reviews and abstracts to profl. jours.; author numerous published poems.

SAFFOLD, KENNETH WAYNE, lawyer; b. Birmingham, Ala., May 30, 1952; s. James Harding and Charlie Mae (Ward) S.; m. Stephanie Burrougs, Mar. 27, 1976; children—Kenneth Wonte, Keary Wayne, Kathryn Elizabeth. B.A. cum laude, Va. Union U., 1974; J.D., Howard U., 1978. Bar: Minn. 1979, Pa. 1980, U.S. Dist. Ct. Minn. 1979, U.S. Ct. Appeals (8th cir.) 1981. Legis. asst., law clk. Dept. Labor, Washington, 1976-78; law clk. U.S. Library of Congress, summer 1977; spl. asst. atty. gen. Minn. Atty. Gen.'s Office, St. Paul, 1978-84; asst. counsel St. Paul Co./Western Life, 1984—; instr. in polit. sci. and law St. Thomas Coll., St. Paul, 1984—; Counsel Minn.-Dakota unit NAACP, 1980-84, St. Paul chpt., 1981-84. Bd. dirs., sec. Pilgrim Fed. Credit Union, St. Paul, 1980-83; trustee Pilgrim Baptist Ch., St. Paul, 1978-84. Mem. Hennepin County Bar Assn., Minn. Minority Lawyers Assn. (bd. dirs. 1980-84, v.p. 1983-84), Omega Psi Phi.

SAFFORD, PHILIP LANE, special education educator, psychologist; b. Cleve., July 3, 1935; s. Clarence William and Georgianne Theresa (Ingersoll) S.; m. Mary Jane Thompson, Aug. 17, 1957; children—Elizabeth Jane, Lynne Ellen. B.A. in English Edn., Ohio Wesleyan U., 1957; M.A. in Edn. and Counseling, Kent State U., 1962; Ph.D. in Edn. and Psychology, U. Mich., 1967. Lic. psychologist, Ohio; cert. tchr., Ohio. Tchr. English and composition Mentor-Bay Village Jr. and Sr. High Schs., 1957-61; dir. edni. therapy Sagamore Hills Child Psychiat. Hosp., Ohio, 1961-63; spl. edn. tchr., coordinator Berea Children's Home, Ohio, 1963-65, trustee, 1980—; U.S. Office Edn. fellow, research asst. ednl. and psychol. program U. Mich., Ann Arbor, 1965-67; prof. edn. Case Western Res. U., Cleve., 1967-74; prof., chmn. spl. edn. Kent State U. Ohio, 1974—; co-dir. Parent Child Learning Ctr., Kent and Cuyahoga Falls, Ohio, 1980—; cons. Soc. Crippled Children Cuyahoga County, also sch. dists. Author: (with D.C. Arbitman) Developmental Intervention With Young Children With Special Needs, 1975; Teaching Young Children With Special Needs, 1978. Contbr. articles to profl. jours. Mem. Gov.'s Adv. Council Spl. Edn., Columbus, 1976-78; bd. govs. Cuyahoga Spl. Edn. Service Ctr., 1976—, Spaulding for Children-Beech Brook, Orange, Ohio, 1978—. Recipient Disting. Educator award Martha Holden Jennings Found., 1982. Mem. Council Exceptional Children (div. on early edn., tchr. edn. div., mental retardation div., council children behavioral disorders, Educator of Yr. 1981), Assn. Persons with Severe Handicaps (exec. council Ohio chpt. 1984—), Phi Delta Kappa, Phi Delta Theta. Democrat. Methodist. Avocation: music, reading, boating. Home: 3276 Elsmere Rd Shaker Heights OH 44120 Office: Kent State U 404 White Hall Kent OH 44242

SAFFRAN, MURRAY, biochemistry educator, author; b. Montreal, Que., Can., Oct. 30, 1924; came to U.S., 1967, naturalized, 1977; s. Isidore Irving and Rebecca Reva (Elimelech) S.; m. Judith Cohen; children—David, Wilma, Arthur, Richard. B.Sc., McGill U., 1945, M.Sc., 1946, Ph.D., 1949. From lectr. to prof. McGill U., Montreal, 1948-69; prof., chmn. Med. Coll. Ohio, Toledo, 1969-80, prof., 1980—. Dozor vis. prof. Ben Gurion U., Israel. Contbr. articles to profl. jours. Ohio Acad. Scis. fellow; Ayerst-Squibb fellow Endocrine Soc. Fellow AAAS. Avocations: sailing, writing. Home: 2331 Hempstead Rd Toledo OH 43606 Office: Med Coll Ohio Dept Biochemistry Toledo OH 43699

SAGADY, DANIEL VICTOR, automotive engineer, engineering consultant; b. Saginaw, Mich., May 16, 1949; s. Fred and Lydia (Leichner) S.; m. Donna Lorraine Budzinski, May 18, 1973; children—Jessica Lorraine, Erika Jane. B.S. in Mech. Engring., Gen. Motors Inst., Flint, Mich., 1972; M.B.A., Oakland U., Rochester, Mich., 1980; M.S. in Indsl. Engring., Wayne State U. Registered profl. engr., Mich. Gen. Motors Inst. coop. student Saginaw Steering Gear div. Gen. Motors, Saginaw, 1967-71, engr., 1971-75, devel. engr., 1975-78; project engr. Ford Motor Co., Dearborn, Mich., 1978-85; staff project engr. Saginaw div. Gen. Motors, Saginaw, Mich., 1985—; engring. cons. Recipient Product Engring. award Saginaw Steering Gear div. Gen. Motors, 1978. Mem. Soc. Automotive Engrs. Republican. Lutheran. Patentee in automotive engring. field. Home: 3185 Sashabaw Oxford MI 48051 Office: Saginaw Div Gen Motors 3900 Holland Saginaw MI

SAGAN, JOHN, automobile company executive; b. Youngstown, Ohio, Mar. 9, 1921; s. John and Mary (Jubinsky) S.; m. Margaret Pickett, July 24, 1948; children—John, Linda, Scott. B.A. in Econs., Ohio Wesleyan U., 1948; M.A., U. Ill., 1949, Ph.D., 1951. With Ford Motor Co., Dearborn, Mich., 1951—, treas., 1966-69, v.p., treas., 1969—; dir. Ford Motor Credit Co., Ford Internat. Capital Corp., Ford Motor Land Devel. Corp., Transcon Ins. Ltd., Am. Road Ins. Co.; chmn. Fed. Res. Bank Chgo., 1981. Trustee, Ohio Wesleyan U., 1964, Com. for Econ. Devel., Oakwood Hosp., Dearborn, Fund for Henry Ford Hosp., YMCA Found., Detroit; bd. dirs. Detroit United Found.; mem. adv. com. Ch. World Service. Served with USNR, 1943-46. Mem. Conf. Bd's Council Fin. Execs., Am. Econ. Assn., Am. Fin. Assn., Fin. Execs. Inst., Phi Beta Kappa, Phi Kappa Phi. Home: 22149 Long Blvd Dearborn MI 48124 Office: Ford Motor Co The American Rd Dearborn MI 48121

SAGASER, DAVID D., insurance company executive; b. Summit, N.J., Jan. 23, 1952; s. Donald D. and Janyce M. (Westcott) S.; m. Carol J. Furst, May 5, 1984; 1 child, David Daniel. B.A., Brown U., 1974; M.B.A., U. Pa., 1977. Tchr., coach Winchendon Sch., Mass., 1974-75; with CIGNA, Phila., 1977—, underwriting mgr., 1984—. Mem. Soc. CPCUs. Home: N26W22325 Birchwood Ct Waukesha WI 53186 Office: CIGNA 2323 N Mayfair Rd Milwaukee WI 53213

SAGER, DONALD JACK, librarian, educator; b. Milw., Mar. 3, 1938; s. Alfred Herman and Sophia (Sagan) S.; m. Sherrill Labaw, Aug., 1960 (div. Feb. 1965); children—Geoffrey Alfred, Andrew Marquis; m. Irene Lynn Sleeth, June 28, 1968. B.S. in English and Am. Lit., U. Wis.-Milw., 1963; M.L.S., U. Wis., 1964. Cert. librarian, N.Y., library adminstr., Ohio, Wis. Dir. Kingston Area Library, N.Y., 1964-66, Elyria Pub. Library, Ohio, 1966-71, Mobile Pub. Library, Ala., 1971-75, Pub. Library of Columbus and Franklin County, Columbus, Ohio, 1975-78; commr. Chgo. Pub. Library, 1978-81; disting. vis. scholar Online Computer Library Ctr., Dublin, Ohio, 1981-82; dir. Elmhurst Pub. Library, Ill., 1982-83; adj. prof. U. Wis.-Milw., 1984—; city librarian and dir. Milw. Publ Library, Milw. County Fed. Library System, 1983—. Author : The American Public Library, 1982; Public Library Administration Planning Guide to Automation, 1983; Participatory Management in Libraries, 1982; Managing the Public Library, 1984. Chmn. United Way campaign, Milw., 1984; bd. dirs. Plymouth Ch., Milw., 1984—, Goethe Inst., Milw., 1984—. Served with U.S. Army, 1954-55. Mem. Pub. Library Assn. (pres. 1982-83), ALA (legis. chmn. 1980-82), Wis. Library Assn. (found. chmn. 1985—), Library Adminstrn. and Mgmt. Assn. (chmn. com. 1979-80), Am. Library Trustees Assn. (bd. dirs. 1983-84). Democrat. Club: Exchange (Milw.) Home: 1560 N Prospect Milwaukee WI 53202 Office: Milw Pub Library 814 W Wisconsin Ave Milwaukee WI 53233

SAGER, ROBERT DAVID, dentist, lectr., cons.; b. Manhattan, Kans., May 17, 1950; s. Robert Frank and Betsy Jane (Otey) S.; B.S. cum laude in Biology, Kans. State U., 1972; D.M.D. with honors, Washington U., St. Louis, 1975. Mem. faculty Dental Sch., Washington U., St. Louis, 1975-76; gen. practice dentistry, St. Louis, 1975-76; outpatient clinic mgr., dept. dentistry Ill. Masonic Med. Center, Chgo., 1977-78, mem. staff, 1977—; hosp. gen. dentistry practice, Chgo., 1977—; clinician, lectr. hosp. dentistry, 1978—; pres. Dentcare Ltd., hosp. dentistry cons., Chgo., 1978—, Dentsystems, Inc., 1979—; pres. Sager Dental Assocs., P.A., 1984—; pres., originator Dr. Toothbrush and Friends Products Co.; mem. staff Swedish Am. Hosp., Rockford, Ill., 1979—, St. Mary's Hosp., Manhattan, 1980—, Meml. Hosp., Manhattan, 1980—; cons. Cook County Hosp., 1979—; guest instr. hosp. gen. practice residency U. Colo. Sch. Dentistry, 1980—; attending dentist Sunset Zoo. Bd. dirs. Riley County Heart Assn. br. Am. Heart Assn., 1980—, v.p., 1984—; chmn. Manhattan Arts Council; mem. curriculum com. Kans. State Univ. Sch. of Interior Design, 1983—. Lic. comml. pilot. Recipient Dentsply Internat. Prosthetic award Dentsply Internat., 1975; Edward R. Hart clin. dentistry award Washington U., 1975. Mem. ADA, Am. Acad. Dental Radiology, Flying Dentists Assn., Acad. Gen. Dentistry, Assn. Hosp. Dentists, Acad. Sports Dentistry (founding mem.), Am. Soc. Dentistry for Children, Pierre Fauchard Acad., Acad. Dentistry for Handicapped (dir. 1980—, treas. 1982—, membership chmn., rep. to ADA Council on hosps. and instl. care 1980—, v.p. 1984—), Kans. Ind. Profl. Assn. (pres. 1983—). Lodges: Masons, Shriners, Odd Fellows. Author: Hospital Dentistry, 1979, Dr. Tooth Brush and Friends Childrens' Books, 1981, Preventive Dentistry Shopper (TV). Home: 1421 Normandy Pl Manhattan KS 66502 Office: 514 Humboldt Plaza Manhattan KS 66502

SAHAKIAN, ALAN VARTERES, electrical engineer, educator; b. L.I., N.Y., Oct. 21, 1954; s. Harold and Mariam Varteres (Garoukian) S.; m. Jill M. Morrison, Aug. 14, 1982. B.S. in Applied Sci. and Physics, U. Wis.-Kenosha, 1976; M.S. in Elec. Engring., U. Wis.-Madison, 1979, Ph.D. in Elec. Engring., 1984. Research asst. elec. and computer engring. U. Wis.-Madison, 1978-79, 80-84; sr. elec. engr. Medtronic, Inc., Mpls., 1979-80; cons. Applied Electronics Cons., Madison, 1982-84; asst. prof. elec. engring. and computer sci. Northwestern U., Evanston, Ill., 1984—. Co-author: Design of Microcomputer-Based Medical Instruments, 1981, Russian edit., 1983. Contbr. articles to profl. jours. Vol. life saver-water safety instr. ARC, Madison, 1973. Mem. IEEE, Sigma Xi. Avocations: ham radio, watchmaking, microscopy, photography. Office: Dept Elec Engring and Computer Sci Tech Inst Evanston IL 60201

SAHLBERG, CHARLES VICTOR, manufacturing company executive; b. Oak Park, Ill., July 2, 1935; s. Carl Victor and Lucile Lynette (Dunn) S.; m. Ruth Erma Stenger, June 22, 1957; children—Jeffrey Lee, Cynthia Lynn, Jennifer Ruth. B.S., Miami U., 1957, M.B.A., 1963. Indsl. engr. Champion Paper Co., Hamilton, Ohio, 1957-61; supr. central services Miami U., Oxford, Ohio, 1961-64; office supr. Moderncote Co., New Castle, Ind., 1964-69; purchasing mgr. New Castle Products, 1969-79; material mgr. Modernfold, New Castle, 1979-83, v.p. material mgmt. Modernfold, 1983—; dir. New Castle Engring., 1979—. Contbr. articles to bus. jours. Pres. First Nighters, New Castle, 1978, YMCA, New Castle, 1980; elder Presbyn. Ch., New Castle, 1984—. Recipient Best Article award Am. Purchasing Soc., 1973, Good Citizenship award Mut. Trust Ins. Co., 1969; Nat. Assn. of Purchasing Mgmt. Presdl. scholar Indpls., 1979. Mem. Indpls. Purchasing Mgmt. Assn. (sec. 1983-84, treas. 1984, 2d v.p. 1985), New Castle C. of C. (v.p. 1985—). Republican. Club: Jaycees (v.p. 1960-61). Lodge: Rotary (pres. 1980-81). Avocations: racquetball; photography; water skiing; softball; reading. Office: Modernfold An Am Standard Co 1711 I Ave New Castle IN 47362

SAHNI, ATAM PARKASH, powder coating company executive, researcher; b. Kuffri, India, Aug. 12, 1937; came to U.S., 1961, naturalized, 1965; s.

Chanan S. and Lajwanti (Suri) S.; m. Veena K. Suri, Feb. 23, 1966; children—Sanjay, Sangeeta. B.Chem. Engring., U. Delhi, India, 1960; M.S. in Chem. Engring., Okla. State U., 1962; postgrad. in chem. engring., NYU 1962-65. Research scientist NYU, 1962-66; sr. research engr. Monsanto Co., Springfield, Mass., 1966-74; dir. research and devel. Ferro Corp., Cleve., 1974—. Patantee in field (Weaver award 1980). Mem. Am. Inst. Chem. Engrs., Assn. for Finishing Processes. Avocations: photography, tennis, sightseeing. Home: 5660 Janet Blvd Solon OH 44139

SAID, MOHSIN M., insurance company executive, consultant; b. Cairo, Egypt, Nov. 7, 1954; came to U.S., 1978, naturalized 1981; s. Mohamed Said and Hanem (Hagag) Mohamoud; m. Therese Hanson, Nov. 7, 1977; children—Sharif Mohsin, Summer. B.A. in Phys. Edn., Cairo U., 1976. Fin. planner Aetna Ins., Milw., 1978-79; ins. exec. Lincoln Fin. Resources, Milw., 1979—; dir. Lincoln Fin. Resources Fin. & Investment Corp., Milw., 1979—. Active Republican Party, Washington, 1983—. Mem. Internt. Assn. Fin. Planners (accredited), Nat. Assn. Life Underwriters (life, Nat. Sales Achievement award, 1981, 82, 83, 84, 85), Nat. Assn. Health Underwriters (life, leading producer roundtable, Nat. Quality award 1981, 82, 83, 84, 85). Club: Athletic. Avocations: soccer; bicycling; travel; tennis, stamp collecting; coin collecting. Home: 14505 Watertown Plank Rd Elm Grove WI 53122 Office: Lincoln Fin Resources Bishops Woods West I Suite 101 150 S Sunnyslope Rd Brookfield WI 53005

SAIDEL, GERALD MAXWELL, biomedical engineering educator; b. New Haven, May 27, 1938. B.Chem.E., Rensselaer Poly Inst., 1960; Ph.D., Johns Hopkins U., 1965. Biomed. engr., researcher VA Med. Ctr., Cleve., 1972—; asst. prof. Case Western Res. U., Cleve., 1967-73, assoc. prof., 1973-81, prof., 1981—. Mem. Biomed. Engring. Soc. (bd. dirs. 1984-87), Am. Inst. Chem. Engrs., Soc. Math. Biology. Office: Case Western Res U Dept Biomed Engring Cleveland OH 44106

ST. AMAND, GERALD EDWARD, real estate development company executive; b. Detroit, June 5, 1944; s. Edward Gerald and Mary (Kreskosky) St. A. B.S. in Fin., U. Detroit, 1966, M.A. in Econs., 1968. Coordinator computer activities Mich. State U. Grad. Sch. Bus. Adminstrn., 1968-82; asst. mgmt. info. systems dir. Melvin Simon and Assocs., Inc., Indpls., 1982—; cons. in field. Recipient Fitzgerald award U. Detroit, 1966. Office: PO Box 7033 Indianapolis IN 46207

ST. CLAIR, JOHN CHARLES, SR., construction executive; b. Indpls., Aug. 26, 1940; s. Jesse H. and Margaret (Wismeier) St. C.; m. Karen Marie Jensen, Oct. 3, 1962; children—John Charles, Michelle Marie. Student Purdue U., 1959-60, Ind. U.-Purdue U., Indpls., 1960-62 Pres., Classic Pool & Spa, Indpls., 1965—. Served with USAF, 1962-67. Mem. Nat. Spa and Pool Inst. (bd. dirs. 1983—, chpt. v.p. and treas. 1976-80, regional v.p. 1985—, judge internat. design awards 1984; Gold Medal Design award 1984, 85, Silver medal 1985, Bronze medal 1984, 85, award of Merit 1979, 84), Central Ind. Pool Service Assn. (charter; v.p. 1970-71, pres. 1971-72, treas., bd. dirs. 1983-85), Nat. Retail Mchts. Assn., Nat. Sporting Goods Assn., Nat. Assn. Home Builders, Ind. Home Builders Assn., Indpls. Landscape Assn., Indpls. C. of C., Better Bus. Bur. Republican. Methodist. Club: Hillcrest Country (Indpls.). Avocations: golfing; boating; skiing. Home: 5006 E 65th St Indianapolis IN 46220 Office: 5294 E 65th St Indianapolis IN 46220

ST. CLAIR, KENNETH HILE, college administrator, business educator; b. Brighton, Colo., June 1, 1927; s. John William and Lida (Dennhardt) St. C.; m. Ida Belle North, Oct. 24, 1948; children—Linda Sue St. Clair Nier, Jeffrey Lynn. B.S., U. Ill.-Urbana, 1956, M.S., 1963. Instr. Gem City Coll., Quincy, Ill., 1952-55; acct. Gray, Hunter, Stenn & Co., Quincy, 1957-59; asst. prof. Cedarville Coll., Ohio, 1959-63, bus. mgr., 1963-82, v.p. bus., 1982—. Treas. Village of Cedarville, 1962-78, councilman, 1978-81. Served with USNR, 1945-46, 50-52. Mem. Nat. Assn. Coll. and Univ. Bus. Officers, Am. Inst. C.P.A.s, Ohio Soc. C.P.A.s, Assn. Bus. Adminstrs. Christian Colls. (v.p. 1974-75, pres. 1976-77). Republican. Baptist. Avocation: classic automobiles. Home: 359 College Hill Dr Cedarville OH 45314 Office: Cedarville Coll 251 N Main St Cedarville OH 45314

ST. JOHN, FRAZE LEE, biology educator; b. Lebanon, Ohio, May 23, 1939; s. Lewis B. and Irene (Loer) St. J.; m. Mary Ellen Kindell, June 9, 1962; children—James, David. B.S. in Edn., Miami U., Oxford, Ohio, 1961; M.A., Ind. U., 1963; Ph.D., Ohio State U., 1970. Instr. Miami U., Oxford, Ohio, 1963-65; research specialist Ohio State U., Columbus, 1969-70; asst. prof. zoology Ohio State U.-Newark, 1970-79, assoc. prof., 1979—; instr. health tech. Central Ohio Tech. Coll., Newark, 1973-83. Educator Licking Alcohol Prevention Program, Licking County, Ohio, 1984—. Mary Osborne fellow Ohio State U., 1966; recipient Good Teaching award Ohio State U.-Newark, 1977. Mem. Ohio Acad. Sci. (v.p. zoology sect. 1980-81), Sigam Xi. Methodist. Avocation: amateur radio. Home: 4067 Milner Rd Newark OH 43055 Office: Ohio State U University Dr Newark OH 43055

ST. JOHN, MICHAEL HAROLD, health services administrator, consultant; b. Erie, Pa., June 1, 1944; s. Harold S. and E. Ruth (Smith) St. J.; m. Jane Ann Russell, Sept. 1, 1967; children—Sharon, Elizabeth, Steven. B.A. in Applied Sociology, Ohio Wesleyan U., 1965; M.S.W. in Social Welfare, U. Wis.-Milw., 1969, postgrad., 1976-79. Correctional counselor Lebanon (Ohio) Correctional Inst., 1966-67; social worker div. corrections State of Wis., 1967-70; liaison tchr. Wis. Sch. for Boys, Wales, 1970-72; community services coordinator Bur. Probation and Parole, Milw., 1972-73; program dir. Jewish Vocat. Services, Milw., 1973-80; dir. dept. social services Sacred Heart Rehab. Hosp., Milw., 1980-81, dir. rehab. services, 1981—; lectr., cons. in field. Pres. bd. dirs. Youth Policy and Law Ctr., Milw.; mem. Exceptional Edn. Task Force, Milw.; bd. treas. Council for the Spanish-Speaking. Mem. Soc. Hosp. Social Work Dirs., Wis. Assn. Rehab. Social Workers (past pres.), Soc. Hosp. Risk Mgmt. Home: 2662 N Grant Blvd Milwaukee WI 53210 Office: 1545 S Layton Blvd Milwaukee WI 53215

ST. JOHN, RALPH C., applied statistics educator; b. Fort Kent, Maine, Aug. 29, 1942; s. Louis A. and Dolores (Daigle) S.; m. Marcie E. Domergue, June 21, 1969; 1 child, Matthew. B.A., U. Maine, 1964; M.A., U. Mass., 1968; Ph.D., U. Wis.-Madison, 1973. Statistician, IBM, Poughkeepsie, N.Y., 1964-68; specialist U. Wis.-Madison, 1968-73; prof. applied stats. Bowling Green State U., Ohio, 1973—. Contbr. articles to profl. jours. Mem. Am. Statis. Assn. (pres. local chpt. 1983-84), Am. Soc. Quality Control (bd. dirs. local sect. 1974—). Avocations: motorcycling, sports. Home: 519 Lorraine Ave Bowling Green OH 43402 Office: Dept Applied Stats OR Bowling Green State U Bowling Green OH 43403

ST. JULIAN, GRANT, JR., microbiologist; b. Beaumont, Tex., Feb. 13, 1931; s. Grant and Leah (Hebert) St. J.; m. Cora Jeanne Wood, Dec. 26, 1955; children—Grant, Andrea Renee, Tanya Suzanne. B.S., Samuel Huston Coll., 1951; B.A., Huston-Tillotson Coll., 1954; M.S., U. Tex., 1957; postgrad. Bradley U., 1964-65, MIT, 1967. Research microbiologist agrl. microbiology unit, fermentation lab. No. Regional Research Ctr., U.S. Dept. Agr., Peoria, Ill., 1961—. Cons. dept. biochemistry U. Oxford (Eng.), Internat. Ctr. Insect Physiology and Ecology, Nairobi, Kenya, 1982. Chmn. Human Relations Commn. Peoria, 1960-64, mem. Fire and Police Commn., 1964-70; chmn. bd. dirs. Peoria Tri-County Urban League, 1969-71; mem. Mayor's Drug Abuse Task Force, 1970-71; bd. dirs. Ill. Arthritis Found, 1970-71, Tri-County Comprehensive Health Planning Commn., 1977; mem. priorities com. Heart of Ill. United Way, 1972-73. Served with U.S. Army, 1952-54. Recipient Cert. of Merit, Human Relations Commn. Peoria, 1963; Humanitarian award State of Ill., 1965; Ralph Bunche Humanitarian award Peoria Bus. Assn., 1966; Paul Schlink Good Govt. award Peoria C. of C., 1968; Disting. Citizen award Urban League, 1976; Cert. of Merit, No. Regional Research Ctr., Peoria, 1979; Disting. Speaker award Am. Chem. Soc., 1980. Mem. N.Y. Acad. Scis., Ill. Acad. Sci., Internat. Invertebrate Pathology, Am. Soc. Microbiology, Ill. Soc. Microbiology, Entomol. Soc. Am., Sigma Xi. Democrat. Roman Catholic. Contbr. 60 articles to profl. jours. Home: 5609 Stephen Dr Peoria IL 61615 Office: 1815 University Peoria IL 61604

SAINT-PIERRE, MICHAEL ROBERT, funeral director, consultant; b. Indpls., July 12, 1947; s. Robert Ross and Gaile Russell (Cousins) S.; m. Betty Carolyn Wilhoit, Jan. 14, 1967; children—Michelle René, Paul Christopher. Student Milligan Coll., 1965-67, Butler U., 1966; B.S., East Tenn. State U., 1969; diploma Ind. Coll. Mortuary Sci., 1970; postgrad. Nat. Found. Funeral Service, 1970, 71, 73, 74, 76, Ind. U., Indpls., 1977. Intern, Hamlett-Dobson, Kingsport, Tenn., 1967-69; pres. J.C. Wilson & Co., Inc., Indpls., 1969—; evaluator/practitioner rep. Am. Bd. Funeral Service Edn., 1980—; prof., trustee Ind. Coll. Mortuary Sci., 1971-76; bd. advisors Nat. Bank Greenwood (Ind.), 1978-80. Contbr. articles to profl. jours. Bd. dirs. Central Ind. Better Bus. Bur., Indpls., 1982—, Adult/Child Mental Health Ctr., Indpls., 1982-85, Allied Meml. Council, Indpls., 1979—; elder Greenwood (Ind.) United Presbyn. Ch., 1976; past mem., treas. bd. dirs. Consumer Info. Bur., Inc.; past mem. bd. dirs. Center for Life/Death Edn., Indpls. Recipient Nat. Bd. Cert., Conf. Funeral Service Exam. Bd., 1970; Disting. Service awards Ind. Coll. Mortuary Sci., Indpls., 1978, Mid Am. Coll. Funeral Service, Jeffersonville, Ind., 1982. Fellow Nat. Found. Funeral Service (pres. alumni assn. 1978); mem. Associated Funeral Dirs. Service Internat. (pres. 1981), Nat. Selected Morticians, Nat. Funeral Dirs. Assn. (practitioner, resource and outreach, edn., supplementary speakers bur. and arbitration coms., chmn. employee/employer task force, chmn. mgmt. practice com.), Acad. Profl. Funeral Service Practice, Ind. Funeral Dirs. Assn. (bd. dirs., pres. 1982-83), Marion County Funeral Dirs. Assn. (pres. 1974), Nat. Eagle Scout Assn. Republican. Presbyterian. Clubs: Valle Vista Country, Skyline. Lodges: Rotary (past pres.; Paul Harris fellow); Masons (sr. deacon 1985); Shriners; Order Eastern Star. Office: Wilson St Pierre Funeral Service 481 W Main St PO 147 Greenwood IN 46142

SAKRY, CLIFF R, writer, publicist, film writer, speaker, trainer, consultant; b. St. Cloud, Minn., Aug. 27, 1914; s. Paul Edward and Monica Sophy (Thomalla) S.; m. Donna Cecilia Barthelemy, Oct. 11, 1946; children—Michelle Marie, Donna Lynnelle, Clifford Mark, Brian John. Student, St. Cloud State U., 1932-38, U. Minn., 1942-43, Harvard U., 1944, St. John's U., 1947, Stanford U., 1951. Reporter, proof reader St. Cloud Daily Times, Minn., 1935-37, columnist, spl. features writer, regional and farm editor, pub. relations dir., 1946-51; spl. features writer/editor AP, 1937-38, regional news corr., 1938-41; news writer, editor, announcer Sta. KFAM (now KNSI), 1938-41, sta. mgr., pub. relations dir., commentator, 1946-51; co-founder, exec. sec. Midwest Conservation Alliance, 1933-34; co-founder, organizer, exec. dir. Minn. Conservation Fedn., 1952-55; radio-TV dir. Olmstead and Foley Advt., Mpls., 1954; founder Minn. Youth Firearms Safety Tng. Program, 1954-55, creative dir., sales, script writer, film dir., musical coordinator Promotional Films, Inc., 1955-66; pub. relations dir. Coll. St. Benedict, dir. Benedicta Arts Ctr., 1966-71; programming mktg. research sales, program coordinator Personal Dynamics, Inc., Mpls., 1971-76; cons. in incentive tng., mktg., 1975—; free-lance writer, 1975—. Author, editor: Boondocks Baseball, 1980; founder, editor: Minn. Out-of-Doors, 1953-55. Author, composer, producer stage musical: Minnesota!, 1949-51, 58, 76, 83 (state award 1949). Author, dir. over 80 documentary films. Contbr. numerous articles to newspapers and magazines, 1934—. TV panelist Sportsmen's Round Table and Minn. Outdoors, 1958-63; co-founder, organizer St. Cloud Blood Donors Guild, 1939-41; vol. Retired Srs. Vol. Program, 1984-85; mem. adv. bd., sr. advocate Whitney Sr. Ctr., St. Cloud, 1981—; mem. St. Cloud's Human Rights Commn., 1983—, St. Cloud Library Bd., 1984—, congressman A. Stangeland Legis. Adv. Com., St. Cloud, 1984-85; co-founder, 1st pres. St. Cloud Community Arts Council, 1970-71; mem. Stearns County Hist. Soc.; active Nat. Wildlife Fedn., del. convs., 1954, 55, 58; founder 2 scholarships St. Cloud State U. Served to lt. (j.g.) USNR, 1941-46; ETO. Recipient Alumni Service award St. Cloud State U., 1983; Robert G. Green Disting. Service award Mpls. Jaycees, 1953; Disting. Service award St. Cloud Jaycees, 1950; Hon. Life Mem. Minn Conservation Fedn., 1955; named Congl. intern, 1983. Roman Catholic. Mem. Minn. Film Producers Assn. (co-founder, pres. 1966). Avocations: music; literature; poetry; golf; politics. Lodge: Kiwanis (Golden K pres. 1983-84). Home and Office: 663 Roosevelt Rd St Cloud MN 56301

SALAFSKY, BERNARD, medical educator, scientist; b. Chgo., Dec. 27, 1935; s. Mandel and Jeanette (Pritikin) S.; m. Marilyn Ann Ritchie, June 18, 1961; children—Joshua, Daniel, David. B.S. in Pharmacy, Phila. Coll. Pharmacy and Sci., 1958; M.S. in Pharmacology, U. Wash., 1961, Ph.D. in Pharmacology, 1962. Instr. U. Wash., Seattle, 1962-64; from asst. prof. to assoc. prof. U. Ill.-Chgo., 1964-70; adj. assoc. prof. U. Pa., Phila., 1970-72; prof. WHO, Geneva, Switzerland, 1973-75; prof. U. Ill.-Rockford, 1977—, dir., 1983—; cons. Biomed. Health Cons., Hong Kong, 1976; external examiner U. Malaya, Malaysia, 1982—. Contbr. articles to profl. jours. Bd. dirs. local devel. corp., Rockford, 1983—. Muscular Dystrophy Assn. spl. fellow, 1972; recipient NIH Prin. Investigator award, 1965-71, 80-83, 84—. Fellow Royal Soc. Tropical Medicine and Hygiene; mem. AAAS, Am. Soc. Pharmacology and Exptl. Therapeutics, Am. Soc. Tropical Medicine and Hygiene. Home: 5730 Clarendon Dr Rockford IL 61111 Office: U Ill Coll Medicine Rockford 1601 Parkview Ave Rockford IL 61107

SALANSKY, PAUL LLOYD, JR., optometrist; b. Washington, Pa., Nov. 20, 1950; s. Paul Lloyd and Betty Jo (Crowley) S.; m. Deborah Louise Soule, June 29, 1974; children—Catherine Ann, Alexa Marie. B.A., Knox Coll., Galesburg, Ill., 1973; O.D., Ill. Coll. Optometry, Chgo., 1977, B.S. in Visual Sci., 1975. Ptnr. Otoe County Optometric Assoc., Syracuse and Nebraska City, Nebr., Shenandoah, Iowa, 1977—. Fellow Am. Acad. Optometry; mem. Eastern Nebr. Optometric Soc. (pres. 1981-82), Nebr. Optometric Assn. (bd. dirs. 1984-86). Republican. Presbyterian. Lodges: Rotary (pres. 1984-85), Jaycees, Elks. Office: Otoe County Optometric Assocs 540 5th St Syracuse NE 68446

SALATA, EDMUND JOHN, university engineering administrator; b. Youngstown, Ohio, May 15, 1934; s. Andrew Albert and Helen S. (Tarajack) S.; m. Clara Carol Chwalik, Mar. 2, 1957; children—Kathleen, Edmund J., Jr., Elaine, Karen, Kevin, Eric. B.E. in Engring., Youngstown, Coll., 1957; postgrad. U. Pitts. Registered profl. engr., Ohio, W.Va. Building code cons. City of Youngstown, 1967-68, asst. dep. dir. of pub. works, 1968-70, dep. dir. pub. works, also city engr., 1969-76; cons., fund raiser Youngstown State U., 1976-77, dean of adminstrv. services, 1977-84, exec. dir. facilities, 1984—. Contbr. articles to profl. jours. Bd. dirs. Youngstown Area Goodwill, 1977—, pres., 1981-82; bd. dirs. Western Res. Transit Authority, 1970-78, Youngstown Planning Commn., 1970-76. Served to lt. U.S. Army, 1957. Mem. Nat. Soc. Profl. Engrs., Ohio Soc. Profl. Engrs. (Young Engrs. award 1969). Democrat. Roman Catholic. Avocations: reading, swimming, hiking. Home: 1255 E Cherokee Dr Youngstown OH 44511 Office: Youngstown State U 410 Wick Ave Youngstown OH 44555

SALAZAR, NINFA ALICIA REYES, janitorial services company executive; b. Dexter, Mo., May 27, 1959; d. Juan Q. and Eloisa (Rodriguez) Reyes; m. Julian Salazar Sr., Sept. 10, 1979; 1 child, Julian Jr. Ed. Prarie State Coll., Sawyer Coll. Bus. With David Temporaries, Chicago Heights, Ill., 1980-82; office mgr. E&B Painting, Harvey, Ill., 1981-82; owner, pres. J&N's Janitorial Services, Chicago Heights, 1982—. Court watcher Cook County Ct. Watcher's Project, Chicago Heights, 1985. Mem. Women in Mgmt., Women's Referral Services, Entrepreneur Assn. Am., Notaries Assn. Am., Chicago Heights C. of C. Avocations: bicycle riding; skating; dancing. Home: 175 Thelma Ln Chicago Heights IL 60411 Office: J&N's Janitorial Service PO Box 353 Park Forest IL 60466

SALERNO, EDWARD ANTHONY, research company executive, stock market analyst; b. Chgo., Sept. 27, 1932; s. Eugene E. and Geraldine (Graziano) S. B.S., Loyola U., Chgo., 1954; M.S., U. Ill., 1959. Dir. research McCormick Co., Chgo., 1966-78, Ill. Co., Chgo., 1979—. Author: You Can Always Trust Your Agent, 1983. Served with U.S. Army, 1954-56. Mem. Chartered Fin. Analysts, Chgo. Analysts Soc. Lodge: Kiwanis (pres. 1976-77). Avocations: writing fiction and nonfiction, poetry. Office: Ill Co 30 N LaSalle Chicago IL 60602

SALES, RAYMOND ALEXANDER, lawyer; b. Nashville, Nov. 17, 1950; s. Desse and Bertha (Bone) S.; m. Harriet J. Hatchett, Feb. 22, 1972 (div. Oct. 1980); 1 child, Raymond Alexander. B.A. in Polit. Sci., Ohio State U., 1971, J.D., 1976, M. City Planning, 1977; LL.M., U. Mo.-Kansas City, 1979. Bar: Mo. 1978, Ill. 1980. Gen. counsel Mid-Am. Regional Council, Kansas City, Mo., 1977-80; participating ptnr. Chapman and Cutler, Chgo., 1980—. Pres. adv. com. Minority Contractors Assn., Kansas City, 1979-80. Mem. ABA, Cook County Bar Assn., Mo. Bar Assn., Nat. Assn. Bond Lawyers. Baptist. Home: 5445 N Sheridan Rd Chicago IL 60640 Office: Chapman and Cutler 11 W Monroe St Chicago IL 60603

SALEWSKY, CHARLES SAMUEL, JR., fire protection company executive; b. Norfolk, Va., Jan. 28, 1956; s. Charles Samual and Virginia Mary (Muollo) S.; B.A. with honors in Fin., Mich. State U., 1978; M.B.A., U. Minn., 1979. Fin. analyst Ford Motor Co., Cleve., 1979-80; mgr. market research Ansul Fire Protection Co., Marinette, Wis., 1980-82, mgr. mkt. research and internat. sales, 1982-83, mgr. planning and info. systems, 1983—; head volleyball coach Marinette Cath. Central High Sch., Marinette, 1982—; cons. health care dept. U. Minn., Mpls., 1978-79, Northwestern Bell Telephone Co., Mpls., 1978-79; Author industry studies. Mem. programming bd. M&M YMCA, Menominee, Mich., 1983—. Mem. Beta Alpha Psi. Roman Catholic. Avocations; Volleyball coaching, tennis, comic book collecting. Home: 800 19th St Apt 2 Menominee MI 49858 Office: Ansul Fire Protection 1 Stanton St Marinette WI 54143

SALIBI, BAHIJ SULAYMAN, neurosurgeon; b. Omdurman, Sudan, May 16, 1922; s. Sleiman Khalil and Salva Ibrahim (Salibi) S.; came to U.S., 1946, naturalized, 1961; B.A., Am. U. Beirut (Lebanon), 1941, M.A., 1944; postgrad. U. Mich., 1946; M.D., Harvard, 1950; m. Margaret Elizabeth Beverley, May 16, 1954; children—Lillian Salwa, Charles Khalil, Ernest Kamal. Intern in pathology and clin. pathology Children's Hosp., Boston, 1950-51, research fellow in neurosurgery, 1956; intern in surgery Barnes Hosp., St. Louis, 1951-52, asst. resident in surgery, 1952-53; resident in neurosurgery St. Lukes Hosp., Chgo., 1953-54; resident in neurosurgery U. Ill. Neuropsychiat. Inst., Chgo., 1954-56, chief resident in neurosurgery, 1955-56; asst. in surgery (neurosurgery) Harvard Med. Sch., Boston, 1956; neurosurgeon Marshfield Clinic, Marshfield, Wis., 1958—; mem. staff St. Joseph's Hosp.; asso. clin. prof. neurol. surgery U. Wis. Med. Sch., Madison. Served as capt. MC, U.S. Army, 1956-58. Diplomate Am. Bd. Neurol. Surgery. Fellow A.C.S.; mem. AMA, Wis. State Med. Soc., Wood County Med. Soc., Congress Neurol. Surgeons, Central Neurosurg. Soc. (pres. 1968-69), Am. Assn. Neurol. Surgeons, Internat. Med. Soc. Paraplegia. Democrat. Episcopalian. Contbr. articles in field to profl. jours. Inventor artery clamp. Home: 1006 W 8th St Marshfield WI 54449 Office: Marshfield Clinic Marshfield WI 54449

SALIGMAN, HARVEY, apparel manufacturing company executive; b. Phila., July 18, 1938; s. Martin and Lillian (Zitin) S.; B.S., Phila. Coll. Textiles and Sci., 1960; m. Linda Powell, Nov. 25, 1979; children—Martin, Lilli Ann, Todd. With Queen Casuals, Inc., Phila., 1960—, v.p., 1966-68, pres., chief exec. officer, 1968-81, chmn., 1981—; pres., chief operating officer Interco Inc., St. Louis, 1981-83, pres., chief exec. officer Interco Inc., St. Louis, 1983—, also dir.; dir. Merc. Bancorp., Inc. Trustee, St. Louis Children's Hosp., Jewish Hosp., St. Louis, St. Louis Art Mus.; bd. dirs. St. Louis Symphony Soc. Mem. Young Pres. Orgn. Clubs: Locust (Phila.); Masons. Office: Interco Inc Ten Broadway Saint Louis MO 63102

SALINGER, RUDOLF M., chemical engineer; b. Berlin, Germany, July 24, 1936; s. Alfred and Paula (Arnfeld) S.; m. Sharon Joyce Norin, June 11, 1961; children—Jay, Sandra. B. in Chem. Engring., Cooper Union, 1958; M.S., U. Wis.-Madison, 1960; Ph.D., U. Cin., 1963. Registered profl. engr., Mich. With research dept. Dow Corning Corp., Midland, Mich., 1964-80, with corp. quality assurance dept., 1980-82, mgr. metall. silicon research, 1982-85 mgr. ceramic program process research, Midland, Mich., 1985—. Contbr. articles to various publs. Patentee in field. Pres. Temple Beth El, Midland, 1968, 78. Mem. Am. Inst. Chem. Engrs., Am. Chem. Soc., Am. Soc. Quality Control, Sigma Xi. Office: Dow Corning Corp PO Box 0995 Midland MI 48686

SALISBURY, ALVIN BURTON, JR., physician; b. Rockford, Ill., Mar. 11, 1922; s. Alvin Burton and Mildred Elizabeth (Scott) S.; student Beloit Coll., 1941-43, Vanderbilt U., 1943-44; M.D., Ohio State U., 1949; m. Cecelia Mitchell, Aug. 26, 1944; m. 2d, Jane Jefford, Aug. 26, 1976; children—Jennifer Lee, Elizabeth Ann, Robert Alvin. Intern, White Cross Hosp., Columbus, Ohio, 1949-50; practice medicine, Fairborn, Ohio, 1952—, Piqua, Ohio, 1979-80; mem. staff Greene Meml. Hosp., Xenia, Ohio; courtesy staff Piqua Meml. Hosp., Miami Valley, St. Elizabeth's hosps., both Dayton, Ohio; founder, pres. Ankh Labs., Inc., Fairborn, 1955-69. Founder, Mus. of Old Northwest Frontier, Lockington, 1970. Served to capt. M.C., AUS, 1943-46, 51-52. Mem. AMA, Miami County Med. Soc., Ohio State Med. Assn. Patentee med. instruments. Editor, pub. Adventures of Col. Daniel Boone (John Filson), 1968. Address: Greater Miami Valley Health Plan 850 E Xenia Dr Fairborn OH

SALITERMAN, LAURA SHRAGER, pediatrician; b. N.Y.C., June 26, 1946; d. Arthur M. and Ida (Wildman) Shrager; A.B. magna cum laude (Greenberg Sci. award 1967), Brandeis U., 1967; M.D. (med. scholarship for merit 1967), N.Y. U., 1971; m. Richard Arlen Saliterman, June 15, 1975; 1 son, Robert Warren. Intern, Montefiore Hosp. and Med. Center, Bronx, N.Y., 1971-72, resident in pediatrics, 1972-74; pediatrician Morrisania Family Care Center, N.Y.C., 1974-75; pediatrician Share Health Plan, St. Paul, 1975—, dir. pediatrics, 1976-82; clin. asst. prof. U. Minn. Med. Sch. Mem. Am. Acad. Pediatrics, Phi Beta Kappa. Club: Oak Ridge. Home: 11911 Live Oak Dr Minnetonka MN 55343 Office: 1020 Bandana Blvd W Saint Paul MN 55108

SALITORE, ROBERT ANGELO, banker, educator; b. Chgo., Nov. 23, 1948; s. James and Josephine (Lipari) S.; m. Judith Marie Jaksich, Aug. 8, 1970; children—Robert Angelo II, Michael. B.A., Loyola U., Chgo., 1972; M.S. in Indsl. Relations, 1976. Asst. dir. personnel Holy Cross Hosp., Chgo., 1977-78; dir. personnel Community Hosp., Munster, Ind., 1978-81; v.p. human resources Bank of Ind., Merrillville, 1981—. Chmn. employment com. Gary Job Service, Ind., 1983—; mem. employment com. Ind. State Job Service, Indpls., 1984—; pres. St. Victor Sch. Bd., Calumet City, Ill., 1984—; personnel com. St. Mary Med. Ctr., Gary, 1983—; mem. Personnel Policy Forum, Bur. Nat. Affairs, Washington, 1985-86. Mem. Am. Soc. Tng. and Devel., Am. Soc. Personnel Adminstrs., No. Ind. Personnel Dirs. Assn., Am. Compensation Assn., Chgo. Personnel Dirs. Assn. Roman Catholic. Avocations: reading; snow skiing; racquetball; photography. Home: 440 Marquette Ave Calumet City IL 60409 Office: 1000 E 80th Ave Merrillville IN 46410

SALM, KURT LEE, structural engineer; b. Chgo., Aug. 13, 1948; s. Charles Eugene and Lorraine Evelyn (Schlichenmaier) S.; m. Marsha Jo Remmers, Jan. 30, 1971; 1 child, Ryan Kurt. B.Arch., U. Ill., 1972; postgrad. DePaul U., 1979-80. Registered structural engr., Ill.; registered architect, Wis. Design engr. Sargent & Lundy, Chgo., 1972-75; chief engr. Nat. Filigree, Countryside, Ill., 1975-79; sr. project engr. Raths, Raths & Johnson Inc., Willowbrook, Ill., 1975—; pres. K.L. Salm Engrs., Woodridge, Ill., 1976—; adv. Schreiber Architects, DeKalb, Ill., 1979—. Author: (with others) Prestressed Concrete Design Handbook, 1984. Mem. Com. to Elect William Murphy Mayor of Woodridge, 1980; adviser com. to Re-elect Fred Foreman Lake County States Atty., Ill., 1980, 84. Mem. Prestressed Concrete Inst., Am. Concrete Inst., AIA, Structural Engrs. Assn. Ill., Gargoyle Soc., Sigma Tau. Republican. Methodist. Avocations: career counseling jr. high sch. students; supr. boy's athletics; stamp collecting; computer programming. Home: 2353 Vista Dr Woodridge IL 60517

SALMERON, BARBARA DOOLITTLE, lawyer; b. Libertyville, Ill., Dec. 14, 1939; d. Albert Ray and H. Eva (Darby) Doolittle; m. Rudolph Salmeron, Jr., June 6, 1959; children—Karyn Edith, Kathryn Felice, Lynda Maria. B.A., Northwestern U., 1976; J.D., Ill. Inst. Tch., 1979. Bar: Ill. 1980, U.S. Dist. Ct. (no. dist.) Ill. 1980. Sec., Hinshaw, et al, Chgo., 1962-69; sole practice, Kenilworth, Ill., 1980—. Mem. Ill. State Bar Assn. Home: 399 Elder Ln Winnetka IL 60093 Office: 420 Green Bay Rd Kenilworth IL 60043

SALO, DENNIS LLOYD, corporate systems director; b. Detroit, Mar. 12, 1944; s. Matt E. and Wilma S. Salo; m. Trudy L. Baker, Aug. 20, 1966; children—Scott, Carrie. B.B.A., Western Mich. U., 1966; M.B.A., U. N.Mex., 1968. Mgr. info. systems devel. Teledyne CAE, Toledo, 1980—. Coach Bedford Women's Softball Assn., Temperance, Mich., 1981-84; mem. adv. com. Vo-Tech Occupational Sch., Adrian, Mich., 1984—. Served to lt. USN, 1968-71. Mem. Am. Prodn. and Inventory Contol Soc., Assn. Systems Mgmt., Delta Sigma Pi. Methodist. Home: 8005 Kingsboro Ct Temperance MI 48182 Office: Tecumseh Products Co 100 E Patterson St Tecumseh MI 49286

SALTER, EDWIN CARROLL, physician; b. Oklahoma City, Jan. 19, 1927; s. Leslie Ernest and Maud (Carroll) S.; B.A., DePauw U., 1947; M.D., Northwestern U., 1951; m. Ellen Gertrude Malone, June 30, 1962; children—Mary Susanna, David Patrick. Intern, Cook County Hosp., Chgo., 1951-53; resident in pediatrics Children's Meml. Hosp., Chgo. and Cook County Hosp., 1956-58; practice medicine specializing in pediatrics, Lake Forest, Ill., 1958—; attending physician Lake Forest Hosp., 1958—, pres. med. staff, 1981-82; attending physician Children's Meml. Hosp., Chgo.; clin. faculty mem. dept. pediatrics Northwestern U. Med. Sch. Served to capt. M.C., U.S. Army, 1954-56. Mem. AMA, Ill. State Med. Soc., Lake County Med. Soc. (pres. 1984), Phi Beta Kappa. Republican. Methodist. Home: 19 N Maywood Rd Lake Forest IL 60045 Office: 800 Westmoreland Rd Lake Forest IL 60045

SALTER, STANLEY JOSEPH, vocal music educator; b. Ada, Ohio, Oct. 7, 1928; s. Stanley Roy and Alpha (Dyson) S.; m. Della Irine Foulkes, Aug. 14, 1949; children—Brickley Lowell, Stanley Elvet, Darryl Lee. B.S., Taylor U., 1950; M.A., Wayne State U., 1964. Tchr. vocal music McGuffey McDonald Schs., McGuffey, Ohio, 1950-51, Ada Village Sch., Ohio, 1951-54; tchr. vocal music Utica Schs., Mich., 1954—, chmn. dept., 1966-77; soloist Detroit Orpheus Club, 1954-64; choir dir. United Meth. Ch., Utica, Mich., 1957-70; Bd. dirs. Community Summer Theatre, Utica, 1967; co-dir. Bicentennial Vesper Choir, 1976; dir. youth musical United Meth. Ch., Sterling Heights, 1983-84. Mem. Soc. Preservation and Encouragement Barbershop Quartet Singing Am. (bd. dirs. 1950-76), Mich. Edn. Assn., Mich. Music Edn. Assn. Avocations: photography; lapidary. Home: 46289 Custer St Utica MI 48087

SALTMARCHE, KENNETH CHARLES, See *Who's Who in America,* 43rd edition.

SALTZMAN, BERNARD EDWIN, environmental health educator, consultant, researcher; b. N.Y.C., June 24, 1918; s. Barnet and Bessie (Sharon) Saltzman; m. Martha Helen Schneider, Apr. 10, 1949; children—Phyllis D. Saltzman, Gregory M., Barbara S. B. Chem. Engring., CCNY, 1939; M.S., U. Mich., 1940; Ph.D., U. Cin., 1958. Registered profl. engr., Ohio. Chem. engr. Joseph E. Seagram Co., Lawrenceburg, Ind., 1940-41; san. engr. USPHS, Mass. and N.Y., 1941-43, Charleston, W.Va., 1944, indsl. hygiene chemist, Bethesda, Md. and Cin., 1945-60, chief of lab., Salt Lake City, 1960-62, dep. chief chem. research and devel. div. air pollution, Cin., 1962-67; prof. environ. health U. Cin., 1967—; cons. Nat. Inst. Occupational Safety and Health, Occupational Safety and Health Adminstrn., Nat. Acad. Sci. Contbr. articles to profl. jours. Mem. Am. Chem. Soc. (Eminent Cin. Chemist award 1978), Am. Indsl. Hygiene Assn., Am. Conf. Govtl. Indsl. Hygienists, Air Pollution Control Assn., ASTM, Assn. Ofcl. Analytical Chemists (Wiley award 1978). Home: 8099 Debonair Ct Cincinnati OH 45237 Office: U Cin Dept Environ Health 3223 Eden Ave Cincinnati OH 45267

SALTZMAN, MELVIN BORIS, physician; b. Bronx, N.Y., Oct. 22, 1950; s. Jonas Ernest and Marion (Severs) S.; m. Louise F. Sobel, June 10, 1973; children—Sarah, Stephanie, Samantha, Michael. B.A. in Biology, CUNY, 1972; D.O., Mich. State U. Coll. Osteo. Medicine, 1975. Diplomate Nat. Bd. Examiners Osteo. Physicians and Surgeons, Am. Osteo. Bd. Internal Medicine, Am. Bd. Internal Medicine with subsplty. in gastronenterology. Intern Zieger-Botsford Osteo. Hosp., Detroit, Farmington Hills, 1975-76, resident in internal medicine, 1976-79; clin. fellow in gastroenterology Yale U. Sch. Medicine, New Haven, 1979-81; staff physician Normandy Osteo. Hosps., North and South, St. Louis, 1981—, DePaul Med. Ctr., St. Louis, 1984—, Jersey Community Hosp., 1984—; del. numerous sci. meetings. Contbr. articles to profl. jours. Mem. Am. Osteo. Assn., Mich. Assn. Osteo. Physicians and Surgeons, Am. Soc. Parenteral and Enteral Nutrition, Mo. Assn. Osteo. Physicians and Surgeons, St. Louis Assn. Osteo. Physicians and Surgeons, Am. Soc. Gastrointestinal Endoscopy. Avocation: photography. Office: Mednorth Med Bldg 8225 S Florissant Rd Suite 8 Saint Louis MO 63121

SALTZMAN, SIDNEY NATHANIEL, information systems executive; b. N.Y.C., Dec. 30, 1946; s. Jack Hyman and Jeanne Sophie (Schwartz) S.; m. Beverly Gail Swift, Mar. 20, 1968; children—Terra Jeanne, Daniel Joseph. B.A., Hiram Coll., 1968; M.B.A., Case Western Res. U., 1972. Systems analyst L.T.V. Corp., Cleve., 1969-73; mktg. rep. Control Data Corp., Cleve., 1973-76; systems project leader B.F. Goodrich Co., Cleve., 1976-79; project mgr. planning and devel. Congoleum Corp., Cleve., 1979-85; mgr. application devel. Internat. Playtex Inc., Dover, Del., 1985—. Fund raiser Pub. TV, Cleve., 1971-83; mem. support group Chem. Abuse Program, Rocky River, Ohio, 1984; Coach Youth Traveling Soccer Team, Rocky River, Ohio, 1983-84. Mem. Assn. Systems Mgmt. (membership com.).

SALTZMAN, WILLIAM, artist; b. Mpls., July 9, 1916. B.S., U. Minn. Asst. dir. U. Minn. Art Gallery, 1946-48; resident artist, also dir. Rochester Art Ctr., Minn., 1948-64; vis. prof. art U. Nebr., Lincoln, 1968; Macalester Coll., St. Paul, 1967-68, assoc. prof. art, vis. prof. art 1969-74, prof. art, 1974. Exhbns. include Calif. Palace Legion of Honor, 1945, Minn. State Fair, 1936-41, 46-58, Mpls. Inst. Art, 1936-41, 59, St. Paul Art Gallery, 1946, 54, 57, Mpls. Women's Club, 1949, 51-58, 62, U. Minn., 1939, San Francisco Mus. Art, 1948, Colo. Springs Fine Arts Center, 1948, Joslyn Art Mus., 1949, 51, 61, 64, Whitney Mus., 1951, Corcoran Gallery Art, 1950, Walker Art Ctr. Travelling exhbn., 1950-52, Carnegie Inst. Tech., 1952, Chgo. Art Inst., 1947, numerous others; one man exhbns. include Little Gallery, Madison, Wis., Waterloo Art Ctr., Iowa, Women's City Club, St. Paul, Luther Coll., Decorah, Iowa, St. Paul Art Ctr., St. Olaf Coll., Rochester Art Ctr., 1948-58, 63, 80, Kilbridge-Bradley Art Gallery, Mpls., U. Nebr., 1950, Stephens Coll., 1950, Carlton Coll., 1951, Dayton Art Inst., Ohio, 1952, Little Studio, N.Y.C., 1960-61, Walker Art Ctr., 1960, Philbrook Art Ctr., Tulsa, retrospective, Tweed Gallery, U. Minn., 1966, Steensland Gallery, St. Olaf Coll., Minn., spl. invitational showing nat. conf., Stained Glass Assn. Am., 1980; maj. works include mural Mayo Clinic Bldg., Rochester, Minn., 1953, stained glass windows, Temple of Aaron Sanctuary, 1956, mural Northwestern Nat. Bank, Rochester, 1957, stained glass Midwest Fed. Bldg., 1968, copper relief Plymouth Congl. Ch., Lincoln, Nebr., 1968, stained glass Holiday Inn Central, Mpls., 1962, chapel at Mpls.-Midwest Fed. Bank Bldg., 1968, Mt. Zion Temple, St. Paul, 1973, brick mural YM-CA-YWCA, Rochester, Minn., 1964, copper sculpture B'nai Abraham Synogogue, St. Louis Park, Minn., 1965, Coast to Coast Stores Hdqrs. Bldg., Edina, Minn., 1978, sculpture in lobby, Lincoln Gen. Hosp., 1967, copper relief sculpture U. Nebr. New Law Sch. Bldg., 1975, 1st Nat. Bank, Sioux Falls, S.D., 1976, Twin Cities Fed. Bank Bldg., Mpls., 1978, Title Ins. Co., Mpls., 1978, copper relief Nationality Cultural Ctr., Internat. Inst., copper relief sculpture Adath Jeshuran Cong., Mpls., 1979, Internat. Isnt., St. Paul, 1980, West St. Paul State Bank, 1980, copper relief chapel doors United Hosps., St. Paul, 1980, stained glass United Hosps. Chapel, St. Paul, 1980, stained glass Vinje Lutheran Ch., Willmar, Minn., 1980, copper sculpture meml. Temple of Israel, Mpls., 1981, stained glass sculpture Osmonics, Minnetonka, Minn., 1981, stained glass mobile Wayzata Bank and Trust Co., Minn., 1981 (recipient awards from Mpls. Inst. Art, 1936, Minn. State Fair, 1937, 40, Walker Art Ctr. 1949, 51), Ch. of Visitation, 1982, Central Luth. Ch., Mpls., 1982, Parkview Ob-Gyn Clinic, St. Paul, 1982, Keller residence, Roseville, Minn., 1983, Mackall, Crounce & Moore Law Offices, 1983. Recipient award Guild for Religious Architecture, 1973, AIA, 1973; Ford Found. grantee, 1966. Mem. Nat. Soc. Mural Painters, Artists Equity Assn., Coll. Art Assn. Home and Office: 19 S 1st St Apt B-802 Minneapolis MN 55401

SALYER, JACK E., lawyer; b. Riverside, Calif., Apr. 6, 1946; s. Gerald W. and Esther (Wilburn) S.; m. Karen A. Tierney, Mar. 12, 1971; children—Scott A., Samantha L., Robert C. B.A., U. Kans.-Lawrence, 1968; J.D., U. Kans. Law Sch., 1975. Bar: Kans. 1975. Atty.-Examiner U.S. Merit Systems Protection Bd., St. Louis, 1975—. Served to staff sgt. USAF, 1968-72. Recipient Superior Performance award U.S. Merit Systems Protection Bd., 1980, 82, 84. Avocations: stamp collecting, reading. Home: 415 Glan Tai Manchester MO 63011 Office: US Merit Systems Protection Bd 1520 Market St Saint Louis MO 63011

SALYERS, ROBERT JUSTICE, See *Who's Who in America,* 43rd edition.

SALZER, RICHARD BROH, gynecologist, educator; b. Huntington, W.Va., July 17, 1927; s. Sydney Broh and Bernice (Meyer); m. Anita E. Canter, Aug. 25, 1955 (dec. Aug. 1962); children—Deborah, Pamela, David; m. Betty Porter. B.S., U. Cin., 1948, M.D., 1950. Diplomate Am. Bd. Ob-Gyn. Intern St. Louis City Hosp., 1950-51; fellow La. State U. Sch. Medicine, 1951, resident Charity Hosp., New Orleans, 1954-57; practice medicine specializing in ob-gyn, Cin., 1957—; assoc. clin. prof. U. Cin. Coll. Medicine, 1957—. Contbr. articles to profl. jours. Bd. dirs. Midwest Found. for Med. Care, 1980—. Served to 1st lt. U.S. Army, 1952-54. Fellow Am. Coll. Obstetricians and Gynecologists; mem. Central Assn. Ob-gyn, Humanistic Studies in Gynecology, Am. Assn. Gynec. Laparoscopists Avocations: sailing, skiing, bicycling. Office: 10496 Montgomery Rd Cincinnati OH 45242

SAMAR, VINCENT JOSEPH, lawyer, philosophy lecturer; b. Syracuse, N.Y., Feb. 12, 1953; s. George Edward and Harriett Helen (Bejnarowicz) S. A.B. in Polit. Sci., Syracuse U., 1975, M.P.A., J.D., 1978; postgrad. in philosophy U. Chgo., 1979—. Bar: N.Y. 1980, U.S. Dist. Ct. (no. dist.) N.Y. 1980, Ill. 1983, U.S. Dist. Ct. (no. dist.) Ill. 1983, U.S. Ct. Appeals (7th cir.) 1983. Law clk. Libit, Lindaurv & Henry, Chgo., 1980-81; philosophy lectr. Roosevelt U., Chgo., 1981-82, St. Xavier Coll., Chgo., 1982-84, Loyola U., Chgo., 1984—; assoc. Foss, Schuman, Drake & Barnard, Chgo., 1983-85; research asst. Cottfield, Ungaretti, Harris & Slavin, Chgo., 1985—. Research asst. Transportation Negligence, 1984. Mem. ACLU, Chgo. Bar Assn., Ill. State Bar Assn., Beta Theta Pi. Home: 3420 N Lake Shore Dr Apt 3K Chicago IL 60657 Office: Cottfield Ungaretti Harris & Slavin 3 First Nat Plaza Chicago IL 60602

SAMBOL, ANTHONY RICHARD, research microbiologist; b. Phoenixville, Pa., June 11, 1956; s. Richard Martin and Delores T. (Handler) S.; m. Kathleen Theresa Formico, July 22, 1977; children—Jeremy Richard, Joshua Martin. B.A., summa cum laude U. Nebr., 1979, M.A., 1981, postgrad., 1981—. Research technologist U. Nebr. Med. Ctr., Omaha, 1978-82, med. technologist, 1982; lab. technician Grand Labs., Inc., Omaha, 1982-83, research scientist, 1983—. Contbr. articles to profl. jours. Scholar U. Nebr., 1978-79, 80-81, U. Nebr. Med. Ctr., 1982-85. Mem. Am. Soc. Microbiology (student), Nebr. Acad. Scis. (student), Sigma Xi. Republican. Roman Catholic. Club: Pre-Veterinary (Lincoln) (curriculum dir. 1976-77). Avocations: family activities. Home: Dept Med Microbiology U Nebr Med Ctr 4001 Wittson Hall 42nd & Dewey Sts Omaha NE 68105 Office: Grand Labs Inc 4436 Ames Ave Omaha NE 68111

SAMBORN, ALFRED H., engineering educator, consulting civil engineer; b. Toledo, Apr. 30, 1917; s. Michael Robert and Minnie (Cousins) S.; m. Miriam Esther Mann, Oct. 12, 1948; children—Michael Robert, Randall Arthur. B.S. in Civil Engring., U. Toledo, 1939; postgrad. Case Sch. Applied Sci., Cleve. 1939-40. Diplomate Am. Acad. Environ. Engrs.; registered profl. engr., Mich., Ohio. Jr. engr. Ward Products Corp., Cleve., 1939-40; structural engr. Builders Structural Steel Co., Cleve., 1940, Giffels & Vallet, Inc., Detroit, 1940-48; pres. Samborn, Stekette, Otis and Evans, Inc., cons. engrs., Toledo, 1948-77, chmn. bd., 1977-83, founder, emeritus, chmn. bd., 1983—; continuing and adult edn. instr., prof. civil engring. U. Toledo, 1984—. Chmn. disaster service com. Toledo Area chpt. ARC; bd. dirs. Toledo Area Govtl. Research Assn., Neighborhood Improvement Found. Toledo. Served to lt. (s.g.) USNR, 1942-46. Mem. Nat. Soc. Profl. Engrs., Ohio Bd. Registration Profl. Engrs. and Surveyors, Nat. Council Engring. Examiners (pres. 1979-80, award merit central zone 1976, Outstanding award 1981), Tech. Soc. Toledo (Outstanding Engr. award 1966), Ohio Soc. Profl. Engrs., Toledo Soc. Profl. Engrs. (Outstanding Engr. award 1966), Ohio Assn. Cons. Engrs. (Disting. Cons. award 1979), Am. Legion, Old Newsboys Goodfellow Assn. (1st v.p. 1980, pres. 1981-82), Tau Beta Pi (Eminent Engr. Mem. award 1977), Phi Kappa Phi (hon.). Jewish. Office: 1001 Madison Ave Toledo OH 43624

SAMMLER, ROBERT LOUIS, chemist; b. Niskayuna, N.Y., Nov. 12, 1953; s. Louis Stanley and Mary Alice (Neverman) S.; m. Carol Elaine Mohler, June 12, 1982. B.S., Rochester Inst. Tech., 1976; postgrad. U. Wis., 1978—. Synthetic polymer chemist Eastman Kodak Co., Rochester, N.Y., 1973-76, analytical chemist, 1976-78; research asst. phys. chemistry U. Wis., Madison, 1980—. Mem. AAAS, Am. Chem. Soc., Sierra Club, Sigma Xi, Alpha Chi Sigma. Office: 1101 University Ave Madison WI 53706

SAMPSON, SCOTT OSCAR, technical writer; b. Mpls., June 26, 1952; s. Sigved Theodore and Elouise Olivia (Torkelson) S.; B.A., Augsburg Coll., 1974; m. Nancy Gayle Hagfors, Oct. 9, 1976. Salesman, Machine Tool Supply Co., Mpls., 1974-77; computer operator, salesman Computer Chrome, Inc., Mpls., 1977-79; mgr. Digi-Slide div. Super Dupes, Inc., Mpls., 1979-82, Tobacco Road Inc., Mpls., from 1981; now self-employed tech. writer tech. manuals and ops. manuals for computer hardware and software. Volunteer, Friend-of-Child, Mpls. Mem. Jaycees. Lutheran. Home: 14015 38th Pl Plymouth MN 55441

SAMPSON, WILLIAM ROBERT, JR., communication and theatre arts educator, administrator; b. Detroit, Apr. 23, 1942; s. William Robert and Alice Juanita (Jones) S.; m. Sharon Kay Miner, Feb. 27, 1970 (div. Jan. 1982); children—William Robert, Michael Stanton; m. 2d, Karin Lee Menzel, Jan. 31, 1983. B.A., Western Mich. U., 1964; M.A., Wayne State U., 1967, Ph.D., 1973. Tchr., Utica Community Schs. (Mich.), 1964-66; instr. Macomb County Community Coll., Mich., 1966-68; asst. prof. Ferris State Coll., Big Rapids, Mich., 1968-72, assoc. prof., 1972-76; assoc. prof. Eastern Mich. U., Ypsilanti, 1976-80; dir. grad. bus. programs, 1978-80, assoc. dean Coll. Bus., 1979-80; chmn., prof. dept. communication and theatre arts U. Wis.-Eau Claire, 1980—; organizational communication tng. and devel. cons. Bd. dirs. Chippewa Valley Theatre Guild. Recipient award Ferris State Coll. Bd. Control, 1972. Mem. Acad. Mgmt., Am. Soc. for Tng. and Devel., Internat. Communication Assn., Speech Communication Assn. Congregationalist. Home: 3245 Noble Dr Eau Claire WI 54701 Office: Dept Communication and Theatre Arts Univ Wis-Eau Claire Eau Claire WI 54701

SAMUEL, ROBERT THOMPSON, optometrist; b. Kansas City, Mo., June 27, 1944; s. Manlius Thompson and Helen Evelyn (Syverson) S. B.A., William Jewel Coll., 1966; postgrad. U. Mo.-Kansas City, 1967, M.S. U. Mo., 1968; D. Optometry, U. Tenn.-Memphis, 1971. Cert. optometrist, Mo. Buyer Recco, Inc., Kansas City, Mo., 1963-67; histology lab. instr. William Jewell Coll., Liberty, Mo., 1965-66; pvt. practice optometry Gladstone, Mo., 1972—. Publicity coordinator Republican Party, Kansas City, Mo., 1975-76; chmn. Save Your Vision Week, Kansas City, 1977; mem. Theatre League of Kansas City, 1976—, Friends of Art, 1985. Recipient Outstanding Young Men of Am. award Jaycees, 1978. Mem. Am. Optometric Assn., Mo. Optometric Assn., Heart of Am. Contact Lens Congress, Smithsonian Assocs. Republican. Lutheran. Lodge: Lions (exec. bd. dirs. Lions Eye Clinic 1974-84, bd. dirs. Lions Eye Clinic 1982—, Outstanding Service award 1973, 74, editor Lions Optometric Ctr. Quar., 1974-84). Avocations: photography, music, piano, swimming. Home: 6325 N Monroe St Gladstone MO 64119 Office: 2700 Kendallwood Pkwy Suite 109 Gladstone MO 64119

SAMUELS, ROBERT T., retail food store chain executive. Pres., chief operating officer First Nat. Supermarkets Inc., Maple Heights, Ohio, also dir. Office: First Nat Supermarkets Inc 17000 Rockside Rd Maple Heights OH 44137*

SAMUELSON, JOHN T., pharmacist; b. Starbuck, Minn., Aug. 18, 1946; s. Lars Milton and Verda Louise (Roberts) S.; m. Nancy Verlee Wade, Sept. 3, 1972; chidlren—Laura Marie, Lynn Elizabeth. B.S. in Pharmacy, N.D. State U., 1969. Registered pharmacist, N.D., Minn. Pharmacy intern St. Francis Hosp., Breckenridge, Minn., 1969-70; pharmacist St. Francis Hosp., Breckenridge, 1972-74; dir. pharmacy, 1974-78; pharmacist in charge Samuelsons' Drug Store, Starburck, Minn., 1978—. dir. pharmacy Minnewaska Dist. Hosp., 1978—; cons. Minnewaska Home, 1978—. Scoutmaster various locations Boy Scouts Am., 1966—; fireman Starbuck Fire Dept. Mem. Am. Soc. Hosp. Pharmacists (dir. pharmacy residency St. Francis Hosp. Breckenridge and N.D. State U. 1977-79), Nat. Assn. Retail Druggists, Minn. State Pharm. Assn., Starbuck C. of C. (bd. dirs. 1980-82, v.p. 1983, pres. 1984), Jaycees (treas. 1979-80), Am. Legion. Lutheran. Home and office: PO Box 398 Starbuck MN 56381

SAN, NGUYEN DUY, psychiatrist; b. Langson, Vietnam, Sept. 25, 1932; s. Nguyen Duy and Tran Tuyet (Trang) Quyen; came to Can., 1971, naturalized, 1977; M.D., U. Saigon, 1960; postgrad. U. Mich., 1970; m. Eddie Jean Ciesielski, Aug. 24, 1971; children—Megan Thuloan, Muriel Mylinh, Claire Kimlan, Robin Xuanlan, Baodan Edward. Intern, Cho Ray Hosp., Saigon, 1957-58; resident Univ. Hosp., Ann Arbor, Mich., 1968-70, Lafayette Clinic, Detroit, 1970-71, Clarke Inst. Psychiatry, Toronto, Ont., Can., 1971-72; chief of psychiatry South Vietnamese Army, 1964-68; staff psychiatrist Queen St. Mental Health Center, Toronto, 1972-74; unit dir. Homewood San., Guelph, Ont., 1974-80; cons. psychiatrist Guelph Gen. Hosp., St. Joseph's Hosp., Guelph; practice medicine specializing in psychiatry, Guelph, 1974-80; unit dir. inpatient service Royal Ottawa (Ont., Can.) Hosp., 1980-84, dir. psychiat. rehab. program, 1985—; asst. prof. psychiatry U. Ottawa Med. Sch., 1980—. Served with Army Republic of Vietnam, 1953-68. Mem. Can. Med. Assn., Can., Am. psychiat. assns., Am. Soc. Clin. Hypnosis, Internat. Soc. Hypnosis. Buddhist. Author: Etude du Tetanos au Vietnam, 1960; (with others) The Psychology and Physiology of Stress, 1969, Psychosomatic Medicine, theoretical, clinical, and transcultural aspects, 1983, Uprooting, Loss and Adaptation, 1984, Southeast Asian Mental Health, 1985. Home: 3309 Riverside Dr Ottawa ON K1V 8N9 Canada Office: 1145 Carling Ave Ottawa ON K1Z 7K4 Canada

SANDAGE, ELIZABETH ANTHEA, advertising educator; b. Larned, Kans., Oct. 13, 1930; d. Curtis Carl and Beulah Pauline (Knupp) Smith; student Okla. State U., 1963-65; B.S., U. Colo., 1967; M.A., 1970; Ph.D. in Communications U. Ill., 1983; m. Charles Harold Sandage, July 18, 1971; children by previous marriage—Diana Louise Danner White, David Alan Danner. Pub. relations rep., editor Martin News, Martin Marietta Corp., Denver, 1960-63, 65-67; retail advt. salesperson Denver Post, 1967-70; instr. advt. U. Ill., 1970-71, vis. lectr. advt., 1977-84; v.p., corp. sec., dir. Farm Research Inst., Urbana, 1984—. Mem. Am. Acad. Advt., Am. Assn. Edn. in Journalism and Mass Communications, Sigma Delta Chi, Kappa Tau Alpha. Republican. Presbyterian. Editor: Occasional Papers in Advertising, 1971; The Sandage Family Cookbook, 1976; The Inkling, Carle Hosp. Aux. Newsletter, 1975-76. Home: 106 The Meadows Urbana IL 61801

SANDBERG, DAVID BRUCE, pharmacist; b. Stanley, N.D., Feb. 23, 1949; s. Orville M. and Harriet (Mortenson) S.; m. Viann E. Herfindahl, May 27, 1972; children—Eric, Ryan, Shaylee. B.S., N.D. State U., 1972. Registered pharmacist N.D. Chief pharmacist Mercy Hosp., Williston, N.D., 1972-74; pharmacist-in-charge B & B Super Drugs, Stanley, N.D., 1974-84; pharmacist-prin. Sandberg Drugs, Stanley, 1984—. Mayor, City of Stanley, 1979—; mem. Moutrail zoning and planning commn., Mountrail County, 1979—; mem. Stanley Ambulance Club (pres. 1977-78). Named one of Five Outstanding North Dakotans, N.D. Jaycees, 1984. Mem. N.D. Pharm. Assn. (v.p. 1st dist. 1984). Republican. Lutheran. Lodge: Lions (pres. 1978-79). Avocations: Woodworking, fishing, hunting, basketball, softball. Office: Sandberg Drug Main St Stanley ND 58784

SANDBERG, RYNE DEE, professional baseball player. Second baseman Chgo. Cubs. Voted Nat. League Most Valuable Player, 1984. Office: Chgo Cubs Wrigley Field Chicago IL 60613*

SANDEFUR, DANIEL LEE, computer company executive; b. New Orleans, Sept. 16, 1951; s. Kenneth Ray and Evelyn Georgia (Evans) S.; m. Deborah Suanne Thomas, Sept. 16, 1981; 1 child, Jason. B.S. Brescia Coll. Quality engr. Gen. Electric Co., Owensboro, Ky., 1978-81; mgr. service logistics Reynolds & Reynolds, Dayton, Ohio, 1981-82, mgr. quality assurance, Cin., 1982-83, mgr. field quality, Dayton, 1983—; quality assurance cons. Dan Com Inc., 1981—. Contbr. articles to profl. jours. Served with USMC, 1969-78. Mem. Am. Soc. Quality Control, Am. Field Service Mgrs. Assn. Democrat. Office: Reynolds & Reynolds PO Box 2608 Dayton OH 45401

SANDEFUR, JOHN EVERETT, real estate company executive; b. Columbus, Ohio, Apr. 20, 1931; s. Everett and Ruth (Montgomery) S.; B.E.E., Ohio State U., 1954; m. Tana Vaseley, June 12, 1954; children—Debra Ann, Jane Ann. Partner, E&J Sandefur Builders, Columbus, 1950-60; v.p. Sandefur Builders, Inc., Columbus, 1960-67, pres., 1967—; pres. Sandefur Co., 1977—. Mem. Columbus Housing Adv. Bd., 1976; bd. dirs. Godman Guild Assn., 1980. Served to 1st lt. USAF, 1955-57. Mem. Nat. Apartment Assn. (v.p. 1979), Nat. Rehab. Assn. (pres. 1979), Ohio Home Builders Assn. (pres. 1968), Columbus Home Builders Assn. (pres. 1962), Tau Beta Pi. Methodist. Clubs: Shriners, Lions. Office: Sandefur Co 935 E Broad St Columbus OH 43205

SANDER, KURT WILLIAM, tax accountant; b. Chgo., May 16, 1955; s. Frederick William and Marilyn Joan (Johnson) S.; m. Marjorie E. Amoroso, Aug. 23, 1980; children—Stephen J., Laurie B. B.S. in Journalism, No. Ill. U., 1979; M.S. in Accountancy, DePaul U., Chgo., 1981. C.P.A., Ill. Writer, photographer Oakton Community Coll., Des Plaines, Ill., 1978-79; sr. tax acct. Price Waterhouse, Chgo., 1981—; auditor North Suburban Evangelical Free Ch., Deerfield, Ill., 1982-83. Treas., bd. dirs. New Moms, Inc., Chgo., 1983—; publicity dir. for conf. Ill. Fedn. for Right to Life, Zion, Ill., 1983. Mem. Am. Inst. C.P.A.s, Ill. C.P.A. Soc. Republican. Office: Price Waterhouse 200 E Randolph Dr Chicago IL 60601

SANDERS, GILBERT OTIS, research psychologist, family therapist, business consultant; b. Oklahoma City, Aug. 7, 1945; s. Richard Allen and Evelyn Wilmoth (Barker) S.; m. Marline Marie Lairmore, Nov. 1, 1969 (dec.); m. Lidia Julia Grados Ventura, Nov., 1985; 1 dau., Lisa Dawn. A.S., Murray State Coll., 1965; B.A., Okla. State U., 1968; M.S., Troy State U., 1969; Ed.D., U. Tulsa, 1974; postgrad. Am. Tech. U., 1978-79, St. Louis U., 1981-85. Chmn. dept. computer sci. Calumet Coll., Whiting, Ind., 1975-78; research psychologist U.S. Army Research Inst., Ft. Hood, Tex., 1978-79; engring. psychologist U.S. Army Tng. and Doctrine Command Systems Analysis Activity, White Sands Missile Range, N.Mex., 1979-80; human factors psychologist, project dir. Applied Sci. Assocs., Inc., Ft. Sill, Okla., 1980-81; behavioral sci. cons., family therapist, Lake St. Louis, 1981-83; research psychologist U.S. Army Records Center, St. Louis, 1981-83; adj. prof. Columbia Coll., St. Louis, 1982-83, U.S. Army command and Gen. Staff Coll., Ft. Leavenworth, Kans., 1982—, Columbia Pacific U., San Rafael, Calif., 1984—; asst. prof. Pittsburg (Kans.) State U., 1983-85; family therapist, bus. cons., Oklahoma City, 1984—; pres. S.W. Mgmt. Assocs., Tulsa and Oklahoma City, 1984—; pres. Am. Bus. Fin. Services of Okla., Tulsa, 1985—. Bd. dirs. Humane Soc. Calumet Area, Hammond, Ind., 1977; mem. No. Ind. Health Systems Agy.'s Com. on Substance Abuse, 1975-78; mem. Ind. State Dept. Mental Health Substance Abuse Task Force, 1977. Served with U.S. Army, 1969-72. Decorated Bronze Star. Mem. Am. Psychol. Assn., Human Factors Soc., Am. Assn. for Counseling and Devel., AAAS, AAUP, N.Y. Acad. Sci., AAAS, Psychol. Assn., Tex. Psychol. Assn., Okla. Psychol. Assn., Okla. Hist. Soc., Assn. Mil. Surgeons U.S., Res. Officers Assn. Baptist. Lodge: Masons. Co-editor (with Elizabeth Todd) Training Effectiveness Analysis, 1980.

SANDERS, HAROLD ARTHUR, clergyman, educator; b. Iowa Falls, Iowa, June 8, 1919; s. Jacob Glenn and Myrtle Lucille (Tarpenning) S.; m. Hazel Luverna Anderson, Apr. 5, 1941; children—Mavis Rae, Harold Arthur, Paul Sidney, David Joshua, John Glenn, James Franklin, Mark Wallace, Alice Lucille, Thomas Ashley. Cert. and Grad. of Theology, Northwestern Schs., Mpls., 1940; B.R.E., Northwestern Theol. Sem., 1941. Ordained to Gospel Ministry, 1941. Pastor, Temple Bapt. Ch., Omaha, 1942-45, First Bapt. Ch., Loup City, Nebr., 1945-49, Rowan & Galt Congl. Ch., Rowan, Iowa, 1949-56, Baileyville Bapt. Ch., Ill., 1956-59, Tabernacle Bapt. Ch., Chgo., 1959-65, First Bapt. Ch., Stillwater, Minn., 1965-74, Grace Bapt. Ch., Des Moines, 1974-79; dean of men, pastoral ministries instr. Grace Coll. of the Bible, Omaha, 1979—; bd. dirs. Conservative Bapt. Fgn. Mission Soc., Wheaton, Ill., 1968-74; pres., bd. dirs. Sunday Sch. Assn., Des Moines, 1975-79; chmn. pastors fellowship Conservative Bapt. Assn. Iowa, 1970-72. Juvenile ct. chaplain Washington County Ct. Systems, Minn., 1967-72; chaplain Ho. of Reps., State of Minn., St. Paul, 1972. Recipient Seal of State of Minn. for dedication and service to Stillwater community and state, 1973. Republican. Avocations; fishing; reading. Home: 1517 S 8th St Omaha NE 68108 Office: Grace Coll of the Bible 1515 S 10th St Omaha NE 68108

SANDERS, JOHN T(ED), state official. Supt. of edn. State of Ill., Springfield. Office: State Supt's Office 100 N 1st St Springfield IL 62777*

SANDERS, WAYNE LAWRENCE, broadcasting company executive; b. Glendive, Mont., June 15, 1954; s. Lawrence Arnold and Emma (Dvorak) S.; Broadcast Communications degree Brown Inst. Broadcasting, 1973; m. Lorna Willer, Sept. 8, 1974; children—Scott Gregory, Mark Jeffrey. Disc jockey Sta. KDIX Radio & TV, Dickinson, N.D., 1970-72, TV account exec., 1973-74; account exec. KFYR-TV, Bismarck, N.D., 1974-80, sales mgr., 1982-84 sales mgr. KQCD-TV, Bismarck div. Meyer Broadcasting Co., Dickinson, 1980-82, gen. mgr., Minot, N.D., 1984—. Roman Catholic. Clubs: K.C., Elks. Home: One 30th St SW Minot ND 58701 Office: Box 1120 Minot ND 58701

SANDERSON, CAROL JEAN, newspaper editor; b. Wichita, June 2, 1932; d. Willis Kenneth and Ruth Anna (Bryant) Hill; student Wichita State U., 1950-52; children—Mark Douglas Brinton, Bambi Lynn Brinton Bird, Mike Douglas Brinton, Todd Douglas Brinton. Sec., bookkeeper United Sch. Dist. 426, Howard, Kans., 1975-77; freelance writer Howard Courant-Citizen, 1975-77, Salina (Kans.) Jour., 1978-80, Scandia (Kans.) Jour., 1978-80; owner, editor Courtland (Kans.) Jour., 1980-84; founder Prairie Valley Empire Newspaper, Belleville, Kans., 1982. Mem. steering com. Courtland PRIDE, 1980-82. Cert. elem. tchr.; recipient PRIDE award Gov. Kans., 1982, 84. Mem. Kans. Press Assn. (awards 1983). Kans. Press Women Assn., Nat. Fedn. Press Women. Lutheran. Home: RR 1 Howard KS 67349 Office: Howard Courant Citizen Howard KS 67349

SANDERSON, SCOTT DOUGLAS, professional baseball player; b. July 22, 1956. Pitcher Chgo. Cubs, 1984—. Office: Chgo Cubs Wrigley Field Chicago IL 60613*

SANDERSON, VIRGINIA KATHRYN, consultant, educational technologist, educator; b. Mpls., Dec. 2, 1943; d. Bruce Harvey and Jeanette Pauline (Dishington) Anderson; B.S. with distinction, U. Minn., 1966; M.S., St. Cloud State Coll., 1974; postgrad. San Francisco State U., U. Wis., St. Cloud U., U. Minn.; m. Wayne Arthur Sanderson, Aug. 16, 1980. Tchr., Columbia Heights (Minn.) Schs., 1966-81, North Park Sch., 1966-71, Valley View Sch., 1971-81; pvt. ednl. technologist, 1981—; project dir. Computerized Record Mgmt. System and Community Skills Bank Service, 1983-84; mem. numerous ednl. coms.; designer, developer ednl. computer programs, 1980-83; resource person Info. Interchange, 1981-83. Contbr. articles to profl. jours. Mem., Fridley City Band, 1968-71. AAUW grantee, 1983-84. Mem. Nat. Assn. Gifted Children, AAUW (edn. com. 1980—, long range planning com. 1981—, state topic com. 1980-82, br. topic chairperson 1981-83), Minn. Assn. Ednl. Data Systems (resource person Speakers Bur., cons. 1983-84), Assn. Ednl. Data Systems, World Future Soc., Sierra Club, Assn. Twin City Ski Clubs, Pi Lambda Theta (planning com. 1985 conv.), Phi Kappa Phi. Lutheran. Clubs: North Star Ski Touring, Sitzmark Ski, Honeywell Ski. Home: 4217 Nancy Pl Shoreview MN 55112

SANDNESS, CLAIRE, agricultural and dairy company executive. Chmn. dir. Land O'Lakes, Inc., Arden Hills, Minn. Office: Land O'Lakes Inc 4001 Lexington Ave N Arden Hills MN 55112*

SANDS, CALVIN DUANE, geologist; b. Penn Yan, N.Y., July 17, 1951; s. Maynard James and Eleanor Louise (Martin) S.; m. Patricia Marie Morse, June 28, 1975; children—Joseph Parker, Michelle Alida, Theresa Louise. B.S., SUNY-Brockport, 1973; M.S. in Geology, U. Wyo., 1976. Certified Profl. Geologist. Geologist, mgr. Am. Stratigraphic Co., Denver, 1976-78; exploration geologist Gulf Oil Co., Casper, Wyo., 1978-80; geologist Mich. Oil Co., Jackson, Mich., 1980-83; geologist, geochemist Mich. Petroleum Geologist, Jackson, Mich., 1983-84; geologist Ladd Petroleum Corp., Jackson, Mich., 1984—; geol., geochem. cons., 1984—. Bd. dirs. Christian Action Com., 1984. Mem. Am. Assn. Petroleum Geologists, Am. Inst. Profl. Geologists. Republican. Christian. Avocations: Cross-country skiing; reading; gardening. Home: 4841 Fleetwood Ln Jackson MI 49201

SANDSNES, ARDEN T., engineering company executive, land surveyor; b. Westby, Wis., May 21, 1934; s. Alf. G. and Beverly B. (Hoff) S.; m. Reeta F. Smith, Aug. 9, 1952; children—Carl M., Terri E. Sandsnes Zimmerman, Eric W. Student Hutchinson Jr. Coll., 1956-57, U. Wis.-Madison, 1957-61. Party chief U.S. C.E., Kansasville, Wis., 1958; land surveyor Alex W. Ely Co., Madison, 1960-64; v.p. Royal Oak Engring. Inc., Madison, 1964—; dep. surveyor, Dane County, 1957-82. Recipient appreciation award U. Wis.-Stout, 1976, appreciation award Madison Bd. Realtors, 1979, appreciation award U. Wis.-Stevens Point, 1980, 81. Mem. Wis. Soc. Profl. Engrs., Am. Congress on Surveying and Mapping, Madison Area Surveyors Council (sec.-treas. 1968-69, pres. 1970), Wis. Soc. Land Surveyors (legis. chmn. 1975-84, pres. 1984, appreciation award 1978), Madison Sports Car Club (chief steward), Midwestern Council Sports Car Clubs (pres.). Lutheran. Avocation: home built aircraft. Home: 4705 Shore Acres Rd Monona WI 53716 Office: Royal Oak Engring Inc 5610 Medical Circle Suite 6 Madison WI 53719

SANDY, WILLIAM HASKELL, training and communications systems company executive; b. N.Y.C., Apr. 28, 1929; s. Fred and Rose S.; A.B., U. Md., 1950, J.D., 1953; postgrad. Advanced Mgmt. Program, Harvard Bus. Sch., 1970-71; m. Marjorie Mazor, June 15, 1952; children—Alan, Lewis, Barbara. Admitted to Md. bar, 1953; planner-writer, account exec., account supr. Jam Handy Orgn., Detroit, 1953-64, v.p., 1964-69, sr. v.p., 1969-71; pres. Sandy Corp., Troy, Mich., 1971—. Bd. govs. Northwood Inst., 1976-80; bd. dirs. Cranbrook Sci. Inst.; mem. nat. exec. council Harvard Bus. Sch., 1985—. Mem. Am. Mktg. Assn. (pres. Detroit chpt. 1975), Am. Soc. Tng. and Devel., Southeastern Mich. Better Bus. Bur. (bd. dirs.), Adcraft Club, Nat. Assn. Ednl. Broadcasters. Clubs: Harvard Bus. Sch. (pres. Detroit club 1983-85), The Hundred. Home: 596 Rudgate Bloomfield Hills MI 48013 Office: Sandy Corp 1500 W Big Beaver Rd Troy MI 48084

SANGHVI, MANOJ KUMAR DALICHAND, oil company executive; b. Morvi, India, Sept. 13, 1928; s. Dalichand Hakubhai and Navalben Jagannath (Sanghani) S.; B.S. with honors, U. Bombay, 1949, B.S. in Tech., 1951; M.S. (Fulbright fellow, Ford Found. scholar), Ohio State U., 1953, Ph.D., 1956; m. Shobhana Hiralal Shah, Apr. 1, 1958; children—Sunil, Parag, Pulin. Came to U.S., 1952. Research fellow Govt. India Council Sci. and Indsl. Research, Bombay, 1951-52; research fellow Ohio State U., Columbus, 1953-55, research asso., 1955-56; project chem. engr. Standard Oil Co. (Ind.), Whiting, Ind., 1956-60; economiste conseil Société Civile Amoco, Paris, 1960-62; chief economist Amoco (U.K.) Ltd., London, 1962-63; econ. adviser-Far East, Amoco Internat. Oil Co., N.Y.C., 1963-65; sr. tech. coordinator Amoco India, Inc., New Delhi, 1965-68; coordinator corporate planning Standard Oil Co. (Ind.), Chgo., 1968-74, sr. coordinator planning and econs., 1974-83, now dir.; dir. Industry Analysis (Internat.), 1983—. Vis. fellow Ohio State U., 1956-57; trustee ILA Found., 1981—, pres., 1984—. Mem. Am. Inst. Chem. Engrs. (chmn. nat. program com., mgmt. sci. 1972-78, chmn. mgmt. group 1980-82), India League Am. (v.p., dir. 1974-81; pres. 1978), Sigma Xi, Phi Lambda Upsilon. Club: Rotary (Chgo.). Contbr. articles to profl. jours. Home: 1024 Heatherfield Lane Glenview IL 60025 Office: 200 E Randolph Dr Chicago IL 60601

SANGMEISTER, GEORGE EDWARD, lawyer, state senator; b. Joliet, Ill., Feb. 16, 1931; s. George Conrad and Rose Engaborg (Johnson) S.; B.A., Elmhurst Coll., 1957; LL.B., John Marshall Law Sch., 1960, J.D., 1970; m. Doris Marie Hinspeter, Dec. 1, 1951; children—George Kurt, Kimberly Ann. Admitted to Ill. bar, 1960, since practiced in Joliet; partner firm McKeown, Fitzgerald, Zollner, Buck, Sangmeister & Hutchison, 1969—; justice of peace, 1961-63; states atty. Will County, 1964-68; mem. Ill. Ho. of Reps., 1972-76, Ill. Senate, 1977—. Chmn. Will County chpt. Salvation Army; chmn. Frankfort Twp. unit Am. Cancer Soc.; former trustee Will County Family Service Agy.; bd. dirs. Joliet Jr. Coll. Found. Served with inf. AUS, 1951-53. Mem. ABA, Ill., Will County bar assns., Am. Trial Lawyers Assn., Am. Legion, Frankfort (past pres.), Mokena chambers commerce, Old Timers Baseball Assn. Lion. Home: S Wolf Rd Mokena IL 60448 Office: 2455 Glenwood Ave Joliet IL 60431

SANISLO, PAUL STEVE, lawyer; b. Cleve., Feb. 8, 1927; s. Paul and Bertha (Kasa) S.; m. Mary Ellen P. Conroy, May 7, 1949; 1 child, Susan J. B.A., Baldwin-Wallace Coll., 1948; J.D., Cleve. State U., 1961. Bar: Ohio 1961, U.S. Dist. Ct. (no. dist.) Ohio 1964. Order clk. Am. Agrl. Chem. Co., Cleve., 1948-52; safety engr. Park Drop Forge Co., Cleve., 1952-62, personnel mgr., 1954-62; assoc. then ptnr. Spohn & Sanislo, L.P.A., Cleve., 1962-81, pres., 1981—; spl. counsel Atty. Gen. Ohio, 1971; arbitrator Am. Arbitration Assn., 1972-78. Mem. Cleve. City Council, 1964-67; trustee Cleve.-Marshall Law Sch., 1962-63; trustee Cleve.-Marshall Ednl. Found., 1963—, pres., 1980-83; mem. Solon City Bd. Edn., Ohio, 1972-83, pres., 1974-83; chmn. Solon Charter Rev. Commn., 1971; past mem., organizer, legal adv. Solon Drug Abuse Ctr.; mem. Cuyahoga County Democratic Exec. Com.; ward leader 29th Ward Dem. Club, 1965-71, also past pres.; trustee Solon Dem. Ward Club, 1972-75. Recipient Disting. Service award City of Solon, 1984, Solon Bd. Edn., 1984, Solon Edn. Assn., 1984. Mem. Bar Assn. Greater Cleve. (Merit Service award 1978-79; chmn. workers compensation sect. 1975—), Ohio Bar Assn., Cuyahoga County Bar Assn., Assn. Trial Lawyers Am., Cleve.-Marshall Law Sch. Alumni Assn. (pres. 1968-69), Hungarian Bus. and Trademen's Club (pres. 1967-68), Cleve. Assn. Compensation Attys. (pres. 1973-76). Democrat. Roman Catholic. Club: Aurora Country (v.p. 1983—) (Ohio). Lodge: KC. Avocations: golf; travel. Office: 710 Standard Bldg Cleveland OH 44113

SANKOVIC, ROY GEORGE, funeral home executive; b. Toronto, Ont., Can., Nov. 11, 1955; came to U.S., 1958, naturalized, 1963; s. Joseph and Lydia (Komar) S.; m. Georgia A. D'Amico, May 16, 1981. Student John Carroll U., 1973-75, Lakeland Community Coll., 1975-77; A.S., Pitts. Inst. Mortuary Sci., 1978. Lic. funeral dir., embalmer, Ohio. With A. Grdina & Sons, Cleve., 1970-80, mgr., 1979-80; mgr. Morasco Funeral Home, Pitts., 1978-79; owner Sankovic-Johnston Funeral Home, Cleve., 1980—. Co-chmn. Waterloo Trade and Devel. Corp., 1982—. Mem. Cuyahoga Funeral Dirs. Assn., Nat. Funeral Dirs. Assn., Ohio Funeral Dirs. Assn., Ohio Embalmers Assn., Cleve. Embalmers Assn., Holy Name Soc. Roman Catholic. Clubs: Forest City Yacht, Slovenian Nat. Benefit Soc., Foresters (trustee). Lodges: Eagles, Moose, Kiwanis. Home and office: 15314 Macauley Ave Cleveland OH 44110

SANNELLA, JOSEPH LEE, industrial science company executive; b. Boston, July 27, 1933; s. Theodore and Anna (Barone) S.; m. Nancy Marshall, June 6. 1959; children—Joseph, SueAnne, Stephen. A.B., Harvard U., 1955; M.S., U. Mass., 1958; Ph.D., Purdue U., 1963; M.B.A., U. Del., 1969. Research chemist FMC, Am. Viscose Div., Marcus Hook, Pa., 1962-67; supr. organic research Ball Corp., Muncie, Ind., 1967-69, mgr. graphic arts, 1969-71, supr. chem. research, 1971-74, dir. research, 1974-85, dir. corp. lab. services, 1985—. Contbr. articles to profl. jours. Patentee in field. Bd. dirs. Big Brothers/Big Sisters of East Central Ind., 1969-78, Easter Seal Soc., 1979—, Ball Employees Credit Union, 1981—, Ball Polit. Action Com., 1976—. Recipient Community Service award Ball Corp., 1984. Mem. Am. Chem. Soc., Soc. Plastic Engrs., Nat. Metal Docorators Soc. Republican. Roman Catholic. Clubs: Del. Country, Muncie (Muncie). Lodge: Kiwanis. Home: 2803 W Woodbridge Muncie IN 47304 Office: Ball Corp 1509 S Macedonia Muncie IN 47302

SANQUIST, GEORGE EDWARD, dentist; b. Pomeroy, Iowa, Nov. 19, 1923; s. John Edward and Sarah Florence (Ivey) S.; m. Nayda Jean Piggott, Oct. 7, 1950 (div. 1979); children—Nancy Elizabeth Sanquist Lamers, George Jr., Mark. Student St. John's U., 1942, St. Thomas Coll., 1943; D.D.S., Marquette U., 1950. Commd. ensign USNR, 1943, advanced through grades to lt. D.C. U.S. Navy, 1954; dental officer U.S. Navy, Washington, Bethesda, Md., 1950-54, instr. U.S. Navy Dental Sch., Bethesda, 1952-54, Marquette U. Dental Sch., Milw., 1954-56; gen. practice dentistry Watertown, Wis., 1956—. Mem. Am. Dental Assn., Wis. Dental Assn., Jefferson County Dental Soc. (pres. and other offices 1954—). Republican. Roman Catholic. Lodge: Rotary. Avocations: sailing; big game hunting; canoeing; camping. Home and Office: 212 N 4th St Watertown WI 53094

SANSBURY, JOHN THADDEUS, lawyer; b. Danville, Ill., Oct. 2, 1929; s. William Joseph and Catherine (Flattery) S.; m. Elizabeth Schmitt, Apr. 23, 1955 (dec. Apr. 1966); children—Stephen, Hugh, Susan, Ellen, Cathleen; m. Peggy Sue McPherson, Dec. 27, 1967; stepchildren—Mark, Scott. B.S., Canisius Coll., 1951; J.D., Fordham U., 1961. Bar: Ohio 1964. Counsel, U.S. Life Co., N.Y.C., 1961-71, atty. Nationwide Ins., Columbus, Ohio, 1961-71; sole practice, Columbus, 1964—. Bd. dirs. Nat. Kidney Found., Columbus, 1967—, pres., 1973; treas. St. Agatha Parish Council, 1974, pres. 1984—. Recipient Service award, Nat. Kidney Found., 1968, 72. Mem. Columbus Bar Assn., Ohio State Bar Assn. Republican. Roman Catholic. Clubs: Swim and Racquet, Racquet. Avocations: gardening; tennis. Home: 2811 Wellesley Dr Upper Arlington OH 43221 Office: 547 E Broad St Columbus OH 43215

SANTANGELO, MARIO VINCENT, dentist, association executive, educator; b. Youngstown, Ohio, Oct. 5, 1931; s. Anthony and Maria (Zarlenga) S.; student U. Pitts., 1949-51; D.D.S., Loyola U. (Chgo.), 1955, M.S., 1960. Instr. Loyola U., Chgo., 1957-60, asst. prof., 1960-66, chmn. dpt. radiology, 1962-70, dir. dental aux. utilization program, 1963-70, assoc. prof., 1966-70, chmn. dept. oral diagnosis, 1967-70, asst. dean, 1969-70; practice dentistry, Chgo., 1960-70; cons. Cert. Bd. Am. Dental Assts. Assn., 1967-76, VA Research Hosp., 1969-75, Chgo. Civil Service Commn., 1967-75; counselor Chgo. Dental Assts. Assn., 1966-69; mem. dental student tng. adv. com. Div. Dental Health USPHS, Dept. Health, Edn. and Welfare, 1969-71; cons. dental edn. rev. com. NIH, 1971-72; cons. USPHS, HEW, Region IV, Atlanta, 1973-76, Region V, Chgo., 1973-77; mem. Commn. on Dental Edn. and Practice, Fedn. Dentaire Internationale, 1984—. Bd. visitors Sch. Dental Medicine, Washington U., St. Louis, 1974-76. Served to capt. USAF, 1955-57. Recipient Dr. Harry Strusser Meml. award NYU Coll. Dentistry, 1985. Fellow Am. Coll. Dentists; mem. Am. Assn. Dental Schs., Odontographic Soc. Chgo., Am. (asst. sec. council dental edn. 1971-81, acting sec. 1981-82, sec. 1982—, asst. sec. commn. on dental accreditation 1975-81, acting sec. 1981-82, sec. 1982—, acting sec. commn. on continuing dental edn. 1981-82, sec. 1982—), Ill., Chgo. dental assns., Am. Acad. Oral Pathology, Am. Acad. Dental Radiology, Am. Acad. Oral Medicine, Omicron Kappa Upsilon (pres. 1967-68), Blue Key, Xi Psi Phi. Contbr. articles to profl. jours. Home: 1440 N Lake Shore Dr Chicago IL 60610 Office: 211 E Chicago Ave Chicago IL 60611

SANTIAGO, EDGARDO, research chemist; b. San Juan, P.R., May 15, 1925; m. Ana C. Becerra, Dec. 23, 1956; children—Edgardo R., Carlos F., Carmen M., Luis A. B.S., U. P.R., 1946; postgrad. Princeton U., 1956-57. Research chemist Econ. Devel. Adminstrn., San Juan, 1946-58, Root Chems., Inc., San Juan, 1958-59; with Owens-Ill., Inc., 1959—, sr. research chemist tech. dept. component products div., Toledo, 1969—. Mem. Am. Chem. Soc., Soc. Plastics Engrs., Colegio de Quimico de P.R., Sigma Xi. Roman Catholic. Research and devel. in carbohydrates, lignin, polymer synthesis, transition metal catalysts, electrochemistry and coatings; patentee transition metal catalysts, electrochemistry, coatings. Home: 1618 Woodhurst Dr Toledo OH 43614 Office: Owens-Ill Inc One Seagate-LDP 30 Toledo OH 43666

SANTMAN, KIM DALE, accountant, hospital financial director; b. Waterloo, Iowa, Dec. 14, 1956; s. Dale Elmer and Beverly Ann (Wendt) S.; m. Robin Rose Boddicker, Apr. 2, 1958. B.S., Iowa State U., 1979. C.P.A., Iowa. Auditor, Ernst & Whinney, Des Moines, 1979-82; fin. dir. Community Meml. Hosp., Clarion, Iowa, 1982—. Mem. Iowa Soc. C.P.A.s, Health Care Fin. Mgmt. Assn. Home: Clarion IA Office: Community Meml Hosp 1316 S Main St Clarion IA 50525

SANTORO, ARLENE TREPTOW, librarian; b. Chgo., Mar. 18, 1938; d. Arthur Ruben and Edna Karoline (Scior) T.; m. August John Santoro, June 27, 1959 (div. Feb. 1970); children—John August, Wayne Arthur. B.A., Blackburn Coll., Carlinville, Ill., 1959; M.A., U. Chgo., 1974. Research asst. Am. Meat Inst./U.Chgo., 1959-63; librarian Frankfort Pub. Library (Ill.), 1966-74, adminstrv. librarian, 1974—; dep. registrar Will County (Ill.), 1975—; cons. to various pub. libraries, Ill., 1983—; mem. Ill. adv. com. State Library, 1980-81. Ill. State scholar, 1971. Mem. ALA, Ill. Library Assn., Beta Phi Mu. Unitarian.

SANTOS, LAVERNE SWINT, dietitian; b. Charleston, S.C., Sept. 7, 1949; d. Charlie and Cora Lee (Lowery) Swint; m. John Santos, Oct. 21, 1971 (div. Mar. 1976). B.S., Hampton Inst., 1978. Registered dietitian. Asst. chief dietitian Bklyn. Jewish Med. Ctr., 1978-80; dir. food service Prospect Hosp., Bronx, N.Y., 1980-82; trouble shooter St. John's Episc. Hosp., Bklyn., 1982-83; food prodn. mgr. Mt. Sinai Hosp., Chgo., 1983, dir. ops., 1983—; nutrition inservice coordinator Lockport Meml. Hosp. (N.Y.), 1982. Author booklet: Your Diet Guide for Longer Life, 1979. Recruiter, Saga Corp.-Hampton Inst. (Va.), 1979; mem. task force Nat. Alliance Bus., Hampton, 1981; fund raiser Sickle Cell Anemia, Hampton, 1978; career day rep. Saga Corp., Hampton, 1980; task force mem. Women in Saga, Kalamazoo, 1984; fund raiser Crusade of Mercy, Chgo., 1984. Recipient Recognition award Saga Corp., 1983. Mem. Am. Dietetic Assn., Greater N.Y. Dietetic Assn. (assoc.), Hampton Inst. Alumni Assn. Democrat. Home: 1919 S Wolf Rd #111 Hillside IL 60162 Office: Mt Sinai Med Ctr Saga Corp 15th & California Chicago IL 60608

SAPARETO, STEPHEN ALAN, cancer research scientist, educator; b. Haverhill, Mass., Oct. 30, 1949; s. Frank Vincent and Alice Loraine (Lambert) S.; m. Sheila Kay Schmeling, June 21, 1972 (div. 1976). B.S. in Physics, U. Mass., 1971; M.S. in Health Physics, Colo. State U., 1973, Ph.D. in Radiation Biology, Cell and Molecular Biology, 1978. Postdoctoral fellow dept. radiology and radiation biology Colo. State U., Ft. Collins, 1977-78; postdoctoral fellow in cancer biology dept. radiology Stanford U., 1978-80; asst. prof. sect. cancer biology, div. radiation oncology Washington U., St. Louis, 1980-82; asst. prof. medicine div. med. oncology Wayne State U., Detroit, 1982-85, assoc. prof. medicine div. med. oncology 1985—; asst. mem. dept. exptl. therapeutics Mich. Cancer Found., Detroit, 1982—, mem. safety com., radiation safety officer, 1982—; dir. Ben Kasle Lab. for Flow Cytometry, 1982—. Recipient Nat. Research Service award USPHS, 1978-79; NSF grantee, 1971; FDA radiation health trainee, 1972-75; mem. exec. com. N.Am. Hypothermia Group, 1985-86. Mem. Radiation Research Soc., Am. Soc. Therapeutic Radiologists, Am. Assn. Cancer Research, Sigma Xi. Contbr. articles to profl. pubs. Office: Mich Cancer Found 110 E Warren Ave Detroit MI 48201

SAPERSTEIN, ESTHER, retired city official; b. Chgo.; ed. Northwestern U.; widow; children—Sidney, Natalie. Mem. Ill. Ho. of Reps., 1957-66; mem. Ill. Senate, 1966-75, chmn. edn. com.; asst. commr. Dept. Human Services, Chgo. Mem. Mayor's Com. on Human Relations, Chgo., Mayor's Juvenile Welfare Com. Chgo.; former pres. Chgo. Region P.T.A.; former sec. Juvenile Protection Assn.; mem. Citizens Adv. Council of Met. Chgo.; chmn. Ill. Commn. Status Women, 1963-83. Ill. chmn. Commn. on Mental Health and Retardation, 1965-83; mem. Ill. Commn. Mental Health and Developmental Disabilities. Alderman, City of Chgo., 1975-83. Bd. dirs. Jewish Community Center of Rogers Park (Ill.), Little City, Chgo. Sch. for Retarded Children, Doctors Gen. Hosp.; mem. Chgo. Area Project, Citizen Sch. Com. Mem. LWV. Democrat. Jewish. Home and Office: 3260 N Lake Shore Dr Apt 12B Chicago IL 60657

SARABIA, ANTONIO ROSAS, lawyer; b. Chihuahua, Mex., June 29, 1913; s. Rafael Rosas and Maria S.; children—Antonio Rosas II, Sean Rosas. B.S. in Chem. Engring., Ind. Tech. Coll., 1942; J.D., U. Chgo., 1949. Bar: Ill. 1950. Assoc. Baker, McKenzie & Hightower, Chgo., 1949-52, ptnr., 1952-62; sole practice, Chgo., 1962-64; sr. assoc. Lord, Bissell & Brook, Chgo., 1964-65, ptnr., 1966-83; faculty mem. Lawyers Inst. John Marshall Law Sch., Chgo., 1962-73. Mem. legis. com. Chgo. Crime Commn., 1971—; bd. dirs. Geographic Soc. of Chgo., 1970-78, 3d v.p., 1978—. Mem. ABA (internat. law sect. 1970—, council 1971-75, budget officer 1972-78), Inter-Am. (membership com.), Ill. State Bar Assn. (internat. law sect. chmn. 1965-66, council 1974-75), Chgo. Bar Assn. (charter flight com. 1961-82, internat. and fgn. law com. 1982—, internat. human rights 1978—, chmn. 1980—), Am. Fgn. Law Assn. (pres. Chgo. br. 1952-59), Am. Arbitration Assn., Mexican Am. Lawyers Assn. Clubs: Univ., Mid-Am. Contbr. articles to profl. jours. Home: 175 E Delaware Pl Apt 7805 Chicago IL 60611 Office: 115 S LaSalle St Suite 2930 Chicago IL 60603

SARANTAKIS, ANTHONY JAMES, advertising executive, consultant; b. St. Louis, Dec. 14, 1949; s. James George and Georgia (Geroulis) S.; m. Christine Carol Dziukala, July 25, 1981. B.S., U. Wis., 1972. Salesman advt. Pubs. Devel. Corp., Skokie, Ill., 1972-75; dist. mgr. Nat. Sch. Bd. Assn., Washington, 1975-77; regional mgr. Cahners Pub., Boston, 1977-80; regional mgr. Irving Cloud Pub., Lincolnwood, Ill., 1980—. Democrat. Greek Orthodox. Home: 1424 Allison Ct Arlington Heights IL 60005 Office: Irving Cloud Pub Co 7300 N Cicero Ave Lincolnwood IL 60646

SARB, FRANCINE MARIE, nurse, educator; b. Goodman, Wis., Oct. 26, 1927; d. Donald Francis and Marie Sylvia (Milos) Jacobson; m. Gordon Lee Sarb, July 26, 1952; children—Mary, Susan. A.S., Eveleth Jr. Coll., 1947; B.S. in Nursing, Marquette U., 1951; M.Ed., U. Ill., 1978. R.N., Wis., Ill. Gen. duty nurse Meth. Hosp., Madison, Wis., 1950-51, evening supr., 1952-53, instr. Sch. Nursing, 1952-53; instr. Luth. Hosp. Sch. Nursing, Moline, Ill., 1954-56; gen. duty nurse Hillman Meml. Hosp., Manteno, Ill., 1959-69; asst. inservice nursing coordinator Freeport (Ill.) Meml. Hosp., 1969-71; health coop. coordinator Freeport Sr. High Sch., 1971-75; health care instr. Stephenson Area Career Ctr., Freeport, 1975—. Religious educator St. Paul Catholic Ch., Peotone, Ill., 1963-69, St. Thomas Aquinas Ch., Freeport, 1969-76; sr. choir mem. St. Joseph Cath. Ch., Freeport; vol. fund raiser Am. Heart Assn., United Cerebral Palsy. Mem. Ill. Vocat. Assn., Ill. Health Occupations Assn., Ill. Coop. Vocat. Edn. Coordinators Assn. (bd. dirs.). Club: Highland Dames (Freeport). Office: Pearl City Rd Freeport IL 61032

SARBINOFF, JAMES ADAIR, periodontist, consultant; b. Indpls., Dec. 29, 1947; s. James Gill and Eileen Sarbinoff; m. Tamara Lynn Griffith, June 6, 1971. A.B. in Zoology, Ind. U., 1970; D.D.S., Ind. U.-Indpls., 1974, M.S. in Dentistry, 1981. Gen. practice dentistry, Indpls., 1974-79; gen. practice periodontics, Indpls., 1981—; cons. Marion County Home, Indpls., 1975-79; instr. clin. dentistry Ind. U. Sch. Dentistry, Indpls., 1974-79, assoc. prof., 1981-82. Editor: Perio Probe, 1981. Chmn. dental div. United Way, Indpls., 1983, 84. Recipient Mosby Scholarship Book award Mosby Pub. Co., 1974. Mem. ADA, Am. Acad. Periodontology, Ind. Dental Assn., Indpls. Dist. Dental Soc. Avocations: skiing; computers. Office: 6801 Lake Plaza Dr A-111 Indianapolis IN 46220

SARGENT, DONALD VIRGIL, gynecologist; b. Bay City, Mich., Apr. 7, 1911; s. Edward Daniel and Nellie Ellen (Brady) S.; B.S., Loyola U., Chgo., 1932, M.D., 1936; m. Helen Marie Van Colen, Feb. 6, 1937; children—Saundra Donahue, Donald Virgil II, Michael, Pamela Richardson. Intern, St. Mary's Hosp., Saginaw, 1936-38, preceptorship, 1938-42, chmn. dept. ob-gyn, 1948-80; practice medicine specializing in gynecology, Saginaw, 1946—; cons. staff Saginaw Gen. Hosp., St. Luke's Hosp., 1948-81; mem. bd. Valley Ob-Gyn Clinic, 1965-81; asso. clin. prof. Mich. State U. Coll. Human Medicine, 1972-83. Served to lt. comdr., M.C., USNR, 1942-46. Diplomate Am. Bd. Ob-Gyn. Fellow ACS, Am. Coll. Obstetricians and Gynecologists; mem. AMA, Mich., Saginaw County med. socs., Mich. Soc. Obstetricians and Gynecologists (council). Roman Catholic. Club: Saginaw. Home: 6355 Weiss Saginaw MI 48603 Office: 926 N Michigan Ave PO Box 3216 Saginaw MI 48605

SARNI, MICHAEL H., resort manager; b. Darien, Conn., June 21, 1934; s. John B. and Mary (Portinova) S.; m. Sheery Lee Greenleaf, Nov. 3, 1971; children—Stephanie, Stephen. B.A. in Hotel Mgmt., Yale U., 1962; exchange student Hotel Sch., Durham, Eng., 1958. Corp. controller Breakers Hotel, Palm Beach, Fla., 1969-72; v.p., gen. mgr. Carlton House Resorts, Orlando, Fla., 1972-75; dir. audit Servico Corp., West Palm Beach, 1975-78; gen. mgr. Mohican Lodge, Perrysville, Ohio, 1978—; cons. Hotel Mgmt. Sch., Miami, Fla., 1977-78; cons. Miami Country Club, Fla., 1977-78; adv. bd. Ashland Coll., Ohio, 1980—. Author: Product Hospitality, 1979. Served to 2nd lt. USMC, 1950-55, Korea. Presbyterian. Avocation: golf. Home: Maple Heights Box A194A Londonville OH 44842

SARNO, JOSEPH ADRIAN, store proprietor; b. Chgo., Feb. 17, 1939; s. Joseph Frederick and Ann Marie (Zaconne) S.; m. June Carol Vaznonis, July 25, 1965; children—Laura Jenine, Jamieson Joseph, Adrienne Joyce. Student, DePaul U., 1965, Amundson City Coll., 1968. With Putman Pub., Chgo., 1957-60; with Sun Electric, Chgo., 1960-61; asst. credit mgr. Wallace Bus. Forms, Chgo., 1964-68; credit supr. Armor-Dial, Inc., Chgo., 1968-73; propr. The Fantasy Shop, Chgo., 1971-78, The Nostalgia Shop, Chgo., 1973-79, Original Comic Art Emporium, Chgo., 1975-78, Comic Kingdom, Chgo., 1979—; pub. The Nostalgia Shop Newsletter, 1975-79, Chgo. Collectors Chronicles, 1978-80, Collectors Bull., 1981-82, Space Acad. Newsletter, 1978—. Contbr. articles and poetry to jours. Author: Poems, 1968; Shattered Dreams, 1978. Served with U.S. Army, 1961-64. Club: Fantasy Collectors of Chgo. Office: Joe Sarno Pub 3905 W. Lawrence Ave Chicago IL 60625

SARTHER, LYNETTE KAY, accountant; b. Terre Haute, Ind., Mar. 16, 1947; d. William Horace and Margaret Jane (Bennett) Alsman; m. William Patrick Sarther, June 7, 1974; 1 dau., Kristen Casey. B.S., Ball State U., 1969. C.P.A., Ohio. Staff acct., office mgr. Arthur Young & Co., Cin., 1969-74; ptnr. Fowler, Alsman & Co., Cin., 1974-75; sr. acct. small bus. John Sullivan, C.P.A., Reston, Va., 1975-77; mgr. small bus. dept. Rippe, Strickling, Kingston & Co., Cin., 1977-79; prin. Lynette K. Sarther, C.P.A., Cin., 1979—; bus. mgr. jour. Woman C.P.A. Mem. Am. Inst. C.P.A.s, Ohio Soc. C.P.A.s, Am. Soc. Women Accts. (bd. dirs., past pres. Cin. chpt., nat. editor Coordinator), Am. Woman's Soc. C.P.A.s, Kindervelt Children's Hosp. Aux. Republican. Methodist.

SARVAY, JOHN THOMAS, sales executive; b. Weirton, W.Va., Apr. 29, 1937; s. George and Anna (Kasich) S.; B.S. in Design, U. Cin., 1961; postgrad. Case Western Res. U., 1963; m. Beth Ann Ogan, July 15, 1961; children—Margaret Louise, Anna Beth, Scott Andrew. Plant mgr., dir. design Altech div. Ravens Metals Products, Parkersburg, W.Va., 1960-63; mgr. applied research Ohio Rubber Co. div. Eagle-Pitcher Corp., Willoughby, Ohio, 1963-65; devel. mgr. Standard Products Co., Cleve., 1965-70; dir. tech. info. group Stirling Homex Corp., Avon, N.Y., 1970-72; dir. corporate design and mktg. services Schlegel Corp., Rochester, N.Y., 1972-77; v.p. mktg. Modernfold, an Am. Standard Co., New Castle, Ind., 1977-79; sr. sales rep. Computervision Corp., Bedford, Mass., 1979—; planning cons. Wirt County (W.Va.), 1962-63. Recipient awards for water color paintings. Mem. Am. Inst. Aeros. and Astronautics, ASTM, Soc. Automotive Engrs., Am. Soc. Metals, Aircraft Owners and Pilots Assn., Confederate Air Force, Nat. Muzzle Loading Rifle Assn., Indsl. Designers Soc. Am., Brit. Airways Exec. Club. Byzantine Catholic. Clubs: Kiwanis (Cleve.); United Red Carpet. Contbr. articles to profl. jours. Patentee in field of archtl. wall and window systems (5). Home: 1200 Ivywood Ct New Castle IN 47362

SASKI, WITOLD, pharmaceutics educator; b. Brest, Poland, Dec. 4, 1909; s. Jerzy Edmund and Teresa Franciszka (Marszalska) S.; came to U.S., 1951; widowed, July 1980. B.A. (equivalent), R. Traugutt Gimnasium, Brest, 1927; B.Sc. in Pharmacy, U. Nebr., 1954; M. in Pharmacy, Stefan Batory U., Poland,

1933; D. Pharmacy, U. Bologna, Italy, 1946; Pharm. Chemist, Brighton Tech. Coll., 1947; diploma in Optometry, Inst. Optical Sci., London, 1950. Registered pharmacist, Eng., Nebr. Profl. pharmacist, Poland, 1933-36; insp. Pharmacy Ministry of Health, Warsaw and Tarnopol, Poland, 1937-39; chief pharmacist Bulstrode Str. Med. Clinic, London, 1947-48; sr. pharmacist Brit. Ministry Health, London, 1948-51; asst. prof. U. Montana, Missoula, 1951-52; asst. prof. to prof. pharmaceutics U. Nebr., Lincoln, 1952-75, prof. emeritus, 1975—. Co-author: Experimental Pharmaceutics, 1961, 4th edit., 1977. Contbr. articles, abstracts to nat. and internat. sci. jours. Mem. editorial bd. Inst. Sci. Info. Current Contents, 1970—. Participant Mayor's Com. for Internat. Friendship, Lincoln, 1970—. Served to 2d lt. Second Polish Corps in 8th Brit. Army, World War II, Italy. Decorated Polish, Italian and Brit. govts.; recipient Lederle Pharmacy awards, 1962, 64, 66; grantee Fulbright, Italy, 1968, USPHS, 1964, 65, 66; U.S. Acad. Scis. Exchange Scientist, Poland, 1970. Fellow Acad. Pharm. Scis.; mem. Polish Inst. Arts and Scis. Am., Nebr. Pharmacists Assn., Great Navy State Nebr. (Adm. 1970), Nebr. Art Assn., Sigma Xi, Kappa Psi, Rho Chi. Avocations: swimming; bicycling; gardening. Home: 2600 S 46 St Lincoln NE 68506

SATARIANO, HARRY JOHN, family therapist; b. Pitts, Nov. 30, 1950; s. Anthony Joseph and Grace Veronica (Bowles) S. B.A., St. Thomas Coll., Sem., 1973; M.S.W., U. Kans., 1977. Lic. specialist clin. social worker Kans.; cert. family therapist. Mem. staff Cath. Social Service, Kansas City, Mo., 1977-79; clin. researcher Community Outreach Program for the Deaf, Tucson, 1979; clin. instr. Children Rehab. Unit, Kans. U. Med. Ctr., Kansas City, 1979—, dir. social work, 1981—, co-founder Neonatal ICU Family Study Inst., 1985; project coordinator Handicapped Child Abuse Prevention Program, RAP Fed. Region VII, 1983-84; staff cons. Head Start Programs, Kansas City, 1980-82; fellow Menninger Found., 1980-82; fed. grant. reviewer HHS. Mem. Am. Assn. Mental Deficiences, Nat. Assn. Auctioneers, Kansas. Assn. Auctioneers. Club: Toastmasters. Home: 4422 W 69th Terr Prairie Village KS 66208 Office: Children's Rehab Unit Room 137 Univ Kans Med Center Olathe Blvd at Rainbow Blvd Kansas City KS 66103

SATINOVER, TERRY KLIEMAN, lawyer; b. Chgo., Apr. 25, 1936; d. Charles D. and Mary (Klieman) Satinover; student Shimer Coll., 1952-54; B.A. cum laude, U. Chgo., 1955, J.D. magna cum laude (Weymouth Kirkland scholar), 1958; m. Richard Rees Fagen, June 15, 1958 (div. June 1970); children—Sharon, Ruth, Elizabeth, Michael. Admitted to Ill. bar, 1970; practice in Chicago, 1971—; partner firm Pope, Ballard, Shepard & Fowle, Chgo., 1971—; mem. inquiry panel Ill. Atty. Registration and Disciplinary Commn., 1971-76. Bd. dirs. Congregation Rodfei Zedec, Charles Satinover Fund. Mem. Am. Friends Hebrew U. Order of Coif, Phi Beta Kappa. Jewish (v.p. congregation). Home: 155 N Harbor Dr Chicago IL 60601 Office: 69 W Washington St Suite 3200 Chicago IL 60602

SATO, SHOZO, artist, educator; b. Kobe City, Japan, May 18, 1933; came to U.S., 1964; s. Takami and Midori Sato; Fine Arts degree, Bunka Gakuin Coll., 1955; diplomas in traditional arts; m. Alice Y. Ogura, June 19, 1975. Dir. Kamakura Ryusei Sch. Fine Arts, Japan, 1959-64; faculty U. Ill., Urbana, 1964-66, 68—, artist-in-residence, prof. art, 1968—, dir. Japan House, 1976—; vis. lectr. colls., univs., 1964—; dir. opera, theatre prodns., 1965—; faculty U. Wis., 1966-67. U. Ill. research grantee on Middle Eastern, Southeastern Asian performing arts, 1974; Hoso Bunk Found. grantee, 1983; co-recipient Poster award for Kabuki Macbeth, Casebook 4, 1979; recipient Joseph Jefferson awards for prodn., direction and costume design for Kabuki Macbeth, Chgo. Theatre Assn., 1982, also award for best costuming for Kabuki Medea, 1984; Designers award for Kabuki Medea poster N.Y. Arts Dirs., 1984; Bay Area Theatre Critics award for best prodn., direction, tech. achievement for Kabuki Medea, 1985; Hollywood Drama-Logue Critics award for outstanding achievement in theatre for Kabuki Medea, 1985; 1st Burlington No. Found. Faculty Achievement award, 1985. Mem. Am. Theatre Assn., Am. Guild Mus. Artists, AAUP, Gold Key (hon.). Author: The Art of Arranging Flowers, 1966; The Appreciation of Oriental Art, 1967; the Art of Sume, 1984. Office: 124 Fine Arts Bldg U Ill Champaign IL 61820

SATTIN, ALBERT, psychiatry and neurobiology educator; b. Cleve., Oct. 5, 1931; s. Sam and Edith (Stolarsky) S.; m. Renee Schnider, Dec. 16, 1962; children—Rebecca Lee, Michael M. B.S., Western Reserve U., 1953, M.D., 1957. Diplomate Am. Bd. Psychiatry and Neurology. Intern Washington U., St. Louis, 1957-58; resident in psychiatry Case-Western Reserve U., Cleve., 1958-62; fellow Dept. Biochemistry, U. London, 1965-66; instr., sr. instr. Case-Western Res. U. Sch. Medicine, 1965-1970, asst. prof. psychiatry and pharmacology, 1970-77; assoc. prof. psychiatry Ind. U. Sch. Medicine, Indpls., 1977-84, assoc. prof. psychiatry and neurobiology, Ind. U. Grad. Sch., 1984—; psychiat. cons. Hooverwood Jewish Home, Indpls., 1981—; dir., Geriatric Psychiatry Clinic, Ind. U. Med. Ctr., Indpls., 1981—; mem. staff R.L. Roudebush VA Med. Ctr., Indpls., 1977—. Contbr. articles to profl. jours. Grantee NIMH, NSF, VA; Am. Psychiat. Assn. fellow, 1969. Mem. Am. Psychiat. Assn., Soc. for Neurosci. Soc. Biol. Psychiatry, Internat. Soc. Neurochemistry. Office: Inst Psychiatric Research 791 Union Dr Ind Univ Med Ctr Indianapolis IN 46223

SATTLER, JOAN LINDA, special education educator; b. Adrian, Mich., Oct. 21, 1947; d. Allen Henry and Ruth Alice (Beyer) M.; m. Edward Lee Sattler, June 7, 1969; children—Linda Grace, Allen Edward, Michael Edward. B.S., Western Mich. U., 1969; Ed.M., U. Ill., 1974, Ed.D., 1977. Cert. elem. and spl. edn. tchr., Nebr., Miss., Ill. Tchr. pub. schs. Springfield, Wis., 1969-70; spl. edn. tchr. Lincoln Pub. Schs., Nebr., 1970-71, Jackson Pub. Schs., Miss., 1971-72; assoc. prof., then chmn. spl. edn. Bradley U., Peoria, Ill., 1977—, assoc. dean Coll. Edn. and Health Scis., 1985—. Assoc. editor Tchr. Edn. and Spl. Edn. jour. 1983—; contbg. editor Ill. Council for Exceptional Children Quar. jour. 1981—. Mem. higher edn. adv. com. Ill. Bd. of Edn., 1979—; mem. sch. bd. Montessori Sch., Peoria, Ill., 1980-81; bd. dirs. Allied Agys., Peoria, 1981-82, Easter Seal Soc., Peoria, 1985. U.S. Office of Edn. fellow, 1972-76; U. Ill. fellow, 1974-76. Mem. Council for Exceptional Children (faculty adviser 1969—), Am. Council for Learning Disabilities, Nat. Council for Accreditation of Tchr. Edn. (team evaluator 1978—), AAUP, Am. Edn. Research Assn, Phi Delta Kappa (del. 1983—, research 1984), Phi Kappa Phi. Unitarian Universalist. Avocations: reading, family activities, piano, organ. Home: 2302 W Bainter Ln Peoria IL 61615 Office: Bradley U Westlake Hall Peoria IL 61625

SAUER, FREDERICK ALBERT, JR., lawyer; b. Pontiac, Mich., Mar. 7, 1929; s. Frederick Albert and Martha Lavina (Witters) S.; m. Frances Louise Jackson, Dec., 1953 (div. June 1960); 1 son, Stephen Dana; m. 2d, Anne Marie Kruizenga, Sept. 7, 1962; children—Stephanie Ann, Mark Frederick. B.A., Albion Coll.-Kalamazoo Coll., 1955; J.D., Detroit Coll. Law, 1958. Bar: Mich. 1958. Ptnr. Sauer & Sauer, Kalamazoo, 1958-60; sole practice, Kalamazoo, 1960-69, 74—; ptnr. Sauer & Tucker, Kalamazoo, 1969-74; lectr. Inst. Continuing Legal Edn., U. Mich. Served with N.G., 1943-44; with USMC, 1947-50; with USAR, 1950-53. Mem. State Bar Mich. (councilman family law sect.), County Bar of Kalamazoo, U.S. Coast Guard Assn. (flotilla staff officer 1983), Sigma Chi, Sigma Ro Sigma. Lutheran. Home: 2455 Kensington Dr Kalamazoo MI 49007 Office: 827 W South St Kalamazoo MI 49007

SAUER, MARY LOUISE, civic leader; b. Chillicothe, Ohio, June 26, 1923; d. Maurice Eichholtz and Sarah Katherine (Kieffer) Steirhilber; B.A. in Edn., Northwestern U., 1945; postgrad. U. Mo., Kansas City, 1963-64, 70-71; m. Gordon Chenoweth Sauer, Dec. 28, 1944; children—Elisabeth Ruth, Gordon Chenoweth, Margaret Louise, Amy Kieffer. Co-chmn., Kansas City Chamber Choir, pres. Kansas City Philharmonic League, 1959-60; pres. women's com. Conservatory of Music, U. Mo., 1963-64; bd. dirs. regional auditions Met. Opera Guild, 1965-69; bd. dirs., program chmn. Nettleton Home, Kansas City, 1976-77; bd. dirs., women's council U. Mo., Kansas City, Univ. Assos.; co-chmn. assos. div. Kansas City Mus. Club. Recipient Distinguished Achievement Internat. Register Profiles award, 1976; Community Leaders and Noteworthy Americans award, Vol. Teaching Assn., 1970-74. Mem. AAUW, Am. Guild Organists, D.A.R., Northwestern U. Alumni Assn., Lyric Opera Guild, Kansas City Musical Club, Mu Phi Epsilon, Kappa Delta. Presbyterian. Producer bicentennial pageant, Under the Liberty Tree, 1976. Home: 830 W 58th Terr Kansas City MO 64113

SAUER, ROBERT WILLIAM, engineering company executive; b. Indpls., Sept. 14, 1941; s. Carl M. and Erma R. (Swaim) S. B.S., Purdue U., 1963; Ph.D., Northwestern U., 1968. With Reuas Engring. Co., Inc., Indpls., 1968—, pres., 1972—; pres. Sauer Realty Co., 1980—. Mem. Am. Soc. Metals, Sigma Xi, Phi Eta Sigma, Alpha Sigma Nu, Sigma Alpha Epsilon, Tau Kappa Beta. Clubs: Columbia; Contemporary. Office: 555 W 16th St Indianapolis IN 46208

SAUNDERS, BRUCE, systems engineer; b. Wichita, Kans., Dec. 12, 1960; s. Leonard Franklin and Carolyn Mae (Hillman) S. Student in elec. engring. tech. Wichita State U., 1977-82. Systems engr. Boeing Mil. Airplane Co., Wichita, 1982—. Eagle scout, Boy Scouts Am., 1976. Mem. IEEE, Wichita Engring. Assn., Assn. Computing Machinery. Clubs: Plane Apple (Wichita); Call-A.P.P.L.E. (Kent, Wash.). Lodge: Order of Arrow (chpt. chief 1976-77). Home: 1717 S Cypress St Apt 412 Wichita KS 67207

SAVAGE, ALFRED DAVID, osteopathic physician; b. Burlington, Iowa, Sept. 21, 1943; s. David Fairlee and Lena Florence (McCracken) S.; m. Debra Jeanne Deierling, Mar. 17, 1976; children—Andria Noelle, David Frank. B.S., Iowa Wesleyan Coll., 1965; M.S., N.E. Mo. State U., 1967; D.O., Des Moines U. Health Scis., 1972. Instr. physics Centerville Community Coll. (Iowa), 1967-68; resident in internal medicine Davenport Osteo. Hosp., 1973-76; emergency room physician Burlington Med. Ctr. (Iowa), 1976-78; pvt. practice osteo. internal medicine, Mt. Pleasant, Iowa, 1978—; med. dir. Henry County Emergency Med. Services, 1980—. Mem. Am. Osteo. Assn., AMA, Am. Heart Assn., Henry County Med. Soc. Mem. Soc. Friends. Home: 301 S Walnut St Mount Pleasant IA 52641 Office: 107 E Madison St Mount Pleasant IA 52641

SAVAGE, BARRY EMERY, lawyer; b. Jackson, Mich., Apr. 19, 1940; s. Herbert E. and Marva V. (Schultz) S.; B.A. in Econ., U. Mich., 1962, J.D., 1965; m. Joyce A. Diaz, Oct. 6, 1977; 1 son by previous marriage, Steven Vincent. Admitted to Ohio bar, 1965, Mich. bar, 1966; practice in Toledo, 1965—; with firm Savage & Lindsley, P.A., Toledo; engaged in real estate investment, 1968—. Mem. Mich. State Bar, Toledo Bar Assn. (chmn. unauthorized practice com. 1970-72), Am. Bar Assn. Clubs: Jolly Roger Sailing (Toledo); Indian Hills Boat (Maumee, Ohio). Home: 4009 River Rd Toledo OH 43614 Office: Savage & Lindsley 228 N Erie St Toledo OH 43624

SAVAGE, DWAYNE CECIL, microbiologist, educator; b. Arco, Idaho, Aug. 8, 1934; s. Cecil Brigham and Pearl Louella (Maynard) S.; m. Norma Jean Bradley, Feb. 14, 1957; children—Marco, Clark. B.S., U. Idaho, 1956; M.A., U. Calif.-Berkeley, 1961, Ph.D., 1965. Asst. prof. dept. microbiology U. Tex., Austin, 1967-69, assoc. prof., 1969-73; assoc. prof. dept. microbiology and Sch. Basic Med. Scis., U. Ill., Urbana, 1973-75, prof. dept. microbiology, 1975—; vis. prof. depts. medicine and microbiology U. Colo. Sch. Medicine, Denver, 1970; cons., researcher in field. Contbr. articles to profl. jours. Served with USN, 1956-59. USPHS, NIH trainee, 1961-62, predoctoral fellow, 1962-65; Rockefeller U. postdoctoral fellow, 1965-67; USPHS grantee, 1968—; recipient U. Ill. Med. Students Golden Apple award, 1974. Mem. Am. Soc. Microbiology, Am. Acad. Microbiology, N.Y. Acad. Scis., Assn. Gnotobiotics, AAAS, Soc. Gen. Microbiology (Eng.), Soc. Intestinal Microbial Ecology and Disease, Sigma Xi. Home: 606 Burkwood Ct E Urbana IL 61801 Office: 131 Burrill Hall 407 S Goodwin U Ill Urbana IL 61801

SAVAGE, FRED WILLIAM, sales executive; b. Cleve., May 28, 1939; s. Frank W. and Anne (Sypos) S.; m. Erna A. Hamacher, May 28, 1964; children—Frank Fredric, Kirsten Erna. Student Ohio U., 1957-58, Baldwin-Wallace Coll., 1966-69. Dist. sales mgr. Hertz Truck Div., Cleve., 1970-75; lease account mgr. Ryder Truck Rental, Cleve., 1976-80; rental mgr. Lend Lease Truck Rental, Cleve., 1980-81, sta. mgr., 1981-82, regional sales mgr., Worthington, Ohio, 1982—; sales cons. Leaseway Transp., Cleve., 1975. Served with M.I., U.S. Army, 1962-66. Republican. Baptist. Avocations: history; golf; jogging. Home: 450 W Wilson Bridge #330 Worthington OH 43085

SAVAGE, GUS, congressman, newspaper columnist, editor and publisher; b. Detroit, Oct. 30, 1925; s. Thomas and Mollie (Wilder) S.; B.A. in Philosophy, Roosevelt U., 1951; postgrad. Chgo.-Kent Coll. Law, 1951-53; m. Eunice King, Aug. 4, 1946; children—Thomas James, Emma Mae. Editor, Am. Negro Mag., 1955-56, Woodlawn Booster, Chgo., 1961-65, Bull. Newspaper, 1963-65; asst. editor Ill. Beverage Jour., 1956-59; editor, pub. Westside Booster, Chgo., 1959-60; editor Citizen Newspapers, Chgo., from 1965; pub. The Chgo. Weekend Newspaper, from 1974; mem. 97th-99th congresses from Ill. 2d Dist. Chmn., Protest at the Polls, 1963, Coalition for a Black Mayoral Candidate, 1977. Served with USAAF, 1943-46. Recipient Vol. Service award Steelworkers Ad Hoc Com., 1969; Citizenship award Operation PUSH, 1976; medal of Merit City of Chgo., 1976; Journalism award Nat. Newspaper Pubs. Assn., 1978; Disting. Achievement award Chatham Bus. Assn., 1979. Mem. Orgn. for S.W. Communities (pres. 1969-70), Chgo. League Negro Voters (founder, campaign mgr. 1958-59). Democrat. Author pamphlets. Office: 1743 E 87 St Chicago IL 60617 also 1121 Longworth House Office Bldg Washington DC 20515*

SAVARD, DENIS, professional hockey player. Ctr., Chgo. Blackhawks., NHL. Office: Chgo Blackhawks 1800 Madison Ave Chicago IL 60612*

SAVOY, SUZANNE MARIE, nurse; b. N.Y.C., Oct. 18, 1946; d. William Joseph and Mary Patricia (Moclair) Savoy. B.S., Columbia U., 1970; M.N., UCLA, 1978. R.N. Staff nurse MICU, transplant Jackson Meml. Hosp., Miami, Fla., 1970-72; staff nurse MICU Boston U. Hosp. (Mass.), 1972-74; staff nurse MICU VA Hosp., Long Beach, Calif., 1974-75; staff nurse MIRU Cedars-Sinai M.C., Los Angeles, 1975-77; critical care clin. nursing specialist Anaheim Meml. Hosp., (Calif.), 1978-81; practitioner, instr. Rush-Presbyn.-St. Luke's Med. Ctr. Coll. Nursing, Chgo., 1982—; edn. cons. Critical Care Services, Inc., Orange, Calif., 1979-81. Author article on the craniotomy patient. Mem. Am. Assn. Neurosci. Nurses (treas. Ill. chpt. 1983-85), Am. Assn. Critical Care Nurses (bd. dirs. Long Beach chpt. 1981-82), No. Am. Nursing Diagnosis Assn., Sigma Theta Tau. Roman Catholic. Office: Office: Rush-Presby St Luke's Med Ctr 1753 W Congress Pkwy Chicago IL 60612

SAWALL, ROGER LEE, construction equipment company executive; b. Chgo., Mar. 13, 1944; s. Howard Arnold and Mary Beatrice (Worley) S.; m. Judith Kaye Dale, Nov. 24, 1946; children—Stephen Dale, Christopher Lee. B.S. in Elec. Engring., Mich. Tech. U., 1966; postgrad., Northeastern U., 1967-68; Wayne State U., 1976-78, Bay de Noc Community Coll., 1979-81. Assoc. engr. Raytheon Co., Waltham, Mass., 1966-68; project engr. Gen. Motors Corp., Milw., 1969-71, sr. project engr., Warren, Mich., 1972-78; asst. chief engr. Harnischfeger Corp., Escanaba, Mich., 1979-81, chief engr. product devel., 1981—. Cub Scout leader Clinton Valley council Boy Scouts Am., 1972-76, chmn. Cub Scouts, 1976-78. Mem. Soc. Automotive Engrs., Constrn. Industry Mfrs. Assn. Republican. Home: 7262 S Lake Bluff 05 Dr Gladstone MI 49837 Office: Harnischfeger Corp 2525 14th Ave N Escanaba MI 49829

SAWINSKI, VINCENT JOHN, chemistry educator; b. Chgo., Mar. 28, 1925; s. Stanley and Pearl (Gapinski) S.; B.S., Loyola U., 1948, M.A., 1950, Ph.D., 1962; m. Florence Whitman, Aug. 24, 1952; children—Christine Frances, Michael Patrick. Instr., asst. prof. chemistry, physiology and pharmacology Loyola U., Chgo., 1949-67; supervisory research chemist VA, Hines, Ill., 1961-66; assoc. prof. chemistry, phys. sci. Chgo. City Coll., 1967-71, prof., 1971—, chmn. phys. sci. dept. Wright campus, 1971—. Served with U.S. Army, 1945-46. Fellow AAAS, Am. Inst. Chemists; mem. Am. Chem. Soc., N.Y. Acad. Sci., Nat. Sci. Tchrs. Assn., Sigma Xi. Contbr. articles to profl. jours. Home: 1945 N 77th Ct Elmwood Park IL 60635 Office: 3400 N Austin Ave Chicago IL 60634

SAWYER, CAROL ANNE, foodservice scientist, educator, researcher, dietitian; b. Chgo., Oct. 11, 1942; d. John Paul and Louise (Lonabough) Beringer; m. Henry William Dahl, Dec. 22, 1962; children—Deanna Lyn, Henry Michael; m. 2d, James William Sawyer, Jan. 1, 1982. M.S. in Food Sci., U. Wis., 1977, Ph.D. in Food Sci., 1979. Registered dietitian. Health aide ACTION program, Washington, 1972-73; nutrition cons. WIC program, Oneida, Wis., 1974; instr. food sci. U. Wis., Madison, 1974-79, research asst., 1974-79; asst. prof. Mich. State U., East Lansing, 1979—; cons. in field. Commr. East Lansing Fine Arts Commn., 1980-83; mem. Ingham County Task Force on Hunger and Nutrition, 1983—. Mary Rose Swartz fellow Am. Dietetic Assn. and Nutrition Found., Inc., 1978. Mem. Inst. Food Technologists, Am. Dietetic Assn., Internat. Microwave Power Inst., Omicron Nu. Methodist. Author: Microwave Ovens-Theory and Use in Foodservice, 1983; contbr. numerous articles to profl. publs. Office: Mich State U 334 Food Sci Bldg East Lansing MI 48824

SAWYER, GEORGE ALBERT, technology company executive; b. N.Y.C., Apr. 20, 1931; s. George Albert and Jeanette (Simmons) S.; m. Betty Ann Hartenstein, Dec. 11, 1954 (dec. Dec. 1981); children—Nancy, Jeffrey, Debra; m. Carol Haedtler, June 25, 1983; children—Jon, Christopher. B.A. with high honors, Yale U., 1953. Nuclear systems supplier Babcock & Wilcox, Lynchburg, Va., 1963-65; mgr. marine systems NUS corp., Rockville, Md., 1965-67; mgr. program devel. Battelle Meml. Inst., Richland, Wash., 1967-69; environ. systems mgr. Bechtel, Inc., San Francisco, 1969-75; pres., chief exec. officer J.J. McMullen Assocs., N.Y.C., 1976-81; asst. sec. of navy Dept. Navy, Washington, 1981-83; exec. v.p. Gen. Dynamics Corp., St. Louis, 1983—, also dir.; mem. acad. adv. bd. U.S. Naval Acad., 1984—. Co-inventor consolidated nuclear steam generator, 1965. Served to lt. comdr. USN, 1953-62. Recipient Recognition of Achievement award Dept. Navy, 1983. Mem. Am. Bur. Shipping (bd. mgrs.), Soc. Naval Architects and Marine Engrs. Republican. Episcopalian. Office: Gen Dynamics Corp Pierre Laclede Ctr Saint Louis MO 63105

SAWYER, HAROLD SAMUEL, congressman, lawyer; b. San Francisco, Mar. 21, 1920; s. Harold S. and Agnes (McGugan) S.; LL.B., U. Calif.-Berkeley, 1943; m. Marcia C. Steketee, Aug. 26, 1944; children—Stephen R., David H., Keary W., Mariya Sinclair. Admitted to Calif. bar, 1943, Mich. bar, 1946, D.C. bar, 1978; practiced in Grand Rapids, Mich.; mem. firm Warner, Norcross and Judd, 1950-76, 85—, chmn., 1969-75; pros. atty. Kent County (Mich.), 1975-76; mem. 95th-98th congresses from 5th Mich. dist. Vice pres., dir. Grand Hotel, Mackinac Island, 1957-76; chmn. bd. Citation Cos., Inc., Grand Rapids, 1953-77, Kysor Indsl. Corp., Cadillac, Mich., 1960-77. Spl. legal counsel Gov. Romney, 1962; mem. Mich. Law Revision Commn., 1967-76. Pres., bd. dirs. D. A. Blodgett Home for Children, 1950-61. Served to lt. (j.g.) USNR, 1941-45. Fellow Internat. Acad. Trial Lawyers (dir. 1964-72), Internat. Soc. Barristers, Am. Coll. Trial Lawyers, Am. Bar Found.; mem. Am. Law Inst. Home: 4100 14 Mile Rd Rockford MI 49341 Office: 900 Old Kent Bldg Grand Rapids MI 49503

SAWYER, JOHN, professional football team executive; s. Charles Sawyer; children—Anne, Elizabeth, Catherine, Mary. Pres., part-owner Cin. Bengals, NFL; pres. J. Sawyer Co., Ohio, Miss., Mont., Wyo. Home: Cincinnati OH Office: 1 E 4th St Cincinnati OH 45202

SAWYER, THOMAS HARRISON, health, physical education and recreation educator; b. Norwich, N.Y., Apr. 5, 1946; s. Harrison Donald and Daughn (Geer) S.; m. Kathleen Ann Daly, July 5 1969; children—Shawn Thomas, Meghan Daly. B.S., Springfield Coll., 1968, M.P.E., 1971; Ed.D. Va. PolyTech Inst., 1977. Instr. health, phys edn., recreation Va. Mil. Inst., Lexington, 1969-72, asst. prof., 1972-75, assoc. prof., 1975-79; dir. recreation center U. Bridgeport, 1979-81; assoc. prof., head dept. Mont. Tech. Inst, Butte, 1981-84; prof., chmn. phys. edn. dept. Ind. State U., Terre Haute, 1984—. cons. Mont. Fitness, Butte, 1981-84, ARC, Mont., 1981-83. Contbr. articles to profl. jours. Bd. dirs. YMCA, Butte, 1981-84; mem. Sch. Bd. Dist. 1, Butte, 1982-84; mem. bd. dirs. Vocation Edn. Council Mont., 1983-84. NDEA scholar, 1968; recipient Founder's award Alcohol Services, Buena Vsita, Va., 1979, Vol. Safety award ARC, Conn., 1981, Red Triangle, YMCA, Butte, 1982. Mem. AAHPER and Dance, Mont. Assn. Health, Phys. Edn. and Recreation, Dance, Nat. Assn. Sports Offcls. Office: Sch Phys Edn Ind State U Terre Haute IN 47809

SAWYER, THOMAS HARRY WINFIELD, lawyer; b. Chgo., May 16, 1948; s. Carleton Amos and Maxine Ruth (Boone) S. B.S. magna cum laude, Ind. State U.-Terre Haute, 1970; J.D. magna cum laude, Ind. U., 1973. Bar: Ill. 1973, U.S. Dist. Ct. (no. dist. Ill.) 1973, U.S. Ct. Appeals, 1977, U.S. Supreme Ct. 1980. Legal intern NASA, Washington, summer 1972; assoc. law firm Arnstein, Gluck, Weitzenfeld & Minow, Chgo., 1973-74; mem. legal staff Ill. Bell Tel. Co., Chgo., 1974-83; regional atty. AT&T, Chgo., 1983—. Mem. Republican Nat. Com. 500 Club, Lyric Opera Guild, Adler Planetarium. Mem. ABA, Ill. State Bar Assn., Chgo. Bar Assn., Order of Coif. Republican. Baptist. Home: 235 S Oakland Ave Villa Park IL 60181 Office: 1 E Wacker Dr Suite 2432 Chicago IL 60601

SAX, JOSEPH LAWRENCE, legal educator; b. Chgo., Feb. 3, 1936; s. Benjamin Harry and Mary (Silverman) S.; m. Eleanor G. Gettes, June 17, 1958; children—Katherine Elaine, Valerie Beth, Anne-Marie. A.B., Harvard U., 1957; J.D., U. Chgo., 1959. Bar: U.S. Supreme Ct., 1960, Mich. 1966. Atty., Washington, 1959-62; asst. prof. U. Colo., 1962-64, assoc. prof., 1965-66; prof. law U. Mich., Ann Arbor, 1966—, Philip A. Hart Disting. Univ. prof., 1982—; vis. prof. U. Calif.-Berkeley, 1965-66, U. Utah, 1977, U. Paris I, France, 1982-83; fellow Ctr. Advanced Study Behavior Scis., 1977-78; vis. prof. Stanford U., 1985. Served with USAF, 1960-66. Recipient Resource Def. award Nat. Wildlife Fedn., 1981; Biennial Book award U. Mich., 1981; Elizabeth Haub award U. Brussels, 1979; Conservation award Am. Motors, 1976, Environment Quality award U.S. EPA, 1975; named Conservationist of Yr., Detroit Audubon Soc., 1981; William O. Douglas award Sierra Club, 1984. Author: Water Law Planning and Policy, 1967; Waters and Water Rights, 1968; Defending the Environment, 1971; Mountains Without Handrails, 1981; Legal Control of Water Resources, 1985. Home: 1220 Fair Oaks St Ann Arbor MI 48104 Office: U Mich Law Sch Ann Arbor MI 48109

SAX, MARY RANDOLPH, speech pathologist; b. Pontiac, Mich., July 13, 1925; d. Bernard Angus and Ada Lucile (Thurman) TePoorten; B.A. magna cum laude, Mich. State U., 1947; M.A., U. Mich., 1949; m. William Martin Sax, Feb. 7, 1948. Supr. speech correction dept. Waterford Twp. Schs., Pontiac, 1949-69; lectr. Marygrove Coll., Detroit, 1971-72; pvt. practice speech and lang. rehab., Wayne, Oakland Counties, Mich., 1973—; mem. sci. council stroke Am. Heart Assn. Grantee Inst. Articulation and Learning, 1969, others. Mem. Am. Speech-Lang.-Hearing Assn., Mich. Speech Pathologists in Clin. Practice, Mich. Speech-Lang.-Hearing Assn. (com. community and hosp. services), Mich. Heart Assn., AAUW, Internat. Assn. Logopedics and Phoniatrics (Switzerland), Founders Soc. of Detroit Inst. Arts, Mich. Humane Soc., Theta Alpha Phi, Phi Kappa Phi, Kappa Delta Pi. Contbr. articles to profl. jours. Home and Office: 31320 Woodside Franklin MI 48025

SAXTON, KATHY PINKSTAFF, lawyer; b. Indpls., Mar. 8, 1942; d. Kenneth Ellsworth and Mary Margaret (Spence) Pinkstaff; children—Amy, Michael, John. B.A., Depauw U., 1964; J.D., Northwestern U., 1979. Bar: Ill. 1979, U.S. Dist. Ct. (no. dist.) Ill. 1979. Assoc. Wildman, Harrold, Allen & Dixon, Chgo., 1979—. Mem. ABA, Ill. State Bar Assn., Phi Beta Kappa. Home: 260 Fairview Ave Winnetka IL 60093 Office: Wildman Harrold Allen & Dixon 1 IBM Plaza Chicago IL 60611

SAY, MARLYS MORTENSEN (MRS. JOHN THEODORE SAY), supt. schs.; b. Yankton, S.D., Mar. 11, 1924; d. Melvin A. and Edith L. (Fargo) Mortensen; B.A., U. Colo., 1949, M.Ed., 1953; adminstrv. specialist U. Nebr., 1973; m. John Theodore Say, June 21, 1951; children—Mary Louise, James Kenneth, John Melvin, Margaret Ann. Tchr. Huron (S.D.) Jr. High Sch., 1944-48, Lamar (Colo.) Jr. High Sch., 1950-52, Norfolk Pub. Sch., 1962-63; Madison County supt., Madison, Nebr., 1963—. Mem. N.E.A. (life), Am. Assn. Sch. Adminstrs., Dept. Rural Edn., Nebr. Assn. County Supts. (pres.), Nebr. Elementary Prins. Assn., AAUW (pres. Norfolk br.), N.E. Nebr. County Supts. Assn. (pres.), Assn. Sch. Bus. Ofcls., Nat. Orgn. Legal Problems in Edn., Assn. Supervision and Curriculum Devel., Nebr. Edn. Assn., Nebr. Sch. Adminstrs. Assn. Republican. Methodist. Home: 4805 S 13th St Norfolk NE 68701 Office: Courthouse Madison NE 68748

SAYLES, RONALD LYLE, computer executive; b. Waukesha, Wis., Oct. 12, 1936; s. Burton Lyall and Sophia (Lapaz) S.; m. Fumiko Soeda, Jan. 15, 1957. B.S. in Secondary Edn., U. Wis.-Milw., 1978. Computer operator Mortgage Assocs., Milw., 1966-71, Kohl's Food Stores, Wauwatosa, Wis., 1971-83; supr. computer ops. Kohl's Dept. Stores, Brookfield, Wis., 1983—. Author articles on old time radio programs. Vol. Jim Moody for Congress 1984, Shirley Krug for State Asembly, 1984. Served with USN, 1954-57. Mem. Milw. Zool. Soc., Am. Film Inst., Smithsonian Instn., Wis. Hist. Soc., Milw. Area Radio Enthusiasts, U. Wis.-Milw. Alumni Assn. (life). Democrat. Mormon. Home: 4278 N 53d St Milwaukee WI 53216 Office: 2315 N 124th St Brookfield WI 53005

SAZUNIC, BERNARDITA, airline sales manager; b. Antofagasta, Chile, Dec. 12, 1948; came to U.S., 1960, naturalized, 1967; s. Antonio and Marina (Krstinic) S. B.A., U. Ill., 1972. Dist sales mgr. Lan Chile Airlines, Chgo., 1972—. Avocations: skiing; white water rafting; adventure travel; reading. Office: Lan Chile Airlines 333 N Michigan Ave Chicago IL 60601

SCANLAN, FRANK ALLEN, component engineer; b. Evanston, Ill., July 30, 1929; s. Allen Joseph and Marie Magdalen (Merk) S.; m. Marilyn Elenor Heuel, June 27, 1964; children—Kevin Francis, Brian William. Component engr. Oak Industries, Crystal Lake, Ill., 1956-83, T.R.W. Electronics Assemblies Div., Wheeling, Ill., 1983—. Com. chmn. Blackhawk council Boy Scouts Am., 1979-84. Served to sgt. U.S. Army, 1951-53, Korea. Recipient Disting. Community Service award Crystal Lake Jaycees, 1982, Founders award Boy Scouts Am., 1982, Cert. of Achievement, Am. Heart Assn., 1981. Republican. Roman Catholic. Home: 434 Porter Ave Crystal Lake IL 60014 Office: TRW Electronic Assemblies Div 661 Glenn Ave Wheeling IL 60090

SCELSI, MICHAEL ANDREW, investment executive; b. Chgo., May 15, 1940; s. Andrew Guy and Carmela (Altier) S.; m. Pamela Marie Reichle, Feb. 17, 1968; children—Lisa, Jill, Michael, Jennifer. B.S. in Fin., U. Ill., 1962. Fin. trainee Ford Motor Co., Chicago Heights, Ill., 1963-65; budget analyst Allstate Ins. Co., Northbrook, Ill., 1965-70; controller Meredith Corp., Chgo., 1970-71, Singer Co.-Graflex, Morton Grove, Ill., 1971-72; investment portfolio mgr. Benefit Trust Life, Chgo., 1972—; dir. B.T.L. Credit Union, Chgo.; pres., dir. Klee Corp., Lombard, Ill. Author, pub. H & R Scelsi Tax and Market Letter, 1983. Vice pres. Young Republicans, Niles Twp., Ill., 1966; treas. Allstate Crusade of Mercy, Skokie, Ill., 1967; chmn. B.T.L. Pub. Involvement Com., Chgo., 1983; treas. Cub Scout pack 235, Mt. Prospect, Ill., 1983—. Served with U.S. Army, 1962-68. U. Ill. scholar, 1958. Fellow Life Mgmt. Inst.; mem. Investment Analysts Soc., Alpha Chi Rho. Roman Catholic. Clubs: Arlington Tennis, B.T.L. Tennis (pres. 1974-78), Goferbrokers (pres. 1970-73). Avocations: tennis; golf; show business. Home: 1203 Linden Ln Mount Prospect IL 60056 Office: Benefit Trust Life Ins Co 1771 Howard St Chicago IL 60626

SCHAAF, JAMES HOWARD, See *Who's Who in America,* 43rd edition.

SCHABEL, DONALD ALBERT, retired lawyer, investor; b. Hammond, Ind., July 22, 1927; s. Francis William and Kathleen (Conroy) S.; A.B., Ind. U., 1948; J.D. cum laude, Harvard, 1951; m. Amelia Llana Agtarap, Oct. 7, 1967; children—Victoria Eileen, Donald Albert. Admitted to N.Y. bar, 1952, Ind. bar, 1954; asso. Milbank, Tweed, Hope & Hadley, N.Y.C., 1951-53; asso. Buschmann, Krieg, DeVault & Alexander, Indpls., 1954-57, partner, 1957-60; partner Buschmann, Carr & Schabel, 1961-75; individual practice law, 1976-85. Mem. cts. div. Ind. Jud. Study Commn., 1973-83. Served with USNR, 1945-46. Roman Catholic. Club: Columbia (Indpls.). Home: 4455 Broadway Indianapolis IN 46205

SCHABER, EILEEN ZELMA, social services coordinator; b. DuBois City, Ind., Mar. 18, 1924; d. John George and Matilda Margaret (Harder) Seitz; m. William George Schaber, Oct. 16, 1948 (dec.); children—Carl John, Janet, Eric, Dorothy, William, Robert, Elaine. Student Butler U., 1948-49, Vincennes U., 1978-79. Activities dir., vol. coordinator, dept. supr. Northwood Good Samaritan Ctr., Jasper, Ind., 1974—; corr. Jasper Herald, 1964—. Mem. Sesquicentennial Celebration Com., Haysville, Ind., 1966; planning com. chmn. 125th Anniversary Celebration, St. Paul's Luth. Ch., Haysville, 1973, Social Ministry Program chmn., 1968-71; fundraiser heart and mental health assns.; bd. dirs. DuBois County Council on Aging and Aged. Mem. Ind. Activities Dirs. Assn. (charter), DuBois County Republican Women's Orgn. (2d v.p., chaplain). Devised turnip kraut cutter and recipes.

SCHACHT, HENRY BREWER, diesel engine mfg. co. exec.; b. Erie, Pa., Oct. 16, 1934; s. Henry Blass and Virginia (Brewer) S.; B.S., Yale U., 1956; M.B.A., Harvard U., 1962; m. Nancy Godfrey, Aug. 27, 1960; children—James, Laura, Jane, Mary. Sales trainee Am. Brake Shoe Co., N.Y.C., 1956-57; investment mgr. Irwin Mgmt. Co., Columbus, Ind., 1962-64; v.p. fin. Cummins Engine Co., Inc., Columbus, 1964-66, v.p., central area mgr. internat., London, 1966-67, group v.p. internat. and subsidiaries, 1967-69, pres., Columbus, 1969-77, chmn., chief exec. officer, 1977—; dir. CBS, ATT, Chase Manhattan Bank. Trustee Com. Econ. Devel., Urban Inst., Brookings Inst., Conf. Bd. Served with USNR, 1957-60. Mem. Bus. Council, Council Fgn. Relations, Tau Beta Pi. Republican. Home: 4300 N Riverside Dr Columbus IN 47201 Office: 432 Washington St Columbus IN 47201

SCHACHT, JAMES WILLIAM, state insurance regulation executive; b. Aurora, Ill., Nov. 24, 1941; s. Robert William and Violet Elnora (Sandholm) S.; m. Carol Mae Kleinwachter, June 25, 1966; children—Susan, Justina, Edward, Max and James. B.S. in Acctg., Walton Sch. Commerce, 1964; student Northwestern U., 1965-67, No. Ill. U., 1959-60, Elmhurst Coll., 1960-62. Adminstr., Ill. Ins. Dept., Springfield, 1964—, dep. dir., 1974-78, chief dep. dir., 1978-82, 83—, acting dir., 1982-83. Editor: Accounting Practices Manual-Fire & Casualty Cos., 1974; Accounting Practices Manual-Life and Health Cos., 1974. Contbr.: Financial Regulation in Illinois, 1977, Financial Regulation in Illinois: An Update, 1981. Contbr. articles to profl. jours. Cubmaster Boy Scouts Am., Springfield, 1981-83. Served with U.S. Army, 1966-72. Methodist. Avocations: golf; tennis; running. Home: RR 1 Box 265C Petersburg IL 62675 Office: State of Ill Dept Ins 320 W Washington Springfield IL 62767

SCHAEFER, JON PATRICK, lawyer; b. Fremont, Ohio, Nov. 20, 1948; s. Ellsworth Joseph and Lois Ann (Fought) S.; m. Kathryn Louise Koch, Aug. 21, 1971; children—Heather Marie, Matthew Thomas. B.S., Bethel Coll., 1971; J.D., Memphis State U., 1974. Bar: Ohio 1974, U.S. Dist. Ct. 1977, U.S. Ct. Appeals 1977. V.p. McKown, Schaefer & McKown Co., Shelby, Ohio, 1974-84; sole practice, Shelby, 1984—; acting mcpl. judge City of Shelby, 1982—; dir. Rodon Inc., Shelby, 1982—; law dir. City of Shelby, 1976-80. Exec. com. Richland County Democratic Club, Mansfield, Ohio, 1977; mem. Shelby Dem. Club, 1974—; bd. dirs. Shelby Heart Assn., 1976-77; sec. Most Pure Heart of Mary Parish, 1985—. Mem. ABA, Ohio State Bar Assn., Ohio Trial Lawyers Assn., Richland County Bar Assn., Huron County Bar Assn. Lodges: Shelby Sertoma (pres. 1981-82), K.C. (council 1968, Grand Knight 1982-84, dist. gov. 1985—), Jr. Order Mechanics. Avocations: Fishing; boating; reading. Home: 131 Parkwood Dr Shelby OH 44875 Office: 68 W Main St Shelby OH 44875

SCHAEFER, JOSEPH ROBERT, JR., architectural design company executive, consultant; b. Des Moines, Feb. 13, 1949; s. Joseph Robert and Janet Marie (Walker) S.; B.A., Drake U., 1980; m. Paula Jannine Middleton, July 16, 1977. Sect. supr. Hygiene Lab. U. Iowa, 1971-79; owner, pres. Archtl. Graphic Services, Inc., Des Moines, 1978—; plan adminstr. Bankers Life Ins. Co., 1979-80; ins. employment cons. Key Employment Inc., Des Moines, 1981—. Historian Sherman Hill Restoration Assn., Des Moines, 1978-80; mem. Drake Neighborhood Assn., Des Moines. Republican. Methodist. Home: 1319 23d St Des Moines IA 50311 Office: 1001 Office Park Rd West Des Moines IA 50265

SCHAEFER, PATRICIA, librarian; b. Ft. Wayne, Ind., Apr. 23, 1930; d. Edward John and Hildegarde (Hormel) Schaefer; B.Music, Northwestern U., 1951; M.Music, U. Ill., 1958; A.M.L.S., U. Mich., 1963. With U.S. Rubber Co., Ft. Wayne, Ind., 1951-52; sec. to promotion mgr. Sta. WOWO, Ft. Wayne, Ind., 1952, sec. to program mgr., 1953-55; coordinator publicity and promotion Home Telephone Co., Ft. Wayne, 1955-56; sec. Fine Arts Found., Ft. Wayne, 1956-57; library asst. Columbus (Ohio) Pub. Library, 1958-59; audio-visual librarian Muncie (Ind.) Pub. Library, 1959—, asst. library dir., 1981—; chmn. Ind. Library Film Circuit, 1962-63; treas. Ind. Library Film Service 1969-70, 83—; mem. exec. com. Eastern Ind. Area Library Services Authority; mem. trustees adv. council Milton S. Eisenhower Library, Johns Hopkins U.; cons. in field; weekly columnist Library Lines, Muncie Evening Press, 1981-83; dir. Franklin Electric Co., Inc. Bd. dirs. Muncie Symphony Assn., 1964-74, 85—; mem. adv. com., bookshop dir. Midwest Writers Workshop, 1976-77; sec. Del. County Council for the Arts, 1978-79, pres., 1979-81, bd. dirs., 1985—; bd. dirs. Muncie YWCA, 1977-82, 84—, treas., 1981-82; gen. chmn. Ind. Renaissance Fair, 1978-79; program annotator Muncie Symphony Orch., 1963—, East Central Ind. Community Singers, 1980—; pres. Muncie Matinee Musicale, 1965-67; past pres. Ind. Film and Video Council; mem. community adv. com. Ball Bros. Found. Mem. Ind. Library Assn., ALA, (council 1983-84), Nat. League Am. Pen Women (pres. Muncie br. 1974-78), Am. Recorder Soc., Northeastern Ind. Recorder Soc., Delta Zeta, Mu Phi Epsilon. Republican. Roman Catholic. Clubs: Riley-Jones, Altrusa (1st v.p. 1985-86) (Muncie). Contbr. articles to profl. jours. Home: 405 S Tara Ln Muncie IN 47304 Office: 200 E Main St Muncie IN 47305

SCHAEFER, PAUL STEVEN, lawyer; b. Kalamazoo, Feb. 8, 1953; s. Julius Herman and Carole (Long) S.; m. Marguerite Sue Goss, July 12, 1975; 1 dau., Katharine Lind. B.A. in History, Mich. State U., 1975; J.D., Thomas M. Cooley Sch. Law, 1979. Bar: Mich. 1979. Staff atty. Delta Area Legal Services, Lansing, Mich., 1979; staff atty. Prison Legal Services, Jackson, Mich., 1979-82, Legal Aid of Central Mich., Lansing, 1982-83, UAW-GM Legal Services Plan, Lansing, 1983—. Organizer Westside Neighborhood Assn., Lansing, 1981-83. Mem. Nat. Lawyers Guild (pres. 1982, State Bar Mich. (defender services and systems com. 1982-84). Office: UAW-GM Legal Services Plan 417 Seymour Ave Suite 6 Lansing MI 48933

SCHAEFFER, GERALD, educational administrator; b. Boonville, Mo., Nov. 13, 1945; s. Hugo Eugene and Mary Lou (Hale) S.; Ph.D., U. Mo.-St. Louis, 1978. Instr. psychology St. Louis Community Coll., Florissant Valley, Mo., 1975-78; chmn. dept. psychology Blackburn Coll., Carlinville, Ill., 1979-81; assoc. dean instrn. St. Louis Community Coll., Florissant Valley, Mo., 1981—. Mem. Ferguson (Mo.) Planning Commn. Served with U.S. Army, 1965-69. Mem. Am. Psychol. Assn., Midwest Psychol. Assn., Mo. Vocat. Assn., Mo. Acad. Sci. Home: 1216 Stein Rd Ferguson Acres MO 63135 Office: 3400 Pershall Rd Saint Louis MO 63135

SCHAFF, HARTZELL VERNON, cardiac surgeon; b. Holdenville, Okla., Feb. 24, 1948; s. Hartzell Vernon and Ruth N. (Stuckey) S.; m. Voni Faith Schafer, Mar. 3, 1973; children—Brynn, Leslie, Sarah, Matthew. Student U. Okla., 1966-69, M.D., 1973. Diplomate Am. Bd. Surgery, Am. Bd. Thoracic Surgery. Intern dept. surgery Johns Hopkins Hosp., Balt., 1973-74, asst. resident, 1974-75, fellow cardiovascular surg. research lab., 1975-76, sr. asst. resident, 1976-78, resident cardiac and thoracic surgery, 1978-80; cons. thoracic and cardiovascular surgery, asst. prof. surgery Mayo Med. Sch., Rochester, Minn., 1980—. Recipient L.G. Moorman award, 1973; George D. Zuidema Resident Research award, 1980. Fellow ACS, Am. Coll. Cardiology, Assn. for Acad. Surgery, Am. Heart Assn., Soc. Univ. Surgeons, Soc. for Thoracic Surg. Edn., Sigma Xi, Phi Eta Sigma, Alpha Omega Alpha. Republican. Episcopalian. Contbr. articles to profl. jours., chpts. to books. Home: 425 SW 9th Ave Rochester MN 55902 Office: 200 1st St SW Mayo Clinic Rochester MN 55905

SCHAFFER, EDWARD VINCENT, orthopedic surgeon, educator; b. N.Y.C., Nov. 17, 1924; s. Arthur E. and Mary L. (Reagan) S.; m. Mary Jo Carroll, Jan. 21, 1977; 1 dau., Paula. B.S., Manhattan Coll., 1944; M.D., N.Y. Coll. Medicine, 1948. Diplomate Am. Bd. Orthopedic Surgery. Intern, City Hosp., N.Y.C., 1948-49; resident Ind. U. Med. Ctr., Indpls., 1952-55; practice medicine, specializing in orthopedic surgery, Indpls.; mem. faculty Ind. U.Med. Ctr., 1957—, prof., 1963—; chmn. dept. orthopedic surgery Community Hosp., 1982—. Mem. Mayor's Adv. Staff for Pub. Safety. Served to maj. M.C., USAF, 1950-53. Mem. Am. Acad. Orthopedic Surgeons, Clin. Orthopedic Soc., Ind. Orthopedic Soc. Roman Catholic. Club: Skyline. Contbr. articles to profl. jours. Home: 4524 W 131st St Westfield IN 46074 Office: 5626 E 16th St Indianapolis IN 46218

SCHAFFER, HARWOOD DAVID, clergyman; b. Dayton, Ohio, Oct. 15, 1944; s. Phillip David and H. Ruth (Scheid) S.; B.S. in Math., Ohio State U., 1965; M.Div., Hartford Sem. Found., 1969; m. Polly Anna Francis, May 6, 1983; children—Rosita, Virginia, Chandra, Karen, Amy, Laura. Ordained to ministry United Ch. of Christ, 1969; chaplain, tchr. Austin Sch., Hartford, Conn., 1967-71; asst. pastor S. Congl. Ch., Middletown, Conn., 1967-71; pastor Trinity United Ch. of Christ, Hudson, Kans., 1971-79, Emma Lowery United Ch. of Christ, Luzerne, Mich., 1979-82, First Congregational United Ch. of Christ and Scambler Union United Ch. of Christ, Pelican Rapids, Minn., 1982—; area counselor 17/76 Achievement Fund of United Ch. of Christ, 1974-75; mem. Western Assn. council Kans.-Okla. Conf., United Ch. of Christ, 1971-74, 76-79, sec.-treas., 1971-74, chmn. ch. and ministry com., 1976-79; mem. various bds. Mich. Conf., United Ch. of Christ, 1979-82; Am. camp mgr. Joint Archaeol. Expdn. to Tel Aphek/Antipatris, Israel, 1978, 80. Bd. govs. Austin Sch., Hartford, 1970-71; mem. Stafford County Democratic Central Com., 1976-79, Oscoda County Dem. Com., 1980-82; mem. Stafford Council Overall Econ. Devel. Planning Com., 1976-79, chmn., 1977-79; mem. Oscoda County Housing Commn., 1979-82. Club: Rotary. Home: 321 1st St SE Pelican Rapids MN 56572 Office: PO Box 313 Pelican Rapids MN 56572

SCHAFFER, JACK, state senator; b. Chgo., Oct. 12, 1942; s. Raymond and Francis (Barter) S.; divorced; children—Neal, Todd, Ryan. B.S., No. Ill. U., 1965. Plant mgr. Oak Mfg. Co., Crystal Lake, Ill., 1967-68; auditor McHenry County, Ill., 1968-72; U.S. senator from Ill., 1972—, Rep. caucus chmn., 1985—. Served to sgt. U.S. Army, 1965-67. Lodge: Rotary. Office: 56 N Williams St Crystal Lake IL 60014

SCHAFFER, THEODORE RICHARD, clergyman; b. Phila., Apr. 30, 1932; s. Warren Holcomb and Anna Elizabeth (Hess) S.; m. Marian Suzanne Shaffer, Dec. 17, 1955; children—James Warren, Marian Elizabeth, Heather Ruth. B.A., Gettysburg Coll., 1958; B.Div., Luth. Sch. Theology, Gettysburg, 1961. Ordained to ministry Lutheran Ch., 1961. Pastor Calvary Luth. Parish, Hempstead, Md., 1961-64, St. Matthew Luth. Ch., Kitchener, Ont., Can., 1964-73, Emanuel Luth. Ch., Bradford, Pa., 1973-84; pastor, dir. pub. relations and devel. Shepherd of the Valley Luth. Home and Retirement Ctr., Niles, Ohio, 1984—; mem. faculty Waterloo Luth. Sem., Ont., part-time, 1968-72; pres. Kitchener-Waterloo Council Chs., 1967-71; campus pastor U. Pitts.-Bradford, 1973-83; sec.-treas. Coalition of Ohio Luth. Agys., 1984—; cons. for pub. relations and fund devel. Scoutmaster Boy Scouts Am., East Lansdowne, Pa., 1951-54; sec. Jr. C. of C., Hempstead, 1962-64; mem. Bradford Area Sch. Bd., 1978-82, Niles Recovery Coalition for Tornado Relief. Mem. Assn. Luth. Devel. Execs. Republican. Avocations: gardening; model trains; home handyman. Home: 3950 Longhill Dr Se Warren OH 44484 Office: Shepherd of the Valley Lutheran Home and Retirement Center 1462 Hillcrest Dr Apt 4 Niles OH 44446

SCHAFFER, THOMAS ALAN, lawyer; b. Cleve., June 28, 1947; s. Wilbur Eugene and Dorothy Jane (Kershaw) S.; m. Gail Helen Scarborough, Aug. 23, 1970 (div. 1975); m. Susan Elizabeth Most, Sept. 24, 1977; 1 son, Griffin Thomas. B.A. in History, U. Mich., 1969; J.D., U. Cin., 1972. Bar: Ohio. Assoc. Graham, Schaffer & West, Cin., 1972-76; pub. defender Dayton, Ohio, 1976-78; sole practice law, Dayton, 1978-83; mem. firm Sutton, Overholser & Schaffer, Dayton, 1983—. Served to capt. USAF, 1969-73. Mem. Nat. Assn. Criminal Def. Lawyers, Ohio Bar Assn., Dayton Bar Assn. (chmn. criminal law com. 1980-82), Ohio Acad. Trial Lawyers, Assn. Trial Lawyers Am. Avocations: skiing; music; golf; tennis. Home: 641 Ridgedale Rd Dayton OH 45406 Office: Sutton Overholser & Schaffer 1700 First National Plaza Dayton OH 45402

SCHAIBLE, TODD DOUGLAS, administrator, clinical psychologist; b. Hanover, Pa., Jan. 3, 1946; s. Wesley and Wilma Helen (Potts) S.; m. Carol Ann Clutter; 1 child, Trent Douglas. B.A., Clark U., 1968; M.A., W. Va. U., 1970, Ph.D., 1972. Lic. psychologist, Mo. Intern. Tex. Research Inst. Mental Health, Houston, 1971-72; program dir. Community Mental Health Ctr., Inc., Huntington, W.Va., 1972-74; ctr. dir. Rappahannock-Rapidan Mental Health Ctr., Culpeper, Va., 1974-76, exec. dir., 1976-77; exec. dir. Burrell Ctr., Springfield, Mo., 1977—; cons. adminstrn. and mktg. Contbr. articles to profl. jours. Mem. Pvt. Industry Adv. Council on Bus., Labor and Tng., Springfield, 1981-83; bd. dirs. Ozarks Regional council Boy Scouts Am., 1984-87. NIMH grantee; Alcohol and Drug Abuse Mental Health Adminstrn. grantee. 1973-82. Mem. Springfield C. of C. (bd. dirs. 1984—), Med. Group Mgmt. Assn., Assn. Mental Health Adminstrs., Mo. State Coalition Community Mental Health Ctrs. (sec.-treas. 1978-79, vice chmn. 1980, chmn. 1981-83). Methodist. Avocations: music, reading. Office: Burrell Ctr Inc PO Box 1611 SSS 1300 Bradford Pkwy Springfield MO 65805

SCHALM, VIRGINIA RUTH, educator, fiber artist, herberest; b. Highland Park, Mich., Mar. 23, 1945; d. Alfred Carl Frederick and Ruthanna (Brinkman) S. B.A., Western Mich. U., 1967, M.A., 1968. Cert. tchr., Mich. Life guard, instr. swimming WSI, City of Frankfort, Mich., 1966-67; tchr. art, phys. edn. Southfield Pub. Schs., Mich., 1967—, coach girls swim, 1968-79, coach girls volleyball, 1969-70, chmn. phys. edn. dept., 1978, 80; profl. spinner, weaver, dyer Clawson, Mich., 1981—; artist, herberist Sheep & Tepee, Clawson, 1981—. Prin. works include Jenny Lynn and pile woven rug, 1967, shown 1967-68 at Western Mich. U., olive texture woven coat, 1975, Jaguar Concours program cover design, 1976, Cat's Paws woven coverlet block, 1983, orange and brown strip woven afgan, 1985. Work featured in Jaguar Indicator of Mich. magazine, 1979. Recipient 1st, 2d, and 3d place awards, Most Improved award Jaguar Concours, 1977-84. Mem. Aerobic Internat. Research Soc. (top 10 swimmers 1979), Handweavers Guild of Am., Mich. League of Handweavers, Detroit Handweavers and Spinners (chmn. evening guild 1977-84), Benzie County Weavers and Spinners, Mich. Handspinners Guild (chmn. spinaround 1983—), Herb Assocs., Jaguar Affiliates Group of Mich., Les Amis du Vin (regional dir. 1979-81), Am. Wine Soc. (chmn. home wine making 1984-85). Avocations: wine; cars; swimming. Home: 1046 W Selfridge Blvd Clawson MI 48017 Office: Southfield High Sch 24675 Lasher Rd Southfield MI 48034

SCHAPER, LAURENCE TEIS, civil engineer; b. Beloit, Kans., Oct. 6, 1936; s. Harry Weber and Pauline (Teis) S.; married Marcia Sue Abmeyer, Aug. 20, 1960; children—Ross Michael, Neil Mitchell. B.S. In Agrl. Engring., Kans. State U., 1959; M.S.C.E., Stanford U., 1962; M.S. in Environ. Health Engring., U. Kans., 1968. Registered profl. engr., Ind., Kans., Ill., Mo., Md., Oreg., S.C., Calif. Jr. engr. Kans. Water Resources Bd., Topeka, 1959-60; jr. civil engr. Calif. Div. of Hwys., San Franciso, summer, 1961; civil engr. Black & Veatch Engrs.-Architects, Kansas City, Mo., 1962-84, ptnr., 1985—. Author: Transfer Station Chapter, 1985. Elder, Southminster Presbyterian Ch., 1966—; mem. adv. bd. Shawnee Mission Pub. Schs., Johnson County, Kans., 1973-78; city councilman City of Prairie Village (Kans.), 1978-82; bd. dirs. Pub. Service TV Sta., Kansas City, 1975-80. Served with USNR, 1959-68. Fellow ASCE (pres. Kansas City sect. 1975); mem. Am. Pub. Works Assn. (Kansas City met. chpt. pres. 1975), Am. Water Works Assn. (Mo. sect. chmn. 1985—), Mo. Soc. Profl. Engrs. (dir. 1981-83), Am. Acad. Environ. Engrs. (diplomate). Republican. Presbyn. Avocation: reading. Home: 4701 W 66th Terr Prairie Village KS 66208 Office: Black & Veatch Engrs-Architects 1500 Meadow Lake Pkwy Kansas City MO 64114

SCHARP, CAROL ANN, choreographer, educator; b. Ypsilanti, Mich., Aug. 9, 1940; d. John Lewis and Mary Vivian (Altherr) Keeney; m. Jack Laurel Scharp, June 14, 1958; children—Kathryn Elaine, Mark Aaron. Student ballet, Randazzo Studio, Ypsilanti, 1950-60, Harkness, Joffrey, Briansky and Eglevsky Schs., N.Y.C., 1960-83; student U. Mich., 1977; pvt. studies C. Flynn and Mme. Darvash, N.Y.C., 1982. Tchr. ballet Chapelle Sch., Ypsilanti, 1968; owner, dir. C.A.S. Ballet Theatre Sch., Ann Arbor, Mich., 1975—; dance dir., mem. steering com. Explorer Scouts, Boy Scouts Am., 1981; dir. Ann Arbor Ballet Theatre, Adrian Coll. Ballet Acad.; regional field judge Nat. Ballet Achievement Fund, 1983. Choreographer 17 prodns. including: Carnival of the Animals, 1982; Midsummer Night's Dream, 1982; Carmen, 1983; Beauty and the Beast, 1983; Nutcracker, 1983. Ruth Mott Fund grantee, 1983. Mem. Mich. Dance Assn., Washtenaw Council for Arts. Presbyterian. Office: 548 Church St Ann Arbor MI 48104*

SCHATZ, ALBERT GERARD, judge; b. Omaha, Aug. 4, 1921; s. Albert A. and Elizabeth C. (Howland) S.; A.B., Nebr. U., 1943; LL.B. Creighton U., 1948; m. Mary Jean Murray, Feb. 14, 1944 (dec. Aug. 1978); children—Gregory M., Thomas G., Philip H., Mary C., Ann L., Jane E.; m. 2d, Donna Reese Kennedy, June 30, 1980; stepchildren—E. Ann Walker, James A.C. Kennedy III, Catherine R. Kennedy, Michael R. Kennedy, Jean M. Kennedy. Admitted to Nebr. bar, 1948; law clk. to judge Ct. Appeals for 8th Circuit, Omaha, 1948-50; partner firm Gross, Welch, Vinardi, Kauffman & Schatz, Omaha, 1950-73; judge U.S. Dist. Ct. for Nebr., Omaha, 1973—. Mem. exec. com. Jud. Conf., from 1980. Served to capt. USMCR, 1943-46. Mem. Am., Omaha, Nebr. State bar assns., Am. Coll. Trial Lawyers, Am. Judicature Soc., Omaha Press Club, Sigma Nu. Republican. Roman Catholic. Clubs: Omaha Country, Rotary. Home: 8721 Capitol Ave Omaha NE 68114 Office: PO Box 607 Omaha NE 68101

SCHATZMAN, BARD IRWIN, psychologist, vocational resource educator; b. St. Louis, Feb. 13, 1950; s. Herman Murray and Eugenia (Bierman) S.; m. Linda Sally Brasch, Mar. 22, 1980; 1 dau., Laura Ann. B.S., Westminster Coll., 1972; M.S., Central Mo. State U., 1974. Registered, lic. psychologist, Mo.; cert. tchr., Mo. Intern psychologist Farmington State Hosp. and Presbyn. Home for Children, 1974; clin. psychologist Fulton State Hosp. (Mo.), 1974-75; vol. Butterfield Youth Services, Marshall, Mo., 1976-78; clin. psychologist Marshall State Sch. and Hosp., 1976-79; clin. psychologist II, St. Louis Developmental Disabilities Treatment Ctr., 1979-80; surrogate parent Juludrive Ctr. for Autistic Children, St. Louis, 1980; cons. psychologist St. John's Mercy Med. Ctr. chem. dependency dept., 1979-81; psychologist Div. Family Services, St. Louis, 1979—; pvt. practice psychology, St. Louis, 1978—; asst. prof., vocat. resource educator and counselor disabled students St. Louis Community Coll., Forest Park, 1982—. Mem. Gov.'s Com. Employment of Handicapped, 1982—. Named Counselor of Yr., St. Louis Community Coll. at Forest Park, 1983. Mem. Am. Assn. Mental Deficiency, Am. Assn. Counseling and Devel., St. Louis Assn. Counseling and Devel. (pres. elect), Mo. Vocat. Spl. Needs Assn. (Outstanding Achievement award for Jr. Colls. 1984-85), Am. Psychol. Assn., Mo. Psychol. Assn., Soc. St. Louis Psychologists, Mo. Vocat. Assn., Mo. Vocat. Spl. Needs Assn., Assn. on Handicaped Student Services Program in Post-Secondary Edn., Mo. Coll. Personnel Assn., Assn. Labor-Mgmt. Adminstrs., Cons. on Alcoholism, ACLU. Jewish. Home: 6677 Berthold St Louis MO 63139-3318 Office: 5600 Oakland St Saint Louis MO 63110

SCHAUB, CALVIN JOHN, life insurance agent; b. Kewaskum, Wis., July 2, 1938; s. Calvin George and Verna Magdalena (Spoerl) S.; m. Patricia Ann Petzold, Aug. 19, 1961; children—Craig C., Mark F., Amy E. B.A. in German and Sociology, Lakeland Coll., Sheboygan, Wis., 1960; M.A. in German and Edn., U. Wis.-Madison, 1967; student German Inst., Lewis and Clark Coll., Munich, W.Ger., 1969; cert. audio-visual U. Wis.-Oshkosh, 1976. Tchr. German, Clinton Community Schs., Wis., 1960-63; tchr. German, Ripon Pub. Schs., Wis., 1963-82, audio-visual dir., 1975-82; self-employed carpenter, Ripon, Wis., 1969-84; ins. agt. Equitable Fin. Services, Ripon, 1982—. Pres. ch. council Our Saviour's United Ch. of Christ, Ripon, 1973-79; mem. ch. council, 1983—; advisor, v.p. Ripon chpt., cons. Am. Field Service, 1967—; gen. chmn. Ripon Area United Way, 1984; pres. Lakeland Coll. Alumni Assn. Bd., Sheboygan, Wis., 1980-82, Mem. Nat. Assn. Life Underwriters (nat. quality award 1984). Mem. Ch. of Christ. Club: Optimist (Ripon, Wis.) (pres. 1975-76). Lodge: Rotary. Avocations: carpentry; reading; camping; hiking; cross country skiing. Home: 411 Joy Ave Ripon WI 54971

SCHAUER, THOMAS ALFRED, insurance company executive; b. Canton, Ohio, Dec. 24, 1927; s. Alfred T. and Marie A. (Luthi) S.; B.Sc., Ohio State U., 1950; m. Joanne Alice Fay, Oct. 30, 1954; children—Alan, David, Susan, William. Ins. agt., Canton, 1951—; with Schauer & Reed Agy., 1951—, Kitzmiller, Tudor & Schauer, 1957—, Webb-Broda & Co., 1971—, Foglesong Agy., 1972—; pres. Ind. Ins. Service Corp. Akron, Dover and Canton, Canton, 1964—, Laurenson Agy., 1978—, Wells-Williams, 1978—, J.D. Craig Agy., 1981—dir. Central Trust Co. NE Ohio (N.A.). Chmn., Joint Hosp. Blood Com., 1974; bd. dirs. Better Bus. Bur., Canton, 1970—, chmn., 1979-80; bd. dirs. dist. YMCA, 1974, v.p., 1975-82, pres., 1982-84; bd. dirs. Hosp. Bur. Central Stark City, 1972-78; vice chmn. bd. Aultman Hosp., 1981-84, chmn., 1984—. JMS Found., 1968—; bd. dirs. United Way, 1974—, pres., 1976-78; mem. distbn. com. Stark County Found., 1977—, chmn. distbn. com.; 1984—; adv. bd. Malone Coll., 1979—; trustee Kent State U., 1980—, N.E. Ohio Univs. Coll. Medicine, 1983—; past trustee Canton Urban League, Boys Village (Smithville, Ohio), Canton Art Inst., Buckeye Council Boy Scouts Am. Served with USNR, 1946-48. C.L.U., C.P.C.U. Mem. Chartered Ins. Inst. London, Nat. Assn. Mfg., Am. Soc. C.P.C.U.'s, Am. Soc. C.L.U.s, Am. Mgmt. Assn., Assn. Advanced Life Underwriters, Am. Risk and Ins. Assn., Am. Soc. Pension Actuaries, Stark County Accident and Health Underwriters (past pres.). Clubs: Canton, Brookside Country, Atwood Yacht. Home: 1756 Dunbarton Dr NW Canton OH 44708 Office: Carnegie Library Bldg 236 3d St SW Canton OH 44702

SCHAUM, JAMES HOWARD, hospital administrator; b. Lodi, Ohio, Apr. 4, 1946; s. Howard Leroy and Effie Irene (Jacot) S.; m. Kathryn Anderson, June 20, 1970; children—Jonathan James, Benjamin Anderson, Robert Howard. B. in Pharmacy, West Va. U., 1969; M.S. in Hosp. and Health Service Adminstrn., Ohio State U., 1979. Registered pharmacist, Ohio, Ind. Pharmacist, store mgr. Revco Discount Drug Stores, Van Wert, Ohio, 1969-71, Akron, Ohio, 1972, Massillon, Ohio, 1972-73, Wooster, Ohio, 1973-77; asst. adminstr. profl. services Med. Center Hosp., Chillicothe, Ohio, 1979-83, assoc. adminstr., 1983-84, sr. assoc. adminstr., 1985—. Pres. YMCA, 1982, 83; mem. ARC. Named Jaycee of the Yr., 1982, Outstanding Dist. Dir. Mem. Am. Coll. Hosp. Adminstrs., Am. Hosp. Assn., Ohio Hosp. Assn., Central Ohio Health Adminstrs. Assn. Republican. Presbyterian. Clubs: Elks, Jaycees (assoc., past state dir., treas.), Rotary. Home: 377 Shannon Dr Chillicothe OH 45601 Office: Medical Center Hospital 272 Hospital Rd Chillicothe OH 45601

SCHEALL, JACK JAMES, air purification company executive; b. Saginaw, Mich., Dec. 15, 1920; s. Jacob and Lena (Fischer) S.; m. Norma Leitow, Oct. 11, 1941; children—Theodore J. B.A., Ind. No. U., 1974. Exec. Boy Scouts Am., Saginaw, Mich. Mt. Pleasant, Mich., Charleston, W.Va., Georgetown,

Ohio, Cin., Lima, Ohio, 1956-68; bus. dir. Jr. Achievement, Indpls., 1968-73, exec. dir., Wichita, Kans., 1973-82; bus. owner Air Purification Kans., Wichita, 1982—. Served with C.E., U.S. Army, 1943-46, PTO. Club: Model A (Wichita). Lodges: Kiwanis (pres. 1979-80, lt. gov. 1978-79), Masons. Avocation: restoration of historic homes. Home: 1063 N Market St Wichita KS 67214 Office: Air Purification Kans 1063 N Market St Wichita KS 67214

SCHEANWALD, MARJORIE DIANA, medical office administrator; b. Toledo, Sept. 27, 1926; d. August G. and Henrietta H. (Helbing) S.; student public schs., Saginaw, Mich. Bookkeeping machine operator Sugar Beet Products, Gen. Office, Saginaw, 1944-46; bookkeeping machiner operator Heavenrich's, Saginaw, 1946-53, sec. to pres., 1953-56; receptionist/sec. pvt. med. office, Saginaw, 1956-72; office mgr., asst. corp. sec. Valley Ob-Gyn Clinic, Saginaw, 1972—, also dir. Mem. Med. Group Mgrs. Assn., Am. Assn. Med. Assts., Mich. Med. Group Mgmt. Assn. Republican. Presbyterian. Home: 311 S Wheeler St Saginaw MI 48602 Office: 926 N Michigan St Box 3216 Saginaw MI 48605

SCHEELE, ROY MARTIN, educator; b. Houston, Jan. 10, 1942; s. Elmer Martin and Hazel Ilene (McChesney) S.; m. Frances McGill Hazen, June 26, 1965; children—Evan Mathew, Christof Andrew. B.A., U. Nebr., 1965, M.A. in English, 1971; postgrad. U. Tex.-Austin, 1965-66. Instr. English, U. Tenn., Martin, 1966-68; research librarian Weldon Kees collection Bennett Martin Pub. Library, Lincoln, Nebr., 1969-70; instr. English, Theodor Heuss Gymnasium, Waltrop, W. Ger., 1974-75; lectr. Classics, Creighton U., 1977-79; vis. instr. Classics, U. Nebr., Lincoln, 1980-81; instr. English as a second lang. Midwest Inst. for Internat. Studies, Doane Coll., Crete, Nebr., 1982—; poet-in-the-schs. program, Nebr. Arts Council, 1976—. Pres. Lincoln chpt. Save the Niobrara River Assn., 1980-81. Recipient Ione Gardner Noyes poetry awards U. Nebr., Lincoln, 1962, 64; 1st prize for poetry John G. Neihardt Found., 1983. Mem. Nebr. Tchrs. English to Speakers of Other Langs./Nebr. Assn. Bi-lingual Educators, Royal Oak Found., Smithsonian Assocs., Nature Conservancy. Democrat. Presbyterian. Author: (poetry) Grams and Epigrams, 1973; Accompanied, 1974; Noticing, 1979; The Sea-Ocean, 1981; Pointing Out the Sky, 1985. Home: 2020 S 25th St Lincoln NE 68502

SCHEFF, RONALD KEVIN, marketing executive; b. Springfield, Ohio, Apr. 13, 1943; s. Edwin V. and Gladys P. (Lineback) S.; m. Carol S. Fry; children—Sheryl, Robert, Catherine. Assoc. Engring. Tech., U. Toledo, 1966, B.B.A., 1971; M.B.A., Bowling Green State U., 1980. Process engr. Dana Corp., Toledo, Ohio, 1966-73, mfg. supr., Northwood, Ohio, 1973-75, project coordinator, Ottawa Lake, Mich., 1975-77, account mgr., Southfield, Mich., 1977-80, mgr. new market devel., Ft. Wayne, Ind., 1980-82; mktg. mgr. Auburn Gear Inc., Ind., 1982—. Asst. scout master Fort Wayne council Boy Scouts Am., 1981-84, also chmn. advancement com. Mem. Soc. Automotive Engrs. Lutheran. Club: Auburn Gear Employees (pres. 1983-84). Avocations: golfing, boating, swimming, camping, bridge. Office: Auburn Gear Inc Auburn Dr Auburn IN 46706

SCHEHL, DAVID ALTON, artist, educator; b. Wheeling W.Va., June 21, 1947; s. Wilbert A. and Grace Ellen (Garrett) S.; m. Pamela K. Shutt, July 27, 1974. B.A., Malone Coll., 1974; M.A., Ohio U., 1980. Cert. visual art instr., Ohio, Pa., Colo., W.Va. Gallery asst. Canton (Ohio) Art Inst., 1972-74; instr. art high schs., 1974-79, 1980-82, Ohio U., Athens, 1979-80; comml. artist Anthony Art & Advt., Coyne Printing Inc., 1970—; free lance comml. artist, 1970—, Mill View Studio, 1983—. Served with U.S. Army, 1966-68; Vietnam. Decorated Bronze Star. Mem. Profl. Arts Assn. Canton, Canton Art Inst. (hon.), Ohio Assn. Supervision and Curriculum Devel., Ohio Arts and Crafts Guild, Knox County Hist. Soc. Home: 310 Smith Ave NW Canton OH 44708

SCHELKOPF, RUSSELL LEROY, veterinarian; b. Geneva, Nebr., June 30, 1930; s. Isaac Newton and Lena Mildred (Schrock) S.; student Nebr. Wesleyan U., 1947-48; B.S., U. Nebr., 1952, M.S., 1954; Ph.D., Iowa State U., 1958, D.V.M., 1958; m. Bernice Elaine Nuss, Aug. 26, 1951; children—Michael, Charles, Steven. Veterinarian, Hall Vet. Clinic, Elburn, Ill., 1958-59; pvt. practice vet. medicine, Sycamore, Ill., 1959—. Pres., Illini Farms, Inc., Sycamore, 1970—, Schelkopf, D.V.M., Sycamore, 1970—; sec.-treas. Cornhusker Agr. Assos., Inc., Shickley, Nebr., 1969—; sec. Cornhusker Cattle Co., Shickley, 1971—. NSF fellow, 1954-58. Mem. Am., Ill. vet med. assns., Ill. C. of C. Home: 229 Somonauk St Sycamore IL 60178 Office: Bethany Rd Sycamore IL 60178

SCHELL, DAVID LAURENCE, health care administrator; b. Cleve., Dec. 16, 1954; s. Paul Lewis and Winifred Rose (Cermak) S.; m. Annette G. Lorenz, June 5, 1976; children—Joshua David, Jeremy Ryan. B.S. in Health Services Mgmt., Ferris State Coll., 1977; M.B.A., Grand Valley State Coll., 1983. Lic. nursing home adminstr., Mich. Mental health adminstr. Cambridge Devel. Ctr., Ohio, 1977-78; facilities planner Cambridge Mental Health & Devel. Ctr., 1978-81; adminstr. Meadowbrook Care Ctr., Holland, Mich., 1981-82; dir., adminstr. Resthaven Patrons, Inc., Holland, Mich., 1982—; adminstrv. intern Reed City Hosp., Mich., 1977; gerontology instr. Muskingum Tech. Coll., Zanesville, Ohio, 1980. Mem. Mich. Non-Profit Homes Assn. (com. chmn.), Am. Hosp. Assn., Mich. Gerontology Assn., Holland Area C. of C. (rep.). Republican. Club: Golconda Investment (asst. fin. advisor). Avocations: sailing; skiing. Home: 197 W 21st St Holland MI 49423 Office: Resthaven Patrons Inc 5 E 8th St Holland MI 49423

SCHELLHAMMER, THERESE ANN, lawyer; b. Washington, D.C., June 3, 1955; d. Rudolph Matthew and Alberta Myree (Towery) S. A.A., Prince George's Community Coll., 1975; B.S., U. Md., 1977; J.D., U. Mo., 1980. Bars: Mo. 1980, U.S. Dist. Ct. (ea. dist.) Mo. 1980. Staff atty. S.E.Mo. Legal Services, Poplar Bluff, 1980-81; assoc. Little, Million & Terando, Poplar Bluff, 1981-83; ptnr. Little, Million, Terando & Schellhammer & Assocs., Poplar Bluff, 1983—. Mem. Mo. Trial Lawyers Assn., Assn. Trial Lawyers Am., Nat. Orgn. Soc. Security Claimants Reps. Roman Catholic. Office: Little Million Terando Schellhammer & Assocs PO Box 518 Poplar Bluff MO 63901

SCHEMA, DOUGLAS, educator; b. Rapid City, S.D., Dec. 3, 1953; s. Ernest Anton and Nima (Bursik) S. B.A. in History and Art, Bellevue Coll., 1977; M.A., U. Mo., 1981; postgrad. Creighton U., 1982. Mfrs. rep. Midwest Supply Co., Des Moines, 1974-75; library staff U. Nebr., Omaha, 1977-79; staff supr. Health Scis. Library, Creighton U., 1979-81; teaching asst. Am. History Studies, U. Mo., Columbia, 1979-81; instr. European history Bellevue Coll., 1981-82; instr. continuing edn. div. U. Nebr., Omaha, 1983—. Contbr. articles to profl. jours. Tech. Advisor Dakota Territorial Mus., 1981-84; mem. speakers bur. Nishnabotna Girl Scout Council. Named Toastmaster of Yr., 1976. Mem. Illuminating Engring. Soc. North Am., State Hist. Soc. Mo., Nat. Trust for Historic Preservation. Methodist. Lodge: Toastmasters (pres. 1974). Home: 711 Grace St Council Bluffs IA 51501

SCHEMBECHLER, GLENN EDWARD (BO), See *Who's Who in America,* 43rd edition.

SCHEMMEL, JEFFREY WILLIAM, lawyer; b. Sioux Falls, S.D., Feb. 19, 1954; s. O. William and Shirlee (Buckmeier) S.; m. Lori Lee Wenk, July 16, 1977; children—Justin William, Jonathan Ray. B.S., Kans. State U., 1976; J.D., Washburn U., 1979. Bar: Kans. 1979, U.S. Dist. Ct. Kans. 1979, U.S. Ct. Appeals (10th cir.) 1979. Corr., Time Mag., summer 1976; law clk. Sabatini Law Firm, Topeka, 1977-79, assoc., 1979-82; head track coach Washburn U., Topeka, 1979-80; mem. Hannah, Waggener, Vinent, Wright & Schemmel, Topeka, 1982-83; sole practice, Topeka, 1983—. Bd. cereal malt beverage lic. rev. City of Topeka, 1984—; pres. Quail Creek Home Owners Assn., Topeka, 1978-79; treas. Topeka Baseball Fedn., 1982—. Recipient Bik 8 Scholarship Medallion, Kans. State U., 1975-76. Mem. ABA, Kans. Bar Assn., Assn. Trial Lawyers Am., Kans. Trial Lawyers Assn., Phi Eta Sigma (Mike Ahearn award 1976), Jaycees. Democrat. Roman Catholic. Clubs: Cedar Crest Country. Home: 2118 Brookfield St Topeka KS 66614 Office: 510 W 10th St Topeka KS 66612

SCHEMMEL, RACHEL ANNE, food science and human nutrition educator, researcher; b. Farley, Iowa, Nov. 23, 1929; d. Frederic August and Emma Margaret (Melchert) Schemmel. B.A., Clarke Coll., 1951; M.S., U. Iowa, 1952; Ph.D., Mich. State U., 1967. Dietitian, Children's Hosp. Soc., Los Angeles, 1952-54; instr. Mich. State, U., East Lansing, 1955-63, from asst. prof. to prof. food sci., human nutrition, 1967—. Author: Nutrition Physiology and Obesity, 1980. Contbr. articles on obesity, clin. nutrition to profl. jours. Recipient Disting. Alumni award Mt. Mercy Coll., 1971. Mem. Am. Inst. Nutrition, Inst. Food Technologists, Am. Diet Assn. (pres. Mich. and Lansing 1975-76), Brit. Nutrition Soc., Soc. for Nutrition Edn. Roman Catholic. Home: 1341 Red Leaf Ln East Lansing MI 48823 Office: Dept Food Sci and Human Nutrition Dept Pediatrics Mich State U East Lansing MI 48824

SCHENCK, HANS UWE, chemical company executive; b. Munich, Germany, Aug. 24, 1942; came to U.S., 1981; s. Gerhard and Anna Amanda (Joeckel) S.; m. Gabriele Damm, May 5, 1967; children—Sandra Bettina, Corinna Elena. B.S., Free U. Berlin, 1964, Ph.D., 1969; M.S., Tech. U. Stuttgart (Germany), 1967. Research asst. Free U. Berlin, 1969-70; mem. research staff BASFAG, Ludwigshafen, Germany, 1970-75, group leader polymeric auxs. research and devel., 1975-77, group leader coating resin research and devel., 1977-81; v.p. research and devel. BASF Wyandotte Corp., Parsippanny, N.J., 1981—. Mem. adv. com. Mich. Molecular Inst. Mem. Am. Chem. Soc., Indsl. Research Inst., Soc. Chem. Industry, Comml. Devel. Assn., Sigma Xi. Club: Gross Ile (Mich.) Golf and Country. Contbr. articles to profl. jours.; patentee in field.

SCHENK, BOYD F., diversified corporation executive. Pres., chief operating officer IC Industries, Inc., Chicago; chmn. Pet, Inc., subs., St. Louis. Office: IC Industries Inc One Illinois Ctr Chicago IL 60601*

SCHENK, QUENTIN FREDERICK, social worker, psychologist, educator; b. Ft. Madison, Iowa, Aug. 25, 1922; s. Fred Edward John and Ida Margaret Caroline (Sabrowsky) S.; B.A., Willamette U., 1948; M.S., U. Wis., 1950, M.S.S.W., Ph.D., 1953; m. Emmy Lou Willson, May 23, 1970; children—Fred (dec. 1972), Patricia, Karl, Martha. Asst. prof. U. Wis., Madison, 1953-55; assoc. prof. U. Mo., Columbia, 1955-61; Fulbright sr. lectr., Italy, 1959-60; prof., chmn. dept. social work U. Wis., Milw., 1961-63, dean Sch. Social Welfare, 1963-68, co dir. U. Wis. project to Brazil, specialist Ford Found., Addis Ababa, 1968-71; spl., cons. World Council Chs., Africa, 1971; prof. social welfare U. Wis., Milw., 1971—; pvt. practice social psychology, 1971—; lectr., cons. Alderman, City of Cedarburg, Wis., 1975-81, mayor, 1981-85; mem. Cedarburg Planning Commn., Public Works Commn., Landmark Preservation Soc., bd. dirs. Milw. Central City Shelter. Served with USNR, 1942-46. Decorated 3 Air medals, D.F.C. Knapp grad. fellow, 1950. Mem. Am. Sociol. Assn., AAUP, Council Social Work Edn., Aircraft Owners Pilots Assn., Am. Legion, Cedarburg Fireman's Assn., Nat. Trust Hist. Preservation. Author: (with E.L. Schenk) Pulling Up Roots, 1978; Welfare, Society and the Helping Professions, 1981. Contbr. articles profl. jours. Home: Box 31 W61 N439 Washington St Cedarburg WI 53012 Office: U Wis Milwaukee WI 53201

SCHENK, RICHARD BUTLER, II, pathologist; b. Cleve., July 20, 1949; s. Richard Butler and Rosaneil (Reynolds) S.; m. Jeanne Annette Palzkill, Jan. 1, 1977; children—Melissa, Tyler. B.A., Wesleyan U., Middletown, Conn., 1971; M.D., Stanford U., 1975. Diplomate Am. Bd. Pathology. Intern, then resident Stanford U. Hosp., Calif., 1975-77; fellow in pathology M.D. Anderson Hosp., Houston, 1977-79; resident St. Luke's Episcopal Hosp., Houston, 1979-80; pathologist Carle Clinic Assn., Urbana, Ill., 1980—; med. adv. bd. Champaign County Regional Health Resources Ctr., Urbana, Ill., 1983—. Commr. Urbana Plan Commn., Ill., 1983; bd. dirs. Am. Cancer Soc., Champaign, Ill., 1981—; committeeman Champaign County Republicans, Ill., 1982-83. Fellow Internat. Acad. Pathology, Coll. Am. Pathologists, Am. Soc. Clin. Pathologists; mem. AMA, Ill. State Med. Soc. Club: Champaign Country. Avocations: golf; literature. Office: Carle Clinic Assn 602 W University Ave Urbana IL 61801

SCHENKEN, JERALD RUDOLPH, pathologist, educator; b. Detroit, Oct. 11, 1933; s. John Rudolph and Lucile (Jerald) S.; m. Charlotte Elizabeth Sutherland Parker, Aug. 8, 1959; children—John Rudolph II, Elizabeth Jerald, Thomas Parker. B.A., Tulane U., 1954, M.D., 1958. Diplomate Am. Bd. Pathology, Spl. Comp. in Clin. Chemistry. Resident in pathology Charity Hosp., New Orleans, 1959-63, assoc. pathologist, 1963-65; pathologist Methodist and Children's Hosp., Omaha, 1965-74, dir. dept., 1974—; pres. Pathology Ctr., P.C., Omaha, 1981—; instr. Tulane U. Med. Sch., 1962-65; instr. U. Nebr. Coll. Medicine, 1965-67, asst. prof., 1967-72, assoc. prof., 1972-75, mem. grad. faculty, 1975—, clin. prof. pathology, 1975—; clin. prof. pathology Creighton U. Sch. Medicine, Omaha, 1978—; pres. Am. Bd. Pathology, 1983-84; mem. med. devices standards mgmt. bd. Am. Nat. Standards Inst., 1978-82, mem. exec. com., 1980-82. Mem. editorial bd. Human Pathology, 1976-78, Am. Jour. Clin. Pathology, 1976-79, 81—. Editor Nebr. Med. Jour., 1982—, CAPitol SCAN, 1980-82, also monographs on pathology of lab. animals, 1982—. Editor: (with J.B. Fuller) Instrumentation Workshop Manual, 1967; (with others) Laboratory Instrumentation, 1980; Clinical Pathology Case Studies, 3d edit., 1975. Contbr. articles to profl. jours. Mem. Nebr. State Nursing Home Adv. Council, 1982-83; bd. dirs. Nebr. Meth. Hosp. Found., 1983—; mem. pres.'s adv. council U. Nebr., 1984—; vice-chmn. com. White House Conf. on Aging, 1981; mem. adv. com. Office of Tech. Assessment, 1984—. Fellow ACP, Am. Soc. Clin. Pathologists, Coll. Am. Pathologists; mem. Coll. Am. Pathologists (Pathologist of Yr. 1983, nat. legis. com. 1971-80, chmn. 1972-80), Am. Soc. Clin. Pathologists (chmn. council clin. chemistry 1969-71, commn. edn. 1982—), Nebr. Assn. Pathologists (pres. 1971-72), Met. Omaha Med. Soc. (chmn. program com. 1971-72, 83—, exec. bd. 1982—, legis. com. 1970-72), Nebr. Med. Assn., AMA (vice-chmn. council legis. 1982-84, chmn. 1984—), Am. Assn. Blood Banks, Am. Soc. Cytology, Internat. Acad. Pathology, Internat. Life Scis. Inst., Soc. Pediatric Pathology, Alpha Omega Alpha. Republican. Episcopalian. Avocations: tennis; golf. Home: 115 N 54th St Omaha NE 68132 Office: PO Box 14424 Omaha NE 68114

SCHERER, VICTOR RICHARD, physicist; b. Poland, Feb. 7, 1940; came to U.S., 1941, naturalized, 1951; s. Emanuel and Florence B. Scherer; B.S. magna cum laude, CCNY, 1960; M.A., Columbia U., 1962; Ph.D., U. Wis., Madison, 1974; m. Gail R. Dobrofsky, Aug. 11, 1963; children—Helena Cecille, Markus David. Health physics asst. Columbia U., N.Y.C., 1961-63; research asst. dept. physics U. Wis., Madison, 1967-74, project asso., project mgr. Inst. for Environ. Studies, World Climate-Food Research Group, 1974-78, specialist computer systems Acad. Computing Center, 1978—; concert pianist; tchr., promoter contemporary composers. AEC fellow, 1960-61. Mem. Am. Phys. Soc., Am. Meteorol. Soc., Am. Soc. Agronomy, Assn. Computing Machinery, Nat. Computer Graphics Assn., AAAS, Sigma Xi, Phi Beta Kappa. Researcher in particle physics, agroclimatology, soil-yield relationships and computer graphics. Office: Academic Computing Center U Wis Madison WI 53706

SCHERICH, ESTHER ANNE, educator, editor; b. New Haven, Dec. 15, 1943; d. Millard and Esther (Petersen) Scherich; B.A., Oreg. State U., 1966; M.A., U. Oreg., 1970, D.Arts, 1973, Ph.D., 1975. Sec. dept. English, U. Oreg., Eugene, 1966-69, research asst., 1969-70, teaching fellow in English, 1970-75; manuscript editor Moody Bible Inst., 1977-83, 84—; vis. asst. prof. English, Wheaton (Ill.) Coll., 1983-84. Mem. Women in Communications, Am. Bus. Women's Assn., MLA, Am. Soc. Eighteenth Century Studies, Conf. on Christianity and Lit., P.E.O., Kappa Delta. Republican. Episcopalian. Home: 821 N Washington Wheaton IL 60187 Office: Moody Bible Inst 820 N LaSalle St Chicago IL 60610

SCHERMER, LLOYD G., publishing company executive. Pres., dir. Lee Enterprises, Inc., Davenport, Iowa. Office: Lee Enterprises Inc 130 E 2nd St Davenport IA 52801*

SCHERNITZKI, PAUL THOMAS, hospital pharmacy administrator; b. Omaha, Sept. 22, 1951; s. Thomas G. and Edith A. S.; m. Ann Maria Chappell, Aug. 18, 1973; children—Rebecca Ann, Paul Scott. B.S. in Pharmacy, U. Mo.-Kansas City, 1974; M.S. in Pharmacy, U. Ariz., 1979. Registered pharmacist, Mo., Iowa, S.D., Ariz. Staff pharmacist Methodist Med. Ctr., St. Joseph, Mo., 1974-78; postgrad. resident Ariz. Health Scis. Ctr., Tucson, 1978-79; dir. pharmacy Des Moines Gen. Hosp., 1979-85; dir. pharmacy Rushmore Nat. Health Systems, Rapid City, S.D., 1985—; mem. pharmacy adv. bd. Iowa Healthcare Purchasing Council, Am. Healthcare Systems. Am. Assn. Poison Control Ctrs. research fellow, 1978. Mem. Am. Soc. Hosp. Pharmacists. Lutheran. Office: 353 Fairmont Blvd Rapid City SD 57701

SCHERRMAN, EMMETT JOHN, leasing co. exec.; b. Farley, Iowa, Mar. 28, 1932; s. Francis Xavier and Mary Philomena (Kelly) S.; m. Mary Ann Barry, Jan. 29, 1953; children—Ellen A. Yaneff, Michael E., Jeffrey F., Mark B., Mary P. B.A., Loras Coll., 1953. With Scherrman Motor Co., Dyersville, Ind., 1955-57; with LeaseAmerica Corp., Cedar Rapids, Iowa, 1958—, pres., 1977—; mem. faculty Nat. Installment Banking Sch., U. Colo.; dir. Iowa Nat. Mut. Ins., Mid-Am. Mut. Fund, Inc., Mid-Am. High Growth Fund, Inc., Oak Hill Engring. Inc., MorAmerica Fin. Corp. Pres., United Way of Ea. Iowa; chmn. trustees Mt. Mercy Coll. Served with AUS, 1953-55. Mem. Am. Assn. Equipment Lessors (chmn. Ind. Constituent Forum). Republican. Roman Catholic. Clubs: Cedar Rapids Rotary, Cedar Rapids Country, Pickwick, K.C. (4th degree). Home: 3614 Bever Ave SE Cedar Rapids IA 52403 Office: 4333 Edgewood Rd NE Cedar Rapids IA 52499

SCHEU, JAMES RICHARD, appliance company official; b. Evansville, Ind., Mar. 3, 1944; s. Leo J. and Mary Ruth (Lannert) S.; m. Patricia Glenn Grant, Sept. 7, 1943; children—Teresa Ann, Tamara Kaye, Jeffrey Michael. B.A. in Chemistry, U. Evansville, 1969, M.B.A., 1972. Lab. technician Whirlpool Corp., Evansville, 1963-69, environ. engr., 1969-72, facilities and environ. engr., 1972-74, supr. quality lab., 1974-75, supr. final assembly quality control, quality engr., 1975-77, supr. customer assurance, 1977-80, mgr. customer assurance, 1980-82, dir. refrigeration group products, sales, 1982-84, mgr. retail mktg. Benton Harbor, Mich., 1984—. Contbr. numerous articles to profl. publs. Mem. vis. council Newburgh Medco Ctr., 1977; bd. dirs. Newburgh Youth Sports Assn.; pres. Soccer Bd., 1979-84. Mem. Am. Soc. Quality Control, Assn. Home Appliance Mfrs., Sigma Xi. Roman Catholic. Club: Whirlpool Management; Foremans. Office: 2000 US 33 N Benton Harbor MI 49022

SCHEUBLE, PHILIP ARTHUR, JR., controls and valve company executive, management consultant; b. N.Y.C., Sept. 25, 1919; s. Philip Arthur and Elsa (Kunkel) S.; m. Katharine Paul Aman, Jan. 19, 1946; children—James, Paul, Katharine, Pamela. B.Engring., CUNY, 1939; M.B.A., U. Toledo, 1950. Registered profl. engr., Ohio, Wis. Asst. group exec. A.O. Smith Corp., Milw., 1951-54, mgr. mfg. staff, 1954-57; with Vapor Corp. subs. Brunswick Co., Niles, Ill., 1957—, corp. v.p., 1959—, group exec., 1969-78; pres. GPE Controls Co., Morton Grove, Ill., 1978—; dir. Nihon Regulator Co., Tokyo. Mem. naval air adv. council Office Asst. Sec. Navy, 1949-62. Served to comdr. USNR, 1941-46. Mem. ASME, Am. Mktg. Assn., Indsl. Mktg. Assn. (chmn. 1967-68, pres. 1966-67), Sci. Apparatus Makers Assn. (dir.), Fgn. Policy Assn. N.Y. (dir.). Episcopalian. Clubs: Glenview (Golf, Ill.), Union League (Chgo.); Michigan Shores (Wilmette, Ill.). Office: 6511 W Oakton St Morton Grove IL 60053

SCHEURER, WILLIAM EDWIN, JR., psychologist; b. South Bend, Ind., Sept. 5, 1946; s. William Edwin and Patricia Jane (Felix) S.; m. Susan Lynn Mailloux, June 6, 1970; children—Katherine, Margaret. B.S., Ball State U., 1968, M.A., 1972; Ph.D., Mich. State U., 1977. Lic. psychologist, Mich. Probation officer Marion County Juvenile Ct., Indpls., 1968-72; therapist Starr Commonwealth for Boys, Albion, Mich., 1972-73; psychologist Ingham County Probate Ct., Lansing, Mich., 1973-77; psychologist Lansing Psychol. Assocs., East Lansing, Mich., 1977—; psychologist in pvt. practice. Mem. Am. Psychol. Assn., Mich. Psychol. Assn., Nat. Register for Health Service Providers in Psychology. Home: 1226 S Genesee Dr Lansing MI 48915 Office: Lansing Psychol Assocs East Lansing MI 48823

SCHEY, RALPH E., manufacturing executive; b. Cleve., 1924. B.S., Ohio U., 1948; M.B.A., Harvard U., 1950. Sales trainee Leisy Brewing Co., 1950-51; indsl. engr. Gen. Motors Corp., 1951; exec. v.p. Clevite Corp., 1951-69; pres. Joseph, Mellen & Miller Inc., 1969-71; venture capital activities, 1971-74; pres. and chief operating officer Scott & Fetzer Co., Cleve., 1974—, chmn. bd. and chief exec. officer, dir., 1974—, pres., 1985—; dir. Hauserman Co. Served with AUS 1943-45. Office: Scott & Fetzer Co Inc 28800 Clemens Rd Westlake OH 44145*

SCHIAPPACASSE, RICHARD HENRY, physician; b. Warren, Mich., June 9, 1948; s. Henry Louis and Eva (Kurdilla) S.; m. Dee Ann Lynn Houdek, Dec. 1, 1973; children—Michael, Angela. B.S., Wayne State U., 1969, M.D., 1973. Diplomate Am. Bd. Internal Medicine, Am. Bd. Tropical Medicine. Intern St. John's Hosp., Detroit, 1973, resident internal medicine 1973-76; fellow in infectious disease William Beaumont Hosp., Royal Oak, Mich., 1976-78; practice medicine Meml. Med. Ctr., Sterling Heights, Mich., 1978—; chief Div. Infectious Disease, Detroit Macomb Hosps., 1980—, chmn. infection control, 1979—; cons. Macomb County Health Dept., Mt. Clemens, Mich., 1978—. Author computer program First Aid, 1983; contbr. articles to profl. jours. Mem. Families for Children, Southfield, Mich., 1982—, Humane Soc. Southeastern Mich., 1983—. Haemophilus Grantee Eli Lily and Co., 1984. Fellow ACP; mem. AMA (Physican Recognition award 1977, 80, 83), Am. Coll. Tropical Medicine, Infectious Disease Soc. Am., Am. Soc. Internal Medicine, Phi Beta Kappa. Club: Mich. Atari Computer Enthusiasts (Southfield). Avocation: computers. Home: 12916 Easton Ct Utica MI 48087 Office: 36300 Van Dyke Sterling Heights MI 48077

SCHICK, JOSEPH SCHLUETER, educator; b. Davenport, Iowa, Mar. 23, 1910; s. Charles and Johannah (Schlueter) S.; grad. Browne and Nichols Sch., Cambridge, Mass., 1927; B.A., U. Iowa, 1931; M.A., U. Chgo., 1932, Ph.D., 1937. English instr. U. Iowa, 1935-36; prof. English, U. Minn.-Duluth, 1938-42, 45-46; lectr. Am. lit. Caserta Tech., Italy, 1945; Merit prof. English, Ind. State U., 1946-76. Served from pvt. to sgt. U.S. Army, 1942-45, cryptanalyst Signal Intelligence. Mem. Am. Assn. U. Profs., Modern Lang. Assn. Am., Iowa, Ind. hist. socs., Phi Sigma Iota, Blue Key. Author: The Early Theater in Eastern Iowa, 1939; also articles profl. jours. Exhibited paintings Swope Gallery, Terre Haute, 1953, 55, 79, 80. Patentee on cobber. Home: 248 S 26th St Dr Terre Haute IN 47803

SCHICK, ROBERT LEROY, fire chief; b. Davenport, Iowa, July 13, 1940; s. Lester Roy Schick and Annabel Marzee (Bonbrake) Kirkman; m. LaVern Florence Rhode, Aug. 9, 1960 (dec. June 1972); children—Sheryl Lee, Lynn Marie; m. Mary Louise Smith, Oct. 2, 1973. Student Palmer Jr. Coll., 1970, Scott Community Coll., 1976, Muscatine Community Coll., 1977. Chief Davenport Fire Dept., 1983—. Bd. dirs. Illowa chpt. ARC, Rock Island, Ill., 1983—. Mem. Internat. Assn. Fire Chiefs, Mo. Valley Fire Chiefs (state v.p. 1984—), Iowa Paid Fire Chiefs Assn., Nat. Fire Prevention Assn., Iowa Soc. Fire Service Instrs. (past bd. dirs.). Lutheran. Lodges: Rotary (com. chmn. 1985), Moose (bldg. chmn. 1965—). Home: 2230 W Columbia St Davenport IA 52804 Office: Davenport Fire Dept 331 Scott St Davenport IA 52801

SCHIFF, HERBERT HAROLD, See *Who's Who in America,* 43rd edition.

SCHIFMAN, EDWARD JOSEPH, marketing executive; b. Kansas City, Mo., Mar. 10, 1949; s. Herman H. and Dorothy (Price) S.; m. Vicki F. Wellner, Aug. 8, 1971; children—Michael Aaron, Lori Ann. B.F.A., U. Kans., 1972; M.B.A., Internat. U., 1978. Product coordinator Aladdin Industries, Nashville, 1972-76; mgr. devel. Kenner Products, Cin., 1976-78; product mgr. Clopay Corp., Cin., 1978-80; v.p. mktg. I.D.I., Kansas City, Kans., 1981-84, pres., 1984—. Patentee mailbox, game board apparatus (2), cart, mounted planter box. Recipient awards Samsonite Corp., Indsl. Design Soc. Am. Mem. Sales and Mktg. Execs. Republican. Jewish. Club: Kansas City (Mo.). Lodge: B'nai B'rith. Avocations: photography, weightlifting, woodworking. Home: 9017 W 113th St Overland Park KS 66210 Office: 5101 Richland Ave Kansas City KS 66106

SCHILLER, MARY ROSITA, allied health educator; b. Mich., June 14, 1936; d. Edmund Martin and Julia Catherine (Greiner) S.; B.S., Mercy Coll., Detroit, 1959; M.S., Mich. State U., 1966; Ph.D. (Hattie Margaret Anthony fellow, Mich. Home Econs. Assn. scholar, Mary Swartz Rose fellow, Hazel Williams Lapp fellow, provisional univ. dissertation yr. fellow), Ohio State U., Columbus, 1972. Joined Sisters of Mercy, Roman Cath. Ch., 1952; dietetic intern Henry Ford Hosp., Detroit, 1959-60; hosp. dietitian Mercy Community Hosp., Manistee, Mich., 1960-62; adminstrv. dietitian St. Lawrence Hosp., Lansing, Mich., 1962-66; from instr. to asso. prof. Mercy Coll., 1966-78, program dir. dietetics, 1972-78; prof. dietetics, dir. med. dietetics div. Ohio State U., Columbus, 1978—, also acting dir. Sch. Allied Med. Professions, 1983-85; pres. Detroit Dietetic Assn., 1969-70; chmn. nutrition com. Mich. Heart Assn., 1975-76; mem. task force dietetic edn. VA, 1975-77. Mem. Am. Dietetic Assn. (chmn. commn. accreditation 1978-79, program chmn. region IV council edn. 1975-76, editorial reviewer jour. 1975—; Mary Zahasky Meml. scholar 1977), Nutrition Today Soc., Am. Soc. Allied Health Professions, Soc. Nutrition Edn., Am. Soc. Health Manpower Edn. and Tng., Ohio Dietetic Assn. (chmn. 1980-81), Ohio Home Econs. Assn., Columbus Dietetics Assn. Author articles in field. Office: 1583 Perry St Columbus OH 43210

SCHILLHORN-VAN-VEEN, TJAART WILLEM, veterinary parasitology educator, college dean; b. Uithuizen, Netherlands, Dec. 6, 1940; came to U.S., 1979; m. Karla Suzanna, 1971. Student Agrl. U., Wageningen, Netherlands, 1958-61; D.V.Sci., State U. Utrecht, Netherlands, 1968, D.V.M., 1970, D.V. Sci., 1981. Postdoctoral fellow State U. Utrecht, 1970; vet. expert Fgn. Aid Dept., Netherlands, assigned to Zaria, Nigeria, 1970-78; vis. asst. prof. Mich State U., East Lansing, 1979-81, assoc. prof., 1981—, asst. dean Coll. Vet. Med., 1983—; co-founding dir. Probe-tek Inc., Lansing, Mich., 1982—; cons. in field. Contbr. articles to profl. jours. Pres. Dutch Vet. Student Orgn., Utrecht, Netherlands, 1966-67; founding sec. Nigerian Assn. Parasitology, 1977. Recipient agrl. and indsl. grants, 1975—. Mem. World Assn. Advancement of Vet. Parasitology, Am. Assn. Vet. Parasitology, AAAS, Overseas Devel. Inst. Club: Samaru Sports and Social (Zaria, Nigeria) (sec. 1974-76). Home: Haslett MI Office: Mich State U A-12 Vet Clinic East Lansing MI 48824

SCHILLING, JOHN MICHAEL, golf course association executive; b. Hiawatha, Kans., Nov. 23, 1951; s. George H. and Darlene J. (Wachter) S.; m. Pamela S. Hischke, Sept. 5, 1969; children—John II, James. Student Highland Coll., 1971-72; B.S. in Journalism, U. Kans., 1974. Assoc. editor Kans. Electric Coops., Topeka, 1975-76, editor, 1976-79; editor Golf Course Supts. Assn. Am., Lawrence, Kans., 1978-79, mktg. dir., 1979-83, exec. dir., 1983—. Contbr. articles to profl. jours. Mem. Am. Soc. Assn. Execs., Nat. Assn. Expn. Mgrs., Am. Advt. Fedn., Topeka Advt. Club, U.S. Golf Assn., Nat. Golf Found. (bd. dirs.), Internat. Assn. Golf Adminstrs. Republican. Lutheran. Club: Alvamar Country (Lawrence). Avocations: golf, boating, coaching, breeding dogs, reading, computers. Home: 3934 NW Morley S Topeka KS 66618 Office: Golf Course Supts Assn Am 1617 St Andrews Dr Lawrence KS 66044

SCHILLING, KATHERINE LEE TRACY, educator; b. Mitchell, S.D., May 31, 1925; d. Ernest Benjamin and Mary Alice (Courier) Tracy; B.A., Dakota Wesleyan U., 1947; M.A., U. S.D., 1957; postgrad. U. Wyo., U. Nebr., Kearney State Coll.; m. Clarence R. Schilling, Oct. 14, 1951; 1 dau., Keigh Leigh. Tchr. elem. and secondary schs., also colls., S.D. and Nebr.; now with specially funded project for disadvantaged children Winnebago Indian reservation, Nebr. Mem. staff S.D. Girls' State, 1950-51; mem. S.D. Gov.'s Com. on Library, Nebr. Gov.'s Com. on Right to Read. Recipient Outstanding Tchr. award S.D. High Sch. Speech Tchrs., 1966. Mem. NEA, Nebr., Thurston County (pres.) edn. assns., Winnebago Tchrs. Assn., Delta Kappa Gamma. Clubs: Internat. Toastmistress (internat. dir. 1963-65, Mitchell Toastmistress of Year 1959), Order Eastern Star. Contbr. articles to profl. jours., also poetry. Home: 39 S Harmon Dr Box 578 Mitchell SD 57301 Office: Winnebago Public Sch Nebr Indian Community Coll Winnebago NE 68071

SCHILTZ, EUGENE JOSEPH, lawyer; b. Chgo., Aug. 7, 1956; s. Eugene Michael and Mary Catherine (Pieroni) s. B.S. in Polit. Sci. and History, Ill. State U., 1977; J.D., U. Chgo., 1981. Bar: Ill. 1981, U.S. Dist. Ct. (no. dist.) Ill. 1981, U.S. Ct. Appeals (7th cir.) 1981. Assoc. Freeman, Atkins & Coleman, Chgo., 1982-84, Robert F. Coleman & Assocs., 1985—. Mem. Ill. State Bar Assn., Chgo. Bar Assn., Chgo. Council Fgn. Relations. Office: Robert F Coleman & Assocs 600 Three First Nat Plaza Chicago IL 60602

SCHIMMOLLER, RICHARD EDMUND, osteopathic physician; b. Dayton, Ohio, Apr. 4, 1929; s. Raymond Louis and Anna Mae (Hartley) S.; m. Gay Lee Mahan, Dec. 29, 1956; children—Terry, Cristy, Becky. Student U. Dayton, 1946-47, Kent State U., 1953-55; D.O., Chgo. Coll. Osteopathy (now Chgo. Coll. Osteo. Medicine), 1960. Diplomate Am. Coll. Gen. Practitioners in Osteo. Medicine and Surgery. Intern, Still Meml. Hosp., Jefferson City, Mo., 1960-61; gen. practice osteo. medicine, Camdenton, Mo., 1961-63, Columbus, Ohio, 1963—; mem. staff Doctors Hosp., Columbus; mem. health adv. bd. Blue Cross, Blue Shield, Ohio. Served to sgt. USAF, 1948-52. Mem. Am. Osteo. Assn., Ohio Osteo. Assn., Chgo. Coll. Osteo. Medicine and Surgery Alumni Assn. Am. Coll. Osteo. Gen. Practitioners, Columbus Acad. Osteo. Medicine, Iota Tau Sigma. Club: Brookside Country (Worthington, Ohio). Home: 6694 Merwin Rd Worthington OH 43085 Office: 5109 W Broad St Columbus OH 43228

SCHINDLER, JOEL MARVIN, scientist, medical educator; b. N.Y.C., Oct. 27, 1950; s. Herbert and Margot (Rosenberg) S.; m. Myra Ellen Krupkin, Aug. 9, 1974; 1 child, Abbe Meryl. B.Sc., Hebrew U., 1973, M.Sc., 1975; Ph.D., U. Pitts., 1978; student U. Rochester, 1969-71. Postdoctoral fellow Roche Inst. Molecular Biology, Nutley, N.J., 1978-81; mem. grad. program in devel. biology Children's Hosp. Research Found., Cin., 1981—; asst. prof. dept. anatomy and cell biology U. Cin. Coll. Medicine, 1981—. Contbr. articles to profl. jours. Mem. exec. bd. Leadership Council, Jewish Fedn. Cin., 1982—. Recipient Acad. awards Faculty Sci., Hebrew U., 1973-75; Irwin Cohen scholar, 1974-75; Mellon fellow, 1977-78; Roche postdoctoral fellow, 1978-81; Am. Cancer Soc. grantee, 1982-83, 84-85; Elsa U. Pardee Found. grantee, 1983-84; NSF grantee, 1983—. Mem. Soc. for Devel. Biology, Am. Assn. Anatomists, Am. Soc. Cell Biology, AAAS, Am. Israel Pub. Affairs Com. Office: Univ Cin Coll Medicine ML 521 231 Bethesda Ave Cincinnati OH 45267

SCHLAFLY, PHYLLIS STEWART, author, lawyer; b. St. Louis, Aug. 15, 1924; d. John Bruce and Odile (Dodge) Stewart; m. Fred Schlafly, Oct. 20, 1949; children—John F., Bruce S., Roger S., Liza S. Forshaw, Andrew L., Anne V. B.A., Washington U., St. Louis, 1944, J.D., 1978; M.A., Radcliffe Coll., 1945; LL.D., Niagara U., 1976. Bar: Ill. 1979. Author, pub. Phyllis Schlafly Report, 1967—; broadcaster Spectrum, CBS Radio Network, 1973-78; commentator Matters of Opinion Sta. WBBM, Chgo., 1973-76; syndicated columnist Copley News Service, 1976—; TV commentator Cable News Network, 1980-83. Del., Republican. Nat. Conv., 1956, 64, 68, 84, alt., 1960, 80; pres. Ill. Fedn. Rep. Women, 1960-64; 1st v.p. Nat. Fedn. Rep. Women, 1964-67; mem. Ill. Commn. on Status of Women, 1975—; nat. chmn. Stop ERA, 1972—; pres. Eagle Forum, 1975—; mem. Adminstrv. Conf. of U.S., 1982—; mem. Pres. Reagan's Def. Policy Adv. Group, 1980. Recipient 10 Honor medals Freedoms Found.; Brotherhood award NCCJ, 1975; named Woman of Achievement in Pub. Affairs, St. Louis Globe-Democrat, 1963; named most influential woman in U.S. in social action World Almanac, 1982; one of 10 most admired women in world Good Housekeeping, 1977—. Mem. ABA, Ill. Bar Assn., DAR (nat. chmn. Am. history 1965-68, nat. chmn. bicentennial com. 1967-70, nat. chmn. nat. def. com. 1977-80, 83—), Phi Beta Kappa, Pi Sigma Alpha. Author: A Choice Not an Echo, 1964; The Gravediggers, 1964; Strike from Space, 1965; Safe Not Sorry, 1967; The Betrayers, 1968; Mindszenty The Man, 1972; Kissinger on the Couch, 1975; Ambush at Vladisvostok, 1976; The Power of the Positive Woman, 1977; editor: Equal Pay for Unequal Work, 1984; Child Abuse in the Classroom, 1985. Address: 68 Fairmount Alton IL 62002

SCHLEGEL, DICK REEVES, lawyer, judge; b. Bloomfield, Iowa, Mar. 4, 1922; s. Verne John and Helen Elizabeth (Reeves) S.; m. Maxine Glenn, Apr. 4, 1943; children—Richard R., Mary Patricia Wilson, Robert Glenn. B.A., U. Iowa, 1948, J.D., 1950. Bar: Iowa 1950. Ptnr. Barnes & Schlegel, Ottumwa, Iowa, 1950-78; judge 8th Jud. Dist. Iowa, 1978-82, Iowa Ct. Appeals, 1982—. Served with USAF, 1942-50. Decorated Air medal. Mem. ABA, Iowa Bar Assn., Ottumwa Bar Assn., Iowa Acad. Trial Lawyers, Iowa Def. Counsel, Assn. Trial Lawyers Iowa, Iowa Judges Assn. Presbyterian. Club: Ottumwa Country. Lodge: Masons. Office: State Capitol Court of Appeals Des Moines IA 50319

SCHLEGEL, EDWARD JOHN, heavy machinery manufacturing company executive; b. Peoria, Ill., Apr. 7, 1922; s. Edward John and Anna (Endres) S.; m. Teresa Ann Radosevich, Apr. 17, 1948; children—Christine, Susan. B.S.B.A., Bradley U., 1947. Mng. dir. Caterpillar of Australia Ltd., Melbourne, 1966-70, chmn. Caterpillar Mitsubishi Ltd., Sagamihara-shi, Japan, 1970-73, v.p. Caterpillar Tractor Co., Peoria, Ill., 1973-75, exec. v.p., 1975—, dir., 1978—; dir. NCR Corp., Dayton, Ohio, Comml. Nat. Bank, Peoria. Trustee, Bradley U., Meth. Med. Ctr. Ill., Peoria. Office: Caterpillar Tractor Co 100 NE Adams St Peoria IL 61629

SCHLIESMAN, LEONARD JAMES, JR., paper research chemist; b. Milbank, S.D., Apr. 19, 1942; s. Leonard Jacob and Ida Emily (Erne) S.; m. Marygrace Benson, May 6, 1967; children—Marie, Philip, Angela. B.S., S.D. State U., 1964; M.S., Inst. Paper Chemistry, 1966; M.B.A., U. Wis.-Oshkosh, 1974. Analytical chemist U. S.D., Vermillion, summers 1963-64; project chemist Consol. Papers, Inc., Wisconsin Rapids, Wis., 1967-76, research chemist project devel., 1976—. Local chmn. K.C. Tootsie Rool Drive, 1974—. Recipient award Consol. Papers Patent Club, 1974. Mem. TAPPI, Phi Kappa Phi. Roman Catholic. Club: Wood County Rifle and Pistol. Lodge: K.C. Patentee in field. Home: 1310 16th St N Wisconsin Rapids WI 54494 Office: Consolidated Papers Inc Wisconsin Rapids WI 54494

SCHLIMGEN, ROBERT JOSEPH, college dean; b. Parkston, S.D., June 4, 1942; m. Carol Koob; children—Mark, Mike, Jeff. B.S. in Edn., So. State Coll., 1964; M.S. in Sch. Adminstrn., S.D. State U., 1968; Ed.D., U. Nebr., 1982. Bus. instr. and coach White Ind. Sch. Dist., S.D., 1964-66, Clear Lake Ind. Sch. Dist., S.D., 1966-67; jr. and sr. high sch. prin. Ponca Pub. Schs., Nebr., 1967-71; dean students N.E. Nebr. Tech. Coll., Norfolk, 1971-72; dean community services, 1972-85; cons. Kans. State U., Lawrence, 1976, S.E. Mo. State U., Springfield, 1980, Nebr. Dept. Edn., Lincoln, 1980. Chmn. Nebr. Community Services Council, 1974-75, 1978-79, 1982-83; bd. dirs. Big Bros./Big Sisters Northeast Nebr., pres., 1978-79; bd. dirs. Community Concern Norfolk, 1975—; Legal and Human Rights Com. Office Mental Retardation, 1980-83; Nebr. Adult Edn. Rev. Panel; Nebr. State Planning and Evalution com., 1982—. Named to Outstanding Young Men Am., 1977. Mem. Adult and Continuing Assn. Nebr., Mo. Valley Adult Edn. Assn., Nat. Assn. Pub. Continuing and Adult Edn., Council for Occupational Edn., Northeast Nebr. Sch. Supt. Assn., Am. Assn. Adult and Continuing Edn. (regional v.p. 1982—). Home: 904 Andy's Lake Rd Norfolk NE 68701

SCHLOEMER, PAUL GEORGE, diversified manufacturing company executive; b. Cin., July 29, 1928; s. Leo Bernard and Mary Loretta (Butler) S.; m. Virginia Katherine Grona, Aug. 28, 1954; children—Michael, Elizabeth, Stephen, Jane, Daniel, Thomas. B.S. in Mech. Engring., U. Cin., 1951; M.B.A, Ohio State U., 1955. Research and devel. engr. Wright Patterson AFB, Dayton, Ohio, 1951-52, R&D officer, 1952-57; resident engr. Parker Hannifin Corp., Dayton, also Eastern area mgr., Huntsville, Ala., 1957-65, v.p. aerospace group, Irvine, Calif., 1965-77, pres. aerospace group, 1977, corp. v.p., 1978-81, exec. v.p., 1981, pres., Cleve., 1982—, also chief exec. officer, also dir. Active United Way, Orange, Calif.; bd. dirs. Orange County council Boy Scouts Am., 1973-82, John Carroll U., University Heights, Ohio, 1982; trustee Hoag Hosp., Orange County, 1980-82. Served to capt. USAF, 1952-53. Recipient Silver Beaver award Boy Scouts Am., 1976. Mem. Aircraft Industry Assn. (bd. govs.). Republican. Roman Catholic. Club: Big Canyon Country. Office: Parker Hannifin Corp 17325 Euclid Cleveland OH 44112*

SCHLOSS, NATHAN, real estate research corporation executive; b. Balt., Jan. 14, 1927; s. Howard L. and Louise (Levi) S.; B.S. in Bus., Johns Hopkins U., 1950; m. Rosa Montalvo, Mar. 1, 1958; children—Nina L., Carolyn D. Buyer, Pacific coast merchandise office Sears Roebuck & Co., Los Angeles, 1955-60, staff asst. econ. research dept., Chgo., 1960-63; sr. market analyst corp. research dept. Montgomery Ward & Co., Chgo., 1963-65; research mgr. real estate dept. Walgreen Co., Chgo., 1970-72; v.p. research and planning Maron Properties Ltd., Montreal, Que., Can., 1972-74; corp. economist, fin. analyst Real Estate Research Corp., Chgo., 1974—, v.p., treas., chief fin. analyst, 1982—; cons. economist, since 1965—; mem. com. on price indexes and productivity Bus. Research Adv. Council of Bur. Labor Stats., Dept. Labor, 1979—, also chairperson com. on employment and unemployment. Mem. Plan Commn., Village of Wilmette, Ill., 1975-77, tech. adv. com. on employment and tng. data Ill. Employment and Tng. Council, 1979-82; mem. tech. adv. com. Ill. Job Tng. Coordinating Council, 1983—. Mem. Am. Mktg. Assn., Nat. Assn. Bus. Economists, Lambda Alpha. Contbr. articles on fin. and market analysis of real estate to profl. jours. Home: 115 Hollywood Ct Wilmette IL 60091 Office: 72 W Adams St Chicago IL 60603

SCHLOTTERER, WILLIAM LEE, osteopathic physician; b. Shelby, Ohio, Mar. 6, 1955; s. Karl Leo and Phyllis Ray (Stewart) S.; m. Cindy Marla Groh, Oct. 5, 1983. B.S. in Zoology with honors, Kent State U., 1976; D.O., Ohio U. Coll. Osteo. Medicine, 1980; postgrad. U. Toledo, 1983—. Intern, Parkview Hosp., Toledo, 1980-81; dir. Rainbow Clinic, Woodville, Ohio, 1981-83; emergency dept. physician Central Ohio Emergency Services, 1983—. Civilian draft and mil. counselor, 1973-74; water safety instr., Akron, Ohio, 1973-75; dir. Radix Christian Workshop Relief Program for Skeels-McElrath, 1975-76. Summer fellow in disaster contingency planning in Appalachian Ohio, 1977; mem. exec. bd. Muskingum Valley Boy Scout Council, 1983—. Recipient Sandoz award for scholarship and community service, 1978. Mem. Am. Osteo. Assn., Ohio Osteo. Assn. Am. Coll. Emergency Physicians, Toledo Acad. Osteo. Medicine (sec.). Jewish. Club: Mensa. Home: 1500 N 11th St Cambridge OH 43725

SCHLOUGH, LAWRENCE JOSEPH, dairy farmer; b. Menomonie, Wis., Jan 28, 1941; s. Edwin Francis and Edna Mary (Denning) S.; m. Sherrie Lee Condit, May 23, 1964; children—Rebecca, Curtis, Tamara, Chad, Patrica. Dairy farmer, Menomonie, 1960—; dir. Farmers Credit Union, Menomonie, 1979-84; del. Tri-State, Menomonie, 1980—; chmn. June Dairy Month, Menomonie, 1981. Recipient Holsum Bakery Salute award, 1981, 84, Dairy Production award, Tri-State, 1981, 83, 84. Mem. Farmers Union, F.F.A. Alumni Assn. Republican. Roman Catholic. Club: Dunn County Holstein Breeders. Lodges: Moose, KC (Knight of Yr. 1977, Grand Knight 1981-83). Avocations: golf; softball. Home and Office: Rural Route Box 9 Menomonie WI 54751

SCHMEDA, JOHN ANTHONY, dentist; b. Chgo., Mar. 1, 194l; s. John Peter and Constance (Palmeri) S.; m. Sue Anne Stuckey, Aug. 8, 1964; children—Jill, Peter, Kelly Anne. D.D.S., Loyola U., Chgo., 1965. Gen. practice dentistry, Des Plaines, Ill., 1967—; cons. Mazarethville Nursing Home, Des Plaines, 1978—, Holy Family Health Ctr., Des Plaines, 1982—; staff Holy Family Hosp., Des Plaines, 1980—; dir. Legis. Interest Com. Ill. Dentists, Springfield, 1982—. Served to capt. USAF, 1965-67. Fellow Acad. Gen. Dentistry; mem. Am. Dental Assn., Ill. State Dental Soc. (exec. council 1985-88), Chgo. Dental Soc. (pres. Northwest suburban br. 1984-85). Roman Catholic. Avocations: golf; skiing. Home: 1027 W Mallard Dr Palatine IL 60067 Office: 1400 Golf Rd #125 Des Plaines IL 60016

SCHMELING, JOHN PETER, university administrator, clergyman; b. Beach, N.D., Oct. 31, 1938; m. Susan Ellen Reinhart, Aug. 10, 1976; children—John R., Heather, Kirsten, Linda, Kim, Erich. B.S., Dickinson State Coll., 1961; M.Div., Wartburg Theol. Sem., 1968; M.S., Ind. State U., 1970, Ph.D., 1977; student U.S. Army Chaplain Sch., 1967, 72, Command and Gen. Staff Coll., 1977. Ordained to ministry Lutheran Ch., 1968. Radio operator Dickinson Police Force, N.D., 1960-61; tchr. German, head basketball and track coach Riverdale High Sch., N.D., 1961-64; tchr. German, Western Dubuque High sch., Epworth, Iowa, 1964-67; commd. 2d lt. U.S. Army Res., 1963, advanced through grades to lt. col., 1985; served as chaplain 604th Mil. Police Battalion, Terre Haute, Ind., 1968-76, staff chaplain 4th Brigaid, 70th Div., Camp Atterbury, Ind., 1976—; pastor Trinity Lutheran Ch., Linton, Ind., 1968-74; interim pastor St. John Evang. Luth. Ch., Shelbyville, Ill., 1975—; asst. prof. religion, European history, social work Vincennes U., Ind., part-time 1970, asst. prof., 1974-77, assoc. prof., 1977-82, prof., 1982—, chmn. social sci. div., 1978-81, v.p. instructional services, dean faculty, 1981—; v.p. Nat. Luth. Campus Ministry, Ind. U., 1972; clergyman Am. Luth. Ch., 1968—, mem. support to ministries com. Ill. dist., 1982—, sec., 1984; Title III field reader U.S. Dept. Edn., 1983, 85; facilitator Vincennes U. in Europe, 1984; lectr. in field. Contbr. articles to profl. jours. Participant Ind. Black Legis. Caucus on Higher Edn., 1984; mem. adv. bd. Salvation Army. NDEA scholar, 1962-63; Advanced Instl. Devel. Programs grantee 1978; Vincennes U. fellow, 1980. Mem. Inter Luth. Com. Wabash Valley, Linton Ministerial Assn. (pres. 1972), Greater Vincennes Ministerial Assn., Mil. Chaplains Assn. (life), Res. Officers Assn. (life), AAUP, Ind. Assn. Pub. Continuing and Adult Edn., Nat. Hist. Soc., Am. Angus Assn., Assn. Ednl. Communications and Tech., Community Coll. Social Sci. Assn., Ind. Assn. Social Work Edn., Nat. Assn. Social Workers, Am. Assn. Community and Jr. Colls., Ind. Acad. Social Scis., Ind.-Ky. Luth. Brotherhood, Am. Council Edn., CAUSE, Ind. Assn. Historians, Assn. Ednl. Data Systems, North Central Assn. Colls. and Schs. (cons. evaluator 1982—), Am. Assn. Higher Edn., Nat. Council Instructional Adminstrs. (State of Ind. coordinator 1984—), Civil War Roundtable, Phi Sigma Pi, Phi Delta Kappa (sec. Illiana chpt. 1981, v.p. programs 1982, v.p. membership 1983, pres. 1984, del. 1984, 85). Office: Vincennes U 1002 N 2d St Vincennes IN 47591

SCHMETZER, ALAN DAVID, psychiatrist; b. Louisville, Sept. 3, 1946; s. Clarence Fredrick and Catherine Louise (Wootan) S.; m. Janet Lynn Royce, Aug. 25, 1968; children—Angela Beth, Jennifer Lorraine. B.A., Ind. U., 1968, M.D., 1972. Diplomate Am. Bd. Psychiatry and Neurology. Intern, Ind. U. Hosps., Indpls., 1972-73, resident, 1972-75; dir. clinics PCI, Inc., Anderson, Beech Grove and Kokomo, Ind., 1975-79; psychiat. cons. Community Addiction Services Agy., Indpls., 1975-80; instr. psychiatry in primary care Family Practice Residency Programs, St. Francis Hosp., St. Vincent's Hosp. and Ind. U. Hosps., Indpls., 1975—; med. dir. Child Guidance Clinic of Marion County, Indpls., 1980-81; chmn. psychiatry dept. St. Francis Hosp., Beech Grove, 1980-82; med. dir. Crisis Intervention Unit, Midtown Mental Health Center and coordinator emergency psychiat. services Ind. U. Med. Ctr., Indpls., 1980—, also asst. prof. psychiatry. Served to maj. Ind. N.G., 1972-79. Decorated Army Commendation medal; recipient Physicians Recognition award AMA, 1978; Residents award for outstanding teaching 1985. Fellow Am. Psychiat. Assn.; mem. AMA, Ind. Med. Assn., Marion County Med. Soc., Am. Psychiat. Assn., Ind. Psychiat. Soc., Am. Orthopsychiat. Assn., Am. Acad. Clin. Psychiatry, Alpha Phi Omega, Phi Beta Pi, Psi Chi, Alpha Epsilon Delta. Presbyterian. Club: Athenaeum Turnverein. Author: Crisis Intervention: The Psychotic Assaultive Patient, a videotape and workbook, 1981; Crisis Intervention: The Suicidal Patient, 1981. Office: 1001 W 10th St Indianapolis IN 46202

SCHMID, FREDERICK, fire chief; b. Ann Arbor, Mich., June 20, 1928; s. Harry H. and Lucille (Schaible) S.; m. Marilyn Etzel, May 8, 1948; children—Elizabeth Ann, Jennette Irene, Thomas Frederick. Firefighter, Ann Arbor (Mich.) Fire Dept., 1951-60, lt., 1960-67, asst. fire chief, 1967-74, fire chief, 1974—; fire chief Silver Lake Fire Dept., 1956—; mem. adv. bd. fire tech. Washtenaw Community Coll., 1969; chief fire rescue service Washtenaw County Emergency Preparedness, 1974—. Mem. Ann Arbor Zoning Bd. Appeals, 1974—; mem. Ann Arbor Housing Bd. Appeals, 1974—. Mem. Washtenaw County Mut. Aid Assn. (pres.), Internat. Assn. Fire Chiefs, Mich. Fire Chiefs Assn., Southea. Fire Chiefs Assn. Lodge: Elks. Office: 111 N 5th Ave Ann Arbor MI 48104*

SCHMIDT, ALBERT DANIEL, utilities company executive; b. Alpena, S.D., Nov. 16, 1925; s. Ernest Otto and Dorothea Marie Augusta S.; student Miami U., Oxford, Ohio, 1943-45; B.S. with honors in Elec. Engring., S.D. Sch. Mines and Tech., 1949; m. Joyce Bernice Anderson, Nov. 24, 1946; children—Roxanne Rae Schmidt Eisen, Janet Jaye Schmidt Foss. With Northwestern Public Service Co., 1949—, v.p. ops., Huron, S.D., 1958-65, pres., chief exec. officer, 1965-80, chmn., chief exec. officer, 1980—, dir.; mem. adv. bd. North Central dist. Norwest Bank, S.D. Trustee, Huron Coll., 1970-73; past chmn., mem. exec. com. Mid-Continent Area Power Pool; past trustee N. Am. Electric Reliability Council. Served with USNR, 1943-46. Named Man of Yr., S.D. Electric Council, 1979; Boss of Yr., Huron Jaycees, 1979; Disting. Service award Nat. Food and Energy Council, 1982. Mem. N. Central Electric Assn. (exec. com.), Food and Energy Council (past dir., past chmn.), Nat. Assn. OTC Cos. (past sec., past dir.), U.S. Bus. and Indsl. Council (dir.), S.D. C. of C. (past dir.), S.D. Council Econ. Edn. (dir.), Nat. Assn. Electric Cos. (past dir.), Am Gas Assn. (past dir.), Midwest Gas Assn. (past pres.), S.D. Electric Council, S.D. Engring Soc., Huron C. of C. Republican. Lutheran. Clubs: Elks, Masons, Huron Country. Office: Northwestern Public Service Co Northwestern Nat Bank Bldg Huron SD 57350

SCHMIDT, ARTHUR IRWIN, steel fabricating co. exec.; b. Chgo., Sept. 9, 1927; s. Louis and Mary (Fliegel) S.; student Colo. A. and M. Coll., 1946-47; B.S. in Aero. Engring., U. Ill., 1950; m. Mae Rosman, July 25, 1950;children—Jerrold, Cynthia, Elizabeth, Richard. Sec. Rosman Iron Works, Inc., Franklin Park, Ill., 1950—. Served with USNR, 1944-46, 51-52. Mem. N.W. Suburban Mfrs. Assn., Iron League Chgo., Ill. Mfrs. Assn., U. Ill. Alumni Assn. Mem. B'nai B'rith (trustee, past pres. Lincolnwood). Home: 3601 Golf Rd Evanston IL 60203 Office: 9109 Fullerton Ave Franklin Park IL 60131

SCHMIDT, C. OSCAR, JR., manufacturing company executive; b. Cin.; s. C. Oscar and Charlotte A. (Fritz) S.; m. Eugenia Hill Williams, June 29, 1944; children—Carl O., Christopher R., Milton W., Eugene H., Juliana R. B.S.M.E., U. Cin.; M.B.A., Harvard U.; student in animal husbandry Rutgers U.; L.H.D., Sterling Coll. Registered profl. engr., Ohio. Apprentice, Am. Can Co.; engr. Cin. Shaper; dir. Cin. Butchers' Supply Co., asst. to pres., v.p. prodn., v.p., gen. mgr., exec. v.p., pres., treas., chmn. bd.; dir., pres. BEC, Inc.; Cin. Renderers Assn., Winger Boss Co.; dir. Cin. Refrigerator and Fixture Works, Dixie Rendering Co., Ky. Chem. Industries, Inc., Mille Lacs Products Co., others. Contbr. articles to profl. jours. Patentee in field; lectr. in field. Trustee Deaconess Hosp.; ruling elder Wyo. Presbyn. Ch., ruling elder, commr. Cin. Presbytery, Ecclesiastical Order Com.; mem. Cin. Art Mus., Friends Pub. Library, Hamilton County Soc. Crippled Children, Hamilton County Soc. Prevention Cruelty to Animals; mem. fin. com. Nat. United Cerebral Palsy Assn.; mem. rev. com. United Funds Cin. Served to capt. U.S. Army, 1940-45. Recipient Silver Beaver award Boy Scouts Am., 1969, Harman award Boy Scouts Am., Disting. Engring. Alumnus award U. Cin., 1969, others. Mem. Am. Oil Chemist Soc., Am. Ordnance Assn., Engr. Soc. Cin., Am. Assn. Indsl. Mgmt., Air Pollution Soc., Cin. Indsl. Inst., Cin. C. of C., Meat Industry Supply and Equipment Assn., Nat. Assn. Mfrs., Nat. Metal Trades Assn., Meat Machinery Mfrs. Inst., Nat. Parks Assn., Zool. Soc. Cin., others. Club: Wyo. Golf. Lodges: Masons, Rotary. Home: 405 Meadow Ln Cincinnati OH 45215 Office: Cin Butchers Supply Co Box 16098 5601 Helen St Elmwood Pl Cincinnati OH 45216

SCHMIDT, CHARLES EDWARD, JR., lawyer; b. Chgo., Nov. 7, 1937; s. Charles Edward and Dorothy Faris S.; B.S. cum laude, Fla. State U., 1960; J.D., Northwestern U., 1964; m. Virginia Hamilton, Dec. 16, 1978; children—Debora, Cathy, Kim, Julie, Ginger, Jennifer, Kiki. Admitted to Ill. bar, 1965; v.p. Community Centers, Chgo., 1961-67; tax shelter mgr. Merrill Lynch, Chgo., 1967-76; mem. firm Shaheen, Lundberg & Callahan, Chgo., 1964-67; chmn. Ill. Racing Bd., Chgo., 1977-82; owner Sunrise Farm Thoroughbreds. Pres., coach Northbrook (Ill.) Speed Skating Club, 1975-77; bd. dirs. Am. Hearing Impaired Hockey Assn., Big Bros.-Big Sisters, Chgo.; chmn. Northbrook Village Caucus Com. Served with U.S. Army, 1956-57. Mem. Nat. Assn. State Racings Commns. (pres.), Thoroughbred Breeders and Owners Assn. Republican. Clubs: Barrington Hills Country, Sunset Ridge Country. Office: 160 N LaSalle Chicago IL 60064

SCHMIDT, GUNTER, dentist; b. Nuremberg, Germany, Aug. 22, 1913; s. Willy and Irma (Treumann) S.; m. Corinne Mitchell, May 26, 1944; children—Carol, Linda. Student U. Munich, 1932-33, U. Wurzburg, 1933; D.D.S., Washington U., St. Louis, 1937. Gen. practice dentistry, St. Louis, 1937-59, Clayton, Mo., 1959—; dentist Shriner's Hosp. for Crippled Children, 1938-43; staff dentist Jewish Hosp., 1938-78, sr. dentist 1978—. Past chmn. United Fund Dental Div., Arts and Edn. Fund Dental Div.; mem. adv. com. on dental technologies St. Louis Community Coll. Served to maj. AUS, 1943-46. Recipient Diamond Pin award, Am. Acad. Oral Medicine, 1976; Gold medal Greater St. Louis Dental Soc., 1985; Am. Acad. Oral Medicine fellow, 1964; Am. Coll. Dentists fellow, 1980. Mem. ADA, Am. Acad. Oral Medicine (past pres., sec., trustee), Am. Soc. Geriatric Dentistry (past pres.). Pierre Fauchard Acad., Acad. Gen. Dentistry, Fedn. Dentaire Internat., St. Louis Soc. Dental Sci., Mo. Dental Assn. (chmn. council on legislation, Disting. Service award 1985). Clubs: Temple Emanuel Men's (founder), Temple Israel Men's (past pres.). Past editor Newsletter of Am. Acad. of Oral Med., Greater St. Louis Dental Soc. Bull., contbr. articles in field to profl. jours. Home: 15 Princeton Pl University City MO 63130 Office: 225 S Meramec Ave Suite 311 Clayton MO 63105

SCHMIDT, JAMES CARL, service executive; b. Urbana, Ill., Feb. 11, 1955; s. Glenn Wilmer and Anna (Hyland) S.; m. Darlene Elizabeth Molner, June 26, 1983. Student in French classic and provincial culinary arts Uberon Coll., France, 1975, French inst. technique du vin Maison du Vin, France, 1975; Profl. chef magna cum laude, Modern Gourmet, 1976. Sr. Chef Chez La Mere Madeleine, Newton Centre, Mass., 1975-77; exec. chef, wine buyer London Chop House and Caucus Club, Detroit, 1977—, exec. gen. mgr., 1977-83; cons. J. Schmidt Enterprises, Detroit, 1983—. Author numerous cooking articles. Names to Honor Roll, Am. Chefs Food & Wine Mag., 1983, Restaurant of Yr. Met. Detroit, 1984, Who's Who in Am. Food (1 of 15 chefs elected), Cooks Mag., 1984; recipient Ivy award Restaurant and Instns. Mag., 1978. Mem. Am. Inst. Food and Wine, Am. Culinitry Fedn. Roman Catholic. Office: London Chop House 155 W Congress Detroit MI 48226

SCHMIDT, JAMES GARDINER, manufacturing company executive; b. Berwyn, Ill., Feb. 19, 1947; s. Raymond John and Margaret (Gardiner) S.; m. Martha Evelyn Crews, June 19, 1971; children—Steven, Sarah. B.S.M.E., Purdue U., 1969; M.B.A., U. Chgo., 1980. Mgr. contracts Rockwell Internat.,

Chgo., 1974-76, dir. customer credit, 1976-77, controller newspaper, 1977-79, dir. fin. ops., 1979-81, controller, dir. Ikegai-Goss Corp., Tokyo, 1981-83; v.p. corp. devel. Fed. Signal Corp., Oak Brook, Ill., 1983-84, v.p. fin. and adminstrn., Burr Ridge, Ill., 1984—. Office: 140 E Tower Dr Burr Ridge IL 60521

SCHMIDT, NEIL JOSEPH, pharmacist, educator; b. St. Louis, Dec. 16, 1949; s. Waring Edward and Angalina Mary (Colton) S.; m. Margaret Susan Nack, July 31, 1971; children—Christopher, Tracy, Stephen. B.S. in Pharmacy, St. Louis Coll. Pharmacy, 1973; M.A., Webster U., 1985. Registered pharmacist, Mo., Ill. Staff pharmacist Venture Pharmacy, Kirkwood, Mo., part-time 1975-81, St. John's Mercy Med. Ctr., Creve Coeur, Mo., 1973—; instr. hosp. pharmacy St. Louis Coll. Pharmacy, 1983—; guest speaker radio and TV. Mgr. Ballwin Athletic Assn., Mo., 1980-84, div. coordinator, 1981-84; chmn. com. Cub Scout Pack 627, Boy Scouts Am., Ballwin, 1981-83, cubmaster, 1985; soccer coach Holy Infant Parish, 1978-80. Mem. St. Louis Soc. Hosp. Pharmacists (Hosp. Pharmacist of Yr. 1979, pres. 1977-78), Mo. Soc. Hosp. Pharmacists (pres. 1983-84, pres. research and edn. found. 1984-85), Am. Soc. Hosp. Pharmacists (student adv. panel 1984), Mo. Pharm. Assn. Democrat. Roman Catholic. Club: Holy Infant Men's. Avocations: Sherlock Holmes, Civil War novels, baseball, soccer, scouting. Home: 532 Golfwood Dr Ballwin MO 63021 Office: St Johns Mercy Med Ctr 615 S New Ballas Rd Creve Coeur MO 63141

SCHMIDT, RETA MAE, educator; b. Sturgeon Bay, Wis., Oct. 15, 1933; d. Vernon Edward Olson and Gertrude Jennie Johnson; m. Frederick James Schmidt, June 28, 1968 (div. 1975); 1 dau., Mary Ann. Student U. Wis., 1952-53, Prospect Hall Secretarial Sch., Milw., 1953-54; B.S. in Elem. Edn., U. Wis.-Oshkosh, 1958. Tchr., Racine (Wis.) Pub. Schs., 1958-59, Neenah (Wis.) Pub. Schs., 1959-68, Broward Pub. Schs., Ft. Lauderdale, Fla., 1968-69; tchr. Sturgeon Bay (Wis.) Pub. Schs., 1978—, 1st grade tchr. Sunrise Elem. Sch., 1978—. Mem. Wis. Edn. Assn., NEA, Internat. Platform Assn. Republican. Mem. Moravian Ch. Club: Order Eastern Star. Home: 845 S 16th Ct Sturgeon Bay WI 54235 Office: Sunrise Sch Sturgeon Bay WI 54235

SCHMIDT, ROBERT, civil engineer; b. Ukraine, May 18, 1927; came to U.S., 1949, naturalized, 1956; s. Alfred and Aquilina (Konotop) S.; B.S., U. Colo., 1951, M.S., 1953; Ph.D., U. Ill., 1956; m. Irene Hubertine Bongartz, June 10, 1978; 1 son, Ingbert Robert. Engr., C.E., U.S. Army, Omaha, 1951-52; asst. prof. theoretical and applied mechanics U. Ill., Urbana, 1956-59; assoc. prof. civil engring. U. Ariz., Tucson, 1959-63; prof. engring. mechanics U. Detroit, 1963—, chmn. dept. civil engring., 1978-80. Recipient 4 research grants NSF. Mem. ASCE, ASME (cert. of recognition), Am. Acad. Mechanics(founding mem.), Am. Soc. Engring. Edn., AAUP, Indsl. Math. Soc. (pres. 1966-67, 81-84), Sigma Xi. Editor Indsl. Math., 1969—; contbr. numerous articles to tech. and sci. jours. Research on linear and nonlinear theory of elasticity and methods of analysis. Office: College of Engineering University of Detroit Detroit MI 48221

SCHMIDT, WILLIAM ALEXANDER, physician, lawyer; b. Mpls., Sept. 23, 1947; s. Herbert William and Kathleen (Campbell) S.; m. Elizabeth Ann Tinkham, Sept. 7, 1968. B.S. in Medicine, U. Minn., 1975, M.D., 1976; J.D., William Mitchell Coll. Law, 1981. Bar: Minn. 1982, U.S. Dist. Ct. Minn. 1982, U.S. Ct. Appeals (8th cir.) 1982. Intern Northwestern Hosp., Mpls., resident 1976-78; practice medicine specializing in internal medicine, Mpls.; mem. law firm Peterson, Gray & Shoahan, Ltd., St. Paul; mem. staff Met. Med. Ctr., Mpls. Served with U.S. Army, 1967-70; S.E. Asia. Fellow am. Coll. Legal Medicine; mem. Rho Chi. Republican. Club: Mpls. Athletic. Lodge: Kiwanis. Office: Professional Bldg Suite 208 Minneapolis MN 55402

SCHMIDTLEIN, EUGENE FRANCIS, college dean; b. Springfield, Mo., July 28, 1927; s. Matthew and Anna (Beier) S.; m. Mary Holland, Aug. 17, 1957; children—Mary, Norma, Rachel. B.A., Conception Coll., 1950; M.A., Notre Dame U., 1956; Ph.D., U. Mo., 1962. Instr. Stephens Coll., Columbia, Mo., 1959-65;' dept. head history, 1965-79, div. head social sci., 1965-79, dean faculty, 1979—. Served to ensign USN, 1952-54, Korea. Roman Catholic. Office: Dean Faculty Stephens Coll Columbia MO 65215

SCHMITT, DENNIS LEE, veterinarian; b. Springfield, Mo., Nov. 25, 1947; s. Ivan Lee and Helen Elizabeth (Dickens) S.; m. Phyllis June Sell, July 14, 1967; children—Brian Lee, Brock Alan. B.S. in Agrl. Edn., U. Mo., 1969, M.S. in Dairy Husbandry, 1974, D.V.M., 1978. Vocat. agr. instr., Forsyth, Mo., 1969-71, Willard, Mo., 1972-73; pvt. practice vet. medicine ltd. to bovine reprodn., Republic, Mo., 1978—; staff veterinarian Dickerson Park Zoo, Springfield, Mo.; ptnr. S&S Transplants, 1982—; owner Reproductive Resources, 1985—; adj. faculty S.W. Mo. State U. Mem. AVMA, Am. Fertility Soc., Mo. Vet. Med. Assn., Theriogenology Soc., Internat. Embryo Transplant Soc. Mem. Ch. of Christ. Home and office: Route 2 Box 188 Republic MO 65738

SCHMITZ, MARY ELLEN, executive housekeeper; b. Centerville, Iowa, Dec. 11, 1938; d. Leonard J. and Thelma LaVelle (Thompson) Clarke; m. Lawrence H. Schmitz, Feb. 17, 1962. Student, Drake U., 1957-58, Okla. Ctr. for Continuing Edn., Okla. U., 1976. Registered exec. housekeeper. Sec., McHale, Cook & Welch, law offices, Indpls., 1964-66, U.S. Steel, Bettendorf, Iowa, 1966-67; sec. to personnel dir. Ottumwa Hosp. (Iowa), 1968-72, dir. housekeeping, 1972—; part time instr. community coll. Named Laundry Mgr. of Yr., Iowa chpt. Nat. Assn. Instl. Laundry Mgrs., 1977. Mem. Nat. Exec. Housekeepers Assn. (registered). Roman Catholic. Office: Ottumwa Hosp 1001 E Pennsylvania Ave Ottumwa IA 52501

SCHMITZ, PAUL ARTHUR, utilities exec.; b. Wadesville, Ind., Jan. 24, 1936; s. Moses and Lorena Elizabeth (Hoell) S.; B.S., Evansville Coll., 1958; M.B.A., U. Evansville, 1968; m. Clara Ethel Reimann, June 8, 1962; children—Eric Earl, Eva Emily. With So. Ind. Gas and Electric Co., Evansville, 1961-68, mgr. taxes and ins., 1969-74, asst. comptrller, 1974-75, asst. comptroller, asst. treas., 1975-76; vice gen. mgr. fin. Big Rivers Electric Corp., Henderson, Ky., 1976-81, asst. gen. mgr., 1981—. Vice chmn. allocations com. Southwestern Ind. United Way, 1975-76. Served with U.S. Army, 1959-60. Mem. Ind. Electric Assn. (vice chmn. joint acctg. com. 1976), Am. Inst. C.P.A.'s, Ky. Soc. C.P.A.'s, Ind. Soc. C.P.A.'s, Nat. Assn. Accts. Mem. United Ch. of Christ. Club: Petroleum. Home: 1420 Stierly Rd Wadesville IN 47638 Office: Big Rivers Electric Corp 201 3d St Henderson KY 42420

SCHMITZ, ROGER ANTHONY, chemical engineering educator, administrator; b. Carlyle, Ill., Oct. 22, 1934; s. Alfred Bernard and Wilma Afra (Aarns) S.; m. Ruth Mary Kuhl, Aug. 31, 1957; children—Jan Joy, Joni. B.S. in Chem. Engring., U. Ill., 1959; Ph.D. in Chem. Engring., U. Minn., 1962. Prof. chem. engring. U. Ill.-Urbana, 1962-79; chmn. dept. chem. engring. U. Notre Dame, Ind., 1979-81, Keating-Crawford prof., 1979—, dean Coll. Engring., 1981—; cons. Amoco Chems., Naperville, Ill., 1966-77; vis. prof. Calif. Inst. Tech. and U. So. Calif., 1968-69. Contbr. articles to profl. jours. Served with U.S. Army, 1953-55, ETO. Guggenheim Found. fellow, 1968. Mem. Am. Inst. Chem. Engrs. (A.P. Colburn award 1970, R.H. Wilhelm award 1981), Am. Chem. Soc., Am. Soc. Engring. Edn. (George Westinghouse award 1977), Nat. Acad. Engrs. Roman Catholic. Home: 16865 Londonberry Ln South Bend IN 46635 Office: Coll Engring U Notre Dame Notre Dame IN 46556

SCHMITZ, THOMAS MATHIAS, lawyer; b. Cleve., June 1, 1938; s. Augustine A. and Lenora C. (Gerhart) S.; m. Gloria E. Sabo, June 6, 1964; children—Christopher T., Susan T. B.S. in Chem. Engring., Case Inst. Tech., 1961; J.D., Cleve.-Marshall Law Sch., 1967; M.B.A. in Internat. Mgmt., Baldwin-Wallace Coll., 1985. Bar: Ohio 1967, U.S. Patent Office 1968; registered profl. engr., Ohio. Sr. engr. E.F. Hauserman Co., Cleve., 1964-67; patent atty. B.F. Goodrich Co., Akron, Ohio, 1967-69; assoc. Slough & Slough, Cleve., 1969-72; sr. patent atty. SCM Corp., Cleve., 1972-84, gen. patent counsel, 1984—. Contbr. articles to profl. jours. Bd. dirs. Fontbonne Home, Lakewood, Ohio, 1981—. Mem. Cleve. Patent Law Assn. (bd. dirs. 1975-83, pres. 1985—), Ohio State Bar Assn., Am. Patent Law Assn. Avocation: golf. Home: 17228 Ernadale Ave Cleveland OH 44111 Office: SCM Corp 900 Huntington Bldg 925 Euclid Ave Cleveland OH 44111

SCHMUCK, KENNETH ERNEST, dentist; b. Freeman, S.D., June 13, 1929; s. Ernest Henry and Martha Elizabeth (Haar) S.; m. Judith Lavaune Sonnichsen, Nov. 26, 1960; children—Robyn Lynn, Tobin Lee, Terry Lee, Jaymee Janelle. A.B., Augustana Coll., 1951; D.D.S., Marquette U., 1959. Pvt. practice dentistry, Sioux Falls, S.D., 1959—; bd. dirs. S.D. Fluoridation Com., Pierre, 1967, 68; mem. policy council Head Start, Sioux Falls, S.D., 1974, 75; bd. dirs. Dental Health Council, Pierre, S.D., 1977-81. Vice pres. St. John's Luth. Ch., Sioux Falls, 1978-79, pres., 1980-82; v.p. Zion Luth. Ch., Sioux Falls, 1985. Served with USAF, 1951-55; PTO. Recipient recognition cert. Head Start, Sioux Falls, 1974-75. Mem. Am. Dental Assn., S.D. Dental Assn., S.E. S.D. Dental Soc. (pres. 1976-77), Omicron Kappa Upsilon (soc. key 1959). Republican. Avocations: woodworking; golfing; hunting; fishing. Home: Rural Route 3 Box 74 Sioux Falls SD 57106 Office: 1509 S Minnesota St Suite 3 Sioux Falls SD 57105

SCHMUCKER, RUBY ELVY LADRACH, nurse, educator; b. Sugarcreek, Ohio, Nov. 17, 1923; d. Walter F. and Carrie M. (Mizer) Ladrach; R.N., Aultman Hosp., Canton, Ohio, 1945; B.S. in Nursing, U. Akron, 1970, M.S. in Edn., 1973; children—Gary, David, Barbara, Steven. Gen. duty nurse, head nurse Aultman Hosp., 1945-47, part-time, 1950-62, instr. nursing, 1962-64, 69-74; instr. nursing Coll. Nursing, U. Akron (Ohio), 1974-76; instr. div. nursing edn. Children's Hosp., Akron, 1976-78; psychiat. nurse and supr. Massillon (Ohio) State Hosp., 1978-80, cons. to nursing dept., 1980—, dir. nursing edn., 1981-84; supr. Molly Stark Hosp. and psychiat. nurse Cuyahoga Falls Gen. Hosp., 1984—; cons. Stark-Tuscarawas Counties Student Nurses Assn., 1973-74. Health chmn. Avondale Sch. PTA, Canton, 1956, mem. coms., 1954-70; vol. instr. home nursing courses ARC, 1959-62, instr. CPR, 1979—. Cert. psychiat. nurse. Mem. Aultman Hosp. Sch. Nursing Alumni Assn., Am. Nurses' Assn., Nat. League Nursing, Am. Personnel and Guidance Assn., Am. Coll. Personnel Assn., U. Akron Alumni Assn., Alpha Sigma Lambda. Mem. Ch. of Christ. Home: 4214 Bellwood Dr NW Canton OH 44708 Office: 1900 23d St Cuyahoga Falls OH

SCHMUTZ, JOHN FRANCIS, lawyer; b. Oneida, N.Y., July 24, 1947; s. William L. and Rosemary S.; m. H. Marie Roney, June 7, 1969; children—Gretchen, Jonathan, Nathan. B.A. cum laude, Canisius Coll., 1969; J.D. cum laude, Notre Dame U., 1972; LL.M., George Washington U., 1975. Bar: Ind. 1972, U.S. Ct. Mil. Appeals 1972, U.S. Tax Ct. 1973, D.C. 1975, U.S. Supreme Ct. 1975. Legislation and major projects officer Office Judge Adv. Gen., 1972-74; appellate atty. U.S. Army Legal Services Agy., 1974-75; assoc. Ice, Miller, Donadio & Ryan, Indpls., 1976-77; staff atty. Burger Chef Systems, Inc., Indpls., 1977-78, sr. atty., 1979, asst. chief legal counsel, 1978-70, chief legal counsel, 1980, v.p., gen. counsel, sec., 1981—; dir., v.p. Bursan Credit Union; dir. Food Service and Lodging Inst.; dir., v.p. Blahs, Inc., RIX Systems, Inc., Burger Chef Distributive Corp.; v.p. Hardee's Food Systems, Inc. Mem. ABA, Fed. Bar Assn., Ind. Bar Assn., D.C. Bar Assn., Indpls. Bar Assn., Am. Assn. Corp. Counsel, Nat. Restaurant Assn. Republican. Roman Catholic. Lodge: K.C. Exec. editor Notre Dame Law Rev., 1971-72. Home: 3231 Van Tassel Dr Indianapolis IN 46240 Office: PO Box 927 Indianapolis IN 46206

SCHNATTER, RICHARD FLYNN, health care executive; b. Jeffersonville, Ind., May 15, 1933; s. John Clement and Marie Agnes (Patrick) S.; m. Georgia Lee Clifford, Jan. 30, 1964. B.S., U. Ky., 1955. Pres. Apoth-A-Care, Jeffersonville, 1966-69; dir. process mgmt. Extendicare, Inc. (now Humana, Inc.), Louisville, 1969-77; exec. v.p. Hosp. Mgmt. Assocs., 1977-79; pres. Flynn James Co., Jeffersonville, 1979—; chmn. bd. Ambulatory Surg., Inc., 1982—; mng. ptnr. Med. Investors, 1982—. Dir. Riverside Water Co., 1979—, Gateway Med., St. Louis, 1984—. Served with USN, 1955-57. Republican. Roman Catholic. Avocations: golf, oenology; bridge; chess. Home: 2203 Augusta Dr Jeffersonville IN 47130 Office: Ambulatory Surg Inc 106 W Court Ave Jeffersonville IN 47130

SCHNEDE, BRENDA LEE, educator; b. Davenport, Iowa, Apr. 9, 1944; s. Donald Dean and Bernice Ramona (Bartscher) S. B.A. cum laude in English and Spanish, U. Iowa, 1966; M.A. in English and Am. Lit., Northwestern U., 1973. Cert. tchr., supr., Ill. Tchr. English, Oak Park and River Forest (Ill.) High Sch., 1966—, head English dept., 1982—, dir. English dept. Gifted Program, 1980—; tchr. Midwest talent search Northwestern U., 1983—, curriculum cons., 1983—; conf. speaker. Mem. Art Inst. Chgo., Chgo. Opera Theater Soc., Friends of Downtown. Named Outstanding Woman of Yr., U. Iowa Faculty and Adminstrn., 1966. Mem. Nat. Council Tchrs. of English, Ill. Assn. Tchrs. of English, Mortar Bd., Phi Beta Kappa, Kappa Kappa Gamma. Editor: Chicago Performs, A Guide to Theatre and Dance, 1977. Home: 340 W Diversey Pkwy Chicago IL 60657 Office: Oak Park and River Forest High Sch 201 N Scoville St Oak Park IL 60302

SCHNEIDER, CHARLES STANLEY, aircraft company executive; b. Granite City, Ill., Sept. 5, 1936; s. Stanley Thomas and Dobrilla (Muntyan) S.; divorced; children—Charlene Haynes, Cheryl. B.E.E., U. Mo.-Rolla, 1959; postgrad. Wichita State U. Engr. Boeing Mil. Airplane Co., Wichita, Kans., 1959-75. program mgr., 1975—. City councilman, Derby, Kans., 1972-74. Served to 1st lt. U.S. Army, 1963-65. Mem. IEEE (sr.), Am. Helicopter Assn., Am. Mgmt. Assn., AIAA, Derby Jaycees (pres. 1971-72). Republican Avocations: golf; photography. Home: 837 Sunrise Derby KS 67037 Office: Boeing Mil Airplane Co 3801 S Oliver Wichita KS 67210

SCHNEIDER, DONALD NORMAN, pharmacist, educator; b. Point Clinton, Ohio, Jan. 7, 1945; s. Norman Edward and Leilia Luela (Lamalie) S.; m. Sharon Kay Asbury, Dec. 23, 1972; children—Kristen Renee, Erinn Dawn. B.S., U. Toledo, 1969; M.S., Ohio State U., 1971. Registered pharmacist, Ohio. Asst. dir. pharmacy Riverside Hosp., Columbus, Ohio, 1971-77, assoc. dir. pharmacy, 1977—; adj. asst. prof. U. Toledo, Ohio, 1979—; asst. clin. prof. Ohio State U., Columbus, 1981—. Co-chmn. Ohio Pharmacy's Centennial Celebration, Columbus, 1984. Recipient Merck award Merck & Co., 1969. Mem. Am. Soc. Hosp. Pharmacists, Ohio Soc. Hosp. Pharmacists (pres. 1984-85), Ohio State Pharm. Assn., Central Ohio Soc. Hosp. Pharmacists (pres. 1975-76), Rho Chi. Republican. Roman Catholic. Avocations: woodworking; gardening; cross country skiing; guitar playing. Home: 3248 Braidwood Dr Columbus OH 43220 Office: Riverside Methodist Hosp 3535 Olentangy River Rd Columbus OH 43214

SCHNEIDER, HAROLD WILLIAM, educator, editor; b. Redwood County, Minn., Feb. 26, 1926; s. William Theofeld and Bertha Augusta (Mell) S.; B.A., U. Minn., 1950, postgrad., 1952-56; m. Mary Bell Willis, July 7, 1956. Teaching asst. U. Minn., 1954-56, instr. English, 1956-61; instr. English, Kans. State U., Manhattan, 1961-68, asst. prof. English, 1969-85, assoc. prof., 1985—. Mem. creative writing adv. panel Kans. Cultural Arts Commn., 1969-81, film adv. panel, 1971-76; mem. Manhattan Library Bd., 1981—. Served to master sgt. U.S. Army, 1950-52. Mem. MLA (rep. del. assembly 1979-82), AAUP, ACLU, Phi Beta Kappa (v.p. Alpha assn. Kans. 1971-72, pres. 1973-74), Lambda Alpha Psi. Lutheran. Mng. editor Critique: Studies in Modern Fiction, 1956-61, adv. editor, 1961-64; editor Kans. Mag., 1967-68, Kans. Quar., 1968—. Contbr. articles to profl. jours. Home: 1405 Nichols St Manhattan KS 66502

SCHNEIDER, LAMARR EDYTHE, marketing and advertising consultant, restauranteur; b. Cleve., Apr. 15, 1943; d. Charles E. and Elaine E. (Smith) Spencer; m. William J. Schneider, Aug. 31, 1973 (div.); children—RoxAnne, Michelle. B.A. in Journalism, U. Minn., 1966. Asst. dir. Pennington County Housing Authority, Rapid City, S.D., 1973-76; dir. news and pub. affairs Sta. KTOQ, 1976-79; dir. research Intermountain Research, 1979—; owner, mgr. Families Sub Shop; owner Catering by LaMarr; pres. Schneider & Assoc. Mem. Nat. Fedn. Press Woman, S.D. Advt. Fedn., Nat. Assn. Housing and Renewal Ofcls., S.D. Restaurant Assn., Am. Bus. and Profl. Womens Assn., Rapid City C. of C. Baptist. Office: PO Box 8042 Rapid City SD 57701

SCHNEIDER, NORMAN RICHARD, veterinary toxicologist; educator; b. Ellsworth, Kans., Mar. 28, 1943; s. Henry C. and Irene C. (Ney) S.; B.S., Kans. State U., 1967, D.V.M., 1968; M.S. (Air Force Inst. Tech. fellow), Ohio State U., 1972; m. Karen Marjorie Nelson, July 1, 1968; 1 son, Nelson R. Commd. capt. U.S. Air Force, 1968, advanced through grades to maj., 1976; base veterinarian Goose AB, Labrador, Can., 1968-70; veterinary scientist/toxicologist Armed Forces Radiobiology Research Inst., Bethesda, Md., 1972-76; vet. toxicologist Aerospace Med. Research Lab., Wright-Patterson AFB, Dayton, Ohio, 1976-79; assoc. prof./vet. toxicologist dept. vet. sci. U. Nebr., Lincoln, 1979—, adj. assoc. prof. dept. pharmacodynamics and toxicology U. Nebr. Med. Ctr.; chief environ. health services 155th Tactical Reconnaissance Group, Nebr. Air Nat. Guard, Lincoln, 1979—. Decorated Joint Services Commendation medal; diplomate Am. Bd. Vet. Toxicology. Mem. Am. Coll. Vet. and Comparative Toxicologists, Nebr. Vet. Med. Assn., Kans. Vet. Med. Assn., AVMA, Am. Assn. Vet. Lab. Diagnosticians, Assn. Ofcl. Analytical Chemists, N.G. Assn. U.S., N.G. Assn. Nebr., Alliance Air N.G. Flight Surgeons, N.G. Environ. Health Assn., Assn. Mil. Surgeons U.S., N.Y. Acad. Scis., Council Agrl. Sci. and Tech., Alpha Zeta, Phi Zeta, Am. Legion, Nat. Rifle Assn., FarmHouse Fraternity. Roman Catholic. Home: Route 1 Box 70 Ceresco NE 68017 Office: Vet Diagnostic Center Lincoln NE 68583

SCHNEIDER, PHILIP JAMES, pharmacist, educator; b. Toledo, Aug. 29, 1947; s. Stanley Dale and Marcella (Degan) S.; m. Candace Gentile, May 27, 1972; children—Gretchen, Karl. B.S., U. Wis., 1970; M.S., Ohio State U., 1975. Asst. dir. pharmacy Ohio State U. Hosp., Columbus, 1975-78, assoc. dir., 1978—; pres. Clin. Pharm. Cons., 1982—; Assoc. clin. prof. pharmacy and medicine Ohio State U. Editor-in-chief Nutrition in Clin. Practice. Mem. Am. Soc. Hosp. Pharmacists, Am. Soc. Parenteral and Enteral Nutrition (bd. dirs. 1982—), Central Ohio Soc. Hosp. Pharmacists, Ohio Soc. Hosp. Pharmacists, Am. Pharm. Assn. Avocations: sailing; running. Home: 835 Chelsea Ave Columbus OH 43209 Office: Ohio State U Hosp 410 W 10th Ave Columbus OH 43210

SCHNEIDER, PHILIP JOE, jeweler, pearl wholesaler; b. Cleve., Oct. 18, 1956; s. Henry and Irene (Blier) S.; m. Marla Sue Sideman, Nov. 1, 1981. Student Cleve. State U., 1974-76; B.B.A., Ohio State U., 1979. Cert. in diamonds Gemological Inst. Am. Sales rep. Berendsohn AG, Chgo., 1979-81, Dun & Bradstreet, Chgo., 1981-84; account mgr. CGA Computer, Inc., Chgo., 1984-85; owner, mgr. Precious Jewelry Stones, Buffalo Grove, Ill., 1984—; pres. Phil Marc Ltd., pearl wholesalers, 1985—. Pres. Men's Club of Congregation B'nai Shalom, Buffalo Grove, 1983-84; bd. dirs. Congregation B'nai Shalom Temple. Named Sales Rep. of Yr., Dun & Bradstreet, 1982, 83. Mem. Data Processing Mgmt. Assn. Cleve. State Hockey Club (pres. 1975-77). Avocations: hockey; golf; drawing; traveling. Home: 1012 Crofton Ln Buffalo Grove IL 60090 Office: Pearls of the Orient Phil Marc Ltd 5 N Wabash St Apt. 1607 Chicago IL 60602

SCHNEIDER, STEVEN EUGENE, training counselor, educator; b. Swansea, Ill., Nov. 9, 1952; s. Alvin Peter and Marie M. (Wimmer) S.; m. Sheryl Marie Deitz, May 8, 1976; children—Sarah Abigail, Benjamin Issac. A.A. in English, Belleville Area Coll., 1972; B.A. in Teaching of English, U. Ill., 1974. Cert. secondary tchr., Ill. Tchr. St. Dominic Sch., Breese, Ill., 1975-79, St. Albert Sch., Fairview Heights, Ill., 1979-81; chief deputy county clk. St. Clair County, Belleville, Ill., 1981-82, dir. property mgmt. Housing Authority, 1982-83, tng. counselor, Intergovernmental Grants Dept., 1983-85, recruitment specialist, 1985—; mem. steering com. Belleville Diocesan Speech League, 1979-80, chmn., 1980-81; mem. Kaskaskia Reading Council, Centralia, Ill., 1975-79. Dir. (community theatre production) Stop the World I Want to Get Off, 1983; writer, dir. (play) A Christmas Play, 1977, The Christmas Caper, 1978. Pres. Belleville Community Theatre, 1974; bd. dirs. Comet Productions Inc.-Community Entertainment Services, 1983, pres., 1984-86. Mem. U. Ill. Alumni Assn., So. Ill. Arts Assn. (resource devel. com. 1985). Democrat. Roman Catholic. Club: St. Peter Cathedral Men's Choir (Belleville) (sec. 1984). Avocations: camping; reading; amateur/community theater. Home: 301 Anna St Swansea IL 62221 Office: Saint Clair County Intergovernmental Grants Dept 512 E Main St Belleville IL 62221

SCHNEKLOTH, HUGO ALLAN, farm company executive, state legislator; b. Eldridge, Iowa, Apr. 24, 1923; s. Hugo William and Sophia (Rusch) S.; m. Mildred Lois Blunk, Feb. 8, 1947; children—John Allan, Doris Schnekloth Dittmer. Grad. high sch., Davenport, Iowa. Pres. Schnekloth Farms Inc., Eldridge, 1980—; mem. Iowa Gen. Assembly, Des Moines, 1977—, chmn. house ways and means com., 1981-82; chmn. Iowa Farm Bur. Beef Adv. Com., Des Moines, 1974-76; dir. Central Scott Telephone Co., Eldridge, 1975—. Pres. Scott County (Iowa) Farm Bur., 1960-61. Mem. Farm Bur., Iowa Cattlemen's Assn., Izaak Walton League. Republican. Lutheran. Lodge: Kiwanis (v.p. 1965) (Davenport). Home and Office: Rural Route 1 Box 87 Eldridge IA 52748

SCHNELLER, GEORGE CHARLES, chiropractor; b. St. Louis, Feb. 22, 1921; s. Michael Alois and Eleanora Christine (Weber) S.; m. Dorothy Virginia Doran, Mar. 6, 1943; children—George Charles, Judith Ann. D. Chiropractic, Mo. Chiropractic Coll., 1946, Ph.Chiropractic, 1946. Ordained priest Anglican Orthodox Ch., 1973. Gen. practice chiropractic, St. Louis, 1946—; chiropractic staff Lindell Hosp., St. Louis; faculty Mo. Chiropractic Coll., 1947-51, dean, 1957-61. Fellow Internat. Chiropractors Assn.; mem. Mo. Acad. Chiropractors (pres. 1970-75), Dist. One Mo. State Chiropractic Assn. (pres. 1952). Clubs: Kiwanis (past pres. Maplewood, Mo.), Moose. Office: 3538 Jamieson Ave Saint Louis MO 63139

SCHOCH, RICHARD ALLAN, distillery company executive; b. Chgo., Jan. 13, 1931; s. Harry Hanson and Helen M. (Johnson) S.; m. Sally Ann Davis, July 7, 1962; children—Bret, Bradley, Kari Ann, Brandon. Student Evanston Jr. Coll., 1950-51; Northwestern U., 1951-52. Asst. state mgr. (Mich.) Coty Cosmetics, N.Y.C., 1952-56; state mgr. (Mich.) Tussy Cosmetiques, N.Y.C., 1956-61; sales mgr. Chgo., Jack Daniel Distillery Co., Nashville, 1962-66, Ill. state mgr., 1966-71, regional sales mgr., 1971-82, v.p., 1982—. Pack master Boy Scouts Am., Wilmette, Ill., 1975, 77, 78. Presbyterian. Home: 1427 Gregory Ave Wilmette IL 60091

SCHOELLHORN, ROBERT A., pharmaceutical company executive; b. Phila., 1928; grad. Phila. Coll. Textiles and Sci., 1957. With Am. Cyanamid Co., 1947-73; pres. Lederle Labs., 1971-73; with Abbott Labs., North Chicago, Ill., 1973—, exec. v.p. hosp. group, 1973-76, pres., 1976-81, chief operating officer, 1976-79, chief exec. officer, 1979—, chmn. bd., 1981—, also dir. Address: Abbott Labs Abbott Park North Chicago IL 60064

SCHOEMEHL, VINCENT CHARLES, JR., mayor St. Louis; b. St. Louis, Oct. 30, 1946; s. Vincent Charles and Lucille Mary (Miller) S.; B.A. in History, U. Mo., St. Louis, 1972; m. Lois Brockmeier, Sept. 18, 1971; children—Timothy, Joseph. Alderman, City of St. Louis, 1975-81, mayor, 1981—. Clubs: Lions, Ancient Order Hibernians. Democrat. Roman Catholic. Office: City Hall Saint Louis MO 63103

SCHOENBAUM, DONALD HARRY, theatre director, producer, consultant; b. Yonkers, N.Y., Jan. 3, 1926; s. Irving and Beatrice (Rubin) S.; m. Geraldine Cain, Aug. 15, 1947 (div. Jan. 1981); children—Mark, Robert, Andrew; m. Patricia J. Nygaard, Feb. 14, 1983. Student NYU, 1943-44, U. So. Calif., 1946-47. Ind. producer, 1951-62; mng. dir. Trinity Square Repertory Theater, Providence, 1963-65, The Guthrie Theater, Mpls., 1965—; dir. Theatre Communications Group, N.Y.C., 1983—; bd. dirs. Am. Arts Alliance, Washington, 1976-82, Sta. KTCA-TV, Mpls., 1975-81; chmn. theater program panel NEA; cons. Nat. Research Ctr., N.Y.C., Found. for Am. Profl. Theater, Minn. State Arts Bd. Served to cpl. USAF, 1944-46. Ford Found. fellow, 1965, grantee, Hawaii, 1963. Mem. League Resident Theaters (pres. 1977-81). Office: The Guthrie Theater 725 Vineland Pl Minneapolis MN 55403

SCHOFIELD, ROBERT EDWIN, history of science educator; b. Milford, Nebr., June 1, 1923; s. Charles Edwin and Nora May (Fullerton) S.; m. Mary-Peale Smith, June 20, 1959; 1 son, Charles Stockton Peale. A.B., Princeton U., 1944; M.S., U. Minn., 1948; Ph.D., Harvard U., 1955. Research asst. Fercleve Corp. and Clinton Labs., Oak Ridge, 1944-46; research assoc. Knolls Atomic Power Lab., Gen. Electric Co., 1948-51; asst. prof., then assoc. prof. history U. Kans., Lawrence, 1955-60; mem. faculty Case Western Res. U., Cleve., 1960-79, prof. history of sci., 1963-72, Lynn Thorndike prof. history of sci., 1972-79; prof. history Iowa State U., Ames, 1979—; mem. Inst. Advanced Study, 1967-68, 74-75; Sigma Xi nat. lectr., 1978-80. Author: The Lunar Society of Birmingham, 1963; Scientific Autobiography of Joseph Priestley: Selected Scientific Correspondence, 1966; Mechanism and Materialism: British Natural Philosophy in a Age of Reason, 1970; (with D.G.C. Allan) Stephen Hales: Scientist and Philanthropist, 1980. Served with AUS, 1945-46. Fulbright fellow, 1953-54; Guggenheim fellow, 1959-60, 67-68. Mem. Am. Phys. Soc., History of Sci. Soc., Soc. History Tech., Midwest Junto History of Sci., Royal Soc. Arts, Am. Soc. 18th Century Studies, Acad. Internat. d'Histoire des Scis. (corr.). Home: 3209 Woodland St Ames IA 50010 Office: Dept History Iowa State U Ames IA 50011

SCHOLER, DAVID MILTON, education administrator; b. Rochester, Minn., July 24, 1938; s. Milton Norris and Bernice Gladys (Anderson) S.; m. Jeannette Faith Mudgett, Aug. 16, 1960; chidlren—Emily and Abigail. B.A., Wheaton Coll., 1960, M.A., 1964; B.D., Gordon Div. Sch., 1964; Th.D., Harvard Div. Sch., 1980. Ordained to ministry Am. Baptist Churches U.S.A., 1966. Asst. prof. N.T., Gordon-Conwell Theol. Sem., South Hamilton, Mass.,

1969-75, assoc. prof. N.T., 1975-81; dean of sem., prof. N.T., No. Bapt. Theol. Sem., Lombard, Ill., 1981—. Author: Nag Hammadi Bibliography 1948-69, 1971, Basic Bibliographic Guide for New Testament Exegesis, 1973. Asst. editor: Encyclopedia of Modern Christian Missions: the Agencies, 1967. Mem. Catholic Biblical Assn., Nat. Assn. Bapt. Profs. Religion, N.Am. Patristic Soc., Soc. Bibl. Lit., Studiorum Novi Testamenti Societas. Baptist. Home: 266 South Myrtle Ave Villa Park IL 60181 Office: Northern Baptist Theol Sem 660 E Butterfield Rd Lombard IL 60148

SCHOLFIELD, KEITH WALTER, real estate broker, insurance agent; b. Eldorado, Kans., Sept. 29, 1936; s. Gene L. and D. Earlyne (Shaw) S.; m. Rochelle Lane English, June 9, 1957; children—Mark K., Julie Lee. B.S. in Bus., U. Kans., 1959. Owner, pres. Keith Scholfield Agy., Inc., Augusta, Kans., 1960—. Pres. Augusta Unified Sch. Dist. 402, 1983-85; Augusta Md. Complex, 1980-82; chmn. Butler County Planning Bd., Kans., 1974. Mem. Nat. Assn. Realtors, Butler County Bd. Realtors, Augusta C. of C. (pres. 1969). Republican. Lodge: Optimist. Avocation: tennis. Home: 1922 Moyle Ave Augusta KS 67010 Office: 606 Walnut St Augusta KS 67010

SCHOLZ, RICHARD F., police chief; b. Milw., Aug. 22, 1938; s. Charles Erwin and Elizabeth (Grafenauer) S.; m. Mary Jean Basich, Apr. 4, 1959 (div. June 1983); children—Richard C., Randall J., Russell. G., Robert A.; Cheryl Lynn Cline, Dec. 30, 1983; stepchildren—Matthew, Michelle, Michael, Meghan. A.A., Marquette U., 1969; B.A., 1975; M.S., U. Wis.-Milw., 1979. FBI Nat. Acad. cert. Patrolman, Milw. Police, 1960-67; sgt. Muskego Police Dept., Wis., 1967-70, lt., 1970-78, chief, 1978—; mem. tng. com. Waukesha County, Wis., 1979—. Cubmaster, Potawatomi council Boy Scouts Am., New Berlin, Wis., 1971-74; bd. dirs. New Berlin Schs., 1980-83. Mem. Wis. Chiefs Police Assn. (tng. com. 1982—); Internat. Chiefs Police Assn.; Waukesha County Chiefs Assn. (pres. 1981). Methodist. Avocations: bowling, golf, reading, motorcycling. Office: W183 S8150 Racine Ave Muskego WI 53150

SCHONEMAN, J.A., insurance company executive. Chmn., chief exec. officer, dir. Wausau Ins. Co., Wausau, Wis. Office: Wausau Ins Co 2000 Westwood Dr Wausau WI 54401*

SCHOPEN, PETER FRANCIS, pest control company executive; b. Evanston, Ill., Oct. 20, 1946; s. Peter N. and Eugene M. (Howard) S.; m. Jean Marie Alsbury, Jan. 15, 1968 (div. 1976); children—Peter Francis, Sonja Katherine, Dayle Evelyn, Drake Andrew; m. Sandra Marie Firestone, Aug. 12, 1978; children—Anita Nina Nuter, Eric Channing. Student Columbia Sch. Broadcasting, Chgo., 1970. Cert. pest controller, Ill. Acct., bookkeeper Electric Hose and Rubber Co., Skokie, Ill., 1967-70; mgr. sales and service Orkin Exterminating Co., Glenview, Ill., 1970-73; pres. Mid Central Pest Control Inc., Algonquin, Ill., 1973—. Pres. H.E.L.P. (hwy. emergency orgn.), Wilmette, 1968-69. Served with U.S. Army, 1964-67; ETO. Home: 639 S 2d St West Dundee IL 60118

SCHOPMEYER, HERMAN H(ENRY), industrial chemist, manufacturing company executive; b. Poland, Ind., Nov. 18, 1904; s. Frank August and Elizabeth Louise (Huckeriede) S.; m. Margaret R. Sharp, June 29, 1934; children—Karl Arthur, William P. (dec.), Robert C. Ph.D. in Biophys. Chemistry, Iowa State U., 1930. Tech. dir. Nat. Distillers Products Corp., N.Y.C., 1930-36; asst. mgr. Am. Maize Products Corp., Hammond, Ind., 1936-50; dir. research Internat. Milling Corp., Mpls., 1950-65, with Archer Daniel Midland, Cedar Rapids, Iowa, 1965—, now v.p., tech. dir. corn sweetener div. Mem. Am. Chem. Soc., Am. Assn. Cereal Chemists, Sigma Xi, Alpha Chi Sigma, Phi Lambda Upsilon. Republican. Methodist. Club: Elmcrest Country (Cedar Rapids). Contbr. articles to profl. jours.; patentee in field. Home: 379 Red Fox Rd SE Cedar Rapids IA 52403 Office: PO Box 1450 Cedar Rapids IA 52406

SCHORER, GALVIN EARL, psychiatrist, educator; b. Sauk City, Wis., June 29, 1919; s. William C. and Anna H. (Walser) S.; m. Avis L. Dagit, July 21, 1950 (div. 1959); m. Marilyn C. Parish, July 8, 1961. B.A., U. Wis.-Madison, 1939; M.A., U. Chgo., 1941, Ph.D., 1948; M.D., U.Wis.-Madison, 1955. Diplomate Am. Bd. Psychiatry and Neurology. Intern, Detroit Receiving Hosp., 1955-56; resident Lafayette Clinic, Detroit, 1956-59; asst. prof. English, No. Mich. Coll., Marquette, 1948-50; prof. Wayne State U., Detroit, 1959—; dir. tng. Lafayette Clinic, Detroit, 1976—. Contbr. articles to profl. publs. Reader, commn. Episcopal Ch. and Diocese of Mich., Detroit and Grosse Pointe, 1957—. Served to capt. USAF, 1942-46. Fellow Am. Psychiat. Assn.; mem. AMA. Lodge: Masons. Avocations, Hunting; basketball. Home: 770 Bedford Grosse Pointe Park MI 48230 Office: 951 E Lafayette Detroit MI 48230

SCHOTTELKOTTE, ALBERT JOSEPH, broadcasting executive; b. Cheviot, Ohio, Mar. 19, 1927; s. Albert William and Venetta (Mentrup) S.; student pub. and parochial schs.; m. Virginia Louise Gleason, July 2, 1951; children—Paul J., Carol Ann, Linda Louise, Joseph G., Matthew, Louis A., Martha Jane, Amy Marie, Mary Jo, Ellen Elizabeth, William H., Michael E. Wtih Cin. Enquirer, 1943-61, successively copy boy, city-wide reporter, columnist, 1953-61; news broadcaster WSAI radio, Cin., 1953-59; news broadcaster WCPO radio-TV, 1959—, dir. news-spl. events, 1961-83, sta. dir., 1983—; gen. mgr. news div. Scripps-Howard Broadcasting Co., 1969-81, v.p. for news, 1971-81, sr. v.p., 1981—; Trustee, Scripps-Howard Found. Served with AUS, 1950-52. Recipient Nat. CD award for reporting on subject, 1958. Mem. Radio-TV News Dirs. Assn. Roman Catholic. Clubs: Maketewah Country, Cin. Home: 7647 Pineglen Dr Cincinnati OH 45224 Office: 500 Central Ave Cincinnati OH 45202

SCHOTTENHEIMER, MARTY, professional football coach. Head coach Cleve. Browns, NFL. Office: Cleveland Browns Cleveland Stadium Cleveland OH 44114*

SCHRADER, ALFRED EUGENE, lawyer; b. Akron, Ohio, Nov. 1, 1953; s. Louis Clement and Helen Maye (Eberz) S.; m. Cathy Diane Fincher, Apr. 17, 1982; children—Eric Brian, Angela Diane. B.A. in Polit. Sci. magna cum laude, Kent State U., 1975; J.D., Ohio State U., 1978. Bar: Ohio 1978, U.S. Dist. Ct. (no. dist.) Ohio 1978, U.S. Ct. Appeals (6th cir.) 1985. Dep. clk. Summit County Clk. of Cts., Akron, 1972-74; sole practice, Akron, 1978—; spl. counsel Bath Twp., Ohio, 1980—; law dir. Northamptian Twp., Ohio, 1983—, Franklin Twp., Ohio, 1984—, Twinsburg Twp., Ohio, 1981—; spl. counsel Richfield Twp., Ohio, 1983-85. Trustee Springfield Twp., Ohio, 1973—, pres., 1975, 79, 82; mem. Summit County Annexation Com., Ohio, 1981-85; mem. Summit County Jail Study Commn., 1983, 84; mem. adv. bd. Springfield Schs., 1975. Mem. Akron Bar Assn. (v.p. legis. com. 1981-82), Ohio Bar Assn., Summit County Twp. assn. (exec. com. 1983—), Ohio Twp. Assn. (exec. com. 1983—). Democrat. Roman Catholic. Home: 3344 Brunk Rd Akron OH 44312 Office: 411 Wolf Ledges Pkwy Akron OH 44311

SCHRAFFENBERGER, LUELLA KATHERINE, nurse; b. Monticello, Iowa, Jan. 15, 1914; d. Lou A. and Matilda (Jacobs) Oltman; R.N., South Shore Hosp., Chgo., 1936; cert. in nursing adminstrn. Baylor U., 1938; m. Howard Edward Schraffenberger, Apr. 30, 1949; 1 dau., Lou Ann. Operating room supr. Mahaska County Hosp., Oskaloosa, Iowa, 1938-40, Ottumwa (Iowa) Gen. Hosp., 1940-41, Moline (Ill.) Public Hosp., 1941-42, Swedish Hosp. of Mpls., 1942-43; operating room supr., clin. instr. Sch. Nursing, South Shore Hosp., Chgo., 1943-52, asst. dir. nurses, 1953-64, dir. nursing service, 1965-82, adminstrv. dir. spl. adminstrv. projects, 1983—. Blood drive vol. ARC, Homewood and Flossmoor, Ill., 1971—. Recipient 35 Years of Service award South Shore Hosp., 1978. Mem. Am. Nurses Assn. (cert. nursing adminstr.), Am. Soc. Nursing Service Adminstrs., Am. Hosp. Assn., Ill. Nurses Assn., Chgo. and Suburban Dirs. Council, South Shore Hosp. Sch. Nursing Alumni Assn. (past pres.). Republican. Lutheran. Club: Dixie Oaks Bus. and Profl. Women's (rec. sec. 1978-79, Woman of Achievement 1978). Office: 8015 S Luella Ave Chicago IL 60617

SCHRAGE, JOHN FREDERICK, information systems educator; b. Granite City, Ill., Mar. 5, 1947; s. Raymond Joe and Rose Marie (Luksan) S.; m. Diane Louise Dressel, Sept. 8, 1973; children—Jason Christopher, Mariam Elizabeth. B.S., So. Ill. U., 1969, M.S., 1973; Ph.D., Mich. State U., 1978. Programmer, analyst So. Ill. U., Edwardsville, 1972-73, assoc. prof. mgmt. info. systems 1978—, scis. coordinator MIS faculty, 1978-84, chmn. dept. mgmt. info. systems, 1984—; asst. mgr., operator Mobile CAI Lab. Penn State U., University Park, 1973; data processing instr. Muskegon (Mich.) Community Coll., 1973-76; asst. prof. computer tech. Purdue U., Ft. Wayne, Ind., 1976-78; word processor Computer Systems, Resource Mgmt. U.S. Army. Sec., treas. Aid Assn. for Lutherans, Troy, Ill., 1979-81; elder St. Paul Lutheran Ch., Troy, 1982—. Served with U.S. Army, 1969-71; USAR, 1971—. Recipient Cert. Merit Am. Legion, 1968; cert. systems profl. Mem. Am. Inst. Decision Scis., Assn. for Computing Machinery, Assn. Ednl. Data Systems, Assn. Systems Mgmt., Am. Mgmt. Assn., Data Processing Mgmt. Assn., EDP Auditors Assn., Pi Omega Pi, Sigma Pi, Alpha Phi Omega (advisor 1979—). Lutheran. Contbr. articles to profl. jours. Home: 617 Brentmoor Dr Troy IL 62294 Office: Campus Box 106 Bldg II Edwardsville IL 62026

SCHRAMM, DAVID NORMAN, astrophysicist, educator; b. St. Louis, Oct. 25, 1945; s. Marvin and Betty (Math) S.; S.B. in Physics, MIT, 1967; Ph.D. in Physics, Calif. Inst. Tech., 1971; m. Melinda Holzhauer, 1963 (div. 1979); children—Cary, Brett; m. 2d, Colleen Rae, 1980. Research fellow in physics Calif. Inst. Tech., Pasadena, 1971-72; asst. prof. astronomy and physics U. Tex., Austin, 1972-74; assoc. prof. astronomy, astrophysics and physics, mem. staff Enrico Fermi Inst., U. Chgo., 1974-77, prof., 1977—, Louis Block prof. phys. scis., 1982—, chmn. dept. astronomy and astrophysics, 1978-84, cosmologist in residence Fermilab, 1982-84; vis. fellow Inst. Theoretical Astronomy, Cambridge, Eng., 1972; vis. prof. Stanford U., 1977; Philips lectr. Haverford (Pa.) Coll., 1977; vis. fellow Japan Soc. for Promotion of Sci., 1979; Hubert Humphrey lectr., Macaelester, Minn., 1981; Richtmeyer lectr. Am. Assn. Physics Tchrs., 1984; lectr. Adler Planetarium, 1976—; Vollmer Fries lectr. Rensselaer Poly. Inst., Troy, N.Y., 1984; J. and N. David lectr. U. Nebr., 1985; mem. adv. and policy coms. Dept. Energy, Nat. Acad. Scis.; mem. Chgo. task force on high tech.; cons. and lectr. in field; frequent radio and TV talk show guest. Trustee Aspen Ctr. for Physics. Investigator grants NSF, NASA, Smithsonian Instn., Dept. Energy. Sloan Found. scholar, 1963-67; NDEA fellow, 1967-71; NSF fellow, 1970-71; U.S. nat. Graeco-Roman Wrestling champion, 1971. Fellow Am. Phys. Soc., Meteoritical Soc.; mem. Am. Astron. Soc. (exec. com. 1977-78, sec.-treas. 1979—; Helen B. Warner prize 1978), Astron. Soc. Pacific (Robert J. Trumpler award 1974), Internat. Astron. Union (various commns.), Sigma Xi (nat. lectr. 1983-85). Contbr. articles to profl. jours.; co-editor: Explosive Nucleosynthesis, 1973, Physical Cosmology, 1980, Essays in Nuclear Astrophysics, 1981, Fundamental Problems in the Theory of Stellar Evolution; editor: Supernovae, 1977, Theoretical Astrophysics Series; co-author: Advanced States of Stellar Evolution, 1977; editorial com. Ann. Rev. Nuclear Sci., 1976-80; assoc. editor Am. Jour. Physics, 1978-81, Physics Reports, 1981; commentor Comments on Nuclear and Particle Physics, 1985-86; columnist Outside Mag. Clubs: Am. Alpine, Quadrangle, X. Home: 155 N Harbor Dr 5203/5204 Chicago IL 60601 Office: Astronomy and Astrophysics Center U Chgo 5640 S Ellis Ave Chicago IL 60637

SCHRAMM, FREDERIC BERNARD, lawyer; b. Cleve., June 3, 1903; s. A. Bernard and Flora Frederica (Leutz) S. B.S., Case Inst. Tech., 1925; J.D., George Washington U., 1931; LL.M., Western Res. U., 1955. Bar: U.S. Patent Office 1930, D.C. 1931, Ohio 1944, N.Y. 1933, Calif. 1957. Patent atty. Gen. Electric Co., Schenectady, 1925-42; ptnr. Richey & Watts, Cleve., 1942-54, Kendrick, Schramm & Stolzy, Los Angeles, 1954-60, Schramm, Kramer & Sturges, Cleve., 1960-72, Schramm & Knowles, Cleve., 1972-80; instr. Fenn Coll., 1973-74, Cleve. Marshal Law Sch., Cleve. State U., 1974-75. Mem. ABA, Cleve. Bar Assn., Am. Patent Law Assn., Cleve. Patent Law Assn., IEEE, Sigma Xi, Eta Kappa Nu, Tau Beta Pi. Clubs: Kiwanis (Shaker Heights, Ohio); Univ., Torch (Cleve.). Author: Handbook on Patent Disputes, 1974; contbr. articles to law jours. Office: 3570 Warrensville Center Rd Suite 201 Cleveland OH 44122

SCHRAMM, RICHARD MARTIN, sales and marketing executive; executive; b. Bklyn., Apr. 15, 1940; s. Harold Matthew and Elizabeth Ann (Hitt) S.; m. Camille K. Khoury, Apr. 24, 1964; children—Christine, Carolyn, Catherine. Student U. San Francisco, 1957-59; B.A., Columbia U., 1961. Nat. sales mgr. 3M Co., 1970-75; dir. mktg. Hollingsworth Co., 1975-79; coach N.Y. Nets profl. basketball, 1967-69; pres. Sol. Term. Mfrs. Assn., N.Y.C., 1972-75; dir. sales and mktg. Mega diamond Industries Inc., 1979-83, Baumgold Diamond Co. Inc., 1983—; dir. Indsl. Diamond Assn., Columbia, S.C., 1982—. Mem. Am. Mgmt. Assn., Chgo. Execs. Club. Author: Marketing - Keys to Successful Selling, 1983.

SCHRECK, EDWARD WILLIAM, medical educator, osteopathic physician; b. Columbus, Ohio, June 19, 1948; s. Victor Charles and Margaret Louise (Trapp) S.; m. Mary Noreen Martens, July 4, 1970; children—Christopher, Douglas, Jennifer. B.S., U. Notre Dame, 1970; D.O., Chgo. Coll. Osteo. Medicine, 1975. Cert. Am. Osteo. Bd. Gen. Practice. Intern, Doctors Hosp., Columbus, 1975-76; gen. practice osteo. medicine with John R. Bowling, D.O., Lancaster, Ohio, 1976-80; dir. Vinton County Health Clinic, McArthur, Ohio, 1981—; asst. prof. family medicine Ohio U., Athens, 1981—; med. dir. Athens chpt. ARC; chmn. rev. com. area VIII Physician Standard Rev. Orgn. Mem. Vinton County Bd. Health, 1981-86. Served to capt. USAR, 1983. Named Outstanding Intern in Family Practice, Doctors Hosp., Columbus, 1976. Mem. Am. Osteo. Assn., Am. Acad. Osteopathy, Am. Coll. Gen. Practitioners Osteo. Medicine, Ohio Osteo. Assn. Republican. Roman Catholic. Clubs: Kiwanis, K.C. Author weekly column on family health problems pub. nationwide newspapers. Office: Ohio U Coll Osteo Medicine Room 245 Athens OH 45701

SCHREIBER, HARRY, JR., management consultant; b. Columbus, Ohio, Apr. 1, 1934; s. C. Harry and Audrey (Sard) S.; B.S., Mass. Inst. Tech., 1955; M.B.A., Boston U., 1958; m. Margaret Ruth Heinzman, June 12, 1955; children—Margaret Elizabeth, Thomas Edward, Amy Katherine. Accountant truck and coach div. Gen. Motors Corp., Pontiac, Mich., 1955; instr. Mass. Inst. Tech., 1958-62; pres. Data-Service, Inc., Boston, 1961-65; pres. Harry Schreiber Assos., Wellesley, Mass., 1965; mgr., nat. dir. merchandising Peat, Marwick, Mitchell & Co., N.Y.C., 1966-70, partner, Chgo., 1970-75; chmn. bd. Close, Martin, Schreiber & Co., 1975-83; partner Deloitte Haskins & Sells, 1983—. Staff, Work Simplification Conf. Lake Placid, N.Y., 1960-61. Served to 1st lt. AUS, 1956-58. Mem. Am. Inst. Indsl. Engrs. (chmn. data-processing div. 1964-66, chpt. v.p. 1961, 65, chmn. retail industries div. 1976-78), Com. Internat. Congress Transp. Confs., Assn. for Computing Machinery, Assn. for Systems Mgmt., Inst. Mgmt. Scis., Retail Research Soc., Retail Fin. Execs., Nat. Retail Mchts. Assn. (retail systems specifications com.), Food Distbn. Research Soc. (dir. 1972—, pres. 1974), Internat. Trade Club, Japan-Am. Soc. Chgo., Chgo. Assn. Commerce and Industry. Republican. Methodist. Clubs: MIT Faculty; Skokie Country; Hidden Creek; Army and Navy (Washington); Plaza (Chgo.). Home: 12137 Stirrup Rd Reston VA 22091 Office: 200 E Randolph Dr Chicago IL 60601

SCHREIBER, JOAN EMELIA, social studies educator; b. La Porte City, Iowa, Feb. 24, 1928; d. Louie and Dorathea Magdalena (Lange) Schreiber; student U. Iowa, 1945-46; B.A., Iowa State Tchrs. Coll., 1949; M.A., State Coll. Iowa, 1960; Specialist in Edn., U. No. Iowa, 1963; Ph.D., U. Iowa, 1967. Tchr. Cedar Rapids (Iowa) public schs., 1949-59; ednl. cons. Cass County, Atlantic, Iowa, 1961-63; asst. prof. Edn. Augustana Coll., Rock Island, Ill., 1963-65; asst. prof. history Ball State U., Muncie, Ind., 1966-69, assoc. prof., 1969-74, prof., 1974—, social studies coordinator, 1968—, pres. univ. senate, 1979-80; social studies program developer for Scott, Foresman. Mem. Ind. State Social Studies Adv. Com., 1974—, Ind. State Tchr. Edn. Adv. Council, 1974-75. Mem. Nat., Ind. (pres. 1974-75) councils social studies, AAUP, Ind. Acad. Social Scis., AAUW, Del. County (Ind.) Hist. Soc., Pi Lambda Theta, Pi Gamma Mu, Phi Delta Kappa. Author: (with Lloyd L. Smith) Social Studies K-6: A Guide for Curriculum Revision, 1971; program author social studies textbooks and supplementary materials for kindergarten through grade 7. Contbr. editor Social Studies Teacher. Contbr. articles to profl. jours. Home: 30 Eucalyptus Dr Route 12 Muncie IN 47302 Office: History Dept Ball State U Muncie IN 47306

SCHREIER, LEONARD, allergist, immunologist; b. Detroit, June 3, 1934; s. Alexander and Fanny (Wayne) S.; M.D., U. Mich., 1959, M.S. in Internal Medicine, 1965; m. Barbara Gay Hirsch, Aug. 11, 1956 (div. June 1980); children—Eric Marvin, Jordan Scott, Barry Andrew; m. Raquel Lucia Cruz, July 11, 1981. Intern, Sinai Hosp., Detroit, 1959-60, resident in internal medicine, 1960-63; fellow in allergy and immunology U. Mich., 1963-65; practice medicine specializing in allergy and immunology, Detroit, 1965-66, Pontiac, Mich., 1968—; staff St. Joseph Mercy Hosp., Pontiac, acting chmn. dept. medicine, 1980-81; asst. clin. prof. medicine Wayne State Coll. Medicine, 1976—. Served with M.C., U.S. Army, 1966-68. Diplomate Am. Bd. Internal Medicine, Am. Bd. Allergy and Immunology. Fellow Am. Acad. Allergy. Jewish. Contbr. articles to med. jours. Office: 1555 Woodward Ave Suite 101 Bloomfield Hills MI 48013

SCHREIER, THOMAS STEPHEN, accounting firm executive; b. St. Paul, Oct. 13, 1936; s. Mathew Henry and Sophie Marcella (Wesolawski) S.; m. Mary Rae Billstein, Oct. 21, 1961; children—Thomas Stephen, John, Jennifer, Martin. B.A., Coll. St. Thomas, St. Paul, 1960. C.P.A., Minn. Staff acct. Sevenich & Co., C.P.A.s, St. Paul, 1958-61; sr. acct. Boulay & Co., C.P.A.s, Mpls., 1962-67; ptnr. Schreier & Mazanec, C.P.A.s, St. Paul, 1967-71; mng. ptnr. Schreier, Heimer, Kosbab & Co., C.P.A.s, St. Paul, 1972—; cons. Bus. Furniture, Inc., Mpls., 1981—; dir. Schaak Electronics Inc., St. Paul. Trustee, treas. Children's Hosp., St. Paul, 1980—; trustee St. Thomas Acad., St. Paul, 1981—. Republican. Roman Catholic. Club: North Oaks Country (St. Paul). Avocations: golf; reading; gardening. Home: 15 Lily Pond Rd Saint Paul MN 55110 Office: Schreier Heimer Kosbab & Co CPAs 3570 N Lexington Ave Saint Paul MN 55112

SCHRICKEL, DENISE MARIE, pharmacist; b. Toledo, Ohio, Apr. 10, 1955; d. Jack and Norma (Rieck) Schrickel. B.S. in Pharmacy, U. Toledo, 1978. Registered pharmacist, Ohio. Pharmacist, Lane Drugs div. People Drug Stores, Toledo, 1975—. Mem. Lambda Kappa Sigma. Republican. Lutheran. Avocations: Genealogy. Office: Lane Drug 2600 Sylvania Ave Toledo OH 43613

SCHRIPSEMA, JACK ALAN, hotel administrator; b. Holland, Mich., Mar. 11, 1951; s. John J. and Janet (Sneller) S.; m. Rita Jean Nonnamaker, June 11, 1973; children—John Jay, Kelly Lynn. B.A., Mich. State U., 1973. Asst. dir. convention service Westin Hotel, Detroit, 1977-79; dir. hospitality Wayne Community Coll., Detroit, 1979-80; asst. dir. Mich. State U. Student Union, East Lansing, Mich., 1980; sales mgr. Amway Grand Plaza Hotel, Grand Rapids, Mich., 1980-82, nat. sales mgr., 1982-84, dir. sales, 1984—. Mem. Meeting Planners Internat., Am. Soc. Assn. Execs., Mich. Soc. Assn. Execs., Mich. Meeting Planners Internat. (com. chmn.), Hotel Sales Mgmt. Assn. Republican. Mem. Dutch Reformed Ch. America. Lodge: Kiwanis. Avocations: Card collecting; golf, fishing, boating, tennis. Office: Amway Grand Plaza Hotel Pearl at Monroe Grand Rapids MI 49428

SCHRODER, BARRY CHARLES, lawyer; b. La Porte, Ind., Apr. 26, 1955; s. Charles William and Veronica Helen (Bigda) S.; m. Nancy Lee Vincent, Sept. 6, 1980. B.A., Mich. State U., 1977; J.D., Wayne State U., 1980. Bar: Mich. 1980, U.S. Dist. Ct. (we. dist.) Mich. 1980, U.S. Ct. Appeals (6th cir.) 1983. Assoc., Rhoades, McKee & Boer, Grand Rapids, Mich., 1980—. Democrat. Roman Catholic. Office: Rhoades McKee & Boer 611 Waters Bldg Grand Rapids MI 49503

SCHROEDER, ALFRED GUSTAV, state supreme court justice; b. Newton, Kans., June 5, 1916; s. Gustav D. and Grete (Janzen) S.; student Bethel Coll., Newton, 1933-35; B.S. with high honors, Kans. State Coll., 1937; J.D., Harvard U., 1940; m. Katheryn Marie Diel, Aug. 8, 1942; children—John Scott, Hedy Marie, Marilyn Sue. Bar: Kans. 1940. Sole practice law, Newton, 1940-42, also farm mgr.; judge Probate and County Ct., Harvey County, Kans., 1947-53, 9th Jud. Dist. Ct. Kans., 1953-57; justice Kans. Supreme Ct., 1957—, chief justice, 1977—; chmn. Kans. Jud. Council, 1963-79; mem. exec. council, chmn. jury mgmt. com. Conf. of Chief Justices. Bd. dirs. Kans. Council Chs., 1962-66; mem. Freedoms award Jury Freedoms Found., 1959, 68; mem. So. Assn. Conglist Chs. Kans., moderator 1956. Served to capt. USAAF, 1942-46. Mem. Am., Kans. bar assns., Phi Kappa Phi, Alpha Zeta. Republican. Home: 825 Buchanan St Topeka KS 66606 Office: State House Topeka KS 66612

SCHROEDER, CHARLES EDGAR, business executive; b. Chgo., Nov. 17, 1935; s. William Edward and Lelia Lorraine (Anderson) S.; B.A. in Econs., Dartmouth Coll., 1957, M.B.A., 1958; m. Martha E. Runnette, Dec. 30, 1958; children—Charles Edgar, Timothy Creighton, Elizabeth Linton. Security analyst Miami Corp., Chgo., 1960-69, treas., 1969-77, pres., 1978—, dir., 1969—; security analyst Cutler Oil & Gas Corp., Chgo., 1960-69, treas., 1969-77, pres., 1978—, dir., 1969—; dir. Nat. Blvd. Bank Chgo., 1969—, chmn. bd., 1981—; chmn. bd. Blvd. Bancorp, Inc., 1984—; dir. Nat.-Standard Co., Niles, Mich. Assoc., Northwestern U., Evanston, Ill., 1975—; trustee 1st Presbyn. Ch. of Evanston, 1968—, Wayland Acad., Beaver Dam, Wis., 1982—; bd. dirs. Presbyn. Home, Evanston, 1979—. Served as lt. (j.g.) USN, 1958-60. Mem. Fin. Analysts Soc. Chgo., Beta Theta Pi. Clubs: Chicago, Mid-Am. (Chgo.); Glen View (Ill.) Golf; Michigan Shores (Wilmette, Ill.); Casque and Gauntlet. Office: 410 N Michigan Ave Chicago IL 60611

SCHROEDER, HENRY WILLIAM, publisher; b. Cleve., Sept. 7, 1928; s. Henry and Esther Julia (Kamman) S.; m. Elizabeth Churbuck, Aug. 15, 1977; children—Joy, Bill, Stephen; m. Dorothy Hildebrand, Aug. 18, 1956 (div.); children—Susan Schroeder Olson, Katherine Jean. B.S., U. Wis., 1957, M.S., 1959. Info. dir. Wis. Farm Bur., Madison, 1960-63; asst. dir. pub. relations Credit Union Internat., Madison, 1963-65; editor, co-pub. Verona Press (Wis.), 1966—, also v.p. Southwest Suburban Publs., Inc., 1966-80; co-pub. Fitchburg Star, 1974—, also pres. Southwest Suburban Publs. and Schroeder Publs., Inc.; pub. Blade-Atlas, Blanchardville, Wis., 1977-83; pres., pub. Leader Publ. Corp., Evansville, Wis., 1981—. Mem. Gov.'s UN Commn., 1974. Served with USNR, 1949-53. Mem. Wis. Newspaper Assn. (pres. 1983-84), Wis. Newspaper Assn. (dir. 1973-86), Madison Press Club, Nat. Newspaper Assn. (govt. affairs conf., mem. services com.), Verona C. of C. (pres. 1970). Republican. Lodges: Optimists, Masons (master 1970), Shriners. Office: Verona Press 120 W Verona Ave Box 6 Verona WI 53593

SCHROEDER, PAUL HILLER, JR., shoe company executive; b. Melrose, Mass., Sept. 3, 1942; s. Paul H. and Elizabeth (Soule) S.; m. Judith Lea Ide, June 13, 1964; 1 child, Susan. B.A., Beloit Coll., 1964. Cert. data processor. Programmer, Northwestern Mutual Life Ins., Milw., 1964-66; instr. Inst. Computer Programming, Milw., 1966-67; dir. data processing, real estate, ops. Weyenberg Shoe Co., Milw., 1967—; cons. Mfrs. Box Co., Milw., Mfrs. Chem. Co., Milw. Unit chmn. United Fund, Milw., 1976; bus. advisor Milw. Art Mus., 1982-83. Mem. Am. Contract Bridge League (life master), Mensa. Avocations: bridge; gravity theory; sailing. Home: S76 W13070 Cambridge Ct Hales Corners WI 53130 Office: Weyenberg Shoe Co 234 E Reservoir Ave Milwaukee WI 53201

SCHROEDER, ROBERT ANTHONY, lawyer; b. Bendena, Kans., May 19, 1912; s. Anthony and Nanon (Bagby) S.; LL.B. cum laude, U. Kans., 1937; m. Janet Manning, Nov. 21, 1936; 1 son, Robert Breathitt. Admitted to Mo. bar 1937; atty. Allstate Ins. Co., Chgo., 1937-38; asso. firm Madden, Freeman, Madden & Burke, Kansas City, Mo., 1938-48; partner firm Swofford, Schroeder & Shankland, Kansas City, 1948-59; owner law offices Robert A. Schroeder, 1959-67; partner firm Schroeder & Schroeder, 1967—; chmn. 16th Circuit Bar Com., 1972-80; commr. 16th Jud. Selection Com., 1974-80; commr. Appellate Jud. Selection Com. of Mo., 1980—; v.p. Roxbury State Bank (Kans.), 1954-72, pres., 1972-77, chmn. bd., 1977—, also dir.; pres., dir. Douglas County Investment Co.; chmn. bd., dir. Mark Twain Bank Noland Independence, Mo. Vice pres. Mo. Found., 1965-70; pres. Mo. Bar Found., 1970-73; trustee Kans. U. Law Sch. Soc.; hon. trustee Kansas City Art Inst.; bd. dirs. Mo. Inst., 1983—. Fellow Am. Bar Found., Am. Coll. Probate Counsel, Kans. U. Law Soc., Harry S. Truman Library Inst. (hon.); mem. Mo. Bar (co-chmn. continuing legal edn. com. 1958-59, chmn. fin. planning subcom. 1958-59, gov. 1959-67, chmn. public edn. com. 1965-66, pres. 1965-66, chmn. cts. and jud. com. 1971-72, Pres.'s award 1972), Am. (state chmn. standing com. on membership 1961-62, mem. lawyer referral com. 1966-70, Ho. of Dels. 1967-71, vice chmn. Mo. bench and bar com. 1968-71, mem. bench and bar com. 1971-83), Kans. (hon. life), Kansas City (pres. 1957-58, chmn. exec. com. 1957-58, judicial recommendations com. 1957-58, 69-70, public relations com. 1958-60, medico-legal com. 1962-64, law day com. 1964-65, lawyer welfare and placement com. 1966-72, program com. 1969-70, pre-paid legal services 1975-77, Achievement award 1976, Merit award) bar assns., Am. Judicature Soc. (dir. 1967-69), Greater Kansas City Kans. U. Law Sch. Alumni Assn. (pres. 1963-64), Delta Tau Delta, Phi Delta Phi (pres. 1936-37), Order of Coif. Clubs: Executives, Chancellor's (U. Kans.); Masons. Author: Twenty-Five Years Under the Missouri Plan; Twenty-Five Years Experience with Merit Judicial Selection in Missouri. Assoc. editor Kans. Law Jour., 1935-37. Office: 11324 Madison Kansas City MO 64114

SCHROEDER, TERRI LEA, city manager, educator; b. Elgin, Ill. Mar. 11, 1955; d. Earl and Caroline Louise Christiansen. Student William Rainey Harper Coll., 1973-77; B.S. in Edn., No. Ill. U., 1977, M.A. in Pub. Adminstrn., 1979. Lic. pub. water supply operator Ill. EPA Class C; cert. water treatment plant operator Iowa Dept. Environ. Quality Grade I. Tchr., English, Sch. Dist. 202, Plainfield, Ill., 1977-78; adminstrv. asst. to village mgr. Village of Deerfield (Ill.), 1978-79; asst. village mgr. Village of Lincolnshire (Ill.), 1979-81, village mgr., 1981-82; city mgr. City of Iowa Falls (Iowa), 1982—; cons. exec. dir. Lake County Youth Service Bur., Lake Villa, Ill., 1979-80; communications and pub. relations coordinator Univ. Health Ctr., DeKalb, Ill., 1977-78; legal asst. Winnebago County Legal Aid, Rockford, Ill., spring 1979; feature speaker KIFG Radio Sta., fall 1982. Trustee, mem. budget com. 1st Congl. Ch., Iowa Falls, 1982—; founder, bd. dirs. Iowa Falls 2000, 1984—; founder Iowa Falls Arts Council, 1984; bd. dirs., mem. leadership com. Com. of 80's Iowa Falls, 1982—; mem. DeKalb Human Relations Commn., 1977-79; lobbyist for Student Assn. on Higher Edn. Appropriations, 79th Gen. Assembly, Washington; chairperson for polit. awareness week, DeKalb, 1977; mem. Gov.'s Com. on Future Iowa Growth, 1984. Named Iowa's Young Career Woman of 1982-83, Iowa Fedn. Bus. Profl. Women, 1983; named Outstanding Young Working Woman, Glamour Mag., 1984; Esper A. Peterson Found. scholar, 1976-79; Gen. Assembly scholar. Mem. Bus. Profl. Women (Young Career Woman, chmn. dist. IV northwest Iowa 1983—), Internat. City Mgmt. Assn. (assoc.), Iowa City Mgmt. Assn. (newsletter editor 1983-84), North Central Iowa City Mgmt. Assn. (founder, exec. bd. dirs.), Mcpl. Fin. Officers Assn., Am. Pub. Works Assn., Internat. Mcpl. Clks. Home: 315 Estes St Iowa Falls IA 50126 Office: City of Iowa Falls IA 315 Stevens St PO Box 698 Iowa Falls IA 50126

SCHROEDER, WILLIAM ROBERT, state official; b. Chgo., May 7, 1945; s. William August and Anna Marie (Aufmuth) S.; B.S., Loyola U., Chgo., 1967; student John Marshall Law Sch., Chgo., 1967-69; m. Margaret Mary Bray, June 22, 1968; children—William Robert, Jennifer Anne. With firm Peterson, Bogucki and Beck, Chgo., 1967-69, Commerce Clearing House, Chgo., 1969-71; with Cook County (Ill.) Bur. Adminstrn., 1971-83, tng. dir. dept. personnel, 1976-83; exec. asst. to Ill. State Treas., 1983—; mem. adv. council masters program in adminstrv. sci./public agy. adminstrn. program U. Ill., Chgo., 1980—. Bd. dirs. Leaning Tower YMCA, 1975—, vice chmn., 1978-81, chmn., 1981—; chmn. fund raising St. Constance Roman Cath. Ch., Chgo., 1977-78; coach Norwood Park Boys Baseball, 1979-82; bd. dirs. 45th Ward Regular Democratic Orgn., 1968—; sec. bus. adv. council Copernicus Found., 1982—. Recipient various service certs. Mem. Intergovtl. Tng. Assn. Chgo. (v.p. 1978), Am. Soc. Public Adminstrn. (sec. Chgo. chpt. 1980-81, pres. 1981, nat. council rep. 1984—), Ill. Correctional Assn. (dir. 1979-80; cert. commendation 1981), Am. Soc. Tng. and Devel., Gentlemen Sportsmen Striders, Polish Nat. Alliance (dir. Chgo. chpt. 1980-81), Chgo. Soc. Club: Moose. Office: 160 N La Salle St Room 815 Chicago IL 60601

SCHROER, EDMUND ARMIN, utility company executive; b. Hammond, Ind., Feb. 14, 1928; s. Edmund Henry and Florence Evelyn (Schmidt) S.; B.A., Valparaiso U., 1949; J.D., Northwestern U., 1952; children—James, Fredrik, Amy, Lisa, Timothy, Suzanne. Admitted to Ind. bar, 1952; practiced in Hammond, 1952—; assoc. Crumpacker & Friedrich, 1952; ptnr. Crumpacker & Schroer, 1954-56; assoc., then ptnr. Friedrich, Petri & Tweedle, 1957-62; partner Schroer & Eichhorn, 1963-66; ptnr. Schroer, Eichhorn & Morrow, Hammond, 1967-77; pres., chief exec. officer No. Ind. Public Service Co., Hammond, 1977—, chmn., 1978—; asst. dist. atty. No. Ind., 1954-56; dir. Edison Electric Inst.; mem. coms. Am. Gas Assn.; dir., mem. exec. com. Ind. Electric Assn.; dir. Harris Bank Corp. Trustee Nat. Electric Reliability Council; vice chmn. East Central Reliability Council; trustee Sch. Bd., Munster, Ind., 1969-71, pres., 1971; fin. chmn. Republican Party, Hammond, 1958-62; del. Ind. Rep. Conv., 1958, 60, 64, 66, 68. Mem. ABA, Fed. Bar Assn., Fed. Power Bar Assn., Ind. Bar Assn. (bd. mgrs. 1969-71), Hammond Bar Assn. (pres. 1966-67). Am. Judicature Soc. Lutheran. Lodge: Rotary (pres. Hammond club 1968). Office: No Ind Pub Service Co 5265 Hohman Ave Hammond IN 46320*

SCHROTT, JANET ANN, social worker, training analyst, consultant; b. Cleve., Dec. 11, 1941; d. Louis Vincent and Amelia Jane (Lauko) Cupolo; B.A., Flora Stone Mather Coll. of Case Western Res. U., 1963, M.S. in Social Adminstrn., 1974; m. Norman Schrott, July 25, 1964. Research asst. Aging Baseline Study, HEW Grant, Miami, Fla., 1964-65; caseworker Div. Social Services, Cuyahoga County Welfare Dept., Cleve., 1965-72, protective services supr., 1974-78; dir. social services Luth. Housing Corp., Cleve., 1973-74; dir. travelers aid services and quality assurance Center for Human Services, Cleve., 1978-85; tng. analyst Cleve. Electric Illuminating Co., Perry, Ohio. Bd. dirs. adv. council Adult Rehab. Services, Salvation Army, 1978-85. Cuyahoga County Welfare Dept. grantee, 1972-74. Mem. Assn. MBA Execs., Acad. Cert. Social Workers, Nat. Assn. Social Workers, Am. Humane Soc., Brookings Inst., Nat. Geographic Soc., Travelers Aid Assn. Am. (bd. dirs., Steering com. 1982-85), Theta Phi Omega. Club: Zonta. Home: 25925 Lake Rd Bay Village OH 44140 Office: Perry Tng Center PO Box 97 Mail Zone TEC Perry OH 44081

SCHROTT, NORMAN, clinical social worker; b. N.Y.C., Jan. 26, 1938; s. Walter Quido Otto and Anna (Klein) S.; B.A. in Sociology, Cleve. State U., 1972; M.S. in Social Planning and Adminstrn. (grantee State of Ohio 1974-76), Case Western Res. U., 1976; m. Janet Ann Cupolo, July 25, 1964. Adminstrv. specialist div. social services Cuyahoga County Welfare Dept., Cleve., 1972-74, foster care specialist, 1976-79, child abuse supr., 1979-80, protective services supr., 1980—. Served with U.S. Army, 1962-65. Mem. Acad. Cert. Social Workers, Nat. Assn. Social Workers, Nat. Conf. Social Welfare, Am. Public Welfare Assn., Am. Acad. Polit. and Social Scis., Nat. Audubon Soc., Am. Orchid Soc. Club: Kiwanis. Home: 25925 Lake Rd Bay Village OH 44140 Office: 3955 Euclid Ave Cleveland OH 44115

SCHRUM, JOHN MARTIN, investment company executive, educator; b. Woodward, Iowa, Dec. 6, 1932; s. Peter Friedrich and Anita (Warner) S.; m. Marilyn Jean Lister, Aug. 9, 1975; children—Rachel Ann, Heidi Marie, Joshua Martin. B.S. in Agrl. Edn., Iowa State U., 1959; M.S. in Agrl. Edn., Purdue U., 1961. Cert. sch. adminstr., Iowa, 1966. Tchr. jr. high and high sch., Coggon, Iowa, 1962-63, Parkersburg, Iowa, 1963-68; broker R.G. Dickinson Co., Cedar Falls, Iowa, 1968-71, Packers Trading Co., Waterloo, Iowa, 1971-72, A.G. Edwards, Waterloo, 1972—, dir. Geerlings Feed Co., Waterloo, 1975-82, Corn Country Beef Co., Dike, Iowa, 1976-77. Republican precinct chmn., Cedar Falls, 1976—. Served with U.S. Army, 1954-56. Lutheran. Avocations: travel; politics; reading. Home: 3703 McClain Dr Cedar Falls IA 50613

SCHUBERT, ELIZABETH M(AY), paralegal adminstrv. asst.; b. Hamilton, Ohio, Sept. 10, 1913; d. A(ndreas) Gordon and Grace Symmes (Laxford) S.; B.S. in Edn. cum laude, Miami U., 1933. Sec., Beta Kappa Nat. Frat., Oxford, Ohio, 1931-38; adminstrv. asst. to dir. Ohio State Employment Service, Columbus, 1938-45, supr. procedures, 1945-47; adminstrv. asst. to pres. Schaible Co., Cin., 1948-50; paralegal adminstrv. asst. to Gordon H. Scherer, Atty.-at-Law, mem. U.S. Congress, U.S. del. to UN, U.S. rep. to exec. bd. UNESCO, Paris, 1950—. Mem. Phi Beta Kappa. Republican. Presbyn. Home: 1071 Celestial St Apt 1701 Cincinnati OH 45202 Office: 2103 Highland Tower Cincinnati OH 45202

SCHUBERT, WILLIAM HENRY, educator; b. Garrett, Ind., July 6, 1944; s. Walter William and Mary Madeline (Grube) S.; B.S., Manchester Coll., 1966; M.S., Ind. U., 1967; Ph.D., U. Ill., 1975; m. Ann Lynn Lopez, Dec. 3, 1977; 1 dau., Heidi Ann; children by previous marriage—Ellen Elaine, Karen Margaret. Tchr., Fairmount, El Sierra and Herrick Schs., Downers Grove, Ill., 1967-75; clin. instr. U. Wis., Madison, 1969-73; teaching asst., univ. fellow U. Ill., Urbana, 1973-75; asst. prof. U. Ill., Chgo., 1975-80, assoc. prof., 1981-85, prof., 1985—, coordinator secondary edn., 1979-82; coordinator instructional leadership, 1979-85, dir. grad. studies Coll. Edn., 1983-85, coordinator grad. curriculum studies, 1985—; vis. assoc. prof. U. Victoria (B.C., Can.), summer 1981. Mem. Profs. of Curriculum (factotum 1984-85), Soc. for Study of Curriculum History (founding mem., sec.-treas. 1981-82, pres. 1982-83), Am. Ednl. Research Assn. (chmn. creation and utilization of curriculum knowledge 1980-82, program chmn. curriculum studies div. 1982-83), John Dewey Soc., Assn. for Supervision and Curriculum Devel. (steering com. of curriculum com. 1980-83), Am. Ednl. Studies Assn., Soc. for Profs. of Edn., Nat. Soc. for Study of Edn., Phi Delta Kappa, Phi Kappa Phi (pres. U. Ill.-Chgo. chpt. 1981-82). Clubs: Masons, Scottish Rite. Author: Curriculum Books: The First Eighty Years, 1980; editor: (with Ann Schubert) Conceptions of Curriculum Knowledge: Focus on Students and Teachers, 1982; (with Short and Willis) Toward Excellence in Curriculum Inquiry, 1985; Curriculum: Perspective, Paradigm, and Possibility, 1986; mem. editorial bd. Ednl. Studies, Ednl. Theory, Phenomenology Pedagogy, Teaching Edn.; cons. editor Jour. Curriculum and Supervision; contbr. articles to profl. publs. Home: 1642 E 56th St Chicago IL 60637 Office: Coll Edn U Ill Chgo Box 4348 Chicago IL 60680

SCHUCHTER, SIDNEY LAZARUS, physician; b. N.Y.C., June 9, 1925; s. Philip and Beatrice (Teplitz) S.; m. Doris Brown, Mar. 24, 1954 (div. 1978); children—Lynn, Janet, Philip. A.B., Syracuse U., 1948; M.D., Chgo. Med. Sch., 1952. Diplomate Am. Bd. Internal. Medicine, Nat. Bd. Med. Examiners. Intern, Phila. Gen. Hosp., 1952-53; resident physician Cleve. Clinic, 1953-56, asst. staff physician, 1956-57; staff internist VA Hosp., Nashville, 1957-58; staff internist Met. Hosp., Detroit, 1958-63, chief dept. medicine, 1963-69; internist Detroit Indsl. Clinic, Southfield, Mich., 1969—; clin. instr. Frank E. Bunts Ednl. Inst., Cleve., 1956-57; adj. clin. instr. Dept. Medicine, Wayne State U., 1960—. Contbr. articles to med. jours. Served to 1st lt. U.S. Army, 1943-46. Fellow Am. Coll. Physicians; mem. Am. Heart Assn., AMA, Am. Rheumatism Assn., Wayne County Med. Soc. Home: 2370 Somerset Blvd Troy MI 48084 Office: 20755 Greenfield Southfield MI 48075

SCHUDT, JOSEPH ARTHUR, civil engineer; b. Chgo., Apr. 16, 1938; s. Joseph August and Pauline (Pelley) S.; m. Jean Carol Falkenthal, Dec. 30, 1961; children—Joseph, Eric, Karl. B.C.E., U. Notre Dame, 1959; M.A. in Environ. Mgmt. Gov.'s State U., 1976. Registered engr., Ill., Ind., Mo., Mich., Fla.; registered land surveyor, Ill. Project mgr. J.A. Schudt & Assocs., Matteson, Ill., 1959-72; prin., 1972-81, pres., 1981—. Com. chmn. Marian High Sch. Lay Adv. Bd., Chicago Heights, Ill., 1985, sec., 1986; mem. St. Mary's Parish Council, Park Forest, Ill., 1986. Served to capt. USAR, 1959-69. Mem. Ill. Soc. Profl. Engrs. (pres. 1979-80, nat. dir. 1976—, Ill. award 1985), Nat. Soc. Profl. Engrs., ASCE, Am. Water Works Assn., Central States Water Pollution Control Fedn. Roman Catholic. Club: Prestwick Country. Home: 1017 Prestwick Dr Frankfort IL 60423 Office: Joseph A Schudt & Assocs 3920 W 216th St Matteson IL 60423

SCHUENKE, DONALD JOHN, insurance company executive; b. Milw., Jan. 12, 1929; s. Ray H. and Josephine P. (Maciolek) S.; Ph.B., Marquette U., 1950, LL.B., 1958; m. Joyce A. Wetzel, July 19, 1952; children—Ann, Mary. Bar: Wis. 1958. Spl. agt. Nat. Life of Vt., 1958-59; real estate rep. Standard Oil Co. of Ind., Milw., 1959-63; atty. Northwestern Mut. Life Ins. Co., Milw., 1963-65, asst. gen. counsel, 1965-74 v.p., gen. counsel, sec., 1974-76, sr. v.p. investments, 1976-80, pres., 1980—, chief operating officer, 1981-83, chief exec. officer, 1983—; dir. Badger Meter, Inc., Competitive Wis., Inc., No. Telcom Ltd., Mortgage Guaranty Ins. Corp., INROADS/Milw., Inc., Regis Group, Inc., Grand Ave. Corp. Bd. dirs. Milw. Symphony Orch., Milw. Art Mus., Marquette U., Med. Research Fund, Com. for Econ. Devel. Milw. Redevel. Corp., Wis. Taxpayers Alliance, Milw. Regional Med. Ctr., Milw. Boys and Girls Club; mem. adv. council Am. Heart Assn.; mem. pres.'s adv. council Cardinal Stritch Coll.; bd. dirs., v.p. Greater Milw. Com. Mem. Wis. Bar Assn., Met. Milw. Assn. Commerce (bd. dirs.), Am. Council Life Ins. Club: University (bd. dirs.) (Milw.). Office: Northwestern Mut Life Ins Co 720 E Wisconsin Ave Milwaukee WI 53202

SCHUERHOLZ, JOHN BOLAND, JR., professional baseball executive; b. Balt., Oct. 1, 1940; s. John Boland and Maryne (Wyatt) S.; m. Ellen Louise Lawson, June 21, 1963, 1 dau., Regina Marie Reagan; m. Karen Louise Wiltse, Sept. 18, 1978; 1 son, Jonathan Lawrence. B.E., Towson State U., 1962; student Loyola Coll. (Md.), 1964-66. Tchr., 1962-66; adminstrv. asst. Balt. Orioles, 1966-68; adminstrv. asst. Kansas City Royals, 1968-70, asst. farm dir., 1970-75, farm dir., 1975, dir. scouting and player devel., 1976-79, v.p. player personnel, 1979-81, exec. v.p., gen. mgr., 1981—. Served with AUS, 1966-72. Lutheran. Office: PO Box 1969 Kansas City MO 64141*

SCHUETTE, BILL, U.S. congressman; b. Midland, Mich., Oct. 3, 1953. B.S.F.S., Georgetown U., 1976; J.D., U. San Francisco, 1979; student U. Aberdeen, Scotland, 1974-75; Bar: Mich. 1981. Mich. field coordinator Bush for Pres. Com., 1979, campaign mgr., Fla., 1979-80, nat. dir. del. ops., 1980; polit. dir. Reagan-Bush Presdl. campaign, Mich., 1980; sole practice law, Midland, 1981-84; mem. 99th Congress from 10th Mich. Dist., 1985—. Del., Mich. State Republican Conv., 1972, 74, 82; mem. Midland County Rep. Exec. Com., 1982. Address: 415 Cannon House Office Bldg Washington DC 20515*

SCHUH, JOHN HOWARD, educational administrator, higher education and student affairs educator; b. Cleve., July 29, 1947; s. Howard John and Elfreide Marie (Wachcic) S.; m. Linda Kay Rezin, June 30, 1973; 1 child, Kimberly Chrisette. B.A., U. Wis.-Oshkosh, 1969; M. Counseling, Ariz. State U., 1972, Ph.D., 1974. Residence complex dir. Ariz. State U., Tempe, 1970-72, asst. dir. housing, adj. prof., 1972-78; dir. residence life Ind. U., Bloomington, 1978-82, asst. dean, assoc. prof., 1982-84, assoc. dean, assoc. prof., 1984—; cons. to colls. and univs., 1977-85. Editor: Programming and Activities in College and University Residence Halls, 1977; (with G.S. Blimling) Increasing the Educational Role of Residence Halls, 1981; A Handbook for Student Group Advisers, 1984. Contbr. articles to profl. jours., chpts. to books. Presenter to profl. confs. Served to capt. USAR, 1973. Recipient Outstanding Research award Am. Coll. Personnel Assn. Commn. III, 1983, 84. Mem. Assn. Coll. Housing Officers (exec. bd. 1977-81, 85—, chmn. legis. issues 1983-85), Am. Coll. Personnel Assn. (mem. media editorial bd. 1979—, govtl. relations com. 1984—, Commn. III dir. 1979-82). Methodist. Avocations: TAC cert. track official, golf; swimming; gardening. Home: 825 Plymouth Rd Bloomington IN 47401 Office: Ind U 801 N Jordan Room 210 Bloomington IN 47405

SCHUL, BILL DEAN, psychological administrator, author; b. Winfield, Kans., Mar. 16, 1928; s. Fred M. and Martha Mildred (Miles) S.; B.A., Southwestern Coll., 1952; M.A., U. Denver, 1954; Ph.D., Am. Internat. U., 1977; m. Virginia Louise Duboise, Aug. 3, 1952; children—Robert Dean, Deva Elizabeth. Reporter and columnist Augusta (Kans.) Daily Gazette, 1954-58, Wichita (Kans.) Eagle-Beacon, 1958-61; Kans. youth dir. under auspices of Kans. Atty. Gen., 1961-65; Kans. state dir. Seventh Step Found., Topeka, 1965-66; mem. staff Dept. Preventive Psychiatry, Menninger Found., Topeka, Kans., 1966-71; dir. cons. Center Improvement Human Functioning, Wichita, 1975—; author: (with Edward Greenwood) Mental Health in Kansas Schools, 1965; Let Me Do This Thing, 1969; (with Bill Larson) Hear Me, Barabbas, 1969; How to Be An Effective Group Leader, 1975; The Secret Power of Pyramids, 1975; (with Ed Pettit) The Psychic Power of Pyramids, 1976, Pyramids: The Second Reality, 1979; The Psychic Power of Animals, 1977; Psychic Frontiers of Medicine, 1977. Bd. dirs. Recreation Commn., Topeka, United Funds, Topeka, Adamic Inst., Trees for Life; mem. adv. bd. Clayton U. Served with USN, 1945-46. Recipient John H. McGinnis Meml. award for Nonfiction, 1972, Am. Freedom Found. award, 1966, Spl. Appreciation award Kans. State Penitentiary, 1967. Mem. Acad. of Parapsychology and Medicine, Kans. Council for Children and Youth (pres. 1965-66), Assn. for Strenghtening the Higher Realities and Aspirations of Man (pres. 1970-71), Smithsonian Inst. Club: Lions (pres. 1957). Address: Rural Route 3 Winfield KS 67156

SCHULDT, JOHN CHARLES, SR., safety director, consultant; b. Blue Island, Ill., Apr. 16, 1937; s. Elmer A. and Marion G. (Meier) S.; m. Alice Marie Biedronski, Sept. 13, 1958; children—John, Joe, Christine. B.B.A., U. Toledo, 1966. Cert. safety profl. Supr. Malanco Inc., Blue Island, 1958-61; gen. supr. Alton Boxboard, Chgo., 1961-64; safety supr. Gen. Motors Co., Defiance, Ohio, 1964—; cons.; tchr. four county vocat. sch. Mem. Northwestern Ohio Safety Council. Mem. Nat. Safety Council, Am. Foundrymen Soc., Am. Soc. Safety Engrs., Defiance C. of C. Republican. Roman Catholic. Club: Kettenring Country. Lodges: Rotary, Elks. Office: Central Foundry Defiance OH 43512

SCHULFER, ROCHE EDWARD, arts administrator; b. Hammond, Ind., Sept. 26, 1951; s. Thomas Florian and Tess (Ronk) S.; m. Arlene Lencioni, June 2, 1973 (div. 1979). B.S. in Econs., U. Notre Dame. Bos office asst. Goodman Theatre, Chgo., 1973-74, asst. to mng. dir., 1974-77, gen. mgr., 1977-80, mng. dir., producer, 1980—. Mem. exec. com. League of Resident Theatres, Chgo., 1981, 83; pres. League of Chgo. Theatres, 1983—; dir. Remains Ensemble, Chgo., Lawyers for Creative Arts, Chgo. Office: Goodman Theatre Chicago Theatre Group 200 S Columbus Dr Chicago IL 60603

SCHULLER, CAROLE ADELE, nurse; b. Youngstown, Ohio, Dec. 15, 1941; d. Raymond Thomas and Isabelle Mae (Woods) Logan; m. Donald Edward Schuller, June 22, 1963; children—D. Geoffrey, T. Douglas, J. Eric. Diploma St. Luke's Hosp., Cleve., 1962. Night charge nurse psychiatry St. Luke's Hosp., Cleve., 1962; head nurse psychiatry, 1963; charge nurse med.-surgery Timken Mercy Med. Ctr., Canton, Ohio, 1964, charge nurse orthopedics, 1970, nurse, 1973-76, charge nurse gynecology, 1976-81, asst. dir. materials mgmt. central sterile supply, 1981, pvt. duty nurse, 1968—; ARC nurse, Canton, 1970—; indsl. nurse Hoover Co., North Canton, 1971-74. Mem. Assn. Advancement Med. Instrumentation, Am. Hosp. Assn., Internat. Assn. Hosp. Central Service Mgrs., St. Luke's Alumna Assn. Republican. Lutheran. Clubs: Branhaven Tennis, Lake Cable Recreation Assn. Office: Timken Mercy Med Ctr 1320 Timken Mercy Dr Canton OH 44708

SCHULTZ, ALFRED WAYNE, talent agy. owner; b. Spooner, Wis., Feb. 4, 1929; s. Edward Everett and Hilma Amelia (Henderson) S.; m. Glenda Sharon Holmberg, Oct. 3, 1954 (div.); 1 son, Mark Wayne. Student U. Wis., 1946-49, Supr., Synder's Drug Store, Mpls./St. Paul, 1951-55; owner, operator Wagon Wheel Cafe and Hotel Warren Cafe, Warren, Minn., 1955-57; mgr. Walgreen Co., Chgo., 1957-63; owner, operator Al Schultz Talent Agy., Waukegan, Ill., 1963—; co-owner Seeing Is Believing, video taping, Waukegan, 1981—. Mem. Am. Fedn. Musicians, Internat. Theatrical Agys. Assn. Lutheran. Home: 2538 N Linden Ave Waukegan IL 60087 Office: 38328 N Sheridan Rd Waukegan IL 60087

SCHULTZ, BRYAN CHRISTOPHER, dermatologist, educator; b. Evergreen Park, Ill., June 29, 1949; s. Warren H. and Norinne A. (McNamara) S.; m. Cathleen T. Fitzgerals, May 14, 1977; children—Carrie T., Megan C., Erin L. B.S., Loyola U., Chgo., 1971; M.D., Loyola Stritch Sch. Medicine, 1974. Diplomate Am. Bd. Dermatology. Intern St. Joseph's Hosp., Chgo., 1975; resident Northwestern U., Chgo., 1976-79; asst. clin. prof. Loyola U., Maywood, Ill., 1979—; practice medicine specializing in dermatology, Oak Park, Ill., 1979—; oons. dermatologist West Suburban Hosp., Oak Park Hosp., Gottlieb Hosp., Westlake Hosp., St. Joseph Hosp., 1979—. Author: Office Practice of Skin Surgery, 1985. Patentee surgical instrument. Contbr. articles to sci. publs. Supr., founder pub. awareness program for skin cancer Loyola U. Stritch Sch. Medicine, 1983—. Mem. Am. Acad. Dermatology, Am. Soc. Dermatologic Surgery, Internat. Soc. Dermatologic Surgery, Soc. Investigative Dermatology, Chgo. Dermatologic Soc., AMA (del. intern and resident sect. 1975), Ill Dermatologic Soc. (exec. com. 1981, chmn. membership com. 1983-84), N.Y. Acad. Scis., ACP, Acad. Cutaneous Surgery, Internat. Soc. Tropical Dermatology, Soc. Cosmetic Chemists, Royal Soc. Medicine, Alpha Sigma Nu. Office: Affiliates in Diseases and Surgery of Skin S C 1159 Westgate Oak Park IL 60301

SCHULTZ, CHARLES ALBERT, theatre educator, historian, director; b. Seattle, Mar. 4, 1941; s. Edmund Anton and Helen D. (Beall) S.; m. Patricia Bowers, June 1, 1963; children—Todd Matthew, Vaughn Andrew, Cynthia Kristine. B.S., Bowling Green U., 1963, Ph.D. (teaching fellow), 1970; M.A., U. Ill., 1964. Profl. actor Wagon Wheel Playhouse, Ind., 1963; tchr., speech dir. Northmont High Sch. (Ohio), 1964-66; dir. theatre, assoc. prof. speech Dickinson (N.D.) State Coll., 1970-74; head theatre div. U. Dayton (Ohio), 1974-76; chmn. dept. theatre N.W. Mo. State U., Maryville, 1976—; mng. dir. Sosondowah-Gov.'s Players of N.D., 1972-74; founder, mng. dir. Popcorn Playhouse, Dayton, 1974-76; artistic and coordinating dir. Creative Arts Prodns., St. Joseph, Mo., 1983; dir. children's theatre; cons. Mem. State bd. Area Commn. on Higher Edn., 1985; chmn. bd. Wesley Found., 1985. Lay leader Methodist chs., Mo., N.D. Recipient Disting. Achievement in Theatre award Bowling Green U., 1963, Outstanding Achievement in TV Directing, 1962, Outstanding Educator award Fireland campus, 1970; Disting. Faculty Service award Dickinson State Coll., 1974; Outstanding Contbr. to Drama award, Dayton, 1976; Mo. Com. for Humanities grantee, 1977, 82; Ohio Arts Council grantee, 1975. Mem. Am. Theatre Assn., Speech Communications Assn., Speech and Theatre Assn. Mo., Mid-Am. Theatre Alliance, Omicron Delta Kappa, Alpha Psi Omega, Theta Alpha Phi, Rho Sigma Mu. Lodge: Rotary (dir. club service) (Maryville). Contbr. articles to profl. jours. Home: 1004 W Cooper Maryville MO 64468 Office: NW Mo State U Maryville MO 64468

SCHULTZ, GWEN MANETTE, geography educator, writer, publisher; b. Milwaukee; d. Herbert A. F. and Aurelia (Nickel) S. B.A., U. Wis.-Madison, 1944, M.A., 1950. Assoc. prof. geography Wis. Geol. and Natural History Survey, U. Wis-Madison, 1969—; owner Reading Gems, Madison, 1972—; owner Hammock & Inglenook, Madison, 1981—. Author: Ice Age Lost (Council for Wis. Writers 1st place award 1975); Icebergs and Their Voyages (Council for Wis. Writers 1st place award 1976); Glaciers and the Ice Age; The Blue Valentine; The Bucky Badger Story; Wisconsin's Foundations (1st place award Nat. League Am. Pen Women 1979). Contbr. articles, fiction, revs., poetry to mags. and profl. jours. Friend of Libraries and Hist. Soc., Mem., Council for Wis. Writers (v.p. 1976-84), Authors Guild, Assn. Am. Geographers, AAUP, Am. Quaternary Assn., Wis. Acad. Scis., Arts and Letters, Wis. Archaeol. Soc. Home: 111 W Wilson St Apt 201 Madison WI 53703 Office: Wis Geol and Natural History Survey Univ Wis Madison WI 53706

SCHULTZ, JEFFREY ERIC, optometrist; b. Cleve., Jan. 28, 1948; s. Albert I. and Lenore (Aster) S.; m. Nancy Lynne Wachs, July 5, 1970; children—Brian David, Amy Robin. B.S. in Zoology, Ohio State U., 1970, O.D., 1974, M.S. in Physiol. Optics, 1974. Lic. optometrist, Ohio, Fla. Research asst. Ohio State U. Coll. Optometry, Columbus, 1970-74, clin. instr., 1974-75; gen. practice optometry, Cleve., 1975—. Contbr. articles to profl. jours. Mem. Ohio Optometric Assn. (continuing edn. com. 1976—, chmn. sports vision com. 1977-79, Optometric Recognition award 1978), Fla. Optometric Assn., Am. Optometric Assn. (Optometric Recognition award 1980, 82—, charter mem. contact lens sect. 1982—, mem. sports vision sect. 1983—), Am. Acad. Optometry, Nat. Eye Research Found., Council Sports Vision, Vision Conservation Inst., Better Vision Inst., Ohio Contact Lens Soc., Beta Sigma Kappa. Lodge: Masons. Avocations: Philately, fine art collecting. Office: 5706 Turney Rd Garfield Heights OH 44125

SCHULTZ, JOHN LEO, univ. adminstr.; b. Cape Girardeau, Mo., Feb. 1, 1931; s. Louis J. and Norma E. (Shivelbine) S.; B.S. magna cum laude, Southeast Mo. State Coll., 1954, B.S. in Edn. magna cum laude, 1957; M.S. in Edn., So. Ill. U., 1959, Ed.S., 1965; Ph.D. Open U., 1977; postgrad. U. Chgo., 1960-63, U. Tenn., 1954, Louisville Sem., 1953, U. Mo., 1977; m. Carole Nelle Sparks, Aug. 19, 1959; children—Elizabeth Ann (dec.), Deborah Lorraine. Asst. in guidance and counseling Community High Sch., Downers Grove, Ill., 1959-60; dir. curriculum research Sch. Dists. 58 and 59, Downers Grove, 1960-64; adminstrv. supr. student employment program So. Ill. U., Carbondale, 1964-65; adminstrv. asst. and prof. psychology Jefferson Coll., Hillsboro, Mo., 1965-66; registrar Cornell Coll., Mt. Vernon, Iowa, 1966-67, asst. prof. edn., 1966-67; registrar, sec. to exec. faculty Sch. Medicine, Washington U., St. Louis, 1967—, asst. prof., 1967—, asst. dean acad. adminstrn., 1976—, registrar Barnes Hosp. Med. Staff, 1967—, lectr. resident program in orthodontics Sch. Dental Medicine, 1970—; cons. Fed. Aid Coordinating Services, Inc., Chgo., 1965-67, Washington, 1966-67; dist. rep. to sch. improvement program U. Chgo., 1960-63; evaluative cons. Health Care Specialists, Inc., St. Louis. Pres. Internat. Forum, Open U., 1977-79; bd. dirs. St. Louis Neighborhood Health Ctr., Inc. Served with U.S. Army, 1954-56. Mem. Am. Ednl. Research Assn., Am. Assn. Coll. Registrars and Admissions Officers (chmn. profl. schs. com. 1975-76), Midwestern Psychol. Assn., Mo. State Tchrs. Assn., NEA, Nat. Soc. for Study Edn., Am. Assn. U. Adminstrs., Am. Assn. Higher Edn., Assn. Am. Med. Colls., Phi Kappa Phi, Kappa Delta Pi, Phi Delta Kappa. Lutheran. Author: (with George J. Fuka) New Education Interaction Curriculum Model, 1966; author curriculum studies; contbr. articles to profl. publs. Office: Washington Univ School Medicine 660 S Euclid Ave Saint Louis MO 63110

SCHULTZ, LOUIS WILLIAM, state supreme court justice; b. Deep River, Iowa, Mar. 24, 1927; s. M. Louis and Esther Louise (Behrens) S.; student Central Coll., Pella, Iowa, 1944-45, 46-47; LL.B., Drake U., Des Moines, 1949; m. D. Jean Stephen, Nov. 6, 1949; children—Marcia, Mark, Paul. Admitted to Iowa bar; claims supr. Iowa Farm Mut. Ins. Co., Des Moines, 1949-55; partner firm Harned, Schultz & McMeen, Marengo, Iowa, 1955-71; judge U.S. Dist. Ct. 6th Dist. Iowa, 1971-80; justice Iowa Supreme Ct., 1980—; county atty. Iowa County, 1960-68. Served with USNR, 1945-46. Mem. Am. Bar Assn., Iowa Bar Assn. (bd. govs.), Iowa Judges Assn. (pres.). Republican. Lutheran. Office: 610 Jefferson Bldg Iowa City IA 52242*

SCHULTZ, RHONA BERKOWITZ, law school administrator; b. Chgo., Feb. 4, 1949; d. Herman C. and Harriet (Pozner) Berkowitz; m. Jay L. Schultz, Aug. 24, 1971. B.S. in Communications with high honors, U. Ill., 1970; postgrad. DePaul U. Coll. Law, 1972. Pub. info. coordinator Ill. Arts Council, Chgo., 1970-71; dir. pub. relations Goodman Theatre, Chgo., 1971-76; asst. exec. dir. Nature Conservancy, Chgo., 1976-80; pub. relations cons. Rhona

Schultz & Assocs., Chgo., 1976-80; dir. devel. and alumni The John Marshall Law Sch., Chgo., 1980—. Active Acad. Festival Theatre, Lake Forest, Ill., 1973-78, Wisdom Bridge Theatre, Chgo., 1977-80; mem. Joseph Jefferson Awards Com., Chgo., 1978-79; com. mem. Chgo. Internat. Theater Festival; mem. Central States campaign com. Morris Animal Found., Englewood, Colo., 1982—. Mem. Nat. Soc. Fundraising Execs., Assn. Am. Law Schs. (instl. advancement com.). Jewish. Clubs: Publicity of Chgo.; Chgo. Beagle (Godley, Ill.). Office: The John Marshall Law Sch 315 S Plymouth Ct Chicago IL 60604

SCHULTZ, THEODORE WILLIAM, retired educator, economist; b. Arlington, S.D., Apr. 30, 1902; s. Henry Edwward and Anna Elizabeth (Weiss) S.; grad. Sch. fo Agr., Brookings, S.D., 1924; B.S., S.D. State Coll., 1927, D.Sc. (hon.), 1959; M.S., U. Wis., 1928, Ph.D., 1930; LL.D., Grinnell Coll. 1949, Mich. State U., in 1962, U. Ill., 1968, U. Wis., 1968, Cath. U. Chile, 1979, U. Dijon, France, 1981, N.C. State U., 1984; m. Esther Florence Werth; children—Elaine, Margaret T., Paul. Mem. faculty, Iowa State Coll., Ames, 1930-43, prof., head dept. econs. and sociology, 1934-43; prof. econs. U. Chgo., 1943-72, chmn. dept. econs., 1946-61. Charles L. Hutchinson Disting. Service prof., 1952-72, now emeritus. Econ. adviser, occasional cons. Com. Econ. Devel., U.S. Dept. Agr., Dept. State Fed. Res. Bd., various congl. coms., U.S. Dept. of Commerce, FAO, U.S. Dept. of Def. (in Germany 1948), Fgn. Econ. Adminstrn. (in U.K. and Germany 1945), IBRD, Resources for the Future, Twentieth Century Fund, Nat. Farm Inst., and others. Dir. Nat. Bur. Econ. Research, 1949-67; research dir. Studies of Tech. Assistance in Latin Am., also bd. mem. Nat. Planning Assn.; chmn. Am. Famine Mission to India, 1946; studies of agrl. developments in central Europe and Russia, 1929, Scandinavian countries and Scotland, 1936, Brazil, Uruguay and Argentina, 1941, Western Europe, 1955; research fellow Center Advanced Study in Behavioral Sci., 1956-57. Recipient Nobel prize in econs., 1979. Fellow Am. Acad. Arts and Scis., Am. Farm Econs. Assn., Nat. Acad. Scis.; mem. Am. Farm Assn., Am. Econ. Assn. (pres. 1960, Walker medal 1972), Royal Econ. Soc., Am. Philos. Soc., also others. Author: Redirecting Farm Policy, 1943; Food for the World, 1945; Agriculture in an Unstable Economy, 1945; Production and Welfare in Agriculture, 1950; The Economic Organization of Agriculture, 1953; Economic Test in Latin America, 1956; Transforming Traditional Agriculture, 1964; The Economic Value of Education, 1963; Economic Crises in World Agriculture, 1965; Economic Growth and Agriculture, 1968; Investment in Human Capital: The Role of Education And of Research, 1971; Human Resources, 1972; Economics of the Family; Marriage, Children, and Human Capital, 1974; Distortions of Agricultural Incentives, 1978; Investing in People: The Economics of Population Quality, 1981; co-author: Measures for Economic Development of Under-Developed Countries, 1951. Editor: Distortions of Agricultural Incentives, 1978; editor Jour. of Farm Economics, 1939-42. Contbr. articles to profl. jours. Home: 5620 Kimbark Ave Chicago IL 60637

SCHULTZ, WILLIAM LOUIS, financial consultant; b. Manitowoc, Wis., Nov. 25, 1923; s. William G. and Linda (Geisler) S.; student Cornell U., 1945-46; B.S., M.S., U. Wis., 1950; postgrad. George Williams Coll., 1951; m. Grace G. Parrott, Nov. 12, 1949; children—William A., Robert L., James R., Timothy P., Thelma A. Dir. phys. edn. Madison (Wis.) YMCA, 1949-51; exec. dir. Keokuk (Iowa) YMCA, 1952-53; dir. Oshkosh (Wis.) YMCA, 1953-57; met. exec. dir. Madison YMCA, 1957-72; exec. dir. Circus World Mus., Hist. Sites Found., Inc., Baraboo, Wis., 1972-84; cons. Campaign Assocs. of YMCA of U.S.; sports cons. D.B. Frampton Co. Columbus, Ohio; circus cons. Genis Book of Records (London). Pres. Inter-Service Club Council of Madison, Phys. Dirs. Soc. Midwestern YMCA's; bd. dirs. Madison and Baraboo Chambers of Commerce; pres. Inter-Agy. Assn. United Way of Madison. Served with USMC, 1943-46. Inducted into Lake Michigan Shore Sports Hall of Fame, 1979. Mem. Showfolks of Am., YMCA Phys. Dirs. Soc., N. Am. YMCA Profl. Soc. Methodist. Club: Rotary, Elks. Nat. open singles paddleball champion, 1962; nat. open singles racquetball champion, 1968; mem. U.S. Marine Corps Boxing and Wrestling Team, Cornell U. Wrestling Team; capt. U. Wis. Gymnastic Team; U.S. rep. to World Council of YMCA's on Phys. Edn. Home: Bonnie Oaks Estate Rural Route 3 Portage WI 53901 Office: 426 Water St Baraboo WI 53913

SCHULZ, DALE METHERD, pathologist; b. Fairfield, Ohio, Oct. 20, 1918; s. Jerome Charles and Minnie Irene (Metherd) S.; m. Dorothy Ann Hartman, June 14, 1947; children—Ann Huston, Stephen Metherd. B.A., Miami U., Oxford, Ohio, 1940; M.S., Washington U., St. Louis, 1942, M.D., 1949. Diplomate Am. Bd. Pathology, 1954. Research chemist Tretolite Co., St. Louis, 1942-45; intern, then resident in pathology Barnes Hosp., St. Louis, 1949-51; fellow in pathology Ind. U., Indpls., 1951-53, asst. prof. pathology Sch. Medicine, 1953-58, assoc. prof., 1958-62, prof., 1962-66, clin. prof., 1966-85; pathologist Meth. Hosp., Indpls., 1966-85. Bd. dirs. Allisonville Civic Assn.; past pres. Cedar Knolls Assn. Served as capt. U.S. Army, 1955-57. Grantee Riley Meml. Assn., 1954-64, USPHS, 1964-71. Mem. Am. Assn. Pathologists, Internat. Acad. Pathology. Republican. Presbyterian. Author: (with others) Principles of Human Pathology, 1959; patentee. Home: 9540 Copley Dr Indianapolis IN 46260 Office: Methodist Hospital Indianapolis IN 46202

SCHULZ, VALDYN, retail executive; b. 1929; married. With Red Owl Stores, Inc., 1959-73; exec. v.p. Nat. Tea Co., Rosemont, Ill., 1973-76, pres., chief exec. officer, 1976—. Office: Nat Tea Co 9701 W Higgins Rd Rosemont IL 60018*

SCHULZE, ERWIN EMIL, See *Who's Who in America,* 43rd edition.

SCHUMACHER, DALE FREDERICK, credit union administrator; b. Litchfield, Ill., Aug 24, 1948; s. Harold Frederick and Marilyn Faye S.; m. Deborah Ann Brodie, Nov. 14, 1970 (div. 1978); m. 2d Patricia Ann McLaughlin, Nov. 23, 1979; 1 child, Dominique J. B.S., Purdue U., 1977. Quality control supr. Coin Acceptors, St. Louis, 1968-72; loan officer Purdue Employees Fed. Credit Union, West Lafayette, Ind., 1973-78; asst. mgr. Mopac Credit Union, St. Louis, 1978-80; pres., treas. SIU Credit Union, Carbondale, 1980—. Mem. govs. bd. Credit Union Advisors, Springfield, Ill., 1983—; Served with USN, 1978-79. Mem. Am. Mgmt. Assn., Credit Union Exec. Soc., Ill. Credit Union League. Lutheran. Avocations: golf; computer programming. Home: PO Box 184 Cambria IL 62915 Office: SIU Credit Union PO Box 2888 Carbondale IL 62902

SCHUMACHER, FERDINAND MATHIAS, holding company executive; b. Kleve, Germany, Mar. 1, 1939; came to U.S., 1963, naturalized, 1968; s. Josef Peter and Maria Schumacher; B.A. in Bus., U. S.Fla., Tampa, 1969; m. Alberta Louise Seldomridge, Dec. 9, 1967. Staff asso. Joseph Schlitz Brewing Co., Milw., 1969-79; v.p. ops., dir. Isoco Ltd., Pewaukee, Wis., 1979-81; pres. Global Trading, Milw., 1980—, Global Beverage, Inc., Edison, N.J., 1985. Adv., Jr. Achievement Milw., 1976; treas. Alliance Française Milw., 1978-80. Republican. Roman Catholic. Office: 12714 W Hampton Ave Butler WI 53007

SCHUMACHER, JOSEPH STUART, foundry consultant; b. Hillsboro, Ohio, June 7, 1912; s. Ernest W. and Helen H. (Hussey) S.; student Denison U., 1930-32; B.S., Ohio State U., 1935; m. Dorothy Jene Lamb, July 24, 1937; 1 son, Joseph Stuart. Metallurgist, Cin. Milacron, Cin., 1935-44; tech. dir., v.p. The Hill & Griffith Co., Cin., 1944-69; pres. J. Schumacher & Co., Cin., 1969-72, 77—; tech. dir. Internat. Minerals & Chem. Corp., Libertyville, Ill., 1972-77; former dir. H.W. Dietert Co., Detroit; v.p. Exec. Cons. Assn., 1978—; cons., speaker to industry, 1944—. Registered profl. engr., Ohio. Fellow Inst. Brit. Foundrymen; mem. Am. Foundrymen's Soc. (chpt. chmn. 1949, award of Sci. Merit 1967, Gold medal 1974, Silver Anniversary award 1983), Sigma Chi. Club: Masons. Patentee in field. Contbr. articles to profl. jours., papers to profl. confs.; cons. editor The Foundry Mag., 1968—. Home: 205 Rivershire Apt 512 Linconshire IL 60015

SCHUMANN, HAROLD ELMER, telephone service analyst; b. Pinconning, Mich., Nov. 19, 1939; s. Elmer William and Regina (Rezler) S.; m. Patricia Hycki, Feb. 8, 1958; children—Rick, Randy, Rodney, Roger, Ronald. Graduate Pinconning High Sch. Line man Contel Telephone Co., Pinconning, 1958-60, repairman, 1960-69, plant supr., 1969-75, service ctr. supr., 1975-81, telephone service anaylst, 1985—. Emergency med. technician No. Bay Ambulance Service, 1969; chief fire dept., Pinconning, 1971, pres. Booster Club, 1965. Roman Catholic. Lodge: Lions (pres. 1969). Home: 3805 Fraser Rd Pinconning MI 48650

SCHUMM, BROOKE, III, lawyer; b. Romulus, N.Y., Apr. 1, 1956; s. Brooke Jr. and Elizabeth (Holenweg) S.; B.S., Cornell U., 1977; J.D., U. Mich., 1980. Bar: Ill. 1980, U.S. Ct. Appeals (7th cir.) 1980, Calif. 1981, U.S. Dist. Ct. (no. dist.) Ill. 1981, U.S. Dist. Ct. (no. dist.) Calif. 1981. Atty. Standard Oil Co. (Ind.), Chgo., 1980-84; assoc. Lord, Bissell & Brook, Chgo., 1984—. Named to Outstanding Young Men Am. U.S. Jr. C. of C., 1978. Mem. Chgo. Bar Assn. (atty. battered women's panel 1981—), ABA, Ill. State Bar Assn., Comml Law League Am., Am. Inst. Indsl. Engrs., U.S. Naval Inst. Democrat. Home: 835 Judson Ave Evanston IL 60202 Office: 115 S LaSalle Chicago IL 60603

SCHURMEIER, L. JON, health systems executive; b. Elgin, Ill., Feb. 17, 1937; s. LeRoy H. and June (Zorn) S.; B.A., DePauw U., Greencastle, Ind., 1959; M.B.A., U. Pitts., 1960, M.H.A., 1970; m. Donna Kay Cunningham, Apr. 1, 1961; children—Kristin, Darla, Steffany. From merchandiser to mgr. Carson, Pirie, Scott & Co., Chgo., 1963-67; adminstrv. extern Presbyn.-St. Luke's Hosp., Chgo., 1967-68; adminstrv. resident, then asst. adminstr. Cin. Gen. Hosp., 1969-72; asso. adminstr. S.W. Gen. Hosp., Middleburg Heights, Ohio, 1972-81, adminstr., 1981-85, system pres., 1985—; asst. clin. prof. U. Pitts.; dir., officer OHMS Health Mgmt. Services, Inc.; regent OSDVS; dir., officer Hudson Younglife, 1981-85; chmn. bd. trustees Central Hosp. Service; dir., officer Emerald Health Network, Westside Imaging Ctr.; bd. dirs. Hospac, 1981—; mem. Hudson (Ohio) Com. Emergency Health Care. Pres. Olde Towne Colony Homeowners Assn., 1979; ch. lay leader, Hudson, 1973-76, trustee, 1981-84; bd. dirs. Hudson Girls-Womens Softball League, 1980—; village councilman, 1984. Served with U.S. Army, 1961-63. Recipient recognition award Seven Hills Neighborhood Houses, Cin., 1972. Fellow Am. Coll. Hosp. Adminstrs.; mem. Hosp. Fin. Mgmt. Assn., Am. Public Health Assn., Health Care Adminstrs. N.E. Ohio, DePauw U. Alumni Assn., U. Pitts. Alumni Assn. Health Adminstrn. (pres. 1976), Middleburg C. of C. Clubs: Hudson, Western Res. Tennis. Author articles in field. Home: 49 Keswick Dr Hudson OH 44236 Office: 18697 E Bagley Rd Middleburg Heights OH 44130

SCHUSTER, EUGENE IVAN, venture capital executive; b. St. Louis, Dec. 8, 1936; s. David Theodore and Anne (Kalisher) S.; B.A., Wayne State U., 1959, M.A., 1962; postgrad. U. Mich., 1959-62, (Fulbright scholar) Warburg Inst., U. London, 1962-65, Courtauld Inst., U. London and London Sch. Econs., 1962-65; m. Barbara Zelmon, June 22, 1958 (div.); children—Joseph, Sarah, Adam. Lectr. art history Wayne State U., Detroit, 1959-62, Eastern Mich. U., Ypsilanti, 1960, Rackham extension U. Mich., 1961, Nat. Gallery, London, 1962-65; owner London Art Gallery, Detroit, 1965—; chmn. bd. Venture Funding Ltd. Recipient Distinguished Alumni award Wayne State U., 1968. Mem. Founders Soc., Detroit Inst. Arts, Detroit Art Dealers Assn., Art Appraisers Assn. Am. Home: 25425 Dennison Franklin MI 48025 Office: Venture Funding Ltd 321 Fisher Bldg Detroit MI 48202

SCHUSTER, HANS JAKOB, food chain executive; b. Winterthur, Switzerland, Aug. 9, 1949; came to U.S., 1980; s. Karl Otto and Gertrud Rosa (Wartmann) S.; M.B.A., Bus. Sch., Zurich, Switzerland, 1974. EDP analyst/programmer Nat. Cash Register Co., Zurich, 1970-71; controller, treas. Metro Internat. AG, Zug, Switzerland, 1974-76, asst. mgr. to internat. chief fin. officer, sr. exec. 1976-80; v.p. Metro Cash & Carry, Inc., Hillside, Ill., 1980—. Bd. dirs. condominium assn. in Chgo. Served to capt. Swiss Army, 1969-80. Mem. Am. Mgmt. Assn., Swiss-Am. C. of C., Vereinigte Zuenfte zur Gerwe und zur Schuhmachern (Zurich). Club: Rotary. Home: 201 E Chestnut St Chicago IL 60611 Office: 250 N Mannheim Rd Hillside IL 60162

SCHWAB, BRADLEY WAGONER, neurotoxicologist; b. Blue Island, Ill., Mar. 2, 1950; s. Robert William and Nevada Maureen (Fox) S.; m. Margaret Mary Shaughnessy, Aug. 21, 1976; children—Mary Claire, Robert Shaughnessy. B.S. in Pharmacy, Northeastern U., 1973; M.Sc., Harvard U., 1977; Ph.D., U. Tex., 1981. Research assoc. Albert Einstein Coll. Medicine, Bronx, N.Y., 1981-83; sr. research assoc. U. Mich., Ann Arbor, 1983-84, asst. research scientist toxicology lab., 1984—; con. Nat. Acad. Scis., Washington, 1984—. Contbr. chpts. in books, articles to profl. jours. Mem. AAAS, Soc. for Neurosci., N.Y. Acad. Scis., Rho Chi, Phi Kappa Phi. Office: Toxicology Program U Michigan 1420 Washington Heights Ann Arbor MI 48109-2029

SCHWAB, EILEEN CECILIA, psychology educator; b. Bklyn., Nov. 20, 1952; d. Peter Van Pelt and Madeleine (Guilfoyle) Schwab; m. Howard Charles Nusbaum, Apr. 8, 1979. B.A., Coll. of Mt. St. Vincent on Hudson, 1970; postgrad. Columbia U., 1977; Ph.D, SUNY-Buffalo, 1981. Grad. asst., teaching asst. SUNY-Buffalo, 1977-81, instr., 1979; instr. D'Youville Coll., 1980; vis. asst. prof. Ind. U., Bloomington, 1981-83, research assoc., 1982-83; human factors cons. AT&T Info Systems, Indpls., 1983—. Contbr. articles to profl. jours. N.Y. State Regents scholar, 1970-74; SUNY-Buffalo award for excellence in teaching, 1980. Mem. Acoustical Soc. Am., AAAS, Am. Psychol. Assn., Cognitive Sci. Soc., Human Factors Soc., Sigma Xi. Jewish. Office: AT&T Info Systems Indianapolis IN 46250

SCHWAB, STEVE J., physician; b. Cape Girardeau, Mo., Jan. 20, 1953; s. Norman J. and Virginia Louise (Schaefer) S.; m. Carol A. Schermann, May 31, 1975. B.S., Southeast Mo. State U., 1975; M.D. with honors, U. Mo., 1979; Diplomate Am. Bd. Internal Medicine, Am. Bd Nephrology. Intern U. Kans.; resident in internal medicine U. Kans. Med. Ctr., Kansas City, 1979-82; fellow in nephrology, renal div., Washington U., Barnes Hosp., St. Louis, 1982-84, asst. attending physician and cons. nephrologist, 1984—, attending nephrologist Chromalloy Am. Dialysis Ctr., 1984—, dir. Renal Diagnostic Ctr. and Renal Outpatient Clinics, 1984—, instr. medicine, 1984-85, asst. prof., 1985—. Contbr. articles to profl. jours. Am. Heart Assn. clinician scientist, 1984—; Nat. Kidney Found. fellow, 1982. Mem. ACP, Am. Soc. Nephrology, Am. Fedn. Clin. Research, Internat. Soc. Nephrology, Nat. Kidney Found. (profl. council), Am. Heart Assn. (sci. council), Alpha Omega Alpha. Office: Renal Div Washington U Barnes Hosp 660 S Euclid Ave Saint Louis MO 63110

SCHWALB, HOWARD RAY, geologist; b. Chgo., Mar. 19, 1924; s. Robert Henry and Ethel Ann (Fick) S.; m. Carol Lee Cathcart, Aug. 15, 1947 (dec. July 1954); m. Phyllis Ann Gentry, Aug. 1, 1957; children—Allen Howard, Steven Ray. B.S., U. Ill., 1949; postgrad. U. Colo., 1949-50. Asst. geologist Ill. Geol. Survey, Champaign, 1951-56, acting head oil and gas sect., 1979—; sr. geologist Phillips Petroleum Co., Evansville, Ind., 1956-61; regional geologist Texota Oil Co., Evansville, 1963-65; cons. geologist, Evansville, 1965-66; sr. geologist Ky. Geol. Survey, Henderson, 1966-79; lectr. U. Evansville, 1963-76; prin. investigator eastern gas shale project U.S. Dept. Energy, Morgantown, W.Va., 1968-71, New Madrid study group NRC, Washington, 1976-81. Contbr. articles and maps to geol. lit. Served with USAAF, 1943-46. Recipient Rock Hound award U. Mo.-Rolla, 1981. Mem. Am. Assn. Petroleum Geologists (pres. eastern sect. 1980-81, A.I. Levorsen award 1983), Interstate Oil Compact Commn., Soc. Econ. Paleontologists and Mineralogists, Ill. Acad. Sci., Sigma Xi. Republican. Home: 1904 Sadler Dr Champaign IL 61821 Office: Ill State Geol Survey 615 E Peabody Dr Champaign IL 61820

SCHWANHAUSSER, ROBERT ROWLAND, aerospace industry executive, engineer; b. Buffalo, Sept. 15, 1930; s. Edwin Julius and Helen (Putnam) S.; m. Mary Lea Hunter, Oct. 17, 1953 (div. 1978); children—Robert Hunter, Mark Putnam; m. Beverly Bohn Allemann, Dec. 31, 1979. S.B. in Aero. Engring., MIT, 1952. With Teledyne Ryan Aero., San Diego, 1954-74, v.p. internat. requirements, 1977-79, v.p. Remotely Piloted Vehicles programs, 1979-81; pres. Condur, La Mesa, Calif., 1973-74; v.p. bus. devel. All Am. Engring., 1976-77; v.p. advanced programs Teledyne Brown Engring., Huntsville, Ala., 1981-83; pres. Teledyne CAE, Toledo, Ohio, 1983—. Bd. dirs. Riverside Hosp., Toledo, 1985. Served to lt. USAF, 1952-54. Fellow AIAA (Outstanding Contbn. to Aerospace award 1971); mem. Assn. Unmanned Vehicle Systems (Pioneer award 1984), Nat. Mgmt. Assn. (Silver Knight of Mgmt. award 1972), Air Force Assn., Am. Def. Preparedness Assn., Nat. Rifle Assn., Navy League, Theta Delta Chi. Republican. Presbyterian. Clubs: Greenhead Hunting (Pine Valley, Calif.); Inverness (Toledo); Maumee River Yacht (Ohio); Gulf Shores Country (Ala.). Avocations: boating; hunting, skiing, golf. Home: 28765 East River Rd Perrysburg OH 43551 Office: Teledyne CAE 1330 Laskey Rd Toledo OH 43612

SCHWARK, HOWARD EDWARD, civil engineer; b. Bonfield, Ill., Aug. 31, 1917; s. Edward F. and Florence M. (Schultz) S.; student St. Viators Coll., Bourbonnias, Ill., 1935-37; B.S., U. Ill., 1942; m. Arlene M. Highbarger, Sept. 28, 1940. Asst. to county supt. hwys. Ford County (Ill.), 1941-43; engr. E. I. DuPont de Nemours Co., 1942; asst. county supt. hwys. Kankakee County (Ill.), 1946-52, county supt. hwys., 1952-82; dir. 1st Bank of Meadowview, Kankakee Devel. Corp.; adviser county rds. FHWA, 1973-82. Co-chmn., Republican Finance Com., 1962-66; pres. Kankakee Park Dist., 1959-70; mem. tech. adv. com. to Ill. Transp. Study Commn., 1975-82; trustee, pres. Azariah Buck Old People's Home; mem. exec. bd. Rainbow council Boy Scouts Am.; bd. dirs. Soil and Water Conservation Service, 1967-74. Served with AUS, 1943-46. Recipient Disting. Alumnus award Civil Engring. Alumni Assn. U. Ill., 1975; Disting. Service award U.S. Dept. Transp., 1982; Spl. Achievement award as road adv. for Region 5, FHWA, 1982 Mem. Nat. Assn. County Engrs. (life mem., v.p. North Central region 1979-81, Urban County Engr. of Yr. award 1982), Ill. Soc. Profl. Engrs., Ill. Assn. County Supts. Hwys. (life mem., pres. 1970), Ill. Engring. Council (pres. 1971-72), Am. Road and Transp. Builders Assn. (life mem., dir. county div. 1969-75, dir. 1975-81, pres. county div. 1975; Outstanding Service award transp. ofcls. div. 1981, Ralph R. Bartelsmeyer award 1983), Kankakee Area C. of C. (dir. 1960-74), Am. Soc. Profl. Engrs., Western Soc. Engrs., Twp. Ofcls. Ill., Freelance Photographers Assn., Ill. Wildlife Fedn. Lutheran. Clubs: Rotary, South Wilmington Sportsman. Home: 1051 W Vanmeter Kankakee IL 60901

SCHWARTZ, ALLAN MARVIN, physician; b. Cleve., July 17, 1941; s. Oscar and Ida (Madam) S.; m. Sandra Beverly Lynn Slade, Dec. 18, 1966; children—Marnie, Jordan. B.S., Ohio No. U., 1964; D.O., Kansas City Coll. Osteo. Medicine, 1968. Intern, Oakland Gen. Hosp., Madison Heights, Mich., 1968-69, resident in internal medicine, 1969-71; fellow U. Mich. Med. Ctr., Ann Arbor, 1971-73; practice medicine specializing in pulmonary medicine, Madison Heights; mem. staff Oakland Gen. Hosp., Redford Community Hosp. Fellow Am. Coll. Chest Physicians. Jewish. Avocation: skiing. Home: 3517 Valleyview Lane West Bloomfield MI 48033 Office: Allan Schwartz 27301 Dequindre Madison Heights MI 48071

SCHWARTZ, CLYDE STEVAN, dentist, dental services executive; b. St. Louis, Feb. 14, 1937; s. Mitchell and Esther (Kriesman) S.; m. Ruth Distler; children—Rebecca, Melissa. B.A., Washington U., 1958; M.A., So. Ill., 1962; Ph.D., George Washington U., 1969; D.D.S., U. Mo., 1975. Asst. prof. U. Minn. Hosp. Sch., 1970-72; pub. health servant Nat. Health Service Corp., Clear Lake, S.D., 1977-80; dir. dental services Woodward State Hosp. Sch., Iowa, 1980—. Contbr. articles to profl. jours. Bd. dirs. Des Moines Pvt. Sch., 1981-82; rules com. del. Polk County Democratic Conv., Iowa, 1980, 83. Served to lt. comdr. USPHS, 1977-80. Mem. Assn. Instl. Dentists. Democrat. Avocations: writing poetry and children's books, teaching science and mathematics to gifted children. Home: 315 51st St Des Moines IA 50312 Office: Woodward State Hosp Sch Woodward IA 50276

SCHWARTZ, GERHART ROBERT, university dean and official; b. Berne, Ind., Apr. 11, 1917; s. Peter D. and Elizabeth (Nussbaum) S.; m. Josephine Ruth Zehr, Aug. 15, 1944; children—Robert Arthur, Susan Jo Schwartz Lavin. B.S., Ball State U., 1942; M.S., Ind. U., 1948, Ed.D., 1952. Asst. to registrar Ball State U., Muncie, Ind., 1939-42; staff counselor Ind. U., Bloomington, 1946-48, dean of students office, 1946-51, asst. dir. student activities, 1949-50, acting dir. student activities, 1950-51; dean students Mankato State U., Minn., 1951-62; dean of students Western Ill. U., Macomb, 1963-68, v.p. student affairs, 1969-76, prof. grad. faculty, 1977—; participant profl. confs. Author: The Effect of a Reading Deficiency on a Student's Scholastic, Social and Emotional Adjustment in College, 1952; The Prospective Teacher Looks at Guidance, 1961. Mem. exec. bd. Mankato Adult-Youth Council, 1955-60; bd. dirs. Mankato YMCA, 1956-62, United Fund, Mankato, 1960-63, Macomb, 1965-67, Mental Health Ctr., Macomb, 1980—, pres., 1981-83; mem. adv. com. on guidance, counseling and testing State Dept. Edn., Minn., 1959-62. Recipient Outstanding Service award Mankato State YMCA, 1956-63, Mental Health Bd., Fulton-McDonough Counties, 1981; Outstanding Contribution award Mankato State U., 1962-63; honored as founder Ind. Coll. Personnel Assn., 1973. Served to lt. comdr. USNR, 1943-46. Mem. Am. Assn. Counseling and Devel. (life mem.), Ill. Assn. Counseling and Devel. (parliamentarian 1981-83), Nat. Assn. Student Personnel Adminstrs. (Commn. III; editor newsletter), Am. Coll. Personnel Assn., Nat. Vocat. Guidance Assn., Ill. Coll. Personnel Assn. (founding mem., treas. 1966-67, pres. 1967-68), NEA, Assn. Higher Edn., Blue Key, Phi Delta Kappa, Pi Gamma Mu, Pi Omega Pi, Sigma Tau Delta, Alpha Phi Gamma, Theta Chi. Presbyterian. Lodges: Elks, Rotary, Masons. Avocations: photography; sailing; horseback riding. Home: West Adams Rd Macomb IL 61455

SCHWARTZ, HAROLD ALBERT, newspaper executive; b. Troy Center, Wis., July 7, 1913; s. Albert Andrew and Mae Estelle (Flanagan) S.; m. Anne Lynch Powers, Aug. 22, 1938; children—Weldon Harold, Lynn Siobhan. Ph.B., Marquette U., 1935. Temporary reporter AP, 1935; with Milw. Jour., 1935-62, Milw. Jour. and Sentinel, 1962—, circulation dir. Jour. and Sentinel, 1970—, v.p., dir. Newspapers Inc., 1970—, v.p., dir. The Jour. Co., 1970—; mem. adv. com. U. Wis. Journalism Inst. Mem. Wis. Equal Rights Council, 1968—; bd. dirs., chmn. fin. com. Northtown Planning and Devel. Council, 1974; bd. dirs. Commandos Project I, Milw. Childrens' Outing Assn., Sunrise Nursing Home for Sr. Blind; mem. Shorewood Citizen Task Force; bd. dirs. Amigos de las Americans; bd. mgrs. Central YMCA, 1975, also bd. dirs.; mem. adv. council Ind. Living Project, also chmn. pub. edn. com., 1975. Recipient Disting. Service award Circulation Mgrs. Assn., 1970, Commandos, Inc., 1973, Journalism By-Line award Marquette U., 1974, Alumnus of Yr. award, 1981; decorated knight Order Northern Star (Sweden). Mem. Central States Circulation Mgrs. Assn. (bd. dirs., Herbert Gilmore exemplary service award 1975), Wis. Circulation Mgrs. Assn. (Frank Thayer award 1975), No. States Circulation Mgrs. Assn. (bd. dirs., 2d v.p.), Internat. Circulation Mgrs. Assn. (bd. dirs. 1972, chmn. research com.; pres. 1979, chmn. bd. 1980), Am. Newspaper Pubs. Assn. Found. (nat. readership council 1977-78), Wis. Newspaper in Edn. Com. (chmn.), Milw. Press Club, Allied Authors (past pres.), Bookfellows Milw. (past pres.), Wis. Council Writers, Crown and Anchor Soc., Wis. Elem. Prins. Assn. (hon. life), Marquette U. Alumni Assn. (pres. 1966-77), Met. Milw. C. of C., Sigma Delta Chi, Alpha Omega Nu. Roman Catholic. Club: South Shore Yacht. Home: 3800 N Newhall St Milwaukee WI 53211 Office: 333 W State St Milwaukee WI 53201

SCHWARTZ, JACOB JACK, government and commercial marketing and business consultant; b. Bklyn., May 8, 1918; s. Abraham and Gussie (Steigman) S.; B.B.A., St. John's U., Bklyn., 1939; m. Jenette Shorr, Mar. 18, 1945; children—Robin, Stanley, Alan. Sr. cost accountant Kay Mfg. Corp., Bklyn., 1939-42; mgr., comptroller Shores Cafe, Dearborn, Mich., 1946-55; owner, operator Jack's Food Box, Oak Park, Mich., 1955-58; accountant, line supr. Detroit Ordinance Dist. (now Detroit Procurement Dist.), 1958-60, from contract price analyst to supervisory price analyst Fin. Services Div., 1960-72, acting chief, 1972-73, pricing and fin. officer, dir. contract adminstrn. directorage, 1973-75, dir. contract adminstrn., chief fin. services div., 1975-77; asst. dist. dir. SBA of Mich., Detroit, 1976-78; cons. Cadillac Gage Co. subs. Excello Corp., Mich., 1979—; founder Schwartz & Parynik, 1982—. Vice-pres., Louis Stone Found., 1965-76, Joint Meml. Day Assn., Detroit, 1985—. Served with USAAF, 1942-46. Recipient numerous awards, including awards Louis Stone Found., 1950-76, Govt. Contracts Assn., 1960-76, City of Detroit, 1961-62, State of Mich., 1962, U.S. Def. Supply Agy., 1964-75, Detroit Pub. Schs., 1966, Fed. Bar Assn., 1972. Mem. Govt. Contracts Assn. (v.p. 1969-71, treas., 1972-84), Engring. Soc. Detroit, Am. Def. Preparedness Assn., Allied Vets. Council (pres. 1985—, Gold award 1970, 82, 83), Am. Legion, Jewish War Vets. (mem. nat. exec. com. 1976-77, Man of Year 1966). Home: 27405 Fairfax St Southfield MI 48076

SCHWARTZ, LEONARD PAUL, management consultant; b. N.Y.C., Feb. 16, 1934; s. Theodore M. and Rose (Diamond) S.; m. Harriet Gale Meltz, Sept. 7, 1958 (div. Feb. 1966); children—Andrea Pearl, Gary Martin; m. 2d, Carolyn Rand, May 1, 1970; children—Sarah Roselyn, Daniel Lee. A.B., U. Miami, 1956, student law, 1958-59; student Inst. Fin., N.Y.C., 1959-60. Cert. Inst. Cert. Profl. Bus. Cons. Registered rep., Walston & Co., Miami, Fla., 1959-62; owner, operator shoe store, Margate, N.J., 1962-65; regional mgr. Gulf Am. Land Corp., Miami, 1965-69; pres. Profl. Econs. & Mgmt., Inc., Cin., 1969—; condr. seminars; tchr. residency programs. Pres. North Miami Beach Jaycees, 1961. Served to 2d lt. USAF, 1956-68. Recipient 2d place Spoke award Fla. Jaycees, 1961, Achievement in Editorial Excellence award Physician's Mgmt. Mag., 1978, Mem. Nat. Assn. Bus. Economist, Soc. Med.-Dental Mgmt. Cons. (dir. 1976-78, pres. 1980-81, Pres.' award 1983), Inst. Cert. Profl. Bus. Cons. (trustee 1983). Democrat. Jewish. Clubs: Mercedes Benz (Cin.); K.P. (Atlantic City). Contbg. editor Physician's Mgmt. and Dental Mgmt. mags.; contbr. articles to profl. jours. Office: 800 Compton Rd Unit 11 Cincinnati OH 45231

SCHWARTZ, MICHAEL ALAN, lawyer; b. Bklyn., Jan. 26, 1948; s. Murray N. and Frances (Goldenstein) S.; m. Sara Oltarz, Dec. 8, 1973; children—Carl, Justin. B.A., L.I. U., 1968; J.D., Fordham U., 1972. Bar: N.Y. 1972, U.S. Dist. Ct. (so. and ea. dists.) N.Y. 1974, U.S. Ct. Appeals (2d cir.) 1975, U.S. Ct. Mil. Appeals 1976, U.S. Supreme Ct. 1976, Mich. 1980, U.S. Dist. Ct. (ea. dist.) Mich. 1980, U.S. Ct. Appeals (6th cir.) 1980. Tchr. pub. schs., N.Y.C., 1968-72;

asst. dist. atty. Kings County, Bklyn., 1973-76; dep. chief counsel Com. on Grievances, Assn. Bar City of N.Y., 1976-79; grievance adminstr. Mich. Atty. Grievance Commn., Detroit, 1979—; adj. prof. law U. Detroit, 1980—, Wayne State U., 1983—. Mem. Wayne County Mediation Tribunal, 1984; Democratic committeeman Westchester County (N.Y.), 1977-79. Served to 2d lt. U.S. Army, 1971-73. Mem. ABA (com. on ethical considerations, criminal justice sect.), State Bar Mich., Oakland County Bar Assn., Internat. Assn. Jewish Lawyers and Jurists, Nat. Orgn. Bar Counsel. Office: Suite 600 Marquette Bldg 243 W Congress St Detroit MI 48226

SCHWARZENTRAUB, JANET KAY, educator; b. St. Louis, Sept. 5, 1954; d. Ralph Joseph and Marjorie Kathryn (Dodds) Schockey; m. Craig L. Schwarzentraub, Dec. 16, 1979. B.S. in Edn., Ill. State U., 1976; M.Ed., U. Ill., 1979. Tchr. elem. schs., Kankakee, Ill., 1976-79; tchr. history and reading pub. schs., Morton, Ill., 1979—. Vol. Springfield Hosp. Charity Golf Classic. Mem. Ill. Sci. Tchrs. Assn., Ill. Reading Council, Delta Delta Delta (dist. pres., award). Roman Catholic. Home: 106 Liberty Morton IL 61550

SCHWELLER, DONALD GEORGE, lawyer; b. Dayton, Ohio, Oct. 13, 1930; s. Edmund Francis and R. Helen (Trace) S.; m. Mary Elizabeth Jauch, Sept. 1, 1956; children—Susan S., Stephen G., Ellen M., Peter C. B.A., U. Dayton, 1952; J.D., U. Cin., 1957; LL.M. in Taxation, NYU, 1958. Bar: Ohio 1957. Vice-pres., ptnr. Pickrel, Schaeffer & Ebeling, Dayton, 1958—. Contbr. articles to profl. jours. First pres. Dayton Opera Assn., 1961-62. Served to 1st lt. U.S. Army, 1953-55, Korea. Fellow Am. Coll. Probate Counsel; mem. Ohio State Bar Assn. (bd govs. probate and trust law sect.). Republican. Roman Catholic. Club: Dayton Bicycle. Avocations: tennis; antique collecting. Home: 1819 Southwood Ln Dayton OH 45419 Office: Pickrel Schaeffer & Ebeling 2700 Kettering Tower Dayton OH 45423

SCHWEMM, JOHN BUTLER, See *Who's Who in America,* 43rd edition.

SCHWEMMER, EUNICE JEAN, educational administrator; b. Benton, Kans., July 12, 1923; d. Theodore and Edith Blanche (Phares) Bachelder; m. Eldon H. Schwemmer, May 10, 1943; children—Vickie Mosteller, Ken, Jane. A.B. in Edn., Wichita State U., 1960, M. Ed., 1970; Ph.D., Kansas State U., 1978. Tchr. Wichita (Kans.) Schs., 1953-60, El Dorado (Kans.) Schs., 1960-71; reading tchr. El Dorado Schs., 1973; learning disabilities tchr. Butler County (Kans.) Sch. Bd. Council, 1973-75; instr. Emporia (Kans.) State U., 1975-78; learning disabilities coordinator Wichita Pub. Schs., 1978-80; learning disabilities coordinator, dir. media ctr. High Plains (Kans.) Edn. Cooperative, 1980—; instr. Northwestern State U., Alva, Okla., summers 1982, 84. cons. Butler County Community Coll. Murdock Twp. (Kans.) 4-H rep. Title VI-B media ctr. grantee, 1981. Mem. United Sch. Adminstrs. Kans., Kans. Assn. Spl. Educators, Kans. Assn. Supervision and curriculum Devel. (nat. conf. del.), Assn. Children with Learning Disabilities (Kans. pres. 1981-84). Republican. Baptist. Club. Moose Aux. Home: 1126 Skelly St El Dorado KS 67042 Office: 919 Zerr Rd Garden City KS 67846

SCHWINN, EDWARD R., JR., bicycle and exercise equipment manufacturing company executive; B.A., U. Denver, 1972. Adminstrv. asst. to exec. v.p. Schwinn Bicycle Co., Chgo., 1972-74, v.p. corp. devel., 1974-79, pres., chief operating officer, 1979—, dir. 1974—. Office: Schwinn Bicycle Co 1856 N Kostner Ave Chicago IL 60639

SCLAROFF, ALLEN, oral and maxillofacial surgeon; b. Mt. Holly, N.J., Nov. 28, 1945; s. Martin and Lillian (Shapiro) S.; m. Janet Lee Bernstein, July 25, 1981; children—Linsey Marisa, Megan Elyse. B.A., U. Colo.-Boulder, 1968; D.D.S., Temple U., 1972; cert. in oral and maxillofacial surgery, Washington U., St. Louis, 1978. Diplomate Am. Bd. Oral and Maxillofacial Surgery. Dir. grad. edn. oral and maxillofacial surgery Washington U., St. Louis, 1978—. Fellow Am. Assn. Oral and Maxillofacial Surgeons. Home: 1032 Medoc Ct Chesterfield MO 63017 Office: Univ Oral and Maxillofacial Surgeons 16432 Barnes Pavilion Saint Louis MO 63110

SCOGGINS, SAMUEL MCWHIRTER, lawyer; b. Shreveport, La., May 8, 1950; s. Thomas Samuel and Virginia Benton (Vaughn) S.; B.A. with honors, Denison U., 1972; J.D., U. Va., 1975. Bar: Ohio, U.S. Dist. Ct. (so. dist.) Ohio. Assoc., Frost & Jacobs, Cin., 1975-82; ptnr., 1982—. Vice chmn. Dan Beard chpt. Nat. Eagle Scout Assn., Cin., 1980—; trustee Hyde Park Community United Methodist Ch., Cin., 1982—, Stepping Stones Ctr. for Handicapped, Cin., 1982—. Mem. ABA, Cin. Bar Assn., Ohio State Bar Assn. Clubs: Cin. Country, Univ. (Cin.). Office: Frost & Jacobs 2500 Central Trust Ctr 201 E 5th Cincinnati OH 45202

SCOGGINS, SHIRLEY LOIS, typographical engineer; b. Dearborn, Mich., Mar. 27, 1929; d. Frederick August Andrew and Anna Marie Elizabeth (Pletz) Morris; student Slippery Rock Tchrs. Coll., 1948, Ind. State Tchrs. Coll., 1949-50; children—Bruce Edward, Michael Albert. Detailer, atomic power div. Westinghouse, Pitts., 1956-64, detailer, research, 1961-64; designer Computer Peripherals, Inc., Rochester, Mich., 1964-78, mgr. documentation control, 1978-82; engr. centronics Data Computer Corp., Rochester, 1982—. Mem. Am. Soc. Profl. and Exec. Women, Am. Bus. Womens Assn. Republican. Lutheran. Home: 30134 Fink St Farmington Hills MI 48024 Office: Centronics Data Computer Corp 1480 N Rochester Rd Rochester MI 48063

SCORCA, MARC AZZOLINI, arts administrator; b. Rockville Centre, N.Y., Sept. 20; s. Louis G. and Rosalie (Tascarella) S. B.A. magna cum laude in History and Music, Amherst Coll. Dir. mktg. Opera Co. of Phila., 1979-80; adminstrv. asst. N.Y.C. Opera, 1980-81, dir. spl. events, 1981-84; mng. dir. Chgo. Opera Theatre, 1984—; dir. Pa. Opera Theater, Phila.; dir., treas. Chgo. Music Alliance. Home: 3270 N Lake Shore Dr Chicago IL 60657 Office: Chgo Opera Theater 410 S Michigan Ave Chicago IL 60605

SCOTT, ALICE HOLLY, library administrator; b. Jefferson, Ga.; d. Frank David and Annie (Colbert) Holly; m. Alphonso Scott, Mar. 1, 1959; children—Christopher Scott, Alison Scott. A.B., Spelman Coll., 1957; M.L.S., Atlanta U., 1958; Ph.D., U. Chgo., 1983. Librarian Woodlawn Br., Chgo., 1959-60, br. head, Chgo., 1961-72, dir. Woodson Regional Library, Chgo., 1974-77, dir. community relations Chgo. Pub. Library, 1977-81, dep. commr., 1982—. Mem. ALA (councilor 1982-85), Ill. Library Assn., Chgo. Library Club. Office: Chicago Pub Library 425 N Michigan Ave Chicago IL 60611

SCOTT, BETTY ANN, advertising agency executive; b. Canton, Ohio, May 23, 1949; d. Charles M. and Betty M. (Barthel) S. Student Kent State U., 1967-75. Asst. art dir. Goodway Pub., Ft. Lauderdale, Fla., 1968-69; layout and design artist Creative Universal, Detroit, 1969-70; owner, pres., account exec. Scott & Assocs., Canton, 1971—; owner, pub. Focus mag., 1978—; owner Beauty Master, Inc., 1984—; owner Nail Place, 1982—. Chmn. enshrinee com. Pro Football Hall of Fame, 1979-82, active display com., 1971-82; bd. dirs. Canton Ballet. Recipient Public Service award Mayor Stanley Cmich, Canton, 1980. Mem. Indsl. Marketers of Cleve., Network of Akron/Canton, Canton C. of C., Internat. Advt. Assn., Am. Mktg. Assn., Profl. Bingo Players Assn. (pres.), Internat. Platform Assn., Akron/Canton Advt. Club. Republican. Home: 5601 Liberty Rd Bentleyville OH 44022 Office: 4041 Batton Dr NW Suite 215 North Canton OH 44720

SCOTT, DARREL JOSEPH, hospital administrator; b. Indpls., Sept. 12, 1947; s. Hubert Norris and Beverly June (Hiatt) S.; m. Janice L. Meredith, June 21, 1969; children—Andrew, Brennan. B.A., Ind. U., 1969, M.H.A. with high honors, 1971. Planning assoc. Ind. Hosp. Assn., Indpls., 1970-72; asst. dir. Welborn Bapt. Hosp., Evansville, Ind., 1972-77, AMA, Chgo., 1977-78; adminstr., chief exec. officer King's Daus. Hosp., Madison, Ind., 1978—; mem. Ind. Emergency Med. Services Commn., 1974-75. Bd. dirs. Jefferson County United Way, 1979—; res. dep. Jefferson County Sheriff's Dept., 1980—; chair coms. Trinity United Methodist Ch., Madison, 1982—. Fellow Am. Coll. Hosp. Adminstrs.; mem. Ind. Hosp. Assn. (council). Republican. Home: Rt 5 Madison IN 47250 Office: King's Daughters Hosp 112 Presbyterian Ave Madison IN 47250

SCOTT, DAVID C., manufacturing company executive; b. Akron, Ohio, 1915; B.Sc. in Chem. Engring., U. Ky., 1940, D.Sc. (hon.), 1971; LL.D. (hon.), Marquette U., 1980. Owner engring. cons. firm. Inst. Tech. Research, 1940-42; exec. Gen. Electric Co., 1945-63, mgr. power tube plant, Schenectady, 1954-60, gen. mgr. cathode ray tube dept., Syracuse, 1960-63; v.p., group exec. several subs. Colt Industries Inc., 1963-65, exec. v.p., dir., 1965-68; pres. Allis-Chalmers Corp., Milw., 1968-69, chmn. bd., chief exec. officer, 1969-83, chmn. bd., 1984—; dir. First Wis. Corp., Martin Marietta Corp., Travelers Corp., Humana, Inc., Harris Corp., Royal Crown Cos. Founding mem. Rockefeller U. Council; mem. exec. com. U.S. sect. Egypt-U.S. Bus. Council; mem. German Dem. Republic-U.S. Bus. Council; vice chmn., dir. Nat. Council for U.S.-China Trade; mem. adv. council Coll. Engring., U. Ky.; mem. exec. com., chmn. export adminstrn. subcom. Pres.'s Export Council; bd. dirs. Farm and Indsl. Equipment Inst.; bd. dirs., mem. devel. council Nigeria-U.S. Bus. Council; bd. dirs., exec. com. Council of Ams., Americas Soc.; pres. David C. Scott Found.; trustee U. Ky. Office: Allis-Chalmers Corp 1205 S 70th St PO Box 512 Milwaukee WI 53201

SCOTT, DAVID KNIGHT, educational administrator, physics and chemistry educator; b. North Ronaldsay, Scotland, Mar. 2, 1940; came to U.S., 1973; s. William and Mary Jane (Knight) S.; m. Kathleen Louise Smith, May 28, 1967; children—Wendelin Kay, Kelvin William Marshall, Jeremy Knight. B.Sc. in Physics, U. Edinburgh, Scotland, 1962; Ph.D., Oxford U., Eng., 1966. Research fellow Balliol Coll., U. Oxford, Eng., 1967-73; sr. scientist Lawrence Berkeley Lab., U. Calif., Berkeley, 1973-79, dir. Cyclotrol Lab., 1978-79; Hannah prof. physics and chemistry Mich. State U., East Lansing, 1979—, assoc. provost, 1983—; assoc. dir. research Nat. Superconducting Cyclotron Lab., Mich. State U., 1982-83. Editor: International Conference on Nucleus-Nucleus Collisions, 1983. Contbr. articles to profl. publs. Grierson fellow, 1958; Chalmers fellow, 1962. Fellow Am. Phys. Soc. (div. nuclear physics); mem. Phi Beta Kappa, Phi Kappa Phi, Tau Sigma. Presbyterian. Home: 340 Walbridge Dr East Lansing MI 48823 Office: Office of Provost Mich State U East Lansing MI 48824

SCOTT, EUGENE DYER, military school superintendent, former air force officer; b. Thomasville, Ga., Nov. 25, 1927; s. Allan D. and Catherine (Russell) S.; m. Joanne Buckner, Nov. 17, 1956; children—Braddock Buckner, Leslie Buckner. B.A., U. of South, 1948; M.S., George Washington U., 1968; grad. Air Command and Staff Sch., 1962, Naval War Coll., 1968. Commd. 2d lt. U.S. Air Force, 1948, advanced through grades to brig. gen., 1975; served in Fed. Republic Germany and Libya, 1950-53; squadron exec. officer, Ching Chuan Kang Air Base, Taiwan, 1968-70; chief missile and space ops. br., strategic div., Directorate of Ops., Hdqrs. U.S. Air Force, Washington, 1971-73; comdr. 390th Strategic Missile Wing, Davis-Monthan AFB, Ariz., 1973-75, 47th Air Div., Fairchild AFB, Washington, 1975-76; dep. dir. ops. Nat. Mil. Command Ctr., Orgn. Joint Chiefs of Staff, 1976-77, chief studies, analysis and gaming agy., 1977-79, ret., 1979; dir. devel. Tex. Mil. Inst., San Antonio, 1979-80; supt. Howe Mil. Sch., Ind., 1981—. Decorated D.S.M., Air medal, Air Force Commendation medal with four oak leaf clusters, Mertorious Service medal, others. Mem. Nat. Assn. Episcopal Schs. (governing bd. 1983—), Assn. Mil. Colls. and Schs. (exec. com. 1984—), Blue Key, Kappa Sigma, Alpha Psi Omega. Lodge: Kiwanis. Republican. Episcopalian. Home: 602 Union St Howe IN 46746 Office: Howe Mil Sch Academy Pl Howe IN 46746

SCOTT, GEORGE MATTHEW, state supreme ct. justice; b. Clark, N.J., Sept. 14, 1922; s. Francis Patrick and Harriet Ann (O'Donnell) S.; B.S., U. Minn.; J.D., William Mitchell Coll. Law; m. Joyce E. Hughes, July 26, 1947; children—Dan, Neil, Brian, George Matthew, Sheila. Admitted to Minn. bar; practice law, 1951-55; dep. atty. gen. State of Minn., 1955; atty. Hennepin County, Mpls., 1955-73; justice Minn. Supreme Ct., St. Paul, 1973—. Trustee William Mitchell Coll. Del. Democratic Nat. Conv., 1960; campaign chmn. Hubert H. Humphrey for Senator, 1960. Served with AUS, 1942-45. Mem. Am., Minn. bar assns., Nat. Dist. Atty's. Assn. (pres. 1964-65), Am. Legion. Roman Catholic. Club: Optimists. Contbr. articles to profl. jours. Office: 228 Minnesota State Capitol Saint Paul MN 55155 *

SCOTT, IRENA MCCAMMON, biologist; b. Delaware, Ohio, July 31, 1942; d. James Robert and Gay (Nuzum) McCammon; B.Sc., Ohio State U., Columbus, 1965; M.S., U. Nev., Las Vegas, 1972; Ph.D., U. Mo., Columbia, 1976; m. John Watson Scott, Dec. 6, 1969. Teaching and research asst. U. Nev., 1970-72; research asst. U. Mo., 1972-76; researcher Cornell U., 1977-78; asst. prof. biology St. Bonaventure (N.Y.) U., 1978-79; researcher Ohio State U., 1979—, Batelle Meml. Inst., 1980—. Grantee St. Bonaventure U. Mem. AAAS, Am. Physiol. Soc., Am. Dairy Sci. Assn., Mo. Acad. Sci., Ohio State U. Astronomy Club, Verse Writers Guild Ohio, Olentangy Poets, Mensa, Sigma Xi, Gamma Sigma Delta. Contbr. articles to profl. jours. Home: 6520 Bale Kenyon St Galena OH 43021 Office: 310 Hamilton Hall Ohio State U Columbus OH 43210

SCOTT, JULES FRANKLIN, advertising executive; b. Chgo., May 22, 1920; s. Jules Franklin and Helen Veronica (Kasmer) S.; B.S., Northwestern U., 1942; postgrad. U.S. Naval Acad., 1941; 1 son, Mark S. Copywriter, Montgomery Ward & Co., 1946-47, catalog advt. mgr., 1947-56; creative dir. Carter & Galantin Advt. Agy., 1956-59; creative dir., account supr. Hammett & Gillespie Advt. Agy., 1964-68; corp. dir. advt., sales promotion, and public relations Vaughan-Jacklin Corp., Downers Grove, Ill., 1968-84; pres. Advantage Promotions, Chgo., 1984—. Former scoutmaster Boy Scouts Am.; former treas. P.T.A.; pres. Homeowner Assn. Served to lt. comdr., USNR, 1941-45; ETO, PTO. Writer short stories; contbr. articles to hort. trade publs. Home: 946 Dartmouth Dr Wheaton IL 60187

SCOTT, LORRAINE ANN, association executive; b. Cleve., Dec. 14, 1947; d. Harry F. and Ann Mae (Dolecek) Dufek; m. John William Scott, Jan. 4, 1969; 1 son, Bruce. B.B.A., Dyke Coll., Cleve., 1967. Acct., Fulton, Reid & Staples, Cleve., 1967-69; acct., data control Nat. City Bank, Cleve., 1969-70; asst. treas. Independence (Ohio) Bd. of Edn. 1978-80; exec. dir. Nat. Frat. of Phi Gamma Nu, Cleve., 1980—. Mem. Am. Soc. Assn. Execs. Republican. Lutheran. Editor Phi Gamma Nu mag., 1980—.

SCOTT, MITCHELL GEORGE, scientific company research manager, immunologist; b. St. Louis, June 30, 1952; s. George Jules and Delores Jean (Rascher) S.; m. Barbara Ann Frey, Aug. 2, 1975; children—Katherine, Jennifer. A.B., Washington U., St. Louis, 1974, Ph.D., 1982; M.S., U. Mo.-St. Louis, 1977. Lab technologist, instr. Barnes Hosp., St. Louis, 1974-77; postdoctoral fellow Sch. Medicine, Washington U., St. Louis, 1982-84, postdoctoral clin. chemistry trainee dept. pathology, 1982-84; research mgr. Mallinckrodt, Inc., St. Louis, 1984—. Contbr. articles to profl. jours. NIH Stephen Morse fellow, 1977-80. Mem. Am. Assn. Clin. Chemistry (cert.). Avocations: photography; tennis; snow skiing; bicycling. Home: 12404 Mathews St Sunset Hills MO 63127 Office: Mallinckrodt Inc 675 McDonnell Blvd St Louis MO 63134

SCOTT, PATRICIA LOUISE, sign manufacturing executive; b. Chgo., Feb. 13, 1946; d. Gerald E. and Grace B. (Hauser) Doyle; m. Gregory L. Marshall (dec. 1967); 1 child, Gregory L. II; m. Don Scott, May 13, 1978. Student Harper Jr. Coll., 1978-82. Adminstrv. asst. Sweda Internat., Chgo. and Des Plaines, Ill., 1969-73; asst. credit mgr. Oce Industries, Chgo., 1974-77; gen. office clk. Nutheme Co., 1977-78, gen. mgr. 1978-83, pres., 1983—. Office: Nutheme Co 1461-D Lunt Ave Elk Grove Village IL 60007

SCOTT, RALPH C., physician, educator; b. Bethel, Ohio, June 7, 1921; s. John Carey and Leona (Laycock) S.; B.S., U. Cin., 1943, M.D., 1945; m. Rosemary Ann Schultz, June 26, 1945; children—Susan Ann, Barbara Lynne, Marianne. Intern Univ. Hosps., U. Iowa, 1945-46; resident, asst. dept. pathology U. Cin. Coll. Medicine, 1948-49, fellow internal medicine, 1949-53, fellow cardiology, 1953-57, mem. faculty, 1950—, 76-82, 85—. medicine, 1968—; staff clinics Cin. Gen. Hosp., 1950-75, clinician in internal medicine, 1952-75, dir. cardiac clinics, 1965-75, attending physician med. service, 1958—; staff VA Hosp., Cin., 1954—, cons., 1961—; attending physician Med. Service, Christian R. Holmes Hosp., Cin., 1957—; attending staff USAF Hosp., Wright Patterson AFB, 1960—; staff Good Samaritan Hosp., Cin., 1961—, cons., 1967—; staff Jewish Hosp., Cin., 1957—, cons., 1968—; cons. Children's Hosp., Cin., 1968—; attending physician Providence Hosp., Cin., 1971—. Served from 1st lt. to capt., AUS, 1946-48. Nat. Heart Inst. grantee, 1964-68, 67-74, 76-82, 85. Diplomate Am. Bd. Internal Medicine (subsplty. cardiovascular disease). Fellow ACP, Am. Coll. Cardiology, Am. Coll. Chest Physicians; mem. AMA, Ohio State Med. Assn., Cin. Acad. Medicine, Central Soc. Clin. Research, Am. Heart Assn. (fellow council clin. cardiology), Cin. Soc. Internal Medicine, Heart Assn. Southwestern Ohio, Am. Fedn. for Clin. Research, Internat. Cardiovascular Soc., Sigma Xi, Alpha Omega Alpha, Phi Eta Sigma, Phi Chi. Contbr. articles to med. jours. Editorial bd. Am. Heart Jour., 1967-79, Jour. Electrocardiology, 1967—; editor Electrocardiographic-Pathologic Conf., Jour. Electrocardiology, 1967—, Clin. Cardiology and Diabetes, 5 vols., 1980-81. Home: 2955 Alpine Terr Cincinnati OH 45208 Office: Room 7157 Med Scis Bldg Univ Cincinnati Med Center 231 Bethesda Ave Cincinnati OH 45267

SCOTT, REBECCA ANDREWS, biology educator; b. Sunny Hill, La., June 4, 1939; d. Hayward and Dorothy (Nicholson) Andrews; m. Earl P. Scott, June 8, 1957; children—Stephanie Scott Dilworth, Cheryl L. B.S., So. U., 1962; M.S., Eastern Mich. U., 1969. Biology tchr., Detroit, 1966-68; sci. tchr. Ann Arbor (Mich.) Pub. Schs., 1968-69; biology tchr. North High Sch., Mpls., 1972—, advisor Jets Sci. Club. Pres. LWV of St. Anthony County, 1981-83, treas., 1984-86. Mem. Nat. Sci. Tchrs. Assn., Minn. Sci. Tchrs. Assn., Iota Phi Lambda. Democrat. Presbyterian. Home: 3112 Wendhurst Ave Minneapolis MN 55418 Office: 1500 James Ave N Minneapolis MN 55411

SCOTT, ROBERT ALLYN, educational administrator; b. Englewood, N.J., Apr. 16, 1939; s. William D. and Ann. F. (Waterman) S.; B.A., Bucknell U., 1961; Ph.D., Cornell U., 1975; m. Phyllis Virginia Brice, Mar. 23, 1963; children—Ryan Keith, Kira Elizabeth. Mgmt. trainee Procter & Gamble Co., Phila., 1961-63; asst. dir. admissions Bucknell U., Lewisburg, Pa., 1965-67; asst. dean Coll. Arts and Scis., Cornell U., Ithaca, N.Y., 1967-69, assoc. dean, 1969-79, prof. anthropology, 1978-79; dir. acad. affairs Ind. Commn. for Higher Edn., Indpls., 1979—; pres.-elect Ramapo Coll. N.J., 1985—; lectr. U. Philippines, 1964-65; cons. to Sta. WSKG Public TV and Radio, 1977-79; cons. to various colls. and univs., pubs., 1966—; mem. curriculum adv. com. Ind. Bd. Edn., 1984—; mem. Lilly Endowment Thinktank, 1984—. Trustee, Bucknell U., 1976-78, First Unitarian Ch., Ithaca, 1970-73, 78-79, chmn., 1971-73, Unitarian Universalist Ch. of Indpls., 1980—. Served with USNR, 1963-65. Spencer Found. research grantee, 1972, Exxon Edn. Found. research grantee, 1977. Fellow Am. Anthrop. Assn.; mem. Assn. Study Higher Edn., Am. Sociol. Assn., Am. Assn. Higher Edn., Higher Edn. Colloquim (chmn. 1982-84), Bucknell U. Alumni Assn. (dir. 1971-80, pres. 1976-78), Indpls. Com. on Fgn. Relations, Phi Kappa Psi, Phi Kappa Phi. Clubs: Ithaca Yacht; Econs. of Indpls. Contbr. articles to sociol., ednl. and popular publs.; author books and mongraphs; editorial bd. Cornell Rev., 1976-79; book rev. editor Coll. and Univ., 1974-78; cons. editor Change mag., 1979—; cons. editor Jour. Higher Edn., 1985—; exec. editor Saturday Evening Post book div. Curtis Pub. Co., 1982—. Office: 143 W Market St Indianapolis IN 46204

SCOTT, ROBERT EUGENE, experimental pathologist, educator; b. Terre Haute, Ind., Oct. 19, 1941; s. Virgil E. and Catherine (Mindrup) S.; m. Harriet Phillips, June 26, 1965; children—David, Anna. B.S., Vanderbilt U., 1963, M.D., 1967; Diplomate Am. Bd. Pathology. Resident in pathology Vanderbilt U., 1967-69; staff assoc. NIH, Bethesda, Md., 1969-71; asst. prof., then assoc. prof. pathology U. Minn., Mpls., 1971-75; prof. pathology, head sect. expl. pathology Mayo Clinic, Rochester, Minn., 1975—. Contbr. 100 articles on carcinogenesis to profl. jours. Served as capt. USPHS, 1969-71. Mem. Am. Assn. Pathologist, AAAS, Internat. Differentiation Soc., Internat. Acad. Pathology, Am. Assn. Cancer Research, Am. Soc. Cell Biol., Internat. Cell Cycle Soc. Office: 511b Guggenheim Bldg Mayo Clinic Rochester MN 55901

SCOTT, ROBERT GENE, lawyer; b. Montague, Mass., Aug. 29, 1951; s. Edwin Ray and Barbara Agnes (Painchaud) S.; m. Laura Beth Williams, May 27, 1978; 1 child, Jason Robert. B.S., U. Notre Dame, 1973, M.S., 1975; postgrad. U. Tex. Med. Br., 1975-76; J.D., U. Notre Dame, 1980. Bar: Ind., U.S. Dist. Ct. (no. dist.) Ind. 1980, Mo. 1981, U.S. Dist. Ct. (we. dist.) Mo. 1981, U.S. Patent Office 1980. Asst. women's basketball coach U. Notre Dame, Ind., 1977-80; assoc. atty. Oltsch, Knoblock & Hall, South Bend, Ind., 1980-81; atty. Swanson, Midgley, et al, Kansas City, Mo., 1981-82; exec. adminstr. Council of Fleet Specialists, Shawnee Mission, Kans., 1982-83; atty. Levy & Craig, Kansas City, Mo., 1983—. Precinct Committeeman Johnson County Republican Party, Kans., 1983-84. Mem. ABA, Ind. Bar Assn., Mo. Bar Assn., Kansas City Bar Assn., Kansas City Lawyers Assn. Republican. Roman Catholic. Club: Notre Dame of Kansas City (pres. 1985-86). Home: 9405 Dice Ln Lenexa KS 66215 Office: Levy & Craig 916 Walnut St Bldg 400 Kansas City MO 64106

SCOTT, ROGER DAN, insurance company executive; b. Ottawa, Kans., Feb. 25, 1951; s. True Roger and Helen Louise (Mages) S.; m. Sally Jo Cox, Apr. 8, 1972; children—Christopher, Marcy, Amy. Student Clark's Bus. Coll., Topeka, 1969-70. Asst. underwriter Taylor & Co. Gen. Agy., Topeka, 1970-73; personal lines mgr. Northwestern Nat. Ins. Co., Topeka, 1973-76; underwriting mgr. Kans. Mut. Ins. Co., Topeka, 1976-80, exec. mgr., 1980—; sec.-treas. Midwest Rating and Service Bur., Inc., McPhearson, Kans., 1984—. Fund raising com. Kans. Ins. Edn. Found., Topeka, 1983-84; chmn. Kans. Com. on Arson Prevention, Topeka, 1983—; co. fund raising chmn. United Way of Topeka, 1980—. Mem. Kans. 1752 Club, Profl. Ins. Agts., Ind. Ins. Agts. Kans., Kans. Assn. Property and Casualty Ins. Cos. (pres. 1982-83), Topeka Underwriters Assn. Republican. Roman Catholic. Home: 6335 W 11th Topeka KS 66615 Office: Kans Mut Ins Co PO Box 1247 Topeka KS 66601

SCOTT, RONALD HUBERT, physician, surgeon; b. Rocky Ford, Colo., Jan. 3, 1912; s. Robert Hetherington and Bessie Estelle (Searls) S.; m. Hazel Louise Wiler, Aug. 15, 1937; 1 child Ronalyn Louise Scott Yeary. A.B., Western State Coll., 1935; D.O., Kirksville Coll. Osteo. Medicine, 1945; postgrad. Kans. U-Med. Ctr., 1970-82. Practice osteo. medicine specializing in geriatrics, Sullivan, Mo., 1947—; Sullivan Community Hosp. Dir. Presbyn. Chancel Choir, Sullivan Community Chorus, 1956-85; bd. dirs. Dist. CII Sch., Sullivan, Mo., 1957-72, pres. bd., 1960-70. Fellow Internat. Coll. Gen. Practitioners; mem. Am. Acad. Osteopathy, Am. Osteo. Assn., (life), Mo. Osteo. Assn. (life; trustee 1957-72), Am. Coll. Gen. Practitioners, Psi Sigma Alpha. Republican. Presbyterian. Lodges: Rotary (pres. 1959-60, dist. gov. 1965-66), Odd Fellows. Home: 131 Meredith Ln Sullivan MO 63080

SCOTT, THEODORE, firechief; b. Racine, Ohio, Sept. 28, 1935; s. George Engel Scott and Marie Lorena (Polk) Holman; m. Sharon Patricia Gunther, Oct. 24, 1959; children—Sonya, Lynn, Linda, Rachel L. A.A., Washtenaw Community Coll., 1972; B.A., with honors, Madonna Coll., 1974. Firefighter, Wayne-Nankin Fire Dept., Wayne, Mich., 1959-63; capt. Westland Fire Dept., Mich., 1967-77, battalion chief, 1977-80, chief, 1980—; instr. ARC, 1967—; fire tng. adv. Firefighters Tng. Council State of Mich., 1981—; instr. Washtenaw Community Coll., Ann Arbor, Mich., 1970-71. Chmn. Summer Festival, Westland, 1976; precinct Elections, Westland, 1976, Dist. Judge Election campaign, Westland, 1978; supt. Sunday Sch., Episcopal Ch., Westland, 1974-81; bd. dirs. YMCA, Westland, 1984—. Recipient Fireman of Yr. award Westland Jaycees, 1978. Mem. Southeastern Mich. Fire Chiefs (pres. 1985), Mich. Fire Chiefs Assn., Internat. Assn. Fire Chiefs, Wayne County Fire Chiefs (v.p. 1983-84). Lodge: Goodfellows (pres. 1979-80). Mason. Avocations: sailing; high power rifle competitor. Office: Westland Fire Dept 36485 Ford Rd Westland MI 48185

SCOTT, THEODORE R., lawyer; b. Mt. Vernon, Ill., Dec. 7, 1924; s. Theodore R. and Beulah (Flannigan) S.; A.B., U. Ill., 1947, J.D., 1949; m. Virginia Scott, June 1, 1947; children—Anne Scott Sheyka, Sarah Scott Buckland, Daniel, Barbara Scott Gomon. Admitted to Ill. bar, 1950; law clk. to Judge Walter C. Lindley, U.S. Ct. Appeals, 1949-51; asso. Spaulding Glass, 1951-53, Loftus, Lucas & Hammand, 1953-58, Ooms, McDougall, Williams & Hersh, 1958-60; partner McDougall, Hersh, & Scott and predecessor, 1960— (all Chgo.). Served to 2d lt. USAAF, 1943-45; ETO. Decorated Air medal. Mem. ABA, Ill., Chgo., 7th Circuit (past pres.) bar assns., Am. Coll. Trial Lawyers, Legal Club Chgo., Law Club Chgo., Patent Law Assn. Chgo. (past pres.), Phi Beta Kappa. Club: Union League (Chgo.); Exmoor Country (Highland Park, Ill.). Home: 1569 Woodvale Ave Deerfield IL 60015 Office: 135 S LaSalle St Chicago IL 60603

SCOTT, WALTER, JR., See *Who's Who in America,* 43rd edition.

SCOTT, WALTER DILL, industrial company executive; b. Chgo., Oct. 27, 1931; s. John Marcy and Mary Louise (Gent) S.; student Williams Coll., 1949-51; B.S., Northwestern U., 1953; M.S., Columbia, 1958; m. Barbara Ann Stein, Sept. 9, 1961; children—Timothy Walter, David Frederick, Gordon Charles. Cons. Booz, Allen & Hamilton, N.Y.C., 1956-58; assoc. Glore, Forgan & Co., N.Y.C., 1958-63, partner, Chgo., 1963-65; partner Lehman Bros., Chgo., 1965-72, sr. partner, 1972-73, also dir.; assoc. dir. econs. and govt. Office Mgmt. and Budget, Washington, 1973-75; sr. v.p. internat. and fin. Pillsbury Co., Mpls., 1975-78, exec. v.p., 1978-80, also dir.; pres., chief exec. officer Investors Diversified Services, Inc., Mpls., 1980-84, group mng. dir. Grand Met. PLC, 1984—; chmn. Grand Met U.S.A., 1984—; dir. JWT Group, Inc.

Chmn. adv. council Kellogg Grad. Sch. Mgmt., Northwestern U. Served to lt. (j.g.) USN, 1953-56. Clubs: Woodhill; Minneapolis.

SCOTT, WILLIAM PAUL, lawyer; b. Staples, Minn., Nov. 8, 1928; A.L.A., U. Minn., 1949; B.S.L., St. Paul Coll. Law, 1952, J.D., 1954; m. Elsie Elaine Anderson, Feb. 7, 1968; 1 son, Jason Lee; children by previous marriage—William P., Mark D., Bryan D., Scott; stepchildren—Thomas J. (dec.), Terri L. Berg. Bar: Minn. 1954. Atty. right of way div. Minn. Hwy. Dept., 1945-52, civil engr. traffic and safety div., 1953-55; practice law Arlington, Minn., 1955-61, Gaylord, Minn., 1963-67; sr. partner firm Scott Law Offices and predecessors, Pipestone, Minn., 1967—; probate, juvenile judge Sibley County, Minn., 1956-61; Minn. pub. examiner, 1961-63; county atty. Sibley County, 1963-68, city atty., Pipestone, 1978—. Formerly nat. committeeman Young Rep. League; Sibley County Rep. chmn., 1961. Served with USMCR, 1946-50; from 2d lt. to lt. col. USAF Res., 1950-77; ret. Recipient George Washington Honor medal Freedoms Found., 1970, 72. Mem. Am., Minn. bar assns., Mensa, V.F.W., DAV, Am. Legion, Air Force Assn., Res. Officers Assn., U.S. Supreme Ct. Bar Assn. Mason (32 deg., Shriner). Home: Box 704 Pipestone MN 56164 Office: Park Plaza Offices Pipestone MN 56164

SCOTT, WINFIELD JAMES, marketing executive; b. Worcester, Mass., Jan. 4, 1933; s. Gherald Dean and Helen L. S.; B.A., Norwich U., 1955; postgrad. Marquette U., 1961-62; m. Betty Joan Price, June 29, 1957; children—Mary Jo, Susan Elizabeth. With sales dept. Norton Co., Worcester, 1956, sales rep. Chgo. dist., 1957, sales supr. Wis. dist., 1960-71; founder, pres. The Abrasive Group, Wauwatosa, Wis., 1971—; co-founder, pres. Indsl. Supply Group, Menomenee Falls, Wis.; ad hoc prof. mktg. U. Wis. Extension. Mem. Abrasive Engring. Soc. (co-gen. chmn. internat. conf.), Nat. Small Bus. Assn., Wis. Mfrs. and Commerce, Ind. Bus. Assn. Wis., Met. Milw. Assn. Commerce, Nat. Fedn. Ind. Bus. Republican. Episcopalian. Author: Modern Machine Shop, 1967. Home: 11037 W Derby Ave Wauwatosa WI 53225 Office: PO Box 13244 Wauwatosa WI 53213

SCRIBNER, MARGARET ELLEN, school evaluator and administrator, consultant; b. Pana, Ill., Oct. 20, 1948; d. William M. and Bertrice Faye (Springman) S.; m. John E. McNeal, Aug. 15, 1977 (div. Oct. 1981). B.S. in Social Work, Spaulding U., 1970. Coordinator Gov.'s Inaugural Com., Springfield, Ill., 1972; sch. evaluation specialist Ill. State Bd. of Edn., Chgo., 1970—; dir. on bd. and corp. sec. Ventura 21, Inc., Roselle, Ill., 1984—. Mem. Uptown Community Orgn., Chgo., 1978-80; charter mem. and organizer Margate-Ainslie Block Club, Chgo., 1979-80. Recipient cert. of Recognition, Ill. State Bd. of Edn., Springfield, 1975, 77, 78. Mem. Bus. and Profl. Women of Chgo., (historian 1978-79), Internat. Leadership Training Inst. (cert. 1974). Republican. Roman Catholic. Clubs: Ill. Athletic (Chgo. 1983—), Brookwood Country (Wooddale, Ill. 1977-81, 83—). Avocations: golf; clarinet; water colors; racquetball. Office: Ill State Bd of Edn 100 W Randolph Suite 14-300 Chicago IL 60601

SCRIVNER, JOYCE KAY, computer programmer/analyst; b. Denver, June 12, 1950; d. Mansil Wayne and Harriet Lorraine (Webster) S.; S.S.T.P., Colo. Sch. Mines, 1967; student U. Colo., 1968-72; student Mich. State U., Clarion, 1974; B.S.C.S., Purdue U., 1976. Clk., U.S. Book Exchange, Washington, 1972-73, Govt. Printing Office, Washington, 1973-74; programmer SCADA group Leeds & Northrup Corp., North Wales, Pa., 1976-78; programmer-/analyst Energy Mgmt. Systems div. Control Data Corp., Mpls., 1979-84; design automation engr. Mercury div. Sperry Corp., Mpls., 1984—; adminstr. Down Under Fan Fund, 1981-83; chmn. Plergbcon, Mpls., 1982. Mem. World Sci. Fiction Conv. Staff, 1977, 78, 80, 81, 83, 84; chairperson art show Minicon, Mpls., 1980-81, 83. Down Under Fan Fund grantee, 1981. Mem. Assn. Women in Computing (program v.p. 1982-83), Minn. Sci. Fiction Assn., IEEE Computer Assn. Editor mags.: Gypsy, 1979—, Of Such Are Legends Made, 1978—. Office: 2300 Berkshire Ln Minneapolis MN 55441

SCULLIN, RICHARD OWEN, artist; b. Cleve., Jan. 5, 1935; s. Harry Joseph and Mary Ellen (Moran) S.; children—Maureen, Carrie, Kathleen, Mathew. Student Cleve. Inst. Art. Artist, Advance Art, Cleve., 1952-54, Pitt Studio, 1954-56, Federmann, Adams, Cleve., 1956-65, New Center Studio, Detroit, 1965-67; artist, owner McNamara Assocs., Inc., Detroit, 1967-79; artist, owner Scullin & Assocs., Inc., Union Lake, Mich., 1979—; dir. Graphic Artist Guild, Detroit, 1967-74. Recipient various awards including: Andy award, 1981. Mem. Mich. Watercolor Soc., Nat. Watercolor Soc. Republican. Home and Office: 6603 Blue Spruce Ct Union Lake MI 48085

SCULLY, JOHN EDWARD, JR., banker; b. Chgo., Jan. 18, 1943; s. John Edward and Ann Berenice (Allenbrand) S.; m. Mary Julia Purvin, June 11, 1966; children—Melissa, Julie, John Edward III. B.A., U. Notre Dame, 1964; M.A., DePaul U., 1966. Supr., No. Trust Co., Chgo., 1968-69, with personnel dept., 1969-74, personnel officer, 1974-77, bond investment officer, 1977-80; asst. v.p. First Nat. Bank of Chgo., 1980-82, v.p., 1982—; instr. Am. Inst. Banking, 1972—. Served with USAR, 1964—, col. Res. Mem. Am. Soc. Personnel Adminstrs., Employment Mgrs. Assn., Res. Officers Assn., Mil. Order World Wars, Assn. U.S. Army. Republican. Roman Catholic. Club: Riverside Swim. Avocations: running, stamp collecting. Home: 258 Lawton Rd Riverside IL 60546 Office: First Nat Bank of Chicago Chicago IL 60670

SEAL, GREGORY MORRIS, management consultant; b. Buffalo, Feb. 23, 1948; s. Maynard A. and Sally (Latak) S.; m. Victoria Ghearing, Mar. 30, 1974; children—Allyson Marie, Alexander Michael. B.A. in Econs., Colgate U., 1970. Cert. mgmt. cons., systems profl. Systems analyst Procter & Gamble, Cin., 1970-73, group mgr., 1973-76; ptnr. Touche Ross & Co., Cleve., 1976—. Contbr. articles retail and mfg. systems Regional pres. Big Bros./Big Sisters Am., Cin., 1976, bd. dirs., Phila., 1975-76, v.p., Cin., 1973-76. Mem. Inst. Mgmt. Cons., Soc. Info. Mgmt. Home: 226 S Park St Aurora OH 44202 Office: Touche Ross 1801 E 9th St Cleveland OH 44114

SEALY, ZOE WEST, artistic director, dance instructor, choreographer; b. Mobile, Ala., Dec. 19, 1939; d. Henry Carver and Margaret (Griffith) West; m. William Francis Sealy, Dec. 12, 1968; children—Charles Lee, Michael Henry. Student U. Ala., 1958-59. Dancer, Mobile Civic Ballet, 1963-65, Crescent City Ballet, New Orleans, 1957-59; tchr./dancer Arthur Murray Studios, Mobile, Pensacola, Fla., 1966-68; co-dir. Studio Dance Arts, Mpls., 1970-72, founder, artistic dir. Zoe Sealy Dance Ctr., Mpls., 1972—, Minn. Jazz Dance Co., Mpls., 1976—; dance tchr. U. Minn. Mpls., 1984—; choreographer Morris Park Players, Mpls., 1970-75; dance instr. Gulf Coast Dance Seminar, Mobile, Ala., 1980-84; panel mem. Minn. Ind. Choreographers Alliance/McKnight Fellowship, Mpls., 1984-85. Choreographer: Rhapsody in Blue, 1977; Classique Moderne, 1978; Tribute, 1979; XI Commandment: Dance, 1982; Under the Influence, 1985. Pres., PTA, Mpls., 1971-72. Recipient 1st Place Tchrs. trophy (regional competition) Arthur Murray Studios, 1968, 2d Place Tchrs. trophy (world competition), 1968. Mem. Profl. Dance Tchrs. Assn., Minn. Ind. Choreographers Alliance. Republican. United Methodist. Avocations: tennis, swimming. Office: Zoe Sealy Dance Center 1815 E 38th St Minneapolis MN 55407

SEAMAN, WILLIAM RICE, lawyer; b. Newton, Mass., Sept. 3, 1909; s. William Grant and Laura Owen (Rice) S.; m. Martha Elizabeth Steed, May 14, 1949; children—Diane Whitten, John Terrell. A.B., DePauw U., 1930; LL.B., Harvard U., 1933. Bar: Ohio 1933, U.S. Dist. Ct. (so. dist.) Ohio 1935, U.S. Ct. Appeals (6th cir.) 1935. Assoc., Frost & Jacobs, Cin., 1933-42, 46-49, ptnr., 1950-79, of counsel, 1980—. Councilman Indian Hill Village, Cin., 1943-54, vice mayor, 1955; trustee Citizens Devel. Com., 1952-53. Served to lt. Comdr. USN, 1942-46, ETO. Decorated Bronze Star. Mem. Cin. Bar Assn., Ohio Bar Assn., ABA, Cincinnatus Assn. (pres. 1951). Republican. Methodist. Club: University. Lodge: Rotary. Home: 8875 Fawn Meadow Ln Cincinnati OH 45242 Office: First & Jacobs 2500 Central Trust Ctr Cincinnati OH 45202

SEARBY, EDWARD RAY, college dean; b. Evansville, Ind., Mar. 5, 1924; s. Harry Edward and Clara Winnifred (Deane) S.; m. Laura Jean Schnitz, May 10, 1945; children—Reta, Steven, Carol. B.S. in Mech. Engring., Purdue U., 1949; M.B.A., Ind. U., 1954; Ed.D., No. Ill. U., 1967. Vice pres. bus. Coll. DuPage, Glen Ellyn, Ill., 1967-70; exec. v.p. Honeggers & Co., Inc., Fairbury, Ill., 1970-71; chmn. bus. div. Waubonsee Community Coll., Sugar Grove, Ill., 1971-73; pres. Kaskaskia Coll., Centralia, Ill., 1973-76; dean instrn. Highland Community Coll., Freeport, Ill., 1976—; sec. Highland Community Coll. Found., Freeport, Ill., 1976—. Bd. dirs. Girl Scouts Am., Freeport, 1982—. Served to sgt. U.S. Army, 1943-45, ETO. Lodge: Rotary (Freeport). Avocations: golf; farming; auto restoration. Home: 709 Santa Fe Dr Freeport IL 61032

SEARLE, DANIEL CROW, retired medical and health services company executive; b. Evanston, Ill., May 6, 1926; s. John Gideon and Frances Louise (Crow) S.; B.S., Yale, 1950; M.B.A., Harvard, 1952; m. Dain Depew Fuller, Sept. 2, 1950; children—Anne Searle Meers, Daniel Gideon, Michael Dain. With G.D. Searle & Co., Chgo., 1938—, successively staff asst. to v.p. charge fin. and mfg., asst. sec., sec., 1952-59, v.p., 1961-63, exec. v.p., 1963-66, pres., chief ops. officer 1966-70, pres., chief exec. officer, 1970-72, chmn. exec. com., from 1972, chmn. bd., 1977-85, dir., 1964—; dir. Harris Trust & Savs. Bank, Chgo., Utilities Inc., Maynard Oil Co., Jim Walter Corp. Bd. dirs. Evanston Hosp., Assocs. of Harvard Bus. Sch.; trustee Northwestern U., Art Inst. Chgo., WTTW, Channel 11, Chgo., Hudson Inst., Indpls., Com. for Econ. Devel. Served with USNR, World War II. Republican. Episcopalian (vestry). Clubs: Indian Hill (Winnetka, Ill.); Shoreacres (Lake Bluff, Ill.); Chicago, Commercial (Chgo.); Seminole Golf; Augusta Nat. Golf; Old Elm (Highland Park, Ill.); Jupiter Island (Fla.). Avocations: golf, flying. Office: GD Searle & Co PO Box 1045 4711 Golf Rd Skokie IL 60076

SEARLE, DANIEL GIDEON, venture capital executive; b. Evanston, Ill., Jan. 23, 1953; s. Daniel Crow and Dain Depew (Fuller) S.; m. Nancy Roberta Schneider, Aug. 15, 1976; children—Kristin Anne, Gideon Paul. B.S. in Sociology, Vanderbilt U., 1975; M.M. in Fin., Northwestern U., 1983. Mgmt. trainee G.D. Searle & Co., Skokie, Ill., 1975-77; asst. product mgr. Searle Pharms., Chgo., 1977-78, pharm. sales rep., 1978-79; mem. mktg. research staff Searle Pharms., Chgo., 1979; mgr. internal control Searle Pharm. Group, Skokie, 1979-83, mgr. records mgmt., 1983-84; assoc. Karl Kinship Capital Corp., Skokie, 1984—. Trustee Allendale Sch., Lake Villa, Ill., 1977—, Shedd Aquarium, Chgo., 1982—. Mem. Chgo. Venture Capital Club, Ducks Unlimited (chmn. North Shore sponsor chpt. 1983—). Republican. Episcopalian. Clubs: Glen View (Golf, Ill.); Indian Hill (Winnetka, Ill.). Avocations: wine collecting; duck hunting; golf; reading in management. Office: Earl Kinship Capital Corp 4711 Golf Rd Skokie IL 60076

SEASTRAND, ROBERT HOWARD, door manufacturing executive; Columbus, Ohio, June 25, 1947; s. Robert Emil Seastrand and Dorothy (Taynor) Seastrand Groves; m. Yvonne Kay Newsom, May 18, 1984; children by previous marriage—Tammy, Chad; stepchildren—Deanna, Greg, Lora, Kristi. Student Clark U., 1953-61, Thomas Jefferson U., 1958-61, West Tech. Coll., 1961-64. From installer to ptnr. Jordan Door Corp., Columbus, Ohio, 1968-80; sales staff Jay Door Co, Zanesville, Ohio, 1980-83, McHenry Enterprises, Zanesville, 1983-85; Midwest sales mgr. Provene Roll Door Co., Marietta, Ga., 1985—. Served with U.S. Army, 1964-67. Democrat. Lodge: Elks. Avocations: racquetball; bowling; fishing. Home: 317 N High St New Lexington OH 43764

SEATON, GEORGE LELAND, former utility co. exec., civic worker; b. Sunny South, Calif., Feb. 9, 1901; s. Frank H. and Charity Jane (Lee) S.; B.S.E.E., Iowa State U., 1923; A.A. (hon.), Coll. DuPage; m. Mildred Irene Sandall, Aug. 14, 1926; children—Robert Lee, James Mann, Mary Seaton Martin. Engr., Gen. Electric Co., Ft. Wayne, Ind., 1923; with Ill. Bell Telephone Co., Chgo., 1923-66, asst. v.p., 1952-64, v.p., 1964-66, ret., 1966. Mem. Hinsdale (Ill.) Bd. Edn., 1941-47; chmn. Chgo. council Boy Scouts Am., 1958-63; chmn. exec. com. Gt. Books Found., Chgo., 1965—; treas. Disciples Div. House, U. Chgo., 1945—, mem. vis. com. U. Chgo. Div. Sch., 1977—; mem. Ill. Fair Employment Com., 1961-69; chmn. Coll. DuPage, 1966-72. Served to 2d lt. C.E., USAR, 1923-28. Recipient Silver Beaver award Boy Scouts Am., Silver Antelope award. Mem. Western Soc. Engrs., Am. Statis. Assn. Republican. Mem. Christian Ch. (Disciples of Christ). Clubs: Union League (Chgo.); Hinsdale Golf, Econ. Home: 6110 S County Line Burr Ridge IL 60521

SEBASTIAN, JAMES JOSEPH, real estate development company executive; b. Warren, Ohio, Apr. 20, 1947; s. James V. and Julie M. S.; B.S., Ohio State U., 1969; M.B.A., Colo. U., 1977; m. Molly M. Moline, June 14, 1975. Mgr. sales/engring. Werner Constrn. Co., Columbus, Ohio, 1971-77; dir. adminstrv. services Red Roof Inns, Columbus, Ohio, 1977-78; pres. James J. Sebastian Co., Inc., real estate developers, cons. and brokers, Columbus, 1978—. Mem. Nat. Republican Com. Mem. Am. Mgmt. Assn., Assn. M.B.A. Execs., Columbus Builders Exchange. Clubs: Columbus Athletic; Little Turtle Country; Amateur Radio Relay League, Tournament Players, Sawgrass Country, St. Augustine Yacht. Home: 103 Nob Hill Dr Gahanna OH 43230 Office: 81 S 5th St Columbus OH 43215 also Camachee Islanu Saint Augustine FL 32084

SEBASTIAN, JOHN FRANCIS, chemistry educator; b. San Diego; s. John Francis and Martha Klazina (Van der Linde) S.; m. Sandra Mary Thompson, Aug. 12, 1967; children—Byron David, Colin Alan. B.S., San Diego State U., 1961; Ph.D., U. Calif.-Riverside, 1965. NIH postdoctoral fellow Northwestern U., Evanston, Ill., 1965-67; asst. prof. chemistry Miami U., Oxford, Ohio, 1967-72, assoc. prof. chemistry, 1972-80, prof. chemistry, 1980—. Research Corp. grantee, 1968; NSF grantee, 1972. Mem. Am. Chem. Soc., Royal Chem. Soc., AAAS, Sigma Xi. Contbr. articles to sci. jours. Office: Dept Chemistry Miami U Oxford OH 45056

SEBASTIAN, STUART, choreographer; b. Dayton, Ohio, July 26, 1950; s. Virginia (Lorah) S.; B.A. magna cum laude, Am. U., 1976. Profl. dancer, 1965—; prin. dancer Nat. Ballet of Washington, 1972-73; choreographer Met. Opera, Royal Winnipeg Ballet, Washington Ballet, others; speaker for USIA in Russia and Eastern Europe; now dir./prin. choreographer Dayton Ballet, 1980—; choreographer operas, off-Broadway musicals, ballets. Mem. dance panel Ohio Arts Council. U.S.-U.K. grantee, 1977; Ford Found. scholar 1963-68 scholar Tex. Christian U., 1968-70. Mem. Assn. Ohio Dance Cos. (dir.), Nat. Assn. Regional Ballet (dir.), Am. Guild Mus. Artists. Office: 140 N Main St Dayton OH 45402

SEBEOK, THOMAS A., linguist, author, educator; b. Budapest, Hungary, 1920; came to U.S., 1937, naturalized, 1944; B.A., U. Chgo., 1941; M.A., Princeton U., 1943, Ph.D., 1945. Mem. faculty Ind. U., Bloomington, 1943—, Disting. prof. linguistics, 1967-78, Disting. prof. linguistics and semiotics, 1978—, prof. anthropology, founder dept. Uralic and Altaic studies, prof. Uralic and Altaic studies, dir. Uralic and Altaic Lang. and Area Center, dir. Air Force lang. tng. program; vis. prof. various univs. in U.S. and Europe, 1946—; lectr. English, French, German or Hungarian on linguistics to various univs. and acads. in U.S., Can., Europe and Asia; cons. to Ford Found., Guggenheim Found., U.S. Office Edn., NSF, Wenner-Gren Found. for Anthrop. Research; mem. council of consultants Hungarian Research Center, 1975—; mem. com. on linguistics and psychology Social Sci. Research Council, com. on sociolinguistics, 1963-64; U.S. mem. internat. organizing com. Internat. Congress of Fenno-Ugrists, 1965—; founder and chmn. Com. on Linguistic Info. Numerous fellowships and grants including: Fulbright grant, 1966, 71, NSF fellow, 1966-67; Nat. Endowment for Humanities fellow; Johns Hopkins Centennial scholar, 1975; Exchange prof. of Nat. Acad. Scis. with Acad. Scis. of USSR, 1973. Fellow Am. Folklore Soc., AAAS, Am. Anthrop. Assn., Culture Learning Inst., Netherlands Inst. for Advanced Study, N.Y. Acad. Scis., Linguistic Soc. Am. (pres. 1975, dir. Linguistic Inst. 1964, mem. com. of pres. 1982—); mem. Toronto Semiotic Circle (hon.), Deutsche Gesellschaft fur Semiotik, Assn. for Philosophy of Sci., Psychotherapy and Ethics, Fedn. Am. Scientists, Internat. Soc. for History Rhetoric, Central States Anthrop. Soc. (past pres.), Semiotic Soc. Am. (exec. dir. 1976-80, editorial bd. 1976—, pres. 1984), Indpls. Zool. Soc. (edn. adv. com.), Am. Assn. for Machine Translation and Computational Linguistics (exec. bd. 1964-66), Animal Behavior Soc., Internat. House of Japan, Internat. Brotherhood Magicians, Sigma Xi. Clubs: Cosmos, University (Chgo.); Bloomington Country. Author, co-author hundreds of papers and reviews in field, 1942—, also numerous books, including: The Sign & Its Masters, 1979; The Play of Movement, 1981; I Think I Am a Verb, 1985; editor books in field; contbr. to ency. Home: 1104 Covenanter Dr Bloomington IN 47401 Office: PO Box 10 Ind U Bloomington IN 47402

SEBRING, ELIZABETH STREET, medical technologist; b. Akron, Ohio, June 17, 1929; d. John Northcott and Dorothy (Hastings) Street; m. Gerald Wayne Sebring, Mar. 13, 1948; children—Richard Lawrence, David Street. B.S., U. Akron, 1952. Cert. med. technologist. Research assoc. Mpls. War Meml. Blood Bank, 1966—. Bd. dirs. Pillsbury-Waite Neighborhood Services, Inc., 1981—, sec., 1982—. Mem. Am. Assn. Blood Banks, Minn. Assn. Blood Banks. Episcopalian. Contbr. articles on blood research to profl. jours. Home: 2320 Nottingham Ct Minnetonka MN 55343

SEDERBURG, WILLIAM ALBERT, state senator; b. Chadron, Nebr., Aug. 1, 1947; s. Marion E. and Viola A. (Shalender) S.; m. Joyce I. Witte, July 29, 1972; children—Matthew E., Kari A. B.S., Mankato State Coll., 1969; M.A., Mich. State U., 1972, Ph.D., 1974. Faculty, dept. polit. sci. Mich. State U., East Lansing, 1973-75; dir. research House Republican Office, Lansing, Mich., 1975-78, exec. dir., 1978; mem. Mich. Senate, Lansing, 1979—, mem. appropriations com., 1983—, chmn. higher edn. and tech. com. Bd. dirs. Lutheran Social Services Mich. NSF fellow, 1970-73. Mem. Phi Beta Kappa, Kappa Delta Pi. Republican. Contbr. articles to profl. jours. Office: 805 Farnum Bldg Lansing MI 48909

SEDGWICK, DOUGLAS LARRY, industrial executive; b. Tisdale, Saskatchewan, Oct. 25, 1937; s. Clifton James and Evelyn Henrietta (Clarke) S.; m. Rosemary Ellen Harrup, Sept. 13, 1958; children—David Stanley, Julie Lynn. B.S.M.E., U. Saskatchewan, 1960; cert. indsl. mgmt. McMaster U., 1968. Prodn. supr. Steel Co. of Can., Hamilton, Ont., 1960-62; mfg. mgr. Tungsol of Can., Bramalea, Ont., 1962-65; mfg. mgr. Tridon Ltd., Burlington, Ont., 1965-73, v.p. ops., 1973-75, pres., 1975-82; v.p. planning Magna Internat. Inc., Markham, Ont., 1983—; dir. Idea Corp. Ont.; dir. Ont. Ctr. for Auto Parts Tech.; cons. fed. govt. task force on auto industry in Can., 1978. Founding mem. exec. com., bd. dirs. Children's Oncology Care Ont., 1979-81; established Ronald McDonald House, Toronto, 1981. Mem. Engring. Inst. Can., Assn. Corp. Growth, Automotive Parts Mfrs. Assn. (dir. 1976—, chmn. 1981-83). Clubs: Port Credit Yacht, Caledon Ski. Home: 130 Aintree Terrace Oakville ON L6J 5J3 Canada Office: Magna Internat Inc 36 Apple Creek Blvd Markham ON L3R 4Y4 Canada

SEDGWICK, RAE, psychologist; b. Kansas City, Kans., Apr. 7, 1944; d. Charles and Helen (Timmons) Sedgwick. R.N., Bethany Sch. Nursing, 1965; B.S., U. Iowa, 1967; M.A., U. Kans., 1970, Ph.D., 1972. Cert. psychologist, Kans. Med./surg., orthopedic and obstet. nurse, Iowa City, Iowa, 1965-67; with Community Mental Health Nursing, Kansas City, Kans., 1967-68; specialist Lab. Edn., Washington, 1971-72; adj. clin. staff community psychiatry, 1975-76; coordinator Health C.A.R.E. Clinic, Pa. State U., 1974-76; head grad. program in community mental health nursing and family therapy, Pa. State U., 1974-76, asst. prof., 1972-76; pvt. practice psychology, Bonner Springs, Kans., 1976—; cons. in field.; staff Bethany Med. Ctr., Kansas City, Kans., Cushing's Meml. Hosp., Leavenworth, Kans., St. John's Hosp., Leavenworth; del. Internat. Council Nurses, Frankfurt, Germany. Active Am. Heart Assn.; city councilwoman Bonner Springs; mem. Kans. Internat. Women's Yr. Commn. Recipient Outstanding Young Woman award, U. Kans., Bus. and Profl. Women's Club scholar. Fellow Am. Orthopsychiat. Assn.; mem. AAAS, Am. Assn. Psychiatric Services for Children, Am. Group Psychotherapy Assn. (dir.), Am. Nurses Assn., Am. Psychol. Assn., Anthrop. Assn. for Study of Play, Council of Advanced Practitioners in Psychiat. Mental Health Nursing, Kans. Psychol. Assn., Council Nurse Researchers, Sigma Theta Tau. Republican. Methodist. Club: Pilot. Author: Family Mental Health, 1980; The White Frame House, 1980; contbr. articles to profl. jours. KS 66012

SEDIA, JOHN MICHAEL, lawyer; b. Buffalo, Aug. 29, 1954; s. Pasquale Joseph and Anne Marie (Delollis) S.; m. Rosemary Piccirilli, Sept. 24, 1983. A.B. in Journalism and Spanish, Ind. U., 1976; J.D., 1979. Bar: Ind. 1979, U.S. Dist. Ct. (no. dist.) Ind. 1979. Assoc. Saul I. Ruman & Assocs., Hammond, Ind., 1979-80, Bainbridge & Tweedle, Highland, Ind., 1980-83; ptnr. Tweedle & Sedia, Highland, 1983—. Ind. U. Alumni Assn. scholar U. Ind., Bloomington, 1976. Mem. Justinian Soc. Lawyers (treas. N.W. Ind. chpt. 1983—), Ind. U. Alumni Assn., Ind. State Bar Assn., Blue Key, Pi Kappa Alpha. Roman Catholic. Home: 653 Wellington Dr Dyer IN 46311 Office: Tweedle & Sedia 2633 45th St Highland IN 46322

SEDLACEK, RICHARD JOHN, educational adminstrator; b. Crete, Nebr., Oct. 20, 1930; s. John Frank and Louise (Chrastil) S.; m. Patricia Joy Kindschi, June 1, 1952; children—Douglas Richard, Cheryl Ann. B.A., Doane Coll., 1952; M.A., U. Nebr., 1958. Tchr. English, Crete High Sch., 1954-57, jr. high prin., 1957-59, sr. high prin., 1959-65; sr. high prin. North Platte High Sch., Nebr., 1965—. Mem. Nebr. Gov.'s Task Force on Excellence in Edn.; mem. Nebr. Vocat. Adv. Commn.; chmn. fund drive United Way, 1984; hon. life mem. PTA; mem. adv. council Nebr. Ednl. TV. Served to cpl. U.S. Army, 1952-54. Mem. Nat. Assn. Secondary Sch. Prins., Nebr. Council Sch. Adminstrs., Nebr. State Assn. Secondary Sch. Prins. (pres. 1971-72), Nebr. Schoolmasters. Republican. Methodist. Lodge: Rotary (pres. 1982-83); Elks. Avocations: golf; boating. Home: 802 Spruce Ave North Platte NE 69101 Office: North Platte Sr High Sch 1000 W 2d St North Platte NE 69101

SEEBERT, KATHLEEN ANNE, international trade consultant; b. Chgo.; d. Harold Earl and Marie Anne (Lowery) S.; M.A., U. Notre Dame, 1976; M.M., Northwestern U., 1983. Publs. editor ContiCommodity Services, Inc., Chgo., 1977-79, supr. mktg., 1979-82; dir. mktg. MidAm. Commodity Exchange, 1982-85; internat. trade cons. to Govt. of Ont., Can., 1985—; guest lectr. U. Notre Dame. Registered commodity rep. Mem. Futures Industry Assn. Am. (treas.). Republican. Roman Catholic. Clubs: Young Executives, Notre Dame of Chgo., Northwestern Mgmt. of Chgo. Office: 208 S LaSalle St Suite 1806 Chicago IL 60604

SEED, NEYSA E., transducer manufacturing company executive; b. Fort Wayne, Ind., Dec. 28, 1929; d. Freeman Ray and Irma Ileen (Cary) Imhof; m. Aniese Edward Seed, June 21, 1952; children—Kathryn, Susan, Edward. B.Music in Edn., U. Mich., 1953. Designer Imhof's Flower Shop, Edon, Ohio, 1945-47, mgr., designer, 1947-49; salesperson J.C. Penney co., Toledo, Ohio, 1974-75; office mgr. Toledo Transducers, Inc., Toledo, 1976-77, purchasing mgr., 1977—. Pres. Longfellow Mothers, Toledo, 1969-70. Avocations: genealogy; poetry; choirs and music; antiques; biking. Office: Toledo Transducers Inc 3525 Monroe St Toledo OH 43606

SEEFELT, EDWARD ROBERT, optometrist; b. Milladore, Wis., Mar. 24, 1926; s. Charles F. and Hattie Ann (Tonn) S.; m. Mary Arilla Higley, Aug. 13, 1955; children—Ellen Louise, Susan Ann. B.S. in Optometry, No. Ill. Coll. Optometry, 1950, O.D., 1951; M.S. in Physiol. Optics, Ind. U., 1962, postgrad., 1968-70. Lic. optometrist, Wis. Practice optometry, Marshfield, Wis., 1955-57; commd. 2d lt. U.S. Air Force, 1952, advanced through grades to lt. col., 1970; served as clin. and research optometrist in Japan, Europe, U.S., 1952-74; ret., 1974. Author: The Seefelt Family History, 1983; also profl. articles. Mem. Amherst Junction Zoning Com., Wis., 1984. Mem. Am. Acad. Optometry, Ret. Officers Assn., Mensa. Republican. Lutheran. Lodge: Lions (Iola, Wis.) (sec. 1977-78). Avocation: writing. Home: 1370 County T Amherst Junction WI 54407

SEEFLUTH, AUGUST RAYMOND, business consultant; b. Geridge, Ark., Aug. 7, 1922; s. August Theodore and Clara Eunice (Dunham) S.; student Air Force tech. and flying schs., 1943, 48, 52, Wright State U., 1961-65; m. Nan. L. Morgan, Oct. 3, 1942; children—Nancy, Ted, Karen, Scott. Served as 2d lt. U.S. Army Air Force, 1942-45, to maj. U.S. Air Force, 1947-65; electronic warfare instr. Keesler AFB, Miss., 1952-57; service in W. Ger. and Eng., 1958-61, group leader Aero. System Div., Wright-Patterson AFB, Ohio, 1961-65; ret., 1965; mgr. new bus. devel. TRACOR, Inc., Austin, Tex., 1965-70; regional mktg. mgr. Lundy Electronics & Systems, Pompano Beach, Fla., 1970-73; prin. Seefluth & Assos., Dayton, Ohio, 1973—, Raymond Tech., Inc., Dayton, 1983—, Quality Communications Corp., Dayton; owner, operator Sta. WYNO, Nelsonville, Ohio, 1984. Tchr. adult classes 1st United Meth. Ch., Troy, Ohio. Decorated Air medal; recipient commendation U.S. Army, 1957, RAF, 1960, Luftwaffe, 1959, NATO, 1960. Mem. Air Force Assn., Am. Def. Preparedness Assn., Assn. Old Crows. Author various tech. studies, reports, primarily on USAF electronic ops. Home: 102 Finsbury Ln Troy OH 45373 Office: 4130 Linden Ave Dayton OH 45432

SEEHAUSEN, RICHARD FERDINAND, architect; b. Indpls., Mar. 17, 1925; s. Paul Ferdinand and Melusina Dorothea (Nordmeyer) S.; student DePauw U., 1943-44, Wabash Coll., 1944, State U. Iowa, 1944; B.Arch., U. Ill., 1949; m. Phyllis Jean Gates, Dec. 22, 1948; children—Lyn, Dirk. Ptnr., Johnson, Kile, Seehausen & Assocs., Inc., architects, engrs., Rockford, Ill., 1949-82, pres., 1974-82; pres. Richard F. Seehausen-Architect, Inc., 1983—. Mem. com. jail planning and constrn. standards Bur. Detention Facilities, Ill. Dept. Corrections, 1970-73; analyst Fed. Fall-Out Shelter, 1962—. Bd. dirs. Rockford Boys Club. Served with USNR, 1943-45, USAF, 1949. Mem. AIA (dir. No. Ill. chpt. 1966-68, 75—, pres. chpt. 1978—), Lambda Chi Alpha. Lutheran. Mason (Shriner), Kiwanian. Club: Forest Hills Country (gov.

1970-72), Prin. works include No. Ill. U. Center, also Health Service Bldg., DeKalb, Winnebago County Courthouse, Rockford, St. Mark Luth. Ch., Rockford, Christ Meth. Ch., Rockford, 1st Presbyn. Ch., Rochelle, Ill., McHenry County Ct. House, Woodstock, Ill., Stephenson County Courthouse, Freeport, Ill., Ogle County Pub. Safety Bldg., Rochelle, DeKalb High Sch., Page Park Spl. Edn. Sch., Rockford, Social Security bldgs. in Racine, Sheboygan, Oshkosh and Janesville, Wis., Freeport YWCA Bldgs., renovation of Carroll County Ct. House, DeKalb Area Retirement Center; renovation Old Winnebago County Courthouse. Rockford, Rockford Mut. Ins. Home Office Bldg., Willows Personal Care Ctr., Rockford, others. Home: 36 Briar Ln Rockford IL 61103 Office: Am Nat Bank Bldg Rockford IL 61104

SEELY, STEVEN WELLMAN, banker; b. Lansing, Mich., Jan. 20, 1951; s. William Charles and Virginia Marian (Wellman) S.; B.A., Mich. State U., 1973; M.B.A., Central Mich. U., 1979; m. Catherine Marie Sheets, Feb. 19, 1970; children—Christopher Steven, Patrick Michael. Lending mgmt. ofcl. Am. Bankcorp Inc., Lansing, 1973-75, dir. advt., 1975-77; dir. mktg. services BancOhio Nat. Bank, Columbus, 1977-82, v.p., dir. corp. mktg. and sales mgmt., 1982—; speaker, cons. Sales trainer United Way, Lansing, 1973-77, solicitor, Columbus, 1977—; active Salesian Center/Boys Club, 1978-80. Recipient numerous advt. and mktg. awards, including: Addy award, 1978; Gold Key award Incentive Mfrs. Rep. Assn., 1978; Bank Mktg. Assn. Best of TV award, 1979, 82, Best of Bank Mktg. Assn. advertising awards (2); Buckeye Mktg. award, 1980. Mem. Am. Mktg. Assn., Bank Mktg. Assn., Columbus Sales Exec. Club, Mich. State U., Central Mich. U. alumni assns., U.S. Golf Assn., Volkswagen Club Am. Republican. Roman Catholic. Home: 1845 Ashland Ave Upper Arlington OH 43212 Office: 155 E Broad St Columbus OH 43251

SEFTON, CYNTHIA DOREEN, business education educator, financial planner, consultant; b. Cin., Oct. 21, 1947; d. Archie and Ruth (Jollie) Bolton; m. James Richard Sefton, Mar. 15, 1969 (div.). B.S. in Edn., U. Cin., 1969, M.Ed. in Bus. Edn., 1975. Tchr. high sch. vocat. bus., Cin., 1969-75; asst. prof. bus. edn. U. Cin., 1975—; bus. and office tchr. educator Ohio Dept. Edn., 1975—; owner CDS Enterprises, human resources devel. cons., 1980—; ptnr. Transcendence, 1981—; adv. Office Edn. Assn., Cin. Inst. Career Alternatives; center mgr. Loving Relationships Tng., 1981—; seminar leader; awareness cons. Mem. Am. Vocat. Assn., Ohio Vocat. Assn., Am. Soc. Tng. and Devel., Ohio Bus. Tchrs. Assn., S.W. Ohio Word Processing Adminstrv. Support Group (hon.), Women's Network, Delta Pi Epsilon (pres. Delta chpt.), Zeta Tau Alpha. Methodist. Club: Metropolitan Exchange (Cin.). Home: 3438 Ferncroft Dr Cincinnati OH 45211

SEGAL, JOAN SMYTH, library association executive; b. Bklyn., Sept. 14, 1930; d. John Patrick and Anna Catherine (Green) Smyth; m. William Segal, June 25, 1955; children—Harold M., Nora A. B.A., Douglass Coll., Rutgers U., 1951; M.S. in L.S., Columbia U., 1955; Ph.D., U. Colo., 1978. Librarian, Math Inst., NYU, 1955-58, Western Interstate Commn. for Higher Edn., Boulder, Colo., 1970-76; library cons., Boulder, 1976-78; resource sharing program mgr. Bibliog. Ctr. for Research, Denver, 1978-80, exec. dir., 1980-84; exec. dir. Assn. for Coll. and Research Libraries, ALA, Chgo., 1984—; trainer library automation, group devel., resource sharing; cons. in field. Contbr. articles to profl. publs. Named Colo. Librarian of Yr., Colo. Library Assn., 1984. Mem. Am. Soc. Info. Sci., Colo. Ad Hoc Interlibrary Loan Com., Colo. Library Assn., Spl. Libraries Assn. (chmn. edn. div. 1981-82, bd. dirs. 1983—), Assn. of Specialized and Coop. Library Agys. (various coms.), OCLC Users Council, OCLC Network Dirs. (chmn. 1983), Mountain Plains Library Assn., ALA, Library of Congress Network Adv. Com. Office: Assn Coll and Research Libraries Div ALA 50 E Huron St Chicago IL 60611

SEGHI, PHILLIP DOMENIC, professional baseball team executive; b. Cedar Point, Ill., 1918; student Northwestern U., 1931-34. Former infielder profl. baseball teams; mgr. minor league teams Pitts. Pirates, 1946-48; with Cleve. Indians Am. League baseball team, 1949-55, 71—, mgr. minor league teams Fargo-Moorhead, Green Bay, 1949-55, v.p., dir. player personnel, 1971-72, v.p., gen. mgr., 1973—; scout Cin. Reds, 1956-58, farm dir., 1958-68; farm dir. Oakland A's, 1968-71. Office: Cleveland Stadium Cleveland OH 44114*

SEGNAR, S.F., pipeline company executive. Chmn., pres., chief exec. officer, dir. Internorth, Inc., Omaha. Office: Internorth Inc 2223 Dodge St Omaha NE 68102*

SEHNKE, ERROL DOUGLAS, geologist; b. Superior, Wis., Mar. 14, 1943; s. Henry Herman and Athlyn Marion (Westlund) S. B.S., U. Wis., 1965; M.S., U. Mich., 1969. Jr. geologist Aluminum Co. of Am., Phoenix, 1971-72, exploration mgr. Alcoa-Fairview Mining, Derbyshire, Eng., 1972-74, project geologist Alcoa-Cimca, San Jose, Costa Rica, 1974-77, sr. geologist Alcoa-Chelsea Properties, Phoenix, 1977-80, staff geologist Alcoa-Suralco, Moengo, Suriname, 1980-83, projects mgr. Alcoa-Western Mining Ltd., Rio de Janiero, Brazil, 1983—. Mem. Soc. Mining Engrs. of AIME, Geol. Soc. Am., Am. Soc. Photogrammetry. Home: PO Box 3007 Superior WI 54880 Office: Aluminum Co of Am 1501 Alcoa Bldg Pittsburgh PA 15219

SEIBERLING, JOHN FREDERICK, congressman; b. Akron, Ohio, Sept. 8, 1918; s. J. Fred and Henrietta S.; student Staunton (Va.) Mil. Acad.; grad. with honors Harvard U., 1941; LL.B., Columbia U., 1949; m. Elizabeth Behr, 1949; children—John B., David P., Stephen M. Admitted to N.Y. bar, 1950, Ohio bar, 1955; asso. firm, N.Y.C., 1949-54; specialist antitrust law Goodyear Tire & Rubber Co., Akron, 1954-70; mem. 92d-99th congresses from 14th Ohio dist., chmn. interior subcom. on pub. lands. Served to maj. AUS, 1942-46. Decorated Legion of Merit, Bronze Star; also decorations France, Belgium. Mem. Akron Bar Assn. Democrat. Address: 1225 Longworth House Office Bldg Washington DC 20515

SEIGER, DANIEL ALTER, pharmaceutical research and development company executive, real estate company executive; b. Cleve., Aug. 9, 1932; s. Isidore and Lillian (Kritzer) S.; m. Marcia Suzanne Levine, Aug. 21, 1955; children—Sherri Beth Seiger Davis, Sanford Bernard. B.Sc., Toledo U., 1954; B.B.A., Fenn Coll., 1957; M.Sc., Northwestern Coll., Tulsa, 1976, Pharm. D., 1979. Registered pharmacist, Ohio. Mgr., Miller's Inc., Cleve., 1955-63; pres. Seiger Realty, Cleveland Heights, Ohio, 1963—; pres. Southside Drugs, Inc., Cleve., 1972-80, Andanco Labs., Inc., Cleveland Heights, 1980—; v.p. The Am. Dietics Co., Cleve., 1984—cons. pharms.; dir. EJBL Pharm., Cleve., 1972-80, Evans Devel., Aurora, Colo., 1976—, Natanya Properties, Cleve., 1977-79. Patentee cough and cold medication for cardiac and diabetic patients, preventative for herpes; author: Preventing S.T.D.'s., 1982; author abstracts, clin. papers, 1960—. Vice pres. Am. Red. Magen David, Ohio, 1976-78; chmn. Ohio Council Gov.'s Phys. Fitness, 1978; pres. Village Residents, Inc. Ohio, 1979; vice chmn. Ohio Ednl. Drug Council, 1981. Recipient Presdl. citation HEW, 1977, commendation Cleve. City Council, 1979, Breath of Life award Am. Red Magen David, 1980. Fellow AAPP; mem. Am. Pharm. Assn. (pres. Toledo chpt. 1953-54, Gavel award 1954), Alpha Zeta Omega (pres. Toledo chpt. 1954-55), Ohio State Pharm. Assn., Greater Cleve. Growth Assn. Lodge: B'nai B'rith. Home: 3830 Severn Rd Cleveland Heights OH 44118

SEIKEL, GEORGE R., engineer; b. Akron, Ohio, Nov. 30, 1933; s. George R. and Lucile (Riley) S.; m. Alice Hudak, Mar. 2, 1957 (div. 1982); children—Linda Ann Seikel Slife, Mary Elizabeth, George R. B.S. magna cum laude, U. Notre Dame, 1955, M.S. in Engring. Mechanics, 1957. With NASA, 1956-81, mgr. MHD Systems and MHD Project office, 1978-81 founder, pres. SeiTec, Inc., Cleve., 1982—; organizer, chmn. sessions for various nat., internat. meetings; lectr. in field; faculty U. Notre Dame, 1955-57. Active Boy Scouts Am., Rocky River, Ohio, 1975-79; pres. St. Christophers PTA, Rocky River, 1973-74; prin., tchr. religion program St. Christopher High Sch., 1965-70. Recipient NASA Outstanding Achievement and Group Achievement awards; U. Notre Dame teaching fellow, 1955-57; ASME Grad. Study award, 1955; U. Notre Dame scholar, K.C. Ednl. Trust Fund, 1950-55. Mem. AIAA (chmn. plasmadynamics and lasers tech. com. 1980-83), Sigma Xi. Democrat. Roman Catholic. Club: Notre Dame Alumni. Contbr. articles to profl. jours. Office: PO Box 81264 Cleveland OH 44181

SEILER, CHARLOTTE WOODY, ret. educator; b. Thorntown, Ind., Jan. 20, 1915; d. Clark and Lois Merle (Long) Woody; A.A., Ind. State U., 1933; A.B., U. Mich., 1941; M.A., Central Mich. U., 1968; m. Wallace Urban Seiler, Oct. 10, 1942; children—Patricia Anne Bootzin, Janet Alice Seiler. Tchr. elem. schs., Whitestown, Ind., 1933-34, Thorntown, Ind., 1934-37, Kokomo, Ind., 1937-40, Ann Arbor, Mich., 1941-44, Willow Run, Mich., 1944-46; instr. English div. Delta Coll., University Center, Mich., 1964-69, asst. prof., 1969-77, ret., 1977; organizer, dir. Delta Coll. Puppeteers, 1972-77. Treas., Friends of Grace A. Dow Meml. Library, 1974-75, 77-79, corr. sec., 1975-77; mem. Midland Art Assn.; adv. bd. Salvation Army, 1980-85, sec., 1984-85; leader Sr. Ctr. Humanities program Midland Sr. Ctr., 1978—. Mem. Am., Mich. Library Assn., AAUW (fellowship honoree 1979), Midland Symphony League, Pi Lambda Theta, Chi Omega. Presbyterian. Clubs: Tuesday Review (pres. 1979-80), Seed and Sod Garden. Home: 5002 Sturgeon Creek Pkwy Midland MI 48640

SEILER, RANDOLPH JOHN, lawyer; b. Mobridge, S.D., July 7, 1946; s. Matthew Walter and LaVaun L. (Huber) S.; m. Patricia Marie Graff, Apr. 26, 1969; children—Christopher Michael, Jeffrey Matthew. B.S., U. Nebr.-Omaha, 1973; J.D., U. S.D., 1980. Bar: S.D. 1980, U.S. Dist. Ct. S.D. 1980, U.S. Ct. Appeals (8th cir.) 1981. Dir. Div. Law Enforcement Assistance, Pierre, S.D., 1974-77; law clk. U.S. Dist. Ct. S.D., 1980-81; ptnr. Krause, Seiler & Cain, Mobridge, S.D., 1981—. Editor-in-chief S.D. Law Rev., 1979-80. Pres., Community Fund, Mobridge, 1982-84; bd. dirs. Mobridge Hosp., 1983. Mem. S.D. State Bar Assn. (pres. young lawyers sect. 1984-85), ABA, Assn. Trial Lawyers Am., Walworth County Bar Assn., VFW, Jaycees (bd. dirs. 1982, disting. service award 1984). Democrat. Roman Catholic. Club: Mobridge Country (bd. dirs. 1983-85, pres. 1985). Lodges: Rotary (bd. dirs. 1982-85), Moose. Home: 617 W 1st Ave Mobridge SD 57601 Office: Krause Seiler & Cain Box 490 Mobridge SD 57601

SEILER, WALLACE URBAN, chem. engr.; b. Evansville, Ind., Aug. 31, 1914; s. Samuel Alfred and Anna Beatrice (Grossman) S.; student U. Evansville, 1932-34; B.S., Purdue U., 1937; postgrad. U. Mich., 1945-46; m. Charlotte Woody, Oct. 10, 1942; children—Patricia Anne, Janet Alice. With Dow Chem. Co., 1937-80, engr., Midland, Mich., 1937-39, cons. research engr., Ann Arbor, Mich., 1939-49, tech. service engr., Midland, 1950-55, mgr. solvents field service, 1955-64, contract research and devel. specialist, 1964-80. Mem. Am. Chem. Soc., AAAS, Am. Inst. Chemists, Sigma Xi, Tau Beta Pi, Phi Lambda Upsilon. Home: 5002 Sturgeon Creek Pkwy Midland MI 48640

SEILER, WALTER ADOLPH, banker; b. Grand Island, Nebr., Dec. 2, 1941; s. Walter Armin and Mary Anne (Fritz) S. B.A., U. Nebr., 1963. Asst. trust officer Guardian State Bank and Trust Co., Alliance, Nebr., 1967-80, trust officer, 1980—, dir. Guardian Banshares, Inc., 1980—. Mem. Alliance Pub. Library Bd., 1982—; treas. Alliance Pub. Library Found., 1983—; mem. Am. Field Service Com., Alliance, 1980—; chmn. Box Butte County chpt. ARC, Alliance, 1970-73; chpt. advisor Order of DeMolay, 1971—; chmn. program adv. com. Nebr. Ednl. TV, Alliance, 1981—; co-chmn. fund dr. Box Butte Gen. Hosp., Alliance, 1974. Decorated Legion of Honor, Internat. Supreme Council, Order of DeMolay, 1973. Mem. Kappa Sigma (Grand Master, No. Platte Valley Alumni chpt. 1975—). Republican. Presbyterian Ch. (treas. Alliance 1969—). Lodges: Kiwanis (pres. Alliance 1973), Masons, Eastern Star, Scottish Rite (Alliance-Consistory 1973—, rank of insp. gen. 33 deg. Supreme Council) Nebr. Scottish Rite Found. (bd. dirs. 1983—). Office: Guardian State Bank Trust Co 224 Box Butte Ave Alliance NE 69301

SEIPEL, RANDIE DIANE, technologies manager; b. Lima, Ohio, Dec. 24, 1952; d. William Franklin and Vera Eunice (O'Dell) Selover; m. Lewis Craig Seipel, June 21, 1975. B.S., Miami U., Ohio, 1975; M.A., Central Mich. U., 1978. Program adminstr. Gould, Inc., Glen Burnie, Md., 1977-79; fin. analyst Ross Labs. div. Abbott Labs., Columbus, Ohio, 1979-80, mgr. distributed technologies, 1980—; cons., lectr. in field. Named Young Career Woman, Bus. and Profl. Women, 1981-82. Mem. Central Ohio Council Office Automation, Assn. Info. Systems Profls., Bus. and Profl. Women. Office: 625 Cleveland Ave Columbus OH 43216

SEIPEL, RICHARD ALAN, insurance agent; b. Columbus, Ohio, Mar. 11, 1953; s. William J. and Mary J. (Tompkins) S.; B.S. in Agr., Ohio State U., 1975, M.S. in Agr., 1980; m. Debra Sue Hand, June 9, 1973; 1 son, Joseph. Vocat. agr. tchr., Future Farmers Am. advisor Greenville (Ohio) High Sch., 1976-81; 4-H agt. Darke County, Ohio Coop. Extension Service, 1981-83; field agt. K.C. Ins., 1983—; tchr. adult hort. classes, Youth Employment Tng. Program. Parliamentarian Village of Wayne Lakes, Ohio, also mem. rules com., 1981-83; bd. dirs., sec. Darke Econ. Found.; initiated neighborhood watch program, Wayne Lakes; dist. advancement chmn. Boy Scouts Am. Named one of 8 Outstanding Young Agr. Tchrs., State of Ohio, 1980; recipient awards for publs. Ohio Vocat. Agr. Tchrs. 30 Minute Club, 1978-80. Mem. Ohio State U. Alumni Assn. (life). Roman Catholic. Clubs: Rotary, K.C. Home: 3612 Scenic Dr Greenville OH 45331 Office: 3612 Scenic Dr Greenville OH 45331

SEITZ, CHRISTINE MARY, export-import company executive; b. Chgo., Dec. 2, 1946; d. Arch Francis and Anne Marie (Wall) Gott; m. James Edmond Fish, Dec. 28, 1968; 1 son, James Edmond; m. 2d, Daniel Bruce Seitz, Nov. 28, 1978; stepchildren—J. Michelle, Shane D. B.A., St. Mary's Coll., Notre Dame, Ind., 1968. Research asst., lobbyist fin. and research div. Ind. State C. of C., Indpls., 1976-77, cons. public employee pension com., 1977; staff assoc. public service div. Ind. U. Sch. Public and Environ. Affairs, Indpls., 1977, asst. dir., 1977-79; exec. dir. Allen County Econ. Opportunity Council, Inc., Ft. Wayne, Ind., 1979-81; adminstrv. mgr. Midland, Inc., Ft. Wayne, 1981—; lectr. in field. Mem. Ft. Wayne Energy Consortium, 1980-82, Ft. Wayne Dist. Heating Assesment Group, 1981-82. Mem. Ind. C. of C. (cons. lobbyist 1977, 78, 79), Ft. Wayne Big Bros.-Big Sisters (sec. to bd. dirs. 1982—), Ft. Wayne Women's Bur. (dir. 1983—), Ft. Wayne Future, Machine and Equipment Mfrs. Assn., Credit Mgrs. Export Group, LWV, Fin. Credit-Internat. Bus. Assn., Ft. Wayne Urban League. Home: 3036 Tonawanda Ct Fort Wayne IN 46815 Office: 4211 Clubview Dr Fort Wayne IN 46801

SEITZ, MARTIN GEORGE, physical scientist; b. St. Louis, May 12, 1944; s. Frank Herman and Mary (Casalone) S.; m. Marilyn S. Pues, Jan. 26, 1967; children—Christian Martin, Amy Elizabeth. B.S. in Engring. Physics, U. Mo.-Rolla, 1966; Ph.D., Washington U., 1971. Research fellow Carnegie Inst. Washington, 1970-73; sr. engr. Singer Simulation Products, Silver Spring, Md., 1973-74; scientist Argonne Nat. Lab., Ill., 1975—; leader group in applied and basic exptl. programs for energy use and waste disposal; peer rev. large tech. programs. Active Paul Simon Senator campaign, DuPage County, 1984, Allen Dixon, Senator Campaign, 1982. U. Mo. research fellow, 1964; NDEA fellow, 1966; Coop. Research awardee Am. Geophys. Union, 1974, Bartlesville Energy Tech. Ctr., 1984. Mem. AAAS, Am. Geophys. Union, Bartlesville Energy Tech. Ctr. Avocations: fgn. langs.; sailing; prospecting. Home: 218 8th St Downers Grove IL 60515 Office: Argonne Nat Lab 9700 S Cass Ave Argonne IL 60439

SEITZ, MELVIN CHRISTIAN, JR., distributing company executive; b. Indpls., Aug. 9, 1939; s. Melvin Christian and Francis Sue (Lee) S.; m. Bette Louise Pierson, May 5, 1941; children—David, Mark, Keith, Cindy. Student Butler U., 1957-60. Salesman, Service Supply Co., Inc., Indpls., 1963-71, sec.-treas., 1971-74, v.p., 1974-81, exec. vp., 1981-83, pres., 1983—. Treas., Franklin Twp. High Sch. Bldg. Corp., Franklin Central High Sch. Booster Club. Served with U.S. Army, 1960-63. Mem. Nat. Fastener Distributor Assn., Sigma Nu. Republican. Mem. Disciples of Christ. Lodges: Masons, Shriners. Home: 4716 Northeastern Ave Wanamaker IN 46239 Office: 603 E Washington St Indianapolis IN 46202

SEITZ, T. MYRON, educator; b. Hutchinson, Kans., Feb. 21, 1945; s. Herbert Arron and Sara Justina (Nickel) S.; m. Sarah Anna Phillips, Aug. 4, 1967; children—Sonya Dawn, Darrell Alan. B.S., Sterling Coll., Kans., 1967; M.S., Emporia State U., 1969. Tchr., Ellinwood Pub. Schs., Kans., 1967—. Trustee, Ellinwood City Library Bd., 1978—, sec., 1980-82, pres., 1982-84, past treas. Ellinwood Cub Scouts. Mem. Nat. Council Tchrs. English, Internat. Reading Assn., Ellinwood Tchrs. Assn. (past pres., treas.), Nat. Campers and Hikers Assn., Christian Motorcyclists Assn. Baptist (Sunday sch. supt. 1979-80, deacon 1981-83). Clubs: Good Sam. Lodge: Lions (dir., past pres. Ellinwood Club). Avocations: camping, boating, cycling, traveling. Home: 313 E 4th St Box 322 Ellinwood KS 67526 Office: Ellinwood Pub Schs Box 368 Ellinwood KS 67526

SELBREDE, HERBERT, dairy products company executive. Pres. dir. Wisconsin Dairies Co-op, Baraboo, Wis. Office: Wis Dairies Co-Op Route #3 Hwy 12 W Baraboo WI 53913*

SELBY, ROBERT BRUCE, accounting and economics educator; b. Colby, Kans., Nov. 18, 1950; s. Bruce Ocie and Marilyn Marie (Smith) S.; m. Patricia Louise Sattler, June 1, 1973; 1 dau., Jennifer Louise. B.S., Fort Hays State U., 1972, M.S., 1978. Tchr. Paradise High Sch., Kans., 1972-74, Ashland High Sch., Kans., 1974-77; instr. Fort Hays State U., Kans., 1977-78; instr. dept. bus. and econs. Colby Community Coll., Kans., 1978—. Mem. Kans. Assn. Community Colls., Phi Beta Lambda, Phi Kappa Phi. Republican. Roman Catholic. Avocations: piano; sports. Office: Colby Community Coll 1255 S Range Colby KS 67701

SELDEN, JOSEPH BARR, hospital administrator; b. Providence, Oct. 10, 1943; s. William Kirkpatrick and Mary Virginia (Barr) S.; m. Joan Carol Hanson, Sept. 9, 1967; children—Brian Glenn, Beth Carol. B.A., Denison U., 1966; M.A., U. Iowa, 1968. Asst. to exec. dir. Group Health Assn. Am., Washington, 1971-72; asst. adminstr. Children's Hosp. Med. Ctr., Cin., 1972-76; adminstr. Longview State Hosp., Cin., 1976-78; asst. adminstr. Hillside Hosp., Warren, Ohio, 1978-79, chief exec. officer, 1979-84; with AMI Fin. Corp., Youngstown, Ohio, 1985—; corp. mem. Trumbull Meml. Hosp., 1981—; surveyor Commn. on Accreditation of Rehab. Facilities. Served to lt. USN, 1978-81. Mem. Am. Coll. Hosp. Adminstrs., Am. Hosp. Assn., Nat. Rehab. Assn., East Ohio Hosp. Assn. (chmn. reimbursement com. 1981-83, govt. hosp. com. 1980-84), Ohio Assn. Rehab. Facilities (v.p. 1982-83), Warren Library Assn. Methodist. Clubs: Kiwanis (dir. 1980—). Home: 9074 Altura Dr NE Warren OH 44484 Office: AMI Fin Corp City Ctr One Suite 410 Youngstown OH 44503

SELFRIDGE, CALVIN, lawyer; b. Evanston, Ill., Dec. 20, 1933; s. Calvin Frederick and Violet Luella (Bradley) S.; B.A., Northwestern U., 1956; J.D., U. Chgo., 1960. Admitted to Ill. bar, 1961; trust officer Continental Ill. Nat. Bank & Trust Co. Chgo., 1961-71; individual practice law, Chgo., 1972-76; mem. firm Howington, Elworth, Osswald & Hough, Chgo., 1976-79; individual practice law, 1979—; pres., dir. Des Plaines Pub. Co., Northwest Newspapers Corp. Pres., bd. dirs. Scholarship Fund Found., 1965—; trustee, sec. Lawrence Hall Sch. for Boys, 1982—. Served with AUS, 1959. Mem. Chgo., Am., Ill. bar assns., Law Club Chgo., Legal Club Chgo., Chi Psi, Phi Delta Phi. Republican. Congregationalist. Clubs: Attic (gov., sec.), Univ. Racquet (treas., former gov.) (Chgo.); Balboa (Mazatlan); Indian Hill Country. Home: 1410 N State Pkwy Chicago IL 60610 Office: 135 S LaSalle St Suite 2120 Chicago IL 60603

SELIG, ALLAN H. (BUD), profl. baseball team exec.; b. Milw., July 30, 1934; s. Ben and Marie Selig; grad. U. Wis. at Madison, 1956. With Selig Chevrolet, West Allis, Wis., 1959—, pres., 1966—; part owner Milw. Braves became Atlanta Braves 1965), 1963-65; co-founder Teams, Inc., 1964; co-founder Milw. Brewers Am. League baseball team, 1965, owner, pres., 1970—. Served with AUS, 1956-58. Address: care Milwaukee Brewers Milwaukee County Stadium Milwaukee WI 53214

SELK, JOHN ELWOOD, civil engineer; b. Boulder, Colo., Aug. 3, 1949; s. William E. and MaryAnne (Severin) S.; m. Sally Jane Harshaw, June 8, 1974; children—Benjamin William, Hannah May. B.S. in Civil Engring., U. Kans., 1972, M.S. in Civil Engring., 1981. Registered profl. engr., Kans., Colo., Mo.; registered land surveyor, Kans. Civil engr. Kans. Dept. Transp., Topeka, 1972-78; dir. engring. Peters, Williams & Kubota, Lawrence, Kans., 1978-79; owner, mgr. Landplan Engineering, Lawrence, 1979—. Mem. Am. Congress on Surveying and Mapping, ASCE, Inst. Transp. Engrs., Kans. Soc. Land Surveyors. Republican. Roman Catholic. Avocations: golf; softball; bowling; flying. Home: 2203 Princeton Blvd Lawrence KS 66044 Office: Landplan Engineering, PA 2500 W 6th Lawrence KS 66044

SELL, NANCY JEAN, chemistry and physics educator; b. Milw., Jan. 18, 1945; d. Homer Paul and Jeanette Rose (Karrels) S. B.A., Lawrence U., 1967; M.S., Northwestern U., 1968, Ph.D., 1971; postgrad. Inst. Paper Chemistry, Appleton, Wis., 1982—. Registered profl. engr., Wis. Teaching asst. Northwestern U., Evanston, Ill., 1967-71; asst. prof. U. Wis.-Green Bay, 1971-77, assoc. prof., 1977-82, prof. Coll. Environ. Sci., 1982—; pres. N.J. Sell & Assocs., Green Bay, 1984—. Author: Industrial Pollution Control: Issues and Techniques, 1981; (with others) Energy: A Conceptual Approach, 1985. Contbr. articles to profl. jours. Patentee in field. Recipient Excellence in Scholarship award U. Wis., Green Bay, 1982; named Alumnus Honoris, Clintonville Sr. High Sch., Wis., 1982. Mem. Am. Chem. Soc. (local chmn.), TAPPI, ASTM (com. chmn. 1981—), Sigma Xi (local chmn.). Avocation: dog training. Home: 3244 Peterson Rd Green Bay WI 54301 Office: U Wis Green Bay ES317 Green Bay WI 54301

SELLECK, ROBERT W., soft drink bottling company executive; b. 1921; ed. Flint Jr. Coll.; married. Salesman, Coca-Cola Co., Inc., 1941-52; propr. R.W. Selleck Distbg. Co., 1953-56; mktg. dir. Pepsi-Cola Gen. Bottlers, Inc., Chgo., 1956, v.p. sales, 1956-59, sr. v.p. mktg., 1959-68, exec. v.p. mktg., mem. exec. com., mem. finance com., 1968-70, sr. exec. v.p., chief operating officer, mem. exec. com., mem. finance com., 1970-72, pres., chief operating officer, 1972-75, pres., chief exec. officer, 1975—, also mem. exec. com., dir.; dir. Bubble Up Co., Dad's Root Beer Co., Midas Internat. Corp., IC Products Co. div. IC Industries, United Nat. Bank. Served with AUS, 1942-45. Mem. Ill. Soft Drink Assn. (bd. dirs.), Nat. Soft Drink Assn. (bd. dirs.). Office: 1745 N Kolmar Ave Chicago IL 60639

SELLERS, DEBORAH ANN CALLAWAY, nurse, educator; b. Oceanside, Calif., Mar. 12, 1956; d. Harold Cecil and Donna June (Mears) Callaway; m. Jeffery Douglas Sellers, Aug. 7, 1976. B.S. in Nursing, U. Kans., Lawrence, 1978; M.N. in Nursing, 1984. Charge nurse U. Kans. Med. Ctr., Kansas City, 1978; occupational health nurse Bendix Corp., Kansas City, Mo., 1979, Hallmark Cards Co., 1979, Bus. Industry Group, 1980; pvt. duty nurse, 1980-82; asst. dir. health services SLH Mgmt. Systems, Kansas City, Mo., 1983-84; instr. Research Coll. Nursing, Kansas City, Mo., 1984—; disaster nurse ARC, Kansas City, Mo., 1982—; site coordinator Greater Kansas City Health Fair, 1981. Co-author health care handbook. Co-chmn., Mental Health Assn. Johnson County, Overland Park, Kans., 1983; block capt. Neighborhood Watch Group, Mission, Kans., 1983. Mem. U. Kans. Nurses Alumni Assn., Greater Kansas City Assn. Occupational Health Nurses (sec. 1980-82, v.p. 1982-83), Kans. State Nurses Assn. (dist. 2 nominating com. 1983-84), Assn. Grad. Students Nursing (sec.-treas. 1981-82), LWV, U. Kans. Alumni Assn. Club: Med. Mates of U. Kans. (2d v.p. 1983-84, class rep. 1984-85) (Kansas City). Home: 9158 Somerset Overland Park KS 66207

SELLERS, MARGARET REGULAR, personnel administrator; b. Pendleton, S.C., Sept. 28, 1935; d. Daniel and Annie Mae (Morris) Regular; B. Gen. Studies, Wayne State U.; M.P.A., Western Mich. U.; m. Thomas James Sellers, Jan. 22, 1955; children—Loren Sellers Jackson, Sharon Elizabeth. Various positions Detroit Public Library, 1951-72, asst. dir. personnel, 1972-74, asso. dir. personnel, 1974-77; dir. personnel Wayne County Community Coll., Detroit, 1977-80; dir. personnel Mich. Dept. Natural Resources, 1980—; chmn. Mich. Personnel Dirs. Council, 1981-82; mem. adv. com. Classified Exec. Service, State of Mich.; lectr. in field. Trustee, Rehab. Inst., 1980-81; bd. dirs. minority apprentice program Mich. State U. Md. fellow, 1973. Mem. Internat. Personnel Mgmt. Assn. U.S. (exec. bd. Mich. chpt. 1977—, pres. Mich. chpt. 1978, v.p. central region 1980-81, pres. region 1981, exec. council, central region rep. 1983-85), ALA (adv. office library personnel resources), Mich. Public Employer Labor Relations Assn. (exec. bd. 1977, program com. 1980). Baptist. Office: Dept Natural Resources PO Box 30028 Lansing MI 48909

SELTZ, PAUL HERMAN, insurance executive; b. McIntosh, Minn., Oct. 28, 1921; s. Paul Julius and Regina Margaret (Nibbe) S.; m. Mildred DeHaan, Aug. 16, 1947; children—Paul, Kathryn, Karen, Sandra. A.A., U. Minn., 1942; student St. Paul Coll. Law, 1946-48. Asst. sec. St. Paul Hosp. and Casualty Co., 1946-48; sec. Des Moines Casualty Co., 1948-56; pres. Nat. Travelers Life Co., Des Moines, 1979—, Am. Travelers Assurance Co. Mem. bd. control Concordia Coll., St. Paul, 1958-72; trustee Luth. Ch. Found., St. Louis, 1983. Served with AUS, 1943-46. Mem. Des Moines C. of C., Am. Council Life Ins. Republican. Lutheran. Clubs: Des Moines, Des Moines Golf and Country. Home: 1909 74th St Des Moines IA 50322 Office: 820 Keosauqua Way Des Moines IA 50308

SELTZER, EARL CHARLES, real estate developer; b. Chgo., Aug. 18, 1922; s. Nathan and Fannie (Lipofsky) S.; m. Mary Frances Denton, Aug. 20, 1942; children—Stephen C., David S. M.S., Washington U., St. Louis, 1948. Head Seltzers Dept. Store, 1948-82; pilot and self-employed in aircraft sales,

Hillsboro, Ill., 1956—; real estate developer, prin. Earl Seltzer Enterprises, Hillsboro, Ill., 1958—; dir. Hillsboro Nat. Bank Mem. St. Louis Met. Area Airport Authority, 1972—. Served to lt. USN, 1942-46; PTO. Mem. Hillsboro C. of C. (pres. 1965). Am. Legion, VFW. Club: Country. Lodge: Moose. Home: 904 Smith Ln Hillsboro IL 62049

SELTZER, PHYLLIS ESTELLE, artist, designer; b. Detroit, May 17, 1928; d. Max and Lillian (Weiss) Finkelstein; m. Gerard Seltzer, May 30, 1953; children—Kim, Hiram. B.F.A., U. Iowa, 1952; postgrad. U. Mich., 1954-55, Cast Western Res. U., 1966-70. Program coordinator Cleve. State U., 1969-71; with Lake Erie Coll., Painesville, Ohio, 1970-72; art interior designer, Dalton, Van Dijk, Johnson, Cleve., 1973-74; pvt. practice designer, Cleve., 1975—; solo show: Vixseboxse Art Galleries, Cleve., 1983; group shows include: Hunterton Art Ctr. Print Exhbn., Clinton, N.J., Bonfoeys on the Sq., Cleve., 1978; Georgetown Coll., Ky., Mitchell Mus. Mt. Vernon, Ill., Music, Assn. Am. Artists, N.Y.C., 1979; Trumbull Art Guild, Warren, Ohio, 1980; New Orgn. for Visual Arts, Lake Erie Coll., Painesville, Ohio, Spaces, Cleve., Gt. Lakes Regional Art Exhbn., Cleve., Generative Systems, Tri-C Coll., Cleve., NOVART, Central Nat. Bank, Cleve., 1981; Nationwide Gallery, Columbus, Ohio, Cleve. Art Festival Catalogue, 1983; Mansfield Art Ctr., Art Acad. Cin., NOVA Regional Exhbn., Cleve., 1984; represented collections: Ctr. for Contemporary Art, Cleve., Denis Conley Gallery, Akron, Ohio, Vixseboxse Gallery, Cleve., Associated Am. Artists, N.Y.C., Old Detroit Gallery, Cleve., A.M. Sachs Gallery, N.Y.C.; represented in collections including: UCLA, U. Man., Can., U. Mass., Obelisk Gallery, Boston, Bklyn. Art Mus., Akron Art Inst., Dayton Art Mus., Nat. Gallery Art, Ottawa, Can., Minn. Mus. Art, Bullor Mus., Youngstown, Ohio, Stouffer's Inn on the Square, Nat. City Bank, Cleve., Rax Inc., Columbus, Cleve. Clinic, Cleve. Mus. Art. Vice pres. New Orgn. Visual Arts, Cleve. Mem. Cleve. Print Club (pres. 1982-84). Home: 11225 Harborview Dr Cleveland OH 44102 Office: 1400 W 10th St Cleveland OH 44112

SELZER, CHARLES LOUIS, retired superintendent schools; b. Homestead, Iowa, Dec. 21, 1914; s. Louis Carl and Caroline (Shoup) S.; B.A. cum laude, Coe Coll., 1935; M.A., State U. Iowa, 1950, postgrad., 1951—; m. Louis Kippenhan, Mar. 9, 1935; 1 dau., Patricia Madelyn (Mrs. Robert Carstensen). Tchr., prin., coach Amana (Iowa) High Sch., 1935-50; supt. Amana Community Schs., 1950-83, ret., 1983; mem. Grant Wood Spl. Edn. Commn.; guest lectr. U. Iowa, 1978, 79, 80; past dir. Amana Telephone Co., Amana Woolens, Inc.; dir. Title V Area X Edn. TV and Media. Mem. Iowa County Bd. Narcotics and Drug Edn.; mem. Area X Iowa Agy. on Aging; bd. dirs. Amana Hist. Preservation Com.; bd. dirs. Amana Travel Council; mem. Iowa County Info. and Referral Center; pres. Amana Community Chest, 1951-53; mem. adv. bd. Kirkwood Coll.; mem. Iowa County Crime Commn.; former justice of peace Iowa County. Cited by Iowa Legislature for service to edn., charitable and civic activities, 1980. Mem. Nat. Assn. Sch. Adminstrs., Associated Sch. Adminstrs. (mem. European study tour 1976), Iowa Assn. Sch. Adminstrs. (past pres., chmn. ethics bd.), NEA, Iowa Edn. Assn., Iowa County Supt.'s Assn., Joint County Area X Supts. Assn. (legis. com.), Iowa Peace Officers Assn., Iowa Hist. Soc. (pres. 1965-67), Iowa County Schoolmasters Assn. (past pres.), Phi Beta Kappa. Mem. Amana Ch. Soc. (trustee, elder, pres. 1971—). Clubs: Homestead Welfare (past pres., sec.), Cedar Rapids Toastmasters (hon.), Elks, Masons (32 deg., Shriner), El Kahir. Translator Amana documents, catechism and testimonies; columnist Amana News Bulletin; author Amana Coop. plan. Home: Homestead IA 52236 Office: Middle IA 52307

SEMEGEN, PATRICK WILLIAM, lawyer; b. Akron, Ohio, Dec. 23, 1946; s. Stephen T. and Jane F. (Schmiedel) S.; m. Joann Kucharski, Jan. 10, 1975; children—Michael, Peter. B.S. in Econs., U. Pa., 1968; J.D., U. Mich., 1971. Bar: Ohio 1971, Calif. 1974. Chief crim. div. Summit County Prosecutor, Akron, Ohio, 1972-74; sole practice, Akron, and San Diego, 1974-77; litigation counsel Beneficial Corp., Peapack, N.J., 1977-81; v.p. gen. counsel, sec. Western Auto Supply Co., Kansas City, Mo., 1981—, also dir. Contbr. articles to profl. jours. Served to capt. USAR, 1968-71. Mem. ABA, Internat. Franchise Assn., Am. Fin. Services Assn., Am. Corp. Counsel Assn. Democrat. Office: Western Auto Supply Co 2107 Grand Ave Kansas City MO 64108

SEMLER, JERRY D., insurance company executive. Pres., chief operating officer Am. United Life Ins. Co., Indpls. Office: Am United Life Ins Co One W 26th St Indianapolis IN 46206*

SEN, ASHISH KUMAR, urban scientist, educator; b. Delhi, India, June 8, 1942; came to U.S., 1967, naturalized, 1985; s. Asoka Kumar and Arati S.; B.S. with honors, Calcutta U., 1962; M.A., U. Toronto, 1964, Ph.D., 1971; m. Colleen Taylor. Research asso., lectr. geography Northwestern U., Evanston, Ill., 1967-69; asst. prof. Coll. Urban Scis., U. Ill., Chgo., 1969-73, assoc. prof., 1973-78, prof., 1978—, acting dean coll. urban scis., 1977, dir. Sch. Urban Scis. 1977-78; pres. Ashish Sen and Assocs., Chgo., 1977—. Mem. Transp. Research Bd. Transp. Research Forum, Am. Statis. Assn., Inst. Math. Statistics, Am. Soc. Planning Ofcls., Regional Sci. Assn. Hindu. Contbr. articles to profl. publs. statistics, transp. Home: 2557 W Farwell Ave Chicago IL 60645 Office: Sch Urban Scis U Ill Chicago IL 60680

SENGPIEHL, PAUL MARVIN, state official; b. Stuart, Nebr., Oct. 10, 1937; s. Arthur Paul and Anne Marie (Andersen) S.; B.A., Wheaton (Ill.) Coll., 1959; M.A. in Pub. Adminstrn., Mich. State U., 1961; J.D., Ill. Inst. Tech.-Chgo. Kent Coll. Law, 1970; m. June S. Cline, June 29, 1963; children—Jeffrey D., Chrystal M. Bar: Ill. 1971, U.S. Supreme Ct. 1982. Adminstrv. asst. Chgo. Dept. Urban Renewal, 1962-65; supr. Ill. Municipal Retirement Fund, Chgo., 1966-71; mgmt. officer Ill. Dept. Local Govt. Affairs, Springfield, 1971-72, legal counsel, Chgo., 1972-73; spl. asst. atty. gen. Ill. Dept. Labor, Chgo., 1973-76; asst. atty. gen. Ct. of Claims div. Atty. Gen. of Ill., 1976-83; hearing referee Bd. Rev., Ill. Dept. Labor, 1983-84; local govt. law columnist Chgo. Daily Law Bull., 1975—; instr. polit. sci. Judson Coll., Elgin, Ill., 1963. Republican candidate for Cook County Recorder of Deeds, 1984. Mem. Ill. Bar Assn. (local govt. law sect. council 1973-79, vice chmn. 1976-77, co-editor local govt. newsletter 1976-77, chmn. 1977-78, editor newsletter 1977-78, state tax sect. council 1979-82, 84—), Chgo. Bar Assn. (local govt. com., chmn. legis. subcom. 1978-79, sec. 1979-80, vice chmn. 1980-81, chmn. 1981-82, state and mcpl. tax com.), Am. Judicature Soc., Am. Soc. Public Adminstrn., Internat. Platform Assn., John Ericsson Republican League Ill. (state sec. 1983—, sec. Cook County 1982—). Republican. Baptist (vice chmn. deacons 1973-76, 79-80, moderator 1983—). Home: 727 N Ridgeland Ave Oak Park IL 60302

SENGSTOCK, CHARLES AUGUST, JR., public relations executive; b. Chgo., Aug. 21, 1932; s. Charles August and Vivian Louise (Comstock) S.; m. Norma Joann Halseth, Oct. 24, 1959. B.S. in Journalism, U. Ill., 1954; postgrad. U. Chgo., 1959-61. Radio announcer, news reporter Sta. WSOY, Decatur, Ill., 1954, 1956-57; news writer, editor Sta. WGN, Chgo., 1957-59; pub. relations assoc. Ill. Inst. Tech. Research Inst., Chgo., 1959-61; dir. pub. relations, dir. mktg. Cenco Instruments Corp. subs. Soiltest, Inc., Chgo., 1961-68; dir. corp. pub. relations Motorola, Inc., Western Region, 1968-73, dir. corp. pub. relations Motorola, Inc., 1973—. Served to lt. U.S. Army, 1954-56. Mem. Pub. Relations Soc. Am. Presbyterian. Club: Chgo. Press. Office: 1303 E Algonquin Rd Schaumburg IL 60196

SENHAUSER, DONALD A(LBERT), pathologist; b. Dover, Ohio, Jan.30, 1927; s. Albert Carl and Maude Anne (Snyder) S.; student U. Chgo., 1944-45; B.S., Columbia U., 1947, M.D., 1951; grad. with honors U.S. Naval Sch. Aviation Medicine, 1953; m. Helen Brown, July 22, 1961; children—William, Norman. Intern, Roosevelt Hosp., N.Y.C., 1951-52; resident Columbia-Presbyn. Hosp., N.Y.C., 1955-56, Cleve. Clinic, 1956-60; instr. in pathology Columbia U., 1955-56; fellow in immuno-pathology Middlesex Hosp. Med. Sch., London, 1960-61; mem. dept. pathology Cleve. Clinic Found, 1961-63; asso. prof. pathology U. Mo., 1963-65, prof., asst. dean Sch. Medicine, 1969-70, dir. teaching labs., 1968-70, prof., vice-chmn. dept. pathology, 1965-75; prof. pathology, chmn. dept. pathology, Ohio State U. Coll. Medicine, 1975—, prof. Sch. Allied Med. Professions, 1975—; dir. labs. Ohio State U. Hosps., 1975—; bd. dirs. Columbus area chpt. ARC, 1978-82; cons. in field; WHO-AMA Vietnam med. edn. project mem. U. Saigon Med. Sch., 1967-72; vis. scientist HEW, 1972-73; acting dir. Central Ohio Regional Blood Center, 1976-79. Served as capt. M.C., USNR, 1944-45, 52-55; China, Korea. Recipient Lower award Bunts Ednl. Found., 1960; diplomate Am. Bd. Pathology. Fellow Coll. Am. Pathologists (chmn. com. edn. resources 1977-78, gov. 1980—); mem. Am. Soc. Clin. Pathologists, Assn. Pathology Chairmen, Am. Assn. Pathology, Internat. Acad. Pathology, Assn. Am. Med. Colls., Am. Assn. Blood Banks, Ohio Soc. Pathologists (gov. 1979—), AAAS, Ohio Hist. Soc., Columbus Art League, Sigma Xi. Lutheran. Club: Masons Co-editor: Proc. 2d Midwest Conf. on the Thyroid, 1967, 3d, 1968, 5th, 1970; mem. editorial bd. Am. Jour. Clin. Pathology, 1965-76; contbr. articles to profl. jours. Office: 333 W 10th Ave Columbus OH 43210

SENN, SHIRLEY ANN, realtor, educator; b. Rockford, Ill., Dec. 12, 1933; d. Ralph Elwood and Almeda Lucille (Williams) Truitt; m. Rodney Charles Senn, June 9, 1957; children—Heather Ann Senn Von Ehr, Hillary Ann. B.S. in Edn., Ill. State U., 1958; postgrad. No. Ill. U., 1957, 64. Cert. elem. tchr., Ill. Tchr., East Aurora, Ill., 1956-59; substitute tchr. in pub. schs., West Aurora, Ill. 1960-66, Oswego, Ill., 1973-83; tchr. in pub. schs., West Aurora, 1966-71; real estate sales assoc. Charles B. Doss & Co., Aurora and Montgomery, Ill., 1981—. Mem. Aurora Bd. Realtors, Ill. Assn. Realtors, Nat. Assn. Realtors. Republican. Presbyterian. Clubs: Oswegoland Garden, Italian Am. (Aurora). Lodge: Women of Moose (Aurora chpt.). Home: 44 Circle Dr W Montgomery IL 60538 Office: Charles B Doss & Co 23 Boulder Hill Pass Montgomery IL 60538

SENSENBRENNER, FRANK JAMES, JR., congressman; b. Chgo., June 14, 1943; s. Frank James and Margaret Anita (Luedke) S.; B.A. in Polit. Sci., Stanford U., 1965; J.D., U. Wis., 1968; m. Cheryl Warren, Mar. 26, 1977; children—Frank James, III, Robert Alan. Bar: Wis. 1968, U.S. Supreme Ct. 1972. Mem. firm McKay & Martin, Cedarburg, Wis., 1970-75; asst. to Congressman J. Arthur Younger of Calif., 1965, to majority leader Wis. Senate, 1966-68; mem. Wis. Assembly, 1969-75; mem. Wis. Senate, 1975-79, asst. minority leader 1977-79; mem. 96th-99th Congresses from 9th Dist. Wis. Mem. Riveredge Nature Center, 1970—. Mem. North Shore Republican Club, 1964-82, Waukesha County Rep. Party, 1982—, Wis. Fedn. Young Reps., 1957-79. Recipient Robert Taft award Midwest Fedn. Coll. Rep. Clubs, 1969. Mem. Am. Inst. Parliamentarians, Phi Alpha Delta. Episcopalian. Home: PO Box 186 Menomonee Falls WI 53051 Office: 2444 Rayburn House Office Bldg Washington DC 20515

SENTURIA, RICHARD HARRY, financial planning company executive; b. West Frankfort, Ill., Aug. 14, 1938; s. Irwin J. and Frances (Persow) S.; student So. Ill. U., 1956-57; student Bus. Sch., Washington U., St. Louis, 1957-59, 60-61, Law Sch., 1959-60; m. Ilene M. Bluestein, Dec. 24, 1961; children—Beth, Philip, Laura. From registered rep. to asst. mgr. Dempsey-Tegeler & Co., Inc., St. Louis, 1961-70; asst. mgr. E.F. Hutton & Co., Inc., St. Louis, 1970; sales promotion, research analyst Stix & Co., St. Louis, 1970-74; v.p. in charge sales promotion, tng., seminars, product acquisition, br. mktg. for tax shelter dept. R. Rowland & Co., St. Louis, 1976-79; pres., chief exec. officer Investment Capital Assocs., Creve Coeur, Mo., 1979—; mem. faculty continuing edn. seminar U. Kansas City Dental Sch., 1978; gen. partner Downtown Devel. Assocs., Ltd., 1980—, Riverside Hotel Investments, Ltd., 1981—; v.p. Wharfside Devel. Co., Riverside Landing Parking Systems, Inc.; tchr. numerous adult evening schs., St. Louis area, 1961—. Founding mem., dir. Traditional Congregation of Creve Coeur, 1964-72; bd. dirs. Forsyth Sch., 1977—, B'nai Amoona Congregation, 1980—, St. Louis chpt. Am. Jewish Congress, 1981—. Served with U.S. Army, 1961-62. Mem. Internat. Assn. Fin. Planners. Home: 425 Shadybrook Dr Creve Coeur MO 63141 Office: Suite 304 707 N 2d St Saint Louis MO 63102

SENZAI, MOHAMMAD DAUD, agronomist, educator, researcher; b. Kabul, Afghanistan, Oct. 14, 1941; s. Mir Ahmad and Bibi (Hanifa) S.; m. Hamida Gulpana Kaboojan, June 19, 1969; children—Farid, Fahim, Farhad. B.S., Kabul U., 1965; M.S., Am. U., Beirut, Lebanon, 1968; Ph.D., U. Wis., 1978; postgrad. Internat. Tng. Ctr., Delft, Netherlands, 1970. Teaching and research asst. Kabul U., 1965, instr., 1968-69, asst. prof., 1970-73; agrl. stats. cons., interpreter USAID, Kabul, 1973-74; assoc. prof. agronomy Kabul U., 1978-80; assoc. prof. Wilmington (Ohio) Coll., 1981-83; crop and soil cons., 1984—; cons. IDEA Ctr., Jeddah, Saudi Arabia, 1980. Afghan Govt. scholar, 1961-65; U.S. Govt. scholar, 1965-68, 75-78; Dutch Govt. fellow, 1969-70; FAO fellow, 1973. Mem. Am. Soc. Agronomy, Soil Sci. Soc. Am., Weed Sci. Soc. Am., Afghan Natural Sci., Delta Tau Alpha (advisor). Moslem. Contbr. articles to profl. jours. Home and Office: 400 Linton Dr Wilmington OH 45177

SEPPALA, KATHERINE SEAMAN, business exec., clubwoman; b. Detroit, Aug. 22, 1919; d. Willard D. and Elizabeth (Miller) Seaman; B.A., Wayne State U., 1941; m. Leslie W. Seppala, Aug. 15, 1941; children—Sandra Kay, William Leslie. Mgr. women's bldg. and student activities adviser Wayne State U., 1941-43; pres. Harper Sports Shops, Inc., 1947—, chmn. bd., treas., sec., 1985—; partner Seppala Bldg. Co., 1971—. Mich. service chmn. women grads. Wayne State U., 1962—, 1st v.p., fund bd., active Mich. Assn. Community Health Services, Inc., Girl and Cub Scouts; mem. Citizen's adv. com. on sch. needs Detroit Bd. Edn., 1957—, mem. high sch. study com., 1966—; chmn., mem. loan fund bd. Denby High Sch. Parents Scholarship; bd. dirs., sec. Wayne State U. Fund; precinct del. Rep. Party, 14th dist., 1956—, del. convs. Recipient Ann. Women's Service award Wayne State U., 1963. Recipient Alumni award Wayne State U., 1971. Mem. Intercollegiate Assn. Women Students (regional rep. 1941-45), Women Wayne State U. Alumni (past pres.), Wayne State U. Alumni Assn. (dir., past v.p.), AAUW (dir. past officer), Council Women as Public Policy Makers (editor High lights) Denby Community Ednl. Orgn. (sec.), Met. Detroit Program Planning Inst. (pres.), Internat. Platform Assn., Detroit Met. Book and Author Soc. (treas.), Myasthenia Gravis Assn., Mortar Bd. (past pres.), Karyatides (past pres.), Anthony Wayne Soc., Alpha Chi Alpha, Alpha Kappa Delta, Delta Gamma Chi, Kappa Delta (chmn. chpt. alumnae adv. bd.). Baptist. Clubs: Zonta (v.p., dir.); Detroit Boat; Les Cheneaux. Home: 22771 Worthington Saint Clair Shores MI 48081 Office: 17157 Harper Detroit MI 48224

SERAFINI, DANIEL JOHN, mathematics educator, personnel supervisor; b. Detroit, Dec. 28, 1947; s. Gilbert Joseph and Dorothy (Tanari) S.; m. Mary Jane Flaherty, Aug. 2, 1969; children—Daniel, Gina, Lisa. A.A., Ill. Valley Community Coll., 1967; B.S., Ill. State U., 1969, M.S., 1974; cert. in organizational dynamics George Williams Coll., Downers Grove, Ill. Cert. tchr., Ill. Grand. asst. Ill. State U., Normal, Ill., 1969-79; instr. math. Putnam County High Sch., Granville, Ill., 1970-79, Ill. Valley Community Coll., LaSalle, Ill., 1977-79; plant statistician B. F. Goodrich Chem., Henry, Ill., 1979-83, personnel supr., 1983—. Chmn., Aid to Leukemia Stricken Am. Children, Putnam County, Ill., 1971-79; bd. dirs. Putnam County Sch. Bd., 1981-83, pres., 1983—. Mem. Ill. Valley Quality Circles, Peru, Ill., Central Ill. Indsl. Assn., Central Ill. Personnel Club, LaSalle, Ill. Democrat. Roman Catholic. Avocations: photography; reading; writing; music; fishing. Home: 418 Hennepin St Granville IL 61326

SEREDA, JOHN WALTER, JR., lawyer, adult education educator; b. Chgo., Dec. 27, 1952; s. John W. and Theresa M. (Karlowicz) S.; m. Sharon Anne Bonior; 1 child, Amanda Marie. B.A., DePaul U., 1975, J.D., 1978. Bar: Ill. 1978, U.S. Dist. Ct. (no. dist.) Ill. 1978, U.S. Dist. Ct. (no. dist.) Ind. 1978. Assoc. S. David Friedlander, Calumet City, Ill., 1978-81; sole practice, Chgo., 1981—; instr. adult edn. Prairie State Coll., 1983—. Mem. ABA, Ill. State Bar Assn., Chgo. Bar Assn., South Suburban Bar Assn., South West Bar Assn., Trial Bar of U.S. Dist. Ct. Roman Catholic. Office: 11732 S Western Ave Chicago IL 60643

SEREWICZ, ANTHONY JOHN, auditor; b. Evanston, Ill., Oct. 6, 1928; s. Albert E. and Caroline M. Serewicz; m. Dolores A. Rash, Aug. 18, 1956; children—Thomas, Ruth, Mary, David, Linda, Susan. B.A., St. Joseph's Coll., Ind., 1950; M.B.A., DePaul U., 1960. Cert. internal auditor. Regional audit mgr. Montgomery Ward & Co., Chgo., 1962—. Served with U.S. Army, 1951-53; Korea. Mem. Inst. Internal Auditors. Roman Catholic. Avocation: gardening. Home: 657 Green Brier Ln Crystal Lake IL 60014 Office: One Montgomery Plaza Chicago IL 60671

SERNETT, RICHARD PATRICK, lawyer; b. Mason City, Iowa, Sept. 8, 1938; s. Edward Frank and Loretta M. (Cavanaugh) S.; B.B.A., U. Iowa, 1960, J.D., 1963; m. Janet Ellen Ward, Apr. 20, 1963; children—Susan Ellen, Thomas Ward, Stephen Edward, Katherine Anne. Admitted to Ill. bar, 1965; with Scott, Foresman & Co., Glenview, Ill., 1963-80, house counsel, asst. sec., 1967-70, sec., legal officer, 1970-80; v.p. law, sec. SFN Cos., Inc., Glenview, Ill., 1980-83, sr. v.p., sec., gen. counsel, 1983—; dir. Data Acquisition Services, Inc., San Marcos, Calif., Can. Pub. Corp., Toronto, Ont., Can.; mem. adv. panel on internat. copyright U.S. State Dept., 1972-75. Bd. dirs. Chgo. Assn. Retarded Citizens, 1983—. Mem. Am. (chmn. copyright div. sect. patent, trademark and copyright law 1972-73), Ill. (chmn. copyright law com. 1978-79), Chgo., bar assns., Am. Patent Law Assn. (chmn. copyright matters com. 1972-73, bd. mgrs. 1981-84), Patent Law Assn. Chgo. (chmn. copyright com. 1972-73, 77-78, bd. mgrs. 1979-81), Copyright Soc. U.S.A. (trustee 1972-75, 77-80), Am. Judicature Soc., Am. Soc. Corporate Secs., Assn. Am. Pubs. (chmn. copyright com. 1972-73, vice chmn. 1973-75), Phi Delta Phi, Phi Kappa Theta. Club: Metropolitan (Chgo.). Home: 2071 Glendale Ave Northbrook IL 60062 Office: 1900 E Lake Ave Glenview IL 60025

SERRA, RUDOLPH ANTHONY, lawyer, social worker, communications consultant; b. Mt. Clemens, Mich., Aug. 7, 1955; s. Rudolph Albert and Shirley Marie (Kozen) S. B.S., Central Mich. U., 1976, M.A. in Human Communications, 1977; J.D., Wayne State U., 1983. Bar: Mich. 1983, U.S. Dist. Ct. (ea. dist.) Mich. 1983. Regional dir. Mich. Lung Assn., Saginaw, 1977-78; area mgr. U.S. Congressman Albosta, Owosso, Mich., 1978-80; community organizer Neighborhood Service Orgn., Detroit, 1980-82; clk. Mich. Ct. Appeals, Detroit, 1982-83, staff atty., 1983-84; assoc. Summers, Schwartz, Silver & Schwartz, Southfield, Mich., 1984—. Contbr. articles to profl. jours. Democratic candidate for Mich. Ho. of Reps. from 89th Dist., 1978; chmn. Ferndale Dem. Club, Mich., 1981—; chmn. 17th Dist. Mich. Young Dems., Ferndale, 1982—; pub. info. officer Polit. Office Watchers, Oakland County, Mich., 1982-84. Recipient Top Speaker awards Motor City Debate Tournament, U. Detroit, Wayne State U., Pi Kappa Delta Nat. Debate Tournament, Precinct Worker honor Mich. Dem. Party, 1979, 84. Mem. Mich. Personnel and Guidance Assn., Mich. Assn. Specialists in Group Work, Assn. Trial Lawyers Am. (winner trial advocacy contest 1982, 83), ABA (winner client counseling competition 1983). Home: 560 Farmdale Ferndale MI 48220 Office: Sommers Schwartz Silver & Schwartz 26555 Evergreen St Southfield MI 48076

SERSTOCK, DORIS SHAY, microbiologist, club woman; b. Mitchell, S.D., June 13, 1926; d. Elmer Howard and Hattie (Christopher) Shay; B.A., Augustana Coll., 1947; Blood Bank tng. course, Washington, 1963; postgrad. U. Minn., 1966-67, Duke, summer 1969, mycology tng. Communicable Disease Center, Atlanta, 1972; m. Ellsworth I. Serstock, Aug. 30, 1952; children—Barbara Anne, Robert E., Mark D. Bacteriologist, civil service positions, S.D., Colo., Mo., 1947-52; research bacteriologist U. Minn., 1952-53; clin. bacteriologist Dr. Lufkin's Lab., 1954-55; chief technologist St. Paul Regional Blood Center of A.R.C., 1959-65; microbiologist, then microbiologist in charge mycology lab. VA Hosp., Mpls., 1968—; instr. Coll. Med. Scis., U. Minn., 1970-79, asst. prof. Coll. Lab. Medicine and Pathology, 1979—; key speaker confs. Mem. Richfield Planning Commn., 1965-71. Recipient scholarship Am. Assn. U. Women, 1966; Ann. Distinctive Alumni medallion award Augustana Coll., 1977; Superior Performance cert. Mpls. VA Med. Center, 1978, 82; Golden Spore award Mycology Observer mag., 1985; named to Exec. and Profl. Hall of Fame, 1966; fellow Augustana Coll., Sioux Falls, S.D. Mem. Minn. Planning Assn., Am. Soc. Microbiology, Minn. Inter Lab. Microbiol. Assn. Republican Lutheran. Clubs: Richfield Women's Garden (pres. 1959), Wild Flower Garden (chmn. 1961). Author articles in field. Home: 7201 Portland Ave Richfield MN 55423 Office: VA Hospital Minneapolis MN 55417

SERVICE, PAMELA FLOY, museum curator; b. Berkeley, Calif., Oct. 8, 1945; d. Forrest Leroy and Floy Elma (Fleming) Horner; m. Robert Gifford Service, July 8, 1967; 1 child, Alexandra Floyesta. B.A., U. Calif.-Berkeley, 1967; M.A., U. London, 1969. Mus. publicist Ind. U., Bloomington, 1970-72; museum curator Monroe County Mus., Bloomington, 1977—. Author: Winter of Magic's Return, 1985; A Question of Destiny, 1986. Columnist for Bloomington Herald Telephone, 1980—. County historian Ind. Hist. Soc., 1981—; precinct committeeman Monroe County Democratic Party, Ind., 1976-78; del. Democratic State Conv., Ind., 1978, 82, 84, Dem. Nat. Conv. Ind., 1984; councilman City Council, Bloomington, 1979—. Recipient Annual Conservation award Sassafras Audubon Soc., 1984. Mem. Phi Beta Kappa. Methodist. Avocations: writing; painting; acting; canoeing. Home: 419 N Washington St Bloomington IN 47401 Office: Monroe County Hist Mus 202 E 6th St Bloomington IN 47401

SESSIONS, WILLIAM CRIGHTON, lawyer; b. Columbus, Ohio, Sept. 22, 1904; s. Frank Lord and Jane (Crighton) S.; B.S., Mass. Inst. Tech., 1926; J.D., Western Res. U., 1930; m. Marian Eloise Hill, June 16, 1931; children—Elizabeth (Mrs. Thomas V. A. Kelsey), Margaret (Mrs. Frank K. Penirian). Admitted to Ohio bar, 1930, since practiced Cleve.; mem. Bosworth, Sessions & McCoy 1941-79, Pearne, Gordon, McCoy and Granger, then Pearne, Gordon, Sessions, McCoy, Granger and Tilberry, 1979—. Mem. alumni council, ednl. council, corp. devel. com. M.I.T. Mem. fiscal adv. com. Cleve. YWCA. Bd. trustees Cleve. Health Mus. Mem. Internat. Patent and Trademark Assn., Am. Judicature Soc., Am., Cleve. (pres. 1963-64) patent law assns., Am., Cleve. bar assns., Newcomen Soc., Cleve. Engring. Soc., Bluecoats, Phi Gamma Delta. Republican. Clubs: Union, Clifton, Westwood Country, Rowfant, Rockwell Springs Trout. Home: 15710 West Shore Ct Lakewood OH 44107 Office: 1200 Leader Bldg Cleveland OH 44114

SESTINA, JOHN E., fin. planner; b. Cleve., Mar. 17, 1942; s. John J. and Regina Sestina; B.S., U. Dayton, 1965; M.S. in Fgn. Service, Am. Coll, 1982; m. Mary Barbara Jezek, Dec. 20, 1970; 1 dau., Alison. With Sestina and Assocs., Inc., Columbus, Ohio, 1967—. Mem. Soc. Ind. Fin. Advisers (past pres., Fin. Planner of Yr. award 1982), Internat. Assn. Fin. Planners, Nat. Assn. Personal Fin. Advisors (pres.), Inst. Cert. Fin. Planners. Author: Complete Guide to Professional Incorporation, 1970; contbr. articles to profl. jours.; contbr. weekly fin. planning segment AM Columbus, WOSU-AM, 1979—. Office: 3726 Olentangy River Rd Columbus OH 43214

SESTRIC, ANTHONY JAMES, lawyer; b. St. Louis, June 27, 1940; s. Anton and Marie (Gasparovic) S.; B.A., Georgetown U., 1962; J.D., Mo. U., 1965; m. Carol F. Bowman, Nov. 24, 1966; children—Laura Antonette, Holly Nicole, Michael Anthony. Bar: Mo. 1965, U.S. Tax Ct. 1969, U.S. Supreme Ct. 1970, U.S. Ct. Appeals (8th cir.) 1965, U.S. Ct. Appeals (7th cir.) 1984, U.S. Dist. Ct. Mo. 1966. Law clk. U.S. Dist. Ct., St. Louis, 1965-66; partner firm Sestric, McGhee & Miller, St. Louis, 1966-77, Fordyce & Mayne, 1977-78; spl. asst. to Mo. atty. gen., St. Louis, 1968; hearing officer St. Louis Met. Police Dept. Mem. St. Louis Air Pollution Bd. Appeals and Varience Rev., 1966-73, chmn., 1968-73; mem. St. Louis Airport Commn., 1975-76; dist. vice chmn. Boy Scouts Am., 1970—. Bd. dirs. Full Achievement, Inc., 1970-77, pres., 1972-77; bd. dirs. Legal Aid Soc. of St. Louis, 1976-77, Law Library Assn. St. Louis, 1976-78; v.p. bd. St. Elizabeth Acad., 1985-86. Mem. ABA (state chmn. judiciary com. 1973-75, circuit chmn. com. condemnation, zoning and property use 1975-77, standing com. bar activities 1982-85), Chgo. Bar Assn., Fed. Bar Assn., Lawyers Assn., Am. Judicature Soc., Mo. Bar (vice chmn. young lawyers sect. 1973-76, bd. govs. 1974-77), Bar Assn. Met. St. Louis (chmn. young lawyers sect. 1974-75, exec. com. 1974-83, pres. 1981-82). Club: Mo. Athletic. Home: 3967 Holly Hills Blvd Saint Louis MO 63116 Office: 1015 Locust St Saint Louis MO 63101

SEVCIK, JOHN GEORGE, business executive; b. Chgo., May 15, 1909; s. Joseph and Rose (Kostal) S.; J.D., DePaul U., 1939, LL.D., 1958; B.S.C., Central YMCA Coll., 1945; M.B.A., U. Chgo., 1947; M.P.L., John Marshall Law Sch., 1950, LL.M., 1954; LL.D., St. Mary's Coll., Ill. Benedictine Coll., 1960; m. Rose Vanek, Mar. 27, 1934; children—Joanne, John Wayne. Asso., Burton Dixie Co., 1925—, dir., 1942—, pres., 1949-72, vice chmn. bd., 1972—; admitted to Ill. bar, 1940, since practiced law; chmn. bd. Financial Marketing Services Inc., 1971—; gen. mgr. McCormick Pl., Chgo., 1971-80; chief exec. officer Chgo. Investment Corp., 1980—; dir. Central Nat. Bank Chgo., Brunswick Corp., Bus. Capitol Corp. Mem. bd. govs. Chgo. Furniture Mart; dir. Nat. Cotton Batting Inst.; mem. editorial bd. Bedding mag. Commr., Pub. Bldgs. Commn. Chgo.; chmn. adv. bd. Chgo. Youth Commn.; mem. adv. com. Chief Justice Municipal Ct. Chgo.; active work Boy Scouts; gen. finance chmn. Chgo. Cerebral Palsy Assn., 1956; mem. exec. bd. Nat. Conf. Christians and Jews; mem. Bd. Edn. Berwyn, Ill. Vice chmn. bd. trustees St. Procopius Coll.; mem., chmn. lay bd. trustees, mem. legal bd. trustees DePaul U.; mem. lay bd. trustees Rosary Coll., chmn. bd., 1966-70; asso. mem. lay bd. St. Xavier Coll., mem. adv. council Sch. of Bus.; citizens bd. U. Chgo.; adv. bd. St. Mary's Coll.; bd. dirs. MacNeal Meml. Hosp.; vice chmn. bd. Ill. Coll. Podiatric Medicine, 1968—; trustee John Marshall Law Sch. Chgo. Mem. Am. Judicature Soc., Am., Ill. bar assns., Nat. Assn. Bedding Mfrs. (pres. 1959-60), Ill. Mfrs. Assn., Furniture Club Am., AAUP, Internat. Assn. Auditorium Mgrs., DePaul U., John Marshall (pres. 1968-71) alumni assns. Phi Alpha Delta, Beta Gamma Sigma. Clubs: Executives, Economic, Union League. Address: Chgo Investment Corp 29 E Madison Chicago IL 60602

SEVERS, ERIC ROBERTSON, lawyer; b. Oberlin, Ohio, Sept. 5, 1948; s. Grover Lawrence and Carol Suzanne (Beachler) S.; m. Diane Marie Reams,

Sept. 8, 1984. B.A. in Econs., Denison U., 1970; J.D., Cleve-Marshall Law Sch., 1975. Bar: Ohio 1975, Fla. 1975, U.S. Dist. Ct. (no. dist.) Ohio 1975. Ptnr., Severs & Boylan Co., L.P.A., Elyria, Ohio, 1975—; city solicitor City of Oberlin, 1980—. Vice-chmn. Oberlin Civil Service Commn., 1976-79. Mem. ABA, Ohio State Bar Assn., Lorain County Bar Assn., Fla. Bar Ohio Mcpl. Attys. Assn., Nat. Inst. Mcpl. Law Officers. Lodge: Kiwanis (pres. 1977-78). Home: 136 Shipherd Circle Oberlin OH 44074 Office: Severs & Boylan Co L P A 28 Lake Ave Elyria OH 44035

SEVY, NAN HARRIS, educator; b. Tazewell, Tenn., Dec. 13, 1930; d. James Milton and Margaret Lee (Rasnick) Harris; m. Robert H. Sevy, Aug. 25, 1951; children—Bruce, Patricia, Laura, Alan. A.B. in English, Berea Coll., 1952; postgrad. Calif. State U., 1970; M.Ed., Nat. Coll. Edn., 1977. Cert. tchr. Tchr., curriculum cons., gifted program coordinator, spl. programs coordinator Sch. Dist. 89, Glen Ellyn, Ill., 1970—; adj. faculty McGaw Grad. Sch., Nat. Coll. Edn.; treas. No. Ill. Planning Commn. for Gifted Edn. Recipient Honorary Life Service award PTA. Mem. Assn. for Supervision and Curriculum Devel., Nat. Assn. for Gifted, Ill. Council for Gifted, Delta Kappa Gamma. Republican. Office: 799 Roosevelt Rd Bldg 6 Suite 15 Glen Ellyn IL 60137

SEWALL, EDWARD REEVES, manufacturing company executive; b. Mpls., Dec. 20, 1927; s. Edward Bradstreet and Lorena (Reeves) S.; m. Barbara Overton, Apr. 21, 1951; children—Stephen, Katherine, David. B.S., Yale U., 1950. With Sewall Gear Mfg. Co., St. Paul, 1951—, v.p., 1965-80, exec. v.p., 1980—; dir. GMI, Ltd., Bermuda. Bd. dirs. YMCA. Mem. Am. Gear Mfrs. Assn. (pres. 1983-84). Republican. Presbyterian. Clubs: North Oaks Golf (St. Paul). Home: 148 W Pleasant Lake Rd North Oaks MN 55110 Office: 705 Raymond Ave St Paul MN 55114

SEWARD, BARRY LEE, health care executive; b. Peoria, Ill., Nov. 19, 1941; s. Arley and Beulah May ('Elmore) S.; m. Patricia Carol Parker, July 27, 1963; children—Susan Diane, Michael Blake. B.A. in Health and Phys. Edn., U. Mo., 1975. Recreation therapy asst. Barnes Med. Ctr., St. Louis, 1961-62, recreation leader, 1962-66, recreation dir., 1966-67; activities dir. Swope Ridge Health Care Ctr., Kansas City, Mo., 1967-70, adminstrv. asst., 1970-71, asst. adminstr., 1971-72, adminstr., 1972-75, exec. dir., 1975-79; dir. met. services, v.p. sales and promotions, corp. v.p. pub. affairs and promotion, pres. downtown subs. Research Health Services System, Kansas City, 1979—; preceptor grad. Studies in health services mgmt. U. Mo., 1978; mem. Mo. Statewide Health Coordinating Council, 1977-78; spl. adviser White House Conf. on Aging, 1980-81. Mem. bd. of aldermen, mayor pro tem City of Raytown (Mo.), 1981-83; Republican candidate for U.S. Ho. of Reps., 1982. Recipient Meritorious Service plaque Mo. Therapeutic Recreation Soc., 1967; cert. of commendation Gov.'s Task Force on the Older Missourian, 1971; Past Pres. award Mo. Park and Recreation Assn., 1972; award of Merit, Chgo. chpt. Soc. for Tech. Communication, 1975. Mem. Am. Hosp. Assn., Am. Coll. Health Care Adminstrs. (Best in Display of Distinction award 1977). Republican. Baptist. Clubs: Carriage, Sertoma. Co-pub. Images of Greatness, 1977. Home: 11009 E 85th St Raytown MO 64138 Office: Research Health Services System 6400 Prospect Ave Suite 308 Kansas City MO 64132

SEWARD, JOHN EDWARD, JR., insurance company executive; b. Kirksville, Mo., June 12, 1943; s. John Edward and Ruth Carol (Connell) S.; B.S. in Fin., St. Joseph's Coll., 1968; children—Mitch, J.J. Mgr. acctg. services Guarantee Res. Life Ins. Co., Hammond, Ind., 1964-69; asst. controller Gambles Ins. Group, Mpls., 1969-71, N.Am. Cos., Chgo., 1971-73; pres., dir. mem. exec. com. Home & Auto. Ins. Co., Chgo., 1975-83; pres., dir., mem. exec. com. Universal Fire & Casualty Ins. Co., 1983—; pres. Dynasty Health Club, Park Lane Ins. Agy., Mussels, Inc., 1983—. Bd. dirs. Calumet council Boy Scouts Am., 1979—, Teddy Bear Club for Shriners Hosp., 1979-81, Chgo. Baseball Cancer Charities, 1981—. F.L.M.I., C.L.U., C.P.C.U. Home: 9549 Prairie Ave Highland IN 46322 Office: 800 Mac Arthur Blvd Munster IN 46321

SEWELL, IKE, restauranteur; b. Wills Point, Tex., Sept. 9, 1903; s. Ike and Monte (Rice) S.; m. Florence Lenore Davis, Apr. 8, 1939. Student U. Tex., 1924-27. With Am. Airlines, 1928-32; v.p. Fleischmann Distilling Corp., Chgo., 1933-65; owner, chief exec. officer Pizzeria Uno, Inc., Chgo., 1943—, Pizzerie Due, Inc., Chgo., 1955—, Su Casa Mexican Restaurant, Chgo., 1963—, Saxet Corp. real estate, Chgo., 1957—, Sewell Corp., Chgo., 1974—; dir. Forman Realty Corp., Bismarck Hotel Corp. Bd. dirs. One Hundred Club Cook County, Sigma Chi Found. Clubs: Tavern, Chgo. Athletic, Casino, Everglades, Beach. Home: 1420 Lake Shore Dr Chicago IL 60610 also 100 Royal Palm Way Palm Beach FL 33480 Office: 619 N Wabash Ave Chicago IL 60611

SEYMOUR, JACK LEROY, manufacturing company executive; b. Pana, Ill., July 10, 1931; s. Roy Kenneth Seymour and Pauline Lucille (Jones) Everman; m. Wilma Lee Horne, Nov. 12, 1955; children—Danny Ray, Debra Elaine. Enlisted U.S. Navy 1948, retired, 1968; plant mgr. Inter Auto Machines, Perrysburg, Ohio, 1967-72; aircraft carborator technician Borg Warner Co., Decatur, Ill., 1972-81; retired, 1981. Creator, chmn. Armed Forces Meml., 1983, Civil War Maml., 1985, Mem. VFW (sr. vice cmdr. Pana chpt. 1980-81, post comdr. 1981-82, 85-86, post sec. 1982-85, jr. vice comdr. dist. chpt. 1983-84, sr. vice comdr. 1984, spl. aide-de-camp to nat. comdr. 1983-84), Ill. Wildlife Fedn. (dist. dir. 1977-78). Republican. Lutheran. Club: Pana Sportmen (sec. 1977). Lodge: Elks. Avocations: gardening, historical research of Pana area. Home: 6 S Pine St Pana IL 62557

SEYMOUR, ROBERT KENNETH, architect; b. Detroit, Nov. 27, 1948; s. Kenneth John and Ann Margaret (Nikolits) S.; B.Arch. magna cum laude, U. Detroit, 1973, M.Arch., 1974. Draftsman, W.P. Lindhout, Livonia, Mich., 1965-66; draftsman, designer Architects Assoc., Southfield, Mich., 1970-71, 73; designer Hubble, Roth & Clark, Bloomfield Hills, Mich., 1971-72; designer, job capt. Clark W. Corey, Westland, Mich., 1973; cons. designer Cement Enamel Devel., Redford, Mich., 1973-74; prin., Robert K. Seymour, Architect, Livonia, 1975—. Author: Hill House Documentation, 1978. Archtl. advisor Hist. Commn., Livonia, 1976-81; chmn. Detroit United Railway Sta. Restoration Com., Livonia, 1977-79; chmn. Hist. Preservation Commn., Livonia, 1978-80; adv. Bldg. Trades Adv. Com., Livonia, 1980—. Recipient Mayor's proclamation City of Livonia, 1982, cert. of honor Am. Soc. Body Engrs., Detroit, 1966. Mem. AIA, Mich. Soc. Architects, Assn. for Preservation Tech., Nat. Council Archtl. Registration Bds., Livonia Hist. Soc. (Heritage award 1984), Blue Key (life). Club: 1st Pa. Regiment (Livonia) (founder, pres. 1974-83). Avocations: hunting; fishing; wood carving; photography.

SHABAZ, JOHN C., federal judge; b. West Allis, Wis., June 25, 1931; s. Cyrus D. and Harriet T. S.; children by previous marriage, Scott J., Jeffrey J. B.A., U. Wis.; LL.B., Marquette U. Bar: Wis. Judge, U.S. Dist. Court. (western dist.) Wis. Office: US Dist Court Western Dist Wis 120 N Henry St Madison WI 53701

SHABAZZ, ABDULALIM, mathematics educator; b. Bessemer, Ala., May 22, 1927; s. Lewis and Mary (Roberson) Cross; A.B., Lincoln U. of Pa., 1949; M.S., M.I.T., 1951; Ph.D., Cornell U., 1955; m. Della Café, Feb. 22, 1968; children—Markus, Suad. Mathematician, Cornell Aero. Lab., Buffalo, 1952-53; instr., teaching fellow Cornell U., 1953-55; mathematician metals research lab. Electro Metall. Co., Niagara Falls, N.Y., 1955; asst. prof. math. Tuskegee Inst., 1956-57; assoc. prof., chmn. dept. math. Atlanta U., 1957-63; minister Muhammad Mosque 4, dir. edn. Muhammad U. Islam 4, Washington, 1963-75; dir. edn. World Community of Al-Islam in West, 1975, dir. adult edn., 1975-82; mem. Imam Consultation Bd., Masjid Elijah Muhammad, 1976-77; resident Imam Masjid Wali Muhammad, Detroit, 1979-82; assoc. prof. math. Ummul Qura U., Makkah, Saudi Arabia, 1982—; mem. Council of Imams Am. Muslim Mission, 1979-82, Midwest regional Imam, 1979-82; adj. prof. math. Union Grad. Sch., Yellow Springs, Ohio, 1975-82; ednl. columnist Bilalian News, Chgo., 1975-82. Mem. Census Advisory Com. on Black Population for 1980 Census, 1973-80. Served with USAAF, 1946-47. Mem. Am. Math. Soc., Math. Assn. Am., Am. Soc. Engring. Edn., Nat. Inst. Sci., AAAS, Assn. Muslim Scientists and Engrs., Nat. Alliance of Black Sch. Educators, Sigma Xi. Home: PO Box 21721 Detroit MI 48221 Office: Ummul Qura U Dept Math PO Box 3711 Makkah Saudi Arabia

SHACKELFORD, DOUGLAS ANDREW, industrial contracting and distributing company executive; b. Columbus, Ohio, Jan. 13, 1948; s. Joseph Andrew and Juanita Belle (Welling) S.; B.A. in Biology and Chemistry, Ohio Dominican Coll., 1973; m. Mary Jo Hatem, Dec. 14, 1968; children—Joseph Jonathan, Andrew. Maintainance mgr. Allen Refractories Co., Columbus, 1970-74, job foreman, 1974-76; tech. adv. refractories CE Cast Indsl. Products, Inc., Oak Park, Ill., 1976-78, sales rep., Wis., 1978-80; br. mgr. Jay L. Angel, Inc., Lima, Ohio, 1980—, corp. sales mgr., 1981—; now dist. rep. process chemicals div. Nalco Chem. Co., Oak Brook, Ill. Bd. dirs. St. Vincent's Children's Center, Columbus, 1976-78, St. Francis Children's Activity and Achievement Center, Milw., 1978-80; mem. endowment com. St. Coletta Sch., Jefferson, Wis. Mem. Am. Foundrymen's Soc. (chmn. apprenticeship com. Southeastern Wis. chpt. 1979-80).

SHADUR, MILTON I., See *Who's Who in America,* 43rd edition.

SHAFER, JON MERVIN, writer, farmer; b. Lima, Ohio, Nov. 15, 1944; s. Howard Lewis and Emma Lois (Day) S.; m. Linda Jo Smith, July 3, 1968 (div. 1972); m. Rebecca Ellen McDowell, Jan. 1, 1983. Student, Regional Council for Internat. Edn., Basel, Switzerland, 1965-66; B.A., Ohio No. U., 1967; M.A., U. Minn., 1977. Mem. community faculty Metro State U., St. Paul, 1972-77; dir. cable project Am. Friends Service Com., Mpls., 1973; dir. communications program Metro Council, St. Paul, 1974-77; farmer Shafer Family Farm, Cloverdale, Ohio, 1979—; instr. Defiance Coll., Ohio, 1980; dir. Putnam County Council on Aging, Ottawa, Ohio, 1983-85; cons. in field. Author: Annotated Bibliography on Cable Television, 1972, 6 edits.; (booklet) Education and Cable TV: A Guide, 1973; Toward A Sustainable Ohio, 1982. Contbr. chpts. to books, articles to profl. jours. Trustee, Community Action Commn., Findlay, Ohio, 1983-85. Ohio No. U. Acad. scholar, 1963-67; named Hon. Ohio Green Thumber, Ohio Green Thumb, 1984. Mem. Inst. Alternative Agr., Ohio Farmers Union (state del. 1984-85), Ohio Gerontol. Soc., Ohio Ecol. Food and Farm Assn. (v.p. 1980, 85). Democrat. Quaker. Address: Route 2 Box 40A Cloverdale OH 45827

SHAFFER, ALFRED GARFIELD, service organization executive; b. Sunbury, Pa., Jan. 5, 1939; d. Alfred G. and Betty Marjorie (Vogel) S.; m. Nancy Jane Dawson, Aug. 29, 1976. B.S., Susquehanna U., 1961. Cert. tchr., Pa. Tchr., Danville Sch. Dist. (Pa.), 1962-69; mgr. club service Kiwanis Internat., Chgo., 1969-74, dir. program devel., 1974-81, dir. program services, Indpls., 1982-85, dir. spl. services, 1985—; corp. affairs cons. Nat. Easter Seal Soc., Chgo., 1981-82; adminstr. Circle K Internat., Chgo., 1982; mem. Pres.'s Com. on Employment of Handicapped, 1983—; sec. Kiwanis Club of Northwest Indpls., 1983-85. Chmn. adv. council 70001 Ltd., Indpls., 1984—. Named Kiwanian of Yr., 1966, 85; recipient Gold Key of Service, Pa. Dist. Key Clubs, 1964; Outstanding Service Kiwanis Club, Chgo., 1981. Lutheran. Lodges: Kiwanis (Selinsgrove, Pa.; pres. 1964; lt. gov. Pa. 1966-67; pres. Chgo. 1970-72). Home: 5688 N Broadway Indianapolis IN 46220 Office: Kiwanis Internat 3636 Woodview Trace Indianapolis IN 46268

SHAFFER, HARRY GARD, JR., advertising executive; b. Clearfield, Pa., Apr. 6, 1932; s. Harry Gard and Harriet (McCloskey) S.; m. Janet Evelyn Bayliss, Nov. 10, 1961 (div. Apr. 1972); children—Lynne, Harry Gard, Karen; m. 2d, Geraldine Louise Adams, Dec. 12, 1976. B.S., U. Hawaii, 1957. Account exec. K.M. & G., Inc., Pitts., 1959-61; account supr. Sykes Advt., Inc., Pitts., 1961-64; v.p., media dir. Carlton Advt. Co., Pitts., 1964-70; account supr. M & F Advt., Inc., Cleve., 1970-72; exec. v.p. Palm & Patterson, Cleve., 1972-78; pres. Shaffer Shaffer Shaffer, Cleve., 1979—; exec. sec. Florists Assn. of Greater Cleve., 1976—. Creative dir. TV program Singing Angels Sing America, 1975 (Best TV Entertainment Spl. award). Capt. Hawaii Olympic Ocean Swimming and Surfing Team, Melbourne, Australia, 1956; pub. relations dir. Swimming Hall of Fame, Fort Lauderdale, Fla., 1967-71. Served with USMC, 1951-54. Recipient Bronze medal Australian Surf Life Sav. Assn. Mem. Mensa. Republican. Presbyterian. Clubs: Singing Angels, Cleve. Ad; Pitts. Ad, Pitts. Athletic. Lodge: Masons, Shriners. Home: 10301 Lake Ave Apt 222 Cleveland OH 44102 Office: Shaffer Shaffer Shaffer Inc 226 Hanna Bldg Cleveland OH 44115

SHAFFER, JANE REGINA, association executive; b. Peoria, Ill., June 4, 1933; d. Archie Henry and Ethel Rose (Pedreyra) Hall; student public schs., Peoria; m. Roy Alvin Shaffer, Jan. 31, 1955; children—Jamie Shaffer Hinson, Roy Michael, Shawn Rene. Sec.-treas. Diverco Corp., Winter Haven, Fla., 1957-70; sec.-treas. Mansyco Corp., Peoria, 1971; dir. div. activities Profl. Photographers Am., Des Plaines, Ill., 1972—. Chmn. Beautification Com. Fla., 1968-69. Recipient Honor certs. Indsl. div. Questioned Document Examiners, Inc., 1977, Am. Soc. Photographers, 1978; Nat. award Profl. Photographers Am., 1981, 84. Mem. Evidence Photographers Internat. Council (hon.; Honor cert. 1976), Am. Photog. Artisans Guild (hon.; Honor cert. 1977). Home: 530 Springside Ln Buffalo Grove IL 60090 Office: Profl Photographers Am 1090 Executive Way Des Plaines IL 60018

SHAFFER, KIM ALLAN, lawyer; b. Pipestone, Minn., Dec. 17, 1952; s. Harold K. and Norma A. Shaffer; m. Janet B. Flagg, June 1, 1974; 1 child, Allan J. B.A., Macalester Coll., 1975; J.D., U. Minn., 1979. Bar: Minn. 1979. Atty. Somsen, Dempsey & Schade, New Ulm, Minn., 1979—. County chmn. Brown County Independent Republicans, Minn., 1981-83; trustee Minn. 4H Found., St. Paul, 1981—; pres. Food Emergency Distbrs., Inc., New Ulm, 1984; bd. dirs. New Ulm Bus. Dists., Inc., 1983—, pres., 1985. Mem. ABA, Minn. State Bar Assn., New Ulm C. of C. (bd. dirs. 1985—). Mem. United Ch. Christ (pres. 1982). Club: Sertoma (pres. 1983-84) (New Ulm). Office: Somsen Dempsey Schade PO Box 38 New Ulm MN 56073

SHAFFER, RONALD LEE, architect; b. Kansas City, Kans., June 1, 1947; s. Charles Edward and Ruth Marie (Mitchell) S.; m. B. Jeannine Hensley, May 1, 1971; 1 child, Whitney Leigh. B.Arch., Kans. State U., 1970. Registered architect 8 states. Architect, Duncan Architects, Kansas City, Mo., 1970-77; assoc. James E. Taylor & Assocs., Kansas City, 1977-79; owner RLS Architects, Shawnee Mission, Kans., 1979—. Bd. dirs. Mid-Continent Small Bus. United, Kansas City, 1984. Named Disting. pres. Kiwanis, 1982-83. Mem. AIA, Internat. Council Bldg. Ofcls., Merriam C. of C. (bd. dir.), Kansas City C. of C. Clubs: Pika Investment (pres.). Home: 4113 W 67 Terr Prairie Village KS 66208 Office: RLS Architects 6750 Antioch Rd Suite 110 Shawnee Mission KS 66204

SHAFRAN, LINDA E., business executive; b. Cleve., July 2, 1949; d. Manual and Marion (Baruch) Shafran. B.A. in Journalism, Ohio State U., 1971, M.A. in Linquistics, 1973. Vice pres. Consol. Internat., Inc., Columbus, Ohio, 1975—. Mem. Columbus C. of C. Jewish. Office: Consol Internat Inc 2020 Corvair Ave Columbus OH 43207

SHAHIDI, FREYDOON, mathematician, mathematics educator; b. Tehran, Iran, June 19, 1947; came to U.S., 1971; s. Manoochehr and Aghdas (Shahidi) S.; m. Guity Ravai, Sept. 21, 1977; 1 child, Alireza. B.S., Tehran U., 1969; Ph.D., Johns Hopkins U., 1975. Vis. mem. Inst. for Advanced Study, Princeton, N.J., 1975-76, 83-84; vis. asst. prof. Ind. U., Bloomington, 1976-77; asst. prof. Purdue U., West Lafayette, Ind., 1977-82, assoc. prof. math., 1982—; vis. asst. prof. U. Toronto, Ont., Can., 1981-82. Contbr. articles to jours. including Am. Jour. Math., Compositio Mathematica, Duke Math. Jour., Mathematische Annalen. Served to 2nd lt. C.E. Iran, 1969-71. NSF grantee, 1977-79, 79—; XL grantee, Purdue Research Found., 1981. Mem. Am. Math. Soc. Moslem. Avocation: Music. Home: 624 Kent Ave West Lafayette IN 47906 Office: Dept Math Purdue Univ West Lafayette IN 47907

SHAIN, IRVING, university administrator; b. Seattle, Jan. 2, 1926; s. Samuel and Selma S.; B.S. in Chemistry, U. Wash., 1949, Ph.D., 1952; m. Mildred R. Udell, Aug. 31, 1947; children—Kathryn A., Steven T., John R., Paul S. Instr. dept. chemistry U. Wis., Madison, 1952-54, asst. prof., 1954-59, asso. prof., 1959-61, prof., 1961—, vice chancellor, 1970-75, chancellor, 1977—, provost, v.p. for acad. affairs U. Wash., Seattle, 1975-77; dir. Olin Corp. Served with U.S. Army, 1943-46. Fellow AAAS; mem. Am. Chem. Soc., Internat. Soc. Electrochemistry, Electrochem. Soc., Sigma Xi, Phi Beta Kappa, Phi Kappa Phi, Phi Lambda Upsilon. Office: 158 Bascom Hall Univ Wis Madison WI 53706

SHAKESPEAR, HORACIO, auto engr., consultant; b. Rosario, Argentina, May 26, 1922; s. Valentin and Julia (Carbajo) S.; came to U.S., 1956, naturalized, 1962; C.E., Universidad del Litoral, Rosario, 1945; m. Mary Rita Gonzalez, Feb. 12, 1947; children—Ann Mary, Paul, Michael, George, Julie Rose, Daniel. Partner civil engring. firm, Rio Negro, Argentina, 1946-47; asst. chief vehicle maintenance Public Works Dept. Buenos Aires, 1948-53; asst. gen. mgr. Crisoldinie steel co., Quilmes, Argentina, 1953-55; chief explt. engr. Industrias Kaiser Argentina, 1956; sr. designer Chevrolet Engring., Gen. Motors Tech. Center, 1956-57, engr., 1957-65, asst. staff engr., 1965-69, staff engr., engring. staff advanced products, 1970-82; mgr. Multi-D Cons., 1982—. Served as 1st lt. Argentinian Air Force, 1948. Mem. Soc. Auto Engrs., Societe des Ingenieurs de l'Automobile. Roman Catholic. Patentee in automotive chassis and body systems and components. Office: 4141 Wendell Rd West Bloomfield MI 48033

SHAMBAUGH, GEORGE ELMER, III, internist; b. Boston, Dec. 21, 1931; s. George Elmer and Marietta Susan (Moss) S.; B.A., Oberlin Coll., 1954; M.D., Cornell U., 1958; m. Katherine Margaret Matthews, Dec. 29, 1956; children—George, Benjamin, Daniel, James, Elizabeth. Gen. med. intern Denver Gen. Hosp., 1958-59; research fellow physiologic chemistry U. Wis., Madison, 1967-69; asst. prof. medicine Northwestern U. Med. Sch., Chgo., 1969-74, assoc. prof., 1974-81, prof., 1981—; mem. Center for Endocrinology, Metabolism and Nutrition, 1969—; chief endocrinology and metabolism VA Lakeside Med. Center, Chgo., 1974—; attending physician Northwestern Meml. Hosp., Chgo., 1969—. Served with M.C., U.S. Army, 1959-67. NIH spl. postdoctoral fellow, 1967-69; Schweppe Found. fellow, 1972-75; diplomate Am. Bd. Internal Medicine. Fellow ACP; mem. Am. Fedn. Clin. Research, Sci. Research Soc. Am., Endocrine Soc., Am. Thyroid Assn., Am. Physiol. Soc., Am. Inst. Nutrition, Am. Soc. Clin. Nutrition, Central Soc. Clin. Research, Inst. Medicine Chgo., Taipei Internat. Med. Soc. (pres. 1960), Sigma Xi, Nu Sigma Nu. Contbr. articles to text books and profl. jours. Home: 530 S Stone Ave LaGrange IL 60525 Office: VA Lakeside Med Center 333 E Huron St Chicago IL 60611 also Northwestern Med Faculty Found 222 E Superior St Chicago IL 60611

SHAMES, MICHAEL CHARLES, stock options trading company executive; b. Omaha, Sept. 15, 1938; s. Frank Aaron and Anne (Smolowitz) S.; m. Abby Louise Graff, May 21, 1967; 1 dau., Amanda Anne. Student Pace U., 1957-60, N.Y. Inst. Fin., 1960-61. Registered rep. N.Y. Stock Exchange. Page, reporter N.Y. Stock Exchange, N.Y.C., 1955-61; account exec. Newburger Loeb & Co., N.Y.C., 1966-70; stock trader Godnick, Inc., 1970-73; pres., chief exec. officer M.C.S. Options, Inc., Chgo., 1973—; mem. N.Y. Futures Exchange, N.Y.C., 1980—, Chgo. Bd. Options Exchange, 1973—. Served with USAF, 1961-65. Mem. Fretted Instrument Guild Am. (bd. dirs. 1973—), Train Collectors Assn. Am., Am. Numismatic Assn., Planetary Soc. Am. Republican. Methodist. Home: 3240 Lake Shore Dr Chicago IL 60657 Office: MCS Options Inc 327 S LaSalle St Chicago IL 60604

SHANAFIELD, HAROLD ARTHUR, educator; b. South Bend, Ind., Nov. 26, 1912; s. Harry Bacon and Anna (Paulsen) S.; B.A., U. Notre Dame; M.S.J., M.A., Northwestern U.; M.Ed., Chgo. State U.; m. Margaret Ann Goodman, Nov. 23, 1939; 1 son, Harold A. Copy editor Chgo. Herald Am., 1945-46; night picture editor Chgo. Sun-Times, 1946-47; mng. editor Elec. Dealer, Chgo., 1947-52; editor, mgr. Florists' Transworld Delivery News, Detroit, 1952-61; asst. mng. editor AMA Jour., Chgo., 1961-62; asst. dean Northwestern U., Chgo.-Evanston campus, evening divs., 1962-73; with Chgo. Bd. Edn., 1973—. Vice chmn., bd. visitors Freedoms Found. at Valley Forge. Served to capt. USCG, 1945—. Bd. dirs. Northwestern U. and Alumni Council, Am. Bus. Writing Assn., Assn. Evening Univs., Quill and Scroll (lifetime faculty mem.), Nat. Sojourners (pres. Chgo. chpt. 1971), Ind. Soc. Chgo. (resident v.p. 1975—), U.S. Coast Guard League (nat. comdr. 1954-55, 59-60, Res. Officers Assn., Am. Legion, Delta Mu Delta, Phi Chi Theta, Delta Sigma Pi, Sigma Delta Chi, Iota Sigma Epsilon. Clubs: Masons, Shriners (pres. 1970), KT (comdr. 1981), Chgo. Press, Chgo. Headline; Star Craft of Ill. (sec. 1972-77, pres. 1977-78). Editor Scottish Rite publs., 1976—, News of Medinah Temple, 1984—. Home: 2515 Marcy Ave Evanston IL 60201

SHANDS, COURTNEY, JR., lawyer; b. St. Louis, Mar. 17, 1929; s. Courtney and Elizabeth W. (Jones) S.; m. Frances Jean Schellfeffer, Aug. 9, 1952; children—Courtney, E.F. Berkley, Elizabeth; m. 2d, Nancy Bliss Lewis, Oct. 25, 1980. A.B., Washington U., St. Louis, 1951; LL.B., Harvard U., 1954. Bar: Mo. 1954, U.S. Supreme Ct. 1962. Assoc. Thompson and Mitchell, St. Louis, 1954-62, ptnr. 1962-63; ptnr. Thompson, Walther and Shewmaker, St. Louis, 1963-69, Kohn, Shands, Elbert, Gianoulakis and Giljum, 1970—; dir. Daniel and Henry Co., Tripos Assocs., Inc., The St. Louis Fund, Inc., Trustee Frank G. and Florence V. Bohle Scholarship Found., Edward Chase Garvey Meml. Found.; bd. dirs. Mark Twain Summer Inst., Citizenship Edn. Clearing House. Mem. ABA, Mo. Bar Assn., Bar Assn. of St. Louis, Selden Soc. Republican. Episcopalian. Clubs: Noonday, Racquet, St. Louis. Home: 507 Taylor Ave Kirkwood MO 63122 Office: Kohn Shands et al 411 N 7th St Saint Louis MO 63101

SHANE, PETER MILO, law educator, lawyer; b. Oceanside, N.Y., July 12, 1952; s. Albert and Ann (Semanoff) S.; m. Martha Elisabeth Chamallas, June 27, 1981; 1 child, Elisabeth Ann. A.B., Harvard U., 1974; J.D., Yale U., 1977. Bars: N.Y. 1978, U.S. Ct. Appeals (5th cir.) 1978, D.C. 1979, U.S. Ct. Appeals (8th cir.) 1983, U.S. Supreme Ct. 1984. Law clk. to judge U.S. Ct. Appeals (5th cir.), New Orleans, 1977-78; atty.-advisor Office of Legal Counsel, U.S. Dept. Justice, Washington, D.C., 1978-81; asst. gen. counsel Office of Mgmt. and Budget, Washington, D.C., 1981; assoc. prof. law U. Iowa, Iowa City, 1981-85, prof. law, 1985—; adj. lectr. Am. U., Washington, D.C., 1979-80; vis. prof. law Duke U., Durham, N.C., 1986; cons. U.S. Dept. Edn., Washington, D.C., 1980; cooperating atty. Iowa Civil Liberties Union, Des Moines, 1982—. Mem. Central Com. of Johnson County, Iowa Democratic Party, Iowa City, 1982—. Old Gold Summer fellow U. Iowa, 1981-84, fellow Mellon Found., Aspen Inst. Humanistic Studies, 1982. Mem. ABA (sect. adminstrv. law com. on govt. orgn. and separation of powers vice-chmn. 1983—). Jewish. Office: Univ Iowa Coll Law Iowa City IA 52242

SHANK, DAVID L., public relations executive; b. Muncie, Ind., Mar. 22, 1949; s. George Myers and Sidney Augusta (Shroyer) S.; m. Marilyn Louise Chance, June 6, 1971; children—Brendon, Andrew. B.S. in Edn., Ind. U., 1972. Acct. exec. Sta. KSSS, Colorado Springs, Colo., 1972-75, Henry & Henry Advertising, 1975-76; dir. pub. relations Garrison, Jasper, Rose, Indpls., 1976-79, BDP Co., 1979—; freelance writer, photographer. Bd. dirs. Central Ind. Better Bus. Bur., 1979—, Indpls. Symphony Orch.; mem. Wayne Twp. Schs. Human Rights Com. Recipient Community Relations award E. Central Pub. Relations Soc., 1978. Mem. Public Relations Soc. Am. (past pres. Hoosier chpt.), Indpls. Art League (dir.). Mem. Christian Ch. (Disciples of Christ).

SHANK, STEPHEN GEORGE, toy manufacturing company executive, lawyer; b. Tulsa, Dec. 6, 1943; s. Louis Warren and Lillian Margaret (Swift) S.; m. Judith Frances Thompson, July 17, 1966; children—Susan, Mary. B.A., U. Iowa, 1965; M.A. (Woodard Wilson fellow) Tufts U., 1966; J.D., Harvard U., 1972. Mem., Dorsey, Marquart, Windhorst, West & Halladay, Mpls., 1972-74; gen. counsel Tonka Corp., Hopkins, Minn., 1974-78, sec., 1974-79, pres., chief exec. officer, Spring Park, Minn., 1979—; mem. Dorsey, Windhorst, Hannaford, Whitney & Halladay, Mpls., 1978-79; asst. prof. William Mitchell Coll. Law, 1974-77. Bd. govs. Methodist Hosp. Served with U.S. Army, 1966-69. Mem. Toy Mfrs. Am. Roman Catholic.

SHANNON, DONALD SUTHERLIN, accounting educator; b. Tacoma Park, Md., Dec. 28, 1935; s. Raymond Corbett and Elnora Pettit (Sutherlin) S.; B.A., Duke, 1957; M.B.A., U. Chgo., 1964; Ph.D., U. N.C., 1972; m. Virginia Ann Lloyd, June 24, 1961 (div.); children—Stacey Eileen, Gail Allison, Michael Corbett; m. 2d, Kay Powe, Dec. 30, 1977; stepchildren—Christopher, Bonnie Bertelson. Mem. auditing staff Price Waterhouse & Co., N.Y.C., 1957-61; sr. accountant Price Waterhouse, Chgo., 1964-65; instr. Duke U., Durham, N.C., 1964-69; asst. prof. bus. adminstrn. U. Ky., Lexington, 1969-76, assoc. prof., 1976-81; assoc. prof. acct. Depaul U., Chgo., Ill., 1981—. Served with AUS, 1958-59, 61-62. Mem. Ky. Soc. C.P.A.s, Am. Inst. C.P.A.s, Western Finance Assn., Am. Finance Assn., Beta Gamma Sigma. Office: DePaul U Acct Dept 25 E Jackson Blvd Chicago IL 60604

SHANNON, STIRLEY ALTON, manufacturing executive; b. St. Louis, Feb. 15, 1935; s. Charles Henry and Gladys Pearl S.; A.B. in Elem. Edn., Harris U., St. Louis; M.A. in Elem. Adminstrn., Washington U., St. Louis; Ph.D. in Supervision and Gen. Adminstrn., St. Louis U., 1975; children—Susan Lee, Stacey Ann, Steven Michael. Prin. City of St. Louis, 1963-65, Mehlville Sch. Dist., St. Louis, 1965-71, dir. personnel, 1971-75, asst. supt., 1975-79, asso. supt., 1979-84; pres. Compu-Vision, Inc., St. Louis, 1984—. Mem. Am. Assn. Sch. Adminstrs., Am. Assn. Sch. Personnel Adminstrs., Phi Delta Kappa. Cert. tchr., prin., supt., Mo. Home: 5652 Chessmount Dr Saint Louis MO 63129 Office: 1835 Beltway Dr Saint Louis MO 63114

SHAPIRO, HAROLD DAVID, lawyer, educator; b. Chgo., Apr. 15, 1927; s. Charles Bernard and Celia Deborah (Nierenberg) S.; m. Beatrice Barbara Cahn, June 6, 1950; children—Matthew D., Michal Ann, Nicholas J. S.B., Northwestern U., 1949, J.D., 1952. Bar: Ill. 1952. Adminstrv. asst. Ill. Dept. Fin., 1952; assoc. Sonnenschein Carlin Nath & Rosenthal, Chgo., 1953-59, ptnr., 1959—; lectr. Northwestern U. Sch. Law, 1959-70, Edward A. Harriman lectr., 1970-83, Edward A. Harriman adj. prof., 1984—. Bd. dirs. Schwab Rehab. Ctr., Chgo., 1960-65, mem. exec. com., 1965—, pres., 1973-76; trustee, pres. Schwab Rehab. Ctr. Found., 1979—; v.p. bd. trustees Northwestern U. Sch. Law Alumni Assn., 1982, pres., 1983-84; trustee One-to-One Learning Ctrs., Winnetka, Ill., Music Ctr. of North Shore, Chgo.; trustee, mem. exec. com., sec. Jr. Achievement Chgo. Served with USN, 1945-46; PTO. Mem. ABA, Ill. State Bar Assn., Chgo. Bar Assn., Chgo. Council Lawyers, Legal Club Chgo. (exec. com., pres.), Law Club Chgo., Order of Coif. Democrat. Jewish. Clubs: Standard, Cliff Dwellers, Metropolitan (Chgo.); Lake Shore (Glencoe, Ill.); Princeton of N.Y. Home: 34 Linden Ave Wilmette IL 60091 Office: 8000 Sears Tower Chicago IL 60606

SHAPIRO, JOAN ISABELLE, laboratory administrator, nurse; b. Fulton, Ill., Aug. 26, 1943; d. Macy James and Frieda Lockhart; m. Ivan Lee Shapiro, Dec. 28, 1968; children—Audrey, Michael. R.N., Peoria Methodist Sch. Nursing, Ill., 1964. Nurse, Grant Hosp., Columbus, Ohio, 1975-76; nurse Cardiac Thoracic and Vascular Surgeons Ltd., Geneva, Ill., 1977—, mgr. non-invasive lab., 1979—. Mem. Soc. Non-invasive Technologists, Kane County Med. Soc. Aux. (pres. 1983-84, adviser, 1984-85). Lutheran. Office: Cardiac Thoracic and Vascular Surgeons Ltd 123 South St PO Box 564 Suite 100 Geneva IL 60134

SHAPIRO, MAYNARD IRWIN, physician, educator; b. Chgo., Dec. 18, 1914; B.S., U. Ill., 1937, C.M., 1939, M.D., 1940; 1 dau., Juli Ann. Intern, Mt. Sinai Hosp., Chgo., 1939-40, resident, 1940-41; practice medicine specializing in family practice, Chgo., 1946—; active staff dept. family practice Jackson Park Hosp., dir. dept. phys. medicine and rehab., pres. med. staff, 1975-77, also v.p. acad. affairs; past clin. asst. surgery, Mt. Sinai Hosp.; prof. family medicine Chgo. Med. Sch. Past bd. dirs. Family Health Found. Am.; past pres., past bd. dirs. Inst. Sex Edn.; past mem. regional adv. group Ill. Regional Med. Program; past chmn. profl. adv. council Nat. Easter Seal Soc.; bd. dirs. Citizens Alliance for VD Awareness, Jackson Park Hosp. Found. Fellow Am Occupational Med. Assn., Acad. Psychosomatic Medicine, Am. Geriatrics Soc., Central States Soc. Indsl. Medicine and Surgery, Inst. Medicine Chgo.; mem. AMA (ho. of dels.), Ill. (ho. of dels.), Chgo. (council) med. socs., Chgo. Found. Med. Care (pres.), Am. Acad. Family Physicians (pres. 1968-69), Ill. Acad. Family Physicians (past pres.) Pan Am. Med. Assn., Am. Congress Rehab. Medicine, Assn. Hosp. Med. Edn., Am. Acad. Med. Adminstrs., Assn. Am. Med. Colls., Soc. Tchrs. Family Medicine, Ill. Soc. Phys. Medicine and Rehab., Chgo. Soc. Phys. Medicine and Rehab., Chgo. Soc. Indsl. Medicine and Surgery (past pres.), Nat. Med. Vets. Soc. Home: 1700 E 56 St #3609 Chicago IL 60637 Office: 7531 Stony Island Ave Chicago IL 60649

SHAPIRO, ROBERT DONALD, management consultant; b. Milw., Sept. 11, 1942; s. Leonard Samuel and Adeline Ruth (Arnovitz) S.; B.S. with honors, U. Wis., 1964; m. Karen Jean Hubert, Apr. 14, 1979; children—Lee Evan, Stacy Ellen, Jenifer Erin, Tracy Elizabeth, Jeffrey Eric. Cons. actuary Milliman & Robertson, Inc., Milw., 1965-80; dir. Life Ins. Cons., TPF&C, Milw., 1980—. C.L.U. Fellow Soc. Actuaries, Conf. Actuaries in Public Practice; mem. Am. Acad. Actuaries. Contbr. articles to profl. lit. Home: 4923 N Oakland Ave Milwaukee WI 53217 Office: 310 W Wisconsin Ave Suite 1104 Milwaukee WI 53203

SHAPIRO, STEVEN ROBERT, osteopathic physician, hospital executive; b. N.Y.C., Oct. 6, 1942; s. Mack and Sylvia (Warshaw) S.; m. Dawn Michelle Vermette, Oct. 19, 1980; children—Jacqueline, Robyn, Marnie, David. B.S., U. Mich.-Ann Arbor, 1965; D.O., Coll. Osteo. Medicine and Surgery, Des Moines, 1969. Intern, Flint (Mich.) Osteo. Hosp., 1969-70; practice osteo. medicine, Flint, 1970—; mem. Flint Osteo. Hosp., 1970—, chmn. dept. gen. practice, 1976-78, vice chief of staff, 1978-82, chief, 1982-84, v.p. for med. affairs, 1984—; assoc. prof. family medicine Mich. State U. Mem. Am. Osteo. Assn., Mich. Assn. Osteo. Physicians and Surgeons, Am. Coll. Gen. Practitioners, Osteo. Gen. Practitioners Mich. Jewish. Office: G-3422 Flushing Rd Flint MI 48504

SHARMA, PIYARE LAL, electrical engineering educator, researcher; b. Srinagar, Kashmir, India, Apr. 17, 1945; s. Nand Lal and Yachawati S.; m. Sarojini Handoo, Aug. 9, 1969; children—Rajesh, Reetu. B.E.E., J and K U., India, 1967; M.Tech. in Elec. Engring., Indian Inst. Tech., New Delhi, 1973; Ph.D.E.E., U. Akron, 1982. Assoc. lectr. elec. engring. Regional Engring. Coll., India, 1967-71, lectr., 1973-78; asst. prof. elec. engring. U. Detroit, 1982—; researcher. Mem. IEEE, Sigma Xi. Hindu. Home: 24358 Rensselaer St Oak Park MI 48237 Office: Electrical Engineering University of Detroit Detroit MI 48221

SHARP, ALLEN, See *Who's Who in America*, 43rd edition.

SHARP, CARL EDWIN, podiatrist; b. Findlay, Ohio, Aug. 15, 1942; s. Roscoe William and Donna Delores (Schade) S.; student Bowling Green State U., 1960-62; B.S. in Anatomy, Ohio State U., 1965, B.S. in Pharmacy, 1970; D.P.M., Ohio Coll. Podiatric Medicine, 1975; m. Kathleen Blanche O'Connell, Dec. 28, 1968; children—Geoffrey Alan, Ryan Devon, Cameron Grannon. Med. and surg. resident Foot Clinic, Youngstown, Ohio, 1975-76; pvt. practice podiatric medicine, Worthington, Ohio, 1976—; mem. surg. staff Doctors Hosp., Columbus, Ohio, 1980-85; assoc. staff Riverside Meth. Hosp.; cons. Friendship Village Dublin/Columbus, Mayfair, Columbus Colony, Wesley Glen. Trustee Central Ohio Diabetes Assn., chmn. constitution com. Mem. Am. Podiatry Assn., Am. Acad. Podiatric Sports Medicine, Am. Pharm. Assn., Ohio Podiatry Assn. (chmn. public edn. and info. com. 1979-81, pres. central acad. 1980-81), Alpha Epsilon Delta. Republican. Clubs: Sawmill Athletic, Arlington Court, Breakfast Sertoma. Home: 2392 Sovron Ct Dublin OH 43017 Office: 37 E Wilson Bridge Rd Worthington OH 43085

SHARP, HOMER GLEN, dept. store exec.; b. Cleve., July 3, 1927; s. Homer David and Kathleen (Hawkins) S.; diploma Parsons Sch. Design, 1945; student Am. Acad. Art, 1947; m. JoAnn Harbour, Aug. 29, 1947; children—David Lee, Terry Glen. Trimmer window display Marshall Field & Co., Chgo., 1946-55, mgr. interior display, 1955-68, display dir., 1968-70, store design and display dir., 1970—, v.p. design and display div., 1971—. Served with USMCR, 1945-46. Recipient Nat. Assn. Display Industries award outstanding achievements, 1973. Mem. Chgo. Assn. Commerce and Industry, Chgo. Council Fgn. Relations, Chgo. Athletic Assn., Nat. Retail Mchts. Assn. (visual merchandising com.), Western Assn. Visual Merchandising (retail adv. com.). Methodist (chmn. pastor parish relations com.). Office: Marshall Field & Co 111 N State St Chicago IL 60690

SHARP, MARY LUCILLE PEDEN, educational administrator; b. Kansas City, Mo., May 29, 1929; d. Clarence Allen and Laura Winifred (Henley) Peden; B.S., Missouri Valley Coll., 1950; M.Ed., Central Mo. State U., 1970; m. Richard Calvin Sharp, June 23, 1951; children—Richard Calvin, Robert Parker, Allen Russell Howland. Classroom tchr., Kans., Mo. and Wash., 1950-69; reading specialist Kansas City (Mo.) Public Schs., 1969-74, adminstr. remedial reading program, 1974-76, cons. K-6 grades, 1976-77, instr. facilitator, 1977-80, prin. elem. schs., 1980—; speaker in field. Active local Boy Scouts Am., 1960-68, PTA, 1950—. Mem. Internat. Reading Assn. (treas. Kansas City chpt. 1975), Nat. Assn. Elem. Sch. Prins., Mo. Assn. Elem. Sch. Prins., Kansas City Assn. Elem. Sch. Prins. (pres. 1984-85), Assn. Supervision and Curriculum Devel., Kansas City Sch. Adminstrs. Assn. (rec. sec. 1983-84), Phi Delta Kappa, Delta Kappa Gamma (editor 1978-80, chmn. chpt. profl. affairs com. 1980-82, chmn. chpt. selective recruitment 1982-84). Episcopalian.

SHARPE, GARY LEWIS, medical equipment company executive; b. Circleville, Ohio, Feb. 19, 1947; s. Harold Eugene and Erma Marie (Lathouse) S.; m. Connie Mae Hahn, Nov. 27, 1971; children—Bethany Lynn, Kyle Lewis. B.A., Ohio State U., 1970; M.B.A., Xavier U., Cin., 1978. With Philips Roxane Labs., Inc. subs. N.Am. Philips, Columbus, Ohio, 1970-78, dir. govt. and contract sales, 1971-78; v.p., treas. Health Care Logistics, Inc., Circleville, Ohio, 1978-82 pres., treas. 1983—; hosp. cons.; sec. Nat. VA Pharm. Adv. Council, 1979-81. Chmn., pres., bd. dirs. Brown Meml. Nursing Home, Circleville; pres. Bethel Lutheran Ch., Grove City, Ohio, 1978-79. Served to 1st lt. Med. Service Corps, U.S. Army, 1967-68. Mem. Am. Hosp. Assn., Am. Soc. Hosp. Pharmacists. Republican. Compiler, editor: Pharmacy Management Systems, 1977; inventor, designer new lines of hosp. carts, cabinets, and spl. packaging. Office: PO Box 25 Circleville OH 43113

SHARPE, MARJORIE JOHNSTON, association executive; b. Toronto, Ont., Can.; came to U.S., 1968; d. Charles Franklin and Dorice Phoebe (Brown) Johnston; m. Alex B. Sharpe, July 27, 1968; 1 son, Gordon Franklin Cheesbrough. B.A., U. Toronto, 1951; postgrad. U. Toronto, York U., Northwestern U. Tchr., North York Bd. Edn., Toronto, 1959-68; pres. Marjorie J. Sharpe & Assocs., Barrington, Ill., 1977-81; exec. dir. Am. Dental Hygienists Assn., Chgo., 1981-84; ad hoc com. voluntarism nat. task force Kellogg Found. Mem. Nat. Assembly, Nat. Voluntary Health and Social Welfare Orgns. for Juvenile Justice Collaboration; bd. dirs. Vis. Nurse Assn., 1979-82, Taylor Inst., 1979-82, Hull House Assn., 1979-82. Recipient commendation for Landmark Commn., City of Woodstock. Mem. Acad. Mgmt., Am. Soc. Assn. Execs., Chgo. Soc. Assn. Execs., Indsl. Relations Research Assn. Club: Lake Barrington Shores Golf. Home: 224 Timber Ridge LBS Barrington IL 60010 Office: 444 N Michigan Ave Suite 3400 Chicago IL 60611

SHARPE, MELVIN LEE, JR., public relations educator, consultant; b. Oklahoma City, Apr. 9, 1936; s. Melvin L. and Dorothy Jean (Shipman) S. B.S., Okla. State U., 1958, M.S., 1962; Ed.D., U. Fla., 1973. Info. specialist U.S. Dept. Agr. Mktg. Info. Service, Dallas, 1953; reporter Guthrie (Okla.) Daily Leader, 1960; publs. editor Okla. State U. Info. Services, Stillwater, 1961-66; news editor Inst. Food and Agrl. Scis., U. Fla., Gainesville, 1962-64, asst. to pres., 1964-69, asst. to dir. Inst. Higher Edn., 1970-73; asst. to chancellor, assoc. dir. personnel and faculty relations State Univ. System of Fla., Tallahassee, 1974-76; asst. prof. journalism, coordinator pub. relations sequence U. Tex., Austin, 1976-81; assoc. prof. journalism, coordinator pub. relations sequence Ball State U., Muncie, Ind., 1981—. Bd. dirs. Muncie Area ARC, 1982—; mem. Muncie Clean City Adv. Com., 1981. Served with U.S. Army, 1958-60. Kellogg fellow, 1973; Alcoa Faculty fellow, 1980; recipient spl. recognition for contbns. to Dept. of Journalism, U. Tex., 1981; award for contbn. to student govt. U. Fla. Faculty and Adminstrn., 1967. Mem. Pub. Relations Soc. Am. (accredited, Hoosier, Indpls. and NE Ind. chpts., Outstanding Achievement in Teaching Pub. Relations award Austin chpt. 1981, chmn. continuing edn. bd. 1985—, newsletter editor educators' sect. 1985—, bd. dirs. educators sect. 1985—), Tex. Pub. Relations Assn., Assn. Educators in Journalism and Mass Communications, Internat. Pub. Relations Assn., Muncie-Delaware County C. of C. (pub. relations com. 1981—). Democrat. Methodist. Author: (with Sam Black) Practical Public Relations, 1983; edn. editor IPRA Rev., 1983—; mem. editorial rev. com. Pub. Relations Rev., 1983—; contbr. articles to profl. jours. Home: 1806 N Alden Rd Muncie IN 47304 Office: Dept of Journalism Ball State U Muncie IN 47306

SHARTLE, STANLEY MUSGRAVE, civil engineering executive, land surveyor; b. Brazil, Ind., Sept. 27, 1922; s. Arthur Tinder and Mildred C. (Musgrave) S.; m. Anna Lee Mantle, Apr. 7, 1948 (div. 1980); 1 child, Randy; m. Maralyn Delores Leibensperger, Feb. 14, 1982. Student Purdue U., 1947-50. Registered profl. engr., Ind. Dep. county surveyor Hendricks County (Ind.), Danville, 1944-50, county engr., surveyor, 1950-54, county hwy. engr., 1975-77; staff engr. Ind. Toll Rd. Commn., Indpls., 1954-61; chief right of way engring. Ind. State Hwy. Commn., Indpls., 1961-75; owner, civil engr. Shartle Engring., Stilesville, Ind., 1977—; right of way engring. cons. Gannett Fleming Transp. Engrs., Inc., Indpls., 1983—. Author: Right of Way Engineering Manual, 1975; Musgrave Family History, 1961; Shartle Genealogy, 1955. Recipient Outstanding Contbn. award Hendricks County Soil and Water Conservation Dist., 1976. Mem. Am. Congress Surveying and Mapping (life), Nat. Soc. Profl. Surveyors, Ind. Soc. Profl. Land Surveyors (charter, bd. dirs. 1979), Nat. Geneal. Soc. (Quarter Century club), Republican. Avocations: astronomy, genealogy, geodesy. Home and Office: Shartle Engring Rural Route 1 Box 33 Stilesville IN 46180

SHAW, CLAYTON THOMAS, physician, air force officer; b. Brockton, Mass., Aug. 24, 1941; s. Arthur Wesley and Evelyn Victoria (Meter) S.; m. Janice Elaine Paulding, Aug. 10, 1963; children—Jeffrey Wayne, Kristin Beth. B.S., Mass. Coll. Pharmacy, 1963, M.S., 1965; M.A. in Sociology, U. Mass., 1969, M.A. in Pub. Health, 1967, M.A.T. in Edn., 1971; D.O., Coll. Osteo. Medicine, 1974; B.A. in Bus., Bellevue Coll., 1984. Diplomate Am. Bd. Family Practice, Am. Bd. Osteo. Bd. Ob-Gyn. Surgery. Intern, Malcolm Grow Med. Ctr., Washington, 1974-75, resident in family practice, 1975-77, fellow in family practice, 1977-78; resident in ob-gyn. Tripler Army Med. Ctr., Honolulu, 1980-82; commd. officer U.S. Air Force, 1974, advanced through grades to lt. col., 1984; served Andrews AFB, Washington, 1974-78, W. Ger., 1978-79, Honolulu, 1980-82; chief dept. ob-gyn U.S. Air Force Hosp., Omaha, 1982—; asst. prof. family practice Creighton U., Omaha, 1982—, instr. ob-gyn, 1982—. Contbr. articles to med. jours. Mem. Am. Osteo. Assn., Am. Acad. Family Practice, Am. Coll. Osteo. Ob-Gyn. Republican. Baptist. Lodge: Mason. Avocation: golf. Home: 1801 Tobin Trail Garland TX 75043 Office: USAF Hosp Offutt AFB Omaha NE 68113

SHAW, CLIFFORD RAY, chemical corporation executive; b. Hallsville, Tex., Jan. 25, 1956; s. Roosevelt and Ruby Lee (Boyd) S.; m. Glynda Kathleen Mills, June 21, 1980; 1 dau., Katharyn Lynn. B.S. in Elec. Engring., Prairie View A&M U., 1980. Process engr. E.I. DuPont de Nemours & Co., Inc., Fort Madison, Iowa, 1981-83, 1st line supr., 1983—. Mem. IEEE, NAACP. Democrat. Baptist. Office: E I DuPont de Nemours & Co Inc 35th St and Ave H Fort Madison IA

SHAW, DANNY WAYNE, educator; b. Detroit, Jan. 18, 1947; s. George L. and Nina Margarete (Smith) S.; m. 2d Nancy Rivard Shaw, Feb. 29, 1980; 1 dau., Christina Marie. B.S., Wayne State U., 1973, M.Mus., 1975, Ed.S., 1979, Ph.D., 1982. Tchr. Dearborn Pub. Schs. (Mich.), 1973-74, Lincoln Park (Mich.), Schs. 1974—; pres. System Support Services, Lincoln Park, 1982—; research asst. Wayne State U., 1980-81, now adj. faculty; adj. faculty Marygrove Coll., Detroit, 1984. Mem. music adv. panel Mich. Council Arts, 1976-84. Served with USMC, 1965-68; Vietnam. Decorated Vietnam Service medal, Nat. Def. Service medal Presdl. Unit citation, Campaign medal Republic of Vietnam; recipient cert. for outstanding acad. achievement Mich. Ho. Reps., 1975. Mem. NEA, Am. Mgmt. Assn., Wayne State U. Alumni Assn., Phi Delta Kappa. Lodge: Masons. Home: 1999 Church Pl Trenton MI 48183

SHAW, DAVID LAWRENCE, lawyer; b. Bklyn., Feb. 7, 1943; s. Arthur Morris and Ray (Epstein) S.; m. Myrna Ann Hurwitz, June 21, 1964; children—Brian Lowell, Leslie Beth. A.B. with distinction, U. Mich., 1963, J.D. with distinction, 1966. Bar: Ill. 1966. Assoc., Mayer, Brown & Platt, Chgo., 1966-70; v.p. counsel Kaufman & Broad Homes, Chgo., 1970-72; ptnr. Wexler, Siegel & Shaw Ltd., Chgo., 1972-83, Neiman & Grais, Chgo., 1983—. Bd. dirs. Jewish United Fund, Chgo., 1977-84, Jewish Fedn., 1977-84; mem. exec. com. Leadership Devel. Com. Council Jewish Fedns., N.Y.C., 1978-82; vice-chmn. young leadership cabinet United Jewish Appeal, N.Y.C., 1977-82, mem. nat. campaign cabinet, 1984—. Recipient Young Leadership award Jewish Fedn. Met. Chgo., 1977; Service award Young Leadership Cabinet, United Jewish Appeal, 1981. Mem. ABA, Ill. Bar Assn., Chgo. Bar Assn., Chgo. Council Lawyers. Jewish. Club: Briarwood Country (Deerfield, Ill.).

SHAW, EDWARD JAMES, physician; b. N.Y.C., Oct. 22, 1914; s. Samuel Johnson and Adele (Herndon) S.; B.A., Columbia U., 1934, M.D., Yale U., 1937; m. Huguette Adele Herman, Apr. 19, 1965; children—Edward James, Emily K., Barbara A. Intern Bellevue Hosp., N.Y.C., 1937-38, resident surgery, 1938-39; resident surgery N.Y. Post Grad. Sch. and Hosp., N.Y.C., 1939-41; chief surg. services U.S. Army Sta. Hosp., Plattsburg Barracks, N.Y., 1941-42, chief gen. surg. sect. 69th Sta. Hosp., North Africa, 1942-44, comdg. officer and chief surgeon 16th Sta. Hosp., Wiesbaden, Ger., 1945-46; chief resident surgeon New Rochelle (N.Y.) Hosp., 1946-47; practice medicine specializing in gen. surgery, New Rochelle, 1947-52; chief resident surgery Lawrence and Meml. Hosp., New London, Conn., 1952-53; chief resident and surgery resident Doctors Hosp., N.Y.C., 1953-54, attending surgeon, 1954-65; practice medicine specializing in gen. surgery, N.Y.C., 1954-65, St. Louis, 1965-67; chief surgeon Sutter Clinic, St. Louis, 1967-71; practice medicine specializing in surgery and occupational medicine, St. Louis, 1971—; mem. surg. staffs Luth. Hosp., St. Louis, Incarnate Word Hosp., St. Louis, Alexian Bros. Hosp., St. Louis, St. Elizabeth Hosp., Granite City; asst. clin. prof. N.Y. Med. Coll., N.Y.C., 1954-65; asst. attending surgeon Flower Fifth Ave. Hosp., N.Y.C., 1954-65; assoc. attending surgeon Met. and Bird S. Coler hosps., N.Y.C., 1954-65; pres. Shaw Surg. Clinic, St. Louis and Granite City, 1975-85. Served with AUS, 1941-44, U.S. Army, 1944-46. Diplomate Am. Bd. Surgery, Am. Bd. Abdominal Surgery. Fellow ACS, Southwestern Surg. Congress, Internat. Coll. Surgeons, St. Louis Soc. Colon and Rectal Surgeons, N.Y. Acad. Medicine; mem. Am. Soc. Colon and Rectal Surgeons, Am. Occupational Med. Assn., Am. Geriatrics Soc., Central States Soc. Occupational Medicine, Aerospace Med. Assn., Pan Am. Med. Assn., St. Louis Met. Med. Assn. (del. to Mo. Med. Assn. 1978-83), Mo. Med. Assn., AMA, Mo. Surg. Soc., Assn. Mil. Surgeons U.S., N.Y. Acad. Gastroenterology, Club: Yale of St. Louis. Home: 3105 Longfellow Blvd Saint Louis MO 63104 Office: Barnes Sutter Healthcare 819 Locust St Saint Louis MO 63101

SHAW, JACK PARKS, computer software company executive, consultant; b. Lockhart, Tex., Mar. 8, 1941; s. Millard and Janie (Parks) S.; m. Merrillyn Griffith, Aug. 24, 1963; children—Myra, Mark. Cons. System Devel. Corp., Milw., 1978-80; pres. Diamond Software, Inc., Cedarburg, Wis., 1980—. Mem. Assn. Computing Machinery, Am. Mensa. Office: Diamond Software Inc W73 N726 Locust Ave Cedarburg WI 53012

SHAW, JOHN STEWART, superintendent schools; b. Oklahoma City, Feb. 3, 1931; s. Merril Henry and Orda Luella (Stewart) S.; m. Betty Ann Hercheck, Jan. 1, 1953; children—John Randall, Terri Lynn, Kimberley Ann. B.S., Central State Coll., 1953; M.Ed., U. Okla., 1957, Ed.D., 1964. Supt. Goodwell Pub. Schs., Okla., 1960-62; adminstrv. asst. U. Okla., Norman, 1962-64; asst. prof. lab. sch. Pittsburg State U., Kans., 1964-75; supt. Unified Sch. Dist. 455, Cuba, Kans., 1975-80, Unified Sch. Dist. 395, LaCrosse, Kans., 1980-83; supt., prin. Unified Sch. Dist. 280, Morland, Kans., 1983—; pres. N. Central Spl. Edn. Coop., Concordia, Kans., 1976-78; v.p. Sch. for Quality Edn., Rozel, Kans., 1977—. Author: Readings for Beginning Teacher, 1970. Scoutmaster Coronado council Boy Scouts Am., 1983, staff mem. Nat. Camp Sch., 1975, staff mem. wood badge, 1983, staff mem. nat. jamboree, 1977, scouter of the month, 1972, golden sun award, 1974, vigil honor, 1980, dist. award of merit, 1985. Served with USNR, 1947-60. Mem. Am. Assn. Sch. Adminstrs., United Sch. Adminstr., Kans. Assn. Sch. Adminstrs. (com. mem. 1984-85), Phi Delta Kappa (pres. 1962-63), Kappa Delta Pi. Democrat. Methodist. Lodge: Lions, Masons. Avocations: golf; Indian lore; music; camping. Home: Box 403 Morland KS 67650 Office: Unified Sch Dist 280 Box 226 Morland KS 67650

SHAW, JUDITH MARILYN, hospital association executive; b. Newark, Aug. 19, 1944; d. Louis H. and Sara C. (Wilson) Kaye; m. John M. Shaw, Sept. 5, 1965; children—Michael, Steven. B.A., Smith Coll., 1966. Pub. relations dir. ARC Blood Program, Phila., 1974-76; mgr. pub. relations services Am. Hosp. Assn., Chgo., 1978-80, pub. relations dir., 1980—. Named Communicator of Yr., Internat. Assn. Bus. Communicators, Chgo., 1982. Mem. Pub. Relations Soc. Am., Publicity Club of Chgo. Office: Am Hosp Assn 840 N Lake Shore Dr Chicago IL 60611

SHAW, PAUL CHARLES, III, psychotherapist, educator; b. Charleston, W.Va., Mar. 16, 1938; s. Paul Charles and Mildred Gail (Ray) S.; m. Nancy Mathias, June 3, 1981; 1 son, Patrick. B.A., Morris Harvey Coll., 1962; M.A., Mich. State U., 1964; Ph.D., Pa. State U., 1973. Research dir. U. Pitts., 1970-73; assoc. prof., dir. Wright State U., Dayton, Ohio, 1973-83; psychotherapist Good Samaritan Hosp. and Health Ctr., Dayton, 1982—. Bd. dirs. Daymont West Community Mental Health Ctr., 1978; mem. City of Trotwood Action Commn., 1975-79. Trainee NIH, 1966. Mem. Am. Psychol. Assn., Am. Soc. Clin. Hypnosis, Am. Assn. Sex Educators, Counselors and Therapists. Contbr. articles to profl. jours. Home: 305 W Sherry Dr Trotwood OH 45426 Office: Good Samaritan Hospital Dayton OH 45406

SHAW, ROBERT EUGENE, minister, administrator; b. Havre, Mt., Apr. 8, 1933; s. Harold Alvin and Lillian Martha (Kruse) S.; m. Marilyn Grace Smit, June 14, 1957; children—Rebecca Jean, Ann Elizabeth, Mark David, Peter Robert. B.A., Sioux Falls Coll., 1955; M.Div., Am. Baptist. Sem. of West, 1958; D.D. (hon.), Ottawa U., 1976, Judson Coll., 1984. Ordained to ministry Am. Bapt. Chs. U.S.A., 1958; pastor First Bapt. Ch., Webster City, Ia., 1958-63, Community Bapt. Ch., Topeka, Kans., 1963-68; sr. pastor Prairie Bapt. Ch., Prairie Village, Kans., 1968-78; pres. Ottawa U, Kans., 1978-83; exec. minister Am. Bapt. Chs. Mich., East Lansing, 1983—; mem. gen. bd. Am. Bapt. Chs. U.S.A., Valley Forge, Pa., 1972-80, nat. v.p., 1978-80; nat. v.p. Am. Bapt. Minister Council, Valley Forge, 1969-72, nat. pres., 1972-75; trustee Northern Bapt. Theol. Sem., Lombard, Ill., 1983—; mem. nat. exec. com. Am. Bapt. Adminstrs. Colls. and Univs., 1980-82; bd. dirs. Kans. Ind. Colls. Assn., 1980-82. Trustee Kalamazoo Coll., Mich., 1983—, Judson Coll, Elgin, Ill., 1983—; dir. Webster City C. of C., 1961-62, Ottawa C. of C., 1980-82. Office: Am Baptist Chs of Michigan 4610 S Hagadorn Rd East Lansing MI 48823

SHAW, RUSSELL CLYDE, lawyer; b. Cleve., Mar. 19, 1940; s. Clyde Leland and Ruth Arminta (Williams) S.; B.S., Ohio State U., 1962; J.D., Ohio State U., 1965; m. Jane Ann Mohler, Feb. 15, 1969; children—Christopher Scott, Robin Nicole, Curtis Russell. Admitted to Ohio bar, 1965, U.S. Supreme Ct. bar, 1968; asso. mem. firm Thompson, Hine & Flory, Cleve., 1965, 69-74, partner, 1974—. Mem. Geauga United Way Services Council, 1980—, officer, 1982—, chmn. (chief vol. officer), 1984—; trustee United Way Services of Cleve., 1983—. Served to capt. AUS, 1965-69. Mem. ABA, Fed. Bar Assn., Ohio Bar Assn., Nat. Lawyers Club, Old English Sheepdog Club Am. (nat. officer 1972-74), Fedn. Ohio Dog Clubs (pres. 1978-82), Sugarbush Kennel Club (pres. 1975-78, 81—), Midwest Pension Conf., Delta Sigma Phi (nat. officer 1975—, nat. officer Found. 1978—, trustee Found. 1983—). Club: President's (Ohio State U.) Office: 1100 National City Bank Bldg Cleveland OH 44114

SHAW, WILBURN WALTER, computer programmer/analyst; b. Los Angeles, Nov. 5, 1946; s. James Antony Shaw and Edna Charlotte (Bowles) Shaw Shambly; m. Sandra Stewart, July 1, 1981. B.S. in Chemistry, Ky. State U., 1978; A.S. in Data Processing, Washington U., St. Louis, 1981; A.A. in Bus. Adminstrn., St. Louis Community Coll., 1984. Chem. operator Swift Chem. Co., Chesapeak, Va., 1973-75; quality control analyst Champale Brewery, Norfolk, Va., 1975-76; programmer Human Resources, Frankfort, Ky., 1978, McDonnall Douglas, St. Louis, 1978-80; programmer/analyst Jewish Hosp. St. Louis, 1980—. Served with USN, 1965-67. Ashland Oil Co. minorities scholar, 1976. Home: 2134 Empire Ct Saint Louis MO 63136 Office: Jewish Hosp Saint Louis 216 Kings Hwy Blvd Saint Louis MO 63107

SHAY, KENNETH GRANT, financial executive; b. Oak Park, Ill., Sept. 25, 1942; s. Kenneth John and Anne Marie (Caruso) S.; m. Elizabeth Anne Smith, June 26, 1971; children—Jonathan, Sarah, Carrie. B.A., U. Ill., 1965, M.S., 1966. Analyst Lincoln Nat. Bank, Chgo., 1968-72; salesman Loeb Rhoades, Chgo., 1972-77; v.p. Blyth Eastman Dillon, Chgo., 1977, Paine Webber, Chgo., 1979-81, Dean Witter Reynolds, Inc., Chgo., 1981-85, Morgan Stanley, Chgo., 1985—. Nominating com. Mid. North Assn., Chgo. Mem. Chartered Fin. Analyst, Chgo. Analysts Soc. (bd. dirs. 1983-86), Phi Beta Kappa. Roman Catholic. Clubs: Chgo. Athletic, River, Midtown. Home: 2130 Cleveland St Chicago IL 60614 Office: Morgan Stanley 115 S La Salle St Chicago IL 60603

SHEA, DENNIS GERARD, data processing executive; b. Portland, Maine, July 22, 1946; s. William G. and Hylda (Payne) S.; m. Jacque T. Stok, Oct. 18, 1969; children—Brian, Adam, Jason, Kevin. B.S. in Computer Sci. and Supervision, Purdue U., 1976. Data processing mgr. Welsh Bros. Hammond, Ind., 1968-76; AJP Foods, Calumet City, Ill., 1976-82; project mgr. Sealy Inc., Chgo., 1982—. Served with USAF, 1964-68. Home: 417 Kristina Bourbonnais IL 60914 Office: Sealy Inc 525 W Monroe St 21st Fl Chicago IL 60606

SHEA, DONNA MIKELS, public relations company executive; b. Marion, Ind., Sept. 27, 1924; d. Ora Elmer and Susan (Dinius) Mikels; m. Cortland William Shea, Apr. 27, 1951; children—Kevin, Kelly. Student Ind. U.-Butler. Reporter Leader-Tribune, Marion, 1941-45; stringer UPI, Ind. and Midwest, 1941-45; asst. city editor, reporter Indpls. Times, 1945-54; writer various syndicated publs., 1945-54; pub. relations dir. Community Service Council, Indpls., 1956—; pres. Donna M. Shea, Inc., pub. relations firm, Indpls., 1979—; cons. Indpls. Marriott; cons. communications/pub. relations field to various agys., seminars and courses; charter com. mem., adminstr. ann. CASPER awards to central Ind. news media, community service agys., 1953—; creator, charter com. mem. ABACUS awards, Indpls., 1983—. Civic worker, 1956—; former mem. bd. Family Service Assn.; Subcom. co-chmn. Nat. Sports Festival Opening Ceremony, 1981; com. mem. Internat. Conf. on Cities, 1973. Recipient numerous state, regional, nat. journalism awards, 1940's, 50's; Big Story award, 1956; hon. CASPER award, Indpls. Mayor's proclamation Donna Mikels Shea Day, 1979; Nat. Pub. Relations award Marriott Hotels, 1977. Mem. Pub. Relations Soc. Am., Alliance to Vis. Nurse Home Health

Care Assn. (charter). Episcopalian. Clubs: Indpls. Press (dir.), Skyline, Players, Lambs (Indpls.) Editor, pub. News Media Handbook, 12th edit., 1985. Home: 245 E Westfield Blvd Indianapolis IN 46220 Office: 1828 N Meridian St Indianapolis IN 46202

SHEA, ELAINE EVANS, civic association executive; b. Ithaca, N.Y., Aug. 1, 1935; d. William Arthur and Genevieve (Covert) Evans; A.A., Stephens Coll., 1955; m. Michael Henry Shea, June 28, 1956; children—Elizabeth Ann, Linda Evans, William Michael. Writer, film previewer Sta. KWTV, Oklahoma City, 1955-56; exec. dir. Save the Tallgrass Prairie, Inc., Shawnee Mission, Kans., 1974—; dir. Grassland Heritage Found. Bd. dirs. Kans. Natural Resource Council; registered lobbyist; pres. Porter Sch. PTA, 1969; leader Girl Scouts; tchr. Sunday Sch., shepherd deacon Village United Presbyn. Ch.; tract chmn. Am. Cancer Soc., 1982; mem. Gov.'s Adv. Commn. Environment, 1983; U.S. del. Internat. Conf. Future Nat. Parks, W.Ger., 1983. Recipient Environ. Quality award EPA, 1978. Clubs: Stephens Coll. Dinner (pres. 1966), Prairie Planters Garden (pres. 1972), Kansas City Country. Editor: Tallgrass Prairie News, 1974—. Home: 6025 Cherokee Dr Shawnee Mission KS 66205 Office: 4101 W 54th Terr Shawnee Mission KS 66205

SHEARER, JUANITA MITCHELL, bookstore executive; b. Chgo., Sept. 8, 1921; d. George Harold and Helen Elliott (Coleman) Mitchell; 1 child, Carolyn Kay. Student pub. schs., Downers Grove, Ill. Sec., Wire operator Wayne Hummer & Co., 1941-43; asst. buyer coats and suits Mandel Bros., Chgo., 1943-49; resident buyer Allied Stores, 1953-56; corr. Commerce Clearing House, 1957-58; owner, mgr. Renaissance Books, Lake Forest Ill., 1982—. Mem. Nat. Assn. Female Execs. Home: 1491 Everett Rd Lake Forest IL 60045 Office: Renaissance Books 1491 Everett Rd Lake Forest IL

SHEARER, LESLIE MARTIN, air freight company executive; b. Columbus, Ohio, Jan. 18, 1941; s. Ernest Franklin and Anna (Luise) S.; m. Renee Easton, Mar. 21, 1970 (div.); m. 2d Sally Jean Banning, Sept. 3, 1978; children—Bradley, Martin. B.A. in Polit. Sci., W.Va. U., 1963; postgrad. Johann Goethe U., Frankfurt, W.Ger., 1963-65, Am. Inst. Fgn. Trade, Glendale, Ariz., 1965-66. Internat. salesman Exportadora of Ill., Chgo., 1968-69; internat. customer service agt. Emery Air Freight, Chgo., 1969-70; sales rep. Seaboard World Airlines, Chgo., 1970-72; v.p. internat. sales Bor Air Freight, Chgo., 1972-73; internat. freight salesman Service By Air, Elk Grove, Ill., 1973-75; internat. exec. Air-Line AirFreight Ltd., Bensenville, Ill., 1975—. Hon. commr. agr. Ind. Div. Internat. Markets, Indpls., 1979. Mem. Animal Air Transp. Assn. (bd. dirs. 1975). Lutheran. Home: 419 Greenwood Dr Barrington IL 60010 Office: Air-Line Air Freight Ltd 554 N York Rd Bensenville IL 60106

SHEARROW, GEORGE GORDON, oil company executive, geologist; b. Chillicothe, Ohio, June 23, 1926; s. George Frederick William and Doretha Gordon (Phillips) S.; m. Evelyn Alice Rohlfs, June 17, 1948; children—Gordon Edward, Charles Alan, George Frederick. B.S. in Geology, Mich. State U., 1950. Geologist Mo. Geol. Survey and Water Resources Div., Rolla, 1950-51; head subsurface, oil and gas sects., dept. natural resources Div. Geol. Survey, Columbus, Ohio, 1951-60; cons. geologist, Worthington, Ohio, 1960-68; dist. geologist, Quaker State Oil Refining Corp., Parkersburg, W.Va., 1968-80, mgr. geology and land, Columbus, 1980-82, mgr. geology, 1982, mgr. geology and exploration, 1983—; v.p. Quaker State Western Corp. subs. Quaker State Oil Refining Corp., Columbus, 1982—. Contbr. articles to profl. jours. Served with USN, 1944-46. Fellow Ohio Acad. Sci.; mem. Am. Inst. Profl. Geologists, Am. Assn. Petroleum Geologists (dist. rep.), Appalachian Geol. Soc., Ohio Geol. Soc. (pres. 1977-78), Ohio Oil and Gas Assn. (trustee 1966-68). Republican. Club: Petroleum (trustee). Lodges: Masons, Shriners (pres. 1975). Avocations: hunting; fishing. Home: 6457 Masefield St Worthington OH 43085 Office: Quaker State Western Corp 6161 Busch Blvd Columbus OH 43229

SHEBILSKY, PAUL MARTIN WALTER, optometrist; b. Argentine, Kans., Sept. 30, 1895; s. John and Pauline Wihelmina (Moltz) Przybylski; grad. Needles Inst. Optometry, 1923; D. Optometry, No. Ill. Coll. Ophthalmology and Otolaryngology, 1926; m. Esther Margaret Wortman, Dec. 27, 1931. Practice optometry, Fairbury, Nebr., 1923-26, Strong City, and Burlington, Kans., 1926-29, Emporia, 1929-77. Served with USNR, 1917-19. Mem. Am., Kans. optometric assns., Am. Legion, Vets. World War I, Kans. Hist. Soc. (life), Beta Sigma Kappa. Congregationalist. Mason, Kiwanian (pres. 1937). Club: Outlook. Editor: Kans. Optometric Journal, 1944-52. Home: 1502 Sherwood Way Emporia KS 66801

SHEETS, RICHARD MARSHALL, land reclamation, waste management company executive; b. Urbana, Ill., Mar. 21, 1940; s. Robert Marshall and Verna Louise (Hollingsworth) S.; student U. Ill., 1958-61, U. Philippines, 1963; m. Linda Scheu Vetter, May 7, 1977; children—Sally A., John Marshall; 1 stepson, Jason Erik Vetter. Supervisory and asso. scientist Ill. State Natural History Survey, 1967-71; state mktg. dir. Diener Stereo, Inc., 1971-72; mktg. dir. Illini Union U. Ill., 1972-74; project dir., site mgr. C-V Solid Waste Mgmt. Group, 1974-76; owner, mgr. R.M. Sheets Devel. Co., Champaign, Ill., 1976—; chmn., pres. Western Lion Co., Inc., 1981—. Coordinator George Bush for Pres., Champaign, 1980. Served with U.S. Army, 1961-64. Mem. Ill. Land Improvement Contractors, Nat. Wildlife Fedn., Nature Conservancy, Am. Security Council, Am. Def. Preparedness Assn., Nat. Audubon Soc., Mensa. Illustrator in field. Home and Office: 1609 Parkhaven Dr Champaign IL 61820

SHEETS, THOMAS WADE, lawyer; b. Decatur, Ind., July 23, 1956; s. Lewis Lindberg and Mary Alice (Lee) Hoffman S. Student Purdue U., 1974-75; B.S. in Edn., Ind. U.-Fort Wayne, 1978; J.D., Valparaiso U., 1981. Bar: Ind. 1981, U.S. Dist. Ct. (so. dist.) Ind. 1981, U.S. Dist. Ct. (no. dist.) Ind. 1982. Sole practice, Decatur, Ind., 1981—; pub. defender, Decatur, 1981-82; dep. pros. atty. 26th Jud. Cir., Decatur, 1982—. Chmn. bd. Adams County Red Cross, 1984; v.p. bd. dirs. Adams/Wells chpt. Big Bros./Big Sisters, 1984. Recipient Am. Jurisprudence award Lawyers Coop. Pub. Co., 1979. Mem. Assn. Trial Lawyers Am., Ind. State Bar Assn., Adams County Bar Assn. (pres. 1985-86). Delta Theta Phi (bailiff 1980-81). Democrat. Lutheran. Home: Route 8 Box 187 Decatur IN 46733 Office: 146 S 2d St PO Box 70 Decatur IN 46733

SHEFFIELD, LESLIE FLOYD, agricultural educator; b. Orafino, Nebr., Apr. 13, 1925; s. Floyd L. and Edith A. (Presler) S.; B.S. with high distinction in Agronomy, U. Nebr., 1950, M.S., 1964; postgrad. U. Minn., summer 1965; Ph.D., U. Nebr., 1971; m. Doris Fay Fenimore, Aug. 20, 1947; children—Larry Wayne, Linda Faye (Mrs. Bernard Eric Hempelman), Susan Elaine (Mrs. Randy Thorman). County extension agt. Lexington and Schuyler, Nebr., 1951-52; exec. sec. Nebr. Grain Improvement Assn., 1952-56; chief Nebr. Wheat Commn., Lincoln, 1956-59; exec. sec. Great Plains Wheat, Inc., market devel., Garden City, Kans., 1959-61; asst. to dean Coll. Agr., U. Nebr. at Lincoln, 1961-66, supt. North Platte Expt. Sta., 1966-71, asst. dir. Nebr. Coop. Extension Service, Nebr. Agrl. Expt. Sta., Lincoln, 1971-75, asst. to vice chancellor Inst. Agr. and Natural Resources, 1975-84, also extension farm mgmt. specialist and assoc. prof. agrl. econs., 1975—; v.p. U. Nebr. Found., 1982—; sec.-treas. Circle 4S-L Acres, Wallace, Nebr., 1973—. Cons. econs. of irrigation in N.D., Minn., S.D. and Brazil, 1975, Sudan, Kuwait and Iran, 1976, People's Republic of China, 1977, 81, Can., 1977, 78, 79, 80, Mex., 1978, 79, Argentina, 1978, Hong Kong, 1981, Japan, 1981. Served with U.S. Army, 1944-46; ETO. Recipient Hon. State Farmer award Future Farmers Am., 1955, Hon. Chpt. Farmer award, North Platte chpt., 1973; fellowship grad. award Chgo. Bd. Trade, 1964; Agrl. Achievement award Ak-Sar-Ben, 1969; NASA research grantee, 1972-77; Citizen award U.S. Dept. Interior Bur. Reclamation, 1984; Pub. Service award for contbns. to Nebr. agr. Nebr. Agribus. Club, 1984. Mem. Am. Agrl. Econs. Assn., Am., Nat., Nebr. (Pres.'s award 1979) water resources assns., Nebr. Irrigation Assn., Nebr. Assn. Resource Dists., Am. Soc. Farm Mgrs. Rural Appraisers, Orgn. Profl. Employees of U.S. Dept. Agr., Lincoln C. of C. (chmn. agrl. com. 1974-77), Gamma Sigma Delta, Alpha Zeta. Club: Rotary (dir. 1965-66). Editor: Procs. of Nebr. Water Resources and Irrigation Devel. for 1970's, 1972; contbg. editor Irrigation Age Mag., St. Paul, 1974—. Contbr. articles to various publs. Home: 3800 Loveland Dr Lincoln NE 68506 Office: 223 Filley Hall U Nebraska-Lincoln Lincoln NE 68583

SHELDON, BERT LEROY, gas company executive; b. Dunkirk, Ohio, July 7, 1931; s. Russell Holmes and Marian Juanita (Sherrick) S.; m. Martha Mae Spearman. Grad. high sch. Pres. Sheldon Gas Co., Dunkirk, 1979—; pres. R. H. Sheldon & Son, Inc., Dunkirk, 1979—. Served with USAF, 1950-56. Mem. Ohio Gas Assn. (pres. 1977). Lodges: Masons, Elks. Avocations: fishing; hunting; flying. Home and Office: 13213 Blanchard T R 50 Dunkirk OH 45836

SHELDON, NANCY WAY, management consultant; b. Bryn Mawr, Pa., Nov. 10, 1944; d. John Harold and Elizabeth Semple (Hoff) W.; m. Robert Charles Sheldon, June 15, 1968. B.A., Wellesley Coll., 1966; M.A., Columbia U., 1968, M.Philosphy, 1972. Registered pvt. investigator, Calif. Mgmt. cons. ABT Assocs., Cambridge, Mass., 1969-70; mgmt. cons. Harbridge House, Inc., 1970-79, Los Angeles, 1977-79, v.p., 1977-79; mgmt. cons., pres. Resource Assessment, Inc., 1979—; ptnr., real estate developer Resource Devel. Assocs., 1980—; ptnr. Anubis Group, Ltd., 1980—. Author: Social and Economic Benefits of Public Transit, 1973. Contbr. articles to profl. jours. Columbia U. fellow, 1966-68; recipient Nat. Achievement award Nat. Assn. Women Geographers, 1966. Mem. Am. Mining Congress, Am. Inst. Mining, Metall. and Petroleum Engrs., Nat. Wildlife Fedn., Nat. Audubon Soc., Nature Conservancy, World Wildlife Fund (charter mem.), Nat. Assn. of Chiefs of Police, Grad. Faculties Alumni Assn. Columbia U., DAR. Clubs: Mt. Kenya Safari; Wellesley (Los Angeles). Office: 1431 Washington Blvd Suite 2108 Detroit MI 48226

SHELLY, ARLENE MARIE, claim examiner; b. Grand Island, Nebr., Nov. 4, 1933; d. Willis James and Marie Elizabeth (Montague) Prowett; m. Jack Howard Shelly, Oct. 31, 1951; children—Patricia Marie, Jac, Howard. Student Am. Inst. Ins., Omaha. Cert. profl. ins. woman. File clk. (claims) Mut. of Omaha, 1952-54, Nat. Indemnity Co., Omaha, 1973-74, clerical supr., 1974-79, subrogation examiner, 1979-82, claims examiner, 1982—. Mem. Ins. Women of Omaha (dir., treas., chmn. pub. relations, long range planning com.; Claims Woman of Yr.). Republican. Presbyterian.

SHELTON, SANDRA MARY, medical supplies company official; b. Knoxville, Tenn., Sept. 6, 1943; d. Claude Earl and Mary Jane (Eblen) Hudson; m. John E. Shelton, Feb. 17, 1973; children—Ingrid, Eric, David. Community health rep. health and welfare div. Met. Life Ins. Co., N.Y.C., 1968; dist. mgr. statis. research div. Research Triangle Inst., Research Triangle Park, N.C., 1968-73; sales rep. Lederle Pharms. div. Am. Cyanamid Co., Pearl River, N.Y., 1973-76; with Mallinckrodt Inc., St. Louis, 1976—, S.E. regional mgr. diagnostic div., 1979, assoc. product mgr., 1981-82, product mgr., 1982-84, sr. product mgr., 1984-85, bus. dir., 1985—. Home: PO Box 12596 Creve Coeur MO 63141

SHENEFELT, PHILIP DAVID, dermatologist; b. Colfax, Washington, July 31, 1943; s. Roy David and Florence Vanita (Cagle) S.; m. Suzanne Hanna, June 4, 1971; children—Elizabeth, Sara. B.S. with honors, U. Wis.-Madison, 1966, M.D., 1970, M.S. in Adminstrv. Medicine, 1984. Intern U.S. Naval Hosp., Bethesda, Md., 1970-71; practice medicine specializing in dermatology Oregon Clinic, Wis., 1975; resident in dermatology U. Wis. Hosp., Madison, 1975-78, staff, 1985—; dermatologist Univ. Health Service, U. Wis.-Madison, 1978—, VA Hosp., Madison, 1982-85. Mem. vestry St. Andrews Ch., Madison, 1980-83. Served to lt. comdr. USN, 1969-74. Kellogg fellow, 1980-82. Mem. AMA, State Med. Soc. Wis., Am. Acad. Dermatology, Chgo. Dermatol. Soc., Wis. Dermatol. Soc. Episcopalian. Home: 2759 Florann Dr Madison WI 53711 Office: Univ Health Service 1552 University Ave Madison WI 53711

SHENKAROW, BARRY, See *Who's Who in America,* 43rd edition.

SHEPARD, BOOTH, lawyer, horse breeder; b. Cin., May 6, 1916; s. Lee and Pearl (Blizzard) S.; m. Allyn Johnson, June 25, 1948; children—Sarah Shepard Cohen, Randall B., David L. Student U. Coll. Southwest, Exeter, Eng., 1937; B.A., Denison U., 1938; LL.B., U. Cin., 1941. Bar: Ohio 1941, U.S. Dist. Ct. (so. and we. dists.) Ohio 1946, U.S. Supreme Ct. 1959. Ptnr. Shepard, Hilton, Clifton, Linnenberg & Rust, Cin.; counsel Cin. Met. Housing Authority, 1966—. Pres. bd. edn. Indian Hill Exempted Sch. Dist., Ohio, 1962-70. Served to lt. (s.g.) USN, 1941-45. Mem. ABA, Ohio Bar Assn., Cin. Bar Assn. Clubs: University (bd. govs. 1949-55), Literary (Cin.). Avocations: golf; squash; ornithology; forestry; woodworking. Office: Shepard Hilton Clifton Linnenberg & Rust 3700 Carew Tower 441 Vine St Cincinnati OH 45202

SHEPARD, RANDALL TERRY, state supreme court judge; b. Lafayette, Ind., Dec. 24, 1946; s. Richard S. and Dorothy I. (Donlen) S.; B.A. cum laude, Princeton U., 1969; J.D., Yale U., 1972. Admitted to Ind. bar, 1972, U.S. Dist. Ct. for So. Dist. Ind., 1972; spl. asst. to under sec. U.S. Dept. Transp., Washington, 1972-74; exec. asst. to mayor City of Evansville (Ind.), 1974-79; judge Vanderburgh Superior Ct., Evansville, 1980-85; justice Ind. Supreme Ct., 1985—; instr. U. Evansville, 1975-78; cons. Marston Robling, Inc., Evansville, 1980-81. Regional vice chmn. bd. advs. Nat. Trust for Historic Preservation, 1980—, now chmn. bd. advisors, trustee; chmn. State Student Assistance Commn. of Ind., 1980—; vice chmn. Vanderburgh County Republican Central Com., 1977-80; mem. state adv. com. Vincennes U., 1983—, Acad. Arts and Scis., U. Evansville, 1983—. Recipient Friend of Media award Cardinal States chpt. Sigma Delta Chi, 1979; Disting. Service award Evansville Jaycees, 1982. Mem. Fed. Bar Assn., Ind. Bar Assn., Ind. Judges Assn. Republican. Methodist. Clubs: Princeton (N.Y.); Capitol Hill (Washington); Evansville Petroleum. Author: Preservation Rules and Regulations, 1980; contbr. articles to profl. publs. Home: 1403 SE 2d St Evansville IN 47713 Office: 304 State House Indianapolis IN 46204

SHEPARD, RICHARD CHARLES, real estate investment executive; b. St. Louis, Feb. 2, 1934; s. Joseph M. and Evelyn A. (Hill) S.; m. Judith Ann Diesem, Oct. 3, 1959; children—Richard Scott, Bradley Stephen, Stephanie Ann, Matthew John. B.S.M.E., Washington U., St. Louis, 1955; M.B.A., St. Louis U., 1959. Registered profl. engr., Mo. Student designer Union Electric Co., St. Louis, 1955-56, engr., 1956-66, sr. engr., 1966-68; v.p. Linclay Corp., St. Louis, 1968-70, exec. v.p., 1970-80, pres., 1980—. Mem. St. Louis Regional Commerce and Growth Assn.; bd. dirs. Good Shepherd Sch. for Children, St. Louis, Served to 2d lt. U.S. Army, 1956. Mem. Urban Land Inst. (council), Internat. Council Shopping Ctrs., Pi Tau Sigma, Tau Beta Pi. Republican. Roman Catholic. Club: St. Louis. Avocations: travel; reading. Home: 9 Fordyce Ln Saint Louis MO 63124 Office: Linclay Corp 1030 Woodcrest Saint Louis MO 63141

SHEPHERD, DAVID H., management consultant; b. Indpls., June 13, 1943; s. Mary C. Shepherd; B.B.A., U. Cin., 1966; M.B.A., Butler U., 1969; m. Jonnie L. Sandlin, Aug. 31, 1974; children—Kellie, Mary Martha. Systems analyst Link Belt div. FMC, Indpls., 1966-68, supr. standard cost acctg., 1968-69; with Touche Ross Co., Detroit, 1970-79, Cleve., 1979-83, ptnr., 1979-83; v.p. Milton Allen & Assocs., 1983—; Trustee, Bus. Edn. Alliance, Detroit. Bd. dirs. Town of Westchester (Mich.), 1977-78. Cert. mgmt. cons. Mem. Inst. Mgmt. Consultants, Am. Prodn. and Inventory Control Soc., Am. Mgmt. Assn., Fin. Execs. Inst., Assn. Accts. Clubs: Detroit Athletic (fin. com.), Oakland Hills Country, Shaker Heights Country. Office: 1717E 9th St Suite 300 Cleveland OH 44114

SHEPHERD, ELSBETH WEICHSEL, operations engineer; b. Youngstown, Ohio, Dec. 5, 1952; d. Richard Henry and Lesley Frances (Lynn) Weichsel; B.S. in Math., Carnegie-Mellon U., 1974; M.B.A., U. Cin., 1978; m. Gordon Ray Shepherd, Aug. 28, 1976. Asst. indsl. engr. Armco, Inc., Middletown, Ohio, 1974-76, asso. indsl. engr., 1976-78, indsl. engr., 1978-82, sr. ops. engr., 1982—. Mem. news mag. staff Jr. League Cin., 1980-81; vol. Miami Purchase Assn. Am. Iron and Steel Inst. fellow, 1978-81. Mem. Soc. Women Engrs. (pres. sect. 1981-82, provisional regional dir. 1983-84), Assn. Computing Machinery, Am. Inst. Indsl. Engrs. (v.p. services, pres. elect 1984-85), Tech. Socs. Council (2d v.p. 1984, treas. 1983). Home: 6255 Howe Rd Middletown OH 45042 Office: 1801 Crawford St Middletown OH 45043

SHEPHERD, ROY JAMES, III, financial planner, pension analyst; b. Jacksonville, Fla., Dec. 27, 1942; s. Roy James, II and Willie Martha Marion (Griffith) S.; student Ohio State U., 1960, Rio Grande (Ohio) Coll., 1962-63; m. Patricia Ann Taggart, Nov. 1, 1980. Area mgr. Massey Ferguson, Ltd., Lansing, Mich., 1970-72; ordinary agt. Prudential Ins. Co., Columbus, Ohio, 1972-76, brokerage mgr., 1976-77; ptnr. Davis Agy., Pomeroy, Ohio, 1977-78; owner, operator Arlington Ins. Service, Columbus, 1978-84; owner, prin. Canterbury Fin. Strategies, 1985—; cons. Minority Devel. Corp., Inc.; composer gospel music. Served with Army N.G., 1964—. Decorated Army Commendation Medal; recipient DeMolay Cross of Honor; named Outstanding Sales Underwriter, also recipient Nat. Quality award Nat. Assn. Life Underwriters; named hon. Ky. Coll. Mem. Profl. Ins. Agts. Assn. Am., Nat. Assn. Life Underwriters, Ins. Econs. Soc. Am., Enlisted Assn. Army N.G., Amvets. Episcopalian. Clubs: Masons, Odd Fellows. Playwright: (with others) Life of Christ, 1982. Home: 5687 Brinkley Ct Columbus OH 43220 Office: 5025 Arlington Centre Blvd Columbus OH 43220

SHEPLEY, ETHAN ALLEN HITCHCOCK, JR., banker. Vice chmn., dir. Boatmen's Bancshares, Inc., St. Louis, Boatmen's Nat. Bank of St. Louis. Office: Boatmen's Nat Bank of Saint Louis 100 N Broadway Saint Louis MO 63102*

SHEPPARD, RALPH, university business executive; b. Lake City, Fla., Oct. 15, 1930; s. Lee Wesley and Marie (Sherman) S.; m. Estella Wright, June 20, 1958; children—Ralph Norman, Ralphael Willetta, Winston Wright. B.S., Bethune Cookman Coll., 1959; postgrad. Volusia County Community Coll., 1962, U. Ky., 1967-68, 72, El Centro Coll., 1971, Xavier U., Cin., 1973, Central Mich. U., 1976, Central State U., 1980. Agt., debit mgr. Central Life Ins. Co. Am., 1959-63; bus. mgr. Edward Waters Coll., Jacksonville, Fla., 1963-65; bus. mgr., student fin. aid officer Wiley Coll., Marshall, Tex., 1965-69; budget officer Bishop Coll., Dallas, 1969-72; controller Wilberforce (Ohio) U., 1972-73; asst. bus. mgr./comptroller Central State U., Wilberforce, 1974-77, dep. bus. mgr., 1977-78, bus. mgr., 1978—. Football, basketball, baseball coach Little League, Xenia, Ohio, 1973-76; bd. dirs. budget com. Third Baptist Ch., Xenia, 1977-82, mem. deacon bd., 1977-81. Served with AUS, 1951-53. Decorated Bronze Star, Purple Heart. Mem. Nat. Assn. Colls. and Univs. Bus. Officers, Phi Delta Kappa, Alpha Phi Alpha (v.p. Chi Lambda chpt. 1982-83). Republican. Club: Optimist (sec./treas. Wilberforce chpt.). Home: 35 Hardacre Dr Xenia OH 45385 Office: Office Fin Central State U Wilberforce OH

SHER, NEAL ANDREW, physician, ophthalmic surgeon; b. N.Y.C., Jan. 17, 1949; s. Max H. and Rita (Rubin) S.; m. Judith Lee Luck, Sept. 2, 1970; children—Melissa, Cynthia. B.A., Boston U., 1967, M.D., 1971. Diplomate Am. Bd. Ophthalmology. Intern U. Minn., Mpls., 1971-72; staff assoc. NIH, Bethesda, Md., 1972-75; resident ophthalmology U. Minn., 1975-78; fellow Moorfields Eye Hosp., Mpls., 1979; practice medicine specializing in ophthalmology, Mpls., 1979—. Contbr. articles to profl. jours. Served to lt. comdr. USPHS, 1972-75. Fellow Am. Acad. Ophthalmology; mem. Mpls. Ophthalmologic Soc. (pres. 1983). Avocation: photography. Home: 2837 Glenhurst Saint Louis Park MN 55416 Office: 1750 Med Arts Bldg Minneapolis MN 55402

SHERBURNE, PAUL VERNON, educational organization executive; b. Menomonie, Wis., Jan. 2, 1948; s. Marvin Dale and Irene Ann (Steinbring) S.; m. Patricia Jo Armstrong, Sept. 23, 1977; 1 son, Andrew Armstrong. B.A., Macalester Coll., 1974; cert. of completion, Humphrey Inst., U. Minn., 1982. Photographer St. Paul, 1972-76; program dir. World Press Inst., St. Paul, 1976-80, exec. dir., 1980—; founder, pub., Topic mag., 1982—. Home: 1283 Dayton Ave Saint Paul MN 55104 Office: World Press Institute Macalester College 1600 Grand Ave Saint Paul MN 55105

SHERE, DENNIS, newspaper publisher; b. Cleve., Nov. 29, 1940; s. William and Susan (Luskay) S.; m. Maureen Jones, Sept. 4, 1965; children—Rebecca Lynn, David Matthew, Stephen Andrew. B.S. in Journalism, Ohio State U., 1963, M.S., 1964. Reporter, Dayton Daily News (Ohio), 1966-69; asst. prof. journalism Bowling Green State U., 1969-70; fin. editor Detroit News, 1970-72, night city editor, 1972-73, city editor, 1973-75; editor The Journal Herald, Dayton, 1975-80; publisher Springfield (Ohio) News-Sun, 1980-83; pub. Dayton Newspapers, Inc., 1983—. Served with AUS 1964-66. Mem. Dayton C. of C. Baptist. Office: 45 S Ludlow St Dayton OH 45401

SHERFEY, GERALDINE RICHARDS, educational administrator; b. Pontiac, Mich., Dec. 11, 1929; d. William and Ethel (Spurr) Richards; m. William E. Sherfey, Aug. 4, 1950 (div.); children—Emily J., Laura A., Susan E., William E. B.S., Ind. State U., 1963, M.S., 1965; Ed.S., U. Ga., 1973, Ed.D., 1978. Biology/gen. sci. instr. Hammond (Ind.) Tech.-Vocat. High Sch., 1963-65; advanced biology instr. Griffith (Ind.) Sr. High Sch., 1965-70, dept. chmn. grades K-12, acting sci. cons., 1968-70; mgr. sch. programs (asst. supt. for curriculum and instrn.) Greenville (S.C.) Pub. Schs., 1972-73; instr. edn. Purdue U., Calumet Campus, Hammond, Ind., 1973-75; guest lectr. Purdue U. Calumet Campus and Ind. U. N.W., Gary, 1975-78; sci. instr. grades 7 and 8, Spohn Middle Sch., Hammond, 1975-78, prin. A.L. Spohn Elem./Middle Sch., 1978-80, adminstrv. asst. for curriculum and instruction Hammond Schs., 1980-82, coordinator vocat. program devel./extended programs, 1982—. Ind. State U. teaching fellow, 1964-65; U. Ga. grad. asst., 1970-72. Mem. World Council for Curriculum and Instruction, Assn. for Supervision and Curriculum Devel., Nat. Sci. Tchrs. Assn., Nat. Middle Schs. Assn., Ind. Middle Schs. Assn. Democrat. Roman Catholic. Contbr. articles to profl. jours. Home: 540 W 56th Ave Merrillville IN 46410 Office: 5727 Sohl Ave Hammond IN 46320

SHERIDAN, PATRICIA ELVIRA O'DOWDA MARTIN, lawyer, educator; b. Oak Park, Ill., Sept. 18, 1939; d. Harold Arpin and Elvira Eba Ada (Anderson) Martin; m. Robert Bliss Sheridan, Mar. 28, 1964 (div. June 8, 1984); children—Jeffrey Bliss, Susanne Elvira O'Dowda, Barbara Jean Arpin. Student U. Ill.-Chgo., 1957-59; B.A. cum laude, Elmhurst (Ill.) Coll., 1961; postgrad. Lewis U. Coll. Law, 1978-79; J.D. magna cum laude, No. Ill. U., 1982. Tchr. cert.; bar: Ill. 1982, U.S. Dist. Ct. 1982, U.S. Ct. Appeals (7th cir.) 1982. Tchr. elem. sch., Elmhurst, Ill., 1961-64, Glen Ellyn, Ill., 1964-66; coordinator arts and crafts Elmhurst Park Dist., 1963; assoc. Stephen D. Helm, Naperville, Ill., 1982-84; sole practice, Glen Ellyn, Ill., 1984—. Casenotes and comments editor No. Ill. U. Law Rev., 1981-82; contbr. articles to profl. jours. Co-dir. Valley View Arboretum Civic Assn., Glen Ellyn, 1975-76; rec. sec. Glen Ellyn Republican Women's Club, 1976-77; chmn. Com. for Round Meadow Park, Glen Ellyn, 1976-77; co-chmn. land and water com. Valley View Arboretum Civic Assn., Glen Ellyn, 1976-78. Recipient Alumni Assn. Achievement award, Outstanding Woman Student Leader award, 1981, Corpus Juris Secundum award No. Ill. U., 1982; Leslie A. Holmes scholar, 1981-82. Mem. ABA, Ill. Bar Assn., Ill. Trial Lawyers Assn., DuPage County Bar Assn., DuPage Assn. of Women Lawyers, Naperville Heritage Soc., Chgo. Council Fgn. Relations, AAUW, LWV, Tau Epsilon Rho. Home: 3 S 201 Arboretum Rd Glen Ellyn IL 60137 Office: 3S 201 Arboretum Rd Glen Ellyn IL 60137

SHERIDAN, WILLIAM COCKBURN RUSSELL, bishop; b. N.Y.C., Mar. 25, 1917; s. John Russell Fortesque and Gertrude Magdalene (Hurley) S.; student U. Va.-Charlottesville; A.B., Carroll Coll., 1939; M.Div., Nashotah House Theol. Sem., 1942, D.D., 1966; cert. St. Mary's Grad. Sch. Theology, 1966; S.T.M., Nashotah House Theol. Sem., 1968, D.C.L., 1984; m. Rudith Treder, Nov. 13, 1943; children—Elizabeth Sheridan Beeler, Margaret Sheridan Wilson, Mary Sheridan Janda, Peter, Stephen. Ordained deacon and priest Episcopal Ch., 1943; asst. priest St. Paul's Ch., Chgo., 1943-44; rector Gethsemane Ch., Marion, Ind., 1944-47, St. Thomas's Ch., Plymouth, Ind., 1947-72; bishop of Episcopal Diocese of No. Ind., 1972—. Vice pres. bd. trustees Nashotah House Theol. Sem.; pres. bd. trustees Howe (Ind.) Mil. Sch. Author: Journey to Priesthood, 1952; Between Catholics, 1966. Home: 2502 S Twyckenham Dr South Bend IN 46614 Office: 117 N Lafayette Blvd South Bend IN 46601

SHERIFF, ALFRED PEARSON, III, association executive; b. Cadiz, O., July 2, 1927; s. Alfred P. and Edyth (Aiken) S.; B.A., Washington and Jefferson Coll., 1949; LL.B., Western Res. U., 1955; J.D., Case-Western Res. U., 1968; m. Margaret Ann Edwards, Aug. 2, 1967; children—Richard A., Thomas E., David G., Nancy G. Bar: Ohio 1956. With trust devel. div. Central Nat. Bank, Cleve., 1955-61; asst. to exec. v.p. Delta Tau Delta, Indpls., 1961-65, exec. v.p., 1965-82; pres. Delta Tau Delta Ednl. Found., 1982—. Bd. govs. Western Res. Sch. Law, 1960; mem. Washington and Jefferson Coll. Devel. Council, 1968-70; mem. Bd. Police Commrs., 1975-78; bd. dirs. Symphony Orch., 1980-84, Boys Clubs Greater Indpls. Mem. Am., Ohio, Cleve. bar assns., Am. Soc. Assn. Execs., Frat. Execs. Assn. (pres. 1975-76), Newcomen Soc., Summit Soc. N.Am., Delta Tau Delta, Phi Alpha Delta. Republican. Presbyterian. Lodges: Masons, KT, Shriners, Rotary. Club: Indianapolis Athletic. Contbr. articles to mags. Home: 11825 Rolling Springs Dr Carmel IN 46032 Office: Suite 324 4740 Kingsway Dr Indianapolis IN 46205

SHERK, LORRAINE MARTHA, nursing school administrator; b. Washington, Mo., Nov. 1, 1922; d. William Frederick and Martha Wilhelmenia (Dierking) Meyer; m. George W. Sherk, Sept. 13, 1947; 1 son, George W. Student Central Mo. State U., 1940-42; diploma summa cum laude St. Luke's Sch. Nursing, St. Louis, 1945; B.S.N., Washington U., 1947, M.A.Ed. with Eliot honors, 1963. Registered profl. nurse, Mo. Staff and pvt. duty nurse St. Francis Hosp., Washington, 1956-57; office nurse, Washington, 1946-56; instr. St. Luke's Sch. Nursing, St. Louis, 1957-62, assoc. dir., 1962-70, dir., 1970—. Contbr. articles to nursing jours. Mem. Assembly Hosp. Schs. (governing council 1978-81), Fedn. for Accessible Nursing Edn. and Licensure (chmn. 1983-84), Nat. League Nursing (chmn. bd. rev. for diploma programs 1972-78, mem. appeal panel), Mo. League Nursing (Outstanding Service award 1981), Mo. Citizens for Life, Am. Cancer Soc., St. Louis Heart Assn., Kirkwood Hist. Soc., Humane Soc. of Mo., Kappa Delta Pi. Presbyterian (deacon). Avocations: traveling; spectator sports; needlepoint; knitting; reading. Home: 643 E Jefferson Ave Kirkwood MO 63122 Office: St Lukes Sch Nursing 5555 Delmar Blvd Saint Louis MO 63112

SHERMAN, ELEANOR B., social worker; b. Chgo., Apr. 23, 1926; d. Alonzo and Sylvia (Burney) Barksdale; B.A., Howard U. 1954; M.S.W., Jane Addams Sch. Social Work, 1975; 1 child, Sylvia Ann Sherman Evans. Caseworker, Ill. Dept. Public Aid, Chgo., 1960-65, supr., 1965-66, intake supr., 1966-73, service supr., 1975—; dir. Meals on Wheels; lectr. in child abuse prevention Speakers Bur., Inc., 1979—, bd. dirs., 1970—. Contact person hunger task force Episcopal Diocese Chgo.; dir./coordinator Meals on Wheels program Bread for the World. Mem. Nat. Assn. Univ. Women (fin. sec. 1976-80), Acad. Social Workers, Am. Public Welfare Assn., Ill. Welfare Assn., Nat. Assn. Social Workers (Ill. chpt. del., bd. dirs. Ill. chpt., Chgo. area dist. program chmn.), Chgo. Met. Bus. and Profl. Women's Club (found. chmn., named Woman of Achievement 1983), Internat. Visitor's Ctr., Internat. Social Welfare Assn., Howard U. Alumni Assn., U. Ill. Alumni Assn., Bread for the World. Office: 8001 S Cottage Grove Ave Chicago IL 60619

SHERMAN, HUNTER B., clergyman, educator; b. Long Beach, Calif., Aug. 30, 1943; s. Hunter B. and Mary Rawls (French) S.; B.A., Calif. State U., Long Beach, 1965; postgrad. Bapt. Bible Coll., 1965-66; M.Div., Talbot Theol. Sem., 1970; Ph.D., Calif. Grad. Sch. Theology, 1976; m. Louisa Ann Stahl, June 27, 1964; children—Whitnae Nicolle, Garrett Hunter. Prof., Bapt. Bible Coll., Springfield, Mo., 1970—, chmn. Bible dept., 1975-78, acad. dean, 1979-83; pastor Bellview Bapt. Ch., Springfield, 1983—. Mem. Soc. Bibl. Lit., Am. Assn. Collegiate Registrars, Am. Schs. Oriental Research, Israel Exploration Soc., Oriental Inst. U. Chgo. Author: Must Babylon Be Rebuilt, 1970; The Biblical Concept of Babylon, 1976. Recipient Audrey Talbot Meml. award Talbot Theol. Sem., 1970. Office: 628 E Kearney St Springfield MO 65802

SHERMAN, IAN MATTHEW, lawyer; b. Chgo., Apr. 30, 1953; s. George and Vivian K. (Soffran) S.; m. Barbara Jan Smiley, Aug. 6, 1978; children—Wendy Joyce, Wesley Jacob. A.B., U. Ill., 1975; J.D., Boston U., 1978. Bar: Ill. 1978, U.S. Dist. Ct. (no. dist.) Ill. 1978, U.S. Ct. Appeals (7th cir.) 1984. Assoc. Rooks, Pitts & Poust, Chgo., 1978—. Participant Youth Motivation Program, Chgo. Pub. High Schs., 1982, Vol. Legal Services Inst., Chgo., 1982—. Mem. Chgo. Bar Assn. (cert. appreciation 1983), Ill. Bar Assn., Workers' Compensation Lawyers Assn., Phi Beta Kappa, Phi Kappa Phi. Home: 512 S Vail St Arlington Heights IL 60005 Office: Rooks Pitts Poust 55 W Monroe St Suite 1500 Chicago IL 60603

SHERMAN, MARY DOLORES, college dean; b. Nashville, Jan. 20, 1934; m. George S. Sherman, Jr., Mar. 10, 1970. B.S., Tenn. State U., 1955; M.S., So. Ill. U., Carbondale, 1963; Ed.D. in Ednl. Adminstrn. and Supervision, Loyola U., 1984. Tchr., Carbondale (Ill.) Pub. Schs., 1957-62; tchr., librarian Gary (Ind.) Pub. Schs., 1963-70, Chgo. Pub. Schs., 1970-72; resident coordinator, supr. student teaching Western Ill. U., Macomb, 1972-79; dean arts and scis. Richard J. Daley City Coll., Chgo., 1980-82, dean instrn., 1982—. Mem. Adv. Council for LaRabida-Dropout Prevention Tng. Project; bd. dirs. Pilgrim Day Care Center. Recipient award of meritorious service LaRabida Hosp., 1982; Outstanding Educator award Dentist's Wives Club Chgo., 1982. Mem. Nat. Assn. Tchr. Edn., Assn. Supervision and Curriculum Devel., Phi Delta Kappa. Office: 7500 S Pulaski Rd Chicago IL 60652

SHERREN, ANNE TERRY, chemistry educator; b. Atlanta, July 1, 1936; d. Edward Allison and Annie Ayres (Lewis) Terry; m. William Samuel Sherren, Aug. 13, 1966. B.A., Agnes Scott Coll., 1957; Ph.D., U. Fla.-Gainesville, 1961. Grad. teaching asst. U. Fla., Gainesville, 1957-61; instr. Tex. Woman's U., Denton, 1961-63, asst. prof., 1963-66; research participant Argonne Nat. Lab., 1973-80; assoc. prof. chemistry N. Central Coll., Naperville, Ill., 1966-76, prof., 1976—. Clk. of session Knox Presbyn. Ch., 1976—, ruling elder, 1971—. Mem. Am. Chem. Soc., Am. Inst. Chemists, AAAS, AAUP, Ill. Acad. Sci., Sigma Xi, Delta Kappa Gamma, Iota Sigma Pi (nat. pres. 1978-81, nat. dir. 1972-78). Presbyterian. Contbr. articles to field to profl. jours. Office: N Central Coll Naperville IL 60566

SHERWOOD, JAMES MICHAEL, advertising agency executive; b. New Castle, Ind., Sept. 27, 1948; s. Everett Russell and Dorothy Jean (Jackson) S.; m. Nanette Faye Harris, Jan. 5, 1980; 1 son, Kyle Dennis. Sports editor Kettering-Oakwood Times, Kettering, Ohio, 1968-69; asst. sports editor Palladium-Item, Richmond, Ind., 1970-71, Courier Tribune, Bloomington, Ind., 1971-72; editor, co-publisher Graphic Publications, Greenville, Ohio, 1972-75; mgr. mktg. services, mgr. sales promotion, nat. sales mgr., div. mgr., dir. sales devel. Shopsmith, Inc., Vandalia, Ohio, 1975-81; dir. mktg. Bench-Mark Tool Co., Jefferson City, Mo., 1981-83; v.p., dir. client services The Parhelion Group, Dayton, Ohio, 1983—. Office: 3636 Dayton Park Dr Dayton OH 45414

SHERWOOD, NORMAN PAUL, army education administrator; b. Spokane, Wash., Feb. 10, 1943; s. Lynn Marvin and Ethel Belle (Miller) S.; m. Kim Yu, June 19, 1970; children—Suni, Jody. B.A. in Polit. Sci., U. Wash., 1966; D.Edn., U. So. Calif., 1982. Pub. relations officer Korea Regional Exchange, Seoul, 1969-71; editor, writer Dept. Navy, Honolulu, 1972-73; edn. services officer Dept. Army, Korea., 1973-79; edn. coordinator Army Recruiting Command, Portland, Oreg., 1979-81, dir. edn., Honolulu, 1981-83; mgr. testing program Hdqrs. U.S. Army Recruiting Command, Fort Sheridan, Ill., 1983—; tchr. ESL, adviser Asia-Pacific Social Cultural Found., Seoul, 1969. Served to sgt. U.S. Army, 1966-69. Recipient Journalism award Dept. Navy, 1971; commendation Dept. Army, 1980, 81, 82, 83; nominated Fed. Employee of Yr., 1982. Mem. Am. Personnel and Guidance Assn., Mil. Edn. Counselors Assn., Phi Delta Kappa. Club: Pusan (Korea) Flying. Methodist. Editor, writer The Pointer, Barbers Point, Hawaii, 1971-73; newspaper columnist Korea Herald, Seoul, 1970; contbr. Korea Times, Seoul, 1969-71. Office: PO Box 203 Education Programs Br Hdqrs US Army Recruiting Command Fort Sheridan IL 60037

SHEVELL, STEVEN KING, psychology educator; b. Los Angeles, Apr. 25, 1950; s. Richard S. and Lorraine M. (King) S.; m. Jeanne Cay Marsh, Oct. 3, 1976. A.B. with distinction, Stanford U., 1973, M.S. in Engring.-Econ. Systems, 1973; M.A. in Stats., U. Mich., 1975, M.A. in Psychology, 1975, Ph.D., 1977. Asst. prof. dept. behavioral scis. U. Chgo., 1978-83, assoc. prof., 1984—; mem. statis. working group NRC, 1979-82; mem. NSF sensory physiology and perception adv. panel, 1986—. Contbr. articles to profl. jours. NSF fellow, 1973-76, 80—; Nat. Eye Inst. trainee, 1977, grantee, 1983—. Mem. Optical Soc. Am. (tech. group chmn. 1986—), Assn. Research in Vision and Ophthalmology, AAAS, Soc. Math. Psychology, Psychometric Soc., Phi Beta Kappa, Sigma Xi. Office: U Chgo 5848 S University Ave Chicago IL 60637

SHEWARD, CLARENCE WILLIAM, gaseous diffusion company executive; b. Jackson County, Ohio, Feb. 6, 1942; s. Delmar Jay and Mildred Alice (Rapp) S.; B.S., U.S. Air Force Acad., 1964; M.B.A., Capital U., 1980; m. Ann Carlisle, June 4, 1965; children—Heather Lynn, Bethany Dawn. Commd. 2d lt. U.S. Air Force, 1964, advanced through grades to capt., 1972, resigned, 1972; plant engr. Jackson Corp. (Ohio), 1972-76; div. safety coordinator Goodyear Atomic Corp., Piketon, Ohio, 1976-78, supr. maintenance services, 1979-83, supt. uranium ops., 1983-85, supt. security, 1985—; tchr. Rio Grande (Ohio) Community Coll., 1980—; mem. adv. bd., Buckeye Hills Vocational Center, 1976-78; deacon, elder local Presbyterian Ch. Decorated D.F.C. with 2 oak leaf clusters, Air medal with 9 oak leaf clusters. Mem. Improvement Inst., Am. Assn. M.B.A. Execs., Assn. Grads. U.S. Air Force Acad. Republican. Club: Lions. Office: PO Box 628 Piketon OH 45331 Home: 1739 Harrison Rd Jackson OH 45640

SHIBLEY, FREDERIC JAMILE, glass company executive; b. Copperhill, Tenn., May 7, 1946; s. George Toufic and Adele (George) S.; B.S. cum laude in Mktg., U. Tenn., 1968; m. Andrea Mannal Haug, Sept. 27, 1969; children—Robert Liggett, Andrew Williamson. Sales trainee Owens Corning Fiberglas, Raleigh, N.C., Miami, Fla., 1968-69, salesman, Cleve., 1969-72, salesman, Chgo., 1973-74, nat. mktg. mgr., Toledo, 1974-77, mgr. shingle mktg. sect., 1977-78, product line mgr. residential roofing, 1978-79, product and facilities devel. mgr. residential roofing, 1979-80, product and market mgr., residential roofing, 1980-84, venture specialist new bus. ops., 1984—; asst. mgr. Shibley's Fabric Center, Dayton, Tenn., 1972-73. Scoutmaster, Boy Scouts Am., Dayton Tenn., 1973; advisor Jr. Achievement, Toledo, 1978-80. Mem. Asphalt Roofing Mfrs. Assn. (residential roofing com. 1980-84), Phi Sigma Kappa, Phi Kappa Phi, Delta Sigma Pi, Beta Gamma Sigma. Club: Masons. Home: 3738 Edgevale Rd Toledo OH 43606 Office: Owens Corning Fiberglas Corp 1 Levis Sq Toledo OH 43659

SHIBLEY, GREGORY JOSEPH, lawyer; b. Toledo, Ohio, Jan. 9, 1956; s. Joseph D. and Roberta Ann (Thew) S. A.B. magna cum laude, Princeton U., 1977; J.D. cum laude, Harvard U., 1980. Bar: D.C. 1980, Ohio 1981, Fla. 1982. Assoc., Howrey & Simon, Washington, 1980-82, Shumaker, Loop & Kendrick, Toledo, 1982-84; prin. Shibley Co., L.P.A., Toledo, 1984—. Mem. ABA, Assn. Trial Lawyers Am., Ohio Assn. Trial Lawyers, D.C. Bar, Fla. Bar, Ohio State Bar Assn., Toledo Bar Assn., Phi Beta Kappa. Home: 2168 Rockspring Rd Toledo OH 43614 Office: National Bank Bldg Toledo OH 43604

SHIEH, CHING LONG, structural engineer, researcher; b. Tainan, Taiwan, Jan. 24, 1948; came to U.S., 1973, naturalized, 1983; s. Yen-Chy and Jean (Tsai) S.; m. Shu-Hui Chuang, June 24, 1978; 1 dau., Lisa. B.S. in Civil Engring., Cheng Kung U.-Taiwan, 1970; M.S. in Civil Engring., Nat. Taiwan U., 1973; Ph.D. in Structural Engring., U. Fla., 1975. Registered profl. civil engr., Republic of China; registered profl. structural engr., Ill. Fla. Research asst. U. Fla., Gainesville, 1973-75; vis. scholar Northwestern U., Evanston, Ill., 1976-77; structural engring. specialist Sargent & Lundy Engrs., Chgo., 1978-80, sr. structural engring. specialist, 1980—, assigned trainer for engrs. analysis and design nuclear power plants People's Republic of China, 1983. Mem. ASCE, Mid.-Am. Chinese Sci. and Tech. Assn. (bd. dirs.). Contbr. tech. papers and reports to internat. jours. Home: 5031 Greenleaf St Skokie IL 60077 Office: 55 E Monroe St 18P65 Chicago IL 60603

SHIEL, LAUREL ELIZABETH, interior designer; b. Benton, Ill., Nov. 4, 1955; d. Suzanne (Reinardy) McReynolds; m. William A. Shiel, Dec. 27, 1980. B.S. in Interior Design with honors, U. Wis.-Madison, 1977. Interior designer Carson Pirie Scott & Co., Chgo., 1978-79, Walgreen Co., Deerfield, Ill., 1979-80, J. Cotey Inc., Northbrook, Ill., 1980-83; facilities planner Teradyne, Deerfield, 1983—; mem. ednl. assistance com. Inst. Bus. Designers, Chgo., 1982-83. Mem. Internat. Facility Mgmt. Assn. (affiliate). Episcopalian. Avocations: reading; running; tennis; travel; modern dance; Office: Teradyne Inc Telecommunications Div 1405 Lake Cook Rd Deerfield IL 60015

SHIELDS, ALBERT BLAIR, business analyst and planner; b. Columbus, Ohio, Aug. 27, 1952; s. Albert Blair Shields and Patricia (Hanley) Newlon; m. Joyce Kainz, May 27, 1978; 1 child, Bridget. B.A. in Math. and Econs., Denison U., 1974; M.B.A. in Ops. Research, U. Mich., 1976. Account exec. ADP Network Services, Dearborn, Mich., 1976-77, dist. mgr., Denver, 1977-79, mgr. business analysis, Ann Arbor, Mich., 1979—. Vice pres. Potomac Towne Condo Assn., West Bloomfield, Mich., 1980-83. Recipient All Ohio Football award Ohio High Sch. Athletic Assn., 1969; Denison U. fellow, 1983-84. Mem. Am. Assn. Individual Investors. Avocations: golf; football; investing. Home: 1140 Nielsen Ct Apt 6 Ann Arbor MI 48105 Office: ADP Network Services 175 Jackson Plaza Ann Arbor MI 48106

SHIELDS, GUY LEE, manufacturing company marketing executive; b. Indpls., Oct. 16, 1957; s. Paul Powers and M. Geraldine (Welscher) S.; m. Rita Jean Blossom, Aug. 3, 1979. B.A., John Carroll U., 1981; M.B.A., Baldwin-Wallace Coll., 1984. Quality control technician Leece-Neville Co., Cleve., 1976-81; mktg. mgr. Cole Consumer Products Co., Cleve., 1981-82; mktg. mgr. Curtis Industries, Eastlake, Ohio, 1983-84; market research mgr. Blue Cross and Blue Shield of Northern Ohio, Cleve., 1984—. Mem. Delta Mu Delta. Republican. Roman Catholic. Home: 1342 W 95th St Cleveland OH 44102 Office: 2060 East 9th St Cleveland Ohio 44115

SHIER, WAYNE THOMAS, pharmacy educator, researcher, editor; b. Harriston, Ont., Can., Dec. 1, 1943; s. Clayton and Margaret Agnes (Pritchard) S.; m. Gloria Cumagan Bulan, May 31, 1969; children—John Thomas, Maria Teresita, Anna Christina. B.Sc., U. Waterloo (Can.), 1966; M.S., U. Ill., 1968, Ph.D., 1970. Research asst. bioscis. div. NRC of Can., Ottawa, 1965-66; research assoc. Salk Inst. Biol. Studies, La Jolla, Calif., 1970-72; asst. research prof., chmn. cell biology lab. Salk Inst. Biol. Studies, 1972-80; assoc. prof. Coll. Pharmacy, U. Minn., 1979-85, prof., 1985—, dir. grad. studies in pharmacognosy, 1985—; vis. prof. U. Philippines Coll. Medicine, Manila, 1985; cons. Tokyo Tanabe Co., 1985; Cancer Research Fund Labs., London, 1973. Durnham jr. fellow in oncology Am. Cancer Soc., 1970-72; research grantee Nat. Inst. Allergy and Infectious Diseases, 1972, Nat. Cancer Inst., 1974, 77, Nat. Inst. Gen. Medicine, 1985, NSF, 1980, 85, Cystic Fibrosis Found., 1979, Com. to Combat Huntington's Disease, 1983, Am. Heart Assn., 1983, 85, Nat. Inst. Gen. Medicine, 1985. Mem. Am. Soc. Biol. Chemists, AAAS, Am. Soc. Cell Biology, Internat. Soc. Toxinology, Am. Chem. Soc., N.Y. Acad. Scis., Soc. Toxicology, Acad. Pharm. Scis., Sigma Xi. Roman Catholic. Founding editor Jour. Toxicology-Toxin Revs., 1979—; contbr. articles to profl. jours., chpts. to books; patentee in field. Home: 1715 Heritage Ln New Brighton MN 55112 Office: 8 168 Health Sciences Unit F University of Minnesota 308 Harvard St SE Minneapolis MN 55455

SHIH, CHIA HSIN, electrical power engineer; plasma physicist; b. Peking, China, Mar. 8, 1941; s. Shao and Hen Feng (Wen) S.; came to U.S., 1966, naturalized, 1977; B.S., Nat. Taiwan U., 1963; M.S., U. Toronto, 1966; Ph.D., Poly Inst. Bklyn., 1971; m. Grendy P. Wang, Oct. 10, 1970; children—Willard C., Loren C. Registered profl. engr., Ohio. Asst. engr. Stanford Linear Accelerator Center, summer 1967; engr., sr. engr. Am. Electric Power Service Corp., 1970, 76-77; mgr. elec. research, N.Y.C., now Columbus, Ohio, 1978—; lectr. math. dept. Chinese Naval Acad.; adj. lectr. elec. engring. dept. CCNY; NRC Can. research asst. Mem. IEEE (sr.), Bioelectromagnetics Soc., Sigma Xi. Contbr. chpts. to Handbook of Electrical and Computer Engineering, articles to engring. jours. Office: AEP 1 Riverside Plaza Columbus OH 43216

SHIMANDLE, FRANCIS EDWARD, advertising agency executive, writer, illustrator; b. Chgo., Nov. 20, 1942; s. Leonard Thomas and Margaret Frances (Voda) S.; m. Sally Ann Callanan, Sept. 5, 1963 (dec. July 1975); children—Shannon Mary, Del Francis, Tara Janine; m. Constance D. Baker, June 26, 1976 (div. Feb. 1984); 1 child, Christopher Jaime. Student Chgo. Acad. Fine Arts, 1960-61. Prin. v.p., The Art Guys, Inc., Evansville, Ind., 1967-69; art dir. Albert Jay Rosenthal & Co., Chgo., 1969-70; exec. art dir. Rothenberg, Feldman & Moore, Chgo., 1970-73; creative dir. Scussell/Miller, Chgo., 1973-76, PGM, Inc., Chgo., 1976-83; prin. Our Co., Inc., Chgo., 1983—. Co-author, illustrator: Chocolate Mooselaneous, 1984. Songwriter popular songs. Recipient awards in field. Roman Catholic. Club: Naturals Social and Athletic (sec. 1981-83) (Chgo.). Home and Office: 411 S Sangamon St Apt 6-D Chicago IL 60607

SHIMMEL, ROBERT GILHAM, dermatologist; b. Jackson, Mich., Feb. 23, 1930; s. Earl Clinton and Alta Stewart (Reid) S.; m. Janice Marie Evely, Oct. 12, 1957; children—Anne E., Thomas R., Amie S., Elizabeth A. B.A., Albion Coll., 1951; D.O., Chgo. Coll. Osteopathic Medicine, 1955. Diplomate Am. Osteo. Bd. Dermatology. Intern Chgo. Osteo. Hosp., 1955-56; dermatology preceptor Chgo. Osteo. Hosp., 1956-59; pvt. practice dermatology, Riverview, Mich., 1959—; cons. Riverside Osteo. Hosp., Trenton, Mich., 1959—; clin. prof. Mich. State U. Coll. Osteo. Medicine, Lansing, 1972—. Diplomate Nat. Bd. Examiners for Osteo. Physicians and Surgeons. Fellow Am. Osteo. Coll. Dermatology (pres. 1963-64, sec. 1969-74); mem. Am. Osteo. Assn., Mich. Osteo. Soc. Dermatologists (pres. 1969-70), Mich. Assn. Osteo. Physicians and Surgeons, Inc., Acad. Dermatology, Wayne County Osteo. Assn. Republican. Presbyterian. Avocation: running. Home: 19891 Parke Ln Grosse Ile MI 48138 Office: 17171 Fort Box 2070 Riverview MI 48192

SHINER, DAVID, philosophy educator; b. Tiberias, Israel, July 26, 1951; came to U.S., 1952, naturalized, 1952; s. Harry and Natalie (Schaeffer) S. B.A. in Philosophy, Temple U., 1973, M.A. in Philosophy, 1974; Ph.D. in Philosophy, Pacific Western U., 1983. Faculty Shimer Coll., Waukegan, Ill., 1976—; prof. philosophy, 1979—; dir. Shimer Coll., Oxford, Eng., 1979-80, program, 1983-84; co-dir. Young Scholars Program, 1982—. Author: (monograph) The New Science of Gregory Bateson, 1983. NEH fellow, 1982; recipient Top Instr. Humanities award Shimer Coll., 1978-81, 83-84. Mem. Ill. Philos. Assn. Avocations: musician; chess player. Home: 426 N Sheridan Waukegan IL 60079 Office: Shimer Coll PO Box A 500 Waukegan IL 60079

SHIPMAN, CHARLES DARREL, university dean; b. Kilgore, Nebr., Apr. 19, 1924; s. Marion Samuel and Margaret Louise (Hill) S.; m. Eva June Holm, Aug. 24, 1952; children—Gregory Kent, Brian Dean; m. 2d, Dorothy Ann Pringle, Aug. 27, 1978; 1 stepson, Dana Drew. B.S., U. Nebr.-Lincoln, 1950, M.E., 1951, Ed.D., 1957. Supt., Thomas County High Sch., Thedford, Nebr., 1951-56; asst. prof. tchr. edn. Dana Coll., Blair, Nebr., 1957-58; asst. prof. ednl. adminstrn. Ball State U., 1958-61, adminstrv. asst. to chmn. div. edn., 1961-65, asst. dean Tchrs. Coll., 1965-74, 76—; dep. dir. Nat. Right to Read Program, Office of Edn., Washington, 1974-75, acting dir., 1975-76; cons. Dept. of Def. Schs., W.Ger., 1967, Am. Schs., Bolivia, 1969-70; dir. 12 state tech. asst. team Office of Edn., 1972-74; mem. nat. adv. bd. Fund for Improvement of Postsecondary Edn., U.S. Dept. Edn., 1983-86. Served with USNR, 1943-46. Recipient Outstanding Service award Phi Delta Kappa, 1973; Outstanding Service award Right to Read Program, P.R., 1976; named Hon. Sec. of State, State of Ind., 1983. Mem. Assn. Supervision and Curriculum Devel., Nat. Assn. Tchr. Educators, Phi Delta Kappa. Methodist. Club: Elks. Author: (with others) American Cooperative Schools in Bolivia, The Ball State Report, 1970; Kindergarten Overseas, a Study of the Requirements for Establishing Kindergarten as Part of the Department of Defense Overseas Dependent Schools, 1967; A Look at the Administrative Structure of Education in England, An Onsite Report, 1980. Office: 1008 Teachers College Ball State University Muncie IN 47306

SHIPMAN, ROBERT OLIVER, journalism educator; b. Flushing, N.Y., Feb. 13, 1920; s. Bertram Francis and Elydia Page (Foss) S.; m. Dorothy Jeanille Hadden, Nov. 2, 1944; children—Robert Hadden, Virginia Anne, Gary Oliver, Bertram Francis. A.B. in English cum laude, Bowdoin Coll., 1947; M.S. in Journalism, Columbia U., 1948. Copy editor Christian Sci. Monitor, Boston, 1948-52; instr. journalism Pa. State U., 1952-56; asst. prof. journalism Principia Coll., Elsah, Ill., 1956-59; asst. to pres. Daycroft Sch., Stamford, Conn., 1959-60; asst. dean journalism Columbia U., 1960-66; communications exec. Christian Sci. Ch., Boston, 1968-74; dir. Mass Communications Inst., Mankato State U., 1975—; gen. mgr. Columbia Journalism Rev., N.Y.C., 1961-66; cons. ROS Internat., Darien, Conn., 1966-68, Medfield, Mass., 1974-75. Contbr. articles to profl. jours. Mem. lang. arts adv. com. Darien Pub. Schs., Conn., 1962-66; founding pres. Morgan Meml. Goodwill Assocs., Boston, 1950-52; past chmn. bd. dirs. Darien Christian Sci. Ch., Conn. Served to capt. JAGC, U.S. Army, 1941-46. Mem. Soc. Profl. Journalists (pres. N.Y.C. chpt. 1964-65, pres. So. Minn. chpt. 1978-79), Assn. Edn. in Journalism, Internat. Soc. Weekly Newspaper Editors. Club: Minn. Press. Avocations: reading, biking, gardening. Home: 308 Davis St Mankato MN 56001 Office: Mass Communications Inst Mankato State U Mankato MN 56001

SHIPPERT, STAN HARRY (TONY), telephone company executive, real estate broker; b. Dixon, Mo., July 11, 1930; s. Harry Winfield and Livonia (Humphrey) S.; m. Betty Louise Good, Dec. 30, 1950; children—Garry, Terry, Shari, Cary. B.A., Rockhurst Coll., 1970. Installation foreman Southwest Bell Telephone Co., Kansas City, Mo., 1963-65, wire chief, Liberty, Mo., 1965-70, outside plant foreman, Liberty, 1970-77, installation force mgr., Independence, Mo., 1977-81, plant foreman, Parkville, Mo., 1981-84, plant foreman, community relations mgr., Liberty, 1984—. Trustee Liberty Hosp. Dist.; bd. dirs. New Liberty Hosp. and Med. Corp. Served with U.S. Army, 1951-53, Far East. Recipient State Farmer Degree, Future Farmers Am., 1947. Mem. Telephone Pioneers (bd. dirs. 1978-79). Democrat. Baptist. Lodge: Kiwanis (v.p. 1970-77, mem. bd. dirs., 1970—, pres. 1977, 84—). Avocations: fishing, hunting, beekeeping, farming, gardening. Home: 812 Park Ln Liberty MO 64068 Office: Southwest Bell Telephone Co Liberty MO 64068

SHIRAEF, JOHN DRAGON, educator; b. Phila., Apr. 18, 1912; s. John and Rose (Kret) S. Tchr., Cass Tech. High Sch., Detroit, 1936-43; newspaperman Detroit Times, 1943-47; tchr.-lectr. on Russia, Europe, 1947—. Innovator compressed methods of speech for sch. lectures. Served with U.S. Army, 1943-44. Mem. Internat. Platform Assn. Republican. First Am. lectr. to travel to Russian villages off-limits to foreigners. Office: 2001 N Center Rd Suite 315 Flint MI 48506

SHIRER, MARTHA QUISENBERRY, feed grains company executive; b. Louisville, Mar. 3, 1915; d. Thomas Edwin and Quinlan (Hanna) Quisenberry; m. Richard V. Pelton, 1935 (div. 1955); m. William L. Shirer, 1972 (div. 1977); children—Martha Pelton Lanier, E. Williams Pelton, Catherine E. Pelton, Suzanne Walker Pelton. B.A., Mt. Holyoke Coll., 1936. Dir., officer Neveridle Corp., Hinsdale, Ill., 1963—, pres., treas., 1980—, mgr., 1983—. Mem. Chgo. Council Fgn. Relations, Chgo. Farmers' Club. Clubs: Mt. Holyoke of Chgo., Mt. Holyoke of Berkshire County (Mass.). Home and office: 5719 S Washington St Hinsdale IL 60521 Home: 62 Cliffwood St Lenox MA 01240

SHIVELY, KENNETH ORION, lawyer; b. Dayton, Ohio, Apr. 26, 1926; s. John H. and Dorothy E. (Gerstner) S.; m. Pauline R. Fecho, Oct. 22, 1955 (div. Aug. 1972); children—Elaine L., Randall K.; Marie Catherine Elliott, July 16, 1977. B.A., Otterbein Coll., 1950; LL.B., U. Mich., 1952. Bar: Ohio 1952. Asst. atty. City of Dayton, 1952-55; assoc. Shively, Shively & Shell, Dayton, 1955-58, ptnr., 1958—. Mem. YMCA; bd. dirs. Otterbein Coll. Devel., Westerville, Ohio. Served with USN, 1944-46. Mem. Dayton Bar Assn., Montgomery County Estate Planning Council. Democrat. Methodist. Lodges: Optimist (Dayton) (pres. 1979), Masons, Shriners. Avocations: golf; fishing; tennis; bridge. Home: 113-C N Village Dr Centerville OH 45459 Office: 1630 Kettering Tower Dayton OH 45423

SHOBER, ROGER DALE, computer/finance executive; b. Superior, Wis., Aug. 18, 1938; s. Arthur Leonard and Pearl Hazel (White) S.; m. Beverly Ann Enerson, Sept. 21, 1963; children—Dawn, Dana, Dyan. B.S., U. Wis.-Superior, 1960. Engr., Control Data Corp., Boston and Los Angeles, 1961-65, sales mgr., Seattle, St. Louis and Denver, 1965-75, region v.p., Mpls., 1975-78, v.p. West Europe, Brussels, Belgium, 1978-80, v.p. industry mktg., Mpls., 1982-83; sr. v.p. bus. services, Mpls., 1983—; v.p. Peripheral Products, Mpls., 1980-82, policy com., Mpls., 1980—; dir. Magnetic Peripherals, Inc., Mpls., Dayflo, Irvine, Calif. Served with USAR, 1960-66. Republican. Roman Catholic. Clubs: Edina Country, Decathalon (Bloomington, Minn.).

SHOEMAKER, HELEN E. MARTIN ACHOR, civic worker; b. Houston, Mar. 24, 1915; d. Earl L. and Blanche L. (Williams) Martin; A.B., Anderson (Ind.) Coll., 1960, LL.D., 1978; m. Harold E. Achor, Oct. 11, 1935; children—Dianne Achor Johnston, Lana Achor Dean; m. Robert N. Shoemaker, May 19, 1972. Resident dir. Anderson Coll., 1967-69, dir. alumni services, 1969-72; legis. counsel Ind. Colls. and Univ. Ind., 1970-72; spl. asst. Center Public Service, Anderson, 1973-77, spl. asst. to dean for acad. devel., 1977-78. Sec.-treas. Ind. State Library and Hist. Bldg. Expansion Commn., 1973-78; mem. com. region VII, Girl Scouts U.S.A., 1958-66; adv. council fin. aid to students Office Edn. HEW, 1976-78. Mem. Ind. Ho. of Reps. from Madison County, 1968-70; v.p. Ind. Fedn. Women's Republican Clubs, 1945-46; treas. Nat. Fedn. Women's Rep. Clubs, 1947-51; Rep. precinct vice chmn. Madison County, 1946-68, vice chmn., Anderson, 1967-68; bd. dirs. Urban League Madison County, 1969-76; adv. com. Georgetown U. Grad. Sch. Acad. in Public Service, 1976-83; mem. adv. com. on sex discrimination Ind. Civil Rights Commn., 1978-83; trustee Anderson Coll., 1978-85; bd. dirs. Opportunities Industrialization Center, Inc., Madison County, 1980-84, Ind. Acad. Public Service, 1981-83, Women's Alternatives Inc., Anderson, 1982—; mem. exec. com. devel. bd. St. John's Med. Center, Anderson, 1981—. Recipient William B. Harper award Urban League Madison County, 1975; named Sagamore of Wabash, State of Ind., 1979. Hon. mem. Anderson Symphony Orch. Guild; mem. LWV (dir. Madison County 1973-76, 78-84), Anderson Council Women, Anderson Fine Arts Center (treas. women's league 1984—). Mem. Ch. of God. Lodge: Ladies of Kiwanis (pres. 1985—) (Anderson). Home: 707 Dresser Dr Anderson IN 46011

SHOEMAKER, MORRELL MCKENZIE, JR., architect; b. Granville, Ohio, Aug. 25, 1923; s. Morrell McKenzie and Ruth (Doehleman) S.; B.Arch., Cornell U., 1945. Archtl. designer Mundie, Jensen & McClurg, Chgo., 1946-49; chief architect Laramore & Douglass, Chgo., 1949-53; partner McClurg, Shoemaker & McClurg, Chgo., 1953-67, McClurg, Shoemaker, Chgo., 1967-74; pvt. investor, 1975—. Registered architect, Ill. Mem. AIA, Soc. Am. Registered Architects, Nat. Council Archtl. Registration Bds., Nat. Soc. Archtl. Hist. (life), Landmark Preservation Council, Nat. Trust for Historic Preservation, Newberry Library Assocs., Chgo. Natural History Mus. (life), Chgo. Hist. Soc. (life), Chgo. Orch. Assn. (life), Ill. Soc. Architects, Art Inst. Chgo. (life), Ill. St. Andrews Soc., Victorian Soc. Republican. Presbyn. (elder, trustee). Clubs: Cornell of Chicago; The Cliff Dwellers. Author: Five Walks In and Around Chicago's Famous Buildings, 1969. Editor: The Building Estimator's Reference Book, 20th edit., 1980. Home: 1310 N LaSalle Dr Chicago IL 60610

SHOEMAKER, ROBERT LEWIS, optometrist; b. Elkhart, Ind., Dec. 22, 1928; s. W. Albert and Annetta (Wilson) S.; m. Alice Marie Amick, Aug. 7, 1954; children—Mark Amick, Scott Robert. Student DePauw U., 1946-48, Ind. U., 1948-49; O.D., Pa. Coll. Optometry, 1953. Diplomate Nat. Bd. Optometry. Cons. Wayne Twp. Sch. System, Indpls., 1970-73, Warren Twp. Sch. System, 1972-73, Ind. Dept. Pub. Instrn., 1974-84, Ind. Boy's Sch., Ind. Dept. Correction, Indpls., 1972—; guest lectr. Butler U., Ind. U., Ind. Central Coll., 1972-80, U. Ill., Bradley U., Congress European Optometric Socs., Paris, 1975. Mem. editorial council Jour. Optometric Vision Therapy, 1970-72. Contbr. articles to profl. jours. Bd. dirs. Prisoners Aid By Citizens' Effort, Indpls., 1968-72, Meridian St. Methodist Ch., 1982—. Served as cpl. U.S. Army, 1953-55. Fellow Am. Acad. Optometry (pres. Ind. chpt. 1979-81); mem. Coll. Optometrists in Vision Devel. (bd. dirs. 1971-73), Ind. Optometric Assn. (Ind. Optometrist of Yr. 1970), Am. Optometric Assn. Republican. Avocation: photography. Home: 718 E 57th St Indianapolis IN 46220 Office: 6225 N Broadway Indianapolis IN 46220

SHONS, ALAN RANCE, plastic surgeon, educator; b. Freeport, Ill., Jan. 10, 1938; s. Ferral Caldwell and Margaret (Zimmerman) S.; A.B., Dartmouth Coll., 1960; M.D., Case Western Res. U., 1965; Ph.D. in Surgery, U. Minn., 1976; m. Mary Ella Misamore, Aug. 5, 1961; children—Lesley, Susan. Intern, U. Hosp., Cleve., 1965-66, resident in surgery, 1966-67; research fellow transplantation immunology U. Minn., 1969-72; resident in surgery U. Minn. Hosp., 1972-74; resident in plastic surgery NYU, 1974-76; asst. prof. plastic surgery U. Minn., Mpls., 1976-79, assoc. prof., 1979-84, prof., 1984; dir. div. plastic and reconstructive surgery U. Minn. Hosp., St. Paul Ramsey Hosp., Mpls. VA Hosp., 1976-84; cons. plastic surgery St. Louis Park Med. Center, 1980-84; prof. surgery Case Western Res. U., Cleve., 1984—; dir. div. plastic and reconstructive surgery Univ. Hosps. Cleve., 1984—. Served to capt. USAF, 1967-69. Diplomate Am. Bd. Surgery, Am. Bd. Plastic Surgery. Fellow ACS (chmn. Minn. com. on trauma); mem. Am. Soc. Plastic and Reconstructive Surgeons, Am. Assn. Plastic Surgeons, Minn. Acad. Plastic Surgeons (pres. 1981-82), AMA, Soc. Head and Neck Surgeons, Am. Assn. Surgery Trauma, Transplantation Soc., Plastic Surgery Research Council, Am. Soc. Aesthetic Plastic Surgery, Am. Soc. Maxillofacial Surgeons, Am. Assn. Immunologists, Soc. Exptl. Pathology, Am. Burn Assn., Am. Cleft Palate Assn., Am. Soc. Nephrology, Assn. Acad. Surgery, Pan Am. Med. Assn., Central Surg. Assn., Minn. Med. Assn., Mpls. Surg. Soc., Ramsey County Med. Soc., Sigma Xi. Office: 2074 Abington Rd Cleveland OH 44106

SHOOP, GEORGE JEROME, agronomist; b. Phila., Dec. 25, 1933; s. Hamilton Wright and Helen (Johnson) S.; A.A., Ferrum Jr. Coll., 1953; B.S., Va. Poly. Inst., 1958, M.S., 1961; Ph.D., Pa. State U., 1967; m. Joe Ann Starowsky, Mar. 1, 1974; children—Elizabeth Ann, Richard Jerome. Research scientist rep. Eli Lilly & Co., Greenfield, Ind., 1966-72, Delray Beach, Fla., 1972-74, Brasil, 1973, Peoria, Ill., 1974-80, Indpls., 1980-82, St. Louis, 1982-85, Balt., 1985—. Spl. dep. sheriff Hancock County, Ind., 1971-72, Palm Beach County, Fla., 1973-74. Served with AUS, 1953-55. Mem. Am. Soc. Agronomy, Weed Sci. Am., North Central Weed Sci. Soc. (dir. 1971, chmn. research com. 1977, chmn. hon. membership com. 1984), Sigma Xi, Gamma Sigma Delta, Phi Sigma, Phi Epsilon Phi. Republican. Methodist. Mason (Shriner), Order Eastern Star, Hon. Order Ky. Cols. Contbr. articles to profl. jours.

SHOOP, RICHARD ARTHUR, management consultant, statistician; b. Salem, Ohio, Sept. 2, 1945; s. Richard Alan and Jayne (Courtney) S.; m. Mary E. Johns, May 4, 1966 (div. Oct. 1977); children—Geoffrey, Christopher; m. Carol Ann Bent, June 1, 1978; children—Meredith, Lauren, Kara. B.S., Kent State U., 1967, M.S., 1968, Ph.D. in Math., 1973. Cert. quality engr. Assoc. prof. math. Kent State U., Ohio, 1968-83; pres. R.A. Shoop & Assocs., Kent, 1984—; quality control cons. to industry. Author: Intuitive Calculus, 1973; Statis. Process Control, 1984. Mem. Am. Statis. Assn., Am. Soc. Quality Control, Am. Math. Soc., Sigma Xi. Avocation: trumpet. Home: 206 N Willow St Kent OH 44240 Office: PO Box 3203 Kent OH 44240

SHOPHER, WILLIAM EUGENE, manufacturing company executive; b. St. Louis, Jan. 22, 1926; s. Joseph E. and Tuna (Blakeburn) S.; student St. Louis U., 1946-47, Washington U., 1955-56, Harvard Grad. Sch. Bus., 1965; m. Emogean J. Smith, Feb. 3, 1946; children—Patricia Ann, Jacqulyn Marie. Dir. purchasing Cherry-Burrell, Cedar Rapids, Iowa and Chgo., 1963-68; with Weyerhaeuser Co., 1968-74, mgr. purchasing systems and training, Tacoma, Wash., 1968-72; dir. purchasing Lockwood Corp., Gering, Nebr., 1974—; pres. Cons. Internat.; lectr. U. Wis. Mgmt. Extension Div., Madison, 1966—. Pres. bd. dirs. Scottsbluff/Gering United Way, 1979-80, bd. dirs., 1979-82; mem. edn. adv. com. Chadron State Coll. Vocat. Sch.; bd. dirs. Western Nebr. unit Am. Cancer Soc., 1980—; mem. Scottsbluff/Gering Clean Communities Commn., 1981-83. Served with USNR, 1944-46, 51-52. Mem. Nat. Assn. Purchasing Mgrs. (steel exec. com. 1979—), Scottsbluff/Gering C. of C. (chmn. edn. com. 1977-78, 81-83, dir. 1984—). Contbr. articles to profl. jours. Office: PO Box 160 Gering NE 69341

SHORT, DARRYL ALAN, sports talent agency executive; b. Detroit, Oct. 5, 1959; s. Thomas and Betty Jean (Walker) S.; m. Denise Golden Carson, Dec. 3, 1983. Student Wayne State U., 1985—. Inspector quality control Ford Motor Co., Dearborn, Mich., 1978-80; law librarian Recorder's Ct., Detroit, 1980—; v.p., co-owner Sportsitis, Inc., Detroit, 1983—. Mem. Young Democrats 1st Dist., Detroit, 1981—, Founders Soc. Detroit Art Inst., 1984—. Lutheran. Avocations: ice skating; reading; baseball; music. Office: Sportsitis Inc 1450 Penobscot St Detroit MI 48226

SHORT, IRENE THERESA, office automation consultant; b. St. Louis, Oct. 31, 1936; d. William H. and Anna E. (Weidinger) Volmert; m. James Robert Short, June 11, 1960; children—Douglas James, Brenda Marie. B.A. cum laude, Fontbonne Coll., St. Louis, 1979; A.A.S., Meramec Community Coll., 1977, A.A., 1975. Instr., VA Vocat. Rehab., St. Louis, 1975-77; systems analyst McDonnell Douglas Corp., St. Louis, 1979-81; fin. systems analyst Nat. Marine, St. Louis, 1981-82; cons. Networking Resources, St. Louis, 1982-83; pres. Profl. Office Automation, Inc., St. Louis, 1983—; cons. Jewish Vocat. Employment Service, Metro Tng. Ctr., Occupational Tng. Ctr. (all St. Louis), 1983-84. Mem. Assn. Systems Mgmt. (chmn. publicity com. 1982-84), Assn. Women in Computing (charter; v.p. 1979-80), Phi Theta Kappa, IBM-PC Users Group. Roman Catholic. Avocation: tennis. Home: 9550 Tiber Dr Saint Louis MO 63123

SHORTRIDGE, DOUGLASS RONALD, lawyer; b. Indpls., July 3, 1931; s. Norman Howard and Lillian (Painter) S.; B.S., Purdue U., 1953; LL.B., Ind. U., 1959; divorced; 1 dau., Sylvia. Bar: Ind. 1959. Dep. atty. gen. State of Ind., 1959-60; practice in Indpls., 1960—; propr. Douglass R. Shortridge P.C., 1972—. Served as officer U.S. Army, 1953-56. Mem. ABA, Am. Judicature Soc., 7th Fed. Circuit Bar Assn., Ind. Bar Assn., Indpls. Bar Assn. (pres. 1974), Iron Key, Sigma Delta Chi, Tau Kappa Alpha, Phi Gamma Delta. Republican. Episcopalian. Clubs: Woodstock, Univ., Columbia, Traders Point Hunt, Crooked Stick Golf. Home: 1473 Prestwick Ln Carmel IN 46032 Office: 1 Indiana Sq Suite 2250 Indianapolis IN 46204

SHOTWELL, VIRGINIA LAMBETH, career education administrator; b. N.Y.C., Dec. 2, 1924; d. Edgar Leigh and Marion Arleen (Maddrea) Lambeth; m. John Ralph Shotwell, June 22, 1947; children—Donna Lynn, JoAnn. B.A., U. Richmond (Va.), 1946; M.A., Trinity Coll., 1972; postgrad. U. Hartford, Governors State U. Asst. buyer Thalhimers Dept. Store, Richmond, 1946-47; adminstrv. asst. Kodak Park, Rochester, N.Y., 1947-49; tchr., Rocky Hill and Hartford (Conn.), 1967-75; prof. Prairie State Coll., Chicago Heights, Ill., 1975-77, Ind. U. Northwest, Gary, 1975—; career edn. coordinator Rich Twp., Matteson, Ill., 1979—; career cons. Region 9 Career Guidance Ctr., Thornton Coll., Ill. Bd. dirs. Family Service and Mental Health; coordinator Network Clergy Spouses Internat. Mem. Am. Vocat. Assn., Ill. Assn. Local Adminstrs., NEA, Vocat. Edn. Assn. (bd. dirs. work-edn. council), Nat. Council Tchrs. English, AAUW, LWV, Phi Delta Epsilon. Office: 242 S Orchard Dr Park Forest IL 60466

SHOULDERS, PATRICK ALAN, lawyer; b. Evansville, Ind., Mar. 26, 1953; s. Harold Ray and Jeanne Marie (Nicholson) S.; m. Lisa Lou Iaccarino, July 12, 1975; children—Samantha Alain, Andrew Patrick. B.A., Ind. U., 1975, J.D. magna cum laude, 1978. Bar: Ind. 1978, U.S. Dist. Ct. (so. dist.) Ind. 1978, U.S. Ct. Appeals (7th cir.) 1979. Assoc. Kahn, Dees, Donovan & Kahn, Evansville, Ind., 1978-81, ptnr., 1981—; adj. prof. law of evidence U. Evansville, 1980-82; mem. instl. rev. bd. St. Mary's Med. Ctr., Evansville, 1980—. Pres. Evansville Parks Found., 1982-83, Vanderburgh Law Library Found., Evansville, 1983-84; bd. dirs. Evansville Mus. Arts and Sci., 1982—; mem. Bd. Park Commrs., Evansville, 1984—. Recipient Cert. of Achievement, City of Evansville, 1982, Civic Service award Ind. Assn. Cities and Towns, 1983. Mem. ABA (litigation sect.), Ind. State Bar Assn., Ind. Trial Lawyers Assn., Seventh Cir. Bar Assn., Evansville Bar Assn. (pres. 1984-85). Methodist. Club: Democrats for Better Govt. (bd. dirs. 1981-83). Home: 417 S Alvord Blvd Evansville IN 47714 Office: Kahn Dees Donovan & Kahn 305 Union Fed Bldg PO Box 3646 Evansville IN 47735

SHREVE, GREGORY MONROE, university administrator; b. Munich, West Germany, Aug. 3, 1950; came to U.S., 1951; s. Joyce L. and Rosa (Zerweiss) S.; m. Joan Marie Nelson, Dec. 29, 1971; 1 dau., Jessica Corrine. B.A., Ohio State U., 1971, M.A., 1974, Ph.D., 1975. Asst. prof. anthropology Kent State U., East Liverpool, Ohio, 1975-80, assoc. prof., East Liverpool and Burton, 1980—, asst. dean, 1978-80, dean, 1981—; pres. Structured Software Systems, Burton, 1982—; vis. prof. Karl Marx U., Leipzig; pres. Logitech, Inc., Chesterland, 1985—. Author: Genesis of Structures, Vols. I and II, 1975, 83; contbr. articles to profl. jours. Fellow Am. Anthrop. Assn., Am. Folklore Soc., Assn. for Computing Machinery, Soc. Hist. Archaeology. Lodge: Rotary. Advocation: collector 19th century Am. ceramics. Home: 14649 Evergreen Dr Burton OH 44021 Office: Kent State U Geauga Campus 14111 Claridon-Troy Burton OH 44021

SHREWSBURY, CAROLYN ANN, political science educator; b. Wichita, Kans., Mar. 28, 1943; d. Richard Charles and Virginia Lee (Martin) Mundell; m. Walton Scott Shrewsbury, July 18, 1969. B.A., U. Chgo., 1965; M.A., U. Okla., 1968, Ph.D., 1974. Asst. prof. polit. sci. Mankato (Minn.) State U., 1968, assoc. prof., 1975-79, prof., 1979—, chmn. women's studies, 1978-83. Mem. Region Nine Subcom. on Human Resources, 1981—. Bush grantee, 1983-84; recipient Outstanding Faculty award Mankato State Student Ambassadors, 1982. Mem. Am. Polit. Sci. Assn., Nat. Women's Studies Assn. (nat. task force on service-learning), Midwest Polit. Sci. Assn., Minn. Women in Higher Edn. (dir. 1980-82), NOW, Delta Kappa Gamma. Contbr. articles to profl. jours. Home: 135 Hawaiian Dr Mankato MN 56001 Office: PO Box 7 Mankato State U Mankato MN 56001

SHROPSHEAR, GEORGE, surgeon; b. Chgo., Nov. 28, 1905; s. George and Ella (Baxter) S.; B.S., U. Ill., 1929, M.D. (Julius Rosenwald fellow), 1931, M.S., 1931; m. Evelyn L. Harris, Feb. 19, 1936, children—Lois, Doris, George III, Joan, Norman J. Intern, Provident Hosp., Chgo., 1931-32, jr. attending surgeon, 1935-42, asso. attending surgeon, 1945-49, sr. attending, 1949—, chmn. dept. surgery, 1955-57, pres. med. staff, 1964-67; fellow gen. edn. bd. in proctology with preceptorship, Provident Hosp., 1933-36; resident surgery Cook County Hosp., Chgo., 1942-45. Med. supt. Cook County Jail, Chgo., 1960-62. Mem. Drug Abuse Council, 1971. Bd. dirs. Ill. Council Continuing Med. Edn. Diplomate Am. Bd. Surgery. Fellow A.C.S., Chgo. Surg. Soc., Am. Soc. Colon and Rectal Surgeons; mem. AAAS, AMA (merit certificate 1966), Ill., Chgo. med. socs., Sigma Xi. Home: 5129 S Drexel Ave Chicago IL 60615 Office: 1525 E 53d St Chicago IL 60615

SHTOHRYN, DMYTRO M., librarian, educator; b. Zvyniach, Ukraine, Nov. 9, 1923; came to U.S., 1950, naturalized, 1955; m. Mykhailo and Kateryna (Figol) S.; student Ukrainian Free U., Munich, W. Ger., 1947-48; M.A. in Slavic Studies, U. Ottawa (Can.), 1958, B.L.S. summa cum laude, 1959, Ph.D. in Ukrainian Lit., 1970; m. Eustachia Barwinska, Sept. 3, 1955; children—Bohdar O., Liudoslava V. Slavic cataloger U. Ottawa, 1959; cataloger Can. Nat. Research Council Library, 1959-60; mem. faculty U. Ill., Champaign-Urbana, 1960—, prof. library adminstrn., 1975—, head Slavic cataloging, 1964—, lectr. Ukrainian lit., 1969—, chmn. Ukrainian Research Program, 1984—; vis. prof. U. Ottawa, summer 1974; vis. prof. Ukrainian Free U., 1977, 82-83, prof., 1984—; assoc. prof. Ukrainian Catholic U., Rome, 1978—. Recipient Silver medal Can. Parliament, 1959, Glorier Soc. Can. award, 1959. Mem. Am. Assn. Advancement Slavic Studies, Assn. Advancement Ukrainian Studies (charter, pres. 1981—), ALA, Shevchenko Sci. Soc. (exec. com. 1977—), Ukrainian Library Assn. Am. (pres. 1972-76, 82—), Ukrainian Acad. Arts and Scis. in U.S., Ukrainian Hist. Assn. (exec. com. 1981—), Internat. I. Franko Soc. (pres. 1978-82), Permanent Conf. Ukrainian Studies (chmn. 1979-80), Am.-Ukrainian Assn. U. Profs. (exec. com. 1977—), Ukrainian Writers Soc., Delta Tau Kappa. Mem. Ukrainian Catholic Ch. Compiler: (biographical directory) Ukrainians in North America), 1975; author articles. Editor: Catalogue of Publications of the Ukrainian Academy of Sciences 1918-1930, 1966; newsletter Slavic sect. ALA, 1969. Office: Slavic and East European Library U Ill 1408 W Gregory Dr Urbana IL 61801

SHUEY, HERBERT ERSLA, protective services official; b. Peola, Kans., Feb. 15, 1942; s. Herbert Henry and Elizibeth Louise (Craig) S.; m. Julianne Charno, Aug. 22, 1975 (div. Dec. 1, 1980); m. Gene Marie Patterson, Oct. 3, 1981. B.A., U. Mo.; M.A., U. Mo.-Kansas City, postgrad.; postgrad. U. Kans. Work evaluator Johnson County Mental Retardation Dept., Lenexa, Kans., 1970-71, houseparent, Olathe, Kans., 1971-72, dir. recreation, Lenexa, 1971-74; tchr. Kansas State Sch. Deaf, Olathe, 1973-76; adv. bd. 1981—; policeman, detective Johnson County Sheriff's Dept., Olathe, 1976—; chmn. adv. bd. Johnson County Mental Health, Olathe, 1980—; cons. Child Protection, Johnson County, 1982—. Contbr. articles to profl. jours. Mem. Friends of Zoo, Kansas City, 1976, Friends of Art, Kansas City, 1977. Served with U.S. Army, 1963-67. Recipient Cert. of Appreciation, Child Protection, Johnson County, 1984, Service award Lion's Club, 1977, Service award Optimist Club, 1979. Mem. Nat. Sheriff's Assn. Republican. Club: Viet Nam Vets. (Kansas City). Avocations: history; bridge. Office: Johnson County Sheriff's Dept Courthouse Olathe KS 66061

SHUFELT, JOHN MARSHALL, psychologist; b. Campbell, N.Y., Nov. 13, 1913; s. Jesse Fremont and Nettie Louise (Reed) S.; m. Aug. 11, 1943; children—John Marshall, Lynne Shufelt Cook. B.A., Colgate U., 1936; Ed.D., Wayne State U., 1963; grad. Episc. Theol. Sem., 1946. Cert. psychologist, Mich. Tchr. sci., high sch., Caguas, P.R., 1936-37; tchr. sci. Grace High Sch., N.Y.C., 1938-40; tchr. sci., asst. prin. Lago High Sch., Aruba, N.W.I., 1941-43; assoc. St. Andrew's Episcopal Ch., Ann Arbor, Mich., 1946-48; canon Cathedral Ch. of St. Paul, Detroit, 1948-60; rector St. John's Epis. Ch., Royal Oak, Mich., 1960-69; cons. psychologist in pvt. practice, 1969-77; dir. research PMH, Inc., Bloomfield Hills, Mich., 1977—. Served to ensign USNR, 1943-45. Mem. Phi Beta Kappa. Clubs: Econ. (Detroit); Rotary (Bloomfield Hills). Home: 3120 Coolidge Hwy Royal Oak MI 48072 Office: PMH Inc 2550 Telegraph Rd Suite 200 Bloomfield Hills MI 48013

SHUGAN, STEVEN MARK, marketing educator; b. Chgo., Apr. 21, 1952; s. David Lester and Charlotte Rose Shugan; B.S. in Chemistry, So. Ill. U., 1973, M.B.A., 1974; Ph.D. in Managerial Econs. and Decision Scis. (fellow), Northwestern U., 1978; m. Irene H. Ginter, Dec. 16, 1973; 1 son, Adam Joshua. Lectr. Grad. Sch. Mgmt., Northwestern U., Evanston, Ill., 1976-77; asst. prof. bus. adminstrn. Grad. Sch. Mgmt., U. Rochester (N.Y.), 1977-79; asst. prof. mktg. Grad. Sch. Bus., U. Chgo., 1979-82, assoc. prof., 1982—; chmn., organizer sessions numerous nat. confs., 1979—; cons. various cos., 1976—; chmn. Mktg. Sci. Conf., 1983. Mem. Am. Mktg. Assn., Ops. Research Soc. Am., Assn. for Consumer Research, Inst. Mgmt. Scis., Am. Statis. Assn. Contbr. articles and revs. to profl. jours., chpts. to books; assoc. editor Mgmt. Sci.; mem. editorial bd. Mktg. Sci. Jour. Office: 1101 E 58th St Chicago IL 60637

SHULA, ROBERT JOSEPH, lawyer, medical clinic executive, travel agency executive; b. South Bend, Ind., Dec. 10, 1936; s. Joseph Edward and Bertha Mona (Buckner) S.; m. Gaye Ann Martin, Oct. 14, 1978; children—Deirdre Regina, Robert Joseph II. B.S. in Bus., Ind. U., 1958, J.D., 1961. Bar: Ind. 1961. Ptnr. Bingham Summers Welsh & Spilman, Indpls., 1965—, sr. ptnr., 1982—; mem. faculty Nat. Inst. Trial Advocacy; guest lectr. Brit. Medicine and Law Soc., 1979, Ind. U. Sch. Law; medico-legal lectr. Ind. U. Schs. Medicine, Dentistry, and Nursing; pres. Meridian Women's Clinic, Inc., Indpls.; v.p. Fifth Season Travel, Inc., Indpls. Bd. dirs. Arts Insight, Indpls.; pres. Oriental Arts Soc., Indpls., 1975-79; trustee Indpls. Mus. Art, 1975-78, life trustee, 1984—; bd. dirs. Ind. Repertory Theatre, Indpls., 1982—, vice chmn., 1984—; v.p., bd. dirs. Flanner House of Indpls., Inc., 1977—. Served to maj. JAGC, USAFR, 1961-65. Mem. Indpls. Bar Assn., Ind. State Bar Assn., Fed. Bar Assn., ABA, Bar Assn. 7th Fed. Circuit, Assn. Trial Lawyers Am., Am. Law Inst., Am. So. Appraisers. Democrat. Episcopalian. Clubs: Indpls. Athletic, Woodstock Country (Indpls.). Home: 4137 N Meridan St Indianapolis IN 46208 Office: One Indiana Sq 2700 Ind Tower Indianapolis IN 46204

SHULER, DANIEL GLENN, chemical company executive; b. June 15, 1954; s. Daniel Phillip and Nina Joyce (Nave) S.; m. Nancy Ann Guffey, June 22, 1974. B.S., Western Ky. U., 1982. Communications specialist Med. Ctr. at Bowling Green, Ky., 1975-82; geological cons. Geocore, Bowling Green, 1982-83; dist. rep. NALCO Chem. Co., Sugarland, Tex., 1984—. Served with Army N.G., 1974-80. Decorated Expert Field Medic badge, Army Commendation medal. Mem. Am. Assn. Petroleum Geologists. Republican. Roman Catholic. Avocations: golf; jogging; racquetball. Home: 205 W Ash St Robinson IL 62454 Office: NALCO Chem Co 2309 G N Kentucky Ave Evansville IN 47711

SHULMAN, AVERY NEAL, optometrist, educator; b. Chgo., Mar. 16, 1949; s. Paul Frank and Adeline (Geller) S.; m. Joyce Lynn Ross, Mar. 18, 1973; children—Daniel, Scott, Amy. Student U. Ill., 1967-68; B.S., Ill. Coll. Optometry, 1970, O.D. cum laude, 1972; M.P.H., U. Ill.-Chgo., 1973. From instr. to asst. prof. Ill. Coll. Optometry, Chgo., 1973-79; optometrist Cole Nat. Corp., Chgo., 1979-84; optometrist, dir. profl. services Eyewear Factory, Schaumburg, Ill., 1984—. Editor: Pre-clinic Laboratory Manual, 1977. Contbr. articles to profl. jours. Grantee USPHS, 1972-73. Mem. Nat. Eye Research Found., Tomb and Key. Democrat. Jewish. Lodge: B'nai B'rith. Avocations: golf; bowling; reading. Home: 805 Sutton Dr Northbrook IL 60062 Office: Eyewear Factory G122 Woodfield Mall Schaumburg IL 60195

SHUMATE, DOROTHY LEE, pharmacist; b. Oak Hill, W.Va., Feb. 4, 1956; d. Garland Lee and Betty Alice (Perry) Pugh; m. David Keith Shumate, Mar. 14, 1981. Student Concord Coll., 1974-76; B.S. in Pharmacy, W.Va. U., 1979. Registered pharmacist. Pharmacist, Rural Acres Pharmacy, Beckley, W.Va., 1979-81, Beckley Hosp., 1979, Fairway Drug, Addison, Ill., 1981-82, Martin Ave. Pharmacy, Naperville, Ill., 1982—. Mem. Am. Pharm. Assn., AAUW, Rho Chi, Gamma Beta Phi, Alpha Chi, Lambda Kappa Sigma. Republican. Mem. Ch. of the Brethren. Avocations: Ping pong; piano; organ; racquetball. Home: Bethany Seminary Oak Brook IL 60521

SHUMATE, MACK HARRIS, coal company executive; b. Northfork, W.Va., Feb. 11, 1922; s. Furchas M. and Bessie (Whittington) A.; m. Helen Angela Schaffer, July 5, 1947; children—Mack H. Jr., Monroe, David, Loren. Student, Va. Poly. Inst., Blacksburg, 1941-43; B.S. in Mining Engring., W.Va. U., 1947. Registered profl. engr., W.Va., Colo., N.Mex. Asst. gen. mgr., mine supt. Island Creek Coal Co., Holden, W.Va., 1947-52; gen. supt., div. gen. mgr., chief engr. Truax Traer Coal Col., Chgo., 1952-62; chief engr., gen. mgr. underground mines Truax Traer div. Consol. Coal Co., 1962-66; gen. mgr. underground mines, asst. to pres. Consol. Midwest div. subs. CONOCO, 1966-69; v.p. engring. Zeigler Coal Co., Des Plaines, Ill., 1969-74; sr. v.p. engring. and planning Zeigler Coal Co. subs. Houston Natural Gas Corp. 1974—, also dir.; dir. Jefferson Oil Co., Riverside Farms. Served to 2d lt. USAF, 1943-45; ETO. Decorated Air medal with cluster. Recipient Fin. Chmn. award Buckskin council Boy Scouts Am., 1957. Mem. Soc. Mining Engrs. of Am. Inst. Mining Engrs., Rocky Mountain Mining Inst., Ill. Mining Inst., Ill. Geol. Survey (chmn.), Ill. Coal Assn. (bd. dirs.). Republican. Methodist. Clubs: Chgo. Coal and Traffic Exchange; Thorngate Country (Deerfield, Ill.). Lodges: Masons, Shriners. Contbr. various tech papers on underground mining practices to profl. jours. Office: 2700 River Rd Des Plaines IL 60018

SHUMWAY, SPENCER THOMAS (TOM), industrial distributing company executive; b. Bronxville, N.Y., May 31, 1943; s. Floyd Mallory Shumway and Margaret (Rabling) Shumway McAvoy; m. Alicia Fain, Apr. 10, 1965 (div. Dec. 1970); 1 dau., Erin Linn; m. 2d Bonnie Lee Shuppert, Dec. 20, 1975; children—Kristen Marie, Megan Nichole. Student pub. and pvt. schs., Lake Forest, Ill., Culver, Ind., Morristown, N.J. Adminstrv. asst. City of Lake Forest, 1960-64; corp. buyer Rogers Park Auto Parts (Ill.), 1964-66; br. mgr. Bearing Hdqrs. Co., Broadview, Ill., 1966-71; dist. mgr. Berry Bearing Co., Chgo., 1971—. Mem. South Bend Purchasing Mgmt. Assn. (sec. 1980-82), Nat. Assn. Purchasing Mgrs. Republican. Presbyterian. Lodge: Soc. Cin. (successor mem.). Home: 11002 Maumee Dr Granger IN 46530 Office: Bearings Service Co 412 E Sample St South Bend IN 46634

SHUPERT, ANN ELAINE, personnel manager; b. Indpls., Oct. 16, 1948; d. Harlan B. and Audrey Miller (Watson) Shupert. B.A. in Sociology, Hanover Coll., 1971; M.B.A., Butler U., 1976. Dep. for penalties Ind. Employment Security Div., Indpls., 1975-78; personnel asst. Rand McNally & Co., Indpls., 1978-82; personnel mgr. Resort Condominiums Internat. Indpls., 1982—. Vol. jr. symphony women's orgn. Indpls. Symphony, 1980—; vol. Ptnrs. 2000; bd. dirs. Whitehall Corp., 1982—. Mem. Assn. M.B.A. Execs., Am. Soc. Personnel Adminstrs., Am. Compensation Assn., Nat. Assn. Female Execs., Nat. Mgmt. Assn., P.E.O. Office: 9333 N Meridian PO Box 80229 Indianapolis IN 46280

SHURY, VERA, security services company executive, insurance agency executive; b. Bremen, Ger., Dec. 7, 1939; came to U.S., 1951; d. Werner and Lisa Mali Magda Karla (Stege) Vujovic; m. Donald Shury, June 9, 1962 (div. Jan. 1984); children—Lisa, Donald. Student Fenn Coll., 1959-62, Ursuline Coll., 1977-81. Gen. agt. A-1 Bonding, Cleve., 1963-83; pres. State Alarm Systems, 1979-84, A-Aalavera Surety, Inc., Cleve., 1983—; pres. Liberty Sci., Inc., 1984—. Lobbyist Cleve. Growth Assn., 1982. Mem. No. Ohio Bail Assn. (pres. 1979-83), Beta Sigma Phi. Republican. Office: 1234 Standard Bldg 1370 Ontario St Cleveland OH 44113

SIDDIQI, MOHAMMED SHAHID, accountant; b. Hyderabad, India, Jan. 18, 1942; s. Mohammed Masood and Majeedunissa S.; B.Comm., Osmania U., 1963; m. Azra Sultana, Oct. 18, 1968; children—Rubina, Zarina, Razeena, Majid. Acct., William Offenbach Ltd., London, 1965-66; chief acct. Aronstead Ltd., London, 1966-68; controller M. Loeb Ltd., Ottawa, 1968-74; public acct. A-1 Income Tax Co., Ottawa, 1974-78; controller Top Rank Enterprises, Inc., Ottawa, 1980-81, acct., tax cons. Avon Income Tax Service, Inc., Nepean, Ottawa, 1981—. Chaderghat Coll. scholar, 1959. Mem. Brit. Inst. Mgmt., Brit. Soc. Commerce, Assn. Indsl. and Comml. Accts., Nat. Soc. Public Accts., Inst. Internal Auditors, Nat. Soc. Accts. for Coops., Nat. Assn. Accts., Am. Mgmt. Assn., Can. Inst. Mgmt., Am. Acctg. Assn., Am. Chartered Inst. Fin. Controllers and Adminstrs. Office: 145 Craig Henry Dr Nepean Ottawa ON K2G 3Z8 Canada

SIDES, GEORGE E., brokerage account executive; b. Highspire, Pa., Aug. 27, 1934; s. Robert E. and Gertrude M. (Kearns) S.; m. Virginia R. Pihl, June 21, 1957 (div. June 1983); children—Jeanine M., Kathryn M., Rebecca E., Robert O., G. Samuel. B.S. in Bus., Drexel U., 1957. Registered rep. Mktg. ofcl. IBM, N.Y.C., 1957-70, F.S. Smithers, N.Y.C., 1970-74, Spencer-Trask, Chgo., 1974-83; account exec. Blunt Ellis & Loewi, Chgo., 1983—. Republican precinct capt., Winnetka, Ill., 1978-83; mem. Winnetka Caucus, 1979; exec. v.p. Winnetka PTA, 1980. Served with U.S. Army, 1958-60. Episcopalian. Home: 148 Glencoe Rd Glencoe IL 60022 Office: Blunt Ellis & Loewi 9933 Lawler Ave Skokie IL 60077

SIDLE, WILLIAM CHRISTOPHER, geologist; b. Montclair, N.J., Aug. 15, 1951; s. Kermit Edward and Helen Marie (O'Gorman) S. B.S. in Geology, U. Idaho, 1973; M.S. in Geology, Portland State U., 1979. Registered geologist, Oreg. Mine geologist Bunker Hill Mining Co., Kellogg, Idaho, 1973-77; hydrologist U.S. Geol. Survey, Portland, Oreg., 1978-80; engring. geologist Found. Scis., Inc., Portland, 1980-81; sr. geologist Gulf Research and Devel. Co., Houston, 1981-84; tech. mgr. radioactive waste dept. U.S. Dept Energy, Columbus, Ohio, 1984—; cons. No. Energy Resources Co., Portland, 1977-78. Author: U.S. Geological Survey Resources of Oregon, 1980. Contbr. articles to profl. jours. Scout leader Columbia Pacific council Boy Scouts Am., 1978-80, Sam Houston council, 1981-83. Ruth Klein Mineralogy Meml. Fund grantee, 1979. Mem. Am. Assn. Petroleum Geologists, Geol. Soc. Am., Geothermal Resources Council, Geochem. Soc., Am. Inst. Profl. Geologists (cert.). Republican. Roman Catholic. Avocations: model railroading, spelunking, lighthouse photography, chess, running, ice skating. Home: PO Box 12394 Columbus OH 43212 Office: US Dept Energy Salt Repository Project Office 505 King Ave Columbus OH 43201

SIEBEN, JAMES GEORGE, adjudant general of Minnesota; b. Hastings, Minn., Apr. 19, 1924; s. Harry A. and Irene H. (Buckley) S.; student U. Minn., Stanford U.; m. Charlotte Jean Gove, July 10, 1954; children—James, Lisa, Terrance. Served as enlisted man AUS, 1942-45; commd. 2d lt. N.G., advanced through grades to maj. gen.; served as 1st lt. U.S. Army, 1951-52; comdt. Minn. Mil. Acad.; now adj. gen. Minn. Mem. NG Assn. of U.S., Adj. Gen's Assn., Am. Legion, VFW. Decorated Silver Star medal with oak leaf cluster, Purple Heart, Bronze Star medal, Combat Inf. badge, Minn. Commendation medal, Minn. medal for merit, Norwegian Disting. Service medal; comdr. Royal Order St. Olav, others. Office: Veterans Service Bldg Saint Paul MN 55155*

SIEBENMANN, NANCYLEE ARBUTUS, hospital administrator, nurse; b. Ladysmith, Wis., Oct. 12, 1933; d. Herbert O. and Arbutus H. (Ruckdashel) Hartig; m. John F. Siebenmann, Apr. 13, 1957; children—John Hart, Lori Jean. Diploma St. Luke's Sch. Nursing, Duluth, Minn., 1954; B.S. in Nursing Adminstrn., U. Minn., 1957; M.A. in Nursing Adminstrn., U. Iowa, 1971. R.N., Iowa. Staff nurse St. Luke's Hosp., 1954, U. Minn., Mpls., 1955-57, Iowa Meth. Hosp., Des Moines, 1957; head nurse pre/post surg. unit St. Luke's Hosp., Cedar Rapids, Iowa, 1957-59, instr., asst. dir. St. Luke's Sch. Nursing, 1960-71, assoc. adminstr. St. Luke's Hosp., 1974-80, v.p. corp. devel. adminstrn., 1980-82, staff asst. to pres.; v.p. St. Luke's Health Resources; founding chmn. and dir. B.S. in Nursing Program, Coe Coll., Cedar Rapids, 1972-74; lectr. in field. Mem. Small Bus. Adv. Council; bd. dirs. ARC (local chpt.). Recipient USPHS grantee, 1956, 57, 71. Mem. Am. Coll. Hosp. Adminstrs., Am. Hosp. Assn. (del.-at-large 1979-82, mem. council on nursing 1980-83), Sigma Theta Tau. Republican. Lutheran. Contbr. articles to profl. publs. Office: St Lukes Methodist Hosp 1026 A Ave NE Cedar Rapids IA 52402

SIEBER, BRADLEY CARLTON, insurance agency executive, insurance consultant; b. Cleve., Oct. 6, 1946; s. Carl Jefferson and Anna Marie (Skapura) S.; m. Diane Marie Krysa, Nov. 25, 1980. Degree in Mktg. Mgmt., Cleve. State U., 1969. Sales mgr. CNA Ins., Cleve., 1969-71; br. mgr. A.I.G. Group, N.Y.C., 1971-74; v.p., gen. mgr. Thomas J. Unik Co., Cleve., 1974—; advisor, cons. Cleve. Police Patrolmans Assn., 1977—; mem. agts. adv. council Midwestern Group, Cin., 1981-83. Democrat. Russian Orthodox. Office: Thomas J Unik Co 2900 Chester Ave Cleveland OH 44114

SIECK, HAROLD F., state legislator; b. Pleasant Dale, Nebr., Feb. 29, 1916; ed. public schs.; m. Elise Meinberg, Feb. 8, 1942; children—Thomas, Barbara, Roger, Gerald, Annette. Farmer; mem. Nebr. Legislature, 1978—. Bd. dirs. Seward County (Nebr.) Rural Power Dist.; chmn. Lower Platte S. NRD; Democratic precinct committeeman. Lutheran.

SIEFKER, GREGORY WILLIAM, broadcasting executive; b. Alma, Mich., May 2, 1945; s. Joseph Leonard and Lorna Helen (Gallagher) S.; m. Carol J. Adams, Apr. 19, 1968; children—Neil Gregory, Jennifer Jo, Anthony Jon. Grad. Brown Inst., 1966. Announcer Sta. WAAM, Ann Arbor, Mich.; news dir. Sta. WSDS, Ypsilanti, Mich.; news reporter Sta. WKZO-TV, Kalamazoo; cost estimator Rieth Riley Constrn., Kalamazoo; owner, operator Siefker Broadcasting Co., St. Louis, Mich. Bd. dirs. St. Louis Downtown Devel. Authority, 1980-84; scoutmaster Lake Huron Area Council Boy Scouts Am. Recipient Scouting Spirit award Lake Huron Area Council, 1983, Minuteman award State of Mich., Gratiot County, 1985. Mem. St. Louis C. of C. Mem. Church of Christ Ch. Lodges: Lions, Rotary. Home: 2620 N Baldwin Ithaca MI 48847 Office: Siefker Broadcasting Corp 4170 N State Alma MI

SIEGEL, HOWARD JACOB, aerospace technical executive; b. N.Y.C., Oct. 19, 1929; s. Murray L. and Jean (Malino) S.; m. Frances Marie Goldstein, June 17, 1951; children—Michael B., Nancy E., David L. B.S. in Mining Engring., U. of Ky., 1951, M.S. in Metall. Engring., 1955. Research assoc. Ky. Research Found., Lexington, 1953-55; engr., mgr. McDonnell Aircraft Co., St. Louis, 1955—; instr. Washington U., St. Louis, 1956-66; cons. NASA, Washington, 1965-76, U.S. Air Force, Washington, 1972-73; lectr. Served to 1st lt., USAF, 1951-53. Recipient Engr. of Yr. award MCAIR-Mfg., 1977. Fellow Am. Soc. for Metals; mem. AIAA. Avocations: tennis. Home: 14147 Forestvale Dr Chesterfield MO 63017

SIEGEL, ROBERT H., lawyer; b. Cin., Nov. 16, 1945; s. Samuel and Ruth (Jacobson) S.; m. Deborah Michelle Lowenstein, Dec. 27, 1969; children—Robyn Jessica, Emily Gayle, Todd Justin. B.A., U. Cin., 1968; J.D., Salmon P. Chase Law Sch., 1975. Bar: Ohio 1975. Atty. City of Cin., 1975-79; mem. firm Furer, Moskowitz, Siegel & Mezibov, 1978-83, Smith & Schnacke, 1983—; title agt. Chgo. Title Ins. Co. and Title Ins. Co. Minn., Cin., 1983—. Trustee, Orthodox Home for the Aged, 1978—. Mem. Nat. Health Lawyers Assn., Ohio Land Title Assn., ABA, Ohio Bar Assn., Cin. Bar Assn., Omicron Delta Epsilon. Jewish. Club: Crest Hills Country (v.p. bd. trustees 1982—). Lodge: Masons. Avocations: golf; tennis. Home: 6 Hickory Hollow Cincinnati OH 45241 Office: Smith & Schnacke 2900 DuBois Tower Cincinnati OH 45202

SIEH, MAURINE KAY, nurse; b. Leon, Iowa, Sept. 28, 1950; d. Vernon Charles and Dorothy Maxine (Akes) Dobson; B.S. in Nursing, N.E. Mo. State U., 1972; m. Robert Hans Sieh, Nov. 18, 1972; children—Robert Carter, Jennifer Clarissa. Charge nurse psychiat. unit St. John's Hosp., Springfield, Mo., 1972-74; public health nurse Will County Health Dept., Joliet, Ill., 1974-75; unit nurse Mental Health Inst. Mentally Retarded Children, Park Forest, Ill., 1977-79; instr. Lamaze method childbirth, Topeka, Kans., 1981; staff nurse, co-chmn. nursing standards com. Menninger Found., Topeka, 1980-81; staff nurse, prenatal educator Ob/Gyn Clinic, U. Miss. Med. Ctr., Jackson, 1981—; instr. Lamaze method childbirth, 1981—. Mem. Am. Soc. Psychoprophylaxis in Obstetrics, Nat. League of Nursing, Internat. Childbirth Edn. Assn., Nat. Arbor Day Found., Smithsonian Instn., Nature Conservancy, Audubon Soc. Mem. Brethren Ch.

SIEKMANN, REM OWEN, business developer; b. Grosse Pointe Farms, Mich., Dec. 15, 1954; s. Harold John and Joan Hoffman (Henritzy) S.; m. Kathleen Eleanor Lake, Jan. 20, 1979; 1 child, Sarah Lake. B.S.E. cum laude, Duke U., 1976; M.B.A., U. Chgo., 1983. Registered profl. engr. Mfg. devel. engr. Baxter Travenol Labs., Deerfield, Ill., 1976-78, sr. devel. engr., 1978-79, prin. engr., 1979-80; project engr. Am. Covertors div. Am. Hosp. Supply Corp., Evanston, Ill., 1980-83; new product planning mgr. Am. Hosp. Supply Corp., 1983-84, sr. bus. analyst, 1984-85, mgr. bus. devel., 1985—. Patentee in field. Patroller Nat. Ski Patrol System, 1969—. Mem. Inst. Environ. Sci., Nat. Soc. Profl. Engrs., ASTM (contbr. F01.10 subcom. 1981-84). Presbyterian. Home: 739 S Cook St Barrington IL 60010 Office: American Hospital Supply Corp One American Plaza Evanston IL 60201

SIEMENS, STEPHEN KENNETH, college president; b. Ft. Dodge, Iowa, Apr. 21, 1952; s. Kenneth Marinus and Harriett Lucille (Ruberg) S.; m. Barbara Jean Price, Dec. 22, 1972; children—Staci Jean, Leisl Suzanne, Christopher Stephen. B.A. in Christian Edn., Ozark Bible Coll., 1974; postgrad. Ky. Christian Coll., 1984—. Student prof. Ozark Bible Coll., Joplin, Mo., 1971-74, prof., 1974-75; prof. Platte Valley Bible Coll., Scottsbluff, Nebr., 1975-77; prof. Iowa Christian Coll., Des Moines, 1977-81, pres., 1982—. Author: Shake Your Head Yes, 1985. Contbr. numerous articles to publs. Pres. Iowa Sunday Sch. Assn., Des Moines, 1981—; deacon Rising Sun Ch. of Christ, 1978—. Mem. Pres.'s Assn., Am. Mgmt. Assn. Republican. Lodge: Kiwanis (Outstanding Service award 1976). Avocations: fishing, wood working, camping, writing, gardening. Home: 6478 NE 5th Ave Runnells IA 50237 Office: Iowa Christian Coll 2847 Indianola Ave Des Moines IA 50315

SIERAWSKI, JOSEPH JAMES, manufacturing company executive; b. Royal Oak, Mich., Aug. 31, 1956; s. Francis John and Rose Frances (Serge) S.; m. Nancy Lynn Quasarano, July 19, 1980; 1 dau., Mary Katherine. B.A., Detroit, 1979. Stock worker II, State of Mich., Lincoln Park, 1977-79; contract adminstr. Evans Products, Inc., Grand Rapids, Mich., 1980-82; material control mgr. Alloy Tek, Grandville, Mich., 1982—. Mem. Am. Prodn. and Inventory Control Soc., Grand Rapids Jaycees. Democrat. Roman Catholic. Avocations: golf; volleyball; skiing; reading; ice skating. Home: 4585 Bellewood Ct Caledonia MI 49316 Office: Alloytek Inc 2900 Wilson Ave Grandville MI 49418

SIERLES, FREDERICK STEPHEN, psychiatrist, educator; b. Bklyn., Nov. 9, 1942; s. Samuel and Elizabeth (Meiselman) S.; A.B., Columbia, 1963; M.D., Chgo. Med. Sch., 1967; m. Laurene Harriet Cohn, Oct. 25, 1970; children—Hannah Beth, Joshua Caleb. Intern, Cook County Hosp., Chgo., 1967-68; resident in psychiatry Mt. Sinai Hosp., N.Y.C., 1968-69, Mt. Sinai Hosp., Chgo., 1969-71, chief resident, 1970-71; staff psychiatrist U.S. Reynolds Army Hosp., Ft. Sill, Okla., 1971-73; assoc. attending psychiatrist Mt. Sinai Hosp., Chgo., 1973-74; instr. psychiatry Chgo. Med. Sch., 1973-74, dir. undergrad. edn. in psychiatry, 1974—, asst. prof., 1974-78, assoc. prof., 1978—; cons. psychiatry Cook County Hosp., 1974-79, St. Mary of Nazareth Hosp., 1979-84; chief Mental Health Clinic, North Chicago (Ill.) VA Hosp., 1982-85, chief psychiatry service, 1983-85. Served to maj., M.C., U.S. Army, 1971-73. Recipient Ganser Meml. award Mt. Sinai Hosp., 1970; Prof. of Year award Chgo. Med. Sch., 1977, 80, 83; N.Y. State Regents scholar, 1959-63; NIMH grantee, 1974-83; Chgo. Med. Sch. grantee, 1974-83. Diplomate Am. Bd. Psychiatry and Neurology. Mem. Am. Psychiat. Assn., Assn. Interns and Residents Cook County Hosp., Assn. Dirs. Med. Student Edn. in Psychiatry (exec. council 1985—), Nat. Assn. VA Physicians (sec.-treas. North Chgo. chpt. 1985—), Nat. Assn. VA Chiefs of Psychiatry, Alpha Omega Alpha, Phi Epsilon Pi. Editor textbook Clinical Behavioral Science, 1982; co-author textbook General Hospital Psychiatry, 1985; contbr. articles to profl. jours. Office: Chicago Medical School 3333 Green Bay Rd North Chicago IL 60064

SIEVERT, ROBERT ALBERT, clergyman, secondary school administrator; b. Watertown, Wis., May 20, 1935; s. Hubert A. and Ada L. (Frey) S.; B.A., Northwestern Coll., 1958; Div.M., Wis. Lutheran Sem., 1963; M.A., Coll. of St. Thomas, 1980; m. Jean Ann Ihde, Oct. 11, 1964; children—Julie Ann, Sharyn Jean, Scott Robert, Deanne Lyn. Instr., Northwestern Luth. Acad., Mobridge, S.D., 1960-61; ordained to ministry Wis. Evang. Luth. Synod, 1964; pastor Luth. chs. Montrose, Minn., 1964-68, Onalaska, Wis., 1968-71; prin. Saint Croix Luth. High Sch., West St. Paul, Minn., 1971-84, supt., 1984—; mem. Minn. Dept. Edn. Nonpublic Sch. Study Com., 1972-82, 85—; dir. pub. relations Western Wis. Dist., Wis. Evang. Luth. Synod, 1969-71. Mem. bd. control Luther High, Onalaska, Wis., 1969-71, chmn., 1970-71; mem. Minn. Dist. Bd. for Info. and Stewardship, Wis. Evang. Luth. Synod, 1965-68; bd. dirs. Minn. Ind. Sch. Fund, 1976-79, 84—, treas., 1985—. Mem. Nat. Assn. Secondary Sch. Prins., Minn. Assn. Pvt. Sch. Adminstrs., Assn. Luth. High Schs. (pres. 1976-78), Assn. for Supervision and Curriculum Devel.

SIGERSON, CHARLES WILLARD, JR., insurance company executive; b. Biloxi, Miss., Mar. 6, 1945; s. Charles Willard and Eugenia (Linstad) S.; m. Elizabeth Ann Moss, Dec. 9, 1967; children—Anthea Louis, Andrew Charles. B. in Gen. Studies, U. Nebr.-Omaha, 1971. Pres., owner, Sigerson Ins. Agy., Inc., Omaha, 1973—; v.p., treas Ms. Liz, Inc., 1983—. Pres. Floyd Rogers Diabetic Found., Lincoln, Nebr., 1981—; mem. Douglas County Stand-by Draft Bd., Omaha, 1982—; staff mem. Hal Daub for Congress, Omaha, 1980; chmn. Douglas County Republican Com., Omaha, 1982-83; mem. exec. com. Nebr. Rep. Com., Lincoln, 1982-83. Served to staff sgt. USAF, 1964-71. Recipient Cosmopolitan of Yr. award I-80 Cosmopolitan Club, 1982, Patrick Hodgins award I-80 Cosmopolitan Club, 1983, Legion of Honor award State Farm Ins. Co., 1984. Mem. Nat. Assn. Health Underwriters (Leading Producers Round Table award 1983, 84), Nat. Assn. Life Underwriters. Presbyterian. Club: I-80 Cosmopolitan (Omaha). Lodges: Rotary Internat., Elks, Masons. Avocations: genealogy; antique book and newspaper collecting; coin collecting. Home: 11435 Grand Circle Omaha NE 68164 Office: Sigerson Ins Agy Inc 10766 Fort St Omaha NE 68134

SIGLER, CAROL JEAN, educator; b. New Castle, Ind., July 19, 1949; d. Robert Sheldon and Ruth (Brooks) S. B.S., Ball State U., 1971, M.A., 1974. Elem. sci. tchr. Greenfield-Central Community Schs., Greenfield, Ind., 1971—. Chancel choir dir. Wilkinson United Methodist Ch., Ind., 1972-80; dir. music Trinity Park United Meth. Ch., Greenfield, 1981—. Students recipient 50 awards including 6 overall championships Central Ind. Regional Sci. Fair, 1974-84. Mem. Alph Delta Kappa (pres. Ind. Alpha Delta chpt. 1984—). Avocation: computer programming. Home: Rural Route 6 Box 224 Greenfield IN 46140 Office: Lincoln Park Sch North and School Sts Greenfield IN 46140

SIKORSKI, GERRY, congressman; b. Breckenridge, Minn., Apr. 26, 1948; s. Elroy and Helen S.; m. Susan Erkel, Aug., 1974; 1 dau., Anne. B.A. summa cum laude, U. Minn., 1970, J.D. magna cum laude, 1973. Bar: Minn. 1973; assoc. law firm Opperman & Pacquin, Mpls., from 1973; mem. Minn. State Senate, 1976-82, majority whip, 1980-82; mem. 98th-99th Congresses. Office: 414 Cannon House Office Bldg Washington DC 20515

SIKORSKI, RICHARD ANTHONY, equipment manufacturing exeutive; b. Cleve., June 23, 1934; s. John P. and Laura M. (Jankowski) S.; m. Diane H. Walker, May 1, 1965; children—Richard A., Stephanie O., William N. B.S. in Mech. Engring., Cleve. State U., 1972. Macinist, Sikorski Tool Co., Cleve., 1952-55; design draftsman Lester Engring. Co., Cleve., 1956-58, indsl. engr., 1959-64, mgr. indsl. engring., 1964-69; chief indsl. engr. Cast Equipment div. Combustion Engring. Co., Cleve., 1969-72, mgr. prodn. and inventory, 1973-74, v.p. mfg., 1974-82; gen. mgr., power systems plant Combustion Engring., East Chicago, Ind., 1983—. Mem. Am. Mgmt. Assn., Am. Productivity Ctr. Roman Catholic. Club: Chgo. Yacht.

SIKYTA, CURTIS ALLEN, lawyer; b. Lincoln, Nebr., Aug. 23, 1948; s. Curtis James and Margaret Louise (Jacobs) S.; m. Marcella Rose Rudloff, Jan. 5, 1974; children—Heather Lea, Jacob Nathaniel. Student, John F. Kennedy Coll., 1966-68; B.A., U. Nebr., 1975, J.D., 1978. Bars: Nebr. 1978, U.S. Dist. Ct. Nebr. 1978. Law clk. Hecht, Sweet, Alesio & Rierden, Lincoln, Nebr., 1977-78; assoc. J. Marvin Weems, P.C., Ord, Nebr., 1978-80; ptnr. Weems & Sikyta, P.C., Ord, 1980; sole practice, Ord, 1980—; mem. jud. nominating com. 20th Dist. Nebr., 1983—; dir. Arcadia State Bank, Nebr. Pres., founder activities com. Our Lady of Perpetual Help Parish, Ord, 1979-81; administrator trust fund St. Mary's Sch., Ord, 1980—, founder endowment fund, 1984; co-chmn. Ord Centennial Com., 1981; parish rep. Diocesan Synod, Grand Island, Nebr., 1983. Mem. ABA, Nebr. Bar Assn., Valley County Bar Assn., Assn. Trial Lawyers Am., Nebr. Assn. Trial Attys., Am. Legion, Ord C. of C. (bd. dirs. 1981-82). Republican. Roman Catholic. Home: 418 S 17th St Ord NE 68862 Office: 314 S 14th St Ord NE 68862

SILBAJORIS, FRANK RIMVYDAS, Lithuanian studies educator; b. Lithuania, Jan. 6, 1926; s. Pranas and Elzbieta (Bagonaviciute) S.; m. Milda Z., July 27, 1955; children—Victoria Silbajoris-Pollock, Alex. B.A. in English, Antioch Coll., 1953; M.A. in Russian, Columbia U., 1955, Ph.D. in Russian, 1962. Instr. Oberlin Coll. (Ohio), 1957-61, asst. prof., 1961-63; assoc. prof. Ohio State U., Columbus, 1963-67, prof., 1967—; pres. Inst. Lithuanian Studies; cons. Internat. Research and Exchanges Bd., 1977, 78, 79; cons. NEH; dir. NEH summer seminars for coll. tchrs., 1975, 77, for high school tchrs., 1983, 84. John Hay Whitney opportunity fellow, 1953-54; Ford Found. fgn. study and research fellow, 1954-56; Inter-Univ. travel grantee, 1963-64; Lithuanian Community prize lit. criticism, 1982; Woodrow Wilson fellow Kennan Found., 1984. Mem. Inst. Lithuanian Studies, Assn. Advancement Baltic Studies (pres. 1973-74), Am. Assn. Tchrs. Slavic and East European Languages, Am. Assn. Advancement Slavic Studies. Author: The Versification Theories of Trediakovskij, Lomonosov and Kantemir, 1968; Perfection of Exile: Essays on Lithuanian Literature in the West, 1970; editor: Second Conf. on Baltic Studies: Summary of Procs., 1970; Lituanistikos Instituto 1973; metu suvaziavimo darlai, 1975; The Architecture of Reading: Essays on Russian Literary Theory and Practice, 1976; Encounters in Reading, 1979; Zodziai ir prasme: Essays on Modern Soviet Lithuanian Literature, 1983; co-author, editor: Mind Against the Wall: Essays on Lithuanian Culture Under Soviet Occupation, 1983. Home: 4082 Ruxton Ln Columbus OH 43220 Office: Dept Slavic Languages Ohio State U Columbus OH 43210

SILBERMAN, ALAN HARVEY, lawyer; b. Chgo., Oct. 22, 1940; s. Milton J. and Mollie E. (Hymanson) S.; m. Margaret Judith Auslander, Nov. 17, 1968; children—Elena, Mark. B.A. with distinction, Northwestern U., 1961; LL.B., Yale U., 1964. Bar: Ill., 1964, U.S. Dist. Ct. (no. dist.) Ill., 1966, U.S. Ct. Appeals (7th cir.) 1970, (5th and 9th cir.) 1977, U.S. Supreme Ct. 1978, (D.C. cir.) 1979, (4th cir.) 1980, (11th cir.) 1981, (3rd cir.) 1982. Law clk. U.S. Dist. Ct., Chgo., 1964-66; assoc. Sonnenschein Carlin Nath & Rosenthal, Chgo., 1964-71, ptnr., 1972—; mem. antitrust adv. bd. Bur. Nat. Affairs, Washington D.C., 1985—. Contbr. articles to profl. jours. Bd. dirs., v.p., sec. Camp Ramah in Wisc., Inc., Chgo., 1966—; bd. dirs. Nat. Ramah Commn., Inc. of Jewish Theol. Sem. Am., N.Y.C., 1970—. Mem. Ill. State Bar Assn. (chmn. antitrust sect. 1975-76), ABA (chmn. antitrust sect. FTC com. 1981-83, chmn. nat. insts. 1983-85, mem. council antitrust sect. 1985—. Home: 430 Oakdale Glencoe IL 60022 Office: Sonnenschein Carlin Nath & Rosenthal 8000 Sears Tower Chicago IL 60606

SILBERMAN, CARL MORRIS, physician; b. Phila., Aug. 7, 1946; s. Emanuel Harry and Sylvia (Cohen) S.; B.A., Temple U., 1968; M.D., Jefferson Med. Coll., 1972. Resident, Cooper Med. Center, Camden, N.J., 1974-76; fellow in cardiology Northwestern U. Hosp., Chgo., 1977-79; practice medicine specializing in cardiology, Chgo., 1979—; asst. prof. medicine dept. cardiology Chgo. Med. Sch., 1979—; dir. cardiology unit Naval Regional Med. Center, North Chicago, Ill.; dir. coronary care unit Cook County Hosp., Chgo.; cons. in cardiology 11th Naval Dist., Cook County Hosp. Diplomate Am. Bd. Internal Medicine, Sub-bd. Cardiovasular Disease. Fellow Am. Coll. Chest Physicians, Am. Coll. Angiographers, Am. Coll. Cardiology; mem. AMA, Chgo. Med. Assn., Ill. Med. Assn., A.C.P. Home: 2734 N Seminary Ave Chicago IL 60614 Office: 2734 N Seminary St Chicago IL 60614

SILBERSTEIN, ROSS LYMAN, paint company executive; b. Star City, Ark., Jan. 5, 1930; s. Ross Lyman and Thelma Bernice (McGraw) S.; m. Mary Elizabeth Witherspoon, Aug. 11, 1962; children—William Brett, Elizabeth Kate. B.S., U. Ark., 1952, M.S., 1956. Chemist Sherwin-Williams, Dallas, 1955-56, prodn. supt., 1956-69, plant mgr., Ga., 1969-74, project mgr., Cleve., 1975, v.p. automotive aftermath div., dir. mfg., Richmond, Ky., 1975—; cons. Chmn. industry United Way, 1978; bd. dirs., 1981-82; chmn. major gifts com. Served with U.S. Army, 1952-54. Republican. Baptist. Club: Internat. Lions. Contbr. articles to profl. jours.

SILER, JAMES FRANCIS, vocational educator; b. Defiance, Ohio, June 23, 1942; s. Victor Francis and Margaret Louise (Holman) S.; m. Jean Ellen Kemerer, June 24, 1967; children—Heather Lynne, Kelby James, Perry Wynn. Student Bowling Green State U., 1962-64; B.S. in Edn., U. Toledo, 1982. Electric motor repairman Bryan Electric Co. (Ohio.), 1960-64; maintenance man B.F. Goodrich Co., Woodburn, Ind., 1969-77; vocat. educator in indsl. elecricity Vantage Joint Vocat. Sch., Van Wert, Ohio, 1977—; journeyman instrument maintenance United Rubber Works Union; asst. football coach Hicksville High Sch. Pres. Hicksville Little League, 1980—, Hicksville Athletic Boosters, 1982—; coach pony league baseball, 1974—; high sch. baseball and basketball ofcl., Ohio. Served with USAF, 1964-68; Vietnam. Decorated Air Force Commendation, Air medal. Recipient Am. Math. Assn. medal, 1960. Mem. Am. Vocat. Assn., Ohio Vocat. Assn., Vocat. Indsl. Clubs Am., Nat. Assn. Trade and Indsl. Educators, Kappa Delta Phi, Iota Lambda Sigma. Democrat. Roman Catholic. Clubs: KC, Kiwanis, VFW, Am. Legion, Nat. Rifle Assn.

SILJANDER, MARK DELI, congressman; b. Chgo., June 11, 1951; s. William A. and Evelyn (Deli) S.; B.S., Western Mich. U., 1972, M.A., 1973. Distbr., dealer Rustic Homes, Timber Lodge Redwood Homes, also Chalet Homes, Three Rivers, Mich., from 1973; trustee Fabius Twp. (Mich.), 1973-76; mem. Mich. Ho. of Reps. from 42d Dist., 1976-80; mem. 97th-99th congresses from 4th Dist. Mich. Mem. Nat. Assn. Towns and Twps., Mich. Conf. Polit. Scientists, Mich. Twps. Assn. (past dir.), Christian Fellowships, Jaycees, Grange. Republican. Office: 137 Cannon House Office Bldg Washington DC 20515

SILKAITIS, RAYMOND PAUL, medical device company executive, pharmacist; b. St. Charles, Ill., Dec. 22, 1949; s. Mitch and Irene S.; m. Rasa Maria Domarkas, June 5, 1976; children—Rimas, Danius. B.S. in Pharmacy, U. Ill.-Chgo., 1973; Ph.D. in Pharmacology, U. Health Scis./Chgo. Med. Sch., 1977. Registered pharmacist, Ill. Formulation chemist R.I.T.A. Chem. Corp., Crystal Lake, Ill., 1971-73; clin. pharmacist U. Ill. Hosp., Chgo., 1974-77; asst. dir. pharmacy MacNeal Meml. Hosp., Berwyn, Ill., 1977-78; sr. clin. research assoc. Abbott Labs., North Chicago, Ill., 1978-80; assoc. dir. clin. affairs Zimmer, Inc., Warsaw, Ind., 1980—; cons. Huron Prodns., Burbank, Calif., 1976. Editorial staff mem., photographer Ateitis Mag., 1976. Contbr. articles on cosmetics and perfumery, brain research, life scis. to profl. jours. Sprague scholar U. Health Scis./Chgo. Med. Sch., 1976. Mem. Soc. Clin. Trials, Bioelectromagnetics Soc., Am. Soc. Hosp. Pharmacists (alt. del. 1975). Roman Catholic Avocations: photography; woodworking; dancing; electronics; arts. Home: 5326 Kindig Dr South Bend IN 46614 Office: Zimmer Inc PO Box 708 Warsaw IN 46580

SILLICK, JOHN FRANCIS, automotive company executive; b. San Francisco, Dec. 25, 1934; s. John Joseph and Margaret Ann (Mullaney) S.; m. Antonia Ella Bowron, Aug. 28, 1954; children—Belinda, Susan, John. B.A., San Francisco State Coll., 1961. Mgr. Standard Oil of Calif., San Francisco, 1953-61; mgr. spl. vehicles Gen. Motors Corp.-Chevrolet Div., Los Angeles, 1962-74, Detroit, 1974—. Pres., Lone Pine Rd. Estates Improvement Assn., Bloomfield Hills, Mich., 1983, 84. Recipient Man of Yr. award Recreation Vehicles Assn., 1971. Served with U.S. Army, 1954-56. Mem. Recreation Vehicle Industry Assn., Mich. Mobile Home and Recreational Vehicle Inst. Republican. Lodges: Elks, Masons. Office: Chevrolet Motor Div 30007 Van Dyke Ave Room 228-04 Warren MI 48090

SILLS, WILLIAM HENRY, III, investment banker; b. Chgo., Jan. 2, 1936; s. William Henry, II and Mary Dorothy (Trude) S.; A.B., Darmouth Coll., 1958; M.A., Northwestern U., 1961; m. Ellen Henriette Gervais, Apr. 24, 1971; children—William Henry, IV, David Andrew Henry. Stockbroker, Bache & Co., Chgo., 1961-65; investment banker Chgo. Corp., Chgo., 1965-79; chmn. bd. Rail Fund Corp., Chgo., 1979-83; with First of Mich. Corp., 1983—; gen. ptnr. Algenia Ranch, Island Park, Idaho, dir. S&S S.S. Lines, Inc., Pacific Enteprises GSW Corp. Chmn., Geneva Lake (Wis.) Area Joint Transit Commn., 1974-78, Com. to Amend Wis. Constn. for Transp., 1977; mem. Walworth County (Wis.) Overall Econ. Devel. Planning Com., 1977-78, Walworth County Transp. Planning Com., 1975-80; pres. Wis. Coalition for Balanced Transp., 1976—; chmn. exec. com. Republican Party Wis., 1978-82. Served with USMCR, 1956-59. Mem. Am. Soc. Traffic and Transp., Am. Short Line R.R. Assn., Am. Soc. Equipment Lessors, Am. Public Transit Assn., Ill. Public Transit Assn., Nat. Rifle Assn. (benefactor mem.), Wis. Rifle and Pistol Assn., Idaho State Rifle and Pistol Assn., Ill. State Rifle Assn., Field Mus., Am. Mensa Assn., Internat. Soc. Philosophic Enquiry, Kappa Beta Phi, Delta Kappa Epsilon. Episcopalian. Clubs: Lake Geneve Country Lake Geneva Yacht (vice commodore), U.S. Yacht Reserve Union Cert. Judge, Skeeter Ice Boat, Delavan Sportsman; Chgo. Lions Rugby Football, Chgo. Area Rugby Football Union Referees Soc. Author papers in field. Home: 760 Lake Shore Dr Rural Route #1 Box 150 A Lake Geneva WI 53147 Office: 135 S LaSalle St Suite 1740 Chicago IL 60603

SILSBY, PHILLIP R., educational adminstrator; b. East St. Louis, Ill., Oct. 5, 1947; s. Elmer Nelson and Anna Louise (Melton) S.; m. Connie Rae Watson, June 8, 1968; children—Gregory Michael, Jacqueline Renee. B.S., Ill. State U., 1969; A.A., Belleville Area Coll., 1967; M.A., So. Ill. U., 1973. Tchr. O'Fallon High Sch., Ill., 1969-72; tchr., prin. Waterloo High Sch., Ill., 1972—; tchr. Belleville Area Coll., Ill., 1973-80, Menard Penitentiary, Chester, Ill., 1973-79; vocat. dir. Waterloo High Sch., Ill., 1983—, in-service dir., 1983—. Dir. Full Gospel Tabernacle, Fairview Heights, Ill., 1983—, Christian Missionary Assn., Tulsa, 1982—. Recipient Those Who Excel teaching award Ill. State Bd. Edn., 1976; Chevelair award Tancred chpt. Order DeMolay, Belleville, Ill., 1967. Mem. Assn. Curriculum and Supervision, Nat. Assn. Secondary Sch. Prins., Ill. Prins. Assn. (dir.-elect. 1983-86). Lodge: Lions (pres. 1984-85). Home: 632 James St Waterloo IL 62298 Office: Waterloo High Sch Bellefontaine Dr Waterloo IL 62298

SILVER, GEORGE, metal trading and processing company executive; b. Warren, Ohio, Dec. 17, 1918; s. Jacob and Sophie (Bradlyn) S.; m. Irene Miller, Aug. 5, 1945. Student U. Ala., 1938; B.A., Ohio U., 1940, postgrad. law sch., 1940-41; grad. Adj. Gen. Sch., 1944. Pres., Riverside Indsl. Materials, Bettendorf, Iowa, 1947-70, Metalpel subs. Continental Telephone Co., Bettendorf, 1970-71, Riverside Industries Inc., Bettendorf, 1971—; now pres. Scott Resources Inc., Davenport, Iowa; founder Iowa Steel Mills (name changed to North Star Steel), Cargill and Wilton. Mem. Nat. UN Day Com., 1975-83. Served to capt. AC, U.S. Army, 1941-46, 50-51; Korea. Mem. Nat. Assn. Recycling Industries (co-chmn. nat. planning com., bd. dirs.), Copper Club, Paper Stock Inst. Am. (mem. exec. com.), Bur. Internat. de la Recuperation (chmn. adv. com.), Mining Club N.Y.C., Phi Sigma Delta. Republican. Jewish. Clubs: Outing, Hatchet Men's Chowder and Protective Assn., Crow Valley Country. Lodge: Elks (Davenport). Contbr. articles to profl. jours.

SILVERGLADE, DAVID SAMUEL, pediatric dentist, educator; b. Chgo.; s. Louis J. and Mary (Kaplan) S.; m. Laura Forst, Sept. 1, 1968; children—Elisa, Janna, Ilana. Student U. Ill., 1964-67; D.D.S., Northwestern U., 1971. Resident

Columbus Children's Hosp. (Ohio), 1973-75, chief resident, 1974-75, now attending staff; practice dentistry specializing in pediatrics, Columbus, 1975—; clin. asst. prof. Ohio State U., Columbus, 1980—; cons. staff Univ. Hosp.; cons. Project Headstart. Trustee Columbus Hebrew Sch. Served to capt. USAF, 1973-75. Mem. ADA, Ohio Dental Assn., Ohio Soc. Pediatric Dentistry, Columbus Dental Soc., Am. Soc. Dentistry for Children, Alpha Omega (pres. Columbus). Office: 5320 E Main St Columbus OH 43213

SILVERMAN, DEBORAH ANN WAIDNER, dietitian, educator, consultant; b. Columbus, Ohio, July 8, 1950; d. Otto Charles and Eileen C. (Herderick) Waidner; m. Gary Harvey Silverman, Dec. 18, 1977. B.S. in Med. Dietetics, Ohio State U., 1972; M.S. in Health Planning/Adminstrn., U. Cin., 1979; postgrad. Eastern Mich. U., 1981—. Registered dietitian. Chief project nutritionist Ohio Dept. Health, Columbus, 1972-78; clin. dietitian Mt. Carmel East Hosp., Columbus, 1973-77 (part-time); instr. pediatric nurse assoc. program Mt. St. Joseph Coll., Cin., 1974-78; nutritionist Drs. Hallet, Bressler and Schaeffer, Columbus, 1975-78; nutritionist maternal and child health Ind. State Bd. Health, Indpls., 1978-79; relief clin. dietitian U. Mich. Hosps., Ann Arbor, 1980—; nutrition cons. St. Joseph Mercy Hosp., Ann Arbor, 1983—; instr. coordinated undergrad. curriculum in gen. dietetics Eastern Mich. U., Ypsilanti, 1979—; cons., lectr. in field. Recipient Josephine Nevins Keal award Eastern Mich. U., 1981. Mem. Am. Dietetic Assn., Am. Pub. Health Assn., Am. Soc. Parenteral and Enteral Nutrition, Nutrition Today Soc., Soc. Nutrition Edn., Mich. Dietetic Assn., Ann Arbor Dist. Dietetic Assn., Dietetic Educators Practice Group of Mich. Dietetic Assn., Dietetic Educators Practice Group and Dietitians in Critical Care of Am. Dietetic Assn. Jewish. Author manuals for dietetic courses at univ. Office: Dept Human Environ and Consumer Resources Eastern Mich Univ Ypsilanti MI 48197

SILVERMAN, RICHARD BRUCE, chemist, biochemist, educator; b. Phila., May 12, 1946; s. Philip and S. Ruth (Simon) S.; m. Barbara Jean Kesner, Jan. 9, 1983; children—Matthew, Margaret, Philip. B.S., Pa. State U., 1968; M.A., Harvard U., 1972, Ph.D., 1974. Postdoctoral fellow Brandeis U., Waltham, Mass., 1974-76; asst. prof. Northwestern U., Evanston, Ill., 1976-82, assoc. prof., 1982—; cons. Procter and Gamble Co., Cin., 1984; mem. adv. panel NIH, Bethesda, Md., 1981, 83, 85. Contbr. articles to profl. jours. Patentee in field. Served with U.S. Army, 1969-71. Recipient Career Devel. award USPHS, 1982—; DuPont Young Faculty fellow, 1976, Alfred P. Sloan Found. fellow, 1981—; grantee various govt. and pvt. insts., 1976—. Mem. AAAS, Am. Chem. Soc., Am. Soc. Biol. Chemists. Avocations: tennis, family interactions. Office: Dept Chemistry Northwestern U 2145 Sheridan Rd Evanston IL 60201

SILVEY, JAMES MADISON, JR., ins. company executive; b. Willow Springs, Mo., Aug. 16, 1909; s. James M. and Mary V. (Garlett) S.; m. Ivis Louise Love, May 29, 1930; children—James M., Marilyn Rose. Grad. LaSalle Extension U., 1933. Bookkeeper, Farmers Coop. Exchange, South Gifford, Mo., 1928-32; mgr. Coop. Elevator, Vandalia, Mo., 1932-33; auditor Mo. Farmers Assn., Inc., Columbia, 1933-34; mgr. Farmers Coop. Exchange, 1934-35; acct. Mo. Farmers Assn. Milling Co., Springfield, 1935-38, mgr. ins. dept. central coop., supply div., 1938-46; pres. Mo. Farmers Assn. Ins. Co. (name now Shelter Ins. Co.), 1946-64; pres. Silvey Corp. and Silvey Ins. Cos., Columbia, Mo., 1964—. Past pres. bd. trustees Mo. Sch. Religion; past trustee Columbia Coll., Lenoir Meml. Home; trustee Christian Coll. Mem. Nat. Assn. Ind. Insurers (past v.p.). Home: 2909 W Broadway Columbia MO 65201 Office: 3301 W Broadway Columbia MO 65201

SILVIA, JOHN EDWIN, financial economist; b. Providence, Sept. 22, 1948. B.A., magna cum laude, in Econs., Northeastern U., 1971, Ph.D. in Econs., 1980. M.A. in Econs., Brown U., 1973. Research asst. Boston Mcpl. Research Bur., 1969-70; cons. Mass. Pub. Finance Project, 1973; assoc. tech. staff Mitre Corp., Bedford, Mass., 1974-75; instr. econ. St. Anselm's Coll., Manchester, N.H., 1977-79; asst. prof. Ind. U., Indpls., 1979-82; econ. research officer Harris Bank, Chgo., 1982-83; v.p., fin. economist Kemper Fin. Services, Chgo., 1983—. Contbr. numerous articles to profl. jours. Mem. Am. Econ. Assn., Am. Fin. Assn., Nat. Assn. Bus. Economists. Home: 913 Turnbridge Circle Naperville IL 60540 Office: Kemper Fin Services 120 S LaSalle St Chicago IL 60603

SIMACEK, MILO JAMES, woodcrafter, industrial technology educator; b. Montgomery, Minn., June 6, 1930; s. Matt and Emma (Koldin) S.; B.S., Mankato State U., 1952, also postgrad.; M.S., Eastern Ky. U., 1969; postgrad. St. Cloud State U., Winona State U., River Falls State U.; m. Lois Mae Davis, Dec. 26, 1955; children—Michele, Mark, David, Scott. Tchr., St. Anns Sch., Wabasso, Minn., 1955-56; tchr. indsl. tech., chmn. dept. Hastings (Minn.) High Sch., 1956—; owner, mgr. Artistry With Wood, Hastings, 1960—; also designer, builder houses. Mem., chmn. Hastings City Planning Commn., 1979—; founding pres. Hastings United Fund. Served with M.C. AUS, 1952-54. Silver Beaver award Boy Scouts Am., 1980, Minn. Indsl. Arts Tchr. of Yr. award, 1981. Mem. Am. Legion (comdr. 1976), Jaycees (senator), Minn. Indsl. Arts Assn. (pres. 1985-86), Am. Indsl. Arts Assn., Minn. Edn. Assn., NEA, Internat. Wood Collectors Soc., DAV, VFW. Roman Catholic. Clubs: Lions, Hastings Snowmobile, Snow Patrol. Home: 1041 W 4th St Hastings MN 55033 Office: 11th and Pine Sts Hastings MN 55033

SIMCOX, EDWIN JESSE, state official; b. LaPorte, Ind., Jan. 12, 1945; s. J. Willard and Rachel (Gibbs) S.; A.B. in Govt. and Econs., Ind. U., 1967, J.D., 1971; m. Sandra Sue Stephenson, Aug. 30, 1970; 1 son, Edwin Jesse. Sec., Ind. Hwy. Commn., 1969-71, Public Service Commn. Ind., 1971; chief dept. Office Reporter Supreme Cts. and Jud. Ct. Appeals Ind., 1973-78; sec. of state State of Ind., Indpls., 1978—. Sec., Ind. Republican Central Com., 1972-77; chmn. Ind. Rep. Platform Com., 1980; chmn. adminstrv. bd. White Harvest United Methodist Ch., 1975-76, 80-81. Mem. ABA, Ind. Bar Assn., Indpls. Bar Assn., Nat. Assn. Secs. State (sec. 1981-82, pres. 1984-85). Lodges: Kiwanis, Masons, Shriners. Author man. for conduct mcpl. campaigns, 1975, Republican precinct man., 1975. Office: 201 State House Indianapolis IN 46204*

SIMLER, CECIL MURL, osteopathic physician; b. Youngstown, Mo., Sept. 29, 1915; s. Roy Earl and Rosa Belle (Weber) S.; m. Shirley Jeannette Cauby, Nov. 23, 1939; children—Janice Coleen Barnes, Murl Royburn. D.O., Kirksville Coll. Osteo. Medicine, 1941. Pvt. practice family osteo. medicine, Gorin, Mo., 1942—. Mayor, City of Gorin, 1953-73; coroner Scotland County, 1952-68. Mem. N.E. Mo. Osteo Assn. Democrat. Baptist. Club: Masons. Address: Jackson & Arcadia Sts Gorin MO 63543

SIMMONS, CLINTON CRAIG, construction company executive; b. Cleve., Nov. 25, 1947; s. Benjamin F. and Catharin (Thornton) R.; m. Cheryl LeRoy, June 16, 1973; 1 child, Eric. B.S. in Bus. Adminstrn., Miami U., Oxford, Ohio, 1969. Specialist employee and community relations Euclid Lamp Plant, Gen. Electric Co., Wickliffe, Ohio, 1970-75; employee and indsl. relations rep. Bailey Controls Co., Wickliffe, 1975-78; mgr., coll. recruiting Gen. Tire and Rubber, Akron, Ohio, 1978-81, profl. staffing coordinator, 1981-82; regional human resource mgr. Gilbane Bldg. Co., Cleve. 1982—. Past chmn. orgn. and extension com. Newton D. Baker Dist., Greater Cleve. council Boy Scouts Am., 1970-71; bd. edn. commr. Villa Angela High Sch., Cleve., 1983—; founder, advisor Explorer Post, Gilbane Bldg. Co., Cleve., 1984—. Recipient commendation Nat. Alliance of Bus., Akron, 1979, Community Service award WJW-Northwest Orient Airlines, 1975. Mem. Cleve. Employee's Equal Opportunity Assn., Am. Soc. Personnel Adminstrn., Mid-West Coll. Placement Assn. (chmn. rubber industry com. 1979-81), Ctr. for Human Services (v.p., trustee), Urban League of Cleve., Alpha Phi Alpha. Democrat. Roman Catholic. Home: 24400 Emery Rd Warrensville Heights OH 44128 Office: Gilbane Bldg Co Central Region 2000 E 9th St Cleveland OH 44115

SIMMONS, ROBERT WAYNE, tire and rubber manufacturing company executive; b. Sayre, Okla., July 1, 1946; s. Ova Wayne Simmons and Verna L. Simmons-Harris; m. Mari Melissa Reeves, Aug. 12, 1974; children—Tia Michelle, Ashley Megan. A.A., Bacone Jr. Coll., Muskogee, Okla., 1967; B.S. in Zoology, Northeastern Okla. State U., 1970. Drilling fluid engr. Baroid Engrng. Co., Houston, 1970-71; sales rep. GAF Corp., Cape Girardeau, Mo., 1971-79, product engr., N.Y.C., 1979-80, assoc. prodn. mgr., 1980, mktg. mgr., 1980-81; midwest regional sales mgr. Gen. Tire & Rubber Co., Toledo, 1981-81, nat. sales mgr., bldg. products group mgr., 1983-85, dir. mktg. coated fabric group, 1985—. Served with USMC, 1968-69. Recipient Pres. Club award GAF Corp., 1976; named hon. capt. Girardeau Navy, 1979. Mem. Constrn. Specification Inst., Roofing Industry Ednl. Instn., Am. Mgmt. Assn., Phi Sigma Epsilon. Democrat. Lutheran. Lodges: Rotary (sec./treas. Cape Girardeau club 1978), Masons, Shriners, Elks. Author: Super System, Maintenance & Repair, Roofing Manual, 1981. Office: Gen Tire & Rubber Co PO Box 875 3729 Twinning St Toledo OH 43696

SIMMS, BRENDA ELAINE, nurse; b. Carrollton, Ill., Mar. 17, 1949; d. Carl Eugene and Mary M. (McGiffen) Rodgers; m. Richard Michael Simms, Jan. 21, 1967; children—R. Michael, Cori Leigh. A.D.N., Ill. Central Coll., 1982; student Coll. of St. Francis, 1983—, Bradley U., 1984—. Lic. practical nurse, Ill. Nurse's aide St. Francis Hosp., Peoria, Ill., 1971-72; lic. practical nurse, 1973-74, 78-82, R.N., 1978—; cert. surg. technician Methodist Hosp., Peoria, 1978. Bd. dirs. Assn. Ileti/Colitis Found., Peoria, 1983—. Exposition Gardens scholar, 1981. Mem. Assn. Cert. Surg. Technicians, Assn. Gastrointestinal Assts., Student Nurse Assn. Democrat. Mennonite. Club: Morton Gymnastic Center Booster (v.p. 1982-83). Home: 333 S Mississippi Morton IL 61550 Office: St Francis Med Center 530 NW Glen Oak Peoria IL

SIMON, DANA LESLIE, anesthesiologist, pain consultant; b. Halifax, N.S., Feb., 9, 1952; came to U.S., 1962, naturalized, 1972; s. Stanley M. and Joyce (Aronoff) S.; m. Ronit Dermansky, June 19, 1977; 2 children—Ariel, Shira. B.S. with highest distinction, valedictorian, U. Ariz., 1972; M.D., Northwestern U., 1977. Diplomate Am. Bd. Anesthesiology. Anesthesia resident Northwestern U., Chgo., 1977-80; pain fellow U. Va. Pain Ctr., Charlottesville, 1980-81; dir. pain block ctr. Mercy Hosp., Des Moines, 1983—, pain cons., 1981—, med. staff, 1981—. Contbr. articles to profl. jours. Bd. dirs. Bur. Jewish Living, Des Moines, 1983—. NIH grantee, 1984—. Mem. Am. Soc. Anesthesiologists, Am. Soc. Regional Anesthesia, Internat. soc. Study of Pain, AMA, Am. Israel Polit. Action Com. Lodge: B'nai B'rith Hillel. Avocations: Mid-East history; philately; reading; music; sports. Office: Med Ctr Anesthesiologists PC 421 Laurel #202 Des Moines IA 50314

SIMON, ELLEN MCMURTRIE, microbiology educator; b. Norristown, Pa., Mar. 29, 1919; d. Harry Gordon and Sue Wood (Hamill) McMurtrie; m. Joseph Simon, Sept. 13, 1954; 1 child, Debra Ann. A.B., Ursinus Coll., 1940; M.S., U. Wis., 1952, Ph.D., 1955. Research assoc. bacteriology U. Wis.-Madison, 1955-58; research assoc. zoology, U. Ill.-Urbana, 1963-64, research asst. prof., 1964-76, vis. asst. prof. microbiology, summers 1975-76, fall, 1976 research scientist genetics and devel., 1977—, vis. assoc. prof., summers, 1977-79, vis. lectr., 1985-86; researcher in genetics, cryobiology and aging of ciliated protozoa. Acitve 4-H, 1965-73. Recipient B.A. Beach award Wis. Vet. Med. Assn., 1954. Mem. Am. Soc. Microbiology, Soc. Indsl. Microbiology, Soc. Cryobiology, Soc. Protozoologists, U.S. Fedn. Culture Collections (exec. bd. 1977-79). Home: 1801 S Anderson St Urbana IL 61801 Office: Univ Ill 515 Morrill Hall 505 S Goodwin Urbana IL 61801

SIMON, HERB, professional basketball executive. Co-owner, Ind. Pacers, Indpls. Office: Ind Pacers 2 W Washington St Suite 510 Indianapolis IN 46204*

SIMON, LEWIS BRYANT, financial executive, steel fabrication and erection executive; b. Chgo., Oct. 12, 1940; s. M. Phillip and Rosalyne L. (Ballin) S.; m. Sherrill A. Miller, Feb. 2, 1963; children—Scott Terrence, Johanne Michele. B.S.C.E., U. Ill., 1963; M.B.A. in Fin., Calif. State U.-Long Beach, 1967. Pres., chief exec. officer, dir. TigerAir, Chgo., 1971-76; exec. v.p., dir. AAR Corp., Elk Grove Village, Ill., 1976-78; group v.p. Avis, Inc., Garden City, N.Y., 1978-79; pres. S-J Fin. Corp., Barrington, Ill., 1978—; chmn. SR Industries Corp., Schaumburg, Ill., 1984—; v.p., ptnr. Realty Unltd., Inc., Barrington, Ill., 1980—; fin. cons. Bombardier, Inc., Que., Can., 1984; sr. v.p., cons. Winthrop Fin. Corp., Boston, 1981-84; cons. FSC Corp./FS Airlease, Inc., Pitts., 1979-84; dir. Am. Risk Transfer Ins. Co., Bermuda, Presdl. Airways, Inc., ARTEX Ins., Dallas. Bd. dirs. Chgo. Jesters Hockey Orgn. Mem. Internat. Soc. Transport Aircraft Traders (founding officer), Central Steel Fabricators Assn., Ill. Rd. Builders Assn., Iron League Chgo. Jewish. Clubs: Riding of Barrington Hills (Ill.); Bit and Bridle (Barrington, Ill.); Barrington Area Figure Skating (pres., bd. dirs.). Avocations: show horses, men's hockey, racquetball. Office: SR Industries Corp 1100 Wiley Rd Schaumburg IL 60196

SIMON, MELVIN, professional basketball executive. Co-owner Ind. Pacers. Office: Ind Pacers 2 W Washington St Suite 510 Indianapolis IN 46204*

SIMON, MORDECAI, See *Who's Who in America*, 43rd edition.

SIMON, PAUL, senator; b. Eugene, Oreg., Nov. 29, 1928; s. Martin Paul and Ruth (Troemel) S.; student U. Oreg., 1945-46; student Dana Coll., Blair, Nebr., 1946-48, LL.D., 1965; D.Litt., McKendree Coll. (Ill.), 1965; D.C.L., Greenville Coll., 1968; LL.D., Concordia Coll., 1969, Lincoln Coll., 1969, Loyola U., Valparaiso U., 1976; m. Jeanne Hurley, Apr. 21, 1960; children—Sheila, Martin. Pub., Troy (Ill.) Tribune, 1948-66; mem. Ill. Ho. of Reps., 1955-63, Ill. Senate, 1963-69; lt. gov. Ill., 1969-73; mem. faculty Sangamon State U., 1972-73; lectr. John F. Kennedy Inst. Politics, Harvard U., 1973; mem. 94th-98th Congresses from 24th Dist. Ill.; U.S. senator from Ill., 1985—. Bd. dirs. Wheatridge Found., McKendree Coll. Served with CIC, U.S. Army, 1951-53. Recipient Am. Polit. Sci. Assn. award, 1957; named Best Legislator 7 times. Mem. Luth. Human Relations Assn., Am. Legion, V.F.W., NAACP, Urban League, Sigma Delta Chi. Lutheran. Lion. Author: Lovejoy: Martyr to Freedom, 1964, Lincoln's Preparation for Greatness, 1966, A Hungry World, 1966; (with Jeanne Hurley Simon) Protestant-Catholic Marriages Can Succeed, 1967; You Want to Change the World? So Change It, 1971; (with Arthur Simon) The Politics of World Hunger, 1973 The Glass House: Politics and Morality in the Nation Capitol; writer weekly column Sidelights from Springfield, 1955-72, P. S/Washington, from 1975; contbr. articles to periodicals, including Saturday Rev., Harper's, The New Republic. Home: Carbondale IL 62901 Office: 462 Dirksen Senate Office Bldg Washington DC 20510*

SIMON, SEYMOUR, justice Supreme Court Illinois; b. Chgo., Aug. 10, 1915; s. Ben and Gertrude (Rusky) S.; B.S., Northwestern U., 1935, J.D., 1938; LL.D. (hon.), John Marshall Law Sch., 1982; m. Roslyn Schultz Biel, May 26, 1954; children—John B., Nancy Harris, Anthony Biel. Admitted to Ill. bar, 1938; spl. atty. Dept. Justice, 1938-42; practice law, Chgo., 1946-74; judge Ill. Appellate Ct., Chgo., 1974-80, presiding justice 1st Dist., 3d Div., 1977-79; justice Ill. Supreme Ct., 1980—. Mem. Bd. Commrs. Cook County, 1961-66, pres., 1962-66; pres. Cook County Forest Preserve Dist., 1962-66; mem. Pub. Bldg. Commn., City Chgo., 1962-67. Alderman, 40th ward, Chgo., 1955-61, 67-74, Democratic ward committeeman, Chgo., 1960-74. Bd. dirs. Schwab Rehab. Hosp., 1961-71, Swedish Covenant Hosp., 1969-75. Served with USNR, 1942-45. Decorated Legion of Merit; recipient citation for distinguished service North Park Coll., Chgo., 1967, 9th Ann. Pub. Service award Tau Epsilon Rho, 1963; Alumni award of Merit, Northwestern U., 1982; Hubert L. Will award Am. Vets. Com., 1983 Mem. ABA, Ill., Chgo. bar assns., Chgo. Hist. Soc., Izaak Walton League, Chgo. Hort. Soc., Phi Beta Kappa Assocs., Order of Coif. Clubs: Standard, Variety (Chgo.). Office: Supreme Ct Bldg Springfield IL 62706 also 3088 Richard J Daley Ctr Chicago IL 60602

SIMONETT, JOHN E., state supreme court justice; b. Mankato, Minn., July 12, 1924; B.A., St. John's U., 1948; LL.B., U. Minn., 1951; m. Doris Simonett. Practice law, Little Falls, Minn., 1951-80; assoc. justice Supreme Ct. of Minn., 1980—. Office: Supreme Ct State Capitol Saint Paul MN 55155*

SIMONSEN, VERNER MARVIN, osteopathic ophthalmologist and otorhinolaryngologist; b. Rome, N.Y., Nov. 3, 1931; s. Verner Marvin and Pauline Ann (Whitmeyer) S.; m. Cleona Eleanor Brooks, June 2, 1959; children—Kristine Pauline Simonsen Monas, Karin Diane. B.S., St. Lawrence U., 1953; D.O., Kirksville Coll. Osteopathy and Surgery, 1959. Intern Greencross Gen. Hosp., Cuyahoga Falls, Ohio, 1959-60; resident in ophthalmology and otorhinolaryngology Detroit Osteo. Hosp., 1962-65; practice osteo. medicine specializing in ophthalmology and otorhinolaryngology, Toledo and Perrysburg (Ohio), 1965—; mem. staff Parkview Hosp., also chmn. dept. ophthalmology and otorhinolaryngology; mem. staff Riverside Hosp., St. Luke's Hosp., Maumee, Ohio; instr. Ohio U. Coll. Osteopathy. Fellow Osteo. Coll. Ophthalmology and Otorhinolaryngology (cert.); mem. Toledo Dist. Osteopathy, Am. Osteo. Assn., Ohio Osteo. Assn., Ohio Med. Assn., Physician for Golden Gloves Boxing of Toledo. Republican. Methodist. Club: Brandywine Country. Lodges: Elks, Masons, Shriners. Home: 2865 Byrnwyck W St Maumee OH 43537 Office: 27121 Oakmead Dr Suite B Perrysburg OH 43551

SIMONSON, MARILYN DIANE, business educator; b. Buffalo County, Wis., Feb. 11, 1936; d. Walter S. and Hilda (Hilgert) Schlawin; m. Byron Dean Simonson, May 23, 1970; children—Tia, Carisa. B.E., Wis. State U.-Whitewater, 1957; postgrad. Winona State U., 1963; M.A., U. Minn., 1969. Cert. tchr., Wis., Minn. Sec., registrar Wis. State U.-Superior, 1957-58; tchr. pub. schs., Wis. and Minn., 1958-70; instr. Lakewood Community Coll., White Bear Lake, Minn., 1970—, head dept. secretarial sci., 1970—, mem. curriculum task force, 1983-84. Publicity chair St. Anthony Middle Sch. PTA, Minn., 1984-85, pres. elect, 1985-86; pres. Wilshire Park PTA, St. Anthony, 1985-86; mem. St. Anthony Lang. Arts Evaluation Com, 1984-85; mem. Christian edn. com. Christ the King Luth. Ch., New Brighton, Minn. Mem. Minn. Community Coll. Faculty Assn., Delta Pi Epsilon. Democrat. Lutheran. Avocations: needlework; reading. Home: 3327 Skycroft Dr Saint Anthony MN 55418 Office: 3401 Century Ave N White Bear Lake MN 55110

SIMPSON, BARBARA L., educational administrator; b. Cleve., Apr. 6, 1947; d. Curley and Cora (Chambliss) Brown; children—Michelle, Crystal, Twilla. B.S., Ohio State U., 1964; M.S. in Ednl. Media, Kent. State U. (Ohio), 1971, M.S. in L.S., 1971. Adminstrv. supr. Cleve. pub. schs., 1968-72; librarian Cuyahoga Community Coll., Cleve., 1972-75, coordinator, 1975-77, interim dir., 1977-78, asst. dean, 1978-80, dir., 1980—; cons. Dembsy Assocs., Boston, 1967-81; editorial cons. Max Pub. Co., N.Y.C., 1967-81; cons. reader U.S. Office Edn., Washington, 1979-80; editorial cons. Jossey-Bass Pub. Co., 1979. Cons. editor Probe, 1975, Sch. Media Ctr., 1968, Booklist, 1969. Recipient Phillips award Kent. State U., 1970. Mem. ALA, Higher Edn. Reps., Oral History Soc. Clubs: Concerned Parents (pres. 1984) (Beachwood, Ohio); Jr. League (vice chmn. 1981, 83) (Cleve.); Women's City Club. Office: Cuyahoga Community Coll (Eastern) 4250 Richmond Rd Warrensville Township OH 44122

SIMPSON, DAVID, electronics/electrical company executive; b. Ceres, Fife, Scotland; s. David and Mary Wallace S.; m. Isobel F. Taylor, July 1952 (dec.); 1 child, Ann Mary; m. Janice Hilbert, June 3, 1980; children—Jeanne Marie, David James Wilpault. Student Dundee Tech. Coll., 1949-52, London U., 1953-54. Mng. dir. Hewlett-Packard Ltd., Scotland, 1962-69; group dir. George Kent Ltd., Cambridge Instrument Co., Ltd., Luton, Cambridge, Eng., 1969-75; mng. dir. Gould Advance Ltd., Eng., 1975-77; v.p. instruments div. Gould, Inc., Cleve., 1977-78, v.p. electronics group, Chgo., 1978-79, pres., chief operating officer, 1979-84, vice chmn. bd., 1984—. Served with British Royal Signals, 1945-49. Fellow Insts. Elec. Engrs. (U.K.), Instn. Electronic and Radio Engrs. (U.K.); mem. Brit. Inst. Mgmt., Am. Mgmt. Assn. Club: Savile (London). Office: Gould Inc 10 Gould Center Rolling Meadows IL 60008

SIMPSON, HOWARD MATTHEW, textbook publisher; b. Peoria, Ill., Apr. 29, 1918; s. Laurens Luther and Pearl Claudia (Howard) S.; m. Kathryn Lucia Jacquin, Nov. 25, 1948; children—John Niehaus, James Patrick (dec.), Cory Jane, Michael Howard, David Matthew, Dana Kathleen. Student U. Ill., 1937-41. Shipping clk. Manual Arts Press, Peoria, Ill., 1933-37, advt., 1945-49, salesman, 1946-53, dir., 1949-83; advt. mgr. Chas. A. Bennett Co., Inc. (formerly Manual Arts Press), 1949-53, sales mgr., 1953-64, treas., 1962-72, v.p., 1970-75, pres., 1975-83, cons., 1983-85, dir., 1949-83, cons., 1983-85; organizer, dir., sec., pres. CABCO, Inc., Peoria, 1964-76. Mem. exec. bd. W.D. Boyce council Boy Scouts Am., Peoria, 1966—, rep. nat. council, 1985—; mem. capital projects com. United Way Peoria, 1978-80, spl. fund raising com., 1978-80; mem. YMCA Leader Luncheon Com., 1981-83. Served to capt., cav. armor U.S. Army, 1941-46; Africa, Italy. Decorated Purple Heart, 6 battle stars; recipient Silver Beaver award Boy Scouts Am., Peoria, 1969, also Order of Arrow. Mem. Am. Legion, Pi Beta Alpha, The Ship, Sigma Alpha Epsilon. Clubs: Kiwanis (dir. 1966-68) Willow Knolls Country (Peoria).

SIMPSON, JACK BENJAMIN, medical technologist, business executive; b. Tompkinsville, Ky., Oct. 30, 1937; s. Benjamin Harrison and Verda Mae (Woods) S.; student Western Ky. U., 1954-57; grad. Norton Infirmary Sch. Med. Tech., 1958; m. Winona Clara Walden, Mar. 21, 1957; children—Janet Lazann, Richard Benjamin, Randall Walden, Angela Elizabeth. Asst. chief med. technologist Jackson County Hosp., Seymour, Ind., 1958-61; chief med. technologist, bus. mgr. Mershon Med. Labs., Indpls., 1962-66; founder, dir., officer Am. Monitor Corp., Indpls., 1966-77; mng. partner Astroland Enterprises, Indpls., 1968—, 106th St. Assos., Indpls., 1969-72, Keystones Ltd., Indpls., 1970-82 Delray Rd. Asso., Ltd., Indpls., 1970-71, Allisonville Assocs. Ltd., Indpls., 1970-82, Grandview Assocs. Ltd., 1977—, Rucker Asso., Ltd., Indpls., 1974—; mng. partner Raintree Assos., Ltd., Indpls., 1978—, Westgate Assos., Ltd., Indpls., 1978—; pres., dir. Topps Constrn. Co., Inc., Bradenton, Fla., 1973—, Acrouest Corp., Asheville, N.C., 1980—, Alpha Systems Resource, Inc., Shelbyville, Ind., 1985—; dir. Indpls. Broadcasting, Inc. Mem. Am. Soc. Med. Technologists (cert.), Indpls. Soc. Med. Technologists, Ind. Soc. Med. Technologists, Am. Soc. Clin. Pathologists, Royal Soc. Health (London), Internat. Platform Assn., Am. Mus. Natural History. Republican. Baptist. Clubs: Columbia of Indpls.; Harbor Beach Surf, Fishing of Am., Marina Bay (Fort Lauderdale, Fla.). Lodge: Elks. Office: 7729 Rucker Rd Indianapolis IN 46250

SIMPSON, JEROME MORRIS, public utility executive; b. Grand Rapids, Mich., Aug. 22, 1927; s. Cecil Asa and Aileen (Morris) S.; m. Doris Mae Sjaarda, Jan. 10, 1951; children—Blaise Patricia, Pamela Sue Gomez. B.S.E.E., Tri-State U., 1953. Personnel supr. Consumers Power Co., Battle Creek, Mich., 1961-65, asst. region supt., Saginaw, Mich., 1965-68, region supt. Battle Creek, 1968-75, gen. supt. adminstrv. services, Jackson, Mich., 1975-78, plant supt., Muskegon, Mich., 1978-79, gen. mgr. West Olive, Mich., 1979—. Pres. United Arts Council, Battle Creek, 1971-74, Civic Theatre, Battle Creek, 1969; mem. steering com. Calhoun County Republican Orgn., 1972-75. Served with USNR, 1945-51. Mem. IEEE. Congregationalist. Club: Birchwood Farm Golf and Country. Avocations: golf, skiing, boating, fishing. Home: 7977 Margaret St West Olive MI 49460 Office: Consumers Power Co 17000 Croswell St West Olive MI 49460

SIMPSON, RICHARD COLLINS, lawyer; b. Dayton, Ohio, May 19, 1947; s. Gustavus Sailer and Ruth Evelyn (Collins) S.; m. Susan Carol Alschbach, July 20, 1970; children—Lia S., Cara N., Caitlin E. B.A. in Econs., Mich. State U., 1969; J.D., U. Mich., 1972. Bar: Ohio 1972. Ptnr. Bricker & Eckler, Columbus, Ohio, 1972—; dir. Capitol Poly Bag Inc., Columbus, 1982—; mem. steering com. Nat. Bond. Atty. Workshop, Chgo., 1981. Contbr. articles to profl. jours. Mem. Columbus Bar Assn., ABA. Republican. Methodist. Club: Athletic (Columbus), Scioto Country (Columbus). Avocation: book collector. Home: 1669 Roxbury Rd Columbus OH 43212 Office: Bricker & Eckler 100 E Broad St Columbus OH 43215

SIMS, KENNETH J., JR., marketing executive; b. Cleve., Dec. 13, 1935; s. Kenneth J. and Ella (Gibbons) S.; B.S., Thiel Coll., 1958; m. Gail McKelvey, June 30, 1962; children—Kelly, Lori. Tchr. history, English public schs., Aurora, Ohio, 1959-62; tchr. history, asst. basketball coach public schs., Wickliffe, Ohio, 1962-63; tchr. govt., head basketball coach public schs., Aurora, 1963-69; with Detrex Chem. Industries, Inc., 1969-84, field sales mgr. chem. div., 1976-78, sales mgr., Ashtabula, Ohio, 1978-84; v.p. mktg. Norben Co., Willoughby, Ohio, 1984—. Sec., City Status Commn., Aurora, 1966; vice chmn. Aurora Planning Commn., 1967-71. Served with U.S. Army, 1958-59. Mem. Cleve. Chem. Assn., Columbus Chem. Assn., St. Louis Chem. Assn. Episcopalian. Home: 33840 Country View Ln Solon OH 44139

SINCLAIR, VIRGIL LEE, JR., lawyer, writer; b. Canton, Ohio, Nov. 10, 1951; s. Virgil Lee and Thelma Irene (Dunlap) S.; m. Judy Ann Montgomery, May 26, 1969 (div. Mar. 1980); children—Kelly, Shannon. B.A., Kent State U., 1973; J.D., U. Akron, 1976; postgrad. Case Western Res. U., 1979. Adminstr. Stark County Prosecutor's Office, Canton, 1974-76; mem. faculty Walsh Coll., Canton, 1976-78; asst. pros. atty. Stark County, Canton, 1976-77; ptnr. Amerman Burt Jones Co. LPA, Canton, 1976—; legal adviser Mayor's Office, City of North Canton, Ohio, 1978-79; referee Stark County Family Ct., Canton, 1981. Author: Law Enforcement Officers' Guide to Juvenile Law, 1975; Lay Manual of Juvenile Law, 1976. Editor U. Akron Law Rev. Contbr. to Ohio Family Law, 1983. Contbr. articles to profl. jours. Mem. North Canton Planning Comm., 1979-82; bd. mgrs. North Canton YMCA, 1976—, Camp Tippecanoe, Ohio, 1981—; profl. adviser Parents Without Partners, 1980—; spl. dep. Stark County Sheriff Dept., 1983—; trustee Palace Theatre Assn., Canton, 1982—. Recipient Disting. Service award U.S. Jaycees, 1984. Mem. ABA, Ohio Bar Assn., Stark County Bar Assn. (lectr. 1984), Ohio Trial Lawyers Assn., Assn. Trial Lawyers Am., Nat. Dist. Attys. Assn., Delta Theta Phi (bailiff 1976; nat. key winner 1975-76), Jaycees. Republican. Methodist. Lodge: Elks. Home: 7794 Angel Dr NW North Canton OH 44720 Office: Amerman Burt & Jones Co LPA 624 Market Ave N Canton OH 44702

SINGER, JOEL DAVID, political science educator; b. N.Y.C., Dec. 7, 1925; s. Morris Louis and Anne (Newman) S.; m. Kathleen Manninen, July 23, 1983; children from former marriage—Kathryn Louise, Eleanor Anne; stepchildren—Benjamin Charles, Daniel Gold. B.A., Duke U., 1946; Ph.D., NYU, 1956. Instr. dept. govt. NYU, 1954-55; instr. Vassar Coll., Poughkeepsie, N.Y., 1955-57; vis. fellow social relations Harvard U., Cambridge, Mass., 1957-58; vis. asst. prof. polit. sci. U. Mich., Ann Arbor, 1958-60, sr. scientist Mental Health Research Inst., 1960-83, assoc. prof. polit. sci., 1964-65, prof., 1965—, coordinator world politics program, 1969-75, 81—; vis. faculty U.S. Naval War Coll., 1960; vis. prof. U. Oslo (Norway) Inst. Social Research 1963-64; vis. fellow, prof. Carnegie Endowment for Internat. Peace and Grad. Inst. Internat. Studies, Geneva, Switzerland, 1967-68; vis. prof. ZUMA, U. Manheim (W.Ger.), 1976; mil. cons. in field. Served with USNR, 1943-66. Ford Found. fellow, 1956, grantee, 1957-58; Phoenix Meml. Fund research grantee, 1959, 81-82; Fulbright research scholar U. Ohio, 1963-64; Carnegie Corp. research grantee, 1963-67; NSF research grantee, 1967-76, 78-83; Guggenheim research grantee, 1978-79. Mem. Am. Polit. Sci. Assn., Internat. Polit. Sci. Assn. (chmn. conflict and peace research com.), Internat. Studies Assn. (pres. 1985-86), Internat. Soc. Polit. Psychology, Internat. Soc. for Research on Aggression, Social Sci. History Assn., Peace Sci. Soc., Internat. Peace Research Assn., Consortium on Peace Research Edn. and Devel., AAAS, Fedn. Am. Scientists, Union Concerned Scientists, Arms Control Assn., Com. for Nat. Security, Am. Com. East-West Accord, SANE, World Federalist Assn. Author: Financing International Organization: The United Nations Budget Process, 1961; Deterrence, Arms Control, and Disarmament: Toward a Synthesis in National Security Policy, 1962, 2d edit., 1984; (with Melvin Small) The Wages of War, 1816-1965; A Statistical Handbook, 1972; (with Susan Jones) Beyond Conjecture in International Politics: Abstracts of Data-Based Research, 1972; (with Dorothy LaBarr) The Study of International Politics: A Guide to Sources for the Student, Teacher and Researcher, 1976; The Correlates of War, Vol. I, 1979, Vol. II, 1980; (with Melvin Small) Resort to Arms: International and Civil War, 1816-1980, 1982; contbr. chpts. to books, anthologies and articles to profl. jours.; mem. editorial bd. Jour. of Conflict Resolution, 1959—; Polit. Sci. Rev., 1971—; Conflict Mgmt. and Peace Sci., 1978—; Etudes Polemologiques, 1978—. Office: Dept Polit Sci U Mich Ann Arbor MI 48109

SINGER, STANLEY THOMAS, JR., engineering administrator; b. Detroit, June 29, 1933; s. Stanley Thomas and Agnes Frances (Maciejewski) S.; m. Iris Josephine Bandmann, Nov. 12, 1960; children—Stanley Thomas III, Eric Herms. B.B.A. U. Detroit, 1966; M.A. Central Mich. U., 1977. Tool designer Gen. Motors Corp., Detroit, 1951-55, prodn. engr., 55-62; prodn. engr. Ford Motor Co., Utica, Mich., 1962-64, research engr., 1964-67, engring. mgr., Dearborn, 1967—. Exec. bd. Detroit Area Council Boy Scouts of Am., 1967—. Recipient Silver Beaver award Boy Scouts Am., 1984, St. George Emblem, Catholic Ch., 1984. Mem. Soc. Automotive Engrs., Engring. Soc. of Detroit, Soc. Mfg. Engrs., Delta Sigma Pi. Republican. Roman Catholic. Clubs: Detroit Yacht, Hillcrest Country. Lodge: K.C. Avocations: skiing, flying, boating.

SINGLETON, FRED WALTER, educational administrator; b. LaPorte, Ind., Nov. 26, 1940; s. Ward Allen and Irene Amy (Wicks) S.; m. Donna Jean Hampton, May 27, 1963; children—Loren Renee, Erin Kathleen. B.A. in Polit. Sci., Colo. Coll., 1963, M.A. in Polit. Sci. and History, 1971; Specialist D. Ednl. Adminstrn., So. Ill. U., 1980. Tchr. Highland Community Schs., Ill., 1964-73, asst. prin., 1973-80, prin., 1980—; cons. Adminstrv. Use of Computers, 1981—. Mem. city planning commn., Highland, 1973-75; legis. aide State Rep., Highland, 1972-76; city councilman, Highland, 1975-83. Named Outstanding Young Educator, Highland Jaycees, 1972; Rotary Internat. exchange fellow, 1972; scholar Royalton Coll. Internat. Scholars, 1972, Taft scholar Ind. State U., Terre Haute, 1977. Mem. Nat. Assn. Secondary Sch. Prins., Ill. Prins. Assn., Phi Delta Kappa. Lodge: Rotary (pres. 1976-77). Home: 46 Cardinal Ln Highland IL 62249 Office: Highland High Sch 1500 Troxler Ave Highland IL 62249

SINGSIME, GRACE SMOCK, catering company executive; b. Chgo., Nov. 22, 1924; d. Albert William and Martha Krueger (Manke) Smid; m. Alvin E. Singsime, Apr. 16, 1966 (dec.); 1 dau., Stacey G. Smock, stepchildren—Delores Singsime De Lellis, Mardi Singsime Schlondrop, Deane A. Owner mgr. Smock's Yankee Doodle Restaurant-Gracious Catering, Milw., 1953-59, Grace Smock-Gracious Catering, Milw., Elm Grove, Wis., 1959—. Mem. Internat. Food Service Exec. Assn. (Food Service Exec. of Yr. Milw. br. 1978), Elm Grove Bus. Assn., Waukesha Old Car Club. Mem. Order Eastern Star. Home: S 36 W 26579 Velma Dr Waukesha WI 53186 Office: Grace Smock Gracious Catering 890 Elm Grove Rd Elm Grove WI 53122

SINHA, DEVENDRA PRASAD, veterinarian, state laboratory administrator; b. Patna, India, Jan. 3, 1936; came to U.S., 1968, naturalized, 1971; s. Mohan Lal and Prameshwari (Devi) S.; m. Chandra Kanta, June 9, 1957; children—Renu, Ajit, Daisy; B.V.Sc. and A. H., Bihar U. (India), 1959; M.S., U. Mo., 1969; Ph.D., Ohio State U., 1973. Lic. veterinarian, Ohio. Veterinarian, State Govt. Bihar, 1959-68; research asst. U. Mo., 1968-70; research assoc. Ohio State U., 1970-73; microbiologist Ohio Dept. Agrl. Labs., Reynoldsburg, 1973-74, veterinarian, 1974—, dir. vet. microbiology lab., animal diseases diagnostic lab., 1974—. Bihar U. merit acad. scholar, 1955-59. Mem. Ohio Vet. Med. Assn., Am. Soc. Vet. Clin. Pathology, Am. Assn. Vet. Lab. Diagnosticians, Am. Soc. Microbiology, Gamma Sigma Delta. Research and pubs. in field. Home: 696 Stow Pl Reynoldsburg OH 43068 Office: 8995 E Main St Reynoldsburg OH 43068

SINNER, GEORGE A., governor of North Dakota; b. Casselton, N.D., May 29, 1928; m. Jane S.; 10 children. B.S. in Philosophy, St. John's U., 1950. Ptnr., Sinner Brothers and Bresnahan, Casselton, N.D.; mem. N.D. State Senate, 1962-66; mem. N.D. Ho. of Reps., 1982-84, chmn. Fin. and Taxation Com., 1983; gov. State of N.D., 1985—. Mem., N.D. State Bd. Higher Edn., 1967-74, chmn., 1970; first chmn. No. Crops Inst., Fargo, N.D.; mem. N.D. Pub. Broadcasting Council, 1968-73; mem. Greater N.D. Assn. Bd.; first chmn. S.E. Regional Mental Health and Retardation Clinic; del. N.D. Constl. Conv., 1972. Served with USAF, 1951-52. Mem. Red River Valley Sugar Beet Growers Assn. (pres. 1975-79). Mem. Democratic Party. Address: State Capitol Bismarck ND 58501

SINOR, DENIS, orientalist; b. Kolozsvar, Hungary, Apr. 17, 1916; s. Miklos and Marguerite (Weitzenfeld) S.; B.A., U. Budapest, 1938; M.A., U. Cambridge (Eng.), 1948; D. hon. causa, U. Szeged, 1971. Asst., Institut des Hautes Etudes Chinoises, U. Paris, 1941-45; attaché de recherches Centre de la Recherche Scientifique, Paris, 1946-48; lectr. Cambridge U., 1948-62; prof. Uralic and Altaic studies and history Ind. U., Bloomington, 1962—, disting. prof., 1975—, chmn. dept. Uralic and Altaic studies, 1963-81; dir. U.S. Office of Edn. Inner Asian and Uralic Nat. Resource Center, 1963—; dir. Asian Studies Research Inst., 1967-79, dir. Research Inst. Inner Asian Studies, 1979-81; v.p. UNESCO Commn. for Preparation History of Civilizations of Central Asia, 1981—. Recipient Arminius Vámbéry Meml. medal; Guggenheim fellow, 1968-69, 81-82; scholar-in-residence Rockefeller Found. Study Center, Villa Serbelloni, Bellagio, 1975; recipient grants Am. Council Learned Socs., 1962, Am. Philos. Soc., 1963, U.S. Office Edn., 1969-70; Nat. Endowment for Humanities, 1980-82; gold medalist Permanent Internat. Altaistic Conf., 1983 Fellow Korosi Csoma Soc. (hon.); mem. Am. Oriental Soc. (pres. 1975-76, chmn. Inner Asian regional com. 1968—), Permanent Internat. Altaistic Conf. (sec. gen. 1960—), Royal Asiatic Soc. Gt. Britain and Ireland (hon. sec. 1952-62), Societas Uralo Altaica (v.p. 1964—), Assn. Asian Studies (chmn. devel. com. Inner Asian studies 1973-79), Tibet Soc. (pres. 1967-69), Mongolia Soc. (chmn. bd. 1964—), Internat. Union Orientalists (past sec.), Am. Hist. Assn., Société Asiatique, Société de Linguistique, Deutsche Morgenlandische Gesellschaft, Hungarian Acad. Scis. (hon.). Clubs: United Oxford and Cambridge U. (London); Cosmos (Washington), Explorers (New York). Served with Forces Françaises de l'Interieur, 1943-44, French Army, 1944-45. Author: Introduction a l'étude de l'Eurasie Centrale, 1963; History of Hungary, 1959; Inner Asia, 1969; Modern Hungary, 1977; Inner Asia and Its Contact with Medieval Europe, 1977; contbr. articles to profl. jours.; editor Jour. Asian History, 1967—; Cambridge History of Inner Asia, Handbook of Uralic Studies. Office: Inner Asian and Uralic Nat Resource Ctr Goodbody Hall 101 Ind Univ Bloomington IN 47405

SINOR, DONNA KAY, lawyer; b. Cozad, Nebr., Sept. 5, 1952; d. Floyd Virgil and Arlene Caroline (Morris) S.; m. Steve E. Bowen, Oct. 27, 1984. B.S., U. Nebr., 1973, J.D., 1984. Bar: Nebr. 1984, U.S. Dist. Ct. Nebr. 1984. Tchr. Lincoln Pub. Schs., Nebr., 1973-81; researcher student Research Service, Lincoln, 1982-84; student coordinator Community Legal Edn., Lincoln, 1982-84; assoc. Nelson and Harding, Lincoln, 1984—. Recipient Outstanding Sophomore Woman award U. Nebr., 1971-72. Mem. Lincoln Bar Assn., Nebr. State Bar Assn., ABA, Nebr. Assn. Trial Attys., Assn. Trial Lawyers Am., Alpha Lambda Delta. Office: Nelson and Harding PO Box 82028 Lincoln NE 68501

SINOR, LYLE TOLBOT, immunohematologist; b. Columbus, Ga., May 24, 1957; s. Claude F. and Bessie (Anderson) S.; m. Jessie Jonette Rader, May 19, 1979; children—Meghan Elizabeth, Mollie Renee. B.G.S. in Microbiology, U. Kans., 1979, B.S. in Med. Tech., 1980, Ph.D. in Immunohematology, 1983. Cert. med. technologist. Staff med. technologist U. Kans. Med. Ctr., Kansas City, 1980-82; sr. staff research scientist Community Blood Ctr., Kansas City, Mo., 1982—. Author: Nonisotopic Immunoassays in Blood Group Serology, 1982; also articles. Patentee method of detecting an immunol. reaction. McPike scholar, 1983; SPEAS Found. grantee, 1983. Mem. Am. Soc. Clin. Pathologists (assoc.), Am. Assn. Pathologists, Am. Assn. Blood Banks, Internat. Soc. Blood Transfusion, N.Y. Acad. Scis. Republican. Methodist. Avocations: computers; tropical fish. Office: Community Blood Ctr 4040 Main St Kansas City MO 64111

SINYKIN, STEPHEN GEOFFREY, dentist; b. Mpls., Aug. 9, 1933; s. Edward Esser and Beverly Jeannette (Heiman) S.; m. Jacqueline Sue Strom, Feb. 19, 1965; children—Troy Gavin, Nicole Beth, Ryan Harris. B.S., U. Minn., 1956, B.A., 1956, D.D.S., 1958. Pvt. practice dentistry, Mpls., 1960—; pres., owner Mobil Dent, Ltd., Mpls., St. Paul, 1978—. Contbr. articles to profl. jours. Mem. Hist. Preservation Bd., Edina, Minn., 1982-83, Adv. Bd. Health, Edina, 1984-86. Served to capt. USAF, 1958-60. Recipient Meritorious Service award Minn. Dental Assn., 1984. Mem. Am. Soc. Geriatric Dentistry Am. Soc. Dentistry for Children (pres. Minn. chpt. 1973-74), ADA (preventive dentistry award 1974), Acad. Gen. Dentistry (pres. met. chpt. 1969-70), Alpha Omega (cert. of merit 1979). Jewish. Avocations: sculpture; gardening; flying; fishing; power boating. Office: 7250 France St S Edina MN 55435

SIPOS, PETER ANDRE, marketing and promotions company executive, consultant; b. Ft. Wayne, Ind., Sept. 18, 1958; s. Endre Francis and Mariann (Kertesz) S. B.S. in Chemistry, Purdue U., 1981. Asst. research chemist Central Soya, Ft. Wayne, summer 1976, 77; prodn. worker United Techs., Ft. Wayne, 1978; process chemist Monsanto Co., St. Louis, 1979; tech. sales rep. Procter & Gamble, Cin., 1981-84; pres. ANR Enterprises, Chgo., 1984—, Lena McLorin Designs, Chgo., 1985—; dir. Leroy Singleton Designs, Chgo., 1984—; sales and mktg. cons. David Condit, Inc., Chgo. Inventor HPLC method for vitamin D3 determination. Author articles and paper in field. Mem. Chgo. Council Fgn. Relations, 1983-84, Art Inst. of Chgo., 1983-84. Alpha Chi Sigma scholar, 1981. Mem. Am. Oil Chemists Soc., Soc. Advancement of Material Process Engring., Am. Chem. Soc. (pres. student affiliate 1980-81), Iowa Chem. Soc. (founding 1977), Phi Kappa Alpha. Club: Barclay (Chgo.). Avocations: art; chess; running; sailing; scuba diving. Home: 70 E Walton Suite 6C Chicago IL 60611

SIRENO, PETER JAMES, university administrator, businessman; b. Englewood, N.J., Oct. 18, 1941; s. James Joseph and Felicia Ann (Fascé) S.; m. Ellen Sue McIntyre, Aug. 18, 1963; children—Lisa, Felicia, Maria. B.S., N.E. Mo. State Coll., 1964, B.S.E., 1966, M.A., 1967; Ed.D. (HEW fellow 1971-73), U. Mo., 1973. Salesman, Tidewater Oil Co., N.Y.C., 1964-65; asst. prof. Mo. Western Community Coll., St. Joseph, 1967-71; dist. mgr. Fin. Programs and Fin. Assurance, Kansas City, Mo., 1968-71; dir. career programs Northeast Mo. State U., Kirksville, 1973-83; dean instructional services Dodge City Community Coll. (Kans.), 1983—. v.p., dir. Hungry Peddler, Inc., Kirksville, Mo., 1980-82; pres. Universal Research, Tng. and Cons. Assocs., Kirksville, 1981—; cons. in field. Pres. Mary Immaculate Parish Council, 1978-81; ex-officio mem. bd. edn. Mary Immaculate Elem. Sch., 1978-81; coach Kirksville Little League, 1978-80; bd. dirs. Coll. Park Homeowners Assn., 1977-80; chmn. Northeast Mo. Regional Manpower Adv. Council, 1978-82; mem. adv. bd. Labor Mgmt. and Econ. Devel. Com., 1982-83. HEW grantee, 1975-77; Mo. Research Coordinating Unit grantee, 1976; Mo. Dept. Natural Resources grantee, 1980; Mo. Pvt. Industry Council/ Mo. Dept. Manpower Planning spl. grantee, 1982. Mem. Mo. Assn. Community Jr. Colls., Mo. Assn. Adult and Continuing Edn., Am. Vocat. Assn., Am. Tech. Edn. Assn., Mo. Tchrs. Assn., Phi Delta Kappa, Pi Omega Pi. Roman Catholic. Contbr. articles to profl. jours. Office: Dodge City Community Coll 14th St and 50 Hwy Dodge City KS 67801

SIRMANS, DAN LAMAR, personnel administrator; b. Durham, N.C., July 13, 1941; s. Horace Lamar and Juanita (Fort) S.; B.B.A., Ga. State U., 1967; m. Sandra Elaine Bridges, Dec. 27, 1962; children—Todd Anthony, Elizabeth Anne. Asso. engr. Western Electric Co., Inc., Atlanta, 1962-67, sr. tng. specialist, St. Louis, 1968-74; dir. tng. and devel. ITT Aetna Corp., Denver, 1975-77; dir. personnel ITT Fin. Corp., St. Louis, 1978-79, dir. adminstrn., 1979-81; dir. employment Gen. Dynamics Communications, St. Louis, 1981-82; dir. human resources United Techs. Communications, 1982-83; v.p. human resources United Tech. Communication, 1983—. Mem. Am. Soc. for Tng. and Devel., Am. Soc. Personnel Adminstrn., Am. Mgmt. Assn., St. Louis Indsl. Relations Assn., Ind. Telephone Pioneer Assn., N.Am. Telephone Assn. Personnel Council, Assn. Human Resources Mgmt. and Orgn. Behavior, Orgn. Devel. Inst.

SISKEL, EUGENE KAL (GENE), film critic; b. Chgo., Jan. 26, 1946; s. Nathan W. and Ida (Kalis) S.; B.A., Yale U., 1967; postgrad. Dept. Def. Info. Sch., 1968; m. Marlene Iglitzen, 1980; 1 child, Kate Adi. Film critic Chgo. Tribune, 1969—; movie critic WBBM-TV, Chgo., 1974—; co-host Sneak Previews, PBS Network, 1978-82; co-host At the Movies, WGN-TV, Chgo., 1982—. CORO Found. fellow, 1968. Mem. Acad. TV Arts and Scis., Sigma Delta Chi. Clubs: Yale, Culver; Arts (Chgo.). Office: care Chicago Tribune 435 N Michigan Ave Chicago IL 60611

SISLER, MAYNARD LEE, physician, retired naval officer; b. Massillon, Ohio, Aug. 12, 1923; s. George Turner and Audrey Augusta (Athey) S.; student Washington Missionary Coll., 1939-40, Shepherd State Tchrs. Coll., 1941, U. So. Calif., 1950-51, Long Beach (Calif.) City Coll., 1948-50; B.S., Northwestern U., 1953, M.D., 1956; m. Sandra Ellen Byrd, Mar. 24, 1977; children by previous marriage—Suzanne, Judith, Kathleen, Mary Elizabeth, Maynard Lee, Leandra; 1 stepdau., Kim Wilburn. Intern, Passavant Meml. Hosp., Chgo., 1956-57; resident U.S. Naval Hosp., St. Albans, N.Y., 1958-61; practice medicine specializing in internal medicine, 1957—; commd. lt. M.C., U.S. Navy, 1957, advanced through grades to comdr., 1968; gen. med. officer U.S. Naval Acad., 1957-58; mem. staff U.S. Naval Hosp., Memphis, 1961-63; head gen. medicine U.S. Naval Hosp., San Diego, 1963-66, head sick officer quarters, 1968-69; chief of medicine U.S. Naval Hosp., Corpus Christi, 1966-68; resigned, 1969; assoc. with Med. Group, Internal Medicine Assocs., Palm Springs, Calif., 1969-70, Dunmire-Cash Clinic, Kennett, Mo., 1970-73; dir. Saturday Clinic, Parma, Mo., 1973-74; pvt. practice internal medicine, Kennett, 1973—; chief of stall Denihler Meml. Hosp., Kennett, 1981-83, chief of medicine, 1983—. Served with USN, 1941-50. Recipient Freedoms Found. award, 1963, 66, 67; Stitt award U.S. Naval Hosp., San Diego, 1966. Diplomate Am. Bd. Internal Medicine. Fellow A.C.P.; mem. Mo. State, Dunklin County med. socs., Royal Soc. Medicine (London). Author: A Large Slice of Life, Carved Into Poetry, 1974; contbr. numerous poems and essays to various newspapers and mags.; editorial editor Dunklin County Press, 1974—. Home: 217 College Ave Kennett MO 63857

SISSON, BETTY LOU, real estate broker; b. Burbank, Calif., Apr. 21, 1934; d. Harvey Orville and Isabel Marion (Melville) Angermeir; student pub. schs., Burbank; m. Everett A. Sisson; children—James Harvey, William Frank. Sales assoc. Rich Port Realtors, Oak Brook, Ill., 1971-76, sales mgr., 1976-78, v.p., 1978—; exec. v.p. Selected Properties, Inc., Oak Brook, 1979—, Midwest Club Co., Oak Brook, 1980-84, Am. Growth Industries, Oak Brook, 1981—, Guildcrest Furniture Industries, Inc., Peru, Ind., 1984—. Mem. Nat. Assn. Realtors, Realtors Nat. Mktg. Inst. Grad. Realtors Inst., DuPage Bd. Realtors, Oak Brook Assn. Commerce and Industry, U.S. Power Squadron Women's Aux. Republican. Club: Michigan City Yacht. Home: 1405 Burr Ridge Club Burr Ridge IL 60521

SISSON, EVERETT ARNOLD, diversified industry executive; b. Chgo., Oct. 24, 1920; s. Emmett B. and Norma (Merbitz) S.; A.B., Valparaiso U., 1942; postgrad. Yale, 1944; children—Nancy Lee Genz, Elizabeth Anne Levy. Sales mgr. Ferrotherm Co., Cleve., 1946-51, Osborn Mfg. Co., Cleve., 1951-56; dir. sales Patterson Foundry & Machine Co., East Liverpool, Ohio, 1956-58; mgr. sonic energy products Bendix Corp., Davenport, Iowa, 1958-60; pres., chief exec. officer, dir. Lamb Industries, Inc., Toledo, 1960-65, Lehigh Valley Industries, Inc., N.Y.C., 1965-66, Am. Growth Industries, Inc., Chgo., 1966—, Workman Mfg. Co., Chgo., 1966-69, Am. Growth Devel. Corp., Chgo., 1968—, Am. Growth Mgmt. Corp., Oak Brook, Ill., 1970—, Oak Brook Club Co., 1969—; chmn. Guildcrest Furniture Industries, Inc., Peru, Ind., 1976—, chmn. bd. Century Life Am., Waverly, Iowa; dir. Telco Equipment Leasing Corp., Chgo., Wis. Real Estate Investment Trust, Chgo., Hickory (N.C.) Furniture Co., Sunstates Corp., Jacksonville, Fla., 1982—, Opelika Mfg. Corp., Chgo., 1982—, Greater Heritage Corp., Lincolnwood, Ill., 1982—. Pres., City Council Mayfield Heights, Ohio, 1952-57. Adviser to bd. trustees Valparaiso U., 1960-69; bd. regents Calif. Luth. Coll. Served to capt. USAAF, 1943-46. Fellow Calif. Luth. Coll.; mem. Am. Mgmt. Assn., Cleve. Engring. Soc., Pres. Assn., Chgo. Power Squadron, Tau Kappa Epsilon. Clubs: Michigan City Yacht; Chgo Yacht; Burr Ridge; Gt. Lakes Cruising. Home: 1405 Burr Ridge Club Burr Ridge IL 60521 Office: 1550 Spring Rd Oak Brook IL 60521

SISSORS, DANIEL LELAND, immunologist, researcher; b. Evanston, Ill., Feb. 15, 1949; s. Jack Z. and L. Imogene (Kleinschmidt) S.; m. Mary Ann Finlon, Aug. 3, 1974; children—Christopher, Abigail. B.S., U. Ill., 1971, M.S., 1974, Ph.D., 1978. Research assoc. Case Western Res. U., Cleve., 1978-84, sr. research assoc. Sch. Medicine, 1984—. Contbr. articles to sci. jours. Mem. AAAS, Am. Chem. Soc., Sigma Xi. Democrat. Mem. Soc. of Friends. Avocations: music, photography, camping, computer programming. Home: 2126 Renrock Cleveland Heights OH 44118 Office: Case Western Res U Cleveland OH 44118

SIT, EUGENE C., investment executive; b. Canton, China, Aug. 8, 1938; s. Hom Yuen and Sue (Eng) S.; B.S.C., DePaul U., 1960, postgrad. Grad. Sch. Bus., 1962-65; m. Gail V. Chin, Sept. 14, 1958; children—Ronald, Debra, Roger, Raymond, Robert, Richard. Fin. analyst Commonwealth Edison, Chgo., 1960-66, fin. asst. to chmn. finance com., 1966-68; asso. portfolio mgr. Investors Stock Fund, Investors Diversified Services, Mpls., 1968-69; portfolio mgr. IDS New Dimensions Fund, Mpls., 1969, v.p., portfolio mgr., 1970-72; v.p., sr. portfolio mgr. IDS New Dimensions, IDS Growth Fund, Mpls., 1972-76; pres. IDS Adv., 1976-77, pres., chief exec. officer, 1977-81; chief exec. officer IDS Trust Co., 1979-81; chmn., chief exec. officer IDS Adv./Gartmore Internat. Ltd., 1979-81; pres., chief exec. officer Sit Investment Assos., Inc., Mpls., 1981—; chmn., pres., dir. New Beginning Income and Growth Fund, New Beginning Growth Fund, New Beginning Investment Res. Fund, New Beginning Yield Fund. Bd. dirs. Loring-Nicollet Bethlehem Community Centers. Minn. C.P.A., Ill.; chartered fin. analyst. Mem. Am. Inst. C.P.A.s, Inst. Chartered Fin. Analysts (trustee), Fin. Analysts Fedn., Twin Cities Soc. Security Analysts, Investment Analysts Soc. Chgo. Presbyterian. Clubs: University (N.Y.C.); Chicago; Minneapolis; Edina Country. Home: 6216 Braeburn Circle Edina MN 55435 Office: 1714 First Bank Pl West Minneapolis MN 55402

SITA, MICHAEL JOHN, pharmacist, educator; b. St. Louis, Apr. 28, 1953; s. Julianne Gail Sita; m. Nora Ann Dillon, June 1, 1974; 1 child, Michael John. B.S., St. Louis Coll. Pharmacy, 1976; M.B.A., So. Ill. U., 1983. Registered pharmacist, Mo., Ill. Staff pharmacist Lutheran Med. Ctr., St. Louis, 1976-78, asst. chief pharmacist, 1978-81, adminstrv. coordinator pharmacy services, 1981-85; dir. pharmacy services Jefferson meml. Hosp., 1985—; instr. St. Louis Coll. Health Careers, 1983—; relief pharmacist Dolgins Apothecary, St. Louis, 1976—. Author/editor Pharmacy Capsule quar., 1977—. Mem. St. Louis Soc. Hosp. Pharmacists, Mo. Soc. Hosp. Pharmacists, Mo. Pharm. Assn., Am. Soc. Hosp. Pharmacists, Am. Pharm. Assn., Am. Soc. Parenteral and Enteral Nutrition. Avocations: carpentry; rehabbing. Home: 6325 Pernod Ave Saint Louis MO 63139 Office: PO Box 350 Crystal City MO 63019

SITHOLE, ELKIN THAMSANQA, music educator; b. Newcastle, S.Africa, Apr. 14, 1931; came to U.S. 1965; s. Abner Mqiniseni and Elda (Mthanti) S.; m. Regina Thembi Buthelezi, June 1, 1934; children—Bongiwe, Linda, Jozana, Siyabonga. Tchrs. diploma St. Francis Coll., S.Africa, 1949; B.A., Natal U. (S.Africa), 1962; licentiate Royal Coll. Music, London, 1966; B. Mus., Hartt Coll., Hartford U., 1967; M.A. Wesleyan U., 1968; Ph.D., Queens U., Belfast, U.K., 1976. Cert. singing tchr., London. Tchr. S.Africa High Schs., 1950-64; prof. music ethnomusicology Northeastern Ill. U., Chgo., 1968—. Recipient Brit. Council Award, 1965, award UN Ednl. and Fellowship Program, 1967-68. Mem. Soc. Ethnomusicologists, Music Educators Nat. Conf. Methodist. Author: Kithi Kwa Zulu (poetry), 1981, Izithakazelo (Zulu family names), 1982; contr. articles on African, black music to publs. composer Zulu choir songs. Office: 700 E Oakwood St Chicago IL 60653

SIVE-TOMASHEFSKY, REBECCA, public affairs executive; b. N.Y.C., Jan. 29, 1950; d. David and Mary (Robinson) Sive; B.A., Carleton Coll., 1972; M.A. in Am. History, U. Ill., 1975; m. Clark Steven Tomashefsky, June 18, 1972. Asst. to librarian Am. Hosp. Assn., Chgo., 1973; researcher Jane Addams Hull House, Chgo., 1974; instr. Loop Coll., Chgo., 1975, Columbia Coll., Chgo., 1975-76; cons. Am. Jewish Com., Chgo., 1975, Center for Urban Affairs, Northwestern U., Evanston, Ill., 1977, Ill. Consultation on Ethnicity in Edn., 1976, Modern Lang. Assn., 1977; dir. Ill. Women's History Project, 1975-76; guest speaker at various ednl. orgns., 1972—; exec. dir. and founder Midwest Women's Center, Chgo., 1977-81; exec. dir. Playboy Found., 1981-84; dir. pub. affairs Playboy Enterprises, Inc., 1983—; dir. NOVA Health Systems, Woodlawn Community Devel. Corp.; instr. Roosevelt U., Chgo., 1977-78; dir. spl. projects Inst. on Pluralism and Group Identity, Am. Jewish Com., Chgo., 1975-77; cons. Nat. Women's Polit. Caucus, 1978-80; adv. bd. urban studies program Asso. Colls. Midwest. Mem. steering com. Ill. Commn. on Human Relations, 1976; mem. structure com. Nat. Women's Agenda Coalition, 1976-77; del.-at large Nat. Women's Conf., 1977; mem. Ill. Gov.'s Com. on Displaced Homemakers, 1979-81; mem. Ill. coordinating com. Internat. Women's Year; coordinator Ill. Internat. Women's Year Photg. Exhbn., 1977; mem. steering com. Women for Mondale-Ferraro; mem. Ill. Employment and Tng. Council; mem. employment com. Ill. Com. Status Women; mem. Ill. Human Rights Commn., 1980—; bd. dirs. Nat. Abortion Rights Action League and NARAL Found., Midwest Women's Center, Jewish Fund for Justice, Chgo. Labor Inst., Chgo. Film and Video Studio Found., Nat. Network Grantmakers; chair United Negro Coll. Fund Telethon; mem. adv. bd. Citizens Participation Project. Recipient award for outstanding community leadership YWCA Met. Chgo., 1979; Woman of Distinction, Chgo. Urban League, 1984; Kizzy award, 1983; others. Mem. ACLU, Women in Founds., Women's Inst. for Freedom of Press (asso.). Contbr. articles on women in Am. history to profl. publs.; editor Ill. Women's Agenda Newsletter, 1975-79. Office: 919 N Michigan Ave Chicago IL 60611

SIZEMORE, DONALD DEAN, statistician; b. Detroit, Oct. 21, 1951; s. Charles Stanley and Rilda Marie (Schoneman) S.; m. Rhonda Lynn Smith, May 12, 1973; children—Rebecca Lynn, Christopher Dean. B.S., U. Mich., 1973; M.B.A., Eastern Mich. U., 1982. Geog. analyst Hwy. Safety Inst., Ann Arbor, Mich., 1970-73; staff asst. Mich. Bell Telephone Co., Southfield, 1973-76, statistician, Detroit, 1976-78, sr. statistician, 1978—; high sch. vis. lectr., Ann Arbor, 1983—. Chmn. adv. bd. Northside Community Ch., Ann Arbor, 1976-77. Mem. Am. Statis. Assn., Math. Assn. Am., Beta Gamma Sigma. Republican. Baptist. Avocations: speleology; space exploration; civil war; fishing; camping; tennis. Home: 3216 Baylis Dr Ann Arbor MI 48104 Office: Mich Bell Telephone Co 444 Michigan Ave Room 1440 Detroit MI 48226

SKAALERUD, BJORN DAVID, retail furniture design executive; b. Feiring, Norway, Oct. 7, 1931; came to U.S. 1948, naturalized 1954; m. Anne Signe Solberg, Aug. 1, 1953 (div. 1975); children—Karin Signe Deger, Lisbeth, Pia Ann; m. Sunny Orlina, Sept. 13, 1975. Student Bklyn. Coll., 1952, Bklyn. Poly. U., 1953-55. Sales mgr. Royal System, Inc., N.Y.C., 1959-61, Dux, Inc., Burlingame, Calif., 1961-63; pvt. practice, N.Y.C., 1963-73; product mgr. Standard Oil Ind., Chgo., 1973-76; sales mgr. Eidsvold Mobel, Norway, 1976-79; tng. coordinator Scandinavian Design, Evanston, Ill., 1979—; bd. dirs. Norway Am. Hosp., Chgo., 1971-73. Recipient Woodbadge Tng. award Boy Scouts Am., 1964. Republican. Lutheran. Clubs: Norwegian (Bklyn.) (pres. 1969); Sons of Norway (Chgo.). Lodge: Masons. Avocations: golf, Norwegian language instruction. Home: 4720 Madison St Skokie IL 60076 Office: Scandinavian Design Inc 820 Church St Evanston IL 60201

SKADBURG, NORMAN DEAN, banker; b. Clarion, Iowa, Oct. 27, 1947; s. Percy Melvin and Ina Mae (Spangler) S.; m. Erma Louise Johnson, Dec. 29, 1968; children—Julie Ann, Jill Kristine. B.S., Iowa State U., 1969, M.S., 1971;

diploma Iowa Sch. Banking, U. Iowa, 1976, Commercial Lending Sch., U. Okla., 1979, Grad. Sch. Banking, U. Wis., 1983. Vocat. agr. instr. Williamsburg Community Schs., Iowa, 1969-71; v.p. Farmers Trust & Savs. Bank, Williamsburg, 1971-75; v.p. Poweshiek County Nat. Bank, Grinnell, Iowa, 1975-81; pres. Farmers State Bank, Stanhope, Iowa, 1984—, First State Bank, Webster City, Iowa, 1981—; dir. Ankeny State Bank, Iowa, Iowa Bankers Ins. Services, Inc., Des Moines, 1984—. Vice pres. Webster City Devel. Corp., 1982-85, pres., 1985—, treas. Trinity Luth. Ch., 1983—; sec. Williamsburg Community Devel. Corp., 1973-75. Recipient Key Man award Williamsburg Jaycees, 1974; Gov.'s Leadership award Iowa Community Betterment Program, State of Iowa, 1980; named Outstanding Young Alumnus, Iowa State U., Ames, 1981. Mem. Am. Bankers Assn., Nat. Ind. Bankers Assn., Am. Inst. Banking (v.p., dir. 1972-75, top student 1973), Iowa Ind. Bankers Assn., Iowa Bankers Assn. (dir. 1984—), Grinnell C. of C. (pres. 1980), Webster City C. of C. (pres. 1983-84), Alpha Zeta, Gamma Sigma Delta. Republican. Lutheran. Club: Ruritan (Grinnell, Iowa) (pres. 1979). Lodge: Rotary (dir., v.p. 1982-85). Avocations: golf; jogging; traveling; singing. Home: 604 Oak Park Dr Webster City IA 50595 Office: First State Bank 505 2d Ave Webster City IA 50595

SKAFF, DUANE LEE, utilities company executive; b. Sioux City, Iowa, Mar. 14, 1939; s. George A. and Delia B. Skaff; m. Wanda A. George, Aug. 28, 1966; children—Vince, Matt, Suzanne. B.S., Morningside U., 1962. Lineman Northwest Bell Telephone, Sioux Falls, S.D., 1965-66, acct., Omaha, 1966-70, staff analyst, 1973-79, mgr., 1979—. Sec., treas. Springville Fire Dept., Omaha. Served with USMC, 1962-64. Recipient Best Speaker award 1983. Mem. Internat. Mgrs. Assn. (pres. 1980-81). Club: Toastmasters (Able award 1982, gov. 1980-81). Lodges: Shriners, Papillion. Avocations: golf, swimming, auto collection. Home: 8624 N 57th St Omaha NE 68152 Office: Northwestern Bell Telephone 100 S 19th St Omaha NE 68102

SKAMSER, ERIK BENDIK, clin. social worker; b. Chgo., Sept. 22, 1947; s. Bruce Robb and Mary K. (Kwiek) S.; B.S. in Edn., No. Ill. U., DeKalb, 1970; M.S.W., U. Ill., Urbana-Champaign, 1976. Ward adminstr. Elgin (Ill.) State Hosp., 1970-73; cons. Ill. Dept. Children and Family Services, summer 1975; sch. social worker Danville (Ill.) public schs., 1975-76, Union Ridge Sch., Harwood Heights, Ill., 1976-78; clin. supr. Hull House Assn., Des Plaines Valley Community Center, Summit, Ill., 1978—; clin. social worker Child Sexual Abuse Treatment and Tng. Center Ill., Inc., 1980-85; field instr. Sch. Social Service Adminstrn., U. Chgo., 1980-83, Jane Addams Coll. Social Work, U. Ill., Chgo., 1981—; psychotherapist in pvt. practice, 1982—; founder, exec. dir. Chgo. Adolescent & Family Treatment Assn., founder, exec. dir., 1984—. Cert. social worker, Ill. Mem. Acad. Cert. Social Workers, Nat. Assn. Social Workers. Office: 56 E Oak St Chicago IL 60611 also CAFTA 30 N Michigan Ave Suite 715 Chicago IL 60602

SKAPEK, GUSTAVE JOHN, chemical company executive; b. Middletown, Ohio, Feb. 12, 1937; s. Gustav and Mary (Biel) S.; m. Frances Mary Skapek, Apr. 11, 1959; children—Gustave Charles, Stephen Xavier, Mary Jane, Amy Theresa. B.S. in Chemistry, Purdue U., 1958; M.B.A., Cleve. State U., 1976. Tech. sales rep. Diamond Shamrock, Chgo., Los Angeles, 1966-70, product-/bus. mgr., Cleve., 1970-74, div. material mgr., 1974-78, internat. purchasing mgr., 1978-81, mgr. purchasing, 1981-83; dir. material mgmt. Sherwin-Williams Co., Cleve., 1983—; cons. in field; lectr. in field. Contbr. articles to profl. jours. Ambassador Jr. Achievement, Cleve., 1980-83; team capt. United Way, Cleve., 1979-82; bus. auditor Cuyahoga County Purchasing Function, Cleve., 1982. Served to 1st lt. U.S. Army, 1959-60. Loyola U. Acad. scholar, 1955. Mem. Am. Chem. Soc., Nat. Assn. Purchasing Mgmt., Soc. Plastic Industry, Cleve. Chem. Assn. (pres.), Pentelicus, Scabbard and Blade, Beta Gamma Sigma. Roman Catholic. Lodge: K.C. Address: 3302 Ingleside Rd Shaker Heights OH 44122

SKARDA, EDWARD JAMES, sales and marketing executive; b. Chgo., Sept. 10, 1942; s. Edward Joseph and Vilma Rose (Heydanek) S.; m. Nancy Ann Byfield, May 23, 1970; children—Nicole Ann, Edward Byfield. B.A., U. Ill., 1965; M.A., No. Ill. U., 1970. Area sales mgr. Chgo. Tribune, 1969-73; sr. sales rep. Cheshire/Xerox, Mundelein, Ill., 1973-74, mgr. European ops., Munich, W.Ger., 1975-77, new product mgr., Mundelein, 1977-78; gen. mgr. Jay Retail Systems, Ltd., Toronto, Can., 1978-82; North Central sales mgr. Alpha Microsystems, Irvine, Calif., 1983—; cons. Nat. Computer Syndicate, Wheeling, Ill., 1983. Author: Four Artists on Horseback, 1970. Served to 1st lt. U.S. Army, 1965-67. Lodge: Rotary. Home: 511 W Hintz Rd Arlington Heights IL 60004

SKARR, CLIFFORD ALLEN, pharmacist; b. Oak Park, Ill., Aug. 20, 1941; s. Thaddeus and Dolores (Trunk) S.; m. Joanne Beth Morlock, June 22, 1963 (div. 1979); children—Brett Clifford, Jennifer Anne, Todd Joseph; m. Cathy Ellen Skoczek, July 21, 1984. B.S., U. Ill., 1962; postgrad. Coll. Pharmacy, Drake U., 1962-64. Pharmacist, Snyder Drug, Hoffman Estates, Ill., 1964-71; owner, pharmacist Town Square Pharmacy, Schaumburg, Ill., 1971-84. Mem., chmn. Olde Schaumburg Ctr. Commn., Village of Schaumburg, 1976-84, mem. Bd. Health, 1975-84; mem. Bd. Health Hoffman Estates (Ill.), 1968-71. Mem. Phi Delta Chi. Republican. Lutheran. Office: Town Square Pharmacy 311 Townsquare Schaumburg IL 60193

SKATZES, DAWERANCE HORACE, retired educator; b. Delaware, Ohio, Aug. 21, 1914; s. Carl Henry and Eulalia (Strickler) S.; B.S., Ohio U., 1951, M.Ed., 1954; postgrad. Ohio State U., 1958-59, 67-73, Muskingum Coll., 1965-66; m. Ruth Helen Jones, Apr. 1, 1941 (div. June 1949); children—Thelma Ruth Skatzes Moore, Elta Anne Skatzes George, Carl Alvin, Neatha Elaine Skatzes Marler, August Brent; m. 2d, Mildred M. Stillion, Feb. 18, 1975. Transient laborer, 1932-36; enrollee Civilian Conservation Corps, Price, Utah, 1936-37; unit clk. Soil Conservation Service, Price, 1938-41; field office mgr. Hunt & Frandsen, Gen. Contractors, Elko, Nev., 1942-44; boiler operator, supt. bldgs. and property Delaware (Ohio) City Schs., 1946-49; tchr. South Zanesville (Ohio) High Sch., 1951-54, 58-59; supt. Wills Local Sch. Dist., Old Washington, Ohio, 1954-58, Somerset (Ohio) Sch., 1959-60; prin. Adamsville (Ohio) Elem. Sch., 1960-61; supt. Quaker City (Ohio) Sch. Dist., 1961-62; prin. Valley High and Elementary Sch., Buffalo, Ohio, 1962-66; tchr. Columbus City Schs., 1967-74. Mayor, Old Washington, Ohio, 1975-79, clk.-treas., 1982—; Democratic candidate state rep., 1960-74. Served with U.S. Army, World War II. Mem. Nat. Soc. Study of Edn., Am. Assn. Sch Adminstrs., Nat. Council Tchrs. of Math., Acad. Polit. and Social Sci., Ohio Hist. Soc., Am. Legion, Am. Def. Preparedness Assn., Assn. U.S. Army, 37th Div. Vets. Assn., Kappa Delta Pi. Clubs: Eagles, Elks, Moose, Masons, Shriners. Home: Old Washington OH 43768-0265

SKELTON, ISAAC NEWTON, IV, congressman; b. Lexington, Mo., Dec. 20, 1931; s. Isaac Newton and Carolyn (Boone) S.; A.B., U. Mo., 1953, LL.B., 1956; m. Susan B. Anding, July 22, 1961; children—Ike, Jim, Page. Admitted to Mo. bar, 1956; practiced in Lexington; pros. atty. Lafayette County, Mo., 1957-60; spl. asst. atty. gen. Mo., 1962-65; mem. Mo. Senate from 28th dist., 1970-76; mem. 95-99th Congresses from 4th Mo. Dist. Chmn., Lafayette County Tom Eagleton for Senator campaign, 1968. Active Cub Scouts. Mem. Phi Beta Kappa, Sigma Chi. Democrat. Mem. Christian Ch. Lodges: Masons, Shriners, Elks. Office: 2453 Rayburn House Office Bldg Washington DC 20515*

SKELTON, JOSEPH RICHARD, lawyer; b. Coschocton, Ohio, Nov. 27, 1949; s. Richard and Marjorie Grace (Kreider) S. B.A., U. Notre Dame, 1971; J.D., U. Akron, 1974. Bar: Ohio, 1974. Ptnr. Pomerene, Burns & Milligan, Coshocton, Ohio, 1973—; law dir. City of Coshocton, 1979—; village solicitor Conesville, Ohio, 1983—; dir. Hancock Mortgage Co., Inc., Coshocton. Vice chmn. Democratic Party, Coshocton, 1983—; bd. dirs. Hopewell Adv. Bd., Coshocton, 1984—, ARC, Coshocton, 1984—. Served to maj. Ohio N.G., 1971—. Mem. ABA, Ohio State Bar Assn., Coshocton County Bar Assn., Ohio Assn. Twp. Trustees, Roman Catholic. Lodges: K.C. (grand knight 1981-84, trustee 1984—), Elks. Avocations: golf, softball, swimming. Home: 859 Chestnut St Coshocton OH 43812 Office: Pomerene Burns & Milligan 309 Main St Coshocton OH 43812

SKIDMORE, GAIL, librarian, bibliographer; b. New London, Conn., Oct. 9, 1945; d. Alvin Morrell and Lorraine (Leighton) S. B.F.A., Ill. Wesleyan U., 1967; M.A. in Speech, U. Ill.-Chgo., 1976; M.A. in L.S., Rosary Coll., 1980. Adjudicator, Ill. Unemployment Ins., Chgo., 1969-79; librarian Truman Coll., Chgo., 1981—. Editor: From Radical Left to Extreme Right. Mem. ALA, Assn. Coll. and Research Libraries. Office: Truman Coll 1145 W Wilson St Chicago IL 60640

SKIDMORE, JAMES WILLIAM, SR., chief of police; b. Pitts., Mar. 21, 1937; s. James Richard and Elizabeth (Legge) S.; m. Helen Margret Kaminski, Feb. 26, 1955; children—Richard, Sharon, James, Jr., Suzanne, Lynn. A.S. in Police Adminstrn. Sci., Allegheny County Community Coll., 1971; B.A. in Adminstrn. of Justice, U. Pitts., 1974; student in criminal justice, FBI Nat. Acad., 1976; cert. of achievement in criminal justice, U. Va., 1976. From police officer, sgt., detective, lt. to comdr. Mt. Lebanon Police Dept., Pa., 1959-78; chief of police West Band Police Dept., Wis., 1978—; instr. criminal justice Waukesha County Tech. Inst.-Moraine Park Tech. Inst., Waukesha-Fond du Lac, Wis., 1978—; advisor, law enforcement bd. chmn. Moraine Park Tech. Inst., Fond du Lac, 1978—; faculty Allegheny County Community Coll., 1972-78; lectr. U. of Ind. of Pa. Recruit Tng. Acad., 1975-76. Pres., West Bend Little League, 1981-85; mem. Gideons Internat., West Bend, 1983. Served with USMC, 1955-59. Recipient Law Enforcement Commendation medal Sons of Am. Revolution, 1983. Mem. Internat. Chiefs of Police Assn., Nat. Chiefs of Police Assn., Wis. Chiefs of Police Assn., Waukesha County Chiefs of Police Assn. (pres. 1980-82). Republican. Presbyterian. Lodges: Masons, Shriners. Avocations: sports; golf; running; hist. books and research. Home: 723 Pennsylvania Ave West Bend WI 53095 Office: Chief of Police West Bend Police Dept 325 N 8th Ave West Bend WI 53095

SKIEST, EUGENE NORMAN, chemical company executive; b. Worcester, Mass., Feb. 2, 1935; s. Hyman Arthur and Dorothy Ida (Brickman) S.; m. Toby Ann Aisenberg, Aug. 14, 1957 (div. 1973); children—Jody, Daniel, Nancy; m. Carol Tata, Nov. 26, 1974. B.S., Mass. Coll. Pharmacy, 1956; M.S., U. Mich., 1958; Ph.D., 1961. Research chemist Foster Grant Co., Leominster, Mass., 1961-62; sr. research chemist Thompson Chem. Co., Atteboro, Mass., 1962-64; pres. C&S Polymers, Westminster, Mass., 1965-66; group leader Borden Chem. Co., Leominster, 1966-69, devel. mgr., 1969-77, dir. devel. and applications, 1976-78; assoc. dir. quality assurance and compliance Borden, Inc., Columbus, Ohio, 1978-79, dir. quality assurance and compliance, 1979-81, corp. tech. dir. chems., 1981-84, corp. tech. dir., 1984—, co. rep. to Ind. Research Inst., 1983—. Contbr. articles, papers to profl. publs. Patentee in field. Bd. dirs. Pickawillany Assn., Westerville, Ohio, 1981. Mem. Am. Chem. Soc., Soc. Plastics Engrs., Formaldehyde Inst. (chmn. tech. com. 1979-84, bd. dirs. 1981), Chem. Mfrs. Assn. (chmn. task force 1983—), Nat. Paint and Coating Assn., Synthetic Organic Chem. Mfg. Assn. (govt. affairs com. 1979-83), Soc. Plastics Industries (vinyl toxicology subcom. 1978-82, vinyl acetate task force 1980-82, chmn. ad hoc packaging risk assessment com. 1978-81). Club: Continental Tennis. Avocations: tennis, reading, sports. Home: 5053 Chuckleberry Ln Westerville OH 43081 Office: Borden Inc 960 Kingsmill Pkwy Columbus OH 43229

SKINNER, DAVID BERNT, surgeon; b. Joliet, Ill., Apr. 28, 1935; s. James Madden and Bertha Elinor (Tapper) S.; B.A. with high honors, U. Rochester (N.Y.), 1958, D.Sc. (hon.), 1980; M.D. cum laude, Yale U., 1959; m. May Elinor Tischer, Aug. 25, 1956; children—Linda Elinor, Kristin Anne, Carise Berntine, Margaret Leigh. Intern, then resident in surgery Mass. Gen. Hosp., Boston, 1959-65; sr. registrar thoracic surgery Frenchay Hosp., Bristol, Eng., 1963-64; teaching fellow Harvard U. Med. Sch., 1965; from asst. prof. surgery to prof. Johns Hopkins U. Med. Sch., also surgeon Johns Hopkins Hosp., 1968-72; Dallas B. Phemister prof. surgery, chmn. dept. U. Chgo. Hosps. and Clinics, 1972—; mem. President's Biomed. Research Panel, 1975-76; mem. Comm. Diagnostic Radiology, 1979—; past cons. USPHS, Office Surgeon Gen. U.S. Navy. Elder, Fourth Presbyn. Ch., Chgo., 1976—; bd. visitors Cornell U. Med. Ctr., 1980—. Served to maj. M.C., USAF, 1966-68. Grantee NIH, 1968—; John and Mary Markle scholar acad. medicine, 1969-74. Diplomate Am. Bd. Surgery (dir. 1974-80), Am. Bd. Thoracic Surgery. Fellow ACS; mem. Am., Western, So. surg. assns., Soc. Univ. Surgeons (pres. 1978-79), Am. Soc. Artificial Internal Organs (pres. 1977), Soc. Surg. Chmn. (pres. 1980-82), Am. Assn. Thoracic Surgery, Soc. Vascular Surgery, Soc. Thoracic Surgery, Soc. Surgery Alimentary Tract, Am. Coll. Chest Physicians, Central Surg. Soc., Assn. Acad. Surgery, Halsted Soc., Soc. Clin. Surgery (pres.-elect 1984), Soc. Pelvic Surgeons, Phi Beta Kappa, Alpha Omega Alpha. Clubs: Quadrangle (Chgo.); Cosmos (Washington). Co-author: Gastroesophageal Reflux and Hiatal Hernia, 1972. Editor Jour. Surg. Research, 1972-82, Current Topics in Surg. Research, 1969-71. Contbr. profl. jours., chpts. in books. Home: 5490 South Shore Dr Chicago IL 60615 Office: 950 E 59th St Chicago IL 60637

SKINNER, GILBERT P(RESLEY), respiratory therapist, hospital administrator; b. Detroit, Jan. 14, 1942; s. Garfield Presley and Blanche Charlotte (Palmer) S.; children—Vernon Richard, Erika Danielle, Gilbert Presley. A.S., Highland Park Community Coll., 1971; B.S.Ed., U. Mich., 1975. Staff respiratory therapist Presbyn. Hosp., San Francisco, project dir. asst. U. Pacific, 1975-77; staff respiratory therapist Harper Hosp., Detroit, 1977-79; mgr. cardiopulmonary services Annapolis Hosp., Wayne, Mich., 1979—; instr. Washtenaw Community Coll., 1982—; mem. respiratory therapy adv. com. Washtenaw Community Coll., Highland Park Community Coll. Pres. bd. dirs. Central Wayne County (Mich.) Am. Cancer Soc. Served with M.C., U.S. Army, 1966-68. Mem. Am. Thoracic Soc., Mich. Soc. Respiratory Therapy (dist. rep., chmn. pub. relations), Am. Assn. Respiratory Therapy. Office: 33155 Annapolis Wayne MI 48184

SKINNER, JASPER DALE, II, prototype equipment co. exec.; b. Ainsworth, Nebr., July 11, 1947; s. Jasper Dale and Marilyn Fawn (Thompson) S.; B.A., U. Nebr., Lincoln, 1969, M.S., 1971, Ph.D., 1974; m. Ethel Marie Baysinger, Oct. 30, 1966; 1 dau., Cliti Eleta Nokomis. Extension entomology technician U. Nebr., Lincoln, 1969-70, research asso. agronomy dept., 1974-75; asst. entomologist Internat. Crops Research Inst. for Semi-arrid Tropics, Hyderabad, India, 1975-76; dir., chief designer Slatem & Tunlaw, Lincoln, 1976—. Regent's scholar, 1964-65; NDEA Title IV fellow, 1970-73. Fellow Internat. Biog. Assn.; mem. Nat. Rifle Assn., Sigma Xi, Phi Eta Sigma. Democrat. Lutheran. Office: PO Box 94993 Lincoln NE 68509

SKINNER, ROLLAND GENE, electric company executive; b. Ogallala, Nebr., Apr. 15, 1941; s. Neal Ray S. and Mildred Fay (Dowlar) Brill; m. Patricia Ann Worley, June 18, 1965; children—Shardel Shae, Brett Deon, Keri Lynn. Student, U. Wyoming. 1960-62. Lineman, meter reader Nebr. Pub. Power Dist., Ogallala, 1964-69, local rep., 1969-73; lineman Northwest Rural Pub. Power Dist., Hay Springs, 1973-74, ops. mgr., 1974-81, mgr., 1981—; speaker in field. Chmn. Tri-State Strategic Load Bldg. Comn., Denver, 1982—; mem. mgm. adv. com. Basin Electric G&T., Bismark, N.D., 1984—; Mem. Hay Springs Fire Dept., 1965-83, pres., 1972. Served to sgt. USNG, 1963-69. Mem. Nebr. REA Mgrs. Assn., Tri-State G&T Mgrs. Assn., Hay Springs C. of C. (pres. 1972), Nebr. Job Tng. and Safety Com., Nebr. Inter-Industry Electric Council, Am. Legion. Democrat. Methodist. Lodges: Masons, Elks. Home: PO Box 416 224 N Post St Hay Springs NE 69347 Office: Northwest Rural Pub Power Dist PO Box 249 S Hwy 87 Hay Springs NE 69347

SKLODOWSKI, ROBERT LEON, judge; b. Chgo., Sept. 10, 1935; m. Dolores Villadonga; children—Edward, Jenni, Andrea, Robert Jr. A.A., Morton Jr. Coll., 1956; B.A., Roosevelt U., 1957; J.D., Chgo. Kent Coll. Law, 1959; postgrad. Nat. Jud. Coll., 1978-82. Bar: Ill. 1959. Asst. atty. Gen. State Ill., 1959-60; ptnr. Schlaeger & Sklodowski, Niles, Ill., 1960-69; mng. ptnr. McLennon, Sklodowski, Nelson & White, Park Ridge, Ill., 1969-76; trial judge Criminal Div. Circuit Ct., Cook County, Ill., 1976-78; Repeat Offender Call Criminal Ct., Cook County, 1979—. Author: Prisoners Rights Handbook, 1980. Contbr. articles to profl. jours.; TV and radio appearances. Recipient award Merit Cruzada De Amour, Dominican Republic, 1971, cert. merit Polish Am. Congress, 1972. Mem. Ill. State Bar Assn., Ill. Trial Lawyers (bd. mgrs. 1972-76, hon.), Northwest Suburban Bar Assn. (pres. 1969-70, Edward Julian Bieg award 1980), Northwest Bar Assn. (Man of Month award 1979). Home: 2285 Landwehr Rd Northbrook IL 60062 Office: Criminal Ct Cook County Room 404 2600 S California Ave Chicago IL 60608

SKOLNICK, VIVIAN BLAIR, clinical psychologist; b. Norfolk, Va., Apr. 20, 1929; d. Morris L. and Pauline (Kleinstein) Blair; m. Irving H. Skolnick, Aug. 16, 1949; children—Blair, Sarelle. B.A., Chgo. State U., 1969; M.S., Ill. Inst. Tech., 1971, Ph.D. in Psychology, 1974. Registered psychologist, Ill. Psychologist, chief withdrawal section Ill. Drug Abuse Program, Chgo., 1971-73; head psychologist drug withdrawal program, U. Chgo., 1973-74; clin. assoc. U. Ill., Chgo., 1981—; pvt. practice psychology, Chgo., 1974—; cons. in field. Mem. Chgo. Psychoanalytic Psychology Assn., Am. Personnel and Guidance Assn., Am. Psychol. Assn., Chgo. Assn. Psychoanalytic Psychology, Am. Soc. Clin. Hypnosis, Soc. Clin. and Exptl. Hypnosis, Nat. Register Health Service Providers, Am. Mental Health Aid to Israel (nat. bd. mem.). Contbr. articles to profl. jours. in field. Office: 180 N Michigan Ave Chicago IL 60601

SKOWRONSKI, FRED STANLEY, banker; b. Chgo., Oct. 27, 1918; s. Joseph and Bernice (Toczek) S.; m. Lois Elaine Lundgren, Nov. 19, 1941; children—Barbara Y. Link, Joan E. Tippet, Terri, Rita M. Pusateri. Student, Ill. Coll. Commerce 1937-38, Wilbur Wright Jr. Coll., 1938-40, Am. Inst. Banking, 1950-51. With Mfrs. Bank of Chgo., 1948—, asst. v.p., 1974—. Treas., Vets. Assistance Commn. of Cook County and Combined Vets. Assn. Ill., 1970-85; v.p., bd. dirs. Polish Mus. Am. Served with USAAF, 1942-45. Recipient Chgo. Clearing House Honor award, 1951; Meritorious awards and citations from AMVETS, Cath. War Vets., DAV, Jewish War Vets., Marine Corps League, Mil. Order Purple Heart, Paralyzed Vets. Am., VFW, others. Mem. Polish Nat. Alliance, Polish Roman Cath. Union, Polish Alma Mater of Am. (pres. 1980-88), Polish Legion of Am. Vets. (nat. treas. 1950-86). Roman Catholic. Lodges: Elks, Kiwanis, Holy Name Soc. Home: 5229 W Melrose St Chicago IL 60641 Office: 1200 N Ashland Ave Chicago IL 60622

SKRAMSTAD, HAROLD KENNETH, JR., museum administrator, consultant, lecturer; b. Washington, June 3, 1941; s. Harold K. and Sarah (Shroat) S.; m. Susan Chappelear, Dec. 28, 1963; children—Robert, Elizabeth. A.B., George Washington U., 1963, Ph.D., 1971. Asst. dir. Am. Studies Program, Smithsonian Instn., 1969-71; spl. asst. to dir. Nat. Mus. Am. History, 1971, chief spl. projects, 1971-72, chief exhibits programs, 1972-74; dir. Chgo. Hist. Soc., 1974-80; pres. The Edison Inst., Henry Ford Mus., Greenfield Village, Dearborn, Mich., 1981—; mem. Joint Com. on Landmarks of Nat. Capital, 1972-82; mem. Chgo. Commn. Hist. and Archtl. Landmarks, 1975-80. Trustee, Kendall Coll., 1976-80, Coll. of Art and Design, Ctr. for Creative Studies, Detroit, 1981—; bd. dirs. Met. Detroit Conv. and Visitors Bur., 1981—, Detroit Symphony Orch., 1981—, Detroit Grand Opera Assn., 1981—. Mem. Am. Assn. Museums (v.p. 1984—). Clubs: Detroit; Cosmos (Washington). Office: The Edison Inst Henry Ford Mus/Greenfield Village 20900 Oakwood Blvd Dearborn MI 48121

SKULINA, THOMAS RAYMOND, lawyer; b. Cleve., Sept. 14, 1933; s. John J. and Mary B. (Vesely) S.; A.B., John Carroll U., 1955; J.D., Case Western Res. U., 1959, LL.M., 1962. Bar: Ohio 1959, U.S. Supreme Ct. 1964, ICC bar 1965. Mem. Skulina & Stringer, Cleve., 1967-72, Riemer Oberdank and Skulina, 1978-81, Skulina, Fillo, Walters & Negrelli, 1981-84, Fillo, Ristau, Drain & Skulina, 1984—; atty. Penn Central Transp. Co., Cleve., 1960-65, asst. gen. atty., 1965-78, trial counsel, 1965-76; with Consol. Rail Corp., 1976-78; tchr. comml. law Practicing Law Inst., N.Y.C., 1970. Income tax and fed. fund coordinator Warrensville Heights, Ohio, 1970-77; spl. counsel City of N. Olmstead (Ohio), 1971-75; pres. Civil Service Commn., Cleve., 1977—; spl. counsel Ohio Atty. Gen., 1983—. Served with U.S. Army, 1959. Mem. Nat. Assn. R.R. Trial Counsel, Internat. Assn. Law and Sci., ABA, Cleve. Bar Assn., Ohio Bar Assn., Fed. Bar Assn. Democrat. Roman Catholic. Clubs: River Run Racquet, Lakewood Country. Contbr. articles to legal jours. Home: 3162 W 165th St Cleveland OH 44111 Office: 1520 Standard Bldg Cleveland OH 44113

SKUTT, VESTOR JOSEPH, See *Who's Who in America,* 43rd edition.

SKYLES, BARNETT, educational administrator; b. Chgo., Nov. 17, 1926; s. Elisha Barnett Skyles and Margaret Lucile (Anderson) Proctor; m. Shawnelle Whitaker, Aug. 5, 1950; 1 son, Christopher. B.Edn. with honors, Chgo. State U., 1962, M.S., 1973. Cert. tchr., counselor, Ill. Transfer clk. U.S. Post Office, Chgo., 1948-62; tchr. elem. sch., Chgo. Bd. Edn., 1962-69, guidance counselor, 1969-83, administrator, 1983—; counselor U. Ill., Chgo., 1969-83. Served to sgt. U.S. Army, 1945-46; Germany. Recipient Excellence in Teaching award W. Norbert Engles Sch., 1968; Cert. Merit, 1977, Outstanding Service award Parent Edn. Council, 1979; Award of Distinction, Local Sch. Council, 1979. Mem. Elem. Sch. Counselors Council, Chgo. Afro-Am. Tchrs. Assn., Phi Delta Kappa. Methodist. Club: Chgo. Assembly.

SLADE, LLEWELLYN EUGENE, lawyer, engineer; b. Carroll, Iowa, May 1, 1911; s. Llewellyn and Mary (Veach) S.; m. Jane England Dickinson, June 8, 1945; 1 dau. by previous marriage, Yvonne Slade Tidd. B.S. in Elec. Engring., Iowa State U., 1938, M.S., 1942; J.D., Drake U., 1951. Registered profl. engr., Iowa. With Iowa Power and Light Co., Des Moines, 1940-68, exec. v.p., dir., 1964-68; cons. Nebr. Pub. Power Dist. nuclear project, 1964-76; pvt. practice exec. counselor, atty., profl. engr., arbitrator, 1968—; mem. panel of arbitrators U.S. Fed. Mediation and Conciliation Service, Am. Arbitration Assn.; organizing chmn., trustee Des Moines Metro Transit Authority; bd. dirs. West Des Moines Devel. Corp., Theta Chi Corp. Mem. Fed. Bar Assn., ABA, Iowa Bar Assn., Polk County Bar Assn., Nat. Soc. Profl. Engrs., Iowa Engring. Soc. Lutheran. Clubs: Men's Garden of America, Embassy (Des Moines). Lodge: Masons (32 deg.), Shriners, Rotary. Home: 5833 Pleasant Dr Des Moines IA 50312 Office: 400 Hubbell Bldg Des Moines IA 50309

SLAGER, RONALD DALE, wholesale-retail company executive; b. Kalamazoo, Mich., Oct. 16, 1952; s. Robert Peter and Ruth M. Slager; student Western Mich. U., 1970, Mich. State U., 1971. Sales rep. Investors Diversified Services, Mpls., 1971-73; sales rep., sales mgr. Dykema Office Supply, Kalamazoo, 1973-77; owner, mgr. Stage Lighting Distbrs., Kalamazoo, 1974-75; co-founder The Hearing Aid Center of Kalamazoo, 1976-78; v.p., sec., dir. Hearing Aid Centers of Am., Inc., Kalamazoo, 1978—; prin. R Slagers' Assocs., Kalamazoo, 1983—; treas., MLR Inc., Kalamazoo, 1980-82; ptnr. AZO Investments, Kalamazoo, 1983—; v.p. HARC Mercantile Ltd., 1984—; dir. Wizen Products Co., Consumer High Tech. mem. Mich. State Bd. Hearing Aid Licensing, 1981—. Bd. dirs. Kalamazoo Youth for Christ, 1973, Youth Opportunities Unltd. Kalamazoo, Inc., 1980—, Milwood Little League, 1982-84; advisor Jr. Achievement, Kalamazoo, 1978-79; mem. pvt. industries Council Youth Steering Com. Mem. Hearing Industries Assn., Am. Mgmt. Assn., Ad Club Kalamazoo, Sales and Mktg. Execs., Kalamazoo C. of C., Ind. Businessmen Assn., A.G. Bell Assn. for Deaf, Better Hearing Inst., Am. Auditory Soc., Mich. Mfrs. Assn., Council on Assistive Devices and Listening Systems (co-founder), Reformed Ch. Club: Sertoma (pres. 1976-77, chmn. 1977-78, dist. gov. N.W. Ohio-Mich. dist. 1978-79), Kazoo Ink (prin. 1985). Home: 6481 East S Ave Scotts MI 49088 Office: 3130 Portage Rd Kalamazoo MI 49003

SLATER, JAMES MICHAEL, surgeon; b. Fort Wayne, Ind., Jan. 18, 1947; s. Fred Lyman and Vera (Van Houten) S.; m. Sue Ellen Anderson, Sept. 6, 1969; children—Jessica Sue, Emily Michael. B.S., Purdue U., 1969; M.S., cum laude in Inorganic Chemistry, Eastern Mich. U., 1971; D.O., Kirksville Coll. Osteo. Medicine, 1975. Diplomate Am. Bd. Surgery. Intern, Flint (Mich.) Osteo. Hosp., 1975-76, resident in gen. surgery, 1977-81; practice medicine specializing in gen. surgery; pvt. practice Whitley County Gen. Hosp., Columbia City, Ind., 1975-76; pres. Whitley Med. Assocs., Columbia City, 1975-76; attending physician Gen. Hosp., Lapeer, Mich., 1979-80; mem. staff Jackson (Mich.) Osteo. Hosp., 1982—, chief of staff, 1983-84, 85-86, chmn. dept. surgery, 1983-84. Named Outstanding Surg. Resident, Flint Osteo. Hosp., 1981; March of Dimes fellow; Stewart fellow. Mem. Am. Osteo. Assn., Genessee County Osteo. Soc., Southeastern Mich. Osteo. Assn., Sigma Sigma Phi. Contbr. articles to profl. jours.

SLATER, JAN S., business executive; b. Fairbury, Nebr., Oct. 1, 1956; d. Calvin Francis and June Marie (Howell) S. A.S., S.E. Community Coll., 1976; B.A., Hastings Coll., 1978. Pub. relations dir. Performing Artists, Omaha, 1978-80; owner J. Slater & Assocs., Omaha, 1980-82; asst. dir. advance and promotion Pacesetter Corp., Omaha, 1982—. Chmn. Hastings Coll. Alumni Assn., 1983-85. Mem. Omaha Fedn. Advt. (bd. dirs. 1983—), Graphic Artists Guild (bd. dirs. 1982-83). Republican. Presbyterian. Avocation: racquetball. Home: 3403 N 93d St Omaha NE 68134 Office: Pacesetter Corp 4343 S 96th St Omaha NE 68127

SLATKIN, LEONARD, conductor; b. Sept. 1; s. Felix Slatkin and Eleanor Aller; began violin study, 1947, piano study with Victor Aller and Selma Cramer, 1955, composition study with Castelnuovo-Tedesco, 1958, viola study with Sol Schoenbach, 1959; conducting study with Felix Slatkin, Amerigo Marino and Ingolf Dahl; attended Ind. U., 1962, Los Angeles City Coll., 1963, Juilliard Sch. (Irving Berlin fellow in musical direction), beginning 1964; student of Jean Morel and Walter Susskind; hon. doctorates St. Louis Conservatory, Washington U., U. Mo.-St. Louis. Conducting debut as asst. condr. Youth Symphony of N.Y., Carnegie Hall, 1966; asst. condr. Juilliard Opera Theater and Dance Dept., 1967; asst. condr. St. Louis Symphony Orch., 1968-71, assoc. condr., 1971-74, music dir., condr., 1979—; founder, music dir. and comdr. St. Louis Symphony Youth Orch., beginning 1969; debut with Chgo. Symphony Orch., 1974, N.Y. Philharmonic, 1974, Phila. Orch., 1974; European debut with Royal Philharmonic Orch., 1974; debut with USSR orchs., 1976-77; prin. guest condr. Minn. Orch., beginning 1974, summer artistic dir., 1979-84; music dir. New Orleans Philharmonic Symphony Orch., 1977-78, musical adv., 1979-80; guest condr. orchs. throughout world; former vis. asst. prof. music Washington U., St. Louis; initiated Friday afternoon lecture series; hosted weekly radio program. Office: care Mariedi Anders Artist Mgmt 535 El Camino Del Mar San Francisco CA 94121 also St Louis Symphony Orch Powell Symphony Hall 718 N Grand Blvd Saint Louis MO 63103

SLATTERY, JAMES CHARLES, congressman; b. Atchison, Kans., Aug. 4, 1948; s. Charles B. and Rose M. (O'Connell) S.; m. Linda Smith. Student Netherlands Sch. Internat. Econs. and Bus., 1969; B.S. in Polit. Sci., Washburn U., 1970, LL.B., 1974. Economist Kans. Dept. Labor, 1970-72; salesman Love & Robb, Realtors, Topeka, 1973-77; sales mgr. Love & Robb, Inc., 1976; pres. Brosius & Slattery, Inc., Topeka, 1977; mem. Kans. Ho. Reps., 1972-78, chmn. Democratic policy com., 1974-76, speaker pro tem, 1977-78; mem. 98th-99th Congresses from 2d Dist. Kans. Pres. Washburn Coll. Young Democrats, 1968; campaign aide to U.S. Rep. William R. Roy, Kans., 1972, 74. Served with Kans. Army N.G., 1970-75. Netherlands exchange student, 1968. Mem. Washburn U. Alumni Assn., Phi Delta Theta. Roman Catholic. Office: 1431 Longworth House Office Bldg Washington DC 20515

SLAUGHTER, DIANA TERESA, psychology educator; b. Chgo., Oct. 28, 1941; d. John Ison and Gwendolyn Malva (Armstead) S. B.A., U. Chgo., 1962, M.A., 1968, Ph.D. in Devel. and Clin. Child Psychology, 1968. Instr. psychiatry Howard U. Sch. Medicine, Washington, 1967-68; research assoc., asst. prof. Yale U. Child Study Ctr., New Haven, 1968-70; asst. prof. human devel. and edn. U. Chgo., 1970-77; assoc. prof. sch. edn. Northwestern U., Evanston, Ill., 1977—; vis. assoc. prof. Afro-American studies U. Ill., Champaign, 1980-81; mem. governing council Soc. for Research in Child Devel., 1981—; chair Social Policy Com. Chgo. affiliate Nat. Black Child Devel. Inst., 1982-85. Recipient Pi Lambda Theta doctoral thesis award, 1969; Nat. Inst. Edn. grantee, 1983. Mem. Soc. for Research in Child Devel., Am. Ednl. Research Assn., Am. Psychol. Assn., Assn. Black Psychologists, Delta Sigma Theta. Contbr. monograph in field; editorial bd. Jour. Black Psychology. Office: 2003 Sheridan Rd Evanston IL 60201

SLAYTON, ALICE HOGAN, educator; b. Florence, Ala., Oct. 7, 1944; d. Milton Earl and Mary Edith (Horsfield) Hogan; m. Arthur Joseph Slayton, Feb. 19, 1966; children—Arthur, Amy Catherine. B.A., Converse Coll., 1967. Tchr. AB4 Skol Bridgeport, W.Va., 1972-76; tchr., San Benito Sch., Humacao, P.R., 1976-80; tchr. Wesley Pre-Sch., Fostoria, Ohio, 1980—; mem. Fostoria Econ. Devel. Assn. Excellence in Edn. Com., 1983—. Author (booklet) Moving to Puerto Rico, 1976. Mem. Fostoria City Sch. Bd. 1982—, v.p., 1983, pres., 1984. Recipient 1st place award W.Va. Fedn. of Women's Clubs, 1975, 76. Mem. AAUW, Ohio Sch. Bd. Assn. Republican. Episcopalian. Avocations: reading, needlework, photography. Home: 1206 Woodrow Wilson Dr Fostoria OH 44830 Office: Wesley Pre School Van Buren Fostoria OH 44830

SLAYTON, RANSOM DUNN, consulting engineer; b. Salem, Nebr., Mar. 10, 1917; s. Laurel Wayland and Martha Ellen (Fisher) S.; B.S. with distinction, U. Nebr., 1938; postgrad. Ill. Inst. Tech., 1942, DePaul U., 1945-46; m. Margaret Marie Ang, Sept. 25, 1938; children—R. Duane, David L., Sharon J. Slayton Manz, Karla M. Slayton Fogel, Paul L. With Western Union Telegraph Co., Lincoln, Nebr., 1937-38, St. Paul, 1938-40, Omaha, 1940, Chgo., 1940-45; asst. prof. elec. engring. Chgo. Tech. Coll., 1945-46; with Teletype Corp., Chgo. and Skokie, Ill., 1946-82, lectr., China and Japan, 1978, 79, 80. Active vol. civic orgns., numerous ch. offices. Mem. IEEE (sr.; numerous coms.), IEEE Communications Soc. (parliamentarian 1972-80, 82—, vice chmn. terminals com. 1980-82, chmn. 1983-84). Patentee in field. Home: 1530 Hawthorne Ln Glenview IL 60025

SLEEMAN, MARY (MRS. JOHN PAUL SLEEMAN), librarian; b. Cleve., June 28, 1928; d. John and Mary Lillian (Jakub) Gerba; B.S., Kent State U., 1965, M.L.S.; m. John Paul Sleeman, Apr. 27, 1946; children—Sandra Sleeman Swyrydenko, Robert, Gary, Linda. Supervising librarian elem. schs. Nordonia Hills Bd. Edn., Northfield, Ohio, from 1965, now dist. elem. librarian; children's librarian Twinsburg (Ohio) Pub. Library, 1965-66. Mem. ALA, Ohio Sch. Librarians Assn., NEA, Summit County Librarians Assn., Storytellers Assn., North Eastern Ohio Tchrs. Assn. Methodist. Home: 18171 Logan Dr Walton Hills OH 44146 Office: 115 Ledge Rd Northfield OH 44067

SLEIGHTER, JAMES CARTER, educational administrator; b. Morgantown, Ind., Dec. 1, 1929; s. James Thurman and Zora (Zimmerman) S.; m. Lois Marie Bowers, June 24, 1951; children—Patsy Ann, Carle Jean. B.S., Franklin Coll., 1952; M.S., Butler U., 1957. Math tchr. Mt. Auburn High Sch., Ind., 1952-55; math tchr., guidance counselor Whiteland High Sch., Ind., 1955-59, high sch. prin., 1959—. Mem. Ind. Secondary Sch. Adminstrs., Phi Delta Kappa. Lodges: Kiwanis, Masons, Eastern Star. Avocation: fishing. Home: Rural Route 1 Box 146 Whiteland IN 46184 Office: Whiteland Community High Sch 300 Main St Whiteland IN 46184

SLEMMONS, ROBERT SHELDON, architect; b. Mitchell, Nebr., Mar. 12, 1922; s. M. Garvin and K. Fern (Borland) S.; B.A., U. Nebr., 1948; m. Dorothy Virginia Herrick, Dec. 16, 1945; children—David (dec.), Claire, Jennifer, Robert, Timothy. Draftsman, Davis & Wilson, architects, Lincoln, Nebr., 1947-48; chief designer, project architect Office of Kans. State Architect, Topeka, 1948-54; asso. John A. Brown, architect, Topeka, 1954-56; partner Brown & Slemmons, architect, Topeka, 1956-69; v.p. Brown-Slemmons-Kreuger, architects, Topeka, 1969-73; owner Robert S. Slemmons, A.I.A. & Assos., architects, Topeka, 1973—. Cons. Kans. State Office Bldg. Commn., 1956-57; lectr. in design U. Kans., 1961. Bd. dirs. Topeka Civic Symphony Soc., 1950-60. Served with USNR, 1942-48. Mem. AIA (Topeka pres. 1955-56, Kans. dir. 1957-58, mem. com. on architecture for justice), Topeka Art Guild (pres. 1950), Kans. Council Chs. (dir. 1961-62), Greater Topeka C. of C., Downtown Topeka, Inc. Presbyn. (elder, chmn. trustees). Kiwanian (pres. 1966-67). Prin. archtl. works include: Kans. State Office Bldg., 1954, Topeka Presbyn. Manor, 1960-74, Meadowlark Hills Retirement Community, 1979, Shawnee County Adult Detention Facility, 1985. Office: 1515 1 Townsite Plaza Topeka KS 66603

SLICK, JEWEL CHERIE, consulting service administrator, nurse; b. Poplar, Mont., June 13, 1934; d. Ralph and Charity Ruth (Reddoor) Wing; R.N., St. Luke's Hosp., Kansas City, Mo., 1955; m. Virgil Slick, May 31, 1970; 1 dau., Cherie Ann. Pvt. duty nurse, 1958—; advocate for Am. Indians, 1969—; owner Am. Indian Cons. Service, Des Moines, 1980—; mem. Des Moines Human Rights Commn., 1974-77, 82—, Gov. Iowa Interstate Indian Council, 1975-77, Nat. Indian Bd. Alcoholism, 1975-78; bd. dirs. Des Moines YWCA, 1981—. Mem. Iowa Nursing Assn., Nat. Assn. Female Execs. Democrat. Address: 3610 Columbia St Des Moines IA 50313

SLIVE, STEVEN HOWARD, lawyer; b. Queens, N.Y., July 1, 1950; s. Theodore Hertzel and Jean Rhoda (Blatt) S.; m. Harriet Weinmann, Sept. 3, 1982. B.G.S., Ohio U., 1972; J.D., Cleve. State U., 1976. Bar: Ohio 1976. Dir. legal clinic Free Med. Clinic of Greater Cleve., 1977-81; ptnr. Slive & Slive, Cleve., 1981—. Trustee Guardian Ad Litem Adv. Bd. Cuyahoga County, Cleve., 1982-84, chmn., 1984—; vol. atty. Free Med. Clinic Greater Cleve., 1981—; bd. dirs. ACLU, 1983-84; trustee Cleve. State U. Mem. Greater Cleve. Bar Assn., Ohio State Bar Assn., Cuyahoga County Bar Assn., Cleve. Marshall Coll. Law Alumni Assn. (trustee 1984—). Democrat. Jewish. Avocations: basketball; jogging; photography. Home: 2648 Eaton Dr University Heights OH 44118 Office: 800 Engrs Bldg 1365 Ontario St Cleveland OH 44114

SLOAN, MARY LOVE STRINGFIELD, interior designer; b. Waynesville, N.C., Aug. 7, 1947; d. Thomas and Harriet (Coburn) Stringfield; m. Hugh Johnston Sloan, III, Feb. 12, 1982; 1 stepchild, Kathleen Sloan Gebhart. B.S., U. Tenn., 1973. Staff designer Omnia Design, Inc., Charlotte, 1973-79; dir. planning and design Counterpoint, Inc., Knoxville, 1979-81; coordinator interior design Ohio State U. Hosps., Columbus, 1981—; instr. Central Piedmont Community Coll., Charlotte, 1978, U. Tenn., Knoxville, 1980. Bd. dirs., pres. ECO, Inc., Charlotte, 1977, 79. Sec. Young Democrats Club, Charlotte, 1978; rep. to state bd. Women's Polit. Caucus, Knoxville, 1980. Mem. Inst. Bus. Designers (nat. trustee 1978-79, v.p. Tenn. chpt. 1980, Cert. of Appreciation 1980), Assn. Univ. Interior Designers (sec. 1983-85, v.p. 1985—), U. Tenn. Alumni Assn. (sec. 1984-85). Republican. Methodist. Clubs: Women's Guild Opera Columbus, World Future Soc., Sierra, Ohio Preservation Alliance. Avocations: travel; gardening; opera; theatre; philately. Home: 758 N Park St Columbus OH 43215 Office: Ohio State U Hosps 410 W 10th Ave Columbus OH 43210

SLOAN, MICHAEL LEE, computer company engineer; b. Chgo., Jan. 24, 1944; s. Robert Earl Sloan and Cyril (Lewis) Glass; m. Claudia Ann Schultz, Sept. 27, 1969. B.S. in Physics, Roosevelt U., 1966, M.S., 1971. Tchr. physics Glenbard West High Sch., Glen Ellyn, Ill., 1966-79; computer cons. Midwest Visual, Chgo., 1979-82; sr. engr. Apple Computer, Rolling Meadows, Ill., 1982—; asst. prof. Roosevelt U., 1971-73; instr. Harper Coll., Palatine, Ill., 1984. Author: AppleWorks: The Program For the Rest of Us, 1985. Bd. dirs. Youth Symphony Orch., Chgo., 1977-78; trustee Body Politic Theatre, Chgo., 1979-80. Home: 411 W Park Ave Wheaton IL 60187 Office: Apple Computer Inc 5655 Meadowbrook Ct Rolling Meadows IL 60008

SLOCUM, LEE ROBERT, lawyer; b. Cin., Feb. 26, 1952; s. Robert Ewing and Margaret Catherine (Langen) S.; m. Victoria Ann Vassolo, May 3, 1975; children—Randall F., Nicholas L. B.A., U. Cin., 1974; J.D., Chase Coll. Law, 1978. Bar: Ohio 1978, U.S. Dist. Ct. (so. dist.) Ohio 1978. Law clk. Hamilton County Ct. Common Pleas, Cin., 1975-79; sole practice, Cin., 1979—; asst. prosecutor Hamilton County Prosecutor's Office, Cin., 1979—. Mem. 26th Ward Republican Club, Cin., 1974-83, bd. dirs., 1983; mem. Green Twp. Rep. Club, Hamilton County, Ohio, 1984—, Hamilton County Rep. Club, Cin., 1984—. Mem. Cin. Bar Assn. Office: Hamilton County Prosecutor 1000 Main St Cincinnati OH 45202

SLOCUM, STEPHEN GLENNON, ophthalmologist; b. St. Louis, May 22, 1950; s. Glennon F. and Agnes (Ahrens) S.; m. Ailleen Cassegrain Livaudais, Dec. 3, 1977; children—Glennon, Sarah. M.D., St. Louis U., 1975. Diplomate Am. Bd. Ophthalmology. Practice medicine specializing in ophthalmology, St. Louis, 1979—. Fellow ACS, Am. Acad. Ophthalmology; mem. AMA. Roman Catholic. Avocation: Piano. Office: Stephen G Slocum MD 1034 S Brentwood Blvd Saint Louis MO 63117

SLOMOVITZ, CARMI MALACHI, newspaper consultant; b. Detroit, Aug. 22, 1933; s. Philip and Anna J. (Gandal) S.; m. Sharron Lorraine Max; 1 child, Randy David. Student Wayne State U., 1951-53. Mng. dir. Jewish News, Detroit, 1960-84, corp. v.p., 1980-84, corp. sec., co-pub., 1974-84, cons., 1984—. Pres. Jewish Nat. Fund Council Met. Detroit, 1978-80; bd. dirs. Jewish Assn. Retarded Citizens, Detroit chpt. Red Magen David for Israel; emeritus mem. nat. exec. com. Zionist Orgn. Am.; pres. Zionist Orgn. Detroit, 1965-67, Detroit Zionist Fedn., 1970-71; mem. Friends of Truman Library. Served with U.S. Army, 1953-56. Recipient Am. Red Magen David Humanitarian award, Helping Hand award, 19—. Mem. Am. Jewish Hist. Soc., Assn. for Welfare Soldiers in Israel, Detroit Inst. Arts Founders Soc., Hadassah Assocs., Jewish Hist. Soc. of Detroit, Detroit Technion Soc. (bd. dirs.), U.S. Golf Assn., Jewish War Vets., Southfield C. of C. Clubs: Boca West, Hundred, Knollwood Country, Nat. Press, Congregation Shaarey Zedek Men's, Tournament Players. Home: 5000 Town Ctr Apt 1705 Southfield MI 48075

SLONEKER, JOHN G., insurance company executive. Chmn., chief operating officer, dir. Ohio Casualty Corp. and Ohio Casualty Ins. Co., Hamilton, Ohio. Office: Ohio Casualty Corp 136 N 3d St Hamilton OH 45025*

SLOTKIN, DONALD, meat processing company executive; b. Long Branch, N.J., 1936; ed. Harvard U., 1958. Pres., chief exec. officer John Morrell & Co., Northfield, Ill. Office: John Morrell & Co 191 Waukegan Rd Northfield IL 60093*

SLOTKIN, HUGO, food products executive; b. Bklyn., June 12, 1912; s. Somuel and Fanny (Rivkin) S.; m. Babette Walsey, Sept., 1935; children—A. Donald, Mitchell, Curtis, Todd. Student L.I. U., 1931. Joined Hygrade Food Products Corp., 1931, dir. 1934, asst. sec., 1935, v.p., asst. sec., 1936-49, pres., 1949-68, chmn. bd., 1956-69; owner Hy Meadow Farms, Holly, Mich., 1956—; pres. K & K Provisions Inc., Lake Worth, Fla., 1972-77; dir. Nathans Famous, N.Y.C., 1969-78; sr. v.p., dir. United Brands Co., 1977—; chmn. bd. John Morrell & Co., Chgo., 1977—; pres., chmn., mem. exec. com., dir. Chgo. Bd. Trade; vice chmn., mem. exec. com., dir. Am. Meat, Inst. Bd. dirs. Sinai Hosp., Detroit, United Found., Project Hope. Mem. inedible animal fats adv. com. W.P.B., 1943. Mem. Eastern Meat Packers Assn. (past pres.), Clubs: Bankers of Am.; Lawyers (N.Y.C.); Franklin Hills Country (Franklin, Mich.); Standard (chgo. and Detroit); Harmonie (N.Y.C.); Banyan Golf (Palm Beach, Fla.). Home: John Morrell & Co 191 Waukegan Rd Northfield IL 60093*

SLOUP, JOHN EDWARD, cooperative manager; b. Enid, Okla., Dec. 20, 1923; s. Edward and Matilda (Troska) S.; m. Alice Irmagard Graf, Sept. 6, 1947; children—Ronald Evan, Donald Alan, Roderick Dean, Curtis Gene. B.S., Okla. State U., 1948. Agrl. extension agt. Phillips County, Kans., 1948-52, Marion County, Kans., 1952-60; field specialist Farmland Industries, McPherson, Kans., 1960-61; merchandiser for State of Kans., Farmland Industries, Kansas City, 1961-66, div. gen. mgr., Kansas City, Mo., 1966—; dir. Kan. Fertilizer and Chem. Inst., Inc. Served with U.S. Army, 1943-46. Recipient Agri-Bus. Service award Kans. Fertilizer and Chem. Inst., 1977; Exceptional Performance award Farmland Securities, 1979; Circle of Excellence awards Farmland Industries, 1977, 78. Mem. Coop Council, County Agt. Assn., C. of C., VFW, Am. Legion, Alpha Zeta. Republican. Lutheran. Home: 508 S Park St McPherson KS 67460 Office: 1070 County Rd McPherson KS 67460

SLOWIKOWSKI, NORBERT STANLEY, management consultant; b. Chgo., Aug. 7, 1938; s. Stanley and Bernice (Olejniczak) S.; m. Mary Kay Brennan, Oct. 14, 1961; children—Annemarie, Eileen, Edward, Timothy. B.S., Loyola U., Chgo., 1961, M.S., 1965. Supr. personnel research Chgo. Police Dept., 1961-65; nat. dir. manpower devel. McDonald's Corp., Oak Brook, Ill., 1965-75; pres. Slowikowski & Assocs., Darien, Ill., 1975—. Contbr. articles to profl. jours. Roman Catholic. Avocation: jogging. Office: Slowikowski & Assocs 7900 Cass Ave Darien IL 60559

SMALE, JOHN GRAY, See *Who's Who in America,* 43rd edition.

SMALL, ARTHUR A., JR., state senator, lawyer; b. Brunswick, Maine, Oct. 14, 1933; B.A., Bowdoin Coll.; M.A., J.D., U. Iowa. m. Mary Jo O'Callaghan, Nov. 26, 1960; children—Peter, Martha, Arthur. Former mem. Iowa Ho. of Reps.; now mem. Iowa State Senate; mem. firm Mears Zimmermann & Mears, Iowa City. Office: State Capitol Des Moines IA 50319 also Mears Zimmermann & Mears 209 E Washington St Iowa City IA 52240

SMALL, GILBERT STANLEY, oral surgeon; b. N.Y.C., May 27, 1929; s. Jack and Mildred S.; m. Rosalie Franklin; children—Curtis, Rebecca, Judy, Toby. B.A., Hobart Coll., 1950; D.D.S., Columbia U., 1954; postgrad. in oral surgery Washington U., 1956, Mt. Carmel Mercy Hosp., Detroit, 1957-59. Research assoc. U. Mich., Ann Arbor, 1964-68, clin. asst. prof., 1968-83, clin. assoc. prof., 1983—; mem. staff St. Joseph Mercy Hosp., Ann Arbor, 1964—, Saline Community Hosp., Mich., 1964—, Beyer Meml. Hosp., Ypsilanti, Mich., 1964—. Contbr. articles to profl. publs. Founding mem. Temple Beth Emeth, Ann Arbor, 1964—; bd. dirs. NCCJ, 1968-70. Served to comdr. USNR, 1954-70. Fellow Am. Coll. Dentists; mem. Washtenaw Dental Soc. (chmn. ethics com. 1970-73), Mich. Dental Assn., ADA (mem. adv. com. commn. on grad. edn. 1981—), Am. Assn. Oral and Maxillofacial Surgery (v.p. 1979-80, pres., 1981-82), Mich. State Soc. Oral and Maxillofacial Surgery (mem. com. profl. standards 1970-71, mem. anesthesia and emergency com. 1973-75, chmn. ethics com., 1982—), Chalmers J. Lyons Acad. Oral Surgery (pres. 1977-79), Am. Rose Soc. Club: Barton Hills Country (bd. dirs. 1978-80). Avocations: golf, jogging. Home: 2780 Provincial Dr Ann Arbor MI 48104 Office: 1303 Packard St Ann Arbor MI 48104

SMALL, LARRY ALAN, medical center official; b. Springfield, Ill., Nov. 23, 1946; s. Walter Alan and Kathleen Joyce (White) S.; m. Barbara Leona Murphy, Aug. 14, 1971; children—Patrick Alan, Erin Leona. Student Springfield (Ill.) Coll., 1965-67, George Williams Coll., Downers Grove, Ill., 1968-69; B.A. in Biol. Sci., So. Ill. U., Carbondale, 1971, M.S. in Edn., 1975. Cert. tchr., Ill. Media specialist Ill. Office Edn., Springfield, 1971-73; grad. asst. So. Ill. U., 1973-75; media specialist Lake-McHenry Regional Project, Gurnee, Ill., 1975-76; dir. media resources Meml. Med. Ctr., Springfield, 1976—; free lance media producer video, slides and photography; cons. equipment. Mem. adv. bd. communications program Capital Area Vocat. Ctr., Springfield. Recipient hon. mention award Kodak Internat. Snapshot Contest, 1973, Best of Show award in employee photography Meml. Med. Ctr., 1979, 1st place award, 1980. Mem. Internat. TV Assn. (sec. local chpt.), Health Scis. Communications Assn., Soc. Broadcast Engrs., Springfield Advt. Club, Meml. Med. Ctr. Mgmt. Club (pres.). Office: 800 N Rutledge St Springfield IL 62781

SMALL, RICHARD ALLAN, radiologist; b. Detroit, Jan. 31, 1941; s. Henry and Sadie (Nuchims) S.; m. Leanne Dorothy Trost, June 11, 1963; children—Brian Joel, Scott Andrew. B.A. in Psychology, U. Mich., 1963; M.D., Chgo. Med. Sch., 1968. Diplomate Am. Bd. Radiology. Intern, William Beaumont Hosp., Royal Oak, Mich., 1968-69, resident in diagnostic radiology, 1969-72; practice medicine specializing in diagnostic radiology Woodland Med. Group, P.C., Detroit, 1972—, dir. div. diagnostic ultrasound, 1982—. Served with USAR, 1960-66. Mem. AMA, Mich. State Med. Soc., Wayne County Med. Soc., Am. Coll. Radiology, Mich. Radiol. Soc., Am. Inst. Ultrasound in Medicine. Club: Wabeek Country (Bloomfield Hills, Mich.) Office: 22341 W Eight Mile Rd Detroit MI 48219 also 49135 W Twelve Mile Rd Novi MI 48050

SMALL, RICHARD DONALD, travel company executive; b. West Orange, N.J., May 24, 1929; s. Joseph George and Elizabeth (McGarry) S.; A.B. cum laude, U. Notre Dame, 1951; m. Arlene P. Small; children—Colleen P., Richard Donald, Joseph W., Mark G., Brian P. With Union-Camp Corp., N.Y.C., Chgo., 1952-62; pres. Alumni Holidays, Inc., 1962—, AHI Internat. Corp., Des Plaines, Ill., 1962—, All Horizons, Inc., 1982—; chmn. AHI, Inc., 1982—. Club: University (Chgo.). Home: 191 Sheridan Rd Winnetka IL 60093 also 2202 Wailea Elua Wailea Maui HI 96753 Office: 1st Nat Bank Bldg 701 Lee St Des Plaines IL 60016

SMALLWOOD, GLENN WALTER, JR., utility company marketing representative; b. Jeffersonville, Ill., Oct. 12, 1956; s. Glenn Walter and Darlene Ruth (Zeller) S.; B.S. in Bus. Adminstrn., SE Mo. State U., 1978. Customer service advisor Union Electric Co., Mexico, Mo., 1979—; instr. Mexico Vo-Tech Sch., 1981; panelist on home design Mo. Extension Service, 1984. Coordinator local United Way, 1984. Mem. Am. Mktg. Assn., Nat. Eagle Scout Assn., Copper Dome Soc., Boy Scouts Am. Alumni Family, Mexico area C. of C. Lodges: Optimist (cert. appreciation 1982, youth appreciation award 1974), Kiwanis (cert. appreciation 1984). Avocations: music; spectator sports; baseball; basketball; tennis. Office: Union Electric Co 321 W Promenade Mexico MO 65265

SMALS, GEORGE WILLIAM, company executive; b. Buena Vista, Va., Nov. 8, 1934; s. George R. and Ruby L. (Lynn) S.; m. Roberta M. Field, Oct. 6, 1957; children—Ellen, Michael, Laura. B.A., Wheaton Coll., 1956; M.B.A., U. Chgo., 1972. Mgr. quality control Reeves Bros., Inc., Buena Vista, Va., 1957-62, distbn. mgr. Skokie, Ill., 1962-68; mgr. blanket div. Samuel Bingham Co., Chgo., 1968-76; product mgr. Roberts & Porter, Des Plaines, Ill., 1976-82; product mgr. blankets Dayco Corp., Dayton, Ohio, 1982—. Served with U.S. Army, 1956-57. Mem. Chgo. Litho Club (assoc., award 1980). Republican. Home: 1020 S Hamlin St Park Ridge IL 60068 Office: Dayco Corp 1539 Jarvis St Elk Grove IL 60007

SMEDAL, DAVID OLAF, dentist; b. Madison, Wis., July 20, 1932; s. Agnar Tengel and Edith Marie (Oldenburg) S.; m. Janice Ruth Kirby, July 30, 1955; children—Susan, Eric, Kristi. Student U. Wis.-Madison, 1950-53; D.D.S., Northwestern U., 1957. Instr. Northwestern U. Dental Sch., Chgo., 1957-58; pvt. practice dentistry Stoughton, Wis.; chief dental staff Stoughton Community Hosp., 1970-71. Treas. Stoughton Bd. Edn., 1963-68; pres. Christ Luth. Endowment Found., 1968-75, 80-85. Mem. Dane County Dental Assn., ADA, Northwestern U. Dental Study Club Wis. (pres. 1970-71), Stoughton C. of C. Clubs: Stoughton Lions (pres. 1967-68), Stoughton Country (rep. 1983-85). Lodge: Sons of Norway. Home: 724 Pine St Stoughton WI 53589 Office: 218 S Forrest St Stoughton WI 53589

SMEDINGHOFF, THOMAS J., lawyer; b. Chgo., July 15, 1951; s. John A. and Dorothy S.; m. Mary Beth Smedinghoff. B.A. in Math., Knox Coll., 1973; J.D., U. Mich., 1978. Bar: Ill. 1978, U.S. Dist. Ct. (no. dist.) Ill. 1978. Assoc. McBride, Baker & Coles and predecessor McBride & Baker, Chgo., 1978-84, ptnr., 1985—. Author: Computer Software Legal Reference Manual, 1985. Mem. Chgo. Bar Assn. (chmn. computer law com. 1984-85), Ill. State Bar Assn., ABA, Computer Law Assn., Assn. Computing Machinery. Office: McBride Baker & Coles Three First Nat Plaza Suite 3800 Chicago IL 60602

SMEDLEY, ALFRED BROADBELT, public relations executive; b. Media, Pa., June 13, 1927; s. Alfred Broadbelt and Frances Baker (Jones) S.; m. Mary Eleanor Burns, June 9, 1951; children—Lynn Smedley Jennings, Laurie Smedley Slinger, Steven A., Thomas A., Kristina L. B.S., Temple U., Phila., 1952. Reporter/columnist Fairchild Publs., Upper Darby News, Phila., 1952-57; v.p. APCL&K Pub. Relations, Phila., 1957-61; v.p. Burson-Marsteller, N.Y.C., 1961-65, v.p., asst. gen. mgr., Chgo., 1971—; dir. corp. communications Scott Paper Co., Phila., 1965-71. Served with USN, 1944-47. Mem. Pub. Relations Soc. Am. (Silver Anvil award, 1971), Nat. Investor Relations Inst., Soc. Profl. Journalists. Club: Glen Oak Country (Glen Ellyn, Ill.), Chgo. Press, Chgo. Athletic, Pickwick (Niles, Mich.). Office: 1 E Wacker Dr Chicago IL 60601

SMILEY, BOB EUGENE, marketing educator; b. Bloomington, Ind.; s. James Robert Smiley and Dorothy Helen (Harding) Smiley Parrott; m. Effie B. Mowery, Aug. 17, 1956; children—Brent Eugene, Bryan Edward. A.A., Fullerton Community Coll., 1968; B.A., Calif State U.-Fullerton, 1970, M.B.A., 1971; Ph.D., Purdue U., 1978. Instr. mktg. Santa Ana Coll. Calif., 1971-72; grad. instr. Purdue U., West Lafayette, Ind., 1972-73; asst. prof. econs., Wabash Coll. Crawfordsville, Ind., 1973-79; prof. mktg. Ind. State U., Terre Haute, Ind., 1979—. Contbr. articles on experiential learning to profl. jours. County chmn. Myers for Congress, 1980, 82. Recipient Outstanding Instr. award Purdue U., 1973. Mem. IEEE, Am. Mktg. Assn., Wabash Valley Mktg. Assn. (chmn. orgn. com., pres. 1980-82, bd. dirs. 1982—), Assn. for Bus. Simulation and Experiental Learning (v.p., exec. dir. 1982-85), Midwest Mktg. Assn., Midwest Case Writers Assn., Ind. Assn. Social Scientists, Ind. Commn. for Humanities, Beta Gamma Sigma (sec. 1983—), Alpha Kappa Psi. Republican. Lodge: Kiwanis. Avocations: bowling, swimming, gardening, reading. Office: Ind State U Dept Mktg Terre Haute IN 47809

SMILEY-DURANT, SANDRA JACQUELINE, nurse; b. Milw., Apr. 1, 1954; d. Thomas and Edna Theresa (Balcerak) Smigelski; m. Lary A. Durant, Aug. 6, 1977 (annulled 1979); 1 dau., Jocelyn Anne. Student U. Wis.-Milw., 1972-75, Tex. Christian U., 1975-77; B.S.N., Marquette U., 1981. Staff nurse ICCU St. Lukes Hosp., Milw., 1981-82; staff nurse III, med. cardiology unit Mt. Sinai Med. Center, Milw., 1982-85; staff nurse cardiology unit St. Mary's Hosp., Milw., 1985—. Mem. Kosciuszko Park Fourth of July Commn., 1972—; pres. Kosciuszko Park Commn., 1982-83; active Presdl. Classroom for Young Ams., 1972—. Mem. Am. Nurses Assn., Assn. Critical Care Nurses, Assn. Marquette U. Women, Kappa Delta. Democrat. Roman Catholic. Home: 2415 S 10th St Milwaukee WI 53215

SMITH, ALAN DUANE, industrial arts educator; b. South Bend, Ind., Aug. 30, 1949; s. Duane Eugene and Nancy Elizabeth (McLaren) S.; m. Michele Ann Kolb, Aug. 4, 1979; 1 child, Erica Michele. B.S. cum laude, Western Mich. U., 1971; M.A., Central Mich. U., 1977. Tchr. Peace Corps, Ethiopia, 1971-73; tchr. Frankenmuth Sch. Dist., Mich., 1974—; chairperson com. on excellence in edn., 1983—. Author: (with others) Teaching Industrial Arts, 1973. Chairperson sign com. Bavarian Festival Frankenmuth, Mich., 1977-78. Named Region II Mich. Indsl. Arts Tchr. of Yr., 1985. Mem. Mich. Indsl. Edn. Soc., Indsl. Edn. Assn. (sec. 1968-69, pres. 1969-70), Epsilon Pi Tau (treas. 1970-71), Omicron Delta Kappa. Home: 6840 Junction Bridgeport MI 48722 Office: E F Rittmueller Middle Sch 965 E Genesee Frankenmuth MI 48734

SMITH, ALICE ELIZABETH, hospital services executive, clinical educator; b. Coral Gables, Fla., Sept. 24, 1948; d. Thomas and Alva Elizabeth (Zebendon) S.; m. Philip Edward Smith, June 26, 1971, 1 child, Eve Elizabeth. Cert. elementaire Le Cordon Bleu, Paris, 1969; B.A. in Home Econs., The Western Coll., 1970; postgrad. U. Dayton, 1972-73; dietetic intern Miami Valley Hosp., Dayton, Ohio, 1973-74; M.S. in Nutrition, No. Ill. U., 1978. Tchr. Miami Dade Jr. High, Opa Locka, Fla., 1970-71; food service coordinator Mercy Med. Ctr., Springfield, Ohio 1972-73; pub. health nutritionist Chgo. Bd. Health, 1974-78; assoc. dir. clin. dietetics Children's Meml. Hosp., Chgo., 1980-84, asst. clin. prof. U. Ill., Chgo., 1983—; dir. clin. dietetics Children's Meml. Hosp., Chgo., 1985—; liaison rep. Am. Acad. Pediatrics Com. on Nutrition, Am. Dietetic Assn., Chgo., 1981—. Contbr. articles to profl. jours.

Vol. 8th Day Ctr. for Justice, Chgo., 1976-77. Grantee Mead Johnson Nutritional Co., 1983—. Mem. Am. Dietetic Assn., Clin. Nutrition Mgmt. Practice Group (newsletter editor, 1983-84), Chgo. Dietetic Assn. Am. Soc. Parenteral and Enteral Nutrition, Dietitians in Pediatric Practice. Avocations: Creative cookery, indoor gardening. Office: Children's Meml Hosp 2300 Children's Plaza Chicago IL 60614

SMITH, ARTHUR E., counseling educator, vocational psychologist; b. St. Louis, Feb. 28, 1926; s. Lee L. and Dorothea M. (Debrecht) S.; m. Jane C. Dooley; children—Greg, Laura, Terry, Chris. B.S., St. Louis U., 1949, M.Ed., 1951, Ph.D., 1962. Diplomate Am. Bd. Vocational Experts; lic. psycholgist. Tchr., counselor St. Louis Pub. Schs., 1949-60; Evening Coll. dir. and assoc. prof., St. Louis U., 1960-66; grad. dean St. Mary's Coll., Notre Dame, Ind., 1966-68; chmn. behavioral studies U. Mo., St. Louis, 1968—; pres. Clayton Bus. Sch., St. Louis, 1983—; dir. Affiliates in Psychology and Counseling, St. Louis, 1970-78. Contbr. articles to profl. jours. Served with USNR, 1944-46, PTO. Recipient Recognition award Am. Soc. Tng. Dirs. and Am. Personnel and Guidance Assn. Mem. Am. Assn. Counseling and Devel. (pres. St. Louis 1965), Nat. Voc. Guidance Assn., Assn. Counselor Educs. and Supvs., Am. Coll. Voc. Experts, Nat. Rehab. Assn. (pres. St. Louis 1979-80, Recognition award 1980). Office: Univ Mo 8001 Natural Bridge St Louis MO 63121

SMITH, BARNELL GEORGE, ednl. adminstr.; b. Chgo., Dec. 15, 1944; s. LeMoyne and Lazora (Shelton) S.; B.S., Loyola U. Chgo., 1967, M.S., 1969, Ed.D., 1977; children—Christina, Barnell George. Exec. dir. Marillac Settlement House, Chgo., 1963-65; tchr Holy Angels Sch., Chgo., 1965-66, asst. prin., 1966-67; founder, chief adminstr. Acad. of St. James Coll. Prep., Chgo., 1966—, instr. psychology, sociology, interpersonal relations, 1967—. Active Boy Scouts Am.; advisor Key Club, 1967-78; active Operation Push, U. Ill. Minority Affairs. Recipient Soc. Disting. Am. Students Nat. Approval award, 1980, 81; Malcom X Coll. Citation of Merit, 1973; Award of Merit, E. Garfield Park Citizen Com., 1969; Humanitarian award African Meth. Episcopal Ch., 1977; Community Service award City of Chgo., 1976. Mem. NAACP, Nat. Assn. Sec. Sch. Prins., Nat. Cath. Edn. Assn., Chgo. Council Exceptional Children, Phi Delta Kappa. Clubs: Wellington Phi Esses Frat., Kiwanis (internat. adv. com. S.E. Area). Address: 7550 S Phillips St Chicago IL 60649

SMITH, BETTY MURNAN, educator; b. Indpls., Sept. 11, 1921; d. Carl J. and Helene Alice (Stephens) Murnan; B.A. (cum laude) in English, Butler U., 1944; M.A. in English, State U. Iowa, 1950; m. Richard Norman Smith, Oct. 21, 1951; children—Allegra Louise Smith Jrolf, Timothy Dwight and Michael Murnan (twins). Tchr. Kingsford (Mich.) High Sch., 1944-46, Bosse High Sch. Evansville, Ind., 1946-48; instr. English, Ely (Minn.) Jr. Coll., 1950-51; acting instr. English, U. Wis. at Milw., 1961-66; instr. English, U. Wis. Center-Waukesha County, 1966-70, asst. prof., 1970-81, asso. prof., 1981—, mem. faculty senate, 1981—; lectr. in field. Co-prin. Hdqrs. Freedom Mil. Sch. Boycott, 1963; bd. dirs. Waukesha Symphony Orch., 1969-72; sec. Waukesha Equal Opportunity Commn., 1970-73; bd. dirs. Waukesha Civic Theatre, 1973-74. Recipient Community Service award U. Wis., Waukesha, 1979. Mem. AAUP (pres. chpt. 1969-70), Modern Lang. Assn., Midwest Modern Lang. Assn., Nat., Wis. councils tchrs. English, Am. Fedn. Tchrs. (treas. Milw. chpt. 1962-66), Assn. Univ. Wis. faculties, Kappa Delta Pi, Sigma Tau Delta. Presbyterian (ruling elder). Contbr. poetry to mags. Home: 1128 Oxford Rd Waukesha WI 53186 Office: Univ Wis Waukesha County 1500 University Dr Waukesha WI 53186

SMITH, CARL BERNARD, educator, writer; b. Dayton, Ohio, Feb. 29, 1932; s. Carl R. and Elizabeth Ann (Lefeld) S.; m. Virginia Lee Cope, Aug. 30, 1958; children—Madonna, Anthony, Regina, Marla. B.A., U. Dayton, 1954; M.A., Miami U., Oxford, Ohio, 1961; Ph.D., Case Western Res. U., 1967. Tchr., Cathedral Latin High Sch., Cleve., 1954-57; customer corr. E.F. MacDonald Co., Dayton, 1958-59; tchr. Kettering (Ohio) High Sch., 1959-61; editor Reardon Baer Pub. Co., Cleve., 1961-62; tchr./researcher Case Western Res. U., Cleve., 1962-65, Cleve. Pub. Schs., 1966-67; asst. prof. edn. Ind. U., Bloomington, 1967-69, assoc. prof., 1970-72, prof., 1973—. Pres. Bd. Edn., St. Charles Sch., Bloomington, 1976-80. Recipient Sch. Bell award NEA, 1967. Mem. Internat. Reading Assn., Nat. Council Tchrs. of English, Assn. Supervision and Curriculum Devel., Am. Ednl. Research Assn., Phi Delta Kappa. Republican. Roman Catholic. Author: Reading Instruction through Diagnostic Teaching, (Pi Lambda Theta Best Book in Edn. award, 1972; Getting People To Read, 1978; sr. author: Series r, 1983; Teaching Reading and Writing Together, 1984. Home: 401 S Serena Ln Bloomington IN 47401 Office: Sch Edn Ind U Bloomington IN 47405

SMITH, CARL EDWIN, electronics company executive; b. Eldon, Iowa, Nov. 18, 1906; s. Seldon L. and Myra (Hutton) S.; B.S. in E.E., Iowa State U., Ames, 1930; M.S. in E.E., Ohio State U., 1932, E.E., 1936; m. Hannah B. McGuire, Sept. 3, 1932; children—Larc A., Darvin W., Barbadeen Jo, Margene Sue, Ada Kay, Ramona Lee. Draftsman, Iowa Electric Co., Fairfield, summer 1929; student engr. RCA Victor Co., Camden, N.J., 1930-31; engr. Radio Air Service Corp., Cleve., 1932; radio operator WGAR, Cleve., 1933; engr. United Broadcasting Corp., Cleve., 1933-36, asst. chief engr., 1936-41, chief engr., 1941-45, v.p., 1946-53; owner, mgr. Carl E. Smith Consulting Radio Engrs., Cleve., 1953-80; pres. Smith Electronics, Cleve., 1956—; founder Cleve. Inst. Electronics Inc., 1934, chmn. ednl. com., 1970—. Recipient Dist. Achievement citation Iowa State U., 1980. Served with Office of Chief Signal Officer, U.S. Army, World War II. Recipient Dist. Alumnus award Ohio State U., 1974. Registered profl. engr., Ohio. Fellow IEEE (life), Radio Club Am.; mem. Cleve. Engring. Soc., Brecksville C. of C. Republican. Presbyterian. Ch. Am. Author 49 books including: Directional Antenna Patterns, Theory and Design of Directional Antennas, Applied Mathematics, Communications Circuit Fundamentals; Contbr. articles to tech. jours. Patentee electromech. calculators; elliptical polarization electromagnetic energy radiation systems; slotted cylindrical antenna; three-slot cylindrical antenna; spiral slot antenna; low loss antenna system. Home: 8704 Snowville Rd Cleveland OH 44141 Office: 8200 Snowville Rd Cleveland OH 44141

SMITH, CARL G., food manufacturing company executive; b. Hesperia, Mich., Jan. 2, 1921; s. Frank W. and Lydia S.; m. Viola Converse Smith, July 3, 1942; children—Carlin, Gail, Kevin, Kimberly. B.S., Mich. State U., 1942. Vice pres. Gerber Products Co., Fremont, Mich., 1964-76, exec. v.p., 1976-78, pres., 1978-82, pres., chief exec. officer, 1982-83, chmn. bd., chief exec. officer, 1983—; dir. Old Kent Bank of Fremont, 1978—. Served to capt., U.S. Army, 1942-46. Recipient Disting. Alumni award Mich. State U., 1964; named Mich. Industrialist of the Year, Impression 5, 1983. Mem. Nat. Food Processors Assn. (chmn.), Mich. C. of C. (dir.), U.S. C. of C., Grocery Mfrs. Am. Republican. Club: Rotary. Lodge: Masons. Office: Gerber Products Co 445 State St Fremont MI 49412

SMITH, CARLYLE SHREEVE, anthropologist; b. Great Neck, N.Y., Mar. 8, 1915; s. Harold William and Lulu (Allen) S.; B.A., Columbia U., 1938, Ph.D., 1949; Litt.D. (hon.), U. S.D., 1979; m. Judith Eva Pogany, May 2, 1942; children—Evan Shreeve, Pamela Anne. Unit supr. archaeol. survey W.P.A. of Nebr. and La., 1939, 40-41; asst. Hudson Valley Archeol. Survey, Vassar Coll., 1940; curator div. anthropology Mus. Natural History, U. Kans., Lawrence, 1947-68, prof. anthropology, 1947-80, prof. and curator emeritus, 1981—; archaeologist Norwegian Archaeol. Expdn. to Easter Island and East Pacific, 1955-56; participant internat. anthrop. congresses, 1949-64; Rica, cons. Lindblad Travel, Inc., 1967-80. Mem. Kans. Hist. Sites Bd. of Rev., Topeka, 1970-83; lectr. Norwegian Am. Line, Prudential Cruises, Royal Viking Line, 1983—. mem. div. behavioral scis. NRC, 1961-64. Served with USAF, 1943-46. NSF grantee, 1960-67; Nat. Park Service grantee, 1950-76; Am. Philos. Soc. grantee, 1960, 64. Fellow Am. Anthrop. Assn., Co. Mil. Historians; mem. Soc. for Am. Archaeology (1st. v.p. 1954-55), Soc. for Hist. Archaeology, Am. Ethnol. Soc., Explorers Club, Sigma Xi. Editor: U. Kans. Publs. in Anthropology, 1969-73; adv. editor N.Am. Archaeologist, 1979—; contbr. articles and revs. to scholarly jours.; author: Archaeology of Coastal New York; Carlyle S. Smith Archaeol. Labs. named in his honor at Nassau County Mus. Natural History, Glen Cove, N.Y., 1967. Home: 2719 Harvard Rd Lawrence KS 66044

SMITH, CAROLE PROCHASKA, clinical psychologist, consultant; b. Cleve., Mar. 21, 1940; d. Charles J. and Harriet (Behm) Prochaska; m. Walter E. Smith, Dec. 27, 1961; children—Gregory, Patrick, Thomas. B.A. summa cum laude, Notre Dame Coll.-Ohio, 1961; M.A. John Carroll U., Cleve., 1965; Ph.D., Kent State U., Ohio, 1980. Lic. psychologist, Ohio. Tchr. social studies South Euclid-Lyndhurst Ohio Sch. Dist., 1961-62; lectr. history Notre Dame Coll.-Ohio, South Euclid, 1965-66; registrar Old Colony Montessori Sch., Hingham, Mass., 1970-73; practice clin. psychologist, Stow, Ohio, 1980—. Mem. Hudson (Ohio) bd. edn., 1980—, v.p., 1982—. Mem. Am. Psychol. Assn., Ohio Psychol. Soc., Cleve. Psychol. Assn., Am. Soc. Clin. Hypnosis. Democrat. Roman Catholic. Office: 3435 Kent Rd Stow OH 44224

SMITH, CHERYL B., university clinic and office administrator; b. Chgo., May 12, 1947; d. James Henry and Mildred Myrna (Johnson) Briscoe; m. Wendell James Smith, Sept. 21, 1968 (div.); 1 dau., Rachel Louise; m. 2d Alfred James Scrutchings, Dec. 31, 1983. B.S., Wilson Jr. Coll., 1967. With Ill. Bell Telephone Co., 1965, Marshall Field & Co., Chgo., 1965-66, Standard Oil Co., Chgo., 1966-69, CNA Ins. Co., Chgo., 1971-73; co-producer talk show WBBM-TV, Chgo., 1973-74; asst. media planner Post-Keyes-Gardner, Chgo., 1974-78; office adminstr. Katz TV/Radio Rep., Chgo., 1978-79; clinic coordinator/office mgr. U. Chgo., 1979—. Mem. St. Thomas Alumni, Home and Sch. Assn. Democrat. Roman Catholic. Club: Hyde Park Neighborhood. Office: 5841 S Maryland Chicago IL 60637

SMITH, CHRISTINE, early childhood educator, counselor; b. St. Louis, July 26, 1948; d. James Bryant and Mamie Lee (Stewart) Bryant; m. John Jefferson, Oct. 5, 1968; children—Michelle Lynn, Andrea Denise, Jevon Jefferson. B.S. in Edn., So., Ill. U., 1976, M.S., 1980. Cert. tchr., Ill. Mem. staff Southwestern Bell Telephone Co., St. Louis, 1966-68; with Union Electric, St. Louis, 1968-71; acct. Monsanto Chem. Co., Sauget, Ill., 1971-73; tchr. early childhood edn., counselor social service East St. Louis Bd. Edn., Ill., 1976—; mem. steering com. early childhood edn. So. Ill. U., 1976—. Vol. Hospice for Cancer Patients, East St. Louis, 1984—; mem. Mo. State Choir, St. Louis, 1981—, sec., 1981—. Mem. Zeta Phi Beta. Democrat. Home: 1135 S 9th St Saint Louis MO 63104

SMITH, CLYDE SHARPE, educator; b. Paris, Ky., Mar. 24, 1938; s. William Warren and Anna Lee (Leggett) S.; m. Ann Lewis, Aug. 17, 1963; children—William Thomas, Elizabeth Ann. B.S., Eastern Ky. U., 1960; M.A., Ohio State U., 1965. Sci. tchr. Bethel-Tate High Sch., Ohio, 1960-64, Jefferson Jr. High Sch., Champaign, Ill., 1965-72, Central High Sch., Champaign, 1972—; faculty Inst. Environ. Exploration, Urbana, Ill., summer 1982. Lay/elder University Place Christian Ch., Champaign, 1970—; bd. dirs. Ill. Disciples Found., Champaign, 1968—; mem. adminstrn. dept. Christian Ch. Ill.-Wis., 1985. Named Lay Person of Yr., Champaign-Urbana Jaycees, 1980. Mem. Champaign Fedn. Tchrs., Ill. Fedn. Tchrs., NEA, Ill. Assn. Chemistry Tchrs. Democrat. Club: Key. Lodge: Kiwanis (bd. dirs.). Avocations: home computers; photography. Home: 24 Lake Park Dr Champaign IL 61821 Office: Central High Sch 610 W University Champaign IL 61820

SMITH, CYNTHIA ANNE, information specialist; b. Akron, Ohio, Nov. 28, 1944; d. Thomas and Lois Eileen (Lowry) Ignizio; m. Michael Wallace Smith, Aug. 26, 1967; children—Andrea Lynne, Jessica Clare. B.S., Kent State U., 1966; postgrad. Akron U., 1967-68. Asst. research librarian Goodyear Tire & Rubber Co., Akron, 1966-70, asst. to dir. research, 1971-77, staff research lit. chemist, 1978-82, staff info. specialist, 1983—. Office: Goodyear Tire & Rubber Co 1144 E Market St Dept 450D Akron OH 44316

SMITH, DALE MICHAEL, podiatrist; b. Chgo., Sept. 16, 1943; s. Harley Francis and Marion (Kucaba) S.; m. Barbara Ann Thomas, Oct. 25, 1975. A.A., Morton Coll., 1965; D. Podiatric Medicine, Ill. Coll. Podiatric medicine, 1970. Diplomate Am. Bd. Podiatric Surgery. Pvt. practice in podiatry, Chgo., 1970—. Mem. Ill Hosp. Licensing Bd., Springfield, 1982—. Fellow Am. Coll. Foot Surgeons; mem Ill. Podiatry Soc. (bd. dirs. 1976—, pres. 1982-83), Midwest Podiatry Conf. (pres. 1984—). Avocation: Building and restoring automobiles. Office: 4901 W 25th St Cicero IL 60650

SMITH, DANIEL JOSEPH, vocational educator, school administrator; b. Mpls., Mar. 14, 1949; s. Benjamin Harrison and Anna Jeanette (Dahlstrom) S.; m. Katherine Louise Alexander, June 26, 1971. B.S. with distinction, U. Minn., 1971. Tchr. graphic arts St. Louis Park Sr. High Sch. (Minn.), 1971-73; mgr. printing div. Royal Australian Coll. Gen. Practitioners, East Melbourne, 1973-76; instr. vocat. graphic arts and drafting Falls Sr. High Sch., International Falls, Minn., 1976-77; instr. Carver-Scott Co-op Ctr., Chaska, Minn., 1977—, dir. vocat. programs, 1982—. Mem. Am. Vocat. Assn., In-Plant Printing Mgmt. Assn., Minn. Vocat. Assn., Minn. Assn. Secondary Vocat. Adminstrs., Internat. Graphic Arts Edn. Assn., Vocat. Indsl. Clubs Am. (exec. bd. Minn. chpt. 1979-83), Eden Prairie Jaycees (treas. 1984-85). Office: 401 E 4th St Chaska MN 55318

SMITH, DARWIN EATNA, paper manufacturing company executive; b. Garrett, Ind., Apr. 16, 1926; s. K. Bryant and Hazel (Sherman) S.; B.S. in Bus. with distinction, Ind. U., 1950; LL.B. cum laude, Harvard, 1955; m. Lois Claire Archbold, Aug. 19, 1950; children—Steven, Pamela, Valerie, Blair. Admitted Ill. bar, 1955, Wis. bar, 1958; asso. firm Sidley, Austin, Burgess & Smith, Chgo., 1955-58; with Kimberly-Clark Corp., Neenah, Wis., 1958—, gen. atty., 1960-62, v.p., 1962-67, v.p. fin. and law, 1967-70, pres., 1970—, chmn., chief exec. officer, 1971—. Served with AUS, 1944-46. Mem. Am., Wis. bar assns., Am. Legion. Presbyn. Mason (32). Office: Kimberly-Clark Corp Neenah WI 54957

SMITH, DAVID ANTHONY, motor manufacturing company executive; b. Spring Grove, Ill., Nov. 4, 1941; s. Elmer P. and Isabelle M. (Meyer) S.; m. Beverly J. Hildinger, July 6, 1963; children—Sheryl, Kimberly, Michael. B.S. in Elec. Engring., Milw. Sch. Engring., 1964. Quality and inspection supr. to design engr. Heppner Mfg., Round Lake, Ill., 1959-68; design engr. Boding Electronic, Chgo., 1968-69; design engr., gen. product mgr. RAE Corp., McHenry, Ill., 1969—. Pres. bd. edn. Richmond Burton Community High Sch., 1981—. Mem. Small Motor Mfrs. Assn., Northwest Internat. Trade Club. Roman Catholic. Lodge: Moose. Home: 3909 Overton Dr Richmond IL 60071 Office: RAE Corp 5801 W Elm St McHenry IL 60050

SMITH, DAVID WESLEY, orthopedic surgeon; b. Piqua, Ohio, Sept. 21, 1937; s. Richard and Harriet Smith; student Ohio Wesleyan U., 1958; D.O., Kirksville Coll. Osteo. Medicine, 1962; m. Tanzy J. Smith, May 21, 1962; children—Douglas M., Dyanna. Intern, Doctors Hosp., Columbus, Ohio, 1962-63, resident in orthopedic and traumatic surgery, 1963-66; practice medicine specializing in orthopedic surgery, Columbus, 1966-67, Massillon, Ohio, 1967—; pres. Tri County Orthopedic Surgeons, Inc.; mem. staff, chmn. dept. surgery Doctors Hosp.; clin. asso. prof. orthopedics Ohio U.; adj. clin. instr. orthopedic surgery Kansas City Coll. Osteo Medicine. Diplomate Am. Osteo. Bd. Surgery. Fellow Am. Coll. Osteo. Surgeons, Am. Osteo. Acad. Orthopedics (past pres.); mem. Eighth Dist. Acad. Osteo. Medicine. Office: 3244 Bailey St NW Massillon OH 44646

SMITH, DAVID WILLIAM, research engineer; b. Lebanon, Ind., Aug. 6, 1945; s. Milburn Francis and Mildred Lois (Bowman) S.; m. Sharon Ann Pritchett, Aug. 28, 1971; children—Beth Ann, Kara Lynn. B.S., Purdue U., 1967, M.S., 1969; Ph.D., U. Ill., 1974. Registered profl. engr., Ill. Research engr. Deere & Co. Tech. Ctr., Moline, Ill., 1973—. Served with U.S. Army, 1969-71. Mem. Am. Soc. Agrl. Engrs. (Young Researcher award 1982), Soc. Automotive Engrs., Sigma Xi, Tau Beta Pi. Republican. Methodist. Co-author: Tractors and Their Power Units. Home: 120 39th Ave East Moline IL 61244 Office: Deere & Co Tech Ctr 3300 River Dr Moline IL 61265

SMITH, DELANEY GERARD, JR., computerized automation company executive; b. Versailles, Ky., Aug. 10, 1954; s. Delaney Gerard and Lottie America (Burns) S. B.E.E., Cleve. State U., 1977; postgrad. Case Western Res. U., 1985—. Report writer Polytech Inc., Cleve., 1972; systems engring. trainee Motorola, Inc., Parma, Ohio, 1973-76; product engr. Gould Instrument Co., Cleve., 1977-79; sr. application engr. Allen-Bradley Co., Highland Heights, Ohio, 1979-82, sr. product engr., 1982—. Inventor (algorithm) PLC-3 PID Controller, 1982. Guitarist (record album) Nat. Conv. Gospel Choirs and Choruses, Orlando, Fla., 1982, Chgo., 1983. Dep. registrar Cuyahoga County Bd. Elections, Ohio, 1984. Mem. Instrument Soc. Am., Nat. Tech. Assn. (chmn. 1976-77), Greater Cleve. Choral Chpt. (young adult treas. 1982-83). Baptist. Avocations: bicycling, martial arts, guitar playing, songwriting, wood working. Home: 4361 Clarkwood Pkwy Warrensville OH 44128 Office: Allen-Bradley Co 747 Alpha Dr Highland Heights OH 44143

SMITH, DONALD ARCHIE, business executive, consultant; b. Dayton, Ohio, Feb. 23, 1934; s. Archie Ford and Catherine Rosella (Rabold) S.; m. Joan Sandra Speedie, May 18, 1955; children—Douglas Alan, Keith Cameron, Deirdre Lynn, Neal Ramsey. B.A. in Sci. and Math., Harvard U., 1956; cert. Indsl. Coll. of Armed Forces, 1971. Nuclear research and project engr. N.Am. Aviation Co., 1956-62; fin. software specialist Nat. Cash Register, 1962-63; mgr. systems engring. N.Am. Aviation, 1963-67; mgr. bus. planning, mktg. services and pub. relations N.Am. Rockwell, Columbus, Ohio, 1967-72, mgr. internat. sales and mktg., 1968-73; mgr. stratetic planning Rockwell Internat. Corp., Columbus, 1973-76, program mgr. Condor weapons system, 1976-77, dir. guided bomb programs, 1977-78, dir. bus. devel. and legis. liaison, 1978-80; v.p. fin. applied tech. group Arvin Industries, Columbus, Ind., 1980-84; v.p. fin. Calspan Corp., Columbus, 1980-82, v.p. fin. and adminstrn., 1982-84, chief fin. officer, treas., dir., 1983-84; bus. dir. Franklin United Meth. Home, 1984—; dir. Calspan Field Services Inc., Arvin Automation, Inc., Echo Sci., Inc.; ops. research cons., 1962-64; instr. math. Sinclair Coll., Dayton, Ohio, 1961-63; mem. U.S.-U.K. Bipartite Com. on Nuclear Weapons, 1958-61; industry chmn. Mil. Specifications and Standards Rev. Com., 1972-79. Pres., trustee Columbus Arts Guild, 1980-83; treas., dir. Franklin United Methodist Home, 1982—; auditor First United Meth. Ch., 1981-84; past pres., treas., trustee Players Theatre of Columbus, 1975-80; v.p. Ohio Assn. of U.S. Army, 1979-80; dist. commr. Boy Scouts Am., 1970-73, cubmaster, 1965-70; squadron comdr. CAP, 1976; chmn. Commn. on Racism in Columbus Pub. Schs., 1972. Recipient Nat. award Jr. Achievement, Inc., 1954; Letters of Commendation govt. agys., Am. Def. Preparedness Assn., Boy Scouts Am., 1958-78; Leadership award Nat. Mgmt. Assn., 1979. Mem. AIAA (nat. chmn. soc. and aerospace tech. com. 1980-83, nat. pub. policy com.), Royal Inst. Nav., Nat. Mgmt. Assn. (v.p., trustee), Nat. Rifle Assn. (life mem.), SAR, Palatines to Am. Clubs: Harrison Lake Country, Aviation Unltd. (Columbus), Harvard of Ind.; Army and Navy. Lodges: Masons, Shriners. Contbr. articles to profl. jours. Home: 301 Sunset Dr Columbus IN 47201 Office: 1070 W Jefferson St Franklin IN 46131

SMITH, DONALD CAMERON, physician, educator; b. Peterborough, Ont., Can., Feb. 2, 1922; s. James Cameron and Clarice (Leighton) S.; came to U.S., 1952, naturalized, 1960; M.D., Queen's U., Kingston, Ont., 1945; M.Sc., U. Toronto (Ont.), 1948; m. Jean Ida Morningstar, Sept. 11, 1946; children—Douglas Frazer, Scot Earle, Donald Ian. Intern, Victoria Hosp., London, Ont., 1944-45; fellow in physiology U. Toronto, 1947-48; asst. med. dir. East York-Leaside (Ont.) Health Dept., 1949-50; exec. dir. Kent County (Ont.) Health Dept., 1950-52; Commonwealth Fund fellow in pediatrics U. Mich., 1952-55, asst. prof. maternal and child health, research asso. in pediatrics, 1955-57, asso. prof. maternal and child health, asso. prof. pediatrics, 1957-61, prof. maternal and child health, prof. pediatrics, 1961—, dir. Child Health Center, 1955-62, 64-72, chmn. dept. health devel., 1964-72; chmn. health policy bd. Mich. Dept. Corrections, 1975—; prin. adviser on health and med. affairs Gov. Mich., 1972-78; dir. Mich. Dept. Mental Health, Lansing, 1974-78; prof. psychiatry and behavioral scis. Northwestern U., Chgo., 1979—; sr. med. advisor Sisters of Mercy Health Corp., 1978—; mem. Pub. Health Adv. Council, 1982—, v.p. for accreditation Joint Commn. on Accreditation of Hosps., 1979-81; mem. Profl. Rev. Orgn. of Mich., 1983—. Served to lt. Royal Canadian Navy, 1945-47. Diplomate Am. Bd. Pediatrics, Am. Bd. Preventive Medicine. Fellow Royal Coll. Physicians (Can.) Am. Acad. Pediatrics (chmn. com. legislation 1966-72), Am. Pub. Health Assn. (chmn. sect. maternal and child health 1968-70); mem. AMA, Mich. State Med. Soc., Midwest Soc. Pediatric Research, Delta Omega (nat. pres. 1966-68). Contbr. articles to profl. publs. Office: 28550 Eleven Mile Rd Farmington Hills MI 48018

SMITH, ERIC CRAIG, construction executive; b. Washington, Nov. 27, 1945; s. Craig Champney and Mary Elizabeth (Leinen) S.; B.A., Brown U., 1967; M.B.A., Wharton Sch., U. Pa., 1971; m. Nancy Mercer Bishop, Feb. 10, 1973; children—Jordan Leinen, Ian Eric, Edward Craig. Acct., Arthur Young & Co., C.P.A.s, N.Y.C., 1971-74; partner, cons. Fails & Assos., Ltd., Raleigh, N.C., 1974-79; v.p., dir. Fishel Co., Columbus, Ohio, 1979—; dir. V.O.G., Inc., Tractor Parts & Equipment Co.; instr. Fails Mgmt. Inst., Raleigh. Served with USN, 1967-70; Vietnam. C.P.A., N.Y. State. Mem. Am. Inst. C.P.A.s, N.Y. State Soc. C.P.A.s, Builders Exchange Columbus. Republican. Clubs: Swim and Racquet (Columbus); Brown. Editor, contbr. Contractor's Digest, 1974-79. Home: 2636 Berwyn Rd Columbus OH 43221 Office: 1170 Kinnear Rd Columbus OH 43212

SMITH, EUGENE VALENTINE, chemical engineer; b. Ossian, Ind., Jan. 7, 1924; s. Keith R. and Clona M. (Valentine) S.; B.S. in Mech. Engring., Purdue U., 1948; s. Maxine Louise Byerly, May 19, 1945; children—Penelope Ann, Rebecca Jo Smith Schinderle. Mech. engr., plant engr. Stanolind Oil and Gas Co., Midwest, Wyo., 1948-54; sr. project engr. Amoco Chems. Corp., Brownsville, Tex., 1954-57, asst. chief plant engr., Texas City, Tex., 1957-61, ops. supr., 1961-65, supt. ops., Joliet, Ill., 1965-71, tech. dir., 1972—. Trustee Jesse Walker United Meth. Ch., 1968—, pres. trustees, 1972-74, v.p. bd., 1978—; mem. Will-Grundy Mfg. Environ. Control Commn., 1965—; dir. Homeowners Assn., 1971-74. Served with USAAF, 1943-45. Mem. ASME (past pres. Texas City chpt.), Am. Inst. Chem. Engrs. (dir. Joliet sect. 1976—), Assn. Energy Engrs., Three Rivers Mfg. Assn., Joliet C. of C., Pi Tau Sigma, Tau Beta Pi. Republican. Home: 2504 Chevy Chase Dr Joliet IL 60435 Office: PO Box 941 Joliet IL 60434

SMITH, EVANGELINE CHRISMAN DAVEY (MRS. ALEXANDER MUNRO SMITH), civic worker; b. Kent, Ohio, May 30, 1911; d. Martin Luther and Berenice Murl (Chrisman) Davey; A.B. (Scholar), Wellesley Coll., 1933; postgrad. Akron U., 1933-34; m. Alexander Munro Smith, Oct. 5, 1935; children—Berenice Jessie Smith Hardy, Diantha Barret Smith Harris, Letitia Amy Smith Manley. Sec., Davey Tree Expert Co., Kent, 1934, dir., 1962-73, mem. dirs. adv. com., 1973-76; dir. Davey Investment Co., Kent, 1982-84; trustee Davey Investment Trust, 1984—. Trustee, Kent Free Library, 1957-77, pres., 1961-63; trustee Patton House, 1966-68, 79-81, historian, 1981—; mem. women's assn. Robinson Meml. Hosp., 1947—, mem. women's assn. governing bd., 1947-68; co-founder Kent council Girl Scouts U.S.A., sec., 1941-45; mem. Kent State U. Pres's. Club, 1976—, Kent State U. Chestnut Soc., 1977—. Mem. Am. Legion Aux., D.A.R. (chpt. regent, 1966-68, registrar, 1973—), Daus. Am. Colonists (regent, 1978-80, registrar 1980—), Colonial Dames XVII Century (librarian), Kappa Kappa Gamma, Phi Sigma Soc. Congregationalist. Clubs: Akron Area Wellesley, Akron Woman's City. Home: 260 Whittier Ave Kent OH 44240

SMITH, FRANCIS THOMAS, III, health center administrator; b. Detroit, June 14, 1934; s. Francis Thomas, Jr. and Maxine (Greene) S.; A.B., Hope Coll., Holland, Mich., 1960; M.H.A. (Nat. Tb Assn. grad. fellow 1960), Wayne State U., Detroit, 1961; m. E. Jane Fawcett, July 30, 1983; children—Thomas John, Karen Marie. Program devel. cons., dir. patient service programs Ill. Tb Assn., Springfield, 1961-63; exec. dir. Peoria (Ill.)-Stark County Tb Assn., 1963-66; adminstr. Allied Agys. Ctr.-Peoria County Bd. Care and Treatment Mentally Deficient Persons, Peoria, 1966—; cons. exec. dir. Ill. Assn. Maternal and Child Health, 1972-84; cons. exec. sec. Downstate Ill. Pediatric Soc.; mem. tri-county project rev. com. Ill. Health Systems Agy. Mem. program and budget com. Heart of Ill. United Way, 1970-78; mem. Forest Park Found., 1971—; bd. dirs. Tower Park, Inc., 1975, Council Responsible Driving, 1976-79; lay leader First United Meth. Ch., Peoria, 1979-80, chmn. adminstrv. bd., 1981-82. Served with USNR, 1953-57. Mem. Am. Soc. Public Adminstrn. (chpt. charter mem., past chpt. pres.), Am. Assn. Mental Deficiency, Nat. Rehab. Counseling Assn., Bldg. Owners and Mgrs. Assn., Nat. Rehab. Assn., Ill. Rehab. Assn., Ill. Public Health Assn. Republican. Lutheran. Clubs: Peoria Rotary, Masons, Shriners. Contbr. articles to profl. jours. Office: 320 E Armstrong Ave Peoria IL 61603

SMITH, FRANK EARL, association executive; b. Fremont Center, N.Y., Feb. 4, 1931; s. Earl A. and Hazel (Knack) S.; m. Caroline R. Gillin, Aug. 14, 1954; children—Stephen F., David S., Daniel E. B.S., Syracuse U., 1952. With Mellor Advt. Agy., Elmira, N.Y., 1954-55; asst. mgr. Assn. Commerce, Elmira, 195-56, Binghamton C. of C., N.Y., and mgr. Better Bus. Bur., Broome County, N.Y., 1956-60; exec. vp. Chemung County C. of C., Elmira, 1960-65, Schenectady County C. of C., N.Y., 1965-69, Greater Cin. C. of C., 1969-78; pres. Greater Detroit C. of C., 1978—. Served to 1st lt. USAF, 1952-54. Mem. C. of C. Execs. Mich., Am. C. of C. Execs. (past chmn.), N.Y. State C. of C. Execs. (past pres.), Ohio C. of C. Execs. (past pres.), C. of C. U.S. (dir., past chmn. nat. bd. regents Inst. Orgn. Mgmt.). Presbyterian. Clubs: Detroit, Detroit Athletic, Renaissance, Lochmoor Golf, Hidden Valley-Otsego Ski. Home: 45 Renaud Rd Grosse Pointe Shores MI 48236 Office: Greater Detroit C of C 150 Michigan Ave Detroit MI 48226

SMITH, FRANKLIN ADAMS, physician; b. Worcester, Mass., June 27, 1934; s. Daniel Southwick and Evelyn Hart (Freeland) S.; m. Irmeli Inez Kola, Jan. 4, 1964; children—Christofer Adams, Erika Raili, Rolf Holbrook. B.S. cum laude, Bates Coll., 1956; M.D., Tufts U., 1960. Diplomate Am. Bd.

Internal Medicine. Commd. ensign U.S. Navy, 1956, advanced through grades to capt., ret., 1980; intern U.S. Naval Hosp., Chelsea, Mass., 1960-61, resident in internal medicine, 1964-67; mem. staff in internal medicine U.S. Naval Hosp., Great Lakes, Ill., 1967-69, asst. chief medicine, 1969-73; chief of medicine Naval Regional Med. Ctr., Great Lakes, 1973-80; asst. v.p., assoc. med. dir. Aid Assn. for Lutherans, Appleton, Wis., 1980—; med. dir. Community Alcohol Services, Inc., Appleton, 1980-83; asst. prof. medicine Chgo. Med. Sch., North Chicago, Ill., 1975-80. Bd. dirs. Appleton Wrestling Club, 1983—; active Appleton Alliance for Arts, 1982—. Mem. ACP, AMA, State Med. Soc. Wis., Outagamie County Med. Soc., Assn. Life Ins. Med. Dirs. Am., Appleton MacDowell Male Chorus (music com. 1982). Lodge: Aid Assn. Lutherans (v.p. br. 1981-83). Avocations: playing cello; chorus; tennis. Office: Aid Assn Lutherans 4321 N Ballard Rd Appleton WI 54919

SMITH, GARRETT EDWARD, dental laboratory administrator; b. Viola, Ark., Feb. 24, 1945; s. Raymond George and Exie (Rand) S.; m. Vivienne Kay Smith, June 10, 1968 (div. Aug. 1976); 1 child, Robert Garrett; m. Josipene Lenna Leone, Nov. 6, 1977 (div. May 1983). Student pub. schs., Viola, Ark. Dental lab. technician Dysart Dental Lab., Kansas City, Mo., 1963-65, Caldwell Dental Clinic, Ft. Riley, Kans., 1968-77; dental lab. technician, owner Smitty's Crown and Bridge Lab., Manhattan, Kans., 1971-76, Garrett's Dental Ceramic Lab., Manhattan, 1977—. Recipient Certs. of Achievement, Julius Aderer, Inc., Chgo., 1966, J.F. Jelenko Co. Inc., Armonk, N.Y., 1967, DAV, Ft. Riley, Kans., 1968, Baylor Acad. Dentistry, Dallas, 1971, Nat. Safety Council, Ft. Riley, 1972, Outstanding Performance award Armed Forces, Ft. Riley, 1971. Baptist. Lodge: Masons. Avocations: snow skiing, water skiing, hunting, fishing, restoring classic autos. Office: Garrett's Dental Ceramic Lab Manhattan KS 66502

SMITH, GARY K., design engineer, owner manufacturing company; b. Delphos, Kans., Jan. 13, 1938; s. Gerald A. and Marjorie N. (Harper) S.; m. Mary Jo Pitlick, June 6, 1959; children—Nancy K., Donna L., Gary A. Grad. Delphos High Sch., 1956; assoc. degrees in Business and in Aerospace, USAF, 1973, 1976. Served with U.S. Air Force as aircraft maintenance and deputy base procurement officer, 1957-77, ret., 1977 electrician El Dorado R. V. Inc., Minneapolis, Kans., 1978-79, engr., 1979-80, plant design engr., 1980—; owner pick-up topper mfg. co. Mem. Christian Ch. Home: 206 E 2d St Minneapolis MN 67467 Office: 1200 W 10th St Minneapolis MN 67467

SMITH, GEOFFREY RAND, lawyer, communications company executive; b. Xenia, Ohio, Sept. 23, 1945; s. Clayton Sherman and Jeanne (Savage) S.; m. Kathryn Estadt, Apr. 20, 1968; children—Susan Liegh, Geoffrey Rand II, Jennifer Kathryn. B.S., Troy State U., 1971; J.D., Capital U., 1974. Bar: Ohio 1974. Ombudsman City of Columbus, Ohio, 1974-75, asst. pros. atty., 1975-77; sole practice, Columbus, 1977—; sec., corp. counsel Westerville Communications, Inc., Columbus, 1982—, Westerville Broadcasting Fla., Inc., Tampa, 1982—, Communications III, Inc., Columbus, 1984—. Contbg. author Capital U. Law Rev., 1974. Pres. Franklin County Republican Lawyer's Club, Columbus, 1978-79; mem. Rep. Presdl. Task Force, Washington, 1984. Served to 1st lt. U.S. Army, 1967-71, Viet Nam. Decorated Bronze Star, Air medal with 12 oak leaf clusters, Army Commendation medal. Mem. Columbus Bar Assn., Acad. Trial Lawyers Am., Ohio Trial Lawyers Assn., Ohio State Univ. Pres.'s Club. Methodist. Club: University (Columbus). Avocations: swimming; skiing. Home: 2417 Abington Rd Columbus OH 43221 Office: 350 E Broad St Suite 300 Columbus OH 43215

SMITH, GEORGE CURTIS, lawyer, judge; b. Columbus, Ohio, Aug. 8, 1935; s. George B. and Dorothy R. S.; m. Barbara Jean Wood, July 10, 1963; children—Curt, Geof, Beth Ann. B.A., Ohio State U., 1957, J.D., 1959. Bar: Ohio 1959. Asst. city atty. City of Columbus, 1959-62; exec. asst. to Mayor of Columbus, 1962-63; asst. atty. gen. State of Ohio, 1964; chief counsel to pros. atty. Franklin County, Ohio, 1965-70, pros. atty., 1971-80; judge Franklin County Mcpl. Ct., Columbus, 1980-85; judge Franklin County Common Pleas Ct., 1985—. Trustee Central Ohio sect. Am. Lung Assn.; trustee Leukemia Soc. Central Ohio; men's bd. Project Hope; trustee Crime Solvers Anonymous, Teen Challenge, Inc.; pres. Young Republican Club, 1963, Buckeye Rep. Club, 1968; exec. com. Franklin County Rep. Party, 1971-80. Recipient Superior Jud. Service award Supreme Ct. Ohio, 1980, 81, 82, 83, 84; Resolution of Honor, Columbus Bldg. and Constrn. Trades Council, 1980; award Eagles, 1980; Mem. Ohio Pros. Attys. Assn. (life, pres., Ohio Prosecutor of Yr, Award of Honor, Leadership award), Columbus Bar Assn., Ohio Bar Assn., Assn. Trial Lawyers Am., Ohio Common Pleas Judges Assn., Ohio Mcpl.-County Judges Assn. 2d v.p., trustee). Presbyterian. Clubs: Columbus Athletic (pres., dir.), Columbus Maennerchor, Germania, Lawyers of Columbus (pres. 1975), Shamrock. Lodges: Fraternal Order Police Assocs., Eagles, Masons, Shriners. Office: Franklin County Common Pleas Ct 369 S High St Columbus OH 43215

SMITH, GLENN M., dentist; b. Gary, Ind., Mar. 12, 1947; s. Morgan B. and Virginia E. (Shepherd) S.; m. Diane Ruth Bontrager, June 3, 1973; 1 child, Erick Glenn. B.S., Ind. U.-Bloomington, 1969; D.D.S., Ind. U.-Indpls., 1972. Councilman, Montpelier City Govt., Ind., 1980—, council pres., 1984—. Fellow Internat. Coll. Dentists; mem. Am. Soc. Geriatric Dentistry, Pierre Fauchard Acad., Am. Dental Assn., Acad. Gen. Dentistry, Ind. Dental Assn. (trustee 1981—), Ind. U. Alumni Assn. (life), Montpelier C. of C., Psi Omega. Republican. Methodist. Lodge: Kiwanis (pres. 1976-77). Avocations: photography; hiking; reading. Home: 533 S Adams St Montpelier IN 47359

SMITH, GLORIA ANN, English and German educator; b. Hartington, Nebr., Mar. 13, 1943; d. Robert Vernon and Evelyn Lucille (Jensen) Lind; m. Kenneth Frank Smith, June 13, 1965; children—Jennifer Ann, David Kenneth. B.S., S.D. State U., 1965; M.A., U. S.D., 1981. Instr. Dakota Wesleyan U., Mitchell, S.D., 1972-83, asst. prof., 1983—. Pres. Mitchell Sch. Bd., 1982—, mem., 1979—. Woodrow Wilson Found. fellow, 1965; Briggs Found. scholar, 1962-65; F.O. Butler scholar, 1961. Mem. Associated Sch. Bd. S.D., Phi Kappa Phi, Sigma Tau Delta, Delta Kappa Gamma. Democrat. Lutheran. Avocations: Gardening; camping; reading; sewing. Home: Rural Route 5 Box 225 Mitchell SD 57301 Office: Mitchell Sch Dist 17-2 117 E 4th Ave Mitchell SD 57301

SMITH, GREGORY JOSEPH, psychologist; b. N. Canton, Ohio, Dec. 27, 1951; s. Joseph Ernest and Dorothy (Uber) S.; m. Marcia K. Broemsen, June 9, 1973. B.A., Kent State U., 1975; M.A., SUNY-Binghamton, 1975, Ph.D., 1981. Jr. research asst. Kent (Ohio) State U., 1973-75; sr. research asst. SUNY-Binghamton, 1975-79, intern Office of Provost for Grad. Studies, 1979-80; asst. prof. Case Western Res. U., Cleve., 1980-84; managerial psychologist PRADCO, 1983—; asst. prof. Kent State U., Ohio, 1984—; cons. in field. Mem. Am. Psychol. Assn., Am. Assn. Sci., Eastern Psychol. Assn., Internat. Soc. Devel. Psychobiology, Midwestern Psychol. Assn., N.Y. Acad. Sci. Contbr. articles to profl. jours. Office: Dept Psychology Kent State Univ Kent OH 44242

SMITH, GUY RAYMOND, JR., accountant; b. Chgo., June 9, 1931; s. Guy Raymond and Anna Mary (Stepanek) S.; m. Carol Grace Heilbrun, Aug. 16, 1958; children—Ruth Elizabeth Kadykowski, Russell Guy. B.A. in Acctg., Mich. State U., 1958, M.B.A., 1976. Cert. personal property examiner, Mich. Field agt. IRS, Detroit, 1958-64; life underwriter Mfrs. Life, Detroit, 1964-66; auditor Chrysler Corp., Highland Park, Mich., 1966-67; fin. analyst Fed. Mogul Corp., Southfield, Mich., 1967-68, tax acct., 1968-82, property tax adminstr., 1982—. Author: One Branch of Captain John Smith and Margaret from 1698, 1978. Music arranger Transcriptions of Civil War Music for Modern Wind Ensemble, 1981. Asst. condr. St. Clair Shores Symphony Orch., Mich., 1963; musician Grosse Pointe Symphony Orch., Mich., 1964; bd. dirs. Mount Clemens Symphony Orch., 1967; founder, condr. Novi Community Concert Band, Mich., 1972; condr. Livonia Community Band, Mich., 1977; condr., arranger 5th Mich. Regt. Band, 1979; mem. formation com. Cub Scout Pack 239, Ottawa Council Boy Scouts Am., 1971; subcom. chmn. needs assessment com. Novi Community Schs., 1973; chmn. Novi Citizens Ad Hoc Fin. Com., 1974; incorporator, officer, bd. dirs. Village Oaks Homeowners Assn., Novi, 1971, Village Oaks Common Areas Assn., 1972, Novi Found. for Performing Arts, 1975; councilman City of Novi, 1977—; campaign mgr. mayoralty, council and sch. bd. candidates, Novi, 1973-79; polit. adviser council and county commr. candidates, 1976, 80. Served as cpl. U.S. Army, 1952-54. Recipient Disting. Citizens Service award City of Novi, 1975. Mem. Inst. Property Taxation, SCV, Augustan Soc., Hereditary Order of Armigerous Augustans, Nat. Soc. SAR, Gen. Soc. Mayflower Descs., Colonial Order of Crown, Plantagenet Soc., Magna Charta Barons, Heraldry Soc. U.S.A., Soc. of Descs. Knights of Most Noble Order of Garter, Mo. Hist. Soc., Phi Mu Alpha. Presbyterian. Avocations: music, genealogical research, heraldry. Home: 22638 Chestnut Tree Way Novi MI 48050

SMITH, HAROLD HASKEN, university administrator; b. Cin., Mar. 16, 1942; s. Harold C. and Ruth V. (Hasken) S.; m. Karen A. Willis, Dec. 20, 1969; children—Amy Elizabeth, Andrew David, Anne Cameron. A.B., Centre Coll., 1964; M.B.A., Am. U., 1968. Admissions counselor Centre Coll., Danville, Ky., 1964-66, assoc. dir. admissions, 1968-70, dir. admissions, 1970-73, dean admissions, 1973-80, v.p., dean students, 1980-83, lectr. econs. mgmt., 1973-80; v.p. devel. Muskingum Coll., New Concord, Ohio, 1983—; cons. in edn. Dir. Boyle-Mercer County (Ky.) YMCA, 1979-83; bd. dirs. Southeast Ohio. Symphony Orch., 1983—, Renew Environment of New Concord, 1983—. Recipient Disting. Chmn. awards Rotary Found., 1981-82. Mem. Council Ind. Ky. Colls. and Univs., Nat. Assn. Student Personnel Adminstrs., Am. Coll. Personnel Assn., Cambridge C. of C. (bd. dirs. 1984—), Nat. Assn. Coll. Admissions Counselors. Presbyterian (elder). Lodge: Rotary (pres. 1979-80, dist. gov.'s rep. 1981-82). Office: Muskingum College New Concord OH 43762

SMITH, HERBERT MICHAEL, pharmacist; b. Cin., June 27, 1951; s. Herbert and Mary Elizabeth (Turner) S.; m. Carmen Smith, Mar. 21, 1981; children—Herbert, William, Christopher, Kendra. B.A. in Biology, Capital U., 1975; B.S. in Pharmacy, Ohio State U., 1980, M.S. in Pharm. Adminstrn., 1982. Registered pharmacist. Store mgr. Churches Fried Chicken Inc., Columbus, Ohio, 1976-77; intern Childrens Hosp., Columbus, 1977-80; tchrs. asst. Ohio State U., Columbus, 1980-82; staff pharmacist Mt. Carmel Hosp., Columbus, 1980-82; VA Hosp., Cleve., 1983—; system, pharmacy directive Revco Drug Store Inc., Twinsburg, Ohio, 1982—. Recruiter Ohio State Coll. of Pharmacy, Columbus, 1978-80; com. chmn. Student Adv. Com., Columbus, 1980. Recipient Outstanding Acad. Performance award Office of Minority Affairs, Columbus, 1980, Outstanding Achievement award Med. Arts Club, Columbus, 1980. Mem. Cleve. Pharm. Assn. (com. mem. 1984—), Rho Chi (Rho Chi Key award, 1981). Democrat. Baptist. Home: 881 Montford St Cleveland Heights OH 44121 Office: Revco Drug Store Inc 1925 Enterprise Pkwy Twinsburg OH 44087

SMITH, ISABEL FRANCIS, financial planner; b. Detroit, May 21, 1935; d. Edward Hugh and Isabel Francis (Winegar); m. Lawrence Smith, June 7, 1958; children—Mark, Hugh, Claire. Student, Newton Coll., 1953-54; B.A., U. Mich., 1957, M.A., 1958, postgrad., 1975-76. Registered investment adviser, SEC; cert. fin. planner. Tchr., Edison Sch., Hazel Park, Mich. and Warren Valley Sch., Dearborn, Mich., 1958-61; counselor Riverside High Sch., Dearborn Hts., Mich., 1961-62; pres. Isabel Francis Smith Ltd., Birmingham, Mich., 1980—, Integrated Fin. Strategies, Ltd., Birmingham, 1980—; registered rep., dist. mgr. Investors Diversified Services, Oak Park, Mich., 1978-80; instr. Henry Ford Community Coll., Oakland County Community Coll., Schoolcraft Community Coll. (all Mich.), 1979—; cons. to women's orgns., 1977—; writer, radio and TV personality. Lectr., trustee Bloomfield Twp. Library; founder Interlochen Friends, Vol. Network for Women. Recipient Heart of Gold award United Found., 1976; Outstanding New Rep. award Investors Diversified Services, 1979. Mem. Registry Fin. Planning Practitioners, AAUW, League Women Voters, Nat. Assn. Profl. Saleswomen, Internat. Assn. Fin. Planners (past pres. S.E. Mich. chpt.), Inst. Cert. Fin. Planners (regional dir., nat. dir.), Nat. Assn. Life Underwriters, Nat. Assn. Women Bus. Owners, Birmingham-Bloomfield C. of C., Interlochen Alumni Assn. (award, past pres.), U. Mich. Alumni Assn., Detroit Symphony League, Phi Beta Kappa (nat. chmn., past pres. Detroit assn., mem. exec. com., Pres.'s award Detroit assn.), Pi Lambda Theta. Clubs: Women's Economic, Village Women's, Birmingham Women's Ctr. Home: 7110 Paterese St Birmingham MI 48010 Office: 30200 Telegraph Rd Suite 466 Birmingham MI 48010

SMITH, JAMES DOUGLAS, architect; b. Chgo., May 14, 1943; s. Lyman Douglas and Hallie Marie (Sanders) S.; m. Anita Louise Metzger, June 24, 1967; 1 child, Elisa Marie. B.Arch. with honors (Lydia Bates scholar 1964-66, Schlaeder Meml. scholar 1966-67, Deeter-Ritchey-Sipple fellow 1967, A. Epstein meml. scholar 1967-68), U. Ill., 1968; certificate with honors Ecole des Beaux Arts, Fontainbleau, France, 1967; Planner, Northeastern Ill. Planning Commn., Chgo., 1966, Dept. Devel. and Planning, Chgo., 1968-69; archtl. designer A. Epstein Internat., Chgo., 1969-72; architect-planner, partner Smith-Kureghian & Assos., Chgo., 1972-77; city architect City of Gary (Ind.), 1977-79; v.p. H. Seay Cantrell Assos., Inc., Architects, 1979—; planning dir. Indsl. Council/N.W. Community, Chgo., 1972; urban planning cons. Nathan-Barnes & Assos., Chgo., 1972—; prin. works include Sheraton Hotel, Gary, Gary Hotel Renovation, Pub. Safety Bldg., Gary, Multi-Modal Transp. Center, Gary; co-designer Hyatt Regency Hotel, Chgo.; other city and comml. rehab. plans; co-author bldg. code; bd. dirs. Ind. Archtl. Found., 1981—. Precinct del. 44th Ward Assembly, Chgo., 1973—, chmn. services com., 1973-74, chmn. steering com., 1974—, campaign area chmn., 1974-76; bd. dirs. Ind. Archtl. Found.; mem. grant rev. jury Ind. Arts Commn., 1983, adv. panel design arts, 1982-83, 84-85. Named an Outstanding Young Man Am., 1974; registered architect, Ill., Ind., Mich., Mo.; lic. real estate broker, Ind. Mem. AIA (sec. planning com. 1972-75, dir. chpt., bd. dirs. 1983-84), Ind. Soc. Architects (bd. dirs. 1984—), Internat. Platform Assn., Prestressed Concrete Inst., Constrn. Specifications Inst., Nat. Council Archtl. Registration Bds., Chgo. Assn. Commerce and Industry, Gargoyle Soc. (membership chmn. 1968), Scarab, Sigma Tau. Home: 1215 W Wellington St Chicago IL 60657 Office: 522 Broadway Suite 212 Gary IN 46402 also 8943 S Stony Island Chicago IL 60617

SMITH, JAMES PERRY, educator; b. Southwest City, Mo., Aug. 15, 1933; s. Eual Clay and Susan Marie (Perry) S.; m. Molly Jayne Smith, Aug. 21, 1955; children—James Duston, Rebecca Dawn. B.S., Okla. State U., 1960; M.S., Ark. U., 1963. Cert. life vocat. agr. tchr., Mo. Instr. animal sci. dept. Okla. State U., Stillwater, 1964-69; sec. Okla. Quarter Horse Assn., 1969-73, vocat. agr. instr. McDonald County High School, Anderson, Mo., 1978—; processor Teledyne, Neosho, Mo., 1974-78. Show supt. McDonald County Fair Bd.; mem. McDonald County Extension Council, Econ. Security Corp., road commr. Buffalo spl. dist.; bd. dirs., Sunday Sch. supt. Goodman United Meth. Ch. Served to sgt. U.S. Army, 1955-57. Recipient Pres.'s award for outstanding vocat. agr. tchr., 1979. Mem. Am. Vocat. Assn., Mo. Vacat. Assn., Mo. Cattleman's Assn. Contbr. articles to profl. jours. Office: McDonald High School Anderson MO 64831

SMITH, JAMES WARREN, pathologist, microbiologist, parasitologist; b. Logan, Utah, July 5, 1934; s. Kenneth Warren and Nina Lou (Sykes) S.; m. Nancy Chesterman, July 19, 1958; children—Warren, Scott. B.S., U. Iowa, 1956, M.D., 1959. Diplomate Am. Bd. Pathology. Intern, Colo. Gen. Hosp., Denver, 1959-60; resident U. Iowa Hosps., Iowa City, 1960-65; asst. prof. pathology U. Vt., Burlington, 1967-70; prof. pathology Ind. U., Indpls., 1970—. Contbr. articles to profl. jours. Served to lt. comdr. USN, 1965-67. Recipient Oustanding Contbrn. to Clin. Microbiology award South Central Assn. Clin. Microbiology, 1977. Fellow Coll. Am. Pathologists (chmn. microbiology resource com. 1981—), Infectious Disease Soc. Am., Royal Soc. Tropical Medicine and Hygiene; mem. Am. Soc. Clin. Pathology, Am. Soc. Microbiology, Am. Soc. Tropical Medicine and Hygiene, AMA. Office: N340 University Hosp Ind U Med Ctr 926 W Michigan St Indianapolis IN 46223

SMITH, JEFFREY EARL, lawyer; b. Dayton, Ohio, Apr. 20, 1941; s. Harold Leslie and Ruth Winifred (Otto) S.; m. Sue Ellen Dils, Sept. 1, 1962; children—Laura Ann, Cynthia Carol, Jeffrey Thomas. B.S. in Bus. Adminstrn., Miami U., 1963; M.B.A., U. Dayton, 1965; J.D., Chase Sch. Law, 1969. Bar: Ohio 1969, Mich. 1970. Personnel dir. Gen. Motors Chevrolet Div., Warren Mich., 1976-81; sr. atty. Armco Inc., Middletown, Ohio, 1981—. Mem. Ohio Bar Assn., ABA. Avocations: all sports. Home: 4684 Westmeath Ct Middletown OH 45042 Office: Armco Inc 713 Curtis St Middletown OH 45042

SMITH, JERRY MILFORD, fire chief; b. DuQuion, Ill., Jan. 13, 1943; s. Milford Robert and Diza Ira (Crawshaw) S.; m. Marilyn Sue Hill, Dec. 30, 1963 (div. May 1976); Barbara Ann Lodge, Mar. 13, 1981; children—Jerry Robert, Annette Kathleen, Joshua Charles, Amanda LuAnn. Cert. Emergency Med. Technician, Bend Lake Coll., 1968. Vol. fireman Pinckneyville Firemans Assn., Ill., 1966-68, asst. fire chief, 1968-79, fire chief, 1979—. Fellow Nat. Fire Protection Assn., Ill. Fire Chiefs Assn., Ill. Profl. Firefighter Assn., Egyptian Fire Fighters Assn. So. Ill., Coal Belt Fire Protective Assn. So. Ill. Apostolic. Lodge: Optimist (pres. 1974, lt. gov. 1975-76). Avocations: hunting, water skiing, fishing camping, demoderby. Home: 203 St Louis PO Box 312 Pinckneyville IL 62274 Office: Pinckneyville Fire Dept 110-114 S Walnut St Pinckneyville IL 62274

SMITH, JEWELL GRACE, librarian; b. St. Joseph, Mo., Apr. 11, 1922; d. John William and Verda Jewell (Ballew) Minor; m. Frank B. Smith, Mar. 21, 1948 (div.); children—Barry, Craig, Doane, Alan. Student St. Joseph Jr. Coll., 1939-40; B.A., William Jewell Coll., 1944; M.L.S., Tex. Women's U., 1962. Tchr.-librarian, Horton, Kans., 1945-47, Hiawatha, Kans., 1947-48, Weston, Mo., 1952-53, Sabetha, Kans., 1953-56, Mansfield, Mo., 1956-58, Cabool, Mo., 1958-61; asst. dir. Daniel Boone Regional Library, 1962-65; reference librarian Ozark Pioneer Library System, Springfield, Mo., 1965-67; asst. dir. Springfield-Greene County Library, Springfield, Mo., 1967-77, dir., 1977—; supply tchr. library sci. S.W. Mo. State U., 1969-70, 72-73; chmn. Mo. Libraries Network Bd., 1978-80; program chmn. Mo. Library Assn. Conf., 1969. Mem. Springfield Area Librarians Assn., Mo. Library Assn., ALA. Democrat. Office: 397 E Central St Springfield MO 65802

SMITH, JOHN BURNSIDE, See *Who's Who in America,* 43rd edition.

SMITH, JOHN CLARENCE, professional model maker; b. Massillon, Ohio, May 15, 1930; s. John Samual and Pearl S.; m. Erna Aab, Nov. 5, 1960; children—J. Christopher, James Walter, Robert Anthony. Student pub. schs., Massillon. Refinery worker Ashland Oil Co., Canton, Ohio, 1949-51; model maker NASA-Lewis Flight Propulsion Lab., Cleve., 1954-57; owner, operator Scale Craft Models, Massillon, 1957—; model maker Gates Learjet Corp., 1970—, Cessna Aircraft Co., 1983—. Mem. Clinton Community Concert Band, 1979—, Canton Community Band, 1983—; mem. exec. bd. Boys Club, Massillon, 1969-72; mem. exec. bd. dirs. local band Parents Club, 1977-82. Served with U.S. Army, 1951-53. Mem. Acad. Model Aeronautics (leader mem., contest dir.), Cleve. Aeromodel Soc. Club: Optimist (past pres.). Contbg. editor Am. Aircraft Modeler Mag., 1969-74; works represented in Nat. Air and Space Mus., Smithsonian Instn. Home and Office: 960 Brenner Ave NW Massillon OH 44646

SMITH, KENT ERNEST, non-profit organization executive; b. Oak Park, Ill., May 21, 1939; s. James Paul and Jane Louise (Gardner) S.; m. Pamela Ann Streich, Sept. 11, 1965; children—Julie Ellen, Stephen Paul. B.S. in Journalism, U. Ill., 1961. Producer, writer pub. service programming Sta. WLW-TV, Cin., 1965-67; radio/TV news writer producer Sta. WGN, Chgo., 1967-69; TV news producer, writer, project planner Sta. WLS-TV, Chgo., 1969-78; exec. dir. Spina Bifida Assn. Am., Chgo., 1978—. Bd. advisors Council For Disability Rights, Chgo.; treas. Elmhurst Instrumental Music Boosters. Served with U.S. Army, 1961-65. Mem. Am. Soc. Assn. Execs., Chgo. Soc. Assn. Execs., Chgo. Headline Club, Sigma Delta Chi. Mem. United Ch. of Christ (elder). Home: 472 Prairie Ave Elmhurst IL 60126 Office: 343 S Dearborn St 317 Chicago IL 60604

SMITH, KURT LAWRENCE, petroleum geologist; b. Buffalo. B.S. in Geology, Wichita State U., 1983. Petroleum geologist No. Lights Oil Co., Wichita, Kans., 1982—. Mem. Am. Assn. Petroleum Geologists (jr.). Office: No Lights Oil Co 212 N Market Suite 400 Wichita KS 67202

SMITH, LARRY GORDON, educator, business consultant; b. Gary, Ind., Aug. 14, 1944; s. Gordon Henry and Loretta Elaine (Reglein) S.; m. Joyce Evelyn Lohrman, June 11, 1966; 1 son, Kenneth Gordon. B.S.Ed., N.E. Mo. State U., 1966, M.A., 1976. With U.S. Steel Co., Gary, Ind., 1964-66; asst. mgr. B. Dalton Booksellers, St. Louis, 1967-69; tchr. Riverview Gardens Schs., St. Louis, 1968-81; mgr. Mid-Am. Theatres, St. Louis, 1980-83, cons., 1983—; tchr., adminstr. Ft. Zumwalt Sch. Dist., O'Fallon, Mo., 1980—. NSF grantee, 1971-72; Allen Scovell scholar, 1977; N.E. Mo. State U. Music scholar, 1962-65. Mem. Nat. Assn. Secondary Sch. Prins., Mo. Assn. Secondary Sch. Prins., Phi Delta Kappa, Alpha Phi Sigma, Kappa Delta Pi, Blue Key. Republican. Home: 2416 Saint Robert Ln Saint Charles MO 63301 Office: Fort Zumwalt Sch Dist 110 Virgil St O'Fallon MO 63366

SMITH, LUCY EDNA, educator; b. Tuscaloosa, Ala., Feb. 21, 1928; d. Jesse S. and Pinkie R. (Brown) S. B.S., Ala. State U.; M.Ed., U. Ill.; Ph.D., St. Louis U. Tchr., supr. elem. grades, Cahokia, Ill. Active YWCA. Mem. Assn. Supervision and Curriculum Devel., Am. Fedn. Tchrs. (rep.), NAACP, Stillman Coll. Alumni Assn., U. Ill. Alumni Assn., St. Louis U. Alumni Assn., Zeta Phi Beta. Deomocrat. Club: Nat. Tuscaloosa (nat. v.p.). Lodge: Order Eastern Star. Home: 2915 Trendley Ave East Saint Louis IL 62207 Office: Penniman Sch Cahokia IL 62206

SMITH, LYNN HOWARD, manufacturing company executive; b. Ft. Wayne, Ind., Mar. 9, 1936; s. Lester Earl and Catherine Lois (McCurdy) S.; student Ind.-Purdue U. Extension, Ft. Wayne, 1956-57; grad. Internat. Harvester Tech. Sch., 1961; m. Jean Marie Bauman, Sept. 2, 1955; children—Julie, Linnett, Jeffery, Lisa. Methods engr. Jervis Corp., Grandville, Mich., 1964-67; project engr. Twigg Industries, Martinsville, Ind., 1967-70; project engr. Tri Industries, Terre Haute, Ind., 1970-74; tool and mfg. engr. Berko Electric Mfg. Co., Peru, Ind., 1974-77, fabrication supt., 1977-78, mgr. mfg. engring., 1978-79, plant supr., 1979; chief project engr. Tube Processing Corp., Indpls., 1979-85, Tube Forming and Mfg. Corp., Lebanon, Ind., 1985—; cons. Groteness Machine Works, Chgo. Pres. Harlan (Ind.) Days Assn., 1962; adv. Jr. Achievement, Terre Haute, Ind., 1972-73. Named Jr. Achievement Adv. of Yr., Terre Haute Jr. Achievement, 1973. Methodist. Clubs: Berko Mgmt., Masons (Harlan lodge master 1964), Shriners. Developed proprietary spot welding process and equipment, 1966, proprietary high temperature brazing process, 1970-74; developer, editor Berko Electric Mfg. Procedures Man., 1975-79. Home: Rural Route 1 Box 269-A Peru IN 46970 Office: 312 E Thompson St PO Box 311 Lebanon IN 46052

SMITH, MARTIN BROOKS, JR., health care executive; b. Whiteville, N.C., Feb. 14, 1947; s. Martin Brooks and Pearl Louise S.; m. Regina Patricia Stopczywski, Dec. 18, 1971; m. Carolyn Marie Vogt, Apr. 14, 1981; 1 son, Martin Brooks III; 1 stepdau. Allison Rebecca Williams. Commd. U.S. Air Force, 1966, advanced through grades to capt., 1977; chief ops. 1st aeromed. squadron Pope AFB, N.C., 1975-77; resigned, 1977; v.p., gen. mgr. Indsl. Health Services, Cin., 1977-79; pres. M.B. Smith & Assocs., Cin., 1979-81; v.p. United Healthcare Systems, Inc., Kansas City, Mo., 1981-82, pres., 1983—; pres. EquiMed, Inc., Overland Park, Kans., 1985—. Mem. Am. Hosp. Assn., Am. Mktg. Assn., Emergency Medicine Mgmt. Assn. (charter). Republican. Club: Blue Hills Country.

SMITH, MARYANN PATRICIA YODELIS, academic administrator, journalism educator; b. Sioux City, Iowa, Dec. 19, 1935; d. Joseph Anthony and Mary Sophie (Galas) Yodelis; m. Kim Rhodes Smith, May 14, 1977; 1 stepchild, Lisa. B.A., Briar Cliff Coll., 1963; M.A., U. Wis.-Madison, 1969, Ph.D., 1971. Tchr. St. Mary High Sch., Remsem, Iowa, 1960-62; asst. dir. admissions Briar Cliff Coll., Sioux City, 1962-64, asst. to acad. dean, 1964-65, dir. publs. and publicity, 1965-67; from teaching asst., lectr. to assoc. prof. U. Wis.-Madison, 1967-81, prof. journalism, 1981—, assoc. vice chancellor of academic affairs, prof., 1978—; asst. prof. Ind. U., Bloomington, 1971-72; mem. media-law relations com. Wis. State Bar, 1976—. Contbr. articles to profl. jours. and book chpts. Recipient Chancellors award U. Wis., 1975. Mem. Journalism Council (pres. 1983-85), Assn. for Edn. in Journalism and Mass Communication (exec. com. 1977-79), Internat. Communications Assn., Orgn. Am. Historians, Soc. Profl. Journalists. Roman Catholic. Clubs: Tempo, Weavers Guild. Office: Assoc Vice Chancellor Acad Affairs U Wis Madison 166 Bascom Hall 500 Lincoln Madison WI 53711

SMITH, MERCY A(NN), insurance agent, consultant; b. Akron, Ohio, Aug. 26, 1953; d. Bryant Ralph and Mary Ann (Mettle) S.; m. Randall C. Allen, Oct. 21, 1977 (div. Dec. 1979). Student pub. schs., Salem, Ohio. Claims clk. Prudential Ins. Co., Youngstown, Ohio, 1971-73, Grange Casualty, Niles, Ohio, 1973-75; ins. agt. Moreman-Yerian Co., Youngstown, 1975-79, Met. Life Ins. Co., Warren, Ohio, 1979-81; account asst. F.B. Hall & Co., Youngstown, 1981-83; account exec. M.W. Early Ins. Assocs., Canton, Ohio, 1983—. Mem. Nat. Assn. Ins. Women (asst. regional dir. region IV 1982-83), Ins. Women Youngstown (Ins. Woman of Yr. 1982), Ohio Ins. Inst. (speakers bur.). Republican. Episcopalian. Office: MW Early Ins Assocs 1944 Whipple NW Canton OH 44708

SMITH, MICHAEL BARUCH, earth scientist, consultant; b. West Point, N.Y., Sept. 5, 1956; s. Stephen Harrison Smith and Jean Carol (Sweany) Nekola. B.S. in Geology, Marietta Coll., 1978; M.A. in Geography, Ohio U., Athens, 1985, M.S. in Environ. Studies, 1985. Geologist, United Nuclear Corp., Gallup, N.Mex., 1978-80, Mid Eastern Geotech, Marietta, Ohio, 1980-81;

petroleum geologist Towner Petroleum, Cambridge, Ohio, 1981-82; cons. geologist, oil and gas, Albany, Ohio, 1982—; assoc. dir. Scalia Lab. for Atmospheric Analysis, Ohio U., Athens, 1984—. Mem. Am. Assn. Petroleum Geologists. Home: Route 2 Box 124 B Albany OH 45710 Office: Ohio U Geography 601 Porter Hall Athens OH 45701

SMITH, MICHAEL DALE, insurance agency executive; b. Rensselaer, Ind., Sept. 17, 1953; s. Hamlin Henry and Phyllis Joan (Hall) S.; m. Gretchen Zuege, Sept. 1, 1973; children—Mandy, Joshua. Grad. Internat. Coll., 1973. Mem. mgmt. program Household Fin. Corp., 1973-74; owner Credit Bur. Rensselaer, 1974-79; pres. Smith Realty, Rensselaer, 1974—; v.p., owner Consol. Ins. Agy., Rensselaer, 1975—. Precinct committeeman Republican party, Rensselaer, del. state conv., 1978, 82. Mem. Ind. Ins. Agts., Soc. Cert. Ins. Counselors (cert.), Profl. Ins. Agts. Assn., Rensselaer C. of C. (past v.p.). Lodges: Rotary (dir. 1982—), Masons, Shriners (Rensselaer). Home: PO Box 1 Rensselaer IN 47978 Office: 116 W Washington St Rensselaer IN 47978

SMITH, NANCY MCCLAIN, psychologist; b. Batesville, Ind., June 24, 1948; d. R. Stanley and Marjorie J. (Littell) M.; m. William F. Smith, May 7, 1976. B.A., Ball State U., 1970, M.A., 1971; Ph.D., Ind. State U., 1977. Cert. in pvt. practice, Ind., Ohio; lic. sch. psychologist, Ind., Mich. Instr. ednl. psychology Ball State U., Muncie, Ind., 1973-74, 81—; psychometrist New Castle (Ind.) Community Schs., 1974-75; psychologist, career edn. coordinator, dir. psychol. services Ind. Sch. for Deaf, Indpls., 1977-81; psychologist Adult & Child Mental Health Ctr., Indpls., 1981—; pvt. practice psychology, 1981—; cons. Mich. Sch. for Deaf, 1978-79. Mem. adv. council Deaf Rehab. Services, Wayne County, Mich., 1978-79; del. Conf. on Future of Sch. Psychology, 1981. Mem. Am. Psychol. Assn., Ind. Psychol. Assn., Nat. Assn. Sch. Psychologists, Soc. Personality Assessment, Nat. Assn. for Deaf, Phi Delta Kappa. Contbr. articles to profl. jours. Home: 8263 Harcourt Apt 234D Indianapolis IN 46260

SMITH, NEAL EDWARD, congressman; b. Hedrick, Iowa, Mar 23, 1920; s. James N. and Margaret M. (Walling) S.; student U. Mo., 1945-46, Syracuse U., 1946-47; LL.B., Drake U., 1950; m. Beatrix Havens, Mar. 23, 1945; children—Douglas, Sharon. Farmer, Iowa, 1937—; admitted to Iowa bar, 1950; practiced in Des Moines, 1950—; atty. 50 sch. bds. in Iowa, 1953—; asst. county atty. Polk County, Iowa, 1951; mem. 86th-92d Congresses from 5th Dist. Iowa, 93d-99th Congresses from 4th Dist. Iowa. Chmn. Polk County Bd. Social Welfare, 1954-56; pres. Young Democratic Clubs Am., 1953-55. Served with AUS, World War II. Decorated Air medal with 4 oak leaf clusters, Purple Heart. Mem. Am. Bar Assn., Farm Bur., Farmers Union., DAV. Club: Masons. Office: 2373 Rayburn House Office Bldg Washington DC 20515

SMITH, OTHA WILLIAM, softball association administrator; b. Omaha, Aug. 31, 1925; s. Otha William and Alice Hattie (Clark) W.; m. Audra Ellen Barnes, June 27, 1943; children—Michael Eugene, Pamela Jo, Rocella Ann. Grad. high sch., Wisner, Nebr. Ptnr. Smith & Clark Trucking, Brekendrige, Colo., 1947-49; dept. mgr. Gamble Skogmo, Inc., Fremont, Nebr., 1952-67; dist. mgr. Century Mfg. Co., Mpls., 1968-80; ecex. dir. Nebr. Softball Assn., Fremont, 1980—, also pres., 1965-76; v.p. Amateur Softball Assn. Am., 1971-72, 81-82, 85—; founder, pres. Nebr. Sports Council, 1984—. Founder, Women's Coll. World Series, 1969, Nebr. Softball Scholarship Program, 1974, Nebr. Softball Hall of Fame, 1977. Served as pvt. U.S. Army, 1941-45. Named Admiral, Great Navy of Nebr., State of Nebr., 1977; named to Nebr. Softball Hall of Fame, 1980. Mem. Nebr. Congress Parents and Tchrs. (life) Nebr. Parks and Recreation Assn. (spl. award 1983), Am. Legion (comdr. 1955-56). Republican. Lodges: Lions (pres. 1984-85). Avocations: fishing; golf. Home: 1840 N C St Fremont NE 68025

SMITH, PATRICIA ANN, lawyer; b. Cin., Oct. 31, 1953; d. Raymond Joseph and Ruth Jane (Kief) S. B.B.A., U. Cin., 1975, J.D., 1978. Bar: Ohio 1979. Staff atty. Ohio Bur. Workers' Compensation, Columbus, 1979-81, asst. law dir., 1981—; sole practice, Cin. and Columbus, 1979—. Active, League Women Voters, Columbus, 1980-82; dir. community involvement Columbus Jaycee Women, 1981-82, treas., 1982. Mem. Columbus Bar Assn. (past mem. workers' compensation, unauthorized practice law and notary pub. coms.), Mensa (local exec. com.), Phi Alpha Delta. Home: 1989 W Fifth Ave Apt E Columbus OH 43212 Office: Ohio Bur Workers' Compensation 246 N High St Columbus OH 43215

SMITH, PATRICIA O'DONNELL, diabetes educator, nurse; b. New Rochelle, N.Y., Apr. 3, 1933; d. Lester Haywood and Isabel (Snyder) O'Donnell; m. John James Smith, July 10, 1955; children—Kim Patricia, Karen Leslie Smith Kramer. Diploma, New Rochelle Hosp. Sch. Nursing, 1954; B.S. in Nursing summa cum laude, Worcester State Coll., 1978. Staff nurse New Rochelle Hosp., 1954-55; pediatric office nurse Norman Survis M.D., New Rochelle, 1955-57; staff nurse New Rochelle Hosp., 1959-62, Glover Hosp., Needham, Mass., 1971-78, diabetic resource nurse, 1978-81, outpatient teaching nurse, 1978-81; diabetes supr., clinician/educator Jewish Hosp., Cin., 1982—; co-sponsor, educator Eastern Hills Diabetes Support Group, Cin., 1983-84. Recipient Med. Theory award New Rochelle Hosp. Sch. Nursing, 1954. Fellow Am. Diabetes Assn.; mem. Am. Diabetes Educators Cin. Republican. Episcopalian. Lodge: Eastern Star. Home: 2860 Lengel Rd Cincinnati OH 45244 Office: Jewish Hosp Burnet Ave Cincinnati OH 45229

SMITH, PAULINE ROSALEE, educational administrator, consultant; b. Lawton, Okla., July 16, 1928; d. Robert Paul and Elsie (Tahkofper) Chaat; A.A., Cameron State U., 1948; B.S., Okla. State U., 1950, M.S., 1960; m. Clodus R. Smith, June 25, 1950; children—Martha Lynn, William Paul, Paula Diane. Tchr., public schs., Bradley, Okla., 1950-52, Booker, Tex., 1953-54, Candor, N.Y., 1957-59, Silver Spring Md., Burtonsville, Md., 1961-74; project mgr. Indian Edn. Services, Cleveland City Schs., 1977-83; vis. instr. Cleve. State U., 1978-83. Bd. dirs. Women Space, 1977-81, Council Econ. Opportunity, Cleve., 1981-83; mem. ACCESS bd. Cuyahoga Community Coll.; chmn. Lau Adv. Task Force Cleve. City Schs., 1979-80. Recipient Career Woman of Achievement award Cleve. YWCA, 1979. Mem. AAUW (pres. Cleve. 1981), Indian Edn. Assn. Ohio (pres. 1981), Nat. Indian Edn. Assn. (bd. dirs. 1983—), Citizens League Cleve., Assn. Childhood Edn., Assn. Supervision and Curriculum Devel., Phi Delta Kappa. Democrat. Methodist. Clubs: Zonta, Womens City, Women's Law Fund (bd. dirs. 1981—). Home: Box 338 Rio Grande OH 45674

SMITH, PETER WILSON, symphony administrator; b. Utica, N.Y., Mar. 15, 1938; s. Stanley W. and Frances (Brown) S.; m. Kay Gardner, 1960 (div. 1972); children—Juliana, Jennifer; m. Lynn Perrott, 1976. B.Mus., U. Mich., 1965. Asst. mgr. Indpls. Symphony, 1966-67; asst. mgr. St. Louis Symphony, 1967-68; exec. dir. Norfolk Symphony, Va., 1968-72; ops. mgr. Buffalo Philharmonic, 1972-74; ops. adminstr. Carnegie Hall Corp., N.Y.C., 1974-76; mng. dir. Fort Wayne Philharmonic, Ind., 1976-85; gen. mgr. Grand Rapids Symphony, Mich., 1985—. Served to airman 1st class USAF, 1961-64. Mem. Met. Orch. Mgrs. Assn. (pres. 1979-81), Am. Symphony Orch. League. Office: Grand Rapids Symphony 415 Exhibitors Plaza Grand Rapids MI 49503

SMITH, PHILIP LAWRENCE, physiology educator; b. Brunswick, Maine, June 19, 1949; s. Oscar Samuel and Mary Anna (Utecht) S. B.A., U. Maine, 1972, M.S., Northeastern U., 1975, Ph.D., 1978. Postdoctoral fellow U. Chgo., 1978-79, U. Tex.-Houston, 1979-81; asst. prof. physiology U. Kans., Kansas City, 1981—. Contbr. articles to profl. jours. Served with U.S. Army, 1970-76. USPHS research grantee, 1982; Am. Heart Assn. research grantee, 1983. Mem. Am. Physiol. Soc., Soc. Gen. Physiologists, N.Y. Acad. Sci., Phi Kappa Phi. Methodist. Office: Dept Physiology 39th and Rainbow Kansas City KS 66103

SMITH, PHYLLIS ALYSE, edn. coordinator; b. Dayton, Ohio, Jan. 7, 1926; d. Harold Hamlin and Georgia Alice (Williams) Shaw; B.Ed., U. Dayton, 1960; m. Lee Wilford Smith, May 5, 1947, (dec.); children—Patricia Antoinette, Christi Collette. Clk., Wright-Patterson AFB, Ohio, 1947-54; sec., bookkeeper Atlantic Bldrs., Inc., Dayton, 1954-58; tchr. Dayton Bd. Edn., 1960-73; edn. coordinator Dayton Newspapers, Inc., 1973—, mem. Jour. Herald Newspaper in Edn. Program; mem. Area XI Right to Read Com., Mem. Nat. Council Tchrs. English, Nat. Council Social Studies Ohio, Assn. of Supervision and Curriculum Devel., Career Guidance Inst., NAACP, Urban League, Alpha Kappa Alpha. Episcopalian. Clubs: Order Eastern Star, Nat. Epicureans Inc. Home: 1505 Bryn Mawr Dr Dayton OH 45406 Office: The Commerical Appeal 495 Union Ave Memphis TN 38103

SMITH, RICHARD JAY, orthodontist, educator; b. Bklyn., Aug. 10, 1948; s. Benjamin and Miriam (Cohen) S.; m. Linda Sharon Harris, Aug. 22, 1970; children—Jason Andrew, Owen Harris, Hilary Rachele. B.A., Bklyn. Coll., CUNY, 1969; M.S. in Anatomy, Tufts U., 1973, D.M.D., 1973; Ph.D. in Anthropology, Yale U., 1980. Asst. clin. prof. orthodontics U. Conn., Farmington, 1976-79; asst. prof. U. Md., Balt., 1979-81, assoc. prof., 1981-84; prof. orthodontics, biomed. sci. and pathology, chmn. dept. orthodontics, adj. prof. anthropology Washington U., St. Louis, 1984—, cons. orthodontics Cleft Palate and Craniofacial Anomalies Team, 1984—; vis. assoc. prof. cell biology Sch. Medicine, Johns Hopkins U., Balt., 1980-84. Editor-in-chief Jour. Balt. Coll. Dental surgery, 1981-84. Contbr. numerous articles in orthodontics, anthropology, comparative biology to profl. jours. Am. Fund for Dental Health dental tchr. tng. fellow, 1977-78; NIH postdoctoral fellow, 1978-79. Mem. ADA, Alumni Assn. Student Clinicians (bd. govs. 1984—, Alan J. Davis award 1983), Am. Assn. Orthodontists, Am. Assn. Phys. Anthropologists, Internat. Assn. Dental Research, Internat. Primatological Soc. Home: 816 S Bemiston Ave Clayton MO 63105 Office: Washington U Sch Dental Medicine 4559 Scott Ave Saint Louis MO 63110

SMITH, ROBERT B., hospital administrator; b. Downey, Calif., Feb. 9, 1937; m. Judith Smith; 2 children. B.S., Calif. State U.-Northridge, 1963; M.B.A., Calif. State U.-Long Beach, 1970; Cert. in Hosp. Adminstrn., Ohio State U., 1978. Adminstrv. trainee Los Angeles County Chief Adminstrv. Office, 1963-64, adminstrv. aid, 1964-66, adminstrv. analyst, 1966; mem. staff Los Angeles County-Harbor-UCLA Med. Ctr., 1966-71; adminstr. Los Angeles County Wesley Hosp., 1971-72; adminstr. UCLA Med. Ctr., 1972-74; exec. dir. Los Angeles County-U. So. Calif. Med. Ctr., 1974-75; dir. hosp. and clinics U. Calif.-Davis Med. Ctr., 1975-79, assoc. clin. prof., 1975-79; chief exec. officer U. Mo.-Columbia Hosp. and Clinics, 1979—; cons. and lectr. in field. Contbr. articles to profl. jours. Mem. Am. Coll. Hosp. Adminstrs., Mo. Hosp. Assn. (vice chmn. research policy com.), C. of C. (bd. dirs. Columbia, Mo. 1982-84), Calif. Hosp. Assn., Sacramento-Sierra Hosp. Assn. (treas. exec. com. 1975-79), Hosp. Council So. Calif. (com. chmn. 1971-74). Address: 1W17 Hosp and Clinics U Mo Columbia MO 65211

SMITH, ROBERT EARL, dentist; b. Merryville, La., Oct. 30, 1932; s. Matthew Robert and Lottie Viola (Johnson) S.; m. Kathryn Isabel Tilly, June 4, 1953; children—Victoria Lynn Stretch, Robert Brent. B.S., U. Okla., 1954; D.D.S., U. Mo.-Kansas City, 1958. Gen. practice dentistry, Kansas City, 1958—. Mem. ADA, Mo. Dental Assn., Kansas City Dist. Dental Soc. (pres. 1975), Kansas City Dental Abstract Study Club (pres. 1968). Episcopalian. Clubs: Saddle and Sirloin (Leawood, Kans.) (pres. 1980-81); Mission Valley Hunt (Stilwell, Kans.) (v.p.). Avocations: horseback riding; foxhunting. Home: 8814 Alhambra Dr Prairie Village KS 66207

SMITH, ROBERT JOHN, office equipment co. exec.; b. Indpls. Feb. 4, 1927; s. Samuel R. and Rosemary (Berry) S.; B.S. in Bus., Butler U., 1950; M.S., U. Pitts., 1951; m. Arlene Ann Sondgerath, Aug. 19, 1950; children—Pat and Michael (twins), Kathleen, Daniel, Timothy, Robert. Sales agt. Marchant Calculating, Lafayette, Ind., 1951-54; founder, pres. Smith Office Equip. Co., Lafayette, 1955—. Mem. St. Thomas Ch. adv. bd., Lafayette, 1960-63; pres. Lafayette Area Parochial Fund dr., 1968. Served with U.S. Army, 1945-47. Decorated Army Commendation medal. Named Man of the Yr., Marchant Calculators, 1953; Gestetner Outstanding Dist. Dealer, 1968. Mem. Lafayette C. of C., Nat. Office Machine Assn., Nat. Office Products Assn. Democrat. Roman Catholic. Clubs: K.C., Lafayette Country. Home: 3521 S 100 St E Lafayette IN 47905 Office: 311 Sagamore Pkwy N Lafayette IN 47904

SMITH, ROBERT MASON, university official, management consultant; b. Fort Sill, Okla., May 5, 1945; s. Arnold Mason and Lillyan (Scott) S.; m. Ramona Lynne Stukey, June 15, 1968; children—David, Angela. B.A., Wichita State U., 1967; M.A., Ohio U., 1968; Ph.D., Temple U., 1976. Debate coach Princeton U. (N.J.), 1971-73; dir. oral communication Wichita State U. (Kans.), 1973-77, chmn. dept. speech communication, 1974-77, assoc. dean Coll. Liberal Arts and Scis., 1977-80, 81—, assoc. dean Univ. Coll. and Continuing Edn., 1981—; spl. asst. Office of Sec., U.S. Dept. HHS, Washington, 1980-81; cons. in field. Contbr. articles to profl. jours. Trustee, Leadership Kans., 1982—; bd. dirs. Sedgwick County unit Am. Heart Assn., 1982—; pres. Citizen Participation Council, Wichita, 1981—; bd. dirs. planning div. Sedgwick County United Way, 1981—. Recipient Univ. Leadership award Wichita State U., 1978; Kans. Leadership award Kans. Assn. Commerce and Industry, 1982; Excellence in Teaching award Council for Advancement and Support of Edn., 1984; HHS fellow, 1980. Mem. Am. Forensic Assn. (editorial bd. 1973-79), Kans. Speech Communication Assn. (Outstanding Coll. Speech Tchr. award 1977, pres. 1978), Assn. Communication Adminstrn. (chmn. profl. devel. com. 1980), Am. Mgmt. Assn., Am. Conf. Acad. Deans., Internat. Communication Assn., Phi Kappa Phi, Phi Eta Sigma, Delta Sigma Rho-Tau Kappa Alpha, Beta Theta Pi. Republican. Baptist. Home: 553 N Fountain Wichita KS 67208 Office: Office of Dean Coll Liberal Arts and Scis Wichita State Univ Wichita KS 67208

SMITH, ROBERT RANDALL, retail food store executive; b. Lancaster, Pa., Oct. 12, 1943; s. Robert Allen and Maude Mabel (Gardner) S.; m. Judy Anne Weaver, Sept. 9, 1968; children—Christopher Andrew, Bowen Timothy, Prescott Chandler. Student, Boston U., 1961. Vice pres. Robert A. Smith & Son, Realtors-Appraisers, Lancaster, 1968-74; exec. v.p. Horst & Lichty Ltd. Sporting Goods, Lancaster, 1974-75; exec. dir. Lancaster Parking Authority, 1975-79; mktg. mgr. Penn Dairies, Inc., Lancaster, 1979-82; mktg. dir. P.D.Q. Food Stores, Inc., Madison, Wis., 1982—. Mem. adv. bd. Lancaster County Planning Commn., 1970-72; dir. youth league YMCA, Lancaster, 1974-76. Recipient Community Service award Lancaster YMCA, 1975. Mem. Nat. Assn. Realtors, Nat. Assn. Convenience Stores, Pa. Food Mchts. Assn., Am. Mktg. Assn. (compensation panel), Sales and Mktg. Execs. Internat. Presbyterian. Clubs: Lancaster Country, Hamilton. Home: 7621 Westchester Dr Middleton WI 53562 Office: PO Box 5068 Madison WI 53705

SMITH, ROBERT STANLEY, librarian; b. Pitts., Sept. 4, 1943; s. Robert L. and Helen J. (Kalinoski) S. B.A., Duquesne U., 1966; M.L.S., U. Pitts., 1967, advanced cert. in library sci., 1976. Br. mgr. Cuyahoga County Pub. Library, Cleve., 1971-82, automation coordinator, 1982-84; city librarian Livonia Pub. Library, Mich., 1984—. Annotator: Fiction for Youth, 1977. Pres., Berea Community Ctr., Ohio, 1975; chmn. steering com. Youth Services Coordinating Council, Cleve., 1983; treas. SW Youth Council, Berea, 1984; bd. dirs., Oakway Symphony Orch., Livonia, 1985. Mem. ALA (council 1981-85), Mich. Library Assn. Home: 28475 W Chicago St Livonia MI 48150 Office: Livonia Pub Library 32901 Plymouth Rd Livonia MI 48150

SMITH, ROBERT STEVE, refinery construction project manager; b. Springfield, Mo., June 29, 1943; s. Fred A. and Helen G. (Whitehead) S.; m. Linda Ann Payne, Jan. 8, 1966; children—Barry S., Gregory J., Sean F. B.S. in C.E., Mo. Sch. Mines and Metallurgy, 1965. Registered profl. engr., Kans. Project engr. Shell Oil Co., Deer Park, Tex., 1965-69; sales mgr. air pollution control Koch Engring. Co., Inc., Wichita, Kans., N.Y.C., 1972-74; pres. R. S. Smith & Assoc., Wichita, 1974-77; sr. project egr. Litwin Engrs., Wichita, 1977-84, project mgr., 1984—. Vice pres. Third Order St. Francis, Wichita, 1979-81, pres. Midwest region, 1981; v.p. St. Anthonys Parish Council, Wichita, 1983-84, pres., 1984-85. Mem. Tau Beta Pi, Phi Kappa Phi, Republican. Roman Catholic. Home: 1844 N Turquoise St Wichita KS 67212 Office: Litwin Engrs & Constructors Inc 110 N Market St Wichita KS 67212

SMITH, ROBERT W., consumer research executive; b. Rochester, N.Y., Sept. 17, 1942; s. Paul V. and Ethel M. (Hornbuckle) S.; m. Jo Ann Tomlin, Aug. 22, 1964; children—Jeff, Kent. B.A., Wichita State U., 1965; M.S., Ga. State U., 1979. Mgr. Market Facts, Chgo., 1964-71, Theo Hamm, St. Paul, 1971-72; systems analyst Anderson Clayton Co., Dallas, 1972-73; mgr. Coca Cola U.S.A., Atlanta, 1973-81; v.p. Maritz Mkt. Research Co., Fenton, Mo., 1981-84; dir. Decision Support Services, Eden Prairie, Minn., 1984—. Mem. Am. Mktg. Assn., Am. Statis. Assn. Democrat. Episcopalian. Home: 841 Oriole Ln Chaska MN 55318 Office: Decision Support Services 11000 W 78th St Eden Prairie MN 55344

SMITH, ROGER BONHAM, automotive manufacturing company executive; b. Columbus, Ohio, July 12, 1925; s. Emmet Quimby and Bess (Obetz) S.; m. Barbara Ann Rasch, June 7, 1954; children—Roger Bonham, Jennifer Anne, Victoria Belle, Drew Johnson. Student U. Mich., 1942-44, B.B.A., 1947, M.B.A., 1949. With Gen. Motors, Detroit, 1949—, treas., 1970-71, v.p. charge fin. staff, 1971-73, v.p., group exec. in charge of non-automotive and def. staff, 1973-74, exec. v.p., 1974-75, vice chmn. fin. com., 1975-81, chmn., chief exec. officer, 1981—. Trustee Cranbrook Ednl. Community, Bloomfield Hills, Mich., Mich. Colls. Found., Detroit; mem. Bus. Council; mem. planning and policy com. Bus. Roundtable. Served with USNR, 1944-46. Mem. Motor Vehicle Mfrs. Assn. (chmn., bd. dirs.). Clubs: Detroit, Detroit Athletic; Orchard Lake Country (Mich.); Bloomfield Hills Country (Mich.); Links (N.Y.C.). Office: 3044 Grand Blvd Detroit MI 48202

SMITH, ROGER PERRY, physician, educator; b. Tucson, Jan. 31, 1949; B.S., Purdue U., 1969; B.S.M., Northwestern U., 1969, M.D., 1972; m. Barbara Ann Nason, May 25, 1974; children—Scott Andrew, Jeffrey Todd. Intern, Chgo. Wesley Meml. Hosp., 1972-73; resident in Ob-Gyn, Northwestern Meml. Hosp.-McGaw Med. Center, 1973-76, Prentice Women's Hosp. and Maternity Center, Chgo., 1973-76; clin. asst. prof. Sch. Clin. Medicine, U. Ill., Champaign-Urbana, 1979—; attending staff Carle Found. Hosp., Urbana, 1976—; mem. courtesy staff Burnham City Hosp., Mercy Hosp., McKinley Hosp., Paris (Ill.) Community Hosp. Fellow Am. Coll. Obstetricians and Gynecologists; mem. Central Assn. Ob-Gyn (Community Hosp. award 1979, 83), Am. Inst. Ultrasound in Medicine, Assn. Advancement of Med. Instrumentation, Am. Fedn. Clin. Research, Ill. Obstetrical and Gynecol. Soc. (asst. sec. 1976-79, sec., 1979—), Ill. Assn. Maternal and Child Health, AMA, Ill. State Med. Soc., Chgo. Med. Soc., Champaign County Med. Soc., Mensa. Contbr. articles to profl. jours. Home: 2204 Galen Dr Champaign IL 61821 Office: Dept Obstetrics and Gynecology Carle Clinic Assn 602 W University Ave Urbana IL 61801

SMITH, RUTH HUNTER, lawyer; b. Columbus, Ohio, Dec. 23, 1949; d. Richard F. and Bernice E. (Strawser) Hunter; m. Joel T. Smith (div. 1972); 1 child, Jason. B.S.Ed. Ohio State U., 1973, Juris Doctor, 1977. Bar: Ohio 1977. Tchr. Columbus Pub. Schs., 1973-74; cons. Franklin County Mcpl. Ct., Columbus, 1975-76; research asst. Ohio State U. Coll. Law, Columbus, 1976, law clerk Vorys, Sater, Seymour, Columbus, 1976-77; legal counsel John W. Galbreath & Co., Columbus and Denver, 1977—lctr. Northwest Ctr. Profl. Ed., Portland, Oreg., 1984. Vol. Am. Cancer Soc., Columbus, 1984, Mother's March of Dimes, Columbus, 1984-85. Milton R. Bierly scholar, 1972; Ohio State U. Coll. Law scholar, 1974-76. Mem. ABA, Ohio State Bar Assn., Columbus Bar Assn., Franklin County Women Lawyers Assn. Republican. Roman Catholic. Office: John W Galbreath & Co 180 E Broad St Columbus OH 43215 also 1560 Broadway Denver CO 80202

SMITH, STEVEN DICKINSON, electronics co. exec.; b. Indpls., Sept. 13, 1953; s. Gerald Dickinson and Dorothy Jane S.; m. Carol G. B.S. in Bus., Ind. U., 1976. Mech. engr., ops. mgr. Mouron & Co., Indpls., 1972-74; mech. engr. Carson Mfg. Co., Indpls., 1974-75; mfg. mgr. Internat. Energy Mgmt. Corp., Indpls., 1975-78; founder, 1978, since pres. Manutek, Inc., Indpls. Mem. IEEE, Indpls. C. of C., Sports Car Club Am. Republican. Presbyterian. Office: 8108 Zionsville Rd Indianapolis IN 46268

SMITH, THOMAS DWIGHT, telephone company executive; b. Chariton, Iowa, Nov. 30, 1938; s. Harold and Carrie Smith; m. Janet E. Hess; 1 child, Michael S. B.B.A., U. Iowa, 1962; M.B.A., Creighton U., 1968. With Northwestern Bell Telephone Co., 1962—, mgmt. trainee, Des Moines, 1962, asst. toll supr., 1963, asst. acct., Omaha, 1963, acctg. supr., 1965, 66, 67, dist. acctg. mgr. revenue, Omaha, data processing, Omaha, 1969, data systems cons., Omaha, 1971, gen. data systems supr., Omaha, 1972-75, asst. comptroller, Omaha, 197-80, treas., Omaha, 1980-83, v.p. advanced info. markets, Omaha, 1983, v.p., chief exec. officer-Iowa, Des Moines, 1983—; dir. internal auditing AT&T, 1978, Bankers Trust, Des Moines, mem. audit com., loan com. Trustee Drake U.; bd. dirs. United Way, Des Moines Metro YMCA, Social Settlement Assn. of Omaha, Omaha Awareness and Action; mem. Greater Des Moines Com; chmn. Des Moines YWCA Strategic Adv. Com.; exec. bd. dirs. Mid Iowa Council Boy Scouts Am.; mem. Am. Heart Assn. Corp. Cabinet; mem. utilities adv. com. Iowa Coll. Found.; v.p. Omaha Symphony Council; mem. exec. com. program, planning and budget com. United Way of the Midlands. Mem. Iowa Telephone Assn. (bd. dirs.), Greater Des Moines C. of C. (bd. dirs., exec. com. of bus. and urban devel.), Am. Mgmt. Assn., Beta Gamma Sigma. Avocations: golf; hunting; physical fitness. Home: 2417 70th Pl Des Moines IA 50322 Office: Northwestern Bell Telephone Co 909 High St Des Moines IA 50309

SMITH, THOMAS EDWARD, social welfare educator; b. Kamakura, Japan, Dec. 5, 1951; came to U.S., 1968; s. Robert L. and Aki (Sato) S. B.S., U. Wash., 1975, M.S.W., 1978, Ph.D., 1982. Crisis counselor Valley Gen. Hosp., Renton, Wash., 1975-76; research asst. Child Devel. and Mental Retardation Ctr., Seattle, 1977-81; instr. Sch. Social Welfare, U. Wis.-Milw., 1981-82, asst. prof., 1982-85, assoc. prof., 1985—; clinician, mem. faculty Family Service of Milw. Seattle Drug Commn. grantee, 1981-82. Mem. Nat. Assn. Social Workers, Acad. Cert. Social Workers, Council on Social Work Edn., Am. Assn. Marriage and Family Therapy (clin. mem.). Contbr. numerous articles to profl. jours. Office: Dept Social Welfare U Wis-Milw PO Box 786 Milwaukee WI 53201

SMITH, THOMAS HAMILTON, IV, optometrist; b. Cedar Rapids, Iowa, Dec. 20, 1943; s. Thomas Hamilton and V. Darlene (Foster) S.; m. Sheryl Ann Cochran, June 17, 1967; children—Tom, Chad, Lynn. O.D., Ill. Coll. Optometry, 1968. Pvt. practice optometry, Chgo., 1968-69, Fergus Falls, Minn., 1969-76, 81—; optometrist Profl. Corp., Fergus Falls, 1976-81. Pres. Otter chpt. Izaak Walton League, 1983. Fellow Coll. Optometrists in Vision Devel.; mem. Am. Optometric Assn., Minn. Optometric Assn., Am. Acad. Optometry. Republican. Baptist. Avocation: photography. Home: 314 N Whitford Fergus Falls MN 56537 Office: 210 N Cascade Box 96 Fergus Falls MN 56537

SMITH, VIRGINIA DODD, congresswoman; b. Randolph, Iowa, June 30, 1911; d. Clifton Clark and Erville (Reeves) Dodd; A.B., U. Nebr., 1936; m. Haven N. Smith, Aug. 27, 1931. Nat. pres. Am. Country Life Assn., 1951-54; nat. chmn. Am. Farm Bur. Women, 1954-74; dir. Am. Farm Bur. Fedn., 1954-74, Country Women's Council; world dep. pres. Assn. Country Women of World, 1962-68; mem. Dept. Agr. Nat. Home Econs. Research adv. com., 1960-65; mem. Crusade for Freedom European Inspection tour, 1958; del. Republican Nat. Conv., 1956, 72; bd. govs. Agrl. Hall of Fame; mem. Nat. Livestock and Meat Bd., 1955-58, Nat. Commn. Community Health Services, 1963-66; adv. mem. Nebr. Sch. Bds. Assns., 1949; mem. bd. edn. Nebr. State Colls., 1950-60; mem. Nebr. Territorial Centennial Commn., 1953, Gov.'s Commn. Status of Women, 1964-66; chmn. Presdl. Task Force on Rural Devel., 1969-70; mem. 94th-99th Congresses from 3d Dist. Nebr., mem. appropriations com., agr., energy and water subcoms., ranking mem. minority agr. appropriations com. Vice pres. Farm Film Found., 1964-74. Recipient award of Merit, D.A.R., 1956; Disting. Service award U. Nebr., 1956, 60; award for best public address on freedom, Freedom Found., 1966; Eyes on Nebr. award Nebr. Optometric Assn., 1970; Internat. Service award Midwest Conf. World Affairs, 1970; Woman of Achievement award Nebr. Bus. and Profl. Women, 1971; selected as 1 of 6 U.S. women Govt. France for 3 week goodwill mission to France, 1969; Outstanding 4H Alumni award Iowa State U., 1973, 74; Nebr. Ak-Sar-Ben award, 1983; Watchdog of Treasury award, 1976, 78, 80, 82, 84, 85; Guardian of Small Bus. award, 1976, 78, 80, 82, 84, 85; Farm Safety award Nat. Safety Council, 1983. Mem. AAUW, Delta Kappa Gamma (state hon. mem.), Beta Sigma Phi (internat. hon. mem.), Chi Omega, P.E.O. (past pres.). Methodist. Clubs: Bus. and Profl. Women, Order of Eastern Star. Good Will ambassador to Switzerland, 1950. Office: 2202 Rayburn House Office Bldg Washington DC 20515

SMITH, WALLACE BUNNELL, physician, church official; b. Independence, Mo., July 29, 1929; s. William Wallace and Rosamond (Bunnell) S.; A.A., Graceland Coll., Lamoni, Iowa, 1948; B.A., U. Kans., 1950, M.D., 1954; m. Anne M. McCullough, June 26, 1956; children—Carolyn, Julia, Laura. Intern, Charity Hosp. of La., 1955; resident in medicine, U. Kans. Med. Center, 1958, resident in ophthalmology, 1959-62; pvt. practice medicine specializing in ophthalmology, 1962-76; ordained to ministry Reorganized Ch. of Jesus Christ of Latter Day Saints, 1945; asso. pastor Walnut Park Congregation, Independence, Mo., 1966-1970, Pleasant Heights Congregation, Independence, 1975-76, center stake pres., 1969-71, president-designate Reorganized Ch. of Jesus Christ of Latter Day Saints, 1976-78, pres., 1978—; clin. asso. U. Kans. Med. Center, 1962-76; dir. Pacific Land Devel. Assn. Pres., bd. trustees Independence Sanitarium and Hosp.; trustee Am. Lung Assn., West Mo.; mem. 21st century com. Independence City Council. Served to lt. M.C., USNR, 1955-58. Diplomate Am. Bd. Ophthalmology. Fellow Am. Acad. Ophthalmology, A.C.S.; mem. AMA, Jackson County Med. Soc., Independence C. of C.,

Phi Beta Pi. Club: Rotary. Home: 337 Partridge Independence MO 64055 Office: Auditorium Box 1059 Independence MO 64051

SMITH, WALTER DELOS, accountant; b. Rensselaer, Ind., June 7, 1936; s. Walter Myron and Evelyn Geraldine (Murphy) S.; m. Yvonne Marie Dietz, Sept. 24, 1960; children—Michele, Michael, Kevin, Bryan, Denise, Derek. B.S. in Acctg., Walton Sch. Commerce, Chgo., 1960. C.P.A., Wis., Ill. Acct. Frazer & Torbet C.P.A.s, Chgo., 1960-66; asst. controller Rath-Packing Co., Waterloo, Iowa 1966-68; controller, treas. DeLeuw, Cather & Co., Chgo., 1968-72; corp. controller Mohawk Data Scis., Utica, N.Y., 1972-75; mgmt. cons. Walter D. Smith & Assocs., New Hartford, N.Y., 1975-76; v.p., gen. mgr. Flambeau-Plastics, Baraboo, Wis., 1976-83; prin. Walter D. Smith, C.P.A., Baraboo, 1983—; owner, pres. Fine Cabinet Shop, Inc., Baraboo, 1983—; mem. adv. panel U. Wis., Madison and Whitewater, 1981—; dir. Trachte Bldg. Systems, Madison. Pres. Downers Grove Drug Abuse Council, Ill., 1972; mem. Baraboo Area Opportunity Devel. Com., 1983—; bd. dirs. New Hartford Sch. Dist., 1974-76, Baraboo Sch. Dist., 1980-83. Served with AUS, 1955-56, Korea. Mem. Nat. Assn. Accts. (bd. dirs. 1966-67), Baraboo Toastmasters. Republican. Roman Catholic. Lodge: Kiwanis. Home: 809 Iroquois Circle Baraboo WI 53913 Office: Walter D Smith CPA 307 Oak St PO Box 15 Baraboo WI 53913

SMITH, WARD, manufacturing company executive; lawyer; b. Buffalo, Sept. 13, 1930; s. Andrew Leslie and Georgia (Ward) S.; student Georgetown U., 1948-49; A.B., Harvard, 1952; LLB., J.D., U. Buffalo, 1955; m. Gretchen Keller Diefendorf, Oct. 29, 1960; children—Jennifer Hood, Meredith Ward, Jonathan Andrew, Sarah Katherine. Admitted to N.Y. bar, 1955, Mass. bar, 1962, Ohio bar, 1977; asso. firm Lawler & Rockwood, N.Y.C., 1959-62; sec., gen. counsel Whitin Machine Works, Whitinsville, Mass., 1962-66; sec., White Consol. Industries, Inc., Cleve., 1966-69, v.p., 1967-69; sr. v.p. 1969-72, exec. v.p., 1972-76, pres., chief adminstrv. officer, 1976-84, pres., chief operating officer, 1984—; also dir.; dir. Centran Corp., Sundstrand Corp., N.Am. Coal Corp. Trustee Case-Western Res. U., Cleve. Orch., Univ. Hosps.; pres., trustee Cleve. Orch. Served to lt. USNR, 1955-59. Mem. ABA, N.Y. State Bar Assn. Clubs: Pepper Pike, Country (Pepper Pike, Ohio); Union (Cleve.). Office: 11770 Berea Rd Cleveland OH 44111

SMITH, WILBUR LAZEAR, radiologist, researcher, educator; b. Warwick, N.Y., Oct. 11, 1943; s. Wilbur and Betty (Norris) S.; m. Rebecca Rowlands, June 19, 1965; children—Jason, Daniel, Joanna, Noah, Ethan. B.A., SUNY-Buffalo, 1965, M.D., 1969. Diplomate Am. Bd. Radiology, Am. Acad. Pediatrics. Intern Buffalo Children's Hosp., 1969-71; resident Cin. Gen. and Children Hosp., 1971-74; asst. prof. Ind. U., Indpls., 1975-78, assoc. prof., 1978-80, acting dir. pediatric radiology, 1979-80; assoc. prof. U. Iowa, Iowa City, 1980-82, prof., 1982—, dir. med. edn. radiology, 1980—, dir. pediatric radiology, 1980—. Contbr. articles to profl. jours. Served with USAR, 1969-77. Recipient Merke Prize Medicine award SUNY, 1968, Wurlitzer Prize Medicine SUNY, 1968. Mem. Am. Coll. Radiology, Soc. Pediatric Radiology (chmn. syllibus com. 1984, mem. program com. 1984—), Radiol. Soc. N.Am., Johnson County Med. Soc. Avocations: photography; amateur soccer coach. Office: Dept Radiology Clinic U Iowa Newton Rd Iowa City IA 52242

SMITH, WILDA MAXINE, history educator; b. Gove, Kans., May 17, 1924; d. Corwin Leroy and Mabel Luzelle (Roberts) Smith. A.B. in History, Ft. Hays Kans. State Coll., 1953, M.S., 1957; Ph.D., U. Ill., 1960. Tchr. pub. schs., Gove County, Kans., 1943-49; tchr. history Hays High Sch., Kans., 1953-57; asst. prof. history Ft. Hays Kans. State Coll., 1960-63, assoc. prof., 1963-66, prof. history, 1966—, chmn. dept. history, 1981—. Contbr. articles to profl. jours. Mem. Kans. Com. for Humanities, Topeka, 1982—; bd. dirs. Kans. Hist. Soc., 1982—. U. Ill. fellow, 1958-60; named Prof. of Month, Student Council, Ft. Hays State Coll., 1965, W.C. Wood award, 1975; Pilot award, Srs. and Alumni Assn. Bd., 1984. Mem. Orgn. Am. Historians, Nat. Women's Studies Assn. (nat. coordinating council, 1977-80), Kans. History Tchrs. Assn. (exec. bd. 1973), ACLU, Common Cause, LWV, NOW, Ft. Hays Faculty Assn. (pres 1966-67), Phi Kappa Phi (pres. 1967-68). Avocations: fishing; traveling. Home: 2924 Walnut Hays KS 67601 Office: Fort Hays State U 600 Park St Hays KS 67601-4099

SMITH, WILLIAM STANLEY, construction company executive; b. Chgo., July 7, 1933; s. Stanley William and Lillie Lou (Peck) S.; m. Susan D. Dixson, Dec. 21, 1957; children—Cynthia Elizabeth, Nancy Anne, Christine Louise. B.A., Beloit Coll., 1955. Indsl. relations mgr. Container Corp. Am., Chgo., 1955-60; v.p. Crampton, Inc., 1960-78, pres., 1978—. Mem. Archtl. Woodworkers Inst., Nat. Club Assn. Republican. Presbyterian. Clubs: Glen Oak Country, Perry Park Country. Home: 844 Woodland Dr Glen Ellyn IL 60137 Office: Crampton Inc 7437 S Vincennes Chicago IL 60621

SMITH, WILLIAM WAYNE, businessman, consultant; b. Uniontown, Pa., Aug. 5, 1926; s. Wayne W. and Mable D. (Keller) S.; m. Phyllis Marie Schumacher, Aug. 25, 1955; children—Sherilyn M., James W. B.A., Am. U., Washington, 1949; B.Th., Grace Sem., 1952. Vice pres. Potomac Oxygen Co., Alexandria, Va., 1961-82; pres. Merrywood Homes, Winona Lake, Ind., 1973-83; cons. Brethren Home Missions, Winona Lake, 1980—. Vol. ARC, Warsaw, Ind., 1966. Mem. Nat. Assn. Evangelicals. Republican. Grace Brethren. Avocation: collect classic automobiles. Home: 411 Auditorium Blvd Winona Lake IN 46590

SMITH, WORTHINGTON LEHURAY, transportation exec.; b. Tacoma, Feb. 12, 1925; s. Worthington C. and Doris (LeHuray) S.; B.A., Yale, 1950; M.A., U. Minn., 1953; postgrad. Harvard Bus. Sch., 1967; m. Elizabeth Ann Getzoff, June 30, 1950; children—Worthington R., Scott, Nancy. With Great No. R.R., 1954-70; with Burlington No., Inc., Seattle and St. Paul, 1970-72; pres. Chgo., Milw., St. Paul & Pacific R.R., Chgo., 1972-79, pres., chief exec. officer, 1979—, also dir. Served with AUS, 1943-46, 51-52. Mem. Nat. Freight Traffic Assn., Am. Soc. Traffic and Transp., Traffic Club Chgo., Western Ry. Club. Club: Met. (Chgo.). Office: Chgo Milw St Paul & Pacific RR 516 W Jackson Blvd Chicago IL 60606

SMITHBURG, WILLIAM DEAN, food products company executive; b. Chgo., July 9, 1938; s. Pearl L. and Margaret L. (Savage) S.; B.S., DePaul U., 1960; M.B.A., Northwestern U., 1961; m. Alberta Hap, May 25, 1963; children—Susan, Thomas. Research analyst Leo Burnett Co., 1961-63; sr. account exec. McCann-Erickson, Inc., 1963-66; with Quaker Oats Co., Chgo., 1966—, v.p., 1971, pres. foods div., 1975, corp. exec. v.p., 1976-79, pres., chief operating officer, 1979-81, pres., chief exec. officer, 1981-83, chmn., chief exec. officer, 1983—, also dir. Served with USAR, 1959-60. Roman Catholic. Office: Quaker Oats Co 345 Merchandise Mart Plaza Chicago IL 60654*

SMITHER, JESS P., oil company executive; b. Indpls., Apr. 19, 1922; s. Jess P. and Ethie (Hicks) S.; m. Edith May Sullivan, Dec. 27, 1943; children—John M., Sharon S., Richard A. B.S. in Chemistry, Ind. Central U., 1953. Chemist, D-A Lubricant Co., Inc., Indpls., 1953-60, chief chemist, 1960-65, mgr. prodn. and research, 1965-70, v.p. prodn. and research, 1970-77, sr. v.p., 1977—. Contbr. articles to profl. jours. Mem. Ind. Lubricant Mfrs. Assn. Republican. Methodist. Club: Valle Vista Country (Greenwood). Lodges: Shriners, Masons. Avocations: computers; golf. Home: 1085 Fiesta Dr Greenwood IN 46142 Office: D-A Lubricant Co Inc 1340 W 29th St Indianapolis IN 46206

SMITHMIER, DENNIS WILLIAM, lawyer; b. Independence, Mo., Oct. 28, 1943; s. Henry Benjamin and Opal Alice (Thomas) S.; m. Gail Ruth Lampshire, July 29, 1967; children—Lynn, Amy, Matthew. A.A., Los Angeles Harbor Coll., 1969; B.A., Calif. State U.-Dominguez Hills, 1971; J.D., U. Mo.-Kansas City, 1974. Bar: Mo. 1974. Counselor U.S. Bur. Prisons, Kansas City, Mo., 1972-74; assoc. Campbell, Erickson, Cottingham, Morgan & Gibson, Kansas City, 1974-75; sole practice, Lawson, Mo., 1975—; dir. Summit Ford Inc., Mo., Lawson Industries Inc., Mo.; mcpl. ct. judge City of Cameron, Mo., 1983—. Mem., pres. Bd. Edn. Lawson R-XIV Sch. Dist., 1977—. Served with USN, 1962-66. Mem. Mo. Bar Assn., ABA, Ray County Bar Assn., 8th Circuit Bar Com. Democrat. Roman Catholic. Avocations: restoration of classic cars, farming, horseback riding. Office: 407 N Pennsylvania St Lawson MO 64062

SMITS, DAVID PAUL, optometrist; b. Appleton, Wis., Aug. 19, 1949; s. Paul Francis and Elaine Clara (Reetz) S.; m. Jayne Cheryl Bouressa, Oct. 9, 1976; children—Neil, Todd. B.S., St. Norbert Coll., 1971; O.D., Ohio State U., 1974. Lic. optometrist, Wis. Pvt. practice optometry, Little Chute, Wis., 1974-80, Sterling Optical, Appleton, Wis., 1980—. Sensenbrenner scholar, 1970; E.F. Wildermuth scholar, 1973; hon. scholar Wis. Optometric Assn., 1972, 74. Fellow Beta Sigma Kappa, Epsilon Psi Epsilon (Beta chpt.); mem. Am. Optometric Assn., Wis. Optometric Assn. (bd. dirs. 1975-78), Fox Cities Optometric Soc. (pres. 1975-78), Ohio State U. Alumni Assn. Club: Jaycees (Little Chute). Lodge: K.C. (Kimberly, Wis.). Avocations: Reading; camping; fishing. Home: 806 Rosehill Rd Kaukauna WI 54130 Office: 1251 Valley Fair Mall Appleton WI 54911

SMOLINSKI, LEONA MARIE, nurse, educator; b. Chgo., Dec. 8, 1924; d. Michael and Rose (Sands) S.; grad. Cook County Sch. Nursing, 1946; B.S. in Nursing Edn., Loyola U., Chgo., 1952; M.A., U. Chgo., 1957; D.N.Sci., Cath. U. Am., 1975. Staff nurse Cook County Hosp., U. Ill. Hosp., 1946-48; instr. Hurley Hosp. Sch. Nursing, Flint, Mich., 1951-53; staff nurse U. Chgo. Billings Hosp., 1956-57; asst. prof. Sch. Nursing, U. Oreg., Portland, 1957-59; asst. prof. Sch. Nursing, Loyola U., Chgo., 1959-62, asso. prof., 1962—, chmn. dept. med.-surg. nursing, 1968-71, acting dean Sch. Nursing, 1969, dir. grad. program in nursing, 1976-78; cons. in field. Treas., Adelante, Inc., 1978-79; mem. Edgewater Community Council, Chgo.; bd. dirs. Ill. Citizens for Better Care, 1981—, sec. exec. com., 1983; mem. adv. council, ret. sr. vol. program Hull House Assn. Chgo., 1982—. Recipient Pres.'s medallion Loyola U., Chgo., 1970; Loyal and Disting. Service award Loyola U. Med. Center, 1979. Mem. Am. Nurses Assn., Ill. Nurses Assn. (commr. human rights 1977-79), Midwest Alliance Nursing, AAAS, Nurse Faculty Devel. in Midwest, Sigma Theta Tau (pres. Alpha Beta chpt. 1980-82). Roman Catholic. Home: 5855 N Sheridan Rd Chicago IL 60660 Office: 6525 N Sheridan Rd Chicago IL 60626

SMOOT, THURLOW, lawyer; b. Glendive, Mont., Dec. 30, 1910; s. Marvin A. and Ivah (Cook) S. J.D., U. Colo., 1933. Trial examiner NLRB, Washington, 1937-47; sole practice, Cleve., 1947—. Contbr. articles to profl. jours. Served to 1st lt. U.S. Army, 1942-45. Mem. Greater Cleve. Bar Assn., Cuyahoga County Bar Assn., Ohio State Bar Assn. Democrat. Home: 12700 Lake Ave #2003 Lakewood OH 44107 Office: 118 St Clair Ave #806 Cleve OH 44114

SMUTZ, DOROTHY DRING, pianist, music educator; b. Kansas City, Mo.; d. Johnson and Emma L. (Mack) Dring; studied with Walter Goff, Sterling, Colo., Dr. Ernest R. Kroeger, St. Louis, E. Robert Schmitz, San Francisco, Paul Badura-Skoda, U. Wis.; postgrad. Kroeger Sch. Music, 1926-28; m. Harold Turk Smutz, Oct. 27, 1930 (dec. Sept. 1976); 1 son, Robert Allen. Radio, TV appearances, also concerts, recitals; soloist St. Louis Philharmonic, St. Louis Little Symphony, St. Louis Symphony orchs.; harpsichordist St. Louis Bach Soc., 1940-44; piano, clavichord, seminars and master classes for tchrs., 1946—; debut Town Hall, N.Y.C., 1949; guest artist, forum leader Okla. Music Tchrs. Assn., 1950; guest artist, workshop cons. Okla., Nebr., Kans. music tchrs. assns.; mem. faculty, adjudicator Nat. Guild Piano Tchrs.; artist-in-residence recital and master classes Concordia Coll., Bronxville, N.Y., 1979, Jefferson Coll., Hillsboro, Mo., 1981; vis. artist in piano Webster Coll. (now Webster U.), St. Louis, 1981-82, faculty, 1983-84; lectr., guest artist various assns. convs.; dir. tchrs. clinic and workshop, So. Ill. U., 1963; guest artist, condr. workshop music dept. Coll. William and Mary, 1973; mem. piano faculty St. Louis Conservatory Music, 1974-80; analyst J.S. Bach Seminars, also lecture recitals, 1982—. Mem. Nat. Music Tchrs. Assn. (cert.) Mo. (cert.; exec. bd., Bach lectr., recital 1980), Nat. (mus. theory com. 1962-64, adjudicator West Central div. 1979) music tchrs. assns., St. Louis Piano Tchrs. Round Table, Suburban Community Concerts Assn. (exec. bd. 1951-57), Mu Phi Epsilon. Presbyterian. Home: 619 Hollywood Pl Webster Groves MO 63119

SNAGE, ALEXANDER MICHAEL, II, chemical engineer; b. Detroit, June 18, 1948; s. Edward and Helen Louise (Ammar) S.; B.S. in Chem. Engring., Wayne State U., 1970; m. Loretta Strenk, May 2, 1970; 1 son, Bryan Alexander. Asst. chemist Nelson Chems., Detroit, 1965-69; process chem. engr. Monsanto Co., Trenton, Mich., 1970-74, mfg. chem. process supr., Augusta, Ga., 1974-78, process chem. engring. supr., Trenton, 1978-82, also chmn. supervisory com. Monsanto Fed. Employees Credit Union, 1980-82; supt. custom chem. mfg. plant Monsanto Co., Dayton, Ohio, 1982-85, product mgr. new tech. devl. dept., 1985—. Mem. Am. Inst. Chem. Engrs. (sec. Dayton chpt), Inst. Food Technologists, Inst. Environ. Scis., Tau Beta Pi. Roman Catholic. Home: 16312 Fullerton Meadows Ellisville MO 63011 Office: Monsanto Co 800 N Lindbergh Blvd Saint Louis MO 63167

SNAIDER, ALAN HOWARD, pharmacist, consultant; b. Bronx, N.Y., Aug. 18, 1951; s. Nathan and Sylvia (Fleischer) S.; m. Margaret Mary Crelly, Feb. 24, 1973; children—Brandon Cole, Megan Elizabeth, Lauren Anne. B.A. in Biochemistry, SUNY-Plattsburgh, 1973; cert. bus., Fla. Atlantic U., 1974; B.A. in Pharmacology, Ohio State U., 1980. Instr. biology Palm Beach Jr. Coll., Fla., 1976-77; pharmacist Super X Corp., Columbus, Ohio, 1980-82; pharmacist, cons. Rite Aid Corp., Columbus, 1982—; counselor Poison Control, Columbus, 1982—. Chmn. Crime Prevention, Columbus, 1980-81; cons. Substance Abuse Columbus Police Dept., 1981—, Substance Abuse Com., Columbus, 1982, Gov.'s Council to Prevent Drug Abuse, 1983; mem. Peer Rev. Com., Columbus, 1980. Recipient award Clinton County Rotary Club, 1971, award Century Club, 1972. Mem. Ohio State Pharm. Assn., Am. Pharm. Assn., Nat. Assn. Retail Druggists. Democrat. Jewish. Avocations: football, fishing. Home: 188 Aldrich Rd Columbus OH 43214 Office: Rite Aid Corp 3000 E Broad St Columbus OH 43209

SNEED, MARIE ELEANOR WILKEY, retired educator; b Dahlgren, Ill., June 12, 1915; d. Charles N. and Hazel (Miller) Wilkey; student U. Ill., 1933-35; B.S., Northwestern U., 1937; postgrad. Wayne State U., 1954-60, U. Mich., 1967; m. John Sneed, Jr., Sept. 18, 1937; children—Suzanne (Mrs. Geoffrey B. Newton), John Corwin. Tchr. English, drama, creative writing Berkley (Mich.) Sch. Dist., 1952-76. Mem. Mich. Statewide Tchr. Edn. Preparation, 1968-72, regional sec. 1969-70; mem. Pleasant Ridge Arts Council, 1982—, Pleasant Ridge Parks and Recreation Commn., 1982—. Mem. NEA, Mich., Berkley (pres. 1961-62) edn. assns., Oakland Tchr. Edn. Council (exec. bd. 1973-76), Student Tchr. Planning Com. Berkley (chmn. 1971-72), Phi Alpha Chi, Pi Lambda Theta, Alpha Delta Kappa, Alpha Omicron Pi. Club: Pleasant Ridge Woman's (pres. 1980-83, dir. 1983—). Home: 21 Norwich Rd Pleasant Ridge MI 48069

SNEED, SHERRIE LYNN, clergy, educator, psychotherapist; b. Knoxville, Tenn., Apr. 17, 1954; d. Charles Herbert and Ann Marie (Maloney) S. B.A., U. Tenn., 1975; postgrad. Hamma Sch. Theology, 1975-78; M.Div., Trinity Luth. Sem., 1979; D.Min. in Pastoral Care and Counseling, Luth. Sch. Theology, 1983. Ordained to ministry Lutheran Ch., 1979. Counselor, Clark County Mental Health Satellite, New Carlisle, Ohio, 1975-76; bookstore bibliographer Hamma Sch. Theology, Springfield, Ohio, 1976-77; asst. to pastor Wittenberg U., Springfield, Ohio, 1977-78; interim pastor Rocky Point Chapel, Springfield, 1978-79; pastor Robinson-Sulphur Luth. Parish, St. Paul Luth. Ch., North Robinson, Ohio, 1979-81, St. John Luth. Ch., Sulphur Springs, Ohio, 1979-81; vice-pastor First Luth. Ch., Galion, Ohio, 1980-81; tchr. Unity Cath. High Sch., Chgo., 1981-82; tchr., dept. head Acad. of our Lady, Chgo., 1982-84; interim pastor St. Thomas Luth. Ch., Chgo., 1983-84, pastor, 1984—; marriage and family therapist West Suburban Counseling and Ednl. Service, Luth. Social Services Ill., Wheaton, 1984—; mem. Ohio Synod Task Force on Women in the Ch., 1979-81, Ohio Synod Ednl. Ministry Team, 1980-81, Ill. Synod Ednl. Ministry Team, 1984—; retreat dir. various chs. in Ohio and Ill., 1981—; stewardship cons. Ohio Synod Stewardship Team, 1980-81; supply pastor Ill. Synod, Luth. Sch. Theology, 1981-83; marriage and family therapist. Cons., instr. Contact, 24-hour hotline, Bucyrus, Ohio, 1980-81; CPR instr., area coordinator Mid-Am. chpt. ARC, Chgo., 1983—. Vol. dep. registrar Cook County Bd. Elections, 1984—. Mem. Am. Acad. Religion, Soc. Bibl. Lit., Bucyrus Area Ministerial Assn., South Shore Ministerial Assn., South Shore Council Chs. Democrat. Lutheran. Home: 1606 E Hyde Park Blvd Chicago IL 60615 Office: St Thomas Luth Ch 8000 S Jeffery Blvd Chicago IL 60617

SNELGROVE, JAMES LEWIS, physicist; b. Cookeville, Tenn., Jan. 9, 1942; s. Clarence Predew and Alma Louise (Youmans) S.; m. Alice Temple Medley, Sept. 11, 1965; children—Anne Caroline and Sarah Margaret (twins). B.S., Tenn. Poly. Inst., 1964; M.S., Mich. State U., 1966, Ph.D., 1968. Asst. physicist Argonne Nat. Lab., Ill., 1968-72, physicist, 1972—. Contbr. articles to profl. jours. Deacon Knox Presbyn. Ch., Naperville, Ill., 1972-74, elder, 1976-78. NASA grad. fellow Mich. State U., 1964, NSF grad. fellow Mich. State U., 1967. Mem. Am. Phys. Soc., Am. Nuclear Soc., Sigma Xi, Phi Kappa Phi. Presbyterian. Avocations: jogging; softball; reading. Home: 8S263 College Rd Naperville IL 60540 Office: Argonne Nat Lab 9700 S Cass Ave Argonne IL 60439

SNELL, ALAN HAROLD, optometrist; b. Liberty, Nebr., June 22, 1940; s. J. Harold and Elizabeth (Finney) S.; m. Phyllis Lea Moses, Aug. 25, 1963; children—Lennah, Michelle, Dawn. B.A., Tarkio Coll., 1963; O.D., Pacific U., 1966. Optometrist, Dr. Watts-Snell, Leavenworth, Kans., 1966-69; practice optometry, Leavenworth, 1969-72, Lansing, Kans., 1972—. Mem. sch. bd. Lansing Sch. Dist. #469, Kans., 1981—, pres., 1985. Mem. Am. Optometric Assn. (sports sect., contact lens sect.), Kans. Optometric Assn., Heart Am. Contact Lens Assn., Leavenworth Area C. of C. (bd. dirs., 2d v.p. 1985). Republican. Home: Rural Route 3 Box 216 C Leavenworth KS. 66048 Office: Holiday Plaza Box 210 Lansing KS 66043

SNELL, THADDEUS STEVENS, III, building materials manufacturing company executive, lawyer; b. Ida Grove, Iowa, Feb. 23, 1919; s. Thaddeus Stevens and Catharine (Noble) S.; m. Mary Ward, Nov., 1951 (div. 1965); children—William, Kathleen, Pamela, Debra, Robert; m. 2d, Gloria Cramer Brent, July, 1966 (dec. 1981); m. 3d, Eleanor Larson Hawes, Nov. 24, 1982. B.S., Northwestern U., 1941, postgrad. Law Sch., 1941-42; postgrad. U.S. Naval Acad. Postgrad. Sch., 1944-45; LL.B., Yale U., 1947. Bar: Ill. 1948, Iowa 1948. Assoc., Keck, Mahin & Cate and predecessors, Chgo., 1947-58, ptnr., 1959-71; v.p., corp. counsel U.S. Gypsum Co., Chgo., 1971-82, v.p., gen. counsel, 1982-84; v.p., gen. counsel USG Corp., 1984—. Deacon, Glenview (Ill.) Community Ch., 1958-61; pres. Kenilworth (Ill.) Citizens Adv. Com., 1973-74; mem. Chgo. Crime Commn. Served to lt. USNR, 1942-46. Mem. ABA, Ill. Bar Assn., Iowa Bar Assn., Chgo. Bar Assn., Legal Club Chgo., Am. Judicature Soc. Clubs: Univ., Met. (Chgo.); Sunset Ridge Country (Northbrook, Ill.); Masons (Ida Grove). Home: 724 Maclean Ave Kenilworth IL 60043 Office: 101 S Wacker Dr Chicago IL 60606

SNELLER, TODD CALVIN, state alcohol fuel programs administrator; b. Vallejo, Calif., Mar. 17, 1952; s. Robert Calvin and Marjorie Jean (Kurfman) S.; m. Mary Lynn Morgan, Oct. 30, 1976; 1 dau., Kristin Lynn. B.S., Nebr. Wesleyan U., 1975. Adminstrv. asst. N.E. Gasohol Com., Lincoln, Nebr., 1976-78; indsl. cons. N.E. Dept. Economic Devel., Lincoln, Nebr., 1978-79; adminstr. Nebr. Gasohol Com., Lincoln, 1979—; bd. dirs. The Renewable Fuels Assn., Washington. Alt. energy advisor Southeast Community Coll., Milford, Nebr., 1982, 83. Mem. Nebr. Indsl. Developers Assn., Theta Chi (pres. bldg. corp.). Episcopalian. Office: 301 Centennial Mall So Mall Level Lincoln NE 68509

SNEVEL, HOWARD FRANKLIN, JR., lawyer; b. Cleve., Aug. 4, 1927; s. Howard F. and Florence E. (Tucker) S.; m. Erma I. Alt, Apr. 22, 1947 (div. May 1974); 1 child, James F.; m. Anna B. Strete, June 15, 1974. J.D., Cleve.-Marshall Sch., 1952. Bar: Ohio 1952, U.S. Dist. Ct. (so. dist.) Ohio 1975, U.S. Supreme Ct. 1974. C.P.C.U. Claims atty., mgr. Nationwide Ins. Co., Raleigh, N.C., 1963-69, reins. claim mgr., Columbus, Ohio, 1969-71, atty. medicare, 1980—; dir. ins. AMA, Chgo., 1971-72; sole practice, Worthington, Ohio, 1972-80. Contbr. articles to profl. jours. Served with USAAF, 1944-46. Mem. Ohio State Bar Assn. (sec. ins. law com. 1980—), Columbus Bar Assn. (chmn. ins. com. 1980-82), Am. Coll. Legal Medicine. Avocation: boating. Home: 5822 Falmouth Ct Worthington OH 43085 Office: Nationwide Ins Co 1 Nationwide Plaza Columbus OH 43215

SNIDER, C. STEVEN, school administrator; b. Terre Haute, Ind., May 16, 1947; s. Charles L. and Barbara M. (Figg) S.; m. Cheryl Ann Lubbehusen, June 7, 1969. B.S., Ind. State U., 1969, M.S., 1972, Ph.D., 1977. Tchr./adminstr. North Newton Sch. Corp., Morocco, Ind., 1969-73; prin. South Central Sch. Corp., Union Mills, Ind., 1973-75; asst. prin./instrn. Penn High Sch., Mishawaka, Ind., 1977-79, prin., 1979-83; supt. schs. FRHC Sch. Corp., Hope, Ind., 1983-85; supt. schs. LaPorte Community Sch. Corp., 1985—; Ind. State U. adminstrv. intern; conf. speaker; lectr., condr. workshops in field. Bd. dirs. Jr. Achievement, 1980-83, Bartholomew County unit ARC; adv. mem. No. Ind. Sch. Band, Orch. and Vocal Assn., 1979-82, Ind. U.-South Bend Sec. Sch., 1979-82; mem. chancellor's adv. com. Purdue North Central U., 1985—. Recipient award of merit Jr. Achievement, 1982. Mem. Nat. Assn. Secondary Sch. Prins., Nat. Soc. Study Edn., Assn. for Supervision and Curriculum Devel., Council for Basic Edn., Nat. Assn. Student Activity Advisors, Ind. Assn. for Supervision and Curriculum Devel., Nat. Orgn. Legal Problems In Edn., LaPorte C. of C. (bd. dirs. 1985—), Phi Delta Kappa. Presbyterian. Lodges: Elks, Kiwanis, Lions. Contbr. articles to profl. jours.

SNIDER, LARRY DALE, optometrist; b. Webb City, Mo., Aug. 5, 1952; s. Jack William and Virginia Ellenor (Bilquist) S.; m. Jean Elizabeth Brown, June 10, 1978; children—Kate Elizabeth, Ann Whitney. Student Mo. So. Coll., Joplin, 1970-72; O.D., So. Coll. Optometry, Memphis, 1976. Pvt. practice optometry, Harrisonville, Mo., 1976—. Chmn. bldg. com. Harrisonville United Meth. Ch., 1979—; mem. Econ. Devel. Com., Harrisonville, 1983-84. Mem. Am. Optometric Assn., Optometric Soc. Greater Kansas City (bd. dirs. 1977-82), Mo. Optometric Assn. (bd. dirs. 1983-84, sec.-treas. 1984—), Harrisonville C. of C. (pres. 1983). Club: Twin Pines Country (bd. dirs. 1981-83). Lodge: Lions. Avocation: Golf. Home: 1700 Twin Oaks Dr Harrisonville MO 64701 Office: PO Box 446 Harrisonville MO 64701

SNIDER, PATRICIA ANN, college counselor; b. Fremont, Ohio, Sept. 7, 1937; d. Millard Alfred and Mary (Danchisen) Snider. B.S. in Edn., Bowling Green State U., 1959; M.Ed., Ohio U., 1963. Instr. St. Joseph Coll., Emmitsburg, Md., 1959-61; grad. asst. tchr. Ohio U. Athens, 1961-63; head resident advisor Western Ill. U., Macomb, Ill., 1963-67; counselor Morton Coll., Cicero, Ill., 1967—. Author: (with others) Community College Career Alternatives Handbook, 1979; Women on their Way-A Guide for Women Returning to School, 1984. Contbr. articles to profl. jours. Bd. dirs. Cicero chpt. Am. Cancer Soc.; flotilla vice comdr. U.S. Coast Guard Aux., 1969-82. Recipient Faculty Mem. of Yr. award Morton Coll. Endowment Found., 1982. Mem. Am. Assn. for Counseling and Devel., Nat. Acad. Advisors Assn., Nat. Assn. for Women Deans, Adminstrs. and Counselors, Ill. Assn. for Counseling and Devel., Nat. Coll. Personnel Assn., Ill. Coll. Personnel Assn. Roman Catholic. Avocations: Reading; fishing. Home: 1540 S 59th Ct Cicero IL 60650 Office: Morton Coll 3801 S Central Ave Cicero IL 60650

SNODERLY, JOHN ALLEN SHELBY, lawyer; b. Akron, Ohio, June 6, 1929; s. William E. Snoderly and Alma (Shelby) Snoderly Sebaugh Ostroff; m. Donna Gover (div.); children—Lynn Marie, John II, Catherine C., Elizabeth; m. Joyce Evelyn Poth (div.); 1 child, Rebecca N.; m. B. Catherine Barnett, May 22, 1975. A.A., Tenn. Wesleyan Coll., 1948; B.A., U. Akron, 1952, J.D., 1959. Bar: Ohio 1959. Sole practice, Akron, 1959—. Trustee Akron Law Library, 1962-82, Lakemore Meth. Ch., Akron, 1973-85. Served with USAF, 1949-50. Mem. Akron Bar Assn., Ohio State Bar Assn. Avocations: farming; flying; golfing; fishing; camping. Office: 77 E Mill St Akron OH 44308

SNODGRASS, PHILIP JAMES, internist, educator; b. Janesville, Wis., Nov. 3, 1927; s. Philip Nulton and Dorothy (Bonnett) S.; m. Marjorie Alice Lagemann, June 21, 1952; children—Martha, Jennifer, Amy, Emily. A.B., Harvard U., 1949, M.D., 1953; postgrad. MIT, 1957-59. Diplomate Am. Bd. Internal Medicine, Am. Bd. Gastroenterology. Intern Peter Bent Brigham, Boston, 1953-54, resident, 1956-57; postdoctoral fellow, 1957-59, sr. asst. resident, 1959-60, chief resident, 1961-63, fellow, 1960-64, chief gastroenterology div., 1963-73; chief med. service VA Hosp., Indpls., 1973—; prof. Ind. U., Indpls., 1973—; cons., lectr. in field. Contbr. chpts. to books, articles to profl. jours. Served as lt. USNR, 1954-56. Grantee USPHS, 1963-73, Hartford Found., 1971-74, VA, 1973-84. Fellow ACP; mem. Am. Gastroenterology Assn., Am. Assn. Study Liver Disease, Central Soc. Clin. Research, Am. Soc. Biol. Chemists, Am. Inst. Nutrition. Club: Harvard (Indpls.) (pres. 1980-82, chmn. schs. 1982—). Avocations: sculling, traveling, swimming. Home: 1481 W 10th St Indianapolis IN 46202 Office: VA Med Ctr 111 1481 W 10th St Indianapolis IN 46202

SNOW, DORCAS LAVINA, piano teacher; b. Brecksville, Ohio, July 27, 1902; d. Harry Ward and Alice Phebe (Noble) S. Tchrs. certificate, diploma Cleve. Sch. Music, 1923. Tchr. pvt. piano, Brecksville, Ohio, 1923—; mem. Profl. Piano Quartette, 1923. Recipient award City of Brecksville, 1973. Sr. Citizen award, 1974; Heritage award Brecksville Lions Club, 1982. Mem. Nat. Music Tchrs. Assn., Ohio Music Tchrs. Assn., Cleve. Piano Tchrs. Club. Mem. United Ch. of Christ. Author: To the City of Brecksville, 1980; Dear Brecksville, 1981; In and Out of Brecksville, 1982; Follow the Sleighbells to Brecksville Square; The Pre School Rhythm Band and their Shows 1933-1946. Home: 8942 Elm St Brecksville OH 44141

SNOWDEN, GENE, state senator; b. Huntington, Ind., Apr. 7, 1928; s. Ben W. and Anna L. (Orr) S.; student Olivet Nazarene Coll., Kankakee, Ill., 1948-49; m. Carol J. Replogle, Aug. 26, 1949; children—Connie J., Barbara J. and Beverly J. (twins), Jodi Ann. Office mgr. Weaver Popcorn Co., Huntington, 1949-50; operator grocery store, Huntington, 1951; dept. mgr. Montgomery Ward & Co., Huntington, 1951-54; appliance and TV dept. mgr. Wolf & Dessauer Dept. Store, Huntington, 1954-58; life ins. underwriter, Huntington, 1958—; mem. Ind. Ho. of Reps. from 10th Dist., 1964-66, Ind. Senate from 17th Dist., 1966—, pres. pro tem, 1979-80, asst. pres. pro tem, 1981-82; mem. Huntington County Council, 1962-64. Trustee Olivet Coll., 1968—. Huntington Coll., 1965. Recipient Disting. Service award Ind. Jaycees, 1960. Mem. Nat. Soc. State Legislators (past pres., chmn. bd. govs.). Republican. Mem. Nazarene Ch. Club: Huntington Optimists (charter pres.). Office: 18 W Washington St Huntington IN 46750

SNOWDEN, PATRICIA LOCKWOOD, gallery curator; b. Atchison, Kans., Aug. 22, 1923; d. Charles Howard and Harriet Lovejoy (Kinney) L.; m. Pennell E. Snowden, Mar. 5, 1946; children—Susan, Katherine, Pennell, Dinah. B.F.A., U. Kans., 1944. Curator, Muchnic Gallery, Atchison, 1974—. Former mem. Kans. Art Commn. Mem. Atchison Art Assn. Republican. Episcopalian. Avocations: painting; ceramics; weaving and spinning; knitting. Home: RR2 Box 12 Atchison KS 66002 Office: Muchnic Gallery 704 N 4th Atchison KS 66002

SNYDER, ANN CATHERINE, exercise physiologist, educator; b. Lansing, Mich., July 16, 1951; d. Warren G. and Ann Catherine (Dearing) S. B.S., Western Mich. U., 1973; M.Ed., Bowling Green State U., 1975; M.A., Mich. State U., 1979; Ph.D., Purdue U., 1982. Asst. prof. exercise physiology, Ball State U., Muncie, Ind., 1982—. Contbr. articles to tech. jours. Internat. Inst. Sports Medicine research grantee, 1984-85. Mem. Am. Coll. Sports Medicine, Am. Alliance of Health, Phys. Edn., Recreation and Dance, Muncie Jaycee Women (pres. 1984). Methodist. Avocations: Cross-country skiing; bicycling; running. Home: Route 9 Box 189 Muncie IN 47302 Office: Ball State Univ Human Performance Lab Muncie IN 47306

SNYDER, CHARLES ROYCE, sociologist, educator; b. Haverford, Pa., Dec. 28, 1924; s. Edward D. and Edith (Royce) S.; B.A., Yale U., 1944, M.A., 1949, Ph.D., 1954; m. Patricia Hanson, June 30, 1951; children—Stephen Hoyt, Christiana Marie, Constance Patricia, Daniel Edward. Mem. staff Yale Center Alcohol Studies, 1950-60; asst. prof. sociology Yale U., 1956-60; prof. sociology So. Ill. U., Carbondale, 1960-85, prof. emeritus, 1985—, chmn. dept., 1964-75, 81-85; vis. prof. human genetics Sackler Sch. Medicine, Tel Aviv U., 1980; cons. behavioral scis. tng. com. Nat. Inst. Gen. Med. Scis., NIH, 1962-64; mem. planning com., chmn. program 28th Internat. Congress Alcohol and Alcoholism, 1964. Mem. theol. commn. United Ch. of Christ, 1964-71. Served with USNR, World War II. Fellow Am. Sociol. Assn.; mem. Soc. Study of Social Problems (v.p. 1963-64, rep. to council Am. Sociol. Assn. 1964-66), Midwest Sociol. Soc. (dir. 1970—), AAUP. Author: Alcohol and the Jews, 1958; editor: (with D. J. Pittman) Society, Culture and Drinking Patterns, 1962; editorial bd. Quar. Jour. Studies on Alcohol, 1957-83; asso. editor Sociol. Quar., 1960-63. Home: 705 Taylor Dr Carbondale IL 62901

SNYDER, COOPER, state senator; b. Blanchester, Ohio, July 10, 1928; s. Harry C. and Marion E. (Sprague) S.; m. Dorothy B. Blakeney, 1949; children—Marianne Snyder Macke, Phillip, Emily Snyder Steer, Harry, Elizabeth. Student Ohio U., 1947, Wilmington Coll., 1948-49. Mem. Ohio State Senate from Dist. 14. Mem. Phi Kappa Tau. Republican. Methodist. Lodges: Rotary, Shriners. Office: 6508 Springhill Rd Hillsboro OH 45133

SNYDER, GARY RONALD, hospital administrator; b. Akron, Ohio, May 7, 1946; s. Harry H. and Zola S.; B.A., Calif. State Coll., Northridge, 1970; M.P.H., U. Mich., 1972; m. Francine Susan Snyder, Sept. 2, 1972; children—Mark Kenneth, Joel Martin. Dir. for health New Detroit, Inc., 1972-74; dir. planning Comprehensive Health Planning Council, 1974-76; cons. HEW, Chgo., 1976-78; mem. Chgo. Bd. Trade, 1976-78; dir. plan devel. and coordination Comprehensive Health Planning Council, Detroit, 1978-83; exec. v.p. Warren Hosp. Corp., 1983—. Chmn., Am. Cancer Soc., Detroit, 1973-76; bd. dirs. Neighborhood Service Orgn., Jewish Family Service, Warren Hosp. Ctr., Mich. Psychiat. Services Corp. Recipient Exceptional Service citation Calif. State Colls., 1970. Mem. Am. Public Health Assn., Am. Health Planning Assn., Am. Mgmt. Assn., Planning Execs. Inst., Am. Hosp. Assn. Home: 5522 Beauchamp Pl Dr West Bloomfield MI 48033 Office: 21230 Dequindre Rd Warren MI 48091

SNYDER, JAMES WILLIAM, JR., sales exec.; b. South Bend, Ind., Mar. 16, 1948; s. James William and Marjorie Jane (Blakeman) S.; B.B.A., Northwood Inst., 1970; m. Sharon Ann Wallace, Aug. 22, 1970; children—Erin Elizabeth, Stephanie Wallace. Sales mktg. rep. Jim Snyder Sales Co., Grosse Pointe Woods, Mich., 1970-72, v.p., 1972-75, sr. v.p., treas., 1975—, dir., 1972—; v.p. sales and mktg., dir. Country Sales, Inc., 1983—. Bd. dirs. Northwood Inst. Alumni; active St. John Men's Hosp. Guild, 1971—, Grosse Pointe Woods Police and Fire Aux., 1971—. Mem. Am. Mgmt. Assn., Soc. Advanced Mgmt., Soc. Plastic Engrs., Am. Soc. Body Engrs., Founders Soc. Detroit Inst. Arts, Automotive Old Timers. Republican. Roman Catholic. Clubs: Detroit Athletic, Detroit Golf, Grosse Pointe Yacht, Grosse Pointe Crisis, The Players; White Hall (Chgo.). Home: 75 Fordcroft Grosse Pointe Shores MI 48236 Office: 17200 E Ten Mile Rd Suite 120 East Detroit MI 48021

SNYDER, JOEL JAY, architect; b. Columbus, Ohio, Feb. 21, 1949; s. Joel Rice and Gloria (Mertz) S.; m. Christine Ann Wittmann, Mar. 13, 1982; 1 child, Austin Wittmann. B.Sc., Ohio State U., 1972; postgrad. U. Ky., 1977, Harvard U., 1982. Registered architect, U.K., Ohio, N.Y., Pa., Ky., W.Va. Intern architect Eschliman & Assocs., Columbus, Ohio, 1968-70, Acock, Trees & White, 1970, County Architects Office of Northamptonshire, Northampton, Eng., 1971, Ireland & Assocs., Columbus, 1972-73, Holroyd & Myers, 1973; architect Brubaker/Brandt, Inc., 1974-75, Feinknopf, Feinknopf, Macioce & Schappa, 1976; prin. Joel J. Snyder, AIA, Architect, 1977—; pres. JS Assocs., 1982—; assocs. Sims Cons. Group, Lancaster, Ohio, 1983—; adj. prof. Ohio State U., Columbus, 1985—; mem. bd. advisors Ohio Bank and Savs. Co. Mem. AIA (chpt. sec., treas. 1985—), Architects Soc. Ohio, Urban Land Inst., Am. Planning Assn., Constrn. Specifications Inst., Royal Inst. Brit. Architects, Inst. Urban Design. Republican. Clubs: Columbus, Scioto Country. Avocations: travel; tennis; history. Home: 1892 Suffolk Rd Columbus OH 43221 Office: 744 S High St Columbus OH 43206

SNYDER, MICHAEL ALAN, public relations exec.; b. Ft. Wayne, Ind., Aug. 8, 1953; s. Raymond Nicholas and Mary Marceil (Isenbarger) S.; B.A. in English, Ind. U., 1975, B.A. in Media Communications, 1975. Editor, art dir. Univ. Publs., Ft. Wayne, 1974-76; assoc. pub. Times Group Newspapers, New Haven, 1976-78; editor, creative dir. Ft. Wayne and Metro Mags., 1978-80; dir. Office of Pub. Affairs, ARC Regional Hdqrs., Ft. Wayne, 1980-84; dir. corp. communications Lincoln Nat. Corp., Ft. Wayne, 1984—; instr. Ind. U.; cons. United Way, N.E. Ind. Emergency Med. Service. Mem. task force on minorities and media Urban League, 1980—; bd. dirs. Tara Neighborhood Assn., 1977—; mem. Mayor's Govt. Reorgn. Study Com., 1975; bd. dirs. Ft. Wayne Ednl. TV Found.; chmn. arts and letters com. Ind. U. Recipient Fourth Estate award Am. Legion, 1976, 11 awards for writing, editing, photography and art Ind. Collegiate Press Assn. Mem. Ind. U. Alumni Assn. (dir.), Internat. Assn. Bus. Communicators, Pub. Relations Soc. Am. Roman Catholic. Editor: Return to Learning, 1977; composer: Who Will Roll Away the Stone, 1972; The Writer, To Your Side and A Song for Rhonda, all 1979; Ride, Sally Ride, 1983. Home: 136 E Essex Ln Fort Wayne IN 46825 Office: 1300 S Clinton St Fort Wayne IN 46801

SNYDER, M(ILTON) JACK, engineering administrator; b. Columbus, Ohio, Oct. 12, 1921; s. Terry Bennett and Maude Emilie (DeLong) S.; m. Miriam Elise Schwab, Jan. 15, 1944; children—Stephen Jack, Carol Gabrielle. B.S. in Chemistry, Ohio State U., 1943. Research engr. Battelle Meml. Inst., Columbus, 1943-50, assoc. sect. mgr., 1950-65, sect. mgr., 1965-70, mgr. dept., 1970-74, program mgr., 1974—. Contbr. articles to profl. jours. Pres., trustee Grandview Heights Pub. Library, Ohio, 1970—. Recipient Wason Medal. Fellow Am. Ceramic Soc.; mem. Nat. Inst. Ceramic Engrs., Am. Chem. Soc., Am. Concrete Soc., Sigma Xi. Republican. Methodist. Office: Battelle Columbus Labs 505 King Ave Columbus OH 43201

SNYDER, RICHARD GERALD, research scientist, administrator, educator, consultant; b. Northampton, Mass., Feb. 14, 1928; s. Grant B. and Ruth (Putnam) S.; m. Phoebe Jones, Mar. 2, 1949; children—Dorinda, Sherrill, Paul, Jeff, Jon, David. Student Amherst Coll., 1946-48; B.A., U. Ariz., 1956, M.A., 1957, Ph.D., 1959. Diplomate Am. Bd. Forensic Anthropology. Teaching asst. dept. anthropology U. Ariz., Tucson, 1957-58, assoc. research engr. Applied Research Lab., Coll. Engring., 1958-60, mem. staff Ariz. Transp. and Traffic Inst., 1959-60, assoc. prof. systems engring., 1960; chief phys. anthropology Civil Aeromed. Research Inst., FAA, Oklahoma City, 1960-66, research pilot, 1962-66, acting chief Protection and Survival Labs., 1963-66; mgr. biomechanics dept. Office of Automotive Safety Research, Ford Motor Co., Dearborn, Mich., 1966-68, prin. research scientist, 1968; assoc. prof. anthropology U. Mich., Ann Arbor, 1968-73, prof., 1973—, research scientist Hwy. Safety Research Inst., 1968—, head biomed. dept., 1969-84, dir. NASA Ctr. of Excellence in Man-Vehicle Systems, 1984—; adj. assoc. prof. U. Okla., 1963; research assoc. Zoller Lab. U. Chgo., 1964-65, research assoc. dept. anthropology, 1965-67; assoc. prof. Mich. State U., East Lansing, 1967-68; cons. U.S. Air Force, Aerospace Med. Research Labs., Nat. Acad. Scis., U.S. Dept. Transp., Mooney Aircraft Corp., Office Naval Research Dept. Navy, Am. Biodynamics Corp., numerous others. Assoc. editor: Jour. of Communication, 1961-63; cons. editor: Jour. of Biomechanics, 1967-81; mem. editorial bd.: Product Safety News, 1973—. Contbr. chpts. to books and numerous articles to profl. jours. Judge, Internat. Sci. Fair, Detroit. 1968; mem. council Explorer Scouts, Ann Arbor, 1968-70. Served to 1st lt. USAF, 1949-54; Korea. Recipient Met. Life award, Nat. Safety Council, 1970; Arch T. Colwell Merit award, Soc. Automotive Engrs., 1973; Award for Profl. Excellence Aerospace Med. Assn., 1978; Admiral Luis de Flores Flight Safety award, Flight Safety Found., 1981. Fellow Aerospace Med. Assn., Royal Anthrop. Inst., AAAS, Am. Anthropl. Assn., Am. Acad. Forensic Scis., AIAA (assoc.); mem. Am. Assn. Phys. Anthropologists, Ariz.-Nev. Acad. Sci., Survival and Equipment Assn., Assn. Aviation Psychologists, Am. Inst. Biol. Scis., Soc. Automotive Engrs., Mich. Acad. Arts Sci. and Letters, Internat. Mustang Pilots Soc., Internat. Soc. Aircraft Safety Investigators, Am. Assn. Automotive Medicine, Aerospace Physiologists Soc., Mich. Soc. Med. Research, Sigma Xi, Beta Beta Beta. Republican. Congregationalist. Avocations: aviation, aerospace medicine, forensic anthropology. Home: 2945 Newport Rd Ann Arbor MI 48103 Office: NASA Ctr of Excellence in Man-Systems Research U Mich 222UMTRI Ann Arbor MI 48109

SNYDER, RONALD WARREN, marketing research and development company executive; b. Phila., Feb. 6, 1947; s. Ronald Clark and Bertha Elizabeth S.; A.A.S., Gloucester County Coll., Sewell, N.J., 1972; B.S.B.A., Loyola U., Paris Extension, 1974, M.B.A., 1983. Owner, operator Eagle Advt., Inc., Springfield, Mo., 1973-74; profl. adventurer, 1974-78; chmn. bd., chief exec. officer Overseas Research & Devel. Inc., Springfield, 1979—; Mo. coordinator Vietnam Vets. in Bus., 1979-82; mem. U.S. Senatorial Bus. Adv. Bd.; mem. nat. adv. bd. NSC. Served with USAR, 1966-69; Vietnam. Decorated Purple Heart, Combat Inf. badge. Mem. Am. Mgmt. Assn., Solar Lobby, Am. Assn. Small Research Cos., Internat. Shooters Devel. Fund, Nat. Rifle Assn., Assn. M.B.A. Execs., Internat. Soc. Financiers, Springfield Area C. of C. Republican. Lutheran. Editor Vanguard mag., 1971-72. Home: Route 2 Box 294-A Everton MO 65646 Office: PO Box 267 Jewell Sta Springfield MO 65801

SNYDER, SUSAN ALICE, counselor, educator; b. Toledo, Nov. 19, 1959; d. Alfred Edward and Miriam Virginia (Hedges) S. B.A., Bowling Green State U., 1980, M.A., 1982. Dir. residence life Urbana Coll., Ohio, 1981-82, asst. dean students, 1982-84; acad. counselor DeVry Inst. Tech., Columbus, Ohio, 1984—. Author: (with others) Urbana Coll. Student Handbook, 1982. Mem. Am. Assn. for Counseling and Devel., Ohio Coll. Personnel Assn. (presenter 1984, mem. task force 1984—), Nat. Acad. Advising Assn., Business and Profl. Women Club, Great Lakes Assn. Coll. and Univ. Housing Officers. Office: DeVry Inst Tech 1350 Alum Creek Dr Columbus OH 43209

SNYDER, THOMAS JOHN, osteopath; b. Monticello, Iowa, June 19, 1950; s. John Arvid and Laura Emma (Dirks) S.; m. LuAnne Carole Horner, June 17, 1972; children—Rachael, Mark, Andrea. B.A., Coe Coll., 1975; D.O., U. Osteo. Medicine, 1978. Cert. in internal medicine. Intern, Davenport Osteo. Hosp., Iowa, 1978-79; resident in internal medicine Normandy Hosp., St. Louis, 1979-82; asst. prof. U. Osteo. Medicine, Des Moines, 1982-83; staff physician Davenport Med. Ctr., Iowa, 1983—; staff physician Mercy Hosp., Davenport, 1984—, St. Lukes Hosp, Davenport, 1984—, Illini Hosp., Silvis, Ill., 1984—. Contbr. articles to profl. jours. Bd. dirs. Am. Cancer Soc., Scott County, 1984. Served with USMC, 1968-71. Mead Johnson fellow, 1982. Mem. Am. Heart Assn., Am. Lung Assn., Am. Diabetes Assn., Iowa Osteo. Med. Assn., Scott County Osteo. Assn. Lutheran. Avocation: running. Office: 3906 Lillie Ave Suite 1 Davenport IA 52806

SOAT, DOUGLAS MARC, insurance company executive; b. Milw., July 29, 1947; s. Harry Harold and Doris Louise (Morgan) S.; m. Lynn Ann Ross, Dec. 23, 1972; children—James Douglas, Jennifer Lynn. B.A. in Psychology (scholar), Cornell U., 1969; M.S. in Clin. Psychology, Marquette U., 1974, Ph.D. in Ednl. Psychology, 1974; M.B.A., U.Wis.-Whitewater, 1981. Lic. psychologist, Wis. Teaching asst. dept. psychology and ednl. psychology Marquette U., Milw., 1969-71, 72-74; psychol. asst. Curative Workshop, Milw., 1971-72; psychometric asst. Milw. Pub. Schs., 1971-72; dir. edn. and staff devel. Am. Appraisal Assocs., Milw., 1974; mgr. employee devel. and personnel adminstrn. Parker Pen Co., Janesville, Wis., 1974-78; v.p. employee devel. Sentry Insurance, Stevens Point, Wis., 1978—; pres., dir. Catalyst Profls. Inc. a Sentry Enterprise, Stevens Point, 1983—; instr. Blackhawk Tech. Inst., Janesville, 1975-77; tng. coordinator United Way, Rock County, Wis., 1977. Com. chmn. Mushkodany Dist. Portage County Boy Scouts Am., 1981—. Mem. Am. Psychol. Assn. (indsl./organizational psychology div.), Am. Soc. Tng. and Devel. (orgn. devel. div.), Insurance Co. Edn. Dirs. Soc., Alliance Am. Insurers (edn. com.), Wis. Pschol. Assn., Am. Personnel and Guidance Assn., Cornell U. Alumni Secondary Schs. Com., Phi Delta Kappa, Psi Chi (v.p. Marquette U. chpt. 1971), Sigma Pi. Clubs: Cornell of Wis., Stevens Point Country. Contbr. articles to profl. jours. Home: 1303 Crossbow Dr Stevens Point WI 54481 Office: 1800 N Point Dr Stevens Point WI 54481

SOBEL, HOWARD BERNARD, osteopathic physician; b. N.Y.C., May 15, 1929; s. Martin and Ella (Sternberg) S.; m. Ann Louise Silverbush, June 16, 1957 (dec. May 1978); children—Nancy Sobel Schumer, Janet Sobel-Medow, Robert; m. Irene S. Miller, June 8, 1980; stepchildren—Avner Saferstein, Daniel Saferstein, Naomi Saferstein. A.B., Syracuse U., 1951; D.O., Kansas City Coll. Osteopathy and Surgery, 1955. Intern, Zieger Osteo. Hosp., Detroit, 1955-56; gen. practice medicine, Redford Twp., Mich., 1956-74, Livonia, Mich., 1974—; chief of staff Botsford Gen. Hosp., Farmington, Mich., 1978; mem. faculty Mich. State U. Coll. Osteo. Medicine, 1969—, clin. assoc. prof. family practice, 1973—. Mem. exec. and med. adv. coms. United Health Orgn. Mich.; mem. VD Action Com., Mich.; apptd. to assist impaired osteo. physicians Mich., 1983; bd. dirs. Med. Rev. Orgn. Wayne County, Physicians Rev. Orgn. Wayne County. Mem. Am. Osteo. Assn. (ho. of dels. 1981-83), Mich. Assn. Osteo. Physicians and Surgeons (ho. of dels.), Am. Coll. Osteo. Rheumatologists, Coll. Am. Osteo. Gen. Practitioners, Osteo. Gen. Practice Mich., Wayne County Osteo. Assn. (past pres.). Jewish. Home: 6222 Northfield West Bloomfield MI 48033 Office: 28275 Five Mile Rd Livonia MI 48154

SOBELSOHN, DAVID C., law educator; b. N.Y.C., May 13, 1953; s. William and Hermine (Schwartz) S. B.A., U. Chgo., 1974; J.D. cum laude, Boston U., 1977. Bar: Calif. 1978, Ill. 1979. Teaching fellow Stanford U. Law Sch., Calif., 1977-78; assoc. Jenner & Block, Chgo., 1979-81; asst. prof. law Case Western Res. U., Cleve., 1981-85; vis. assoc. prof. law U. Detroit, 1985—. Cons. Ill. Coalition Against Death Penalty, Chgo., 1979-82, NOW, Chgo., 1979-81, Edn. for Freedom of Choice, Cleve., 1981-83. Democrat. Jewish. Home: 1431 Washington Blvd Detroit MI 48226 Office: U Detroit Law Sch 651 E Jefferson Ave Detroit MI 48226

SOBIERAY, RICHARD JOSEPH, architect, health care consultant; b. Lucernemines, Pa., July 20, 1940; s. Joseph Stanley and Anna Louise (Brodrick) S.; m. Gerry Muskus, May 16, 1964; children—Richard, Michael, Robyn. B.S. in Architecture, U. Cin., 1970. Cert. Nat. Council Archtl. Registration Bds.; registered architect, Ind., W.Va. Project architect Lewis & Shimer Architects, Inc., Indpls., 1970-74; pres. Richard J. Sobieray Architects, Inc., Indpls., 1974—; pres. Boyd/Sobieray Assocs., Indpls., 1975—; cons. health care. Served with U.S. Army, 1960-63. Mem. Am. Soc. Health Planners, Am. Hosp. Assn., AIA (cert.), Nat. Council Archtl. Registration Bds., Ind. Soc. Architects, Nat. Fire Protection Assn., Cons. Engrs. Ind., Am. Arbitration Assn., Indpls. C. of C. Clubs: Kiwanis, Shriners. Office: 6810 N Shadeland Ave Indianapolis IN 46220

SOBOLESKI, RENEE MAXINE, educator; b. International Falls, Minn., Jan. 27, 1937; d. Max Paul and Elaine Josephine (LaValley) Goulet; m. Frank Joseph Soboleski, Jan. 12, 1973; children—Beth E. Madison, Bonnie I. LaJambe, Barbara L. Cassibo. A.S., Rainy River Community Coll., 1968; B.S., Bemidji State U., 1970, M.S., 1976. Spl. edn. tchr. International Falls (Minn.) Sch. Dist. 361, 1970-78, elem. edn. tchr., 1978-84; now spl. edn./EMH tchr. Backus Middle Sch. Sunday Sch. tchr. Sr. high sch. students. Mem. Minn. Fedn. Tchrs. (bd. dirs., negotiating com. 1980-84), Cat Fanciers Assn. AAUW. Clubs: Gen. Federated Women's (v.p. 1972-74, pres., 1974-76), Ice Box Twirlers Square Dance (International Falls, Minn.). Home: Route 8 Box 121 International Falls MN 55649 Office: Alexander Baker Middle Sch International Falls MN 56649

SOGNEFEST, PETER WILLIAM, manufacturing company executive; b. Melrose Park, Ill., Feb. 4, 1941; s. Peter and Alvera E. Sognefest; B.S. in E.E., U. Ill., 1964, M.S. in E.E., 1967; m. Margaret Brunkow, Aug. 15, 1964; children—Scott, Brian, Jennifer. Elec. engr. Magnavox Corp., Urbana, Ill., 1964-67; sr. fellow, mgr. research, United Techs. fellow Mellon Inst., Pitts., 1967-71; gen. mgr. for semicondr. ops. United Techs., Pitts., 1971-77; v.p. indsl. electronics unit Motorola Inc., Schaumburg, Ill., 1977-84; pres., chief exec. officer Digital Appliance Controls, Inc., Hoffman Estates, Ill., 1984—, also dir.; dir. Two-Six Inc. Mem. IEEE, U. Ill. Elec. Engring. Alumni Assn. (pres. 1984), Covey Property Owners Assn. (pres. 1982). Republican. Presbyterian (pres. bd. deacons 1981). Clubs: Univ., Longue Vue. Patentee in field. Home: 4 Back Bay Rd Barrington IL 60010 Office: 2401 Hassell Rd Hoffman Estates IL 60195

SOKOL, ROBERT JAMES, obstetrician, gynecologist, educator; b. Rochester, N.Y., Nov. 18, 1941; s. Eli and Mildred (Levine) S.; B.A. with highest distinction in Philosophy, U. Rochester, 1963, M.D. with honors, 1966; m. Roberta Sue Kahn, July 26, 1964; children—Melissa Anne, Eric Russell, Andrew Ian. Intern, Barnes Hosp., Washington U., St. Louis, 1966-67, resident in obstetrics and gynecology, 1967-70, asst. in obstetrics and gynecology, 1966-70, research asst., 1967-68, instr. clin. obstetrics and gynecology, 1970; Buswell fellow in maternal fetal medicine Strong Meml. Hosp., U. Rochester, 1972-73, asst. prof., asso. obstetrician and gynecologist, 1972-73; fellow in maternal fetal medicine Cleve. Met. Gen. Hosp., Case Western Res. U., Cleve., 1974-75, asso. obstetrician and gynecologist, 1973-83, asst. prof. obstetrics and gynecology, 1973-77, asst. program dir. Perinatal Clin. Research Center, 1973-78, co-program dir., 1978-82, program dir., 1982-83, acting dir. obstetrics, 1974-75, co-dir., 1977-83, assoc. prof., 1977-81, prof., 1981-83, asso. dir. dept. ob-gyn, 1981-83; prof., chmn. dept. ob-gyn Wayne State U., Detroit, 1983—; dir. C.S. Mott Ctr. Human Growth and Devel., Detroit, 1983—; past pres. med. staff Cuyahoga County Hosps.; chief ob-gyn Hutzel Hosp., Detroit, 1983—; mem. profl. adv. bd. Educated Childbirth, Inc., 1976-80; cons. NIH task forces and Nat. Clearinghouse for Alcohol Psychosocial Research rev. com. Nat. Inst. Alcohol Abuse and Alcoholism, 1981—, Nat. Inst. Child Health and Human Devel., Health Resources and Services Adminstrn.; assoc. examiner Am. Bd. Ob-Gyn. Mem. pres.'s leadership council U. Rochester, 1976-80. Served from capt. to maj. M.C., USAF, 1970-72. Diplomate Nat. Bd. Med. Examiners, Am. Bd. Obstetrics and Gynecology, Sub-Bd. Maternal-Fetal Medicine. Mem. Am. Coll. Obstetricians and Gynecologists, Soc. Gynecologic Investigation, Perinatal Research Soc., Assn. Profs. Gyn-Ob, Behavioral Teratoloy Soc., Research Soc. Alcoholism, AMA, Royal Soc, Medicine, Wayne County Med. Soc., Mich. State Med. Soc., Soc. Perinatal Obstetricians, Central Assn. Ob-Gyn, Research Soc. Alcoholism, Phi Beta Kappa Alpha Omega Alpha. Republican. Jewish. Contbr. articles and chpts. to med. jours. and books; reviewer several med. jours.; mem. editorial bd. Jour. Perinatal Medicine, 1985—; researcher computer applications in perinatal medicine, alcohol-related birth defects, cardiac and neuro-physiology. Home: 5200 Rector Ct Bloomfield Hills MI 48013 Office: Hutzel Hosp Dept Ob-Gyn 4707 St Antoine Blvd Detroit MI 48201

SOKOLL, MARTIN DAVID, physician, educator; b. Harrisville, Ohio, Oct. 14, 1932; s. Frank and Leocadia (Pesta) S. B.S., Coll. Steubenville, 1954; M.D., U. Pitts., 1958. Diplomate Am. Bd. Anesthesiology. Intern St. Margaret Meml. Hosp., Pitts., 1958-59; resident Mercy Hosp., Pitts., 1959-61; asst. prof. U. Iowa, Iowa City, 1963-67, assoc. prof. anesthesiology, 1968—. Contbr. chpts. to books and articles to profl. jours. Pres. Johnson County Med. Soc., 1983—. Served as capt. USAF, 1961-63. USPHS research fellow, 1967. Mem. Am. Soc. Anesthesiologists (dist. dir. 1982—), Am. Soc. Pharmacology and Exptl. Therapeutics, AAAS, N.Y. Acad. Sci., Assn. Univ. Anesthetists. Roman Catholic. Avocations: jogging; pianist. Office: Dept Anesthesia U Iowa Iowa City IA 52242

SOLBERG, ELIZABETH TRANSOU, public relations executive; b. Dallas, Aug. 10, 1939; d. Ross W. and Josephine V. (Perkins) Transou; m. Frederick M. Solberg, Mar. 8, 1969; 1 son, Frederick W. B.J., U. Mo., 1961. Reporter, Kansas City (Mo.) Star, 1963-70, asst. city editor, 1970-73; reporter spl. events, documentaries Sta. WDAF-TV, Kansas City, Mo., 1973-74; prof. dept. journalism Park Coll., Kansas City, Mo., 1975-76, advisor, 1976-79; mng. ptnr. Fleishman-Hillard, Inc., Kansas City, Mo., 1979—. Mem. Kansas City Commn. Planned Indsl. Expansion Authority, 1974—; mem. long-range planning com. Heart of Am. council Boy Scouts Am., 1980-82; mem. Clay County (Mo.) Devel. Commn., 1979—; bd. govs. Citizens Assn., 1975-82. Recipient award for contbn. to mental health Mo. Psychiat. Assn., 1973. Mem. Pub. Relations Soc. Am. (nat. honors and awards com., co-chmn. Silver Anvil Com. 1983; Silver Anvil award 1979-82), Mo. C. of C. Pub. Relations Council, Kansas City C. of C., Pi Beta Phi. Clubs: Jr. League, Kansas City, Carriage, Central Exchange. Office: One Crown Ctr Suite 507 Kansas City MO 64108

SOLBERG, NELLIE FLORENCE COAD, artist; b. Sault Ste. Marie, Mich.; d. Sanford and Mary (McDonald) Coad; m. Ingvald Solberg, Aug. 24, 1930; children—Jeanne Elaine Solberg Unruh, Walter Eugene, Kay Louise Solberg Link. B.A., Minot State Tchrs. Coll., 1930; M.A., N.D. State U., 1963; postgrad. Wash. State U., 1960, U. Wyo., 1964, St. Cloud Coll., 1971. Tchr. Bismarck Elem. Schs., N.D., 1954-63, art dir. high sch., 1963-72; instr. art Bismarck Jr. Coll., 1964-67; cons. Bismarck Art Assn. Galleries, 1973-79, State Capitol Galleries, 1973-78; dir. arts festivals including Statewide Religious Arts Festival, Bismarck, 1969-85, State Treas.'s Gallery, 1977, N.D. State Capitol, Bismarck, 1973-78; co-dir. Indian Art Show, Nat. Congress Am. Indians, Bismarck, 1963. One-woman shows include Minot State Coll., 1963, Dickinson State Coll., 1964, Jamestown Coll., 1964, U. N.D., Valley City State Coll., Bismarck Jr. Coll., 1963, 65, 68, 69, N.D. State U., 1970, 74, Linha Gallery, Minot N.D., 1972, 74-77, Bank of N.D., 1972-74, 76-77, Elan Gallery, 1982; exhibited in group shows at Gov. John Davis Mansion, 1960, Concordia Coll., Moorhead, Minn., 1965, N.D. Capitol, 1968, 69, Gov. William Guy Mansion, 1971, Internat. Peace Gardens, 1969. Mem. Indian Culture Found., 1964—, Civic Music Assn., 1942—; religious arts com. Conf. Chs., 1973; bd. dirs. Citizens for Arts, 1978-81. Recipient numerous awards including Gov.'s award for arts, 1977, Gov. Allen Olson award, 1982, Gov.'s award Bismarck Art Show, 1982, Dakota Northwestern Bank award, 1983, Dr. Shari Orser Purchase award Religious Arts Festival, 1984, William Murray award Religious Arts Festival, 1984; named N.D. Woman Artist of Yr., 1974. Mem. Bismarck Arts and Galleries Assn. (membership com.), Bismarck Art Assn. (charter, Honor award 1960, pres. 1963-64, 71-72), Jamestown Art Assn., Linha Gallery (Minot), Nat. League Am. Pen Women (pres. N.D. 1964-66, pres. Medora br. 1972-74, treas. 1975—), Mpls. Soc. Fine Arts, P.E.O. (pres. chpts. 1967-69), Bismarck Vets, Meml. Library (life), Soc. Preservation Gov.'s Mansion (charter, bd. dirs.), Sigma Sigma Sigma. Republican. Lodges: Zonta, Order of Eastern Star. Home: 925 N 6th St Bismarck ND 58501 Office: 1021 N 6th St Bismarck ND 58501

SOLBERG, RONALD DEAN, bank public relations executive; b. Tracy, Minn., Jan. 20, 1941; s. Adolph Tedeman and Helen Marie (Swanjord) S.; m. Norma Shearon Dick, Aug. 3, 1962; children—Barrett R., Jerrell C. Student, St. Olaf Coll., 1958-60; B.S., Mankato State U., 1962, B.A., 1962. Tchr. English and journalism Tech. High Sch., St. Cloud, Minn., 1962-69; dir. publs. and pub. relations Central Minn. Ednl. Research and Devel. Council, St. Cloud, 1969-70; coordinator sch. info. Downers Grove Schs., Ill., 1970-73; dir. communications Inst. Real Estate Mgmt., Chgo., 1973-75; dir. pub. relations Million Dollar Round Table, Des Plaines, Ill., 1975-77; staff media rep. Standard Oil Co. of Ind., Chgo., 1977-79; press relations adminstr. Continental Bank, Chgo., 1979-81, corp. affairs officer, mgr. retail advt., 1981-83, 2d v.p., 1983—. Chmn.

fin. com., first asst. treas. Woodhaven Lakes Assn., 1982, v.p., 1984—. Mem. Pub. Relations Soc. Am. (chpt. pres.-elect 1984, chpt. pres. 1985, nat. chmn. technologies task force). Democrat. Unitarian. Home: 1032 61st St Downers Grove IL 60516 Office: Continental Bank 231 S LaSalle St Chicago IL 60697

SOLEM, MAIZIE ROGNESS, educator; b. Hendricks, Minn., Nov. 8, 1920; d. John A. and Nora Adeline (Engelstad) Rogness; B.A., Augustana Coll., 1942; postgrad. George Washington U., 1955-57, Wright State U. 1970-71; M.Ed., Miami U., Oxford, Ohio, 1970-71; Ed.D., U. S.D., 1976; postgrad. U. Calif., 1978. Tchr., LeMars, Iowa, 1942-43, Internat. Children's Centre, Bangkok, Thailand, 1952-53, George Washington U., Washington, 1957, Fairfax (Va.) schs., 1956-58, Maxwell AFB Sch., Montgomery, Ala., 1963-66; tchr., librarian Central High Sch., Madison, S.D., 1943; dir., tchr., supr. remedial reading tchrs. City schs., Fairborn, Ohio, 1966-71; Title I resource tchr. L.B. Anderson Elem. Sch., Sioux Falls, S.D., 1971-73; primary coordinator Instructional Planning Center, Sioux Falls, 1973-77; curriculum coordinator Sioux Falls public schs., 1973—. Mem. adv. bd. Ret. Sr. Vol. Program, 1974-78, publicity chmn., 1975-78; mem. adv. bd. Vol. Action Center, 1976-78, mem. service com., 1974-78; chmn. exec. bd. Augustana Fellows, 1979-81; scholarship chmn. LaSertoma, 1979-80; active various drives including Heart Fund, Muscular Dystrophy, Cancer Fund; bd. regents Augustana Coll., 1984—. Recipient S.D. Gov.'s award for vol. of yr. in edn., 1984, Leader Luncheon award in field of professions YWCA, 1984. Mem. AAUW, Sch. Adminsrs. S.D. (v.p. 1977-78), Assn. Supervision Curriculum Devel. (pres. 1976-78, nat. exec. council 1979-82), Nat. Assn. Supervision Curriculum Devel. (bd. dirs. 1977-79; mem. nat. selection com. 1977-78), Assn. Childhood Edn. Internat., S.D. Assn. Elem. Prins., Elem., Kindergarten, Nursery Sch. Edn., Nat. Assn. Edn. Young Children, Sioux Land Assn. for Edn. Young Children, NEA, S.D. Edn. Assn., Nat. Council Social Studies, Internat. Reading Assn., S.D. Tchrs. Maths. Orgn., S.D. Assn. Supervision and Curriculum Devel., Orton Soc. Republican. Lutheran. Home: 1600 North Dr Box 911 Sioux Falls SD 57101 Office: 201 E 38th St Sioux Falls SD 57102

SOLENBERGER, IRA DALE, accountant; b. Douglas, N.D., Mar. 21, 1918; s. Harry Hale and Ragnhildt (Knudtsen) S.; B.B.A., U. Minn., 1947; m. Emma I. Peterson, July 8, 1944; 1 son, David R. With Ernst & Whinney, Kansas City, Mo., 1951-83; pvt. accts. and taxes, 1983—; mgr. tax dept. Treas., Greater Kansas City People to People Council. Served with U.S. Army, 1943-46. C.P.A., Mo. Mem. Am. Inst. C.P.A.s, Mo. Soc. C.P.A.s, Estate Planning Council Kansas City, Heart of Am., Japan-Am. Soc. Republican. Congregationalist. Clubs: Kansas City, Blue Hills Country. Home and Office: 7933 Roe Ave Prairie Village KS 66208

SOLIE, TIMOTHY LEE, lawyer; b. Mpls., Aug. 21, 1958; s. Emory Arthur and Margaret Joan (O'Neil) S.; m. Anne Elizabeth DeVout, Feb. 7, 1981; 1 child, Jenna Elizabeth. B.S. in Bus. Adminstrn., U. N.D., 1979; J.D., William Mitchell Coll. Law, 1982. Bar: Minn. 1982. Acctg. clk. Equico Lessors, Mpls., 1979-81; law clk. then ptnr. Gaasedelen & Solie, Mpls., 1981-83; ptnr. Solie & Solie, Mpls., 1983—. Group home counselor Summit House II, St. Louis Park, Minn., 1982-84; foster parent New Life Homes, 1984—; del. Ind. Republican Party, Mpls., 1984—; deacon Shiloh-Bethany Presbyterian Ch., Mpls., 1983—; vol. atty. Christian Legal Soc., Mpls., 1982—, Legal Advice Clinic, Mpls., 1982-83. Mem. Minn. Bar Assn., Phi Beta Si. Office: Solie & Solie 200 Mar-Ten Bldg 921 Marquette Ave Minneapolis MN 55402

SOLLENBERGER, DONNA FITZPATRICK, educational administrator; b. Tuscola, Ill., Jan. 13, 1949; d. Vincent Norman and Marian Louise (Mumbower) Fitzpatrick; student U. Kans., 1968-70; B.A., Sangamon State U., 1971, M.A., 1974; 1 child, Shannon. Tchr., Springfield (Ill.) S.E. High Sch., 1971-74; public info. officer Ill. Dept. Transp., Springfield, 1974-75; exec. asst. to dir. Ill. Dept. Conservation, Springfield, 1975-76; adminstrv. asst. to chmn. dept. surgery So. Ill. U. Sch. Medicine, Springfield, 1976-80, asst. to chmn. dept. surgery, 1984—; instr. communications Lincoln Land Community Coll., Springfield, part-time, 1976-77, instr. English, 1980-84. Mem. Springboard Arts Council. Recipient Conservation Merit award Ill. Dept. Conservation, 1976. Mem. Nat. Council Tchrs. of English, Springfield Art Assn., Delta Gamma Alumnae Assn. Morman. Home: 1930 Whittier St Springfield IL 62704 Office: 801 N Rutledge St Springfield IL 62702

SOLOMON, MARK RAYMOND, law educator, lawyer; b. Pitts., Aug. 23, 1945; s. Louis Isadore and Fern Rhea (Josselson) S. B.A., Ohio State U., 1967; M.Ed., Cleve. State U., 1971; J.D. with honors, George Washington U., 1973; LL.M. in Taxation, Georgetown U., 1976. Bar: Ohio, Mich. Assoc., Butzel, Long, Gust, Klein & Van Zile, Detroit, 1976-78; dir., v.p. Shatzman & Solomon, P.C., Southfield, Mich., 1978-81; prof., chmn. tax and bus. law dept., dir. M.S. in Taxation Program, Walsh Coll., Troy, Mich., 1981—; of counsel in tax matters Meyer, Kirk, Snyder and Safford, Bloomfield Hills Mich., 1981—; adj. prof. law U. Detroit, 1977-81. Editor: Cases and Materials on Consolidated Tax Returns, 1978. Mem. ABA, Mich. Bar Assn., Ohio Bar Assn., Phi Eta Sigma. Clubs: Kiwanis. Avocation: bridge (life master). Home: Apt 102 2109 Golfview Dr Troy MI 48084 Office: Meyer Kirk Snider and Safford Suite 100 100 W Long Lake Rd Bloomfield Hills MI 48013

SOLOMON, MARTIN B., computer science educator. B.S. in Commerce, U. Ky., 1955, M.B.A., 1960, Ph.D. in Bus. and Econs., 1967. Instr. Coll. Commerce, U. Ky., 1960-67; assoc. prof. dept. bus. adminstrn., 1967-82, acting chmn. computer sci. dept., 1967-69; research assoc. U. Ky. Computing Ctr., 1960-62, mgr. ops. and systems, 1962-64, asst. dir., 1964-67, dir., 1967-82; prof. computer and info. sci. Ohio State U., Columbus, 1982—, dir. acad. computing, 1982—; cons. in field; vis. scientist ACM and NSF, 1964-65. Co-author: (with Michael Kennedy) Eight Statement PL/C (PL/ZERO) Plus PL/ONE, 1972, Ten Statement Fortran Plus Fortran IV, 1975, Ten Instruction PASCAL, 1982. Contbr. articles to profl. jours. Chmn. HASP project SHARE, 1968-69, bd. dirs., 1969-70, treas., 1970-72; mem. higher edn. info. systems com. So. Regional Edn. Bd., 1968-71; bd. dirs. CUMREC, 1975-78; bd. dirs. CAUSE, 1981-84, program chmn., 1982; mem. Ohio Bd. Regents Computer Task Force, 1983-84. Mem. Assn. Computing Machinery, Am. Econs. Assn., Internat. Word Processing Assn. Office: Ohio State U Instrn and Research Computer Ctr 1971 Neil Ave Columbus OH 43210

SOLOMON, MICHAEL, civil engr., former univ. ofcl., cons.; b. Youngstown, Ohio, Oct. 27, 1921; s. Steve and Maria (Kulynch) S.; B.E., Youngstown U., 1957; M.S., U. Akron, 1962; m. Myrtle C. Chapman, July 7, 1957. Various positions constrn., also press operator Youngstown Paint Chrysler Corp., 1946-50; hwy. insp. Ohio Hwy. Dept., Youngstown, 1953; engr.-surveyor Mahoning Valley San. Dist., Youngstown, summers 1954, 57; Mahoning County San. Engring. Dept., Youngstown, 1957-67; asst. prof. civil engring. Youngstown U. (now Youngstown State U.), 1957-67; project mgr. san. engring., municipal engring. Mosure & Syrakis Co., Ltd., Youngstown, 1967-80; dir. phys. plant Youngstown State U., 1980-83; ret., 1983. Served with U.S. Army, 1942-46 to capt. C.E., 1942-53. Registered profl. engr., Ohio. Decorated Bronze Star. Mem. ASCE, Sigma Tau.

SOLTI, GEORG, conductor; b. Budapest, Hungary, Oct. 21, 1912; s. More and Theres (Rosenbaum) S.; ed. Budapest Music High Sch.; D.Music (hon.), Harvard U., Yale U., Greenville U., Rochester U., Oxford (Eng.) U., Leeds (Eng.) U., Surrey (Eng.) U., De Paul U.; m. Hedi Oechsli, October 29, 1946; m. 2d, Anne Valerie Pitts, Nov. 11, 1967. Musical asst. Budapest Opera House, 1930-33, condr., 1934-39; pianist (refugee) Switzerland, 1939-45; gen. music dir. Bavarian State Opera, Munich, Germany, 1946-52, Frankfurt (Germany) Staatstheater, 1952-60; mus. dir. Royal Opera House Covent Garden, London, 1961-71, Chgo. Symphony Orch. 1969—; prin. condr., artistic dir. London Philharmon. Orch., 1977-83, condr. emeritus, 1983—; pianist Concours Internat., Geneva, 1942; guest condr. various orchs.; condr. Salzburg Festival, Bayreuth, Edinburgh and Glyndebourne festivals, Vienna State Opera, Paris Opera, Vienna Philharmonic, Berlin, London, N.Y. Philharmonic orchs., Amsterdam, Concertgebouw, orchs. in San Francisco, Hollywood, Los Angeles, St. Louis & Ravinia (Ill.) Park, Chgo., Chgo. Lyric Opera. Decorated Great Cross of German Republic; comdr. Order Brit. Empire; knight Order Brit. Empire, comdr. Legion Honor (France); recipient grand prix du Disque Mondiale, 1959, 62, 63, 64, 66, 70, 77, 24 Grammy awards, 1963-85. Fellow Royal Coll. Music (hon.). Address: Chgo Symphony Orch 220 S Michigan Ave Chicago IL 60604

SOLTIS, ROBERT ALAN, lawyer; b. Gary, Ind., Jan. 30, 1955; s. George William and Frances Marie (Jakob) S. A.B. (scholar), Ind. U., 1977; J.D. DePaul U., 1982. Bar: Ill. 1982, Ind. 1982, U.S. Dist. Ct. (no. dist.) Ill. 1982,

---

U.S. Dist. Ct. (No. and so. dists.) Ind. 1982, U.S. Ct. Apls. (7th cir.) 1983, U.S. Dist. Ct. Trial (no. dist.) Ill. 1984, Ind. Indsl. Bd. 1982; lic. instrument-rated pilot. Photographer, Herald Newspapers, Merrillville, Ind., 1971-72; dep. coroner Lake County, Ind., 1972-78, spl. dep. sheriff, 1972-78; dep. coroner, Monroe County, Ind., 1975-76; area dir. Mayors Office of Urban Conservation, Gary, Ind., 1977-80; title examiner Law Bull. Title Services, Chgo., 1980; field clm. rep. Employers Ins. of Wausau, River Forest, Ill., 1980-82; assoc. Perz & McGuire, P.C., Chgo., 1982-84, McKenna Storer Rowe White & Farrug, Chgo., 1984—. Dir. pub. info. Am. Cancer Soc., Gary, 1977-79, Monroe County unit, 1975-76; pres. Gary Young Democrats, 1977-78; bd. dirs. N.W. Ind. Urban League; precinct committeeman Democratic Party, Gary, 1978-82; chmn. Com. to Retain State Rep. William Drozda, 1978-82. Recipient Outstanding Reporter award Lake County Mayor of Dimes, 1973; Disting. Service award Am. Cancer Soc. Ind. Div., 1975, 76. Mem. ABA, Chgo. Bar Assn., Ill. State Bar Assn., Ind. State Bar Assn., Lawyer-Pilots Bar Assn., Glen Park Jaycees (pres. chpt. 1977), Ind. U. Alumni Assn. (life). Roman Catholic. Club: Slovak (Gary). Co-host twice weekly TV show: Cancer and You, Bloomington, Ind., 1975-76; contbr. articles in field of cancer. Home: 1711 W 105th Pl Chicago IL 60643 Office: 135 S LaSalle Suite 4200 Chicago IL 60603

SOMERICK, NANCY MARIE, communication educator, consultant; b. Barberton, Ohio, Sept. 16, 1945; d. Anthony Lawrence and Margaret Marie (Patrick) Somerick. B.S. cum laude, Ohio U., 1967, Ph.D., 1974; M.A., Kent State U., 1969. Communication dir. Kent State U. Stark Campus, Canton, Ohio, 1973-74; asst. prof. Cleve. State U., 1974-77; officer, pub. relations mgr. BancOhio/Akron Nat. Bank, Akron, 1977-78; asst. prof. U. Akron, 1978-83, assoc. prof. communication, 1983—; cons. Wadsworth Pub. Co., Belmont, Calif., 1981, 84, West Pub. Co., Mpls., 1982. Author Case Studies in Public Relations: the Profession and the Practice, 1983; contbr. articles and book revs. to profl. jours.; mem. editorial bd. Coll. Press Rev., 1980. Pub. relations cons. to community orgns., Summit County, Ohio, 1978-84; founder, adviser Pub. Relations Student Soc. Am., U. Akron, 1978-86; mem. County Bd. of Visitors, Summit County, 1980-83; judge contest for high sch. students Ohio Press Women's Assn., 1981. Recipient Merit award for teaching Cleve. State U. Dept. Communication, 1976; adviser of yearbook with 1st place rating Am. Scholastic Press Assn., 1983. Mem. Pub. Relations Soc. Am., Internat. Assn. Bus. Communicators, Internat. Communication Assn., Women in Communications, Assn. Edn. in Journalism, Akron Press Club, Akron Advt. Club, Sigma Delta Chi. Democrat. Roman Catholic. Home: 908 E Robinson Ave Barberton OH 44203 Office: Univ Akron Dept Communication Akron OH 44325

SOMERS, WILLIAM WESTLEY, optometric educator, environmental vision consultant, visual training specialist; b. Chgo., Oct. 19, 1947; s. George William and Norma Jean (West) S. B.S.c., Ohio State U., 1969, O.D., 1971, M.S., 1973, Ph.D., 1977. Diplomate Nat. Bd. Examiners Optometry. Grad. teaching assoc. Ohio State U. Coll. Optometry, Columbus, 1971-76, clin. instr., 1971-76; instr. Columbus Inst. Tech., 1976; asst. prof. Ind. U. Sch. Optometry, Bloomington, 1977—; cons. Visual Display Terminal Hazards, Ind. Bell Telephone Co., Bloomington, 1983, Can. Captioning Devel. Agy., Montreal, Que., 1984; spl. cons. vision Goodman, Eden, Millender & Bedrosian, Detroit, 1983; cons. Environ. and Occupational Vision - VDT Safety, St. Louis, 1984; cons. Devel. Tng. Ctr., Bloomington, 1983-84. Co-author: Vision Training Manual: Lectures and Laboratories, 1982. Contbr. articles to profl. jours. Alt. mem. Ind. Gov.'s Commn. on Handicapped, Indpls., 1980; cons. Brown County Community Sch. Corp., Nashville, Ind., 1982; mem. Monroe County Amateur Radio Emergency System and SKYWARN, Bloomington, 1982-84; panelist Community Service Council's Forum on Reading Disabilities, Bloomington, 1980. Am. Optometric Found. fellow, 1973-74; research grantee Ind. U., 1977; named Optometry Prof. Yr., Ind. U. Student Optometric Assn., 1980. Mem. Am. Optometric Assn., Am. Acad. Optometry, Ind. Optometric Assn. (Optometric Concern for Ednl. Concern div.), Stonebelt Optometric Soc., Beta Sigma Kappa. Baptist. Avocations: private pilot, amateur radio, astronomy, softball, cross-country skiing. Office: Ind U Sch Optometry 800 E Atwater Ave Bloomington IN 47405

SOMERVILLE, RONALD LAMONT, biochemistry educator; b. Vancouver, B.C., Jan., Feb. 27, 1935; came to U.S., 1957; s. Thomas Lennox and Vivian May (Code) S.; m. Joyce Elizabeth Crowe, May 4, 1955; children—Gregory, Kenneth, Gordon, Victoria, Daniel. B.A. with honors, U. B.C., 1956, M.S.c., 1957; Ph.D., U. Mich., 1961. Vis. scholar Stanford U., 1961-64; asst. prof., U. Mich., 1964-67; assoc. prof. biochemistry Purdue U., West Lafayette, Ind., 1967-77, prof. biochemistry, 1977—; cons. NIH, 1982—, Monsanto Co., St. Louis, 1983—, Genex Corp., Gaithersburg, Md., 1980-84. Author/editor: Amino Acids: Biosynthesis and Genetic Regulation, 1983. Contbr. articles to profl. jours. Patentee in field. Served to lt. Royal Can. Navy Res., 1952-57. C.T. Huang lectr. U. Hong Kong, 1983. Mem. Am. Soc. Biol. Chemists, Genetics Soc. Am., Am. Soc. Microbiology. Office: Dept Biochemistry Purdue U West Lafayette IN 47907

SOMIT, ALBERT, university president; b. Chgo., Oct. 25, 1919; s. Samuel and Mary (Rosenblum) S.; A.B., U. Chgo., 1941, Ph.D., 1947; m. Leyla D. Shapiro, Aug. 31, 1947; children—Scott H., Jed L. Prof. polit. philosophy N.Y. U., 1945-65; chmn. dept. polit. sci. State U. N.Y. at Buffalo, 1966-69, exec. v.p., 1970-80, acting pres., 1976-77; pres. So. Ill. U., Carbondale, 1980—; fellow Netherlands Inst. Advanced Study, 1978-79; Nimitz prof. polit. philosophy U.S. Naval War Coll., 1961-62. Served with AUS, 1950-52. Author: (with Joseph Tanenhaus) The Development of American Political Science: From Burgess to Behavioralism, 1967, rev., 1982; (with Tanenhaus) American Political Science: A Profile of a Discipline, 1964; Political Science and the Study of the Future, 1974; Biology and Politics: Recent Explorations, 1976; (with others) The Literature of Biopolitics 1963-1977, 1978. Home: Stone House Douglas Dr So Ill U Carbondale IL 62901

SOMMER, JOSEPH THOMAS, magnetic coil company executive; b. Chgo., Apr. 23, 1941; s. Joseph J. and Solveig E. S.; m. Barbara Carol Homer, Dec. 17, 1965; children—Joseph Thomas, Jeffrey Todd. B.S., U. Ill., 1964. With Magnetic Coil Mfg. Co., Chgo., 1964—, exec. v.p., 1972—; mgmt. cons. Head swim coach YMCA, Camp Duncan, Volo, Ill.; bd. dirs. YMCA Camp Duncan. Mem. Sigma Chi (bd. dirs. chpt.).

SOMMER, THOMAS PETER, JR., data processing company executive; b. Evanston, Ill., Jan. 21, 1952; s. Thomas Peter and Nancy Lois (Hager) S.; m. Mary Diane Pienkowski, Aug. 17, 1973; children—Thomas Peter III, Daniel Clayton. B.A., Washington U., St. Louis, 1974, M.B.A., 1976. Account mgr. Automatic Data Processing, Inc., Chgo., 1976-79, tng. specialist, Ann Arbor, Mich., 1979-81, supr. software product devel., 1982—. Asst. treas. Webster United Ch. of Christ, Ann Arbor, 1984-85. Mem. Am. Soc. Tng. and Devel. (data base mgr. 1980-81). Republican. Office: Automatic Data Processing Inc 175 Jackson Plaza Ann Arbor MI 48106

SOMMERS, PAUL ALLEN, health care executive; b. Marshfield, Wis., Apr. 9, 1945; s. Frank Albert and Rosalie Bertha (Steffen) S.; B.S., U. Wis., 1967; M.S., So. Ill. U., 1969, Ph.D., 1971; m. Carol Ann Newsom, June 10, 1967; children—Eric Paul, Marc Allen. Instr. health/phys. edn. Wisconsin Rapids (Wis.) public schs., 1967-68; instr. dept. health/phys. edn. So. Ill. U., Carbondale, 1968-69, research asst. dept. spl. edn., 1969-70, instr., 1970-71; evaluation cons. Minn. State Dept. Edn., St. Paul, 1971-72; dir. Spl. Edn. Services-Coop. Edn. Service Agy. 4, Cumberland, Wis., 1972-73; dir. spl. edn. services Wausau (Wis.) Dist. public schs., 1973-75; dir. liaison edn. affairs Comprehensive Child Care Center, Marshfield (Wis.) Clinic and Med. Found., 1975-80; instr. exeptional children U. Wis., Stevens Point, 1973-79, Milton (Wis.) Coll., 1973-79; exec. dir. Comprehensive Child Care Center, asst. adminstr. Gundersen Clinic, LaCrosse, Wis., 1980-85; chief adminstrv. officer Ramsey Clinic, St. Paul, 1985—; field editor div. spl. edn. and rehab. U.S. Dept. Edn., 1982—. Bd. dirs. Midstate Epilepsy Ctr., 1976-78, Neurodevel. Inst. for Cerebral Palsy, Wausau Med. Center, 1973-80; bd. dirs. mem. policy com. Sunburst Youth Homes for Emotionally Disturbed, 1975-80, Wis. Assn. Perinatal Centers, 1976-79. Recipient Disting. Service award Epilepsy Assn., 1980; Nat. Doctoral Honors fellow, 1970-71; State of Ill. Masters Honors fellow, 1969-70; State of Wis. scholar, 1966-67, many grants. Mem. Am. Public Health Assn., Nat. Council Adminstrs. of Spl. Edn., Wis. Council Adminstrs. of Spl. Edn. (exec. officer 1975-76), Council for Exceptional Children, Am. Assn. on Mental Deficiency, United Cerebral Palsy Assn. Am., United Cerebral Palsy Assn. Wis., Nat. Epilepsy Assn., Wis. Epilepsy Assn. (pres. Midstate Ctr. 1978-80), Easter Seal Soc. Wis. (v.p. 1978-79), Wis. Assn. Perinatal Centers, Wis. Assn. Children with Learning Disabilities (profl. adv.

---

bd. 1983—), Am. Med. Group Practice Assn. (mktg. com. 1983—), Med. Group Mgmt. Assn. Lutheran. Contbr. articles to profl. jours. and books. Home: 221 13th Ave S Onalaska WI 54650 Office: 1836 South Ave LaCrosse WI 54601

SOMS, ANDREW PETER, mathematics educator; b. Riga, Latvia, Mar. 7, 1938; came to U.S., 1950, naturalized, 1956; s. Peter and Elsa S.; B.S. with high honors in Math. (Disting. Alumni fellow 1956-60), Mich. State U., 1960; M.S. in Math. (Woodrow Wilson fellow 1960-61), U. Wis., Madison, 1961, M.S. in Statistics (Wis. Alumni Research Found. fellow 1968-70), 1970, Ph.D. in Statistics (fellow 1970-71), 1972. Statistician, Mich. State Dept. Health, Lansing, 1961-62, Delco Electronics, Milw., 1962-68; computer scientist Burroughs, Wayne, Pa., 1973; sr. statistician G.D. Searle & Co., Skokie, Ill., 1973-75; asso. prof. dept. math., U. Wis., Milw., 1975—; vis. asst. prof. Math. Research Center, summer 1978, fall 1979; cons. pharm. firms. Research grantee U. Wis., Milw., 1976-77, 77-78; Office Naval Research co-grantee, 1979-82. Mem. Am. Statis. Assn., Biometrics Soc., Inst. Math. Stats., Statis. Soc. Can. Contbr. papers in field to sci. publs. Home: 401 N Eau Claire Madison WI 53705 Office: Dept Math U Wis-Milw PO Box 413 Milwaukee WI 53201

SON, BENJAMIN SANTOS, physician; b. Rizal, Philippines, Jan. 6, 1939; came to U.S., 1963, naturalized, 1975; s. Liam and Lydia Carmelo (Santos) S.; m. Diane Margaret Richards, Dec. 12, 1970. A.A., Far Eastern U., Manila, 1957, M.D., 1962. Diplomate Am. Bd. Internal Medicine (Cardiovascular Disease). Intern, St. Elizabeth Hosp., Elizabeth, N.J., 1963; resident in internal medicine Albert Einstein Med. Ctr., Phila., 1964-66; fellow in cardiology Wayne County Gen. Hosp., Eloise, Mich., 1967-68, clin. cons. in cardiology, 1968-72; clin. instr. medicine U. Mich. Med. Sch., Ann Arbor, 1968-72; cons. cardiology Southwestern Mich. Health Care Assn., St. Joseph/Benton Harbor, Mich., 1972—. Bd. dirs. Mich. Heart Assn., Twin City Symphonic Soc. Fellow Am. Coll. Cardiology; mem. Am. Heart Assn., AMA. Home: 2110 Arrowhead Tr Saint Joseph MI 49085 Office: Southwestern Michigan Health Care Assn 777 Riverview Dr Benton Harbor MI 49022

SONGER, STEVEN WAYNE, insurance agent; b. Anderson, Ind., Jan. 10, 1949; s. Robert Neal and Dorothy Mae (Keesling) S.; m. Diane Lee Tabla, Feb. 1, 1975; children—Marquis, Micah. B.S., Ind. State U., 1971, M.S., 1977. Asst. dept. sports info. Ind. State U., Terre Haute, 1971-72; tchr. Anderson Community Schs., 1972-73; order clk. Gen. Motors Corp., Anderson, 1973-74; coordinator confs. and non-credit programs Ind. State U., 1974-83; equities registered rep. Equitable Life Assurance Soc. U.S., Terre Haute, 1983—; player agt. profl. athletes. Chmn. Brentwood Subdivs., Terre Haute, Leadership Terre Haute; vol. Wabash Valley United Way campaign. Recipient All-State Baseball Player award Ind. chpt. Nat. Baseball Congress, 1970, 73; Frat. Advisor of Yr. award Ind. State U., 1978. Mem. Nat. Assn. Life Underwriters, Assn. Repr. Profl. Athletes, Nat. Assn. Collegiate Dirs. Athletics, Nat. Assn. Athletic Mktg. and Devel. Dirs., Theta Chi (regional advisor). Home: Rural Route 51 Box 902 Terre Haute IN 47805 Office: 1110 Ohio St Terre Haute IN 47807

SONNINO, CARLO BENVENUTO, mfg. co. exec.; b. Torino, Italy, May 12, 1904; s. Moise and Amelia S.; Ph.D., U. Milano (Italy), 1927, LL.B., 1928; m. Mathilde Girodat, Jan. 21, 1949; children—Patricia, Frederic, Bruno. Dir. research Italian Aluminum Co., Milan, 1928-34; pres. Laesa Cons. Firm, Milano, 1934-43; tech. adviser Boxal, Fribourg, Switzerland, 1944-52, Thompson Brand, Rouen, France, 1972-76; materials engring. mgr. Emerson Electric Co., St. Louis, 1956-72, sr. staff scientist, 1972—; prof. metall. engring. Washington U., St. Louis, 1960-68, U. Mo. at Rolla, 1968—; cons. Monsanto Chem. Co., other major firms U.S., Europe. Decorated knight comdr. Italian Republic. Fellow Am. Soc. Metals, ASTM, Sigma Xi, Alpha Sigma Mu (hon.). Patentee process for synthetic cryolite; mfr. 1st aluminum cans in world, 1940; patentee in field metallurgy corrosion. Home: 7206 Kingsbury Blvd Saint Louis MO 63130 Office: Emerson E and S div Emerson Electric Co 8100 W Florissant St Saint Louis MO 63136

SOPER, GEORGE EBEN, hospital administrator, physical therapist; b. Mason City, Iowa, July 3, 1938; s. George Eben and Helen Margaret (Towle) S.; m. Jannis Esther Boardman, Aug. 15, 1959; children—Jennifer, Jonathon; m. 2d, Sharona Kapff, Apr. 18, 1970; children—Teresa, Jessica. B.A., U. No. Iowa, 1961; M.A., U. Iowa, 1967, Ph.D., 1976. Cert. phys. therapy, U. Iowa. Tchr., coll. community schs., Cedar Rapids, Iowa, 1961-64; chief, phys. therapist Myrtue Meml. Hosp., Harlan, Iowa, 1966-69; supr. phys. therapy U. Iowa Hosp. Sch., Iowa City, 1969-71; dir. phys. therapy U. Iowa Hosps. and Clinics, Iowa City, 1971-80; v.p. Meml. Hosp. of South Bend (Ind.), 1980—; clin. instr. phys. therapy Washington U., St. Louis, 1973-80, Northwestern U., 1974-80; mem. multipurpose adminstrv. ctr. rev. com., NIH, Dept. HEW, 1978-80; mem. Allied Health Professions Research Com. Nat. Arthritis Found., 1981-83; mem. in field. Bd. dirs. St. Joseph Council for Retarded, South Bend, 1982-84. Recipient Olive Farr Disting. Service award Iowa Phys. Therapy Assn., 1978. Mem. Am. Phys. Therapy Assn. (dir. 1977-80, sec. 1980-83), Am. Phys. Therapy Assn. (Ind. Chpt.), Am. Hosp. Assn. Republican. Club: Knollwood Country (Granger, Ind.). Contbr. articles to profl. jours.; cons. editor Allied Health and Behavioral Scis., 1977-81. Office: Meml Hosp 615 N Michigan St South Bend IN 46601

SORAWAT, SALLY ANN, pharmacist, nursing home consultant; b. Jamestown, N.D., Nov. 14, 1951; d. Donald Albert and Bernice Hazel (Brophy) Odenbach; m. Sutin Sorawat, Oct. 5, 1974; children—Stacey Albert, Eva Udon. B.S. in Pharmacy, N.D. State U., 1974. Registered pharmacist, N.D. Intern, City Pharmacy, Fergus Falls, Minn., 1973-75; pharmacist Medina Drug, N.D., 1975-76; pharmacist, owner Hatton Pharmacy, N.D., 1976—. Mem. bd. edn. St. John Ch., Hatton, N.D., 1984—. Mem. N.D. Pharm. Assn. Lutheran. Avocations: reading; crochet. Office: Hatton Pharmacy 505 7th St Hatton ND 58240

SOREMEKUN, MAURICE ADEKUNLE EBUN, obstetrician, gynecologist, medical center administrator; b. Lagos, Nigeria, Nov. 5, 1939; came to U.S., 1959; s. Joseph Oladipo Ebun and Jemima Oladuni (Cocker) S.; m. Sophronia Janet White, June 17, 1981; children—Yomi, Jadesola. B.S., W.Va. Wesleyan Coll., 1963; M.Sc., U. Western Ont. (Can.), 1968; M.D., U. Mich., 1974. Diplomate Am. Bd. Ob-Gyn. Intern, Wayne State U. Affiliated Hosps., Detroit, 1974-76; resident SUNY-Upstate Med. Ctr. Syracuse, 1978-80; active staff Kaiser Permanente Med. Ctr., Cleve., 1978-80, dir. in-patient maternity services, 1981—. Fellow Am. Coll. Ob-Gyn, Royal Soc. Medicine (affiliate); mem. AMA, Cleve. Med. Soc., Ohio State Med. Assn., Acad. Medicine Cleve., Am. Assn. Gynecological Laparoscopy. Office: Kaiser Permanente Med Ctr 2475 Martin Luther King Jr Dr Cleveland OH 44120

SORGEN, RICHARD JESSE, architect; b. Toledo, Ohio, Aug. 4, 1945; s. William C. and Frances Louise (Lederhaus) S.; m. Ellen Kathleen Mumma, Aug. 19, 1972; children—Brian Richard, Neal Andrew. B.S. in Arch., U. Mich., 1972, M.Arch. with high distinction, 1973, postgrad. U. Toledo, 1974, 80. Registered architect, Ohio, Pa. Designer, Schauder & Martin, Architects, Toledo, Ohio, 1972; project mgr. Sanborn, Steketee, Otis and Evans, Toledo, 1972-76; v.p. Harris Builders, Inc., Toledo, 1977; assoc. Sanzenbacher, Miller, Troy, Dansard. Ltd., Toledo. 1977; partner The Richard Troy Partnership, Toledo, 1977-83; prin. Richard Jesse Sorgen, AIA, Toledo, 1983—. Solicitor, United Way Campaign com., 1981; adminstrv. bd. Epworth United Meth. Ch. 1981-82. Served with USN, 1965-69. Recipient Scholastic award AIA and AIA Found., 1972. Mem. AIA (nat. design com.). Architects Soc. Ohio (trustee 1980), Toledo Mus. Art, Nat. Council Archtl. Registration Bds. Clubs: Sylvania Country, Rotary, Elks. Maj. works incl.: Toledo Engring. Co. Hdqrs., YMCA, Oregon, Ohio, Ohio Citizens Bank, Owens Tech. Coll., others. Office: 2326 Pemberton Dr Toledo OH 43606

SORIANO, DANILO BUENAFLOR, neurosurgeon; b. Manila, May 15, 1938; s. Restituto F. and Leonisa (Buenaflor) S.; B.S., U. Phillippines, 1957, M.D., 1962; m. Lydianila S. San Pedro, Sept. 5, 1964; children—Brian, Perry, Jennifer. Intern. St. Francis Hosp., Pitts., 1962-63; teaching fellow, resident in neurosurgery U. Pitts., 1964-66; asst. instr. neoranatomy Albert Einstein Coll. Medicine, 1966-67, neurosurgery, 1968-69, instr. neurosurgery, 1969-70; chief of neurosurgery Queens Hosp. Center, N.Y., 1970-73; asst. prof. neurosurgery SUNY-Stony Brook, 1972; chief of neurosurgery Hempstead Gen. Hosp., 1972-74; neurosurgeon Palos Community, Holy Cross, Central Community hosps. Recipient William C. Menninger award; NIH research fellow. Diplomate Am. Bd. Neurosurgery. Fellow ACS; mem. Am. Assn. Neurol. Surgeons, Congress Neurol. Surgeons, Internat. Coll. Surgeons, AMA, Chgo.,

Ill. med. socs., Central Neurosurg. Soc., Soc. Functional Neurosurgery, Mensa, U.S. Chess Fedn., Phi Kappa Phi, Phi Sigma. Republican. Roman Catholic. Contbr. articles profl. jours. Research on spinal cord physiology, spasticity, pain. Composer: I Endure (Voice and Piano), 1960; Silangan Quartet (2 Violins, Viola, Cello), 1976. 1st violinist SW Symphony Orch.; mem. Chamber Music Players, Chinquapin Hills String Quartet; concertmaster St. Xavier Chamber Orch. Office: 6600 W College Dr Palos Heights IL 60463

SORKIN, ALEX, optometrist; b. Chgo., Aug. 6, 1937; s. Sidney and Nettie (Horwitz) S.; B.S., Ill. Coll. Optometry, 1963, Dr. Optometry, 1964. Mem. faculty Ill. Coll. Optometry, 1964-66; gen. practice optometry, Chgo., 1964-66, Champaign, Ill., 1972—; researcher and lectr. contact lens design and fitting; supr. research clinic Wesley-Jessen, Inc., Chgo., 1969-72; attending staff dept. ophthalmology Cook County Hosp., Chgo., 1971-72; optometry officer med. service corps U.S. Army, U.S. Army Hosp., Nurnberg, Bavaria, Germany, 1966-68; preceptor Pa. Coll. Optometry, 1979—; Judge Chgo. Pub. Schs. Sci. Fair, 1965, 66; classical music annotator Sta. WTWC-FM, 1973-76; chmn. sect. on eye photography Nat. Eye Research Found., 1969-72, traveling lectr., 1969—, vice chmn. sect. keratoscopy, 1973—; bd. dirs. Cancer Coop., 1977—, pres., 1978-81. Bd. dirs. Champaign-Urbana Symphony, 1980—. Recipient service award Cancer Coop., 1981; cert. in contact lenses Nat. Eye Research Found., recipient Service Recognition award, 1980. Mem. Am. Optometric Assn., Ill. Optometric Assn. (exec. council 1978—, v.p. edn. 1980—, chmn. membership task force 1979-80), East Central Ill. Optometric Assn. (pres. 1978-80), Aircraft Owners and Pilots Assn., Ill. Pilots Assn. Contbr. articles to profl. jours. Home: 1210 W Union St Champaign IL 61821 Office: 605 S Wright St Champaign IL 61820 also 201 E Sangamon Ave Rantoul IL 61866

SOSTROM, SHIRLEY ANNE, organizational communications cons. co. exec., educator; b. Billings, Mont., Dec. 22, 1933; d. Jack Kenneth and Edith Ester (Bates) Thompson; student U. Wyo., 1951-59; B.Sc., No. Ill. U., 1966; M.A., Central State U., 1970; Ph.D., Ohio State U., 1976; m. John Philip Sostrom, July 11, 1950; children—John David, Kristen Ingrid, Edith May. Tchr. various high schs., Ohio, Mont., 1966-74; with Carroll Coll., Helena, Mont., 1972-74; lectr. linguistics and writing Sinclair Coll., 1976-78; program coordinator Sch. Public Adminstrn., Ohio State U., Columbus, 1978-80; lectr. English and journalism Muskingum Coll., 1980-81; pres. Sostrom Assocs., pub. relations cons., Columbus, 1979—; prin., dir. human resource services, officer The Sims Cons. Group, Lancaster, Ohio, 1983—; prof. Grad. Sch. Adminstrn., Capital U., Columbus, 1980—. Mem. Women's Poetry Workshop, Am. Assn. for Tng. and Devel., Internat. Assn. Bus. Communicators, Internat. Materials Mgmt. Soc. (v.p. communications), Am. Soc. Public Adminstrn., Ohio State U. Alumni Assn., Phi Delta Kappa. Republican. Club: Zonta. Author chpts. and articles on pub. relations and bus.; contbr. poetry to mags. Home: 99 E Weber St Columbus OH 43202 Office: 2199 E Main St Columbus OH 43209 also PO Box 646 919 E Fair Ave Lancaster OH 43130

SOUCIE, WILLIAM GEORGE, food scientist, biochemistry researcher; b. Missoula, Mont., Mar. 20, 1942; m. Mary Kathleen King, July 23, 1966; children—william, Danielle, Michelle, Laura. B.A., Carroll Coll., 1964; M.A., Incarnate Word Coll., 1968; Ph.D., N.C. State U., 1973; postgrad. U. Colo., 1973-76. Research scientist Kraft Research and Devel., Glenview, Ill., 1976-77, group leader, 1977—; lectr. Coll. Lake County, Grays Lake, Ill., 1981-83. Author sci. articles. Active Woodland Sch. Bd., Grays Lake, 1980. Served with USAF, 1965-69. NIH research fellow, 1969-73. Mem. Am. Oil Chemists Soc. Avocations: Camping; hiking; photography; swimming; sailing. Office: Kraft Research and Devel 801 Waukegan Rd Glenview IL 60025

SOUDER, HERSHEL RAY, computer educator; b. Cin., July 8, 1944; s. William August and Luella (Lanter) Goering; m. Roberta Jean Horton, Jan. 4, 1978; 1 child, Kathryn. B.B.A., U. Cin., 1971, M.B.A., 1972, Ph.D., 1983. Vice pres. Complete Systems, Inc., Cin., 1972-76; chmn. bd. Visionnaire Inc., Cin., 1976-77; pres. R3M Inc., Cin., 1977-79; prof. computer edn. No. Ky. U., Highland Heights, 1981—; Mng. ptnr. ltrs Cons., Cin., 1976—; dir. Robinson Mitchell Assocs., Cin. Author: Simple Linear & Multiple Regression, 1982. Contbr. articles to profl. jours. Served to capt. AUS, 1963-69. Mem. Data Processing Mgmt. Assn. (v.p. 1983-84, outstanding service award 1983), Nat. Edn. Found. (regent 1984—), Inst. Indsl. Engrs., Assn. Computing Machinery, DAV, Smithsonian Instn. Republican. Presbyterian. Home: 475 Purcell Ave Cincinnati OH 45205 Office: Sch Bus No Ky U Highland Heights KY 41076

SOULAK, JOSEPH HAROLD, publishing executive; b. Adams, Wis., Mar. 25, 1932; s. Harold Joseph and Mary I. (Turski) S.; A.B., Providence Coll., 1960; postgrad. Boston U., 1960, Roosevelt U., 1969; m. Leanora Galante, Sept. 1, 1956 (div. Oct. 1971); 1 dau., Deborah; m. Judith A. Sharpe, Oct. 1975. Sports editor Lakeland Pubs., Grayslake, Ill., 1960-62, news editor, 1962-64, mng. editor, 1964-65; news editor Pawtuxet Valley Times, West Warwick, R.I., 1964; mgr. pub. relations Bastian-Blessing Co., Chgo., 1966-68; publs. mgr. Ryerson Steel, Chgo., 1969; dir. news services Ency. Brit., Inc., Chgo., 1969-75; pub., editor South Milw. Voice-Jour., Cudahy Free-Press, The Bay Viewer, Suburbanite (all South Milw.), 1975—; editor PR/Chicago, 1969-75; sec. Wis. Spectacle of Music, Inc., 1977; columnist, writer Waukegan (Ill.) News Sun, 1969-75. Mem. Lake County Safety Commn., 1961-65; mgr. pub. relations for Ill. Senator, 1964-75. Served with USN, 1952-56; Korea. Mem. Nat. Newspaper Assn., Wis. Press Assn., S. Milw. Assn. Commerce (dir., pres. 1976-85); Chgo. Press Club. Club: Kiwanis (dir. 1983). Home: 1332 Manitoba South Milwaukee WI 53172 Office: 723 Milwaukee Ave South Milwaukee WI 53179

SOVA, GREGORY, lawyer; b. Detroit, Aug. 6, 1951; s. Walter Andrew and Virginia Mildred (Boniakowsky) S.; m. Margaret Janice Armbruster, Aug. 19, 1972; children—Brett Gregory, Lauren Gabrielle. B.A., U. Mich., 1973; J.D., U. Toledo, 1976. Bar: Ohio 1976. Assoc. Duffey & Henning, Toledo, 1976-78; staff atty. First Fed. Savs. and Loan Assn., Toledo, 1978-81, asst. gen. counsel, 1981-83, asst. sec., 1983-84, asst. v.p., 1984—. Mem. ABA, Toledo Bar Assn. Roman Catholic. Home: 6534 Millbrook Maumee OH 43537 Office: 701 First Federal Plaza Suite 400 Toledo OH 43624

SPAETH, HERBERT HELLMUT, internat. mktg. specialist; b. Bandjermasin, Indonesia, Aug. 28, 1930; came to U.S., 1956, naturalized, 1970; s. Erwin Alfred and Elisabeth (Fanderl) S.; Diploma in Indsl. Mgmt., Bus. Coll., Nuernberg (W. Ger.) 1952. Exec. asst. Acme Mfg. Co., Detroit, 1958-72; internat. relations dir. Acme-Murray Way Internat., Detroit, 1973-75; dir. internat. mktg. Fraser Automation, Sterling Heights, Mich., 1977-78; asso. H.M. Seldon Co., investment realtors, Detroit, 1979—; cons. to indsl., legal and investment firms, 1975—. Mem. Am. Mgmt. Assn., Detroit Bd. Realtors, Christian Bus. Men's Com. U.S.A. Club: Rotary. Home: 770 Withington St Ferndale MI 48220 Office: HM Seldon Co 500 The Penobscot Bldg Detroit MI 48226

SPAETH, NICHOLS, state government official. Atty. gen. State of N.D., Bismarck. Office: Office of the Atty Gen State Capitol Bldg 1st Floor Bismarck ND 58505*

SPAETH, ROBERT LOUIS, college administrator; b. St. Cloud, Minn., Mar. 22, 1935; s. Louis John and Thecla Josephine (Stueve) S.; m. Elizabeth Ann Stoltz, Aug. 16, 1958; children—Catherine, Ann, Thomas, Caroline, Judith, Margaret. B.S., summa cum laude St. John's U., 1959; postgrad. U. Ill., 1959-60, U. Wis., 1961-62. Tchr. Cathedral High Sch., St. Cloud, Minn., 1960-61; math. writer Ednl. Research Council Greater Cleve., 1962-63; tutor St. John's Coll. Annapolis, Md., 1963-79; dean Coll. Arts and Scis., St. John's U., Collegeville, Minn., 1979—. Author: No Easy Answers: Christians Debate Nuclear Arms, 1983; A Dean Speaks His Mind: Exhortations On Liberal Education, 1984; The Church and a Catholic's Conscience, 1985. Editor Coll. Teaching; bd. dirs. Catholicism in Crisis. Alderman Annapolis City Council, 1973-79; mem. Minn. Democratic-Farmer-Labor Party State Central Com., 1978-84. Served with U.S. Army, 1954-56. Democrat. Roman Catholic. Home: Rural Route 3 St Joseph MN 56374 Office: St Johns U Collegeville MN 56321

SPAHR, JON RAY, judge; b. New Castle, Ind., Sept. 20, 1939; s. Marvin M. and Virginia (Allaback) S.; m. Mary Jane Barr, Aug. 24, 1963; children—Jennifer, Julie, Joel. B.S. in Bus., Miami U., 1961; J.D., Ohio State U., 1964; student Nat. Jud. Coll., 1983. Bar: Ohio 1964, U.S. Dist. Ct. Ohio 1965. Ptnr., McDonald, Robinson, Spahr & Noecker, Newark, Ohio, 1964-79; judge Licking County Mcpl. Ct. (Ohio), 1979-82, Licking County Common Pleas Ct., 1983—. Contbr. articles to newspapers. Bd. dirs. Licking County United Way, 1983—, Big Bros. Mem. Newark Jaycees (Outstanding Young Man award 1971), ABA, Ohio Bar Assn., Licking County Bar Assn., Ohio Common Pleas Judges Assn. Republican. Presbyterian. Lodges: Elks, Masons, Rotary (bd. dirs.). Avocations: running; gardening; golf; tennis; skiing; fishing. Office: Licking County Common Pleas Ct Courthouse Newark OH 43055

SPALDING, JOHN ARTHUR, architect; b. Chgo., Sept. 29, 1948; s. Arthur Rudolph and Bernice Matilda (Bork) S.; m. Victoria Jean Dillon, June 22, 1968; 1 dau., Lisa Marie. Student Ill. Inst. Tech., 1966-70; B.S. in Archtl. Engring., Chgo. Tech. Inst., 1971. Registered architect, Wis. Apprentice architect Arnold May Builders, Inc., Richmond, Ill., 1971-75; v.p. archtl. div. Cooper Architects/Engrs., Rice Lake, Wis., 1976-82; owner Spalding Architects, Rice Lake, 1983—. Mem. Diocese of Superior Commn. on Art and Architecture. Mem. AIA, Wis. Soc. Architects, Constrn. Specifications Inst., Am. Arbitration Assn. Roman Catholic. ch. renovation project pub. in Wisconsin Architect mag. Home: Route 5 Woodland Vista Rice Lake WI 54868 Office: PO Box 681 431 S Main St Rice Lake WI 54868

SPANGLER, JIMMY LEE, city official; b. Hillsdale, Mich., Dec. 5, 1950; s. Eben L. and Jean (Rothlisberger) S.; m. Joyce E. Heller, July 22, 1972; children—Christopher E., Joshua R. B.C.E., Mich. State U., 1973. Registered profl. engr., Mich. Plant engr. Wash. Suburban Sanitary Commn., Hyattsville, Md., 1973-76; asst. supt. City of Pontiac, Mich., 1976-79; wastewater div. supt. City of Lansing, Mich., 1979—. Mem. Water Pollution Control Fedn. (Hatfield award 1983), Nat. Soc. Profl. Engrs., Mich. Water Pollution Control Assn. Methodist. Avocations: camping; hunting; playing with children. Office: Wastewater Div 1625 Sunset Ave Lansing MI 48917

SPARGO, WILLIAM GILBERT, mechanical engineer; b. St. Louis, May 9, 1925; s. Roy and A. Margaret (Schneider) S.; m. Erna K. Nottmeier, June 6, 1954; children—Janice, Darryl. B.M.E., Tulane U., 1947. Registered profl. engr., Mo. Mgr. engring. Anheuser Busch Cos., Inc., St. Louis, to 1983, mgr. packaging equipment devel., 1983—. Patentee process for filling beer containers. Served to lt. (j.g.) USNR, 1945-47, PTO. Mem. ASME (chmn. beverage subcom. of food drug and beverage equipment com. 1972—), Master Brewers Assn. Am., Soft Drink Technologists Assn. Lodges: Masons, Elks. Home: 9154 Cordoba Ln Crestwood MO 63126

SPARKS, ALLEN KAY, electronics company executive; b. Chgo., Sept. 26, 1933; s. Allen Kay and Violet Elsie (Lindstrom) S.; m. Nina Suzanne Bade, Nov. 5, 1955; 1 child, Alison Claire. A.B. in Chemistry, Ripon Coll., 1955; Ph.D. in Chemistry, Case Inst. Tech., 1960. Dir. chem. research Signal Co., Des Plaines, Ill., 1972-75, v.p. tech. chem. div., East Rutherford, N.J., 1975-76, v.p. ops. Chem. div., 1976-78; v.p., gen. mgr., 1978-80, v.p., gen. mgr. Norplex Div., LaCrosse, Wis., 1980-85, pres., 1985—; dir. Norplex Hong Kong, Ltd., Norplex France SARL, Paris, Norplex U.K. Ltd., Northampton, Eng. Contbr. articles to profl. jours. Patentee in field. Bd. advisors Viterbo Coll., LaCrosse, Wis., 1982—; bd. dirs. Elk Grove Twp. Republicans, Ill., 1971-74; pres Dist. 59 Bd. of Edn., Elk Grove, 1968-74; area chmn. Des Plaines Community Chest, 1964. Allied Corp. fellow Case Inst. Tech., 1958-60. Mem. LaCrosse C. of C., Sigma Xi. Avocations: travel, photography, swimming, golf. Home: Rt 1 Box 247M-8 LaCrescent MN 55947 Office: Signal Co Norplex Div 1300 Norplex Dr PO Box 1448 La Crosse WI 54601

SPARKS, BILLY SCHLEY, lawyer; b. Marshall, Mo., Oct. 1, 1923; s. John and Clarinda (Schley) S.; A.B., Harvard, 1945, LL.B., 1949; student Mass. Inst. Tech., 1943-44; m. Dorothy O. Stone, May 14, 1946; children—Stephen Stone, Susan Lee, John David. Admitted to Mo. bar, 1949; partner Langworthy, Matz & Linde, Kansas City, Mo., 1949-62, firm Linde, Thomson, Fairchild Langworthy & Kohn, 1962—. Mem. Mission (Kans.) Planning Council, 1954-63; mem. Kans. Civil Service Commn., 1975—. Mem. dist. 110 Sch. Bd., 1964-69, pres., 1967-69; mem. Dist. 512 Sch. Bd., 1969-73, pres., 1971-72; del. Dem. Nat. Conv., 1964; candidate for representative 10th Dist., Kans., 1956, 3d district, 1962; treas. Johnson County (Kans.) Dem. Central com., 1958-64. Served to lt. USAAF, 1944-46. Mem. Kansas City C. of C. (legis. com. 1956-82), Am., Kansas City bar assns., Mo. Bar, Law Assn. Kansas City, Harvard Law Sch. Assn. Mo. (past dir.), Nat. Assn. Sch. Bds. (mem. legislative com. 1968-73), St. Andrews Soc. Mem. Christian Ch. (trustee). Clubs: Harvard (v.p. 1953-54), Kansas City (Kansas City, Mo.); Milburn Golf and Country. Home: 8517 W 90th Terr Shawnee Mission KS 66212 Office: City Center Sq 12th and Baltimore Sts Kansas City MO 64105

SPARKS, JACK DAVID, appliance manufacturing company executive. Chmn., pres., chief exec. officer Whirlpool Corp., Benton Harbor, Mich., also dir. Office: Whirlpool Corp Adminstrv Ctr Benton Harbor MI 49022*

SPARKS, (THEO) MERRILL, entertainer, translator, poet; b. Mount Etna, Iowa, Oct. 5, 1922; s. David G. and Ollie M. (Hickman) S.; student U. Besancon (France), 1945; B.A., U. So. Calif., 1948; postgrad. U. Iowa, 1948-51, Columbia U., 1951-52. Entertainer as singer, pianist, Los Angeles, Midwest, Fla., N.Y., N.J. areas, 1953—. Served with AUS, 1942-46. Co-recipient P.E.N. transl. award, 1968, Cross of Merit with Vernon Duke for cantata Anima Eroica, Order of St. Brigida, Rome, 1966. Mem. Am. Fedn. Musicians, Authors Guild, Am. Guild Authors and Composers, Modern Poetry Assn., Iowa Friends of the Library, Iowa Geneal. Soc. Composer songs including Sleepy Village, 1942, A Heart of Gold, 1956, Anima Eroica, 1971, An Italian Voyage, 1976, O Come and Join the Angels, 1982, Ballad of Ollie and Bart, 1983; poems pub. in mags. including Western Rev., Choice, South & West, N.Y. Rev. Books; poems included in: Arts of Russia, Primer of Experimental Poetry; co-editor, co-translator (with Vladimir Markov) Modern Russian Poetry, 1966. Club: Rotary. Home: Mount Etna IA 50855 Office: 4620 SE 4th St #104 Des Moines IA 50315

SPATHELF, STEPHEN EDWARD, financial executive, cash management consultant; b. Phila., June 12, 1947; s. Walter Edward and Margaret Ada (Shuttleworth) S.; m. Susan Kathaleen Hall, Sept. 14, 1974; children—Jennifer Susanne, Jonathan Edward. B.S. in Acctg. and Math., U. Dubuque, 1969. C.P.A., Ill. Asst. sr. acct. Deloitte, Haskins & Sells, Chgo., 1969-70; sr. acct. Friedman, Galen & Co., Chgo., 1970-72; asst. treas., sec. Nat. Student Mktg. Corp., Chgo., 1972-76; controller, treas. Arthur Frommer Enterprises, Inc., N.Y.C., 1976-78; asst. treas. Playboy Enterprises, Inc., Chgo., 1978-84, treas., 1984—. Chmn. bd. dirs. Transitional Living Programs, Inc., 1979-81. Mem. Am. Inst. C.P.A.s. Office: 919 N Michigan Ave Chicago IL 60611

SPAUN, WILLIAM BECKER, lawyer; b. Atchison, Kans., Aug. 22, 1913; s. Floyd and Bertha (Becker) S.; J.D., U. Mo., Kansas City, 1936; m. Sidney Clyde Collins, Sept. 13, 1930 (dec.); 1 dau., Theon Spaun Martin; m. 2d, Mary Louise Robinson, Aug. 5, 1948 (dec.); children—William Becker, Mary Lou Spaun Montgomery, Robert R., Sarah Jean Fletcher, Shirley Anne. Admitted to Mo. bar, 1937; U.S. Supreme Ct., 1960; practice law, Hannibal, 1937—; charter mem. World Peace Through Law Center, participant Washington conf., 1965. Regional fund chmn. ARC, 1961, nat. staff mem., 1943-44, nat. vice chmn. fund campaigns, 1963-64, local chpt. chmn., 1977-82; govt. appeal agt. SSS, 1968-72, chmn., 1972—. Recipient award for meritorious personal service WW II from ARC. Fellow Am. Coll. Probate Counsel, Harry S. Truman Library Inst. (hon.); mem. Am., Tenth Jud. Circuit (pres. 1958-60) bar assns., Mo. Bar (chmn. Law Day 1961, asso. editor jour. 1942-43), Am. Judicature Soc., Scribes. Republican. Home: 2929 McKinley St Hannibal MO 63401 Office: 617A Broadway Hannibal MO 63401 also PO Box 1169 Hannibal MO 63401

SPEAR, PAUL WILBURN, church administrator; b. Crawfordsville, Ind., Feb. 13, 1926; s. Perry Wilburn and Lula Bell (Calder) Godbye; m. Lythia Paulean Flick, Feb. 13, 1944; children—Paula Jean Spear Reeves, Priscilla Sue. B.A., Olivet Nazarene Coll., 1954. Bookbinder, R. R. Donnelly & Sons, Crawfordsville, 1944-50; employment mgr. A.O. Smith Corp., Kankakee, Ill., 1954-68; dir. personnel and services Ch. of the Nazarene Internat. Hdqrs., Kansas City, Mo., 1968—; bd. dirs. Faith Village, Lenexa, Kans., 1981—, Southtown Council, Kansas City, Mo., 1982—. Contbg. author: Church Building Source Book, 1980. Bd. dirs. Southtown Council, Kansas City, Mo., 1982-83, 83-84. Served with USN, 1944-46; PTO. Fellow Nat. Assn. Ch. Bus. Adminstrs. (regional v.p. Dallas, 1982); mem. Am. Mgmt. Soc., Am. Soc. Personnel. Republican. Home: 700 E 90th St Kansas City MO 64131 Office: Ch of the Nazarene 6401 The Paseo Kansas City MO 64131

SPEARS, CHESTER ARTHUR, pathologist; b. Tulsa, Okla., Aug. 16, 1950; s. Chester and Clarice (Parker) S.; m. Sydney Spruill; children—Christy, Kelly. B.S., Southwestern State Coll., 1970; M.D., St. Louis U., 1976. Intern St. Louis U. Hosp., 1976-77; resident Mo. Bapt. Hosp., 1977-78, U. Okla. Hosp., 1978-80; pathologist Newman Meml. Hosp., Emporia, Kans., 1980—. Mem. Coll. Am. Pathologists, Am. soc. Clin. Pathologists. Methodist. Home: 2630 Westridge Dr Emporia KS 66801 Office: Newman Meml Hosp Lab Dept 12th & Chestnut Sts Emporia KS 66801

SPEARS, JANET E., educator; b. Chambersburg, Ill., Sept. 5, 1933; d. Enoch E. and Marguerite Irene (Riley) Downey; A.A., Black Hawk Coll., 1978; B.S. (Chris Hoerr scholar), Bradley U., 1980; postgrad., St. Ambrose Coll., 1981-84; m. Keith A. Spears, July 6, 1952; children—Bruce, Roger, Darci, Paul. Secretarial positions Kewanee Machinery Conveyor (Ill.), 1951-52, William E. Trinke, atty., Lake Geneva, Wis., 1952-53, Walworth Co., Kewanee, 1968-72; adminstrv. asst. Kewanee Pub. Hosp., 1972-75; asst. personnel dir. Davenport (Iowa) Osteo. Hosp., 1980-81; bus. mgr. Franciscan Med. Center, Rock Island, Ill., 1981; bus. prof. Black Hawk Coll., Kewanee, 1981—. Mem. Am. Mgmt. Assn., Soc. Advancement Mgrs., AAUW, Nat. Assn. for Female Execs., Kewanee Pub. Hosp. Assn., Kewanee Art League, Phi Chi Theta. Republican. Methodist (ch. liturgist and Sunday sch. tchr., mem. adminstrv. council). Clubs: Henry County Republic Women, Annawan Jr. Women's (pres. 1964-65), United Fairview Women. Home: Rural Route 1 Sheffield IL 61361 Office: Black Hawk Coll East Campus PO Box 489 Kewanee IL 61443

SPECTER, MELVIN H., lawyer; b. East Chicago, Ind., July 12, 1903; s. Moses and Sadie (Rossuck) S.; A.B., U. Mich., 1925; J.D., U. Chgo., 1928; m. Nellie Rubenstein, Feb. 1, 1927; children—Lois, Michael Joseph. Admitted to Ind. bar, 1928; individual practice law, East Chicago, Ind. 1928—. Bd. dirs. ARC (chpt. chmn. 1940-46), Community Chest Assn., Salvation Army Adv. Bd., pres., 1930-35; bd. dirs. Vis. Nurse Assn., pres., 1943-44; bd. dirs. East Chgo. Boys Club, 1958-65; trustee East Chicago Pub. Library, 1956-80, pres., 1957-67; pres. Anselm Forum, 1957-58; chmn. Brotherhood Week NCCJ, East Chicago, 1958-61; exec. bd. Twin City council Boy Scouts Am.; city chmn. U. Chgo. Alumni Found. Fund, 1951-55. Awarded James Couzen Medal for Inter-collegiate debate, U. Mich., 1924; citation for distinguished pub. service, U. Chgo. Alumni Assn., 1958. Citizenship award Community Chest Assn., 1965. Mem. Am. Ind. (del.), East Chicago (pres. 1942-44) bar assns., Am. Judicature Soc., Comml. Law League Am., Community Concert Assn. (dir. 1950-55), Wig and Robe Frat., Phi Beta Kappa, Delta Sigma Rho. Elk (exalted ruler 1945), K.P., Kiwanian (dir. 1946, 49-51, 52-55, pres. 1961); mem. B'nai B'rith. Home: 4213 Baring Ave East Chicago IN 46312 Office: 804 W 145th St East Chicago IN 46312

SPEERHAS, REX ANTHONY, hospital pharmacist; b. Beaver Falls, Pa., Sept. 8, 1951; s. Franklin William and Edith Irene (Rimoldi) S.; m. Karen Marie Lyons, Oct. 12, 1974; 1 dau., Audra Brooke. B.S. in Pharmacy, Duquesne U., 1974. Registered pharmacist. Pharmacy intern Med. Ctr. Beaver County, Beaver, Pa., 1972-73; hosp. pharmacist, Cleve. Clinic, 1974—; pharmacology instr. Cleve. State U., 1977-79. Capt. Am. Heart Assn. fund drive, Westlake, Ohio, 1981—; mem. St. Ladislas Ch. Health Commn., Westlake, 1983—, mem. choir, 1976—. Named Hosp. Pharmacist of Yr., Pfizer Pharms. and Ohio Soc. Hosp. Pharmacists, 1984. Mem. Am. Soc. Hosp. Pharmacists, Ohio Soc. Hosp. Pharmacists (council on profl. affairs 1981—), Cleve. Soc. Hosp. Pharmacists (treas. 1978-80, pres. 1980-81, service award 1982, 83, 84). Democrat. Roman Catholic. Avocations: golf; gardening. Home: 2100 Berkeley Dr Westlake OH 44145 Office: Cleve Clinic Hosp Pharmacy 9500 Euclid Ave Cleveland OH 44106

SPEIR, KENNETH GUINTY, lawyer; b. Peabody, Kans., June 22, 1908; s. John and Bessie (Guinty) S.; student Colo. Coll., 1926-28; LL.B., Kans. U., 1931; children—Helen Ann, Patricia Jane, Elizabeth Eve; m. 2d, Shirley Whittemore. Admitted to Kans. bar, 1931, N.Mex. bar, 1932, U.S. Supreme Ct. bar, 1943; practiced in Albuquerque, 1932-34, Newton, Kans., 1934—; county atty. Harvey County (Kans.), 1939-41; Judge 9th Jud. Dist. Kans., 1941-44; dir. counsel 1st Fed. Savs. Bank of Newton; counsel Hesston Corp., Midland Nat. Bank, Newton. Mem. Kans. Bd. Health, 1950-51; bd. dirs., gen. counsel Hesston Found., Inc. Served as lt. col. USMCR, 1942-46, Res. ret. Mem. Am., N.Mex., Kans., Harvey County bar assns., Am. Legion, VFW. Republican. Lutheran. Lodge: Elks. Home: 1411 Hillcrest Rd PO Box 546 Newton KS 67114 Office: PO Box 546 809 Main St Newton KS 67114

SPENCE, JOHN D(ANIEL), consultant, real estate broker; b. Lethbridge, Alta., Can., May 18, 1915; s. Benjamin Abner and Clara May (Fullerton) S.; came to U.S., 1915, naturalized, 1943; A.B., Grinnell Coll., 1938; LL.D. (hon.), Rockford Coll., 1979; m. Phyllis Saxton Johnson, Feb. 4, 1939; children—Susan Kathleen Spence Glassberg, John Daniel. With Container Corp. Am., 1938-54, v.p., 1949-54; Lanzit Corrugated Box Co., 1954-64; dir. devel. Rockford (Ill.) Coll., 1964-65, v.p. devel., 1965-77, acting pres., 1977-79; bus. and edn. cons., 1980—; broker Hart Realtors of Rockford. Mem. land adv. council Winnebago County Forest Preserve, 1975—; chmn. Severson Dells Adv. Council, 1976—; mem. community adv. bd. WNIU-FM, No. Ill. U., 1981—; trustee Keith Country Day Sch., 1971-81; trustee Children's Home Rockford, 1973-76, Rockford Art Assn., 1980-83, Rockford Highview Retirement Home Assn.; bd. dirs. John Howard Assn., until 1974, Pecatonica Prairie Path, 1975—; Recipient Karl C. Williams award Rockford Coll. Alumni Assn., 1980; Service above Self award Rockford Rotary, 1980. Mem. Ill. C. of C. (com. for respect law enforcement 1967-72), Rockford C. of C. (dir. 1966-72). Republican. Club: Univ. (Chgo.). Lodge: Lions. Home and Office: 6710 Woodcrest Pkwy Rockford IL 61109

SPENCER, ALAN GERALD, film and audiovisual producer, genealogist; b. Youngstown, Ohio, Mar. 16, 1941; s. David and Esther (Sohmer) Shwartz; m. Marylin Joyce Camberg, June 16, 1968; children—Bennett Colin, Ronna Lynn. B.S. in Edn., Ohio U., 1963; M.A., Central Mich. U., 1966. Cert. tchr., Ill. Tchr., Paul C. Bunn Sch., Youngstown, 1963-65; radio newscaster WBBW Radio, Youngstown, 1963-65; tchr. Coleman Intermediate Sch. (Mich.), 1965-66; tchr., resource dir. Crow Island Sch., Winnetka, Ill., 1966-74; producer, dir. The Spot Shop, Chgo., 1974-81; exec. producer Williams/Gerard Prodns., Chgo., 1981—. Editor: Search, 1981—, Internat. Quar. Researchers Jewish Geneaology; producer, dir. ednl. films, documentaries; contbr. articles to mags. Recipient Best Ednl. Film award Chgo. Internat. Film Festival, 1975. Mem. Jewish. Geneal. Soc. of Ill. (bd. dirs. 1981—). Jewish. Office: Williams/Gerard Prodns 420 N Wabash 5th Floor Chicago IL 60611

SPENCER, EDSON WHITE, manufacturing company executive; b. Chgo., June 4, 1926; s. William M. and Gertrude (White) S.; student Princeton U., 1943, Northwestern U., U. Mich., 1944; B.A., Williams Coll., 1948; B.A., Oxford (Eng.) U., 1950, M.A., 1950. With Sears, Roebuck & Co., 1951-54, Venezuela and Mpls., 1954; with Honeywell, Inc., 1954—, dir. exports, 1964-65, v.p. fgn. ops., 1965-69, exec. v.p., 1969-74, pres., 1974-78, chief exec. officer, 1974—, chmn. bd., 1978—. Mem. Mpls. C. of C., St. Paul Com. Fgn. Relations, Mpls. Citizens League, Phi Beta Kappa. Office: Honeywell Inc 2701 4th Ave S Minneapolis MN 55408*

SPENCER, ETTA LORRAINE, nurse; b. East St. Louis, Ill., July 3, 1928; d. Leonard and Matilda Leola (Wiggins) Richie; R.N., St. Mary's Infirmary, 1949; m. Thomas Lee Spencer, Aug. 20, 1960; 1 son, Kevin. Staff, operating room nurse St. Mary's Infirmary, East St. Louis, 1949-55; night charge nurse Firmin Deslage Hosp., St. Louis, 1955-59; operating room nurse John Cochran VA Hosp., St. Louis, 1957-62; operating room supr. Centreville Twp. Hosp., East St. Louis, 1962—. Mem. City Bd. Health Rev., Mem. Am. Nurses Assn., Ill. Nurses Assn., 10th Dist. Nurses Assn., Assn. Operating Room Nurses, Black Nurses Assn. Democrat. Baptist. Lodge: Lioness. Home: 519 N 22d St East Saint Louis IL 62205 Office: Centreville Twp Hosp 5900 Bond Ave East Saint Louis IL 62207

SPENCER, GARY DALE, chief police; b. Monte Vista, Colo., Sept. 3, 1949; s. Bob and Helen Eloise (Martz) Simpson; m. Myrna Ellen Willmore, July 6, 1969; children—Daniel Dale, Jeffrey Paul, Sheila Diane. Student various schs., intermittently, 1968—. Shop foreman Tripple M Chinehilla Cage Co., Omaha, 1964-67; acct. Commodore Corp., Omaha, 1967-70; patrolman Fremont Police Dept., Nebr., 1970-78; dir. Southeast Nebr. Ct. Alcohol Program, Beatrice, Nebr., 1978-79; chief of police Falls City, Nebr., 1979—. Den leader Falls City Webelos, 1981-82; bd. dirs. Southeast Nebr. Alcohol Program, 1978-85, mem. adv. council, 1980-85. Recipient awards including State of Nebr. Gov.'s award, 1980, Dist. Experts award Nat. Rifle Assn., 1981, Disting. Service award, 1985; Pedestrian Safety awards AAA Motor Club, 1979-84. Mem. Am. Guild of Hypnotherapists, Internat. Assn. Chiefs of Police, Nat. Assn. Chiefs Police, Police Officers Assn. Nebr., Internat. Order Eagle, Nebr. Assn. Notary Pubs.,

Internat. Order Forresters, Nebr. Assn. Alcoholism Counselors, Falls City Jaycees (pres. 1984—, Outstanding Service award 1982, 83, Keyman award 1983-84). Republican. Mem. Christian Ch. Clubs: Falls City Lion, Eagle. Home: 2618 Schoenheit St Falls City NE 68355

SPENCER, JAMES EARL, architect; b. Brookfield, Mo., Oct. 1, 1948; s. Watson C. and Elizabeth M. (Gosney) S.; m. Nancy M. Street, Apr. 17, 1976; children—Eric John, Brian James. B.Arch., Ill. Inst. Tech., 1972. Registered architect, Ill. Project mgr. Standard Oil Co., Chgo., 1972-76, mgr. archtl. services, 1976—; v.p. Standard Oil Realty Corp., Chgo., 1976—. Trustee, St. Michaels Lutheran Ch. Mem. AIA, Internat. Facility Mgrs. Assn. (sec. Chgo. chpt.), Pi Kappa Phi, Alpha Pi. Office: 200 E Randolph Dr Chicago IL 60601

SPENCER, JOSEPH STEWART, mfg. co. exec.; b. Kilbirnie, Scotland, Apr. 26, 1922; s. Hugh Morrison and Mary (MacInnes) S.; A.B., Harvard, 1948; M.B.A., Columbia, 1950. Tax accountant, asst. to treas., asst. treas., sec.-treas. Union Spl. Corp., 1950-78, v.p., sec., 1978—. Served with AUS, 1942-45. Mem. Am. Soc. Corp. Secs., Ill. C. of C., Ill. St. Andrew Soc., Chgo. Assn. Commerce and Industry. Presbyn. Home: 1450 Astor St Chicago IL 60610 Office: 400 N Franklin St Chicago IL 60610

SPENCER, MICHAEL SHEA, author, educator, business executive; b. Oak Park, Ill., Sept. 12, 1949; s. Frank L. and Helen T. (Zezulak) S.; m. Susan C. Switzer, Dec. 27, 1971; children—Kathleen M., Cynthia M., Kelsey S. B.S., So. Ill. U.-Carbondale, 1971; M.B.A., So. Ill. U.-Edwardsville; M.A., U. No. Iowa, 1980. Cert. tchr., Iowa. Supr. inventory planning John Deere Engine Works, Waterloo, Iowa, 1976-78, systems analyst, 1978-80, master scheduler, 1980-81, mgr. inventory control, 1982—; ptnr. Lancer Cons. Group, Cedar Falls, Iowa, 1983—; adj. prof. econs. U. No. Iowa, 1978-83. Served to capt. USAF, 1972-76. Decorated Air Force Commendation medal; So. Ill. U.-Carbondale resident fellow, 1970, 71. Mem. AAUP, Am. Prodn. and Inventory Control Soc. (v.p. Region V). Home: 421 W Seerley Blvd Cedar Falls IA 50613 Office: John Deere Engine Works Bos 5001 Waterloo IA 50704

SPENCER, PATRICIA TRUMBO, city official; b. Montgomery, Ala., Dec. 12, 1938; d. Thurman Louis and Virginia Mae (Trumbo) Ward; m. Douglas Spencer, Apr. 30, 1958 (div.); children—Patricia Denise, Douglas Jerome, Wilfred Trumbo. Student Ala. State U., 1956-58, Wayne State U., 1974-77. With City of Detroit Water and Sewerage Dept., 1966—, tng. specialist, 1974—; cons. Nat. Sch. Bd. Assn., Nat. Alliance Black Sch. Educators, 1974-83. Mem. Detroit Bd. Edn., 1973—; v.p. Nat. Caucus Sch. Bd. Mems., 1981-83; mem. screening com. for U.S. Mil. Acad., Sen. Carl Levin, Mich., 1981-84; mem. trio adv. com. Oakland U., 1982-86 Recipient Spirit of Detroit award Mayor and City Council, 1982, Testimonial Resolution, State Senate and Gov., 1982, Service award Detroit Bd. Edn., 1979. Mem. Nat. Alliance Black Sch. Educators (chmn. commn. spl. projects adminstrn.), NAACP, Ala. State Alumni, Gamma Phi Delta. Democrat. Baptist. Club: Elmwood Citizens Dist. Council. Auditorium at M.L. King Jr.-Sr. High Sch., Detroit, named in her honor, 1982. Home: 3777 Buena Vista St Detroit MI 48238 Office: 735 Randolph St Suite 1109 Detroit MI 48226

SPENCER, THOMAS HALSEY, materials engineer, researcher; b. Chgo., Aug. 9, 1932; s. William John and Thelma Helen (McKee) S.; m. Ellen Sharemet, Nov. 2, 1957; children—Jeffrey William, Claudia Jean, Cynthia Joan, Gregory Robert. B.S., Ill. Inst. Tech., 1970; M.S., U. Ill.-Chgo., 1980, Ph.D., 1985. Experimentalist Ill. Inst. Tech. Research Inst., Chgo., 1955-62; staff engr. Bunker-Ramo Corp., Broadview, Ill., 1962-70; devel. engr. Bell Telephone Labs., Cicero, Ill., 1970-73; sr. engr. AT&T Tech., Chgo., 1973—. Contbr. articles to profl. jours. Mem. Am. Inst. Metall. Engrs., Am. Soc. Metals., Internat. Soc. Hybrid Microelectronics, Sigma Xi. Avocations: oil painting; travel; long distance swimming. Home: 29 W 377 Crabtree Ln Warrenville IL 60555 Office: AT&T Tech Inc Hawthorne Station Chgo IL 60623

SPENCER, WALTER WILLIAM, clinical chemist, consultant; b. Mansfield, Ohio, Nov. 10, 1933; s. Walter Frederick and Anna Caroline (Otto) S.; m. Margaret Sidney Wardian, Sept. 5, 1964; children—James William, Mary Margaret. B.S., Heidelberg U., Tiffin, Ohio, 1955; M.S., Purdue U., 1958, Ph.D., 1960. Registered clin. chemist. Clin. chemist St. Elizabeth Med. Ctr., Dayton, Ohio, 1961—; clin. asst. prof. U. Dayton, 1969-75, clin. assoc. prof., 1975-80; treas. Clin. Chemistry Cons., Inc., Dayton, 1976—; cons. VA Hosp., Dayton, 1984—. Contbr. chpts. to books, articles to profl. publs. Chmn. Kettering Bd. Community Relations (Ohio), 1974-82; bd. dirs. Dayton Area Diabetic Assn., 1974-80, Dayton Area Cystic Fibrosis Assn., 1981—. Named Vol. of Yr., United Health Way, Montgomery County, Ohio, 1980, Dayton Area Diabetic Assn., 1980. Fellow AAAS; mem. Am. Assn. Clin. Chemists (Bernard J. Katchman award Ohio Valley Sect. 1977), Sigma Xi. Roman Catholic. Lodge: K.C. (Knight of Yr. Council 4022 Kettering 1984). Avocations: fishing; hiking; bowling; bicycling. Home: 933 Ingersol Dr Dayton OH 45429 Office: St Elizabeth Med Center 601 Edwin C Mosses Blvd Dayton OH 45429

SPENCER, WILLIAM EDWIN, telephone company executive, engineer; b. Kansas City, Mo., Mar. 22, 1926; s. Erwin Blanc and Edith Marie (Peterson) S.; student U. Kansas City, 1942; A.S., Kansas City Jr. Coll., 1945; B.S. in E.E., U. Mo., 1948; postgrad. Iowa State U., 1969; m. Ferne Arlene Nieder, Nov. 14, 1952; children—Elizabeth Ann, Gary William, James Richard, Catherine Sue. With Southwestern Bell Telephone Co., Kansas City, Mo., 1948-50, Topeka, 1952-61, sr. engr., 1966-69, equipment maintenance engr., 1969-76, engring. ops. mgr., 1976-79, dist. mgr., 1979—; mem. tech. staff Bell Telephone Labs., N.Y.C., 1961-62, Holmdel, N.J., Force, 1984—, U.S. Senatorial Club, 1985—. Served with AUS, 1950-52. Recipient best Kans. idea award Southwestern Bell Telephone Co., 1972, cert. of appreciation Kans. Miss Teen Pageant, 1984. Registered profl. engr., Kans. Mem. Kans. Engring. Soc., Nat. Soc. Profl. Engrs., IEEE, Topeka Engrs. Club (past pres.), Nat. Geog. Soc., Kans. Hist. Soc., Am. Assn. Ret. Persons, U. Mo.-Columbia Alumni Assn., Nat. Travel Club. Republican. Patentee in field. Home: 3201 MacVicar Ct Topeka KS 66611 Office: 220 E 6th St Topeka KS 66603

SPERLICH, HAROLD KEITH, See *Who's Who in America,* 43rd edition.

SPERRY, JAMES EDWARD, anthropologist, historical society administrator; exec.; b. Weeping Water, Nebr., May 17, 1936; s. John Edward and Augusta Anea (Frandsen) S.; student Bethany Coll., Lindsborg, Kans., 1953-55; A.B. in Art and Anthropology, 1962, M.A. in Anthropology, U. Nebr., Lincoln, 1965; m. Gail Louise Killen, Sept. 26, 1964; 1 son, Patrick Reuben. Teaching asst. dept. anthropology U. Nebr., Lincoln, 1961-63, instr., 1964-65; research archeologist State Hist. Soc. N.D., Bismarck, 1965-69, supt., 1969—; sec. N.D. Heritage Found., 1973-76; mem. N.D. Lewis and Clark Trail Council, 1969—, sec., 1970, chmn., 1971; N.D. historic preservation officer, 1969-84, 85; N.D. state records coordinator, 1975—. Mem. Theodore Roosevelt Rough Rider Award Com., 1969—, N.D. Natural Resources Council, 1969—. Served with USAF, 1956-59. Am. Assn. State and Local History fellow, 1967; Bush Found. fellow, 1984. Mem. Sigma Xi, Delta Phi Delta, Sigma Gamma Epsilon. Methodist. Editor: N.D. History: Jour. of No. Plains, 1969-73; contbr. numerous articles and reports to profl. publs. Office: ND Heritage Center Bismarck ND 58505

SPEZIA, MICHAEL JOSEPH, osteopathic physician and surgeon, educator; b. St. Louis, Sept. 8, 1950; s. Anthony Louis and Annabelle (Schauer) S.; m. Joyce Louvre Henson, Oct. 28, 1978; 1 child, Michelle. B.A., U. Mo., 1972; D.O., Kansas City Coll. Osteo. Medicine, 1977. Intern Normandy Osteo. Hosp., St. Louis, 1977-78, clin. teaching faculty, 1978—; practice medicine specializing in family practice and osteo. medicine, St. Louis, 1977—; adj. clin. faculty Kirksville Coll. Osteo. Medicine, 1978—, Tulsa Coll. Osteo. Medicine, 1978—, Kansas City Coll. Osteo. Medicine, 1978—. Adv. bd. Forest Park Community Coll., St. Louis, 1984—; patron St. Louis Zool. Assn., 1984—. Mem. Am. Osteo. Assn., St. Louis Assn. Osteo. Physicians and Surgeons, Mo. Assn. Osteo. Physicians, Am. Coll. Osteo. Gen Practioners, Am. Osteo. Assn. of Scleprotherapy, Fraternal Order Police (assoc.). Roman Catholic. Lodge: K.C. (4th degree). Avocations: classic auto restoration, road rallys. Home: 3008 Ridgeview St Saint Louis MO 63121 Office: 23 Normandy Shopping Ctr Saint Louis MO 63121

SPHIRE, RAYMOND DANIEL, anesthesiologist; b. Detroit, Feb. 12, 1927; s. Samuel Raymond and Nora Mae (Allen) S.; B.S., U. Detroit, 1948; M.D., Loyola U., Chgo., 1952; m. Joan Lois Baker, Sept. 5, 1953; children—Suzanne M., Raymond Daniel, Catherine J. Intern, Grace Hosp., Detroit, 1952-53, Harvard Anesthesia Lab., Mass. Gen. Hosp., 1953-55; attending anesthesiologist Grace Hosp., 1955-72, dir. dept. inhalation therapy, 1968-70; sr. attending anesthesiologist, dir. dept., dir. dept. respiratory therapy Detroit-Macomb Hosps. Assn., 1970—, trustee, 1978—, chief of staff, 1980—; clin. asst. prof. Wayne State U. Sch. Medicine, 1967—; clin. prof. respiratory therapy Macomb County Community Coll., Mt. Clemens, Mich., 1971—. Examiner, Am. Registry Respiratory Therapists, 1972—; insp. Joint Rev. Com. Respiratory Therapy Edn., 1972—; Served with AUS, 1944-45; as 1st lt. M.C., USAF, 1952. Diplomate Am. Bd. Anesthesiology. Fellow Am. Coll. Anesthesiologists, Am. Coll. Chest Physicians; mem. AMA, Am., Wayne County (pres. 1967-69), socs. anesthesiologists, Am. Assn. Respiratory Therapists, Soc. Critical Care Medicine. Clubs: Detroit Athletic, Country of Detroit, Severance Lodge. Co-author: Operative Neurosurgery, 1970; First Aid Guide for the Small Business or Industry, 1978. Home: 281 Lake Shore Rd Grosse Pointe Farms MI 48236 Office: 119 Kercheval St Grosse Pointe Farms MI 48236

SPICE, DENNIS DEAN, state univeresity official, financial consultant; b. Rochester, Ind., Feb. 7, 1950; s. Donnelly Dean and Lorene (Rhodes) S.; m. Linda Kay Buehler, Oct. 1, 1971; 1 dau., Kristie Lorene. A.A., SUNY, Albany, 1974; B.A., Eastern Ill. Univ., 1978; M.B.A., Univ. Ill., Urbana, 1985. Cert. systems profl., 1984. Employee benefits mgr. Eastern Ill. Univ., Charleston, 1977-80; disbursements officer State Univs. Retirement System, Champaign, Ill., 1980-81, asst. exec. dir. adminstrn., 1981—; pres., cons. Executive Managerial Bus. Assocs., Inc., Champaign, 1984—. Served to staff sgt. USMC, 1968-77; Vietnam. Mem. Data Processing Mgmt. Assn. (v.p. 1982-83), Nat. Assn. Accts., Assn. Systems Mgmt., Am. Cons. League. Republican. Home: Rural Route 3 Box 39 Champaign IL 61821 Office: State Univs Retirement System 50 Gerty Dr Champaign IL 61820

SPICER, EMILY TAYLOR, educational administrator; b. Versailles Ky., July 25, 1926; d. Larry Duncan and Arega (Twyman) Harris; m. Mac Cecil Watkins; 1 son, Mac Duncan Watkins; m. 2d, Roy James Spicer, Dec. 18, 1976. B.S. in Edn., U. Cin., 1948, M.Ed., 1963. Tchr., Lincoln Heights High Sch., Cin., 1958-59, Heinold Jr. High Sch., Cin., 1959-62, Aiken High Sch., Cin., 1962-65, counselor, 1965-68; guidance coordinator Woodward High Sch., Cin., 1968-71, asst. prin., 1976-78; prin. Merry Jr. High Sch., Cin., 1976-78, Taft High Sch./Queen City Vocat. Ctr., Cin., 1978-81; dir. staff devel. Cin. Pub. Schs., 1981-82; dir. secondary edn., Cin., 1982—. Bd. dirs. YMCA, YWCA, Black Career Women, Inc.; bd. youth services juvenile ct.; mem. planning com. Cin. Presbytery. Recipient Outstanding Profl. Woman award Iota Phi Lambda, 1977; Outstanding Educator award Ohio Elks Assn., 1979; YMCA Black Achiever award Cin. Bd. Edn., 1979; Service in Edn. award NAACP, 1980; YWCA Career Woman Achiever award, 1980; Ethelrie Harper human relations award Cin. Human Relations Commn., 1980; Cin Enquirers One of Ten Women of Yr. award, 1980; Service to Edn. and Community award Shriners, 1981; featured on TV show PM Mag., 1978. Mem. Ohio Assn. Supervision and Curriculum Devel., Ohio Edn. Assn., NEA, Cin. Assn. Adminstrs. and Suprs., Nat. Assn. Secondary Sch. Prins., NAACP, Delta Kappa Gamma, Delta Sigma Theta, Phi Delta Kappa. Clubs: Top Ladies of Distinction, Woman's City. Home: 11289 Lockport Ct Cincinnati OH 45240 Office: 230 E 9th St Cincinnati OH 45202

SPICER, JAMES WARREN, pharmaceuticals company executive; b. Massillon, Ohio, July 22, 1953; s. Warren Harding and Eileen Mary (McLaughlin) S.; m. Antonia Marie Andriotto, Dec. 4, 1976; children—James Warren, Andrew Barclay. B.A. cum laude, W.Va. U.-Morgantown, 1975. Instr. lab. human physiology, cellular molecular biology W.Va. U.-Morgantown, 1974-75, surg. technician (Am. Heart Assn. Dept. Pharmacology grantee), 1975-76; trainee med. sales Bowman Drug Co., Canton, Ohio, 1976-77; rep. med. sales Pennwalt Corp., Rochester, N.Y., 1977-80, hosp. sales rep., sales trainer, various locations, 1980-82, dist. sales mgr., Pitts., Canton, W.Va., Columbus, Youngstown, 1982—. Editor, Dist. 207 Newsletter Smoke Signals, 1980-81. Pres., Massillon (Ohio) Young Republicans Club, 1971-72; mem. Canton Council for Exceptional Children, 1976—; head coach Masontown (W.Va.) Midget Football, 1972, 73. Mem. Beta Beta Beta, Alpha Epsilon Delta. Republican.

SPICKARD, PAUL R., historian, educator; b. Seattle, June 20, 1950; s. Donald Elliot and Mary Alice (Adkins) S.; m. Rowena Fong, June 9, 1974; children—Naomi, Daniel. Student, U. Wash., 1970-71, Gordon-Conwell Sem., South Hamilton, Mass., 1973; A.B., Harvard U., 1973; M.A., U. Calif.-Berkeley, 1976, Ph.D., 1983. Instr., Solano Coll., Suisun City, Calif., 1980; acting instr. U. Calif.-Berkeley, 1981; lectr. San Francisco State U., 1981; asst. prof. Bethel Coll., St. Paul, 1981-84, assoc. prof., 1984—; bd. dirs. Midwest China Ctr., St. Paul, 1982—; mem. World Service Assocs., St. Paul, 1984—, assoc. dir., 1984-85. Contbr. articles to profl. jours. Trustee Sunrise Preschool, San Francisco, 1979-81; chmn. Sunset Chinese Bapt. Ch., San Francisco, 1980-81. Recipient undergrad. prize fellowship Charles Warren Ctr., Harvard U., 1972; McCormack fellow U. Calif., 1978-80. Mem. Orgn. Am. Historians, Am. Hist. Assn., Conf. on Faith and History, Asian Am. Studies Assn., Immigration History Soc., Assn. of Asian Scholars. Democrat. Baptist. Avocations: basketball; running; backpacking. Home: 1197 Hague Ave Saint Paul MN 55104 Office: Bethel Coll 3900 Bethel Dr Saint Paul MN 55112

SPIDELL, PATRICK JAMES, labor relations executive; b. Traverse City, Mich., Dec. 20, 1946; s. Edward Arthur and Charlotte Ester (Weathers) Hickey; m. Cathy Sloan, Mar. 21, 1969; 1 child, Christy. B.A. in Police Adminstrn., Madonna Coll., Livonia, Mich., 1979, B.A. in Sociology, 1979; M.A. in Pub. Adminstrn., Central Mich. U., 1986. Police officer Detroit Police Dept., 1966-73, Clinton Twp. Police, Mount Clemens, Mich., 1973-83; labor relations rep. Police Officers Assn. Mich., Livonia, 1978—, exec. bd., 1978—. Dir. sales Clinton Twp. Goodfellows, Mount Clemens, 1982. Mem. Clinton Twp. Police Officers Assn. (pres. 1975-83), Indsl. Relations Research Assn. (Detroit chpt.), Cousteau Soc., Acad. Sci. Fiction, Fantasy and Horror Films (co-chmn. state chpt.). Lodge: Clinton Valley Kiwanis (pub. relations dir. 1984—). Avocations: Science fiction memorabilia collecting, radio controlled modeling, golf. Home: 2806 Bamlet Royal Oak MI 48067 Office: Police Officers Assn Mich 28815 W 8 Mile Rd Suite 103 Livonia MI 48152

SPIEGEL, S. ARTHUR, judge; b. Cin., Oct. 24, 1920; s. Arthur Major and Hazel (Wise) S.; m. Louise Wachman, Oct. 31, 1945; children—Thomas, Arthur Major II, Andrew, Roger Daniel. B.A., U. Cin., 1942; LL.B., Harvard U., 1948; postgrad. in acctg. and philosophy Cin. Evening Coll., 1949. Bar: Ohio 1948, U.S. Ct. Appeals (6th cir.), U.S. Dist. Ct. (so. dist.) Ohio. Assoc., Kasfir and Chalfie, Cin., 1948-52, Benedict, Bartlett & Shepard, Cin., 1952-53, Gould & Gould, Cin., 1953-54; ptnr. Gould & Spiegel, Cin., 1954-59; assoc. Cohen, Baron, Druffel & Hogan, Cin., 1960-61; ptnr. Cohen, Todd, Kite & Spiegel, Cin., 1961-80; judge U.S. Dist. Ct. So. Dist. Ohio, Cin., 1980—. Served with USMC, 1942-45. Mem. ABA, Ohio Bar Assn., Cin. Bar Assn. Fed. Bar Assn. Democrat. Jewish. Office: 832 US Courthouse and PO Bldg 5th St and Walnut St Cincinnati OH 45202

SPILLANE, RICHARD JEROME, utility co. mgr., alcoholism cons.; b. Chgo., Nov. 13, 1935; s. Jerry and Helen (Kelly) S.; B.S.C., Loyola U., Chgo., 1957, M.Mgmt., 1959; student in alcoholism counseling Central States Inst. on Addiction, 1975; advanced safety cert. Nat. Safety Council, 1976; m. Annette Busse, Feb. 11, 1961; children—Mary Ellen, Patrick, John, Joseph, Kathleen, Susan, Daniel, Michael, William, Mary Anne, David. Steel salesman A. M. Castle, Franklin Park, Ill., 1959-62; with Ill. Bell Telephone Co., 1962—, employment mgr., Oak Brook, 1971-73, personnel mgr., 1973-75, mgmt. tng. mgr., Hinsdale, 1977—; cons. occupational alcoholism, Oak Park, 1975—; guest lectr. numerous colls., hosps., agys.; bd. govs. Ill. Alcoholism Cert. Bd.; counselor/lectr. Driving While Intoxicated Program, Suburban Cook County, Ill., 1975; mem. Ill. Task Force on Cert., 1976-80; chmn. profl. coms. Served to 1st lt. U.S. Army, 1957-59. Recipient Presdl. award Ill. Bell Telephone, 1979, Community Leadership-Alex award, 1979; Ill. Combined House/Senate commendation, 1978, Ill. Task Force on Cert. award, 1980; Leadership awards ARC, 1981, Am. Cancer Soc., 1982; cert. alcoholism counselor, Ill. Mem. Assn. Labor Mgmt. Cons. on Alcoholism (pres.), Ill. Alcoholism Counselor Alliance (gov.), Nat. Alcoholism Counselors Assn., Am. Soc. Safety Engrs., Ill. Alcoholism and Drug Dependence Assn., Antique Airplane Assn. Roman Catholic. Research in interpersonal aspects of human behavior. Home: 320 Wisconsin Oak Park IL 60302 Office: 12 Salt Creek Ln Hinsdale IL 60521

SPILLER, HARRY LEE, sheriff, law enforcement educator; b. Marion, Ill., July 3, 1945; s. Ralph and Goldie (Johnson) S.; m. Shirley Beasley, Aug. 6, 1967; 1 child, Lisa. A.S., John A. Logan Coll., 1978; B.S. in Adminstrn. of Justice, So. Ill. U., 1980, B.A. in Polit. Sci., 1980, M.P.A., 1982. Dep. sheriff Williamson County Sheriff's Dept., Marion, Ill., 1974-79, sheriff, 1982—; mem. security police John A. Logan Coll., Carterville, Ill., 1979-82, instr. law enforcement, 1980—. Mem. VFW, Am. Legion. Home: Rural Route 5 Box 150A Marion IL 62959 Office: Sheriff's Dept Williamson County 200 E Jefferson Marion IL 62959

SPINDEL, ROBERT J., financial consultant, investment advisor; b. St. Louis, June 19, 1946; m. Joyce Ann Sharp. A.A., St. Louis Community Coll., 1970; C.L.U., Am. Coll. 1978, Chartered Fin. Cons., 1980. Acctg. and fin. specialist U.S. Air Force, 1960-64; acct. Siegel, Robert, Plating and Co., St. Louis, 1965-70; life underwriter New England Life, St. Louis; 1970-75; pres., owner Spindel, Van Ittersum & Co., St. Louis, 1976—; mem. Estate Planning Council of St. Louis, 1975—. Contbr. articles on fin. and tax planning to profl. jours. Served to sgt. USAF, 1964-70. Life and quality mem. Million Dollar Round Table; charter mem. Registry Fin. Planning Practioners; mem. Internat. Assn. for Fin. Planning, Fin. Profls. Adv. Panel. Republican. Mem. United Ch. of Christ. Club: Mo. Athletic. Avocation: fishing

SPINK, GORDON CLAYTON, osteopathic physician; b. Lansing, Mich., Jan. 6, 1935; s. John Clayton and Marian (Taylor) S.; m. Jane Miller Frisbee, Nov. 26, 1960; children—John, Anne. B.S., Mich. State U., 1957, Ph.D., 1966, D.O., 1975. Instr. Research Electron Microscope Lab., Mich. State U., 1962-66, dir., 1966-72, asst. prof. Pesticide Research Ctr., 1966-71, dir., Electron Microscope Lab. Osteo Medicine 1972-74, clin. asst. prof. dept. family medicine, 1975-76, assoc. prof., 1976—, unit III coordinator osteo. medicine, 1977-80, co-dir. preceptor program, 1978-80; acting asst. dean grad. and continuing med. edn. in osteo. medicine, 1980; research collaborator Brookhaven Nat. Lab., Upton, N.Y., 1969; intern Osteo. Hosp., Flint, Mich., 1976, dir. med. edn., 1976, 80-82; dir. med. edn. Lansing Gen. Hosp., Mich., 1982-84. Bd. dirs. devel. fund Mich. State U., 1981-85; mem. Okemos Sch. Bd., Mich., 1983. Served with USAF, 1958-60. NIH fellow 1972-73. Mem. Am. Osteo. Assn., Mich. Osteo. Physicians and Surgeons Assn., Maine Osteo Assn., Assn. Osteo. Dirs. Med. Edn., Am. Heart Assn. (Mich. affiliate), Mich. Sch. Health Assn., Am. Med. Soccer Assn. (sec., treas.), Am. Soc. Cell Biology, AAAS, Electron Microscope Soc., Mich. Assn. Osteo. Dirs. Med. Edn., Mich. Council Grad. Med. Edn., Mich. State U. Coll. Osteo. Med. Alumni Assn. (past chmn.), Sigma Xi. Home: 3910 Sandlewood Dr Okemos MI 48864 Office: Mich State U Fee Hall East Lansing MI 48824

SPINNER, LEE LOUIS, accountant; b. Hillsboro, Ill., Nov. 9, 1948; s. John Louis and Clara Mae (Brown) S. B.S. in Acctg., U. Ill., 1971, M.A.S. in Acctg., 1972; M.S. in Taxation, DePaul U., 1983. C.P.A., Ill. Sr. tax acct. Ernst & Whinney, Chgo., 1972-78; dir. tax returns and audits Sunbeam Corp., Chgo., 1978-82; dir. tax compliance Sara Lee Corp., Chgo., 1982-83; mgr. tax compliance AM Internat., Inc., Chgo., 1983—; instr. tax tng. program Ernst & Whinney, 1975-78. Tax advisor Sta. WIND, Call Your Acct., Chgo., 1977-78; sec. Grant Park Accts. Softball League, Chgo., 1976-77. Mem. Ill. C.P.A. Soc., Am. Inst. C.P.A.s. Democrat. Roman Catholic. Club: Top Social Athletic (Chgo.). Lodges: Moose, K.C. Home: 9332 Landings Ln Des Plaines IL 60016 Office: AM Internat Inc 333 W Wacker Dr Chicago IL 60606

SPIRE, ROBERT M., state attorney general; b. Omaha, Sept. 20, 1925; B.S., Harvard U., 1949, J.D., 1952; student Juilliard Sch. of Music, 1952. C.P.A., Nebr.; D.H.L. (hon.), U. Nebr.-Omaha, 1971. Ptnr., Ellick, Spire & Jones, Omaha; adj. assoc. prof. med. jurisprudence U. Nebr. Coll. Medicine, 1968-84; atty. gen. State of Nebr., Lincoln, 1985—; mem. Nebr. Fourth Jud. Dist. Com. on Inquiry, 1959-81, vice chmn., 1974-81. Contbr. articles to profl. jours. Mem., Gov.'s Citizens Commn. for Study of Higher Edn. in Nebr., 1984. Served with U.S. Army, 1943-46. Recipient numerous awards for profl. and civic contbns. including: Spl. Contbn. to Black Heritage award, Omaha Black Heritage Series, 1983; Urban League of Nebr. Whitney M. Young Meml. award, 1983. Fellow Am. Bar Found.; mem. Am. Judicature Soc. (bd. dirs. 1983-84), ABA (spl. com. on lawyers' pub. service responsibility 1983-84), Am. Guild Organists, Nebr. State Bar Assn. (pres. 1981-82), Nebr. Continuing Legal Edn. (pres. 1978-80), Urban League Nebr. (bd. dirs. 1977-80), Omaha Bar Assn. (pres. 1978-79), Legal Aid Soc. Omaha (bd. dirs. 1971-79, pres. 1972-75). Address: State of Nebr Dept of Justice Office of Atty Gen Lincoln NE 68509

SPITZIG, NORMAN J., JR., club administrator, consultant; b. Cin., Jan. 6, 1950; s. Norman J. and Alice H. (Wilken) S.; m. Cody Pollock, Feb. 6, 1982; children—Adam A., Mark C. A.B. magna cum laude, Boston Coll., 1972; M.A., Ohio State U., 1974. Asst. mgr. Scioto Country Club, Columbus, Ohio, 1974-76; mgr. Losantiville Country Club, Cin., 1976-81; gen. mgr. Ft. Wayne Country Club, Ind., 1981—; cons. K&S Enterprises, Inc., Ft. Wayne, 1981—. Contbg. author: Club Management Operations, 1984; also articles. Mem. Club Mgrs. Assn. Am. (textbook com. 1984, co-ednl. chmn. Ohio Valley chpt. 1982-83, pres. Greater Cin. 1981, bd. govs. Ohio Valley chpt. 1978-79, Best Country Club Luncheon Menu award 1978). Avocations: marathoning; cross-country skiing. Home: 7122 Woodhue Ln Ft Wayne IN 46804 Office: Ft Wayne Country Club 5221 Covington Rd Ft Wayne IN 46804

SPIVACK, JOHN MICHAEL, history educator; b. N.Y.C., June 22, 1942; s. Abraham Henry and Tybel Sonya (Berman) S.; m. Patricia Kay Dwyer, June 15, 1962 (div.); m. Patricia Susan Calhoon, June 13, 1980. B.A., Columbia U., 1964; J.D., U. Fla., 1967, M.A.T., 1973, Ph.D., 1978; LL.M., NYU, 1968. Bar: Fla. 1968, Ga. 1969, Pa. 1971. Labor atty. Smith, Currie & Hancock, Atlanta, 1968-70; mem. firm Handler, Gerber & Widmer, Harrisburg, Pa., 1970-71; teaching assoc. U. Fla., Gainesville, 1972-78, adj. asst. prof. social sci., 1978-79; asst. prof. history Bellevue Coll., Nebr., 1979-83, assoc. prof., 1983—. Mem. Internat. Affairs Com. Omaha, 1981—. Mem. Am. Hist. Assn., Orgn. Am. Historians, Pa. Bar Assn., NCCJ, Phi Kappa Phi. Democrat. Avocations: racquetball; reading; travel. Home: 7607 S 45th Ave Omaha NE 68157 Office: Bellevue Coll Wright Way at Galvin Rd Bellevue NE 68005

SPIVAK, PETER BEECHING, lawyer; b. Phila., Jan. 9, 1934; s. Alexander Avery and Marguerite Elizabeth (Beeching) S.; m. Anne Dorothy Markley, Jan. 3, 1974; children—Jeffrey, Michele, Peter. B.A., Ohio Wesleyan, 1955; J.D., Northwestern, 1957. Bar: Mich. 1957. Asst. U.S. atty. gen. Detroit, 1957-59; law clk. to presiding judge U.S. Dist. Ct., 1959-60; sole practice, Detroit, 1960-64; chmn. Mich. Pub. Service Commn., Lansing, 1964-68; judge Mich. Common Pleas and Cir. Ct., Wayne County, 1968-81, presiding judge, 1971-72; sole practice, 1981—; founding chmn., commr. USFL; pres. Mich. Panthers, Detroit, 1982-83. Contbr. articles to profl. jours. Chmn. Wayne County Republican Comm., Mich., 1962-64, Assocs. of Detroit Inst. of Arts, 1980—; bd. dirs. Music Hall Ctr. for Performing Arts, 1972—, chmn., 1972-74; trustee alumni regent Northwestern U., 1980—, Friends of , Pub. Library, 1972—, Detroit Symphony, 1980; Recipient Disting. Service award NAACP, Detroit, 1973. Mem. ABA (forum com. on sports and entertainment law), Mich. Bar Assn., Mystery Writers of Am. Clubs: Detroit, Detroit Athletic. Avocations: theatre; film; music, sports. Home: 1 Alger Pl Grosse Pointe MI 48230 Office: 2580 Penobscot Bldg. Detroit MI 48226

SPLETE, HOWARD HENRY, JR., counselor educator; b. Watertown, N.Y., Nov. 7, 1931; s. Howard Henry and Minnie Bertha (Peterjohn) S.; m. Marlene Barbara Rebits Mar. 4, 1961; children—Andrew, Charles, Nancy. B.A., St. Lawrence U., 1953; M.S., Syracuse U., 1956; Ph.D., Mich. State U., 1968. Counselor pub. schs., N.Y., Mich., Fed. Republic Germany, 1958-70; counselor educator Wayne State U., Detroit, 1970-78, Oakland U., Rochester, Mich., 1978—. Served with U.S. Army, 1953-55. Mem. Am. Assn. Counseling and Devel. (cert.), Mich. Personnel and Guidance Assn. (Disting. Service award 1979), Internat. Assn. Ednl. and Vocat. Guidance. Author: The Consulting Process 1975; Career Development, 1975; Counseling: An Introduction, 1984. Office: Oakland U 524 O'Dowd Hall Rochester MI 48063

SPOHN, WILLIAM DUANE, chemical company executive; b. Tucson, Apr. 20, 1951; s. George William, Jr., and Catherine Sheila (Richards) S.; m. Carolyn Jo Bailey, June 2, 1973; 1 son, Michael William. B.S. in Indsl. Engring. magna cum laude, B.B.A. magna cum laude, U. Cin., 1974; postgrad. U. So. Calif., 1977-78, Ohio State U., 1981—. Project engr. Rockwell Internat., Allegan, Mich., 1974-75, project mgr., Ashtabula, Ohio, 1975-77; sr. mfg. engr. Mattel, Inc., City of Industry, Calif., 1977-78; chief engr. Kenner Products, Cin., 1978-81, corp. engr., 1981-83; dir. mfg. Franklin Chem. Industries, Columbus,

Ohio, 1983—; tchr. prodn. and inventory control techniques. Mem. Spring Grove Assn. Fellow Am. Prodn. and Inventory Control Soc. (cert.); mem. Am. Inst. Indsl. Engrs., Beta Gamma Sigma. Roman Catholic. Club: Indoor Soccer Acad. (Columbus). Office: 2020 Bruck St Columbus OH 43207

SPOOR, WILLIAM HOWARD, food products company executive. Chmn. Pillsbury Co., Mpls., also dir. Office: Pillsbury Co 200 S 6th St Minneapolis MN 55402*

SPRANDEL, DENNIS STEUART, management consulting company executive; b. Little Falls, Minn., June 1, 1941; s. George Washington and Lucille Margaret (Steuart) S.; A.B., Albion Coll., 1963; M.Ed., U. Ariz., 1965; Ph.D., Mich. State U., 1973. Grad. teaching asst. U. Ariz., Tucson, 1964-65; dir. athletics, Owen Grad. Center Mich. State U., East Lansing, 1965-68; prof., dir. student teaching Mt. St. Mary's Coll., 1968-70; exec. dir. Mich. AAU, 1974-81, mem. numerous nat. coms., 1974-81; mem. U.S. Olympic Com., 1974-77; pres., chmn. bd. Am. Sports Mgmt., Ann Arbor, 1976—, Am. SportsVision, 1981—, Am. Sports Research, 1977—, Sprandel Group, 1984—; pres. Nat. Sports & Entertainment, Inc., 1984—, Sprandel Assocs., 1984—; bd. dirs. Nat. Golden Gloves, 1980—, Port Huron TV Project, 1985—; pres. Detroit Golden Gloves Charities; pres. adminstrv. bd. Detroit Golden Gloves, 1985—; Bd. dirs. Mich. Sports Hall of Fame, 1976—; Cons. in field. Recipient Detroit Striders award, 1978; Emerald award, 1979; World TaeKwonDo award, 1979; Detroit Spl. Olympics award, 1978; Community Service award Mich. State U., 1985. Mem. Am. Soc. Assn. Execs., Nat. Assn. Phys. Edn. in Higher Edn., AAHPER, Nat. Recreation and Parks Assn., Internat. Boxing Fedn., N.Am. Boxing Fedn., U.S. Boxing Assn., World Boxing Assn., World Boxing Council, Nat. Assn. for Girls and Women in Sport, Psi Chi. Contbr. articles to profl. jours. Home: 1530 Pine Valley Apt 5 Ann Arbor MI 48104 Office: 27208 Southfield Rd Suite 3 Lathrup Village MI 48076

SPRIGGS, ROBERT PAUL, oil and gas drilling company executive, engineer; b. Muskogee, Okla., July 4, 1932; s. Paul Snow Spriggs and Hazel Alpha (Dawson) Binda; m. Betty Nell Culver, Dec. 12, 1954 (div. 1971); children—Paul David, Sandra Lee, Mary Sue; m. Berna Dene Vance, Aug. 31, 1973; 1 child, Lori Lynn Lessenden. B.S. in Petroleum Engring., U. Okla., 1954. Registered profl. engr., Tex., Kans. Engr. Humble Oil & Refining, Baytown, Tex., 1954-59; profl. engr. D.R. McCord & Assocs., Dallas, 1959-63, G.L. Yates & Assocs., Wichita, Kans., 1965-69; v.p. Energy Res. Group, Wichita, 1969-78; ops. mgr. Beren Corp., Wichita, 1978-79; pres. Midco Drilling, Inc., Wichita, 1979—, also dir.; dir. Midco Petroleum Tech., Wichita, 1983—. Patentee wireline extension hanger. Union Oil Tex. scholar, 1953. Mem. Soc. Petroleum Engrs., AIME, Am. Assn. Petroleum Geologists. Republican. Methodist. Clubs: Crestview Country, Wichita Ski (treas. 1975-76). Avocations: fishing; scuba diving; skiing; flying. Office: Midco Drilling Inc 125 N Market Suite 1250 Wichita KS 67202

SPRINGER, HARRY AARON, surgeon; b. El Paso, Tex., Nov. 23, 1937; s. Moses David and Louise (Fessinger) S.; m. Nancy K. Springer, Sept. 1, 1958 (div. 1977); children—Rhonda Springer Levin, Michael R., Steven. m. Mavis Leona Springer, May 4, 1980. D.D.S., Northwestern U., 1960; M.D., U. Tex., 1964. Diplomate Am. Bd. Plastic Surgery. Intern Cook County Hosp., Chgo., 1964-65, resident in gen. surgery, 1964-69; resident in plastic surgery Northwestern U., 1968-71; practice medicine specializing in plastic surgery, Evanston, Ill. Contbr. articles to med. jours. Served with USAR, 1981-84. Fellow ACS; mem. Am. Soc. Plastic and Reconstructive Surgeons, AMA, Ill. State Med. Soc. (2d v.p. 1985-86), Chgo. Med. Soc. (pres. 1983-84, trustee 1983—). Office: Aesthetic Surgery Ltd 800 Austin Suite 610 Evanston IL 60202

SPRINGER, IRVING MOXLEY, real estate company executive; b. Indpls., Aug. 3, 1915; d. George Barret and Charlotte Stewart (Scott) Moxley; m. William Albert Diven, Jr., Feb. 25, 1942; 1 son, Michael Moxley; m. 2d, Frank C. Springer, Jr., Feb. 17, 1951. Student Smith Coll., Columbia U. Pres. Scott-Carey Realty Co., Indpls., 1982—. Trustee, Indpls. Mus. of Art; founding pres. Clowes Hall Women's Com.; chmn. grounds com. Eli Lilly Bot. Garden, Indpls.; bd. dirs., chmn. Garden Club Am.; mem. allocations com. United Way, Central Ind.; founder ARC Motor Corps., Indpls.; bd. dirs. Planned Parenthood, Central Ind. Recipient medal of merit Garden Club of Am. Republican. Presbyterian. Clubs: Progressive, Woodstock, Colonial Dames of Ind., Dramatic (Indpls.). Home: 5763 Sunset Ln Indianapolis IN 46208

SPRINGER, NEIL A., heavy equipment manufacturing company executive; b. Fort Wayne, Ind., May 2, 1938; s. Roy V. and Lucille H. (Gerke) S.; m. Janet M. Grotrian, Sept. 3, 1960; children—Sheri Lynn, Kelly Jean, Mark Allen. B.S., U. Ind., 1960; M.B.A., U. Dayton, 1966; C.P.A., U. Ill., 1975. With Internat. Harvester, 1966—, staff asst. acctg., Bridgeport, Conn., 1966-68, asst. plant comptroller, Ft. Wayne, Ind. 1968-70, staff asst., Chgo., 1970-75, asst. corp. comptroller, 1975-77, v.p. fin., 1977-79, v.p., gen. mgr. trucks, 1979-81, pres. truck group, 1981-84, pres., chief operating officer Internat. Harvester, 1984—; dir. Century Life Ins., Highway Users Fedn., 1981-82. Bd. dirs. Lutheran Home for Aged, Arlington Heights, Ill. Mem. Ill. C.P.A. Soc. Lutheran. Office: Internat Harvester Co 401 N Michigan Ave Chicago IL 60611

SPRINGER, RAYMOND LOUIS, lawyer, manufacturing company executive; b. Louisville, June 8, 1913; s. Byron Marcellus and Louise (Pitts) S.; m. Jane Dorsey, Sept. 4, 1953. J.D., U. Louisville, 1936. Bar: Ky. 1936. Asst. office mgr., atty. Fed. Land Bank of Louisville, 1930-41; asst. gen. mgr. H.T. Colling Co., Cin., 1949-51, v.p., gen. mgr., 1951-56; pres. Auto Sun Products Co., Cin., 1956—; metal finishers rep. Nat. Indsl. Pollution Control Council, 1971. Served to maj. AUS, 1941-46, U.S. Army, 1946-49, col. Res. ret. Mem. Fed. Bar Assn., Ret. Officers Assn., Mil. Order of World Wars, Ky. Bar Assn., C. of C., Nat. Assn. Metal Finishers (pres. 1967-69, Silvio C. Taormina award 1972), Metal Finishers Found. (pres. 1972-74), Sigma Delta Kappa. Clubs: Kenwood Country, Jaguar; Brit. Auto Racing; Masons, K.T. Home: 7100 Ragland Rd Cincinnati OH 45244

SPRINGER, TIMOTHY JON, ergonomic consulting company executive; b. Fort Wayne, Ind., Nov. 12, 1952; s. Daniel Christian and Mabel Ann (Fuhrman) S.; m. Joyce Eileen McAllister, Sept. 1, 1973; children—Laura Trese, Benjamin Jon. Student, U.S. Naval Acad., 1970; B.A., Augustana Coll., 1974; M.A., U. S.D., 1976, Ph.D., 1978. Research asst. Dept. Transp., Vermillion, S.D., 1974-77, S.D. Hwy. Patrol, Pierre, 1977-78; assoc. research adminstr. State Farm Ins., Bloomington, Ill., 1978-82; assoc. prof. psychology Ill. State U., Normal, 1979-80; pres. Springer Assocs., Inc., St. Charles, Ill., 1982—. Contbr. articles to profl. jours. Mem. Human Factors Soc., Environ. Research and Design Assn. Office: Springer Assocs Inc 1405 W Main St PO Box 1159 Saint Charles IL 60174

SPROSTY, ALLAN ELMER, JR., textile manufacturing executive; b. Columbus, Ohio, Aug. 24, 1948; s. Allan Elmer and Donna Mae (Leslie) S.; m. Lucille Gambrill, Feb. 14, 1975; children—Jenniffer Regan, Jaklyn Krista, Matthew Allan. B.S. in Psychology, Denison U., 1970. Mgt., Side Door, Phoenix, 1978-80, Lakeland Golf Equipment, Cleve., 1970-71; v.p. Gen. Bag Corp., Cleve., 1971-77, 80-83, Triple S Corp., Cleve., 1979—. Caseworker Big Bros., Cleve., 1981—. Mem. Textile Bag Mfrs. Assn., Textile Bag Processors Assn., Mktg. Assn. Clubs: Cleve. Athletic; Westwood Country, Rotary Internat., Bluecoats. Office: Gen Bag Corp 3368 W 137th St Cleveland OH 44111

SPROUSE, GARY LEE, sales executive; b. St. Louis, Dec. 22, 1938; s. Grady Louis and Eleanor May S.; student (working scholar 1959-61), Central Meth. Coll., 1959-61; B.S.B.A., Washington U., St. Louis, 1963; M.B.A., Central Mich. U., 1968; m. Donna Sue Green, July 27, 1963; children—Anne Elizabeth, Gregory Herbert. Staff mgmt. asst. Western Electric Co., St. Louis, 1963-65; with Dow Corning Corp., 1965-82, regional sales mgr., Englewood Cliffs, N.J., 1972-74, gen. mgr. SE Asia, Hong Kong, 1974-78, regional sales mgr., Chgo., 1978-82; dir. sales Olin Water Services, Overland Park, Kans., 1982—. Served with U.S. Army, 1957-58. Republican. Episcopalian. Clubs: Bull Valley Hunt, Am. Hardware, Elks. Home: 11519 Hadley Overland Park KS 66210 Office: 9393 W 110th St 51 Corporate Woods Overland Park KS 66210

SPURGEON, PAUL EDMUND, JR., lawyer; b. Mt. Vernon, Ohio, Feb. 24, 1948; s. Paul Edmund and Elsie Marie (Burch) S.; m. Linda Rae Feasel, Sept. 12, 1970; children—Jeffrey Paul, Chad Aaron, Sara Nicole. B.S., Ohio State U., 1970; J.D., Capital U., 1976. Bar: Ohio 1976, U.S. Dist. Ct. (so. dist.) Ohio 1976, U.S. Supreme Ct. 1980. Tchr. Plain Local Schs., New Albany, Ohio, 1970-72; trust officer Bank One, Columbus, Ohio, 1973-78; city prosecutor City of Mt. Vernon, 1978-81; ptnr. Zelkowitz, Barry & Cullers, Mt. Vernon, 1981—. Mem. Knox County Republican. Fin. Com., Mt. Vernon, 1983—. Mem. Ohio State Bar Assn. (natural resources com. 1979—), Knox County Bar Assn. (pres. 1984-85), Mt. Vernon Jaycees (pres. 1981-82), Mt. Vernon C. of C. Methodist. Office: Zelkowitz Barry & Cullers 121 E High St PO Box 28 Mount Vernon OH 43050

SPURRELL, FRANCIS ARTHUR, animal disease genetics educator, researcher; b. Independence, Iowa, Apr. 13, 1919; s. John Arthur and Evangeline (Francis) S.; m. Joy Dibble, Dec. 24, 1942; 1 dau., Margaret Joy. B.S. in Animal Husbandry, U. Wis., 1941; D.V.M., Iowa State Coll., 1946; Ph.D., U. Minn., 1955. Lic. in vet. medicine, Minn. County livestock agt. U. Wis. Extension, Fond Du Lac, 1946; veterinarian Land-O-Lakes Breeders Coop., 1947; instr. in vet. anatomy U. Minn., St. Paul, 1947-49, instr. in vet. obstetrics, 1949-55, assoc. prof. vet. radiology, 1955-62, prof. vet. radiology, 1962-68, prof. theriogenology, 1968—, dir. Summer Inst. in Radiation Biology, 1960-64. Trustee Master Eye Found., Minnetonka, Minn., 1950—, treas., 1980—. Served with Vet. Service, AUS, 1941-43. Mem. Am. Coll. Vet. Radiology (charter), Minn. Vet. Med. Assn., N.Y. Acad. Sci., Minn. Pure Bred Dog Breeders Assn., Minn. Humane Soc. Lutheran. Designer livestock data base mgmt. system Systems Therio, 1974, 80, 82; research in race-track computer systems; designer equine racing mgmt. control systems, 1983, 84, 85. Office: 1988 Fitch Ave PO Box 8137 Saint Paul MN 55108 also Master Eye Found 10709 Wayzata Blvd Minnetonka MN 55343

SPYKMAN, ERIK DAVID, lawyer; b. Amsterdam, The Netherlands, Nov. 4, 1954; s. Gordon John and Eleanor Bernice (Hendriksen) S.; m. Jennifer Sprunger, June 2, 1978. B.A., Calvin Coll., 1977; J.D., U. Notre Dame, 1980. Bar: Ind. 1980, Mich. 1981, U.S. Dist. Ct. (no. and so. dists.) Ind. 1980, U.S. Ct. Appeals (7th cir.) 1984. Assoc. Stuart & Branigin, Lafayette, Ind., 1980-85, ptnr., 1985—. Bd. dirs. Lafayette Neighborhood Housing Services, Inc., Ind., 1983-85. Mem. ABA, Ind. State Bar Assn., Tippecanoe County Bar, State Bar Mich., Christian Legal Soc., Computer Law Assn. Office: Stuart & Branigin 801 Life Bldg Lafayette IN 47902

SQUILLANTE, MARC DAVID, osteopathic physician; b. Balt., Aug. 2, 1955; s. Alphonse M. and Diana J. (Keilman) S.; m. Carol Ann Galeazzi, May 29, 1982. B.S. in Pharmacy with distinction, U. Iowa, 1978; D.O., Coll. Osteo. Medicine and Surgery, Des Moines, 1981. Intern, Des Moines Gen. Osteo. Hosp., 1981-82; resident in emergency medicine St. Francis Med. Ctr., Peoria, Ill., 1982-84, also chief resident in emergency medicine U. Ill.-Peoria and St. Francis Med. Ctr., Peoria, 1983-84. Mem. Am. Coll. Emergency Physicians, Am. Osteo. Assn., Emergency Medicine Residents' Assn., Rho Chi. Office: East Liverpool City Hosp 425 W 5th St East Liverpool OH 43920

SQUIRES, SANDRA KAY, special educator, consultant; b. Glendive, Mont., June 3, 1944; d. Ralph E. and M. Elouise (Cabbage) S.; m. James A. Boland, June 19, 1965 (div. May 1, 1980); children—Michael F., Jennifer L. B.S. in Elem. Edn., Eastern Mont. Coll., 1966; M.A. in Mental Retardation, Colo. State Coll., 1969; Ed.D. in Mental Retardation, U. No. Colo., 1972. Cert. elem. tchr., Mont., Okla., Colo. First grade tchr. Billings Pub. Sch., Mont., 1966-67; spl. edn. tchr. Ft. Benning Children's Schs., Ga., 1967-68, Comanche County United Cerebral Palsy Assn., Lawton, Okla., Weld Bd. Coop. Services, Ault, Colo., 1970; instr. Loretto Heights Coll., Denver, 1972; instructional materials specialist Rocky Mountain Instructional Materials Ctr., Greeley, Colo., 1971-72, asst. prof., 1973-74; dir. career edn. for Mentally Handicapped Weld Bd. Coop. Services, LaSalle, Colo., 1974-77; asst. prof. Colo. State U., Ft. Collins, 1978; sr. project assoc. Pa. State U., Bur. of Edn. for Handicapped, Washington, 1979; asst. prof. Wash. State U., Pullman, 1979-81; assoc. prof., chmn. counseling and spl. edn. U. Nebr. Omaha, 1981—; pres. Ednl. Cons. Enterprises Inc., Greeley, 1974-79; speaker, cons. univs., local, state, and federal agencies, profl. orgns. U.S. and Canada, 1972—; sec., treas. Squires, Inc., Glendive, Mont., 1980—. Co-editor, editor (newsletter) Inservice Consultant, 1974-77. Author training manuals, monograph, children's books. Contbr. articles to profl. jours. Polit. action network coordinator Nebr. Fedn. Council for Exceptional Children, Omaha, 1982-85. Recipient Robert G. Sando award Eastern Mont. Coll., 1966. Mem. Internat. Council Exceptional Children, Internat. Div. on Career Devel. (sec. 1976-79, v.p. 1979-80, pres.-elect 1980-81, pres. 1981-82), Internat. Council of Adminstrs. in Spl. Edn. Tchr. Edn., Phi Delta Kappa. Home: 681 S 85th St Omaha NE 68114 Office: Dept Counseling & Spl Edn Univ Nebraska Omaha NE 68182

SRAWLEY, JOHN EWART, science and engineering consultant; b. Birmingham, Eng., Aug. 14, 1921; came to U.S., 1952, naturalized, 1957; s. William Ewart and Lottie Elizabeth S.; m. Helene Hill, Jan. 9, 1946; children—Jane Margaret, John Ewart, B.Sc. with 1st honors U. London, 1949, D.Sc., 1969. Chartered engr., Eng. Apprentice, BCIRA, Birmingham, Eng., 1938-40; sr. asst. metallurgist, Halesowen, Eng., 1940-41; research metallurgist Mond Nickel Co., Birmingham, Eng., 1949-50; sr. sci. officer BCIRA, Redditch, Eng., 1950-52; head strength of materials br. NRL, Washington, 1956-63; sect. head, sci. cons. NASA, Lewis Research Ctr., Cleve., 1963-83; sci. and engring. cons., North Olmsted, Ohio, also worldwide, 1983—; lectr. Lehigh U., Del. Research Corp., also cons.; cons. U.S. Air Force, U.S. Army, U.S. Navy, NRC, AEC, others. Served as pilot Royal Air Force, 1941-46. ASTM fellow and recipient Award of Merit, 1971. Fellow Inst. Metals; mem. Fedn. Am. Scientists, ASTM, Am. Soc. Metals, Sigma Xi. Democrat. Unitarian. Contbr. articles to profl. jours.

STAAL, DENNIS RAY, financial consultant; b. Chadron, Nebr., Aug. 26, 1948; s. Raymond L. and Betty L. (Gold) S.; m. Pamela J. Grantham, June 11, 1971; children—David, Suzann. B.S., U. Nebr., 1970. C.P.A., Nebr., S.D. Fin. cons. Health Planning, Omaha, 1973-77; acct. Arthur Andersen & Co., Omaha, 1971-73; pres. Wulf Oil Corp., Chadron, 1977-81; controller Advanced Cattle Tech., Cody, Nebr., 1981-82, High Plains Genetics, Piedmont, S.D., 1982-84; fin. cons., Rapid City, S.D., 1984—. Mem. Am. Inst. C.P.A.s. Republican. Roman Catholic. Lodges: Kiwanis (treas. 1980), K.C., Elks. Home: 3512 Powderhorn Dr Rapid City SD 57702 Office: Box 835-10 Piedmont SD 57769

STAAS, JOHN WILLIAM, psychologist, educator; b. Freeport, Ill., July 28, 1942; s. William Franklin and Lucille Ann (Harney) S.; A.A., Cerritos Jr. Coll., 1962; student Calif. State U., Fullerton, 1962-63; B.S., No. Ill. U., 1964; M.A., U. Mo., Kansas City, 1966; postgrad. in Psychology, Bowling Green State U., 1966-67, Wayne State U., 1969-71; m. Zee L. Kinman, children—Laura Christine, Kevin Gregory. Research asst. Kansas City Mental Health Found., 1965-66; asst. psychologist Peace Corps., U. Mo., Kansas City, 1966; research asso. Kans. U. Med. Center, 1965; staff psychologist Kansas City Found. for Exceptional Children, 1965-66; asst. prof. psychology Mary Manse Coll., Toledo, 1967-70; asso. prof. psychology Monroe County (Mich.) Community Coll., Monroe, 1970—; pvt. practice clin. psychology, Toledo, 1968—; cons. psychologist Rescue, Inc., 1968-71, Holy Spirit Sem. and Vocat. Office Toledo Cath. Charities, 1971-77, Dr. S.N. Petas, Med. Clinic, Toledo, 1972-76; cons. clin. psychologist Toledo Mental Hygiene Clinic, 1967-74; clin. psychologist, adj. med. staff St. Charles Hosp., Oregon, Ohio, 1977—; cons., workshops on non-verbal communication and psychology of multiple personalities, 1976—. Named Tchr. of Year, Monroe County Community Coll., 1975-76, 78-79, 82-83; registered psychologist; lic. psychologist, Ill., Ohio; cert. hypnotist. Mem. Am. Psychol. Assn., Assn. for Advancement of Psychology, Ill. Psychol. Assn., Assn. for Advancement of Behavior Therapy, N.W. Ohio Psychol. Assn., N.W. Ohio Clin. Hypnosis Assn., NEA, Mich. Edn. Assn., Phi Theta Kappa (spl. tchr.'s award 1973, hon. mem.). Roman Catholic. Club: Heatherdowns Country (Toledo). Author script Voice of Am. Radio. Home: 4125 Greenglen Rd Toledo OH 43614 Office: 1455 S Raisinville Rd Dept Psychology Monroe MI 48161 also 5321 Southwyck Blvd Suite L Briarwood Medical Center Toledo OH 43614

STAATS, BRUCE ALBERT, medical educator, physician; b. Lincoln, Nebr., May 5, 1946; s. Laura Elizabeth (Longacre) S.; m. Brenda Lynn Nicholson, June 5, 1971; children—Emily Christine, Peter Michael. B.S., U. Nebr., 1968, M.D., 1971; M.S., U. Minn., 1980. Diplomate Am. Bd. Internal Medicine, Am. Bd. Pulmonary Disease. Intern Los Angeles County Hosp.-U. So. Calif., 1971-72; resident Mayo Clinic, Rochester, Minn., 1974-79, asst. prof. medicine, 1979—. Stewardship chmn. Congl. Ch., Rochester, Minn., 1981-83. Served to capt. M.C., USAF, 1972-74. Mem. Am. Thoracic Soc., Am. Physiol. Soc., Phi Beta Kappa, Sigma Xi. Avocation: photography. Home: 6930 Buckthorn Rd NW Rochester MN 55901 Office: Mayo Clinic 200 1st St SW Rochester MN 55905

STACH, JAMES EDWARD, data processing administrator; b. Browerville, Minn., Apr. 8, 1937; s. Edward Louis and Mary Hattie (Buhl) S.; m. Catherine Dorothy Williams, Sept. 17, 1960; children—Robert, Ellen, Mary Kay. B.A. in Bus. Adminstrn., Met. State U., St. Paul, 1983. Cert. data processor Inst. Certification of Computer Profls. Computer operator Econ. Lab. Inc., St. Paul, 1955-60, computer programmer, 1960-64, payroll supr., 1964-67, indsl. salesman, 1967-71, computer ops. supr., 1971-73, computer ops. mgr., 1973-78, data ctr. mgr., 1978-83; data processing cons. INTEC Systems, Inc., West Palm Beach, Fla., 1983—. Served with USAR, 1958-64. Named Outstanding Bus. Advisor of the Yr., Inroads, Mpls./St. Paul, 1979-80. Mem. Data Processing Mgmt. Assn., Volkfest Assn. Minn. Republican. Roman Catholic. Home: 2186 Upper Afton Rd Saint Paul MN 55119 Office: 400 Australian Ave West Palm Beach FL 33401

STACHURA, ROBERT DEAN, automotive supply manufacturing company executive; b. Columbus, Nebr., Sept. 5, 1942; s. John Barney and Martha Betty (Mimick) S.; m. Jane Marie Bougger, Oct. 5, 1963; children—Kristine Marie, Karen Jean, Nicole Lynn. B.S. in Bus., Kearney State Coll., 1979; student Platte Coll., 1973. Indsl. engr. Dale Electronics Inc., Columbus, 1963-73; indsl. engr. Douglas & Lomason Co., Columbus, 1973-79, production mgr., 1979-80, plant supt., 1980-81, plant mgr., 1981-84, plant mgr. 2 plants, Columbus, Red Oak, Iowa, 1984—. Mem. Columbus C. of C. (bd. dirs. 1983-84). Democrat. Roman Catholic. Lodge: Optimist (pres. 1983-84). Home: 3355 36th Ave Columbus NE 68601 Office: PO Box 879 Columbus NE 68601

STACK, DANIEL JAMES, III, elementary school administrator; b. Detroit, Dec. 12, 1946; s. Daniel J. and Margaret A. (Maloney) S.; m. Marion Jeanne Wasko, Nov. 26, 1971. B.A., St. Bernard Coll., 1969; M.A., Mich. State U., 1974; Ed.S., Wayne State U., 1981. Cert. elem. tchr., Mich. Elem. tchr. Pier Sch., Coloma, Mich., 1969-71, prin. 1971-80; prin. Eaman Sch., Benton Harbor, Mich., 1972-80, Clymer Sch., Coloma, 1973, Coloma Elem. Sch., 1980—; coordinator spl. edn. services Coloma Community Sch. Dist.; dir. summer migrant program; mem. adv. council Mich. Migrant Edn. Mem. Spl. Edn. Dirs. and Coordinators Council, Mich. Elem. and Middle Sch. Prins. Assn. (cert. sch. adminstr. 1981), Nat. Assn. Elem. Sch. Prins., Phi Delta Kappa. Clubs: K.C., Elks. Home: 5189 Riverview St Coloma MI 49038 Office: Coloma Elementary School West St Box 218 Coloma MI 49038

STACK, ROBERT J., librarian; b. Milw., Apr. 18, 1949; s. James Jerome and Ann (McIntaggart) S.; m. A. Christine Nelson, Nov. 24, 1972; children—Amanda, Matthew. B.A., Lakeland Coll., 1971; M.L.S., U. Wis.-Madison, 1974. Asst. dir. Clinton (Iowa) Pub. Library, 1975-78; dir. Granite City Pub. Library, Ill., 1978—; mem. adv. com. for LTA program Lewis & Clark Community Coll., Godfrey, Ill., 1981-83. Mem. Ill. Library Assn., ALA, Beta Phi Mu. Club: Rotary (sec. 1982-84, v.p. 1984-85, pres. 1985-86). Office: Granite City Public Library 2001 Delmar St Granite City IL 62040

STACK, STEPHEN S., manufacturing company executive; b. DuPont, Pa., Apr. 25, 1934; s. Steve and Sophie (Baranowski) Stasenko; B.S.M.E., Case Western Res. U., 1956; postgrad. Syracuse U. Mech. engr. Kaiser Aluminum, Erie, Pa., 1956-58; instr. Gannon U., Erie, 1958-60, Syracuse (N.Y.) U., 1960-61; engring. supr. A. O. Smith Corp., Erie and Los Angeles, 1961-66; gen. mgr. Am. Elec. Fusion, Chgo., 1966-67; mgr. new products Maremont Corp., Chgo., 1967-69; dir. market planning Gulf and Western Ind., Bellwood, Ill., 1969-71; mgmt. and fin. cons. Stack & Assos., Chgo., 1971-76; pres. Seamcraft, Inc., Chgo., 1976—; mem. Ill. Legis. Small Bus. Conf., 1980; mem. Mfrs. Polit. Action Com., 1983-85, Gov.'s Small Bus. Adv. Commn., 1984-85. Active Easter Seals Telethon, Sem. Townhouse Assn., Lincoln Park Conservation Assn., Sheffield Neighbors Assn. Registered profl. engr., Ill. Recipient Am. Legion award, 1948; Case Western Res. U. Honor Key, 1956, Eagle Scout award, 1949. Mem. Ill. Mfrs. Assn., Small Mfrs. Action Council, Am. Mgmt. Assn., Pres.' Assn., Blue Key, Beta Theta Pi, Theta Tau, Pi Delta Epsilon. Clubs: Chgo. Execs., East Bank, Chgo. Corinthian Yacht, Fullerton Tennis (pres. 1971-79), Fullerton Tennis (treas. 1979-83), Mid-Town Tennis, Lake Shore Ski (v.p. 1982). Patentee in liquid control and metering fields. Office: 932 W Dakin St Chicago IL 60613

STACKERT, RICHARD DENNIS, dentist; b. Gary, Ind., Mar. 9, 1946; s. Thomas Elmer and Camille Jesse (Smith) S.; m. Karen Jean Wineinger, Aug. 22, 1969; children—Jill Nicole, Jeffrey Richard, Faith Ann. Student The Citadel, Charleston, S.C., 1964-66; A.B. in Chemistry, Ind. U., 1968, D.D.S., Ind. U.-Indpls., 1972. Gen. practice dentistry, Valparaiso, Ind., 1972—; dental staff Beatty Meml. Hosp., Westville, Ind., 1972-74; cons. nursing homes, Valparaiso, 1978-80. Mem. ADA, Northwest Ind. Dental Soc., Porter County Dental Soc., Jaycees. Evangelical. Club: Valparaiso Golf. Avocations: marathon running, golfing, making precious metal jewelry. Home: 106 N Wild Rose Ct Valparaiso IN 46383 Office: Med Arts Bldg 2102 E Evans Ave Valparaiso IN 46383

STACKHOUSE, DAVID WILLIAM, JR., furniture systems installation contractor; b. Cumberland, Ind., Aug. 29, 1926; s. David William and Dorothy Frances (Snider) S.; B.S., Lawrence Coll., Appleton, Wis., 1950; m. Shirley Pat Smith, Dec. 23, 1950; 1 son, Stefan Brent. Indsl. designer Globe Am. Co., Kokomo, Ind., 1951-53; product designer, chief engr. L.A. Darling Co., Bronson, Mich., 1954-66; contract mgr. Brass Office Products, Indpls., 1966-73; mfrs. rep., Nashville, Ind., 1973-78; mktg. exec. Brass Office Products, Inc., Indpls., 1978-80; office furniture systems installation contractor, 1980—. Precinct committeeman Republican Party. Served with USNR, 1944-46; PTO. Mem. Bldg. Owners and Mfrs. Assn. (past pres. Indpls. chpt.), Brown County Bd. Realtors, Beta Theta Pi. Anglican. Clubs: Lions, Kiwanis (past v.p.), Masons, Shriners. Patentee interior structural systems. Home: Rural Route 3 Box 324 Nashville IN 47448

STACKLEY, DENNIS DUANE, sheriff; b. Eldorado, Kans., Mar. 12, 1959; s. Fred L. and Ethel Joanne (Walters) S.; m. Phyllis Ann Perks, Sept. 1, 1979, children—Charity Ann, Aaron Duane. Grad. high sch. Jailer, dispatcher Butler County Sheriff's Dept., Eldorado, Kans., 1977-78, dep. sheriff, 1978-80; patrolman II, Wellington Police Dept., Kans., 1980-81, sgt., 1981; undersheriff Barber County Sheriff's Dept., Medicine Lodge, Kans., 1981-82, sheriff, 1982—. Mem. Nat. Sheriffs Assn., Internat. Assn. Identification. Republican. Lodge: Lions (Medicine Lodge). Avocations: electronics, photography, beekeeping. Home: Sheriff's Quarters Medicine Lodge KS 67104 Office: 124 E Washington St Medicine Lodge KS 67104

STACY, RALPH WINSTON, rehabilitation engineering scientist, university administrator; b. Middletown, Ohio, Feb. 6, 1920; s. Wayne and Elvira (Gillum) S.; m. Marjorie Jayne Shepard, Mar. 19, 1943; children—William B., Susan M. B.Sc.Ed., Miami U., Oxford, Ohio, 1942; M.Sc., Ohio State U., 1947, Ph.D., 1948. From asst. prof. to prof. physiology Ohio State U., Columbus, 1948-61; prof. and dir. biomath. and bioengring., U. N.C., Chapel Hill, 1961-69; dir. tech. services Cox Heart Inst., Dayton, Ohio, 1969-72; chmn. dept. physiology So. Ill. U., Carbondale, 1972-77; dir. human studies EPA, Chapel Hill, 1977-82; research dir. Nat. Ctr. Rehab. Engring., Wright State U., Dayton, 1983—. Author books, including: Essentials of Biological and Medical Physics, 1955; Modern College Physiology, 1966; also numerous articles, 1947—. Editor books, including: Computers in Biology and Medicine, 4 vols., 1965-72. Served to 1st lt. USAAF, 1942-46. Grantee NIH, 1948-84, Am. Heart Assn., 1948-84. Mem. Am. Physiol. Soc., Biophys. Soc. (charter, treas. and bd. dirs. 1955—), Bioengring. Soc. Roman Catholic. Avocations: painting, etching, writing. Home: 700 W 6th Ave Middletown OH 45044 Office: Wright State U Nat Ctr for Rehab Engring Dayton OH 45435

STAFFORD, JOHN M., food products company executive. Pres., chief exec. officer Pillsbury Co., Mpls., also dir. Office: Pillsbury Co 200 S 6th St Minneapolis MN 55402*

STAFFORD, ROBERT GARY, lawyer; b. Columbus, Ohio, Dec. 30, 1938; s. Don Edward and Elizabeth (Penn) S.; m. Patricia Ruth Redding, Mar. 19, 1960; 1 child, Stephanie Anne. B.E.E., Ohio State U., 1961; J.D. Capital U., 1968. Bar: Ohio 1968. Engr., Ohio Branch Telephone, Columbus, 1961-68; assoc. Means, Bichimer, Burkholder & Baker, Co., L.P.A., Columbus, 1968—; adj. prof. Capital U., 1973-78. Recipient Merit award Ohio Legal Ctr. Inst., 1972. Mem. Columbus Jaycees, Ohio State Bar Assn., Columbus Bar Assn.,

Ohio Soc. Profl. Engrs. (trustee 1973-74, Young Engr. of Yr. award 1971, Outstanding Service award 1977). Republican. Methodist. Club. University. Avocations: computers; amateur radio. Home: 201 Saint Pierre Worthington OH 43085 Office: Means Bichimer Burkholder & Baker Co LPA 42E Gay St 14th Floor Columbus OH 43215

STAFFORD, THOMAS JANEWAY, ophthalmologist, educator; b. Detroit, Jan. 9, 1934; s. Frank Williams John and Bertha May (Arthur) S.; m. Jean Lois Whitten, June 21, 1958; 1 child, Alan. Student Cornell U., 1951-54; M.D., U. Mich., 1958. Diplomate Am. Bd. Ophthalmology. Intern Harper Hosp., Detroit, 1958-59; resident Kresge Eye Inst., Detroit, 1959-60, King County Hosp., Seattle, 1960-62, Children's Orthopedic Hosp., Seattle, 1960-62; fellow U. Miami Bascom Palmer Eye Inst., Fla., 1965-66; practice medicine specializing in ophthalmology, Evanston, Ill., 1966—; sr. attending surgeon Children's Meml. Hosp., Chgo., 1969—, Evanston Hosp., 1973—; researcher ind. ophthal. studies, 1966—; asst. prof. clin. ophthalmology Northwestern U., Chgo., 1974—. Commr. Zoning Amendment Com., Evanston, 1982—. Served to lt. comdr. USNR, 1962-64. Fellow Am. Acad. Ophthalmology (Honor award 1983), ACS, AMA; mem. Ill. State Med. Soc., Chgo. Med. Soc., Assn. for Research in Vision and Ophthalmology, Am. Assn. of Ophthalmology, Ill. Assn. Ophthalmology. Congregationalist. Home: 1206 Croft Ln Evanston IL 60202 Office: 636 Church St Evanston IL 60201

STAHL, C. DAVID, pharmaceutical sales representative, pharmacist; b. Toledo, Oct. 24, 1952; s. Marrit Nathaniel and Nellye Blanche (Herrell) S.; m. N. Lynn Stout, May 7, 1977; children—Courtney Lynn, Andrew David. B.S. in Pharmacy, U. Toledo, 1975. Registered pharmacist, Ohio. Intern, Shaffer Pharmacy, Toledo, 1969-72, Toledo Hosp., 1972-74; pharmacist intern Lane Drug Co., Toledo, 1974-76; pharmacist, owner Shaffer Pharmacy, Sylvania, Ohio, 1976-81; pharm. sales rep. Ayerst Labs. div. Am. Home Products Corp., N.Y.C., 1981—. Mem. Ohio State Pharm. Assn. (student dir. 1974-75, chpt. pres. 1972-73, Student award 1975), N.W. Ohio Pharm. Reps. Assn. (coms.), Toledo Acad. Pharmacy, Alpha Zeta Omega (Outstanding Undergrad. award 1975, various offices local and nat. 1972-78), Pi Kappa Phi (chpt. pres. 1974-75). Republican. Avocations: racqetball; tennis; basketball; computers. Home: 2262 Kingston Dr Maumee OH 43537

STAHL, CARROLL CLIFFORD, II, investment management company executive, consultant; b. Danville, Pa., Mar. 13, 1948; s. Carroll Clifford and Mildred Geneva (Vingling) S.; m. Amy F. Seesholtz, Aug. 25, 1972 (div. 1976) m. Betty Jean Green, June 21, 1980; 1 stepson, Ronald Lee. B.B.A., The Citadel, 1970. Asst. bond mgr. First Nat. Bank of East Pa., Wilkes-Barre, 1970-74; mgr. equities, v.p. investments Armco Inc., Middletown, Ohio, 1974-82; pres., chief investment officer C-S Capital Advs., Inc., Cin., 1982—. Mem. Cin. Fin. Analysts Fedn. Chpt. Mem. Assembly of God Ch. Avocations: snow skiing; autograph collecting; reading. Home: 8137 Timbertree Way West Chester OH 45069 Office: C-S Capital Advisors Inc 8150 Corporate Park Dr Suite 224 Cincinnati OH 45242

STAHL, CLAUD LAWRENCE, screen co. exec.; b. Pierceton, Ind., Feb. 4, 1928; s. Lawrence Nay and Minnie Alice (Bareham) S.; student Internat. Corr. Sch., 1948-52, Purdue U., 1967-71; grad. Ind. Coll. Auctioneering, 1975; m. Betty Rose Nichols, Oct. 23, 1948; children—Bradley Rene, Belinda Jane. With Gatke Corp., Warsaw, Ind., 1946-55, R. T. Brower Co., Pierceton, Ind., 1955-57; with Da-Lite Screen Co., Inc., Warsaw, 1957—, personnel mgr., 1976—. Interim bd. mem. Whitko Community Sch., 1966-68, treas., 1967; active Boy Scouts Am., Warsaw, 1946-49, Jr. Achievement, 1976-79; bd. dirs. Kosciusko Community Hosp., Warsaw, 1967-81; trustee Washington Twp., 1963-71. Served with Ind. N.G., 1948-52. Mem. Kosciusko County Hist. Soc. (1st pres. 1965-66), Ind. Auctioneers Assn., Ind. Personnel Mgrs. Assn., Ind. C. of C. (com. on occupational health and safety 1980—). Democrat. Methodist. Clubs: Lions, Masons, Shriners, Order Eastern Star. Inventor reversible boat oars. Home: 207 W Elm St Pierceton IN 46562

STAHL, DULCELINA ALBANO, hospital administrator, educator, nurse; b. Bacarra, Ilocos Norte, Philippines, Aug. 10, 1943; came to U.S., 1967, naturalized, 1978; d. Rosalino and Jovita (Acosta) Albano; m. Wendelin Walter Stahl, Nov. 16, 1968; children—Astania, Bryan, Larraine. Cert. nurse adminstr. Dir. nursing Mary Thompson Hosp., Chgo., 1970-71; asst. dir. nursing U. Ill. Hosp., Chgo., 1971-72; faculty sch. nursing South Chgo. Community Hosp., Chgo., 1972-75; dir. nursing Bethany Hosp., Chgo., 1975-80; sr. assoc. adminstr. Olympia Fields Osteo. Med. Ctr., Ill., 1980-85; adminstr. program devel., ambulatory and patient care services CCOM Hosps., 1985—; faculty nursing mgmt. nat. seminars, 1984—; faculty Prairie State Coll., Chgo., 1981—. Author: (with others) Cancer Nursing, 2d edit., 1982. Contbr. articles to profl. jours. Bd. dirs. Hospice Suburban S., Olympia Fields, 1983—; mem. adv. com. Prairie State Coll. Nursing Edn., 1981—, Thornton Community Coll. Nursing Edn., South Holland, Ill., 1981—. Mem. Inst. Ethics Life Scis., Am. Mgmt. Assn., Ill. Soc. Nurse Adminstrs., League Nursing, Ill., Am. Nurses Assn., Ill. Nurses Assn., Am. Cath. Philos. Assn., Philippine Nurses Assn. Chgo. (bd. dirs. 1980—). Avocations: swimming; singing; dancing; writing poetry. Home: 2269 Post Rd Northbrook IL 60062 Office: Olympia Fields Osteo Med Ctr 20201 S Crawford Ave Olympia Fields IL 60461

STAHL, GERALD RALPH, lawyer, writer; b. Grand Rapids, Mich., Dec. 7, 1955; s. Gerald Lawrence and Mary Helene (Hauenstein) S.; m. Elizabeth JoAnne Hunt. B.B.A., Western Mich. U., 1978; J.D., Gonzaga U., 1981. Bar: Mich. 1982, U.S. Dist. Ct. (we. dist.) Mich. 1982, Ill. 1983. Assoc. Sharpe, Ganz & Henderson, Spokane, Mich., 1979-81, Pinsky, Smith & Soet, Grand Rapids, 1981-82; sole practice, Grand Rapids, 1982—; instr. Grand Rapids Jr. Coll., 1984—. Author: The Will To Survive, 1984. Mem. Assn. Trial Lawyers Am., Grand Rapids Bar Assn., Chgo. Bar Assn., Mich. Trial Lawyers Assn. Club: Kent County Republican Party 400.

STAHL, RAYMOND EARL, research chemist; b. Chgo., Feb. 21, 1936; s. Arthur Daniel and Gladys Hazel (Lockwood) S.; Ph.B., Northwestern U., 1971. Technician-coatings formulator DeSoto Inc., Chgo., 1956-62, sr. chemist, research chemist, sr. research chemist, research asso., 1967-73; group leader metal finishes Adcote div. Morton Chem. Co., Chgo., 1962-66; tech. dir., cons. Am. Indsl. Finishes Co., Chgo., 1966-67; staff scientist, research assoc. Dexter-Midland Co., Waukegan, Ill., 1973—. Served with U.S. Army, 1954-56; PTO. Fellow Am. Inst. Chemists; mem. Société de Chimie Industrielle, Am. Chem. Soc., Am. Inst. Physics, Am. Phys. Soc., AAAS, Ill. Acad. Sci., Am. Statis. Assn., Am. Math. Assn., Fedn. Socs. Paint Tech., Am. Mgmt. Assn., Am. Platform Assn., Nat., Ill. rifle assns. Republican. Inventor chem. coatings. Home: 2207 Rolling Ridge Ln Lindenhurst IL 60046 Office: Dexter-Midland Co E Water St Waukegan IL 60085

STAHLMAN, LEROY EDWARD, pharmacist; b. Washington, Mo., Oct. 17, 1951; s. Earl Ruben and Mildred Henrietta (Bone) S.; m. Barbara Ann Knoernschild, Aug. 11, 1973; children—Jennifer Lee, Michael Leroy, Jonathan Edward. B.S. in Applied Math., U. Mo.-Rolla, 1974, B.S. in Pharmacy, Creighton U., 1977. Pharmacist Whaley East End Drugs, Jefferson City, Mo., 1977-79, Osco Drugs, Jefferson City, 1979-82; chief pharmacist Medicare Glaser, Jefferson City, 1983-84; pharmacist Super D, Jefferson City, 1984—. Active Faith Lutherans for Life, Jefferson City, 1984; elder Faith Luth. Ch., Jefferson City, 1985. Recipient Eagle Scout award Boy Scouts Am. Mem. Mo. Pharm. Assn. Avocations: softball, woodworking, fishing, hunting. Home: 2000 Meadow Ln Jefferson City MO 65101 Office: Super D 1404 Missouri Blvd Jefferson City MO 65101

STAINBROOK, JAMES RALPH, JR., educator; b. Indpls., Dec. 8, 1936; s. James Ralph, Sr., and Alta Marie (Doty) S.; m. Margaret Ann McKinley, June 21, 1959; children—Susan Ann, Steven James. A.B., Butler U., Indpls., 1959; M.A., U. Wis., Madison, 1964; Ed.D., Ind. U., Bloomington, 1970. Cert. Latin tchr., secondary sch. adminstr., counselor guidance and social studies, Ind. Tchr. Indpls. public schs., 1963-68; teaching asst. Ind. U., 1968-70; prof. edn. Ball State U., Muncie, Ind., 1970—. Served as officer USAF, 1959-62. Mem. Assn. Teacher Educators, Assn. for Supervision and Curriculum Devel., Phi Delta Kappa, Kappa Delta Pi, Phi Kappa Phi. Republican. Methodist. Clubs: Scottish Rite, Shriners. Masons. Contbr. numerous articles to profl. jours. Home: 8225 Lockwood Ln Indianapolis IN 46217 Office: Teachers College 822 Ball State U Muncie IN 47306

STAIR, DAVID LEROY, college athletic administrator, educator, coach; b. Syracuse, N.Y., Apr. 15, 1945; s. Arthur Leroy and Bernice Lucile (Eroh) S.; m. Carol Joyce Costanzo, Sept. 12, 1964; children—Pamela Joy, David Paul. A.S., Broome County Community Coll., 1965, A.A., 1971; B.S., SUNY-Cortland, 1973, M.S., 1974; Ed.D., U. Ark., 1981. Ptnr. Stair Builders Constrn. Co., 1965-70; tchr.-coach Ilion (N.Y.) High Sch., 1974-76; assoc. prof. phys. edn., coach Evangel Coll., Springfield, Mo., 1976-82, athletic dir., 1982—; grad. asst. U. Ark., 1980-81. SUNY-Cortland grad. fellow, 1973-74. Mem. Am. Alliance for Health, Phys. Edn., Recreation and Dance, Nat. Assn. Intercollegiate Athletic Coaches, Nat. Assn. Intercollegiate Athletic Dirs. Mem. Assembly of God Ch. Office: 1111 N Gleastone Springfield MO 65802

STALEY, HUGH ARTHUR, lawyer; b. Shelby County, Ohio, Mar. 28, 1900; s. Edwin Leonidas and Etta (Arbogast) S.; m. Catherine McVay, Aug. 6, 1927 (dec. Oct. 1976); children—Dorothy Anne Staley Lafferty, Jean Louise Staley Hanes, David Edwin, Tom McVay; m. Kathryn Bailey, Nov. 4, 1977. J.D., Ohio No. U., 1926. Bar: Ohio 1926. Ptnr. Staley & Smith, Greenville, Ohio, 1926-29, Murphy & Staley, Greenville, 1929-48, Spidel, Staley, Hole & Hanes predecessor firm Spidel, Staley & Hole, Greenville, 1950—; pros. atty. Darke County, Greenville, 1937-41. Author: (booklet) Greenville United Methodist Church, 1952. Bd. dirs. Civil Service, Greenville, Recipient Silver Beaver award Boy Scouts Am., 1949, Outstanding Achievement award Ohio No. U., 1965, Service award, 1967, Disting. Alumni award Pettit Coll. Law, Ohio No. U., 1985. Mem. Darke County Bar Assn., ABA. Lodges: Rotary (pres. 1950-51), Internat. Order Odd Fellows (grand master 1949-50). Home: 1213 Sugar Maple Dr Greenville OH 45331 Office: 507 S B Broadway Greenville OH 45331

STALLARD, RICHARD ELGIN, dentist, health administrator; b. Eau Claire, Wis., May 30, 1934; s. Elgin Gale and Caroline Francis (Betz) S.; B.S., U. Minn., 1956, D.D.S., 1958, M.S., 1959, Ph.D., 1962; m. Norma Ann Woock, Oct. 15, 1956 (dec. 1973); children—Rondi Lynn, Alison Judith; m. 2d, Jaxon Shirley Sandlin, May 2, 1974; 1 son, Elgin Sandlin. Co-dir. periodontal research Eastman Dental Ctr., Rochester, N.Y., 1962-65; prof., head dept. periodontology Sch. Dentistry, U. Minn., Mpls., 1965-68, adj. prof. pub. health, 1976—; asst. dir. Eastman Dental Ctr., 1968-70; prof. anatomy Boston U. Sch. Medicine, asst. dean Sch. Grad. Dentistry, dir. clin. research center Boston U. Sch. Grad. Dentistry, 1970-74; dental dir., head dept. periodontology Group Health Plan, Inc., St. Paul, 1974-79; sec. Minndent, Inc., Mpls., 1980-82; dental dir. Horizon Dental Assocs., P.A., Mpls., 1981-82; dental dir. Arrowhead Dental Services, Ltd., 1982—; cons. U.S. Air Force, 1968-78, U.S. Navy, 1971-75, Republic of Kenya, 1984—, Hamad Gen. Hosp., Doha, State of Qatar, 1984—; mem. tng. grant com. NIH/Nat. Inst. Dental Research, 1969-72; edn. cons. Project Vietnam, AID, Saigon, 1969-74; mem. grants and allocations com. Am. Fund for Dental Health, 1976-81. Recipient Meritorious Achievement citation for dental research and edn. Boston U., 1970. Fellow Am., Internat. colls. dentists, Internat. Congress Oral Implantologists (diplomate, pres. 1980-81), Acad. Gen. Dentistry; mem. Am. Acad. Periodontology (pres. 1974), Am. Acad. Dental Spltys. (pres. 1971-75), Am. Pub. Health Assn., Omicron Kappa Upsilon, Sigma Xi. Club: Alumni (Mpls.). Author preventive dentistry textbook; contbr. articles to profl. jours.; editor The Implantologist, Jour. Mktg./Mgmt. for Professions; assoc. editor Acta de Odontologia Pediatrica. Home: 4200 W 44th St Edina MN 55424 Office: 7645 Metro Blvd Minneapolis MN 55435

STALLARD, WAYNE MINOR, lawyer; b. Onaga, Kans., Aug. 23, 1927; s. Minor Regan and Lydia Faye (Randall) S.; B.S., Kans. State Tchrs. Coll., Emporia, 1949; J.D., Washburn U., 1952; m. Wanda Sue Bacon, Aug. 22, 1948; children—Deborah Sue, Carol Jean, Bruce Wayne (dec.). Admitted to Kans. bar, 1952 pvt. practice, Onaga, 1952—; atty. Community Hosp. Dist. No. 1, Pottawatomie, Jackson and Nemaha Counties, Kans., 1955—; Pottawatomie County atty., 1955-59; city atty. Onaga, 1953-79; atty Unified School Dist. 322, Pottawatomie County, Kans., 1966-83. Bd. dirs. North Central Kans. Guidance Center, Manhattan, 1974-78; atty. Rural Water Dist. No. 3, Pottawatomie County, Kans., 1974—. Fund dr. chmn. Pottawatomie County chpt. Nat. Found. for Infantile Paralysis, 1953-54. Served from pvt. to sgt., 8th Army, AUS, 1946 to 47. Mem. ABA, Pottawatomie County, Kans. bar assns., Onaga Businessmen's Assn., Am. Judicature Soc., City Attys. Assn. Kan. (dir. 1963-66), Phi Gamma Mu, Kappa Delta Pi, Delta Theta Phi, Sigma Tau Gamma. Conglist. Mason (Shriner); mem. Order Eastern Star. Address: Onaga KS 66521

STALLMAN, MICHAEL DAVID, accountant; b. Cedar Rapids, Iowa, Dec. 20, 1946; s. Carl David and Mary Elaine (Weland) S.; m. Dorothy E. Risdal, June 14, 1969; children—John M., Cheryl E., Susan K. B.A., Loras Coll., 1969. C.P.A., Iowa. Ptnr. McGladrey, Hendricson & Pullen, Cedar Rapids, 1969—. Pres., treas. Regis LaSalle High Sch. Found., Cedar Rapids, 1984—; asst. treas., bd. dirs. Hawkeye Area Council Boy Scouts Am., 1984—; bd. dirs. Discovery Village Corp., Cedar Rapids, 1984—; chmn. com. fin. St. Judes Ch. Corp., Cedar Rapids, 1984—. Mem. Am. Inst. C.P.A.s, Iowa Soc. C.P.A.s (com. fed. tax 1979, pres. bd. dirs. Hawkeye chpt. 1978), Cedar Rapids Area Estate Planning Council (pres., bd. dirs. 1980). Roman Catholic. Lodges: Rotary (v.p. 1980-84), K.C. (treas. 1982-84). Avocations: hunting, fishing, woodwork. Home: 3204 Ravenwood Terr NW Cedar Rapids IA 52405 Office: 10th Fl MNB Bldg Cedar Rapids IA 52401

STALNAKER, ARMAND CARL, insurance company executive; b. Weston, W.Va., Apr. 24, 1916; m. Rachel J. Pickett; children—Timothy, Thomas. B.B.A., U. Cin., 1941; M.A., U. Pa., 1945; Ph.D., Ohio State U., 1951. With Gen. Am. Life Ins. Co., St. Louis, 1963—, chmn. bd. dirs., 1974—, also dir.; prof. mgmt. Sch. Bus., Washington U., St. Louis, 1982—. Office: Gen Am Life Ins Co 700 Market St Saint Louis MO 63101

STAMM, THOMAS JAMES, ophthalmologist, surgeon; b. Chgo., Oct. 26, 1904; s. John Charles and Jane M. (McCue) S.; m. Katheryn (Mary) Heringer, May 24, 1947; 1 child, Thomas Mark. B.A. Loyola U., Chgo., 1926, M.D., 1946; M.A., St. Louis U., 1932. Diplomate Am. Bd. Ophthalmology. Intern Cook County Hosp., Chgo., 1946-47, resident in ophthalmology, 1950-51. Assoc., attending vol. Cook County Hosp., 1942-79; assoc. prof. ophthalmology Loyola U. Stritch Sch. Medicine, Maywood, Ill., 1952—. Served as capt. M.C., U.S. Army, 1947-49. Mem. AMA, Ill. State Med. Soc., Chgo. Med. Soc., Chgo. Ophthal. Soc. (pres. 1965-66). Roman Catholic. Avocations: golf; gardening. Home: 1845 77th Ave Elmwood Park IL 60635 Office: 7544 North Ave Elmwood Park IL 60635

STAMM, WILLIAM, city fire chief; b. Milw., Nov. 7, 1916; s. Jacob Herman and Florence (Buetler) S.; m. Etelka Ann Wittmann, June 4, 1938; 1 dau., Charlene Anita Stamm Wussow. A.Fire Tech., Milw. Area Tech. Coll., 1964. With Milw. Fire Dept., 1940—, fire lt., 1948-50, fire capt., 1950-59, bn. chief, 1959-62, dep. chief, 1962-70, chief, 1970—. Bd. dirs. ARC, Good Samaritan Hosp., St. Francis Children's Activity and Achievement Ctr. Recipient State Firefighter of Yr. award Schlitz Brewery, 1971, Disting. Service award Ptnr. of Ams., 1973; named Nat. Fire Chief of Yr., Dictograph Co., 1980. Mem. Met. Fire Chiefs, Internat. Assn. Fire Chiefs (exec. bd. metro com.), Milw. County Fire Chiefs, So. Wis.-No. Ill. Fire Chiefs, Joint Council Nat. Fire Service Orgns. (past chmn.). Club: Milw. Athletic. Lodges: Eagles (Nat. Firefighter of Yr. award 1972), Masons, Shriners. Contbr. articles to profl. jours. Office: 711 W Wells St Milwaukee WI 53233*

STAMP, JAMES ALLEN, fin. cons., accountant; b. Salem, Ohio, Nov. 3, 1942; s. Elmer Richard and Fae L. (Andre) S.; B.A., Mt. Union Coll., Alliance, Ohio, 1966; postgrad. in acctg. U. Akron, 1967-68; m. Margaret Jane Boski, June 19, 1966; children—Shawn R., Heather L., Eric L. Telegrapher, CB&Q R.R., Chgo., 1960-62; draftsman Sterling-Salem Corp., Salem, 1962-63; credit mgr. Sears, Roebuck & Co., Alliance, 1964-66; acct. Ernst & Ernst, Akron, Ohio, 1966-70; area sales coordinator Bestline Products, Akron, 1970-73; budget dir. Timken Mercy Hosp., Canton, Ohio, 1973-76; dir. fin. Green Cross Gen. Hosp., Cuyahoga Falls, Ohio, 1977-78; practice public acctg., Norton, Ohio, 1978—; pres., chief exec. officer Stim-A-Kron Inc.; dir. Norton Fish Co. Inc., Inc., Ashtabula Fish & Chips Inc., Tech Pow'r Inc., Shema, Inc.; Frye & Assocs. Inc.; founder Boardroom Exchange Assn. Sponsor, sponsor Norton Nat. Little League Baseball and Softball; mem. Senatorial Bus. Adv. Bd. C.P.A., Ohio. Mem. Nat. Assn. Accts. (Mem. of Yr., 1980, dir. 1978-81), Ohio Soc. C.P.A.s, Internat. Platform Assn., Hosp. Fin. Mgmt. Assn., Am. Mortgage Brokers Assn. Republican. Methodist. Home: 3405 Mark Ln Norton OH 44203 Office: PO Box 1216 Norton OH 44203

STAMPER, DONALD LEE, emergency room physician; b. Middletown, Ohio, July 22, 1938; s. Chester Arthur and Garnet (Williams) S.; m. Beverly Jean Sticklen, Dec. 19, 1964; children—Amy Elizabeth, Melissa Kathleen. A.B., Miami U., Oxford, Ohio, 1968; D.O., Kansas City (Mo.) Coll. Osteo. Medicine, 1972. Patrolman, Middletown Div. Police, 1960-68; intern Grandview Hosp., Dayton, Ohio, 1972; ptnr. Franklin Family Clinic (Ohio), 1973—; police surgeon, Middletown; mem. staff Grandview Hosp. Capt., Middletown Police Res., 1982. Served with USN, 1955-59. Named Boss of Yr., Dayton Dist. Acad., 1978, Outstanding Citizen, City of Middletown, 1981. Mem. Ohio Osteo. Assn., Dayton Dist. Acad. Osteo. Medicine, Internat. Assn. Chiefs of Police, Alpha Phi Omega, Sigma Sigma Phi, Psi Sigma Alpha. Republican. Baptist. Home: 6119 Brookshire Ln Franklin OH 45005 Office: Franklin Family Clinic 10 Stadia Dr Franklin OH 45005

STANBERY, ROBERT CHARLES, veterinarian; b. Conneaut, Ohio, Apr. 5, 1947; s. Robert James and Ruth Virginia S.; student Miami U., Oxford, Ohio, 1965-67; D.V.M., Ohio State U., 1971; m. Constance Ann Coutts, July 24, 1971; 1 son, Scott Andrew. Veterinarian, Lexington (Mass.) Animal Hosp., 1971-74, Avon Lake Animal Clinic Inc. (Ohio), 1974-76; pres., treas. Bay Village Animal Clinic Inc. (Ohio), 1976—. Mem. AVMA, Ohio Vet. Med. Assn., Animal Hosp. Assn. Cleve. Acad. Vet. Medicine, Lorain County Vet. Assn. Internat. Platform Assn., Bay Village C. of C. (bd. dirs., pres.), U.S. Jaycees. Fundamentalist Christian. Home: 309 Timberlane Dr Avon Lake OH 44012 Office: 627 Clague Rd Bay Village OH 44140

STANDEFER, JOHN HOADLEY, financial executive; b. Marshalltown, Iowa, May 25, 1937; s. Joe Milton and Lorene F. (Hoadley) S.; Student U. Iowa, 1956; B.S., Drake U., 1964; m. Mary Therese Higgins, Aug. 31, 1963; children—John Hoadley, Jack, James, Jean. Staff auditor Peat, Marwick, Mitchell & Co., Des Moines, 1964-67; audit mgr. Cloutier, Sanders & Clifford, Des Moines, 1967-69; gen. acctg. mgr. Massey Ferguson Inc., Des Moines, 1969-73; corp. audit mgr. J.I. Case Co., Racine, Wis., 1973-74, controller internat. div., 1974-81, asst. to sr. v.p. fin., 1981-83; v.p., controller Candasco, Inc., Rosemont, Ill., 1983-85; v.p. fin. Scholle Corp., Northlake, Ill., 1985—. Mem. United Way budget com., Racine, 1980; mem. Willow Crest Community Ch., South Barrington, Ill. Served with USN, 1957-61. C.P.A., Iowa. Mem. Am. Inst. C.P.A.s, Iowa Soc. C.P.A.s. Republican. Home: 4195 Crimson Dr Hoffman Estates IL 60195 Office: 200 W North Ave Northlake IL 60164

STANFORD, MELVIN JOSEPH, university dean, management consultant; b. Logan, Utah, June 13, 1932; s. Joseph Sedley and Ida Pearl (Ivie) S.; B.S. (First Security Found. scholar), Utah State U., 1957; M.B.A. (Donald Kirk David fellow), Harvard U., 1963; Ph.D., U. Ill., 1968; m. Linda Barney, Sept. 2, 1960; children—Connie, Cheryl, Joseph, Theodore, Emily, Charlotte, Charles, Sarah. Asst. audit supr. Utah Tax Commn., Salt Lake City, 1958-61; acct. Haskins & Sells, Boston, 1961-62; acctg. staff analyst Arabian Am. Oil Co., Dhahran, Saudi Arabia, 1963-66; teaching and research asst. U. Ill., Urbana, 1966-68; asst. prof. Brigham Young U., Provo, Utah, 1968-69, assoc. prof., 1969-74, prof. bus. mgmt., 1974-82; dean Coll. Bus., Mankato (Minn.) State U., 1982—; vis. prof. mgmt. European grad. programs Boston U., Heidelberg, Germany, 1975-76; co-chmn. Commn. for Joint Program Rev. with U. Costa Rica, 1984; mgmt. and fin. cons. Served with USAF, 1951-55. Mem. Strategic Mgmt. Soc., Acad. Mgmt., Case Research Assn. (v.p.) 1985—), SAR (pres. Utah Soc. 1978-79, nat. trustee 1979-81), Alpha Kappa Psi, Phi Kappa Phi. Mem. Ch. Jesus Christ of Latter-day Saints. Club: Kiwanis. Author: New Enterprise Management, 1975, 82; Management Policy, 1979, 2d edit., 1983; contbr. cases to textbooks, articles to profl. jours. Address: 221 Crestwood Dr North Mankato MN 56001

STANG, PHILIP DAVID, manufacturing executive; b. Providence, Dec. 20, 1946; s. Robert Fredrick and Norma (Hawkins) S.; m. Dianne Alice Henninger; children—Anne-Marie, Laurie, Rebecca. B.B.A., Bryant Coll., 1973, M.B.A., 1976. Asst. chief mfg. control Gen. Dynamics/Electric Boat, Groton, Conn., 1974-77; sr. corp. ops. cons. ITT Grinnell Corp., Providence, 1977-82; mgr. mfg. controls ITT Blackburn Corp., St. Louis, 1982, corp. materials mgr., 1983; dir. materials Seco Products, Washington, Mo., 1983-84; dir. ops. Seco Products/BIH Foodservice, Washington, Mo., 1984—; conf. reviewer Am. Prodn. and Inventory Control Soc., 1985. Town committeeman East Greenwich Republican Town Com., 1976-82; sponsor Spl. Olympics of R.I., Kingston, 1979-82. Served with USAF, 1965-68. Mem. Am. Prodn. and Inventory Control Soc., Small Mfg. Spl. Interest Group, Repetitive Mfg. Spl. Interest Group, Nat. Assn. Purchasing Mgmt., Mapics Support Group, Bryant Coll. Alumni Assn. Republican. Avocations: sailing; golf; antiques; gourmet foods/cooking. Home: 722 Henry Ave Manchester MO 63011 Office: Seco Products BIH Foodservice Old Hwy 100 E Washington MO 63090

STANGE, JAMES HENRY, architect; b. Davenport, Iowa, May 25, 1930; s. Henry Claus and Norma (Ballhorn) S.; m. Mary Suanne Peterson, Dec. 12, 1954; children—Wade Weston, Drew Dayton, Grant Owen. B.Arch., Iowa State U., 1954. Registered architect, Iowa, Nebr., Kans., Mo., Okla. Designer, Davis & Wilson, Lincoln, Nebr., 1954-62, v.p., 1962-68; v.p., sec. Davis, Fenton, Stange, Darling, Lincoln, Nebr., 1968-76, pres., 1976—, chmn., 1979—. Pres. Lincoln Ctr. Assn., 1979, pres. Capitol Assn. Retarded Citizens, 1972; 1st vice chmn. United Way Campaign, 1985. Recipient Honor award Conf. on Religious Architecture, 1969, also numerous state and nat. awards from archtl. orgns. Mem. AIA (regional AIA design award 1976, pres. Nebr. soc. 1968, v.p., 1967, treas. 1965, sec. 1966, bd. dirs. 1964-65, com. architecture for Health), Am. Assn. Health Planners, Interfaith Forum on Religion, Art, Architecture, Lincoln C. of C. (bd. dirs. 1982). Republican. Presbyterian. (deacon 1960, chmn. bd. trustees 1968, elder 1972). Club: Executives (pres. 1972). Home: 3545 Calvert St Lincoln NE 68506 Office: 211 N 14th St Lincoln NE 68508

STANGELAND, ARLAN INGHART, congressman; b. Fargo, N.D., Feb. 8, 1930; s. Inghart and Pearle (Olson) S.; student pub. schs., Moorhead, Minn.; m. Virginia Grace Trowbridge, June 24, 1950; children—David, Beth, Brian, Jean, Todd, Jeffrey, Stuart. Farmer, Barnesville, Minn., 1951—; mem. Minn. Ho. of Reps., 1966; mem. 95th-99th Congresses from 7th Minn. Dist. Pres., Barnesville PTA, 1965-66; sec. Republican Party of Wilkin County (Minn.), 1960-65, pres., 1965-66. Recipient N.D. State U. Agriculturalist award for community service, 1976. Mem. Minn. Shorthorn Assn. (dir.). Lutheran. Office: 1526 Longworth House Office Bldg Washington DC 20515

STANICH, GEORGE, microwave communications educator; b. Cleve., Feb. 1, 1943; s. Dick D. and Anne (Uminski) S.; m. Grace Ann Gulley, Oct. 10, 1964; children—Deborah Rene, Terrence Brent. Cert. vocat., indsl. tchr. Enlisted U.S. Air Force, 1961; ret., 1982; sr. tech. tng. instr. Motorola Co., Schaumburg, Ill., 1982—. Author course microwave concepts, 1982. Recipient Honor award Freedoms Found. at Valley Forge, 1970. Republican. Mem. Ch. of Christ. Office: Motorola 1301 Algonquin Schaumburg IL 60196

STANICH, RONALD, dentist; b. Barberton, Ohio, June 23, 1947; s. Ralph and Martha (Pavkov) S.; m. Claudia Ann Curry, Feb. 26, 1972; 1 child, Sarah Diane. B.S. in Biology, B.A. in Secondary Edn., U. Akron, 1970; D.D.S., Ohio State U., 1977. Gen. sci. tchr. Akron pub. schs., Ohio, 1971-72, physics, chemistry tchr., 1973-74; gen. practice dentistry, Canal Fulton, Ohio, 1977—. Bd. dirs. Northwest Stark Sr. Citizens Ctr., Canal Fulton, 1984—; rep. Ohio Dental Polit. Action Com., Columbus, 1984—. Served with USAF, 1972-73, Ohio Air N.G., 1973-80. Recipient Jaycee disting. service award, 1984. Mem. Stark County Dental Assn. (bd. dirs. 1983—), Ohio Dental Assn., ADA, Ohio N.G. Assn., N.G. Assn. U.S., Assn. Mil. Surgeons of U.S., Canal Fulton Area C. of C. (pres. 1983, Bus. Person of Yr. 1982). Republican. Clubs: Cascade, University (Akron). Lodges: Rotary (pres. 1980-81, bd. dirs. 1980—), Masons. Avocations: flying, reading, sports. Office: 2184 Locust St Canal Fulton OH 44614

STANIEC, MARJAN PETER, associate judge; b. Chgo., Aug. 1, 1914; s. Hipolit and Mary (Rulikowski) S.; m. Mary M. Hobbs, Oct. 21, 1977; children—Wayne P., Joyce, Carol Ann, William, Joseph G. J.D., Catholic U. Am., 1941, LL.M., 1942, J.D., 1957. Bar: D.C. 1941, U.S. Ct. Appeals (D.C. cir.) 1941, U.S. Supreme Ct. 1959, Ill. 1970, U.S. Dist. Ct. (ea. dist.) Ky., U.S. Dist. Ct. (ea. dist.) Wis., U.S. Ct. Appeals (7th cir.), U.S. Dist. Ct. (no. dist.) Ill. Adminstr., Social Security Adminstrn., various midwestern states, 1940-68; dep. regional dir. HEW, Chgo., 1968-76; assoc. judge Ill. Circuit Ct. Cook County, Chgo., 1976—; lectr. legal topics; co-producer, host TV program WCIU-TV, Chgo., 1965-68. Mem. Chgo. Adv. Council Aging, 1957—, vice chmn., 1978-82; mem. pub. edn. com. Ill. div. Am. Cancer Soc., 1966—; active numerous civic orgns.; nat. del. to White House Conf. on Aging, 1981; mem. forum subcom. Met. Chgo. Coalition on Aging, 1981-83. Recipient meritorious service citation Fed. Govt., 1944, 49, disting. service award Back of Yards Council, 1965, citation in Congl. Record, 1967, outstanding service citation

Am. Cancer Soc., 1974, 75, outstanding performance in fed. service citation Fed. Exec. Bd., 1975, cert. of merit Sec. of HEW, 1976, outstanding service award Ill. Citizens for Better Care, 1982, Humanitarian award Central Lions Club, Chgo., 1982, numerous others. Mem. Ill. Jud. Conf., Ill. Judges Assn. (bd. dirs. 1984-87), Fed. Bar Assn. (pres. Chgo. chpt. 1963-64, nat. v.p. 1964-65), Chgo. Bar Assn. (mental health and adoption coms. 1978—), N.W. Suburban Bar Assn., West Suburban Bar Assn., Advocates Soc. (award of merit 1966), Polish Nat. Alliance, Chgo. Soc., Sigma Delta Kappa. Lodges: Lions, Moose. Co-author: Are You Planning To Live the Rest of Your Life, 1965; columnist Chgo. Daily Law Bull., 1963—; bi-weekly columnist Your Social Security, Chgo. Tribune, 1965-67. Home: 5707 N New Hampshire Ave Chicago IL 60631

STANIFER, DEBORAH LYNN, educational administrator; b. Bellaire, Md., Sept. 28, 1945; d. Ralph Eugene and Evelyn Martha (Zellman) S.; m. Arvy Kavaliauskas, Aug. 6, 1983. B.S., Wayne State U., Detroit, 1967, M.Ed., 1970. Tchr. Detroit Pub. Schs., 1969-70; counselor Wayne State U., 1970-73, dir. student activities, 1974-81, assoc. dir. student ctr. and program activities, 1981—. Sec. Women of Wayne Alumni Assn., Detroit, 1983, treas., 1984. Mem. Am. Coll. Unions Internat., Nat. Assn. Women Deans, Adminstrs. and Counselors, Am. Coll. Personnel Assn. (dir. 1979-81), Mich. Coll. Personnel Assn. (pres. 1983-84). Avocations: traveling, bicycling. Office: Wayne State U 351 Student Ctr Detroit MI 48202

STANISLAO, JOSEPH, college dean, engineering educator, industrial engineer, consultant; b. Manchester, Conn., Nov. 21, 1928; s. Edguardo and Rose (Zaccaro) S.; m. Bettie Chloe Carter, Sept. 6, 1960. B.S., Tex. Tech. U., 1957; M.Sc., Pa. State U., 1959; D.Engring. Sci., Columbia U., 1970. Registered profl. engr., Mass. Asst. engr. Naval Ordnance Research Lab., University Park, Pa., 1958-59; asst. prof. N.C. State U., Raleigh, 1959-61; dir. research and devel. Darlington Fabrics Corp., Pawtucket, R.I., 1961-62; asst. prof. indsl. engring. U. R.I., Kingston, 1962-68, assoc. prof., 1968-71, prof., 1971; prof. indsl. engring., chmn. dept. Cleve. State U., 1971-75; prof. indsl. engring., dean Coll. Engring. and Architecture, N.D. State U., Fargo, 1975—, acting v.p., asst. to pres., 1981-84, dir. engring. computer ctr. for tech. transfer, 1984; cons. indsl. engr. Served with USMC, 1948-51. Recipient Sigma Xi award U. R.I., 1968, Recognition award USAF, Fargo, N.D., 1979, ROTC Appreciation award USAF, N.D. State U., 1982; named to Order of Engr., 1976. Mem. Inst. Indsl. Engrs. (sr.), ASME, Am. Soc. Engring. Edn., Phi Kappa Phi. Republican. Roman Catholic. Lodges: Lions, Elks. Contbr. chpts., numerous articles on engring., mgmt., econs. to profl. publs., 1959—. Home: 3520 Longfellow Rd Fargo ND 58102 Office: Engring Ctr ND State U Coll Engring and Architecture Fargo ND 58105

STANKEWICZ, MARY JANE, retail executive, consultant; b. Cleve., May 16, 1944; d. George John and Mary Grace (Millen) Biros; m. Ben Andrew Stankewicz, Aug. 1, 1964; children—Renee Lynn, Ben Anthony, Heather Janette. Owner, operator Cornerstone Book & Gift Shoppe, Strongsville, Ohio, 1983—. Advisor, Holy Trinity Youth Group, Bedford Heights, Ohio, 1971-75; pres. Bedford Co-op Nursery Schs., 1971; officer Citizens League of Bedford Heights, 1975; bd. dirs. Womankind, Inc., Bedford, 1976-78. Mem. Christian Booksellers Assn., Ohio Right to Life Soc. Roman Catholic. Office: Cornerstone Book & Gift Shoppe 13500 Pearl Rd Strongsville OH 44136

STANLEY, RICHARD HOLT, consulting engineer; b. Muscatine, Iowa, Oct. 20, 1932; s. Claude Maxwell and Elizabeth Mabel (Holthues) S.; m. Mary Jo Kennedy, Dec. 20, 1953; children—Lynne Elizabeth, Sarah Catherine, Joseph Holt. B.S. in Elec. Engring., Iowa State U., 1955, in Mech. Engring., 1955; M.S. in San. Engring., U. Iowa, 1963. Registered profl. engr., Iowa, other states. With Stanley Cons. Inc., Muscatine, 1955—, exec. v.p., 1968-71, pres., 1971—, also dir.; dir. Stanley Cons. Ltd., Liberia; vice-chmn. HON Industries, Inc.; chmn. Middle West Service Co., 1981—, Nat. Constrn. Industry Council, 1978, Com. Fed. Procurement Archtl./Engring. Services, 1979; pres. Eastern Iowa Community Coll., Bettendorf, 1966-68; mem. adv. council Coll. Engring., Iowa State U., Ames, 1969—, chmn., 1979-81. Bd. dirs., pres. Stanley Found., Muscatine; bd. dirs. Muscatine United Way, 1969-75; bd. dirs. Iowa State U. Meml. Union, 1968-83; bd. govs. Iowa State U. Achievement Found., 1982—; bd. dirs. U. Dubuque, Iowa, 1977—. Served with C.E., AUS, 1955-57. Recipient Young Alumnus award Iowa State U. Alumni Assn., 1966; Disting. Service award Muscatine Jaycees, 1967; Profl. Achievement citation Coll. Engring., Iowa State U., 1977; named Sr. Engr. of Yr., Joint Engring. Com. of Quint Cities, 1973. Fellow Iowa Acad. Sci., Am. Cons. Engrs. Council (pres. 1976-77); mem. Cons. Engrs. Council Iowa (pres. 1967), Nat. Soc. Profl. Engrs., ASME, ASCE, IEEE, Am. Soc. Engring. Edn., Iowa Engring. Soc. (John Dunlap-Sherman Woodward award 1967, Disting. Service award 1980, pres. 1973-74), C. of C. U.S. (constrn. action council 1976—), Tau Beta Pi, Eta Kappa Nu, Phi Kappa Phi, Pi Tau Sigma. Presbyterian (elder). Lodge: Rotary. Contbr. articles to profl. jours. Home: 601 W 3d St Muscatine IA 52761 Office: Stanley Bldg Muscatine IA 52761

STANLEY, SANDRA ORNECIA, former educational administrator, educational diagnostician, researcher, consultant; b. Jersey City, July 6, 1950; d. McKinley and Thelma Louise (Newberry) S.; B.A., Ottawa U., 1972; postgrad. Jersey City State Coll., 1973; M.S.Ed., U. Kans., 1975, Ph.D. (fellow), 1980; now med. student St. George U. Sch. Medicine, Grenada, W.I. Dir., head tchr. Salem Baptist Accredited Nursery Sch., Jersey City, 1972-73; spl. edn. instr. Joan Davis Sch. Spl. Edn., Kansas City, Mo., 1975-76; instructional media/materials trainee U. Kans. Med. Center, Kansas City, 1976-77; research asst., 1977-79; research asst. U. Kans., Lawrence, 1979; dir., coordinator tng. and observation Juniper Gardens Children's Project, Bur. Child Research, U. Kans., Kansas City, 1979-82, co-adv. master students, from 1977, doctoral students, from 1980, ednl. diagnostician, tutorial and prescriptive specialized services, from 1980; cons. YWCA, 1980, Dept. Spl. Edn. and Inst. Research in Learning Disabilities, U. Minn., from 1980. Recipient plaque Salem Bapt. Nursery Sch., 1973, achievement recognition Jersey Jour. Newspapers, Jersey City, 1981; Easter Seal Scholarship grantee, 1975. Mem. Council Exceptional Children, Div. Children with Learning Disabilities, Black Caucus - Minority Exceptional Children, Assn. Supervision and Curriculum Devel., Women's Ednl. Network, Coll. Women Inc., Nat. Assn. Female Execs., Easter Seal Soc. Crippled Children and Adults Mo., Women's Ednl. Soc. of Ottawa U., Internat. Platform Assn., Democrat. Baptist. Author: The Relationship Between Learning Disabilities and Juvenile Delinquency: A Link Based on Family and School, 1980; How much —Opportunity to Respond— does the minority disadvantaged student receive in school?, 1983; co-author: Allocating opportunity to learn as a basis for academic remediation: A developing model for teaching, 1981; also instructional manuals ednl. research papers. Contbr. articles to profl. jours.

STANLEY, WILLIAM ELDON, surgeon; b. Mercer, Mo., Aug. 16, 1947; s. Richard H. and Alta B. (Cox) S.; m. Lynda Akeright, May 31, 1969; children—Darrell, Patrick. Student N.E. Mo. State Tchrs. Coll., 1965-67; B.S., U. Iowa, 1969; D.O., Kirksville Coll. Osteo. Medicine, 1973. Diplomate Am. Bd. Thoracic Surgery. Intern, Des Moines Gen. Hosp., 1973-74, resident in gen. surgery, 1974-77; resident in cardiovascular and thoracic surgery Cleve. Clinic, 1977-79; practice osteo. medicine specializing in cardiac, vascular and thoracic surgery, Des Moines, 1979—; mem. staff, chmn. dept. surgery Des Moines Gen. Hosp.; adj. clin. assoc. prof. surgery U. Osteo. Medicine and Health Scis. Mem. Am. Osteo. Assn., Am. Coll. Osteo. Surgeons, Iowa Soc. Osteo. Physicians and Surgeons. Contbr. articles to profl. jours. Home: 8028 NE 46th Ave Altoona IA 50009 Office: 1440 E Grand Ave Suite 1A Des Moines IA 50316

STANLEY, WILLIAM STEPHEN, pharmacist; b. Athens, Ohio, Nov. 29, 1954; s. Joseph and Ida Mae (Brown) S. B.S. in Zoology, Ohio U., 1977; B.S. in Pharmacy, Ohio No. U., 1981. Registered pharmacist, Ohio, W.Va. Pharmacist Brown Drug Co., Springfield, Ohio, 1981, Village Pharmacy, Middleport, Ohio, 1983-84; staff pharmacist Appalachian Regional Hosps., Man, W.Va., 1981-83, Hosp. Pharmacies Inc., Hocking Valley Community Hosp., Logan, Ohio, 1985—. Mem. Nat. Rifle Assn. Democrat. Methodist. Lodge: Masons. Avocations: running; skiing; ice skating; playing piano; reading. Home: Rt 1 40292 SR 33 Shade OH 45776

STANTON, JEANNE FRANCES, retired lawyer; b. Vicksburg, Miss., Jan. 22, 1920; d. John Francis and Hazel (Mitchell) S.; student George Washington U., 1938-39; B.A., U. Cin., 1940; J.D., Salmon P. Chase Coll. Law, 1954. Admitted to Ohio bar, 1954; chief clk. Selective Service Bd., Cin., 1940-43; instr. USAAF Tech. Schs., Biloxi, Miss., 1943-44; with Procter & Gamble, Cin., 1945-84, legal asst., 1952-54, head advt. services sect. legal div., trade practices dept., 1954-73, mgr. advt. services, legal div., 1973-84, ret., 1984. Team capt. Community Chest Cin., 1953; mem. ann. meeting com. Archaeol. Inst. Am., 1983. Mem. AAAS, Am., Ohio (chmn. uniform state laws com. 1968-70), Cin. (sec. law day com. 1965-66, chmn. com. on preservation hist. documents 1968-71) bar assns., Vicksburg and Warren County, Cin. hist. socs., Internat. Oceanographic Found., Otago Early Settlers Assn. (asso.), Intercontinental Biog. Assn., Cin. Lawyers, Cin. Women Lawyers (treas. 1958-59, nominating com. 1976). Clubs: Terrace Park Country; Cincinnati, Lawyers of Cin. (exec. com. 1978—, sec. 1980—, 1st v.p. 1982, pres. 1983). Home: 2302 E Hill Ave Cincinnati OH 45208

STANTON, WILLIAM ALSPAUGH, retired educator; b. Chgo., Mar. 9, 1924; s. Robert Hart and Sue Margaret (Alspaugh) S.; m. Mary Claire Bechtold, July 9, 1982; children—Susan C., David William, Donald F. B. Vocat. Edn., La. State Coll., 1957; M.A. in Edn., Long Beach State Coll., 1960; Ed.D., UCLA, 1967. Lic. radio engr., FCC. Dean vocat. tech. edn. Coll. of Redwoods (Calif.), 1966-68; assoc. prof. indsl. edn. Purdue U., West Lafayette, Ind., 1968-75; chmn. dept. vocat. edn. U. Cin., 1975-78, prof. edn., 1978-85, prof. emeritus, 1985—; cons. desktop computers. Served with USAF, 1942-45, 47-50. Sr. Fulbright scholar, Cyprus, 1972-73; Fulbright exchange prof., France, 1978. Mem. IEEE, Phi Delta Kappa. Roman Catholic. Author: Pulse Technology, 1964, Polish transl., 1966. Home: 7558 Montgomery Rd Apt 2 Cincinnati OH 45236

STAPLES, DANNY LEW, state senator; b. Eminence, Mo., Apr. 1, 1935; s. Harvey R. and Edna O. (Smith) S.; m. Barbara Ann Salisbury, 1967; children—Jeannine Staples Spurgin, Janet Staples Reisk, Robin Staples Morgan, Joe Shaffer, Richard. Student Southwest Mo. State U., 1952-54, Ark. State U., 1954. Mem. Mo. State Ho. of Reps., 1977-82, Mo. State Senate, Dist. 20, 1983—. Democrat. Methodist. Mem. Sigma Pi. Office: Route 3 Box 18 Eminence MO 65466

STAPLES, LAURANCE STARR, JR., manufacturing company executive; b. Kansas City, Mo., Jan. 31, 1931; s. Laurance Starr and Bertha Marie (Schaefer) S.; B.S. in Gen. Engring., U. Ill., 1956; m. Barbara Ruth Hazard, Oct. 5, 1957; children—Laurance Starr, III, Mary Ruth. Mgr. applied products Marley Co., Kansas City, Mo., 1957-69; dir. customer service Tempmaster Corp., Kansas City, 1969-71; sales rep. Kansas City Equipment Co., Kansas City, 1971; sales mgr. Havens Cooling Towers div. Havens Steel Co., Kansas City, 1971-73; with L.S. Staples Co., Kansas City, 1974-81, pres., 1974-81; v.p. field sales Marley Cooling Tower Co., Mission, Kans., 1981—; cons. Butler Mfg. Co., Kansas City, 1971. Superwalk chmn. safety and communications March of Dimes, Kansas City, Mo., 1972—, mem. gen. bd., 1977, 79; bd. dirs. Heart of Am. Radio Club, Kansas City, 1978-80; Master of servers St. Paul's Episcopal Ch., Kansas City, 1959-65, vestryman, 1967-73, treas., 1975-81; stewardship officer Episc. Diocese W. Mo., 1980-81, mem. diocesan council, 1981-83, jr. warden, 1982, sr. warden, 1983-84. Served with U.S. Army, 1953-55. Mem. ASHRAE (chpt. pres. 1980-81, energy mgmt. Region IX 1981-84, regional chmn., bd. dirs. 1984), Am. Soc. Mech. Engrs., Kansas City Engrs. Club, Refrigeration Engring. and Tech. Assn., Tau Kappa Epsilon. Episcopalian. Clubs: Heart of America Radio, Kansas City VHF (pres. 1961-62, corp. agt., trustee). Home: 425 W 49th Terr Kansas City MO 64112 Office: 5800 Foxridge Dr Mission KS 66201

STAPLETON, ELLA MAE, educational administrator; b. Detroit, Feb. 20, 1928; d. Thomas Daniel Lee and Dilsie (Christian) Jimerson; m. James Foster Stapleton, Nov. 29, 1953; children—James, Maureen, B.A., Mich. State Normal Coll., 1949; M.A., U. Mich., 1963; Ed.S., Wayne State U., 1974, Ed.D., 1981. Tchr., counselor, asst. prin., prin. Detroit Pub. Schs., 1949-79; instr. Wayne State U., 1979, LaVerne Coll., 1977-80, Regis Coll., Newton, Mass., 1976, Boston State U., 1978, East Strausburg U., Allentown, Pa., 1978-79, Elizabethtown Coll., N.J., 1980; region asst. supt. Detroit Pub. Schs., 1979-83; lectr. various schs. 1971-81. Vol. ARC, United Negro Coll. Fund; active NAACP, Detroit Urban League, YWCA, Nat. Alliance Females for Urban Concerns. Mem. Am. Assn. Sch. Adminstrs. (Valiant Woman award 1981), Assn. Suprs. and Curriculum Developers, New Profl. Women's Network, Alpha Kappa Alpha. Democrat. Episcopalian. Clubs: Carrousel Women's, Bridge-A-Dears. Home: 19405 Warrington Dr Detroit MI 48221 Office: 4400 Oakman Blvd Detroit MI 48204

STAPLETON, ROBERT J., industrial executive; b. Ft. Wayne, Ind., Jan. 9, 1922; s. Clarence Albert and Eva Elizabeth (Grashoff) S.; A.B., Valparaiso U., 1946; M.S., U. Wis., 1947; postgrad., U. Mich., 1943, Columbia U.; m. Marilyn Jeane Stinchfield, Sept. 7, 1946; children—Jan Elizabeth, Jill Leigh, Robert Guy. Indsl. devel. rep. Commonwealth Edison Co., Chgo., 1947-55; mng. dir., sec. Clinton Devel. Co. (Iowa), 1955-63; mgr. Cordova (Ill.) Indsl. Park, No. Natural Gas Co., 1963-69; exec. dir. Elgin (Ill.) Econ. Devel. Commn., 1969-71; exec. dir. Jobs div. IVAC, LaSalle, Ill., 1971-77; pres. Scioto Econ. Devel. Corp., Portsmouth, Ohio, 1977-83; pres. Clinton Area Devel. Corp., 1983—; pvt. practice as indsl. devel. cons., 1947—. Past pres., dir. Ill. Devel. Council. Served to lt (j.g.), USNR, 1942-46; capt. Res. ret. Certified indsl. developer. Mem. Res. Officers Assn., Naval Res., Assn. Am. Soc. Planning Ofcls., Am. (v.p., dir.), Mid. Am. Econ. Devel. Council (past v.p., dir.) devel. councils, Nat. Assn. Corp. Real Estate Execs., Urban Land Inst., Indsl. Devel. Research Council (past chmn., dir., advanced profl. assoc.), Ohio Devel. Assn. (past pres., dir.), Council Urban Econ. Devel., Clinton C. of C., Valparaiso U. Lettermen's Assn., Iowa Profl. Developers Assn., Wis. Alumni Assn. Republican. Lutheran. Clubs: Rotary, Clinton Country. Office: Wilson Bldg Clinton IA 52732

STARK, HARRY D., electronic company executive; b. Gregory, S.D., Apr. 21, 1908; s. Otto George and Anna Elizabeth Stark; E.E., U. Minn., 1933; m. Myrle Mae Miller, Feb. 10, 1934; children—Mary Ann, Judith Kay, Richard Miller. Partner, N.W. Radio Supply Co., Mpls., 1934-37; with Stark Electronics Supply, Inc., Mpls., 1938—, now chmn., pres. Mem. Nat. Electronics Distbrs. Assn. (nat. sec., mem. exec. bd.), Electronic Distbrs. Research Inst. (pres., dir.), Council of Ind. Mgrs. Clubs: Athletic (Mpls.); Spectators, Masons. Office: 401 Royalston Ave Minneapolis MN 55405

STARK, THEODORE EUGENE, JR., janitorial supplies distributor; b. Mpls., Jan. 17, 1930; s. Theodore Eugene and Mary Alice (James) S.; m. Edith Patricia McColl, May 7, 1955; children—Theodore Eugene, Karen Ann, Peter McColl. A.B., Bucknell U., 1953. Ptnr., Theodore Stark & Co., C.P.A., Mpls., 1955-62; pres., owner, chief exec. officer Dalco Corp., Mpls., 1968—, v.p., treas., 1962-68; owner, treas., chmn. bd. Am. Rug Laundry, Mpls., 1971-77; treas. Standardized Sanitation Systems, Inc., Burlington, Mass., 1971-73, dir., 1972—; chmn. SSS Inc., 1980-82; dir. First St. Anthony Bank. Treas. Wooddale PTA, Edina, Minn., 1967-68; bd. dirs. Colonial Ch. of Edina Found., 1975-80; trustee Colonial Ch., 1972-74, 76-79. Served to capt. USMCR, 1953-56. Mem. Edina C. of C. (dir. 1965-80), Minn. Golf Assn. (dir. 1969—, pres. 1982—), Phi Kappa Psi. Clubs: Mpls. Athletic, Gyro, Edina Country, Olympic Hills Country. Home: 4621 Townes Circle Edina MN 55424 Office: 3010 Broadway NE Minneapolis MN 55143

STARKEY, EDWARD DAVID, academic librarian; b. Oswego, N.Y., Oct. 21, 1942; s. Edward Davidson and Eileen (Heaney) S.; m. Paulette Schaller, Aug. 17, 1968; children—Brendan, Elyane. B.A., Stonehill Coll., 1965; postgrad. Gregorian U., Rome, Italy, 1965-66; M.A. in Lit., SUNY-Albany, 1968; M.S. in L.S., U. Ky., 1976; M.A. in Religion, U. Dayton, 1985. Tchr., Voorheesville (N.Y.) High Sch., 1968-70, Lees Jr. Coll., Jackson, Ky., 1970-73, The Lexington (Ky.) Sch., 1973-75; coll. librarian Urbana (Ohio) Coll., 1976-79; head reference U. Dayton (Ohio) Library, 1979—, mem. grad. council, 1982—, mem. grievance com., 1980—; cons. librarian Porter, Wright, Morris & Arthur, Dayton, Ohio, 1982—; mem. accreditation com. North Central Assn., 1979. HEW nat. teaching fellow, 1970-72; Library Services and Constrn. Act grantee Urbana Coll., 1978-79. Mem. Acad. Library Assn. Ohio (pres. 1983-84), Ohio Multitype Library Coop. Com. (vice-chmn. 1980-83), Ohio Council Library and Info. Services, Dayton-Miami Valley Consortium (mem. exec. bd. 1976-79). Roman Catholic. Home: 4409 Grayson St Kettering OH 45429 Office: U Dayton Library Dayton OH 45469

STARKS, GREGORY CHARLES, obstetrician, gynecologist, educator; b. Greenville, Miss., Jan. 25, 1948; s. Maurice and Bernice Livita (McGoy) S.; m. Janet Marie Adams, May 29, 1970; children—David, Christopher, Geoffrey. M.D., Jefferson Med. Coll., Phila., 1973; postgrad. Case Western Res. U., 1973-79. Intern, Univ. Hosps., Cleve., 1973-74, resident in ob-gyn, 1974-78; asst. prof. ob-gyn Case Western Res. U., 1979, U. Mo.-Kansas City, 1979—; chief ob-gyn Group Health, Inc., Kansas City, 1979-81; dir. ob-gyn Research Med. Ctr., Kansas City, 1981—. Bd. dirs. Quincy Research Inst., Kansas City, Mo., 1982—, Planned Parenthood Kansas City, 1981—. Am. Cancer Soc. research grantee and scholar, 1968-69; Robert Wood Johnson Found. scholar, 1969-71. Fellow Am. Coll. Ob-Gyn; mem. Am. Fertility Soc., Southwest Clin. Soc., Mo. Med. Soc. Democrat. Methodist. Club: Indian Creek Racquet (Kansas City). Contbr. articles to profl. publs.

STARNER, ROBERT NEIL, insurance company executive; b. Alexandria, Minn., Nov. 23, 1947; s. Robert Franklin and Ruth Maxine (Ness) S.; m. LuAnn Marie Cartwright, Oct. 11, 1975; children—Joshua Lee, Leslie Marie. B.A., U. Minn.-Morris, 1969. Programmer, Aid Assn. for Lutherans, Appleton, Wis., 1969-72, systems specialist, 1972-76, systems devel. mgr., 1976-84, dir., 1984—. Chmn. AAL United Way Campaign, Appleton, 1974. Served with U.S. Army 1970-72. Mem. Soc. Preservation and Encouragement of Barber-shop Quartet Singing in Am., Inc. (treas. 1978-83, program v.p. 1983-84, sec. 1984-85, pres. 1985, BOTY award Appleton Wis. chpt. 1977), Data Processing Mgmt. Assn. Lutheran. Avocation: gardening. Home: Rt 2 Box 180 Hortonville WI 54944

STARNES, JAMES WRIGHT, lawyer; b. East St. Louis, Ill., Apr. 3, 1933; s. James Adron and Nell (Short) S.; student St. Louis U., 1951-53; LL.B., Washington U., St. Louis, 1957; m. Helen Woods Mitchell, Mar. 29, 1958 (div. 1978); children—James Wright, Mitchell A., William B. II. Bar: Mo. 1957, Ill. 1957. Assoc. Stinson, Mag & Fizzell, Kansas City, Mo., 1957-60, partner, 1960—; ptnr. Mid-Continent Properties Co., 1959—, Fairview Investment Co., Kansas City, 1971-76, Monticello Land Co., 1973—; sec. Packaging Products Corp., Mission, Kans., 1972—. Bd. dirs. Mo. Assn. Mental Health, 1968-69; bd. dirs. Kansas City Assn. Mental Health, 1966-78, pres., 1969-70; bd. dirs. Heed, 1965-73, 78-82, pres., 1966-67, fin. chmn. 1967-68; bd. dirs. Kansas City Halfway House Found., exec. com., 1966-69, pres., 1966; bd. dirs. Joan Davis Sch. for Spl. Edn., 1972—, v.p., 1972-73, 79-80, pres., 1979-82; bd. dirs. Sherwood Ctr. for Exceptional Child, 1977-79, v.p., 1978-79. Served with arty. AUS, 1957. Mem. Am., Mo., Kansas City bar assns., Kansas City Lawyers Assn. Presbyterian (deacon). Mem. adv. bd. Washington U. Law Quar., 1957—. Home: 3715 W 63d St Mission Hills KS 66208 Office: 2100 Charter Bank Center Kansas City MO 64105

STAROSTOVIC, EDWARD JOSEPH, JR., engineer, engineering company executive; b. Chgo., Apr. 8, 1933; s. Edward J. and Esther Ruth (Guinee) S.; m. Marilyn Ann Mucek, June 23, 1956; children—Lynn, Ann, Karen, Susanne. B.A., Ill. Inst. Tech., Chgo., 1958. Registered profl. engr., Wis. Owner, Structural Plywood Co., Chgo., 1958-60; engr., mgr. Wausau Homes Inc., Wis., 1960-72; engr., exec. v.p. PFS Corp., Madison, Wis., 1972-78, engr., pres., 1978—; bd. dirs. Wood Heating Alliance, Washington, 1982—; del. U.S.-USSR Tech. Exchange Agreement, Washington, 1977—. Mem. editorial rev. bd. Automation in Housing, 1973—. Chmn. Wausau Area Regional Plan Commn., 1967. Served with U.S. Army, 1953-55, Korea. Recipient E. Kurtz award Nat. Assn. Bldg. Mfrs., 1972. Mem. Nat. Soc. Profl. Engrs., Nat. Inst. Bldg. Scis., Am. Soc. Quality Control, Forest Products Research Soc., Internat. Assn. Elec. Inspectors, ASTM. Office: PFS Corp 2402 Daniels St Madison WI 53704

STARR, BRYAN BARTLETT, profl. football coach; b. Montgomery, Ala., Jan. 9, 1934; s. Benjamin B. and Lula I. (Tucker) S.; B.S., U. Ala., 1956; m. Cherry Morton, May 8, 1954; children—Bart, Bret. Quarterback, Green Bay Packers, Nat. Football League, 1956-71, asst. coach, 1972, gen. mgr., head coach, 1975—; owner, operator Bart Starr Lincoln-Mercury automobile dealership, Birmingham, Ala.; gen. ptnr. RAL Asset Mgmt. Group, Brookfield Wis.; dir. Sentry Ins. Active in fundraising for numerous charities. Played in NFL Pro-Bowl after 1960, 61, 62, 66 seasons; NFL Passing Leader, 1962, 64, 66; NFL Player of Yr., 1966; Super Bowl Most Valuable Player, 1967, 68; named to Nat. Profl. Football Hall of Fame, 1977. Methodist. Co-author: Quarterbacking, 1967; Perspective on Victory, 1972. Office: RAL Asset Mgmt Group 1025 S Moorland Rd Brookfield WI 53005

STARR, JOHN PHILIP, insurance company executive; b. Kansas City, Kans., Jan. 19, 1933; s. John Wilbur and Martha Jane (Phillips) S.; m. Katherine Barry Mann, Oct. 15, 1960; children—John Robert, James Philip. A.B., Princeton U., 1955; M.B.A., Wharton Coll., Phila., 1956. C.L.U. Asst. to mng. dir. R.B. Jones & Sons, Inc., Kansas City, Mo., 1959-64, mgr. life and health div., 1964-69; v.p. fin., dir. R.B. Jones Corp., Kansas City, Mo., 1969-74, pres. employee plans, 1974-76, sr. v.p., dir., 1976-79; v.p. Alexander & Alexander, Kansas City, Mo., 1979—; dir. Corp. Woods Bank, Overland Park, Kans. Cons. editor: Group Insurance Handbook, 1965. Trustee St Luke's Hosp., Kansas City, Mo., 1977—; v.p. ops. Heart of Am. council Boy Scouts Am., 1983-84, exec. v.p., 1985; pres. Pembroke-Country Day Sch., Kansas City, Mo., 1980-81. Served to capt. U.S. Army, 1957-59. Named to Summit Club, Alexander & Alexander, 1982, 83; recipient Silver Beaver award Boy Scouts Am., 1985. Mem. Shepherd's Ctr. (bd. dirs.), Nelson-Atkins Mus., Am. Coll. Life Underwriters, Care-For, Inc. Republican. Episcopalian. Club: Mercury (Kansas City, Mo.). Avocation: competitive ballroom dance.

STARR, STEPHEN FREDERICK, See *Who's Who in America*, 43rd edition.

STARTZMAN, JEFFREY PAUL, lawyer; b. Columbus, Ohio, Apr. 28, 1956; s. Thomas Lloyd and Catherine Elizabeth (Shaw) S.; m. Donna Jean Srail, Dec. 16, 1978. B.A. summa cum laude with honors, Ohio State U., 1976, J.D., 1979. Bar: Ohio 1979, U.S. Dist. Ct. (so. dist.) Ohio 1982. Clk. Pub. Utilities Commn. Ohio, Columbus, 1977-78; intern CIA, Langley, Va., 1978; staff atty. Dayton Power & Light, Ohio, 1979-80; asst. pros. atty. Montgomery County Prosecutor's Office, Dayton, 1980—. Adviser Miami Valley Explorers council Boy Scouts Am., 1981, mem. exec. com. 1983; mem. exec. com. Montgomery County Democratic Party, Dayton, 1981—; bd. dirs. Ohio Family Support Assn., Bowling Green, 1983—. Mem. Ohio State Bar Assn., Dayton Bar Assn. (subcom. chmn. 1979—), Phi Beta Kappa. Home: 9987 Bannon Ct Miamisburg OH 45342 Office: Montgomery County Prosecutor's Office 14 W 4th St Suite 290 Dayton OH 45402

STAUB, JAMES RICHARD, chiropractor; b. Peoria, Ill., Apr. 22, 1938; s. John and Dorothy Christine (Benson) S.; student Bradley U., 1956-60, U. Wis., 1972; D.Chiropractic, Palmer Coll. Chiropractic, 1972; B.A., Columbia Coll., 1977; m. Sandra Lee Herman, Dec. 21, 1958 (div. July 1979); children—Gary James, Gregory Alan; m. 2d, Sheryl Ann Vander Velde, Nov. 17, 1979. Asst. to mgr. A & J Lumber Co., Peoria Hts., Ill., 1956-60; with Central Ill. Light Co., Peoria, 1961-69; pvt. practice chiropractic, Valparaiso, Ind., 1972—. Missionary to Haiti, Ch. of Nazarene, 1984; minister of music South Haven Ch. of Nazarene, 1985. Recipient certificate of merit Palmer Coll. Chiropractic Clinic, 1972. Mem. Valparaiso Bus. and Profl. Couples Club (chmn. 1974-75), Internat., Am., Ky., Ind., Porter County (v.p. 1975-76), N.W. Dist. Ind. (sec. 1975-76), Christian chiropractic assns., Palmer Coll. Alumni Assn. (Ind. pres. 1974-79), Internat. Acad. Preventive Medicine, N.W. Ind. Comprehensive Health Planning Council, Phi Mu Alpha. Home: 811 E Chicago St Valparaiso IN 46383 Office: 1402 E Evans Ave Valparaiso IN 46383

STAUDE, PETER, resort executive; b. Gmunden, Austria, Feb. 9, 1944; came to U.S., 1958, naturalized, 1965; s. Leonard Staude and Hildegard (Steiner) Whitman; m. Wanda Fay Mosier, May 20, 1976; 1 child, Rachael. Resident mgr., gen. mgr. Tan-Tar-A Resort, Osage Beach, Mo., 1960-76; v.p., gen. mgr. Olympia Resort, Oconomowoc, Wis., 1976-78; owner, operator Staude's Trucking, Ft. Wayne, Ind., 1978-80; gen. mgr. Hilton Inn, Kansas City, 1980-83, Holiday Inn, Lake Ozark, Mo., 1983—; chmn. hotel and restaurant vocat. tech. Platt County Vocat.-Tech. Sch., Mo., 1983. Served as staff sgt. USAF, 1966-70. Mem. Lake Assn. (bd. dirs. 1984-85), Mo. Hotel Assn. (bd. dirs. 1982-83, 84-85), Mo. Travel Council (bd. dirs. 1984—). Avocations: snow skiing, tennis, swimming. Home: PO Box 648 Osage Beach MO 65065 Office: Route 1 Box 45 Lake Ozark MO 65049

STAUFFER, LEE DALLAS, public health educator; b. Wisner, Nebr., Mar. 20, 1929; s. Lee Henry and Myrtle Ann (Schulz) S.; m. Donna Lois Frederickson, Aug. 27, 1952; children—Karl, Lisa, Dane, Kristian. B.S., U. Nebr., 1951; M.P.H., U. Minn., 1956. Registered sanitarian, Minn. Various teaching and sanitarian positions U. Minn., Mpls., 1952-62, asst. prof., asst. dir. sch. pub. health, 1962-66, dean sch. pub. health, 1970-82, assoc. prof., 1982—; dep. health officer City of Coon Rapids, Minn., 1960-64; exec. sec. Am. Coll. Health Assn., Coral Gables, Fla., 1966-68; exec. dir. postgrad. edn. Coll. Med. Scis., Mpls., 1968-70; mem. Met. Health Bd., St. Paul, 1970-73; trustee, pres. Northlands Regional Med. Program, St. Paul, 1970-78; counselor, v.p., pres.

Council Edn. for Pub. Health, Washington, 1974-80. Mem. Contbr. articles to profl. jours. trustee, pres. North Suburban San. Sewer Dist., Spring Lake Park, Minn., 1962-66; mem., v.p., pres. sch. bd., St. Anthony, Minn., 1969-73; chmn. Am. Field Service Club, St. Anthony, 1976-78. Served with USMC, 1946-47; served as midshipman USNR, 1947-48. Recipient spl. recognition award Am. Coll. Health Assn., 1976, Sch. Pub. Health award, 1983; named adm. Nebr. Navy, 1982. Fellow Am. Pub. Health Assn. (gov. council 1983—); mem. Nat. Acad. Sanitarians (founder, diplomate, bd. dirs. 1970-73), Nat. Assn. Pub. Health Policy (sec., environ. health council 1984—), Nat. Environ. Health Assn. (registered, Cert. Merit 1971), Minn. Environ. Health Assn. (chmn. registration com. 1962-66, Sanitarian of Yr. 1971), Assn. Sch. Pub. Health (sec.-treas. 1980-82). Democrat. Lutheran. Club: Campus (Mpls.). Avocation: music. Home: 300 Croft Dr NE Minneapolis MN 55418 Office: Sch Pub Health Univ Minn Box 197 Mayo Hosp 420 Delaware St SE Minneapolis MN 55455

STAUFFER, PETER WALLACE, newspaper executive; b. Topeka, Kans., Sept. 6, 1947; s. Stanley Howard and Suzanne (Wallace) S.; m. Anne Blade, May 12, 1979; 1 child, Caroline Suzanne. Student Shattuck Sch., Faribault, Minn.; B.A., U. Kansas., postgrad. Sch. Journalism. Reporter, Kansas City Kansan, Kans., 1972-73; summer relief writer AP, Kansas City, Mo., 1974; Washington corr. Topeka Capital-Jour., 1974-76; editor, gen. mgr. Glenwood Post, Glenwood Springs, Colo., 1977-82; publisher The Examiner, Independence, Mo., 1982—; dir. Commerce Bank of Independence. Served to 1st lt. USMC, 1969-72. Mem. Am. Newspaper Pubs. Assn., Inland Daily Press Assn., Mo. Press Assn., Sigma Delta Chi. Republican. Episcopalian. Office: The Examiner 410 S Liberty St Independence MO 64050

STAUFFER, RICHARD LA VERGNE, art educator, sculptor, glassblower; b. New Cambria, Kans., Apr. 1, 1932; s. Kenneth L. and Mary (Bell) S.; m. Mary Hake, Aug. 23, 1953; children—Brad, Bridgett, Brendy. B.S., Kans. State Tchrs. Coll., 1955; M.S., Kans. U., 1962. Tchr. art Emporia City Schs., Kans., 1957-62; prof. art Emporia State U., 1962—; judicator Scholastic Art Awards, Wichita, Kans., 1984—. Pres. Friends of Art, Emporia, 1970; chmn., trustee Congl. Ch., 1985. Served with U.S. Army, 1955-57. Recipient HM award Kans. Designer Craftsman, 1972, Smokey Hill Art, 1976, Juror's award Art Inc., 1984; named Outstanding Art Educator, Nat. Art Edn. Assn., 1984, Govs. Artist Arts Commn., 1985. Fellow Art Glass Directory, Kans. Sculpture Assn. (regional adviser 1983-87, Group Sculpture Design prize, 1984); mem. Kans. Artist Craftsman Assn. (treas. 1973-77), Kans. Art Edn. Assn. (editor 1984-88). Democrat. Avocations: sports, archeology. Home: 2001 Lincoln St Emporia KS 66801 Office: Emporia State U 12th Commercial St Emporia KS 66801

STAUFFER, STANLEY HOWARD, newspaper and broadcasting executive; b. Peabody, Kans., Sept. 11, 1920; s. Oscar S. and Ethel L. (Stone) S.; m. Suzanne R. Wallace, Feb. 16, 1945 (div. 1961); children—Peter, Clay, Charles; m. Elizabeth D. Priest, July 14, 1962; children—Elizabeth, Grant. A.B., U. Kans., 1942. Assoc. editor Topeka State Jour., 1946-47; editor, pub. Santa Maria Times (Calif), 1948-52; rewriter copy editor Denver Post, 1953-54; staff mem. AP, Denver bur., 1954-55; exec. v.p. Stauffer Publs., Inc., 1955-69; gen. mgr. Topeka Capital-Jour., 1957-69; pres. Stauffer Communications, Inc., Topeka, 1969—; dir. Yellow Freight System, Inc., 1st Nat. Bank Topeka, Newspaper Advt. Bur., Gt. Lakes Forest Products Ltd., Past pres. Topeka YMCA; past chmn. adv. bd. St. Francis Hosp.; mem. Met. Topeka Airport Authority; trustee William Allen White Found., Menninger Found., Midwest Research Inst. Served as officer USAAF, 1943-45. Named Chpt. Boss of Yr., Am. Bus. Women's Assn., 1976; Outstanding Kans. Pub., Kappa Tau Alpha, 1980; Legion of Honor, DeMolay, Topeka Phi of Yr., 1971. Mem. Kans. Press Assn. (past pres.), Inland Daily Press Assn. (past dir.), Air Force Assn. (past pres. Topeka), Kans. U. Alumni Assn. (past dir.), Kans. C. of C. and Industry (past chmn.), Topeka C. of C. (dir.), Phi Delta Theta (past chpt. pres.), Sigma Delta Chi (past chpt. pres.). Episcopalian. Clubs: Topeka Country, Topeka Town, Topeka Press (past pres.). Office: Stauffer Communications Inc 6th St and Jefferson St Topeka KS 66607

STEAD, JAMES JOSEPH, JR., securities company executive; b. Chgo., Sept. 13, 1930; s. James Joseph and Irene (Jennings) S.; B.S., DePaul U., 1955, M.B.A., 1957; m. Edith Pearson, Feb. 13, 1954; children—James, Diane, Robert, Caroline. Asst. sec. C. F. Childs & Co., Chgo., 1955-62; exec. v.p., sec. Koenig, Keating & Stead, Inc., Chgo., 1962-66; 2d v.p., mgr. midwest municipal bond dept. Hayden, Stone Inc., Chgo., 1966-69; sr. v.p., nat. sales mgr. Ill. Co. Inc., 1969-70; mgr. instl. sales dept. Reynolds and Co., Chgo., 1970-72; partner Edwards & Hanly, 1972-74; v.p., instnl. sales mgr. Paine, Webber, Jackson & Curtis, 1974-76; v.p., regional instl. sales mgr. Reynolds Securities, Inc., 1976-78; sr. v.p., regional mgr. Oppenheimer & Co., Inc., 1978—; instr. Mcpl. Bond Sch., Chgo., 1967—. Served with AUS, 1951-53. Mem. Security Traders Assn. Chgo., Nat. Security Traders Assn., Am. Mgmt. Assn., Municipal Finance Forum Washington. Clubs: Executives, Union League, Municipal Bond, Bond (Chgo.); Olympia Fields Country (Ill.); Wall Street (N.Y.C.). Home: 20721 Brookwood Dr Olympia Fields IL 60461 Office: One S Wacker Dr Chicago IL 60606

STEADMAN, JACK W., professional football executive; b. Warrenville, Ill., Sept. 14, 1928; s. Walter Angus and Vera Ruth (Burkholder) S.; B.A., So. Methodist U., 1950; m. Martha Cudworth Steinhoff, Nov. 24, 1949; children—Thomas Edward, Barbara Ann, Donald Wayne. Accountant, Hunt Oil Co., Dallas, 1950-54; chief's acct. W.H. Hunt, Dallas, 1954-58; chief acct. Penrod Drilling Co., Dallas, 1958-60; gen. mgr. Dallas Texans Football Club, 1960-63; gen. mgr. Kansas City Chiefs Football Club, 1963-76, exec. v.p., 1966-76, pres., from 1976; pres. Mid-Am. Enterprises (Worlds of Fun), Kansas City, from 1982; v.p. First Fidelity Investment Trust, Kansas City; dir. Ct. Council; exec. com., bd. dirs. Starlight Theatre Assn., Kansas City; bd. dirs. Kansas City chpt. Fellowship Christian Athletes, 1976, chmn. finance com., 1977; bd. dirs. YMCA, Am. Royal Assn.; mem. exec. com., bd. dirs. Heart of Am. United Way, campaign chmn., 1979; adv. trustee Research Med. Center, Kansas City; deacon Leawood Bapt. Ch. Mem. Greater Kansas City C. of C. (dir. from 1976, chmn. world's fair com. 1976, v.p. membership 1978). Clubs: Kansas City Downtown Rotary, Kansas City, 711 Inner, Brookridge Country (Kansas City). Office:Kansas City Chiefs 1 Arrowhead Dr Kansas City MO 64129*

STECKLER, WILLIAM ELWOOD, judge; b. Mt. Vernon, Ind., Oct. 18, 1913; s. William Herman and Lena (Menikheim) S.; LL.B., Ind. Law Sch., 1936; J.D., 1937; LL.D., Wittenberg U., Springfield, Ohio, 1958; H.H.D., Ind. Central Coll., 1969; m. Vitallas Alting, Oct. 15, 1938; children—William Rudolph, David Alan. Admitted to Ind. bar, 1936, practiced in Indpls., 1937-50, mem. firm Key & Steckler; pub. counselor Pub. Service Commn., State Ind., 1949-50; judge U.S. Dist. Ct. So. Dist. Ind., 1950—. Served as seaman USN, 1943. Recipient Disting. Alumni Service award Ind. U., 1985, Ind. U. Sch. Law, 1985. Mem. Am., Fed., Ind., Indpls. bar assns., Am. Judicature Soc., Nat. Lawyers Club, Jud. Conf. U.S., Am. Legion, Order of Coif, Sigma Delta Kappa. Democrat. Lutheran. Mason (33 deg., Shriner). Club: Indianapolis Athletic. Home: 30 Jurist Ln Lamb Lake Trafalgar IN 46181 Office: US Courthouse 46 E Ohio Indianapolis IN 46204

STEEL, GEORGE BRADFORD, JR., brokerage company executive; b. S.I., N.Y., July 28, 1921; s. George Bradford and Beatrice (Morris) S.; m. Kathleen Howe, Apr. 24, 1952; children—George D., John T. Student U. N.C., 1939-40; A.B., Middlebury Coll., 1943. Dist. sales mgr. Comptometer Corp., Lansing, Mich., Indpls., 1950-59; owner, pres. George B. Steel & Assocs., Indpls. 1958—; pres. Planned Investment Co. Inc., Indpls., 1958—. Bd. dirs. Better Bus. Bur., Citizens Forum. Served to lt. USNR, World War II. Mem. Nat. Assn. Accts., Adminstrv. Mgmt. Soc., Assn. Fin. Planners, Nat. Assn. Securities Dealers, Navy League, Nat. Fedn. Ind. Businessmen. Republican. Episcopalian. Clubs: Columbia, Downtown Kiwanis, Service (Indpls.); Woodland Country (Carmel). Office: 300 E Fall Creek Park N Indianapolis IN 46205

STEELE, CLEMENT JOSEPH, computer professional; b. Waukon, Iowa, June 16, 1937; s. Burnill William and Susan Lois (Stubstad) S.; student Marquette U., 1955-56; B.A., Loras Coll., 1961; postgrad. Ill. Inst. Tech., 1964, Lawrence U., 1966, U. Wyo., 1971, U. Iowa, 1972, U. Wis., 1973-76; M.S., Rutgers U., 1968; m. Mary Jane Valley, Aug. 11, 1962; children—Maureen, Teresa, Daniel. Tchr. math. Jefferson Jr. High Sch., Dubuque, 1961-63, Lake Forest (Ill.) High Sch., 1963-67, Campion Acad., Prairie du Chien, Wis., 1968-73; math. supervisory intern Milw. public schs., 1973-74; teaching asst., research asst. U. Wis., Madison, 1974-76; research and evaluation cons. Keystone Area Edn. Agy., Dubuque, 1976-77; instructional computer cons., computer center dir. Keystone Area Edn. Agy., 1977-83, coordinator computer services, 1983—; guest lectr. in research Clarke Coll., 1978-83; instr. Loras Coll., 1979-81; adj. prof. No. Ill. U., 1983—. Served with U.S. Army, 1961. Named Outstanding Young Educator, Wis. Jaycees, 1972; NSF grantee, 1973-74. Mem. Iowa Assn. for Ednl. Data Systems (bd. dirs. 1980-82), Nat. Council Tchrs. Math., Nat. Council Suprs. Math., Iowa Council Tchrs. Math., Tri-State Data Processing Assn., Phi Delta Kappa. Roman Catholic. Club: Lions. Contbr. articles to profl. jours. Home: 2371 Carter Rd Dubuque IA 52001 Office: 1473 Central Ave Dubuque IA 52001

STEELE, DARRELL STANLEY, veterinarian; b. Treynor, Iowa, Sept. 30, 1917; s. Carroll Chester and Hazel Lydia (Redman) S.; D.V.M., Kans. State U., 1939; m. Betty Jean Guyot, Feb. 1, 1936; children—Richard, Suzanne. Dir. small animal biol. products Pitman Moore Co., Zionsville, Ind., 1939-41; practice veterinary medicine specializing in small animals, Mpls., 1947—; pres. Minn. Veterinary Exam. Bd. Trustee North Methodist Ch., Mpls., 1959-63, chmn. ofcl. bd., 1961-63. Served to lt. col. U.S. Army, 1941-47; col. USAF, Res. Mem. Am., Minn. veterinary med. assns., Am., Met. (pres. 1956-57), animal hosp. assns., Midwest Small Animal Assn. (pres. 1958-59, Distinguished Service award 1960), Kans. State U. Vet. Alumni Assn. (pres. 1970), Res. Officers Assn. Clubs: Minn. 100 (v.p. 1978-79, pres. 1980-81), Midland Hills Country (pres. 1959-60), Masons, Jesters, Shriners. Home: 584 Westwood Village Saint Paul MN 55113 Office: 1332 Marshall St NE Minneapolis MN 55413

STEELE, HILDA HODGSON, retired home economist, consultant; b. Wilmington, Ohio, Mar. 24, 1911; d. George and Mary Jane (Rolston) Hodgson; A.A., Wilmington Coll., 1931, B.S., 1935; M.A. in Home Econs. Edn., Ohio State U., 1941; postgrad. Ohio U., 1954, Miami U., 1959; m. John C. Steele (dec. Jan. 1973). Tchr., Brookville (Ohio) Elementary Sch., 1932-37; tchr. home econs. Lincoln Jr. High Sch., Dayton (Ohio) Pub. Schs., 1937-40, coordinator home econs. dept., traveling exptl. home econs. tchr., 1940-45, supr. home econs., 1945-81, cons., 1981—; program dir. Family Life Adult Disadvantaged Program, 1969-81. Mem. Ohio Farm Electrification Com., 1964-66. Mem. town and country br. career com. Miami Valley br. YMCA, 1948-59. Adv. bd. Dayton Sch. Practical Nursing, 1951—; adv. com. Dayton Miami Valley Hosp. Sch. Nursing, 1951-63; jr. adv. com. Montgomery County chpt. ARC, 1940-80; mem. com. United Appeal, 1970—; bd. dirs. (Ohio) FHA-HERO, 1979-81. Mem. Dayton area Nutrition Council, Am. Home Econs. Assn. (del. 1961), Ohio Home Econs. Assn. (chmn. elementary and secondary edn. com. 1947-51, co-chmn. ann. conv. 1961-77, mem. housing and equipment coms. 1965-68, chmn. found. com. 1979-81), Dayton Met. Home Econs. Assn. (pres. 1949-50, 60-61); Nat., Ohio edn. assns., Ohio Council Local Adminstrs., Dayton Sch. Adminstrs. Assn., Elec. Women's Round Table (pres. 1960-61), Dayton City Sch. Mgmt. Assn. (charter), Ohio Vocat. Assn. (Disting. Service award 1981), Am. Vocat. Edn. Assn., Ohio Vocat. Edn. Assn., Phi Upsilon Omicron (hon.). Mem. Ch. of Christ. Mem. Order Eastern Star. Club: Zonta (pres. Dayton 1950-52). Research in pub. sch. food habits, 1957. Home: 1443 State Route 380 Xenia OH 45385

STEELE, IRA MAI, ednl. adminstr.; b. Cleve., June 24, 1952; s. Ira Jefferson and Audria Mai Steele; student Cuyahoga Community Coll., Cleve., 1969-71; B.S. in Elem. Edn., Tenn. State U., 1973; M.S. in Elem. Edn., Ind. U.-Purdue U., Indpls., 1977; supervision and adminstrn. cert. Butler U., 1984. Tchr. elem. sch., Danville, Ill., 1973-74, Columbia, Tenn., 1974-75; facilitator Center for Leadership Devel., Indpls., 1977-79; tchr. elem. schs. Indpls. Public Schs., 1975-80, Title VII multicultural tng. specialist dept. human relations, 1980-81, Title VI in-service tng. cons., 1981-82; coordinator Project Strive, summer 1983; saleswoman, 1982—; del. Ind. Tchrs. Conf., 1977-79. Vice precinct committeeman Indpls. Democratic Com., 1976—; mem. youth adv. council Center for Leadership Devel., 1975—. vice chmn. Indpls. Polit. Action Com., 1977-78; senate coordinator Sch. 81, Operation P.U.S.H., Indpls., 1980; vol. cons. Center Twp. Young Citizens, Indpls., 1980-81. Named hon. sheriff and bailiff Marion County, Indpls., 1978; recipient recognition award Indpls. Public Schs. Bd. Sch. Commrs., 1980, plaque of appreciation Center for Leadership Devel., 1981. Mem. Assn. for Supervision and Curriculum Devel., Soc. for Intensified Edn. (Outstanding Classroom Tchr. award 1980), Ind. Tchrs. Assn. (music multicultural com. 1980-82), Tenn. State U. Alumni (v.p., scholarship chmn. Indpls. chpt. 1979-82), Indpls. Edn. Assn. (profl. relations chmn. 1978-79). Methodist. Clubs: The Committee, Elks. Home: 6010 W Lake South Dr Indianapolis IN 46224 Office: 1849 Pleasant Run Pkwy South Dr Indianapolis IN 46202

STEELE, JOHN ROBERT, lawyer; b. Chattanooga, July 16, 1951; s. James Russell and Hazel Virginia (Meyers) S.; m. Susan Faye Nielsen, Aug. 22, 1970; children—Amanda, Corey James. B.A., U. Central Fla., 1974; J.D., U. S.D., 1978. Bar: S.D. 1978, U.S. Dist. Ct. S.D. 1979. Pres., Steele Law Office, Plankinton, S.D., 1978—; state's atty. Aurora County, Plankinton, 1978—; city atty., Plankinton, 1980-84; adminstrv. hearing officer S.D. Dept. Edn., Pierre, 1978—; adj. instr. Dakota Wesleyan U., Mitchell, S.D., 1979—. Chmn. bd. trustees Plankinton United Methodist Ch., S.D., 1981-82; state committeeman Aurora County Democratic Com., Plankinton, 1982-85. Mem. ABA, Nat. Dist. Attys. Assn., S.D. Bar Assn., S.D. State's Atty. Assn. Democrat. Methodist. Home: 107 Vine St Plankinton SD 57368 Office: Steele Law Office PC 405 S Main St Plankinton SD 57368

STEEN, DONALD MARINER, agri-business executive; b. Scottsbluff, Nebr., Mar. 24, 1924; s. Clarence Guido and Jean Mabel (Whipple) S.; m. Bonnie Jeanne Jirdon, Oct. 30, 1946; children—John Robert, William Gary. Student U. Nebr., 1941-42; B.Sc., U.S. Merchant Marine Acad., 1981. Pres., Blue J. Feeds, Inc., 1970-81, Jirdon Wyoming Inc., 1970-80, Wyo. Chem., Inc., 1975-80, Chems. Internat. Ltd., 1974-79, Jirdon Livestock Co., Morrill, Nebr., 1983—; cons. Allied Chem. Corp.; chmn. bd. PAB Nebr. Natural Resources Commn., 1981. Chmn., Gov.'s Forward Nebr. Task Force, 1982; state vice chmn. Nebr. Republican Party, 1975. Served to lt. USN, 1943-46. Recipient Outstanding Community Service award Am. Feed Mfrs. Assn., 1975; Service to Handicapped, Goodwill Industries of Wyo., 1979, others. Mem. Am. Legion, Nebr. Water Resources Assn. (pres. 1982), Nebr. Assn. Commerce and Industry (v.p. 1981). Presbyterian. Clubs: Rotary, Stockgrowers, Masons, Shriners, Elks. Patentee liquid protein supplement, artificial protein, liquid fire retardent. Office: PO Box 456 Morrill NE 69358

STEEN, JAN PHAFF, div. pres. Umie/Dayton, banker; b. Frederiksberg, Denmark, Jan. 31, 1935; s. Thomas S.; and Else S.; B.A., Copenhagen State Coll., 1954; M.B.A., Copenhagen Comml. U., 1956; 1 dau., Sara. Trainee, East Asiatic Co., Copenhagen, 1954; adminstrv. asst. USAF Base Exchange, Sondrestrom AFB, Greenland, 1959-60; purchase sales mgr., Royal Greenland Trade Dept., Copenhagen, 1960-63; comml. attache Royal Danish Consulate Gen., Kuwait, 1964-65; asst. v.p., mgr. Privatbanken Copenhagen, 1966-69; internt. mgr. Winters Nat. Bank & Trust Co., Dayton, Ohio, 1969-71, asst. v.p., 1971-73, v.p., div. mgr., 1973-77, sr. v.p., 1977-83; pres. JPS Export-Import Trading, 1982-85; internat. fin. cons., 1982-85; corp. v.p., regional internat. mgr. ComericA Bank Internat., Dayton, 1985—. Pres., Dayton Council World Affairs, 1977-79; gov. Ohio Adv. Council Internat. Trade, 1974-78; treas. So. Ohio Dist. Export Council, 1975; bd. dirs. Dayton Opera Assn., 1977-83. Served to capt. Royal Danish Army, 1956-58. Danish Dept. Commerce Export fellow, 1964. Mem. Dayton C. of C. (chmn. world trade council 1974-75) Fgn. Credit Ins. Assn. (midwest adv. com. 1980—), Bankers Assn. Fgn. Trade, Robert Morris Assos., Res. Officers Assn. (hon.). Clubs: Royal Danish Yacht, Dayton Racquet. Contbr. articles to profl. jours. Home: 8344 Towson Blvd Miamisburg OH 45342 Office: ComericA Bank International Gem Plaza Dayton OH 45402

STEEN, LOWELL HARRISON, physician; b. Kenosha, Wis., Nov. 27, 1923; s. Joseph Arthur and Camilla Marie (Henriksen) S.; B.S., Ind. U., 1945, M.D., 1948; m. Cheryl Ann Rectanus, Nov. 20, 1969; children—Linda C., Laura A., Lowell Harrison, Heather J., Kirsten M. Intern, Mercy Hosp.-Loyola U. Clinics, Chgo., 1948-49; resident in internal medicine VA Hosp., Hines, Ill., 1950-53; practice medicine specializing in internal medicine, Hammond, Ind., 1953—; pres., chief exec. officer Whiting Clinic; mem. sr. staff St. Catherine Hosp., East Chicago, Ind.; staff Community Hosp., Munster, Ind.; bd. commrs. Joint Commn. Accreditation of Hosps. Served with M.C., AUS, 1949-50, 55-56. Recipient Disting. Alumni Service award Ind. U., 1983. Fellow ACP; mem. AMA (trustee 1975, chmn. bd. trustees 1979), Ind. Med. Assn. (pres. 1970, chmn. bd. 1968-69), World Med. Assn. (dir. 1978-82, chmn. bd. 1979-82, del. World Assembly 1978-82), Ind. Soc. Internal Medicine (pres. 1963), Lake County Med. Soc. Presbyterian. Home: 8800 Parkway Dr Highland IN 46322 Office: 2450 169th St Hammond IN 46323

STEFFEN, ALFRED JOSEPH, environmental engineer, consultant; b. Milw., Aug. 4, 1911; m. Nancy Olive Benage, Sept. 26, 1936; children—Carol, Mary, Paul. B.S., U. Wis.-Madison, 1933. Registered profl. engr., Wis. Dist. engr. Wis. State Bd. Health, Madison, 1934-42; chief environ. engr. Wilson & Co., Chgo., 1946-65; v.p., mgr. Ralph B. Carter Co., Hackensack, N.J., 1965-70; assoc. prof. civil engring. Purdue U., West Lafayette, Ind., 1970-77; pres., owner Steffen Environ. Engrs. West Lafayette, 1978—. Contbr. articles to profl. jours. Served to major C.E. U.S. Army, 1942-46. Mem. Am. Acad. Environ. Engrs. (diplomate), Water Pollution Control Fedn. (pres. 1964-65). Lutheran. Home and Office: 2863 Ashland St West Lafayette IN 47906

STEFFY, GARY ROBERT, lighting design company executive; b. Lancaster, Pa., Feb. 6, 1954; s. George Robert and Ann Louise (Eshleman) S. B. Archtl. Engring., Pa. State U., 1977. Research engr. Owens-Corning Fiberglas, Granville, Ohio, 1977-79; lighting designer Smith, Hinchman & Grylls, Detroit, 1979-82; pres. Gary Steffy Lighting Design, Ann Arbor, Mich., 1982—. Contbr. articles to profl. jours. Mem. Internat. Assn. Lighting Designers, Illuminating Engring. Soc. N. Am. Republican. Lutheran. Avocation: stamp collecting. Office: Gary Steffy Lighting Design Inc 3003 Washtenaw Ave Suite 3 Ann Arbor MI 48104

STEGMEYER, CHARLES HARLEY, lawyer; b. Belleville, Ill., Oct. 7, 1941; s. Charles Fred and Mildred Augusta (Schmitz) S.; m. Jo Ann Bloomer, June 20, 1964 (dec. 1978); children—Nicole, Nichelle, Noelle; m. 2d Cynthia Ann Kelso, Mar. 20, 1982. B.A., Washington U., St. Louis, 1963, J.D., 1966. Bar: Ill. 1966. Mem. firm Karns & Starnes, East St. Louis, Ill., 1966-70, Karns, Starnes, Nester & Stegmeyer, 1970-74, Dixon, McDonnell, Starnes, Nester & Stegmeyer, 1974-76, Storment, Stegmeyer & Read, 1976-83; ptnr. Stegmeyer & Stegmeyer, Belleville, Ill., 1983—; chief asst. State's Atty., St. Clair County, Ill., 1966-76, Randolph County, Ill., 1968-72, Perry County, Ill., 1968-72. Mem. ABA, Ill. Bar Assn., Am. Trial Lawyers Assn., St. Clair County Bar Assn., East St. Louis Bar Assn. (pres.), Ill. Trial Lawyers Assn. Clubs: Mo. Athletic, St. Clair Country, Elks. Home: 121 Country Club Pl Belleville IL 62223 Office: 114 E Lincoln St Belleville IL 62220

STEHMAN, FREDERICK BATES, gynecologic oncologist, educator; b. Washington, July 20, 1946; s. Vernon Andrew and Elizabeth Coats (Bates) S.; m. Helen Sellinger, July 17, 1971; children—Christine Renee, Eileen Patricia, Andrea Kathleen, Lara Michelle. A.B., U. Mich., 1968, M.D., 1972. Diplomate Am. Bd. Ob-gyn. Resident in ob-gyn. U. Kans. Med. Ctr., Kansas City, 1972-75, resident in surgery, 1975-77; fellow in gynecol. oncology UCLA, 1977-79; asst. prof., attending staff Ind. U. Med. Ctr., Indpls., 1979-83, assoc. prof., 1983—, chief gynecol. oncology, 1984—. Author: (with B.J. Masterson and R.P. Carter) Gynecologic Oncology for Medical Students, 1975; also articles. Nat. Cancer Inst. grantee, 1981—. Fellow Am. Coll. Obstetricians and Gynecologists, ACS (chpt. dir. 1984—); mem. AMA, Am. Soc. Clin. Oncology, Am. Cancer Soc., Ind. Med. Assn., Assn. Profs. Gynecology and Obstetrics, Central Assn. Obstetricians and Gynecologists, Gynecol. Oncology Group, K.E. Krantz Soc., Marion County Med. Soc., Radiation Therapy Oncology Group, Soc. Gynecol. Oncologists, Western Assn. Gynecol. Oncologists, Phi Chi. Office: Ind U Med Ctr 926 W Michigan St N262 Indianapolis IN 46223

STEIL, GORDON ELWYN, perforated materials manufacturing company executive; b. Garner, Iowa, Feb. 17, 1920; s. Jacob Nicholas and Mabel (Rasmus) S.; m. Nathalie B. Knox, Dec. 5, 1942; children—Mark, Blythe, Linda. B.S. in C.E., Iowa State U., 1942. With Curtis-Wright Aircraft Corp., Buffalo, 1942-44; with Page Engring. Co., McCook, Ill., 1946-72; pres. Harrington & King Perforating Co., Inc., Chgo., 1972—; pres., dir. H&K South, Cleveland, Tenn.; pres., dir. H&K West, San Jose, Calif. Pres., River Forest Park Bd., 1975-78; mem. River Forest Traffic Commn., 1972-75. Served with USNR, 1944-46. Mem. ASME, Am. Mgmt. Assn. Republican. Presbyterian. Clubs: Union League, Big Foot Country. Patentee in field. Office: 5655 W Fillmore St Chicago IL 60644

STEIN, ADLYN ROBINSON (MRS. HERBERT ALFRED STEIN), jewelry company executive; b. Pitts., May 8, 1908; d. Robert Stewart and Pearl (Geiger) Robinson; Mus.B., Pitts. Mus. Inst., U. Pitts., 1928; m. F. J. Hollearn, Nov. 14, 1929 (dec.); children—Adlyn (Mrs. Brandon J. Hickey), Frances (Mrs. Ralph A. Gleim); m. Allen Burnett Williams, Dec. 5, 1955 (dec.); m. Herbert Alfred Stein, Nov. 28, 1963 (dec. Oct. 1980); 1 dau., Rachel Lynn (Mrs. Stephen M. Kampfer). Treas., R. S. Robinson, Inc., Pitts., 1947—. Mem. Tuesday Musical Club, Pitts.; mem. women's com. Cleve. Orch. Mem. DAR. Republican. Anglican. Clubs: Duquesne, University, South Hills Country (Pitts.); Lakewood Country, Clifton (Cleve.). Home: 22200 Lake Rd Cleveland OH 44116 Office: Clark Bldg Pittsburgh PA 15222

STEIN, ARNOLD, retail executive; b. Bronx, N.Y., Mar. 12, 1936; s. Jacob and Jennie (Mark) S.; m. Linda Sheryl DePoy; children—Rhonda Sheryl, Kristyn Marie, Jeremy Jacob. A.S. in Bus. Adminstrn., Vincennes U., 1955; B.B.A., Ind. U., 1957. Mgmt. trainee Sears Roebuck & Co., Massillon, Ohio, 1957-63, asst. store mgr., Newark, Ohio, 1963-65, Mid-Central Zone staff field rep., Dayton, Ohio, 1966-71, store mgr., Tiffin, Ohio, 1971-73, Elkhart, Ind., 1973-76, St. Louis, 1976-84, Fox Valley Store, Chgo., 1984—; pres. Tiffin Shopping Ctr. Assn., 1972, Pierre Moran Shopping Ctr. Assn., Elkhart, 1974-75, Crestwood Plaza Shopping Ctr. Assn., Mo., 1977-82. Bd. dirs. Urban League, Elkhart, 1974, Campfire Inc., St. Louis, 1983-84, United Way, Tiffin, 1973; mem. Heidelberg U. Assocs., Tiffin, 1973. Served with U.S. Army, 1959-60. Recipient Others award Salvation Army, Tiffin, 1973. Mem. Tiffin C. of C., Elkhart C. of C., St. Louis C. of C. Lodges: Masons, Shriners, Order Eastern Star, Royal and Select Masters. Avocations: sailing; racquetball; physical fitness.

STEIN, ELEANOR BANKOFF, judge; b. N.Y.C., Jan. 24, 1923; d. Jacob and Sarah (Rashkin) Bankoff; m. Frank S. Stein, May 27, 1947; children—Robert B., Joan Jenkins, William M. Student, Barnard Coll., 1940-42; B.S. in Econs., Columbia U., 1944; LL.B., NYU, 1949. Bar: N.Y. 1950, Ind. 1976, U.S. Supreme Ct. 1980. Atty. Hillis & Button, Kokomo, Ind., 1975-76, Paul Hillis, Kokomo, 1976-78, Bayliff, Harrigan, Kokomo, 1978-80; judge Howard County Ct., Kokomo, 1980—; co-juvenile referee Howard County Juvenile Ct., 1976-78. Mem. Republicans Women's Assn. Kokomo, 1980—; bd. dirs. Howard County Legal Aid Soc., 1976-80; commn. mem. Kokomo Bd. Human Relations, 1967-70. Mem. law rev. bd. NYU Law Rev., 1947-48. Mem. Am. Judicature Soc., Ind. Jud. Assn., Nat. Assn. Women Judges, ABA, Ind. Bar Assn., Howard County Bar Assn. Jewish. Clubs: Kokomo Country, Altrusa. Home: 3204 Tally Ho Dr Kokomo IN 49602 Office: Howard County Ct Howard County Courthouse Kokomo IN

STEIN, GERTRUDE EMILIE, educator, pianist, soprano; b. Ironton, Ohio; d. S.A. and Emilie M. (Pollach) Stein; Mus.B., Capitol Coll. Oratory and Music, 1927; B.A., Wittenberg Coll., 1929, M.A., 1931, B.S. in Edn., 1945; Ph.D., U. Mich., 1948; piano and voice student Cin. Coll. Conservatory Music; cert. in piano Cin. Coll. Music, 1939. Music supr. Centralized County Schs. Ohio, Williamsburg, 1932-37; dir. jr. high sch. music, 1937-68, elem. music, 1968-71; mem. faculty Adult Evening Sch. Springfield (Ohio) Public Schs., 1951-68; head dept. music, asso. prof. piano and music edn. Tex. Lutheran Coll., Seguin, 1948-49. Donor, founder Rev. Dr. and Mrs. Samuel A. Stein Meml. Funds, 1955—. Mem. AAUW, Am. Symphony Orch. League, NEA, Ohio Edn. Assn., Ohio Assn. Supervision and Curriculum Devel., Council for Exceptional Children, Assn. Tchr. Educators, Ohio Assn. Adult Educators, Associated Council Arts, Met. Opera Guild, Soc. Educators and Scholars, Am. Film Inst., Ohio Music Tchrs. Assn., Nat. Story League, Music Tchrs. Nat. Assn., Music Educators Nat. Conf., Nat. Assn. Schs. Music, Nat. Fedn. Music Clubs (spl. mem. Ohio), Amateur Chamber Music Players, Women's Assn. Springfield Symphony Orch., Springfield Authors Guild, Nat. Fedn. Bus. and Profl. Women, Zonta Internat., Phi Kappa Phi (hon.), Pi Lambda Theta (hon.). Lutheran. Club: Fortnightly Musical (Springfield). Contbr. articles to profl. jours.; research in field. Home: 133 N Lowry Ave Springfield OH 45504

STEIN, JOEL A., lawyer, educator; b. N.Y.C., Nov. 4, 1949; s. Henry J. and Belle Pearl (Weiss) S.; m. Michele A. Grimaldi, July 5, 1981; children—Benjamin Julius, Leah Danielle. B.A. in English, SUNY-Buffalo, 1974; J.D., U. Chgo., 1978. Bar: Ill. 1978, U.S. Dist. Ct. (no. dist.) Ill. 1978, D.C. 1979, Calif. 1980. Asst. state's atty. Cook County, Chgo., 1978-82; assoc. Laser, Schostok, Kolman & Frank, Chgo., 1982—; adj. prof. Chgo.-Kent Law Sch., 1980—.

Chmn. bd. Ashford Homeowners Assn., Westmont, Ill., 1984. Mem. Ill. Bar Assn., Ill. Appellate Lawyers Assn., Chgo. Bar Assn. Office: Laser Schostok Kolman & Frank 189 W Madison St Chicago IL 60602

STEIN, MICHAEL JOHN, health care consultant; b. Chgo., Mar. 26, 1942; s. James R. and Helen E. (Waterhouse) S. B.A. in Math., DePaul U., 1964; M.S. in Mgmt., Northwestern U., 1976. Chief mgmt. research sect. Def. Atomic Support Agy., Albuquerque, 1966-67, dir. edn. and tng. programs, 1967-68; mgr. med. assistance program Cook County, Chgo., 1969-72; dir. med. services program No. Cook County, 1972-73; dir. med. services City of Chgo. Programs, 1973-74; spl. cons. for health care Ill. State Legislature, Markham, Ill., 1974-79, dir. health programs Ill. Legis. Adv. Com., Chgo., 1980; fin. cons. Hyatt Med. Mgmt. Services, Inc., Chgo., 1981-82; sr. cons. Mediflex Systems, Evanston, Ill., 1983—; cons. in mgmt. Recipient disting. service award for uncovering fraud in fed. med. care programs Chgo. Assn. Commerce and Industry, 1977. Mem. Am. Hosp. Assn., Grad. Mgmt. Assn., Am. Coll. Hosp. Adminstrs., Chgo. Health Execs. Forum, Chgo. Zool. Soc., Northwestern U., DePaul U. alumni assns., Chgo. Council Fgn. Relations, Beta Alpha Psi. Club: Century. Home: 3044 W Addison St Chicago IL 60618 Office: 140 S Dearborn St Chicago IL 60603

STEIN, PAUL DAVID, cardiologist; b. Cin., Apr. 13, 1934; s. Simon and Sadie (Friedman) S.; B.S., U. Cin., 1955, M.D., 1959; m. Janet Louise Tucker, Aug. 14, 1966; children—Simon, Douglas, Rebecca. Intern, Jewish Hosp., Cin., 1959-60, med. resident, 1961-62; med. resident Gorgas Hosp., C.Z., 1960-61; fellow in cardiology U. Cin., 1962-63, Mt. Sinai Hosp., N.Y.C., 1963-64; research fellow in medicine Harvard Med. Sch., Boston, 1964-66; asst. dir. cardiac catheterization lab. Baylor U. Med. Center, Dallas, 1966-67; asst. prof. medicine Creighton U., Omaha, 1967-69; asso. prof. medicine U. Okla., Oklahoma City, 1969-73; prof. research medicine U. Okla. Coll. Medicine, Oklahoma City, 1973-76; dir. cardiovascular research Henry Ford Hosp., Detroit, 1976—. Am. Heart Assn. Council on Clin. Cardiology fellow, 1971, Council on Circulation fellow, 1972. Fellow Am. Coll. Cardiology, Am. Coll. Chest Physicians; mem. Am. Physiol. Soc., Central Soc. Clin. Research, ASME. Author: A Physical and Physiological Basis for the Interpretation of Cardiac Auscultation: Evaluations Based Primarily on Second Sound and Ejection Murmurs, 1981; contbr. articles to profl. jours. Office: Henry Ford Hosp 2799 W Grand Blvd Detroit MI 48202

STEINBACH, ALAN HENRY, church official; b. St. Louis, Aug. 5, 1930; s. John Emil and Erna (Gieselmann) S.; m. Ruth A. Wischmeier, June 28, 1953; children—Steven, Carol. B.S., Concordia Coll., 1952; M.A., San Diego State U., 1957; M.Sci. Teaching, U. Ariz., 1964; Ph.D., U. Tex., 1968. Sch. prin., San Diego, 1952-61; prof. chemistry St. John's Coll., Winfield, Kans., 1961-70, acad. dean, 1970-78; v.p., acad. dean Bethany Coll., Lindsborg, Kans., 1979-85; mem. exec. staff Bd. Profl. Edn1. Services, Luth. Ch.-Mo. Synod, 1985—. ednl. cons. Kans. Dist. Lutheran Ch.-Mo. Synod, 1979-85. Mem. Total Community Devel., Winfield, 1970-72; bd. dirs. Kans. Dist., Lutheran Ch.-Mo. Synod, 1973-85; vice chmn. Cowley County chpt. Am. Cancer Soc., 1975-76; chmn. Kans. Corrections Ombudsman Bd., 1976-84. Named Winfield Citizen of Month, Optimist Club, 1978. Mem. Am. Assn. for Higher Edn., Nat. Sci. Tchrs. Assn., Phi Delta Kappa. Lodge: Rotary (Winfield). Contbr. chpts. to books, publs. in field. Home: 518 E Essex Saint Louis MO 63122 Office: Internat Hdqrs Luth Ch-Mo Synod 1333 S Kirkwood Saint Louis MO 63122

STEINDLER, HOWARD ALLEN, lawyer; b. Cleve., June 12, 1942; s. Sidney and Lois Jean (Rosenberg) S.; m. Shirley Weinstein, Oct. 26, 1973; children—Rebecca, Allison, Daniel. B.S., Miami U.-Oxford, Ohio, 1964; J.D., Ohio State U., 1967. Bar: Ohio 1967. Mem. firm Benesch, Friedlander, Coplan & Aronoff, Cleve., 1967—. Office: Benesch Friedlander Coplan & Aronoff 1100 Citizens Bldg Cleveland OH 44114

STEINER, MAURICE EARLE, marketing and retailing educator; b. Meigs County, Ohio, Jan. 18, 1920; s. Emory Earl and Lola Marie (Eblin) S.; m. Irene Gloria Hamilton, May 9, 1953; children—Earle Hamilton, Kay Marie. B.S. in Commerce, Ohio U., 1948; M.B.A., Harvard U., 1950. Buyer, Higbee Co., Cleve., 1950-53; store mgr. Bonwit Teller, Inc., Cleve., 1953-59; div. mdse. mgr. Carlisle-Allen Co., Ashtabula, Ohio, 1959-78; assoc. prof. mktg. and retailing Ferris State Coll., Big Rapids, Mich., 1978—. Served with USAAF, 1942-45. Mem. Am. Mktg. Assn., Delta Sigma Pi. Republican. Methodist. Lodges: Masons, Shriners. Home: 1796 Westview Dr NE Warren OH 44483 Office: Ferris State Coll Big Rapids MI 49307 also 319 N Warren Ave Big Rapids MI 49307

STEINERT, ROCKY BRENT, counseling therapist; b. Miles City, Mont., June 11, 1951; s. Irvin Earl and Barbara Fae (Archer) S.; m. Marilyn Joyce Backman, June 15, 1974; children—Brent, Jeremy, Angela, Melissa. B.A., N.W. Bible Coll., 1973; M.S., No. State Coll., Aberdeen, S.D., 1978. Tchr., adminstr. Internat. Bible Coll., Moose Jaw, Sask., Can., 1973-77; counselor Presentation Coll., Aberdeen, S.D., 1978-84; counseling therapist, Aberdeen, 1980—; dir. Profl. Counseling Services, Aberdeen, 1984—. Mem. Am. Assn. Counseling and Devel., Am. Coll. Personnel Assn., Am. Mental Health Counselors Assn., Assn. for Religious and Value Issues in Counseling. Republican. Mem. Ch. of God. Club: Missions (Minot, N.D.) (pres. 1971-73). Avocations: tennis, guitar playing, coin/stamp collecting. Home: 423 N Lincoln St Aberdeen SD 57401 Office: Profl Counseling Services 422 5th Ave SE Aberdeen SD 57401

STEINIGER, (IRENE) MIRIAM LARMI, child development specialist; b. Weirton, W.Va., Dec. 20, 1916; d. (Kustaa) Edward and Aune Ellen (Raitanen) Larmi; B.S. in Edn., Ohio State U., 1936; M.A., Miami U., Oxford, Ohio, 1964; Ed.D., U. Cin., 1975; m. Erich W. Steiniger, June 6, 1941; children—Erika, Fredrik, Anthony, Karsten, Theron. Tchr., Ohio Sch. for Deaf, Columbus, 1937-41, 44-46; tchr. English and lit. Mason (Ohio) High Sch., 1955-56; tchr. elementary schs., Hamilton, Ohio, 1956-59, tchr. of deaf, Hamilton Pub. Schs., 1959-63, speech and hearing therapist, 1963-70; tchr.-cons. for neurologically handicapped, Hamilton, 1970-72; cooperating tchr. Tchr. Tng. Program, Miami U., Hamilton, 1970-72; vis. asst. prof., adj. vis. prof. U. Cin., 1972-75, asst. prof., 1975-79; asst. dir. presch. programs Cin. Center for Devel. Disorders, 1975-79; dir. Children's Diagnostic Center, Inc., Butler County, Ohio, 1979-83; ret., 1983; early childhood diagnostic cons., 1983—; teaching cons. Perceptual Motor Workshops, Miami U., 1970, 71; dir., planner tchr. tng. projects and workshops Hamilton City Schs., 1965, 68, 69, 71. Vice pres. Talawanda Bd. Edn., Oxford, Ohio, 1968-72; pres., chmn. coms. LWV, Oxford; ednl. com. Butler County Mental Hygiene Assn.; leader Girl Scouts U.S.A., Dan Beard council Boy Scouts Am.; chmn. Early Childhood Edn. Task Force, SW Ohio Early Childhood Coalition Task Force on Certification; Sunday sch. tchr. Lutheran Ch.; mem. CORVA. Recipient ann. action award Action for Handicapped, 1983; ACT award ACTion for Handicapped, Inc., 1983; Martha Holden Jennings Found. grantee, 1968; grantee Ohio Dept. MR/DD and Ohio DD Planning Council, 1981-83. Mem. Butler County (pres. 1969, legis. chmn. 1964—, dir. 1964—), Ohio, Nat. councils exceptional children, Am. (cert.), Cin., Ohio, Nat. speech and hearing assns., Tri-County (certificate of appreciation 1974), Ohio, Nat. assns. for children with learning disabilities, Nat., Ohio, Cin. assns. for edn. of young children, Butler County Assn. Edn. Young Children, Day Care and Child Devel. Council Am., Inter-Univ. Council for Exceptional Children, AAUP, Delta Kappa Gamma. Democrat. Contbr. to Piagetian research book. Home: 208 Beechpoint Dr Oxford OH 45056

STEINLE, LEONARD GEORGE, educational administrator; b. Russell, Kans., July 17, 1932; s. George and Martha Elizabeth (Galyardt) S.; m. Nancy Ann Ruehlen, June 12, 1955; children—Lenette, Kirk, Brad, Melanie. B.M.E., Bethany Coll., 1954; M.M.E., Vandercook Coll. Music, 1959; M.S., Pittsburg State U., Kans., 1965; Ed.D., U. Kans., 1974. Tchr., prin. schs. Kans., 1954-68; supt. schs. Baldwin City Unified Sch. Dist., Kans., 1968-72; grad. teaching asst. U. Kans., Lawrence, 1972-74; supt. schs. Independence Unified Sch. Dist., Kans., 1974-82; tchr. Independence Community Coll., 1982, dean fin. affairs, 1983-85; supt. schs. Arkansas City Unified Sch. Dist., Kans., 1985—; chmn. North Central Evaluation Teams, Arma and Altamont, Kans., 1977, 79; bd. dirs. Kans. Assn. Sch. Adminstrs., Topeka, 1978-82. Author booklet: Selecting a Supt., 1980. Bd. dirs. Blue Cross, Topeka, 1981-83. Mem. Independence C. of C. (pres. 1982), Am. Assn. Sch. Adminstrs., Kans. Assn. Community Coll. Bus. Ofcls., Phi Delta Kappa. Republican. Methodist. Lodges: Rotary (pres. 1981), Lions (pres. 1978). Avocations: music; sports events; gardening. Home: 1109 N B St Arkansas City KS 67005 Office: Arkansas City Unified Sch Dist 119 W Washington Arkansas City KS 67005

STEINMETZ, DONALD WALTER, state supreme court justice; b. Milw., Sept. 19, 1924; B.A., U. Wis., 1949, J.D., 1951. Admitted to Wis. bar, 1951; individual practice law, Milw., 1951-58; asst. city atty. Milw., 1958-60; 1st asst. dist. atty. Milwaukee County, 1960-65; spl. asst. atty. gen. Wis., 1965-66; judge Milwaukee County Ct., 1966-80; assoc. justice Wis. Supreme Ct., 1980—; chmn. Wis. Bd. County Judges; sec.-treas. Wis. Bd. Criminal Ct. Judges; mem. State Adminstrv. Commn. Cts., Chief Judge Study Com., Fin. Reporting Com., Study Com. TV and Radio Coverage in Courtroom. Pres., South div. High Sch. Old Timers. Mem. ABA, Wis. Bar Assn., Milw. Bar Assn., Am. Judicature Soc. Clubs: Milw. W, Nat. W. Office: Supreme Ct Wis State Capitol Madison WI 53702

STEINMETZ, RICHARD, geologist, petroleum company executive; b. Cuxhaven, Germany, Aug. 3, 1932; s. Carl Steinmetz and Florence (Beaver) Faust; m. Janet Elaine Berkshire, Aug. 21, 1954; children—Charles, Carolyn, Christopher. B.A. with honors, Princeton U., 1954; M.S., Pa. State U., Pa., 1957; Ph.D., Northwestern U., 1962. Asst. prof. geology Tex. Christian U., Ft. Worth, 1967-71; staff research scientist Amoco Research Ctr, Tulsa, 1971-77; sr. staff geologist Amoco Prodn. Co., Denver, 1977-80, regional cons. geologist, New Orleans, 1980-83, regional geologist, 1983-84, asst. mgr. geology, Chgo., 1984—. Contbr. articles to profl. jours. Mem. AAAS, Am. Assn. Petroleum Geologists (editor 1983-85), Soc. Econ. Paleontologists and Mineralogists. Republican. Presbyterian. Clubs: Princeton (Chgo.) (Tulsa) (pres. 1975-76). Avocations: hiking; skiing; travel. Home: 260 E Chestnut St Chicago IL 60611 Office: Amoco Prodn Co Code 4701 PO Box 5340-A Chicago IL 60680

STEINMETZ, ROBERT FRANCIS, lawyer; b. Cleve., Oct. 12, 1950; s. William C. and Winifred A. (Jones) S.; m. Barbara Nan Dean, Aug. 4, 1979; children—Timothy Robert, Nan Elizabeth. B.A., Bowling Green U., 1972; postgrad. Cleve. State U., 1973; J.D., Ohio State U., 1976. Bar: Ohio, U.S. Dist. Ct. (no. dist.) Ohio. Router, Ford Motor Co., Brook Park, Ohio, 1972-73; sole practice law, Fairview Park, Ohio, 1976—; guardian ad litem Cuyahoga County Juvenile Ct., Cleve., 1980—, Cuyahoga County Domestic Relations Ct., Cleve., 1984—; mem. Legal Aid Soc. Vol. Services, Cleve., 1977—. Water safety instr. ARC, YMCA and YWCA, Cleve., 1981—; lector St. Patrick's West Park Roman Catholic Ch., Cleve., 1983—; mem. St. Patrick's Liturgical Planning Commn., Cleve., 1983-84. Recipient Recognition for Services-Guardian ad Litem Project and Legal Aid Soc., Cuyahoga County Commrs. Mem. West Shore Writers. Avocations: sailing, alpine and Nordic skiing, water skiing, writing. Home: Cleveland OH Office: Robert F Steinmetz & Assoc 19443 Lorain Rd Fairview Park OH 44126

STEINMEYER, NANCY LEE, artist; b. Carlinville, Ill., Feb. 12, 1956; d. Elwood E. and Nancy L. (Schmitt) S. Student Western Ill. U., 1974-78; grad. Rockland Ctr. for Internat. Studies, Colchesterm Eng., 1984. Art lectr. So. Ill. high schs., 1974-82; mem. faculty Western Ill. U. Coll. Fine Arts, Macomb, 1978; co-founder, coordinating artist Ann. Art Affair, Raymond, Ill., 1979; vis. artist Rembrandt Soc., 1982. One man shows include Kean-Mason Gallery, N.Y.C., 1982, Springboard Gallery, Springfield, Ill., 1982; exhibited in group shows at Joy Horwich Gallery, Chgo., 1981, Sioux City Art Ctr., Iowa, 1983, Winner's Circle Gallery, Van Nuys, Calif., 1983, Internat. Art Competition, Los Angeles, 1984, Evanston Art Ctr., Ill., 1985; illustrator book: The Old Town, 1977. Western Ill. U. grantee, 1974-78. Mem. Internat. Fine Arts Guild, Chgo. Artist Coalition, Women's Caucus for Art. Home and Studio: 7729 N Ashland Ave Chicago IL 60626

STEINREICH, OTTO SELICK, surgeon; b. N.Y.C., Mar. 13, 1914; s. George and Ida (Mayer) S.; A.B., U. N.C., 1934; M.D., Med. Coll. Va., 1938; m. Helen Natalie Bane, June 19, 1938; children—Michael Martin, Steven Carl. Intern, Newark City Hosp., 1939-41; resident surgery St. Thomas Hosp., Akron, Ohio, 1946-48; practice medicine specializing in surgery, Akron, 1948—; med. staff St. Thomas Hosp., dir. med. edn., chmn. div. surgery; mem. staff Akron Gen. Hosp., Akron City Hosp., Akron Children's Hosp. Bd. dirs. Jewish Welfare Fund, Jewish Family Service, Akron Jewish Center; trustee Summit Portage Area Health Edn. Network, Region Six Peer Rev. Orgn. Served to capt. M.C. AUS, 1941-46. Diplomate Am. Bd. Surgery. Fellow A.C.S., Internat. Coll. Surgeons; mem. AMA, Council of Deans (assoc. dean clin. scis.), Northeastern Ohio Univs. Coll. Medicine, Summit County Med. Soc. (bd. dirs. Ind. Med. Plan), Zeta Beta Tau, Phi Lambda Kappa. Jewish (pres. congregation). Contbr. articles to profl. jours. Home: 433 Delaware Ave Akron OH 44303 Office: 475 N Howard St Akron OH 44310

STELLER, ARTHUR WAYNE, ednl. adminstr.; b. Columbus, Ohio, Apr. 12, 1947; s. Fredrick and Bonnie Jean (Clark) S.; B.S., Ohio U., 1969, M.A., 1970, Ph.D., 1973. Tchr., Athens (Ohio) City Schs., 1969-71; curriculum coordinator, tchr. Belpre (Ohio) City Schs., 1971-72; prin. elem. schs., head tchr. learning disabilities South-Western City Schs., Grove City, Ohio, 1972-76; dir. elem. edn. Beverly (Mass.) Pub. Schs., 1976-78; adj. prof. Lesley Coll., Cambridge, Mass., 1976-78; coordinator spl. projects and systemwide planning Montgomery County Pub. Schs., Rockville, Md., 1978-80; asst. supt. elem. edn. Shaker Heights (Ohio), 1980—. Charles Kettering Found., IDEA fellow, 1976, 78, 80; Nat. Endowment Humanities fellow; 1977. Mem. Am. Assn. Sch. Adminstrs., Nat. Assn. Elem. Sch. Prins., Nat. Assn. Edn. Young Children, Nat. Sch. Pub. Relations Assn., Assn. Supervision and Curriculum Devel., Internat. Soc. Ednl. Planning, Nat. Soc. Study Edn., Nat. Planning Assn., Council Basic Edn., Ohio Assn. Elem. Sch. Adminstrs., Buckeye Assn. Sch. Adminstrs., Ohio Assn. Supervision and Curriculum Devel., Ohio U. Alumni Assn. (nat. dir. 1975-78, pres. Central Ohio chpt. 1975-76, pres. Mass. chpt. 1976-78, life mem. trustee's acad.), World Future Soc., Tau Kappa Epsilon Alumni Assn. (regional officer Mass. 1976-78), Kappa Delta Pi (life), Phi Delta Kappa (life). Methodist. Contbr. articles to profl. jours.; author: Educational Planning for Educational Success; editor: Effective Instructional Management. Office: 15600 Parkland Dr Shaker Heights OH 44120

STELLER, DEBORAH ANN, educational administrator; b. Cleve., Nov. 21, 1947; d. Milton John and Sarah (Valek) Hasselo; m. Arthur Wayne Steller, Aug. 14, 1981. B.S., Fla. State U., 1970; M.Ed., Miss. State U., 1973, Ed.D., 1979. Grad. asst. instl. research, Miss. State U., 1973-74; elem. sch. tchr./team leader Tampa (Fla.) Pub. Schs., 1970-76, curriculum specialist II, 1976, curriculum intervention specialist, 1976-79, elem. curriculum supr., 1979-81; prin. Nordonia Hills City Sch. Dist., Northfield, Ohio, 1981—; cons. U. South Fla. Center for Econ. Edn., 1978. Active Friends of Shaker Hts. Pub. Library, Lomond Community Assn. Selected for Proctor and Gamble Leadership Inst. Consumer Edn., 1979; Freedoms Found. scholar, 1982. Mem. Shaker Hts. Hist. Soc., LWV, Cleve. Chi Omega Alumnae Assn., Miss. State Alumnae Assn., Fla. State Alumni Assn., Ohio Alliance for Arts in Edn., Assn. for Supervision and Curriculum Devel., Am. Assn. Sch. Adminstrs., Nat. Assn. Elem. Prins., Phi Delta Kappa. Democrat. Mem. Ch. of Christ. Club: Nordonia Boosters. Home: 17929 Sherrington St Shaker Heights OH 44122 Office: 9130 Shepard Rd Macedonia OH 44056

STELLERS, THOMAS JOE, educational administrator; b. Dover, Ohio, May 22, 1940; s. Joseph A. and Jane Elizabeth (Stieber) S.; m. Carol Jean Crichton, Aug. 28, 1971. B.S. in Edn., Bowling Green State U., 1962; postgrad. U. Pitts., 1963-64, So. Ill. U., 1965; M.Ed., Kent State U., 1968, Ph.D., 1973. Cert. tchr., high sch. prin., supt., Ohio. Biology tchr., yearbook advisor Austintown-Fitch High Sch., Austintown, Ohio, 1962-71, 72-74; univ. fellow Kent (Ohio) State U., 1971-72; supr. middle schs., supr. sci., Mahoning County Schs., Youngstown, Ohio, 1974-76, dir. adminstrv. services and mgr. data processing, 1976—; instr. yearbook workshops Kent State U., 1968-71, Northwood Inst. and Delta Coll., Mich., 1971-72; chmn. beginning computer awareness Ohio Statewide Ednl. Computer Fair, 1982, 84; mem. software adv. com. Ohio Dept. Edn. Edn. chmn. Am. Cancer Soc., 1977, United Way, 1979, 80; cooordinator Mahoning County Health Promotion Program. Recipient No. One award Ohio's Project Leadership. Mem. Ohio Ednl. Data Systems Assn. (pres.), Ohio Ednl. Computer Mgmt. Council (bd.), Ohio Com. for Ednl. Info. Systems, Nat. Sci. Tchrs. Assn. (task force for establishing clearinghouse for research evaluation instruments), Ohio Ednl. Assessment Program (panel mem.), Buckeye Assn. Sch. Adminstrs., Phi Delta Kappa, Sigma Phi Epsilon. Mem. Christian Ch. (Disciples of Christ). Home: 2405 Vollmer Dr Youngstown OH 44511 Office: 2801 Market St Youngstown OH 44507

STELLOS, MARIE HELEN, educational adminstrator; b. Highland Park, Mich., July 15, 1925; d. Demosthenes A. and Marie C. (klotz) Stylianopoulos; 1 son, Jamie A. B.S. in Chemistry, Wayne State U.; J.D., U. Detroit; M.Ed., Ph.D., St. Louis U.; postgrad. U. Mich., U. Detroit, U. St. Louis, U. Mo. Bank teller, Detroit; compensation claims supr. Am. Assn. Ins. Cos., Detroit; staff research engring. div. Chrysler Engine Div., Highland, Mich.; friend of court Wayne County (Mich.) Circuit Ct., Detroit; claims supr. Mass. Bonding and Ins. Co., St. Louis; tchr. St. Louis pub. schs.; adminstrv. asst. Sumner High Sch., St. Louis, also asst. dir. magnet schs. program; now asst. prin. Cleveland High Sch., St. Louis. Active Opera Theatre St. Louis, St. Louis Symphony Soc., Friends of Art Mus., Nat. Council Negro Women (recipient numerous awards), NAACP, Urban League, Am. Bus. Women's Clubs. Recipient Appreciation award Cleveland High Sch. Mem. Sigma Gamma Rho, Phi Delta Kappa. Contbr. articles to profl. jours. Home: 3441 Shendandoah St Saint Louis MO 63104 Office: Cleveland High School 4352 Louisiana St Saint Louis MO 63111

STELMACH, WALTER JACK, physician, medical education administrator; b. Kansas City, Kans., Mar. 7, 1926; s. Jacob and Stella (Wanchuk) S.; m. Patricia Ann Scherrer, June 19, 1948; children—Christopher Stephen, Cheryl Anne, Jeffrey David. B.A., U. Mo.-Kansas City, 1949; M.D., Kans. U.-Kansas City, 1953. Diplomate Am. Bd. Family Practice (bd. dirs. 1980—, exec. com. 1980-82, pres. 1983). Intern, St. Mary's Hosp. and Children's Mercy Hosp., Kansas City, Mo., 1953-54; practice family medicine, Kansas City, Mo., 1954-74; clin. prof. medicine, Sch. Medicine U. Mo., Kansas City, 1974—, asst. dean, chmn. council on evaluation, 1974-75, chmn. dept. community and family medicine Truman Med. Ctr., 1977-80; chmn. sect. gen. practice Baptist Meml. Hosp., 1969-71, pres. med. staff, 1967-68, dir. Family Practice Residency Program, 1974—, chmn. Residency Assistance Program Project Bd., 1975-80; preceptor Sch. Medicine, U. Mo., Columbia; chmn. sect. family practice Research Hosp., 1969-71; participant Ditchley Park Conf. on Devel. of Health Services and Med Care, Brit., Can., U.S., 1972; mem. Grad. Med. Edn. Nat. Adv. Com., 1976-80, chmn., 1976-78; bd. dirs. Council of Med. Specialty Socs., 1979-81, pres., 1980-81; chmn. Council for Med. Affairs, 1981. Pres. Family Health Found. Am., 1980—; trustee U. Mo., Kansas City, 1981. Served with USN, 1943-46. Recipient John G. Walsh award, 1981, Max Cheplove award, 1981, Alumni award, U. Mo., Kansas City, 1981. Charter fellow Am. Acad. Family Physicians (del. 1969-74, mem. commn. on edn. 1971-76, chmn. 1974-75, 75-76, dir. 1974-77, chmn. bd. dirs. 1976-77, pres. 1978-79); mem. AMA, Mo. State Med. Assn. (del. 1964-73), Mo. Acad. Family Physicians (bd. dirs. 1966-69, pres. 1973-74), Kansas City Acad. Family Physicians (pres. 1965-66), Jackson County Med. Soc. (sec. 1960-61), Southwest Clin. Soc. (sec. 1967-68, bd. dirs. 1967-69, assoc. dir. clinics 1972-73, dir. clinics 1975), Kansas City Acad. Medicine, Kans. U. Med. Alumni (1st v.p. 1972-73), Alpha Omega Alpha. Mem. Unity Ch. Contbr. articles to med. jours., presentations to profl. confs. Home: 5252 Sunset Dr Kansas City MO 64112 Office: 6601 Rockhill Rd Kansas City MO 64131

STENE, DENNIS CARTER, podiatrist; b. Elgin, Ill., Aug. 1, 1944; s. Arvin and Erna Wanda (Loechelt) S.; D.P.M., Ill. Coll. Podiatric Medicine, 1967; m. Carol Jean Gray, May 25, 1974. Pvt. practice podiatry, Bensenville, Ill., 1967-69, Rockford, Ill., 1969-70, Elgin, Ill., 1969—. Active Norwegian Lutheran Bethesda Home Assn. Mem. Am. Podiatry Assn., Ill. Podiatry Soc., Alumni Assn. Ill. Coll. Podiatric Medicine. Republican. Lutheran. Clubs: Masons (worshipful master 1973), Shriners, Scottish Rite, York Rite. Home: 1785 Joseph Ct Elgin IL 60120 Office: 100 E Chicago St Elgin IL 60120

STENERSON, DOUGLAS C., educator; b. Barron, Wis., Aug. 29, 1920; s. Christopher P. and Maxine Miliam Ureal (Dalton) S.; m. Marjorie Barrows, Jan. 11, 1957. A.B. magna cum laude, Harvard U., 1942, I.A., 1943; M.A., U. Minn., 1947, Ph.D., 1961. Asst. prof. English, U. Miami, Coral Gables, Fla., 1955-57; asst. prof. English, Macalester Coll., St. Paul, 1958-59; asst. prof. English, Winona State (Minn.) Coll., 1959-63, assoc. prof., 1963-67, dept. head, 1966-67; assoc. prof. Roosevelt U., Chgo., 1967-68, prof. English, Am. studies, grad. adviser, 1968-84, prof. emeritus, 1984—; cons. North Central Assn. for Colls. and Secondary Schs., 1970—; cons. NEH, 1972-74. Served with U.S. Army, 1943-46. So. Fellowships grantee, 1957-58; Fulbright vis. prof., Finland, 1965-66; recipient McKnight Found. humanities award, 1961; Ill. Humanities Council grantee, 1982. Mem. Am. Studies Assn., MLA, AAUP. Democrat. Author: H.L. Mencken: Iconoclast from Baltimore, 1971; contbr. chpts. to books and articles to profl. jours.

STENNER, JOHN MARTIN, health care administrator; b. N.Y.C., Jan. 31, 1939 s. John and Kathrine (Conley) S.; m. Sheila J. VanWart, May 15, 1965; children—Andrea, Douglas, Brett. B.B.A. summa cum laude, Govs. State U., Park Forest, Ill., 1981; M. Health Services Adminstrn., Webster U., St. Louis, 1984. Enlisted U.S. Navy, 1956 advanced through grades to command master chief; fin. mgmt. asst. Hdqrs. Naval Dental Clinic, Norfolk, Va., 1968-70; head med. materials mgmt. Marine Corps Air Sta., Iwakuni, Japan, 1970-71; adminstrv. asst. Marine Corp Base Twentynine Palms, Calif., 1971-76; head, operating mgmt. asst. Hdqrs. Naval Regional Dental Ctr., San Diego, 1977-78; head mgmt. info. systems Naval Regional Dental Ctr., Great Lakes, Ill., 1978—. Mem. mil. adv. com. USO of Chgo., 1978—; chmn. mem. fin. com. Citizens Adv. Com., Dist. 123, North Chgo. Community High Sch., 1979-84. Mem. Am. Coll. Hosp. Adminstrs. (student), Am. Hosp. Assn., No. Ill. Health Adminstrs. Forum.

STENZEL, PAULETTE LYNN, business law educator, lawyer; b. Ypsilanti, Mich., July 9, 1951; d. Paul and Juanita Ilene (Harrison) S.; m. John C. Scherbarth, Aug. 26, 1978. B.A., Albion Coll., 1972; J.D., Wayne State U., 1979. Bar: Mich. 1979. Tchr. French and Spanish, Albion Schs., Mich., 1972-74. Gaylord Schs., Mich., 1974-76; staff atty. S.E. Mich. Legal Services, Adrian and Jackson, 1979-81; sole practice, Southfield, Mich., 1981-82; asst. prof. bus. law Mich. State U., East Lansing, 1982—. Mem. Mich. Bar Assn., Women Lawyers Assn. Mich., Am. Bus. Law Assn., Mid-West Bus. Law Assn., Inghan County Bar Assn., Mich. Scholars in Coll. Teaching, Mortar Bd., Phi Beta Kappa. Office: Mich State U 116 Olds Hall East Lansing MI 48824

STEPHAN, ROBERT T., attorney general of Kansas; b. Wichita, Kans., 1933; B.A., J.D., Washburn U.; married; 1 son, 3 daus. Bar: Kans. 1957. Judge Wichita Mcpl. Ct., 1963-65; judge Sedgwick County Dist. Ct., 1965-78; atty. gen. State of Kans., 1979—. Bd. dirs. state and county Am. Cancer Soc., hon. crusade chmn. state div., 1979-81; mem. adv. bd. Big Bros.-Big Sisters, Cath. Social Services; trustee Kans. chpt. Am. Leukemia Soc.; bd. dirs. Parents Against Leukemia and Malignancies Soc., Accent on Kids, Kans. Day Club; hon. state chmn. Lions Club Journey for Sight, 1985; chmn. Kans. Spl. Olympics Corp. Giving Club, hon. chmn. bd. dirs. Topeka Athletic League. Named Kans. Trial Judge of Year, Kans. Trial Lawyers Assn., 1977. Mem. Am. Judges Assn., Am. Judicature Soc., ABA, Kans. Bar Assn., Nat. Assn. Attys. Gen. (exec. com., chmn. Midwest region, pres.-elect nat. assn.), Kans. Dist. Judges Assn. (pres. 1977-78), Kans. Jud. Conf. (chmn. 1977). Republican. Club: Wagonmasters. Lodges: Elks, Moose, Scottish Rite. Office: Office of Atty Gen Judicial Center Topeka KS 66612*

STEPHANS, DANIEL JAMES, architect; b. LaCrosse, Wis., Apr. 23, 1948; s. Charles Jack and Beuhla Mae (Naas) S.; m. Lori Lynn Steffen, May 25, 1968; 1 child; m. Audrey Ann Cecka, Nov. 12, 1976. B.Arch., Iowa State U., 1971. Lic. architect, Wis., Minn., Ind., Wyo., Iowa, Kans., S.C., Mont., N.D.; cert., Nat. Council Architects Registration Bd. Architect trainee Larson & Darby, Architects, Rockford, Ill., 1971-72; architect, constrn. mgr. Larson & Tetzlaff, Architects, Rockford, Ill., 1972-76; architect, job capt. archtl. dept. Am. Med. Bldg., Milw., 1976; architect Studio Three Enterprises Inc., Tomah, Wis., 1976-79; pvt. practice architecture D.J. Stephans, Warrens, Wis., 1976—; constrn. mgr. RDS Inc., Madison, Wis., 1979; assoc. Sieger Architects, Madison, 1984. Past pres. Village of Warrens; sponsor Girl Scouts Am. troops. Recipient Merit award Wis. Dept. Natural Resources archtl. design competition, 1983; Concrete Design award Wis. Ready-mix Concrete Assn., 1984. Mem. AIA, Wis. Soc. Architects, Nat. Rifle Assn., Wis. Rifle and Pistol Assn., Internat. Shooter Devel. Fund, Nat. Fedn. Ind. Bus., Internat. Platform Assn. Club; 3d Wheel Inc. Developer numerous projects in field. Home and Office: 3560 Breckinridge Ct Apt 6 Madison WI 53713

STEPHENS, ALAN CHILDS, lawyer; b. Soda Springs, Idaho, July 1, 1951; s. Ellwood Jay and Gertrude (Childs) S.; m. Glenn Ann Jernigan, Aug. 21, 1973; children—Casey, Christopher Alan, Craig Matthew, Cathryn, Andrew Jay. B.A., Brigham Young U., 1975; J.D., U. Idaho, 1978. Bar: Idaho 1978, U.S. Dist. Ct. Idaho 1978. Ptnr. Moorer, Stephens & Westberg, Moscow, 1978-80; lectr. bus. law Washington State U., Pullman, 1979-80; assoc. St. Clair, Hiller, Wood & McGrath, Idaho Falls, Idaho, 1980-84; jr. ptnr. St. Clair, Hiller, Wood, McGrath, St. Clair & Baker, 1984—. Scout leader Boy Scouts Am., Moscow, Idaho, 1977, 81; knot-hole baseball coach, Idaho Falls, Idaho,

1982-84. Recipient Coll. Law Found. scholarship U. Idaho, 1976, George Warren scholarship, 1977. Mem. Idaho State Bar Assn., ABA, Assn. Trial Lawyers Am., Idaho Trial Lawyers Assn. Republican. Mormon.

STEPHENS, CAROLYN KING, sales manager; b. Milw., Mar. 5, 1940; d. David B. and Winifred H. (Hamel) King; m. John A. Stephens, June 24, 1961; children—Allison K., John W., Matthew D., Stephanie C. B.A. in English and Drama cum laude, Milw.-Downer Coll., 1962; postgrad. in English, U. Wis.-Milw., 1968, M.B.A., 1980. Mem. faculty Milw. Area Tech. Coll., 1970-72; fundraising coordinator Nat. Congl. Campaign Salaried Staff, 1974; dir. community relations Cardinal Stritch Coll., 1975-80; gen. mgr. Milw. Ballet, after 1981-84; now corporate sales and mktg. mgr. Personnel Pool, Milw. Trustee Lawrence U.; elder United Presbyn. Ch. Office: 828 N Broadway Milwaukee WI 53202

STEPHENS, CHARLES GUSTON DURBROW, physician, farmer; b. Mountainburg, Ark., July 27, 1913; s. Clive and Ida May (Renfroe) Durbrow; m. Jennie Madeline Costello, June 21, 1936; children—Joan Shirley, Diann Elizabeth, Thomas Michael; m. 2d, Millie Cjeka, Apr. 6, 1968. D.O., Univ. Health Scis., 1938; apprentice in gen. surgery Lakeside Hosp., 1943-48; resident in clin. surgery Allgemines Krankenhaus, Linz, Austria, 1954; resident in basic sic. and lab. surgery, Coll. Osteo. Physician and Surgeons, 1950; gen. chmn. Nat. Child Health Conf. and Clinic, 1941-42; gen. practice osteo. medicine, Kansas City, Mo., 1937—; chief surg. staff Cass County Meml. Hosp., Harrisonville, Mo., 1983. Pres. bd. Paseo Methodist. Ch., 1953. Mem. Nat. Wildlife Fedn., Nat. Geog. Soc., Ducks Unlimited, Mo. Prairie Found., Am. Mus. Natural History, Mo. Audubon Soc., Nat. Audubon Soc., Greater Kansas City Dahlia Soc., Am. Osteo. Assn., Mo. Osteo. Assn., Jackson County Osteo. Assn. (pres. 1943), Coll. Osteo. Surgeons (life mem.), Alumni Found. of Kansas City Coll. Osteopathy (pres. 1942). Democrat. Lodges: Lions (charter mem. Alpha Kansas City, Mo.), Westport Masons, Shriners. Home: RR 1 Clear Creek Farm Cleveland MO 64734 Office: 400 E Red Bridge Rd Kansas City MO 64131

STEPHENS, GERALD D., insurance company executive; b. Peoria, Ill., June 17, 1932; m. Helen Marie Davis. B.B.A., with honors in Ins., U. Wis., 1955. Vice pres. H.O. Stephens & Sons, Inc., Peoria, 1958-65; pres., dir. RLI Ins. Co., Peoria, 1965—; dir. numerous businesses and ins. agys. Dir. adv. bd. St. Francis Hosp., 1983—. Served as 2d lt. U.S. Army, 1955-58. Mem. Peoria Jr. C. of C. (past dir.), Peoria C. of C., Soc. C.P.C.U. (nat. dir., regional v.p., past pres. Central Ill. chpt.), Beta Theta Pi. Clubs: Creve Coeur (Ill.); Country of Peoria. Home: 9127 N Frye Rd Peoria IL 61615 Office: 9025 N Lindbergh Dr Peoria IL 61615

STEPHENS, JEWELLEAN DANDY, nurse; b. Birmingham, Ala., June 30, 1940; d. Jesse and Mae (Stevenson) Dandy; m. William Clark, Apr. 11, 1964; 1 child, William Christopher. R.N., Grady Meml. Sch. Nursing, Atlanta, 1960; student Columbia Union Coll., Ohio, 1983—. Cert. nurse adminstr. Staff nurse VA Hosp., Birmingham, Ala., 1962-64; head nurse VA Med. Ctr., Dayton, 1966-71, nursing supr., 1974—; motivational speaker. Leader, Boy scouts Am., 1982—. Served to maj. USAR, 1974—. Recipient Spl. Achievement medal USAR, 1984. Mem. Nat. Assn. Female Execs., Am. Nurses Assn. (scholar 1984), Res. Officers Assn., Am. Mil. Surgeons U.S., Nurses Orgn. VA (recruiter). Roman Catholic. Club: Toastmistress (Dayton). Avocations: reading; sewing; aerobics; film. Home: 1029 Newpark Dr Englewood OH 45322

STEPHENS, LARRY RALPH, history educator, publisher; b. Council Bluffs, Iowa, Nov. 10, 1940; s. Ralph L. and Agnes Leona (Fitzsimmons) S.; m. Betty Jean Tally, Aug. 29, 1965; children—Tally Jill, Libby Gail, Tyler Lane. B.A. in Ministry, Nebr. Christian Coll., Norfolk, 1964, B.Theology, 1964; M.A. in History, Fort Hays Kans. State Coll., 1968. Instr. history Northeast Mo. State U., Kirksville, 1968-73, asst. prof., 1974—; pub. Lancaster Excelsior Newspapers, Mo., 1980—. Author: Long Branch Lake Historical Resources: A History, 1975. Bd. dirs. preservation com. Friends of St. Mary's, Kirksville, 1977—; campaign mgr. county clerk candidate and sheriff candidate; bd. dirs. Mo. Com. Humanities, NEH, 1984—. Mem. Am. Hist. Assn., Am. Assn. State and Local History, Campus Vols. of Kirksville. Democrat. Mem. Christian Ch. (Disciples of Christ). Lodge: Masons. Avocations: acting, gardening, raising Bantam chickens, square dancing. Home: Route 2 Box 304A Kirksville MO 63501 Office: Social Sci Dept Northeast Mo State U Kirksville MO 63501

STEPHENS, PATRICK JOHN, university administrator; b. Baldwin, Wis., Sept. 16, 1948; s. Michael Joseph and Mary E. (Walsh) S.; m. Joanne Marie Meuler, Aug. 8, 1970; children—Kelley, Shannan, Sean, Casey. B.S., U. Wis.-LaCrosse, 1971. Tchr. Kiel Pub. Schs., Wis., 1970-71; salesman Fidelity Union Ins. Co., LaCrosse, 1971-79; deferred-giving officer U. Wis.-LaCrosse Found., 1979-84; dir. devel. U. Wis.-LaCrosse, 1984—. Recipient Charles Kulp Jr. award U.S. Jaycees, 1982, Ambassador award, 1985; Jaycee Statesman award Wis. Jaycees, 1982. Mem. Nat. Soc. Fund Raising Execs. (bd. dirs.), Council for Advancement and Support Edn., Onalaska Area Jaycees (pres. 1972—), LaCrosse Area C. of C. (com. chmn. 1984—), Delta Sigma Phi (pres. local chpt. 1980-85, nat. Gordian Knot award 1978). Republican. Roman Catholic. Clubs: LaCrosse Plugs, Shamrock (v.p.) (LaCrosse). Lodge: K.C. Home: W6094 County Rd T Holmen WI 54636 Office: U Wis 1725 State St Room 215 LaCrosse WI 54601

STEPHENS, RAY GARRETT, accounting educator; b. Rocky Mount, N.C., Oct. 17, 1943; s. Alvin Ray Stephens Jr. and Nancy (Garrett) Adams; m. Jean Joyner, July 25, 1970; children—Heather, Wendy, Adam. A.B., U. Ga., 1965; M.B.A., East Carolina U., 1975; D.B.A., Harvard U., 1978. C.P.A., Ohio. Comml. lender Planters Nat. Bank, Rocky Mount, 1969-73; asst. prof. acctg. Ohio State U., Columbus, 1978-84, assoc. prof., 1984—; dir. Va. Electronic and Lighting Corp., Urbana, Ohio, 1983—; exec. dir. Ohio Mut. Assistance Group C.P.A.s, Columbus, 1984—. Author: Uses of Financial Information in Bank Lending Decisions, 1980. Contbr. articles to profl. jours. Served to lt. USN, 1965-68. Mem. Ohio Soc. C.P.A.s (sec. Columbus chpt. 1984—), Am. Acctg. Assn. Methodist. Home: 6722 Masefield St Worthington OH 43085 Office: Ohio State U 1775 Coll Rd Columbus OH 43210

STEPHENS, ROBERT ALLAN, service agency executive; b. St. Louis County, Mo., Jan. 15, 1937; s. Charles Franklin and L. Pearl (Cales) Stephens; B.A., Mo. Valley Coll., 1958; M.S., Nova U., 1984; m. Carolyn Beth Hurst, Aug. 26, 1956; children—Shari Lee, Beth Ann. Claims supr. Gen. Am. Life Ins. Co., Pitts., 1958-61, underwriting mgr., St. Louis, 1961-67, dist. sales mgr., Oklahoma City and St. Louis, 1967-69; dist. sales mgr. New Eng. Life, Dallas, 1969-71; exec. dir. Goodland Presbyn. Children's Home, Hugo, Okla., 1971-74; exec. dir. Beech Acres, Cin., 1974—. Mem. Hamilton County Juvenile Ct. Rev. Bd., 1975-83; mem. Hamilton County Youth Service Coordinating Council, 1979-83; legis. bd., Southeastern Ecumenical Ministries Manor, 1976-81, bd. dirs., 1980-82; mem. Clermont County Mental Health Bd., 1980-85, vice chmn., 1981, chmn., 1982-85; mem. Clermont County Youth Service Coordinating Council, 1980-83, Clermont County Juvenile Ct. Adv. Bd., 1980-81. Named Nat. United Presbyterian Man of Mission, 1978. Mem. Nat. Assn. Homes for Children (dir. 1975-80), Ohio Assn. Child Caring Agys. (dir. 1975-80, pres., 1978-79). Presbyterian. Club: Exchange (pres. 1980-81, Book of Deeds award 1984). Home: 1258 Maplecrest Ct Amelia OH 45102 Office: 6881 Beechmont Ave Cinncinnati OH 45230

STEPHENSON, HOWARD GRANT, lawyer; b. Jacksonville, Fla., Sept. 11, 1949; s. C. B. and June Louise S.; m. Stephanie Suzann Kruathaupt, June 17, 1977; 1 child, Katherine L. B.A., Ohio U., 1971; J.D., Ohio State U., 1979. Bar: Ohio 1979, U.S. Dist. Ct. (so. dist.) Ohio 1980, U.S. Dist. Ct. (no. dist.) Ohio 1983. Assoc. Porter, Wright, Morris and Arthur, Columbus, Ohio, 1979—. Mem. ABA, Ohio State Bar Assn. Office: Porter Wright Morris & Arthur 37 W Broad St Columbus OH 43215

STEPHENSON, ROBERT ELGIN, JR., state official; b. Washington, Apr. 25, 1937; s. Robert Elgin and Clara Virginia (Edwards) S.;m. Shirley Jane Nichols, Feb. 11, 1963; children—Gregory Keith, Rhonda Joy, Dawn Michelle, Marsha Lynn. Student, Marion Jr. Coll., 1958, Lincoln U., 1980. Buyer, SEMCO, Huntsville, Ala., 1965-72; purchasing agt. Helena Corp., Hoover, Ala., 1972-74, Astro Space Lab., Huntsville, 1974-77; mgr. purchasing State of Mo., Jefferson City, 1977—. Scoutmaster N. Ala. council Boy Scouts Am., Huntsville, 1965-72, Mid-Mo. council, Jefferson City, 1977-79. Served with USMC, 1954-57. Recipient Mo. State Employee of Month award, 1985. Mem. Nat. Inst. Govtl. Purchasing (cert.), Mo. Assn. State Purchasing Ofcls. (Cronin award 1984). Mormon. Avocations: scouting; fishing. Home: 127 W Haven Dr Jefferson City MO 65101 Office: State of Mo Div Purchasing W High St Jefferson City MO 65102

STEPHENSON, SANDRA SCHRIER, mental health administrator, social worker; b. Bucyrus, Ohio, Sept. 18, 1947; d. Edward Alfred and Marjorie Rita (Fellers) Schrier; 1 child, Jan Alan. B.S. in Social Work, Ohio State U., 1974, M.S.W., 1975, M.A. in Pub. Adminstrn., 1980. Lic. in massage therapy, Ohio. Research asst. Ohio State U., 1972; vol. services coordinator North Central Mental Health, Columbus, Ohio, 1975-76, consultation and edn. team coordinator, 1976-78; coordinator residential services Columbus Area Mental Health, 1978-79, coordinator partial hospitalization/daytreatment, 1979-80; ptnr. Trux Stephenson Tng. Seminars for Mgmt., Columbus, 1980-81; exec. dir. Capital Care Women's Ctr., Columbus, 1980-83; assoc. exec. dir. Southeast Mental Health, Columbus, 1983—; mem. adj. faculty Ohio State U., 1976—, Capital U., 1983—. Mem. planning council Olentangy Dist. council Boy Scouts Am., 1977; bd. dirs. Choices for Victims of Domestic Violence, 1978-79; mem. Task Force on Women's Issues, 1979-81; bd. dirs. Nat. Abortion Rights Action League, 1981-82. Recipient DAR Citizenship award, 1965; Merit Scholar award Ohio State U., 1973; Pacesetter award Coll. Adminstrv. Scis., Ohio State U., 1974. Mem. Ohio State U. Coll. Social Work Alumni Assn., Am. Assn. Partial Hospitalization, Assn. Mental Health Adminstrs., Phi Kappa Phi. Democrat. Contbr. articles to profl. jours. Home: 190 W California Ave Columbus OH 43202 Office: 1455 S 4th Columbus OH 43207

STERKEL, ROGER DUANE, sheriff; b. Bayard, Nebr., June 6, 1939; s. George and Emma (Burbach) S.; m. Judith Ann Middleswart, Nov. 11, 1961; children—Bradley Duane, Clinton Dean. Student pub. schs., Bridgeport, Nebr. Farmer, Bridgeport, 1961-68; patrolman Bridgeport Police Dept., 1973-74; dep. sheriff Morrill County, Bridgeport, 1975-78, sheriff, 1979—. Mem. State of Nebr. Jail Standards Commn. Named Officer of Yr., Sheriffs and Peace Officers Nebr., 1983; recipient Enforcement award Gov. of Nebr., 1984; Nat. Child Safety Council award, 1980, 1982, 1984. Mem. Nebr. Sheriffs Assn. (3rd v.p. 1982-84). Republican. Lutheran. Lodges: Lions, Eagles. Home: Route 1 W Bridgeport NE 69336

STERN, ANDREW MICHAEL, lawyer; b. Covington, Ky., June 28, 1949; s. Joseph F. and Matilda I. (Domaschko) S.; m. Eileen Marie Beringer, Dec. 28, 1973; 1 child, Mary Kathryn. B.A. in Biology and Psychology, Thomas More Coll., 1976; J.D., No. Ky. U., 1980. Bar: Ky. 1980, Ohio 1981, U.S. Dist. Ct. (ea. and we. dists.) Ky. 1981, U.S. Dist. Ct. (ea. dist.) Tex. 1982. Jud. clk. U.S. Dist. Ct. (ea. dist.) Ky., Covington, 1980; sole practice, Covington, 1980-83; assoc. White, Getgey & Meyer, Cin., 1983—; instr. torts, research and investigation Am. Inst. Paralegal Studies, Inc., Cin., 1981—. Served to sgt. USMC, 1968-72, Vietnam. Named Outstanding Young Men Am., Jaycees, 1981. Mem. Ky. Bar Assn., Ohio Bar Assn., Fed. Bar Assn., ABA (litigation sect. admiralty com.), Cin. Bar Assn., Am. Judicature Soc. Democrat. Home: 122 Highland Ave Fort Thomas KY 41075 Office: White Getgey & Meyer Co LPA Adam Riddle House 2021 Auburn Ave Cincinnati OH 45219

STERN, CLARENCE AMES, historian, educator; b. McCluskey, N.D., Jan. 6, 1913; s. Adam M. and Minnie (Krieger) S.; A.B. (salutatorian), Eastern Mich. U., 1934; M.A., Wayne State U., 1938; postgrad. LaSalle Extension U., 1947-49; Ph.D., U. Nebr., 1958; m. Kathleen Gober, Feb. 20, 1946. Tchr. social sci. Ecorse (Mich.) Pub. Schs., 1934-37; tchr. history and social sci. Detroit Pub. Schs., 1937-42, River Rouge (Mich.) Pub. Schs., 1954-55; asst. prof. history and polit. sci. Coll. Engring., Lawrence Inst. Tech., Detroit, 1946-50; asst. dept. history U. Nebr., 1951-53; asso. prof. history polit. sci. Wayne (Nebr.) State Coll., 1958-65; asso. prof. constl. and polit. party history U.S. and Europe, U. Wis., Oshkosh, 1965—, asso. prof. history U. Wis., Fond du Lac, 1975—, chmn. history dept; chmn. div. social scis., grant proposal reviewer Nat. Endowment Humanities, 1978—; polit. sci. expert Nat. Council Social Studies. Served with USAAF, 1942-46; ETO. Ford Found. Am. Polit. Sci. Assn. grantee U. Ind., 1962; hon. fellow Harry S. Truman Library Inst. Fellow Intercontinental Biog. Assn., Anglo-Am. Acad. (hon.), Internat. Inst. Community Service; mem. AAUP (pres. chpt. 1964-65), Orgn. Am. Historians, Am. Polit. Sci. Assn., ACLU, Phi Alpha Theta, Pi Gamma Mu, Kappa Delta Pi. Author: Republican Heyday: Republicanism Through the McKinley Years, 1962, 69; Resurgent Republicanism: The Handiwork of Hanna, 1963, 68; Golden Republicanism: The Crusade for Hard Money, 1964, 70; Protectionist Republicanism: Republican Tariff Policy in the McKinley Period, 1971. Home: 1625 Elmwood Ave Oshkosh WI 54901 PO Box 2294 Oshkosh WI 54903

STERN, DOUGLAS DONALD, foundry company official, consultant, educator; b. New London, Wis., Apr. 29, 1939; s. Sylvester S. and Gretchen W. S.; m. Karen Mari Holm, June 11, 1960 (div. 1983); children—Randal, Richard, Robert, Russell. B.S. in Bus. and Math., U. Wis.-Oshkosh, 1962. With Neenah Foundry Co. (Wis.), 1962—, indsl. engr., 1962-65, dir. indsl. engring., 1965-73, gen. supt. Plant 3, 1973-83, plant mgr. Plant 2, 1983—; cons. FMC, Lenox; instr. Fox Valley Tech. Inst., Leach; dir. Dura Products. Coach. Neenah Baseball, 1976—, treas., 1976—; pres. Our Savior's Lutheran Ch., 1971, treas. Found., 1983. Recipient Neenah Football Rocket award, 1981. Mem. Am. Foundrymen's Soc. (speaker's award 1976, pres. N.E. Wis. chpt.), Am. Inst. Indsl. Engrs. (past pres. and bd. dirs.), Nat. Foundry Assn. (indsl. engring. com.). Republican. Author student workbook: Operations Analysis, 1983. Home: 946 Hickory Ln Neenah WI 54956 Office: 2121 Brooks Ave Neenah WI 54956

STERN, PAUL G., computer and business machinery manufacturing company executive. Pres., chief operating officer Burroughs Corp., Detroit. Office: Burroughs Corp Burroughs Place Detroit MI 48232*

STERN, PETER JOSEPH, orthopaedic surgeon; b. Cin., May 16, 1944; s. Joseph Smith and Mary Stern, m. Sandra Schoening, May 28, 1970; children—Kimberly Anne, Joseph Smith, Lisa. B.A., Williams Coll., 1966; M.D., Washington U., St. Louis, 1970. Diplomate Am. Bd. Orthopaedic Surgery. Intern, Beth Israel Hosp., Boston, 1970-71; resident Mass. Gen. Hosp., Boston, 1975-77; asst. prof. orthopaedic surgery Cin. Coll. Medicine, 1979-83, assoc. prof. orthopaedic surgery, 1983—. Served with M.C., USAF, 1972-74. Fellow ACS; mem. Am. Soc. Surgery Hand, Am. Acad. Orthopaedic Surgeons. Jewish. Contbr. articles to profl. publs. Home: 5780 Drewry Farm Ln Cincinnati OH 45243 Office: 231 Bethesda Ave Suite 5707 Cincinnati OH 45267

STERNBERGER, STEPHEN JEFFREY, insurance company executive; b. Indpls., May 26, 1949; s. Robert Sidney and Sandra Sue (Knoy) S.; B.S.Ed., Ind. U., 1971; m. Valerie Dale Garbrecht, July 31, 1971. Tchr., coach, Pike Twp. (Ind.) Schs., 1971-74; agt. Mass. Mut. Ins. Co., Indpls., 1974-75; dir. adminstrn. Compensation Systems, Inc., Indpls., 1975; author, cons. Pictorial Publishers, Inc., Indpls., 1975-83; v.p. advanced underwriting and mktg. services United Presdl. Life Ins. Co., 1983—; v.p. Ind. Assn. Health Underwriters, Indpls., 1974-75. Registered health underwriter (R.H.U.), C.L.U.; recipient Heart Fund Solicitors award, 1979. Mem. Indpls. Assn. Life Underwriters, Indpls. Assn. Health Underwriters, Nat. Assns. Life and Health Underwriters, Estate Planning Council Indpls., Am. Soc. C.L.U.s, Am. Soc. Tng. and Devel., Assn. for Advanced Life Underwritng, Internat. Assn. Fin. Planning, Am. Mgmt. Assn. Ind. U. Alumni Assn., Pi Kappa Alpha. Republican. Unitarian. Club: Ind. U. Varsity. Author: Advanced Underwriting Training Course, 1978; Estate Planning Training Course, 1979; Pension Planning Training Course, 1981; Business Insurance Basics, 1982; contbr. articles to profl. jours. Home: 4343 Idlewild Ln Carmel IN 46032 Office: PO Box 2498 217 Southway Blvd E Kokomo IN 46902

STEUBINGER, RICHARD PAUL, mortgage company executive, real estate company executive; b. Peoria, Ill., Mar. 17, 1927; s. Paul L. and Edna M. (Wier) S.; m. Helen M. Roedell, Nov. 4, 1951 (div. 1968); children—Connie, Linda, Richard, Jr., Cathy; m. Jonnee M. Johnson, Feb. 18, 1978; 1 child, Shawnda. Student Bradley U., 1944-48. Lic. real estate broker, Ill. Owner, pres. Holiday Store, Peoria, 1948-57; pres. Lynnhurst Devel. Co., Peoria, 1957-80, Pioneer Realty Co., Peoria, 1959—, Tri-County Mortgage Co., Peoria, 1983—. Pres. Counseling and Family Service, Peoria, 1981; chmn. Am. Heart Assn., Peoria, 1981-82. Served with USN, 1945-46. Mem. Bradley U. Alumni Assn. (pres. 1982-83, Pres. award 1982), Nat. Assn. Realtors. Lutheran. Lodge: Kiwanis (Leadership award 1979, pres. 1979). Home: 4518 Hetherwood Peoria IL 61615 Office: Tri-County Mortgage Ltd 6816 Frostwood Peoria IL 61615

STEVENS, CHARLES THOMAS, psychologist; b. Nevada, Mo., Oct. 25, 1932; s. Glenn Monroe and Edna Estelle (Thomas) S.; B.S. in Agr., S.W. Mo. State U., 1955, B.S. in Psychology, 1974, M.S. in Guidance and Counseling, 1974; Ph.D. candidate, U. Mo., Columbia; m. Helen Louise Utterback, Dec. 27, 1953; children—Mark Thomas, Diana Lynn, Eric Allen. Served as enlisted man U.S. Army N.G., 1954-55; commd. 2d lt., 1955, advanced through grades to lt. col. inf., 1969; ret., 1971; vets. benefits counselor U. Mo. Counseling Center, Columbia, 1977-79; dir. Bur. for Blind, State of Mo., Jefferson City, 1979-84; field rep. Nat. Fedn. of Blind, 1984—; cons., counselor visually impaired coll. students, 1975-78; guest lectr. on blindness; state pres. Nat. Fedn. of the Blind, 1977-79. Decorated Legion of Merit, Bronze Star with V, Army Commendation Medal with V, 2 Purple Hearts; Cross of Galantry (Vietnam); grantee Handicapped Manpower Availability Survey. Mem. Am. Personnel and Guidance Assn., Mem. Christian Ch. Club: Lions. Home and Office: 1203 Fairview Rd Columbia MO 65203

STEVENS, FREDDIE JAMES, educational adminstrator; b. St. Louis, Sept. 1, 1946; s. Willie and Ruby Bernice S. A.B., Harris Tchrs. Coll., St. Louis, 1969; M.A., St. Louis U., 1974; Advanced Cert. Studies, U. Mo., St. Louis, 1982. Dir., Pruitt-Igoe Summer Program, 1969-71; behavior modifier Program to Improve Sch. Attendance, 1974-75; tchr. Banneker dist. St. Louis Pub. Schs., 1969-75, asst. prin. Wyman Sch., 1975-76, Clay Sch., 1976-78, Cupples Sch., 1978-80, Stevens Middle Sch., 1980-82, acting prin. Cupples Sch., 1982—; tutor Carr Lane Community Sch., 1978-79; elem. prin. Gundlach Summer Sch., 1980; coordinator Stevens Middle After Sch. Program, 1981-82. Mem. City-Wide Youth Council, Human Devel. Corp., St. Louis, 1969, 71; chmn. Pruitt-Igoe Youth Council, 1969. Mem. Nat. Middle Sch. Assn., Assn. Supervision and Curriculum Devel., St. Louis Adminstrs. Assn., Phi Delta Kappa. Methodist. Home: 3530 Laclede Ave Saint Louis MO 63103 Office: Saint Louis Pub Schs Cupples Elem Sch 4908 Cote Brilliante Saint Louis MO 63113

STEVENS, HAROLD RUSSELL, physician; b. Detroit, Nov. 18, 1930; s. Harold Russell and Etheleen Mae (Stone) S.; A.B., Albion Coll., 1951; M.D., U. Mich., 1955; m. Karen Lee Leathers; children—Kirk Russell, Martha Lee, Kori Lynn, Kelly Lou. Intern Toledo Hosp., 1955-56, resident in anesthesiology 1960-62, attending anesthesiologist, 1962—, med. dir. respiratory therapy, 1966—, chmn. dept. anesthesiology, 1983, research asso. Inst. Med. Research, 1965-70; practice medicine specializing in anesthesiology, respiratory therapy, Toledo, 1962—; med. dir. respiratory therapy U. Toledo, 1971—, prof. respiratory therapy, 1974—; asst. clin. prof. Med. Coll. Ohio, Toledo, 1971—; dir. anesthesiology Mercy Hosp., Toledo, 1968-79, med. co-dir. respiratory therapy, 1969-83; dir. intensive care unit Toledo Hosp., 1975—. Health councilor Community Planning Council Northwestern Ohio, 1970-71. Trustee Maumee Valley Found. Served to capt. M.C., USAF, 1957-59. Diplomate Am. Bd. Anesthesiology. Mem. Acad. Medicine Toledo and Lucas County (councilor 1970-71), Am., Ohio med. assns., Am. Assn. Respiratory Therapy, Internat. Anesthesia Research Soc., Am., Ohio (pres. 1982-83), Toledo (pres. 1971) socs. anesthesiologists, Phi Beta Kappa, Alpha Omega Alpha. Clubs: Masons (32 deg.), Shriners; Inverness, Toledo. Contbr. articles to profl. jours. Office: 3939 Monroe St Toledo OH 43606 Home: 4204 Northmoor Rd Toledo OH 43606

STEVENS, JEFFREY BRYAN, toxicologist, educator; b. Bay City, Mich., Jan. 14, 1948; s. John B. and Dona Marie (Spinner) S.; m. Polly Perkins, Dec. 29, 1984. B.S., Mich. State U., 1970, M.S., 1970; Ph.D., Cornell U., 1976. Postdoctoral fellow U. Iowa, Iowa City, 1976-80; asst. prof. U. Minn., Mpls., 1980—; cons. No. States Power Co., Mpls., 1982—, Minn. State Health Dept., Mpls., 1981—, various law firms, Mpls., St. Paul, 1982—. Author: General Environment Toxicology, 1982, Health Risk Assessment, 1983. Recipient New Investigator award Nat. Inst. Environ. Health Scis., 1981; Faculty Excellence award U. Minn., 1982, 83; grantee Am. Lung Assn., 1982. Avocations: tennis, skiing. Home: 3042 Benjamin St NE Minneapolis MN 55418 Office: 1115 Mayo Bldg 420 Delaware St SE Minneapolis MN 55455

STEVENS, MARJORIE, librarian; b. Calhoun County, Mich., Jan. 1, 1923; d. Will Oliver and Ethel Grace (Frye) Rundle; m. Paul Andrew Stevens, Mar., 1940 (dec. Mar. 1971); children—Lorainne Marie, Norman Douglas, Clare Eugene, Janice May, Sandra Kay, Garry Alan, Maynard Carl, Lynn Carol, Ronald Paul. B.A., Olivet Coll., 1982; M.S.L., Western Mich. U., 1977. Clk., Olivet (Mich.) Coll. Library, 1960-75, acquisitions technician, 1976-78, acquisitions and govt. documents librarian, 1978-80, acquisitions and fed. govt. documents librarian, 1980—, also archivist, audio-visual instr. Mem. Mich. Archival Assn., Women's Soc. Christian Service. Methodist.

STEVENS, MARK OLIVER, superintendent of schools; b. Youngstown, Ohio, Mar. 9, 1948; s. Paul E. and Janet L. (Weisert) S.; m. Kelline Ann White, June 28, 1975. M.A. in Ednl. Adminstrn., Ohio State U., 1978, M.A. in Pub. Adminstrn., 1979, postgrad., 1979—. Tchr., coach Austintown (Ohio) Schs., 1972-74, Bexley City (Ohio) Schs., 1974-78; grad. adminstrv. asst. to assoc. dean for program devel. Ohio State U., Columbus, 1978-80; asst. prin. Groveport Madison (Ohio) Local Schs., 1980, supt., 1981—. Pres., Coll. Edn. adv. council Ohio State U., 1982—; mem. Greater Groveport Human Needs Com., 1982—, Citizens Opposing Noise, 1982—, Coalition for Local Adminstrn. Schs., 1983, Franklin County Sch. Funding Task Force, 1981—. Recipient Ross-Gainer award Ohio State U., 1971, Martin W. Essex award, 1980, Ednl. Achievement award, 1982, Dir.'s award Southeast Columbus Mental Health Ctr., 1983; Dan. H. Eikenbury fellow, 1980. Mem. Buckeye Assn. Sch. Adminstrs. (Ednl. Leadership award 1984), Am. Assn. Sch. Adminstrs., Ohio Local Supts. Assn., Franklin County Supts. Assn. (pres. 1983-84), Sigma Phi Epsilon (pres. 1970-71, alumni pres. 1974-80), Phi Delta Kappa (pres. 1983-84). Unitarian. Club: Bexley Celebrations. Lodge: Lions. Contbr. chpts. to books, articles to profl. publs. Home: 2543 Bryden Rd Columbus OH 43209 Office: 5055 S Hamilton Rd Groveport OH 43125

STEVENS, PATRICIA CAROL, university administrator; b. St. Louis, Jan. 11, 1946; d. Carroll and Juanita Donohue; A.B., Duke U., 1966; M.A., U. Mo.-Kansas City, 1974, Ph.D., 1982; m. James H. Stevens, Jr., Aug. 27, 1966 (div. Mar. 1984); children—James H. III, Carol Janet. Tchr. math, secondary schs., Balt., St. Louis, Shawnee Mission, Kans., 1966-71; lectr. U. Mo., Kansas City, 1975-76, research asst. affirmative action, 1976-79, coordinator affirmative action, 1979-82, instl. research assoc., 1982-84, acting dir. affirmative action and acad. personnel, 1984; dir. institutional research Lakeland Community Coll., 1984—. Bd. dirs., v.p. Am. Cancer Soc. Jackson County, 75—; bd. dirs. PTA, 1975-77. Recipient Outstanding Service and Achievement award U. Mo. Kansas City, 1976; Jack C. Coffey grantee, 1978; Cream Rose Outstanding Service award Delta Gamma, 1970. Mem. Nat. Council Tchrs. Math, Assn. Supervision and Curriculum Devel., Women's Equity Project, Nat. Assn. Student Personnel Adminstrs., Women's Network, Phi Delta Kappa, (pres.), Phi Kappa Phi, Pi Lambda Theta, Delta Gamma (v.p.). Home: 7454 Blueridge Dr Concord OH 44060 Office: Lakeland Community Coll Mentor OH 44060

STEVENS, VIOLETE LEE, technology coordinator; b. China, June 2, 1942; came to U.S., 1961, naturalized, 1973; d. Y.C. and C.Y.B. (Chang) L.; m. Rex R. Stevens, May 16, 1970. A.A., Georgetown Jr. Coll., 1963; B.S., Viterbo Coll., 1965; M.S., San Jose State Coll., 1967. Research assoc., tech. coordinator, Dow Chem. Co., Midland, Mich., 1967—; mem. industry adv. bd. Eastern Mich. U. Patentee in field (15); contbr. articles to profl. jours. Mem. industry adv. bd. Eastern Mich. U. Mem. Assn. Finishing Processes (bd. dirs.), Am. Chem. Soc., Nat. Paint and Coatings Assn (industry adv. bd.), Steel Structures Painting Council. Republican. Roman Catholic. Avocations: candle making; hiking; woodworking; canoeing. Office: Dow Chem Co 2020 W H Dow Ctr Midland MI 48640

STEVENS, WILLIAM LOUIS, Episcopal bishop; b. Yuba City, Calif., Jan. 12, 1932; s. Ralph Fremont and Elsie Mae (Schultz) S.; B.A., San Francisco State Coll., 1953; M.Div. Gen. Theol. Sem., 1956. Ordained priest, Episcopal Ch.; curate St. Luke's Ch., San Francisco; sr. curate St. Savior's, London, Order of the Holy Cross, N.Y.; rector St. Benedict's Ch., Plantation, Fla. to 1980; bishop Episcopal Diocese of Fond du Lac (Wis.), 1980—. Trustee, Nashotah Ho. Sem.; bishop visitor Sisterhood of the Holy Nativity; mem. Nat. Right to Life Com. Office: PO Box 149 Fond du Lac WI 54935

STEVENSON, BILLY MORRIS, chief of police; b. Ramsey, Ark., Dec. 18, 1932; s. Morris Andrew and Versa Mae (Stewart) S.; m. Phyllis Lucille, Aug. 15, 1958; children—Jeffery, Lisa, Julie. Grad. Bastrop High Sch., La., 1951. Chief of police Cozad Police Dept., Nebr., 1980—. Served with USAF, 1951-75. Mem. VFW, Am. Legion, Nat. Assn. Chiefs of Police. Club: Optimist. Lodge:

Masons. Home: 505 E 14th St Cozad NE 69130 Office: Cozad Police Dept 229 E 8th St Cozad NE 69130

STEVENSON, RICHARD ANDREW, finance educator, consultant; b. Utica, N.Y., Aug. 5, 1938; s. Edward D. and Doris Stevenson; m. Sheila Vaughn, Aug. 12, 1967; children—Daniel, Maura, Susan. B.B.A., St. Bonaventure U., 1961; M.B.A., Syracuse U., 1962; Ph.D., Mich. State U., 1965. Chartered fin. analyst. Research analyst Household Fin., Chgo., 1965-67; prof. fin. U. Iowa, Iowa City, 1967—, dept. chmn., 1981—, bd. dirs., chmn. Univ. Credit Union. Author: (with others) Fundamentals of Investments, 1984; Asset-Liability Management for Credit Unions, 1984; Fundamentals of Finance, 1980. Contbr. articles to profl. jours. Mem. adv. bd. Iowa Sch. Banking, 1977—; treas. Bicyclists of Iowa City, 1982—. Ford Found. fellow, 1963-65. Mem. Am Fin. Assn., Des Moines Soc. Fin. Analysts, Inst. Chartered Fin. Analysts, Fin. Mgmt. Assn. (bd. dirs. 1978-80), Midwest Fin. Assn. (pres. 1983-84). Avocations: biking, reading. Office: U Iowa Coll of Bus Iowa City IA 52242

STEVENSON, RICHARD MARSHALL, chemist; b. Detroit, July 2, 1923; s. Richard Ambrose and Jeanne Margaret (Marshall) S.; B.S. cum laude, Detroit Inst. Tech., 1947; postgrad. Wayne State U.; m. Marion Ignatius Byrne, Feb. 13, 1944; children—Michael Richard, Mark Alan. Chemist, Udylite Corp. div. Oxy Metal Industries, Warren, Mich., 1959-76; pres. Richard M. Stevenson & Co., Cons. Chemists, Grosse Pointe, Mich., 1976—; research dir. Detroit Plastic Molding Co., Sterling Heights, Mich., 1978—. Served with USN, 1944-46. Fellow Am. Inst. Chemists; mem. Am. Chem. Soc., Am. Electroplaters Soc., Am. Contract Bridge League. Patentee in electrodisposition of metals. Home: 2179 Allard Ave Grosse Pointe MI 48236 Office: 6600 E 15 Mile Rd Sterling Heights MI 48077

STEVENSON, ROBERT JAMES, aircraft company executive, consultant, designer; b. Watertown, S.D., Oct. 30, 1916; s. Robert William and Bessie (Schooley) S.; m. Oma Nell Smith, Dec. 27, 1943 (div. Oct. 1957); children—Robert William, Thomas Richard, Timothy James; m. 2d, Kimary Elizabeth Leonard, Nov. 4, 1957; children—Leonard Franks, Randall James, Romney Jan. Student Oreg. U., 1936-38. Bush pilot Peterson Flying Service, Anchorage, 1945-46; v.p. No. Consol. Airlines (Wein Alaska) Anchorage, 1947-56, also dir.; pres. Arctic Air Cargo, Anchorage, 1956-60; pres. Cal-Nat Airways, Inc., Grass Valley, Calif., 1960-71, also dir.; pres. Engine Air Ltd., St. Louis, 1971—, also dir.; cons. aviation; designer aircraft accessories. Bd. dirs. Assorted Charities Nevada County (Calif.), 1963-70, Community Concert Assn., Grass Valley, 1966-71; co-chmn. Senator Chappie Election Com., 6th Dist., Calif., 1967-71; coordinator Friends of Reagan Election Com., Nevada County, Calif., 1970. Served to 1st lt. USAAF, 1942-45; South Africa, ETO, Asia. Mem. Nat. Air Tanker Assn. (sec. 1960-71), Quiet Birdmen Internat. Republican. Club: 20/30 (pres. 1938-40) (Salem, Oreg.). Home: 12144 Gravois Saint Louis MO 63127 Office: Engine Air Ltd Inc Lambert Field PO Box 10385 Saint Louis MO 63145

STEVENSON, THOMAS HERBERT, management consultant; author; b. Covington, Ohio, Oct. 16, 1951; s. Robert Louis and Dolly Eileen (Minnich) S.; m. Pamela F. Blythe, Mar. 10, 1979. B.A., Wright State U., 1977. Teaching asst., research asst. Wright State U., 1975-77; teaching asst. Bowling Green State U., 1978; loan officer Western Ohio Nat. B Bank & Trust Co., 1979-80, asst. v.p. adminstrs., 1981-82, v.p. mgmt. services div., 1983-85; v.p., bank mgmt. cons. Young & Assocs., Inc., 1985—; mem. exec. com. Owl Electronic Banking Network, 1981—; mem. adv. bd. Upper Valley Joint Vocat. Sch. for Fin. Instns., 1981—. Mem. Community Bankers Polit. Action Com. Served to cpl. USMC, 1972-73. Recipient George Washington Medal of Honor, Freedom's Found., 1974. Mem. Am. Inst. Banking (adv. bd. 1982—), Am. Bankers Assn., Bank Adminstrn. Inst., Ind. Bankers Assn. Am., Ohio Bankers Assn., Community Bankers Assn. Ohio. Republican. Mem. Ch. of Brethren. Club: Eagles. Contbr. articles in field to profl. jours. Home: 516 1/2 N High St Covington OH 45318 Office: 102 N High St Covington OH 45318

STEVOFF, AUDREY LAZNICKA, investment analyst, telecommunications specialist; b. Chgo., Dec. 13, 1934; d. Frank and Bessie (Srp) Laznicka; m. Nick Spiro Stevoff, Dec. 26, 1970; children—Nadine, Sheryl. B.S. in Acctg., U. Ill., 1956; M.B.A., Northwestern U., 1965. Acct. Arthur Andersen & Co., Chgo., 1956; statistical analyst Standard Oil (Ind.), Chgo., 1956-66; public utility analyst Harris Trust & Savs. Bank, Chgo., 1966-71; telecommunications analyst Duff & Phelps, Inc., Chgo., 1982—, asst. v.p., 1984—. Mem. Investment Analysts Soc. Chgo. (chmn. membership com. 1985-86), Inst. Chartered Fin. Analysts (cert.), Fin. Analysts Fedn., Pub. Utility Securities Club Chgo. (treas. 1968-69, sec. 1969-70). Club: Women's Assn. 1st Presbyterian Ch. Deerfield (treas. 1978-79, v.p. 1980-81, pres. 1981-82). Avocations: golf, travel, arts and crafts, attending concerts and theater. Office: Duff & Phelps Inc 55 E Monroe St Chicago IL 60603

STEWARD, WELDON CECIL, architecture educator; b. Pampa, Tex., Apr. 7, 1934; s. Weldon C. and Lois (Maness) S.; m. Mary Jane Nedbalek, June 9, 1956; children—Karen A., W. Craig. Cert. architecture and planning Ecole des Beaux Arts, Fontainebleau, France, 1956; B.Arch., Tex. A&M U., 1957; M.Arch., Columbia U., 1961. Designer, Perkins & Will, Architects, White Plains, N.Y., 1961-62; asst. prof. Sch. Arch., Tex. A&M U., 1962-67, assoc. chmn., 1966-69, assoc. dean, prof. Coll. Environ. Design, 1969-73; prof., dean Coll. Architecture U. Nebr., Lincoln, 1973—; project dir. Imo State Univ. Planning, Nigeria, 1981—; co-chmn. nat. coordinating commn. AIA/NCARB Internship, 1980-81; profl. advisor Nat. Design Competition, Wick Alumni Ctr., Lincoln, 1981. Mem. Nat. Com. for U.S.-China Relations, N.Y.C., 1981—; ednl. cons. Peoples Republic of China, 1979, 84. Served to capt. USAF, 1957-60. Columbia U. Grad. fellow, 1960. Fellow AIA; mem. Nebr. Soc. Architects (bd. dirs. 1977—), Archtl. Found. Nebr. (treas. 1981—), Assn. Collegiate Schs. Architecture (bd. dirs. 1975-79), Tau Sigma Delta, Phi Kappa Phi. Avocations: handball; downhill skiing; tennis; water skiing. Home: 1250 Aldrich Rd Lincoln NE 68510 Office: Coll Architecture U Nebr Lincoln NE 68588-0106

STEWART, BEVERLY JEAN, exercise and aerobic instructor, choreographer; b. Bellingham, Wash., Aug. 15, 1951; d. Cecil Wilbur and Ida Catherine (Gobatto) Brann; m. David Miles Stewart, May 15, 1976; 1 son, John. B.A., Wash. State U., 1973. Cert. YMCA, Nat. Dance Assn., CPR. Exercise instr. Sausalito, Calif., 1974-76; instr. slim and trim and fitness fantasia Missouri Valley Family YMCA, Bismarck, N.D., 1977-80; owner, dir. Fitness Unltd., Bismarck, 1981—; trainer instrs. Bismarck parks; lectr. in field. Mem. YMCA, leader vol. classes. Named Vol. of Yr., Ctr. for Ind. Living, 1982. Mem. Internat. Dance-Exercise Assn., Working Women's Network. Roman Catholic. Coordinator exercise routines, style shows. Home and office: 622 W Thayer Ave Bismarck ND 58501

STEWART, BILL J., design engineer, educator; b. Jasper, Ala., July 31, 1950; s. Robert Lee and Catherine Mae (Stewart) S.; m. Ellen Kay Blackwell, July 17, 1976; children—Chris, Schnette, Stephany, Stephen, Carmen. A.A., Johnson County Community Coll., 1976; B.S., Avila Coll., 1980; M.A., Webster U., 1982. Repair clk. supr. Southwestern Bell, Kansas City, 1979-80, installation supr., 1980-82, repair supr., 1982-83, design engr., 1983—; instr. Nat. Coll., Kansas City, Kans. Mem. Black Democrat Caucus, Topeka, Kans., 1983. Served with U.S. Army, 1970-73. Mem. Christian Ch. Avocations: horseback riding, jogging. Home: 5335 Dearborn St Mission KS 66202

STEWART, ERNEST WILLIAM, market research executive; b. Kansas City, Kans., Oct. 16, 1950; s. Ernest William Davey and Elizabeth Jeannette (Forbes) S.; m. Deborah Gayle Hofling, Dec. 8, 1979; 1 dau., Catherine Soteldo. Student S.W. Mo. State U., 1968-71; B.S. in Communications, Lindenwood Coll., 1972; M.A. in Bus. Adminstrn. and Mktg., Webster U., 1982. Youth news editor St. Louis County Star, Overland, Mo., 1965-67; corr. St. Louis Post-Dispatch, 1971-72; writer/news editor Sta.-KMOX, St. Louis, 1972-73; reporter, then news editor St. Charles (Mo.) Jour., 1973-76; editorial dir. Ednl. Media Inc., St. Charles, 1976; dir. mem. relations St. Louis Tchrs. Credit Union, 1976-79; pub. relations rep. Mercantile Bancorp., St. Louis, 1979-82; dir. mktg. research Nat. Decorating Products Assn., St. Louis, 1982—; tchr. seminars, condr. workshops in journalism, mktg.; cons. advt. agys. Recipient cert. excellence for best news story Suburban Newspapers Am., 1975, cert. appreciation Vocat. Indsl. Clubs Am., 1974, Pioneer award Mo. Credit Union League, 1978; named hon. Ky. col. Mem. Am. Mktg. Assn., Direct Mktg. Club St. Louis, Webster U. Alumni Assn. (long-range planning commn. 1982—, bd. dirs. 1983—). Episcopalian. Author: SBA publ. starting a Retail Decorating Products Business. Contbr. numerous articles to decorating-products industry trade publs. Home: 415 George Ave Kirkwood MO 63122 Office: 1050 N Lindbergh Saint Louis MO 63132

STEWART, GARY VINCENT, manufacturing company executive; b. Toledo, Oct. 29, 1949; s. Wilmer and Rosalie (Nash) S.; m. Karen Elaine Patterson, Aug. 31, 1969; children—Gary, Vincent, Markus, Sharon. B.S. in History, Canisius Coll., 1972; M.S. in Adminstrn. and Supervision, U. Toledo, 1980. Pres. SPC Electronics, Inc., Toledo, 1984—; dir. Seagate Devel. Corp. Mem. NAACP. Democrat. Baptist. Lodge: Rotary. Avocations: golfing, fishing, tennis. Home: 2319 Grelyn St Toledo OH 43615 Office: SPC Electronics Inc 1946 N 13th St Toledo OH 43624

STEWART, MICHAEL OSBORNE, university administrator; b. Sacramento, Aug. 25, 1938; s. Morris Albion and Marjorie Cathryn (McFarlin) S.; m. Lucille Arnette Cooper, June 11, 1961; children—Heather, Blaine. B.A., U. Calif.-Berkeley, 1960, M.A., 1961; Ph.D. Kans. State U., 1972. Asst. dean of students San Jose State U., Calif., 1965-66; assoc. dean of students Fort Hays State U., Kans., 1966-71, asst. v.p. acad. affairs, dir. instl. research, 1971-74; v.p. adminstrn. Peru State Coll., Nebr., 1974-79, U. S.D., Vermillion, 1979-82; v.p. bus. affairs, treas. Lawrence U., Appleton, Wis., 1982—; v.p., sec., treas. Lawrence Corp. Wis., 1983—. Mem. editorial bd. College and University Business Administration, 4th edit., 1981-82. Contbr. articles to profl. jours. Bd. dirs., chmn. Youth Care Inc., Hays, 1969-74. Served to capt. U.S. Army, 1961-65. Alumni scholar U. Calif.-Berkeley, 1956-57; NDEA fellow, 1967-68. Mem. Kans. Assn. Student Personnel Adminstrn. (pres. 1970-71), Am. Assn. Univ. Adminstrns. (bd. dirs. 1979-82, chmn. audit budget com. 1982—), Nat. Assn. Coll. Bus. Officers, Central Assn. Coll. Bus. Officers (idea exchange, publs. and host coms. 1974—), Theta Chi (nat. chaplain, sec. 1972-80). Democrat. Episcopalian. Lodge: Kiwanis (bd. dirs. Auburn club 1974, Appleton club 1984—). Avocation: tennis. Office: Lawrence Univ 115 S Drew St PO Box 599 Appleton WI 54912

STEWART, PAUL ARTHUR, management consultant; b. Greensburg, Ind., Sept. 28, 1955; s. John Arthur and Alberta Jeannette (Densford) S.; m. Susan Rhodes, Dec. 20, 1975. B.S., Purdue U., 1976; postgrad. Harvard Bus. Sch., 1985—. Grad. asst. Purdue U., West Lafayette, Ind, 1976-77; asst. treas. Stewart Seeds, Inc., Greensburg, Ind., 1977-82, sec./treas., 1982-84; founder, owner PASCO Group, mgmt. and computer cons. to seed cos., 1979—; cons. on computer software to seed cos., govt., 1979—. Mem. Greensburg-Decatur County Bd. of Airport Commrs., 1980-85, pres., 1980, 81, 83; mem. Decatur County Data Processing Bd., 1982-85. Mem. Ind. Seed Trade Assn. (dir. 1982—, v.p. 1983-84, pres. 1984—, chmn. legis. com. 1982-83), Am. Seed Trade Assn. (legis. com. 1983-85), Alpha Gamma Rho. Republican. Presbyterian. Home: 2 Soldiers Field Park #810 Boston MA 02163-1723 Office: Pasco Group PO Box 607 Greensburg IN 47240

STEWART, ROBERT F., international diversified company executive; b. Gardner, Mass., Aug. 6, 1927; s. Arlington Kenneth and Edith (Fletcher) S.; m. Joan Marshall, June 23, 1951; children—Carolyn Stewart, Eleanor Heidbrink. B.E.E., Worcester (Mass.) Poly. Inst., 1950, Ph.D. (hon.), 1979; student Babson Coll., Wellesley, Mass., 1951. Vice-pres. Litton Industries, Hartford, Conn., 1964-71; v.p., pres. indsl. products Rockwell Internat., Pitts., 1971-75; sr. v.p. United Technologies, Hartford, Conn., 1975-78; pres. Arlen Realty, N.Y.C., 1978-79; sr. exec. v.p. IC Industries, Chgo., 1979—; dir. Cross & Trecker Corp. Trustee, Worcester Poly. Inst. Clubs: Chicago, Economic (both N.Y.C. also Chgo.), Glen View. Office: IC Industries Inc 111 E Wacker Dr Chicago IL 60601

STEWART, TRENT ANTHONY, pharmacist; b. Cin., Dec. 10, 1954; s. Philip Howard and Essie Mae (Kilgore) S. B.S., U. Cin., 1978. Registered Pharmacist. Staff pharmacist Kettering Med. Ctr., 1978-81; staff pharmacist St. Elizabeth Med. Ctr., Dayton, Ohio, 1981-83; sales rep. Eli Lilly & Co., Portland, Oreg., 1983-84; mgr. pharmacy Dunbar Pharmacy and Med. Supply, Inc., Dayton, 1984-85; intravenous admixture pharmacist Dayton VA Med Ctr., 1985—. Sponsor, Big Bros. and Big Sisters of Dayton, 1981. Mem. Dayton Area Soc. Hosp. Pharmacists (sec. 1985), Ohio Soc. Hosp. Pharmacists, Cin. Pharm. Soc. Democrat. Roman Catholic. Club: Dayton Indoor Tennis. Home: 1769 Sheltering Tree Dr West Carrollton OH 45449 Office: Dayton VA Med Ctr 4100 W 3d St Dayton OH 45428

STEWART, VIRGINIA KAMPP (MIMI), public relations executive; b. Oak Park, Ill., Dec. 12, 1939; d. Hubert Eugene and Virginia (Dalton) Kampp; student Northwestern U., 1957-59, Rosary Coll., 1959-60; m. Henry Lawrence Stewart III, Apr. 7, 1961; children—John Hubert, Peter David, Michael Edward. Asst. editor Internat. Altrusan, 1961-64; free-lance writer, 1964-71; editor Wheaton (Ill.) Leader, 1971-73; assoc. dir. pub. relations Central DuPage Hosp., Winfield, Ill., 1973-78, dir. pub. relations, 1978-83; v.p. pub. relations Healthcorp Affiliates, Naperville, Ill., 1983—. Founder The Art Fair, Pitts., 1970; chmn. judges Daily Jour. Ad Craft, 1975-82; chmn. Wheaton City Council Nominating Assembly, 1976; bd. dirs. Community Nursing Service DuPage County, 1976-83; mem. Wheaton Plan Commn., 1979—, chmn., 1983. Named Editor of Yr., Ill. Press Assn., 1972; Profl. Woman of Yr., Bank of Wheaton, 1976; recipient Ron Brinkman award Wheaton C. of C., 1982. Mem. Am. Soc. for Hosp. Pub. Relations, Acad. Hosp. Pub. Relations (sec. 1979-80, dir. 1980— pres. 1984), Ill. Hosp. Pub. Relations Soc., Chgo. Hosp. Pub. Relations Soc., Greater Wheaton C. of C. (dir. 1973-81, Brinkman award 1982). Republican. Clubs: Service (Chgo.), Altrusa. Home: 1103 N President St Wheaton IL 60187 Office: Healthcorp Affiliates 1151 E Warrenville Rd Naperville IL 60566

STEWART, W. RODERICK, manufacturing company executive; b. Norwood, Ohio, Mar. 22, 1916; s. Raymond Forrest and Estelle Marie (Keller) S.; B.B.A., U. Cin., 1939; m. Dolores Faye Doll., Apr. 15, 1944; 1 dau., Sharon Marie. Owner, dir. Music by Roderick Orch., 1934-49; v.p. Cin. Lithographing Co., 1949-63; owner, pres. Concrete Surfacing Machinery Co., Cin., 1963-71, Bossert Machine Co., Cin., 1963-71, R & C Tool & Mfg., Amelia, Ohio, 1970-71, Bourbon Copper & Brass, Cin., 1968-71; pres. Stewart Industries, Inc., Cin., 1971-80, chmn. bd., chief exec. officer, 1980—; pres. Printing Machinery Co., Cin., 1976—; pres. Stewart Safety Systems, Inc., 1981—. Chmn., dir. Greater Cin. & Ky. chpt. Nat. Hemophilia Found., 1976-80; del. White House Conf. Small Bus., 1980. Served with USNR, 1942-45. Mem. Cin. C. of C. (Small Businessman of Yr. 1980), Engring. Soc. Cin., Sales and Mktg. Execs., Assn. Equipment Distbrs., Lambda Chi Alpha. Republican. Presbyterian. Clubs: Rotary, Masons (Shriner), Royal Jesters, Maketewah Country, Northport Point Golf, Cin. (Man of Yr. 1979), Officers of World Wars. Home: 220 Linden Dr Cincinnati OH 45215 Office: Stewart Industries Inc 7234 Blue Ash Rd Cincinnati OH 45236

STEYER, FRANCIS JAMES, food company executive; b. Fostoria, Ohio, Jan. 26, 1935; s. Francis Albert and Helen Lucille (Smith) S.; m. Marilyn Ann Thiel, June 8, 1957; children—Laura, Denise, Lisa, Brian. B.S., Ohio State U., 1957. Produce buyer, store mgr. Kroger Co., Toledo, Ohio, 1960-65, advt. mgr., Pitts., 1965-67, zone mgr., Detroit, 1967-70; exec. v.p. Cardinal Foods, Inc., Columbus, Ohio, 1970-79; pres. Dublin Food Gallery, Ohio, 1979-83; pres., chief exec. officer Food Gallery Supermarkets, Columbus, 1983—; ptnr. Steyer Assocs., Worthington, Ohio, 1984—. Info. officer U.S. Naval Acad., Annapolis, Md., 1982—; bd. dirs. Dublin Arts Council, 1984—. Served with USN, 1957-60, comdr. USNR. Republican. Roman Catholic. Club: Navy League. Lodge: Rotary. Office: Food Gallery Supermarkets 5975 E Main St Columbus OH 43213

STEYER, RAYMOND JAMES, II, computer programmer; b. Downers Grove, Ill., Aug. 11, 1950; s. Raymond James and Jeane Olga (Wensch) S.; m. Karen Sue Jones, Mar. 3, 1984; 1 child, William Christopher. B.A. in Math. and Physics, Beloit (Wis.) Coll., 1972. Sr. programmer No. Trust Co., Chgo., 1972-75; v.p. software dept. Child Inc., Lawrence, Kans., 1975-77, also dir, 1976; sr. analyst/programmer Zurich Ins. Co., Chgo., 1977; programmer technician Montgomery Ward, Chgo., 1977-78; sr. systems engr. Econorex Systems, Kansas City, Mo., 1978-81; system engr. Electronic Data Systems, Kansas City, Mo., 1981-82; cons., 1980—; sr. analyst Universal Systems Am., Overland Park, Kans., 1984—. Mem. Math. Assn. Am., Assn. Computing Machinery. Roman Catholic. Home: 4517 E 112th St Kansas City MO 64137 Office: PO Box 24538 Kansas City MO 64131

STICKLER, IVAN, dairy products company executive. Pres., dir. Mid-Am. Dairymen, Inc., Springfield, Mo. Office: Mid-Am Dairymen Inc PO Box 1837 SS Station Springfield MO 65805*

STICKLER, ROBERT BROWN, surgeon; b. Red Oak, Iowa, Aug. 24, 1917; s. Archie Jay and Lois (Brown) S.; m. Charlotte Hill, Nov. 23, 1920; chilren—Linda Elizabeth, Robert Hill. B.S., U. Iowa, 1941, M.D., 1941. Diplomate Am. Bd. Surgery. Intern, Iowa Methodist Hosp., Des Moines, 1941-42; resident U.S. Army, 1942-45; with Iowa Meth. Hosp., 1945-47, S.W. Iowa Hosp., Iowa City, 1947-50; pvt. practice medicine specializing in surgery, Des Moines, 1950—; mem. staff, mem. teaching staff Iowa Meth. Hosp.; mem. staff Iowa Luth. Hosp., Mercy Hosp., Broadlawn Hosp. Bd. dirs. various civic orngs.; active Tallcorn council Boy Scouts Am. Served to maj. U.S. Army, 1942-45. Fellow ACS; mem. AMA, Iowa State Med. Assn., Polk County Med. Assn., Iowa Acad. Surgery. Congregationalist. Clubs: Wakonda (Des Moines); Garden of the Gods (Colorado Springs, Colo.). Contbr. articles to med. jours. Home: 2626 Sioux Run Des Moines IA 50321 Office: 1418 Woodland Ave Des Moines IA 50309

STICKNEY, JOHN MOORE, lawyer; b. Cleve., Apr. 8, 1926; s. Isaac Moore and Alicia Margaret (Burns) S.; m. Elfriede von Rebenstock, Oct. 4, 1958; children—Michaela B., Alicia J., Thomas M. A.B., Western Res. U., 1948, L.L.B., 1951. Bar: Ohio 1952. Sole practice, Cleve., 1952-79; ptnr. Burgess, Steck, Andrews & Stickney, Cleve., 1979—; pres. Scranton-Averell, Inc., Cleve., 1979—. Trustee Cleve. Music Sch. Settlement, 1967—, Salzedo Sch. Harp, Cleve., 1962—, Bishop Brown Fund, Cleve., 1981—; co-trustee Margaret & Edwin Griffiths Trusts, Cleve., 1968—. Served with USNR, 1945-46. Mem. ABA, Ohio State Bar Assn., Cleve. Bar Assn., Republican. Episcopalian. Club: Hermit (Cleve.). Avocation: woodworking. Office: Burgess Steck Andrews & Stickney 1140 Terminal Tower Cleveland OH 44113

STICKNEY, TRUMAN MANVILLE, engineer; b. Crookston, Minn., Dec. 2, 1922; s. Truman Leander, and Thora (Hagen) S.; m. Bernice Lillian Wheeler, Apr. 14, 1951; children—George, Jeffrey, Sandra. B.S. in Aerospace Engring., U. Minn., 1944, B.E.E., 1948. Research scientist NASA, Cleve., 1948-56; engring. supr. Aero Research Instrument Co., Chgo., 1956-60; project engr. Cook Electric Co., Chgo., 1960-63; sr. design engr. Rosemount, Inc., Eden Prairie, Minn., 1963-84, prin. design engr., 1984—. Contbr. articles to sci. jours Patentee high temperature measuring probe. Chmn. U.S. Savs. Bonds campaigns Rosemount plants, 1985. Served with USN, 1944-46, PTO. Assoc. fellow Am. Inst. of Aeros. and Astronautics (chmn. twin cities chpt. 1976). Republican. Presbyterian. Club: Spartan Speakers (Richfield, Minn.) (pres. 1972). Avocations: duck hunting, classical music. Home: 2409 W 97th St Bloomington MN 55431

STIEHL, CHARLES WILLIAM, physician, surgeon; b. South Milwaukee, Wis., Apr. 23, 1924; s. Carl Ernst and Marjorie (Simon) S.; B.S., Northwestern U., 1942, B.M., M.D., 1947; m. Sarah D. Harding, Dec. 20, 1945 (div. Oct. 1957); children—Patti (Mrs. Christopher Philbin), Carl Harding, Sarah Ann; m. 2d, Edith Ann Mauer, Nov., 1967; 1 dau., Edith Ann. Intern, Columbia Hosp., Milw., 1947-48; resident St. Mary's Hosp., Milw., 1948-49; physician and surgeon Algoma (Wis.) Clinic, 1950-66; chief surgery Algoma Meml. Hosp., 1964—; mem. dir. Heil Co., Milw. owner Von Stiel Wine, Inc., Algoma, 1961—; pres. S & M Real Estate Corp., Algoma, 1958—. Mem. Sch. Bd., 1954-58. Served with USNR, 1942. Mem. Wis., Kewaunee County (past pres.) med. socs., Wis. Coll. Emergency Physicians (pres.), Acad. Indsl. Medicine, Beta Theta Pi, Nu Sigma Nu. Lutheran. Author emergency medicine computer dictation software program. Originator Von Stiehl natural cherry wine, stabilization natural cherry wine, aging wrap. Home: 2740 W Forest Home Ave Milwaukee WI 53215 Office: 2740 W Forest Home Milwaukee WI

STIEWE, GERHILD GERTRAUD, German and Spanish educator; b. Aussig, Czechoslovakia, Sept. 26, 1933; came to U.S. 1956, naturalized 1961; d. Ludwig and Herta (Walter) Eiselt; m. Rainer Hermann Stiewe, Feb. 6, 1955; children—Barbara Ann, Carl Werner. B.A. magna cum laude, U. Minn., 1966, B.S. with high distinction, 1966, M.A., 1968, Ph.D., 1979. Teaching asst. U. Minn., Mpls., 1967-70; instr. German and Spanish, Inver Hills Community Coll., Inver Grove Heights, Minn., 1970—. Vol. lang. instr. Hubert Humphrey Job Corps. Ctr.; adviser St. Paul Learning Ctr. Recipient Outstanding Educator's award Inver Hills Community Coll. Student Assn. Mem. Am. Assn. Tchrs. Spanish and Portuguese (treas. Minn. chpt. 1984—), Am. Assn. Tchrs. German, Am. Council Teaching Fgn. Langs., Phi Beta Kappa, Sigma Delta Pi, Lambda Alpha Psi. Roman Catholic. Avocations: music; theater; reading; volleyball; gymnastics. Home: 2465 Londin Ln Maplewood MN 55119 Office: Inver Hills Community Coll 8445 College Trail Inver Grove Heights MN 55075

STIGLER, GEORGE JOSEPH, economist, educator; b. Renton, Wash., Jan. 17, 1911; s. Joseph and Elizabeth (Hungler) S.; m. Margaret Mack, Dec. 26, 1936 (dec. Aug. 1970); children—Stephen, David, Joseph. B.B.A., U. Wash., 1931; M.B.A., Northwestern U., 1932; Ph.D., U. Chgo., 1938; Sc.D., Carnegie Mellon U., 1973, U. Rochester, 1974, Helsinki Sch. Econs., 1976, Northwestern U., 1979; LL.D., Brown U., 1980. Asst. prof. econs. Iowa State Coll., 1936-38; asst. prof. U. Minn., 1938-41, asso. prof., 1941-44, prof., 1944-46, Brown U., 1946-47; prof. econs. Columbia, 1947-58; Walgreen prof. Am. instns. U. Chgo., 1958—, dir. Center Study Economy and the State, 1977—; lectr. London Sch. Econs., 1948; vice chmn., dir. Securities Investor Protection Corp., 1971-74; dir. Chgo. Bd. Trade, 1980-83. Author: Production and Distribution Theories, 1940, The Theory of Price, 1946, Trends in Output and Employment, 1947, Five Lectures on Economic Problems, 1949, (with K. Boulding) Readings in Price Theory, 1952, Trends in Employment in the Service Industries, 1956, (with D. Blank) Supply and Demand for Scientific Personnel, 1957, The Intellectual and the Market Place, 1964, 84, Essays in the History of Economics, 1965, The Organization of Industry, 1968, (with J.K. Kindahl) The Behavior of Industrial Prices, 1970, The Citizen and the State, 1975. The Economist as Preacher, 1982; Editor: Jour. Polit. Economy, 1972—; Contbr. articles to profl. jours. Mem. atty. gen.'s. com. for study anti-trust laws, 1954-55; mem. Blue Ribbon Def. Panel.; Trustee Carleton Coll. Recipient Nobel prize in econs., 1982; Guggenheim fellow, 1955; fellow Center for Advanced Study in Behavioral Scis., 1957-58. Fellow Am. Statis. Soc., Econometric Soc., Nat. Acad. Sci.; mem. Am. Econ. Assn. (pres. 1964), Royal Econ. Soc. Am. Philos. Soc., History of Econs. Soc. (pres. 1977), Mt. Pelerin Soc. (pres 1977-78). Office: U Chgo 1101 E 58th St Chicago IL 60637

STILLMAN, MIKELE GARFIELD, city official; b. Cleve., Aug. 14, 1938; d. Howard R. and Dorothy L. (Garfield) Rome; A.A., William Woods Coll., 1958; postgrad. Edgewood Coll., 1970, U. Wis., Madison, 1974—; children—Eva, Eric, Amea, Sarah. Spl. events dir. H.S. Manchester's, Inc., Madison, 1962-66; public service dir. WISC-TV, Madison, 1966-72; placement services dir. Goodwill Industries, Madison, 1974-80; instr. mktg. Madison Area Tech. Coll., 1963-73; clin. asso. Vocat. Rehab. Program, U. Wis., 1977-80; events coordinator Concourse/Mall, City of Madison, Dept. Public Works, 1980—; cons., trainer Dane County Affirmative Action Office; cons. employee tng. State of Wis., 1980—; chairperson Dane County Sect. 504 Team; adv. council Women's Resource Center; mem. contract compliance com. State Wis., 1979-80. Developer spl. program for juvenile offenders, 1963-70; bd. dirs. United Way, 1968; city rep. to coordinate Swiss Festival with Swiss Govt., Zurich, 1965; appted. by Gov. to document renovation of exec. residence on film, 1968; bd. dirs. YWCA, 1979-81, Capitol Farmers' Market Inc., 1983—; publicity chmn. Internat. Yr. of Disabled, 1981; chmn. publicity com. Dane County June Dairy Month Promotion, 1983—. Recipient Outstanding Service award for public broadcasting, 1971; Outstanding Pub. Service award Wis. Assn. Retarded Citizens, 1983. Mem. Nat. Rehab. Assn., Wis. Rehab. Assn., Job Placement for Handicapped Assn., Wis. Assn. Vocat. and Adult Edn., Phi Beta. Editor WIRE Rehab. Newsletter for Wis., 1977-78, Mall/Concourse News, 1983—. Contbr. articles to newspapers and jours., poetry to Jewish Heritage, Wis. State Jour., Capital Times. Office: 510 Ciemons Ave Madison WI 53704

STINSON, SCOTT LINNELL, doctor of chiropractic; b. Goldsboro, N.C., Nov. 24, 1956; s. Phillip Cedric and Arlene Joan (Linnell) S.; m. Renette Mary Grandstrand, June 23, 1984. Student St. Cloud State U., 1974-78; D.Chiropractic, Northwestern Coll. Chiropractic, 1982. Lic. chiropractor, Minn. Gen. practice chiropractic medicine, cert. sports physician, Inver Grove Heights, Minn., 1982—. Pres. Chiropractic Communications Group, St. Paul, 1985; student Leadership South St. Paul, 1984-85. Mem. Am. Chiropractic Assn., Minn. Chiropractic Assn. (com. chmn. 1984—), Am. Soc. Chiropractic Orthopedists, Northwestern Coll. Chiropractic Alumni Assn. Avocations: rugby; running; reading; fishing. Office: Cahill Chiropractic Office 5972 Cahill Ave Inver Grove Heights MN 55075

STIRITZ, WILLIAM P., food company executive. Chmn., pres., chief exec. officer Ralston Purina Co., St. Louis, also dir. Office: Ralston Purina Co Checkerboard Sq St Louis MO 63164*

STIRLING, JAMES PAULMAN, investment banker; b. Chgo., Mar. 30, 1941; s. Louis James and Beverly Louise (Paulman) S.; m. Ellen Adair Foster, June 6, 1970; children—Elizabeth Ginevra, Diana Leslie, Alexandra Curtiss. A.B., Princeton U., 1963; M.B.A., Stanford U., 1965. Vice-pres. corp. fin. Kidder, Peabody & Co., Inc., N.Y.C./Chgo., 1965-71, 84—; dir. internat. investments Sears Roebuck & Co., Chgo./London, 1971-75, 77-84; asst. to sec. commerce U.S. Dept. Commerce, Washington, 1976-77. Pres. Jr. Bd. Chgo. Symphony, 1968-70; trustee Chgo. Symphony, 1970-75; trustee Northwestern Meml. Hosp., Chgo., 1985—. Mem. Investment Analysts Soc., Bond Club of Chgo, Nat. Econs. Honor Soc. Episcopalian. Clubs: Chgo., Racquet (Chgo.); Onwentsia (Lake Forest, Ill.). Office: Kidder Peabody & Co Inc 125 S Wacker Dr Chicago IL 60606

STITCH, MORTON, aerospace company executive; b. N.Y.C., Aug. 26, 1929; s. Milton and Gussie (Levine) S.; m. Lois Eileen Algren, Nov. 21, 1952; children—Merryl Lynn, Mark Alan, Frank Brian, Douglas Bruce. B.E.E., CCNY, 1950. Jr. engr. Cons. & Designers, Inc., 1950, Teletone TV, 1950; engr. Arma Corp., 1951; div. mgr. Hazeltine Corp., Little Neck, N.Y., 1953-61; with McDonnell Aircraft Corp., St. Louis, 1961-68, group mgr. reliability, 1964-66, sect. mgr. reliability, 1966-68; with McDonnell Astronautics Co. (became McDonnell Douglas Astronautics Co.-St. Louis div. 1968), 1966—, chief effectiveness engr., 1975-76, mgr. harpoon product assurance, 1976-77, dir. product assurance, 1977—; pres. Advanced Healthcare Systems, St. Louis, 1982—, Stitch Mgmt. Enterprises, St. Louis, 1982—; dir. Larken Industries Ltd., Kansas City, Mo. Bd. dirs., sec. bd. Normandy Osteo. Hosp., St. Louis, 1974-84. Served as 1st lt. USAF, 1951-53. Fellow AIAA; mem. IEEE (sr.), Electronic Industries Assn. Avocations: computer programming; medical electronics. Home: 23 N Walling Dr Saint Louis MO 63141 Office: McDonnell Douglas Corp J S McDonnell Blvd Saint Louis MO 63134

STIVER, JAMES FREDERICK, pharmacist, health physicist, administrator; b. Elkhart, Ind., Jan. 27, 1943; s. Melvin Hugh and Pauline Anna (Schrock) S.; m. Joan Louise Trindle, Aug. 14, 1965; children—Gregory James, Richard Frederick, Kristin Louise, Elizabeth Ann. B.S. in Pharmacy and Pharm. Scis., Purdue U., 1966, M.S., 1968, Ph.D., 1970. Lic. pharmacist, Ind., N.D. Asst. prof. N.D. State U., Fargo, 1969-73, assoc. prof., 1973-76, radiol. safety officer, 1969-76; radiation safety officer KMS Fusion Inc., Ann Arbor, Mich., 1976-80; mgr., pharmacist Kroger Sav-On Pharmacy Co., Elkhart, Ind., 1980-81; pharmacist Elkhart Gen. Hosp., 1981; environ. regulatory affairs adminstr. Upjohn Co., Kalamazoo, Mich., 1981—; cons., lectr. Mem. Emergency Med. Service, Jefferson Township, Elkhart County, 1981—; mem. Trinity Luth. Ch., Goshen, Ind. Mem. Am. Pharm. Assn., Ind. Pharmacists Assn., N.D. Pharm. Assn., Am. Chem. Soc., Health Physics Soc., Internat. Radiation Protection Assn., Am. Biol. Safety Assn., N.Y. Acad. Scis., AAAS, Kappa Psi, Rho Chi, Phi Lambda Upsilon, Sigma Xi. Lodge: Masons. Contbr. articles, abstracts to publs. Home: 59089 SR15 Goshen IN 46526 Office: Upjohn Co Kalamazoo MI 49001

STOCKDALE, DAVID CLYDE, lawyer; b. Canton, Ohio, Mar. 10, 1950; s. Clyde Edison and Mary Margaret (Bremkamp) S.; m. Judith Ann Weizenecker, Apr. 24, 1982. A.B., Ohio U., 1972, M.A., 1973; J.D. U. Cin., 1976. Bar: Ohio 1976. Ptnr. Aronoff, Rosen & Stockdale and predecessor Aronoff & Rosen, Cin., 1976—; law dir. City of Mt. Healthy, Ohio, 1978-79. Editor: U. Cin. Law Rev., 1975-76. Contbr. articles to profl. jours. pres. City Council, Mt. Healthy, 1982-83, mayor, 1984—. Mem. ABA, Cin. Bar Assn., Phi Beta Kappa. Republican. Roman Catholic. Home: 7935 Seward Ave Mount Healthy OH 45231 Office: 425 Walnut St #1400 Cincinnati OH 45202

STOCKLAND, WAYNE LUVERN, nutritionist; b. Lake Lillian, Minn., May 4, 1942; s. Gaylord Luvern and Betty (Springstein) S.; m. Jerrilyn Jean Stockland, June 5, 1971; children—Lisa, Renee, Eric. B.S., U. Minn., 1964, Ph.D., 1969. Research asst. U. Minn., St. Paul, 1969, research fellow, 1969-70; research nutritionist Internat. Multifoods, Courtland, Minn., 1970-75, research nutritionist and statis. mgr., 1975-76, dir. animal nutrition research, 1976—. Contbr. articles to profl. jours. Pres., Courtland Vol. Fire Dept., 1979-83, Courtland Businessmen's Assn., 1974-84; mem. Courtland City Council, 1978-82. Mem. Am. Soc. Animal Sci., Am. Dairy Sci. Assn., Poultry Sci. Assn., Am. Inst. Nutrition, N.Y. Acad. Sci., Assn. Ofcl. Analytical Chemists. Republican. Lutheran. Lodge: Lions. Avocations: bowling; woodworking; fishing. Home: 421 Riverview Dr Courtland MN 56021 Office: Internat Multifoods Supersweet Research Farm Courtland MN 56021

STOCKMAN, RICHARD OWEN, manufacturing company executive; b. Plymouth, Ind., Oct. 9, 1930; s. Samuel Seth and Emma Gail (Amones) S.; student public schs.; children—Gary Blake, Roxanne, John Jay. Field service specialist Worthington Corp., Harrison, N.J., 1955-63; service mgr., product engr. Haskon, Inc., Warsaw, Ind., 1963-70; mgr. customer service DePuy div. Bio Dynamics Co., Warsaw, 1970-80; dir. ops. Kellogg Industries, Jackson, Mich., 1981-84, v.p. ops., 1984—; instr. Ind. Vocat. Tech. Coll. Served with USN, 1948-52. Clubs: Masons, Shriners. Home: 1104 Tanbark W Jackson MI 49203 Office: 159 W Pearl St Jackson MI 49201

STOCKTON, EUGENE LESLIE, lawyer; b. Oceanside, Calif., Jan. 15, 1953; s. Leslie Eugene and Ruth Elaine (Salzmann) S.; m. Pamela Steadly Cook, Mar. 31, 1984; children—Jessica, Catherine, Daniel. B.A., Augustana Coll., 1975; J.D., U. Dayton, 1978. Bar: Ill. 1978. Asst. states atty. Lee County, Ill., 1978-80, states atty., 1980—; dir. Petunia Festival Corp., Dixon, Ill., 1978-79, legal counsel, 1980—. Bd. dirs. NW Criminal Justice Comm., Dixon, 1980—; active Ogle-Lee Crimestoppers, Oregon, Ill., 1981—. Mem. ABA, Ill. State Bar Assn., Ill. States Attys. Assn., Am. Judicature Soc., Chgo. Bar Assn. Republican. Lodge: Lions (treas. 1983-84, sec. 1984-85, 3d v.p. 1985-86). Home: 618 E 2d St Dixon IL 61021 Office: Lee County States Atty PO Box 462 Dixon IL 61021

STODDARD, MICHAEL EUGENE, pharmacist; b. Council Bluffs, Iowa, Dec. 28, 1956; s. Noel Freemont and Kathryn E. (Wolfe) S. B.S. in Pharmacy, Drake U., 1979, M.B.A., 1984; M.D. candidate U. Iowa, 1984—. Registered pharmacist, Iowa. Pharmacist, Creighton U., Omaha, 1980-81, U. Tex./M.D. Anderson Hosp. and Tumor Inst., Houston, 1981-82, U. South Fla., Tampa, 1982-83; home health care cons., Iowa City, 1984—. Mem. Iowa Med. Soc., AMA (student), Sheishen Ki Karate Union, Sigma Iota Epsilon. Republican. Avocations: karate; photography; marathon running. Home: 620 12th Ave Apt #6 Coralville IA 52241

STOEBNER, DONALD, pharmacist; b. Eureka, S.D., July 29, 1947; s. Raymond E. and Norma (Neuharth) S.; m. Bonnie Lee McNeil, Dec. 27, 1969; children—Jodie Marie, Joseph. B.S., U. N.D., 1969; B.S. in Pharmacy, N.D. State U., 1977. Registered pharmacist, N.D., Wis. Tchr., Oriska Pub. Schs., N.D., 1969-70, Braddock Pub. Schs., N.D., 1970-74, Streeter Pub. Schs., N.D., 1974-75, Jud. Pub. Schs., N.D., 1975-76; owner, pharmacist Carson Pharmacy, Carson, N.D., 1977-82; owner, pharmacist Solar Town Pharmacy, Soldiers Grove, Wis., 1982—. Bd. dirs. Jacobson Meml. Hosp., Elgin, N.D., 1980-82, Kickapoo Valley Assn., La Forge, Wis., 1982—, Grant County Hist. Soc., Leith, N.D., 1978-82, Kickapoo Exchange, Gays Mills, Wis., 1983—. Mem. N.D. Pharm. Assn., Wis. Pharm. Assn., Fedn. Ind. Bus., Carson Mchts. Assn. (past pres.). Republican. Methodist. Club: Soldiers Grove Lions (treas. 1983—). Avocations: coin collecting, stamp collecting, barbed wire collecting, hunting, fishing. Home: Box 94 Soldiers Grove WI 54655 Office: Solar Town Pharmacy Passive Sun Dr Soldiers Grove WI 54655

STOECKMANN, ETHEL DOLORES, fin. exec.; b. N.Y.C., July 4, 1922; d. Albert Lewis and Ethel Carol (Wade) Infantas; student public schs., N.Y.C.; m. Sept. 17, 1944; 1 son, Robert W. Sec./treas. Stoeckmann Land Co., Inc., Baudette, Minn., 1972—, Stoeckmann Ranches, Inc., Red Bluff, Calif., 1976—, Stoeckmann Farms, Inc., Pecos Tex., 1977—, dir., 1951—; partner Stoeckmann & Co., 1972—, S & S Enterprises, Baudette, 1976—, Stoeckmann Investment Co., Red Bluff, 1976—. Democrat.

STOELTING, JOHN ALBERT, advertising agency executive; b. Vincennes, Ind., Sept. 11, 1936; s. Floyd William and Virginia Marie (Weiler) S.; B.B.A., U. Cin., 1959. Dist. group mgr. Ohio Nat. Life Ins. Co., Washington and Cin., 1959-63, life ins. agt., 1963-65; service and fund dir. Am. Cancer Soc., Cin., 1965-68; account exec. Shulman Advt., Cin., 1968-71; pres. Advt. Mgmt. Inc., Cin., 1971-80; dir. mktg. services Dektas & Eger Advt., Cin., 1980-81, v.p., 1981—; career resource advisor U. Cin., 1977—. Mem. Greater Cin. exec. council City of Hope, 1975-79; trustee Coll. Ednl. and Charitable Found., 1976—; mem. U. Cin. Greek Affairs Council. Mem. Am. Advt. Fedn., Bus./Profl. Advt. Assn., Delta Sigma Pi, Pi Delta Epsilon, Pi Kappa Alpha (dist. pres. 1960-66, Pres.'s Service award 1978, Disting. Service award Cin. chpt. 1979, dir. alumni assn. 1959-67, 74—, sec. 1979-80). Roman Catholic. Clubs: Cincinnatus, Advt. of Cin. (treas. 1978—; Disting. Service award 1983). Editor, Pi Kappa Alpha Newsletter, 1957-60, contbr., 1962-66, 75—. Office: 1077 Celestial St Cincinnati OH 45202

STOFER, JOHN MILTON, JR., history and government educator; b. Lakewood, Ohio, Nov. 17, 1935; s. John Milton and Lillian Caroline (Tinnerman) S.; m. Anna Marie Gerig, June 10, 1974 (div. June 1984). B.A., Colgate U., 1958; student Syracuse U., 1958-59; M.Edn., Kent State U., 1966; J.D., U. Akron, 1976. Cert. elem. tchr., Ohio. Tchr., Greene Local Schs., Smithville, Ohio, 1960—. Served with Army NG, 1959-65. Recipient Tchr. of Yr. award Greene Local Edn. Assn., 1980; Jennings scholar, 1984. Mem. Greene Local Edn. Assn. (pres. 1970-71, 81-82), Ohio Edn. Assn., NEA, Ohio Hist. Soc., Nat. Hist. Soc. Mem. Christian Ch. (Disciples of Christ). Avocations: running; physical fitness; reading; investments; cats. Home: 2340 H Cardinal Ct Wooster OH 44691 Office: Greene Middle Sch 484 E Main St Smithville OH 44677

STOKELY, WILLIAM BURNETT, III, business executive; b. Los Angeles, Sept. 18, 1940; s. William Burnett and Tamara S.; m. Kay Haslett July 25, 1962; children—William Burnett Stacy Ivie, Shelley Kay, Clayton Frank. Pres., The Stokely Co. and Stokely Affiliated Fin. Enterprises, Inc.; past chmn., chief exec. officer Stokely-Van Camp, Inc.; dir. Instries Portela, C. por A., Casa Linda, C. por A., Navarette, D.R., Mchts. Nat. Bank & Trust Co., Indpls. Pres., William B. Stokely, Jr. Found.; bd. dirs. Indpls. Conv. and Visitors Bur., St. Vincent Hosp. R&D Found., Indpls.; mem., past chmn. U. Tenn. Devel. Council, Knoxville; past chmn. bd. visitors Berry Coll., Rome, Ga.; mem. pres.'s council Brebeuf Sch. Indpls.; bd. dirs. Ind. Inst. Agr., Food and Nutrition, Inc., Internat. Inst. Sports Medicine; past chmn. Met. Indpls. campaign U.S. Savs. Bonds; mem. bus. adv. council U. Tenn. Mem. Ind. Canners Assn. (past pres.), Young Pres. Orgn., Penrod Soc. Indpls. (past pres.), Indpls. Mus. Art, Children's Mus. Indpls., U.S. C. of C. (dir., regional vice-chmn.), Newcomen Soc. N.Am., Kappa Sigma, Omicron Delta Kappa. Clubs: Economic (dir.), Hundred (dir.), University, Indpls. Athletic, Skyline (Indpls.); Crooked Stick Golf, Carmel Racquet (Carmel, Ind.). Office: 8900 Keystone Crossing Suite 1010 Indianapolis IN 46240

STOKES, LOUIS, congressman; b. Cleve., Feb. 23, 1925; s. Charles and Louise (Stone) S.; student Western Res. U., 1946-48; J.D., Marshall Law Sch., Cleve., 1953; LL.D. (hon.), Wilberforce U., 1969; Shaw U., 1971, Morehouse Coll., Meharry Coll. Medicine, Oberlin Coll.; m. Jeanette Francis, Aug. 21, 1960; children—Shelley, Louis C., Angela, Lorene. Admitted to Ohio bar, 1954, practiced in Cleve.; mem. firm Stokes, Character, Terry and Perry, from 1966; mem. 91st-99th Congresses from 21st Dist. Ohio, mem. Budget Com., Appropriations Com.; chmn. Select Com. King/Kennedy Assassinations, House Ethics Com.; dean Ohio Dem. del.; lectr. in field. Mem. internat. adv. council African Am. Inst. Served with AUS, 1943-46. Recipient numerous awards for civic activities. Mem. Am., Ohio (past chmn. criminal justice com.) bar assns., Nat. Assn. Def. Lawyers Criminal Cases (dir.), Fair Housing (dir.), Urban League, Citizens League, John Harlan Law Club, ACLU, Kappa Alpha Psi. Democrat. Club: Plus (Cleve.). Lodges: Masons (33 deg.). Office: 2304 Rayburn House Office Bldg Washington DC 20515*

STOLEE, MICHAEL JOSEPH, education educator, consultant; b. Mpls., Aug. 22, 1930; s. Gullik R. and Adeline J. (Thomason) S.; m. Marilyn Sandbo, June 7, 1952; children—Margaret Kay, Anne Marie. B.A., St. Olaf Coll., 1952; M.A., U. Minn., 1959, Ph.D., 1963. Assoc. dean edn. U. Miami, Coral Gables, Fla., 1970-75, prof., 1963-75; dean Sch. Edn., U. Wis.-Milw., 1975-84, prof., 1975—; acting assoc. headmaster U. Sch. Milw., 1985—; cons. sch. desegregation HEW, U.S. Dept. Justice, White House, NAACP, NAACP Legal Def. Fund, ACLU, states and sch. dists., Boston, Miami, Fla., Chgo., Phila., San Francisco, Mpls., Dallas, St. Louis, Pitts., Los Angeles, 1965—. Named Disting. Alumnus, St. Olaf Coll., Northfield, Minn., 1972. Mem. Am. Assn. Colls. Tchr. Edn. (govt. relations com. 1980-83), Phi Delta Kappa (area coordinator 1984—, pres. Milw. chpt. 1984-85). Democrat. Lutheran. Avocations: gardening, philately, photography. Home: 7033 N Lombardy Rd Milwaukee WI 53217 Office: U Wis-Milw PO Box 413 Milwaukee WI 53201

STOLNITZ, GEORGE JOSEPH, economist; b. N.Y.C., Apr. 4, 1920; s. Isidore and Julia (Jurman) S.; B.A., CCNY, 1939; M.A., Princeton U., 1942, Ph.D., 1952; m. Monique J. Delley, Aug. 26, 1976; children—Cindy, Wendy, Dia. Statistician, U.S. Bur. Census, 1940-41; research asso. Office Population Research, Princeton U., 1948-56; asst. prof. econs. Princeton U., 1953-56; prof. econs. Ind. U., Bloomington, 1956—; vis. research scholar Resources for the Future, 1965-67; dir. Ind. U. Internat. Devel. Research Center, 1967-72; prin. officer population and econ. devel. UN, N.Y.C., 1976-78; cons. Ford Found., Rockefeller Found., UN, U.S. Congress, U.S. Dept. Energy, Dept. Commerce, Dept. State, HEW; vis. lectr. univs.; cons. to pvt. industry. Served to capt. USAF, 1942-46. NSF fellow, 1959-60. Mem. Am. Econ. Assn., Am. Statis. Assn., Econometric Soc., Population Assn. Am. (pres. 1983), Internat. Union for Sci. Study Population, Phi Beta Kappa. Club: Cosmos (Washington). Author: Life Tables from Limited Data: A Demographic Approach, 1956; editor: World Population: The Look Ahead, 1968; Concise Report on World Population: New Beginnings and Uncertain Ends, 1979; contbr. articles to profl. jours. Home: 2636 Covenanter Ct Bloomington IN 47401 Office: Dept Econs Ind Univ Bloomington IN 47405

STOLTE, LARRY GENE, computer processing company executive; b. Cedar Rapids, Iowa, Sept. 17, 1945; s. Ed August and Emma Wilhelmena (Tank) S.; B.B.A. with highest distinction (FS Services scholar), U. Iowa, 1971; m. Rebecca Jane Tappmeyer, June 13, 1970; children—Scott Edward, Ryan Gene. Tax and auditing acct. McGladrey Hendrickson & Co., Cedar Rapids, 1971-73; v.p. TLS Co., Cedar Rapids, 1973—, also dir. Served to sgt. USMC, 1964-67. C.P.A., Iowa, Ill., Mo., Minn., Mich., Wis.; cert. mgmt. acct. Mem. Nat. Assn. Computerized Tax Processors (pres.), Nat. Assn. Accts., Am. Inst. C.P.A.'s, Am. Mgmt. Assn. Republican. Methodist. Home: 2107 Linmar Dr NE Cedar Rapids IA 52402 Office: TLS Co 425 2d St SE PO Box 1686 Cedar Rapids IA 52406

STOLTZ, CHARLES EDWARD, meat packing company executive; b. Dubuque, Iowa, July 31, 1936; s. Edward and Bertha (Klingenberg) S.; B.S. in Bus. Adminstrn., U. Dubuque; M.A., U. Iowa; m. Jean Wahlert, Aug. 20, 1964; children—Jennie, Michael, John, Charles II. Salesman, Am. Can Co., 1961-62; v.p. Dubuque Packing Co., 1965, exec. v.p., to 1977, pres., 1977—, chmn., 1982—; dir. Dubuque Bank & Trust Co., Am. Trust and Savs. Bank. Trustee U. Dubuque, United Fund, Boys Club. Served with USMC, 1956-58. Office: Dubuque Packing Co Suite 200 7171 Mercy Rd Omaha NE 68106

STOLTZFUS, CONRAD MARTIN, virologist; b. Ft. Dodge, Iowa, Oct. 19, 1942; s. Chris Martin and Elizabeth (Graber) S.; m. Charlotte Marie Kivisto, Aug. 19, 1965; children—Katharine Anne, Mark Frederick. Student Goshen Coll., 1960-62; B.A., U. Colo., 1966; Ph.D., U. Wis., 1971. Postdoctoral fellow Roche Inst., Nutley, N.J., 1971-73; asst. prof. Vanderbilt U., Nashville, 1973-79, assoc. prof., 1979; assoc. prof. dept. microbiology U. Iowa, Iowa City, 1979-85, prof., 1985—. Author jour. articles. Nat. Cancer Inst. research career devel. awardee, 1976, research grantee, 1981—. Mem. Am. Soc. Microbiology, Am. Soc. Virology, AAAS, Sigma Xi, Phi Beta Kappa. Avocations: running; amateur astronomy. Home: 1641 Derwin Dr Iowa City IA 52240 Office: Dept Microbiology U Iowa Iowa City IA 52242

STONE, IRVING I., See *Who's Who in America,* 43rd edition.

STONE, J. W., superintendent schools; b. Fortescue, Mo., Nov. 6, 1927; s. Perry Allen and May (Murrah) S.; B.S., NW Mo. State Coll., 1956; M.A., U. Mo., Kansas City, 1957, also postgrad. Farmer, Fortescue, Mo., 1944—; instr. Craig (Mo.) R-III High Sch., 1957-59; supt. schs., Holt County, Oregon, Mo., 1959-61, Craig R-III Sch. Dist., 1961—; del. to Hungary, USSR, Internat. Edn. Soc., 1968; mem. Mo. Adv. Council on Vocat. Edn., 1983—. Dist. dir. ARC, 1954—, bd. dirs. Midland Empire region, 1979—; bd. dirs. Heart Assn., Crippled Children's, March of Dimes, Tb Soc., 1954—; mem. Town Bd., Fotescue, Mo., 1962-78; mayor City of Fortescue, 1968-78; chmn. Holt County Citizens Council, 1979—; vice chmn. Wesley Found., NW Mo. State U., 1970—; mem. regional empire com. bd. Girl Scouts, 1973-75; mem. com. Mo. Council Public Higher Edn., 1973; regional dir. Mo. Vocat. Rehab., 1967—; chmn. bd. NW Mo. Community Services, 1980—. Mem. 6th Congressional Dist., 1960—, 6th Congressional Legis. Dist., 1960—, Mo. Republican State Com., 1960—; chmn. Holt County Rep. Central Com., 1954—; state com. del. to inauguration Pres. Reagan, 1981; mem. Balance of State Planning Council, State of Mo., 1981—. dir. OEO Corp.; sec.-treas. NW Mo. Econ. Opportunity Corp., Maryville, Mo., chmn. bd., 1969-79; v.p. Mo. Council Chs., 1948-50; dir. Camps and Conf., W. Mo. Conf., United Meth. Ch., 1965—, mem. bd. adminstrv. fin., 1972—; mem. Selective Service Bd. Mo. Region I, 1982, Appeals Bd. Western half of Mo., 1983; U.S. del. World Meth. Council Meeting, Dublin, 1976, Honolulu, 1981; Maryville dist. trustee Meth. Ch., 1960—. World del. Meth. Conf., Oslo, Norway, 1961; del. United Meth. Ch. Mo. West Conf. to World Meth. Council Evangelism, Jerusalem, 1974; world del. representing U.S. on Christian Edn., Tokyo, 1958; U.S. del. Comparative and Internat. Edn. Soc., Round-the-World, 1970, S. Am., 1971. Served with AUS, 1950-52. Mem. NEA, Nat., Mo. State assns. sch. adminstrs., Mo. State, Holt County (past pres.) tchrs. assns., Pi Omega Pi, Kappa Delta Pi, Tau Kappa Epsilon. Methodist (dist. lay leader 1968—). Clubs: Masons (32 deg., Shriner), Order Eastern Star. Home: Fortescue MO 64452 Office: Craig MO 64437

STONE, JOHN TIMOTHY, JR., author; b. Denver, July 13, 1933; s. John Timothy and Marie Elizabeth (Briggs) S.; student Amherst Coll., 1951-52, U. Mex., 1952; B.A., U. Miami, 1955; m. Judith Bosworth Stone, June 22, 1955; children—John Timothy, George William. Sales mgr. Atlas Tag, Chgo., 1955-57; br. mgr. Household Fin. Corp., Chgo., 1952-62; pres. Janeff Credit Corp., Madison, Wis., 1962-72; pres. Recreation Internat., Mpls., 1972-74; pres. Continental Royal Services, N.Y.C., 1973-74; author: Mark, 1973; Going for Broke, 1976; The Minnesota Connection, 1978; Debby Boone So Far, 1980; (with John Dallas McPherson) He Calls Himself "An Ordinary Man", 1981; Satiacum, The Chief Who's Winning Back the West, 1981; The Great American Treasure Hunt, 1983; Runaways, 1983; (with Robert E. Gard) Where The Green Bird Flies, 1984; dir. Madison Credit Bur., Wis. Lenders' Exchange. Served with CIC, U.S. Army, 1957-59. Mem. Sigma Alpha Epsilon. Republican. Presbyterian. Clubs: Minarani, African First Shotters. Home: 1009 Starlight Dr Madison WI 53711 Office: Wordworks PO Box 5562 Madison WI 55705

STONE, NEIL JOSEPH, cardiologist, educator, researcher; b. Chgo., Dec. 17, 1944; s. Milton J. and Margery (Berstein) S.; m. Karla Saxon, May 4, 1975; children—Scott, Adam, Lauren. B.S. in Medicine, Northwestern U., 1966, M.D. in Medicine with honors, 1968. Diplomate Am. Bd. Internal Medicine, Am. Bd. Cardiovascular Diseases. Intern, then resident Peter Bent Brigham Hosp., Boston, 1968-70; staff assoc. NIH, Bethesda, Md., 1970-73; chief resident Northwestern Meml. Hosp., Chgo., 1973-74; fellow in cardiology Northwestern Med. Sch., Chgo., 1974-75, asst. prof., 1975-80, assoc. prof. medicine, 1981—; lectr. Cook County Grad. Sch., Chgo., 1976—. Author: Fat Chance, 1980. Contbr. publs. and chpts. in books to med. jours. Recipient Award of Yr., Chgo. Dietetic Assn., 1978, Teaching Attending of Yr. award Northwestern Med. Sch., 1979. Fellow ACP, Am. Coll. Cardiology, Am. Heart Assn. (council arteriosclerosis), Council Clin. Cardiology, Inst. Med.; mem. Chgo. Heart Assn. (nutrition sub com. 1979—), Northwestern Med. Sch. Alumni Council (pres. 1981-83). Jewish. Avocations: golf, stamps. Home: 1341 Edgewood Ln Winnetka IL 60093 Office: 707 N Fairbanks Ct Suite 1210 Chicago IL 60611

STONE, PAUL ALLEN, electronic company executive; b. Springfield, Ill., July 7, 1932; s. Carroll Lee and Besse Marie (Shumate) S.; m. Doris Alma Altwine, Oct. 12, 1952 (dec. 1970); children—Lee Allen, Lynette Marie; m. Mary Ann Schribner, June 26, 1972. B.E.E., TriState Coll., 1958. Project engr. Heath Co., Benton Harbor, Mich., 1959-62; sales mgr., elec. engr. Utah Electronics, Huntington, Ind., 1962-65; sales mgr. R.T. Bozak Mfg. Co., Norwalk, Conn., 1969-70, Elpa Mktg., New Hyde Park, N.Y., 1970-72; mfg. rep. Paul Stone Sales, Indpls., 1972—. Co-author software, 1981, 82. Patentee in field. Served to staff sgt. USAF, 1952-56. Republican. Presbyterian. Club: Toastmasters (v.p. 1982-83). Lodge: Shriners, Masons. Avocations: flying; music. Office: Paul Stone Sales Co Inc 5174 Allisonville Rd Indianapolis IN 46205

STONE, ROGER WARREN, container manufacturing company executive. Chmn., chief exec. officer Stone Container Corp., Chgo., also dir. Office: Stone Container Corp 360 N Michigan Ave Chicago IL 60601*

STONE, W. CLEMENT, insurance executive; b. Chgo., May 4, 1902: s. Louis and Anna M. (Gunn) S.; student Detroit Coll. Law, 1920, Northwestern U., 1930-32; LL.D., Monmouth Coll., 1963; H.H.D., Interlochen Arts Acad., 1964; Litt.D., Coll. Chiropractic, Lombard, 1969; H.H.D. (hon.), Whitworth Coll., 1969, S.W. Baptist Coll., 1970, Lincoln Coll., 1970; LL.D., Whittier Coll., 1973, Detroit Coll. Law, 1983; D. Pub. Service, Salem Coll., 1974; m. Jessie Verna Tarson; children—Clement, Donna (dec.), Norman. Chmn. bd., dir. Combined Internat. Corp.; chmn. bd. Combined Ins. Co. Am., Chgo.; chmn., dir. Combined Life Ins. Co. N.Y., Albany, W. Clement Stone PMA Communications, Inc.; chmn. bd. Combined Opportunities, Inc., Chgo.; chmn. bd., chief exec. officer, dir. Combined Ins. Co. Wis. (merged into CICA), Fond du Lac; organizer Combined Mut. Casualty Co., 1940, pres. 1940-47; dir. Alberto-Culver Co.; chmn. bd. Success, The Mag. for Achievers; Chgo. Hon. chmn. bd. Chgo. Boys' Club, named Chicagoan of Yr., 1980; mem. nat. exec. com. Boys Club Am.; chmn. bd. W. Clement and Jessie V. Stone Found.; chmn. bd. trustees Internat. Council on Edn. for Teaching; trustee George Williams Coll.; bd. govs. Chgo. Heart Assn.; bd. dirs., mem. Lyric Guild, Lyric Opera Chgo.; pres., trustee Religious Heritage Am.; mem. exec. com. Internat. Fedn. Keystone Youth Orgns.; hon. trustee So. Baptist Coll.; trustee Urol. Research Found., Coll. Medicine U. Utah; chmn. trustees Interlochen Arts Acad. and Nat. Music Camp. Recipient Horatio Alger award, 1963; Church Layman of the Year award, 1968; nominee Nobel Peace Prize, 1981. Mem. Adler Planetarium Soc., Chgo. Assn. Health Underwriters Chgo., Am. Life Ins. Assn., Soc. Midland Authors, United Shareholders Am. (mem. nat. policy adv. com.), Art Inst. Chgo. (life), Northwestern U. Alumni Assn., Ill. C. of C., Chgo. Ednl. TV Assn. (trustee), Insts. Religion and Health (chmn. bd.), Alpha Kappa Psi. Presbyn. Clubs: Masons; Chicago Press, John Evans, Executives, Michigan Shores Country. Author: (with Napoleon Hill) Success Through a Positive Mental Attitude; (with Norma Lee Browning) The Other Side of the Mind: The Success System that Never Fails. Office: 222 N Dearborn Chicago IL 60601

STONE, WILLIAM BRUHN, English educator; b. Milw., May 31, 1929; s. William Herbert and Martha Emily (Bruhn) S.; B.A. with gen. honors, U. Chgo., 1948, M.A., 1957; m. Jane Bergman, Mar. 13, 1953; children—David, Daniel, Joyce. Instr. English, U. Ky., Lexington, 1958-61, Wis. State U., LaCrosse, 1961-62; lectr. English, Ind. U. N.W., Gary, 1962-71, 80—; asst. dir. composition U. Ill., Chgo., 1976-80; editorial cons. various pubs. Active member Amnesty Internat. U.S.A. Served with AUS, 1952-54; Korea. Mem. AAUP, Assn. Tchrs. Advanced Composition (v.p. 1984—), Conf. Coll. Composition and Communication, Midwest Modern Lang. Assn., MLA, Nat. Council Tchrs. of English, Rhetoric Soc. Am., Anthony Powell Soc. (sec.-treas. 1983—), U.S. Chess Fedn., ACLU. Editor: Anthony Powell Communications, 1977-79; editorial bd. Jour. Advanced Composition, 1979—, contbg. editor, 1984—. Contbr. articles, revs. and poetry to profl. jours., articles to ency. Home: 5704 S Kenwood Ave Chicago IL 60637 Office: Indiana University Gary IN 46408

STONEKING, LEWIS WILLIAM, college dean; b. Hannibal, Mo., July 5, 1923; s. Lewis Levi and Arlene (Wolfgram) S.; m. Lena Precup, Nov. 24, 1949; children—Lewis Michael, Leslie Myron, Lisa Arlene, Lori Ann. B.A., Harris Tchrs. Coll., 1950, M.A., Ball State U., 1957, Ed.D., Ind. U., 1960. Cert. supt., curriculum dir., elem. tchr., secondary tchr. Tchr. St. Louis Pub. Schs., 1950-54; tchr. secondary sch. University City Pub. Schs., Mo., 1954-56, Anderson Pub. Schs., Inc., 1956-57; asst. prof. edn. Ball State U., Muncie, Ind., 1956-57; vis. lectr. Ind. U., Bloomington, 1959-60; prof. edn. George Peabody Coll. Tchrs., Nashville, 1960-65; vis. prof. edn. Central Washington State Coll., Ellensburg, 1969, Eastern Washington State Coll., Cheney, 1967; chmn. dept. edn. Parsons Coll., Fairfield, Iowa, 1965-72; dean Coll. Edn., U. Wis.-Whitewater, 1972—. Author: Modern Elementary Mathematics, 1966. Contbr. articles to profl. jours. Served as tech. sgt. USMC, 1943-46. Mem. NEA, Assn. Childhood Edn. Internat. (editorial bd.) Lodge: Rotary. Office: U Wis 800 W Main St Whitewater WI 53190

STONER, ELAINE BLATT, chemical patent literature analyst; b. Bklyn., Dec. 31, 1939; d. Joseph and Ann (Wertentheil) Blatt; m. Clinton Dale Stoner, Apr. 18, 1965; children—Robert, Michael. B.S., Bklyn. Coll., 1961; Ph.D., U. Calif.-Berkeley, 1965. NIH postdoctoral fellow U. Wis., 1964-65; with Chem. Abstracts Service, Columbus, Ohio, 1965—, sr. editor, 1976—. Mem. Am. Chem. Soc., Sigma Xi. Home: 1014 Kenway Ct Columbus OH 43220 Office: PO Box 3012 Columbus OH 43210

STONER, RALPH BOYD, company controller; b. Mt. Pleasant, Pa., Oct. 13, 1939; s. Lyle Hunt and Mary Jane (Boyd) S.; m. Nancy Jane Hayden, Dec. 20, 1960 (div. 1971); children—Stephen H., Robert M.; m. Sharalyn Sue Durr, May 4, 1978; 1 child, Kenneth Durr. B.S. in B.A., W.Va. U., 1961; M.B.A., Kent State U.-Ohio, 1971. With Firestone Tire, Akron, 1961-66; sec., controller Firestone Singapore, 1966-69; corp. acct. Firestone Tire, Akron, 1969-72, adminstrv. asst. to pres., 1972-74; controller NDM Corp., Dayton, 1974—. Mem. Nat. Assn. Accts., Miami Valley Mgmt. Assn. Republican. Avocations: computer programming; investment analysis; auto mechanics; bowling; jogging. Home: 47 Dorchester Dr Dayton OH 45415 Office: NDM Corp 3040 E River Rd Dayton OH 45439

STORM, RANDAL HALL, educational bookstore administrator; b. Indpls., July 12, 1953; s. Ronald S. Storm and Fayetta R. (Hall) Storm Davis; m. Linda Sue Chambers, May 8, 1976; children—David R., Emily F. Student Edison Jr. Coll., 1971-72, Lincoln Christian Coll., 1973-75. Bookstore mgr. Lincoln Christian Coll., Ill., 1981—. Elder Lincoln Christian Ch., 1983—; cast mem. Lincoln Community Theater, 1979, 81, 83, 85. Mem. Nat. Assn. Coll. Stores, (cert.), Ill. Assn. Coll. Stores (membership chmn. 1984, treas. 1985). Democrat. Mem. Christian Ch. Club: Kiwanis (Lincoln). Avocation: music, photography. Home: 501 Oglesby Ave Lincoln IL 62656 Office: Lincoln Christian Coll Bookstore 100 Campus View Dr Lincoln IL 62656

STORY, BENJAMIN SPRAGUE, clergyman; b. Cleve., Apr. 24, 1924; s. Benjamin S. and Jean Dale (Marshall) S., Sr.; m. Cleo Josephine Davis, Jan. 7, 1944; children—Benjamin S., III, Willard E., Constance Ann. B.B.A., U. Minn., 1949; postgrad. Presbyn. Theol. Sem., 1975. Sales mgr. Town and Country Real Estate, Louisville, Ky., 1951-78; pres., owner Ben Story Apt. Rentals, Jeffersonville, Ind., 1967-79; priest Episcopalian Ch. Diocese of Indpls., 1978—; social minister Episcopal Ch., Daviess and Jackson Counties, Ind., 1978—. Served with AUS, 1943-46. Mem. Louisville Apt. Assn. (bd. dirs. 1972—, pres. 1974). Republican. Club: Seymour Country (Ind.). Lodge: Elks. Avocations: travel; reading; theater; radio control flying; swimming; scuba diving; boating. Home: 648 Parkwood Dr Jeffersonville IN 47130

STOTLAR, BRIAN SCOTT, accountant; b. Davenport, Iowa, July 3, 1951; s. Robert Lawrence and Muriel Eleanor (Johnson) S.; m. Carol Ann McCutcheon, Dec. 30, 1982; children—Liza Ann Verhelst, Nathan Robert. B.A. in Acctg., St. Ambrose Coll., 1974. C.P.A., Ill., Wis. Acct. Coopers & Lybrand Assocs., Chgo., 1974-78; ptnr. Baillies, Denson, Erickson & Smith, Madison, Wis., 1978-85; shareholder Stotlar & Stotlar, S.C., Madison, 1985—. Mem. Am. Inst. C.P.A.s (team capt. peer rev. 1982-84), Wis. Inst. C.P.A.s (chmn. competence aid com. 1983-85), Exchange Club. Republican. Presbyterian. Avocation: golf. Home: 5030 Regent St Madison WI 53705 Office: Stotlar & Stotlar SC 702 N Blackhawk Ave Madison WI 53705

STOTTLEMYER, HERBERT LEE, retired city letter carrier; b. Anderson, Ind., May 9, 1926; s. Herbert and Alice Catherine (Seybert) S.; m. Carolyn Sue Stohler, Oct. 26, 1952. Student Gen. Motors Inst. Tech., 1944. Apprentice toolmaker Delco Remy, Anderson, 1943-45; farm machinery mechanic, Case Farm Machinery, Anderson, 1945-48; semi-skilled machinist Pierce Governor Co., Anderson, 1948-53; cable splicers helper, Gen. Telephone, Anderson, 1953-55; city carrier U.S. Postal Service, Anderson, 1955-85. Served with U.S. Army, 1950-51. Mem. Nat. Federated Craft (nat. sec. 1970—). Mem. United Ch. Christ. (past trustee, deacon). Lodges: Kentucky Colonels, Masons. Avocations: gardening; sports; traveling; reading. Home: 5824 S Ridge Rd Anderson IN 46011 Office: Nat Federated Craft 5824 S Ridge Rd Anderson IN 46011

STOTTLEMYRE, DONNA MAE, jewelry store executive; b. Mystic, Iowa, Nov. 11, 1928; d. Clarence William and Nina Alene (Millizer) Clark; m. Robert Arthur Stottlemyre, May 8, 1946; children—Roger Dale, Amber Anita, Tamra Collette. Owner, operator Donna's Dress Shop, Unionville, Mo., 1973-76, Donna's Jewelry Box and Bridal Boutique, Unionville, 1978—. Sunday sch. tchr. First Baptist Ch., Unionville, Bible sch. tchr.; 4H Club judge County Fair, Unionville. Mem. C. of C. Avocations: sewing; flower arranging. Home: 217 N 14th Unionville MO 63565 Office: Donna's Jewelry and Bridal 1610 Main Unionville MO 63565

STOUP, ARTHUR HARRY, lawyer; b. Kansas City, Mo., Aug. 30, 1925; s. Isadore and Dorothy (Rankle) S.; student Kansas City (Mo.) Jr. Coll., 1942-43; B.A., J.D., U. Mo., 1950; m. Kathryn Jolliff, July 30, 1948; children—David C., Daniel P., Rebecca Ann, Deborah E. Admitted to Mo. bar, 1950, D.C. bar, 1979; pvt. practice law, Kansas City, Mo., 1950—; mem. firm Stoup & Thompson; mem. Lawyer to Lawyer Consultation Panel-Litigation, 1976—; chmn. U.S. Merit Selection Com. for Western Dist. Mo., 1981. Chmn. com. to rev. continuing edn. U. Mo., 1978-79; trustee, pres. U. Mo. at Kansas City Law Found., 1979-82; trustee U. Kansas City, 1979—. Served with USNR, 1942-45. Recipient Alumni Achievement award U. Mo.-Kansas City Alumni Assn., 1975. Fellow Internat. Soc. Barristers, Am. Bar Found.; mem. Kansas City (pres. 1966-67), Mo. (bd. govs. 1967-76, v.p. 1972-73, pres.-elect 1973-74, pres. 1974-75), Am. (ho. of dels. 1976-80) bar assns., Lawyers Assn. Kansas City, Mo. Assn. Trial Attys., Assn. Trial Lawyers Am. (sustaining mem.), So. Conf. Bar Pres.'s (life), Mobar Research Inc. (pres. 1978—), Phi Alpha Delta Alumni (justice Kansas City area 1955-56, William H. Pittman hon. award Lawson chpt. 1974), Tau Kappa Epsilon. Mem. B'nai B'rith. Clubs: Optimists (pres. Ward Pkwy. 1961-62, lt. gov. Mo. dist. internat. 1963-64); Sertoma. Home: 9002 Western Hills Dr Kansas City MO 64114 Office: Home Savs Bldg Kansas City MO 64106

STOUT, DONALD EVERETT, real estate developer and appraiser; b. Dayton, Ohio, Mar. 16, 1926; s. Thorne Franklin and Lovella Marie (Sweeney) S.; B.S., Miami U., 1950; m. Gloria B. McCormick, Apr. 10, 1948; children—Holly Sue, Scott Kenneth. Mgr. comml.-indsl. div. G.P. Huffman Realty, Dayton, 1954-58; leasing agt., mgr. Forest Park Plaza, Dayton, 1959-71; developer 1st transp. center for trucking in Ohio; pres. devel. cos. Sunderland Falls Estates, Wright Gate Indsl. Mall, Edglo Land Recycle, Grande Tierra Corp., Dayton and Eastwood Lake Lodge/Marina; pres. Donald E. Stout, Inc. Served with AUS, 1944-45, USN, 1945-46. Named Outstanding Real Estate Salesman in Dayton, Dayton Area Bd. Realtors, in Ohio, Ohio Bd. Realtors, 1961. Licensed real estate broker, Ohio, U.S. Virgin Islands. Mem. Dayton Area Bd. Realtors (founder; 1st pres. salesman div. 1959, dir. 1959-60), Nat. Assn. Real Estate Bds., Soc. Real Estate Appraisers (sr. real estate appraiser, dir. chpt. 1959-60, pres. chpt. 1964), Am. Inst. Real Estate Appraisers, Nat. Assn. Rev. Appraisers (charter), Soc. Indsl. Realtors, Appraisal Inst., Res. Officers Assn., C. of C., Phi Delta Theta. Clubs: Masons (32 deg.), Shrine, Dayton Racquet. Contbr. articles to profl. jours. Home: 759 Plantation Ln Dayton OH 45419 Office: 1336 Woodman Dr Dayton OH 45432

STOUT, GLENN EMANUEL, meteorologist, educator; b. Fostoria, Ohio, Mar. 23, 1920; s. Glen Hosler and Eva Myrtle (Barkley) S.; B.S., Findlay (Ohio) Coll., 1942, D.Sc., 1973; cert. U. Chgo., 1942, 46; m. Helen Lucille Beery, Nov. 15, 1942; children—Bonnie Gywnn, Steven Owen. Instr., U. Chgo., 1943; head atmospheric sci. sect. Ill. State Water Survey, Urbana, Ill., 1947-69, 71-73; sci. coordinator NSF, 1969-71; prof. environ. studies U. Ill., 1973—, dir. Water Resources Center, 1973—. Bd. dirs. Salvation Army, Champaign County, 1979—; bd. govs. Univ. YMCA, 1979—; mem. Ill. Gov.'s Task Force on State Water Plan, 1980—; bd. dirs. Univ. Council Water Resources, 1983—; mem. U.S. com. Internat. Hydrologic program UNESCO. Served with USNR, 1942-52. Mem. Am. Meteorol. Soc., Am. Geophys. Union, Am. Water Resources Assn., N.Am. Lake Mgmt. Soc., Internat. Water Resources Assn. (pres. U.S. geog. com. 1979-83, exec. dir. 1984—), AAAS, Ill. Acad. Sci., Sigma Xi (sec. U. Ill. chpt. 1981-84, pres. 1985—, chmn. nat. meeting 1984). Methodist. Club: Kiwanis (pres. Champaign-Urbana 1979-80, lt. gov. Div. 26, 1982-83). Editor-in-chief: Water Internat., 1981-85, sec. gen., 1986—. Office: University of Illinois 208 N Romine St Urbana IL 61801

STOUT, GORDON HOWARD, computer systems executive, consultant; b. Northville, Mich., Dec. 8, 1939; s. Leslie Harold Stout and Wilma Elizebeth (Bell) Stull; m. Judith Kay Sieberg, June 21, 1957; children—Debra Lynn, Mark Douglas, Jeffrey Todd, Jonathan Paul. B.A., So. Ill. U., 1964; postgrad., U. Ky., 1966, Purdue U., 1966. Tchr. math., sci. Evansville Day Sch., Ind., 1964-66; sci. programmer Monsanto Research, Miamisburg, Ohio, 1966-68; sci. programmer, analysis Duriron Co., Dayton, Ohio, 1968-69, mgr. programming engrng. analysis, 1969-77, mgr. programming, ops., 1977-81, asst. dir. info. systems, 1981—; systems cons. dir. Hipple Lab.-Cancer Research, Kettering, Ohio, 1983—; analyst, programmer Carousel Dance Studio, Dayton, 1984—. Sec., chmn. edn. com. Dayton Christmas Schs. Inc., 1972-82. NIH grantee, 1966. Mem. Assn. Systems Mgmt. Republican. Baptist. Avocations: swimming, scuba diving, ballroom dancing. Home: 1401 Kin Richard Pkwy West Carrollton OH 45449 Office: Duriron Co Inc PO Box 11 . 425 N Findlay Dayton OH 45401

STOVER, JAMES R., manufacturing company executive; b. Marion, Ind., 1927; B.M.E., Cath. U. Am., 1950; LL.B., George Washington U., 1955; married. Project engr. Eisenhauer Mfg. Co., 1950-51; patent examiner U.S. Patent Office, Washington, 1951-55; with Eaton Corp., Cleve., 1955—, hydrostatics program coordinator, Marshall, Mich., 1968-69, plant mgr., 1969-71, gen. mgr., 1971-73, gen. mgr. engineered fasteners div., 1973-74, group v.p. indsl. and security products, 1974-77, corp. exec. v.p. ops., 1977-78, vice-chmn., chief operating officer transp. products, 1978-79, pres., chief operating officer, 1979—, also dir.; dir. Nat. City Corp., Nat. City Bank, White Consol. Industries, Leaseway Transp. Co., Ohio Bell Telephone Co. Bd. dirs. Greater Cleve. Growth Assn., Hwy. Users Fedn. Mem. U.S. C. of C. (bd. dirs.). Office: Eaton Corp Eaton Center Cleveland OH 44114

STOWE, CHARL KENNETH, lawyer; b. Champaign, Ill., Oct. 4, 1951; s. Carl Henry and June Maydon (Wood) S. B.A., Greenville Coll., 1974; M.A., So. Ill. U., Edwardsville, 1975; Ph.D., St. Louis U., 1978; J.D., So. Ill. U., Carbondale, 1981. Bar: Ill. 1981, U.S. Dist. Ct. (so. and cen. dists.) Ill. 1981, U.S. Ct. Appeals (7th cir.) 1981, U.S. Supreme Ct. 1984. Mem. history dept. Kaskaskia Coll., Centralia, Ill., 1970-74, Greenville Coll., Ill., 1972-74, So. Ill. U., Edwardsville, 1974-75, St. Louis U., 1975-78; ptnr. Stowe & Stowe, Greenville, 1981—. Home and Office: 611 Ward Greenville IL 62246

STRADLEY, NORMAN HENRY, ceramic engineer; b. Newark, Ohio, June 28, 1924; s. Edward Foster and Catherine Leah (Keller) S.; m. Margaret Jeanne Coy, Nov. 27, 1947; children—Edward Ray, Pamela Jeanne. B.S., Ohio State U., 1949, M.S., 1949; student U. Va., 1943-44. Registered profl. engr., Tenn. Research fellow Ohio State U. Found., Columbus, 1949; research engr., group supr. Minn. Mining & Mfg. Co., St. Paul, 1950-59; tech. and supervisory research positions Am. Lava Corp., Chattanooga, 1960-75; product devel. specialist 3M Co., 1976-81; patent liaison 3M Co., St. Paul, 1982—; cons. in field. Served to maj. USAFR, to 2d lt. USAF, 1943-46. Fellow Am. Ceramic Soc., Am. Inst. Chemists; mem. Nat. Inst. Ceramic Engrs., Keramos, Sigma Xi, Tau Beta Pi, Sigma Gamma Epsilon, Sigma Nu. Club: Lions (dist. gov. 1982-83). Contbr. articles to profl. jours.; patentee in field. Home: 740 Nightingale Blvd Stillwater MN 55082 Office: 3M Co 3M Center Saint Paul MN 55101

STRAHLER, VIOLET RUTH, educational administrator; b. Dayton, Ohio, Sept. 30, 1918; d. Ezra F. and Bertha (Daniels) S. A.B. magna cum laude, Wittenberg U., 1944; M.A., Miami U., Ohio, 1959; Ed.D., Ind. U., 1972. Cert. tchr., supt., Ohio. Tchr. Miamisburg Pub. Schs., Ohio, 1944-51; tchr., counselor Dayton Pub. Schs., 1952-66, supr. sci. and math. curriculum, 1967-72, acting asst. supt. curriculum, 1972-73, exec. dir. curriculum services, 1973—; instr. U. Dayton, Miami U., 1959-74; ednl. cons. Author and co-author numerous textbooks, lab. guides. Editor newsletter Ohio Jr. Acad. Sci., 1950-52. Contbr. articles to profl. jours. Mem. Dayton/Montgomery County Arson Task Force; trustee Dayton Mus. Natural History. Ford Found. fellow, 1952-53. Mem. NOW, Am. Assn. Sch. Adminstrs., Buckeye Assn. Sch. Adminstrs., Assn. Supervision and Curriculum Devel., Am. Chem. Soc., Nat. Sci. Tchrs. Assn. (life), Ohio Acad. Sci., Phi Delta Kappa. Methodist. Home: 5340 Brendonwood Ln Dayton OH 45415 Office: 4280 N Western Ave Dayton OH 45427

STRAIGHT, BONNIE JEAN, information systems consultant; b. Inglewood, Calif., Nov. 17, 1942; d. James A. and Evelyn Mae (Ash) Reeser; m. Richard Leroy Straight, Aug. 12, 1966. B.A., DePaul U., 1985; student N. Central Coll., Naperville, Ill., 1965-66, El Centro Coll., Dallas, 1970-72. Programmer analyst Assn. Logos Bookstores, Ann Arbor, Mich., 1975-78, Spring Arbor Distbrs., Ann Arbor, 1978-79; systems rep. Honeywell Info. Systems, Southfield, Mich., 1979-80; programmer analyst Mfg. Data Systems, Inc., Ann Arbor, 1980-81; data processing mgr. Callaghan & Co., Wilmette, Ill., 1981-84; dir./cons. Dunham Systems Corp., Roselle, Ill., 1984-85; pres., cons. The Alpha Group, Chgo., 1985—. Vol., Peace Corps/Nat. 4-H Found., Brazil, 1963-65; elder 1st Presbyn. Ch., Evanston, Ill., 1985—; deacon Univ. Reformed Ch., Ann Arbor, 1980-81. NSF/Tex. Women's U. grantee, 1971. Mem. Women in Mgmt., Assn. Systems Mgmt. (chpt. treas. 1982, v.p. 1983), Christian Ministries Mgmt. Assn. Avocations: fiber arts, literature; Bible studies; humanitarian issues. Home: 1860 Sherman Ave #15E Evanston IL 60201 Office: The Alpha Group 1860 Sherman Ave #15E Evanston IL 60201

STRAIGHT, WILLIAM GILBERT, hospital administrator, consultant; b. St. Petersburg, Fla., Feb. 1, 1931; s. Alfred and Wilma Ruth (Brooks) S.; m. Carol Joyne Goodner, Sept. 15, 1950; children—Joyce Lynette, Toni Marie Straight Davis. B.S. in Bus. Adminstrn., So. Coll., Collegedale, Tenn., 1960; postgrad., Franklin U., 1977, U. Dayton, 1979. Adminstr., Watkins Meml. Hosp., Ellijay, Ga., 1963-68; regional systems mgr. United Med. Labs., Portland, Oreg., 1968-73; assoc. adminstr. Harding Hosp., Worthington, Ohio, 1974-80; adminstr. Windsor Hosp. (Mo.), 1980-81; sr. v.p. Battle Creek Adventist Hosp. (Mich.), 1981—; design cons. to psychiatric hosps., mental health ctrs. Trustee Good Samaritan Hospice, Battle Creek, 1981—, Moberly Regional Med. Ctr. (Mo.), 1980-81; former mem. County Disaster Planning Commn.; bd. dirs. New Day, Inc., Berrian Springs, Mich., 1983—. Served with U.S. Army, 1956-58. Recipient Outstanding Achievement award Harding Hosp., 1977, Top Three award U.S. Army Med. Corps., 1956. Mem. Am. Coll. Hosp. Adminstrs., Epsilon Delta Chi. Lodge: Lions. Home: 406 WahWayTay See Way Battle Creek MI 49015 Office: Battle Creek Adventist Hosp 165 N Washington Ave Battle Creek MI 49016

STRANAHAN, ROBERT A., JR., manufacturing company executive; b. Toledo, 1915. With Champion Spark Plug Co., 1935—, v.p., 1949-54, pres., 1954-85, chmn. bd. and chief exec. officer, dir., 1962—; chmn. bd., dir. Baron Drawn Steel Corp., Anderson Co.; pres., dir. Hellertown Mfg., Iowa Industries, P B Mktg. Office: Champion Spark Plug Co Inc 900 Upton Ave PO Box 910 Toledo OH 43661*

STRAND, GAIL CHRISTINE, pharmacist; b. Mankato, Minn., May 12, 1955; d. Stanley John and Mildred T. (Chlian) Hadac; m. Timothy John Strand, Sept. 17, 1983. B.S. in Pharmacy, S.D. State U., 1978. Registered pharmacist, Minn. Pharmacist Volness Drug Store, Lake Crystal, Minn., 1978-79, Corner Drug Store, LeSueur, Minn., 1978-79, Merwin Drug Store #4, Maple Grove, Minn., 1979-81, Erickson Valu Drug Store, St. Peter, Minn., 1981—. Vol. VFW Aux., St. Peter, 1973—, Ladies Guild St. Peter's Ch., 1984—. Mem. Am. Pharm. Assn., Minn. Pharm. Assn. Republican. Roman Catholic. Lodge: Redmen (Pochohontas 1982—). Avocations: sewing; crewel work; quilting; cooking. Home: 1413 Winona St Saint Peter MN 56082

STRAND, JOHN ARTHUR, III, manufacturing company executive; b. LaCrosse, Wis., Feb. 18, 1950; s. John A. and Grace S.; B.A., U. Wis., LaCrosse, 1972; m. Laurie R. Gibson, Aug. 7, 1971; children—Kathryn, John IV. With Seven-Up Bottling of LaCrosse, 1972—, v.p., 1978-81, pres., 1981—; pres. Route Acctg. Mgmt. Systems. cons. data processing. Mem. Nat. Soft Drink Assn., Wis. Soft Drink Assn., Nat. Seven-Up Developers Assn. Clubs: Masons, Shriners. Office: 2041 Avon St LaCrosse WI 54601

STRAND, ROBERT JAMES, state revenue administrator; b. Madison, Wis., Oct. 14, 1938; s. Ernest Strand and Doris Eleanor (Erickson) Strand Frydenlund; m. Karen Faye Thorne, Dec. 30, 1960; children—Shelley Dawn, Derrick Robert. B.S. in Econs., U. Wis., 1962. Cert. assessor, Wis. Salesman Pillsbury Co., Milw., 1962-64; with Wis. Dept. Revenue, Madison, 1964—, asst. to div. adminstr., 1970-77, spl. asst. to bur. dir., 1977—, chmn. statewide adv. com. on assessor continuing edn., 1980—. Vice pres. Elvejham Parent Tchrs. Orgn., Madison, 1972; chmn. Buckeye Evang. Free Ch., Madison, 1976; mem. exec. bd. Timberlee Christian Ctr., East Troy, Wis., 1978-80. Served with Air N.G., 1956-62. Mem. North Central Regional Assn. Assessing Officers (planning com. 1982-83). Home: 5305 Greenbriar Ln Madison WI 53714 Office: Wis Dept Revenue 125 S Webster St Madison WI 53702

STRANDBERG, FLOYD ALVIN, educational administrator; b. Muskegon, Mich., Aug. 11, 1948; s. Gerald and Elizabeth (Lofton) S.; m. Sandra Kay McSorley, Dec. 20, 1969; children—Kevin, Jennifer. B.A., Western Mich. U., 1970; M.A., Central Mich. U., 1972, Ed.S., 1984. Counselor Ferris State Coll., Big Rapids, Mich., 1970-73; tchr. Big Rapids Schs., 1973-78, Morley-Stanwood Schs., Morley, Mich., 1978-80; prin. Baldwin Middle Sch., Baldwin Community Schs., Mich., 1980-84, Baldwin High Sch., 1984—. Served to 1st lt. U.S. Army, 1966-70. Mem. Western Mich. Prin. Assns. (pres. 1982-84). Republican. Mem. United Ch. of Christ. Club: Western Mich. Athletic Assn. (Big Rapids). Avocation: running. Home: Route 1 Box 318 Reed City MI 49677 Office: Baldwin Schs 525 W 4th St Baldwin MI 49304

STRANDHAGEN, ADOLF GUSTAV, engineering educator; b. Scranton, Pa., May 4, 1914; s. Daniel Peter and Theresa Ann (Lylick) S.; m. Lucile E. Perry, Aug. 22, 1941; children—Karen, Gretchen. B.S., U. Mich., 1939, M.S., 1939, Ph.D., 1942. Asst. prof., research physicist Nat. Def. Research Council, Carnegie Inst. Tech. and Princeton U., 1942-46; assoc. prof. engrng. sci. U. Notre Dame, 1946-50, prof., 1950—, chmn. dept. engrng. sci., 1950-68; cons. U.S. Navy Mine Def. Lab., 1961-67; temporary staff U.S. Navy David Taylor Model Basin, 1958-60. Recipient Outstanding Engr. award St. Joseph chpt. ASME, 1958. Mem. Soc. Naval Architects and Marine Engrs. (mem. panel H-10 ship maneuvering 1965-75), Soc. Engrng. Sci., ASME. Assoc. editor Jour. Vehicle Dynamics, 1972-80, Bull. on Ship Maneuvering, 1975; contbr. research papers and reports on hydrodynamics, ship maneuvering, applied math., probability theory to profl. jours. Office: Coll Engring Univ Notre Dame Notre Dame IN 46556

STRANG, CHARLES DANIEL, See *Who's Who in America,* 43rd edition.

STRANG, DURWOOD STANLEY, tax commissioner; b. Marshall County, Ind., July 30, 1924; s. Dolph R. and Lila G. (Miller) S.; m. Agnes Jean Friend; 1 dau., Diane. Diploma in Gen. Acctg., South Bend (Ind.) Coll. Commerce, 1943; B.S.C., Internat. Bus. Coll., Ft. Wayne, Ind., 1948. Acct., Studebaker Corp., South Bend, 1954-64; field auditor Ind. Bd. Tax Commrs., Indpls., 1964-66, no. supr., 1966-67, commr., 1967—. Served with U.S. Army, 1943-46, 50-51. Decorated Bronze star. Mem. Internat. Assn. Assessing Officers, Am. Legion. Democrat. Methodist. Lodges: Odd Fellows, Moose. Home: 867 Golfview Terr Plainfield IN 46168 Office: 201 State Office Bldg Indpls IN 46204

STRANSKY, TERRY ELLIOT, geologist; b. N.Y.C., July 25, 1951; s. Howard Wolf and Sandra (Glick) S.; m. Renee Gail Greenwald, Dec. 1, 1974; children—Scott Jason, Elissa Joy. B.S. in Geology, Bklyn. Coll., 1972, M.A. in Geology, 1977. Cert. profl. geologist, Ind. Geologist, U.S. Army Corps. Engrs., Cin., 1977—; expert witness. Contbr. articles to profl. jours. Served with U.S. Army, 1972-74. Mem. Assn. Engring. Geologists, Internat. Soc. for Rock Mechanics, Am. Assn. Petroleum Geologists. Avocations: mineral collecting; coaching and refereeing youth soccer; reading. Home: 5803 Jeb Stuart Dr Milford OH 45150 Office: US Army Corps of Engrs 5851 Mariemont Ave Cincinnati OH 45227

STRASSER, DON DAVIS, automobile sales executive; b. Burnettsville, Ind., Mar. 13, 1944; s. Thomas Robert Sr. and Margaret Estelle (Regan) S.; m. Sharon Sue Smith, May 31, 1964. Grad., Burnettsville High Sch., 1962. Salesman Dave Mason Oldsmobile-Cadillac, Logansport, Ind., 1977-79, Greg Rudd Oldsmobile-Cadillac, 1979-81, Bill Timberman Motor Sales, 1981-84; owner, mgr. Don Strasser Motor Sales, Logansport, 1984—. Active Cass County Mental Health Assn., Cass County United Way, Logansport. Served with U.S. Army, 1966-68, Vietnam. Mem. Cass County C. of C., Cass County Churchmen United. Methodist. Lodges: Kiwanis (pres. 1980-82), Eagles. Avocations: electronics repair; bowling; automobile repair. Office: Don Strasser Motor Sales Inc Logansport IN 46947

STRASSER, KURT ALBERT, township official; b. Chgo., Nov. 6, 1942; s. Carl Joseph and Mary Eugena (Gifford) S.; m. Martha Etta Adams, Sept. 20, 1962; children—Dawn, Adam, Sarah. Cert. in acctg. and bus. adminstrn. McBride Bus. Coll., Dallas, 1963. Cert. assessing officer, rev. appraiser, Ill. Dep. assessor York (Ill.) Twp., 1973-75; appraiser DuPage County (Ill.), 1975-77; chief dep. assessor Addison Twp. (Ill.), 1977-82, assessor, 1982—; tchr. Ill. Property Assessment Inst. Past pres. DuPage Young Reps. (Ill.); past treas. Ill. State Young Reps.; Rep. committeeman Addison (Ill.) Twp. Served to 2d lt. USAF, 1961-62. Mem. Internat. Assn. Assessing Officers, Am. Fed. Appraisers, Ind. Fee Appraisers, Paralyzed Vets. Am., DAV. Roman Catholic. Lodges: Wood Dale Lions; Moose; Masons (32d deg.) (Chgo. and Lombard, Ill.). Office: Township Addison 121 E Fullerton Ave Addison IL 60101

STRATTON, FREDERICK P., JR., manufacturing company executive; b. Milw., 1939. B.S., Yale U.; M.B.A., Stanford U., 1963. With Arthur Andersen & Co., 1963-65, Robert W. Baird & Co. Inc., 1965-73; asst. service mgr. Briggs & Stratton Corp., Wauwatosa, Wis., 1973-75, asst. sales mgr., 1975, mgr. sales and service adminstrn., 1976, v.p. adminstrn., now pres. and chief exec. officer, 1977—; dir. Allen Bradley Co., Marine Corp., Pabst Brewing Co., Weyenberg Mfg. Co. Office: Briggs & Stratton Corp 3300 N 124th St Wauwatosa WI 53222*

STRATTON, WILLIAM GRANT, banker; b. Ingleside, Ill., Feb. 26, 1914; s. William J. and Zula (Van Wormer) S.; B.A., U. Ariz., 1934; hon. degrees John Marshall Law Sch., North Central Coll., Shurtleff Coll., 1954, Bradley U., Lincoln Coll., 1955, Elmhurst Coll., 1956, Lincoln Meml. U., 1957, So. Ill. U., U. Ariz., 1958; Mem. U.S. Congress from Ill., 1941-43, 47-49; treas. State of Ill., 1943-45, 51-53, gov., 1953-61; livestock farmer, Cantrell, Ill., 1954-70; ins. bus., Chgo., 1965-68; asst. to pres. Canteen Corp., Chgo., 1968, v.p. corp. relations, 1968-81, dir., 1981-84; v.p. Chgo. Bank of Commerce, 1984—; dir. Dartnell Corp. Chmn., Interstate Oil Compact Commn., 1955, Nat. Gov.'s Conf., 1957; pres. Council State Govts., 1958; mem. Lincoln Sesquicentennial Commn., 1958, Fed. Adv. Commn. Intergovtl. Relations, 1959, Ill. Task Force on Higher Edn., 1970-71, Ill. Legis. Reapportionment Commn., 1971; regent Lincoln Acad. of Ill., 1966—; del. Rep. Nat. Conv., 1952, 56, 60, 76; former chmn. bd. trustees Robert Morris Coll., Carthage, Ill.; mem. adv. council U. Toledo Coll. Bus. Adminstrn., 1976-79; bd. dirs. Mundelein Coll., Chgo., 1976—, Davenport Coll., Grand Rapids, Mich., 1976—, Nat. Inst. Foodservice Industry, 1975-78, Kemper Charitable and Ednl. Found., Chgo. Better Bus. Bur., Chgo. Crime Commn., pres. USO, Chgo., 1984-85, chmn. bd., 1985—; co-chmn. Ill. Election Reform Commn., 1985. Served to lt. (j.g.) USNR, 1945-46; PTO. Mem. Chgo. and Ill. Restaurant Assn. (chmn. 1977—), Ill. C. of C. (dir. 1976—), Am. Legion, Amvets, Mil. Order World Wars (comdr. Chgo. chpt. 1971-72), Nat. Inst. Foodservice Industry (pres. 1979-80), Delta Chi. Methodist. Club: Executives (Chgo.) (bd. dirs. Lodges: Masons (33 deg.), Rotary (pres. Chgo. 1979-80). Home: 3240 N Lake Shore Dr Chicago IL 60657 Office: Chgo Bank of Commerce 225 N Michigan Ave Chicago IL 60601

STRAUMAN, GERALD DAVID, optometrist; b. Pekin, Ill., Aug. 3, 1950; s. Russell Raymond and Jennie Arlene (Holland) S.; m. Susan Frazier, July 6, 1974; 1 child, Michael Richard. O.D., Ill. Coll. Optometry, 1976. Gen. practice optometry, Havana, Ill., 1976—. Bd. dirs. Havana Library, 1978. Mem. Nat. Eye Research Found. Roman Catholic. Club: Optimists. Lodges: Elks, K.C. Avocations: jogging, aerobics, racquetball, woodworking. Home: 529 N Promenade Havana IL 62644 Office: 108 E Market St Havana IL 62644

STRAUSBAUGH, J(OHN) DEAN, judge; b. Columbus, Ohio, Aug. 27, 1918; s. Harold Dale and Ethel Minerva (Dean) S.; m. Mary Elizabeth Smith, Aug. 30, 1949; children—Elizabeth Ann O'Boyle, John Dean, Jr. B.A., Duke U., 1940; postgrad. in Indsl. Adminstrn., Bus. Sch. Harvard U., 1943; J.D., U. Mich., 1947. Bar: Ohio 1948. Sole practice, Columbus, Ohio, 1948-54; reading clk. Ohio Ho. of Reps., 1950-54; 1st asst. City Atty's Office, Columbus, 1954-55; judge Franklin County Mcpl. Ct., Columbus, 1955-68, 10th Dist. Ct.

Appeals, Columbus, 1968—. Bd. dirs. Mt. Carmel Hosp., Columbus; past pres. Columbus Area Community Mental Health Ctr., 1970-73, Columbus Area Council on Alcoholism and One-to-One; mem. adv. bd. Franklin County Leukemia Soc., Alcoholism Prevention Bd., Columbus Dept. Health; bd. dirs. Community Agy. for Labor and Mgmt.; mem., past governing bd. 1st Community Ch.; past bd. dirs., v.p. Catholic Social Services. Served to lt. USN, 1943-46. Recipient Disting. Service award Columbus Jaycees, 1955. Mem. Ohio State Bar Assn., Columbus Bar Assn., Ohio Cts. of Appeals Assn. (chief justice 1983), Ohio Mcpl. Judges Assn. (pres. 1966-69), Delta Tau Delta. Republican. Club: University (pres.). Home: 1228 Kenbrook Hills Dr Columbus OH 43220 Office: Tenth Dist Ct Appeals 369 S High St Columbus OH 43215

STRAUSS, PAUL LEONARD, lawyer; b. Syracuse, N.Y., July 2, 1956; s. Bernard S. and Carol Maxine (Dunham) S.; m. Marlies Ann Carruth, Sept. 4, 1982. B.A. summa cum laude with highest honors in History of Ideas, Williams Coll., 1978; J.D., Yale U., 1981. Bar: Ill. 1981, U.S. Dist. Ct. (no. dist.) Ill. 1981, U.S. Ct. Appeals (7th cir.) 1984. Assoc. Davis, Miner, Barnhill & Galland, Chgo., 1981—. Mem. Chgo. Council Lawyers (state jud. evaluation com. 1983—), Phi Beta Kappa. Home: 5300 South Shore Dr Apt 122 Chicago IL 60615 Office: Davis Miner Barnhill & Galland 14 W Erie St Chicago IL 60610

STRAUSS, ROBERT FREDRICK, amusement company executive; b. Des Moines, May 9, 1930; s. William Andrew and Ruth Almeda Strauss S.; m. India Viola Crawford, June 11, 1951 (div. 1969); children—Vicki L., Yvonne M.; m. Beverly Jean Wray, June 23, 1961; children—Robert W., Thomas E. Student Des Moines Tech. Sch. Service engr. SCM, Des Moines, 1952-55; maintenance technician Abbott Labs., North Chicago, Ill., 1955-63; sales rep. Herschberger Truck and Equipment Co., Mundelein, Ill., 1963-65; Western regional sales mgr. D-Fab Engring. Co., Montgomeryville, Pa., 1965-67; gen. mgr. Terra Equipment Co., Mundelein, 1967-78; pres. Circus Promotions Corp., Cary, Ill., 1978—; corp. officer RSP Promotions, Cary, 1980—; ptnr. CICS, Deerfield, Ill., 1967—. Patentee in field. Served with U.S. Army, 1950-52. Republican.

STRAUSS, WILLIAM VICTOR, lawyer; b. Cin., July 5, 1942; s. William Victor and Elsa (Lovitt) S.; m. Linda Leopold, Nov. 9, 1969; children—Nancy T., Katherine S. A.B. cum laude, Harvard U., 1964; J.D., U. Pa., 1967. Bar: Ohio 1967. Ptnr. Strauss, Troy & Rehulmann Co., L.P.A., Cin., 1969—; pres. Security Title and Guaranty Agy., Inc., Cin., 1982—. Mem. Cin. C. of C. Housing Com., 1980—; dir. Pro-Seniors, 1985—. Mem. Cin. Bar Assn., Ohio State Bar Assn., ABA. Avocations: tennis; music; world affairs. Home: 40 Walnut Ave Wyoming OH 45215 Office: Strauss Troy & Ruehlmann Co LPA 2100 Central Trust Ctr 201 E 5th St Cincinnati OH 45202

STRAWHECKER, PAUL JOSEPH, fundraiser, association executive; b. Omaha, Oct. 31, 1947; s. John Leslie and Leone Francis (Kalamaja) S.; student St. Joseph's Sem., 1963-67, Blessed John Neumann Coll., 1967-68; B.A., Creighton U., 1970, student Law Sch., 1971-73; M.P.A., U. Nebr., 1980; m. Margaret Ellen Baumann, Aug. 31, 1974; children—Risa Nicole, Ryan John. Research specialist Mayor's Office, City of Omaha, 1970, spl. asst. to mayor, 1971, mgr. spl. programs, 1972-73; dir. spl. resources Father Flanagan's Boys Home, Boys Town, Nebr., 1974-81; v.p. for devel. Luth. Hosps. and Homes Soc. of Am., Fargo, N.D., 1982—. treas. Credit Union, 1975; clk., treas., liaison officer Village of Boys Town, 1974-81; writer Am. Soc. Planning Ofcls.; past owner The Wooden Spoon Ltd., Omaha. Chmn. Met. Area Planning Agency Council Ofcls. Goals Com. for Human Services, 1976; mem. Omaha/Douglas County Criminal Justice Commn., 1977-80; mem. adv. com. Douglas County Office on Children Youth; chmn. urban affairs com. Met. Area Planning Agy. Mem. Nat. Assn. Fund Raising Execs. (cert., pres. N.D. area chpt., bd. dirs.), Nat. Assn. Hosp. Devel. (speaker 1983), Internat. City Mgmt. Assn. (speaker 1971), Phi Kappa Psi. Roman Catholic. Home: 3901 River Dr Fargo ND 58103 Office: Luth Hosps and Homes Soc PO Box 2087 Fargo ND 58107

STRAWN, EARL HOWARD, city official; b. Lancaster, Ohio, Mar. 1, 1937; s. Howard H. and Florence A. Strawn; m. Julia A. Phillips, June 14, 1963. Student Columbus Tech. Inst., 1977. With Lancaster & Carroll Elevator Co., 1955-63; with Ohio Dept. Transp., Lancaster, 1963—, service-safety dir., 1980—. Bd. advisors Salvation Army: precinct committeeman Republican Party. Served with U.S. Army, 1957. Mem. Ohio Assn. Pub. Safety Dirs. (trustee), Buckeye State Sheriff Assn., Fraternal Order of Police Assn., C. of C. Methodist. Clubs: Lions, Elks, Order of Ky. Cols., Masons, Shriners. Home: 445 Hilltop Dr Lancaster OH 43130 Office: 104 E Main St Lancaster OH 43130

STRECKER, LOUIS FREDERICK, III, marketing company executive; b. St. Louis, Feb. 21, 1942; s. Louis F. and Helen M. (Reiser) S.; m. Carol A. Meyer, Sept. 6, 1965. B.A., U. St. Louis, 1963; postgrad. Washington U., St. Louis, 1963-65. Sales mgr. Rayfax div. Litton Industries, St. Louis, 1966-70, regional mgr., Columbus, Ohio, 1970-73; regional mgr. C. ITOH, Columbus, 1973-76; v.p. Govtl. Interiors, St. Louis, 1976-80; owner, pres. Contract Design Products, St. Louis, 1980—; cons. furniture mfg. firms, Iowa, 1983—, Ill., 1984—; guest speaker U. Mo. Sch. Design, Columbia and St. Louis, 1984. Served with N.G., 1965-69. Mem. Midwest Travelers, Nat. Office Products Assn. Avocations: golf; chess. Office: Contract Design Products Suite 306 7700 Clayton Rd Saint Louis MO 63117

STREETMAN, JOHN WILLIAM, III, museum official; b. Marion, N.C., Jan. 19, 1941; s. John William, Jr. and Emily Elaine (Carver) S.; B.A. in English and Theatre History, Western Carolina U., 1963; cert. in Shakespeare studies Lincoln Coll., Oxford (Eng.) U., 1963; m. July 15, 1967 (div.); children—Katherine Drake, Leah Farrior, Burgin Eaves. Founding dir. Jewett Creative Arts Center, Berwick Acad., South Berwick, Maine, 1966-70; exec. dir. Polk Pub. Mus., Lakeland, Fla., 1970-75; dir. Mus. Arts and Sci., Evansville, Ind., 1975—; chmn. mus. adv. panel Ind. Arts Commn., 1977-78. Mem. Am. Assn. Museums, Assn. Ind. Museums (bd. dirs.). Episcopalian. Office: 411 SE Riverside Dr Evansville IN 47713

STREICH, ARTHUR HAROLD, business exec.; b. Mpls., Apr. 22, 1925; s. Herman Henry and Rose (Anderson) S.; B.A. in Journalism, Macalester Coll., 1952; m. Arlene June Ostlund, Aug. 30, 1947; children—Jennifer Streich Hallam, Jack, Paula Jo. Partner, S&E Publs., St. Paul, 1952-55; asst. sec. Northwestern Lumbermans Assn., 1955-57; gen. mgr. Nat. Electronics Conf., 1957-59; public relations exec. Mullen & Assos., Inc., Mpls., 1959-60; investment adviser Dempsey Tegeler & Co., Inc., Mpls., 1960-63; regional sales mgr. Dreyfus Corp., 1963-68; regional v.p. Anchor Corp., Chgo., 1968-69; regional v.p. wholesale sales and mgmt. Dreyfus Sales Corp., Chgo., 1969-72; regional v.p. Crosby Corp., Chgo., 1972-73; regional sales mgr. John Nuveen & Co., Chgo., 1973-74; owner Fin. Planning Services Co., Wayzata, Minn., 1974—. Republican candidate for mayor St. Paul, 1952. Served with USN, 1942-46. Mem. Nat. Assn. Security Dealers (registered prin.), Nat. Speakers Assn. Republican. Mem. Evang. Free Ch. Club: Toastmasters (Disting. Toastmaster). Address: 14431 Wellington Rd Wayzata MN 55391

STRENGER, JAN ELIZABETH, social worker; b. Lake Forest, Ill., Jan. 6, 1954; d. Donald Sell and Mona Elizabeth (Benson) S.; B.A., Yankton Coll., 1976. Supr., counselor Lewis/Clark Mental Health Center, Yankton, S.D., 1976-78, acting program adminstr., 1978; case mgr. Yankton Area Adjustment Tng. Center, 1978-80, program dir., 1980—; cons. S.D. Human Service Center. Mem. Gov.'s Task Force on Dual Diagnosis/DD Offenders. Cert. in behavior mgmt. techniques, U. S.D.; cert. mental retardation profl., S.D. State Adjustment Tng. Services; cert. trainer Mandt System. Coach, Yankton Spl. Olympics Team. Mem. Am. Assn. Mental Deficiency, Nat. Rehab. Assn., Assn. for Retarded Citizens. Republican. Presbyterian. Home: 416 E 16th St Yankton SD 57078 Office: Yankton Area Adjustment Tng Center 909 W 23d St Yankton SD 57078

STRESEN-REUTER, FREDERICK ARTHUR, II, mining company executive; b. Oak Park, Ill., July 31, 1942; s. Alfred Proctor and Carol Frances (von Pohek) S.-R.; cert. in German, Salzburg Summer Sch., 1963; B.A., Lake Forest Coll., 1967. Mgr. advt. Stresen-Reuter Internat., Bensenville, Ill., 1965-70; mgr. animal products mktg. Internat. Minerals & Chem. Corp., Mundelein, Ill., 1971-79, dir. animal products mktg., 1979—; pres. Brit. Iron Ltd., 1984—; lectr. mktg. U. Ill., 1977, Am. Mgmt. Assn., 1978; cons. mktg. to numerous agrl. cos., 1973—. lectr. Trustee, governing mem. Library Internat. Relations, Chgo. Recipient cert. of excellence Chgo. 77 Vision Show, 1977; Silver Aggy award, 1977; spl. jury gold medal V.I., N.Y. Internat. film festival awards, 1977; CINE Golden Eagle, 1980; Bronze medal N.Y. Internat. Film Festival, 1981, Silver medal, 1982; Silver Screen award U.S. Indsl. Film Festival, 1981. Mem. Nat. Feed Ingredients Assn. (chmn. publicity and publs. 1976), Nat. Agrl. Mktg. Assn. (numerous awards), Am. Feed Mfrs. Assn. (citation 1976, public relations com., conv. com.), Nat. Agrl. Mktg. Assn., Mid-Am. Commodity Exchange, World Expeditionary Assn. (London), USCG Aux., U.S. Naval Inst., Am. Film Inst., Rolls-Royce Owners Club, Vanden Plas Owners Club. Episcopalian. Club: Sloane (London). Contbr. articles to profl. jours. Home: Thaxmeade Farm Lock Box 89 Lake Forest IL 60045 Office: 421 E Hawley St Mundelein IL 60060

STREVEY, RICHARD I., bank official; b. Grand Haven, Mich., May 17, 1952; s. Richard I. and Betty Mae (Gardner) S.; m. Jeanne Marie Reeths, July 24, 1976; children—Adam, Sarah. B.B.A., Grand Valley State Colls., Allendale, Mich., 1975. Asst. v.p., auditor Manistee Bank and Trust Co. (Mich), 1976—; adj. prof. cost acctg. West Shore Community Coll., Scottville, Mich., 1977. Chmn. Manistee World of Arts and Crafts, 1980, Manistee County Headlee for Gov. Com., 1982. Mem. Manistee Jaycees (Jaycee of Yr. 1981, pres. 1981-82, chmn. bd. dirs. 1982-83), Manistee County C. of C. (treas. 1981-83). Avocations: writing, gardening. Home: 1731 Cherry Manistee MI 49660 Office: Manistee Bank and Trust Co 375 River St Manistee MI 49660

STRIBLING, FRANK LLEWELLYN, JR., consultant, tax service company executive; b. San Diego, June 6, 1939; s. Frank Llewellyn and Bliss May (Johnson) S.; m. Iva Mae Wright, Feb. 15, 1964; children—Alan, Darren. B.S. in Chemistry, San Diego State U., 1962; M.B.A. in Fin., U. Mo.-Kansas City, 1974. Process devel. engr. DuPont, Chattanooga, 1964-67; asst. to quality control mgr. Baxter Labs., Kingstree, S.C., 1967-68; quality control coordinator Mobay Chem. Corp., Kansas City, 1968-81; mng. asst. research and devel. West-Agro Chem. Inc., Kansas City, 1981-83; pres. Stribling Tax Service Inc., Raytown, Mo., 1979—; cons., 1983—. Served as seaman USN, 1962-64. Mem. Am. Soc. for Quality Control (cert. quality engr. 1980). Mem. Reorganized Ch. Latter Day Saints (ordained minister, elder).

STRICKLAND, FREDERICK WILLIAM, JR., osteopathic physician, educator; b. Kansas City, Mo., Aug. 24, 1944; s. Frederick William and Ardene (Graves) S.; Student Coffeyville Jr. Coll., 1962-64; B.A. in Biology, Southwestern Coll., Winfield, Kans., 1966; M.A. in Ecology, Drake U., 1976; D.O., Coll. Osteo. Medicine and Surgery, Des Moines, 1978. Diplomate Am. Bd. Osteo. Medicine, Am. Osteo. Bd. Gen. Practice. Tchr. pub. schs., Oklahoma City and Des Moines, 1967-75; instr. Area XI Community Coll., Des Moines and AnKeny, Iowa; biomed. communications technician Coll. Osteo. Medicine and Surgery, Des Moines, 1975-77; electrocardiogram technician Des Moines Gen. Hosp., 1976-78, intern, 1978-79, resident in family practice, 1979-80, mem. staff, 1980—; gen. practice osteo. medicine, Des Moines, 1980—; mem. staff Des Moines Gen. Hosp., Mercy Hosp. Med. Ctr.; clin. dir., student trainer Coll. Clinics East and West, U. Osteo. Medicine and Health Scis., Des Moines, 1980—, assoc. prof. family medicine, 1980—. Chmn. bd. Des Moines Osteo. Employees Credit Union; active NAACP, People United to Save Humanity, SCLC, Still Nat. Osteo. Mus.; physician mem. Iowa Pharmacy Commn., 1984—; del. Democratic Nat. Conv., 1984; mem. Des Moines Plan and Zoning Commn., 1985—. Served to capt. M.C., Iowa Army N.G., 1979—. Recipient Found. Builder award Southwestern Coll., Winfield, Kans., 1978; disting. service award Corinthian Bapt. Ch., Des Moines, 1978. Mem. Am. Acad. Osteopathy, Iowa Found. for Med. Care, Osteo. Physicians and Surgeons, Assn. Mil. Surgeons of U.S., Assn. Army Flight Surgeons, Am. Coll. Gen. Practitioners Osteo. Medicine and Surgery, Arthritis Found., Omega Psi Phi, Sigma Sigma Phi. Democrat. Baptist. Home: 4910 Country Club Des Moines IA 50312 Office: 1300 21st St Des Moines IA 53111

STRIEFSKY, LINDA ANN, lawyer; b. Carbondale, Pa., Apr. 27, 1952; d. Leo James and Antoinette Marie (Carachilo) S.; m. James Richard Carlson, Nov. 3, 1984. B.A. summa cum laude, Marywood Coll., 1974; J.D., Georgetown U., 1977. Bar: Ohio 1977. Assoc., Thompson, Hine and Flory, Cleve., 1977—. Loaned exec. United Way of Northeast Ohio, Cleve., 1974. Mem. Am. Bar Found., ABA (mem. real estate fin. com. 1980—), Ohio State Bar Assn. (bd. govs. real estate property sect.), Greater Cleve. Bar Assn. (chmn. bar applicants com. 1983-84, exec. council young lawyers sect. 1982-85, chmn. 1984-85, mem. exec. council real property sect. 1980-84; Merit Service award 1983, 85), Pi Gamma Mu. Democrat. Roman Catholic. Office: Thompson Hine and Flory 1100 Nat City Bank Bldg Cleveland OH 44114

STRIETLEMEIR, DON, fire chief. Fire chief City of Indpls. Office: Indianapolis Fire Dept Office of the Fire Chief Indianapolis IN 46204*

STRINGER, VALERIE ANN, nurse; b. Massillon, Ohio, Nov. 21, 1957; d. Louise Weldon and Carol Ann (Barnes) Stringer. Diploma nursing, Mercy Sch. Nursing, 1982. R.N., Ohio. Nurse asst., nurse Doctor's Hosp., Massillon, 1978-83; nurse Massillon Community Hosp., 1983—; pianist, composer. Democrat. Home: 327 Fairlawn SW Massillon OH 44646

STRIZEK, JAN, graphic designer; b. Berwyn, Ill., June 11, 1947; d. William J. and Rose F. (Jana) S.; B.F.A., No. Ill. U., 1969. Prin. Strizek Design, Chgo., 1980—. Recipient awards for design excellence N.Y. Art Dirs. Club, Women in Design, Inst. of Bus. Designers 1st annual effective product brochure and binder competition, 1984. Mem. Women in Design (treas. Chgo. 1980-81), Soc. Typographic Arts (treas. Chgo. 1980-81, v.p. 1981-82), AIA (affiliate). Prodn. of graphics, textiles and flat pattern design for archtl. and interior installations. Office: 213 W Institute Pl Chicago IL 60610

STROBEL, RUDOLF GOTTFRIED KARL, biochemist; b. Kiessling Thuringia, Germany, Feb. 7, 1927; came to U.S. 1958, naturalized 1968; s. Karl M.F. and Frida L. (Weber) S.; m. Josefine M. Haunschild, Sept. 2, 1958; children—Wolfgang R., Christine B., Oliver K., Roland W. B. Sci., U. Regensburg, Bavaria, 1953; Dipl. Chem., U. Munich, Fed. Republic Germany, 1956, Ph.D., 1958. Biochemist, The Procter & Gamble Co., Cin., 1958-75, group leader, 1975-81, sect. head, 1981—. Patentee in fields of flour tech., emulsion tech., coffee aroma and flavor tech., tea and fruit juices. Mem. Am. Chem. Soc., Assn. Scientifique Internat. du Café, Internat. Apple Inst. Avocations: Farming; gardening; pomology; machine design and repair. Office: The Procter & Gamble Co 6110 Center Hill Rd Cincinnati OH 45224

STROHL, RODNEY NEAL, telephone company executive; b. Burlington, Iowa, Nov. 25, 1944; s. Clarence Orville and Helen Lillian (Burgner) S.; m. Dorothy Elaine Gillen, Dec. 28, 1963; children—Todd Gregory, Rodney Brian, Chad Owen. B.A. in Bus. and Econs., Southwestern Coll., 1966. With personnel assessment ctr. Southwestern Bell Telephone Co., Topeka, Kans., 1970-71, mem. gen. hdqrs. staff, St. Louis, 1971-73, bus. office ops. supr., Topeka, 1973-75, mgmt. devel. supr., Topeka, 1975-76, dist. mgr., Hays, Kans., 1976-79, dist. mgr. residence service ctr., Mission, Kans., 1979—; dir. employee polit. action com., Topeka, 1983—, advisor community relations team, Mission, 1979—. Bd. dirs. Pvt. Industry Council-Job Tng., Kansas City, Kans., 1983, Nekan Bell Credit Union, Topeka, 1984—; chmn. adminstrv. com. Pvt. Partnership Act-Job Tng., Kansas City, 1983; chmn. Ellis County United Way campaign, Hays, Kans., 1978. Named Key Man Chanute Jaycees (Kans.), 1970; recipient Outstanding Citizen award Wichita Police Dept., 1971. Mem. Overland Park C. of C., Kansas City C. of C., Lenexa C. of C., Shawnee C. of C., Olathe C. of C., U. Kans. Alumni Assn. Republican. Methodist. Club: Speakers Bur. (Mission). Lodge: Rotary (Shawnee Mission). Home: 6923 Widmer Rd Shawnee KS 66216 Office: Southwestern Bell Telephone Co 5960 Dearborn Mission KS 66202

STROMBERG, DONALD RICHARD, music educator; b. Des Moines, Jan. 23, 1940; s. Donald Laverne and Mary Elizabeth (Shultice) S.; m. Eleanor Brindle, Aug. 21, 1963; children—Daniel Richard, Emily Jane. B.A., U. No. Iowa, 1963; Mus.M., Northwestern U., 1965; Ph.D., 1974; postgrad. Denver U., 1975, U. Minn., 1975, Memphis State U., 1975-77. Vocal music tchr. Reinbeck (Iowa) Community Schs., 1963-64; tchr. choral music Evanston (Ill.) Twp. High Sch., 1965-69; faculty mem. Grand View Coll., Des Moines, 1970-78, prof. music, 1970-78; assoc. prof. music U. S.D., Vermillion, 1978—. Mem. Am. Orff-Schulwerk Assn., Sioux Valley Orff Assn. (pres. 1962-63), Music Educators Nat. Conf., NEA, S.D. Music Educators Assn., S.D. Edn. Assn., Orgn. Am. Kodaly Educators, Midwest Kodaly Music Educators Assn., Nat. Consortium for Computer-Based Music Instrn., Assn. for Devel. Computer-Based Instructional Systems, Phi Mu Alpha Sinfonia, Phi Delta Kappa. Baptist. Choral composer: Sing, Shout and Praise, 1981, Psalm 100, 1981, Sing to the Lord of Harvest, 1981. Office: Mathews Williams & Assocs 28 Triangle Park Dr Cincinnati OH 45246

STROMBERG, GREGORY, printing ink company executive; b. Milw., Feb. 10, 1948; s. Clifford Norman and Margaret Betty (Hoover) S.; m. Gail Elizabeth Steinbach, Aug. 22, 1970; children—Christopher, Brian, Ellen. B.S., Marquette U., Milw., 1970. Office contact salesman Continental Can Co., Milw., 1970-78; sales rep. Sun Chem. Co., Milw., 1978-82; v.p., gen. mgr. Acme Printing Ink Co., Milw., 1982—; exec. v.p. Can. operation Acme Printing Ink Can. Ltd., 1985—; pres. Toobee Internat., Inc., Milw., 1981—. Author: Toobee Air Force Flight Training Manual, 1983. Advisor Milw. Jr. Achievement, 1974; sponsor Muscular Dystrophy, 1983; asst. com. mem. Toys for Tots, Children's Hosp., Milw., 1983. Mem. Sales and Mktg. Execs. of Milw., Am. Mgmt. Assn. Home: 6931 N 99th St Milwaukee WI 53224 Office: Acme Printing Ink Co Milwaukee WI 53218

STROMQUIST, PETER S., broadcasting station executive; b. Duluth, Minn., Nov. 14, 1952; s. John W. and Janet E. (Stubbee) S.; B.A., St. Olaf Coll., 1974; m. Jane E. Phleger. Former account exec. Sta. WIZM, LaCrosse, Wis., agy. account exec. Sta. KSTP, Mpls., sr. account exec. Plough Broadcasting, Chgo., gen. sales mgr. Sta. KIRL, St. Louis; pres., chmn. bd. Stromquist Broadcast Services, Mpls., 1979—. Mem. Am. Film Inst., Minn. Broadcasters Assn., Iowa Broadcasters Assn., N.D. Broadcasters Assn., S.D. Broadcasters Assn. Episcopalian. Home: 3064 Parkwild Bettendorf IA 52722

STRONG, DOROTHY MAE, educational administrator; b. Memphis, Feb. 3, 1934; d. John Harrison and Willie Beatrice (Hawkins) Swearengen; B.S. in Edn., Chgo. State U., 1958; M.A. in Math. Edn., 1964; Ed.D., Nova U., 1985; m. Joseph Nathaniel Strong, Mar. 19, 1953; 1 dau., Joronda Ramette. Elem. and secondary tchr. Chgo. Pub. Schs., 1958-65, dir. math., 1976—; cons. math, 1965-76; instr. Chgo. State U., 1969-71; mem. Commn. on Tchr. Edn., Task Force on Math. in Urban Centers, Ill. Basic Skills Adv. Council, Nat. Inst. Edn. Conf. on Basic Skills; mem. council acad. affairs Coll. Bd., v.p., 1983—; bd. dirs. Allendale Sch. for Boys, 1974—. Pres. youth dept. Midwest dist. United Pentecostal Council, Assemblies of God Inc., 1979—. Recipient Edn. PaceSetter award President's Nat. Adv. Council on Supplementary Centers, 1973. Mem. Assn. Supervision and Curriculum Devel., Nat. Council Tchrs. Math., Nat. Council Suprs. Math. (sec. chpt. 1973-75, pres. chpt. 1977-79), Elem. Sch. Math. Advs. Chgo. Area, Met. Math. Club, Math. Club Chgo. and Vicinity, Nat. Alliance Black Sch. Educators, Ill. Council Tchrs. Math., Delta Sigma Theta, Kappa Delta Pi, Kappa Mu Epsilon. Author: Modern Mathematics Structure and Use-Spirit Masters, 1977; author Chgo. Public Schs. curriculum materials; contbr. articles to profl. publs.; coordinator devel. numerous curriculum guides. Home: 2820 Paris Rd Olympia Fields IL 60461 Office: 1819 W Pershing Rd 6C-SE Chicago IL 60609

STRONG, JEROME ANTON, political science consultant; b. Muskegon, Mich., Aug. 18, 1947; s. Ben and Anna Belle (Childress) S.; m. Deborah Deon, July 28, 1968; 1 dau., Simone Yvette. B.S., U. Mich., 1976, M.A. in Polit. Sci., 1978. Research assoc. Inst. Social Research, U. Mich., Ann Arbor, 1976-80, Joint Center for Polit. Studies, Washington, 1977—; adminstrv. asst. Mich. State Senator Ann Arbor, 1983-84; exec. asst. to state budget dir. for legis. liaison Mich. Dept. Mgmt. and Budget, Lansing, 1984—; founder SAJ Research, Inc., 1980—; instr. polit. sci. Washtenaw Community Coll., 1980-81. Mem. state central com. Mich. Democratic Party, 1976-83; vice chmn. Ypsilanti Democratic Party, 1980-82, Washtenaw County Democratic Party, 1984—; bd. dirs. ACLU, Washtenaw County, alternate State of Mich. ACLU. Mem. Mich. Soc. Gerontology, Gerontol. Soc., Am. Polit. Sci. Assn., Am. Assn. Budget and Program Analysis, NAACP, Midwest Polit. Sci. Assn. Roman Catholic. Lodges: Masons, Shriners, KC. Home: 921 Pleasant Dr Ypsilanti MI 48197 Office: Mgmt and Budget Lewis Cass Bldg Lansing MI 48909

STRONG, JOHN DAVID, insurance company executive; b. Cortland, N.Y., Apr. 12, 1936; s. Harold A. and Helen H. S.; m. Carolyn Dimmick, Oct. 26, 1957; children—John D., Suzanne. B.S., Syracuse U. (N.Y.), 1957. With Kemper Group, 1957—, empire div. sales mgr., 1972-74, exec. v.p. Fed. Kemper Ins. Co., Decatur, Ill., 1974-79, pres., dir., 1979—; dir. Pershing Nat. Bank. Mem. adv. council Sch. Bus. Millikin U., 1975-79; bd. dirs. United Way of Decatur and Macon County, Ill., 1976-79, campaign chmn., 1978-79, pres. bd., 1979-81; pres. United Way of Ill., 1981-83; bd. dirs. Decatur-Macon County Econ. Devel. Found., 1983—; bd. dirs. Ill. Ednl. Developmental Found., 1983—, pres., 1985—. Served to capt. USAR, 1958-69. Mem. Metro Decatur C. of C. (dir. 1977-80, 2d vice chmn. 1981-82, 1st vice chmn. 1982-83, chmn. 1983-84), Alpha Kappa Psi. Club: Decatur (dir. 1980-83, pres. 1983), Country of Decatur. Office: 2001 E Mound Rd Decatur IL 62526

STRONG, RUSSELL ARTHUR, university administrator; b. Kalamazoo, Apr. 20, 1924; s. Walter A. and Dana (Sleeman) S.; m. June Thomas, Aug. 17, 1946; children—William W., Jonathan T., David R., Christopher C., Timothy B. State editor Kalamazoo Gazette, 1948-51; dir. pub. info. Western Mich. U., Kalamazoo, 1951-63, dir. alumni relations, 1979-84, dir. devel. research, 1984—; univ., editor Mich. State U., East Lansing, 1963-66; dir. news and info. Davidson Coll., N.C., 1966-74; univ. editor Wake Forest U., Winston-Salem, N.C., 1974; dir. info. services Wright State U., Fairborn, Ohio, 1975-76; dir. coll. relations St. Andrews Presbyn. Coll., Laurinburg, N.C., 1976-79. Author: First Over Germany; Biographical Directory, Command and Staff Officers, U.S. 8th Air Force, 1942-45. Contbr. articles to profl. jours., chpts. to books. Served to 1st lt. U.S. Army Air Force, 1943-45. Decorated D.F.C., Air medal with three oak leaf clusters. Mem. Air Force Assn., 8th Air Force Hist. Soc., 306th Bomb Group Hist. Assn. (editor, historian, sec.), 8th Air Force Meml. Mus. Found. (v.p. 1983-84). Methodist. Club: Torch. Home: 2041 Hillsdale Kalamazoo MI 49007 Office: Alumni Ctr Western Mich U Kalamazoo MI 49008

STROSS, ROBERT MARSHALL, JR., marketing and management development executive; b. Dayton, Ohio, May 24, 1943; s. Robert Marshall and Christine (Noland) S.; m. Charlane JoAnn Colip, Aug. 20, 1966 (div.); children—Andy, Betsy; m. 2d, Ruth Ann Lenhard, Dec. 21, 1974; children—Sandy, Kelly, Kerry. B.A. in Psychology, DePauw U., 1965; M.B.A., Mich. State U., 1970. Ops. mgr. Marriott In-Flite Services, Washington, 1970-73; dir. Tng. and Planning W.T. Sistrunk & Co., Lexington, Ky., 1974-79; dir. orgn. mgmt., develop. Wetterau, Inc., St. Louis, 1979-84; dir. mktg. Wetterau, Inc., 1984, v.p., 1985—. Supt. ch. sch. St. Timothys Episcopal Ch., Creve Coeur, Mo., vestryman, 1985—. Served to capt. USAF, 1965-69; Vietnam. Recipient Robert E. Crouch Meml. award DePauw U., 1965. Mem. Am. Soc. Tng. and Devel. (pres. chpt. 1978-79; Service award, 1982), Internat. Platform Assn. Republican. Episcopalian. Home: 11445 N Forty Dr Saint Louis MO 63131 Office: 8920 Pershall Rd Hazelwood MO 63042

STROTZ, ROBERT HENRY, university chancellor; b. Aurora, Ill., Sept. 26, 1922; s. John Marc and Olga (koerfer) S.; student Duke U., 1939-41; B.A., U. Chgo., 1942, Ph.D., 1951; LL.D. (hon.), Ill. Wesleyan U., 1976, Millikin U., 1979; m. Margaret L. Hanley; children by previous marriage—Vicki, Michael, Frances, Ellen, Ann. Mem. faculty Northwestern U., Evanston, Ill., 1947—, prof. econs., 1958—, dean Coll. Arts and Scis., 1966-70, pres. univ., 1970-85, chancellor, 1985—; vice chmn., dir. Nat. Merit Scholarship Corp.; past chmn., dir. Fed. Res. Bank Chgo.; dir. First Ill. Corp., Ill. Tool Works Inc., Norfolk So. Corp., MidCon Corp., Mark Controls Corp.; chmn. Council Postsecondary Accreditation. Bd. dirs. McGaw Med. Center of Northwestern U.; hon. trustee Northwestern Meml. Hosp.; life trustee Mus. Sci. and Industry, Field Mus. Nat. History. Served with U.S. Army, 1943-45. Fellow Econometric Soc.; mem. Am. Econ. Assn., Econometric Soc. (council 1961-67), Royal Econ. Soc. Clubs: Old Elm (Ft. Sheridan, Ill.); Chicago, Commercial, Economic, University, Standard, Tavern (Chgo.); Glen View (Ill.); Bohemian (San Francisco). Mng. editor Econometrica, 1953-68; econometrics editor Internat. Ency. Social Scis., 1962-68; editor Contbns. to Econ. Analysis, 1955-70. Office: 633 Clark St Evanston IL 60201

STUARK, BARBARA IRENE, retail management executive; b. Chgo., Mar. 19, 1948; d. Frank R. and Irene Julia (Wojnicki) S. Ph.B., Northwestern U., 1973, cert. in computer sci., 1985; C.B.A., Keller Grad. Sch. Mgmt., Chgo., 1978. Buyer, Goldblatts, Chgo., 1974-79; outside sales rep. Raymor/Moreddi, Ridgefield, N.J., 1979-80; div. mgr. Lord & Taylor-Water Tower Place, Chgo., 1980-83; dir. pub. merchandising Field Mus. of Natural History, Chgo., 1983—. Mem. Nat. Assn. Female Execs. Roman Catholic. Club: Northwestern of Chgo. Office: Mus Stores Field Mus Natural History Roosevelt Rd and Lake Shore Dr Chicago IL 60605

STUART, CLARENCE, industrial supply company executive; m. Dorothy Stuart; children—Darryl, Tony, Clarence. Founder, pres. Sentry Comml. & Indsl. Supply Co., Ft. Wayne, Ind., 1975—. Del. Gov.'s Small Bus. Conf., Ind.; mem. Com. of 24, Mayor's Commn. on Minority Bus., Ft. Wayne; bd. dirs. Ind. Supplier's Devel. Council, Jr. Achievement, Leadership Prayer Breakfast, Allen County; chmn. Ch. Bldg. Com.; mem. loan com. Ft. Wayne Econ. Devel. Address: Sentry Commercial and Industrial Supply 1321 E Wallace ST Fort Wayne IN 46803

STUART, JOSEPH MARTIN, art center administrator; b. Seminole, Okla., Nov. 9, 1932; s. Arch William and Lillian (Lindsey) S.; B.F.A. in Art, U. N.Mex., 1959, M.A. in Art, 1962; m. Signe Margaret Nelson, June 18, 1960; 1 dau., Lise Nelson Pope. Dir., Roswell (N.Mex.) Museum and Art Center, 1960-62; curator U. Oreg. Mus. Art, 1962-63; dir. Boise (Idaho) Gallery Art, 1964-68, Salt Lake (City) Art Center, 1968-71, S.D. Meml. Art Center, Brookings, 1971—; prof. art S.D. State U., 1971—; represented in permanent collections: Coll. Idaho, Eureka Coll., Salt Lake Art Center, Sioux City (Iowa) Art Center, U. N.Mex. Art Mus., West Tex. State U. Served with USN, 1951-55. Mem. Am. Assn. Museums, Artists Equity, Coll. Art Assn., Phi Kappa Phi. Unitarian. Author: Index of South Dakota Artists, 1974; Art of South Dakota, 1974; author numerous exhbn. catalogs. Office: SD Meml Art Center Brookings SD 57007

STUART, WILLIAM CORWIN, federal judge; b. Knoxville, Iowa, Apr. 28, 1920; s. George C. and Edith (Abram) S.; student Chariton Jr. Coll., 1937-38; A.B., U. Iowa, also J.D., 1942; m. Mary Elgin Cleaver, Oct. 20, 1946; children—William Corwin, Robert Cullen, Melanie Rae, Valerie Jo. Bar: Iowa. Practice law, Chariton, 1946-62; city atty., Chariton, 1946-47; justice Iowa Supreme Ct., 1962-71; U.S. dist. judge So. Dist. Iowa, 1971—. Mem. Iowa Senate, 1953-61. Served with USNR, 1943-45. Mem. Am. Legion, Am., Iowa bar Assns., Am. Judicature Soc., Order of Coif, Phi Kappa Psi, Phi Delta Phi, Omicron Delta Kappa. Presbyterian (elder). Clubs: Masons, Shriners. Office: US Dist Ct E 1st and Walnut Sts Des Moines IA 52818

STUBBLEFIELD, JOHN WILLIAM, cosmetology schools and salon executive; b. Decatur, Ill., Oct. 20, 1940; s. John H. and Florence E. (Chrysler) S.; m. Brenda J. Hyle, June 4, 1961 (div. Dec. 1980); children—Kristi, John J., Lisa, Stacy; m. Kathy E. Farrier, Oct. 20, 1984. Student Milliken U., 1 yr. Dir., Decatur Sch. Cosmetology, 1963-67; pres. Mr. John's Sch. Cosmetology, Decatur, 1967-83, Mr. John's Schs. of Cosmetology Inc., Decatur and Springfield, Ill., 1983—; dir. lic. testing services, 1982-83. Chmn. Maroa Bicentennial Com. (Ill.), 1975-76; commr. Lincoln Trails council Boy Scouts Am., Decatur, 1979—; advisor Jr. Achievement, Decatur, 1973-75, Ill. Dept. Corrections Vast Program, Decatur, 1973-74. Recipient Silver Beaver award Boy Scouts Am., 1981, awards Ill. Jaycees, 1977, 78. Mem. Ill. Hairdresser and Cosmetology Assn. (1st v.p. 1982-84, pres. 1984-86, dir. 1980-84), Ill. Cosmetology Council (vice chmn. 1982-83). Methodist. Lodge: Kiwanis (dir. Decatur). Home: PO Box 428 Forsyth IL 62535 Office: Mr Johns Sch Cosmetology Inc 304 E Adams Springfield IL 62701

STUCKEY, RICHARD JORIAN, accounting company executive; b. Reading, Eng., Jan. 6, 1943; came to U.S., 1965; s. Derek Richard and Gladys Muriel (Saunders) S.; B.Sc. with gen. honors, U. London, 1965; M.B.A., Stanford U., 1967; m. Lois Ilene Engel, July 3, 1976. Cons., Arthur Andersen & Co., San Francisco, 1967-76, world hdqrs. mgr. advanced practices, Chgo., 1976-81, ptnr., 1981—; lectr. Golden Gate U., San Francisco, 1974-76; speaker mini/microcomputer systems. Mem. Assn. for Computing Machinery, Stanford Grad. Sch. Assn., King's Coll. London Assn. Clubs: Cliff Dwellers, Chgo. Yacht. Contbr. articles in field to profl. publs. Home: 2101 N Bissell St Chicago IL 60614 Office: Arthur Andersen & Co 33 W Monroe St Chicago IL 60603

STUCKI, JACOB CALVIN, pharmaceutical company executive; b. Neillsville, Wis., Nov. 30, 1926; s. Benjamin and Ella S.; m. Naomi Bersch, Nov. 24, 1948; children—Marcia, Heidi, J. Christopher. B.S., U. Wis., 1948, M.S., 1951, Ph.D., 1954. Research endocrinologist, William S. Merrell Co., 1954-57; research endocrinologist Upjohn Co., Kalamazoo, 1957-60, mgr. endocrinology research, 1960-61, mgr. pharmacology research, 1961-68, asst. dir. biochem. research, 1968-69, dir. adminstrn. and support ops., 1969-81, dir. pharm. R&D, 1981, v.p. pharm. research, 1981—; mem. acad. corp. liaison program NRC; bd. dirs. NRC Space Applications Bd. Bd. dirs., trustee, pres. Lift Found.; bd. dirs., pres., treas. Planned Parenthood Assn. Kalamazoo County, Inc.; chmn. housing task force Community Services Council/Community Chest; bd. dirs. Kalamazoo Arts Council; mem. human subjects instl. rev. bd. Western Mich. U.; bd. govs. Rackham Found., Mich. State U.; mem. econ. adv. council Mich. Democratic party. Served with USN, 1944-46. Mem. AAAS, Soc. Exptl. Biology and Medicine, Endocrine Soc., Project Mgmt. Inst., Nat. Assn. Biomed. Research (bd. dirs.), Pharm. Mfrs. Assn., Indsl. Research Inst., Internat. Assn. Study of Interdisciplinary Research, Gamma Alpha, Sigma Xi. Contbr. numerous articles to profl. jours. Office: Upjohn Co Pharm Research Div 301 Henrietta St Kalamazoo MI 49001

STUCKI, WARREN WILLIS, broadcast engineer; b. Helena, Mo., Nov. 1, 1921; s. William W. and Ella May (Thomann) S.; m. Georgia Lee Blakley, Jan. 9, 1943; children—Warren Douglas, Roger Blake. Student Northwest Mo. State Tchrs. Coll., 1939-40, U. Utah, 1943-44. Radio mechanic Am. Airlines, St. Joseph, Mo., 1946-47, St. Joseph Aviation Sales, 1947; owner Airadio Service, St. Joseph, 1947-48; engr. Sta. KFEQ, KFEQ-TV; with Sta. KFEQ, 1948-72, chief engr., 1969-72; chief engr. Sta. KXCV-FM, Northwest Mo. State U., 1972—; guest lectr. Served in U.S. Army, 1942-45. Recipient Bohlken award Northwest Mo. State U., 1980. Mem. Soc. Broadcast Engrs. (sr. charter mem.), Nat. Inst. Cert. Engring. Techs. (sr. engring technician). Baptist. Office: Sta KXCV Northwest Mo State U Maryville MO 64468

STUDEBAKER, JAMES DALE, optometrist; b. Dayton, Ohio, Feb. 3, 1940; s. Paul Wenger and Marjorie Alice (Hedges) S.; m. Lana Sue Mills, Sept. 5, 1959; children—Joseph, Peter, Susan, Samuel, Jesse. Student Manchester Coll., 1961; B.S. in Optometry, Ind. U., 1962, M.S. in Optometry, 1963; D.O., Ohio State U., 1977. Gen. practice optometry, Englewood, Ohio, 1963—; nat. bd. advisors Cooper Vision Optics, San Jose, Calif., 1983—. Past bd. dirs. Northmont Bd. Edn., Englewood, 1966-72. Mem. Miami Valley Soc. Optometrists, Ohio Optometric Assn., Am. Optometric Assn., Am. Optometric Found. (life mem.), Studebaker Family Assn. (past mem. bd. dirs.). Democrat. Avocations: fishing, farming, photography, gardening. Home: 811 N Main St Union Ohio Office: 639 W National Rd Englewood Ohio 45322

STUDER, GARY ALLEN, business forms company executive; b. Peoria, Ill., Dec. 10, 1945; s. Walter Raymond and Thelma Patricia (Jones) S.; m. Judith May Hamilton, Sept. 27, 1969. B.A., Drake U., 1967; M.S. in Bus. Adminstrn., Ind. U., 1973. Fin. analyst Gen. Electric Co., Schenectady, 1969-71; systems analyst Assocs. Computer Services, South Bend, Ind., 1971-77; dir. mgmt. services Form Systems, Inc., St. Louis, 1977—; mem. faculty Am. Mgmt. Assns., 1979-80; mem. editorial rev. bd. Jour. Systems Mgmt., Assn. Systems Mgmt. Bd. dirs. Schenectady Bus. Opportunity Corp., 1970. Served with U.S. Army, 1967-69. Mem. Drake U. Nat. Alumni Assn. (bd. dirs. 1981—), Schenectady Jaycees (sec.-treas. 1970-71), Am. Fin. Services Assn., Internat. Consumer Credit Assn., St. Louis Council World Affairs, Mo. Hist. Soc., Delta Sigma Pi. Contbr. articles to profl. jours.

STUDWELL, WILLIAM EMMETT, librarian; b. Stamford, Conn., Mar. 18, 1936; s. Alfred Theodore and Mary Alice (Baker) S.; m. Ann Marie Stroia, Aug. 28, 1965; 1 dau., Laura Ann. B.A., U. Conn., 1958, M.A., 1959; M.S.L.S., Cath. U. Am., 1967. Tech. abstracter Library of Congress, Washington, 1963-66; asst. editor decimal classification office, 1966-68; head librarian Kirtland Community Coll., Roscommon, Mich., 1968-70; head/prin. cataloger No. Ill. U., DeKalb, 1970—, chmn. library building and conservation com., 1981—; mem. U.S. Adv. Com. to Chemistry Sects., Universal Decimal Classification, 1968-72; chmn. Adv. Group to Library Research Ctr., Urbana, Ill., 1982-84; advisor on subject headings Subject Cataloging Div., Library of Congress, 1984—. Author: Chaikovskii, Delibes, Stravinski, 1977; Christmas Carols, 1985; Adolphe Adam and Leo Delibes, 1986; contbr. articles on music history and library sci. to profl. jours. Co-founder Infertility Forum Support Group, Rockford, Ill., 1978. Mem. Ill. Assn. Coll. and Research Libraries (mem. exec. bd. 1980—, newsletter editor 1980—), Ill. Library Assn. (newsletter adv. com. 1983-85). Lodge: Kiwanis. Home: Rural Route 1 Box 88A Sycamore IL 60178 Office: Univ Libraries No Ill U DeKalb IL 60115

STUEBER, RAYMOND JAMES, architect; b. Cleve., Nov. 15, 1926; s. Raymond William and Lillian (Spitzel) S.; m. Mary Joyce Thornbury, Apr. 16, 1943; children—Robin, Cheryl, Kim, Kyle, Toni. Student Kent State U., 1945; B.A. Ohio State U., 1951. Cert. architect. Architect, W. B. Huff, Akron, Ohio, 1951-53; prin. architect Derr & Stueber, Akron, 1953-76; v.p. Keith Haag & Assocs. Architects, Cuyahoga Falls, Ohio, 1976-79; v.p. John Dellagnese & Assocs. Inc., Akron, 1979—; archtl. design instr. Kent (Ohio) State U., 1955-56. Served with U.S. Army, 1945-47. Mem. Nat. Council Archtl. Registration Bds., AIA, Architects Soc. Ohio, Constrn. Specification Inst. Home: 2545 Meloy Rd Kent OH 44240 Office: 2725 Abington Rd Akron OH 44313

STUMPF, LOWELL C(LINTON), artist-designer; b. Canton, Ill., Dec. 8, 1917; s. Oral Baxter and Marie (Dawson) S.; grad. Chgo. Acad. Fine Arts; student L'Ecole de Beaux Arts, Marseille, France, 1945; m. Jacqueline Jeanne Charlotte Andree Lucas, Sept. 5, 1945; children—Eric Clinton, Roderick Lowell. Staff artist Internat. Harvester Co., Chgo., 1939-42, Nugent-Graham Studios, Chgo., 1945-47; free lance artist, designer, Chgo., 1947—. Served with AUS, 1942-45; NATO USA, ETO. Mem. Artist Guild Chgo., Internat. Platform Assn. Contbr. sci. and tech. illustrations, maps to Compton's Pictured Ency., Rand McNally & Co., Macmillan Co., Scott, Foresman & Co., Ginn & Co. textbooks, World Book Year Book, Field Enterprises Sci. Yearbooks, Childcraft Ann. and Library, World Book Dictionary. Home and Office: 7N161 Medinah Rd Medinah IL 60157

STURGEON, PAULINE RUTH, editor; b. Centralia, Mo., Sept. 4, 1907; d. William Arthur and Ruth Jane (Cook) Sturgeon. B.J., U. Mo.-Columbia, 1929, B.A., 1977. Staff, Centralia Fireside Guard, 1956-60; feature writer Columbia Daily Tribune (Mo.), 1960-66; editor The Russell Record, (Kans.), 1967—. Mem. Kans. Press Women, Fedn. Press Women, DAR, Sigma Delta Chi. Club: Bus. and Profl. Women's. Address: The Russell Record 802 N Maple St Russell KS 67665

STURGES, SIDNEY JAMES, pharmacist, educator, investment and development company executive; b. Kansas City, Mo., Sept. 29, 1936; s. Sidney Alexander and Lenore Caroline (Lemley) S.; m. Martha Grace Leonard, Nov. 29, 1957 (div. 1979); 1 child, Grace Caroline; m. Gloria June Kitch, Sept. 17, 1983. B.S. in Pharmacy, U. Mo., 1957, post grad., 1959; M.B.A. in Pharmacy Adminstrn., U. Kans., 1980; Ph.D. in Bus. Adminstrn., Pacific Western U., 1980. Registered pharmacist, Mo., Kans.; registered nursing home adminstr., Mo.; cert. vocat. tchr., Mo. Pharmacist, mgr. Crown Drugs, Kansas City, Mo., 1957-60; pharmacist, owner Sav-On-Drugs and Pharmacy, Kansas City, 1960-62; ptnr. Sam's Bargain Town Drugs, Raytown, Mo., 1961-62; pharmacist, owner Sturges Drugs DBA Barnard Pharmacy, Independence, Mo., 1962—; pres., owner Sturges Med. Corp., Independence, Mo., 1967-1977, Sturgess Investment Corp., Independence, 1967-1978, Sturwood Investment Corp., Independence, 1968—, Sturges Agri-Bus. Co., Independence, 1977—, Sturges Devel. Co., 1984—; instr. pharmacology Penn Valley Community Coll., 1976-84; instr., lectr. various clubs and groups. Contbr. articles to profl. jours. Bd. dirs. Independence House, 1981-83; mem. Criminal Justice Adv. Commn., Independence, 1982—. Recipient Outstanding award Kans. City Alcohol and Drug Abuse Council, 1982. Mem. Mo. Sheriffs Assn., Mo. Pharm. Assn. (pharmacy dr. 1981), Mo. Found. Pharm. Care, U. Mo. Alumni Assn. Home: 16805 Cogan Rd Independence MO 64055 Office: Sturges Co 13701 E 35th St Independence MO 64055

STURM, DIETER HANS, publicist, special effects expert; b. Milw., Sept. 15, 1955; s. Dieter Hans and Gertrude Norma (Zielke) S. Student U. Wis.-Milw., 1973-75, Marquette U., 1974-76. Proto-type design, prodn. engr. Venture Computer Systems, New Berlin, Wis., 1972-73; dir. promotions and pub. relations Malrite Broadcasting Co., Milw., 1973-81; pub. relations mgr. Playboy Clubs Internat., Lake Geneva, Wis., 1981-82; corp. pub. relations dir. TSR, Inc., Lake Geneva, 1982—; free-lance spl. effects tech. cons., designer. Mem. steering com. Toys for Tots program; judge Jr. Achievement Talent Search. Mem. Visual Music Alliance, Creative Communications Council, Spl. Effects Internat. (founder), Broadcasters Promotion Assn. Democrat. Lutheran. Author manual: Laser Light Entertainment Optic Techniques, 1982. Home: Route 2 Box 242 Lake Geneva WI 53147 Office: PO Box 756 Lake Geneva WI 53147

STURM, JEFFREY CLINTON, lawyer, consultant; b. Newton, Kans., Aug. 26, 1951; s. Samuel H. and Betty Lou (DuFriend) S.; m. Liane Gina Alley, Aug. 1, 1980; children—Lindsey Ann, Camille Nicole. B.A., Wichita State U., 1975; J.D., Washburn U., 1978. Bars: Kans. 1979, U.S. Dist. Ct. Kans. 1979, U.S. Ct. Appeals (10th cir.) 1979. Assoc. Render & Kamas, Wichita, Kans., 1979-81; sole practice, Wichita, 1981-84, ptnr. Reals & Sturm, Wichita, 1984-85; sole practice, 1985—; officer McKelso, Sturm & Assocs., Wichita, 1978—. Mem. Assn. Trial Lawyers Am., Kans. Bar Assn., Kans. Trial Lawyers Assn., Wichita Bar Assn. Republican. Baptist. Home: 2922 Wilderness Wichita KS 67226 Office: 330 N Main St Wichita KS 67202

STURROCK, IAN TYNDALE, university official; b. Birmingham, Ala., Dec. 22, 1943; s. Ian William and Margaret (Sloss) S.; m. Lynette Russell, Apr. 3, 1971; 1 child, Emily Margaret. B.S., Birmingham So. Coll., 1965; M.A., U. Ala., 1968, Ph.D., 1972. Cert. fund raising exec. Dir. recruitment Birmingham So. Coll., Ala., 1965-68, dean students, 1968-70; dir. inst. devel., Dickinson Coll., Carlisle, Pa., 1972-74; vice chancellor devel. U. Tenn., Chattanooga, 1974-80; v.p. devel. and univ. relations Bradley U., Peoria, Ill., 1980—. Author, producer ednl. TV series College Life, 1967. Contbr. articles to profl. publs., chpts. to books. Vice pres. fin. W.D. Boyce council Boy Scouts Am.; mem. exec. bd. First Federated Ch., Peoria; mem. Midwest Contbns. Forum. Mem. Council for Advancement and Support of Edn., Nat. Soc. Fund Raising Execs. (nat. bd. dirs. 1983—, pres. central Ill. chpt. 1982), Omicron Delta Kappa, Phi Eta Sigma, Kappa Delta Pi. Republican. Presbyterian. Clubs: Mount Hawley Country (Peoria); Creve Coeur. Lodge: Rotary. Office: Bradley U 1501 W Bradley Ave Peoria IL 61625

STURTEVANT, RUTHANN PATTERSON, anatomy educator, researcher; b. Rockford, Ill., Feb. 7, 1927; d. Joseph Hyelmun and Virginia (Wharton) Patterson; m. Frank M. Sturtevant, Mar. 18, 1950; children—Barbara (dec.), Jill Sturtevant Rovani, Jan Sturtevant Cassidy. B.S., Northwestern U., 1949, M.S., 1950; Ph.D., U. Ark., 1972. Instr. Ind. State U., Evansville, 1965-72; asst. prof. Ind. U. Sch. Med., Evansville, 1972-74; lectr. Northwestern U. Med. Sch., Chgo., 1974-75; asst. prof. Loyola U. Med. Sch., Maywood, Ill., 1975-81, assoc. prof., 1981—. Ad hoc reviewer for several profl. jours.; contbr. articles to profl. jours. and books. Mem. Mayor's Commn. High Tech., Chgo., 1982-84. Grantee NIH, 1981, 83, Potts Found., 1983, Distilled Spirits Council U.S., 1984. Mem. Am. Assn. Anatomists, Internat. Soc. Chronobiology, Internat. Soc. Biomed. Research on Alcoholism, Am. Soc. Pharmacology and Exptl. Therapeutics, Soc. Exptl. Biology and Med. Avocations: underwater photography, scuba diving. Home: 1868 Mission Hills Ln Northbrook IL 60062 Office: Loyola Univ Med Ctr 2160 S 1st Ave Maywood IL 60153

STUTESMAN, BARRY SCOTT, entertainment and broadcast producer; b. Flint, Mich., Nov. 18, 1953; s. Virgil Milton and Shirley Naomi (Popps) S.; m. Karen Ann Nelson, Feb. 14, 1980 (div. 1982). Grad. Northeast Mich. Acad. Broadcast Arts, 1971. Staff announcer Sta. WHSB, Alpena, Mich., 1971-72, Sta. WDBI, Tawas City, Mich., 1980-81; news dir. Sta. WBMB, West Branch, Mich., 1972-79, Sta. WKLT, Kalkaska, Mich., 1979-80, Sta. WJEB-WGMM, Gladwin, Mich., 1980; program dir. Cable Channel 13, Rose City, Mich., 1981-82, Sta. WBMB-WBMI, West Branch, 1983-84; gen. mgr. Great No. Recovery Inc., Rose City, 1982-83, v.p., 1982-83; producer B&B Prodns., Prudenville, Mich., 1982-83; co-creator, producer Mich. Record Rev., Lupton, Mich., 1984—. Producer: (half hour radio mag.) Spectrum, 1974 (honorable mention Mich. AP 1974), (daily cable TV series) Northern Michigan Horizons, 1983, (daily morning TV show) Good Morning Rose City, 1983; co-producer, writer: (daily satellite network radio series) Michigan Record Review, 1985. Recipient Outstanding Local News Coverage award Mich. AP, 1974. Home: Box 272 Rose City MI 48654 Office: Michigan Record Review Box 250 Lupton MI 48635

SUBRAMANIAN, SETHURAMAN, scientist, researcher; b. Mattur, Tamilnadu, India, May 16, 1940; came to U.S., 1970, naturalized, 1978; s. P. Sethuraman and Rajalakshmi (Panchanathan) S.; m. Ananthi Gopala Krishnan, Jan. 29, 1969; children—Sumathi, Sukanya, Mekhala. B.Sc., U. Madras, India, 1960, M.Sc., 1965; Ph.D., Indian Inst. Tech., Kanpur, 1969; M.B.A., Ind. U. South Bend, 1985. Research assoc. U. Kans., Kansas City, 1970-74; research physicist Naval Med. Research Inst., Bethesda, Md., 1974-75; vis. scientist NIH, Bethesda, 1975-82; sr. research scientist Miles Labs., Elkhart, Ind., 1982—. Contbr. articles to profl. jours. and chpts. to books. Fellow AEC, 1963-65, NRC, 1974-75. Mem. Am. Chem. Soc. (chmn.-elect St. Joseph Valley sect. 1985), Am. Soc. Biol. Chemists (elected), Miles Sci. Forum (chmn. 1984). Avocations: reading, tennis, classical music. Home: 54648 Glenwood Park Dr Elkhart IN 46514 Office: Miles Labs Inc PO Box 932 Elkhart IN 46515

SUCHNER, ROBERT, sociology educator; b. Detroit, Jan. 8, 1944; s. Raymond William and Dorothy Muriel (Pickett) S.; m. Patricia Maxine Jones, Aug. 20, 1965; children—Sheryl Michelle, Kathryn Stacey. B.A., Western Mich. U., 1966; M.S., U. Wis., 1968, Ph.D., 1972. Asst. prof. sociology No. Ill. U., DeKalb, 1970-78, assoc. prof., 1978—, dept. chmn., 1981-84. Co-author: Citizenship in an Age of Science, 1980; contbr. articles to profl. jours. Mem. Am. Sociol. Assn., Midwest Sociol. Soc. (state dir. 1984—), Ill. Sociol. Assn. Avocation: tennis. Home: 426 Gayle St DeKalb IL 60115 Office: No Ill U Dept Sociology 815 Zulauf Hall DeKalb IL 60115

SUDBRINK, JANE MARIE, sales and marketing executive; b. Sandusky, Ohio, Jan. 14, 1942; niece of Arthur and Lydia Sudbrink. B.S., Bowling Green State U., 1964; student in cytogenetics Kinderspital-Zurich, Switzerland, 1965. Field rep. Random House and Alfred A. Knopf Inc., Mpls., 1969-72, Ann Arbor, Mich., 1973, regional mgr., Midwest and Can., 1974-79, Canadian rep., mgr., 1980-81; psychology and ednl. psychology adminstrv. editor Charles E. Merrill Pub. Co. div. Bell & Howell Corp., Columbus, Ohio, 1982-84; sales and mktg. mgr. trade products Wilson Learning Corp., Eden Prairie, Minn., 1984—. Mem. Am. Ednl. Research Assn., Nat. Assn. Female Execs. Lutheran. Home: 6730 Vernon Ave Edina MN 55436 Office: Wilson Learning Corp 6950 Washington Ave S Eden Prairie MN 55344

SUDHEENDRA, RAO, cardio-thoracic and peripheral vascular surgeon; b. Bangalore, India, Aug. 25, 1941; came to U.S., 1965, naturalized, 1978; s. K. Ragothama and R. Nagaratnamma Rao; m. Sarala S. Krishna, Sept. 19, 1971; children—Deepak, Kiran. Diploma in Intermediate Sci., Chemistry, Botany and Zoology with honors, U. Mysore, India, 1958, B.Medicine, B.Surgery, 1964. Diplomate Am. Bd. Surgery. Houseman in medicine, surgery, pediatrics, radiology, ophthalmology, anesthesiology, obstetrics, gynecology, dermatology and dental surgery Med. Coll. Hosps., Mysore, 1964-65; sci. officer dept. surgery Atomic Energy Establishment India, Bombay, 1965; intern St. Frances Community Health Ctr., Margaret Hague Maternity Ctr., Jersey City, 1965-67; resident in surgery, clin. instr. surgery Methodist Hosp. Bklyn., SUNY-Kings County Hosp., Bklyn., 1967-71; resident in thoracic and cardiovascular surgery La. State U.-Charity Hosp. La., New Orleans, 1971-73; clin instr. surgery La. State U. Med. Ctr., New Orleans, 1972-73; assoc. attending surgeon div. cardiovascular surgery Hamot Med. Ctr., Erie, Pa., 1973-76; cons. cardiovascular surgery Shriner's Hosp. for Crippled Children, Erie, 1973-76; chief dept. thoracic and cardiovascular surgery, dir. vascular lab. Trumbull Meml. Hosp., Warren, Ohio, 1976—; active attending thoracic and cardiovascular surgery, dir. vascular lab. St. Joseph Riverside Hosp., Warren, 1976—; cons. thoracic and cardiovascular surgery Warren Gen. Hosp., 1976—; attending surgeon Youngstown Hosp. Assn., Ohio, 1982—; dir. Angiosonics Vascular Lab., Warren. Bd. dirs. Trumbull County br. Eastern Ohio chpt. Am. Heart Assn. Fellow ACS, Internat. Coll. Surgeons, Am. Coll. Angiology; mem. James D. Rives Surg. Soc., Ohio Thoracic Soc., Trumbull County Med. Soc., Ohio State Med. Assn., AMA, Am. Assn. Critical Care Medicine, Non-Invasive Vascular Technologists (adv. bd. local chpt.), World Med. Assn. (assoc.). Avocation: tennis. Office: 1216 E Market St Warren OH 44483

SUEDHOFF, CARL JOHN, JR., lawyer; b. Fort Wayne, Ind., Apr. 22, 1925; s. Carl John and Helen (Lau) S.; B.S., U. Pa., 1948; J.D., U. Mich., 1951; m. Carol Mulqueeney, Apr. 10, 1954; children—Thomas Lau, Robert Marshall, Mark Mulqueeney. Admitted to Ind. bar, 1951; assoc. Hunt & Mountz, Fort Wayne, 1951-54; partner Hunt, Suedhoff, Borrorr & Eilbacher, and predecessors, 1955—; officer, dir. Inland Chem. Corp., Fort Wayne, 1952-81; pres., dir. Lau Bldg. Co., Fort Wayne, 1951-78, S.H.S. Realty Corp., Toledo, 1960-78; officer, dir. Inland Chem. P.R., Inc., San Juan, P.R., 1972-81, Summit Resource Mgmt., Inc., also others. Mem. Allen County Council, 1972-76, pres., 1974-76; mem. Allen County Tax Adjustment Bd., 1973-74, N.E. Ind. Regional Coordinating Council, 1975-76; bd. dirs. YMCA, Fort Wayne, 1961-63. Served with AUS, 1943-45. Mem. VFW (comdr. 1958-59), Am., Ind., Allen County bar assns., Beta Gamma Sigma, Phi Delta Phi, Psi Upsilon. Republican. Lutheran. Clubs: Univ. Michigan (pres. 1965-66), Friars, Fort Wayne Country, Mad Anthony's. Office: 900 Paine Webber Bldg Fort Wayne IN 46802

SUELFLOW, AUGUST ROBERT, historical institute administrator, educator; b. Rockfield, Wis., Sept. 5, 1922; s. August Henry and Selma Hilda (Kressin) S.; m. Gladys I. Gierach, June 16, 1946; children—August Mark, Kathryn Lynn Du Bois. B.A., Concordia Coll., Milw., 1942; B.Div., M.Div., Concordia Sem., St. Louis, 1946, fellow, 1947, S.T.M., 1947; Div.D., Concordia Sem., Springfield, Ill., 1967. Asst. curator Concordia Hist. Inst., St. Louis, 1946-48, dir., 1948—; guest lectr. Concordia Sem., St. Louis, 1952-69, adj. prof., 1975—, chmn. hist. theology dept., 1975-81; asst. pastor Luther Meml. Ch., Richmond Heights, Mo., 1948-56, Mt. Olive, St. Louis, 1958-75; archivist Western Dist. Luth. Ch.-Mo. Synod, 1948-66, archivist Mo. Dist., 1966—; instr. Washington U., St. Louis, 1967—. Mem. Am. Assn. Museums, Nat. Trust for Hist. Preservation, Soc. Am. Archivists, Orgn. Am. Historians, Western History Assn., Luth. Acad. for Scholarship, Luth. Hist. Conf. Lutheran. Author: A Preliminary Guide to Church Records Depositories, 1969; Religious Archives: An Introduction, 1980; Heart of Missouri, 1954; cons., contbr. Lutheran Cyclopedia; contbr. Ency. of the Lutheran Ch., 1965. Assoc. editor Concordia Hist. Inst. Quar., 1950—; Archives & History: Minutes and Reports, 1952—; editor: Directory of Religious Hist. Depositories in America, 1963; Luth. Hist. Conf. Essays and Reports, 1964—; series editor: Selected Writings of C.F.W. Walther, 6 vols., 1981; vol. editor, translator: Walther's Convention Essays, vol. III, 1981. Office: 801 DeMun Ave Saint Louis MO 63105

SUH, EDWARD KITACK, social work educator, geriatric service consultant; b. Seoul, Korea, Sept. 21, 1940; came to U.S., 1971; s. Jungwhan and Samduck (Shin) S.; m. Jennifer Moonsun Kim, Nov. 8, 1975; children—Bernard Boongbi, Jonnathan Yongbi. B.A., Seoul Nat. U., 1965, M.A., 1967; M.S.P., Boston Coll., 1973; Ph.D., Brandeis U., 1978. Lectr., Ministry of Health and Social Affairs, Korea, 1967-69, Seoul Nat. U., also Song-sim Coll. for Women, 1969-71; asst. prof. U. Maine, Orono, 1978-79; asst. prof. social work U. No. Iowa, Cedar Falls, 1979—; social work cons. Sunnycrest Nursing Ctr., Dysant, Iowa. Served with arty. Army Republic of Korea, 1961-63. U. No. Iowa research grantee, 1980. Mem. Council on Social Work Edn., Nat. Assn. Social Workers, Am. Inst. Planners, Am. Pub. Health Assn. Democrat. Roman Catholic. Contbr. articles to profl. jours. Home: 316 E 10th St Cedar Falls IA 50613 Office: University Northern Iowa Cedar Falls IA 50613

SUKOVATY, JACK EDWARD, environmental control executive; b. Lincoln, Nebr., Jan. 24, 1948; s. William Milo and Hilda Marie (Houser) S.; m. Barbara Gail Lanman, Aug. 22, 1971; children—Aniece Ellen, Reece William. B.S. in Agronomy, U. Nebr., 1970, M.S. in Soil Sci., 1973. Research technician U. Nebr., Lincoln, 1970-73; agrl. insp. Nebr. Dept. Environ. Control, Lincoln, 1973-75, sect. chief Non Point Sources, 1975-76, chief Agrl. Div., 1976—; owner, mgr. farm, Southeast, Nebr., 1975—. Mem. council Sheridan Lutheran Ch., Lincoln, 1984—. Mem. Gamma Sigma Delta Alpha Gamma Rhoo (property mgr. 1983—). Democrat. Avocations: fishing, hunting, camping, boating. Office: Dept Environ Control PO Box 94877 Lincoln NE 68509

SUKYS, PAUL ANDREW, law educator, lawyer, consultant; b. Cleve., Feb. 7, 1948; s. Vitus John and Catherine Louise (Corsi) S.; m. Brenda Dee Stitzlein, Sept. 16, 1983. B.A., John Carroll U., 1970, M.A., 1972; J.D., Cleve. State U., 1980. Bar: Ohio 1980. Instr. John Carroll U., Cleve., 1970-72, Fairmount Ctr. Creative and Performing Arts, 1971-72; asst. prof. English, North Central Tech. Coll., Mansfield, Ohio, 1972-80, assoc. prof. law, 1980-84, prof. law, 1984—; newspaper cons., 1972-76, lit. cons., 1973-77, pub. relations coordinator, 1984—. Campaign mgr. Johns for Councilman Com., Mansfield, 1973. Recipient Am. Jurisprudence award Bancroft Whitney Co., 1978, 79, William K. Gardner award Cleve. State U., 1979, Sidney A. Levine award Cleve. State U., 1979. Mem. AAUP (com. chmn. Ohio Conf. 1974-75, v.p. local chpt. 1974-75), Am. Bus. Law Assn., Associated Writing Program. Home: 660 Lexington Ave Mansfield OH 44907 Office: North Central Tech Coll 2441 Kenwood Circle Mansfield OH 44901

SULG, MADIS, corporate planning executive; b. Tallinn, Estonia, May 25, 1943; came to U.S., 1950; s. Hans Eduard and Erika (Turk) S.; m. Mary Diane Detellis, Dec. 30, 1967; children—Danielle Marie, Michaella Erika. S.B., MIT, 1965, S.M., 1967. Mgr. bus. planning Converse Rubber Co., Wilmington, Mass., 1971-75; mgr. planning and devel. AMF, Inc., Stamford, Conn., 1975-78; sr. v.p. planning and devel. Bandag, Inc., Muscatine, Iowa, 1978—; pres. Muscatine Natural Resources Corp., 1981—. Served with U.S. Army, 1968-70. Mem. Am. Inst. Decision Scis., N.Am. Soc. Corp. Planning, Inst. Mgmt. Scis., Ops. Research Soc. Am. Club: Country (Davenport, Iowa). Home: 4855 Rambling Ct Bettendorf IA 52722 Office: Bandag Inc Bandag Ctr Muscatine IA 52761

SULLIVAN, ANTONY THRALL, foundation executive, consulting firm official; b. New Haven, Nov. 7, 1938; s. Francis Joseph and Jazel Mae (Thrall) S.; m. Marjory Elizabeth Kuhn, May 5, 1962; children—Sandra Lincoln, David Thrall. B.A., Yale U., 1960; M.A., Columbia U., 1961; Ph.D., U. Mich., 1976. History instr. Internat. Coll., Beirut, 1962-67; counselor U. Mich., Ann Arbor, 1968-69; program officer, corp. sec. Earhart Found., Ann Arbor, 1969—; dir. Near East Support Service, Ann Arbor, 1980—. Author: Thomas-Robert Bugeaud, France and Algeria, 1784-1849: Politics, Power and the Good Society, 1983. Chmn. bd. trustees Adventure Sch., Birmingham, Mich., 1982-85. Mem. Middle East Studies Assn., Middle East Inst., Nat. Assn. Arab Americans. Republican. Episcopalian. Club: Liberty Tennis. Home: 908 Westwood Ann Arbor MI 48103 Office: Earhart Found 2929 Plymouth Rd Suite 204 Ann Arbor MI 48105

SULLIVAN, BARRY, banker; b. Chgo., Mar. 7, 1939; s. J. Barry and Marta (Yokubat) S. B.S. in Bus. Adminstrn., Northwestern U., 1961. With trust dept. Continental Ill. Nat. Bank & Trust Co. of Chgo., 1961—, trust officer, 1970-80, 2d v.p., 1980—. Mem. Art Inst. Chgo. (life). Home: 15322 West Fair Ln Libertyville IL 60048 Office: Continental Ill Nat Bank & Trust Co Chgo 213 S LaSalle St Chicago IL 60697

SULLIVAN, DENNIS MICHAEL, lawyer; b. Manitowoc, Wis., June 25, 1953; s. Raymond Earl and Olive Lauraine (Skauge) S.; m. Janice Susan Walicki, June 28, 1980; 1 son, Brian Joseph. B.S. with distinction, U. Wis.-Madison, 1975, J.D., 1980. Bar: Wis. 1980, U.S. Dist. Ct. (we. dist.) Wis. 1980, U.S. Ct. Appeals (7th cir.) 1984. Assembly page Wis. Assembly, Madison, 1975-76; project specialist Wis. Clin. Cancer Ctr., Madison, 1976-77; ptnr. Herrick, Hart, Duchemin, Danielson & Guettinger, Eau Claire, Wis., 1980—. Mem. Wis. Bar Assn., Wis. Acad. Trial Lawyers, Eau Claire County Bar Assn. Roman Catholic. Home: 1511 Frederic St Eau Claire WI 54701 Office: Herrick Hart Duchemin Danielson & Guettinger PO Box 167 116 W Grand Ave Eau Claire WI 54702

SULLIVAN, DONALD JOHN, corporation executive, health care management consultant, publisher; b. Ont., Can., Apr. 18, 1939; s. John Donald and Mary (Mintenko) S.; m. Kate Hoisington, Oct. 27, 1962; children—Jeffrey, Daniel, Jennifer. B.S. in Indsl. Engring., Mich. Tech. U., 1965; M.S.A., Wayne State U., 1966. Project dir. NASA, 1963; Ohio rep. Am. Hosp. Assn., 1968; pres. Health Care Systems Inc., Columbus, Ohio, 1969-75; v.p. Chi Systems, Ann Arbor, Mich., 1973-75; pres. D. J. Sullivan & Assocs. Inc., Ann Arbor, Mich., 1975—, Health Care Pub., DJS Properties & Investments. Bd. dirs. Adventure Sch. for Learning Disabilities, Bloomfield Hills, Mich. Recipient awards for activities in field. Mem. Am. Coll. Hosp. Adminstrs., Hosp. Systems Mgmt. Soc., Hosp. Fin. Mgmt. Assn., Nat. League Nurses, Am. Assn. Hosp. Cons., Nat. Hosp. Planning Assn. Developer physician-hosp. programs. Office: 407 N Main Ann Arbor MI 48104

SULLIVAN, FRANK BERNARD, fraternal benefit society executive; b. Butte, Mont., July 17, 1919; s. Michael Jack and Mary Ellen (Sullivan) S.; m. Louise Lorraine Goss, Oct. 4, 1945; children—Michael, Roberta. B.A., Gallaudet Coll., Washington, 1941; LL.D. (hon.), 1978. Tchr. S.D. Sch. for Deaf, 1941-42; W. Va. Sch. for Deaf, 1942-44; insp. Firestone Tire and Rubber Co., Akron, Ohio, 1944-45; pres. Nat. Fraternal Soc. of the Deaf, 1967-84; mem. Conf. Ednl. Adminstrs. Serving the Deaf; trustee Gallaudet Coll. bd. dirs. Nat. Captioning Inst., Falls Church, Va. Recipient awards Ill. Parents of Hearing Impaired, 1976, Gallaudet Coll. Alumni Assn., 1979. Editor The Frat, official publ. of Nat. Fraternal Soc. of the Deaf.

SULLIVAN, JOHN FREDERICK, construction company executive; b. Chgo., Aug. 17, 1927; s. John Frederick and Dorothy (Horter) S.; m. Jeanne Wise, June 25, 1955; children—Cathy, Julie, John, Matthew, Margaret, Molly. B.A. in Bus. Adminstrn. and Banking, Colo. Coll., 1949; B.S. in Mech. Engring., U. Ill., 1957. Mem. sales staff Becker Equipment & Supply, Chgo., 1950-51; field erector Babcock & Wilcox, Chgo., 1951-54; with A & M Insulation Co., Chgo., 1957—, asst. supt., 1957-71, field supt., 1971-82, v.p. constrn., 1973—, dir., 1977—. Bd. dirs. Village Mgrs. Assn., Oak Park, Ill., 1968-83. Served with USNR, 1945-46, lt. Res. ret. Mem. Alpha Kappa Psi (life), Phi Gamma Delta, U. Ill. Alumni Assn. Republican. Roman Catholic. Club: Oak Park. Home: 619 Fair Oaks Oak Park IL 60302 Office: 2614 N Clybourn Ave Chicago IL 60614

SULLIVAN, JOHN LEONARD, public utility executive; b. Kansas City, Kans., Aug. 29, 1923; s. Leonard Riley and Katherine Bell (Singleton) S.; corr. student Internat. Accts. Soc., 1951-57; B.A., Ottawa U., 1982; m. Mary Jane Sechrest, Apr. 13, 1947; children—Kay Cheryl, Patricia Lee, John Michael. Acct., Kansas City, Suburban Water Co., Inc., 1947-57; acct. Water Dist. 1 of Johnson County, Mission, Kans., 1957-60, chief acct., office mgr., 1960-69, asst. controller, 1970, dir. fin., 1970—; acctg., fin. mgmt. cons. for small businesses, 1962—. Served with USNR, 1942-46. Mem. Adminstrv. Mgmt. Soc. (pres. Kansas City chpt. 1971-72, asst. area dir. 1972-73, Diamond Merit award 1975), Am. Water Works Assn., Nat. Assn. Accts., Overland Park (Kans.) C. of C. Presbyterian. Club: Sertoma (life, steering com. Theater in Park project 1976-78). Contbr. articles to Adminstrv. Mgmt., Public Works. Home: 9618 Nieman Pl Overland Park KS 66214 Office: Water Dist 1 Johnson County 5930 Beverly St Mission KS 66202

SULLIVAN, LAWRENCE JOSEPH, pension consultant; b. Springfield, Mass., Jan. 28, 1928; s. William Joseph and Anne Catherine (Duquette) S.; m. Mary Patricia Sullivan, June 6, 1953; children—Bernard, Robert, Joane, Mary, Patricia. B.S., Am. Internat. Coll., 1954. Sales rep. Liggett & Meyers, Springfield, Mass., 1954-56; with Mass. Mutual Life Ins. Co., Oak Brook, Ill., 1956—, now sr. group pension cons., Chgo.; investment chmn. Twenty-Fifty Trust, Wheaton, Ill., 1983—. Served with U.S. Army, 1945-56. Republican. Roman Catholic. Clubs: Wheaton North Fan, Irish Am. (pres. 1974-75). Home: 505 Hawthorne Blvd Wheaton IL 60187 Office: Mass Mutual Life Ins Co 8700 W Bryn Mawr Ave Suite 720 S Chicago IL 60631

SULLIVAN, MICHAEL WILLIAM, business executive; b. Evanston, Ill., Oct. 13, 1945; s. Edward Joseph and Marion Katherine (Brady) S.; m. Mary Ellen Quay, June 15, 1968; children—Michael Edward and Mary Ellen (twins). B.S.B.A., Xavier U., Cin., 1967. Asst. sales acctg. mgr. Victor Comptometer, Chgo., 1971-73, fin. analyst, 1973-75; sales adminstrn. mgr. Victor Graphic Systems, Chgo., 1975-76; controller Infolink Corp., Northbrook, Ill., 1976-77; regional adminstrv. mgr. Savin Corp., Elk Grove, Ill., 1977-83; ops. mgr. Tek-Aids Industries, Arlington Heights, Ill., 1983-84; regional dist. mgr. AMP Products Corp., Schaumburg, Ill., 1983-84. Mem. Planning Execs. Inst., Ill. Jaycees (regional dir. 1980, personnel v.p. 1981), Wheeling Jaycees (pres. 1978). Republican. Roman Catholic. Office: 1100 W Irving Park Rd Schaumburg IL 60193

SULLIVAN, PATRICK FLORENCE, clinical psychologist; b. Freeport, Ill., Nov. 26, 1942; s. Florence Leo and Magdalene Anne (Heinl) S.; student St. Benedict's Coll., 1960-63; B.A., U. Iowa, 1965, M.A., 1967; Ph.D., U. Vt., 1972; m. Jeanne Margaret Hildebrandt, Aug. 22, 1964 (div. 1983); children—Suzanne Colleen, Daniel Florence, Sarah Elizabeth; m. Jane Pauline Martin Michka, Apr. 6, 1984. Clin. psychology intern Des Moines Child Guidance Center, VA Hosp., 1967-68; instr., counselor Albion (Mich.) Coll., 1968-70; instr. U. Vt., 1971-72; clin. psychologist, program mgr. Polk County Mental Health Center, Des Moines, 1972-75; asst. prof. Grand View Coll., Des Moines, 1975-79; dir. criminal justice treatment unit Adapt, Inc., Des Moines, 1975-76; pvt. practice clin. psychology, Des Moines, 1975—; cons. Des Moines Police Dept., Iowa Dept. Pub. Safety; cons., v.p. Polk County Rape-Sexual Assault Care Center. Commr. West Des Moines Park Bd., 1976-79, chmn., 1977-79; mem. City of West Des Moines Comprehensive Plan Com., 1978; bd. dirs. West Des Moines Community Sch. Dist. Mem. Am. Psychol. Assn., Iowa Psychol. Assn. (pres. 1980-81, mem. exec. council 1978-82), Midwestern Psychol. Assn., Central Iowa Psychol. Assn., Am. Soc. Psychologists in Pvt. Practice, Assn. Advancement Psychology. Contbr. articles to profl. jours. Office: 1601 22d St Suite 210 West Des Moines IA 50265

SULLIVAN, ROBERT TERRENCE, financial executive; b. Evergreen Park, Ill., Mar. 24, 1947; s. Robert Eugene and Mary (Moran) S.; m. Jeanne R. King, May 26, 1972; 1 son, Robert T. B.S., Roosevelt U., 1974; M.B.A., U. Chgo., 1977. Dir. patient acctg. Community Meml. Hosp., LaGrange, Ill., 1972-75; asst. controller Evangelical Hosp. Assocs., Oak Lawn, Ill., 1975-77; treas. Evang. Hosps. Corp., Oak Brook, Ill., 1977—; asst. treas. Evang. Health Systems Corp., Oak Brook, 1983, Evang. Services Corp., Oak Brook, 1982-83; treas. Good Shepherd Manor, Barrington, Ill., 1982-83. Asst. treas. Peace Meml. Manor, Downers Grove, Ill., 1981-83, Immanuel Residences, Downers Grove, 1982-83; mem. stewardship bd. First Congl. Ch. LaGrange (Ill.), 1983; mem. Nat. Republican Com., 1980-84. Mem. Ch. of Christ. Clubs: Yacht (Chgo.); LaGrange (Ill.) Country. Office: Evangelical Hosps Corp 2025 Windsor Dr Oak Brook IL 60521

SULLIVAN, RONALD E(UGENE), manufacturing company executive; b. Terre Haute, Ind., Mar. 25, 1938; s. Charles R. and Stella M. (Rector) S.; B.S., Ind. State U., 1960, M.S., 1967. Basketball coach public high schs., DeMotte, Bunker Hill and Ossian, Ind., 1960-69, asst. prin., Union City, Ind., 1970; sales mgr. Charles W. Rice & Co., Union City, 1970-71, exec. v.p., part owner, after 1976, now pres., owner; dist. sales mgr. Hamilton Industries, Two Rivers, Wis., 1972-76. Organizer, Union City Summer Recreation Program, 1970. Mem. Nat. Sch. Supply Equipment Assn., Am. Sch. Bus. Ofcls. Methodist. Clubs: Elks (Union City); Masons, Shrine, Scottish Rite. Home: 626 Pearl St Box 305 Union City IN 47390 Office: 201 S Columbia St Union City IN 47390

SULLIVAN, WILLIAM DONALD, insurance executive; b. Monongahela, Pa., Jan. 19, 1939; s. William Donald and Esther Jane (Jones) S.; m. Beatrice Barbara Trolier, Aug. 12, 1961; children—Beth, Kelly. B.S., Pa. State U., State College, 1960; M.S. in Adminstrn., George Washington U., 1973. C.P.C.U., C.L.U. Mgmt. devel. supt. State Farm Ins. Co., Bloomington, Ill., 1972-74, div. mgr., Costa Mesa, Calif., 1974-78, exec. asst., Bloomington, 1978-80, dep. regional v.p., West Lafayette, Ind., 1980—. Pres. Jr. Achievement, Lafayette, Ind., 1984—; chmn. stewardship com. Covenent Presbyterian Ch., Lafayette, 1983-84; pres. Camelot Homeowners Assn., Lafayette, 1983-84. Mem. Lafayette C. of C. (chmn. various coms. 1980—). Republican. Avocations: flying, golfing, fishing. Home: 1309 King Arthur Dr Lafayette IN 47905 Office: State Farm Ins Cos 2550 Northwestern Ave West Lafayette IN 47901

SULLIVAN, WILLIAM TIMOTHY, pharmaceutical company executive, consultant; b. Hurley, Wis., Mar. 31, 1922; s. Patrick J. and Hazel C. (Hunt) S.; m. Meriam C. Keister, May 11, 1946; children—Barbara, William Timothy, Deborah, Patrick J., Mary Ellen. A.A., Gogebic Jr. Coll., 1941; B.S. in Chem. Engring., U. Mich., 1943. Registered profl. engr., Ill. Process engr. Abbott Labs., North Chicago, Ill., 1943-53, devel. engr., 1957-64, maintenance mgr., 1964-68, dir. engring., 1968—; process engr. Podbielniak, Inc., Chgo., 1953-57. Village trustee, Libertyville, Ill., 1973-83; active Solid Waste Adv. Com., Lake County, Ill., 1983-84, Regional Planning Commn., Lake County, 1984-85. Recipient Abbott Ann. Research award, 1962. Fellow Am. Inst. Chem. Engrs.; mem. Am. Inst. Plant Engrs. (v.p. region III 1980, Plant Engr. of Yr. award 1972). Roman Catholic. Avocations: civic work; golf; swimming; snorkel; scuba. Home: 1035 Harms Rd Libertyville IL 60048

SULLY, IRA BENNETT, lawyer; b. Columbus, Ohio, June 3, 1947; s. Bernie and Helen Mildred (Koen) S.; m. Nancy Lee Pryor, Oct. 2, 1983. B.A. cum laude, Ohio State U., 1969, J.D. summa cum laude, 1974. Bar: Ohio 1974, U.S. Dist. Ct. (so. dist.) Ohio 1974. Assoc. Schottenstein, Garel, Swedlow & Zox, Columbus, 1974-78; atty. Borden Inc., Columbus, 1978-80; sole practice, Columbus, 1980—; instr. Real Estate Law Columbus Tech. Inst., 1983—; title ins. agt. Sycamore Title Agy., Columbus, 1983—. Commentator Sta. WOSU, Columbus, 1980. Treas. Leland for State Rep., Columbus, 1982, 84; asst. treas. Pamela Conrad for City Council, Columbus, 1979; bd. dirs. Research Franklin County Celeste for Gov., Columbus, 1978. Mem. Columbus Bar Assn., ABA. Democrat. Jewish. Club: Agonis (Columbus). Avocations: running, coin collecting. Home: 305 E Sycamore Columbus OH 43206 Office: 844 S Front St Columbus OH 43206

SULTAN, WILLIAM WOODROW, JR., industrial and medical diagnostic consultant; b. Cleveland, Miss., Sept. 26, 1943; s. William Woodrow and Mary Helen (Burdine) S.; B.S. in Biology/Chemistry, Delta State U., 1964; M.S. in Microbiology/Biochemistry, Miss. State U., 1966; M.B.A., Lake Forest Sch. Mgmt. (Ill.), 1979; m. Gloria Herbison, Dec. 19, 1965; children—William Woodrow III, Jennifer Rebecca. Commd. 2d lt. USAF, 1966, advanced through grades to capt., 1968; chief of microbiology 5th Epidemiol. Lab., Manila, 1967-70; chief microbiology lab. Wright-Patterson AFB, Ohio, 1970-71; resigned, 1971; microbiologist Abbott Labs., North Chicago, Ill., 1971-72, sr. microbiologist, 1973-75, group leader, 1975-77, mgr. tech. support, 1978, mgr. mfg., 1978-81; pres. ME-DI-CO, Inc., med. diagnostic cons., Waukegan, Ill., 1981—, UTI-tect, Inc., med. diagnostic mfrs.; v.p. mktg. Zeta Digital Systems, computer applications products mfrs. Vice chairperson, Waukegan Housing Authority, 1977—; mem. Community Action Council, 1980-82; active local United Methodist ch., 1970—; Waukegan Soccer Assn., 1977—; mem. Waukegan Area Crime Stoppers, 1983—, vice chmn., 1985. NASA fellow, 1964-66; recipient Presdl. award Abbott Labs., 1975, 77, 78. Mem. Am. Soc. Microbiology, Am. Prodn. and Inventory Control Soc., Am. Mgmt. Assn., Res. Officers Assn., Phi Mu Alpha Sinfonia, Delta State U. Alumni Assn. Democrat. Contbr. articles to profl. jours. Home: 314 Douglas Ave Waukegan IL 60085 Office: 2233 Northwestern Ave Waukegan IL 60087

SUMMERS, BRIAN KEITH, music educator; b. Christopher, Ill., Feb. 16, 1959; s. James J. and Geneva Loretta (Stowers) S.; m. Susan Elizabeth Derry, May 8, 1982. A.A., Rend Lake Jr. Coll., 1979; B.Mus., Eastern Ill. U., 1981. Tchr. music Sesser Unit Schs., Ill., 1982-83; tchr. vocal music Benton Consol. High Sch., Ill., 1983—; dir. music Pyramid Players, Benton, Ill., 1977—; minister music Park Ave Bapt. Ch., Mt. Vernon, Ill., 1983-84; instr. vocal music Rend Lake Coll., Ina, Ill., 1982—; dir. Rend Lake Community Chorus, Ina, 1982—. Co-dir. Pyramid Players Community Theatre, Benton, 1977—; dir. Rend Lake Coll. Community Chorus, Ina, 1982—. Recipient Community Service award Sta. WMCL, 1984. Mem. Music Educators Nat. Conf., Am. Choral Dirs. Assn., NEA, Ill. Music Educators. Baptist. Club: Franklin County Arts Assn. (treas. 1983-84). Home: 410 S DuQuoin St Benton IL 62812 Office: Benton Consol High Sch 511 E Main St Benton IL 62812

SUMMERS, H. MEADE, JR., lawyer; b. St. Louis, Mar. 12, 1936; s. H. Meade and Josephine Elizabeth (Hicks) S.; A.B., Brown U., 1958; J.D., U. Mich., 1961; m. Bonnie Barton, Sept. 2, 1960; children—H. Meade III, Elizabeth Barton. Admitted to Mo. bar, 1961, U.S. Supreme Ct. bar; practiced in St. Louis, 1961—; assoc. Thompson & Mitchell, St. Louis, 1960-67. Chmn., Mo. Adv. Council on Hist. Preservation, 1973-78; mem. exec. com. Am. Revolution Bicentennial Commn. of Mo., 1973-76; mem. Thomas Hart Benton Meml. Homestead Commn., 1976-77, co-founder, v.p., bd. dirs. Mo. Heritage Trust, Inc., 1976-79; mem. Estate Planning Council St. Louis; mem. Old Post Office Landmark Com., St. Louis, 1969—; mem. exec. com. St. Louis-St. Louis County Commn. on Equal Ednl. Opportunities, 1968-74; chmn. legis. com. City of Ladue (Mo.), 1976—; bd. dirs. Landmarks Assn. St. Louis, 1969—, pres., 1972-73, counselor, 1973—; mem. St. Louis County Hist. Bldgs. Commn., 1971-83; bd. advisers Churchill Sch., St. Louis, 1977—; mem. Preservation Task Force of East-West Gateway Coordinating Council, 1976-80, Gateway Preservation Com., 1981-83; vice chmn. Clayton Twp. Republican Club, 1970-73. Mem. ABA, Mo., St. Louis County, St. Louis Met. (spl. com. on jud. reform 1975-76) bar assns., Nat. Trust Historic Preservation, Preservation Action, State Hist. Soc. Mo., Mo. Hist. Soc. (trustee 1978—), Market Preservation Inc., St. Louis Met. C. of C. (edn. com. 1964-74, chmn. com. 1972-74), Beta Theta Pi, Phi Delta Phi. Lodge: Rotary. Home: 42 Woodcliffe Rd Ladue MO 63124 Office: 7777 Bonhomme Ave Saint Louis MO 63105

SUMMERS, RICHARD MICHAEL, lawyer; b. Cleve., Apr. 4, 1954; s. Marcia Faye (Brucker) Summers. B.S. in Bus. Adminstrn., John Carroll U., 1976; J.D., Ohio Northern U., 1980. Bar: Ohio 1980. Assoc. Shane, Shane, Caravona & Behrens, Cleve., 1980-83; ptnr. Shane, Caravona, Behrens & Summers, Cleve., 1983-84, Share, Shane & Summers, 1984—; personal cons. to Orange Village (Ohio) chief of police, Bentleyville (Ohio) chief of police, 1983—. Named One of Cleve.'s Most Interesting People, Cleve. Mag., 1983. Mem. Am. Trial Lawyers Assn., Cleve. Bar Assn., Ohio State Bar Assn., Cuyahoga County Bar Assn. Democrat. Jewish. Club: Northeast Yacht (sec.) (Cleve.). Home: 29400 Harvard Rd Orange Village OH 44122 Office: Shane Shane & Summers Co LPA 1460 Illuminating Bldg Cleveland OH 44113

SUMMERSETT, KENNETH GEORGE, psychiatric social worker, educator; b. Marquette, Mich., Mar. 9, 1922; s. Frank Elger and Ruth H. (Fairbanks) S.; B.S., No. Mich. U., 1948, M.A. in Sociology, 1964; M.S.W., Wayne State U., 1951; student U. Puget Sound, 1942-43; m. Vivian M. Wampler, June 17, 1950; children—Nancy M., Kenneth R., Mark G. With Mich. Dept. Mental Health, 1950—, Marquette (Mich.) Child Guidance Clinic, 1950-52; chief psychiat. social worker Battle Creek (Mich.) Child Guidance, 1952-54; dir. social services Newberry (Mich.) State Hosp., 1954-66, dir., cons. social services, 1966-73, adminstrv. dir. community psychiatry, 1973—, mental health exec., 1975-82, dir. community services div., 1975-82; extension prof. sociology dept. No. Mich. U., 1962-70; lectr. sociology Lake Superior State Coll., 1968—; pvt. practice marriage and family counseling, 1982—. Mem. Upper Peninsula Mental Health Planning Com., 1964-65, Mich. Task Force Com. Mentally Retarded, 1964-65, Upper Peninsula Mental Health Com. for Comprehensive Health Planning, 1972-75, Mich. Dept. Mental Health Legis. Planning Com. Release Planning, 1975—. Bd. dirs. Eastern Upper Penninsula Mental Health Clinic, v.p., 1970-72; bd. dirs. Luce County Extension Program, sec. bd., 1972-75; bd. dirs. Luce County Social Services, 1983—. Served with AUS, 1943-46. Certified marriage counselor. Mem. Nat. Assn. Social Workers (chmn. upper Peninsula chpt. 1957-59, 64-65, vice chmn. 1972-73), Acad. Cert. Social Workers, Mich. County Social Services Assn., Theta Omicron Rho. Clubs: Lions (pres. 1959-60), Elks (maj. projects chmn. 1968-70). Author various articles pub. in profl. jours. Home: 217 W Truman Blvd Newberry MI 49868

SUMNER, RICHARD LEE, geologist; b. Indpls., Nov. 13, 1950; s. Fredric Dean and Barbara Ellen (Bredell) S.; m. Jacki Lynn Cales, Nov. 19, 1972; children—Russell Raymond, Matthew Gregory. B.S. in Geology, Ball State U., 1975; M.S. in Geology, So. Ill. U., 1977. Exploration geologist Shell Oil Co., Houston, 1977-79; devel. geologist Union Oil Co., Olney, Ill., 1979-80; cons. geologist, Olney, 1980—. Contbr. articles to profl. jours. Mem. Republican Senatorial Inner Circle, Washington, 1983; sustaining mem. Rep. Nat. Com., Washington, 1980-85. Served with U.S. Army, 1969-71, Vietnam, Decorated Bronze Star (2), Army Commendation medal, Air medal. Mem. Am. Assn. Petroleum Geologists, Southeast Asia Petroleum Exploration Soc. Clubs: Petroleum (Olney) (v.p. 1983-84), U.S. Senatorial (Washington). Home: 1260 Hall St Olney IL 62450 Office: 1146 W Main Olney IL 62450

SUMNER, STEVEN PAUL, office systems company executive; b. Evanston, Ill., June 15, 1950; s. Edmund George and Mary (Cook) S.; m. Donna Marie Zucchero, July 26, 1975; 1 son, Steven Joseph. B.S. in Bus. Adminstrn. and Mktg., U. Mo., 1973. With Datamax, St. Louis, 1973—, controller, 1977-78, controller, exec. v.p., 1978-79, pres., chief exec. officer, 1979—; mem. dealer adv. council Sharp Electronics, 1977-78; mem. distbr. adv. com. A. B. Dick, Chgo., 1980-81. Named Bus. Person of Week, Sta. KEZK, St. Louis, 1982. Mem. Young Pres.'s Orgn., Nat. Office Machines Dealer Assn., St. Louis Regional Commerce and Growth, Mo. C. of C. Republican. Presbyterian. Club: Old Warson Country (St. Louis). Office: Datamax Office Systems Inc 2121 Hampton Saint Louis MO 63139

SUMNICHT, FRANCIS HENRY, learning innovation center exec.; b. Appleton, Wis., Dec. 25, 1921; s. Henry August and Rose Marie (Honeck) S.; B.S., Marquette U., 1948; m. Patricia Beth Gambsky, Feb. 4, 1964; children—Nancy Lee, Vern, Christopher, Shawn, Eric, Heidi. Advt. and display mgr. Sears Roebuck, Appleton, 1948-51; sec., founder Advance Industries Inc., electronics, Appleton, 1951-70; postmaster, Appleton, 1956-72; sec., founder A-1 Builders, Inc., Appleton, 1954—; partner Sumnicht Supply Co., Appleton, 1951-71; pres., dir. Children's Learning Innovation Center, Inc., Appleton, 1973; direct distbr. Amway, 1975—. Mem. E. Central Wis. Regional Planning Comm., 1974-75; treas. History Alive Inc., hist. mus. found., 1973—; co-founder nat. Pray for Peace movement, 1948. Sec., Outagamie County Republican Com., 1951-55; Wis. chmn. Young Republicans, 1952. Bd. dirs. Sumnicht Charitable Found., 1968—, Outagamie County Hist. Soc., 1948—. Served with USCGR, 1942-46. Mem. Am. Mgmt. Assn., Soc. Advancement Mgmt. (regional v.p. 1971-74, 77-79), Am. Soc. Personnel Adminstrn., V.F.W., Am. Legion, Catholic War Vets. K.C., Nat. Accountants Assn. Clubs: Butte des Morts Country. Home: 325 W Michigan St Appleton WI 54911 Office: 325 W Michigan St Appleton WI 54911

SUNDBERG, COLLINS YNGVE, funeral director; b. DeKalb, Ill., May 29, 1911; s. Axel and Sophia (Collin) S.; student Worsham Coll. Mortuary Sci., 1937-38; m. Norma E. Johnson, June 20, 1942. Partner, Sundberg Funeral Home, Rockford, Ill., 1952—; pres. Col-Nor Corp., Rockford, 1961—. Pres. Winnebago County Humane Soc.; active Goldie B. Floberg Center for Children. Served with USNR, 1942-45. Mem. Nat., Ill., No. Ill. funeral dirs. assns., Am. Vets. (comdr. Rockford post), Rockford C. of C., Rockford Hist. Soc., Swedish Hist. Soc. Am. Legion, VFW. Republican. Lutheran. Clubs: Navy of U.S.A., Pyramid, John Ericsson (past pres.), Rock River Kennel (past pres., dir.) (Rockford); Forest Hills Country. Lodges: Masons, Shriners, Moose, Odd Fellows. Home: 5431 Einor Ave Rockford IL 61108 Office: 215 N 6th St Rockford IL 61107

SUNDBERG, NORMA ELIZABETH JOHNSON (MRS. COLLINS Y. SUNDBERG), funeral director; b. Rockford, Ill.; d. Conrad Walfred and Olga (Pierson) Johnson; student Brown's Bus. Coll., 1928-30; m. Collins Y. Sundberg, June 20, 1942. Partner Sundberg Funeral Home, Rockford, Ill., 1952—; sec.-treas. ColNor Corp., Rockford, 1961—. Mem. Winnebago County Women's Republican Club, 1948—, v.p., 1956, 57; active Goldie B. Floberg Center for Children. Mem. Nat., Ill. funeral dirs. assns., Swedish Hist. Soc., Jenny Lind Soc., Am. Legion Aux., Humane Soc. Aux., Humane Soc., Women of Moose. Lutheran. Mem. Order Eastern Star, Order White Shrine of Jerusalem, Daus. of the Nile. Clubs: Zonta (bd. dirs. 1962-64), Rockford Woman's; Forest Hills Country. Home: 5431 Einor Ave Rockford IL 61108 Office: 215 N 6th St Rockford IL 61107

SUNDEM, DEBORAH DIANE, educator; b. Valley Springs, S.D., Oct. 30, 1955; d. Harlowe and LaVane Dorothy (Stoltenberg) S. Diploma secretarial sci. U. S.D., 1974; B.S., S.D. State U., 1979. Clk.-typist Minnehaha County Extension Office, Sioux Falls, S.D., 1974-75; coll. work study Extension Home Econs. Specialists, S.D. Coop. Extension Service, S.D. State U., Brookings, 1976-78; home econs. tchr. Sandhills Pub. Sch., Dunning, Nebr., 1979—; chpt. adv. Future Homemakers Am., 1979—. Mem. Am. Home Econs. Assn., NEA, Nat. Assn. Vocat. Home Econs. Tchrs., Am. Vocat. Assn., Nebr. State Edn. Assn., Nebr. Vocat. Home Econs. Assn., Nebr. Vocat. Assn. Democrat. Lutheran. Home: Box 4 Dunning NE 68833

SUNDERLAND, LANE VON, college dean; b. Horton, Kans., Feb. 27, 1945; s. Raymond Lafayette and Eunice (McCrerey) S.; m. Linda Gilna, June 3, 1967; children—Danielle, Celeste. B.A., Kans. State U., 1967; M.A., U. Wash., 1968; Ph.D., Claremont Grad. Sch., 1972. Asst. prof. polit. sci. Knox Coll., Galesburg, Ill., 1972-78, assoc. prof., chmn. polit. sci. dept., 1978-83, assoc. dean, 1983—, faculty chmn., 1976-79; cons., evaluator NEH, Washington, 1984. Author: Obscenity: The Court, The Congress and the President's Commission, 1974. Contbr. articles to profl. jours. Recipient Philip Green Wright Disting Teaching award Knox Coll., 1975; Haynes Dissertation fellow Claremont Grad. Sch., 1971-72; research fellow NEH, 1979-80. Mem. Midwest Assn. Pre-law Advisors (exec. com. midwest region 1983-85), Phi Kappa Phi, Phi Eta Sigma. Baptist. Home: 1173 N Academy Galesburg IL 61401 Office: Knox Coll College Box K136 Galesburg IL 61401

SUNSERI, ALBERT JOSEPH, preventive health educator, communications consultant; b. Pitts., Apr. 22, 1942; s. Salvatore R. and Agnes S.; m. Sandra Jane Swank, Aug. 20, 1967; children—Reid Allan, Jason Charles; m. 2d Joan Kruc, May 8, 1982. B.S., U. Pitts., 1965, M.Ed., 1966, Ph.D., 1972. Cert. tchr., Pa. Asst. prof. edn., biol. scis. Point Park Coll., Pitts., 1970-75; dir. edn. Heart Attack Prevention Program, Chgo. Heart Assn., 1975-78, co-prin. investigator Chgo. Heart Health Curriculum Project, 1978—; communications cons. Nat. Heart, Lung and Blood Inst. research grantee, 1979-83. Mem. Am. Sch. Health Assn., Am. Pub. Health Assn., Assn. Supervision and Curriculum Devel., Internat. Union Health Educators. Contbr. articles to profl. jours. Home: 611

S Ridge Ave Arlington Heights IL 60005 Office: Chgo Heart Assn 20 N Wacker Dr Chicago IL 60606

SUPALLA, DONALD DEAN, educational administrator; b. Mankato, Minn., Mar. 9, 1948; s. Robert George and Betty Jane (Schroeder) S.; m. Stephanie Ann Walvoord, Apr. 17, 1971; children—Michelle, Kristen. A.A., Rochester Community Coll., 1968; B.S., Winona State U., 1971, M.S., 1975. Instr. bus. edn. Rochester Area Vocat. Tech. Inst., Minn., 1972-83, bus. office, tech. coordinator, 1983—, instr. adult edn., 1975—. Instr. vocat. edn. Winona State U., Minn., 1984—. Mem. steering com. Jefferson Sch. Council, Rochester, 1982. Mem. Minn. Bus. Educators (state treas. 1978-80), Southeast Minn. Bus. Educators (exec. bd. 1974—, pres. 1976-78), Minn. Assn. Area Vocat. Tech. Insts. (fiscal mgr. 1984—), Nat. Bus. Edn. Assn., Am. Vocat. Assn., Minn. Vocat. Assn. Democrat. Roman Catholic. Home: 1906 NE 3d Ave Rochester MN 55904 Office: Rochester Area Vocat Tech Inst 1926 SE 2d St Rochester MN 55904

SURA-THOMSON, WENDY, automotive executive; b. Detroit, Nov. 29, 1950; d. John Paton and Dorothy Ann (Sura) Thomson; m. William Edward Thomas, Sept. 1, 1979; 1 dau., Brittany Nicole (dec.). Student Mich. State U., 1968-70; B.B.A., U. Miami (Fla.), 1973; postgrad. U. Chgo., 1977; M.S., Fla. State U., 1977. Pension fund mgr. Centel, Chgo., 1977-79; auditor Gen. Motors Fisher Body Div., Warren and Grand Blanc, Mich., 1979-81, gen. supr. gen. acctg., Flint and Grand Blanc, 1981-82, div. staff asst., Warren, 1982-83, treas. staff, Gen. Motors, Detroit, 1983-84, comptroller's staff, 1984—. Mem. Assn. M.B.A. Execs., Beta Gamma Sigma, Lambda Delta, Phi Kappa Phi. Club: Choral Creations (treas. 1981-83) (Oxford, Mich.). Office: Gen Motors Corp 12-257 GM Bldg 3044 W Grand Blvd Detroit MI 48202

SURILLO, THEODOSIA VAZQUEZ, educator; b. Yabucoa, P.R., Mar. 19, 1950; d. Rogelio and Agustina (Solis) Surillo; m. Robert Therion Bullock, Nov. 8, 1981 (div.). B.A., John Carroll U., 1973; M.Ed., Baldwin Wallace Coll., 1979. Cert. in adminstrn. and supervision. Day care dir. Spanish Am. Com. Day Care Ctr., Cleve., 1975-77; tchr. corps intern Cleve. Pub. Schs., 1977-79, resource cons., tchr., 1980-82, tchr. Spanish, 1979-80, 82—. Active Hispanic Community Devel. Task Force, 1980—. Recipient Secondary Bilingual Program service award, 1982. Democrat. Roman Catholic. Home: 2863 Avondale Cleveland Heights OH 44118 Office: John Adams High School 3817 E 116th St Cleveland OH 44105

SURRIDGE, (EDGAR) DONALD, osteopathic physician; b. Geneva, Ohio, Nov. 15, 1926; s. Edgar Donald and Mary Elizabeth Bruce (Schnitzler) S.; m. Patricia A. Murphy; children—Victoria Lynn Merrick, Wendy Lee. Student, Youngstown U., 1946-47; A.B., Miami U., Oxford, Ohio, 1950; D.O. Kirksville Coll. Osteo. Medicine, 1954. Cert. manipulative medicine. Intern, Mt. Clemens (Mich.) Gen. Hosp., 1954-55; sole practice specializing in manipulative medicine, North Jackson, Ohio, 1955—; mem. staff Youngstown (Ohio) Osteo. Hosp. 1955—, chmn. dept. physical medicine, rehab., 1963-70, chmn. dept. osteo. structure and diagnosis, 1965-79; mem. Physicians Adv. Bd. Mahoning County Valley Planning Agy. Served with USN, WWII. Fellow Am. Acad. Osteopathy (bd. govs., structural consultation service com., chmn. endowment com.); mem. Am. Osteo. Assn., Ohio Osteo. Assn., Mahoning County Osteo. Soc. (pres. 1968-70), Cranial Acad. (bd. trustees). Republican. Clubs: Redbrook Boat (Ashtabula), Saxon, Scottish Rite Valley (Youngstown), Masons. Contbr. articles to profl. jours. Home: 5625 Tarrytown Ln Youngstown OH 44515 Office: 439 S Salem Warren Rd North Jackson OH 44451

SUTCLIFFE, RICHARD LEE (RICK), professional baseball player. Pitcher Chgo. Cubs. Recipient Nat. League Cy Young Meml. award, 1984. Office: Chgo Cubs Wrigley Field Chicago IL 60613*

SUTHERLAND, PAUL HOWARD, financial planner; b. Detroit, Mar. 6, 1955; s. Dale Edwin and Mary (Waddell) S.; m. Kimberly Creamer, June 21, 1980. Grad. Resources Acad., Denver, 1982. Tchr., Solar Sch., Suttons Bay, Mich., 1974; agt. Golden Rule Assocs., Sutton Bay, 1974-78, ptnr., 1978-79, owner 1979—; founder Pension Service Design Inc., Sutton Bay, 1981—; mng. exec. Integrated Recources Equity Corp., Suttons Bay, 1981—; founder Fin. and Investment Mgmt. Group, 1983—; lectr. in field. Recipient Fin. Writers awards Fin. Planners Mag., 1981. Mem. Internat. Assn. Fin. Planners, Nat. Assn. Life Underwriters, Nat. Assn. Health Underwriters, Suttons Bay C. of C. (dir. 1983). Club: Suttons Bay Rotary. Contbr. articles to profl. jours. and nat. mags. Home: Route 1 Box 73 Suttons Bay MI 49682 Office: PO Box 40 417 Saint Joseph Suttons Bay MI 49682

SUTTER, BRIAN, professional hockey player. Left wing St. Louis Blues, NHL. Office: St Louis Blues 5700 Oakland Ave Saint Louis MO 63110*

SUTTON, PATRICIA MARLENE, jewelry store executive; b. Goodland, Kans., July 1, 1953; d. Richard L. and Betty D. (Wright) Roth; 1 child, Kelli M. Reinbold. Student pub. schs., Dodge City. Salesperson (part-time) Roth Jewelers, Dodge City, Kans., 1966-72, Vernon Jewelers, Salina, Kans., 1972-73; salesperson, 1973-76, mgr., 1976—. Bd. dirs. Greater Downtown Salina Inc., 1981—, 2d v.p., 1985—, promotion com., 1984—. Mem. Kans. Jewelers Assn., Salina C. of C. (retail activities com. 1984-85). Republican. Avocations: scuba diving; fishing; archaeology. Office: Vernon Jewelers of Salina 123 N Santa Fe Salina KS 67401

SUYEMATSU, KIYO, music librarian, music educator; b. Casper, Wyo., Apr. 17, 1926; d. Benjamin Tschuchio and Masa S. B.Mus., U. Colo., 1949, M.Mus., 1963; M.A., U. Denver, 1970. Sec., Bur. of Reclamation, Casper, Wyo., 1949-51; sec. Marathon Oil Co., Casper, 1951-61; accompanist, piano tchr., Casper, 1949-61; instr. music Mankato (Minn.) State U., 1963-70, music librarian, music instr., 1970—; asst. condr. Women's Choir, Casper, 1956-61; pianist Kiwanis Club, Casper, 1956-61. Mem. negotiating council faculty bargaining unit State Univs. of Minn. Mem. Music Educators Nat. Conf., Music Library Assn., Minn. Edn. Assn., Sigma Alpha Iota (faculty adviser), Delta Kappa Gamma. Office: Performing Arts Ctr Mankato State U Mankato MN 56001

SVENSON, ROBERT HENRY, mechanical engineer; b. Balt., May 31, 1921; s. Robert Henry and Miriam (McElhose) S.; m. Shirley Foltz, Feb. 21, 1964; children by previous marriage—Peg, John, Karin, Tom, Ted. B.S. in Mech. Engring., Auburn U., 1944. Registered profl. engr., Ohio. Engr., B.F. Goodrich Co., Akron, Ohio, 1945-51; plant engr. B.F. Goodrich Co., Bogota, Colombia, 1951-57, project engr., fgn. countries, 1957-64, project mgr., Australia, other countries, 1964-80, project dir., Guadalajara, Mex., 1981-83; spl. cons. B.F. Goodrich Co., Ft. Wayne, Ind., 1984—. Scout leader Boy Scouts Am., Akron, 1970-74. Mem. Nat. Soc. Profl. Engrs., ASME (chmn. 1975-76; recipient 100th anniversary medal for outstanding service to chpt. 1976), Pi Tau Sigma, Alpha Phi Omega. Republican. Christian Scientist. Club: Pinehurst Country. Avocations: philately; bowling; golfing. Home: 2376 Burnham Rd Akron OH 44313 Office: B F Goodrich Co D/6012 500 S Main St Akron OH 44313

SVOBODA, ANGELA MAE, educator; b. Central City, Iowa, Apr. 10, 1929; d. Frank Joseph and Ann Marie (Vrba) S. Student Coe Coll., 1953-55; B.S. in Commerce, U. Iowa, 1956; M.S. in Edn., U. Mich., 1961; postgrad. U. No. Iowa, U. Iowa, Coe Coll., Appalachian State U. Exec. sec. I.O.A. Foods, Cedar Rapids, Iowa, 1947-53; departmental asst. to head bus. edn. dept. Coe Coll., Cedar Rapids, 1954-55; bus. tchr. Burlington (Iowa) Sr. High Sch., 1956-59; bus. tchr., office edn. coordinator Washington Sr. High Sch., Cedar Rapids, 1959—; public speaker. Mem. Iowa Office Edn. Assn., Iowa Vocat. Edn. Assn., Am. Vocat. Assn., Iowa Bus. Edn. Assn., Cedar Rapids Edn. Assn., Iowa State Edn. Assn., NEA (life), U. Iowa Alumni Assn. (life), Cedar Rapids Edn. Assn. (sec.), Profl. Secs. Inc., Daus. of Isabella (past pres. Cedar Rapids, past state v.p.), Czech Heritage Found., Pi Omega Pi, Delta Pi Epsilon, Delta Kappa Gamma. Democrat. Roman Catholic. Club: Quota (1st v.p. Cedar Rapids 1976-77, sec.-treas. dist. 7, 1975-76). Home: 4280 Cottage Pkwy SE Cedar Rapids IA 52403 Office: 2205 Forest Dr SE Cedar Rapids IA 52403

SVOBODA, RICHARD FRANK, accountant, writer; b. Cleve., June 25, 1926; s. Frank William and Mary Elizabeth Violet Stanczak, June 28, 1947; children—David, Joan, Daniel, Douglas, Wendy. Student, Baldwin-Wallace Coll., 1944-47, Case Western Res. U., 1948. Acct. Resterneir Co., Cleve., 1947-49; salesman Continental Baking Co., Cleve., 1949-51; asst. controller Cleve. Press., 1951-82, Sritek, Inc., Brecksville, Ohio, 1983—; baseball writer U.P.I., Cleve., 1966—; dir. Fourth Estate Credit Union, Cleve., 1970-82. Author: Baseball, Your Father's Favorite Game, 1982. Served with USN, 1944-46. Mem. Baseball Writers Assn. Am. (sec.-treas. 1968—, chmn. 1974), Sports Media Cleve. (treas. 1983—), Basketball Writers Assn. Am., Fedn. Musicians. Republican. Roman Catholic. Avocations: music, sports Home: 9421 Sladden Ave Garfield Heights OH 44125 Office: Sritek Inc 6615 W Snowville Rd Brecksville OH 44141

SWAIM, GLENN EUGENE, health care products company executive; b. Detroit, Mar. 20, 1942; s. Charles Miller and Margaret Ann (Swigart) S.; m. Lynn Ann Fortuna, Aug. 26, 1966 (div. Sept. 1976); children—Timothy, Thomas, Christine; m. Diane Phyllis Hayna, Nov. 20, 1976; children—Jeannette, Kathryn. B.S., Pa. State U., 1964; M.B.A., Fairleigh Dickinson U., 1972. Engr. Parke, Davis Co., Detroit, 1965-72; engr., sec. mgr. Ortho Diagnostics Inc., Raritan, N.J., 1972-74; project mgr. Kitchens of Sara Lee, Deerfield, Ill., 1974-78; mgr. mfg. engring. Abbott Labs., North Chicago, Ill., 1978—. Chmn. Bus. and Econ. Devel. Commn., Vernon Hills, Ill., 1980-82; pres. bd. edn. Hawthorn Community Consol. Dist. 73, Vernon Hills, Ill., 1983—. Mem. Am. Inst. Indsl. Engrs. (chpt. v.p. 1972-73), Am. Soc. Mfg. Engrs. (program chmn. 1975). Club: Detroit Yacht (social chmn. 1968-70). Lodge: Lions. Avocations: sailboat racing; skiing. Home: 1104 Swinburne Pl Vernon Hills IL 60061 Office: Abbott Labs Dept 73W AP4A Routes 137 and 43 Abbott Park IL 60064

SWAIMAN, KENNETH FRED, pediatric neurologist, educator; b. St. Paul, Nov. 19, 1931; s. Lester J. and Shirley (Ryan) S.; B.A. magna cum laude, U. Minn., 1952, B.S., 1953, M.D., 1955, postgrad., 1956-58, (fellow pediatric neurology) Nat. Inst. Neurologic Deseases and Blindness, 1960-63; children—Lisa, Jerrold, Barbara, Dana. Intern, Mpls. Gen. Hosp., 1955-56; resident pediatrics U. Minn., 1956-58, neurology, 1960-63; asst. prof. pediatrics, neurology U. Minn. Med. Sch., Mpls., 1963-66, assoc. prof., 1966-69, prof., dir. pediatric neurology, 1969—, exec. officer, dept. neurology, 1977—, mem. internship adv. council exec. faculty, 1966-70. Cons. pediatric neurology Hennepin County Gen. Hosp., Mpls., St. Paul-Ramsey Hosp., St. Paul Children's Hosp. Chmn. Minn. Gov.'s Bd. for Handicapped, Exceptional and Gifted Children, 1972-75; mem. human devel. study sect. NIH, 1976-79, guest worker NIH, 1978-81. Served to capt. M.C., U.S. Army, 1958-60. Diplomate Am. Bd. Psychiatry and Neurology, Am. Bd. Pediatrics. Fellow Am. Acad. Pediatrics, Am. Acad. Neurology (rep. to nat. council Nat. Soc. Med. Research); mem. Soc. Pediatric Research, Central Soc. Clin. Research, Central Soc. Neurol. Research, Internat. Soc. Neurochemistry, Am. Neurol. Assn., Minn. Neurol. Soc., AAAS, Midwest Pediatric Soc., Am. Soc. Neurochemistry, Child Neurology Soc. (1st pres. 1972-73, Hower award 1981), Internat. Assn. Child Neurologists (exec. com. 1975-79), Profs. of Child Neurology (pres. 1978-80), Phi Beta Kappa, Sigma Xi. Author (with Francis S. Wright) Neuromuscular Diseases in Infancy and Childhood, 1969, Pediatric Neuromuscular Diseases, 1979; (with Stephen Ashwal) Pediatric Neurology Case Studies, 1978, 2d edit., 1984; editor: (with John A. Anderson) Phenylketonuria and Allied Metabolic Diseases, 1966; (with Francis S. Wright) Practice Pediatric Neurology, 1975, 2d edit., 1982; mem. editorial bd. Annals of Neurology, 1977-83, Neurology Update, 1977-81, Pediatric Update, 1977—, Brain and Devel., 1980—, Neuropediatrics, 1983—; editor-in-chief Pediatric Neurology; contbr. articles to sci. jours. Home: 420 Delaware St SE Minneapolis MN 55455 Office: U Minn Med Sch Dept Pediatric Neurology Minneapolis MN 55455

SWAIN, RALPH ADRIAN, mass communication educator, audio-video consultant; b. Gulfport, Miss., June 14, 1943; s. Ralph Brownlee and Su Zan (Noguchi) S.; m. Wendy Anne Humphreys, Jan. 13, 1974; children—Nathan Humphreys, Ethan Ralph, Alexander Adrian. B.A., Colo. State U., 1967, M.A., 1972; postgrad. U. Pitts., 1977-80. News dir. Sta. KCSU-FM, Ft. Collins, Colo., 1971-72; reporter Sta. KCOL-AM, Ft. Collins, 1972-73; news dir. Sta. KOWB-AM, Laramie, Wyo., 1973-76; instr. journalism U. Wyo., Laramie, 1975-77; reporter Sta. WTOV-TV, Steubenville, Ohio, 1978-80; dir. pub. communications Wheeling (W.Va.) Coll., 1977-80; chmn. dept. mass communications Briar Cliff Coll., Sioux City, Iowa, 1980—; TV producer, video cons. Served with U.S. Army, 1967-70; Vietnam. Decorated Army Commendation medal; recipient Best Newsroom of 1974 award Wyo. Assn. Broadcasters, 1974, Best News award Intermountain Radio Network, 1974, 75, 76, Mark of Excellence award Sigma Delta Chi, 1977. Mem. Investigative Reporters and Editors, Am. Film Inst., Sigma Delta Chi. Club: Sioux City Press. Office: Briar Cliff Coll Sioux City IA 51104

SWALLEY, GARY WILLIAM, history educator; b. East St. Louis, Ill., Nov. 22, 1951; s. William Carter and Janiece Lucille (Roustio) S. B.A., So. Ill. U., 1974. Teaching intern Edwardsville (Ill.) Sch. Dist., 1976; substitute tchr. Edwardsville Jr. High Sch., 1977, tchr. English, social studies jr. high sch., 1977—. Valley Forge Freedoms Found. scholar, 1979; Tchrs. medal Valley Forge, 1982. Mem. Nat. Council Social Studies, Edwardsville Edn. Assn., Rotary Fellowship Group Study Exchange. Methodist. Office: Edwardsville Jr High Sch St Louis Rd Edwardsville IL 62025

SWAN, HARRY DAVID, private investigator, design engineer, personnel and criminal justice consultant; b. Rochester, N.Y., Feb. 25, 1926; s. Harry and Florence (Ellison) S.; m. Pauline E. Gunnison, May 20, 1950 (div.); children—David, Lynne. A.S. in Commerce, Henry Ford Community Coll., Dearborn, Mich., 1965; B.S. in Criminal Justice, Madonna Coll., Livonia, Mich., 1977; M.A. in Criminal Justice, U. Detroit, 1980. Lic. pvt. investigator, Ky. Design checker Chrysler Corp., Highland Park, Mich., 1953-64, Hydramatic div. Gen. Motors, Ypsilanti, Mich., 1980, AC Spark Plug div. Gen. Motors, Flint, Mich., 1981, Alliance-Renault-AMC, Detroit, 1982; design engr. Corvette-Chevrolet, Gen. Motors, Warren, Mich., 1983; chief exec. officer Covert Intelligence Agy. and Covert Pvt. Police, Lexington, Ky., 1983—. Served with USAAF, 1944-45. Mem. Sports Car Club Am., Delorean Internat. Club. Democrat. Presbyterian. Designer automotive chassis innovations, 1953-83. Address: 411 S Woodward Suite 1013 Birmingham MI 48011

SWAN, HERBERT SIEGFRIED, communications mfg. exec.; b. Montclair, N.J., Jan. 2, 1928; s. Herbert S. and Alma (Oswald) S.; grad. Phillips Exeter Acad., 1945; A.B. in Econs. and Bus. Adminstrn., Lafayette Coll., 1949; m. Roberta J. Whitmire, July 2, 1960; 1 dau., Roberta Allyson. Advt. supr. TV receiver dept. Gen. Electric Co., Syracuse, N.Y., 1954-55; copywriter Bresnick Co. advt. agy., Boston, 1955-58; sr. copywriter J.T. Chirurg Advt. Agy., Boston, 1958-59; advt. mgr. agrl. chems., indsl. minerals div. Internat. Minerals & Chem. Corp., Skokie, Ill., 1959-61; editor Motorola Newsgram, direct indsl. advt. mgr. Motorola, Chgo., 1962-68; dir. pub. info. Motorola Communications & Electronics, Schaumburg, Ill., 1968-71, mgr. indsl. advt. and sales, 1971-73, mgr. field merchandising, 1973—. Served with USAF, 1950-54. Mem. Community Radio Watch (nat. coordinator 1967-68). Home: Box 1192 Barrington IL 60010 Office: 1300 E Algonquin Rd Schaumburg IL 60172

SWAN, RONALD DAVID, university police chief, criminal justice educator; b. St. Louis, Mar. 2, 1943; s. David Percy and Dorothea Prudence (Myers) S.; m. Cheryl Ann Ramey, May 11, 1972; children—Ronald David II, Brendan Daniel. A.A.S., Hannibal-LaGrange Coll., 1964; B.S. in Adminstrn. Justice, U. Mo.-St. Louis, 1973; M.A., Webster U., 1974; B.S., SUNY-Albany, 1982; postgrad. New Scotland Yard. Maj., Hillsdale Police Dept.; Mo., 1968-71; chief police, Beverly Hills, Mo., 1971-77, Monticello, Ill., 1977-83, Ill. State U., Normal, 1983—; part-time instr. criminal justice St. Louis Community Coll., Forest Park, 1975-77, St. Mary's Coll., of O'Fallon, Mo., 1975-77, Columbia Coll., Mo., 1976-77, Parkland Coll., Champaign, Ill., 1980—, Richland Community Coll., Decatur, Ill., 1982—. Contbr. articles to profl. Recipient Medal of Distinction City of Monticello. Mem. Brit. Acad. Forensic Scis., Acad. Criminal Justice Scis., Internat. Assn. Chiefs of Police, Ill. Assn. of Chiefs of Police, Am. Soc. Criminology. Methodist. Home: 102 Sheringham Normal IL 61761 Office: Ill State U Police Dept 700 W College Normal IL 61761

SWANGER, STERLING ORVILLE, appliance manufacturing company executive; b. Battle Creek, Iowa, Jan. 5, 1922; s. Orville M. and Alma Louise (Messing) S.; m. Maxine O. Hindman, July 2, 1950; 1 son, Eric. B.S., Iowa State U., 1947; student U. Va., 1965. Registered profl. engr., Iowa. Indsl. engr. Maytag Co., Newton, Iowa, 1947-52, methods engr., 1952-54, asst. chief methods engr., 1954-57, chief methods engr., 1957-68, mgr. prodn. engring., 1968-71, mgr. engring., 1971-74, asst. v.p. mfg., 1974-75, v.p. mfg., 1975—, also dir. Mem., Newton Planning and Zoning Commn., 1966-70; trustee Newton Skiff Hosp. Served with AUS 1943-46. Mem. Nat. Soc. Profl. Engrs., Iowa Engring. Soc., Nat. Mgmt. Assn., Am. Mgmt. Assn., Am. Ordnance Assn. Republican. Presbyterian. Clubs: Newton Country, Elks.

SWANN, HAROLD DENVER, railroad executive; b. Huntington, W.Va., Jan. 28, 1933; s. Stonewall Jackson and Zama Janette (Minor) S.; m. Lillian Mae Perkins, Dec. 20, 1957; children—Crystal Livette, Harold David. B.Engring. Sci., Marshall U., 1960, M.B.A., 1971. Gen. engr. research and devel. U.S. Air Force, Dayton, Ohio, 1960-61; engr., U.S. C.E., Huntington, W.Va., 1961; supt. finishing and shipping Novamont Corp., Neal, W.Va., 1961-63; engr. Chessie System, Huntington, 1963-73, mgr. labor relations, Balt., 1973-80, gen. plant mgr., Huntington, 1980-85; asst. gen. mgr. Loco Heavy Shops, 1985—. Served with USN, 1951-55, Korea. Mem. Locomotive Maintenance Officers Assn. Republican. Baptist. Avocation: hunting. Home: Route 2 Box 93 South Point OH 45680 Office: Chessie System PO Box 1800 Huntington WV 25718

SWANSON, ALFRED BERTIL, orthopedic surgeon; b. Kenosha, Wis., Apr. 16, 1923; s. O.P. and Esther (Person) S.; m. Genevieve deGroot, Dec. 7, 1969; 1 child, Eric Alfred; children by previous marriage—Karin Louise, Miles Raymond. B.S., U. Ill., 1944, M.D., 1947. Diplomate Am. Bd. Orthopedic Surgery. Intern St. Luke's Hosp., Chgo., 1947; spl. tng. orthopedic surgery Ill. Crippled Children's Hosp. Sch., Chgo., 1948, St. Luke's Hosp., 1949, Northwestern U. Med. Sch., 1950, Ind. U. Med. Ctr., 1951; practice medicine specializing in orthopedic surgery, Grand Rapids, Mich., 1954—; chief orthopedic and hand surgery tng. program Grand Rapids Hosp., and chief hand surgery fellow, orthopedic research dir. Blodgett Meml. Hosp., Grand Rapids, 1958—; chief of staff Mary Free Bed Children's Hosp. and Orthopedic Ctr., Juvenile Amputee Clinic; prof. surgery Mich. State U., Lansing; lectr. throughout world. Author: Implant Resection Arthroplsty in the Hand and Extremities, 1973; also articles. Inventor implants for replacement of arthritic joints. Served with USNR, 1944-45, to capt. M.C., U.S. Army, 1952-54. Decorated Medal of Honor (Vietnam); recipient Profl. Medicine award Mich. Internat. Council, 1977, Nat. Vol. Service citation Arthritis Found., 1984, U. Ill. Alumni Achievement award, 1985. Fellow ACS; mem. Am. Med. Writers Assn., AMA (Disting. Service award 1966, 69), Am. Acad. Orthopedic Surgeons, Pan Am. Med. Assn., Assn. Mil. Surgeons U.S., Brit. Club Surgery of Hand, Italian Soc. Surgery of Hand, Internat. Fedn. Socs. Surgery of Hand (sec. gen. 1978-83, pres. 1983—), Am. Soc. Surgery of Hand (pres. 1979-80), Am. Orthopedic Assn., Am. Orthopedic Foot Soc., Mich. Med. Soc. (Disting. Service award 1966, Nat. Pres.'s award 1979, 84), Japanese Soc. Hand Surgery, Brazilian, Latin Am., Chilean, Peruvian, Argentinian, Belgian, Turkish Socs. Orthopedic Surgery and Traumatology, Soc. Am. Inventors, Airplane Owners and Pilots Assn., others. Congregationalist. Club: Blythefield Country (Grand Rapids). Lodge: Rotary. Office: 1900 E Wealthy St Grand Rapids MI 49506

SWANSON, ALICE MAY, educator, musician, agriculturist; b. Bloomington, Ill., July 31, 1937; d. Charles Victor and Agnes (Funk) S.; student Ill. State U., summers 1957-58, 61; B.A., Eureka Coll., 1959, postgrad., 1978-79; M.Ed., U. Ill., 1964, postgrad., 1976-77; postgrad. Ind. U., 1979-80. Elem. tchr., public schs., Rossville, Ill., 1958-61; elem. tchr. Rantoul (Ill.) City Schs., 1961-72, reading specialist, 1972—, yearbook coordinator, 1968—; mem. tchr. liaison council Center for Study Reading, U. Ill., Champaign, 1977—; cons. Becoming a Nation of Readers, 1985. Choir dir. Evangelical Covenant Chs. Am., Paxton, Ill., 1976—. Recipient several publ. awards. Mem. Internat. Reading Assn. (nat. conv. del. 1978), Assn. Supervision and Curriculum Devel., Orton Soc. (nat. del. 1979), Ill. Reading Council. Republican. Music arranger; developer reading programs; writer poetic verses; designer small farm equipment. Home: Maple Grove Farm Rural Route 1 Paxton IL 60957 Office: 400 E Wabash Ave Rantoul IL 61866

SWANSON, ARTHUR P., architect; b. Chgo., Nov. 25, 1906; s. Paul William and Ida (Mord) S.; B.S., Ill. Inst. Tech., 1929; m. Jean M. Lillyquist, Feb. 4, 1939; children—Paul W., Lynn Virginia (Mrs. Thomas Wilson), Carol Jean (Mrs. David Robbin), Christine Mary, Carl John. With N. Max Dunning Co., Chgo., 1929-32, Douglas Aircraft Co., Chgo., 1941-42; pvt. practice architecture, Des Plaines, Ill., 1932-41, Chgo., 1943-59, Skokie, Ill., 1959-66, Rosemont, Ill., 1966—; v.p. O'Hare Inn, Chgo., 1959-71. Registered architect, Ill. Mem. AIA, Am. Srs. Golf Assn., Western Srs. Golf Assn. (dir.). Clubs: Architects (past pres.) (Chgo.); Bobolink Golf; Quail Ridge (Fla.). Prin. works include O'Hare Inn, Des Plaines, 1959, Win Schuler Restaurants, Mich., 1960—, O'Hare East Office Bldg., Rosemont, 1966, Gen. Mills Office Bldg., Internat. Harvester, Ft. Wayne, O'Hare Internat. Transp. Center Office Bldg., Rosemont, 1968, Nat. Assn. Ind. Insurers Office Bldg., Des Plaines, 1971. Home: 1454 Estate Ln Glenview IL 60025 Office: 9501 W Devon Ave Rosemont IL 60018

SWANSON, DAVID H(ENRY), economist, educator; b. Anoka, Minn., Nov. 1, 1930; s. Henry Otto and Louise Isabell (Holiday) S.; B.A., St. Cloud State Coll., 1953; M.A., U. Minn., 1955; m. Suzanne Nash, Jan. 19, 1952; children—Matthew David, Christopher James. Economist area devel. dept. No. States Power Co., Mpls., 1955-56, staff asst., v.p. sales, 1956-57, economist indsl. devel. dept., 1957-63; dir. area devel. dept. Iowa So. Utilities Co., Centerville, 1963-67, dir. econ. devel. and research, 1967-70; dir. New Orleans Econ. Devel. Council, 1970-72; div. mgr. Kaiser Aetna Texas, New Orleans, 1972-73; dir. corp. research United Services Automobile Assn., San Antonio, 1973-76; pres. Lantern Corp., 1974-79; adminstr. bus. devel. State of Wis., Madison, 1976-78; dir. Center Indsl. Research and Service, Iowa State U., Ames, 1978—, mem. mktg. faculty Coll. Bus. Adminstrn., 1979—; dir. Iowa Devel. Commn., 1982-83; mem. adv. bd. Iowa Venture Capital Fund, 1985—; dir. Applied Strategies Internat. Ltd., 1983—; chmn. Iowa Curriculum Assistance System, 1984-85. Mem. Iowa Airport Planning Council, 1968-70; mem. adv. council office Comprehensive Health Planning, 1967-70; mem. adv. council Ctr. Indsl. Research and Service, 1967-70, New Orleans Met. Area Com., 1972-73; mem. Dist. Export Council, 1978—; mem. region 7 adv. council SBA, 1978—; dir. Mid-Continent R&D Council, 1980-84; chmn. Iowa del. White House Conf. on Small Bus., 1980; chmn. Gov.'s Task Force on High Tech., 1982-83; chmn. Iowa High Tech. Council, 1983—; adv. com. U. New Orleans, 1971-73; county finance chmn. Republican Party, 1966-67; bd. dirs. Greater New Orleans Urban League, 1970-73, Indsl. Policy Council, 1984—; mem. Iowa Gov.'s Export Council, 1984—; v.p. Iowa Sister State Friendship Com., 1985. Served with USAF, 1951-52. C.P.C.U. Mem. Nat. Assn. Mgmt. Tech. Assistance Ctrs. (pres.), Tech. Transfer Soc. (bd. dirs. 1984—), Nat. Univ. Continuing Edn. Assn., Internat. Council Small Bus. Republican. Episcopalian. Clubs: Rotary, Toastmasters (past pres.). Home: 1007 Kennedy Dr Ames IA 50010 Office: Iowa State U Ames IA 50011

SWANSON, DENNIS LEROY, environmental scientist; b. N.Y.C., Sept. 8, 1937; s. Stewart and Katherine (Danilik) S.; m. Janice Lee Bohn, Jan. 12, 1980. B.S., U. Minn., 1968; M.P.A., Western Mich. U., 1984. Fisheries scientist U. Minn.-St. Paul, 1968-72; asst. dir. Toxic Materials Office, Mich. Dept. Natural Resources, Lansing, 1972-81, regional biologist, 1982-83, chief environ. assessment dept., 1983—; environ. advisor Mich. Toxic Substance Commn., Lansing, 1981. Author: A Review of EPA Quality Criteria for Water, 1979. Contbr. articles to profl. jours. Mem. AAAS, Am. Fisheries Soc. (cert. fisheries scientist), Water Pollution Control Fedn., Am. Soc. Pub. Adminstrn., Soc. Environ. Geochemistry Health, Am. Soc. Linmology and Oceanography. Avocations: fishing, hunting, skiing, powerboat racing, scuba diving. Office: Mich Dept Natural Resources PO Box 30028 Lansing MI 48909

SWANSON, DWIGHT HAROLD, retired utility company executive; b. Princeton, Minn., Aug. 13, 1919; s. Arthur B. and Signe C. (Odelius) S.; B.S. in Elec. Engring., Purdue, 1948; m. Audrey C. Myers, May 30, 1946; children—Mark Alan, Nancy Joan. With Central Ill. Electric & Gas Co., 1939-42; various positions including field engr., div. engr. Commonwealth Edison Co., Chgo., 1948-60; div. v.p., then mktg. v.p. Pub. Service Ind., Kokomo and Plainfield, 1961-69; pres., chief exec. officer, dir. Iowa Power & Light Co., Des Moines, 1969-70, pres., chmn. bd., 1970-84, ret., 1984, now dir., mem. exec. com.; chmn. bd., chief exec. officer Iowa Resources Inc., Des Moines, 1983—; dir. Bankers Trust Co., Des Moines, Bankers Life, Des Moines. Past chmn. Food and Energy Council. Mem. pres.'s council Purdue U.; bd. dirs. Central Bapt. Theol. Sem., Iowa Meth. Health Found., Des Moines; bd. govs. Living History Farms Found. Iowa. Iowa State U. Found. Served with USNR, 1942-46. Mem. Edison Electric Inst. (pres. 1978), Greater Des Moines C. of C., Missouri Valley Electric Assn. (pres. 1972), Iowa Engring. Soc., Kokomo Fine Arts Assn. (pres. 1967). Lodge: Rotary (pres. Kokomo 1967-68). Home: Grand Ave #309 Des Moines IA 50312

SWANSON, FRANK WILLIAM, manufacturing consulting executive; b. Chgo., Dec. 28, 1946; s. Arthur B. and Alice M. (Balles) S.; B.S.E., No. Ill. U., 1968; m. Grace Palmenco, May 10, 1974; children—Edsel, Gemma, Jewelia,

Maricel, Dawn, Kristin. Mgr., C.E. Niehoff, Chgo., 1977-79; materials mgr. Raymond Control Systems, St. Charles, Ill., 1979-83; dir. materials TSR, Inc., 1983-84; v.p. mfg. cons. Orb Systems, Inc., 1984-85; pres. Frank W. Swanson & Assocs., 1985—; instr. Harper Coll. Served with AUS, 1968-70. Mem. Am. Prodn. and Inventory Control Soc. (cert. inventory mgr., pres. Fox River chpt. 1981, chmn. bd. dirs. Region XIII 1982-84, v.p. edn. programs 1984—), Fox Valley Purchasing Soc., Am. Materials Mgmt. Soc. Republican. Lutheran. Home and office: 5174 Cypress Ct Lisle IL 60532

SWANSON, G. MARIE, epidemiologist; b. Defiance, Ohio, Aug. 28, 1943; d. Gordon U. and Doris M. (Dunbar) Rowe; m. Russell H. Swanson, Jan. 28, 1978. B.A., Wayne State U., 1967, M.A., 1969, Ph.D., 1974; M.P.H., Johns Hopkins U., 1983. Instr. dept. sociology and anthropology U. Windsor, (Ont., Can.), 1970-71; instr. dept. sociology Wayne State U., 1969-75; project dir. Social Conflict and Homicide Studies, Detroit Police Dept., 1973-75; chief Evaluation Unit, Mich. Cancer Found., Detroit, 1976-77, chmn. dept. social oncology, 1977-82, dir. Div. Epidemiology, 1982—; assoc. dir. Epidemiology Comprehensive Cancer Ctr. Met. Detroit, 1980—; mem. Chronic Disease Adv. Com., State of Mich., 1980—; mem. rev. coms. Nat. Cancer Inst., 1982-83, mem. Working Group on Behavioral Aspects of Screening and Early Detection Cancer, 1983, mem. support rev. com. Cancer Ctr., 1984—; cons. Social Conflict Task Force, Detroit City Council, 1974-76, U.S. Conf. Mayors, 1975, Subcom. On Crime, Com. on Judiciary, U.S. Ho. of Reps., 1975. Ctrs. for Disease Control grantee, 1979, 80-83; Nat. Cancer Inst. grantee, 1977—; Nat. Inst. Occupational Safety and Health grantee, 1984-87. Fellow Am. Coll. Epidemiology; mem. Am. Assn. Cancer Research, Soc. Epidemiol. Research, AAAS, Am. Sociol. Assn., Am. Pub. Health Assn., Internat. Assn. Cancer Registries. Democrat. Contbr. articles to profl. jours. Office: 110 E Warren Detroit MI 48201

SWANSON, LILLIAN LOUISE, nurse, bookkeeper; b. Woodland Ville, Mo., July 6, 1915; d. Homer Lee and Elsie (Mead) Claxton; m. Frank Martin, Feb. 23, 1930 (dec. 1938); children—Homer, John, Samuel Martin; m. Ashley Glenn Skeen, Feb., 1939 (div. 1942); children—Patricia VanBooven, Larry Skeen; m. Vernon Lewis Swanson, June 1, 1949; 1 child, Michael Frederick, 1 stepchild, Wayne Swanson. Student of various practical nursing courses. Lic. practical nurse, Mo. Nurse aide Ellis Fischel Cancer Hosp., Columbia, Mo., 1941-54, licensed practical nurse, 1954-59; office nurse, bookkeeper Charles A. Leech, M.D., Columbia, 1961—. Recipient Disting. Service award Mo. Gov.'s Office, 1962. Mem. Nat. Assn. Lic. Practical Nurses, Nat. Assn. Practical Nurse Edn. and Service, Mo. State Assn. Lic. Practical Nurses (state membership chmn. 1963-64, 78-82, chmn. state nominating com. 1984—), Columbia Lic. Practical Nurses (pres., sec., bd. dirs., nominating, edn., membership, publicity coms., chmn. legis. com.). Democrat. Methodist. Avocations: reading; sewing.

SWANSON, NORMA THEISEN, corporate financial officer; b. Mpls., June 4, 1933; d. John L. and Marion A. (Groschen) Theisen; m. Arthur J. Swanson, Nov. 11, 1952; children—Denise, Ken, Dave, John, Jerry, Gary. Grad. high sch., Mpls. Corp. officer Art's Superette, Inc., Fridley, Minn., 1968-70; credit clk. Unity Hosp., Fridley, 1970; office mgr. Bryant-Franklin Corp., Mpls., 1970-75; acct. Authorized Cons., Mpls., 1976; mng. ptnr. Theisen B Partnership, Mpls., 1982—; corp. officer Bossaire, Inc., Mpls., 1982—. Past mem. W. Broadway Project area com., Mpls. Mem. West Broadway Bus. Assn. Republican. Roman Catholic. Home: 361 Rice Creek Terr Fridley MN 55432 Office: Bossaire Inc 415 W Broadway Minneapolis MN 55411

SWANSON, PAUL JOHN, JR., finance educator; b. Crawfordsville, Ind., May 10, 1934; s. Paul John and Helen (Bath) S.; student DePauw U., 1952; B.S. in Accountancy, U. Ill., 1959, B.S. in Econ. and Fin., 1960, M.S. in Fin., 1962, Ph.D., 1966. Grad. teaching asst. U. Ill., Urbana, 1960-65, grad. research asst., 1964-65; asst. prof. finance U. Cin., 1965-67, assoc. prof., 1967—, prof.-in-charge dept. quantitative analysis, 1967-68; pres. Paul Swanson and Assocs., Inc., 1983—; cons. local bus. and govt. agencies. Served with AUS, 1956-58. Mem. Nat. Def. Exec. Res., Inst. Mgmt. Scis. (past pres. Miami Valley chpt.), Ops. Research Soc. Am., Am., Midwest finance assns., Fin. Analysts Soc., Inst. Chartered Fin. Analysts, Am. Statis. Assn., Delta Chi, Delta Sigma Pi. Republican. Episcopalian (vestryman, chmn. TV ministry com. 1983—; mem. fin. com.). Home: 3441 Telford St Cincinnati OH 45220

SWANSON, RICHARD CARL, electronics company executive; b. Mpls., Feb. 21, 1937; s. Carl E. and Signa Alvilde (Omodt) S.; m. Carol Jeneve Youngquist, Aug. 31, 1960; children—Michael S., Dale K., Brian R.C., Kimberly A. B.E.E., U. Minn., 1960. Sales engr. Honeywell, Mpls., 1958-60; engr. Am. Monarch, Mpls., 1960-62; regional mgr. Semiconductor Specialists, Bloomington, Minn., 1962-67; pres., owner Indsl. Components Inc., Edina, Minn., 1967-76, Electronic Tool Supply, Inc., Burnsville, Minn., 1976—; cons. Terado Corp., St. Paul, 1959-64. Contbg. author: Select Semiconductor Circuits, 1960. Patentee in field. Scoutmaster, Boy Scouts Am., St. Paul, 1967—, tng. chmn., 1977-79, dist. chmn., 1979-82. Served with USAFR, 1958-62. Recipient Silver Beaver award Boy Scouts Am., 1982, Dist. Award of Merit, 1979, others. Mem. Soc. Mfg. Engrs. Republican. Lutheran. Lodge: Optimists. Home: 110 Shoshoni Trail Apple Valley MN 55124 Office: Electronic Tool Supply Inc 755 E Cliff Rd Burnsville MN 55337

SWANSON, ROBERT MARTIN, medical center administrator; b. Bell, Calif., Oct. 14, 1940; s. Harold M. and Elsie Lorraine (Allison) S.; A.B., Long Beach (Calif.) State Coll., 1963; M.A., U. Iowa, 1965; Ph.D., UCLA, 1970; m. Katharine Vivian Martin, Feb. 16, 1980. Dir., Office of Mental Health Research, U. Iowa, Iowa City, 1966-70; research dir. Health Planning Council, St. Paul, 1970-73; exec. dir. Kansas City (Mo.) Health Plan, 1973-75; asst. dir. St. Louis U. Hosps., 1975-80; asst. v.p. and chief planning officer St. Louis U. Med. Ctr., 1981—; dir. Organizational Research & Devel. Corp., Kansas City, Group Health Plan Greater St. Louis, Group Health Plan Found.; clin. prof. St. Louis U. Grad. Program in Health and Hosp. Adminstrn., 1980—; adj. prof. Webster Coll., St. Louis, 1975-82; spl. cons. to Kansas City (Mo.) Health Dept., 1974-75; tech. cons. Health Services Adminstrn., HEW, 1973-75; coordinator St. Louis Community-Univ. Conf., 1977-80; mem. health affairs task force Mo. Catholic Conf., 1977. Sec. to holy synod Eastern Orthodox Catholic Ch. in Am. Named Adm. in Nebr. Navy, 1971; State of Iowa grantee, 1969. Mem. Nat. Assn. Hosp. Devel. (cert.), Am. Mgmt. Assn., Soc. for Advancement Mgmt., N.Am. Soc. Corp. Planners, Internat. Platform Assn., Advt. Club Greater St. Louis, Zeta Beta Tau. Republican. Orthodox Catholic. Contbr. articles on health services to profl. jours. Office: 3556 Caroline St Saint Louis MO 63104

SWANSON, SUSAN KATHLEEN, management information professional, dog breeder; b. Evergreen Park, Ill., July 11, 1950; d. George Bernard and Betty Jayne (Caughey) Reynolds; m. Richard Carl Swanson, Aug. 26, 1978. B.B.A., Loyola U., Chgo., 1972. Statis. analyst Blue Cross Assn., Chgo., 1972-75; mgr. sales adminstrn. Omron Corp. Am., Chgo., 1975-76, mgr. external accts., Schaumburg, Ill., 1976-77, mgr. systems and programming, 1977—; speaker IBM Seminars, Rolling Meadows, Ill., 1982—. Mem. Illini Search and Rescue, 1984. Mem. Data Processing Mgmt. Assn. Republican. Roman Catholic. Club: American Chesapeake. Avocations: Hunting, fishing, collecting Western American art. Office: Omron Business Systems 1300 N Basswood St Schaumburg IL 60195

SWANSTROM, KATHRYN RAYMOND, conv. mgmt. exec.; b. Milw., Sept. 5, 1907; d. William Hyland and Jessie Viola (Bliss) Raymond; student Bryant and Stratton Bus. Coll., 1927-28; m. Luther D. Swanstrom, Aug. 27, 1937; 1 son, William Hyland Raymond. Caterer, Racine, Wis., 1926; field rep., asst. mgr. Master Reporting Co., 1936-52; dir., sec. Diesel-Ritter Corp., 1942-46; pres. Kay C. Raymond Assos., 1952—; v.p., treas. Kenneth G. MacKenzie Assos., 1954—. Asst. sec. nat. com. U.S.A. 3d World Petroleum Congress, 1950-51. Sec. Ridge Civic Council, 1940-60; sec. Police Traffic Safety Com.; state chmn. legislation Ill. Congress Parents and Tchrs., 1943; Rep. state central committeewoman, 1938-44, asst. ofcl. reporter Rep. Nat. Conv., 1940-48. Mem. Anti-Cruelty Soc., AIM, Soc. Mayflower Descs. (dep. gov. gen.), Soc. Sons and Daus. of Pilgrims (3d v.p.), Soc. Daus. of Colonial Wars (nat. sec.), DAR (ofcl. timekeeper), Nat. Geog. Soc., ASTM, Ladies Oriental Shrine N. Am., Founders, Patriots (nat. councillor), Aux. Ancient Honorable Arty. Co. of Boston (nat. pres. 1977-80), John Alden Kindred, Internat. Platform Assn., Nat. Hugenot Soc. (pres. gen. 1979-83), Pi Omicron (nat. pres. 1950-54). Republican. Episcopalian. Clubs: Beverly Hills Woman's, Crescendo. Address: 9027 S Damen Ave Chicago IL 60620 also 3 Old Hill Farms Rd Westport CT 06880

SWARTZ, EDWARD MORTON, dentist; b. Chgo., June 11, 1938; s. Aaron and Frances (Marc) S.; B.S., U. Chgo., 1960; D.D.S., U. Ill., 1963; m. Carol Swartz; children—Arden, Alan, Heidi, Lisa, Melanie. Practice dentistry, Niles, Ill., 1965—; cons. Triton Coll. Served with AUS, 1963-65. Mem. Am. Dental Assn., Am. Analgesia Soc., N.W. Acad. Applied Dental Econs., Acad. Gen. Dentistry (past editor Ill. Pulse), Niles C. of C., U.S. Judo Assn. Club: Rotary (pres. Niles-Morton Grove 1979-80). Contbg. author: Bloom's Textbook Histology; contbr. articles profl. publs.; author, lectr. relative analgesia in modern dentistry. Home: 708 Clearwater Ct Wheeling IL 60090 Office: 7942 W Oakton St Niles IL 60648

SWARTZ, JACK, association executive; b. Dodge City, Kans., Nov. 24, 1932; s. John Ralph and Fern (Cave) S.; m. Nadine Ann Langlois, Aug. 4, 1956; children—Dana, Shawn, Tim, Jay. A.A., Dodge City Community Coll., 1953; student St. Mary of Plains Coll., 1953-55, 58; B.A. in Econs., Washburn U., 1974, B.B.A., 1973. Vice pres. D.C. Terminal Elevator Co., Dodge City, Kans., 1957-65; exec. v.p. Kans. Jaycees, Hutchinson, 1965-68, Kans. Assn. Commerce and Industry, Topeka, 1968-82; pres. Nebr. Assn. Commerce and Industry, Lincoln, 1982—. Served with U.S. Army, 1955-57. Named Outstanding Local Pres. in State, Kans. Jaycees, 1961; Outstanding Young Man of Yr., Dodge City Jaycees, 1961; Outstanding State Vice Pres., U.S. Jaycees, 1962, Outstanding Nat. Dir., 1963. Mem. Am. Soc. Assn. Execs. (cert.), Am. Chamber Commerce Execs. (cert.), Nebr. Chamber Commerce Execs. (sec.-treas.), Nebr. Soc. Assn. Execs. (dir.), Nebr. Fedn. Bus. Assns. (v.p. 1984—). Republican. Roman Catholic. Lodge: Rotary. Home: 2744 Laurel St Lincoln NE 68502 Office: Nebr Assn Commerce and Industry 1320 Lincoln Mall PO Box 95128 Lincoln NE 68509

SWARTZ, ROBERT DALE, newspaper publisher; b. Flint, Mich., Dec. 2, 1925; s. Harry C. and Mattie B. (Jespersen) S.; student Flint Jr. Coll., 1946-48; m. Idamae K. Stiehl, Nov. 2, 1946; children—Timothy J., Mary Swartz Smith, Kathleen Swartz Tupper, Dale R. With Flint Jour., 1949-58, controller, 1960-63, pub., 1979—; with Grand Rapids (Mich.) Press, 1958-60, advt. mgr., 1963-79. Trustee Butterworth Hosp., Grand Rapids, 1968-78, McLaren Gen. Hosp., Flint, 1978—, Flint Area Conf. Bd., 1979—; pres. bd. dirs. Salvation Army, Grand Rapids, 1964-78, trustee, Flint, 1979—, chmn. adv. bd., 1984—; pres. Jr. Achievement, Grand Rapids, 1966-78; mem. Health Systems Agy. for Western Mich., 1976-78; bd. dirs. Kent Med. Found., 1973-78, YMCA, 1972-78, Flint United Way, 1979—. Served with U.S. Army, 1944-46. Recipient Salvation Army Others award, 1978; Jr. Achievement award, 1976; Am. Legion 4th Estate award, 1972. Mem. Flint Area C. of C. (trustee 1979—, chmn. bd. 1983-85), Am. Newspapers Pubs. Assn., Mich. Press Assn., Inland Press Assn. Clubs: Flint City, Flint Golf, Univ., Rotary. Home: 1603 Apple Creek Trail Grand Blanc MI 48439 Office: 200 E First St Flint MI 48502

SWARTZ, WILLIAM JOHN, See *Who's Who in America*, 43rd edition.

SWARTZLANDER, GLENN CARROLL, osteopathic pediatrician; b. Toledo, Aug. 19, 1943; s. Glenn C. and Virginia Mae (Hartman) S.; m. Patricia A. Wenzel, Aug. 28, 1965; children—Christi A., Kurt D. A.A., Muskegon Community Coll., 1963; B.S., Central Mich. U., 1966; D.O., Kansas City Coll. Osteopathy and Surgery, 1970. Intern, Muskegon (Mich.) Gen. Hosp., 1970-71; gen. practice medicine, Ravenna, Mich., 1971-72; resident in pediatrics Grand Rapids Osteo. Hosp. (Mich.), and Butterworth Hosp., Grand Rapids, 1973-75; practice medicine specializing in pediatrics, Muskegon, 1975—; chief of staff Muskegon (Mich.) Gen. Hosp., 1984—; clin. assoc. prof. pediatrics W.Va. Sch. Osteo. Medicine. Pres. Westshore Heart Assn., 1977, 79, adviser Multicap Presch. program, 1975-82; mem. SCAN com. Protective Services Muskegon County; committeeman Boy Scouts Am., 1980—; soccer coach Tri-Cities Soccer League, 1979—. Mem. Western Mich. Pediatric Soc., Mich. Assn. Osteo. Physicians and Surgeons, Am. Osteo. Assn., Am. Coll. Osteo. Pediatricians (sr.). Republican. Mem. Ref. Ch. Am. Home: 18690 Pinecrest St Spring Lake MI 49456 Office: 1828 Oak Ave Muskegon MI 49442

SWEARINGEN, JOHN ELDRED, bank holding co. exec., former oil company executive; b. Columbia, S.C., Sept. 7, 1918; s. John Eldred and Mary (Hough) S.; m. Bonnie L. Bolding, May 18, 1969; children by previous marriage—Marcia L. Swearingen Pfleeger, Sarah K. Swearingen Origer, Linda S. Swearingen Evans. B.S., U. S.C., 1938, LL.D. (hon.), 1965; M.S., Carnegie-Mellon U., 1939, D.Eng. (hon.), 1981. Chem. engr. research dept. Standard Oil Co. (Ind.), Whiting, Ind., 1939-47; various positions Amoco Prodn. Co., Tulsa, 1947-51; gen. mgr. prodn. Standard Oil Co. (Ind.), Chgo., 1951, dir., 1952, v.p. prodn., 1954, exec. v.p., 1956, pres., 1958, chief exec. officer, 1960-83, chmn. bd., 1965-83; chmn., chief exec. officer, Continental Illinois Corp., Chgo., 1984— dir. Lockheed Corp., Chase Manhattan Corp. Mem. adv. bd. Hoover Instn. on War, Revolution and Peace, from 1967; trustee Carnegie Mellon U., from 1960, DePauw U., 1966-81, Chgo. Orchestral Assn., 1973-79; bd. dirs. McGraw Wildlife Found., 1964-75, Automotive Safety Found., 1959-69; chmn. Automotive Safety Found., 1962-64; bd. dirs. Hwy Users Fedn. for Safety and Mobility, 1969-75, Northwestern Meml. Hosp., from 1965. Decorated Order of The Taj, Iran; commendatore Dell'Ordine Del Merito Della Repubblica Italiana; recipient Washington award Western Soc. Engrs., 1981, Trustees award John F. Kennedy Ctr. for Performing Arts, 1982. Fellow Am. Inst. Chem. Engrs.; mem. Am. Petroleum Inst. (dir. from 1958, chmn. 1978-79), Nat. Petroleum Council (chmn. 1974-76), Am. Inst. Mining, Metall and Petroleum Engrs. (Charles F. Rand Meml. gold medal 1980), Conf. Bd. (sr.), Am. Chem. Soc., Nat. Acad. Engring., Phi Beta Kappa, Sigma Xi, Omicron Delta Kappa, Tau Beta Pi. Clubs: Mid-Am., Chgo., Racquet (Chgo.); Links (N.Y.C.); Bohemian (San Francisco); Eldorado Country (Palm Springs); Old Elm (Lake Forest, Ill.); Glen View (Ill.) Golf. Office: Continental Illinois Corp 231 S La Salle St Chicago IL 60697

SWEAT, ROBERT LEE, veterinary medical scientist, virologist; b. Lamar, Colo., June 8, 1931; s. James B. and Ora L. (Wile) S.; m. Barbara J. Shaffer, Mar. 15, 1953; children—Michael J., Deborah L. B.S., Colo. State U., 1954, D.V.M., 1956; M.S., U. Nebr., 1962, Ph.D., 1966. Vet. virologist, U. Nebr., Lincoln, 1958-66, Norden Labs., Lincoln, 1967; vet. med. scientist U. Idaho, Caldwell, 1968-70; vet. virologist Ft. Dodge Lab. (Iowa), 1970—. Vet. rep. Nebr. State Bd. Health, 1966-67; trustee Sioux Falls Coll., 1983—. Served to 1st lt. Vet. Corps, U.S. Army, 1956-58. Mem. AVMA, Iowa Vet. Med. Assn., Nebr. Vet. Med. Assn., Am. Assn. Bovine Practitioners, AAAS. Baptist. Avocation: Camping. Home: 1371 N 14th St Fort Dodge IA 50501 Office: Fort Dodge Labs PO Box 518 Fort Dodge IA 50501

SWEEN, GOODWIN EDWARD, veterinary drugs company executive; b. Hurley, S.D., Dec. 5, 1919; s. Emil and Eva Mae (Masters) S.; m. Shirley Gylaine Shafer, Apr. 17, 1947; children—Donald, Richard, Jann. Owner, operator Sween Drug Co., Sioux Falls, S.D., 1946-50; with sales mgmt. Charles Pfizer & Co., N.Y.C., 1950-63; product. mgr. Diamond Labs, Inc., Des Moines, 1963-70. Served with U.S. Army, 1941-46. Democrat. Lutheran. Avocation: golf. Office: Vet-Vax Inc 109 E 2d St Bonner Springs KS 66012

SWEENEY, ASHER WILLIAM, state justice; b. Canfield, Ohio, Dec. 11, 1920; s. Walter W. and Jessie K. S.; student Youngstown Coll., 1939-42; LL.B., Duke U., 1948; m. Bertha Englert, May 21, 1945; children—Randall, Ronald, Gary, Karen. Commd. 2d lt. U.S. Army, 1950, advanced through grades to col., 1965; ret., 1968; admitted to Ohio bar, 1949; chief Fed. Contracting Agy., Cin., 1965-68; corp. lawyer, 1968-76; justice Ohio Supreme Ct., 1977—. Active Boy Scouts Am. Decorated Bronze Star, Legion of Merit; named to U.S. Army Hall of Fame, Ft. Benning, Ga., 1981. Mem. Ohio Bar Assn., Am. Legion Phi Delta Phi. Democrat. Roman Catholic. Office: 30 E Broad St Columbus OH 43215

SWEENEY, HILDA MAE, nurse, infection control coordinator; b. Arenac County, Mich., Sept. 17, 1937; d. Edward L. and Irene M. (Yacks) Smith; m. Joseph Francis Sweeney, Nov. 7, 1959; children—Linda Sweeney Slayden, Timothy, Gary, Bryan. Diploma St. Mary's Hosp. Sch. Nursing, Saginaw, Mich., 1959. Staff nurse various depts. Huron Meml. Hosp., Bad Axe, Mich., 1960-74, infection control coordinator, 1975—, employee health coordinator, 1980—; tchr. emergency medicine. Roman Catholic parish religion tchr. and coordinator, 1975-78; 4-H leader, Elkton, Mich.; mem. Mich. Farm Bur. Mem. Mich. Nurses Assn., Huron Dist. Nurses Assn. (pres.), Mich. Soc. Infection Control, Thumb Area Infection Control Coordinators (organizer), Confrat. Christian Mothers, Popple Trail Blazers Conservation Club, Home Extention Club. Home: 2165 Moore Rd Elkton MI 48731 Office: Huron Meml Hosp 1100 S Van Dyke St Bad Axe MI 48413

SWEENEY, J. GRAY, American art historian, curator, educator; b. Jacksonville, Fla., Nov. 20, 1943; s. John M. and Mary (Gray) S.; m. Karrie J. Knecht, Aug. 24, 1981; 1 child, James Gray Flournoy. B.A. magna cum laude, U. N.Mex., 1968; M.A., Ind. U., 1969, Ph.D., 1975. From asst. prof. to assoc. prof. Grand Valley State Coll., Allendale, Mich., 1971—; guest curator Muskegon Mus. Art, Mich., 1978-83, Grand Rapids Art Mus., Mich., 1976, 77, 81; research assoc. Tweed Mus. Art, Duluth, Minn., 1980-82; sr. fellow Nat. Mus. Am. Art, Smithsonian Inst., Washington, 1984—. Author, curator exhbn. and catalog Themes in American Painting, 1977, Artists of Grand Rapids, 1981, Great Lakes Marine Painting, 1983. Author: Tweed Museum of Art, 1982; Muskegon Museum of Art, 1980. Grantee Ind. U., 1970-71, Kress Found. Ind. U., 1967-68, Ford Found. U. N.Mex., 1966-68. Mem. Coll. Art Assn. Am., Am. Assn. Museums. Avocation: Sailing. Office: Grand Valley State Coll Art and Design Dept Allendale MI 49401

SWEENEY, JAMES LEE, government defense supply center official; b. Rocky River, Ohio, Mar. 23, 1930; s. John H. and Mary J. (Walkinshaw) S.; B.B.A., Case-Western Reserve, 1959; m. Marion J. Ridley, Oct. 4, 1958; children—John A., James L. Cost acct. AFB, Dayton, Ohio, 1959-62; acct. Def. Electronics Supply Center, Dayton, 1962-64, budget analyst, 1964-67, budget officer, 1967-74, supervisory budget analyst, 1974-82, supervisory mgmt. analyst, 1982, supervisory program analyst, 1983—; pres. 3001 Hoover Inc.; Mem. tax adv. com. Dayton-Montgomery County, 1967-70; bd. dirs. Dayton Human Relations Commn., 1970-74, Model Cities Housing Corp., 1972-74, M & M Broadcasting Co., Ohio Valley Broadcasting Co., 1979-81; vestryman St. Margaret's Episcopal Ch. Served with U.S. Army, 1952-54. Recipient Public Service award Def. Electronics Supply Center, 1972; Meritorious Civilian Service award, 1981; Unity award in Media, Lincoln U., 1982-83. Mem. Alpha Phi Alpha. Producer, commentator Spl. Community Report Sta. WHIO-TV, twice weekly 1970-76, daily, 1976—, producer, commentator Spotlight. Home: 743 Argonne Dr Dayton OH 45408 Office: DESC-LSP Dayton OH 45444

SWEENEY, RICHARD THOMAS, librarian; b. Atlantic City, Jan. 22, 1946; s. Harry A. and Margaret (McArdle) S.; B.A., Villanova U., 1967; M.A., Glassboro State Coll., 1970; M.L.S., Drexel U., 1972; m. Virginia Beschen, Aug. 26, 1967; children—Meghan, Moira, Thomas, Maureen. Tchr., Holy Spirit High Sch., Absecon, N.J., 1967-69; librarian Central Jr. High Sch., Atlantic City, 1969-70; dir. Atlantic City Free Public Library, 1971-76; mem. faculty Glassboro State Coll. Grad. Sch. Library Sci., 1973-74; dir. Genesee County Library, Flint, Mich., 1976-79; exec. dir. Public Library of Columbus and Franklin County, Columbus, Ohio, 1979—. Mem. Columbus Area Cable TV Adv. Com.; mem. adv. bd. Kent State U. Mem. ALA, Ohio Library Assn., Met. Library Dirs., Franklin County Dirs. Club: Rotary. Office: 28 S Hamilton Rd columbus OH 43213*

SWEET, FREDERICK, ob-gyn scientist, educator; b. N.Y.C., May 15, 1938. B.S., Bklyn. Coll., CUNY, 1960; Ph.D. in Organic Chemistry, U. Alta. (Can.), 1968. Instr. chemistry and chem. tech. Bronx Community Coll., CUNY, 1962-64, asst. prof. chemistry and chem. tech., 1968-70; instr. dept. extension U. Alta., Edmonton, 1966-67; research assoc. ob-gyn U. Kans. Sch. Medicine, Kansas City, 1970-71; research asst. prof. ob-gyn Washington U. Sch. Medicine, St. Louis, 1971-76, co-dir. NIH program project, 1974-80, research assoc. prof., 1976-80, mem. com. on admissions, 1979—, assoc. prof., 1981-82, prof., 1982—; vis. prof. chemistry So. Ill. U., Edwardsville, 1976—. Sci. advisor to Unit #10 Sch. System of Greater St. Louis, Post Dispatch, Monsanto Sci. Fair, 1977-81. NIH grantee, 1974-79; Nat. Acad. Scis. Internat. Sci. Exchangee, 77-78, 79; NATO sr. research fellow, 1974-76, 77-79. Mem. Am. Chem. Soc., Chem. Inst. Can., AAAS, Endocrine Soc., N.Y. Acad. Scis., Soc. for Gynecol. Investigation. Contbr. numerous articles on gynecol. research and biochemistry to profl. jours. Home: 406 Polo Dr Clayton MO 63105 Office: Washington U Sch Medicine 4911 Barnes Hosp Pl St Louis MO 63110

SWEET, PHILIP WHITFORD KIRKLAND, JR., banker; b. Mt. Vernon, N.Y., Dec. 31, 1927; s. Philip Whitford Kirkland and Katharine (Buhl) S.; A.B., Harvard U., 1950; M.B.A., U. Chgo., 1957; m. Nancy Frederick, July 23, 1950; children—Sandra Harkness, Philip Whitford Kirkland, III, David A.F. With No. Trust Co., Chgo., 1953-84, sr. v.p. bond dept., 1968-74, exec. v.p. bank, 1974-75, pres., dir., 1975-81, chmn., chief exec. officer, dir., 1981-84; pres., dir. No. Trust Corp., 1975-81, chmn., chief exec. officer, 1981-84. Treas., trustee Chgo. Sunday Evening Club; vis. com. U. Chgo. Council on Grad. Sch. Bus. and Divinity Sch.; trustee Chgo. Zoological Soc., Rush-Presbyn.-St. Luke's Med. Center; bd. dirs., Protestant Found. Greater Chgo.; mem. adv. com. United Negro Coll. Fund. Clubs: Econ. (dir.), Attic, Chgo., Comml., Commonwealth (Chgo.); Onwentsia, Shoreacres (gov.), Old Elm.

SWEEZY, JOHN WILLIAM, political party official; b. Indpls., Nov. 14, 1932; s. William Charles and Zuma Frances (McNew) S.; B.S. in Mech. Engring., Purdue U., 1956; M.B.A., Ind. U., 1958; student Butler U., 1953-54, U. Ga., 1954-55, Ind. Central Coll., 1959; m. Carole Suzanne Harman, July 14, 1956; children—John William, Bradley E. Design, test engr. Allison div. Gen. Motors Corp., Indpls., 1953-57; power sales engr. Indpls. Power & Light Co., 1958-69; dir. pub. works City of Indpls., 1970-72; chmn. Marion County Republican Central Com., 1972—; mng. partner MCLB Co., Indpls., 1972—; dir. Lorco Engring., Indpls. Bd. dirs. Indpls. Humane Soc.; chmn. 11th Dist. Rep. Com., 1970, 73—; chmn. Nat. Assn. Urban Rep. County Chmn.; alt. del. Rep. Nat. Conv., 1968, del., 1972, 76, 80, del., mem. credentials com., 1984; mem. credentials com., 1980; mem. Rep. Nat. Com., 1984—, exec. com., 1984—; mem. Warren Schs. Citizens Screening Com., 1958-72. Served with AUS, 1953-55. Mem. Mensa, Sigma Iota Epsilon. Home: 166 N Gibson Indianapolis IN 46219 Office: 14 N Delaware St Indianapolis IN 46204

SWIFT, DOLORES MONICA MARCINKEVICH (MRS. MORDEN LEIB SWIFT), public relations executive; b. Hazleton, Pa., Apr. 3, 1936; d. Adam Martin and Anna Frances (Lizbinski) Marcinkevich; student McCann Coll., 1954-56; m. Morden Leib Swift, Dec. 18, 1966. Pub. relations coordinator Internat. Council Shopping Centers, N.Y.C., 1957-59, Wendell P. Colton Advt. Agy., N.Y.C., 1959-61, Sydney S. Baron Pub. Relations Corp., N.Y.C., 1961-65, Robert S. Taplinger Pub. Relations, N.Y.C., 1965-66; prin. Dolores M. Swift, Pub. Relations, Chgo., 1966—. Bd. dirs. Welfare Pub. Relations Forum, 1971-79, treas., 1975-77; mem. pub. relations adv. com. Mid-Am. chpt. A.R.C., 1973—; mem. women's com. Mark Twain Meml., 1968-69; pub. relations dir. N.J. Symphony, Bergen County, 1969-70, mem. pub. relations/-promotion com.; mem. Wadsworth Atheneum, 1968-69; bd. dirs. Youth Guidance, 1972-75; mem. NCCJ Labor, Mgmt. and Pub. Interest Conf., 1977—; mem. pub. relations com. United Way/Crusade of Mercy, 1979-80, 83. Mem. Pub. Relations Soc. Am. (accredited, chmn. subcom. Nat. Center for Vol. Action 1971-72, pub. service com. Chgo. chpt. 1971-72, dir. 1975—, chmn. counselors sect. 1976-77, assembly del. 1976, 79-81, sec. 1977-78, v.p. 1978-79, pres.-elect 1979-80, pres. 1980-81, Midwest dist. chmn. 1984, nat. bd. dirs. 1985—, host chpt. chmn. 1981 conf., chmn. Midwest Dist. Conf. 1983). Clubs: Women's (publs. chmn. Englewood, N.J., 1970-71); Publicity (chmn. pub. info. com. 1975-76) (Chgo.). Editorial bd. Pub. Relations Jour., 1978. Address: 525 Hawthorne Pl Chicago IL 60657

SWIGART, SCOTT ALLEN, pharmacist, educator; b. Omaha, Jan. 24, 1956; s. Warren Russell and Janice Marguerite (Shinrock) S.; m. Cynthia Louise Keagel, Nov. 26, 1977; 1 child, Kimberly. B.S., Wayne State Coll., 1979; Pharm.D., U. Nebr.-Omaha, 1982. Lic. pharmacist, Nebr. Monitor poison control Mid Plains Regional Poison Control Ctr., Omaha, 1980-82; pharmacy resident in pediatrics U. Nebr.-Omaha, 1982-83, clin. instr., 1983-84, assoc. prof., 1984—; clin. pharmacist U. Nebr. Hosp., 1983—. Contbr. articles to profl. jours. Mead Johson Pharm. Co. grantee, 1982. Mem. Am. Soc. Hosp. Pharmacists, Great Plains Perinatal Orgn. Republican. Congregationalist. Home: 10812 Taylor Omaha NE 68164 Office: U Nebr Coll Pharmacy 42d St and Dewey Ave Omaha NE 68105

SWIGERT, ALICE HARROWER (MRS. JAMES MACK SWIGERT), civic worker; b. Montrose, Pa., Dec. 18, 1908; d. Lewis Titcomb and Margaret (Ayars) Harrower; student U. Tenn., 1927-29; m. James Mack Swigert, July 7, 1931; children—Oliver, David Ladd, Sally Harper (Mrs. Swigert Hamilton). Sec. to profs. Harvard Law Sch., Cambridge, Mass., 1932-35; pub. relations U. Chgo. Press, 1935-36. Mus. panoramas chmn. Cin. Symphony Orch. Women's Com., 1963-65; founder, treas. Citizens Crusade, 1967-77; vol. Children's Convalescent Hosp., 1969-75; founder, corr. sec. New Life for Girls, Inc., Cin., 1971-75, trustee, 1971-82, hon. trustee and adv. 1982—. Mem. adv. council Ohio Presbyn. Home, 1973-75; trustee emeritus Cin. Speech and Hearing Center; trustee, scholarship chmn. 3 Arts Scholarship Fund, 1972-75; Mem.

DAR, Mensa, Chi Omega. Republican. Presbyterian. Clubs: Cincinnati Womans, Cincinnati Country, Queen City, Town. Home: 196 Green Hills Rd Cincinnati OH 45208

SWINDLEHURST, RICHARD JOHN, financial services and data processing company executive; b. Carbondale, Pa., Feb. 23, 1946; s. John R. and Marian (Fletcher) S.; m. Chalene Beth Varner, Aug. 3, 1968; children—Amy Varner, Christina Ann, William John. B.S. in Physics, Pa. State U., 1968; M.B.A., Wharton Sch., U. Pa., 1978. Sr. assoc. engr. IBM, Fishkill, N.Y., 1968-71; sr. mktg. rep., cons. Control Data Corp., Phila., 1971-80; dist. sales mgr. Data Gen. Corp., Blue Bell, Pa., 1980-81; gen. mgr. Chase Manhattan Bank, Phila., 1981-82; v.p. Savs. & Loan Data Corp., Cin., 1982—. Pres., Providence Chapel, Ref. Episcopal, Mt. Laurel, N.J., 1980, bd. dirs., 1972-82; dir. sch. bd. The King's Christian Sch., Haddon Heights, N.J., 1976-82; com. chmn. N.Y. and Phila. synod Ref. Episcopal Ch., 1979-81. Recipient profl. awards. Mem. Planning Execs. Inst., N.Am. Soc. Corp. Planning, Am. Mgmt. Assns. Presbyterian. Club: Sycamore Soccer (coach 1982—) (Montgomery, Ohio). Avocations: travel, photography, bridge, soccer coaching, outdoor activities. Home: 11515 Applejack Ct Cincinnati OH 45249 Office: 11279 Cornell Park Dr Cincinnati OH 45242

SWINFORD, EILEEN MARY, educational administrator; b. Chgo., Oct. 5, 1932; d. George Michael Gerald and Lulu Jeannette (Winecoff) M'Gonigle; m. Carson Leon Swinford (div.); children—Sherly Eileen, Kedric Leon, Carson Blake. B.S., Eastern Ill. U., 1970; M.S., Nat. Coll. Edn., 1983. Tchr., Catlin Community Dist. Schs., 1957—, coordinator gifted edn., tchr., 1978—; cons. in-service tng. for tchrs. Mem. Vermilion County CETA Adv. Com., 1979—. Mem. Ill. Edn. Assn. (bd. dirs. 1977-81, chairperson profl. excellence 1977-81), NEA, Ill. Gifted Educators. Democrat. Lutheran. Home: 1102 Loraine St Danville IL 61832 Office: Box B Catlin IL 61817

SWING, GAEL DUANE, college president; b. LaPorte County, Ind., Mar. 13, 1932; s. William Edward and Dorothy Ruth (Jessup) S.; A.B., Franklin (Ind.) Coll., 1954; M.S., Ind. U., 1963; m. Sandra Sue Scott, Apr. 13, 1957; children—Scott, Kristie, Janet. Sales rep. Burroughs Corp., Indpls., 1954; successively dir. placement and admission counselor, dir. admissions, bus. mgr., v.p. devel. Franklin Coll., 1954-69; dir. spl. program services Office Devel., Washington U., St. Louis, 1969-73; exec. v.p. North Central Coll., Naperville, Ill., 1973-75, pres., 1975—; dir. Comml. Resources, Inc.; mem. Ill. Bd. Higher Edn. Non-Pub. Adv. Com. Recipient Alumni citation Franklin Coll., 1975. Mem. Fedn. Ind. Ill. Colls. and Univs. (exec. com.), Council West Suburban Colls. (dir.), United Methodist Found. (dir.), Asso. Colls. Ill. (chmn.), Ednl. and Instl. Ins. Adminstrs. (bd. dirs.), Council Advancement and Support of Edn. Methodist. Club: Naperville Country. Home: 329 S Brainard St Naperville IL 60540 Office: North Central Coll Naperville IL 60566

SWISHER, LOUISE DUNCAN, hosp. adminstr.; b. New Castle, Ind., Dec. 5, 1917; d. Paul Joseph and Dollie (Downey) Duncan; student Ind. Bus. Coll., 1936-37, Ind. U.-Purdue U., Indpls., 1972-73; m. Paul W. Swisher, Jan. 24, 1937; children—Janet Mackenzie, Charles Duncan, Paula Schelm. Clk.-treas. Town of Mooresville (Ind.), 1942-53; mgr. bus. officer Comer Hosp., Mooresville, 1953-61; asst. adminstr. Comer-Kendrick Hosp., Mooresville, 1961-72; adminstr. Kendrick Meml. Hosp. Inc., Mooresville, 1972—. Vice chmn. Republican Party, Morgan County, Ind., 1956—; sec. 6th Dist. Ind. Republicans, 1972—. Mem. Adminstrv. Mgmt. Soc., Am. Coll. Hosp. Adminstrs., Am. Bus. Women's Assn., Am. Med. Record Librarians Assn., Am. Hosp. Assn., Nat. Assn. Physicians Nurses. Quaker. Clubs: State Assembly Women's, Order of Eastern Star. Home: Rural Route 2 Box 1 Mooresville IN 46158 Office: Kendrick Meml Hosp Inc 1201 Hadley Rd Mooresville IN 46158

SWITZ, MARY ANN, funeral home executive; b. Massillon, Ohio, July 1, 1944; d. Harold Homer and Margaret Ann (Abel) Hartel; m. David Lee Switz, Oct. 13, 1962 (div. 1970); children—Bethany Lynne, Philip David. Student Cleve. Inst. Music, 1974-75, Cuyahoga Community Coll., Cleve., 1976—. Sec., Calvin Woodward, Atty., Warren, Ohio, 1969-73, Univ. Circle Research Center, Cleve., 1973-74; program coordinator Univ. Circle Center Community Programs, Cleve., 1974-77; bus. office mgr. Johnson-Romito Funeral Homes, Bedford, Ohio, 1977—; dir. music Luth. Ch. of Covenant, Maple Heights, Ohio, 1982—. Mem. bd., accompanist, keyboard prin. Chagrin Valley Choral Union, and Orch., Cleve., 1981—; accompanist, concertmistress Solon Players Community Theatre and Orch. (Ohio), 1981-83. Mem. Nat. Assn. Female Execs., Chagrin Valley Choral Union, Am. Guild Organists. Lutheran. Home: 17304 Mapleboro Ave Maple Heights OH 44137 Office: Johnson-Romito Funeral Homes 521 Broadway Ave Bedford OH 44146

SWOPE, SCOTT RAY, osteopathic physician, educator; b. Dayton, Ohio, Sept. 21, 1936; s. Fred L. and Miriam F. (Fowler) S.; m. Judith K. Igelman, Aug. 9, 1958; children—Bradley, Todd, Julie, Jennifer. B.S., Purdue U., 1958; D.O., Kirksville (Mo.) Coll. Osteo. Medicine, 1962. Intern, Grandview Hosp., Dayton, 1962-63; practice osteo. medicine specializing in family practice and sports medicine, Springboro, Ohio, 1963—; ptnr. Swope and Jones, 1963—; mem. staff Grandview Hosp., chief of staff, 1978; mem. staff Southview Hosp., Kettering Hosp., Sycamore Hosp.; faculty Ohio U. Coll Osteo. Medicine; asst. coroner Warren County, Ohio; researcher McNeil Pharm. Co. Mem. Clearcreek Bd. Edn., 1978—; mem. Clearcreek Fire Dept. and Life Squad. Recipient Springboro (Ohio) High Sch. Principal's award, 1980; named Ohio Outstanding Team Physician, Ohio State Med. Assn. and Ohio High Sch. Athletic Assn., 1983. Mem. Am. Osteo. Assn., Am. Coll. Gen Practitioners, Ohio Osteo. Assn., Dayton Osteo. Assn., Am. Osteo. Acad. Gen. Practitioners, Am. Osteo. Acad. Sports Medicine, Nat. Athletic Trainers Assn. (med. advisor), Kirksville Alumni Assn. (past pres.). Mem. United Ch. of Christ. Office: Swope and Jones 780 W Central Ave Springboro OH 45066

SWOPES, REGINA, publisher, songwriter; b. Chgo., Mar. 7, 1955; d. Nelson and Mildred Laura (Taylor) S. B.Econs., Northeastern Ill. U., 1984. Co-founder Swift Record Co., Chgo., 1979, Regis Music Publs., Chgo., 1980, Regis Publs., Chgo., 1982—. Mem. Broadcast Music Inc. Roman Catholic. Feature writer: After-Five Mag., 1978-79. Home: 833 N Leclaire Ave Chicago IL 60651

SY, BENJAMIN MANGAOANG, physician; b. Pangasinan, Philippines, July 23, 1940; came to U.S., 1973, naturalized, 1980; s. Kim and Juliana (Mangaoang) S.; m. Erlinda Ocampo, June 15, 1965; children—Noel O., Eileen O., Benerva O. B.S., U. Philippines, 1959; M.D., Far Eastern U., 1965. Inhalation therapist St. Anne's Hosp., Chgo., 1973; intern West Suburban Hosp., 1974; resident Grant Hosp., Chgo., 1975-77; physician employee Swedish Am. Hosp., Rockford, Ill., 1977-80; clinic mgr., physician Savanna (Ill.) Med. Ctr., 1980-82; pres. med. staff Savanna City Hosp., 1982—, sec. med. staff, 1984-85 Pres., Carroll County unit Am. Cancer Soc., 1981-83, chmn. profl. edn. com., 1981-83; mem. Interchurch Council, Savanna, 1979-81; mem. adminstrv. bd., fin. com. Savanna United Meth. Ch., 1984-85. Mem. AMA (Physician's Recognition award 1983), Ill. Med. Soc. (rep. interstate ins. exchange 1984-85), Carroll County Med. Soc. (pres. 1980-82) (del. to Ill. Med. Soc. 1984-85), Blackhawk Area Ind. Practice Assn. (bd. dirs. N.W. Ill. 1984-85), C. of C. of Savanna. Republican. Lodge: Rotary (chmn. youth exchange Savanna 1984-85, v.p. 1985-86). Home: 258 N Loop St Savanna IL 61074 Office: 333 Chicago St Savanna IL 61074

SYFERT, SAMUEL RAY, librarian; b. Beecher City, Ill., July 20, 1928; s. Fred and LaVonne Mildred (High) S.; B.S. in Edn., Eastern Ill. U., 1957, M.S., 1961; M.S. in Edn., Calif. Christian U., 1979. Tchr. bus. Geneseo (Ill.) Community Unit schs., 1957-59; tchr. English, Bethany (Ill.) Community Unit schs., 1961-77, sch. librarian, 1977—; bd. dirs., treas. Marrowbone Twp. Library, Bethany, 1978-84, sec., 1984-85, pres., 1985—. Served with AUS, 1950-52. Named Tchr. of Yr. in Moultrie County (Ill.), 1975. Mem. NEA, ALA, Ill. Edn. Assn., Ill. Library Assn., Bethany C. of C. (sec. 1977-81, pres. 1982), Am. Legion. Republican. Mem. Christian Ch. (Disciples of Christ) (bd. chairperson). Home: Box 402 Bethany IL 61914 Office: Box 97 Bethany IL 61914

SYKES, CATHERINE, educator; b. Bowman, S.C., Feb. 19, 1942; d. Martha (Jones) S.; B.S., Clarion State Coll., 1964; M.A.T., Oakland U., 1973; Ed.S., Wayne State U., 1981; m. Barry Sykes, Dec. 23, 1966; children—Barry Jabbar, Brent Justin. Tchr., Freedom (Pa.) High Sch., 1964-67; reading specialist Pontiac (Mich.) Schs., 1967-75, curriculum analyst, 1975-78, staff devel. specialist, 1978—; human resource devel. trainer; cons. Tide Project, Wayne State U. Trustee Macedonia Missionary Baptist Ch., 1978—, also young adult usher, bd. divs. Project for Equal Ednl. Rights, Urban League. Mem. NAACP (nat. dir. membership), Nat. Assn. Negro Bus. and Profl. Women's Clubs (nat. 2d v.p.), Mich. Council Tchrs. English, Assn. Supervision and Curriculum Devel., Mich. Assn. Supervision and Curriculum Devel., NEA, Mich. Edn. Assn., Pontiac Edn. Assn., Mich. Ednl. Research Assn., Assn. Tchrs. English, Mich. Reading Assn., Mich. Assn. Middle Sch. Educators, Nat. Alliance Black Sch. Educators, Mich. Alliance Black Educators, Alpha Kappa Alpha. Home: 1172 Eckman St Pontiac MI 48057 Office: 1051 Arlene St Pontiac MI 48058

SYLVESTER, TERRY LEE, business manager; b. Cin., June 12, 1949; s. Wilbert Fairbanks and Jewell S.; B.S. in Bus. Accounting, Miami U., Oxford, Ohio, 1972; M.B.A. in Fin., Xavier U., Cin., 1983; m. Janet Lynn Brigger, Nov. 29, 1975; children—Carisa, Laura, Jason, Katherine. Staff accountant Alexander Grant & Co., C.P.A.'s, Cin., 1972; treas., controller Imperial Community Developers, Inc., Cin., subs. of Chelsea Moore Devel. Corp., 1972—; controller home bldg. div. Chelsea Moore Devel. Corp., 1978—; controller, chief fin. officer Armstrong Cos., apt. mgmt., 1978-79, Dorger Investments, Cin., 1979-81, Delta Mechanical Constructors, Inc., Fairfield, Ohio, 1981-83; bus. mgr. Oak Hills Local Schs., Cin., 1983—. Home: 31 Woodmont Ct Fairfield OH 45014 Office: 6479 Bridgetown Rd Cincinnati OH 45248

SYLVESTRI, MARIO FRANK, educational administrator; b. San Francisco, Mar. 26, 1948; s. Bennie and Carolina Elizabeth (D'Amante) S.; m. Mary Catherine Gurnee, Feb. 16, 1985. A.A. in Chemistry and Biology, Coll. San Mateo, 1969; B.A. in Chemistry and Biology, Coll. Notre Dame, Belmont, Calif., 1970; B.S. in Pharmacy, Creighton U., 1973; M.S., U. Pacific, Stockton, Calif., 1976, Pharm.D. summa cum laude, 1976. Instr. dept. pharmaceutics U. Pacific, 1974-75; teaching asst. U. Nebr. Med. Ctr., Omaha, 1977; research fellow Creighton U., Omaha, 1980-82, instr. div. allied health scis., 1981-82, asst. dir., 1982-83, asst. dean, 1983-84, 84—, dir. continuing edn., 1984—; pres. bd. dirs. Nebr. Council Continuing Pharm. Edn., 1984—; chmn. com. on continuing edn. Nebr. State Bd. Pharmacy, 1984—. Contbr. articles to profl. publs. Recipient Eli Lilly Achievement award, 1973; grantee Cutter Labs., 1973-74, U. Pacific, 1974-76, U. Nebr. Med. Ctr., 1979-80, 83-84, Squibb Research and Devel., 1984-85; Nat. Achievement Rewards for Coll. Scientists scholar, 1976; Robert Lincoln McNeil Meml. fellow, 1977-80. Mem. Am. Pharm. Assn., AAAS, Am. Soc. Hosp. Pharmacists, Am. Soc. Allied Health Professions, Am. Assn. Colls. of Pharmacy, Greater Omaha Pharmacists Assn. (bd. dirs. 1984—), Rho Chi. Avocations: cooking, racquetball. Home: 15006 Cuming St Omaha NE 68154 Office: Creighton U Sch Pharmacy and Allied Health Professions California at 24th St Omaha NE 68178

SYMINGTON, STUART, JR., company executive; b. Rochester, N.Y., June 12, 1925; s. Stuart and Evelyn (Wadsworth) S.; m. Janey Belle Studt, June 21, 1949; children—Anne Wadsworth, William Stuart, Sidney Studt, John Sante. B.A., Yale U., 1950; LL.B., Harvard Law Sch., 1953. Bar: Mo. Clk., Arnold, Fortas & Porter, Washington, summer 1951; assoc. firm Simpson, Thacher & Bartlett, N.Y.C., 1953-56; assoc., ptnr. Stolar, Kuhlmann & Meredith and successor firms, St. Louis, 1956-62; founding ptnr. Guilfoil, Symington, Petzall & Shoemake, St. Louis, 1962-82; counsel Thompson & Mitchell, St. Louis, 1983; v.p., gen. solicitor Union Pacific System, St. Louis, 1983—. Dir., St. Louis Regional Commerce and Growth Assn., Downtown St. Louis, Inc.; hon. counsul of France at St. Louis; mem. Zoning and Planning Commn., City of Ladue, Mo.; chmn. Kammergild Chamber Orch.; mem. chancellor's council U. Mo., St. Louis; bd. dirs. James S. McDonnell USO, St. Louis World Affairs Council, St. Louis Merc. Library Assn.; trustee John W. Barriger III Library, Mo. State Hist. Soc., Supreme Ct. of Mo. Hist. Soc. Served with U.S. Army, 1943-46; ATO; ETO; PTO. Recipient Dept. Army Outstanding Civilian Service medal, 1970. Mem. D.A.V., Assn. U.S. Army (chpt. dir.), Delta Kappa Epsilon. Lodge: Masons, Shriners. Episcopalian. Address: 210 N 13th St 22nd Floor Saint Louis MO 63103

SYMMONDS, MARGARET GISONDI, state ofcl.; b. Gloversville, N.Y., Mar. 21, 1929; d. Harvey and Dorothy (Desmond) Gisondi; B.S., Columbia U., 1957; 1 dau., Nina Lucia. Adminstrv. asst. to dean of grad. faculties Columbia U., N.Y.C., 1951-53; tchr. public schs., N.Y.C., 1956-63; sect. supr. Basic Systems, Inc., N.Y.C., 1963-64; writer Holt, Rinehart and Winston, 1964-65; free lance writer, 1966-71; partner Hasty Pudding Catering Service, Macomb, Ill., 1972-74; exec. dir. Ill. Commn. on Status of Women, Springfield, 1974-80; exec. Ill. Dept. Children and Family Services, Springfield, 1980-82, Ill. Dept. Commerce and Community Affairs, Springfield, 1982—. Mem. coordinating com. Internat. Women's Yr., 1976-77, Ill. del. nat. conf., 1977; mem. Gov.'s Adv. Com. on Statewide Displaced Homemakers Program, 1979-82, mem. adv. bd. Ill. Women's History Week, 1980; mem. Adv. Council Edn. Handicapped Children, 1980-81; mem. health edn. adv. com. Ill. Bd. Edn., 1981-82, early childhood services com., 1980-81; mem. Ill. Council on Nutrition, 1982—. Mem. Nat. Women's Polit. Caucus, AAUW, Ill. Women's Polit. Caucus (past dir.), Springfield Women's Polit. Caucus. Republican. Unitarian. also 12 Elmo Dr Macomb IL 61455 Office: Ill Dept Commerce and Community Affairs 320 W Washington St Springfield IL 62706

SZABO, LAJOS, architect; b. Debrecrn, Hungary, Sept. 2, 1931; came to U.S., 1956, naturalized, 1961; s. Laszlo and Margit S.; m. Wilhelmina Alida Gerritsen, Dec. 13, 1958; children—Lajos L., Marcus R., Margit R. B.S., U. Budapest, Hungary, 1956. Registered architect, 28 states. With R.C. Kempton Architect, Columbus, Ohio, 1958-61, Benham, Richards & Armstrong Architects, Columbus, 1961-64, Urban and Calabretta, Columbus, 1964-66; pres. Lajos Szabo, AIA, Columbus, 1966—. Mem. AIA, Architects Soc. Ohio, Constrn. Specification Inst., Inst. Profl. Designers, Inst. Bus. Designers. Republican. Methodist. Avocations: gardening; swimming; skiing. Home: 1234 W 1st Ave Columbus OH 43212 Office: 995 Safin Rd Columbus OH 43204

SZEKELY, MICHAEL ERNEST, lawyer; b. Lorain, Ohio, Feb. 13, 1949; s. Ernest Frank and Concetta (Alessandro) S.; B.A., Miami U., Oxford, Ohio, 1971; J.D., Cleve.-Marshall Coll., 1974. Bar: Ohio 1974. Legal intern Legal Aid Soc., Elyria, Ohio, 1973-74, staff atty., 1974; prosecutor Elyria Solicitor's Office, 1974—; sole practice, Elyria, 1979—; instr. Lorain County Community Coll., Elyria, 1979-80. Pres. Lorain County Young Democrats, 1977—; mem. Lorain County Exec. Com., 1977—; asst. ward leader Elyria Dem. Com., 1980-84, ward leader, 1984—; councilman St. Michael's Ch., Lorain, 1977-83; mem. Lorain County Bd. Mental Retardation and Devel. Disabilities. Mem. Ohio Bar Assn. (criminal law com., traffic law com.), Lorain County Bar Assn., Ohio Byzantine Catholic. Clubs: Lorain County, Golf Assn. Avocations: golf, tennis, alpine skiing, traveling, chess. Home: 2280 W River Road Apt B-10 Elyria OH 44035 Office: 375 Broad St Elyria OH 44035

SZOTT, FRAN STANLEY, floor covering consultant and executive; b. LaSalle, Ill., Apr. 10, 1939; s. Henry Leo and Stella Esther (Witalka) S.; m. Sheila Marie Studzinski, June 27, 1983; children—Kathy Ann, Gary Lee. Student Ill. State U., 1957, Ray-Vogue Sch., 1959; cert. Chgo. Sch. Interior Design, 1960. Interior design cons. Szott's of Peru (Ill.), 1960-65, installation cons., 1965-70, buyer, sales mgr., 1970-75, adminstrv. mgr., 1975-78, personnel mgr., 1978-79, v.p., acting mgr., 1979—. Asst. mgr., mgr. Peru Youth Baseball, 1969-76; mgr. Babe Ruth League, Peru, 1976-77; mgr. com. Peru Airport Com., 1983; city rep. for state beautification, Peru, 1982; sec. Northview Parents Club, Peru. Roman Catholic. Lodges: Elks, K.C. Home: 4th at Creek Bed Trail Peru IL 61354 Office: Rt 51 and Wenzel Rd Peru IL 61354

SZPREJDA, EVELYN A., international marketing executive; b. Green Bay, Wis., Nov. 30, 1944; s. John O. and Pearl (Cwiak) S.; Student U. Wis., 1962-63, 67-68, U. Minn., 1975-77; B.A., Coll. St. Thomas, 1980. Various adminstrv. positions Campbell-Mithun Advt., Mpls., 1968-71; adminstrv. asst. Internat. div. First Nat. Bank Mpls., 1971-73; ops. adminstr. Far East ops. Medtronic Inc., Mpls., 1973-76, mktg. coordinator, 1976-78, market adminstrn. specialist Internat. div., 1978-79, mgr. internat. market planning and adminstrv. mgr., 1979-80, mgr. internat. market info. and research, 1980-81; dir. market research and planning Gibsongroup, Inc., Mpls., 1981-82; trade ops. devel. mgr. Control Data Commerce Internat., Mpls., 1982-83; mktg. mgr. healthcare products, 1983-84; dir. planning and new program devel. First Internat. Corp., Mpls., 1984-85; mgr. IXI World Trade Corp., 1985—; instr. Coll. St. Thomas, 1984—; export cons., 1981—; ptnr. Intermar Group Ltd., 1985—. Mem. Minn. Gov.'s Task Force on Internat. Bus. Edn., 1983-84. Recipient Bus. Woman Leader award YMCA, 1980. Mem. Am. Mktg. Assn., Internat. Advt. Assn., Japan Am. Soc. Minn. (sec. 1981-82), Mpls. C. of C. (world trade com.), Minn. World Trade Assn. (bd. dirs. 1980, pres. 1983—). Roman Catholic. Club: Greenway Athletic. Home: 121 S Washington Ave 1310 Minneapolis MN 55401 Office: PO Box 26344 Park Station Minneapolis MN 55426

SZYMANSKI, DAVID JOHN, recreation educator; b. Adams, Mass., Feb. 17, 1951; s. John Gabriel and Flora Kathryn (Nowak) S.; m. Elizabeth Ann Knotts, July 22, 1978; children—Kate Emily, Laura Elizabeth. A.A., St. Thomas Jr. Coll., 1970; B.A., Niagara U., 1972; M.A., Coll. St. Rose, 1973; student U. Iowa, 1975-77; Re.D., Ind. U., 1986. Project coordinator Spl. Project Grant, N.Y. State Edn. Dept., Albany, 1973-75; instr. U. Iowa, Iowa City, 1975-77; vis. lectr. dept. recreation and park adminstrn. U. Mo., Columbia, 1978; asst. prof. dept. health, phys. edn. and recreation U. Kans.-Lawrence, 1978-82; vis. asst. prof. dept. recreation and park adminstrn. U. Mo.-Columbia 1982-83, asst. prof., 1983-85; park ranger U.S. Army Corps Engrs.; dir. Youth Conservation Corps, Lawrence, Kans. Vol., Wakarusa Twp. Vol. Fire Dept., Boone County Fire Dept., Douglas County Ambulance Service; instr. CPR, Am. Heart Assn., Kans. also Mo. Mem. Nat. Therapeutic Recreation Soc., AAHPERD, Nat. Consortium Phys. Edn. and Recreation for Handicapped, Soc. Park and Recreation Educators, Mo. Park and Recreation Assn. Republican. Roman Catholic. Home: 1036 Jana Dr Lawrence KS 66044

TABACCHI, FRED LAWRENCE, vacuum cleaner company executive; b. Kelly, N. Mex., Aug. 10, 1917; s. Carlo F. and Dora M. (Katzenstein) T.; m. Laura Mae Doebbeling, Dec. 23, 1944; children—Loretta Tabacchi Johndrow, Larry W., Terri Beth Tabacchi Gardner. Student pub. schs., Tucson; bus. adminstrn. student Alexander Hamilton Inst., 1950-51. With Hoover Co., 1937—; sr. v.p., 1964-66, exec. v.p., 1966-75, pres., chief operating officer North Canton, Ohio, 1975-82, pres., chief operating officer Hoover Worldwide Corp., 1975-78, vice chmn., 1978; pres., dir. Hoover Co. Ltd., Can., 1975-82, Hoover Mexicana (Sa de CV), 1975-82; dir. Hoover Ltd., U.K., 1974—; dir. Hoover Indsl. y Comml. SA, 1976-82, Chemko Comml. Product, 1979-82; dir., exec. com. Hoover Co., 1982—, also dir. Hoover plc (U.K.). Gen. chmn. Buckeye council Boy Scouts Am. Capital campaign, 1983; bd. dirs. Mount Union Coll., Alliance, Ohio, United Negro Fund, 1971; campaign chmn. Jr. Achievement, 1980; mem. U.S.-Mex. C. of C., pres., chmn. bd., 1977-79, bd. dirs., exec. com. 1977. Mem. Vacuum Cleaner Mfg. Assn. (pres. 1973-75, exec. com. 1979—). Clubs: Brookside Country (Canton); Skyline Country (Tucson). Office: PO Box 2818 North Canton OH 44720

TABER, MARGARET RUTH STEVENS, educator, engineer; b. St. Louis, Apr. 29, 1935; d. Wynn Orr and Margaret (Feldman) Stevens; B. Elec. Engring., Fenn Coll (now Cleve. State U.) 1958, B. Engring. Sci., 1958; postgrad. Western Res. U., 1959-64; M.S. in Engring., U. Akron, 1967; Ed.D., Nova U., 1976; m. William J. Taber, Sept. 6, 1958. Engring. trainee Ohio Crankshaft Co., Cleve., 1954-57, devel. engr., 1958-64, tng. dir., 1963-64; instr. elec.-electronic engring. tech. Cuyahoga Community Coll., Cleve. 1964-67, asst. prof., 1967-69, assoc. prof., 1969-72, prof., 1972-79, acad. unit leader engring. tech., 1977-79; assoc. prof. elec. engring. tech. Purdue U., West Lafayette, Ind., 1979-83, prof., 1983—; lectr. Cleve. State U., 1963-64. Bd. dirs. West Blvd. Christian Ch., deaconess, 1974-77, elder, 1977-79; deacon Federated Ch., 1981-84; mem. acad. adv. bd. Cleve. Inst. Electronics, 1981—. NSF grantee, 1970, 71, 72, 73, 78. Registered profl. engr., Ohio. Mem. IEEE, Soc. Women Engrs. (sr.; counselor Purdue chpt. 1983-85), Am. Bus. Women's Assn. (ednl. chmn. 1964-66), Nat. Rifle Assn., Am. Soc. Engring. Edn., Am. Tech. Edn. Assn., Tau Beta Pi (hon.). Author: (with Frank P. Tedeschi) Solid State Electronics, 1976; (with Eugene M. Silgalis) Electric Circuit Analysis, 1980; (with Jerry L. Casebeer) Registers, (with Kenneth Rosenow) Arithmetic Logic Units, Timing and Control, Memory Units, 1980; Architecture and Operation, 1984; Programming I: Straight Line, 1984; contbr. articles to profl. jours. Home: 3036 W State Rd 26 West Lafayette IN 47906 Office: Knoy Hall of Techology West Lafayette IN 47907

TABET, JOSEPH A., orthopedic surgeon; b. Beirut, Lebanon, Mar. 30, 1942; came to U.S., 1968, naturalized, 1973; s. Abdallah Sakhr and Hneineh (Fadel) T.; m. Kathe G. Wintercorn, Sept. 27, 1975; children—Randa, Alia, Aboudi. B.Sc., Am. U. Beirut, 1961, M.D., 1966. Diplomate Am. Bd. Orthopedic Surgery. Intern, Am. Univ. Hosp., Beirut, 1966, resident in gen. surgery, 1966-68; resident in gen. surgery Buffalo Gen. Hosp., 1968; resident in orthopedic surgery Northwestern U., Chgo., 1969-72; practice medicine specializing in orthopedic surgery, Chgo., 1972—; teaching staff Children's Meml. Hosp., Chgo., 1972-74, Loyola U., Mercy Med. Ctr., Chgo., 1976—. Mem. Am. Acad. Orthopedic Surgeons, ACS, AMA, Inst. Medicine of Chgo., Oriental Inst. Chgo. Home: 11933 W 79 St Burr Ridge IL 60525 Office: 6925 W Archer Ave Chicago IL 60638

TACCHI, DENNIS GERARD, architect, consultant; b. St. Louis, Aug. 16, 1955; s. Joseph Mario and Josephine Louise (Garavaglia) T.; m. Karen Marie Mueller, May 27, 1978. A.Arch., Meramec Community Coll., 1975; B.Archtl.-Tech., Washington U., 1982. Registered architect, Mo.; cert. Nat. Council Archtl. Registration Bds. Project architect Mackey & Assocs., St. Louis, 1975-82; prin. ARCHITECTUS, St. Louis, 1982—. Mem. AIA (mem. St. Louis chpt., pub. relations com. 1982-83). Roman Catholic. Avocations: drawing; swimming; hiking; photography; travel. Office: ARCHITECTUS 1611 Ann Ave St Louis MO 63122

TACKOWIAK, EUGENE CHARLES, insurance public relations executive; b. East Troy, Wis., June 1, 1923; s. Valentine Walter and Mary Anne (Sokolowski) T.; m. Bernadine Van Engel, June 12, 1954; children—Mary Virgine, Bruce Joseph, Janine Ann Baretta, Edith Christine, Paula Jane. B.A. in Journalism, Marquette U., 1950. Reporter, editor Milw. Sentinel, 1951-62; mng. editor Am. Sch. Bd. Jour., 1962-67; info. and publs. dir. Wis. Dept. Pub. Instrn., 1967-69; v.p. pub. relations Wis. Ins. Alliance, Madison, 1969—; lectr. colls., tech. schs., high schs.; consumer cons. Mem. Gov.'s Com. Safety 1967-69, Gov.'s Com. Ins., 1976-80; bd. dirs. Wis. Consumer League, 1979—. Served with USNR, 1943-46; PTO. Recipient W.R. Hearst Reporting award, 1957; award of excellence Nation's Schs., 1964, award of distinction, 1970, cert. of excellence Sch. Mgmt., 1969, 70; Outstanding Service award Wis. Driver Tng., 1974. Mem. Pub. Relations Soc. Am., Nat. Assn. Ins. Info. Dirs., Madison Press Club, Nat. Sch. Pub. Relations Assn. Roman Catholic. Club: Madison (Wis.). Home: 210 Eddy St Madison WI 53705 Office: 121 E Wisconsin St Madison WI 53703

TAECKENS, DIANNE ELAINE, newspaper executive; b. Flint, Mich., Nov. 29, 1946; d. Richard Ernest Taeckens and Shirley Joanne (Currie) Hooper; m. Kenneth J. Mulder, Oct. 4, 1974. A.A.S., Mott Community Coll., Flint, Mich., 1966; B.S. in Bus. Adminstrn., Central Mich. U., Mount Pleasant, 1969; M.B.A., U. Mich., 1978. C.P.A., Mich. Jr. acct. Ernst & Ernst, Detroit, 1969-70; acct. Dupuis & Ryden, P.C., Flint, 1971-77; asst. controller The Flint Jour., 1977-79, controller, 1979—; instr. U. Mich.-Flint, 1973, 74. Mem. Am. Inst. C.P.A.s, Mich. Assn. C.P.A.s, Internat. Newspaper Fin. Execs., Flint Women's Forum. Home: 2025 Stoney Brook Ct Flint MI 48507

TAECKENS, DOUGLAS RICHARD, plastics mfg. co. exec.; b. Flint, Mich., May 9, 1950; s. Richard Ernst and Shirley Joanne (Currie) T.; B.B.A., U. Mich., 1972, M.B.A., 1985. m. Pamela Kay Webb, Sept. 29, 1984; children—James, April. Mem. sales dept. Helmac Products Corp., Flint, 1972-74, Southwest regional mgr., Dallas, 1974-76, nat. sales mgr., Flint, 1976-78, v.p. sales and mktg., 1978—. Mem. Sales and Mktg. Execs. Club, Nat. Assn. Service Merchandising, Gen. Mdse. Distbrs. Council, U. Mich. Alumni Assn. Republican. Office: PO Box 73 Flint MI 48501

TAFLIN, CHARLES OLAF, civil engineer; b. McIntosh, Minn., July 4, 1934; s. Carl E. and Selma O. (Hagen) T.; m. Marlys R. Melberg, June 14, 1958; children—Daniel, David, Mary. B.S. in Engring., U. Minn., 1956, postgrad., 1956-58. Registered profl. engr., Minn. Project engr. Mpls. Water Works, 1958-65, supt. planning and engring., 1967-75, supt. plant ops., 1975—; environ. engr. Schoell & Madsen, Hopkins, Minn., 1965-66; mem. faculty U. Minn., 1975-76. Served to 1st lt. U.S. Army, 1958-62. Mem. Internat. Water Supply Assn., Am. Water Works Assn. (Fuller award 1976). Home: 10811 French Lake Rd Champlin MN 55316 Office: Minneapolis Water Works 4300 Marshall St NE Minneapolis MN 55421

TAFT, JOHN AILES, JR., hospital executive; b. Evanston, Ill., Aug. 6, 1927; s. John Ailes and Mildred (Bent) T.; m. Portia Downs, June 20, 1952; children—Sarah, Peter, Andrew, Mary. B.S., Northwestern U., 1947, M.H.A., 1957; M.B.A., Dartmouth Coll., 1950. Adminstrv. asst. Chgo. Wesley Meml. Hosp., 1954-57; v.p. Delnor Hosp., St. Charles, Ill., 1957-61, pres., 1961—. Bd. dirs. Fox Valley Hospice, 1979—, Health Systems Agency, Cary, Ill., 1983—.

Served with USNR, 1945-46. Fellow Am. Coll. Hosp. Adminstrs.; mem. Ill. Hosp. Assn. (dir. 1978-82, 84—), Chgo. Hosp. Council (dir. 1982—). Office: Delnor Hosp 975 N 5th Ave St Charles IL 60174

TAFT, ROBERT, JR., lawyer, former U.S. senator; b. Cin., Feb. 26, 1917; s. Robert A. and Martha (Bowers) T.; B.A., Yale U., 1939; LL.B., Harvard U., 1942; m. Blanca Noel, 1939 (dec.); children—Robert A., Sarah B. Taft Jones, Deborah Taft Boutellis, Jonathan D.; m. 3d, Joan M. Warner, 1978. Admitted to Ohio bar; assoc. firm Taft, Stettinius & Hollister, Cin., 1946-51, ptnr., 1951-63, 77—; dir. Taft Broadcasting Co.; mem. Ohio Ho. of Reps., 1955-62, majority floor leader, 1961-62; mem. 88th Congress at-large from Ohio; mem. 90th-91th Congresses from 1st Ohio Dist.; U.S. senator from Ohio, 1971-76; practice law in Washington and Cin., 1976—. Trustee Children's Home Cin., Inst. Fine Arts; bd. dirs. World Affairs Council D.C.; trustee Robert A. Taft Inst. Govt., Population Crisis Com., Draper Fund; mem. Com. on Present Danger; bd. advisors Patterson Sch. Diplomacy and Internat. Commerce, U. Ky. Served with USNR, 1942-46. Mem. Am., Ohio, Cin. bar assns. Republican. Clubs: Camargo, Racquet, Lit., Queen City (Cin.); Alibi. Home: 4300 Drake Rd Cincinnati OH 45243 Office: 1620 I St NW Washington DC 20006 also 1800 First Nat Bank Center Cincinnati OH 45202

TAGHERT-BERGSTROM, NICOLE MARY, film producer; b. Alexandria, Egypt, Jan. 24, 1949; came to U.S., 1957, naturalized, 1962; d. Francis and Betty Katherine (Moffatt) Taghert; m. Erick A. Bergstrom, June 23, 1985. Student, Mills Coll., 1966-68; B.A., Northwestern U., 1970, M.A., 1973. Stylist, producer Sedelmaier Films, Chgo., 1977-80; art dir. PBS feature, Any Friend of Nicholas Nickeby, Rubicon Prodns., Evanston, Ill., 1981; producer Film, 1983-84; exec. producer, ptnr. Cinetex Inc., Chgo., 1984—; dir., writer, ptnr. In Camera Prodns., 1981-83. Translator: Secret Doors of the Earth (J. Bergier), 1975. Club: Chgo. Yacht. Avocations: stretching the language of our awareness, understanding through film and writing. Office: Cinetex Inc 1254 N Lake Shore Dr Chicago IL 60610

TAIRA, FRANCES SNOW, nurse educator; b. Glasgow, Scotland, Feb. 27, 1935; came to U.S., 1959, naturalized, 1964; d. Thomas and Isabel (McDonald) Snow; m. Albert Taira, June 20, 1962; children—Albert, Deborah, Paul. B.S.N., U. Ill., 1974, M.S.N., 1976; Ed.D., No. Ill. U., 1980. Staff nurse various hosps., 1959-73; instr. nursing Triton Coll., 1976-81; asst. prof. nursing Loyola U., Chgo., 1981—. Mem. Am. Nurses Assn., Ill. Nurses Assn. (pres. 19th dist. 1982-84), U. Ill. Nursing Alumni Assn., Sigma Theta Tau, Phi Delta Kappa. Roman Catholic. Author: Aging: A Guide for the Family, 1983; contbr. articles to profl. jours. Home: 404 Atwater Ave Elmhurst IL 60126 Office: Loyola U Lake Shore Campus 6525 N Sheridan Rd Chicago IL 60626

TAKACS, ANDREW JOSEPH, manufacturing executive; b. Toledo, July 20, 1933; s. Andrew Joseph and Ann Marie (Masney) T.; B.B.A. in Journalism and Bus. Adminstrn., U. Toledo, 1956, B.E. in Social Sci., 1957, M.E. in Polit. Sci., 1961; m. Anne Louise Schlicher, Nov. 10, 1956; children—Michael, David, Karen. Publicity dir. City of Toledo, 1954-56; reporter Toledo Times, 1954-56; asso. news dir. Sta. WSPD Radio-TV, Toledo; pub. relations Toledo Scale, 1957-59; with Whirlpool Corp., 1959—, mgr. community relations Clyde (Ohio) div., 1959-61, pub. relations asst., Benton Harbor, Mich., 1962-63, mgr. pub. affairs, 1963-66, mgr. legis. affairs, 1966-67, dir. govt. affairs, 1967-70, dir. govt. and urban affairs, 1970-73, dir. pub. affairs, 1973-78, v.p. pub. and govt. relations, 1978—; trustee Whirlpool Found.; chmn., dir. Whirlpool Opportunities, Inc. Mem. Washington reps. Bus. Roundtable, mem. corp. responsibility and govt. regulation task force. Trustee, Twin Cities Area Cath. Sch. Fund, Inc. Served with U.S. Army, 1957, 61-62. Mem. Assn. Home Appliance Mfrs. (chmn. govt. bd., strategic planning com., trustee polit. action com.; leadership award 1980), Am. Acad. Polit. and Social Sci., NAM (govtl. issues com.), U.S. C. of C. (pub. affairs com.), Pub. Relations Soc. Am., Twin Cities C. of C. (dir., exec. com., chmn. govt. relations legis. com.), Roman Catholic. Clubs: Berrien Hills Country, Chgo. Press, Capitol Hill. Office: 2000 US 33 N Benton Harbor MI 49022

TAKESHITA, TAKUO, metallurgist; b. Takase, Kagawa, Japan, Aug. 13, 1941; came to U.S., 1966; s. Takanosuke and Kazue (Morikawa) Hosokawa; m. Setsuko Shinohara, Nov. 24, 1970; children—Akiko, Marie, Taro, Sachiko. B.S., U. Tokyo, 1965; Ph.D., SUNY-Stony Brook, 1970. Chemist, Sumitomo Chem., Japan, 1965-72; research assoc. U. Pitts., 1972-74; research asst. prof. U. Pitts., 1974-77; vis. metallurgist Ames Lab., Iowa State U., 1977-78, assoc. metallurgist, 1978—. Mem. Am. Phys. Soc., Am. Soc. for Metals, Sigma Xi. Contbr. articles to sci. jours.; patentee.

TALABA, LINDA, artist, lecturer, educational administrator; b. Detroit, July 15, 1943; d. Laszlo and Irma Leona (Fairles) T.; m. John Albert Cummens, Aug. 28, 1964; 1 child, Michael Sean Cummens. B.F.A., Ill. Wesleyan U., 1965; M.F.A., So. Ill. U., 1973. Inst. Shawnee Coll., Ullin, Ill., 1969, So. Ill. U., Carbondale, Ill., 1971-73; Lincoln Land Community Coll., Springfield, Ill., 1975-77, Coll. Lake County, Grays Lake, Ill., 1984; guest lectr., instr. Sangamon State U., Springfield, 1975-76; dir. art sch. Suburban Fine Arts Ctr., Highland Park, Ill., 1984—; exhbn. juror U. Ill., Springfield, 1976, Springfield Art Fair, 1979. Illustrator and editor: Lakeland's Paradise, 1961; illustrator: The Black Book, 1964-65; co-author and illustrator: Helping Your Doctor, 1985. One-woman shows: The Rotunda, City Hall, Highland Park Art 80, Unitarian Art Fair, 1980, Suburban Fine Arts Ctr., 1982, Deerfield Courts Gallery, Lake Cook Plaza, Deerfield, Ill., 1983-85. Fundraiser Am. Cancer Soc., Lake County Branch, Ill., 1982—; sec. and fundraiser Dist. 113 Orch., Lake County, Ill., 1981-83; alumni fundraiser Ill. Wesleyan U., Bloomington, Ill., 1968-81. Research grantee Smithsonian Inst., Nat. Scholarship, 1972; recipient Boston Mus. Printmaker's award, 1965, Ball State U. award, 1975, Ill. State Mus. Craftsman's award, 1975. Mem. AAUW (nominating com. 1985—, book chmn. 1983), Am. Recorder Soc., Soc. Concerned Scientists, Suburban Fine Arts Ctr. (bd. dirs. 1983—), North Shore Art League, Art Inst. Chgo. Club: Deerfield Courts. Avocations: poetry, writing, racquetball, biking, cross country skiing, walking. Home: 1316 Oxford Rd Deerfield IL 60015 Office: Suburban Fine Arts Ctr 777 Central Ave Highland Park IL 60035

TALBOT, ARDITH ANN, bookstore administrator, homemaker; b. Superior, Nebr., Mar. 11, 1933; d. Charles H. and Dolly Eunice (Ryan) Snell; m. Richard Charles Talbot, Oct. 17, 1954; children—Richard Daryl, Robert Charles. B.A. in Edn., Kearney St. Coll. Cert. secondary tchr., Nebr., Iowa. Tchr. English Juniata High Sch., Nebr., 1957-59, Hudson High Sch., Iowa, 1962-68; bookstore owner Sutherland, Marshalltown, Mason City, all Iowa, 1971—. Fundraising chmn. Waterloo council Girl Scouts of Am., Hudson, Iowa, 1965; project chmn. Christian Women's Assn., Mason City, Iowa, 1966; pres. Christian Fed. Women's Club, Hudson, 1978. Mem. Christian Booksellers Assn. Republican. Avocations: Reading; traveling; antique collecting. Home: 14 N Boulder Nora Springs IA 50401 Office: Alpha Book & Gift 111 W State Mason City IA 50401

TALBOT, DAVID JOHN, broadcast journalist, educator; b. Peoria, Ill., Aug. 28, 1949; s. Russell Roberts and Emma Martha (Bossman) T.; m. Patricia Ann Cushing, Sept. 19, 1975. B.A., U. Ill., 1971, postgrad. Inst. Labor and Indsl. Relations, 1971-73. Broadcast journalist WMBD-AM-FM/TV, Peoria, 1968-71, WILL-TV, Urbana, Ill., 1971-73, WDWS, Champaign, Ill., 1973—; lectr. U. Ill., Urbana, 1980—; cons. Recipient Sigma Delta Chi awards, 1975, 76. Mem. Ill. Newsbroadcasters Assn. (dir. 1979-80), Soc. Profl. Journalism (regional pres. 1975-77), Radio TV News Dirs. Assn., Alpha Epsilon Rho. Home: 116 W Florida Ave Urbana IL 61801 Office: Sta WDWS PO Box 677 Champaign IL 61820

TALBOT, GERRI JOAN, office supply company executive; b. Detroit, Feb. 8, 1935; d. Leo and Helen (Mazur) Mankowski; m. James J. Wallace, Sept. 8, 1956 (dec. 1968); children—Thomas, Lynn, Carol, Laurence, John; m. Edgar A. Talbot, May 29, 1971; stepchildren—Edgar, Rochelle, Marilyn, Caryn, Elizabeth, Rhonda. A.A., Henry Ford Community Coll., 1953; B.S. in Dental Hygiene, U. Mich., 1955. Dental hygienist in pvt. practice, Dearborn, Mich., 1956-58, 64; entrepreneur, co-owner, pres. Paper Tiger Books and Office Supplies, Inc., Livonia, Mich., 1974—. Counselor, Crisis Counseling Ctr., Harper Woods, Mich., 1984. Mem. Nat. Office Products Assn., C. of C., Lifespan. Republican. Home: 784 Springfield Dr Northville MI 48167 Office: Paper Tiger 33460 Seven Mile Rd Livonia MI 48152

TALKINGTON, ROBERT VAN, state senator; b. nr. Patrick, Tex., Aug. 23, 1929; s. William Henry and Nannie J. (Patrick) T.; A.A., Tyler Jr. Coll., 1949; B.S., U. Kans., 1951, LL.B., 1954, J.D., 1971; m. Donna Jill Schmaus, Mar. 25, 1951; children—Jill Talkington McCaskill, Jacki T. Chase, James, Thomas, Lisa. Admitted to Kans. bar, 1954; county atty., Allen County, 1957-63; city atty., Moran, 1968; mem. Kans. Ho. of Reps. from 10th Dist., 1969-73; mem. Kans. Senate from 12th Dist., 1973—, v.p., 1977-81, majority leader, 1981-85, pres., 1985—. Chmn. Republican Party, Allen County, 1964-68, state treas., 1964-66. Trustee, Iola Pub. Library, 1962-70; mem. adv. bd. Greater U. Fund, U. Kans., 1967-72. Served with CIC, AUS, 1954-56. Mem. Am. Legion, Sigma Alpha Epsilon, Phi Delta Phi. Clubs: Masons, Shriners, Elks. Home: 20 W Buchanan St Iola KS 66749 Office: 20 N Washington St Iola KS 66749

TALLAN, NORMAN M., research and development executive, engineer; b. Newark, N.J., Sept. 24, 1932; s. Max and Anna (Barer) T.; m. Joan Judith Harnett, Aug. 24, 1958; children—Mitchell Matthew, Eric Michael, Mark David, Daniel Elan. B.S., Rutgers U. 1954; M.S., Ohio State U., 1955; Ph.D., Alfred U., 1959. Sr. scientist AFWAL Materials Lab, Wright-Patterson AFB, Dayton, Ohio, 1976-77, acting chief, metals nd ceramics div., 1977-78, chief scientist, 1978-82; spl. asst. to dep. for technology Office of Asst. Sec. of Air Force, Washington, 1982-83; chief metals and ceramics div. AFWAL Materials Lab, Dayton, 1983—. Editor: Electrical Conductivity in Ceramics, 1974. Fellow Am. Ceramic Soc.; mem. Am. Phys. Soc., N.Y. Acad. Scis. Home: 3743 Greenbay Dr Dayton OH 45415 Office: Materials Lab AFWAL/MLL Wright-Patterson AFB Dayton OH 45433

TALLCHIEF, MARIA, ballerina; b. Fairfax, Okla., Jan. 24, 1925; d. Alexander Joseph and Ruth Mary (Porter) T.; student pub. schs., Calif.; A.F.D. (hon.), Lake Forest Coll., Colby Coll., 1968, Ripon Coll., 1973, Boston Coll.; D.F.A. (hon.), Smith Coll., 1981, Northwestern U., 1982, Yale U., 1984; hon. degree St. Mary of the Woods Coll., 1984; m. Henry Paschen, Jr., June 3, 1957; 1 dau., Elise. Joined Ballet Russe de Monte Carlo, 1942; prima ballerina N.Y.C. Ballet, 1947-60; guest star Paris Opera, 1947; prima ballerina Am. Ballet Theater, 1960; with N.Y.C. Ballet Co., until 1965; now artistic dir. Chgo. City Ballet; guest star Royal Danish Ballet, Copenhagen, 1961. Recipient Achievement award Women's Nat. Press Club, 1953; Dance mag. award, 1960; Capezio award, 1965; named Hon. Princess Osage Indian Tribe, 1953; Disting. Service award U. Okla., 1972; Jane Addams Humanitarian award Rockford Coll., 1973; award Dance Educators Am., 1956. Mem. Nat. Soc. Arts and Letters.

TALLEY, FREDERICO JEROME, JR., university adminstrator; b. Phila., Mar. 4, 1957; s. Frederico Jerome and Laila Faye (Corley) T. B.A., Dickinson Coll., 1978; M.A., Bowling Green State U., 1980. Cert. secondary tchr., Pa. Acad. advisor Wright State U., Dayton, Ohio, 1980-81, dir. orientation, 1984—; coordinator student activities Ohio U., 1981-84, asst. to dean students, 1983-84. Big brother Carlisle Big Bros. and Big Sisters, Pa., 1976. Mem. Am. Coll. Personnel Assn., Am. Assn. Counseling and Devel., Assn. Non-White Concerns in Personnel and Guidance, Ohio Coll. Personnel Assn. Democrat. Baptist. Avocations: photography; creative writing; piano; racquetball. Office: Wright State Univ 122 Student Services Dayton OH 45435

TAMBURRINO, MARIJO BERNADETTE, psychiatrist; b. Mansfield, Ohio, Jan. 10, 1952; d. Jospeh David and Rosemary (Nicita) T.; m. Ronald Anthony McGinnis, Sept. 24, 1977. B.S. summa cum laude, Ohio State U., 1974; M.D., Med. Coll. Ohio, 1977. Intern, Med. Coll. Ohio, Toledo, 1978, resident, 1981, asst. prof. psychiatry, 1981—. Mem. Northwest Ohio Psychiat. Assn. (program chmn. 1981-83, pres. 1983—), Am. Med. Women's Assn. (sec. 1979-81), Ohio State Med. Assn., AMA. Office: Med Coll Ohio Dept Psychiatry Arlington Ave CS #10008 Toledo OH 43699

TANAKA, STEPHANIE MASAE, geologist; b. St. Louis, Oct. 13, 1958; d. George Masayuki and Mitzi Mitzue (Nakao) T. B.S. in Geology and Geophysics, U. Mo.-Rolla, 1981. Geologist-oil shale Phillips Petroleum Co., Lexington, Ky., 1980, Denver, 1981; geologist-oil and gas Cities Service Co., Tulsa, 1982-83; geologist-minerals Amselco Exploration Inc., St. Peters, Mo., 1983—. Mem. Am. Assn. Petroleum Geologists, Geol. Soc. Am., Sigma Gamma Epsilon, Alpha Chi Sigma. Lutheran. Avocations: skiing, horseback riding, travelling. Office: Amselco Exploration Inc 14 Algana Dr St Peters MO 63376

TANCULA, THOMAS NICHOLAS, labor relations specialist; b. Chgo., Mar. 14, 1956; s. Bruno Walter and Virginia (DiPrizio) T.; m. Judith Lynn La Haye, July 24, 1982. B.A., Elmhurst Coll., 1981. With Chgo., Milw., St. Paul & Pacific R.R. Co., Chgo., 1978—, asst. labor relations officer, 1981, labor relations officer, 1981-82, mgr. labor relations, 1982-85; labor relations specialist NIRCRC/METRA, Chgo., 1985—; author, negotiator labor agreement Internat. Brotherhood of Firemen and Oilers, 1983. Mem. Ill. Ry. Mus., Union, Ill., 1977. Mem. Ry. Fuel and Operating Officers Assn., Chgo. R.R. Car Assn. (mem. audit com. 1984), Air Brake Assn., Car Dept. Officers Assn. Roman Catholic. Avocations: photography; railroad history. Home: 1206 Scarlet Ct Addison Il 60101 Office: NIRCRC/METRA 547 W Jackson Blvd Chicago IL 60606

TANDON, JAGDISH SINGH, pollution control co. exec.; b. New Delhi, India, Apr. 3, 1940; s. Mool C. and Vidya V. (Somra) T.; came to U.S., 1961, naturalized, 1973; B.Sc., U. Delhi, 1961; M.S., U. Minn., 1963, postgrad., 1963-67; m. Monika Dettmers, May 12, 1967; 1 son, Hans Peter. Mgr. mech. collector div. Aerodyne Corp., Hopkins, Minn., 1968-69; dir. control systems div. Environ. Research Corp. div. Dart Industries, St. Paul, 1969-70; gen. mgr. pollution control systems div. George A. Hormel & Co., Coon Rapids, Minn., 1970-77; pres. Am. Envirodyne div. Pettibone Corp., Chgo., 1977-78; dir. mktg. MMT Environ. Inc., St. Paul, 1978-80; pres. Environ. Cons., Northbrook, 1980—; pres. Am. Environ. Internat. Inc., Northbrook, 1982—; instr. U. Minn. Inst. Tech.; vis. scientist Nat. Center Atmospheric Research, Boulder, Colo. Mem. ASCE, Air Pollution Control Assn., Am. Foundry Soc. Contbr. pollution control articles to profl. lit. Home: 1344 Southwind Dr Northbrook IL 60062

TANGEMAN, ROGER LEE, retail executive; b. Celina, Ohio, Sept. 12, 1948; s. Philip J. and Philomena Tangeman. Grad. high sch. Coldwater, Ohio. Stockchaser, Fort Recovery Industries, Ohio, 1967-72; head receiver Halterman, Inc., Coldwater, 1973—. Chmn. com. Combined Charities, Coldwater, 1980, 84, Bishop Relief Fund, Coldwater, 1982; bd. dirs. Coldwater Boosters, 1984—; mem. com. Precious Blood Soc., St. Henry's Ch., 1979—; asst. coach Fort Recovery Girls Softball, 1972-74; sec.-treas. Coldwater Jr. Bowling Assn., 1980—; sec.-treas. Coldwater Men's Bowling Assn., 1980—. Mem. Coldwater Jaycees (bd. dirs. 1977-78, v.p. 1978-79, state bd. dirs. 1979-80, chpt. pres. 1981-82, dist. dir. 1982-83, chmn. Spl. Olympics com. 1984, chmn. pub. relations 1976-77, numerous awards), Celina Jaycees (charter, state dir. 1983). Roman Catholic. Lodge: KC (Coldwater) (chmn. com. 1981-82). Avocations: bowling; spectator sports. Home: 725 W Walnut St Coldwater OH 45828

TANGEN, NEIL RALPH, lawyer; b. Glenwood, Minn., Aug. 26, 1952; s. Ralph Vernon Wallace and Joanna Marie (Phelps) T. Student Willmar Jr. Coll., 1970-71; B.A., U. Minn., 1973; J.D., Hamline U., 1976. Bar: Minn. 1979, U.S. Dist. Ct. Minn. 1979, U.S. Ct. Appeals (8th cir.) 1979. Law clk. St. Cloud Legal Services, Little Falls, Minn., 1978-79; staff atty. Anishinabe Legal Services, Cass Lake, Minn., 1979-83; assoc. Marshall & Marshall, Hoffman, Minn., 1984-85; sole practice, 1985—. Home: 1215 2d St NE Glenwood MN 56334

TANIN, GARY STEVEN, songwriter, producer, electronics consultant; b. Milw., Sept. 19, 1952; s. Ananij and Natalie (Holowinsky) T. Student U. Wis., 1970-72. Rec. with Odessa Records, 1969, Vera Records, 1972, 75, 76, 81; rec., produced numerous records, albums; pub. 29 songs. Active drug and alcohol abuse work. Recipient certs. Milw. Psychiat. Hosp. for work in drug and alcohol field, 1981, 82, 83, 84. Mem. Country Music Assn., Nat. Acad. Rec. Arts and Scis. (voting mem.), Broadcast Music Inc. Home: PO Box 10181 Milwaukee WI 53210

TANNEBAUM, SOL, optometrist; b. Brest-li-tovsk, Poland, Apr. 2, 1924; came to U.S., 1929; m. Marilynn Etta Barshay, June 1949; children—Ross David, Lisa Rose. B.S., Roosevelt U., 1959; O.D., Ill. Coll. Optometry, 1948; postgrad., U. Ind., 1959, Ohio State U., 1958, Pa. State Coll. Optometry, 1955; M.H.S., Gov.'s State U., 1981. Practice optometry, Park Forest, Ill., 1954-75, Olympia Fields, Ill., 1975—; clin. assoc. Ill. Coll. Optometry, Chgo., 1970—; assoc. editor Jour. Am. Optometric Assn., 1966—; vis. prof. European Coll. Optometry, 1973; participant coop. eye project with ophthalmology and nursing Dominican Republic; del. eye/vision exch. project to People's Republic of China, 1985. Chmn. visual health com. Park Forest Health Council, 1961—, South Suburban Pub. Sch. Coop., 1966; chmn. Sight and blind com. Park Forest Lions Club; bd. dirs. Family counseling Service South Cook County, 1966-69, Health Careers Council Ill., 1967-72. Contbr. articles to profl. jours. Served with USNR, 1945-46. Fellow Am. Acad. Optometry; mem. Am. Optometric Assn., Ill. Optometric Assn. (editor jour. 1969-71, mem. child vision care com. 1973), Assn. Optometric Editors, Optometric Hist. Soc. (trustee), Assn. Optometric Editors. Lodge: Lions. Avocations: swimming; racquetball; skiing. Home: 2620 Oakwood Dr Olympia Fields IL 60461 Office: 2555 Lincoln Hwy Olympia Fields IL 60461

TANNENBERG, DIETER E. A., business equipment manufacturing company executive; b. Chevy Chase, Md., Nov. 24, 1932; s. Wilhelm and Margarete (Mundhenk) T.; B.S. in Mech. Engring., Northwestern U., 1959; m. Ruth Hansen, Feb. 6, 1956; 1 dau., Diana. Supervising engr. Flexonics div. Calumet & Hecla, Inc., Chgo., 1959-61, chief engr., 1961-63, program mgr. advanced space systems, 1963-65, dir. mfg. services, 1965-67; dir. mfg. engring. SCM, Cortland, N.Y., 1967-69; tech. dir. internat. Singer Co., N.Y.C., 1969-71; v.p. ops., internat. Addressograph-Multigraph Corp., Cleve., 1971-74; mng. dir. Addressograph Multigraph GmbH, Frankfurt/M., Germany, 1974-78; v.p., gen. mgr. Europe, Middle East and Africa, AM Internat., Inc., Chgo., 1978-79, pres. AM Bruning div., 1979-82, corp. v.p., 1981-83, corp. sr. v.p., 1983—; pres. AM Multigraphics, 1982—; chmn. AM Internat. GmbH, Frankfurt; dir. Mathias Bauerle GmbH, St. Georgen, Germany, 1972-75. Served with M.I., U.S. Army, 1953-56. Registered profl. engr., Ill., N.Y., N.J., Conn., Ohio, Wis., Ind. Mem. ASME, Nat. Soc. Profl. Engrs., Assn. Reprodn. Materials Mfrs. (dir. 1979-82, v.p. 1980-82), Nat. Assn. Quick Printers (bd. dirs. 1982-84), Nat. Printing Equipment and Supplies Mfg. Assn. (dir. 1983—), Computer and Bus. Equipment Mfg. Assn. (dir. 1983—), Pi Tau Sigma. Contbr. chpt. to Handbook of Modern Manufacturing Management, 1970. Patentee in field. Office: Multigraphics div AM Internat Inc 1800 W Central Rd Mount Prospect IL 60056

TANNER, JIMMIE EUGENE, college dean; b. Hartford, Ark., Sept. 27, 1933; s. Alford C. and Hazel Ame (Anthony) T.; m. Carole Joy Yant, Aug. 28, 1958; children—Leslie Allison, Kevin Don. B.A., Okla. Baptist U., 1955; M.A., U. Okla., 1957, Ph.D., 1964. Assoc. prof. English, Franklin Coll., Ind., 1964-65; prof. English, Okla. Bapt. U., Shawnee, 1958-64, 65-72; v.p. acad. affairs Hardin-Simmons U., Abilene, Tex., 1972-78, La. Coll., Pineville, 1978-80; dean William Jewell Coll., Liberty, Mo., 1980—. Contbr.: The Annotated Bibliography of D.H. Lawrence, 1982. Mem. Shawnee Sch. Bd., 1966-72; mem. edn. commn. So. Bapt. Conv., 1967-72. So. Fellowships Fund fellow, 1960-61; Danforth fellow, 1962-63. Mem. AAUP, MLA. Democrat. Baptist. Avocations: tennis; photography. Home: 609 Lancelot Dr Liberty MO 64068 Office: William Jewell College Liberty MO 64068

TANNER, MARTIN ABBA, statistics and human oncology educator; b. Highland Park, Ill., Oct. 19, 1957; s. Meir and Esther Rose (Bauer) T.; m. Anat Talitman, Aug. 14, 1984. B.A., U. Chgo., 1978, Ph.D., 1982. Asst. prof. stats. and human oncology U. Wis., Madison, 1982—, also dir. lab.; cons. Kirkland & Ellis, 1980-82. Contbr. articles to profl. jours. Recipient New Investigator Research award NIH, 1984; NSF grantee, 1983. Fellow Royal Statis. Soc.; mem. Am. Statis. Assn., AAAS, Mensa, Sigma Xi. Avocations: classical guitar; mideval poetry. Office: Biostatistics-6th Floor 420 N Charter St Madison WI 53706

TANSEY, ROBERT PAUL, SR., pharmaceutical chemist; b. Newark, Apr. 27, 1914; s. William Austin and Charlotte E. (Endler) T.; m. Natalie C. McMahon, Feb.22, 1941; children—Barbara, Carol, Robert, David. B.S., Rutgers U., 1938, M.S. in Pharm. Organic Chemistry, 1950. Sect. head Schering Corp., Bloomfield, N.J., 1953-58; mgr. research Strong Cobb Arner, Inc., Cleve., 1958-63; tech. dir., v.p. Vet. Labs., Inc., Lenexa, Kans., 1963-84, cons., 1984—. Registered pharmacist, N.J., Mo., Ohio. Contbr. articles to profl. jours. Patentee in field (5). Mem. Am. Pharm. Assn., Rho Chi, Kappa Psi. Club: Toastmasters (cert.). Home: 11141 Glen Arbor Rd Kansas City MO 64114

TAPLETT, LLOYD MELVIN, human resources management consultant; b. Tyndall, S.D., July 25, 1924; s. Herman Leopold and Emiley (Nedvidek) T.; B.A., Augustana Coll., 1949; M.A., U. Nebr., 1958; postgrad. S.D. State U., U. S.D., U. Iowa, Colo. State U.; m. Patricia Ann Sweeney, Aug. 21, 1958; children—Virginia Ann, Sharon Lorraine, Carla Jo, Carolyn Patricia, Catherine Marie, Colleen Elizabeth. Tchr., Sioux Falls (S.D.) public schs., 1952-69; with All-Am. Transport Co., Sioux Falls, 1969-78, Am. Freight System, Inc., Overland Park, Kans., 1978-79; dir. human resources and public relations, corp. affirmative action compliance ofcl. Chippewa Motor Freight Inc., Sioux Falls, 1979-80; human resource and mgmt. cons., 1980-81; mgr. Sioux Falls Job Services, 1981—; chmn. Chippewa Credit Union; mem. adv. bd. dirs. Nelson Labs., Sioux Falls 1981-82; evening mgmt. instr Nat. Coll., Sioux Falls, 1981—, chmn. adv. com., 1984—. Past bd. dirs. Jr. Achievement, United Way, Sioux Vocat. Sch. for Handicapped; past mem. Gov.'s Adv. Bd. for Community Adult Manpower Planning; chmn. bus. edn. adv. com. Sioux Falls Public Schs., 1982—; chmn. adv. com. South East Area Vocat. Sch., 1982—. Served to capt. USMC, 1943-46, 50-52. Recipient Liberty Bell award S.D. Bar Assn., 1967; Sch. Bd. award NEA/Thom McAn Shoe Corp., 1966; named Boss of Yr., Sioux Falls, 1977; cert. tchr. and counselor, S.D. Mem. Am. Soc. for Personnel Adminstrn. (accredited personnel mgr., S.D. dist. dir. 1980-84), Am. Trucking Assn., NEA (life mem., Pacemaker award), S.D. Edn. Assn. (life), Sioux Falls Personnel Assn. (past pres.), Sales and Mktg. Club Sioux Falls, Sioux Falls Traffic Club, VFW (life), Am. Legion. Republican. Roman Catholic. Clubs: Toastmasters (past gov. dist. 41, Disting. Toastmaster award, Outstanding Toastmaster award dist. 41, Hall of Fame 1977), Elks. Contbr. articles to nat. mags. Office: 3932 S Western Ave Sioux Falls SD 57105

TAPP, JUNE LOUIN, psychology educator; b. N.Y.C.; d. R.B. Louin and Ann Revier-Wacholder. B.A., magna cum laude in Sociology, U. So. Calif., 1951, M.S. in Ednl. Psychology, 1952; Ph.D. in Psychology, Syracuse U., 1963. Registered psychologist Ill. Instr. ednl. psychology and psychology St. Lawrence U., Canton, N.Y., 1952-55, adminstrv. asst. to dean Moran Crime Inst., 1954-60; asst. instr. in citizenship Maxwell Grad. Sch., Syracuse (N.Y.) U., 1955-56; tutor in psychology and sociology Albert Schweitzer Coll., Churwalden, Switzerland, 1957-58; asst. prof. psychology Harvey Mudd Coll., Claremont, Calif., 1961-64, organizer Behavioral Scis. program, 1961-64; lectr./cons. Indian Coll. Youth Project, U. Poona (India), 1963-64; asst. prof., research assoc. Com. on Human Devel., U. Chgo., 1964-67, assoc. prof. in social scis., 1967-72, faculty assoc. Com. South Asian Studies, 1968-72, co-investigator, project investigator, adminstr. Children's Socialization into Compliance Systems, 1965-70; sr. research social scientist Am. Bar Found., Chgo., 1967-72, affiliated scholar, 1972-74; fellow in law and psychology Harvard U. Law Sch., Cambridge, Mass., 1971-72; prof. psychology U. Calif.-San Diego, La Jolla, 1976-78, provost Revelle Coll., 1976-78, chmn. humanities program, 1976-77, chmn. law and society program, 1977-78; prof. child psychology and criminal justice studies, adj. prof. law, adj. prof. family studies U. Minn., Mpls., 1972—; participant U. Calif.-Irvine Mgmt. Inst., 1977; cons. and lectr. to profl. confs. and symposiums. Author: (with F. Krinsky) Ambivalent America: A Psycho-political Dialogue, 1971, (with F.J. Levine) Law, Justice and Individual in Society, 1977. Mem. editorial bds. numerous profl. jours.; manuscript reviewer for numerous profl. jours. Contbr. articles to profl. jours., chpts. to books. Mem. numerous civic, govtl. and profl. orgns. Recipient numerous civic and profl. awards; grantee in psychology and law from numerous profl. and govtl. agys. and orgns. Fellow Am. Psychol. Assn. (council 1981-84, chmn. com. on structure and function 1983-85); mem. Am. Council Edn., Am. Psychology-Law Soc. (pres. 1972-73), Soc. Psychol. Study Social Issues (pres. 1978-79), Soc. Research Child Devel., Internat. Assn. Polit. Psychology (trustee 1980-84), Assn. Advancement Psychology, Interam. Soc. Psychology (U.S. rep. 1981,. v.p. for sci. programs 1983—), Internat. Assn. Cross-Cultural Psychology, AAAS, Am. Legal Studies Assn., Internat. Assn. Philosophy Law and Social Philosophy (exec. com. 1974-75), Internat. Sociol. Assn., Law and Soc. Assn.(sec. 1973-79, trustee 1980-82), Soc. Exptl. Social Psychology. Address: Inst Child Devel 51 E River Rd U Minn Minneapolis MN 55455

TARGOWSKI, STANISLAW PYTKOWSKI, veterinarian, microbiologist; b. Nagorzyce, Poland, Nov. 13, 1940; came to U.S., 1967; naturalized, 1980; s. Waclaw Pytkowski and Maria Targowski; m. Hanna Pawlowski, Dec. 28, 1970. DVM, U. Warsaw, 1963; M.S., U. Wis., 1969, Ph.D., 1972. Diplomate Am. Coll. Veterinary Microbiologists. Research asst. U. Wis., Madison, 1967-72; research assoc. Purdue U., Lafayette, Ind., 1972-74; asst. prof. SUNY, Buffalo,

1974-78; assoc. prof. Ohio State U., Columbus, 1978-82; research leader Nat. Animal Disease Ctr., Ames, Iowa, 1982—. Contbr. articles to profl. jours. and chpts. to books. Grantee Am. Cancer Soc., NIH, USDA Sci. Fdn. and Adminstrn. Mem. Am. Assn. Immunologists, N.Y. Acad. Sci. AVMA, Am. Coll. Veterinary Microbiologists (bd. govs. 1982—). Democrat. Roman Catholic. Home: RR 1 Ames IA 50010 Office: Nat Animal Disease Ctr Dayton Ave P O Box 70 Ames IA 50010

TARKOWSKY, CYNTHIA ANN, pharmacist; b. Hanover, Pa., Apr. 28, 1956; d. Donald David and Donna Lou (Berkheimer) Wagner; m. John Tarkowsky, Sept. 2, 1979; 1 child, Stefanie Marie. B.S. in Pharmacy, Ohio No. U., 1979. Pharmacist, asst. mgr. Super-X Drugs, Inc., Mansfield, Ohio, 1979—. Mem. N.W. Ohio Pharm. Assn. Republican. Ukrainian Orthodox. Avocations: traveling; tennis. Home: 1596 Royal Oak Dr Mansfield OH 44906 Office: Super-X Drug Store 750 W 4th St Mansfield OH 44906

TARKOWSKY, JOHN, lawyer; b. Cleve., Jan. 16, 1954; s. Mykola and Antanina (Lape) T.; m. Cynthia Ann Wagner, Sept. 2, 1979; 1 dau., Stefanie Marie. B.A., Baldwin-Wallace Coll., 1975; J.D., Ohio No. U., 1978. Bar: Ohio 1978, U.S. Dist. Ct. (no. dist.) Ohio 1979. Ptnr. Baran & Baran Co. L.P.A., Mansfield, Ohio, 1978—; mng. atty. Tarkowsky-Baran Legal Services, Mansfield, 1978—. Mem. ABA, Richland County Bar Assn., Ohio State Bar Assn., Assn. Civil Trial Attys., Delta Theta Phi. Republican. Ukrainian Orthodox. Lodges: Kiwanis, Elks. Home: 1596 Royal Oak Dr Mansfield OH 44906 Office: Baran & Baran Co LPA 3 N Main St Mansfield OH 44902

TARLETON, BENNETT, arts administrator; b. Wadesboro, N.C., Apr. 9, 1943; s. Claude Bennett and Frances Brama (Covington) T.; m. Victoria Jane Smith, Jan. 29, 1977; children—Catherine Victoria, William Wiley. B.A. in English with honors, U. Mo., 1965; M.A. in Teaching, Harvard U., 1966; postgrad. U. Mo., 1969-71. Secondary English tchr. Great Neck Schs., N.Y., 1966-69; adminstrv. asst. U. Mo., Columbia, 1969-71; curriculum developer, coordinator CEMREL, Inc., St. Louis, 1971-76; coordinator Nat. Aesthetic Edn. Learning Ctr., Kennedy Ctr., Washington, 1976-79; dir. Alliance for Arts Edn., Kennedy Ctr., Washington, 1979-82; exec. dir. Dance St. Louis, 1982-83, Tenn. Arts Commn., Nashville, 1984—; arts edn. cons. U. Mich., Nat. Inventory Conf. on Learning Resources Related to East Asia, Nat. Com. Arts for Handicapped, U. Va. Sch. Edn., Fla. Dept. State; arts cons. Mo. Arts Council, Mississippi River Festival, Am. Film Festival, St. Louis Art Mus., Washington U. Film Arts Soc.; host Tenn. Arts!, Sta. WDCN-TV. Contbr. film reviews and criticism to profl. jours. Editor newsletter Alliance for Arts Education, 1980-82. Contbr. to KWMU-FM and WPLN-FM radio. Episcopalian. Club: Harvard (N.Y.C.). Home: 133 Taggart Ave Nashville TN 37205 Office: Tennessee Arts Commission 320 6th Ave N Suite 100 Nashville TN 37219

TARM, FELIX, internist, medical researcher; b. Tallinn, Estonia, May 22, 1939; came to U.S., 1950, naturalized, 1960; s. Feliks and Eugenia (Semyonov) T.; m. Kay A. Mallicoat, Sept. 2, 1962; children—Susan A., Michael V., Viktor F. M.D., U. Iowa, 1965. Diplomate Am. Bd. Internal Medicine. Intern Med. Coll. Va., Richmond, 1966; fellow Mayo Clinic, Rochester, Minn., 1970-73, assoc. cons., 1973; physician, researcher, cons. Internal Medicine Specialists PA, Hutchinson, Kans., 1973—; lectr. Hutchinson Hosp. Corp., 1973—. Mem. editorial bd. jour. Postgrad. Medicine, 1979. Contbr. articles to profl. jours. Served to maj. U.S. Army, 1967-70. Recipient Outstanding Achievement in Internal Medicine award Mayo Found., 1973; FDA grantee; Mem. Mayo Clinic Assn., AMA (Physician's Recognition award, 1983), Am. Soc. Internal Medicine. Libertarian. Avocations: writing poetry; racquetball. Home: 43 Linksland Hutchinson KS 67502 Office: Internal Medicine Specialists PA 2020 N Waldron Hutchinson KS 67502

TAROSKY, ROBERT EUGENE, cons. engr.; b. New Kensington, Pa., Apr. 29, 1942; s. Frank John and Mary Wanda (Bartos) T.; B.S. in Mech. and Aerospace Engring., Ill. Inst. Tech., 1970; m. Verna May Lucci, Feb. 1, 1964 (dec. 1976); m. 2d, Diane Carol Baran, Feb. 25, 1978; children—Michele Lynn, Renata Elizabeth. With Tuthill Pump Co., Alsip, Ill., 1963-68; with Gen. Environments Corp., Morton Grove, Ill., 1970-75, staff engr., 1970-75, cons. engr., 1975-79; with Hazard Engring. Inc., Morton Grove, 1975—, v.p., 1979—. Registered profl. engr., Ill. Mem. Nat. Soc. Profl. Engrs., Ill. Soc. Profl. Engrs., Soc. Automotive Engrs. Home: 818 N Kennicott Ave Arlington Heights IL 60004 Office: Hazard Engring Inc 6208 Lincoln Ave Morton Grove IL 60053

TARPY, THOMAS MICHAEL, lawyer; b. Columbus, Ohio, Jan. 4, 1945; s. Thomas Michael and Catherine G. (Sharshal) T.; m. Mary Patricia Canna, Sept. 9, 1967; children—Joshua Michael, Megan Patricia, Thomas Canna, John Patrick. A.B., John Carroll U., 1966; J.D., Ohio State U., 1972. Bar: Ohio 1969, U.S. Dist. Ct. (so. dist.) Ohio 1972, U.S. Dist. Ct. (no. dist.) Ohio 1974, U.S. Ct. Appeals (6th cir.) 1982. Assoc. Vorys, Sater, Seymour & Pease, Columbus, 1969-76, ptnr., 1977-85. Chmn. Columbus Graphics Commn., 1980; mem. Columbus Area Leadership Program, 1975. Served with U.S. Army, 1969-75. Mem. ABA, Ohio State Bar Assn., Columbus Bar Assn. Office: Liebert Corp 1050 Dearborn Dr Box 29186 Columbus OH 43229

TARRANT, MARGARET ELIZABETH, lawyer; b. Springfield, Mass., July 15, 1952; d. James Joseph and Kathleen (O'Brien) T.; m. Michael Patrick Carlton, Sept. 20, 1980. B.A., Franklin & Marshall Coll., 1974; J.D., George Mason U., 1978; LL.M., London Sch. Econs. and Pol. Sci., 1984. Bar: Va. 1979, Wis. 1981. Trial atty. U.S. Dept. Justice Criminal Div., Washington, 1979-81; asst. dist. atty. Milwaukee County, Wis., 1981—. Mem. Va. State Bar Assn., Wis. State Bar Assn. Democrat. Roman Catholic. Home: 2572 N Prospect Ave Milwaukee WI 53211 Office: Milwaukee County Dist Attys Office 821 W State St Milwaukee WI 53233

TARTOF, DAVID, medical educator, researcher; b. Detroit, Sept. 15, 1945; s. Herman Harry and Margaret (Bensie) T.; m. Linda Abbey Yee, May 9, 1970; children—Rachel, Sara. B.S., Mich. State U., 1966; M.D., U. Mich., 1970; Ph.D., U. Chgo., 1978. Diplomate Am. Bd. Internal Medicine, Am. Bd. Rheumatology. Intern, U. Ill.-Chgo., 1970-71, med. resident, 1973-75; research fellow U. Chgo., 1975-78, rheumatology fellow, 1978-80, asst. prof. medicine, 1980—; mem. med. bd. Ill. Lupus Soc., Chgo., 1983—. Contbr. articles to profl. jours. Served to capt. U.S. Army, 1971-73; Viet Nam. Research fellow Chgo. Community Trust, 1982. Mem. Am. Rheumatism Assn., Am. Assn. Immunologists, Sigma Xi. Avocation: Photography. Home: 1640 E 50th St Apt 18B Chicago IL 60615 Office: Univ Chicago 950 E 59th St Chicago IL 60637

TARVER, MAE-GOODWIN, consulting company executive; b. Selma, Ala., Aug. 9, 1916; d. Hartwell Hill and R. Louise (Wilkins) T.; B.S. in Chemistry, U. Ala., 1939, M.S., 1940. Project supr. container shelflife Continental Can Co., Inc., Chgo., 1941-48, project engr. stats., 1948-54, quality control cons., research statistician, 1954-77; pres., prin. cons. Quest Assocs., Ltd., Park Forest, Ill., 1978-81; adj. assoc. prof. biology dept. Ill. Inst. Tech., Chgo., 1957-81. Bd. dirs. Ash Street Coop., Park Forest, Ill., 1976-85. Fellow Am. Soc. Quality Control (Joe Lisy award 1961, Edward J. Oakley award 1975, E.L. Grant award 1983); mem. Inst. Food Technologists, Soc. Women Engrs., Am. Statis. Assn., Sigma Xi. Home: 130 26th St Park Forest IL 60466

TASCH, ALCUIN (BUD) MARTIN, advertising and public relations agency executive; b. Oak Park, Ill., Apr. 21, 1924; s. John Leo and Anne Catherine (Smith) T.; m. Joyce Madden, Jan. 17, 1955; children—Cuin, Gail, Martin, William, Robert. Student Idaho State Tchrs. Coll., 1943, U. Okla., 1944. Ptnr., co-founder Aerial Photography, Chgo., 1946-60; pres. Alcuin Tasch & Co., River Forest, Ill., 1958—, Cuill Advt. Co., Chgo., 1963—. Served to lt. comdr. AC, USN, World War II. Decorated Air medal, 6 others. Mem. Naval Commandery, Naval Airmen of Am. (past nat. comdr. 1949-50). Republican. Roman Catholic. Clubs: Press, Germania. Home and Office: 7979 Chicago Ave River Forest IL 60305

TASKER, FRED L., physician, educator; b. Gloucester, Mass., May 13, 1931; s. Fred L. and Frances C. (Spiller) T.; m. Edna May Taylor, June 27, 1955; children—Gregory Allen, Patricia Ann, Cynthia Ann, Jennifer Sue. B.S., Calvin Coll., Grand Rapids, Mich., 1961; M.S. in Physiology and Pharmacology, U. N.D., 1963; M.D., U. Kans.-Kansas City, 1966. Intern, Wesley Med. Ctr., Wichita, 1966-67, resident in surgery, 1967-68; dir. emergency room and dept. St. Joseph Hosp., Wichita, 1969-70; resident in ophthalmology Eye & Ear Hosp., Pitts., 1970-73; practice medicine specializing in ophthalmology, Sandusky, Ohio, 1973—; chief of staff Good Samaritan Hosp., Sandusky, 1982-83; clin. asst. prof. surgery Med. Coll. Ohio, Toledo, 1975—; cons. ophthalmologist Providence Hosp., Meml. Hosp., Sandusky. Served with USAF, 1950-54. Mem. AMA, Ohio State Med. Assn., Erie County Med. Soc., Am. Acad. Ophthalmology, Internat. Assn. Ophthalmic Surgeons, Sigma Xi. Republican. Club: Nat. Wildlife Assn. Contbr. article in field. Office: 521 W Perkins Ave Sandusky OH 44870

TASSANI, SALLY MARIE, marketing and graphics communications executive; b. Teaneck, N.J., Dec. 30, 1948; d. Peter R. and Marie I. T. Grad. Am. U., 1970; B.A., Am. U., 1970. Elem. tchr., Washington, 1970-73; asst. prodn. and promotion mgr. First Nat. Bank of Chgo., 1973-74; exec. dir. Jack O'Grady Graphics, Inc., Chgo., 1974-76; creative dir. Dimensional Mktg., Inc., Chgo., 1976-78; pres. Nexus, Inc., Chgo., 1978—. Mem. Women in Healthcare, Women in Design, Am. Mgmt. Assoc. Office: 233 E Erie St Suite 708 Chicago IL 60611

TATARU, TERRY L., lawyer; b. Canton, Ohio, Mar. 20, 1948; s. John N. and Colleen June (John) T.; m. Roberta S. Mitchell, Oct. 10, 1980; 1 stepchild, Heather Mitchell. B.A., Bowling Green U., 1971; J.D., Capital U., 1975. Bar: Ohio 1975. Asst. atty. gen. State of Ohio, Columbus, 1975-77; sole practice, Columbus, 1977—; staff atty. Legal Clinic, Capital U., Columbus, 1980; spl. counsel Ohio Atty. Gen.'s Office, Columbus, 1977—. Mem. ABA, Ohio Bar Assn., Columbus Bar Assn., Assn. Trial Lawyers Am., Ohio Acad. Trial Lawyers, Franklin County Trial Lawyers Assn. Home: 1901 King Ave Upper Arlington OH 43212 Office: 137 E Livingston Ave Columbus OH 43215

TATE, DAVID GENE, health sciences educator, psychotherapist; b. Lafayette, Ind., Feb. 9, 1946; s. Vernon Eugene and Marjorie Glenn (Powell) T.; m. Maureen Ann Krug, Mar. 11, 1972; 1 child, Ryan Churchill. B.S., Purdue U., 1970, M.S., 1980, Ph.D., 1985. Instr., Purdue U., West Lafayette, Ind., 1979-80, instr., supr. in counseling personnel services, 1980-82, instr. edn., 1982-84, grad. instr. health scis., 1984—, dir. clin. med. tech. program, dir. student services Sch. Health Scis., 1985—; dir. student services St. Joseph's Coll., Rensselaer, Ind., 1981-82; cons. Warren Co. Sheriff's Dept., Williamsport, 1984—; adj. faculty Ind. Affiliated Clin. Hosps., 1985; nat. liaison mem. Am. Personnel Guidance Assn., Washington, 1982. Pres., County Park and Recreation Bd., Williamsport, 1983—; co-founder Tippecanoe Council on Alcohol Abuse Lafayette chapt., 1983; co-founder 360 House for Alcohol Abuse, Purdue Univ., 1984; precint committeeman Republican Party, Warren County, 1984—. Mem. Menninger Found., Am. Assn. for Counseling and Devel., Am. Psychol. Assn., AMA (curriculum edn. com.), Eta Sigma Gamma, Sigma Iota, Omicron Delta Kappa, Kappa Delta Pi, Theta Xi. Clubs: Health Sci. (Purdue) (advisor 1984—), Grad. Student Orgn. (Purdue) (pres. 1984—). Avocations: weightlifting; classical music; match pistol shooting. Home: 307 E Monroe St Williamsport IN 47993 Office: Sch of Health Science Purdue Unif Pharmacy Bldg #156 West Lafayette IN 47906

TATE, JEAN FRANK, chemist; b. Roseland, Ark., Nov. 19, 1941; s. Jean Virgil and Peggy (Brady) T.; m. Leila Joyce Livingston, Aug. 17, 1962; children—Gene F., Rebecca L., Jonathan W. B.S. in Chemistry, U. Mich., 1963. Exptl. chemist Buick Motor Div., Flint, Mich., 1963-72; sr. chemist USS Chemicals, Ironton, Ohio, 1976—. Pres. bd. Wheelersburg Local Schs., Ohio, 1984, bd. v.p., 1982, 83-85; exec. com. Ohio Sch. Bds. Assn., South East Region, 1985, chmn., 1985. Mem. Am. Chem. Soc., Ohio Sch. Bds. Assn. Home: 1566 Lawson St Wheelersburg OH 45694 Office: Wheelersburg Local Sch Dist Wheelersburg OH 45694

TATE, PAUL HAMILTON, airline executive, accountant; b. Canton, Ohio, Apr. 7, 1951; s. James C. and Grace E. (Polivy) T.; m. Donna Lynn Mueller, Sept. 23, 1978; 1 child, Tiffany. B.A., Northwestern U., 1973, M.M., 1975. C.P.A., Ill. Page, U.S. Ho. of Reps., Washington, 1967-69; auditor U.S. Gen. Acctg. Office, Chgo., 1974; mgr. cons. Arthur Young & Co., Chgo., 1975-80; controller Midway Airlines, Chgo., 1980-83, v.p. adminstrn., controller, 1984—. Mem. Am. Inst. C.P.A.s. Office: Midway Airlines Inc 5700 S Cicero Ave Chicago IL 60638

TATEL, FREDRIC STEVEN, pediatric dentist; b. Chgo., Aug. 10, 1943; s. Louis Leonard and Helen Dorothy (Aronson) T.; m. Faye Judith Goldfarb, July 23, 1967; children—Jennifer Beth, Samuel Gilbert. Student, Northwestern U., 1961-63; D.D.S., 1967. Lic. pediatric dentistry, Ill. Intern and resident Children's Hosp., Pitts., 1967-68. Practice pediatric dentistry, Northbrook, Ill., 1969—, Glenwood, Ill., 1972—. Mem. ADA (Cert. of Recognition 1979), Ill. Dental Assn., Chgo. Dental Assn., Am. Soc. Dentistry for Children, Am. Acad. Pediatric Dentistry, Ill. Acad. Pediatric Dentistry, Am. Dental Vols. for Israel (life). Avocations: sports; art; music. Office: Fredric S Tatel DDS 18430 S Halsted St Glenwood IL 60425

TATOOLES, CONSTANTINE JOHN, cardiovascular and thoracic surgeon; b. Chgo., May 7, 1936; B.S., Albion (Mich.) Coll., 1958; M.S. in Physiology, Loyola U., Chgo., 1961, M.D., 1961; m. Betty Ann, Jan. 30, 1960; children—Julie Denise, Anton John, Jon William. Research asst. Loyola U., 1958-59, research asso., 1959-60; intern U. Chgo. Hosps., 1961-62, resident in surgery, 1962-68, instr. in surgery, 1966-68; clin. assoc. surgery Nat. Heart Inst.; sr. registrar in surgery Gt. Ormond St. Hosp. for Children, London, 1968-69; practice medicine specializing in cardiovascular and thoracic surgery, Chgo., 1969—; asst. prof. surgery and physiology, Loyola U., 1969-73, attending surgeon, 1969-73; asso. attending surgeon thoracic and cardiovascular surgery Cook County Hosp., Chgo., 1969-73, chmn. dept. cardio-thoracic surgery, 1969-78, attending surgeon, 1970, lectr. in cardiac surgery, 1970; chief cardiovascular and thoracic surgery Abraham Lincoln Sch. Medicine, U. Ill., Chgo., 1973-74, asso. prof. surgery, 1973-76, prof. surgery, 1976; attending surgeon U. Ill., 1973; chmn. dept. cardiothoracic surgery St. Francis Hosp., Evanston, Ill., 1977-78, St. Mary's of Nazareth Hosp., Chgo., 1981—; chmn. Chgo. Inst. for Heart and Lung, 1972; chmn. bd. Penda Corp., Portgage, Wis., 1981-85; pres., chmn. Am. Family Life Ins. Assn., Chgo.; mem. Chgo. Bd. Trade. Fellow A.C.S., Am. Coll. Cardiology, Am. Coll. Chest Physicians (chmn. motion picture div., 1975-76); mem. Am. Assn. Thoracic Surgery, Am. Heart Assn. (council on cardiovascular surgery), AMA, Am. Thoracic Soc., Assn. for Acad. Surgery, Chgo. Heart Assn. (council on cardiovascular surgery), Chgo. Med. Soc., Chgo. Surg. Soc., Ill. State Med. Soc., Inst. of Medicine Chgo., Royal Soc. Medicine London (Eng.), Soc. Thoracic Surgeons, Chgo. Thoracic Soc. (pres. 1981), A.G. Morrow Soc. (exec. dir.), Warren J. Cole Soc. Contbr. to films in field, articles to profl. publs. Office: 800 Austin St Evanston IL 60202

TATTERSALL, PAUL A., commodities exchange executive; b. Pawtucket, R.I., Sept. 23, 1934; s. Roger A. and Doris (Darling) T.; m. Patricia A. Gallaher, Apr. 30, 1960; children—Jennifer, Sarah. B.A., Weleyan U., 1956; M.B.A., Columbia U., 1958. Media industry marketing mgr. IBM, White Plains, N.Y., 1957-71; asst. gen. mgr. The Washington Post, Washington, 1971-75; sr. v.p. Mpls. Star and Tribune Co., 1975-81; pres. Mpls. Grain Exchange, 1982—, also dir.; dir. Nat. Futures Assn., Chgo., 1982—. Bd. dirs. Mpls. Orchestral Assn. Served to sgt. U.S. Army, 1958-64. Club: Minneapolis. Home: 4802 Golf Terr Edina MN 55424 Office: Mpls Grain Exchange 400 S 4th St Minneapolis MN 55415

TAUB, ROBERT GOLDE, ophthalmologist; b. Chgo., Sept. 16, 1928; m. Sheila K. Kaplan, June 15, 1952; children—Jay, Susan, Jodie. B.S., Northwestern U., 1949, M.D., 1951; M.S. in Ophthalmology, U. Minn., 1955. Diplomate Am. Bd. Ophthalmology. Intern Michael Reese Hosp., Chgo., 1951-52; fellow in ophthalmology Mayo Clinic, Rochester, Minn., 1952-55; instr. ophthalmology Northwestern U., Chgo., 1955-65, assoc., 1965—; cons. Armour Research Div., 1955-59; attending ophthalmologist Columbus Hosp., Cuneo Hosp., Children's Meml. Hosp., Chgo. Contbr. articles to profl. jours. Bd. dirs. Nat. Eye Research Found.; mem. Michigan City Area Sch. Bd., Ind., 1970-82. Fellow ACS; mem. Mayo Clinic Alumni Assn. (pres. 1969-70), Phi Beta Kappa, Sigma Xi, Alpha Omega Alpha, Phi Rho Sigma. Jewish. Home: 666 N Lake Shore Dr Chicago IL 60611 Office: Taub Taub Taub & Taub Ophthalmology 6 N Michigan Ave Chicago IL 60602

TAUKE, THOMAS J., congressman; b. Dubuque, Iowa, Oct. 11, 1950; B.A., Loras Coll., 1972; J.D., U. Iowa, 1974. Mem. firm Curnan, Fitzsimmons, Schilling and Tauke, 1976-80; mem. Iowa Ho. of Reps., 1975-79; mem. 96th-99th Congresses from 2d Dist. Iowa. Chmn., Dubuque County Republican Com., 1972-74, 2d Congressional Dist. Rep. Com., 1974-77; trustee Mt. Mercy Coll. Mem. Iowa Bar Assn., Dubuque County Bar Assn., Cedar Rapids C. of C., Dubuque C. of C. Roman Catholic. Club: Rotary. Office: 2244 Rayburn House Office Bldg Washington DC 20515

TAURMAN, EUGENE, corporation executive; b. Monte Vista, Colo., Mar. 8, 1936; s. Louis Frederick and Ruth W.E. (Langshaw) T.; m. Carol Ann Taurman, June 21, 1939; children—Jonathan Patrick, Sarah Jane. A.A., Riverside City Coll., 1956; B.S. in Indsl. Engring., U. Calif., 1959. Indsl. engr., Los Angeles, 1959-61, sr. indsl. engr. (MSA), Pitts., 1961-65; application engr. Bendix, Elmira, N.Y., 1966-68, with products, 1968-72, dir. mktg., South Bend, Ind., 1972-82; exec. v.p., gen. mgr. Hayes Ind. Brake Inc., Mequon, Wis., 1984—. Mem. Soc. Automotive Engrs., Mequon C. of C. Republican. Presbyterian. Office: Hayes Ind Brake Inc 5800 W Donges Bay Rd Mequon WI 53092

TAUSCHER, MICHAEL JOHN, lawyer; b. Chgo., Aug. 24, 1955; s. John Walter and Mary Claire (Cline) T.; m. Kathleen Loretta Mancuso, May 26, 1984. B.S. with high honors, Mich. State U., 1977; J.D. cum laude, Wayne State U., 1980. Bar: Mich. 1980, U.S. Dist. Ct. (ea. dist.) Mich. 1980, Fla. 1981, U.S. Ct. Appeals (6th cir.) 1981. Assoc. Jenkins, Nystrom & Sterlacci, Southfield, Mich., 1980-84, Damm & Smith, P.C., Detroit, 1984—. Roman Catholic. Office: Damm & Smith PC 400 Renaissance Ctr Suite 2300 Detroit MI 48243

TAVENOR, ALBERT SAMUEL, tire company executive; b. Indpls., Feb. 10, 1926; s. William Earnest and Martha (Brunner) T.; m. Wilma Mae Rooker, Sept. 5, 1947; children—Albert Paul, Janet Ruth Tavenor Heath, Thomas Joseph. B.S., Purdue U., 1946; M.S., Butler U., 1948. Dir. quality assurance Uniroyal Tire Co., Detroit, 1976-79, factory mgr., 1979-81, v.p. research and devel., Troy, Mich., 1981-84, v.p. ops., 1984—. Patentee in field. Served to lt. (j.g.) USN, 1944-46. Republican. Congregationalist. Avocation: stamp collecting. Home: 21356 Littlestone Rd Harper Woods MI 48225 Office: Uniroyal Tire Co 3290 W Big Beaver Rd Suite 200 Troy MI 48225

TAYLOR, ANNA DIGGS, judge; b. Washington, Dec. 9, 1932; d. Virginius Douglass and Hazel (Bramlette) Johnston; m. S. Martin Taylor, May 22, 1976; children—Douglass Johnston Diggs, Carla Cecile Diggs. B.A., Barnard Coll., 1954; LL.B., Yale U., 1957. Bar: Mich. 1961. Atty. Office Solicitor, Dept. Labor, 1957-60; asst. prosecutor Wayne County (Mich.), 1961-62; asst. U.S. atty. Eastern Dist. of Mich., 1966; ptnr. firm Zwerding, Maurer, Diggs & Papp, Detroit, 1970-75; asst. corp. counsel City of Detroit, 1975-79; U.S. dist. judge Eastern Dist. Mich., Detroit, 1979—; adj. prof. labor law Wayne State U. Law Sch., Detroit, 1976-77. Trustee Receiving Hosp. Detroit, Met. Hosp., Detroit, Detroit Sci. Ctr., Planned Parenthood League, Detroit, Neighborhood Service Orgn., Detroit Symphony, Sinai Hosp., Episcopal Diocese of Mich., United Found., Community Found. Southeastern Mich. Mem. Fed. Bar Assn., Nat. Lawyers Guild, State Bar Mich., Wolverine Bar Assn., Women Lawyers Assn. Mich. Democrat. Episcopalian. Office: 211 Fed Courthouse Detroit MI 48226

TAYLOR, BOWEN EVERITT, physician; b. Scottsbluff, Nebr., Feb. 18, 1919; s. Ross V. and Anna Marie (Eacritt) T.; m. Caroline S. Thompson, Sept. 4, 1940; children—John, Bruce, Jean, Steven, Nancy, Scott. A.B., U. Nebr., 1940, M.D., 1943; M.S. in Medicine, U. Minn., 1950. Practice internal medicine and cardiology West Point, Nebr., 1946, Lincoln Clinic, Nebr., 1951—; resident Mayo Found., Rochester, Minn., 1947-51; asst. prof. internal medicine U. Nebr., Omaha, 1963—; chief staff Bryan Meml. Hosp., Lincoln, 1975-76. Served to capt. M.C., U.S. Army, 1944-46. Recipient Mayo Found. Alumni award, 1950. Fellow ACP (gov. Nebr. chpt. 1980-84), Am. Coll. Cardiology (gov. Nebr. chpt. 1960-63), Council Clin. Cardiology of Am. Heart Assn.; mem. Am. Soc. Internal Medicine, Nebr. Soc. Internal Medicine (pres. 1960-61), Nebr. Heart Assn. (pres. 1963-64), Lancaster County Med. Soc. (pres. 1980-81), AMA, Nebr. Med. Soc., Sigma Xi, Phi Gamma Delta, Phi Rho Sigma. Avocations: gardening, hunting. Home: 1310 Crestdale Rd Lincoln NE 68510 Office: Lincoln Clinic PC POB 81009 3145 O St Lincoln NE 68501

TAYLOR, CHARLES LEE, ceramic company official; b. Sedalia, Mo., Jan. 27, 1953; s. Charles Emil and Margaret Francis (Maples) T.; m. Sherry Ann Summers, Aug. 16, 1971. B.B.A., Central Mo. State U., 1980. Shift mgr. Pitts. Corning Corp., Sedalia, 1976-79, supr. quality control, 1979-81, mgr. quality and environ. control, 1981-84, mgr. quality and environ. control and process, 1984—. Roman Catholic. Home: Route 1 Box 98 Smithton MO 65350 Office: Pitts Corning Corp PO Box 716 Sedalia MO 65301-0716

TAYLOR, DALE, advertising executive; b. N.Y.C., Dec. 25, 1945; s. John Elsworth and Lannie (Haynes) T.; m. Toni Taylor, Aug. 17, 1968; children—Anne, Dale, Amelia. B.J., Northwestern U., 1967, M.J., 1968. Dir. communication Searle Anaalytic Co., Vhgo., 1973-75; exec. v.p. Arnold, Hinton, Hoff, Chgo., 1975-77; v.p. Abelson Frankle, Chgo., 1977-81; pres. Abelson Taylor, Chgo., 1981—. Served to sgt. AUS, 1968-70: Korea. Mem. Biomed. Mktg. Assn. (bd. dirs. 1985). Home: 249 Colony Ct Bloomingdale IL 60108 Office: Abelson Taylor 35 E Wacker Dr Chicago IL 60601

TAYLOR, DANIEL JENNINGS, classics educator; b. Covington, Ky., Sept. 1, 1941; s. William Jennings and Tabitha Louise (Thompson) T.; m. Donna Baker, Aug. 2, 1966; children—Karissa Louise, Narella Edna. B.A., Lawrence Coll., 1963; M.A., U. Wash., 1965, Ph.D., 1970. Instr. Univ. Ill., Urbana, 1968-70, asst., 1970-74; asst. prof. Lawrence U., Appleton, Wis., 1974-78, assoc. prof., 1978—; v.p. Lawrence U., Appleton, 1977-78, 1980-81; exec. sec., treas. Latin League Wis., Appleton, 1975—. Author Declinatio, 1975. Mem. editorial bd. Historiographia Linguística, Ottawa, Ont. Can., 1973. Contbr. articles to profl. jours. Fellow NEH, Florence, Italy, 1980-81. Mem. Am. Philol. Assn. (Excellence in Teaching award 1983), Am. Classical League, Archeol. Inst. Am., Wis. Acad. Scis., Arts & Letters, Mortar Bd., Eta Sigma Phi. Home: 2 Winona Ct Appleton WI 54911 Office: Lawrence Univ Box 599 Appleton WI 54912

TAYLOR, DAVID GEORGE, banker; b. Charlevoix, Mich., July 29, 1929; s. Frank Flagg and Bessie (Strayer) T.; m. Helen Alexander, Jan. 14, 1978; children—David, Amy. B.S., Denison U., 1951; M.B.A., Northwestern U., 1953. With Continental Ill. Nat. Bank and Trust Co. Chicago, 1961—, asst. cashier, 1961-64, 2d v.p., 1964-66, v.p., 1966-72, sr. v.p., 1972-74, exec. v.p., 1974-80, exec. v.p., treas., 1980-83, vice chmn., 1983-84, 84—, chmn., 1984. Mem. Dealer Bank Assn. Com. on Glass-Steagall Reform, 1985—. Bd. dirs. Evanston Hosp., Glenbrook Hosp.; trustee Art Inst. Chgo., 1981—; advisor J.L. Kellogg Grad. Sch. Mgmt., Northwestern U., 1984—. Served to lt. USN, 1953-56. Mem. Pub. Securities Assn. (bd. dirs. 1977-78, chmn. 1977, treas. 1978), Govt. and Fed. Agys. Securities Com. (chmn. bd. dirs. 1982-83), Assn. Res. City Bankers (asset/liability com/govt. relations com. 1983—), Assn. Bank Holding Cos., Internat. Monetary Conf. Republican. Presbyterian. Office: Continental Ill Nat Bank and Trust Co Chicago 231 S LaSalle St Chicago IL 60697

TAYLOR, DAVID RIDDLE, JR., advertising executive; b. Waycross, Ga., May 21, 1948; s. David Riddle and Martha Eleanor (McNary) T.; m. Carole Ann Fitzpatrick, July 11, 1970; children—Michelle, Caroline, David John. B.B.A., Kent State U., 1970; M.B.A., U. Dayton, 1977. Advt. asst. DAP, Inc., Dayton, Ohio, 1970-72, merchandising services coordinator, 1972-74, asst. product mgr., 1974-76; account exec. Parker Advt. Co., Dayton, 1976-80, v.p., 1980-82, v.p., dir., 1982—. Mem. Miami Valley Mil. Affairs Assn., Sales and Mktg. Execs. Assn., Dayton Advt. Club, Am. Assn. Advt. Agys. Republican. Methodist. Clubs: Patrons; Sycamore Creek Country (Springboro, Ohio); Quail Run Racquet (Kettering, Ohio); Optimists Internat. (bd. dirs. 1973-81, v.p. 1979-81). Avocations: golfing, swimming, skiing, tennis. Home: 6230 Millbank Dr Dayton OH 45459 Office: Parker Advt Co 3077 S Kettering Blvd Dayton OH 45439

TAYLOR, DONALD, diversified capital goods manufacturing company executive; b. Worcester, Mass., June 2, 1927; s. John A.B. and Alice M. (Weaver) T.; B.S. in Mech. Engring., Worcester Poly. Inst., 1949; grad. Mgmt. Devel. Program, Northeastern U., 1962, Advanced Mgmt. Program, Harvard U., 1979; m. Ruth L. Partridge, June 2, 1950; children—Linda Taylor Robertson, Donald, Mark, John. Various managerial positions Geo. J. Meyer Mfg. Co., 1951-69; pres. Geo. J. Meyer Mfg. div. A-T-O Inc., 1969; exec. v.p. Nordberg div. Rex Chainbelt, Inc., 1969-73; v.p. ops. Rexnord Inc., 1973-78, pres. Nordberg machinery group, 1973-78, pres., chief operating officer, 1978-85, vice chmn., chief exec. officer, 1985—; dir. Harnischfeger Corp., Johnson Controls Inc., Marine Corp., Marine Nat. Exchange Bank. Mem. adv. bd. Center for Mgmt. Devel., Northeastern U.; bd. dirs., vice chmn. Met. Milw.

YMCA; mem. Nat. Council YMCA's; bd. dirs. Milw. Symphony Orch.; div. chmn. Milw. United Way Campaign, 1971, unit chmn., 1972; campaign co-chmn. United Performing Arts Fund, 1976. Served with USNR, 1945-46, 50-54. Registered profl. engr., Mass. Mem. ASME. Clubs: Milw. Country, Milw. Athletic, Town, Univ. (Milw.). Office: Rexnord Inc 350 N Sunny Slope Brookfield WI 53005

TAYLOR, DONALD FRANCIS, manufacturing company executive; b. Milw., May 14, 1914; s. Francis Edwin and Anna L. (Gatien) T.; m. Eileen M. Weber; children—Sandra M. Taylor Annis, Richard L. Student Merrill Comml. Coll., U. Wis., Marquette U. Pres., Taylor Insulation Co., Merrill, Wis., Bay Insulation Co., Green Bay, Wis., Basic Wire Products, Columbus, Ohio; chmn. bd. Merrill Mfg. Corp. Mem. Wis. State C. of C. (past pres.), U.S. C. of C. (past dir.), Wis. Assn. Mfrs. and Commerce (dir.). Republican. Roman Catholic. Clubs: Wausau (Wis.); Merrill Rotary (past pres.) Home: N 2790 Taylor Dr Merrill WI 54452 Office: 236 S Genesee St Merrill WI 54452

TAYLOR, EDMUND EUGENE, metrologist; b. Eaton, Ind., May 30, 1924; s. Howard and Guila Beatrice (Barley) T. D.Sc. in Elec. Engring., Sussex Coll. Tech., Eng., 1983. Electronic insp. Farnsworth TV Corp., Marion, Ind., 1942-43; radio facsimile developer RCA, Indpls., 1943-44; elec. metrologist Mallory Components Group, Indpls., 1944—; owner, chief engr. Taylor Elec. Lab., Indpls., 1943—; curator, historian, archivist Ed Taylor Radio Mus., Indpls., 1973—. Author: Taylorvision, 1984. Contbr. articles to profl. jours. Patentee in field. Mem. Instrument Soc. Am., Internat. Soc. Profl. Inventors, Antique Wireless Assn., Tesla Coil Builders Assn., Ind. Hist. Radio Soc. (founder), Indpls. Radio Club, Mallory Mgmt. Club, Am. Guild Organists, Am. Theatre Organ Soc., Ind. Jaguar Club. Home: 245 N Oakland Ave Indianapolis IN 46201 Office: Mallory Components Group 3029 E Washington St Indianapolis IN 46206

TAYLOR, GENE, congressman: b. nr. Sarcoxie, Mo., Feb. 10, 1928; student S.W. Mo. State Coll., Springfield; m. Dorothy Wooldridge, July 26, 1947; children—Linda Kay, Larry Eugene. Mayor, Sarcoxie, 1954-60; mem. 93d-99th Congresses from 7th Mo. Dist. Republican nat. committeeman, 1966-72. Mem. Mo. N.G., 1948-49. Mem. Mo., Sarcoxie chambers commerce. Methodist. Lodges: Masons, Shriners, Lions. Office: 2134 Rayburn House Office Bldg Washington DC 20515

TAYLOR, HARRY MARSHALL, purchasing dir.; b. Bartonville, Ill., June 19, 1920; s. Harry H. and Ruth V. (Church) T.; student public schools; m. Lucille E. Staley, Sept. 4, 1955; children—Ronald Lee, Connie Sue. Apprentice machinist Caterpillar Tractor Co., 1939-42, journeyman machinist, 1942-45; journeyman machinist E.M. Smith & Co., Peoria, Ill., 1945-74, gen. mgr., 1974-78, purchasing dir., 1978—. Served with USMCR, World War II. Mem. Soc. Mfg. Engrs., Nat. Rifle Assn., Travelers Protective Assn., Audubon Soc., Am. Legion (post comdr. 1951-52, 71-72, fin. officer 1972—). Methodist. Clubs: Spoon River Sportsmen Forty and Eight, Wildlife, Franklin, Hamilton. Office: 826 W Detweiller Dr Peoria IL 61615

TAYLOR, HOWARD RICHARD, JR., former health care organization adminstrator; b. Cleve., Sept. 22, 1919; s. Howard Richard and Ednajean (Wallace) T.; A.B., Allegheny Coll., 1941; m. Barbara MacDonald Shenk, Oct. 18, 1946; children—Margaret Jean Shenk Taylor, Susan McDonald Taylor Scherbel, Lynne Wallace Taylor. Reporter, Butler (Pa.) Eagle, 1941; account exec. Griswold-Eshleman, Cleve., 1946-47; asst. to pres. and v.p. Fenn Coll., Cleve., 1950-56; asst. to pres. Carling Brewing Co., Cleve., 1956-60; owner, pres. Howard Richard Taylor & Assocs., Pub. Relations, Cleve., 1961-71; dir. devel. and pub. relations Cleve. Clinic Fedn., 1971-79, exec. asst. to chmn. bd. govs., 1979-85. Trustee, Cleve. Health Mus., 1954-60; trustee Cleve. Center for Alcoholism, 1957-68, pres., 1965-68; trustee Beech Brook, Cleve., 1972—, Fairfax Found., Cleve., 1972—, Center for Human Services, Cleve., 1976-80. Served with USMC, 1941-45, 47-50. Decorated Silver Star, Bronze Star with oak leaf cluster. Mem. Nat. Assn. Hosp. Devel., Am. Mktg. Assn. Republican. Presbyterian. Clubs: Country, Union. Home: 31100 Fairmount Blvd Pepper Pike OH 44124

TAYLOR, JACK PAUL, superintendant of schools; b. Wapakonata, Ohio, Jan. 27, 1931; s. George T. and Frieda (Moeller) T.; B.S., Bowling Green State U., 1953, M.S., 1954; Ph.D., Ohio State U., 1966; m. Berneda Florence Ruck, Dec. 27, 1953; children—Thomas Roberts, Carole Jane. Sr. social studies instr., guidance Perrysburg (Ohio) Schs., 1954-56; high sch. prin. Liberty Center Schs., 1956-59; supt. schs., Crestline, Ohio, 1959-62, Xenia, Ohio, 1964-67, Saginaw, Mich., 1967-76, Shaker Heights, Ohio, 1977-82, Omaha, 1982-84; exec. Cleve. Pub. Schs., 1984-85; supt. schs. City of Waukegan, Ill., 1985—; coordinator Sch. Mgmt. Inst., Columbus, Ohio; vis. prof. Central State U.; adj. prof. Cleve. State U.; cons. grad. faculty Ohio State U.; host Taylor on Edn. Show Cox Cable, Omaha. Co-author: Who Runs America's Schools. Pres., Future Tchrs. Ohio, 1952; mem. Library Bd., Crestline, 1959-62; mem. Human Relations Commn., Mayor's Com. Concern; chmn. Nat. Consortium on Ednl. Evaluation. Mem. exec. com. Young Republicans Ohio, 1950-54. Chmn. edn. div.; bd. dirs. United Way of Midlands; bd. dirs. United Fund, Jr. Achievement, YMCA; mem. exec. com. Cuyahoga Council for Handicapped Children; mem. Lt. Gov.'s Task Force on Edn.; pres. Saginaw Symphony Assn.; trustee United Appeal Crestline, Shaker Lake Regional Nature Center; bd. dirs. Ohio Adminstrs.; mem. planning com. Boy Scouts Am., Omaha. Action Com. Recipient Worth McClure award Am. Assn. Sch. Adminstrs., 1964; E.E. Lewis award in edn. Ohio State U., also Frontier's Internat. service award of year, 1973. Mem. Xenia Area C. of C. (dir.), Distributive Edn. Clubs Am. (past nat. v.p.), Mich. Middle Cities Edn. Assn. (pres.), Bowling Green State U. Alumni Assn. (trustee), Buckeye Assn. Sch. Adminstrs. (legis. com.), Ohio Soc. N.Y., Delta Tau Delta, Omicron Delta Kappa, Pi Sigma Alpha, Phi Delta Kappa. Mem. United Ch. Christ. Rotarian. Club: Edliners (pres.) (Ohio State U.). Home: 901 Sunset Terr Waukegan IL 60087 Office: 1201 N Sheridan Rd Waukegan IL 60085

TAYLOR, JACKSON H., songwriter, music publisher, record producer; b. Madison, Wis., Nov. 26; s. Thomas Hayhurst and Margaret Jackson (Tucker) T.; m. Louise Ann Talma, June 20, 1964. Student U. Wis.-Madison; grad. Automation Inst., Milw., 1964. Profl. singer and musician with The Stratosonics and other groups, 1961-64; automobile salesman, 1965-69; songwriter, 1970—, affiliated with Broadcast Music, Inc., 1973—; founder and owner Play Me Records, 1974—, Superjack Music, pub., 1976—. Recipient Hall of Fame award, 1969; Legion of Leaders award, 1969; winner numerous profl. songwriting competitions, 1974-83. Mem. U.S. Ski Assn., Nat. Thespian Soc. Composer more than 100 songs; author: The Professional Approach to Selling Your Songs, 1979; inventor Doggie-Sox, 1983.

TAYLOR, JAMES EDWARD, insurance company executive; b. Cin., June 18, 1947; s. Victor E. and Charlotte M. (Sowers) T.; m. Martha A. Ennis, July 2, 1966 (div. 1980); children—James D., Cherie L.; m. Phyllis J. Stubbers, Aug. 8, 1981. B.S., U. Cin., 1979. Computer operator Union Central Life Ins. Co., Cin., 1965-66; mgr. data processing ops. Ohio Nat. Life Ins. Co., Cin., 1970—. Served with USAF, 1966-70. Mem. Assn. Systems Mgmt., Data Processing Mgmt. Assn. Avocations: reading; home computers. Home: 2430 Whitewood Ln Cincinnati OH 45239 Office: Ohio Nat Life Ins Co 237 William H Taft Rd Cincinnati OH 45219

TAYLOR, JAMES IRVIN, engineering educator, traffic engineering consultant; b. Clyde, Ohio, Jan. 14, 1935; s. Irvin William and Blanche Marie (Wright) T.; m. Patricia Elizabeth Eaton, Jan. 28, 1956; children—Elizabeth Ann, Stanton James. B.S. in C.E., Case Inst. Tech., 1956, M.S. in C.E., 1962; Ph.D., Ohio State U., 1965. Registered profl. engr., Ohio; Registered Surveyor, Ohio. Research assoc. Ohio State U.-Columbus, 1961-65; mgr. environ. scis. HRB-Singer, Inc., State College, Pa., 1966-68; prof. civil engring. Pa. State U., 1968-76; chmn. dept. civil engring. U. Notre Dame, 1976-82, assoc. dean engring., 1982—; cons. traffic engring., 1974—. Contbr. articles to tech. jours. Recipient G. Brooks Earnest award, Case Inst. Tech., 1956. Mem. ASCE (recipient mead prize 1962), Am. Soc. Photogrammetry (recipient presdl. citation 1971), Inst. Transp. Engrs., Am. Soc. Engring. Edn., Am. Rd. and Transp. Builders Assn. (div. pres. 1978-79, dir. 1979—). Republican. Roman Catholic. Avocations: travelling, reading. Home: 16838 Colony Dr South Bend IN 46635 Office: Univ Notre Dame 257 Fitzpatrick Hall Notre Dame IN 46556

TAYLOR, JERRY ALAN, osteopathic physician; b. Detroit, July 12, 1939; s. Harry and Ann (Skolnick) T.; m. Laura Dorsey, June 18, 1972; children—Megan, Erin. Student, Wayne State U., 1957-61, U. Detroit, 1960-61, U. Mich., 1960; M.D., Coll. Osteo. Medicine and Surgery, Des Moines, 1965. Intern, Botsford Gen. Hosp., Farmington, Mich., 1965-66; sole practice, Garden City, Mich., 1966-67; resident in orthopedic surgery Doctors Hosp., Columbus, Ohio, 1969-71, Botsford Gen. Hosp., Farmington, Mich., 1971-73; fellow in hand surgery Grace Hosp., Detroit, 1972-73; pvt. practice medicine, specializing in hand surgery, Southfield, Mich., 1973—; mem. staff Botsford Gen. Hosp., Farmington Hills, Mich., Oakland Gen. Hosp., Madison Heights, Mich. Served to lt. comdr. USNR, 1967-69. Fellow Am. Osteo. Acad. Orthopedic Surgery, Am. Osteo. Coll. Surgeons; mem. Am. Osteo. Acad. Orthopedics (dir. hand surgery sect.), Am. Osteo. Assn., Am. Assn. Hand Surgery, Mich. Acad. Osteo. Orthopedic Surgeons, Mich. Assn. Osteo. Physicians and Surgeons, Oakland County Osteo. Assn., Detroit Acad. Orthopedic Surgeons. Contbr. articles to profl. jours. Office: 20905 Greenfield St Suite 602 Southfield MI 48075

TAYLOR, JOHN R., insurance company executive. Pres., chief exec. officer, dir. Bankers Life Co., Des Moines, Iowa. Office: Bankers Life Co 711 High St Des Moines IA 50307*

TAYLOR, JOYCE GERALDINE, educator; b. Gibsland, La., June 16, 1929; d. Lonnie Howard and Beattie (Williams) Lewis; B.S., Mercy Coll., Detroit, 1968; M.Ed., Wayne State U., 1972, Ed.S., 1976; children by previous marriage—Bruce A., Joyce Annette, Gloria, Billy. Tchr. elem. schs., Detroit Public Schs., 1968—. Mem. Detroit Fedn. Tchrs. (bldg. rep. 1981—), Nat. Assn. Supervision and Curriculum Devel., Mich. Assn. Supervision and Curriculum, Am. Fedn. Tchrs. Home: 9655 Whitcomb St Detroit MI 48227 Office: 20601 W Davison St Detroit MI 48223

TAYLOR, LINDA WALLACE, accountant, financial consultant; b. Marion, Ind., Jan. 27, 1948; d. Eugene Winfred and Christina Iris W.; m. Kenneth Taylor, Apr. 21, 1975; 1 dau., Jacqueline. B.A., Ind. U., 1972, M.B.A., 1975. Mgmt. trainee Internat. Harvester, Ft. Wayne, Ind., 1970-73; sales rep. Aetna Life & Casualty, Indpls., 1973-75; acct. Fisher Body div. Gen. Motors, Detroit, 1977—, sr. cost estimator, 1982—. Active United Fund Found., NAACP. Nat. Merit scholar, 1967-70; Consortium fellow for grad. studies, 1973-75. Mem. Nat. Assn. Profl. Women, Delta Sigma Theta. Baptist. Home: 10007 Cheyene Detroit MI 46832

TAYLOR, LYNN BOGGESS, college associate dean; b. South Bend, Ind., Aug. 13, 1945; d. Jean B. (Petree) Slaughter. B.A., Western Mich. U., 1967; M.Ed., Kent State U., 1977, Ph.D., 1984. Counselor, Cuyahoga Valley CMHS, Ohio, 1979-83; dir. counseling, assoc. dean students Hiram Coll., Ohio, 1983—; cons. Womenshelter, Kent, Ohio, 1977; instr. Kent State U., 1978. Presenter numerous presentations at profl. conferences. Vol. Akron City Hosp. Emergency Room, Ohio, 1983. Mem. Nat. Assn. Women Deans, Adminstrs., and Counselors (exec. bd. 1978-79, nominations com. 1982—), Ohio Assn. Women Deans, Adminstrs., and Counselors, Am. Coll. Personnel Assn., Am. Assn. Counseling and Devel. Club: Ohio Pinto (sec.). Avocation: exhibiting horses. Home: 1930 Cambridge Dr Kent OH 44240 Office: Hiram Coll Bates Hall Hiram OH 44234

TAYLOR, LYNN FRANKLIN, lawyer; b. Hutchinson, Kans., Sept. 25, 1945; s. Lynn F. and Rebecca Ellen (Jones) T.; m. Kathryn Ruth Achterberg, May 31, 1968; children—Laura Jeanne, Deborah Lynne, Amelia Ruth. B.A., Doane Coll., 1967; J.D., U. Kans., 1975. Bar: U.S. Tax. Ct. 1975, Kans. 1975, U.S. Supreme Ct. 1978. Assoc. Payne & Jones Chartered, Overland Park, Kans., 1975—; city atty. City of DeSoto, Kans., 1979—; mcpl. judge City of Olathe, Kans., 1980-85. Author: Inheritance and Other Estate Taxes, 1980. Bd. dirs. Olathe United Way, Inc., 1978—, chmn., 1981—; pres. Olathe Area C. of C., 1984. Served to lt. USNR, 1968-72. Mem. ABA, Kans. Bar Assn., Order of Coif. Republican. Episcopalian. Home: 502 E Cedar St Olathe KS 66061 Office: Payne & Jones Chartered PO Box 25625 Overland Park KS 66225

TAYLOR, MARK ROBERT, hospital administrator; b. Pontiac, Mich., Jan. 10, 1952; s. Robert Vincent and Zetta Elanore (Jarrard) T.; m. Marianne Coronado, July 7, 1950; children—Benjamin, Christopher, Bethany. B.A., Hillsdale Coll., 1974; M.Health Service Adminstrn., U. Mich., 1983. Asst. dir. personnel Saginaw (Mich.) Osteo. Hosp., 1975-77; dir. personnel Chelsea (Mich.) Community Hosp., 1977-83; v.p. St. Lukes Hosp., Saginaw, 1983—. Bd. dirs. Chelsea United Way, 1981-82. Recipient Share Our Savs. award Mich. Hosp. Assn., 1980; Pres.'s award Hosp. Personnel Adminstrs. Assn. S.E. Mich., 1981-82. Mem. Am. Coll. Hosp. Adminstrs., Am. Soc. Hosp. Personnel Adminstrs., Indsl. Relations Research Assn., Am. Hosp. Assn. Republican. Roman Catholic. Home: 308 S Macomb St Manchester MI 48158 Office: St Lukes Hosp 700 Cooper St Saginaw MI 48602

TAYLOR, MARY LOU, health science educator; b. Springfield, Mo., Sept. 19, 1931; s. Floyd Monroe and Mary Etta (James) Robards; m. Allen Gwyn Taylor, Dec. 24, 1955. B.S., Drury Coll., 1954; M.A., U. Mo-Kansas City, 1965; Ph.D., Kansas State U., 1983. Registered nurse Staff nurse Springfield Baptist Hosp., Mo., 1954-55; instr., part-time supr. nursing service Trinity Luth. Hosp. Sch. Nursing, Kansas City, Mo., 1955-60, asst. dir., 1960-64, dir. 1964-70; coordinator nursing program. Johnson County Community Coll., Overland Park, Kans., 1970-74, 75-84, dir. Nat. and Health Related Sci., 1984—; program officer Pub. Health Service HEW, Kansas City, 1974-75; adv. com. nursing degree programs, Kansas, Mo., 1975—; cons., vis. com. Kans. State Bd. Nursing, Topeka, Kans., 1975—; regional vis. bd. rev. Nat. League Nursing Council Diploma Program, N.Y.C., 1964-70; mem. Council of Assoc. Degree Programs, N.Y.C., 1982-84. Contbr. articles to profl. jours. Mem. nominating credentials com. Mid-Am. Health Systems Agy., Kansas City, 1979; bd. dirs. Faith Handicap Village, Overland Park, Kans. 1981—; mem. adv. panel health care Padgett-Thompson, Inc., Overland Park, 1982; mem. Press Room Presdl. Debate LWV, Kansas City, 1984. Recipient Recognition of Leadership and Service award Trinity Luth. Hosp. Med. staff, 1970; named Kans. Nurse of Month, Kans. State Nurses Assn., 1981. Mem. Am. Nurses Assn. (numerous offices 1954—), Kans. State Nurses' Assn. (numerous offices 1954—), Nat. League Nursing (nominations com. 1982-84), AAUW, Phi Delta Kappa (offices 1981—), Beta Beta Beta, Sigma Theta Tau, Phi Kappa Phi, Kappa Delta Alumni Assn. Avocations: golf; antiques. Home: 7200 W 99 St Overland Park KS 66212 Office: Johnson County Community Coll 12345 Coll at Quivira Overland Park KS 66210

TAYLOR, MAUREEN SULLIVAN, lawyer; b. Chgo., Nov. 4, 1942; d. Jeremiah Patrick and Eileen Therese (Ricker) Sullivan; m. Terrence Joseph Taylor, June 26, 1965; children—Michael, Mary Ellen, Kevin, Jeffrey. B.A., Marycrest Coll., 1963; student Fgn. Language Inst., Loyola U.-Mundelein, 1964; J.D., No. Ill. U., 1982. Bar: Ill. 1982, U.S. Dist. Ct. (no. dist.) Ill. 1982. Tchr. French, all levels of edn., Ill., 1963-77; legal intern U.S. Atty.'s Office, Chgo., 1981-82; teaching asst. No. Ill. U., Glen Ellyn, 1981-82; assoc. Benjamin Hyink & Assocs., Chgo., 1982-83, Haskin, Mindel, Faermark & Sotos, Wheaton, Ill., 1983—. Recipient Am. Jurisprudence award No. Ill. U., 1980. Mem. ABA, Ill. State Bar Assn., DuPage County Bar Assn., Women's Bar Assn., Phi Alpha Delta. Roman Catholic. Home: 21 W 184 22nd St Lombard IL 60148 Office: Haskin Mindel Faermark & Sotos 219 E Wesley Wheaton IL 60187

TAYLOR, ORA CHRISTINE, educator; b. Junction City, La., 1931; d. Jesse Rogers and Ruby Beatrice (Brown) Ross; B.S., U. Ark., 1952; M.Ed., Wayne State U., 1962; summer fellow in math. U. Ill., 1973; m. Tillman Taylor, Jan. 28, 1953 (div. 1984); 1 child, Krasne. Tchr. math. Detroit Public Schs., 1952—, supr. middle sch. math., 1969-83, head adminstrv. unit Emerson Middle Sch., 1983—, dir. metric edn. project, 1978-79, dir./author/contbr. various curriculum materials/projects; part-time faculty Wayne State U., Detroit, 1980-81; metric estimation coordinator Mich. Sci. Olympiad. Dir., We Care Summer Program, Detroit United Community Services, 1979, 80; dir. Christian edn. Greater St. Mark Baptist Ch.; dir. youth activities Bapt. State Congress, 1979-81, mem. faculty, 1979; also mem. choir, Sunday sch. tchr., leader Bapt. Tng. Union Group local ch. Mem. Nat. Council Tchrs. Math., Assn. Curriculum Supervision and Devel., Nat. Alliance Black Sch. Educators, Mich. Council Tchrs. Math., Detroit Area Council Math. Tchrs., Mich. Assn. Curriculum Supervision and Devel., Metro Detroit Area Black Sch. Educators, Alpha Kappa Mu. Editor/contbg. author: Alternative Learning Activities, 1974. Home: 18700 Sorrento Detroit MI 48235 Office: 932 Schools Center Bldg 5057 Woodward Ave Detroit MI 48202

TAYLOR, PAT, editor, publisher; b. Williamson, W.Va., Sept. 10, 1924; s. Walter M. and Willie (Cox) T.; m. Adeline Irene Reynolds, Jan. 9, 1955; children—Charles, Sharon. B.J., U. Tex., 1945. Reporter, Circleville Herald (Ohio), 1945-46; news editor Hays Daily News (Kans.), 1946-55; editor, pub. Western Times, Sharon Springs, Kans., 1955-57, Ellis County Farmer, Hays, 1957-59; editor, owner Norton Daily Telegram (Kans.), 1960-68; publisher Ellis Rev., (Kans.), 1970-83; editor Ellis County Star, Hays, 1968—; publicist Kans. Oil Industry, 1982—. Chmn., Kansans for Kennedy, Hays, 1959-60. Recipient 1st place news reporting award Inland Daily Press Assn., 1963, also 1st place awards Kans. Press Assn. Pentecostal Methodist. Office: Ellis County Star 708 Main St Hays KS 67601

TAYLOR, PATRICIA ANN, occupational therapist; b. Allegan, Mich., Sept. 15, 1922; d. John William and Grace Adele (Burnett) Exton; B.S., Milw.-Downer Coll., 1944; diploma in Occupational Therapy, Lawrence U., 1945; M.S., U. Mich., 1976; m. Ernest Taylor, Mar. 19, 1954; children—Sally, Carolyn, Steven, David, John. Asst. prof. phys. medicine U. Wis., 1946-49; dir. activity therapy Menninger Found., Topeka, 1949-53; supr. occupational therapy VA, Fayetteville, N.C., 1956-66; coordinator activity therapy Mich. Dept. Mental Health, Northville, 1966-75; clin. instr. Eastern Mich. U. and Wayne State U., 1967-75; curriculum cons. Ohio State U., 1969-70, Wayne State U., 1976-77; rehab. cons. Kans. Dept. Mental Health, Topeka, 1950-54. Civilian occupational therapist U.S. Army Hosps., 1945-46, recreation cons., Korea, 1953; dir. service club Pope AFB, N.C., 1954-55; mem. Southeastern Mich. adv. council White House Conf. on Aging, 1981. Recipient Civilian Merit award Hdqrs. Korean Communications Zone, 1953, Mich. Civil Service award, 1968. Mem. Nat. Assn. Retarded Citizens, Mich. Soc. Gerontology, Am. Occupational Therapy Assn. (bd. mgmt. 1950-53), Older Women's League. Episcopalian. Contbg. editor Am. Jour. Occupational Therapy, 1950-53. Address: 2477 Sandalwood Circle Ann Arbor MI 48105

TAYLOR, RAY, state senator; b. Steamboat Rock, Iowa, June 4, 1923; s. Leonard Allen and Mary Delilah (Huffman) T.; student U. No. Iowa, 1940-41, Baylor U., 1948-49; m. Mary Allen, Aug. 29, 1924; children—Gordon, Laura Rae Taylor Hansmann, Karol Ann Taylor Flora, Jean Lorraine Taylor Mahl. Farmer, Steamboat Rock, Iowa, 1943—; mem. Iowa Senate, 1973—; bd. dirs., sec. Am. Legis. Exchange Council, 1979—. Sec., Hardin County Farm Bur., 1970-72; mem. Iowa div. bds. Am. Cancer Soc.; chmn. Am. Revolution Bicentennial Com. Mem. Steamboat Rock Community Sch. Bd., 1955-70; coordinator Republican youth, 1968-72. Bd. dirs. Faith Bapt. Bible Coll.; pres. Am. Council Christian Chs.; chmn. Iowans for Responsible Govt. Mem. Wildlife Club. Baptist. Address: Steamboat Rock IA 50672

TAYLOR, RICHARD LAVERN, computer company executive; b. Dayton, Ohio, Mar. 8, 1950; s. William Edward and Beatrice (Long) T.; B.S. (Ill. State scholar), No. Ill. U., 1972; M.B.A., U. Cin., 1973; m. Jacqueline Madigan, Aug. 19, 1972; children—Kristen Nicole, John William. Sr. staff coordinator Muscular Dystrophy Assn., Chgo., 1968-71; asst. buyer fashionwear McAlpins Co., Cin., 1972-73; internat. sales engr. Honeywell Inc., Mpls., 1973-75, mktg. rep., Boston, 1975-77; chief product devel. analyst Ford Motor Corp., Dearborn, Mich., 1977-78, chief program analyst forward model strategy planning, emissions, and fuel economy, 78-80; sr. cons., dir. mktg. industry mfg. Control Data Corp., Mpls., 1980, now mng. dir. sales mfg. industry CAD/CAM, Internat. Computer Systems. dir. Yo Choma, Inc.; cons. Minn. Minority Bus. League; lectr. Hennepin Coll. Asso. adviser explorers council Boy Scouts Am.; mem. Hennepin County CETA Adv. Council, 1980—. U. Cin. fellow, 1972-73. Mem. Am. Mgmt. Assn. Engring. Soc. Detroit, Soc. Automotive Engrs., Am. Mktg. Assn., Assn. MBA Execs., Delta Sigma Pi, Phi Beta Lambda. Democrat. Roman Catholic. Club: Ski Unlimited. Home: 8241 Oregon Rd Bloomington MN 55438 Office: 8100 34th Ave S Minneapolis MN 55440

TAYLOR, RICHARD LEE, lawyer; b. Des Moines, Mar. 23, 1954; s. Glen Charles and Erma Arlene Taylor; m. Robin Sue Warren, July 6, 1979. B.S., Iowa State U., 1976; J.D., Drake U., 1979. Bar: Iowa 1979, Ill. 1980, U.S. Dist. Ct. (so. dist.) Iowa 1979. Staff atty. Am. Farm Bur. Fedn., Park Ridge, Ill., 1979-82; corp. atty. United Fed. Savs. Bank, Des Moines, 1982—. Mem. ABA, Iowa State Bar Assn., Polk County Bar Assn., Des Moines Civic Ctr. Republican. Presbyterian. Office: United Fed Savs Bank 400 Locust Des Moines IA 50308

TAYLOR, ROBERT ELMER, oil, gas and chemical co. exec.; b. Durango, Colo., Aug. 21, 1935; s. Lloyd B. and Helen Golda (McGee) T.; B.S. in Mktg., Brigham Young U., 1957; m. Dorene Smith, June 20, 1956; children—Shereen, Bryan, David, Dean. Economic analyst, distbn. mgr., mktg. services mgr. El Paso Products Co., 1957-68; dir. diversification InterNorth, Inc., 1968-69, mktg. mgr., Des Plaines, Ill., 1970-73, v.p. petrochems. mktg. div., 1974-81, v.p., bus. dir. petrochems. No. Petrochem Co., Omaha, 1982—; dir. Calcasieu Chem. Corp., Lake Charles, La.; tchr. evening sch. U. Tex., El Paso, 1960-64, Odessa (Tex.) Coll., 1965-68. Mem. Nat. Petroleum Refiners Assn. (bd. dirs., petrochem. com.), Am. Inst. Chem. Engrs., S.W. Chem. Assn. Republican. Mormon. Home: 1559 Elm Northbrook IL 60062 Office: 2223 Dodge St Omaha NE 68102

TAYLOR, ROBERT LEE, automobile company executive, educator; b. Adrian, Mich., Jan. 9, 1944; s. Jack Raleigh and Virginia Dixon (Oakes) T.; m. Janice Grace George, Dec. 9, 1961; children—Robin, Lynne, David. A.A., Siena Heights Coll., 1974, B.A., 1976. With computer operation Gen. Parts div. Ford Motor Co., Rawsonville, Mich., 1965-66, prodn. monitoring supr. Saline Plant, Mich., 1966-75, methods and systems analyst, Ypsilanti Plant, Mich., 1975-77, data processing supr. Milan Plant, Mich., 1977-82, sr. systems analyst Plastics, Paint and Vinyl div., Wixom, Mich., 1982-85; systems engr. Electronic Data Systems, Warren, Mich., 1985—; instr. data processing Siena Heights Coll., Adrian, 1985—. Commr. Tecumseh Planning Commn., Mich., 1976-80, vice-chmn., 1981-82; trustee Tecumseh Bd. Edn., 1981-82, sec., 1983-84, chmn. citizens adv. com., 1983, chmn. computer adv. com., 1984, chmn. policy com., 1983-84; chmn. Tecumseh Area Laymen's Assn., 1983; mem. exec. com. Lenawee County Republican party, Adrian, 1982-85, precinct del., 1982-85, chmn. computer com., 1984-85; state del. State of Mich., 1983-85; founding advisor, Sunday Sch. supt. Evang. Free Ch., Adrian, 1984-85; asst. Sunday Sch. supt. Berean Baptist Ch., Adrian, 1980-83; tchr. mentally impaired, 1977-83; deacon, Sunday Sch. supt., Grace Bible Ch., Tecumseh, 1973-76; chmn. bd. deacons First Bapt. Ch., Tecumseh, 1970-71, youth advisor, 1968-71, Layman of Yr., 1970; vice chmn. Tecumseh Area Crusade for Christ, 1973. Served with USAF, 1961-65. Mem. Computer and Automated Systems Assn. (sr.), Soc. Mfg. Engrs. Republican. Avocations: golf; geneology. Home: 603 Outer Dr Tecumseh MI 49286 Office: 7000 Chicago Rd Room 1312 Warren MI 48090

TAYLOR, ROBERT MALCOLM, physician; b. Detroit, Sept. 13, 1924; s. Malcolm Edgar and Mary Estelle (Trevarthen) T.; m. Lorna Elaine Mundt, June 21, 1947; children—Robert M., Jill Anne, Sara Jo. M.D., Wayne State U., 1948. Diplomate Am. Bd. Internal Medicine. Intern Harper Hosp., Detroit, 1948-49; resident Crile VA Hosp., Western Reserve U., Cleve., 1950-53; chmn. dept. internal medicine Burns Clinic, Petoskey, Mich., 1955—. Served to capt. U.S. Army, 1949-50, PTO, 1953-55. Fellow ACP, ACCP; mem. Am. Soc. Internal Medicine (del. 1977-81), Mich. Soc. Internal Medicine (pres. 1979-81), No. Mich. Med. Soc. (pres. 1964-65), Mich. State Med. Soc. (del. 1977-81), AMA, Alpha Omega Alpha. Republican. Presbyterian (elder). Club: Birchwood Farm Golf & Country (Harbor Springs, Mich.). Avocations: tennis; golf; skiing; fly fishing. Home: 2431 Greenbriar Rd Harbor Springs MI 49740 Office: Burns Clinic Petoskey MI 49770

TAYLOR, SAMUEL GALE, III, physician, educator, administrator; b. Elmhurst, Ill., Sept. 2, 1904; s. Samuel Gale Jr. and Anna J. (Mead) T.; m. Eleanor Roberts, June 1, 1938 (dec. 1978); children—Constance Taylor Blackwell, John W., Samuel Gale IV.; m. Jocelyn Pierson (Kennedy), Apr. 21, 1979. Student Chgo. Latin Sch., 1912-23; B.A., Yale U., 1927; M.D., U. Chgo. (Rush U.), 1932. Diplomate Am. Bd. Internal Medicine. Research fellow Cook County Hosp., Chgo., 1935-39; assoc. in medicine U. Chgo., Rush Sch., 1935-41; asst. prof. U. Ill., Chgo., 1941-46, assoc. to prof., 1946-73; prof. medicine Rush U., Chgo., 1973-78, prof. emeritus, 1978—; dir. Rush Cancer Ctr., 1972-74, Ill. Cancer Council, Chgo., 1974-76. Contbr. more than 100 articles to profl. publs. Pres. Ill. Cancer Council, 1973; chmn. med. adv. com. Chgo. Vis. Nurses Assn.; vestry Ch. Holy Spirit, Lake Forest, Ill., 1960-65. Endowed chmn. in oncology in his name Rush Med. Sch., 1978; recipient Disting. Service award Am. Cancer Soc., 1973. Fellow ACP (life mem., chmn. cancer com. 1975-78), Am. Soc. Clin. Oncology (bd. dirs. 1970); mem. Endocrine Soc., Surg. Oncology Soc., liason mem. ACS. Republican. Episcopalian. Clubs: University (Chgo.); Onwensia (Lake Forest, Ill.). Home: PO Box

646 Lake Forest IL 60045-646 Office: Rush Univ 1750 W Harrison St Chicago IL 60612

TAYLOR, SCOTT MAXFIELD, department store executive; b. Evanston, Ill., Aug. 13, 1953; s. Brett Maxfield and Gretchen Pauline (Porter) T., Jr. B.A., Coe Coll., 1975; M.Mgmt., Northwestern U., 1977; M.S.C., New Sem., 1985. Sales mgr. Daytons, Mpls., 1977-78, asst. buyer, 1978-79; store mgr. Brett's Dept. Store, Mankato, Minn., 1979-80, buyer jr. dept., 1981-83, v.p., 1981—, div. mdse. mgr., 1984—, also dir. Bd. dirs. Blue Earth County Hist. Soc., Mankato, 1984—, Mankato Area Conv. and Visitors Bur., 1985—. George F. Baker scholar, 1975. Mem. Omicron Delta Epsilon. Republican. Presbyterian. Lodge: Kiwanis (bd. dirs. 1984—). Avocation: curling. Home: Box 3642 Mankato MN 56002 Office: Bretts Dept Stores Box 609 Mankato MN 56002

TAYLOR, STEPHANIE ANN, pharmacist; b. Greenfield, Ind., Apr. 4, 1958; d. Loren DeVerl and Helen Gene (Scott) Kirkpatrick; m. Curtis James Taylor, Aug. 4, 1979. B.S. in Pharmacy, Purdue U., 1981. Registered pharmacist, Ind. staff pharmacist Porter Mem. Hosp., Valparaiso, Ind., 1981—. Mem. Am. Soc. Hosp. Pharmacists, Am. Pharm. Assn., Ind. Pharm. Assn., Phi Kappa Phi. Mem. Ch. of Christ. Avocations: cooking; music; reading; crafts. Home: 1427 N Tremont Rd Chesterton IN 46304

TAYLOR, THOMAS ROGER, educational consultant, educator; b. Urbana, Ill., May 31, 1945; s. Thomas and Ora Wilma T.; m. Beverly Milam, Dec. 19, 1981. B.S., U. Ill., 1967; M.A., So. Ill. U., 1972, Ph.D., 1980. Tchr., Mt. Vernon (Ill.) Schs., 1967-71; cons. Ill. Dept. State, 1971-74; dir. Area Service Ctr. for Gifted Children, South Cook County, Ill., 1975-79; prof. urban edn. Govs. State U., 1975-79; cons. Ednl. Cons. Assocs., Denver, 1977-82, also dir.; pres. Curriculum Design for Excellence, Oak Brook, Ill.; sr. ptnr. T & H Investments, Hinsdale, Ill. Vice-pres. Mt. Vernon Community Coll. Orch. Named Ky. Col., 1979. Mem. U. Ill. Alumni Assn. (dir. 1967-71), NEA, Ill. Edn. Assn. (bd. dirs.), Nat. Assn. Gifted Children, World Council for Gifted, Assn. Childhood Edn. Internat., Profl. Assn. Diving Instrs., Nat. Rifle Assn., Phi Delta Kappa. Clubs: Demolay. Contbr. in field. Home: 1907 Midwest Club Pkwy Oak Brook IL 60521

TAYLOR, WILLIAM HENRY, lawyer, political consultant; b. Waukegan, Ill., Feb. 6, 1954; s. William Henry and Patricia (Rockingham) T. B.A., Cornell Coll., Mount Vernon, Iowa, 1979; J.D., Northwestern U., 1979. Bar: Ill. 1980, U.S. Dist. Ct. (no. dist.) Ill. 1980. Staff asst. Congressman R. McClory, Washington, 1975-76; Iowa dir. Birch Bayh for Pres., 1976; assoc. Peterson, Ross, Schloeb & Seidel, Chgo., 1979-82, Sachnoff, Weaver & Rubenstein Ltd., Chgo., 1983—; mem. nat. field staff Ted Kennedy for Pres., 1979-80; field dir. Cuyahoga, Springer for Gov., Cleve., 1982; No. Calif. field dir. Tom Bradley for Gov., San Francisco, 1982; dep. dir. Mondale/Ferraro campaign, Ill., 1985. Author: Grassroots Campaign Manual for Progressive Candidates, 1983. Orgn. adviser A. Phillip Randolph Inst., Cedar Rapids, Iowa, 1975-76; del. Iowa Democratic Conv., 1974, 76; alt. del. Dem. Nat. Conv., N.Y.C., 1976; chmn. Young Dems., Cornell Coll., 1974-76; bd. dirs. Progressive Chgo. Area Network, 1983, Demicco Youth Services, 1984, Citizens Utility Bd., 1984. Named Outstanding Young Men Am., U.S. Jaycees, 1977, 80. Mem. Ill. State Bar Assn., Chgo. Council Lawyers. Office: Sachnoff Weaver & Rubenstien Ltd 30 S Wacker Dr Suite 2900 Chicago IL 60611

TAYLOR-GORDON, ELAINE, marketing executive, writer; b. N.Y.C.; d. Harry Benjamin and Gertrude Schneider; m. Morton Gordon (div.); children—Jennifer, Heather; m. 2d G. Laurence Patterson, Sept. 17, 1977. B.A. in Speech, U. Vt.; postgrad. Bernard Baruch Sch. Bus., 1976-78. Dir. sales devel. Revlon, Internat., N.Y.C., 1974-76; v.p. mktg. Puritan Fashions Corp., N.Y.C., 1976-79; dir. mktg. Foley's Houston, 1979-82; v.p. advt. and sales promotion, B. Dalton Bookseller, Mpls., 1982-84; v.p. mktg. services Izod, Ltd., N.Y.C., 1984—. Bd. dirs. Minn. Opera, New Dance Ensemble, Minn. Named YWCA Woman of Yr., 1980; recipient cert. of appreciation Assn. for Advancement of Mexican-Ams., Houston, 1980. Mem. Fashion Group Minn. Author: The Businesswoman's Guide to 30 American Cities, 1982.

TAZELAAR, EDWIN JOSEPH, II, insurance company executive; b. Chgo., June 16, 1947; s. Edwin Joseph and Nancy Annette (DeStevens) T.; grad. N.W. Police Acad., 1971; student Harper Coll., 1974-76; m. Mary Anne Marnul, July 3, 1982; children—Bradley James, Marcus Thomas, Edwin Joseph III; stepchildren—Brian Thomas, Bradley Louis Siok. Police officer Village of Hoffman Estates (Ill.), 1971-77; assoc. Am. Family Life Assurance Co. of Columbus, Ga., 1977; dist. mgr., 1978, regional mgr., Palatine, Ill., 1979-83; state mgr. Capitol Am. Life Ins., Deerfield, Ill., 1983—; store mgr. Robert Hall Clothes, Chgo., 1968-71. Served with U.S. Army, 1966-68. Recipient Patrol Achievement award Village of Hoffman Estates, 1973; Cert. of Achievement Lake County Dept. Ct. Services, 1985; Fireball award Am. Family Life Assurance Co., 1977, co. awards, 1977, 78, named to President's Club, 1978. Mem. Am. Mgrs. Assn., Internat. Platform Assn. Roman Catholic. Home and Office: 1345 Somerset Ave Deerfield IL 60015

TEACH, GARY LEE, accountant; b. Troy, Ohio, Mar. 2, 1947; s. Lester E. and Janet I. (Hirsch) T.; m. Glenda L. McKim, May 9, 1969; children—Gary Lee, Jr., Sara R. Student, Ohio State U., 1965-67; B.S. in Acctg., Bliss Coll., 1969; M.B.A., Xavier U., Cin., 1971. C.P.A., Ohio. Plant acct. Hobart Corp., Troy, 1971-73; controller Leisure Lawn, Inc., Dayton, Ohio, 1973-77, v.p., gen. mgr., 1974-77; dir. fin. and adminstrn. United Way of Dayton, 1977-83; mng. ptnr. Teach, Sturgeon & Assocs., Troy, 1980—. Pres. Troy Dollars for Scholars, 1975. Mem. Am. Inst. C.P.A.s, Ohio Soc. C.P.A.s, Internat. Assn. Fin. Planners, Nat. Assn. Accts., Soc. Advancement Mgmt. (pres. 1978-79). Republican. Presbyterian. Lodge: Masons. Home: 480 Birchwood Ct Troy OH 45373 Office: Teach Sturgeon & Assocs CPAs 1560 McKaig Ave Troy OH 45373

TEACHOUT, GERALD EUGENE, tourist attraction executive; b. Shenandoah, Iowa, Oct. 12, 1924; s. Lowell Frank and Anna Mary (Newman) T.; m. Darlene Marie Nelson, June 29, 1947; children—Anna Marie, Bruce, Bryan, Brent. B.S. in Mil. Sci., U. Md., 1958; student San Antonio Jr Coll., 1956-58, S.D. Sch. Mines and Tech., 1972-75. Command pilot USAF, 1950-71; owner and operator Black Hills Petrified Forest, Piedmont, S.D., 1963—; chmn. Gov.'s Steering Com. on Tourism, Pierre, S.D., 1972-74. Mem. Piedmont Valley Assn., 1972—, Retirees Affairs Council, Ellsworth AFB, S.D., 1978—. Served to lt. col. USAF, 1943-71. Numerous mil. awards and decorations. Mem. Assn. S.D. Mus. (bd. dirs.), Ellsworth Heritage Found. (pres. 1984—), S.D. Archeol. Soc. (pres. 1981-84), Ret. Officers Assn. (past pres.), Rapid City C. of C. Republican. Methodist. Lodge: Lions (v.p. and pres. 1983-85) Piedmont. Avocations: woodworking; silver-smithing; photography; travel. Home: Piedmont Rt Box 766 Piedmont SD 57769

TEAL, MARY DURDEN, music educator; b. Monroe, La., May 13, 1924; d. Yancy Harvey and Minerva Lucinda (Reeks) D.; m. Laurence Lyon Teal, Dec. 21, 1957. B.S. in Music Edn., Northwestern State Coll., Natchitoches, La., 1945; M.Mus. in Music Edn., U. Mich., 1955, Ph.D. in Music Edn., 1964. Pvt. tchr. piano and voice, Bastrop, La., 1946-51; tchr. vocal music Pub. Schs. Bastrop, 1951-53, Ann Arbor (Mich.), 1954-58; lectr. in music edn. U. Mich., Ann Arbor, 1955-58; tchr. piano Teal Sch. Music, Detroit, 1958-66; lectr. music Eastern Mich. U., Ypsilanti, 1965-69, assoc. prof., 1969-77, prof. 1977—. Cons. Am. music history, gen. music edn. Mem. Mich. Music Educators Assn. (editor Mich. Music Educator 1978—; award of Merit 1982), Music Educators Nat. Conf., AAUW, Sonneck Soc., Mich. Hist. Soc., Women's Research Club U. Mich., U. Mich. Sch. Music Alumni Soc. (chairperson bd. govs.), Univ. Alumni Assn. U. Mich. (nat. dir.), Sigma Alpha Iota (Rose of Honor 1974). Methodist. Author: (with Lawrence W. Brown) The Effect of the Civil War on Music in Michigan, 1965; Elements of Music for the Classroom Teacher, 1972; contbr. articles to profl. publs., vocal arrangements to: Birchard Music Series, Book 8, 1959. Home: 2671 Bedford Rd Ann Arbor MI 48104 Office: Dept Music Eastern Mich U Ypsilanti MI 48197

TEARE, WILLIAM TAGGART, JR., dentist; b. Beaumont, Tex., May 27, 1943; s. William Taggart and LaMerle (Smith) T.; m. Elexandra Jean Fisher, Nov. 22, 1975; children—Shane, Nikki. D.D.S., Ind. U., 1967. Pvt. practice dentistry, Evansville, Ind., 1969—. Served with USNR, 1967-69. Mem. ADA, Ind. Dental Assn., First Dist. Dental Soc. (pres.-elect 1984). Roman Catholic. Club: Rotary. Avocations: Flying, scuba diving. Office: 1421 N Main St Evansville IN 47711

TEASDALL, ROBERT DOUGLAS, neurologist, educator; b. London, Ont., Can., Dec. 9, 1920; came to U.S., 1950; s. Douglas Rupert and Marjorie (Irvine) T.; m. Veronica Publow, July 17, 1948; children—Mary Susan, Robert Douglas. M.D., U. Western Ont., 1946, Ph.D., 1950. Diplomate Am. Bd. Psychiatry and Neurology. Resident in neurol. medicine Johns Hopkins Hosp., Balt. City Hosps., Balt., 1950-54; instr. thru assoc. prof. neurol. medicine Johns Hopkins U., Balt., 1954-73; clin. prof. neurology U. Mich., Ann Arbor, 1975—; chief neurologist Henry Ford Hosp., Detroit, 1974-79, staff neurologist, 1979—. Contbr. articles on clin. neurology and neurophysiology to profl. jours. Fellow Am. Acad. Neurology; mem. Am. Physiol. Soc., Am. Neurol. Assn., Mich. Neurol. Assn. Home: 16240 N Park Dr Southfield MI 48075 Office: Henry Ford Hospital 2799 W Grand Blvd Detroit MI 48202

TEBBEN, SHARON LEE, chemistry educator; b. Fairfield, Iowa, Oct. 15, 1943; d. Richard Paul and Arline Marie (Sires) Brandt; m. E. Marvin Tebben, Sept. 7, 1963; children—Laurel Ann, Leslie Kay, Paul Marvin. B.S., Mankato State U., 1965; M.S., U. Wyo., 1973. Chemistry tchr. San Diego City Schs., 1965-68, Alhambra City Schs., Calif., 1968-70; teaching asst. U. Wyo., Laramie, 1970-73; faculty Presentation Coll., Aberdeen, S.D., 1974—, chmn. dept. chemistry, 1975—. NDEA fellow, 1971-73. Mem. AAUW, Am. Chem. Soc., Phi Kappa Phi, Alpha Lambda Delta. Republican. Avocations: tennis; painting; writing; travel. Office: Presentation Coll 1500 N Main St Aberdeen SD 57401

TEBO, ALBERT ROBERTSON, editor, technical writer, physicist; b. New Orleans, Nov. 1919; s. Albert R. and Sallie R. (Watson) T.; m. Edith M. Janssen, June 3, 1950; children—Mary Virginia Tebo Grimes, Fontaine F., Catherine Anne. B.S., Tulane U., 1940, M.S., 1948; postgrad. U. Va., 1948-52. Physicist U.S. Army Electronics Research and Devel. Labs., Ft. Monmouth, N.J., 1952-78; assoc. editor Cahners Pub. Co., Chgo., 1979-83; sr. contbg. editor PennWell Pub. Co., Littleton, Mass., 1983—. Contbr. articles to profl. jours. Served to maj. USMC, 1940-45, ETO, PTO. Mem. Optical Soc. Am., IEEE, Laser Inst. Am., Soc. Photo-Optical Instrumentation Engrs., Soc. for Info. Display. Presbyterian. Home: 3100 N Sheridan Rd Apt 12A Chicago IL 60657 Office: Laser Focus Mag 119 Russell St Littleton MA 01460

TEDONI, STEVEN JAMES, county police official; b. St. Louis, Aug. 13, 1952; s. Thomas H. and Rosemary (Thiess) T.; A.A., Meramec Community Coll., 1972; B.S. in Adminstrn. Justice, U. Mo.-St. Louis, 1974; M.B.A., Webster U., 1983. Police officer St. Louis County Police, Clayton, Mo., 1974—, adminstrv. aide to supt., 1979-80, dir. bur. office services, 1980—; cons. InfoPro Inc., Clayton, 1983—. Vice pres. Gravois Gardens Improvement, Affton, Mo., 1982. Mem. Assn. Info. System Profls. Roman Catholic. Avocations: tennis; racquetball, music. Office: St Louis County Police Dept 7900 Forsyth Clayton MO 63105

TEEGARDEN, KENNETH LEROY, See *Who's Who in America,* 43rd edition.

TEEPLE, HOWARD MERLE, educator; b. Salem, Oreg., Dec. 29, 1911; s. Charles and Eltruda (Branchflower) T.; m. Gladys Windedahl, Oct. 26, 1947; M.A. in L.S., U. Chgo., 1963, Ph.D., 1955. Farmer, 1938-47; research asst. Emory U., 1955-57; vis. instr. Bexley Hall, 1957-58; assoc. prof., chmn. dept. religion W.Va. Wesleyan Coll., 1958-61; ind. researcher, 1961-62; librarian order/reference depts. Deering Library, Northwestern U., Evanston, Ill., 1963-69; head reference dept. Douglas Library, Chgo. State U., 1969-77; exec. dir. Religion and Ethics Inst., Evanston, 1973—. Mem. Soc. Bibl. Lit. Democrat. Author: The Mosaic Eschatological Prophet, 1957; The Literary Origin of the Gospel of John, 1974; The Noah's Ark Nonsense, 1978; The Historical Approach to the Bible (cert. of recognition NCCJ), 1982; video producer Conflicts over the Bible, The Quest to Understand the Bible, both 1985; contbr. articles to profl. jours. Home: 400 Main St Evanston IL 60202 Office: Religion and Ethics Inst PO Box 664 Evanston IL 60204

TEEPLE, WADE IRVING, social services official; b. Bay Mills, Mich., Oct. 27, 1943; s. Frank Clinton and Sarah Lillian (Marshall) T.; m. Barbara Teresa Teeple, June 27, 1975; 1 dau., Tracy Noel. Ed. pub. schs. Comml. fisherman Brown Fisheries, Whitefish Point, Mich., 1966-72; police officer Bay Mills Indian Community, Brimley, Mich., 1974-79, tribal pres., 1979-84; adminstrv. asst. Mich. Indian Child Welfare Agy., 1984—. Mem. Chippewa/Ottewa Fisheries Mgmt. Authority; mem. steering com. Native Am. Rights Fund, Boulder, Colo.; vice chmn. Inter-Tribal Council Mich., Sault Ste. Marie. Served with U.S. Army, 1962-65. Democrat. Methodist. Home: Route 1 Box 312 Brimley MI 49715 Office: Mich Indian Child Welfare Agy 120 Ridge St PO Box 537 Sault Sainte Marie MI 49783

TEGTMEYER, GAMBER FREDERICK, neurologist; b. Milw., July 23, 1933; s. Gamber Frederick and Margaret Louise (Brown) T.; m. Audrey Mae Hippe, Apr. 30, 1961; children—David, Kenneth, Thomas. A.B., Kenyon Coll., Gambier, Ohio, 1955; M.D., Columbia U., 1959. Diplomate Am. Bd. Psychiatry and Neurology. Intern, U. Wis. Hosps., Madison, 1959-60, resident, 1960-63; chief neurology Shepard AFB, Wichita Falls, Tex., 1963-65; pres. Madison Neurol. Ctr., 1970—; chief of staff Madison Gen. Hosp., 1984—; assoc. clin. prof. neurology U. Wis. Med. Sch., Madison, 1980—. Bd. dirs. Civic Music Assn., Madison, 1978-80. Served as capt. USAF, 1963-65. Fellow Am. Acad. Neurology; mem. Wis. Neurol. Soc. (pres. 1982-83). Presbyterian. Home: 6334 Landfall Dr Madison WI 53705 Office: Madison Neurol Ctr SC 20 S Park St Madison WI 53715

TEHOLIZ, LEO, arts and humanities educator, artist; b. Windsor, Ont., Can., July 1, 1920; came to U.S., 1923, naturalized, 1934; s. Peter and Xenia (Tahill) Teholizoff; children—Lyn, Wendy, Peter Arnold. B.Design, U. Mich., 1949, M.F.A., 1951; diploma Indsl. Coll. Armed Forces, 1961. Artist, sign painter Newman Sign Co., Hamtramck, Mich., 1937-39; display artist Display-Rite, Inc., Detroit, 1939-40; studio art asst. McLaughlin Studios, Detroit, 1940-42; comml. artist, cartoonist, advt. artist, illustrator freelance, Mich., 1945-54, Creative Arts Studio, Washington, 1951; art editor Mich. Gargoyle, U. Mich. humor mag., Ann Arbor, 1947-49; teaching asst. U. Mich., 1948-49, instr. 1950-51, staff art asst. ednl. TV devel. program, 1950-51; staff research analyst Johns Hopkins U., Chevy Chase, Md., 1951-52; lectr. Fgn. Service Inst. U.S. State Dept., Washington, 1961; ednl. specialist, audio-visual specialist, tng. officer, graphical analysis officer, pubs. officer U.S. Govt., Washington, 1952-68; prof. arts and humanities West Shore Community Coll., Scottville, Mich., 1968—, chmn. div. humanities and fine arts 1972—. Author: (with others) The Make-Up and Production of Russian Newspapers and Printed Media, 1952. Contbr. articles, illustrations, cartoons to profl. jours. mags., newspapers. Various one-man shows of paintings and drawings, 1936-82, final exhbn. 50 yr. retrospective at West Shore Community Coll., 1982. Chmn. Mason County chpt. ARC, Ludington, Mich., 1973—. Served with USNR, 1942-45, ETO. U. Mich. fellow, 1950-51; recipient U.S. Govt. Cert. of Commendation, 1963. Mem. Mason County Hist. Soc. (bd. dirs. 1970-72), Tau Sigma Delta. Lodge: Optimists. Home: 1914 S Lakeshore Dr Ludington MI 49431 Office: West Shore Community Coll 3000 N Stiles Rd Scottville MI 49454

TEI, TAKURI, accountant; b. Korea, Feb. 25, 1924; s. Gangen and Isun (Song) T.; came to U.S., 1952, naturalized, 1972; diploma Concordia Theol. Sem., 1959; B.D., Eden Theol. Sem., 1965; M.Ed., U. Mo., 1972; m. Maria M. Ottwaska, Dec. 1, 1969; 1 dau., Sun Kyung Lee. Partner, Madeleine Ottwaska & Assos., St. Louis, 1968—; pres. TMS Tei Enterprises Inc., Webster Groves, Mo., 1969—; instr. Forest Park Community Coll. Mem. Am. Coll. Enrolled Agts. (pres. 1976—), Am. Accounting Assn., Am. Taxation Assn., Assn. Asian Studies, NAACP. Republican. Lutheran. Home and office: 7529 Big Bend Blvd Webster Groves MO 63119

TEICH, RALPH DONALD, printing company executive; b. Chgo., May 24, 1925; s. Curt and Anna (Neither) T.; B.S., Northwestern U., 1949; m. Joan Martha Laurine (div. Sept. 1965); children—Deborah, Lawrence, Cheryl, Fred Teich Anderson; m. Elizabeth Perrizo, Jan. 20, 1968. Pres., R-Dit Enterprises, Inc., Curt Teich & Co., Inc. Past fund raising area chmn. A.R.C., Glencoe, Ill., Community Chest, Glenview, Ill., N. Shore Country Day Sch., Winnetka, Ill.; active Art Inst., Lyric Opera; past bd. dirs. Chgo. Ballet, Curt Teich Found.; past bd. dirs., v.p., pres. Mid-Am. Ballet Found. of Ill., past dir. Interstate Bd.; cons., bd. dirs. Lake County Mus. Spl. Collection. Mem. Am. Friends Austria (dir. 1965-72), Chgo. Hist. Soc. (life), Power Squadron, Field Mus. Natural History (life), Chgo. Art Inst. (life), Balzekas Mus. Lithuanian Art, Lake Forest Hist. Soc., Gleassner House. Lutheran (deacon, v.p. 1966-73). Mason (32 deg., Shriner). Clubs: Executives, University, Michigan Shores (Chgo.); Waukegan Yacht. Lodges: Masons (32 deg.), Shriners. Home: 700 S Ridge Rd Lake Forest IL 60045 Office: PO Box 169 Lake Forest IL 60045

TEICHER, HARRY, chemist; b. N.Y.C., Jan. 11, 1927; s. Hyman C. and Lena Teicher; m. Charlotte Ann Leavy, June 17, 1951; children—Howard, Mark, Joel. B.S., Queens Coll., 1948; M.S., Syracuse U., 1950, Ph.D., 1953. Research chemist Monsanto Co., Miamisburg, Ohio and Everett, Mass., 1953-57, research group leader, St. Louis, 1957-80, research mgr., 1980—. Served with USAF, 1946-47. Mem. Am. Chem. Soc., Inst. Food Technologists, Am. Assn. Cereal Chemists. Jewish.

TEICHERT, CARLOS, microbiologist, quality assurance specialist; b. Mexico City, Apr. 15, 1948; s. Pedro Carlos and Consuelo Maria (Del Valle) T.; m. Maria del Consuelo Del Valle, 1 son, Joseph Albert; m. Cheryl Ann Stai, Aug. 7, 1981; 1 dau., Erika Marie. B.A., U. Miss., 1969; M.S. in Microbiology, Miss. State U., 1976. Research asst. Miss. State U., Starkville, 1973-78, teaching asst., 1973-75; quality assurance supr. Quaker Oats Co., Pascagoula, Miss., 1978-79; mgr. quality assurance Ross Labs., Sturgis, Mich., 1979-81, divisional mgr. compliance assurance, Columbus, Ohio, 1983—; dir. quality assurance Fisher Cheese Co., Wapakoneta, Ohio, 1984—; v.p. Lutriplate, Inc., Starkville, 1983—; pres. Stai-Teichert Assocs., Columbus, 1983—; sr. cons. T&C Bacteriol. Cons., Starkville, Miss. and Columbus, 1973-83. Served to capt. U.S. Army, 1970-73; Vietnam. Decorated Bronze Star with V; Cross of Gallantry, Unit Civic Actions medal (both Republic Viet Nam). Mem. N.Y. Acad. Scis., Inst. of Food Tech., AAAS, Soc. Indsl. Microbiology, Am. Soc. Quality Control. Republican. Presbyterian. Lodge: Elks. Contbr. articles to profl. pubs. Home: 3205 Greens Lima OH 45805 Office: PO Box 409 Wapakoneta OH 45895

TEJADA, PAUL, health care administrator; b. N.Y.C., Jan. 12, 1945; s. Nicanor T. and Dorothy Virginia (Doraman) T.; m. Evalyn Lawther Foot, Dec. 30, 1966; children—Dan, Jennifer, Carrie, Melissa. B.A. in Govt., Lake Forest Coll., 1966; M.S. in Hosp. Adminstrn., U. Minn., 1973. Asst. adminstr. Riverview Hosp., Wisconsin Rapids, Wis., 1973-77; adminstr. St. Olaf Hosp., Austin, Minn., 1977-82; adminstr. Alton Meml. Hosp. (Ill.), 1982—. Bd. dirs. Piasa Council Boy Scouts Am., Alton, Ill., 1983—, ARC, Alton, 1983—. Mem. Am. Coll. Hosp. Adminstrs., Am. Mgmt. Assn., Hosp. Fin. Mgmt. Assn., Am. Mktg. Assn. Episcopalian. Lodge: Rotary (Austin, Minn.).

TELANDER, RICHARD DAVID, vocational educator; b. Milaca, Minn., Nov. 15, 1941; s. William L. and Agnes C. (Rolstad) T.; m. Sandra K. Miller, Sept. 23, 1962; children—Karen, Mark, Kaye. Student Mankato (Minn.) Vocat. Tech. Inst., 1960-62. Lic. post secondary instr., Minn. Foreman tool room Midtex Inc., Mankato, Minn., 1961-69; shop foreman Amdevco Engring., Mankato, 1969-72; product mgr. North Star Concrete, Mankato, 1973; instr. tool and die Alexandria (Minn.) Tech. Inst., 1973—, com. chairperson profl. devel., 1983—. Named Educator of Yr., Alexandria Tech. Inst., 1982-83. Mem. Minn. Trade and Industry Assn. (pres.), Minn. Vocat. Assn., Am. Vocat. Assn., Minn. Edn. Assn. Lutheran. Club: Viking Sportsmen (Alexandria).

TELL, A. CHARLES, lawyer; b. Chgo., May 9, 1937; s. William K and Virginia S (Snook) T.; m. Wendy Thomsen, June 16, 1962; children—Tracey, Melissa, A. Charles, Jr. A.B., Dartmouth Coll., 1961; J.D., Ohio State U., 1963. Ptnr. George, Greek, King & McMahon, Columbus, Ohio, 1964-78, Baker & Hostetler, Columbus, 1978—; dir. Kaplan Trucking Co., Cleve. Editor Your Letter of the Law, 1984. Contbr. articles to profl. jours. Served with U.S. Army, 1958-60. Mem. ABA, Am. Judicature Soc., Ohio State Bar Assn., Columbus Bar Assn., Transp. Lawyers Assn. (pres. elect 1985). Republican. Presbyterian. Clubs: City (pres. 1985), Columbus Country (trustee 1985-87), Athletic. Office: Baker & Hostetler 65 E State St Suite 2200 Columbus OH 43215

TELLERMAN, JUDITH SILVERMAN, clinical psychologist. B.A., Brandeis U.; M. Reading Edn., Harvard U.; M.S., Ph.D. in Psychology, Boston Coll. Intern, Michael Reese Hosp., supr. tng. in psychotherapy for interns, research assoc. Psychosomatic and Psychiat. Research Inst.; cons. Gary Community Mental Health Ctr., Meth. Hosp., Gary, Sealy Inc., AFL-CIO Displaced Workers Program, GSA, Ill. CPA Soc.; leader workshops; now staff psychologist and adminstr. Roosevelt U., Chgo.; pvt. practice clin. psychology, Chgo.; sch. psychologist, reading and learning disabilities specialist, educator; mem. attending staff Barclay Hosp., Chgo. Interviews on local and nat. radio programs. Home: 2020 Lincoln Park W 38J Chicago IL 60614 Office: 55 E Washington St Suite 1601 Chicago IL 60602

TELLING, EDWARD RIGGS, retail, insurance, real estate, financial services, international trade executive; b. Danville, Ill., Apr. 1, 1919; s. Edward Riggs and Margaret Katherine (Matthews) T.; Ph.B., Ill. Wesleyan U., 1942, LL.D., 1978; m. Nancy Hawkins, Dec. 29, 1942; children—Edward R. III, Pamela Telling Grimes, Kathryn Telling Bentley, Nancy Telling O'Shaughnessy, Thomas Cole. With Sears, Roebuck & Co., 1946—, store mgr., 1954-59, zone mgr., 1960-64, mgr. met. N.Y.C. area ops., 1965-67, adminstrv. asst. to v.p. Eastern ter., Phila., 1968, v.p. Eastern ter., 1969-74, exec. v.p. Midwestern ter., Chgo., 1974-75, sr. exec. v.p. field, Chgo., 1976-77, chmn., chief exec. officer, 1978—, also dir.; dir. Dart & Kraft, Inc., Dean Witter Intercapital Funds, Cox Communications, Inc., Ill. Tool Works Inc. Bd. dirs. Sears-Roebuck Found.; chmn. bd. Savs. and Profit Sharing Fund of Sears Employees; mem. Bus. Council. Served to lt. USN, 1941-45. Clubs: Chicago, Old Elm, Commercial, Economic. Office: Sears Tower Chicago IL 60684

TELLONI, JOHN LOUIS, clergyman; b. Lorain, Ohio, Mar. 7, 1950; s. Dominic Louis and Mildred Suzanne (Mihok) T.; m. Mary Susan Cutka, Aug. 12, 1979; children—John Michael, Stephen Andrew. B.S. Ed., Bowling Green State U., 1972; M. Div., Concordia Theol. Sem., Ft. Wayne, Ind., 1977; postgrad. Concordia Sem., St. Louis, 1972-73, Lutheran Sch. Theology, Chgo., 1983. Ordained to ministry Luth. Ch., 1977; pastor St. Paul Evang. Luth. Ch. of Whiting (Ind.), 1977; interim pastor Martin Luther Ch. of Gary (Ind.), 1979-80, St. John Luth. Ch. of Whiting, 1981-83; dir. Luth. Retirement Village, Crown Point, Ind.; sec. student welfare bd., mem. youth bd. St. Paul Evang. Luth. Ch. dist. Luth. Ch.-Mo. Synod, chmn. gen. pastoral conf., 1983; dir. action group, forward in remembrance spl. appeal Luth. Ch.-Mo. Synod, 1980-81; lay youth del. to Luth. Ch.-Mo. Synod Conv., 1975; pres. central dist. Internat. Luther League, dist. Luth. Ch.-Mo. Synod, 1969-74, mission dir., 1974-75, v.p., 1975-81. Trustee, Luth. Haven, Oviedo, Fla. Democrat. Columnist Wheat & Chaff mag., 1969-70; editor The Courier, 1983; newsletter The Herald, 1979. Home: 1809 Atchison Ave Whiting IN 46394 Office: St Paul Evang Luth Ch 1801 Atchison Ave Whiting IN 46394

TEMIN, HOWARD MARTIN, biological sciences educator; b. Phila., Dec. 10, 1934; B.A., Swarthmore (Pa.) Coll., 1955, D.Sc. (hon.), 1972; Ph.D., Calif. Inst. Tech., 1959, postdoctoral fellow, 1959-60; D.Sc. (hon.), N.Y. Med. Coll., 1972, U. Pa., 1976, Hahnemann Med. Coll., 1976, Lawrence U., 1976, Temple U., 1979, Med. Coll. Wis., 1981. Asst. prof. oncology U. Wis., Madison, 1960-64, assoc. prof., 1964-69, USPHS research career devel. award Nat. Cancer Inst., 1964-74, prof. oncology, 1969—, Wis. Alumni Research Found. prof. cancer research, 1971-80, H.P. Rusch prof. cancer research, 1980—, Am. Cancer Soc. prof. viral oncology and cell biology, 1974—, Steenbock prof. biol. scis., 1982—; mem. virology study sect. NIH, 1971-74, spl. virus cancer program tumor virus detection segment working group Nat. Cancer Inst., 1972-73; mem. adv. com. to dir. NIH, 1979-83; sci. adv. Stehlin Found., Houston, 1972—; cons. working group on human gene therapy NIH Recombinant DNA Adv. Com., 1984—. Recipient Warren Triennial prize Mass. Gen. Hosp., 1971, Spl. Commendation, Wis. Med. Soc., 1971, Pap award Papanicolaou Inst., Miami, Fla., 1972, Bertner award M.D. Anderson, Houston, 1972, U.S. Steel Found. award in molecular biology Nat. Acad. Scis., 1972, Waksman award Theobald Smith Soc., 1972, Am. Chem. Soc. award in enzyme chemistry, 1973, Modern Medicine award for disting. achievement, 1973, Griffuel prize Assn. Devel. Recherche Cancer, Villejuif, 1973, G.H.A. Clowes Lectureship award Am. Assn. for Cancer Research, 1974, Gairdner Found. Internat. award Toronto, 1974, Albert Lasker award in basic med. research, 1974, Nobel prize for physiology or medicine, 1975, Lucy Wortham James award in basic research Soc. Surg. Oncologists, 1976, Alumni Disting. Service award Calif. Inst. Tech., 1976; Lila Gruber Research award Am. Acad. Dermatology, 1981; New Horizons for Radiologists lectr. Radiol. Soc. N.Am., 1968, Harry Shay Meml. lectr. Fels Inst., Phila., 1973, Dyer lectr. NIH, 1974, Harvey lectr., 1974; Charlton lectr. Tufts U. Med. Sch., 1976; Hoffman-La Roche lectr. Rutgers U., 1979; Yoder honor lectr. U. Tacoma, 1983; Bitterman

Meml. lectr., N.Y.C., 1984; Cetus lectr. U. Calif., 1984; Dupont lectr. Harvard Med. Sch., 1985; lectr. Japanese Found. Promotion Cancer Research, 1985. Fellow Am. Acad. Arts and Scis.; mem. Nat. Acad. Sci., Am. Philos. Soc., Wis. Acad. Sci., Arts and Letters (hon.). Assoc. editor: Jour. of Cellular Physiology, 1966-77, Cancer Research, 1971-74; mem. editorial bd. Jour. of Virology, 1971—, Intervirology, 1972-75, Archives of Virology, 1975-77, Procs. Nat. Acad. Scis., 1975-80, others. Office: McArdle Lab 450 N Randall St U Wis Madison WI 53706

TEMPEL, EUGENE RAYMOND, foundation administrator, speaker, researcher; b. St. Meinrad, Ind., Mar. 30, 1947; s. Charles Xavier and Bernadette Scholastica (Otto) T.; m. Mary Jo Ekerle, May 24, 1969; children—Jonathan, Jason, Zachary. B.A. in English and Philosophy, St. Benedict Coll., 1970; M.A. in English, Ind. U., 1973, Ed.D. in Higher Edn., 1985. Asst. prof. English, Vincennes U., Ind., 1970-77, dir. Jasper Ctr., 1973-77; v.p., dean of faculty Three Rivers Community Coll., Poplar Bluff, Mo., 1977-80; dir. external affairs Ind. U., Bloomington, 1980-83; exec. dir. for Indpls. Ind. U. Found., 1983-85, v.p., 1985—; bd. dirs. devel. cons. Marian Heights Acad., Ferdinand, Ind., 1973—; devel. cons. Ind. Agrl. Inst., Indpls., 1985. Author (study) Decline in Small Colleges, 1984. Commr. Jasper Community Arts Commn., Ind., 1975-77; mem. Mingo Community Relations Council, Poplar Bluff, 1977-80; vol. Indpls. Symphony, 1985. Mem. Indpls. C. of C., Council for Advancement and Support Edn., Am. Assn. Higher Edn. Democrat. Roman Catholic. Club: Athletic (Indpls.). Lodge: Rotary. Avocations: soccer parents, sailing. Home: 7277 Hawthorne Ln Indianapolis IN 46250 Office: Ind U Found 355 N Lansing St Indianapolis IN 46202

TEMPLIN, ROBERT JAMES, automobile company executive; b. Toronto, Ont., Can., Dec. 9, 1927; came to U.S., 1934; s. Albert Alexander and Elizabeth Lydia (Zingle) T.; m. Peggy Ann Wyatt, July 15, 1974; children—Patricia E., Lucie E., R. James. B.Chem.Engring., Rensselaer Poly Inst., 1947. Registered profl. engr., Mich. Asst. chief engr. Cadillac Motor Car Div., Detroit, 1965-69, chief engr., 1973-84; tech. dir. Gen. Motors Research Lab., Warren, Mich., 1969-70; spl. asst. to pres. Gen. Motors Corp., Detroit, 1970-72; dir. advanced design and process Buick Olds Cadillac Group, Warren, Mich., 1984—; mem. Rensselaer Council, Troy, N.Y., 1979—; cons. Ordnance Corps, U.S. Army, Yuma, Ariz., 1950-51, Washington-Heidelberg, 1954. Patentee in field of air pollution control Mem. Soc. Automotive Engrs. Republican. Avocations: amateur radio; photography; scuba. Office: Buick Olds Cadillac Advanced Design and Process Tech Ctr Bldg W-3 Warren MI 48090

TEN EICK, ROBERT EDWIN, cardiac electrophysiology educator; b. Port Chester, N.Y., Oct. 14, 1937; s. Arthur Ray and Viola (Spence) T.; m. Mary Louise Costa, July 1, 1962; children—Matthew, Andrew. B.S. in Chemistry, Columbia U., 1963, Ph.D. in Pharmacology, 1968. Guest investigator The Rockefeller U., N.Y.C., 1968; asst. prof. Northwestern U., Chgo., 1968-74, assoc. prof., 1974-80, prof., 1980—; vis. prof. Universitat des Saarlandes, Homburg, W. Ger., 1974-75. Contbr. articles to profl. jours.; speaker profl. symposia. Grantee NIH USPHS, 1975—, Am. Heart Assn., 1976-81, Chgo. Heart Assn. 1969-75. Mem. Am. Soc. Pharmacology and Exptl. Therapeutics, Am. Physiol. Soc., Am. Heart Assn. (Basic Sci. Council sect.), Cardiac Muscle Soc., Cardiac Electrophysiol. Soc. Avocations: tennis; swimming; sailing; wind surfing; camping. Office: Northwestern Univ Med Sch 303 E Chicago Ave Chicago IL 60611

TENER, THOMAS NORMAN, utility company executive; b. Tulsa, Feb. 6, 1946; s. Samuel Amaziah and Ruth (Cassidy) T.; m. Myra Russek, July 1, 1977; children—Thomas Norman, William Christian, Trula Ruth. B.A., U. Tulsa, 1968. Acctg. office supr. Southwestern Bell Telephone Co., Tulsa, 1968-69, acctg. mgr., 1969-71, methods acct., St. Louis, 1971-73, asst. dist. acctg. mgr., Wichita, Kans., 1973-75, sr. methods acct., St. Louis, 1975-78, dist. staff mgr., St. Louis, 1978—; mem. part-time faculty St. Louis Community Coll., 1980—; v.p. Arrowhead Info. Services. Mem. Queeny Republican Twp. Club, Des Peres, Mo.; sustaining mem. Rep. Presdl. Task Force, Rep. Senatorial Com., Mo. Rep. Party; bd. dirs. Good Shepherd Found. Episcopalian. Home: 13276 Gateroyal Des Peres MO 63131 Office: Southwestern Bell Telephone Co 1010 Pine Room 1322 Saint Louis MO 63101

TENG, JAMES, chemist; b. Hong Kong, Dec. 4, 1929; came to U.S., 1947. B.S., Tri State U., 1952; M.S., Case Western U., 1965, Ph.D., 1967. Research supr. Nylouge Corp., Cleve., 1953-66; research assoc. Purdue U., West Lafayette, Ind., 1967; research mgr. Anheuser Busch Co., St. Louis, 1968-72, sr. research mgr., 1982-84, dir. process devel., 1984—. Patentee in cellulosic compounds and process, cosmetics, brewing. Mem. Am. Chem. Soc., AAAS, N.Y. Acad. Sci., Master Brewer Assn. Am., Sigma Xi. Avocations: photography; tennis. Home: 11815 Edie and Park Rd Crestwood MO 63126 Office: Anheuser Busch Co 1 Busch Pl St Louis MO 63118

TENG, LEE CHANG-LI, researcher in accelerator physics; b. Peiping, China, Sept. 5, 1926; came to U.S., 1947, naturalized, 1962; s. Tsuey Ying and Chien Min (Ho) T.; m. Nancy Lai-Shen Huang, Sept. 21, 1961; 1 child, Michael Nan-Hao. B.S., FuJen U., Peiping, 1946; M.S., U. Chgo., 1948, Ph.D., 1951. Asst. prof. U. Minn., Mpls., 1951-53; assoc. prof. Wichita State U., Kans., 1953-55; leader accelerator theory group Argonne Nat. Lab., Ill., 1955-62, dir. accelerator div., 1962-67; lectr. U. Chgo., 1964-67; dept. chmn. accelerator theory sect. Fermi Nat. Accelerator Lab., Batavia, Ill., 1967-72, advanced projects, 1974-79, assoc. head accelerator div., 1972—; dir. Synchrotron Radiation Research Ctr., Taiwan, China, 1983—; hon. prof. Beijing Normal U.; chmn. numerous confs., workshops, schs., and coms.; cons. various univs., labs., and cos. Contbr. articles to profl. jours. Recipient Gold medal of Achievement Chinese Ministry of Edn., 1956; Disting. Service award Immigrants Service League, 1963. Fellow Am. Phys. Soc. (exec. com. 1980-82); mem. Academia Sinica (academician), AAUP, Inst. High Energy Physics, Chinese Acad. Sci. (hon. adv.), Chinese Student and Alumni Assn., FuJen Alumni Assn. (hon. chmn.), Phi Tau Phi (pres. 1963-66), Sigma Xi (pres. 1954). Republican. Avocations: violin, tennis, skiing. Home: 400 E 8th St Hinsdale IL 60521 Office: Fermi Nat Accelerator Lab PO Box 500 Batavia IL 60510

TENNANT, CAROLYN GAY, college administrator; b. Janesville, Wis., June 19, 1947; d. Ralph Benjamin and Beverly Jane (Hart) Jenny; m. Raymond Frank Tennant, Dec. 28, 1968. B.A., U. Colo., 1969, M.A., 1973, Ph.D. in Edn1. Adminstrn. and Supervision, 1979. Ordained to ministry Assemblies of God Ch., 1985. Tchr. Adams County Sch. Dist. 12, Denver, 1969-73, spl. programs coordinator, dir. gifted and talented, instr. staff devel., 1978-79; dir. Inst. Cognitive Devel., Denver, 1979-81, Dayton, Ohio, 1981-83; v.p. student life N. Central Bible Coll., Mpls., 1983—. Nat. Inst. Edn. grantee, 1975-78; recipient Fulbright-Hays award, 1981. Mem. Assn. Supervision and Curriculum Devel., Assn. Christians in Student Devel., Nat. Assn. Gifted Children, Colo. Lang. Arts Soc. (treas. 1973-74), Nat. Soc. Study Edn., Nat. Council Tchrs. English, Internat. Reading Assn. Republican. Author: (with H.S. Morgan and M. Gold) Elementary and Secondary Level Programs for the Gifted and Talented, 1980. Office: 910 Elliot Ave S Minneapolis MN 55404

TENNANT, JEFFREY SPENCER, ophthalmologist; b. Frankfurt, Fed. Republic Germany, Feb. 16, 1947; came to U.S., 1947; s. Maurice Marc and Helen Diane (Isenberg) T.; m. Noreen Simona Chertow, May 1, 1983. B.S. in Biology, U. Ill.-Chgo., 1966, M.D., 1970. Intern, Cook County Hosp., Chgo., 1970-71, resident in ophthalmology, 1974, attending physician, 1974-79; attending physician Oak Forest Hosp. (Ill.), 1974-79. Mem. AMA, Ill. State Med. Soc., Chgo. Med. Soc., Am. Intra-Ocular Implant Soc., Ill. Assn. Ophthalmology (pres. 1984—), Am. Acad. Ophthalmology. Office: 4647 W 103d Oak Lawn IL 60453

TENNENT, DAVID MADDUX, retired pharmaceutical company executive, consultant; b. Bryn Mawr, Pa., Oct. 2, 1914; s. David Hilt and Esther Margaret (Maddux) T.; m. Martha Alice Meloy, Apr. 21, 1945; children—Isabel Blythe, Meredith Meloy, David Lambie, Charles Maddux. A.B., Yale U., 1936, Ph.D., 1940. Research asst. Yale U., New Haven, 1940-42; research assoc. Merck Inst., Rahway, N.J., 1942-60; asst. dir. research Hess & Clark div. Richardson-Merrell, Inc. (became Hess & Clark div. Rhodia Inc. 1971, now Rhone Poulenc Inc.), Ashland, Ohio, 1960-63, dir. research and devel., 1963-69, v.p. research and devel. Hess & Clark div. Rhodia Inc., Ashland, 1969-75, cons. vet. affairs Rhodia, Inc., N.Y.C., 1975-79. Contbr. articles to profl. sci. jours. Patentee (6) in field. Trustee Ashland Pub. Library; mem. Street Tree Commn., Ashland. Fellow AAAS, Am. Heart Assn. Council on Arteriosclerosis (retired); mem. Am. Soc. Biol. Chemists, Soc. for Exptl. Biology and Medicine (emeritus), Am. Chem. Soc. (emeritus). Republican. Avocations: travel, woodworking, Bridge. Home: 981 Forest Ln Ashland OH 44805

TENNEY, MARK WILLIAM, environ. engring. cons.; b. Chgo., Dec. 10, 1936; s. William and Frieda (Sanders) T.; B.S., Mass. Inst. Tech., 1958, M.S., 1959, Sc.D., 1965; m. Jane E. Morris, June 1, 1974; children by previous marriage—Scott, Barbara. Design engr. Greeley & Hansen, Engrs., Chgo., 1959-61; asso. prof. civil engring. U. Notre Dame, 1965-73; pres. TenEch Environ. Engrs., Inc., South Bend, Ind., 1973—. Served with C.E., AUS, 1959-60; col. Res. USPHS research fellow, 1961-64. Diplomate Am. Acad. Environ. Engrs. Fellow ASCE; mem. Nat. Soc. Profl. Engrs., Am. Cons. Engrs. Council, Water Pollution Control Fedn., Am. Water Works Assn., Sigma Xi, Chi Epsilon, Phi Delta Theta. Clubs: Ill. Athletic; Lake Macatawa Yacht; Summit. Contbr. articles to profl. jours. Home: 2110 Niles-Buchanan Rd Niles MI 49120 Office: 744 W Washington St South Bend IN 46601

TENNYSON, ROBERT DUANE, education, computer science and psychology educator; b. Culver City, Calif., Aug. 19, 1945; s. Harry Langley and Alise Vivian (Lowder) T.; m. Halyna Hajovy, Sept. 19, 1978. B.S., Brigham Young U., 1967, Ph.D., 1971; M.A., Calif. State U., 1968, M.A., 1969. Tchr., Newhall (Calif.) High Sch., 1967-69; prof. Fla. State U., 1971-74; prof. edn. and psychology U. Minn., Mpls., 1974—, dir. Instructional Systems Lab., 1974—. Fulbright Research scholar, Germany, 1981-82. Fellow Am. Psychol. Assn. Editor Am. Ednl. Research Jour. Contbr. numerous articles to profl. jours. Home: 8710 Hunters Way Apple Valley MN 55124 Office: 159 Pillsbury Dr SE U Minn Minneapolis MN 55455

TEPATTI, ROBERT JAMES, life insurance agent, annuity consultant; b. Hillsboro, Ill., Apr. 17, 1951; s. Antone and Roberta Marie (Marti) T.; m. Terri Ann Clayton, July 7, 1973 (div. 1982); children—Ann Marie, Stephen James. B.A., Greenville Coll., 1973; M.S., Ill. State U., 1974. Cert. fellow Life Mgmt. Inst. with specialization in pension planning Life Office Mgmt. Assn. C.L.U. Teaching asst. Ill. State U. Normal, 1973-74; agt. Mut. and United of Omaha, Springfield, Ill., 1975-77; annuity cons. Horace Mann Life Ins. Co., Springfield, 1977—. Lay leader United Meth. Ch., Riverton, Ill., 1980—. Mem. Fellows Life Mgmt. Inst. Soc. (Central Ill. chpt.); mem. Springfield Assn. Life Underwriters, Ill. Assn. Life Underwriters, Nat. Assn. Life Underwriters, Lodge: Masons. Contbr. tech. articles to profl. publs. Home: 3100 Butler Rd Apt 7 Springfield IL 62703 Office: Horace Mann Life Ins Co 1 Horace Mann Plaza Springfield IL 62715

TEPPER, MARC JEFFREY, corporation manager; b. Chgo., Mar. 19, 1956; s. Samuel and Grace Lael (Goldstein) T.; m. Carolyn Marie Thompson, May 29, 1983. B.S., Colo. State U., 1979. Lab. asst. Environeering, Des Plaines, Ill., 1980-81, research and devel. engr., 1981-82; sales engr. Flex-Kleen, Chgo., 1982-84, regional sales mgr., 1984—; cons. Mem. Air Pollution Control Assn. Republican. Jewish. Avocations: downhill skiing; golf; softball. Office: Flex-Kleen Corp 165 N Canal St Chicago IL 60606

TEPPER, NEAL GARY, counselor; b. Bklyn., Mar. 12, 1951; s. Leon and Bernice Rhoda (Fisher) T. B.A., State U. N.Y., Potsdam, 1972; M.A., U. N.D., 1973, B.S. in Edn., 1985. Group therapist St. Mike's Hosp., Grand Forks, N.D., 1972-73; tchr. courses Center Teaching and Learning, U. N.D., 1973-75, grad. teaching asst. dept. counseling and guidance, 1974-77, intern counselor Counseling Center, 1975-77; practicum guidance counselor Red River High Sch., Grand Forks, 1973-74; mental health clinician IV, Meml. Mental Health and Retardation Center, Mandan, N.D., 1977-79; dir. Children and Family Services for Standing Rock Sioux Tribe, Ft. Yates, N.D., 1978-81; dir. counseling United Tribes Ednl. Tech. Center, 1981-83; counselor Bur. Indian Affairs, Dept. Interior, Fort Totten, N.D., 1983-85; family therapist Lutheran Soc. Services of Minn., Grand Forks, N.D., 1985—. Mem. Am. Personnel and Guidance Assn., N. Central Assn. Counselor Educators Assns., Mental Health Assn., Assn. Edn. of Young Children, N.D. Conf. Social Welfare. Office: PO Box 985 Grand Forks ND 58206 Home: 314 State St Grand Forks ND 58201

TERKEL, STUDS LOUIS, interviewer, author; b. N.Y.C., May 16, 1912; s. Samuel and Anna (Finkel) T.; Ph.D., U. Chgo., 1932, J.D., 1934; m. Ida Goldberg, July 2, 1939; 1 son, Paul. Stage appearances include Detective Story, 1950, A View From the Bridge, 1958, Light Up the Sky, 1959, The Cave Dwellers, 1960; star TV program Studs Place, 1950-53, radio program Wax Mus., from 1945, Studs Terkel Almanac, from 1952, now Studs Terkel Show, Sta. WFMT-FM, Chgo.; master of ceremonies Newport Folk Festival, 1959, 60, Ravinia Music Festival, 1959, U. Chgo. Folk Festival, 1961, others; panel moderator, lectr., narrator films. Program, Wax Museum, winner 1st award as best cultural program in regional radio category Inst. Edn. by Radio-TV, Ohio State U., 1959; recipient Prix Italia, UNESCO award for best radio program East-West Values, 1962; Communicator of Year award U. Chgo. Alumni Assn., 1969. Author: Giants of Jazz, 1956; Division Street America, 1966; (play) Amazing Grace, 1959; Hard Times, 1970; Working, 1974; Talking to Myself, 1977; American Dreams: Lost and Found, 1980; The Good War (Pulitzer prize 1985). Office: 303 E Wacker Dr Chicago IL 60601*

TERRA, DANIEL JAMES, chemical executive; b. Phila., June 8, 1911; s. Louis J. and Mary (DeLuca) T.; B.S., Penn State U., 1931; m. Adeline Evans Richards, Aug. 7, 1937; children—Penny Jane (dec.), James D. Founder, Lawter Chems., Inc., Chgo., 1940, chmn., chief exec. officer, 1964—, also dir.; ambassador-at-large for cultural affairs Dept. State, 1981—. Bd. dirs. Easter Seal Soc., Chgo. Lyric Opera, Chgo. Crime Commn.; trustee Chgo. Orchestral Assn., Dickinson Coll., Roycemore Sch.; adv. council Northwestern U. Grad. Sch. Mgmt., mem. Pres.'s Council Nat. Coll. Edn.; mem. Pres.'s club Loyola U.; bd. dirs. Woodrow Wilson Ctr. for Scholars, Nat. Gallery Art, Washington; exec. com. Ill. Inst. Tech. Research Inst.; mem. Chgo. Commn. Trust, Assos. of Northwestern U., Pres.'s Com. Arts and Humanities; mem. grand council Am. Indian Center Chgo.; mem. univ. council Pa. State U.; mem. Am. arts com. Art Inst. Chgo. Recipient Winthrop Sears medal Chem. Industry Assn., 1972, Disting. Alumnus medal Pa. State U., 1976; decorated comdr. Order Arts and Letters (France). Mem. Clubs: Westmoreland Country (Wilmette, Ill.); Kenilworth; Capitol Hill (Washington); Metropolitan, Chicago, Comml., Casino, Mid-Am. (Chgo.); Lauderdale Yacht (Fort Lauderdale, Fla.); Nat. Arts of N.Y.; Links (N.Y.C.). Office: 990 Skokie Blvd Northbrook IL 60062

TERRELL, WILLIE ANDREW, JR., educator; b. Dayton, Ohio, June 18, 1951; s. Willie A. and Hazel (Wright) T.; B.S., Central State U., Ohio, 1972; Ed.M., Miami U., Ohio, 1977, Wright State U., 1980. Youth advocate Youth Services Bur., Dayton, 1972-76; tchr. social studies Dayton Bd. Edn., 1973-76, 77—; substitute tchr. Hamilton (Ohio) Public Schs., 1977; notary public, Ohio, 1980—. Named Black Man of Yr., Roosevelt Black Awareness Council, 1974. Mem. Assn. for Supervision and Curriculum Devel., Nat. Council Social Studies, NEA, Ohio Council Social Studies, Western Ohio Edn. Assn., Dayton Edn. Assn., Central State U. Alumni Assn., Kappa Delta Pi, Alpha Kappa Mu, Phi Alpha Theta, Omega Psi Phi (Omega Man of Yr. 4th Dist. 1985). Club: Masons. Home: 1721 Radio Rd B-6 Dayton OH 45403 Office: 48 W Parkwood Dayton OH 45403

TERRILL, JAMES SAMUEL, lawyer; b. Ulysses, Kans., Mar. 20, 1916; s. Colyar St. Clair and Carrie Arbuckle (Alexander) T.; m. Nalda Mae Northrup, Oct. 4, 1945; children—Candace Leigh, Hollace Jo. B.A., Kans. U., 1937, LL.B., 1939, LL.D. (hon.), 1975. Bar: Kans. 1939. Atty. County of Hamilton, Syracuse, Kans., 1941-42, 46-52; atty. City of Syracuse, 1941-42; sole practice, Syracuse. Mem. Kans. Bar Assn., Southwest Kans. Bar Assn., Industrial Club (pres. 1946), Syracuse C. of C., Am. Legion, VFW. Democrat. Presbyterian. Lodges: Lions, Rotary, Masons. Home: 307 N Elizabeth Syracuse KS 67878 Office: Northrup Theater Bldg Box 615 Syracuse KS 67878

TERRY, JAMES ANDREW, III, clinical psychologist, administrator, consultant; b. Chgo., July 7, 1935; s. James Andrew and Gussie Ola (Jones) T. B.A. in History, Roosevelt U.; M.S., Ill. Tchrs. Coll., 1966; Ph.D. in Clin. Psychology, Northwestern U., 1978. Cert. high sch. history, supervision, adminstrn., Ill. History tchr. Chgo. Bd. Edn., 1957-63; dir. and supr. jobs project YMCA, Chgo., 1964-68; dir. services Ebony Mgmt. Assocs., Chgo., 1968-69; dir. Englewood Mental Health Clinic, 1969—; cons. to indsl. cos. and agys.; condr. seminars for Ministry Edn. and Culture, Freeport Bahamas. Fellow Northwestern U. Med. Sch.; recipient Health Services award Young Execs. in Politics, 1983. Mem. Am. Psychol. Assn., Ill. Psychol. Assn., Chgo. Psychol. Assn., Musicians Union, Kappa Alpha Psi. Roman Catholic. Contbr. articles to profl. jours. Home: 1916 S Hamlin St Chicago IL 60623 Office: 641 W 63d St Chicago IL 60621

TERRY, LEON CASS, neurologist, educator; b. Northville, Mich., Dec. 22, 1940; s. Leon Herbert and Zella Irene (Boyd) T.; m. Suzanne Martinson, June 27, 1964; children—Kristin, Sean. Pharm. D., U. Mich., 1964; M.D., Marquette U., 1969; Ph.D., McGill U., 1982. Dipolmate Am. Bd. Psychiatry and Neurology. Intern, U. Rochester, N.Y., 1969-70; staff assoc. NIH, 1970-72; resident in neurology McGill U., Montreal, Que., Can., 1972-75, MRC fellow, 1975-78; assoc. prof. U. Tenn., Memphis, 1978-81; prof. neurology U. Mich., Ann Arbor, 1981—, assoc prof. physiology, 1982—; asst. chief neurology VA Med. Ctr., Ann Arbor, 1982—. Contbr. articles to profl. jours., chpts. to books. Served to lt. comdr. USPHS, 1970-72. NIH grantee, 1981-84; VA grantee, 1980—; VA Clin. Investigator award, 1980-81. Mem. Am. Soc. Clin. Investigation, Am. Neurol. Assn., Endocrine Soc., Am. Acad. Neurology. Clubs: Ann Arbor Flyers, UM Flyers. Avocations: pilot; skiing; scuba diving; computers. Office: VA Med Ctr Neurology 127 2215 Fuller St Ann Arbor MI 48105

TERSTEEG, JOHN THOMAS, steel products executive; b. Olivia, Minn., Nov. 24, 1930; s. John Edward and Elizabeth Francis (Mysicka) T.; m. Elizabeth Ann Scheibel, July 10, 1954; children—Theresa, Kathryn, Barbara, Patricia, Marilyn, Joseph, Kari. Pres. Steel Products, Inc., Olivia, Minn., 1968-78, 1980—; pres. Energy World, Inc., Olivia, 1979—; mem. nat. council Behlen Mfg. Co., Columbus, Nebr., 1971-73, pres., 1973-75. Pres. Nat. Farm Orgn., Renville County, 1962-64; dir. Bird Island Twp. Bd., Renville County, 1955-57; dir. Mid-State Aviation, Olivia, 1971-73. Served with U.S. Army, 1951-52. Mem. Minn. Alternative Energy Assn. (dir. 1979-83). Roman Catholic. Clubs: Lions (Olivia). Inventor, flex-bar, 1967. Home: Rural Route 1 PO Box 109 Olivia MN 56277

TERZIC, BRANKO DUSAN, state official, engineer; b. Diepholz, W. Ger., June 19, 1947; came to U.S., 1950; s. Dusan Branko and Olivera (Beljakovic) T.; m. Judith Ware Antonic, Oct. 7, 1978; children—Dusan-Alexander, Elizabeth Alexandra Olivera. B.S. in Energy Engring., U. Wis.-Milw., 1972. With Am. Appraisal Milw., 1970-72, 73-36; engr. Wis. Electric Power Co., Milw., 1972-73; v.p. Assoc. Utility Services, Milw., 1976-79; ptnr. Terzic & Mayer, Milw., 1979-81; mem. Wis. Pub. Service Commn., Madison, 1981—. Chmn. Fifth Congl. Republican Orgn., 1975-77. Decorated comdr. Cross of Merit, Sovereign Mil. Order of Malta, Knight Grand Officer of Crown (Yugoslavia) Knight S.O.M. Constantine and St. George. Mem. Nat. Assn. Regulatory Utility Commrs. (chmn. engring. com. 1982—). Serbian Orthodox. Club: Milwaukee Athletic. Office: PO Box 7854 Madison WI 53707

TESCH, RONALD CARL, educator, school administrator; b. Aurora, Ill., June 25, 1944; s. Carl Erwin and Evelyn (Mietz) T.; m. Karen Lynn Gamble, Aug. 13, 1966; children—Kristoffer, James Robert. B.A., N. Ill. U.; M.A., Mich. State U. Tchr. Plano Jr. High Sch., Ill., 1966-67; tchr. Lake Fenton High Sch., Fenton, Mich., 1967-73, prin. Lake Fenton Jr. High Sch., 1973-76, Lake Fenton High Sch., 1976-79, Ann Arbor Huron High Sch., Mich., 1979—; cons. Edn. Services Bur., Ann Arbor. Contbr. articles to profl. jours. Mem. Genesse Assn. Middle Sch. Educators (pres. 1975-76), Ann Arbor Secondary Council (pres. 1982-83), Assn. Supervision and Curriculum Devel., Nat. Assn. Secondary Sch. Prins., Phi Delta Kappa. Lodge: Rotary. Avocations: tennis; golf; running; sailing. Home: 3272 Bluett Dr Ann Arbor MI 48105

TESCHNER, PAUL AUGUST, JR., lawyer; b. Green Bay, Wis., June 20, 1925; s. Paul August and Helen (Boyington) T.; student U. Wis., 1943-44; B.B.A., Northwestern U., 1949; D.J. with distinction, Ind. U., 1953; m. Barbara Malmstone, June 12, 1948; children—Karen Janette, Paul August III, Tammy Jane; m. Anastasia Ferensen, Oct. 15, 1977. Teaching asso. Northwestern U. Sch. Law, Chgo., 1953-54; admitted to Ind., Ill., U.S. Tax Ct. bars, 1953-54, U.S. Ct. of Claims bar, 1963, U.S. Supreme Ct. bar, 1967, U.S. Ct. Appeals for Fed. Cir. Bar, 1982. Employee Pope & Ballard, Chgo., 1954-57; partner firm Pope, Ballard, Uriell, Kennedy, Shepard & Fowle, Chgo., 1958-72; sr. partner Teschner & Teschner, Chgo., 1972-75; chief exec. officer Teschner Profl. Corp., Chgo., 1975—; instr. tax, constl. and bus. law Elmhurst Coll. Evening Div., 1960-73; adj. prof. legal ethics Ind. U. Sch. Law, Bloomington, 1975-76; lectr. in field. Sec., mem. Village of Hinsdale (Ill.) Zoning Bd. of Appeals, 1966-77, Zoning Commn., 1966-77; mem. Ill. Master Plan Com. on Legal Edn., 1968-69. Served with AUS, 1943-46. Decorated Bronze Star with oak leaf cluster. Mem. Am. (com. on standards tax practice of tax sect. 1966-75), Ind., Ill. (com. on specialization 1968-71, 73-77, chmn. legal edn. and admission to bar com. 1970-72, assembly del. 1972-78, 80—, com. profl. ethics 1973-81, chmn. 1979-80), Chgo. (com. fed. taxation 1958-67, com. legal edn. 1955-80, chmn. com. 1967-68, 76-77), also unauthorized practice com., specialization com., chmn. specialization com. 1976-78), Internat. bar assns., World Assn. Lawyers (founder, life), World Peace Through Law Center, Am. Judicature Soc., Selden Soc., Internat. Platform Assn., Order of Coif, Phi Delta Phi, Beta Alpha Psi. Clubs: Monroe (founding life), Execs. Author: Essays Before Watergate, 1977. Contbr. articles to profl. jours. Home: 316 E 6th St Hinsdale IL 60521 Office: 39 S LaSalle St Chicago IL 60603

TESMER, NANCY ANN STUTLER, librarian; b. Akron, Ohio, Aug. 25, 1934; d. Ernest Lynn and Sophrona Rebecca (Pepper) Stutler; student U. Akron, 1952-54; B.A., Kent State U., 1956; m. Clifford Frank Haines, Aug. 20, 1960 (div.); m. John A. Tesmer, Sept. 10, 1980. Jr. asst. librarian E. Br. Library, Akron, 1956-59; hosp. librarian VA Hosp., Northampton, Mass., 1959-61; med. librarian VA Hosp., Brecksville, Ohio, 1961-65, chief librarian, 1965-73; assoc. chief librarian Cleve. VA Hosp., 1973-75, chief librarian, 1975—. Mem. Med. Library Assn., N.E. Ohio Med. Library Assn., Zeta Tau Alpha. Home: 603 Tollis Pkwy Broadview Heights OH 44147 Office: 10000 Brecksville Rd Brecksville OH 44141

TEW, ARNOLD GERARD, educational administrator; b. Bklyn., Mar. 10, 1938; s. Benjamin and Jean (Abramowitz) T.; m. Sheila Berlow, June 21, 1959; children—Alissa, Debra, JoAnn. B.B.A., The City Coll., N.Y.C., 1958; M.A., Columbia U., 1961; Ph.D., Case Western Res. U., Cleve., 1969. Instr., asst. prof. Fenn Coll., Cleve., 1961-65; asst. assoc. prof. Cleve. State U., Ohio, 1965—, assoc. dean arts and scis., 1966-71, v.p. student services, 1971-83, v.p. adminstrn., student affairs, 1984—. Editor Prentice Hall, 1961. Program chmn. Greater Cleve. council Boy Scouts Am., 1983, div. chmn. Jewish Welfare Fund, Cleve., 1979. Recipient Danforth tchr. award, Danforth Found., 1966; fellow Am. Council Edn, 1970. Mem. Nat. Assn. Coll. and Univ. Bus. Officers, Am. Assn. for Counseling and Devel., Greater Cleve. Growth Assn. Reform Judaism. Avocation: Square dancing. Office: Cleveland State Univ Cleveland OH 44115

TEWKSBURY, DUANE ALLAN, biochemist; b. Osceola, Wis., Oct. 4, 1936; s. Allen and Ethel (Holmquist) T.; m. Jean Marie Dombrock, Aug. 30, 1958 (div.); children—Craig Duane, Randall Duane. B.S., St. Olaf Coll., 1958; M.S., U. Wis., 1960, Ph.D., 1964. Sr. research biochemist Marshfield Med. Found., Wis., 1964—. Contbr. articles to profl. jours. Mem. Am. Soc. Biol. Chemists, AAAS, Am. Chem. Soc. (chmn. 1973, outstanding contributions to chemistry award Central Wis. sect. 1981), Am. Heart Assn. (basic sci. council, council for high blood pressure research, outstanding research award 1979), Wis. Heart Assn. Home: Rt 3 Box 165 Marshfield WI 54449 Office: Marshfield Med Found 510 North St Joseph Ave Marshfield WI 54449

TEYKL, JAMES STEPHEN, lawyer; b. Houston, Dec. 21, 1954; s. Irvin Frank and Marjorie Doris (Johnston) T.; m. Mary Beth Crowson, Apr. 30, 1983. B.A., U. Ill., 1977; J.D., Northwestern U., 1980. Bar: Ill. 1980, U.S. Dist. Ct. (no. dist.) Ill. 1980, U.S. Ct. Appeals (7th cir.) 1981. Assoc. Anthony Scariano & Assocs., P.C., Chicago Heights, Ill., 1980-81; ptnr. Greenberg & Teykl, Park Forest, Ill., 1981—; guest lectr. law Thornton Community Coll., South Holland, Ill., 1982—. Trustee Ill. Community Coll. Dist. 515, Chicago Heights, 1983—; mem. Taxpayers Adv. Bd., Chgo., 1983—. Mem. Ill. Bar Assn., South Suburban Bar Assn., Ill. Community Coll. Trustees Assn., Coalition Polit. Honesty. Episcopalian. Home: 209 Krotiak St Park Forest IL 60466 Office: Greenberg & Teykl 24 Plaza Suite 7 Park Forest IL 60466

TEYRAL, JOHN WALTER, art educator; b. Yaroslav, Ukraine, Soviet Union, June 10, 1912; came to U.S., 1916; s. Alexander and Mary (Hrabenik) T.; m. Valerie Calvert Howard, June 2, 1962 (div. 1982). Student Cleve. Inst. Art, 1928-31, Boston Mus. Sch. Fine Arts, 1934-37, Ecole De La Grande Chaumière, Paris, 1938, Accademia di Belli Arti, Florence, Italy, 1949-50. Tchr. art Cleve. Inst. Art, 1939-77; tchr. art Coll. Club, Cleve., 1977-84. Oil portraits include: Gov. Rhodes of Ohio, 1964, Dr. John S. Millis (pres. Western Res. U., 1956), Lorin Maazel (Cleve. Orch. condr.), 1982, others. Served with AC U.S. Army, 1942-44; N. Africa. Gund travelling scholar Cleve. Inst. Art,

1934; Fulbright grantee, 1939-40; recipient 1st prize Butler Art Inst., 1948; Purchase award Pepsi-Cola Art Competition, N.Y., 1948.

THACKER, GERALD DEAN, wire manufacturing executive; b. Pekin, Ill., Mar. 1, 1935; s. Inest Clayburn and Alice Lucille (Jones) T.; m. Shirley Dean May, Dec. 12, 1953; 1 child, Jeffrey Dean. Various managerial positions Keystone Consol. Industries, Peoria, Rockford, Ill., also Crawfordsville, Ind., 1955-80, 83-85; plant mgr. Midstates Wire Co., Crawfordsville, 1978-80, mgr. engring. and maintenance, 1983-85; mgr. engring. and maintenance Crawford Industries, Crawfordsville, 1980-82; sales rep. Walter Danville Corp., Danville, Ill., 1981-82, Central Ind. Rubber Co., Crawfordsville, 1982-83. Mem. Pyramid Soc., Arabian Horse Club (bd. dirs. Crawfordsville), Mgmt. Club (pres. Crawfordsville). Lodges: Masons (32d degree), Kiwanis. Republican. Avocation: breeding; raising and showing Egyptian related Arabian horses. Home: Rural Route 7 State Rd 47 S Crawfordsville IN 47933 Office: Mid-States Wire Co 510 Oak St Crawfordsville IN 47933

THAIN, JOHN GRIFFITHS, lab. adminstr.; b. Hayes, Middlesex, Eng., Sept. 27, 1937; s. Charles J. and Dilys D. (Griffiths) T.; came to U.S., 1958; student Acton Tech. Coll., 1955-58, Ind. U., 1958-63; A.S. in Bus. Adminstrn., U. New Haven, 1980; m. Jacqueline M. Hart, Nov. 3, 1962; children—Jeremy Guy, Richard Gary, Jennifer Ann. Lab. asst. Castrol Ltd., Hayes, Middlesex, U.K., 1953-58; lab. technician Miles Labs., Inc., Elkhart, Ind., 1958-61, coordinator mfg. records, 1961-67, coordinator packaging devel. and labelling, 1967-72, adminstr. regulatory affairs and inspections, 1972-74, supr. records and auditing, 1974-75, mgr. corp. quality assurance-tng. services, 1976-79, mgr. quality assurance, corp. research, 1979—. Mem. Regulatory Affairs Profl. Soc., Am. Soc. Quality Control. Episcopalian. Home: 59527 Ridgewood Dr Goshen IN 46526 Office: 1127 Myrtle St Elkhart IN 46514

THARP, D(AVID) ROBERT, educational administrator; b. Columbus, Ohio, Apr. 1, 1937; s. George Delmar and Doris Lucille (Forshey) T.; m. Reta Kaye Teets, Aug. 8, 1964; children—Linda Ann, Denise Kay, Beth Michelle. B.S., Otterbein Coll., 1959; M.A., Ohio U., 1967. Cert. elem. tchr., Ohio. Tchr., coach Lakewood Schs., Hebron, Ohio, 1959-61; prin., tchr., coach Licking Valley Local Schs., Newark, Ohio, 1961-68, 83-85, adminstrv. asst., 1966-67; prin. Licking Valley Jr. High Sch., Newark, 1968—; mem. tchr. edn. adv. council Denison U., 1982-84. Contbr. articles to profl. jours. Supt. Sunday sch. Harrison Chapel Ch., Pataskala, Ohio, 1966—, tchr. adult Sunday sch., 1968—; rifle instr. Licking County Boy Scout Camp, Utica, Ohio, 1977; pres. Heath Choir Boosters, Ohio, 1984—. Jennings adminstrv. leadership scholar Martha Holden Jennings Found., 1985-86. Mem. Licking Valley Edn. Assn. (pres. 1963-64), Licking County Edn. Assn. (pres. 1967-68), Ohio Assn. Secondary Sch. Adminstrs., Geneal. Soc. Licking County. Republican. Methodist. Avocations: gardening; canoeing; genealogy; hunting; fishing. Home: 456 Irving Wick E Heath OH 43056 Office: Licking Valley Jr High School 1379 Licking Valley Rd NE Newark OH 43055

THARP, MICHAEL JOHN, dentist; b. Waterloo, Iowa, July 2, 1948; s. Benjamin William and Arlene Iona (Jacklin) T.; m. Patricia Anne Olsen, Mar. 21, 1970; children—Lara, William, Thomas, Melanie. B.A., U. No. Iowa, 1970; D.D.S., U. Iowa, 1974. Pvt. practice dentistry, West Liberty, Iowa, 1974—. Recipient Cert. of Merit, Am. Acad. Medicine, 1974. Mem. ADA, Iowa Dental Assn., Muscatine County Dental Assn. (pres. 1980—), West Liberty C. of C. Lodge: Rotary (pres. 1981). Home: 109 W Gibson St West Liberty IA 52776 Office: 107 W 3d St West Liberty IA 52776

THAYER, CHARLES DEWEY, athletic trainer, paramedic; b. Lewiston, Maine, Aug. 21, 1942; s. George Dewey and Verna Geraldine (Grover) T.; m. Nancy Miller, Apr. 6, 1963 (div.); children—David Scott, Stephen Charles, Gregory Ernest; m. Patricia Ann Joslyn, June 8, 1975; 1 son, Matthew Paul. B.S., U. Maine, 1966; M.S., Ind. U., 1967. Cert. athletic trainer, emergency med. technician. Phys. edn. instr. Nichols Coll., Dudley, Mass., 1967-69; paramedic Paramedic Service Ill., Chgo., 1979—; head trainer Chgo. Black Hawks, 1969—. Active Boy Scouts Am. Mem. Nat. Athletic Trainers Assn., Profl. Hockey Trainers Assn. (v.p. 1971-72, pres. 1972-74, 1981-82), Phi Delta Kappa. Republican. Congregationalist. Office: Chicago Black Hawks 1800 W Madison St Chicago IL 60612

THAYER, ROBERT WILCOX, music educator; b. Detroit, Oct. 26, 1927; s. Willard Charles and Eva Stuart (Missildine) T.; m. Norma Jean Boyd, Dec. 19, 1954; children—Douglas Boyd, Stephen Bruce. B.Music, U. Rochester, 1949; M.M.E., Wichita State U., 1955; Ph.D., U. Iowa, 1971. Elem. and secondary music tchr. pub. and pvt. schs. Waterford Pa., Wichita, Kans., Clearwater, Kans., 1949-53; asst. prof. music Friends U., Wichita, 1953-58; assoc. prof. music Cornell Coll., Mt. Vernon, Iowa, 1958-72; assoc. prof. music SUNY-Potsdam, 1972-73, assoc. dean music, 1973-76, dean music, 1976-82; dean music Coll. Musical Arts Bowling Green State U., Ohio, 1983—; musician French horn and tuben Rochester Philharm. Orch., N.Y., 1949, French horn Erie Philharm. Orch., Pa., 1949-50; solo French horn Wichita Symphony Orch., Kans., 1950-58, Cedar Rapids Symphony Orch., Iowa, 1958-70; adj. instr. horn Wichita State U., 1955-58; cons. Nat. Assn. Schs. Music, Reston, Va., 1978—, accreditation evaluator, 1975—, mem. task force on State Certification, 1981-82; planner, adminstr. Olympic ceremonial music by Crane Sch. Music 1980 Winter Olympic Games, Lake Placid, N.Y., 1980; cons. music edn. Republic of China, 1981. Contbr. articles to profl. jours. Mem. Music Educators Nat. Conf., Coll. Music Soc., Nat. Assn. Sch. Music Grad. Commn., Phi Mu Alpha Sinfonia (sec. Wichita alumni chpt. 1955-58). Democrat. Club: Torch (Toledo). Office: Coll Music Arts Bowling Green State U Bowling Green OH 43403

THEIN, ANTHONY PETER, music educator, administrator; b. Montevideo, Minn., Dec. 28, 1938; s. John Joseph and Rose Katharine (Thissen) T. B.A., St. John's U., 1960; M.M., Ind. U., 1967; Ph.D., U. Minn., 1978. Vocal music dir. Mapleton Pub. Schs. (Minn.), 1960-61; prof. theory, history and voice Mayville State Coll. (N.D.), 1963—, chmn. music dept., 1980-81, chmn. div. humanities and social sci., 1981—; tenor soloist U.S., Can., Europe, 1960—; music adjudicator, N.D., Minn., Can., 1963—. Founding mem., v.p. West Winds Council Arts, Mayville, 1980-81. Bush Found. grantee, 1969-75. Mem. Music Educators Nat. Conf., NEA, Am. Choral Dirs. Assn., Nat. Assn. Tchrs. of Singing. Club: Community. Lodges: Elks, Eagles, K.C. Home: 343 3d Ave NE Mayville ND 58257 Office: Mayville State Coll Mayville ND 58257

THEIS, EDWARD HOWARD, obstetrician, gynecologist; b. Granite City, Ill., Jan. 26, 1934; s. Edward Herman and Lida (Cotter) T.; m. Judy Strutz, June 14, 1960 (div. 1977); children—Tracey, Mark, Lisa; m. Helen Bernier, Aug. 10, 1985. A.B., Washington U., St. Louis, 1956; B.S., U. Ill., 1958, M.D., 1960. Diplomate Am. Bd. Ob-gyn. Intern, Presbyn.-St. Luke's Hosp., Chgo., 1960-61; resident St. Louis Maternity Hosp., 1961-64, St. Louis City Hosp., 1964-65; practice medicine specializing in ob-gyn., Fond Du Lac, Wis., 1965—; mem. staff St. Agnes Hosp. Med. dir. Planned Parenthood of Fond Du Lac, 1979—. Served as lt. comdr. USNR, 1966-68. Mem. AMA, Wis. Med. Soc., Am. Coll. Obstetricians and Gynecologists, Wis. Soc. Obstetricians and Gynecologists (past pres.), Fond Du Lac County Med. Soc. (past pres.), Wis. Perinatal Soc. Republican. Presbyterian. Club: Exchange. Avocations: skiing, camping, auto restoring, model airplanes. Home: 190 Skyway Dr Route 3 Fond Du Lac WI 54935 Office: Sharpe Clinics 92 E Division St Fond Du Lac WI 54935

THEIS, FRANCIS WILLIAM, See *Who's Who in America,* 43rd edition.

THEISEN, JOHN FREDERICK, dentist; b. Omaha, Apr. 10, 1926; s. Francis Frederick and Viola I. (Muldoon) T.; m. Valeria Ruth Schott, Aug. 16, 1952; children—Frank, Mary Jo, Patti. D.D.S., Creighton U., 1953. Gen. practice dentistry, Schuyler, Nebr., 1953—; liaison officer for polit. structure Nebr. Legislature, 1982—. Past. mem. Schuyler City Council; past pres. Catholic Ednl. Bd., Schuyler; past pres. bd. Meml. Hosp., Schuyler. Served to sgt. USAF, 1943-46. Recipient Good Neighbor award Ak-sar-ben, 1966. Mem. Royal Soc. Health, ADA, No. Dist. Dentists Soc., Nebr. Dental Assn., Schuyler C. of C. (past pres.), Am. Legion (post comdr.), VFW, Alpha Sigma Nu. Democrat. Lodges: Rotary, Lions. Avocations: Hunting, fishing, golf. Home: 217 B St Schuyler NE 68661 Office: 214 E 10th St Schuyler NE 68661

THEISMAN, NORMAN AUGUSTINE, hospital personnel administrator; b. St. Libory, Ill., May 9, 1935; s. Henry Herman and Josephine Mary (Jansen) T.; m. Verna Mae Haar, May 30, 1961; children—Lynn Marie, Mark Alan. B.A. in Bus. and Psychology, McKendree Coll., 1966. Acct., Feuren Motor Co., New Athens, Ill., 1960-61, M.B. Gintz, Inc., East Louis, Ill., 1961-65, J.W. Boyle & Co., Belleville, Ill., 1965-69; dir. personnel Christian Welfare Hosp., East St. Louis, 1969-74, St. Elizabeth's Hosp., Belleville, 1974—; mem. adv. com. Intergovtl. Grants Dept., Belleville, 1983—. Ambassador, Belleville Econ. Progress Inc., 1975—, v.p. small bus. council; mem. adv. bd. Comprehensive Employment Act, Belleville, 1974-83; trustee St. Mary's Catholic Ch., Belleville, 1974—. Served with U.S. Army, 1958-60. Mem. Am. Soc. Hosp. Personnel Adminstrn., So. Ill. Hosp. Personnel Assn. (v.p. 1985—), Althoff Cath. High Sch. Assn. (v.p. 1984-85). Republican. Lodge: Belleville Rotary (treas. 1985—). Avocations: golf; camping. Office: St Elizabeths Hosp 211 S 3d St Belleville IL 62220

THEKDI, ARVIND CHHOTALAL, mechanical engineer, researcher; b. Ahmedarad, Gujarat, India, Aug. 5, 1941; s. Chhotalal D. and Shantaben T.; m. Manjula Thekdi, Dec. 14, 1964; children—Hina, Apurva, Anita. B.E., Gujarat U., 1963; M.E., Indian Inst. Sci., 1965; Ph.D., Pa. State U., 1970. Staff engr. Firestone Tire, Bombay, India, 1965-67; research and devel. engr. energy tech. div. Surface Combustion Tech. Ctr., Toledo, Ohio, 1970-73, mgr. thermal systems, 1973-79, asst. dir. devel., 1979-83, dir. research and devel., 1983—. Author: (with others) Advances in Combustion, 1970; Energy Management, 1978. Patentee in field. Mem. ASME, Combustion Inst. Avocations: jogging; computer club projects. Home: 7756 Shaftesbury Dr Sylvania OH 43560 Office: Midland Ross Corp 2375 Dorr St Toledo OH 43607

THELEN, LEON EDWARD, farmer, county official; b. Fowler, Mich., Feb. 5, 1925; s. Joseph William and Anna Rosella (Werner) T.; m. Bertine Ann Cook, June 27, 1953; children—LuAnne, Leon J., Joseph, Edward, Therese, Patrice, Michael, Thomas, Philip. Cert. assessor state of Mich., 1970-83; assessor, adminstr. property taxes Clinton county, Mich., 1969—, equalization dir., 1970—; owner, operator livestock and crop farm, Clinton county, Mich., 1954—; seminar instr., valuation cons. Served with U.S. Army, 1950-53. Mem. Internat. Assn. Assessing Officers, Mich. Assessor Assn., Mich. Assn. Equalization Dirs., County Assessors Assn. Roman Catholic. Lodge: KC. Home: 7340 N DeWitt Rd Saint Johns MI 48879 Office: Court House Saint Johns MI 48879

THENO, DANIEL O'CONNELL, state legislator; b. Ashland, Wis., May 8, 1947; s. Maurice William and Janet Nora (Humphrey) T.; B.S., U. Wis., Madison, 1969; student, Brazil, 1969; m. Sue Burnham, June 16, 1973; children—Scott Patrick, Tad William. Tchr. agr. public schs., Oregon, Wis., 1969-72; mem. Wis. State Senate, 1972—; mem. Wis. Bldg. Commn. Named Superior Hon. Alumni, U. Wis., 1977; recipient Vet. Recognition award, 1978. Mem. Coll. Agr. Alumni Assn., U. Wis. Alumni Assn., Iron Cross Honor Soc. Clubs: Ashland County (Wis.) Republican, Elks, K.C.

THEODORE, WILLIAM JAMES, educational administrator; b. Chgo., Feb. 6, 1947; s. George and Winnie (Stafford) T.; m. Dana Yeargin, Mar. 1, 1980 (div. Nov. 1981). A.B., U. Mich., 1969, A.M., 1972; Ed.S., Wichita State U., 1981. Tchr. Tecumseh High Sch., Mich., 1970-72, Orleans Parish, La., 1972-76; prin. Nickerson sch. dist., Kans., 1980-82; tchr. Jefferson Parish schs., Gretna, La., 1976-80, 1982-83; asst. prin. Arch Blenk High Sch., Gretna, 1983-84; prin., supt., Hillcrest Rural Sch. Dist., Cuba, Kans., 1984—. Mem. Nat. Assn. Secondary Prins., Nat. Assn. Elem. Prins., Kans. Unified Sch. Adminstrs., Kans. Assn. Elem. Prins., Phi Kappa Phi. Avocation: sports. Home: PO Box 85 Agenda KS 66930 Office: Hillcrest Rural Schs PO Box 167 Cuba KS 66940

THERIEN, WILLIAM RUSSELL, automobile dealer; b. Momence, Ill., Sept. 29, 1921; s. William Wilbur and Catherine (Sweet) T.; m. Clairdel Lois Phillips, Jan. 28, 1942; children—Nancy Kaye, Cynthia Joan. Student, St. Joseph's Coll., Rensselaer, Ind., 1940-42, Gen. Motors Mgr. Sch., 1959. Parts and service mgr. W.W. Therien Chevrolet, Momence, Ill., 1945-57, mgr. service, 1957-60, owner, dealer, mgr., 1960-69, pres. W.W. Therien Chevrolet Corp., 1969—; trustee Ill. Automotive Trade Assn. Insurance Trust Bd., Springfield, 1979-83; dir. Momence Fed. Savs. & Loan, Bloomington Fed. Treas., City of Momence, 1948-54; jr. committeeman Ganeer Township, Momence, 1952-60; dir., Momence rep. St. Jude League, Chgo. chpt., 1955-70, chmn. Kankakee (Ill.) County Dinner, 1958-59, 62, 67; dir., sec. lay adv. bd. St. Mary's Hosp., Kankakee, 1964-74; chmn. fund-raising Boy Scouts Am., Momence, 1970; chmn. Momence Area, Kankakee County Community Chest. Served to cpl. U.S. Army, 1942-45, PTO. Recipient 50 Yr. service award Gen. Motors; recognition for work in St. Jude League, Pope Paul, 1960. Mem. Gen. Motors Dealers Planning Commn., Momence C. of C. (past pres., past dir.), VFW, Am. Legion. Republican. Roman Catholic. Clubs: Lions (Momence); Kankakee Country.

THERIOT, EDWARD DENNIS, JR., physicist; b. Baton Rouge, Mar. 19, 1938; s. Edward D. and Beulah (Pace) T.; m. Lee Day, Aug. 25, 1960; children—Sharon, Julie. B.S., Duke U., 1960; M.S., Yale U., 1961, Ph.D., 1967. Postdoctoral fellow CERN, Geneva, 1967-68, Los Alamos Sci. Lab., 1968-69; physicist Fermilab, Batavia, Ill., 1969—. Sec. Wheaton-Warrenville Community Sch. Dist., Wheaton, Ill., 1982, 83, pres., 1984. Mem. Am. Phys. Soc. Home: 427 Bridle Ln Wheaton IL 60187 Office: Fermilab PO Box 500 Batavia IL 60510

THEUNE, GERALD OWEN, optometrist; b. Madison, Wis., Feb. 5, 1952; s. Warren Stanley and Virginia (Bull) T.; m. Susan Marie Boyce, Oct. 8, 1977; 1 child, Ryan James. Student, U. Wis.-Whitewater, 1970-72; B.S., Ind. U., 1974, O.D., 1976. Pvt. practice optometry, Whitewater, 1976—. Mem. Am. Optometric Assn., Wis. Optometric Assn. Lodge: Rotary. Avocations: Skiing, jogging, biking, golf, tennis. Office: Whitewater Vision Ctr 128 N Tratt Whitewater WI 53190

THEYS, FELIX LIONEL, mechanical engineer; b. Beaverdale, Pa., Sept. 18, 1938; s. Felix Joseph and Agnes Celina (Draye) T.; m. Carol Marie Harvanec, May 19, 1962; children—Deborah, Scott, Kristen, Amy. Student in mech. engring. Cleve. State U., 1967-72. Registered profl. engr., Ohio, Ky., Ind., Wis., Calif., Pa., Okla., Fla. Machinist Donn Products, Westlake, Ohio, 1960-64; project engr. Evans & Assocs., Cleve., 1964-72; assoc. Denk-Kish Assocs., 1972-78; cons. engr. F. L. Theys Assocs., 1978—. Chmn. Medina County Bd. Appeals, 1984—. Served with USAF, 1956-60. Mem. Am. Cons. Engrs. Assn., Ohio Assn. Cons. Engrs., Cleve. Cons. Engrs. Council, Smoke Control Assn., ASHRAE. Republican. Mem. United Ch. of Christ (elder). Office: F L Theys Assocs 672 E Royalton Rd Cleveland OH 44147

THICKINS, GRAEME RICHARD, marketing consultant; b. Perth, Australia, Apr. 4, 1946; came to U.S., 1952; s. Richard Percy and Lucie Joy (McDiarmid) T.; m. Jane Elizabeth Bantle, Nov. 6, 1969; children—Jeffrey, Christopher, Sarah. A.A., Austin State Jr. Coll., 1967; postgrad. U. Minn., 1967-70. Editor, prodn. mgr. Data 100 Corp., Edina, Minn., 1970-72; pub. relations and promotion writer, editor MTS Systems Corp., Eden Prairie, Minn., 1972-73; dir. pub. relations services, writer, account exec. Communication Coalition, Inc., Edina, 1973-74; free-lance writer, cons., Mpls., 1974-75; mktg. communications writer, asst. mgr. Medtronic, Inc., Mpls., 1975-77; mktg. services mgr., communications mgr., Am. Med. Systems, Inc., Mpls., 1977-78; account exec. D'arcy-MacManus & Masius, Twin Cities, Minn., 1978; cons. editorial services, corp. communications Control Data Corp., Mpls., 1978-79, mgr. editorial services, 1979, mgr. promotion lit., 1980, mgr. creative services, 1981, mgr. advt. and promotion, systems and services co., 1982; cons. mktg., advt., direct mail, pub. relations, Mpls., 1975-82; pres. GT&A, Inc., advt. and mktg., Mpls., 1982—. Recipient numerous awards and certs. of excellence from various profl. assns. Mem. Advt. Fedn. of Minn., Bus. and Profl. Advt. Assn., Midwest Direct Mktg. Assn., Direct Mktg. Assn., Minn. Graphic Design Assn., Nat. Computer Graphics Assn., Twin Cities IBM Personal Computer Users Group, Phi Gamma Delta. Clubs: Olympic Hills Golf (Eden Prairie); Northwest Tennis (Mpls.); Minn. Entrepreneurs. Avocations: tennis, fishing, swimming, boating. Home and Office: 8135 Kentucky Circle West Bloomington MN 55438

THIEBAUTH, BRUCE EDWARD, advertising executive; b. Bronxville, N.Y., Oct. 30, 1947; s. Bruce and Margaret Evelyn (Wiederhold) T.; student Colby Coll., Waterville, Maine, 1965-66, Pace Coll., 1971; B.A. magna cum laude in Bus. Adminstrn. and Sociology, Bellevue Coll., 1972; m. Sherry Ann Proplesch, Aug. 31, 1968; 1 son, Bruce Revere. Credit mgr. Gen. Electric Credit Corp., Croton Falls, N.Y., 1971; ops. mgr. Bridal Publs., Inc., Omaha, 1972-73; regional mgr. Bridal Fair, Inc., Omaha, 1973-74, sales mgr., 1974-76, chmn. bd., pres., 1976—; dir. Multi-Media Group, Inc., Applied Video Mktg. (AVM, Inc.), Revcom, Inc. Served with USAF, 1966-70; Vietnam conflict. Recipient Nat. Def. Service medal; Somers League citizenship and pub. service award, Somers, N.Y., 1965. Mem. Nat. Small Bus. Assn., Nat. Radio Broadcasters Assn., Nat. Assn. Broadcasters, Airline Passengers Assn., Bellevue Coll. Alumni Assn. Republican. Congregationalist. Office: 8901 Indian Hills Dr Omaha NE 68114

THIEL, MYRON KEITH, food company executive; b. Fergus Falls, Minn., Mar. 24, 1947; s. Clinton Llewellyn and Iris Gladys (Howlett) T.; m. Marsha Jean Randall, Dec. 20, 1969; children—Laurie, Lisa, Christopher. B.B.A., Moorhead State Coll. (Minn.), 1970. Farm sales supr. Northrup, King & Co., Mpls., 1970-73; customer service mgr. Pfizer, St. Louis, 1973-78; dir. mktg. Fed. Intermediate Credit Bank, St. Louis, 1978-79; dir. info. services, Olivia, Minn., 1979-80; advt. mgr. Internat. Multifoods, Mpls., 1980—. Emergency med. technician Olivia Ambulance Service, 1980. Mem. Animal Health Inst. (pub. info. com.), Nat. Agri-Mktg. Assn. Republican. Roman Catholic. Avocations: Fishing, hunting, softball. Home: 14489 96th Ave N Maple Grove MN 55369 Office: Internat Multifoods Multifoods Tower Box 2942 Minneapolis MN 55402

THIEMANN, PAUL P(ETER), department store chain financial executive, lawyer; b. Louisville, Aug. 2. 1927; s. Paul P. and Helen E. (Kern) T.; m. Theresa Duwel; children—Paul P. III, Gerard, Joseph. B.S. summa cum laude, Xavier U., Cin., 1950; LL.B., Salmon P. Chase Coll., 1957. Bar: Ohio 1957. Chief acct. William S. Merrell Co., 1952-57; internat. acct. Vick Chem. Co., 1957-58; tax mgr. Am. Laundry Machinery Co., 1958-60; v.p.-tax planning and adminstrn. Federated Dept. Stores, Cin., 1960-81. v.p.-taxes, 1981—. Mem. exec. com. Com. for Effective Capital Cost Recovery; mem. fin. planning com. Cin. chpt. ARC. Mem. Cin. Bar Assn., Nat. Retail Mchts. Assn. (taxation com.), Am. Retail Fedn. (co-chmn. fed. tax subcom. tax coordinating council), U.S. C. of C. (tax com.), Tax Execs. Inst. (pres. Cin. 1963-64). Office: Federated Dept Stores Inc 7 W 7th St Cincinnati OH 45202

THIES, PATRICK WILLIAM, clinical pharmacist; b. Chgo., May 8, 1956. B.S., U. Iowa, 1979, M.S., 1981. Clin. asst. prof. U. Iowa Coll. Pharmacy, Iowa City, 1981-83; clin. pharmacist Mercy Hosp., Iowa City, 1981-83, St. Mary's Hosp., Streator, Ill., 1983—. Contbr. articles to profl. jours. Riback pharmacokinetic fellow U. Ill. Coll. of Pharmacy, 1984. Mem. Am. Soc. Hosp. Pharmacists, Iowa Soc. Hosp. Pharmacists, Ill. Council Hosp. Pharmacists, Am. Coll. Clin. Pharmacy (assoc.). Roman Catholic. Lodge: K.C. Avocations: aerobic exercise, racquetball. Office: Pharmacy Dept St Mary's Hosp 111 E Spring St Streator IL 61364

THIESSEN, DAN, state senator. Mem. Kans. State Senate from Dist. 15. Republican. Office: R R 1 Independence KS 67301*

THIESSEN, DAVID RAY, educator; b. Winchester, Ky., Aug. 22, 1940; s. Isaac Holzrichter and Margaret Grace (Richards) T.; m. Ximena Ann Brumitt, Aug. 1, 1965; children—Timothy David, Tamara Ximena. B.S., Wheaton Coll., 1962; M.A. in Edn., U. Chgo., 1964; M.S. in Physics, Purdue U., 1970. Cert. tchr., Ill. Tchr. pub. sch., Wheeling, Ill., 1964-84, Deerfield, Ill., 1984—; computer cons. Lake County Computer Tech. Consortium, Grayslake, Ill., 1984, Micro labs., Highland Park, Ill., 1984, Sch. Dist. 214, Mt. Prospect, Ill., 1980-84, Sch. Dist. 113, Highland Park, 1984, Micro Ideas, Glenview, Ill., 1982. Mem. Soccer Parents Com. Arlington Heights, Ill., 1979; soccer coach, 1977-84. Named Outstanding Young Educator, Mt. Prospect Jaycees, 1968, Master Tchr., Gov. Ill., 1984. Mem. NEA, Am. Assn. Physics Tchrs. Republican. Presbyterian. Clubs: Call Apple, Boats/U.S. Avocations: computers, sailing, camping, tennis, racquetball. Home: 215 W Hintz Rd Arlington Heights IL 60004 Office: Deerfield High Sch 1959 N Waukegan Rd Deerfield IL 60015

THIEWES, RONALD CHARLES, tax accountant, lawyer; b. Winona, Minn., July 14, 1946; s. Harold Frank and Marian Rose (Fisher) T.; m. Barbara Ann Erickson, Mar. 16, 1974; children—Joseph Gerard, Mary Elizabeth. B.A., St. Mary's Coll., 1968; J.D., St. Louis U., 1974; LL.M. in Tax, Washington U., St. Louis, 1975. Bars: Mo. 1974, Minn. 1975, U.S. Tax Ct. 1975, U.S. Ct. Claims 1982, U.S. Supreme Ct. 1979. Tax supr. Hurdman & Cranstoun, C.P.A.s, Kansas City, Mo., 1978-79; asst. tax mgr. Kansas City Power & Light Co., 1979-83; tax. mgr. Troupe, Kehoe, Whiteaker & Kent, Kansas City, 1983—. Editor Mo. Taxation Law and Practice, 1981, 82, 85. Contbr. articles to profl. jours. Decorated Silver Star medal. Mem. ABA, Mo. Bar Assn., Kansas City Bar Assn., Kansas City Lawyers Assn. Republican. Roman Catholic. Home: 1408 NW 67th St Kansas City MO 64118 Office: Troupe Kehoe Whiteaker & Kent 900 Penntower Office Ctr 3100 Broadway Kansas City MO 64111

THILL, LEONARD STEPHEN, oil and gas consultant; b. New Albany, Ind., Aug. 3, 1945; s. Leoanrd J. and Doris (Bube) T. B.S. Mech. Engring. Tech., Purdue U., 1975; postgrad. U. So. Calif., 1983. Project engr. Internat. Rubber Co., Louisville, 1975-77; sr. engr. Fluor Corp., Daharan, Saudi Arabia, 1977-78, M.W. Kellog, Algeria, 1978-79, Cherne Corp., New Washington, Ind., 1979-80; Sr. engr., Bechtel Petroleum, Louisville, 1980-81; cons. engr. Mobile Oil Co., Tripoli, Libya, 1981; cons. engr. Ralph M. Parson, Pasadena, Calif., 1981-82; cons. engr. Sirte Oil Co., Marsal el Brega, Libya, 1982; cons. oil and gas engring., New Albany, Ind. Mem. ASME, Nat. Assn. Corrosion Engrs. Home: 1924 Ekin Ave NE Albany IN 47150-1750

THIMMAPPAYA, BAYAR, biochemist; b. Kerala, India, Jan. 3, 1943; s. Shiva and Saraswathi Sharma; m. Sept. 27, 1977; 1 child. B.Sc., Govt. Coll., Mangalore, India, 1961-65; M.Sc., M.S. U., Baroda, India, 1967; Ph.D., Indian Inst. Sci., Bangalore, 1975. Research assoc. Yale U., New Haven, 1975-77, U. Conn. Health Ctr., Farmington, 1977-80; asst. prof. biochemistry Northwestern U.-Chgo., 1981—; established investigator Am. Heart Assn., Dallas, 1982—. NIH grantee, 1981—. Mem. Am. Soc. Microbiology. Office: Northwestern U 303 E Chicago Ave Chicago IL 60611

THINNES, KIMBERLY ANN, nurse; b. Cin., Sept. 19, 1956; d. Robert Louis and Patricia Louise (Staehlin) T. Student Ohio State U., 1974-75; diploma in Nursing, Miami Valley Hosp. Sch. Nursing, Dayton, Ohio, 1979; student Wright State U., 1983-84, Mt. St. Joseph Coll., Cin., 1984—. Registered nurse, Ohio. Primary scrub nurse U. Ala. Hosp., Birmingham, 1980-81; surg. asst. Thoracic and Cardiovascular Assocs., San Antonio, 1981; charge nurse ICU, Kimberly Nurses, San Antonio, 1981-83; nurse surgery/recovery SW Ambulatory Surg. Ctr., San Antonio, 1982-83; charge nurse ICU, Grandview Hosp., Dayton, 1983-84; radiology/spl. procedures nurse, 1984-85, dir. central distbn. and linen distbn., 1985—; lectr. in field; vol. San Antonio Marathon Med. Team, 1982. Coach, coordinator local volleyball teams, 1984-85; co-chmn. campaign United Way, 1985; participant Dayton Battle of Businesses, 1985. Mem. Miami Valley Hosp. Sch. Nursing Alumni Assn., Phi Mu. Club: Excel Investment (treas. 1984-85, Dayton). Address: 865 Oakcreek Dr Dayton OH 45429 Office: Grandview Hosp 405 Grand Ave Dayton OH 45405

THIRUVATHUKAL, KURIAKOSE VARKEY, educator, researcher; b. Shertallay, India, May 1, 1925; came to U.S., 1954, naturalized, 1980; s. Varkey K. and Rosa V. Thiruvathukal; children—George K., Maria K., Cheryl K. B.Sc., Kerala U. (India), 1948; M.S., Boston Coll., 1956; Ph.D., St. Louis U., 1959. Instr., Duquesne U., Pitts., 1959-60; asst. prof. Aquinas Coll., Grand Rapids, Mich., 1960-62, Gonzaga U., Spokane, Wash., 1962-65, Canisius Coll., Buffalo, 1965-68; prof. Lewis U., Romeoville, Ill., 1968—. Home: 2213 Arden Pl Joliet IL 60435

THISSEN, DAVID MICHAEL, psychology educator; b. Fort Dodge, Iowa, Nov. 14, 1949; s. John R. and Shirley A. (Conroy) T.; m. Mary Rita Collinge, June 4, 1971; children—Anne, Paul. B.A., St. Louis U., 1971; Ph.D., U. Chgo., 1976. From asst. prof. to assoc. prof. psychology U. Kans., Lawrence, 1976—; cons. in field. Co-author: Skeletal Maturity, 1975. Contbr. articles to profl. jours. Mem. Psychometric Soc., AAAS, Am. Statis. Assn., Aircraft Owners and Pilots Assn. Avocations: aviation, photography. Office: Dept Psychology U Kansas Lawrence KS 66045

THOENE, JESS GILBERT, pediatrics and biological chemistry educator; b. Bakersfield, Calif., Aug. 4, 1942; s. Gilbert Fredrick and Hazel Elizabeth (Wattenbarger) T.; m. Marijim Stockton, Sept. 1, 1965; B.S. in Chemistry, Stanford U., 1964; M.D., Johns Hopkins U., 1968. Diplomate Am. Bd. Pediatrics, Am. Bd. Med. Genetics. Asst. prof. pediatrics U. Mich., Ann Arbor,

1977-81, assoc. prof., 1981—, asst. prof. biol. chemistry, 1984—. Contbr. articles to profl. jours. Served to maj. USAF, 1971-74. Recipient research grants NIH, FDA, March of Dimes; Travel grant Welcome Found., 1984; fellow Lalor Found., 1974-76. Mem. Midwest Soc. Pediatric Research (counselor 1983—), Soc. Pediatric Research, Am. Soc. Human Genetics, Soc. Inherited Metabolic Disorders, Nat. Orgn. Rare Disorders (v.p. 1982-85, pres. 1985-87). Home: 1308 Brooks Ann Arbor MI 48103 Office: U Mich Dept Pediatrics Kresge II-R 6028 Ann Arbor MI 48109

THOLE, NANCIE JOHNSON, nursing educator; b. Waukegan, Ill., Apr. 3, 1938; d. Albert William and Francis Irene (Carroll) Johnson; m. Jack T. Thole, Apr. 1, 1961; children—Gregory A., Terri Lynn. B.S., George Williams Coll., 1972; M.S., Rush U., 1975; Ed.D., Internat. Grad. Sch., St. Louis, 1983. R.N., Ill. Staff nurse Rush Presbyterian St. Lukes Med. Center, Chgo., 1972-75; nursing educator, Coll. Nursing Lewis U., Romeoville, Ill., 1975—, assoc. prof., 1981-83, prof., 1983—, dir. R.N. degree completion studies, 1982—; cons. Personel Advancement and Career Enrichment, Inc., 1978—. Mem. Am. Nurses Assn., Ill. Nurses Assn., Nat. League for Nursing, Sigma Theta Tau. Office: Lewis Univ Coll Nursing Rt 53 Romeoville IL 60441

THOMAN, MARK EDWARD, physician; b. Chgo., Feb. 15, 1936; s. John Charles and Tasula Mark (Petrakis) T.; A.A., Graceland Coll., 1956; B.A., U. Mo., 1958, M.D., 1962; m. Theresa Thompson, 1984; children—Marlisa Rae, Susan Kay, Edward Kim, Nancy Lynn, Janet Lea, David Mark. Intern, U. Mo. at Columbia, 1962-63; resident in pediatrics Blank Meml. Children's Hosp., Des Moines, 1963-65, chief resident, 1964-65, lt. comdr. USPHS, Washington, 1965-66, cons. in toxicology, 1966-67; chief dept. pediatrics Shiprock (N.Mex.) Navajo Indian Hosp., dir. N.D. Poison Info. Center, also practice medicine, specializing in pediatrics Quain & Ramstad Clinic, Bismarck, N.D., 1967-69; dir. Iowa Poison Info. Center, Des Moines, 1969—; pvt. practice pediatrics, Des Moines, 1969—; sr. aviation med. examiner, accident investigator FAA, 1976—; faculty Iowa State U., U. Iowa, U. Osteo. Sci. and Health; dir. Cystic Fibrosis Clinic, 1973-82; dir. Mid-Iowa Drug Abuse Program, 1972-76; mem. med. adv. bd. La Leche Leauge Internat., 1965—; pres. Medic-Air Ltd., 1976—. Bd. dirs. Polk County Pub. Health Nurses Assn., 1969-77, Des Moines Speech and Hearing Center, 1974-79. Served with USMCR, 1954-58. Recipient N.D. Gov.'s award of merit, 1969; Cystic Fibrosis Research Found. award, 1975, Am. Psychiat. Assn. Thesis award, Diplomate Am. Bd. Pediatrics, Am. Bd. Med. Toxicology (examiner). 1962. Mem. AMA (del. 1970—), Polk County Med. Soc., Iowa State Med. Assn., Aerospace Med. Assn., Soc. Adolescent Medicine, Inst. Clin. Toxicology, Internat. Soc. Pediatrics, Am. Acad. Pediatrics, Cystic Fibrosis Club, Am. Acad. Clin. Toxicology (trustee 1969—, pres. 1982-84), Am. Assn. Poison Control Centers, Nat. Rifle Assn. (life). Republican. Mem. Reorganized Latter-Day Saints Ch. Clubs: Flying Physicians, Aircraft Owners and Pilots Assn., Nat. Pilots Assn. (Safe Pilot award), Hyperion Field and Country. Editor-in-chief AACTION. Home: 6896 NW Trailridge Dr Johnston IA 50131 Office: 1426 Woodland Ave Des Moines IA 50309

THOMAS, ALEXANDER EDWARD, III, research chemist; b. Chgo., May 3, 1930; s. Alexander E. and Ethel E. (Bauer) T.; m. Mary Ann Weiner, Apr. 7, 1956; children—Carol Ann, Laura Jean, Joanne Marie. B.S., U. Ill., 1955; M.S., DePaul U., 1961. Research chemist Glidden Co., Chgo., 1955-58; sect. head analytical chemistry Durkee Foods div. SCM Corp., Chgo., 1958-66, mgr. chem. research, Strongsville, Ohio, 1967-72, mgr. applications research, 1972-78, assoc. dir. applied sci., 1978—. Author tech. articles. Served with U.S. Army, 1952-54. Mem. Am. Chem. Soc., Am. Oil Chemists Soc. Republican. Roman Catholic. Avocations: tennis; golf; fishing. Office: Durkee Foods 16651 Sprague Rd Strongsville OH 44136

THOMAS, BRENDA, bookstore executive; b. Russell, Ky., Mar. 16, 1948; d. Charles X. and Jeannette Frances (Thompson) Calia; m. Evan Thomas, July 11, 1972; children—Alexandra Logan, Jessica Theon, Erin Elizabeth. Dir. Am. Lang. Ctr., Fez, Morocco, 1968-70; proprietor The Bookshop, St. Paul, 1981—. Commr. human rights Roseville, Minn., 1979—; bd. dirs, Quantum Theatre, St. Paul, 1984—. Mem. NOW, ACLU, Amnesty Internat. Avocation: astrology. Office: The Bookshop 2100 N Snelling Ave Saint Paul MN 55113

THOMAS, CAMERON HOUSTON, real estate and insurance executive; b. Omaha, Sept. 26, 1961; s. George Houston and Mercedes (Turner) T. B.S., U. Nebr., 1983. Salesman, Kinney Shoes, Omaha, 1978; clk. typist CETA, Omaha, 1979; bookkeeper Thomas Realty, Omaha, 1980-81; teller, savs. cons. First Fed., Lincoln, Nebr., 1982-83; mgr. Tommie Rose Gardens, Omaha, 1984; exec. v.p. Thomas Real Estate and Ins., Omaha, 1984—. Mem. Omaha C. of C. Home: 10524 Evans Plaza #723 Omaha NE 68134 Office: Thomas Real Estate & Ins Co 2821 Meredith Ave Omaha NE 68111

THOMAS, CHRISTOPHER YANCEY, III, physician, educator; b. Kansas City, Mo., Oct. 27, 1923; s. Christopher Yancey and Dorothea Louise (Engel) T.; m. Barbara Ann Barcroft, June 27, 1946; children—Christopher, Gregg, Jeffrey, Anne. Student U. Colo., 1942-44; M.D., U. Kans., 1948. Diplomate Am. Bd. Surgery. Intern, U. Utah Hosp., Salt Lake City, 1948-49; resident in surgery Cleve. Clinic Found., 1949-52; practice medicine specializing in surgery, Kansas City, Mo., 1954—; mem. staff St. Luke's Hosp., chief of surgery, 1969-70; mem. staff Children's Mercy Hosp.; assoc. prof. surgery U. Mo.-Kansas City Med. Sch. dir. Mission Hills Bank; pres. St. Luke's Hosp. Edn. Found., 1977-83, Med. Plaza Corp., 1977-79, Midwest Organ Bank, 1977-82. Served to capt. M.C., U.S. Army, 1952-54. Fellow ACS; mem. AMA, Southwestern Surg. Congress, Central Surg. Assn., Mo. State Med. Soc., Kansas City Surg. Soc. (pres. 1968), Jackson County Med. Soc. (pres. 1971). Republican. Methodist. Clubs: Kansas City Country, Homestead Country. Editor IMTRAC, investment adv. letter, 1978—. Home: 5830 Mission Dr Shawnee Mission KS 66208 Office: 4320 Wornall Rd Suite 308 Kansas City MO 64111

THOMAS, CLAYTON FLOYD, university administrator; b. Greene, Iowa, July 10, 1936; s. Lloyd C. and Marlys (Kingery) T.; m. Bonnie Brown, Aug. 14, 1955; children—Terry Lee, Brenda Jane. B.A., U. No. Iowa, 1958, M.A., 1959; Ph.D., U. Iowa, 1964. Tchr. Iowa City pub. schs., Iowa, 1959-60, asst. prin., 1960-63; asst. prof. Ill. State U., Normal, 1964-66, assoc. prof., 1966-69, prof., 1969-74, chmn. dept. ednl. adminstrn., 1974-83, prof. ednl. adminstrn., 1983-84, asst. grad. dean, 1984—. Author: Effective Secondary Education, 1966. Contbr. articles to profl. jours. Recipient Fulbright award USIA, 1984. Mem. Am. Assn. Higher Edn., Nat. Soc. Sch. Prins., Ill. Prin. Assn. (exec. officer, bd. dir.), Ill. Assn. Sch. Adminstrs. Lodge: Lions (pres. 1966-67). Home: 802 Smith Dr Normal IL 61761 Office: Graduate Sch Ill State U Normal IL 61761

THOMAS, DENNIS DEE, lawyer, consultant; b. North Platte, Nebr., Mar. 16, 1954; s. Bruce Earnest and Violet Bell (Shill) T.; m. Annette Jo Sheetz, July 10, 1976; children—Marcus Evan, Collin Ellis. B.A. in Edn., Kearney State Coll., 1976; J.D., U. Nebr., 1980. Bar: Nebr. 1980, U.S. Dist. Ct. Nebr. 1980. Assoc. Watkin, Osborne, Keist, Lincoln, Nebr. 1980; atty. Fed. Land Bank, North Platte, 1980—; cons. estate planning. Mem. Lincoln County Bar Assn. Republican. Methodist. Lodge: Sertoma (active American Heritage Day 1984). Home: 816 S York North Platte NE 69101 Office: Fed Land Bank 120 E 12th PO Box 1576 North Platte NE 69103

THOMAS, DONALD CHARLES, university administrator; b. Cin., Sept. 26, 1935; s. Howard G. and Elsie M. (Sack) T.; m. Barbara J. Kindt, Sept. 2, 1957; children—Mark D., Matthew K., Michael J. B.S., Xavier U., 1957; M.S., U. Cin., 1959; Ph.D., St. Louis U., 1968. Instr., Villa Madonna Coll., Covington, Ky., 1961-63; NIH trainee, Washington, 1963-68; asst. prof. Ohio State U., Columbus, 1968-72, assoc. dir. U. Research Found., 1972-77, mem. research com. Coll. Biol. Scis., 1974-77; assoc. dean Wright State U., Dayton, Ohio, 1977-83, assoc. prof. pathology, 1977—, mem. research com. Sch. Medicine, 1977-79, univ. dean, vice provost, 1983—; adminstrv. advisor Nat. Reyes Syndrome Found., Bryan, Ohio, 1975-81; lab. cons. VA Med. Ctr., Dayton, 1978-81. Author: (with others) Molecular Basis of Viral Cancer, 1969. Contbr. articles to profl. jours., chpt. to book. Mem. research adv. com. Children's Hosp. Research Found., Columbus, 1968-77, mem. human subjects rev. com., 1975-77; mem. com. on biomed. ethics Sponsor Group for Confs. on Biomed. Ethics State of Ohio, 1973-77; mem. steering com. Consortium for Cancer Control in Ohio, 1978—, mem. evaluation com., 1980—; mem. pilot research com. Ohio div. Am. Cancer Soc., 1979-82; mem. regents adv. com. for grad. studies Ohio Bd. Regents, 1980—; mem. exec. com. Hospice of Dayton, 1981—, treas., 1981-85; mem. gov.'s tech. task force Ohio Dept. Econ. and Community Devel., 1982-83; bd. dirs. St. Leonard Ctr., Dayton, v.p. bd., 1983-85; mem. Tech. Assistance Panel, Dayton, Ohio. Grantee NIH Rhinovirus Reference Ctr., 1968-72, Dept. Edn. Grad. and Profl. Opportunity Program, 1978-85. Mem. Am. Soc. for Microbiology, AAAS, Licensing Exec. Soc., Fedn. Am. Scientists. Clubs: Woodhaven Swim, Dayton Executive. Office: Office Grad Studies Wright State U 3640 Col Glenn Hwy Dayton OH 45435

THOMAS, EDWARD GLENN, business educator, consultant; b. Bowling Green, Ky., Jan. 18, 1946; s. William Edward and Orangie Lee (Owens) T.; m. Cathy Ann Stanley, Nov. 25, 1974. B.S., Western Ky. U., 1968, M.A., 1970; Ed.D., U. Ky., 1973. Cert. adminstrv. mgr. Asst. prof. Cleve. State U., 1973-77, asst. dean, assoc. prof., 1977-79, dept. chair, prof., 1979-85, assoc. dean, prof., 1985—; cons. pub. cos., 1975—; cons., evaluator Assn. Ind. Colls. and Schs., Washington, 1975—. Contbr. articles to profl. jours. Named Educator of Yr., Cleve. Area Bus. Tchrs. Assn., 1983. Mem. Adminstrv. Mgmt. Soc. (dir. 1983-85, merit and diamond merit awards 1980, 300 Club award 1983, Ambassador award 1984, outstanding chpt. mem. 1981), Office Systems Research Assn. (pres. 1982-83, exec. dir. 1984—), Ohio Bus. Tchrs. Found. (v.p. 1981-82), Ohio Bus. Tchrs. Assn. (historian 1977-79). Club: Toastmasters Internat. (pres. 1981-82) (Cleve.). Avocations: reading; cross country skiing. Home: 286 Fernway Ave Copley OH 44321 Office: Coll Bus Cleve State U E 24th St at Euclid Ave Cleveland OH 44115

THOMAS, FAYE EVELYN J., educator; b. Summerfield, La., Aug. 3, 1933; d. Reginald Felton and Altee (Hunter) Johnson; B.A., So. U., 1954; student Tuskegee Inst., 1958, 69, U. Detroit, summers, 1961, 62, 63, Central Mich. U., summer 1965; M.S., U. Central Ark., 1971; M.S., Cleve. State U., 1979; m. Archie Taylor Thomas, Sept. 8, 1960; 1 son, Dwayne Andre. Tchr., Cullen (La.) Elem. Sch., 1957; tchr. English and social studies Charles Brown High Sch., Springhill, La., 1957-70; tchr. English, Upward Bound Program, Grambling State U., 1968; tchr. English, Springhill (La.) High Sch., 1970; elem. intermediate tchr. Riveredge Elem. Sch., Berea, Ohio, 1971—; tchr. asst. elem. council curriculum and instrn. Berea Sch. Dist., 1984-85. Trustee, Charles Brown Soc. Orgn. EPDA grantee, 1970-71; Internat. Paper Found. grantee, summers 1958, 60; NDEA grantee, summer 1965; Martha Holden Jennings scholar, 1984-85. Mem. NEA, Ohio Edn. Assn., Berea Edn. Assn., N.E. Ohio Tchrs. Assn., Assn. for Supervision and Curriculum Devel., Charles Brown Soc. Orgn. (trustee 1984—), People United to Save Humanity, Black Caucus Nat. Edn. Assn., Ohio Motorists Assn. Democrat. Baptist. Mem. Order Eastern Star. Home: 19353 E Bagley Rd Middleburg Heights OH 44130 Office: 224 Emerson Dr Berea OH 44017

THOMAS, FRANCIS BRIAN, educator; b. Washington, Dec. 21, 1930; s. Cyrus B. and Carolyn C. (Coates) T.; B.S., U. Cin., 1957; M.A., Kent State U., 1966; Ph.D., U. Akron, 1983; m. Diane R. Ruehrwein; children—Teresa Lynn, F. Brian, Leslie Ann, Mark Richard. Prodn. engr. RCA Co., Cin., 1957-59; sci. programmer analyst Lockheed Co., Marietta, Ga., 1959-62; sec. head Applied Computer div. Goodyear Aerospace, Akron, Ohio, 1962-70; dir. computer services U. Akron, 1970—; cons. in field. Served as master sgt. U.S. Army, 1952-54. Decorated Army Commendation medal; recipient Assn. for Systems Mgmt. Systems Man of the Yr. award, 1973, Merit award, 1976, Achievement award, 1978, Disting. Service award, 1981. Mem. Assn. for Systems Mgmt., Assn. for Computing Machinery. Republican. Contbr. articles to profl. jours. Home: 2480 15th St Cuyahoga Falls OH 44223 Office: 302 E Buchtel Ave Akron OH 44325

THOMAS, FRANCIS DARRELL, oil compounder executive; b. Palestine, Ill., Feb. 11, 1928; s. Odin F. and Dorothy (Carrol) T.; B.S., Butler U., 1951; m. Nancy; children—Steven, Bruce, Gail. Regional mgr. Sun Oil Co., Cin., 1955-72; pres. Keenan Oil Co., Cin., 1972-74; gen. mgr. Weatherator Engring. Co., Columbus, Ohio, 1975-76; pres. Nat. Oil and Chem. Co., Hamilton, Ohio, 1976—. Served with USMC, 1946-47. Mem. Ind. Oil Compounders Assn., Assn. Petroleum Re-refiners (past mem. nat. exec. com.), Am. Soc. Lubrication Engrs. (past chmn. Cin. sect.). Republican. Clubs: Clovernook Country, Masons, Shriners. Office: 1000 Forest Ave Hamilton OH 45015

THOMAS, FRANKLIN BAKER, III, accountant, consultant; b. Bryn Mawr, Pa., Oct. 15, 1929; s. Franklin B. and Mary (Rohloff) T.; m. Barbara Renninger, Apr. 12, 1958; 1 child, Bonnie Lynn. A.S., Wharton Sch., U. Pa., 1958; B.Profl. Studies, Elizabethtown Coll., 1984. C.P.A., Pa. Ptnr. Ernst & Whinney, Harrisburg, Pa., 1954-75; v.p., fin. St. Joseph Hosp., Lancaster, Pa., 1975-78; chief fin. officer Wilmington Coll., Ohio, 1978—; self-employed acctg. cons., Lancaster, 1975-78, Wilmington, 1978—; dir. Armstrong Bldg. & Loan Assn., 1975-77. Treas. Tecumseh council Boy Scouts Am., Springfield, 1979-84; bd. dirs., treas. YMCA, Wilmington, 1980-84. Mem. Nat. Assn. Accts. (bd. dirs. 1970-72), Am. Inst. C.P.A.s, Am. Mgmt. Assn., Lodge: Masons. Avocations: model trains; coin collecting, bowling, dancing. Office: Wilmington Coll College Ave Wilmington OH 45177

THOMAS, GEORGE, physician; b. Miklos, Syria, Oct. 22, 1946; came to U.S., 1947; c. Ghattas Deeb and Sameera (Haddad) T.; children—Farrah, Tiffany. B.S., U. Pitts., 1968; D.O., Kirksville Coll. Osteo. Medicine, 1972. Cert. Am. Coll. Gen. Practice. Intern, Still Osteo. Hosp., Jefferson City, Mo., 1972-73; practice medicine, Euclid, Ohio, 1973—; pres. staff Richmond Heights Gen. Hosp., Ohio, 1985—, sec.-treas. staff, 1977-80, v.p. staff, 1980-85. Fellow Am. Coll. Gen. Practitioners; mem. Am. Osteo. Assn., Ohio Osteo. Assn. (treas. 1985), Cleve. Acad. Osteo. Medicine (program chmn. 1982, v.p. 1981-82, pres. 1983-84), Am. Coll. Gen. Pactitioners in Osteo. Medicine and Surgery, Undersea Med. Soc. Avocations: scuba diving. Office: 26151 Euclid Ave Euclid OH 44132

THOMAS, GEORGE WILLARD (BILL), micrographics quality control company executive, consultant; b. York, Pa., Jan. 26, 1927; s. George Washington and Ruth Jeanette (Lukens) T.; m. Juanita Anne Vinson, Feb. 6, 1948; children—Lynn Anne Thomas Nelson, George Willard. Student York Jr. Coll. (Pa.), 1946-47; A.B., Gettysburg Coll. (Pa.), 1949; postgrad. U. Del.-Newark, 1949-51. Physicist, U.S. Navy, Panama City, Fla., 1951-56, Corona, Calif., 1956-71; owner, mgr. MicroFilming Services, Corona, 1971-79; pres. Neoteric Arts, Inc., Corona and Burnsville, Minn., 1972—; pres. MicroD Internat., Corona and Burnsville, 1973—. Contbr. articles in field. Commr. Inland Empire council Boy Scouts Am., Corona. Served with U.S. Navy, 1945-46. Recipient Disting. Merit award Boy Scouts Am., 1974; Merit award So. Calif. Micrographics Assn., 1980. Mem. Nat. Micrographics Assn., Internat. Micrographics Congress, Canadian Micrographics Soc., Am. Records Mgmt. Assn. Republican. Office: Neoteric Arts Inc 15000 County Rd 5 Burnsville MN 55337

THOMAS, HOLLY MARIE, university counselor; b. St. Louis, Nov. 12, 1954; d. Benjamin Robinson and Mariantha (James) Williams; m. Mark Powers Thomas, June 27, 1981. B.S., Denison U., 1977; M.A., Ohio State U., 1979. Cert. counselor. Resident counselor Ohio Wesleyan U., Delaware, Ohio, 1978-79; asst. dean Holy Cross Coll., Worcester, Mass., 1979-81; asst. dir. placement services Wright State U., Dayton, Ohio, 1981-85. Advisor, Southminster Presbyn. Ch. Sr. High Fellowship, 1981—. Mem. Am. Coll. Personnel Assn. (Annuit Coeptis honored participant 1981, membership chmn. commn. VI 1982-85), Ohio Coll. Personnel Assn. (bd. dirs.), Nat. Assn. Student Personnel Adminstrs., Thomas Paine Homeowners Assn. (v.p. 1983-85), Pi Beta Phi (pres. 1984-85). Avocations: gourmet cooking; needle work; skiing; music; movies. Home: 6392 Jason Ln Centerville OH 45459

THOMAS, ISIAH LORD, III, professional basketball player. Guard, Detroit Pistons. Office: Detroit Pistons Pontiac Silverdome 1200 Featherstone Pontiac MI 48057*

THOMAS, JAMES DOUD, mathematics educator, statistical consultant; b. Normal, Ill., Sept. 19, 1937; s. Raymond A. and Mary Alice (Weaner) T.; m. Katherine Elizabeth McDaniel, Jan. 28, 1961; children—Christopher, Laura, Michele, Joseph, Matthew, Stephen. B.S., St. Louis U., 1959, M.S., 1961; M.A., Yeshiva U., 1968; Ph.D., Pa. State U., 1976. Asst. prof. math. Marist Coll., Poughkeepsie, N.Y. and Mt. St. Mary Coll., Neuburg, N.Y., 1960-69; dir. Agrl. Stats. Lab., Pa. State U., University Park, 1969-75; statistician U. Tex., San Antonio, 1976-80; assoc. prof. stats. Sangamon State U., Springfield, Ill., 1980-82; chmn. dept. math. Cardinal Newman Coll., St. Louis, 1982-84; chmn. dept. math. Quincy Coll., Ill., 1984—; cons. stats. and computer State of Ill. Bd. Elections, Springfield, 1982. Mem. Am. Statis. Assn. Home: 411 Washington St Quincy IL 62301 Office: Quincy Coll Dept Math Quincy IL 62301

THOMAS, JAMES KEITH, data processing manager; b. Mpls., Mar. 16, 1953; s. Thomas G. and Joanne K. (Frane) T.; m. Cynthia Jo McPherson, Dec. 1, 1973 (div. Aug. 1978). Grad. high sch. Computer operator NCR Corp., Roseville, Minn., 1977-78; mgr. data processing Am. Bus. Ins., Mpls., 1978-85; mgr. data processing Charter Med. Inc., 1985—. Served with USAF, 1972-76. Republican. Roman Catholic. Avocations: yachting; golf; bowling; fishing. Office: 9900 Bren Rd E Suite 300 Minnetonka MN 55343

THOMAS, JAMES SAMUEL, bishop; b. Orangeburg, S.C., Apr. 8, 1919; s. James and Dessie Veronica (Mark) T.; m. Ruth Naomi Wilson, July 7, 1945; children—Claudia Thomas Williamson, Gloria Jean Randle, Margaret Yvonne Thomas Glaze, Patricia Elaine. A.B., Clafin Coll., 1939, D.D., 1953; B.D., Gammon Theol. Sem., 1943; M.A., Drew U., 1944; Ph.D., Cornell U., 1953; LL.D., Bethune Cookman Coll., 1963, Simpson Coll., 1965, Morningside Coll., 1966, Iowa Wesleyan Coll., Coe Coll., 1968, Westmar Coll., 1970, W.Va. Wesleyan Coll., 1980; L.H.D., Cornell Coll., 1965, Ohio Wesleyan U., 1967, DePauw U., 1969; H.H.D., St. Ambrose Coll., 1970; S.T.D., Parsons Coll., 1972; Baldwin-Wallace Coll., 1977; D.H., Rust Coll., 1975; D.D., Allegheny Coll., 1979; D.Litt., Mt. Union Coll., 1979; D.D., Wofford Coll., 1972, Ohio Northern U., 1983, Asbury Theol. Sem., 1983, Emory U., 1985. Ordained to ministry Methodist Ch., 1944; pastor Orangeburg Circuit, 1942-43, York, S.C., 1946-48; chaplain S.C. State Coll., 1944-46; prof. Gammon Theol. Sem., Atlanta, 1948-53; assoc. sec. Meth. Bd. Edn., 1953-64; bishop Iowa area Meth. Ch., 1964-76; bishop Ohio East area United Meth. Ch., 1976—; pres. Council of Bishops, 1984-85, Gen. Council on Ministries, 1984—; dir. Equitable of Iowa; vis. prof. Perkins Sch. Theology, So. Meth. U., summer 1958, Duke U. Div. Sch., fall 1978. Trustee Baldwin-Wallace Coll., Meth. Theol. Sch. in Ohio, Mt. Union Coll., Ohio Wesleyan U., Otterbein Coll., Copeland Oaks, Elyria Home, Berea Children's Home, St. Luke's Hosp. Office: 8800 Cleveland Ave NW North Canton OH 44720

THOMAS, JAMES WILLIAM, lawyer; b. N.Y.C., May 12, 1949; s. Howard and Alice (Brennan) T.; m. Cecilia Coleman Goad, July 7, 1973; children—James William Jr., Brennan McKinney. B.S., U. Dayton, 1971; J.D., Ohio No. U., 1974. Bar: Ohio 1974, U.S. Dist. Ct. Ohio 1976. Ptnr., Earley & Thomas, Eaton, Ohio, 1974—; village solicitor Village of Lewisburg (Ohio), 1977-81, Village of Verona (Ohio), 1979-81; asst. pros. atty. Preble County (Ohio), 1980-81. Mem. Community Improvement Corp., Eaton. Mem. Preble County Bar Assn. (pres. 1982-84). Republican. Roman Catholic. Club: Eaton County. Lodge: Rotary (dir. 1980—). Avocations: boating; tennis. Home: 761 Vinland Cove Eaton OH 45300 Office: Earley & Thomas 112 N Barron St Eaton OH 45320

THOMAS, JOHN ARLEN, pharmacologist; b. LaCrosse, Wis., Apr. 6, 1933; s. John M. and Eva H. (Nelson) T.; m. Barbara A. Fisler, June 22, 1957; children—Michael J., Jane L. B.S., U. Wis., 1956; M.A., U. Iowa, 1958, Ph.D., 1961. Diplomate Am. Acad. Toxicologic Sci. Instr., U. Iowa, Iowa City, 1961; asst. prof. U. Va., Charlottesville, 1961-64; assoc. prof. Creighton U., Omaha, 1964-67; assoc. prof. W.Va. U., Morgantown, 1968-69, prof. pharmacology 1970-80; v.p. corp. research Travenol Labs., Round Lake, Ill., 1980—. Asst. dean W.Va. Sch. Medicine, Morgantown, 1973-75, assoc. dean, 1973-80, cons. toxicology, 1966-80. Author: (with M.G. Mawhinney) Synopsis of Endocrine Pharmacology, 1978; (with E.J. Keenan) Principles of Endocrine Pharmacology, 1985; editor: (with others) Basic and Clinical Toxicology of Lead, 1985; Endocrine Toxicology, 1985, others. Contbr. articles to profl. publs. Served with U.S. Army, 1951-53. Recipient Cert. of Service, U.S. EPA, 1977. Names Outstanding Alumnus, U. Wis.-La Crosse, 1978; Outstanding Tchr., W.Va. U., 1971. Mem. Endocrine Soc., Soc. Toxicology (councilor), Am. Soc. Pharmacology and Exptl. Therapeutics, Am. Coll. Toxicology, Teratology Soc., Am. Acad. Vet. Pharmacology. Republican. Home: 1304 Woodland Dr Deerfield IL 60015

THOMAS, JOHN RUSSELL, professional football team executive; b. Griffithsville, W.Va., July 24, 1924; s. Ezra Neri and Ada Elizabeth (Sowards) T.; student Ohio State U., 1943-46; m. Dorothy Snyder, Aug. 3, 1945; children—John, Jim. Player, Detroit Lions, 1946-49, mem. coaching staff, 1952-56, scout, 1952-59, mem. radio broadcasting team, 1960-63, dir. player personnel, 1964-66, exec. v.p., gen. mgr., 1967—; asst. coach St. Bonaventure Coll., Olean, N.Y., 1950-51; dir. NFL Properties; mem. NFL Coaches Pension Plan Com. Office: 1200 Featherstone Rd Box 4200 Pontiac MI 48057*

THOMAS, JON CAYSON, financial advisor, real estate developer; b. St. Louis, June 22, 1947; s. Jefferson C. and Edna W. Thomas; B.S., U. Mo., 1971; M.B.A., So. Ill. U., 1978; m. Alma DeBasio, Aug. 31, 1968; children—Jennifer Anne, Jon Cayson, II. Div. mgr. pensions and mut. funds Safeco Securities Co./Safeco Life Ins. Co., St. Louis, 1970-74; v.p. fin. planning dept. A.G. Edwards & Sons, Inc., St. Louis, 1974-77; pres. Intermark Assets Group Inc., St. Louis, 1978—; founder, 1980, thereafter prin. Monetary Mgmt. Group, St. Louis. Cert. fin. planner. Mem. Nat. Assn. Securities Dealers (registered investment advisor), Internat. Assn. Fin. Planners, Inst. Cert. Fin. Planners, Beta Theta Pi. Office: 232 S Meramac Clayton MO 63105

THOMAS, JONATHAN WAYNE, educational administrator, engineering and education consultant; b. Henderson, Ky., Dec. 12, 1950; s. Wayne and Mary (Browning) T.; m. Rhonda G. Thomas, Sept. 20, 1975; children—Rachel, Jarod. A.A.S., Rend Lake Jr. Coll., 1971; B.S., Ind. State U., 1973, M.S., 1974. Chmn. transp. tech. Vocat. Tech. Coll., Evansville, 1977-80, chmn. tech. div., 1980-83, dir. instrn., Sellersburg, 1983—. Contbr. articles to profl. jours. Mem. Soc. Automotive Engrs., Ind. Vocat. Assn., Ind. Vocat. Post-Secondary Edn. Assn. (v.p. 1984—), Epsilon Pi Tau. Avocations: fishing, camping, spelunking, dune buggies. Home: 2305 Allentown Rd Sellersburg IN 47172 Office: Indiana Vocat Tech Coll 8204 Hwy 311 Sellersburg IN 47172

THOMAS, JOSEPH WESLEY, lawyer; b. Detroit, Aug. 16, 1955; s. John Joseph and Geraldine Clare (France) T.; m. Jamie Ann MacKercher, Aug. 16, 1980. B.A., Oakland U., 1977; J.D., Thomas M. Cooley Law Sch., 1980; M.L.T., Georgetown U., 1982. Bar: D.C. 1980, Mich. 1981, U.S. Dist. Ct. D.C. 1981, U.S. Dist. Ct. (ea. dist.) Mich. 1981, U.S. Tax Ct. 1981, U.S. Ct. Appeals (D.C. cir.) 1981, U.S. Ct. Appeals (6th cir.) 1982. Assoc. Dickstein, Shapiro & Morin, Washington, 1980-81; sole practice, Troy, Mich., 1982-83; ptnr. Farhat & Thomas, P.C., Farmington Hills, Mich., 1983—. Office: Farhat & Thomas PC 30777 Northwestern Hwy Farmington Hills MI 48018

THOMAS, KEITH CHARLES, dentist; b. Carroll, Nebr., May 3, 1932; s. David Jenkin and Helen Ivy (Swihart) T.; m. Beatrice Mary Majkut, July 3, 1959; children—David, LouAnn. D.D.S., Creighton U., 1956. Lic. dentist, Nebr. Gen. practice dentistry, USAF, Japan, 1956-59, Chadron, Nebr., 1959—. Pres. Bd. Edn., Chadron, 1982—; mem. Chadron Hosp. Bd., 1969-73. Served to capt. USAF, 1956-59. Mem. West Dist. Dental Soc. (pres. 1974), Nebr. Dental Assn., ADA, Acad. Gen. Dentistry. Republican. Episcopalian. Lodges: Masons, Shriners, Elks, Kiwanis (pres. 1964, lt. gov. 1968). Avocation: golf. Home: 421 Cedar St Chadron NE 69337 Office: 341 Main Chadron NE 69337

THOMAS, KENT RICHARD, biochemistry educator; b. Topeka, Sept. 12, 1948; s. Keith Marshall and Rosemary (Harmon) T.; m. Sandra Jean Wehmeyer, June 17, 1972; 1 child, Jennifer Lynne. B.A., U.N.C.-Wilmington, 1975; Ph.D., Kans. State U., 1980. Grad. research asst. Kans. State U., Manhattan, 1976-80; postdoctoral research assoc. U. Iowa, Iowa City, 1980-82; instr. biochemistry U. Nebr., Omaha, 1982-84, asst. prof., 1984—, sr. mem. immunology council Med. Ctr., 1983—; instr. natural sci. Coll. of St. Mary, Omaha, 1984—; cons. Brandeis Inc., Omaha, 1984—. Author: Toushstone, 1984. Contbr. articles to profl. jours. Contbng. editor various profl. jours. Chmn. Ralston San. Improvement Dist., 1984—. Served with USN, 1968-72. Grantee Nat. Kidney Found., 1982, Nebr. Dept. Health, 1984. Mem. Am. Assn. Coll. Pharmocologists, Nebr. Acad. Scis., Greenpeace Internat., Nat. Wildlife Fedn., Alpha Chi Sigma, Theta Xi. Avocations: Am. history, running, wildlife conservation. Home: 8812 Monroe St Ralston NE 68127 Office: Coll Pharmacy U Nebr Med Ctr 42nd and Dewey Ave Omaha NE 68105

THOMAS, LEWIS JONES, JR., anesthesiology educator, biomedical researcher; b. Phila., Dec. 13, 1930; s. Lewis Jones and Margaretta Eleanore (Schmid) T.; m. Jane E. Priem, June 18, 1955; children—Lewis Jones III., Sarah Jane Thomas Snell. B.S. in Biology, Haverford Coll., 1953; M.D. cum laude, Washington U., St. Louis, 1957. Diplomate Am. Bd. Anesthesiology. Assoc. dir. Biomed. Computer Lab., Wash. U. Sch. Med., 1972-75, assoc. prof. anesthesiology, physiology and biophysics, biomed. engring., 1974—, assoc. prof. elec. engring., 1978—, dir. 1975—; assoc. dir. Inst. Biomed. Computing,

St. Louis, 1983—; cons. Health Resources Admin., Rockville, Md., 1974-75, Nat. Ctr. Health Service Research, Washington, 1978-82. Contbr. articles to profl. jours. and books. Bd. dirs. Bd. Edn., University City, Mo., 1970, 72-73; v.p. Symphony Orch., University City, 1969-78, pres. 1978—. Served to sr. asst. surg. USPHS, 1962-64. Recipient USPHS Research Career Devel. award, 1966. Mem. Am. Heart Assn., AMA, Am. Physiol. Soc., AAAS, Am. Soc. Anesthesiologists, Barnes Hosp. Soc., N.Y. Acad. Scis., St. Louis Metro. Med. Soc. Avocations: music performance, recreational computing. Office: Biomed Computer Lab Washington Sch Med 700 S Euclid St Saint Louis MO 63110

THOMAS, MARK ALAN, real estate developer; b. Beaver Dam, Wis., July 10, 1941; s. Lewis Ellery and Margaret Jane (Griffiths) T.; m. Pamela Sue Humphries, May 27, 1972; children—Graham Elton Earl, Morgan Roland. B.A. in Econ., Lawrence Coll., 1963; M.B.A., Dartmouth Coll., 1965. Mem. fin. staff Ford Motor Co., Dearborn, Mich. and Buenos Aires, Argentina, 1965-69; salesman Weir, Manuel, Snyder & Ranke, Inc., Birmingham, Mich., 1969-74, ptnr., 1974—; ptnr. Caiman Properties, Troy, Mich., 1973—, T.G. Assocs., Birmingham, 1978—; v.p., sec. Stoneleigh Internat., Freeport, Grand Bahama, 1965-71. Bd. dirs. Birmingham Hist. Soc., 1977—; mem. Birmingham Hist. Bd., 1981—. Mem. Nat. Assn. Realtors, Mich. Assn. Realtors, Internat. Real Estate Fedn., Nat. Real Estate Exchange, Birmingham-Bloomfield C. of C. (dir. 1983—). Republican. Methodist. Club: Oakland Hills Country. Home: 175 Baldwin Ave Birmingham MI 48009 Office: 298 S Woodward Ave Birmingham MI 48011

THOMAS, MARTHA MAXINE, educator, counselor; b. Lima, Ohio, Jan. 16, 1940; d. Louis A. and Virginia W. Thomas. B.Sc., Ohio State U., 1964; M.Ed., Xavier U., 1969; M.A., Wright State U., 1978. Tchr., Trotwood-Madison (Ohio) Schs., 1964-66, Beavercreek (Ohio) High Sch., 1966-69; counselor Beavercreek (Ohio) Jr. High Sch., 1969-79, Bellbrook (Ohio) High Sch., 1980-81; career counselor Vandalia-Butler Schs., Dayton, Ohio, 1981—; career edn. counselor Vandalia-Butler City Schs., Vandalia, Ohio. Mem. NEA, Nat. Assn. Secondary Sch. Adminstrs., Assn. Supervision and Curriculum Devel., Ohio Edn. Assn., Vandalia Butler Edn. Assn., Phi Kappa Delta, Kappa Delta Pi. Democrat. Methodist. Office: 600 S Dixie Dr Vandalia OH 45377

THOMAS, MARY IMELDA PLACE, college administrator; b. Grove City, Pa., June 2, 1933; d. John Anthony and Mary E. (Campbell) Place; m. Raymond Joseph Thomas, May 18, 1974. B.S. in Edn., St. John Coll., 1962; M.Ed. in Adminstrn. and Supervision, Kent State U., 1968; student Youngstown State U., Duquesne U., Cath. U., 1976—. Cert. elem. prin., supt., Ohio. Tchr., Youngstown Diocese Cath. Schs., 1956-60, 64-72, Cleve. Diocese, 1960-64; prin. Youngstown Diocese, 1968-72; Title III project dir. Youngstown State U., 1972-75, program devel. specialist, tchr. corps, 1975-78, tchr. placement coordinator, 1978-79, inservice coordinator Sch. Edn., 1980—; cons. in field. Trustee Youngstown YWCA, 1968-77, 82—, Friendly Town, Children and Family Services Orgn., 1972-82; mem. panel Am. Women's Ordination Conf., 1982—. Mem. Am. Assn. for Supervision and Curriculum Devel., Internat. Reading Assn., Cath. Coll. Assn., Assn. for Individually Guided Edn., Internat. Profl. Women's Orgn., Phi Delta Kappa. Contbr. articles to profl. jours. Office: School of Education Youngstown State University Youngstown OH 44555

THOMAS, MICHAEL CRAIG, physician; b. Massillon, Ohio, July 25, 1950; s. Henry Daniel and Margaret Grace (Spangler) T.; m. Karen Raley, June 30, 1973 (div.); children—Matthew Reese, Michael Ryan. B.S. cum laude, Marietta Coll., 1972; M.D., Case Western Res. U., 1976. Intern, Northwestern Meml. Hosps., Chgo., 1978-79; emergency room physician, Lakewood (Ohio) Hosp., 1979-80; dir., chmn. dept. emergency medicine Trumbull Meml. Hosp., Warren, Ohio, 1980—; instr. emergency medicine N.E. Ohio Coll. Medicine; lectr., paramedic program Youngstown State U. Chmn. Trumbull County Paramedic Adv. Com., med. dir. EMT-Advanced Program; trustee Eastern Ohio chpt. Am. Heart Assn. Mem. Am. Coll. Emergency Physicians, Ohio State Med. Soc., Trumbull County Med. Soc., Cleve. Acad. Medicine, Phi Beta Kappa, Omicron Delta Kappa. Methodist. Office: Trumbull Meml Hosp 1350 E Market St Warren OH 44482

THOMAS, PATRICIA GRAFTON (MRS. LEWIS EDWARD THOMAS), educator; b. Michigan City, Ind., Sept. 30, 1921; d. Robert Wadsworth and Elinda (Oppermann) Grafton; student Stephens Coll., 1936-39, Purdue U., summer 1938; B.Ed. magna cum laude, U. Toledo, 1966; postgrad. (fellow) Bowling Green U., 1968; m. Lewis Edward Thomas, Dec. 21, 1939; children—Linda L. (Mrs. John R. Collins), Stephanie A. (Mrs. Andrew M. Pawuk), I. Kathryn (Mrs. James N. Ramsey), Deborah. Tchr., Toledo Bd. Edn., 1959—, tchr. lang. arts Byrnedale Sch., 1976-81. Dist. capt. Planned Parenthood, 1952-53, ARC, 1954-55; mem. lang. arts curriculum com. Toledo Bd. Edn., 1969, mem. grammar curriculum com., 1974; bd. dirs. Anthony Wayne Nursery Sch., 1983—; bd. dirs. Toledo Women's Symphony Orch. League, 1983—, sec., 1985—. Mem. Toledo Soc. Profl. Engrs. Aux., Helen Kreps Guild, AAUW, Toledo Artists' Club, Spectrum, Friends of Arts, Phi Kappa Phi, Phi Delta Kappa, Kappa Delta Pi, Pi Lambda Theta (chpt. pres. 1978—), Delta Kappa Gamma (chpt. pres. 1976-78, area membership chmn. 1978-80, 1st place award for exhbn. 1985). Republican. Episcopalian. Home: 4148 Deepwood Lane Toledo OH 43614

THOMAS, RICHARD C., orchestra executive. Gen. mgr. Milw. Symphony Orch. Office: Milwaukee Symphony Orchestra Uihlein Hall/Performing Arts Ctr 212 W Wisconsin Ave Milwaukee WI 53203*

THOMAS, ROBERT DOUGLAS, accountant; b. Toronto, Ont., Can., Nov. 18, 1924; s. Robert Duncan and Alice Georgina T.; B.Com., U. Toronto, 1946; M.B.A., U. B.C., 1956; m. Anna Clare Washington, Dec. 20, 1946; 1 son, Robert Duncan. Asst. prof. U. B.C., 1951-56; ptnr. Riddell Stead & Co., Toronto, Ont., Can., 1957-59; exec. dir. Can. Inst. Chartered Accts., Toronto, 1960-73, also dir. research, 1960-68, gen. dir. research, 1973—. Decorated Queen's Jubilee medal. Fellow Ont. Inst. Chartered Accts., Order Chartered Accts. Que.; mem. Can. Inst. Internat. Affairs (chancellor's council), Internat. Bus. Council of Can. (chmn. fin. reporting com.), Am. Acctg. Assn. (adv. council internat. sect.), Acctg. Hall of Fame, Victoria Coll. Alumni Assn. (pres. 1973-74), U. Toronto Alumni Assn. (v.p.). Clubs: St. James, Granite. Home: 179 Golfdale Rd Toronto ON M4N 2C1 Canada Office: 150 Bloor St W Toronto ON Canada M5S 2Y2

THOMAS, WILLIAM ARTHUR, lawyer; b. Pitts., Jan. 20, 1939; s. W. Arthur and Ruth Roberna (Mock) T.; 1 child, Gretchen Gale. B.S., Purdue U., 1960; Ph.D., U. Minn., 1967; J.D., U. Tenn., 1972. Bar: Tenn. 1972, Ill. 1980. Research scientist Oak Ridge Nat. Lab., 1967-72; prof. law U. Tenn., Knoxville, 1972-73; research atty. Am. Bar Found., Chgo., 1973-80, 82—; vis. prof. law U. Ill, 1981-82, U. Iowa, 1977, 80. Contbr. articles to legal and sci. jours. Served to 1st lt. USMC, 1960-62. Office: 750 N Lake Shore Dr Chicago IL 60611

THOMAS JIRAUCH, SISTER MARY, nun; b. St. Louis, Sept. 26, 1928; d. Milton B. and Margaret M. (Thomas) Jirauch. B.Nursing, St. Louis U., 1958, M.Hosp. Adminstrn., 1960. Joined Sisters of Divine Providence, 1946. Provincial counsellor, St. Louis, 1970-80; pres. St. Elizabeth Med. Ctr., Granite City, Ill., 1960-84, chmn. bd., 1984—. Contbr. articles to profl. jours. Fellow Am. Coll. Hosp. Adminstrs.; mem. Am. Hosp. Assn., Cath. Health Assn., Ill. Hosp. Assn. (bd. mem.), Ill. Cath. Hosp. Assn. (bd. dirs.). Home: 2100 Madison Ave Granite City IL 62040 Office: St Elizabeth Med Ctr 2100 Madison Ave Granite City IL 62040

THOMPSON, BETTY J., insurance executive; b. Shreveport, La., Jan. 5, 1939; d. Elizabeth (Cross) Linder; m. Albert Harris (div. 1970); children—Charmaine, Kimberly, Mark; m. William H. Thompson. Grad. Spencerian Coll. Bus., 1955. Personnel mgr., payroll dir., advt. cons. Haugan Olson Advt. Inc., 1956-59; coordinator data processing Northwestern Mut. Life Co., 1959-65; setup person Globe Union, Inc., 1965-68; admistrv. asst., newsletter editor, counselor Council on Urban Life, 1968-71; counselor, delinquency diversion program, 1971-73; exec. dir. Project Equality Wis., Inc., Milw., 1973—. Mem. State Health Policy Council, Wis., 1975-81; mem. State Real Estate License Regulation Bd., Wis., 1979-85; bd. dirs. Wis. Heart Assn., Women's Coalition Constr. Project, Catholic Com. Urban Ministry, diaconate Milw. Catholic Archdiocese, St. Anthony Hosp., Milw. br. NAACP; mem. Milw. Human Relations Radio TV Council; mem. adv. com. integration commn. Milw. Archdiocese, Wis. Equal Employment Opportunity Program; mem. com. Harambee Revitilization Project Community Council, Minority Profls., United Negro Coll. Fund drive, United Way Greater Milw. Recipient Outstanding Service Citizen award Milw. Theol. Inst.; Human Rights citation award N.G.; Human Rights award B'nai B'rith; Human Relations award Milw. Commn. Community Relations; Quincentenary award St. Thomas Moore Lawyers Soc. Home: 9150 N Maura Ln Brown Deer WI 53223 Office: Project Equality Wis 1442 N Farwell Ave Suite 210 Milwaukee WI 53202

THOMPSON, CHARLES EDGAR, insurance company executive; b. Kirksville, Mo., Jan. 26, 1944; s. Samuel E. and Carrie N. (Hoffman) T. Sales agt. Londen Ins. Group, Phoenix 1977-79, assoc. regional mgr., 1979-80, regional mgr., 1980, regional v.p., 1980-81, div. v.p., 1981—. Co-editor: History of Elmer, 1976. Mayor, city of Elmer, 1976-78, mem. city council, 1972-76; chmn. Bicentennial Com., 1976, Served with U.S. Army, 1965-67; Vietnam. Named Mgr. of Yr., Londen Ins. Group, 1979, Top Divisional Vice-Pres., 1982, Salesman of Yr., 1980; All Star Honor Roll, Ins. Sales Mag., 1981. Democrat. Home: PO Box 142 Elmer MO 63538 Office: Lincoln Heritage Mktg Ctr 1709 S 5th St Springfield IL 62703

THOMPSON, DALE MOORE, banker; b. Kansas City, Kans., Nov. 19, 1897; s. George Curl and Ruth Anna (Moore) T.; A.B. cum laude, U. Mich., 1920; m. Dorothy Allen Brown, July 2, 1921; 1 son, William Brown (dec.). Trainee, City Bank of Kansas City (Mo.) (now United Mo. Bank, N.A.), 1920-22, asst. cashier, 1922-27, asst. v.p., 1927-30, v.p., 1930-34; v.p. City Bond & Mortgage Co. Kansas City (now United Mo. Mortgage Co.), 1934-43, exec. v.p., 1943-48, pres., 1948-68, chmn. bd., 1968-74, hon. chmn. bd., 1974—, also dir.; chmn., trustee Central Mortgage & Realty Trust, 1972-76, hon. chmn., 1976—; v.p. Regency Bldg. Co., Kansas City. Lectr. Northwestern U. Sch. Mortgage Banking, also Stanford, 1954-62. Mem. Mo. Gov.' Com. on Arts; chmn. Kansas City campaign United Negro Coll. Fund, 1958-59; mem. Mo. Bd. Edn., 1966-82; pres. Kansas City Philharm. Assn., 1944-54, also trustee; trustee U. Kansas City, Conservatory Music Kansas City, Kansas City Art Inst., Kansas City Children's Mercy Hosp.; treas. Kansas City Truman Med. Center, 1962-78. Served with USN World War I. Recipient citation Kansas City C. of C., 1954, Archbishop's Community Service citation, 1954, citation NCCJ, 1965; Mayor's citation, 1955; Pioneer in Edn. award, 1982. Mem. Mortgage Bankers Assn. Am. (nat. pres. 1962-63, Distinguished Service award 1966, life mem. bd. govs.), U. Mich. Alumni Assn. (past dir.), Phi Beta Kappa (pres. Kansas City 1946-49), Trigon, Phi Kappa Psi. Mem. Christian Ch. Clubs: River, University, Indian Hills Country (Kansas City); Monterey Peninsula Country (Pebble Beach, Calif.). Home: 221 W 48th St Kansas City MO 64112 Office: United Mo Bank Bldg Kansas City MO 64106

THOMPSON, DANIEL BUSH, food company executive; b. Cranford, N.J., Dec. 3, 1933; s. John Irvin and Gwenyth (Bruyere) T.; m. Pamela Diane Yeager, Sept. 12, 1959; children—Judith Lynne, Daniel Bush, III. B.A., Washington and Lee U., 1956. Mgmt. trainee Campbell Soup Co., Camden, N.J., 1956-59, asst. mgr. purchasing, 1959-68, dir. container purchasing, 1968-78, asst. plant mgr., Napoleon, Ohio, 1978-82, plant mgr., Chgo., 1982—. Mem. Sch. Bd., Delvan, N.J., 1968. Served to 1st lt. USMCR, 1956-58. Mem. Old Guard Soc. Republican. Presbyterian. Lodge: Elks. Avocations: sailing; tennis. Home: 1511 Arrow Wood Ln Downers Grove IL 60515 Office: Campbell Soup Co 2550 W 35th St Chicago IL 60632

THOMPSON, DAVID ALLEN, pharmaceutical company executive; b. Milbank, S.D., Dec. 4, 1941; s. Lester George and Henrietta Josephine (Gannon) T.; m. Marilyn Marie Selgeby, June 27, 1964; children—Dawn, Virginia, Brian. B.S. in Dairy Sci., S.D. State U., 1964. With Abbott Labs., 1964—, dir. mfg. and engring., Columbus, Ohio, 1972-75, v.p. mfg. and engring., 1975-76, v.p. ops., 1976-81, v.p. corp. materials mgmt., North Chicago, Ill., 1981-82, v.p. personnel, 1982-83, pres. Abbott Diagnostics Div., 1983—. Mem. C. of C. (dir. 1972). Republican. Roman Catholic. Club: Biltmore Country (Barrington, Ill.). Lodge: Rotary (dir. 1972). Office: Abbott Labs Abbott Park IL 60064

THOMPSON, DAVID EUGENE, data processing executive; b. Plainfield, N.J., Dec. 10, 1945; s. Maurice Eugene and Charlotte Ruth (Harrington) T.; B.S., Northwestern U., 1968, postgrad., 1969; postgrad. U. Mich., 1970-71; M.B.A. with distinction, Rockhurst Coll., 1982; m. Beverly J. Johnson, 1983; children by previous marriage—Michael David, Jonathan Paul, Daniel Ethan. Programmer, Ford Motor Co., Chgo., 1968-69; fin. analyst, Detroit, 1969-72, data processing mgr., Norfolk, Va., 1972-77, data processing exec., Kansas City, Mo., 1978—; adj. prof. mgmt. Ottawa U.; cons. in field. Treas., Virginia Beach (Va.) Civic Chorus, 1975-76, pres., 1977; treas. singles ministry Village Presbyn. Ch., 1982, co-chmn., 1983 Mem. Am. Mgmt. Assn., Data Processing Mgmt. Assn. (dir. 1983—, v.p. 1985, Outstanding Dir. award 1984), Am. Mensa. Republican. Home: 7508 W 98th Terr Overland Park KS 66212 Office: PO Box 11009 Kansas City MO 64119

THOMPSON, DAVID JEROME, chemical company executive, biochemist, nutritionist; b. Sand Creek, Wis., July 21, 1937; s. Marshall and Bernice (Severson) T.; m. Virginia Ruth Williams, Aug. 11, 1962; children—Keith D., Craig M. B.S., U. Wis., 1960, M.S., 1961, Ph.D., 1963; M.B.A., U. Chgo., 1975. Research biochemist Internat. Minerals and Chem. Corp., Libertyville, Ill., 1964-68, supr. animal research, 1968-69, dir. tech. service, Mundelein, Ill., 1969-79, sales mgr., 1979-81, v.p. sci. and tech., Northbrook, Ill., 1981-84, v.p. and gen. mgr. Sterwin div., 1984—; cons. Am. Assn. Feed Control Ofcls., 1974-85; com. mem. Nat. Research Council, Nat. Acad. Scis., 1976-80. Co-author: Mineral Tolerance of Domestic Animals, 1980; contbr. articles to profl. jours. Mem. Am. Inst. Nutrition, AAAS, Poultry Sci. Assn., Am. Dairy Sci. Assn., Am. Soc. Animal Sci., Am. Chem. Soc., N.Y. Acad. Scis., Am. Feed Mfrs. Assn. (chmn. nutrition council 1980), Sigma Xi, Gamma Alpha, Phi Lambda Upsilon, Theta Delta Chi. Club: Liberty Road and Track. Avocations: Competitive running; jazz and classical music; art; landscape gardening. Home: 826 Fair Way Libertyville IL 60048 Office: Internat Minerals and Chem Corp 2315 Sanders Rd Northbrook IL 60062

THOMPSON, DENNIS SCOTT, psychiatrist, physician; b. Detroit, June 18, 1943; s. Albert George and Mildred Marie (Mertens) T. B.S., U. Mich., 1965; postgrad. Wayne State U., 1966; D.O., Chgo. Coll. Osteo. Medicine, 1970. Cert. Am. Bd. Neurology and Psychiatry. Asst. prof., psychiatrist U. Ill. Med. Sch., Chgo., 1976-83, Chgo. Coll. Osteo. Medicine, 1983-84; med. dir. Hamilton Ctr., Terre Haute, Ind., 1984. Fellow Am. Acad. Child Psychiatry. Office: Hamilton Center 620 8th Ave PO Box 4323 Terre Haute IN 47804

THOMPSON, DOROTHY BROWN, writer; b. Springfield, Ill., May 14, 1896; d. William Joseph and Harriet (Gardner) Brown; A.B., U. of Kansas, 1919; m. Dale Moore Thompson, July 2, 1921; 1 son, William B. (dec.). Began writing professionally, 1931; contributed verse to nat. magazines and newspapers including Saturday Review, Sat. Eve. Post, Va. Quar. Rev., Poetry, Commonweal, Good Housekeeping and others, author research articles for various historical jours.; poems pub. in over two hundred collections and textbooks; magazines and textbooks pub. in Eng., Australia, New Zealand, Can., India, Sweden; twenty-five in Braille. Leader poetry sect. Writers' Conf., U. Kan., 1953-55, McKendree Coll., 1961, 63, Creighton U., Omaha, 1966; lectr. writers' conf. U. Kan., 1965, Am. Poets Series, Kansas City, Mo., 1973; mem. staff Poets Workshop, Central Mo. State U., 1974; poet-in-schs. residency for Mo. State Council of Arts, 1974—. Received Mo. Writers' Guild Award, 1941, Poetry Soc. Am., nat. and local awards. Mem. Diversifiers, Poetry Soc. Am., Nat. Soc. Colonial Dames, First Families of Va. (Burgess for Mo.). Mem. Christian Ch. Clubs: Woman's City, Filson (Louisville). Author: Subject to Change (poems), 1973. Address: 221 W 48th St Apt 1402 Kansas City MO 64112

THOMPSON, EDWARD FRANCIS, lawyer, municipal judge; b. Yonkers, N.Y., Aug. 29, 1953; s. Edward Francis and Mary Francis (Keating) T. B.A., Manhattanville Coll., 1975; J.D., U. Puget Sound, 1978. Bar: Wis. 1978, U.S. Dist. Ct. (ea. and we. dists.) Wis. 1978, U.S. Ct. Claims 1980, U.S. Ct. Appeals (7th cir.) 1980, U.S. Supreme Ct. 1982. Legal intern Puget Sound Legal Assistance Found., Tacoma, Wash., 1976-78; assoc. Hammett, Williams, Riemer & Thompson and predecessor Hammett, Williams & Riemer, Delavan, Wis., 1978-80, ptnr., 1980-84; mcpl. judge Town of Delavan, 1983—; ptnr., v.p. Clair Law Offices, Delavan, 1984—; atty. chmn. Wis. Patients Compensation Panel, 1982—. Bd. dirs. Delavan-Darien Sch. Dist. Found., 1982—. Mem. ABA, Assn. Trial Lawyers Am., Wis. Bar Assn., Walworth County Bar Assn. (v.p. 1984—), Wis. Acad. Trial Lawyers, Wis. Mcpl. Judges Assn., Walworth County Judges Assn. Home: Route 4 Box 638 Holig Ln Delavan WI 53115 Office: Clair Law Offices SC 617 E Walworth Ave Delavan WI 53115

THOMPSON, FRED WELDON, clergyman, administrator; b. Durant, Okla., Aug. 1, 1932; s. Fredrick Weldon and Mary Mauvolyn (Barnes) T.; m. Lois Bell Reedy, Apr. 25, 1954; children—Alicia Ann, Penny Sue. B.A., Ottawa U., 1954, D.D. (hon.), 1984; B.D., Central Bapt. Theol. Sem., 1958, Th.M., 1959. Ordained to ministry Am. Bapt. Chs. U.S.A., 1956; pastor South Broadway Bapt. Ch., Pittsburg, Kans., 1961-66; campus minister Bapt. Student Union, Pittsburg, 1962-66; area minister Am. Bapt. Ch. Central Region, Topeka, Kans., 1966-77, assoc. exec. minister, exec. minister, 1982—; assoc. gen. sec. Am. Bapt. Chs., Valley Forge, Pa., 1982—. Bd. dirs. Central Bapt. Theol. Sem., Kansas City, Kans., 1982—, Ottawa U., Kans., 1980—, Bacone Coll., Muskogee, Okla., 1974-82; bd. dirs. United Sch. Dist. 503 Sch. Bd., Parsons, Kans., 1971-77, pres., 1973-76. Recipient Ch. and Community award for Outstanding Alumni, Ottawa U., 1979. Mem. Ottawa U. Alumni Assn. (pres. 1977), Central Bapt. Sem. Alumni Assn. (pres. 1964). Office: Am Baptist Chs Central Region 5833 SW 29th St PO Box 4105 Topeka KS 66604

THOMPSON, GEORGE IRVING, data processing official; b. Tuscola, Ill., Sept. 23, 1949; s. Wilbur Wright and Virginia Lorraine (Sibley) T.; m. Debra Jeanne Hayes, June 24, 1978. B.S., Eastern Ill. U., 1971; M.S., U. Ill., 1973; M.B.A., U. Chgo., 1983. Sr. systems engr. Allstate Ins. Co., Northbrook, Ill., 1973-75; sr. systems analyst Kraft Inc., Glenview, Ill., 1975-78; sr. tech. analyst Continental Grain Co., Chgo., 1978-83; data processing mgr. ContiCarriers & Terminals, Des Plaines, Ill., 1983—. Recipient Super-Sleuth award Boole & Babbage, Inc., 1979. Avocations: tennis, running, aerobics. Home: 1128 N Ridgeland St Oak Park IL 60302 Office: ContiCarriers & Terminals Inc 2700 River Rd Des Plaines IL 60018

THOMPSON, GERALD PAUL, public relations counsel; b. Pitts., Jan. 8, 1959; s. Raymond Merton and Dorothy L. (Sabol) T.; m. Deborah Jean Lee, June 12, 1982; B.S. in Communications, Ind. State U., 1981. Account exec. Wabash Valley Ad-Plan, Inc., Terre Haute, Ind., 1981-82; v.p. Orpurt Thompson Communications, Terre Haute, 1982-83; asst. v.p. Howard S. Wilcox, Inc., Indpls., 1983-84; mgr. pub. relations Am. Red Ball Transit Co., Indpls., 1984-85; dir. pub. relations Indpls. Union Sta., 1985—. Republican precinct committeeman, 1983-84. Mem. Pub. Relations Soc. Am., Am. Trucking Assns. (pub. relations council), Internat. Assn. Bus. Communicators, U.S. Jaycees. Home: 1164 E 58th St Indianapolis IN 46220 Office: 200 S Meridian St Suite 400 Indianapolis IN 46225

THOMPSON, GLENN JUDEAN, library science educator; b. Sioux Falls, S.D., Oct. 16, 1936; s. Carl Melvin and Emma Bertina (Johnson) T.; m. Agnes Myrleen Nord, Aug. 23, 1958; children—Christine Faye, Nathan Glenn. B.S., Augustana Coll., Sioux Falls, S.D., 1958; M.A., U. Minn., 1966; Ed.D., U. S.D., 1969. Cert. music tchr., English tchr., librarian, audiovisual dir., Minn. Music tchr. Wayzata Pub. Schs. (Minn.), 1958-63; librarian, audiovisual dir. Perham Pub. Schs. (Minn.), 1963-66; mem. faculty St. Cloud State Coll., (Minn.), 1966-70; mem. faculty U. Wis.-Eau Claire, 1970—, chmn. dept. library sci. and media edn., 1972—. Mem. ALA, Wis. Library Assn., Wis. Ednl. Media Assn., NEA. Republican. Lutheran. Avocation: boating. Home: Route 7 Box 76 Menomonie WI 54751 Office: Library 2044 U Wis-Eau Claire Eau Claire WI 54701

THOMPSON, HOBSON, JR., librarian; b. Tuscumbia, Ala., Sept. 26, 1931; s. Hobson and Marie (BeLue) T.; m. Geneva Elaine Simon, Feb. 14, 1965; children—Michael Stewart, Sharon Marie. B.S.Ed., Ala. State U., 1952; M.S. in Library Sci., Atlanta U., 1958. Head librarian, instr. math Morris Coll., Sumter, S.C., 1954-62; asst. prof. math, head librarian Elizabeth City (N.C.) State U., 1962-74; br. head Chgo. Public Library, Chgo., 1976—. Mem. adv. council librarians Bd. Govs. U. N.C., 1968-74. Served with USN, 1955-57. Mem. ALA, Ill. Library Assn., Am. Topical Assn., Postal Commemorative Soc., Black Am. Philatelic Soc., Omega Psi Phi, Beta Kappa Chi. Democrat. Methodist. Home: 400 E 33d St Apt 212 Chicago IL 60616 Office: Chicago Public Library 115 S Pulaski Rd Chicago IL 60624

THOMPSON, HUGH LEE, educational administrator; b. Martinsburg, W.Va., Mar. 1934; s. Frank Leslie and Althea (Brown) T.; m. Patricia Smith, Oct. 9, 1952; children—Cheryl, Linda, Tempe, Vicki. B.S., B.A. in English and Secondary Edn., Sheperd Coll., Shepherdstown, W.Va., 1952-56; M.A. in Phys. Edn., Pa. State U., 1958; Ph.D. in Higher Edn. Adminstrn., Case Western Res. U., 1969. Grad. asst. Pa. State U., University Park, 1956-57, tchr., 1957-60; tchr. Akron U., Ohio, 1960-62; tchr. Baldwin-Wallace Coll., Berea, Ohio, 1962-66, asst. to pres., asst. prof., 1966-69, dir. instnl. planning, asst. to pres., assoc. prof., 1969-70; coordinator Assoc. Colls. Cleve., 1970-71; pres., prof. Siena Heights Coll., Adrian, Mich., 1971-77; pres. Detroit Inst. Tech., 1977-80; chancellor, prof. Ind. U.-Kokomo, 1980—; cons. to colls. and univs.; dir. Union Bank and Trust Co., Kokomo, Continental Steel Corp., Kokomo. Mem. Nat. Cons. Com. Higher Edn., Luth. Ch. Am.; bd. dirs. ALFALIT, St. Joseph Meml. Hosp., Wittenberg U., Creative Arts council, Holy Cross Luth. Ch., Leadership Kokomo, United Way, Am. Cancer Soc., Kokomo Civic Theater, Kokomo Symphonic Soc., Kokomo Devel. Corp. Recipient Purdue U. Alumni Service award, 1983. Mem. Am. Ednl. Research Assn. (mem. spl. interest group in gen. edn.), Nat. Urban Edn. Assn. Avocations: travel, fishing, swimming; collecting religious art. Home: 2713 S Lafountain St Kokomo IN 46902 Office: Ind U 2300 S Washington Kokomo IN 46902

THOMPSON, JAMES ROBERT, governor of Illinois; b. Chgo., May 8, 1936; s. J. Robert and Agnes Josephine (Swanson) T.; student U. Ill., Washington U., St. Louis; LL.B., No. U., 1959; m. Jayne Anne Carr, June 19, 1976; 1 dau., Samantha. Admitted to Ill. bar; prosecutor, Cook County States Atty.'s Office, Chgo., 1959-64; assoc. prof. Northwestern U. Law Sch., 1964-69; chief dept. law enforcement and pub. protection Atty. Gen.'s Office, 1969-70; asst. U.S. atty. No. Dist. Ill., 1970-71, U.S. atty., 1971-75; gov. Ill., 1977—. Mem. Nat. Govs. Assn. (chmn. 1983—), Republican Govs. Assn. (chmn. 1982). Author: Cases in Common on Criminal Procedure; Cases in Common on Criminal Law; Criminal Law and Its Administration. Office: 207 State House Springfield IL 62706

THOMPSON, JANET ARLENE, educational administrator; b. Belsano, Pa., June 7, 1932; d. Clarence Melvine and Minnie Grace (Williams) Bennett; m. Raymond Duane Thompson, Aug. 20, 1953; children—Renee Darlene, Raymond Duane. B.S. in Edn., Marion Coll., 1954; M.S. in Edn., Ball State U., 1967. Cert. tchr., Ind., Ohio. Elem. tchr. Oak Hill Sch. Dist., Sweetser, Ind., 1958-60, Marion City Schs., Ind., 1960-67; dean students God's Bible Sch., Cin., 1976—; tchr. kindergarten Norwood City Schs., Ohio, 1967-70, 71—. Mem. NEA, Ohio Edn. Assn. Mem. Wesleyan Ch. Office: Gods Bible Sch and Coll 1810 Young St Cincinnati OH 45210

THOMPSON, JOSEPH WARREN, physician, surgeon; b. Wichita Falls, Tex., June 27, 1950; s. Allen Dulaney and Norma Helen (Rinabarger) T.; m. Harriet Ann Weeks, June 19, 1976; div. B.S., S.E. Mo. State U., 1972; D.O., Coll. Osteo. Medicine, Kansas City, Mo., 1976. Diplomate Am. Coll. Gen. Practitioners, Nat. Bd. Osteo. Med. Examiners. Intern, Normandy Hosp., St. Louis, 1976-77, resident in family practice, 1977-79; pvt. practice medicine, St. Louis, 1979—; program dir. family practice residency, 1982—. Mem. Mo. Osteo. Assn. (polit. action com.), Am. Osteo. Assn. (com. on edn. and evaluation), Am. Coll. Gen. Practitioners (past pres. Mo. soc.), Mo. Assn. Osteo. Physicians and Surgeons, St. Louis Dist. Assn. Osteo. Physicians and Surgeons. Democrat. Methodist. Lodges: Elks, Masons, Shriners. Office: 3301 Ashby Rd Saint Ann MO 63074

THOMPSON, JUUL HAROLD, lawyer, educator; b. Chgo., May 3, 1945; s. Jules Harold and Ruth Edith (Pudark) T.; m. Elizabeth Jean Bohler, Sept. 20, 1975; children—Michael, Erin, David, Margaret. B.A. in History, U. Chgo., 1967; J.D., U. Ill., 1973. Bar: Ill. 1973. Asst. states atty. Kane County, Ill., 1974-76; ptnr. Beck and Thompson, Batavia, Ill., 1976-82; sole practice, Batavia, 1983—; counsel Batavia Council on Aging, 1979—; counsel, grant chmn. Batavia Social Services Com., 1983—; counsel Programming for Low Income and Urban Services Community Service Agy., Batavia, 1978—; instr. law Elgin Community Coll., Ill., 1981—, Harper Community Coll., Palatine, Ill., 1981-83, Waubonsee Community Coll., Sugar Grove, Ill., 1982, Person Wollinsky C.P.A. Rev. Course, Downers Grove, Ill., 1984. Mem. Holy Cross Parish Council, 1985—. Served as 1st lt. U.S. Army, 1969-71, Vietnam. Decorated Bronze Star (2). Mem. VFW (Batavia comdr. 1979-80, trustee 1985—), Holy Cross Players. Republican. Roman Catholic. Lodge: K.C. Avocations: reading; woodworking; writing. Home: 1220 S Batavia Ave Batavia IL 60510 Office: 150 W Houston St Batavia IL 60510

THOMPSON, LARRY RICHARD, university administrator, law educator; b. Dayton, Ohio, Oct. 15, 1947; s. Theodore Roosevelt and Helen Ruth (Casey) T.; m. Francie Helen Hinson, July 10, 1971 (div.); 1 child, Eric Stephen; m. Patricia Lynn Rowe, Feb. 4, 1984. B.A., Wittenberg U., 1969; M.S., Calif. State U.-Los Angeles, 1973; J.D. summa cum laude, Ohio State U., 1976. Bar: Ohio 1976, U.S. Supreme Ct. 1980. Dir. fin. aid Wilmington Coll., Ohio, 1970-75; assoc. Vorys, Sater, Seymour & Pease, Columbus, Ohio, 1976-81; spl. asst. to pres., adj. prof. law Ohio State U., Columbus, 1981—; v.p., dir. Ohio Teleport Corp., Columbus, 1982—. Mem. ex officio, bd. dirs. Friends of WOSU, Columbus, 1983—; bd. dirs. Combined Health Appeal Central Ohio, Columbus. Mem. Nat. Assn. Coll. and Univ. Attys. (rep. exec. bd. 1984—, chmn. sect. governance and accountability 1981—), Inst. Econ. and Social Dialogue (bd. dirs.), ABA, Ohio State Bar Assn., Columbus Bar Assn., C. of C. Central Ohio (task force for econ. devel. 1984), Order of Coif. Avocations: jogging; travel; reading. Office: Suite 201 190 N Oval Mall Columbus OH 43210

THOMPSON, LEONARD LEROY, theology educator; b. LaFontaine, Ind., Sept. 24, 1934; s. Russell Charles and Ruth Alice (Dyson) T. B.A., DePauw U., 1956; B.D., Drew U., 1960; M.A., U. Chgo., 1963, Ph.D., 1968. Prof. religion Lawrence U., Appleton, Wis., 1968—. Author: Introducing Biblical Literature, 1978. Contbr. articles to theol. publs. Nat. Endowment for Humanities fellow, 1981-82. Mem. Soc. Bibl. Lit., Am. Acad. Religion, Chgo. Soc. Bibl. Research. Office: Lawrence U Appleton WI 54912

THOMPSON, LEROY TAYLOR, writer, security consultant; b. St. Louis, June 3, 1944; s. Earl and Lorraine Margaret (Cooper) T.; m. Gayle Starker, Dec. 21, 1974. B.S. in B.A., S.E. Mo. State U., 1967; M.A. in English, St. Louis U., 1971; postgrad. U. London, 1972-73, Oxford U., Eng., 1973, Edinburgh U., Scotland, 1974. Tchr. English, Ritenour Schs., Overland, Mo., 1968-69, 71-72, 74-84; instr. English, St. Louis U., 1969-71; security cons., 1971-84. Contbg. editor: Combat Handguns, 1982-84, Gun Week, 1981-84, AMI, 1983-84. Author: Uniforms of the Elite Forces, 1982; Uniforms of the Vietnam War, 1984; Dead Clients Don't Pay, 1984; U.S. Special Forces, 1984. Served to 1st lt. USAF, 1967-68. Clubs: Chute and Dagger, Soc. Vietnamese Rangers. Avocations: military insignia collecting, military knife collecting, book collecting. Home: 3471 Frontier Rd Festus MO Office: PO Box 67 Mapaville MO 63065

THOMPSON, MARC EDWARD, broker; b. Sacramento, Jan. 4, 1952; s. William Edward and Carmen Sidney (Drollet) T.; m. Ann Iris Milstein, Dec. 30, 1978 (div. Mar. 1981). B.A. in Econs., U. Calif.-Berkeley, 1974; postgrad., Stanford U., 1975. Resident mgr. Clayton Brokerage Co., San Francisco, 1974-77, spread specialist, Chgo., 1977-78, fin. instruments specialist, 1978-80; dir., arbitrage ptnr. Tradelink Corp., Chgo., 1980-83; floor broker, ind. trader Chgo. Bd. Trade, 1983—; v.p. Va. Trading Corp.; dir. Bd. Trade Found., mem. various coms. Sponsor, Chgo. Fgn. Affairs Council; active Chgo. Archtl. Found., Field Mus. Found. Mem. Internat. Monetary Market. Republican. Home: 1444 N Astor St Apt 301 Chicago IL 60610 Office: PO Box 900 141 W Jackson Blvd Chicago IL 60604

THOMPSON, MARCIA BRYANT, real estate associate broker; b. Denver, Nov. 20, 1937; d. Don R. and Marion F. (Miall) Bryant; m. Richard H. Thompson, Aug. 27, 1960; children—Richard, Kristen. B.A., U. Mich., 1959; grad. Realtors Inst., 1980. Real estate broker Koenig & Strey Inc., Wilmette, Ill., 1977-83, Baird & Warner, Winnetka, Ill., 1983—. Mem. Ill. Assn. Realtors (life; Million Dollar Club), North Shore Real Estate Bd., Nat. Assn. Realtors. Republican. Episcopalian. Clubs: Kenilworth (Ill.); Old Willow (Northbrook, Ill.) Home:721 20th StWilmetteIL 60091Office: 576LincolnWinnetka IL 60093

THOMPSON, MARK EVANS, lawyer; b. Chgo., Feb. 12, 1955; s. Harry Evans and Blanche Marie (Tanney) T.; m. Janet Cay Mac Donald, June 13, 1981. B.A., Augustana Coll., 1977; J.D., Chgo.-Kent Coll. Law, Ill. Inst. Tech., 1980. Bar: Ill. 1980, U.S. Dist. Ct. (no. dist.) Ill. 1980, U.S. Ct. Appeals (7th cir.) 1981. Asst. state's atty. Cook County, Chgo., 1980-81; dep. dir. dept. adminstrv. hearings Office of Ill. Sec. of State, Chgo., 1981—; lectr. Ill. Inst. for Continuing Legal Edn., Chgo., 1983—. Mem. Maine Twp. Bd. Trustees, Ill., 1981—; mem. Chgo. (Liquor) Lic. Appeal Commn., 1981-83; active Maine Twp. Republican Orgn., 1979—. Named to Outstanding Young Men Am., U.S. Jaycees, 1982. Mem. Nat. Dist. Attys. Assn., Ctr. for Study Presidency. Congregationalist. Home: 1305 Walnut St Des Plaines IL 60016 Office: Office Sec of State 188 W Randolph Chicago IL 60601

THOMPSON, MARY E., chemistry educator; b. Mpls., Dec. 21, 1928; d. Albert C. and Blanche (McAvoy) T. B.A., Coll. St. Catherine, 1953; M.S., U. Minn., 1958; Ph.D., U. Calif.-Berkeley, 1964. Math. and sci. tchr. Derham Hall High Sch., St. Paul, 1953-59; faculty Coll. St. Catherine, St. Paul, 1964—, prof., chmn. dept. chemistry, 1969—. Contbr. articles to profl. jours. Mem. Am. Chem. Soc., N.Y. Acad. Sci., Chem. Soc. London, AAAS, Sigma Xi, Phi Beta Kappa. Democrat. Roman Catholic. Avocations: tennis; biking; camping. Home: 1132 Grand Ave Saint Paul MN 55105 Office: Coll St Catherine 2004 Randolph Ave Saint Paul MN 55105

THOMPSON, MARY EMMA, principal; b. Paris, Ill., Oct. 14, 1933; d. Fred Mascher and Velma (Britton) G.; m. George Elmer Thompson, Aug. 6, 1950 (dec. Aug. 1959); children—Tony, Bobbi Thompson Harris, Gary. A.A., Palm Beach Jr. Coll., 1965; B.S. in Elem. Edn., Fla. Atlantic U., 1966; student So. Ill. U., 1969-71; M.S. in Elem. Edn., Eastern Ill. U., 1975 Ed.S., 1978; student Western Ill. U., 1975-76, 78; Ph.D. in Edn. Adminstrn., Ind. State U., 1985. Elem. tchr. Monroe County Schs., Fla., 1967-68, Pittsfield Dist. 10, Ill., 1968-78; elem. prin. Westfield Dist. 105, Ill., 1978-83; fellow Ind. State U., Terre Haute, 1983-84; chpt. I dir. Westfield Schs., 1979—, prin., 1984—; mem. survey and evaluation teams Ind. State U., Terra Haute, 1983-84. Sponsor Cystic Fibrosis Bike-a-thon, Westfield, 1979-82; mem. Clark County Mental Health Bd., Marshall, Ill., 1979—, treas., 1983—. Mem. Delta Kappa Gamma, Alpha Upsilon, Phi Delta Kappa. Republican. Baptist. Club: 4-H (leader 1967-73) (Pearl, Ill.). Avocations: reading, sewing, crocheting, traveling. Home: Rural Route 1 Box 85 Westfield IL 62464 Office: Westfield High Sch PO Box 218 Westfield IL 62474

THOMPSON, MERNA RUTH, social worker; b. Oconee, Ill., Feb. 25, 1918; d. Edgar and Clara M. (Neathery) Bass; B.A., Wayne State U., 1956; M.A., U. Mich., 1960, Ed.S., 1971; postgrad. Mich. State U., 1978; m. Frank L. Thompson, June 7, 1942 (dec.); children—Carol, Janice (dec.). Elem. classroom tchr., Ill., 1938-42, Walled Lake (Mich.) Schs., 1954-59, sch. social worker, 1959-81; cons. in field; coordinator spl. edn. programs. Mem. Youth Assistance Camping Program Com., 1975-76. Cert. social worker. Mem. Mich. Assn. Emotionally Disturbed Children, Nat. Assn. Social Workers, Mich. Assn. Sch. Social Workers, Mich. Soc. Mental Health, NEA, Mich. Edn. Assn., Walled Lake Edn. Assn. Baptist (Sunday sch. tchr., class sec.-treas.). Home: 2159 Decker Rd Apt 17 Walled Lake MI 48088

THOMPSON, OTIS EUGENE, state official; b. West Plains, Mo., June 17, 1923; s. Othel Albert and Mable Grace (Laffoon) T.; m. Patricia Foster, June 18, 1950; children—Kenneth Foster, Wallis Laffoon, John Patrick. Underwriter, v.p. Nat. Automobile and Casualty Co., Los Angeles, 1968-76; gen. mgr. Ozark Industries, Inc., West Plains, 1976-78; cons. Mo. Dept. Elem. Secondary Edn., Jefferson City, 1978-80; dir. Mo. Dept. Edn., Extended Employment Workshop, Jefferson City, 1980—; mem. adv. bd. Nat. Head Injury Found., 1982—; cons. Mo. Sheltered Workshop Mgrs. Assn., 1980—. Precinct capt. Arcadia, Calif., 1970-75; pres. Republican Club, 1974-75. Served with U.S. Army, 1943-46. Recipient Outstanding Employer award Vocat. Rehab., 1977. Mem. Am. Mgmt. Assn., Mo. State Tchrs. Assn., Kappa Alpha Alumni Assn. Republican. Presbyterian. Clubs: Gyro, Rotary (v.p.), Masons, Shriners. Home: 664 Senate Ct Jefferson City MO 65101 Office: 117 Commerce St PO Box 480 Jefferson City MO 65102

THOMPSON, PAT A., training consultant evaluator; b. St. Louis, May 16, 1955; d. George Luther and Wenona (Phillips) T.; m. Ralph Mark Thomas, Jan. 10, 1981. B.A., Tex. Tech U., 1975; M.A., U. Nebr., 1976, Ph.D., 1980. Evaluator FIPSE project U. Nebr., 1976-79, Lincoln Pub. Schs., Nebr., 1979-80; asst. prof. U. Nebr., Lincoln, 1979—; assoc. research scientist Am. Insts. Research, Palo Alto, Calif., 1980-82; owner, sr. ptnr. Evaluation Tng. Cons., Lincoln, 1982—; cons. various fin. insts., health care agys. Contbr. articles to profl. jours. Mem. NOVA Bus. Profl. Women (sec.-treas. 1983—), Am. Soc. for Tng. and Devel. (treas. Lincoln chpt. 1985—), Bank Mktg. Assn. Roman Catholic. Home: 3220 S 29th St Lincoln NE 68502 Office: Evaluation Tng Cons 261 N 8th St Suite 210 Lincoln NE 68508

THOMPSON, PAUL LELAND, artist; b. Buffalo, Iowa, May 20, 1911; s. Buell and Flora Elizabeth (Steen) T.; student Calif. Sch. Fine Arts, 1932-34, Corcoran Sch. Art, 1944-45; m. Phyllis McGregor, June 15, 1953; 1 dau., Leslie Ruth. One-man shows Internat. Galleries, Washington, 1946, M. Knoedler Co. Inc., 1954, Unitarian Ch., Plainfield, N.J.; 1975, Cin. Art Club, 1978, others; exhibited group shows Seattle Art Mus., 1937, Honolulu Acad. Art, 1933, Corcoran Biennial Nat. Painting Exhbn., 1945, San Francisco Palace of Legion of Honor, 1948, San Francisco Art Mus., 1948, NAD Nat. Watercolor Exhbn., 1956, Hunterdon County Art Center, Clinton, N.J., 1968; executed two murals Shiloh Baptist Ch., Plainfield, N.J.; represented in permanent collections Barry's Art Gallery, Scotch Plains, N.J., Cin. Bell Collection, The Heritage Gallery, Cin. Recipient Soc. Washington Artists prize, 1946; Washington Times Herald award, 1947. Mem. Artists Equity N.Y., Cin. Art Club, Cin. McDowell Soc., Am. Inst. Conservation Works of Art. Home: 314 Ludlow Ave Cincinnati OH 45220 Office: 3412 Telford St Cincinnati OH 45220

THOMPSON, PAUL WOODARD, research ecologist; b. Manchester, N.H., May 21, 1909; s. Gordon H. and Helen M. (Woodward) T.; m. Dorothy Bobisuthi, Oct. 23, 1936; children—Jane Susan Thompson Babbitt, Nancy R. B.S., U. Ill., 1930, M.S. in Chemistry, 1932; postgrad. in nuclear chemistry U. Chgo., 1933-36. Chemist, Ill. State Water Survey, Urbana, 1930-32; research chemist Sherwin Williams Paint Co., Chgo., 1935-39, Acme White Lead & Color, Detroit, 1939-42, Ethyl Corp., Detroit, 1942-71; fellow, research assoc. Cranbrook Inst. Sci., Bloomfield Hills, Mich., 1952—; cons. ecology Mich. Dept. Natural Resources, 1979—, others. Author: Plants of Oakland County, Michigan, 1959; Vegetation and Plants of Sleeping Bear, 1984; Vegetation and Plants of Huron Mountains, Michigan, 1976; also articles. Recipient Oakleaf award The Nature Conservancy, 1975; Charles Viol fellow, 1933, 34. Mem. Am. Forestry Assn., Am. Chem. Soc., Mich. Bot. Club (big tree com.). Presbyterian. Avocations: swimming; skiing, hiking; photography. Home: 17503 Kirkshire Rd Birmingham MI 48009 Office: Cranbrook Inst Sci PO Box 801 Bloomfield Hills MI 48013

THOMPSON, PETER RUSSELL, construction and development company executive; b. N.Y.C., Dec. 12, 1921; s. Alfred Peter and Edythe Morris (Helfenstein) Swoyer; m. Elizabeth Smith Park, Oct. 23, 1948 (dec. 1971); children—Sharon F., Peter Russell, Elizabeth Park; m. Elizabeth Ann Edwards, Jan. 28, 1973. B.E. in C.E., Yale U., 1947. Engr., Gulf Oil Corp., N.Y.C., 1947-49, Gilbane Bldg. Co., Providence, 1949-52; sales engr. Masonite Corp., Providence, 1952-53; regional sales mgr. Nat. Homes Corp., Lafayette, Ind., 1953-58; exec. v.p. Inland Homes Corp., Piqua, Ohio, 1958-61; pres. Mid-Continent Properties, Inc., Piqua, 1962—; pres., dir. Mid-Continent Bldg. Corp.; dir. Miami Citizens Nat. Bank; v.p., dir. DTS Thoroughbred, Inc. Chmn., Piqua Planning Commn., 1967-74; mem. Ohio Housing Devel. Bd., 1971-74; mem. adv. com. on truth in lending to Bd. Govs., FRS, 1971-76; trustee Miami Valley Health Systems Agy., 1980; vice chmn., trustee Dettmer Hosp. and Found.; bd. dirs. Piqua YMCA; past pres., bd. dirs. Piqua United Fund. Served to lt. AUS, 1943-46; ETO. Decorated Air medal; recipient Man of Yr. awards Piqua Jaycees, Piqua C. of C. Mem. Nat. Assn. Home Builders (dir. 1965-78), Ohio Home Builders Assn. (trustee, past pres.), Miami County Home Builders Assn. (life dir., past pres.), Piqua C. of C. (past pres., past dir.). Republican. Episcopalian. Clubs: Piqua Country (past pres., dir.), Rotary (past pres., dir.), Yale of Dayton. Office: 322 W Water St Piqua OH 45356

THOMPSON, PHEBE KIRSTEN, physician; b. Glace Bay, N.S., Can., Sept. 5, 1897; d. Peter and Catherine (McKeigan) Christianson; M.D., C.M. Dalhousie U., Halifax, N.S., 1923; m. Willard Owen Thompson, M.D., June 21, 1923 (dec. Mar. 1954); children—Willard Owen, Frederic, Nancy, Donald. Came to U.S., 1923, naturalized, 1937. Intern Children's Hosp., Halifax, N.S., 1922-23; asst. biochemistry, dept. applied physiology Harvard Sch. Pub. Health, 1924-26; asst. and research fellow in medicine, thyroid clinic, Mass. Gen. Hosp., Boston, 1926-29; asst. in metabolism dept. (endocrinology) Rush Med. Coll. of U. Chgo. and The Central Free Dispensary Chgo., 1930-46; assoc. with husband in practice medicine, Chgo., 1947-54; mng. editor Jour. Clin. Endocrinology and Metabolism, 1954-61, cons. editor, 1961-65; editor Jour. Am. Geriatrics Soc., 1954-82; cons. editor Endocrinology, 1961-65; free-lance editor and writer. Recipient Thewlis award Am. Geriatrics Soc., 1966; cert. of appreciation Am. Thyroid Assn., 1966. Fellow Am. Med. Writers' Assn. (adv. com. 1955-60, v.p. Chgo. 1962), Am. Geriatrics Soc., Gerontological Soc. Am.; mem. Endocrine Soc., AAAS, Am. Genetic Assn., Am. Pub. Health Assn., Ill. Pub. Health Assn., Ill. Acad. Scis., Art Inst. Chgo. (life), Chgo. Hist. Soc. (life). Clubs: Univ.; Harvard; Canadian (corr. sec. 1968-73; mem. bd. 1973-76). Address: 2300 Lincoln Park W Chicago IL 60614

THOMPSON, RAYMOND LOUIS, JR., data systems executive; b. Des Moines, Nov. 8, 1946; s. Raymond Louis and Harriet (Eldred) T.; m. Deborah Jessica Eisenberg, July 5, 1970; children—Rachel, Rebekah, David. Student Kans. U., 1964-67; B.S. in Bus. Mgmt., Drake U., 1972. Cert. data processer; cert. systems profl. Mgr. data processing Funeral Security Plans, Kansas City, Mo., 1972-75, City of Olathe, Kans., 1978-84; supr. licensing Ozark Nat. Life, Kansas City, 1975-76; mgr. credit systems and procedures Western Auto, Kansas City, 1976-78; mgr. data systems fin. planning United Data Services, Inc., Overland Park, Kans., 1984—; speaker internat. confs. Served with USNR, 1967-69. Recipient Cert. Accounting Conformance, Mcpl. Fin. Officers Assn., Olathe, 1979. Mem. Data Processing Mgmt. Assn., Assn. System Mgrs., Assn. Computer Users, Urban Regional Info. Systems Assn. Republican. Lodge: Optimists. Avocations: home improving; wood working. Office: United Data Services Inc 5454 W 110th St Overland Park KS 66207

THOMPSON, RICHARD RAYMOND, stockbroker; b. Jerseyville, Ill., Mar. 4, 1941; s. Raymond Oscar and Ruby (Starkay) T.; m. Carol Sue Rhoades, Sept. 11, 1965; children—Patricia Sue, Matthew J. B.S.B.A., So. Ill. U., 1970. Cert. fin. planner. Acct. Merc. Trust Co., St. Louis, 1970-73; v.p., dir. Slayton Pontius & Co., Alton, Ill., 1973-82; v.p. Newhard, Cook & Co., Alton, 1982—; dir. Germania Fla., 1978-84, adv. dir., 1984—; dir. Germania Fin. Corp., Alton. Bd. dirs. Easter Seal Soc., Alton, 1979—, pres., 1983-85; mem. exec. bd. Piasa Bird council Boy Scouts Am., 1980—; deacon 1st Assembly of God Ch., Wood River, Ill., 1973—; councilman Evang. Coll., Springfield, Mo., 1979—. Served with U.S. Army, 1966-68. Mem. Greater Alton C. of C. Republican. Lodge: Rotary (pres. East Alton 1981-82). Home: 60 Dugger St East Alton IL 62024 Office: Newhard Cook & Co 502 First Nat Bank Bldg Alton IL 62002

THOMPSON, ROBERT BRUCE, sales executive; b. Detroit, Mar. 4, 1950; s. Russell J. and Alice M. (Ash) T.; m. Diane M. Parker, Oct. 10, 1970 (div. Apr. 1976). Assoc. in Tool and Product Design, Ferris State Coll., 1970. Tool and die maker Greenville Tool & Die, Mich., 1970-71; engrng. mgr. Alma Plastics Co., Mich., 1971-79; dist. sales mgr. Epco, Inc., Fremont, Ohio, 1979-81; dir. mktg. Centrex Corp., Findlay, Ohio, 1982-83; regional sales mgr. Hunkar Labs., Cin., 1983—. Mem. Soc. Plastics Engrs., Pi Kappa Alpha. Republican. Roman Catholic. Club: Optimist (Greenville, Mich.). Lodge: Elks. Avocation: pvt. pilot. Home: 415 Charity Circle Apt 124 Lansing MI 48917 Office: Hunkar Labs 7007 Valley Ave Cincinnati OH 45244

THOMPSON, ROBERT EUGENE, ophthalmologist, hospital administrator; b. Battle Creek, Mich., June 5, 1934; s. Leo LaVerne and Maybelle (James) T.; m. O. Tamzon Brumbaugh, Nov. 30, 1957; children—John Robert, T. Elizabeth, Michael James. B.S., Northwestern U., 1955, M.D., 1959. Diplomate Am. Bd. Ophthalmology. Intern, Akron City Hosp., Ohio, 1959-60; resident Cleve. Clinic, 1960-63; practice medicine, specializing in ophthalmology, 1963—; chmn. dept. ophthalmology Akron City Hosp., 1975—, now also mem. hosp. exec. com.; assoc. prof. ophthalmology Northeastern Ohio Univs. Coll. Medicine, 1977—; mem. physician adv. com. quality assurance and peer rev. Physicians Peer Rev. Orgn.'s Health Care Rev. Systems Inc. Active Great Trail council Boy Scouts Am., 1982—. Fellow ACS, Am. Acad. Ophthalmology. Republican. Roman Catholic. Clubs: Fairlawn Country, Portage Country. Avocation: Golf. Home: 156 Sand Run Rd Akron OH 44313 Office: The Profl Ctr Suite 508 75 Arch St Akron OH 44304

THOMPSON, RONALD L., railroad equipment and services company executive; b. Detroit, June 17, 1949; m. Cynthia Bramlett; 2 children. B.B.A. with distinction, U. Mich., 1969; M.S., Mich. State U., 1972, Ph.D., 1975. Research assoc. and assoc. prof. Va. State Coll., Bur. Econ. Research and Devel., Petersburg, 1974-75; asst. prof. Old Dominion U., Norfolk, Va., 1975-77; chmn. bd., chief exec. officer Evaluation Technologies, Inc., Arlington, Va., 1977-78; gen. mgr. Puget Sound Pet Supply Co., Inc., Seattle, 1978-79; pres. R.L. Thompson and Assocs., Inc., Seattle, 1977-80, Gen. R.R. Equipment & Services, Inc., East St. Louis, Ill., 1980—, R & R Steel Supply, Inc., St. Louis, 1983—. Bd. dirs. St. Louis Regional Commerce and Growth Assn., 1983—; chmn. Partnership with Youth campaign, Monsanto YMCA, 1983-85; mem. spl. events adv. bd. State of Ill. Address: 7 Waterman Pl Saint Louis MO 63112

THOMPSON, ROSEMAE M. SCHENCK, hospital executive; b. Hannibal, Mo., Apr. 17, 1923; d. Raina and Mallie Elizabeth (Dickerson) Murphy; m. Albert F. Schenck, July 26, 1942 (dec.); children—Loretta Schenck Grunden, Elizabeth Schenck Barnes; m. Herbert J. Thompson, Dec. 24, 1983. Instr. airplanes Curtiss Wright Aircraft Co., 1942-45; bookkeeper Internat. Shoe Co., Hannibal, Mo., 1951-65; purchasing agt. Levering Hosp., Hannibal, 1967—. Mem. Am. Legion Aux. (past post pres.); Assn. Hosp. Purchasing Materials Mgmt. Greater St. Louis, N.E. Mo. Med. and Dental Soc. (past pres.), Bus. and Profl. Women (past pres.), Epsilon Sigma Alpha (past pres. Loveland, Colo.), Bowling Assn. Monday Night Hannibal Ladies League (pres. 1969-81). Home: Ideal Villa Sub Div 158 Janapas Dr Hwy 61 S Hannibal MO 64301 Office: 1734 Market St Hannibal MO 63401

THOMPSON, RUSSELL VERN, school district superintendent; b. Clarinda, Iowa, Feb. 24, 1934; s. Vern Russell and Parrie Lee (Pricer) T.; m. Ruth Ann Steeve, Apr. 1, 1956; children—Kevin Lee (dec.), Lisa Kim, Russell Vern II (dec.). B.S., N.W. Mo. State U., 1956; M.Ed., U. Mo., 1960, Ed.D., 1968; postdoctoral Columbia U., 1977. Lic. ednl. adminstr., Mo. Tchr., chmn. dept. Hickman High Sch., Columbia, Mo., 1957-62, asst. prin., 1962-63, prin., 1963-65; dir. secondary edn. Columbia pub. schs., Mo., 1965-69, asst. supt., 1969-76, supt., 1976—; vis. assoc. prof. U. Mo., Columbia, 1972—. Contbr. articles to pamphlets and profl. jours. Pres., bd. dirs. Columbia United Way, Mo., 1970—; bd. dirs. Indsl. Devel. Bd., Columbia, 1976—; chmn. Mo. Edn./Bus. Ptnrs. Program, 1984—. Named Outstanding Young Man of Yr., Jaycees, Columbia, 1970; named Disting. Leader, Kiwanis Internat., 1974; One of Top 100 Exec. Educators of N.Am., The Exec. Educator, 1984. Mem. Am. Mgmt. Assn., Am. Assn. Sch. Adminstrs., Mid-Am. Assn. Supts., Mo. Assn. Sch. Adminstrs. (pres. 1983-84), Phi Delta Kappa (Gamma chpt. 1967-68). Lodges: Kiwanis (pres. 1970-71), Rotary (pres.-elect. 1985). Avocations: horseback riding; reading; swimming; golf. Home: Box 11 Route 4 Columbia MO 65203 Office: Columbia Pub Sch District Adminstrn Bldg 1818 W Worley Columbia MO 65203

THOMPSON, THOMAS JAMES, mechanical design engineer, consultant; b. Red Wing, Minn., Nov. 6, 1956; s. Dale James and Marlene Yvonne (Sylvander) T.; m. Teresa Marie Pfau, Aug. 28, 1981; 1 child, Blake. B.S., N.D. State U., 1979. Registered profl. engr., Minn., Wis. Mech. engr. I & S Engrs., Inc., Mankato, Minn., 1979—; dir. Mankato Builders Exchange, 1982—. Mem. ASME (assoc.), ASHRAE (assoc.), Nat. Soc. Profl. Engrs. Lodge: Elks. Home: 125 Atwood Dr Mankato MN 56001 Office: I and S Engrs Inc 329 N Broad St Mankato MN 56001

THOMPSON, VERONA MARGARET COOPER, publishing company executive; b. Exeter, Calif., Apr. 1, 1932; d. Sidney Benjamin and Verona Mason (Gibson) Cooper; m. Robert William Thompson, Oct. 23, 1953; children—Robin Ann, Ren Allen. B.A., Linfield Coll., 1952. Dir. mktg. Eden Pub. House, St. Louis, 1977-78; v.p., dir. merchandising and mktg. Christian Bd. Publ., St. Louis, 1978—, CBP Press, 1978—. Mem. Direct Mail Mktg. Assn., Exec. Female Assn. Republican. Mem. United Ch. of Christ. Avocations: Painting; clothes designing; reading. Home: 3860 Woodcrest Dr Florissant MO 63033 Office: Christian Bd Publ PO Box 179 Saint Louis MO 63166

THOMPSON, WALLACE CLAUDE, dentist; b. West Point, Nebr., Mar. 29, 1924; s. Claude Landis and Edith Cecilia (Herrmann) T.; m. Mildred Imogene Taylor, Nov. 21, 1942; children—Claudia H., Judith S., Mildred C., Landis K. B.S., U. Nebr., 1949, D.D.S., 1951. Gen. practice dentistry, West Point, 1953-59, Chadron, Nebr., 1959-64; dentist State of Nebr., Lincoln, 1964-65; dentist VA, Grand Island, Nebr., 1965-85, chief dental services, 1979-85. Pres. Chadron Sch. Bd., 1962. Served to capt. USAF, 1952-53. Mem. ADA, Hall County Dental Assn. Republican. Lutheran. Lodges: Masons, Shriners, Commandery. Home: 2425 N Wheeler St Grand Island NE 68801

THOMPSON, WILLIAM LAY, bilolgical science educator; b. Austin, Tex., Feb. 16, 1930; s. William Henry and Dora (Lay), T.; m. Retta Catherine Maninger, Sept. 14, 1958; children—Stephen Patrick, Catherine Irene, Mark Douglas. B.A., U. Tex., 1951, M.A., 1952; Ph.D., U. Calif.-Berkeley, 1959. Assoc., U. Calif.-Berkeley, 1958-59; asst. prof. Wayne State U., Detroit, 1959-65, assoc. prof., 1965-71, prof., 1971—; cons. Levitt and Sons, Lake Success, N.Y., 1973. Editor: Enjoying Birds in Michigan, 1970. Editor, The Jack-Pine Warbler jour., 1971-75. Served with U.S. Army, 1955-57. NSF grantee, 1962, 65. Fellow AAAS; mem. Am. Ornithologists Union, Am. Soc. Zoologists, Animal Behavior Soc. Home: 37 Wellesley Dr Pleasant Ridge MI 48069 Office: Dept Biol Sci Wayne State Detroit MI 48202

THOMPSON, W(ILMER) LEIGH, research laboratory executive, researcher; b. Shreveport, La., June 25, 1938; s. Wilmer Leigh and Mary Bissell (McIver) T.; m. Maurice Eugenie Horne, Mar. 27, 1957; 1 child, Mary Linton Bounetheau. B.S., Coll. Charleston, 1958; M.S. in Pharmacology, U. S.C., 1960, Ph.D., 1963; M.D., John Hopkins U., 1965. Diplomate Am. Bd. Internal Medicine. Intern, Johns Hopkins Hosp., 1965-66, resident, 1966-67, 69-70; staff assoc. NIH, Bethesda, Md., 1967-69; asst. prof. medicine and pharmacology Johns Hopkins U., Balt., 1970-74; prof. medicine, assoc. prof. pharmacology Case Western Res. U., Cleve., 1974-82, head critical care and clin. pharmacology, 1974-82; exec. dir. Lilly Research Labs., Eli Lilly & Co., Indpls., 1982—. Editor: Critical Care Medicine, 1983. Editor: State of the Art: Critical Care, 1980-83. Served to sr. surgeon USPHS, 1967-69. Burroughs Welcome Fund scholar 1975; recipient Faculty Devel. award Pharm. Mfrs. Assn. Found. Fellow ACP; mem. Soc. Critical Care Medicine (pres. 1981-82), Central Soc. Clin. Research, Am. Soc. Pharmacology and Exptl. Therapeutics, Am. Soc. Clin. Pharmacology and Therapeutics. Episcopalian. Office: Lilly Research Labs Lilly Corp Ctr Indianapolis IN 46285

THOMS, PAUL EDWARD, educational administrator, music education consultant; b. Louisville, Apr. 16, 1936; s. B. C. and Augusta T.; m. Marion Carol Cox, Aug. 16, 1958; children—Monica, Melinda. B.M., U. Ky., 1958; M.M., Miami U., Oxford, Ohio, 1965; postgrad. Ind. U., Millikin U., Calif. State Coll., Baldwin-Wallace Conservatory, Ohio State U. Rural music supr., Brown County, Ohio, 1958-60; dist. music coordinator, choral dir. Fairfield (Ohio) City Schs., 1960-82, curriculum coordinator, 1982—. Recipient Ohio Senate Resolution, mayoral proclamation and Bd. Edn. resolution establishing Paul Thoms Day; named One of Ten Most Outstanding Sch. Music Dirs. in U.S. and Can., Sch. Musician mag. Mem. Ohio Music Edn. Assn. (pres.), Tri-M (pres. bd. dirs.). Contbr. articles to profl. jours. Home: 128 S D St Hamilton OH 45013 Office: 5050 Dixie Hwy Fairfield OH 45014

THOMSEN, LANNY DEAN, pharmacist; b. Red Cloud, Nebr., May 22, 1949; s. Wayne Francis and Adeline Doris Thomsen; m. Julie Ann Linnemeyer, Aug. 30, 1969; children—Amanda Susan, Alexis Ann. B.S. in Pharmacy, U. Nebr., 1975. Registered pharmacist, Nebr., Ill. Pharmacist, Dekoven Drug, Chgo., 1975-76, Farrell Drug, McCook, Nebr., 1976-83; pharmacist, ptnr. A.&M. Rexall Drug, McCook, 1983—; monitor continuing edn. for pharmacists U. Nebr.-McCook, 1984—. Mem. Retail Task Force McCook, 1978—; vol. United Fund Drive, McCook, 1980—; pres. Task Force on Domestic Violence, McCook, 1983—. Mem. McCook C. of C. (bd. dirs. 1980-83), Nebr. Pharmacists Assn., Nat. Assn. Retail Druggists, Amateur Trapshooting Assn. Republican. Lutheran. Clubs: McCook Gun (pres. 1980-83). Lodges: Jaycees, Elks. Avocations: Hunting, fishing, trap shooting, bridge, motorcycling, water and snow skiing. Home: Star Route McCook NE 69001 Office: A & M Rexall 205 Norris Ave McCook NE 69001

THONEY, ROGER NEIL, electrical engineer; b. Cin., Mar. 29, 1954; s. Albert Phillip and Margaret Ann (Erb) T.; B.S.E.E., U. Ky., 1976, M.B.A., 1981; M.S. in Elec. Engring., Ohio State U., 1977. Registered profl. engr., Ky. Elec. engr. Procter & Gamble Co., Cin., 1977-80; engr. Cin. Gas and Electric Co., 1981-83, acting planning dir. nuclear engring. dept. W.H. Zimmer Nuclear Power Stu., 1983-84; sr. assoc. engr. facilities engring. IBM Corp., 1984—. Ohio Elec. Utilities Inst. fellow, 1976; Eagles Nat. scholar U. Ky. Coll. Bus. and Econs., 1981. Recipient Outstanding Sr. Elec. Engring. award U. Ky. Dept. Elec. Engring., 1976, Jr. Elec. Engring. award, 1975. Mem. IEEE, Am. Mktg. Assn.

THORN, DAVID LEE, industrial engineer; b. Carthage, Mo., Oct. 12, 1955; s. Lloyd Lewis and Maggie Louise (Boyer) T.; m. Dallas Leigh Kirk, July 21, 1978; 1 child, Andrew Robert. B.S. in Engring. Mgmt., U. Mo.-Rolla, 1977. Tech. asst. Inland Steel, East Chicago, Ind., 1978-80; indsl. engr. Eagle Picher, Joplin, Mo., 1980-81, LOF Vickers, Joplin, 1981; regional sales mgr. Ingersoll-Rand, Baxter Springs, Kans., 1981—. Mem. U.S. Waterjet Assn., Robotics Internat. Republican. Baptist. Avocations: softball; racquetball. Office: Ingersoll-Rand 22122 Telegraph Southfield MI 48037

THORN, WILLIAM ELWOOD, environmental services administrator; consultant; b. Duquoin, Ill., June 27, 1936; s. Sylvan Elwood and Margaret Thorn; m. Iris Ann Cargal, Dec. 15, 1964; 1 son, Jonathon; m. 2d, Karen Dillon, Nov. 9, 1974; children—Matthew, Karen. B.A., McKendree Coll., Lebanon, Ill., 1976; M.A., Webster U., St. Louis, 1977. Joined U.S. Air Force, 1956; personnel supt. various locations, ret., 1976; asst. mgr. housekeeping MediService, Springfield, Mo., 1976-77; bus. mgr. II, Chester Mental Health Ctr. (Ill.), 1977-80; dir. environ. services Alexian Bros. Hosp., St. Louis, 1980—, also cons. Alexian Bros. Corp. Am.; instr. U. Mo., St. Louis. Decorated Bronze Star medal. Mem. Nat. Exec. Housekeepers Assn. (cert.), Mo. Hosp. Adminstrv. Housekeepers Soc., Mo. Assn. Hosp. Central Supply Personnel, VFW. Republican. Mem. Christian Ch. Lodge: Elks. Office: Alexian Bros Hosp 3933 S Broadway St Louis MO 63118

THORNBROUGH, A.A., farm, industrial and construction equipment manufacturing company executive. Chmn., dir. Massey-Ferguson, Inc., Des Moines. Office: Massey-Ferguson Inc 1901 Bell Ave Des Moines IA 50315*

THORNBURGH, DANIEL ESTON, university official; b. Terre Haute, Ind., Sept. 17, 1930; s. Lester D. and Dorothy (Green) T.; m. M. Adrianne Ames, Aug. 11, 1956; children—Debra Kay Thornburgh Considine, Stewart Beckett, Malcolm Noble. B.S., Ind. State U., 1952; M.A., U. Iowa, 1957; Ed.D., Ind. U., 1980. Reporter Terre Haute Star, 1952; publicity dir. Simpson Coll., Indianola, Iowa, 1955-57; info. dir. Marshall U., Huntington, W.Va., 1957-59; info. dir. Eastern Ill. U., Charleston, 1959-65, chmn., prof. journalism, 1965-84, dir. univ. relations, 1984—; pub. Casey Banner Times, Ill., 1967-69. Editor: (with others) Interpretative Reporting Workbook, 1982. Mem. Charleston City Council, 1973-77; active Ill. Recreation Council, Springfield, 1979—; pres. Coles Hist. Soc., Charleston, 1972-74. Served with U.S. Army, 1952-54. Named Outstanding Advisor, Council Coll. Publs. Advisors, 1971. Mem. Charleston C. of C. (area man of yr. award 1971), Pub. Relations Soc. Am., Council Advancement and Support Edn., Sigma Delta Chi. Democrat. Methodist. Lodges: Masons, Elks, Rotary (pres. Charleston 1976-77). Avocations: Tennis; writing. Home: 1405 Buchanan Ave Charleston IL 61920 Office: Eastern Ill U Old Main 111 Charleston IL 61920

THORNE, FRANCIS XAVIER, real estate broker, builder; b. Hays, Kans., Dec. 20, 1925; s. Francis Xavier and Blanche M. (Gabriel) T.; B.S. in Bus. Adminstrn., Rockhurst Coll., 1949; student U. Minn., 1944-46; m. Kathleen Marie Keller, Feb. 11, 1950; children—Mary, Beverly, Christine, Frank Xavier III, Mark, Joseph, Teresa, Anne, Rosemary, Catherine. Real estate broker, Leavenworth County, Kans., 1973—; owner, operator Francis X. Thorne Realty, Lansing and Leavenworth, Kans., 1974-75; founder Del. Land Devel., Inc., 1977—, Xavier Custom Homes, Inc., 1979—. Mem. Lansing Planning Commn. Served to lt. (j.g.) USNR, 1946-50. Cert. residential broker Nat. Assn. Realtors; mem. Inst. Residential Mktg.; named Boss of Yr., Am. Bus. Women's Assn., 1977. Mem. Nat. Assn. Realtors, Nat. Assn. Real Estate Appraisers, Kans. Assn. Realtors, Leavenworth County Bd. Realtors, Kansas City Home Builders Assn., Sales and Mktg. Council, Inst. Residential Mktg., Home Builders Assn. Am., Leavenworth C. of C. (dir. 1980). Democrat. Roman Catholic. Lodges: K.C., Eagles, Kiwanis. Home: Box 117H Rural Route 2 Leavenworth KS 66048 Office: 100 Highland Rd Lansing KS 66043

THORNS, JOHN CYRIL, JR., art educator; b. Denver, Apr. 14, 1926; s. John Cyril and Margaret Bertha (Hallauer) T.; m. Catherine Gallagher (dec.); children—Karen Patricia, Jennifer Ruth (dec.). B.A., Ft. Hays State U., 1950; M.A., Ind. U., 1952; M.F.A., U. Iowa, 1953. Instr. dept. art Ft. Hays State U., Hays, Kans., 1954-57, asst. prof., 1957-61, assoc. prof., 1961-63, prof., 1963—, chmn. dept. art, 1973—; numerous exhibns.; designer First Presbyn. Ch., Hayes, 1973-75; designer Campanile, Ft. Hays State U. Pres., Hays Arts Council, 1971-73, 85-88, bd. dirs., 1985-88; bd. dirs. Ellis County Hist. Soc., Hays, 1971-73. Served with USNR, 1944-46. Recipient Gov.'s Artist award Kans. Arts Comm., 1985-86. Mem. Kans. Watercolor Soc. (bd. dirs. 1976-78), Soc. Painters West, Delta Phi Delta (editor Palette 1966-70, nat. pres. 1970-73), Phi Kappa Phi, Phi Delta Kappa. Avocations: Creative work; gardening. Home: Cornado Estates 500 W 36th St Hays KS 67601 Office: Dept Art Ft Hays State U 600 Park St Hays KS 67601

THORNTON, ANDRE, professional baseball player. First baseman Cleve. Indians. Office: Cleve Indians Cleveland Stadium Cleveland OH 44114*

THORNTON, JOHN MICHAEL, physics educator; b. Youngstown, Ohio, Nov. 2, 1951; s. James Michael and Mary Vera (Beil) T.; m. Judith Ann Pokrivnak, June 21, 1980. B.S., Youngstown State U., 1973; M.S., U. Dayton, 1976. Technician, Rasor Assocs., Dayton, Ohio, summer 1974; grad. teaching asst. U. Dayton, 1973-75; lectr. Sinclair Community Coll., Dayton, part-time 1975-77; assoc. prof. physics, head dept. Stark Tech. Coll., Canton, Ohio, 1977—; occasional text book reviewer Benjamin/Cummings, 1978—, E. Merrill Co., 1982, Prentice-Hall Co., 1985—, Saunders Coll. Pub., 1985—. Mem. Dist. Sci. Fair Council, Stark County, Ohio, 1981—. Mem. Am. Assn. Physics Tchrs., Ohio Assn. Two-Year Colls. (sec. 1983-85), Planetary Soc., Sigma Phi Sigma. Democrat. Roman Catholic. Avocations: astronomy; microcomputers. Office: Dept Physics Stark Technical College 6200 Frank Ave NW Canton OH 44720

THORNTON, WILLIAM CARL, retail executive; b. Amarillo, Tex., Feb. 5, 1943; s. Marion Van and Dorothy Elaine (Hodges) T.; m. Sandra Kay Baker, Jan. 23, 1965; children—John William, Jena. B.B.A., Tex. Tech U., 1965. Retail trainee Sears, Roebuck & Co., Dallas, 1965-68, mdse. mgr., 1968-70, asst. group market mgr., Chgo., 1970-74, nat. mktg. mgr., 1974-78, buyer infant apparel, 1978—. Mem. Sch. Bd. Dist. 61, Darien, Ill., 1978-82; co-pres. Eisenhower Jr. High Band Boosters, Darien, 1981-82, Downers Grove South Mustang Band Boosters (Ill.), 1984-85. served with USAR, 1961. Mem. Kappa Sigma. Republican. Methodist. Club: Tech Retail (Tex. Tech U.). Avocations: Scuba diving, photography. Home: 1817 Gigi Ln Darien IL 60559 Office: Sears Roebuck & Co D/629 Sears Tower Chicago IL 60684

THORPE, NEAL OWEN, biology educator; b. Wausau, Wis., Sept. 8, 1938; s. George Theodore and Gunvor Elvira (Riiser) T.; m. Kay Agnes Dustin, June 25, 1960; children—Lisa Kaye, Heather Leigh, Peter Neal. B.A., Augsburg Coll., 1960; Ph.D., U. Wis., 1964. Regional dir. grants Research Corp., Mpls., 1973-74; assoc. prof. biology Augsburg Coll., Mpls., 1967-79, prof., 1979—, chmn. dept., 1975—. Author: Cell Biology, 1984. Am. Heart Assn. fellow, 1966-67; NIH fellow, 1965-66. Avocations: maple syrup production; flying. Office: Dept Biology Augsburg Coll Minneapolis MN 55454

THORSEN, MARIE KRISTIN, radiologist, educator; b. Milw., Aug. 1, 1947; d. Charles Christian and Margaret Josephine (Little) T.; m. James Lawrence Troy, Jan. 7, 1978; children—Katherine Marie Troy, Megan Elizabeth Troy. B.A., U. Wis., 1969; M.B.A., George Washington U., 1971; M.D., Columbia U., 1977. Diplomate Am. Bd. Radiology. Intern, Columbia-Presbyn. Med. Ctr., N.Y.C., 1977-78, resident dept. radiology, 1978-81; fellow computed body tomography Med. Coll. Wis., Milw., 1981-82; asst. prof. radiology, 1982—; staff radiologist Milwaukee County Med. Complex, Froedtert Luth. Meml. Hosp., VA Hosp., Milw., 1982—. Contbr. articles to profl. jours. Mem. Am. Coll. Radiology, Am. Inst. Ultrasound Medicine, Radiol. Soc. N.Am.

THORSON, DOUGLAS YOUNG, economist, educator; b. Winthrop, Minn., May 13, 1933; s. Hugo William and Goldie (Elenore) T.; m. Rachael Ann Thorson, June 23, 1957; children—Scott, Teri, Blake. B.A., Gustavus Adolphus Coll., 1955; M.A., U. Nebr., 1957; Ph.D., U. Wis., 1961; postdoctoral student Harvard U., 1966-67. Asst. prof. econs. Bradley U., Peoria, Ill., 1960-64, assoc. prof., 1964-69, prof., 1969—, chmn. dept., 1973—. Contbr. articles to profl. publs. Mem. Gov.'s Blue Ribbon Tax Reform Com., Chgo., 1982-83. Guggenheim fellow, 1966-67; recipient Profl. Excellence award Bradley U., 1975. Mem. Nat. Tax Assn., Am. Econs. Assn. Club: Rotary. Avocations: Bridge; bowling; jogging. Office: Econs Dept Bradley U Peoria IL 61625

THORSON, MILTON ZENAS, paint and varnish company executive; b. Thorsby, Ala., Oct. 26, 1902; s. Theodore T. and Emma (Hokanson) T.; student Am. Inst. Banking, extension courses U. So. Calif.; m. 3d, Helen Lob, Aug. 31, 1978. Chief teller Tenn. Valley Bank, Decatur, Ala., 1919-28; teller Security First Nat. Bank, Los Angeles, 1928-29; with Red Spot Paint & Varnish Co., Inc., Evansville, Ind., 1929-60, chmn. exec. bd., dir., 1961-79; chmn. exec. bd. Owensboro Paint & Glass Co. (Ky.), former mem. Regional Export Expansion Council, U.S. Dept. Commerce. Mem. Audubon Soc., Nat. Paint and Coatings Assn. (hon.), Soc. Plastic Engrs. (Plastic Industry Pioneer). Republican. Club: President's of U. Evansville (life). Contbr. tech. articles profl. jours. Home: Box 418 Evansville IN 47703 also 527 Harbor Dr Key Biscayne FL 33149 Office: 110 Main St Evansville IN 47701

THORSON, NANCY ANN, health care manager, consultant; b. Oak Hill, Ohio, May 11, 1939; d. Clarence and Mary (Harrell) Harless; m. James M. Thorson, Sr.; 1 son, James M. B.F.A., Ohio U., 1961. With Good Samaritan Med. Ctr., Zanesville, Ohio, 1967—, dir. speech pathology/audiology dept., 1967-79, asst. dir. rehab. ctr., 1979-80, dir. community relations, 1980-82, communication/liasion specialist, 1982—. Bd. dirs. Zanesville Civic League; mem. Zanesville City Sch. Bd., Zanesville Vocat. Sch. Bd. Named Outstanding Sch. Bd. Mem. Southeastern Ohio, 1983. Mem. Ohio Soc. Hosp. Pub. Relations, Am. Soc. Hosp. Pub. Relations, Ohio Sch. Bd. Assn., Nat. Sch. Bd. Assn., C. of C. Protestant. Club: Republican of Zanesville. Home: 533 Cambridge Ave Zanesville OH 43701 Office: Good Samaritan Medical Center 800 Forest Ave Zanesville OH 43701

THORSTEINSON, ARNI CLAYTON, real estate company executive; b. Rosetown, Sask., Can., Oct. 14, 1948; s. Johann Thorsteinson and Mayme Thorsteinson Griffiths; m. Susan Jane Glass, Oct. 28, 1984. B.Commerce with honors, U. Man., Winnipeg, Can., 1969. Chartered fin. analyst. Securities analyst Richardson Securities Can., Winnipeg, 1969-72, underwriting exec., 1972-76; exec. v.p. Shelter Corp. Can., Winnipeg, 1976-79; pres. Shelter Can. Holdings Ltd., Winnipeg, 1979—; dir. Unicorp Resources Ltd., Calgary, Alta., Can., Onex Capital Corp., Toronto, Ont., Can., Montreal Trust Co., Global Communications Ltd., Toronto, CanWest Broadcasting Ltd., Winnipeg, CanWest Communications Inc., Winnipeg, Fed. Industries Ltd., Winnipeg. Mem. Inst. Chartered Fin. Analysts (trustee 1974-76), Young Pres.' Orgn., Fin. Analysts Fedn. Progressive Conservative. Clubs: Manitoba, St. Charles Country (Winnipeg). Avocations: golf; boating; travelling; reading. Home: 12D-221 Wellington Crescent Winnipeg MB R3M 0R1 Canada Office: Shelter Can Holdings Ltd 2600 Seven Evergreen Pl Winnipeg MB R3L 2T3 Canada

THROCKMORTON, PHYLLIS MARIE, accountant; b. Bloomington, Ill., Jan. 28, 1929; d. Loren D. and Hazel M. (Daly) McGrew; m. Peter E. Throckmorton, June 30, 1948; children—Ann Marie, Carla Louise, Peter E. A.A., Normandale State Jr. Coll., 1970; B.S., Ohio State U., 1977. Lic. pub. acct. Owner acctg. service, Columbus, Ohio, 1970-80; tax cons., 1970—. state examiner for auditor State of Ohio, Columbus, 1980—. Mem. Am. Soc. Women Accts. Home: 15943 Hawn Rd Plain City OH 43064 Office: 88 E Broad St Columbus OH 43215

THRONE, JAMES LOUIS, plastics engineering consultant; b. Cleve., July 10, 1937; s. Charles George and Clara Elizabeth (Kieffer) T.; m. Jean Ruth Anderson, Aug. 22, 1959; children—Michael William, Barbara Jean. B.S. in Chem. Engring., Case Inst. Tech., 1959; M.S., U. Del., 1961, Ph.D., 1964. Registered profl. engr., Ill., Ohio. Research engr. E.I. duPont de Nemours, Wilmington, Del., 1963-64; assoc. prof. chem. engring. Ohio U., Athens, 1964-68; supr. plastics processing Am. Standard, New Brunswick, N.J., 1968-72; vis. prof. engring. U. Wis.-Milw., 1972-73; dir. plastics research Beloit Corp., Wis., 1973-74; research assoc. Amoco Chems. Corp., Naperville, Ill., 1974-85, engring. cons., 1985—; prof. Food Engring. Orgn. Am. States, Campinas, Brazil, 1973. Author: Plastics Molding, 1973; Plastics Process Engineering, 1979; Thermo forming, 1985. Contbr. articles to profl. jours. Patentee in field. Recipient Man of Yr. award Jaycees, 1971. Fellow Plastics and Rubber Inst., Soc. Plastics Engrs. (div. chmn. 1979-80, councilor 1980-83; Man of Yr. 1982); profl. mem. Soc. Plastics Industry. Club: Naperville Art League (pres. 1982-84). Avocation: exhibiting artist. Home: 109 Springwood Dr Naperville IL 60540 Office: One Naperville Plaza Suite 441 Naperville IL 60540

THRUNE, NICHOLAS JOSEPH, pharmacist; b. Winona, Minn., Mar. 7, 1951; s. Raphael Joseph and Betty Jean (Stuck) T. B.S. in Pharmacy, U. Minn., 1977. Pharmacist intern Highland Drug Ct., St. Paul, 1975-76; pharmacist intern Group Health Inc., St. Paul, 1976-77, pharmacist, 1977-78, pharmacist-in-charge, Maplewood, Minn., 1978—. Mem. supervisory com. Group Health Fed. Credit Union, Roseville, Minn., 1982—; mem. exec. bd. Hosp. and Nursing Home Employee Union, Mpls., 1983—; pres. Profl. and Tech. Health Sect. Local 113, Mpls., 1984—. Roman Catholic. Clubs: Group Health Social (treas. 1983—); Rose Comml. Bowling (pres. 1983—). Avocations: softball; golf; bowling; fishing; travelling. Home: 1065 N Chatsworth Saint Paul MN 55103 Office: Group Health Inc 2165 White Bear Ave Maplewood MN 55109

THUEME, WILLIAM HAROLD, educator; b. St. Clair, Mich., Sept. 4, 1945; s. Harold Arthur and Delphine Betty (Buhl) T.; m. Nora Kathleen Koning, May 8, 1971; children—Benjamin William, Rebecca Kathleen. Student Port Huron Jr. Coll., 1963-64; B.A., Mich. State U., 1967, M.A., 1969; postgrad. Oakland U., 1971, U. Mich., 1971, San Francisco State U., 1975, U. Hawaii, 1975. Cert. tchr., Mich. Tchr. pub. schs., Charlotte, Mich., 1967-69, Ann Arbor, Mich., 1969—; fgn. travel coordinator Ambassadors Abroad Program, Amsterdam, Netherlands, 1968—; regional driver coordinator for Southeastern Mich., Avis Rent a Car, 1983—. Elections coordinator Eaton County (Mich.) Republican Party, 1968; mem. troop com. Troop 210, Boy Scouts Am., Ypsilanti; elders quorum instr., sec., exec. sec. Ch. of Jesus Christ of Latter-day Saints, 1976-81, adult spl. interest coordinator, 1982—, Sunday Sch. sec. Ann Arbor stake, 1983—; mem. Mich. Mormon Concert Choir, 1977—. Recipient Spl. Recognition award Reagan Presdl. Campaign, 1981. Mem. NEA, Mich. Edn. Assn., Internat. Reading Assn., Washtenaw Reading Council, Southeastern Mich. Reading Assn., Mich. Reading Assn., Assn. for Supervision and Curriculum Devel., Ann Arbor Edn. Assn., Am. Security Council, Nat. Geog. Soc., Am. Film Inst., Nat. Rifle Assn., Tri-County Sportsman League, Sigma Alpha Eta. Club: Washtenaw Sportsmen's (Ypsilanti). Lodge: Optimist (v.p. and dir. 1975-78) (Ann Arbor). Office: 401 N Division St Ann Arbor MI 48104

THUENTE, DAVID JOSEPH, computer science educator, researcher; b. Ossian, Iowa, Mar. 17, 1945; s. Frank William and Mary Francis (Lansing) T.; m. Mary Helen Ernst, July 15, 1967; children—Daniel, Michael. B.S., Loras Coll., 1967; M.S., U. Kans., 1969, Ph.D., 1974. Asst. prof. Purdue U., Fort Wayne, Ind., 1974-78, assoc. prof., 1979—; researcher Argonne Nat. Lab., Ill., 1976, 80, 83; mem. tech. staff MITRE Corp., Bedford, Mass., 1981-82; cons. in field. Contbr. articles to profl. jours. NDEA fellow, 1967-72, Argonne Nat. Lab. fellow, 1976, 80, 83; Purdue U. fellow, 1975, 81. Mem. Assn. Computing Machinery, Soc. Indsl. and Applied Math., Ops. Research Soc. Am., Ops. Research Soc. Ireland, Math. Programming Soc. Avocations: skiing, basketball, investing. Home: 5905 Heywood Cove Fort Wayne IN 46815 Office: Ind-Purdue U at Fort Wayne 2101 Coliseum Blvd East Fort Wayne IN 46805

THULIN, ADELAIDE ANN, design company executive, interior designer; b. Chgo., Nov. 15, 1925; d. Martin Evold and Kathleen Marie (Glennon) Peterson; m. Frederick Adolph Thulin, Jr., Aug. 18, 1945; children—Frederick, Kristin, Mary, Margaret, Francis, Peter, Andrea, Charles, Joseph, Kathleen, James, Suzanne, Patricia. Student Northwestern U., 1943-46; A.A. in Interior Design, Harper Coll., 1977. Asst. production mgr. Cruttenden & Eger, Chgo., 1946; editor Mt. Prospect Independent, Ill., 1960; real estate salesperson Homefinders, Northwest Chgo. suburbs, 1965-67; asst. v.p. advt. Littelfuse, DesPlaines, Ill., 1965-67; owner, pres. Applied Design Assocs., Mt. Prospect, 1977—; career day speaker local high schs., 1982—. Author, editor monthly newsletter Women's Archtl. League, 1983—, The Binnacle, CYC, 1979-81. Organizer, Mother's March of Dimes, Mt. Prospect, 1953-54; mem. Vols. for Stevenson, 1952, 56, Citizens for Douglas, 1954, Citizens for Kennedy, 1960; mem. Fair Review Council, Chgo., 1983-84; mem. 13th Congl. Dist. Democratic Women's Club, publicity chmn. 1957-58; mem. Chgo. Symphony Orchestra Chorus, 1972; del. Ill. Statehouse Conf. on Small Bus., 1984, 85. Mem. Ill. Devel. Council, Ind. Bus. Assns. Ill., Women's Archtl. League (publicity chmn. 1964-65), Mt. Prospect C. of C. Roman Catholic. Avocations: reading for print-handicapped on CRIS radio; choral singing. Home: 4 S Owen St Mt Prospect IL 60056 Office: Applied Design Assocs Ltd 200 E Evergreen Ave Mount Prospect IL 60056

THURMAN, JAMES WINSTON, children's home executive, investment and insurance consultant; b. Marshall, Mo., Sept. 22, 1943; s. Ewell S. and Katherine P. (Arend) T.; m. Gail A. Snyder, Oct. 7, 1966; children—Cynthia D., Christopher M. B.S. in Bus., S.W. Mo. State U., 1966. Registered prin. Nat. Assn. Security Dealers; lic. ins. broker, Mo. Sr. staff supr. traffic dept. Southwestern Bell Telephone Co., St. Louis, 1966-70; v.p., sec. K.W. Chambers & Co., St. Louis, 1970-77; assoc. exec. dir. fin., treas. Presbyterian Children's Services, Inc., Farmington, Mo., 1977—. Elder Richmond Heights Presbyn. Ch.; chmn. bd. Coll. Sch., Webster Groves, Mo. Mem. Nat. Soc. Fund Raising Execs. Republican. Home: 105 Turf Ct Webster Groves MO 63119 Office: 412 W Liberty St Farmington MO 63640 also 7339 Lindbergh Dr Richmond Heights MO 63117

THWAITS, JAMES ARTHUR, diviersified products company executive; b. London, 1923. Student East Hampshire Tech. Coll., 1939, Woolwich Poly., 1942, Borrough Poly, 1944. With Minn. Mining and Mfg. Co., St. Paul, 1949—, v.p. engring. and mfg. internat. div., 1964-68, div. v.p. Afro-Asian and Can. areas, 1968-72, group v.p. tape and allied products, 1972-74, group v.p. internat., 1974, corp. v.p. and pres. internat. ops., 1975-81, pres. internat. ops. and corp. staff services, dir., 1981—. Mem. Inst. Elec. Engrs. (London). Office: Minn Mining and Mfg Co Inc 3M Center PO Box 3388 St Paul MN 55101*

TIBBETTS, JACK HOLLIS, lawyer; b. Chgo., June 16, 1954; s. Frank Hollis and Marguerite Rachael (Troyer) T. B.A., Northwestern U., 1976; J.D., 1979. Bar: Ill. 1979; U.S. Dist. Ct. (so. dist.) Ill. 1980. Staff atty., housing law coordinator Land of Lincoln Legal Assistance Found., Inc., Mount Vernon, Ill., 1979—; mem. Ill. Statewide Housing Task Force, Chgo., 1981—. Mem. Ill. State Bar Assn. (council real estate law sect. 1982-83, 83-84, lectr. 1983), Jefferson County Human Services Networking Council. Democrat. Mormon. Office: Land of Lincoln Legal Assistance 1212 Main St Mount Vernon IL 62864

TIBERI, DOMINIC, civic worker; b. Introdacqua, Aquila, Italy, July 31, 1906; came to U.S., 1912; s. Louis and Filomena (Monaco) T.; m. Wincey M. DePeso, Aug. 28, 1937; children—Louis E., Nancy J. Tiberi Scott. Student pub. schs., Columbus, Ohio. Chain maker Ohio Malleable Iron Co., 1922-23; with Pa. R.R. and Penn Central, 1923-71, office mgr., master mechanic, office mgr., supt., also recreation and athletic dir., 1948-53; head football coach St. Charles High Sch., 1943-49, asst. football coach, 1949-58. Gen. chmn. Columbus Day Celebrations, 1952, transp. chmn., 1954. Named Citizen of Yr., Am.-Italian Golf Assn., 1975. Club: Agonis (sec. 1971—). Home: 1003 Kenwood Ln Columbus OH 43220

TICHENOR, ROBERT WOODROW, physician; b. St. Louis, Sept. 1, 1914; s. Robert Anderson and Willie Mae (Wooley) T.; B.S., St. Louis Coll. Pharmacy, 1939; A.B., Washington U., St. Louis, 1941, M.D., 1943; m. Letitia Bernice Youngman, May 20, 1935; children—Trebor Jay, Bruce Harding. Intern, resident St. Louis City Hosp., 1944-45; practice medicine, Sappington, Mo., 1946—; mem. staff St. Joseph, St. Anthony hosps. Served to 1st lt. M.C., AUS, 1945-46. Fellow Am. Acad. Family Physicians; mem. St. Louis (past pres.), Mo., Am. acads. family physicians, Pan-Am., AMA (recognition award for continuing med. edn. 1983), Mo., St. Louis med. assns., St. Louis German Shepherd Club (past pres.), Am. Kennel Club (conformation judge), Miss. Valley Kennel (pres.), German Shepherd Dog Club Am. (past dir.). Club: Washington University. Home: 175 Misty Manor Rd Fenton MO 63026 Office: 11521 Gravois St Sappington MO 63126

TICKTIN, HAROLD, banker, lawyer; b. Chgo., Aug. 6, 1936; s. Joseph J. and Reva (Schwartz) T.; B.S., Ill. Inst. Tech., 1958; J.D., Chgo. Kent Coll. Law, 1964; m. Judith Brown, May 25, 1975; children—Jodi, David, Stephen. Admitted to Ill. bar, 1964; staff atty. Legal Aid, 1964-66; individual practice law, Wheaton, Ill., 1966—; chmn. bd., pres. First Nat. Bank of Wheaton, 1975—. Served with AUS, 1959-60. Mem. Am. Bankers Assn., Chgo. Bar Assn. Club: East Bank. Office: 1275 Butterfield Rd Wheaton IL 60187

TICKTIN, HAROLD, lawyer; b. Cleve., June 19, 1927; s. Charles and Lena (Bernstein) T.; m. Muriel Bergida, Dec. 23, 1951 (div.); children—Laurie Ann, Daniel Saul, Philip Adam, Robert Eli; m. 2d, Ellen Ruth Horwin, May 1, 1983. B.A., Ohio State U., 1950; J.D., Case Western Res. U., 1953. Bar: Ohio 1953. Practice, Cleve., 1953—; ptnr. firm Ticktin & Corwrich, 1958-66; sole practice, 1966-69; ptnr. firm Ticktin & Baron, 1969—; adj. prof. law Cleve. State U., 1968-79. Pres. Euclid Jewish Ctr., 1960-61, Nationalities Services Ctr., 1970-72, No. Ohio Council Am. Jewish Congress, 1974-77; bd. dirs. Ohio CLU, 1970-75, Cleve. Coll. Jewish Studies, 1962—; bd. govs. Case Western Res. U. Law Sch., 1963-66, Central YMCA Cleve., 1982—. Served with USN, 1945-46. Mem. Cleve. Bar Assn., Cuyahoga County Bar Assn., Ohio Bar Assn., Am. Profs. for Peace in Middle East. Democrat. Contbr. articles on religion, culture, politics to numerous popular and special interest publs. Home: 13800 Fairhill Apt 215 Shaker Heights OH 44120 Office: 1621 Euclid Ave Suite 930 Cleveland OH 44115

TIDABACK, DAVID PAUL, vocational educator; b. LaSalle, Ill., Mar. 2, 1950; s. Robert and Margaret (Spriet) T.; m. Karen Buttel, Aug. 2, 1981; children—Melissa, Sean. A.S. in Structural Design, Morrison Inst. Tech., 1970; B.S. in Indsl. Edn., No. Ill. U., 1979. Cert. postsecondary tchr., Ill. Drafter, U.S. Steel Corp., Chgo., 1970-71; estimator Chemetron Corp., Chgo., 1971-72, Midwesco Enterprise Inc., Chgo., 1972-76; tchr. Stephenson Area Career Ctr., Freeport, Ill., 1979-81, Highland Community Coll., Freeport, 1979—; cons. Competency Based Individualized Ednl. Consortium. Mem. Ill. Vocat. Assn., Ill. Indsl. Educators Assn., Am. Indsl. Arts Assn., Am. Vocat. Assn., Am. Inst. Drafting and Design, Ill. Tech. Drafting Tchrs. Assn., Nat. Computer Graphics Assn., Nat. Tech. Educators Assn., Nat. Mgmt. Assn. Club: Freeport Mgmt. Office: Highland Community Coll Pearl City Rd Freeport IL 61032

TIERNEY, EUGENE FRANCIS, lawyer, air force reserve officer; b. Hartford, Conn., Sept. 26, 1930; s. William Albert and Katherine Mary (Egan) T.; m. Cynthia Jane Palen, May 25, 1957; children—Gwyn C., Alison S. B.A., U. Conn., 1953, L.L.B., U. Conn.-Hartford, 1956, M.B.A., 1966. Bar: Conn. Claims adjuster Allstate Ins. Co., West Hartford, Conn., 1956-57, 60-63, claims examiner, 1963-65; claims atty. Nationwide Ins., Hamden, Conn., 1965-70, regional claims atty., Memphis, 1970-73, claims staff atty., Columbus, Ohio, 1973—; bd. dir. N.Y. Med. Malpractice Ins. Assn., N.Y.C., 1978-83, Air Force Logistics Command, Judge Adv. Res., Wright Patterson AFB, Dayton, Ohio, 1973-82; mem. Air Force Logistics Command Judge Adv. Res. Exec. Bd., 1979-82. Drafted first arson reporting statute for Ohio, 1976 (later became model law adopted by all 50 states). Pres. Worthington Resource Ctr., 1984—; mem. Concerned Citizens of Worthington Sch. Dist., 1984—. Served as 1st lt. USAF, 1957-60, to lt. col. USAFR. Mem. Ohio Assn. Civil Trial Attys. (edn. chmn. 1978-84, trustee 1980—, editor 1984—). Republican. Lutheran. Clubs: Worthington Men's (pres. 1981-82), Del. Golf (Ohio). Avocation: golf. Home: 219 Northigh Dr Worthington OH 43085 Office: Nationwide Ins Co One Nationwide Plaza Columbus OH 43216

TIERNO, EDWARD GREGORY, insurance company executive; b. Latrobe, Pa., Oct. 9, 1948; s. Frank Albert and Mary Christine (Santarelli) T.; m. Emily Mittacos, Nov. 27, 1971. B.A., Youngstown State U., 1970; postgrad. Indiana U. Pa., 1969. Tchr., coach Youngstown (Ohio) Bd. Edn., 1970-74; liability supr., mktg. rep. Underwriters Adjusting Co., Youngstown and Southfield, Mich., 1974-78; ins. risk mgr. McNicholas Transp. Co., Youngstown, 1978-82; pres. Ins. Claim Service, Youngstown, 1982—. Pa. Higher Edn. Assn. scholar, 1966-70. Mem. Common Carrier Conf. Irregular Route Carriers, Ohio State Claims Assn., Ohio Assn. Ind. Adjusters, Youngstown Claims Assn. (pres., scholarship chmn. 1981-82), Nat. Assn. Ind. Insurance Adjusters, Youngstown C. of C., Order of Ahepa. Greek Orthodox. Lodge: Kiwanis. Author: Ohio Comparative Negligence, An Overview, 1980. Co-author: How to Collect An Insurance Claim, 1984. Home: 7002 Youngstown-Pittsburgh Rd Poland OH 44514 Office: 1749 S Raccoon Rd Suite 3 Youngstown OH 44515

TIESZEN, LAURENCE A., accounting and business instructor, accountant; b. Sioux Falls, S.D., June 13, 1937; s. Jacob A. and Tina A. (Wiens) T.; m. Mabel Ann Voss, July 21, 1962; children—Paul, Michelle, Mark, Marissa. B.A., Sioux Falls Coll., 1959; M.A., Mankato State U., 1965; postgrad. U.

Mo.-Kansas City, U. Nebr., U. Minn., Mankato State U. Tchr. bus. Hills (Minn.) Pub. Sch., 1961-63, Met. Jr. Coll., Kansas City, Mo., 1965-68; dept. chmn. bus edn. Augustana Coll., Sioux Falls, S.D., 1968-73; instr. acctg. Pipestone Area Vocat. Tech. Inst., 1973-74; dir. edn. services and asst. personnel Sioux Valley Hosp., 1974-77; instr. bus. Mankato (Minn.) Area Vocat.-Tech. Inst., 1977—. Served with USAR, 1959-65. Mem. Mankato Tchrs. Assn., Minn. Tchrs. Assn., Nat. Tchrs. Assn., Mankato Vocat. Tchrs. Assn., Minn. Vocat. Tchrs. Assn., Am. Vocat. Tchrs. Assn., Delta Pi Epsilon. Republican. Home: 1031 Orchard Rd Mankato MN 56001 Office: 1900 Lee Blvd North Mankato MN 56001

TIGGES, JOHN THOMAS, writer, musician; b. Dubuque, Iowa, May 16, 1932; s. John George and Madonna Josephine (Heiberger) T.; student Loras Coll., 1950-52, 57, U. Dubuque, 1960; m. Kathryn Elizabeth Johnson, Apr. 22, 1954; children—Juliana, John, Timothy, Teresa, Jay. Clk. John Deere Tractor Works, Dubuque, Iowa, 1957-61; agt. Penn Mut. Life Ins. Co., Dubuque, 1961-74; bus. mgr., bd. dirs. Dubuque Symphony Orch., 1960-68, 71-74; v.p., sec. Olson Toy and Hobby Inc., 1964-66; pres. JKT Inc., 1978-82; research specialist Electronic Media Services (Scripp-Howard); violinist. Author: (novels) The Legend of Jean Marie Cardinal, 1976; Garden of the Incubus, 1982; Unto the Altar, 1985; Kiss Not the Child, 1985; Voice of the Nightmare, 1985; The Immortal, 1986; (plays) No More-No Less, 1979, We Who Are About to Die, 1979; radio plays: Valley of Deceit, 1978, Rockville Horror, 1979, The Timid, 1982; TV drama: An Evening with George Wallace Jones, 1982; biographies: George Wallace Jones, 1983, John Plumbe Jr., 1983; co-author history book: The Milwaukee Road Narrow Gauge: The Bellevue, Cascade & Western, Iowa's Slim Princess, 1985; co-author: They came from Dubuque, 1983; co-author, editor: A Cup and a Half of Coffee, 1977; editorial asst. Julian Jour.; interviewer, spl. reporter Editorial Assocs., 1982-84; columnist Memory Lane; syndicated columnist Tough Trivia Tidbits; tchr. creative writing Northeast Iowa Tech. Inst.; co-founder Dubuque Symphony Orch., 1960; founder Julien Strings, 1972, Dubuque Sch. of Novel, 1978, Northeast Iowa Writers Workshop, 1981; co-host Big Broadcast Radio Program, WDBQ Radio, 1979-82; co-founder Sinnipee Writers Workshop, 1985. Founder, bus. mgr. Dubuque Pops Orch., 1957. Recipient Nat. Quality award, 1966-70, Carnegie-Stout Library World of Lit. honors award, 1981. Fellow World Lit. Acad.; mem. Nat. Writers Club (profl.), Iowa Authors, Am. Fedn. Musicians, Internat. Platform Assn., Toy Train Collectors Club. Roman Catholic. Office: PO Box 902 Dubuque IA 52001-0011

TILLMAN, STAN MARCELINUS, optometrist; b. St. Meinrad, Ind., Sept. 3, 1937; s. Cornelious Tillman and Mildred (Denning) Sandage; m. Jan Boerste, July 20, 1963; children—Alicia, Scott, Kurt. O.D., Ind. U., 1963. Diplomate Am. Bd. Optometry. Ptnr., Drs. Denning, Tillman, Weyer, Evansville, Ind., 1963—. Pres., St. John's Bd. Edn., Newburgh, Ind., 1978-83, Boys Club of Evansville, 1982-83. Mem. Ind. Optmetric Assn. (pres. sect. 1971-72), Am. Optmetric Assn., Evansville Jaycees (pres. 1971-72). Republican. Roman Catholic. Clubs: Serra (pres. 1985) (Evansville); Rolling Hills Country (sec. 1983-85) (Paradise). Lodge: Kiwanis. Avocation: Golf. Home: 4600 Elm Dr Newburgh IN 47630 Office: 605 Main St Evansville IN 47708

TILLMAR, ARVID RICHARD, insurance company executive; b. Louisville, Nov. 4, 1943; s. Arvid Roscoe and Sarah Louise (Honaker) T.; m. Mary Patricia Keating, Nov. 25, 1967; children—Patrick Richard, Sarah Catherine. B.A. in Bus., Bellarmine Coll., 1966. Pres., T/N & Assocs., Inc., Milw., 1972-78; health care mgmt. cons., Milw., 1978-79; sr. v.p. Galbraith & Green/James, Milw., 1979-82; exec. v.p., regional benefits dir. James Benefits/Fred S. James & Co. of Wis., Inc., Milw., 1981-83, exec. v.p., 1983-84; pres., profit ctr. mgr. Fred S. James & Co. of Wis., Inc., Milw., 1984—; mem. Greater Milw. Employee Benefit Council, 1981-84. Bd. dirs. Douglas F. McKey Christmas Club, Milw., 1978—, Marquette Univ. High Sch., Milw., 1983—. Mem. Self Ins. Inst. Am. (legis. and regulatory com.), Wis. Assn. Mfrs. and Commerce (health care cost mgmt. com.). Republican. Roman Catholic. Club: Ozaukee Country (bd. dirs. 1983—) (Mequon, Wis.). Office: 330 E Kilbourn Ave Suite 450 Milwaukee WI 53202

TILLOTSON, JOSEPH HUGH, banker; b. Marshall, Mo., Nov. 27, 1944; s. Joseph Andrew and Virginia C. (Fisher) T.; m. Carolyn Kay Coleman, Apr. 10, 1965; children—Ricky Lynn, Ronald Lynn. Student pub. schs., Independence, Mo. Asst. mgr. CIT Fin. Services, Lawton, Okla., 1970-72; regional supr. Avco Fin. Services, Chgo., 1972-79; div. v.p. Unity Savs Assn., Chgo., 1979-82; sr. v.p. Talman Home Savs. & Loan, Chgo., 1982-83; exec. v.p., chief operating officer USA Consumer Credit Corp., Burbank, Ill., 1983—, also dir. Bd. dirs. New Horizon Center for Profoundly Handicapped and Retarded, Chgo., 1982-83. Served with AUS, 1961-70. Decorated Air medal with cluster, Bronze Star with cluster and V device. Mem. Inst. Savs. Instns., U.S. League Savs. Instns. (nat. com. on consumer lending). Republican. Baptist.

TILLOTSON, RAYMOND JENNISON, rancher; b. Shields, Kans., Mar. 1, 1904; s. Warren Jackson and Bessie (Jennison) T.; B.S., Kans. State U., 1929; M.S., Iowa State U., 1931; m. Amy C. Jones, Aug. 28, 1929; children—Don R., Paul J., Betty (Mrs. Kenneth L. Milford), Peggy (Mrs. Edwin J. Tajchman). Rural service engr. Kans. Gas & Elec. Co., Newton, 1929-30; asst. agrl. engr. Soil Conservation Service, U.S. Dept. Agr., Iowa, Mo., Kans., 1934-43; owner, operator ranch, Shields, Kans., 1944—. Mem. dist. bd. Lane County Soil Conservation, 1944-69, chmn., 1949-55; mem. Extension Council Bd., 1966-70, chmn., 1967-70. Mem. Am. Soc. Agrl. Engrs., Am. Soc. Range Mgmt., Kans. Livestock Assn., Kans. Wheat Growers Assn., Lane County Farm Bur. (dir. 1962-66), Kans. Master Farmer (pres. 1971), S.W. Kans. Gem and Mineral Soc. (pres. 1971-72, show chmn. 1977), Kans. Anthrop. Soc. (dir. 1974-76), Lane County Hist. Soc. (pres. 1956-57, dir. 1958-81). Methodist. Clubs: Masons, Rotary (pres. 1979-80). Home: Shields KS 67874

TILSON, STEPHEN FREDERICK, lawyer; b. Madison, Tenn., June 18, 1949; s. Charles Everett and Mary Nola (Milburn) T.; m. Dawn Elaine Garverick, June 21, 1975; children—Andrea Linet, Eric Stephen. B.A. cum laude, Ohio Wesleyan U., 1971; J.D. cum laude, Ohio State U., 1974. Bar: Ohio 1974, U.S. Dist. Ct. (so. and no. dists.) Ohio 1975. Sole practice, Columbus, Ohio, 1974-75; mem. Petri, Hottenroth, Garverick & Tilson Co. L.P.A., Galion, Ohio, 1975—. Bd. dirs. Crawford County Community Health Bd., Bucyrus, Ohio, 1979-82, chmn. personnel, 1981-82; bd. dirs. Galion Community Ctr. YMCA, 1982—, chmn. gifts, 1984. Mem. Comml. Law League, Crawford County Bar Assn., Galion Area C. of C. Democrat. Lutheran. Lodge: Kiwanis. Avocations: Fishing, music, stamp collecting, art. Home: 725 Grove Ave Galion OH 44833 Office: 126 S Market St Galion OH 44833

TILUS, DARRELL DUANE, electrical engineer; b. Buffalo, S.D., May 5, 1943; s. Waino and Anna Mary T.; B.S. in Elec. Engring., Mich. Tech. U., 1967; M.B.A., Webster U., 1978; m. Nancy Lee Barlow, Aug. 29, 1964; children—Duane Tod, Troy Darrell. Avionics engr. Trans World Airlines, Kansas City, Mo., 1967-70, project avionics engr., 1972—; engr. Black & Veatch, Cons. Engrs., Kansas City, 1971-72; bd. dirs. TWA Employees' Council, 1985-86. Mem. Nashua Sch. Bldg. Com., 1973-75. Mem. IEEE. Republican. Mem. Assembly of God Ch. (bd. mem. 1984-86, ednl. dir. 1979-84). Home: 1014 NE 97th St Kansas City MO 64155 Office: PO Box 20126 Kansas City MO 64195

TIMBERLAKE, CHARLES EDWARD, historian, educator; b. South Shore, Ky., Sept. 9, 1935; s. Howard E. and Mabel V. (Collier) T.; B.A. in History, Berea (Ky.) Coll., 1957; cert. Claremont Grad. Sch., 1958; M.A. in History, Claremont Grad. Sch., 1962; Ph.D. (Nat. Defense Fgn. Lang. fellow), U. Washington, Seattle, 1968; m. Patricia Perkins, Dec. 23, 1957; children—Mark B., Daniel E., Eric C. Tchr. history Barstow (Calif.) High Sch., 1959-60, Claremont (Calif.) High Sch., 1960-61; research bibliographer Far Eastern and Russian Inst., U. Wash., Seattle, 1961-62, teaching asst. dept. history, 1962-64; asst. prof. dept. history U. Mo., Columbia, 1967-73, assoc. prof., 1973-81, prof., 1981—, editor dept. newsletter, 1972, dir. undergrad. studies, 1973-74, departmental honors dir., 1975—, coordinator honors interdisciplinary program in social and behavioral scis., 1976—; guest lectr. Soviet affairs various schs. and radio TV programs, 1967—. Internat. Research and Exchange Bd. sr. exchange scholar, USSR, 1971; Earhart Found. fellow, 1972, U. Mo. Research Council fellow, 1978; Am. Council Learned Socs. fellow, USSR, 1978; Nat. Endowment for the Humanities grantee, 1979. Mem. Am. Hist. Assn., Am. Assn. for the Advancement of Slavic Studies (dir. 1980-82, 85—, chmn. council regional affiliates 1981-82, 85-86, rep. Central Slavic Conf. 1979—, pres. Central Slavic Conf. 1969, 77, 84), Rocky Mountain Assn. for Slavic Studies. Editor, contbr. Essays on Russian Liberalism, 1972; Detente: A Documentary Record, 1978; contbr. articles on modern Russian history to periodicals and lit. jours. Home: Route 4 Box 173 Columbia MO 65201 Office: History Dept Univ Missouri Columbia MO 65211

TIMKEN, W. ROBERT, JR., manufacturing company executive; b. 1938; B.A., Stanford U., 1960; M.B.A., Harvard U., 1962; married. With Timken Co. (formerly The Timken Roller Bearing Co.), Canton, Ohio, 1962—, asst. to v.p. sales, 1964-65, dir. corp. devel., 1965-68, v.p., 1968-73, vice-chmn. bd., chmn. fin. com., 1973-75, chmn. bd., chmn. fin. com., 1975—, also dir. Office: Timken Co 1835 Dueber Ave SW Canton OH 44706*

TIMMINS, RICHARD HASELTINE, foundation executive, educator; b. Ottumwa, Iowa, Jan. 24, 1924; s. Isaiah Phillip and Nellie Mae (Haseltine) T.; m. Jean Ardelle Moore, Feb. 16, 1946 (dec.); 1 dau., Cynthia Lea; m. Mischelle Christene Talley Mitchell, Aug. 10, 1983. B.A., U. Iowa, 1948, M.A., 1956; Ed.D., Columbia U., 1962. Cert. jr. coll. adminstr., Iowa. Vice-pres. Tarkio (Mo.) Coll., 1962-68; pres. Huron (S.D.) Coll., 1968-74; exec. dir. Council Chiropractic Edn. and Found. Chiropractic Edn. and Research, Des Moines, 1974-76; pres. Western States Coll., Portland, Oreg., 1976-79; exec. dir. N.D. Community Found., Bismarck, 1979-81, pres., 1981; pres. S.D. Assn. Pvt. Colls., 1968-71; chmn. bd. Colls. Mid-Am. Inc., 1972-74; pres. S.D. Edn. Assn. Dept. Higher Edn., 1974. Mem. adv. com. higher edn. Midwestern Conf., Council State Govts., 1969-71. Served as capt. USAF, 1943-45, U.S. Army, 1948-54. Am. Assn. Fund Raising Councils fellow, 1960-62. Mem. Am. Legion, Sigma Delta Chi, Kappa Tau Alpha, Kappa Delta Pi, Phi Delta Kappa. Presbyterian. Clubs: Omaha, Rotary. Lodges: Masons, Shriners, Elks. Contbr. to books and profl. jours. Home: 919 E Central Bismarck ND 58501 Office: 2900 E Broadway Suite 8 Bismarck ND 58501

TIMMONS, BESS SPIVA, foundation executive, education advocate; b. Galena, Kans., Oct. 12, 1901; d. George Newton and Bess (Tamblyn) Spiva; m. Leroy Kittrell Timmons, Sept. 2, 1922 (dec. 1954); children—Robert L., George S., Judith Ann Timmons Spears. Grad. Monticello Coll., 1921. Mem. George N. Spiva scholarship com. Pittsburg State U., Kans., 1951—; pres. Bess Spiva Timmons Found., Pittsburg, 1967—; donor Univ. Scholarship Trusts in Kans., Mo., Wyo., 1967—; mem. Timmons Chapel Com., Pittsburg, 1966—. Author: Yesterday, 1976. Life mem., past pres. Salvation Army Adv. Bd., Pittsburg, 1930's—; charter mem., past pres. Pittsburg State U. Endowment Assn., 1951—; sec. Mt. Carmel Found., Pittsburg, 1984—. Mem. Altrusa Internat. (hon.). Republican. Presbyterian.

TIMMONS, TIMOTHY ALAN, property leasing executive; b. Logansport, Ind., Dec. 4, 1955; s. George Richard and Patsy Lou (Baker) T.; m. Tamara Lynn Herriford, Nov. 15, 1980; 1 child, Tyler Alan. B.S. in Mgmt. and Adminstrn., Ind. U.-Indpls. Gen. mgr. Logansport Mall, Ltd., 1979-81; gen. mgr. Chessler Mgmt. Co., Kalamazoo, 1981-83, property mgr., 1983-84; dir. leasing and mktg. Meyer C. Weiner Co., Kalamazoo, 1984—, v.p., 1985—. Mem. Inst. Real Estate Mgmt. (West Mich. chpt.). Roman Catholic. Avocations: golf; basketball; weight lifting. Office: Meyer C Weiner Co 200 Mall Dr Portage MI 49081

TIMOTHY, (MICHAEL NEGREPONTIS), See *Who's Who in America,* 43rd edition.

TING, CHIHYUAN CHARLES, chemist; b. Tsingtao, China, Feb. 1, 1947; came to U.S., 1971, naturalized, 1979; s. Shu-Ren and Shu-Yin (Yin) T.; m. Margaret An, Aug. 6, 1971; children—Michelle, Michael. B.S., Fu-Jen U., Taipei, Taiwan, 1970; M.S., Wilkes Coll., 1973; Ph.D., Pa. State U., 1978. Research specialist Monsanto, St. Louis, 1977—. Patentee in field. Mem. Am. Chem. Soc., Sigma Xi. Avocations: Reading, music, sports. Office: Monsanto 800 N Lindbergh Blvd Saint Louis MO 63167

TINSLEY, STEPHEN JAMES, real estate developer; b. Chgo., Nov. 7, 1950; s. Milton and Phylis (Silverman) T.; m. Bibi Lewison, May 21, 1978; children—Lauren, Susan. B.S., U. Ill., 1974; M.A., U. Chgo., 1976. Sales mgr. Am. Invesco, Chgo., 1976-77; v.p. Met. Structures, Chgo., 1977-80; sr. v.p. Alter Group, Wilmette, Ill., 1980—. Contbr. articles to profl. jours. Mem. Urban Land Inst., Chgo. Office Leasing Brokers Assn., Real Estate Bd. Office: The Alter Group 2000 Glenview Rd Wilmette IL 60091

TIPPING, HARRY A., lawyer; b. Bainbridge, Md., Nov. 2, 1944; s. William Richard and Ann Marie (Kelly) T.; m. Kathleen Ann Palmer, July 12, 1969; 1 child, Christopher A. B.A., Gannon U., 1966; J.D., U. Akron, 1970. Bar: Ohio. Asst. law dir. City of Akron, Ohio, 1971-72, chief asst. law dir., 1972-74; ptnr. Gillen, Miller & Tipping, Akron, 1974-77, Roderick, Myers & Linton, Akron, 1977—. Chmn., Bd. of Tax Appeals, City of Fairlawn, Ohio, 1979-81, mem. merger com., 1980-82. Served with USCGR, 1966-72. Mem. Akron Bar Assn., Ohio Bar Assn., ABA, Ohio Acad. Trial Lawyers, Assn. Trial Lawyers Am., Defense Research Inst., Am. Arbitration Assn. Republican. Roman Catholic. Clubs: Fairlawn Country (Ohio); Cascade (Akron). Office: Roderick Myers & Linton 300 Centran Bldg Akron OH 44308

TIPPLE, ROBERT BERNARD, violinist, violin maker, composer; b. Bloomington, Ill., Mar. 29, 1913; s. Robert W. and Jeanette M. (Dixon) T.; m. Wilma Irene Hazel, Dec. 28, 1966. Spl. degree in violin, Am. Conservatory Mus., Chgo., 1935; studied under noted violin masters. Toured extensively in U.S. as concert violinist; piano technician, profl. tuner, Steinway and Baldwin, St. Louis, 1966-73, Aeolian Corp., St. Louis, 1966-73; violin appraiser collector, maker, prop. Tipple Violin Shop, Mt. Vernon, Ill., 1973—; tchr. violin-making, piano tech. Served with 728th Army Airforce band, 1943-45. Mem. Nat. Piano Technicians Guild, ASCAP. Mem. Christian Ch. Research into the varnish processes of Italian violin makers, 1550-1750. Produces replicas of world's greatest violins for concert artists. Home and Office: 1132 Bel Aire Dr Mount Vernon IL 62864

TIPTON, CLYDE RAYMOND, JR., research institute executive; b. Cin., Nov. 13, 1921; s. Clyde Raymond and Ida Marie (Molitor) T.; B.S., U. Ky., 1946, M.S. (Haggin fellow), 1947; m. Marian Gertrude Beushausen, Aug. 6, 1942; children—Marian Page Cuddy, Robert Bruce. Research engr. Battelle Meml. Inst., Columbus, Ohio, 1947-49, sr. tech. adviser, 1951-62, coordinator corporate communications, 1969-73, v.p. communications, 1973-75, asst. to pres., 1978-79, v.p., corp. dir. communications and public affairs, 1979—; staff mem. Los Alamos Sci. Lab., 1949-51; dir. research Basic, Inc., Bettsville, Ohio, 1962-64; asst. dir. Battelle Pacific N.W. Labs., Richland, Wash., 1964-69; pres., trustee Battelle Commons Co. for Community Urban Redevel., Columbus, 1975-78. Secretariat, U.S. Del., 2d Internat. Conf. on Peaceful Uses Atomic Energy, Geneva, Switzerland, 1958; cons. U.S. AEC in Atoms for Peace Program, Tokyo, Japan, 1959, New Delhi, India, 1959-60, Rio de Janeiro, Brazil, 1961. Bd. dirs., past pres. Pilot Dogs; bd. dirs. Central Ohio United Negro Coll. Fund, Columbus Assn. for Performing Arts, Central Ohio Resource Bd. CARE; bd. dirs., asst. sec.-treas. Pilot Guide Dog Found. bd. dirs., past pres. Architects Soc. Ohio Found. bd. dirs., past pres. Greater Columbus Arts Council, Jazz Arts Group; trustee, chmn. bd. Battelle Scholars Program Trust Fund; bd. govs. Battelle Youth Sci. Program. Served with USAAF, 1943. Sr. fellow Otterbein Coll., 1978. Mem. AAAS, Am. Mgmt. Assn., Am. Soc. Metals, Public Relations Soc. Am., Nat. Soc. Profl. Engrs. (vice chmn. central region), Ohio Soc. Profl. Engrs. (treas.), Profl. Engrs. in Industry (vice chmn. central region), Ohio Acad. Sci., Sigma Xi, Alpha Chi Sigma. Episcopalian. Lion. Clubs: Athletic (Columbus, Washington). Editor: Jour. Soc. for Nondestructive Testing, 1953-57; The Reactor Handbook, Reactor Materials, vol. 3, 1955, vol. 1, 1960; Learning to Live on a Small Planet, 1974; author: How to Change the World, 1982; patentee in field. Home: 2354 Dorset Rd Columbus OH 43221 Office: 505 King Ave Columbus OH 43201

TIPTON, KAREN YVONNE, insurance company official; b. Indpls., Mar. 26, 1951; d. Charles Luther and Minerva Ethel (Mumford) Tipton; m. William Harold Hardy, Nov. 3, 1979 (div. Mar. 1983). B.A. in Spanish and German, U. Evansville (Ind.), 1973; M.P.A., Roosevelt U., 1981. Telephone claims adjuster Allstate Ins. Co., Lincolnwood, Ill., 1974-75, casualty field adjuster, 1975-76, casualty field specialist, Gurnee, Ill., 1976-78, staff claims rep., Gurnee, 1978-80, Arlington Heights, Ill., 1980-81, sr. claims rep., 1981—, trainer Ptnrs. Workshop, Allstate Ins. Co., Skokie, Ill., 1983—. Vice pres. Echo Mag. Inc. (Spanish edit.), 1980-81. Recipient Claims Employee award Allstate Ins. Co., 1979; cert. law for the claimsmen, 1975. Mem. Alpha Kappa Alpha. Democrat. Methodist. Home: 5137 Winona Ln Gurnee IL 60031 Office: Allstate Ins Co 1051 W Rand Rd Arlington Heights IL 60004

TIPTON, RICHARD JAMES, optometrist; b. Memphis, Oct. 19, 1946; s. Henry Field and Mildred (Hawkins) T.; m. Linda Easterwood, Sept. 26, 1968 (div. 1981); 1 dau., Laura Diane. B.S., Ark. State U., 1968; O.D., So. Coll. Optometry, Memphis, 1972. Lic. optometrist, Ark., Mo. Sole practice optometry, Jonesboro, Ark., 1974-77, Cape Girardeau, Mo., 1980—; assoc. William S. Wright, Cape Girardeau, 1977-80. Served to capt. AUS, 1972-74. Mem. Am. Optometric Assn., Mo. Optometric Assn., S.E. Mo. Optometric Assn. Methodist. Clubs: Kiwanis (past pres.), Lions. Avocations: Bowling, golf, woodworking. Address: 2609 Themis St Cape Girardeau MO 63701

TISCHLER, IRWIN WOLF, osteopathic physician and surgeon, educator; b. N.Y.C., June 15, 1945; s. Henry A. and Sylvia (Solomonick) T.; m. Cheryl Behl, Dec. 27, 1973; children—Julie, Mark, Jason. B.A., Bethany Coll., 1967; D.O., Chgo. Coll. Osteo. Medicine, 1971. Diplomate Am. Coll. Osteo. Internists. Sr. fellow dept. hematology Cook County Hosp., Chgo., 1974-75; dir. sect. hematology and oncology Chgo. Coll. Osteo. Medicine and Chgo. Osteo. Med. Ctr., 1975-81; co-chmn. cancer com. Candell Meml. Hosp., Libertyville, Ill., 1981-82, now mem. staff; practice internal medicine, specializing in hematology and oncology, Vernon Hills, Ill., 1981—; mem. staff Highland Park Hosp. (Ill.); adj. assoc. prof. medicine Chgo. Coll. Osteo. Medicine. Mem. AMA, Am. Osteo. Assn., Am. Soc. Internatl Medicine, Ill. Med. Soc., Am. Cancer Soc. (dir.). Mem. editorial bd. Jour. Postgrad. Medicine. Contbr. articles to osteo. med. jours.

TISDALE, THOMAS EDWARD, engineer; b. Chgo., Mar. 14, 1942; s. Eugene Ephriam Tisdale and Modena (Hess) Pulliam; m. Mary Ellen Szarowicz, July 25, 1959 (div. Apr. 1977); children—Elizabeth Marie, Julie Anne, Thomas Edward. B.S. in Mech. Engring., San Jose State U., 1963; postgrad. Ill. Inst. Tech., 1966, U. Chgo. Engr., Cook Research Co., Morton Grove, Ill., 1963-65, Dale & Assocs., Chgo., 1965-69; project engr. U.S. Army, Charlestown, Ind., 1969-74, Sundstrand Corp., Rockford, Ill., 1974-77; project mgr. FMC Corp., San Jose, Calif., 1977-79; engr. Abbott Labs., North Chicago, Ill., 1979—; cons. Dept. Energy, Idaho Falls, Idaho, 1977-79. Contbr. articles on engring. to profl. jours. Chmn. No. Ill. Heart Assn., Rockford, 1976, 77; mem. Young Republicans of Ill., Oak Park, 1968, 69. Mem. Soc. Mfg. Engrs. (cert.), ASME, Am. Def. Preparedness Assn., Robotics Internat. (cert. robotics engr.). Roman Catholic. Lodges: Eagles, Masons. Home: 827 Chatham Elmhurst IL 60126 Office: Abbott Labs AP4A/04B North Chicago IL 60064

TISTHAMMER, DANA JEAN, librarian; b. Des Moines, Nov. 8, 1924; d. Kenneth James and Mary Daniela (Haskell) Catterson; m. Arne Gutru Tisthammer, Sept. 4, 1947. B.A., U. Nebr., 1948; B.S. in Library Sci., Tex. State Coll. for Women, 1954. Order librarian So. Meth. U., Dallas, 1955-57; head acquisitions Pius XII Meml. Library, St. Louis U., 1957-65, head tech. services, 1965-69, asst. dir., 1969—. Mem. AAUP, ALA, Phi Beta Kappa, Beta Phi Mu. Republican. Methodist. Home: 504 E Polo Dr Clayton MO 63105 Office: St Louis U Pius XII Meml Library 3655 W Pine Blvd Saint Louis MO 63108

TITLE, MONROE MORRIS, hospital administrator; b. Bklyn., Oct. 6, 1918; s. Joseph and Helen (Sonnenberg) T.; m. Sylvia Title, Jan. 7, 1942 (div. 1972); 1 child, Diane; m. Sylvia Schlossberg, July 10, 1983. B.A., CCNY, 1939; M.A., U. Mich., 1941, M.S.W., 1941. Adminstr. Brent Gen. Hosp., Detroit, 1953-64, Woodside Med. Ctr., Pontiac, Mich., 1964-65, Park Community Hosp., Detroit, 1965-66; adminstr. North Detroit Gen. Hosp., 1966—; instr., dir. health care adminstrn. program Oakland Community Coll., Bloomfield Hills, Mich., 1979—; instr., chmn. dept. nursing home adminstrn. Applied Mgmt. and Tech. Ctr., Wayne State U., Detroit, 1969-81, field instr. Sch. Social Work, Detroit, 1978—; chmn. com. shared services Greater Detroit Area Hosp. Council, 1974-79. Pres. Westbrook Manor Neighborhood Assn., Farmington Hills, Mich., 1980-82. Fellow Am. Coll. Hosp. Adminstrs. (life); mem. Mich. Assn. Community Hosps. and Physicians (sec. 1980-82), Am. Pub. Health Assn., Am. Assn. Hosp. Planning, Am. Arbitration Assn. (arbitrator 1982—), Hamtramck C. of C. (pres. 1985). Lodge: Rotary (v.p. 1985-86). Avocations: chess; writing. Home: 28960 Lorikay St Farmington Hills MI 48018

TITUS, LARRY REED, electronics manufacturing company executive; b. Warren, Ohio, May 15, 1943; s. Leland R. and Elma A. (Gotthardt) T.; m. Barbara J. Kinnison, Sept. 8, 1962; children—Mary Jane, Rebecca Lynn, Debra Sue. B.B.A., Loyola U., Chgo., 1980; M.B.A., U. Chgo., 1984. Mgr. mgmt. info. systems ITT-Grinnell, 1974-78, ITT, 1978-81; mgr. mgmt. info. systems fixed div. Motorola Inc., Schaumburg, Ill., 1981-84, dir. internat. mgmt. info. systems, 1984—. Vice pres. Joint Vocat. Edn., Warren, 1974; pres. Warren Sch. System, 1976; bd. dirs. Homeowners Assn., Palatine, Ill., 1984. Mem. Assn. System Mgmt. (bd. dirs. 1972-76), Data Processing Mgmt. Assn. (v.p. 1968-74), Nat. Assn. Accts. Republican. Club: Loyola U. Alumni. Lodge: Moose. Avocations: sports; reading. Office: Motorola Inc 1301 E Algonquin Rd Schaumburg IL 60196

TIWANA, NAZAR HAYAT, librarian; b. Kalra, India, Nov. 27, 1927; came to U.S., 1965; s. Khizar Hayat and Sultan (Bibi) T.; m. Sita Sarware Sahgal, Jan. 24, 1951; children—Yasmine, Omar. B.A. in Econs., Pembroke Coll., Cambridge, Eng., 1947; M.A. in L.S., U. Chgo., 1971. Reference librarian Chgo. Pub. Library, 1973-75, adminstrv. asst., 1975-76; adult services librarian Rogers Park Library, Chgo., 1976-79; dir. America's Ethnic Heritage Program, Chgo., 1979-81; head dept. Hild Regional Library, Chgo., 1981-83; spl. staff asst. White House Conf. on Libraries and Info. Services, Washington, 1979; del. Ill. White House Conf. Librarian and Info. Services, 1978; del. State Dept. Adv. Conf. on Exchange of Internat. Info., Washington, 1979. Author: (with Don Schabel) Integrated Rural Information Systems, 1976. Assoc. Newberry Library, Chgo., 1981—. Recipient Spl. Service award Friends of Chgo. Pub. Library, 1979. Mem. ALA, Internat. Fedn. Library Assns., Spl. Libraries Assn., Ill. Libraries Assn., Art Inst. Chgo., Field Mus., Beta Phi Mu. Club: Chgo. Library. Home: 2620 W Pratt Blvd Chicago IL 60645

TOBIAS, PAUL H., lawyer; b. Cin., Jan. 5, 1930; s. Charles H. and Charlotte (Westheimer) T.; m. Toni Laboiteaux, Sept. 5, 1964 (div. 1975); 1 child, Eliza; m. Phyllis A. Vlach, Jan. 15, 1984. A.B., Harvard U., 1951, LL.B., 1958. Bar: Ohio 1958. Assoc. Stoneman & Chandler, Boston, 1958-62, Goldman, Cole & Putnick, Cin., 1962-76; ptnr. Tobias & Kraus, Cin., 1976—; instr. U. Cin. Law Sch., 1975-78. Contbr. articles to profl. jours. Commr. Cin. Park Bd., 1974-81; mem. Cin. Human Relations Commn., 1980-85. Mem. ABA, Ohio Bar Assn., Cin. Bar Assn., Phi Beta Kappa. Democrat. Jewish. Club: University (Cin.). Home: 15 Hill and Hollow Ln Cincinnati OH 45208 Office: Tobias & Kraus 105 E 4th St 911 Clopay Cincinnati OH 45020

TOBIAS, RICHARD CHARLES, science educator, consultant; b. Chgo., Sept. 12, 1937; s. Joseph and Genevieve (Stwora) T.; m. Marian Jeanette Johnson, June 4, 1966; children—Timothy Richard, Denise Marie. B.S. in Edn., U. Wis.-River Falls, 1959, M.S. in Edn., 1968; D.Arts, U. No. Colo., 1976. Cert. tchr., Minn., Wis. Instr. sci. Webster (Wis.) Sr. High Sch., 1962-66, Burnsville (Minn.) Sr. High Sch., 1966—, chmn. sci. dept., 1985—; cons. product devel. 3M, St. Paul, 1980-84. Mem. steering com. North Central Assn. Com. Schs., 1974-78, chmn., 1981-84. Contbr. articles to profl. jours. Active Indianhead council Boy Scouts Am., 1980—. Served with U.S. Army, 1960-62. Recipient Tchr. Intern Program award St. Paul C. of C., 1980-81. Mem. Am. Soc. Parasitologists, Assn. Biology Tchrs., Minn. Sci. Tchrs. Assn., Minn. Acad. Sci., Minn. Edn. Assn., NEA (life), Sigma Xi. Democrat. Roman Catholic. Home: 4337 Onyx Dr Eagan MN 55122

TOBIN, CALVIN JAY, architect; b. Boston, Feb. 15, 1927; s. David and Bertha (Tanfield) T.; B.Arch., U. Mich., 1949; m. Joan Hope Fink, July 15, 1951; children—Michael Alan, Nancy Ann. Designer, draftsman Arlen & Lowenfish, architects, N.Y.C., 1949-51; with Samuel Arlen, N.Y.C., 1951-53, Skidmore, Owings & Merrill, N.Y.C., 1953; architect Loebl, Schlossman & Bennett, architects, Chgo., 1953-57; v.p. Loebl, Schlossman & Hackl, 1957—. Chmn., Jewish United Fund Bldg. Trades Div., 1969; chmn. AIA and Chgo. Hosp. Council Com. of Hosp. Architecture, 1968-76. Chmn. Highland Park (Ill.) Appearance Rev. Commn., 1972-73; mem. Highland Park Plan Commn., 1972-78; mem. Highland Park City Council, 1974—, mayor pro tem, 1979—; bd. dirs. Young Men's Jewish Council, 1953-67, pres., 1967; bd. dirs. Jewish Community Centers Chgo., 1973-78. Served with USNR, 1945-46. Mem. AIA (2d v.p. Chgo. chpt.), Pi Lambda Phi. Jewish. Clubs: Standard, Highland Park Country. Archtl. works include Michael Reese Hosp. and Med. Center, 1954—, Prairie Shores Apt. Urban Redevel., 1957-62, Louis A. Weiss Meml. Hosp., Chgo., Chgo. State Hosp., Central Community Hosp., Chgo., Gottlieb Meml. Hosp., Melrose Park, Ill., West Suburban Hosp., Oak Park, Ill., Thorek

Hosp. and Med. Center, Chgo., Shriners Hosp., Chgo., Water Tower Pl., Chgo., also numerous apt., comml. and community bldgs. Home: 814 Dean Ave Highland Park IL 60035 Office: 845 N Michigan Ave Chicago IL 60611

TOBIN, ILONA L., psychologist, marriage/family counselor, sex educator and counselor, consultant; b. Trenton, Mich., Apr. 15, 1943; d. Frank John and Marjorie Cathalean (Lines) Kotyuk; m. Roger Lee Tobin, Aug. 20, 1966. B.A., Eastern Mich. U., 1965; M.A., 1968; M.A., Mich. State U., 1975; Ed.D., Wayne State U., 1978. Tchr., counselor Willow Run Pub. Schs., Ypsilanti, Mich., 1966-72; prof. Macomb County Community Coll., Mt. Clemens, Mich., 1974-79; psychotherapist Identity Center, Inc., Mt. Clemens, 1974-79; dir. treatment Alternative Lifestyles, Inc., Orchard Lake, Mich., 1979-80; psychologist Profl. Psychotherapy and Counseling Ctr., Farmington Hills, Mich., 1980-83; pvt. practice clin. psychology, Birmingham, Mich., 1983—; lectr. Wayne State U., Detroit, 1977—; recruitment dir. Upward Bound Eastern Mich. U., Ypsilanti, 1969-72. Co-chmn. Birmingham Families in Action, 1982-83; bd. dirs. HAVEN-Oakland County's Physical and Sexual Abuse Ctr. and Oakland Area Counselors Assn., 1984—; mem. exec. bd., v.p. personnel Birmingham Community Women's Ctr., 1984—, also dir.; mem. adv. bd. Woodside Med. Ctr. for Chemically Dependent Women, 1984—. NIMH fellow, 1976; Wayne State U. scholar, 1976-78. Mem. Am. Psychol. Assn., Mich. Psychol. Assn., Am. Assn. Sex Educators, Counselors and Therapists, Am. Assn. for Counseling and Devel., Pi Lambda Theta, Phi Delta Kappa. Unitarian. Clubs: Birmingham Bus. Womens.

TOBIN, LARRY MICHAEL, newspaper publisher; b. Kansas City, Mo., Feb. 4, 1946; s. Charles Adrian and Allyn Fern (Lamar) T.; m. Kathleen Ann Branen, Feb. 8, 1975; children—Kerry William, Kelly Melissa. Student Marquette U., 1964-68. Asst. dir. alumni funds Marquette U., Milw., 1969-70; various legis. positions State Capitol, Madison, Wis., 1970-73; dir. mem. services Wis. Electric Coop. Assn., Madison, 1973-77; legis. coordinator, asst. mgr. Wis. Newspaper Assn., Madison, 1977-80; publisher Jefferson Banner, Wis., 1980-81, Tomahawk Leader, Wis., 1982—; v.p. Wis.-Mich. Pubs., Eagle River, Wis., 1982—; dir. Tomahawk Investors, Inc. Chmn., Tomahawk Tomorrow Action Com., 1983—, Tomahawk Community Cleanup Campaign, 1983—; Mem. Dane County Bd. Suprs., Madison, 1975-78; bd. dirs. North Central Wis. Private Industry Council, Rhinelander, 1983—. Mem. Wis. Newspaper Assn., Nat. Newspaper Assn., Tomahawk Regional C. of C. (pres. 1983-84, interim pres. 1985). Club: Ducks Unlimited (Tomahawk). Avocations: hunting, fishing, bowling, wood carving. Home: W7273 Ridge Rd Tomahawk WI 54487 Office: Tomahawk Leader PO Box 345 315 W Wisconsin Ave Tomahawk WI 54487

TOBIN, RICHARD LARDNER, journalism educator; b. Chgo., Aug. 9, 1910; s. Richard Griswold and Anne (Lardner) T.; m. Sylvia Cleveland, Oct. 11, 1937; 1 child, Mark Cleveland. B.A., U. Mich., 1932. Reporter, editor, war corr., asst. to pub. N.Y. Herald Tribune, 1932-56; dir. news ABC, N.Y.C., 1945-46; asst. to pres. Campbell Soup Co., N.J., 1957-59; mng. editor, exec. editor, assoc. pub., sr. v.p. Saturday Rev. mag., N.Y.C., 1960-76; assoc. prof. Columbia U., N.Y.C., 1940-52; Riley prof. journalism Ind. U., Bloomington, 1977—. Author: Invasion Journal, 1944; Golden Opinions, 1948; The Center of the World, 1951; Decisions of Destiny, 1961; Tobin's English Usage, 1985. Nat. pub. relations chmn. Citizens for Eisenhower, 1955-56. Recipient Disting. Alumnus award U. Mich., 1964; named to Journalism Hall of Fame, U. Mo., 1968. Republican. Episcopalian. Clubs: University, Pilgrims (N.Y.C.). Avocations: gardening; music; English usage. Office: Ind U Bloomington IN 47405

TOBIN, RONALD LEROY, pharmacist, chemist; b. Kansas City, Mo., Nov. 9, 1946; s. Jack O. and Helen Nadine (Rabon) T.; m. Sue O. Klepper, July 16, 1942; children—David Lee, Kathleen Suzanne. B.S. in Pharmacy, U. Mo.-Kansas City, 1975; P.D. (hon.), Sch. Pharmacy, Kans. U., 1980. Registered pharmacist, Mo., Kans. Pharmacist, owner Ron's Pharmacy, Blue Springs, Mo., 1979—. Mem. Mayor's Council, Blue Springs, 1983-84. Served with USAF, 1966-70. Eagle Scout, Boy Scouts Am., 1960. Democrat. Baptist. Home: 1408 Deer Run Trail Blue Springs MO 64015 Office: Ron's Pharmacy 1700 N 7 Hwy Blue Springs MO 64015

TODD, EUGENIA J. KORCHEVSKY, business executive; b. Newark; d. Joseph and Mary (Leczse) Korchevsky; student Montclair State Tchrs. Coll.; B.S., Jersey City State Tchrs. Coll., 1947; R.N., Jersey City Med. Center, 1947; m. Robert Louis Todd, May 10, 1948; children—Robert Joseph, John Burton. Clk., Irvington (N.J.) Jewish Cemetery, 1938-39; marker Bamberger's Dept. Store, Newark, 1940-41; sec. Graybar Electric Co., Newark, 1942-43, Orbachs Dept. Store, Newark, 1943-44, Montclair State Tchrs. Coll., 1943-44; sec., grad. supr., nurse Jersey City Med. Center, 1944-47; nurse Mountainside Hosp., Montclair, N.J., 1947-49, VA Hosp., Dearborn, Mich., 1949-51; cons. Home and Hawkeye Nursing Registry, Burlington, Iowa, 1955-59; v.p., sec., treas. North Hill Med. Bldg. Corp., Burlington, 1960—; journalist Mediapolis News; columnist Mediapolis Monitor, Mediapolis Memories. Den leader Boy Scouts Am., Burlington, 1955-65. Mem. Art Guild (life, patron), Nat. Wildlife Fedn., Am. Geriatrics Soc., Nat. Parks and Conservation Assn., Smithsonian Assos., Nat. Hist. Soc. Club: Crystal Lake (Ill.). Office: 608 Prairie St Mediapolis IA 52637

TODD, JOHN JOSEPH, justice state supreme court; b. South St. Paul, Minn., Mar. 16, 1927; student St. Thomas Coll., 1944, 46-47; B.S. in Law, U. Minn., 1949, LL.B., 1950; m. Dolores Shanahan, Sept. 9, 1950; children—Richard, Jane, John. Bar: Minn. 1951. Ptnr. Thuet & Todd, South St. Paul, 1951-72; assoc. justice Minn. Supreme Ct., St. Paul, 1972—; mem. Minn. Tax Ct., 1966-72. Served with USN, 1945-46. Mem. Minn. Trial Lawyers Assn., First Dist. Bar Assn. Minn. (pres. 1969-70), Minn. Bar Assn. Office: Supreme Ct 225 State Capitol Saint Paul MN 55155*

TODD, JOHN ODELL, ins. co. exec.; b. Mpls., Nov. 12, 1902; s. Frank Chisholm and Mary Mable (Odell) T.; A.B., Cornell U., 1924; C.L.U., Am. Coll., 1933; m. Katherine Sarah Cone, Feb. 21, 1925; children—John Odell, George Bennett. Spl. agt. Equitable Life Assurance Soc., Mpls., 1926-28; ins. broker, Mpls., 1928-31; spl. agt. Northwestern Mut. Life Ins. Co., Mpls., 1931-38, Evanston, Ill., 1938—; ptnr. H.S. Vail & Sons, Chgo., 1938-43, Vail and Todd, gen. agts. Northwestern Mut. Life Ins. Co., 1943-44; sole gen. agt., Chgo., 1944-51; pres. Todd Planning and Service Co., life ins. brokers, 1951—; founder, chmn., prin. John O. Todd Orgn. Inc., Exec. Compensation Specialists and Cons., 1970—; faculty lectr. C.L.U. Insts., U. Conn., 1952-53, U. Wis., 1955-57, U. Calif., 1956, U. Hawaii, 1966; host interviewer ednl. Films Series of the Greats, 1973-74. Pres. Evanston (Ill.) 1st. Ward Non-Partisan Civic Assn., 1956-57; trustee Evanston Hist. Soc., 1973-76. Recipient Golden Plate award Am. Acad. Achievement, 1969; Huebner Gold medal for contbn. to edn., 1978; named Ins. Field Man of Year, Ins. Field Pub. Co., 1965; Ill. Room in Hall of States dedicated to him by Am. Coll., 1981. Mem. Nat. Assn. Life Underwriters (John Newton Russell award 1969), Assn. Advanced Life Underwriters (pres. 1963-64), Am. Coll. Life Underwriters (trustee 1957-78), Chgo. Life Underwriters Assn. (dir. 1938-41, Disting. Service award 1984), Northwestern Mut. Spl. Agts. Assn. (pres. 1955-56), Life Agy. Mgrs. Assn. (dir. 1945-48), Northwestern Mut. Assn. Agts. (pres. 1957-58), Chgo. Life Trust Council, Million Dollar Round Table (pres. 1951, qualifier 50 consecutive yrs.), Psi Upsilon, Sphinx Head. Republican. Clubs: Evanston Univ.; Glen View; Mpls. Author: Taxation, Inflation and Life Insurance, 1950; Ceiling Unlimited, 1965, 5th edit., 1984; contbg. author to text Huebner Foundation, 1951.

TODD, LINDA KAY, retirement housing industry executive, consultant; b. Kansas City, Mo., Nov. 6, 1946; d. Grover Eugene and Beatrice May (Cramer) Fanning; m. James Todd (div. 1980); children—Christopher, Paul, Kevin. Student U. Mo.-Kansas City, 1965-66. Lic. pvt. pilot single engine. Vice pres. advt., mktg. and adminstrn. Christian Services, Inc., Kansas City, Mo., 1973-81; exec. v.p. Mktg. and Media Services, Inc., Lee's Summit, Mo., 1982—; active nat. seminars on mktg. and promoting retirement communities. Mem. Direct Mail Mktg. Assn., Am. Assn. Housing Aging, Nat. Council on the Aging, Am. Assn. Ret. Persons, Lee's Summit C. of C. Home: 3507 Lake Dr Lee's Summit MO 64063 Office: 512 S 291 Lee's Summit MO 64063

TODD, ZANE GREY, utility executive, electrical engineer; b. Hanson, Ky., Feb. 3, 1924; s. Marshall Elvin and Kate (McCormick) T.; student Evansville Coll., 1948-49; B.S.E.E. summa cum laude, Purdue U., 1951, D. Engring., 1979; postgrad. U. Mich., summer 1965; m. Marysnow Stone, Feb. 8, 1950 (dec. 1983); m. 2d, Frances Z. Anderson, Jan. 6, 1984. Fingerprint classifier FBI, 1942-43; electric system planning engr. Indpls. Power & Light Co., 1951-56, spl. assignments supr., 1956-60, head elec. system planning, 1960-65, head substa. engring., 1965-68, head distbn. engring., 1968-70, asst. to v.p., 1970-72, v.p., 1972-74, exec. v.p., 1974-75, pres., 1975-76, chmn. bd., pres., 1976-81, chmn. bd., chief exec. officer, 1981—, also dir.; pres., chmn. IPAL CO Enterprises, Inc., 1984—; chmn. bd., chief exec. officer Mid-Am. Capital Resources, Inc., 1984—; gen. mgr. Mooresville Pub. Service Co., Inc. (Ind.), 1956-60; dir. Mchts. Nat. Bank Mchts. Nat. Corp., Am. States Ins. Cos., Consumers Credit Counseling Service. Mem. adv. bd. St. Vincent Hosp., Salvation Army, Clowes Hall; bd. dirs. 500 Festival Assocs., Commn. for Downtown, United Way of Greater Indpls., Corp. Community council, Environ. Quality Control; Ind. chmn. U.S. Savs. Bond Program; chmn. bd. trustees Ind. Central U.; bd. govs. Asso. Colls. Ind.; mem. adv. bd., trustee Christian Theol. Sem.; chmn. YMCA Found. Served with AUS, 1943-47. Recipient Distinguished Alumnus award Purdue U., 1976. Fellow IEEE (past chmn. com. application probability methods, past chmn. power systems engring. com.); mem. Indpls. (dir.), Ind. (dir.), Mooresville (past pres.) chambers commerce, Nat. Soc. Profl. Engrs., Ind. Soc. Profl. Engrs., Power Engring. Soc., ASME, Am. Mgmt. Assn. (gen. mgmt. council), NAM (dir.), Ind. Electric Assn. (dir., chmn. 1976-77), Assn. Edison Illuminating Cos. (bd. dirs.), Newcomen Soc. (Ind. chmn.), Eta Kappa Nu, Tau Beta Pi. Clubs: Indianapolis Athletic (bd. dirs.), Meridian Hills Country, Columbia, Skyline (bd. govs.); La Coquille (Palm Beach). Lodge: Rotary. Contbr. to tech. jour. Originator probability analysis of power systems reliability. Home: 7645 Randue Ct Indianapolis IN 46278 Office: 25 Monument Circle Indianapolis IN 46204

TOEBE, KENNETH WILBURT, resort owner; b. Woodville, Wis., Feb. 13, 1935; s. Wilburt William and Lucille Laura (Lopas) T.; m. Carol Jean Odegard, Nov. 14, 1981. B.S., U. Wis.-Oshkosh, 1958; M.A., Eastern Mich. U., 1961. Cert. tchr., Wis. English tchr. Cement City Schs., Mich., 1960-62, Kaukauna Community Schs., Wis., 1962-68, Hayward Community Schs., Wis., 1968-75; resort owner, operator Sunset Lodge, Hayward, 1966—; chmn. English dept. Hayward Community Schs., 1969-75. Pres. Northwest Territories tourism orgn., Wis., 1981—; v.p. Hayward Lakes Resort Assn., 1984—, sec., treas. 1973-79; pres. Lost Land-Teal Resort Assn., Hayward, 1978-80. Recipient Outstanding Service award Hayward Lakes Resort Assn., 1979. Mem. Muskies, Inc. (v.p. Hayward Lakes chpt. 1978-81, sec.-treas. 1981-83, bd. dirs. 1984—), Am. Birkebeiner Ski Found., Fresh Water Fishing Hall of Fame (charter), Humane Soc. U.S. World Concern, Christian Blind Mission Internat. Lutheran. Lodge: Masons. Avocations: reading; music; travel; skiing; swimming. Home and Office: Route 7 Hayward WI 54843

TOERING, MYRON DEAN, lawyer; b. Hospers, Iowa, Jan. 11, 1948; s. Mince and Nellie (Steenhoven) T.; m. Marla Joy Kleinhesselink, Aug. 23, 1974; children—Mickey, Matthew. B.B.A., U. Iowa, 1975, M.A., 1976; J.D., U. Tulsa, 1979. Bar: Iowa 1979. C.P.A., Iowa. Acct. Arthur Young Co., Tulsa, 1978; clk. Dyer, Power, Marsh, Tulsa, 1978-79; trust officer Am. State Bank, Sioux Center, Iowa, 1979-80; sole practice, Sioux Center, 1980—; sec. Hospice of Sioux County Inc., Sioux Center, 1984—; mem. adv. bd. Mid-Sioux Opportunity Inc., Remsen, Iowa, 1984—. Councilman Sioux Center City Council, 1983; v.p. Sioux Center PTA, 1983—. Served as sgt. USAF, 1967-71. Chester Phillips scholar U. Iowa, 1975. Mem. Christian Legal Soc., Iowa State Bar Assn., Sioux Center C. of C. Democrat. Mem. Reformed Ch. Am. Lodge: Lions. Home: 1115 Eastside Dr Sioux Center IA 51250 Office: 128 3d St NW Sioux Center IA 51250

TOFTELAND, BRUCE CARLYN, dentist; b. Harvey, N.D., Mar. 15, 1956; s. Donald Morris and Y. Georgine (Goodman) T.; m. Joan Marie Hofland, July 25, 1981. Student U. N.D., 1974-78; D.D.S., Creighton U., 1982. Assoc. dentist Worthington Dental Ctr., Minn., 1982-84; sole practice, Fargo, N.D., 1984—; dir. dental care for hosp. bedridden Worthington Regional Hosp., Minn., 1983-84. Mem. ADA, Acad. Gen. Dentistry, Am. Profl. Practice Assn., S.E. Dist. Dental Soc. N.D., S.W. Dist. Dental Soc. Minn. Lutheran. Avocations: camping; fishing; hunting; canoeing; cross-country skiing; recreational sports. Office: 210 Black Bldg Fargo ND 58102

TOFTNER, RICHARD ORVILLE, chemical company executive; b. Warren, Minn., Mar. 5, 1935; s. Orville Gayhart and Cora Evelyn (Anderson) T.; B.A., U. Minn., 1966; M.B.A., Xavier U., 1970; m. Jeanne Bredine, June 26, 1960; children—Douglas, Scott, Kristine, Kimberly, Brian. Sr. economist Federated Dept. Stores, Inc., Cin., 1967-68; dep. dir. EPA, Washington and Cin., 1968-73; mgmt. cons. environ. affairs, products and mktg., 1973-74; prin. PEDCo Environ., Cin., 1974-80; trustee PEDCo trusts, 1974-80; pres. ROTA Mgmt., Inc., Cin., 1980-82; gen. mgr. CECOS, 1982—; real estate developer, 1980—; adj. prof. U. Cin.; lectr. Grad. fellowship rev. panel Office of Edn., 1978—; advisor, cabinet-level task force Office of Gov. of P.R., 1973; subcom. Nat. Safety Council, 1972. Served with AUS, 1954-57. Mem. Am. Inst. Cert. Planners, Soc. Advancement Mgmt., Water Pollution Control Fedn., Engring. Soc. Cin., Cin. C. of C. Republican, Lutheran. Clubs: Columbia (Indpls.); Bankers (Cin.). Contbr. articles to mgmt. planning and environ. to periodicals, chpts. in books; developer Toxitrol. Home: 9175 Yellowwood Dr Cincinnati OH 45239 Office: 11475 Northlake Dr Cincinnati OH 45242

TOKAR, MAUREEN TANSEY, architect; b. Cin., Mar. 4, 1931; d. Bernard Joseph and Cecile Marie (Sunman) Tansey; B.S. in Architecture, U. Cin., 1955; m. Edward Tokar, June 29, 1974. Job capt. Hixson, Tarter & Merkel, Cin., 1964-68; dir. interior architecture Ferry & Henderson, Springfield, Ill., 1968-72; project coordinator Skidmore, Owings & Merrill, Chgo., 1972-76; rev. architect Ill. Capital Devel. Bd., Chgo., 1977-82; v.p. Planning and Design Cons., 1975—. Active, Art Inst. Chgo. Mem. AIA, Chgo. Women in Architecture, Alpha Omicron Pi. Club: Chgo. Altrusa.

TOLCHINSKY, PAUL DEAN, organizational psychologist; b. Cleve., Sept. 30, 1946; s. Sanford M. and Frances (Klein) T.; children—Heidi E., Dana M. B.A. in Bus. Adminstrn., Bowling Green State U., 1971; Ph.D. in Organizational Behavior, Purdue U., 1978. Mgmt. trainer Detroit Bank and Trust Co.; tng. and devel. Babcock & Wilcox Co., Barberton, Ohio, 1973-75; internal cons. Gen. Foods, Inc., West Lafayette, Ind., 1975-77; prof. Fla. State U., Tallahassee, 1978-79, U. Akron, Ohio, 1979-81; prin. Performance Devel. Assocs., Cleve., 1981—; adj. prof. Bowling Green State U., 1981-82. Served in U.S. Army, 1966-69; Vietnam. Mem. Am. Psychol. Assn., Cert. Cons. Internat., Acad. Mgmt. Contbr. numerous articles to profl. jours. Home: 939 Aintree Park Apt 203 Cleveland OH 44143

TOLEDO-PEREYRA, LUIS HORACIO, transplant surgeon; b. Nogales, Ariz., Oct. 19, 1943; s. Jose Horacio and Elia Elvira (Pereyra) T.; m. Marjean May Gilbert, Mar. 21, 1974; children—Alexander Horacio, Suzanne Elizabeth. B.S. magna cum laude, Regis Coll., 1960; M.D., U. Mex., 1967, M.S. in Internal Medicine summa cum laude, 1970; Ph.D. in Surgery, U. Minn., 1976. Rotating intern Hosp. Juarez, U. Mex., 1966; resident in internal medicine Instituto Nacional de la Nutricion, U. Mex., 1968, 70; resident in gen. surgery U. Minn., 1970-76; resident in thoracic and cardiovascular surgery U. Chgo., 1976-77; dir. surg. research Henry Ford Hosp., Detroit, 1977-79, co-dir. transplantation, 1977-79; chief transplantation, dir. surg. research Mt. Carmel Mercy Hosp. Med. Ctr., Detroit, 1979—; instr. biochemistry and internal medicine U. Mex., 1963, 68. Recipient Outstanding Achievement award U. Mex., 1961, 64, 67; Resident Research award Assn. Acad. Surgery, 1974; Cecil Lehman Mayer Research award Am. Coll. Chest Physicians, 1975. Mem. AMA, Transplantation Soc., Assn. Acad. Surgery, Am. Soc. Nephrology, Am. Assn. Immunologists, Am. Physiol. Soc., Soc. Exptl. Biology and Medicine, Am. Soc. Artificial Organs, European Dialysis and Transplantation Assn., Am. Diabetes Assn., European Soc. Study of Diabetes. Roman Catholic. Club: Groose Pointe Yacht. Guest editor various med. and transplant jours.; editor bd. Dialysis and Transplantation, 1979—; contbr. over 200 articles on organ preservation, transplantation and other surg. and med. related areas to profl. jours.

TOLIVER, C.R., fashion coordinator; b. Chgo., Aug. 4, 1952; d. William Saunders and Amo B. (McWhorter)-Evans; m. Steve N. Toliver, July 2, 1969 (div. July 1980); 1 dau., Stephanie Monique. Telephone operator Ill. Bell Telephone Co., Chgo., 1979-82; owner, pres. Ceci, fashion coordinating, Chgo., Lacquered Images, Ltd., 1979—; chmn. Adaptations, entertainment service and cons. firm, not-for-profit, 1984—. Mem. Cosmopolitan C. of C., Notaries Assn. Ill., Am. Mus. Natural History, Am. Film Inst., Nat. Assn. Female Execs. Democrat. Roman Catholic. Office: PO Box 19161 Chicago IL 60619

TOLL, ROBERTA DARLENE (MRS. SHELDON S. TOLL), social worker; b. Detroit, May 14, 1944; d. David and Blanche (Fischer) Pollack; B.A., U. Mich., 1966; M.S.W., U. Pa., 1971; m. Aug. 11, 1968; children—Candice, John, Kevin. Dir. counselors Phila. Family Planning, Inc., 1971-72; psychologist Lafayette Clinic, Detroit, 1972-73; social worker Project Headline, Detroit, 1973-75; pvt. practice social work, Bloomfield Hills, Mich., 1975—; adj. prof. U. Detroit, Oakland Community Coll. Bd. dirs. Detroit chpt. Nat. Council on Alcoholism. Cert. social worker, Mich. Fellow Masters and Johnson Inst.; mem. Nat. Assn. Social Workers. Democrat. Club: Franklin Hills Country. Home and office: 640 Lone Pine Hill Rd Bloomfield Hills MI 48013

TOLLESON, RICHARD L., meat products company executive. Vice chmn. Oscar Mayer & Co., Madison, Wis. Office: Oscar Mayer & Co PO Box 7188 Madison WI 53707*

TOLMAN, DAN EDWARD, oral and maxillofacial surgeon; b. Silver Creek, Nebr., Aug. 9, 1931; s. Nathaniel Edward and Virginia (West) T.; m. Suzanne Nelson, June 8, 1957; 1 dau., Kimberly Suzanne. B.S.B.A., U. Nebr., 1953, B.Sc. in Dentistry, 1957, D.D.S., 1957; M.S.D., U. Minn., 1961. Diplomate Am. Bd. Oral and Maxillofacial Surgery. Resident, Mayo Grad. Sch. Medicine, Rochester, Minn., 1959-62; practice dentistry specializing in oral and maxillofacial surgery, Rochester, 1965—; cons. sect. dentistry and oral surgery Mayo Clinic, Rochester, 1965-66; instr. Mayo Grad. Sch. Medicine, U. Minn., 1966-70, asst. prof. dentistry, 1970-73, asst. prof. Mayo Med. Sch., 1973-78, assoc. prof., 1978—; mem. staff Mayo Clinic; mem. adv. group Northlands Regional Med. Program, 1969-71; mem. panel, div. ednl. resources and programs Assn. Am. Med. Colls., 1976—. Contbr. articles to profl. jours.; editor Jour. Oral Surgery, 1974-81. Mem. nominating com. Minn. Cancer Council, 1978-79, 1st vice chmn., 1980, chmn., 1981, 82, 83, Minn. Dental Assn. rep. 1978—; bd. dirs. Minn. div. Am. Cancer Soc., 1973-82, 83-84, v.p., pres. elect, 1979-80, pres. Minn. div., 1980-81, bd. dirs. Olmsted County Unit, 1972-81, chmn. standing crusade com., 1979-80; active Olmsted County Republican Party, 1968-72; pres.-elect Jefferson PTA, 1970-71, mem. scholarship com. Rochester Council, 1970-71; mem. benevolence com. 1st Presbyn. Ch., 1984—. Served with USAF, 1956-65; served to col. USAR, 1979—. Recipient cert. merit Am. Soc. Dentistry for Children, 1957; Nat. Divisional award Am. Cancer Soc., 1983; named hon. Adm., Nebr. Navy, 1953. Fellow Internat. Assn. Oral Surgeons, Am. Coll. Dentists; mem. Am. Assn. Oral and Maxillofacial Surgeons (trustee 1978-82, presdl. adv. com. 1982-83), Midwestern Soc. Oral and Maxillofacial Surgeons (sec.-treas. 1973-78, v.p. 1978-79, pres.-elect 1979-80, pres. 1980-81, 81-82, nominating com. 1981—, chmn. com. 1984—), Minn. Soc. Oral and Maxillofacial surgeons (constl. and by-laws com. 1984—), Minn. Dental Assn. (Meritorious Service citation 1978, 81, rep. to Minn. Cancer Council 1978—), Zumbro Valley Dental Soc. (Olmsted County welfare com. 1967-68, community dental health com. 1970-71), Am. Bd. Oral and Maxillofacial Surgery (adv. com. 1975-78), ADA, Southeastern Dist. Dental Soc., Am. Acad. Dental Radiology, U. Nebr. Alumni Assn., Mayo Alumni Assn., Milw. Dental Forum (hon.), Am. Assn. for Cancer Edn., Sigma Chi. Lodges: Masons (32 degree), Shriners. Home: 2709 Merrihills Dr SW Rochester MN 55901 Office: Mayo Clinic Dept Dentistry 200 1st St SW Rochester MN 55905

TOLMAN, SUZANNE NELSON, psychologist; b. Omaha, Nov. 8, 1931; d. Raymond LeRoy and Lottie (Kerns) Nelson; B.A. with distinction in Spanish, U. Nebr., Omaha, 1951; M.A., U. Nebr., Lincoln, 1952, Ph.D., 1957; m. Dan Edward Tolman, June 8, 1957; 1 dau., Kimberly Suzanne. Research asst. U. Nebr., Lincoln, 1951-52; tchr. Omaha Pub. Schs., 1952-53, counselor, high sch. instr. history and English, 1953-59; instr. psychology U. Nebr., Omaha, 1957-59; social service worker Mayo Clinic, Rochester, Minn., 1959-60; instr. psychology U. Tampa, 1962-63; sch. psychologist Sch. Dist. 535, Rochester, 1966—. Bd. dirs. Jefferson PTA, Rochester, 1966-68; bd. dirs., sec. Family Consultation Center, Rochester, 1970-76; bd. dirs. Olmsted County (Minn.) Council Coordinated Child Care, 1971-75, pres., 1973-75; bd. dirs. Olmsted County Assn. Mental Health; pres. condr.'s com. Rochester Symphony, 1977-78. Mem. Minn., Rochester edn. assns., Minn. Sch. Psychologists, Rochester Civic Music Guild (pres. 1981-82), Am. Psychol. Assn., AAUW, Zumbro Valley Dental Aux. (pres. 1970-71), Phi Delta Kappa, Alpha Lambda Delta, Alpha Delta Kappa, Psi Chi, Chi Omega. Presbyterian. Club: Order Eastern Star. Home: 2709 Merrihills Dr Rochester MN 55901 Office: Ind Sch Dist 535 Rochester MN 55901

TOLT, LESTER THOMAS, lawyer; b. Cleve., Feb. 20, 1928; s. Thomas and Mary (Petrie) T.; m. Florance Mae Citino, Feb. 3, 1952; children—Susan, Amy, Thomas. B.B.A., Western Res. U., 1950; J.D., Cleve. State U., 1963. Bar: Ohio 1963; C.P.A., Ohio. Sole practice, Cleve., 1956—. Served with USN, 1946-47, 50-52. Mem. ABA, Am. Inst. C.P.A.s, Ohio Bar Assn., Cleve. Bar Assn., Ohio Soc. C.P.A.s. Avocation: marathon running. Home: 5057 Hampton Dr North Olmsted OH 44070 Office: Terminal W Park Bldg 4239 W 150th St and I-71 Cleveland OH 44135

TOMAZI, GEORGE DONALD, electrical engineer; b. St. Louis, Dec. 27, 1935; s. George and Sophia (Bogovich) T.; B.S. in E.E., U. Mo., Rolla, 1958, Profl. E.E. (hon.), 1970; M.B.A., St. Louis U., 1965, M.S. in E.E., 1971; m. Lois Marie Partenheimer, Feb. 1, 1958; children—Keith, Kent. Project engr. Union Electric Co., 1958-66; dir. corp. planning Gen. Steel Industries, 1966-70; exec. v.p. St. Louis Research Council, 1970-74; exec. v.p. Hercules Constrn. Co., St. Louis, 1974-75; project dir. Mallinckrodt, Inc., St. Louis, 1975—. Active Nat. Kidney Found.; bd. dirs. U. Mo. Devel. Council; elder Lutheran Ch. Served with U.S. Army, 1959-61. Registered profl. engr., Mo., Ill., Wash., Ohio, Calif. Mem. Nat. Soc. Profl. Engrs., IEEE, Japan-Am. Soc., AAAS, Am. Inst. Chem. Engrs., Am. Def. Preparedness Assn., U. Mo. Alumni Assn. (dir. 1972-78), Sigma Pi Frat. Clubs: Engrs. (v.p. 1981—), Rotary (St. Louis). Author: P-Science: The Role of Science in Society, 1972; The Link of Science and Religion, 1973. Home: Mallinckrodt Inc PO Box 5840 Florissant MO 63033 Office: 675 McDonnell Blvd Saint Louis MO 63134

TOMCZAK, STARR LYN, lawyer; b. Gaylord, Minn., Mar. 7, 1947; d. Edward Leo and Elaine Mae (Sylvester) T. B.A., Carleton Coll., 1969; M.A., Northwestern U., 1971; J.D., NYU, 1975. Bar: N.Y. 1978, Ill. 1983. Law clk. U.S. Ct. Appeals (4th cir.), Richmond, Va., 1976-77; assoc. Cravath, Swaine & Moore, N.Y.C., 1977-82; ptnr. Sonnenschein Carlin Nath & Rosenthal, Chgo., 1982—; vis. asst. prof. law NYU, N.Y.C., 1981. Editor, contbg. author: Corporate and Commercial Finance Agreements, 1984; editor NYU Law Rev., 1973-75. AAUW fellow NYU, N.Y.C., 1974-75. Mem. ABA (com. on devel. in bus. financing sect. corp., banking and bus. law), Chgo Bar Assn. (com. on corp. law), Ill. State Bar Assn., Order of Coif.

TOMHAVE, JONATHAN, artist, marketing executive; b. Hibbing, Minn., Dec. 6, 1946; s. Wesley G. and Anne (Rukavina) T.; m. Beverly Korstad, Oct. 15, 1977; children—Anna Mercedes, Dane Stefan. B.S., U. Minn., 1969, B.A. summa cum laude, 1971; M.A., U. Mich., 1972. Program coordinator U. Minn., Mpls., 1970-71, 72-73; pres. Jonathan Studios, Mpls., 1974—. Editor: (mag.) Academy, 1970-71. Illustrator: The Family Caregivers Manual, 1984. Mem. Am. Soc. Interior Designers, AIA, Phi Beta Kappa. Roman Catholic. Avocations: tennis; weight lifting; reading. Office: Jonathan Studios 1628 Oakways Wayzata MN 55391

TOMKO, CAROLE W., manufacturing company official; b. Columbus, Ohio, Dec. 3, 1954; d. Paul Arthur and Nancy Anne (McGinnis) Wherry; m. Michael Paul Tomko, Jr., May 9, 1981. B.A. in Sociology, U. Cin., 1977; J.D., Ohio State U., 1980. Bar: Ohio 1981. Legal intern State of Ohio, Columbus, 1979-81; employment supr. Federated Dept. Stores, Columbus, 1981-83; mgr. employee relations Standard Register Co., Newark, Ohio, 1983—. Mem. Newark Area Safety Council, 1983—, v.p., 1984—; mem. Pvt. Industry Council. Recipient Mortar Bd. award U. Cin., 1976. Mem. Central Ohio Personnel Assn., Personnel Mgmt. Assn. Home: 153 Clinton Heights Columbus OH 43202 Office: Standard Register Co PO Box 400 Newark OH 43055

TOMLINSON, FEROL MARTIN, educator; b. Woodstock, Ill., Sept. 21, 1931; d. Clinton E. and Minnie Ada (Tremere) Martin; m. Henry Sawyer Tomlinson, June 27, 1953; children—Lynn Tomlinson Lenker, Lee Eleanor. B.S., U. Ill., 1953; cert. reading specialist, Nat. Coll. Edn., 1966, cert. learning ctr. media specialist, 1977. Tchr. McHenry (Ill.) Sch. Dist., 1953-55, Johnsburg Sch. Dist. 12, 1958-63, tchr. remedial reading, 1965-67, dir. learning ctr., 1970-83; head tchr. Ringwood (Ill.) Sch., 1977-83; dir. Dist. 12 Summer Sch., 1965-68. Active McHenry Circle Club, 1953-72, 4-H; sec.-treas. Assoc. Milk Producers Ill., 1967-75; sec.-treas. McHenry County Lamb and Wool Producers, 1978-81. Named Outstanding Delta Zeta Alumnae, U. Ill., 1968; recipient service award Assoc. Milk Producers Ill., 1974; named Dist. 12 Tchr. of Yr.,

1978. Mem. U. Ill. Alumnae Assn., NEA, Ill. Edn. Assn., Johnsburg Tchr. Assn., (past officer), DAR, Delta Kappa Gamma (sec. 1972-76), Delta Zeta (past chpt. pres.). Republican. Methodist. Lodge: Eastern Star. Home: 2505 N Martin Rd McHenry IL 60050 Office: 4700 School Rd Ringwood IL 60072

TOMLINSON, HARRY JUSTIN, pharm. co. exec.; b. Indpls., Mar. 21, 1918; s. Harry M. and Mildred Elizabeth (Sparks) T.; student U. Mex., 1938; B.A., Ind. U., 1939; postgrad. U. Chile, 1940-41, N.Y. U., 1949-51; m. Christina Soulias, Dec. 1, 1951; children—Margaret Anne, Alice Emily, Christina Maria. Corr., UP, 1940-41, N.Y. Herald Tribune, S. Am., 1942-43; with W. R. Grace & Co., 1946-57, dir. public relations, N.Y.C., 1953-57; pres. Cuban-Am. Research & Investment, Havana Cuba, 1957-60; mgr. public relations Upjohn Co., Kalamazoo, 1961-75, adminstr. corp. contbns., 1975—. Served with U.S. Army, 1943-46. Mem. Public Relation Soc. Am., Explorers. Home: 10239 Fox Hollow Portage MI 49081 Office: 7000 Portage Rd Kalamazoo MI 49001

TOMS, MILLIAN MCKAY, accountant; b. Detroit, Jan. 27, 1942; d. Thomas Stanley and Mildred McKay (Stone) Dean; m. Richard A. Stan, July 20, 1963 (div. 1969) 1 dau., Michele Anne Stan. Grad. Internat. Accts. Soc., 1968. C.P.A., Mich. Sr. acct. Plante & Moran, C.P.A.s, Southfield, Mich., 1967-76; pvt. practice acctg., Royal Oak, Mich., 1976—. Contbr. articles to profl. jours. Vol. Detroit-Renaissance Found., Detroit, 1983-85 Mem. Mich. Assn. C.P.A.s (chmn. small practitioners 1981-83, vice chmn. 1979-81, chmn. monthly meeting group Southfield 1978—, vice chmn. pvt. cos. practice div. 1985—), Am. Women's Soc. C.P.A.s, Am. Inst. C.P.A.s, Royal Oak C. of C. (fin. com.). Clubs: Women's Econ., Toastmasters. Office: 521 9th St Royal Oak MI 48067

TONGREN, JOHN DAVID, computer security company executive, consultant; b. Erie, Pa., Dec. 1, 1942; s. John Corbin and Alice Jeanette (Jones) T.; m. Nancy Cowie, Aug. 28, 1965 (div. Dec. 1972); 1 son, Jon Eric; m. Kathleen McKay, Feb. 14, 1981. B.A., DePauw U., 1964; M.B.A., U. Mich., 1965. Cert. info. systems auditor. Cost study coordinator U. Louisville, 1971-72; sr. internal auditor Westinghouse Co., Columbus, Ohio, 1972-74, corp. audit mgr.-audit systems, Pitts., 1974-78; mgmt. cons. Alexander Grant & Co., Chgo., 1978-79, nat. dir. computer audit, 1979-81; pres. Tongren & Assocs., Chgo., 1981—; dir. edn. EDP Auditors Found., Chgo., 1983—. Vice-pres. Saddle Lake Property Owners Assn., Grand Junction, Mich., 1983. Mem. EDP Auditors Assn. (pres. Pitts. chpt. 1975-76), Inst. Internal Auditors, Nat. Assn. Accts., Inst. Mgmt. Acctg. (cert.). Office: Tongren & Assocs 502 W Roscoe St Suite 3N Chicago IL 60657

TONI, DOMENIC LOUIS, automotive technology company executive; b. Highland Park, Ill., June 17, 1950; s. Fred A. and Erma (Vigetti) T. A.B., Loyola U., Chgo., 1973; M.B.A., DePaul U., 1978. Internat. mktg. mgr. United Tech. Automotive, Breda, Netherlands, 1979—. Inventor anti-theft system. Mem. Fluid Power Soc. (cert.), Am. Assn. M.B.A. Execs. Roman Catholic.

TONTHAT, KIMSAM, music educator; b. Vietnam, Apr. 1, 1936; d. Kiem and Nghia (Hoang) Vu; m. Phu Tonthat, Mar. 11, 1957; children—Kim-Khanh Trent, K. Hoang Hickman, Cuong, Mike. Mus.B., Philippine Women's U., 1962; M.A., in Music, Denver U., 1969. Cert. music tchr., Nebr. Instr. piano Saigon Conservatory, 1963-66; music tchr. Am. schs., Saigon, 1963-65; now tchr. piano, voice, Kearney, Nebr. Mem. Nat. Tchrs. Assn., Nebr. Music tchrs. Assn., Kearney Music Tchrs. Assn. (program chmn.). Baptist. Clubs: Faculty Wives' Assn., Christian Women Assn. Home: 3311 10th Ave Kearney NE 68847

TOOPS, RICHARD ALAN, commodity broker, game company executive, music publisher; b. Apr. 1, 1942; s. Glynn Herbert and Mary Jane (Clampitt) Toops; m. Diane C. Kolettes; 1 son, Philip. Student Roosevelt U., Chgo., 1962-65. Pres. Flaky Crust Music Pubs., Chgo., 1968—; commodity broker Chgo. Bd. Trade, 1971-83; gen. ptnr. Total Games, Inc., Chgo., 1981—; stock index broker N.Y. Futures Exchange, 1982—; mem. Broadcast Music, Inc. Inventor board game Multinational; composer pop songs. Mem. N.Y. Futures Exchange, N.Y. Coffee, Sugar and Cocoa Exchange, Chgo. Bd. Trade.

TOOPS, TIMOTHY RAY, superintendent schools; b. Dayton, Ohio, Aug. 18, 1948; s. Warren George and Reecie Reva T.; m. Constance Kathleen Amon, Aug. 28, 1970; children—Michele, Laura. B.E., Marion Coll., 1970; M.Ed., Wright State U., 1976; Ed.S., U. Dayton, 1983. Cert. tchr., prin., supt., Ohio, 1983. Tchr., Troy (Ohio) City Schs., 1970-80; prin., dir. fed. programs Bethel Local Schs., Tipp City, Ohio, 1980—. Dir. Christian edn., bd. dirs. Methodist Ch. Served with AUS, 1970-77. Mem. Ohio Elem. Sch. Prins. Assn., Nat. Elem. Sch. Adminstrs., Phi Delta Kappa.

TOOT, J. F., JR., See *Who's Who in America,* 43rd edition.

TOOTIKIAN, LAWRENCE PETER, marketing research executive; b. Cleve., Dec. 18, 1931; s. Jack P. and Marie (Turabian) T.; B.B.S., Northwestern U., 1954; m. Christine Mink, Oct. 7, 1980. Research analyst WGN, Inc., Chgo., 1960-61; research mgr. WBBM-TV, Chgo., 1962-63, WLS-TV, Chgo., 1963-64, Fawcett Pubs., Chgo., 1967-72; pres. Research U.S.A., Inc., Chgo., 1972—. Served with U.S. Army, 1955-57. Mem. Am. Mktg. Assn., Nat. Agrl. Mktg. Assn., Soc. Nat. Assn. Pubs., Western Pubs. Assn., Chgo. Assn. Commerce and Industry, Chgo. Council Fgn. Relations, Fla. Mag. Assn., Am. Soc. Assn. Execs. Clubs: Executives, Chgo. Press, Chgo. Media Research (pres. 1976-77). Contbr. articles to profl. jours. Office: 100 E Ohio St Chicago IL 60611

TOPPER, JOSEPH RAY, See *Who's Who in America,* 43rd edition.

TOPPING, CHARLES G., JR., health care company executive; b. Bklyn., Dec. 6, 1940; s. Charles G. and Eleanor H. (Martin) T.; m. Elizabeth J. Sachs, June 21, 1969; children—Charles R., Brian D. B.A., Notre Dame, 1963, M.B.A., Columbia U., 1968. Dir. mktg. Oral B div. Cooper Labs., Bedford Hills, N.Y., 1971-73, gen. mgr. consumer div., Parsippany, N.J., 1973-75; v.p. mktg. Chayes Virginia, Evansville, Ind., 1975-78; gen. mgr. Teledyne Getz, Elk Grove Village, Ill., 1978-80, pres. 1980—. Served to lt. USN, 1963-67. Office: Teledyne Getz 1550 Greenleaf Ave Elk Grove Village IL 60007

TORCHINSKY, ALBERTO, mathematics educator, dean; b. Buenos Aires, Argentina, Mar. 9, 1944, came to U.S., 1966, naturalized, 1978; s. Naum and Sara (Gurvich) T.; m. Massoumeh Hosseinzadeh, Aug. 31, 1969; children—Cyrus, Darius. Ph.D. in Math., U. Chgo., 1971. Prof. math. Ind. U., Bloomington, 1975—; dean office Latino affairs, 1981—; dir. Educatec, Indpls., 1983-84. Author: Weighted Hardy Spaces, 1984; contbr. articles to profl. jours. Vice pres. Middle Sch. PTA, Bloomington, 1982-83; coordinating com. high sch. parent group, Bloomington, 1984—. Mem. Inst. Advanced Studies (Princeton, N.J.), Math. Analysis Centre (Canberra, Australia), Nat. Chicano Council on Higher Edn., Ind. Nat. Assn. Bilingual Edn. Home: 117 N Park Ridge Rd Bloomington IN 47405 Office: Office Latino Affairs Meml Hall W 109 Bloomington IN 47405

TORDOFF, HARRISON BRUCE, zoologist, ecology educator; b. Mechanicville, N.Y., Feb. 8, 1923; s. Harry F. and Ethel M. (Dormandy) T.; B.S., Cornell U., 1946; M.A., U. Mich., 1949, Ph.D., 1952; m. Jean Van Nostrand, July 3, 1946; children—Jeffrey, James. Curator Inst. of Jamaica, Kingston, 1946-47; instr. U. Kans., Lawrence, 1950-52, asst. prof., 1952-57, asso. prof., 1957; asst. prof. U. Mich., Ann Arbor, 1957-59, asso. prof., 1959-62, prof., 1962-70; prof. ecology U. Minn., Mpls., 1970—, dir. Bell Mus. Natural History, 1970-83. Served with USAAF, 1942-45. Decorated D.F.C., Air medals (17). Fellow Am. Ornithologists Union (pres. 1978-80); mem. Nature Conservancy (chmn. bd. Minn. chpt. 1975-77), Wilson Ornithol. Soc. (editor 1952-54), Cooper Ornithol. Soc. Contbr. articles to profl. jours. Home: 6 Chickadee Ln North Oaks Saint Paul MN 55110 Office: 10 Church St SE Minneapolis MN 55455

TORGERSON, LARRY KEITH, lawyer; b. Albert Lea, Minn., Aug. 25, 1935; s. Fritz G. and Lu (Hillman) T. B.A., Drake U., 1958, M.A., 1960, LL.B., 1963, J.D., 1968; M.A., Iowa U., 1962; LL.M., U. Minn., 1969; Columbia U., 1971, U. Mo., 1976; PMD, Harvard U., 1973, Ed.M., 1974. Bar: Minn. 1964, Wis. 1970, Iowa 1970, U.S. Tax Ct. 1971, U.S. Supreme Ct. 1972, U.S. Dist. Ct. Minn. 1964, U.S. Dist. Ct. (no. dist.) Iowa 1971, U.S. Dist. Ct. (ea. dist.) Wis. 1981, U.S. Ct. Appeals (8th cir.) 1981. Asst. corp. counsel First Bank Stock Corp., Mpls., 1963-67; v.p., trust officer Nat. City Bank, Mpls., 1967-69; sr. mem. Torgerson Law Firm, Northwood, Iowa, 1969—; chmn. Internat. Investments, Mpls., 1983—; pres. Torgerson Investments, Northwood, 1984—. Mem. ABA, Am. Judicature Soc., Iowa Bar Assn., Minn. Bar Assn., Wis Bar Assn., Mensa, Psi Chi, Circle K, Phi Alpha Delta, Omicron Delta Kappa, Pi Kappa Delta, Alpha Tau Omega, Pi Delta Epsilon, Alpha Kappa Delta. Lutheran.

TORKELSON, HENRY JOHN, educator, advisor; b. Hiawatha, Kans., Jan. 19, 1921; s. Tonie and Emilie (Hansen) T.; m. Mary Elizabeth Yaussi, Nov. 23, 1944. A.A.S., Iowa Lakes Community Coll., 1974; B.S., Mankato State U., 1975. Territory dir. Ford Motor Co., Kansas City, Mo., 1947-63, service rep., 1967-83; instr. Iowa Lakes Community Coll., Emmetsburg, 1963—; counselor, adv. bd. Served with U.S. Army, 1944-46. Recipient Nat. Master Tchr. Award, 1982. Mem. Am. Vocat. Assn., Iowa Vocat. Assn., Assn. Diesel Specialists, Am. Legion, VFW. Republican. Lutheran. Lodge: Masons. Home: Rural Route 2 Box 876 Deming NM 88030 Office: 3200 College Dr Emmetsburg IA 50536

TORRES, ANTHONY IGNATIUS, educator; b. Chgo., July 5, 1929; s. Anastasio and Bivina (Garcia) T.; B.S., No. Ill. U., 1954; M.Ed., DePaul U., 1956, Ed.S., 1958; Ed.D., Loyola U., Chgo., 1973. Tchr., Chgo. Public Schs., 1954-66; adminstr. Ill. Office of Edn., 1966-72; prin. Park Ridge (Ill.) Public Schs., 1972-76; dir. personnel Prairie State Coll., Chicago Heights, Ill., 1976-77; supt. schs., River Grove, Ill., 1977-79, Sauk Village, Ill., 1979—. Bd. govs. United Republican Fund; mem. Ill. Ednl. Facilities Authority, 1979—; bd. dirs. United Way Suburban Cook County, 1981—; bilingual chmn. Nat. Adv. and Coordination Council, 1984—. Recipient Those Who Excel award Ill. State Bd. Edn., 1978. Mem. Am. Assn. Sch. Adminstrs., Ill. Assn. Sch. Adminstrs., Am. Assn. U. Adminstrs., Phi Delta Kappa (Service award Loyola U. chpt.). Club: Columbia Yacht (Chgo.). Contbr. articles to profl. jours., column on edn. to local newspapers. Home: 1700 N North Park Chicago IL 60614

TORTORICI, JOSEPH ANTHONY, realtor; b. Cleve., June 16, 1935; s. Anthony Joseph and Janet (Ettari) T.; m. Roberta Sue Penn, May 17, 1957; children—Carole, Joan, Jean. B.A., Kent State U., 1957; A.A., Cuyahoga Community Coll., 1977. Territory mgr. Nestle Co., Inc., Cleve., 1958-61; div. mgr. Helene Curtis Inc., Cleve., 1961-63; regional mgr. Bacardi Imports, Inc., Cleve., 1963; realtor HGM-Hilltop Realtors, Cleve., 1977—. Named Hillcrest Rotarian of Yr., 1981. Mem. Nat. Assn. Realtors, Ohio Assn. Realtors, Cleve. Area Bd. Realtors, Distillers Reps. Orgn. Ohio (pres. 1973-74). Republican. Roman Catholic. Lodges: Fraternal Order of Police Assocs., KC, Rotary. Home: 1387 S Lyn Circle South Euclid OH 44121 Office: 5035 Mayfield Rd Lyndhurst OH 44124

TOSTO, LOUIS FRANK, retail lumber manager; b. Chgo., Mar. 20, 1948; s. Michael Angelo and Eleanor Elizabeth (Caster) T.; student William Penn Coll., Oskaloosa, Iowa, 1966-67, North Park Coll., Chgo., 1967-68, William R. Harper Community Coll., Palatine, Ill., 1968-70. Produce mgr. Jewel Cos. Inc., Chgo., 1964-72; sales rep. Internat. Playtex Corp., N.Y.C., 1972-74; asst. field supr. Southland Corp., Chgo., 1974-75; asst. mgr. Ace Hardware, Elk Grove Village, Ill., 1975-78; asst. store mgr. Edward Hines Lumber Co., Villa Park, Ill., 1978—. Vol. fireman Elk Grove Village Fire Dept., 1969—; bd. dirs. Elk Grove Community Services and Mental Health Bd., 1977-81; founder Elk Grove Village Jayteens, 1977—, Elk Grove Village's Village Fair, 1977—; chmn. Elk Grove Village Youth Services Com., 1978-81; co-mem. Congregation of Alexian Bros., Roman Cath. Ch., 1982—; chaplain Alexian Bros. Med. Ctr., Elk Grove Village, 1983—. Mem. Nat. Retail Hardware Assn., Elk Grove Village Jaycees (dir. 1976-78, pres. 1979-80, ambassador 1983—). Club: Elks. Home: 1507 Armstrong Ln Elk Grove Village IL 60007 Office: 600 N Villa Ave Villa Park IL 60181

TOTH, DAVID SCOTT, podiatrist; b. Cleve., Jan. 5, 1952; s. Joseph Francis and Margaret Judy (Kovacs) T.; B.A., Coll. of Wooster, 1973; D.P.M., Ohio Coll. Podiatric Medicine, 1977; m. Donna Georgene Dolch, July 19, 1975; children—David Scott, Jennifer Theresa. Resident Ohio Coll. Podiatric Medicine, 1978; asso. Dr. Marvin Z. Arnold, Maple Heights, Ohio, 1977-78; practice podiatric medicine, Brecksville, Ohio, 1978—; mem. staff Wayne Gen. Hosp., Geauga Community Hosp., Huron Rd. Hosp.; chmn. bd. K.T.E. Found.; lectr. profl. seminars; cons. Geauga Fitness Ctr., Chardon, Ohio, 1982—, Scandinavia Health Spa, Broadview Heights, Ohio, also various high sch. sports programs; guest appearances on local cable TV programs. Bd. dirs. Geauga County chpt. Am. Cancer Soc., 1983—. Recipient Order of Battered Boot award March of Dimes, 1975. Fellow Acad. Ambulatory Foot Surgery; mem. Am. Podiatry Assn., Ohio Podiatry Assn. (geriatrics com. 1984-85), N.E. Ohio Acad. Podiatric Medicine (sec. 1984-85, v.p. 1985-86), Am. Coll. Sports Medicine, Alumni Assn. Ohio Coll. Podiatric Medicine (dir. 1981—, trustee 1981-85, v.p. 1985-87 chmn. scholarship com.), Kappa Tau Epsilon (treas. 1976-77, Outstanding Alumni award), Pi Delta (treas., 1976-77). Roman Catholic. Contbr. articles on foot surgery to profl. jours. Home: 13050 Kenyon Dr Chesterland OH 44026 Office: 7650 Chippewa Rd Suite 205 Brecksville OH 44141 also 100 Parker Ct Chardon OH 44024

TOURNELL, WILLIAM NATHAN, dentist; b. Grand Rapids, Mich., Dec. 29, 1922; s. William Nathaniel and Hattie Christina (Appel) T.; m. Katherine Leona Drake, July 20, 1946; children—Nancy, Mark, Meredith, Miriam. A.S., Grand Rapids Jr. Coll., 1943; D.D.S., U. Mich., 1946. Lic. dentist, Mich. Bd. dirs. North Park Coll. and Theol. Sem., Chgo., 1967-71; deacon, chmn. bd. trustees Evang. Convenant Ch. Served to lt. (j.g.) USN, 1943-45, 1946-48. Mem. West Mich. Dental Soc. (chmn. peer rev. com. 1979-81), ADA, Kent County Dental Soc. Office: William N Tournell DDS 4500 Cascade Rd SE Grand Rapids MI 49506

TOURTILLOTT, ELEANOR ALICE, nurse, educational consultant; b. North Hampton, N.H., Mar. 28, 1909; d. Herbert Shaw and Sarah (Fife) T. Diploma Melrose Hosp. Sch. Nursing, Melrose, Mass., 1930; B.S., Tchrs. Coll., Columbia U., 1948, M.A., 1949; edn. specialist Wayne State U., 1962. Gen. pvt. duty nurse, Melrose, Mass., 1930-35; obstet. supr. Samaritan Hosp., Troy, N.Y., 1935-36, Meml. Hosp., Niagara Falls, N.Y., 1937-38, Lawrence Meml. Hosp., New London, Conn., 1939-42, New Eng. Hosp. for Women and Children, Boston, 1942-43; dir. H. W. Smith Sch. Practical Nursing, Syracuse, N.Y., 1949-53; dir., founder assoc. degree program Henry Ford Community Coll., Dearborn, Mich., 1953-74, project dir. USPHS, 1966-71; prin. cons., initial coordinator Wayne State U. Coll. Nursing, Detroit, 1975-78; cons. curriculum design, modular devel., instructional media Tourtillott Cons., Inc., Dearborn, Mich., 1974—; mem. Mich. Bd. Nursing, Lansing, 1966-73, chmn., 1970-72; condr. numerous workshops on curriculum design, instructional media at various colls., 1966—; mem. rev. com. for constrn. nurse tng. facilities, div. nursing USPHS, 1967-70, mem. nat. adv. council on nurse tng., 1972-76. Served to capt. Nurse Corps, U.S. Army, 1943-48; ETO. Recipient Disting. Alumnae award Tchrs. Coll. Columbia U., 1974, Spl. tribute 77th Legislature Mich., 1974, Disting. Alumnae award Wayne State U., 1975, Disting. Service award Henry Ford Community Coll., 1982. Mem. Melrose Hosp. Sch. Nursing Alumnae, Am. Nurses Assn., Nat. League Nursing (chmn. steering com. dept. assoc. degree programs 1965-67, bd. dirs. 1965-67, 71-73, mem. assembly constituent leagues 1971-73, council assoc. degree programs citation 1974), Mich. League for Nursing (pres. 1969-71), Tchrs. Coll. Alumnae Assn., Wayne State U. Alumnae Assn., Phi Lambda Theta, Kappa Delta Pi. Republican. Contbg. author: Patient Assessment-History and Physical Examination, 1977-81; contbr., chpts., articles, speeches to profl. publs.

TOUSEY, LOUANN HOLLY, nurse administrator; b. Oconto Falls, Wis., Dec. 5, 1943; d. Gordon John and Ethel Judith (Kopitzke) T.; m. Richard E. Orchard, Aug. 23, 1964 (div.); 1 dau., Kaia Michelle. Lic. practical nurse Hinsdale (Ill.) Sanitarium and Hosp., 1963; B.S. in Nursing, U. Wis., 1974; M.S. in Health Services Adminstrn., Coll. St. Francis, Joliet, Ill., 1984. Emergency and surgery supr. Community Meml. Hosp., Oconto Falls, 1963-71; night supr. Manor House of Madison Nursing Home (Wis.), 1975; shift supr. Algoma (Wis.) Meml. Hosp. and Long Term Care Unit, 1975-76, dir. patient care services, 1976-82; dir. nursing service Langlade Meml. Hosp., Antigo, Wis., 1982—; cons. nursing adminstrn. Rural Health Systems, Chgo. Chairperson Kewaunee County (Wis.) Health Careers Adv. Com., 1978-82. Mem. Am. Orgn. Nurse Execs., Wis. Orgn. Nurse Execs., Am. Soc. Nursing Service Adminstrs., Wis. Soc. Nursing Service Adminstrs. (sec. 1981-82, pres. 1984-86), Am. Nurses Assn. (cert. nurse adminstr.), Wis. Nurses Assn., Northeastern Wis. Emergency Med. Services Council, Am. Indian Nurses Assn., Dist. 4 Nursing Service Council for Long Term Care. Home: 1106 Arctic St Antigo WI 54409 Office: Langlade Meml Hosp 112 E 5th Ave Antigo WI 54409

TOUSSAINT, JACK LAYTON, hospital administrator; b. Allerton, Iowa, Nov. 25, 1924; s. Harry Lorenz and Verda Leota (Layton) T.; m. Betty Lucille Eppel, Nov. 24, 1944 (dec. Mar. 1969); children—John Steven, Carol Diane; m. Diane Nadine Bernard, Mar. 18, 1978. B.S. in Commerce, State U. Iowa, 1949, M.A. in Hosp. Adminstrn., 1954. Adminstrn. intern U. Iowa, Iowa City, 1953-54, adminstrn. resident, 1954-55, dir. admitting, research assoc., 1955-62; asst. supt. St. Luke's Hosp., Cedar Rapids, Iowa, 1963-75, assoc. dir., 1975-80, sr. v.p., 1980—; bd. dirs. Iowa Statewide Family Practice Tng. Program, Iowa City, 1975-79, Family Service Agency, Cedar Rapids, 1974-79, Dental Health Clinic, Cedar Rapids, 1978—, St. Paul's United Meth. Ch., Cedar Rapids, 1984—; active United Way, 1970; mem. Cedar Rapids Care Ctr. Rev. Com., 1978, Orthopedic Physicians Asst. Adv. Com. 1972-79; mem. adv. com. County Health Ctr. Medically Indigent, 1977. Served with U.S. Army, 1943-46. Mem. Am. Coll. Hosp. Adminstrs., Am. Hosp. Assn. (life), Pi Omega Pi. Republican. Methodist. Avocations: travel; fishing; reading. Home: 435 Memorial Dr SE Cedar Rapids IA 52403 Office: St. Luke's Hosp 1026 A Ave NE Cedar Rapids IA 52402

TOW, MARK RANDALL, pharmacist; b. Rensselaer, Ind., May 21, 1952; s. Ralph F. and Gladys May (Duley) T.; m. Cathie J. White, Nov. 27, 1970 (div. 1972); 1 son, John Mark; m. Donna Jean Hayden, Dec. 30, 1972; children—Jaclyn Suzanne, Jillian Leanne. Student U.S. Coast Guard Acad., 1970; B.S. in Pharmacy, Purdue U., 1975. Registered pharmacist. Apprentice pharmacist Ribordy Drug, Knox, Ind., 1972-75; asst. mgr. Hook's Drugs, Winamac, Ind., 1975-78, mgr., 1978-85, buyer, promotions coordinator, 1985—; cons. pharmacist Winamac Nursing Home, 1978-82; extern instr. Sch. Pharmacy, Purdue U., 1980-84. Republican. Nazarene. Lodge: Rotary (past sec., treas., v.p., pres. 1984—). Office: Hook Drug Co Inc 2800 Enterprise St Indianapolis IN 46226

TOWE, NANCY ELLEN CARPENTER, electronics manufacturing company executive; b. Kildav, Ky., July 28, 1941; d. John Henry and Nora Jenny (Snyder) Carpenter; m. Marshall Towe, Sr., Dec. 1, 1958 (div. 1981); children—Marshall, Jr., Michael Lee. A.A.S. in Mktg. Mid-Mgmt., McHenry Community Coll., 1981; B.A. in Orgnl. Psychology, Nat. Coll. Edn., 1982. Switchboard operator Malibu Answering Service, Chgo., 1964-71; corr. Seaboard Life Ins. Co., Chgo., 1972-74; sales corr. Chgo. Miniature div. Gen Instrument Co., Chgo., 1975-77; product mgr. Oak Industries, Crystal Lake, Ill., 1978-82; pres., chief exec. officer Lamptronix Co., Ltd., Crystal Lake, 1982—; speaker in field. Den mother Chgo Area council Boy Scouts Am., 1970-75; active Pierce Sch. PTA, Chgo., 1973; mem. Lake in the Hills Property Owners Assn., 1978-82; founder Woodstock Ctr. for Women, Ill., 1982. Recipient Disting. Service scroll Ill. Congress PTA, 1973. Mem. Women in Electronics, Nat. Network of Women in Sales, Aerospace Lighting Inst., Crystal Lake C. of C. (bd. dirs.). Congregationalist. Home: 102 Hunter's Path Lake in the Hills IL 60102 Office: Lamptronix Co Ltd 85 N Williams Crystal Lake IL 60102

TOWER, RAYMOND C., chemical executive; b. N.Y.C., Feb. 20, 1925; s. Raymond C. and Elinor (Donovan) T.; B.S., Yale U., 1945; m. Jaclyn Bauerline, Feb. 7, 1948; children—Raymond, Patricia, Christopher, Robert, Mary, Michael, Victoria. Research chemist Westvaco Chem. Co., 1946-48; various mktg.and mgmt. positions FMC Corp., N.Y.C., 1948-67, exec. v.p., mgr. chem. group, 1967-77, pres. FMC Corp., Chgo., 1977—, also dir.; dir. Firestone Tire & Rubber Co., Household Internat., Evanston Hosp. Corp., Inland Steel Co.; trustee 5 investment trusts under mgmt. of Goldman Sachs & Co. Trustee, Ill. Inst. Tech.; bd. govs. IIT Research Inst.; assoc. Northwestern U.; bd. dirs. United Way of Chgo. Served to lt. USNR, 1944-46, 51-53. Mem. Chem. Mfrs. Assn., Chgo. Assn. Commerce and Industry (dir.), Machinery and Allied Products Inst. (exec. com.), Nat. Safety Council (trustee), Soc. Chem. Industry, Aerospace Industries Assn. (bd. govs.), Chgo. Council Fgn. Relations (mem. Chgo. com.), Alpha Chi Sigma. Clubs: Chicago, Commercial, Economic, Mid-America (Chgo.); Glen View. Office: FMC Corp 200 E Randolph Dr Chicago IL 60601

TOWNER, LAWRENCE WILLIAM, historian, librarian; b. St. Paul, Sept. 10, 1921; s. Earl Chadwick and Cornelia (Mallum) T.; B.A., Cornell Coll., Mt. Vernon, Iowa, 1942, L.H.D., 1965; M.A., Northwestern U., 1950, Ph.D. (Hearst Found. fellow), 1955, L.H.D., 1965; LL.D., Lake Forest Coll., 1965; m. Rachel Eleanor Bauman, Nov. 28, 1943; children—Wendy Kay Towner Yanikoski, Kristin Anne Towner Moses, Lawrence Baumann (dec.), Elizabeth Gail, Peter Mallum, Michael Chadwick. History master Chgo. Latin Sch., 1946-47; instr., asst. prof. history Mass. Inst. Tech., Cambridge, 1950-55; asso. prof. history Coll. William and Mary, 1955-62; librarian and dir. Newberry Library, Chgo., 1962—, pres., 1975—. Vis. prof. Northwestern U., summer 1957, 68-72; dir. Inst. for Hist. and Archival Mgmt., Radcliffe Coll., Harvard U., 1959; Center for Study History of Liberty In Am. fellow Harvard U. 1961-62. Chmn. Williamsburg Area Interracial Study Group, 1960-61; mem. Ill. Humanities Council, 1974-78, chmn., 1976-78; mem. adv. bd. Who's Who in Am.; trustee Grinnell (Iowa) Coll., 1966-72, Chgo. Latin Sch., 1970-72, Mus. Contemporary Art, 1972-75; mem. council Eleutherian Mills-Hagley Found., 1976-79, Fedn. Pub. Programs in Humanities, 1977-79; adv. bd. Papers of George Washington, Papers of Benjamin Franklin, Papers of James Madison. Served to 1st lt., pilot AUS, 1943-46. Mem. Am. Hist. Assn. (mem. council 1973-75), Orgn. Am. Historians, Am. Antiquarian Soc., Colonial Soc. Mass., Mass. Hist. Soc., Bibliog. Soc. Am., Modern Poetry Assn. (trustee, pres.). Clubs: Harvard (N.Y.C.); Columbia Yacht, Cosmos, Caxton, Econ., Tavern, Arts. Author: An Uncommon Collection of Uncommon Collections: The Newberry Library, 1970, 76; (with A.N.L. Munby) The Flow of Books and Manuscripts, 1969. Editor: William and Mary Quar.: A Mag. of Early Am. History, 1955-62, A Summary View of the Rights of British America by Thomas Jefferson, 1976; bd. editors Jour. Am. History, 1965-68, America, History and Life, 1965-82. Office: 60 W Walton St Chicago IL 60610

TOWNSEND, EARL CUNNINGHAM, JR., lawyer, author, composer; b. Indpls., Nov. 9, 1914; s. Earl Cunningham and Besse (Kuhn) T.; Rector scholar De Pauw U., 1932-34; A.B., U. Mich., 1936, J.D., 1939; m. Emily Macnab, Apr. 3, 1947; children—Starr (Mrs. John R. Laughlin), Vicki M. (Mrs. Christopher Katterjohn), Julia E. (Mrs. Edward Goodrich Dunn, Jr.), Earl Cunningham III, Clyde G. Bar: Ind. 1939, Mich. 1973, U.S. Supreme Ct., U.S. Ct. Appeals (4th, 6th, 7th cirs.), U.S. Dist. Ct. (no. and so. dists.) Ind., U.S. Dist. Ct. (ea. dist.) Va., U.S. Dist. Ct. (ea. dist.) Mich.; diplomate Am. Bd. Trial Advocates (Ind. pres. 1982-85). Sr. ptnr., founder Townsend & Townsend, Indpls., 1940-69, Townsend, Hovde & Townsend, Indpls., 1970-79, Townsend, Hovde, Townsend & Montross, 1979-85; Townsend, Yosha & Cline, 1985—; ptnr. Townsend, Laughlin & Townsend, Roscommon, Mich., 1973—; dep. prosecutor, Marion County, Ind., 1942-44; radio-TV announcer WIRE, WFBM, WFBM-TV, Indpls., 1940-49, 1st TV announcer 500 mile race, 1949, 50; Big Ten basketball referee, 1940-47; lectr. trial tactics U. Notre Dame, Ind. U., U. Mich., 1968-79; owner Tropical Isle Palm Tree Farms, Key Biscayne, Fla., Terney-Townsend Historic House, Roscommon, Mich.; founder, v.p., treas. Am. Underwriters, Inc., Am. Interinsurance Exchange, 1965-70; mem. Com. to Revise Ind. Supreme Ct. Pattern Jury Instructions, 1975-84; faculty chmn. personal injury trials in Ind., Ind. Continuing Legal Edn. Forum, Ind. Bar Found., Ind. U. Sch. Law, Indpls. and Bloomington, U. Notre Dame, Valparaiso U. Sch. Law, 1981. Founder, life fellow Roscoe Pound Am. Trial Lawyers Found., Cambridge, Mass.; co-founder, dir. Meridian St. Found.; mem. fin. and bldg. coms., bd. dirs., later life trustee Indpls. Mus. Art; trustee Cathedral High Sch., Indpls., Ind. State Mus.; fellow Meth. Hosp. Found.; trustee Cale J. Holder Scholarship Found., Ind. U. Law Sch., mem. dean's council, 1984—. Recipient Ind. Univ. Writers Conf. award, 1960; Hanson H Anderson medal of honor Arsenal Tech. Schs., Indpls., 1971; named to Council Sagamores of Wabash, 1969, Ind. Basketball Hall of Fame; hon. chief Black River-Swan Creek Saginaw-Chippewa Indian tribe, 1971—. Fellow Ind. Coll. Trial Lawyers (pres. 1984—), Internat. Acad. Trial Lawyers, Internat. Soc. Barristers; mem. Ind. Trial Lawyers Assn. (pres. 1963-64, life dir.), Am. (com. trial techniques 1964-76, com. aviation and space 1977—, tort and ins. practice com. 1985—), Ind. State (del. 1977-79, aviation and space law com. 1982—), Indpls., 34th Jud. Circuit Mich. bar assns., State Bar Mich., Am. Judicature Soc., Assn. Am. Trial Lawyers (v.p. Ind. 1959-60, bd. govs. 7th jud. circuit 1966-68, asso. editor Jour. 1964-80), Bar Assn. 7th Fed. Circuit, Lawyers Assn. Indpls., Am. Arbitration Assn. (nat. panel), Ind. Archeol. Soc. (founder, pres.), Genuine Indian Relic Soc. (co-founder, chmn. frauds com.), Marion County/Indpls. Hist. Soc. (life dir.), Ind. Hist. Soc., Trowel and Brush Soc. (hon.) U. Mich. Pres.'s Club, U. Mich. Victors Club (charter), Soc. Mayflower Descs. (gov. 1947-49), Key Biscayne C. of C. (bd. dirs.), ASCAP, Indpls. C. of C., Ind. C. of C., Delta Kappa Epsilon, Phi Kappa Phi. Republican. Methodist. Clubs: Players; U. Mich. (local pres. 1950); Columbia; Indianapolis Athletic; Key Biscayne Yacht; Masons (32 deg., Shriner). Author: Birdstones of the North

American Indian, 1959; also articles in legal and archeol. fields; composer Moon of Halloween. Home: 5008 N Meridian St Indianapolis IN 46208 Office: 151 E Market St Indianapolis IN 46204 also 603 Lake St Roscommon MI 48653

TOWNSEND, HAROLD GUYON, JR., publishing company executive; b. Chgo., Apr. 11, 1924; s. Harold Guyon and Anne Louise (Robb) T.; A.B., Cornell U., 1948; m. Margaret Jeanne Keller, July 28, 1951; children—Jessica, Julie, Harold Guyon III. Advt. salesman Chgo. Tribune, 1948-51; gen. mgr. Keller-Heartt Co., Clarendon Hills, Ill., 1951-62; pub. Santa Clara (Calif.) Jour., 1962-64; pres., pub. Dispatch-Tribune newspaper Townsend Communications, Inc., Kansas City, Mo., 1964—; dir. United Mo. City Bank. Chmn., Suburban Newspaper Research Commn., 1974—; dir. Certified Audit Bur. of Circulation, 1968-72. del. Rep. Nat. Conv., 1960; chmn. Mission Hills Rep. Com., 1966-77; bd. dirs. Kansas City Jr. Achievement, 1966-68, Kansas City council Girl Scouts U.S.A., 1969-71, Kansas City council Boy Scouts Am., 1974, Kansas City chpt. ARC, 1973-79, Kansas City Starlight Theater, Clay County (Mo.) Indsl. Commn.; treas., trustee Park Coll., Parkville, Mo., 1970-78. Mem. adv. com. North Kansas City Hosp.; bd. dirs. Taxpayers Research of Mo., 1978—, Nelson Gallery Friends of Art, 1980-85. Served with inf. AUS, World War II. Mem. Kansas City Advt. and Sales Club, Kansas City Press Club, Suburban Press Found. (pres. 1969-71), Suburban Newspapers Am. (pres. 1976-77), Kansas City Printing Industries Assn. (pres., dir.), Printing Industries of Am. (pres. non-heatset web sect. 1980-82), North Kansas City C. of C. (dir., pres. 1964-70), Univ. Assocs. (treas. 1977-80), Sigma Delta Chi, Pi Delta Epsilon, Phi Kappa Psi. Clubs: University (treas. 1977); Indian Hills Country; Hinsdale (Ill.) Golf; Mission Valley Country, Field (Sarasota, Fla.). Home: 6321 Norwood Rd Mission Hills KS 66208 Office: 7007 NE Parvin Rd Kansas City MO 64117

TOWNSEND, J. RUSSELL, JR., insurance executive; b. Cedar Rapids, Iowa, Nov. 21, 1910; s. J. Russell and Mabel (Ferguson) T.; B.S., Butler U., 1931; M.B.A., U. Pa., 1933; m. Virginia Holt, Aug. 1, 1938; 1 son, John Holt. Registered health underwriter. Field asst. Equitable Life Ins. Co. Iowa, 1933-50, gen. agt., 1950-69, gen. agt. emeritus, 1969—; mng. asso. J. Russell Townsend & Assos., 1969—; assoc. prof. emeritus bus. adminstrn. Butler U., Indpls., 1982; cons. Ind. Dept. Ins., 1948-50; mem. Ind. Ho. of Reps., 1946-48, Ind. Senate, 1956-64; lectr., writer ins. field. Chmn. Indpls. Bicentennial Com., 1975-76; pres. Indpls. Jaycees, 1940. Served with USNR, 1942-46; lt. comdr. Res. ret. Recipient 25-year teaching award Am. Coll. C.L.U.s, 1960; Alumni Achievement award Butler U., 1979. Mem. Indpls. chpt. C.L.U.s (past pres.), Ind. Life Underwriters Assn. (past v.p.), Ret. Officers Assn. (past pres. Indpls. chpt.), Ind. Soc. Assn. Execs., Naval Res. Assn., Navy League U.S., Am. Soc. C.L.U.'s, AAUP, Am. Soc. Risk and Ins., Ind. Acad. Sci., Sales and Marketing Execs. Council, U.S. Naval Inst., Phi Delta Theta (past pres. Indpls. alumni club). Republican. Presbyterian. Clubs: Columbia, Meridian Hills Country, Indpls. Literary, Kiwanis (dir. Ind. Found., lt. gov. Ind. dist. internat. 1975-76), Indpls. Press, Ft. Harrison Officers, Masons, Sojourners (Indpls); Army and Navy (Washington); Crystal Downs Country (Frankfort, Mich.) Contbr. articles to trade mags. Home: 8244 N Pennsylvania St Indianapolis IN 46240 Office: 906 Investors Trust Bldg 107 N Pennsylvania St Indianapolis IN 46204

TOWNSEND, PAMELA GWIN, business educator; b. Dallas, Aug. 24, 1945; d. William Thomas and Doris (Gwin) T.; B.A. with distinction in Econs. (Univ. scholar), U. Mo., Kansas City, 1977, M.B.A. (Outstanding Acctg. Grad.), 1980; m. Rae R. Jacobs, July 5, 1975. Real estate sales assoc. KEW Realtors, Austin, Tex., 1967-70; staff mktg. asst. Lincoln Property Co., Dallas, 1970-72; dir. mktg. Commonwealth Devel. Co., Dallas, 1972-73; v.p. market analysis Fin. Corp. N.Am., Kansas City, 1973-75; asst. prof., dir. dept. acctg. Park Coll., Parkville, Mo., 1980—, on leave to Kansas U. Ph.D. program. Coordinator, IRS VITA Program; mem. Friends of Art, Nelson Gallery; mem. Mo. Repertory Theater Guild; Underwriter Folly Theater. C.P.A., Kans.; lic. real estate broker, Tex., Mo., Kans. Mem. Am. Inst. C.P.A.s, Kans. Soc. C.P.A.s, Mo. Soc. C.P.A.s, Am. Acctg. Assn., Nat. Assn. Accts., Beta Alpha Psi Alumnae (pres. 1982), Beta Gamma Sigma, Phi Kappa Phi, Omicron Delta Epsilon, Alpha Chi Omega, Mortar Bd. Episcopalian. Columnist, Tax Tips, Platte County Gazette, 1981. Home: 2604 University St Lawrence KS 66044 Office: Summerfield Hall U Kans Lawrence KS 66044

TOWNSEND, RICHARD ARTHUR, state financial official; b. Lincoln, Ill., Jan. 10, 1958; s. Henry Albert and Lillian (Washington) T.; m. Deborah Elaine Hitchcock, May 14, 1983; 1 dau., Britney Patrice. B.B.A., Western Mich. U., 1980; A.A. in Fin., Davenport Bus. Coll., Grand Rapids, Mich., 1982; postgrad. M.B.A. work Grand Valley State Coll. Asst. br. mgr. Union Bank & Trust Co. N.A., Grand Rapids, 1980-83, br. bank mgr., 1983-84; asst. debt adminstr. Dept. Treasury, State of Mich., Lansing, 1984—. Vice chmn. program dept. social services Youth Companionship Program, Grand Rapids, 1981-82; asst. sec., treas. Paul I. Philips Block Orgn., Grand Rapids, 1982; advisor, sponsor Kent County Jr. Achievement, Grand Rapids, 1983. Baptist. Avocations: racquetball; basketball; tennis; bowling. Home: 6211 Beechfield Dr Lansing MI 48910 Office: Mich Dept of Treasury 1st Floor Treasury Bldg PO Box 15128 Lansing MI 48901

TOWNSEND, WILLIAM BEACH, consultant health and welfare; b. Cleve., Mar. 16, 1910; s. Henry Burton and Helen (Malley) T.; B.A., Western Res. U., 1932, M.A., 1948; m. Colette Marie Sheehan, Dec. 28, 1937; 1 son, Eric Beach. Employment supr. Cleve. Asso. Charities, 1933-40; exec. dir. Cleve. Soc. Crippled Children, 1940-79; adminstr. William B. Townsend Rehab. Inst. (formerly Heman Rehab. Inst.), 1940-79. Registrar of Camp Cheerful, 1940-79; cons. to aux. Soc. for Crippled Children, 1942-79; cons. Lakewood (Ohio) Draft Bd., 1948— (fed. commendation award for 15 years service); adv. bd. Cuyahoga Assn. Retarded Children; budget com. Health Council; mem. occupational planning com. Ohio Citizens Council for Health and Welfare; v.p. Madonna Hall, 1954-56; pres. Cath. Youth Orgn., 1938-42; trustee Cath. Child Guidance Bur., 1956-62; gov. Lakewood Safety Council; pres. Citizens Juvenile Council; dir. Council Retarded Child, 1952-55, Cleve. Health Council, 1947—, Council Human Relations, 1955—. Treas. Mayor's Com. Employment of Handicapped, 1944-62; adviser F.S.R.C., Rehab. Internat., United Torch Services-Speakers' Bur. Agy.; nat. trustee Nat. Council for Handicapped; mem. Buckeye-Woodland Community Congress, No. Ohio Area Coordinating Com., United Torch Exec. Adv. Com., 1975—; sec.-gen. Stop the Arms Race; mem. Cleve. Sr. Council. Served with Transp. Corps, AUS, 1945-46; PTO. Recipient distinguished service award and Man of year award Cleve. and U.S. Jaycees, 1943; 25-Year commendation U.S. Selective Service, 1973; 1st Ann. Dedicated Service award Nat. Council for Handicapped, 1975; proclamation Mayor of Lakewood, 1975; proclamation of congratulations City of Cleve., 1975; resolution of commendation Ohio Ho. of Reps., 1975; resolution United Way Sers., 1978; plaque Am. Legion, 1978; resolution U.S. Ho. of Reps., others. Mem. Council for Exceptional Children, Nat. Conf. Social Work, Am. Camping Assn. (sec. Ohio sect.), Ohio Rural Health Assn., Easter Seal Execs. Assn., Western Res. U. Alumni Assn., Early Settlers Assn. (life.), Advt. Fedn. Am., Cleve. Counsellors Assn. (pres.), Para-Progressives (hon.), Am. Legion, Cleve. Advt. Club, Nat. Publicity Council, Rehab. Internat. (U.S. del. Stockholm Conv. 1951), Cleve. C. of C., Lake Erie Jr. Mus., Ohio Assn. Workers for Blind, Rehab. Internat., Cleve. Council World Affairs, Greater Cleve. Growth Assn., Fedn. for Community Services (rep. assembly), Friends Cleve. Zoo, Cleve. Health Mus., Nat., Ohio (exec. bd. 1958—) rehab. assns., Cleve. Citizens League, Cleve. Mus. Art, Am. Acad., Am. Mus. Natural History, New Eng. Soc. Western Res. (life), Western Res., Lakewood (dir.), 120 Cleve. hist. socs., League Ohio Sportsmen, Frostville Mus., Cleve. Inst. Music, Human Soc. U.S., Nat. Council Cath. Men, Postal Commemorative Soc., New Eng. Soc. Western Reserve, Smithsonian Instn., Am. Acad. Polit. and Social Sci., Council Rehab. Center Execs., Defenders of Wildlife, Olmsted Hist. Soc., Cleve. Ballet, Garfield Perry Stamp Club, Am. Legion. Roman Catholic. Clubs: City, Mid-Day, Communicators, Auto, Rotary (Cleve.). Home: 1107 Nicholson Ave Lakewood OH 44107

TOZZER, JACK CARL, civil engr., surveyor; b. Marion, Ohio, Jan. 5, 1922; s. Carl Henry and Henrietta (Schellenbaum) T.; B.C.E., Ohio No. U., 1944; children—Brent Jack, Hal Jack; m. Aleta C. Lehner, July 14, 1974. Pres. firm Tozzer & Assos. Inc., Marion, 1948—; county engr. Marion County, Ohio, 1964—; city engr. Marion, 1959, Galion, Ohio, 1960—. Cons. civil engr. Mem. consultants bd. Coll. Engring. Ohio No. U., 1970, recipient Order of Engr., 1971; v.p. Marion Community Improvement Corp.; mem. Marion County Regional Planning Commn. Served with USNR, 1944-46. Registered profl. engr., Ohio, Fla., registered surveyor, Ohio. Fellow ASCE; mem. Nat. Soc. Profl. Engrs., Marion C. of C., Cons. Engrs. Ohio, Profl. Land Surveyors Ohio, Ohio, Marion County (past dir.) hist. socs., Delta Sigma Phi. Lutheran (past trustee). Elk. Home: 307 Forest Lawn Blvd Marion OH 43302 Office: 299 Clover Ave Marion OH 43302

TRABAND, CHARLES MARLOW, lawyer; b. Sandusky, Ohio, Feb. 8, 1950; s. Charles Marlow and Margaret Jean (Mattey) T.; m. Margaret Mary Fitzgerald, Sept. 9, 1972; children—Joseph Matthew, Kathryn Marlow, Margaret Anna. B.A., U. Toledo, 1972, J.D., 1977. Bar: Ohio 1978. Indsl. relations counsel Owens-Corning Fiberglas, Toledo, 1977-82, indsl. relations adviser, 1982—. UAW Walter Reuther scholar U. Toledo, 1977. Mem. ABA, Ohio Bar Assn., Toledo Bar Assn. Republican. Roman Catholic. Office: Owens-Corning Fiberglas Fiberglas Tower-3 Toledo OH 43659

TRACY, EUGENE ARTHUR, utility executive; b. Oak Park, Ill., Dec. 14, 1927; s. Arthur Huntington and Emily Margaret (Groff) T.; B.S. in Bus. Adminstrn., Northwestern U., 1951; M.B.A., DePaul U., Chgo., 1958; m. Irene Walburga Kacin, June 30, 1951; children—Glen Eugene, Diane Emily Tracy Champion, Janet Freda. With Peoples Gas Light & Coke Co., Chgo., 1951—, pres., 1977—, chmn., chief exec. officer, 1981—, also dir.; pres., dir. North Shore Gas Co., Waukegan, Ill., 1977—, chmn., chief exec. officer, 1981—, also dir.; chmn., pres., chief exec. officer Peoples Energy Corp., Chgo., 1981—, also dir. Bd. dirs. Central YMCA Community Coll., Chgo., 1971—, treas., 1972-77, chmn. bd., 1977-79, vice chmn. bd., 1981—; treas. St. David's Episcopal Ch., Glenview, Ill., 1970-79; bd. dirs. Civic Fedn. Chgo., 1976-77, Jr. Achievement, Chgo., 1978—; trustee Taxpayers Fedn. Ill., 1973-77; trustee Inst. Gas Tech., Chgo., 1978—, chmn., 1984—; trustee Mus. Sci. and Industry, Chgo., 1981—, De Paul U., 1982—; bd. dirs. United Way of Chgo., 1983—. Served with U.S. Army, 1946-47. Mem. Am. (dir. 1979-85), Midwest (dir., chmn. 1985—) gas assns., Chgo. Assn. Commerce and Industry (dir. 1979-85, dir. Central Area com. 1981-85). Clubs: Economic, University, Chicago, Comml. (Chgo.); Sunset Ridge Country (Northbrook, Ill.). Office: 122 S Michigan Ave Chicago IL 60603

TRACY, LOUIS EDWARD, lawyer; b. Franklin, Ohio, May 5, 1927; s. John Edward and Ruby (Burkhardt) T.; m. Estelle Mary Purdy, Dec. 1, 1951; children—John P., Guy R., Bridget A., Mary C. J.D., Notre Dame U., 1949, Ph.D., 1951. Bar: Ohio 1952, U.S. Dist. Ct. (so. dist.) Ohio 1953. Dir. law City West Carrollton, Ohio, 1952-67; founder, sr. ptnr. Tracy & Tracy, 1967—; officer, dir. Lake of the Woods Club, Farmersville, Ohio. Pres. West Carrollton Civic Improvement Corp., 1982—. Recipient Cert. Appreciation award Miami Valley council Boy Scouts Am., 1961, City West Carrollton, 1968. Mem. Dayton Bar Assn., C. of C. (bd. dirs. 1955). Roman Catholic. Lodges: Rotary, K.C., Masons, Shriners. Home: 26 E Blossom Hill Rd West Carrollton OH 45449 Office: PO Box 156 31 E Central Ave West Carrollton OH 45449

TRACY, MARY ELIZABETH, librarian; b. Joliet, Ill., Aug. 18, 1922; d. Charles Joseph and Catherine (Fay) Tracy; B.A. cum laude, Coll. St. Francis, 1944; M.A., Rosary Coll., 1958. Tchr., librarian Joliet pub. schs., 1944-52, 54-61, Am. schs., Bremerhaven and Frankfurt, Germany, 1952-54; librarian Central Campus Joliet Twp. High Sch., 1961—; chmn. Joliet Local Archives Com., 1981-83. Sec., v.p., and mem. adv. bd. Alumnae of the Coll. of St. Francis. Mem. Am., Ill. Library Assns., Ill. Assn. for Media in Edn., Ill. Audio-Visual Assn., Will County Library/Media Assn. (pres. 1976), Joliet Jr. Cath. Woman's League (pres. 1950-51). Home: 1010 Glenwood Ave Joliet IL 60435 Office: 201 E Jefferson St Joliet IL 60432

TRAEGER, BARBARA SHIELDS (MRS. JOHN E. TRAEGER), hospital official; b. Pitts., Oct. 19, 1932; d. Marshall Charles and Margaret Helen (Ward) Shields; B.A. in English, Ripon Coll., 1954; postgrad. U. Chgo., 1971; m. John E. Traeger, Apr. 30, 1971; children by previous marriage—Cynthia, Charles R., Henry. Dir. pub. relations Chgo. unit Am. Cancer Soc., 1964-65; asst. bur. pub. info. Am. Hosp. Assn., Chgo., 1966-68; dir. pub. relations U. Chgo. Hosps. and Clinics, 1968-72; dir. pub. relations Evanston Hosp. Corp., Ill., 1972—; mem. adv. bd. Profiles in Mktg. Recipient excellence award Am. Inst. Graphic Arts, 1975, 76, recognition of achievement Nat. Publs. Assn., 1975, MacEachern award, 1972, 73, 74, 75, 79, 80, 85, award Type Dirs. Club, 1970, excellence award Modern Publicity, 1972; Outstanding Editorial Achievement award Chgo. Assn. Bus. Communicators, 1978, 79, 80, 81, 82, 83; Best Internal Publ. award Suburban Press Club, 1979, 80, 82; Best Mags., Best 4-color brochure awards, 1983, 84, 85; Silver Touchstone award Am. Soc. Hosp. Pub. Relations, 1983; Gold Touchstone award, 1985; others. Mem. Assn. Am. Med. Colls., Am. Soc. Hosp. Pub. Relations (chmn. mktg. com., mem. accreditation com., chmn. budget com. 1981-83, Horizons com. 1983), Acad. Hosp. Pub. Relations (seminar chmn. 1974, dir. 1976, pres. 1978-79, dir. 1980-81, 82-83), Ill. Hosp. Assn. (ann. meeting com. 1977, 78, 79), Press Council of McGaw Med. Center of Northwestern U., Pub. Relations Soc. (chmn. mktg. com.) Chgo. Hosp. Council. Club: Publicity (Chgo.). Contbr. articles to Hosps. jour., chpt. to book; mem. editorial adv. bd. Profiles in Hosp. Mktg. Home: Box 381 Winnetka IL 60093 Office: 2650 Ridge Ave Evanston IL 60201

TRAFICANT, JAMES A., U.S. congressman; b. Youngstown, Ohio, May 8, 1941; s. James A. and Agnes T.; m. Patricia Choppa; 2 children. B.S. in Edn., U. Pitts., 1963; M.S. in Adminstrn., Youngstown State U., 1973, M.S. in Counseling, 1976. Dir., Mahoning County Drug Program, Ohio, 1971-81; sheriff, Mahoning County, 1981-85; mem. 99th Congress from 17th Dist. Ohio, 1985—, mem. pub. works and transp. com., sci. and tech. com.; cons. and lectr. in drug and alcohol abuse. Initiator: Parent Awareness Group, Ohio, to educate families on drug and alcohol abuse. Recipient Outstanding Citizen award Mahoning County, Youngstown Fraternal Order of Police, 1980; Outstanding Service award Inner City Helping Hand Inc., 1984. Democrat. Roman Catholic. Address: 128 Cannon House Office Bldg Washington DC 20515 also 11 Overhill Rd Youngstown OH 44512 also 918 Youngstown-Warren Rd Niles OH 44446

TRAINOR, JAMES BERNARD, window manufacturing company executive; b. Allentown, Pa., May 4, 1940; s. Leo Patrick and Irene Cecelia (Hartman) T.; m. Gertrude Nellie Sidenstick, Dec. 26, 1964; children—Audrey Ann, Gloria Jean. B.A., St. Joseph's Coll., Rensselaer, Ind., 1962. Prodn. scheduler RCA, Indpls., 1966-72; prodn. control mgr. Machine-Rite, La Grange, Ind., 1972-73, Abbott Labs., Rocky Mount, N.C., 1973-76; materials mgr. Electra, Indpls., 1976-77; corp. prodn. control mgr. Solo Cup, Urbana, Ill., 1977-84; dir. materials Caradco Corp., Rantoul, Ill., 1984—; instr. Parkland Coll., Champaign, Ill., 1979—. Mem. steering com. Parkland Coll., 1983-85. Mem. Am. Prodn. and Inventory Control Soc. (founder Ill. chpt., cert., pres. 1983-84). Roman Catholic. Avocations: jogging; softball; guitar. Home: 2307 Barberry Dr Champaign IL 61821 Office: Caradco Corp 201 Evans Dr Rantoul IL 61866

TRAMILL, JAMES LOUIS, psychology educator; b. Clarksville, Tenn., July 25, 1945; s. Louis H. and Mable Louise (Clark) T.; m. Jeannie Klienhammer, May 19, 1982; 1 child, Lacey Taylor. B.S., Austin Peay State U., 1967, M.A., 1977; Ph.D., U. So. Miss., 1981. Tchr., Montgomery (Tenn.) County Bd. Edn., 1968-77; instr. Austin Peay State U., 1977-78; assoc. prof. ednl. psychology Wichita State U., 1980—. Mem. Am. Psychol. Assn., Am. Ednl. Research Assn., Soc. Research in Child Devel., Assn. Psychol. and Ednl. Research in Kans. (pres. 1980-82). Home: 7523 E 26th St Wichita KS 67226 Office: Wichita State U PO Box 28 Wichita KS 67208

TRAMMELL, ALAN STUART, professional baseball player. Shortstop Detroit Tigers. Office: Detroit Tigers Tiger Stadium Detroit MI 48216*

TRANDAHL, EDWARD JOSEPH, railroad company executive; b. Springfield, Minn., Apr. 2, 1939; s. Joe E. and Ann Agnes (Newman) T.; m. Sandra Marlene Jederberg, Dec. 28, 1961; children—Carmen Lee, Kristin Therese. B.S. in Journalism, S.D. State U., 1964. Reporter, Huron (S.D.) Daily Plainsman, 1964-65; city editor Mitchell (S.D.) Daily Republic, 1965-66; editor, mgr. Norwood (Minn.) Times, 1966-68; mng. editor Estherville (Iowa) Daily News, 1968-70; reporter Omaha World-Herald, 1970-77; editor mag. Union Pacific R.R., Omaha, 1977-80, mgr. media relations, pub. relations dept., 1980-81, system dir. spl. projects for dept., 1981—. Bd. dirs. Met. Sci. and Engring. Fair, 1982-83; campaign mgr. for Office County Commr., 1978; chmn. S.D. Coll. Young Republicans, 1960, Douglas County Rep. Com., 1960; chmn. state com. Nebr. Operation Lifesaver. Served with AUS, 1961-63. Recipient Iowa Outstanding Newspaper 1st place local news, 1969, 1st place sch. news awards, 1969, 1st place spot news writing award Iowa AP, 1970. Mem. Assn. R.R. Editors (1st place mag. awards 1978, 80), Internat. Assn. Bus. Communicators (1st place award 1979), Pub. Relations Soc. Am. Republican. Roman Catholic. Clubs: Omaha Press, Variety of Nebr. (dir. 1984-85). Home: 5108 Webster St Omaha NE 68132 Office: Room 100 Public Relations Dept Union Pacific System 1416 Dodge St Omaha NE 68179

TRANKINA, LEONARD VINCENT, hotel executive, consultant; b. Chgo., June 27, 1936; s. Leonard A. and Kathryn A. (Ihm) T.; m. Virginia A. Taylor, Dec. 16, 1965; 1 child, Robin Anna. Gen mgr. Stockyard Inn-Internat. Amphitheatre, Chgo., 1971-73; food and beverage cons. Arlington Hotel, Hot Springs, Ark., 1973-79, State of Ark., Little Rock, 1974-79; gen. mgr. Pheasant Run Corp., St. Charles, Ill., 1979-81, Mackinac Hotel, Mackinac Island, Mich., 1981—; cons. in field. Author: The Way Out Plan, 1973; Welcome to the Hotel Industry, 1975; A Little to Do with Wines, 1979. Mem. Mich. C. of C., Mackinac Island C. of C., Hotel Sales Mgrs. Assn. (pres. 1969), Front Office Mgrs. Assn., Wine and Food Soc. Club: Sons of Italy. Lodge: Elks. Avocations: writing, comedy writing, commercial art, musician, gourmet chef. Office: Mackinac Hotel Mackinac Island MI 49757

TRANQUILLI, ROLAND ANTHONY, JR., electrical company executive; b. Springfield, Ill., May 20, 1941; s. Roland A. and Marian I. (Peters) T.; B.S. in E.E., Wayne State U., 1969; M.B.A., Ill. Benedictine Coll., 1984; m. Paulette I. Pritula, Mar. 25, 1967; children—Ronald Scott, Tammy Lyn. Engr. printing instrumentation and control Safran Printing Co., Detroit, 1966-70; with Western Electric Co., Naperville, Ill., 1970—, engr. spl. projects devel., 1970-76, sr. engr., 1979-80, project engr. mfg. communication switching systems, 1976-80, mgr. engring., 1980-82, processor product mgr., 1982—; microprocessor coordinator Western Electric Co., No. Ill. Works, Lisle, 1974-76, vice-chmn. X3T9 standards com. for minicomputers, 1980-84. Mktg. and exec. adv. Jr. Achievement, Lisle, 1979-81. Served with USAF, 1960-64. Recipient Spl. Achievement Engring. award Western Electric Co., 1980. Mem. IEEE, Am. Motorcycle Assn., Instrument Soc. Am. Office: AT&T 4513 Western Ave Lisle IL 60532

TRANTER, TERENCE MICHAEL, lawyer; b. Cin., Nov. 26, 1944; s. John Lawrence and Florence Ellen (McGann) T.; m. Doris Ann Tepe, June 22, 1968; children—Amy, Terry, Michael, Christopher. A.B., Georgetown U., 1966; J.D., U. Cin., 1969. Bar: Ohio 1969, U.S. Dist. Ct. (so. dist.) Ohio 1969, U.S. Ct. Appeals (6th cir.) 1969. Asst. atty. gen. State of Ohio, Cin., 1970-71; sole practice law, Cin., 1969—; mem. Ohio Ho. of Reps., Columbus, 1976—. Vice chmn. Hamilton County Democratic Exec. Com., Cin., 1984—. Mem. ABA, Ohio Bar Assn., Cin. Bar Assn., Cin. Ins. Bd., Ohio Bd. Realtors, Cin. Bd. Realtors. Democrat. Roman Catholic. Lodge: K.C. Home: 7303 Fair Oaks Dr Cincinnati OH 45237

TRAVIS, EUGENE CHARLES, investment banker; b. Chgo., May 2, 1920; s. Eugene Charles and Claire Patricia T.; m. Grace Elizabeth Koerner, Dec. 6, 1944; children—Richard Bruce, Diane Grace, Patricia Kay, Eugene Charles, Michael Allen. M.B.A., U. Chgo., 1953. Mcpl. bond analyst and trader Continental Ill. Nat. Bank, Chgo., 1937-49; mcpl. bond underwriting and trader Harriman Ripley, Chgo., 1949-60; dir. inst. sales and mcpl. bond dept. Hayden, Stone & Co., Chgo., 1960-62, v.p., 1962-63, div. v.p., dir., 1963-69, dir. nat. inst. sales, 1966-69; 1st v.p. Shearson, Hammill & Co., San Francisco, 1969-71; chmn., mng. dir. Travis, Weiner & Housman, San Francisco, 1972—; mng. dir. Mesirow & Co., Chgo., 1972—; founder The Exempters, 1949; gov. Midwest Stock Exchange, Chgo., 1966-70. Served with USNR, 1944-46. Mem. Am. Fin. Assn., Newcomen Soc. Clubs: Attic, Union League, Bond of Chgo., Mcpl. Bond of Chgo. Lodges: Masons, Shriners. Home: 754 N Waukegan Rd Lake Forest IL 60045 Office: Mesirow & Co 135 S LaSalle St Chicago IL 60603

TRAXLER, BOB, congressman; b. Kawkawlin, Mich., July 21, 1931; B.A. in Polit. Sci., Mich. State U., 1953; LL.B., Detroit Coll. Law, 1959; children—Tamara, Brad, Sarah. Bar: Mich. Prosecutor Bay County, Mich., 1960-62; mem. 93d-98th Congresses from 8th Mich. Dist., mem. appropriations com.; mem. Mich. Ho. of Reps., 1962-73. Mem. ABA, Mich. Bar Assn., Bay County Mental Health Soc. Episcopalian. Office: 2366 Rayburn House Office Bldg Washington DC 20515

TRAYNOR, JOHN THOMAS, JR., lawyer; b. Devils Lake, N.D., June 14, 1955; s. John Thomas and Kathryn Jane (Donovan) T. B.A., U. N.D., 1977, J.D., 1980. Bar: N.D., 1980, U.S. Dist. Ct. N.D. 1980. Assoc., Traynor & Rutten, Devils Lake, N.D., 1980-82; ptnr Traynor, Rutten & Traynor, Devils Lake, 1982—; mcpl. judge, Devils Lake, 1983-84; dir. 1st Ins. Agy., Devils Lake, 1984—. Editor Law Rev., U. N.D., 1979-80. Bd. dirs. Community Devel. Corp., Devils Lake, 1983—, treas. 1984; pres. Lake Region Devel. Corp., 1983-84, bd. dirs. 1983—. Recipient Book award, Am. Jurisprudence, 1980. Mem. ABA, N.D. Bar Assn., N.E. Jud. Dist. Bar Assn., Lake Region Bar Assn. (pres. 1980-83), Devils Lake C. of C. (dir. 1982—), Jaycees. Republican. Roman Catholic. Lodges: Rotary, KC, Elks (officer 1982—). Home: Box 838 Devils Lake ND 58301 Office: Traynor Rutten & Traynor 509 5th St Devils Lake ND 58301

TREASH, HAROLD THEODORE, fund raising executive; b. Pontiac, Ill., Feb. 14, 1918; s. Walter Alden and Nanie Rosetta (Aker) T.; m. Sally Leona Crader, Apr. 26, 1942; children—Myra Catherine, Anya Rae. B.Ed., Ill. State U., 1941. Program dir YMCA, Springfield, Ill., 1941-44, program edn. dir., Boston, 1944-51, program edn. dir., Hartford, Conn., 1951-54; field rep. Ward Dreshman & Reinhardt, Inc., N.Y.C., 1954-64, v.p., N.Y.C., Worthington, Ohio, 1964-73, pres., Worthington, 1973-81, chmn. bd., 1981—. Mem. Am. Assn. Fund Raising Counsel (bd. dirs.). Republican. Mem. United Ch. of Christ. Avocation: tennis. Office: Ward Dreshman & Reinhardt Inc 6660 N High St Worthington OH 43085

TREFZGER, JOHN DENNIS, clergyman; b. Peoria, Ill., Sept. 4, 1923; s. Charles Joseph and Dorothy Angelica (Trockur) T.; m. Marilyn Lestilie Wilson, June 9, 1946; children—Richard C., James E., Robert T. Student Bradley U., 1941-43; B.A., Eureka Coll. (Ill.), 1948; M.D., Lexington Theol. Sem. (Ky.), 1951; D. Ministry, Christian Theol. Sem., Indpls., 1978; D.D. (hon.), Eureka Coll., 1965. Ordained to ministry Christian Ch., 1948. Sr. pastor First Christian Ch., Waukegan, Ill., 1951-57, Bloomington, Ill., 1957-73, 80-83, South Bend, Ind., 1973-80, Bloomington, Ind., 1980-83; regional minister Christian Ch. Ill./Wis., Bloomington, 1984—; pres. bd. trustees Eureka Coll., 1964-70; chmn. ecumenical concerns commn., Christian Ch. Ind., 1978-82; vice moderator Christian Ch. Ind., 1982-84. Author: Reading the Bible With Understanding, 1978. Contbr. articles to profl. publs. Chmn. United Way Fund Drive, Bloomington, 1972. Served to sgt. USAAC, 1942-46; CBI. Paul Harris fellow, 1983. Mem. Disciples of Christ Hist. Soc., Council on Christian Unity of Christian Ch. (Disciples), Coll. Profl. Christian Ministers Ill., Cursillo, Theta Phi. Lodges: Masons, Rotary. Avocations: Astronomy, athletics camping, fishing, travel. Office: Christian Ch Ill/Wis 1011 N Main St Bloomington IL 61701

TREJBAL, HELEN VICTORIA, hospital administrator; b. St. Louis, Oct. 7, 1917; d. Victor and Theresa (Valdhans) T. Student Shurtleff Coll., 1934-36, Washington U., St. Louis, 1945-60. Legal sec., St. Louis, 1936-40; sec. to administr. Mo. Bapt. Hosp., St. Louis, 1940-50, adminstrv. asst., 1950-72, asst. adminstr., 1972-80, v.p., 1980—. Mem. Literacy Council of Greater St. Louis, 1978-84, sec., 1981-82, tutor, 1979; Sunday sch. tchr., Southwest Bapt. Ch., St. Louis, 1936—, co-chmn. stewardship com., 1979-80, chmn., 1979-80, 82-85, chmn. constn. com., 1979-81, 82-83; Mo. rep. stewardship commn. So. Bapt. Conv., 1975-83, vol. missionary to Alaska, Home Mission Bd., 1982, Colo., 1985; mem. rev. com. Mo. Bapt. Conv., 1979-82, mem. exec. bd. Woman's Missionary Union, 1958-64; pres. Mo. Bapt. Bus. Women's Fedn., 1958-61, dir. Sunday sch. tng., 1945-47; life mem. Mo. Bapt. Hosp. Aux., 1970—; mem. Mo. Bapt. Hosp. Pacesetters, 1972—. Mem. Am. Hosp. Assn. Pub. Relations Soc., Southside Bus. and Profl. Women's Club (named outstanding career woman 1982). Club: Soroptimist Internat. Office: Missouri Baptist Hosp 3015 N Ballas Rd Saint Louis MO 63131

TREMBLEY, SUSAN JANE, science educator, paleontologist; b. Wadsworth, Ohio, Feb. 5, 1931; d. Gilbert Peter and Miley Caroline (Witchey) Glossen; m. Robert Joseph Barcus, Apr. 9, 1950 (dec. June 1967); children—Gilbert, Hugh, Paul; m. 2d, Marion Henry Trembley, Nov. 11, 1968. B.A. magna cum laude, U. Akron, 1971, M.S., 1974. Cert. tchr., Ohio. Research asst. Yoder Bros. Inc., Barberton, Ohio, 1959-65; teaching asst. paleontology Cleve. Community Coll., 1972-73; teaching asst. geology, asst. to dir. environ. studies dept. U. Akron (Ohio), 1973-77; tchr. sci. Stow (Ohio) City Schs., 1977—; environ. cons. Harrison Hills Assn., Carrollton, Ohio, 1974-76, pres., 1976—.

Named tchr. of Yr., Stow Workman High Sch., 1981-82; Martha Holden Jennings grantee, 1972; U. Akron scholar, 1969-71; Jennings Found. scholar, 1981-82. Mem. Geol. Soc. Am., Nat. Sci. Tchrs. Assn., Nat. Educators Orgn., Ohio Acad. Sci., Stow Tchrs. Assn., Sigma Xi, Phi Alpha Theta. Office: Stow City Schs 3732 Darrow Rd Stow OH 44224

TRENNEPOHL, GARY LEE, finance educator; b. Detroit, Dec. 6, 1946; s. Leo Donald and Wilma Mae (Tiensvold) T.; m. Sandra K. Yeager, June 9, 1968; children—Paige E., Adrienne A. B.S., U. Tulsa, 1968; M.B.A., Utah State U., 1971; D.B.A., Tex. Tech U., 1976. Asst. prof. aero. studies Tex. Tech U., Lubbock, 1972-74; asst. prof. fin. Ariz. State U., Tempe, 1977-80, assoc. prof., 1980-82; prof. U. Mo., Columbia, 1982—, dir. Sch. Bus., 1984—. Author: An Introduction to Financial Management, 1984. Contbr. articles to profl. jours. Assoc. editor Jour. Fin. Research, 1983—. Served to capt. USAF, 1968-72. Decorated Commendation medal with oak leaf cluster, Vietnam Service medal. Mem. Fin. Mgmt. Assn., So. Fin. Assn., Southwestern Fin. Assn. (dir. 1983—, v.p. 1985), Midwest Fin. Assn. Republican. Lutheran. Home: 112 Sappington St Columbia MO 65203 Office: U Mo Coll Bus 228 Middlebush Hall Columbia MO 65211

TRENT, VIRGINIA RATCLIFF, public relations executive, musician; b. Jasper, Tex., June 3, 1931; d. Bennett S. and Emma L. (Mason) Ratcliff; B. in Music Edn., Lindenwood Coll., 1952; M. in Music Edn., U. Tex., 1953; postgrad. Westminster Choir Coll., 1953, Organ Inst., Mass., 1953, Hardin Simmons U., 1954; m. William Franklin Trent, June 30, 1956; children—Deborah Ratcliff, Faye Brabson. Dir. choral music San Angelo (Tex.) Public Schs., 1953-54; dir. music First Meth. Ch., San Angelo, 1953-54; dir. religious edn. and organist First Meth. Ch., Jasper, Tex., 1954-55; dir. choral music Hillcrest High Sch., Dallas, Tex., 1955-56; organist and dir. music Salem Meth. Ch., St. Louis, 1962-71; dir. public relations Mallinckrodt Inst. Radiology, Washington U. Sch. Medicine, St. Louis, 1971—; pianist-recitalist tours in St. Louis Community, 1956—. Pres., Ladue Chapel Nursery Sch. Bd., 1965-66; mem. aux. bd. St. Louis Conservatory and Sch. for the Arts, 1979—; Ladue Residential chmn. Arts and Edn. Fund Drive, 1965; mem. St. Louis Symphony Rotograuvre Com., 1977-80; music chmn. St. Louis Symphony Music Marathon Gala, 1981. Recipient Disting. Alumni award Lindenwood Coll., 1982. Mem. Am. Assn. Hosp. Public Relations Dirs., Internat. Assn. Bus. Communicators, Advt. Club of Greater St. Louis (bd. govs. 1984-85), Advt. Fedn. of St. Louis (pres. 1983-84, bd. dirs. 1984-85, Club Achievement award 1982-83, Pub. Service award 1983, Flair award 1982, Person of yr. award 1985), Am. Guild of Organists, Nat. Soc. Arts and Letters, Nat. Fellowship of Meth. Musicians, Hosp. Public Relations Soc. of St. Louis, Women's Assn. of the St. Louis Symphony Soc. (exec. bd. 1960-75, pres. jr. div. 1960-62), Lindenwood Coll. Alumnae Assn. (nat. v.p. 1962-64), Am. Hosp. Assn., Advt. Club Greater St. Louis (bd. govs. 1984-85), Mu Phi Epsilon. Republican. Presbyterian. Contbg. writer and editor Focal Spot, 1971—. Home: 41 N Clermont Ln St Louis MO 63124 Office: 510 S Kingshighway St Louis MO 63110

TRENT, WENDELL CAMPBELL, hospital administrator; b. Sneedville, Tenn., Nov. 1, 1940; s. William Campbell and Inez Hall (Daugherty) T.; m. Donna Lee Posey, May 31, 1964. B.A., Berea Coll, 1963; M.P.H., U.C.L.A., 1971; Ph.D. in Pub. Adminstrn., Nova U., 1980. Assistantship U.S. Pub. Health Service, U.C.L.A., 1969; pres. Lockwood MacDonald Hosp., Metoskey, Mich., 1971-75, Allegan Gen. Hosp., Mich., 1975-79, Bethany Meth. Hosp., Chgo. 1979-84, St. Ansgar Hosp., Moorhead, Minn., 1984—; chmn., bd. trustees Midwest Home Health Care, Fargo, N.D., 1984—; mem. Health Adv. Com., State of Tenn. Contbr. articles to profl. jours. Served to maj. USAF, 1963-69. Decorated Bronze Star. Fellow Am. Coll. Hosp. Adminstrs. (article of year com.); mem. Minn. Hosp. Assn. (legis. affairs com. 1984). Republican. Presbyterian. Club: Moorhead Country. Lodge: Rotary. Avocations: photography; amateur radio. Home: 2818 S Rivershore Dr Moorhead MN 56560 Office: St Ansgar Hosp 715 N 11th St Moorhead MN 56560

TRIBBLE, RICHARD WALTER, oil and gas company executive, investment executive; b. San Diego, Oct. 19, 1948; s. Walter Perrin and Catherine Janet (Miller) T.; m. Joan Catherine Sliter, June 26, 1980. B.S., U. Ala.-Tuscaloosa, 1968; student Gulf Coast Sch. Drilling Practices, U. Southwestern La., 1977. Stockbroker, Shearson, Am. Express, Washington, 1971-76; ind. oil and gas investment sales, Falls Church, Va., 1976-77; pres. Monroe & Keusink, Inc., Falls Church, Columbus, Ohio, 1977—. Served to cpl. USMC, 1969-71. Mem. Va. Oil and Gas Assn. (charter), Ohio Oil and Gas Assn., Soc. Petroleum Engrs. (asoc.), Ohio Geol. Soc. Am. Republican. Methodist. Club: Petroleum (Columbus).

TRIDLE, ROBERT JAY, county official, chemical engineer; b. Deadwood, S.D., July 11, 1953; s. Clarence Marvin and Dorothy Opaline (Shields) T.; m. Deanne Rose Nowell, Nov. 20, 1982. B.S. in Chemistry, S.D. Sch. Mining and Tech., 1981. Chemist, Homestake Mining Co., Lead, S.D., 1980-81; CD coordinator Lawrence County, Deadwood, S.D., 1982—; communications coordinator Lawrence County Fire Adv., Deadwood, 1982—. Musician, v.p. No. Black Hills Soc. for Preservation Performing Arts, Deadwood, 1984. Served with U.S. Army, 1976-79. Republican. Club: Lawrence County Search and Rescue (Deadwood). Lodge: Moose. Avocations: snow skiing, camping. Home: 514 Sunnyhill St Lead SD 57754 Office: Lawrence County Civil Defense 78-80 Sherman Deadwood SD 57732

TRIMBLE, KAREN ILLINGWORTH, career consulting executive; b. Lafayette, Ind., June 16, 1954; d. Robert LaVerne and Betty Mae (Long) Illingworth; B.S. in Office Adminstrn. cum laude (scholar), Ind. State U., Terre Haute, 1975; postgrad. in bus. adminstrn. Butler U., 1981—; m. Tony L. Trimble, Aug. 30, 1975. Sec. to dir. sales The Studio Press, Inc., Indpls., 1976-78; exec. sec. to pres. Indpls. Conv. and Visitors Bur., 1978-79, conv. services mgr., 1979-80, bus. mgr., 1980-83, dir. bus. office, 1983—; cons. Career Cons. Indpls., Inc., 1983, office mgr., 1984—. instr. Clark Coll., Indpls., 1979-82. Active United Way campaigns, 1978, 80. Cert. profl. sec. Mem. Am. Bus. Women's Assn. (enrollment event com. 1978, rec. sec. 1979), Exec. Women Internat. (membership com., audit com.). Roman Catholic. Office: 107 N Pennsylvania Suite 404 Indianapolis IN 46204

TRIPATHI, BRENDA JENNIFER, ophthalmology researcher, educator; b. Rochford, Essex, Eng., July 5, 1946; came to U.S., 1977, naturalized, 1983; d. Charles Edward and Kathleen Lane; m. Ramesh Chandra Tripathi, May 20, 1969; children—Anita, Paul. B.S. with honors, U. London, 1967, Ph.D., 1971. Research asst. Univ. Coll. Hosp., London, 1967-69; lectr. pathology U. London, 1969-77; research assoc. (asst. prof.) U. Chgo., 1977-84, research assoc. (assoc. prof.) ophthalmology, 1984—, asst. prof. lectr., 1979-84, assoc. prof. lectr., 1984—, ocular microbiologist dept. ophthalmology, 1977—; cons. Krogh Found. NSF. Contbg. editor Exptl. Eye Research, Cornea, Lens Research, Ophthalmic Research. Contbr. over 100 articles and communications to profl. jours., chpts. to books. Recipient Outstanding Citizen award Chgo. Citizenship Council, 1984. Named co-prin. investigator Med. Research Council, 1973-76, Nat. Eye Inst. USPHS, 1981; named prin. investigator Nat. Soc. to Prevent Blindness, 1978-80. Mem. N.Y. Acad. Scis., AAAS, Am. Acad. Ophthalmology (assoc.), Assn. for Research in Vision and Opthalmology, Midwest Soc. Electron Microscopists, Assn. Indians in Am. (life), Assn. Research Scientists, Sigma Xi. Office: Univ Chgo 939 E 57th St Chicago IL 60637

TRIPLEHORN, CHARLES A., entomology educator, curator; b. Bluffton, Ohio, Oct. 27, 1927; s. Murray E. and Alice Irene (Lora) T.; m. Wanda Elaine Neiswander, June 12, 1949; children—Bradley Alyn, Bruce Wayne. B.S., Ohio State U., 1949, M.S., 1952; Ph.D., Cornell U., 1957. Asst. prof. entomology U. Del., Newark, 1952-54; teaching asst. Cornell U., Ithaca, N.Y., 1954-57; asst. research prof. Ohio Agrl. Research and Devel. Ctr., Wooster, 1957-62; asst. prof. Ohio State U., Columbus, 1962-63, assoc. prof., 1963-67, prof., 1967—; entomologist UAID, Brazil, 1964-66. Active Boy Scouts Am.; pres. Wheaton Club of Columbus, 1971. Fellow Royal Entomol. Soc. London; mem. Entomol. Soc. Am. (pres. north central br. 1983, pres. 1985), Washington Entomol. Soc., Kans. Entomol. Soc., Soc. Systematic Zoologists, Coleopterists Soc. (pres. 1975). Republican. Methodist. Club: Pres.'s (Ohio State U.). Co-author: Introduction to the Study of Insects, 1981; contbr. numerous articles to profl. jours. Home: 3943 Medford Sq Columbus OH 43220 Office: 1735 Neil Ave Columbus OH 43210

TRIPODI, MARY ANN, physical education educator; b. Massillon, Ohio, Feb. 3, 1944; d. Domenico A. and Margaret P. (Cicchinelli) T. B.S., Kent State U., 1966, M. Ed., 1970, postgrad., 1981—. Instr. phys. edn. Canton (Ohio) South High Sch., 1966-69; instr. health and phys. edn. Notre Dame Coll., Cleve., 1969-71; instr. health and phys. edn. U. Akron (Ohio), 1971-80, coordinator women's sports clubs, 1971-79, asst. prof. health and phys. edn., 1980—, asst. to dir. athletics, 1979-85, asst. athletic dir., 1985—, head coach women's volleyball, 1971-75, head coach women's basketball, 1971-81, dir. coaching workshops, 1981—; cons. Ohio Female Athletic Found., 1982-83. Mem. AAHPER and Dance, Nat. Assn. Phys. Edn. Coll. Women, Fin. Aid and Ethics and Eligibility (chmn. 1974-80), Midwest Assn. Phys. Edn. Coll. Women, Ohio Assn. Health, Phys. Edn., Recreation and Dance, Ohio College Assn. (chmn. elect curriculum div. women's phys. edn. sect. 1971, mem.-at-large 1972), Ohio Assn. Intercollegiate Sports for Women (N.E. dist. commr. 1974-77), Ohio Female Athletic Found. (trustee, v.p.), Cleve. Women's Phys. Edn. and Recreation Assn., Pi Lambda Theta, Delta Psi Kappa. Roman Catholic. Contbr. articles to profl. jours. Clubs: University, Touchdown, Varsity A Assn. (Akron, Ohio). Home: 1303 Cedarwood Dr Kent OH 44240 Office: Jar Annex U Akron Akron OH 44325

TRIPP, THOMAS NEAL, lawyer, political consultant; b. Evanston, Ill., June 19, 1942; s. Gerald Frederick and Kathryn Ann (Siebold) T.; m. Ellen Marie Larrimer, Apr. 16, 1966; children—David Larrimer, Bradford Douglas, Corinne Catherine. B.A. cum laude, Mich. State U., 1964; J.D., George Washington U., 1967. Bar: Ohio 1967, U.S. Ct. Mil. Appeals 1968, U.S. Supreme Ct. 1968. Sole practice, Columbus, Ohio, 1969—; real estate developer, Columbus, 1969—; chmn. bd. Black Sheep Enterprises, Columbus, 1969—; vice chmn. bd. Sun Valley-Elkhorn Assn., Idaho, 1983—, Sawtooth Sports, Ketchum, Idaho, 1983—; legal counsel Wallace F. Ackley Co., Columbus, 1973—. Trustee Americans for Responsible Govt., Washington, GOPAC; mem. Peace Corps Adv. Council, 1981—; mem. U.S. Commn. on Trade Policy and Negotiations, 1985—; campaign mgr., fin. chmn. Charles Rockwell Saxbe, Ohio Ho. of Reps., 1974, 76, 78, 80; campaign mgr. George Bush for Pres., 1980, nat. dep. field dir., 1980; regional co-chmn. Reagan-Bush, 1984, mem. nat. fin. com., 1984; mem. Victory '84 Fin. Com. Served to capt. U.S. Army, 1967-69. Fellow Pi Sigma Alpha; mem. Phi Delta Phi. Republican. Avocations: swimming; tennis; skiing; writing. Home and Office: 5420 Clark State Rd Gahanna OH 43230

TRISCHLER, FLOYD D., real estate executive, consultant; b. Pitts., Aug. 31, 1929; s. Edward C. and Margaret (Sirlin) T.; m. Gloria N. Fusting, June 30, 1951; children—Thomas J., John D., Annette M., Nannette L., Rene L., Denise M. B.S., U. Pitts., 1951; postgrad. San Diego State U., 1953-56, postgrad. in bus. adminstrn., 1963-69. Cert. master real estate cons. Program dir. Whittaker Corp., San Diego, 1963-71; exec. v.p. Turner Devel., Indpls., 1971-73; pres. Guadelupe Developers, Inc., Indpls., 1973-78; pres. Iroquois Realty, Inc., Indpls., 1978—, also dir; cons. NASA, Huntsville, Ala., 1963-69, Rincon Indian Reservation, Escondido, Calif., 1969-71, Promotora Ritco, Cancun, Mex., 1985. Author publs. Patentee in polymer chemistry. Vol. Central State Hosp., Indpls., 1984—; notary pub., Indpls., 1980—; mem. Scottish Rite Chorus; mem. nat. publicity com. Nat. Pow-wow VII, 1985. Mem. Nat. Assn. Home Builders, Indpls. Builders Assn., Indpls Bd. Realtors, Ind. Bd. Realtors, Nat. Assn. Real Estate Cons., Midwest Cherokee Alliance. Republican. Roman Catholic. Lodges: Masons, Tecumpseh. Home: 8249 Filly Ln Plainfield IN 46168 Office: Iroquois Realty Inc 8249 Filly Ln Plainfield IN 46168

TROMBLE, WILLIAM WARNER, university official; b. Madrid, Nebr., June 15, 1932; s. Ralph A. and Edna Belle (Warner) T.; m. Joella Jane Boone, Sept. 2, 1954; children—Gina Gayle, Lori Lynne, William Warner. A.B., Asbury Coll., 1953; Mus.M., Mich. State U., 1960; Ph.D., U. Mich., 1968. Assoc. prof. music Spring Arbor Coll., Mich., 1966-70, Olivet Nazarene Coll., Kankakee, Ill., 1970-77; dir. alumni affairs Houghton Coll., N.Y., 1977-81; dir. gifts Spartanburg Meth. Coll., S.C., 1981-83; asst. dir. alumni and devel. Ball State U., Muncie, Ind., 1983—. Composer: Freedom Overture for symphony orch., 1960. Author: The American Intellectual and Music, 1968. Compiler, editor: Alumni Information Guide, 1979; co-editor Hymns of Faith and Life, 1976. Mem. Council for Advancement and Support Edn., Phi Mu Alpha. Lodge: Rotary. Avocations: writing; tennis; travel. Home: 4308 Kings Row Muncie IN 47304 Office: Alumni and Devel Programs Ball State U 700 N McKinley St Muncie IN 47306

TROMBOLD, WALTER STEVENSON, supply company executive; b. Chanute, Kans., June 21, 1910; s. George John and Margaret (Stevenson) T.; m. Charlotte Elizabeth Kaufman, Dec. 28, 1941; children—Joan Kleitsch, Lynn Oliphant, Walter Steven, David George, Charles Phillip. B.S. in Bus., U. Kans., 1932; A.A., Iola Jr. Coll., 1930; spl. degree, Balliol Coll., Oxford U., 1943. Asst. mgr. S.H. Kress & Co., 1932-38; counselor Penn Mut. Life Ins. Co., 1938-41; with Reid Supply Co., Wichita, Kans., Kansas City, Mo., 1946—, now pres., chmn. bd. Bd. dirs., officer YMCA, 1922—; merit badge councilor Boy Scouts Am.; bd. dirs. Camp Fire Girls; life mem. PTA, 1953—, pres., 1952; chmn. personnel adv. bd. City of Wichita (Kans.), 1956—; commr. Gen. Assembly Presbyn. Ch. U.S.A., past deacon, elder, trustee; commr. Synods of Mid Am., Presbytery of So. Kans.; assoc. chmn. Nat. Laymen's Bible Week, 1972—. Served to lt. comdr. USN, 1942-46. Recipient various awards including Honor Man Wichita Swim Club, 1970; Disting. Service award to Youth YMCA, 1970; Service award to Swimmers Kansas City High Sch. Activities, 1975. Mem. Kans. U. Alumni Assn. (life), Kans. C. of C., Wichita C. of C., Sales and Mktg. Execs. (bd. dirs., v.p.), Textile Care and Allied Trades Assn., Alpha Tau Omega. Clubs: Old Timer (sec., treas. 1964—, Honor Man of Yr. 1977), Wichita Racquet, Knife and Fork Internat. (bd. dirs., v.p.), University (chmn. bd., v.p.). Lodges: Rotary, Masons (32 deg.). Republican. Home: 340 Hillsdale Wichita KS 67230

TROPEA, LEONARD ANTHONY HENRY, educator; b. Youngstown, Ohio; s. Anthony F. and Esther C. (Marinelli) T.; B.A. in English, Ohio State U., 1959; B.Sc. in Zoology, 1959; postgrad. Kent State U., Youngstown State U.; m. Anita R. Vacca; children—Richard, Linda, James, Robert, Maria, Teresa, Leonard II, Paul, Martin. Free lance writer, Youngstown, Ohio, 1960-62; tchr. Struthers (Ohio) City Schs., 1962-75, dir. adult edn., 1968-75. Treas. pres. Youngstown Writers, 1960-63; sec. Serra Internat. Orgn., 1973-75. Named Tchr. of Yr. in U.S., 1975. Mem. NEA, Ohio State, Struthers (pres.) edn. assns., Nat. Sci. Assn., Internat. Reading Assn. Jennings Scholar, 1965-66. Home: Tall Pines 90 Charles Ave Youngstown OH 44512 Office: Manor Sch Struthers OH 44471

TROPPITO, CHARLES C., JR., toxic waste management-chemical manufacturing detoxifying reagents executive; b. Kansas City, Mo., Sept. 14, 1947; s. Charles C. and Philomene (Magness) T.; B.A., U. Mo., Kansas City, 1970, M.P.A., 1975; m. Mary A. Barthelmass, June 7, 1969; children—Christopher M., Laurie A. Bond underwriter Reliance Ins. Co., Kansas City, Mo., 1969-70; title examiner trainee St. Paul Title Ins. Co., Kansas City, 1970-71; adminstrv. asst. to mayor/plan commn. City of Leawood (Kans.), 1971-75; dir. adminstrn. and budget City of Prairie Village (Kans.), 1975-78; chief adminstrv. officer, budget dir. City of Urbana (Ill.), 1978-83; guest lectr. U. Ill., Urbana; mem. adj. faculty public adminstrn. Columbia Coll., Kansas City; treas., bd. dirs. Urbana Promotion Com., 1980-81; mem. planning com. Sch. Adminstrn., U. Mo., Kansas City, 1976; mem. bd. Champaign-Urbana High Tech. Devel. Group, 1980; mem. faculty adv. com. grad. program in pub. adminstrn. U. Ill., Urbana. Recipient various certs. of appreciation. Mem. Internat. City Mgmt. Assn., Mcpl. Fin. Officers Assn., Am. Public Works Assn. Lutheran. Club: Rotary. Author papers, reports on pub. adminstrn. and hazardous waste regulations. Office: 2108 Wyandotte Kansas City MO 64108

TROTTER, RICHARD DONALD, psychologist, clergyman, consultant; b. Grand Island, Nebr., June 9, 1932; s. P. Dean and Ethel Dell (Masters) T.; m. Kathleen Marie Tyler, Apr. 10, 1966; children—Terri Marie, Nancy Lee, Laurel Lynn. Student U. Wis.-Madison, 1950; B.S., U. Nebr., 1968; M.Div., Iliff Sch. Theology, Denver, 1970; Ph.D., Southwest U., Phoenix, 1974; D.H.L. (hon.), London Inst., 1973. Ordained to ministry United Meth. Ch., 1971. Sr. pastor, 1st United Meth. Ch., Miller, S.D., 1970-73; pvt. practice counseling and therapy, Rapid City, S.D., 1974-78; sr. pastor Canyon Lake United Meth. Ch., Rapid City, 1978-80; theologian in residence Collins Ctr., Portland, Oreg., 1981-83; counselor, therapist Wellspring Inc., Marion, Inc., 1983—, also dir. Author: 40,000 Pounds of Feathers, 1970; 'Til Divorce Do Us Part, 1982. Mem. council City of West Lincoln, Nebr., 1960-61, mayor, 1962; mem. Rapid City Bd. Edn., 1977-80, pres., 1979-80; bd. dirs. Marion Civic Theatre, 1984—. Served with USAF, 1949-52. Named hon. col. Cody Scouts of North Platte, 1965; recipient Service award Rapid City Bd. Edn., 1980. Mem. Nat. Council Family Relations, Sex Info. and Edn. Council, Assn. for Humanistic Psychology, Am. Assn. Marriage and Family Therapists, Nat. Assn. Social Workers, Assn. for Transpersonal Psychology, U. Nebr. Alumni Assn. Democrat. Avocations: philately, sports officiating, acting. Home: 1106 Windsor Dr Marion IN 46952

TROUB, DONALD LESLIE, osteopathic physician; b. Camden, N.J., May 7, 1944; s. Nathan Lawrence and Mildred (Goldberg) T.; m. Sarah Jane Haynes, June 23, 1968; 1 dau., Leslie Shannon. B.A. in Biology, U. Tenn., 1967; postgrad. Tenn. Tech. U., 1967-68; D.O., Chgo. Coll. Osteo. Medicine, 1974. Diplomate Nat. Bd. Examiners Osteo. Physicians and Surgeons, Am. Bd. Emergency Medicine. Intern Mt. Clemens Gen. Hosp. (Mich.), 1974-75, emergency physician, 1976-82; emergency physician Providence Hosp., Novi, Mich., 1982—, med. dir. emergency room, 1982—; former clin. instr. Mich. State U., Des Moines Coll. Osteo. Medicine. Fellow Am. Coll. Emergency Physicians; mem. Am. Osteo. Assn. Jewish. Office: 39500 W Ten Mile Rd Novi MI 48050

TROUP, WILLIAM ROGER, physician; b. Dallas, Mar. 3, 1944; s. Roger Chenot and Natalie Florene (Valkus) T.; m. Violet Marie Packard, Aug. 19, 1967; children—Cristine, Denise, Danae. Student Wheaton Coll., 1963-65; M.D., U. Colo.-Denver, 1969. Diplomate Am. Bd. Family Practice. Intern, St. Francis Hosp., Wichita, Kans., 1969-70; practice medicine specializing in family practice, Walsh, Colo., 1970-84, Johnson, Kans., 1984—; mem. staff Walsh Dist. Hosp., 1970—, chief of staff, 1976-84; mem. staff S.E. Colorado Hosp., Springfield, 1972—, chief of staff, 1976-78; chief of staff Stanton County Hosp., 1984—. Dep. coroner Baca County, Colo., 1970-84; mem. Walsh Pub. Sch. Bd. Edn., 1974-81, v.p., 1978-81. Mem. AMA, Colo. Med. Soc., Am. Acad. Family Practice, S.E. Colo. Med. Soc. (pres. 1978-80, v.p. 1980-82). Methodist. Club: Prairie Twisters Sq. Dance (Walsh). Office: 101 E Greenwood St Johnson KS 67855

TROUT, STEVEN RUSSELL, professional baseball player. Pitcher Chgo. Cubs. Office: Chgo Cubs Wrigley Field Chicago IL 60613*

TROUT, WILLIAM JOHN, lawyer, media executive; b. Des Moines, Nov. 5, 1937; s. William Benedict and Theresa Elizabeth (McCabe) T.; m. Barbara Anne, Nov. 19, 1960; children—Christopher Paul, Mary Theresa, Michael Joseph, Robert George. Student Marquette U., 1957-59; J.D., Drake U., 1962. Bar: Iowa 1962, U.S. Supreme Ct. 1976. Of counsel Iowa Legislature, Des Moines, 1962-63; ptnr. Coppola, Trout, Taha & Gazzo, Des Moines, 1963—; pres. Independence Broadcasting Corp., Des Moines, 1979—; treas. Iowa Met. Water & Sewer Cos., Des Moines, 1976-79. Bd. dirs. Dowling-St. Joseph Ednl. Ctr., West Des Moines, 1982—. Mem. Iowa Bar Assn. Democrat. Roman Catholic. Lodge: KC (grand knight 1964-66). Avocations: fishing; tennis. Office: Coppola Trout Taha & Gazzo Court III Bldg 111 3rd St Des Moines IA 50309

TROUTMAN, BRUCE WEBER, osteopathic physician; b. Dayton, Ohio, Mar. 15, 1947; s. H. Eugene and Margaret (Weber) T.; m. Kay Stevens, May 16, 1981. B.S., Ohio State U., 1969; D.O., Chgo. Coll. Osteo. Medicine, 1973. Intern Zieger Botsford Hosp., Detroit, 1974; osteo. physician Shelby Dale Clinic, Utica, Mich., 1974-75, Lane-Swayze Clinic, Almont, Mich., 1975-77, Knollwood Clinic, Lapeer, Mich., 1977—; physician reviewer Profl. Rev. Orgn., Genesee, Lapeer, Shiawassee counties, Mich., 1976—; med. dir. two health maintenance orgns., 1984—; cons. health maintenance orgns. Mem. Am. Osteo. Assn., Mich. Assn. Osteo. Physicians and Surgeons, Lapeer Osteo. Soc., Nat. Bd. Osteo. Examiners,,Group Health Assn. Am. (med. dirs. div.), Lapeer C. of C. (bd. dirs. 1983-84). Republican. Lutheran. Lodge: Optimists (bd. dirs. 1981-83, 85—, v.p. 1983-84). Avocations: photography; cross country skiing; raising wild animals; landscaping. Home: 2033 Gray Rd Lapeer MI 48446 Office: Knollwood Clinic 1259 N Main St Lapeer MI 48446

TROUTNER, JOANNE JOHNSON, computer resource educator, consultant; b. Muncie, Ind., Sept. 9, 1952; d. Donal Russel and Lois Vivian (Hicks) Johnson; m. Lary William Troutner, May 17, 1975. B.A. in Media and English, Purdue U., 1974, M.S. in Edn., 1976. Media specialist Lafayette Sch. Corp. (Ind.), 1974-77, 81-83, computer resource tchr., 1983-84; media specialist, Tippecanoe Sch. Corp., Lafayette, Inc., 1984-85, ednl. computer coordinator, 1985—; tchr. English, Minot Pub. Schs. (N.D.), 1978-79, media specialist, 1979-81; vis. prof. continuing edn. U. S.C., Columbia, summer 1983; instr. Purdue U., West Lafayette; vis. prof. continuing edn. U. N.D. Author: The Media Specialist, The Microcomputer and the Curriculum, 1983; contbr. materials rev. column Sch. Library Media Quar.; computer literacy columnist Jour. Computers in Math. and Sci. Teaching. Active Greater Lafayette Leadership Acad. Alumni Group, 1983—. Mem. Assn. Media Educators (chmn. computer div. 1982-84), Am. Assn. Sch. Librarians (sec. 1983-84), Nat. Assn. Ednl. Computing (adv. bd. 1982—, dist. dir. 1982—), ALA, Phi Beta Kappa. Home: 3002 Roanoke Circle Lafayette IN 47905 Office: Klondike Middle High 3310 N 300 W West Lafayette IN 47906

TROWBRIDGE, DEANNA G., educator; b. Chadron, Nebr., Mar. 12, 1955; d. Dean C. and Eldora (Tyree) Trowbridge. B.S. in Edn., Chadron State Coll., 1978, M.S. in Bus. Adminstrn., 1981. Asst. buyer The Other Half, Chadron, 1977-78; tchr. bus. and home econs., Norfolk (Nebr.) High Sch., 1978-80; grad. asst. Chadron State Coll., 1980-81, instr., 1981, asst. dir. Nebr. Bus. Devel. Ctr., Chadron, 1981—; county fair judge. Parliamentarian, Toastmasters Internat.; sec. Christian Responsibility Exec. Com.; mem. United Methodist Ch. Pastor Parish Relations com.; active Am. Legion Aux. Mem. Am. Vocat. Assn., Am. Home Econs. Assn., Nat. Bus. Edn. Assn., Phi Beta Lambda, Sigma Delta Nu. Club: Order of Does. Home: 358 Shelton St Chadron NE 69337 Office: Chadron State Coll 10th and Main Sts Chadron NE 69337

TROXEL, LARRY LEE, retail building materials and ready-mixed concrete products company executive; b. Battle Creek, Mich., Apr. 18, 1942; s. Emerald V. and Melba Lucille (Church) T.; student Kellogg Community Coll., 1960-62; m. Marilyn Jean Richman, Feb. 2, 1963; children—Jodi Lyn, Karla Sue, Ronna Kay. Mgr., V.E. Troxel & Sons, Inc., Battle Creek, 1960-68, corp. sec., gen. mgr., 1973-81; also dir.; mgr. Lumber div. Wickes Corp., Saginaw, Mich., 1968-73; pres. L-M Troxel Services, Inc., Battle Creek, 1981—; pres. V.E. Troxel & Sons, Inc., Battle Creek, 1982—. Constable, Emmett Twp., 1976-80, trustee, 1984—; mem. Calhoun County Citizens Coalition Against Crime, 1976-79; advisor Jr. Achievement South Central Mich., 1979-80; v.p. West End Devel. Assn. of Battle Creek, 1984—. Recipient Spoke award Battle Creek Jaycees, 1975, Spark Plug award, 1976, 77, 78; named Outstanding Young Man of the Yr., Dale Carnegie, 1977. Mem. Battle Creek Area C. of C. Republican. Baptist. Club: Optimists (pres. 1967-68). Address: 13084 Hoyt Dr Battle Creek MI 49017

TROZZOLO, ANTHONY MARION, chemist, educator; b. Chgo., Jan. 11, 1930; s. Pasquale and Francesca (Vercillo) T.; B.S., Ill. Inst. Tech., 1950; M.S., U. Chgo., 1957, Ph.D., 1960; m. Doris C. Stoffregen, Oct. 8, 1955; children—Thomas, Susan Trozzolo Hecklinski, Patricia, Michael, Lisa, Laura. Asst. chemist Chgo. Midway Labs., 1952-53; asso. chemist Armour Research Found., Chgo., 1953-56; mem. tech. staff Bell Labs., Murray Hill, N.J., 1959-75; Charles L. Huisking prof. chemistry U. Notre Dame, 1975—; chmn. Gordon Research Conf. Photochemistry, 1964; vis. prof. Columbia U., N.Y.C., 1971, U. Colo., Boulder, 1981; lectr. Faculty Scis., U. Leuven (Belgium), 1983; vis. lectr. AEC fellow, 1951; NSF fellow, 1957-59; Phillips lectr. U. Okla., 1971; P.C. Reilly lectr. U. Notre Dame, 1972; C. L. Brown lectr., Rutgers, 1975; Sigma Xi lectr., Bowling Green, 1976, Abbott Labs., 1978; M. Faraday lectr. No. Ill. U., 1976; F.O. Butler lectr. S.D. State U., 1978; Chevron lectr. U. Nev., Reno, 1983; Plenary lectr. 8th Internat. Symposium on Free Radicals, 1967, 7th Internat. Symposium on Photochemistry, 1978; vis. lectr. Max Planck Inst. Biophysikalische Chemie, Göttingen, Germany, 1978, 82, 83, Staudinger Inst. Makromoleculare Chemie, Freiburg, Germany, 1978, Max Planck Inst. Strahlenchemie, Mülheim an d Ruhr, Ger., 1983, U. Louvain, Belgium, 1983; Coronado lectr. Am. Chem. Soc., 1980. Fellow N.Y. Acad. Scis. (chmn. chem. scis. sect. 1969-70, Halpern award 1980), AAAS, Am. Inst. Chemists; mem. Am. Chem. Soc. (Disting. Service award St. Joseph Valley sect. 1979), AAUP, Gordon Research Conf. Council, Sigma Xi. Roman Catholic. Asso. editor Jour. Am. Chem. Soc., 1975-76; editor Chem. Reviews, 1977-84; editorial adv. bd. Accounts of Chem. Research, 1977—; cons. editor McGraw-Hill Ency. Sci. and Tech., 1982—; patentee; contbr. articles to profl. jours. Home: 1329 E Washington St South Bend IN 46617 Office: U Notre Dame Notre Dame IN 46556

TRUDELL, THOMAS JEFFREY, hospital administrator, educator; b. New Britain, Conn., May 13, 1941; s. Raymond Joseph and Clara (Rule) T.; m.

Sandra Robinson, Oct. 9, 1965; children—Christopher Thomas, Nicole Elizabeth. A.B. in Econs., Providence Coll., 1963; M.B.A., Northeastern U., 1965; M.H.A., Yale U., 1975. Staff acct., United Aircraft Co., East Hartford, Conn., 1965; ops. analyst Am. Cyanamid Co., Wayne, N.J. 1968-70; materials mgr., v.p. St. Vincent's Med. Ctr., Bridgeport, Conn., 1970-76; v.p. profl. services Newport Hosp. (R.I.), 1977-78, v.p. planning and program devel., 1979-81; pres., chief exec. officer Marymount Hosp., Garfield Heights, Ohio, 1981—; prof. Salve Regina Coll., 1977—. Active Boys Scouts Am., YMCA; bd. dirs. Emerald Health Network; chmn. bd. dirs. Alliance for Access, 1981—; bd. dirs. Hosp. Coop. Linen Services. Served to capt. U.S. Army, 1966-68; Thailand. Named to Lt. of Yr., St. Louis Soc. Engrs., 1967. Mem. Am. Coll. of Hosp. Adminstrs., Greater Cleve. Hosp. Assn., Acad. of Med. Adminstrs., Am. Hosp. Assn., Ohio Hosp. Assn., Catholic Conf. Ohio, Am. Legion, DAV. Club: Exchange. Lodge: Rotary. Office: Marymount Hosp 12300 McCracken Rd Garfield Heights OH 44125

TRUSHEIM, H. EDWIN, insurance company executive; b. Chgo., 1927; grad. Concordia Coll., 1948, Northwestern U., 1950. Pres., chief exec. officer Gen. Am. Life Ins. Co., St. Louis; dir. Angelica Corp. Bd. dirs. Inc., Civic Progress, St. Louis Area Boy Scouts Am., St. Louis Symphony Orch., United Way Greater St. Louis, Washington U. Mem. Am. Council Life Ins. (dir.), Regional Commerce and Growth Assn. (dir.). Office: Gen Am Life Ins Co PO Box 396 Saint Louis MO 63166

TRUTTER, JOHN THOMAS, urban consultant, retired telephone company executive; b. Springfield, Ill., Apr. 18, 1920; s. Frank L. and Frances (Mischler) T.; A.B., U. Ill., 1942; postgrad. Northwestern U., U. Chgo.; m. Edith English Woods, June 17, 1950; children—Edith English II, Jonathan Woods. With Ill. Bell Telephone Co., Chgo., 1946-55, 58-85, gen. traffic mgr., 1959-62, asst. v.p. pub. relations, 1962-65, asst. v.p. suburban ops., 1965-67, gen. mgr. north suburban ops., 1967-69, v.p. pub. relations, 1969-71, v.p. operator services, 1971-80, v.p. community affairs, 1980-85; pres. John T. Trutter Co. Inc., urban cons., Chgo., 1985—; mem. personnel relations staff AT&T, N.Y.C., 1955-58; dir. State Nat. Bank Evanston (Ill.); dir. adv. bd. Alford & Assocs., 1983—; lectr. gen. semantics. Mem. City of Evanston Zoning Amendment Bd., 1968-70; mem. regional bd. NCCJ, Chgo., 1963-83, v.p., chmn. exec. com., 1969-73, presiding co-chmn., 1973-83, nat. trustee, 1967-83, mem. nat. exec. com., 1979-83, life trustee, 1983; active Met. Crusade Mercy, 1968-72; mem. adv. bd. Citizenship Council Met. Chgo., 1969—; mem. exec. bd. Chgo. Area council Boy Scouts Am., 1969-75; trustee Children's Home and Aid Soc. Ill., 1970—, v.p., 1975-79, pres., 1979-81, also chmn. centennial com., life trustee, 1983—; pres. Hull House Assn., 1983—1972-74, hon. chmn. 90 Year Fund, 1979-82, life trustee, 1981—; bd. dirs., exec. com., pres. United Cerebral Palsy Greater Chgo., 1972-77, chmn., 1977—; v.p., nat. campaign chmn. United Cerebral Palsy Assns., 1977-83, steering com. nat. telethon, 1978; bd. dirs. Chgo. Conv. and Tourism Bur., 1979—, exec. com., 1981—, vice-chmn., 1982-84; bd. dirs. Chgo. Council Fgn. Relations, 1968-74; bd. dirs. Nat. Minority Purchasing Council, 1976-80, nat. treas., 1976-77; mem. com. on case flow Cook County Circuit Ct., 1979-81; chmn. blue ribbon com. truancy in Chgo. schs., 1979-80; task force chmn. Chgo. United Inc., 1971-81, treas., 1981—; mem. Chgo. Mayor's Task Force on High Tech., 1982-83; mem. Chgo. Crime Commn., dir., 1976—, chmn. membership com., v.p., 1981, chmn. Chgo. Law Enforcement Week, 1982; bd. dirs. Lyric Opera Chgo., 1976—, hon. vice chmn. Orch. of Ill., 1981—; chmn. bd. dirs. Chgo. City Ballet, 1981-83, chmn. emeritus, 1983—; bd. dirs. North Communities Health Plan, sec., 1979-81; chmn. adv. bd. Pru Care, Inc., HMO, 1981—; exec. bd. Northwestern U. Library, council, treas., 1983-85; trustee U. Ill. YMCA, 1970-81; mem. adv. council U. Ill. Coll. Commerce and Bus. Adminstrn., 1982-85; bd. dirs. Upper Ill. Valley Assn., 1982-85; benefit chmn. Vatican Arts Council Chgo., 1983; mem. nat. devel. com. Providence St. Mel High Sch.; chmn. adv. council Chgo. West Project, 1983-85; mem. Ill. Econ. Devel. Commn., 1984-85, Spl. Commn. on Adminstrn. of Justice in Cook County, 1984—; bd. dirs., mem. exec. com. Chgo. City Coll. Found., 1984—; bd. dirs. English Speaking Union, 1985—. Served to lt. col. AUS, 1942-46; CBI. Recipient Laureate award Lincoln Acad. Ill., 1980-81; Outstanding Exec. Leadership award Nat. Soc. Fund-Raising Execs., 1979; decorated Legion of Merit, China medal. Mem. Sangamon County Hist. Soc. (pres. 1961-62), Pub. Relations Soc. Am., Ill. State Hist. Soc. (v.p. 1978-80, pres.-elect 1985—), Abraham Lincoln Assn. (dir. 1983—), Lincoln Acad. of Ill. (regent 1983 chancellor 1984—), Chgo. High Tech. Assn. (bd. dirs. 1984—), Ill. C. of C. (dir. 1983—), Chgo. High Tech. Assn. (dir. 1984—), Alpha Sigma Phi (Nat. award Delta Beta Xi). Clubs: Mid-America, Tavern (bd. govs. 1978-81), Economic, City (Chgo.) (v.p. 1984—). Co-author: Handling Barriers in Communications, 1957; The Governor Takes a Bride, 1977. Contbr. articles to profl. jours. Home: 630 Clinton Pl Evanston IL 60201 Office: 225 W Randolph St Chicago IL 60606

TRYBER, THOMAS ANTHONY, JR., dairy foods company executive; b. Rapid City, S.D., May 18, 1943; s. Thomas A. and Rose Mary Tryber; student pub. schs., Racine, Wis; m. Kathleen M. Kober, May 25, 1963. Supr. cost and budgets J.I. Case, Racine, 1971-74, mgr. cost and budget control, 1974-77, fin. systems analyst, Wichita, Kans., 1977-78, mgr. systems and data processing, 1978-81; mgr. systems and data processing Steffens Dairy Foods Co., Inc., Wichita, Kans., 1982—. Mem. Data Processing Mgmt. Assn., Am. Prodn. Inventory Control Soc. Home: 1324 Crestline Wichita KS 67202 Office: 700 E Central Wichita KS 67208

TRYLCH, SCOTT WILLIAM, psychologist; b. Flint, Mich., Jan. 23, 1948; s. Donald Kent and Merodean Virginia (Harvie) T.; m. Darlene Sue Harris, May 12, 1973; children—Jason, Jeremy. M.A., Central Mich. U., 1972; Ed.D., Western Mich. U., 1982. Therapist, Genessee County Community Mental Health, Flint, Mich., 1972-73; clin. psychologist Cath. Family Service, Saginaw, Mich., 1973-81; intern Mott Children's Health Ctr., Flint, 1981-82; clin. supr., clin. psychologist Cath. Family Service, Saginaw, 1982—; pvt. practice psychology, 1984—. Mem. Am. Psychol. Assn., Am. Soc. Clin. Hypnosis, Am. Orthopsychiat. Assn., Mich. Assn. Profl. Psychologists, Soc. Personality Assessment, Mich. Soc. for Psychoanalytic Psychology, Mich. Psychol. Assn., Mich. Assn. Alcoholism and Drug Abuse Counselors, Mich. Burn Team. Office: 710 N Michigan St Saginaw MI 48602 also 120 N Michigan Ave Suite 220 Saginaw MI 48602

TSAI, TENLIN SIE, biochemist; b. Shanghai, China, June 15, 1948; came to U.S., 1969, naturalized, 1980; m. Steve Y.H. Tsai, Dec. 23, 1973; children—Miranda, Justin. Ph.D., U. Ill., 1974. Postdoctoral fellow U. Ill.-Chgo., 1974-75; research assoc. U. Ill., Urbana, Ill., 1975-78; sr. enzymologist United Techs./Packard Instrument Co., Downers Grove, Ill., 1979-83, research and devel. mgr., 1983—. Author: International Symposium of Bioluminescence and Chemiluminescence, 1981, 84; Methods of Enzymatic Analysis, 1984. Contbr. articles to profl. jours. Patentee in field. Recipient Indsl. Research award Tech. Pub., 1984; NIH research fellow, 1974; Natural Sci. scholar Taiwan Ministry Edn., 1968. Mem. AAAS, Am. Assn. Clin. Chemistry, Am. Fedn. Clin. Research, Sigma Xi. Office: United Techs/Packard Instrument Co 2200 Warrenville Rd Downers Grove IL 60515

TSALIKIAN, EVA, physician; b. Piraeus, Greece, June 22, 1949; came to U.S., 1974; d. Vartan and Arousiak (Kasparian) T. M.D., U. Athens, 1973. Research fellow U. Calif.-San Francisco, 1974-76; resident pediatrics Children's Hosp., Pitts., 1976-78, fellow endocrinology, 1978-80; research fellow Mayo Clinic, Rochester, Minn., 1980-83; asst. prof. dept. pediatrics U. Iowa, Iowa City, 1983—. Fellow Juvenile Diabetes Found., 1978-80, Heinz Nutrition Found., 1980-81; recipient Young Physician award AMA, 1977. Mem. Am. Diabetes Assn. Home: 1217 Dolan Pl Iowa City IA 52240 Office: Dept Pediatrics U Iowa Iowa City IA 52242

TSUKAMOTO, JACK TORU, library service educator, catalog librarian, consultant; b. Marugame, Japan, Jan. 3, 1931; came to U.S., 1954; s. Shigeru and Kinue (Yokota) T.; m. Nobuko Ohashi, Nov. 25, 1968 (div. 1979). B.A., Shikoku Christian Coll., 1954; B.A., Austin Coll., 1955; M.A., U. Tex.-Austin, 1960, M.L.S., 1962, Ph.D., 1976. Catalog librarian U. Tex.-Austin, 1961-63; asst. librarian Monmouth Coll. (Ill.), 1963-66; asst. prof. Japanese, Washington U., St. Louis, 1968-71; assoc. prof. library service Ball State U., Muncie, Ind., 1971—; dir., founder Tamagawa In USA, Monmouth, 1965-69; cons. Galaxy Systems, Inc., Washington, 1978—. Editor: Library Instruction, 1979. Shikoku Christian Coll. scholar, 1950-54; Bd. World Missions Presbyterian Ch. fellow, 1954-57; NDEA fellow, 1969-71. Mem. ALA, Assn. for Asian Studies, Linguistic Soc. Am., Japan Library Assn., Com. on East Asian Libraries. Home: 4305 Tillotson Muncie IN 47304 Office: Ball State U Library Muncie IN 47306

TUASON, RICARDO MAURICIO, general and hand surgeon; b. Bangued, Abra, Philippines, Nov. 27, 1938; s. Gabriel Barba and Mary (Foster) T.; m. Daisy Thiele Delgado, May 14, 1966. M.D., Univ. East, Manila, 1965. Diplomate Am. Bd. Surgery. Intern Ch. Home & Hosp., Balt., 1966-67, resident in surgery, 1967-71; fellow in hand surgery Cook County Hosp., Chgo., 1971-72; surgeon St. Joseph's Hosp., Bloomington, Ill., 1972-73; practice medicine specializing in hand surgery, Muncie, Ind., 1973—. Fellow ACS, Internat. Soc. Microsurgery, Am. Soc. Liposuction Surgery; mem. Del.-Blackford Med. Soc. Republican. Roman Catholic. Home: 4110 Riverside Ave Muncie IN 47304 Office: 420 W Washington St Muncie IN 47305

TUCKER, DENNIS CARL, library director; b. St. Louis, Oct. 17, 1945; s. Carl Ernest and Elsa Grace (Witt) T.; m. Maria Teresa Guillermina Castro, Dec. 6, 1975; children—Dennis Andrés, William Alexandro, Eric Scott. B.S., S.E. Mo. State U., 1967, M.A.T., 1974; M.L.S., U. Mo., 1983. Tchr. English, Univ. Autó. de Sinaloa, Culiacán, Mexico, 1971-73, Academia de Idiomas, 1974-76; owner, dir. Academia Logos, Mazatlán, Mexico, 1976-77; tchr. English, U. Américas, Cholula, Mexico, 1977-78; tchr. English and Spanish, Rifle High Sch. (Colo.), 1978-79; librarian Webb Jr. High Sch., East Prairie, Mo., 1980-83; dir. library Bethel Coll., Mishawaka, Ind., 1983—. Sec.-treas. S.E. Mo. Dept. Sch. Librarians, Cape Girardeau, 1980-82. Writer, photographer El Periódico del Noroeste, 1975-76. Recipient Kodak Internat. Newspaper Snapshot award, 1975. Mem. ALA, Ind. Coop. Library Services Authority (dir. 1983—), Area Library Services Authority (dir. 1983—), Christian Writers Club Michiana (v.p. 1984, pres. 1985), Sigma Tau Delta. Home: 17745 Tollview South Bend IN 46635 Office: Library Bethel Coll 1001 W McKinley Mishawaka IN 46545

TUCKER, GEORGE LEON, surgeon; b. New York, N.Y., Dec. 30, 1931; s. Max and Sally (Feiden) T.; m. Beverly Jean Irvine, June 15, 1963; children—Melodie Jean Monroe, Jason Patrick, Jonathan Paxson. A.B., Columbia U., 1952; M.D., Harvard U., 1956. Diplomate Am Bd Surgery. Intern, then resident Barnes Hosp., St. Louis, 1956-63, asst., assoc. surgeon, 1963—; chief surgeon St. Luke's Hosp., Chesterfield, Mo., 1983—; successively instr., asst-prof., assoc. prof. clin. surgery Washington U. Sch., St. Louis, 1963—. Contbr. articles to profl. jours., 1963—. Served to lt. M.C., USNR. Fellow Am. Coll. Surgeons; mem. Mo. State Surg. Soc. (pres. 1983-84), Barnes Hosp. Soc. (pres. 1982-83), Mo. chpt. ACS (councillor 1983—), AMA, St. Louis Surg. Soc. Episcopalian. Clubs: University, Racquet (St. Louis). Avocations: aviation; computer programming. Office: St Luke's Hosp 224 Woods Mill Rd S Chesterfield MO 63017

TUCKER, ROBERT ALLEN, communications executive; b. Pitts., Mar. 14, 1926; s. Newman Wallace and Helen Virginia (Stanley) T.; m. Jean Ardith Graves, Aug. 16, 1947; children—Robert Allen, Rebecca A., Douglas E., Kevin A. B.S. in Mktg., U. Pitts., 1950; LL.B., 1954; postgrad. Purdue U. Sch. Bus. Nat. sales mgr., dir. mktg. Fed. Plastics, Chgo., 1955-60; exec. v.p. Trindle Products, Ltd., Chgo., 1960-70; nat. v.p. sales Spl. Products div. Panasonic, 1971-75; internat. pres. Tele-Communications Radio, Inc., Des Plaines, Ill., 1975—. Nat. v.p. Young Republicans, 1961-62; pres. Young Reps., 1962-63. Served with USMC, 1942-46. Radio Club Am. fellow. Mem. Profl. Communications Dealers Assn. (pres.), Am. Police Communications Officers, Communications Mktg. Assn., Nat. Assn. Bus. and Ednl. Radio, IEEE (assoc.). Methodist. Clubs: Radio of Am., Sertoma (pres. 1961-63). Home: 98 East Ave Park Ridge IL 60068 Office: 960 Rand Rd Des Plaines IL 60016

TUCKER, SHERIDAN GREGORY, child psychiatrist, clinical psychopharmacologist; b. Bossier City, La., Feb. 26, 1950; s. William Samuel and Marie Regina (Nevarez) T.; m. Jaylene Dale Lambert, Dec. 30, 1977; children—Julia Elizabeth, Elliott Thomas. B.S., U. Mo.-Kansas City, 1972; M.D., U. Kans., 1975. Diplomate Am. Bd. Psychiatry and Neurology. Resident in psychiatry U. Kans., Kansas City, 1975-78. chief dept. psychiatry U.S. Army, Ft. Polk, La., 1978-80; fellow dept. psychiatry Kans. U. Med. Ctr., Kansas City, 1980-82, clin. asst. prof., 1984-85; staff dir. div. adolescent services Kans. Inst., Olathe, 1985; child psychiatrist Psychiat. and Psychol. Cons., Prairie Village, Kans., 1985—. Served to maj. U.S. Army, 1980-82. Decorated Army Commendation medal, 1980. Mem. Am. Acad. Child Psychiatry, Am. Acad. Clin. Psychiatrists, Am. Psychiat. Assn., N.Y. Acad. Scis., Assn. Child Psychology and Psychiatry. Republican. Episcopalian. Avocation: computing. Office: Psychiat and Psychol Cons 4121 W 83rd St Prairie Village KS 66208

TUCKER, THOMAS LESTAL, college official; b. Galatia, Ill., Nov. 6, 1937; s. Loren Denny and Ruth Edna (Dodd) T.; m. Patricia Sue Wheeler Parke, Feb. 22, 1958; m. Karen Sue Kraemer, Feb. 10, 1968; children—Patricia Sue Bixby (dec.), Debra Lynn, Thomas Lestal, Christina Mae. B.S., So. Ill. U., 1979; M.A., Webster Coll., 1983. Enlisted in USN, 1956; tng. mgr. Coll. Lake County, Naval Tng. Schs., Great Lakes, Ill., 1980—. Mem. Am. Vocat. Assn., Am. Legion. Roman Catholic. Lodges: Masons, Moose. Home: 411 E Schaumburg Rd Streamwood IL 60103 Office: Bldg 236 Room 349 SSC NTC Great Lakes IL 60088

TUCKER, THOMAS RANDALL, engine company public relations executive; b. Indpls., Aug. 6, 1931; s. Ovie Allen and Oris Aleen (Robertson) T.; A.B., Franklin Coll., 1953; m. Evelyn Marie Armuth, Aug. 9, 1953; children—Grant, Roger, Richard. Grad. asst. U. Minn., 1953-54; dir. admissions, registrar Franklin Coll., 1954-57; trainee Cummins Engine Co., Inc., Columbus, Ind., 1957-58; supr. community relations, 1958-61, mgr. community relations, 1961-64, mgr. pub. relations, 1964-68, dir. pub. relations, 1968—. Mem. Bd. Sch. Trustees Bartholomew County, Ind., 1966-72, pres., 1968-69; chmn. Bartholomew County Sch. Reorgn. Com., 1964-65; chmn. legis. com. Ind. Sch. Bd. Assn., 1970-71; mem. Ind. State Bd. Edn., 1977—; treas. Bartholomew County Republican Central Com., 1960-80; bd. dirs. Bartholomew County Hosp. Found., 1966-70, pres., 1968; trustee, chmn. ednl. policy com. of bd. trustees Franklin Coll.; bd. dirs. The Hoosier Salon. Recipient Distinguished Service award Columbus (Ind.) Jr. C. of C., 1965; named One of Five Outstanding Young Men, Ind. Jr. C. of C., 1965. Mem. Pub. Relations Soc. Am., Columbus C. of C., Kappa Tau Alpha, Phi Delta Theta, Sigma Delta Chi. Lutheran. Club: Rotary. Home: 4380 N Riverside Dr Columbus IN 47203 Office: Box 3005 Columbus IN 47202

TULER, DONALD THOMAS, educational administrator; b. Milw., March 5, 1936; s. Frank John and Irene Ann (Ptasynski) T.; m. Arlene Mary Guckenberger, July 7, 1956; children—Debra, Denise Tuler Scott, Michael. B.S., U. Wis.-Milw., 1958, M.S., 1963, Ed.S., 1976; Ph.D., U. Wis.-Madison, 1983. Tchr. elem. grades, pub. schs., Wis., 1958-67; dir. instrn. Glendale-River Hills pub. schs. (Wis.), 1967-72; asst. supt. Greendale pub. schs. (Wis.), 1972-73; prin. middle sch., elem. sch. Franklin Sch. Dist. 5 (Wis.), 1973-77; supt., dist. adminstr. Merton Sch. Dist. (Wis.), 1977-78; supt. schs. Nekoosa Sch. Dist. (Wis.), 1978-82, Port Washington Pub. Schs. (Wis.), 1982—; instr. edn. and reading, U. Wis. system, 1965-76; cons. reading, reading research Coop. Ednl. Service Agy. 19, Milw., 1970-72; cons. Harper & Row Pubs., 1984—; cons. leadership and mgmt. evaluation; pvt. tutor. Active Positive Youth Devel. Initiative. Mem. Assn. Supervision and Curriculum Devel. (bd. dirs. 1970-72), Am. Assn. Sch. Adminstrs., Wis. Assn. Sch. Dist. Adminstrs. (chmn. mgmt. team com.) Internat. Reading Assn. U. Wis. Alumni Assn., Phi Delta Kappa. Lodges: Rotary, KC (Council).

TULLMAN, HOWARD ALLEN, lawyer, entrepreneur; b. St. Louis, June 27, 1945; m. Judith K. Zindell, Apr. 18, 1983; children—Jamie B., Thea. B.A. cum laude, Northwestern U., 1967, J.D. with distinction, 1970. Bars: Ill. 1970, U.S. Dist. Ct. (no. dist.) Ill. 1970, U.S. Ct. Appeal (7th cir.) 1971, U.S. Supreme Ct. 1974. Assoc. Levy and Erens, Chgo., 1970-73, ptnr., 1974-81; pres. Hat Communications Co., Chgo., 1979—, Cert. Collateral Corp., Chgo., 1980—; arbitrator Am. Arbitration Assn., Chgo., 1976—; lectr. Grad. Bus. Sch., Northwestern U.; dir. Chestnut Foods, Inc., Chgo., Cert. Collateral Corp. Chmn.-assoc. editor Northwestern Law Rev., 1969. Contbr. articles to profl. jours. Mem. men's council Mus. Contemporary Art, Chgo., 1974—. Ford Found. fellow 1968. Mem. ABA, Ill. State Bar Assn., Chgo. Bar Assn., Order of Coif. Home: 219 W Concord Ln Chicago IL 60614 Office: Cert Collateral Corp 640 N LaSalle St Chicago IL 60610

TUMANIS, SUSAN KAY, marketing executive, consultant, writer; b. Sturgis, Mich., Mar. 10, 1949; d. Merritt W., Sr. and Marion A. (Stevens) T. B.A. in Journalism, Mich. State U., 1971; postgrad. In English Lit., Oakland U., 1979-80; completed various mgmt. courses, seminars. Gen. mgr. Orchard Mall, West Bloomfield, Mich., 1976-78, Trappers Alley Festival Market Place in Greektown, Detroit, 1985; asst. gen. mgr. Tel-Twelve Shopping Ctr., Southfield, Mich., 1978-80; mktg. dir. Wonderland Shopping Ctr., Livonia, Mich., 1980-84; account exec. Anthony M. Franco PR, Detroit, 1984-85, Simons Michelson Zieve, Inc., 1985—; instr. in shopping ctr. mktg. and promotion Oakland Community Coll.-Orchard Ridge, Farmington Hills, Mich.; reporter The Oakland Press, Pontiac, Mich., 1973-75, The Associated Press, Detroit, 1973; reporter, mag. editor, wire editor The Sandusky Register, Ohio, 1972-73. Contbr. articles to profl. jours. Editor Youth Today Page, Battle Creek Enquirer and News, 1965-71. Vol. Reuther for Congress, 1973; vol. Washtenaw County Commr. Kathleen Fojtak, 1973; co-chmn. Walled Lake Christmas Treelighting Com., 1975; mem. pub. relations com. Walled Lake Annual Waterfest Com., 1975, Mich. Artrain, Milford, 1976; pub. relations dir., treas. Roberts for State Rep. 24th Dist., 1976, co-mgr., 1980; mem. bi-centennial research com. Walled Lake and Commerce Township Cemeteries, 1976; mem. West Oakland League of Women Voters, 1976-77 (nominated state pub. relations chmn.); chmn. West Bloomfield Mich. Week Parade com., 1977, 78; press coordinator High-Am.-Detroit News Balloon Festival, Rochester, Mich., 1980; bd. dirs. Miss Livonia Scholarship Pageant, 1983, West Bloomfield Symphony Orchestra, 1978, West Bloomfield High Sch. Co-operative Edn. Adv. Council, 1977, 78. Mem. Greater West Bloomfield C. of C. (sec. 1977-78), Nat. Writer's Club (adv. bd. mem. 1970, 71), Livonia C. of C. (bd. dirs. 1984), Sigma Delta Chi (recipient Mark of Excellence 1971). Democrat. Episcopalian. Avocations: gravestone rubbings (tracing); sailing. Home: 874 Village Green Ln #2083 Pontiac MI 48054

TUNCA, JOSH COSKUN, physician, educator; b. Istanbul, Turkey, July 19, 1943; came to U.S., 1968, naturalized, 1978; s. Ahmet and Hikmet Emine Tunca; M.D., Cerrahpasa Med. Sch., Istanbul, 1968; m. Nilgun Musoglu, May 1, 1970; 2 sons, Alper, John. Intern, New Hanover Meml. Hosp., Wilmington, N.C., 1968-69; resident in obstetrics and gynecology Bowman-Gray Sch. Medicine, Wake Forest U., Winston-Salem, N.C., 1969-73, chief resident, 1972-73; fellow gynecol. oncology Emory U. Sch. Medicine, Atlanta, Ga., 1973-75; practice medicine specializing in ob-gyn (gynecol. oncology) Morgantown, W.Va., 1975-77; dir. gynecol. oncology W.Va. U. Sch. Medicine, 1975-77, asst. prof. ob-gyn, 1975-77; asst. prof. ob-gyn, assoc. dir. gynecol. oncology U. Wis., Madison, 1977-82; assoc. prof., dir. gynecol. oncology U. Ill. Coll. Medicine, Chgo., 1982—; practice medicine specializing in ob-gyn, 1982-84. Am. Cancer Soc. Jr. Faculty Clin. fellow, 1978-79; diplomate Am. Bd. Ob-Gyn. Mem. Am. Coll. Ob-Gyn, Soc. Gynecol. Oncology, Am. Soc. Clin. Oncology, N.Y. Acad. Scis., AMA. Contbr. articles in field to med. publs. Home: 100 Sequoia Lane Deerfield IL 60015 Office: 2510 Dempster Suite 112 Des Plaines IL 60016

TUNGATE, JAMES LESTER, lawyer; b. Columbus, Ohio, Sept. 27, 1947; s. Ernest O. Jr. and Diantha (Woltz) T.; m. Susan Sumner, Aug. 25, 1973; 1 child, Edward Ernest. B.S., Ill. Wesleyan U., 1969; M.A., Northwestern U.-Ill., 1970, Ph.D., 1972; J.D., U. Ill.-Urbana, 1979; hon. D.H.L., London Sch. (Eng.), 1972. Bar: Ill. 1979, U.S. Supreme Ct. 1985. Spl. instr. Northwestern U., Evanston, Ill., 1971; prof., chmn. Loyola U., New Orleans, 1971-76; state dir. News Election Service, New Orleans, 1972-74; dir. Inst. Religious Communications, New Orleans, 1974-76; asst. to state's atty. Iroquois County, Watseka, Ill., 1978; ptnr. Tungate & Tungate, Watseka, 1979—; media cons. Inst. Politics, New Orleans, 1973-76; legal cons., lectr. Iroquois Mental Health Ctr., Watseka, 1980—; lectr. law Kankakee Community Coll., Ill., 1982. Author: Romantic Images in Popular Songs, 1972; Readings in Broadcast Law, 1975. Dir. Iroquois Mental Health Ctr., 1980—; chmn. Iroquois County chpt. ARC, 1982-84, 85—; dir. Iroquois Republican Council, 1983—. Recipient Internat. Radio and TV Found. award; Harnow scholar U. Ill., 1976. Mem. Ill. Bar Assn., Iroquois County Bar Assn. (Law Day chmn.), Chgo. Bar Assn., Assn. Trial Lawyers Am., Am. Film Inst., Pi Alpha Delta. Republican. Methodist. Lodges: Masons (master 1982-83), Elks. Home: 454 S 5th St Watseka IL 60970 Office: Tungate & Tungate PO Box 337 Watseka IL 60970

TUNIS, SANDRA SIMMONS, health services administrator; b. Fort Wayne, Ind., Mar. 18, 1948; d. Robert Walter and Martha Louise (Krueckeberg) Simmons; m. Ronald Ellis Tunis, Aug. 22, 1970; 1 dau., Kristin Marie. B.A. in Microbiology with distinction Ind. U., 1970; A.A. in Nursing with highest distinction Ind. U.-Kokomo, 1975. R.N., Ind., Wis.; cert. swimming ofcl. Microbiology lab. asst. Ind. U., Bloomington, 1968-70; microbiologist Meml. Hosp., Logansport, Ind., 1970, student nurse, 1973-75, staff nurse, 1975, night charge nurse obstetrics, 1976, nurse epidemiologist, quality assurance coordinator, 1977-85; health services adminstr. HealthReach Health Maintenance Orgn., Milw., 1985—; lectr. at continuing edn. workshops; cons. to various infection control practitioners; mem. Ind. U.-Kokomo Nursing Adv. Bd.; preceptor for baccalaureate nursing students Purdue U. Active Logansport community ch. choir. Mem. Ind. State Nurses Assn. (vol. program rev. for continuing edn.), Assn. for Practitioners in Infection Control (pres. Ind. chpt. 1984), Ind. Assn. Quality Assurance Profls., Wis. Assn. Quality Assurance Profls., Assn. for Continuity of Care, Ind. U. Alumni Assn. (active extern program), Phi Beta Kappa, Psi Iota Xi (pres. Alpha Xi chpt.). Democrat. Lutheran. Home: 150 E Chateau Milwaukee WI 53217 Office: HealthReach 2266 N Prospect Suite 612 Milwaukee WI 53202

TUOMI, DONALD, scientific firm executive, materials scientist, consultant; b. Willoughby, Ohio, Sept. 12, 1920; s. August and Lempi (Kannasta) T.; m. Ruth Elaine Campbell, May 23, 1923; children—Donna Jean, Mary Ellen. B.S. in Chemistry, Ohio State U., Columbus, 1943; Ph.D. in Phys. Chemistry, 1952. Research scientist Manhattan Project, SAM Labs., Columbia U., 1943-45; staff mem. MIT Lincoln Lab., Cambridge, 1953-54; research scientist Research Lab. T.A. Edison Corp., West Orange, N.J., 1955-59, T.A. Research Lab., McGraw Edison Corp., West Orange, 1959-61; mgr. solid-state physics Borg-Warner Research Ctr., Des Plaines, Ill., 1961-78, sr. scientist, 1978-83; pres. Donald Tuomi Ph.D. and Assocs. Ltd., Arlington Heights, Ill., 1983—; vis. indsl. sci. lectr. Am. Chem. Soc., Am. Inst. Physics, Indsl. Research Inst.; lectr. in field. Lay del. United Methodist Ch. Ann. Conf.; active Nuclear Freeze, Clergy and Laity Concerned, Common Cause. Recipient award of Merit Chgo. Tech. Soc. Council, 1973. Fellow Am. Inst. Chem., AAAS; mem. Am. Phys. Soc., Am. Chem. Soc., The Electro-Chem. Soc. (Battery Div. award 1968), Am. Crystallographic Soc., Sigma Xi. Conbtr. articles in field to profl. jours. Patentee thermo electric energy conversion, batteries, polymers. Home: 221 S Illinois Dr Arlington Heights IL 60005 Office: 103 N Arlington Heights Rd Arlington Heights IL 60004

TURCOTTE, MARGARET JANE, nurse; b. Stow, Ohio, May 17, 1927; d. Edward Carlton and Florence Margaret (Hanson) McCauley; R.N., St. Thomas Hosp., Akron, Ohio, 1949; m. Rene George Joseph, Nov. 24, 1961 (div. June 1967); 1 son, Michael Lawrence. Mem. nursing staff St. Thomas Hosp., 1949-50; pvt. duty nurse, 1950-57; polio nurse Akron's Children Hosp., 1953-54; mem. nursing staff Robinson Meml. Hosp., Ravenna, Ohio, 1958-67, head central service, 1963-67; supr. central service Brentwood Hosp., Warrensville Heights, Ohio, 1967, emergency med. technician. Mem. St. Thomas Hosp. Alumni Assn. Democrat. Roman Catholic. Home: 6037 Highview St Lot 14-F Ravenna OH 44266 Office: 4110 Warrensville Center Rd Warrensville Heights OH 44122

TUREK, FRED WILLIAM, educator; b. Detroit, July 31, 1947. B.S., Mich. State U., 1969; Ph.D., Stanford U., 1973. Postdoctoral fellow U. Tex., Austin, 1973-75; asst. prof. Northwestern U., Evanston, Ill., 1975-80, assoc. prof., 1980-83, prof. dept. neurobiology and physiology, 1983—. Contbr. articles to profl. jours. NIH grantee, 1978-83, 78-83. Fellow AAAS; mem. Endocrine Soc., Neurosci. Soc., Am. Physiol. Soc., Soc. Study of Reprodn. Home: 990 N Lakeshore #33D Chicago IL 60611 Office: Dept Neurobiology and Physiology Hogan Bldg Evanston IL 60201

TURINO, BRUCE ROBERT, chiropractor; b. Marquette, Mich., Feb. 9, 1950; s. Robert Walter and Helen Marian (Koskinen) T.; m. Mary Catherine Downs, Aug. 21, 1971; 1 son, Brandon John. B.S., Palmer Coll. Chiropractic, 1978, Dr. of Chiropractic, 1978. Orderly, Bell Meml. Hosp., Ishpeming, Mich., 1973-75; chiropractor, prin. Turino Chiropractic Ctr., Ishpeming, 1978—; lectr. in field. Served with USNR, 1969-73. Mem. Internat. Chiropractic Assn., Mich. State Chiropractic Assn., Mich. Chiropractic Council, Am. Legion. Roman Catholic. Lodges: Kiwanis, Elks. Home: 215 S Rose St Ishpeming MI 49849 Office: 587 Washington St Ishpeming MI 49849

TURK, ALICE ELAINE, banker; b. Cleve., June 15, 1948; d. Melton Norman and Alice Loretta (Paulus) McConnell. Student Sch. Banking, U. Wis., 1981. Acct., Soc. Nat. Bank, Cleve., 1968-78, asst. treas., 1978-79, sr. fin. systems officer, 1979-82, v.p., mgr. acctg. and fin. systems, 1982—. Recipient cert. merit YWCA, 1980, profl. excellence award, 1983. Mem. Bank Adminstrn. Inst.,

Am. Inst. Banking. Democrat. Roman Catholic. Office: 127 Public Square Cleveland OH 44114

TURNBULL, CHARLES VINCENT, hospital administrator; b. Mpls., May 13, 1933; s. Charles Vivien and Lucille Frances (Dallas) T.; B.A. in Sociology, U. Minn., 1960, M.S.W., 1962; m. Gloria Marlene Tilley, July 21, 1956; children—Charlene Kay, Charles Vincent, Terry Lucille, Mary Marlene. Unit dir. mental health treatment service Cambridge (Minn.) State Hosp., 1962-67, dir. rehab. therapies, 1967-68, program dir., 1973-74; program dir. Minn. Valley Social Adaptation Center, St. Peter, 1968-73; chief exec. officer Faribault (Minn.) State Hosp., 1974-84; adminstr. Minn. Vets. Home, Mpls. and Hastings, 1984—; program cons. Rochester (Minn.) Social Adaptation Center, 1970-71; cons. St. Louis State Sch. and Hosp., 1973-74. Chmn., United Fund Drive, St. Peter, 1971; scoutmaster Boy Scouts Am., 1973-75; co-chmn. Faribault Bicentennial Horizons Subcom., 1975-76; mem. Minn. Developmental Disabilities Planning Council, 1975, chmn. comprehensive planning subcom., 1977-78; chmn. Cannon River Adv. Council, 1978-79; pres. Riverbend Nature Center, 1981—; mayor Village of Lexington (Minn.), 1962-64; candidate for U.S. Ho. of Reps. from 2d Dist. Minn., 1972, 74. Served with USMC, 1953-56. Mem. Am. Assn. Mental Deficiency. Mem. Democratic-Farm-Labor Party. Lutheran. Home: Route 3 Box 169 Faribault MN 55021 Office: Minn Vets Home 5101 Minnehaha Ave S Minneapolis MN 55417

TURNER, DONALD WILLIAM, dental educator, researcher; b. St. Louis, Jan. 24, 1931; s. Glenn Rolwes and Helen Ursula (Kuhn) T.; m. Mary Ellen Shaughnessy, June 29, 1957; children—Joan, Ann, Glenn, Thomas, Mark, Timothy. B.S., Washington U., St. Louis, 1957, D.D.S., 1960; Ph.D., U. Md., 1974. Gen. practice dentistry, Mexico, Mo., 1960-64; commd. lt. U.S. Navy, 1964, advanced through grades to capt., 1982; dental officer U.S. Navy, 1964-82; assoc. prof. Northwestern U., Chgo., 1982—; guest lectr. Okla. U., Oklahoma City, 1983—. Decorated Bronze Star. Fellow Internat. Coll. Dentists; mem. Am. Assn. Dental Research (pres. Washington chpt. 1979-80), ADA, Internat. Assn. Dental Research. Roman Catholic. Avocation: Civil War literature and history. Office: Northwestern U Dental Sch 240 E Huron St Chicago IL 60611

TURNER, EVAN HOPKINS, museum adminstrator; b. Orono, Maine, Nov. 8, 1927; s. Albert Morton and Percie Trowbridge (Hopkins) T.; m. Brenda Winthrop Bowman, May 12, 1956; children—John W., Jennifer H. A.B., Harvard U., 1949, M.A., 1950, Ph.D., 1954. Head docent service Fogg Mus., 1950-51; curator Robbins Art Collection of Prints, Arlington, Mass., 1951; teaching fellow fine arts Harvard U., 1951-52; lectr., research asst. Frick Collection, N.Y.C., 1953-56; gen. curator, asst. dir. Wadsworth Atheneum, Hartford, Conn., 1956-59; dir. Montreal Mus. Fine Arts, Que., Can., 1959-64, Phila. Mus. Art, 1964-77, Ackland Art Mus., Chapel Hill, N.C., 1978-83; adj. prof. U. N.C., Chapel Hill, 1978-83; adj. prof. art history U. Pa., Phila., 1964-77; dir. Cleve. Mus. Art, 1983—. Benjamin Franklin fellow Royal Soc. Arts. Mem. Assn. Art Mus. Dirs., Coll. Art Assn., Am. Assn. Mus., Am. Fedn. Arts. Clubs: Union (Cleve.); Century Assn. (N.Y.C.); Unitatian (Franklin Inn-Phila.).

TURNER, FRED L., fast food restaurant company executive; b. 1933; student Drake U.; married. With McDonald's Corp., Oak Brook, Ill., 1957—, v.p. ops., 1958-67, exec. v.p., 1967-68, pres., chief adminstrv. officer, 1968-73, chief exec. officer, 1973-77, chmn. bd., chief exec. officer, 1977—, also dir. Served with U.S. Army, 1943-45. Office: McDonald's Corp McDonald's Plaza Oak Brook IL 60521

TURNER, GLENN FORREST, office supply company executive; b. Lake Forest, Ill., Nov. 7, 1954; s. Forrest Eugene and Lottie Cathryn (Abshire) T. B.S., No. Ill. U. Instr. Ill. Inst. Diving, Glen Ellyn, Ill., 1978-83; mem. sales staff Suburban Office Supply, Crystal Lake, Ill., 1970-73, mgr., 1973-77, v.p., 1977—; co-founder Kiss Research & Devel. Co., Marengo, Ill., 1984—. Mem. Ill. Retail Mchts. Assn., Nat. Office Products Assn., U.S. C. of C., Cousteau Soc. Avocations: flying; scuba diving; woodworking. Home: 127 N Main St Crystal Lake IL 60014 Office: Suburban Office Supply Inc 125 N Main St Crystal Lake IL 60014

TURNER, GREGORY SCOTT, jeweler; b. Harrisonburg, Va., June 23, 1950; s. Waldo Neil and Margaret (Yoder) T.; m. Lana Eileen Hostetler, June 26, 1976 (div. Apr. 1985); children—Tara Dawn, Gregory Seth; m. Mary Jo Schumacher, June 22, 1985. A.S. in Bus. Mgmt., Blue Ridge Community Coll., 1974; grad. State Tech. Inst. and Rehab. Ctr., 1980. Cert. horologist, jeweler. Brick mason G. Swick Co., Broadway, Va., 1966-69; bus. mgr. Turner Constrn., Broadway, 1971-73; watch repairman D. Isham Repair Service, Kinde, Mich., 1976-77; watchmaker John Ballas Jeweler, Pueblo, Colo., 1980-81; owner Greg Turner Jewelers, Hartville, Ohio, 1981—. Mem. Lake Twp. Zoning Appeals Bd., Hartville, 1985. Mem. Nat. Wheelchair Athletic Assn., Hartville Jaycees. Republican. Mem. Pentecostal Ch. Avocations: swimming; fishing; flying; cars. Home: 2171 Green St Hartville OH 44632 Office: Greg Turner Jewelers 137 S Prospect St PO Box 988 Hartville OH 44632

TURNER, HERMAN NATHANIEL, JR., educator; b. St. Louis, Nov. 6, 1925; s. Herman Nathaniel and Rosie Mae (Williams) T.; B.S., Bradley U., Peoria, Ill., 1951; m. Terrance Diane Parker, Oct. 5, 1980; children by previous marriage—Anthony, Mark, Herman Nathaniel III, Erik; stepchildren—Marian, Mariesta and Melita Simmons. Cartographic aide Aero. Chart and Info. Center, St. Louis 1953-54; mathematician White Sands Proving Ground, N.Mex., 1954-55; tchr. math., Caruthersville, Mo., 1961-62, Phila., 1956-59, East Moline, Ill., 1965-66, N.W. High Sch., St. Louis, 1968-84, Visual and Performing Arts High Sch., St. Louis, 1984, Vashon High Sch., St. Louis, 1984—. Area coordinator Operation Brightside (city clean-up campaign), St. Louis, 1982-83. Served with USMC, 1944-46. Named Tchr. of Yr., N.W. High Sch., 1980; Community Worker citation St. Louis Voice mag., 1982; cert. math. tchr., Mo., Ill., N.Y., Pa., N.J.; recipient cert. of appreciation Kiwanis Club of East Moline, 1965; named Tchr. of Month, N.W. High Sch., 1979. Fellow Internat. Biog. Assn., Am. Biog. Inst. (nat. bd. advs.), Anglo-Am. Acad. (hon.); mem. Math. Assn. Am., Am. Math. Soc., Am. Fedn. Tchrs. Democrat. Presbyterian. Club: East Moline Kiwanis. Home: 5917 Emma Ave Saint Louis MO 63136 Office: Vashon High Sch 3504 Bell Ave Saint Louis MO 63106

TURNER, JOHN GOSNEY, See *Who's Who in America,* 43rd edition.

TURNER, JOHN WHITFIELD, JR., endocrinologist; b. Texarkana, Ark., June 13, 1944; s. John W. and Nancy (Williamson) T.; m. Valerie Anne Chamberlain, June 23, 1966; children—Melissa, Delaney. B.A., Franklin and Marshall Coll., 1966; Ph.D., Cornell U., 1970. Postdoctoral researcher UCLA Med. Sch. and Brain Research Inst., 1971; instr. Med. Coll. Ohio, Toledo, 1971-72, asst. prof., 1973-79, assoc. prof., 1979—; vis. assoc. prof. UCLA Med. Sch., 1983. Author: Restricted Environmental Stimulation and Self-Regulation, 1985. Contbr. articles to profl. jours. Dir. Human Sexuality Program in Medicine, Reprodn. Clinic, Med. Coll. Ohio, 1975—. Grantee NIH, U.S. Dept. Interior, Med. Coll. Ohio, pvt. founds., Animal Welfare Inst. Mem. Flotation Tank Assn., Internat. Restricted Environ. Stimulation Therapy Investigators Soc., Soc. Study Reprodn., Sigma Xi. Democrat. Mem. Christian Ch. Avocations: Mountaineering, hiking, guitar, auto mechanics, writing. Office: Medical Coll Ohio Dept Physiology CS 10008 Toledo OH 43699

TURNER, RICHARD BARRY, communications executive; b. Phoenix, Nov. 18, 1940; s. John Richard and Elizabeth Ross (Barry) T.; B.S., Northwestern U., 1962; M.S., Ariz. State U., 1968. Gen. mgr. Arie Crown Theatre, Chicago, 1974; co. mgr., assoc. dir. pub. relations, editor Lyric Opera News, Lyric Opera of Chgo., 1974-81; dir. info. services and advt. Sta. WTTW-TV, Chgo., 1981-85; dir. communications Chgo. Community Trust, 1985—. Past chmn. Joseph Jefferson awards comm.; founding pres. bd. dirs. Wisdom Bridge and Travel Light Theatres, Steppenwolf Theatre, Hubbard Street Dance; mem. assocs. bd. U. Chgo. Cancer Research Found. Club: Arts (Chgo.). Office: 208 S La Salle St Chicago IL 60604

TURNER, RICHARD LEE, JR., lawyer, real estate broker; b. Sendai, Japan, July 6, 1955; s. Richard L. and Ruth (Barron) T.; m. Anita Jo Dlabal, Aug. 11, 1979; 2 children—Joseph Adam, Genevieve Lee. B.S. in Edn., No. Ill. U., 1977; J.D. with honors, DePaul U., 1981. Bar: Ill. 1981, U.S. Dist. Ct. (no. dist.) Ill. 1981. Tchr. spl. edn. DeKalb Sch. Dist. 428, Ill., 1977-78; legal intern DeKalb County States Atty., Sycamore, Ill., 1979-81; assoc. Minnihan, Smith & Brown, Sycamore, 1981-82, Burns and Carlson, DeKalb, Ill., 1982-83; ptnr. Burns, Cronauer & Turner, DeKalb, 1984—. Big bro. Big Bros. and Big Sisters, DeKalb County, Ill., 1983-84; mem. DeKalb County Bd. Health, 1982—. Recipient Am. Jurisprudence award AmJur Pub. Co., 1979; Law Found. grantee Gonzga Law Sch., 1979. Mem. ABA, Assn. Trial Lawyers Am., Ill. State Bar Assn., Ill. Trial Lawyers Assn., DeKalb County Bar Assn. (sec.-treas. 1983-84), DeKalb Jaycees, Phi Alpha Delta. Lodges: KC (chancellor adv. 1982-83), Kiwanis. Home: 120 Charter St DeKalb IL 60115 Office: Burns Cronauer & Turner 1017 N 1st St DeKalb IL 60115

TURNER, THEODORE HOWARD, educational administrator; b. Wierton, W.Va., July 24, 1924; s. James Howard and Alice Josephine (Newsome) T.; m. Iva Mae Smithers, June 2, 1951; children—Marcia Lynn, Amy Kathleen. B.S., Ohio State U., 1950; B.Mus., 1950; M.Ed., U. Cin., 1956. Tchr. music, Lockland, Ohio, 1950-56, Cin., 1956-57, Columbus, Ohio, 1957-66; jr. high sch. prin., Columbus, 1966-69, high sch. prin., 1969-74, interim supt., Columbus, 1982, asst. supt., 1974—. Served with U.S. Army, 1943-46; ETO. Mem. Nat. Assn. Jazz Educators, Nat. Alliance Black Sch. Educators, Am. Assn. Sch. Adminstrs., Assn. Curriculum and Supervision Devel., Music Educators Nat. Conf., U.S. Tennis Assn., NAACP, Columbus Com. Mental Health, Columbus Leadership Conf., PUSH, Phi Mu Alpha, Phi Delta Kappa.

TURNER, TIM, historic preservation executive; b. Mpls., July 2, 1948; s. Lawrence Frank and Lois Muriel (Hedlund) T.; m. Elizabeth Ann Christensen, Aug. 2, 1969; 1 child, Jennifer Marie. B.A., U. Nebr., 1972. Editorial asst. Nebr. Hist. Soc., Lincoln, 1972-73, curator hist. sites, 1973-76; preservation planner Nat. Trust for Historic Preservation, Oklahoma City, 1976-79, asst. dir., Chgo., 1979-80, regional dir., 1981—; dir. Neighborhood Devel. and Conservation Ctr., Oklahoma City, 1978-79; vice chmn. Coalition Neighborhood Assns., Oklahoma City, 1978-79. Mem. adv. com. Friends of Downtown Chgo., Ill., 1982—. Democrat. Roman Catholic. Avocation: golf. Office: Nat Trust for Historic Preservation 407 S Dearborn Suite 710 Chgo IL 60605

TURNHAM, YALE THOMAS, educator; b. Independence, Mo., Dec. 12, 1948; s. Yale and Marjorie Wilma (Lyness) T. B.A. in Music, B.S. in Psychology, Central Mo. State U., 1975. Cert. tchr., Mo. Child care worker Ozanam Home for Boys, Kansas City, Mo., 1973-75; tchr. Pilot Grove (Mo.) High Sch., 1978-79; tchr. behaviorally disordered Knob Noster (Mo.) Pub. Schs., 1979-80; spl. services tchr., vocat. adjustment coordinator Crest Ridge High Sch., Centerview, Mo., 1980—; ordained to ministry Ch. of Gospel Ministry, 1983. Bd. dirs. Indsl. Services Contractors, Inc. Warrensburg, Mo., 1979—. Mem. Internat. Reading Assn., Mo. State Tchrs. Assn., Phi Mu Alpha. Home: PO Box 463 Warrensburg MO 64093 Office: Route 2 Box 94 Centerview MO 64019

TURNQUIST, DANA DEE, office administrator; b. Crosby, Minn., Nov. 15, 1943; d. Robert Louis and Valerie June (Lefebvre) Vranish; student U. Minn., Duluth, 1961-63, 74-79; m. Kenneth E. Turnquist, Sept. 14, 1963; children—Christopher Paul, Brett Eric. Dir. Youth Activities Ctr., Goeppingen, Germany, 1966-67; office mgr. Hickory Lodge, Crosby, 1968; adminstrv. asst. to pres. Key Finders, Inc., St. Paul, 1976-77; personnel adminstr. Gray, Plant, Mooty, Mooty & Bennett, Mpls., 1978-81; pres. Minn. Legal Adminstrs. Assn., 1982-83. United Way coordinator, 1978-80. Mem. Minn. Legal Office Adminstrs. Assn. (pres. 1982-83), Am. Bus. Women's Assn., Assn. Legal Adminstrs., Devonshire Homeowners Assn. Lutheran. Home: 3040 Devonshire Dr Woodbury MN 55125 Office: Gray Plant Mooty Mooty Bennett 300 Roanoke Bldg Minneapolis MN 55402

TURRIFF, CLARENCE JOSEPH, chemical executive; b. Green Bay, Wis., Apr. 22, 1920; s. Charles Henry and Dorinda (Quatsoe) T.; B.S., St. Norbert Coll., 1941; m. Gladys Cecelia Hoenslaar, Apr. 30, 1942; children—Barbara Ann Turriff Shiple, Thomas Joseph, Susan Clare Turriff Leichtman, Terry Lynn, Mary Lee. Buyer, McKesson & Robbins, Inc., Chgo., 1946-48; br. mgr. McKesson Chem. Co., Chgo., 1948-53, dist. mgr., 1953-58; pres., chief exec. TAB Chem. Inc., Chgo., 1958—, owner, chief exec. officer, 1979—; dir. 1st Nat. Bank Western Springs. Served to maj. AUS, 1941-46. Mem. Chgo. Drug and Chem. Assn. (dir. 1963—, pres. 1970). Republican. Roman Catholic. Clubs: Sugar Mill (Fla.) Country; LaGrange (Ill.) Country. Home: 5631 Lawn Dr Western Springs IL 60558 also 228 Live Oak Ln Sugar Mill Country Club Estates New Smyrna Beach FL 32069 Office: 4801 S Austin Ave Chicago IL 60638

TURRILL, SHELDON LEE, geologist, consultant; b. Marietta, Ohio, Nov. 15, 1932; s. Harry Austin and Marie Evelyn (Morris) T.; m. Marlene Ann Stanley, Sept. 7, 1957; children—Sheldon L. Jr., Alison Ann, Amie Michelle. B.S., Ohio U., 1958, M.S., 1960. Geologist Texaco Inc., Columbus, Ohio, 1960-63, pvt. cons. geologist, Columbus, 1963—. Served with USAF, 1950-54. Mem. Ohio Geol. Soc. (pres. 1978), Am. Assn. Petroleum Geologists (cert.), Am. Inst. Profl. Geol. Scientists (cert.), Ohio Oil and Gas Assn. (trustee 1979-84). Avocations: hunting; fishing; golf. Home: 4936 Wintersong Ln Westerville OH 43081 Office: 3592 Corporate Dr Columbus OH 43229

TURSSO, DENNIS JOSEPH, business executive; b. St. Paul, Apr. 13, 1939; s. Joseph Bias and Cecelia Beatrice (Solheid) T.; m. Sharon Ann Benike, June 6, 1964 (div. 1975); 1 son, Jason Bradford; m. 2d, Jacqueline Mary Hoffmann, Oct. 19, 1977; children—Shannon and Missey Michele (twins). Student U. Minn., 1959-61. Sales mgr. Sten-C-Labl Inc., St. Paul, 1958-65; salesman Dymo Industries, Berkeley, Calif., 1965-68; with Dawson Patterson, St. Paul, 1968—; pres., chief exec. officer Tursso Cos. holding co., St. Paul, 1980—; dir. Summit Nat. Bank, St. Paul. Advisor SBA, St. Paul, 1981-83. Recipient Star Club sales awards Dymo Industries, 1966, 67. Mem. Nat. Fed. Ind. Bus., Soc. Packaging Engrs., St. Paul C. of C. (cert. of merit). Clubs: St. Paul Athletic, St. Paul, University, Minnesota, Decathlon, Pool and Yacht. Address: Tursso Cos 223 Plato Blvd E Saint Paul MN 55107

TUSCHMAN, JAMES MARSHALL, steel company executive, lawyer; b. Toledo, Nov. 28, 1941; s. Chester and Harriet (Harris) T.; B.S. in Bus., Miami U., Oxford, Ohio, 1963; J.D., Ohio State U., 1966; m. Ina S. Cheloff, Sept. 2, 1967; children—Chad Michael, Jon Stephen, Sari Anne. Admitted to Ohio bar, 1966, since practiced in Toledo; ptnr. Shumaker, Loop & Kendrick, 1966-84; a founder, sr. prin. Jacobson Maynard Tuschman & Kalur, Toledo, Cleve., Cin. and Columbus, Ohio, 1984—, also mem. mgmt. com.; chmn. bd., sec. Tuschman Steel Co., Toledo, 1969-76; vice chmn. bd. Kripke Tuschman Industries, Inc., 1977—; chmn. bd., sec. Toledo Steel Supply Co., 1969—; ptnr. Starr Ave. Co., Toledo; gen. counsel Toledo subs. bd. PIE Mut. Ins. Co. Trustee, Maumee Valley Country Day Sch., Jewish Welfare Fedn. of Toledo. Mem. Am., Ohio, Toledo bar assns., Nat. Assn. R.R. Trial Counsel, Def. Research Inst., Soc. Hosp. Attys., Zeta Beta Tau, Phi Delta Phi. Jewish (past trustee, v.p., treas. temple). Clubs: Glengary Country, Toledo. Home: 5240 Coldstream Rd Toledo OH 43623 Office: 4 Sea Gate 9th Floor Toledo OH 43604

TUSZYNSKI, SHERRY LEE, medical instrumentation company executive; b. Monroe, La., Sept. 24, 1942; d. Lee Edward and Lyda Fern (Epley) Trahan; m. Jack Price, Mar., 1961; m. Robert Allen Tuszynski, Dec. 26, 1969; 1 son, Bruce Lee. B.A. in Econs., Ind. U., 1969. Sales analyst Puritan-Bennett Corp., Westmont, Ill., 1973-76, mgr. sales analysis, 1976, sales rep., 1976-82, dist. sales mgr., 1982—. Mem. Alpha Mu Gamma. Office: Puritan-Bennett 26 Plaza Dr Westmont IL 60559

TUTEN, RICHARD KIRBY, mechanical engineer; b. Columbia, S.C., Jan. 9, 1933; s. Raphael O. and Ethelyn (Kirby) T.; m. Jane Houchens, Feb. 23, 1974; 1 child, Amy Marie; m. Virginia Cory, Aug. 1, 1964 (dec. Aug. 1973). B.S., U. S.C., 1955. Engr., E.I. DuPont, Nashville, 1955; engr., Gen. Electric Co., Cin., 1957—, program mgr., 1976-83, design mgr., 1983—. Patentee engine mounting. Mem. Planning Commn. Montgomery, 1984, Landmarks Commn., 1984. Republican. Baptist. Avocations: sailing; fishing. Home: 10561 Adventure Ln Montgomery OH 45242 Office: Gen Electric 1 Neumann Way Cincinnati OH 45215

TUTTLE, ROBERT D., industrial products manufacturing company executive. Chmn., pres., chief exec. officer, dir. Sealed Power Corp., Muskegon, Mich. Office: Sealed Power Corp 100 Terrace Plaza Muskegon MI 49443*

TWEED, THOMAS EDWARD, corporate executive; b. Mason City, Iowa, Aug. 11, 1942; s. Selmer Theodore and Clarissa F. (Dahl) T.; m. Rita Lorainne Johnson, Nov. 26, 1964; children—Nancy Anne, Michael Thomas. Student U. Iowa. Sales rep. CIBA Pharmaceutical, Summit, N.J., 1968-73; regional mgr. Ludlow Corp., Ware, Mass., 1973-81; pres. Heart Medical, Inc., Hanover Park, Ill., 1982—. Bd. dirs. Evangel. Retirement Homes/Friendship Village of Schaumburg, Chgo. and Schaumburg, Ill., 1982—; pres. Lord of Life Lutheran Ch., Schaumburg, 1984. Served as HM3 USN, 1960-63. Republican. Avocations: music; photography. Home: 11124 Court G Hanover Park IL 60103 Office: PO Box 241 Bloomingdale IL 60108

TWELLS, JOHN LAWRENCE, manufacturing and distributing company executive; b. Flint, Mich., Feb., 1934; s. Robert and Margaret Shaw (MacKillop) T.; B.B.A., U. Toledo, 1957; postgrad. Marquette U., 1975; M.B.A., Columbia Pacific U., 1981, D.B.A., 1983; m. Mary Jane Jentzen, Nov., 1961; children—Linda, John Lawrence, Robert William. Lab., terr. mgr., nat. accounts rep. Motorcraft/Autolite div. Ford Motor Co., Dearborn, Mich., 1950-63; dist. mgr., regional sales mgr. MOPAR div. Chrysler Corp., Detroit, 1963-67; asst. gen. mgr. NAPA Genuine Parts Co., Atlanta, 1967-68; gen. mgr. John MacKillop and Co., Inc., Poland, Ohio, 1968—; mgr. replacement parts Baker Material Handling Corp., a joint venture of Linde AG (W.Ger.) and United Technologies Corp., Cleve., 1976-78, gen. sales mgr. Amweld Bldg. Products div. Am. Welding & Mfg. Co. subs. Hoover Universal, Inc., Niles, Ohio, 1978-82, asst. gen. mgr., 1982, gen. mgr., 1983—; lectr. in field. Deacon, Immanuel Presbyterian Ch., Milw., 1974-76. Served with U.S. Army, 1957-59. Recipient Disting. Mktg. award Sales and Mktg. mag., 1980. Mem. Am. Prodn. and Inventory Control Soc., Constrn. Specifications Inst., Sales and Mktg. Execs. Internat., Am. Inst. Indsl. Engrs., Am. Def. Preparedness Assn., Am. Legion, VFW, Tau Kappa Epsilon. Republican. Lodge: Rotary. Contbr. articles on microfiche, inventory control, personnel selection, motivation and evaluation to profl. jours. Home: 8996 Sherwood Dr NE Warren OH 44484 Office: PO Box 5214 Poland OH 44514

TWITCHELL, HANFORD MEAD, printing company executive; b. N.Y.C., Dec. 17, 1927; s. Hanford Mead and Virginia (Sterry) T.; m. Inge Dyring Larsen, Mar. 15, 1969; 1 son, Robert. Student Princeton U., 1948-50. Writer, corr., translator, Europe and Latin Am., 1954-61; prodn. mgr. Pace Publs., Los Angeles, 1962-69, Scott & Scott, Santa Monica, Calif., 1969-71; sales mgr. Noll Printing Co., Huntington, Ind., 1971-78, mktg. dir., 1978-80, v.p., 1980—. Served with U.S. Army, 1950-53. Episcopalian. Club: Orchard Ridge Country (Ft. Wayne, Ind.). Office: Noll Printing Co 100 Noll Plaza Huntington IN 46750

TWITCHELL, MARY CATHERINE, communications educator, speech pathologist; b. Rapid City, S.D., Nov. 20, 1938; d. Marvin Ernst and Marcella Mae (Rollins) Finger; m. Robert Twitchell Apr. 19, 1962 (div. July 1982); children—John Andrew, Anthony James. B.A., U. S.D., 1961, M.A., 1965; postgrad. Mich. State U., 1965-67, 69, 83—. Speech and hearing clinician pub. schs., Aberdeen, S.D., 1961-62, Rapid City, 1962-63, Laramie, Wyo., 1966-67; instr., clin. supr. U. S.D., Vermillion, 1967-74, speech and hearing clinic coordinator, 1975—, asst. prof. communication disorders, 1980—; grad. asst. U. S.D., 1964, Mich. State U., 1965, 66, 69, 83. Mem. Am. Speech-Hearing-Lang. Assn. (cert. clin. competence in speech/lang. 1965), S.D. Speech Hearing Assn., S.D. Nu Voice Club-Am. Cancer Soc., Council Higher Edn., Council Univ. Suprs. Practicum in Speech Lang. Pathology and Audiology. Democrat.

TWYMAN, JACK, wholesale grocery executive. Chmn., pres., chief exec. officer, chief operating officer, dir. Super Food Services, Inc., Dayton, Ohio. Office: Super Food Services Inc 3185 Elbee Rd Dayton OH 45439*

TYAGI, NARENDRA SINGH, surgeon; b. Nangola, India, Jan. 12, 1945; s. Tilak Ram and Jagwati (Tyagi) T.; M.D., All India Inst. Med. Scis., New Delhi, 1966; m. Shashi Tyagi, June 26, 1970; children—Rachana, Renuka, Ashutosh. Intern Ellis Hosp., Schenectady, N.Y., 1968; resident in gen. surgery St. Joseph Mercy Hosp., Pontiac, Mich., 1970-73; dir. Pontiac Med. Scis. Research Labs., 1973-74; dir. intensive care unit Oakland Med. Center, Pontiac, 1973-74; active attending physician St. Joseph Mercy Hosp., Pontiac, 1973—, now chmn. dept. surgery; dir., v.p. Pontiac Emergency Care Group. Chmn. ad-hoc com. Bharatiya Temple, 1975, sec. bd. trustees, 1976. Recipient C. Walton Lilliehei award Pontiac Med. Sci. Research Lab., 1971, Charles G. Johnston award Detroit Surg. Assn., 1971-72; Frederick A. Coller award Mich. chpt. A.C.S., 1972. Diplomate Am. Bd. Surgery. Fellow A.C.S., Internat. Coll. Surgeons; mem. Mich. State, Oakland County med. socs., Am. Coll. Emergency Physicians. Developer sling suture technique for use in tracheal surgery. Home: 4209 Margate Ln Bloomfield Hills MI 48013 Office: 909 Woodward Ave Pontiac MI 48053

TYBOUT, ALICE MARIE, educator; b. Ann Arbor, Mich., Dec. 2, 1949; d. Richard Alton and Rita Harris (Holloway) T. B.A. in Bus. Adminstrn., Ohio State U., 1970, M.A. in Consumer Behavior, 1972; Ph.D. in Mktg., Northwestern U., 1975. Academic counselor Coll. Adminstrv. Scis. Ohio State U., 1970-72; research asst. Northwestern U., Evanston, Ill., 1972-74, asst. prof. mktg. and transp., 1975-81, asso. prof., 1981-85, prof., 1985—, J.J. Kellogg research prof. Kellogg Grad. Sch. Mgmt., 1980-81 Buchanan research prof. Kellogg Grad. Sch. Mgmt., 1983-84, Gen. Foods research prof., 1985-86; instr. bus. U. Chgo., 1974-75; cons. Am. Bankers Assn., AT&T, Sears Retailing scholar, 1969. Mem. Am. Mktg. Assn., Assn. Consumer Research (treas. 1982, 83, co-chmn. 1982, 85 confs.). Mem. editorial bd. Jour. Mktg., 1979-81, Jour. Bus. Research, 1980—, Jour. Mktg. Research, 1981-85, Jour. Consumer Research, 1982—; Co-editor: Advances in Consumer Research, Vol. 10; contbr. articles to profl. jours. Office: Department of Marketing 2001 Sheridan Rd Evanston IL 60201

TYLER, KENNETH DEAN, II, educator, historian; b. Iowa City, Iowa, Dec. 12, 1944; s. Kenneth Dean and Ethelmae (Safley) T.; m. Mary Ann Dumas, Aug. 8, 1970; children—Sarah Kinyon, Elizabeth Flynn. B.S.Ed., Drake U., 1967; M.S.Ed., No. Ill. U., 1972, Ed.D., 1982. Tchr., adminstr. Downers Grove (Ill.) Elem. Sch. Dist. 58, 1967—; student teaching supr. No. Ill. U., DeKalb, 1973-74. Mem. Assn. Supervision and Curriculum Devel., Ill. Assn. Supervision and Curriculum Devel., NEA, Phi Delta Theta. Author: The Educational Life and Work of Charles A. McMurry: 1872-1929, 1982; The School-Within-A-School Approach to Interdisciplinary Team Teaching, 1972.

TYLER-SLAUGHTER, CECIL LORD, housing relocation specialist; b. Peoria, Ill., Oct. 15, 1958; s. William Albert and Verline Marie (Tyler) Scott. Student Ill. State U., 1974-78. Adminstrv. intern Ill. State U., Normal, 1974-76; child care coordinator Community Action Agency, Peoria, 1976-79; program coordinator Learning Tree Prep. Sch., Peoria, 1980-83; housing relocation specialist Salvation Army, Peoria, 1984—. Investigative reporting journalist Face to Face, 1982; interviewer radio news format, 1983. Cons. NAACP, Peoria, 1984; leader 4H Club, Peoria, 1980-83; election judge Peoria Democratic Party, 1984. Recipient 4H Silver Clover Leadership award, 1983, Save the Children Spl. Honor Mayor Office, Atlanta, 1981; White House fellow Presdl. Commn., 1983. Mem. George Washington Carver, ARC, Smithsonian Inst. Orthodox Jewish. Home: 1904 Grand View Peoria Heights IL 61614 Office: Central Ill Eastern Iowa Salvation Army Hdqrs 413-415 Adams NE Peoria IL 61612

TYRRELL, KARINE, documentation analyst; b. Saarbrucken, Germany, Nov. 4, 1940; came to U.S., 1968, naturalized, 1978; d. Eduard and Charlotte (Faber) Ambrosius; B.A., McMaster U., Can., 1964; M.A., So. Ill. U., 1972, Ph.D., 1984; m. James Tyrrell, Aug. 27, 1964 (div. 1979); 1 child, Dalton. Tchr., Hamilton (Ont., Can.) Sch. Bd., 1964-65, Ottawa (Ont., Can.) Sch. Bd., 1966-68; research asst. U.S. Grant Assos., So. Ill. U., Carbondale, 1973-74, teaching asst. 1974-77, dissertation fellow, 1977-78; tech. writer Action Data Services, St. Louis, 1979-80, Boeing Computer Services, Wichita, Kans., 1980—. Home: 1235 S Pershing Ave Wichita KS 67218 Office: 3801 S Oliver M/S K12-07 Wichita KS 67210

TYSINGER, PHILIP LINDSEY, automotive executive, advertising agency executive; b. Durham, N.C., Jan. 31, 1948; s. Elmo Lindsey Tysinger and Gladys Virginia (Tysinger) Barringer; m. Linda Ilene Donahey, Aug. 7, 1970; 1 child, Erin Nichole. Student Campbell Coll., 1966-68; B.B.A., Washburn U., 1974. Advt. mgr. KTPK Radio, Topeka, 1974-84 ptnr., 1982-84; ptnr. KINA Radio, 1979-85, B&T Advt., Topeka, 1985—; sr. v.p. Ed Bozark Chevrolet, Topeka, 1985—. Served with USAF, 1968-72. Mem. Jr. Achievement of Northeastern Kans. (bd. dirs. 1979—), Profl. Advertisers Club Topeka (pres. 1978-79), Topeka Blood Bank (bd. dirs. 1984—), Sales and Mktg. Execs. of Topeka (Outstanding Salesman award 1978, 80, bd. dirs. 1980-84), Topeka C.

of C. Republican. Methodist. Office: Ed Bozarth Chevrolet 3731 S Topeka St Topeka KS 66609

TYSL, GLORIA JEANNE, history educator, consultant, researcher; b. Chgo., Apr. 17, 1931; d. Anton Otto and Myrtle Geraldine (Voborsky) T. B.A., Mt. Marty Coll., Yankton, S.D., 1960; M.A., De Paul U., Chgo., 1967; Ph.D., Ind. U., Bloomington, 1976. Tchr., Sacred Heart Acad., Lisle, Ill., 1950-67; prof. history Ill. Benedictine Coll., 1968-74, 78—, acad. dean and dean of faculty, 1974-78; cons. to Nat. Endowment Humanities. NSF fellow, 1967, Carnegie fellow, 1976, NEH fellow, 1981-82. Mem. Am. Hist. Assn., Catholic Hist. Assn., Brit. Hist. Assn., English Hist. Assn., N.W. Suburban Arts Council, Chgo. Council on Fgn. Relations, AAUW, Am. Assn. Higher Edn., Am. Council Edn. Roman Catholic. Home: 1045 Mayfield Ln High Point Hoffman Estates IL 60195 Office: Ill Benedictine Coll Lisle IL 60532

TYSON, FREDERICK JACKSON, rubber products company executive; b. Amarillo, Tex., Oct. 10, 1943; s. Newby Claude and Virginia Louise (Sterne) T.; m. Linda Elaine Nipper, Aug. 18, 1967 (div. 1979); 1 dau., Melinda Ruth; m. 2d Shirley J. Burris, Apr. 1, 1983. Student West Tex. State U., 1963-65, Okla. State U., 1967; Tech. illustrator E-Systems, Inc., Greenville, Tex., 1967-72; art services supr. North Electric Co., Galion, Ohio, 1972-77, Cin. Electronics Corp., Evendale, Ohio, 1977-80; dir. graphic art services Dayco Corp., Dayton, Ohio, 1980—; v.p. mktg. and sales Puls Digital Info., Inc., San Antonio, 1982—. Contbr. articles to profl. jours. Mem. Internat. Plastic Modeler Soc., Republican. Methodist. Avocations: model building; painting; reading. Home: 8377 E State Route 571 New Carlisle OH 45344-9633 Office: Dayco Corp 333 W First St Dayton OH 45401

TYSON, JOHN C., academic administrator; b. Richlands, Va., Aug. 4, 1951; s. Issac McKnight and Catherine (Rutledge) T.; m. Rogenia LaVerne Motley, Nov. 24, 1973. B.S.Ed., Concord Coll., 1972; M.L.S., U. Ill., 1976; M. Pub. Adminstrn., W.Va. U., 1979; D.Arts candidate Simmons Coll., 1984. Cert. mgmt. cons. Spanish tchr. Fairview Jr. High Sch., Bluefield, W.Va., 1972-73; circulation librarian Concord Coll., Athens, W.Va., 1973-75; reference librarian W.Va. U., Morgantown, 1976-77; pub. services librarian U. Wis.-Parkside, Kenosha, 1977-79; archives librarian Wentworth Inst. Tech., Boston, 1982; asst. dir. planning, adminstrn., devel. No. Ill. U., Dekalb, 1979—; pres. John Tyson & Assocs., Dekalb, 1979—. Supt. Lilly Grove Baptist Ch., Squire, W.Va., 1968; faculty advisor Minority Student Union U. Wis.-Parkside, 1977-79; pub. speaker Toastmaster's Internat., Dekalb, 1979—. HEA Title II B Doctoral fellow, 1982; Wentworth fellow, 1982. Mem. ALA (councilor-at-large 1984—, exec. bd. 1985, exec. bd. Black Caucus 1982-84), Ill. Library Assn., Alpha Mu Gamma (sec., treas. 1970-71), Kappa Delta Pi, Blue Key Nat. Honor Frat., Alpha Phi Alpha. Baptist. Author: Materials and Methods for Business Research, 1980; Basic Library Skills, 1979. Editor: Staff Devel. Column in LAMA Newsletter, 1981—. Office: No Ill Univ 415 Founders Meml Library Dekalb IL 60115

TYSON, KIRK W. M., business consultant; b. Jackson, Mich., July 2, 1952; s. George Carlton and Wilma Marion (Barnes) T.; m. Janice Lynn Lorimer, Aug. 25, 1979. B.B.A., Western Mich. U., Kalamazoo, 1974; M.B.A., DePaul U., Chgo., 1982. C.P.A., Ill. Bus. cons. Arthur Andersen & Co., Chgo., 1974—. Pres., Chgo. Jr. Assn. Commerce and Industry Found., 1977-79; active Easter Seals Soc., 1977, Am. Blind Skiing Found., 1977-78, Jr. Achievement, 1976-77, United Way Met. Chgo., 1979-80, Urban Gateways, 1975. Mem. Am. Inst. C.P.A.s, Ill. C.P.A. Soc., Planning Execs. Inst., N.Am. Soc. Corp. Planning, Alpha Kappa Psi (Disting. Service award 1982). Lutheran. Home: 7615-C Bristol Ct Woodridge IL 60517 Office: Arthur Andersen & Co 33 W Monroe St Chicago IL 60603

UBELL, DAVID ANTHONY, machinery manufacturing company executive; b. Canton, Ill., Sept. 24, 1937; s. William C. Jr. and Anna M. (Sepich) U.; m. Sharon Elaine Fletcher, Oct. 6, 1956; children—David Anthony, Michael, Julie, Chris, Jane. Student Canton Community Coll., 1966-67, Spoon River Coll., 1984. Prodn. scheduler Internat. Harvester Co., Canton, Ill., 1955-83, security supr., 1983—; dir. Canton, Works Club, 1959-60. Mem. Youth Council City of Canton, Ill., 1974. Served to Sp/2 U.S. Army, 1956-58; Korea. Mem. Am. Legion. Democrat. Roman Catholic. Lodges: Moose, Elks. Home: 105 E Myrtle St Canton IL 61520 Office: Internat Harvester Co 260 E Elm St Canton IL 61520

UBERT, HOWARD JOSEPH, computer company manager; b. Hays, Kans., July 21, 1941; s. Roderick and Eleanor (Sander) U.; m. Joyce Ann Michel, Feb. 1, 1964; children—Kevin Paul, Gregory Michael, Kathleen Ann. B.S. in Elec. Engring., Kans. State U., 1964; postgrad. U. Ala.-Huntsville, 1965-66. Systems engr. Indsl. Nucleonics (now AccuRay Corp.), Columbus, Ohio, 1967-68, area sales mgr., 1969-73, regional mgr., 1973-76, mgr. internat. tire industry, 1976-78; eastern regional mgr. energy Measurex Corp., Cupertino, Calif., 1978-81; v.p. sales August Systems, Tigard, Oreg., 1981-82; regional mgr. Indsl. Data Terminals, Westerville, Ohio, 1982-83, field sales mgr., 1983-84, nat. sales mgr., 1984—. Bd. dirs. Worthington (Ohio) Parks and Recreation Com.; v.p., sec., treas. Cardinal Boosters, Worthington; pres. Worthington High Sch. PTA. Served to capt. U.S. Army, 1964-67. Mem. Instrument Soc. Am., IEEE, Soc. Plastics Engrs., ASME, Worthington Jaycees (Outstanding Jaycee Committeeman 1973). Republican. Roman Catholic. Home: 6425 Meadowbrook Circle Worthington OH 43085 Office: 173 Heatherdown Rd Westerville OH 43081

UCHIMOTO, TADASHI TED, book binding and mailing firm exec.; b. Stockton, Calif., Feb. 3, 1918; s. Kometaro and Shitsu (Hanaoka) U.; grad. high sch., Hiroshima, Japan, Stockton; m. Hamako Oye, Feb. 11, 1943 (dec. Apr. 1966); 1 son, Dennis Den; m. 2d, Mitsu Miyazaki, Mar. 5, 1967. Founder, Gen. Mailing Service and Sales Co., Inc., Chgo., 1945—. Mem. Japanese Am. Assn. Chgo. (pres.), Chgo. Hiroshima Kenjinkai (pres.). Home: 5515 N Francisco Ave Chicago IL 60625 Office: 2620 W Washington Blvd Chicago IL 60612

UDELL, JON GERALD, business educator; b. Columbus, Wis., June 22, 1935; s. Roy Grant and Jessie M. (Foster) U.; m. Susan Smykla, June 12, 1960; children—Jon Jr., Roy Steven, Susan Elizabeth, Bruce Foster, Alan Joseph, Kenneth Grant. B.B.A., U. Wis., 1957, M.B.A., 1958, Ph.D., 1961. Instr., asst. prof., assoc. prof. U. Wis.-Madison, 1959-68, prof. bus., 1968—, assoc. dir. and dir. Bur. Bus. Research and Service, 1963-75, assoc. dir. Univ-Industry Research Program, 1967-77, Irwin Maier prof. bus., 1975—; dir., chmn. bd. Fed. Home Loan Bank of Chgo., 1982—; dir. Research Products Corp., Madison, Wis. Electric Power Co., Milw. Author: Successful Marketing Strategies in American Industry, 1972; The Economics of the American Newspaper, 1978; Reporting on Business and the Economy, 1981; Marketing in An Age of Change, 1981. Chmn. funding Madison Boychoir, 1983-84; chmn. Consumer Adv. Council, State of Wis., 1972-74; mem. Gov.'s Council of Econ. Devel., Wis., 1967-73; v.p. Madison C. of C., 1976. Recipient Gov.'s citation for service, 1969, 71, Sidney S. Goldish award, 1973; named Wisconsinite of Yr. Wis. State C. of C., 1973, Mktg. Man of Yr. So. Wis. chpt. Am. Mktg. Assn., 1976. Mem. Am. Mktg. Assn., Bus.-Edn. Coordinating Council (pres. 1979-80, bd. dirs.), Wis. for Research (bd. dirs.), Wis. Assn. Mfrs. and Commerce (trustee Bus. World 1981—). Presbyterian. Club: Faculty Roundtable (chmn. 1970-71). Lodge: Rotary. Home: 5210 Barton Rd Madison WI 53711 Office: Sch Bus U Wis 1155 Observatory Dr Madison WI 53706

UEDA, CLARENCE TAD, pharmacy educator, pharmaceutical scientist, researcher; b. Kansas City, Mo., July 6, 1942; s. Don Takao and Grace Yukiko (Furukawa) U.; m. Judith Katsuko, Feb. 20, 1971; children—Kimi Rei, Marc Ryan. A.A., Contra Costa Coll., 1963; Pharm. D., U. Calif.-San Francisco, 1967, Ph.D., 1974. Asst. prof. U. Nebr.-Omaha, 1974-77, assoc. prof., 1977—, chmn. dept. pharmaceutics, 1976—, dir. clin. pharmacokinetics Cardiovascular Ctr., 1976-80; cons. Sandoz, Ltd., Basel, Switzerland, 1982-85. Author, co-author research articles and book chpts. USPH trainee, San Francisco, 1973-74; grantee Am. Heart Assn., 1975-82, 84-85, Sandoz Found., 1983-85. Fellow Am. Coll. Clin. Pharmacology; mem. Am. Soc. Clin. Pharmacology Therapeutics, Am. Pharm. Assn., Acad. Pharm. Sci., Am. Assn. Colls. Pharmacy. Office: U of Nebr Coll Pharmacy 42d and Dewey Ave Omaha NE 68105

UEHLING, BARBARA STANER, univ. adminstr.; b. Wichita, Kans., June 12, 1932; d. Roy W. and Mary Elizabeth (Hilt) Staner; B.A. in Psychology, U. Wichita, 1954, Ph.D., 1958; M.A., Northwestern U., 1956; D.H.L. (hon.) Drury Coll., 1978; LL.D. (hon.), Ohio State U., 1980; children—Jeff, David. Mem. faculty, research fellow Emory U., 1964-69; mem. faculty Oglethorpe U., Atlanta, 1959-64; adj. prof. psychology U. R.I., 1969-71; mem. faculty Roger Williams Coll., 1970-71, acad. dean, 1972-74; dean arts and scis. Ill. State U., 1974-76; provost U. Okla., 1976-78, chancellor U. Mo., Columbia, 1978—; dir. Merc. Bancorp. Inc.; adv. dir. Merc. Trust Co.; dir. Meredith Corp.; mem. adv. council pres. Assn. Governing Bds., 1981—. Bd. dirs. United Way, Columbia; trustee Carnegie Council for Advancement Teaching. NIMH fellow, 1966-69. Mem. Am. Assn. Higher Edn. (past pres.), Nat. Council on Ednl. Research (dir.), Resources for the Future (bd. dirs.), Am. Council on Edn. (dir.), Sigma Xi, Phi Kappa Phi. Mem. editorial bd. Nat. Forum Mag. Office: 105 Jesse Hall Univ Mo Columbia MO 65211

UELAND, ARNULF, JR., wholesale lumber and plywood company executive; b. St. Paul, June 21, 1920; s. Arnulf and Louise (Nippert) U.; m. Rebecca Prentiss Lucas, Oct. 29, 1943. Student Dartmouth Coll., 1938-40; B.A., U. Minn., 1943. Mem. sales staff Long-bell Lumber Co., Longview, Wash., 1948-49, Winton Lumber Sales Co., Mpls., 1949-50; asst. mgr. Hayes Lucas Lumber Co., Mankato, Minn., 1950-53; owner, mgr. Ueland Lumber Sales Co., Mankato, 1953-73, pres., 1974—. Mayor, City of North Mankato, 1969-72; mem. Minn. Senate, 1973-80; mem. Mankato Planning Commn., 1961-67, Mankato Charter Commn., 1965-67; mem. exec. com. Blue Earth County Republican Com., 1965-67; chmn. Mankato Rep. Com., 1961-65; chmn. Nicollet County Rep. Com., 1969-71, 2d Dist. Rep. Com., 1971-73; mem. Minn. Rep. Central Com., 1969-73; del. Rep. Nat. Conv., 1972; sec. Mankato Symphony Orch. Assn., 1964-65. Served with USN, 1943-46. Mem. Greater Mankato Area C. of C., U. Minn. Alumni Assn., Dartmouth Alumni N.W., Acad. Polit. Sci., Ret. Officers Assn., Am. Legion, St. Paul-Mpls. Com. on Fgn. Relations. Alpha Delta Phi. Congregationalist. Clubs: Minneapolis, U. Minn. Alumni; Mankato Golf; University (St. Paul) Lodges: Sons of Norway, Nordmanns Forbundet, Elks, Rotary (pres. 1965-66). Home: 2013 Roe Crest Dr North Mankato MN 56001 Office: PO Box 1028 Mankato MN 56002

UGAI, SUSAN MARIE, lawyer; b. North Platte, Nebr., Jan. 4, 1956; d. Norman F. and Alice T. (Nakada) U. B.A., U. Nebr., 1978, J.D., 1981. Bar: Nebr. 1981, U.S. Dist. Ct. Nebr. 1981. Law clk. intern Nebr. Dept. Aging, Lincoln, 1979-81; city atty. City of North Platte, 1981-85; legal services developer Nebr. Dept. Aging, Lincoln, 1985—. Mem. adv. bd. Salvation Army, North Platte, 1981-85; chmn. edn. and prevention com. Sexual Assault Task Force, 1984-85; mem. North Platte Area Women's Council, 1983—; mem. Women in Transition/Displaced Homemaker Adv. Bd., 1982-85. Mem. ABA (exec. com. young lawyers div. com. on delivery legal services to elderly 1983—, young lawyers div. award Achievement 1984), Nat. Inst. Mcpl. Law Officers (chmn. Nebr. 1983-85), Nebr. State Bar Assn. (co-vice chairperson young lawyers sect. com. on delivery legal services to elderly 1981—), Lincoln County Bar Assn., Nat. Fedn. Bus. and Profl. Women (local treas. 1984-85, dist. YCW chmn. 1984-85, State PAC chmn. 1985-86). Democrat. Episcopalian. Club: Altrusa (North Platte). Office: Nebr Dept on Aging PO Box 95044 Lincoln NE 68509

UGOAGWU, BARBARA JACKSON, chemist; b. Birmingham, Ala., June 24, 1952; d. Louis and Elizabeth J. Davis; lab. cert. Cook County Grad. Sch. Medicine, Chgo., 1969; A.S. with honors (DeWitt Wallace Found. scholar 1972), Central Y Coll., Chgo., 1973; health cert. with honors (Health Edn. Corps. scholar 1976) Harvard U., 1976; B.S. in Biology and Chemistry, Roosevelt U., Chgo., 1977; m. Marcel C. Ugoagwu, Aug. 13, 1976; 1 dau., Vanlynette Bridget. Clin. chemistry technician Ill. Masonic Hosp., Chgo., 1969-70; med. research supr. Ill. Inst. Tech. Research Inst., Chgo., 1970-71; lead poison screening supr. Chgo. Dept. Health, 1972-76; med. coordinator Blue Cross/Blue Shield, Chgo., 1978—; tchr., cons. in field. Mem. Lab. Medicine Assn., Am. Chem. Soc., Harvard U. Alumni Assn., Roosevelt U. Alumni Assn., Park Forest South Women's Assn. (dir. 1981), AAUW, Phi Theta Kappa, Delta Tau. Democrat. Roman Catholic. Home: 759 Burr Oak Ln Apt 2K Park Forest South IL 60466 Office: 10233 S Racine Ave Chicago IL 60643

UHL, PATRICK EUGENE, pharmacist, management company executive; b. Sioux City, Iowa, Apr. 30, 1953; s. Lester R. and Gertrude A. (Garvin) U.; m. Carolyn Rae McArthur, Mar. 7, 1983. Student Creighton U., 1971-73, B.S. in Pharmacy, 1976. Clk., stocker Hindy Dinky, Omaha, 1972-74; pharmacy intern Immanuel Hosp., Omaha, 1974-75; pharmacist Walgreen Drug Co., Council Bluffs, Iowa, 1975—; owner Corn Crazy, Omaha, 1984—; pres., chmn. bd. dirs. U.S. Mgmt., Inc., Omaha, 1984—. Mem. Omaha C. of C., Greater Omaha Pharmacist Assn., Nebr. Pharmacy Assn. Democrat. Roman Catholic. Lodge: Kiwanis. Avocations: camping; hunting; stained glass; collecting antiques. Home: 3516 N 93d Ave Omaha NE 68134 Office: US Mgmt Inc 12281 W Center Rd Omaha NE 68144

UHLENHOPP, ELLIOTT LEE, chemistry educator; b. Hampton, Iowa, Dec. 8, 1942; s. Harvey Harold and Elizabeth Christine (Elliott) U.; m. Frances Ann Gragg, June 24, 1967; children—Andrew Cummings, Amy Grace. B.A., Carleton Coll., 1965; Ph.D., Columbia U., 1971; postgrad. Damon Runyan fellow U. Calif.-San Diego, 1971-73. Research chemist U. Calif.-San Diego, 1973-74; asst. prof. chemistry Whitman Coll., Walla Walla, Wash., 1974-77; asst. prof. Grinnell Coll., Iowa, 1977-80, assoc. prof., 1980—; asst. prof. biochemistry Rush Med. Coll., Chgo., 1978-82. Contbr. articles to profl. jours. Mem. Am. Chem. Soc., AAAS, Iowa Acad. Sci., Phi Beta Kappa, Sigma Xi. Home: 1515 Spencer St Grinnell IA 50112 Office: Grinnell Coll Chemistry Dept PO Box 805 Grinnell IA 50112

UHLENHOPP, HARVEY HAROLD, justice state supreme court; b. Butler County, Iowa, June 23, 1915; s. Henry Harold and Charlotte Ellen Wade (Green) U.; A.B., Grinnell Coll., 1936, LL.D., 1973; J.D., U. Iowa, 1939; m. Elizabeth Christine Elliott, June 20, 1940; children—Elliott Lee, John Cummings. Admitted to Iowa bar, 1939; county atty. Franklin County (Iowa), 1947-50; mem. Iowa Ho. of Reps., 1951-52; dist. judge Iowa, 1953-70; justice Iowa Supreme Ct., Des Moines, 1970—. Served with USCG, 1943-46. Mem. ABA, Iowa Bar Assn., Am. Law Inst., Am. Judicature Soc. (dir. 1965-67), Inst. Jud. Adminstrn. Contbr. articles to legal jours. Active ct. improvement. Office: PO Box 341 Hampton IA 50441*

UHRIG, FREDERIC GEORGE, police officer; b. Hoboken, N.J., Sept. 11, 1941; s. Vivian and Margaret Rose (Lotsey) U.; m. Alice Winnefred Spears, Oct. 10, 1970 (div. Dec. 1978). A.A. in Criminal Justice, Barton County Community Coll., 1979. Policeman, Junction City Police Dept. (Kans.), 1969-72, detective, 1972-73, detective sgt., 1975, detective lt., 1975-79, detective capt., 1979—; dir. Rape Crisis Advocates, Junction City, 1979—. Served with U.S. Army, 1960-68. Mem. FBI Nat. Acad. (assoc.), Am. Fedn. Police, Kans. Peace Officers Assn., Am. Soc. Indsl. Security, Internat. Assn. Chiefs of Police, Am. Legion. Republican. Home: 1006 N Price St Junction City KS 66441 Office: Junction City Police Dept 700 N Jefferson Junction City KS 66441

UHRIK, STEVEN BRIAN, psychotherapist; b. Chgo., June 30, 1949; s. George Steven and Elizabeth Gertrude Beisse (Will) U.; B.A., No. Ill. U., 1973; M.S.W., U. Ill., 1980. Vocat. coordinator O. H. Industries div. Opportunity House, Inc., Sycamore, Ill., 1970-79; clin. social worker, family counselor Rockford (Ill.) Meml. Hosp., 1979-81, co-dir. devel. chronic pain program, 1979-80; social worker West Suburban Kidney Center, S.C., Oak Park, Ill., 1981—; social work cons. Continental Health Care, Ltd., Oak Park, 1981—; pres. Personal Consultation, Elmhurst, Ill., 1983—; pub. relations cons. Dekalb County Villages, Inc., 1975-76. Recipient award Dekalb-Sycamore Human Relations Commn., 1974; developed patient edn. program for dialysis patients and family members Nat. Kidney Found. of Ill. Mem. Nat. Assn. Social Workers, Single Profl. Soc., Omicron Delta Kappa, Alpha Kappa Delta. Office: 159 Sunnyside Elmhurst IL 60126

UICKER, JOSEPH BERHARD, engineering company executive; b. State College, Pa., Mar. 29, 1940; s. John Joseph and Elizabeth Josephine (Flint) U.; m. Mary Catherine Howze, June 5, 1965 (div. Oct. 1971); children—Patricia, Suzzane; m. Janet Ann Ballman, Sept. 22, 1973. B.S.M.E., U. Detroit, 1963, M.S., 1965. Registered profl. engr., Mich. Engr., Smith Hinchman & Grylls, Detroit, 1964-72, chief mech. engr. health facilities, 1972-73, asst. dir. health facilities, 1973-75, v.p., dir. mech. engring., 1975-82, v.p., dir. profl. staff, 1983—, also dir.; dir. Smith Group, Detroit, 1984—. Served to capt. U.S. Army, 1966-67. Mem. Nat. Soc. Profl. Engrs., ASME, ASHRAE, Soc. Am. Mil. Engrs. Clubs: Engring. Soc., Athletic (Detroit). Avocations: golf; photography; gardening. Home: 14585 Lamphere Detroit MI 48223 Office: Smith Hinchman & Grylls 455 W Fort Detroit MI 48226

UIHLEIN, HENRY HOLT, refrigeration mfg. co. exec.; b. Milw., Aug. 17, 1921; s. Herman Alfred and Claudia (Holt) U.; B.A., U. Va., 1946; m. Marion Struss, June 13, 1942; children—James Christopher, Richard A., Philip John, Henry Holt. Pres., gen. mgr. Ben Hur Mfg. Co., Milw., 1947-62; pres. Ouictrez Inc., Fond duLac, Wis., 1955-60; pres., gen. mgr., dir. U-Line Corp., Milw., 1962—, chmn. bd., 1977—; pres., dir. Jensen Service Co., 1962—; pres. U-Line Internat. Corp. Bd. dirs. Herman A. Uihlein Found., Inc., 1955—. Served with USMC, 1943-45. Named to Wis. Ice Hockey Hall of Fame, 1978. Christian Scientist. Clubs: Milw., Athletic, Milw. Country. Contbr. articles to profl. jours. Home: 8500 Green Bay Ct N Milwaukee WI 53209 Office: 8900 55th St N Milwaukee WI 53223

ULAKOVICH, RONALD STEPHEN, development company executive; b. Youngstown, Ohio, Nov. 17, 1942; s. Stephen G. and Anne (Petretich) U. B.S., Indsl. Engring. Coll., 1967; M.S., Ill. Inst. Tech., 1969. Methods engr. Supreme Products, Chgo., 1964-66; pres. Contract Chair, 1966-70; v.p. sales Amrep Corp., Rosemont, Ill., 1970-73; pres. Condo Assoc., Ltd., Arlington Heights, Ill., 1973—. Mem. Am. Assn. Investors, Apt. Owners Assn., Real Estate Soc. of Syndicators and Investors. Roman Catholic. Home: 510 Van Buren St East Dundee IL 60118

ULBRICHT, ROBERT E., lawyer, savings and loan executive; b. Chgo., Dec. 1, 1930; s. Emil Albert and Vivian June (Knight) U.; m. Betty Anne Charleson, June 20, 1953; 1 dau., Christine Anne. A.B., U. Ill., 1952, M.A., 1953; J.D., U. Chgo., 1958. Bar: Ill. 1958, U.S. Dist. Ct. (no. dist.) Ill. 1959. Research atty. Am. Bar Found., Chgo., 1957-59; asst. trust counsel Continental Ill. Nat. Bank & Trust Co., Chgo., 1959-60; assoc. law firm Cummings and Wyman, Chgo., 1960-68; gen. atty., sec., sr. v.p. Bell Fed. Savs. & Loan Assn., Chgo., 1968—; instr. Aurora Coll., Coll. DuPage. Mem. nominating com. Dist. 41 Sch. Bd., 1970-71, vice chmn., 1971; chmn. dist. area fund raising Glen Ellyn council Girl Scouts Am., 1970. Bd. dirs. Glen Ellyn (Ill.) Pub. Library, 1979-85, pres., 1983-84. Served with AUS, 1953-55. Mem. Chgo. Bar Assn., Ill. Bar Assn., ABA. Clubs: Glen Oak Country, Glen Ellyn Tennis. Bd. editors Chgo. Bar Record, 1970-73; contbr. articles to legal jours. Office: 79 W Monroe St Chicago IL 60603

ULIN, WALTER MAURICE, greeting card company executive; b. Boston, May 6, 1933; s. Charles and Helene Marion (Platt) U.; m. Carole Deborah Kaplan, Jan. 29, 1959; children—Jeffrey Charles, Wendy Ellen. B.A. magna cum laude, Harvard U., 1954, M.B.A. with honors, 1958. Product mgr. Colgate Palmolive Co., N.Y.C., 1958-62; mgmt. cons. Harbridge House Inc., Boston, 1962-67, v.p., 1967-73; v.p. corporate planning and devel. Hallmark Cards Inc., Kansas City, Mo., 1973—. Vice pres. Kansas City Philharmonic, Mo., 1977-82; bd. advisors U. Mo.-Kansas City Sch. Bus. Adminstrn., 1982—. Mem. Greeting Card Assn. (v.p. 1982-83, pres. 1984). Clubs: Harvard/Radcliffe of Kansas City; Homestead Country (Shawnee Mission, Kans.). Avocations: travel, tennis, photography. Home: 3710 Wyncote Ln Shawnee Mission KS 66205 Office: Hallmark Cards Inc PO Box 580 Kansas City MO 64141

ULRICH, REINHARD, educator, clergyman; b. Treysa, Germany, July 1, 1929; came to U.S., 1949, naturalized, 1959; s. Karl and Martha (Hubach) U.; m. Helen E. Neuhaus, June 10, 1952; children—Martin K., Joan M., Karl R. B.A., Lakeland Coll., 1951, LL.D. (hon.), 1984; B.D., Mission House Theol. Sem., 1953; S.T.M., Luth. Sch. Theology, 1960, S.T.D., 1963. Ordained minister United Ch. Christ. Instr., Lakeland Coll., Sheboygan, Wis., 1951-53, prof., 1964—, chmn. dept. philosophy and religion, 1964—, chmn. div. humanities, 1973—; pastor Saron United Ch., Sheboygan, 1953-56, Eden United Ch., Chgo., 1953-64; interim pastor United Ch. of Christ; lectr. in field. Author: (with W. Jaberg et al) A History of Mission House/Lakeland, 1962; transl. Church as Dialogue, 1968; Theology of Play, 1972; also articles. Bd. dirs. Howards Grove Bd. Edn., Wis., 1974—, pres., 1979—. Mem. Wis. Assn. Sch. Bds. (bd. dirs. 1982—, v.p. 1983-84, pres. 1985), AAUP, Am. Philos. Assn. Office: Lakeland Coll Box 359 Sheboygan WI 53081

ULRICH, WILLIAM JOHN, history educator; b. Columbus, Ohio, Nov. 1, 1920; s. Fred William and Cornelia (Stephens) U.; m. May Fern Moore, Oct. 5, 1957; B.A., Ohio State U., 1942, M.A., 1948, Ph.D., 1959. Instr., John Carroll U., Univ. Heights, Ohio, 1959-61, asst. prof., 1961-68, assoc. prof., 1968-73, prof. history, 1973—, chmn. dept. history, 1965—. Mem. Orgn. Am. Historians, So. Hist. Assn., Ohio Acad. History, Western Res. Hist. Soc., Am. Catholic Hist. Assn., Phi Alpha Theta. Roman Catholic. Avocations: music; stamp collecting. Office: Dept History John Carroll Univ University Heights OH 44118

ULSETH, HAROLD ALLYN, clergyman, educator; b. Mpls., July 19, 1928; s. Harold A. and Helen Dorothy (Allyn) U.; m. Marilyn June Johnson, June 25, 1960; children—Linda Marie, Pamela June. B.A., U. Minn., 1954, B.S., 1965, M.A., 1973; B.D., Chgo. Theol. Sem. and U. Chgo., 1968. Ordained to ministry Congregational Ch. (now United Ch. of Christ), 1959. Minister, Eden Prairie Methodist Ch., Minn., 1955-57, Minnewashta United Ch. Christ, Excelsior, Minn., 1958-62; tchr. sci. Mpls. Pub. Schs., 1965—. Author numerous children's stories. Minister, counselor Alcohol Anonymous, Mpls., 1959-62; mem. Mayflower Ch. Bd. Benevolences, Mpls., Augsburg Coll. Parents Bd., Mpls.; bd. dirs. Minn. Am. Swedish Council, Mpls. Served with USN 1952-54. Mem. Twin Cities East Assn. (Minn. conf.), Minn. Fedn. Tchrs. Home: 5704 Colfax Ave S Minneapolis MN 55419 Office: Field Elem Sch 4645 4th Ave S Minneapolis MN 55409

UMANA, ROSEANN FRANCES, psychologist; b. N.Y.C., July 17, 1947; d. Salvatore and Palma Marie (Sciacca) U. B.S. in Psychology, Mich. State U., 1969; M.A. in Clin. Psychology, Ohio State U., 1971, Ph.D., 1979. Lic. psychologist, Ohio. Psychol. assoc. Central Ohio Psychiat. Hosp., Columbus, 1973-74; family crisis specialist Columbus (Ohio) Area Community Mental Health Ctr., 1974-75; exec. dir. Open Door Clinic, Columbus, 1975-83; pvt. practice clin. psychology, Columbus, 1979—; adj. instr. sch. social work Ohio State U., Columbus, 1978-84; cons. child assault prevention project Women's Action Collective, 1980-84; psychol. cons. Ohio Bur. Disability Determination, 1984—. Treas., Calico's, Women's Cultural Arts Ctr., Columbus, 1983—. Mem. Am. Psychol. Assn., Ohio Psychol. Assn., Central Ohio Psychol. Assn. Democrat. Author: Crisis in the Family, 1980. Home: 127 E Kelso Rd Columbus OH 43202 Office: 3840 N High St Columbus OH 43214

UMBACH, DALE EDWARD, statistics educator, researcher; b. Cin., Jan. 21, 1950; s. Albert Clarence and Audrey Claire (Geiser) U.; m. Nancy Lee Grossheim, Aug. 27, 1971; children—Erin Elizabeth, Amy Therese. B.A. in Math., U. Cin., 1972; M.S. in Stats., Iowa State U., 1974, Ph.D. in Stats., 1976. Asst. prof. stats. U. Okla., 1976-79; asst. prof. Ball State U., Muncie, 1979-83, assoc. prof., 1983—. Contbr. articles to profl. jours. Grantee Ball State U., 1982, 84—. Mem. Inst. Math. Stats., Am. Statis. Assn., Mu Sigma Rho. Lodge: Moose. Avocations: Photography, racquetball. Office: Ball State U Dept Math Scis Muncie IN 47306

UNDERDAHL, NORMAN RUSSELL, microbiologist; b. Freeborn County, Minn., June 5, 1918; s. Knut and Maria (Stoa) U.; m. Bernice Eleanor Nagle, Aug. 29, 1948; 1 child, Kimbra. B.A., St. Olaf Coll., Northfield, Minn., 1941; M.S., U. Minn., 1948. Research assoc. Hormel Inst., Austin, Minn., 1946-55; asst. prof. microbiology U. Nebr.-Lincoln, 1955-60, assoc. prof., 1960-68, prof., 1968-82, prof. emeritus, 1982—. Author: SPF Swine, 1973. Contbr. numerous articles to profl. jours., chpts. to books. Served with USN, 1942-46, PTO. Named Hon. Veterinarian, Nebr. Vet. Med. Assn., 1961; recipient Service award Nebr. Specific Pathogen Free Assn., 1971, Nat. Specific Pathogen Free Accrediting Assn., 1974. Mem. Soc. Am. Microbiologists, Conf. Research Workers Animal Disease, Nat. Swine Repopulation Assn. (sec.-treas. 1964—), AVMA (assoc.), Am. Legion, Sigma Xi, Gamma Sigma Delta. Republican. Lutheran. Avocations: restoring antique furniture; travel; fishing; collecting antiques. Home: 935 N 67th St Lincoln NE 68505 Office: Dept Vet Sci U Nebr Lincoln NE 68583

UNDERHILL, GLENN MORIS, physics educator; b. Trenton, Nebr., Oct. 30, 1925; s. George Frederick and Anna Mabel (Jackson) U.; student McCook Jr. Coll., 1942-44; B.S., Kearney State Coll., 1955; M.A. in Physics, U. Nebr., 1957, Ph.D., 1963; m. F. Susan Ann Day, Dec. 27, 1958; children—G. Mark, Rachel S., Sterling D., Gretchen E., Cynthia A., Enoch M. Grad. asst. U. Nebr., Lincoln, 1955-59, instr., 1960-62; assoc. prof. Kearney (Nebr.) State Coll., 1963-67, planetarium dir., 1966—, prof. physics, 1967—, head dept. physics and phys. sci., 1971-77; vis. lectr. various univs.; lectr. in field. Mem. Riverdale (Nebr.) Village Bd., 1978—, chmn. bd., 1978—. Recipient Council of Deans Service award Kearney State Coll., 1983. Mem. Am. Phys. Soc., Am. Assn. Physics Tchrs., Nebr. Acad. Sci., AAAS, Sigma Xi, Lambda Delta Lambda, Sigma Tau Delta, Kappa Delta Pi. Republican. Mem. Ch. of God. Contbr. articles to profl. jours. Home: PO Box 70 Riverdale NE 68870 Office: Kearney State Coll Kearney NE 68847

UNDERHILL, LEE, philosophy educator, minister; b. Wells, Kans., Oct. 19, 1919; s. Lee and Ruth Agnes (Adee) U.; m. Inez Dorrine Jones, June 1, 1941; children—Janet Lorraine, Warren Lee. B.A., Ft. Hays Kans. State Coll., 1941; B.D., Drew Theol. Sem., 1945; Ph.D., Drew U., 1957; postdoctoral Princeton U., Union Theol. Sem., Columbia U., 1964-66. Ordained to ministry United Methodist Ch., 1945. Pastor chs., N.J., Pa. and Kans., 1941-50; prof. philosophy and religion Iowa Wesleyan Coll., Mt. Pleasant, 1950-54; pastor Woodrow Meth. Ch., S.I., N.Y., 1954-57; prof., chmn. dept. philosophy Coll. Idaho, Caldwell, 1957-60; prof. Meth. studies Dubuque Theol. Sem., Iowa, 1960-72; prof. philosophy and religion Hastings Coll., Nebr., 1972—. Mem. Hastings Area Arts Council, 1979-83. Tipple scholar, 1955. Mem. Am. Philos. Assn., Am. Acad. Religion, Soc. Creativity in Philosophy, Iowa Ann. Conf. United Meth. Ch. Avocations: photography; philately; book collecting; travel. Home: 420 W 10th St Hastings NE 68901 Office: Hastings College Hastings NE 68901

UNDERWOOD, EARL FREDERICK, JR., clergyman; b. Ft. Smith, Ark., Aug. 31, 1943; s. Earl Fredrick and Pearl Lucille (Kukuk) U.; m. Laura Ruth Anderson, July 23, 1967; 1 child, Ray Charles. B.A., Huron Coll., 1968; M.Div., Louisville Presbyterian Sem., 1971. Ordained to ministry Presbyn. Ch., 1971. Pastor, Faith Pres. Ch., Brandon, S.D., 1971-76, Riverside Presbyn. Ch., Sioux Falls, S.D., 1971-76, Akron Plymouth Presbyn. Ch., Iowa, 1976-79, Meml. Presbyn. Ch., Marysville, Kans., 1979—. Author (booklet) Family Budgeting, 1984; (genealogy) From Vilson Germany to Linn Kansas, 1980. Editor (geneology) Reedy Family Assn., 1980-84. Treas., Pride Marysville Kans., 1982-84. Mem. Iowa Genealogy Soc. (Outstanding Genealogist award 1975), Blue Valley Genealogy Soc. (pres. 1980-82, v.p. 1983-84). Avocation: Bridge; genealogy. Home: 808 N 12th St Marysville KS 66508 Office: Meml Presbyn Ch 200 N 10th St Marysville KS 66508

UNDERWOOD, ROBERT LEIGH, venture capitalist; b. Paducah, Ky., Dec. 31, 1944; s. Robert Humphreys and Nancy Wells (Jessup) U.; B.S. with gt. distinction (Alcoa scholar), Stanford U., 1965, M.S. (NASA fellow), 1966, Ph.D. (NSF fellow), 1968; M.B.A., U. Santa Clara, 1970; m. Susan Lynn Doscher, May 22, 1976; children—Elizabeth Leigh, Dana Whitney. Research scientist, project leader Lockheed Missiles & Space Co., Sunnyvale, Calif., 1967-71; spl. asst. for engring. scis. Office Sec., Dept. Transp., Washington, 1971-73; sr. mgmt. assoc. Office Mgmt. and Budget, Exec. Office Pres., 1973; with TRW Inc., Los Angeles, 1973-79, dir. retail nat. accounts, 1977-78, dir. product planning and devel., 1978-79; pres., chief exec. officer OMEX, Santa Clara, Calif., 1980-82; v.p. Heizer Corp., Chgo., 1979-85; v.p. No. Trust Co., pres. No. Capital Corp., Chgo., 1985—; dir. OMEX; mem. adv. com. indsl. sci. and tech. innovation NSF. Mem. AIAA, IEEE, Sigma Xi, Phi Beta Kappa, Tau Beta Pi, Beta Gamma Sigma. Elder, Presbyterian Ch., 1978-79. Clubs: Union League Chgo.; Manasquan River Yacht (Brielle, N.J.). Contbr. articles to profl. jours. Home: 59 Woodley Rd Winnetka IL 60093 Office: 50 S La Salle St Chicago IL 60675

UNFER, LOUIS, JR., geologist, educator; b. Bayard, Iowa, Jan. 18, 1923; s. Louis and Beulah Marie (Teskey) U.; m. Lois June Havel, Jan. 30, 1954; children—Robert Louis, Roberta Louise. B.S., U. Ill., 1948; M.A., U. Wyo., 1951. Cert. geologist. Research asst. Ill. State Geol. Survey, Urbana, 1949-54; geologist Carl Bays & Assocs., Urbana, 1954-57; instr. Southeast Mo. State U., Cape Girardeau, Mo., 1957-60, asst. prof., 1960-68, assoc. prof. geology, 1968—. Served to col. USAR, 1946-79. Fellow Geol. Soc. Am; mem. Nat. Assn. Geology Tchrs. (exec. council 1967), Am. Assn. Petroleum Geologists, Am. Inst. of Profl. Geologists (exec. com. 1977), Assn. Mo. Geologists (pres. 1980), Big Rivers Area Geol. Soc. (pres. 1975). Methodist. Lodge: Moose. Avocations: bowling; camping; hiking; rock, mineral, and fossil collecting. Home: 1632 N West End Blvd Cape Girardeau MO 63701 Office: Southeast Mo State U Cape Girardeau MO 63701

UNGAR, IRWIN ALLAN, botany educator; b. N.Y.C., Jan. 21, 1934; s. Isidore and Gertrude (Feigeles) U.; m. Ana Celia Del Cid, Aug. 10, 1959; children—Steven, Sandra, Sharon. B.S., CCNY, 1955; M.A., U. Kans.-Lawrence, 1957, Ph.D., 1961. Instr., U. R.I., Kingston, 1961-62; asst. prof. Quincy Coll., Ill., 1962-66; asst. prof. Ohio U., Athens, 1966-69, assoc. prof., 1969-74, prof. botany, 1974—, chmn. dept., 1984—; panelist Nat. Sea Grant Program, 1984—; grant proposal reviewer NSF, 1980-84; manuscript reviewer Am. Jour. Botany, 1972-84, Bot. Gazette, 1976-84. Contbr. articles to profl. jours. NSF grantee, 1974-76, 76-78, 80-83. Fellow Ohio Acad. Sci.; mem. Bot. Soc. Am., Ecol. Soc. Am., AAAS, Sigma Xi. Home: 44 Walker St Athens OH 45701 Office: Ohio Univ Athens OH 45701

UNGER, DAVID JAMES, engineering mechanics educator; b. East St. Louis, Ill., Feb. 1, 1952; s. Anthony and Stella (Borkowski) U.; m. Carolyn Elizabeth Stilwell, Feb. 21, 1981. B.S., St. Louis U., 1973; M.S., U. Ill., 1976, Ph.D., 1981. Researcher dept. chem. engring. U. Minn., Mpls., 1981-82; asst. prof. engring. mechanics Ohio State U., Columbus, 1982—. Contbr. articles to profl. jours. NSF grantee, 1984—. Mem. ASME, AIAA, AAAS, Am. Acad. Mechanics, Ohio Acad. Sci. Office: Ohio State U Dept Engring Mechanics 155 W Woodruff Ave Columbus OH 43210

UNNEWEHR, LEWIS EMORY, electrical engineer; b. Berea, Ohio, Sept. 27, 1925; s. Emory Carl and Ivy May (Lewis) U.; B.S.E.E., Purdue U., 1946; M.S.E.E., U. Notre Dame, 1952; m. L. Jean Affleck, Aug. 22, 1948; children—David, Laura, Janet, Chris. Assoc. prof. Valparaiso U. (Ind.), 1949-55; research engr. Franklin Inst., Phila., 1955-57; assoc. prof. Villanova (Pa.) U., 1957-61; sr. design engr. Garrett Corp., Los Angeles, 1961-66; mem. research staff Ford Motor Co., Dearborn, Mich., 1966-81; dir. research and devel. Lima Energy Products (Ohio), 1981-84; dir. advanced electronics dept. Allied Automotive Tech. Ctr., Troy, Mich., 1984—. Author: (with S.A. Nasar) Electromechanics and Electric Machines, 1979; Electric Vehicle Technology, 1982; contbr. articles to profl. jours.; patentee in field. Lay del. Central United Meth. Ch., Detroit, 1978-80. Mem. IEEE (vice-chmn. electronics transformer tech. com.), Sigma Xi. Democrat. Methodist. Lodges: Elks, Optimists. Home: 31093 Fairfax Dr Birmingham MI 48009 Office: 900 W Maple Rd Troy MI 48084

UNO, HIDEO, pathologist, medical educator; b. Tokyo, Nov. 28, 1929; came to U.S., 1969; s. Yoshinori and Hana (Uno) U.; m. Shoko Ohashi; children—Takeshi, Yayoi. M.D., Yokohama Med. Coll., Japan, 1955, Ph.D., 1961. Asst. prof. Yokohama City U., 1961-64, assoc. prof., 1968-69; instr. Jefferson Med. Coll., Phila., 1964-66; vis. scientist Oreg. Primate Research Ctr., Beaverton, 1966-68, scientist, 1970-79; sr. scientist Wis. Primate Research Ctr., Madison, 1979—, head pathology div., 1979—; adj. assoc. prof. dept. pathology, U. Wis. Med. Sch., Madison, 1980—. Grantee Oreg. Med. Found., 1976, Upjohn Co., 1982-85. Counselor Japanese Histochemistry and Cytochemistry; mem. Am. Assn. Pathologists, Internat. Acad. Pathology, Soc. Investigative Dermatology, Am. Assn. Anatomists. Club: Internat. House of Japan (Tokyo). Avocation: music. Home: 3722 Ross St Madison WI 53705 Office: Wis Reg Primate Research Ctr U Wis 1223 Capitol Ct Madison WI 53706

UNOWSKY, R(OUL) DAVID, bookseller, publisher; b. St. Paul, May 9, 1942; s. Reuben T. and Evelyn (Cooperman) U.; m. Rolla Jean Breitman, Mar. 22, 1964; children—Lee Samuel, Steven Philip. B.A., U. Minn., 1964. Lab. asst. Lab. for Research in Social Relations, U. Minn.-Mpls., 1964; v.p., treas. Louis Distbg. Co., Mpls., 1964-70; owner Hungry Mind Bookstore, St. Paul, 1970—; dir. Minn. Revs., Mpls., 1984—, Mpls. Rev. of Baseball, 1984—; founder Hungry Mind Reading Series, St. Paul, 1975—. Editor, pub.: Odd Fodder, 1983; Summa, 1983; Conservation of Matter, 1983. Past bd. dirs., sec., treas., v.p. Talmud Torah of St. Paul, 1977—; mem. Human Rights Commn., Robbinsdale, Minn., 1968-69; organizer Jewish Book Fair-Jewish Ctr., St. Paul, 1982—. Recipient Best Bookstore award Downtowner, 1984, Mpls. Mag., 1979. Mem. Upper Midwest Booksellers Assn. (pres. 1983-85), Am. Booksellers Assn. (assn. devel. com. 1984—), Grand Ave. Bus. Assn. Democrat. Avocations: baseball; softball; reading. Home: 1704 Bohland Ave Saint Paul MN 55116 Office: Hungry Mind 1648 Grand Ave Saint Paul MN 55105

UNRUH, ALLEN DALE, chiropractor, mail order marketer; b. Conistota, S.D., June 16, 1948; s. Henry H. and Albena (Schmidt) U.; m. Leslee Joy Bonrud; children—Nathan, Nakia, Chace, Amber, Cash. D.C., Nat. Coll. of Chiropractic, 1970. Gen. practice chiropractic medicine, Sioux Falls, S.D., 1970—. Author therapeutic exercise booklets, newspaper columns, edn. phamplets, tape courses. Del., Republican Nat. Conv. from S.D., 1984; speaker Nat. Right to Life Conv., Kansas City, 1984; creater 24 Hour Abortion Info. Hotline, The Alpha Ctr. for Women. Mem. S.D. Chiropractic Assn., Am. Chiropractic Assn., Nat. Speakers Asn., S.D. Jaycees (Speakup award, 1974). Avocations: reading; writing. Home: 2801 Kinkade Ln Sioux Falls SD 57103 Office: Chiropractic Arts Ctr 600 N Western Ave Sioux Falls SD 57104

UNRUH, PAUL E., optometrist; b. Kobe, Japan, Jan. 12, 1955; s. Verney L. and Belva (Waltner) U.; m. Christine S. Andres, Aug. 14, 1976; children—Zachary Andres, Nicholas Andres. B.S., Bethel Coll., Kans., 1977; O.D., U. Houston, 1982. Lic. optometrist, Kans. Practice optometry, Hillsboro, Kans., 1982—. Mem. adv. com. Parkside Nursing Home, Hillsboro, 1984-85; mem. bldg. com. Salem Hosp., Hillsboro, 1984-85. Mem. Am. Optometric Assn., Kans. Optometric Assn. (zone treas. 1982-84), Hillsboro C. of C. (bd. dirs. 1985). Mennonite. Lodge: Kiwanis (bd. dirs. 1983-85) (Hillsboro). Office: 132 S Main St Hillsboro KS 67063

UPCRAFT, JOHN OLIN, geologist; b. Mt. Vernon, Ill., June 10, 1958; s. Frederick James and Huram Maxfield (Turner) U.; m. Diana Carol Sampson, Sept. 1, 1979; children—Jennifer Leigh, Melissa Kay. A.A., Rend Lake Jr. Coll., 1980. Draftsman, Gen. Radiator, Mt. Vernon, 1976-78, salesman, 1978-79; geol. draftsman Brehm Oil Co., Mt. Vernon, 1979-82; geol. technician Orion Energy Corp., Mt. Vernon, 1982—; cons. in field. Vol. Okwa Valley council Boy Scouts Am., 1980-82. Brehm Found. scholar, 1980-82. Mem. Am. Assn. Petroleum Geologists, Ill. Geol. Survey. Lodge: Optimist (Mt. Vernon). Avocations: music performance; fishing; hunting; shooting; boating. Home: 2023 College Mt Vernon IL 62864

UPDYKE, GERALD DEAN, mining company executive; b. Zanesville, Ohio, Apr. 19, 1921; s. Lee H. and Maebelle M. (Link) U.; m. Alma Jean Boyer, Dec. 31, 1941; children—Linda Jean, Gerald Bruce. Student public schs., Philo, Ohio. Driller, Indsl. Gas and Oil Co., Zanesville, 1939-52; maintenance supt. Central Ohio Coal Co., Cumberland, 1952-69; service and erection engr. Marion Power Shovel Co. (Ohio), 1969-74; mgr. maintenance, eastern div. Peabody Coal Co., Evansville, Ind., 1974; div. gen. mine supt. Central Ohio Coal Co., Cumberland, 1974—. Served with Q.M.C., U.S. Navy, 1942-45; PTO. Mem. AIME, Zanesville C. of C., Am. Legion. Methodist. Clubs: Elks, (Zanesville); Masons, Shriners (Columbus, Ohio). Home: 3964 Darcie Dr Zanesville OH 43701 Office: PO Box 98 Cumberland OH 43732

UPHOFF, JAMES KENT, education educator; b. Hebron, Nebr., Sept. 1, 1937; s. Ernest John and Alice Marie (Dutcher) U.; m. Harriet Lucille Martin, Aug. 6, 1962; 1 child, Nicholas James. B.A., Hastings Coll., 1959; M.Ed., U. Nebr., 1962, Ed.D., 1967. Tchr., Walnut Jr. High Sch., Grand Island, Nebr., 1959-65, dept. chmn., 1962-65; instr. dept. edn. U. Nebr., Lincoln, 1965-66; curriculum intern Bellevue (Nebr.) Pub. Schs., 1966-67; asst. prof. edn. Wright State U., Dayton, Ohio, 1967-70, assoc. prof., 1970-75, prof. edn., 1975—, co-dir. pub. edn. religion studies ctr., 1972-75, dean br. campuses, 1974-79, dir. lab. experiences, 1982—; vis. prof. U. Dayton, 1968-69. Phi Delta Kappa scholar, 1969. Mem. adv. com. pub. edn. fund Dayton Found., 1985—. Mem. NEA, Ohio Edn. Assn. (devel. commn.), Western Ohio Edn. Assn. (pres. 1974-75, exec. com. 1979—), Assn. Supervision and Curriculum Devel. (dir. 1974-79), Ohio Assn. Supervision and Curriculum Devel. (v.p. 1972-73), Nat. Council Social Studies (religion com.), Ohio Council Social Studies (profl. concerns com.), Dayton Area Council Social Studies (pres. (1970-71, 85-86), LWV Greater Dayton (edn. dir. 1981—), Ohio Council Chs. (edn. com. 1973-75), Phi Delta Kappa (chpt. pres. 1983-84), Kappa Delta Pi. Republican. Lutheran. Clubs: Rotary (editor; dir. 1974-79), Optimist (pres. 1983-85). Contbr. chpts. to books and articles to profl. jours. Home: 150 Spirea Dr Dayton OH 45419 Office: 320 Millett Edn Wright State U Dayton OH 45435

UPTON, KEVIN JOHN, public relations executive; b. N.Y.C., Jan. 3, 1947; s. John Joseph and Muriel Agnes (Weiss) U.; m. Theresa Ann Malone, Aug. 13, 1967; children—Kirsa, Bryn. Student, Notre Dame U., 1965-67; B.A., Ind. U., 1973; M.A., U. Wis., 1977. Instr. dept. polit. sci. Carroll Coll., Waukesha, Wis., 1975-77; dir. devel. Wis. Center for Pub. Policy, Madison, Wis., 1977-79; asst. to mayor Madison, 1979-80; pres. Upton, Boelter & Lincoln, Madison, 1980-83; v.p. mktg. Credit Union Nat. Assn. and CUNA Service Group, Inc., 1983—. Mem. Pub. Relations Soc. Am. Democrat. Club: Madison. Home: 7209 Branford Lane East Madison WI 53717 Office: 5710 Mineral Point Rd Madison WI 53701

UPTON, LAURENCE ROGER, educational administrator, consultant; b. Keene, N.H., Aug. 27, 1947; s. Roger James and Fannie Helen (Seppa) U. B.A. summa cum laude, U. N.H., 1969; M.S., Purdue U., 1973; postgrad. U. Minn. Instr. human devel. U. N.H., Durham, 1971-72; research asst. psychology Purdue U., West Lafayette, Ind., 1972-74; program evaluation specialist U. Minn., Mpls., 1974-76, student activities cons., coordinator program on human issues and values, 1976-79, asst. coordinator admissions Coll. Liberal Arts, 1980—; researcher exptl. psychology, 1975—; tech. edn. cons. U. Research Consortium, Mpls., 1984—; presenter conf. papers. Dist. del. Democratic Farmer Labor Party, Mpls., 1976, 80, 84. Granite State Merit scholar, 1965-69, Ford Found. scholar, 1967-69; NSF trainee, 1969-71. Mem. Ctr. Research in Human Learning, Midwestern Psychol. Assn., Am. Assn. Counseling and Devel., Am. Coll. Personnel Assn., Minn. Coll. Personnel Assn., Phi Beta Kappa, Phi Kappa Phi, Psi Chi, Pi Gamma Mu, Pi Mu Epsilon. Unitarian. Office: U Minn Coll Liberal Arts 49 Johnston Hall 101 Pleasant St SE Minneapolis MN 54455

UPTON, LUCILE MORRIS (MRS. EUGENE V. UPTON), writer; b. Dadeville, Mo., July 22, 1898; d. Albert G. and Veda (Wilson) Morris; student Drury Coll., 1915-16, S.W. Mo. State U., 1917-20; m. Eugene V. Upton, July 22, 1936 (dec. July 1947). Pub. sch. tchr., Dadeville Mo., 1917-19, Everton, Mo., 1920-22, Roswell, N.Mex., 1921-23; tchr. creative writing Adult Edn. div. Drury Coll., 1947-52; reporter Denver Express, 1923-24, El Paso (Tex.) Times, 1924-25, Springfield (Mo.) Newspapers, Inc., 1926-64, writer weekly hist. column, 1942-82. Mem. Springfield City Council, 1967-71, Springfield Hist. Sites Bd., 1972-78. Recipient Heritage award Mus. of Ozarks, 1978; named Woman of Achievement Woman's div. Springfield C. of C., 1967; named to Greater Ozark Hall of Fame, Sch. of Ozarks, Point Lookout, Mo., 1980. Mem. Mo. Writers Guild (past pres.), State Hist. Soc. Mo. (life), Greene County (Mo.), White River Valley hist. socs., Nat. Fedn. Press Women, Mo. Press Women. Congregationalist. Author: Bald Knobbers, 1939; (booklet) Battle of Wilson's Creek, 1950; co-author: Nathan Boone, the Neglected Hero, 1984; contbr. short stories, articles to mags., newspapers. Home: 1305 S Kimbrough Springfield MO 65807

URBACH, FREDERICK LEWIS, chemistry educator; b. New Castle, Pa., Nov. 21, 1938; s. Lewis Loraine and Helen Myrtle (Spann) U.; m. Carrie Marie Grimm, June 26, 1960; children—Deborah Ann, Allison Jean. B.S., Pa. State U., 1960; Ph.D., Mich. State U., 1964. Research assoc. Ohio State U., Columbus, 1964-66; asst. prof. Case Western Res. U., Cleve., 1966-73, assoc. prof., 1973-80, prof., 1980—. Contbr. articles to profl. jours. and book chpts. Mem. Am. Chem. Soc. Methodist. Office: Dept Chemistry Case Western Res U Cleveland OH 44106

URBAN, THOMAS N., agricultural products company executive. Chmn., pres., chief executive officer, dir. Pioneer Hi-Bred Internat., Inc., Des Moines. Office: Pioneer Hi-Bred Internat Inc 400 Locust 700 Capital Square Des Moines IA 50309*

URBAN, WILLIAM LAWRENCE, history educator; b. Monroe, La., Dec. 31, 1939; s. David Osterfund and Grace Margaret (Doane) U.; m. Jacquelynn Juvenal, Mar. 28, 1965; children—Ilsake, Elke, Karl. B.A., U. Tex., 1961, M.A., 1964, Ph.D, 1967; postgrad U. Hamburg, W.Ger., 1964-65; Jagiellonian U., Cracow, Poland, 1973. Asst. prof. history U. Kans., Lawrence, 1965-66; prof., chmn. dept. Monmouth Coll., Ill., 1966—; vis. prof. Fort Hays Kans State Coll., 1971; dir. Assn. Colls. Midwest Program, Florence, Italy, 1974-75; dir. translation project Nat. Endowment Humanities, 1978-79. Author: Juvenal-Juvinall-Juvenile: a family history, 1972; The Baltic Crusade, 1975; The Prussian Crusade, 1980; The Livonian Crusade, 1981 (Dr. Arthur Pusksow award 1983); Narcissus and The Faceless Man, 1984; (with others) A History of Monmouth College through its Fifth Quarter-Century, 1979. Translator: (with others) The Livonian Rhymed Chronicle, 1977; The Chronicle of Balthasar Russow. Contbr. articles to profl. jours. Grantee Fulbright Found., 1975-76, Deutsche Akademische Austauschdenst, 1983. Mem. Assn. Advancement Baltic Studies, Medieval Acad. Am., Am. Hist. Assn., Eta Sigma Phi, Phi Alpha Theta, Zeta Beta Tau (citation of merit 1971). Democrat. Mem. Society of Friends. Home: 1062 E 2d Ave Monmouth IL 61462 Office: Monmouth Coll 700 E Broadway Monmouth IL 61462

URBANIAK, DAVID LEE, restaurant exec., microfilm co. exec.; b. Dearborn, Mich., May 5, 1944; s. Joseph Frank and Ethel (Behnke) U.; student Western Mich. U., 1964-65; m. Sally Joanne Dexter, July 25, 1964; children—Matthew James, Bethany Lyn. Foreman, McGraw Edison, Albion, Mich., 1964-70; gen. foreman ITT Hancock, Jackson, Mich., 1970-76; owner Sal's 5th Ave. Restaurant, Michigan Center, Mich., 1976—; founder, pres. Automatic Microfilm Co., Michigan Center, 1978—. Mem. Leoni Bus. Assn. (co-founder 1977, chmn. 1977-81). Lutheran. Home: 484 Ballard St Jackson MI 49201 Office: 115 5th St Michigan Center MI 49254

URBOM, WARREN KEITH, judge; b. Atlanta, Nebr., Dec. 17, 1925; s. Clarence A. and Anna Myrl (Ireland) U.; A.B., Nebr. Wesleyan U., 1950; J.D., U. Mich., 1953; m. Joyce Crawford, Aug. 19, 1951; children—Kim Marie Urbom Rager, Randall, Allison Lee, Joy R. Admitted to Nebr. bar, 1953; mem. firm Baylor, Evnen, Baylor, Urbom & Curtiss, Lincoln, 1953-70; U.S. dist. judge, 1970—, chief judge Dist. of Nebr., Lincoln, 1972—. Del., Gen. Conf., United Meth. Ch., 1962, 76, 80; pres. Lincoln YMCA, 1965-66; chmn. bd. govs. Nebr. Wesleyan U., 1975-80. Mem. Am., Nebr., Lincoln bar assns., Am. Coll. Trial Lawyers. Clubs: Masons, Shriners. Office: 100 Centennial Mall N Federal Bldg Lincoln NE 68508

URION, DAVID KENDALL, mathematics and computer science educator; b. Seattle, Sept. 23, 1943; s. Kendall Dwight and Mary Elizabeth (Slaughter) U.; m. Marilyn Vogler, July 31, 1965; children—Seth David, Franklin August. B.A., Culver-Stockton Coll., 1965; M.S., Miami U., Oxford, Ohio, 1967; Ph.D., U. Md.-College Park, 1976. Instr. math. Miami U., Middletown, Ohio, 1967-68, U.S. Naval Acad., Annapolis Md., 1970-74; curriculum developer Somerset Sch., Washington, 1974-76; assoc. prof., chmn. dept. math. Marymount Coll., Salina, Kans., 1976-82; prof. chmn. dept. Winona State U., Minn., 1982—; curriculum cons. Riverhaven Sch., Winona, 1983—. Editorial adviser jour. Computer Instructor, 1984—. Served to lt. USNR, 1968-76. Mem. Nat. Council Tchrs., Math. Assn. Am.. Democrat. Unitarian Universalist. Avocations: running; french horn; vocal music. Office: Dept Math and Computer Sci Winona State U Winona MN 55987

URNESS, CAROL LOUISE, librarian; b. Wilmington, Calif., Apr. 8, 1936; d. Carl Bernard and Dorothy Luverne (Skow) U. Student St. Olaf Coll., 1954-55; B.A., U. Minn.-Mpls., 1957, M.A., 1960, Ph.D., 1982. Librarian, U. Minn.-Mpls. Libraries, 1957-64, librarian, asst. curator James Ford Bell Library, 1964—. Editor: A Naturalist in Russia, 1968; The American Revolution, 1976. Mem. Soc. History of Discoveries (adv. editor), Hakluyt Soc., Soc. Bibliography of Natural History, ALA, Assocs. of James Ford Bell Library. Lutheran. Club: Ampersand. Home: 1026 NE 23 Ave Minneapolis MN 55418 Office: James Ford Bell Library Univ Minn 309 19th Ave S Minneapolis MN 55455

URQUHART, SYLVESTER MICHAEL, dentist, pharmacist; b. Ramer, Ala., Nov. 19, 1928; s. Willie Arthur and Emma Lee (Gamble) U.; m. Mary Elizabeth Williams, Dec. 29, 1954; 1 child, Sylvia Marie. B.S. in Pharmacy, Xavier U., 1949; D.D.S., U. Detroit, 1956. Pharmacist, Anderson Drugs, Detroit, 1949-51, Sam's RX Drugs, Detroit, 1951-56, 74-77; pvt. practice dentistry, Detroit, 1959-73, Highland Park Health Dept., Mich., 1978-79, W.J. Maxey Boys Tng. Sch., State of Mich., Whitmore Lake, 1979—. Served to capt. USAF, 1956-58. Roman Catholic. Avocations: reading, bridge. Home: 13615 Cloverlawn St Detroit MI 48238 Office: WJ Maxey Boys Tng Sch Box 349 Whitmore Lake MI 48189

URSEM, RICHARD EDWARD, fluid power distributing company executive; b. Detroit, Nov. 3, 1932; s. William A. and Adelaide J. (Schwering) U.; m. Joanne Clare Hones, May 12, 1956; children—William R., DeLourde M., Brian E., Keith A. (dec.), Devra J., Durene J. B.S. in Engring. Adminstrn., U. Detroit, 1955. Salesman, F. & W. Ursem Co., Cleve., 1957-65, sales mgr., 1965-74; pres. Ursem Co., Cleve., 1974—; mem. adv. council C.A. Norgren Co., Denver, 1976-78. Contbr. bi-monthly article Safari mag., 1980-81. Served to 1st lt. AUS, 1955-57. Named State Conservationist of Yr., League Ohio Sportsmen, 1984. Mem. Mem. Fluid Power Distbrs. Assn. (charter), Fluid Power Soc., Safari Club Internat. (govt. affairs com. 1980—, pres. 1980-81, Outstanding Mem. 1980-81), Nat. Rifle Assn. (life), Quiet Birdmen (pres. Ohio 1977). Republican. Roman Catholic. Club: Cleveland Yachting. Avocations: aviation; boating; hunting sports. Office: Ursem Co 1548 W 117th St Cleveland OH 44107

USERA, JOHN JOSEPH, chemistry educator, researcher, consulting systems analyst; b. Cleve., Mar. 18, 1941; s. Libertad Vivas and Beatrice (Ramirez) U.; m. Maria Bernadette Borszich, Sept. 6, 1969; children—Helen E., Karena M., Pamela Y. B.S., Black Hill State Coll., 1971, B.S. in Edn., 1972; M. Natural Sci., U. S.D., 1978, M.A., 1980; Ph.D., Kans. State U., 1984. Registered analytical chemist, Kans.; cert. secondary sch. chemistry tchr., S.D. Teaching asst. S.D. Sch. Mines, Rapid City, 1973-74; sci./math. instr. Shannon County Schs., Batesland, S.D., 1971-73; chemistry/physics instr. Bon Homme Sch. Dist., Tyndall, S.D., 1974-81; chemistry lectr. U. S.D., Springfield, 1979-80; chemistry prof. Labette Community Coll., Parsons, Kans., 1981—; dir. forensic lab. Labette Community Coll., 1982—. Author: Science Anxiety, 1984. Contbr. articles to profl. jours. Served to sgt. USMC, 1965-69, Viet Nam. Named S.D. Tchr. of Yr., S.D. Edn. Assn., 1980. Fellow Am. Inst. Chemists; mem. Am. Chem. Soc., Am. Chem. Soc. (analytical chemistry sect.), Two-Yr. Coll. Chemistry Conf., Nat. Sci. Tchrs. Assn., Kans. Edn. Assn., NEA; Kans. Sci. Tchr. Assn., Sigma Delta Nu, Pi Mu Epsilon. Roman Catholic. Lodge: K.C. Avocations: computers; reading; classical music. Home: 3102 Briggs Parsons KS 67357 Office: Labette Community Coll 200 S 14th St Parsons KS 67357

UTES, FRANK ALAN, osteopathic physician; b. Chgo., Apr. 20, 1951; s. Frank Edward and Esther (Rowoldt) U.; m. Karen Marie Younker, June 23, 1973; children—Christine, Julia, Laura. B.S. in Chemistry, U. Ill., 1973; D.O., Chgo. Coll. Osteo. Medicine, 1978. Intern Lansing (Mich.) Gen. Hosp., 1978; gen. practice osteo. medicine, Winamac, Ind., 1979—; mem. staff Pulaski Meml. Hosp., Winamac, 1979—, chief obstetrics, 1981—; pres. Utes Family Practice, Inc., Winamac. Mem. Am. Osteo. Assn., Ind. Assn. Osteo. Physicians and Surgeons, Pulaski County Med. Assn. Club: Kiwanis.

UTLEY, DANALD EMERSON, principal; b. Henderson Ky., Dec. 29, 1932; s. George Letcher and Mable (Allen) U.; m. Jo Ann Whitledge, Sept. 1, 1955; children—Yvonna C. Utley Pardus, Gregg Emerson. B.S., Western Ky. U., 1955; M.S., Ind. U., 1963. Tchr., Evansville-Vand Sch. Corp., Ind., 1960-70, counselor, 1970-73, prin., 1973—. Served to capt. USAF, 1956-63, PTO. IDEA fellow Charles F. Kettering Found. Mem. Phi Delta Kappa. Democrat. Baptist. Lodge: Mason (33 degree) (treas. 1980—). Avocation: sailing. Home: 2087 Polaris Ave Evansville IN 47715 Office: Evans Middle Sch 837 Tulip Ave Evansville IN 47711

UTRECHT, JAMES DAVID, lawyer; b. Camp Polk, Ia., May 23, 1952; s. James C. and Susan (McDevitt) U.; m. Karen Lee Kelly, Aug. 17, 1975; 1 child, Ann Elizabeth. B.B.A., U. Cin., 1974, J.D., 1977. Ptnr., Shipman, Utrecht & Dixon, Troy, Ohio, 1977—; asst. law dir. City of Troy, 1984—.Chmn. Miami County Reagan-Bush Com. (Ohio), 1984. Mem. Miami County Bar Assn., Ohio Bar Assn., ABA, 1/2 Republican. Roman Catholic. Clubs: Troy Jaycees (dir. 1983-84), Troy Rotary. Lodge: Elks. Home: 2299 Pleasantview Dr Troy OH 45373 Office: Shipman Utrecht & Dixon 12 S Plum St Troy OH 45373

UTZ, EUGENE JOSEPH, lawyer; b. Cin., July 27, 1923; s. Edward Joseph and Frances (Kraemer) U.; m. Gertrude Ellen Bernert, Nov. 27, 1948; children—Eugene Joseph II, Gary Lee, Marcia Ann, Marianne. B.B.A., U. Cin., 1949; J.D., Chase Coll. Law, 1953. Bar: Ohio 1953, U.S. Dist. Ct. Ohio 1955, U.S. Ct. Appeals (6th cir.) 1960, U.S. Supreme Ct. 1970. Sole practice, Ohio, 1953—; judge Hamilton County Ct., Ohio, 1963-68. Served with U.S. Army, 1943-45, ETO. Mem. Ohio Bar Assn., Cin. Bar Assn. Republican. Roman Catholic. Club: Maketewah (Cin.) (v.p., pres. 1980-82). Lodge: Elks. Avocation: golf. Home: 7865 Shawnee Run Rd Indian Hill OH 45243 Office: 1306 Fourth and Walnut Bldg 36 E 4th St Cincinnati OH 45202

VAAL, JOSEPH JOHN, JR., psychologist; b. St. Louis, Nov. 19, 1947; s. Joseph John and Dorothy Jane (Collett) V.; B.A., Lawrence U., 1969; M.A. in Psychology, Western Mich. U., 1971; Ph.D., Columbia Pacific U., 1981; m. Patricia Gail Winkler, Apr. 24, 1982; 1 child, Lauren Elizabeth. Tchr. spl. edn. KVISD Title VI Program, Kalamazoo, 1970, Mannheim Pub. Schs., Franklin Park, Ill., 1971; sch. psychologist Wheaton (Ill.) Pub. Schs., 1971-79; dir. office continuing edn. Rush-Presbyn.-St. Luke's Med. Ctr., Chgo., 1979-81; adj. instr. Grad. Sch. Nat. Coll. Edn., Evanston, 1972-81; spl. edn. due process hearing officer Ill. Bd. Edn., Springfield, 1978—; dir. ednl. services Healthcare Fin. Mgmt. Assn., Oak Brook, Ill., 1981-84; psychologist Vaal and Assocs., Evanston, Ill., 1984—. Mem. Ill. Sch. Psychologists Assn., Nat. Assn. Sch. Psychologists. Office: 612 Sheridan Rd Evanston IL 60202

VACTOR, HOWARD, industrial engineer; b. Cleve., July 6, 1924; s. Sam and Effie Vactor. B.S., U. Ill., 1948; postgrad. in Sci., Columbia U., 1950. Registered profl. engr., Ohio. Prodn. asst. Club-Mate Sportwear Co., Cleve., 1951-52; staff indsl. engr. Am. Greetings Inc., Cleve., 1956-58; prin., indsl. engr. Midwest Assocs., Cleve., 1958—. Mem. productivity task force Case Western Res. U., Cleve.; mem. tech. adv. com. Lakeland Community Coll.; indsl. cons. Goodwill Industries Cleve.; mem. citizens adv. bd. N.E. Ohio Devel. Ctr.; founding mem. Playhouse Square Assn. Served with USAF, 1944-46. Decorated Air medal, Bronze Star with two oak leaf clusters. Mem. Internat. Materials Mgmt. Soc. (sr. mem.), Inst. Indsl. Engrs. (officer Cleve. chpt.), Cleve. Engring. Soc. Republican. Club: Cleve. Athletic. Home: 15810 Van Aken Shaker Heights OH 44120 Office: 6900 Granger Rd Cleveland OH 44131

VAGNIERES, ROBERT CHARLES, architect; b. Chgo., Oct. 2, 1932; s. Alfred and Elsa (Krueger) V.; B.Arch., U. Ill., 1955; m. Dorothy Lee Wandrey, June 13, 1953; children—Robert, Krista, Ross, Pam. Draftsman, Robert Soellner, Architect, Park Forest, Ill., 1957-59; asso. mem. firm Joel Robert Hillman, Architect, Chgo., 1959-71; partner Hillman Vagnieres & Assos., Chgo., 1972-75; owner, prin. Robert C. Vagnieres Architect Ltd., Olympia Fields, Ill., 1975-79; cons., 1979—; cons. hotel planning and constrn.; cons. Sheraton Naperville Hotel, 1980, Vista Internat. Hotel, N.Y.C., 1981. Served to lt., C.E., U.S. Army, 1955-57. Mem. AIA. Prin. works include Chgo. City Centre, 1976, Sheraton Plaza Hotel, Chgo., 1971, Homewood-Flossmoor (Ill.) High Sch., 1977. Home: 1410 N State Pkwy Chicago IL 60610

VAIDYA, HEMANT CHUNILAL, medical researcher; b. Ahmedabad, Gujarat, India, Jan. 21, 1954; came to U.S., 1982; s. Chunilal Balashanker and Hervidya V.; m. Smita Hemant, May 28, 1979; children—Maitri, Jalpa. B.S., Gujarat U., 1974; M.S., Maharaja Sayajirao U., India, 1976; Ph.D. in Microbiology, Sardar Patel U., India, 1982. Demonstrator in microbiology Gujarat Coll., 1976-78; research technician Sardar Patel U., Gujarat, 1978-82; research assoc. Washington U. Sch. Medicine, St. Louis, 1982—. Contbr. articles to profl. jours. Hindu. Avocations: classical oriental music; sports; volleyball; cricket. Home: 4617B Gustine Terr Saint Louis MO 63116 Office: Washington U Med Sch Box 8118 660 S Euclid St Saint Louis MO 63116

VAIL, IRIS JENNINGS, civic worker; b. N.Y.C., July 2, 1928; d. Lawrence K. and Beatrice (Black) Jennings; grad. Miss Porters Sch., Farmington, Conn.; m. Thomas V.H. Vail, Sept. 15, 1951; children—Siri J., Thomas V.H. Jr., Lawrence J.W. Exec. com. Garden Club Cleve., 1962—; mem. women's council Western Res. Hist. Soc., 1960—; mem. jr. council Cleve. Mus. Art, 1953—; chmn. Childrens Garden Fair, 1966-75, Public Square Dinner, 1975; bd. dirs. Garden Center Greater Cleve., 1963-77; trustee Cleve. Zool. Soc., 1971—; mem. Ohio Arts Council, 1974-76, pub. sq. com. Greater Cleve. Growth Assn.; mem. endangered species com. Cleve. 200 Soc. Recipient Amy Angell Collier Montague medal Garden Club Am., 1976, Ohio Gov.'s award, 1977. Episcopalian. Clubs: Chagrin Valley Hunt, Cypress Point, Kirtland Country, Union, Colony, Women's City of Cleve. (Margaret A. Ireland award). Home: Hunting Valley Chagrin Falls OH 44022

VAIL, JOE FRANKLIN, marketing company executive; b. Indpls., Mar. 24, 1928; s. Frank Albert and Trixie May (Hawley) V.; B.S., Purdue U., 1951; m. Margaret Louise Warne, Nov. 24, 1984; 1 son, Kevin Joe. Treas., Apex Corp., Indpls., 1953-60; owner, operator Bus. Service Co., Indpls., 1961-63; partner Pulse Publs., Indpls., 1963-64; pres. Unique, Inc., Indpls., 1965-70; owner, operator Mid-Am. Advt. Co., Indpls., 1970-73; pres. Mid-Am. Mktg., Inc., Indpls., 1973—; editor, pub. Land Opportunity Rev., 1970—. Mem. Chgo. Assn. Direct Mktg., Nat. Fedn. Ind. Bus., Indpls. C. of C. Am. Bus. Club. Clubs: John Purdue, Masons. Author: Keys to Wealth, 1971; Your Fortune in Mail Order, 1972; How to Get Out of Debt and Live Like a Millionaire, 1977; Money-Where It Is and How To Get It, 1981. Home: 8228 E 13th St Indianapolis IN 46219 Office: 1150 N Shadeland Ave Indianapolis IN 46219

VAIL, ROBERT WILLIAM, consulting company executive; b. Columbus, Ohio, Oct. 29, 1921; s. Robert David Dmitri and Dorothy (Mosier) Vail; student Ohio State U., 1938-39; m. Martha Henderson, Apr. 7, 1939; children—William N., Veronica Vail Fish, David A., Ashley M., Victor H., Lorelei Hird, Hilary W. Chemist, Barnebey-Cheney Engring. Co., 1941-44; sr. chemist Pa. Coal Products Co., Petrolia, 1944-51; abrasive engr. Carborundum Co., Niagara Falls, N.Y., 1951-54; tech. sales Allied Chem. Corp., Cleve., 1954-59; head research lab. U.S. Ceramic Tile Co., Canton, Ohio, 1960-62; sales mgr. Ferro Chem. div. Ferro Corp., Walton Hills, Ohio, 1962-70; pres. R. William Vail Inc., Cleve., 1970-72; mgr. tech. services Manpower Inc., Cleve., 1972-74; owner, mgr. Vail, Shaker Heights, Ohio, 1974-78; sr. cons. Hayden, Heman, Smith & Assos., Cleve., 1978-83; owner Vail, Newbury, Ohio, 1983—. Recipient Am. Security Council Bus. Citizenship Competition Excellence award, 1967. Mem. Amateur Radio Relay League. Republican. Presbyterian. Lodges: Masons, Scottish Rite, Al Koran Shrine. Author: Teardrops Falling, 1963; contbg. author: Ency. of Basic Materials for Plastics, 1967. Home: Box 516 Newbury OH 44065 Office: 14871 Highview Newbury OH 44065

VAIL, THOMAS VAN HUSEN, publisher, editor; b. Cleve., June 23, 1926; s. Herman Lansing and Delia (White) V.; A.B. cum laude in Polit. Sci., Princeton U., 1949, H.H.D., Wilberforce U., 1964; L.H.D., Kenyon Coll., 1969, Cleve. State U., 1973; m. Iris Jennings, Sept. 15, 1951; children—Siri, Thomas Van Husen, Lawrence J.W. Reporter, Cleve. News, 1949-53, polit. editor, 1953-57; bus. dept. Cleve. Plain Dealer, 1957-61, v.p., 1961-63, pub., editor, 1963—, pres., 1970—, also dir.; pres., dir. Art Gravure Corp., Ohio, AP, 1968-74; mem. U.S. Adv. Commn. on Info., Nat. Adv. Commn. on Health Manpower, Pres.'s Commn. Observance 25th Anniversary UN. Dir., past pres. Cleve. Conv. and Visitors Bur.; chmn. Nat. Brotherhood Week, 1969; bd. dirs. Greater Cleve. Growth Assn.; mem. distbn. com. Cleve. Found.; trustee Clinic Found., No. Ohio region NCCJ, Downtown Cleve. Corp. Com. for Econ. Devel. Served to lt. (j.g.) USNR, 1944-46. Recipient Nat. Human Relations award NCCJ, 1970, Man of Yr. award Sales and Mktg. Execs. of Cleve., 1976; Ohio Gov.'s award, 1982; Downtown Bus. Council recognition award Greater Cleve. Growth Assn., 1983. Mem. Am. Newspaper Pubs. Assn., Am. Soc. Newspaper Editors, Sigma Delta Chi. Clubs: Cleve. Athletic, Union (Cleve.); Kirtland Country (Willoughby, Ohio); Cypress Point (Pebble Beach, Calif.); Bohemian (San Francisco); Nat. Press (Washington); Chagrin Valley Hunt (Gates Mills, Ohio). Home: Hunting Valley Chagrin Falls OH 44022 Office: 1801 Superior Ave Cleveland OH 44114

VAIL, VICTOR ALANZO, communications company executive; b. Lewiston, Minn., Feb. 22, 1938; s. John Langdon and Frances Olga (Gaulke) V.; m. Renate Elisabeth Bausch, Oct. 20, 1957 (div. 1964); 1 child, Wayne V.; m. Sherriann Gloria Daniels, Oct. 1, 1966; children—Tamara D., Vickiann G., Daniel T. Student, Winona State Coll., 1956, Rochester Community Coll., 1972-74. Electronic technician Admiral Corp., Harvard, Ill., 1961-65; electronic technician Telex Communication, Rochester, Minn., 1965—, indsl. engr., 1970-75, prodn. engring. mgr., 1975-85, custom hearing aid ops. mgr., 1985—. Bd. dirs. Warren Cemetery Assn., Lewiston, 1967—. Served with USAF, 1956-61. Named Sportsman of Year, Lewiston Sportsman Club, 1982, recipient Farmer Sportsmen award, 1983, 84. Mem. Minn. Conservation Fedn. (sec. 1983-84, dir.), Turn in Poachers (dir. 1981-84), Bob White Quail Soc. Lutheran. Club: Lewiston Sportsman's (pres. 1978-83). Avocations: Conservation; hunting; fishing; coin collecting. Home: Route 1 Box 75 Lewiston MN 55952 Office: Telex Communications 1620 Industrial Dr NW Rochester MN 55901

VAINISI, JEROME ROBERT, professional football executive, lawyer; b. Chgo., Oct. 7, 1941; s. Anthony A. and Marie (Delisi) V.; m. Doris Mary Lane, Nov. 14, 1964; children—Mary Terese, Jerome A., John A., Mark E., Melissa P. B.S. in Bus. Adminstrn., Georgetown U., 1963; postgrad. in law Loyola U., 1963-64; J.D., Chgo. Kent Coll. Law, 1969. Bar: Ill. 1969. News and sports dir. Sta. WRAM, Monmouth, Ill., 1964-65; tax acct., office mgr. Arthur Andersen & Co., Chgo., 1965-72; successively controller, corp. asst. sec., treas. Chgo. Bears Football Club, Inc., 1972-83, v.p., gen. mgr., 1983—; dir., chmn. bd. Forest Park Nat. Bank (Ill.), 1978—; v.p. NFL Ins. Ltd., 1984—. Roman Catholic.

VAJDA, JANETTE ANNE, psychiatric nursing educator; b. Cleve., May 22, 1954; d. Alex Francis and Catherine Helen (Hermann) V. B.S. in Nursing, U. Akron, 1976; postgrad. in psychiat./mental nursing Kent State U., 1984-85. Case mgr., counselor West Side Community Mental Health Ctr., Cleve., 1976-81; psychosocial nursing instr. Cleve. Met. Gen. Hosp. Sch. Nursing, 1981—.

VAJPEYI, DHIRENDRA KUMAR, political science educator; b. Farrukhabad, India, Feb. 7, 1936; s. Shree Narayan and Savitri (Mishra) V.; m. Georgia Kay Norris, May 21, 1983. M.A., Lucknow U. (India), 1958, M.A. in Publ. Adminstrn., 1961; M.A., Mich. State U., 1968, Ph.D., 1971. Asst. prof. Inst. Public Adminstrn. India, 1961-64; research assoc. Centre for Study Developing Socs. India, 1964-66; mem. faculty U. No. Iowa, Cedar Falls, 1969—, assoc. prof. polit. sci., to 1979, prof., 1979—. Author: Modernization and Social Change in India, 1979; Government and Politics in India (with Baljit Singh), 1981; contbr. articles to professional journals. Am. Inst. Indian Studies postdoctoral sr. fellow, 1976; Smithsonian Inst. grantee, 1978; Inst. Internat. Edn. grantee, 1969; Inst. Internat. Agr. and Nutrition Mich. State U. grantee, 1968. Mem. Iowa Polit. Conf. (pres. 1982-83), Assn. Asian Studies, Assn. Advancement Policy, Research and Devel. Clubs: Beverly Hills Country (Cedar Falls); Rotary. Home: 1913 Four Winds Dr Cedar Falls IA 50613 Office: Univ No Iowa Dept Polit Sci Cedar Falls IA 50614

VALANCE, MARSHA JEANNE, library director, story teller; b. Evanston, Ill., Aug. 2, 1946; d. Edward James, Jr. and Jeanne Lois (Skinner) Leonard; m. William George Valance, Dec. 27, 1966 (div. 1976); 1 dau., Marguerite Jeanne. Student Northwestern U., 1964-66; A.B., UCLA, 1968; M.L.S., U. R.I., 1973. Children's librarian trainee N.Y. Pub. Library, N.Y.C., 1968-69; reference librarian Action Meml. Pub. Library (Mass.), 1969-70; mgr. The Footnote, Cedar Rapids, Iowa, 1976-78; assoc. editor William C. Brown, Dubuque, Iowa, 1978-79; library dir. Dubuque County Library, Dubuque, 1979-81; library dir. G.B. Dedrick Pub. Library, Geneseo, Ill., 1981-84; library dir. Grand Rapids Pub. Library, Minn., 1984—; workshop coordinator, participant, sect. chmn. profl. confs. Co-author: Mystery, Value and Awareness, 1979; Pluralism, Similarities and Contrast, 1979; contbr. articles to publs. Troop leader Mississippi Valley Council Girl Scouts U.S.A., Cedar Rapids, 1976-78; mem. liturgy com. St. Malachy's Roman Catholic Ch., Geneseo, 1983; com. judging clinic 4-H, Moline, Ill., 1984. Iowa Humanities Bd. grantee, 1981. Mem. ALA, Minn. Library Assn., Iowa Libraries of Medium Size (sec. 1981), Northlands Storytelling Network, Alliance Info. and Referral Services, DAR (constn. chmn. 1983-84), Am. Morgan Horse Assn., Mississippi Valley Morgan Horse Club, North Central Morgan Assn., Alpha Gamma Delta. Club: Geneseo Jr. Women's (internat. chmn. 1983-84). Home: 925 NW 2d Ave Grand Rapids MN 55744 Grand Rapids Pub Library 21 E 5th St Grand Rapids MN 55744

VALAUSKAS, CHARLES C., lawyer; b. Chgo., Nov. 14, 1952; s. Edward A. and Madeline (Markovich) V.; m. Linda S. Kawano, Nov. 6, 1977. B.S., U. Ill., 1977; J.D., DePaul U., 1981; LL.M., Northwestern U., 1985. Bar: Ill. 1981, U.S. Dist. Ct. (no. dist.) Ill. 1981. Research assoc. John Shedd Schweppe Found., Chgo., 1981-84; assoc. Karon, Morrison & Savikas, Ltd., Chgo., 1984—. Contbr. articles to profl. jours. State of Ill. Gov.'s fellow, 1979; Nat. Wildlife Fedn. fellow, 1980; Research and Edn. Fund fellow Northwestern U., Chgo., 1982; MacChesney Fund grantee Northwestern U. Law Sch., Chgo., 1983. Home: 205 Marengo St Forest Park IL 60130 Office: 5720 Sears Tower 233 S Wacker Dr Chicago IL 60606

VALENTINE, MARJORIE PARKS, psychologist, consultant; b. Chattanooga, Apr. 20, 1928; d. Leon C. and Marjorie (Atlee) Parks; m. Andrew Jackson Valentine, July 20, 1949; children—Rawson J., Atlee Ann, Sarah. B.A., U. Tenn., 1949; M.A., George Washington U., 1954; Ph.D., Am. U., 1977. Lic. psychologist, D.C., 1981. Sch. psychologist Escambia County Schs., Pensacola, Fla., 1962-65, dir. Headstart Program, 1965; sch. psychologist Arlington (Va.) Pub. Schs., 1966-79; instr. U. Va. Regional Ctr., 1975-76; research affiliate Program on Women, Northwestern U., 1979-82; assoc. Cassell, Rath and Stoyanoff, Ltd., Evanston, Ill., 1981—; adj. faculty Seabury-Western Seminary, 1984—. Bd. dirs., mem. exec. com. Chicago Commons, 1980—. Mem. Am. Psychol. Assn., Ill. Psychol. Assn. Republican. Episcopalian. Club: Junior League of Evanston. Address: 1091 Sheridan Rd Winnetka IL 60093

VALENTINE, PHILIP WILLIAM, optometrist; b. Piqua, Ohio, July 14, 1941; s. M. Richard and Virginia L. (Agenbroad) V.; m. Susan J. Barnhart, July 10, 1965; children—Sara, Carolyn, Ashley, David. O.D., Ohio State U., 1965. Practice optometry, Sidney, Ohio, 1968—. Pres., Upper Valley Joint Vocat. Sch. Bd., Piqua, 1974-76, Sidney Bd. Edn., 1976-78, Adminstrv. Bd. Methodist Ch., Sidney, 1983-84. Served to capt. U.S. Army, 1966-68. Mem. Ohio Optometric Assn. (mem. edn. com. 1970-72). Republican. Clubs: Epicurean, Stock (Sidney). Lodge: Masons (pres. Shelby County shrine 1972-73). Avocations: duck and pheasant hunting; reading; traveling; gourmet cooking. Home: 132 Woodhaven Dr Sidney OH 45365 Office: 737 Spruce Ave Sidney OH 45365

VALENTINE, RALPH JAMES, chemical engineer; b. Mahwah, N.J., May 11, 1922; s. Richard Van and Matilda (Fisher) V.; m. Irene M. Sandberg, Feb. 13, 1944; children—Ralph James, Dorothy June, Leonard Bradley, Christine Marie. B.Chem. Engring., Pratt Inst., 1943; postgrad Stevens Inst. Tech., 1948-51, Case Inst. Tech., 1952, Fairleigh Dickinson U., 1965-67. Registered corrosion specialist. Devel. engr. AT&T, 1946-49; chem. process engr. Lederle Labs. div. Am. Cyanamid Co., Pearl River, N.Y., 1949-51, asst. supt. chem. prodn., 1951-52, corrosion and materials engr., 1952-56, sr. chem. engr. design and constrn. chem. and prodn. facilities, cons. corrosion and materials engring. problems, 1956-73, sr. chem. project engring. mgr. Cyanamid Engring. and Constrn. div., Wayne, N.J., 1973-81; sr. engring. project mgr., corrosion cons. Upjohn Co., Kalamazoo, 1981—. Elder, v.p. consistory, del. to gen. synod Reformed Ch. Am. Served to capt. USAAF, 1943-46. Fellow Am. Inst. Chemists; mem. Nat. Assn. Corrosion Engrs., Structural Steel Painting Council, Sea Horse Inst. Lodge: Vasa Order Am. (past N.J. dist. master). Home: 173 Parkland Terr Portage MI 49002 Office: Upjohn Co 7171 Portage Rd Kalamazoo MI 49001

VALERIAN, ROBERT J., lawyer; b. Cleve., Jan. 13, 1943; s. Joseph M. and Clara M. (Petti) V.; m. Dorothy Janusko, Mar. 20, 1965; children—Lisa, Christopher, Daniel. B.S. in Fgn. Service, Georgetown U., 1964; J.D., Case Western Res. U., 1976. Bar: Ohio 1976. Assoc. Kahn, Kleinman, Yanowitz & Arnson, Cleve., 1976-81, ptnr., 1981—. Mem. exec. com. Cuyahoga County Democratic Com., 1979—; active Catholic Diocese Cleve., 1982—, Cath. Endowment Trust Fund. Served with USAF, 1964-73; maj. USAFR. Decorated D.F.C., Air medal, Meritorious Service medal. Mem. ABA, Ohio Bar Assn. Roman Catholic. Home: 3320 Avalon Rd Shaker Heights OH 44120 Office: Kahn Kleinman Yanowitz & Arnson 1300 Bond Ct Bldg Cleveland OH 44114

VALERIO, MICHAEL ANTHONY, financial executive; b. Detroit, Sept. 20, 1953; s. Anthony Rudolph and Victoria (Popoff) V.; m. Barbara Ann Nabozny, Oct. 8, 1983. B.A., U. Mich-Dearborn, 1975. C.P.A., Mich. Jr. acct., Carabell, Bocknek C.P.A.s, Southfield, Mich., 1975-76; sr. acct. Purdy, Donovan & Beal, C.P.A.s, Detroit, 1976-77; mgr. Buctynck & Co., C.P.A.s, Southfield, 1978-79; controller Transcontinental Travel, Harper Woods, Mich., 1979-80; exec. v.p. Holland Cons., Inc., Detroit, 1980—. Mem. Mich. Assn. C.P.A.s, Am. Inst. C.P.A.s, Acctg. Research Found., Mich. Assn. of Professions. Roman Catholic. Office: Holland Consulting Inc 260 Edison Plaza Detroit MI 48226

VALERIUS, FREDERICK MICHAEL, special education administrator; b. Cin., Jan. 22, 1947; s. Frederick Anthony and Marian Gertrude (Gundlach) V.; m. Joyce Ann Rupp, July 12, 1974; children—Jillian Marie, Christina Ann. B.S. in Edn., U. Cin., 1969, M.Ed., 1971. Qualified mental retardation profl., Ohio. Instr., Hamilton County Bd. Mental Retardation, Cin., 1969-70; instr. Butler County Bd. Mental Retardation, Hamilton, Ohio, 1970-72, instr. supr., 1972-75, dir. ednl. services, 1976-79; asst. supt. program services Butler County Bd. Mental Retardation and Devel. Disabilities, Fairfield, Ohio, 1980—. Mem. Am. Assn. Mental Deficiency (membership chmn. Ohio chpt.), Assn. Curriculum and Supervision Devel., Profl. Assn. Retardation Ohio (pres. 1974-75). Office: 155 Donald Dr Fairfield OH 45014

VALINCY, THOMAS DERRICK, manufacturing company executive; b. Cleve., Jan. 17, 1951. B.A., Kent State U., 1975; Assoc. Mfg. Control, Cuyahoga Community Coll., Cleve., 1980; M.B.A., Baldwin-Wallace Coll., 1983. Fin. cons., Cleve., 1970-77; mfg. analyst NCR, Cleve., 1977-79. Sperry Univac, Cleve., 1980-82; strategy analyst Hoover Co., Canton, Ohio, 1983—; pres. Productivity II, Cleve., 1982—; lectr. Author, editor; A Practitioner's Guide to Production and Inventory Control, 1983. Recipient Man of Yr. award Am. Prodn. and Inventory Control Soc., 1981, 82. Mem. Am. Prodn. and Inventory Control Soc. (exec. v.p. 1982, pres. 1983-84), Inst. Indsl. Engrs. (dir. 1982—). Roman Catholic. Club: Aquamarine. Home: 4313 Elmwood Rd South Euclid OH 44121

VALLADARES, NAVIJA, physician; b. Camaguey, Cuba, Nov. 14, 1950; came to U.S., 1960, naturalized, 1969; d. Roger Peter and Navija (Achkar) V. Student U. Montpellier, France, summer 1969; B.S. in Biology, Youngstown State U., 1972; postgrad. Universidad Autonoma de Barcelona, Spain, 1972-75; M.D., Universidad Central del Este, Dominican Republic, 1977; diplomas in ob-gyn, cardiology, psychiatry, neurology. Resident in family practice Mercy Hosp., Toledo, Ohio, 1981-84; jr. lab. technician St. Elizabeth Hosp., Youngstown, Ohio, 1970-72; emergency room vol. Mahonig chpt. Red Cross Hosp., Youngstown, 1971-72; extern dept. pathology Youngstown Hosp. Assn., 1974; clin. clk. VA Hosp., Miami, Fla., 1978; house doctor ob-gyn, pediatrics, medicine Surger Riverside Hosp., Toledo, 1978-79; with family practice residency program Mercy Hosp., Toledo, 1981-84; pvt. practice Valladares Family Practice Ctr., Orlando, Fla., 1985—. Author: Incidence of Uterine Myomas in Five Hospitals in Miami, 1977. Consultant: Incidence and Causes of Congestive Heart Failure and Pulmonary Edema in 10 Patients on Peritoneal Dialysis, 1979. Instr. Introduction to a Career in Medicine, St. Elizabeth Hosp., 1968; sec. Future Physicians Club; sec. Youngstown Philiantric Soc., 1971; tutor Youngstown State U. Recipient Award of Distinction, State Bd. Edn., 1969, award for companionship, efficiency, integrity as a med. student, 1977; named Best Female Student, 1977. Fellow Am. Bd. Family Practice (cert.); mem. Ohio State Med. Assn., AMA, Am. Assn. Family Physicians, Speech Club (speechmaster), United Nations Assn. Roman Catholic.

VALLERA, DANIEL ATTILIO, therapeutic radiology educator, cancer and transplantation researcher; b. East Liverpool, Ohio, Oct. 13, 1951; s. Jesse Anthony and Mary Sue (Frank) V. B.S., Ohio State U., 1973, M.S., 1975, Ph.D., 1978. Asst. prof. therapeutic radiology and lab. medicine and pathology U. Minn., 1980-84, assoc. prof., 1984—. Leukemia Soc. Am. scholar, 1983; Minn. Med. Found. spl. research grantee, 1982; recipient Am. Cancer Soc. Jr. Faculty award, 1983, Hubert H. Humphrey Cancer Research award, 1981. Mem. Am. Assn. Immunologists, Transplantation Soc., Assn. Minn. Immunologists. Roman Catholic. Office: Dept Therapeutic Radiology Univ Minn Box 367 Mayo Meml Bldg 420 Delaware St SE Minneapolis MN 55455

VAMOS, FLORENCE MARIE, lawyer; b. N.Y.C., Apr. 9, 1934; d. Joseph Salvatore and Louise Marie (Riccio) Calabro; m. Joseph S. Vamos, Sept. 20, 1952. B.A. magna cum laude, U. Minn., 1974; J.D., William Mitchell Coll. Law, 1978. Bar: Ind. 1978, Mich. 1982, U.S. Dist. Ct. (ea. dist.) Mich. 1982, U.S. Dist. Ct. (no. dist.) Ind. 1979, U.S. Dist. Ct. (so. dist.) Ind. 1978. Sole practice, South Bend, Ind., 1978—, Edwardsburg, Mich., 1982—. Office: Suite 303 Lafayette Bldg 115 S Lafayette Blvd South Bend IN 46601

VAN AKEN, WILLIAM RUSSELL, lawyer; b. Shaker Heights, Ohio, Dec. 1, 1912; s. William J. and Florence E. (Swallow) Van A.; m. Dorothy Harrison, Apr. 27, 1940; children—Nancy, William R. (dec.), Mary Alice, Dorothy Louise, William J. II. B.S., Lafayette Coll., 1934; LL.B., Western Res. U., 1937. Bar: Ohio 1938. Practiced in Cleve., 1938—; mem. firm Van Aken, Bond, Withers, Asman & Smith, 1949—; pres. William J. Van Aken Orgn., Inc., 1951-72; dir., v.p. Ohio Bar Title Ins. Co. Co-author: Ohio Practice-Real Estate Transactions; author: Buckeye Barristers - The First Hundred Years of the Ohio State Bar Association, 1980. Assoc. editor Baldwin's Ohio Legal Forms, 1962. Trustee, chmn. bd. Ohio Bar Automated Research Corp.; v.p., trustee Ohio Info. Com.; mem. Ohio Legislature, 1943-44, 47-48, Shaker Heights City Council, 1951-55, Ohio Republican Central and Exec. Com., 1954-65, Cuyahoga County Rep. Central Com., 1942-64; pres. bd. trustees Heather Hill, Inc., 1970-78; trustee Shaker Hist. Soc., pres., 1964-66, 70-71; trustee Ohio Legal Ctr. Inst., 1971-77; bd. mgrs. Heights YMCA, 1942-73. Fellow Am. Bar Found., Ohio Bar Found. (trustee, pres. 1971-77); mem. Am. Judicature Soc., Apt. and Home Owners Assn. (trustee, past pres.), ABA, Ohio Bar Assn. (council dels., pres. 1958-59), Nat. Conf. State Bar Founds. (pres. 1977-79, trustee 1979—), Am. Coll. Real Estate Lawyers, Northeastern Ohio Intermus. Council (chmn. 1968-70, trustee 1968—, vice chmn. 1977), Cleve. Fedn. Realty Interests, Cleve. Real Estate Bd. (pres. 1957, trustee 1953-58), Greater Cleve. Growth Assn., Ohio Hist. Soc., Western Res. Hist. Soc., Early Settlers Assn. (v.p.), Phi Gamma Delta (gen. counsel 1969-72). Delta Theta Phi. Presbyterian. Clubs: Union, Mid-Day, Skating (Cleve.); Univ. (Columbus). Lodge: Rotary. Home: 22299 Douglas Rd Shaker Heights OH 44122 Office: Nat City Bank Bldg Cleveland OH 44114

VAN ALLEN, MAURICE WRIGHT, physician, neurology educator, administrator; b. Mt. Pleasant, Iowa, Apr. 3, 1918; s. Alfred Maurice and Alma E. (Olney) Van A.; m. Janet Marjorie Hunt; children—David, Martha, Evalyn, Jonathan. B.A., Iowa Wesleyan U., 1939; M.D., U. Iowa, 1942. Diplomate Am. Bd. Neurol. Surgery, Am. Bd. Psychiatry and Neurology. From asst. prof. to prof. Coll. Medicine U. Iowa, 1959—, head dept. neurology, 1974—. Author: Pictorial Manual of Neurologic Tests, 1967. Contbr. articles to profl. jours. Served to capt. USMC, 1943-45. Fellow Am. Acad. Neurology; mem. Am. Neurol. Assn., AMA (del. 1972-80), Alpha Omega Alpha. Republican. Episcopalian. Avocations: orchidology; collecting ancient coins; wordworking. Home: 354 Lexington Ave Iowa City IA 52240 Office: Univ Hosp Iowa City IA 52242

VAN ALTEN, PIERSON JAY, immunology educator; b. Grand Rapids, Mich., Feb. 21, 1928; s. Daniel and Anna (Zuidema) Van A.; m. Lucille Westendorp, June 30, 1953; children—Faith, Daniel J. B.A., Calvin Coll., 1950; M.S., Mich. State U., 1955, Ph.D., 1958. Research fellow UCLA, 1958-60; asst. prof. anatomy U. Ill.-Chgo., 1960-65, assoc. prof., 1965-73, prof., 1973—; vis. prof. U. Minn., Mpls., 1966-67; U. Bern, Switzerland, 1973-74. Contbr. articles to profl. jours. Contbg. author books in field. Served with U.S. Army, 1951-53. Fellow Am. Cancer Soc., N.Y.C., 1973-74; grantee United Cerebral Palsy, N.Y.C., 1965-68, John A. Hartford Found., N.Y.C., 1973-76, Nat. Cancer Inst., Bethesda, Md., 1976-82. Mem. Fedn. Am. Socs. Exptl. Biology, Reticuliendothelial Soc. (treas. 1979-80), Am. Soc. Immunologists (rep. Life Scis. Research office 1975-81), Am. Assn. Anatomists, Transplantation Soc., AAAS. Mem. Christian Reformed Ch. Avocation; model trains. Home: 140 Fairview Elmhurst IL 60126 Office: Dept Anatomy U Ill PO Box 6998 Chicago IL 60680

VAN ANDEL, BETTY JEAN, household products company executive; b. Mich., Dec. 14, 1921; d. Anthony and Daisy (Van Dyk) Hoekstra; A.B., Calvin Coll., 1943; m. Jay Van Andel, Aug. 16, 1952; children—Nan Elizabeth, Stephen Alan, David Lee, Barbara Ann. Elementary sch. tchr., Grand Rapids, Mich., 1943-45; service rep. and supr. Mich. Bell Telephone Co., Grand Rapids, 1945-52; dir.-stockholder Amway Corp., Grand Rapids, 1972—. Treas., LWV, 1957-60; chmn. Eagle Forum, Mich., 1975—; bd. dirs. Christian Sch. Ednl. Found., Pine Rest Christian Hosp., Mem. Nat. Trust Hist. Preservation, St. Cecelia Music Soc., Smithsonian Assos. Republican. Club: Women's City of Grand Rapids. Home: 7186 Windy Hill Rd SE Grand Rapids MI 49506 Office: PO Box 172 Ada MI 49301

VAN ANDEL, JAY, corporation executive; b. Grand Rapids, Mich., June 3, 1924; s. James and Nella (Vanderwoude) Van A.; student Pratt Jr. Coll., 1945, Calvin Coll., 1942, 46, Yale, 1943-44; D.B.A. (hon.), No. Mich. U., 1976, Western Mich. U., 1979; LL.D. (hon.), Ferris State Coll., 1977; m. Betty J. Hoekstra, Aug. 16, 1952; children—Nan, Stephen, David, Barbara. Formerly engaged in aviation, restaurant and mail order businesses; co-founder, chmn. bd. Amway Corp., Ada, Mich.; chmn. bd. Amway Can., Ltd., Amway Australia, Amway Mgmt. Co., 1970—, Amway U.K. Ltd., Amway Germany, Amway Hong-Kong, Amway France, Amway Malaysia, Amway Japan,

Amway Netherlands, Amway Hotel Properties, Mut. Broadcasting System, Nutrilite Products Inc.; dir. Mich. Nat. Bank, Lansing, Van Andel & Flikkema Motor Sales, Grand Rapids. Mem. adv. council Nat. 4H Found.; chmn. Mich. Republican Finance Com.; mem. Nat. Rep. Finance Com.; trustee, Ferguson Hosp., Grand Rapids, Hillsdale Coll., Citizens Research Council Mich.; nat. bd. govs. USO; bd. dirs. Hudson Inst., N.Y.; chmn. Citizens Choice, Netherlands Am. Bicentennial Commn., Mich. Senate Trust; pres. Van Andel Found. Served to 1st lt. USAAF, 1943-46. Recipient Disting. Alumni award Calvin. Coll., 1976; Freedom Found. award. Mem. Soap and Detergent Assn. (dir.), U.S. C. of C. (past chmn. bd.). Mem. Christian Reformed Ch. (elder). Clubs: Penisular; Cascade Hills; Lotus; Capitol Hill (Washington); Macatawa Bay Yacht (Holland, Mich.); La Mirador (Switzerland). Home: 7186 Windy Hill Rd Grand Rapids MI 49506 Office: 7575 E Fulton Rd Grand Rapids MI 49355

VAN AS, WILLIAM OLIVER, financial executive; b. Rochester, N.Y., Aug. 21, 1947; s. Robert Augustine Vanas and Virginia Marie (Bartold) Weden; m. Caroleah V.W. Van As, Aug. 23, 1969; children—Jennifer, William Robert. A.B.A., Rochester Bus. Inst., 1968; B.S. in Bus. Adminstrn., Tri-State U., Angola, Ind., 1970; M.B.A., Ind. No. U., Marion, 1979. Acct., Consumers Power Co., Jackson, Mich., 1971-72, gen. acct., 1972-74, sr. acct., 1974-76, savs. and stock plans supr., 1976-78, benefit systems coordinator, 1978-79, mgr. benefit fin. adminstrn. Sundstrand Corp., Rockford, Ill., 1979-83; mgr. benefit planning The Firestone Tire & Rubber Co., Akron, Ohio, 1983—. Mem. Employee Benefits Assn. No. Ill. (chmn. 1981-82), Internat. Found. Employee Benefit Plans, Employee Benefits Council Cleve. Republican. Lutheran. Address: 1003 W Abbey Dr Medina OH 44256

VAN ATTA, RALPH EDWARD, clinical psychologist, consultant in forensic psychology; b. Columbus, Ohio, July 24, 1933; s. Clarence Dell and Wilma (Davidson) V.; m. JoAnn Luce, Sept. 15, 1962; children—Katherine, Karen, Ralph Davidson, Sarah. B.S., Ohio State U., 1955, M.A., 1960, Ph.D., 1964. Lic. psychologist, Wis., Ill. Nat. Register Health Service Providers in Psychology, diplomate Am. Bd. of Psychotherapy. Intern, Ohio State Counseling Ctr., Columbus, 1962; clin. psychology intern Norwich (Conn.) Hosp., 1963; asst. prof., psychologist U. Tex., 1964-69; assoc. prof., psychologist, So. Ill. U., Carbondale, 1969-72; dir., prof. dept. psychol. services U. Wis.-Milw., 1972-80; exec. dir. Behavioral Medicine Assocs., Waukesha, Wis., 1978—; pres. Behavioral Medicine Wis., Ltd., 1984—; mem. Panel Forensic Experts, Counties of Waukesha and Milwaukee, Wis. Served to 1st lt. U.S. Army, 1955-57. Named Disting. Mil. Student Ohio State U., 1955. Mem. Am. Psychol. Assn., Wis. Soc. Clin. and Cons. Psychologists, Wis. Psychol. Assn., Am. Acad. Psychotherapists. Contbr. articles to profl. jours. Office: Behavioral Medicine Assocs 1519 Summit Ave Waukesha WI 53186

VAN BECELAERE, ROBERT MORRIS, engineering executive; b. Kansas City, Mo., Sept. 2, 1941; s. Emil Alidor and Margaret Mary (Vinckier) Van B.; m. Mary Elizabeth Daniel, June 5, 1964; children—Susan, Mike, Laura. B.E.E., Finlay Engring. Coll., 1960. Vice pres. engring. Tempmaster, Kansas City, 1963-76, Rusking Mfg. Co., Grandview, Mo., 1976—. Patentee in field. Served with USNR, 1963-69. Mem. ASME (chmn. CONAGT sub-com. 1981—). Roman Catholic. Home: 7627 Chadwick St Prairie Village KS 66208 Office: Ruskin Mfg Co 3900 Dr Greaves Rd Grandview MO 64030

VAN BELKUM, THOMAS GERALD, lawyer; b. Grand Rapids, Mich., Aug. 16, 1951; s. Gerald and Carol (Afton) Van B.; m. Kathleen Ann Murphy, Sept. 13, 1980. B.A.A., Western Mich. U., 1973; J.D., Detroit Coll. Law, 1978; B.B.A. cum laude (hon.), Western Mich. U., 1973. Bar: Mich. 1979, Ill. 1979, U.S. Dist. Ct. (ea. and we. dists.) Mich. 1980, U.S. Dist. Ct. (no. dist.) Ill. 1980. Atty., J.T. Ryerson & Son, Inc., Chgo., 1978-80; assoc. Baxter & Hammond, Grand Rapids, 1980-83, Moll, Desenberg, Bayer & Behrendt, Detroit, 1983—. Mem. ABA, Mich. Trial Lawyers Assn., Mich. Bar Assn., Ill. State Bar Assn. Methodist. Office Moll Desenberg et al 600 Renaissance 13th Floor Detroit MI 48243

VAN BODEGRAVEN, ARTHUR, management consultant; b. Hammond, Ind., Aug. 4, 1939; s. Arthur and Hilda (Boersma) V.; m. Phyllis Ann Laucis, Feb. 4, 1967; children—Julie, Elizabeth, David, Jonathan. B.S., Purdue U., 1961. Data processing mgr. Inland Steel Co., Chgo., 1964-68; data processing cons. Lybrand, Ross Bros. & Montgomery, Chgo., 1968-71; systems dir. Hirsh Co., Skokie, Ill., 1971-72; mgr. productivity cons. Coopers & Lybrand, Chgo., 1973-75, dir. productivity cons., Columbus, Ohio, 1975-83, regional dir. resource productivity cons., 1983—; speaker to various orgns., 1969—. Contbr. articles to various publs. Campaign worker various local Rep. campaigns, 1962—. Served with U.S. Army, 1961-64. Mem. Inst. Indsl. Engrs., Assn. Systems Mgmt., Data Processing Mgmt. Assn. Republican. Club: University (Columbus). Home: 7630 Ashworth St Worthington OH 43085 Office: Coopers & Lybrand 100 E Broad St Columbus OH 43215

VAN BORTEL, JAMES ALAN, food service management company executive; b. Palmyra, N.Y., Oct. 14, 1935; s. Marvin Peter and Margaret Nelly (Blankenburg) Van B.; m. Barbara Jean Campbell, July 16, 1960; children—Scott, Brett, Grant. B.A. in Econs., Mich. State U., 1959. Gen. mgr. Stouffer Foods Corp., Cleve., 1959-68; pres., chief operating officer Service Systems Corp., Oak Brook, Ill., 1968—. Served with U.S. Army, 1959-62. Mem. Ill. Restaurant Assn. (dir. 1976-79, adv. com. 1979-84, edn. com. 1974-76). Republican. Mem. Christian Reformed Ch. Clubs: Naperville Country, Dairymen's Country. Office: Service Systems Corp 2605 W 22nd St Oak Brook IL 60521

VAN BROOKER, MARGE MARY, data processing company executive; b. Lawrence, Mass., Jan. 14, 1923; d. Alvin Bernard and Mary Theresa (Donovan) Kane; m. Irving C. Van Brooker, May 19, 1945 (dec. Dec. 1981); children—Denise, Damien, Deborah, Danette, Daniel. Student Cin. Bus. Coll., 1940-41, U. Cin., 1941-43; B.A., Oxford Coll., Ohio, 1944. Profl. model, singer, dancer, Cin., 1939-45; co-owner Black Angus Prodns., Plymouth, Ill., 1945-78; owner, operator Regis Kennels, Plymouth, 1960-70; supr. Western Ill. U., Macomb, 1964-71, adminstrv. asst., 1971-83; owner, operator OMO Datamation Enterprises, Macomb, 1983—. Organizer, Mother's March of Dimes, Plymouth, 1948-50; leader Two Rivers council Girl Scouts U.S.A., 1953; ofcl. McDonough County, Ill., 1985—. Mem. Nat. Sec. Assn., Profl. Bus. Women, Am. Legion (adjutant 1982-85, adjutant 14th dist. 1983-84, adjutant 3rd div. 1985—), Am. Legion Aux. Served with USMC, 1943-45. Republican. Roman Catholic. Avocations: target shooting; antiques; interior decorating; golf; tennis. Home and Office: 210 Arlington Dr Macomb IL 61455

VAN BRUNT, MARCIA ADELE, social worker; b. Chgo., Oct. 21, 1937; d. Dean Frederick and Faye Lila (Greim) Slauson; student Moline (Ill.) Pub. Hosp. Sch. Nursing, 1955-57; B.A. with distinguished scholastic record, U. Wis., Madison, 1972, M.S.W. (Fed. tng. grantee), 1973; M.O.E. Bartholomew; children—Suzanne, Christine, David. Social worker div. community services Wis. Dept. Health Social Services, Rhinelander, 1973, regional adoption coordinator, 1973-79, chief adoption and permanent planning no. region, 1979-83, asst. chief direct services and regulation no. region, 1983-84, adminstr., clin. social worker No. Family Services, Inc.; counselor, public speaker, cons. in field of clin. social work. Home: 5264 Forest Ln Route 1 Box 2262 Rhinelander WI 54501 Office: Box 697 Rhinelander WI 54501

VANBUSKIRK, EDMUND L., ophthalmologist; b. Fort Wayne, Ind., Oct. 15, 1907; s. Edmund Michael and Louise Henrietta (Swartz) VanB.; m. Dorothy Elizabeth Deming, Jan. 30, 1930; children—Nancy Louise Stevens, Joan Elizabeth Tanner, Edmund Michael II. B.A., Albion Coll., 1929; B.S., Ind. U., 1932; M.D., Ind. U.-Indpls., 1933. Diplomate Am. Bd. Ophthalmology. Intern, St. Vincent's Hosp., Indpls., 1933-44; resident in ophthalmology Ind. U. Med. Ctr., Indpls., 1934-46; ophthalmologist Arnett Clinic, Lafayette, Ind., 1936-77; practice medicine specializing in ophthalmology, Lafayette, 1977—; chief ophthalmology Lafayette Home Hosp., Ind., 1983—, prin. investigator, 1983—. Mem. editorial bd. Ind. State Med. Jour. 1939-44. Bd. dirs. Wabash Valley Assn. Hist. Preservation, Ind. Selective Service System, 1943-46, William Ross Tb. Sanitarium, 1946-56; mem. com. Greater Lafayette Conf. Health, Edn. and Welfare; pres. West Lafayette Bd. of Health, 1940-82, St. Elizabeth Hosp. Med. Staff Recipient Selective Service cert. appreciation Pres. of U. S. Republican. Episcopalian. Clubs: Skyline (Indpls.), Lafayette Country. Lodge: Elks. Office: 2500 Ferry St Suite 301 Lafayette IN 47904

VANCE, CHARLES CLARK, retired public relations executive; b. Streator, Ill., Mar. 18, 1918; s. Charles Clayton and Elizabeth V.; m. Mary Ellen Wheeler, Nov. 8, 1941; children—Penny Lee. Student pub. schs. Reporter, Ill. State Register, Springfield, 1946-49; dir. Ill. State Fair Publicity, Springfield, 1949-53; v.p., Mayer & O'Brien, Inc., Chgo., 1953-62, Buchen Pub. Relations, Chgo., 1962-71; dir. corp. communications Joslyn Mfg., Chgo., 1971-75; dir. news media Nat. Assn. Realtors, 1975-79; dir. pub. relations Nat. Safety Council, Chgo., 1979-85. Served with USAF, 1943-46. Decorated Air medal. Author: Boss Psychology; Manager Today, Executive Tomorrow. Mem. Soc. Profl. Journalists, Am. Soc. Journalists and Authors, Chgo. Headline Club, Chgo. Press Club, Hump Pilots Assn., Pub. Relations Soc. Am., Sigma Delta Chi. Republican. Home: 207 Gold St Park Forest IL 60466

VANCE, JOAN EMILY JACKSON (MRS. NORVAL E. VANCE), educator; b. Anderson, Ind., Feb. 25, 1925; d. Virgil S. and Hannah (Hall) Jackson; B.S., Ball State U., 1947, M.A., 1955; m. Norval E. Vance, Aug. 17, 1955; 1 son, Bill E. Tchr. art and phys. edn. Winchester (Ind.) High Sch., 1948-50, 50-52, Wheatfield (Ind.) Elem. Sch., Wheatfield High Sch., 1952-54; tchr. Eaton (Ind.) Elementary Sch. and High Sch., 1954—; tchr. elem. art, Elwood, Ind., 1954—, bilingual-bi-cultural migrant sch., summers 1969—; exhibited in group shows at Erica's Gallery, John Herron. Anderson Fine Art Ctr., state shows, street fairs. Mem. council Hoosier Salon, Indpls. Mus. Art. Recipient First prize Anderson Fine Arts Center show, 1975, 77. Mem. Nat. Art Edn. Assn., Western Art Edn. Assn., Ind Art Edn. Assn. (council), Ind. Art Tchrs. Assn. (mem. council), Anderson Art League (pres. 1967-68, 76—) Anderson Soc. Artists (v.p.), Ind. Weavers Guild, Elwood Art League (pres. 1960-70), Brown County Gallery, Brown County Guild, Ind. Artists and Craftsmen Assn., Delta Kappa Gamma, Delta Theta Tau. Home: Route 1 Box 68 Frankton IN 46044 Office: Elwood Community School State Rd 13 N Elwood IN 46036

VANCE, TERRY, interior designer; b. Cleve., Sept. 22, 1929; d. Toby and Edith (Zulli) Gesualdo; m. Edward Francis Vance, May 26, 1951; children—Victoria, Deborah, David, Rebecca, Sarah, Barbara. B.A., Case Western Res. U., 1951. Interior designer Bonhard Interiors, Cleve., 1968-80; pres., interior designer Terry Vance, Inc., Shaker Hts., Ohio, 1980—. Mem. Am. Soc. Interior Designers. Office: Terry Vance Inc 18740 Chagrin Blvd Shaker Heights OH 44122

VAN CLEAVE, PETER, underwriting and foundation consultant; b. Evanston, Ill., May 18, 1927; s. Wallace and Katherine M. (Ziesing) Van C.; m. Barbara Adams, Dec. 30, 1960; 1 dau., Claire. B.S., Northwestern U., 1949. Prodn. mgr. F.L. Jacobs Co., Traverse City, Mich., 1949-50; asst. to ambassador U.S. embassy, Rio de Janeiro, Brazil, 1953-55; with James S. Kemper & Co., Chgo., 1955-83, vice chmn., 1965-83; pres. Peter Van Cleave & Assocs., Inc., Chgo., 1983—; prin. Donor's Mgmt. Services; underwriting mem. Lloyds of London, also cons.; dir. Marley Holdings, Inc. Trustee Newberry Library, Chgo.; bd. dirs. Ill. Ins. Exchange, Lyric Opera, Chgo. Served with U.S. Army, 1950-52. Mem. Nat. Assn. Security Dealers, Northwestern U. Alumni Assn. (pres.). Republican. Clubs: Chicago; Bohemian (San Francisco); University, Glen View (Chgo.); City of London (London); The Casino. Home: 71 E Bellevue Pl Chicago IL 60611 Office: Suite 2336 35 E Wacker Dr Chicago IL 60601

VAN CLEVE, JOHN WOODBRIDGE, research chemist; b. Kansas City, Mo., Nov. 22, 1914; s. Horatio Phillips and Leslie Gertrude (Allen) Van C.; m. Ethel Dannenmaier, Feb. 7, 1947; children—John Walter, Julia Ann, Mark David. B.S., Antioch Coll., 1937; Ph.D., U. Minn., 1951. Research fellow C. F. Kettering Found. for Study Chlorophyll and Photosynthesis, Yellow Springs, Ohio, 1937-40; research chemist Aluminum Co. Am., East St. Louis, Ill., 1943-48, No. Regional Research Ctr., U.S. Dept. Agr., Peoria, Ill., 1951—. Contbr. articles to various publs. Mem. Am. Chem. Soc., AAAS, N.Y. Acad. Sci., Sigma Xi. Republican. Presbyterian. Home: 903 W Meadows Pl Peoria IL 61604 Office: Northern Regional Research Center US Dept Agriculture 1815 N University St Peoria IL 61604

VAN CURA, BARRY JACK, ballet dancer, choreographer; b. Berwyn, Ill., Nov. 13, 1948; s. John J. and Eleanor (Knize) Van C.; m. Anna Baker Miller, Aug. 18, 1979; children—Anamarie, Anthony, Victoria. B.F.A., N.C. Sch. Arts, Winston-Salem. Trainee, Rebeccah Harkness Found., 1972; dancer, soloist Chgo. Ballet and Lyric Opera, 1970-74, Milw. Ballet, 1974-75; dir., choreographer Ballet Midwest, Chgo., 1977-84; dir. Nat. Acad. of Dance, Champaign, Ill., 1979-81; dir., choreographer Chattanooga Ballet, 1984—; mem. part-time faculty U. Ill., Champaign, 1980-82; resident choreographer theatre dept., Youngstown U., Ohio, 1984-85; choreographer Allegheny Coll., Meadville, Pa. 1984-85; cons. on dance Warren Dance Ctr., Ohio, 1983-84. Choreographer; Firebird/Gemstones, 1984, Liebeslieder/Interlude, 1983, Seasons/Canon/Congregation, 1979; Tribute to the Beatles, 1980. Founder Friends of Ballet Midwest, Youngstown, 1982, Chattanooga Ballet Guild, 1984; Ohio Arts Council grantee, 1983, 84. Mem. Assn. Ohio Dance Co. (trustee 1983-85), Nat. Assn. Regional Ballet, Southeastern Regional Ballet Assn. Buddhist. Office: 1915 S 59th Ave Cicero IL 60650

VANDAHM, THOMAS EDWARD, economics educator; b. Chgo., Feb. 20, 1924; s. Thomas and Sarah (Toren) VanD.; m. Lois I Stanton; 1 child, Ruth E. A.B., Hope Coll., 1948; M.A., U. Mich., 1949; Ph.D., 1959. Asst. prof. econs. bus. Central Coll., Pella, Iowa, 1950-53, Augustana Coll., Rock Island, Ill., 1954-55, Hope Coll., Holland, Mich., 1955-60, Ill. U., Edwardsville, 1960-64; prof. econs. Carthage Coll., Kenosha, Wis., 1964—. Author: Money and Banking, 1975. Contbr. articles to profl. jours. Served to cpl. U.S. Army, 1943-46. Ford Found fellow, 1969. Mem. Midwest Econs. Assn. Lodge: Kiwanis (sec. 1976-79, pres. elect 1985—). Home: 4103 Taft Rd Kenosha WI 53142 Office: Carthage Coll 2001 Alford Dr Kenosha WI 53141

VAN DAM, DORIS MAY, wastewater treatment plant official; b. Grand Rapids, Mich., Jan. 27, 1924; d. John Henry and Alice (Small) De Vries; m. Lloyd Arie Voshel, Oct. 30, 1946 (div. 1969); children—David Voshel, Anne Voshel Nudo; m. Ernest D. Van Dam, Jan. 27, 1971. Teaching diploma Sherwood Acad., 1943; student Calvin Coll., 1944-49. Chief chemist, engr. City of Grand Rapids, Mich., 1944-73; gen. mgr. Grand Haven-Spring Lake Wastewater Treatment Plant, Grand Haven, Mich., 1973—; mem. mgmt. adv. group EPA, 1977-79. Contbr. articles to tech. jours. Chmn. trustees North Ottawa Community Hosp., Grand Haven; mem. exec. bd. W. Cen. Mich. Hosp. Council, 1983—; gen. campaign chmn. Tri-Cities United Fund Drive, 1977, 82; trustee Grand Haven Area Community Found., 1983—. Mem. Mich. Water Pollution Control Assn. (past pres.), Water Pollution Control Fedn. (dir. 1981-84, mem. exec. bd 1981). Republican. Mem. Reformed Ch. Am. Clubs: Spring Lake Country, Century. Avocation: Music. Home: 10975 Lakeshore West Olive MI 49460 Office: Grand Haven-Spring Lake Wastewater Plant 1525 Washington St Grand Haven MI 49417

VAN DE KREEKE, JEFFREY ROBERT, financial executive, accountant; b. Sheboygan, Wis., Apr. 23, 1957; s. Robert and Betty Jane Van De K.; m. Lynda Lou Stuckmann, Oct. 23, 1982. B.B.A., U. Wis.-Eau Claire, 1979. C.P.A., Wis. Auditor Ernst and Whinney, Milw., 1979-84; chief fin. officer New Berlin Meml. Hosp., Wis., 1984—. M.R. Detling Meml. scholar, 1975. Mem. Am. Inst. C.P.A.s, Wis. Inst. C.P.A.s, Health Care Fin. Mgmt. Assn., Phi Kappa Phi, Phi Eta Sigma. Home: 9412 W Palmetto Ave Wauwatosa WI 53222 Office: New Berlin Meml Hosp 13750 W National Ave New Berlin WI 53151

VAN DELLEN, KENNETH J., geology educator, editorial and educational consultant; b. Ionia, Mich., May 24, 1937; s. Jerrian and Anna (Terpstra) VanD.; m. Pearl Kiel, Aug. 21, 1959; children—Lisa Anne, Kara Jane. B.A., Calvin Coll., 1958; M.S. in Zoology, Mich. State U., East Lansing, 1961; M.S. in Geology, U. Mich., 1978. Tchr. biology and chemistry Southwest Minn. Christian High Sch., Edgerton, Minn., 1958-59; tchr. Fitzgerald Jr.-Sr. High Sch., Warren, Mich., 1961-65; prof. Macomb Community Coll., Warren, Mich., 1965—. Mem. Geol. Soc. Am., Am. Assn. Petroleum Geologists, Nat. Assn. Geology Tchrs., Mich. Basin Geol. Soc., Mich. Acad. Sci., Arts and Letters. Mem. Christian Reformed Ch. Advocation: Photography. Home: 1018 Nottingham Rd Grosse Pointe Park MI 48230 Office: Macomb County Community Coll 14500 12-Mile Rd Warren MI 48093

VAN DEMARK, ROBERT EUGENE, orthopedic surgeon; b. Alexandria, S.D., Nov. 14, 1913; s. Walter Eugene and Esther Ruth (Marble) Van D.; S.B., U. S.D., 1936; A.B., Sioux Falls (S.D.) Coll., 1937; M.B., Northwestern U., 1938, M.D., 1939; M.S. in Orthopedic Surgery, U. Minn., 1943; m. Bertie Thompson, Dec. 28, 1940; children—Ruth Elaine, Robert, Richard. Interne Passavant Meml. Hosp., Chgo., 1938-39; fellow orthopedic surgery, Mayo Found., 1939-43; 1st asst. orthopedic surgery Mayo Clinic, 1942-43; orthopedic surgeon Sioux Falls (S.D.), 1946—; attending orthopedic surgeon McKennan Hosp., pres. med. staff, 1954, 70, attending orthopedic surgeon Sioux Valley Hosp., pres. staff, 1951-52; clin. prof. orthopedic surgery U. S.D., 1953—, adj. prof. orthopedic anatomy, 1983; med. dir. Crippled Children's Hosp. and Sch.; chief hand surgery clinic VA Hosp., Sioux Falls. Served from lt. to maj. AUS, 1943-46. Recipient Alumni Achievement award U. S.D., 1977, faculty recognition award Med. Sch., 1980; named Disting. Citizen of Yr., S.D. Press Assn., 1978; diplomate Am. Bd. Orthopedic Surgery. Fellow A.C.S. (pres. S.D. chpt. 1952, 1953); mem. Am. Assn. Med. Colls., Assn. Orthopaedic Chmn., Am. Acad. Orthopedic Surgery, Clin. Orthopedic Soc., Am. Assn. Hand Surgery, Assn. Mil. Surgeons U.S., Am. Acad. Cerebral Palsy, S.D. Med. Assn. (pres. 1974-75), Sioux Falls Dist. Med. Soc., S.A.R., 500 1st Families Am., Sigma Xi, Phi Chi Alpha Omega Alpha. Lutheran. Clubs: Optimist; Minnehahn Country. Editor S.D. Jour. Medicine. Contbr. to med. jours. Home: 2803 Ridgeview Way Sioux Falls SD 57105 Office: 1301 S 9th Ave Suite 400 Sioux Falls SD 57105

VAN DEMARK, RUTH ELAINE, lawyer; b. Santa Fe, N. Mex., May 16, 1944; d. Robert Eugene and Bertha Marie (Thompson) Van D.; m. Leland Wilkinson, June 23, 1967; children—Anne Marie, Caroline Cook. A.B., Vassar Coll., 1966; M.T.S., Harvard U., 1969; J.D. with honors, U. Conn., 1976. Bar: Conn. 1976, U.S. Dist. Ct. Conn. 1976, Ill. 1977, U.S. Dist. Ct. (no. dist.) Ill. 1977, U.S. Supreme Ct. 1983, U.S. Ct. Appeals (7th cir.) 1984. Instr. legal research and writing Loyola U. Sch. Law, Chgo., 1976-79; assoc. Wildman, Harrold, Allen & Dixon, Chgo., 1977-84, ptnr., 1984—. Assoc. editor Conn. Law Rev., 1975-76. Mem. adv. bd. Horizon Hospice, Chgo., 1978—; del.-at-large White House Conf. on Families, Los Angeles, 1980; mem. adv. bd. YWCA Battered Women's Shelter, Evanston, Ill., 1982—; vol. atty. Pro Bono Advocates, Chgo., 1982—; bd. dirs. New voice Prodns., 1984—. Recipient Vol. of Yr. award Jr. League Evanston, 1983-84. Mem. ABA, Ill. Bar Assn., Conn. Bar Assn., Chgo. Bar Assn., Appellate Lawyers Assn. Ill., Women's Bar Assn. Ill., AAUW, Jr. League Evanston. Clubs: Chgo. Vassar (pres. 1979-81), Cosmopolitan (N.Y.C.). Home: 1127 Asbury Ave Evanston IL 60202 Office: Wildman Harrold Allen & Dixon 1 IBM Plaza Chicago IL 60611

VANDEMOTTER, PETER ALAN, electrical engineer; b. N.Y.C., Apr. 11, 1955; s. John Stephen and Barbara Frances (Mechling) V.; m. Linda Sue Ruesch, Apr. 24, 1977; 1 child, Scott David. B.S. in Elec. Engring., Rose-Hulman Inst., 1977. Engr., Commonwealth Edison, Chgo., 1977-78; project engr. Underwriters Lab., Northbrook, Ill., 1978-80; elec. engr. Fluor Corp., Chgo., 1980-81, HOH Engrs., Chgo., 1981—. Mem. IEEE, Des Plaines Area Jaycees (sec. 1984). Avocations: photography; train watching. Home: 837 Hollywood St Des Plaines IL 60016 Office: HOH Engrs 180 N Wabash St Chicago IL 60601

VANDENBERGHE, MARY ELIZABETH, market research director; b. Syracuse, N.Y., Feb. 4, 1959; d. Kenneth John and Rosalie (Nash) Zill; m. Loren Dale VandenBerghe. B.A. in Advt., Mich. State U., 1981. Sales asst. Ann Arbor News, Mich., 1981-82, sales rep., 1982; data collection coordinator Group 243 Design, Ann Arbor, 1982-83, sr. analyst, 1983-84, market research mgr., 1984—. Mem. Am. Mktg. Assn., Female Executives Am., Adcrafters of Detroit, Mktg. Research Assn.

VANDENDORPE, MARY MOORE, social scientist, educator; b. Chgo., June 2, 1947; d. Era William and Mary Desales (Dobis) M.; m. James Edward Vandendorpe, Aug. 16, 1969; 1 dau., Laura Marie. A.B., St. Louis U., 1969; M.S., Ill. Inst. Tech., 1975, Ph.D., 1980. Copywriter, Spiegel Inc., Chgo., 1969-72; adj. instr. Lewis U., Romeoville, Ill., 1976-79, asst. prof., 1980—. Mem. Am. Psychol. Assn., Gerontol Soc., Chgo. Psychol. Assn. (dir. 1979—, pres. 1982—), Naperville Heritage Soc., Psi Chi. Office: 213 Science Dept Lewis U Romeoville IL 60441

VANDERGRIFF, LELAND EDWARD, software engineering executive; b. Bonne Terre, Mo., Oct. 9, 1949; s. Williard C. and Alta Mae (Jarrette) V.; m. Alice Lynn Merton, Mar. 20, 1976; 1 dau., April Michelle. B.S.E.E. with honors, U. Mo.-Rolla., 1971; M.S.E., U. Pa., 1975. Registered profl. engr., Iowa. Mem. tech. staff RCA Corp., Adv. Tech. Labs., Camden, N.J., 1971-75; design engr. Fisher Controls, Marshalltown, Iowa, 1975-76, sr. design engr., 1976-79, engring. specialist, 1980—. Curator's scholar U. Mo., 1967. Mem. Assn. for Computing Machinery, IEEE Computer Soc., Tau Beta Pi, Eta Kappa Nu. Republican. Baptist. Office: RA Engel Tech Center PO Box 11 Marshalltown IA 50158

VANDER JAGT, GUY, congressman; b. Cadillac, Mich., Aug. 26, 1931; s. Harry and Marie (Copier) Vander J.; A.B., Hope Coll., 1953; B.D., Yale U., 1957; LL.B., U. Mich., 1960; postgrad. U. Bonn (Germany), 1955-56; m. Carol Doorn, Apr. 4, 1964; 1 dau., Virginia Marie. Admitted to Mich. bar, 1960; practice in Grand Rapids; mem. firm Warner, Norcross & Judd, 1960-64; mem. Mich. Senate, 1964-66; mem. 89th-98th Congresses from 9th Mich. Dist.; mem. ways and means com., trade and select revenue measures subcoms.; chmn. Nat. Republican Congressional Com.; keynote speaker Rep. Nat. Conv., Detroit, 1980. Named One of Five Most Outstanding Young Men in Mich., Mich. Jr. C. of C., 1956. Republican. Mem. Hope Coll. Alumni Assn. Washington (pres.). Home: Luther MI 49656 Office: 2409 Rayburn House Office Bldg Washington DC 20515

VANDER KOOI, DARYL JAY, speech communication educator; b. Grandville, Mich., July 27, 1940; s. David J. and Edith (Woodwyk) Vander K.; m. Maris Elaine Hager, Dec. 16, 1960; children—Michelle Elaine, Dalaine Joy, David Shane. A.B., Calvin Coll., 1963, postgrad., 1965; postgrad. Coll. Great Falls, 1966; M.S., Mont. State U., 1971, Ed.D., 1979; postgrad. U. Iowa-Iowa City, 1973, U. S.D.-Vermillion, 1974. Tchr., Hope Protestant Christian Sch., Grandville, Mich., 1961-62; tchr., forensic coach Manhattan Christian High Sch. (Mont.), 1963-70; forensic coach, tchr. communications, chmn. dept. Dordt Coll., Sioux Center, Iowa, 1971—. NDEA grantee, 1966. Mem. Central States Speech Assn., Speech Communication Assn., Iowa Communication Assn., Assn. Ref. Communication (v.p., chmn. steering com.). Republican. Mem. Christian Ref. Ch. Contbr. articles to communication, scholastic jours. Office: Dordt Coll Sioux Center IA 51250

VANDERLAAN, RICHARD B., marketing company executive; b. Grand Rapids, Mich., Sept. 2, 1931; s. Sieger B. and Helen (Kerr) V.; cert. liberal arts Grand Rapids Jr. Coll., 1952; cert. mech. engring. U. Mich., 1955; cert. indsl. engring. Mich. State U., 1960; cert. Harvard Bus. Sch., 1970; m. Sally E. Conroy, Mar. 26, 1982; children—Sheryl Vanderlaan DeWitt, Pamella Vanderlaan De Vos, Brenda. Tool engr. Four Square Mfg. Co., Grand Rapids, 1950-60; sales engr. Ametek, Lansdale, Pa., 1960-63; br. mgr. J.N. Fauver Co., Grand Rapids, 1964-68; v.p. Fauver Co. subs. Sun Oil Co., Grand Rapids 1968-76, exec. v.p., 1976-80; pres. House of Printers, Inc., 1980-82, also dir.; pres. Richard Vanderlaan Assocs., 1982—. Bd. dir. Am. Cancer Soc.; eagle scout. Industries Mich., Grand Rapids C. of C., Sales and Mktg. Execs., Grand Rapids Power Squadron. Republican. Clubs: Peninsular, Macatawa Bay Yacht, Birmingham Country, Oakland Hills Country. Office: 22157 Metamora Dr Birmingham MI 48010

VANDERPLOEG, KENNETH PAUL, business executive; b. Grand Rapids, Mich., Oct. 26, 1941; s. Frederick and Eva Mae (Harvey) Vander P.; m. Sue Ann Tornga, Sept. 6, 1963; children—Laura E., Michele Ann. A.A.S., Grand Rapids Jr. Coll., 1962; B.B.A., Western Mich. U., 1964. Asst. controller Lawndale Industries, Aurora, Ill., 1969-72; asst. controller Cracker Jack, Chgo., 1972-74; controller IMS Internat., Ambler, Pa., 1974-76, Cummins Allison Corp., Glenview, Ill., 1976-78; v.p., chief exec. officer Quickprint, Downers Grove, Ill., 1978—. Served with U.S. Army, 1966-68. Methodist. Club: Rotary (Downers Grove) (bd. dirs. 1982-84, treas. 1985-86). Office: Quickprint 415 Ogden Ave Downers Grove IL 60515

VANDERPOOL, WARD MELVIN, management and marketing consultant; b. Oakland, Mo., Jan. 20, 1917; s. Oscar B. and Clara (McGuire) V.; M.E.E., Tulane U.; m. Lee Kendall, July 7, 1935. Vice pres. charge sales Van Lang Brokerage, Los Angeles, 1934-38; mgr. agrl. div. Dayton Rubber Co., Chgo.,

1939-48; pres., gen. mgr. Vee Mac Co., Rockford, Ill., 1948—; pres., dir. Zipout, Inc., Rockford, 1951—, Wife Save Products, Inc., 1959—; chmn. bd. Zipout Internat., Kenvan Inc., 1952—, Shevan Corp., 1951—, Atlas Internat. Corp.; pres. Global Enterprises Ltd., Global Assos. Ltd.; chmn. bd. Atlas Chem. Corp., Merzart Industries Ltd.; trustee Ice Crafter Trust, 1949—; dir. Atlas Chem. Internat. Ltd., Shrimp Tool Internat. Ltd.; mem. Toronto Bd. Trade. Mem. adv. bd. Nat. Security Council; mem. Presdl. Task Force, Congressional Adv. Com. Mem. Internat. Swimming Hall of Fame. Mem. Nat. (dir. at large), Rock River (past pres.) sales execs., Sales and Mktg. Execs. Internat. (dir.), Am. Mgmt. Assn., Rockford Engring. Soc., Am. Tool Engrs., Internat. Acad. Aquatic Art (dir.), Am. Inst. Mgmt. (pres. council), Am. Ordnance Assn., Internat. Platform Assn., Ill. C. of C. Clubs: Mason, Shriners, Jesters, Elks, Rockford Swim, Forest Hills Country, Exec., Elmcrest Country, Pyramid, Dolphin, Marlin. Home: 374 Parkland Dr SE Cedar Rapids IA 52403 Office: Box 242A Auburn St Rd Rockford IL 61103 also 120 Adelaide St W St W Suite 16 Toronto ON Canada also Richview Rd Toronto ON Canada

VANDERROEST, ROBERT D., dentist; b. Kalamazoo, June 21, 1927; s. Richard and Emma (Stuut) VanderR.; m. Ruth A. Zwart, July 17, 1950; children—Lynn Carol, Karen Lee, Julie Diane, Steven Robert. D.D.S., U. Mich., 1954. Practice dentistry, Portage, Mich., 1954—; trustee Am. Nat. Bank, Portage, 1979—; mem. dental hygiene adv. bd. Kalamazoo Valley Community Coll., 1974-78; bd. dirs. Mich. Acad. Dentistry for the Handicapped, 1980-83; lectr. Pres., Portage Pub. Schs. Bd. Edn., 1956-70, Kalamazoo Valley Intermediate Sch. System Bd., 1970—, Mich. Assn. Retarded Children, 1984—. Served with C.E., U.S. Army, 1946-48. Recipient Community Service award Assn. Retarded Children, 1979; deacon Bethany & Reformed Ch., 1961-64, elder, Southridge Reformed Ch., 1976-79. Mem. Kalamazoo Valley Dental Soc. (pres. 1962-63), ADA, Mich. Dental Assn. (Dental Citizen of Yr. 1984). Lodges: Optimists (pres. 1960), Rotary (Portage). Avocations: hunting; stamp collecting; photography; sailing; power boating. Home: 7603 Primrose Ln Portage MI 49081 Office: 200 E Centre Ave Portage MI 49081

VANDER WAL, KENNETH LEE, accounting firm executive; b. Oskaloosa, Iowa, Aug. 19, 1947; s. Cornie and Antoinette Pauline (Rietveld) Vander W.; m. Cindy De Prenger, May 29, 1970; children—Sonja Leigh, Steven Craig, David Alan, Daniel Jay, Kevin Mark. Student Dordt Coll., 1965-67; B.A., U. Iowa, 1967-69; M.B.A., George Washington U., 1976. C.P.A.; cert. info. systems auditor. EDP plans and ops. officer U.S. Army, Washington, 1970-72; ops. research supr., 1972-77; tech. support rep. Applications Software, Inc., Oak Brook, Ill., 1977-79; computer auditor Ernst & Whinney, Chgo., 1979-84, ptnr., 1984—. Deacon, Wheaton Christian Reformed Ch., Ill., 1979-82, Sunday sch. supt., 1984. Served to lt. U.S. Army, 1969-71. Mem. EDP Auditors Assn. (highest score worldwide on cert. exam.), Ill. Soc. C.P.A.s, Am. Inst. C.P.A.s. Office: Ernst & Whinney 150 S Wacker Dr Chicago IL 60606

VAN DER WEELE, ROBERT ANTHONY, transportation company official; b. Kalamazoo, Jan. 18, 1931; s. Anthony and Meryl Eunice (Ellard) Van Der W.; B.S., Western Mich. U., 1958; m. Marilyn Ruth Martin, Aug. 16, 1953; children—Susan, Brian, Joel. Sta. agt. United Airlines, Toledo, 1958-59; traffic mgr., prodn. control supr. Brown Trailer div. Clark Equipment Co., Michigan City, Ind., 1959-62; truck fleet mgr. J.I. Case Co., Racine, Wis., 1962-67; br. mgr. Saunders Leasing System, Detroit, 1967-74; transp. mgr. Amway Corp., Ada, Mich., 1974-77; dir. transp. Havi Corp., Lemont, Ill., 1977-80; dist. mgr. Lend Lease Transp. Co., Columbus, Ohio, 1980—. Mem. Republican Precinct Com., 1964-67. Served with USAF, 1950-53. Mem. Pvt. Truck Council Am., Ill. Trucking Assn., Pvt. Carrier Conf. Episcopalian. Clubs: Rotary (past v.p.), Masons, Elks. Home: 1865 Lane Ave Columbus OH 43229 Office: 4079 Lyman Rd Hilliard OH 43026

VANDE WALLE, GERALD WAYNE, justice N.D. Supreme Ct.; b. Noonan, N.D., Aug. 15, 1933; s. Jules C. and Blanche Marie (Gits) VandeW.; B.Sc., U. N.D., 1955, J.D., 1958. Admitted to N.D. bar, 1958; spl. asst. atty. gen. State of N.D., Bismarck, 1958-75, 1st asst. atty. gen., 1975-78; justice N.D. Supreme Ct., Bismarck, 1978—; mem. faculty bus. law Bismarck Jr. Coll., 1972-76. Active Bismarck Meals on Wheels; bd. dirs. Bismarck-Mandon Orchestral Assn. Mem. Bar Assn. N.D., Burleigh County Bar Assn., ABA, N.D. Jud. Council, Am. Contract Bridge League, Order of Coif, Phi Eta Sigma, Beta Alpha Psi, Beta Gamma Sigma, Phi Alpha Delta. Roman Catholic. Clubs: Elks, KC. Editor-in-chief N.D. Law Rev., 1957-58. Office: Supreme Ct State Capitol Bismarck ND 58505

VANDEWIELE, MARION CUNNINGHAM, oil company executive; b. Auchterderran, Scotland, Sept. 13, 1944; came to U.S., 1961; d. John Rolland and Marion G. (Johnson) Cunningham; m. Roy L. Shimer, June 20, 1965 (div. Jan. 1970) 1 son, Keith A.; m. 2d, Thomas R. VanDeWiele, Sept. 18, 1970; 1 dau., Jennifer J. Student Commerce Bus. Sch., Macomb Coll., Inst. for Energy Devel., Dallas, 1981. Acctg. supr. Splane Electric Co., Detroit, 1962-70; with assessors' office City of St. Clair Shores (Mich.), 1974-79; v.p. ops. Mid-Am. Oil & Gas Corp., New Baltimore, Mich., 1980—, dir. Mpls., 1981—; co-owner, v.p. 4x4 & More, Inc., St. Clair Shores, Mich. Mem. Petroleum Accts. Soc. of Mich., Mich. Oil & Gas Assn., Ind. Petroleum Assn. Am. Club: Clinton River Boat (Mt. Clemens, Mich.). Lodges: Order of Eastern Star (officer 1980), Women's Aux. Masons.

VAN DYKE, MARC DAVID, university administrative assistant; b. Bloomington, Ind., Mar. 19, 1950; s. LaDonna M. Van Dyke. B.S., Ind. U., 1972. Office dept. mgr. Ind. U., Bloomington, 1976—. Active Monroe County Cancer Soc., 1968—; nat. youth ambassador Am. Cancer Soc., 1971-73; cert. pageant judge Miss Ind./Miss America, 1978—; So. Ind. field dir. Miss Ind. Pageant, Inc., 1979—; exec. dir. Hoosier Hills Scholarship Pageant, 1977—; pageant judge Hoopeston (Ill.) Jaycees Nat. Sweetheart, 1973, 74, 78, 80; bd. dirs. Miss America Pageant, 1980—, Monroe County Fair Assn., 1976—; mem. Ind. Hoosier Devel. Com., 1983. Am. Cancer Soc. Cancer Found. scholar, 1969. Lodge: Masons. Home: 3670 S Walnut St Rd Bloomington IN 47401 Office: 801 N Jordan Ave Bloomington IN 47405

VAN EENENAAM, ROBERT DALE, dentist; b. Holland, Mich., Aug. 7, 1928; s. Charles Richard and Bernice (Vanden Brink) Van E.; m. Mary Catherine Johnson, June 13, 1953; children—Jeffrey Alan, Ann Patrice. B.A., Hope Coll., 1950; D.D.S., U. Detroit, 1954. Pvt. practice dentistry, Kalamazoo. Mem. athletic bd. Portage No. High Sch., Mich., 1956-59; chmn. Reelection Wayne Sackett to Mich. Ho. of Reps., 1970. Served to lt. USN, 1954-56. Mem. ADA, Mich. Dental Assn., Kalamazoo Valley Dental Soc., Psi Omega. Republican. Mem. Reformed Ch. Am. Clubs: Kalamazoo Country, Kalamazoo Power Squadron. Lodge: Elks. Avocations: boating; golf; hooked rugs; hiking; missionary dentistry. Home: 2711 Coachlite St Portage MI 49081 Office: 3907 S Westnedge St Kalamazoo MI 49008

VAN ERT, MELVIN WILLIAM, electrical contracting company executive; b. Carson, Wis., Oct. 25, 1923; s. William and Nellie Van E.; m. Mary Agnes Zimmerman, July 2, 1949; children—Jo Anne, Robert, Paula, Terry, Jane, Chris, Carol, Mary, Julie, Anne. Student Indsl. Tng. Inst., Chgo., 1946-47. Co-owner, Thomas Electric Co., Marshfield, Wis., 1953-64; pres. Van Ert Electric Co. Inc., Wausau, Wis., 1964—. Mem. nat. adv. bd. Am. Security Council. Served with USAF, 1943-46. Mem. Nat. Elec. Contractors Assn. (Wis. dir. 1965—), Am. Legion. Republican. Roman Catholic. Home: 6984 Grotto Ave Rudolph WI 54475 Office: 7019 W Stewart Ave Wausau WI 54401

VAN GILST, BASS, state senator, farmer; b. Marion County, Iowa, Apr. 14, 1911; s. Peter and Nellie (Klien) Van G.; m. Harriet De Bruin, Nov. 26, 1937; children—Ken, Carl, Elaine, Mark, Diane, Joleen. Mem. Iowa Senate, 1965—, Democratic whip, 1975-76, asst. majority leader, 1977-78; mem. State Bd. Regents, 1984—; livestock and grain farmer, Oskaloosa, Iowa; dir. VG Farms. Fund dr. chmn. United Community Services; mem. legis. fiscal com. Capitol Planning Comm. Mem. C. of C., Farm Bur. Mem. Christian Reformed Ch. Club: Oskaloosa Lions (past pres.).

VANHANDEL, RALPH ANTHONY, librarian; b. Appleton, Wis., Jan. 17, 1919; s. Frank Henry and Gertrude Mary (Schmidt) Van H.; B.A., U. Wis., 1946; A.B., U. Mich., 1947; m. Alice Catherine Hogan, Oct. 27, 1945; children—William Patrick, Karen Jean, Mary Jo. Head librarian Lawrence (Kans.) Free Pub. Library, 1947-51, Hibbing (Minn.) Pub. Library, 1951-54; library dir. Gary (Ind.) Pub. Library, 1954-74, Wells Meml. Pub. Library, Lafayette, Inc., 1974-82, Tippecanoe County Library, Lafayette, Ind., 1983-84; mem. Ind. Library Certification Bd., 1969-84, pres., 1982-84; mem. Ind. Library Expansion Commn., 1973-81. Named Ind. Librarian of Year, 1971; Sagamore of Wabash, 1984. Mem. Anselm Forum (sec. 1964, v.p., 1965), ALA, Ind. (pres. 1963-64), Kans. (v.p. 1951) library assns. Lodges: K.C., Rotary. Home: 3624 Winter St Lafayette IN 47905

VANHAREN, ROGER JAMES, English educator; b. Oconto Falls, Wis., Jan. 24, 1939; s. Chester J. and Gladys B. (Thompson) VanH.; m. Marilyn A. Schroeder, July 1, 1961; children—Jill, Tim, Mike, Christopher, Mark. B.S., U. Wis.-Oshkosh, 1961; B.A., U. Wis.-Madison, 1969. Cert. tchr. Tchr. Beaver Dam Pub. Schs., Wis., 1961-74; English tchr., chmn. dept. fine arts Wayland Acad., Beaver Dam, 1974—. Alderman, Beaver Dam City Council, 1970-74; pres. Beaver Dam Community Theater, 1970-71, 84; parish council St. Patrick's Ch., 1979-81. Recipient Outstanding Young Tchr. award Beaver Dam Jaycees, 1969. Roman Catholic. Club: Beaver City Pacers. Lodge: Lions (sec. 1965—). Avocations: Acting, running, softball Home: 223 E 3d St Beaver Dam WI 53916

VANHARN, GORDON LEE, college provost; b. Grand Rapids, Mich., Dec. 30, 1935; s. Henry and Edna (Riemersma) VanH.; m. Mary Kool, June 12, 1958; children—Pamela L., Mark L., Barbara A. B.A., Calvin Coll., 1957; M.S., U. Ill., 1959, Ph.D., 1961. Asst. prof. biology Calvin Coll., Grand Rapids, Mich. 1961-68, prof., 1970-82, acad. dean, 1982-85, provost, 1985—; assoc. prof. biology Oberlin Coll., Ohio, 1968-70; assoc. physiologist Blodgett Meml. Med. Ctr., Grand Rapids, 1970-76; research assoc. U. Va., Charlotteville, 1975-76. Contbr. articles to profl. jours. Mem. sci. adv. com. Gerald R. Ford, 1972-73, Blodgett Hosp. research and review com., 1978—; pres. Grand Rapids Christian Sch. Assn. Bd., 1982-85. Grass Found. fellow, 1969. Mem. AAAS, Am. Assn. Higher Edn., Phi Kappa Phi. Mem. Christian Reformed Ch. Home: 1403 Cornell SE Grand Rapids MI 49506 Office: Calvin Coll Burton St Grand Rapids MI 49506

VAN HOLTEN, DALE GARRETT, food processing company executive; b. Milw., Feb. 27, 1951; s. E. Jerry and Ruth (Wilcox) Van H.; m. Cheryll Kay Meise, Sept. 13, 1980. Student Luther Coll., Decorah, Iowa, 1969-72; A.Bus., Madison (Wis.) Bus. Coll., 1982. With J.G. Van Holten & Son, Waterloo, Wis., 1976—, plant mgr., 1979-82, v.p. mgr., 1982—. Served with U.S. Army, 1972-78. Mem. Am. Mgmt. Assn. Republican. Methodist. Club: Lions (v.p. 1983) (Waterloo). Home: 535 Edison St Waterloo WI 53594 Office: 703 W Madison St Waterloo WI 53594

VAN HOOK, DONALD WAYNE, manufacturing company official; b. Stanford, Ky., June 1, 1938; s. James Orville and Althene Jones Van H.; m. Beverly Gwinn Hennen, Oct. 26, 1963; children—Andrea Gwinn, James Carlton, Alison Lin. B.S., Ohio U., 1960. Asst. advt. mgr. Monarch Marking Systems Co., Dayton, Ohio, 1960-62; copywriter Yeck & Yeck Advt., Inc., Dayton, 1962-64, Deere & Co. Advt., Moline, Ill., 1964-71; supr. indsl. advt. Deere & Co., 1971-72; mgr. European Advt. Centre, Mannheim, W.Ger., 1972-76, mgr. overseas advt., Moline, Ill., 1976-84, mgr. agrl. advt., 1984—. Mem. exec. bd. local council Boy Scouts Am., 1967-71. Served with U.S. Army Res., 1961-67. Recipient awards for indsl. copywriting. Mem. Am. Mgmt. Assn., Assn. Nat. Advertisers, Internat. Advt. Assn., Nat. Agri-Mktg. Assn. Unitarian. Editorial bd. Agri-Mktg., 1981. Home: 1332 42d Ave Rock Island IL 61201 Office: Deere & Co John Deere Rd Moline IL 61265

VAN HOOSER, PARICIA LOU SCOTT, art educator; b. Springfield, Mo., Oct. 4, 1934; d. Arthur Irving and Isoline Elizabeth (Jones) Scott; m. Buckley Blaine Van Hooser, Mar. 28, 1956 (div.); children—Buckley Blaine III, Craig Alan. A.B., Drury Coll., 1956; M.S. in Art, Pittsburg (Kans.) State U., 1968. Gift wrapper, with display dept., advt. dept. Heer's Inc., Springfield; continuity writer sta. KGBX, Springfield, 1953-55; society writer Springfield News & Leader & Press, 1955-56; hostess radio program sta. KSEK, Pittsburg, Kans., 1962-63; tchr. art and home econs. Hurley (Mo.), High Sch., 1956-57; art supr. elem. sch., Mountain Grove, Mo., 1960; tchr. art Hickory Hills Sch., Springfield, 1960-61; tchr. art English jr. and sr. high schs., Baxter Springs, Kans., 1965-75; art coordinator Joplin (Mo.) Elem. Sch. Dist., 1975—; lectr. in field; chmn. for S.W. Mo., Nat. Youth Art Month. Bd. dirs. Spiva Art Ctr.; sec. Parents without Ptnrs.; sec. CV & FE Credit Union; recorder S.W. Mo. Credit Unions. Mem. Joplin Writer's Guild, Writers of the Six Bulls, AAUW (2d v.p. Joplin br.), Assn. Childhood Edn. Internat. (pres. Joplin), Nat. Art Edn. Assn., Mo. Art Edn. Assn., S.W. Mo. Dist. Art Tchrs., NEA, Mo. Edn. Assn., Assn. for Supervision and Curriculum Devel., S.W. Mo. Mus. Assn., Joplin Community Concert Assn., Pittsburg State U. Alumni (sec., treas.), Epsilon Sigma Alpha. Methodist. Club: Cafe au Lait.

VAN HOOSER, RUSSELL EARL, investment company executive, lawyer; b. Clay, Ky., May 27, 1938; s. J. Gordon and Lillie P. (Miller) Van H. B.A. magna cum laude, Kenyon Coll., 1960; postgrad. govt. and internat. affairs John Hopkins U., 1960-61; J.D., Harvard U., 1964. Bar: Mich. 1964. Assoc., McClintock Fulton Donovan and Waterman, Detroit, 1964-66; exec. asst. to commr. ins. State of Mich., 1966-69, commr. ins., 1969-73; v.p. MGIC Investment Corp., Milw., 1973-80, sr. v.p., 1980—, also dir. Woodrow Wilson Fellow John Hopkins U., 1960-61. Mem. Nat. Assn. Ins. Commrs. (pres. 1972-73), State Bar Mich. Republican. Club: Milw. Athletic. Home: 7239 N Barnett Ln Fox Point WI 53217 Office: 250 E Kilbourn St Milwaukee WI 53202

VAN HOOZER, HELEN LUCILLE, instructional designer; b. Shenandoah, Iowa, Jan. 28, 1938; d. George Doak and Hazel Lucille (Burke) Staten; M.A., U. Iowa, 1974; student N.W. Mo. U., N.E. Mo. U., Drake U., Marshalltown Community Coll.; m. Richard Neil Van Hoozer, May 20, 1956; children—Cynthia Diane, Robert Wayne, Randall Gene. Elem. tchr., media dir. Clear Creek Community Schs., Oxford Center, Tiffin, Iowa, 1970-73; media specialist handicapped Midwest Ednl. Resource Center, Coralville, Iowa, 1973-74; instructional designer U. Iowa Coll. Nursing, Iowa City, 1974—. Mem. rules com. John County Democratic Conv., 1976. U. Iowa Fund Spl. Instructional Support grantee, 1978. Mem. Assn. Ednl. Communications and Tech., Iowa Ednl. Media Assn., Assn. Supervision and Curriculum Devel., NOW. Author: (with Alberta A. Tedford) Pharmacology: A Self-Instructional Approach, 1980; (with Lavonne Ruther and Martha Craft) Introduction to Charting, 1982; contbr. articles to profl. jours. Home: Rural Route 1 Kalona IA 52247 Office: Coll Nursing U Iowa Iowa City IA 52242

VAN HOVEN, JAY, insurance company executive; b. Holland, Mich., Aug. 11, 1944; s. Leonard Jay and Mary Helene (Schaap) Van Hoven; m. Nancy L. Voight, June 27, 1975; children—Joshua, Janna, Lydia. B.A., Hope Coll., 1966; student Wayne State U., 1966-68; M.A., No. Mich. U., 1971; postgrad. Mich. State U., 1973-75. Vol., Peace Corps, S.Am., 1968-69; tchr. St. Dunstans Sch., U.S. V.I., 1969-70; community sch. dir. Des Moines Schs., 1970-72; adminstr. Ctr. for Community Edn., Alma, Mich., 1973-75; asst. ombudsman Mich. State U., East Lansing, 1975; fin. mgr. Sch. Nursing, U. N.C., Chapel Hill, 1976-78; desegregation specialist Ind. U., Indpls., 1979-82; ptnr. Westlake Profl. Services, Indpls., 1982—; pres. Med. Specialty Disability Ins. Corp., Indpls., 1983—. Rep., Interurban Coll. and Univ. Consortium, Des Moines, 1971-72; adminstr. Urban Cities, Flint, Mich., 1970; mem. Hispanic Edn., Des Moines, 1971-72; mem. Ind. Community Edn. Adv., Indpls., 1979—. Mott fellow, 1970-71, 73-75. Mem. Phi Delta Kappa. Methodist. Office: Med Specialty Disability Ins Corp 6357 W Rockville Rd Indianapolis IN 46224

VAN KIRK, DONALD JOHN, forensic and consulting engineer; b. Detroit, Jan. 6, 1935; s. Kenneth John and Helen Van Kirk; Asso. in Sci., Henry Ford Community Coll., 1961; B.S. in Elec. Engring., Wayne State U., 1964, M.S. in Engring. Mechanics, 1969; M.B.A., U. Mich., 1975; m. Wyva A. Moore, Apr. 28, 1956; 1 dau., Cheryl Ann. TV technician Sta. WXYZ-TV, Detroit, 1959-60, WTVS-TV, Detroit, 1960-64; product design engr. Ford Motor Co., Dearborn, Mich., 1964-66, research engr., 1969-73, sr. design engr., 1973-84; pres. D.J. Van Kirk P.E. & Assocs., P.C., 1985—; instr. Henry Ford Community Coll. and Ford continuing edn. programs; mgmt. cons. Chmn. bldg. and plans com. Dearborn Hills Home Owners Assn., 1973-75; vol. Consumer Product Safety Com., Washington, 1977; chmn. Consumer Affairs Com., Dearborn, 1977-79; vol. traffic safety com. Dearborn Police Dept., 1979. Served with USN, 1955-59. Recipient Outstanding Student award Wayne State U., 1963-64; Community Service award Ford Motor Co., 1973. Mem. Nat. Soc. Profl. Engrs., Soc. Automotive Engrs., IEEE, Oakland County Traffic Safety Assn., Mich. Soc. Profl. Engrs., Am. Assn. Automotive Medicine, Am. Acad. Forensic Scis. Presbyterian. Clubs: Dearborn Exchange (Outstanding Service award 1974, Man of Yr. award 1975), Masons, Shriners. Patentee cold weather diesel starting aid; contbr. articles to profl. jours. Home: 23917 Rockford Dearborn MI 48124

VAN LAAR, TIMOTHY JON, artist, educator; b. Ann Arbor, Mich., Mar. 3, 1951; s. Jack and Eloise (Holtrop) Van L.; m. Karen Lee DeHaan, June 19, 1972; children—Elise Kristine, Jacob Peter. B.A., Calvin Coll., Grand Rapids, Mich., 1973; M.F.A., Wayne State U., Detroit, 1975. Part-time instr. Wayne State U., Detroit, 1976-77; instr. Calvin Coll., 1977-81; asst. prof. U. Ill.-Champaign, 1981—; resident artist Common Ground for the Arts, Detroit, 1975-77, Urban Inst. Comtemporary Art, Grand Rapids, Mich., 1978. One man shows include Judson Coll., Elgin, Ill., U. Alaska, Roberts Wesleyan Ch., Rochester, N.Y., 1984; exhibited in group shows at Klein Gallery, Chgo., 1983, ARC Gallery, Chgo., 1984, N.A.M.E. Gallery, Chgo., 1985. Mich. Council Arts grantee, 1978; Yaddo fellow, 1985. Mem. Coll. Art Assn. Avocation: Mountaineering. Office: U Ill Sch Art and Design 408 E Peabody Dr Champaign IL 61820

VAN LEUVEN, HOLLY GOODHUE, social scientist, consultant, researcher; b. Salem, Mass., Dec. 2, 1935; d. Nathaniel William and Elizabeth VanClowes (Crowley) Goodhue; m. John Jamison Porter, II, Oct. 16, 1954 (div. 1974); children—Donald J. II, Nathaniel G., Alison A. Dionne, Erin E.; m. Robert Joseph VanLeuven, Dec. 31, 1976. B.A. with honors, Western Mich. U., 1971, M.A. with honors, 1975. Exec. dir. Community Confrontation and Communication Assocs., Grand Rapids, Mich., 1969-73; coordinator tng., research Nat. Ctr. for Dispute Settlement, Washington, 1973; tng. dir. Forest View Psychiat. Hosp., Grand Rapids, 1974; case coordinator Libner, Van Leuven, & Kortering, P.C., Muskegon, Mich., 1982—; talk show host Sta. WTRU-TV, Muskegon, 1985; cons. U.S. Dept. Justice, Washington, 1969-73, No. Ireland Dept. Community Relations, Belfast, 1971; jury selection cons. various law firms in Midwest, 1975—. Contbr. articles to profl. jours. Bd. dirs. Planned Parenthood Western Mich., Grand Rapids, 1964-72, Jr. League Grand Rapids, 1955—, YFCA, Muskegon, 1981-83; chmn. Student Showcase, Inc., Muskegon, 1983—; candidate for Mich. State Rep. 97th Dist., Muskegon, 1978; pres. Planned Parenthood Assn., Muskegon, 1980. Mem. Am. Sociol. Assn. Clubs: Muskegon Country, Century; Women's City (Grand Rapids). Lodges: Zonta, Compass. Home: 966 Mona Brook Rd Muskegon MI 49441 Office: Libner VanLeuven & Kortering PC 400 Comerica Hackley Bank Bldg Box 450 Muskegon MI 49443

VAN LEUVEN, ROBERT JOSEPH, lawyer; b. Detroit, Apr. 17, 1931; s. Joseph Francis and Olive (Stowell) Van L.; student Albion Coll., 1949-51; B.A. with distinction Wayne State U., 1953; J.D., U. Mich., 1957; m. Holly Goodhue Porter, Dec. 31, 1976; children—Joseph Michael, Douglas Robert, Julie Margaret. Admitted to Mich. bar, 1957, since practiced in Muskegon; partner firm Hathaway, Latimer, Clink & Robb, 1957-68, partner McCroskey, Libner & Van Leuven, 1968-81, Libner, Van Leuven & Kortering, 1982—. Bd. dirs. Muskegon Children's Home, 1965-75. Served with AUS 1953-55. Fellow Am. Coll. Trial Lawyers; mem. Trial Lawyers Assn. Am., State Bar Mich. (past mem. council negligence law sect.), Mich. Assn. Professions, Am. Arbitration Assn., Muskegon Urban League, Delta Sigma Phi. Club: Muskegon Country. Home: 966 Mona Brook Muskegon MI 49445 Office: Hackley Bank Muskegon Mall Muskegon MI 49443

VAN LOH, FREDERICK ALVIN, educator; b. Ashton, Iowa, Nov. 28, 1926; s. Jans and Fenna (Luitjens) Van L.; m. Rose Marie Helmers, July 28, 1950; children—Linda Killian, James. Student S.D. State U., summers 1944, 47, 48; B.S., Iowa State U., 1950, M.S., 1964. Lic. tchr., Iowa. Youth asst. Osceola County, summer 1948; tchr. Correctionville High Sch. (Iowa), 1950-51; tchr. vocat. agr. Sheldon Community High Sch. (Iowa), 1951—; advisor Sheldon chpt. Future Farmers Am., 1951—; judge county fairs. Served with U.S. Army, 1944-46. Recipient Regional Dist. Conservation Tchr. award Iowa Soil Conservation Service, 1971, Beresford Quaife award, 1981; hon. Iowa Farmer Degree, 1969, hon. Am. Farmer Degree, 1982. Mem. Nat. Vocat. Agr. Tchrs. Assn., Iowa Vocat. Agr. Tchrs. Assn. (voting del. conf. 1982. Harry R. Schroeder Disting. Iowa Vocat. Agr. Tchr. award 1983, dir. 1982-84), Am. Vocat. Assn., Iowa Vocat. Assn. (voting del. conf. 1982, dir. 1982-84), O'Brien County Farm Bur., Gamma Sigma Delta. Republican. Baptist. Home: 1211 Kahler Ct Sheldon IA 51201 Office: 1700 E 4th St Sheldon IA 51201

VAN MELE, RICHARD JOHN, insurance company executive; m. Debra G.; 3 children. B.S. in Bus. Fin., Notre Dame U.; M.B.A., J.D., Ind. U. Assoc. prof. bus. law Ball State U., Muncie, Ind., 1963-67; dir. research Ind. Legis. Council, 1967-70; dir. legis. research Assocs. Corp. N.Am., 1970-71, v.p. govtl. affairs, 1971-73, v.p. corp. mgmt. affairs, 1975-76, sr. v.p. corp. govtl. and mgmt. affairs, 1976—; pres. Bath, Van Mele & Assocs., Inc., South Bend, Ind., 1976—, dir., 1980—, chief exec. officer, 1983—; former chmn. St. Joseph Govt. Study Commn., former vice chmn. Ind. Toll Rd. Commn.; chief exec. officer Robertson's Dept. Stores, Former pres. Mich. Coll. Commerce. Mem. South Bend-Mishawaka C. of C. (chmn.). Home: 1243 E Jefferson Blvd South Bend IN 46617

VAN METER, JAMES ARIS, utility company executive; b. Lexington, Ky., Jan. 10, 1938; s. James Samual and Frances Roena (Shouse) Van M.; m. Karole Diann Trusty, Jan. 4, 1958; children—Timothy Lee, Denise Lynn, Jeffrey Brian. Assoc. of Sci., Purdue U., 1957. Design group leader United Tech. Ctr., Sunnyvale, Calif., 1960-65; indsl. engring. supr. Westinghouse, Sunnyvale, 1965-67; works mgr. Babcock & Wilcox Co., Mt. Vernon, Ind., 1967-73; v.p. elec. So. Ind. Gas & Electric Co., Evansville, Ind., 1973—. Home: 9710 Middle Mount Vernon Rd Evansville IN 47712 Office: So Ind Gas & Electric Co 20 24 NW 4th St Evansville IN 47741

VAN METRE, DAVID CARL, manufacturing company executive; b. Milw., Dec. 23, 1954; s. Marvin Earl and Beverly Jean (LaRue) Van M.; m. Susan Kay Maurer, Oct. 2, 1976; children—Matthew Edward, Christopher James. B.S. in Ceramic Engring., U. Ill.-Urbana, 1977. Mfg. engr. Babcock & Wilcox, Lynchburg, Va., 1977-78; process engr. Owens/Corning Fiberglas Co., Fairburn, Ga., 1978-84, div. energy and waste recovery specialist, Toledo, 1984—. Mem. Assn. Energy Engrs. Avocations: Electronics; swimming; tennis; racquetball. Home: 6753 Gaines Mill Dr Sylvania OH 43560 Office: Owens/-Corning Fiberglas Co Fiberglas Tower E/9 Toledo OH 43659

VANN, JAMES, wire company executive; b. Badin, N.C., Jan. 26, 1928; m. Lee Vann; children—Stephanie, Sherry Debbie, James, Michael. B.B.A., Davidson Coll., 1950. Sales trainee REA Magnet Wire Co., Inc., Tenn.; sales engr., Atlanta, 1953, mgr. indsl. bldg. products, Pitts., 1960, mgr. nonresidential bldg. product sales, 1962-66, mktg. mgr. bldg. and constrn., dist. sales mgr., Atlanta, 1969, N.W. area and Vancouver ops. mgr., 1976, gen. mgr. Western Australia Ops., Alcoa of Australia, 1980, gen. mgr. alumna div., 1981, pres., Ft. Wayne, Ind., 1982—. Adv. bd. Wash. State U., 1980; bd. dirs. Wash. State Research Council, 1980; bd. dirs. Ft. Wayne Corp. Council, 1985—, Summit Tech. and Research Transfer Ctr., 1985—, N.E. Ind. Bus. Group on Health, 1984-85; 1st v.p., trustee Ft. Wayne Mus. Art; trustee Ft. Wayne Fine Arts Found. Mem. Nat. Elec. Mfrs. Assn. (vice chmn. magnet wire sect.). Clubs: Ft. Wayne Country, Summit, Duquesne. Address: REA Magnet Wire 3600 E Pontiac St PO Box 6128 Fort Wayne IN 46896

VANNATTA, DENNIS ROY, optometrist; b. Cherokee, Iowa, Sept. 3, 1955; s. Darrel Roy and Delores Jean (Jensen) V. Student in pre-optometry U. S.D., 1973-76; B.S. in Visual Sci., Pacific U., 1978, O.D., 1980. Lic. optometrist, Iowa. Hosp. staff optometrist U.S. Navy, Patuxent River, Md., 1980-83; optometrist with Dr. Ralph Danner, Mapelton, Iowa, 1983; pvt. practice optometry, Sioux City, Iowa, 1984—. Served to lt. with USN, 1980-83, USNR, 1983—. Mem. Iowa Optometric Assn., Am. Optometric Assn., Nat. Assn. Professions, Armed Forced Optometric Soc., Siouxland Assn. Bus. and Industry. Republican. Methodist. Club: Siouxland Cosmopolitan. Lodges: Sertoma, Eagles. Avocations: photography; fishing; boating; skiing. Home: 430 South Lynn Dr LeMars IA 51031 Office: 4016 Morningside Ave Sioux City IA 51106

VAN NATTA, ELEANOR SUE POUNDSTONE, nurse; b. Decatur, Ill., Nov. 22, 1932; d. Herbert Lloyd and Blanche Cleo (Zink) Poundstone; diploma in nursing Washington U., St. Louis, 1953, M.S. in Nursing, 1961; B.S. in Nursing, U. Mo., 1956; M.S.Ed., Purdue U., 1970; m. Charles R. Van Natta, Jr., June 12, 1971 (div. 1977); children—Laura, Sue. Staff nurse Barnes Hosp., St. Louis, 1953-54; staff nurse, then head nurse U. Mo. Med. Center, Columbia, 1954-58; instr. Decatur (Ill.) and Macon County Hosp. Sch. Nursing, 1958-60; instr. U. Colo., Denver, 1961-63; asst. prof. U. Mo., Columbia, 1964-66; asst. prof. Forest Park Community Coll., St. Louis, 1967-69; high sch. counselor, Decatur, 1970-71; coordinator diagnostic and evaluation project Comprehensive Devel. Centers, Monticello, Ind., 1975-77; asst. prof. Purdue U. Sch.

Nursing, 1980-84; program supr. for nursing Ind. Vocat. Tech. Coll., Lafayette, 1984—; pres. White County Registered Nurses Orgn., 1975-76. Vol., Twin Lakes Contact, crisis hotline, Monticello, 1975-76; bd. dirs. Tippecanoe County unit Am. Heart Assn., Purdue Women's Caucus, 1983-84; ednl. coordinator Matrix Lifeline, 1981-82. Mem. Am. Nurses Assn., Ind. Nurses Assn., Ind. League for Nursing (bd. dirs. 1984-86), Phi Delta Kappa, Sigma Theta Tau, Kappa Kappa Kappa. Club: Order Eastern Star. Home: 1137 Hillcrest Rd West Lafayette IN 47906 Office: Ind Vocat Tech Coll Lafayette IN 47902

VAN NORMAN, WILLIS ROGER, computer systems researcher; b. Windom, Minn., June 17, 1938; s. Ralph Peter and Thelma Pearl (Bare) Van N.; A.A., Worthington Jr. Coll., 1958; B.S., Mankato State Coll., 1960; m. Irene Anna Penner, Sept. 7, 1959; children—Eric Jon, Brian Mathew, Karin Ruth. Tchr. chemistry, St. Peter, Minn., 1961; tchr., Byron, Minn., 1962, spl. edn., Rochester, Minn., 1963-65; instr. pilots ground sch. Rochester Jr. Coll., 1968-69; with Mayo Clinic, Rochester, 1962—, developer biomed. computer systems, 1974—; instr. Gopher Aviation, 1968-71. Treas., United Methodist Ch. Mem. Mankato State Alumni Assn. (dir.), Minn., Nat. ednl. assns., Internat. Flying Farmers (dir.), Minn Flying Farmers (sec.-treas.), Am. Radio Relay League (mgr. Minn. sect. traffic net), Rochester Amateur Radio Club (pres.). Founder, mgr. Van Norman's Flying V Ranch, 1972—, Van Norman Airport, St. Charles, 1977—. Home: Route 3 Box 25 Saint Charles MN 55972 Office: Mayo Clinic Rochester MN 55901

VAN OOSBREE, CHARLYNE SELMA NELSON, librarian; b. Alta, Iowa, Jan. 19, 1930; d. John Albin and Albertina (Rydstrom) Nelson; m. Anton Van Oosbree, Dec. 30, 1950 (dec. 1965); children—Tina Van Oosbree Taylor, Jon, David. B.S. in English, Iowa State U., 1970; M.L.S., U. Mo., 1973. Hospital librarian Army Hosp., Ft. Leonard Wood, Mo., 1970-72; head sch. library Tng. Sch. for Boys, Boonville, Mo., 1973-76; head br. library Mid-Contninent Pub. Library, Independence, Mo., 1976-82; head base library Whiteman AFB, Mo., 1982—; mem. adv. council U. Mo. Sch. Library and Info. Sci., Columbia, 1978-80, sec., 1978-79; coordinator Writers' Group, Platte Woods, Mo., 1980-82. Contbr. articles to library publ., poems, articles to newspapers. Bd. mem. Tri-County Mental Health Assn., Kansas City, Mo., 1980-82, Park Hill Sch. Adv. Council, Kansas City, 1977-78, Synergy House, Parkville, Mo., 1976-77; mem. youth adv. council Whiteman AFB; counselor Widowed Persons Service, Kansas City, 1977-78. Named SAC Librarian of Yr., 1984; Mo. State Library scholar, 1972. Mem. ALA, Fed. Librarians Round Table, Beta Phi Mu. Home: 339 E Market St Warrensburg MO 64093 Office: Base Library USAF Whiteman AFB MO 65305

VAN RIPER, GUERNSEY, JR., real estate and oil company executive, author; b. Indpls., July 5, 1909; s. Guernsey and Edith (Longley) Van R.; m. Betty Cline, Nov. 14, 1981. A.B., DePauw U., 1930; M.B.A., Harvard U., 1932. Advt. copywriter Sidener & Van Riper, Indpls., 1933-40; editor Bobbs-Merrill Co., Indpls. and N.Y.C., 1941-48; freelance writer children's books, 1949-74; pres. Crooked Stick Devel. Corp., Carmel, Ind., 1972—; pres. Venture Petroleum Drillers (name changed to Vandrill, Inc. 1984), Carmel and Oklahoma City, 1980—, Van Riper Gallery Fine Arts, Inc., 1984—; trustee Ind.-Fla. Realty Trust; author children's books: Lou Gehrig, Boy of the Sandlots, 1949; Will Rogers, Young Cowboy, 1951; Knute Rockne, Young Athlete, 1952; Babe Ruth, Baseball Boy, 1954; Jim Thorpe, Indian Athlete, 1956; Richard Byrd, Boy Who Braved the Unknown, 1958; Yea Coach! Three Great Football Coaches, 1966; The Game of Basketball, 1967; World Series Highlights, 1970; The Mighty Macs, Three Famous Baseball Managers, 1972; Behind the Plate, Three Great Catchers, 1973; (with J. Newcomb and G. Sullivan) Football Replay, 1973; (with S.B. Epstein and R. Reeder) Big League Pitchers and Catchers, 1973; Golfing Greats, 1975. Mem. Authors League of Am. Republican. Methodist. Clubs: Highland Golf and Country, Skyline. Address: PO Box 455 Carmel IN 46032

VAN SANT, R. W., aircraft manufacturing company executive. Pres., chief operating officer Cessna Aircraft Co., Wichita, Kans. Office: Cessna Aircraft Co PO Box 1521 Wichita KS 67201*

VAN SICKLE, BRUCE MARION, judge; b. Bismarck, N.D., Feb. 13, 1917; s. Guy Robin and Hilda Alice (Rosenquist) Van S.; B.S.L., U. Minn., 1941, J.D., 1941; m. Dorothy Alfreda Hermann, May 26, 1943; children—Susan (Mrs. Michael Cooper), John Allan, Craig Bruce, David Max. Admitted to Minn. bar, 1941, N.D. bar, 1946; practiced in Minot, 1947-71; judge U.S. Dist. Ct., 1971—. Mem. N.D. Ho. of Reps., 1957-61. Served with USMCR, 1941-46. Mem. Am., N.D., Northwest, Ward County bar assns., Am. Trial Lawyers Assn., Am. Coll. Probate Counsel, Am. Judicature Soc. Mason (Shriner). Elk. Office: US District Ct PO Box 670 Bismarck ND 58501

VAN SLYKE, DEBORAH PHYLLIS, business executive; b. Rockford, Ill.; d. Harold Walter and Dorothy Violet (Callahan) Johnson; m. Richard Kelley Rodgers, Sept. 3, 1964 (div. Jan. 1973); 1 child, Kristen Elizabeth; m. Alan Van Slyke, May 27, 1978; children—John David, Jason Ross. B.A., Ripon Coll., 1960; M.A., U. Wis., 1961. Asst. librarian First Nat. Bank Chgo., 1963-69; head librarian Montgomery Ward & Co., Chgo., 1971-76, Real Estate Research Corp., Chgo., 1976-77; mgr. record services and word processing Chgo., Rock Island R.R., Chgo., 1977-78; supr. reprographic services Honeywell Inc., Mpls., 1981—. Elder, Valley Presbyn. Ch., Golden Valley, Minn., 1981-83; pres. New Neighbors League, Omaha and Mpls., 1980-83. Mem. Assn. Info. Image Mgrs., Assn. Record Mgrs. and Adminstrs. (2d v.p., treas. 1983-84, v.p. 1984—). Club: St. Paul Athletic. Avocations: cross-country skiing, reading, needlepoint. Home: 310 Cloverleaf Dr North Minneapolis MN 55435 Office: Honeywell Inc 6400 France Ave Minneapolis MN 55432

VAN TASSEL, LEO M., ret. univ. adminstr.; b. Howard City, Mich., Jan. 28, 1912; s. Louis M. and Lillian (Ranshaw) Van T.; A.C., Grand Rapids Jr. Coll., 1933; A.B., Western Mich. U., 1936; M.A., U. Mich., 1942; postgrad. Columbia, 1949; m. Evelyn Loveridge, Nov. 5, 1938; 1 dau., Marilyn. High sch. tchr., Fennville, Mich., 1936-41, Midland, Mich., 1941-45; pub. accountant Ernst & Ernst, Detroit, 1945-46; prof. accounting No. Mich. U., Marquette, 1946-49, v.p., 1949-77, treas. Univ. Found., 1960-68, devel. fund, 1968-77. Mem. Central, Nat. assns. bus. officers, NEA, Mich. Edn. Assn., Assn. Sch. Bus. Ofcls., Delta Sigma Phi. Mason (Shriner). Home: 710 W Kaye St Marquette MI 49855

VAN TIEM, PHILLIP MICHAEL, hospital business administrator; b. Grosse Pointe, Mich., Oct. 4, 1935; s. August Gerard and Margaret Mary (Power) Van T.; B.A., Mich. State U., 1963; postgrad. Wayne State U., 1972-73, U. Detroit, 1974-76; M.A. in Public Adminstrn., Central Mich. U., 1978, M.A. in Health Care Adminstrn., 1983; m. Darlene Miriam Roff, Apr. 4, 1964; children—Bradford, Adrienne. With Gen. Motors Acceptance Corp., 1963-68, credit mgr., 1965-68; comml. sales rep. Goodyear Tire & Rubber Co., 1968-69; mgr. accounts receivable Lansing (Mich.) Gen. Hosp., 1969-70; mgr. patient acctg. Sinai Hosp., Detroit, 1971-72, St. John Hosp., Detroit, 1972-79, asst. controller, 1979-81, dir. patient acctg., 1982—. Bd. dirs. Lansing Gen. Hosp. Credit Union, 1969-70, treas., 1970; chmn. supr. com. Sinai Hosp. Credit Union, 1971-72. Vol. social worker Family to Family Movement, 1965-71; mem. vol. program Mich. Dept. Social Services, 1965-71; chmn. publicity Grosse Pointe Park Civic Assn.; asst. commr. Boy Scouts Am., Lakeshore dist., 1982—. Served with AUS, 1958-60. Recipient hon. mention for suggestion Mich. Hosp. Assn., 1972; Cost Containment award Hosp. Fin. Mgmt., 1978. Mem. Hosp. Fin. Mgmt. Assn. (membership com. 1975-77, social chmn. 1975-77, awards chmn. 1977-78, public relations chmn. 1978-79, dir. 1979-83, chpt. del. for coordinating council 1980-83, vice chmn. 1982-83, placement chmn. 1981-82, Follmer award 1979, Reeves award 1982), Mich. Hosp. Assn. (various coms., publicity chmn. 1983-84), Grosse Pointe Alumnae Assn. (v.p. 1980-81, pres. 1981-82). Roman Catholic. Home: 1310 Kensington Rd Grosse Pointe MI 48230 Office: 22101 Moross Rd Detroit MI 48236

VAN VOORHEES, CURTIS, education educator, consultant; b. Kalamazoo, Dec. 20, 1934; s. Frank Lloyd and Barbara Lorraine (Curtiss) Van V.; m. Florence Elizabeth Raetz, June 14, 1958; children—Megan, Erin. Student Kalamazoo Coll., 1953-54; B.S., Western Mich U., 1957; M.A., No. Ill. U., 1961; Ed.D., Mich. State U., 1968. Prin., counselor Paw Paw Jr./Sr. High Sch., Mich., 1960-63; asst. prin. Chofu High Sch., Japan, 1963-65; assoc. prof. Ball State U., Muncie, Ind., 1967-71; prof. edn. U. of Mich., Ann Arbor, 1971—; pres., chief cons. Meer, Inc., Whitmore Lake, Mich., 1981—, Gen. Motors, Procter & Gamble, Ford, Ashland Oil Co., U. of Mich. Sch. Medicine, 1981—. Author: The Role of Community Education in the School, 1970. Advisor Saline Pub. Schs., Mich., 1981—, U. Mich. Outpatient Services, Ann Arbor, 1982—. Mott fellow, Mott Found., Flint, Mich., 1966-67. Mem. Nat. Community Edn. Assn. (pres. 1973), Am. Assn. Sch. Instrs. and Adminstrs., Am. Assn. Supervision and Curriculum Devel., Mich. Assn. Sch. Adminstrs., Mich. Assn. Supervision and Curriculum Devel. (bd. dirs. 1982—). Avocations: cabinet-making; golf; tennis; fishing; travel; boating. Home: 1189 W 8 Mile Rd Whitmore Lake MI 48189 Office: U Mich 4119 SEB Ann Arbor MI 48109

VAN VOORST, DENNIS J., optometrist; b. Sioux Center, Iowa, Apr. 23, 1949; s. John G. and Eileen (Van't Hul) Van V.; m. Sheryl Dianne Engbers, June 28, 1969; children—Jamison John, Ann Marie. B.S. in Optometry, U. Houston, 1971; O.D., 1973. Practice optometry, Rock Valley, Iowa, 1973—; mem. adv. bd. Bethesda Midwest Mental Health Facility, Orange City, Iowa, 1984—. Mem. Iowa Optometric Assn., Am. Optometric Assn. Republican. Mem. Christian Reformed Ch. Lodges: Lions, Rotary Internat. Avocations: woodworking; Stamp collecting; antique automobile restoration; golf. Address: 704 Fairway Dr Rock Valley IA 51247

VAN VORST, CHARLES BRIAN, health facility administrator; b. Harvey, Ill., June 22, 1943; s. John William and Bessie (Borg) Van V.; divorced; children—Krista Ann, Dirk Brian. B.S., U. Evansville, 1966; M.B.A., George Washington U., 1968. Adminstrv. resident Meth. Hosp., Indpls., 1967-68, adminstrv. asst., 1968-69, asst. adminstr., 1969-71, assoc. adminstr., 1971-72, v.p. ops., 1972-79; pres., chief exec. officer Carle Found., Urbana, Ill., 1979—, Carle Found. Hosp., Urbana, 1979—; clin. asst. prof. Coll. Medicine, U. Ill., Urbana; dir. CarleCare, Inc.; former tchr. bus. adminstrn. Ind. Central U.; past dir., treas. Alpha Home Assn.; former mem. nat. adv. com. on pub. health tng. Dept. Tng., HEW, NIH. Former bd. dirs., med. adv. com., long range planning com. United Meth. Home, Franklin, Ind.; former bd. dirs. Met. Health Council, Inc.; former chmn. fin. com. Community Addiction Services Agy.; chmn. Champaign-Urbana Areawide Emergency Med. Services Council; trustee Ill. Provider Trust; mem. allocation com., chmn. Profl. Services div. United Way campaign, 1982; mem. Urbana Polit. Action Com.; vice chmn. Ill. Health Care Cost Containment Council. WHO fellow, 1973; recipient cert. of excellence Evansville Alumni Assn., 1973. Fellow Am. Coll. Hosp. Adminstrs.; mem. Am. Hosp. Assn., Am. Assn. for Hosp. Planning (bd. dirs.), Health Issues Study Soc. (past pres.), Ill. Hosp. Assn. (teaching hosps. council, governing bd., trustee, exec. com. cost containment com.), Ill. Health Care Containment Council (bd. dirs., vice chmn.), George Washington U. Alumni Assn. for Health Care (pres., exec. com.), Urbana Downtown Promotion Assn., Urbana C. of C. (long range planning com., mem. fin. and econ. devel. coms.). Republican. Methodist. Clubs: Rotary (Champaign), Champaign Country. Contbr. articles to med. jours. Home: 1914 Woodfield Rd Champaign IL 61821 Office: Carle Found 611 W Park St Urbana IL 61801

VAN WAGNER, JEFFREY WILLIAM, lawyer; b. Ravenna, Ohio, Nov. 18, 1953; s. Donald Henry and Vita Mary (Cacioppo) Van W.; m. Janet Marie Van Wagner, Mar. 21, 1982. B.A., John Carroll U., 1976; J.D., Case Western Res. U., 1979. Bar: Ohio 1979. Clk., Turoff & Turoff, Cleve., 1978-79; assoc. Gallagher, Sharp, Fulton, & Norman, Cleve., 1979-83, Ulmer, Berne, Laronge, Glickman & Curtis, Cleve., 1983—; instr. writing and advocacy, Case Western Res. U., Cleve., 1978-79. Mem. ABA, Ohio Bar Assn., Order of Coif. Republican. Roman Catholic. Home: 2051 Miramar Blvd South Euclid OH 44121 Office: Ulmer Berne Laronge Glickman Curtis 900 Bond Court Bldg Cleveland OH 44114

VARDEMAN, STEPHEN BRUCE, statistics educator; b. Louisville, Aug. 27, 1949; s. Bruce Hamilton and Helen Jane (Martin) V.; m. Jo Ellen Nollsch, Aug. 30, 1970; children—Micah Stephen, Andrew David. B.S. with distinction in Math., Iowa State U., 1971, M.S. in Math., 1973; Ph.D. in Stats., Mich. State U., 1975. Asst. prof. stats. Purdue U., West Lafayette Ind., 1975-81; asst. prof. Iowa State U., Ames, 1981-83, assoc. prof., 1983—; cons. Amana Refrigeration Inc., Iowa, 1983—, Hewlett Packard Corp., Palo Alto, Calif., 1984, John Deere Corp., Moline, Ill., 1985. Co-author: (text) Elementary Statistics, 1982. Contbr. papers, revs. to profl. publs. Fin. sec., sunday sch. tchr., presch. Christian edn. coordinator First Evangel. Free Ch., Ames, 1981—; conv. del. Story County Republican Party, 1984. IBM fellow, 1971; grantee Purdue Research Found., 1977, NSF, 1978, 79-80, 82. Mem. Am. Statis. Assn. (com. quality and productivity 1984—, assoc. editor jour. 1984—, nat. program chmn. sect. physical and engring. scis. 1986), Am. Soc. Quality Control, Inst. Math. Stats. Home: 812 Northwestern Ave Ames IA 50010 Office: Stats Dept Iowa State U Snedecor Hall Ames IA 50010

VAREJCKA, JANET FAYE, educational administrator; b. Columbus, Nebr., June 23, 1944; d. John and Blanche (Aringdale) V. B.A. in Edn., Wayne State Coll., 1966; M.S. in History, U. Nebr.-Omaha, 1976, postgrad, 1978. Tchr. history, speech, psychology Logan Community Sch., Iowa, 1967-80; prin. Bennett County High Sch., Martin, S.D., 1980—. Mem. adv. bd. FFA-FHA, Martin, 1980—, State adv. bd. to FHA, 1983-84; mem. Nursing Home Auxilary, Martin, 1984. Mem. Nat. Assn. Secondary Sch. Prins. (com. on small secondary schs.), Sch. Adminstrs. in S.D. (exec. bd. 1985—), S.D. Assn. Secondary Sch. Prins. (regional rep. 1981-84, v.p. 1984-85, pres.-elect 1985), Beta Iota (sec. 1983-84, pres. 1985). Democrat. Methodist. Avocations: reading; guitar. Office: Bennett County High Sch Box 580 Martin SD 57551

VARGA, STEVEN CARL, insurance company official; b. Columbus, Ohio, Jan. 19, 1952; s. Stephen Thomas and Eva Jeney V.; B.A. in Psychology and Philosophy magna cum laude, Carthage Coll., 1977; m. Michelle L. Auld, Nov. 17, 1973; children—Zachary Steven, Joshua Lewis. Service mgr. Chem-Lawn Corp., Columbus, 1972-75; respiratory therapist St. Catherine's Hosp., Kenosha, Wis., 1975-77; policy analyst Nationwide Ins. Cos., Columbus, 1978-79, asst. mgr. Corp. Tng. Center, 1979—, mem. civic action program, 1979—. Mem. Nat. Mental Health Assn., 1972—, v.p. Kenosha County chpt., 1975-77; mem. Franklin County (Ohio) Mental Health Assn., 1978—. Rhodes scholar, 1976-77. Mem. Am. Soc. Tng. and Devel., Soc. Broadcast Engrs., Internat. TV Assn., Am. Assn. Respiratory Therapy, Am. Psychol. Assn., Ins. Co. Edn. Dirs. Soc., Smithsonian Assocs., Am. Film Inst., Carthage Coll. Alumni Assn., Phi Beta Kappa, Psi Chi. Home: 1707 E Dunedin Rd Columbus OH 43224 Office: One Nationwide Plaza Columbus OH 43216

VARGAS, DANIEL JOSEPH, interior designer, furniture company executive; b. Topeka, July 17, 1948; s. Manuel J. and Emily T. (Terrones) V. B.F.A., U. Kans., 1973. Pres., Vargas Fine Furniture, Inc., Topeka, 1985—; designer Everywoman's Resource Ctr., Designers Showhouse, Topeka, 1985. Served with AUS, 1971-73. Mem. Internat. Soc. Interior Designers. Democrat. Roman Catholic. Avocations: music; racquetball; softball. Home: 6847 SW Dunstan Ct Topeka KS 66610 Office: Vargas Fine Furniture Inc 4900 S Topeka Blvd Topeka KS 66609

VARGUS, BRIAN STANLEY, sociologist, educator, political consultant; b. Vallejo, Calif., Aug. 2, 1938; s. Stanley John and Edna Nettie (Rabb) V.; m. Nanci Jean Reginelli, Aug. 29, 1964; children—Jilda, Rebecca, Abigail. B.A., U. Calif.-Berkeley, 1961, M.A., 1963; Ph.D., Ind. U., 1969. Instr., Bakersfield Coll., Calif., 1964-66, Ind. U., Bloomington, 1966-69; asst. prof. U. Pitts., 1969-75; prof. sociology Ind./Purdue U., Indpls., 1975—, dir. publ. opinion labs., 1975—; pres. Opinion Research and Eval., Indpls., 1980—; cons. Bayh, Tabbert & Capehart, Indpls., 1984, Pub. Policy Cons., Bloomington, 1984; polit. analyst, participant radio and TV programs; speaker in field. Author: Reading in Sociology, 3d edit., 1984. Pres. bd. dirs. Greater Ind. Council on Alcholism, Nat. Council on Alcoholism, Indpls., 1982-84; cons. Greater Indpls. Progress Com., 1982, Children's Mus., Indpls., 1984, Gov.'s Task Force on Drunk Driving, Ind., 1984—. Fulbright fellow, 1973, Flynn fellow, 1981; recipient Disting. Service award Greater Council Alcoholism, 1984; recipient numerous research grants. Mem. Am. Sociol. Assn., Am. Assn. Pub. Opinion, Midwest Assn. Publ. Opinion Research, North Central Sociol. Assn. Methodist. Club: Indpls. Press. Avocations: racquetball, reading, swimming. Home: 4084 Rocking Chair Rd Greenwood IN 46142 Office: Ind/Purdue U 425 Anges St Indianapolis IN 46220

VARIS, JOHN, educational administrator, educator; b. Arahovitika Patras, Greece, Oct. 26, 1942; s. William and Dina (Loukopoulos) Varis; m. Diane Carol Maezer, June 12, 1971; children—Jason William, Justin Albert B.S., Bowling Green State U., 1965, M.A., 1970, Ph.D., 1973; postgrad. U. Cin., 1974. Cert. supt., Ohio. Tchr., Anthony Wayne Schs., Whitehall, Ohio, 1969-70; tchr. Oregon City (Ohio) Schs., 1970-72; doctoral fellow Bowling Green State U., 1972-73; prin. Norwood City (Ohio) Schs., 1973-81, asst. supt., 1981—; adj. assoc. prof. Xavier U. Active Sch. Found. Greater Cin., 1976-80, Sherwood Civic Assn., 1979. Served to capt. USAR, 1965-68. Recipient DAR Americanism Medal, 1979; Tchrs. award, Daus. Colonial Wars, 1980; PTA Educator of Yr. award Norwood, Ohio, 1977; Bowling Green State U. fellow, 1972; Mem. Buckeye Assn. Sch. Adminstrs., Assn. Supervision and Curriculum Devel., Ohio Assn. Elem. Sch. Adminstrs., Alpha Sigma Phi, Alpha Phi Omega, Phi Delta Kappa. Greek Orthodox. Contbr. articles to profl. publs. Office: 2132 William Ave Norwood OH 45212

VARMA, VIRENDRA KUMAR, engineer, educator. B.S. in Engring., B.I.T.S., Pilani, India, 1965; M.S., SUNY-Buffalo, 1970; Ph.D., U.Mo.-Columbia, 1983. Registered profl. engr., Mo.; registered profl. structural engr., Pa. Project engr. BSRTC, engring. div., Patna, India, 1966-67, GFC&C, Inc., Cons. Engrs., Harrisburg, Pa., 1969-78; chmn. tech. Mo. Western State Coll., St. Joseph, 1979—; cons. Fuller Engring., St. Joseph, 1984—; ptnr. BKV Civil Engring. Assn., St. Joseph, 1981. Contbr. articles to profl. publs. Chmn. St. Joseph Sts. Standards Com., 1985. Mem. ASCE, Am. Soc. Engring. Edn. Club: Saint Joseph Racquet. Avocations: tennis, pingpong. Home: 4610 Badger Terr Saint Joseph MO 64506

VARNELL, WILLIAM GLENN, insurance company executive, consultant; b. Knoxville, Tenn., Oct. 3, 1945; s. James Henderson and Iva Elizabeth (Williamson) V.; m. Sharon Kay Harley, Aug. 5, 1967; 1 child, Meredith Harley. B.A., Jacksonville U., 1967; M.A., Duke U., 1969. Instr., Jacksonville U., Fla., 1968-70; dir. Blue Cross-Blue Shield, Jacksonville, 1970-81, Worthington, Ohio, 1981—; cons. Preferred Podiatry Ohio, Columbus, 1984. Officer, PTA, Worthington, 1982—, For Excellence in Worthington, 1985; chmn. Directions in Edn. Worthington, 1983; mem. steering com. State Conf. Minority Health, Ohio, 1985. Mem. Am. Statis. Assn., Math. Assn. Am., Am. Med. Care and Rev. Assn., Am. Physics Inst. (v.p. 1964-65), Kappa Delta Pi. Lodge: Masons. Avocations: Woodworking, gardening, camping, travel. Home: 612 Morning St Worthington OH 43085 Office: Community Mutual Ins Co Blue-Cross-Blue Shield 6740 N High St Worthington OH 43085

VARNER, CHARLEEN LAVERNE MCCLANAHAN (MRS. ROBERT B. VARNER), educator, adminstr., nutritionist; b. Alba, Mo., Aug. 28, 1931; d. Roy Calvin and Lela Ruhama (Smith) McClanahan; student Joplin (Mo.) Jr. Coll., 1949-51; B.S. in Edn., Kans. State Coll. Pittsburg, 1953; M.S., U. Ark., 1958; Ph.D., Tex. Woman's U. 1966; postgrad. Mich. State U., summer, 1955, U. Mo., summers 1952, 62; m. Robert Bernard Varner, July 4, 1953. Apprentice county home agt. U. Mo., summer 1952; tchr. Ferry Pass. Sch., Escambia County, Fla., 1953-54; tchr. biology, home econs. Joplin Sr. High Sch., 1954-59; instr. home econs. Kans. State Coll., Pittsburg, 1959-63; lectr. foods, nutrition Coll. Household Arts and Scis., Tex. Woman's U., 1963-64, research asst. NASA grant, 1964-66; asso. prof. home econs. Central Mo. State U., Warrensburg, 1966-70, adviser to Colhecon, 1966-70, adviser to Alpha Sigma Alpha, 1967-70, 72, mem. bd. advisers Honors Group, 1967-70; prof., head dept. home econs. Kans. State Tchrs. Coll., Emporia, 1970-73; prof., chmn. dept. home econs. Benedictine Coll., Atchison, Kans., 1973-74; prof., chmn. dept. home econs. Baker U., Baldwin City, Kans., 1974-75; owner, operator Diet-Con Dietary Cons. Enterprises, cons. dietitian, 1973—. Mem. Joplin Little Theater, 1956-60. Mem. NEA, Mo., Kans. state tchrs. assns., AAUW, Am., Mo., Kans. dietetics assns., Am., Mo., Kans. home econs. assns., Mo. Acad. Scis., AAUP, U. Ark. Alumni Assn., Alumni Assn. Kans. State Coll. of Pittsburg, Am. Vocat. Assn., Assn. Edn. Young Children, Sigma Xi, Beta Sigma Phi, Beta Beta Beta, Alpha Sigma Alpha, Delta Kappa Gamma, Kappa Kappa Iota, Phi Upsilon Omicron. Methodist (organist). Home: Main PO Box 1009 Topeka KS 66601

VARNER, ETHELORIA DOLL, educational administrator; b. Detroit, Aug. 30, 1930; d. Thomas and Vera (Awtrey) Smith; m. Carl A. Varner, May 23, 1950; children—Tanya, Rocklyn Carl. B.S., Boston U., 1949; M.A., Wayne State U., 1960, M.Ed., 1971. Instr. Howard U., Washington, 1949-53, Hampton Inst., 1953-54; asst. to Dr. Lyle Crawford, Wayne State U., Detroit, 1968-70; supr. elem. schs., Washington, 1954-54; prin. Jamieson Elem. Sch., Detroit, 1980—. Bd. dirs., treas. Northwest Community Council, 1969. Named Outstanding Tchr. of Yr., Detroit, 1969; Profl. Growth Ctr. award, 1975. Mem. Met. Soc. Black Ednl. Adminstrs., Guidance Assn. Met. Detroit, Detroit Women Sch. Adminstrs., Nat. Assn. Secondary Sch. Prins., Alpha Kappa Alpha. Roman Catholic. Contbr. articles to profl. jours. Home: 9300 LaSalle Blvd Detroit MI 48206 Office: 2900 W Philadelphia St Detroit MI 48206

VARNER, JEAN MARIE, pharmacist; b. Ft. Benjamin Harrison, Ind., May 9, 1959; d. Fred Franklin and Joanna Mabel (Pope) Blair; m. Dwayne Steven Varner, Aug. 14, 1982; 1 dau., Kathryn. B.S. in Pharmacy, Ohio No. U., 1982. Pharmacy intern Muhlberg Pharmacy, West Chester, Ohio, 1979-82; pharmacist Northedge Pharmacy, Eaton, Ohio, 1982-84; staff pharmacist Richmond State Hosp., Ind., 1984—, mem. quality assurance com., 1984—, mem. pharmacy and therapeutics com., 1984—. Mem. Ohio State Pharm. Assn., Phi Kappa Phi, Rho Chi Pharm. Lutheran. Avocations: reading; golf; tennis; cross stitch.

VARNER, ROBERT BERNARD, educator, counselor; b. Ellsworth, Kans., May 31, 1930; s. Bernard Lafayette and Leota (Campbell) V.; B.S., Kans. State U., Pittsburg, 1952; M.S., U. Ark., 1959; postgrad. Mich. State U., summer 1955, U. Mo., summer 1962, (grantee) U. Kans., 1972-73; m. Charleen LaVerne McClanahan, July 4, 1953. Athletic coach, social sci. tchr. Joplin (Mo.) Sr. High Sch., 1956-63; head social sci. dept. R.L. Turner High Sch., Carrollton, Tex., 1963-66; asst. athletic coach, jr. high sch. social sci. tchr. Warrensburg, Mo., 1966-70; coach, social sci. tchr., Emporia, Kans., 1970-72; asst. cottage dir., counselor Topeka Youth Ctr., 1973—; substitute tchr. Topeka Pub. Schs., 1974—. Recreation dir. Carrollton-Farmer's Br. Recreation Center, Dallas County, Tex., 1964-66; city recreation dir., Warrensburg, Mo., 1966-68. Served with USN, 1953-54. Mem. NEA, Kans. State U.-Pittsburg Alumni Assn., U. Ark. Alumni Assn., Phi Delta Kappa, Sigma Tau Gamma. Democrat. Methodist. Club: Elks. Address: Main PO Box 1009 Topeka KS 66601

VARNER, STERLING VERL, oil company executive; b. Ranger, Tex., Dec. 20, 1919; s. George Virgle and Christina Ellen (Shafer) V.; student Murray State Sch. Agr., 1940, Wichita State U., 1949; m. Paula Jean Kennedy, Nov. 17, 1945; children—Jane Ann, Richard Alan. With Kerr-McGee, Inc., 1941-45, Koch Industries, Inc., Wichita, Kans., 1945—, pres., 1974—; chief operating officer, 1974—, also dir., mem. exec. com.; dir. Fourth Nat. Bank & Trust Co., Dir. Wesley Med. Center, NCCJ. Mem. Assn. Oil Pipelines, Petroleum Industry 25 Year Club, Nat. Petroleum Refiners Assn. Mem. Church of Christ. Clubs: Wichita, Crestview Country. Home: 337 Lynwood Wichita KS 67218 Office: PO Box 2256 Wichita KS 67201

VARNES, DOUGLAS WILLIAM, executive search company executive, speaker; b. Chgo., Oct. 2, 1942; s. Blair and Madeline (Wardan) V.; m. Mary Jean Norton, Aug. 20, 1967 (div. Feb. 1971); 1 child, William Blair; m. Janice Emily Glinka, Mar. 15, 1980; 1 child, Kalyn Kimberly. B.A., Vanderbilt U., 1975; M.B.A., Keller Sch., 1980. Asst. sect. dir. Marshall Fields, Chgo., 1961-65; exec. v.p. Product Communication, Los Angeles, 1970-75; asst. gen. mgr. B. L. Downey Co., Cicero, Ill., 1975-78; div. mgr. Roth Young, Chgo., 1978-82; prin. Search Systems, Oak Brook Ill., 1982-84; pres. Sales & Mktg. Search, Inc., Schaumburg, Ill., 1984—; speaker sales and mktg. motivation seminars; mem. ad hoc membership com. Assn. Finished Products/Soc. Mfg. Engring., Dearborn, Mich., 1983-84. Served to lt. (j.g.) USNR, 1965-68; Vietnam. Recipient appreciation cert. U.S. Navy League, 1965. Mem. Robotics Internat. (sr.), Soc. Mfg. Engring. (sr.). Roman Catholic. Clubs: Lake Shore Ski (pres. 1983-84) (Chgo.); Columbia Yacht. Office: Sales & Mktg Search Inc 1900 E Golf Rd Suite 840 Schaumburg IL 60195

VARNOLD, CECIL BURL, township official; b. Maquon, Ill., Mar. 14, 1912; s. James Martin and Nellie Mae (Smith) V.; m. Ellouise Lorraine Ronesela Conner, Oct. 14, 1943; children—Paul Martin, Richard Mark, Charles Burdette. Rd. commr. Maquon Twp. (Ill.), Maquon, 1939-47, 71-77; owner, operator Varnold Found. & Erection Co., Maquon, 1947-66. Mem. Ill. Assn. Twp. and County Ofcls., Taxpayers Fedn., Internat. Union Operating Engrs. Republican. Methodist. Clubs: Masons, Shriners. Home: PO Box 155 Maquon IL 61458

VARRICCHIO, FREDERICK ELIA, biochemist; b. N.Y.C., May 18, 1938; s. Elia and Anna M. Varricchio; m. Claudette Goulet, Dec. 29, 1962; children—Nicole, Erika. B.S., U. Maine, 1960; M.S., U. N.D., 1964; Ph.D., U. Md., 1966. Assoc. in exptl. pathology Meml. Sloan Kettering Cancer Center, N.Y.C., 1972-77; assoc. prof., dir. grad. studies Life Sci. Center, Nova U., Ft. Lauderdale, Fla., 1977-79; vis. prof. Max Planck Inst. for Ernaehrungsphysiologie Dortmund, W. Ger., 1979; prof., chmn. dept. chemistry Nat. Coll., Lombard, Ill., 1980—; resident assoc. Argonne (Ill.) Nat. Lab., 1980—; faculty research participant Oak Ridge Nat. Lab., 1979—; adj. instr. chemistry Coll. of Du Page, 1980—; clin. prof. biochemistry Loyola U. Dental Sch., 1983—. Am. Cancer Soc. fellow, 1966-68, Deutscher Akademischer Austauschdienst fellow, 1979. Mem. Am. Soc. Biol. Chemists, Am. Assn. Pathologists, Am. Assn. for Cancer Research, Am. Chem. Soc., Sigma Xi, Sigma Chi (sec. N.Y.C. alumni chpt. 1977). Contbr. articles in field to profl. jours. Home: 26 W285 Blackhawk Dr Wheaton IL 60187

VASILAKIS, GEORGE JAMES, dentist; b. Leka, Samos, Greece, Sept. 7, 1943; came to U.S., 1951; s. James George and Mary (Pavlithis) V.; m. Irene Costaras, June 20, 1976; children—Callie, Maria. A.B., Western Res. U., 1965; D.D.S., Case Western Res. U., 1969; M.S. in Gen. Pathology, U. Pitts., 1974. Lab. instr. dept. pathology U. Pitts., 1972-74; asst. prof. Case Western Res. U. Sch. Dentistry, Cleve., 1974-78, assoc. clin. prof., 1978-80; pres., dental practitioner Vasilakis Dental Assocs., Parma, Ohio, 1980—. Contbr. articles to profl. jours. Pres. parish council St. Paul Greek Orthodox Ch., North Royalton, Ohio, 1982-84; bd. dirs. Case Western Res. U. Sch. Dentistry, Cleve., 1982—. Mem. Orgn. Tchrs. Oral Diagnosis, Am. Dental Assn., Am. Orthodontic Soc., Pierre Fouchard Dental Acad., Acad. Gen. Dental Practitioners, Ohio Dental Assn. (alternate del. 1980-84), Psi Omega Dental Alumni (pres. 1982-84), Ahepa. Lodge: Rotary. Home: 11608 Pleasant Ridge Pl Strongsville OH 44136 Office: Vasilakis Dental Assocs 6688 Ridge Rd Parma OH 44129

VASOLD, ARTHUR A., insurance underwriter; b. Saginaw, Mich., Feb. 7, 1941; s. A. Herman and Margaret (Lutz) V.; m. Carole J. Huffman, June 4, 1966; children—Julie, Michael, Candace. B.S., Mich. State U., 1963, M.S., 1968. Chartered life underwriter. Tchr. North Branch Sch., Mich., 1963-66, Rapid River Pub. Sch., Mich., 1967-71; agt. State Farm Ins., Calumet, Mich., 1971—. Trustee Laurium Village, Mich., 1980-83, Copper Country Indsl. Council, Houghton, Mich., 1984. Mem. Copper County Life Underwriters (pres. 1972-73). Lodges: Masons (worshipful master 1979), Elks (exalted ruler). Avocations: farming; skiing; fishing. Home: 117 Iroquois St Laurium MI 49913 Office: State Farm Ins 325 5th St Calumet MI 49913

VASQUEZ, CESAR LUIS, physician; b. Lima, Peru, Sept. 19, 1935; came to U.S., 1978; s. Eulogio and Adelina (Soplin) V.; B.S., San Marcos U., 1954, M.D., 1961; m. Mary Margaret MacAulay, Feb. 7, 1964; children—Roberto Luis, Mario Tonyo, Ian Alexander. Asst. prof., research fellow Inst. Andean Biology, Lima, Peru, 1967-72; assoc. prof. medicine U. San Marcos, Lima, 1972—; med. cons. for Latin Am., Imperial Chem. Industries, Eng., 1969-78; v.p. Vasquez Mgmt. Cons. Internat. Projects, Wadsworth, Ill., 1979—; pres. Vasquez Med. Cons/CME in Peru, 1980—. Colo. Heart Assn. fellow, 1963-64. Mem. Peruvian Heart Assn., Am. Heart Assn., Meeting Planners Internat., N.Y. Acad. Scis., AMA. Roman Catholic. Research on high altitude residents in Peru and Colo., coop. studies on beta-blockers in Latin Am. Home and Office: 38760 Northwoods Dr Wadsworth IL 60083

VASQUEZ, ROSETTA, educational administrator; b. Coldiron, Ky., Feb. 25, 1945; m. Santiago Vasquez, Feb. 3, 1962; 1 child, Cynthia. B.A., Northeastern Ill. U., Chgo., 1976; M.A., Chgo. State U., 1982. Cert. tchr., Ill. Tchr. Chgo. Pub. Schs., 1977-82, human relations specialist, 1982-83, Office Equal Ednl. Opportunity specialist, 1983-84, coordinator trainer inst., 1984—. Chmn. SER-Jobs for Progress, Inc., Chgo., 1980-83. Recipient Dir.'s award SER-Jobs for Progress, Inc., 1973; Chgo. State Acad. Achievement award, 1982. Mem. Phi Delta Kappa (sec.). Home: 2645 S Christina Ave Chicago IL 60623 Office: Chgo Pub Schs Trainer Inst 1819 W Pershing Rd Chicago IL 60609

VATSIS, KOSTAS PETROS, pharmacologist; b. Patras, Greece, May 6, 1945; came to U.S., 1962; naturalized, 1983; s. Petros Dennis and Eugenia (Konstantinopoulou) V.; B.S., Calif. State U.-Long Beach, 1967, M.S., 1969; Ph.D., U. Ill. Coll. Medicine, 1975. Lectr., U. Mich., Ann Arbor, 1976-78; asst. prof. pharmacology Northwestern U., Chgo., 1978-84, assoc. prof., 1984—; cons. U. Ill. Coll. Medicine, Chgo., 1976—. Contbr. articles to sci. jours. NIH grantee, 1980-84; recipient Oral Presentation award Am. Oil Chemistry Soc., 1983. Mem. Soc. Toxicology, Am. Chem. Soc., Am. Soc. Pharmacology and Exptl. Therapeutics (travel award 1984), Sigma Xi. Democrat. Avocations. Fiction, classical music and jazz, sports. Home: 3950 N Lake Shore Dr Apt C-1315 Chicago IL 60613 Office: Northwestern U Med Sch Dept Pharmacology 303 E Chicago Ave Chicago IL 60611

VAUGHAN, DAVID JOHN, distribution company executive; b. Detroit, July 17, 1924; s. David Evans and Erma Mildred V.; A.B., U. Ill., 1950; postgrad. U. Chgo., U. Mo.; m. Anne McKeown Miles, Aug. 21, 1975; children by previous marriage—David John, Melissa Ann, Julia Crawford McLaughlin. Chemist, Midland Electric Colleries, 1950-52; pres. Varrco Distbg. Co., Peoria, Ill., 1953—; prin. David J. Vaughan, investment adv., Peoria, 1970—; investment adviser Fundamentalist Fund; instr. Carl Sandburg Coll., Peoria, 1968—. Served to lt. USAAF, 1942-46, USAF, 1951-52; Korea. Registered investment adv. Mem. Alpha Tau Omega, Phi Eta Sigma, Phi Alpha Delta. Republican. Presbyterian. Clubs: Peoria Country, Northport Point (Mich.); Peoria Skeet, Racquet, Masons, Shriners, Jesters. Home: 4510 N Miller Ave Peoria IL 61614 also 825 Birchwood Point Northport Point MI 49670

VAUGHAN, DELL WILLIAM, publisher, entertainer, broadcast producer; b. Flint, Mich., June 24, 1937; s. Harold Laverne and Evelyn Rose (Doyle) V.; m. Garneta Doris Rose, Mar. 28, 1959; children—Adelbert, Jeffry, Cindy. Student Kirtland Community Coll., 1974. Stockboy, Hamady Bros., Flint, Mich., 1952; lineman Gen. Motors, Flint, 1957-63; truck driver various cos., Flint, 1963-67; pres. Key Constrn., Lupton, Mich., 1967—, Neta Record Co., Lupton, 1982—, Cindy-Jeff Pub. Co., Lupton, 1982—; producer B&B Prodns, Prudenville, Mich., 1983; co-creater, producer Mich. Record Review, Lupton, 1984—. Author and pub. popular songs including Won't You Take My Hand, Soar Like An Eagle, Broken Hearts, Michigan (official song State of Mich.). Served to cpl. USMC, 1954-57. Decorated Nat. Def. medal. Recipient Vol. Services Cert. of Merit, State of Mich., 1984. Mem. Broadcast Music Inc. Avocation: fishing. Home: 3091 Sage Lake Rd Lupton MI 48635 Office: Mich Record Review 3091 Sage Lake Rd Lupton MI 48635

VAUGHAN, SALLY SEDLAK, state agy. adminstr.; b. Springfield, Ill., Jan. 25, 1942; d. Frank A. and Lorraine (Watts) Sedlak. A.A., Gulf Park Coll., 1961; B.A., MacMurray Coll., 1965; M.A., Sangamon State U., 1973. Tchr. remedial reading and English, Pana (Ill.) Jr. High Sch., 1966-67, Springfield High Sch., 1967-70; coordinator community service center Lincoln Land Community Coll., 1974-77; tng. officer Ill. Dept. Aging, Springfield, 1977—; chmn. health and human services Region V Tng. and Edn. Consortium, 1979. Mem. DAR, AAUW, Springfield Art Assn., Jr. League Springfield. Republican. Methodist. Office: 421 E Capitol Springfield IL 62706

VAUGHAN, WILLIAM MACE, environmental specialist; b. Mt. Vernon, N.Y., Aug. 26, 1942; s. William Francis and Nan Louise (Mace) V.; m. Alice Ann Pepper, June 12, 1965; children—David M., Blake E. B.S. in Physics, Wittenberg U., 1964; M.S. in Physics, U. Ill., 1966, Ph.D. in Biophysics, 1969. Research assoc. Washington U., St. Louis, 1969-71; project coordinator Ctr. for Biology of Natural Systems, St. Louis, 1971-74; instr./lectr. Washington U. Engring. Sch., 1973-77; mgr. field services Environ. Measurements, Inc., St. Louis, 1974-78, v.p. services, 1978—; pres., dir. Engring. Mgmt. Info. Corp., St. Louis, 1981-84; sec., dir., cons. EMI Aerodata, St. Louis, 1984—; mgr. Midwest ops. AeroVironment, Inc., St. Louis, 1985—. Chmn. energy com. St. Louis Coalition for the Environment, 1973-79. Mem. Air Pollution Control Assn., AAAS. Lutheran. Avocations: reading; hiking. Office: AeroVironment Inc 8505 Delmar Blvd University City MO 63124

VAUGHN, DONALD WILLIAM, city official, genealogist; b. Yates Center, Kans., Feb. 3, 1930; s. Warren Potter and Edith Vadna (King) V.; m. Wilma Kathryn Morton, Feb. 12, 1950; children—Ronald Dean, Marlene Kay, David Warren. Kans. wastewater treatment cert. Class 4. Operator, Yates Ctr. Water Dept., 1948-53, supt. water, 1953-56; chief operator wastewater treatment City of Lawrence, Kans., 1956-62, plant supr., 1962—. Mem. Kans. Water Pollution Control Assn. (v.p. 1967-68, pres. 1969, William D. Hatfield award 1972), Water Pollution Control Fedn., Douglas County Geneal. Soc. (pres. 1981-83, v.p. 1984). Republican. United Methodist. Avocations: geneaology; photography; organ and piano; sports. Home: 1946 Barker St Lawrence KS 66046 Office: City of Lawrence Wastewater Treatment Plant Box 708 Lawrence KS 66044

VAUGHN, RICHARD ADELBERT, dentist; b. Hamtramck, Mich., Mar. 1, 1935; s. John Oliver and Mildred (Smith) V.; B.S., U. Detroit, 1957, D.D.S., 1961; postgrad. U. Pitts., 1961-64; m. Brenda Farrington, Feb. 18, 1956 (div.); children—Belinda, Richard, Carla; m. 2d, Esther Livingston, Mar. 23, 1974; stepchildren—Ronald Livingston, Andrea Livingston. Practice of dentistry, specializing in oral and maxillofacial surgery, Detroit, 1964— instr. oral surgery U. Pitts., 1962-63; instr. oral and maxillofacial surgery Detroit Gen. Hosp., 1964—, trustee, 1971-79, chmn. superintending com., 1972-73. Mem. Detroit Mayor's Com. Human Resources, Devel. Med. Subcom., Com. Study Med. Care of Indigent; mem. Spl. Admissions Com. U. Detroit Sch. Dentistry; treas., Cub Scouts, Boy Scouts Am., 1966-67, asst. Webelo instr., 1967-68, scoutmaster, 1968-69; trustee, mem. exec. bd. Detroit Med. Center, 1972; bd. dirs. Pres.'s Cabinet, U. Detroit, 1976—. Mem. Gt. Lakes Soc. Oral Surgeons, Am., Nat., Mich., Detroit Dist. (chmn. children's dental health week 1970-71) dental assns., Wolverine Dental Soc. (pres. 1968-69). Am. Dental Soc. Anesthesiology, Detroit Acad. Oral Surgeons, U. Detroit Black Dental Alumni Assn. (chmn. 1974—), U. Detroit Nat. Alumni Assn. (dir. 1973—), Mich. Soc. Oral and Maxillofacial Surgeons. Clubs: Economic, Century (trustee) (Detroit). Home: 1333 Strathcona Dr Detroit MI 48203 Office: 13724 Woodward Highland Park IL 48203

VAWTER, ELVIN GEORGE, retired educational administrator; b. Mansfield, Ohio, Dec. 27, 1925; s. George Samuel and Cosette Mirl (Slick) V.; m. Onnolee Jeanette Morris, Jan. 31, 1948 (div. 1970); children—Gregory Ross, Georgia Lee Vawter Gregory; m. 2d Helen Genevieve Newberry, Dec. 17, 1977. Cert. prin., Ohio. Tchr. Jackson Twp. Schs., Grove City, Ohio, 1948-49, Van Buren Twp. Schs., Kettering, Ohio, 1949-54, Kettering (Ohio) City Schs., 1957-59; purchasing agt. Huber Constrn. Co., Dayton, Ohio, 1954-56; mgr. Jackson County Lumber Co., Ravenswood, W.Va., 1956-57; prin. Moraine Meadows Sch., Kettering, Ohio, 1959-82, ret., 1982. Served with USAF, 1944-45. Mem. NEA (life), Ohio Edn. Assn. (life), Nat. Assn. Elem. Sch. Prins. (conv. discussion leader 1970, cons. 1973), Ohio Assn. Elem. Sch. Prins. (bd. dirs. zone 3 1974-76), Kettering Classroom Tchrs. Assn. (pres. 1953-54), Western Ohio Elem. Prins. Assn. (pres. 1972-74), Phi Delta Kappa. Club: Dayton Pilots'.

VEENHUIS, BRIAN CHARLES, lawyer; b. Flint, Mich., Sept. 14, 1944; s. Melvin Leslie and Carolyn Eileen (Burr) V.; m. Jeanette Carol Barajas, Oct. 17, 1975; children—Erik Brian, Ethan Daniel. B.S. in Edn., Central Mich. U., 1968; J.D., Detroit Coll. Law, 1982. Bar: Mich. 1983, U.S. Dist. Ct. (ea. dist.) Mich. 1983. Clk. Fisher Body, Grand Blanc, Mich., 1966; tchr. North Branch Schs., Mich., 1966-67, Flint Pub. Schs., Mich., 1967-83; sole practice, Flint, 1983—. Mem. staff Reigle for Congress, Flint, 1972, Kildee for Commr., Flint, 1984; dir. Kildee for State Rep., Flint, 1980; student vol. coordinator Carter Townhall Meeting, Flint, 1980; bd. dirs. Social Services for Hearing Impaired, Flint, 1984—. Mem. ABA, State Bar Mich., Mich. Edn. Assn., Genesee County Bar Assn. (com. chair 1983), United Tchrs. Flint (pres. 1973-74). Democrat. Home: 1925 Park Forest Dr Flint MI 48502 Office: 727 S Grand Traverse Flint MI 48502

VEENSTRA, H. ROBERT, cons. engr.; b. Leighton, Iowa, Oct. 21, 1921; s. Henry and Gretta (Vandehaar) V.; B.S. in Civil Engring., Iowa State U., 1947; m. Norena D. Grandia, Sept. 9, 1944; children—Henry Robert, Cynthia L., John N., Mark A. Design engr. Stanley Engring. Co., Muscatine, Iowa, 1947-49, sect. head, 1949-51, project engr., 1951-57, supervising engr., 1957-61; partner Veenstra & Kimm, Engrs. & Planners, West Des Moines, 1961-80; chmn. bd. Veenstra & Kimm, Inc., Engrs. & Planners, West Des Moines, 1980—. Served to capt. AUS, 1942-46. Fellow ASCE, Am. Council Cons. Engrs.; mem. Nat. Soc. Profl. Engrs. (past nat. dir.), Iowa Engring. Soc. (Anson Marston award 1962), Am. Congress on Surveying and Mapping, Cons. Engrs. Council Iowa (past pres.), ASTM, Am. Water Works Assn., Water Pollution Control Fedn., Theta Xi. United Methodist. Club: Masons. Contbr. articles to profl. jours. Office: 300 West Bank Bldg 1601 22nd St West Des Moines IA 50265

VELAER, CHARLES ALFRED, ret. educator; b. Kansas City, Mo., Jan. 25, 1932; s. Charles Alfred and Edna (Bothwell) V.; B.S., Roosevelt U., 1957; M.S., Ill. Inst. Tech., 1960; m. Caryl Ruth Sonnenburg, Nov. 17, 1962; children—Ruth Anne, Charles Alfred. Instr., asst. prof. Roosevelt U., Chgo., 1957-68, asso. prof. physics, 1968-74, ret., 1974; cons. New Horizons Pub., Inc., Chgo. Served with Signal Corps, AUS, 1950-54. Mem. Am. (cons. rosarian 1971—), English, Chgo. Regional (dist. pres. 1966-67, dir. 1968—) rose socs., Am. Inst. Physics. Home: 9636 S Brandt Ave Oak Lawn IL 60453

VENARD, DAVID, banker, consultant, educator; b. Hinsdale, Ill., Nov. 27, 1955; s. Richard T. and Mary R. (Spelich) V.; m. Diane L. Levy, Aug. 5, 1979. B.S. in Acctg. summa cum laude, Bradley U., 1977. C.P.A., Ill. Supr. Ernst & Whinney, Chgo., 1977-84; v.p. fin. Parkway Bank & Trust Co. and First State Bank Chgo., 1984—; pres. Dane Assocs., Inc., Chgo., 1982—, Horizon Systems, 1983—; dir., treas. The Perfect Nut Co., Chgo. Editor, author course manual Bank Operations, Accounting and Auditing, and Bank Profitability, 1983-84. Bd. dirs., treas. Horwitz-Slavin Meml. Cancer Research Found., Northbrook, Ill., 1978-84. Mem. Am. Inst. C.P.A.s (tech. adv. 1984), Ill. C.P.A. Soc. (instr. 1982—, specialized com. banking 1981—), Chgo. Fin. Microcomputer Users Group (dir. 1985—), Delta Upsilon Internatl. (bd. dirs., asst. treas. 1983—), Bradley Delta Upsilon (bd. dirs., pres. 1977—). Republican. Jewish. Club: River (Chgo.). Avocations: skydiving; hang gliding; golf; travel.

VENDER, CARL STANLEY, mining and civil engineer; b. Great Falls, Mont., Jan. 26, 1948; s. Fred and Zelma (Cunnington) V.; m. Mildred Ann Wickstrom, May 26, 1971; children—Charles, Bradley, Michael. A.A. No. Mont. Coll., 1969. Registered profl. surveyor, Mont., N.D. Rodman, Mont. Hwy. Dept., Helena, 1969-70; engr. Knife River Coal, Bismarck, N.D., 1971—. Mem. N.D. Soc. Profl. Surveyors (state officer 1979-84), Nat. Soc. Profl. Surveyors (chmn. com. 1983—), N.D. Soc. Profl. Surveyors (newsletter editor 1979—), Am. Congress Surveying and Mapping (chmn. com. 1983—), Soc. Mining Engrs., Mont. Assn. Profl. Surveyors. Office: Knife River Coal 1915 N Kawaney Dr Bismarck ND 58501

VENEMA, WILLIAM JOHN, pediatrician; b. Grand Rapids, Mich., Feb. 24, 1937; s. Charles J. and Amy Ruth (Van Peenan) V.; m. Carol Ann Duerr, Aug. 19, 1961; children—Charles William, Amy Margaret. B.A., Kalamazoo Coll., 1959; M.D., U. Mich., 1963. Diplomate Am. Bd. Pediatrics. Pediatric intern U. Mich., Ann Arbor, 1963-64, redisent in pediatrics, 1964-66; mem. faculty So. Mich. Area Health Edn. Corp., Kalamazoo, 1968—; pvt. practice medicine specializing in pediatrics, Kalamazoo, 1968—; chief pediatric sect. Bronson Methodist Hosp., Kalamazoo, 1979-81; vol. missionary M.L. Lyles Hosp., Madanapalle, India, 1984. Bd. dirs. Constance Brown Hearing and Speech Ctr., Kalamazoo, 1968-72, Family and Children's Service, Kalamazoo, 1969-74. Served to capt. USAF, 1966-68. Mem. Am. Acad. Pediatrics, West Mich. Pediatric Soc. (pres. 1976-77), Kalamazoo Acad. Medicine (chmn. legis. com. 1982-83), Mich. State Med. Soc. (legis. com. 1981—). Democrat. Contbr. articles to profl. publs. Home: 2125 Sheffield Dr Kalamazoo MI 49008 Office: 517 Pleasant Ave Kalamazoo MI 49008

VENGLARCHIK, ANDREW STEFAN, JR., insurance executive; b. Monaca, Pa., Nov. 23, 1922; s. Andrew Stefan and Mary Martha (Stas) V. Student Western Res. U., 1945-50. Clk. typist Comml. Motor Freight Co., Cleve., 1941; jr. buyer S.K. Wellman div. Abex Corp., Bedford, Ohio, 1941-66; pres. Slovak Gymnastic Union Sokol of U.S.A., East Orange, N.J., 1967-83; pres. Sokol Apts., Inc., Astoria, N.Y., 1975-83, Falcon Apts. Inc., 1967-74, 78-83; adminstrv. mgr. research and devel. Mego Corp., 1979-83. Mem. N.J. Ethnic Communities Congress, N.J. Bicentennial Ethnic Council, Nat. Ethnic Racial Alliance of Am. Revolution Bicentennial Commn., AAU, Nat., N.J. (pres. 1976-77), N.Y. fraternal congresses. Roman Catholic. Club: Slovak Gymnastic Union Sokol of U.S.A., Nat. Slovak Soc. U.S.A. Home: 1226 S New Wilke Rd Arlington Heights IL 60005

VENIT, WILLIAM BENNETT, electrical products company executive, consultant; b. Chgo., May 28, 1931; s. George Bernard and Ida (Schaffel) V.; student U. Ill., Champaign, 1949; m. Nancy Jean Carlson, Jan. 28, 1956; children—Steven Louis, Aprilann. Sales mgr. Coronet, Inc., Chgo., 1952-63, pres., chmn. bd., 1963-74; pres., chmn. bd. Roma Wire Inc., Chgo., 1971-74; pres. Wm. Allen Inc., Chgo., 1972-74; pres., chmn. bd. William Lamp Co., Inc., William Wire Co., Inc., 1974-76; pres., chmn. bd. MSWV, Inc., 1981—; pres. Trio Steel Inc., Chgo.; spl. cons. MacKinney Co. cons. Nu Style Lamp Shade, Chgo. Sunbeam Clock Co., Hackensack, N.J., Moschiano Plating, Chgo., Spartus Corp., Chgo., Seth Thomas, Athens, Ga. Served with Q.M.C., AUS, 1949-52. Mem. Mfr. Agt. Club, Chgo. Lamp and Shade Inst. (dir.). Home: 4850 N Monticello Ave Chicago IL 60625 Office: 5512 W Lawrence Ave Chicago IL 60630 also 320 Suwanee Ave Sarasota FL 33508

VENTO, BRUCE FRANK, congressman: b. St. Paul, Oct. 7, 1940; s. Frank A. and Ann V. (Sauer) V.; B.A., Wis. State U., River Falls, 1965; postgrad. U. Minn., 1966—; m. Mary Jean Moore, Oct. 24, 1959; children—Michael, Peter, John. Tchr. sci., social studies Mpls. pub. schs., from 1965; mem. Minn. Ho. of Reps. from St. Paul 66A Dist., 1971-76, asst. majority leader, vice chmn. jud. com., 1973-76; mem. 95th-99th Congresses from 4th Minn. Dist., chmn. nat. parks and recreation subcom. Mem. legis. rev. com. Minn. Commn. on Future. Del., Democratic Farm Labor party Central Com., from 1972, chmn. Ramsey County Com., from 1972. NSF grantee, 1967-68. Mem. Minn. Fedn. Tchrs., Beta Beta Beta, Kappa Delta Phi. Office: 2433 Rayburn House Office Bldg Washington DC 20515 also 150 Mears Park Place 405 Sibley St Saint Paul MN 55101*

VENTRES, ROMEO JOHN, See *Who's Who in America,* 43rd edition.

VERBECK, WILLARD LEROY, vocational educator; b. Kearney, Nebr., Feb. 27, 1944; s. Raymond E. and Edyn M. (Jarzynka) V.; m. Raeleen Gail Duncan, Aug. 1965; children—Kimberlee Ann, Kellee Jo. B.S. in Bus. Edn., U. Nebr., 1972; M.S. in Vocat. Edn., Kearney State Coll., 1975. Cert. edn. and adminstrn., Nebr., Iowa, S.D. Bus. edn. instr. Alliance and Doniphan Schs., Nebr., 1972-76; adult edn. dir. Alliance City Schs., Nebr., 1976-77; vocat. dir. Edn. Service Unit No 5, Beatrice, Nebr., 1977-78; vocat. asst. dir. Northwestern Iowa Tech. Coll., Sheldon, 1978-79; vocat. dir. Western Dakota Vocat.-Tech., Rapid City, S.D., 1979—. Mem. Econ. Understanding Com., Rapid City, S.D. Served with USCG, 1964-68. Mem. Am. Vocat. Assn. (program developer 1980, award 1981), S.D. Vocat. Assn., Am. Soc. for Personnel Devel., Black Hills Personnel Assn. (pres., v.p., sec. 1982—), C. of C. Roman Catholic. Lodge: Am. Legion. Avocations: home remodeling and woodworking; hunting; fishing; golf. Home: 3705 Western Ave Rapid City SD 57702 Office: Western Vocat Tech Inst 2300 E St Charles St Rapid City SD 57702

VERDUGO, DARIO G., automotive company executive; b. Santiago, Chile, Mar. 28, 1941; came to U.S., 1966; s. Dario B. and Adriana (Gormaz) V.; m. Nancy A. Nikkinen, Dec. 15, 1969 (div. May 1974); m. 2d, Barbara Marie Wickert, Apr. 10, 1977; children—Lindsay A., Julie A., Diana P. B.A. in Econs., U. Chile, Santiago, 1966; M.B.A., U. Calif.-Berkeley, 1968. Fin. analyst Xerox Corp., Rochester, N.Y., summers 1966-67; staff systems analyst Ford Motor Co., Dearborn Mich., 1968-70, staff fin. analyst, 1971-75; mgr. fin. studies Ford Venezuela, 1976-78, treas., Caracas, 1979-80; mgr. internat. fin. Chrysler Corp., Highland Park, Mich., 1980-82, mgr. bus. devel., 1983—; fellow Wolfson Coll., U. Cambridge (Eng.), 1979. Bd. dirs. Foxcroft, Bloomfield Twp., Mich., 1983; mem. Internat. Visitors Council, Detroit, 1984. Mem. Am. Mgmt. Assn. Home: 5590 Fieldston Ct Birmingham MI 48010

VERHOFF, JOHN EDWARD, family physician; b. Columbus, Ohio, Dec. 13, 1934; s. Adolph William and Ruth Mary (Spangler) V.; m. Patricia Ann Boeke, Sept. 1, 1956 (div. Sept. 1976); children—John Edward, Amy, Emily, Timothy; m. 2d, Virginia Lee Ruisinger, Dec. 13, 1979; children—Keith, Kim. B.A., Ohio State U., 1959, M.D., 1959. Diplomate Am. Bd. Family Practice. Intern Mt. Carmel Hosp., Columbus, 1959-60; practice medicine specializing in family practice, Columbus, 1960—; pres. Beechcroft Family Practice Inc.; mem. staff Riverside Meth. Hosp., Mt. Carmel Hosp., St. Ann's Hosp.; mem. faculty Riverside Methodist Hosp., Columbus; clin. asst. prof. Ohio State U. Sch. Medicine. Mem. adv. bd. rehab. div. Indsl. Commn., Columbus. Served as capt. U.S. Army, 1966-68. Mem. Columbus and Franklin County Med. Assn., Ohio State Med. Assn., Central Ohio Acad. Family Physicians, Ohio Acad. Family Physicians, Am. Acad. Family Physicians. Republican. Roman Catholic. Lodge: K.C. Home: 8035 McKitrick Rd Plain City OH 43065 Office: 5797 Beechcroft Rd Columbus OH 43229

VERMEULEN, GERALD DONALD, pathologist; b. Geneseo, Ill., Oct. 3, 1939; s. Lawrence Felix and Esther Margaret (Cummings) V.; student U. Ill., Champaign, 1957-60; M.D., U. Ill., Chgo., 1964. Intern, San Francisco Gen. Hosp., 1964-65; resident in gen. surgery U. Calif., San Francisco, 1965-66; resident in pathology U. Ill. Hosp., Chgo., 1973-77, asst. prof. pathology, 1977-78; dir. labs. Silver Cross Hosp., Joliet, Ill., 1979—. Served with USPHS, 1966-73. Fellow Am. Soc. Clin. Pathologists, Coll. Am. Pathology; mem. Am. Soc. Microbiology, AMA, Ill. State Med. Soc. Contbr. articles to profl. jours. Office: Silver Cross Hospital 1200 Maple Rd Joliet IL 60432

VERNON, ARTHUR E., pharmacist; b. Ashland, Ohio, Sept. 21, 1944; m. Susan Elberty, 1967; children—Elizabeth Anne, Andrew Elberty. B.S. in Pharmacy, Ohio No. U., 1967, postgrad., 1967-84. Registered pharmacist, Ohio. Co-owner Reynolds Drugs, Orrville, Ohio, 1967—. Com. mem. Trinity United Meth. Ch., 1967-84; active Orrville United Way., 1970-84; pres. Orrville Hist. Mus., 1974-85; bd. dirs. Orrville C. of C., 1970-84; active Orrville Revitalization Campaign. Mem. Am. Pharm. Assn., Ohio State Pharm. Assn., Wayne Pharm. Assn. (pres.), Nat. Woodcarvers Club. Lodge: Internat. Orgn. Odd Fellows. Avocations: conservation; reforestation for wildlife; ecology; art, carving. Home: 1185 N Crownhill Rd Orrville OH 44667 Office: 120 N Main St Orrville OH 44667

VERNON, DUANE RICHARD, credit bureau executive; b. Ithaca, Mich., Sept. 3, 1931; s. Wesley Robert and Leah Amelia (Smith) V.; B.A. in Personnel Adminstrn., Mich. State U., 1953; m. Virginia Louise Graff, Apr. 4, 1954 (dec. 1975); children—Rick, Nancy, Mary Jo. Asst. mgr. affiliated divs. Mich. Retailers Assn., Lansing, 1956-59; dir. sales and pub. relations Credit Bur. Greater Lansing, 1959-74, pres., gen. mgr., 1974—; active in enactment Mich. Equal Credit Opportunity Act, 1977; lectr. Mich. State U., Lansing Community Coll., Cooley Law Sch. Pres., Lansing Jaycees, 1961-62; bd. dirs., capital area div. campaign chmn. United Way, Lansing, 1962-68; pres. Lansing Vol. Bur., 1967-68; bd. dirs. Easter Seal Soc. Mid-Mich., 1975-81, Mich. State U. Devel. Council, 1977-81, Camp Highfields, 1977-83; exec. bd. Chief Okemos council Boy Scouts Am.; charter bd. dirs. Mid-Mich. chpt. Nat. Football Found. and Hall of Fame; Mid-Mich. chmn. Olympathon '79. Served with U.S. Army, 1954-56. Recipient Lansing Jaycees Key Man award, 1960, Lansing Outstanding Young Man of Yr. award, 1963, Jaycee Internat. Senator award, 1978; Outstanding Club Pres.'s award Mich. State U. Alumni Assn., 1969; Disting. Alumni award Delta Tau Delta, 1978, Vandervoort Meml. award Downtown Coaches Club of Lansing, 1978, service award Mich. State U. Varsity, Club, 1982, emerald award Mich. State U. Women's Swimming, 1982, others. Mem. Assoc. Credit Burs. Mich. (pres. 1979-80, Gold Key Leadership award 1978, Exec. Achievement award 1979), Pub. Relations Assn. Mich., Retail Credit Grantors Assn. Lansing (pres. 1961-62), Mid-Mich. Personnel Assn., Lansing Assn. Credit Mgmt. (bd. dirs. 1977-79), Lansing Regional C. of C. (bd. dirs. 1981—), Mich. State U. Alumni Club (pres. 1969). Methodist. Clubs: Rotary (pres. 1980-81), Downtown Coaches (bd. dirs. 1979-83, pres. 1983), Greater Lansing Bull-Pen (pres. 1972), Waverly High Sch. Sideliners Athletic Boosters (pres. 1977-79), Waverly Swim (dir. 1977-79), Box 23 of Lansing (chief 1982-83), Lansing Rotary (pres. found. 1981-82). Home: 4315 Wagon Wheel St Lansing MI 48917 Office: 520 S Washington St Lansing MI 48901

VERNON, WALTER NEWTON, III, business executive, lawyer; b. Dallas, Aug. 21, 1935; s. Walter Newton and Ruth (Mason) V.; m. Barbara May Jensen, June 14, 1958; children—Walter Newton, Eric Eugene, Alex Cay. B.B.A., So. Meth. U., 1957, J.D., 1961, LL.M., 1971. Bar: Tex. 1961, Mo. 1966, U.S. Supreme Ct. 1970. Sole practice, Dallas, 1961-63; assoc. counsel Campbell Taggart, Dallas, 1963-73; exec. v.p., sec., counsel, chief exec. officer Kansas City (Mo.) Bd. Trade, 1973-83; pres. Bartlett Futures, Inc., 1983—; writer, speaker on commodity futures and related legal subjects. Mem. Johnston County Wholesale Water Dist. 1 Bd., 1979—, sec., 1979—, chmn. engring. com., 1979-85; mem. Shawnee Mission (Kans.) East Dist. Adv. Bd., 1980—; mem. Shawnee Mission Sch. Bd., 1976-77. Served with M.I., USAR, 1957-63. Mem. ABA, Tex. Bar Assn., Mo. Bar Assn., Kansas City C. of C. (chmn. agri-bus. council 1985—), Futures Industry Assn. Methodist. Contbr. articles to profl. jours. Office: 4800 Main St Suite 460 Kansas City MO 64112

VERSIC, LINDA JOAN, nurse educator, research company executive; b. Grove City, Pa., Aug. 27, 1944; d. Robert and Kathryn I. (Fagird) Davies; m. Ronald James Versic, June 11, 1966; children—Kathryn Clara, Paul Joseph.

R.N., Johns Hopkins Sch. of Nursing, 1965; B.S. in Health Edn., Central State U., 1980. Asst. head nurse, Johns Hopkins Hosp., Balt., 1965-67; staff Nurse Registry Miami Valley Hosp., Dayton, Ohio, 1973—; instr. Miami Jacobs Jr. Coll. Bus., Dayton, 1977-79; pres. Ronald T. Dodge Co., Dayton, 1979—; instr. Warren County (Ohio) Career Center, 1980-84, coordinator diversified health occupations, 1984—. Youth coordinator, Queen of Apostles Community, 1978-80. Active Miami Valley Mil. Affairs Assn.; Oakwood Hist. Soc., Cox Arboretum, Friends of Smith Gardens. Mem. Ohio Vocat. Assn., Am. Vocat. Assn., Vocat. Indsl. Clubs Am. (chpt. advisor 1982—). Roman Catholic. Club: Johns Hopkins, Yugoslav of Greater Dayton. Home: 1601 Shafor Blvd Dayton OH 45419 Office: Ronald T Dodge Co PO Box J Dayton OH 45409

VERSTEGEN, DENNIS ALLAN, manufacturing company executive; b. Appleton, Wis., Aug. 20, 1939; s. John and Irene (Piepenburg) V.; m. Ann Elliott Ferguson, May 10, 1967 (div. May 1972); children—Britt Elizabeth, Ian Ferguson; m. Janice Elaine Lyman, Apr. 27, 1980. B.S. in Indsl. Engring., GMI Inst. Engring and Mgmt., 1961. Program mgr. Olin Corp., East Alton, Ill., 1969-73; sr. program mgr. Accuray Inc., Columbus, Ohio, 1973-76; gen. mgr. Tru-Cor Corp., Menasha, Wis., 1976-79; bus. devel. mgr. Diversified Control Co., Madison, Wis., 1979-80; cost improvement mgr. Rayovac Corp., Madison, 1981-83; mfg. mgr. Columbia Parcar Co., Deerfield, Wis., 1984—; cons., Madison, 1976—. Contbr. articles to profl. jours. Patentee sealing methods. Officer CAP, Wis., Mich., 1955-62; advisor Jr. Achievement, Wis. and Mich., 1965-67, Boy Scouts Am., Mich., 1968. Mem. Inst. Indsl. Engrs. (activity chmn. 1977-78), Soc. Am. Valve Engrs., Soc. Mfg. Engrs., Am. Prodn. and Inventory Control Soc., Nat. Council Corvette Clubs (bd. govs. 1965-66). Avocations: automobile and real estate restoration; flying. Home: 5217 Hammersley Rd Madison WI 53711

VERTICCHIO, RICK, lawyer; b. Litchfield, Ill., July 10, 1953; s. Paul C. and Marge (Lacy) V.; m. Jamie Lee Barry, Feb. 9, 1979; children—Gina Maria, Jonathan Barry. B.A. with honors, Ill. Coll., Jacksonville, 1975; J.D. (3d in class), So. Ill. U., 1978. Bar: Ill. 1978, U.S. Dist. Ct. (cen. and so. dists.) Ill. 1980, U.S. Ct. Appeals (4th cir.), 1980. Mem. Verticchio & Verticchio, Gillespie, Ill., 1978—; asst. pub. defender Macoupin County, 1980—. Editor So. Ill. Law Jour. Recipient William Jennings Bryant award for Polit. Sci., Ill. Coll., 1975; C.J.S. award for Legal Scholarship, 1977; Order of Barrister for Appellate Advocacy, 1978. Democrat. Roman Catholic. Home: 1205 Jane Dr Gillespie IL 62033 Office: Verticchio & Verticchio 100 E Chestnut St Gillespie IL 62033

VERYSER, THOMAS JAMES, dentist; b. Detroit, Apr. 17, 1946; s. H. James and Dorothy M. (Miller) V.; m. Karen Marie Kroha, Nov. 28, 1970; children—Jeffery, Renee. Student Aquinas Coll., 1964-66; D.D.S., U. Detroit, 1970. Pvt. practice dentistry, Ubly and Bad Axe, Mich., 1970—; chief dentistry Huron Meml. Hosp., Bad Axe, 1974—, trustee, v.p., pres., 1976—. Mem. Am. Equilibration Soc., ADA, Acad. Gen. Dentistry, Mich. Dental Assn., Omicron Kappa Upsilon, Alpha Sigma Nu. Roman Catholic. Avocations: boating; skiing; hunting; fishing. Home: N McKichen Rd Bad Axe MI 48413 Office: 1080 S Van Dyke Bad Axe MI 48413

VESPERENY, CATHERINE R., reporter; b. St. Louis, Sept. 7, 1954; d. Thomas E. and Kathy (Henry) Vespereny. B.A. magna cum laude, U. Mo.-St. Louis, 1976. News clk. Christian Sci. Monitor, Boston, 1976; with Post-Dispatch, St. Louis, 1976—, editorial writer, 1979-80, reporter, 1980—. Bd. dirs. St. Louis Journalism Rev., 1982—. Mem. NEA (Horace Mann award Mo. chpt. 1983), Sigma Delta Chi (Con Lee Kelliher award 1983). Club: Investigative Reporters and Editors, Inc. Office: Post-Dispatch 900 N Tucker Blvd Saint Louis MO 63101

VESSENES, PETER, marketing executive; b. Oak Park, Ill., Oct. 16, 1950; s. Daniel John and Theodora (Karedis) V.; m. Katherine Louise Kammerzell, July 28, 1974; children—Peter Joseph, Theodore Jason, Sarah Katherine. B.A., U. Denver, 1976. System cons. Comprehensive Health Planning So. Ill., Carbondale, 1975; pres. PKV Assocs., Black River Falls, Wis., 1976—; pres. Polygon, Inc., Black River Falls, 1981-82; sr. mktg. exec. Computerland, Inc., Madison, Wis., 1983—; product devel. cons. Tex. Instruments, 1983—. Republican. Office: Computerland of Madison 632 Grand Canyon Dr Madison WI 53719

VEST, CHARLES MARSTILLER, university dean, mechanical engineering educator, consultant; b. Morgantown, W.Va., Sept. 9, 1941; s. Marvin Lewis and Winifred Louise (Buzzard) V.; m. Rebecca Ann McCue, June 8, 1963; children—Ann Kemper, John Andrew. B.S.M.E., W.Va. U., 1963; M.S.E., U. Mich., 1964, Ph.D., 1967. Asst. prof. mech. engring. U. Mich., 1968-72, head interferometric holography group Willow Run Labs., 1970-73, assoc. prof., 1972-77, prof., 1977—, assoc. dean acad. affairs Coll. Engring., 1981—; vis. assoc. prof. Stanford U., 1974-75. Recipient Excellence in Research award U. Mich. Coll. Engring., 1980, Disting. Service award, 1972. Fellow Optical Soc. Am.; mem. ASME, Sigma Xi, Tau Beta Pi, Pi Tau Sigma. Presbyterian. Author: Holographic Interferometry, 1979; assoc. editor Jour. Optical Soc. Am., 1982—; contbr. articles to profl. jours. Home: 910 Kuebler Dr Ann Arbor MI 48103 Office: Coll Engineering U Mich Ann Arbor MI 48109

VETTER, DALE BENJAMIN, educator; b. Henry County, Ill., Aug. 11, 1908; s. John and Esther (Soliday) V.; A.B., North Central Coll., 1930; A.M., Northwestern U., 1935, Ph.D., 1946; m. Frona A. Tonkinson, Mar. 28, 1932; children—Sharon, Ione, Judith, Rebecca. Prin. Hooppole High Sch., 1932-35; tchr. Harrison Pub. Sch., 1936-37; teacher-librarian Riverside-Brookfield High Sch., 1937-41; prof. English, Ill. State U., 1941-76, prof. emeritus, 1976—. Exec. com. Midwest English Conf., 1962-76. Mem. Am. Assn. U. Profs., Mod. Lang. Assn. Am., Northwestern U. Alumni Assn., Ill. Am. Soc. 18th Century Studies, Newberry Library Assos. Augustan Reprint Soc., Friends of Milner Library, Newberry Library (fellow). Unitarian. Author articles, Bull. of Friends of Milner Library, Ill. State Normal Bull., Modern Language Notes. Home: 214 W Willow St Normal IL 61761

VETTER, JAMES L., food research association administrator; b. St. Louis, Jan. 26, 1933; s. Charles W. and Dorothy (Smith) V.; m. Rose Marie Gentille, Aug. 21, 1954; children—Douglas John, Debra Dianne. A.B., Washington U., St. Louis, 1954; M.S., U. Ill., 1955, Ph.D., 1958. Food technologist Monsanto Co., St. Louis, 1958-63; dir. research Keebler Co., Elmhurst, Ill., 1963-72; v.p. tech. dir. div. Standard Brands, Franklin Park, Ill., 1972-75; pres. West Tex. Milling, Amarillo, 1975-77; v.p. Am. Inst. Baking, Manhattan, Kans., 1977—; adj. prof. Kans. State U., Manhattan, 1977—; tech. cons. Editor: Adding Nutrients to Foods, 1982; Dairy Products for Cereal Processing, 1984. Contbr. articles to profl. jours. Patentee in field. Bd. dirs., pres. Wharton Manor Nursing Home, Inc., Manhattan, 1980—. Mem. Inst. Food Technologists, Am. Assn. Cereal Chemists (sec. 1983-85), Phi Tau Sigma. Lodge: Kiwanis (dir.). Avocations: photography; golf. Home: 1947 Bluestem Terr Manhattan KS 66502 Office: Am Inst Baking 1213 Bakers Way Manhattan KS 66502

VEY, MILDRED JOANE, educator, nurse; b. Pitts., Mar. 16, 1929; d. Eugene Charles and May Julia (Thunell) V.; B.A. in Math., Benedictine Coll., 1959; M.A. in Math., Montclair State U., 1970; A.A. in Nursing, St. Louis Community Coll. at Forest Park, 1976; postgrad. Peru State Coll., 1963-64, U. Nev., 1964, U. Colo., 1965-66, U. Kans., 1967-68, U. Mo., 1969-70, Creighton U., 1971-72; M.A. in Spl. Edn., St. Louis U., 1984, M.A. in Edn., 1985. Joined Benedictine Order, Roman Catholic Ch., 1948; tchr. math., art, parochial and pub. schs., Kans., Colo., Nebr., Mo., 1949-71; nurse St. Catherine's Hosp., Omaha, 1970-72; nurse Alexian Bros. Hosp., St. Louis, 1975-80; tchr. Continued Edn. Project, Alt. Sch. for Pregnant Girls, St. Louis Pub. Schs., 1978—, head dept., 1978—; oil painter, genealogist. Chairperson United Way, St. Louis, United Negro Coll. Fund, St. Louis, United Black Community Fund. Carnegie Mus. scholar, 1943-46; NSF scholar, 1965-68; Parsons-Blewett scholar, 1979—; cert. tchr., Mo. Mem. Nat. Council Tchrs. Math., Am. Assn. Ret. Persons, Am. Fedn. Tchrs., Math. Club Greater St. Louis, St. Louis U. Alumni, Benedictine Alumni, Montclair Alumni, Forest Park Alumni, Kappa Mu Epsilon. Democrat. Club: Social. Home: PO Box 7391A Saint Louis MO 63177

VIAL, PAUL ROBERT, security advisor; b. Rockford, Ill., May 25, 1956; s. William Robert and Jane Ethyl (Ryden) V.; m. Suzanne Marie Ryan, Nov. 21, 1981. B.A., U. Ill.-Chgo., 1979. Childcare worker Maryville Acad., Des Plaines, Ill., 1979-80; regional security advisor, polygraph examiner Ace Hardware Corp., Oak Brook, Ill., 1980—. Mem. Fgn. Policy Assn. (assoc.), Am. Soc. Indsl. Security. Republican. Congregationalist. Office: Ace Hardware Corp 2200 Kensington Ct Oak Brook IL 60521

VICE, DAVID G., telecommunications company executive. Pres. Northern Telecommunication Can., Ltd., Islington, Ont. Office: Northern Telecommunication Can Ltd 304 The East Mall Islington ON M9B 6E4 Canada*

VICKERS, NAOMI R., real estate manager; b. Anderson, Ind., Mar. 25, 1917; d. Floyd Leroy and Gertrude Marie (Richards) Stamm; m. Robert Ross Vickers (dec.); children—Robert Vernon, Richard Ross, Philip Leroy, Denise (Mrs. Michael Eugene Lennen). Sec., treas. Vickers Fine Homes, Anderson, 1951—, Vickers Apts., 1956—; sec., treas. Comml. Bldgs., 1958—. Mem. Toy Collectors Am. (antique toy train collector). Mem. Order Eastern Star, White Shrine, Madison County Shrine. Home: 2003 E 7th St Anderson IN 46012 Office: 2006 E 7th St Anderson IN 46012

VICKERY, MILLIE MARGARET, photographer, journalist; b. Clinton County, Ind., Apr. 29, 1920; d. Walter L. and Opal M. (Small) Cox; m. Eugene Livingstone Vickery, Dec. 21, 1941; children—Douglas Eugene, Constance Michelle Suski, Anita Sue Ramsey, Jon Livingstone. Student Ind. U., 1938-42, U. Toledo, 1944. Writer, Sheridan News (Ind.), 1937-38; floor mgr. Lamsons Dept. Store, Toledo, 1943-45; receptionist, bookkeeper Office E.L. Vickery, M.D., Lena, Ill., 1946-85; freelance writer-photographer, Lena, 1964—. Author: P.S. I Love You, 1983; editor Pulse of the Doctor's Wife mag., 1966-78; contbg. editor MD's Wife mag., 1964-74; contbr. articles and photographs to various newspapers and mags. Bd. dirs. Highland Coll. Found., Freeport, Ill., 1970—. Recipient Pacesetter award Highland Community Coll., Freeport, 1978; Sweepstake award, several 1st trophies Rockford Cooking Contests (Ill.), 1979-81; Disting. Alumnae award Marion-Adams High Sch., Sheridan, Ind., 1981. Mem. Ill. Woman's Press Assn. (pres. 1971-73, over 40 writing awards, Woman of Achievement award 1984), Nat. Fedn. Press Women (dir. 1971-73, Nat. Woman of Achievement nominee 1984), Ill. State Med. Soc. Aux. (state pres. 1975-76, Ill. Humanitarian of the Yr. award 1984), Ill. Acad. Family Physicians Aux. (state pres. 1976-77), Ill. Press Photographers Assn., Women in Communications, Mortar Board, Delta Delta Delta, Beta Sigma Phi (pres. chpt. 1950, 72, Order of Rose award 1981, internat. award of Distinction 1982, photography award 1982-84). Republican. Mem. Evangel. Free Church. Clubs: Lena Women's, Lena Golf. Lodges: Order Eastern Star, PEO. Home: 602 Oak St Lena IL 61048

VICKREY, ROBERT FISCHER, newspaper/broadcasting executive; b. Mendota, Ill., May 21, 1944; s. Gail Sabin and Marie Augusta (Fischer) V.; m. Barbara Ann Harmon, May 30, 1970; 1 son, Robert James. Student Ill. Valley Community Coll., 1963-64, Dana Coll., 1964. Account exec. Daily News Tribune, La Salle, Ill., 1968-71; account exec. La Salle County Broadcasting Corp., La Salle, 1971-72, sales mgr., 1972-84, v.p., 1984—; v.p. Daily News-Tribune, 1985—. Bd. dirs. United Way of Illinois Valley, 1973-75, mem. public relations com., 1980-82; v.p. No. Ill. Indsl. Devel. Corp.; mem. public relations com. Starved Rock Area council Boy Scouts Am. Served with U.S. Army, 1966-68. Decorated Army Commendation medal; named asst. hon. prof. St. Bede Acad., 1974, hon. prof., 1978. Mem. Nat. Assn. Broadcasters, Radio Advt. Bur., Nat. Radio Broadcasters Assn., Newspaper Advt. Bur., Ill. Valley Area C. of C. (v.p.). Clubs: Wide Waters Yacht (Ottawa, Ill.); Elks. Home: 902 16th St Peru IL 61354 Office: 426 2d St La Salle IL 61301

VICTOR, MICHAEL GARY, physician, lawyer; b. Detroit, Sept. 20, 1945; s. Simon H. and Helen (Litsky) V.; m. Karen Sue Hutson, June 20, 1975; children—Elise Nicole, Sara Lisabeth. Bars: Ill. 1980, U.S. Dist. Ct. (no. dist.) Ill. 1980, U.S. Ct. Appeals (7th cir.) 1981; diplomate Am. Bd. Law in Medicine. Pres., Advocate Adv. Assocs., Chgo., 1982—; mem. clin. faculty Northwestern U. Med. Sch., Chgo., 1982—; sole practice law, Barrington, Ill., 1982—; dir. emergency medicine Loretto Hosp., Chgo., 1980—, St. Josephs Hosp., Chgo., 1985—; v.p. Med. Emergency Services Assocs., Buffalo Grove, Ill. Author: Informed Consent, 1980; Brain Death, 1980; (with others) Due Process for Physicians, 1984. Recipient Service awards Am. Coll. Emergency Medicine, 1973-83. Fellow Am. Coll. Legal Medicine, Chgo. Acad. Legal Medicine; mem. Am. Coll. Emergency Physicians (pres. 1980, med.-legal-ins. council 1980-81, 83-84), ABA, Ill. State Bar Assn., Am. Soc. Law and Medicine, Am. Trial Lawyers Assn., Ill. Trial Lawyers Assn., Chgo. Bar Assn. (med.-legal council 1981-83), AMA, Ill. State Med. Soc. (med.-legal council 1980—), Chgo. Med. Soc. Jewish. Home: 1609 Guthrie Circle Barrington IL 60010 Office: Care MESA 15 S McHenry Rd Buffalo Grove IL 60090

VIDRICKSEN, BEN EUGENE, food service executive, state senator; b. Salina, Kans., June 11, 1927; s. Henry and Ruby Mae Vidricksen; A.B., Kansas Wesleyan U., 1951; m. Lola Mae Nienke, Jan. 20, 1950; children—Nancy, Janice, Ben, Penelope, Jeffery. Field supt. Harding Creamery div. Nat. Dairy Products, Salina, Kans. and O'Neill, Nebr., 1951-53, mgr., 1953-59; ptnr. Vidricksen's Food Service, Salina, 1959—; cons. in field; mem. Kansas Senate, 1979—; mem. Hennessy/U.S. Air Force Worldwide Food Service Evaluation Team, 1978, 79. Mem. Salina Airport Authority, 1972-84, chmn., 1976-77; chmn. Republican Central Com., County of Saline, Kans., 1974-79; adv. council SBA, 1982—; Served with USN, 1945-46. Mem. North Salina Bus. Assn. (past pres.), Kans. Restaurant Assn. (past pres.), Nat. Restaurant Assn. (dir. 1977—), Travel Industry Assn. Kans. (dir.) VFW, Am. Legion. Clubs: Elks, Moose, Eagles, Masons, Shriners. Office: 713 N 11th St Salina KS 67401

VIETOR, HAROLD D., judge. Judge, U.S. Dist. Ct. (so. dist.) Iowa, 1979—. Office: 221 US Courthouse Des Moines IA 50309*

VIEWEG, ROBERT ARTHUR, lawyer; b. New Brunswick, N.J., Aug. 8, 1940; s. Hermann Frederick and Alice (McNulty) V.; B.A., Earlham Coll., 1963; J.D., U. Mich., 1966; m. Jane Edith Johnson, Feb. 24, 1973. Admitted to Mich. bar, 1967; asso. firm Levin, Levin, Garvett & Dill, 1968-72; adminstrv. v.p., gen. counsel Avis Enterprises, 1972-73; atty. firm Helm, Schumann & Miller, 1973-79; partner firm Hoops & Hudson, 1979-80; Keywell & Rosenfeld, Troy, Mich., 1980-81, Carson & Vieweg, 1981—; instr. law Macomb County Community Coll. Active, Detroit Com. Fgn. Relations. Mem. Am. Bar Assn., Mich. Bar Assn., Fed. Bar Assn., Detroit Bar Assn. Republican. Episcopalian. Clubs: Detroit Athletic, Univ., Detroit Boat, Detroit Torch. Office: 860 W Long Lake Rd Suite 200 Bloomfield Hills MI 48013

VIGDAHL, ROGER LEON, research biochemist; b. Mason City, Iowa, Sept. 17, 1935; s. Ansil S. and Irene F. (Carpenter) V.; m. Helene Ann Ries, Mar. 13, 1970; children—Nicholas, Valerie. B.S. in Chemistry, Simpson Coll., 1963; M.S. in Biochemistry, Iowa State U., 1965, Ph.D., 1967. Sr. research chemist Nat. Animal Disease Lab., Ames, Iowa, 1963-67; sr. research biochemist Mead Johnson Co., Evansville, Ind., 1967-73; research specialist Riker Labs., 3M Co., St. Paul, 1973-78, sr. research specialist-biochemistry, 1978—. Contbr. articles to sci. jours. Served with USN, 1954-58. Mem. Am. Chem. Soc. Avocation: racquetball. Home: 50 Michael St Saint Paul MN 55119 Office: 3M Co Saint Paul MN 55101

VIGLIA, EDWIN PETER, JR., radiologic director, educator; b. Joliet, Ill., Nov. 19, 1943; s. Edwin P. and Margaret (Brancato) V.; children—Deanna M., Edwin P., III. Student St. Mary's Sch. Radiologic Tech., 1965-67. Spl. procedures technologist St. Mary's Hosp., Kankakee, Ill., 1965-69; chief technician Fox Children's Center, Dwight, Ill., 1970-72; dir. radiology Kankakee Community Coll., Ill., 1972—. Author: Nursing Assistants, 1983; Introduction to Nursing, 1984. Served with U.S. Army, 1961-64. Mem. Ill. State Soc. Radiologic Technologists (pres. 1980-81), Am. Soc. Radiologic Technologists, Am. Registry Radiologic Tech. Roman Catholic. Home: 184 Anita Dr Bourbonnais IL 60914 Office: Kankakee Community Coll Box 888 Kankakee IL 60901

VILLA, FERNANDO LUIS, gastroenterologist, medical educator; b. Matanzas, Cuba, Oct. 10, 1925; s. Jacinto U. and Rosa E. (Lens) V.; m. Ana Perdomo, June 26, 1955; children—Fernando, Eduardo, Xavier, Luis, Rosemary, Michael, Charles, Maryana. M.D., Havana U., 1951. Intern, Calixto Carcia Univ. Hosp., Havana, 1951-55, Columbus Hosp., Chgo., 1955-56; resident Cook County Hosp., Chgo., 1956-59, fellow in gastroenterology, 1959-60, attending, 1959-76; from instr. to assoc. prof. medicine Loyola U. Med. Sch., Chgo., 1963-76; asst. prof. medicine U. Ill.-Chgo. Med. Ctr., 1976-81, assoc. clin. prof., 1983—; med. dir., chmn. depts. gastroenterology and continuing med. edn. Martha Washington Hosp., Chgo., 1976—. Contbr. articles to profl. jours. Lic. physician, Ill., Ind. Fellow Am. Coll. Gastroenterology; mem. Am. Soc. Gastrointestinal Endoscopy, Chgo. Soc. Gastroenterology, Am. Assn. Study of Liver Disease, Chgo. Med. Soc., Ill. Med. Soc., AMA, Assn. Am. Physicians and Surgones. Recipient Med. award Loyola U., 1966. Initiated peritoneoscopy studies in U.S., 1955; 1st duodenoscopy performed, 1st colonoscopy performed, both 1961; developed gastroduodenoscope, 1961. Home: 3280 Pleasant Run Northbrook IL 60062 Office: 4055 N Western Ave Chicago IL 60618

VILLANUEVA, ANTONIO DEL ROSARIO, research scientist; b. La Union, Philippines, Oct. 17, 1926; s. William Martinez and Pia Guerrero (del Rosario) V.; came to U.S., 1946, naturalized, 1954; B.S., Detroit Inst. Tech., 1961; M.A., Central Mich. U., 1978; Ph.D., Pacific Western U., 1982, Columbia Pacific U., 1984; m. Carmen Emilia Perez, Sept. 5, 1954; children—Yvette, Suzanne. Research asst. Ind. U. Med. Center, Indpls., 1953-54, 1956-57; research asso., research scientist, dir. calcified tissue lab. Henry Ford Hosp., Detroit, 1959—; cons. in field. Served with arty. U.S. Army, 1950-52. Co-recipient Hektoen Gold medal AMA, 1963; Achievement award Lab World, 1979. Mem. AAAS, Am. Soc. Clin. Pathology, Nat. (charter mem., chmn. awards com.), Mich. socs. of histotech., Am. Soc. Med. Tech., P.A.C.E. Sci. Assembly (chmn.), Histochem. Soc., Biol. Stain Commn. Contbr. numerous articles to profl. jours.; developer 2 biol. dyes; editor Jour. of Histotech., 1977. Home: 13101 Oak Park Blvd Oak Park MI 48237 Office: Henry Ford Hosp Detroit MI 48202

VILLAUME, PHILIP GORDON, lawyer; b. St. Paul, Sept. 9, 1949; s. Paul Eugene and Catherine Agnes (Kielty) V.; m. Kay Ann Hanratty, Sept. 30, 1979; children—Cory Philip, Alle Katharine. B.A. magna cum laude, Macalaster Coll., 1972, postgrad., 1972; M. Criminal Justice Program, Mankato State Coll., 1972; J.D., Hamline U., 1979. Bar: Minn. 1979, U.S. Dist. Ct. Minn. 1979, U.S. Supreme Ct. 1984. Probation and parole officer 2d jud. dist., Ramsey County Dept. Ct. Services, St. Paul, 1972-76; pres., owner Villaume Investigative Services, St. Paul, 1977-81; prin. Philip G. Villaume and Assocs., St. Paul and Mpls.; tchr. course Sibley Sr. High Sch., West St. Paul, 1972; instr. course Macalaster Coll., St. Paul, 1974, Maplewood Community Edn. Program, Minn., 1975; instr. legal asst. program Inver Hills Community Coll., Inver Grove Heights, Minn., 1980-82; lectr., vol. atty. Chrysalis Ctr. for Women; bd. mem. Ramsey County Atty. Referral System; bd. dirs. Families in Crisis, Lawyers Concerned for Lawyers, 1985—; apptd. Civil Commitment Def. Project, Fed. Pub. Def. Panel, Ramsey County Criminal Def. Project, Hennepin County Juvenile Def. Project. Mem. ABA, Assn. Trial Lawyers Am., Minn. Trial Lawyers Assn. (edni. coordinator criminal law sect. 1984—, lectr. affirmative bus. communication, continuing legal edn. 1983), Hennepin County Bar Assn., Ramsey County Bar Assn., Nat. Assn. Criminal Def. Lawyers, Alpha Kappa Delta, Sigma Nu Phi. Home: 446 Mount Curve Blvd Saint Paul MN 55105 Office: Shepard Park Office Ctr Suite 180 2177 Youngman Ave Saint Paul MN 55116 also United Labor Ctr Suite 592 312 Central Ave SE Minneapolis MN 55414

VILLEGAS, ROBERTO REGINO, JR., publishing executive; b. Weslaco, Tex., Jan. 25, 1947; s. Roberto Regino and Dominga (Arevalo) V.; m. Judith Ellen Fortner, Dec. 8, 1979; children—Stacy, Adriane, Dagny, Roberto Regino. Assoc. degree in Humanities, SUNY-Albany, 1978. Pub., Lion Enterprises, Walkerton, Ind., 1974—; customer service rep. United Parcel Service, 1978—. Served with U.S. Army, 1966-68. Author: Credo for Future Man—Poems and Poetic Prose, 1981; The Resurrection—A Short Play, 1977. Office: 8608 Old Dominion Ct Indianapolis IN 46231

VINCENT, DONALD ALEX, association executive; b. Ann Arbor, Mich., Sept. 15, 1941; s. Alex James and Gertrude Helen (Alber) V.; m. Caroline L. Kelley, Sept. 25, 1965; children—Bradley, Amy. Student Coll. of Guam, 1963, U. Md., 1963; B.S. in Mktg., Ferris State U., 1969. Cert. assn. exec. Asst. mgr. mem. and chpt. relations Soc. Mfg. Engrs., Dearborn, Mich., 1969-74, mgr. services dept., 1977-79; exec. dir. Computer and Automated Systems Assn., 1979-82; exec. v.p. Robot Inst. Am., Dearborn, Mich., 1982—. Vol., Spl. Olympics, Youth for Understanding. Served with USAF, 1960-64. Mem. Am. Soc. Assn. Execs. Democrat. Methodist. Home: 6110 Wilmer St Westland MI 48185 Office: Robotic Industries Assn PO Box 1366 Dearborn MI 48121

VINCENT, FREDERICK MICHAEL, neurologist, educational administrator; b. Detroit, Nov. 19, 1948; s. George S. and Alyce M. (Borkowski) V.; m. Patricia Lucille Cordes, Oct. 7, 1972; children—Frederick Michael, Joshua Peter, Melissa Anne. B.S. in Biology, Aquinas Coll., 1970; M.D., Mich. State U., 1973. Diplomate Am. Bd. Psychiatry and Neurology. Intern St. Luke's Hosp., Duluth, Minn., 1974-75; resident in neurology Dartmouth Med. Sch., Hanover, N.H., 1975-77, instr. dept. medicine, 1977-78; chief, neurology sect. Munson Med. Ctr., Traverse City, Mich., 1978-84; asst. clin. prof. medicine and pathology Mich. State U., East Lansing, 1978-84, chief sect. neurology Coll. Human Medicine, 1984—; clin. and research fellow neuro-oncology Mass. Gen. Hosp., Boston, 1985; Clin. Fellow in neurology Harvard Med. Sch., Boston, 1985; cons. med. asst. program Northwestern Mich. Coll., Traverse City, 1983-84; neurology cons. radio call-in show Sta. WKAR, East Lansing, 1984. Author: (with others) Neurology: Problems in Office Practice, 1985. Contbr. articles to profl. jours. Fellow NSF, 1969, Nat. Multiple Sclerosis Soc., 1971. Fellow Am. Acad. Neurology, ACP; mem. Am. Fedn. Clin. Research, Am. Soc. Neurol. Investigation, N.Y. Acad. Scis. Democrat. Roman Catholic. Club: University. (East Lansing). Office: Dept Medicine Neurology Sect B-220 Life Scis East Lansing MI 48824

VINCENT, JON STEPHEN, Portuguese and Spanish educator; b. Denver, Feb. 28, 1938; s. Joseph William and Lillian (Diamond) V.; m. Maria Louise Girard, June 13, 1962; children—Sean David, Tanya Maria. B.A., U. N.Mex., 1961, Ph.D., 1970. Instr., U. N.Mex., Albuquerque, 1963-64; asst. prof. U. Kans., Lawrence, 1967-74, assoc. prof., 1974-79, prof., 1979—, assoc. chmn. dept. Spanish, 1974-78, chmn., 1978-82; vis. prof. U. Costa Rica, San Jose, 1972. Author: Joao Guimaraes Rosa, 1978. Assoc. editor Hispania, 1984—; asst. editor Latin Am. Theatre Rev., 1969—; mem. rev. staff World Lit. Today, 1983—. Served with U.S. Army, 1953-56. Mem. MLA (chmn. Luso-Brazilian div. 1982), Am. Assn. Tchrs. Spanish and Portuguese, Latin Am. Studies Assn., Fulbright Am. Republics, Kans. Fgn. Lang. Assn., Am. Republics Adv. Com. Democrat. Avocations: Fishing; hunting. Home: 1104 Centennial Dr Lawrence KS 66044 Office: Dept Spanish and Portuguese U Kansas Lawrence KS 66045

VINCENT, LOYAL ALLEN, school superintendent; b. Long Island, Kans., Dec. 19, 1935; s. Alvin Victor and Marion Eleanor (Parker) V.; m. Vesta Darlene DeBoer, Mar. 30, 1961; children—Steven D., Clayton S., Cameron H. B.S., Ft. Hays State U., 1957; M. S., Pittsburg State U., 1969; Ph.D., Kans. State U., 1978. Tchr., coach Culver Rural High Sch., Kans., 1957-58, Norton pub. schs., Kans., 1960-66; part-time spl. edn. coordinator Norton State Hosp., 1962-66; coordinator vocat. devel. H.I.P. Parsons State Hosp. and Tng. Ctr., Kans., 1966-69; sch. prin. Wamego pub. schs., Kans., 1969-82; sch. supt. Unified Sch. Dist. 448, Inman, Kans., 1982—; condr. workshops in field; also lectr., cons. Contbr. articles to profl. jours. Chmn. bd. Meth. Ch., 1981-82; active Boy Scouts Am. Recipient Modern Woodman Community Service award, 1975, award Dairy Council Greater Kansas City, 1979; named Kans. Prin. of Yr., Kans. Assn. Elem. Sch. Prins., 1977-78, Prin. of Yr., Nat. Assn. Elem. Sch. Prins., 1977-78; others. Mem. United Sch. Adminstrs. Kans. (bd. dirs. 1980-81), Nat. Assn. Elem. Prins., Kans. Assn. Sch. Adminstrs., Kans. Internat. Reading Assn., Ft. Hays State U. Alumni Assn., Kans. State U. Alumni Assn., Phi Delta Kappa. Republican. Lodges: Lions, Masons. Home: Box 475 Bluestem Dr Inman KS 67546 Office: Box 98 Inman KS 67546

VINCENT, ROBERT SHELEY, publishing company executive; b. Binghamton, N.Y., Jan. 27, 1937; s. Leonard Sheley and Martha (Shillinger) V.; m. Patricia Ann Goldie, Apr. 13, 1956 (div. Apr. 1978); m. 2d, Nan Hunter, June 24, 1978; children—Mary Patricia, Robert Sheley II, Jason M., Nathan A. B.A., Syracuse U., 1958. With Ency. Brit., Syracuse, N.Y., 1959-61; nat. sales mgr. Reader's Digest Sales & Services, Inc., Pleasantville, N.Y., 1962-66; with advt. div. Reader's Digest Assn., 1967—, mgr., Detroit, 1981-83, midwest advt. sales dir., Troy, Mich., 1983—. Mem. exec. com. United Found., 1980. Mem. Detroit Adcraft Club. Clubs: Oakland Hills Country (Birmingham, Mich.); Grosse Pointe Yacht (Grosse Pointe Shores, Mich.); Hunters Creek (Metamora, Mich.); Recess (Detroit). Home: 4593 Brightmore Rd Bloomfield Hills MI 48013 Office: Readers Digest Assn 3250 W Big Beaver Rd Suite 333 Troy MI 48084

VINCOLESE, LEROY VINCENT, automotive dealership executive, automotive leasing company executive; b. Chgo. Nov. 3, 1930; s. George Joseph and

Marie Josephine (Novelle) V.; m. Sally Belle, Sept. 29, 1956; children—Laura Lee, Lee Vincent. B.A., U. Ill., 1952. Gen. mgr., sec., treas. Chgo. Auto Sales, Inc., 1954-60; acct. Courtesy Motors Sales, Inc., Chgo., 1960-63, comptroller, 1964-67; co-owner Courtesy Lease-Save Plan, Inc., Schaumburg, Ill., and Colonial Chevrolet, Inc., Schaumburg, 1967—. Pres. Our Lady of Ransom Holy Name Soc., Niles, Ill., 1976-77. Mem. Chevrolet Dealers Assn., Chgo. Auto Trade Assn., Nat. Auto Dealers Assn., Dealer Investment Group (bd. dirs.). Clubs: Park Ridge Country; Columbian of Chgo. (treas. 1983-84). Lodge: Lions (pres. 1974-75). Office: 1100 E Golf Rd Schaumburg IL 60195

VIRKHAUS, TAAVO, symphony orchestra conductor; b. Tartu, Estonia, June 29, 1934; came to U.S., 1949; s. Adalbert August and Helene Marie (Sild) V.; m. Nancy Ellen Herman, Mar. 29, 1969. B.M., U. Miami, 1955; M.M., Eastman Sch. of Music, Rochester, 1957, D.M.A., 1967. Dir. music U. Rochester (N.Y.), also assoc. prof. Eastman Sch., Rochester, 1967-77; music dir., condr. Duluth Superior Symphony Orch. (Minn.), 1977—; guest condr. Rochester Philharmo. and others, 1972—; guest condr. at Tallinn, Estonia SSR, 1978; lectr. U. Minn.-Duluth, U. of Wis.-Superior. Served with U.S. Army, 1957-58, USAR, 1957-61. Recipient Howard Hanson composition award, 1966; Am. Heritage award, JFK Library for Minorities, 1974; Fulbright Scholar, Musickhochschule, Cologne, 1963. Mem. Am. Symphony Orch. League, Condrs. Guild, Am. Fedn. of Musicians. Composer: Violin Concerto, 1966, Symphony No. 1, 1976, Symphony No. 2, 1979. Home: 321 High St Duluth MN 55811 Office: 506 W Michigan St Duluth MN 55802

VIRTUE, JACK DOWN, consulting engineer; b. Sioux City, Iowa, July 23, 1930; s. William Wayne and Ariel M. (Moore). B.S.E., Iowa State U., 1952. Registered profl. engr., Iowa. Ptnr., Virtue & Virtue, Onawa, Iowa, 1960-74; pres. Virtue Engr. P.C., Onawa, 1974—; dir. Pioneer Valley Savs. Bank. Pres. Prairie Gold council Boy Scouts Am., 1976-79; mem. North Central Regional Bd., 1982—. Mem. Monona County Planning and Zoning Com., 1972—; trustee Onawa Pub. Library, 1969. Mem. Iowa Engring. Soc. (N.W. chpt. pres. 1974), Nat. Soc. Profl. Engrs., Soc. Land Surveyors Iowa (dir. 1972-80), Am. Congress Surveying and Mapping. Congregationalist. Lodge: Masons (33 degree). Home: 1004 15th St Onawa IA 51040 Office: Virtue Engr PC Box 99 Onawa IA 51040

VISCLOSKY, PETER J., U.S. congressman; b. Gary, Ind., Aug. 13, 1949; s. John and Helen (Kauzlaric) V. B.S. in Acctg., Ind. U., 1970; J.D., U. Notre Dame, 1973; LL.M., Georgetown U., 1983. Bar: Ind., D.C., U.S. Supreme Ct. Legal asst. Dist. Atty.'s Office, N.Y.C., 1972; assoc. Benjamin, Greco & Gouveia, Merrillville, Ind., 1973-76; assoc. staff Appropriations Com., U.S. Ho. of Reps., Washington, 1976-80, budget com., 1980-82; assoc. Greco, Gouveia, Miller, Pera and Bishop, Merrillville, 1982-84; mem. 99th Congress from Ind., 1985—. Office: US Ho of Reps 1632 Longworth Bldg Washington DC 20515 20515

VISNAPUU, HERK, architect; b. Tartu, Estonia, Apr. 26, 1920; s. Eduard and Lilli (Tarri) Y.; student Nomme Jr. Coll., Estonia, 1938-40, Tech. U., Tallinn, Estonia, 1942-43, Tech. Inst., Stockholm, 1947-48; A.B., Oberlin Coll., 1950; B.Arch., Western Res. U., 1953; children—Lilli, Andres; came to U.S., 1948, naturalized, 1957. Architect, City Stockholm, 1945; with Ernst Gronwal, Stockholm, 1946, Ancher, Gate & Lindgren, Stockholm, 1947, H.K. Ferguson Co., Cleve., 1950-54, Garfield, Harris, Robinson, Schafer, Cleve., 1954-56; partner Visnapuu & Gaede Architects & Planners, Cleve., 1956-74; chmn. bd. Visnapuu Assocs., Inc., Architects and Planners, 1974—. Mem. fine arts adv. com. City of Cleve.; active Cleve. Mus. Art, YMCA. Bd. dirs. Estonian Nat. Com. U.S.A., Estonian Relief Com., Henrik Visnapuu Lit. Found. Recipient nat. award Ch. Archtl. Guild Am., 1962; merit certificate Ohio Prestressed Concrete Inst., 1963; Honor award Architects Soc. Ohio, 1965; Honor award Greater Cleve. Growth Assn., 1971. Registered architect, Ohio, Pa., Ill., Mass., Ind., N.Y., Mich., Fla., Man., Can. Mem. AIA, Royal Archtl. Inst. Can., Korp Sakala (Estonian frat.), Epsilon Delta Rho. Lutheran. Rotarian. Archtl. work exhibited locally and nationally and pub. in nat. archtl. and trade mags. Home: 2886 Kingsley Rd Shaker Heights OH 44122 Office: 333 The Arcade 401 Euclid Ave Cleveland OH 44114

VISSER, AUDRAE EUGENIE, educator, poet; b. Hurley, S.D., June 3, 1919; d. Harry John and Adeline Mae (Perryman) V.; B.S., S.D. State U., 1948; M.A., U. Denver, 1954; 1 son, Harry Gerritt. Tchr. 27 yrs. in S.D., 14 yrs. in Minn. and Japan; tchr. Verdi (Minn.) High Sch., 1974-85; apptd. poet laureat of S.D. by Gov. Richard F. Kneip, 1974. Mem. United Poets Laureate Internat., Nat. League Am. Pen Women, S.D. State Poetry Soc., Nat. Fedn. Press Women, NEA, S.D. Edn. Assn., Minn. Edn. Assn., Bus. and Profl. Women's Clubs, Gen. Fedn. Women's Clubs, AAUW, Delta Kappa Gamma. Democrat. Presbyterian. Author: Rustic Roads, 1961; Poems for Brother Donald, 1974; Meter for Momma, 1974; Poems for Pop, 1976; South Dakota, 1980; Honyocker Stories, 1981. Home: Elkton SD 57026

VISSERS, DONALD NORBERT, fire chief; b. DePere, Wis., Nov. 24, 1928; s. Martin and Nellie (Coenen) V.; m. Helen Ann Kasten, May 17, 1952; children—Mary Kay, Robert. Student St. Norbert Coll., 1947-48. Fire chief City of DePere, Wis., 1973—. Served with USN, 1949-50, U.S. Army, 1952-54, Korea. Mem. Internat. Assn. Fire Chiefs, Wis. Fire Chiefs Assn., Fox Valley Fire Chiefs, Emergency Med. Services Council. Roman Catholic. Lodge: Kiwanis (pres. 1978-79). Avocations: tennis, racquetball, bowling. Home: 803 Mount Olivet Dr DePere WI 54115 Office: DePere Fire Dept 400 Lewis St DePere WI 54115

VISTE, ARLEN ELLARD, chemistry educator; b. Austin, Minn., Aug. 13, 1936; s. Arthur E. and Edith L. (Kehret) V.; m. Elizabeth Ann Lindbeck, June 14, 1959; children—Solveig, David, Mark. B.A., St. Olaf Coll., 1958; Ph.D., U. Chgo., 1962. Asst. prof. chemistry St. Olaf Coll., Northfield, Minn., 1962-63; NSF fellow Columbia U., N.Y.C., 1963-64; asst. prof. Augustana Coll., Sioux Falls, S.D., 1964-68, assoc. prof., 1968-73, prof., 1973—. Mem. Am. Chem. Soc., Royal Soc. Chemistry (London), S.D. Acad. Sci., Midwest Assn. Chemistry Tchrs. in Liberal Arts Colls., Phi Beta Kappa, Sigma Xi. Contbr. articles to profl. jours. Home: 1500 W 30th St Sioux Falls SD 57105 Office: Augustana Coll Chemistry Dept Sioux Falls SD 57197

VISTE, GERALD DELMAR, insurance company executive; b. Foley, Minn., Mar. 29, 1923; s. Martin N. and Mildred E. (Schwartz) V.; A.B., Harvard U., 1947, M.B.A., 1954; m. Marion C. Muller, June 14, 1947; children—Deborah Viste Wetter, John, Nathan. With Wausau Ins. Cos., now pres., chief operating officer, dir.; dir. First Am. Nat. Bank, Wausau, AMRECO, Chgo. Gen. campaign chmn. United Way of Marathon County, 1979, pres., 1982; mem. Wis. Humanities Com., 1973-80, chairperson, 1978-80; trustee Performing Arts Found., 1979-83, pres., 1980-81; mem. council Wis. Acad. Scis., Arts & Letters, 1982—; bd. dirs. U. Wis. Stevens Point Found., 1982—, Wausau Hosp. Ctr., 1984—; bd. visitors U. Wis., 1984—; bd. dirs. Marathon County Hist. Soc., 1982—, pres., 1983—; bd. curators State Hist. Soc. Wis., 1982—; mem. adv. bd. Sigurd Olson Environ. Inst., 1982-83, mem. adv. bd. Northland Coll., 1982—, trustee, 1983—. Served with USAAF, 1942-45. Mem. Ins. Acctg. and Statis. Assn., Acctg. Roundtable. Unitarian (pres. Central Midwest dist. Unitarian Universalist Assn. 1963, pres. North Central Area council 1964). Club: Wausau. Office: 2000 Westwood Dr Wausau WI 54401

VITE, FRANK ANTHONY, realtor; b. Aurora, Ill., Feb. 9, 1930; s. Frank A. and Rose (Cosentino) V.; grad. Marmion Mil. Acad., 1948; student Sch. Mgmt., U. Notre Dame, 1958; D.B.A. (hon.), Hillsdale Coll., 1972; m. Barbara Ann Decio, Oct. 23, 1954; children—Bradley Scott, Mark Steven, Michael Lee, Leslie Ann, Lisa Ann. Plant engr. Lyon Metal Products, Aurora, 1951-52, purchasing agt., 1953-54; became sales mgr., exec. v.p., owner, dir. Skyline Homes, Inc., Elkhart, Ind., 1954; pres., owner B&F Realty, Inc., No. Ind. Appraisal Co., Golden Falcon Homes, Inc.; real estate broker; dir. 1st Nat. Bank, Elkhart, Ind. Trustee Hillsdale (Mich.) Coll.; bd. dirs. Ind. Commn. Higher Edn. Served with AUS, 1952-53, Korea. Mem. Elkhart Bd. Realtors, Nat. Sales Execs. Assn., Ind. Real Estate Assn., Nat. Inst. Real Estate Brokers, Holy Name Soc. Republican. Clubs: K.C. (4 deg.), Knight of Malta, Elks. Home: 23236 Shorelane Elkhart IN 46514 Office: 1300 Cassopolis St Elkhart IN 46514

VITEK, FRANK JOHN, association executive; b. Oak Park, Ill., Aug. 12, 1948; s. Frank John and Marian (Lamberti) V.; m. Bonnie Sue Harmon, July 13, 1970; 1 child, Colin. A.S. in Aviation, U. Ill., 1968, B.S. in Communications, 1970; cert. in assn. mgmt. U. Notre Dame, 1982. Mgr. Western Electric, Cicero, Ill., 1970-75; communications dir. Nat. Automatic Laundry and Cleaning Council, Chgo., 1975-79; asst. exec. dir. Nat. Carwash Council, Chgo., 1977-79; pres. Coin Laundry Assn., Downers Grove, Ill., 1979—; cons. to assns., Chgo., 1978-82. Contbr. articles to profl. mags., jours., 1977—. Press sec. Gray for Ill. Treas., 1979; com. mem. Nat. Fire Protection Assn., 1982-85. Served to lt. USMC, 1967-69. Recipient awards of appreciation U.S. Jaycees, Chgo., 1974-75. Fellow World Ednl. Congress for Laundering and Drycleaning (exec. dir. 1981-85, Meritorious Service award 1977); mem. Am. Soc. Assn. Execs., Chgo. Soc. Assn. Execs., Meeting Planners Internat., Found. Internat. Meetings, Chgo. Area Planners, Laundry Cleaning Council (treas. 1980-85), Chgo. Jr. Assn. Commerce and Industry (bd. dirs. 1972-75), Chgo. Jaycees (v.p. 1973-75). Avocations: sports (skiing, tennis, golf, racketball, and others); reading. Office: Coin Laundry Assn 1315 Butterfield Rd Suite 212 Downers Grove IL 60515

VITULLI, CLARK JOSEPH, auto manufacturing company executive; b. Bklyn., Apr. 2, 1946; s. William and Rosaria (Stallone) V.; m. Jacqueline Pain, June 22, 1968. B.S., U. Fla., 1968. With Chrysler Corp., various locations, 1969—, zone mgr., Los Angeles, 1980-84, nat. mdse. mgr. Dodge div., Detroit, 1984—; mem. dealer licensing div. Fla. Dept. Motor Vehicles, 1978-79. Mem. Am. Mgmt. Assn., Sales and Mktg. Execs. Los Angeles, Adcraft Club of Detroit, Internat. Platform Assn., Mensa, Beta Theta Pi. Home: 633 Hawthorne Birmingham MI 48009 Office: PO Box 857 Detroit MI 48288

VIVIAN, JOHN H., journalism educator; b. Kellogg, Idaho, Apr. 22, 1945; s. Harold H. and Elaine Lucile (Anderson) V. M.S. in Journalism, Northwestern U., 1968; A.B., Gonzaga U., 1967. Newsman, UPI, Spokane, Wash., 1963-64, AP, 1964-72; prof. journalism Marquette U., Milw., 1972-80, N.Mex. State U., Las Cruces, 1980-81; prof. journalism Winona State U., Minn., 1981—, chmn. mass communication dept., 1981—. Pub. Winona Campus Life, 1983—; contbr. articles to profl. jours. Served to capt. USAR, 1968-82. Decorated Army Commendation medal. Mem. Soc. Profl. Journalists, AAUP (state treas. 1978-80), Coll. Media Advisors, Assn. Edn. Journalism, Am. Soc. Journalism Sch. Adminstrs. Home: 322 Market Winona MN 55987 Office: Mass Communication Dept Winona State U Winona MN 55987

VIVONA, DANIEL NICHOLAS, chemist; b. Chgo., Apr. 13, 1924; s. Daniel and Mary Rose (Lamonico) V.; student Chgo. City Coll., 1941-42, 46; B.A., U. Maine, 1951; M.S., Pa. State U., 1953; postgrad. Purdue U., 1953-56; m. Helen Mary Belanger, Sept. 14, 1950; 1 son, Daniel Maurice. Instr. chemistry Purdue U., Lafayette, Ind., 1955-56; with Minn. Mining and Mfg. Co., St. Paul, 1956—, sr. chemist, 1969-79, info. scientist, 1979-81, quality assurance sr. chemist, 1981—. Served with USAAF, 1942-45. Decorated Air medal with oak leaf clusters, DFC. Dow Corning fellow, 1952-53. Mem. Am. Chem. Soc., Phi Beta Kappa. Roman Catholic. Club: Toastmasters. Home: 3253 Kraft Circle North Lake Elmo MN 55042 Office: Minn Mining and Mfg Co 235-1E-14 Saint Paul MN 55144

VOBACH, WILLIAM H., state senator. Mem. Ind. State Senate from Dist. 31, 1983—; practice law, Indpls. Republican. Office: One Indiana Sq Suite 2120 Indianapolis IN 46204

VODERBERG, KURT ERNEST, machinery sales company executive; b. Rendsburg, Germany, Apr. 8, 1921; s. Max Henry and Margarethe (Siedel) V.; m. Louise Collier, May 21, 1948 (div. 1969); children—Paul, John, Mary Beth, Jill; m. 2d, Sophie Dufft, Sept. 5, 1969. B.S. in M.E., Ill. Inst. Tech., 1943; postgrad. Northwestern U., 1944-45. Registered profl. engr., Ill. Asst. master mechanic Danly Machine Co., Cicero, Ill., 1943-47; pres. Dynamic Machine Co., Chgo., 1947-75, pres. Dynamic Machinery Sales, Inc., Chgo., 1975—, pres. Paramount Machinery Sales Co., Chgo., 1982—. Mem. Ill. Soc. Profl. Engrs., Soc. Mfg. Engrs., Tool and Die Inst., Chgo. Assn. Commerce and Industry (mem. com.). Lutheran. Clubs: Michigan Shores, American Turners, German, Glenbrook Shrine. Lodge: Masons. Patentee in field. Home: 1440 Sheridan Rd Apt 706 Wilmette IL 60091 Office: 1800 N Rockwell St Chicago IL 60647

VOEGE, JANIS MACKEY, home economics educator, consultant, researcher, administrator; b. Carbondale, Ill., May 26, 1942; d. Paul Fairless and Lois Violet (Mallory) Mackey; m. Herbert Walter Voege, June 12, 1972; children—Jana R., Mark S., Amy J. B.S., So. Ill. U.-Carbondale, 1963, M.A., 1968; Ph.D., Mich. State U., 1977. With Coop. Extension Service, U. Ill., Champaign-Urbana, 1963-66; grad. asst. So. Ill. U.-Carbondale, 1966-68; prof. Adrian (Mich.) Coll., 1968-72; prof. home econs. Central Mich. U., Mt. Pleasant, 1972—, chmn. dept., 1980-83; resource for CUBES (C. of C./Univ. liaison group). Chmn. ch.-affiliated Day Care Center Bd.; mem. joint council on econ. edn. programs for elderly consumers and high sch. students. Shell Oil grantee, 1969; Coll. Human Ecology grantee, 1976; Am. Home Econs. Assn. fellow, 1975, Kellogg Found./Assn. for Ind. Colls. and Univs. in Mich. grantee, 1971. Mem. Am. Home Econs. Assn. (Premier Class of Leaders 1984), Mich. Home Econs. Assn., Nat. Council on Family Relations, Mich. Council on Family Relations, Am. Council on Consumer Interests, Consumer Educators of Mich., Assn. Consumer Research, Soc. Study Social Problems, World Future Soc., Kappa Omicron Phi, Omicron Nu. Contbr. articles to pubs. in field. Office: 209 Wightman Hall Central Mich Univ Mount Pleasant MI 48859

VOELKER, RONALD GENE, farmer, agricultural instructor; b. Colman, S.D., Feb. 8, 1942; s. John and Mildred Voelker. B.S., S.D. State U., 1965, postgrad., 1969. Agrl. instr. Lake Benton High Sch. (Minn.), 1969—; snowmobile safety instr., coach. Served to capt. U.S. Army, 1965-71. Mem. NEA, Minn. Edn. Assn., Am. Vocat. Assn., Minn. Vocat. Assn., Minn. Vocat. Agr. Instrs. Assn. Minn. Wrestling Coaches Assn., Am. Legion. Lutheran. Club: Lions. Home: 109 East Mathews St Lake Benton MN 56149 Office: Lake Benton High School 101 S Garfield St Lake Benton MN 56149

VOGEL, ARTHUR ANTON, See *Who's Who in America,* 43rd edition.

VOGEL, CARL EDWARD, property administration executive; b. Chgo., Oct. 21, 1919; s. Eugene E. and Madeline (Keim) V.; student Wilson Jr. Coll., Chgo., 1937-39, Northwestern U., 1940-41; m. Frances Stevens Terrell, Mar. 17, 1945; children—Cynthia, Susan, Meredith, Kirkland. With Nat. Bur. Property Adminstrn., Inc., Chgo., 1939—, chmn. bd., exec. v.p., 1958-63, chmn. bd., pres., 1963—; chmn., bd., pres. Kirkland Corp., Chgo., 1969—. Active in local fund-raising drives. Served to 1st lt. USAAF, 1942-46. Mem. Chgo. Assn. Commerce and Industry, Nat. Assn. Rev. Appraisers, Internat. Assn. Assessing Officers, Nat. Tax Assn., Inst. Property Taxation. Clubs: Mid-America (Chgo.); North Shore Country (Glenview). Home: 720 Glenayre Dr Glenview IL 60025 Office: 1824 Prudential Plaza Chicago IL 60601

VOGEL, J. THOMAS, freight forwarding company executive; b. 1946; married. Exec. v.p. Vogel Van & Storage, 1966—; with Allied Van Lines, Inc., Maywood, Ill., 1979—, vice chmn. bd., 1979-80, chmn., 1980—, also dir. Office: Allied Van Lines Inc 25th Ave & Roosevelt Rd Maywood IL 60153*

VOGEL, STEVE GREGORY, controller; b. Lawrence, Kans., Sept. 11, 1951; s. John Joseph and Anne Meredith (Beardsworth) V.; m. Denise Linda, 1984. B.A. in Psychology, Lehigh U., 1973, M.B.A. in Fin., 1974. C.P.A., Pa., Ohio Fin. analyst Ford Motor Co., Pennsaucon, N.J., 1974-76; plant controller Corning GlassWorks, Corning, N.Y., 1976-79; controller Ryder System, Inc., Buffalo, 1979-81, group controller, 1981-82; div. planning Ryder Systems, Inc., Bloomfield Hills, Mich., 1982-83; group controller Guardian Ind., Inc., Upper Sandusky, Ohio, 1983—; fin. cons., 1979—; teaching asst. Dale Carnegie, Buffalo, 1981-82. Recipient James Clark Hayden award Lehigh U., Bethlehem, Pa., 1971, 72, 73. Mem. Mich. Soc. C.P.A.s, Ohio Soc. C.P.A.s, Nat. Assn. Accts. Republican. Roman Catholic. Home: 541 Adams Ln Delaware OH 43015

VOGEL, WALTER, farm equipment company executive; b. Schwaebisch Hall, Germany, Apr. 28, 1928; s. Gustav and Rosa (Barger) V.; m. Lore Jost, June 19, 1959; children—Birgit, Peter, Sabine. Student, Stuttgart U. (Fulbright scholar), U. Mich. With Deere & Co., 1956—, dir. mfg. Europe, Africa and Middle East, 1970, mng. dir. Europe, Africa and Middle East, 1975, v.p., 1975-77, exec. v.p., Moline, Ill., 1979—; mem. adv. council Deutsche Bank, Mannheim. Trustee, Edison Welding Inst. Mem. Am. Soc. Agrl. Engrs., Soc. Mfg. Engrs. (adv. bd.). Office: Deere & Co John Deere Rd Moline IL 61265

VOGT, KENNETH JOHN, lawyer; b. David City, Nebr., Feb. 15, 1914; s. John W. and Myrtle A. (Schaepler) V.; m. Dorothy J. Porter; children—Linda Vogt Musselman, Suzanne Vogt Kaiser. B.Sc. in Bus. Adminstrn., U. Nebr., 1934, J.D., 1937. Bar: Nebr. 1937, Ohio 1952. Sole practice, Dayton, Ohio, 1952—. Served to lt. USN, 1946-48. Mem. Nebr. Bar Assn., Ohio Bar Assn. Democrat. Lutheran. Home: 4709 Sunray Rd Kettering OH 45429 Office: 2801 Far Hills Ave Dayton OH 45419

VOICA, RUDOLPH, psychologist, educator; b. East Chicago, Ind., Aug. 6, 1923; s. Jordan and Anna V.; M.S., Inst. State U., Terre Haute, 1952; postgrad. U. Denver, 1956, Ind. U., Bloomington, 1957, Marquette U., 1959, State U. Iowa, 1962; m. Mary Rita Dusthimer, Sept. 22, 1951; children—Michael, Robert, Joseph. Tchr., counselor Roosevelt High Sch., East Chicago Public Schs., 1952-56; dir. guidance South High Sch., Sheboygan Public Schs., 1957-64; dir. student services U. Wis. Center System, Sheboygan, 1964-70; sr. sch. psychologist Stevens Point Area (Wis.) Public Sch. Dist., 1970—; dist. trainer, resource cons. child abuse and neglect, 1977—. Exec. dir. Portage County chpt. Big Bros. Am., 1972, Sheboygan chpt., 1966-69; instr. evening adult edn. program Hammond (Ind.) Vocat. Tech. High Sch., 1953-56, Sheboygan (Wis.) Vocat.-Tech. Inst., 1959-62; pres. Portage County Assn. Mental Health, 1971-72, exec. com. chmn., 1972-73; v.p. Portage County Council Alcohol and Drug Abuse, 1974-75; bd. dirs. Halfway House, Sheboygan, 1967-68, Head Start Program, Sheboygan, 1967-68. Served with U.S. Army, 1943-46, 50-51. Recipient Wis. Gov.'s Spl. award, 1968. Mem. Am. Psychol. Assn., Am. Personnel and Guidance Assn., Council Pupil Personnel Services, Phi Delta Kappa. Roman Catholic. Home: 714 Maplewood Dr Plover WI 54467 Office: 1900 Polk St Stevens Point WI 54481

VOIGHT, LAWRENCE JOSEPH, clinical social worker, psychotherapist; b. Detroit, Aug. 13, 1958; s. Joseph Robert and Kathleen Nancy (McAtamney) V. B.S.W., Wayne State U., 1980; M.S.W., 1981. Dir. social work services Glen Eden Hosp., Warren, Mich., 1977—; field instr. Wayne State U., Oakland U., U. Mich.; teaching cons. to local law enforcement agys. Mem. Mich. Group Psychotherapy Soc., Soc. of Hosp. Social Work Dirs., Acad. Cert. Social Workers, Nat. Assn. Social Workers. Home: 1916 Yosemite St Birmingham MI 48008 Office: Glen Eden Hosp 6902 Chicago Rd Warren MI 48092

VOIGHT, NANCY LEE (MRS. JAY VAN HOVEN), counseling psychologist; b. Kansas City, Mo., Nov. 24, 1945; d. Paul and Leona Alvina (Schultz) V.; B.A., Wittenberg U., 1967; M.A., Ball State U., 1971; Ph.D., Mich. State U., 1975; m. Jay Van Hoven, June 27, 1975; children—Joshua, Janna, Lydia. Tchr. lang. arts Ashland (Ohio) City Schs., 1967-68; tchr. English, Speedway (Ind.) City Schs., 1969; basic literacy instr. Army Edn. Center, Gelnhausen, W. Ger., 1969-70; individual assistance Bethel Home for Boys, Gaston, Ind., 1970-71; counselor Wittenberg U. Ohio, 1971-72; staff psychologist Ingham County Probate Ct., Lansing, Mich., 1972-74; asst. prof. U. N.C., Chapel Hill, 1975-79, counseling psychologist, 1976-79; psychologist for employee devel. Gen. Telephone Electronics, No. Region Hdqrs., Indpls., 1979-80; behavioral sci. coordinator Family Practice Center, Community Hosp., Indpls., 1980-82; media psychologist Sta. WIFE, Indpls., 1981-82; asst. dir. Chapel Hill Counseling Center, 1980—; dir. Behavior Therapy Ctr., Indpls., 1982—; treas. Med. Specialty Disability Ins. Corp., Indpls., 1982—; psychologist Alternatives to Boys Sch., 1983—; advisor Sex Info. and Counseling Center, Chapel Hill, 1977-79. Chmn. housing bd. U. N.C., 1976-79. Office Edn. grantee, 1977-78, 78-80; Spencer Found. young scholars grantee. Mem. Am. Psychol. Assn., Ind. Psychol. Assn., Assn. Advancement Behavior Therapy, Inst. Rational Living, Soc. Behavioral Medicine, Am. Assn. Marriage and Family Therapists. Lutheran. Author: Becoming, 1978; Becoming: Leader's Guide, 1978; Becoming Aware, 1979; Becoming Informed, 1979; Becoming Strong, 1979; also articles. Home: 600 N High School Rd Indianapolis IN 46224 Office: Behavior Therapy Ctr 6357 W Rockville Rd Indianapolis IN 46224

VOIGT, STEVEN RUSSELL, lawyer; b. Geneva, Nebr., Dec. 29, 1952; s. James L. and Martha A. (Ericksen) V.; m. Barbara J. Molcyk, Apr. 23, 1983. B.S., U. Lincoln, 1975, J.D., 1978. Bars: Nebr. 1978, U.S. Dist. Ct. Nebr. 1978, U.S. Tax Ct. 1980. Assoc. Nye, Hervert, Jorgensen & Watson, P.C., Kearney, Nebr., 1978-80; ptnr. Giese, Butler & Voigt, Kearney, 1980-82, Butler & Voigt, Kearney, 1982—; bd. dirs. Nebr. Lawyers Trust Account Found., Lincoln, 1983—, Western Nebr. Legal Services Corp., 1984—. Mem. ABA, Nebr. Assn. Trial Attys., Assn. Trial Lawyers Am., Buffalo County Bar Assn., Nebr. State Bar Assn. (pres. young lawyers sect. 1982-83), Phi Delta Phi (pres. 1978). Republican. Methodist. Lodges: Sertoma (pres. 1983-84), Masons, Shriners. Home: 3407 Ave F Kearney NE 68847 Office: Butler & Voigt Rovar Park #14-Box 1184 Kearney NE 68847

VOINOVICH, GEORGE V., mayor; b. Cleve., July 15, 1936; m. Janet; 3 children. B.A., Ohio U., 1958; J.D., Ohio State U., 1961 LL.D. (hon.) Ohio U., 1981. Bar: Ohio 1961, U.S. Supreme Ct. 1968. Asst. atty. gen. State of Ohio, 1962-63; mem. Ohio Ho. of Reps., 1967-71; auditor Cuyahoga County (Ohio), 1971-76, county commr., 1977; lt. gov. State of Ohio, 1979; mayor City of Cleve., 1979; trustee U.S. Conf. Mayors, 1983; 1st v.p. Nat. League Cities, 1984; trustee U.S. Conf. Mayors, 1979—; pres. Nat. League Cities, 1985. Recipient cert. of merit Ohio U.; YMCA Disting. Service award, 1984; named Outstanding Young Man, Ohio Jaycees, Cleve. Jaycees. Mem. Omicron Delta Kappa, Phi Alpha Theta, Phi Delta Phi. Republican. Office: Office of Mayor City Hall 601 Lakeside Ave E Cleveland OH 44114

VOLDING, GARY DEAN, mathematics educator, computer software company executive; b. Crystal Lake, Iowa, Oct. 23, 1935; s. Gerald N. and Hazel (McFarland) V.; m. Harriet Jane Stevens, May 4, 1957; children—Michael, Jon, Lori. B.S., Mankato State U., 1959; postgrad. No. Iowa U., 1961-62, Mankato State U., 1966-69. Cert. life tchr., Minn. Tchr. pub. schs., Rockford, Iowa, 1959-62; tchr. math. pub. schs., Shakopee, Minn., 1963-83; founder, pres. Ideal Learning Inc., Shakopee, 1982—; bd. dirs., chmn. long range planning computer center. Elder, Presbyterian Ch., Shakopee; youth recreation worker. Served with U.S. Army, 1954-56. Mem. Nat. Council Tchrs. Math., Assn. Supervision and Curriculum Devel., Shakopee Edn. Assn. (pres.). Club: Masons. Developed method of teaching by integrating microcomputer-tchr.-video into process with built-in testing system. Home: 1044 Fuller Shakopee MN 55379 Office: 327 S Marschall Rd Suite 200 Shakopee MN 55379

VOLK, DAVID LAWRENCE, state treas. S.D.; b. Mitchell, S.D., Apr. 12, 1947; s. Erwin John and Joan M. (Nieses) V.; B.S. in Govt., No. State Coll., Aberdeen, S.D.; postgrad. Augustana Coll., Sioux Falls, S.D. Field rep. Ben Reifel, M.C., 1966-69; state treas. S.D., Pierre, 1972—; commr. Sch. and Pub. Lands. Mem. adv. com. U.S. Commn. on Civil Rights; mem. exec. com. Boy Scouts Am., S.D., S.D. Mental Health Assn. Served with U.S. Army, 1969-71. Decorated Bronze Star medal; named Outstanding Young Republican, 1968. Mem. Nat. Assn. State Treas. (pres.), S.D. Investment Soc., VFW, Am. Legion, Jr. C. of C. Roman Catholic. Club: Elks. Office: State Treas Office Capitol Bldg Pierre SD 57501

VOLKERT, DARLEEN JOYCE, antique bookstore owner; b. Battle Creek, Iowa, Nov. 6, 1930; d. Robert Elbert and Lucille Catherine (Williamson) Volkert. Student Morningside Coll., Sioux City, Iowa, 1949-50. Sales rep. Braniff Internat., Sioux City, other locations, 1951-73; owner, mgr. The Book Barn, South Sioux City, Nebr., 1973—. Named Star Salesman Braniff Internat., 1954. Mem. Bus. and Profl. Women Sioux City (v.p. 1961). Lodge: Zonta Internat. (pres. 1963). Home: Rural Route 1 Box 304 H South Sioux City NE 68776 Office: The Book Barn Rural Route 1 Box 304-H South Sioux City NE 68776

VOLKMER, HAROLD LEE, congressman; b. Jefferson City, Mo., Apr. 4, 1931; ed. St. Louis U.; LL.B., U. Mo., 1955; m. Shirley Ruth Braskett, Aug. 20, 1955; children—Jerry Wayne, John Paul, Elizabeth Ann. Admitted to Mo. bar, 1955; individual practice law, Hannibal; pros. atty. Marion County, 1960-66; mem. Mo. Ho. of Reps., 1966-76, chmn. Judiciary com.; mem. 95th-99th Congresses from 9th Mo. Dist., mem. agr. com., sci. and tech. com.; asst. atty. gen. Mo. Mem. Mo., 10th Jud. Circuit bar assns. Lodges: K.C., Hannibal Lions. Recipient two awards for meritorious pub. service in Gen. Assembly, St. Louis Globe-Democrat. Office: 2411 Rayburn House Office Bldg Washington DC 20515*

VOLLMER, RINA S(ERRANO), emergency physician, medical administrator; b. Cuba; d. Rafael G. and Dora (Jorrin) Serrano; children—Charles, Anna, Paul. M.D., Havana U., 1960, Ohio State U., 1961. Intern Mt. Carmel Med. Ctr., Columbus, Ohio, 1961-62, resident in diagnostic and internal medicine, 1965-66, mem. staff, 1966—; practice medicine specializing in emergency medicine, Columbus, Ohio, 1973—; dir. intermediate care Shaver Med. Ctr.

Active various coms. Bexley Civic Assn. Mem. AMA, Ohio State Med. Assn., Columbus and Franklin County Acad. Medicine (community affairs com.), Cuban Med. Assn. in Exile, Ohio State U. Alumni Assn., Mt. Carmel Hosp. Alumni Assn. Republican. Roman Catholic. Contbr. writings to med. publs. Home: 2454 Brentwood Rd Bexley OH 43209 Office: 793 W State St Columbus OH 43222 also 5677 Scioto Darby Rd Hilliard OH 43026

VOLTMER, MICHAEL DALE, electric company executive; b. Des Moines, July 26, 1952; s. Robert D. and Kathy A. (Miller) V.; m. Joann H. Hove, Sept. 9, 1978; 1 child, Gerad Frank. B.S., Luther Coll., 1974. Founder, pres. Voltmer Electric Co., Decorah, Iowa, 1974—; ptnr. Brown and Assocs., Decorah, 1984—. Chmn. Winneshiek County Republican Party, Decorah, 1982-83, fin. chmn., 1984—; pres. Sunflower Child Care Ctr. Inc., Decorah, 1979-80; mem. Planning and Zoning Commn., City of Decorah, 1983—. Mem. Illuminating Engring. Soc., Nat. Fire Protection Assn. Lutheran. Club: Silvercrest Golf and Country (pres. 1985). Lodge: Elks. Avocations: golf; racquetball. Home: Rural Route 6 Decorah IA 52101 Office: Voltmer Electric Inc 507 W Water St Decorah IA 52101

VOLZ, WILLIAM HARRY, legal educator, consultant; b. Sandusky, Mich., Dec. 28, 1946; s. Harry Bender and Belva Geneva (Riehl) V. B.A., Mich. State U., 1968; A.M., U. Mich., 1972; J.D., Wayne State U., 1975; M.B.A., Harvard U., 1978. Bar: Mich. 1975. Sole practice, Detroit, 1975-77; mgmt. analyst Office of Gen. Counsel, HEW, Woodlawn, Md., 1977; asst., then assoc. prof. bus. law Wayne State U., Detroit, after 1978, interim dean sch. Bus. Adminstrn., 1985, now assoc. prof bus law; cons. Merrill, Lynch, Pierce, Fenner & Smith, N.Y.C., 1980—, City of Detroit law dept., 1982, Mich. Supreme Ct., Detroit, 1981; ptnr. Mich. C.P.A. Rev., Southfield, 1983—. Author: Managing a Trial, 1982; contbr. articles to legal jours. Legal counsel Free Legal Aid Clinic, Inc., Detroit, 1976, Shared Ministries, Detroit, 1981, Sino-Am. Tech. Exchange Council, People's Republic of China, 1982; participant Better Bus. Bur. Arbitration Program, Southfield, 1981. Recipient Disting. Faculty award Wayne State Sch. Bus. Adminstrn., 1982. Mem. ABA, Am. Bus. Law Assn., Amateur Mendicant Soc. (commissionaire 1981—), Golden Key, Alpha Kappa Psi, Beta Alpha Psi. Mem. Reorganized Ch. Latter Day Saints. Clubs: Econ. of Detroit, Harvard Bus. Sch. of Detroit. Home: 3846 Wedgewood Dr Birmingham MI 48010 Office: Wayne State U Sch Bus Adminstrn Cass Ave Detroit MI 48202

VON BAUER, ERIC ERNST, business consulting firm executive; b. LaHabra Heights, Calif., Apr. 12, 1942; s. Kurt Ernst and Margaret Ross (Porter) v.; m. Joyce Ruth Schmidt, Dec. 29, 1973; children—Suzanne Lynn, Katherine Jean. Student Occidental Coll., Los Angeles, 1960-63; M.B.A., U. Chgo., 1973; postgrad. U. Chgo. Law Sch., 1973. Registered rep. Piedmont Internat. Ltd. subs. Piedmont Capital Corp., Frankfurt, W.Ger., 1968-71; fin. adv. trust dept. 1st Nat. Bank Chgo., 1971-72; sec.-treas., controller, Am. Med. Bldgs. Inc., Milw., 1973-75; sr. managing cons. Mgmt. Analysis Ctr., Inc., Chgo., 1975-79; v.p., gen. mgr. corp. fin. adv. services div. Continental Ill. Nat. Bank, Trust Co., Chgo., 1979-82; pres., chief exec. officer The Capital Strategy Group, Inc., Chgo., 1982—; dir., pres. Chgo. chpt. N.Am. Soc. Corp. Planning, 1981—; guest lectr. U. Chgo., Grad Sch. Bus. Bd. dirs. Chgo. chpt. Reading is Fundamental, 1972-73. Served to 1st lt. C.E. U.S. Army, 1964-67. Decorated Army Commendation award. Mem. Assn. Corp. Growth, Midwest Planning Assn., Am. Mgmt. Assn. C. of C. (dir. Chgo. jr. chpt. 1971-73). Presbyn. Club: Rotary (Chgo.) Co-author: Zero Base Planning, Budgeting, 1977; contbr. articles to profl. publs. Home: 28 Carlisle Rd Hawthorn Woods IL 60047 Office: 20 N Wacker Dr Chicago IL 60606

VON BERGEN, PENNIE LEA, lawyer; b. Sterling, Ill., Mar. 19, 1949; d. Donald Leroy and Mary Lou (Hammerle) von B.; m. Michael Joseph Wessels, Aug. 23, 1969. B.S.E.D., No. Ill. U., 1971; postgrad. So. Ill. U., 1972-73, 80-81; J.D. magna cum laude, U. Ill., 1983. Tchr., St. Cornelius Sch., Chgo., 1974-75; social worker Fla. Dept. Children and Family Service, Sanford, Fla., 1978; tchr. Oak Lawn High Sch., Ill., 1975-77, 78-79; La Salle Peru High Sch., LaSalle, Ill., 1979-80; assoc. Ronald F. Coplan, Morrison, Ill., 1984—. Editor: one-woman show Justice?, on tour in Ill., 1983—. Mem. Whiteside County Bd., 1984—; chmn. voters registration Democratic Com. Whiteside County, 1984. So. Ill. U. fellow, 1973. Mem. ABA, Ill. Bar Assn., Assn. Trial Lawyers Am., Whiteside County Bar Assn. Unitarian. Home: 21381 W Lincoln Hwy Sterling IL 61081

VON DOHNANYI, CHRISTOPH, musician, conductor; b. Berlin, Ger., Sept. 8, 1929; s. Hans and Christina (Bonhoeffer) D.; m. Anja Silja, Apr. 21, 1979; children—Julia, Benedikt, Olga. Student, Sch. Law U. Munich (Ger.), Musikhochschule, Fla. State U., Berkshire Music Ctr. Coach, condr., artistic dir. Frankfurt Opera, Ger.; gen. music dir. Lubeck (Ger.), Kassel (Ger.); dir. West German Radio Symphony, Cologne; artistic dir., prin. condr. Hamburg State Opera (Ger.), 1978-84; music dir. designate The Cleve. Orch., 1982-84, music dir., 1984—; guest condr. in U.S. and Europe. Numerous recordings include: 5 symphonies of Mendelssohn with Vienna Philharmonic, opera Lulu, Petrouchka Su9te, Wozzeck. Recipient Richard Strauss prize, Munich; Bartok prize, Hungary; Goethe-Plaket award City of Frankfurt. Office: Severance Hall 11001 Euclid Ave Cleveland OH 44106

VON FISCHER, DAVID WILLIAM, wholesale wine and imported beer company executive; b. Cleve., July 18, 1950; s. William Erhard Carl and Cordelia (Thacker) Von F.; m. Carolyn Bradford Nelson, Apr. 13, 1974; children—Nathaniel David, Sarah Louise. Student Ohio State U., 1968-70; B.A. in Psychology, Ohio U., 1972. With warehouse dept. Excello Wine Co., Columbus, Ohio, 1973-74, with outside sales dept., 1974-83, dir. sales and mktg., 1983—; tchr. creative arts Ohio State U., Columbus, 1983-84; cons. wine merchandising, Columbus, 1974—; lectr. in field, 1974—. Mem. First Community Ch. Club: Marine City Yacht (Marblehead). Avocations: reading; tennis; gardening; sport fishing; boating; jogging. Home: 1893 Bedford Rd Columbus OH 43212 Office: Excello Wine Co 1401 E 17th Ave Columbus OH 43211

VON KLUG, WILLIAM ALAN, professional service executive; b. Topeka, June 7, 1946; s. Francis Gilbert and Velma Mary (Sejkora) Klunk; m. Donna Kay Zaiser, March 20, 1970 (div. April 1974); m. Judith Ann Brower; 1 child, Theresa Elizabeth. Student Washburn U., 1964-66; B.A. St. Cloud State U., Minn., 1971. Dir. relocation Housing Redevel. Authority, St. Cloud, 1970-72; cons. C.R. Pelton & Assocs., St. Paul, 1972-75; pres. Von Klug & Assocs., Mpls., 1975—. Pres. Internat. Right of Way Assn., Mpls., 1984-85, dir., 1985—, pres., 1983-84. Recipient plaque for lecturing Hamline Law Sch., 1976, 78, Internat. Right of Way Assn., 1984. Served to cpl. USMC, 1966-69, Vietnam. Decorated Vietnamese Cross of Galantry. Mem. Nat. Assn. Housing Ofcls. Club: Calhoun Beach, (Mpls.). Avocations: golf; tennis; weight lifting; travel. Office: Von Klug & Associates Inc 4725 Excelsior Blvd Saint Louis Park MN 55416

VON LANG, FREDERICK WILLIAM, librarian, genealogist; b. Scranton, Pa., May 6, 1929; s. Frederick William and Carrie (Brundage) Baron von Lang zu Leinzell; B.S., Pa. State U.-Kutztown, 1951; M.L.S., Syracuse U., 1955; m. Ilsabe von Wackerbarth, July 12, 1960; children—Christoph, Karl Philipp. Librarian, Broughal Jr. High Sch., Bethlehem, Pa., 1951; asst. librarian Bethlehem Public Library, 1952-55; asst. librarian Enoch Pratt Free Library, Balt., 1956-66; library dir. Lehigh County Community Coll., Allentown, Pa., 1966-73, Auburn (Maine) Public Library, 1973-77; dir. St. Joseph (Mo.) Public Library, 1977-79, Hibbing (Minn.) Public Library, 1980—; mem. computer taskforce com. Arrowhead Library System, Virginia, Minn., 1980—; mem. adv. council North Country Library Coop., 1981—. Founding mem., exec. bd., treas. Friends Bethlehem Public Library, 1964-70; mem. exec. bd. Northampton County Assn. for Blind, 1970-72; bd. dirs. St. Joseph Mental Health Soc.; edn. counselor Lehigh Valley br. Lutheran Brotherhood, 1972-73; mem. adv. bd. Salvation Army, Hibbing, 1981—. Mem. Pa. (treas., exec. bd. Lehigh Valley chpt. 1967-70, chmn. community and jr. coll. sect. 1970-71), Maine (legis. com., editor Legis. Manual), New Eng., Mo., Minn. library assns., ALA (council, fed. relations coordinator to Maine Library Assn.), Arrowhead System Council Library Dirs., Bethlehem Jr. C. of C. (past editor, chmn. publs.), Hibbing Hist. Soc. (v.p. 1981-82), Range Geneal. Soc. (pres. 1982-84), S.A.R. (past sec.-treas. bd. mgrs. Valley Forge chpt.), Maine Soc. Mayflower Descs., Soc. Colonial Wars in State Maine, Huguenot Soc. Maine, Bradford Family Compact, Beta Phi Mu. Clubs: Masons (32 deg.), K.T., Shriners, Elks, Order Eastern Star (chpt. patron), Rotary Asso. editor Genealogisches Handbuch des in Bayern immatrikulierten Adels, Vol. 4, 1953. Home: 2129 3d Ave W Hibbing MN 55746 Office: 2020 5th Ave E Hibbing MN 55746

VONRUEDEN, JOHN EDWARD, television station executive; b. Grand Forks, N.D., Jan. 4, 1934; s. John Lawrence and Teresa Margaret (Ackerman) VonR.; m. Joan Alice Schulz, Sept. 15, 1962; children—Jody Lynn, Kurt Michael, Karen Elizabeth. Ph.B., U. N.D., 1955. Sales mgr. Sta. KRYR-AM-FM, Bismarck, N.D., 1966-68, Sta. KFYR-TV, Bismarck, 1968-71; sta. mgr. Sta. KXMB-TV, Bismarck, 1971-79, gen. sales mgr., 1971—; regional sales mgr. 4X TV Network, Bismarck, 1979—; pres. Trans Kakota Advt., Bismarck, 1975—; v.p. Great Plains Video Prodns., Bismarck, 1981—; dir. Audio Visual, Inc., Bismarck; cons., speaker in field. Author: (monthly column) Von on Vin, 1974-83. Commr., Bismarck Park Bd., 1972-76, Bismarck City Commn., 1976-84; nat. committeeman Republican Nat. Com., 1984—; bd. dirs. Young Rep. Nat. Fedn., Fargo, N.D., 1960-66. Served to 1st lt. U.S. Army, 1955-57. Mem. Advt. and Mktg. Club of Bismarck (pres. 1973-74, Ad Person of Yr. 1971, 72, 73), N.D. Broadcasters Assn. (pres. 1976), Nat. Assn. Broadcasters, TV Bur. Advt., Am. Soc. Profl. Cons., Giant Club Meyer Broadcasting Co., (life), Big K Club 4X TV Network (life), Am. Legion. Club: Apple Creek Country (Bismarck) (pres. 1976-77). Lodges: Rotary, KC, Elks. Avocations: banquet speaking, emcee; reading; wine lore. Office: Sta KXMB-TV 1811 N 15th St Box 1617 Bismarck ND 58502

VOORHEES, SUE ITTNER, publisher, editor; b. St. Louis, Sept. 2, 1929; d. William Butts and Mignon Josephine (Morrow) Ittner; m. Alphonso Howe Voorhees, May 14, 1953; children—Kenton Ittner, Janet Ittner Voorhees Lugo, Reed Ittner. A.B. in Bus. Adminstrn., Washington U., St. Louis, B.S. in Bus. Adminstrn., 1951. Asst. soc. editor St. Louis Post dispatch, 1951-54; pub., editor St. Louis Daily Record and St. Louis Countian, 1974—. Chmn. women's com. ABA conv., St. Louis, 1970; women's adv. bd. Continental Bank and Trust Co., St. Louis, 1971-79, Bethesda Hosp., 1981—; lay adv. bd. St. Louis Med. Soc., 1971-74. Mem. Am. Ct. and Comml. Newspapers, Inc. (chmn. pub. notice com. 1983-84, 1st v.p. 1984-85), Met. St. Louis Lawyers' Wives Assn. (1st chmn. 1974-76). Republican. Presbyterian. Club: Jr. League (St. Louis). Office: Daily Record Co 4356 Duncan Ave Saint Louis MO 63110

VORNBROCK, RICHARD PAGE, social worker; b. St. Louis, July 11, 1921; s. Walter Guerdan and Ruth (Page) V.; B.A., U. Mo., 1942; M.S.W., Washington U., St. Louis, 1949; m. Betty Jo Jamieson, Sept. 6, 1947; children—Judith Ann, Richard Page, Betty Marie. Caseworker II, St. Louis city office Mo. Dept. Welfare, 1946-48; psychiat. social worker VA Hosp., Topeka, 1948-53, Minnehaha County Mental Health Center, Sioux Falls, S.D., 1953-58; pvt. practice psychiat. social work, Sioux Falls, 1953-58; instr. sociology Augustana Coll., Sioux Falls, 1955-58; assoc. dir. psychiat. Social Services U. Iowa Hosps and Clinic, Iowa City, 1958-85; pvt. practice psychiat. social work, 1985—; lectr. Sch. Social Work, U. Iowa, 1960-65, instr., 1965—. Served with inf. U.S. Army, 1943-46. Decorated Bronze Star with oak leaf cluster; recipient cert. of appreciation VA, 1953. Mem. Nat. Assn. Social Workers (Social Worker of Yr. 1969), Acad. Cert. Social Workers, Am. Group Psychotherapy Assn., Council Social Work Edn., Nat. Conf. Social Welfare, Register clin. Social Workers, Internat. Assn. Group Psychotherapy, Mental Health Assn., Iowa Human Resources Assn., Social Workers in Health Facilities, Iowa Hosp. Assn. Democrat. Episcopalian. Club: Lions (Iowa City). Home: 1612 Derwen Dr Iowa City IA 52240 Office: 1612 Derwen Dr Iowa City IA 52240

VORYS, ARTHUR ISAIAH, lawyer; b. Columbus, Ohio, June 16, 1923; s. Webb Isaiah and Adeline (Werner) V.; m. Lucia Rogers, July 16, 1949 (div. 1980); children—Caroline S., Adeline Vorys Cranson, Lucy Vorys Noll, Webb I.; m. Ann Harris, Dec. 13, 1980. B.A., Williams Coll., 1945; J.D., Ohio State U., 1949. Bar: Ohio 1949. Since practiced in Columbus: assoc., ptnr. Vorys, Sater, Seymour & Pease, 1949—, sr. ptnr., 1982—; dir. Ohio Casualty Corp., Ohio Casualty Ins. Co., Ohio Security Ins. Co., Pan-Western Life Ins. Co., Shelby Mut. Ins. Co., Vorys Bros., Inc., Wendy's Internat., Inc., other corps.; Supt. of ins., Ohio, 1957-59. Del. Republican Nat. Cov., 1968, 72; trustee, pres. Children's Hosp., Greenlawn Cemetery Assn., Griffith Found. for Ins. Edn., Internat. Ins. Seminars Franklin County Hosp. Commn.; trustee, vice chmn. Ohio State U. Hosps. Served as lt. USMCR, World War II. Decorated Purple Heart. Fellow Ohio State Bar Assn.; mem. ABA, Columbus Bar Assn., Am. Judicature Soc., Am. Soc. Hosp. Attys., Columbus Area C. of C. (dir.), Phi Delta Phi, Chi Psi. Clubs: Rocky Fork Hunt and Country (Gahanna); Columbus Athletic, Capital. Home: 5826 Havens Corners Rd Gahanna OH 43230 Office: 52 E Gay St PO Box 1008 Columbus OH 43216

VORYS, YOLANDA VARGAS, lawyer; b. Tegucigalpa, Honduras, Aug. 24, 1952; came to U.S., 1970; d. Angel D. and Yolanda Pineda de Vargas; m. John C. Vorys, June 19, 1976; 1 dau., Yolanda C. Student Dean Jr. Coll., 1970-71; B.A., Williams Coll., 1974; J.D., Ohio State U., 1981. Bar: Ohio 1981. Translator, Dept. State, Washington, Consulate of Honduras, N.Y.C., Embassy of Honduras, Washington, 1974-77; assoc. Gingher & Christensen, Columbus, Ohio, 1981-84, Vorys Sater Seymour & Pease, Cin., 1984—. Contbr. article to legal jour. Mem. ABA, Ohio Bar Assn., Women Lawyers of Franklin County, Columbus Bar Assn. Home: 800 Farmsworth Ct Cincinnati OH 45202 Office: Vorys Sater et al Suite 2100 Atrium II 221 E 4th St Cincinnati OH 45202

VOSKA, JOSEPH, JR., construction company executive; b. Chgo., July 18, 1930; s. Joseph and Mary (Kulich) V.; married; children—Douglas J., Deborah Leigh, Daryl A., Dennis Joseph, David Andrew. B.Arch., U. Ill., 1952, M.Arch., 1957; postgrad. MIT. Registered architect, Ill., Fla. Nat. planning mgr. Sears Roebuck & Co., Chgo., 1975-79, nat. property mgr., 1979-81, nat. real estate mgr., 1981-83, nat. constrn. mgr., 1983—. Editor: Inland Architect, 1961-65; Nat. Assn. Lutheran Scouters, 1978-83. Contbr. articles to profl. jours. Mem. exec. bd. Northwest Suburban council, Boy Scouts Am., 1974—, v.p., 1982-85; pres. Nat. Assn. Lutheran Scouters, 1978-82; pres. St. Matthews Lutheran Ch., Lake Zurich, Ill., 1982-84. Served to capt. U.S. Army, 1952-54; Korea. Recipient Silver Beaver award Boy Scouts Am., 1977; Lamb award Dept. Nat. Youth Agy. Relationships, Lutheran Council, U.S.A., 1980. Fellow Inst. Store Planners (pres. 1967-68); mem. Nat. Council Archtl. Registration Bds., Internat. Council Shopping Ctrs. (gen. chmn. design and constrn. conf. 1982, 84), Nat. Assn. Rev. Appraisers, Nat. Assn. Corp. Real Estate Execs., Soc. Am. Registered Architects (bd. dirs. 1980), AIA, Ill. Assn. Real Estate Brokers, Chgo. Real Estate Bd., Nat. Inst. Bldg. Sci. Lutheran. Avocations: camping; photography; gardening. Home: 25588 W Miller Rd Barrington IL 60010 Office: Sears Roebuck & Co Sears Tower Chicago IL 60684

VOZAK, FRANK REDIN, III, social worker, educator; b. Alton, Ill., May 12, 1952; s. Frank Henry and Margarita (Redin) V.; m. Terrie Adrienne Rymer, June 30, 1985. B.S. in Social Work, St. Louis U., 1974, cert. environ. studies, 1974, cert. peace studies, 1975, M.S.W., 1975. Cert. assoc. addictions counselor, Ill., Social Worker, Ill. Clin. social work Edward J. Hines Jr. VA Hosp., Hines, Ill., 1977—; social work officer U.S. Army Med. Dept., 1975-77; instr. field work Jane Addams Sch. Social Work, U. Ill., Chgo., 1980—; social work cons. R.D. Traffic Sch., Inc., Aurora, Ill., 1984—. Sec., treas. Mo. Ill., 1984—. Interest Research Group, 1973-74, pres., 1974-75; adult leader Order of Arrow, Boy Scouts Am. Capt. USAR, 1977—; vol. psychotraumatologist disaster services Mid Am. chpt. ARC, 1985—. Mem. Nat. Assn. Social Workers, Ill. Welfare Assn., Acad. Cert. Social Workers, Social Workers in Emergency Medicine (rec. sec. 1983—), Nat. Eagle Scout Assn., Psychosocial Clinicians in Emergency Medicine, Ill. Terminal R.R. Hist. Soc., Nat. Model R.R. Assn., Ill. Ry. Mus., White Pines Model R.R. Club, Gulf Mobile & Ohio Hist. Soc., Nat. Assn. R.R. Passengers, 20th Century R.R. Club, Oak Park Soc. Model Engrs. (sec. 1983—), Am. Youth Hostels, St. Louis U. Alumni Assn., Alton, Hines & Pacific R.R. Hist. Soc., Alpha Sigma Nu. Unitarian. Home: 3655 N Marshfield St Chicago IL 60613 Office: Social Work Service VA Edward J Hines Hospital Hines IL 60141

VREDENBURG, DWIGHT CHARLES, retail company executive. Chmn., chief exec. officer Hy-Vee Food Stores, Inc., Charlton, Iowa, also dir. Office: Hy-Vee Food Stores Inc 1801 Osceola Ave Charlton IA 50049*

VREEMAN, JERRY HEIN, radio-television producer, clergyman; b. Hull, Iowa, May 19, 1950; s. Gerrit William and Nickie Jo (DeVries) V.; m. Coranne Faye Peters, May 26, 1973; children—Joy Christel, Rebecca Sue, Jeremy Evan, Nathan John. B.A., U. Dordt, 1972; M.Div., Calvin Sem., 1976, Th.M., 1976; postgrad. Westminster Sem., 1983. Ordained to ministry Protestant Christian Ref. Ch., 1977. Disc jockey stas. WJBL-AM, Holland, Mich. 1966-68; program dir. Sta. KDCR-FM, Sioux Center, Iowa, 1968-72; producer, assoc. minister broadcasting Back to God Hour, Chgo., 1976-83; producer Radio Today internat. syndication, 1977-83; program dir. ZGBC, Roseau, Dominica, B.W.I., 1980-83; exec. producer Free Man Products, Inc., Lansing, Ill., 1983—; exec. dir. Multimedia Ministries Internat., Lansing, 1983—. Mem. Assn. for Pub. Justice, Assn. Advancement Christian Scholarship, Fellowship Christians in Arts and Media, Assn. Ref. Communication, Nat. Assn. Broadcasters, Nat. Religious Broadcasters, World Assn. Christian Communicators, Broadcast Edn. Assn., Council Chgo. Fgn. Relations. Club: Wimbledon (Palos Heights, ILL.). Publisher, writer children's books including: Little Red, Rennis the Nam, Gorgoyles; (documentary) Issues in American Education; also cassettes, articles, sermons, songs. Office: 18221 Torrance Ave Lansing IL 60438

VUCKOVICH, DRAGOMIR MICHAEL, neurologist; b. Bileca, Yugoslavia, Oct. 27, 1927; s. Alexander J. and Anka (Ivanisevich) V.; came to U.S., 1957; naturalized, 1962; M.D., U. Birmingham, Eng., 1953; m. Brenda Mary Luther, Aug. 23, 1958; children—John, Nicholas, Adrian. Jr. Diplomate Am. Bd. Psychiatry and Neurology, Am. Bd. Pediatrics, Pan Am. Med. Assn. resident in pediatrics Birmingham Children's Hosp., 1954-55; resident med. officer Princess Beatrice Hosp., London, 1955; house physician Hosp. for Sick Children, London, 1955; resident physician Nat. Hosp., London, 1956-57; rotating intern Columbus Hosp., Chgo., 1957-58; resident in neurology and pediatrics VA Research Hosp., Northwestern U. Med. Sch., Chgo., 1958-59, Wesley Meml. Hosp., Chgo., 1959-60, Children's Hosp., 1960-62; practice medicine specializing in neurology, Chgo., 1962—; asso. attending neurologist Children's Hosp., Chgo., 1968—; head, neurology psychiatry Columbus Hosp., Chgo., 1968-81, head of electroencephalography dept., 1969—; v.p. neurosci. Columbus Cuneo Cabrini Med. Center, Chgo., 1981-83, chmn. dept. neurosci., 1981—; head pediatric neurology Loyola U., Chgo., 1970-79, asso. prof., neurology and pediatrics, 1970-77, prof., 1977—. Served with Royal Yugoslav Army, 1942-44, lt. col. Res. Fellow Am. Acad. Pediatrics (sect. neurology), Am. Acad. Neurology, Royal Soc. Health; mem. Am. British med. assns., Soc. Profs. Child Neurology, Am. Med. Electroencephalographic Assn., Royal Coll. Surgeons, Royal Coll. Physicians. Serbian Orthodox. Clubs: Beefeaters, Les Gourmet. Contbr. articles to med. jours. Home: 755 Kipling Pl Deerfield IL 60015 Office: Deerfield Professional Plaza Osterman Ave Deerfield IL 60015

VUILLEMIN, LAWRENCE WILLIAM, lawyer, educator; b. Akron, Ohio, Dec. 24, 1948; s. Alfred Ernest and Rita (Huth) V.; m. Mary Linden Clancey, June 23, 1969 (div. 1976); m. Carol Anne Vinciguerra, June 8, 1979; children—Brett, Betsy. B.A., Notre Dame U., 1970; J.D., U. Akron, 1973. Bar: Ohio 1973, U.S. Dist. Ct. (no. dist.) Ohio 1980. Lectr. in law U. Akron Sch. Law, 1973-80; asst. law dir. City of Cuyahoga Falls, Ohio, 1974; sr. asst. prosecutor Summit County (Ohio), Akron, 1974-80; ptnr. Goldman, Tsarnas & Vuillemin, Akron, 1980-82; assoc. Guy, Mentzer & Towne, Akron, 1982-85; ptnr. Blakemore, Rosen, Meeker & Varian Co., L.P.A., 1985—. Councilman-at-large City of Akron, 1980-82. Recipient Cert. of Appreciation, U.S. Dept. Justice, 1977. Mem. Ohio State Bar Assn., Akron Bar Assn., Omicron Delta Kappa. Democrat. Roman Catholic. Home: 784 Marmont Dr Akron OH 44313 Office: 277 S Broadway Akron OH 44308

VULGAMORE, MELVIN L., college president; b. Springfield, Ohio, July 19, 1935; s. Leo B. and Della M. (McCoy) V.; m. Ethelanne Oyer, Feb. 17, 1957; children—Allison Beth, Sarah Faith. B.A., Ohio Wesleyan U., 1957; B.D., Harvard U., 1960; Ph.D., Boston U., 1963. Prof., chmn. dept. religion Ohio Wesleyan U., Delaware, 1962-78, dean acad. affairs, 1973-78; v.p., provost U. Richmond, Va., 1978-83; pres. Albion Coll., Mich., 1983—; vis. prof. Am. U. Beirut, Lebanon, 1971-72; pres. Va. Inst. for Sci. Research, Richmond, 1978-83; dir. Chem. Bank. Contbr. articles to profl. publs. Mem. Collector's Circle Va. Mus., Richmond, 1978-83; Econ. Devel. Com., Albion, 1983—; mem. Kiwanis Club, Richmond, 1978-83. Mem. Great Lakes Colls. Assn. (exec. com. sec.-treas.), Am. Assn. Higher Edn., N.Am. Tillich Soc., Albion C. of C., Phi Beta Kappa, Omicron Delta Kappa. United Methodist. Clubs: Univ. (N.Y.C.); Detroit Athletic, Detroit Econ.; Country (Battle Creek, Mich.). Lodge: Rotary. Avocations: antique furniture; classic cars; jogging. Office: Albion College Albion MI 49224

VYVERBERG, ROBERT WILLIAM, mental health superintendent; b. Dubuque, Iowa, Dec. 23, 1940; s. William Pifer and Virginia Thelma (Rutger) V.; B.Ed., Ill. Wesleyan U., 1963; M.S., Ill. State U., 1964; Ed.D., No. Ill. U., 1972; m. Mari Ann Jacobs, Nov. 6, 1982; children by previous marriage—Robert William, Benjamin Rutger. Dir. counseling services Crown High Sch., Carpentersville, Ill., 1964-67; dir. outcare services, children and adolescent unit H. Douglas Singer Mental Health Center, Rockford, Ill., 1969-72, dir. psychiat. rehab. and extended care services, 1972-82; region coordinator Services to Elderly, 1978-83; clin. dir. Children's and Adolescent Services, 1982-84, adminstrv. dir., 1982-84; supt. Zeller Mental Health Ctr., 1984—; lectr. crisis theory and crisis intervention No. Ill. U., 1970-84, instr. group counseling and psychotherapy, 1973; cons. Juvenile Justice Personnel Devel. Center, U. Wis., 1977. Mem. Nat. Rehab. Assn., Am. Assn. Counseling and Devel., Am. Rehab. Counselors Assn., Am. Mental Health Counselors Assn., Internat. Assn. Psycho-Social Rehab. Services. Methodist. Home: 4420 Lynnhurst Dr Peoria IL 61615 Office: Zeller Mental Health Center 5407 N Univ Peoria IL 61614

WAAGE, DONALD LANGSTON, public relations executive, banker; b. Minn., Jan. 30, 1925; s. John A. and Amanda O. (Andreas) W.; m. Lori deBrossoit, Sept. 8, 1946; children—Donn, Suzanne Friedman, Bruce, Eric. B.S., St. Cloud U., 1949; M.A., Am. U., 1962. Cert. secondary and coll. tchr., Minn. Reporter, St. Cloud Daily Times, Minn., 1951-54; asst. mgr. fin. and taxation dept., sec. fin. com. C. of C. of U.S., Washington, 1954-60; asst. to bd. dirs., dir. congl. and pub. relations FDIC, Washington, 1960-62; sr. editor fin. reports and pub. Investors Diversified Services, Inc., Mpls., 1962-67; v.p. advertising and pub. relations North Am. Life and Casualty Co., Mpls., 1967-69; dir. fin. and pub. relations Josten's Inc., Mpls., 1969-72; v.p. sales and mktg. Am. Survey Research Corp., Mpls., 1972-77; regional dir. Hwy. Users Fedn., Washington, 1977-83; exec. v.p., ptnr. Coughlan, Trepanier, Waage Assocs., Minnetonka, Minn., 1983—; cons. World Bank, Washington, 1965-70, Republican Nat. Com., Washington, 1974-77; dir. Summit Bank, Bloomington, Minn., 1968-80. Author Mil. history monograph, 1952; contbr. articles on banking to profl. jours. Vice chmn. Mpls. Symphony Orch. fund drive, 1964; chmn. Minnetonka Rep. fund drive, 1970-74; deacon Westminster Presbyn. Ch.; trustee Am. Univ., Washington, 1966-72. Served to maj. with U.S. Army, 1950-53, ETO. Mem. Minn. Press Club, French-Am. C. of C. Club: Wayzata Country; Twin City Polo; Exchequer (first chancellor, founder) (Washington). Avocations: skiing; polo.

WACHEL, LEONARD JOHN, instrumentation company executive; b. East Chicago, Ind., Jan. 2, 1956; s. Walter Frank and Jean Sophie (Kornelik) W.; m. Debra Ellen Scatena, June 27, 1981. B.S. in Chemistry and Physics, Purdue U.-Hammond, 1979; M.B.A. in Fin. and Mktg., U. Chgo., 1982. Owner, Analytical Services Lab., Whiting, Ind., 1973-78; engring. asst. Amoco Oil Co., Whiting, 1978-79, project mgr. tech. services, 1979-81, dept. head process analyzer group, 1981-82; gen. mgr. UIC, Inc., Joliet, Ill., 1982-83, v.p., gen. mgr., 1983—. Author: Process Analyzers, 1982; Automated Stream Analysis for Process Control, vol. 2, 1984. Recipient Nat. Exploration award Explorers Club/Union Carbide, N.Y.C., 1973; Outstanding Achievement award Purdue U., 1978. Mem. Am. Chem. Soc., Instrument Soc. Am., Explorers Club. Avocations: Travel; scuba diving; photography; numismatics. Home: 1700 E 56th St Apt 3902 Chicago IL 60637 Office: UIC Inc 1225 Channahon Rd Joliet IL 60436

WACHOLZ, MARLIN WILLIAM, educator; b. Freeborn County, Minn., Mar. 14, 1936; s. William H. and Erma (Meyer) W.; m. Betty L. Edens, July 2, 1960; children—James, Thomas, John. B.S., U. Minn., 1959, M.A., 1969. Lic. adminstr., tchr. in vocat. edn. Tchr. agr. and adult farm mgmt. Renville (Minn.) High Sch., 1960-77; adminstr. adult vocat. edn. Granite Falls (Minn.) Area Vocat. Tech. Inst., 1977—; tchr. educator Mankato State U., S.W. State U. Served with U.S. Army, 1957-58, 61-62. Named Outstanding Voc-Agr. Tchr. of Minn., Cargill Co. and Mpls. C. of C., 1968. Mem. Minn. Vocat. Assn. (pres. 1975-76), Am. Vocat. Assn., Minn. Vocat. Adminstrs. Assn. (pres. 1983-84), Minn. Vocat. Agr. Instrs. Assn. (pres. 1972-73), Am. Inst. Parliamentarians, Granite Falls C. of C. Lutheran. Club: Granite Falls Golf (pres. 1980-82). Home: 502 11th St Granite Falls MN 56241 Office: AVTI Hwy 212 Granite Falls MN 56241

WACHOWSKI, THEODORE JOHN, radiologist; b. Chgo., Nov. 20, 1907; s. Albert and Constance (Korzeniewski) W.; B.S., U. Ill., 1929, M.D., 1932; m. Barbara F. Benda, June 1, 1931; 1 son, Ted J. Waller. Intern, resident in radiology, asso. radiologist U. Ill. Hosps., 1931-67; clin. prof. radiology U. Ill., 1949-67; radiologist Copley Meml. Hosp., Aurora, Ill., 1935-77, Loretto Hosp., Chgo., 1941-48; practice medicine specializing in radiology, Wheaton, Ill.,

1975-83; ret., 1983. Mem. Radiol. Soc. N.Am. (pres. 1960, Gold medal 1969), Am. Coll. Radiology (pres. 1963, Gold medal 1969), Ill., Kane County med. socs., AMA, Am. Roentgen Ray Soc., Chgo. Radiol. Soc. (past pres., Gold medal 1982). Republican. Club: Glen Oak Country. Contbr. articles to profl. jours. Home: 101 Tennyson Dr Wheaton IL 60187

WACKER, FREDERICK GLADE, JR., manufacturing company executive; b. Chgo., July 10, 1918; s. Frederick Glade and Grace Cook (Jennings) W.; grad. Hotchkiss Sch., 1936; B.A., Yale, 1940; student Gen. Motors Inst. Tech., 1940-42; m. Ursula Comandatore, Apr. 26, 1958; children—Frederick Glade III, Wendy, Joseph Comandatore. With AC Spark Plug div. Gen. Motors Corp., 1940-43, efficiency engr., 1941-43; with Ammco Tools, Inc., North Chicago, Ill., 1947—, pres., chmn. bd., 1948—; founder, 1954, since pres., chmn. bd. Liquid Controls Corp., North Chicago; partner Francis I. duPont & Co., N.Y.C., 1954-70; dir. Moehlenpah Industries, Inc.; condr. Freddie Wacker and His Orch., 1955-70, orch. appeared on TV and radio, recorded for Dolphin Records, Cadet Records. Mem. World Bus. Council, 1971—; chmn. Chgo. chpt. Young Presidents Orgn., 1965-66. Bd. govs. United Republican Fund Ill., 1952-78; trustee Lake Forest Acad., 1956-71; hon. dir. Chgo. chpt. Multiple Sclerosis Soc.; bd. govs. Warren Wilson Coll.; bd. govs. Lyric Opera Chgo., dir., 1963-66; bd. dirs. Trinity Evang. Div. Sch., 1975—, Ch. League Am., 1977-81; bd. dirs., vice chmn. Rockford Inst., 1980—. Served to lt. (j.g.) USNR, 1943-45. Mem. N.A.M., Sports Car Club Am. (pres. 1952-53), Waukegan-North Chgo. C. of C. (dir. 1965-68), Chief Execs. Forum, Chgo. Pres.'s Orgn. (pres. 1972-73), Pres.'s Forum, Am. Motorcycle Assn., Soc. Automotive Engrs., Chgo. Fedn. Musicians (life), Ill. Mfrs. Assn. (dir. 1966—, chmn. bd. 1975), Automotive Hall of Fame (life mem., dir. 1976—). Presbyn. Clubs: Chicago, Racquet (pres. 1960), Econ., Casino, Mid-Am. (Chgo.); Shoreacres (Lake Bluff); Onwentsia (Lake Forest, Ill.); N.Y. Yacht. Home: 1600 Green Bay Rd Lake Bluff IL 60044 Office: 2100 Commonwealth Ave North Chicago IL 60064

WADDELL, OLIVER WENDELL, banker; b. Covington, Ky., 1930. Ed., Duke U., 1954, Rutgers U., 1969. Chmn. bd. chief exec. officer, dir. First Nat. Bank of Cin.; chmn. bd., chief exec. officer First Nat. Cin. Corp.; dir. Myers Y. Cooper Co., Inroads, Inc. Mem. Am. Inst. of Banking. Office: First Nat Bank of Cin 55 E 5th St Cincinnati OH 45201

WADDELL, ROBERT CLINTON, physics educator; b. Mattoon, Ill., Aug. 15, 1921; s. James Franklyn Waddell and Bonnie (Devore) Waddell Richardson; m. Helen Douglas Reynolds, Nov. 28, 1941 (div. 1958); children—Keven, Todd, Nathan; m. Leyla Jane Audi, June 5, 1960. B.S. in Edn., Eastern Ill. U., 1947; M.S., U. Ill., 1948; Ph.D., Iowa State U., 1955. Faculty Eastern Ill. U., Charleston, 1948—, prof. physics, 1960—; research asst. Iowa State U., Ames, 1953-55. Served to ensign USNR, 1942-46. Mem. Am. Assn. Physics Tchrs. (chmn. com. internat. edn. 1978-79), Ill. Assn. Physics Tchrs. (pres. 1968-72), Groupe Internat. De Recherche Sur S'Enseignement De La Physique, Charleston C. of C. Lodge: Elks. Avocation: musician. Home: 9 Circle Dr Charleston IL 61920 Office: Eastern Ill U Charleston IL 61920

WADDLE, DEBRA JOLENE, college residence administrator; b. Larned, Kans., Nov. 6, 1953; d. Conrad Lee and Lois Marlene (Sanders) W. B.S. in Psychology, Emporia State U., 1975, M.S. in Student Personnel Adminstrn., 1977. Residence hall dir. U. Wis.-River Falls, 1977-81; area coordinator Central Mo. State U., Warrensburg, 1981-83; dir. residence Coll. St. Teresa, Winona, Minn., 1983—. Mem. United Telecom Customer Council, 1981-83, co-chmn. faculty relations com. 1981-83. Recipient lifetime membership award Hagestad Union Bd., U. Wis.-River Falls, 1980-81. Mem. Nat. Assn. Student Personnel Adminstrs., Am. Personnel and Guidance Assn., Nat. Assn. Women Deans, Adminstrs. and Counselors, Am. Coll. Personnel Assn., Assn. Coll. and Univ. Housing Officers (mem. personnel training com. 1983-84). Office: Residence Life Office Coll St Teresa Winona MN 55987

WADE, DALE BROOKINS, dentist, educator; b. Columbus, Ohio, July 25, 1940; s. Robert Edward and Louise (Roby) W.; m. Jan Schwiebert, June 22, 1963; children—Geoffrey Edward, Andrew Brookins. M.S., Ohio State U., 1969, D.D.S., 1965. Diplomate Am. Bd. Orthodontics. Asst. clin. prof. Ohio State U., Columbus, 1969—; practice orthodontics, Columbus, 1969—; editor Great Lakes Orthodontic Soc., 1980—, Found. for Orthodontic Research. Contbr. articles to profl. jours. Life mem. Upper Arlington Civic Assn., Columbus, 1980; scoutmaster Troop 180, Central Ohio council Boy Scouts Am., 1984—. Served as lt. USN, 1965-67. Fellow Acad. Internat. Dental Studies; mem. Am. Bd. Orthodontics (Coll. of Diplomates), Edward Angle Soc., Columbus Dental Soc. (pres. 1981), Ohio State U. Orthodontic Alumni Found. (pres. 1972), Omicron Kappa Upsilon. Club: N.W. Sertoma (pres. 1976). Avocations: camping; skiing; photography; jogging; golf. Home: 3120 S Dorchester Rd Columbus OH 43221 Office: 3220 Riverside Dr Columbus OH 43221

WADE, ORMAND JOSEPH, See *Who's Who in America,* 43rd edition.

WADE, RONALD DEAN, optometrist; b. Columbus, Ind., Mar. 11, 1943; s. Paul Edward and Ruby Love (Jackson) W.; m. Beverly Joy Meyer, Jan. 31, 1970; children—Jill, Jeffrey. B.S., Ind. U., 1965, M.O., 1966. Diplomate Nat. Bd. Examiners in Optometry. Practice of optometry, South Bend, Ind., 1970—. Served to lt. USN, 1966-69. Fellow Am. Acad. Optometry; mem. Am. Optometric Assn. (mem. contact lens sect.), Ind. Optometric Assn., North Central Optometric Soc., St. Joseph County Optometric Soc. Republican. Methodist. Club: Knollwood Country (Granger). Avocations: Tennis; golf. Home: 50600 Woodbury Way Granger IN 46530 Office: 810 E Colfax Ave South Bend IN 46617

WADE, ROYCE ALLEN, real estate broker, consultant; b. Medford, Wis., Apr. 30, 1932; s. Charles L. and Mildred H. (Clarin) W.; B.S. (acad. scholar), U. Wis.-Stevens Point, 1954; M.Div., Garrett Theol. Sem., Evanston, Ill., 1960; M.S. in Adult Edn., U. Wis.-Milw., 1968; postgrad. U. Wis.-Madison, 1970-75; m. Corinne Mae Weber, June 30, 1956; children—Suzanne Mae, Debra Ann. Ordained to ministry Methodist Ch., 1960; pastor Richmond (Wis.) Meth. Ch., 1956-58, Asbury United Meth. Ch., Janesville, Wis., 1958-61; tchr., guidance counselor Edgerton (Wis.) High Sch., 1961-62; assoc. pastor Community United Meth. Ch., Whitefish Bay, Wis., 1962-66; pastor Simpson and Gardner United Meth. Chs., Milw., 1966-68; assoc. pastor St. Luke United Meth. Ch., Sheboygan, Wis., 1968-69; pastor Poynette and Inch United Meth. Chs., 1969-74; dir. Adult Study Center, Portage, Wis., 1974-75; dir. growth and devel., dir. Profl. Products & Services, Inc., Sauk City, Wis., 1976-83; realtor Dick Marquardt Agy., Poynette, 1983—; HRD cons., 1983—; curriculum cons. U. Wis. Sch. Nursing, 1974-76, instr. small group seminar, 1974-76, supr. behavioral disabilities student tchrs., 1974-76; adult edn. instr. Wis. Conf. United Meth. Ch., 1964-69. Village trustee, Poynette, 1977-81; mem. Police Aux., Whitefish Bay; bd. dirs. North Shore Council Human Relations, Milw., Inter Faith Council, Milw. Served with C.I.C., AUS., 1954-56. Cert. in pastoral counseling, interpersonal relations; Grad Realtors Inst.; candidate Cert. Resdl. Specialist Mem. Adult Edn. Assn., Am. Soc. Tng. and Devel., Nat. Assn. Realtors, Wis. Realtors Assn., Phi Delta Kappa. Club: Optimist. Research on participation in adult intructional groups using Eriksonian ego-stage theory. Home: 122 E Washington St Poynette WI 53955 Office: 125 N Main St Poynette WI 53955

WADENA, DARRELL EUGENE, Indian tribe executive; b. White Earth, Minn., Nov. 23, 1938; s. John S. and Mary (Peabody) W.; m. Bonnie Londo, Apr. 7, 1959; children—Tony, Ann, Darrell Eugene, Shannon, Tracy, David. Student Minn. pub. schs. Heavy equipment operator Swingen Constrn., Grand Forks, N.D., 1970-73, W.E. Wylie Constrn. Co., Mpls. and Los Angeles, 1962-73; mng. dir. Minn. Chippewa Tribe Constrn. Co., Cass Lake, 1973-76; pres. Minn. Chippewa Tribe; chmn. White Earth Band of Chippewa Indians. Served with U.S. Army, 1956-59. Mem. Internat. Union Operating Engrs. of AFL-CIO, 1962-74. Democrat. Roman Catholic. Office: Box 418 White Earth Reservation White Earth MN 55491*

WAGENAAR, THEODORE CLARENCE, sociology educator; b. Heerhugowaard, Netherlands, July 19, 1948; came to U.S., 1951, naturalized, 1961; s. Henry and Alice (Bouwens) W.; m. Barbara K. Visser, May 26, 1970; 1 child, Keri. A.B., Calvin Coll., Grand Rapids, Mich., 1970; M.A., Ohio State U., 1971, Ph.D., 1975. Cert. elem. sch. tchr., Ohio. Asst. prof. sociology Miami U., Oxford, Ohio, 1975-78, assoc. prof., 1978-82, prof., 1982—; program analyst Nat. Ctr. Edn. Stats., Washington, 1980. Author: Readings for Social Research, 1980; Practicing Social Research, 1982; Readings and Review-Sociology, 1985. Nat. Ctr. Edn.-Stats. grantee, 1981—; recipient Mauksch award Disting. Contbns. to Undergrad. Sociology, 1984. Mem. Am. Sociol. Assn., North Central Sociol. Assn., Pacific Sociol. Assn., Midwest Sociol. Soc., Am. Ednl. Research Assn. Home: 1329 Dana Dr Oxford OH 45056 Office: Miami U Dept Sociology Oxford OH 45056

WAGENER, EUGENE HERBERT, hospital maintenance manager, construction consultant; b. St. Louis, June 13, 1931; s. Edward J. and Carrie (Wochlinger) W.; m. Anna Marie Oswald, Apr. 21, 1956; 1 son Christopher Eugene. Student parochial schs., St. Louis. Supt. maintenance Bussman Fuse Co., 1954-63; supr. Springfield (Mo.) Housing Authority, 1974-76; master mechanic City of Springfield, 1977-78; mgr. maintenance dept. St. Louis U. Hosp., 1979—; cons. constrn., archtl., interior design cos. Served to master sgt. U.S. Army, 1949-54. Decorated Silver Star, Bronze Star, Purple Heart (3). Mem. St. Louis Engring. Assn., Am. Legion, VFW. Roman Catholic. Club: Eagles. Developed innovative procedures and devices for hosp. Home: 11650 Raymond St Spanish Lake MO 63138 Office: St Louis Univ Hosp 1325 S Grand Blvd St Louis MO 63104

WAGENKNECHT, JAMES ROBERT, school principal; b. Smithton, Mo., July 13, 1934; s. Lawrence Everett and Gladys Gertrude (Hoehns) W.; m. Jean Lydell, June 8, 1957; children—Dawn Renee, Holly Beth. B.S. in Edn., Central Mo. State U., 1956; M.S. in Secondary Adminstrn., So. Ill. U., 1966; postgrad. U. Mo.-St. Louis, 1972-75. Tchr. math. Ritenour Sch. Dist., St. Louis, 1958-61, tchr. phys. edn., 1961-70, asst. prin., 1970-82, prin., 1982—. Chmn. park bd. City of Bridgeton, Mo., 1982-84. Served with U.S. Army, 1956-58. Mem. Nat. Assn. Secondary Sch. Prins., Mo. Assn. Secondary Sch. Prins., Nat. Middle Sch. Assn., Mo. Middle Sch. Assn., St. Louis Middle Sch. Assn. Mem. Christian Ch. Lodge: Masons. Avocation: woodworking. Home: 4324 Gladwyn Dr Bridgeton MO 63044 Office: Hoech Middle Sch 3312 Ashby Rd Saint Ann MO 63074

WAGLEY, ROBERT ALLEN, business and public policy educator; b. Chgo., Mar.12, 1939; s. Leonard Marion and Syble Agnes (Thomas) W.; m. Lorraine Janice Murray, June 9, 1962; children—Jennifer, Jocelyn, Shawn. B.S., Ball State U., 1962, M.A., 1968, Ed.D., U. Cin., 1974. Tchr. Wayne Twp. Schs., Dayton, Ohio, 1964-67, head. bus. dept., 1967-69; instr. bus. Wright State U., Dayton, 1969-74, assoc. prof., 1974—, faculty assoc. Ctr. for Corp. Concern, 1983—; research fellow U. Cin., 1971-74; sec. bd. dirs. Wagley Farms, Inc., Muncie, Ind., 1974—. Author: (with others) Readings in Business and Society, 1972; Business and Society '74 and '75, 1974; Management Response to Public Issues Concepts, Cases in Strategy Formulation, 1985. Contbr. articles on social responsibility and corp. reporting to profl. jours. Mem. Acad. Mgmt., World Future Soc., Assn. Pub. Policy Analysis and Mgmt., Pub. Affairs Council, Midwest Bus. Adminstrn. Assn. Republican. Lutheran. Home: 3912 Knollwood Dr Beavercreek OH 45432 Office: Wright State Univ Rike Hall Dayton OH 45435

WAGNER, ALVIN LOUIS, JR., profl. real estate appraiser, cons.; b. Chgo., Dec. 19, 1939; s. Alvin Louis and Esther Jane (Wheeler) W.; student U. Ill., 1958-59; B.A., Drake U., 1962; postgrad. Real Estate Inst., Chgo., 1960-65; m. Susan Carole Fahey, Aug. 14, 1965; children—Alvin Louis III, Robert Percy. Asst. appraiser Oak Park (Ill.) Fed. Savings & Loan Co., 1955-60; v.p. real estate sales A. L. Wagner & Co., Flossmoor, Ill., 1961-63; real estate loan officer, chief appraiser Beverly Bank, Chgo., 1963-67; assoc. real estate appraiser C. A. Bruckner & Assos., Chgo., 1967-70; founder, profl. real estate appraiser and cons. A. L. Wagner & Co., Flossmoor, 1970—. Mem. faculty Am. Inst. Real Estate Appraisers, Chgo., 1974—; instr. real estate appraising Prairie State Coll., Chicago Heights, Ill., 1970—; mem. adv. com. Real Estate Sch., 1972—; community prof. Gov.'s State U., 1977—, founding mem. real estate adv. bd. Mem. Rich Township (Ill.) Personal Services Commn., 1973—; v.p., drive chmn. Flossmoor Community Chest, Crusade of Mercy, 1974-75, pres., 1975-76. Auditor, Rich Township, 1973-77. Governing bd. Glenwood (Ill.) Sch. for Boys, 1973—; chmn. bus. edn. occupational adv. com. Homewood-Flossmoor High Sch., 1977; pres. South Suburban Focus Council; mem. South Suburban Mayors and Mgrs. Bus. and Industry Adv. Council, Flossmore Econ. Devel. Commn. Mem. Am. Inst. Real Estate Appraisers (mem. governing council 1974-75, Profl. Recognition award 1977), Chgo. Assn. Commerce and Industry, Chgo., Homewood-Flossmoor real estate bds., Nat., Ill. assns. realtors, Homewood-Flossmoor Jaycees, Phi Delta Theta (pres. chpt. 1960), Chgo. Phi Delta Theta Alumni Club (pres.), Omega Tau Rho, Lambda Alpha. Clubs: Flossmoor Country, Variety, Rotary, Masons. Mem. editorial bd. Appraisal Jour., 1975—; contbr. articles to real estate jours., also Mobility mag., Mcpl. Econ. Devel. Home: 927 Park Dr Flossmoor IL 60422 Office: 2709 Flossmoor Rd Flossmoor IL 60422

WAGNER, BLAKE DOUGLAS, clergyman; b. Akron, Ohio, Oct. 27, 1931; s. John Ernest and Ruth Etta (Daniel) W.; m. Gere Caryl Fulmer, Aug. 6, 1954; children—Lynn Ann Wagner Wood, Blake Douglas, Jr. B.A., U. Akron, 1953; M.Div., Oberlin Grad. Sch. Theology, 1957; D.Ministry, Vanderbilt U., 1974. Ordained to ministry Methodist Ch., 1957. Pastor Zion Evang. United Brethren, Cuyahoga Falls, Ohio, 1951-53, Montrose Zion Evang. United Brethren Ch., Akron, 1953-59, The Emmanuel Ch., Evang. United Brethren, Lorain, Ohio, 1959-67, The Master's Ch., United Meth. Ch., Euclid, Ohio, 1967-74; sr. pastor Main St. United Meth. Ch., Mansfield, Ohio, 1974—; field rep. The Robert H. Schuller Inst. for Successful Church Leadership, Garden Grove, Calif., 1980—. Pres. Richland County Hospice Assn., Mansfield, 1980—; trustee Make-a-Way Center, Inc., Mansfield, 1984—; mem. exploring com. Johnny Appleseed council Boy Scouts Am., Mansfield, 1983—; participant Ohio State U. Commn. on interprofl. edn. and practice, Columbus. Named life mem. Ohio Pastor's Convocation Ohio Council of Chs., 1973; recipient Dean Thomas Graham award Oberlin Coll. Grad. Sch., Theology, 1957, St. Martin DePorres award Lorain County Catholic Council, 1966, Founders award Ohio Wesleyan U., 1980; Pixley scholar U. Akron, 1952-53. Mem. Inter-Church Council (pres. 1984-85), The Mansfield Ministerial Assn., (pres. 1978-79), East Ohio Conf. United Meth. Ch. (bd. ministry 1984—), Mansfield Dist. Com. on Ministry (chmn. 1983—), Dist. Council on Ministries. Republican. Lodges: Optimist (pres. 1978-79), Masons. Avocations: travel, camping, photography. Home: 516 Fairoaks Blvd Mansfield OH 44907 Office: 230 S Main St Mansfield OH 44903

WAGNER, BRIAN ALLEN, distributing company executive; b. Moline, Ill., Nov. 7, 1958; s. Norbert Herbert and Mary Jane (Carden) W. A.A., Black Hawk Coll., 1976. Gen. mgr. Warren Radio Co., Davenport, Iowa, 1978—. Republican precinct committeeman, Rock Island County, Moline, Ill., 1984. Mem. Tri-City Assn. of Purchasing Mgmt. Presbyterian. Avocations: gardening; collecting political memorabilia. Home: 119 17th Ave East Moline IL 61244 Office: Warren Radio Co 1205 East River Dr Davenport IA 52803

WAGNER, CHARLES ALAN, librarian; b. Elkhart, Ind., Apr. 27, 1948; s. C. Arthur and Lydia M. (Stump) W.; B.A., Manchester (Ind.) Coll., 1970; M.L.S., Ind. U., 1973; m. Marilynn B. Dray, Aug. 17, 1971; children—Sarah, Wendy. Library dir. Peru Public Library, 1973—. Mem. Ind. Library Assn., Plymouth Club Am. Lodge: Rotary. Author articles field. Cartoons appear in comic books, newspapers, mags. Address: 102 E Main St Peru IN 46970

WAGNER, DOROTHY MARIE, court reporting service executive; b. Milw., June 8, 1924; d. Theodore Anthony and Leona Helen (Ullrich) Wagner; grad. Milw. Bus. U., 1944; student Marquette U., U. Wis., Milw. Stenographer, legal sec., Milw., 1942-44; hearing reporter Wis. Workmen's Compensation Dept., 1944-48; ofcl. reporter to judge Circuit Ct., Milw., 1952-53; owner, operator ct. reporting service Dorothy M. Wagner & Assocs., Milw., 1948—; guest lectr. ct. reporting Madison Area Tech. Coll., 1981—; asst. ofcl. reporter State of Wis. Recipient Gregg Diamond medal Gregg Pub. Co., 1950. Mem. Nat. (registered profl. reporter, certificate of proficiency), Wis. shorthand reporters assns., Am. Legion Aux. Roman Catholic. Home: 214 Williamsburg Dr Thiensville WI 53092 Office: 135 Wells St Suite 400 Milwaukee WI 53203

WAGNER, ERIC ARMIN, sociology educator; b. Cleve., May 31, 1941; s. Armin Erich and Florence (Edwards) W. A.B., Ohio State U., 1964; M.A., U. Fla., 1968, Ph.D., 1973. Instr. sociology Ohio U., Athens, 1968-73, asst. prof., 1973-75, assoc. prof., 1975-83, prof., 1983—, chmn. sociology and anthropology, 1974-78, vice chmn. faculty senate, 1982-84. Mem. Am. Sociol. Assn., Internat. Sociol. Assn., Latin Am. Studies Assn., North Central Sociol. Assn., Midwest Assn. for Latin Am. Studies (pres. 1979-80), U.S. Orienteering Fedn. (dir. 1976-82, sec.-treas. 1976-78, v.p. 1979-80, sec. 1980-82), Delta Sigma Phi. Presbyterian. Club: Southeast Ohio Orienteering (Athens). Contbr. articles on Latin Am. sport and society to various publs. Home: Route 5 Box 237 Athens OH 45701 Office: Dept Sociology Ohio U Athens OH 45701

WAGNER, HARVEY L., electric utility company executive; b. Wilkinsburg, Pa., Sept. 13, 1952; s. Samuel Francis and Marjorie Annette (Dick) W.; m. Linda Christine Bauer, July 12, 1975; children—David Robert, Brian James. A.B. in Acctg., Grove City Coll., 1974; M.B.A. in Fin., U. Akron, 1980. Acctg. trainee Ohio Edison Co., Akron, 1974, assoc. acct., 1974-75, coordinating acct., 1975-79, chief acct., 1979-83, asst. comptroller, 1983—. Treas. Advent Lutheran Ch., Uniontown, Ohio, 1979—. Mem. Fin. Mgmt. Assn. Republican. Home: 10630 Scotney Ave Uniontown OH 44685 Office: Ohio Edison Co 76 S Main St Akron OH 44308

WAGNER, JEFFRY TENNANT, banker; b. Columbus, Ohio, April 19, 1954; s. Vincent William and Patricia Joanne (Tennant) W.; m. Amanda Ann Harville, Mar. 29, 1981. B.S. in Fin., Internat. Bus. and Econs., Bowling Green State U., 1976. With controllers office, Transmission and Chassis div. Ford Motor Co., Livonia, Mich., 1977-80; bank officer Huntington Nat. Bank (merged with Reeves Bank and Trust Co., 1982), Dover, Ohio, 1980—; cons. computer use. Mem. budget com. local United Way, 1983—. Recipient Wall St. award Dow Jones, 1976. Mem. Beta Gamma Sigma. Republican. Methodist. Home: 434 E 2d St Dover OH 44622

WAGNER, JOHN GARNET, educator, researcher, consultant; b. Weston, Ont., Can., Mar. 28, 1921; s. Herbert William and Coral (Cates) W.; m. Eunice Winona Kelsey, July 4, 1946; children—Wendie Lynn, Linda Beth. Phar. B., U. Toronto, 1947; B.S. in Phar., U. Sask. (Can.), 1948, B.A. in Chemistry, 1949; Ph.D., Ohio State U., 1952, D.Sc., 1980. Research scientist The Upjohn Co., Kalamazoo, 1953-56, head pharm. research sect., 1956-63, sr. research scientist Med. Research div., 1963-68; prof. pharmacy, asst. dir. research and devel. pharm. service Univ. Hosp., U. Mich., Ann Arbor, 1968-72, prof. pharmacy and Coll. Pharmacy and staff mem. Upjohn Ctr. Clin. Pharm., Med. Sch., 1973-82, Albert B. Prescott prof. pharmacy and staff mem. Upjohn Ctr. Clin. Pharm., 1982—; cons. Upjohn Co., Key Pharms., Inc., Warner Lambert Co. Served with RCAF, 1941-45. Recipient William E. Upjohn award, 1960; Ebert prize Am. Pharm. Assn., 1961; Centennial Achievement award Ohio State U., 1970; Host-Madsen medal Fedn. Internat. Pharmaceutique, 1972; Propter merita medal Czechoslovakian Med. Soc., 1974; Stimulation Research award Acad. Pharm. Scis., 1983; Volwiler Research Achievement award Am. Assn. Colls. Pharmacy, 1983. Mem. Am. Pharm Assn., Acad. Pharm. Sci. (research achievement award 1984, pharmaceutics award 1984), Am. Fedn. Clin. Research, AAAS, Am. Soc. Pharmacology and Exptl. Therapeutics, N.Y. Acad. Scis., Internat. Soc. Study Xenobiotics, Sigma Xi, Rho Chi, Phi Lambda Upsilon. Author: Biopharmaceutics and Relevant Pharmacokinetics, 1971; Fundamentals of Clinical Pharmacokinetics, 1975; contbr. numerous articles to profl. jours.; patentee in field. Office: Upjohn Ctr Clin Pharmacology U Mich Med Ctr Ann Arbor MI 48109

WAGNER, KENNETH A., educational consultant, photographer; b. Union City, Ind., Nov. 30, 1919. A.B., DePauw U., 1941, M.A., 1946; Ph.D., U. Mich., 1951. Instr. botany U. Tenn., Knoxville, 1947-49; asst. prof. Fla. State U., Tallahassee, 1949-54; prof., head biology Old Dominion Coll., Norfolk, Va., 1954-59; sci. coordinator Powell Labs., Gladstone, Oreg., 1959-66; prof. biology N.C. Wesleyan Coll., Rocky Mount, 1966-69, Ferris State Coll., Big Rapids, Mich., 1969-84; mem. Sino-Am. Sci. and Tech. Exchange, China, 1982. Author: (with others) Introduction to Modern Biology, 1972; Under Siege, 1973. Author-photographer ednl. slide sets on erosion, agr., desert ecology; contbr. articles to sci. jours. Instr. U.S. Power Squadron, Oreg., 1962-66; del. Alma Coll. Nat. Conf. on Energy, 1971. Home: 112 Ave D Greenville OH 45331

WAGNER, LYNNITA KAY COATS, court referee, lawyer; b. Celina, Ohio, Jan. 13, 1943; d. Vaughn Daniel Coats and Mary Helen (Baker) Peterson; divorced; children—William A., Whitney Lynn, Adam Vaughn. B.A., Ohio No. U., 1964, J.D., 1967. Bar: Ohio 1967, U.S. Dist. Ct. (so. dist.) Ohio 1971, U.S. Ct. Appeals (6th cir.) 1971. Assoc. McCulloch, Felger, Fite & Gutmann, Piqua, Ohio, 1967-69; ptnr. Huffman & Landis, West Milton, Ohio, 1969-76, Wagner & Wagner, West Milton, 1977-80; sole practice, West Milton, 1980-82; civil asst. Miami County Pros. Office. Troy, Ohio, 1969, 73-74, 76-82; referee Miami Probate and Juvenile Ct., Troy, 1982—; dir. Miami County Custody Rev. Bd., Troy, 1982—. Pres. Union Twp. Republican Womens Club, West Milton, 1972-74; bd. dirs. Migrant Ministry, Tipp City, Ohio, 1970-72, Upper Valley Youth Services Bur., Troy, 1975-76, Dettmer Hosp., Troy, 1977-85, sec., 1981-85; atty. Fish Union Twp., West Milton, 1970—; bd. dirs., atty. Miami County Rehab. Ctr., Piqua, 1972-82. Mem. ABA, Ohio State Bar Assn., Miami County Bar Assn. (sec. 1969-71), Miami Valley Assn. Women Attys. Methodist. Clubs: Miltonian, Dayton Ski. Avocations: skiing; needlework; reading. Home: 111 S Jay St West Milton OH 45383 Office: Miami County Juvenile Ct Miami County Safety Bldg Troy OH 45373

WAGNER, MORRIS, microbiology educator; b. Chgo., Aug. 6, 1917; s. Isador Joel and Ida (Rovner) W.; m. Zelma Zonenberg, Aug. 24, 1947; children—Nana L., Robert D., Joel I., Judith B. B.S., Cornell U., 1941; M.S., U. Notre Dame, 1946; Ph.D., Purdue U., 1966. Lab. technician Snyder Packing Co., Albion, N.Y., 1939; microbiologist Lobund Lab., Notre Dame, Ind., 1943-46; instr. dept. microbiology U. Notre Dame, 1946-51, asst. prof., 1951-54, assoc. prof., 1954-69, prof. microbiology, 1969—; adj. prof. Ind. U. Med. Sch., South Bend Ctr. for Med. Edn., 1977—, cons., 1985. Co-editor; Germfree Research 1985. Contbr. articles to profl. jours. Recipient award of Recognition, Am. Soc. Dentistry for Children, 1981; faculty fellow NSF, 1963; grantee NSF, NASA, NATO, Nat. Inst. Dental Research. Mem. Am. Soc. Microbiology (pres. Ind. chpt. 1967-68), Assn. Gnotobiotics of Am. (bd. dirs.), Internat. Assn. Gnotobiology, Am. Assn. Lab. Animal Sci. Democrat. Jewish. Club: Racquet (South Bend). Lodge: B'nai B'rith. Home: 1940 Briar Way South Bend IN 46614 Office: Lobund Lab U Notre Dame Notre Dame IN 46556

WAGNER, RICHARD, sports consulting executive; b. Central City, Nebr., Oct. 19, 1927; s. John Howard and Esther Marie (Wolken) W.; student public schs., Central City; m. Gloria Jean Larsen, May 10, 1950; children—Randolph Greg, Cynthia Kaye. Gen. mgr. Lincoln (Nebr.) Baseball Club, 1955-58; mgr. Pershing Mcpl. Auditorium, Lincoln, 1958-61; exec. staff Ice Capades, Inc., Hollywood, Calif., 1961-63; gen. mgr. Sta. KSAL, Salina, Kans., 1963-65; dir. promotion and sales St. Louis Nat. Baseball Club, 1965-66; gen. mgr. Forum, Inglewood, Calif., 1966-67; asst. to exec. v.p. Cin. Reds, 1967-70, asst. to pres., 1970-74, v.p. adminstrn., 1975, exec. v.p., 1975-77, exec. v.p., gen. mgr., pres., gen. mgr., 1977-83; pres. RGW Enterprises Inc., Cin., 1978—; pres., dir. N.Platte (Nebr.) Broadcasting, Inc., 1972—, pres., treas. Emporia Broadcasting, Inc., Kans., 1984—. Served with USNR, 1945-47, 50-52. Named Exec. of Yr., Minor League Baseball, Sporting News, 1958. Mem. Internat. Assn. Arena Mgrs. Republican. Methodist. Office: 110 Boggs Ln Suite 280 Cincinnati OH 45246

WAGNER, ROBERT DEAN, greenhouse and garden store owner, clergyman; b. Akron, Colo., July 22, 1926; s. Anton M. and Gertie (Nelson) W.; m. Anneta Lucille Foster, Nov. 15, 1945; children—Joy, Janet, Judith, James. B.Th., San Jose Bible Coll., 1950; B.S. in Edn., Lincoln U., 1969; postgrad. U. Mo., 1971-72. Cert. tchr., Mo.; ordained to ministry Christian Ch., 1944. Minister Christian Ch., Jefferson City, Mo., 1962-69, Benton City, Mo., 1972-77, Auxvasse, Mo., 1983—; owner-mgr. House Plants Unltd., Columbia, Mo., 1977—; pres. Christian Evangelizers, Central Mo., 1983-84. Hybridizer 6 generic crosses of succulent plants in lily family, 1981-84. Republican. Avocations: philately; piano playing. Home: Rural Route 2 Columbia MO 65201 Office: House Plants Unlimited I-70 at Millersburg Exit Columbia MO 65201

WAGNER, ROBERT WALTER, photography, cinema and communications educator, media producer, consultant; b. Newport News, Va., Nov. 16, 1918; s. Walter George and Barbara Anna W.; m. Betty Jane Wiles, Nov. 21, 1948; children—Jonathan R., Jeffrey A., Jennifer J. B.Sc., Ohio State U., 1940, M.A., 1941, Ph.D., 1953. Motion picture writer-dir. Office War Info., N.Y.C. and Washington, 1942-43; writer-dir. Office Coordinator Interam. Affairs for South and Central Am., 1943-44; chief info. Div. Mental Hygiene, Ohio Dept. Pub. Welfare, 1944-46; dir. div. motion pictures Ohio State U., 1946-58, prof. communications, photography and cinema, 1960—; pres. Univ. Film Found., 1979-85; internat. cons. communications; bd. dirs. Am. Film Inst., 1974-81; mem. faculty U. So. Calif., 1958-59, U. P.R., 1961, 66, 68, San Jose State U., 1967, Ariz. State U., 1971, Concordia U., Montreal, Que., Can., 1980, 81,

Danish Nat. Film Sch., 1983, 84. Ency. Brit. fellow, 1953; Sr. Fulbright fellow, Peru, 1976. Fellow Soc. Motion Picture and TV Engrs. (Eastman Gold Medal award 1981); mem. Acad. TV Arts and Scis. (Disting. Service award 1967, Ohiana Pegasus award 1985), Univ. Film/Video Assn. (bd. editors jour. 1975-85, editor jour. 1956-75), Internat. Congress Schs. Cinema and TV (v.p. 1964-82), Assn. Ednl. Communication and Tech. (bd. editors jour. 1976—). Club: Torch (Columbus, Ohio). Author film series: Series of Motion Picture Documents on Communication Theory and New Educational Media, 1966; editor: Education of Film Maker, 1975. Home: 1353 Zollinger Rd Upper Arlington OH 43221 Office: 156 W 19th Ave Ohio State U Columbus OH 43210

WAGNER, ROMAN FRANK, insurance agency executive; b. Sheboygan, Wis., Mar. 16, 1927; s. Roman N. and Clara C. (Ott) W.; B.S. in Bus. Adminstrn., Marquette U., 1950; M.S. in Fin. Services, Am. Coll., 1983 m. Jacqueline Anne Randall, Aug. 13, 1949; children—Kenneth, Katherine, Julie, Lisa, Janine, Jodi, Randall. With Bankers Life Co., Sheboygan, 1950—; spl. agt. Sheboygan Falls (Wis.) Mut. Ins. Co., 1953-54; treas. Sheboygan Town & Country, Inc., 1963—; pres. Roman Wagner Agy., Inc., Sheboygan, 1964—, Scorpio, Inc., Sheboygan, 1979—; instr. Ins. Inst. Am., Lakeshore Tech. Inst., 1966—; condr. workshops in field; mem. Wis. Ins. Agts. Adv. Council, 1974-80. Active, United Fund drs., Sheboygan, 1963-68; mem. City of Sheboygan Police and Fire Commn., 1968-75, sec., 1970-75. Served with USN, 1945-47. Named Wis. Mr. Mut. Agt., 1966; Jaycees Key Man, 1960. Chartered fin. cons. Mem. Sheboygan County Ind. Ins. Agts., Chartered Life Underwriters Soc., Soc. Chartered property and Casualty Underwriters, Am. Inst. Property and Liability Underwriters (mem. ethical inquiry bd. 1982—), Ind. Ins. Agts. of Wis-(Agt. of Yr.-award 1978), Wis. Assn. Life Underwriters, Profl. Ins. Agts. of Wis., Wis. Found. for Ins. Edn. (Disting. Service award 1975), Sheboygan C. of C., Alpha Kappa Psi, Beta Gamma Sigma, Alpha Phi Omega. Republican. Roman Catholic. Clubs: Econ. (pres. 1980), K.C. (4th degree), Rotary (dist. chmn. Belgium Youth Exchange 1981-82). Home: 1120A Aspen Ct Kohler WI 53044 Office: 611 New York Ave Sheboygan WI 53081

WAGNER, THOMAS EDWARD, lawyer; b. Erie, Pa., Dec. 4, 1944; s. Edward W. and Margaret E. (Roscher) W.; m. Maryann Jackman, Aug. 3, 1968; children—Kristen, John, Andrew, Daniel. B.S., U.S. Mil. Acad., 1966; J.D., Vanderbilt U., 1973. Bar: Ohio 1973. Assoc. Calfee, Halter & Griswold, Cleve., 1973-78, ptnr., 1979, 81—; law dir. City of Cleve., 1979-81. Mem. com. fgn. relations Cleve. Council World Affairs, 1975—, trustee, 1985—; mem. vis. com. Coll. Urban Affairs, Cleve. State U., 1982—; trustee Playhouse Sq. Found., 1982—; trustee Greater Cleve. council Boy Scouts Am.; mem. Cuyahoga County Republican Exec. Com., 1981—; trustee Great Lakes Shakespeare Festival, 1982—, Luth. Med. Found., 1982—. Served to capt. U.S. Army, 1966-70. Decorated Bronze Star, Commendation medals. Mem. ABA, Ohio Bar Assn., Greater Cleve. Bar Assn., Cuyahoga County Law Dirs. Assn., West Point Soc. Cleve. Republican. Roman Catholic. Office: Calfee Halter & Griswold 1800 Central Nat Bank Bldg Cleveland OH 44114

WAGNER, WILLIAM STUART, JR., automotive accessory manufacturing company executive; b. Quincy, Ill., May 6, 1947; s. William Stuart and Mary Margaret (Mckinney) W.; m. Patricia Ann Adams, June 10, 1972; children—Kelly Michele, Stephanie Ann. Student Western Ill. U., 1965-67; B.S., Quincy Coll., 1974. Theatre mgr. Kerasotes Theatres, Quincy, 1971-74; sales rep. Packaging Corp. Am. Marshalltown, Iowa, 1974-77; sales mgr. Deflecta-Shield Corp., Corydon, Iowa, 1977-84, v.p. sales, 1984—. Served with U.S. Army, 1968-71. Named Man of Yr. Automotive Merchandising News, 1982. Mem. Automotive Parts and Accessories Assn., Specialty Equipment Mfg. Assn., Automotive Service Industry Assn., Automotive Industry Assn. (Can.), Am. Mgmt. Assn., Tau Kappa Epsilon (treas. 1966-67). Republican. Methodist. Lodge: Masons. Home: Rural Route 2 Box 219A Chariton IA 50049 Office: Deflecta-Shield Corp 314 E Jefferson Corydon IA 50060

WAGONROD, KAREN LOUISE, home economics educator; b. Decatur, Ind., May 11, 1951; d. Rueben Perry Corwin and Evelyn Mary (Sorg) Minerd; m. Dennis A. Wagonrod, June 24, 1978. B.S. in Vocat. Edn., Ball State U., 1973. Home econs. tchr. Wayne Trace local schs., Haviland, Ohio, 1973—; home econs. instr. adult edn. Vantage Joint Vocat. Sch., 1980-81; sewing instr. Buttons & Bolts fabric shop, 1980-81. Mem. Future Farmers Am. (hon.), Am. Vocat. Assn., Ohio Vocat. Assn., Ohio Edn. Assn., Ohio Assn. Future Homemakers Am. (hon.), NEA, Am. Bus. Womens Assn., Quest Inc. (charter). Republican. Methodist. Club: VanWert Womens. Lodge: Woman of the Moose. Home: 746 Airport Ave VanWert OH 45891 Office: RFD 1 Haviland OH 45851

WAGSTAFF, ROBERT K., technical services and applied research executive, nutritionist; b. Murray, Utah, June 29, 1934; s. Keith Amos and Mary (Eva) W.; m. Nancy Burton, Aug. 16, 1957; children—Carolyn, Susan, Martha, Robert, Nathan. B.S., Utah State U., 1958, M.S., 1959; Ph.D., Wash. State U., 1964. Postdoctoral fellow U. Ga., Athens, 1964-65; dir. research and ops. mgr. Pillsbury Farms, Mpls., 1965-71; gen. mgr. Olsen Farms, Quakertown, Pa., 1971-72; exec. v.p. OMI, Inc., North Palm Beach, Fla., 1972-75, Golden Pride, Inc., Berlin, Md., 1975-79; exec. dir. Kemin Industries Inc., Des Moines, 1979—; cons. Pillsbury Co., Mpls., 1964-65; owner Adventure Video, Des Moines, 1984, Dr. Bobs Inc., West Des Moines, 1980—. Contbr. articles to profl. jours. Served to capt. U.S. Army, 1959-61. NSF grantee, 1963. Mem. Poultry Sci. Assn., Am. Sci. Assn., World Poultry Sci. Assn. Republican. Mormon. Avocations: tennis; golf. Home: 1084 Belle Mar Dr West Des Moines IA 50265 Office: Kemin Industries PO Box 70 Des Moines IA 50301

WAHL, ROSALIE E., state justice; b. Gordon, Kans., Aug. 27, 1924; B.A., U. Kans., 1946; J.D., William Mitchell Coll. Law, 1967; children—Christopher Roswell, Sara Emilie, Timothy Eldon, Mark Patterson, Jenny Caroline. Admitted to Minn. bar, 1967; practice in Mpls., 1967-77; assoc. justice Minn. Supreme Ct., 1977—; adj. prof. criminal law U. Minn. Law Sch., 1972-73; clin. prof. William Mitchell Coll. Law, 1973-77; instr., lectr. continuing edn. programs. Mem. Nat. Assn. Women Lawyers, Am. Judicature Soc., ABA (accreditation com. sect. legal edn. and bar admissions, council criminal justice sect.), Minn. Women Lawyers Assn., Nat. Assn. Women Judges Minn. Bar Assn. Address: 230 State Capitol Saint Paul MN 55155

WAHLBERG, EMILY ELAINE, educator; b. Ely, Minn., Nov. 24, 1938; d. Reino Harold and Rachel (Rosdet) Wahlberg. B.S., U. Minn., 1961; M.Ed., U. Ill., 1969. Tchr. sci. Sch. Dist. 228, Midlothian, Ill., 1962—, bowling coach, 1973—. NSF grantee, 1967. Mem. Am. Fedn. Tchrs. (local pres. 1979-80), Bremen Faculty Assn. (pres. 1975-76, 83-84), Nat. Sci. Tchrs. Assn., Nat. Biology Tchrs. Assn. Democrat. Lutheran. Clubs: Bremen Booster, Bremen Twp. Ladies Bowling League (pres.). Home: 6450 W 179th St Tinley Park IL 60477 Office: Bremen High Sch 15203 S Pulaski Midlothian IL 60445

WAHLING, JON B(ARNARD), artist, educator; b. Council Bluffs, Iowa, Apr. 14, 1938; s. Edgar J. and Mada C. (Barnard) W. B.F.A., Kansas City Art Inst. and Sch. of Design, 1962; M.F.A., Cranbrook Acad. Art, 1964; student Haystack Mt. Sch. of Crafts, 1963, 1965. Instr. textiles Columbus Cultural Arts Ctr., Ohio, 1964—. One-man shows include: Ohio Designer Craftsmen Gallery, 1984, Gallery 200, Columbus, 1985; exhibited in group show Ohio Found. on the Arts, 1983-84. Named hon. mem. Central Ohio Weavers Guild; Ohio Arts Council fellow, 1978. Mem. Am. Crafts Council, Ohio Designer Craftsmen (past trustee 1979-83, sec. 1982-83, 20th Anniversary Exhbn. award 1983). Lutheran. Home: 44 Stimmel St Columbus OH 43206 Office: Columbus Cultural Arts Ctr 139 W Main St Columbus OH 43215

WAHLMEIER, JAMES EDWARD, hospital administrator; b. Norton, Kans., Nov. 10, 1954; s. Francis Joseph and Marcella Rose (Campbell) W.; m. Jane Evelyn Carter, July 20, 1973; children—Michael James, Joshua Allan. B.S., Ft. Hays U., Kans., 1978; postgrad. U. Minn., 1982—. Bus. mgr. Trego County-Lemke Meml. Hosp., Wakeeney, Kans., 1979-81, adminstr., 1981—. Bd. dirs. Trego County Cancer Soc., Wakeeney, 1982—; pres. Hospice Trego County, 1984. Served with USN, 1972-76. Mem. Youth Health Care Execs. Republican. Roman Catholic. Lodge: Kiwanis. Avocations: Fishing; hunting; golf. Office: Trego County-Lemke Meml Hosp 320 N 13th St Wakeeney KS 67672

WAHLSTROM, DUANE ELLSWORTH, vocational agriculture educator; b. Grasston, Minn., Oct. 17, 1929; s. Oscar Samuel and Lillian Ida (Olson) W.; m. Georgia Ann Seaman, Sept. 5, 1954; children—Barbara, Beverly, Craig. B.S. in Animal Sci., Agrl. Edn., Iowa State U., 1956. Cert. secondary profl. vocat. technologist, Iowa. Vocat. agrl. tchr. Paton (Iowa) High Sch., 1956-59, Odebolt-Arthur High Sch., 1959-68; mgr. Coop. Elevator, Odebolt, Iowa, 1968-73; feed dept. head Albert City (Iowa) Coop. Elevator, 1973-74; animal sci. instr., Northwest Iowa Tech. Coll., Sheldon, 1974—. mem. adminstrv. bd. Methodist Ch. Served with USN, 1948-52. Mem. Iowa Vocat. Agrl. Tchrs. Assn., Am. Vocat. Assn. Home: 409 7th Ave Sheldon IA 51201 Office: Northwest Iowa Tech Coll Sheldon IA 51201

WAHREN, DOUGLAS, paper research institute executive, researcher; b. Norkoping, Sweden, Mar. 12, 1934; came to U.S., 1979; s. K. Helge and Jane I. C. (Agrell) W.; m. Inger Weleen, Feb. 9, 1957; children—Caroline, Johan. M.S., Royal Inst. Tech., Stockholm, Sweden, 1957, Ph.D., 1960, Dr. Sci. in Paper Tech., 1964, Docent, 1965, Prof. (hon), 1973. Research scientist Beloit Corp., Wis., 1964-65; cons. to paper and paper machine bldg. industries, 1966-73; research asst. to dir. research paper tech. div. Swedish Forest Products Research Lab., Stockholm, 1957-73; prof. paper tech. Royal Inst. Tech., Stockholm, 1970-73; v.p. research AB Karlstads Mekaniska Werkstad, Sweden, 1974-78; v.p. research Inst. Paper Chemistry, Appleton, Wis., 1979—. Contbr. articles to profl. jours. Patentee in field. Fellow TAPPI; mem. Swedish Pulp and Paper Engrs. Assn., U.K. Paper Industry Tech. Assn., Can. Pulp and Paper Assn. Lodge: Rotary. Office: Inst Paper Chemistry PO Box 1039 Appleton WI 54912

WAINSCOTT, JAMES LAWRENCE, accountant; b. LaPorte, Ind., Mar. 31, 1957; s. James J. and Frances J. (Cunningham) W. B.S. magna cum laude, Ball State U., 1979; postgrad. U. Notre Dame. C.P.A., Ind.; cert. mgmt. acct.; cert. internal auditor; cert. info. systems auditor. Sr. auditor Geo. S. Olive & Co., C.P.A.s, Indpls. and Valparaiso, Ind., 1979-82; fin. mgr. Midwest div. Nat. Steel Corp., Portage, Ind., 1982—; cons. Edward J. Wainscott, C.P.A., LaPorte, Ind., 1982—; instr. acctg. Purdue U.-Westville, 1980-82, Valparaiso U., 1980—. Adv., Jr. Achievement, 1984; vol. Am. Cancer Soc., Valparaiso Income Tax Assistance Program, Valparaiso Community/Univ. Campaign; mem. Intertel, Ball State U. Cardinal Connection; mem. N.W. Ind. Open Housing Council; mem. dean's adv. council Valparaiso U. Mem. Ind. C.P.A. Soc. (chmn. chpt. activities com. 1985-86, chpt. bd. dirs. 1983—, chpt. pres. 1984-85), Nat. Assn. Accts. (chpt. bd. dirs. 1982—, chpt. pres. 1983-84; Past Pres. award 1984), Am. Inst. C.P.A.s, Acctg. Research Assn., Am. Acctg. Assn., Inst. Mgmt. Acctg., Inst. Internal Auditors, Soc. Profl. Mgmt. Cons., Assn. M.B.A. Execs., Mensa, Blue Key, Delta Sigma Pi. Roman Catholic. Club: Ducks Unlimited. Avocations: music; chess; coin collecting; sports; travel. Home: 554 Sheffield Dr Valparaiso IN 46383

WAINWRIGHT, WILLIAM NELSON, metal stamping company executive; b. St. Louis, Oct. 21, 1947; s. Nelson William and Mary Colette (Wehner) W.; m. Leslie Ann Bright, Sept. 11, 1976. B.S. in Mech. Engring., Purdue U., 1969. Engr. Northrop Corp., Los Angeles, 1969-72; engr. Wainwright Industries, Inc., St. Peters, Mo., 1972-74, v.p., 1974-78, pres., 1978—. Mem. Soc. Automotive Engrs. Republican. Club: Univ. (St. Louis). Avocations: meteorology; snow and water skiing; hiking; racquet sports. Office: Wainwright Industries Inc 17 Cermak Blvd Box 626 Saint Peters MO 63376

WAITE, LAWRENCE WESLEY, physician; b. Chgo., June 27, 1951; s. Paul J. and Margaret E. (Cresson) W.; m. Courtnay M. Snyder, Nov. 1, 1974; children—Colleen Alexis, Rebecca Maureen. B.A., Drake U., 1972; D.O., Coll. Osteo. Medicine and Surgery, Des Moines, 1975; M.P.H., U. Mich., 1981. Diplomate Nat. Bd. Osteo. Examiners. Intern, Garden City Osteo. Hosp., Mich., 1975-76; practice gen. osteo. medicine, Garden City, 1979-82, Battle Creek, 1982—; assoc. clin. prof. Mich. State U. Coll. Osteo. Medicine, East Lansing, 1979—; dir. med. edn. Lakeview Gen. Osteo. Hosp., Battle Creek, Mich., 1983—; cons. Nat. Bd. Examiners Osteo. Physicians and Surgeons, 1981—. Writer TV program Cross Currents Ecology, 1971; editor radio series Friendship Hour, 1971-72. Bd. dirs., instr. Hospice Support Services, Inc., Westland, Mich., 1981—; mem. profl. adv. council Good Samaritan Hosp., Battle Creek, 1982-83; bd. dirs. Neighborhood Planning Council 11, Battle Creek, 1982—; mem. population action council Population Inst., 1984—. Served to lt. comdr. USN, 1976-79. State of Iowa scholar, 1969. Mem. Aerospace Med. Assn., AMA, Am. Osteo. Assn., Am. Pub. Health Assn., Am. Acad. Osteopathy, Bermuda Hist. Soc. (life). Episcopalian. Avocations: geography; medieval history; genealogy. Home: 140 S Lincoln Blvd Battle Creek MI 49015 Office: 3164 Capital Ave SW Battle Creek MI 49015

WAITE, PAUL J., climatologist, educator; b. New Salem, Ill., June 21, 1918; s. Wesley Philip and Edna Viola (Bartlett) W.; m. Margaret Elizabeth Cresson, June 13, 1943; children—Carolyn, Lawrence. B.E., Western Ill. State U., 1940; M.S., U. Mich., 1966. State climatologist Nat. Weather Service, Des Moines, Madison, 1956-73; meteorologist Nat. Weather Service, 1973-74, 1948-51, 1952-56; dep. project mgr. NOAA, Houston, 1974-76; state climatologist Iowa Dept. Agr., Des Moines, 1976—; adj. prof. geography, geology Drake U., Des Moines, 1970-74, 1976—; asst. dir. Iowa Weather Service, Des Moines, 1959-70, dir. 1970-73; U.S. Dept. Commerce collaborator Iowa State U., Ames, 1959-73. Contbr. articles to profl. jours. and chpts. to bks. Served to 1st lt. USAF, 1942-46, 1951-52, Korea. Recipient NASA Group Achievement Award, 1979. Fellow Iowa Acad. Scis. (Disting. Service award 1983, pres. elect 1985); mem. Am. Assn. State Climatologist (pres. 1977-78), Am. Meteorol. Soc., Nat. Weather Assn. Republican. Club: Toastmasters (Des Moines) (pres. 1980). Lodge: Masons. Avocations: hiking; gardening; photography. Home: 6657 NW Timberline Dr Des Moines IA 50313 Office: State Climatologist Iowa Dept Agriculture Rm 10 Terminal Bldg Des Moines Internat Airport Des Moines IA 50321

WAITKUS, PHILLIP ANTHONY, polymer chemist; b. Sheboygan, Wis., Oct. 27, 1939; s. Felix Anton and Martha Helen (Brotz) W.; B.A., Ripon (Wis.) Coll., 1961; M.A., Wesleyan U., Middletown, Conn., 1963; Ph.D., Tulane U., New Orleans, 1967; m. Audrey Ann Ayo, Jan. 16, 1965; children—Mark Edward, Patrick Anthony. Chemist, Plastics Engring. Co., 1966-70; chief chemist, 1970—. Vice pres., fin. chmn. Sheboygan County Receiving Home, 1970-73; cubmaster, asst. scoutmaster Boy Scouts Am., 1975-79; mem. alumni bd. Ripon Coll., 1970-72. Recipient Scouters Key Boy Scouts Am. Roman Catholic. Club: Sheboygan Noon Optimist (pres. 1969-70). Patentee in field. Home: 336 Clement Ave Sheboygan WI 53081 Office: 3518 Lakeshore Rd Sheboygan WI 53081

WAKEFIELD, JOHN PERSHING, osteopathic physician and surgeon; b. Des Moines, Oct. 25, 1918; s. Walter Edwin and Pearl Evelyn (McCroby) W.; m. DeLores Mae Pechman, Aug. 26, 1967. B.S., Iowa State U., 1942; postgrad., Drake U., 1950-53; D.O., Coll. Osteo. Medicine and Surgery, 1959. Civil engr. Brown Engring. Co., Des Moines, 1946-47; supt. forestry Iowa Conservation Commn., Des Moines, 1947-52; prof. biology Drake U., Des Moines, 1952-57; gen. practice osteo. medicine, Des Moines, 1959—; mem. staff Des Moines Gen. Hosp., tchr. preceptors, 1965-83. Republican precinct chmn., 1974-78; chmn. Citizens' Adv. Com., 1981-82. Served to capt. U.S. Army, 1942-46. Decorated Bronze Star medal; recipient Nat. Service award Des Moines C. of C., 1974. Mem. Am. Osteo. Soc., Iowa Soc. Osteo. Physicians and Surgeons, East High Sch. Alumni Assn. (pres. 1970-71), 2d Inf. Div. Assn. (pres. 1971-74). Unitarian (mem. council). Clubs: Toastmasters, East High Boosters. Author: Laboratory Manual for Nursing Biology, 1955, An ETO Tour Chronology, 1978.

WALBERG, PETER ELON, nuclear power plant engineer, youth director; b. Barberton, Ohio, Apr. 15, 1944; s. Maynard Elon and Daisy Lenore (Gessner) W.; m. Darlene Amanda Fuhre, Apr. 8, 1967; children—Timothy, Joel, Rachel. B.S., U.S. Naval Acad., 1966. Registered profl. engr., Ill. Engr. Ill. Power Co., Decatur, Ill., 1976-82, supervising engr., 1982—. Youth comdr. Awana Youth Orgn., Decatur, Ill., 1983-84. Served to lt. comdr. USN, 1966-76. Mem. ASME. Baptist. Home: 390 Loma Dr Box 57 Forsyth IL 62537 Office: Ill Power Co V-928 PO Box 306 Clinton IL 61727

WALCHER, DWAIN NEWTON, state official, pediatrician; b. Ill., Apr. 7, 1915; s. Jesse Leroy and Lucile Agnes (Newton) W.; m. Emily Jane Jones, Dec. 31, 1939; children—Susan Dair Walcher Reed, David Newton. Student Blackburn Coll., 1933-35; B.S., U. Chgo., 1938, M.D., 1940. Diplomate Am. Bd. Pediatrics. Intern, Ind. U. Med. Ctr., Indpls., 1940-41; intern, asst. resident, then resident in pediatrics Yale U. Sch. Medicine, New Haven Hosp., 1941-44; instr. pediatrics Yale U. Sch. Medicine, 1943-46; asst. prof. pediatrics Ind. U., 1946-52, assoc. prof., 1952-62, prof., 1962-63, clin. prof. health adminstrn. and pediatrics, 1980-82, clin. prof. pediatrics, 1982—; dir. growth and devel. program Nat. Inst. Child Health and Human Devel., NIH, Bethesda, Md., 1963-66, assoc. dir. program planning and evaluation, 1966-69, dir. Inst. Study Human Devel., 1969-78; spl. asst. to provost Pa. State U., 1971-74, sr. adv. for coll. devel. and relations, 1978-80, prof. human devel., 1969-80; spl. asst. for med. ops. Ind. State Bd. Health, Indpls., 1980—; mem. program com. Nat. Easter Seal Soc., 1969-71; cons. Nat. Inst. Child Health and Human Devel., 1969-74; trustee Nat. Easter Seal Research Found., 1968-76, chmn. bd. trustees, 1971-75. Recipient Disting. Service medal Université Rene Descartes, Academie de Paris, 1977; Disting. Alumnus award Blackburn Coll., 1982. Emeritus mem. numerous profl. assns., including Internat. Orgn. for Study Human Devel. (exec. sec.-treas. 1969-82). Presbyterian. Contbr. articles to profl. jours.; co-editor books, including: Mutations: Biology and Society, 1978; Food, Nutrition and Evolution, 1981.

WALD, KATHRYN SONDERMAN, lawyer; b. Chgo., Dec. 20, 1928; d. Carl E. and Mary (Donlon) Sonderman; m. C. Ben Wald, June 26, 1951; children—David, Stephen, Kenneth, Gregg, Barbara. B.A., St. Mary of Woods Coll., 1950; J.D., U. Dayton, 1980. Tchr. math. Alter High Sch., Kettering, Ohio, 1966-75; ptnr. Henley Vaughn Becker & Wald, Dayton, Ohio, 1980—. Home: 4533 Wingview Ln Dayton OH 45429 Office Henley Vaughn Becker & Wald 200 Talbott Tower Dayton OH 45402

WALD, ROBERT MANUEL, physicist; b. N.Y.C., June 29, 1947; s. Abraham and Lucille (Lang) W. A.B., Columbia U., 1968; Ph.D., Princeton U., 1972. Research assoc. U. Md., College Park, 1972-74; research assoc. U. Chgo., 1974-76, asst. prof., 1976-80, assoc. prof., 1980-85, prof., 1985—. Author: Space, Time and Gravity, 1977; General Relativity, 1984. Home: 5514 S Woodlawn Ave Chicago IL 60637 Office: Enrico Fermi Inst U Chgo 5640 S Ellis Ave Chicago IL 60637

WALDBAUM, JANE COHN, art history educator; b. N.Y.C., Jan. 28, 1940; d. Max Arthur and Sarah (Waldstein) Cohn. B.A., Brandeis U., 1962; M.A., Harvard U., 1964, Ph.D., 1968. Research fellow in classical archaeology Harvard U., Cambridge, Mass., 1968-70, 72-73; asst. prof. U. Wis.-Milw., 1973-78, assoc. prof., 1978-84, prof. art history, 1984—, chmn. dept., 1982-85. Author: From Bronze to Iron, 1978; Metalwork from Sardis, 1983; author (with others), editor Sardis Report I, 1975. Contbr. numerous articles to profl. jours. Bd. dirs. Milw. Soc. of Archaeol. Inst., 1973—, pres., 1983-85. Woodrow Wilson Found. fellow, dissertation fellow, 1962-63, 65-66; grantee Am. Philos. Soc., 1972, NEH, summer 1975, U. Wis.-Milw. Found., 1983. Mem. Am. Schs. Oriental Research, Assn. for Field Archaeology, Soc. for Archaeol. Sci., Archaeol. Inst. Am. (exec. com. 1975-77, chmn. com. on membership programs 1977-81, nominating com. 1984, chmn. com. on lecture program 1985—), Phi Beta Kappa. Office: Dept Art History U Wis-Milw PO Box 413 Milwaukee WI 53201

WALDEN, JAMES WILLIAM, accountant, educator; b. Jellico, Tenn., Mar. 5, 1936; s. William Evert and Bertha L. (Faulkner) W.; B.S., Miami U., Oxford, Ohio, 1963; M.B.A., Xavier U., Cin., 1966; m. Eva June Selvia, Jan. 16, 1957; 1 son, James William. Tchr. math. Middletown (Ohio) City Sch. Dist., 1963-67, Fairfield (Ohio) High Sch., 1967-69; instr. accounting Sinclair Community Coll., Dayton, Ohio, 1969-72, asst. prof., 1972-75, asso. prof., 1975-78, prof., 1978—; cons., public acct. Active CAP. Served with USAF, 1954-59. Mem. Butler County Torch Club, Pub. Accountants Soc. Ohio (pres. S.W. chpt. 1972-73), Nat. Soc. Pub. Accountants, Greater Hamilton Estate Planning Council, Beta Alpha Psi. Home: 187 Westbrook Dr Hamilton OH 45013 Office: Sinclair Community Coll 444 W 3d St Dayton OH 45402

WALDEN, RONALD LEE, environmental scientist, geologist; b. Lafayette, Ind., Oct. 2, 1959; s. Edward Gene and Alyce Louise (Whittaker) W. B.S. cum laude, Bowling Green State U., 1982, M.S., 1984. Exploration geologist Kirkwood Oil and Gas, Casper, Wyo., summer 1982; lab technician Bowling Green State U., Ohio, 1982-84; environ. scientist Ohio EPA, Bowling Green, 1984—. Mem. Am. Assn. Petroleum Geologists (jr.), Geology Club Bowling Green State U., Geophysics Soc. Bowling Green State U., Sigma Gamma Epsilon. Democrat. Lutheran. Avocations: sports; exercise; reading; music; travel. Home: 623 Wallace Ave Bowling Green OH 43402 Office: Ohio EPA 1035 Devlac Grove Dr Bowling Green OH 43402

WALDERA, GERALD JOSEPH, political science educator; b. Britton, S.D., June 18, 1931; s. Roman Lawrence and Rosalie Virginia (Jagodzinski) W.; m. Jean Anne Bigelow, Jan. 17, 1959; children—Mark, Michael, Gerald II. B.S., N.D. State U., 1958, M.S., 1960; postgrad. U. Denver, 1960-62. Grad. asst. N.D. State U., 1959-60; teaching fellow U. Denver, 1961-62; asst. prof. social sci. Millikin U., Decatur, Ill., 1962-67; assoc. prof. polit. sci. Dickinson State Coll. (N.D.), 1967—, chmn. social-behavioral sci. div., 1969—. Mem. N.D. Senate, 1982—. Served to 1st lt. USMC, 1952-58; Korea. Mem. Orgn. Am. Historians, Am. Acad. Polit. Sci., N.D. Council Social Sci. Democrat. Lodges: Rotary, Century, Elks, Masons, Shriners, German-Hungarian, Eagles (Dickinson). Home: 942 9th Ave W Dickinson ND 58601 Office: Dickinson State Coll Dickinson ND 58601

WALDING, DEREK JAMES, Canadian government official; b. Rushden, Northamptonshire, Eng., May 9, 1937; s. Howard and Dorothy E. (King) W.; m. Valerie Monica Hatton, Nov. 16, 1957; children—Andrew James, Philip Kimball, Christine Anne. Student pub. schs., Wellingborough, Eng. Optician; mem. gen. election Legis. Assembly, Winnipeg, Man., Can., 1971—, speaker, 1982—. Mem. Royal Can. Legion. Mem. New Democratic Party. Address: 26 Hemlock Pl Winnipeg MB R2H 1L7 Canada

WALDINGER, VIRGINIA KATHLEEN, office automation consulting company executive; b. Newark, Ohio, June 5, 1931; d. Harold and Lucille Kathleen (Gilmore) Boase; m. John Waldinger, June 17, 1960; 1 son, Scott J. Student U. Mich., 1975-78, Wayne State U., 1980. Sec., Ford Motor Co., Dearborn, Mich., 1975-81; tchr. Dearborn Pub. Schs., 1969-81; pres. Electronic Info. Systems, Dearborn, 1980—; cons. Hewlett Parkard, Pinewood, Eng., 1983—; EDS/Systems engr., 1985—; tchr. Oakland Community Coll., 1980-83. Mem. Am. Mgmt. Assn., Am. Bus. Women's Assn., Assn. Info. Systems Profls.

WALDMAN, SIDNEY HERMAN, bookstore executive; b. Albany, N.Y., Oct. 23, 1934; s. Philip Samuel and Jennie (Samuelson) W.; m. Audrey Gail Smith, June 6, 1959; children—Karen Lynn, Eric Joseph. B.S., N.Y. U., 1957. Clk. to asst. dir. N.Y. U. Bookstore, N.Y.C., 1951-61; asst. dir. bookstores Syracuse U. Bookstores, N.Y., 1961-65, dir., 1965-74; mgr. Barnes & Noble at Cleve. State U., 1974-79, pres., chief exec. officer, 1979—. Contbr. articles to profl. jours. Mem. Cleve. Exec. Assn., Nat. Assn. Coll. Stores (past trustee), N.Y. State Assn. Coll. Stores (past pres.), Ohio Assn. Coll. Stores (past pres.). Republican. Unitarian. Office: B & N Inc 2400 Euclid Ave Cleveland OH 44115

WALDO, FRANCIS XAVIER, environmental engineer; b. New Orleans, Mar. 12, 1936; s. Harry Joseph and Louise Alice (Lapeyre) W.; m. Patricia Irene Felter, Aug. 8, 1959; children—Edward, Teresa, Daniel, Annette. B.S.C.E., U. Detroit, 1959; M.S.C.E., U. Tex., 1961. Registered profl. engr., Ohio; diplomate Am. Acad. Environ. Engrs. Civil engr. II, Cin. Water Works, Ohio, 1963-65; prin. engr., assoc. Floyd Browne Assoc., Marion, Ohio, 1965-81; assoc. Jones & Henry Engrs. Ltd., Toledo, 1981—. Com. chmn. Harding area council Boy Scouts Am., 1968-72. Served to 1st lt. C.E., U.S. Army, 1961-63. HEW grantee, 1960-61. Mem. Nat. Soc. Profl. Engrs., Ohio Soc. Profl. Engrs., Toledo Soc. Profl. Engrs., Water Pollution Control Fedn., ASCE, Am. Water Works Assn., Tau Beta Phi, Chi Epsilon. Republican. Roman Catholic. Lodge: K.C. Avocations: power boating; water skiing. Home: 5618 305th St Toledo OH 43611 Office: Jones & Henry Engrs Ltd 2000 W Central Ave Toledo OH 43606

WALDRON, CLARENCE RAYMOND, JR., microbiologist, clergyman; b. Trenton, N.J., Jan. 27, 1940; s. Clarence Raymond and Hilda Gertrude (Dean) W.; m. Joan Lynn Grau, Jan. 6, 1968; children—Kathleen Marie, John David. A.B., Rutgers U., 1961; M.Div., Phila. Div. Sch., 1964; M.S., Rutgers U., 1971, Ph.D., 1985. Ordained priest Episcopal Ch. Rector St. John's Ch., Gibbsboro, N.J., 1964-72, St. James Ch., Edison, N.J., 1972-78; research instr. Rutgers U., New Brunswick, N.J., 1980-83; research microbiologist Campbell Soup Co., Napoleon, Ohio, 1983—. Patentee Cellulose degrading enzymes from Thermophilic actinomycetes; contbr. articles to profl. jours. Pres. Gibbsboro Bd. Health, 1966-70; chmn. Juvenile Conf. Com., Gibbsboro, 1966-70. Mem. Am. Soc. Microbiologists, Soc. Indsl. Microbiologists, N.J. Acad. Sci. Office: Campbell Soup Co Napoleon OH 43545

WALDRON, JOSEPH A., psychologist, educator; b. Batavia, N.Y., Oct. 3, 1943; s. Elsworth T. and Dolores A. (Kanaley) W.; m. Irene M.G. Montgomery, Oct. 31, 1966; children—Wendy, Joelle, Elizabeth. B.A. in Psychology, SUNY-Buffalo, 1972; M.A., Ohio State U., 1973, Ph.D., 1975. Lic. psychologist, Ohio. Head dept. psychology Buckeye Youth Ctr., Ohio Youth Commn., Columbus, 1973-76; chief psychologist Mahoning County Diagnostic and Evaluation Clinic, Youngstown, Ohio, 1976-77; owner Towne Square Psychol. Services, Youngstown, 1976—; assoc. prof. and dir. forensic research lab. Youngstown State U., 1977—; founder Integrated Profl. Systems Inc., Youngstown, 1981, Polymetrics Lab., Youngstown, 1982—. Served with USMC, 1961-65. Mem. AAAS, Acad. Criminal Justice Sci., Mahoning Valley Acad. of Psychologists (pres. 1981-82), Sigma Xi, Kappa Delta Pi. Contbr. articles to profl. jours; developer computer programs in field. Home: 266 Bradford Dr Canfield OH 44406 Office: Polymetrics Lab PO Box 367 Canfield OH 44406

WALES, STEPHEN HENRY, SR., accounting educator; b. Northampton, Mass., Aug. 12, 1932; s. Earl Edward and Doris Rita (Jay) W.; m. Charlotte Beatrice Orner, 1953 (div. 1959); children—Donna Lee, Jay Stephen; m. 2d Patsy Lou Blackwell, Oct. 17, 1960; children—Cynthia Marie, Stephen H. Student, U. Conn., 1951-52; B.B.A., U. Mass., 1959; M.B.A., Ind. U., 1960; postgrad. Purdue U., 1963-68, Earlham Coll., 1963-68, Ferris State Coll., 1968-83. C.P.A., Ind., Mich. Faculty, Ind. U., Bloomington, 1960-68; faculty Ferris State U., Big Rapids, Mich., 1960—, prof. accountancy, 1984—; pvt. practice acctg., Big Rapids, 1965—. Served with USAF, 1950-55. Mem. Am. Inst. C.P.A.s, Nat-Assn. Accts., Am. Acctg. Assn., Mich. Assn. C.P.A.s. Home: Rural Route 1 Box 313-21061-19 Mile Rd Big Rapids MI 49307 Office: B338 Ferris State Coll Big Rapids MI 49307

WALGREEN, CHARLES RUDOLPH, III, retail store executive; b. Chgo., Nov. 11, 1935; s. Charles Rudolph and Mary Ann (Leslie) W.; B.S. in Pharmacy, U. Mich., 1958; m. Kathleen Bonsignore Allen, Jan. 23, 1977; children—Charles Richard, Tad Alexander, Kevin Patrick, Leslie Ray, Chris Patrick; stepchildren—Carlton A. Allen Jr., Jorie L. Allen. With Walgreen Co., Chgo., 1952—, adminstrv. asst. to v.p. store ops., 1965-66, dist. mgr., 1967-68, regional dir., 1968-69, v.p., 1969, pres., 1969-75, chmn., 1976—, also dir. Mem. bus. adv. council Chgo. Urban League. Bd. dirs. Jr. Achievement Chgo., Internat. Coll. Surgeons Hall Fame and Mus. Surg. Scis. Mem. Am. Found. Pharm. Edn., (dir.), Nat. Assn. Chain Drug Stores (dir. 1971—), Ill. Retail Mchts. Assn. (dir. 1966—), Young Pres.'s Orgn., Am., Ill. pharm. assns., Delta Sigma Phi. Clubs: Economic, Commercial, Tavern (Chgo.); Great Lakes Cruising; Yacht and Country (Stuart, Fla.); Exmoor Country (Highland Park, Ill.); Key Largo Anglers (Fla.). Office: 200 Wilmot Rd Deerfield IL 60015

WALHOUT, DONALD, philosophy educator; b. Muskegon, Mich., Aug. 9, 1927; s. Peter and Sena (Kallenkoot) W.; m. Justine Isabel Simon; children—Mark, Timothy, Lynne, Peter. B.A., Adrian Coll., 1949; M.A., Ph.D., Yale U., 1952. Instr. philosophy Yale U., New Haven, 1952-53; prof. philosophy Rockford Coll., Ill., 1953—. Author: Interpreting Religion, 1963; The Good and the Realm of Values, 1978; Festival of Aesthetics, 1978; Send My Roots Rain, 1981; also articles. Mem. Am. Philos. Assn., Am. Soc. Aesthetics, Am. Assn., Philosophy Tchrs., AAUP, U.S. Chess Fedn., Internat. Hopkins Assn. Mem. Presbyterian. Avocation: chess. Office: Dept Philosophy Rockford Coll 5050 E State St Rockford IL 61108

WALI, ANUPAM SOMNATH, microbiologist, researcher, consultant; b. Srinagar, India, Oct. 12, 1951; came to U.S., 1979, naturalized, 1984; s. Somnath N. and Manmohini (Zutshi) W.; m. Neelam Khushu, Jan. 29, 1981; 1 child, Ambika. B.Sc. in Zoology, M.S. U. Baroda, India, 1971, M.Sc. in Microbiology, 1973, Ph.D. in Microbiology, 1978. Asst. lectr. U. Baroda, India, 1974-77, research assoc., 1977-78; research assoc. Temple U., Phila., 1979-80; sr. scientist Hindustan Lever Ltd., Bombay, Ind., 1980-81; sr. research assoc. Johns Hopkins U. Med. Sch., Balt., 1981-83; dir. microbiology/fermentation Promega Biotec Inc., Madison, Wis., 1983—. Univ. Grants Commn. Research fellow, India, 1977-78. Mem. Am. Soc. Microbiology, AAAS, Am. Chem. Soc., Soc. Indsl. Microbiology. Home: 5622 W Lacy Rd Madison WI 53711 Office: Promega Biotec Inc 2800 S Fish Hatchery Rd Madison WI 53711

WALIGORA, ROBERT PAUL, educator; b. Oak Park, Ill., Jan. 4, 1951; s. Edwin S. and Margaret (Hallstrom) W.; m. Elizabeth Aird Snyder, Apr. 28, 1984. B.A. in Journalism, U. Minn., 1983. Hotel mgr. U. Minn. Hosps., Mpls., 1976-78; field rep. Defenders of Wildlife, Washington, 1979-80; admissions clk. U. Minn. Hosps., Mpls., 1980-83; editor The Alley Community Paper, Mpls., 1983-84; edn. dir. Minn. Humane Soc., St. Paul, 1984—. Author: Trapping: A Study of Animal Cruelty, 1981; contbr. articles to profl. jours. Coordinator, founder Friends of Animals and Their Environment, Mpls., 1976—. Avocations: hiking; reading. Home: 2427 10th Ave S Minneapolis MN 55404 Office: Friends of Animals and Their Environment Box 7283 Minneapolis MN 55407

WALINSKI, NICHOLAS JOSEPH, judge; b. Toledo, Nov. 29, 1920; s. Nicholas Joseph and Helen Barbara (Morkowski) W.; B.S. in Engring., U. Toledo, 1949, LL.B., 1951; m. Vivian Melotti, June 26, 1954; children—Marcianne, Barbara, Deanna and Donna (twins), Nicholas Joseph III (dec.). Admitted to Ohio bar, 1951; law dir., Toledo, 1953, police prosecutor, 1953-58, municipal ct. judge, 1958-64, common pleas ct. judge, 1964-70; judge No. dist. Ohio Western div. U.S. Dist. Ct., Toledo, 1970—. Served to capt. USNR, 1942-48. Mem. Am., Toledo, Lucas County bar assns., Am. Legion, V.F.W., Cath. War Vets, Toledo Jr. Bar Assn. (Order of Heel 1970). Office: 1716 Speilbusch St US Courthouse Toledo OH 43624

WALINSKI, RICHARD S., lawyer; b. Toledo, Ohio, May 1, 1943; s. Thaddeus N. and Geniveve E. Walinski. B.A., U. Toledo, 1965, J.D., 1969. Bar: Ohio 1969. Asst. pub. defender, Toledo, 1969-71; spl. counsel Atty. Gen. Ohio, Columbus, 1975-76, chief counsel, 1976-79, spl. counsel, 1979—; cons. Ohio Gen. Assembly Select Com. on Evidence, Columbus, 1979-80. Contbr. articles to profl. jours. Recipient Outstanding Service award Ohio Acad. Trial Lawyers, 1980; Merit award Ohio Legal Ctr. Inst., 1974. Mem. ABA, Toledo Bar Assn. (trustee 1981-82). Clubs: North Cape Yacht (LaSalle, Mich.); Toledo. Home: 31 Exmoor Toledo OH 43615 Office: 900 Adams St Toledo OH 43624

WALKENBACH, RONALD JOSEPH, research foundation executive; b. Hermann, Mo., Mar. 15, 1948; s. Walter Bernard and Lillian Ann (Ochsner) W.; m. Mary McLean Hodge (div. 1981); m. DeAnna Marie Roemer, Oct. 3, 1984. B.S. in Chemistry, Quincy Coll., 1970; Ph.D. in Pharmacology, U. Mo., 1975. Research assoc. U. Va., Charlottesville, 1975-77, U. Mo., Columbia, 1977-78; sr. research investigator Eye Research Found., Columbia, 1978-80, exec. dir., 1980—; asst. prof. dept. pharmacology U. Mo., Columbia, 1978—, dept. ophthalmology, 1978—. Contbr. articles to profl. jours. Scouting coordinator Boy Scouts Am., Columbia, 1980—. Postdoctoral fellow U. Mo., 1974-75, NIH, 1977; NIH grantee, Nat. Eye Inst. grantee, 1978—. Mem. Assn. Research Vision and Ophthalmology, Eye Bank Assn. Am., Sigma Xi. Roman Catholic. Lodge: Lions (2d v.p. 1984—). Avocations: outdoor sports; woodworking. Home: 919 Bourn Ave Columbia MO 65203 Office: Eye Research Found Mo Inc 404 Portland St Columbia MO 65201

WALKER, BLANCHE NELLIE, educator; b. Dadeville, Ala., Apr. 10, 1920; d. Ulsia G. and Ilar (Smith Greathouse; m. Michael William Walker, Nov. 27, 1943 (dec.); children—Margaret Walker Blakey, Kenneth R., Patricia Y. A.A. in Edn., A&I Coll., 1942; B.S., Coll. St. Teresa, 1958; M.A. in Math., Webster Coll., St. Louis, 1975. Classroom tchr. Kansas City (Kans.) Sch. Dist., 1953-54, tchr. math., 1954-55, asst. prin., 1955-57, tchr., 1957-58; tchr. Kansas City (Mo.) Sch. Dist., 1958-70, math. and sci. specialist, 1970-74, math. specialist, 1974—; cons. Named Most Outstanding Elem. Sci. Tchr., Kansas City Met. Area, 1974; recipient Outstanding Achievement in Edn. award Phi Delta Kappa, 1975, 1st grand award intermediate div. Math. Sci, 1977; cert. of merit Sigma Xi, 1974. Mem. Women's C. of C. (past bd. dirs.), NEA, NAACP (life), Phi Delta Kappa, Gamma Beta. Roman Catholic. Club: 20th Century.

WALKER, CHARLES HENRI, lawyer; b. Columbus, Nov. 11, 1951; s. Watson Hershel and Juanita Elizabeth (Webb) W.; m. Amanda Tressel Herndon, June 27, 1981; 1 child, Katrina Della. B.A. magna cum laude, Tufts U., 1973; J.D., Emory U., 1976. Bar: Ohio 1976. Assoc. Bricker & Eckler, and predecessors, Columbus, 1976-81, ptnr., 1982—. Bd. dirs. Salesian Boys Club, Columbus, 1983—, Planned Parenthood Central Ohio, Columbus, 1984—. Mem. ABA, Nat. Bar Assn., Ohio Bar Assn., Columbus Bar Assn., Nat. Assn. R.R. Trial Counsel, Columbus Acad. Alumni Assn. (past pres.). Democrat. Roman Catholic. Clubs: Athletic (Columbus); President's (Ohio State U.). Home: 556 City Park Ave Columbus OH 43215 Office: Bricker & Eckler 100 E Broad St Columbus OH 43215

WALKER, CLIFFORD MILTON, JR., pharmacist; b. Poterdale, Ga., June 14, 1944; s. Clifford M. and Letitia (Hollingsworth) W.; m. Jill Gray, Aug. 8, 1965; children—E. Wade, John S., James M. B.S. in Pharmacy, U. Ga., 1966. Registered pharmacist, Va., N.Y., Ga. Pharmacist Patterson Drug Co., Lynchburg, Va., 1966-68; pharmacist U.S. Air Force, Niagara Falls, N.Y., 1969-70, Ramstein, Fed. Republic Germany, 1970-71; chief pharmacy services U.S. Air Force, Upper Heyford, Eng., 1971-74, Moody AFB, Ga., 1974-80, Wurtsmith AFB, Mich., 1981—. Mem. Am. Soc. Hosp. Pharmacy, Am. Pharm. Assn., Assn. Mil. Surgeons, Air Force Assn. Republican. Baptist. Avocations: reading; agriculture.

WALKER, DALE MAXWELL, city official; b. Big Rapids, Mich., Dec. 18, 1947; s. Lewis M. and Hilma I. (Windquist) W.; m. Joanne Kay Richmond, June 22, 1968; children—Christina Elizabeth, Heather Marie. B.S., Ferris State Coll., 1970; M.B.A., Central Mich. U., 1981. Dir. fin. City of Owosso, Mich., 1970-74; internal auditor John Wesley Coll., Owosso, 1974-76; corp. treas. Mich. Bapt. Homes, Detroit, 1976-77; dir. fin. City of Cadillac, Mich., 1977—; pres. Gospel Bookstore, Inc., Cadillac, 1983—. Bd. dirs. Wexford County United Way, 1980-82, Shiawassee County United Way, 1971-72; sec.-treas. Cadillac Police and Fire Retirement System, 1977—. Fellow Govtl. Fin. Officers Assn. U.S. and Can. (Profl. Achievement award 1984); mem. Mich. Mcpl. Fin. Officers Assn. (bd. dirs. 1983-85), Internat. City Mgrs. Assn., Mich. Mcpl. Treas. Assn. (bd. dirs. 1982-84), Mcpl. Treas. Assn. U.S. and Can. Republican. Baptist. Club: Contry (Cadillac). Avocations: golf; basketball; reading. Home: 901 Lincoln St Cadillac MI 49601 Office: 200 Lake St Cadillac MI 49601

WALKER, DANIEL EUGENE, health care industry executive; b. San Diego, Nov. 24, 1952; s. Russell Eugene and Jerry Mae (Hamilton) W.; m. Jennifer Anne Walker, Aug. 2, 1975 (div. 1982); 1 child, Paul Daniel; m. Sharon Elaine Jackson, July 23, 1983. A.B. cum laude, Humboldt State U., 1974; postgrad. U. S.C., 1975; Ind. Central U., 1979; Ph.D., Purdue U., 1978. Sr. quality control chemist Dow Chem. Co., Indpls., 1979-81; mgr. quality control Dow Instruments and Reagents, Indpls., 1981-82; dir. quality assurance Seragen Diagnostics, Indpls., 1983-84, mgr. internat. sales and mktg., 1984-85; mktg. mgr. Tech Am., Inc., 1985—. Author: Proc. Health Industry Mfrs. Assn. Meeting, 1980. Contbr. articles to profl. jours. Mem. Am. Chem. Soc. Republican. Avocations: Water skiing, sports. Office: Tech Am Inc PO Box 338 Elwood KS 66024

WALKER, DONALD E., funeral home executive; b. Portsmouth, Ohio, July 9, 1930; s. Alva C. and Goldie M. (Hammond) W.; children from previous marriage—Gary W., Timothy A.; m. Cora A. Woodworth, May 17, 1975; 1 child, Donald E. B.A., Olivet Coll., 1967; Mortuary Sci., Cin. Coll. Mortuary Sci., 1974. Minister, Ch. of Nazarene, 1960-70; tchr. jr. high sch. Cardington Schs., Ohio, 1970-71; tchr. spl. edn. Morrow County Schs., Chesterville, Ohio, 1971-73; substitute tchr. Ashtabula County, Jefferson, Ohio, 1973—; funeral dir. Donald E. Walker Funeral Home, Geneva, Ohio, 1974—. Treas. Geneva Grape Jamboree, Ohio, 1976-77; pres. Geneva Sch. Bd., 1984—; mem. adv. council Christian Life Acad., Ashtabula, 1985—. Served to with USAF, 1952-56, Korea. Mem. Geneva C. of C. (pres. 1978-80), Nat. Assn. Funeral Dirs., Ohio Assn. Funeral Dirs., Tri-County Funeral Dirs., Ohio Sch. Bd. Assn. Democrat. Clubs: Boosters, Music. Lodge: Lions (pres. 1982). Avocations: designing and building furniture; reading; bowling. Home: 138 Richard St Geneva OH 44041 Office: 828 Sherman St PO Drawer 349 Geneva OH 44041

WALKER, ELVA MAE DAWSON, cons. health, hosps., aging; b. Everett, Mass., June 29, 1914; d. Charles Edward and Mary Elizabeth (Livingston) Dawson; R.N., Peter Bent Brigham Hosp., Boston, 1937; student Simmons Coll., 1935, U. Minn., 1945-48; m. Walter Willard Walker, Dec. 16, 1939 (div. 1969). Supr. nursery Wesson Maternity Hosp., Springfield, Mass., 1937-38; asst. supr. out-patient dept. Peter Bent Brigham Hosp., Boston, 1938-40; supr. surgery and out-patient dept. Univ. Hosps., Mpls., 1945. Chmn. Gov.'s Citizens Council on Aging, Minn., 1960-68, acting dir., 1962-66, Econ. Opportunity Com. Hennepin County, 1964-69; v.p., treas. Nat. Purity Soap & Chem. Co., 1968-69, pres., 1969-76, chmn. bd., 1976—; cons. on aging to Minn. Dept. Pub. Welfare, 1962-67; mem. nat. adv. Council for Nurse Tng. Act, 1965-69, Com. Status on Women in Armed Services, 1967-70; dir. Nat. Council on the Aging, 1963-67, sec., 1965-67; dir. Planning Agy. for Hosps. of Met. Mpls., 1963—, United Hosp. Fund of Hennepin County, 1955—, Nat. Council Social Work Edn., 1966-68; vice chmn. Hennepin County Gen. Hosp. Adv. Bd., 1965-68; sec. Hennepin County Health Coalition, 1973; chmn. bd. dirs. Am. Rehab. Found, 1962-68, vice chmn., 1968-70; pres. bd. trustees Northwestern Hosp., 1956-59, Children's Hosp. Mpls., 1961-65; dir. Twin Cities Internat. Program for Youth Leaders and Social Workers, Inc., 1965-67; mem. community adv. council United Community Funds and Council Am., Inc., 1968, Nat. Assembly Social Policy and Devel., Inc., 1968—; mem. priorities determination com. United Fund Mpls., 1971; vice chmn. govt. specifications com. Soap and Detergent Assn., 1972-76, vice-chmn. indsl. and instn. com., 1974-76, chmn., 1976-78, bd. dirs., 1974—; candidate for Congress, 3d Minn. Dist., 1966; trustee Macalester Coll., Archie D. and Bertha H. Walker Found.; chmn. St. Mary's Jr. Coll. Bd., 1970-74, 78-80; pres. U. Minn. Sch. Nursing Found., 1958-70. Mem. Am. Pub. Welfare Assn., Mpls. Med. Research Found., Minn. League Nursing (pres. 1971-73), Jr. League Mpls. Democrat. Presbyterian. Home: 3655 Northome Rd Wayzata MN 55391 Office: Nat Purity Soap & Chem Co 110 SE 5th Ave Minneapolis MN 55414

WALKER, FRANK BANGHART, pathologist; b. Detroit, June 14, 1931; s. Roger Venning and Helen Frances (Reade) W.; B.S., Union (N.Y.) Coll., 1951; M.D., Wayne State U., 1955, M.S., 1962; m. Virginia Elinor Granse, June 18, 1955; children—Nancy Anne, David Carl, Roger Osborne, Mark Andrew. Intern Detroit Meml. Hosp., 1955-56; resident Wayne State U. and affiliated hosps., Detroit, 1958-62; assoc. pathologist Detroit Meml. Hosp. and Cottage Hosp., Grosse Pointe, Mich., 1962-84; pathologist, dir. labs. South Macomb Hosp., Warren, Mich., 1966—, Detroit Meml. Hosp., 1984—, Cottage Hosp., Grosse Pointe, Mich., 1984—; pathologist, dir. labs. Jennings Meml. Hosp., Detroit, 1971-79, Alexander Blain Hosp., Detroit, 1971—. Partner Langston, Walker & Assos., profl. corp., Grosse Pointe, 1968—. Instr. pathology Wayne State U. Med. Sch., Detroit, 1962-72, asst. clin. prof., 1972—. Pres. Mich. Assn. Blood Banks, 1969-70; mem. med. adv. com. ARC, 1972-83; mem. Mich. Higher Edn. Assistance Authority, 1975-77. Trustee Alexander Blain Meml. Hosp., Detroit, 1974-83, Detroit-Macomb Hosp. Assn., 1975—; bd. dirs. Wayne State Fund, 1971-83. Served to capt., M.C., AUS, 1956-58. Diplomate Am. Bd. Pathology (trustee bd. 1983—, treas. 1985—). Fellow Detroit Acad. Medicine; mem. Wayne State U. Alumni Assn. (bd. govs. 1968-71), Wayne State U. Med. Alumni Assn. (pres. 1969, trustee 1970-75, distinguished alumni award 1974), Coll. Am. Pathologists, Am. Soc. Clin. Pathologists (sec. 1971-77, pres. 1979-80), Mich. Soc. Pathologists (pres. 1980-81), Econ. Club Detroit, AMA (council on long range planning and devel. 1982—, vice-chmn. 1985—), Wayne County Med. Soc. (pres. 1984-85), Mich. Med. Soc. (bd. dirs. 1981—), Am., Mich. assns. blood banks, Phi Gamma Delta, Nu Sigma Nu, Alpha Omega Alpha. Republican. Episcopalian. Clubs: Detroit Athletic, Lochmoor; Mid-America (Chgo.). Home and office: 47 DePetris Way Grosse Pointe Farms MI 48236

WALKER, GEORGE LENWORTH, dentist; b. Jamaica, W.I., Feb. 6, 1945; s. William Ferguson and Leila (Russell) W.; m. Shirley Murray. B.S. in Biology, U. Ill., 1969; D.D.S., Coll. Dentistry, 1973. Intern, VA Hosp., Chgo., 1973-74, resident gen. practice dentistry, 1973-74; instr. Coll. Dentistry, U. Ill.-Chgo., 1973-74; supr. Dental Center Friendship Med. Center, Chgo., 1974-76; mem. staff Woodlawn Hosp., Chgo., 1974-78, Cermak Hosp., Chgo., 1974-78; pvt. practice dentistry, Chgo., 1976—. Recipient Cert. of Merit, Chgo. Assn. Commerce and Industry, 1975. Mem. ADA, Kenwood-Hyde Park Dental Soc., Lincoln Dental Soc., Kenwood Hyde Park Dental Soc. (corr. 1980-82). Episcopalian. Club: I-C (Chgo.). Lodge: Kiwanis. Home: 1115 S Plymouth Ct 113 Chicago IL 60605 Office: 1623 E 55th St Chicago IL 60615

WALKER, GLENN KENNETH, cell biology educator; b. South Weymouth, Mass., May 15, 1948; s. Kenneth Myles and Esther J. (Tuthill) W. B.S. in Zoology, U. Mass., 1970; M.S. in Cell Biology, No. Ariz. U., 1972; Ph.D. in Cell Biology, U. Md., 1975; NIH postdoctoral fellow U. Mich., 1975-76. Asst. prof. Eastern Mich. U., Ypsilanti, 1976-80, assoc. prof., 1980-85, prof., 1985—; adj. assoc. prof. U. Mich. Med. Sch., Ann Arbor, 1982—; cons. OSHA, 1982—. Contbr. articles to sci. jours. Mem. Washtenaw County Hazardous Substance Commn., 1983-84. Mem. Am. Micros. Soc., Mich. Electron Microscopy Forum, Sigma Xi, Phi Kappa Phi. Democrat. Avocations: running; racquetball; reading. Home: 713 Collegewood Dr Ypsilanti MI 48197 Office: Eastern Mich U Ypsilanti MI 48197

WALKER, JAMES ANDREW, aluminum company executive; b. Toronto, Ont., Can., Mar. 23, 1925; came to U.S., 1960; s. Wilson Gordon and Florence Owena (Godfrey) W.; m. Elizabeth Jennette McDonald, Sept. 20, 1967; children—Scott Robert, John Gordon, Susan Elizabeth. B.A.S. in Civil Engring., U. Toronto, 1951. Constrn. engr. Aluminum Co. Can., Montreal, Que., 1951-53; salesman Alcan Aluminum, N.Y.C., 1953-62; sales mgr. Amax Aluminum Co., N.Y.C., 1962-65; pres., mgr. Ugine-Kuhlman (Paris), N.Y.C., 1965-70; sales mgr. Noranda Aluminum Inc., Westport, Conn. and New Madrid, Mo., 1970-79, v.p. sales, Cleve., 1979—; v.p., dir. Noranda Commodities Inc., N.Y.C., 1976—. Area capt. United Fund, Westport, 1974-75. Republican. Clubs: Nutmeg Curling (gov. 1974-76) (Darien, Conn.); Metropolitan (N.Y.C.). Office: Noranda Aluminum Inc 30100 Chagrin Blvd Suite 100 Cleveland OH 44124

WALKER, JAMES CHARLES, quality control executive; b. Kansas City, Mo., Dec. 28, 1949; s. Kenneth Morris and Shirley (Kinzel) W.; m. Karen Sue Coverstone, Oct. 26, 1974; children—Andrea, Melissa, Stephen. B.S. in Indsl. Mgmt., Purdue U., 1972; postgrad. U. Tenn., 1983. Quality control supr. Copeland Corp., Sidney, Ohio, 1972-73, quality engr., 1973-76, sr. quality engr., 1976-77, quality control mgr., West Union, Ohio, 1977-78; quality assurance mgr. Oster div. Sunbeam Corp., Milw., 1978-79; mgr. quality control Fram div. Allied Corp., Greenville, Ohio, 1979-85, dir. quality assurance Prestolite Motor and Ignition div., Toledo, 1985—. Mem. Am. Soc. Quality Control (cert. quality engr.), Am. Statis. Assn., Soc. Mfg. Engrs., Soc. Automotive Engrs. (affiliate), Inst. for Productivity Through Quality Alumni. Republican. Roman Catholic. Lodge: Elks. Office: Prestolite Motor and Ignition Div Allied Corp Four Seagate Toledo OH 43691

WALKER, JAMES SILAS, college president; b. LaFollette, Tenn., Aug. 21, 1933; s. John Charles and Ruth Constance (Yeagle) W.; m. Nadine Leas Mortenson, May 28, 1954; children—Steven J., David K., Bradley P., Scott C. B.A., U. Ariz., 1954; B.Div., McCormick Theol. Sem., 1956; postgrad. U. Basel, Switzerland, 1956-57; Ph.D., Claremont Coll., 1963. Ordained to ministry Presbyterian Ch., 1956. Asst. paster Central Presbyn. Ch., Denver, 1957-60; prof. Huron Coll., S.D., 1963-66; prof., dean Hastings Coll., Nebr., 1966-83; pres. Jamestown Coll., N.D., 1983—; adj. faculty mem. Luther Northwestern Theol. Sem., St. Paul, 1984—. Author: Theology of Karl Barth, 1963. Bd. dirs. Salvation Army, Jamestown. Rotary Internat. Found. fellow, 1956-57; Nat. Def. Title IV grantee, 1960-63. Mem. Assn. Presbyn. Colls. and Univs. (sec.-treas.), Presbytery of No. Plains. Republican. Lodge: Rotary (dist. 563 gov. 1978-79). Avocations: travel; hunting; photography. Office: Jamestown Coll Box 6008 Jamestown ND 58401

WALKER, JAMES TERRY, museum director, archaeologist; b. Salt Lake City, Nov. 7, 1947; s. William J. and Erma (Shakespear) W.; m. Lucinda Rae Matheny, May 2, 1974; children—James, Timothy, Aaron, Jon. B.S., Brigham Young U., 1973, M.A., 1977. Archaeologist Brigham Young U., Provo, Utah, 1975-77, U.S. Forest Service, Moab, 1976-77; mus. curator Edge of Cedars State Hist. Monument, Blanding, Utah, 1977-81, Pioneer Trail State Park, Salt Lake City, 1981; mus. dir. Sanford Mus., Cherokee, Iowa, 1982—. Mem. Cherokee Adult Edn. Adv. Bd., 1982-85. Mem. Soc. Hist. Archaeology, Iowa Archaeol. Soc. Bd., Iowa Hist. Materials Preservation Soc. Council, Mormon Hist. Soc., Am. Assn. Mus., Cherokee Area Archives (cons., bd. dirs. 1982—), Aurelia Heritage Soc. (cons. 1983-84). Lodge: Kiwanis (pres. 1983-84).

WALKER, JESSIE, writer, photographer; b. Milw.; d. Stuart Richard and Loraine (Freuler) Walker; m. Arthur Griggs, Feb. 5, 1984. B.S., Medill Sch. Journalism, Northwestern U., also M.S. First major feature article appeared in The Am. Home mag., since contbr. numerous articles in nat. mags. including Am. Heritage's Americana, Better Homes and Gardens, McCall's, House and Garden, Good Housekeeping, others; midwest editor Am. Home mag.; contbg. editor Better Homes & Gardens. Mem. Ill. Opera Guild; mem. N. Shore jr. bd. Northwestern U. Settlement, 1949-59. Recipient Dorothy Dawes award for distinguished journalistic coverage in home furnishing, 1976, 77. Mem. Am. Soc. Interior Designers (press mem.), Women in Communications. Author: How to Plan a Trend Setting Kitchen, 1962; How to Make Window Decorating Easy, 1969; Shaker Design-150-year-old Modern, 1972; Good Design—What Makes It Last?, 1973; Junking Made Easy, 1974; Poster Power, 1976; For Collectors Only, 1977; Bishop Hill-Utopian Community 1978; also articles. Photographer cover photo Better Homes & Gardens, Mar. 1980, Oct. 1980, Sept. 1982, Better Homes & Gardens Decorating, spring 1984, cover Country Living, June 1983, Nov. 1983, Jan. 1984, Apr. 1984, Apr., May and July 1985. Address: 241 Fairview Rd Glencoe IL 60022

WALKER, JIMMY NEWTON, corporate company executive; b. Eldorado, Okla., Mar. 6, 1924; s. Edward Lee and Ruby (Dixon) W.; m. Margaret Mare Rice, Sept. 10, 1949; children—Beverly Joan Giberson, Karen Sue Freeburg. Assoc. Engr., Altus Jr. Coll., 1943; student Brown U., 1944; B.S. in Chem. Engring., Oklahoma State U., 1949; M.B.A., U. Chgo., 1963. Research chemist U.S. Gypsum Co., Chgo., 1949-59, lab. mgr., 1959-61, div. mgr. research and devel., Des Plaines, Ill., 1961-66, dir. research and devel., 1966-77, v.p., Libertyville, Ill., 1977-85, v.p. spl. assignments, 1985—; dir. U. Chgo. Div. Sch., 1982—; mem. adv. council NSF, Washington, 1976—; chmn. adv. com. Nat. Bur. Standards, 1977-78. Co-author: Status of Cement Research in U.S., 1979. Com. mem. Econ. Devel. Council, Libertyville, 1982—; mem. exec. bd. Northwest YMCA, Des Plaines, 1975-82; nat. bd. dirs. Am. Baptist Chs., Valley Forge, Pa., 1984—; pres. Chgo. Baptist Assn., 1981-84. Served with USAF, 1943-45. Mem. Am. Chem. Soc., Internat. Bldg. Congress, Indsl. Research Inst. (com. mem. 1968—), Research Dirs. Assn. (officer and pres. 1977-82), Phi Kappa Phi, Phi Lambda Upsilon. Republican. Club: Mission Hills (Northbrook, Ill.). Avocations: reading; golf; hiking; cruising. Office: USG Corp 101 S Wacker Dr Chicago IL 60606

WALKER, JOHN ALVIN, III, pharmacist; b. Rochester, Minn., Apr. 8, 1948; s. John Alvin, Jr. and Ione Louise (Kujath) W.; m. Connie Marie Witt, June 24, 1972 (div. Apr. 1978); m. Teri Jo Ellis, Oct. 13, 1984. B.S. in Pharmacy, U. Iowa, 1972. Lic. pharmacist, Iowa. Intern pharmacy Walgreen's, Racine, Wis., 1972-73; clin. instr. U. Iowa, Iowa City, 1973-81; dir. pharmacy Wayne County Hosp., Corydon, Iowa, 1981—; cons. Seymour Care Ctr., Iowa, 1983—. Contbr. chpts. to books in field, articles to profl. jours. Mem. Focus Drug Abuse Com., Wayne County, 1983—. Mem. Am. Soc. Hosp. Pharmacists, Am. Pharm. Assn. (Chpt. Contbn. award 1982), Shelby Am. Automobile Club, Ducks Unltd. Republican. Methodist. Avocations: skiing; classic automobiles; canoeing; golf. Home: 110 S Greeley St Corydon IA 50060 Office: Wayne County Hosp 417 S East St Corydon IA 50060

WALKER, JUDITH CHRISTOL, lawyer; b. Wisconsin Rapids, Wis., Dec. 16, 1939; d. Max Stanton and Phyllis Lorraine (Hepner) Christol; m. Hermon Benjamin Walker, Sept. 6, 1959 (div. 1976); children—Harold Jennings, Elizabeth Anne, John Hermon, James Bruce. B.A., U. S.D., 1960, M.A., 1967, J.D., 1978. Bar: S.D. 1978, U.S. Dist. Ct. S.D. 1980. Tchr. Spearfish High Sch., S.D., 1969-70; student intern Atty. Gen., Pierre, S.D., summer 1977; sole practice, Sturgis, S.D., 1978—; state's atty. Meade County, Sturgis, 1981—; dir. New Dawn Enterprises, Sturgis, 1984. Author: The Law and the Handicapped, 1977. Vice-chmn. Meade County Republican Central Com., Sturgis, 1979—; clerk of vestry St. Thomas Episcopal Ch., Sturgis, 1980—; pres., parliamentarian S.D. Fedn. Republican Women, 1982—; alternate rep. S.D. Republican Central County, Pierre, 1983—; active Sturgis Area Arts Council, 1981—, Sturgis C. of C., 1983—, Faith Area C. of C., 1982—. Mem. S.D. State Bar Assn. (chmn. juvenile justice com. 1984—), ABA, S.D. State's Atty.'s Assn. (dist. 1 bd. dirs. 1981—), Nat. Dist. Atty.'s Assn., AAUW, Nat. Orgn. victim Assistance, Phi Sigma Iota. Republican. Club: Cowbelles. Home: PO Box 700 Sturgis SD 57785 Office: Meade County States Atty 1000 Main St Sturgis SD 57785

WALKER, KAY L., insurance agent; b. Rigby, Idaho, Dec. 4, 1942; s. Allen H. and Lora (Taylor) W.; B.S., Brigham Young U., 1967; student So. Ill. U., 1967-68, U. Mo., St. Louis, 1968-69; m. Angela Galloway, Jan. 27, 1966; children—Kara, Kindra, Karsten, Kimber, Kenton, Kayla, Kyle. Agt., N.Y. Life, St. Louis, 1970-77; pres. Walker, Morris & Walker, Inc., St. Louis, 1973—; pres. Nauvoo Devel. Inc., 1977—; pres. Halcyon Travel Ltd., 1980—; mng. ptnr. Walker, McElliott & Wilkinson, 1984—. State coordinator Mo.

Citizens Council, 1980—; mem. St. Louis Commn. on Human Relations 1981—. Mem. Nat. Assn. Pension Adminstrs., Life Underwriters Assn., Million Dollar Round Table. Republican. Mormon. Kiwanian. Office: PO Box A 7001 Howdershell Hazelwood MO 63042

WALKER, KENNETH LYNN, lawyer; b. New Haven, Nov. 22, 1948; s. John Charles and Virginia Clare (Lovett) W.; m. Suzanne Kay Thompson, Jan. 27, 1979; 1 child, Katherine Leslie. B.A., Coe Coll., 1969; M.A., New Sch. Social Research, 1973; J.D., U. Iowa, 1975. Bar: Ohio. Assoc. Baker & Hostetler, Cleve., 1975-79; atty. Cole Nat. Corp., Cleve., 1979-84; group counsel TRW, Inc., Cleve., 1984—. Editor Jour. Corp. Law, 1975. Mem. ABA, Ohio Bar Assn. Office: TRW Inc 30050 Chagrin Blvd Cleveland OH 44124

WALKER, NEAL FRANCIS, pharmacist, consultant; b. Crosby, Minn., May 12, 1955; s. Neal Edward and Mary Grace (Lee) W.; m. Kim Kathleen Krier, June 19, 1976; children—Christina Ann, Matthew Neal, Eric Robert. B.S. in Pharmacy, N.D. State U., 1978. Registered pharmacist. Pharmacist Prescription Shoppe Co., Detroit Lakes, Minn., 1978-79; sr. pharmacist White Drug Co., East Grand Forks, Minn., 1979; staff pharmacist Central Mesabi Med. Ctr., Hibbing, Minn., 1979—; cons. Adams Clinic, Hibbing, 1983—. Contbr. articles to profl. Jours. Chmn. Hibbing Commn. on Alcohol and Drug Awareness, 1983—; v.p. Hibbing Mcpl. Band, 1984. Recipient Pvt. Enterprise award Minn. Power, 1984. Mem. Range Area Pharmacists, Minn. Soc. Hosp. Pharmacists, Am. Fed. Musicians, Jaycees (v.p. Hibbing 1983-85; C. William Brownfield award Detroit Lakes chpt. 1979, Outstanding Community Project award Hibbing chpt. 1984). Roman Catholic. Lodge: K.C. Avocations: basketball; cross country skiing; camping. Home: 4111 4th Avenue E Hibbing MN 55746 Office: Central Mesabi Med Ctr 750 E 34th St Hibbing MN 55746

WALKER, PATRICIA ANN, lawyer; b. Latrobe, Pa., Nov. 13, 1953; d. William J. and Sylvia R. (Fradel) W.; m. Ralph E. Jocke, Oct. 8, 1982. A.B., Grove City Coll., 1975; J.D., Cleve.-Marshall Coll. Law, 1981. Bars: Ohio 1981, U.S. Dist. Ct. (no. dist.) Ohio 1981; U.S. Ct. Appeals (6th cir.) 1982; U.S. Supreme Ct. 1985. City clk. City of Broadview Heights, Ohio, 1975-77; claims rep. Soc. Security Adminstrn., Cleve., 1977-81; assoc. Law Offices of Ellis B. Brannon, Sharon Center, Ohio, 1981—. Advisor Divorce Equity, Inc., Cleve. Mem. ABA, Assn. Trial Lawyers Am., Fed. Bar Assn., Nat. Orgn. Soc. Security Claimants' Reps., Ohio State Bar Assn., Ohio Acad. Trial Lawyers, Medina County Bar Assn., Akron Bar Assn., Cuyahoga County Bar Assn., Bar Assn. Greater Cleve., Cleve. Women Lawyers Assn. Democrat. Mem. United Ch. of Christ. Club: Slovenain Nat. Benefit Soc. Office: Law Office of Ellis B Brannon 6294 Ridge Rd PO Box 189 Sharon Center OH 44274

WALKER, RICHARD C., accounting educator; b. Sandusky, Mich., Jan. 23, 1941; s. C.B. and Marion (Cameron) W. B.A., Mich. State U., 1962; M.S., So. Ill. U.-Carbondale, 1964; Sp.A., Western Mich. U., 1978; Ph.D., U. Colo., 1978. C.P.A., cert. mgmt. acct., cert. internat. auditor, cert. cost analyst. Cost supr. Chevrolet-Gen. Motors Corp., Flint, Mich., 1962-63; audit mgr. Horwath & Horwath, Chgo., 1963-64; asst. prof. No. Mich. U., Marquette, 1964-66, Miami U., Oxford, Ohio, 1966-69; assoc. prof. Grand Valley State Coll., Allendale, Mich., 1969-78; prof. acctg. Ind. U., Bloomington, 1978—; cons. various bus. orgns., 1970—. Author: Introduction to Accounting, 1972. Recipient Outstanding Teaching award No. Mich. U., 1965. Mem. Am. Inst. C.P.A.s, Inst. Mgmt. Acctg., Am. Acctg. Assn., Nat. Assn. Accts. (dir. student activities Kokomo, Ind. 1984-85), Ind. C.P.A. Soc., Kokomo C. of C. (various coms.). Methodist.

WALKER, ROBERT COLEMAN, jewelry store executive, watchmaker; b. Hoxie, Ark., Apr. 28, 1925; s. Robert Tony and Ailsie Ann (Coleman) W.; m. Pauline Hudson, Jan. 15, 1944; children—Carrol Jean Walker Fisher, Susan Lee Walker Cox. Student pub. schs. Watchmaker, Gift Chest Jewelers, Poplar Bluff, Mo., 1940-43; watchmaker, mgr. Lane's Jewelry, Malden, Mo., 1945-49; instr. Lane's Sch. Watchmaking, Malden, 1949-51; watchmaker Dale's Jewelry, Carmi, Ill., 1951-53; watchmaker, mgr. Saliba's Jewelry, Charleston, Mo., 1953-80; owner, jeweler Walker's Jewelry, Charleston, 1980—. Served with AUS, 1943-45, ETO. Mem. Am. Watchmaker Inst., Jewelers of Am., Mo. Jewelers and Watchmakers Assn. (bd. dirs., pres. 1973-74), Horological Assn. Mo. (pres. 1961-62). Democrat. Baptist. Avocations: photography; woodworking. Home: 803 S Main St PO Box 253 Charleston MO 63834

WALKER, ROBERT EDWARD, automotive company executive; b. Janesville, Wis., Mar. 18, 1928; s. Peter and Mary Elizabeth (Keegan) W.; m. Thora Irene Stangeland, July 12, 1947; children—Kathryn A. Walker Baker, Karen P. Walker Riley, Barbara G. Walker Fisher, Margaret E. Walker Fleck, Carol L. Walker-Aten. B.S. in Mech. Engring., GM Inst., Flint, Mich., 1955. Mfg. engr. Chevrolet Motor Div., Flint, 1950-60, GM Overseas Ops., Detroit, 1960-64; Bedford truck plant mgr. Vauxhall Motors Ltd. div. GM, Luton, Beds., Eng., 1965-72, Ellesmere Port plant mgr., 1972-74; dir. internat. strategic planning Detroit Diesel Allison div. GM, 1976—. Served to maj. U.S. Army, 1946-60. Republican. Roman Catholic. Avocations: Photography; meteorology-climatology; reading; music. Home: 1851 Jenny Ln Rochester MI 48063

WALKER, RONALD LEE, educator, librarian; b. St. Joseph, Mo., Nov. 1, 1934; s. Arthur Francis and Hilma Dell (Atwood) Walker; m. Patricia Ann Walker, May 15, 1954; children—Mitchell Scott, Matthew Craig, Martin Wayne. B.A., Biola Coll., 1963; M.A., Talbot Theol. Sem., 1976; M.A. in Library Sci., U. Mo., 1983. Ordained to ministry Baptist Ch., 1967; asst. pastor Central Bapt. Ch., Anaheim, Calif., 1963-65; adminstr. Springfield (Mo.) Christian Schs., 1966-72; asst. pastor N.T. Bapt. Ch., Springfield, 1966-72; dir. Faith of Our Fathers Radio Broadcast, Springfield, 1967-71; dir. Sheltering Heights Bible Camp, Springfield, 1967-71; pastor Quint City Bapt. Temple, Davenport, Iowa, 1972-75; prof. Bibl. studies Bapt. Bible Coll., Springfield, 1976—, librarian, 1981—. Pres., Iowa Bapt. Fellowship, 1973-74, state rep., 1973-74. Author: King James Controversy, 1980; editor: The Baptist Church, 1981. Served as sgt. USMC, 1954-57. Mem. ALA. Republican. Baptist. Home: Route 20 Box 205 Springfield MO 65803 Office: Baptist Bible Coll 628 E Kearney St Springfield MO 65803

WALKER, SCOTT BALTZELL, marketing educator; b. Evansville, Ind., June 6, 1957; s. Jessie E. and Mary E. (Hardy) W. B.S., Ind. U., 1979, M.S., 1984. Program specialist Pvt. Industry Council, Evansville, 1979-80; adult edn. coordinator Evansville-Vanderburgh Schs., Evansville, 1980-82, mktg. tchr., 1984—; orientation instr. Ind. U., Bloomington, 1983, internat. student news editor, 1983, career asst., 1983. Named to Hall of Fame, Mktg. and Distributive Edn., 1985. Mem. Ind. Vocat. Assn., Distributive Clubs Am., Kappa Alpha Psi. Home: 1741 S Garvin Evansville IN 47713 Office: William Henry Harrison High Sch 211 Fielding Rd Evansville IN 47715

WALKER, THOMAS STUART, microbiologist, researcher; b. Evansville, Ind., July 16, 1949; s. Thomas Martin and Mary Ruth (Blackburn) W.; m. Andrea Lea Houchin, Aug. 12, 1972; children—Lisa Nicole, Nathaniel Stuart. B.A., Cedarville Coll., 1971; M.S., Ind. U. Sch. Medicine, 1975, Ph.D., 1977; postgrad., Grace Sem., 1984. Postdoctoral fellow U. Va. Coll. Medicine, Charlottesville, Va., 1977, U. South Ala. Sch. Medicine, Mobile, 1978-79; asst. prof. Ball State U., Muncie, Ind., 1979-84; assoc. prof. microbiology Ball State U., Ind. U. Sch. Medicine, 1984—. Contbr. articles to profl. jours. Choir dir. Grace Bapt. Ch., Muncie, 1983-84, adult Sunday sch. tchr., 1980—. Recipient Nat. Research Service award Nat. Cancer Inst. 1979; NSF fellow 1978; NIH grantee 1982—. Mem. Cedarville Coll. Alumni Council (bd. dirs. 1983—) Am. Soc. Microbiology (sec., treas. Ind. br.), Am. Heart Assn. (bd. dirs. Delaware County 1984—), Am. Soc. Rickettsiology, Sigma Xi. Republican. Avocations: golf; basketball; classical guitar. Home: 2008 Alden Rd Muncie IN 47304 Office: Muncie Ctr Med Edn Ball State U Muncie IN 47306

WALKER, WALTER WILLARD, real estate and investments executive; b. Mpls., Dec. 4, 1911; s. Archie Dean and Bertha Willard (Hudson) W.; B.A., Princeton U., 1935; M.D., Harvard U., 1940; postgrad. U. Minn., 1942-48; m. Elva Mae Dawson, Dec. 16, 1939 (div. Oct. 1969); m. Elaine Barbatsis, Mar. 17, 1972. Teaching fellow pathology U. Minn., 1942-48; left medicine, went into bus., 1948; dir. Shasta Forest Co., Redding, Calif., 1951-71, treas., 1954-66, v.p., 1966-71; sec., dir. Barlow Realty Co., Mpls., 1954-67, pres., 1967-77, chmn., 1977-80, sec., 1980-83, v.p., 1983—; sec., dir. Walker Pence Co., 1950-72; sec. Penwalk Investment Co., 1958-72, dir., 1943-72; dir. Craig-Hallum Corp., Mpls., 1954—; adv. bd. Lincoln office Northwestern Nat. Bank, Mpls., 1957-74. Bd. dirs. T.B. Walker Found., 1953-76, v.p., 1954-76; bd. dirs. Minn. Opera Co., 1968-73, Archie D. and Bertha H. Walker Found., 1953—, Mpls. Found., 1962-79, Walker Art Center, 1954-76, United Fund, 1966-72; trustee Abbott-Northwestern Hosp., 1969-77; trustee Children's Health Center, Inc., 1968-73, treas., 1969-73; pres. Found. Services, 1967-73; bd. dirs., exec. com. Minn. Charities Review Council, 1965-74; mem. Hennepin County Capital Budgeting Task Force, 1973-74. Mem. Sigma Xi, Nu Sigma Nu. Methodist. Clubs: Minneapolis; Woodhill Country; Princeton (N.Y.C.); U. Minn. Alumni. Home: 1900 Knox Ave S Minneapolis MN 55403 also 4143 Gulf Dr Sanibel FL 33957 Office: 1121 Hennepin Ave Minneapolis MN 55403

WALKER, WILLIE MARK, electronics engineering executive; b. Bessemer, Ala., Aug. 18, 1929; s. Johnnie and Annie Maimie (Thompson) W.; m. Mae Ruth Fulton, Apr. 28, 1952; children—Patricia Ann, Mark William, Karen Marie. B.E.E., Marquette U., 1958; M.S. in Elec. Engring., U. Wis., 1965. Registered profl. engr., Wis. Devel. technician AC Spark Plug, Milw., 1953-56, project engr., 1956-60, engring. supr., 1960-65; sr. devel. engr. AC Electronics, Milw., 1965-71; sr. prodn. engr. Delco Electronics, Oak Creek, Wis., 1971—; mem. occupational adv. bd. on computer sci. Milw. Area Tech. Coll., 1983—. Author various proprietary reports. Pres., Potawatomi Area council Boy Scouts Am., Waukesha, Wis., 1982-84; loaned exec. United Way of Greater Milw., 1983; usher, minister of communion St. Mary Catholic Ch., Menomonee Falls, Wis., 1967—. Served with USAF, 1949-53. Elected to Black Achievers in Bus. and Industry, Milw. Met. YMCA, 1984; recipient Civic Service award Rotary Club, 1983; Gen. Motors award for Excellence, 1980; St. George award Milw. Archidiocese, 1975; Silver Beaver award Boy Scouts Am., 1973; Black Achiever in Bus. and Industry award YMCA Greater Milw., 1984. Mem. Wis. Soc. Profl. Engrs., Computer Soc. of IEEE, NAACP. Lodges: Lions (chpt. pres. 1979-80, sec. 1974-75); K.C. (recorder 1966-67, advocate 1975-76). Office: Delco Electronics Div Gen Motors Corp 7929 S Howell Ave Oak Creek WI 53154

WALKERDINE, KENNETH MARTIN, mechanical engineering executive; b. Port Hope, Ont., Can., Jan. 7, 1946; came to U.S., 1981. B.M.E., General Motors Inst., 1970; M.B.A., Western Mich. U., 1984. Engr., Gen. Motors, Toronto, Can., 1965-71; with Simpson Industries, Inc., Thamesville, Ont., 1971-81, engring. mgr., Litchfield, Mich., 1981-83, v.p. engring., 1983—. Mem. Beta Gamma Sigma. Office: Simpson Industries Inc 917 Anderson Rd Litchfield MI 49252

WALKUP, MARSHA ANN, interior designer; b. Rolla, Mo., June 13, 1955; d. Wilbur Cline and Doris Ann (Harmon) Batson; m. Eugene Davis Carney, July 8, 1973 (div. 1976); m. Grant William Walkup, Mar. 20, 1982; stepchildren—Teresa Ann, Gregory Wayne, Barton William. B.S. in Interior Design, S.W. Mo. State U., 1979; postgrad. in design, Kans. U., 1985—. Interior designer VA, Leavenworth, Kans., 1980—. Active St. Mary's Coll. Community Cultural Club, Leavenworth, 1983—. Recipient Dir.'s commendation award VA, 1981, Performance award, 1984, 85. Affiliate mem. Inst. Bus. Designers. Democrat. Club: Pilot Internat. (treas. 1984-85). Home: 2408 17th St Terr Leavenworth KS 66048 Office: VA 4th St Trafficway Leavenworth KS 66048

WALL, ARTHUR EDWARD PATRICK, editor; b. Jamestown, N.Y., Mar. 12, 1925; s. George Herbert and Doris (Olmstead) W.; student pub. schs.; m. Marcella Joan Petrine, Nov. 5, 1954; children—John Wright, Marie Ann, David Arthur Edward. Copy editor Worcester (Mass.) Telegram, 1958; Sunday editor Hawaii Island Corr., Honolulu Star-Bull., 1958-60; editor Hilo (Hawaii) Tribune-Herald, 1960-63; Sunday editor Honolulu Advertiser, 1963-65, mng. editor, 1971-72; mng. editor Cath. Rev., 1965-66, editor, 1966-71; editor-in-chief Nat. Cath. News Service, Washington, 1972-76; editor, gen. mgr. The New World (name changed to Chgo. Catholic 1977), Chgo., 1976—, pres., 1979—; pres. New World Pub. Co., 1977—; dir. Noll Printing Co., Inc., Huntington, Ind. Dir. bur. info. Archdiocese Balt., 1965-66; mem. fin. com. Archdiocese Chgo., 1979-82; mem. council Internat. Cath. Union of Press, Geneva, 1972—, v.p., 1974-77. Chmn., Gov.'s Com. Ednl. TV, Honolulu, 1964-65; regent Chaminade Coll., Honolulu, 1959-65, chmn., 1963-65; trustee St. Mary's Sem. and Univ., Balt., 1975-76; bd. dirs. Cath. Journalism Scholarship Fund, 1976—, Our Sunday Visitor, Inc., Huntington, Ind., 1977—; mem. spiritual renewal and devel. com. 41st Internat. Eucharistic Congress, Phila., 1975-76. Named Young Man of Year, Hilo, Hawaii, 1960; recipient St. Francis de Sales award Cath. Press Assn., 1977; Father of Year, Honolulu C. of C., 1964; Spl. award U.S. Cath. Conf., 1980. Mem. Internat. Fedn. Cath. Press Agys. (pres. 1974-77), Internat. Fedn. Cath. Journalists (pres. 1977-80, v.p. 1981-83), Cath. Press Assn. U.S. and Can. (bd. dirs. 1978—), Sigma Delta Chi (past chpt. pres.). Roman Catholic. Clubs: Nat. Press (Washington); Overseas Press (N.Y.C.); Chgo. Press. Author: The Big Wave, 1960; The Mind of Cardinal Bernardin, 1983. Editor: Origins and Catholic Trends, 1972-76. Contbr. articles to mags. Home: 2100 Lincoln Park W Chicago IL 60614 Office: Chicago Catholic 155 E Superior St Chicago IL 60611

WALL, ARTHUR FREDERIK, building contracting company executive; b. Cedar Rapids, Iowa, July 2, 1927; s. Arthur John and Randi Aletta (Bruas) W.; m. Ulla Viola Simonsen, May 29, 1973. B.A., U. Iowa, 1951. Treas., Wall & Co., Cedar Rapids, 1949-55, v.p., 1955-61, pres., 1961—. Served with USAF, 1945-46. Lutheran. Lodge: Cedar Rapids Danish Brotherhood (pres. 1978-82), Danish Brotherhood (pres. Iowa-Minn. dist. 1984-85). Avocations: fraternal lodges; organizing; building. Home: 362 E Post Rd SE Cedar Rapids IA 52403 Office: Wall & Co 1220 6th St SW Cedar Rapids IA 52404

WALL, DENNIS THOMAS, publishing executive; b. Camden, N.J., Dec. 2, 1950; s. James Leo and Roseanna (Pillo) W.; m. Beverly Ann Wall, Apr. 21, 1972; children—Lisa, Linda. A.S., Camden County Coll., 1977; student Glassboro State Coll., 1979-81. Printer, compositer S. Chew & Sons, Camden, N.J., 1969-74; directory prodn. mgr. Datacomp Corp., Phila., 1974-80; sr. project mgr. Macmillan, Inc., Delran, N.J., 1980-82; dir. prodn. systems Standard Rate and Data, Wilmette, Ill., 1983—. Roman Catholic. Office: Standard Rate and Data Service Inc 3004 Glenview Rd Wilmette IL 60091

WALL, ROBERT EVANS, dentist; b. Linton, Ind., Feb. 29, 1948; s. George Arthur and Rosalie Elaine (Francis) W.; m. Christine Lois Huber, May 15, 1982; 1 child, Morgan Sage. B.A., DePauw U., 1970; D.D.S., Ind. U., 1974. Resident VA Hosp., Indpls., 1974-75; staff VA Hosp., North Chicago, Ill., 1975-77; gen. practice dentistry, Madison, Ind., 1977—; on staff King's Daughter's Hosp., Madison, 1977—, Madison State Hosp., 1984—. Pres. Jefferson County Labor/Mgmt. Commn., Madison, 1984—; bd. dirs. Lide White Boys Club, Madison, 1978—, Girls Club Jefferson County, Madison, 1977-83. Mem. ADA, Ind. Dental Assn., Southeastern Ind. Dental Soc. Republican. Methodist. Club: Madison Country (v.p. 1985). Lodge: Elks. Avocations: fishing; golf; travel. Home: 1735 Crozier Ave Madison IN 47250 Office: 753 W Main St Madison IN 47250

WALL, WILLIAM E., See *Who's Who in America,* 43rd edition.

WALLACE, DOUGLAS ALEXANDER, oil company executive, consultant; b. Charlottesville, Va., July 31, 1947; s. Wayne Alexander and Naomi Ruth (Smith) W.; m. Sally Carmichael, Mar. 29, 1969; children—David Alexander, Michael Bruce. B.A., Monmouth Coll., 1975. With prodn. mgmt. dept. Butler Mfg. Co., Galesburg, Ill. 1975-78; sales mgr. Schaeffer Mfg. Co., St. Louis, 1976-84, Primrose Oil Co., Dallas, 1983—; chmn. Preventive Maintenance Design Co., Bettendorf, Iowa, 1976—. Author, manuals in field. Served with USN, 1967-71, Vietnam. Mem. Am. Soc. Lubrication Engrs. (cert.), Soc. Automotive Engrs., Presbyterian. Lodge: Lions. Avocations: scuba diving; camping; flying. Home: 48 Rainbow Dr Bettendorf IA 52722 Office: Preventive Maintenance Design Co 48 Rainbow Dr Bettendorf IA 52722

WALLACE, FRANKLIN SHERWOOD, lawyer; b. Bklyn., Nov. 24, 1927; s. Abraham Charles and Jennie (Etkin) Wolowitz; student U. Wis., 1943-45; B.S. cum laude, U.S. Mcht. Marine Acad., 1950; LL.B., J.D., U. Mich., 1953; m. Eleanor Ruth Pope, Aug. 23, 1953; children—Julia Diane, Charles Andrew. Admitted to Ill. bar, 1954, since practiced in Rock Island; ptnr. firm Winstein, Kavensky, Wallace & Doughty; asst. state's atty. Rock Island County, 1967-68; local counsel UAW at John Deere-Internat. Harvester Plants. Bd. dirs. Tri City Jewish Center; trustee United Jewish Charities of Quad Cities. Mem. ABA Ill. (chmn. jud. adv. polls com. 1979-84), Rock Island County bar assns., Am., Ill. trial lawyers assns., Nat. Assn. Criminal Def. Lawyers, Am. Orthopsychiat. Assn., Am. Judicature Soc., Blackhawk Coll. Found. Democrat. Jewish. Home: 3405 20th St Ct Rock Island IL 61201 Office: Rock Island Bank Bldg Rock Island IL 61201

WALLACE, MELVIN EUGENE, pharmacist; b. Athens, Ohio, May 2, 1951; s. Jack Melvin and Mollie Marie (Howell) W.; m. Doreen Jeanette Miller, June 26, 1976; 1 child, Stephanie Renee. B.S. in Pharmacy, Ohio State U., 1979; B.S. cum laude in Zoology, Ohio U., 1974. Registered pharmacist. Pharmacist, asst. mgr. Super-X Drugs, Zanesville, Ohio, 1979-81; acting dir. pharmacy Pharmacy Systems, Inc., Dublin, Ohio, 1982; staff pharmacist Doctors Hosp., Columbus, Ohio, 1982—. Fellow Ohio State Pharm. Assn. Avocations: Little League coaching; basketball; softball. Home: 4224 Valley Quail Blvd N Westerville OH 43081

WALLACE, RICHARD GORDON, wine company executive; b. Syracuse, N.Y., Aug. 19, 1947; s. Earl Thomas and Jeanne (Dolan) W.; m. Ania Marie Kwiatkowski, Sept. 21, 1985. Grad. Internat. Sch. Mktg. and Mgmt., 1983. Mgr. dist. E & J. Gallo, Syracuse, N.Y., 1970-76; mgr. regional Monsieur Henri Wines, Chgo., 1976-78, v.p., 1978—. Mem. Les Amis du Vin. Republican. Avocations: photography; travel. Office: Monsieur Henri Wines Ltd 9575 West Higgins Rd Rosemont IL 60018

WALLACE, ROBERT FRANCIS, retired business executive; b. Chgo., Sept. 11, 1917; s. Peter A. and Helen Jeanne (Georres) W.; student U. Ill., 1935-37; B.S., Loyola U., Chgo., 1943; m. Harriet Jane Scales, Feb. 9, 1963; children—Warren L., David S. Staff auditor Arthur Andersen & Co., Chgo., 1943-49; pres., chief operating officer Outboard Marine Corp., Waukegan, Ill., 1949-85. Police magistrate, Winthrop, Ill., 1951-55. Bd. dirs. Ole Evinrude Found. Mem. Boating Industry Assn., Internat. Trade Club, Belgian-Am. C. of C., Phi Eta Sigma. Home: 20929 Lakeview Pkwy Mundelein IL 60060

WALLACE, WILLIAM FORBES, dentist; b. Uniontown, Pa., June 13, 1941; s. Paul Forbes and Rosemond Mildred (Williams) W.; m. Lida Ruth Hizey, Dec. 15, 1962; children—Michael William, Christopher William, Julie Lynn. B.S., Ohio State U., 1963, D.D.S., 1967. Commd. capt. U.S. Army, 1968, advanced through grades to comdr.; various dental assignments, 1968-79; officer in charge, Germany, 1979-81; chief dental sci. div., San Antonio, 1981-84; DENTAC comdr., Ft. Leavenworth, Kans., 1984—; adj. asst. prof. dentistry Creighton U., Omaha, 1982-84. Pres. High Sch. PTA, Germany, 1980-81; mem. German-Am. Club, 1979-81. Decorated D.S.M. with two bronze oak leaf clusters. Fellow Acad. Gen. Dentistry; mem. ADA, Fed. Services Bd. Gen. Dentistry (cert.). Republican. Methodist. Clubs: Rod and Gun, Hunt, Quarterback. Avocations: fishing; sports. Home: 26 Summer Pl Ft Leavenworth KS 66027 Office: USA Dental Activities US Army Ft Leavenworth KS 66027

WALLACH, JOHN SIDNEY, library administrator; b. Steubenville, Ohio, Jan. 6, 1939; s. Arthur Martin and Alice Irene (Smith) W.; B.S. in Edn., Kent State U., 1963; M.L.S., U. R.I., 1968; M.P.A., U. Dayton, 1977; m. Jane Springett Wallach, Sept. 21, 1963; children—John Michael, Wendy Anne, Bethany Lynne, Kristen Michele. Dir. Mercer County (Ohio) Dist. Library, Celina, 1968-70; dir. Greene County (Ohio) Dist. Library, Xenia, 1970-77; asst. dir. Dayton and Montgomery County (Ohio) Library, 1977-78, dir., 1979—. Mem. Ohio Com. for Employer Support of Guard and Res.; pres. Dayton Mus. Natural History; bd. dirs., treas. Family Services Assn., Dayton bd. dirs. Ohionet; vice chmn. PAR Council of United Way. Served with U.S. Navy, 1963-68, capt. Res. Mem. ALA, Ohio Library Assn. (dir. 1971-74, pres.), Naval Res. Assn., Res. Officers Assn., Miami Valley Mil. Affairs Assn. Club: Dayton Discussion. Office: 215 E 3d St Dayton OH 45402

WALLACH, MARK IRWIN, lawyer; b. Cleve., May 19, 1949; s. Ivan A. and Janice (Grossman) W.; m. Harriet Kinney, Aug. 11, 1974; children—Kerry Melissa, Philip Alexander. B.A. magna cum laude, Wesleyan U., 1971; J.D. cum laude, Harvard U., 1974. Bar: Ohio 1974, U.S. dist. ct. (no. dist.) Ohio 1974. Law clk. U.S. Dist. Ct., Cleve., 1974-75; assoc. Baker & Hostetler, Cleve., 1975-79; chief trial counsel City of Cleve., 1979-81; assoc. Calfee, Halter & Griswold, Cleve., 1981-82; ptnr., 1982—. Author: Christopher Morley, 1976. Bd. dirs. Citizens League of Greater Cleve., 1978-79; exec. com. mem. Van Aken Project Com., 1982—; pres. Wesleyan Alumni Club Cleve., 1983—. Mem. ABA, Ohio Bar Assn., Cuyahoga County Law Dirs. Assn., Greater Cleve. Bar Assn. Republican. Jewish. Club: Commerce (Cleve.). Avocations: Reading; space exploration; politics. Home: 23538 Duffield Rd Shaker Heights OH 44122 Office: Calfee Halter & Griswold 1800 Central Nat Bank Bldg Cleveland OH 44114

WALLER, DENNIS KEITH, city police official, police educator; b. Garden City, Mich., July 9, 1948; s. Arthur Max and Elizabeth (Gunn) W.; m. Deborah Ruth Schroeder, Nov. 18, 1983; children—Laura Christine, William Max. B.S. in Police Adminstrn., Mich. State U., 1970; M.Sc. in Pub. Adminstrn., Fla. Internat. U., 1975. Cert. police instr., Mich., Fla., N.C. Police officer Dade County Pub. Safety Dept., Miami, Fla., 1971-72; investigator, analyst Carol Mgmt. Co., Miami, 1973-74; asst. comdg. officer S. Miami Police Dept., Fla., 1974-76; coordinator criminal justice program Craven Community Coll., New Bern, N.C., 1976-78; dir. law enforcement tng. Wake Tech. Inst., Raleigh, N.C., 1978-83; chief of police Ripon Police Dept., Wis., 1983—; cons. Fairfield Harbour Police Dept., New Bern, N.C., 1978-81, N.C. State U. Pub. Safety Dept., Raleigh, 1979-80, N.C. State Fairgrounds, Raleigh, 1980-81. Recipient Outstanding Young Man of Am. award Jaycees, 1980, 81. Mem. Fond du Lac County Law Enforcement Execs. Assn. (v.p. 1984, pres. 1985), Wis. Chiefs of Police Assn., Internat. Assn. Chiefs of Police, Law Enforcement Tng. Officers Assn. Wis. Episcopalian. Lodge: Kiwanis. Office: Ripon Police Dept 100 Jackson St Ripon WI 54971

WALLER, EDWARD DENNIS, child psychologist; b. Passaic, N.J., July 28, 1951; s. Edward George and Elizabeth (Eslinger) W.; m. Nancy Varone, Oct. 9, 1977; children—Edward Jason, Megan Anne. B.A. in Psychology, Seton Hall U., 1973; M.A. in Clin. Psychology, U. Dayton, 1976; Ph.D., Ohio State U., 1982. Case mgr. Cox Heart Inst., Kettering, Ohio, 1975-76; psychiat. social worker Passaic County Diagnostic Ctr., Patterson, N.J., 1976-77; counselor South Community Mental Health Ctr., Kettering, Ohio, 1977-78; grad. teaching asst. dept. psychology Ohio State U., Columbus, 1978-81; grad. practicum East Central Guidance Ctr., Columbus, 1979-80; psychology intern Eastern Va. Grad. Sch. Medicine, Norfolk, 1981-82; psychologist, clin. supr. Samaritan Ctr. for Youth Resources, Dayton, Ohio, 1982—; instr. psychology Tidewater Community Coll., Virginia Beach, Va., 1981-82. Mem. Am. Psychol. Assn., Ohio Psychol. Assn., Midwestern Psychol. Assn., Psi Chi, Phi Kappa Phi. Roman Catholic. Office: 5670 Philadelphia Dr Dayton OH 45415

WALLER, LARRY JAMES, chamber of commerce executive; b. Mason City, Iowa, Feb. 27, 1940; s. Franklin James and Bernadine Grace (Van Blair) Kaiser W.; m. Kim Davenport, Nov. 20, 1964; children—Jeffrey Waller, Jennifer Waller. B.Acad. of Orgn. Mgmt., U. Notre Dame, 1976; B.S., Nat. Coll., Rapid City, S.D., 1977. Cert. chamber exec. Iowa. Mgr., SM Fin. Co., Jefferson, Iowa, 1965-67; exec. v.p. Marion C. of C., Iowa, 1967-70; gen. mgr. Billings C. of C., Mont., 1970-71; pres. Rapid City C. of C., S.D., 1971-81, Cedar Rapids Area C. of C., Iowa, 1981—; Colo. bd. regents U.S. C. of C., 1977—; bd. dirs., vice chair Am. C. of C. Execs., 1978-83; pres. Mid-Am. Chamber Execs., 1978; pres. bd. dirs. Iowa C. of C., 1982—. Mem. task force Cedar Rapids Pub. Schs.; bd. dirs. All-Iowa Fair Assn., 1981—; treas. Five Seasons Leadership, Cedar Rapids, 1982—; v.p. Jr. Achievement, Cedar Rapids, 1985. Served with U.S. Army, 1959-62. Recipient numerous speaking awards Toastmasters, Jr. C. of C., Air Force Assn. medal of merit, 1980. Republican. Presbyterian (elder). Club: Rotary (Cedar Rapids). Avocations: golf; reading; youth sports. Home: 3951 Sally Dr NE Cedar Rapids IA 52402 Office: Cedar Rapids Area C of C 424 1st Ave NE Cedar Rapids IA 52401

WALLER, ROBERT MORRIS, health care services company executive; b. Flint, Mich., Jan. 3, 1944; s. Ashton Carr and Nell Kathryn (Morris) W.; m. Sharon L. Waller, July 24, 1965; children—Robert M., Jennifer Anne. B.S. in Bus. Adminstrn., Northwestern U., 1966; M.B.A., Lake Forest Sch. Mgmt., 1984. Area ops. mgr. Am. Hosp. Supply Corp., Evanston, Ill., 1970-72, dir. distbn., 1972-74, v.p. ops., 1974-77, v.p. hosp. services, 1977-82; pres. AHSECO div. Am. Hosp. Supply Corp., Evanston, 1982—. Contbr. articles to profl. jours. Mem. Internat. Mgmt. and Devel. Inst., Washington, 1984—; deacon Presbyn. Ch., Deerfield, Ill., 1974; guest lectr. Northwestern U., 1980-82, U. Colo., Boulder, 1980. Republican. Presbyterian. Home: 588 E Linden Lake Forest IL 60045 Office: Am Hosp Supply Corp 2020 Ridge Ave Evanston IL 60201

WALLER, RONALD WILLIAM, clinical psychologist, educator; b. Decatur, Ill., Feb. 27, 1948; s. Frank William and Fern Lorene (Wilson) W.; 1 dau.,

Angela Ann. Student Eastern Ill. U., 1966-68; B.S. in Psychology, U. Ill., 1970; M.A. in Clin. Psychology, Bowling Green U., 1974, Ph.D., 1981. Psychology cons. Toledo (Ohio) Ct. Diagnostic and Treatment Ctr., 1972-73; psychology intern Galesburg (Ill.) State Research Hosp., 1974-75, psychologist Galesburg Mental Health Ctr. (formerly Galesburg State Research Hosp.), 1975-83; pvt. practice clin. psychology, Galesburg, 1981-83, Lakeside Family Therapy Services, Racine, Wis., 1983—; instr. communication Carl Sandburg Coll., Galesburg, 1981-82; adj. asst. prof Parkside br. U. Wis., Kenosha, 1984—; cons. and lectr. in field. NIMH trainee, 1971. Mem. Am. Psychol. Assn., Ill. Psychol. Assn. Contbr. articles to profl. jours. Office: 5814 Washington Ave Racine WI 53406

WALLER, STEVEN SCOBEE, agriculture educator; b. Indpls., Aug. 29, 1947; s. Claude Victor and Margaret Ann (Scobee) W.; m. Jessie Ellen Simone, Jan. 24, 1970; children—Christina Dee, Scott Steven. A.S., Vincennes U., Ind., 1967; B.S., Purdue U., 1970; Ph.D., Tex. A&M U., 1975. Research fellow Tex. A&M U., College Station, 1974-75; asst. prof. S.D. State U., Brookings, 1975-78, asst. to dir. resident instrn., 1977-78; assoc. prof. U. Nebr., Lincoln, 1978-84, prof., 1985—; chmn. Great Plains Com., 1984—, Range Sci. Edn. Council, 1985—. Assoc. editor Jour. Range Mgmt., 1982-84. Contbr. articles to profl. jours. Mem. Summer Festival Com., Brookings, 1977; coach Lincoln Youth Softball Assn., 1980—. Tom Slick Research fellow, 1974. Mem. Soc. Range Mgmt., Nebr. Forage and Grassland Council (pres. 1981), Nebr. Acad. Sci., Nebr. Soc. Range Mgmt. (pres. elect 1984—), Sigma Xi, Phi Sigma, Beta Rho, Gamma Sigma Delta, Xi Sigma Pi, Phi Theta Kappa. Methodist. Office: U Nebr Dept Agronomy 347 Keim Lincoln NE 68583

WALLESTAD, PHILIP WESTON, physician; b. Madison, Wis., May 14, 1922; s. John Oscar and Dorothy Francis (White) W.; B.A., U. Wis., 1947, M.D., 1954; m. Edith Stolle, Jan. 15, 1949 (div. Mar. 1967); children—Kristin Eve, Ingrid Birgitta, Erika Ann; m. 2d, Muriel Annette Moen, June 22, 1968; children—Thomas John, Scott Philip. Intern, Calif. Lutheran Hosp., Los Angeles, 1954, resident in surgery, 1955-56; gen. practice medicine, Fredonia and Port Washington Wis., 1957-72, Libby, Mont., 1972-74; staff physician VA Hosp., Fort Harrison, Mont., 1974-77, Tomah, Wis., 1977-78, VA Hosp., Iron Mountain, Mich., 1978-84. Served with AUS, 1943-46; ETO; lt. col. USAF Res., 1979-82. Mem. Exptl. Aviation Assn., Am. Legion, DAV, Assn. Mil. Surgeons U.S., Air Force Assn., Am. Security Council, Conservative Caucus, Am. Def. Preparedness Assn., U. Wis. Alumni Assn., Nat. W Club, NRA. Republican. Presbyterian Ch. (elder). Club: Rotary. Home: 1005 Bluff St Kingsford MI 49801 Office: VA Hosp Center H Iron Mountain MI 49801

WALLING, DAVID PERCY, retail sales corporation executive; b. St. Thomas, Ont., Can., Mar. 15, 1932; came to U.S., 1958; s. Percy William and Edith Beulah (Brown) W.; m. Elizabeth Anne Corbett, July 4, 1958; 1 dau., Linda. B.A., U. Western Ont., London, Can., 1955; M.B.A., Mich. State U., 1976. With S.S. Kresge, Detroit, 1958-80, mgr. property acctg., 1965-67, chief acct., 1967-73, asst. controller, 1973-76, v.p. acctg., 1976-80; v.p. corp. acctg. and reporting K-Mart, Troy, Mich., 1980—. Mem. Fin. Execs. Inst., Nat. Assn. Accts., Planning Execs. Inst., Nat. Retail Mchts. Assn. Home: 1457 Ardmoor St Birmingham MI 48010 Office: 3100 W Big Beaver Rd Troy MI 48084

WALLMAN, CHARLES JAMES, former money handling products exec., author; b. Kiel, Wis., Feb. 19, 1924; s. Charles A. and Mary Ann (Loftus) W.; student Marquette U., 1942-43, Tex. Coll. Mines, 1943-44; B.B.A., U. Wis., 1949; m. Charline Marie Moore, June 14, 1952; children—Stephen, Jeffrey, Susan, Patricia, Andrew. Sales promotion mgr. Brandt, Inc., Watertown, Wis., 1949-65, v.p., 1960-70, exec. v.p., 1970-80, v.p. corp. devel., 1980-83, past dir. Mem. exec. bd. Potawatomi council Boy Scouts Am., also former v.p. council; former bd. dirs., pres. Earl and Eugenia Quirk Found., Inc. Trustee, Joe Davies Scholarship Found.; bd. dirs. Watertown Meml. Hosp. Served with armored inf. AUS, 1943-45; ETO. Decorated Bronze Star. Mem. Am. Legion, E. Central Golf Assn. (past pres.), Wis. Alumni Assn. (local past pres.), 12th Armored Div. Assn., Watertown Hist. Soc. (bd. dirs.), Phi Delta Theta. Republican. Roman Catholic. Clubs: Rotary (bd. dirs.), Elk (past officer), Watertown Country (past dir.). Author: Edward J. Brandt, Inventor, 1984. Home: 700 Clyman St Watertown WI 53094

WALLS, JOHN WILLIAM, association executive; b. Knightstown, Ind., Mar. 25, 1927; s. Otto and Ruth (Miller) W.; m. Phyllis Hardin, June 20, 1948; children—Ann, Kathryn, Elizabeth, Timothy. B.A., Ind. U., 1949; M.P.A., Wayne State U., 1955. Various positions with assns. and state and local govt., 1949-62; dep. planning dir. City Planning Dept., Pitts., 1962-65; exec. dir. Greater Indpls. Progress Com., 1965-68; sr. dep. mayor City of Indpls., 1968-73, v.p. govt. and community affairs Mchts. Nat. Bank, Indpls., 1973-78; pres. Ind. State C. of C., Indpls., 1978—; mem. Ind. Job Tng. Coordinating Council, Indpls., 1983; chmn. Council of State Chambers of Commerce, Washington, 1984. Served as sgt. USAAF, 1944-46. Recipient Good Govt. award Indpls. Jaycees, 1970, Brotherhood award NCCJ, 1972. Republican. Mem. Soc. Friends. Clubs: Meridian Hills Country, Columbia (Indpls.). Home: 5465 Far Hill Rd Indianapolis IN 46226 Office: Ind State C of C One N Capitol Suite 200 Indianapolis IN 46204-2248

WALMSLEY, JAMES NAYLOR, hydroponic farmer; b. Rockford, Ill., Sept. 6, 1929; s. James A. and Louella H. (Gage) W.; M. Helga Nimtz, June 23, 1978; children—Kristen V., Tanya J. Student George Washington U., 1949-52, Loyola U., Chgo., 1953-55. Investment banker Hornblower & Weeks, Chgo., 1955-61; pres. Manin Internat. Inc., Chgo., 1961-72; pres. Jinga Hydroponic Farms Ltd., Chgo., 1972—. Mem. U.S. Congl. Adv. Bd., Washington, DC, 1984; mem. Am. Security Council, Washington, DC, 1984. Served with USN, 1949-53. Mem. Royal Hort. Soc. (London), Am. Hort. Soc. Republican. Christian Scientist. Home: 1088 Griffith Rd Lake Forest IL 60045 Office: Jinga Hydroponic Farms Ltd 23 N Genesee St Waukegan IL 60085

WALONICK, DAVID STEVEN, computer consultant company executive; b. Mpls., Mar. 20, 1949; s. Albert L. and Beverlee Ann (Klein) W. Student, U. Minn., 1967-70, Northwestern U., 1971, U. Calif.-Riverside, 1977. Researcher, St. Mary's Jr. Coll., Mpls., 1978-79; research cons. Rainbow Research, Inc., Mpls., 1979, Minn. Inst., Anoka, 1979; dir. mktg. and research Lakewood Publs., Mpls., 1980; pres. Walonick Assocs., Inc., Mpls., 1981—. Mem. Aircraft Owners and Pilots Assn. Author: A Library of Subroutines for the IBM PC, 1983; contbr. articles to profl. jours.

WALSH, EDWARD FRANCIS, business consultant, accountant; b. Chgo., July 11, 1944; s. Patrick J. and Mary J. Walsh; B.B.A., Loyola U., 1967; M.B.A., No. Ill. U., 1969; M.A. in Bus. Adminstrn., Govs. State U., 1976; m. Joan Elizabeth Ambrose, June 26, 1971; children—Erin Ann, Daniel Edward. Teaching asst. No. Ill. U., DeKalb, Ill., 1967-69; mem. faculty dept. bus. Prairie State Coll., Chicago Heights, Ill., 1969-80, prof., 1972-80; owner Walsh Bus. Ops. Cons., Homewood, Ill., 1981—; gen. mgr. Assn. for Health Care, Ltd., Chgo., 1980-82; cons. Allied Tube and Conduit Corp., Harvey, Ill., 1973; acct. Wilkes Besterfield, C.P.A.'s, Olympia Fields, Ill., 1979-80; vis. prof. Govs. State U.; prof. Keller Grad. Sch. Mgmt. Vice chmn. sch. bd. Infant Jesus of Prague Sch., 1985—. C.P.A., Ill. Mem. Ill. C.P.A. Soc., Illiana C.P.A. Soc., Midwest Bus. Adminstrn. Assn., Blue Key, Sigma Iota Epsilon (pres.), Alpha Beta Gamma (nat. pres. 1979-80), Delta Sigma Pi (life, Man of Yr.). Office: 18161 Morris Homewood IL 60430

WALSH, JAMES PATRICK, JR., insurance consultant, actuary; b. Ft. Thomas, Ky., Mar. 7, 1910; s. James Patrick and Minnie Louise (Cooper) W.; comml. engr. degree, U. Cin., 1933; m. Evelyn Mary Sullivan, May 20, 1939. Acct., Firestone Tire & Rubber Co., also Gen. Motors Corp., 1933-36; rep. ARC, 1937, A.F. of L., 1938-39; dir. Ohio Div. Minimum Wages, Columbus, 1939-42; asst. sec.-treas. union label trades dept. AFL, Washington, 1946-53; v.p. Pension and Group Cons., Inc., Cin., 1953—. Mem. Pres.'s Commn. Jud. and Congl. Salaries, 1953, Gov. Ohio Commn. Employment of Negro, 1940, Hamilton (Ohio) County Welfare Bd., 1957—, council long term illness and rehab. Cin. Pub. Health Fedn., 1957-68. Bd. dirs. U. Cin., 1959-67; bd. govs. St. Xavier High Sch., Cin., 1953-65; trustee Newman Fund, Brown Fund; mem. Internat. Found. Employee Benefit Plans, Inc. Served to lt. col. AUS, 1942-46; col. Res. Decorated Legion of Merit, Army Commendation medal with 2 oak leaf clusters; recipient Insignis award St. Xavier High Sch., Cin., 1973, Disting. Alumni award U. Cin.; Disting. Alumni award Covington Latin Sch., 1983; Kevin Barry award. cert. pension cons. Mem. Am. Acad. Actuaries, English Speaking Union, Archives Assn., Cin. Hist. Soc., Germania Soc., High Frontier, Res. Officers Assn. (life), Am. Mil. Retirees Assn. (life), Ret. Assn. for Uniformed Services (life), Am. Legion (life; Americanism award), Navy League (life), Q.M. Assn., VFW (life), Marine Corps League (life), Air Force Assn. (life), Naval Res. Assn. (life), Marine Corps Res. Officers Assn. (life), Amvets (life), Nat. Football Found. and Hall of Fame, Mil. Order World Wars (life), Am. Fedn. State, County and Employees Union, Internat. Alliance Theatrical Stage Employees (life mem.; past sgt. at arms), Internat. Hodcarriers, Bldg. and Common Laborers Union, Ins. Workers Internat. Union, Office Employees Internat. Union, Cooks and Pastry Cooks Local, Friendly Sons St. Patrick (past pres.), Covington Latin Sch. Alumni Assn. (past pres.), Laborers Polit. League Century Club, Soc. for Advancement Mgmt., Def. Supply Assn., Ancient Order Hibernians (past pres.), Assn. U.S. Army, Cursillio, Cin. Council World Affairs, Nat. Hist. Soc., Am. Ordnance Assn., Soc. Am. Mil. Engrs., Am. Arbitration Assn. (nat. community dispute settlement panel, employee benefit claims panel, employees withdrawal liability panel), Order of Alhambra, Allied Constrn. Industries, U. Cin. Alumni Assn. (life), Internat. Assn. Health Underwriters, Health Ins. Council S.W. Ohio, Scabbard and Blade, Greater Cin. Indsl. Relations Research Assn., Zoo Soc., Nat. Council Catholic Men, Archives Assos., Millcreek Valley Assn., Nat. Hist. Soc., Ret. Officers Assn. (past pres. Cin., past pres. Ohio council, mem. nat. bd.), Am. Assn. Ret. Persons, Seneca County Geneal. Soc., Cin. Hist. Soc., Men of Milford, CATS, Smithsonian Assos., Inter Am. Soc., Am. Soc. Pension Actuaries, Internat. Actuarial Assn., Alpha Kappa Psi. Catholic. K.C. (4 deg.), Elk. Clubs: St. Antoninus Athletic, Green Twp. Republican, Republican of Hamilton County (life), War Veterans Republican, Newman (Cin.), Cincinnati (past pres.), Queen City, Nat. Travel, American-Irish, Insiders, U.C. Boosters, Germania Soc., Xavier U. Musketeer, Bengals Touchdown, Global Sportsman, Military. Home: 5563 Julmar Dr Cincinnati OH 45238 Office: 309 Vine St Room 200 Cincinnati OH 45202

WALSH, JEANNE (REGINA) DENISE, business systems analyst; b. Chgo., Sept. 1, 1956; d. Vincent James and Rena Leonita (Baldaccini) W. B.S., Loyola U., Chgo., 1980; M.B.A. candidate Lake Forest Sch. Mgmt., 1982—. Customer service supr. Rand McNally & Co., Skokie, Ill., 1977-80, staff analyst, 1980-81, fin. and ops. analyst, 1981-82, mgr. sales service, planning and telemarketing, 1982-84, sr. bus. systems analyst, 1984—. Mem. Nat. Council Phys. Distribution Mgmt., Am. Telemarketing Assn., Internat. Customer Service Assn. Democrat. Roman Catholic. Avocations: reading, athletics. Office: Rand McNally & Co 8255 N Central Park Skokie IL 60076

WALSH, JOHN BREFFNI, scientist, engineer; b. Bklyn., Aug. 20, 1927; s. George Patrick and Margaret Mary (Rigney) W.; m. Marie Louise Leclerc, June 18, 1955; children—George, John, Darina. B.E.E., Manhattan Coll., 1948; M.S., Columbia U., 1951; postgrad. NYU, 1954-62. Registered profl. engr., N.J. Asst. prof. elec. engring. Columbia U., N.Y.C., 1948-51, asst. dir. electronic research lab., 1953-66; with Rome Air Devel. Ctr., N.Y.C., 1951-53; dep. for research to asst. sec. Dept. Air Force, Washington, 1966-71; sr. staff mem. Nat. Security Council, and asst. to pres.'s sci. adviser, Washington, 1971-72; dep. dir. def. research and engring. Strategic Space Systems, Dept. Def., 1972-77; asst. sec. gen. for Def. Support/NATO, Brussels, 1977-80; prof. systems acquisition mgmt. Def. Systems Mgmt. Coll. and dean. exec. inst., Fort Belvoir, Va., 1980-82, prof. emeritus, 1982—; v.p. chief scientist Boeing Airplane Co., Wichita, Kans., 1982—. Author texts: Electromagnetic Theory and Engineering Applications, 1960; Introductory Electric Circuits, 1960; Elementary and Advanced Trigonometry, 1961; Advanced Trigonometry, 1977. Contbr. articles to profl. publs. Mem. indsl. adv. bd. Wichita State U. Coll. Engring., 1985—; mem. Kans. Advanced Tech. Commn., 1985—. Served with U.S. army, 1946-47. Recipient Exceptional Civilian Service award Dept. Air Force, 1969, Meritorious Civilian Service award Dept. Def., 1971, Outstanding Civilian Employee of Yr. Citation of Honor, Air Force Assn., 1971, Disting. Civilian Service award Dept. Def., 1977, Theodore von Karman award Air Force Assn., 1977. Fellow IEEE, AIAA (assoc.); mem. N.Y. Acad. Scis., Sigma Xi, Eta Kappa Nu. Office: Boeing Mil Airplane Co 3801 S Oliver St Wichita KS 67277

WALSH, KENNETH ALBERT, chemist; b. Yankton, S.D., May 23, 1922; s. Albert Lawrence and Edna (Slear) W.; B.A., Yankton Coll., 1942; Ph.D., Iowa State U., 1950; m. Dorothy Jeanne Thompson, Dec. 22, 1944; children—Jeanne K., Kenneth Albert, David Bruce, Rhonda Jean, Leslie Gay. Asst. prof. chemistry Iowa State U., Ames, 1950-51; staff mem. Los Alamos Sci. Lab., 1951-57; supr. Internat. Minerals & Chem. Corp., Mulberry, Fla., 1957-60; mgr. Brush Beryllium Co., Elmore, Ohio, 1960-72; assoc. dir. tech. Brush Wellman Inc., Elmore, 1972—. Democratic precinct chmn., Los Alamos, 1956, Fremont, Ohio, 1980. Mem. Am. Chem. Soc. (sect. treas. 1956), Am. Soc. for Metals, AIME, Theta Xi, Phi Lambda Upsilon. Methodist. Club: Toastmasters Internat. Patentee in field. Home: 2624 Fangboner Rd Fremont OH 43420 Office: Brush Wellman Inc Elmore OH 43416

WALSH, RONALD LENNOX, cardiologist; b. Detroit, Dec. 18, 1952; s. Lennox Albert and Gloria Maria (Grau) W.; m. Liisa Lydia Johanna Laakso, May 21, 1977. B.S. in Biology, Alma Coll., 1974; D.O., Chgo. Coll. Osteo. Medicine, 1977. Diplomate Am. Bd. Osteo. Med. Examiners, Am. Osteo. Bd. Internal Medicine, Am. Osteo. Bd. Cardiology. Intern, Zieger-Botsford Hosps. Inc., Farmington Hills, Mich., 1977-78; resident in internal medicine Chgo. Osteo. Med. Ctr., 1978-80; fellow in cardiology Loyola U. Med. Ctr., Maywood, Ill., 1980-82; asst. prof. medicine sect. cardiology Chgo. Osteo. Med. Ctr., 1982—; tchr., cons. in cardiology. Recipient Acad. Excellence award Upjohn Co., 1977. Mem. Am. Osteo. Assn., AMA, Am. Coll. Osteo. Internists, Am. Coll. Cardiology, Chgo. Med. Soc., Am. Heart Assn. Presbyterian. Contbr. articles to profl. jours. Office: Chgo Osteo Med Ctr 5200 S Ellis Ave Chicago IL 60615

WALSH, SUSAN FRANCES, psychiatric social worker; b. Fostoria, Ohio, Apr. 5, 1943; d. Edward Doty and Frances Elizabeth (Storey) W.; B.S., Ind. U., 1965; A.M., U. Chgo., 1968, Ph.D., 1984. Instr. social work Northwestern U. Med. Sch., also staff social worker Northwestern Meml. Hosp., Chgo., 1968-75; pvt. practice psychotherapy, Chgo., 1974—; asso. dept. psychiatry Northwestern U., also coordinator outpatient services Inst. Psychiatry, Northwestern Meml. Hosp., 1975-84, asst. to dir. Inst. Psychiatry, 1984-85; lectr. U. Chgo., 1984—; field instr. U. Chgo., U. Ill., Chgo. Circle; pres. Susan Walsh, Ph.D. Ltd. Mem. Nat. Assn. Social Workers. Research on alternative to psychiat. hospitalization. Home: 3180 N Lake Shore Dr Chicago IL 60657 Office: 333 E Ontario St Chicago IL 60611

WALSH, THOMAS J(OSEPH), chemical engineer, educator; b. Troy, N.Y., July 17, 1917; s. Thomas Joseph and Anna (Sharp) W.; B.S., Rensselaer Poly. Inst., 1939, M.S., 1941; Ph.D., Case Inst. Tech., 1949; m. Beatrice Metcalfe Passage, July 12, 1941; 1 dau., Joan Beatrice Waltz. Chem. engr. Standard Oil Co. Ohio, 1941-47; prof. Case Inst. Tech., 1947-61; engr. Lewis Flight Propulsion Lab. NACA, 1951-55; cons. Thompson Ramo Wooldridge, 1955-61, sr. staff specialist, requirements mgr. research applications equipment labs. division, 1961-66; process specialist corp. engring. dept. Glidden-Durkee div. SCM Corp., Cleve., 1966-68, mgr. process engring., from 1968, mgr. environ. conservation, energy coordinator, to 1979, mgr. corp. energy conservation, 1979-80; v.p. Consultex, Inc., 1980—; cons. Glascote Products Co., 1954-61, Hukill Chem., Booth Oil Co., ECA, Inc., Argonne Nat. Lab.; adj. prof. chem. engring. Case Western Res. U., 1980—; adj. prof. chem. engring., spl. lectr. Cleve. State U., 1980-83, prof. chem. engring., 1983—. Pres. Northeastern Ohio Science Fair, Inc. Recipient Junior Tech. award Cleve. Tech. Soc. Council, Merit award Cleve. Chem. Profession. Fellow Am. Inst. Chem. Engrs.; mem. AAAS, Am. Chem. Soc. (trustee), ASCE, AAUP, Cleve. Tech. Socs. Council (past pres.), AIAA, Cleve. Engring. Soc. (gov.), Order of Engr. Home: 32555 Creekside Dr Pepper Pike OH 44124 Office: Stillwell Hall Cleveland State U Cleveland OH 44115

WALSH, THOMAS JOSEPH STEWART, foundry executive; b. Cambusland, Scotland, Sept. 24, 1947; came to U.S., 1958; s. Thomas Bunyan and Agnes Robertson (Russell) W.; m. Lonarta M. Carlson, Oct. 7, 1967; children—Krista Rae, Heather Ann Scott, Thomas Russell. B.S. in Commerce, DePaul U., 1976. Asst. purchasing mgr. Rixson Firemark, Franklin Park, Ill., 1967-72; owner, mgr. T W Industries, Inc., Dundee, Ill., 1972—. Mem. Am. Foundry Soc. Home: 163 Hilltop Ln Sleepy Hollow IL 60118 Office: PO Box 246 Dundee IL 60118

WALSH, WILLIAM JOHN, management consultant, accountant; b. N.Y.C., July 29, 1933; s. Thomas P. and Ann Gertrude (Daley) W.; m. Clare Marie Schenck, Jan. 6, 1956 (div. Dec. 1966); m. Lois Marie Heileman, June 26, 1971; children—Daniel, Patricia, Thomas, Joseph. B.S. in Acctg., U. Cin., 1974; M.B.A., Xavier U., 1977. C.P.A., Ohio. Pub. acct. J.D. Cloud & Co., C.P.A.s, Cin., 1964-67; plant controller Dover Corp., Cin., 1967-69; corp. controller Bardes Corp., Cin., 1969-75; gen. mgr., controller Famous Foods, Richmond, Ind., 1975-76; with LMX, Inc., Cin., 1977—; lectr. acctg. U. Cin., 1980—. Served with USMC, 1952-61. Mem. Court Street Mchts. Assn. (organizer). Roman Catholic. Club: Cin. Athletic. Avocations: basketball; travel. Home and Office: 3328 Bauerwoods Dr Cincinnati OH 45239

WALT, ALEXANDER JEFFREY, surgeon, educator; b. Cape Town, S. Africa, June 13, 1923; came to U.S., 1961, naturalized, 1966; s. Isaac and Lea (Garb) W.; m. Irene Lapping, Dec. 21, 1947; children—John R., Steven D., Lindsay J. M.B., U. Capetown, S. Africa, 1948; M.S. in Surgery, U. Minn., 1956. Diplomate Am. Bd. Surgery. Intern, Groote Schuur Hosp., Cape Town, 1949-50; resident Mayo Clinic, Rochester, Minn., 1952-56; asst. surgeon Groote Schuur Hosp., Cape Town, 1957-61; asst. chief surgery VA Hosp., Dearborn, Mich., 1961-62; chief surgery Detroit Receiving Hosp., 1965-80, Harper-Grace Hosps., Detroit, 1972—; prof., chmn. dept. surgery Wayne State U., Detroit, 1966—; mem. Council Med. Specialty Socs., Chgo., 1982—; mem. exec. com. Am. Bd. Med. Specialties, Chgo., 1983—, treas., 1985—; vice chmn. Am. Bd. Surgery, 1983-85. Co-editor: Management of Trauma, 1975. Editor: Early Care of the Injured Patient, 3d edit., 1982. Served with S. African Army, 1943-45. Mem. Am. Assn. Surgery of Trauma (pres. 1976-77), Central Surg. Assn. (pres. 1977-78), ACS (bd. govs. 1975-81, bd. regents 1984—). Home: 26373 Hendrie Huntington Woods MI 48070 Office: Wayne State U 4201 St Antoine 6-C Detroit MI 48201

WALTER, DAVID PORTER, life insurance company executive; b. Pitts., Oct. 23, 1941; s. George Harrison and Margaret (Lohr) W.; m. Carol Jane Coombs, Aug. 28, 1965; children—David Porter, Grant Harrison, Braden Coombs. B.A., Pa. State U., 1963; postgrad. Colo. Coll., 1964, Ind. U., 1971. Plant mgr. Boise Cascade Corp., 1968-70; sr. mktg. analyst Cummins Engine Co., Columbus, Ind., 1970-72; mgr. research and engring. Ryder System, Inc., Miami, 1973; agt., dist. mgr. Gt. West Life, Grand Rapids, Mich., 1973-81; gen. mgt. Washington Nat. Ins. Co., Grand Rapids, 1981—. Fedn. chief YMCA Indian Guides, 1975-77; mem. allocation and review panel United Way of Kent County and State of Mich. Served with U.S. Army, 1963-68. Decorated Bronze Star medal, Air medal; Vietnamese medal. Mem. Nat. Assn. Life Underwriters, Gen. Agts. and Mgrs. Assn. Republican. Presbyterian. Office: 3351 Claystone St SE Grand Rapids MI 49506

WALTER, ERIC W(ILLIAM), radiologist; b. Abington, Pa., July 4, 1921; s. Erich Max and Minnie (Miller) W.; m. Mar. 15, 1946; children—Eric W., Kathy Lynn, Brian Lee. B.S., Muhlenberg Coll., 1943; M.D., Hahnemann Med. Sch., 1946. Diplomate Am. Bd. Radiology. Intern, Shadyside Hosp., Pitts., 1946-47; gen. practice medicine, Pa. and W.Va., 1949-50; resident in radiology Bismarck Hosp., N.D., 1950-53; radiologist St. Alexis Hosp., Bismarck, 1953-56, Quain & Ramstad Clinic, Bismarck, 1955-56; cons. in radiology Wooster Community Hosp., Ohio, 1956—, sec. staff, 1957-82; attending in radiology Dunlap Meml. Hosp., Orrville, Ohio, 1969—; asst. clin. prof. Med. Sch., Case Western Res. U., Cleve., 1975—. Bd. dirs. Wayne County Soc. Crippled Children, Wooster, 1958—; pub. edn. officer U.S. Coast Guard Aux., Wooster, 1970—. Served to capt. M.C., U.S. Army, 1947-49. Mem. Am. Coll. Radiology, Radiol. Soc. N.Am., Ohio Med. Soc., Wayne County Med. Soc. (pres. 1975). Lodges: Rotary (bd. dirs. Wooster 1969-71), Masons. Home: 1741 Morgan St Wooster OH 44691

WALTER, FRANK S., hospital administrator; b. Denver, June 23, 1926; s. Frank J. and Nancy W. (Sherman) W.; B.S., U. Oreg., 1950; M.B.A., U. Chgo., 1951; m. Carolyn May Cox, July 29, 1949; children—Douglas, Steven, Nancy. Adminstrv. resident Grad. Hosp., U. Pa., Phila., 1950-51, adminstrv. asst., 1951-52, asst. dir., 1952-55; adminstr. Meth. Hosp., Phila., 1955-63, St. Barnabas Hosp., Mpls., 1962-70; pres. Met. Med. Center, Mpls., 1970-83; exec. v.p. HealthOne Corp., 1983—; trustee Blue Cross/Blue Shield of Minn., 1977—. Bd. dirs. Mpls. War Meml. Blood Bank, 1964-70; clin. preceptor U. Minn., 1965—; dir. Downtown Council, 1977—. Served with USAAF, 1944-46. Fellow Am. Coll. Hosp. Adminstrs.; mem. Health Manpower Mgmt. Assn., Upper Midwest Hosp. Assn., Minn. Hosp. Assn. (trustee 1970-78, treas. 1973-74, pres. 1975-76), Twin City Hosp. Assn. (pres. 1970-71). Episcopalian. Club: Kiwanis. Home: 6809 Dovre Dr Edina MN 55436 Office: Exec Vice Pres Health One Corp 80 S 8th St Minneapolis MN 55402

WALTER, JAMES KENT, educational administrator, consultant; b. Kokomo, Ind., Jan. 26, 1948; s. Jack Gibson and Marie (Kaplan) W.; m. Deborah Marie Crouch, Jan. 29, 1968; children—Zachary Fitzgerald, Andrea Marie. B.S., Ind. U., 1970; M.A., Ball State U., 1972, postgrad., 1983—. Tchr. English, Sycamore Middle Sch., Kokomo, 1970-72, dept. head, Right to Read coordinator, 1972-80; head trade and tech. div. Ind. Vocat. Tech. Coll., Kokomo, 1980-81; tchr. English, Haworth High Sch., Kokomo, 1981-84; asst. prin. Kokomo High Sch., 1984—. Contbr. articles to profl. jours. Named Outstanding Educator and Adminstr., Ind. Vocat. Tech. Coll. Student Body, 1981. Mem. NEA, Nat. Council Tchrs. English, Ind. Council Tchrs. English, Ind. State Tchrs. Assn., Kokomo Tchrs. Assn., Nat. Orgn. Legal Problems in Edn., Nat. Assn. Secondary Sch. Prins., Ind. Secondary Sch. Adminstrs., Kokomo Prins. Assn., Assn. for Supervision and Curriculum Devel., Phi Delta Kappa. Club: Elks. Developer programs and curriculum materials for academically and culturally disadvantaged. Office: Kokomo High School 2501 S Berkley Rd Kokomo IN 46902

WALTER, JOSEPH DAVID, tire company research executive, educator; b. Merchantville, N.J., July 6, 1939; s. Joseph and Dorothy Madeline (Schenck) W.; m. Virginia Catherine Burke, July 14, 1962; children—Joseph, Michael, Martin. B.S. with honors, Va. Poly. Inst., 1962, M.S., 1964, Ph.D., 1966; M.B.A., U Akron, 1985. Naval architect Phila. Naval Base, 1962; mech. engr. Litton, Blacksburg, Va., 1963; adj. prof. engring. U. Akron (Ohio), 1975—; research scientist Firestone Co., Akron, 1966-69, research mgr., 1969-74, asst. dir. research, 1974—; instr. Va. Poly. Inst., 1964-66. NSF summer fellow, 1964, 66; NDEA fellow, 1962-65. Mem. ASME, Fiber Soc., AIAA (best paper awards), Tire Soc., Soc. for Exptl. Mechanics, Am. Acad. Mechanics, Am. Chem. Soc. (rubber div.), Phi Kappa Phi, Tau Beta Pi, Pi Tau Sigma, Sigma Pi Sigma, Beta Gamma Sigma. Roman Catholic. Clubs: Torch, Franklin (Akron). Contbr. articles to profl. jours. Home: 343 Barnstable Ave Akron OH 44313 Office: Firestone Tire & Rubber Co 1200 Firestone Pkwy Akron OH 44317

WALTER, NOLA JANICE, rental co. exec.; b. Eau Claire, Wis., Mar. 29, 1934; d. Robert Emmet and Adeline Victoria (Johnson) Rossman; student Dist. 1 Tech. Inst., Eau Claire, 1977-78; 1 dau., Rhea Carol. Exec. sec. W.H. Hobbs Supply Co., Eau Claire, 1952-54; jr. accountant C.A. Irwin Co., Eau Claire, 1954-61; legal sec. various attys. in Eau Claire, Mpls., 1963-73; office mgr. Bearson-Steinmetz Rentals, Eau Claire, 1974—; freelance artist, 1980-81. Recipient Gregg Shorthand certificate of merit, 1952, certs. of award in oil painting, 1977, 78; Gold, Silver and Bronze awards in competitive dancing, 1979, 80, 81. Mem. Nat. Wildlife Fedn., Am. Antiques and Crafts Soc., Nat. Trust for Historic Preservation, Mpls. Soc. Fine Arts, Smithsonian Assos., Am. Film Inst. Democrat. Congregationalist. Home: 825 Barland St Eau Claire WI 54701 Office: 315 E Madison St Eau Claire WI 54701

WALTER, RALPH COLLINS, III, business educator, consultant; b. Hinsdale, Ill., Nov. 25, 1946; s. Ralph Collins and Ethel Marie (Eustice) W.; B.A., Knox Coll., 1969; M.A., Ind. U., 1972; m. Sharon L. Maretta Koop, Aug. 9, 1980. Chartered fin. analyst. Instr., Ind. U. Bloomington, 1971-72; with A.G. Becker, Inc., Chgo., 1973-81, v.p., 1976-81; v.p. Dean Witter Reynolds Co., 1981-82; prof. fin. Northeastern Ill. U., Chgo., 1982—, chmn. dept. fin., acctg. and law, 1983—. Served to capt. U.S. Army, 1973. Woodrow Wilson fellow, 1969, Alfred P. Sloan scholar, 1966-69. Mem. Am. Econ. Assn., Am. Fin. Assn., Fin. Mgmt. Assn., Investment Analyst Soc. Chgo., Phi Beta Kappa. Home: 10501 5th Ave Cutoff LaGrange IL 60525 Office: Northeastern Ill U 5500 N St Louis Ave Chicago IL 60625

WALTER, SCOTT EVERETT, lawyer; b. Springfield, Mass., June 23, 1954; s. Robert L. W. B.A., Drake U., 1977; J.D., St. Louis U., 1980. Bar: Mo. 1980, U.S. Dist. Ct. (ea. dist.) Mo. 1983, Ill. 1984. Asst. pub. defender State of Mo., 1980-81, pub. defender, 1981-83; asst. atty. County of Cape Girardeau, Mo., 1983—; ptnr. Waldron & Walter, Jackson, Mo., 1984—. Mem. ABA, Assn. Trial Lawyers Am., Mo. Assn. Trial Lawyers. Home: 910A Themis Cape Girardeau MO 63701 Office: Waldron & Walter 417 N High Jackson MO 63755

WALTERS, JEFFERSON BROOKS, musician, real estate broker; b. Dayton, Ohio, Jan. 22, 1922; s. Jefferson Brooks and Mildred Frances (Smith) W.; student U. Dayton, 1947; m. Mary Elizabeth Espey, Apr. 6, 1963 (dec. July 22, 1983); children—Dinah Christine Basson, Jefferson Brooks; m. 2d, Carol Elaine Clayton Gillette, Feb. 19, 1984. Composer, cornetist Dayton, 1934—; real estate broker, Dayton, 1948—; founder Am. Psalm Choir, 1965; apptd. deferred giving officer Kettering (Ohio) Med. Ctr., 1982—. Served with USCGR, 1942-45; PTO, ETO. Mem. SAR, Greater Dayton Antique Study Club (past pres.), Dayton Art Inst., Montgomery County Hist. Soc., Dayton Area Bd. Realtors. Presbyterian. Club: Masons (32 deg.). Condr., composer choral, solo voice settings of psalms and poetry Alfred Lord Tennyson; composer Crossing the Bar (meml. performances U.S. Navy band), 1961. Home: 81 Winnet Dr Dayton OH 45415 Office: Classics Realty 53 Park Ave Dayton OH 45419 also Kettering Med Ctr 3535 Southern Blvd Kettering OH 45429

WALTERS, SUMNER JUNIOR, judge; b. Van Wert, Ohio, Oct. 4, 1916; s. Sumner E. and Kittie (Allen) W.; J.D., Ohio No. U., 1940; m. Marjorie Acheson, May 22, 1948; 1 son, Sumner E. Admitted to Ohio bar, 1940; mem. firm Walters & Koch, 1941-42, Stroup & Walters, 1946-68; pvt. practice, Van Wert, 1969-71; mem. firm Walters, Young & Walters, 1971-80; judge Van Wert Mcpl. Ct., 1980—; asst. pros. atty. Van Wert County, 1946-48, pros. atty., 1948-60; acting judge Van Wert Municipal Ct., also asst. city solicitor City of Van Wert, 1962; village solicitor Middle Point, 1960-80. Pres., Van Wert Indsl. Devel. Corp., 1966-76, Humane Soc., 1963—, YMCA, 1962-63; mem. council Camp Fire Girls, 1965-72. Pres. bd. trustees Van Wert County United Fund, 1959-60; trustee United Health Found., Van Wert County Hosp., Van Wert County Found., Marsh Found., Van Wert. Served with Mil. Police, C.I.C., AUS, 1942-45; ETO. Named Outstanding Citizen of Year, Van Wert Jr. C. of C., 1965. Mem. Ohio, Northwestern Ohio (pres. 1957-58), Van Wert County (pres. 1953-55) bar assns., Am. Legion, V.F.W., Sigma Phi Epsilon. Methodist (chmn. ofcl. bd. 1963-64, lay del. Ohio West conf. 1967-79, conf. sec. 1970-71, mem. bd. hosps. and homes, trustee 1983—). Mason (32 deg., Shriner, K.T.), Rotarian (pres. 1966-67). Home: Rt 2 Ohio City OH 45874 Office: 307 Court House Van Wert OH 45891

WALTERS, TOM FREDERICK, manufacturing company official; b. Des Moines, Oct. 18, 1931; s. Basil Leon and Reah E. (Handy) W.; m. Mary Katherine Russell, Dec. 8, 1956; children—Karen E., Juliet M., Thomas R., Alexandra K., Suzanne C. B.A., Beloit Coll., 1953; M.B.A. candidate Northwestern U., 1962-66. Sales and advt. staff Eaton, Yale & Towne, Chgo., 1956-62, prodn. mgr., 1962-65; sr. cons. Cresap, McCormick & Paget, Chgo., 1965-67; materials mgr. Joy Mfg. Co., Michigan City, Ind. 1967-73, gen. mgr., Elk Grove Village, Ill., 1973—; lectr. Contbr. articles to profl. jours. Pres., LaPorte County Young Republicans, Ind., 1970-71; dist. chmn. Boy Scouts Am., 1972; elder, trustee 1st Presbyterian Ch., Libertyville, Ill., 1980-83; mem. village bd. Village of Long Beach, Ind., 1969. Served to lt. (j.g.) USNR, 1953-56; Far East. Mem. Indsl. Compressor Distbrs. Assn. (chmn. com. 1979-84), Constrn. Industry Mfrs. Assn. (bd. dirs., com. chmn. 1975-82), Am. Prodn. and Inventory Control Soc. (chpt. pres. 1970-71), Greater O'Hare Assn. Commerce and Industry, Omicron Delta Kappa, U.S. Power Squadrons. Republican. Presbyterian. Clubs: Abbey Yacht (Lake Geneva, Wis.); Michigan City Yacht (Ind.). Avocations: boating; fishing; skiing; swimming. Home: 766 Kenwood Ave Libertyville IL 60048 Office: Joy Mfg Co 2300 W Devon Ave Elk Grove Village IL 60007

WALTERS, WILLIAM LEROY, physics educator; b. Racine, Wis., Mar. 30, 1932; s. Robert Nicholas and Elsa Bertha (Ahrens) W.; m. Darlene Agnes Kessenich, Feb. 5, 1955; children—Judy, Sandra, Robert, James. B.S., U. Wis., 1954, M.S., 1958, Ph.D., 1961. Asst. prof. U. Wis.-Milw., 1961-62, assoc. prof., 1962-66, prof. physics, 1966—, assoc. dean coll. letters and sci., 1965-67, spl. asst. to chancellor, 1967-68, exec. asst. chancellor, 1968-69, acting dean coll. applied sci. and engring., 1969-70, vice chancellor, 1971-81. Contbr. articles to physics jours. and sci. publs. Pres. Wis. Assn. Lake Dists., Madison, 1982-85. Served with U.S. Army, 1954-56, West Germany. Mem. AAAS, Am. Assn. Physics Tchrs., Am. Phys. Soc., Am. Vacuum Soc., Nat. Assn. State Univ. and Land Grant Colls (council acad. affairs 1976-78, chmn. 1978). Club: Physics (bd. dirs. 1964-67, 82—) (Milw.). Home: 4301 N Morris Blvd Shorewood WI 53211 Office: U Wis PO Box 413 Milwaukee WI 53201

WALTHER, ROBERT NICHOLAS, mechanical engineer, real estate developer; b. Dayton, Ohio, Dec. 4, 1948; s. James Whitmer and Dorothy Bogert W.; m. Arlene Lynn Sintzel, Dec. 5, 1969; children—Richard Ayres, Susan Carolyn Rose. B.S. in Mech. Engring., U. Dayton, 1975; postgrad. Purdue U., Ft. Wayne, Ind. Foreman various depts., plant engr., engring. designer Dayton/Walther Corp., Dayton, Ohio and Orillia, Ont., Can., 1963-74; v.p. ops. Fairview Industries, Inc. (Tenn.), 1975-78; foundry engr. Ford Meter Box Co., Wabash, Ind., 1978-83; pres., developer Fairview Industries, Inc., Wabash, 1980—. Shelter officer CD of Wabash County. Mem. Am. Foundrymen's Soc., Am. Soc. for Metals, Am. Contract Bridge League. Republican. Clubs: Wabash Country, Kiwanis (Wabash). Home: Route 2 Box 30AA Wabash IN 46992

WALTMANN, WILLIAM LEE, mathematics educator; b. Cedar Falls, Iowa, July 5, 1934; s. Leo Herman and Alma Louise (Engel) W.; m. Carol Ann Johnson, July 12, 1958; children—Karen Jean, Ronald Dale, Diane Lynn. B.A., Wartburg Coll., 1956; M.S., Iowa State U., 1958, Ph.D., 1964. Instr. math. Wartburg Coll., Waverly, Iowa, 1958-61, Iowa State U., Ames, 1963-64; from asst. prof. to assoc. prof. Wartburg Coll., 1964-1972, chmn. dept. math and computer sci., 1971—, prof., 1972—; mathematician-programmer White Sands Proving Ground, Las Cruces, N.Mex., 1957. Contbr. articles to profl. jours. Pres. Waverly-Shell Rock PTA, 1969-70; bd. dirs. Waverly Day Care Ctr., 1973-77; trustee, sec. Waverly Mcpl. Hosp., 1976—. Fellow Hill Found., 1975. Mem. Soc. Indsl. and Applied Math., Am. Math. Soc., Math. Assn. Am. (chmn. Iowa 1966-67), Iowa Acad. Sci. (chmn. math. sec. 1966-67), Math. Assn. Am. (gov. Iowa sect. 1980-83). Republican. Lutheran. Lodge: Kiwanis (pres. 1979-80). Avocations: bridge; camping; auto repair. Home: 1904 3d Ave NW Waverly IA 50677 Office: Wartburg Coll Waverly IA 50677

WALTON, ANDREA, nurse; b. St. Joseph, Mo., Dec. 10, 1938; d. Clarence Donald and Camille (Holland) Walton. Diploma, St. Luke's Hosp. Sch. Nursing, 1960; A.A., Mo. Western Coll., 1967; B.A., U. Mo.-Kansas City, 1969, M.A., 1971. Charge and staff nurse St. Luke's Hosp., Kansas City, Mo., 1960-65, charge nurse, 1967-73; pvt. duty nurse Nurses Profl. Registry, St. Joseph, Mo., 1965-67; instr. nursing Mo. Western State Coll., St. Joseph, 1973-76, asst. prof. nursing, 1979—, chmn. admissions com., 1982-84. Served to capt. Nurse Corps, USAF, 1976-79. Mem. Nat. League Nursing, Mo. Vocat. League, Mo. League Nursing, Phi Theta Kappa. Episcopalian. Club: St. Bernard of Am. Office: Mo Western State Coll Dept Nursing 4525 Downs Dr Saint Joseph MO 64507

WALTON, DONALD WILLIAM, author, lecturer; b. Cleve., Aug. 13, 1917; s. William H. and Bertha (Grill) W.; m. Edith J. Robinson, Sept. 27, 1941; 1 child, Scott W. Student Western Res. U., 1936-37, John Huntington Art Sch., Ohio, 1938-39. Copy chief Ross Roy Advt., Detroit, 1946-55; v.p.-creative D.P. Bros. Advt., Detroit, 1956-68; dir. mktg. devel. Franklin Mint, Phila., 1969-73; mng. dir. The Franklin Gallery, Phila., 1974-77; mgr. The Hallmark Collection, Kansas City, Mo., 1978-83; author/lectr., 1984—. Author: Art is to Enjoy, 1963; A Rockwell Portrait, 1978. Co-author/co-dir.: (film) Norman Rockwell (Gold medal N.Y. Film Festival and Internat. Film Festival), 1976. Bd. dirs., v.p. Friends of the Kansas City Library, 1984. Mem. Am. Bus. Communicators Assn., Authors Guild. Presbyterian. Avocation: bridge. Home: 330 E Bridlespur Dr Kansas City MO 64114

WALTON, JAMES EDWARD, agricultural publication executive; b. Macomb, Ill., Dec. 25, 1954; s. Charles Edward and Alice Louise (Pickle) W.; m. Susan Marie Thompson, Aug. 24, 1975. B.S. in Indsl. Mktg., Western Ill. U., 1975. Advt. mgr. Sergeants Western Store, Macomb, 1975-78, Yetter Mfg. Co., Colchester, Ill., 1978-82; gen. mgr. Ind. Agri-News, LaSalle, Ill., 1982—; advisor, dir. Ind.-Ill. Farm Show, Indpls., 1980—, Purdue Farm Show, Lafayette, Ind., 1983—; cons. Pathfinder Systems, Lexington, Nebr., 1982-83. Mem. Nat. Agri-Mktg. Assn. (v.p. membership 1980, founder cornbelt chpt., merit award 1981), Mid-Am. Agri-Mktg. Assn. (founder, pres. 1983). Methodist. Avocations: photography; golf. Office: Agri-News Publs PO Box 688807 Indianapolis IN 46268

WALTON, JOHN RICHARD, health care company executive, health educator; b. Chgo., Apr. 6, 1951; s. Charles Chandler and Dolores Barbara (Oehmen) W.; m. Erika Louise Kingsbury, Sept. 21, 1974; children—Scott, Michael, Tracey. B.S. in Chemistry, Loyola U., 1973; M.H.A., Chgo. Med. Sch., 1979; M.B.A., U. Chgo., 1985. Registered respiratory therapist, cert. respiratory technician, Ill. Various positions respiratory therapy dept. Northwestern Meml. Hosp., Chgo., 1971-76, adminstrv. dir. respiratory therapy dept., 1976-83; pres. John Walton & Assocs., Chgo., 1983—; pres. Respiratory Care Seminars, Chgo., 1983-84; instr. respiratory therapy program Northwestern U. Med. Sch. Recipient Outstanding Young Man of Am. award, 1980; Literacy award Am. Respiratory Therapy Found., 1983. Mem. Am. Assn. Respiratory Therapy (pres., chmn. bd. dirs. 1982, Recognition Plaque award 1982), Ill. Soc. Respiratory Therapy (pres. 1976-77). Author: Clinical Application of Blood Gases, 3d edit., 1983; contbr. chpts. to books, articles to profl. jours. Office: John Walton & Assocs PO Box 1688 Elk Grove Village IL 60007

WALTON, LAURENCE ROLAND, information scientist, librarian; b. Coffeyville, Kans., Mar. 27, 1939; s. Orvile Mac and Zora Laverne W.; B.A. in Chemistry, Okla. State U., 1965; B.S. in L.S., Washington U., St. Louis, 1972; m. Lucretia Jane Mize, June 1, 1963; 1 son, Laurence Roland. Library asst. Stillwater (Okla.) Public Library, 1957-65; tech. librarian Research and Devel. Center, Pet, Inc., Greenville, Ill., 1965-73, mgr. corp. info. center, 1973—. Mem. Spl. Libraries Assn., Am. Soc. Info. Sci., Inst. Food Technologists, Am. Assn. Cereal Chemists, Am. Soc. Microbiologists. Editor: Food Publication Roundup: A Bibliographic Guide, 1977-83. Home: 1516 Marbella Dr Saint Louis MO 63138 Office: Pet Inc 400 S 4th St Saint Louis MO 63166

WALTON, MATT SAVAGE, state geological survey executive, educator, consultant; b. Lexington, Ky., Sept. 16, 1915; s. Matt Savage and Lilias Oleno (Wheeler) W.; m. Kathryn Ann Ralston, Dec. 6, 1939 (div. May 1968); children—Matt Savage III, Kate Johns, Lisa Baar; m. Kay Ann Thorson, June 21, 1969; children—Anne Elizabeth, Owen Hardwick. B.A., U. Chgo., 1936; M.A., Columbia U., 1946, Ph.D., 1951. Geologist U.S. Geol. Survey, Washington, 1941-48, N.Y. State Geol. Survey, Albany, summers 1948-58; instr. Yale U., New Haven, 1948-51, asst. prof. geology, 1951-56, assoc. prof., 1956-65; cons. geology, Denver, 1965-73; prof., dir. Minn. Geol. Survey, U. Minn.-St. Paul, 1973—; regent's lectr. UCLA, 1970-73; dir. Deep Observation and Sampling of the Earth's Continental Crust, Palisades, N.Y., 1984—. Fellow Geol. Soc. Am. Home: 30 Crocus Pl Saint Paul MN 55102 Office: Minn Geol Survey 2642 University Ave Saint Paul MN 55114

WALTON, ROBERT EUGENE, SR., agriculture company executive, geneticist; b. Shattuck, Okla., Jan. 15, 1931; s. Lonnie J. and Marguerite Ruth (Rose) W.; m. Janice Carolyn Graning, Sept. 5, 1959; children—Cynthia Claire, Robert Eugene, John Randolph. B.S. in Agr., Okla. State U., 1952; postgrad. Royal Agr. Coll., Uppsala, Sweden, 1952-53; M.S. in Animal Breeding, Okla. State U., 1956; Ph.D. in Animal Breeding and Genetics, Iowa State U., 1961; cert. in Program Mgmt. Devel., Harvard Bus. Sch., 1970. Gen. mgr. West Hide Farms, Hereford, Eng., 1953-54; asst. prof. dairying U. Ky., Lexington, 1958-62; geneticist Am. Breeders Service, DeForest, Wis., 1962-65, dir. mktg. and breeding div., 1965-67, exec. v.p., 1967-68, pres., 1968—; dir. First Wis. Nat. Bank, Madison, Am. Genetics, Inc., Middleton, Wis., World Dairy Expo, Madison. Developer genetic evaluation system, cattle breeding system. Bd. dirs., v.p. United Way Dane County, Madison, 1983—; bd. dirs. Meth. Hosp., 1972-81, Wis. Rural Leadership Program, 1982—; businessmen's sect. chmn. Wis. Easter Seal campaign, 1978-79. Served to capt. U.S. Army, 1952-62. Recipient awards Newcomen Soc. N.Am., 1976, Okla. 4-H Alumni, 1979; Disting. Service award Wis. State Future Farmers Am., 1979; award of distinction U. Wis., 1980; named Disting. Animal Sci. Alumnus, Okla. State U., 1975; Industry Person of Yr., World Dairy Expo, 1982; All-Time Great Dairyman, Internat. Stockmen's Sch., 1983; Sales and Mktg. Exec. of Yr., Sales and Mktg. Execs. Madison, 1984. Mem. Am. Soc. Animal Sci., Am. Dairy Sci. Assn., Dairy Shrine (co-chmn. nat. fund raising com.), Nat. Assn. Animal Breeders (pres. 1972-74), Cert. Semen Services (pres. 1977-79), Am. Simmental Assn., Biometrics Soc., Nat. Agrl. Mktg. Assn. (Agri-Bus. award 1985), Wis. Agri-Bus. Council (dir. 1972-75), Wis. Beef Improvement Assn. (pres. 1974-75), Greater Madison C. of C. (dir. 1985), Sigma Xi, Alpha Zeta, Omicron Delta Kappa. Republican. Methodist. Club: Madison. Lodge: Rotary. Avocations: gardening; flower growing; photography; book collecting; reading. Home: 4066 Vinburn Rd DeForest WI 53532 Office: Am Breeders Service PO Box 459 DeForest WI 53532

WALZ, BRUCE JAMES, oncologist; b. Waterloo, Ill., Sept. 18, 1940; s. George Frederick and Alberta Emma (Heyl) W.; m. Renata T. Jaeger, Mar. 8, 1970; children—Jennifer Mara, Rachel Elizabeth. A.B., Washington U., 1962, M.D., 1966. Diplomate Am. Bd. Radiology. Intern, St. Luke's Hosp., St. Louis, 1966-67; resident Washington U. St. Louis, 1969-72; instr. Harvard Med. Sch., Boston, 1972-74, Washington U., 1974—. Contbr. articles to profl. jours. Served to lt. comdr. USNR, 1967-69, Vietnam. Harvard Med. Sch. fellow, 1972-73. Mem. AMA, Mo. Med. Soc. (ho. of dels. 1975—), Mo. State Radiol. Soc. (bd. dirs.), St. Louis Metro Med. Assn., Am. Soc. Therapeutic Radiologists and Oncologists, Am. Coll. Radiology, Am. Soc. Clin. Oncologists. Presbyterian. Clubs: Castle Oak (Chesterfield, Mo.), Bath and Tennis, Whittemore House (Clayton, Mo.). Avocations: gardening; wine and beer making. Office: 510 Sikings Hwy Saint Louis MO 63110

WALZER, NORMAN CHARLES, economics educator; b. Mendota, Ill., Mar. 17, 1943; s. Elmer J. and Anna L. (Johnston) W.; m. Dona Lee Maurer, Aug. 22, 1970; children—Steven, Mark. B.S., Ill. State U., Normal, 1966; M.A., U. Ill., 1969, Ph.D., 1970. Research dir. Cities and Villages Mcpl. Problems Com., Springfield, Ill., 1974-84; vis. prof. U. Ill., Urbana, 1977-78; prof. econs. Western Ill. U., Macomb, 1978—, chmn. dept. econs., 1980—. Author: Cities, Suburbs and Property Tax, 1981; Government Structure and Public Finance, 1984; editor: Financing State and Local Governments, 1981. Mem. Am. Econs. Assn., Ill. Econs. Assn. (pres. 1979-80), Mid-Continent Regional Sci. Assn. (v.p. 1984-85). Lodge: K.C. Home: 727 Auburn Dr Macomb IL 61455 Office: Western Ill U Dept Econs Adams St Macomb IL 61455

WALZTONI, MARK WILLIAM, human resources specialist; b. Chgo., May 19, 1954; s. Raymond W. and Rosemary (Wackerle) W.; m. Kathleen Nicole Cornell, Apr. 8, 1978. B.S., Northeastern Ill. U., 1976; M.S. in Indsl. Relations, Loyola U., Chgo., 1980. Adminstrv. mgr. engring. agy., Chgo., 1976-77; corp. recruiter Allstate Ins. Co., Northbrook, Ill., 1977-78; regional personnel mgr. Am. Express, Chgo., 1978-83; asst. v.p. human resources Home Group, Chgo., 1983-85; human resources mgr. Am. Express Co., Chgo., 1985—; cons. Travel Tng. Assocs., Mpls., 1984—; dir. Kingston Cons. Group, Ill., 1984—. Mem. Am. Soc. Personnel Adminsrs. (manuscript reviewer). Baptist. Home: 3737 N Sacramento Ave Chicago IL 60618 Office: Am Express 300 S Riverside Chicago IL 60606

WAMBOLD, FRANKLYN JACOB, III, computer electronics manufacturing executive; b. Kansas City, Mo., Sept. 5, 1935; s. Franklin Jacob Jr. and Hazel Bernadetta (Cullen) W.; m. Patricia Ann Irvin, July 20, 1960; children—Franklin J. IV, Terri D., James V. B.B.A., U. Mo., 1973. Enlisted with U.S. Air Force, 1953, advanced through ranks to master sgt., 1972; ret., 1974; product mgr. R-TEC, Bedford, Tex., 1975-80; mfg. supr. Boeing Electronics, Irving, Tex., 1980-81; mfg. mgr. Litton Data Systems, Lubbock, Tex., 1981-82; v.p. ops. Central Data Corp., Champaign, Ill., 1982—. Decorated Bronze Star (2), Air medal (2). Mem. Inst. Indsl. Engrs., Soc. Mfg. Engs. Republican. Lodge: Masons. Avocations: woodworking; golf; reading. Home: 705 Somerset Circle Saint Joseph IL 61873 Office: Central Data Corp 1602 Newton Dr Champaign IL 61821

WAMPLER, LLOYD CHARLES, lawyer; b. Spencer, Ind., Nov. 4, 1920; s. Charles and Vivian (Hawkins) W.; A.B., Ind. U., 1942, J.D., 1947; m. Joyce Ann Hoppenrath, Sept. 28, 1950 (dec. 1954); 1 dau., Natalie Gay; m. Mary E. Shumaker, Sept. 16, 1982. Admitted to Ind. bar, 1947, U.S. Supreme Ct. bar, 1971; instr. bus. law U. Kans., 1947-49; dep. atty. gen. Ind., 1949-50; mem. legal com. Interstate Oil Compact Commn., 1950; asst. pub. counselor Ind., 1950-53; mem. firm Stevens, Wampler, Travis & Fortin, Plymouth, 1953-83; claim counsel Am. Family Ins. Group, Indpls., 1983—. Mem. Ind. Rehab. Services Bd., 1978—; Democratic nominee for judge Ind. Supreme Ct., 1956. Served with USNR, 1942-46. Mem. Am. Judicature Soc., ABA, Ind. Bar Assn. (bd. mgrs. 1975-77), Marshall County Bar Assn., Ind. Acad. Sci., Ind. Def. Lawyers Assn. (dir. 1967-72, v.p. 1970, pres. 1971-72), Ind., Marshall County (dir. 1969-75) hist. socs., Assn. Ins. Attys. U.S. and Can., Am. Legion, Phi Delta Phi, Delta Sigma Pi. Club: Moose. Home: 4000 N Meridian St Indianapolis IN 46208 Office: 1625 N Post Rd Indianapolis IN 46219

WANATICK, MARY ANN, fund-raising consultant; b. Detroit, June 12, 1929; d. Samuel Tilden and Cilenore Catherine (Smith) Steedman; B.A., U. Toledo, 1951, B.Ed., 1964; m. Michael D. Wanatick, Oct. 30, 1958; 1 child, Robert Michael. Instr. computer and related systems Remington Rand, Inc., Toledo, 1951-54; city dir. New Neighbors League, Toledo, 1954-58; area dir. Relax-a-Cizor, Inc., Toledo, 1966-68; elementary tchr. Toledo Pub. Schs., 1962-65; exec. dir. Arthritis Found., Northwestern Ohio chpt., Toledo, 1968-84. Mem. arthritis adv. com. Ohio Dept. Health; bd. dirs. Toledo Symphony Orch. League, Toledo Opera Guild. Mem. Arthritis Found. Profl. Staff Assn., Barrier Free Toledo Com. (adv. com.), N.W. Ohio Rehab. Assn., Nat. Rehab. Assn., Ohio Rehab. Assn., Ohio Pub. Health Assn., Toledo Execs. Forum (treas.), Ohio Rheumatism Soc., Fund Raising Exec. of N.W. Ohio, Alpha Omicron Pi (pres. Toledo alumni). Club: Zonta (Toledo). Home and Office: 4857 Rudgate Blvd Toledo OH 43623

WANDEL, JOSEPH FRANK, account executive; b. Buffalo, Nov. 28, 1942; s. Joseph Frank and Florence Mary (Gluszkowski) W.; B.S. in Chemistry, Alliance Coll., 1964; postgrad. St. John's U., N.Y.C., 1964-65; M.B.A., Kent State U.; m. Sally Ann Jessen, Feb. 14, 1976; 1 son, Stephen. Chem. sales rep. Emery Industries, Inc., Cin., 1966-79; tech. rep. Glyco Chem. Co., Greenwich, Conn., 1979—; tech. sales engr. Henkel Corp., chem. spltys. div., Maywood, N.J., 1980-84; account exec. Loxiol Lubricants, 1984—. Adv. merit badges Boy Scouts Am. Served with USAR, 1965-72. Mem. Soc. Plastics Engrs., Vinyl Siding Inst., Soc. Plastics Industry, Chem. Mktg. Research Assn., Am. Chem. Soc., Cleve. Chem. Assn., Akron Rubber Group. Republican. Roman Catholic. Clubs: Bishop's Century, Hudson Montessori Parents, Polish Nat. Alliance. Address: 270 Kennedy Blvd Northfield OH 44067

WANDER, HERBERT STANTON, lawyer; b. Cin., Mar. 17, 1935; s. Louis Marvin and Pauline (Schuster) W.; m. Ruth Cele Fell, Aug. 7, 1960; children—Daniel Jerome, Susan Gail, Lois Marlene. A.B., U. Mich., 1957; LL.B., Yale U., 1960. Bar: Ohio 1960, Ill. 1960. Law clk. to judge U.S. Dist. Ct. (no. dist.) Ill., 1960-61; ptnr. Pope Ballard Shepard & Fowle, Chgo., 1961-78, Katten Muchin Zavis Pearl & Galler, Chgo., 1978—; dir. Telephone & Data Systems, Chgo. Contbr. numerous articles to profl. jours. Bd. dirs. Jewish Fedn. Met. Chgo., 1972—, pres., 1981-83; bd. dirs. Jewish United Fund, 1972—, pres., 1981-83, chmn. pub. affairs com., 1984—; former regional chmn. nat. young leadership cabinet United Jewish Appeal; vice chmn. large city budgeting conf. Council Jewish Fedns., 1979-82, bd. dirs., 1980—, exec. com., 1983-84. Mem. ABA, Chgo. Bar Assn., Ill. State Bar Assn., Yale Law Sch. Assn. (exec. com. 1982—), Phi Beta Kappa. Clubs: Standard, Economics (Chgo.); Northmoor Country (Highland Park, Ill.). Home: 2023 Linden Ave Highland Park IL 60035 Office: Katten Muchin Zavis Pearl & Galler 525 W Monroe St Chicago IL 60606

WANG, JOSEPH YUNG-CHYUNG, polymer chemist; b. Fu-san, China, Apr. 1, 1949; came to U.S., 1972; s. Kwan-shih and Jen-Inn (Lieu) W.; m. Mona Min-Huey Hwang, Nov. 14, 1975; 1 child, Karen Kai-Lun. B.S., Tamkang U., 1970; Ph.D., Poly. Inst. N.Y., 1975. Research scientist Miles Lab., Inc., Elkhart, Ind., 1976-83, sr. research scientist, 1984—; assoc. prof. chemistry Fu-Jen U., Taipei, Taiwan, Republic of China, 1978-80. Patentee in field. Mem. Am. Chem. Soc. Avocations: fishing; table tennis; tennis. Home: 2922 Brooktree Court Elkhart IN 46514 Office: Miles Lab Inc 1127 Myrtle St Elkhart IN 46515

WANG, JOSEPHINE L. FEN, physician; b. Taipei, Republic of China, Jan 2, 1948; came to U.S., 1974; d. Pao-San and Ann-Nam (Chen) Chao; m. Chang-Yang Wang, Dec. 20, 1973; children—Edward, Eileen. M.D., Nat. Taiwan U., Taipei, 1974. Diplomate Am. Bd. Pediatrics, Am. Bd. Allergy and Immunology. Intern Nat. Taiwan U. Hosp., 1973-74; resident U. Ill. Hosp., Chgo., 1974-76; fellow Northwestern U. Med. Ctr., Chgo., 1976-78, instr. pediatrics, Chgo., 1978—; cons. Methodist Hosp. Ind., 1979—, Holy Cross Hosp., Chgo., 1978—, St. Anthony Hosp., 1985—. Mem. Am. Acad. Allergy. Office: 9012 Connecticut Dr Merrillville IN 46410 also 6815 W 94th St Oak Lawn IL 60453

WANTLAND, WILLIAM CHARLES, Episcopal bishop; b. Edmond, Okla., Apr. 14, 1934; s. William Lindsay and Edna Louise (Yost) W. B.A., U. Hawaii, 1957; J.D., Oklahoma City Law Sch., 1964; Rel.D., Geneva Theol. Coll., 1976; D.D. honoris cause, Nashotah House, 1983; D.D. honoris causa, Seabury Western Sem., 1983. Bar: Okla. 1964. Atty., Seminole, Okla., 1964-77; atty. gen. Seminole Nation, 1969-72, 75-77; presiding judge Mcpl. Ct., Seminole, 1970-77; ordained deacon, 1963, priest, Episcopal Ch., 1970; vicar St. Mark's Episcopal Ch., Seminole, 1963-77, St. Paul's Episcopal Ch., Holdenville, Okla., 1974-77; rector St. John's Ch., Oklahoma City, 1977-80; consecrated bishop, 1980; bishop Episcopal Diocese of Eau Claire, Wis., 1980—; pres. Wis. Conf. Chs.; adj. prof. probate law Okla. U., 1970-78; Canon law advisor Duquesne U., 1976—. Trustee, Nashotah House, Wis., canon law lectr., 1984—, Okla. Bar Found.; chmn. Okla. Com. to Implement Jud. Reform, 1969-71; cons. Am. Indian Policy Rev. Commn. U.S. Senate, 1973-74; exec. dir. Seminole Housing Authority, 1969; exec. dir. Seminole Nation Indian Housing Authority, 1971. Recipient Supreme Ct. award for Contbn. to Law and Order, 1975. Mem. Okla. Bar Assn., ABA, Am. Judges Assn., Okla. Indian Rights Assn. (pres. 1975-76), Okla. Conf. Mcpl. Judges (pres. 1973); Evang. and Catholic Mission of Episcopal Ch. (pres. 1982-85), Am. Judicature Soc., Soc. Mary, Confraternity of the Blessed Sacrament, Catholic Clerical Union, Clan Lindsay Assn. (regional v.p.), The Living Church Found. Democrat. Author (with William Bishop and Dwaine Schmidt): Oklahoma Probate Forms, 1972; Foundations of the Faith, 1983; Canon Law in the Episcopal Church, 1984. Contbr. articles to profl. and religious jours. Office: 510 S Farwell St Eau Claire WI 54701

WARD, ANTHONY GILES, futures exchange executive; b. Bloomington, Ill., July 16, 1938; s. William V. and Leone J. (Costigan) W.; B.S. in Polit. Sci., Loyola U., Chgo., 1961; postgrad. Sch. Bus., U. Chgo., 1967-68; m. Diane J. Anstett, Jan. 9, 1965; children—Joseph M., Daniel S., Kevin P., Christopher B. Mgmt. asst., sales asst., sales mgr., group sales mgr., mktg. mgr. data communications, Ill. Bell, Chgo., 1965-69; cons. Fry Cons., Chgo., 1969-72; cons., assoc., mng. assoc. Booz, Allen & Hamilton, Chgo., 1972-78; v.p. Space/Mgmt. Programs, Chgo., 1978-83; sr. v.p. ops. Chgo. Merc. Exchange, 1983—. Mem. Businessmen for Loyola U. Served with U.S. Army, 1962-64. Mem. Futures Industry Assn. (bd. dirs. ops. div. Chgo. chpt.). Roman Catholic. Clubs: River, Univ. (Chgo.). Home: 1231 Lake St Libertyville IL 60048 Office: Chgo Merc Exchange Center 30 S Wacker Dr Chicago IL

WARD, ARTHUR DEMETRICE, investment company executive, stock market analyst; b. Chgo., July 20, 1956; s. William B. Ward and Hester Ward Sims; m. Florence Ann Johnson, July 11, 1981; 1 child, Richard Andrew. Portfolio mgr., gen. ptnr. Magnolia Capital Markets, Chgo., 1980—; group chief Nichiren Shoshu Am., Chgo., 1978—; market analyst Mason Investment Group, Chgo., 1983.

WARD, CHESTER VIRGIL, banker; b. Wood River, Ill., Dec. 2, 1949; s. Martin Wesley and Bernadine Fay (Behrer) W.; m. Melinda Jo Temperly, Oct. 6, 1973; 1 dau., Meredith. Student Bradley U., 1968-69; A.A., Columbia Coll., 1984. Mgr., Household Internat., Kansas City, Mo., 1971-76; asst. v.p. So. Ill. Bank, Fairview Heights, Ill., 1976-78; v.p. Bethalto Nat. Bank (Ill.) 1978-84; exec. v.p., chief exec. officer Central Bank of Glen Carbon, Ill., 1984—, dir., 1985—. Bd. dirs. Piasa Bird council Boy Scouts Am., 1980-83, Bethalto Hist. Soc., 1980-83, Easter Seal Soc., Alton, Ill., 1983. Named Outstanding Young Man in Ill., Ill. Jaycees, 1982, Outstanding Young Man Am., U.S. Jaycees, 1983. Mem. Am. Inst. Banking (cert. 1979, 80), Ill. bankers Assn. (cert. 1980, 81, 83), So. Ill. Bank Officers, Bethalto C. of C. (dir. 1978-79, pres. 1979), Wood River C. of C. (dir. 1980-83, pres. 1982), Metro East C. of C. (dir. 1981-82), Edwardsville C. of C. (bd. dirs. 1985), Phi Theta Kappa. Methodist. Lodge: Rotary (bd. dirs. 1978-83, pres. 1982-83) Bethalto). Home: 704 Euclid Pl Alton IL 62002 Office: Central Bank 3601 S Hwy 159 Glen Carbon IL 62034

WARD, DANIEL PATRICK, state judge; b. Chgo., Aug. 30, 1918; s. Patrick and Jane (Convery) W.; student St. Viator Coll., 1936-38; J.D., DePaul U., 1941, D.H.L. (hon.), 1976; LL.D. (hon.), John Marshall Law Sch., 1972; m. Marilyn Corleto, June 23, 1951; children—Mary Jane, John, Susan, Elizabeth Ward. Admitted to Fed. bar, Ill. bar; asst. prof. law Southeastern U., Washington, 1941-42; pvt. practice law, 1945-48; asst. U.S. atty. No. Dist. of Ill., 1948-54, chief criminal div., 1951-54; with firm Eardley & Ward, Chgo., 1954-55; dean Coll. Law, DePaul U., Chgo., 1955-60; states atty. Cook County, Ill., 1960-66; judge Supreme Ct. Ill., 1966—, chief justice, 1976-79; adj. prof. law DePaul U. Coll. Law, 1979—. Chmn., Ill. Courts Commn., 1969-73. Served with AUS, 1942-45. Mem. Am., Fed., Ill., Chgo. bar assns. Roman Catholic. Home: 11000 Kingston Ave Westchester IL 60153 Office: 3083 Richard J Daley Center Chicago IL 60602

WARD, DAVID ALLISON, lawyer; b. Charleston, S.C., Sept. 28, 1951; s. Leslie A. and Leola J. (Erickson) W. B.A. in Math., So. Ill. U., 1973; M.A. in Econs., Western Ill. U., 1975; J.D., Ill. Inst. Tech., Chgo.-Kent Coll. Law, 1983. Bar: Ill. 1983, U.S. Dist. Ct. (no. dist.) Ill. 1983. Economist, Office of Gov., Bur. of Budget, Springfield, Ill., 1975-79; exec. asst. to dir. Ill. Dept. Revenue, Springfield, 1979-80; dir. Ill. Local Govt. Fin. Study Commn., Chgo., 1980-81; assoc. Silets & Martin, Ltd., Chgo., 1983—; summer intern Office of Ill. Atty. Gen., Chgo., 1981; mem. of various govtl. coms., 1978-80. Contbr. articles to profl. jours. Mem. com. Oak Park Republican Organization, 1983—. Pres.'s scholar So. Ill. U., 1969-73. Mem. ABA, Ill. State Bar Assn., Chgo. Bar Assn., Moot Court Soc., Omicron Delta Epsilon. Office: Silets & Martin Ltd 140 S Dearborn Chicago IL 60603

WARD, ELMER L., JR., clothing manufacturing executive; b. 1924. With Palm Beach Co., Cin., 1948—, exec. v.p., 1955-68, pres., 1968-71, pres. and chief exec. officer, dir., 1971—, also chmn. bd., pres. Palm Beach Inc. Office: Palm Beach Co Inc 1290 Ave of Americas New York NY 10104

WARD, JACK DONALD, lawyer; b. Blue Island, Ill., Aug. 14, 1952; s. Sylvan Donald and Beatrice Dorrell (Stackhouse) W.; m. Sharmon Oaks, Nov. 21, 1973; children—Spencer, Julianna, Christopher, Brent. B.S. summa cum laude in Acctg., Brigham Young U., 1975, J.D. cum laude, 1978. Bars: Ill. 1978, U.S. Dist. Ct. (no. dist.) Ill. 1979, U.S. Ct. Appeals (7th cir.) 1982, U.S. Supreme Ct. 1983. Assoc. Reno Zahm Law Firm, Rockford, Ill., 1978-82, ptnr., 1982—. Research asst.: Bogert on Trusts, 5th edit., 1978. Vol. missionary Ch. of Jesus Christ of Latter-Day Saints, Italy, 1971-73; mem. com. for today and tomorrow Rockford Meml. Hosp., 1980—. Mem. ABA, Ill. Bar Assn., Winnebago County Bar Assn., Assn. Trial Lawyers Am., Beta Gamma Sigma. Republican. Club: City of Rockford. Office: Reno Zahm Law Firm 1415 E State St Rockford IL 61108

WARD, MARK ALAN, lawyer; b. Ft. Scott, Kans., Sept. 17, 1956; s. Daniel Sherman and Barbara (Ellen) W.; m. Lisa Ann DiNardo, Sept. 4, 1976. B.A. in Polit. Sci., Pittsburg State U., 1978; J.D., Washburn U., 1981. Bars: Kans. 1981, U.S. Dist. Ct. Kans. 1981. Adminstrv. hearing officer/legal intern Kans. Dept. Revenue, Topeka, 1979-81; gen. counsel Kans. Fire Marshall's Office, Topeka, 1981-82; sole practice, Ft. Scott, 1983—. Author (newsletter) Fire Marshal's Trumpet, 1981-82. Mem. Ft. Scott Parks Adv. Bd., 1983—, Ft. Scott Planning Commn., 1984—. Mem. ABA, Bourbon County Bar Assn. (pres. 1984—), Kansas Bar Assn., Assn. Trial Lawyers Am., Ft. Scott C. of C. Republican. Methodist. Home: 820 S Eddy St Fort Scott KS 66701 Office: 1 1/2 N Main St Suite 1 Fort Scott KS 66701

WARD, RICHARD HURLEY, university administrator; b. N.Y.C., Sept. 2, 1939; s. Hurley and Anna C. (Mittasch) W.; m. Maureen D. Ward, Sept. 3, 1966 (div. Dec. 1982); children—Jeanne M., Jonathan B. B.S., John Jay Coll. Criminal Justice, 1968; M.Crim., U. Calif.-Berkeley, 1969, D.Crim., 1971. Detective, N.Y.C. Police Dept., 1962-70; coordinator student activities John Jay Coll., N.Y.C., 1970-71, dean students, 1971-75, v.p., 1975-77; vice chancellor, prof. criminology U. Ill., Chgo., 1977—; U.S. del. People to People Citizen Ambassador Program in China, 1983; del. to China, Eisenhower Found., 1985; English lang. coordinator Internat. Course Higher Specialization Police Forces, Messina, Italy, 1981, 83, Madrid, 1984, course dir., 1982, 85; chmn. Joint Commn. on Criminology and Criminal Justice Edn. and Standards, 1975-80. Co-author: Police Robbery Control Manual, 1975; author: Introduction to Criminal Investigation, 1975; An Anti-Corruption Manual for Administrators in Law Enforcement, 1979; (with Robert McCormack) Quest for Quality, 1984; gen. editor Foundations of Criminal Justice, 46 vols., 1972-75; editor: (with Austin Fowler) Police and Law Enforcement, Vol. I, 1972; Police and Law Enforcement, Vol. II, 1975; The Terrorist Connection: A Pervasive Network; (newsletter) CJ Internat. Mem. Near West Side Community Conservation Council, 1982—; varsity baseball coach U. Ill., Chgo., 1980-82; varsity baseball coach John Jay Coll. Criminal Justice, N.Y.C., 1971-72. Served to cpl. USMC, 1957-61. Recipient Leonard Reisman award John Jay Coll. Criminal Justice, 1968, Alumni Achievement award, 1978; Richard McGee award U. Calif.-Berkeley Sch. Criminology, 1971; Justice Dept. fellow U. Calif.-Berkeley, 1968-69; Danforth Found. fellow, 1971. Mem. Acad. Criminal Justice Scis. (pres. 1977-78, founders' award 1985), Am. Soc. Pub. Adminstrn., Internat. Assn. Chiefs of Police (chmn. edn. and tng. sect. 1974-75), Sigma Delta Chi. Home: 901 S Ashland Ave Apt 801A Chicago IL 60607 Office: U Ill at Chicago Box 6998 Chicago IL 60680

WARD, STEPHEN ROSBOROUGH, manufacturers' representative; b. St. Louis, Mar. 1, 1948; s. Gershon Albert and Ruth Juanita (Rosborough) W.; m. Susan Lee Charlesworth, June 12, 1970; children—Adam Whitehall, Kathryn Lindsay. B.A., Hope Coll., 1970; M.B.A., Mich. State U., 1973. Mgr. Steak and Ale Restaurants Am. Inc., Atlanta, 1973-75; ptnr. Charlesworth-Imre Assocs., St. Louis, 1975-76, Charlesworth-Ward Assocs., St. Louis, 1977-78, Charlesworth-Ward-Rafferty Assocs., St. Louis, 1978-79; v.p. Charlesworth-Ward-Rafferty, Inc., St. Louis, 1979-82, pres., 1983-85, chmn. bd., 1983-85; pres., chmn. bd. Ward, Raffery & Jacobs, Inc., 1985—; dir. C-W-R Profit Sharing Plan and Trust. Served to capt. Air N.G., 1970-76. Mem. Illuminating Engring. Soc. N.Am., St. Louis Elec. Bd. Trade. Republican. Presbyterian. Club: Town and Country Racquet. Home: 1051 Kenmore Dr Kirkwood MO 63122 Office: 130 W Monroe Ave Saint Louis MO 63122

WARD, THOMAS E., lawyer; b. Bronx, N.Y., Sept. 17, 1938; s. George Francis and Mary Elizabeth (Brennan) W.; m. Eileen Mary Moriarty, Mar. 30, 1964; children—Kevin John, Thomas Brennan. B.S., Fordham U., 1961; LL.B., St. John's U., Bklyn., 1967; LL.M., NYU, 1971. Bar: N.Y. 1967, Ill., 1974. Pension trainee Met. Life Ins. Co., N.Y.C., 1956-61, computer programmer, 1961-67, atty., 1967-77, asst. gen. counsel, Oak Brook, Ill., 1977-79, assoc. gen. counsel, 1979—. Served with U.S. Army, 1961-63. Mem. Chgo. Bar Assn., ABA (sect. corp., banking and bus. law, sect. real property, probate trust law). Republican. Roman Catholic. Lodge: K.C. Avocations: Swimming, reading, travel. Home: 450 Stratford Elmhurst IL 60126 Office: Met Life Ins Co 2021 Spring Rd Suite 300 Oak Brook IL 60521

WARD, WILLIAM EDWARD, museum exhibition designer; b. Cleve., Apr. 4, 1922; s. Edward and Lura Dell (Eckelberry) W.; B.S., Western Res. U., 1947, M.A., 1948; diploma Cleve. Inst. Art, 1947; postgrad. Columbia U., 1950; m. Evelyn Svec, Nov. 12, 1952; 1 dau., Pamela. Mem. staff edn., Oriental depts. Cleve. Mus. Art, 1947—, designer, 1957—, now chief designer; instr. Calligraphy and watercolor Cleve. Inst. Art, 1960—, after 1960, now prof. cons. graphic and installation exhbn. Exhibited in numerous exhbns.; exhbn.; Cleve. Playhouse Gallery, 1984; designer George Gund Collection of Western Art Mus., 1972; Firemen's Meml., Cleve., sculpture design, 1968; designer ofcl. seals Case Western Res. U., also Sch. Medicine, 1969; curator Culcon exhbn. Masterpieces of World Art from Am. Museums, Tokyo and Kyoto, Japan, 1976. Mem. Internat. Design Conf., Aspen, 1959—; mem. Fine Arts Adv. Com. City Cleve., 1966—; mem. mayor's com. for selection of ofcl. seal City of Cleve., 1973. Served with Terrain Intelligence, AUS, 1942-45; CBI. Recipient commn. award City Canvis competition Cleve. Area Arts Council, 1975. Mem. Cleve. Soc. Contemporary Art, Print Club Cleve. Club: Rowfant (Cleve.). Home: 27045 Solon Rd Solon OH 44139 Office: Cleve Mus Art 11150 E Boulevard Cleveland OH 44106

WARDEN, BRUCE LELAND, music publishing company executive; b. Beloit, Wis., July 14, 1939; s. Jack Leland and Violet Matelda (Sampson) W.; m. Judith Ann Guetschow, Sept. 10, 1960; children—Lea Ann, Wendy, Gina, Gary. Student U. Ill., 1957-59; B.S. in Tech., So. Ill. U., 1965; M.S. in Tech./Mgmt., No. Ill. U., 1970; postgrad. U. Ill., 1969-70. Cert. tchr., Ill. Tchr. Rockford (Ill.) pub. schs., 1965-70; with D.R. Johnson Cons. Engring. Co., 1966-67; pres. WGE Prodns., Rockford, 1968-82; v.p. Mark Allen Corp., Rockford, 1970-73; pres. Leland Investment Corp., Rockford, 1972-76; pres. Leland Constrn. Corp., Rockford, 1976—, Forest Hills Investment, Inc., Rockford, 1981—, WGE Record Co., 1967—, WGE Music Pub. Co., Rockford, 1979—. Mem. ASCAP, Am. Fedn. Musicians, Iota Lambda Sigma. Mem. Evangelical Free Ch. Lodge: Lions (Rockford). Office: WGE Music Pub Corp 3311 Carefree St Rockford IL 61111

WARE, BEVERLY GISS, public health educator; b. Chelsea, Mass., June 30, 1933; d. Benjamin and Ruth (Taylor) Giss; m. Robert E. Mytinger, Feb. 19, 1961 (div. 1970); m. 2d, Richard Anderson Ware, Dec. 22, 1972; stepchildren—Alexander, Bradley, Patricia. Student Forsyth Sch. for Dental Hygiene, Boston, 1951-53; B.Ed., Boston U., 1955; M.P.H., U. Mich., 1957; Dr.P.H., UCLA, 1969. Registered dental hygienist, Mass., N.Y. Health educator Grand Rapids-Kent County (Mich.) Health Dept., 1957-59, Denver Dept. Health and Hosps., 1959, Santa Clara County Health Dept., San Jose, Calif., 1960-62; asst. in pub. health U. Hawaii, Honolulu, 1966-68; asst. prof. Calif. State U.-Northridge, 1969-70; asst. prof. U. Mich., Ann Arbor, 1970-76; cardiovascular risk intervention coordinator Ford Motor Co., Dearborn, Mich., 1976-77, corp. health edn. programs coordinator, 1977—; cons. Nat. Cancer Inst., Nat. Heart Lung and Blood Inst.; trainer Am. Occupational Med. Assn., Nurse's Assn. Bd. dirs. Washtenaw County League for Planned Parenthood, 1973-76; bd. dirs., chmn. com. on environ. health Am. Lung Assn. Southeastern Mich., 1982-85. Mem. Am. Pub. Health Assn., Soc. Pub. Health Edn., Soc. Behavioral Medicine, Pi Lambda Theta, Delta Omega. Democrat. Jewish. Club: Women's Economic. Contbr. articles to profl. jours. Home: 16 Haverhill Ct Ann Arbor MI 48105 Office: 900 Parklane Towers W Suite 900 Dearborn MI 48126

WARE, GEORGE HENRY, botanist; b. Avery, Okla., Apr. 27, 1924; s. Charles and Mildred (Eshelman) W.; B.S., U. Okla., 1945, M.S., 1948; Ph.D., U. Wis., 1955; m. June Marie Gleason, Dec. 21, 1955; children—David, Daniel, Patrick, John. Asst. prof. Northwestern State U. of La., Natchitoches, 1948-56, asso. prof., 1956-62, prof., 1962-67; dir. Conservation Sect., No. La. Supplementary Edn. Center, Natchitoches, 1967-68; dendrologist Morton Arboretum, Lisle, Ill., 1968—, adminstr. research group, 1976—; vis. prof. U. Okla., Norman, summers, 1957, 61, 63, 64; adj. prof. Western Ill. U., 1972—; mem. extension faculty George Williams Coll., Downers Grove, Ill., 1969-76, Nat. Coll. Edn., Evanston, Ill., 1972-76. Trustee nomination caucus Coll. of DuPage, Glen Ellyn, Ill., 1974-78; bd. dirs. Kane-DuPage Soil and Water Conservation Dist., 1969—; pres. La. Acad. Scis., 1966-67; bd. dirs. La. State Sci. Fair, 1966. Served with USN, 1942-46. Mem. Ecol. Soc. Am., Soil Conservation Soc. Am., Southwestern Assn. Naturalists (treas. 1963-69), Internat. Soc. Arboriculture, Sigma Xi. Home: 23W 176 Indian Hill Dr Lisle IL 60532 Office: Morton Arboretum Lisle IL 60532

WARKOCZESKI, LARRY STANLEY, lawyer, health care executive, consultant; b. Battle Creek, Mich., Dec. 17, 1951; s. Harold Stanley and Beverly Ann (Gorham) W.; m. Vicki Carol Mandernach, Aug. 31, 1979. B.S. summa cum laude, Western Mich. U., 1974; J.D., Valparaiso U., 1977; M.H.S.A., U. Mich., 1984. Bar: Mich. Adminstrv. asst. to chmn. bd. Alliance Foods, Inc., Coldwater, Mich., 1976-78, gen. counsel, dir. research and devel., 1978-80, v.p., 1979-80; asst. prof. law Eastern Ill. U., Charleston, 1980-82; strategic planner Sarah Bush Lincoln Health Ctr., Mattoon, Ill., 1981-82; atty., health care cons., Ypsilanti, Mich., 1982-84; assoc. Office of Bus. Devel., Catherine McAuley Health Ctr., 1984-85; v.p. corp. devel. Gen. Health Mgmt. Co., 1985—. Bd. dirs. Mich. Internat. Council, East Lansing, 1978-80; spl. agrl. policy advisor Am. Freedom from Hunger Found., Washington, 1978-79; chmn. Union City (Mich.) Village Police Commn., 1978-79, Democratic party, Branch City, Mich., 1980. Recipient Mich. Ho. of Reps. cert. Outstanding Citizenship, 1971. Mem. ABA, Mich. Bar Assn., Midwest Bus. Adminstrn. Assn., Health Care Forum. Address: 14 Mesa Verde Ct Madison WI 53705

WARMS, LEON JAMES, retail executive; b. Phila., Dec. 6, 1920; s. Leon and Viola Regina (Ullman) W.; B.A. in Edn., Washington and Lee U., 1942; postgrad. U. Pa., 1942; m. Ruth Hanstein, Jan. 4, 1947. Jr. exec. trainee, buyer M.E. Blatt Co., Atlantic City, N.J., 1946-48; asst. to gen. mdse. mgr. Strouss, Youngstown, Ohio, 1948-49, div. mdse. mgr., 1949-58; div. mdse. mgr. Charles Livingstons, Youngstown, 1958-61; pres. The Clothes Tree, Youngstown, 1961—, also 3 other stores; instr. mktg. Rutgers U., 1946-47; instr. bus. adminstrn. Youngstown U., 1949-54. Served with USCGR, 1942-46. Mem. Better Bus. Bur., Youngstown C. of C., Kappa Phi Kappa, Zeta Beta Tau. Republican. Jewish. Club: Rotary. Home: 207 Gypsy Ln Youngstown OH 44504 Office: 570 Gypsy Ln Youngstown OH 44505

WARNECKE, RICHARD B., social epidemiology and medical sociology researcher and educator; b. Bklyn., Aug. 23, 1937; s. Robert I. and Althea (Reynolds) W.; m. Barbara Billings, Aug. 24, 1963; children—Mark, Elizabeth. B.S. in Indsl. Relations, Cornell U., 1959; M.A., Colgate U., 1963; Ph.D. in Sociology, Duke U., 1966. Asst. prof. sociology SUNY-Buffalo, 1967-74; assoc. prof. U. Ill.-Chgo., 1974-82, assoc. dir. Survey Research Lab., 1974-82, dir. Survey Research Lab., 1983—; assoc. dir. Ill. Cancer Council, Chgo., 1976-82, assoc. dir. epido cancer ctr., 1983—; cons. Nat. Cancer Inst., Bethesda, Md., 1979—. Contbr. articles to profl. publs. Nat. Cancer Inst. grantee, 1977—. Mem. Am. Sociol. Assn., Soc. Epidemiol. Research, Am. Assn. Pub. Opinion Research, Am. Statis. Assn., Am. Soc. Preventive Oncology. Office: Ill Cancer Council 36 S Wabash Chicago IL 60603

WARNER, CHARLES WILLIAM, JR., real estate broker, developer; b. Columbus, Ohio, Apr. 11, 1928; s. Charles William and Elsie (Burns) W.; m. Marjorie Lucille Dillin, July 20, 1952; children—Belinda Mae, Charles William III. B.Mus., Ohio State U., 1951. With Don M. Casto Orgn., Columbus, Ohio, 1951-69; pres. Chuck Warner & Assocs., Columbus, 1969—. Chancel choir dir. Northwest United Meth. Ch., Columbus, 1963—. Mem. Nat. Assn. Realtors, Ohio Assn. Realtors, Columbus Bd. Realtors, Mansfield Bd. Realtors, Am. Fedn. Musicians. Methodist. Office: Chuck Warner & Assocs 236 E Town St Columbus OH 43215

WARNER, JAMES DANIEL, See *Who's Who in America,* 43rd edition.

WARNER, RICHARD BRADLEY, educational administrator; b. Bklyn., Mar. 7, 1945; s. William John and Anneabelle Marie (Reutzel) W.; m. Mary Francis Hackleman, June 19, 1971; children—Kevin, Matthew, Kathryn. B.S., Springfield Coll., 1967; Ed.M., U. Ill., 1971, Ed.D., 1975. Cert. ednl. adminstr., N.Y., N.J., Ill., N.D. Research asst. Coll. Edn., U. Ill., 1972-74; asst. prin. Flossmoor Jr. High Sch., Ill., 1974-76; prin. Agassiz Jr. High Sch., Fargo, N.D., 1976-79, Fargo South High Sch., 1979—; adj. prof. Tri Coll. U., 1980—. Contbr. articles to profl. jours. Served to staff sgt. USAF, 1968-72. Named Instr. of Yr., U.S. Air Force, 1970. Fellow Charles Kettering Found.; mem. N.D. Assn. Supervision and Curriculum Devel. (pres. 1982—), Am. Assn. Sch. Adminstrs. (corr. site com.). Roman Catholic. Club: Fargo Moorhead YMCA (bd. dirs.). Avocations: cross country skiing, racquetball; reading; traveling. Office: Fargo South High Sch 1840 15th Ave S Fargo ND 58103

WARNKE, GLEN ALVIN, material management executive, consultant; b. St. Paul, Mar. 27, 1942; s. Alvin Gottlieb and Lucille Lydia (Mahle) W.; m. Susan Frieda Kottke, June 28, 1968; children—Dunoon, Lucy, Michael. Student U. Minn., 1962-70; B.A. in Bus. Adminstrn., Columbia Coll., 1976. Cert. practitioner inventory mgmt. Prodn. control analyst visual products 3M, St. Paul, 1968-70, prodn. control supr., Columbia, Mo., 1970-76, material control mgr. electronic products, Columbia, 1976-84, material control specialist staff mfg., St. Paul, 1984—; cons. speaker Sch. Indsl. Engring., U. Mo., Columbia, 1975-77. Vice chmn. better bridges com. Boone County Ct., Columbia, 1979; dir., treas., v.p., pres. Boone County R-IV Sch. Bd., Hallsville, Mo., 1976-82; vice-chmn. Commn. on Role and Status of Women, Mo. East Conf., United Meth. Ch., St. Louis, 1980-84; pres., dir. central region Mo. Sch. Bds. Assn., Columbia, 1979-82. Served with USNR, 1963-68. Mem. Am. Prodn. and Inventory Control Soc. (pres. Mid-Mo. chpt. 1975-76). Republican. Methodist. Avocations: tennis; swimming; skiing; travel; home improvement. Office: 3M Staff Mfg 3M Ctr 525-1W-01 Saint Paul MN 55144

WARREN, CLARENCE JAMES, oil company executive; b. Princeton, Ind., Nov. 12, 1946; s. Marvin James and Lydia Theresa (Judice) W.; B.A. with honors, Western Ky. U., 1969. Sales exec. DuPont Glore Forgan, N.Y.C., 1971-72; supr. So. Triangle Oil Co., Mt. Carmel, Ill., 1972-76; pres. C.J. Warren Oil Co., Inc., Mt. Carmel, 1976—, also dir. Mem. zoning bd. City of Mt. Carmel, 1983—; mem. Republican Presdl. Task Force, 1980—. Served to capt. USAR, 1969-71. Football scholar Western Ky. U., 1964-68. Mem. Ohio Oil and Gas Assn., Ill. Oil and Gas Assn., Ind. Oil and Gas Producers Assn. Methodist. Lodge: Elks. Contbr. articles to profl. publs. Home: 311 E 6th St Mount Carmel IL 62863 Office: 319 Market St Mount Carmel IL 62863

WARREN, JANET ELAINE, librarian; b. Lindsborg, Kans., Sept. 19, 1951; d. Jack Edward and Mildred Louise (Ahlstedt) Beebe; m. Perry DeLong Warren, July 6, 1974; children—Emily Louise, Britta Elizabeth. Student Stephens Women's Coll., 1969-70; B.S. in Edn., Kans. U., 1973; M.L.S., Emporia State U., 1974. Asst. dir. Goodland Pub. Library (Kans.), 1974-75, library dir., 1975—. Sec., Sherman County Day Care Bd., Goodland, 1983; bd. dirs. Sherman County Jr. Miss Program, 1979. Mem. ALA, Kans. Library Assn., Mountain Plains Library Assn., AAUW. Republican. Club: Thalia Women's (pres. 1982-83). Home: Rt 1 PO Box 185 Goodland KS 67735 Office: Goodland Pub Library 8th & Broadway Goodland KS 67735

WARREN, JOE ELLISON, state senator, farmer; b. Silverdale, Kans., Sept. 17, 1912; s. James Edman and Phoebe (Harkelroad) W.; student pub. schs., Arkansas City, Kans.; m. Pauline Goff, Sept. 4, 1931; children—James, Helen Jane. Treas., Spring Creek Twp., 1952-56; mem. Kans. Senate, 1956—, chmn. soil conservation dist., 1956-78, minority caucus chmn. Senate, 1964-72, chmn. livestock subcom. Senate Com. on agr., 1968-72, vice chmn. legis. facilities com., 1972-76, asst. minority leader, 1969-77, caucus chmn., vice chmn. agr. and livestock com., 1974-77, ranking mem. agr. and small bus. com., 1979-84, ways and means com., 1983-85, edn. com., 1985—; farmer, rancher, Maple City, Kans., 1932—. Mem. sch. bd., Common Sch. Dist., Kans., 1936-57; mem. exec. Council Extension Cowley County, Kan., 1956-58; mem. fed. adv. council Bur. Employment Security, U.S. Dept. Labor; mem. Kans. Legis. Council; mem. Gov.'s Com. on Criminal Adminstrn. Recipient numerous awards in field of soil conservation and edn. Address: Route 1 Maple City KS 67102

WARREN, ROBERT WILLIS, See *Who's Who in America,* 43rd edition.

WARRICK, WOODWARD ALFRED, JR., securities company executive; b. Indpls., Jan. 20, 1922; s. Woodward Alfred and Charlotte Miller (Barksdale) W.; m. Janet Anderson, June 14, 1952; children—Cecily Barksdale, Courtney Barron. B.S.E., U. Mich., 1947, M.B.A., 1948. Fin. mgr. Bruce Flournoy Motor Co., Norfolk, Va., 1948-50; statistician Inland Container Co., Indpls., 1950-54, sales mgr., Cin., 1954-62; nat. sales mgr. St. Regis Paper Co., Detroit, 1962-65; v.p. E. F. Hutton & Co., Ann Arbor, Mich., 1965-83; v.p. Prudential-Bache Co., Ann Arbor, 1983—. Patentee automotive glass package. Chmn. bldg com. St. Joseph Mercy Hosp., Ann Arbor, 1973-74. Mem. Phi Delta Theta. Republican. Episcopalian. Clubs: U. Mich. (pres. Cin. 1957-58), U. Mich. M (pres. Ann Arbor 1976-77), Barton Hill Country; Economic (Detroit); Athletic (Indpls.). Office: Prudential-Bache Securities 325 E Eisenhower Pkwy Ann Arbor MI 48104

WARRUM, RICHARD LINDAMOOD, neon design company executive, designer; b. Rushville, Ind., Sept. 18, 1942; s. Robert Paul and Mary Evelyn (Lindawood) W. B.F.A. cum laude, Sch. Chgo. Art Inst., 1965; M.A. in Art History, Ind. U., 1968. Installation designer and asst. registrar Ind. U. Art Mus., Bloomington, 1965-68; asst. to dir. Indianapolis Mus. Art, 1968-70, asst. dir., 1970-75, graphic designer, 1975-78; pres., chief exec. officer Neonics Inc/Light & Space Design, Chgo., 1978—. Editor and graphic designer mus. publs., 1970-75. Mem. Soc. of Friends. Office: Light & Space Design 3324 N Halsted St Chicago IL 60657

WARSHAY, MARVIN, chemical engineer, educator; b. Tel Aviv, Jan. 12, 1934; s. Isaac and Miriam (Lepon) W.; m. Ieda Wilkof Bernstein, Feb. 11, 1962; children—Daniel, Susan, Alisa. B.Ch.E., Rensselaer Poly. Inst., 1955; M.S.Ch.E., Ill. Inst. Tech., Chgo., 1957, Ph.D.Ch.E., 1960. Research and devel. Esso Research & Engring. Co., Linden, N.J., 1960-62; basic researcher NASA Lewis Research Ctr., Cleve., 1962-75, mgr. fuel cell project office, 1975—; adj. prof. chem. engring. Cleve. State U., 1967—. Mem. Cleve. Council on Soviet Anti-Semitism, Police Athletic League of Cleve., Zionist Orgn. Am. Recipient Tech. Utilization award NASA, 1976, dirs. recognition, 1978, 1980, Group Achievement award, 1984. Mem. Am. Inst. Chem. Engrs., Am. Chem. Soc., Electrochem. Soc., Jewish Engrs. and Scientists Club, Sigma Xi. Democrat. Jewish. Lodge: B'nai B'rith. Editor: Progress in Batteries and Solar Cells, 1984. Contbr. articles to profl. jours. Home: 3652 Latimore Rd Cleveland OH 44122 Office: 21000 Brookpark Rd Cleveland OH 44135

WASHAM, TERRENCE CHRISTOPHER, counselor; b. Lima, Ohio, Nov. 12, 1950; s. Ralph Glenn and Francis Ann (DePalma) W.; m. Marcia Michals, May 21, 1977; children—Jennifer, Geoffrey, Matthew. B.S.S.W., Ohio State U., 1976; M.S.S.A., Case Western Res. U., 1978, M.B.A., 1984. Counseling supr. Trumbull County Council on alcoholism, 1978-79; speaker St. Johns and West Shore Med. Clinic, 1980—; mgr. Vets Ctr., VA, Cleve., 1979—; instr. Youngstown State U., 1979; registered rep. Ohio Co., Cleve., 1985—. Mem. West Shore Resource Council, 1980—; bd. dirs. Regional Council on Alcoholism of Cuyahoga, Geauga, Lake and Lorain Counties, 1982—. Served with U.S. Army, 1970-71. Nat. Inst. Alcohol Abuse and Alcoholism grantee, 1976-78. Mem. DAV. Democrat. Roman Catholic. Lodge: Cleve. Rotary. Home: 505 Columbia Rd Bay Village OH 44140 Office: Ohio Co 1127 Euclid Ave Cleveland OH 44114

WASHBURN, GREGORY GEORGE, printing company executive; b. LaGrange, Ill., Jan. 7, 1947; s. George Burton and Doris W.; student U. Notre Dame, 1965-66; B.A. in Bus. Adminstrn., Coe Coll., 1969; m. Sarah Ione Williams, 1983; children—Brian Gregory, Kristin Belle, Clayton Gerard. With mktg. div. Midwest regional office IBM, Chgo., 1969-70; co-owner, v.p. Washburn Graficolor, Inc., Lisle, Ill., 1970—; instr. adult coll. graphic arts program Ill. Benedictine Coll.; co-instr. undergrad. mktg. studies George Williams Coll. Mem. pres.'s adv. council, PAC exec. council Ill. Benedictine Coll. Recipient award Printing Industry Am., 1972, 75, 76, 83; Outstanding Service award Ill. Benedictine Coll., 1978. Mem. Bus./Profl. Advt. Assn., Phi Kappa Tau. Roman Catholic. Clubs: Kiwanis, Rotary. Office: Washburn Graficolor Inc 1975 University Ln Lisle IL 60532

WASHINGTON, CHARLES JOSEPH, manufacturing company executive; b. Indiana, Pa., Oct. 30, 1938; s. Harry J. and Elizabeth D. (Buckley) W.; m. Ruth Elizabeth Popp, June 11, 1960; children—Paul C., Susan M., Mark B.; B.S., Loyola U., 1961; M.B.A., U. Chgo., 1969. Corp staff Timex Waterbury, Conn., 1974-75, gen. mgr., 1975-76; mgr. ops. Optical div. Bell & Howell Co., Chgo., 1976-78; plant mgr. E Z Por div. of Ecko, Wheeling, Ill., 1978-79, Hon Industries, Muscatine, Iowa, 1979-80, v.p., gen. mgr., 1980—. Vice pres. Illowa council Boy Scouts Am., Davenport, Iowa, 1982-84, pres., 1985; bd. dirs. Sheltered Workshop, Muscatine, 1985. Mem. Am. Inst. Indsl. Engrs., Am. Mgmt. Assn. Lodge: Elks. Home: 2005 Circle Dr Muscatine IA 52761 Office: Hon Industries 414 E 3rd St Muscatine IA 52761

WASHINGTON, CONNIE MAE HENDERSON, public administrator; b. Chgo., June 3, 1934; d. Harold Edgar and Lillian Carrie (Haynes) Henderson; m. George Washington, Apr. 7, 1956; children—Sharon Maria, Matthew Anthony. B.A., Chgo. State U., 1981, M.S., 1984. X-ray technician U. Ill. Med. Ctr., Chgo., 1954-58; real estate property mgmt., Chgo., 1958-64; casework supr. Cook County Hosp., Chgo., 1964-67; with Chgo. Housing Authority, 1967—, mgr. 1981—. Mem. AAUW, Nat. Assn. Female Execs., Am. Forum for Internat. Study, Chgo. Archtl. Found., Nat. Assn. Housing and Redevel. Ofcls., Am. Correctional Assn., Phi Alpha Theta. Home: 7951 S Harvard Ave Chicago IL 60620 Office: Chgo Housing Authority 22 W Madison St Chicago IL 60602

WASHINGTON, HAROLD, mayor of Chicago; b. Chgo., Apr. 15, 1922; B.A., Roosevelt U., Chgo., 1949; J.D., Northwestern U., 1952. Admitted to Ill. bar, 1953; practice in Chgo., from 1953; asst. corp. counsel City of Chgo., 1954-58; arbitrator Ill. Indsl. Commn., 1960-64; mem. Ill. Ho. of Reps., 1965-76, chmn. jud. com.; mem. Ill. Senate, 1976-80, chmn. public health, welfare and corrections com.; lectr. urban politics Roosevelt U.; mem. 97th-98th Congresses from 1st Dist. Ill.; mayor City of Chgo., 1983—. Bd. dirs. Suburban SCLC, Mid-South Mental Health Assn.; founder Washington Youth and Community Orgn. Served with USAAF, 1942-46. Mem. Nat. Bar Congresses Ill. Bar Assn., Cook County Bar Assn., NAACP, Urban League, Black Taxpayers Fedn. (founder, past. pres.). Address: Office of Mayor 121 N La Salle St Chicago IL

WASIEKO, ROBERT MICHAEL, recreational vehicle company executive; b. Pitts., Feb. 21, 1934; s. Michael A. and Maria (Barcal) W.; m. Carol A. Donovan, June 28, 1958; children—Karen, Robert. Student U. Ga., 1955-56; B.A., Duquesne U., 1960, postgrad. 1961-62; With Ford Motor Co., Pitts. and Detroit, 1958-72; regional sales mgr. Am. Motors Corp., Detroit, 1972-74, gen. sales mgr., 1974-76; pres. Chinook Internat., Los Angeles, 1976-78; v.p. sales and br. ops. Coachmen R.V. Co., Middlebury, Ind., 1978-80, pres. Sportscoach Corp., sr. v.p. Coachmen Industries, 1980—, mem. exec. com., 1983—; mem. White House Staff, 1972-73. Bd. dirs. Lakeland Hills YMCA, 1967-72. Served with AUS, 1953-54. Mem. Recreation Vehicle Industry Assn., Elkhart C. of C. (dir. govt. com.). Club: Elcona Country.

WASSERMAN, MARVIN, sales and marketing company executive; b. Bklyn., Feb. 16, 1931; s. William and Mary (Moskowitz) W.; A.A., Glendale Coll., 1955; student U. Calif. Extension, Los Angeles, 1964; m. Anita Strain, Jan. 1, 1956 (div. Aug. 1972); children—Steven, Neil, Mark; m. 2d, Mary M. McColgan, Aug. 7, 1981. Machine operator Lockheed Aircraft Co., Burbank, Calif., 1952-55; resident engr., sr. designer Pacific div. Bendix Corp., North Hollywood, Calif., 1955-62, sr. engr. systems div., Ann Arbor, Mich., 1962-64; configuration control coordinator Mich. div. Ling-Temco-Vought, Warren, 1964; sr. gen. engr. liaison Brown Engrng. Co., Inc., Huntsville, Ala., 1964-66; sr. tech. asst. IBM Fed. Systems div. Space Systems Center, Huntsville, 1966-67; sr. engrng. specialist ARINC Research Corp., Ridgecrest, Calif., 1967-68; prin. devel. engr. Honeywell, Inc., Marine Systems Center, West Covina, Calif., 1968-69; sr. value engr. Aerojet ElectroSystems Co., Azusa, Calif., 1969-74; mgr. value engrng. Byron Jackson Pump div. Borg Warner Corp., Vernon Calif., 1974-75; value engr. Ingersoll Rand Co. Proto Tool Div., Fullerton, Calif., 1975-77; v.p. Orosico, Inc., 1976-77; account mgr. McGraw-Hill Pub. Co., Westminster, Calif., 1977-78, regional mgr. Mid-West/Can. region, Chgo., 1978-80; mktg. mgr. aerospace Pyle-Nat., Chgo., 1980; owner, chief exec. officer The Listening Post, 1981—; instr. Grad. Sch. Mgmt., UCLA Extension. Com. chmn. Pack 72, Chikasaw Dist., Tennessee Valley council Boy Scouts Am., 1966-67, mem. awards com. Pack 92, Ridgecrest, 1967-68, mem. spl. projects com. Pack 205, Cypress, Calif., 1969-71. Loaned exec. Jr. Achievement fund raising campaign, 1975. Served with USAF, 1951-52. Recipient Diamond Club award McGraw-Hill Pub. Co., 1978; cert. value specialist. Mem. Soc. Am. Value Engrs. (recipient awards as editor Redstone chpt. newsletter 1966, 67, named Value Engr. of Year 1967, nat. dir. 1967-71, pres. Orange County chpt. 1970-71, nat. v.p. S.W. region 1971-74, gen. chmn. 14th Ann. Nat. Conf. 1974; nat. historian 1976-77), Am. Soc. Performance Improvement (gen. chmn. nat. conf. 1976, v.p. So. Calif. chpt.). Jewish (pres. temple 1971). Contbr. articles to profl. jours. Home: 4555 El Monte Dr Saginaw MI 48603 Office: The Listening Post and Book Co div Listening Post 3097 Bay Plaza Saginaw MI 48604

WATERBURY, JACKSON DEWITT, marketing executive; b. Evanston, Ill., Feb. 4, 1937; s. Jackson D. and Eleanor (Barrows) W.; A.B., Brown U., 1959; m. Suzanne Butler, Aug. 27, 1958 (div. Jan. 1970); children—Jackson D. III, Arthur Barrows; m. Lynn Hardin, Mar. 17, 1971 (div. July 1984). 1 son, Timothy Bradford. Account exec. D'Arcy Advt. Co., St. Louis, 1958-63, Batz-Hodgson-Neuwoehner, Inc., St. Louis, 1963-66; exec. v.p., sec., dir. Lynch, Phillips & Waterbury, Inc., St. Louis, 1966-68; pres. Jackson Waterbury & Co., St. Louis, 1968-73; v.p., partner Vinyard & Lee & Partners, 1973-74; pres. Waterbury Inc., 1975-80, Bright Ideas, Inc., 1977-80; v.p./group supr. Batz-Hodgson-Neuwoehner, St. Louis, 1980-81; sr. v.p. Fawcett McDermott Cavanagh, Honolulu, 1981-82; prin. Waterbury Cons., 1982-84; sr. v.p. account service Kenrick Advt., Inc., St. Louis, 1984—. Football coach Mo. High Sch. All-Stars, 1966-67, St. Louis U., 1968-70; vice chmn. bd. dirs. Hawaii Soccer Assn., 1981-83. Mem. Ducks Unltd., Am. Motorcycle Assn., St. Louis Advt. Producers Assn. (steering com., negotiating com. 1977-80), Nat. Rifle Assn. Beta Theta Pi. Episcopalian. Clubs: Racquet, Pacific, Strathalbyn Farms. Home: 118 N Bemiston Saint Louis MO 63105 Office: 7711 Carondelet #800 Saint Louis MO 63105

WATERS, JAMES MERLIN, electrical engineer; b. Tabor, S.D., Feb. 12, 1926; s. Claude Arthur and Laura Almeda (Mordick) W.; m. Kathleen Mary Carr, Aug. 27, 1949; children—Ann Marie, Joseph M., Thomas J., Michael J. B.S. in Elec. Engring., U. Wis., 1946. Registered profl. engr., Wis., Mich., Minn. Elec. engr. United Engrng. Service, Mpls., 1947-51; sr. profl. engr. Commonwealth Assn. Inc., Jackson, Mich., 1951-61; prin. engr. Mead & Hunt Inc., Madison, 1961-68; pres. Waters & Assoc. Inc., Madison, 1968—. Served to lt. USN, 1943-47; PTO. Mem. IEEE (sr. mem.), Nat. Soc. Profl. Engrs. Republican. Roman Catholic. Club: Kilowatt (pres. 1965-66). Lodge: K.C. (fin. sec. 1953-55). Office: Waters & Assoc Inc 995 Applegate Rd Madison WI 53713

WATERS, THOMAS FRANK, fisheries educator, aquatic biology researcher; b. Hastings, Mich., May 17, 1926; s. Raymond Edward and Ella Joan (Steinke) W.; m. Carol Yonker, June 21, 1953; children—Daniel Frank, Elizabeth Lee, Benton Edward. B.S., Mich. State U., 1952, M.S., 1953, Ph.D., 1956. Biologist, Mich. Dept. Conservation, Vanderbilt, 1956-57; asst. prof. fisheries U. Minn.-St. Paul, 1958-63, assoc prof., 1963-68, prof., 1968—. Author: The Streams and Rivers of Minnesota, 1977. Contbr. articles to sci. jours. Served with USN, 1944-46. Mem. N.Am. Benthological Soc. (pres. 1975-76), Am. Fisheries Soc., Ecol. Soc. Am. Home: 2551 Charlotte St Saint Paul MN 55113 Office: Dept Fisheries and Wildlife U Minn 1980 Folwell Ave Saint Paul MN 55108

WATKINS, CURTIS WINTHROP, artist; b. Pontiac, Mich., Apr. 9, 1946; s. Robert James and Arvella Marquitta (Chenoweth) W.; student Ann Arbor Art Center, 1964-66, Kendall Sch. Design, 1966-68, Kraus Hypnosis Center, 1966, 70, Arons Ethical Hypnosis Tng. Center, 1977; m. Gayle Lynn Blom, Dec. 19, 1975; 1 dau., Darcy Ann. Illustrator, instr. Ann Arbor Art Center, 1969-71; owner, dir. Hypno-Art Research Center and Studio, Howell, Mich., 1971—; research on visualization process of subconscious by doing art work under hypnosis; lectr. hypnosis convs. and schs.; one-man shows include: LeVern's Gallery, 1969, Rackham Gallery, 1973, Hartland Gallery, 1974, Platt Gallery, 1975, Detroit Artists Guild Gallery, 1975, Golden Gallery, 1977, Cromaine Gallery, 1982, Driggett Gallery, 1982, Mill Gallery, 1983, Walnut Street Gallery, 1983; group shows include Mich. All-State Show, 1980, Mich. State Fine Arts Exhibit, 1980, Washington Internat., 1981, Lansing Art Gallery (Mich.), 1981, Capitol City Arts Show, 1981, Mich. Ann., 1981, Mich. Ann., 1982-83; bd. dirs. 9th Ann. Hartland Art Show, 1975, Livingston Arts and Crafts Assn., 1977-79, Hartland Art Council, 1974-78. Recipient numerous awards of excellence in art. Mem. Internat. Soc. Artists, Assn. Advance Ethical Hypnosis, Am. Assn. Profl. Hypnologists, Internat. Soc. Profl. Hypnosis, Internat. Platform Assn. Presbyterian. Home and Studio: 1749 Pinckney Rd Howell MI 48843

WATKINS, H.T., railroad company executive. Chmn., dir. Chesapeake and Ohio R.R., Cleve. Office: Chesapeake and Ohio RR PO Box 6419 Cleveland OH 44101*

WATKINS, JOHN BARR, III, pharmacologist, toxicologist, educator; b. Jacksonville, Fla., Apr. 25, 1953; s. John Barr and Ella Weems (Hawkins) W. B.A. cum laude, Wake Forest U., 1975; M.S., U. Wis., 1977, Ph.D., 1979. Lab. asst. Methodist Hosp., Jacksonville, Fla., summers 1972-75; NIH trainee U. Wis. Sch. Pharmacy, Madison, 1975-79, U. Kasn. Med. Ctr., Kansas City, 1979-82; asst. prof. pharmacology and toxicology Ind. U. Sch. Medicine, Bloomington, 1982—. Marie Christine Kohler fellow U. Wis., 1978-79; Biomed. Research Support grantee, 1982-83; PMA Found. grantee, 1984-86; Am. Diabetes Assn. grantee 1985-86; diplomate Am. Bd. Toxicology. Mem. Am. Chem. Soc., Soc. Toxicology, Am. Soc. Pharmacology and Exptl. Therapeutics, Sigma Xi, Rho Chi. Republican. Presbyterian. Contbr. articles to profl. publs. Office: Ind Univ Med Scis Program Bloomington IN 47405

WATKINS, LLOYD IRION, university president; b. Cape Girardeau, Mo., Aug. 29, 1928; s. Herman Lloyd and Lydia Mina (Irion) W.; m. Mary Ellen Caudle, Aug. 14, 1949; children—John Lloyd, Joseph William, Robert Lawrence. B.S. in Edn., Southeast Mo. State U., 1949; M.S., U. Wis.-Madison, 1951, Ph.D., 1954; D.Hum. (hon.), U. Dubuque, 1978. Tchr., Jackson High Sch., Mo., 1948-50; asst. prof. Moorhead State U., Minn., 1954-56; asst. to assoc. prof. Ohio U., Athens, 1956-66; exec. v.p. Idaho State U., Pocatello, 1966-69; pres. Iowa Assn. Pvt. Colls., Des Moines, 1969-73; pres. West Tex. State U., Canyon, 1973-77, Ill. State U., Normal, 1977—; dir. Bloomington Fed. Savs. and Loan. Contbr. articles to profl. jours.; speaker at convs. Bd. dirs. ISU Found., 1977—; trustee Mennonite Coll. Nursing, Bloomington, 1982—. Recipient Baker Research award Ohio U., 1962. Mem. Am. Assn. State Colls. and Univs. (bd. dirs. 1982—), N.Am. Council Internat. Assn. Univ. Pres. (chmn. 1984—). Presbyterian. Lodge: Rotary (Normal, Ill.). Avocations: reading; fishing; gardening; walking. Home: 1000 W Gregory St Normal IL 61761 Office: Illinois State Univ 308 Hoveyn Hall Normal IL 61761

WATKINS, MARY ANN, rehabilitation institute official; b. Beckley, W.Va., Dec. 20, 1936; d. Gorman Harry and Mabel Hattie (Gray) Shultz; children—Doreen, Cheryl, Rhonda, Michael, Richard. Student Wayne State U., U. Mich. Cert. healthcare materials mgmt. profl. Sec., Beckley Hosp., 1955-56, Appalachian Regional Hosp., Beckley, 1964-67, Pincecreat Hosp., Beckley, 1962-64; sec. social service, personnel, purchasing asst., purchasing dir., materials mgmt. dir. Rehab. Inst., Detroit, 1968—. Chairperson patient care adv. com. Detroit Receiving Hosp.; dir. Med. Center Citizens Dist. Council. Mem. Southeastern Mich. Hosp. Purchasing Assn. (pres.), Am. Hosp. Purchasing Assn., Health care Materials Mgmt. Assn. (sec. Mich. chpt.), Nat. Hosp. Purchasing Assn. Democrat. Baptist. Home: 4611 Chrysler Detroit MI 48201 Office: 261 Mack Detroit MI 48201

WATKINS, MARY JOCQUELINE, city official, real estate salesperson; b. McKeesport, Pa., Mar. 20, 1940; d. Roy Lee and Clidie Lee (Fordham) Hamlin; m. Lucious Delmas East, Apr. 25, 1959 (dec. 1971); children—Robert Maurice, Arona Michelle; m. Al Roy Watkins, July 16, 1975 (div. 1976). B.A., Ind. Christian U., 1970; postgrad. in bus. adminstrn., Ind. U. Northwest Gary, 1972—. Lic. real estate salesperson, Ind. Head cashier J.C. Penney's, Hammond, Ind., 1965-66; lab. technician, nuclear medicine technician St. Margaret's Hosp., Hammond, 1966-70; housing dir. Urban League of N.W. Ind., Gary, 1975-78; cons. Nat. Urban League/HUD, Chgo. region, 1978; adminstrv. asst. Opportunities Industrialization Center, Inc., Gary, 1978-79, chmn. bd., 1981—; community services specialist Bur. Census, Dept. Commerce, Chgo. region, 1979-80; chief property disposition officer, demolition specialist City of Gary, 1980-84, mgr. housing projects, 1984—; lay mem. urban zoning and housing interim study com. Ind. Gen. Assembly, 1976. Sec., v.p. Ind. Fedn. Housing Counselors, 1976-77; vice chmn. Ind. OIC/A State Council, 1982—; Century Club chmn. Calumet council Boy Scouts Am.; 1st v.p. Horace Mann Neighborhood Orgn.; mem. Supervisory com. Gary Mcpl. Fed. Credit Union. Recipient appreciation plaques Gary OIC, 1978, 80, 81, appreciation awards Sch. City of Gary, 1982, OIC/A award, 1982, award Boy Scouts Am., 1980, 81, 82, 83, cert. of recognition Opportunities Acad. Mgmt. Tng., 1982; cert. office of personnel Fed. Govt., 1979. Mem. Bus. and Profl. Women (pres. 1985-86), Ind. Fedn. Bus. and Profl. Women (state membership com.). Office: 824 Broadway Gary IN 46402

WATKINS, SHIRLEY MARRIE, retail store executive; b. Milw., Oct. 9, 1952; d. George Allen and Senora (Sargent) Smith; m. Leslie Kendrick Watkins, Feb. 22, 1975. B.S. in Elem. Edn., Carroll Coll., 1974. Cert. elem. tchr., Wis. Res. group mgmt. trainee Sears, Roebuck & Co., Milw., 1975-76, res. group asst. div. mgr., 1976-77, res. group div. mgr., 1977-80, asst. mdse. mgr., St. Louis, 1980-84, customer convenience mgr., 1984-85. Democrat. Baptist. Avocations: aerobic dancing, reading, bridge. Home: 17107 Elm Dr Hazel Crest IL 60429

WATKINS, WYNFRED CLIFFORD, retail executive; b. Toledo, Ohio, Apr. 15, 1946; s. Clifford Garnet and Blanche Marie (Marr) W.; m. Brenda Joyce Sparks, Mar. 18, 1967; children—Suzan Marie, Tara Edwina. Student Bowling Green State U., 1965-66. Dept. mgr. J.C. Penney Co., Lansing, Mich., 1969-71, dept. mgr., Toledo, 1971-74, dist. merchandise mgr., Toledo, 1974-76, Pitts., 1977-80, regional merchandiser, Pitts., 1976-77, store mgr., Youngstown, Ohio, 1980-84, Florence, Ky., 1984—, coll. recruiter, Toledo, 1972-74, retail career speaker, 1972-74; retail mgmt. advisor Owens Tech. Coll., Toledo, 1973-75. Youth dir. Union Baptist Ch., Youngstown, 1982-84. Mem. NAACP. Democrat. Lodge: Kiwanis. Avocation: tennis. Home: 7475 Kingston View Ct Cincinnati OH 45230 Office: J C Penney Co Inc 6000 Florence Mall Rd Florence KY 41042

WATNEY, WILLARD LYNN, geologist, researcher, administrator; b. Mason City, Iowa, Mar. 6, 1948; s. Willard Vincent and Lucille Mae (Radloff) W.; m. Karen Louise Amundson, Dec. 28, 1970; 1 child, Chris. A.A., No. Iowa Area Community Coll., 1968; B.S. with distinction, Iowa State U.-Ames, 1970, M.S., 1972; Ph.D., U. Kans., 1985. Petroleum geologist Chevron, U.S.A., New Orleans, 1972-76; research assoc. Kans. Geol. Survey, Lawrence, 1976-81, chief geologic investigations, 1981—; cons. petroleum geologist, Lawrence, 1981—; cons. Univs. Field Staff Internat., AID. Contbr. articles to sci. jours. Mem. Am. Assn. Petroleum Geologists, Soc. Econ. Paleontologists and Mineralogists, Soc. Profl. Well Log Analysts, Soc. Petroleum Engrs., Kans. Geol. Soc., Phi Kappa Phi, Sigma Chi. Avocations: snow and water skiing; computer programming. Office: Kans Geol Survey 1930 Constant Ave Campus W Lawrence KS 66046

WATSON, DAVID PARKER, corporation executive; b. Chgo., Dec. 6, 1943; s. David O. and Beatrice (Libbey) W.; m. Maureen Coffee, Feb. 22, 1968; children—Courtney, Spencer. B.S. in History, U. Wis.-Madison, 1966, B.B.A., M.B.A. in Acctg., 1971. C.P.A., Wis. Auditor, Arthur Young & Assoc., Chgo., 1972-73; pres. Hillmark Corp., Madison, Wis., 1973—. Contbr. articles to profl. jours. Mem. various coms. Republican Orgn. Wis., Madison, 1980—; mem. ad hoc com. State Wis. Govs., 1980; bd. regents, 1984—; bd. dirs. Wis. Inkeepers, Milw., 1982-83. Served to capt. USAF, 1966-70. Fellow Am. Inst. C.P.A.s, Wis. Inst. C.P.A.s, Hotel-Motel Assn., Am. Hotel-Motel Assn. (bd. dirs. 1984—), Nat. Apt. Assn., Wis. Apt. Assn. Roman Catholic. Avocations: Boating; walking; reading. Home: 3600 Ritchie Rd Verona WI 53593

WATSON, GARY L., newspaper executive. Pres., pub. Cin. Enquirer. Office: Cin Enquirer 617 Vine St Cincinnati OH 45201*

WATSON, KENNETH FREDERICK, molecular biologist, consultant; b. Pasco, Wash., Feb. 17, 1942; s. Walter Irvin and Isabel Danforth (Frost) W.; m. Janice Pauline Wilson, June 6, 1964; children—Heidi Michelle, Julie Monique. A.B., N.W. Nazarene Coll., 1964; Ph.D., Oreg. State U., 1969. Postdoctoral fellow Columbia U., N.Y.C., 1969-71, instr. human genetics, 1971-72; research fellow Internat. Agy. for Cancer Research, Berlin, 1972-73; from asst. prof. to prof. U. Mont., Missoula, 1973-83; head Lab. Viral Genetics, Abbott Labs, Abbott Park, Ill., 1983—, cons., 1981-83; cons. Life Scis. Inc., St. Petersburg, Fla., 1976-83, Molecular Genetic Resources, Tampa, Fla., 1983—. Bd. regents N.W. Nazarene Coll., 1980-83. Faculty research award Am. Cancer Soc., 1976-81; research grantee USPHS, 1973-83, Am. Cancer Soc., 1976-82. Mem. Am. Soc. Microbiology, N.W. Nazarene Coll. Alumni Assn. (bd. dirs. 1973-83, pres. 1980-83), Sigma Xi. Avocations: fly fishing, skiing, jogging. Office: Abbott Labs Dept 93D/AP9A Abbott Park IL 60064

WATSON, LELAND (LEE) HALE, theatrical lighting designer; b. Charleston, Ill., Feb. 18, 1926; s. Dallas V. and Hazel Emma (Dooley) W.; B.A., State U. Iowa, 1948; M.F.A., Yale U., 1951. Instr., Utah State Agrl. Coll., Logan, 1948-49, Bklyn. Coll., 1952, 54; with CBS-TV, N.Y.C., 1951-55, Polakov Studio Scenic Design, N.Y.C., 1957-62; mem. faculty U. Houston, 1968-71; asst. prof. C.W. Post Coll., L.I.U., 1971-75; guest lectr. Syracuse (N.Y.) U., 1974-75; asso. prof. Purdue U., 1975-81, prof., 1981—; lighting designer Cin. Ballet, 1977-80, also for 27 Broadway prodns. including Diary of Anne Frank, View From the Bridge; numerous Off-Broadway prodns. including The Blacks, Suddenly Last Summer; lighting designer for operas in N.Y.C., Houston, Phila., Balt., Vancouver, Wash., Milw., also dance companies and Seattle World's Fair, 1962; designer sets for 6 Broadway prodns., also prodns. at Washington Arena, indsl. shows. Served with AUS, 1944-45. Decorated Purple Heart; recipient Obie award for Machinal, Show Bus. award 1959. Mem. United Scenic Artists, Internat. Alliance Theatre and Stage Employees, U.S. Inst. Theatre Tech. (pres. 1980-82), Soc. Brit. Theatre Designers, Internat. Assn. Lighting Designers, Am. Soc. Lighting Dirs., Illuminating Engrng. Soc., Am. Theatre Assn., Phi Beta Kappa. Methodist. Co-author: Theatrical Lighting Practice, 1954; columnist, sr. contbg. editor Lighting Dimensions mag.; contbr. articles magazines. Address: 2400 State St Lafayette IN 47903

WATSON, RALPH EDWARD, physician, educator; b. Cin., Apr. 4, 1948; s. John Sherman and Evelyn (Moore) W.; m. Demetra Rencher, Sept. 9, 1972; children—Ralph, Jr., Monifa. B.S., Xavier U., 1970; M.D., Mich. State U., 1976. Diplomate Am. Bd. Internal Medicine. Intern, U. Cin. Med. Ctr., 1976-77; resident in internal medicine U. Cin. Med. Ctr., 1977-79, asst. clin. prof., internal medicine, 1980—. Mem. Nat. Med. Assn., Cin. Acad. Medicine, Ohio State Med. Assn., ACP, Am. Soc. Internal Medicine, Xavier U. Alumni Assn. (bd. govs.). Home: 10597 Toulon Dr Cincinnati OH 45240 Office: Bethesda Oak Profl Ctr 629 Oak St #606 Cincinnati OH 45206

WATSON, RUSSELL JEROME, psychology educator, researcher; b. Martins Ferry, Ohio, Mar. 25, 1948; s. Russell Jerome and Margaret Marie (Diehl) W.; m. Melissa Marie Stillman, July 1, 1978. B.A., North Park Coll., 1970; M.A., Northeastern Ill. U., Chgo., 1972; Ed.D., No. Ill. U., DeKalb, 1982. Instr. speech/communications Glenbrook North High Sch., Northbrook, Ill., 1970-73; instr. psychology Wheaton-Warrenville High Sch., Wheaton, Ill., 1973—; newscaster NBC-TV Chgo., Sta. WMAQ, Everyman talk show, 1978—; instr. psychology Coll. DuPage, Glen Ellyn, Ill., 1982—; dir. biofeedback Hinsdale (Ill.) Hosp. and Sanitarium, 1982—. Mem. Am. Psychol. Assn., Am. Soc. Clin. Hypnosis. Lutheran. Office: Dept Learning and Devel No Ill U DeKalb IL 60115

WATTS, JOHN RANSFORD, university administrator; b. Boston, Feb. 9, 1930; s. Henry Fowler Ransford and Mary Marion (Macdonald) W.; A.B., Boston Coll., 1950, M.Ed., 1965; M.F.A., Yale U., 1953; Ph.D., Union Grad. Sch., 1978; m. Joyce Lannom, Dec. 20, 1975; 1 son by previous marriage, David Allister. Prof., asst. dean Boston U., 1958-74; prof., dean of fine arts Calif. State U., Long Beach, 1974-79; dean and artistic dir. The Theatre Sch. (Goodman Sch. of Drama), DePaul U., Chgo., 1979—; gen. mgr. Boston Arts Festivals, 1955-64; adminstr. Arts Programs at Tanglewood, 1966-69; producing dir. Theatre Co. of Boston, 1973-75. Chmn., Mass. Council on Arts and Humanities, 1968-72; dir., v.p. Long Beach (Calif.) Pub. Corp. for the Arts, 1975-79; mem. theatre panel, Ill. Arts Council, 1981—. Served with U.S. Army, 1953-55. Mem. Mass. Ednl. Communications Commn., Am. Theatre Assn., Nat. Council on Arts in Edn., Met. Cultural Alliance, League Chgo. Theatres, Phi Beta Kappa. Club: St. Botolph (Boston), Cliffdwellers (Chgo.). Office: 804 W Belden Chicago IL 60614

WATTS, MEREDITH WAYNE, JR., political science educator; b. Bloomington, Ill., Apr. 14, 1941; s. Meredith Wayne and Leah Lucille (Stiegman) W.; B.A., Lawrence U., 1962; postgrad. No. Ill. U., 1962-63; M.A., Northwestern U., 1964, Ph.D., 1967; children—David, Christopher. Asst. prof. polit. sci. U. Wis., Milw., 1966-67, 70-74, assoc. prof., 1974-78, prof., 1978—, chmn. dept., 1982—, asst. to chancellor, 1977-79, asst. chancellor, 1979-81. Active United Way, Future Milw. Bd. assocs. Ctr. Biopolit. Research. Served with USAF, 1967-70. Decorated Air Force Commendation medal; Nat. Ctr. Edn. in Politics fellow, 1964; NSF grantee, 1965-66. Mem. Am. Polit. Sci. Assn., Midwest Polit. Sci. Assn., Internat. Polit. Sci. Assn., Internat. Soc. Research on Aggression, Internat. Communication Assn., Soc. Psychophysiol. Research, Internat. Soc. Human Ethology. Author: (with others) Legislative Roll Call Analysis, 1966, State Legislative Systems, 1968; Gender and Biopolitics, 1983; contbr. articles to profl. jours.; editorial bd. Politics and the Life Scis. Home: 2113 E Jarvis St Milwaukee WI 53211 Office: U Wis Milwaukee WI 53201

WATTS, PHILLIP BAXTER, exercise physiologist; b. Charlotte, N.C., Apr. 15, 1951; s. Curtis Pinkney and Vera (Thornburg) W.; m. Annette Diane Glover, May 27, 1973. B.S., E. Carolina U., 1973, M.A., 1974; Ph.D., U. Md., 1980. Cert. instr. Venture Wilderness Inst. Research asst. Sports Medicine Ctr., U. Md., 1975-77; exercise physiologist No. Mich. U., 1978—, dir. Exercise Physiology Lab., 1978—, dir. Cardiac Rehab. Program, 1979—; cons. Great Lakes Sports Acad. No. Mich. U. Faculty Research grantee, 1980-81, 84, 85. Mem. Am. Coll. Sports Medicine (cert. exercise specialist), Sigma Xi. Home: 535 Rock St Marquette MI 49855 Office: Health Phys Edn and Recreation Dept No Mich U Marquette MI 49855

WATTS, ROBERT ALLAN, publisher, lawyer; b. Adrain, Mich., July 4, 1936; s. Richard P. and Florence (Hooker) W.; m. Emily Stipes, Aug. 30, 1958; children—Benjamin H., Edward S., Thomas J. Student DePauw U., 1954-55; B.A., U. Ill., 1959, J.D., 1961. Bar: Ill. 1961. Assoc. Stipes Publishing Co., Champaign, Ill., 1962-67, ptnr., editor, 1967—. Treas., Planned Parenthood, 1976-80; mem. Pres.'s Council, U. Ill.; pres. Friends of Library, U. Ill., 1980-82; bd. dirs. local United Way, 1972-81. Mem. Ill. Bar Assn., U. Ill. Found., Nat. Acad. Arts (bd. dirs. 1983—). Republican. Clubs: Champaign Country; Saugatuck Yacht (Douglas, Mich.). Home: 1009 W University St Champaign IL 61821 Office: Stipes Publishing Co 10-12 Chester St Champaign IL 61820

WAX, DAVID M., orchestra executive. Gen. mgr. Minn. Symphony Orch. Office: Minn Symphony Orch 1111 Nicollet Mall Minneapolis MN 55403*

WEAR, GARY DOUGLAS, public health official; b. Sycamore, Ill., Sept. 26, 1942; s. Marvin Walter Wear and Norma Eileen (Behler) Riske; m. Susan Kathleen Carlson, Mar. 17, 1967 (div.); 1 dau., Jennifer Sue; m. Patricia Anne Crawford, July 14, 1984. Student U.S. Naval Acad., 1963-66; A.S., Rock Valley Coll., 1968; B.A., Judson Coll., 1969; M.A., Western Mich. U., 1974. Quality control engr. Automatic Electric Co., Genoa, Ill., 1966-67; personnel mgr. Flexfab, Inc., Hastings, Mich., 1969-72; dir. Occupational Health Center, Kalamazoo, 1972-74; tng. dir. Mead Corp., Dayton, 1975-76; personnel and labor relations mgr. Office of Substance Abuse Services-Mich. Dept. Pub. Health, Lansing, 1976—; instr. Davenport Coll., Grand Rapids, 1977-79. Instr., ARC, Lansing, 1981-83. Served with USN, USMC, 1961-66. Alumni Assn. scholar, 1973; grantee: Nat. Inst. on Alcohol Abuse and Alcoholism, 1972-74, HHS, 1981. Mem. Profl. Assn. Diving Instrs. (master scuba diver trainer 1983), Am. Soc. for Pub. Adminstrn., Internat. Personnel Mgmt. Assn., Mich. Pub. Health Assn., Mensa. Club: Capitol City Dive (Lansing). Home: 135 W Walnut St Hastings MI 49058 Office: Office Substance Abuse Services Mich Dept Pub Health 3500 N Logan St Lansing MI 48909

WEATHERHEAD, ALBERT JOHN, III, business executive; b. Cleve., Feb. 17, 1925; s. Albert J. and Dorothy (Jones) W.; A.B., Harvard U., 1950, postgrad., 1951; m. Celia Scott, Jan. 1, 1975; children—Dwight S., Michael H., Mary H. Prodn. mgr. Yale & Towne, Stamford, Conn., 1951-54, Blaw-Knox, Pitts., 1954-56; plant mgr. Weatherhead Co., Cleve., 1957-59, gen. mgr., 1959-61, v.p., gen. mgr., 1962-66, gen. sales mgr., 1962-63, v.p. mfg., 1964-66; v.p., dir. Weatherhead Co. of Can., Ltd. 1960-63, pres., chief exec. officer, dir., 1964-66; treas. Weatherchem Corp., 1971-82, pres., dir., 1971—; dir. Weatherhead Co., Protane Corp., L.P.G. Leasing Corp., Leasepac Corp., Leasepac Can., Ltd., Creative Resources, Inc. Mem. Harvard U. com. on univ. resources; trustee Case Western Res. U., mem. resources com., council on research involving human subjects, mem. Univ. Sch. alumni council, trustee Univ. Sch.; mem. vis. com. Ohio U., Athens; v.p. nat. adv. com. Rollins Coll., Winter Park, Fla.; adv. trustee Pinecrest Sch., Ft. Lauderdale, Fla.; mem. capital campaign steering com. Laurel Sch.; trustee Vocat. Guidance and Rehab. Services, Hwy. Safety Found., Arthritis Found.; v.p. Weatherhead Found.; bd. dirs. New Directions Inc., Glenwillow, Ohio; col. CAF. Served with USAAF, 1943-46. Mem. Am. Newcomen Soc., Beta Gamma Sigma (hon.). Clubs: Union (Cleve.); Country (Shaker Heights, Ohio); Ottawa Shooting (Freemont, Ohio); Ocean (Delray, Fla.); Everglades (Palm Beach, Fla); Codrington (Oxford, Eng.). Author: The New Age of Business, 1965. Home: 19601 Shelburne Rd Shaker Heights OH 44118 Office: 2222 Highland Rd Twinsburg OH 44087

WEATHERS, K. RUSSELL, hospital foundation exec., mayor; b. Harrison County, Mo., June 21, 1942; s. William Kenneth and Mildred Grace (Fitzpatrick) W.; B.S., U. Mo., 1964; m. Judith C. Cain, Aug. 12, 1961; children—Vince S., Kent A., Joy L. Tchr. vocat. agr. North Platte High Sch., Dearborn, Mo., 1964-66, Centralia (Mo.) Public High Sch., 1966-67; staff asst. and mem. services staff Farmland Industries, Inc., Kansas City, Mo., 1967-69, formerly dir. services div., exec. dir. mem. public relations staff, 1980-84; exec. dir. Liberty (Mo.) Hosp. Found., 1984—. Asst. scoutmaster Boy Scouts Am., 1975; chmn. ch. bd. Liberty Christian Ch., 1974-75; co-chmn. Mo-Am. Royal Night, 1980—; chmn. Am. Royal 4-H Conf.; mem. council Kansas City Tomorrow, 1980-81; v.p. Ag Hall of Fame, 1980—; v.p. Earnest Shepherd Youth Center, 1976-78, chmn., 1978-80; bd. dirs., vice chmn. Mo. 4-H Found., 1979—; chmn. Liberty Econ. and Preservation Commn., 1980-81; mem. Liberty City Council, 1977-81; mayor City of Liberty, 1981—; Liberty chmn. County Criminal Justice Center Bond Issue, 1980—; mem. Kansas City FFA adv. com.; chmn. 4-H Found., 1983—; mem. sponsoring com. Nat. Future Farmers Am.; mem. Tri-County Mental Health Adv. Bd., Mo. Gov.'s Com. on Community Block Grant and Devel., Clay County Elected Ofcls. Commn., Nat. Ag Day Com., Northland Devel. Com. mem. ARC Blood Doner's Gallon Club, 1980. Recipient Disting. Service award Nat. FFA; hon. awards State Young Farmers Assn. Okla., Iowa, Mo., Kans., Colo., Nebr. Mem. Guest Relations Assn., Mo. Mcpl. League (revenue sharing commn. 1983—, Westgate div. coms.), U. Mo. Alumni Assn., C. of C. Liberty (office site com.), Northland C. of C. (govt. relations com. 1982-83). Club: Internat. Agribus. (v.p. 1979-80, pres. 1980-81). Mem. Christian Ch. Home: 1907 Clay Dr Liberty MO 64068 Office: PO Box 7305 Kansas City MO 64116

WEATHERSBY, GEORGE BYRON, publishing executive; b. Albany, Calif., Dec. 9, 1944; s. Byron and Fannie A. W.; B.S., U. Calif., Berkeley, 1965, M.S., 1966, M.B.A., 1967; S.M., Harvard U., 1968, Ph.D., 1970; m. Linda Rose W., June 29, 1979; children—Deborah Jane, Geoffrey Byron. Assoc. dir. analytical studies U. Calif., Berkeley, 1969-72, also dir. Ford Found. research program, mem. faculty, 1969-72; spl. asst. to U.S. Sec. of State, Washington, 1972-73; dir. research Nat. Commn. on Financing Higher Edn., Washington, 1973-74; assoc. prof. mgmt. Harvard U., 1974-78; commr. higher edn. state of Ind., 1977-83; pres., chief operating officer Curtis Pub. Co., Indpls., 1983—; chmn. bd. Otis

Conner Cos., 1984—, Curtis Media Co., 1984—, Curtis Internat. Ltd., 1984—, Ednl. Skills Corp., 1985—; dir. N.Am. Rubber, Inc. Bd. dirs. U. So. Ind., 1985—. Calif. Regents scholar, 1963-65; NSF fellow, 1966-67; AEC fellow, 1966-67; Kent fellow, 1967-70; White House fellow, 1972-73; named 1 of 100 Outstanding Young Leaders in Higher Edn., Change Mag., 1978, One of Outstanding Young Men of 1976. Mem. Am. Council Edn. Ops. Research Soc. Am., Inst. Mgmt. Scis., Econometrica. Republican. Author books including: Financing Postsecondary Education in the U.S., 1974; Colleges and Money, 1976; editor Change mag., 1981-84; contbr. numerous articles to profl. jours., 1967—; cons. editor Jour. Higher Edn., 1974—. Office: Curtis Pub Co 1000 Waterway Blvd Indianapolis IN 46202

WEATHERSBY, JOSEPH BREWSTER, civil rights administration executive; b. Cin., Nov. 23, 1925; s. Albert and Gertrude (Renfro) W.; m. Louberta Gray, Oct. 28, 1950 (div. Oct. 13, 1980). B.B.A., Salmon P. Chase Coll., 1950; M.Div., Berkley Div. Sch., 1960. Ordained priest Episcopal Ch. Rector St. Mary's Episcopal Ch., Detroit, 1961-68, St. Clement's Episcopal Ch., Inkster, Mich., 1973-74; dir. Saginaw Urban Ministry, Mich., 1969-72, 74-75; dist. exec. Mich. Dept. Civil Rights, Saginaw, 1976—. Served with USMC, 1944-46, PTO. Mem. Alpha Phi Alpha. Democrat. Home: 4392-2 Lakeside Place East Saginaw MI 48603

WEAVER, ARTHUR LAWRENCE, physician; b. Lincoln, Nebr., Sept. 3, 1936; s. Arthur J. and Harriet Elizabeth (Walt) W.; B.S. (Regents scholar) with distinction, U. Nebr., 1958; M.D., Northwestern U., 1962; M.S. in Medicine, U. Minn., 1966; m. JoAnn Versemann, July 6, 1980; children—Arthur Jensen, Anne Christine. Intern U. Mich. Hosps., Ann Arbor, 1962-63; resident Mayo Grad. Sch. Medicine, Rochester, Minn., 1963-66; practice medicine specializing in rheumatology and internal medicine, Lincoln, 1968—; mem. staff Bryan Meml. Hosp., chmn. dept. rheumatology, 1976-78, 82-85, vice-chief staff, 1984—; mem. courtesy staff St. Elizabeths Hosp., Lincoln Gen. Hosp.; mem. cons. staff VA Hosp.; chmn. Juvenile Rheumatoid Arthritis Clinic, 1970—; assoc. prof. dept. internal medicine U. Nebr., Omaha, 1976—; med. dir. Lincoln Benefit Life Ins. Co., Nebr., 1972—; mem. exam. bd. Nat. Assn. Retail Druggists; mem. adv. com. Coop. Systematic Studies in Rheumatic Diseases III. Bd. dirs. Nebr. chpt. Arthritis Found., 1969—; trustee U. Nebr. Found., 1974—. Served to capt., M.C., U.S. Army, 1966-68. Recipient Outstanding Nebraskan award U. Nebr., 1958, also C.W. Boucher award; Philip S. Hench award Rheumatology, Mayo Grad. Sch. Medicine, 1966; diplomate Am. Bd. Internal Medicine, Am. Bd. Rheumatology. Fellow A.C.P. (Nebr. council 1983—); mem. Am., Nebr. socs. of internal medicine, Am. Rheumatism Assn. (com. on rheumatologic practice 1983—, pres.-elect Central region 1983-84, pres. Central region 1984-85; exec. com. 1985—), Nebraska Rheumatism Assn., AMA, Nebr. Med. Assn., Lancaster County Med. Soc., Mayo Grad. Sch. Medicine Alumni Assn., Arthritis Health Professions Assn. (com. on practice 1984—), Nat. Soc. Clin. Rheumatology. Phi Beta Kappa, Sigma Xi, Alpha Omega Alpha, Pi Kappa Epsilon, Phi Rho Sigma. Republican. Presbyterian. Editorial bd. Nebr. Med. Jour., 1982—; contbr. articles to med. jours. Home: 3600 S 40th St Lincoln NE 68506 Office: 2121 S 56th St Lincoln NE 68506

WEAVER, BRUCE EVERETT, osteopathic anesthesiologist; b. Amarillo, Tex., Mar. 5, 1935; s. James C. and Mayvi H. (Smith) W.; m. Barbara Ann Gillespie, June 24, 1961; children—James Laurie, Margaret Carey, Alicia Brooke. B.A., Baylor U., 1957; D.O., Kansas City Coll. of Osteo Medicine, 1969. Diplomate Nat. Bd. Examiners for Osteo Physicians and Surgeons; cert. Am. Osteo Bd. of Anesthesiology. Intern, Lakeside Osteo. Hosp., Kansas City, Mo., 1969-70; resident in anesthesiology, 1970-71; resident Kansas City Coll. of Osteo Medicine (Mo.), 1971-72, asst. prof., 1972-73; attending anesthesiologist St. Luke's Hosp., Kansas City, 1973-74, chief of cardioaccular anesthesiology, 1974-78; chief of cardiovascular anesthesia Boone County Hosp., Columbia, Mo., 1978—, vice chmn. dept. of anesthesia, 1981—. Mem. nat. faculty for advanced cardiac life support Am. Heart Assn., 1982—, mem. bd. dirs. Boone div. pres.-elect Kansas City chpt., 1978-79; deacon Baptist Ch., 1980—. Served with U.S. Army, 1957-59. Fellow Am. Osteo Coll. of Anestesiology (gov., v.p. 1982-83); mem. Am. Osteo Assn., Mo. Assn. Osteo. Physicians and Surgeons, Midwest Osteo. Soc. of Anesthesiologists, Am. Soc. Anesthesiologists, MidAm. Regional Council for Emergency Rescue, Republican. Home: 13 Countryshire Estates Route 5 Columbia MO 65202 Office: Boone Hosp Ctr 1502 E Broadway St PO Box 7041 Columbia MO 65205

WEAVER, CHARLES LYNDELL, JR., architect, consultant, hat company executive; b. Canonsburg, Pa., July 5, 1945; s. Charles Lyndell and Georgia Lavelle (Gardner) W.; m. Ruth Marguerite Uxa, Feb. 27, 1982; 1 son, Charles Lyndell III. B.Arch., Pa. State U., 1969; cert. in assoc. studies U. Florence (Italy), 1968. Registered architect, Pa., Md., Mo. With Celento & Edson, Canonsburg, Pa., part-time 1966-71; project architect Meyers & D'Aleo, Balt., 1971-76, corp. dir., v.p., 1974-76; ptnr. Borrow Assocs.-Developers, Balt., 1976-79, Crowley/Weaver Constrn. Mgmt., Balt., 1976-79; pvt. practice architecture, Balt., 1976-79; cons., project mgr. U. Md., college Park, 1979-80; corp. cons. architect Bank Bldg. & Equipment Corp., Am., St. Louis, 1980-83; dir. archtl. and engring. services Ladue Bldg. & Engring. Inc., St. Louis, 1983-84; v.p., sec. Graphic Products Corp.; vis. Alpha Rho Chi lectr. Pa. State U., 1983; panel mem. Assn. Univ. Architects Conv., 1983. Project bus. cons. Jr. Achievement, 1982-85; mem. cluster com., advisor Explorer Program, 1982-85. Recipient 5 brochure and graphic awards Nat. Assn. Indsl. Artists, 1973; 1st award Profl. Builder/Am. Plywood Assn., 1974; Honor award Balt. chpt. AIA, 1974; Better Homes and Gardens award Sensible Growth, Nat. Assn. Home Builders, 1975; winner Ridgely's Delight Competition, Balt., 1976. Mem. BBC Credit Union (bd. dirs. 1983-85), Vitruvius Alumni Assn., Penn State Alumni Assn., Alpha Rho Chi (nat. treas. 1980-82). Home and Office: 1318 Shenandoah Saint Louis MO 63104

WEAVER, CLARK BRANSON, lawyer; b. Sterling, Ill., Apr. 28, 1934; s. Arthur Eugene and Lois (Clark) W.; m. Janet F. Holzman, Aug. 31, 1957; children—Kim, Tracey, Clark Jr. B.Sc., Ohio State U., 1957; J.D., Salmon P. Chase Coll., 1965. Bar: Ohio 1966. Claims personnel mgr. Allstate Ins. Co., Ohio, 1959-69; ptnr. Lands Kroner & Weaver, Cleve., 1969-82, Weaver, Kolick, Georgeadis & Ernewein Co. L.P.A., Cleve., 1982—. Mem. Strongsville Civil Service, Ohio, 1979-80, Strongsville Charter Commn., 1981; mem. Strongsville City Council, 1981—. Served with U.S. Army, 1957-59. Fellow Ohio Bar Assn. Fedn.; mem. Cleve. Bar Assn., Ohio Bar Assn., Parma Bar Assn. (trustee 1978-80). Republican. Presbyterian. Avocations: model trains; bridge; tennis; golf; volleyball. Home: 11780 River Ridge Rd Strongsville OH 44136 Office: Weaver Kolick Georgeadis & Ernewein Co LPA 910 Citizens Bldg Cleveland OH 44114

WEAVER, JAMES JOHN, utility company executive, consultant, professional racing car driver; b. Prestonsburg, Ky., June 5, 1947; s. Ralph Elmer and Susie (Crum) W. Student Purdue U., 1966-67, 73, 82, Ind.-Purdue U., 1968, Iowa State U., 1979, Community Coll. Denver, 1980; M.Mgmt., J. L. Kellogg Grad. Sch. Mgmt., Northwestern U., 1984. System ops. coordinator Ind. and Mich. Electric Co., Ft. Wayne, Ind., 1975-78; system ops. supr. Tri-State Generation and Transmission Assn. Inc., Thornton, Colo., 1978-79, system ops. and procedures coordinator, asst. project mgr. energymgmt. project, 1979-80; gen. mgr. Jasper County (Ind.) Rural Electric Membership Corp., 1980—; cons. mgmt.; dir. United Utility Supply Coop., Louisville; mem. Nat. Inst. Coop. Edn. faculty Purdue U., 1982. Mem. Ind. Rural Electric Membership Corp. Mgrs. Assn. (pres. 1984-85), Rensselear (Ind.) C. of C., DeMotte C. of C. (bd. dirs. 1981-82). Republican. Presbyterian. Clubs: Curtis Creek Country (Rensselaer); Rotary, Sports Car Am. Home: Rural Route 6 Box 259A Rensselear IN 47978 Office: PO Box 129 Rensselear IN 47978

WEAVER, PHILLIP JAY, municipal recreation director; b. Topeka, Dec. 28, 1957; s. Norman Gene and Doris Arleen (Schnee) W.; m. Lynda Ruth Swanson, June 16, 1984. B.A. in Bus. Adminstrn., Bethany Coll., 1980. Recreation dir. Hugoton Recreation Commn., Kans., 1980—. Mem. Stevens County Council on Aging, Hugoton, 1984. Mem. Nat. Recreation & Parks Assn., Kans. Recreation & Parks Assn. Republican. Methodist. Avocations: golf; softball; skiing; basketball; spectatorsports. Home: 113 W 2nd Box 416 Hugoton KS 67951 Office: Recreation Commission 211 S Madison Hugoton KS 67951

WEAVER, RICHARD L., II, educator; b. Hanover, N.H., Dec. 5, 1941; s. Richard L. and Florence B. (Grow) W.; m. Andrea A. Willis, 1965; children—R. Scott, Jacquelynn M., Anthony K., Joanna C. A.B., U. Mich., 1964, M.A., 1965; Ph.D., Ind. U., 1969. Teaching asst. Ind. U., 1965-68; instr. U. Mass., 1968-69, asst. prof., 1969-74; assoc. prof. speech communication Bowling Green State U., 1974-79, prof., 1979—; vis. prof. U. Hawaii, Manoa, 1981-82. Named Bowling Green's Best Prof., 1980. Mem. Internat. Communication Assn., Speech Communication Assn., Central States Speech Assn., Internat. Soc. Gen. Semantics, Ohio Speech Communication Assn., World Communication Assn., Internat. Platform Assn., Midwest Basic Course Dirs. Conf. Author: (with Saundra Hybels) Speech/Communication, 1974, 2d edit. 1979; Speech/Communication: A Reader, 1975, 2d edit. 1979; Speech/Communication: A Student Manual, 1976, 2d edit., 1979; Understanding Interpersonal Communication, 1978, 2d edit., 1981, 4th edit., 1987; (with Raymond K. Tucker, Cynthia Berryman-Fink) Research in Speech Communication, 1981; Foundations of Speech Communication: Perspectives of a Discipline, 1982; Speech/Communication: Skills, 1982; Understanding Public Communication, 1983; Understanding Business Communication, 1985; Understanding Speech Communication Skills, 1985; Readings in Speech Communication, 1985; Communicating Effectively, 1986; contbr. articles to profl. jours. Home: 9583 Woodleigh Ct Perrysburg OH 43551 Office: Dept Interpersonal and Pub Communication Coll Arts and Scis Bowling Green State U Bowling Green OH 43403

WEAVER, STANLEY B., state senator; b. Harrisburg, Ill., May 23, 1925; student Mich. State Coll., U. Ill.; grad. Ind. Coll. Mortuary Sci.; m. Mary Smith; children—Blake, Sherry. Partner, Weaver-Henderson Funeral Home, Urbana, Ill.; former mem. Ill. Ho. of Reps.; now mem. Ill. Senate; mayor Urbana, 1957-69. Active various civic orgns. Served with USAAF, World War II. Republican: Address: 309 State Capitol Springfield IL 62706

WEBB, CECIL EDWARD, financial executive; b. Memphis, Aug. 26, 1943; s. William Clarence and Beatrice Kathryn Webb; m. Linda Darlene Stephens, Apr. 7, 1968; children—Heidi, Cecil II. B.S., Calif. State U.-Fresno, 1966; M.B.A., Andrews U., 1978. C.P.A. Calif. Asst. bus. mgr. Fresno Adventist Acad., Calif., 1974-76; mgr. student fin. Andrews U., Berrien Springs, Mich., 1976-78; auditor Adventist Health System West, Glendale, Calif., 1978-80; v.p. fin. Hinsdale Hosp., Ill., 1980—; dir. Health Ventures, Inc., Hinsdale; chmn. bd. Hinsdale Med. Enterprises. Bd. dirs. Ctr. Health Promotion, Hinsdale, 1983—. Served with U.S. Army, 1967-69. Mem. Am. Inst. C.P.A.s, Calif. Soc. C.P.A.s, Ill. Soc. C.P.A.s (vice chmn. minority recruitment com. 1983—), Healthcare Fin. Mgmt. Assn. Seventh Day Adventist. Lodge: Rotary. Office: Hinsdale Hosp 120 N Oak St Hinsdale IL 60521

WEBB, FREDERICK WINFIELD, JR., restaurant owner, consultant; b. Portland, Oreg., Dec. 16, 1950; s. Frederick Winfield and Helen Frances (Potter) W. B.A., Gustavus Adolphus Coll., 1973. Tchr., coach Woodbury Jr. High Sch., Minn., 1973-75; owner, operator My Pie, Original Pancake House, Winfield Potter's, Rupert's Am. Cafe and Nightclub, Coco Lezzone's, Mpls., 1975—; owner Webb Enterprises Inc., Golden Valley, Minn., 1975—; restaurant mgmt. cons. NCR 2160, Easy-Bar Liquor System and Payroll Systems, 1981—. Patentee in field. Com. mem. Mr. Basketball Com. Minn., Mpls., 1982—. Recipient First Decade Alumni award Gustavus Adolphus Coll., 1983; named one of Outstanding Young Men of Am., 1983. Mem. Nat. Restaurant Assn., 2160 Users Group, Mpls. C. of C. Republican. Avocations: golf; football; basketball; skiing. Office: Webb Enterprises Inc 5410 Wayzata Blvd Golden Valley MN 55416

WEBB, JAMES B., utility company executive, consultant; b. St. Louis, Mo., July 20, 1944; s. James C. Webb and Rose M. (Davis) Reid; m. Margaret Dawson, June 17, 1967; children—Ann, James. B.Mus.Ed., Lincoln U., 1967. Dist. sales mgr. Southwestern Bell Telephone Co., St. Louis, Mo., 1976-77, gen. mktg. supr., 1977-79, div. staff mgr. planning, 1983—; div. mgr. market mgmt. AT&T, Morristown, N.J., 1979-81, dir. mgr. ventures-market mgmt., 1981-83; vis. prof. Nat. Urban League, N.Y.C., 1976-79. Author: (with others) Financial Support Plan for Schools and Non-Profit Organizations, 1984. Bd. dirs. Child Day Care, Inc., St. Louis, 1978, Consolidated Neighborhood Services, Inc., St. Louis, 1985—, Carver House, Inc., St. Louis, 1985; chmn. bd. adminstrn. Morristown Methodist Ch., 1983. Recipient Achievement award Urban League, 1978, Community Recognition award Carver House, Inc., 1979, Dash-Thompson Achievement award AT&T, 1979, Disting. Leadership and Service award United Negro Coll. Fund, 1983. Fellow Harry S. Truman Library Inst. (hon.), Phi Mu Alpha Sinfonia. Home: 12807 Pleasant Ridge Ct Chesterfield MO 63017 Office: Southwestern Bell Telephone Co One Bell Ctr Room 11-L1 Saint Louis MO 63101

WEBB, KENNETH FRANK, heating and air conditioning equipment company executive; b. St. Louis, Oct. 23, 1942; s. Lawrence Joseph and Helen M. (Klenke) W.; m. Margaret Mary Mehrtens, Feb. 4, 1967; children—Brian, Kim, Andrew. B.A., St. Louis U., 1983; M.A., Webster U., 1984. Product application mgr. Singer Co., St. Louis, 1975-77, tech. communications mgr., 1977-82; tech. communication mgr. Snyder Gen. Corp., Red Bud, Ill., 1982—. Served with USCG, 1961-69. Home: 5432 Stonehurst Dr Mehlville MO 63139 Office: Snyder Gen Corp 401 Randolph Red Bud IL 62278

WEBB, MYRNA RUTH, urban redevelopment administrator; b. Detroit, Oct. 27, 1942; s. Hudson and Harvey Mae (Cole) W.; 1 child, Jonathan Hudson. B.B.A., Detroit Inst. Tech., 1974; postgrad. Wayne State U., 1977-78. Adminstrv. sec. to pres. Motown Record Corp., Detroit, 1968-71; sales rep. Artie Fields Prodn. Co., Detroit, 1971-72; community service worker City of Detroit, 1972; supr. U.S. Census Bur., Detroit, 1972-73; planning supr. Met. Detroit AFL-CIO, 1974-75; adminstr. Med. Ctr. Citizens Dist. Council, Detroit, 1975—. Mem. adminstrv. service com. Comprehensive Health Services of Southeastern Mich., 1978—; trustee Hutzel Hosp., Detroit, 1978-85; vice chmn. Detroit Sub-Area Adv. Council, 1976-79; mem. Detroit Cable Communications Commn., 1982—. Named Outstanding Citizen, City of Detroit, 1980. Mem. Engring. Soc. Detroit, Leadership Detroit I, Nat. Assn. Housing and Redevel. Ofcls. (bd. dirs. Mich. chpt. 1977-83). Lutheran. Club: Progressive Motowners (Detroit) (founding pres. 1982—). Home: 4615 Chrysler Dr Detroit MI 48201

WEBB, O(RVILLE) LYNN, physician, pharmacologist, educator; b. Tulsa, Aug. 29, 1931; s. Rufus Aclen and Berla Ophelia (Caudle) W.; m. Joan Liebenheim, June 1, 1954 (div. Jan. 1980); children—Kathryn, Gilbert, Benjamin. B.S., Okla. State U., 1953; M.S., U. Okla., 1961; Ph.D. in Pharmacology, U. Mo., 1966, M.D., 1968. Diplomate Nat. Bd. Med. Examiners, Am. Bd. Family Practice. Research assoc. in pharmacology U. Okla., 1959-61; research fellow NIH, 1962-66; instr. pharmacology U. Mo., Columbia, 1966-68, asst. prof., 1968-69; intern, U. Mo. Med. Center, 1968-69; family practice, New Castle, Ind., 1969—; mem. staff Henry County Meml. Hosp., New Castle, 1974—; guest prof. pharmacy and pharmacology Butler U. Coll. Pharmacy, Indpls., 1970-75; owner, dir. Carthage Clinic, 1975—; county physician, jail med. dir. Henry County, Ind., 1976—. Recipient Cert. of merit in Pharmacol. and Clin. Med. Research, 1970; Med. Student Research Essay award Am. Acad. Neurology, 1968. Fellow Am. Acad. Family Physicians; mem. AMA (ann. award recognition 1975—), Ind. State Med. Assn., Am. Coll. Sports Medicine, AAAS, N.Y. Acad. Sci., Am. Soc. Contemporary Medicine and Surgery, Festival Chamber Music Soc. (bd. dirs. Indpls. 1981—), Sigma Xi. Clubs: Columbia, Skyline (Indpls.). Lodge: Elks. Author: (with Blissitt and Stanaszek, Lea and Febiger) Clinical Pharmacy Practice, 1972; contbr. articles to profl. jours. Home and office: 420 S Main New Castle IN 47362

WEBB, THOMAS IRWIN, JR., lawyer; b. Toledo, Ohio, Sept. 16, 1948; s. Thomas Irwin and Marcia Davis (Winters) W.; m. Linde Kay Hurst, Aug. 14, 1971; 1 dau., Elisabeth Hurst. B.A., Williams Coll., 1970; postgrad. Boston U., 1970-71; J.D., Case Western Res. U., 1973. Bar: Ohio. Assoc. Shumaker, Loop & Kendrick, Toledo, 1973-79, ptnr., 1979—; dir. Comml. Aluminum Cookware Co., York Oldsmobile, Inc. Council mem. Village of Ottawa Hills, Ohio, 1978—; bd. dirs. Kiwanis Youth Found. of Toledo, Inc. Mem. ABA, Ohio Bar Assn., Toledo Bar Assn., Order of Coif. Republican. Methodist. Clubs: Crystal Downs Country, Toledo (trustee 1984—), Inverness; Williams Club of N.Y. Avocations: skiing; rowing; sailing. Office: Shumaker Loop & Kendrick 1000 Jackson Toledo OH 43624

WEBB, WILLIS EVERETTE, casket company executive; b. Oxford, Miss., Feb. 27, 1947; s. Charles C. and Hazel (Banks) W.; m. Anna Yvonne Edwards, Dec. 6, 1970; 1 dau., Michelle Monee. B.B.A., Chgo. State U., 1976. Sales coordinator Borg & Warner Health Products, Chgo., 1968-71; territory mgr. Amoco Oil Co., Chgo., 1971-76, advt. analyst, 1976-77, heavy oils merchandiser, 1977-80, pricing specialist, 1980-82, petroleum product merchandiser, 1982-83; pres. Ill. Casket Co., Chgo., 1983—. Author: The Story of Our Song, 1983. Bd. dirs. sta. WSSD community radio station, Chgo., 1977—; mem. nominating com. Dollars and Sense Mag. awards banquet, Chgo., 1977; mem. community bd. The Neighborhood Inst., Chgo., 1978. Mem. United Ch. of Christ. Office: Ill Casket Co 700 E 111th St Chicago IL 60628

WEBER, ALBAN, association executive, lawyer; b. Chgo., Jan. 29, 1915; s. Joseph A. and Anna (von Placheck) W.; A.B., Harvard U., 1935, LL.B., 1937; m. Margaret Kenny, Dec. 29, 1951; children—Alban III, Peggy Ann, Gloria, Brian. Admitted to Ill. bar, 1938; mem. firm Weber & Weber, 1937-41; gen. counsel Fgn. Liquidation Commn., State Dept., 1946; trust officer Lake Shore Nat. Bank, Chgo., 1952-55; univ. counsel Northwestern U., Evanston, Ill., 1955-70; pres. Fedn. Ind. Ill. Colls. and Univs., Evanston, 1971-84. Benjamin Franklin Fund, Inc., 1965-75, Northwestern U. Press, Inc., 1965-70; chmn. State Assn. Execs. Council, 1981. Pres. N.E. Ill. council Boy Scouts Am., 1970-71. Alderman, City of Chgo., 1947-51. Served to comdr. USNR, 1941-45, rear adm., 1974. Recipient Silver Beaver award Boy Scouts Am.; Meritorious Service award Loyola U., 1978; Edn. for Freedom award Roosevelt U., 1984. Mem. Nat. Assn. Coll. and Univ. Attys. (pres. 1962), Harvard Law Soc. Ill. (pres. 1984), Navy League (pres. Evanston council 1967-70, Univ. Risk Mgmt. Assn. (pres. 1965), Univ. Ins. Mgrs. (pres.). Clubs: Law, Economics, Harvard, Executives, Chicago Yacht (Chgo.); White Lake Golf, White Lake Yacht. Lodge: Kiwanis (lt. gov.). Home: 1500 Chicago Ave Apt 411 Evanston IL 60201 Office: Schuyler Roche & Zwirner State Bank Bldg Evanston IL 60201

WEBER, ARNOLD R., university president; b. N.Y.C., Sept. 20, 1929; s. Jack and Lena (Smith) W.; m. Edna M. Files, Feb. 7, 1954; children—David, Paul, Robert. B.A., U. Ill., 1951; M.A., M.I.T., 1958, Ph.D. in Econs., 1958. Instr., then asst. prof. econs. MIT, Cambridge, 1955-58; mem. faculty U. Chgo. Grad. Sch. Bus., 1958-69, prof. indsl. relations, 1963-69; asst. sec. for manpower Dept. Labor, 1969-70; exec. dir. Cost of Living Council, 1970; spl. asst. to Pres. Nixon, 1971; Glady C. and Isidore Brown prof. urban and labor econs. U. Chgo., 1971-73; provost Carnegie-Mellon U., 1973-80, dean, prof. labor econs. and pub. policy, 1973-80; pres. U. Colo., Boulder, 1980-85, Northwestern U., Evanston, Ill., 1985—; vis. prof. Stanford U., 1966; assoc. dir. Office of Mgmt. and Budget, Exec. Office of Pres., 1970-71; cons. to numerous govtl. agys. and orgns. Author: (with G.P. Schultz) Strategies for the Displaced Worker, 1966. Contbr. articles to profl. jours. Served to lt. USCGR, 1952-54, PTO. Ford Found. faculty research fellow, 1964-65. Mem. Indsl. Relations Research Assn., Am. Econ. Assn., AAUP, Phi Beta Kappa. Jewish. Home: 639 Central St Evanston IL 60201 Office: 633 Clark St Evanston IL 60201

WEBER, DORIS ETHEL, children's literature specialist; b. St. Louis, Jan. 25, 1911; d. George Clarence and Jesse Theresa (Myers) Wehmeier; m. Orville O. Weber, Sept. 25, 1934; children—Joan Julia, Richard C. B.A., Washington U., St. Louis, 1932; postgrad. U. Mo.-St. Louis. Librarian dept. edn. Main St. Louis Pub. Library, 1963-68; children's lit. specialist, librarian middle sch., cons. library services Mary Inst., St. Louis, 1969-79; area librarian, mem. book selection com. Library Services Ctr., St. Louis Pub. Schs., 1980-81; freelance writer, reviewer, critic books for children and young people St. Louis Globe-Democrat, 1978—; organizer Books Fairs, Mary Inst.-Country Day Schs., 1973-79; mem. Loughborough Internat. Seminars Children's Lit., 1973—; chmn. program Nat. Assn. Ind. Schs. Conf., Chgo., 1977; dir. UN Assn./Webster Coll. Yr. of Child Festival, St. Louis, 1979. Mem. Friends Internat. Bd. Books Young People, Greater St. Louis Library Club (past pres.), Suburban Sch. Library Assn., Mo. Assn. Sch. Librarians, Archeol. Inst. Am., St. Louis Council World Affairs, Alpha Chi Omega. Presbyterian. Address: 42 Frontenac Estates Saint Louis MO 63131

WEBER, FRANK EARL, periodontist; b. New Albany, Ind., Aug. 30, 1932; s. Frank H. and Elizabeth W.; divorced; children—Gregory K., Frank H. B.A., U. Louisville, 1954, D.D.S., 1962; M.S., U. Ky., 1955; postdoctoral specialty Ind. U., 1962-64. Grad. asst. U. Ky., Lexington, 1954-55; ins. underwriter Am. States Ins. Co., Indpls., 1958-60; grad. asst. Ind. U. Sch. Dentistry, 1962-64; practice dentistry specializing in periodontics, Indpls., 1964—; faculty practitioner Ind. U. Sch. Dentistry, 1978—. Contbr. articles to profl. jours. Served with USAF, 1956-58. USPHS scholar, 1959-62; Daman Runyon Cancer Research grantee, 1959-62. Fellow Royal Soc. Health, Acad. Dentistry Internat., Acad. Gen. Dentistry; mem. ADA, Ind. Dental Assn., Indpls. Dist. Dental Soc., Internat. Platform Assn., Nat. Fedn. Ind. Bus., Am. Endodontic Soc., Westside Dental Study Club, Chgo. Dental Soc., Fedn. Advanced Ethical Hypnosis, Acad. Oral Medicine (Merit award 1962), Am. Legion, Omicron Kappa Upsilon, Phi Kappa Phi, Phi Delta (pres. 1961-62) Beta Delta, Omicron Delta Kappa, Delta Sigma Delta (life), Sigma Phi Epsilon (life). Avocations: piloting; golfing; fishing; hunting. Office: Northwest Medical Center 3500 Lafayette Rd Indianapolis IN 46222

WEBER, GEORGE RUSSELL, microbiologist; b. Novinger, Mo., Dec. 29, 1911; s. William and Celia Iciphene (Helton) W.; B.S., U. Mo., 1935; Ph.D., Iowa State Coll., 1940; spl. evening student George Washington U., 1944-45, U. Cin., 1948-49; m. Margaret Carrington Cable, Apr. 19, 1947; children—Jeanine Marie, Michael Elwin. Asst. chemist, expt. sta. U. Mo., 1935-36; teaching fellow in bacteriology Iowa State Coll., 1936-38, asst., 1938-39, teaching asst., 1939-40, instr., 1940-42; bacteriologist USPHS, 1946, sr. asst. scientist, 1947, scientist, 1949, chief sanitizing agents unit, 1949-53; research microbiologist Nat. Distillers & Chem. Corp., 1953-63, research project leader, 1963-73, sr. research microbiologist, 1973-75, research asso., 1975, ret., 1977; lectr. in biology U. Cin., 1969-70. Dir. Ky. br. Nat. Chinchilla Breeders of Am., 1955-57, research chmn., 1958-64; pres. Greater Cin. Chinchilla Breeders Assn., 1957-58, 63-64. Served from 1st lt. to maj. AUS, 1942-46; lt. col. AUS (ret.). Recipient War Dept. citation for control of food poisoning and infection, 1946. Fellow Am. Public Health Assn., Royal Soc. Health (Eng.); mem. AAAS, Am. Soc. Microbiology, Am. Inst. Biol. Scis., Ohio Acad. Sci., N.Y. Acad. Scis., Am. Soc. Profl. Biologists (v.p. 1957-58), Smithsonian Assos., Inst. Food Technologists, Research Soc. Am., Res. Officers Assn. U.S. (exec. council Cin. chpt. 1963-65, chpt. pres. 1966-67), Ret. Officers Assn., Mil. Order World Wars, others, Sigma Xi, Phi Kappa Phi. Patentee animal feed, biol. metal corrosion control. Home: 1525 Burney Ln Cincinnati OH 45230

WEBER, JOHN HERBERT, stone company executive; b. Kitchener, Ont., Can., Oct. 15, 1939; s. Alson M. and A. Loraine (Snyder) W.; m. Donna June Wilson, July 5, 1969; children—Deborah Lynne, David John, John-Michael. B.Sc. in Bus. Adminstrn., Bluffton (Ohio) Coll., 1963. Office mgr. Superior Stone Co., Ltd., Kitchener, 1963-67, v.p., dir., 1967-74, pres., 1974—. Pres., Inter-County Baseball Assn., 1978-80, Kitchener Sports Assn., 1979-80; coach, mgr., mem. exec. bd. boys hockey and baseball programs, Ont. Recipient Past. Pres. award Inter County Baseball, 1982. Mem. Monument Builders N.Am. (v.p. 1981-85), Ont. Monument Builders Assn. (Past Pres. award 1982), Am. Inst. Commemorative Art. Mennonite. Home: 124 Strathcona Crescent Kitchener ON N2B 2W9 Canada Office: Superior Stone Co Ltd 528 Victoria St N Kitchener ON N2H 5G1 Canada

WEBER, MILAN GEORGE, ret. army officer, mgmt. cons.; b. Milw., Oct. 15, 1908; s. Adam George and Frances (Lehrbaumer) W.; B.S., U.S. Mil. Acad., 1931; grad. Coast Arty. and Air Def. Sch., 1938, Nat. War Coll., 1952; m. Mary Agnes Keller, Sept. 2, 1931; 1 son, Milan George. Commd. 2d lt. U.S. Army, 1931, advanced through grades to col., 1944; various army command and staff exec. positions, Philippine Islands, 1932-36, Hawaii, 1938-41, Ft. Monroe, Va., 1936-38; anti-aircraft exec., hdqrs. 3d and 9th armies, U.S., Europe, 1943-45; mem. Gen. Patton's staff, 1944, War Dept. Gen. Staff, 1945-48; mil. adviser to Argentine govt., 1949-51; global strategic planner Joint Chiefs of Staff, 1952-54; comdr. Missile Defense of Norfolk and Hampton Roads, 1954-55; chief of staff advisory group, Japan, 1955-58; dept. comdr. Air Def. Region, Ft. Meade, Md., 1958-60, ret., 1960; mgr. electronic counter measures Loral Electronics Corp., N.Y.C., 1960-62; product mgr. electronic counter measures Hallicrafters Corp. (name changed to Northrop Corp.), Chgo., 1962-64; partner Weber Assos., Mgmt. Cons., Deerfield, Ill., 1964-69; pres. dir. Milan G. Weber Associates, Inc., Deerfield, 1969—; mgmt. cons. to various bus. firms, 1964—; acquisitions and mergers cons. to various corps., 1969—. Chmn. Great Lakes Ecology Assn. Ill., 1974—; chmn. Citizens Com. Honesty in Govt., 1969—; mem. Ill. Drivers Safety Adv. Com., 1975—, Deerfield Library Bd., 1976—, Deerfield Caucus Com., 1978—, Deerfield Energy Adv. Council, 1981—. Decorated Legion of Merit, Bronze Star, Commendation medal with oak leaf cluster. Mem. Assn. Old Crows, West Point Soc. Chgo., Internat. Platform Assn., Assn. Grads. U.S. Mil. Acad., Electronic Counter Measures Assn., Great Lakes Ecology Assn. of the Mil. Clubs: Army Navy, Army Navy Country. Contbr. articles on anti-aircraft arty., air def. and mil. strategy to profl. publs. author of joint strategic capabilities plan; author weekly column on environment, 1977—.

Home: 611 Colwyn Terr Deerfield IL 60015 Office: PO Box 81 Deerfield IL 60015

WEBER, THOMAS LOUIS, financial executive; b. Detroit, July 13, 1941; s. Louis J. and Margaret A. (Harding) W.; m. Mary Martha McGlaughlin, July 18, 1964; children—John, Tim, Meg, Tracy. B.A., U. Detroit, 1964; postgrad. Wayne State U., 1968. Asst. br. mgr. Nat. Bank Detroit, 1964-68; system analyst Chrysler Corp., Detroit, 1968-70; controller Ex-Cell-O Corp., Detroit, 1970-72; v.p. fin. ODL, Inc., Zeeland, Mich., 1972—. Trustee Holland Hosp., 1982—, Holland Ednl. Found., 1984—. Mem. Holland C. of C. Roman Catholic. Avocations: running, sailing. Home: 27 W 25th St Holland MI 49423

WEBER, VIN, congressman; b. Slayton, Minn., July 24, 1952; ed. U. Minn., 1974; m. Jeanie Lorenz, 1979. Pres., Weber Pub. Co., Slayton; co-pub. Murray County Herald; congressional press sec., 1974-75; senatorial sr. aide, 1979-80; mem. 97th-99th Congresses from 2d Dist. Minn. Republican. Address: 318 Cannon House Office Bldg Washington DC 20515

WEBSTER, GEOFFREY EVERETT, lawyer; b. Dalhart, Tex., Jan. 19, 1948; s. Gale Eugene and Mary Nell (Harbour) W.; m. Mary Kay Javaras, Sept. 19, 1971 (div. July 1976); Rose Marie Ellis, July 22, 1977; children—Noah Geoffrey, Benjamin Lee. B.S., Ohio State U., 1970; J.D. magna cum laude, Capital U., 1975. Bar: Ohio 1975. Tchr., McAdams Elem. Sch., New Carlisle, Ohio, 1970-71; clk. G.W. Ankney, Jr. Columbus, Ohio, 1971-73, Ohio atty. gen., Columbus, 1975-76; asst. atty. gen. State of Ohio, Columbus, 1975-76; chief counsel Dept. Pub. Welfare, Columbus, 1977-79; sole practice, Columbus, 1979—; chief counsel Ohio Acad. Nursing Homes, Columbus, 1980—. Mem. Victorian Village Commn., Columbus, 1984—. Served with U.S. Army, 1970-76. Mem. ABA, Columbus Bar Assn., Nat. Health Lawyers Assn., Assn. Trial Lawyers Am., Order of Curia. Republican. Avocations: Reading, gardening. Home: 80 W Starr Ave Columbus OH 43201 Office: 17 S High St Suite 1070 Columbus OH 43215

WEBSTER, JEFFREY LEON, graphic designer; b. Idaho Falls, Idaho, Nov. 23, 1941; s. Leon A. and Marjory M. (McAllister) W.; student Sch. Associated Arts, St. Paul, 1962; m. Judith Kess, Apr. 17, 1965; children—Eric J., Marjorie P. Sci. illustrator Mayo Clinic, Rochester, Minn., 1963-66; layout artist Brown & Bigelow, St. Paul, 1966; graphic designer U. Minn., Mpls., 1966-67, U. Calgary (Alta., Can.), 1967-68; sr. artist Control Data Corp., St. Paul, 1968-70; mem. Idaho State U. Meml. Lectureship Com.; graphic designer Idaho State U., 1970-78; owner, operator studio, Harmony, Minn.; design, advt. and mktg. cons. Mem. Idaho Civic Symphony Bd. Recipient Profl. citation Library Congress, 1976. Artist pub. ednl. exhibits. Home and Office: Route 1 Harmony MN 55939

WEBSTER, WILLIAM L., state government official. Atty. gen. State of Mo., Jefferson City. Office: Office of the Atty Gen PO Box 899 Jefferson City MO 65702*

WEDER, DONALD ERWIN, manufacturing executive; b. Highland, Ill., Aug. 18, 1947; s. Erwin Henry and Florence Louise (Graham) W.; student U. Ill., 1965-66; B.S. summa cum laude, Bradley U., 1969; m. Phyllis Ann Styron; children—Erwin Michael, Andrew Styron, David August, Ann Marie. Pres. Highland Mfg. & Sales Co., 1977—, also dir.; pres. Seven W Enterprises, 1977—, also dir.; pres. LEXCO, 1977—, IMUTEK, 1977—, Pullex, 1977—; dir. 1st Nat. Bank Highland, Ill. Served to capt., inf. AUS, 1969-71. Mem. Zeta Phi, Phi Kappa Phi. Republican. Lodge: Kiwanis. Home: 621 Main St Highland IL 62249 Office: 1111 6th St Highland IL 62249

WEDER, ERWIN HENRY, corp. exec.; b. Highland, Ill., Dec. 13, 1904; s. August and Julia (Brunner) W.; student public schs.; m. Florence Louise (Graham), July 19, 1938; children—Mary Kay, Dona Lee, Donald Erwin, Wanda May, Janet Marie. Office work Highland Dairy Farms, 1923-25; detective Fla. East Coast Hotel Co., 1927-29; auto salesman, broker L.E. Anderson Co., 1930-32; salesman Metal Goods Corp., 1933-41; product devel., sales mgr., pres., then chmn. bd. Highland Supply Corp., 1941—; pres., then chmn. bd., sales and products mgr. Highland Products, Inc., 1948—, Highland Mfg. Co., 1944—; mng. partner, sales and products mgr. Highland Mfg. & Sales Co., 1952—; pres., then chmn. bd. Weder Farms, Inc., 1950—, Quality Motors, Inc., 1946—; sr. ptnr., then chmn. bd. Seven W. Enterprises, 1958—; chmn. bd. Life Extender Corp.; dir. Inland Valley Engring. owner, operator Six Bar X ranch, Jordan, Mont. Mem. St. Louis Media Club. Republican. Clubs: DX-5; Mo. Athletic; Capitol Hill; Masons. Home: 1304 Washington St Highland IL 62249 Office: 6th and Zschokke Sts Highland IL 62249

WEDO, SONDRA LEE, jeweler; b. Cleve., Oct. 25, 1934; d. Forest Lee and Edna Virginia (Childs) Jacobs; m. Angelo Wedo, Oct. 19, 1958; children—Gregory, Michelle, Anthony, Valerie, Victoria. Quality control supr. Ferry Cap and Set Screw Co., Cleve., 1964-67; owner, tchr. San Dee's Mud Hut, Brook Park, Ohio, 1973-77; supr. quality control Ford Motor Co., Brook Park, 1977-81; payroll personnel staff mem. Servomation Corp., Brook Park, 1982-84; owner, pres. Starfire, Brook Park, 1984—; columnist Brook Park News, 1968. Author weekly column Seen N' Heard, 1982-83. Named First Lady, City of Brook Park, 1971-81; recipient 1st Place award for ceramic eggs Ceramic Hobbyist Guild, 1972. Democrat. Roman Catholic. Avocations: golf; sewing; reading; listening to positive thinking tapes. Home: 14069 Park Dr Brook Park OH 44142

WEED, BRENDA CAROL, pharmacist; b. Indpls., May 21, 1956; d. Gene Vinton and Barbara Jacqueline (Boyd) Black; m. Stanley Eugene Weed, Dec. 29, 1979; 1 child, Burton Gene. B.S. in Pharmacy, Butler U., 1980, M.S. in Pharmacology, 1985. Registered pharmacist, Ind. Pharmacist Am. Assn. Retired Persons, Indpls., 1980-82, Kroger Co., Frankfort, Ind., 1982-83; pharmacist, coordinator clin. services Metro Health, Indpls., 1983—. Author (thesis) Nifedipine Effect on Isoproteranol-theophylline Induced Myocardial Lesions, 1985. Mem. Ind. Pharm. Assn., Tri Kappa, Kappa Kappa Gamma. Republican. Avocation: equestrian competition. Home: 8210 E 725 N Brownsburg IN 46112

WEED, EDWARD REILLY, marketing executive; b. Chgo., Jan. 25, 1940; s. Cornelius Cahill and Adelaide E. (Reilly) W.; student Fordham U., 1959-61, Loyola U., 1961-62; m. Lawrie Irving Bowes, Feb. 2, 1969. Account exec. Leo Burnett Co., Chgo., 1961-71; pres. GDC Ad Inc., corporate officer advt. and sales promotion Gen. Devel. Corp., Miami, Fla., 1971-74; v.p., account supr. D'Arcy Mac Manus & Masius, Chgo., 1975; group v.p. mktg. Hart Schaffner & Marx (Hartmarx), Chgo., 1975-82; pres. Hart Services, Inc., 1975-82; v.p. mktg. Tishman, 1983—; dir. First Nat. Bank So. Miami. Trustee, Latin Sch. Found., 1976—; bd. dirs. North Ave. Day Nursery, 1969-73, Santa for Poor, 1975—, Off-the-Street, 1982—, Chgo. Boys' and Girls' Clubs, 1983—. Served with Ill. N.G. Republican. Roman Catholic. Clubs: Tavern, Cliff Dwellers, Saddle and Cycle. Office: 300 S Riverside Plaza Chicago IL 60606

WEESE, HARRY M., architect; b. Evanston, Ill., June 30, 1915; s. Harry E. and Marjorie (Mohr) W.; student Yale U., 1936-37; B.Arch., Mass. Inst. Tech., 1938; m. Kate Baldwin, Feb. 8, 1945; children—Shirley, Kate, Marcia. Fellow Cranbrook Acad. Art, 1938-39; prin. firm Baldwin & Weese, Kenilworth, Ill., 1940-42; with firm Skidmore, Owings & Merrill, Chgo., 1946-47; ind. practice as Harry Weese & Assos., Chgo., 1947—; archtl. cons. fgn. bldgs. program Dept. State, 1973-76. Mem. Pres.'s Citizens' Adv. Com. Recreation and Natural Beauty, 1966-69, Pres.'s Citizens' Adv. Com. Environ. Quality, 1969-71, Gov. Ill. Commn. on Orgn. Ill. Dept. Transp., 1972-74; mem. Nat. Council on Arts, 1974-80; trustee Latin Sch., Chgo. Served as lt. (s.g.) USNR, 1941-45. Fellow AIA (pres. Chgo. chpt. 1975); mem. NAD. Clubs: Arts, Comml., Yacht (Chgo.). Principal projects include Am. Embassy, Ghana; Crown Center Hotel, Kansas City; restoration of Adler-Sullivan Auditorium, Chgo., 1st Bapt. Ch., Columbus, Ind.; metro transit systems various cities; Fed. Correctional Center, Chgo.; Arena Stage Theatre, Washington; Performing Arts Center, Milw.; Performing Arts/Conv.-Exposition Center, Grand Rapids, Mich.; Wolf Point Landings, Chgo.; 200 S. Wacker Bldg., Chgo.; Time and Life Bldg., Chgo.; Am. Embassy Housing, Tokyo; Fed. Triangle Master Plan, Washington. Office: Harry Weese & Assocs 10 W Hubbard St Chicago IL 60610

WEGSCHEID, DARRIL, state senator, manufacturing company executive; b. Watertown, Minn., July 14, 1944; s. Edmund Frank and Anne Marie (Vorderbruggen) W.; m. Carol J. Amberg, Feb. 13, 1965; children—Timothy, Jennifer. B.A. in Math., Coll. of St. Thomas, 1966; M.S. in Ops. Research, U. Pa., Phila., 1968. Systems analyst 3M Co., St. Paul, 1968-72, info. systems mgr., 1972—; mem. Minn. Senate, 1983—. Bd. dirs. Ind. Sch. Dist. 196 Bd., Apple Valley, Minn., 1977-82. Mem. Inst. Mgmt. Sci. (treas. Upper Midwest chpt. 1974-75), Ops. Research Soc. Am. (treas. Upper Midwest chpt. 1974-75), Valley Democrat Farmer Labor Club (chmn. 1975-1977), Delta Epsilon Sigma. Roman Catholic. Office: Minn State Senate Dist 37 Room 309 State Capitol St Paul MN 55155

WEICKER, JACK EDWARD, educational administrator; b. Woodburn, Ind., June 23, 1924; s. Monald Henry and Helen Mae (Miller) W.; A.B., Ind. U., 1947, M.A. (James Albert Woodburn fellow, All-Univ. fellow), 1951; m. Janet Kathryn Thompson, May 29, 1946; children—John H., Kathryn Ann, Jane Elizabeth, Emily Jo. Tchr. history and English, Harrison Hill Sch., Ft. Wayne, Ind., 1947-48, South Side High Sch., Ft. Wayne, 1951-61; counselor, asst. prin. South Side High Sch., 1961-63, prin., 1963—. Mem. Ind. State Scholarship Commn., 1969-77; mem. exec. com. Midwest regional assembly Coll. Entrance Exam. Bd., 1974-77, chmn. nominating com., 1976-77, mem. nat. nominating com., 1979; mem. Midwest Regional Coll. Access Services Com., 1982-84. Chmn., Easter Seal Telethon, Allen County Soc. Crippled Children and Adults, 1982, 83. Recipient award for meritorious service Ball State U., 1980; Outstanding Prin. of Yr. award Ind. Secondary Sch. Adminstrs. Assn., 1981; Rotary Paul Harris fellow, 1985. Mem. Ft. Wayne Prins. Assn., Nat. Assn. Secondary Sch. Prins. (conf. speaker New Orleans 1985), Ind. Secondary Sch. Adminstrs., PTA (life), Phi Beta Kappa, Phi Delta Kappa, Phi Alpha Theta. Mem. Christian Ch. (Disciples of Christ) (moderator of bd. trustees 1975-79). Clubs: Ft. Wayne Rotary (dir. 1973-76, 79—, pres.-elect 1981-82, pres. 1982-83), Quest (dir. 1979-81), Fortnightly (v.p. 1984-85, pres. 1985-86), (Ft. Wayne). Author: (with others) Indiana: The Hoosier State, 1959, 63; (monographs) Due Process and Student Rights/Responsibilities: Two Points of View, 1975; Back to Basics: Language Arts, 1976; College Entrance Exams—Friend or Foe?, 1981; How the Effective Principal Communicates, 1983; Readin', Writin', and Other Stuff, 1984. Home: 5200 N Washington Rd Fort Wayne IN 46804 Office: 3601 S Calhoun St Fort Wayne IN 46807

WEIDNER, TIMOTHY ARNOLD, office equipment and supply dealership executive; b. Racine, Wis., Mar. 28, 1950; s. Richard O. and Lucille (Ruelle) W.; m. Janice Lynn Morgenson, July 22, 1972; children—Sara Ann, Matthew Douglas, Margarette Lucille. B.S., U. Wis.-Kenosha, 1972. Sales rep. N.M.L., Milw., 1973-75; mgr. CFM Inc., Racine, 1975-80, sales rep. AB Dick Products, Racine, 1980-81; gen. mgr., v.p. Bus. Communications, Racine, 1981—. Active RAMAC, Racine; com. mem. Racine Redevel. Corp., 1984. Served with UAAR, 1970-76. Mem. Nat. Machine Dealers Assn. Republican. Lutheran. Lodge: Kiwanis. Home: 2015 Grange Ave Racine WI 53403 Office: Bus Communications 337 Main St Racine WI 53403

WEIGEL, ROBERT LEWIS, JR., printing co. exec.; b. St. Louis, Sept. 7, 1944; s. Robert Lewis and Georgene Nancy (Walbancke) W.; student St. Petersburg Jr. Coll., 1963-64; m. Linda Lee Ross, July 29, 1982; children—Michael, Cathi, Danielle, Larry David. Sec.-treas. Creative Interiors, Clearwater, Fla., 1967-69; office mgr. Consol. Hotel Equipment, Clearwater, 1969; store mgr. Am. Nat. Stores, St. Louis, 1970-72; sec.-treas. Weigel Screen Process, Eureka, Mo., 1972-76, pres., 1976—. Served with U.S. Army, 1964-66. Mem. Nat. Space Inst., Screen Printing Assn., Eureka C. of C. (dir.). Episcopalian. Home: 5 Dreyer PO Box 133 Eureka MO 63025 Office: 141 S Central Eureka MO 63025

WEILAND, DONALD GERARD, lawyer, educator; b. Evanston, Ill., Jan. 29, 1954; s. Francis John and Frances Rita (Summers) W.; m. Sonia I. Rodriguez, Sept. 17, 1983. Student Am. U., 1974; B.A., Ill. Wesleyan U., 1976; postgrad. comparative law study Coll. William and Mary, Exeter, Eng., 1979; J.D., John Marshall Law Sch., 1980. Bar: Ill. 1980, U.S. Dist. Ct. (no. dist.) Ill. 1980, U.S. Ct. Appeals (7th cir.) 1980. Law clk. Ill. Supreme Ct., Bloomington, 1980-81; instr. law John Marshall Law Sch., Chgo., 1981—; sole practice, Chgo., 1981—; hearing officer Ill. Bd. Edn., 1984; staff atty. Holiday Project, Chgo., 1982. Mem. ABA, Ill. State Bar Assn., Chgo. Bar Assn. (co-chmn. nat. moot ct. competition 1984), Assn. Trial Lawyers Am. Democrat. Roman Catholic. Office: 135 S LaSalle Chicago IL 60603

WEILEDER, KENNETH JAY, manufacturing company marketing executive; b. Milw., Nov. 7, 1945; s. Kenneth Joseph and Betty Jane (Havlik) W.; m. Monika Barbara Jaros, Oct. 11, 1969; children—Kenneth Robert, Julianna Jane. Student No. Ill. U., 1963-64, Wis. State U., 1964-66; B.S. in Elec. Engring., Milw. Sch. Engring., 1974. Sales trainee Allen-Bradley Co., Milw., 1974-75, sales engr., Indpls., 1975-78, br. mgr., Erie, Pa., 1978-81, dist. mktg. mgr., Cleve., 1981—. Mem. Sales and Mktg. Execs., Republican. Lutheran. Avocations: photography; golf; racquetball; swimming. Home: 31883 Lynton Ln Solon OH 44139 Office: Allen-Bradley Co 747 Alpha Dr Cleveland OH 44143

WEIMER, FERNE LAURAINE, librarian; b. Valparaiso, Ind., May 28, 1950; d. John Junior and Helen Lorraine (Dillingham) W. A.B. in History, Wheaton Coll., 1972; M.A. in L.S., No. Ill. U., 1974. Cataloger, Lake County Pub. Library, Merrillville, Ind., 1974-77; cataloger Billy Graham Ctr. Library, Wheaton (Ill.) Coll., 1977-79, dir., 1979—. Mem. ALA, Am. Theol. Library Assn., Assn. Christian Librarians, Chgo. Area Theol. Library Assn. (v.p., pres. elect 1985-86), DuPage Librarians Assn. (sec. 1981-82, pres. 1982-83). Office: Billy Graham Ctr Library Wheaton Coll Wheaton IL 60187

WEIMER, JEAN ELAINE, nursing educator; b. Denver, June 8, 1932; d. John and Marquerite Christina (Friehauf) Jacoby; m. James David Weimer, Aug. 5, 1956; 1 dau., Lisa Marie. Diploma in nursing Children's Hosp. Sch. Nursing, Denver, 1953; B.S.N., U. Denver, 1954; M.A., N.Y. U., 1962. R.N., Colo., S.D., N.Y., Ill. Staff nurse Children's Hosp., Denver, 1953-54, head nurse, 1954-56; dir. nursing edn. Yankton (S.D.) State Hosp., 1956-60; instr. Mt. Sinai Hosp. Sch. Nursing, N.Y.C., 1962-63, curriculum coordinator, 1964-67; asst. prof. nursing City Colls. Chgo., 1968-78, assoc. prof., 1978-85, prof., 1985—; co-chmn. nursing dept. Truman Coll., 1984—. NIMH grantee, 1960-62. Mem. Am. Nurses' Assn., Council Advanced Practioners Psychiat. Nursing (dir. R.N. tutoring project), Kappa Delta Pi, Pi Lambda Theta. Mem. United Ch. of Christ. Home: 6171 N Sheridan Rd Apt 2811 Chicago IL 60660 Office: Truman Coll 1145 W Wilson Ave 2824 Chicago IL 60640

WEINACHT, TERRY ALLEN, broadcasting executive; b. Alton, Ill., Dec. 28, 1954; s. Henry and Doris Virginia (Dresch) W.; m. Mary Ann Wyatt, Feb. 14, 1983. B.A. in Mass Communications, Western Ill. U., 1977. Announcer, salesman Sta. KBKB, Ft. Madison, Iowa, 1977-79; gen. mgr., program dir. Sta. KFMO, Flat River, Mo., 1979-81; sales mgr. Sta. KIEE, Harrisonville, Mo., 1981-83; gen. mgr. Sta. WKIN-WZXY, Kingsport, Tenn., 1983-84; ops. mgr. Sta. WKNR-WKFR, Battle Creek, Mich., 1984—. Recipient Gold-Platinum Records A&M Records, Motown Records, CBS Records, 1984-85. Avocations: music; sports; working with charity organizations. Home: 21167 Capital Ave NE Battle Creek MI 49017 Office: WKNR-WKFR Radio 612 Am Bank Bldg Battle Creek MI 49017

WEINBERG, HOWARD JAY, plastic/reconstructive surgeon; b. Chgo., Nov. 28, 1947; s. Benjamin A. and Jean M. Weinberg; m. Ruth Juttstein, June 21, 1970; children—Sara, Aaron. Student Northwestern U., 1965-1968; M.D., Ind. U., 1972. Diplomate Am. Bd. Plastic Surgery. Intern, resident in gen. surgery Presbyn. St. Luke's Hosp., Chgo., 1972-76; resident in plastic surgery U. N.Mex. Hosps.; Albuquerque, 1976-78; fellow in hand surgery U. N.Mex., 1978-79; pvt. practice medicine specializing in plastic and reconstructive surgery, Munster, Ind., 1979—. Mem. Am. Soc. Plastic and Reconstructive Surgeons, AMA. Avocations: golf; tennis; travel; sports cars. Office: 9337 Calumet Ave Munster IN 46321

WEINBERG, RICHARD ALAN, psychologist, educator; b. Chgo., Jan. 28, 1943; s. Meyer and Mollie I. (Soell) W.; m. Gail E. Blumberg Aug. 25, 1964; children—Eric, Brett. B.S., U. Wis., 1964; M.A.T., Northwestern U., 1965; Ph.D., U. Minn., 1968. Lic. cons. psychologist, Minn. Asst. prof. Tchrs. Coll., Columbia U., N.Y.C., 1968-70; prof. ednl. psychology, psychology and child psychology U. Minn., Mpls., 1970—; cons. EPA; reviewer Office of Edn., NSF; guest speaker TV and radio shows. Mem. adv. com. Children's Mus. Minn.; pres.-elect Am. Assn. State Psychol. Bds. Bush found. grantee; NSF grantee; NIH grantee. Fellow Am. Psychol. Assn.; mem. Soc. for Research in Child Devel., Behavior Genetics Soc., Am. Edn. Research Assn., Phi Beta Kappa, Phi Kappa Phi. Author: (with A. Boehm) The Classroom Observer: A Guide for Developing Observation Skills, 1977; (with Scarr and Levine) Understanding Development, 1985; assoc. editor Contemporary Psychology. Office: N 548 Elliott St U Minn Minneapolis MN 55455

WEINER, ELIZABETH ELDER, nursing educator, consultant; b. Louisville, Jan. 17, 1953; s. Edward Leslie and Jeanette (Reynolds) Elder; m. Daniel Lee Weiner, May 18, 1974; children—Brian Edward, Michael Lee. B.S.N., U. Ky., 1975, Ph.D., 1982; M.S.N., U. Cin., 1978. Staff nurse St. Joseph's Hosp., Lexington, 1975-76; staff relief RN Registry, Cin., 1976-78; instr. U. Cin. Coll. Nursing and Health, Cin., 1979-81, asst. prof., level III dept. chmn., 1982—, dir. computer-assisted instrn. project, 1984—; nursing research cons. VA Med. Ctr., Cin., 1983—. Univ. Research Council travel awardee, 1984. Mem. Am. Nursing Assn., AAUP, Assn. Women Faculty, Midwest Nursing Research Soc., Nat. League Nursing, Soc. Research in Nursing Edn., Sigma Theta Tau. Democrat. Methodist. Home: 239 N Colony Dr Edgewood KY 41017 Office: Univ Cin Coll Nursing and Health 3110 Vine St Cincinnati OH 45221-0038

WEINER, GERALD ARNE, stockbroker; b. Chgo., Dec. 20, 1941; s. Irwin S. and Lilyan (Stock) W.; m. Barbara I. Allen, June 18, 1967; children—Rachel Anne, Sara Naomi. B.S.S., Loyola U., Chgo., 1964; student U. Vienna, Austria, 1962-63; M.S., Georgetown U., 1966; postgrad. Ind. U., 1966-72, S.E. Asian Areas cert., 1967. Pacification specialist AID, Laos, 1965; instr. polit. sci. Loyola U.-Chgo., 1970-72; asst. v.p. A.G. Becker & Co., Chgo., 1973-78; sr. v.p. Oppenheimer & Co., Chgo., 1978-83; sr. v.p. J. David Securities, Inc., Chgo., 1983-84; sr. v.p. Dean Witter Reynolds, Chgo., 1984—; v.p. Caputo Literary Properties. Bd. dirs. Spertus Mus. Jewish Culture, Travelers Aid and Immigrant League. Mucia fellow, 1969. Mem. United Schutzhund Clubs Am. Republican. Jewish. Club: East Bank (Chgo.). Office: Dean Witter Reynolds 70 W Madison Chicago IL 60602

WEINER, STEVEN ALLAN, research engineer; b. N.Y.C., June 6, 1942; s. Henry and Arline Anna (Maron) W.; m. Cynthia Avis Brand, July 4, 1971; children—Francesca C., Bryan H. A.B., Columbia Coll., 1963; Ph.D., Iowa State U., 1967; M.B.A., Mich. State U., 1982. Fellow Calif. Inst. Tech., Pasadena, 1967-68; with Ford Motor Co., Detroit, 1968—, mgr. sodium-sulfur battery program, 1973-77, prin. research engr. Mfg. Devel. Ctr., 1982—. Recipient Acad. Excellence award Mich. State U., 1982; Henry Ford Technol. award, 1983; NASA fellow, 1965. Mem. AAAS, Am. Chem. Soc. (Leibmann Meml. award 1959), Am. Inst. Indsl. Engrs., Ops. Research Soc. Am., Sigma Xi, Beta Gamma Sigma, Phi Kappa Phi, Phi Lambda Upsilon. Contbr. sci. articles to profl. publs. Home: 28330 Quail Hollow Rd Farmington MI 48018 Office: 24500 Glendale Ave Detroit MI 48239

WEINGART, WENDY ANNE, clinical data coordinator, researcher, pharmacist; b. Milw., Dec. 28, 1955; d. William Frederick and Bernice Elaine (Igl) W.; m. William Walter Bennewitz, Sept. 22, 1984. B.S. in Pharmacy, U. Wis.-Madison, 1978, M.S. in Pharmacy, 1983. Registered pharmacist; cert. in hosp. pharmacy. Pharmacist Peters Drugs, Milw. 1978-81, cons., 1984-85; pharmacist Meadowood Pharmacy, Madison, Wis., 1978-81; clin. pharmacist U. Wis. Hosp. and Clinics, Madison, 1980-82, clin. asst. prof., 1982-84; research instr., clin. data coordinator, Med. Coll. Wis., Milw., 1984-85; asst. dir. pharmacy Northview Home and Hosp., Waukesha, Wis., 1985—. Coordinator spay-neuter follow-up program Dane County Humane Soc., Madison, 1983-84. Upjohn Co. grantee, 1981. Mem. Am. Soc. Hosp. Pharmacists, Wis. Pharm. Assn., Wis. Soc. Hosp. Pharmacists, Dane County Pharm. Soc. (v.p. 1982-84), Pharmacists Soc. Milw. County, Humane Soc. U.S., Kappa Psi (grad. chpt.), Alpha Sigma Alpha (grad. chpt.). Presbyterian. Lodge: Job's Daus. Avocations: jogging; tennis; cross-country skiing. Office: Northview Home and Hosp 25042 W Northview Rd Waukesha WI 53188

WEINHOLD, JOHN DONALD, educator; b. Kansas City, Mo., Jan. 21, 1935; s. Theophil A. and Magdelene (Spilker) W.; m. Esther Jens, June 8, 1957; children—Kim D., Karmin F., Nathan R. B.S. in Edn., Concordia Tchrs. Coll., Seward, Nebr., 1957; M.A. in Sci., Ball State U., 1962, Ed.D., 1970. Cert. elem. and secondary tchrs., Nebr. Tchr. elem. sch. St. John's Luth. Sch., Arnold, Mo., 1954-55; instr. Concordia High Sch., Seward, 1957, Concordia Luth. High Sch., Fort Wayne, Ind., 1957-62; asst. prof. Concordia Coll., River Forest, Ill., 1962-68; prof. edn., Concordia Coll., Seward, 1968—; cons. in edn. to Luth. Sch. Tchrs.' Confs., N.Y., N.J., Iowa, Miss., Nebr. Aid Assn. for Lutherans fellow, 1966-67. Mem. Luth. Edn. Assn. (nat. dir. 1972-76), Nat. Sci. Tchrs. Assn., Phi Delta Kappa. Lutheran. Contbr. articles on edn. to profl. jours. Home: 604 N Fifth St Seward NE 68434 Office: 800 N Columbia Seward NE 68434

WEINHOLD, VIRGINIA BEAMER, interior designer; b. Elizabeth, N.J., June 21, 1932; d. Clayton Mitchell and Rosemary (Behrend) Beamer; B.A., Cornell U., 1955; B.F.A. summa cum laude, Ohio State U., 1969; M.A. in Design Mgmt., Ohio State U., 1982; divorced; children—Thomas Craig, Robert Scott, Amy Linette. Freelance interior designer, 1969-72; interior designer, dir. interior design Karlsberger and Assos. Inc., Columbus, Ohio, 1972-82; assoc. prof. dept. indsl. design Ohio State U., 1982—; lectr. indsl. design Ohio State U., 1972, 79-80. Bd. visitors Found. for Interior Design Edn. and Research. Mem. Inst. Bus. Designers (chpt. treas. 1977-79, nat. trustee 1979-81, nat. chmn. contract documents com. 1979-84, chpt. pres. 1981-83), Constrn. Specifications Inst., Interior Design Educator's Council, asso. mem. AIA. Prin. works include Grands Rapids (Mich.) Osteo. Hosp., Melrose (Mass.) Wakefield Hosp., Christopher Inn, Columbus, John W. Galbreath Hdqrs., Columbus, Guernsey Meml. Hosp., Cambridge, Ohio, Trinity Epis. Ch. and Parish House, Columbus, Hale Hosp., Haverhill, Mass., others. Author: IBO Forms and Documents Manual. Home: 112 Glen Dr Worthington OH 43085 Office: 128 N Oval Mall Columbus OH 43210

WEINLANDER, MAX MARTIN, retired psychologist; b. Ann Arbor, Mich., Sept. 9, 1917; s. Paul and Emma Carol (Lindemann) W.; B.A., Eastern Mich. Coll., 1940; M.A., U. Mich., 1942, Ph.D., 1955; M.A., Wayne U., 1951; m. Albertina Adelheit Abrams, June 4, 1945; children—Bruce, Annette. Psychometrist, VA Hosp., Dearborn, Mich., 1947-51; sr. staff psychologist Ohio Div. Corrections, London, 1954-55; lectr. Dayton and Piqua Centers, Miami U., Oxford, Ohio, 1955-62; chief clin. psychologist Child Guidance Clinic, Springfield, Ohio, 1956-61, acting dir., 1961-65; clin. psychologist VA Center, Dayton, Ohio, 1964-79; cons. Ohio Div. Mental Hygiene; summer guest prof. Miami U., 1957, 58, Wittenberg U., 1958; adj. prof. Wright State U., Dayton, 1975-76; cons. State Ohio Bur. Vocat. Rehab., Oesterlen Home Emotionally Disturbed Children. Pres. Clark County Mental Health Assn., 1960, Clark County Health and Welfare Club, 1961; mem. Community Welfare Council Clark County, 1964; chmn. Comprehensive Mental Health Planning Com. Clark County, 1964; trustee United Appeals Fund, 1960. Mem. citizens adv. council Columbus Psychiat. Inst., Ohio State U. Served as sgt. AUS, 1942-46. Fellow Ohio Psychol. Assn. (chmn. com. on utilization of psychologists; treas., exec. bd. 1968-71); mem. Am. Psychol. Assn., Ohio Psychol. Assn., Mich. Psychol. Assn., DAV, Pi Kappa Delta, Pi Gamma Mu, Phi Delta Kappa. Lutheran. Lodge: Kiwanis. Contbr. articles to psychology jours. Home: 17185 Valley Dr Big Rapids MI 49307

WEINMANN, RONALD VINCENT, business educator; b. Harvey, N.D., Apr. 14, 1945; s. Vincent R. and Adeline C. (Muscha) W.; m. Loretta Jane Schmaltz, Dec. 28, 1973; children—Shannon, Shane. A.A., N.D. State Sch. Sci., 1971; B.S., N.D. State U., 1974. Asst. mgr. Pierce Co., Fargo, N.D., 1974-76; spl. agt. Lincoln Nat. Life Ins. Co., Fargo, 1976-78; buyer Crane Johnson Co., West Fargo, N.D., 1978-79; small bus. mgmt. instr., coordinator small bus. mgmt. Lake Region Community Coll., Devil's Lake, N.D., 1979—; cons. SBA. Pub. relations dir., dist. commr. Boy Scouts Am., 1980—. Served with USAF, 1967-69. Decorated Air Force Commendation medal; recipient Dist. award of Merit, Boy Scouts Am., 1984. Mem. N.D. Assn. Small Bus. Mgmt. Instrs. (pres.), Nat. Assn. Small bus. Mgmt. Instrs. (past editor), Jaycees (past state officer, mem. internat. senate), N.D. Assn. Acctg. Instrs., VFW. Roman Catholic. Lodge: Eagles. Contbr. articles to profl. jours. Home: 1207 2d Ave W Devils Lake ND 58301 Office: Lake Region Community Coll Devils Lake ND 58301

WEINSTEIN, BARRY STUART, hospital administrator; b. Cin., Dec. 28, 1944; s. Leon B. and Dorothy (Hoffert) W.; m. Julia L. Crouch, Sept. 17, 1971; children—Sarah, Benjamin, Anna. B.A. with honors in Arts and Scis., U. Cin., 1966, M.B.A., 1968. C.P.A. Various positions to mgr. Coopers & Lybrand, Cin., 1968-77; v.p. Children's Hosp. Med. Ctr., Cin., 1977-84, exec. v.p., chief operating officer, 1984—; dir. Cancer Family Care, Cin., 1984—. Bd. dirs. Isaac M. Wise Temple, Cin., 1974—; mem. Cincinnatus Soc. Served with U.S. Army, 1968-74. Fellow Hosp. Fin. Mgmt. Assn. (William G. Folmer award 1980,

Robert H. Reeves award 1984); mem. Am. Coll. Hosp. Adminstrs., Ohio Soc. C.P.A.s, Am. Inst. C.P.A.s, Beta Alpha Psi, Omicron Delta Epsilon. Office: Children's Hosp Med Center Elland and Bethesda Ave Cincinnati OH 45229

WEINSTEIN, GEORGE, accountant, management consultant; b. N.Y.C., Mar. 20, 1924; s. Morris J. and Sara (Broder) W.; m. Shirley Beatrice Greenberg, Sept. 1, 1945; children—Stanley Howard, Jerrald, Sara Belle. B.S., U. Ill., 1944, postgrad. Law Sch., 1944-55; M.B.A., NYU, 1947. Joined Morris J. Weinstein, Groothuis & Co., N.Y.C., 1944, ptnr., 1945-72; ptnr. Weinstein Assocs., N.Y.C. and Milw., 1973—; chmn. Weinstein Assocs. Ltd.; pres. dir. REIT Property Mgrs. Ltd., Milw.; pres. Hudson Valley Corp., WAL Ltd.; dir. Growth Realty Co., Regency Investors. Active United Jewish Appeal, Fedn. Jewish Philanthropies; bd. dirs., founder North Shore Hebrew Acad.; founder, past pres. Gt. Neck (N.Y.) Synagogue; treas. Sarah B. Weinstein Found.; chmn. Lake Park Synagogue; trustee M. Rainville trust; bd. dirs. Milw. Jewish Home, Jewish Nat. Fund, Milw. Hillel Acad. Mem. Am. Inst. Accts., N.Y. Soc. C.P.A.s, Hebrew Immigrant Soc., Tau Delta Phi (nat. treas.), Delta Sigma Phi. Clubs: President's of U. Ill., Westmoreland, Ambassadors of Yeshiva U., Milw. Athletic, Wisconsin; Citrus (Orlando, Fla.). Lodge: Masons (past master). Address: 925 E Wells St Milwaukee WI 53233

WEINSTEIN, LAURENCE ALAN, beverage company executive; b. Madison, Wis., Dec. 3, 1923; m. Frances Lipton; 2 children. B.B.A., U. Wis.-Madison, 1945, J.D., 1947. Bar: Wis. 1947. Pres., Gen. Beverage Sales Co., Madison, Oshkosh, and Eau Claire, Wis., also Gen. Beer Distbrs., Madison, 1951—. Mem. Mayor's Adv. Coms., Madison; bd. regents U. Wis. System, 1984—; bd. dirs. U. Wis. Hosp. and Clinics, Wis. Higher Edn. Adv. Bd., Madison Urban League, Wis. Assn. Alcoholism and Other Drug Abuse, Madison Art Assn.; mem. Wis. Legis. Recodification Com.; voting mem. United Way, Madison; life bd. dirs. Beth El Temple, Madison, Madison Jewish Community Council; past pres. Hillel Student Found., U. Wis. Mem. Wine and Spirits Wholesalers Am. (past pres., bd. dirs.), Nat. Beer Wholesalers Assn. Am. (past pres.), Union Am. Hebrew Congregations (bd. dirs.), Council Jewish Fed. and Welfare Funds (bd. dirs.), Nat. Hillel Commr., Bascom Soc. U. Wis., Madison C. of C. (v.p.), Wis. Alumni Assn., Wis. Law Alumni Assn. Office: PO Box 4326 Madison WI 53711

WEINSTOCK, ROBERT, physics educator; b. Phila., Feb. 2, 1919; s. Morris and Lillian (Hirsch) W.; m. Elizabeth Winch Brownell, Apr. 22, 1950; children—Frank Morse, Robert Brownell. A.B., U. Pa., 1940; Ph.D., Stanford U., 1943. Instr. physics Stanford U., Calif., 1943-44, instr. math., 1946-50, acting asst. prof. math., 1950-54; research assoc. in radar countermeasures Radio Research Lab., Harvard U., Cambridge, Mass., 1944-45; asst. prof. U. Notre Dame, Ind., 1954-58, assoc. prof. math., 1958-59; vis. assoc. prof. math. Oberlin Coll., Ohio, 1959-60, assoc. prof., 1960-66, prof. physics, 1966-83, emeritus prof., 1983—. Author: Calculus of Variations, 1952. Contbr. numerous tech. articles to profl. jours. Fellow Ohio Acad. Sci.; mem. Am. Assn. Physics Tchrs., Am. Phys. Soc., History of Sci. Soc., AAAS, Sigma Xi. Avocations: concert going; reading; walking; travel. Home: 171 E College St Oberlin OH 44074 Office: Dept Physics Oberlin Coll Oberlin OH 44074

WEINZIERL, THOMAS ALLEN, telecommunications, data processing consultant; b. Pitts., Sept. 5, 1951; s. George William and Genevieve Blanche (Nyga) W.; m. Elizabeth Katherine Yost, Dec. 16, 1972; children—Cynthia Ann, Cheryl Lynn, Thomas Michael. B.S. in Engring., U. Ill., Chgo., 1972; M.B.A., DePaul U., 1975. Cert. data processor. Data processing specialist Internat. Harvester, Chgo., 1972-77; supr. data communications, Milw., 1978-79, planning mgr., Chgo., 1980, cons. Blue Cross Blue Shield Milw., 1981—. James scholar U. Ill., 1969-72. Mem. Soc. Mfg. Engrs., Phi Kappa Phi, Delta Mu Delta. Roman Catholic. Home: 3004 Fairwood Ct Wauwatosa WI 53222 Office: Blue Cross Blue Shield United Wis 501 W Michigan St Milwaukee WI 53201

WEINZIMMER, MARK ALAN, printing company executive; b. Chgo., Aug. 10, 1942; s. Franklin S. and Ruth C. (Weintraub) W.; m. Margaret Nava, July 29, 1977. A.A.S. in Printing Mgmt., Rochester (N.Y.) Inst. Tech., 1962. Cert. forms cons., Ill. Pres., Lake Shore Bus. Forms, Chgo., 1962-64, Battye Franklin Corp., Elk Grove, Ill., 1964-74, Syncron Inc., Elk Grove, 1974-77; owner Wild Wood Acres, Spencer, W.Va., 1977-79; v.p. sales and mktg. Gen. Bus. Forms, Skokie, Ill., 1979—. Office: Gen Bus Forms 7312 Niles Center Rd Skokie IL 60077

WEIRAUCH, BERNARD CHAPMAN, supply company executive; b. White County, Ill., Oct. 1, 1912; s. Wenzel Dickison and Viola (Chapman) W.; m. Winifred Kisner, Feb. 9, 1936; 1 dau., Susan Weirauch Stegall. B.S., U. Evansville (Ind.), 1935; postgrad. indsl. distbn. program Harvard U., 1958. Instr., U. Evansville, 1935; field rep. Orr Iron Co., Evansville, 1936-46, sales mgr., 1946-54, v.p., 1954-70; gen. mgr. Ram Supply Co., Evansville, 1970-75, v.p., 1975—. Recipient Sales Mgr. of Yr. award Nat. Sales Execs. Club, 1954. Presbyterian. Clubs: Eagles Country, Central Turners (Evansville). Lodges: Rotary, Masons, Shriners. Author: Selling Benefits and Advantages, 1956; also SBA pubs. Home: 878 Sunset Dr Evansville IN 47713 Office: 1301 W Franklin St PO Box 3038 Evansville IN 47730

WEISBERG, SEYMOUR WILLIAM, physician; b. Chgo., Aug. 5, 1910; s. Isaac and Eda (Provus) W.; B.S., U. Chgo., 1932; M.D., Rush Med. Coll., 1936; m. Ella Sperling, Oct. 16, 1949; children—Gerald, Louise. Intern Michael Reese Hosp.; resident Cook County Hosp., Chgo.; practice medicine specializing in internal medicine, Chgo., 1940—; asso. prof. medicine U. Ill. Coll. Medicine, Chgo.; asso. attending physician Cook County Hosp., 1940-44; chief resident tng. unit Chgo. Regional Office VA; mem. attending staffs Michael Reese Hosp., Chgo., Louis A. Weiss Meml. Hosp., Chgo., St. Joseph Hosp. Served with AUS, 1944-47. Diplomate Am. Bd. Internal Medicine. Mem. AMA, Ill. Med. Soc., Phi Beta Kappa, Alpha Omega Alpha. Office: 2800 N Sheridan Rd Chicago IL 60657

WEISMAN, JOEL, nuclear engineering educator; b. N.Y.C., July 15, 1928; s. Abraham and Ethel (Marcus) W.; m. Bernice Newman, Feb. 6, 1955; 1 son Jay (dec.). B. Chem. Engring., CCNY, 1948; M.S., Columbia U., 1949; Ph.D., U. Pitts., 1968. Registered profl. engr., N.Y., Ohio. Engr., Etched Products Corp., N.Y.C., 1950-51; assoc. engr. Brookhaven Nat. Lab., Upton, L.I., N.Y., 1951-54; sr. engr. to supervisory engr. Westinghouse Electric Corp., PWR div., Pitts., 1954-60; sr. engr. Nuclear Devel. Assocs., White Plains, N.Y., 1960; fellow engr. to mgr. thermal and hydraulic analysis Westinghouse Electric Corp., PWR div., Pitts., 1960-68; assoc. prof. U. Cin., 1968-72, dir. nuclear engring. program, 1979—, prof. nuclear engring., 1972—; cons. to nuclear industry. Pres. Cin. Asian Art Soc., 1982-84; mem. exec. bd. dirs. Cin. Air Pollution League, 1980—. Sr. fellow NATO, 1972; fellow Argonne Nat. Lab., summer, 1980. Fellow Am. Nuclear Soc.; mem. Am. Inst. Chem. Engrs., Ops. Research Soc. Am., Inst. Mgmt. Sci., Sigma Xi. Jewish. Author: (with B. Gottfried) Introduction to Optimization Theory, 1973; (with L. S. Tong) Thermal Analysis of Pressurized WaterReactors, 1970, 2d edit., 1979; (with R. Eckart) Modern Power Plant Engineering, 1985; editor: Elements of Nuclear Reactor Design, 1977, 2d edit., 1983; contbr. numerous articles on nuclear engring. to profl. jours.; patentee in field. Office: Dept Chemical and Nuclear Engring Univ Cin Cincinnati OH 45221

WEISS, JACK RICHARD, graphic designer; b. Lansing, Mich., Mar. 15, 1939; s. Walter Leonard and Mary Elizabeth (Robert) W.; m. Esther Ruskin, July 11, 1963 (div. July 1985); children—Judith, Rachel. B.S., Ill. Inst. Tech., 1965; B.F.A., M.F.A., Yale U., 1967. Designer, Low's Inc., Chgo., 1963-65, Kevin Roche John Dinkeloo Assoc., Hamden, Conn., 1965-67; designer, v.p. Blake & Weiss, Inc., Evanston, Ill., 1967-77; prin., pres. Jack Weiss Assocs., Inc., Evanston, 1977—; tchr. Inst. Design Ill. Inst. Tech., Chgo., 1968-76, vis. lectr., 1978; vis. lectr. Sch. of Art Inst., Chgo., 1982; panelist graphic design history, design and tech. Rochester Inst. Tech., N.Y., 1983, panelist design and tech., 1983. Publisher: The Design Index, 1981-83; contbr. articles Realty & Building, Print, Sign of the Times. Bd. dirs. Earn & Learn, Evanston, 1976—, Design Evanston, 1984—, McGaw YMCA, Evanston, 1984—, Evanston Arts Alliance 1985—. Served to airman 1st class USAF, 1957-61. Recipient design awards Graphic Arts Council Chgo., 1968, 69, Communications Collaborative Chgo., 1969-80, Am. Inst. Graphic Arts, N.Y.C., 1975, Chgo. Book Clinic, 1971, 81, 84, others. Fellow STA (dir. 1969-78, 1st v.p. 1978-79; awards 1965, 67, 81, 83, 84), Am. Inst. Graphic Arts, 27 Chgo. Designers (chmn. 1981-83), Soc. Environ. Graphic Designers. Democrat. Jewish Reconstructionist. Office: Jack Weiss Assocs Inc 820 Davis St Evanston IL 60201

WEISS, LARRY WAYNE, dermatologist; b. Burlington, Colo., Aug. 7, 1942; s. Albert Carl and Martha Margaret (Adolf) W.; m. Ruth Ann Dow; children—Leslie, Nathan, Aaron. B.A., Dana Coll., 1964; Ph.D., U. Minn., 1970, B.S., 1971, M.D., 1972, M.S. in Dermatology, 1975. Diplomate Nat. Bd. Med. Examiners. Intern, Northwestern Hosp., Mpls., 1972-73; resident U. Minn., Mpls., 1973-75; practice medicine, specializing in dermatology, Marshalltown, Iowa, 1976—; mem. staff Marshalltown Area Community Hosp., 1976—. Contbr. articles to profl. jours. Treas., Boy Scouts Am., Marshalltown, 1984—. Mem. Am. Acad. Dermatology, Iowa Dermatol. Soc., Minn. Dermatol. Soc., Am. Soc. Dermatologic Surgery. Lutheran. Avocations: stained glass work; rock and coin collecting; treasure hunting; metal detecting; fishing. Office: 208 E Church St #106 Marshalltown IA 50158

WEISS, MARTIN E., communications and marketing specialist; b. Cleve., Nov. 22, 1926; s. Samuel B. and Margaret (Freedman) W.; B.A., Columbia U., 1947; m. Regina Melville Martyn, Jan. 16, 1983; children—Jack Martyn, Kevin Martyn, Michelle Martyn, Dawn Martyn, Lorraine Frame; children from previous marriage—James L. Weiss, Andrew R. Weiss. Dir. advt. and public relations Del. Floor Products, 1948-52; promotion dir. Street & Smith Publs., 1952-56; editor, publisher Westbury (N.Y.) Times, 1956-73; publisher Edn.-Tng. Market Report, Washington, 1973-75; dir. public relations and publs. AAU/USA, Indpls., 1976-79; dir. communications, mktg. Athletics Congress/USA, Indpls., 1979—. Served with AUS, 1944-46. Mem. Ind. Bus. Communicators. Home: 11654 Buttonwood Dr Carmel IN 46032 Office: 200 S Capitol Ave Suite 140 Indianapolis IN 46225

WEISS, MORRY, See *Who's Who in America,* 43rd edition.

WEISS, RAYMOND LEE, development officer; b. Cleve., Jan. 3, 1955; s. Raymond and Georgia Ellen (Baker) W.; B.S. in Sociology, Capital U., 1983. Child care worker Parmadale Children's Village, Parma, Ohio, 1976-79, asst. dir. edn., 1981-83, asst. dir. research and devel., 1983—; cons. St. Charles Group, Lakewood, Ohio, 1983, 84, 85. Mem. adv. bd. Parma City Schs., 1983—; trustee No. Ohio chpt. Nat. Hemophilia Found., 1984—. Mem. Ohio Council Fund Raising Execs. Avocations: photography; fishing. Home: 6753 State Rd Parma OH 44134 Office: Parmadale Children's Village 6753 State Rd Parma OH 44134

WEISS, SAMUAL, hotel and restaurant company executive; b. Rock Springs, Wyo., Dec. 25, 1924; s. Morris and Alta Weiss; m. Barbara R. Coggan; children—Cathy, Marcy, Karen. B.A. cum laude, U. Mich., 1948; LL.B., Harvard U., 1951. Asst. v.p. Cuneo Press, Inc., Chgo., 1951-68; exec. v.p., treas., dir. Holly's Inc., Grand Rapids, Mich., 1968—; exec. v.p., dir. Holly Enterprises, Inc., Grand Rapids, 1969—, Holly Grills of Ind., South Bend, 1970—, Fare Devel. Corp., Grand Rapids, 1974—. Co-chmn. U.S. Olympic com. Mich., 1976-80; bd. control Intercollegiate Athletics U. Mich., 1982—. Served to 2d lt. USAAF, 1942-46. Mem. Nat. Assn. Corp. Real Estate Execs. (founding), Nat. Restaurant Assn., U. Mich. Alumni Assn. (dir.). Republican. Clubs: Peninsular (Grand Rapids). Home: 3645 Oak Terrace Ct SE Grand Rapids MI 49508 Office: 255 Colrain St SW PO Box 9260 Grand Rapids MI 49509

WEISS, WILLIAM LEE, telecommunications company executive; b. Big Run, Pa., May 21, 1929; s. Harry W. and Dorothy Jane (McKee) W.; m. Josephine Elizabeth Berry, June 3, 1951; children—Susan Leigh Weiss Miller, David William, Steven Paul. B.S. in Indsl. Engring., Pa. State U., 1951. With Bell Telephone Co. of Pa., 1951, v.p. staff, Phila., 1973-74, v.p., gen. mgr. western region, 1974-76, Pitts.; v.p. ops. Wis. Telephone Co., Milw., 1976-78; pres. Ind. Bell Telephone Co., Indpls., 1978-81; pres. Ill. Bell Telephone Co., Chgo., 1981, chmn., 1982-83; chmn., chief exec. Ameritech, 1983—, also dir.; dir. Continental Ill. Nat. Bank, Chgo., Continental Ill. Corp., Abbott Labs., Chgo., Ransburg Corp., Indpls., USG Corp., Chgo. Mem. Gov's Comm. on Sci. and Tech.; chmn. Ill. Council on Econ. Edn.; trustee Mus. Sci. and Industry, Chgo., Northwestern U. The Orchestral Assn., Chgo.; Rush-Presbyn.-St. Lukes Med. Ctr., Chgo.; Chgo. Com. Chgo. Council Fgn. Relations, Ill., Served with USAF, 1951-53. Mem. Western Soc. Engrs., Phi Delta Theta, Tau Beta Pi. Clubs: Country of North Carolina; Chgo., Mid-Am., Comml., Glen View, Old Elm. Office: 30 S Wacker Dr Suite 3800 Chicago IL 60606

WEISSBOURD, BERNICE TARG, publishing executive, editor; b. Chgo., Jan. 25, 1923; d. Max and Fannie (Wexler) T.; m. Barnard BenZion Weissbourd, Oct. 31, 1946; children—Burt, Ruth, Robert, Richard. B.M., Am. Conservatory Music, Chgo., 1943; M.A., Columbia U., 1945. Tchr., Roosevelt U., Chgo., 1945-52; dir. Music for Children, Chgo., 1954-59; supr. King Family Ctr., Chgo., 1967-71; edn. dir. Child Care Ctr., Evanston, Ill., 1972-76; pres. Family Focus, Evanston, Ill., 1976—; pres. Family Resource Coalition, Chgo., 1981—; nat. task force mem. Child Devel. Assocs., Washington, 1984—; bd. dirs. Child Care Action Campaign, N.Y.C., 1984—; cons., lectr. in field. Author: Creating Drop-In Centers: A Family Focus Model, 1979. Editor: Infants: Their Social Environments, 1981. Columnist: Parents mag. Two Year Olds, 1977—. Bd. dirs. Erikson Inst., Loyola U., Chgo., 1965—, Northwestern U. Inst. Psychiatry, Chgo., 1980—; women's bd. dirs. U. Chgo., 1981—; bd. dirs. Expressways Children's Mus., Chgo., 1982—, People for American Way, Washington, 1983—. Named Nat. Hon. Commnr., Internat. Yr. of Child, 1979; recipient YWCA Outstanding Service award, 1981; World of Children award, Chgo. UNICEF, 1983; Outstanding Woman award Nat. Forum for Women, 1985. Fellow Am. Orthopsychiat. Assn.; mem. Assn. Edn. Young Children (v.p. 1983—), Nat. Ctr. Clin. Infant Programs (bd. dirs.), Child Care Action Campaign (bd. dirs.), Am. Pub. Welfare Assn., Chgo. Pediatric Soc. (hon.). Jewish. Office: Family Focus 2300 Green Bay Rd Evanston IL 60201

WEIST, PHILIP FREDRICK, can company executive, building consultant; b. LaRue, Ohio, Feb. 5, 1936; s. Mac Philip and Mildred Lucile (Burdge) W.; m. Le Ann Parish, Feb. 14, 1956; children—Robyn, Rodney, Todd, Renee, Amy. Student pub. schs., LaRue; cert. in quality control Internat. Corr. Schs., 1969. Farmer, 1954-58; with Nat. Can Corp., 1958—, quality control supr., Marion, Ohio plant, 1970-71, dist. mgr. quality control, 1971-72, south central area mgr. quality control, 1972-74, asst. plant mgr. Laporte, Ind., 1974-76, plant mgr. Green Bay (Wis.) plant, 1976—. Bd. dirs. LaRue Retirement Devel. Corp.; mem. Republican Nat. Com. Named State Farmer Ohio, Future Farmers Am., 1953, recipient Am. Farmer Degree Kansas City, Mo. 1957. Mem. Soc. Mfg. Engrs. (Wis. cert.), Green Bay Area personnel Dirs., Green Bay Area C. of C. (mem. speakers bur.). Methodist. Clubs: Rotary (treas.), Traffic, Shriners (past pres.) Green Bay; Masons. Contbg. author co. quality control manuals. Home: 1620 Zita St Des Peres WI 54115

WEIZMAN, SAVINE GROSS, psychologist; b. Cleve., Oct. 28, 1929; d. Isadore and Zelda (Rubenstein) Gross; m. Alvin A. Weizman, Feb. 11, 1951 (dec.); children—Elissa, David, Robert. B.S.Ed., Case Western Res. U., 1951, M.S., 1968, Ph.D., 1975. Lic. psychologist, and sch. psychologist, Ohio Elem. sch. tchr., 1951-54; psychol. staff Cleve. Pub. Schs., 1968-77; child and family therapist Beechbrook Residential Treatment Center for Children, Pepper Pike, Ohio, 1977-79; pvt. practice psychology and psychotherapy specializing in coping with loss, Beachwood, Ohio, 1975—; psychologist orthopedically handicapped program Lake-Geauga Counties, 1972-73; lectr. John Carroll U., 1970-73; asst. prof. psychology Cleve. Inst. Art, 1975-81; lectr. in field of mental health, mourning and bereavement. Mem. behavioral scientists com. Fairmount Temple; trustee Jewish Community Center Mem. Am. Psychol. Assn., Cleve. Psychol. Assn., AAUP. Author: Understanding the Mourning Process, When Your Mate Dies, 1977; About Mourning: Support and Guidance for the Bereaved, 1984; contbr. articles and papers to profl. jours. Office: 3659 Green Rd Suite 211 Beachwood OH 44122

WELCH, E. THOMAS, banker; b. Mpls., Aug. 24, 1938; s. Eugene James and Mary Ellen (Fleming) W.; m. Rita D Czapiewski, July 28, 1962; children—Colleen, Patrick, Katie. B.S. in Bus. Adminstrn., U. N.D., 1962, J.D., 1962. Trust examiner U.S. Dept Treasury, Mpls., 1962-65; sr. v.p. F&M Marquette Bank, Mpls., 1965-84; chief operating officer Resource Bank & Trust, Mpls., 1984—, also dir., 1984—; instr. Nat. Trust Sch. and Nat. Retail Banking Sch., 1976—. Bd. dirs., treas. Mpls. council Girl Scouts U.S.A., 1978—; bd. dirs. United Way, Mpls., 1982—; bd. advisors Retail Banking Sch., 1982—; mem. Mpls. Estate Planning Council (pres. 1970—), Mpls. Pension Council. Roman Catholic. Avocation: Tennis. Home: 900 Elgin Pl Golden Valley MN 55427 Office: Resource Bank & Trust 900 2d Ave S Suite 300 Minneapolis MN 55402-3306

WELCH, JACKIE LEE, financial executive; b. Macomb, Ill., July 24, 1949; s. Wilbur and Mary Kathleen (Hensley) W.; m. Marla Ann Brandon, Mar. 23, 1969; 1 son, Zachary. B.S., Central Mo. State U., 1975. C.P.A., Mo. Sr. auditor Peat Marwick Mitchell & Co., Kansas City, Mo., 1975-77; internal auditor Seaboard Allied Milling Corp., Kansas City, Mo., 1977-79, acctg. mgr., 1979-80; acctg. mgr. Mfa Inc., Columbia, Mo., 1980—. Served with USAF, 1969-73. Decorated Air Force Commendation medal. Mem. Am. Inst. C.P.A.s, Nat. Soc. Accts. for Coops. Republican. Methodist. Club: Kiwanis (program dir. 1983-84, bd. dirs. 1983—). Home: Route 1 Box 6-K Columbia MO 65201 Office: 201 S Seventh Columbia MO 65201

WELCH, PATRICK DANIEL, state senator; b. Chgo., Dec. 12, 1948; s. William C. and Alice (McParland) W.; m. Bonita Lerud, 1972. Student Danville Jr. Coll., 1966-68; B.A., So. Ill. U., 1970; J.D., Chgo. Kent Coll. Law, 1974. Bar: Ill. 1974. Sole practice, Peru, Ill., 1974—; mem. Ill. Senate, 1983—. Del., mem. credentials com. Democratic Nat. Conv., 1976, del., 1980; precinct committeeman Peru Dem. Party, 1976—; treas. Peru Twp. Dem. Central Com., 1976—; mem. Peru Zoning Bd. Appeals, 1977—; del. Dem. Nat. Mid-Term Conf., 1978, 82; committeeman Ill. Dem. Central Com., 1978—, mem. exec. com., 1983—; mem. Peru Citizens' Service Orgn. Recipient Disting. Service award Ill. Bicentennial Commn., 1976. Mem. Ill. Bar Assn., La Salle County Bar Assn. Roman Catholic. Lodges: K.C., Rotary. Office: PO Box 341 Peru IL 61354

WELCH, PAUL E., city official; b. Evanston, Ill., Nov. 6, 1948; s. Robert Ryan and Anne (Donnegan) W.; m. Kathryn A. Wolters, Oct. 17, 1970; children—Jennifer, Colleen, Michael, Kimberly. grad. FBI Nat. Acad., 1982; B.S. in Pub. Adminstrn., Roosevelt U., 1983; M.S. in Mgmt., Cardinal Strictch Coll., 1985. Police officer Evanston Police Dept., 1970-80; chief police Monona Police Dept., Wis., 1981-85; assessor Commn. Law Enforcement Accreditation, Monona 1984—. Served with USN, 1969-70; Vietnam. Recipient Commendation award Evanston Police, 1974; Honorable Mention award Chgo. Police, 1971. Mem. FBI Nat. Acad. Assocs., Nat. Criminal Justice Assn. (charter), Nat. Assn. Chiefs Police, Internat. Assn. Chiefs Police (com. crime prevention), Wis. Chiefs Police Assn., Dane County Police Chiefs Assn., V.F.W. Avocations: sports, home computers. Office: 5211 Schluter Rd Monona WI 53716

WELDON, RAMON NATHANIEL, city official; b. Keokuk, Iowa, July 26, 1932; s. Clarence and Virginia H. (White) W.; m. Betty Jean Watkins, July 24, 1955; 1 child, Ramon N., Jr. Student pub. schs., Keokuk. Patrolman, Keokuk Police Dept., Iowa, 1962-74, detective, 1974-80, capt., 1980-82, chief of police, 1982—. Mem. Keokuk Humane Soc., 1982, Lee County Juvenile Restitution Bd., Ft. Madison, Iowa, 1982, Lee County Health Care Coalition, Ft. Madison, Iowa, 1983; trustee Library Bd., Keokuk, Served with U.S. Army, 1952-54. Mem. Iowa Chief's Assn., Nat. Chief's Assn., Internat. Chief's Assn. Methodist. Lodge: Masons (master 1955). Avocations: racquetball; hunting; basketball; swimming. Home: 2510 Decatur St Keokuk IA 52632 Office: Keokuk Police Dept 1222 Johnson St Keokuk IA 52632

WELDON, VIRGINIA V., medical school administrator, pediatric endocrinologist; b. Toronto, Sept. 8, 1935; came to U.S. 1937; d. John Edward and Carolyn Edity (Swift) Verral; m. Clarence S. Weldon, Nov. 30, 1963; children—Ann Stuart, Susan Shaeffer. A.B. cum laude, Smith Coll., 1957; M.D., SUNY-Buffalo, 1962. Diplomate Am. Bd. Pediatrics. Intern Johns Hopkins Hosp., Balt., 1962-63, resident in pediatrics, 1963-64, fellow in pediatric endocrinology Johns Hopkins U., 1964-67, instr. pediatrics, 1967-68; asst. prof. Washington U., St. Louis, 1968-73, assoc. prof. pediatrics, 1973-79, prof. pediatrics, 1979—, dep. vice chancellor med. affairs, 1983—; gen. clin. research ctrs. adv. com. NIH, Bethesda, Md., 1976-80; research resources adv. council, 1980-84; bd. dirs. Nat. Soc. Med. Research, Washington, 1982. Contbr. articles to profl. jours. Commr. St. Louis Zool. Park, 1983; bd. dirs. United Way Greater St. Louis, 1978—. Fellow Am. Acad. Pediatrics; mem. Inst. Medicine, Assn. Am. Med. Colls. (del., chmn.-elect council acad. socs. 1983), Am. Pediatric Soc., Endocrine Soc., Soc. Pediatric Research, AAU (joint com. health policy), St. Louis Med. Soc., Sigma Xi, Alpha Omega Alpha. Methodist. Home: 4967 Pershing IL Saint Louis MO 63108 Office: Washington U Sch Medicine Box 8106 660 S Euclid Ave Saint Louis MO 63110

WELKER, HENRY ALBERT, II, personnel consulting company executive; b. Detroit, July 22, 1940; s. Henry Albert and Helen Marie (Zindler) W.; m. Teuta Bego, June 11, 1972. B.B.A., U. Detroit, 1970. Cert. personnel cons. Acct. Gen. Motors, Livonia, Mich., 1961-70; account exec. Mgmt. Recruiters, Southfield, Mich., 1971-72; placement dir. Honeywell Inst., Southfield, 1972-73; placement mgr. R. Half Personnel, Southfield, 1973-76; chief exec. officer H. Welker Personnel, Southfield, 1976—; advisor electronic data processing curriculum Oakland Community Coll., Farmington Hills, Mich., 1982—. Served with U.S. Army, 1963-64. Mem. Mich. Assn. Personnel Cons. (chmn. ethics com.). Office: Henry Welker Personnel Inc 24901 Northwestern St Suite 304 Southfield MI 48075

WELL, DON, theological college president; b. Haifa, Israel, July 15, 1937; came to U.S., 1938, naturalized, 1955; s. Ben Zion and Esther (Hill) W.; m. Hedi Esther Friedman, Oct. 5, 1975; children—Avraham B., Shira, Yishai, David S., Tamar L., Hillel. B.A., Roosevelt U., 1959; postgrad. U. Chgo., 1961-66; B.H.L., Hebrew Theol. Coll., 1961, D.H.L., 1977. Ordained rabbi, 1960. Lectr., U. Chgo., 1964-66; research assoc. Nat. Inst. Research in Behavioral Scis., Szold Inst., Jerusalem, Israel, 1966-71, sr. research psychologist, 1966-71; prof. ednl. adminstr. U. Tel Aviv, Ramat Aviv, Israel, 1966-71; assoc. dean Hebrew Theol. Coll., Skokie, Ill., 1971-79, pres., 1981—; exec. asst. to pres. Car-X Mufflers, Chgo., 1979-81. Advisor, Minister of Edn., Govt. Israel, 1968-71. Vice-pres. Religious Zionists of Am., 1978-82. Served with Israeli Def. Forces, 1970-71. NDEA fellow, 1961-64. Mem. Chgo. Rabbinical Council, Rabbinical Council Am., Assn. Profs. Jewish Studies. Jewish Orthodox. Author: Case Book in Educational Administration, 1970; co-editor: Megamot, 1967-70; mem. editorial staff Halachah U'Refuah, 1981, 82, 83; sculptor bronze Jerusalem, 1982. Office: 7135 N Carpenter St Skokie IL 60077

WELLER, LLOYD WAYNE, engineering firm executive; b. Kansas City, Kans., Nov. 27, 1921; s. Lloyd Cecil and Maude Buford (Wahlenmaier) W.; B.S.C.E., Kans. State U., 1944; B.S.S.E., U. Ill., 1945; M.S. Environ. Engring., Kans. U., 1966; m. Lorene Grant DeMuth Eherenmann, June 8, 1979; children—Fredrick Wayne, Courtney Ann; stepchildren—Roy Grant DeMuth, William Barry DeMuth, Karol Gwen DeMuth Padget. Engring. designer Consol. Vultee Aircraft Corp., Fort Worth, 1944; engring. designer Black & Veatch, Kansas City, Mo., 1946-51, project engr., 1951-64, partner, prin. engr., 1964—; bd. govs. Am. Royal. Cubmaster, Kaw council Boy Scouts Am., 1956, asst. scoutmaster, 1958-61, mem. Eagle Bd. Rev., 1960-70; hon. bd. dirs. Rockhurst Coll.; mem. pres.'s club Kans. State U. Served with AUS, 1944-46. Diplomate Am. Acad. Environ. Engrs.; registered profl. engr. Fellow ASCE; mem. Water Pollution Control Fedn., Am. Water Works Assn. (life), Am. Soc. Mil. Engrs., Am. Soc. Mil. Engrs., Nat. Soc. Profl. Engrs., Am. Cons. Engrs. (dir. council 1980-81), Kans. Cons. Engrs. (chmn. 1979-80), Kans. Engring. Soc. (past pres. Eastern chpt., Key Mem. award 1967), Am. Philatelic Soc., Kans. State U. (life), U. Ill. (life), Kans. U. (life), alumni socs., Kansas City Univ. Assocs., Nat. Rifle Assn., Phi Kappa Phi, Sigma Tau, Steel Ring. Republican. Clubs: Homestead Country, Indian Creek Racquet, Woodside Racquet, Overland Racquet, Perry Yacht, Mill Creek Gun; Elephant of Johnson City. Contbr. articles to various tech. jours. Home: 5357 Mission Woods Rd Mission Woods KS 66205 Office: Black & Veatch 1500 Meadow Lake Pkwy Kansas City MO 64114

WELLES, NYDIA LELIA CANOVAS, psychologist; b. Buenos Aires, Argentina, Mar. 30, 1935; came to U.S., 1968, naturalized, 1977; d. Artemio Tomás and Pura (Martínez) Canovas; B.A. in Elem. Edn., Nat. Coll. Edn., Evanston, Ill., 1976; M.A. in Counseling Psychology, Northwestern U., 1977, now postgrad.; m. Lorant Welles, Oct. 21, 1967; 1 son, Lorant Esteban. Tchr. in Argentina, 1954-64; pvt. practice psychology, Argentina, 1964-67; social worker Cath. Charities, Chgo., 1971-75; translator SRA, Chgo., 1975; test adminstr. Ednl. Testing Service, 1975-76; Latin Am. Services supr. Edgewater Uptown Community Mental Health Council, Chgo., 1978—; research asst. Center Family Studies, 1978-79. Mem. Ill. Assn. for Hispanic Mental Health (co-founder), Phi Delta Kappa. Roman Catholic. Author papers in field. Home: 5255 W Winona St Chicago IL 60630

WELLINGTON, ROBERT HALL, See *Who's Who in America,* 43rd edition.

WELLIVER, WARREN DEE, state supreme court justice; b. Butler, Mo., Feb. 24, 1920; s. Carl Winfield and Burdee Marie (Wolfe) W.; B.A., U. Mo., 1945, LL.B., J.D., 1948; m. Ruth Rose Galey, Dec. 25, 1942; children—Gale Dee (Mrs. William B. Stone), Carla Camile (Mrs. Dayton Stone), Christy Marie (Mrs. Norman Sullivan). Admitted to Mo. bar, 1948; asst. pros. atty. Boone County, Columbia, Mo., 1948-54; sr. ptnr. firm Welliver, Atkinson and Eng, Columbia; 1960-74; tchr. law U. Mo. Law Sch., 1948-49; mem. Mo. Senate, 1977-79; justice Supreme Ct. Mo., Jefferson City, 1979—. Mem. Gov. Mo. Adv. Council Alcoholism and Drug Abuse, chmn. drug council, 1970-72; chmn. Task Force Revision Mo. Drug Laws, 1970-71; liaison mem. council Nat. Inst. Alcoholism and Alcohol Abuse, 1972-79. Bd. dirs. Nat. Assn. Mental Health, 1970-79, regional v.p., 1973-75; pres. Mo. Assn. Mental Health, 1968-69, Stephens Coll. Assocs., 1965—; pres. Friends of Library, U. Mo., 1978-79; bd. curators Stephens Coll., 1980—; Democratic county chmn., 1954-64; Served with USNR, 1941-45. Hon. fellow Harry S. Truman Library Inst., 1979—. Fellow Am. Coll. Trial Lawyers, Am. Bar Found.; mem. Am., Mo. (pres. 1967-68), Boone County (pres. 1970) bar assns., Am. Judicature Soc., Am. Legion (past post comdr.), Order of Coif. Clubs: Country of Mo., Columbia Country (past pres.). Home: 3430 Woodrail Terr Columbia MO 65203 Office: Supreme Ct Bldg Jefferson City MO 65101

WELLNITZ, CRAIG OTTO, lawyer, English educator; b. Elwood, Ind., Dec. 5, 1946; s. Frank Otto and Jeanne (Albright) W.; m. Karen Sue Thomas, Apr. 13, 1974; children—Jennifer Suzanne, Anne Katherine. B.A., Purdue U., 1969; M.A., Ind. U., 1972; J.D., Ind. U.-Indpls., 1978. Bar: Ind. 1978, U.S. Dist. Ct. (so. dist.) Ind. 1978, U.S. Supreme Ct. 1983, U.S. Ct. Appeals (7th and Fed. cirs.) 1984. Instr. Danville Jr. Coll., Ill., 1972-74, S.W. Mo. State U., Springfield, Mo., 1974-75; ptnr. Coates, Hatfield & Calkins, Indpls., 1978—; pub. defender Marion County, Ind., 1979—; instr. Ind. Central U., Indpls., 1981-82; mem. adj. faculty dept. English, Butler U., Indpls., 1983—. Columnist: A Jury of Your Peers, 1984—; lectr. The American Legal Justice System, 1984—; The Written Word: The Power of Effective Writing, 1985. Vice committeeman Indpls. Republican precinct, 1978. Postgrad. study grantee S.W. Mo. State U., Springfield, 1975. Mem. Indpls. Bar Assn., Ind. State Bar Assn., ABA, Assn. Trial Lawyers Am., Ind. Trial Lawyers Assn. Methodist. Club: Riviera (Indpls.). Lodge: Elks. Home: 5234 N New Jersey St Indianapolis IN 46220 Office: Coates Hatfield & Calkins 107 N Pennsylvania Suite 902 Indianapolis IN 46204

WELLS, DARRELL GIBSON, plant science educator; b. Pierre, S.D., Feb. 21, 1917; s. Frank Elliot and Anna Wilhelmina (Gibson) W.; m. Lois Ida Hall, Feb. 1, 1946; children—David, Howard, Alan. B.S., S.D. State Coll., 1941; M.S., Washington State Coll., 1943; Ph.D., U. Wis.-Madison, 1949. Asst. in agronomy Washington State U., Pullman, 1943-45; research asst. in plant pathology, U. Wis., Madison, 1945-49; assoc. prof. to prof. agronomy Miss. State U., Starkville, 1949-58, 60-62, advisor Moor Plantation, Ibadan, Nigeria, 1958-60, prof. plant sci. S.D. State U., Brookings, 1962-82; lobbyist in state govt. S.D. Resources Coalition, Pierre, 1984. Contbr. articles to profl. jours. Plant breeder 8 varieties of winter wheat S.D. State U., 1964-82. Mem. Watertown Peace and Justice Ctr., S.D.; bd. dirs. S.D. Resources Coalition, Brookings. Mem. Common Cause, The Nature Conservancy (chmn. S.D. chpt. 1982—). Democrat. Mem. Unitarian Universalist Fellowship, Soc. for Preservation Barbershop Quartet Singing in Am. (Brookings) (show chmn., editor 1974-84). Avocations: barbershop singing; camping; bird watching; gardening; peace. Home: RR4 Box 233 Brookings SD 57006

WELLS, DAVID LEE, mechanical engineering technology educator, manufacturing researcher; b. McKeesport, Pa., Oct. 21, 1936; s. Otis Henry and Ottilie Hilda (Bostak) W.; m. Phyllis Claire Burmester, Mar. 19, 1960 (div. 1972); m. Carol Louise Villars, Dec. 31, 1977; 1 child, Tammie Jo. B.S., in Mech. Engring., Stanford U., 1958, M.S. in Mech. Engring., 1960. Cert. mfg. engr. Materials and mfg. cons. U.S. Air Force, Los Angeles, 1963-64; v.p. Universal Tech. Corp., Dayton, Ohio, 1964-69; pres. Delphi Corp., Dayton, 1969-73; mfg. cons. Wilmington, Ohio, 1973-78; head dept. mech. engring. tech. U. Cin., 1978—; instr. civil and indsl. techs. So. State Coll., Ohio, 1977-78; acting asst. prof. physics Wilmington Coll., 1978; cons. Multinat. Agribus. Systems, Inc., 1979, Ctr. Mfg. Tech., 1981-82, Charles Merrill Publishing Co., 1981, Ohio Med. Instrument Co., 1982, Houghton-Mifflin Pubs., 1983, Cin. Gas & Electric Co., 1983, Gen. Electric Co., 1984. Contbr. articles to profl. jours. and papers to profl. confs. Served as 1st lt. U.S. Air Force, 1960-63. Recipient exemplary leadership plaque Engring. and Sci. Inst. Dayton, 1972. Mem. Accreditation Bd. for Engring. and Tech. (ad hoc visitor for mech. engring. tech. programs 1981—), Am. Soc. Engring. Edn. (chmn. mfg. div. 1983—, dir. profl. interest council 1984—), ASME (chmn. Stanford chpt. 1957-58, vice chmn. mech. tech. in engring. dept. heads com. 1979-82, chmn. 1982-83, chmn. ad hoc task group on mech. engring. tech. accreditation criteria 1980—, engring. edn. bd. 1981-84, Soc. Mfg. Engrs. (mem. edn. com., Computer and Automated Systems Assn., Machine Vision Group, Robotics Inst.), Tau Alpha Pi (faculty adv. 1981-82). Republican. Avocations: military history; wine collecting; art collecting. Office: Dept Mech Engring Tech U Cincinnati 100 E Central Pkwy Cincinnati OH 45210

WELLS, ROGER WARREN, wildlife biologist; b. Pittsburg, Kans., Feb. 20, 1951; s. Warren Eugene and Thelma Irene (Brown) W.; m. Nancy Marie Schauf, Oct. 5, 1974; children—Angela Marie, Diane Christine, Sheila Kathleen. B.S. in Wildlife Biology, Kans. State U., 1973. Area wildlife mgr. Kans. Fish and Game Commn., Independence, Kans., 1973-77, dist. wildlife biologist, Eureka, Kans., 1977-78, wildlife research biologist, Emporia, Kans., 1978—; wildlife cons. Sutherlands, Inc., 1980—. Contbr. articles to profl. jours. Chmn., Lyon County Rural Water Dist. 1, Americus, Kans., 1984—; coordinator Sacred Heart Ch. Marriage Preparation, Emporia, 1984—; bridge team leader Lyon County Marriage Encounter, 1983. Mem. Soc. Range Mgmt., Wildlife Soc. (chpt. sec.-treas.), Quail Unltd., Inc., Ducks Unltd., Kans. Acad. Sci. Prarie Grouse Tech. Council. Republican. Roman Catholic. Avocations: Hunting; fishing; gardening; reading; outdoor photography. Home: 508 7th St Box 26 Americus KS 66835 Office: Kans Fish and Game Commn PO Box 1525 Emporia KS 66801

WELLS, WILLIAM LEROY, clergyman; b. Bion Orville and Pauline (Brashler) W.; m. Mary Jesse Apolinar, June 5, 1965; children—Jeffrey Grant, William LeRoy, Mark Andrew. B.A., Seattle Pacific Coll., 1956; M.Div., Berkeley Bapt. Div. Sch., 1959; D.Min., Pitts. Theol. Sem., 1978. Ordained to ministry, Baptist Ch., 1959; pastor First Bapt. Ch., Hay, Wash., 1959-62, Delta Community Bapt. Ch., Everett, Wash., 1962-66; minister Leadership Devel. program Pitts. Bapt. Assn., 1973-80; exec. minister Wis. Bapt. State Conv., 1980—. Served with AUS, 1966-73. Decorated Bronze Star medal. Democrat. Club: Milwaukee Athletic. Author: Planning for Evangelism in the Local Church, 1978. Office: 15330 W Watertown Plank Rd Elm Grove WI 53122

WELLS, WILLIAM STEVEN, marketing communications consultant, syndicated cartoonist; b. Detroit, Aug. 19, 1945; s. Ronald and Eleanor (Vancea) W.; A.B., Hamilton Coll., 1967; m. Mary Rudolph, Nov. 27, 1969; children—Adam, David. Journalist, New Haven Register, Providence Jour., Detroit Free Press, 1968-75; exec. asst. to Mich. Gov. William Milliken, Lansing, 1975-76; account exec. Fleishman-Hillard, Inc., St. Louis, 1976-78; v.p., mgr. Doremus & Co., Mpls., 1978-80; sr. v.p., mng. dir. Hill & Knowlton, Inc., Mpls., 1980-84; pres. Wells and Co., 1984—; co-author syndicated bus. cartoon strip Executive Suite, United Features Syndicate. Served with USNR, 1968-69. Mem. Nat. Investor Relations Inst., Issues Mgmt. Assn. Republican. Clubs: Minneapolis, Edina Country, Minn. Squash Raquets Assn. Contbr. articles to profl. jours. Office: Wells and Co 1 Main at Riverplace Suite 501 Minneapolis MN 55414

WELTER, HAROLD AUGUSTINE, insurance agency executive; b. La Porte, Ind., Mar. 12, 1945; s. Joseph Leo and Lou Ellen (Atchison) W.; m. Becky Jane Green, Aug. 18, 1973; children—Susan Elizabeth, Laura Jane, Cheryl Lyn, Nathan Joseph. Student, U. Ky.-Fort Knox, 1963-65; diploma Midwestern Broadcasting Sch., 1965. Staff announcer Sta. WRIN, Rensselaer, Ind., 1965-66; program dir. Sta. WLOI, La Porte, 1966-69; gen. mgr. Sta. WKVI, Knox, Ind., 1969-73; press sec. to U.S. Congressman E.F. Landgrebe, Washington, 1973-75; owner, mgr. Harold Welter & Assocs., Knox, 1975—. Trustee Knox Community Sch. Corp., 1978—, pres., 1980-81, 84-85; precinct committeeman Starke County Republican Central Com., Knox, 1982—; del. Rep. State Conv., 1978, 80, 82, 84. Served with U.S. Army, 1963-65. Recipient Prodn. Growth award Equitable Life N.Y., 1977; named to Nat. Leaders Corps, Equitable Life N.Y., 1977. Mem. Million Dollar Round Table, Nat. Assn. Life Underwriters (Nat. Quality award 1980, 81, 82, 84, Nat. Sales Achievement award 1978, 80, 81, 82, 84). Roman Catholic. Avocations: sportscasting; travel. Home: Route #3 Box 85 Knox IN 46534 Office: Harold Welter & Assocs PO Box 195 Knox IN 46534

WELTMAN, HARRY, professional basketball executive. Exec. v.p., gen. mgr. Cleve. Cavaliers. Office: Cleve Cavaliers The Coliseum 2923 Streetsboro Rd Richfield OH 44286*

WELTON, JAMES ARTHUR, transportation broker and consultant; b. Portland, Oreg., Jan. 1, 1921; s. Raymond Patrick and Birdie Vernette (Larson) W.; m. Maverette Lavonne Ness, Aug. 22, 1942 (dec. Nov. 1963); children—Richard, Timothy, Nancy; m. 2d, Marjorie Elaine Page, May 31, 1964; children—Kathleen, William. Student Am. U., 1968. Instr., Inver Hills Jr. Coll., 1975, Normandale Jr. Coll., 1977; with Soo Line R.R., 1938-78, div. supt., Enderlin, N.D., 1962-72, dir. intermodal service, Mpls., 1972-77, dir. labor relations, 1977-78; pres. Welco Driver Leasing, Burnsville, Minn., 1982; pres. Welco Cons., 1981—; transp. and safety cons. United Van Bus Delivery, Mpls., Midwest Truck Leasing, Assoc. Delivery Service, Loeffel-Engstrand Co. Pres., Enderlin (N.D.) City Park Bd., 1962; bd. dirs. Greater N.D. Assn., Bismarck, 1961-62; pres. Big Bros., Shrine Hosp. Crippled Children, Mpls., 1983. Sr. reservist ICC, Washington, 1961-62. Republican. Presbyterian. Home: 2717 Dalridge Circle Burnsville MN 55337 Office: 2601 32d Ave S Minneapolis MN 55406

WELTY, TIMOTHY EDWARD, clinical pharmacist, medical educator; b. Indpls., Nov. 28, 1953; s. Willis Edward and Catherine Louise (Hatfield) W.; m. Connie Lydia Haberstroh, June 27, 1980; 1 dau., Elizabeth Anna. Student Taylor U., 1972-73; B.S. in Pharmacy, Butler U., 1977; M.A. in Religion, Trinity Evang. Div. Sch., 1980; Pharm.D., U. Minn., 1982. Registered pharmacist, Ind., Ill. Staff pharmacist Parkview Meml. Hosp. Ft. Wayne, Ind., 1977-78, Highland Park Hosp., Ill., 1978-80; staff pharmacist St. Paul Ramsey Med. Ctr., 1982-83, research fellow, 1982-83; asst. prof. pharmacology Purdue U., West Lafayette, Ind., 1983-85; clin. pharmacist for neurology/cardiology Meth. Hosp., Indpls., 1985—; co-investigator, asst. clin. research, 1983—. Mem. Am. Soc. Hosp. Pharmacists, Am. Coll. Clin. Pharmacists, Epilepsy Found. Am., Am. Assn. of Colls. of Pharmacy, Ind. Soc. of Hosp. Pharmacists. Mem. Christian and Missionary Alliance Ch. Avocation: photography. Office: Pharmacy Dept Meth Hosp 1604 N Capitol Indianapolis IN 46202

WENDEL, CHARLES HARRY, author, consultant; b. Alburnett, Iowa, Feb. 13, 1939; s. Harry A. and Letha (Risdal) W.; m. N. Kay Gerke, June 26, 1959; children—Steven, Lisa, Rosalyn. Student Concordia Coll., River Forest, Ill. Author: Power in the Past, 1971; Ency. American Farm Tractors, 1979; 150 Years of International Harvester, 1981; American Gas Engines Since 1872, 1983; Nebraska Tractor Tests Since 1920. Bd. dirs. Benton Community Sch. Dist., Van Horne, Iowa, 1982. Mem. Am. Soc. Agrl. Engrs., Midwest Old Threshers, Midwest Gas Engine Assn. (charter mem.). Democrat. Lutheran. Avocation: philately. Address: Old Iron Book Co Rural Route 1 Box 28A Atkins IA 52206

WENDELBURG, NORMA RUTH, composer, pianist, educator; b. Stafford, Kans.; d. Henry and Anna (Moeckel) Wendelburg; Mus.B., Bethany Coll., 1943; Mus.M., U. Mich., 1947; Mus.M., Eastman Sch. Music, 1951, postgrad., 1964-65, 66-67, Ph.D. in Composition, 1969; postgrad. Mozarteum, 1953-54, Vienna Acad. Music, 1955. Asst. prof. music edn., piano Wayne (Nebr.) State Coll., 1947-50, Bethany Coll., Lindsborg, Kan., 1952-53, State Coll., Cedar Falls, Ia., 1956-58; asst. prof. composition, theory, piano Hardin-Simmons U., Abilene, Tex., 1958-66, chmn. grad. com. Sch. Music, 1960-66, founder ann. univ. festival contemporary music, 1959, chmn., 1959—; asso. prof. music Dallas Bapt. Coll., 1973-75; research asst. to dir. grad. studies Eastman Sch. Music, 1966-67; former asso. prof., chmn. dept. theory, composition Southwest Tex. State U.; mem. faculty Friends Bible Coll., Haviland, Kans., 1977-83; guest composer several colls. including U. Ottawa, 1984; appeared as pianist various solo recitals, festivals. Recipient Meet the Composer award N.Y. State Council of Arts, 1979; Composition scholar Composers' Conf. Middlebury (Vt.), 1950, Berkshire Center, 1953; Fulbright award, 1953-55; Residence fellow Huntington Hartford Found., 1955-56, 58, 61; MacDowell Colony, 1958, 60, 70. Mem. Music Tchrs. Nat. Conf., Am. Music Center, MacDowell Colonists, ASCAP, Am. Soc. Univ. Composers, Am. Women Composers, Sigma Alpha Iota. Composer numerous works including Symphony, 1967, Suite for Violin and Piano, 1965, Song Cycle for Soprano, Flutes, Piano, 1974, Music for Two Pianos, 1985, Affirmation, 1982, Interlacings (organ), 1983, others. Address: 2206 N Van Buren Hutchinson KS 67052

WENDT, ELIZABETH WARCZAK, insurance company officer; b. Chgo., Aug. 27, 1931; d. John George and Elizabeth Marion (Jankowski) Warczak; m. John Edward Wendt, Oct. 31, 1953 (div.); children—John Alan, Brian Arthur, James Michael. Student Loyola U.-Chgo., 1951-52; B.S.B.A., St. Mary-of-the-Woods Coll., 1980; postgrad. Chgo. Kent Coll. Law, 1981-82. Asst. to actuary Globe Life Ins. Co., Chgo., 1970-74, asst. compliance officer Globe Life/Ryan Ins. Group, Chgo., 1974—; mem. co. rep. FLMI Soc. Chgo., 1983—; mem. Life A&H Legis. Com. Consumer Credit Ins. Assn., Chgo., 1983—; co. rep., mem. Handout Com. Life & Health Compliance Assn., 1979—. Mem. United Farm Workers Support Com., Chgo. Fellow Life Mgmt. Inst.; mem. Inst. Distaff Execs. Assn., Nat. Assn. Ins. Women (dir. 1981-82) (Chgo.). Democrat. Roman Catholic. Home: 5506 S Madison 11 Hinsdale IL 60521

WENDT, JOHN THOMAS, lawyer, educator; b. Chgo., Mar. 26, 1951; s. William Henry and Virginia (Hauf) W. B.A. summa cum laude in Humanities, U. Minn., 1973, M.A. in Am. Studies, 1981; J.D., William Mitchell, St. Paul, 1977. Bar: Minn., U.S. Dist. Ct. Minn., U.S. Ct. Appeals (8th cir.) 1978. Sole practice, Mpls., 1978—; Hennepin County Ct. arbitrator; instr. U. Minn., Mpls., 1984—, Coll. St. Thomas, St. Paul, 1983—, Lakewood Community Coll., St. Paul, 1983-84; dir. publ. Minn. Continuing Legal Edn., St. Paul, 1982-83. Contbr. articles to profl. jours. Counsel U.S. Aquatics, Inc., Colorado Springs, Colo., 1980—, Gov.'s Task Force on Minn. Sports Festival, Mpls., 1983—, U.S. Amateur Athletic Union, Indpls., 1978-80; bd. govs. U.S. Water Polo, 1983—. Recipient Gov.'s Cert. Commendation for Service, State of Minn., 1984. Mem. ABA (chmn. com. sports and entertainment law, mem. spl. projects, 1982—), Hennepin County Bar Assn. (chmn. sports and entertainment law 1983—), Minn. State Bar Assn. (legal edn. com.). Home: 1630 S 6th St Minneapolis MN 55454 Office: 219 Oliver Ave S Minneapolis MN 55405

WENGER, STEVEN KENNETH, psychology educator, researcher; b. Horton, Kans., June 11, 1945; s. Kenneth Leo and Thelma Elizabeth (Sernes) W.; m. Barbara Jane Youmans, Dec. 23, 1972; 1 child, Noah Christopher. A.S. in Electronic Engring., Central Tech. Inst., 1967; B.A. in Psychology, Washburn U., 1975; M.S. in Psychology, Kans. State U., 1977, Ph.D. in Psychology, 1980. Instr. Kans. State U., Manhattan, 1977-79; asst. prof. psychology MacMurray Coll., Jacksonville, Ill., 1979—, chmn. Dept. Psychology, 1982—. Contbr. articles to profl. jours. Served as staff sgt. U.S. Air Force, 1967-71. Mem. Midwestern Psychol. Assn. (local rep. 1984—), AAUP (v.p. 1984-85, pres. 1985—), Psi Chi, Phi Kappa Phi. Avocation: amateur radio. Home: 803 S Church Jacksonville IL 62650 Office: Mac Murray Coll Psychology Dept Jacksonville IL 62650

WENK, DENNIS CHARLES, insurance company executive; b. Evergreen Park, Ill., Apr. 6, 1952; s. Charles Martin and Barbara Jean (Timmons) W.; m. Manette Jean McReynolds, May 14, 1978; 1 child, Marissa Ann. Student Coe Coll., 1970-72; A.A. in Bus. and data processing, Moraine Valley Community Coll., 1974; B.S. in Computer Sci., No. Ill. U., 1977, M.B.A., 1985. Cert. systems profl.; cert. data processor; cert. info. systems auditor. Programmer, analyst Allied Mills, Inc., Chgo., 1977-78; sr. cons. Consumer Systems, Oakbrook, Ill., 1978-79; acct. mgr. C.B.M., Schaumburg, Ill., 1979-80; EDP audit cons. Beatrice Cos., Chgo., 1980-82; mgr. data ctr. Zurich-Am. Inst. Co., Schaumburg, Ill., 1982—. Author: Management Accounting for MIS. Mem. Assn. Computing Machinery, Computer Measurement Group. Avocations: tennis; racketball; volleyball. Home: 816 Madison Ave St Charles IL 60174

WENSTRAND, THOMAS, agribusiness executive; b. Shenandoah, Iowa, Nov. 25, 1947; s. William Sherwood and Bernice (Liljedahl) W. B.S., Iowa State U., 1970; M.B.A., Harvard U., 1972. Seed mktg. trainee Dekalb AgResearch Inc., Red Oak, Iowa, 1970, mgr. mergers and acquisitions, DeKalb, Ill., 1977-78, mgr. animal ops., 1978-79, mgr. internat. ops., 1979-80; faculty Harvard U. Bus. Sch., 1972-73; asst. to pres. Ariz.-Colo. Land & Cattle Co., Phoenix, 1973-77; pres. Hawkeye Steel Products, Houghton, Iowa, 1981—. Mem. Ariz. Trade Council, 1975-77; mem. Iowa Dist. Export Council, 1981—. Mem. Young Pres.'s Orgn., Livestock Conservation Inst. (bd. dirs. 1984—), Phi Eta Sigma, Alpha Zeta, Gamma Sigma, Delta, Gamma Gamma. Address: Soaring Hawk Pl Mount Pleasant IA 52641

WENSTROM, FRANK AUGUSTUS, state senator, city and county official; b. Dover, N.D., July 27, 1903; s. James August and Anna Petra (Kringstad) W.; student public schs., Carrington, N.D.; m. Mary Esther Pickett, June 10, 1938. In oil bus., Carrington, 1932-38, Williston, N.D., 1938-45; mgr. Williston C. of C., 1945-51; public relations officer 1st Nat. Bank, Williston, 1951-53, mng. officer real estate mortgage dept., 1953-60; exec. officer Northwestern Fed. Savs. and Loan Assn. Williston, 1964-68; spl. cons. Am. State Bank Williston, 1968-73; mem. N.D. Senate, 1957-60, 67—, pres. pro tem, 1973-74; lt. gov. State of N.D., 1963-64; dir., sec. Williston Community Hotel Co., 1950—; chmn. subscriber's com. N.W. dist. N.D. Blue Cross-Blue Shield, 1972—. Mem. Williston Public Housing Authority, 1951—, Williams County Park Bd., 1951—, N.D. Yellowstone-Ft. Union Commn., 1957-64, Legis. Research Council, 1957-60, Legis. Council, 1969-70; del. N.D. 2d Constl. Conv., 1970, pres., 1971-72; Williams County chmn. U.S. Savs. Bonds Com., 1958-69; bd. dirs. N.D. Easter Seals Soc., 1960-75, state pres., 1970-71; bd. advisors Salvation Army, 1960-75; bd. dirs. Univ. Found., U. N.D., Williston Center, 1965—; mem. joint legis. com. Nat. Assn. Ret. Tchrs.-Am. Assn. Ret. Persons, 1975—, chmn., 1979-80. Recipient Liberty Bell award N.D. Bar Assn., 1977, Disting. Service award Bismarck Jr. Coll., 1981; award Nature Conservancy, 1982; Service award Greater N.D. Assn., 1983. Mem. Upper Missouri Purebred Cattle Breeders Assn. (sec.-treas. 1947-62), N.D. Wildlife Fedn. (state pres. 1947-48), Greater N.D. Assn. (dir. 1955-56, mem. Roosevelt Nat. Meml. Park com. 1957-63), U.S. Savs. and Loan League (legis. com. 1965-67). Republican. Congregationalist. Clubs: Rotary, Elks, Masons, Shriners, Order Eastern Star. Office: PO Box 187 Williston ND 58801-0002

WENTE, VERGIE D., state official; b. Decatur County, Kans., Apr. 24, 1936; d. Virgil D. and Hazel (Storer) Wennihan; student Colby Community Coll., 1969; m. Lloyd A. Wente, June 23, 1953 (div. May 1966); children—Allen Charles, Rhonda Marie, Daniel Lloyd, Lynne LaRea. Librarian, N.W. Kans. Library System, Hoxie, Kans., 1968-70; clk. Dist. Ct. Sheridan County, Hoxie, 1971—, chief dist. ct. clk. 15th Jud. Dist., Hoxie, 1977—. Recipient Spl. Recognition, chief Justice Supreme Ct. Kans., 1981. Mem. Nat. Assn. Ct. Adminstrn. (dir. 1982—, chmn. awards com.), Kans. Dist. Ct. Clks. Assn. (state sec.-treas. 1978, state pres. 1980), Kans. Assn. Dist. Ct. Clks. and Adminstrs. (legis. chmn. 1981—), N.W. Kans. Dist. Ct. Clks. Assn. (pres. 1975-77), Kans. Jud. Adminstrs. (spl. mem. clks. and adminstrs. adv. council 1979, 81—), Mem. Ch. of Christ. Home: 1417 Sheridan Ave Hoxie KS 67740 Office: Courthouse Hoxie KS 67740

WENTZIEN, PAUL WARREN, accountant; b. Marshaltown, Iowa, Nov. 4, 1937; s. Irwin H. and Vivian Alice (Walter) W.; m. K. Elaine Armstrong, Dec. 30, 1962; children—Elizabeth, Jennifer, Paul, Margo. B.S. in Commerce, U. Iowa, 1959. C.P.A., Mo. Acct., Arthur Andersen, Chgo., 1959-72, ptnr., Chgo., 1972-79, ptnr., St. Louis, 1979—. Chmn. Chgo. Bible Soc., 1978; treas. Oak Park Housing Center (Ill.), 1977; bd. dirs. Eden Theol. Sem., St. Louis, 1983, Oak Park Pub. Library, 1978. Mem. United Ch. of Christ. Clubs: Mo. Athletic, Sunset Country (St. Louis); Palisades Park Country (Mich.).

WENZEL, FRED WILLIAM, apparel manufacturing executive; b. St. Louis, 1915. Vice pres. H. Wenzel Tent and Duck Co., 1937-61; pres. Hawthorn Finishing Co. Inc., 1952-61; with Kellwood Co., Inc., Chesterfield, Mo., 1961—, chmn. bd. and chief exec. officer, 1964, chmn. bd., pres., 1965-76, chmn. bd. and chief exec. officer, dir., 1976—; dir. Anheuser-Busch Cos. Inc., Merc. Trust Co. N.Am., Merc. Bancorp Inc., United Energy Resources Inc., United Gas Pipe Line Co. Office: Kellwood Co Inc 600 Kellwood Pkwy Chesterfield MO 63017

WENZEL, RICHARD FRANK, educator, consultant; b. Milw., Sept. 10, 1930; s. Theodore Elmer and Corrinne Gladys (Collins) W.; m. Marguerite Patty Lu Anderson, July 12, 1958; children—Peter, Jeremy. B.S., Marquette U., 1952, M.A., 1958. Classroom tchr. Milw. Pub. Schs., 1954-57, speech therapist, 1952-57, supr. community relations, 1957-64, coordinator mass media services, 1964-66, dir. student transp., 1967—; dir. pub. relations Wis. Edn. Assn., 1966-67; cons. pub. relations and transp. Pres. Boesel Scholarship Found., 1967—; chmn. Milwaukee County unit Am. Heart Assn., 1970-72; mem. Milw. Presbytery Commn. on Race and Religion, 1964-67; drama dir. Red Arrow Boys Camp, 1953—. Recipient Disting. Service award Milw. Jaycees, 1964; Outstanding Transp. Supr. award Wis. AAA, 1979; Valuable Vol. award WMVS-TV, 1967. Mem. Wis. Assn. Pupil Transp. (pres. 1975), Wis. Edn. Assn. (pres. nat. pub. relations council 1966), Schoolmasters of Wis. (pres. 1969), Milw. Radio and TV Council (pres. 1966), Friends of Channel 10 (pres. 1967), Wis. Congress Parents and Tchrs. (dir. 1966-69), Wis. Assn. of the Professions (dir. 1967-70), Nat. Safety Council (com. mem. 1979—), Wis. Sch. Pub. Relations Assn. (pres. 1968-70), Nat Assn. Pupil Transp. Lodge: Masons. Producer ednl. series Wis. Ednl. TV Network, 1973; producer-dir. Bicentennial pageant Free and Equal, Milw. Pub. Schs., 1976; producer-dir. radio series High Hopes, 1966-67. Home: 17780 Royalcrest Dr Brookfield WI 53005 Office: 5225 W Vliet St Milwaukee WI 53208

WERGOWSKE, WILLIAM GARY, accountant; b. Cin., Sept. 6, 1941; s. William Leslie and Thelma Leah (Clemons) W.; B.B.A., U. Cin., 1963; M.B.A., Xavier U., 1971; m. Mary Helen Kemper, June 7, 1975. Mem. staff Pension Group Cons.'s, Inc., Cin., 1957-63; methods analyst Western and So. Life Ins. Co., Cin., 1965-73; mgr. mgmt. services and accounting services Main Lafrentz and Co., Cin., 1973-77; pvt. practice accounting, Cin., 1977-79; pres. William G. Wergowske & Co., Inc., C.P.A.s, Cin., 1979—; mem. faculty Coll. Mt. St. Joseph, 1979-80; chmn. bd., pres. Midwest Software, Inc., 1978—; treas. Oil Pit Shop, Inc., 1979-80, Nursing Staff of Louisville, Inc., 1979-80; dir., treas. Simon Winds, Inc., 1981—, Tri-Ax Communications, Inc., 1982-83, Country Wide Communications, Inc., 1982-83. Treas. Home Aid Service of Cin. Community Chest, 1974-77; bd. dirs., treas. Down Syndrome Assn. of Greater Cin., 1981-83, Southwestern Ohio Coalition for Persons with Disabilities, 1982—. Served to 1st lt. Signal Corps, U.S. Army, 1963-65. C.P.A., Ohio. Mem. Nat. Assn. Accountants (v.p. 1976-78), Ohio Soc. C.P.A.'s (cons. systems and EDP), Am. Inst. C.P.A.'s, EDP Auditors Assn. Roman Catholic. Club: Cin. (trustee 1977-79, 2d v.p. 1979). Home: 5519 Lucenna Dr Cincinnati OH 45238 Office: 1958 Anderson Ferry Rd Cincinnati OH 45238

WERLING, DONN PAUL, environmental educator; b. Ft. Wayne, Ind., Oct. 14, 1945; s. Paul Henry and Lydia Sophia (Rebber) W.; m. Diane Mueller, July 11, 1970; 1 child, Benjamin Paul. B.S., Valparaiso U., 1967; M.S., Mich. State U., 1968; M.Ed., Loyola U., 1970; Ph.D., U. Mich., 1979. Dir. nature project Raymond Sch., Chgo. Bd. Edn., 1969-72; dir. Evanston Environ. Assn., Ill., 1973-81; dir. Henry Ford Estate, U. Mich.-Dearborn, 1983—, adj. asst. prof. edn., 1984—; founder N.Am. Voyageur Conf., 1977. Author: Environmental Education and Your School Site, 1973; A School-Community Stewardship Model, 1979; Lake Michigan and Its Lighthouses, 1982. Mem. state master plan com. on environ. edn. State of Ill., Springfield, 1970; mem. adv. com. Ill. Coastal Zone, Chgo., 1978; bd. dirs. Ill. Shore council Girl Scouts U.S.A., 1978-82, Chgo. Maritime Soc., 1982. Recipient Mayor's award City of Evanston, 1976, Russell E. Wilson award U. Mich. Sch. Edn., 1979, Service award Ill. Shore council Girl Scouts U.S., 1978; named to Outstanding Young Men Am., Jaycees, 1975. Mem. Assn. Interpretive Naturalists, Am. Assn. Mus., Great Lakes Lighthouse Keepers Assn. (founder, pres. 1982—), Tourist and Travel Assn. Southeast Mich. (chmn. bd. dirs. 1984—). Club: Prairie (Chgo). Lodge: Kiwanis. Avocations: canoeing; writing; singing bluewater music. Address: Henry Ford Estate Lair Ln U Mich Dearborn MI 48128

WERNER, DONALD, municipal official. Fire chief City of Columbus, Ohio. Office: Columbus Fire Dept Office of the Fire Chief Columbus OH 43215*

WERT, HAL ELLIOTT, JR., history educator; b. Detroit, Apr. 17, 1940; s. Hal Elliott and Frances May (Shadle) W.; m. Tinsley Jane Lowe, Nov. 25, 1978; children—Andrew Elliott, Allison East. B.A., U. Iowa, 1966, M.A., U. Kans., 1974, M.P.H., 1975, Ph.D., 1985. Asst. instr. U. Kans., Lawrence, 1967-71; instr. Kansas City Art Inst., Mo., 1971-74; asst. prof. Kansas City Art Inst., 1975-78, assoc. prof. history, 1979—, dir. Japan Study Abroad, 1977—, dir. Japanese studies program, 1975—. Contbr. articles to profl. jours. Served with U.S. Army, 1960-63. Nat. Def. Fgn. Lang. grantee, 1969; Nat. Teaching fellow, 1972; Alliance of Ind. Colls. of Art grantee, 1984; Hoover Presdl. Library Assn. fellow, 1985. Mem. Soc. Historians of Am. Fgn. Relations, Am.

Com. History of Second World War, Internat. Council Fgn. Relations, Internat. Churchill Soc., Am. Hist. Assn. Democrat. Avocations: campaign buttons; political memorabelia. Home: 1847 Barker Lawrence KS 66044 Office: Kansas City Art Inst 4415 Warwick Blvd Kansas City MO 64111

WERTH, PAMELA ANN, lithographic company executive; b. Beaver Dam, Wis., Aug. 19, 1954; d. William Russell and Clara Mary (Davison) W. B.B.A., U. Wis.-Stout, 1976; postgrad. Printing Inst. Ill., part-time 1979-81, DePaul U., summer 1975, Keller Grad. Sch., Chgo., 1983-84. Adminstrv. asst. Reed Ill. Corp., Chgo., 1977-78; payroll clk. Chgo. Litho Plate Graining Co., Inc., 1978-79, acctg. mgr., 1980-83, treas., 1984—, sec.-treas. subs. Ala. Engraving/-Platemakers, Birmingham, 1981—, treas. subs. Spectracolor, Inc., Milw., 1985—; acct. cons. Relgraphic Systems, Chgo., 1980-81. Sunday sch. tchr. Trinity Luth. Ch., Evanston, Ill., 1978-80; gen. leader 4th Youth Group, Hanover Park, Ill, 1982. Mem. Nat. Assn. Female Execs. Avocations: reading; sewing; travel in U.S.; growing house plants. Home: Apt 215 700 Wellington St Elk Grove Village IL 60007 Office: Chgo Litho Plate Graining Co Inc 3d Floor 549 W Fulton Ave Chicago IL 60606

WERTH, RICHARD GEORGE, chemistry educator; b. Markesan, Wis., Feb. 5, 1920; s. George William and Lillie (Luethe) W.; B.A., Wartburg Coll., 1942; M.S., U. Wis., 1948, Ph.D., 1950; m. Wilma Margaret Lauer, June 2, 1943; 1 son, Gerald Richard, Jr. chemist E.I. duPont de Nemours & Co., Niagara Falls, N.Y., 1942-44, 46; prof. chemistry Concordia Coll., Moorhead, Minn., 1950—, chmn. dept., 1961-69, 74-77; vis. fellow Cornell U., Ithaca, N.Y., 1970-71; vis. scientist Univ. Hygienic Lab., U. Iowa, 1983. Served with USNR, 1944-46. Fellow AAAS, Am. Inst. Chemists; mem. Am. Chem. Soc. (councilor 1964-78, com. on chem. edn. 1971-76), Midwest Assn. Chemistry Tchrs. in Liberal Arts Colls., Soc. Applied Spectroscopy, Minn., N.D. acads. sci., Am. Radio Relay League, Sigma Xi, Phi Lambda Upsilon. Home: 1207 S 7th St Moorhead MN 56560

WERTS, MERRILL HARMON, management consultant; b. Smith Center, Kans., Nov. 17, 1922; s. Mack Allen and Ruth Martha (Badger) W.; B.S., Kans. State U., 1947; M.S., Cornell U., 1948; m. Dorothy Wilson, Mar. 22, 1946; children—Stephen M., Riley J., Todd J., Kelly M. Beef sales mgr. John Morrell & Co., Topeka and Memphis, 1948-53; dir. mktg. Kans. Dept. Agr., Topeka, 1953-55; sec.-treas. Falley's Markets, Inc., Topeka, 1955-58; v.p. S.W. State Bank, Topeka, 1958-65; pres. First Nat. Bank, Junction City, Kans., 1965-78; individual practice mgmt. cons., Junction City, 1978—; mem. Kans. Senate, 1978—; dir. Mid Am. Machine Corp., Stockgrowers State Bank, Maple Hill, Kans., J.C. Housing & Devel., Inc. Mem. Kans. Bank Mgmt. Commn., 1967-71; mem. adv. com. U.S. Comptroller of Currency, 1971-72. Mem. Topeka Bd. Edn., 1957-61; pres. Junction City-Geary County United Fund, 1967-68; pres. Junction City Indsl. Devel., Inc., 1966-72. Trustee Kans. State U. Endowment Assn., Kans. Synod Presbyn. Westminster Found., 1965-72. Served to 1st lt., inf., AUS, 1943-46. Decorated Bronze Star medal, Purple Heart, Combat Inf. badge. Mem. Kans. State U. Alumni Assn. (pres. 1957), Am. Legion, VFW, Kans. Bankers Assn., Assn. U.S. Army, U.S., Kans. (bd. dirs., v.p. 1979-84), Junction City (pres. 1975-76) chambers commerce, Kans. Farm Bur., Kans. Livestock Assn., DAV, Sigma Phi Epsilon. Republican. Presbyterian. Clubs: Masons, Shriners, Rotary (dist. gov. 1973-74). Club: Junction City Country (past pres.). Home: 1228 Miller Dr Junction City KS 66441

WESCHE, BRENDA K., printing company executive; b. St. Louis, Feb. 21, 1956; d. Virgil Frederick Homeyer and Doris (Rueidger) Homeyer Vedder; m. John H. Wesche, May 21, 1977. A.A. in Piano, East Central Coll., Union, Mo., 1977. Bindery worker Speed-E-Way Duplicating, St. Louis, 1978-80; owner, operator B & J Printing, Washington, Mo., 1981—. Mem. United Ch. of Christ. Office: B&J Printing 213 W Main St Washington MO 63090

WESELY, DONALD RAYMOND, state senator; b. David City, Nebr., Mar. 30, 1954; s. Raymond Ely and Irene (Sabata) W.; m. Geri Williams, 1982; 1 child, Sarah. B.A., U. Nebr., 1977. Mem. Nebr. Legislature, Lincoln, 1978—; exec. assoc. Selection Research, Inc., Lincoln, 1984—. Del., Democratic Nat. Conv., San Francisco, 1984. Recipient Friend of Edn. award Nebr. State Edn. Assn., 1982, Disting. Service award Nebr. Pub. Health Assn., 1984; named Mental Health Citizen of Yr., Nebr. Mental Health Assn., 1984, Outstanding Young Man, Nebr. Jaycees, 1985. Roman Catholic. Office: State Capitol Lincoln NE 68509

WESSE, DAVID JOSEPH, university official; b. Chgo., May 5, 1951; s. Herman Theodore and Lorraine Joan (Holland) W.; m. Deborah Lynn Smith, Oct. 11, 1975; children—Jason David, Eric Joseph. A.A., Thornton Coll., 1971; student Purdue U., 1971-72; B.S., Ill. State U., 1973; M.S., Loyola U., 1983. Cert. adminstrv. mgr. Adminstrv. mgr. Reuben H. Donnelley, Chgo., 1974-76, Loyola U., Chgo., 1976-79, Joint Commn. on Accreditation Hosps., Chgo., 1979-81; adminstrv. dir. Northwestern U., Evanston, Ill., 1981—. Pres., bd. dirs. Riverdale Library Dist., 1975, Riverdale Youth Commn., 1975. Recipient Service Recognition award Riverdale Library Dist., 1975. Mem. Adminstrv. Mgmt. Soc. (bd. dirs. Chgo. chpt. 1983—, pres. 1986—), Nat. Assn. Coll. and Univ. Bus. Officers, Lambda Epsilon. Democrat. Lutheran. Home: 207 S Washington St Wheaton IL 60187 Office: Northwestern U 633 Clark St Evanston IL 60201

WESSELS, BURDELL RENSEN, insurance management executive; b. Ellsworth, Minn., Dec. 3, 1939; s. Ralph and Bernadine (Mulder) W.; m. Eileen M. Binzen, Sept. 16, 1961; children—Gail Carmon, Brian Burdell. A.A., U. Minn., 1959. Adminstrv. asst. Cargill Inc., Mpls., 1960-69; dir. ins. Internat. Multifoods, Mpls., 1969-74; pres., founder Corp. Risk Mgrs., Inc., Eden Prairie, Minn., 1974—. Mem. bldg. com. Eden Prairie Presbyn. Ch., 1982-84. Mem. Eden Prairie C. of C. (transp. com. 1982-84, accreditation com. 1984), Risk Ins. Mgmt. Soc. (chpt. bd. dirs. 1973-76), Mpls. Jaycees (treas. 1973-74). Lodge: Lions (sec. 1977-79, pres. 1981-82; Lion of Yr. 1978-79, 81-82) (Eden Prairie). Avocations: travel; spectator football and hockey. Home: 9980 Dell Rd Eden Prairie MN 55344 Office: 7525 Mitchell Rd Eden Prairie MN 55344

WESSNER, KENNETH THOMAS, management services company executive. Chmn., chmn. exec. com. Service Master Industries Inc., Downers Grove, Ill., also dir. Office: Service Master Industries Inc 2300 Warrenville Rd Downers Grove IL 60515*

WESSON, MARY ELIZABETH, office manager; b. Chgo.; d. Claude B. and Madge (Scott) Jeter. Student Ind. U. N.W., Gary, 1957-59; A.A., Ind. State U., 1979. Comml. teller Gary Nat. Bank, 1964-68; exec. sec. Lake County Mental Health Assn., Gary, 1961-64; intake supr. Lake County Dept. Pub. Welfare, Gary, 1970-73; head tchr. Elka Child Care Ctr., Gary, 1968-70; dir.-owner-adminstr. Mel-O-Dee Ln. Infant & Child Care Ctr., Gary, 1973-79; exec. sec. Gary Community Sch. Corp., 1976-79; adminstr. Health Services, Inc., Chgo., 1979-80; human resource systems data coordinator Armak Co., Chgo., 1980—; adminstrv. asst., office mgr. Robinson Bus. Service, Inc., Chgo., 1983—; curriculum coordinator Hayes Day Care Ctr., Gary, 1980—, also staff cons. Mem. Gary Bus. and Profl. Women (charter). Avocations: piano; sewing; arts and crafts; poetry. Home: 544 Roosevelt St Gary IN 46404 Office: Robinson Bus Service Chicago IL 60651

WEST, BYRON KENNETH, banker; b. Denver, Sept. 18, 1933; s. W. Byron and Cecil Bernice (Leathers) W.; m. Barbara Huth, June 25, 1955. A.B., U. Ill., 1955; M.B.A., U. Chgo., 1960. with Harris Bank, Chgo., 1957—, pres., 1980—, chmn., chief exec. officer, 1984—; dir. Motorola, Inc., Schaumburg, Ill.; bd. govs. Midwest Stock Exchange, Chgo. Chmn. bd. trustees U. Chgo.; trustee Rush-Presbyn.-St. Luke's Med. Ctr., Chgo., TRUST, Inc., Chgo.; governing mem. Orchestral Assn., Chgo.; bd. dirs. U. Ill. Found. Served to lt. (j.g.) USN, 1955-57. Recipient award for acad. excellence Wall Street Jour., 1960; named Significant Sig, Sigma Chi, 1981. Mem. Am. Bankers Assn., Assn. Res. City Bankers, Bankers Club, Econ. Club, Phi Beta Kappa. Clubs: Chicago, Commercial, Chgo. Sunday Evening, Commonwealth, University (Chgo.); Old Elm (Ft. Sheridan, Ill.); Skokie Country (Glencoe, Ill.); Pine Valley Golf (N.J.); Country of Fla. Office: Harris Bankcorp Inc 111 W Monroe St Chicago IL 60690

WEST, JACKIE LORRAINE, analyst, computer services consultant; b. Kansas City, Mo., Oct. 14, 1957; d. Everett Raymond and Donna Corraine (Cunningham) Lauderdale; m. Charles Richard West, Dec. 18, 1976; children—Raina Marie, Joshua Thomas. Cert. in EDP, Kansas City Vocat. Tech. Edn. Ctr., 1975; Assoc. Applied Sci. degree, Longview Community Coll., 1980. Sr. analyst Hallmark Cards, Kansas City, 1985—; v.p. Bits, Bytes & Prototypes, Kansas City, 1980—. Chmn. adv. bd. Kansas City Vocat. Tech. Edn. Ctr., 1985—; mem. Hallpack polit. group, 1984-85. Mem. Nat. Assn. Female Execs., Commodore User Group of Kansas City. Democrat. Baptist. Home: 16916 E 4th Terr S Independence MO 64056 Office: Hallmark Cards 25th and McGee Sts Kansas City MO 64141

WEST, RICHARD IRVING, financial exec.; b. Racine, Wis., Feb. 10, 1929; s. Byron S. and Ruth (Wilson) W.; B.S., Wis. State U., 1957; M.B.A., Northwestern U., 1966; m. Virginia M. Hansen, Mar. 16, 1957; children—Ruth Ellen, Sharon Marie, David Richard, Benjamin Thomas. Asst. to dir. finance Ill. Agrl. Assn., Chgo., 1957-60; asst. v.p. Chgo. Med. Sch., 1960-63; treas., bus. mgr. George Williams Coll., Downers Grove, Ill., 1963-70; controller Mayer, Brown & Platt, Chgo., 1970-79; pres. real estate mgmt. co., also bus. cons. firm; v.p. Stratum Five Internat., Inc., 1979—. Served with AUS, 1946-49, USAAF, 1950-51. Mem. Downers Grove C. of C. (dir.), Northwestern U. Grad. Bus. Assn. Home: 826 Birch St Downers Grove IL 60515 Office: 921 Curtis St Downers Grove IL 60515

WEST, ROBERT LEWIS, financial planner; b. Springfield, Ohio, Aug. 18, 1951; s. Robert Leslie and Julia Belle (Early) W.; student Ohio State U., 1969-70, Wright State U., 1971-73; grad. Coll. for Fin. Planning, 1982; m. Helen Marie Isreal, July 24, 1982. Ind. ins. broker and agt., 1973-79; founder Green & West Agy., Columbus, Ohio, from 1977; area sales mgr. Fireman's Fund Am. Life, San Rafael, Calif., from 1979; founder, owner West R L Fin. Planning, Columbus, from 1980; founder, owner Capital Research Services, from 1983; now investment broker, cert. planner McDonald & Co. Securities, Inc., Dayton, Ohio. adj. faculty Coll. Fin. Planning, Denver; cons. in field. Organizer, pres. Children's Christian Research Found. Cert. fin. planner; registered investment advisor. Republican. Lutheran. Home: 56 Waverly Ave Dayton OH 45405 Office: 2460 Kettering Tower Dayton OH 45423

WEST, ROBERT PATRICK, judge; b. Cleve., Aug. 18, 1918; s. Thomas and Helen (Pelka) W.; m. Virginia Hinterschied, June 13, 1940; children—Patrick A., Ginger, Joan M. Krueger, Michael J. Student Ohio State U., 1935-39; B.S., Franklin U., 1948, L.L.B., 1948; J.D., Capital U., 1966. Asst. mgr. Ohio Hotels Protective Assn., Columbus, 1936-40; mem. credit dept. Gen. Motors Acceptance Corp., Columbus, 1940-42; mem. claims dept. Travelers Ins. Co., Columbus, 1942-44; claims mgr. Am. States Ins. Co., Columbus, 1947-55; sr. asst. city atty. City of Columbus, 1955-57; ptnr. West & Holmes, Columbus, 1957-69, Teaford, Bernard, West & Brothers, Columbus, 1969-70; judge Franklin County Mcpl. Ct., Columbus, 1970-80, Franklin County Common Pleas Ct., 1980—; asst. sec., counsel Lake Central Airlines, Indpls., 1957-68; Ohio counsel Allegheny Airlines, Washington, 1968-70. Contbr. articles to profl. jours. Chmn. Ohio Aviation Bd., Columbus, 1962, Ohio Jud. Coll., Columbus, 1976—; mem. Columbus Urban Renewal Commn., 1957, Ohio Bldg. Authority, 1968. Served with armed forces, World War II. Recipient 12 awards for superior, excellent and outstanding jud. service Ohio Supreme Ct., 1971-85. Faculty award Ohio Jud. Coll., 1978. Mem. ABA, Am. Judges Assn., Ohio State Bar Assn. (25-yr. service award aviation law com. 1980), Columbus Bar Assn., Lawyer-Pilots Assn. Republican. Roman Catholic. Club: Athletic (Columbus). Lodge: K.C. Avocation: flying. Home: 345 E Longview Ave Columbus OH 43202 Office: Common Pleas Ct 369 S High St Columbus OH 43215

WEST, RONALD LA VERA, association executive; b. Tampa, Fla., June 11, 1948; s. Henry and Endiak Julia (Lockett) W.; B.A., Shaw Coll., 1971; M.A., Wayne State U., 1973; m. Linda Marie Ronse, Feb. 27, 1975; children—Shelley Lynn, Julia Lea. Counselor, asst. dist. supr. Mich. Dept. Edn., Bur. Rehab., Detroit, 1971-77; with Mich. Dept. Mental Health, Southgate Regional Ctr., 1977-83, counselor, asst. dist. supr., 1977-81, program dir., 1981-83; asst. sec. adminstrn. Kiwanis Internat., 1983—; dir. alternative living services, mem. adv. council Bur. Rehab. Past chmn. and bd. mem. Riverview (Mich.) Zoning Bd. of Appeals, sec. to bldg. commn., 1978—; chmn. project sales Downriver council Boy Scouts Am., 1978-81; bd. dirs. YMCA, Downriver br. Recipient Meritorious Service award Mich. Rehab. Counseling Assn., 1979; Leadership award, Detroit Rehab. Assn., 1976; cert. social worker, Mich. Mem. Am. Personnel and Guidance Assn., Nat. Rehab. Assn., Mich. Rehab. Assn. (dir. 1972—), Detroit Rehab. Assn. (past pres.), Nat. Rehab. Counseling Assn., Great Lakes Region Rehab. Counseling Assn. (past pres.), Mich. Rehab. Counseling Assn. (past pres.), Am. Assn. Mental Deficiency, Omega Psi Phi. Club: Kiwanis (past pres., past lt. gov. Mich. Dist. 1981-82, Kiwanian of Yr. award 1981). Home: 1041 Mohawk Hills Dr Carmel IN 46032 Office: 3636 Woodview Trace Indianapolis IN 46268

WEST, TERENCE DOUGLAS, furniture company design executive; b. Twin Falls, Idaho, Sept. 12, 1948; s. Clark Ernest and Elsie Erma (Kulm) W. B.S., San Jose State U., 1971. Indsl. designer Clement Labs., Palo Alto, Calif., 1970-74, U.S. Govt., Washington, 1974-78; dir. design Steelcase, Inc., Grand Rapids, Mich., 1978—. Com. mem. San Jose Urban Coalition, 1971-72. Mem. Inst. Bus. Designers, Am. Soc. Interior Designers, Found. Interior Edn. and Research, Indsl. Designers Soc. Am., Design Mgmt. Inst. Democrat. Lutheran.

WEST, WILSON HARVEY, automotive executive; b. Detroit, Nov. 4, 1930; s. John Harvey and Leonilda (Barbera) W.; m. Vaughan Evelyn Ouimette, Apr. 19, 1952; children—Jill Marie, Wilson John, Mary Louise. M.E., U. Detroit, 1964. Sr. engr. research and devel. Fisher Body div. Gen. Motors Corp., Warren, Mich., 1967-69, asst. dir. research and devel., 1969-74, asst. chief engr., 1974-78, dir. research and devel., 1978-79, asst. chief engr. Pontiac Motor div., Pontiac, Mich., 1979-82, asst. mgr. forward programs, Detroit, 1982-84, asst. group chief engring., 1984—. Patentee in field. Served with U.S. Navy, 1952-54. Mem. Soc. Automotive Engrs (dir. Detroit sect.), Am. Soc. Body Engrs. (sec., dir.), Engring. Soc. Detroit. Republican. Roman Catholic. Club: Stonycroft Hills Golf and Country (Bloomfield Hills, Mich.). Home: 548 Whitehall Dr Bloomfield Hills MI 48013 Office: General Motors Corp General Motors Bldg W Grand Blvd Detroit MI 48202

WESTBAY, CHARLES DUANE, farm equipment retail and service company executive; b. Yates City, Ill., Dec. 8, 1930; s. Charles Bond and Beatrice Elizabeth (Bates) W.; m. Bonnie Jean Gravitt, Sept. 30, 1950; children—Charles Grant, Shirley Jo, Steven Larry, Bette Jean. Student U. Ill., 1949. Lic. pvt. pilot. With Internat. Harvester Co., Peoria Ill. and Madison, Wis., 1949-59, zone sales mgr., 1951-56, store mgr., 1957-58, nat. del. Dealer Council, 1971-72; pres. Westbay Equipment Co., Galesburg, Ill., 1959—; pres. N.Am. dealer adv. council Versatile Mfg. Co.; owner Westbay Leasing Co., Galesburg; owner, operator Westbay Farms. Chmn. Knox County chpt. Ill. Future Farmers Am. Found., 1977-78. Recipient Hon. Chpt. Farmer's award Future Farmers Am., 1977, 78. Mem. Knox County YMCA, Galesburg Pilots Assn., Aircraft Owners and Pilots Assn. Ill. Retail Farm Equipment Assn. Republican. Methodist. Lodge: Masons. Home: 206 Division Knoxville IL 61448

WESTBROCK, DAVID ANTHONY, endocrinologist; b. Dayton, Ohio, Mar. 27, 1946; s. Raymond John and Mary (Gaier) W.; m. Judy Day; children—Jennifer Elizabeth, David. B.S., U. Dayton, 1968; M.D., Ohio State U., 1972 Diplomate Am. Bd. Internal Medicine, Am. Bd. Endocrinology and Metabolism. Intern, Ohio State U. Hosps., Columbus, 1972-73, resident in internal medicine, 1973-75; fellow in endocrinology and metabolism U. Cin. Hosps., 1975-77; practice medicine specializing in endocrinology and metabolism, Dayton, 1977—; mem. staffs Miami Valley Hosp., Kettering Med. Ctr., St. Elizabeth Med. Ctr.; clin. assoc. prof. medicine Wright State U.; Trustee Am. Diabetes Assn., Dayton. Fellow ACP, mem. Greater Dayton Hormone Soc. (convener). Office: 60 Wyoming St Dayton OH 45409

WESTENFELDER, GRANT ORVILLE, physician, educator; b. Chgo., Jan. 12, 1940; s. Orville L. and Eleanor Jean (Langley) W.; student U. Mich., 1957-60; B.S., Northwestern U. 1961, M.D., 1964; m. Sharon L. Zelesnik, June 22, 1981; children—Mark, Bruce, Natalie; 1 stepdau., Shari. Intern, Evanston (Ill.) Hosp., 1964-65, now sr. attending physician, resident in internal medicine Northwestern U. McGaw Med. Center, 1965-68, fellow in infectious diseases, 1968-70, mem. infectious diseases sect. Med. Sch., 1970—, asst. prof. clin. medicine Northwestern U., 1974-81, asso. prof. clin. medicine, 1981—; asso. chmn. dept. medicine, head div. infectious diseases Evanston Hosp. Corp.; head dept. medicine Glenbrook Hosp., Glenview, Ill. Bd. deacons Trinity Luth. Ch., Evanston, 1970-71. Diplomate Am. Bd. Internal Medicine. Fellow A.C.P., Am. Coll. Chest Physicians; mem. Am. Soc. Microbiology, Am. Fedn. Clin. Research, Infectious Disease Soc. Am., AMA, Chgo. Soc. Internal Medicine, Assn. Practitioners in Infection Control, Am. Soc. Epidemiologists, Surg. Infection Soc., Alpha Kappa Kappa. Office: 2100 Pfingsten Rd Glenview IL 60025 also 2050 Pfingsten Rd Glenview IL 60025

WESTERMEYER, JOSEPH JOHN, psychiatrist, educator; b. Chgo., Apr. 8, 1937; s. Joseph John and Irene B. (McDonagh) W.; m. Rachel Moga, 1962; children—Michelle, Joseph. Student St. Thomas Coll., 1955-57; B.S. in Biology and Chemistry, U. Minn., 1959, M.D., 1961, M.A., 1969, M.P.H., 1970, Ph.D. in Psychiatry (Ginzburg fellow), 1970. Diplomate Am. Bd. Psychiatry Am. Bd. Family Practice. Intern, St. Paul-Ramsey Hosp., 1961-62; gen. practice medicine Payne Ave. Med. Clinic, St. Paul, 1962-65; dep. chief div. pub. health AID, Laos, 1965-67; resident in psychiatry U. Minn., Mpls., 1967-70, mem. psychiatry staff U. Minn. Hosps., 1970—, instr., 1970-71, asst. prof., 1971-74, assoc. prof., 1974-78, prof. psychiatry, 1978—, adj. prof. anthropology, 1979—, adj. prof. psychology, 1979—; vis. prof., lectr. Bemidji State Coll., Brown U., U. Hawaii, U. Calif.-Irvine, Mo. Inst. Psychiatry, Johns Hopkins U., Purdue U., U. S.C., U. Wash. Narcotics Commn. Hong Kong, Mayo Clinic, SUNY-Buffalo, Harvard U., Milw. Med. Coll., U. Okla., U. Mo.; editorial bd. Am. Jour. Drug and Alcohol Abuse, 1973—, Jour. Operational Psychiatry, 1977—, Am. Jour. Pub. Health, 1980-84, Advances in Alcohol and Substance Abuse, 1980—, Alcoholism: Clin. and Exptl. Research, 1980—, Alcohol and Research World, 1981—; social sci. editor Substance Abuse newsletter Assn. Med. Educators and Researchers in Substance Abuse, 1979—; reviewer, book reviewer; lectr., panel participant profl. meetings. Author: A Primer on Chemical Dependency: A Clinical Guide to Alcohol and Drug Problems, 1976; Poppies, Pipes and People: A Study of Opium and Its Use in Laos, 1983; editor: Anthropology and Mental Health, 1976; editor: (with E. Foulks, et al) Transcultural Psychiatry, 1977; contbr. numerous chpts. to books, monographs and articles to profl. jours. Bd. dirs. Indian Guest House, Mpls., 1969-72, Juel Fairbanks House, St. Paul, 1970-73; chmn. ednl. policy com. U. Minn. Med. Sch., 1979-81; mem. Mpls. VA Hosp. for Mental Health and Behavioral Scis. Council, 1976-79; mem. thanatology com. and ethics subcom. U. Minn. Hosps., 1982-84; resource group on alcoholism and other chem. dependencies Minn. State Med. Assn., 1976-81, med. policy com. mental health Minn. Dept. Pub. Welfare, 1978-80; treas., bd. dirs. Acad. Med. Research and Edn. in Substance Abuse, 1976-78; mem. steering com. Soc. Study of Psychiatry and Culture, 1979—; cons. psychosocial research com. Nat. Inst. Alcohol Abuse and Alcoholism, 1981; cons. World Health Orgn., 1979-86, mem. spl. adv. group on drug-alcohol dependence; chmn. sect. mental health and anthropology 9th World Congress Anthropology and Ethnology, Chgo., 1973; mem. sect. transcultural psychiatry World Psychiat. Assn., 1978—. Recipient Meritorious Service award AID, 1967; NIH fellow, summers 1970, 72, 78; U. Minn. grantee, 1971, 74-78, 77-78, 78, 79-80, 79-83, 81; NIMH grantee, 1971-73, 73-75, 80-81; Nat. Inst. Alcohol Abuse and Alcoholism grantee, 1974-75, 74-77; others. Fellow Am. Anthrop. Assn., Am. Assn. Family Practice, Am. Psychiat. Assn.; mem. Minn. State Med. Soc., County Med. Soc., Minn. Psychiatric Assn. (pres. 1984-87, mem. chem. dependency subcom. 1979—), Soc. Med. Anthropology, Assn. Med. Educators and Researchers on Substance Abuse, Am. Med. Soc. on Alcoholism, AAAS, Assn. Behavioral Sci. and Med. Edn., Assn. Acad. Psychiatrists, Am. Pub. Health Assn., Soc. Study of Culture and Psychiatry, Research Soc. on Alcoholism, Alpha Omega Alpha. Home: 1935 Summit Ave Saint Paul MN 55105 Office: Box 393 Mayo 420 Delaware St SE Minneapolis MN 55455

WESTFALL, RICHARD SAMUEL, history educator; b. Ft. Collins, Colo., Apr. 22, 1924; s. Alfred Rensselaer and Dorothy (Towne) W.; m. Gloria Marilyn Dunn, Aug. 23, 1952; children—Alfred, Jennifer, Kristin. B.A., Yale U., 1948, M.A., 1949, Ph.D., 1955; postgrad. London U., 1951-52. Instr. history Calif. Inst. Tech., Pasadena, 1952-53; instr., asst. prof. State U. Iowa, 1953-57; asst. prof. Grinnell (Iowa) Coll., 1957-60, assoc. prof., 1960-63; prof. history of sci., Ind. U., Bloomington, 1963-76, prof. history, 1965-76, Disting. prof., 1976—, chmn. dept., 1967-73. Mem. United Ministry Bd., Bloomington, 1964-73; elder First Presbyterian Ch., Bloomington. Served with USNR, 1944-46. Recipient Pfizer award, 1972, 83; Leo Gershoy award, 1981. Fellow Am. Acad. Arts and Scis., Royal Soc. Lit.; mem. Am. Hist. Assn., AAUP, History of Sci. Soc. (pres. 1976-77), Société Internationale d'Histoire des Sciences. Author: Science and Religion in Seventeenth Century England, 1958; Force in Newton's Physics, 1971; Construction of Modern Science, 1971; Never At Rest: A Biography of Isaac Newton, 1980; editor: (with V.E. Thoren) Steps in the Scientific Tradition, 1969. Home: 2222 Browncliff Rd Bloomington IN 47401 Office: Dept History and Philosophy of Sci Ind U Bloomington IN 47401

WESTHOFF, REGINA SHIDELER, army ammunitions plant buyer; b. Pittsburg, Kans., May 3, 1954; d. Harold James and Joanne Marie (Cosner) Shideler; m. Ren Bradford Westhoff, May 11, 1985. A.A., Ft. Scott Community Coll., 1974. Sec. Western Insurance, Ft. Scott, Kans., 1973-74; jr. clk. Day & Zimmermann, Inc., Parsons, Kans., 1974-75, sr. clk., 1975-77, buyer, 1977-84, sr. buyer, 1984—. Speaker Kiwanis Club, Parsons, 1983. Mem. Labette Community Bus. and Profl. Women (2nd v.p. 1982-83). Avocations: horseback riding; reading. Office: Day & Zimmermann Inc Kansas Div Parsons KS 67357

WESTMAN, ALVIN ADOLPH, accountant; b. Menominee, Mich., Nov. 6, 1930; s. Adolph and Delia (Walander) W.; m. Marilyn E. Borden, June 30, 1956; children—David, Paul, Mark. A.B., Augustana Coll., 1953. C.P.A. Acct., J.L. Clark Mfg. Co., Rockford, Ill., 1955-58; C.P.A., ptnr. Gauger & Diehl, Rockford, 1958-70; C.P.A., ptnr. Peat, Marwick, Mitchell & Co., Rockford, 1970-73, C.P.A., mng. ptnr., 1973-85. Dir. alumni bd. Augustana Coll., 1983; mem. bd. counselors Rockford Coll., 1984. Served with U.S. Army, 1953-55, Japan. Mem. Am. Inst. C.P.A.s, Ill. Soc. C.P.A.s, Nat. Acctg. Assn., Greater Rockford C. of C. (treas., dir., various service awards). Lutheran. Club: Rockford County (treas. 1979-82). Lodge: Rotary. Avocations: Photography; travel. Home: 4501 Lanewood Circle Rockford IL 61108 Office: Peat Marwick Mitchell & Co 120 W State Suite 401 Rockford IL 61101

WESTON, DAWN THOMPSON, artist, researcher; b. Joliet, Ill., Apr. 15, 1919; d. Cyril C. and Vivian Grace Thompson; student (scholar) Penn Hall Jr. Coll., Chambersburg, Pa., 1937-38; B.S., Northwestern U., 1942, postgrad. in reading and speech pathology, 1960-61, M.A. in Ednl. Adminstrn., 1970; postgrad. U. Ill., 1964; student Art Inst. Chgo., 1954, Pestalozzi-Froebel, Chgo., 1955, Phila. Inst. for Achievement Human Potential, 1963; m. Arthur Walter Weston, Sept. 10, 1940; children—Roger Lance, Randall Kent, Cynthia Brooke. Therapist, USN Hosp., Gt. Lakes, Ill., 1940-45; tchr. Holy Child and Waukegan (Ill.) High Schs., 1946-54; elem. and jr. high art dir. Lake Bluff (Ill.) Schs., 1954-58; pioneer ednl. dir. Grove Sch. for Brain-Injured, Lake Forest, Ill., 1958-66, now life mem. corp., chmn. bd., 1984-85; one-woman shows: Evanston Woman's Club, Northwestern U., Deerpath Gallery, Lake Forest; The Hein Co., Waukegan; numerous group shows, 1939-76. Represented in permanent collections: ARC, Victory Meml. Hosp., Waukegan, Sierra Assos., Chgo., numerous pvt. collections U.S., Can., Japan, Africa; works include: Poisonous Plants of Midwest set of etchings for Country Gentleman mag., 1956, Clouds mural, 1981; ind. researcher on shifting visual imagery due to trauma, 1982—. Mem. Presdl. Gold Chain, Trinity Coll., 1979. Named Citizen of Yr., Grove Sch., 1978, room at sch. named in her honor, 1982; cert. tchr., Ill. Mem. Art Inst. Chgo., Deerpath Art League, Pi Lambda Theta. Methodist (del. Ann. Conf. 1982, 83). Research on uneven growth, 1969-70. Home and Office: 349 E Hilldale Pl Lake Forest IL 60045

WESTON, RONALD CURTIS, government executive; b. Lake City, Fla., Jan. 31, 1949; s. Adolphus Alexander and Ethel Lee (Jones) W.; m. Rubydean Jones, Dec. 21, 1970; children—Shuna, Ranieka, Ronald. B.A. in Econs., Fla. A&M U., 1971; M.B.A., Mich. State U., 1985. Lic. residential builder, Mich. Economist HUD, Jacksonville, Fla., 1971-78, dir. econ. market analysis div. Indpls. area office, 1978-79, chief multifamily housing programs, 1979-80, dep. dir. multifamily devel. Detroit area office, 1980-83, dir. housing devel. div., 1983-85, regional housing dir. Chgo. regional office, 1985—. Scoutmaster Detroit Area council Boy Scouts Am., 1983—; trustee Trinity United Meth. Ch., Detroit, 1983—, also chmn. adminstrv. bd. Recipient cert. of appreciation Dennis M. Hertel, U.S. Congressman, 1982. Mem. Kappa Alpha Psi. Clubs: Detroit-Metro Investment, Toastmasters (area gov. 1982-83, lt. gov. Div. A, Dist. 28, 1983-84, winner club, area and div. ann. speech contests Dist. 47, 1977, Dist. 28, 1982, Area Gov. of Yr., Dist. 28, 1982-83, Able Toastmaster 1982). Home: 3472 W 83d St Woodridge IL 60517 Office: Regional Housing Dept Chgo Regional Office HUD Chicago IL

WESTRAN, ROY ALVIN, insurance company executive; b. Taft, Oreg., Apr. 30, 1925; s. Carl A. and Mae E. (Barnhardt) W.; B.B.A., Golden Gate Coll., 1955, M.B.A., 1957; m. Dawn M. Oeschger, Oct. 18, 1952; children—Denise,

Thomas, Michael, Dawna. Mem. sales staff C.A. Westran Agy., Taft, 1946-49; underwriter Fireman's Fund Group, San Francisco, ins. mgr. Kaiser Aluminum Chem., Oakland, 1952-65; pres., dir. Citizens Ins. Co. Am., Howell, Mich., 1967—; pres., dir. Am. Select Ins. Co. and Beacon Ins. Co. Am., Waterville, Ohio, 1969—; v.p. Hanover Ins. Co.; dir. 1st Nat. Bank, Howell. Mem. ins. adv. council Salvation Army, San Francisco, 1957-60; chmn. drive United Fund, 1970. Bd. dirs., exec. com. Portage Trails council Boy Scouts Am., 1970-72; trustee Traffic Safety Assn. Detroit, 1967, Traffic Safety for Mich., 1967; bd. dirs. Cleary Coll., Area Agy. on Aging; mem. adv. bd. Olivet Coll.; mem. bus. adv. council Central Mich. U. Served with AUS, 1943-46. C.P.C.U. Mem. Ins. Inst. Am., Mich. C. of C. (dir. 1968-71), Am. Soc. Ins. Mgmt. (pres. 1960-62), Soc. C.P.C.U. (nat. pres. 1968-69), Mich. Catastrophic Claims Assn. (vice chmn.). Office: 645 W Grand River Howell MI 48843

WESTRICK, WALLACE JOHN, traffic consultant, career advisor; b. Fargo, N.D., May 3, 1948; s. John Fredrick and Vivian Alice (Ellingson) W.; m. Donna Irene Walkinshaw, June 21, 1968; children—Leslyn A., Chad M., Michael J. Student, Mayville State Coll., 1966 to 1968; McGee Tyson Air Base Acad., 1974. Sales and traffic mgr. Red River Commodities, Fargo, N.D., 1974-80; traffic mgr. and sunflower trader Agra-By-Products, Fargo, 1980-81; specialty crops trader Prairie Processing and Handling, Grafton, N.D., 1981-82; Sunflower div. mgr. Kuhn-Fargo, West Fargo, 1983-84; traffic consultant-broker Walvatne Trucking Co., Fargo, 1984—. Pres. Cass Valley North Bd. Edn., Argusville, N.D., 1984-85; fire chief Argusville Vol. Fire Fighters, 1979—; pres., sec., treas., dir., No. Cass Jaycees, Argusville, 1977-83; gen. mgr.-coach Argusville Little League, 1976-84; pres. Cass Valley North PTO, 1978. Served to staff sgt. USAF, 1968-72; mem. N.D. Air N.G., 1972—. Mem. Am. Legion. Home: RR Argusville ND 58005 Office: Walvatne Trucking Co 717 21st St N Fargo ND 58102

WESTROM, ROBERT GEORGE, microfilm and mosquito control co. exec.; b. Des Moines, Feb. 4, 1925; s. Fred William and Grace Marie (Canady) W.; B.A. in Bus. Adminstrn., N. Central Coll., Naperville, Ill., 1951; m. Thelma Jean Robertson, July 1948; children—Dean Robert, Brad Canady, Lee Francis, Jan Lisa. Supt. personnel dept. Studebaker Corp., Chgo., 1951-55; owner, operator Shoe Tree, West Chicago, Ill., 1955-65, Tifa Sales Corp., West Chicago, 1965-79; owner, pres., dir. Microchem, Inc., West Chicago, 1979—. Mem. Bd. Edn. Dist. 94, West Chicago, 1969-80, pres., 1974-78; dep. chief West Chicago Fire Protection Dist., 1971-74. Served with USN, 1942-45. Named Citizen of Yr., West Chicago C. of C., 1957. Mem. Am. Mosquito Control Assn., Ill. Pest Control Assn., Ill. Mosquito Control Assn., Nat. Micrographics Assn., Ind. Sanitarians, Ind. Vector Control Assn., Ill. Sch. Bds. Assn. Republican. Methodist. Club: Rotary (past pres.). Home: 426 E Washington St West Chicago IL 60185 Office: Microchem Inc 185 W Washington St West Chicago IL 60185

WESTROM, RONALD LYLE, personnel manager; b. Aurora, Ill., Nov. 8, 1940; s. Lyle A. and Louise E. (Zander) W.; m. Leona R. Lance, April 23, 1966; children—Janet Caras, Jeffrey, Susan. A.A., Kemper Sch., 1960; B.S. in Bus. Adminstrn., Elmhurst Coll., 1963. Personnel specialist Continental Bank, Chgo., 1965-68; prodn. supr. Johnson & Johnson Corp., Chgo., 1968-72; asst. personnel dir. Capitol Packaging Co., Melrose Park, Ill., 1972-73; personnel dir. Glenview State Bank, Ill., 1973-76; asst. personnel dir. Dr. Scholl, Inc., Chgo., 1976-82; personnel mgr. ITW Spiroid, Chgo., 1982—. Pres., Robbie Fund of Children's Meml. Hosp. Served to 1st lt. USA, 1963-65, Korea. Mem. Am. Soc. Personnel Adminstrs., Midwest Personnel Mgmt. Assn., Midwest Indsl. Mgmt. Assn., No. Ill. Indsl. Assn., Jr. C. of C. (chmn. Spark Club com. 1967). Republican. Episcopalian. Lodge: Elks. Home: 216 North Maple St Mount Prospect IL 60056 Office: ITW Spiroid 2601 North Keeler Ave Chicago IL 60639

WETHINGTON, NORBERT ANTHONY, college administrator; b. Dayton, Ohio, Sept. 14, 1943; s. Norbert and Sophie Lillian W.; B.A., U. Dayton, 1965; M.A., John Carroll U., 1967; postgrad. Baldwin Wallace Coll., 1968-70; m. Martha M. Vannice, Aug. 13, 1966; children—Paula, Mark, Eric, Kristen, Rebecca, Lisa, Bethany. Grad. asst., teaching asso. John Carroll U., Cleve., 1965-67; English tchr. Padua Franciscan High Sch., Parma, Ohio, 1967-70; instr., chmn. dept. tech. writing and speech N. Central Tech. Coll., Mansfield, Ohio, 1970-74; dir. evening div. Terra Tech. Coll., Fremont, Ohio, 1974-80, dir. public and community service technologies, 1980—. Vice pres. Sandusky County Bd. Health, 1979-80. Mem. Am. Vocat. Assn., Ohio Vocat. Assn., Nat. Council Tchrs. English. Democrat. Roman Catholic. Contbr. articles to profl. jours. Home: 1036 Hazel St Fremont OH 43420 Office: Terra Technical College 1220 Cedar St Fremont OH 43420

WETTERAU, THEODORE C., diversified food wholesaler; b. St. Louis, Nov. 13, 1927; s. Theodore C. and Edna (Ehrlich) W.; m. Helen Elizabeth Killion, Feb. 20, 1954; children—T Conrad, Mark Stephen, Elizabeth Killion. B.A., Westminster Coll., Fulton, Mo., 1952, LL.D. (hon.), 1977. With Wetterau, Inc., Hazelwood, Mo., 1952—, dir., 1960—, v.p. mktg., 1960-63, exec. v.p., 1963-70, pres., from 1970, chief exec. officer, 1970—, chmn. bd., 1974—; dir. Centerre Bank of St. Louis, Godfrey Co., Waukesha, Wis. Bd. dirs. Mark Twain Inst., Boy Scouts Am., St. Louis Symphony Soc., Operation Rearch (all St. Louis); trustee Westminster Coll.; adv. bd. St. Louis Salvation Army; mem. Pres.'s Council of Community Assn. Schs. for the Arts, St. Louis. Served with U.S. Army, 1946-47; Korea. Named Man of Month, Progressive Grocer mag., 1966, Sales Exec. of Yr., Sales and Mktg. Execs. St. Louis, 1977; recipient Aggus Disting. Pub. Skrvice award, 1980, Nat. Disting. Service award Am. Jewish Com., 1980, Bus. and Profl. award Religious Heritage of Am., 1980. Mem. Nat. Wholesale Grocers Assn. (gov., past chmn. bd.), Ind. Grocers Alliance (past chmn.), Food Mktg. Inst., U.S. C. of C., Knights of Round Table, Knights of the Cauliflower Ear. Clubs: Univ., Old Warson Country, St. Louis. Office: Wetterau Inc 8920 Pershall Rd Hazelwood MO 63142

WETTERSTROM, EDWIN, engr.; b. Oak Park, Ill., Dec. 20, 1919; s. Frank and Alma (Ekstrom) W.; bus. diploma Wright Coll., 1940; B.S. in Mech. Engring., Ill. Inst. Tech., 1944; M.S. in Engring. Mechanics, Purdue U., 1947, Ph.D., 1951; m. Betty Barbara Chase. Engr., devel. dept. Continental Can Co., 1944-45; staff mem. engring. mechanics dept. Purdue, 1945-51; analytical research engr. research and devel. dept. Graver Tank & Mfg. Co., 1951, cons., 1952—; asst. prof. civil engring. U. Mo., 1952-55; asso. prof. applied mechanics Mich. State U., 1955-57; prof. mech. engring. N.D. State U., 1957-67, U. Toledo, 1967-70, Ind. Inst. Tech., 1970-72, Tuskegee Inst., 1972-74; sr. analytical engr. Westinghouse Air Brake Co., 1974-80, cons. engr., 1980—. Mem. ASME, Am. Soc. Engring. Edn., Sigma Xi. Lutheran. Contbr. articles tech. press. Home: PO Box 157 Washington IL 61571

WHALEN, BRIAN B., manufacturing company executive; b. Chgo., Oct. 7, 1939; s. Donald James and Mary (Ennis) W.; m. Sheila Ann Nolan, June 9, 1967. B.S. in Social Sci., Loyola U., Chgo., 1962. Mem. staff Sen. Everett Dirksen, 1961-62; adminstrv. asst. to Sheriff Cook County, Chgo., 1963-66, Pres. Cook County Bd., 1967-68; exec. asst. to Gov. Ill., Springfield, 1969-73; dir. pub. affairs Internat. Harvester, Chgo., 1973-83, staff v.p. pub. affairs, 1983—. Chmn. Ill. Youth for Goldwater, 1964; campaign mgr. Ogilvie for Cook County Bd. Pres., 1966; deacon Chgo. United, 1979—; bd. dirs. TRUST, Inc., 1981-84; mem. adv. council Local Initiatives Support Corp., 1982—; mem. Ill. Gov.'s Med. Malpractice Task Force, 1984—. Mem. Associated Employers Ill. (chmn. 1984). Office: Internat Harvester 401 N Michigan Ave Chicago IL 60611

WHALEY, THOMAS PATRICK, chemical research executive, consultant; b. Atchison, Kans., Jan. 13, 1923; s. George A. and Anna Theresa (Mueller) W.; m. Betty Maxine McLaughlin, Apr. 22, 1946 (dec. 1968); children—Laura Kathleen, Michael Patrick; m. Jane Esther Wilkinson, Apr. 12, 1969; stepchildren—Charles, Conrad, Christopher, Donna Jane Pioli. B.S. in Chemistry, St. Benedict's Coll., 1943; Ph.D. in Chemistry, U. Kans., 1950. Sr. research assoc. Ethyl Corp., Detroit and Baton Rouge, 1950-62; mgr. inorganic and phys. chemistry Internat. Minerals and Chem. Corp., Libertyville, Ill., 1962-69, dir. analytical and tech. services, 1969-74; tech. dir. Sipi Metals Corp., Chgo., 1974-76; assoc. dir. solar energy Inst. Gas Tech., Chgo., 1976-81, sr. advisor, 1981—; pres. Consanal Corp., Ltd., Deerfield, Ill., 1974—. Co-author 8 tech. books and encys.; editor Chem. Bulletin, 1977-81; contbr. articles to profl. jours.; patentee. Chmn. dist. advancement Northwest Suburban council Boy Scouts Am., 1963-66; chmn. plan commn. Village Govt., Deerfield, 1973-80, chmn. energy council, 1981-83, chmn. Village Ctr. Devel. Commn., 1975—. Served to capt. USAAF, 1943-46. Recipient Key Scouter award Boy Scouts Am., 1967. Mem. Am. Chem. Soc. (dir. Chgo. sect. 1980—, chmn. 1983-84, abstractor 1966—), AAAS, Sigma Xi, Alpha Chi Sigma, Phi Lambda Upsilon. Republican. Roman Catholic. Club: Lions (bd. dirs. Baton Rouge 1962). Avocations: golf; tennis; skiing; piano; civic affairs; bridge. Home: 912 Westcliff Ln Deerfield IL 60015 Office: Inst. Gas Technology 3424 S State St Chicago IL 60616

WHALLEY, RICHARD EARL, furniture manufacturing exec.; b. Kalamazoo, Mich., Aug. 16, 1934; s. Vincent Luke and Ruth (Jacobsen) W.; B.S., Ind. U., 1955; m. Dorothy Tiffany, Aug. 29, 1959; children—Scott, Sharon. Asst. buyer Rike-Kumler Co., Dayton, Ohio, 1955-57; buyer Furniture div. Montgomery Ward & Co., Chgo., 1959-63; div. mdse. mgr. Kroehler Mfg. Co., Naperville, Ill., 1964-69, div. v.p., 1969-70; pres. Pullman Couch Co., Cleveland, Tenn., 1974—; dir. Cleve. Chair Co.; Jackson Mfg. Co. Served with AUS, 1957-59. Mem. Nat. Wholesale Furniture Assn. Republican. Presbyterian. Club: Metropolitan (Chgo.). Home: 893 E Westleigh Rd Lake Forest IL 60045 Office: PO Box 220 1426 Old Skokie Rd Highland Park IL 60035

WHEAT, ALAN DUPREE, congressman; b. San Antonio, Oct. 16, 1951; s. James Weldon and Emogene W. B.A. in Econs., Grinnell Coll., 1972. Economist HUD, Kansas City, Mo., 1972-73, Mid-Am. Regional Council, Kansas City, 1973-75; aide County Execs. Office, Kansas City, 1975-76; mem. Mo. Ho. of Reps., 1977-82; mem. 98th Congress from 5th Dist. Mo. Mem. exec. com. Democratic Study Group; mem. Dem. Caucus Com. on Party Effectiveness; mem. Women's Congl. Caucus, Environ. and Energy Study Conf. Mem. NAACP. Named Best Freshman Legislator, St. Louisan Mag., 1978, One of 10 Best Legislators, Jefferson City News Tribune, 1980, Mo. Times, 1980. Office: 1204 Longworth House Office Bldg Washington DC 20515

WHEELER, BARBARA MONICA, lawyer; b. Chgo., Mar. 20, 1947; d. John Benjamin and Elizabeth (Keife) Wheeler; B.A., St. Dominic Coll., 1969; cert. Lewis U. Sch. Paraprofl. Studies, 1976; J.D., DePaul U., 1980. Gen. supt. Md. Manor Devel. Co., Chgo., 1970-74; v.p. Omega Constrn. Co., Chgo., 1974-78; admitted to Ill. bar, 1980; asst. state's atty. Cook County, Ill. Mem. Bd. Edn., Community High Sch. Dist. 99, DuPage County, 1974-76, pres., 1976—. Mem. Ill. Assn. Sch. Bds., dir.-at-large Tri County div., 1976-77, dir. DuPage div., 1977-78, state dir., 1982—; bd. dirs. Sch. Mgmt. Found. Ill., 1983; mem. task force on purposes of edn. in eighties Nat. Sch. Bds. Assn. Mem. ABA, Ill. Bar Assn., Chgo. Bar Assn., Am. Mgmt. Assn., Phi Alpha Delta. Roman Catholic. Office: 7501 Lemont Rd Woodridge IL

WHEELER, BEVERLY GAIL, physician; b. Fort Knox, Ky., July 15, 1952; d. Jesse Leonard and Magaret (Teabeaut) W.; B.S., Emory U., 1974; M.D., Med. Coll. Va., 1978. Intern, Cin. Gen. Hosp., 1978-79; resident U. Cin. Med. Center, 1979-81, chief resident, 1981-82, fellow in geropsychiatry, 1982-84, asst. prof. psychiatry, 1984—; psychiatrist Rollman's Psychiat. Inst., 1979—; adj. clin. prof. U. Cin., 1982-83. Recipient Upjohn Achievement award for most outstanding intern U. Cin. Med. Center, 1978-79. Mem. AMA, Gerontol. Soc. Am., Am. Assn. Geriatric Psychiatry, Am. Geriatrics Soc., Am. Psychiat. Assn., Ohio Psychiat. Assn., Assn. Advancement Psychiatry, Acad. Medicine Cin. Ohio Med. Assn., Phi Sigma. Presbyterian. Office: Central Psychiatric Clinic 3259 Elland Ave Cincinnati OH 45267

WHEELER, CLARENCE, educational administrator; b. St. Petersburg, Fla., Oct. 17, 1939; s. Mack and Eliza (Crockett) W.; B.A., Morehouse Coll., 1962; M.Ed., DePaul U., 1970; m. Lillie M. Edwards, June 8, 1963; children—Clarence, Andrea Michelle. Recreation therapist children's ward Chgo. State Hosp., 1963-64; tchr. Chgo. Bd. Edn., 1964-72, asst. prin., 1972—. Counselor, YMCA, 1968—, Boys Club, 1964; coach Little League; v.p. Wabash-104th St Block Club, 1972-74; treas. Leisure Time Council, 1979-80. Recipient Coach Forbes award Morehouse Coll. Mem. DePaul U. Alumni Assn., Morehouse Coll. Alumni Assn., Nat. Muliple Sclerosis Soc., Nat. Middle Sch. Assn., Phi Delta Kappa. Club: Chgo. Morehouse Alumni. Episcopalian.

WHEELOCK, SHARON MARIE, newspaper publisher; b. Hyannis, Nebr., June 23, 1938; d. Milton Dwight and Lois Mae (Jones) Thomas; student public schs. Denver and Hyannis; children—Robyn Renee, James Sidney, Londa Sue, Christi Marie, Lance Michael. With Grant County News, Hyannis, 1957—, owner, pub., editor, 1976—. Mem. Nebr. Writers Guild, Nat. Fedn. Press Women, Nebr. Press Assn., Internat. Clover Poetry Assn., Soc. Am. Poets, Sigma Delta Chi. Baptist. Poetry pub. in Best Am. Poems, 1967, Clover Collections and Verse, 1972, 74, 20th Century Poets and Their Poems, 1982. Home: PO Box 134 Hyannis NE 69350 Office: PO Box 308 Hyannis NE 69350

WHELAN, DONALD JOSEPH, fundraising executive; b. Omaha, Nov. 8, 1934; s. Edward Charles and Mary Margaret (Weppner) W.; m. Patricia Jean McCabe, Oct. 1, 1960; children—Donald Joseph, Jr., Timothy, Michael, Mary Kathryn, Theresa, Joseph. B.S. in Journalism, Creighton U., 1957; L.H.D., Duchesne Coll., 1968. Dir. devel. Duchesne Coll. and Acad., Omaha, 1965-68, John Burroughs Sch., St. Louis, 1968—; cons. Sunset Hill Sch., Kansas City, Mo., 1975-78, others; workshop leader. Author, editor: Handbook for Development Officers at Independent Schools, 1979, 2d edit., 1982. Pres. sch. bd. St. Joseph Cath. Ch., Manchester, Mo., 1970-71; pres. parish council St. Clare Cath. Ch., Mo., 1973-75. Served to 1st lt., U.S. Army, 1957-59. Mem. Council Advancement and Support of Edn. (nat. chmn. ind. sch. sect. 1978-81, trustee 1978-81; recipient Steel award 1974, 83, Exceptional Achievement award 1980, Disting. Service award 1980, Robert Bell Crow award 1982). Republican. Lodge: Rotary. Home: 907 Clayworth Dr Manchester MO 63011 Office: John Burroughs Sch 755 S Price Rd Saint Louis MO 63124

WHELAN, JOSEPH L., neurologist; b. Chisholm, Minn., Aug. 13, 1917; s. James Gorman and Johanna (Quilty) W.; student Hibbing Jr. Coll., 1935-38; B.S., U. Minn., 1940, M.B., 1942, M.D., 1943; m. Gloria Ann Rewoldt, June 12, 1948; children—Joseph William, Jennifer Ann. Intern, Detroit Receiving Hosp., 1942-43; fellow neurology U. Pa. Hosp., Phila., 1946-47; resident neurology U. Minn. Hosps., Mpls., 1947-49; chief neurology service VA Hosp., Mpls., 1949; spl. fellow electroencephalography Mayo Clinic, Rochester, Minn., 1951; practice medicine specializing in neurology, Detroit, 1949-73, Petoskey, Mich., 1973-85, Gaylord, Mich., 1985—; chief neurology services Grace, St. John's, Bon Secour hosps., Detroit; cons. neurologist No. Mich. Hosps., Petoskey, Community Meml. Hosp., Cheboygan, Mich., Charlevoix Area Hosp., Mich., Otsego Meml. Hosp., Gaylord; instr. U. Minn. Med. Sch., 1949; asst. prof. Wayne State U., 1957-63; cons. USPHS, Detroit Bd. Edn. Founder, mem. ad hoc Com. to Force Lawyers Out of Govt.; chmn. Reagan-Bush Campaign, Kalkaska County, Mich., 1980. Served to capt. AUS, 1943-46. Diplomate Am. Bd. Psychiatry and Neurology. Fellow Am. Acad. Neurology (treas. 1955-57), Am. Electroencephalography Soc.; mem. Assn. Research Nervous and Mental Diseases, Soc. Clin. Neurologists, Mich. Neurol. Assn. (sec.-treas. 1967-76), AMA, Mich. State Med. Assn., No. Mich. Med. Soc., No. Mich. Hosps. Assn. (trustee 1983-85), AAAS, N.Y. Acad. Sci. Republican. Roman Catholic. Club: Grosse Pointe (Mich.). Contbr. to profl. publs. in field. Home: Oxbow Rural Route 2 Mancelona MI 49659 Office: 847 N Center St Gaylord MI 49735

WHERRY, MERRELL KENNETH, sheriff; b. Faulkton, S.D., May 18, 1928; s. Charles Emmett and Jenney (Sorenson) W.; m. Marion Ann Fought, Oct. 13, 1953; children—Camille, Bruce, Celeste, Bradley, LaVar. Grad. high sch., Faulkton, S.D. Sheriff, Faulkton County, S.D., 1965—. Inventor metal detection attachment. Served with Signal Corps, U.S. Army, 1954-56. Republican. Avocations: Crime scenes; beaches; parks; historical sites. Home: 924 Lafoon Ave Faulkton SD 57438

WHIPPS, EDWARD FRANKLIN, lawyer; b. Columbus, Ohio, Dec. 17, 1936; s. Rusk Henry and Agnes Lucille (Green) W.; B.A., Ohio Wesleyan U., 1958; LL.B., Ohio State U., 1961, J.D., 1968; children—Edward Scott, Rusk Huot, Sylvia Louise, Rudyard Christian. Bar: Ohio 1961. Asso. firm George, Greek, King & McMahon, Columbus, 1961-66; partner firm George, Greek, King, McMahon & McConnaughey, Columbus, 1966-79, McConnaughey, Stradley, Mone & Moul, Columbus, 1979-80, Thompson, Hine & Flory, Columbus, Cleve. and Washington, 1981—; founder, pres. Creative Living Inc., Columbus, 1975—, Community Services Inc., Columbus, 1965—; moderator TV shows Upper Arlington Plain Talk, 1980-83, Bridging Disability, 1981-84, Lawyers on Call, 1982—, U.A. Today, 1982—, The Ohio Wesleyan Experience, 1984—. Mem. Upper Arlington Bd. Edn., 1972-80, v.p., 1975, pres., 1976; bd. alumni dirs. Ohio Wesleyan U., 1975—. Mem. Columbus (chmn. municipal ct. com. 1973-75, chmn. common pleas ct. com. 1979-81, chmn. public relations com. 1981-84), Am., Ohio bar assns., Assn. Trial Lawyers Am., Ohio Acad. Trial Lawyers, Franklin County Trial Lawyers Assn., Am. Judicature Soc., Upper Arlington Area C. of C. (trustee 1979—). Republican. Methodist. Clubs: Lawyers Columbus, Barristers Columbus, Columbus Athletic, Ohio State U. Faculty, Delta Tau Delta (nat. v.p. 1974-76), Touchdown Columbus. Home: 3771 Lyon Dr Columbus OH 43220 Office: 100 E Broad St Columbus OH 43215

WHITAKER, CINDY JO, science educator; b. Waynesville, Mo., Sept. 11, 1957; d. Archie Wythe and Clarice Mae (Jones) W. B.S. in Phys. Edn., Southwest Baptist U., 1981. Cert. tchr., Mo. Phys. edn. tchr., coach Dixon High Sch. (Mo.), 1980-82, sci. tchr. Dixon Middle Sch., 1982—; pres. Dixon Community Tchrs. Assn., 1983-84, 84-85. Mem. AAHPERD, Mo. State Tchrs. Assn., So. Central Dist. Tchrs. Assn. (exec. com.; legis. reception com. Jefferson City 1984, 85), Phi Delta Kappa. Democrat. Mem. Disciples of Christ Ch. Office: Dixon R1 Sch System Hwy 28 Dixon MO 65459

WHITAKER, GLEN LEROY, lawyer; b. Kansas Mo., Feb. 16, 1918; s. Thomas Henderson and Mabel Ella (Bates) W.; m. Doris Kerr, June 18, 1944; children—Krista Jean, James K. B.A. cum laude, U. Mo.-Kansas City, 1938, J.D. cum laude, 1941. Bar: Mo. 1941, U.S. cts. 1942. Dep. indsl. commr. State of Mo., Kansas City, 1949. Elder Country Club Christian Ch., Kansas City, Mo., 1983—. Mem. Mo. Bar (com. council comml. law 1983—), S.R. (patriot of yr. 1980, officer 1966—), Heart of Am. Genealogy Soc. (pres. 1983-85), Kansas City Bar Assn. (chmn. comml. law com. 1958-59). Democrat. Mem. Christian Ch. Lodges: Masons, Shriners. Avocations: genealogy, Revolutionary and Civil War history, Bible. Office: 253 E Bridlespur Dr Kansas City MO 64114

WHITAKER, LOUIS RODMAN, professional baseball player. Second baseman Detroit Tigers. Office: Detroit Tigers Tiger Stadium Detroit MI 48216*

WHITAKER, RONALD MARTIN, engineer; b. Fullerton, Nebr., Jan. 30, 1933; s. Leonard Bert and Margaret Mary (Seely) W.; student Central Tech. Community Coll., Hastings, Nebr., 1977, Franklin U., Columbus, Ohio, 1981 Ohio U., Lancaster; m. Janet Louise Spitz, Apr. 12, 1955; children—Mark David, Jeffrey Keith, Wendy Elaine. Mgr. Spitz Foundry Inc., Hastings, Nebr., 1965-78, Crosier Monastery, 1978; plant engr. Lattimer Stevens Co., Columbus, Ohio, 1978-80, v.p. engring., 1980—; instr. Engr. Ctr., Ft. Belvoir, Va., 1953. Scoutmaster Overland Trails council Boy Scouts Am., Grand Island, Nebr., 1970-78, dist. camping dir., 1975-78, Order of Arrow advisor, 1976-78; extraordinary minister Roman Cath. Ch. Served with C.E. U.S. Army, 1953-55. Decorated Combat Infantryman's Badge, others; cert. mfg. engr.; registered profl. engr. Mem. Soc. Mfg. Engrs. (chmn. sr. mem.), Am. Foundrymen's Soc. (sr.), Nat. Rifle Assn. (endowment mem., cert. firearms instr.), Nebr. Rifle and Pistol Assn. (life mem.), Nat. Reloaders Assn., Central Ohio Council Internat. Visitors, Am Legion, Nat. Eagle Scout Assn., Am. Photog. Soc. Republican. Editorial cons. Plant Engineering mag. Home: 7411 Woodale Dr Carroll OH 43112 Office: 715 Marion Rd Columbus OH 43207

WHITCRAFT, JAMES RICHARD, JR., accountant; b. Muncie, Ind., Jan. 27, 1947; s. James R. and Hazel V. (Garner) W.; m. Pamela D. Imel, July 29, 1977; children—Christopher K., Kelle D. B.S., Ball State U., 1969, M.B.A., 1972. C.P.A., Ind., Mich. Sr. staff accountant Arthur Andersen & Co., Indpls., 1969-77; audit mgr. Holdeman, Fulmer, Elkhart, Ind., 1977-81; owner Dick Whitcraft, CPA, Elkhart, 1981-84; mng. ptnr. Whitcraft & Thomas, C.P.A.s, Elkhart, 1984—. Served with U.S. Army, 1969-71. Mem. Am. Inst. C.P.A.s, Ind. Assn. C.P.A.s, Mich. Assn. C.P.A.s. Republican. Presbyterian. Lodges: Elks, Optimists (pres. 1981-82). Home: 20348 US 12 E Edwardsburg MI 49112 Office: Whitcraft & Thomas CPAs 524 S Second St Elkhart IN 46516

WHITE, BOB MCKNIGHT, grain and transportation company executive; b. Bristow, Okla., Nov. 5, 1949; s. Charles McKnight and Gladys Fern (Allee) White; m. Patricia Sue Avery, Dec. 20, 1969; children—Christopher, Julie. B.B.A., Wichita State U., 1969; A.A., Cowley County Community Coll., 1969; M.B.A., Wichita State U., 1976. C.P.A., Ill. Asst. controller Garvey Internat. Inc., Bloomingdale, Ill., 1975-77, controller, 1977-79, v.p. fin., 1979-81, exec. v.p., 1981-82, pres., 1982—, also dir., 1979—; dir. Garvey Commodities Corp., Chgo., 1979—, Interail Inc., Bloomingdale, 1979—, NW Okla. R.R., Woodward, Okla., 1980—, Pacific Coast Transp. Inc., Bloomingdale, 1980—. Mem. family life com. Baker Methodist Ch., St. Charles, Ill., 1983. Mem. Nat. Assn. Accts. (various offices 1976-83, pres. Chgo. chpt. 1983-84), Ill. Soc. C.P.A.s, Kans. Soc. C.P.A.s. Republican. Clubs: Union League (Chgo.); St. Charles Country (Ill.).

WHITE, BRUCE ALLEN, dentist; b. Kalamazoo, Mich., Sept. 13, 1946; s. Byron E. and Joan Harriet (Spitters) W.; m. Claire Jean Houtman, Mar. 22, 1969; children—Lisa, Kristin, Brian. B.A., Hope Coll., 1968; D.D.S., U. Mich., 1972. Cert. Fin. Planner, Coll. Fin. Planning. Pres., Bruce White D.D.S., P.C., Bay City, Mich., 1974—; treas., ptnr. Haddix Lumber Co., Midland, Mich., 1979—; cons., ptnr. Practice Cons. Group, Phoenix, 1981—; dir. CRW Assocs., Bay City, Mich. Bd. dirs. White Family Found., 1984—. Served to capt. AUS, 1972-74. Mem. Bay Area C. of C., Bay Area Dental Soc. (past pres.), ADA, Acad. Gen. Dentistry, Soc. Occlusal Studies, Inst. Cert. Fin. Planners. Presbyterian (past deacon). Avocation: hunting. Home: 3055 Linden Park Dr Bay City MI 48706 Office: 800 S Euclid St Bay City MI 48706

WHITE, BRUCE WAYNE, statistician; b. Plum City, Wis.; Dec. 3, 1953; s. Wayne Dallas and Elaine Bertha (Shelstad) W.; m. Cheryll Drew Grodem, June 23, 1978; 1 child, Zachary Adam. B.A. in Math., St. Cloud State Univ., 1976; M.A. in Stats., U. Minn., Mpls., 1983. Technician, 3M Co., Hastings, Minn., 1977, St. Paul, 1977-81, statis. technologist, 1981—. Mem. Am. Statis. Assn. Mem. Bible Ch. Club: 3M (St. Paul). Avocations: reading, playing guitar, Bible study. Home: 1311 Edgerton St St Paul MN 55101 Office: 3M Co 3M Ctr Bldg 236-1N-05 St Paul MN 55101

WHITE, C. THOMAS, justice state supreme court; b. Humphrey, Nebr., Oct. 5, 1928; LL.B., Creighton U., Omaha, 1952; m. Joan Jiranek, Oct. 9, 1971; children by previous marriage—Michaela, Thomas, Patrick. Admitted to Nebr. bar, practiced law; judge 21st Dist. Ct. Nebr.; atty. Platte County; justice Supreme Ct. Nebr., 1977—. Mem. Nebr. Dist. Ct. Judges Assn. (pres.), Alpha Sigma Nu, Delta Theta Phi. Address: Nebr Supreme Ct State Capitol Lincoln NE 68509*

WHITE, CAROLYN NEWELL PITT, museum coordinator; b. Bklyn., Oct. 13, 1943; d. Frank Rylands and Winifred Gladys (Nagel) P.; m. John James White II, Aug. 28, 1965; children—Allison Newell, Kevin Brandon. Cert. Evanston Bus. Coll., 1964; B.A., Northwestern U., 1965, M.A., 1967. Showroom rep. Am. Standard, Chgo., 1965; sec. Med. Group of Evanston (Ill.), 1967; instr. Harford Jr. Coll., Bel Aire, Md., 1968; sec. Ayres, Lewis, Norris & May, Ann Arbor, Mich., 1970-71; unit coordinator Am. Cancer Soc., Columbus, Ind., 1979-80; broker assoc. Tipton Lakes Co., Columbus, 1981-84. Bd. dirs. Mayor's Task Force on Status of Women, 1973-74; archtl. tour guide Vis.'s Center 1973-75; chmn. voters service LWV, 1974-75; vol. in pub. and pvt. schs., 1976-81; vol. instr. Columbus Girls Club, 1977; bd. dirs. Indpls. Museum of Art, Columbus, 1981-85, v.p., 1983-84, pres., 1984-85; pres. Mt. Healthy PTA, 1982-83; vol. United Way, 1983; area coordinator Arts Insight. Recipient award Indpls. Museum of Art, 1976. Mem. Am. Assn. Mus., Leadership Bartholomew County, First Tuesday Forum, Delta Zeta. Unitarian-Universalist. Home: 3701 S Poplar Dr Columbus IN 47201 Office: Indpls Mus Art 506 Fifth St Columbus IN 47201

WHITE, DANIEL JOSEPH, lawyer; b. Cleve., May 13, 1953; s. Melvin Marshall and Mary-Jane (Buckley) W. B.S., U. Cin., 1976; J.D. cum laude, Cleve.-Marshall Sch. Law, 1980. Bars: Ohio 1980, U.S. Dist. Ct. (no. dist.) Ohio 1980, U.S. Ct. Appeals (6th cir.) 1982, U.S. Dist. Ct. (so. dist.) Ohio 1983. Assoc. Nurenberg, Plevin, Jacobson, Heller & McCarthy Co., L.P.A., Cleve., 1980-82, Columbus, Ohio, 1983-85, Jacobson, Maynard, Tuschman & Kalur Co., L.P.A., Columbus, 1985—. Mem. Assn. Trial Lawyers Am., Ohio State Bar Assn., Columbus Bar Assn., Defense Research Inst. Roman Catholic. Home: 4770 Shire Ridge Rd W Columbus OH 43220 Office: Jacobson Maynard Tuschman & Kalur Co LPA 175 S Third St Suite 340 Columbus OH 43215

WHITE, EUGENE M., product development executive; b. Laud, Ind., Aug. 2, 1937; s. Robert Herold and Margaret Bell (Ward) W.; A.B. in Philosophy, Ind. U., 1963; children—Michelle, Michael. Founder, pres. Genesis Products,

Ft. Wayne, Ind., 1979—. Dir. conservation caucus Ind. 4th Congl. Dist., 1977-79; alt. del. to Republican Nat. Conv., 1976; pres. Ft. Wayne chpt. Parents without Partners, 1980-81; founder Single/Single Again, 1982. Dept. Energy research grantee, 1979-80. Mem. AAAS, Soc. Mfg. Engrs., Ft. Wayne Astron. Soc., Coptic Fellowship. Republican. Methodist. Patentee in field of mechanics. Home: 1624 Franklin Ave Fort Wayne IN 46808

WHITE, HENRY PAUL, chemist; b. Chgo., Sept. 30, 1921; s. Millard Earl and Juliette Zoe (Kieffer) w.; m. Rhea Mae Parnock, June 4, 1948 (div. Feb. 1958); m. Dolores Esther Carlson, Mar. 1, 1958. A.A., U. Fla., 1943; B.A., Roosevelt U., 1953. Lab. technician Catalin Corp. Am., Calumet City, Ill., Fords, N.J., 1954-55, Chgo. Extruded Metals Corp., Cicero, Ill., 1955-56; chemist quality control Taylor Forge Inc., Cicero, Memphis, 1956-64, 1967-72, Burlington No. R.R., Aurora, Ill., St. Paul, 1964-66, chemist research and devel. Kester Solder Co., Chgo., 1966-67; chemist, fuels analyst No. Ind. Pub. Service Co., Chesterton and Hammond, 1979—. Served with U.S. Army, 1944-46, ETO. Mem. Am. Chem. Soc., Am. Soc. Metals, Lake County Poetry Club (pres. 1980-82), Hoosier Pens Crown Point, 1st Friday Poets NW Ind. Lodge: Masons (marshall 1966-67). Avocations: music; art; writing. Home: 117 Las Olas Dr Crown Point IN 46307 Office: No Ind Pub Service Co 501 Bailly Rd Chesterton IN 46304

WHITE, JOE CHARLES, vocational educator; b. Fayetteville, Ark., May 13, 1949; s. Joseph Bell and Ethel Irene (Kappen) W.; m. Barbara Carol Stanley, Mar. 25, 1972; children—Steven Joseph, Kelli Lynn. B.S. in Indsl. Edn., S.E. Mo. State U., 1972, postgrad., 1979; M.S., Murray State U., 1976; postgrad. U. Mo., 1978, 81. Indsl. edn. tchr. Cairo (Ill.) pub. schs., 1972-73, Ritenour Sch. Dist., Overland, Mo., 1973-76; vocat. edn. tchr. Jefferson Coll., Hillsboro, Mo., 1976-77, dir. vocat. preparation, 1977—; mem. North Central Assn. High Sch. Program Evaluation, 1982—. Mem. Am. Vocat. Assn., Mo. Vocat. Assn., Nat. Assn. Vocat. Spl. Needs Personnel, Mo. Vocat. Spl. Needs Assn., Home Builders Assn., Mo. Assn. Community Jr. Colls. Methodist. Home: Route 1262 Scenic Dr Festus MO 63028 Office: Jefferson Coll Hillsboro MO 63050

WHITE, JUDITH ANN O'RADNIK, social worker; b. St. Paul, Oct. 27, 1943; d. Clarence Edwin and Marcella Ann (Cappelle) O'Radnik; B.A., Quincy Coll., 1965; M.S.W., Ohio State U., 1970; m. Dean H. White, May 22, 1981. Dep. juvenile officer St. Louis Circuit Ct. Juvenile Div., 1965-68; caseworker Ohio Div. Youth Services, Powell, Ohio, 1968-69; supr. intake delinquency juvenile div. St. Louis Circuit Ct., 1970-76, supr. child abuse and neglect unit, 1976—; liaison mem. project for coordination legal and protective services for sexually abused children St. Louis Circuit Atty.'s Office, 1985—. Bd. dirs. Council on Child Abuse and Neglect of Met. St. Louis, 1979-82; mem. St. Louis Task Force on Child Abuse, St. Louis Network on Child Abuse and Neglect. Fed. grantee, 1985—. Mem. Nat. Council Crime and Delinquency, Ohio State U. Sch. Social Work Alumni Assn. Home: 138 Manlyn Dr Kirkwood MO 63122 Office: 920 N Vandeventer Ave Saint Louis MO 63108

WHITE, LARRY CURTIS, osteo. physician; b. Decatur, Ill., May 1, 1941; s. Gerald Curtis and Elizabeth Jane (Moore) W.; B.S., U. Ill., 1963; D.O., Kirksville Coll. Osteo. Medicine, 1970; m. Mary Ann Savage, Aug. 21, 1965; children—Mark, Michelle, Gerald, Barbara. Intern, Riverside Osteo. Hosp., Trenton, Mich., 1970-71; practice osteo. medicine, pres. Romeo (Mich.) Clinic, 1971—; mem. staff, mem. med. exec. com. Crittenton Hosp., 1977—, chmn. med. records com., 1977, vice chmn. dept. family practice, 1977-79, chmn., 1979—. Diplomate Am. Bd. Family Practice. Mem. Am. Osteo. Assn., Mich. Assn. Osteo. Physicians and Surgeons, Am. Acad. Family Physicians, Am. Assn. Family Practice, U. Ill. Alumni Assn., Psi Sigma Alpha, Alpha Phi Omega, Sigma Sigma Phi, Theta Psi, Alpha Kappa Lambda. Methodist. Clubs: Masons, Shriners, K.T. Home: 2250 E Gunn Rd Rochester MI 48063 Office: 241 N Main St Romeo MI 48065

WHITE, LINDA DAMER, educator; b. Springfield, Ill., Dec. 5, 1938; d. J. Fred and Mary Jane (Thurmond) Welsh; B.A., William Jewell Coll., 1959; M.A., Boston U., 1967; Ed.D., U. N.C., Greensboro, 1979; children—Diana, Cynthia and John Damer. Tchr., Kearney (Mo.) Public Schs., 1959-60, Consolidated Sch. Dist. 1, Kansas City, Mo., 1960-63, Wellesley (Mass.) Pub. Schs., 1963-64, Newton (Mass.) Pub. Schs., 1966-67, Smyth County (Va.) Pub. Schs., 1969-72, Washington County (Va.) Pub. Schs., 1973-76, Burlington (N.C.) Pub. Schs., 1978-79; grad. teaching asst. U. N.C., Greensboro, 1977-78; assoc. prof. music Ind. State U., Terre Haute, Ind., 1979—. U. N.C., Greensboro fellow, 1976-77. Mem. Music Educators Nat. Conf., Ind. Music Educators Assn. (exec. bd., pres.-elect), Am. Orff Schulwerk Assn., Pi Kappa Lambda (v.p.), Phi Delta Kappa (v.p.) Clubs: University (pres.), Faculty Women's (pres.). Home: 9048 Arrowood Ct Terre Haute IN 47802 Office: Dept Music Ind State U Terre Haute IN 47809

WHITE, PAMELA KAY, librarian, language educator; b. Ann Arbor, Mich., Sept. 21, 1951; d. Stephen Bruce and Barbara June (Petree) W. B.A., Ind. State U., 1973; M.L.S., 1979. Coop. student, claims rep. Social Security Adminstrn., Balt., 1971, Indpls., 1972, Balt., 1972, Harrisburg, Ill., 1974-75, West Frankfort, Ill., 1975-78; librarian Oakland City-Columbia Twp Pub. Library, Oakland City, Ind., 1979—; tchr. German, Wood Meml. High Sch., Oakland City, Ind., 1983—. Sponsor, advisor Footlight/Puppet Club, Oakland City, 1983—; asst. leader Brownie Troop 458, Oakland City, 1983—. Mem. Ind. Library Assn. (mem. small libraries div. 1980—, treas. 1981-82, pres. 1982-83, mem. children and young people div. 1981—). Baptist. Office: Oakland City-Columbia Twp Pub Library 210 S Main St Oakland City IN 47660

WHITE, RAYMOND JOSEPH, history educator; b. Mpls., Jan. 23, 1930; s. Raymond Adolphus and Helen Amelia (Doles) W.; m. Alice Martha Rothen, May 22, 1954; children—Jon, Jeffery, R. David. B.S., U. Wis.-Milw., 1957, M.S., 1968; Ph.D., U. Wis.-Madison, 1975. Tchr. history Milw. Pub. Schs., 1957—. Served to staff sgt. USAF, 1949-52. Mem. Milw. County Hist. Soc., Nat. Council Social Studies, State Hist. Soc. Wis., Milw. Met. Historians Assn. (founder, pres 1981—), Wis. Assn. for promotion of History (exec. bd.), Assn. for Supervision and Curriculum Devel., Phi Delta Kappa. Author of multi media kit and various ednl. slide tapes. Home: N 63 W 15328 Pocahontas Dr Menomonee Falls WI 53051 Office: PO Drawer 10k Milwaukee WI 53201

WHITE, RICHARD THOMAS, radiology educator; b. Binghamton, N.Y., May 10, 1941; s. William Joseph and Winifred (Murphy) W.; m. Carole Helen Peckham, Mar. 15, 1970; 1 son, Kevin Michael. B.S., SUNY-Binghamton, 1967; D.O., Chgo. Coll. Osteo. Medicine, 1972. Intern, Bi County Hosp., Warren, Mich.; resident Detroit Hosp., Children's Hosp., Detroit, 1973-76; fellow Johns Hopkins Hosp., Balt., 1976; staff radiologist Bi-County Hosp., 1977-79; asst. prof. radiology Mich. State U., East Lansing, 1980—, cons. ultra-sound research, 1980-83, cons. nuclear magnetic research, 1982-83; physician cons. varsity sports, 1980—; cons. handicapped athletes Spl. Olympics, Washington, 1978—. Med. dir. Mich. Spl. Olympics Central Mich. U., Mt. Pleasant, 1977—; bd. dirs. Spl. Olympics, Mt. Pleasant, 1980—; med. advisor Amateur Hockey Assn. USA, Colorado Springs, Colo., 1980—; cons. Detroit Red Wings hockey team, 1977—. Served with U.S. Army, 1959-64. Recipient Outstanding Contbn. award Spl. Olympics, 1980; named Team Physician U.S. Nat. Hockey Team, Mich. Amateur Hockey Assn., 1979, 81, 83. Mem. Am. Coll. Radiology, Am. Coll. Med. Imaging, Am. Coll. Sports Medicine, Am. Inst. Ultrasound in Medicine, Am. Acad. Sci. Clubs: Detroit Red Wing Hockey, Econ. (Detroit).

WHITE, SANDRA JEANNE, elementary school educator; b. Peoria, Ill., May 23; d. Allen Noel Pate and Margaret Lucy (Stout) P.; m. Dale Eugene White Aug. 31, 1957; children—Cynthia Jeanne, Julie Ann Nelson. B.S. in Edn., Western Ill. U., 1967; M.S. in Edn., Ill. State U., 1974. Elem. tchr. Peoria Pub. Schs., 1967—; adj. instr. Ill. Central Coll. Bd. dirs., v.p., chmn. promotions Corn Stock Theatre; chmn. play selection com. Community Children's Theatre; active 1st United Meth. Ch., adminstrv. bd., council ministries, edn. chmn., mem. choir, tchr. Selected for 1981 Social Studies Colloquium Northwestern (Ill.) U., Follett Pub. Co.; Gov.'s Master Tchr. program nominee, 1984. Mem. AAUW, Peoria Edn. Assn., Ill. Edn. Assn., NEA (life), Assn. Supervision, Curriculum Devel., Ill. Assn. Supervision and Curriculum Devel. (editorial bd.), Ill. Assn. Tchr. Educators, Ill. Guidance and Personnel Assn., Ill. Prins. Assn., Delta Kappa Gamma, Phi Delta Kappa (newsletter editor Beta Psi chpt.). Club: Pilot Internat. (Peoria). Office: 1619 W Fredonia Peoria IL 61606

WHITE, STANTON MCCONNELL, SR., newspaper publisher; b. Oklahoma City, Dec. 7, 1923; s. Stephen S. and Mary M. (McConnell) W.; student public schs., Kankakee, Ill.; m. Marcella M. Girard, Sept. 27, 1945; children—Stanton M., Stephen, Jackie, Rick, Shari. Salesman, Daily Jour., Kankakee, Ill., 1950-53, promotion mgr., 1953-54, asst. ad mgr., 1954-56, advt. mgr., 1956-67, advt. dir., asst. gen. mgr., 1967; with Ottawa (Ill.) Daily Times, 1967—, gen. mgr., 1968-69, pub., 1969—, pres., 1979—; dir. Ottawa Pub. Co.; pres., pub. Streator (Ill.) Times-Press, also dir. Bd. dirs. Greater Ottawa United Fund, Ottawa Downtown Devel. Corp. Served with USN, 1940-46; ETO. Mem. Am. Newspaper Pubs. Assn., Internat. Newspaper Advt. Execs., Inland Press Assn., Ill. Press Assn., Chgo. Press Club, C. of C. and Industry (bd. dirs.). Republican. Clubs: Ottawa Boat, Elks. Home: Rural Route 4 Pine Hills Subdiv Ottawa IL 61350 Office: 110 W Jefferson St Ottawa IL 61350

WHITE, THOMAS GREGG, air force officer; b. Fort Worth, July 26, 1955; s. Thomas Arthur and Evelyn Estelle (Nichols) W.; m. Roxanne Marie Josephson, Aug. 28, 1976; children—Jason Thomas, Christina Heather. A.A., Chapman Coll., 1979, B.A. in Psychology, 1980; A.S. in Electronics Tech. Community Coll. of Air Force, 1983. Enlisted as airman basic U.S. Air Force, 1973; advanced through grades to 2d lt., 1983; radar technician 756 radar squadron Finland AFB, Minn., 1974-77, 714 radar squadron, Cold Bay, Alaska, 1977; radar technician 756 radar squadron, Finland AFB, Minn., 1977-80; space systems technician 1970 communications squadron, Woomera, South Australia, 1980-82, 1000 satellite ops. group, Loring AFB, Maine, 1982-84; munitions officer 379 munitions maintenance squadron, Wurtsmith AFB, Mich., 1984—. Mem. Air Force Assn. Lutheran. Avocations: microcomputing; shortwave radio. Home: 8004-A N Alaska Wurtsmith AFB MI 48753 Office: 379 MMS Wurtsmith AFB MI 48753

WHITE, THOMAS LESTER, consulting engineer; b. Youngstown, Ohio, May 30, 1903; s. William Lester and Ethel Mary (Jackson) W.; m. Marion Elizabeth Evans, Sept. 24, 1930 (dec. July 1983); 1 dau., Harrietellen White McKendrick. Tool designer, engr. Comml. Shearing Inc., Youngstown, 1924-26, chief engr., 1926-51, cons. engr., 1951-68, 68—; cons. engr. coal mines, metal mines, hwy., railroad and subway tunnels, Belgium, Portugal, India, Australia, S.Am., Can., others; lectr. various univs. and tech. orgns. Registered profl. engr., Ohio. Fellow ASME (past chmn. petroleum div.); mem. Am. Ry. Engring. Assn., Mahoning Valley Tech. Soc. (named outstanding person 1973). Baptist. Clubs: Kiwanis, Shriners, Masons. Author: (with R.V. Proctor and Karl Terzaghi) Rock Tunneling with Steel Supports, 1946; Earth Tunneling with Steel Supports, 1977. Contbr. articles to profl. jours. Address: 721 W Warren Ave Youngstown OH 44511

WHITE, WILLIAM J., lumber and building products company executive. Pres., chief operating officer Masonite Corp., Chgo. Office: Masonite Corp 29 N Wacker Dr Chicago IL 60606*

WHITE, W(ILLIE) GLENN, counseling psychology educator, counseling psychologist, consultant, researcher; b. Dumas, Ark., Jan. 15, 1933; s. Eugene Lee and Ernestine Cornelius (Jordan) W.; m. Gloria Waters, Jan. 1, 1955; 1 dau., Terry Finister. B.A. in Edn., Harris-Stowe Tchrs. Coll., 1959; M.A., Washington U., St. Louis, 1964; Ph.D., U. Mo., 1974. Lic. psychologist, cert. counselor and tchr., Mo. Tchr., counselor St. Louis Pub. Sch. System, 1959-65; dir. research coordinating unit Mo. Dept. Elem. and Secondary Edn., Jefferson City, 1965-77; asst. prof. edn. U. Mo.-St. Louis, 1977-83, assoc. prof., 1983—; cons. to program devel. and tng. instns. Bd. dirs. Life Crisis Suicide Prevention, 1983-85. Served with U.S. Army, 1953-56. Recipient Career Achievement award Urban League, 1978, Achievement award St. Louis Assn. Counseling and Devel., 1985. Mem. Am. Personnel and Guidance Assn., Am. Psychol. Assn., Assn. Measurement and Evauation, Omega Psi Phi. Baptist.

WHITE, WILLIS SHERIDAN, JR., utilities executive; b. nr. Portsmouth, Va., Dec. 17, 1926; s. Willis Sheridan and Carrie (Culpepper) W.; m. LaVerne Behrends, Oct. 8, 1949; children—Willis Sheridan III, Marguerite Louise White Spangler, Cynthia Diane. B.S., Va. Poly. Inst., 1948; M.S., MIT, 1958. With Am. Electric Power Co. System, 1948—; asst. engr. Am. Electric Power Service Corp., N.Y.C., 1948-52, asst. to pres., 1952-54, office mgr., 1954-57, adminstrv. asst. to operating v.p., 1958-61; div. mgr. Appalachian Power Co., Lynchburg, Va., 1962-66, asst. gen. mgr., Roanoke, Va., 1966-67, asst. v.p., 1967-69, v.p., 1969, exec. v.p., dir., 1969-73; sr. exec. v.p. ops., dir. Am. Electric Power Service Corp, N.Y.C., 1973-75, vice chmn. ops., also dir., chmn. bd., chief exec. officer, 1976—; chmn. bd., chief exec. officer Am. Electric Power Co., 1976—; chmn., dir. Appalachian Power Co., Columbus and So. Ohio Electric Co., Ind. & Mich. Electric Co., Mich. Power Co., Ohio Power Co., Ky. Power Co., Kingsport Power Co., Wheeling Electric Co.; pres., dir. Beech Bottom Power Co., Blackhawk Coal Co., Cardinal Operating Co., Cedar Coal Co., Central Operating Co., Franklin Real Estate Co., Ind. Franklin Realty Co., Mich. Gas. Exploration Co., Price River Coal Co., Kanawha Valley Power Co., So. Appalachian Coal Co., So. Ohio Coal Co., Twin Br. R.R. Co., W.Va. Power Co., Windsor Power HouseCoal Co., Ohio Valley Electric Corp., Ind.-Ky. Electric Corp., AEP Energy Services, Inc., AEP Generating Co.; dir. Irving Bank Corp., Irving Trust Co.; mem. Nat. Coal Council; pres. Internat. Large High Voltage Electric Systems, Paris. Trustee Battelle Meml. Inst., Children's Hosp., Columbus, United Way, Franklin County, Ohio; bd. visitors Va. Poly. Inst. and State U. Served with USNR, 1945-46. Sloan fellow, 1957-58. Mem. Edison Electric Inst. (bd. dirs.), NAM (dir.), IEEE, Eta Kappa Nu. Methodist. Office: American Electric Power 1 Riverside Plaza PO Box 16631 Columbus OH 43216

WHITE, WOODIE W., clergyman Bishop Central Ill. and So. Ill. confs. United Methodist Ch. Office: PO Box 2050 Bloomington IL 61701*

WHITE, ZENOBIA MAXINE, educator; b. Cotton Plant, Ark., Feb. 16, 1933; d. Willie Joe and Johnnie (Jones) Reid; B.S., Drake U., 1951; postgrad. Drake U., 1971-75; m. Harold White, Nov. 3, 1959; children—Claire, William, June Carol, Harold, Robin, Cris Jon, Grace Angela. Exec. sec. Forest Ave Mission, Des Moines, 1960-76; social worker Polk County Dept. Social Services, Des Moines, 1976-77; tchr. public schs. Des Moines Ind. Sch. Dist., 1976—; exec. dir., founder OSACS Inc. Self Actualizing Ctr. for Women, 1979—. Mem. adv. com. State Birth Defects Inst., 1970-81; mem. older worker com. Iowa Commn. on Aging, 1985—. Mem. Assn. Childhood Edn. Am. Office: 1218 21st St Des Moines IA 50311

WHITEHEAD, STEPHEN ELLIOTT, social service administrator; b. Elkhart, Ind., Aug. 18, 1937; s. Clinton Elliott and Lula Lucille (Sommers) W.; m. Carol Jean Miller, Feb. 16, 1962 (div. Nov. 1980); children—Scott Elliott, Kimberly Ann; m. Karen Rose Malmquist, July 10, 1982. B.A., North Central Coll., 1961; M.Div., Garrett Theol. Sem., 1963; cert. Urban Tng. Ctr., Chgo., 1967. Ordained to ministry Methodist Ch., 1964. Asst. pastor Christ United Meth. Ch., Hammond, Ind., 1961-63; pastor Maple Lane United Meth. Ch., South Bend, Ind., 1963-65; dir. Christian Service Ctr., South Bend, 1965-66; founder, co-owner Vanguard Bookstore Ministry, Chgo., 1967-69; rehab. counsel Ill. Dept. Mental Health, Chgo., 1969-70; exec. dir. Christopher House, Chgo., 1970—; bd. mem. United Neighborhood Ctrs. Am., N.Y.C., 1981—, Day Care Action Council, Chgo., 1981—; co-founder, pres. After Sch. Program Lincoln Park, Chgo., 1976-80; co-founder, registered agt. Citizens Alert, Chgo., 1967-69; co-host Midwest New Games Found. Tng., 1980, 82; New Games trainer, 1980—. Treas., Lincoln Sch. Edn. Council, Chgo., 1974; com. mem. 43d Ward Ind. Alderman Campaign, Chgo., 1975; com. mem. State Senate Campaign, 1976. Recipient award Okla. Conf. Christian Chs., 1968; Plaque, Orgn. Citizens Alert, 1982. Mem. Chgo. Fedn. Settlements (dir., sec. 1983). Democrat. Methodist. Home: 515 W Grant Pl Chicago IL 60614 Office: Christopher House 2507 Greenview Ave Chicago IL 60614

WHITEHOUSE, ALTON WINSLOW, JR., oil company executive; b. Albany, N.Y., Aug. 1, 1927; s. Alton Winslow and Catherine (Lyda) W.; B.S., U. Va., 1949, LL.B., 1952; m. Helen MacDonald, Nov. 28, 1953; children—Alton, Sarah, Peter. Admitted to Ohio bar, 1953; assoc. ptnr. McAfree, Hanning, Newcomer, Hazlett & Wheeler, Cleve., 1952-68; v.p., gen. counsel Standard Oil Co. Ohio, Cleve., 1968-69, sr. v.p., 1969-70, pres., chief operating officer, 1970-77, vice chmn. bd., 1977-78, chmn. bd., chief exec. officer, 1978—, also dir., mem. exec. com.; dir. Ohio Bell, Midland-Ross Corp., Cleve. Cliffs Iron Co., Brit. Petroleum Co. p.l.c. Trustee, Cleve. Clinic Found., Case-Western Res. U., Cleve. Mus. Art, Cleve. Mus. Natural History. Mem. ABA, Ohio Bar Assn., Cleve. Bar Assn., Am. Petroleum Inst. Episcopalian. Office: Standard Oil Co 1750 Midland Bldg Cleveland OH 44115

WHITEMAN, NELSON THOMAS, educational administrator; b. Dayton, Ohio, Apr. 18, 1926; s. Chester Ray and Estella (Anderson) W.; m. Donna June Larrimer, Aug. 30, 1947; children—Vickie Lynn Nickles Scott Thomas, Monique Celeste Redwine. B.A., Otterbein Coll., 1951; M.A., Miami U., 1955; postgrad. U. Cin., 1958-59, Wright State U., 1975-76. Tchr., Deerfield Rural Twp. Sch. Dist., Ross County, Ohio, 1951-53; tchr. Patterson Coop. High Sch., Dayton, 1953-57; asst. prin., 1957-66, prin., 1966—. Chmn., Dayton High Sch. Athletic Bd. Control, 1982-83; bd. dirs. Jr. Achievement of Dayton. Served with USAAF, 1944-46. Mem. Ohio Vocat. Assn. (Man of Yr. 1983), Am. Vocat. Assn., Ohio Assn. Secondary Sch. Adminstrs. Republican. Methodist. Home: 5300 Middlebury Rd Dayton OH 45432 Office: 118 E 1st St Dayton OH 45402

WHITENER, VIRGIL SYLVESTER, JR., banker; b. Memphis, Feb. 2, 1931; s. Virgil S. and Nola (Moore) W.; m. LaVerne R. Maze, Jan. 26, 1957; children—David, DeWayne. Asst. v.p. New Era Bank, Fredericktown, Mo., 1960-68; asst. cashier Cape County Bank, Jackson, Mo., 1968-77; asst. v.p. Jackson Exchange Bank, 1977—. Served with USAF, 1951-55. Baptist. Club: Jackson C. of C. (treas. 1974). Lodges: Lions (treas. 1975), Kiwanis (pres. 1983). Home: Route 4 Jackson MO 63755 Office: Jackson Exchange Bank 101 Court St Jackson MO 63755

WHITESELL, TERRY GENE, marketing executive; b. Marion, Ind., Aug. 29, 1939; s. Gene and Margaret (Hoosier) W.; m. Julia L. Kilgus, Sept. 7, 1963; children—Brian, Andrea, Jeffery. Student Ball State U., 1957-61. Buyer Richmond Baking Co. (Ind.), 1961-63; purchasing agt. Dille and McGuire Mfg., Richmond, 1963-65; sales rep. and mgr. P & L Packaging Corp., Midland Container, Richmond, 1965-67; buyer Wayne Corp., Richmond, 1967-68, regional sales mgr., 1968-74, nat. sales mgr., 1974-81, v.p. mktg., 1981—; dir. Richmond Power & Light Co. Mem. City Council Richmond, 1979, 84—; bd. dirs. Jr. Achievement; mem. exec. bd. YMCA, Kullman Youth Ctr.; chmn. United Way Campaign. Mem. Am. Mgmt. Assn. Club: Forest Hills Country. Home: 781 Mikan Dr Richmond IN 47374 Office: PO Box 1447 Richmond IN 47374

WHITESIDE, CAROLYN ANN, correctional officer; b. St. Louis, Mo., July 9, 1949; d. Wyatt and Maggie Mae (Buck) Gilkey; m. Emanuel Charles Whiteside, Oct. 4, 1983; children by previous marriage—Tanya, Robert, Tawania, Aisha. A.A., Black Hawk Coll., 1978; B.A., Marycrest Coll., 1980; postgrad. Augustana Coll. Cert. tchr., Iowa, Ill. Insp., packer, operator Louisiana Plastics, Mo., 1969-73; vice chmn. local AFL-CIO, 1971-72, chmn., 1972-73; line worker Gen. Motors Corp., St. Louis, 1973-74; nurses aide, med. sec. Vis. Nurses Assn., Davenport, Iowa, 1974-76; news reporter, WQAD-TV, Channel 8, Moline, Ill., 1977-79; instr. Black Hawk Coll., Rock Island, Ill., 1981; pre-trial release counselor Dept. Corrections, Davenport, 1981—; radio personality KALA-FM, St. Ambrose Coll., 1981—. Bd. dirs., v.p. HELP Legal Aid, Davenport, 1979—; bd. dirs. Legal Service Corp. Iowa, 1982—; Brownie leader, Davenport, 1980-81; vice chmn. Inner City Devel. Corp., 1981-83; com. mem. United Neighbors Inc., 1981—. Recipient Student Achievement award Continental Ill. Nat. Bank & Trust Co. Chgo., 1976. Mem. Black Profl. Assn., Black Social Workers Assn., Iowa Corrections Assn. (chmn. minority issues com., mem. Spring planning com.). Democrat. Baptist. Home: 515 E Eighth St Davenport IA 52803 Office: 326 W 3d St Suite 507 Kahl Davenport IA 52801

WHITESIDES, ROBERT GENE, manufacturing company executive; b. Jefferson City, Mo., Jan. 31, 1927; s. Rowland F. and Bertha E. (Louthan) W.; m. Lesley M. Echlin, June 1, 1947; children—Thomas, MaryAnn, Laura. Cert. Davenport Bus. Coll., 1948. Salesman DAKE div. JSJ Corp., Grand Haven, Mich., 1960-67, sales, 1967—. Served with USN, 1945-46; PTO. Mem. Am. Supply and Machinery Mfrs. Assn. (pres. 1982-83), Grand Haven C. of C. (pres. 1957). Republican. Methodist. Club: Spring Lake Country (pres. 1980) (Mich.). Avocations: Golf, music. Home: 18295 Holcomb Hills Grand Haven MI 49417 Office: DAKE div JSJ Corp 724 Robbins Rd Grand Haven MI 49417

WHITLOW, MARION VIRGINIA, educator, nurse; b. Johnstown, Pa., May 17, 1929; d. William Sercy and Mary Thelma (Hill) Holton; diploma in nursing St. Francis Hosp., Pitts. 1950; B.S. in Nursing, U. Pitts. 1966; M.S., U. Ind.-Purdue U., Indpls., 1977; m. Emery Whitlow, June 28, 1969; children—Cecily Patterson, Gary Patterson, Carol Patterson Upshur. Staff nurse St. Francis Hosp., 1950-52; staff nurse Mercy Hosp., Johnstown, 1956-58, 60-65, instr. pediatrics, 1966-69; assoc. prof. nursing Purdue U., Westville, Ind., 1980—. Chmn. statewide steering com. to organize family life programs in all African Meth. Episc. chs. in Ind. Mem. AAUW, Am. Nurses Assn., (intercultural council), Am. Nurses Found., Am. Black Nurses Assn., Nat. League for Nursing, Harriet Tubman Nurse Assn. Michigan City (organizer), NAACP (sec. Michigan City 1971-73), Ind. Com. for Blacks in Higher Edn. (charter mem., sec.), Michigan City Bus. and Profl. Women, Sigma Theta Tau. Democrat. Mem. African Methodist Episcopal Ch. Office: Purdue University North Central Westville IN 46390

WHITMAN, DALE A., law school dean; b. Charleston, W.Va., Feb. 18, 1939; m. Marjorie Miller; 8 children. Student, Ohio State U., 1956-59; B.S. in Elec. Engring., Brigham Young U., 1963; LL.B., Duke U., 1966. Bar: Calif. 1967, Utah 1974. Assoc. O'Melveny & Myers, Los Angeles, 1966-67; asst. prof., then assoc. prof. Sch. Law, U. N.C., Chapel Hill, 1967-70; vis. prof. law N.C. Central U., Durham, 1968, 69; vis. assoc. prof. law UCLA, 1970-71; dep. dir. Office Housing and Urban Affairs, Fed. Home Loan Bank Bd., Washington, 1971-72; sr. program analyst FHA, HUD, Washington, 1972-73; prof. law Brigham Young U., 1973-78, 79; vis. prof. law U. Tulsa, 1976, U. Mo., Columbia, 1976; prof. law U. Wash., Seattle, 1978-82, assoc. dean, 1978-79, 81-82; dean U. Mo. Sch. Law, Columbia, 1982—; cons., lectr. in field. Co-author: Low Income Housing, 1971; Cases and Materials on Real Estate Finance and Development, 1976; Real Estate Finance Law, 1979; Cases and Materials on Real Estate Transfer, Finance and Development, 1981; The Law of Property, 1984. Contbr. articles to profl. jours. Home: 1005 Audubon Dr Columbia MO 65201 Office: 116 Tate Hall U Mo Columbia MO 65211

WHITNEY, KENT RALPH NELSON, investment banker; b. Chgo., Nov. 25, 1954; s. Emerson Calhoun and Eileen (Holmberg) W.; B.B.A., Loyola U., Chgo., 1977; m. Arlene Mary Delpino, Apr. 29, 1978; 1 son, Kent Ralph Emerson. C.P.A., Arthur Andersen and Co., Chgo., 1977, Deloitte, Haskins and Sells, Chgo., 1981; stock exchange specialist Rockwell Internat. Corp. Securities, Chgo., 1976-81; pres. Kent Whitney and Co., Inc., Chgo., 1978—; partner Whitney-Pacific Investments, Chgo., 1971—, Post Oak Investments, Chgo., 1979—, Lee Land Co., Chgo., 1980—; dir. Lee Ltd. of Miss., Inc., R. Dwight Whitney Corp., P.S. Fin. Group Inc., Nomura Options Ltd., T and T Originals Ltd., Whitney Bancshares Ltd., N.W. Ordinance Ltd. C.P.A., Ill. Mem. Ill. C.P.A. Soc., Midwest Stock Exchange, Chgo. Bd. Options Exchange; Chgo. Merc. Exchange. Home: 308 E Louis St Sullivan IL 61951 Office: Post Oak Farm Sullivan IL 61951

WHITNEY, WILLIAM KUEBLER, artist; b. New Orleans, July 6, 1921; s. Percy Macklin and Elizabeth (Kuebler) W.; m. Charlotte Armide Lamm; children—Charlene, Alice. B.F.A., Cranbrook Acad. Art, 1949, M.F.A., 1958. Owner, mgr. Whitney Silver Shop, Birmingham, Mich., 1950-58; from instr. to assoc. prof. art Olivet Coll., Mich., 1959-63, prof. 1973-79. Exhbns. include: Corcoran Biennial Am. Art, 1945; Octagon House, Washington, 1972; Detroit Inst. Art, 1949; one-man show: McNeese State Coll., 1984, Battle Creek Sister City exhbn., Takasaki, Japan, 1984. Served to with U.S. Army, 1942-45, PTO. Recipient Bronze medal for Still Life Soc. Washington Artists, 1942; Merit award Mich. Acad. Sci. Arts and Letters, Ann Arbor, 1950. Mem. Mich. Soc. Archtl. Historians, Battle Creek Artists Guild, AAUP., Eaton Art League (v.p. 1984). Avocations: photography. Home and Office: 614 Summer St Olivet MI 49076

WHITSON-SCHMIDT, FRANCES GALE, investments analyst; b. Balt., Oct. 31, 1946; d. Frank Gilson and Frances Elizabeth (Moore) Whitson; B.A., Towson State U., 1967; M.B.A., Northwestern U., 1981; m. Donald Eugene Schmidt. Programmer-analyst Monumental Life Ins., Balt., 1967-72; programmer-analyst United Meth. Bd. of Pensions, Evanston, Ill., 1973-77, sr. systems analyst, 1977-82, asst. gen. sec., 1982-84, asst. treas., 1984—. Vice pres., bd. dirs. Adult Community OutReach Network, 1979—. Democrat. United Methodist. Home: 3212 Otto Ln Evanston IL 60201 Office: 1200 Davis St Evanston IL 60201

WHITTAKER, ROBERT R., congressman; b. Eureka, Kans., Sept. 18, 1939; student U. Kans., 1957-59, Emporia State Coll., summer 1959; B.S., Ill. Coll. Optometry, 1961, O.D., 1962; m. Marlene Faye Arnold, 1963; children—

Steven, Stephanie, Susan. Pvt. practice optometry, 1962-78; dir. Kans. Low Vision Clinic, 1973; mem. Kans. Ho. of Reps., 1974-77; mem. 96th-99th Congresses from 5th Dist. Kans. Precinct committeeman Augusta (Kans.) Republican Com., 1970-74; mem. Augusta City Planning Commn., 1970-74; past chmn., elder Christian Ch. Fellow Am. Acad. Optometry; mem. Am. Optometric Assn., Heart of Am. Contact Lens Soc. (past pres.). Office: 332 Cannon House Office Bldg Washington DC 20515

WHITTAKER, SHARON ELAINE, university adminstrator; b. Gary, Ind., Sept. 6, 1952; d. Robert Earl and Edith Elizabeth (Berry) W. B.A., Howard U., 1974, M.Ed., 1976; Ph.D., Ill. State U., Normal, 1983. Tchr. English, McKinley Tech. High Sch., Washington, 1974-75, Cromwell Acad., Pvt. Sch. for High Ability Students, Washington, 1975-76; residence hall counselor Howard U., Washington, 1976-79; adminstr. Office Residential Life, Ill. State U., Normal, 1979—. Recipient George N. Leighton award Howard U., 1974. Mem. Nat. Assn. Student Personnel Adminstrs., Nat. Assn. Women Deans, Adminstrs. and Counselors, Assn. Coll. and Univ. Housing Officers, Nat. Assn. Personnel Workers, Assn. Black Bus. Women Bloomington/Normal (v.p. 1981—), Phi Beta Kappa, Phi Delta Kappa, Kappa Delta Pi, Alpha Kappa Alpha. Democrat. Pentecostal. Author: What In the Hall is Going On?, 1979. Home: Watterson Towers Clay Apt Normal IL 61761 Office: Office Residential Life Ill State U Normal IL 61761

WHITTEN, BONNIE LEE, property manager; b. Council Grove, Kans., June 3, 1924; d. Charles Vaughn Lloyd and Faye Alice (Bryan) Branic; m. Donald David Whitten, Apr. 18, 1947. Student George Washington U., 1943-45. Mgr. distbn. of recs. War Fin. div. U.S. Treasury, Washington, 1945-46; dental technician Drs. Paul Swanson and Curtis Babcock, Oak Park, Ill., 1947-51; tng. supr. United Airlines, Chgo., 1951-61; dir. consumer services Sperry & Hutchinson Co., N.Y.C., 1961-71; dir. apt. mgmt. Harts Co., Indpls., 1971-77; property adminstr. Basic Am. Industries, Inc., Indpls., 1977-81; dir. condominium mgmt. Barrett & Stokely, Indpls., 1981—. Mem. Pub. Relations Soc. Am., Apt. Assn. Ind., Community Assn. Central Ind., Inc. Republican. Mem. Christian Ch. Club: Plus Investment.

WHITTENBERG, JAMES MATTHEW, physician; b. Libertyville, Ill., Jan. 6, 1939; s. Thomas L. and Bessie M. W.; B.A., So. Ill. U., 1960; M.D., U. Ill., 1964; m. Wilma Derringer, Nov. 8, 1979; children—Kimberly, James Matthew II, Jennifer D. Walter, Kirk Alan. Intern, Springfield (Ohio) City Hosp., 1964-65; practice medicine specializing in family practice, Chester, Ill., 1967—; mem. staff Meml. Hosp. of Chester, Meml. Hosp. of Carbondale; asst. clin. prof. So. Ill. U. Served with M.C., U.S. Army, 1965-67; Vietnam. Decorated Bronze Star, Air medal; diplomate Bd. Med. Examiners. Mem. AMA, Am. Geriatric Soc., Ill. Ob-Gyn Soc., Ill. Med. Soc., Soc. Contemporary Medicine and Surgery, Am. Acad. Family Practice, Royal Soc. Medicine, VFW (life), Am. Legion. Clubs: Chester Country, Moose. Home: 1211 Henrietta Chester IL 62233 Office: 1650 State St Chester IL 62233

WHITTINGTON, NANCY ANN, audit bureau supervisor; b. Mexico, Mo., Nov. 9, 1947; d. James Nugent and Helen Margaret (Grove) Harlow; m. William Warren Weging, June 27, 1970 (dec. Dec. 31, 1975); 1 child, Laura Beth; m. Robert Clifford Whittington, Dec. 1, 1978; 1 child, Jessica Marie. Student Loop Jr. Coll., 1970. Clk. Kemper Ins. Co., Chgo., 1966-68; with membership dept. ADA, Chgo., 1968-71; coordinator membership sevices Am. Acad. Dermatology, Evanston, Ill., 1976-78; supr. publisher statements Audit Bur. Circulations, Schaumburg, Ill., 1980—. Mem. Am. Mgmt. Assn. Roman Catholic. Clubs: Streamwood Booster (bd. dirs. 1981, 83), Streamwood Boys Football (Ill.). Avocations: sewing; crocheting; reading. Home: 127 Woodcrest Circle Streamwood IL 60103 Office: Audit Bur Circulations 900 N Meacham Rd Schaumburg IL 60195

WHITTINGTON, RICHARD OREN, biochemist; b. South Bend, Ind., Nov. 28, 1929; s. Oren Leslie and Edna Caroline (Schlundt) W.; m. Mary Eloise Vargas, Sept. 5, 1959; children—Bruce William, David Richard, Daniel Patrick. B.S., Lake Forest Coll., Ill., 1959; postgrad. Northwestern U., 1960. Research biochemist Abbott Labs., North Chicago, Ill., 1962—. Asst. scoutmaster NE council Boy Scouts Am., 1973-80. Served with U.S. Army, 1951-53. Decorated Bronze Star, UN Service medal; recipient Presdl. award Abbott Labs., 1980, 85, Entrepreneurial award, 1982, Disting. Service award, 1982. Mem. Sigma Xi. Lutheran. Club: Fraternal Order Police. Contbr. articles in field to profl. jours. Home: 297 Westerfield Pl Grayslake IL 60030 Office: 14th St and Sheridan Rd North Chicago IL 60064

WHITTY, MARY JANE, counselor; b. Baraboo, Wis., June 26, 1947; d. Robert Peter and Virginia (Marron) W. B.S. in Edn., U. Wis.-LaCrosse, 1970; M.Counseling, U. Wis.-Whitewater, 1979, M.Sch. Adminstrn., 1980. Cert. tchr., counselor, Wis. Tchr., New Berlin Schs. (Wis.), 1970-78, counselor elem., 1978-80, counselor secondary, 1980—, curriculum chmn. guidance dept., 1982—, chairperson dist. wide curriculum research, 1983. Pvt. counselor parents of terminally ill children, Greendale, Wis., 1980—. Recipient Outstanding Tchr. award Zerox Corp., 1974. Mem. Wis. Guidance Profl. Assn., Nat. Guidance Profl. Assn. Democrat. Roman Catholic. Clubs: Ski, Track (New Berlin) (dir. 1980—), Health.

WHOLF, BEVERLY DEAN, real estate broker; b. Omaha, Mar. 14, 1937; d. Everett Lee and Veronica Dean (Wakefield) Gardner; student U. Kans., 1955; cert. residential specialist; m. Emmett Clark Wholf, Oct. 12, 1956; children—Gordon Dean, Stuart Clark, Alan Ray. Broker, owner E.C. Wholf & Assos., Inc., Realtors, Lee's Summit, Mo., 1976—; pres., dir. Multiple Listing Service Kansas City. Mem. Met. Kansas City Mo. Bd. Realtors (Realtor of Yr. award 1980). Home: 338 SW Marsh Wren Lee's Summit MO 64063 Office: 116 W 3rd St Lee's Summit MO 64063

WIANT, KURT DEVERE, psychologist; b. Lakewood, Ohio, Feb. 24, 1946; s. Lloyd Devere and Martha Louise W.; m. Rita Ellen Krupar, Apr. 8, 1972; children—Kyle, Ethan, Sara. B.S., Kent State U., 1968, M.Ed., 1973, Ed.S., 1975. Tchr. math. Parma (Ohio) Pub. Schs., 1969, Lakewood (Ohio) Pub. Schs., 1969-72; psychologist, adminstr. Berea (Ohio) Pub. Schs., 1972—; pvt. practice psychologist, 1979—. Mem. Nat. Assn. Sch. Psychologists, Ohio Sch. Psychologists Assn., Cleve. Area Sch. Psychologists Assn., Phi Delta Kappa, Kappa Delta Pi. Presbyterian. Home: 3097 Creekside Dr Westlake OH 44145

WICK, CHAD PHILIP, banker; b. Dayton, Ohio, Aug. 17, 1942; s. Daniel Martin and Louella Elizabeth (Greer) W.; student Gen. Motors Inst. Tech., 1960-62; B.B.A., U. Cin., 1965; M.Internat. Mgmt. with honors, Thunderbird Grad. Sch., 1972; m. Gail Elaine Stichweh, Sept. 19, 1964; children—Christine, Aubrey. With Frigidaire div. Gen. Motors Corp., Dayton, 1960-66; asst. v.p. Winters Nat. Bank, Dayton, 1972-75, v.p., Cin., 1975-79; pres. AmeriTrust of Cin., sr. v.p. AmeriTrust Co., 1979-81; exec. v.p., dir. So. Ohio Bank, Cin., 1981-82, pres., chief exec. officer, 1982—. Served to capt. USAF, 1966-71. Trustee, Coll. Mt. St. Joseph, 1980—, Cin., Seven Hills Neighborhood Houses, Inc.; bd. dirs. Cin. Council World Affairs, 1978-81; chmn. bd. dirs. World Affairs Inst.; chmn. bd. trustees Program for Cin. Unitarian. Clubs: Bankers, Coldstream Country, Queen City. Office: 515 Main St Cincinnati OH 45202*

WICKMAN, JOHN EDWARD, library exec.; b. Villa Park, Ill., May 24, 1929; s. John E. and Elsie (Voss) W.; A.B., Elmhurst Coll., 1953; M.A., Ind. U., 1958, Ph.D., 1964; m. Shirley Jean Swanson, Mar. 17, 1951; children—Lisa Annette, Eric John. Instr. English, history Hanover (Ind.) Coll., 1959-62; instr. history Ind. U., Jeffersonville, 1962; asst. prof. history N.W. Mo. State Coll., Maryville, 1962-64; faculty fellow Nat. Center Edn. in Politics, 1964-65; asst. prof. history Purdue U., Fort Wayne, Ind., 1965-66; dir. Dwight D. Eisenhower Library, Abilene, Kans., 1966—. Personal asst. to Gov. Kans., 1964-65. Served with AUS, 1953-55. Congl. fellow, Washington, 1975-76. Mem. Oral History Assn. (past pres.), Am. Soc. Pub. Adminstrn., Western History Assn. (council 1972-75), Am., Kans. State (bd. dirs., past pres.) hist. socs. Office: Dwight D Eisenhower Library Abilene KS 67410

WIDDRINGTON, PETER NIGEL TINLING, See *Who's Who in America,* 43rd edition.

WIDTFELDT, JAMES ALBERT, lawyer; b. O'Neill, Nebr., Nov. 18, 1947; s. Albert Theodore and Gusteva Emma (Peterson) W. B.S., MIT, 1970, M.S., 1970; postgrad. Rensselaer Poly. Inst., 1970-75, Ph.D., 1977; J.D., U. Nebr.-Lincoln, 1978. Bar: Nebr. 1978, U.S. Dist. Ct. Nebr. 1978. Civilian employee Office Naval Research, Troy, N.Y., 1973-75; assoc. Cronin & Hannon, O'Neill, Nebr., 1978-79; sole practice law, Atkinson, Nebr., 1979—. Co-author articles in Jour. Acoustical Soc., 1973-75. Mem. Nebr. Bar Assn., Sigma Xi, Delta Theta Phi, Sigma Pi Sigma. Republican. Methodist. Club: Toastmasters. Lodges: Masons, Shriners. Home: Anncar Route O'Neill NE 68763 Office: 103 State St Atkinson NE 68713

WIECHERT, ALLEN LEROY, university official; b. Independence, Kans., Oct. 25, 1938; s. Norman Henry and Serena Johanna (Steinke) W.; B.Arch., Kans. State U., 1962; m. Sandra Swanson, Aug. 19, 1961; children—Kirstin Nan, Brendan Swanson, Megan Ann. Architect in tng. McVey, Peddie, Schmidt & Allen, Wichita, Kans., 1962-63; architect Kivett & Myers, Kansas City, Mo., 1963-68; asst. to vice chancellor plant planning and devel. U. Kans., Lawrence, 1968-74, asso. dir. facilities planning, 1974-78, univ. dir. facilities planning, 1978—; mem. long range phys. planning com. Kans. Bd. Regents, 1971—; designer, archtl. programmer of ednl. facilities; bd. dirs. Kans. U. Fed. Credit Union, 1972-81, pres. bd., 1974. Chmn. horizons com. Lawrence Bicentennial Commn.; designer Kaw River Trail, 1976; mem. Action 80 Com., 1980-81; mem. standing com. Kans. Episcopal Diocese, 1976-80, pres. com., 1981, mem. diocesan council, 1982-84, chmn. coll. work com., 1982-84; sr. warden Trinity Episc. Ch., Lawrence, 1978-80; trustee Kans. Sch. Religion, 1973-80, 82-85, v.p., 1984, 85; bd. dirs. Trinity Group Care Home, 1973-79; advancement chmn. troop com. Boy Scouts Am., 1981—, vice chmn. Pelathe dist., 1984, chmn., 1985—; sec. Hist. Mt. Oread Fund, Kans. U. Endowment Assn., 1982—. Served to 1st lt. Kans. Air N.G., 1961-67. Lic. architect, Kans.; cert. Nat. Council Archtl. Registration Bds. Mem. AIA, Assn. Univ. Architects, Nat. Hist. Trust. Editor, contbr. to Physical Development Planning Work Book, 1973. Home: 813 Highland Dr Lawrence KS 66044 Office: Office Facilities Planning University of Kansas Lawrence KS 66045

WIECZOREK, GERALD MICHAEL, money manager, stockbroker; b. Ionia, Mich., Apr. 17, 1948; s. Michael J. C. and Betty Lou (Wheeler) W. Investigating security supr. Borman Div., Detroit, 1964-68; dir., chief investigator Counselors Advocate Internat. Inc., Lansing, Mich., 1968-78; pres., legis. agt. Fed. Legis. Consultants, Inc., Washington, 1972-75; pvt. investment cons., 1978; cert. diamond broker Internat. Gems, Ltd., Boston, 1978-79; indsl. and comml. investment real estate specialist, realtor and investment instr., 1978-81; life underwriter, Newark, 1979-81; dir., researcher, computer game theorist Questor Group Unltd., 1980-83; stockbroker Dean Witter Reynolds Inc., Lansing, Mich., 1983—; curator SJ Gallery, 1980—. Statistician, cons., trainer Listening Ear Crisis Intervention Center, East Lansing, Mich., 1974-76, chmn. bd. dirs., dir., 1976-78. Mem. Internat. Commn. of Jurists (Geneva, Switzerland), Council of Internat. Investigators (London), Fin. Analysts Fedn., Investment Analysis Soc., N.Y. Soc. Security Analysts, Am. Econ. Assn., Am. Petroleum Inst., Internat. Chess Fedn. Republican. Author: Questron; contbr. articles to mags. and profl. jours. Office: Dean Witter Reynolds Inc 6105 W St Joseph St Lansing MI 48917

WIEDER, MICHAEL DAVID, real estate developer, lawyer; b. Cleve., Apr. 29, 1944; s. Norman D. and Beatrice T. (Tamler) W.; m. Mildred Carol Altman, Aug. 15, 1970; children—Adam L., Matthew S., Shana C. B.B.A., Western Res. U., 1965; LL.D., Cleve. Marshall Law Sch., 1969. Bar: Ohio 1969, U.S. Dist. Ct. (no. dist.) Ohio 1974, U.S. Supreme Ct. 1978; C.P.A., Ohio. Acct., Scott & Berkman, Cleve., 1965-69; gen. counsel, treas. Shannon Constrn., 1970-78; asst. gen. counsel Developers Diversified, 1979-80; mng. ptnr. Highland Devel. Co., Cleve., 1980—. Contbr. articles to profl. jours. Pres. Bet Sefer Mizrachi of Cleve., 1984—; active Jewish Community Fedn., 1984—; bd. dirs. Young Israel of Cleve., 1984—, Bur. Jewish Edn., 1984—. Mem. Ohio State Bar Assn., Nat. Assn. Securities Dealers. Avocations: Jogging; tennis; baseball; cross country skiing; water skiing. Home: 4625 Birchwold Rd South Euclid OH 44121 Office: Highland Devel 3985 Warrensville Ctr Rd Warrensville Heights OH 44122

WIEDMAN, MARY ELIZABETH, occupational therapist; b. Bonne Terre, Mo., Sept. 12, 1932; d. Edward Carl and Elva (Vinetta) Johnson; student N.W. Okla. State U., 1972-75, postgrad. 1979—; B.S. in Occupational Therapy, U. Okla. Health Sci. Center, 1978; m. Bill B. Wiedman, May 23, 1977; children—Michael Pinkley, Deborah Pinkley Lewis, Mark Pinkley, Susan Pinkley Schneider; stepchildren—Michael Wiedman, Jan Wiedman Schrock, Jill Wiedman Howard. Asst. for tng. Occupational Therapy in Ednl. Mgmt., Oklahoma City and Tulsa, 1981—; pvt. practice pediatric and rehab. therapy, Kiowa, Kans., 1979—; occupational therapy cons. Achenbach Rehab. Center, Hardtner, Kans., 1979—, Cedar Crest Nursing Home, Kiowa; occupational therapist Northwestern Okla. Regional Edn. Service Center, Alva, 1978—; guest lectr. N.W. Okla. State U., 1978-79. Mem. World Fedn. Occupational Therapists, Am. Occupational Therapy Assn., Okla. Occupational Therapy Assn., Kans. Occupational Therapy Assn., Am. Occupational Therapy Found., Council Exceptional Children (charter mem. chpt.), Center Study Sensory Integration Dysfunction, AAUW. Republican. Baptist. Home: 1011 Coats Kiowa KS 67070 Office: 1540 Davis St Alva OK 73717

WIEGAND, ALBERT JOHN, mechanical engineer, developer; b. Hecker, Ill., Jan. 21, 1930; s. William George and Emma (Hepp) W.; m. Bernice Helen Schuchardt, Oct. 15, 1960; children—Eric Gerard, Dawn Charise. B.S. in Mech. Engring., U. Ill., 1952, M.S., 1953. Engring. supr. McDonnell Douglas, St. Louis, 1956-73; city adminstr. City of St. Peters, Mo., 1973-78; mgr. McKelvey Devel., O'Fallon, Mo., 1978-81; pres. Ticon Corp., St. Peters, Mo., 1981—; dir., sec. P.R.&S., Inc., Cons. Engrs., St. Peters, 1978—; pres. Mid-Rivers Realty & Devel. Co., 1982—. Mayor, City of St. Peters, Mo., 1968-73. Served to 1st lt. USAF, 1954-56. Honored by resolution Mo. Senate, 1978. Club: Com. for Civic Progress (pres. 1978-80). Avocations: skiing; traveling; boating. Home: 15 N Service Rd Saint Peters MO 63376 Office: Ticon Corp 349 Mid Rivers Dr Saint Peters MO 63376

WIEGAND, SALLY ALETHA, higher education finance executive; b. Richmond, Calif., Aug. 15, 1944; d. Harold Anton and Cora Aletha (Evans) Olson; m. Charles Thomas Smith, Jr., Aug. 17, 1964 (div. July 1975); children—Charles Thomas III, Abigail Aletha; m. Erich Klepfer Wiegand, Dec. 4, 1982; 1 child, Erich Harold. B.A. in English, U. Ala., 1971. Tchr. English, vice prin. Spencerville Jr. Acad., Md., 1972-73; dir. fin. aid Lacaze Acad., Washington, 1973-74; dir. fin. aid, asst. dean Hood Coll., Frederick, Md., 1975-77; dir. fin. aid Loma Linda U., Calif., 1977-79; supr. loan program Calif. Student Aid Com., Sacramento, 1979-80; v.p. mktg. United Student Aid Funds, Indpls., 1981-85; v.p. fin. aid policy and devel. Superior Tng. Services, Indpls., 1985—; coordinator, originator Career Fair for Adults, Indpls., 1983. Counselor, Planned Parenthood, Sacramento, 1980. Mem. Internat. Assn. Bus. Communicators, Nat. Assn. Student Fin. Aid Adminstrs., Western Assn. Student Fin. Aid Adminstrs. Avocations: reading; doll collecting; swimming. Home: 6814 Brendon Way N Dr Indianapolis IN 46226 Office: Superior Tng Services 3334 Founders Rd Indianapolis IN 46268

WIEHL, JOHN RICHARD, financial executive; b. N.Y.C., Sept. 15, 1947; s. John Jack and Ruth Dorothy (Anderson) W.; m. Michelle Irene McGuire, Sept. 6, 1975 (div. Dec. 1979). A.A.S. in Automotive Tech., SUNY Canton Coll., 1967; B.S. in Acctg., SUNY-Buffalo, 1977; M.B.A., U. Dayton, 1980. Cost acct. Grand Island Biol. Co. (N.Y.), 1974-77; cost acct. Adria Labs., Columbus, Ohio, 1977-79; mgr. fin. planning and cost power tool div. Rockwell Internat. Corp., Bellefontaine, Ohio, 1979-81; corp. mgr. budgets and cost Hancor, Inc., Findlay, Ohio, 1981-84; corp. mgr. fin. info. systems Oneida Molded Plastics, N.Y., 1984—. Served with USN, 1968-71; Vietnam. Decorated Bronze Star; SUNY Edn. Dept. Regents scholar, 1965; Clark Found. scholar, 1965. Mem. N.Y. Acad. Scis. Lutheran. Office: 104 S Warner St Oneida NY 13421

WIEMANN, MARION RUSSELL, JR., biologist, microscopist; b. Chesterton, Ind., Sept. 7, 1929; s. Marion Russell and Verda (Peek) W.; B.S., Ind. U., 1959; 1 dau., Tamara Lee. Histo-research techician U. Chgo., 1959, research asst., 1959-62, research technician, 1962-64; tchr. sci. Westchester Twp. Sch., Chesterton, Ind., 1964-66; with U. Chgo., 1965-79, sr. research technician, 1967-70, research technologist, 1970-79; prin. Marion Wiemann & Assos., cons. research and devel., Chesterton, Ind., 1979—. Served with USN, 1951-53. McCrone Research Inst. scholar, 1968. Mem. Internat. Platform Assn., Field Mus. Natural History (assoc.), AAAS, Soil Sci. Soc. Am., Am. Soc. Agronomy, Crop Sci. Soc. Am., Internat. Soc. Soil Sci. Contbr. articles to profl. jours. Address: PO Box E Chesterton IN 46304

WIERS, BRANDON HELMHOLZ, manufacturing company research and development executive; b. San Francisco, July 31, 1934; s. Walter Benjamin Wiers and Grace Elizabeth (Pleune) MacNaughton; m. Patricia Joan Hollingsworth, May 14, 1960; children—Matthew Dirk, Suesann Elizabeth, Carl John. B.A., Calvin Coll., Grand Rapids, Mich., 1957; PhD., U. Minn.-Mpls., 1964. Staff chemist research and devel dept. Proctor & Gamble, Cin., 1964-69, staff chemist, sect. head internat. div., 1969-74, group leader packaged soap and detergent div., 1974-78, sect. head research and devel. services and research adminstrn., 1979—; instr. phys. chemistry Colo. State Coll., Greeley, 1961, Xavier U., Cin., 1966-67. Contbr. articles to profl. jours. Mem. council, mayor City of Forest Park, Ohio, 1976—; mem. Community Housing Resources Bd., Cin., 1982—; mem. Leadership Cin., 1984—. Recipient Fair Housing award Community Housing Resources Bd., 1984. Mem. Am. Chem. Soc., Am. Statis. Assn., AAAS, Phi Lambda Upsilon. Presbyterian. Club: Forest Park Run/-Walk. Avocation: jogging. Home: 11261 Hanover Rd Forest Park OH 45240 Office: Procter & Gamble Co Miami Valley Labs PO Box 39175 Cincinnati OH 45247

WIERSUM, BRADLEY JOHN, marketing executive; b. Kenosha, Wis., May 10, 1953; s. Russell A. and Delores (Dyutka) W.; m. Karen Louise Johnson, Aug. 27, 1983. B.A., Calvin Coll., 1975; M.B.A., U. Minn., 1980. Quality control supr. Menasha Corp., Neenah, Wis., 1976-78; asst. product mgr. Gen. Mills, Inc., Mpls., 1979-83; mktg. mgr. Malt-O-Meal Co., Mpls., 1983—. Cons., Project Bus./Jr. Achievement, Mpls., 1984, Mgmt. Assistance Project, Mpls., 1983. U. Minn. scholar, 1979. Mem. Am. Mgmt. Assn., Beta Gamma Sigma. Republican. Mem. Christian Reformed Ch. Avocations: reading; wind-surfing; touch football; running; skiing. Home: 13246 Dahlgren Rd Minnetonka MN 55343 Office: Malt-O-Meal Co 2601 IDS Tower Minneapolis MN 55402

WIESE, ROBERT PAUL, principal; b. Milw., Sept. 30, 1925; s. Paul Christian and Teckla Mary Wiese; m. Patricia Ann Nagle Nov. 5, 1927; children—Bradley, Cheryl, Theresa, Margaret, Paul, Michael, Bridget. B.S. in Edn., U. Wis., 1951, postgrad., 1964-66; M.S. in Edn., Marquette U., 1957; postgrad. U. Colo., 1966-74. Tchr., Wis. pub. schs., 1951-1958; high sch. prin. Wis. pub. schs., Oconto Falls, 1958-64, Evansville, 1964-66, New Berlin High Sch., 1966—. Editor mag. The Bulletin, 1970-80. Trustee New Berlin Pub. Library, 1967—; bd. dirs., vice chmn. Holy Apostles Ch., New Berlin, 1974-80. Served with USN, 1943-46; PTO. Recipient Disting. Service award Wis. Prins., 1972, 80. Mem. North Central Assn. Commn. Schs., Nat. Assn. Secondary Prins., Wis. Assn. Secondary Prins., Assn. Wis. Schs. (bd. dirs. 1970-74). Club: Local Partners Ams. (pres. 1974-85). Lodges: Kiwanis (pres. 1962-63), Lions (pres. 1973-74). Avocations: Reading, outdoor sports. Home: 21935 W MacGregor Dr New Berlin WI 53151 Office: New Berlin High Sch 18695 W Cleveland Ave New Berlin WI 53151

WIESEN, ROBERT J., real estate executive; b. Toledo, Sept. 21, 1943; s. James Douglas and Dorothy J. (Korreck) W.; m. Ruzica Marionovic, June 10, 1972; 1 child, Sasha James. B.S., Ind. U., 1965. Salesman Continental Can Co., Chgo., 1965-72; dir. sales and mktg. First Am. Realty, Chgo., 1974-75; v.p. sales Seay & Thomas, Chgo., 1975-78; v.p. investments Golub & Co., Chgo., 1979—; pres. First Am. Equities Inc., Chgo., 1972—; pres. Combined Health Appeal of Am., Hartford, Conn., 1985, also dir. Contbr. articles to pubs. Bd. dirs. Cystic Fibrosis Found., 1978—. Served with Air N.G., 1966-71. Avocations: Sailing; photography. Home: 325 W Belden Ave Chicago IL 60614 Office: First Am Equities Inc 625 N Michigan Ave Suite 2000 Chicago IL 60611

WIESER, JOSEPH ALPHONSUS, educational adminstrator, alcohol and drug abuse consultant; b. Plymouth, Wis., May 29, 1943; s. Alfred A. and Anna Mae (Braun) W.; m. Wendy Mae Brandt, June 30, 1979; children—Adam, Mark; m. Doris Ann Rommelfanger, Jan. 8, 1966 (dec. Nov. 1977). B.S. in Elem. Edn., Lakeland Coll., 1966; M.A. in Elem. Sch. Adminstrn., No. Mich. U., 1971. Tchr. Milw. Pub. Schs., 1966; tchr. New Holstein Pub. Schs., Wis., 1966-74, asst. prin., 1974-77, elem. sch. prin., 1977—; cons. alcohol and other drug abuse, Wis., 1981—; speaker/trainer ETC Trainers, Campbellsport, Wis., 1985—; trainer Community Tng. Assn., Oshkosh, Wis., 1985—; coordinator SPIN Network, New Holstein, Wis., 1984—. chmn. Calumet County Republican party, 1983—; pres. Rds. to Freedom, Inc., Chilton, Wis., 1983—. Mem. Nat. Elem. Sch. Prins. Assn., Assn. Wis. Sch. Adminstrs., Wis. PTA (pres. 1975-76), Sch. Prevention Intervention Network (coordinator 1984—). Roman Catholic. Avocations: computers; antiques; jogging; gardening. Home: 1704 Mayflower St New Holstein WI 53061 Office: New Holstein Elem Sch 2226 Park Ave New Holstein WI 53061

WIESNER, JOHN JOSEPH, retail chain store executive; b. Kansas City, Mo., Mar. 31, 1938; s. Vincent A. and Jane Ann (Hagerty) W.; m. Georgiana Schild, Oct. 17, 1961; children—Susan, John V., Gretchen. B.S. in Bus. Adminstrn., Rockhurst Coll., 1960. Vice pres., controller Fisher Foods, Cleve., 1970-77; asst. corp. controller Richardson Vicks, N.Y.C., 1960-70; sr. exec. v.p. Pamida, Inc., Omaha, 1977-85, vice chmn., chief exec. officer, 1985—. Bd. dirs. Omaha Girls' Club, 1983—, Omaha Area Council on Alcohol and Drug Abuse, 1983—; bd. dirs. Fontenelle Forest, Omaha, chmn., 1983, 84; mem. bd. regents Rockhurst Coll., Kansas City, Mo. Named Bus. Assoc. of Yr., Am. Bus. Women's Assn., 1983. Mem. Nat. Assn. Accts. Republican. Roman Catholic. Clubs: Omaha, Field (Omaha).

WIGG, HELEN JACKSON, chemical manufacturing company executive; b. Wilmington, N.C., June 13, 1941; d. Samuel Patterson Wigg and Josie Lou Wigg DeCover. B.S., N.C. State U., 1963; M.A., Fairfield U., 1972; M.B.A., U. Ct., 1980. Quality assurance dept. head Clairol, Inc., Stamford, Conn., 1966-80; sales rep. Syntex Agribusiness Northeast Territory, 1981-84, mktg. product mgr., Springfield, Mo., 1984—. Vol. U.S. Peace Corps., New Delhi, India, 1964-66. Mem. Am. Mktg. Assn., Springfield C. of C., Am. Bakers Assn. (tech. adv. com.). Republican. Baptist. Clubs: 99'ers (Springfield); U.S. Coast Guard Aux. (Kimberling City, Mo.). Avocations: sailing, boating, skiing. Home: 1419 S Gelven Ave Springfield MO 65804 Office: Syntex Agribusiness Inc 1915 W Sunshine St Springfield MO 65805

WIGGINS, RICHARD HERBERT, investment counselor; b. Chgo., Apr. 14, 1935; s. Herbert Joseph and Lillian May (Sabinske) Killen W.; m. Beth Rose, Mar. 12, 1975; m. Dolores Felcyn (div.); children—Mary Beth, Richard Herbert, Jr. B.S. in Indsl. Mgmt., Wayne State U., 1961. Chartered investment counselor. Investment aide Comerica, Inc., Detroit, 1960-62; investment counselor Heber-Fuger-Wendin, Inc., Detroit, 1962-68; pres. Investors Mgmt. Services, Inc., Birmingham, Mich., 1968—. Fellow Fin. Analysts Fedn.; mem. Fin. Analysts Soc. Detroit, Econ. Club Detroit. Clubs: Birmingham Athletic (Mich.); Huron River (Farmington, Mich.). Avocations: travel; fishing. Home: 30365 Rock Creek Southfield MI 48076 Office: Investors Mgmt Services Inc 700 E Maple Rd Birmingham MI

WIGHTMAN, D. D., hospital administrator; b. Larchwood, Iowa, Nov. 12, 1929; s. Stanley H. and Effie (Middlan) W.; m. Norma Jean Briggs, Dec. 19, 1948; children—Lori, David. B.S., State U. Iowa, 1952, M.H.A., 1954. Resident and fellow in adminstrn. Fitzsimmons Army Hosp., Denver, 1954-55; hosp. adminstr. Boone County Hosp., Iowa, 1956-64, Dakota Hosp., Fargo, N.D., 1964-78, pres., 1978—; mem. N.D. Health Council, Bismarck, 1980—, chmn., 1982-84; sec. Blue Cross of N.D., Fargo, 1973—. Served to capt. U.S. Army, 1954-56. Fellow Am. Coll. Hosp. Adminstrs.; mem. Am. Hosp. Assn., N.D. Hosp. Assn. (past chmn.). Lodge: Lions (bd. dirs.). Home: 1005 South Dr Fargo ND 58103 Office: Dakota Hosp 1720 S University Dr PO Box 6014 Fargo ND 58108-6014

WIKIERA, EDWARD STANLEY, physician; b. Detroit, Dec. 16, 1918; s. Stanley and Bernice (Kubik) W.; B.S., Wayne State U., 1940, M.D., 1944; m. Josephine Warchol, June 14, 1942. Intern, Woman's Hosp., Detroit, 1944-45; gen. resident Detroit Receiving Hosp., 1947, resident in dermatology, 1949-51; resident dermatology VA Hosp., Detroit, 1948; pvt. practice dermatology, Detroit, 1952-56, Dearborn, Mich., 1956—; cons. dermatology Oakwood Hosp., Alexander Blain Hosp., Annapolis Hosp., Wayne, Mich., Delray Gen. Hosp., Outer Drive Hosp., Ford Motor Co. Mem. Nat. Com. for Immigration Reform, 1966, President's Com. on Immigration Reform. Served to capt. AUS, 1945-47. Diplomate Am. Bd. Dermatology and Syphilology, PanAm. Med. Assn. Fellow Am. Acad. Dermatology and Syphilology, Am. Geriatrics Soc.; mem. AMA, Mich., Wayne County med. socs., N.Y. Acad. Scis., N.Am. Clin. Dermatol. Soc., Internat. Soc. Tropical Dermatology, Assn. Am. Med. Colls., Mich. Assn. Professions, Nat. Med. and Dental Assn. Am., Med. Dental Arts Club, Wayne State Alumni Assn., Phi Beta Pi, Alumni Phi Beta Pi. Clubs: Great Dane of America (Conn.); Deutche-Doggen of Germany; Great Dane of

Gt. Britain. Home: 17400 West Outer Dr Dearborn Heights MI 48127 Office: 15120 Michigan Av Dearborn MI 48126

WIKSTROM, GUNNAR, JR., political science educator; b. Quincy, Mass., Apr. 23, 1936; s. Gunnar and Anna Carolina (Nelson) W.; m. Marilyn Mansfield, May 16, 1959; children—Jeffrey Alan, Daryl Lyn, Milton Curtis, Byron Kent. A.B., Tufts U., 1958; B.D., Hartford Sem. Found., 1961; M.A., U. Ariz., 1967, Ph.D., 1973. Ordained to ministry Congregational Ch., 1961; minister United Ch. of Christ-Congregational Chs., Wash. and Minn., 1961-65; asst. prof. polit. sci. No. State Coll., Aberdeen, S.D., 1966-68; grad. asst. U. Ariz., Tucson, 1968-71; asst. prof. div. social sci., philosophy and religion Buena Vista Coll., Storm Lake, Iowa, 1971-74, assoc. prof., 1974-78, prof., 1978—, chmn. div., 1976-78, 82—; dir. Iowa Program Impact, 1976-77. Parliamentarian Buena Vista County Democratic Central Com., 1975—; councilman Storm Lake City, 1977—, chmn. fin. com., 1977—. Lilly Found. fellow, 1978-81; Herbert Hoover Library Assn. grantee, summer 1983. Mem. Am. Soc. for Pub. Adminstrn., Am. Polit. Sci. Assn., Midwest Polit. Sci. Assn., Iowa Assn. Polit. Scientists. Author: Municipal Response to Urban Riots, 1974; co-editor: Municipal Government, Politics, and Policy, A Reader, 1982; contbr. revs. to profl. jours. Home: 915 Russell St Storm Lake IA 50588 Office: Dept Polit Sci Buena Vista Coll Storm Lake IA 50588

WILCOX, LAIRD MAURICE, investigator, writer; b. San Francisco, Nov. 28, 1942; s. Laird and AuDeene Helen (Stromer) W.; student Washburn U., 1961-62, U. Kans., 1963-65; m. Eileen Maddocks, 1962 (div. 1967); children—Laird Anthony IV, Elizabeth Leone; m. 2d, Diana Brown, 1978; 1 dau., Carrie Lynn. With Fluor Corp., Ltd., 1960-62; mgr. office supply store U. Kans., 1963; editor Kans. Free Press, 1963-66; owner, operator Maury Wilcox Constrn. Co., Kansas City, Mo., 1967-70; carpenter foreman various employers, 1974—; semi-profl. genealogist, 1975-78; chief investigator Editorial Research Service, Kansas City, Mo., 1977—; lectr. various fields. Dep. sheriff Wyandotte County, Kans., 1971-75. Fellow Augustan Soc., Acad. Police Sci.; mem. Internat. Brotherhood of Carpenters and Joiners of Am. (officer 1975-82, condr. carpenter's local 61 1977-82), Nat. Rifle Assn., Mensa, ACLU, Internat. Legion of Intelligence, Nat. Coalition Against Censorship, Free Press Assn., SAR, Soc. Mayflower Descs., Mil. Order Loyal Legion of U.S., Nat. Soc. Old Plymouth Colony Descs., St. Andrew Soc. Author: Guide To The American Left, 1970; Guide to The American Right, 1970; Psychological Uses of Genealogy, 1976; Astrology, Mysticism and The Occult, 1978; Directory of the American Right, 1981; Directory of the American Left, 1981; Directory of the Occult and Paranormal, 1981; Guide to the American Right, 1984; Guide to the American Left, 1984; editor Wilcox Report, 1979—. Founder Wilcox Collection on Contemporary Polit. Movements, U. Kans. Libraries. Home and Office: PO Box 1832 Kansas City MO 64141

WILCOX, WILLIAM HOWARD, educational administrator; b. Columbus, Kans., Dec. 5, 1938; s. Floyd Howard and Opal Katharine (Miller) W.; B.S., Pittsburg State U., 1960, M.S., 1965, Ed.S., 1975; Ed.D., U. Mo., 1982; m. Miriam Catharine Malcom Cummins, Feb. 8, 1971; children—Denise Catharine, Mary Janis, John Timothy, Miriam Dee. Tchr., Cherokee High Sch., 1960, St. Paul High Sch., 1961-63, Galena High Sch., 1963-65; prin. Cherryvale (Kans.) Jr. High Sch., 1965-68, prin. sr. high sch., 1968-69, supt. schs., 1969-71; prin. high sch. Joplin, Mo., 1971-79; supt. schs. Louisiana, Mo., 1981—; chmn. adv. bd. Franklin Tech. Area Trade Sch., Joplin; asst. state dir. Com. on Accredited Non Public Schs., U. Mo., 1979-81. City chmn. Heart Fund, 1965-71. Mem. Nat. Assn. Secondary Sch. Prins., Mo. Assn. Secondary Sch. Prins., Assn. Supervision and Curriculum Devel., Am. Fedn. Musicians, Nat. Middle Sch. Assn., Assn. Am. Sch. Adminstrs., Phi Delta Kappa, Kappa Delta Pi, Phi Alpha Theta. Republican. Methodist. Clubs: Lions, Exchange, Rotary, Elks. Home: 120 N A St Louisiana MO 63353 Office: 515 Jackson St Louisiana MO 63353

WILD, STEPHEN KENT, insurance marketing company executive; b. Omaha, Nov. 18, 1948; s. Roger Charles and Marguerite Mae W.; m. Cheryl Katherine Sparano, June 5, 1971; children—Deric Justin, Drew Ian. Student Ottawa U., 1967-68, U. Nebr.-Omaha, 1968-71. Internal auditor Kirkpatrick, Pettis, Smith and Polian, Omaha, 1971-75; fin. planner First Fin. Planning Group, Omaha, 1975-80; mng. gen. agt. E.F. Hutton Life Ins. Co., Omaha, 1980-81; chmn. bd. Nat. Fin. Dynamics, Omaha, 1981—, Securities Am., Inc., 1984—; life ins. cons. Mem. Nat. Assn. Life Underwriters, Internat. Assn. Fin. Planners. Baptist. Club: Highland Country. Home: 16561 Nina Circle Omaha NE 68130 Office: 8420 W Dodge Rd Suite 500 Omaha NE 68114

WILDER, LEROY JOSEPH, JR., environmental engineer, hygiene technologist; b. La Crosse, Wis., Aug. 25, 1954; s. LeRoy Joseph and Bertha Pauline (Benson) W. Assoc. in Applied Sci., Western Wis. Tech. Inst.; B.S., U. Wis.-La Crosse, 1977, postgrad., 1980-81. Environ. engr. Rayovac Corp., Madison, Wis., 1981-85; co-ordinator environ. activities No. States Power Co., Eau Claire, Wis., 1985—; diver-biologist Environ. Impact Survey for Wis. Dept. of Natural Resources and Wis. Dept. Transp., La Crosse, 1977. Mem. Air Pollution Control Assn., Fedn. Environ. Technologists, Nat. Elec. Mfrs. Assn.; Inst. Profl. Assn. Diving Instrs. (rev. com. 1982—), Wis. Utilities Assn., Wis. Mfrs. and Commerce Assn. Lodge: Eagles Avocations: scubadiving; flying; water skiing; camping; golf. Home: 1619 LaCrescent St La Crosse WI 54603 Office: No States Power Co PO Box 8 Eau Claire WI 54702

WILDEY, SHARON ANN, lawyer; b. North Vernon, Ind., June 21, 1943; d. Murrell Edward and Virginia Lorane (Beach) W.; m. Edward Victer Mikesell, Feb. 23, 1975 (div. Apr. 1980); children—Tim, Heather, Brooke, Meredith. B.S., Ind. U., 1972, J.D., 1975. Bar: Ind. Assoc., Luber, Sakaguchi & Wildey, South Bend, 1976-78, Wildey & Forsman, South Bend, 1978-81; founder, pres. Women's Legal Clinic, Inc., South Bend, 1980—. Editor Justicia, 1976. Recipient Roses award Ind. U. Women's Studies, 1979. Mem. Ind. Bar Assn., ABA, Assn. Trial Lawyers Am., Ind. Bar Found., Ind. Women's Polit. Caucus. Democrat. Mem. Soc. Friends. Office: Women's Legal Clinic 630 E Colfax St South Bend IN 46615

WILENS, MICHAEL ENGBER, computer software firm executive, researcher, educator; b. Chgo., Aug. 23, 1953; s. Charles E. and Norma J. (Myers) W. S.B. in Elec. and Computer Engring., MIT, 1975, S.M. in Elec. and Computer Engring., 1976; M.S. in Computer Sci., U. Mich., Ann Arbor, 1979, Ph.D. in Computer Sci., 1984, M.B.A., 1980. Sr. systems analyst Digital Equipment Corp., 1972-73; computer scientist Naval Surface Weapons Ctr., White Oak, Md., 1973-74; teaching asst. elec. engring. MIT, 1975, project mgr. Sloan Sch. Ctr. for Info. Systems Research, 1975-76; teaching fellow computer sci. U. Mich., Ann Arbor, 1976-80, project mgr. Info. Systems Research Group, 1976-80, research asst. Grad. Sch. Bus., 1981, instr. software engring, elec. engring., 1981-82; staff cons. Infosystems Mgmt., Ann Arbor, 1981; pres., chief exec. officer Computerized Office Services, Inc., Ann Arbor, 1982—; cons. mil. services. Instr. fin. planning and control Midwest Assn. of Housing Coops., Ann Arbor. Named for Teaching Excellence U. Mich., 1979. Mem. Assn. of Computing Machinery (reviewer Computing Revs. jour.), IEEE, Ann Arbor Computer Bus. Assn. (pres. 1983), AAAS, Sigma Xi. Home: 200 Orchard Hills Dr Ann Arbor MI 48104 Office: Computerized Office Services Inc 313 N 1st St Ann Arbor MI 48103

WILES, ANN LOUISA, management engineer; b. Williamsport, Pa., Apr. 26, 1951; d. E. Robert and Edna (Leinbach) Buzzell; B.S. summa cum laude in Nursing, U. Mich., 1974; M.B.A., Oakland U., 1980; m. Robert Wiles, May 18, 1974. Public health nurse Huron County Health Dept., Bad Axe, Mich., 1974-76; public health nurse Oakland County Health Dept., Southfield, Mich., 1976-78; mgmt. engr. Mt. Carmel Mercy Hosp., Detroit, 1979-80; mgmt. engr. William Beaumont Hosp. System, Royal Oak, Mich., 1980-83, sr. mgmt. engr., 1983—. Mem. Mich. Hosp. Mgmt. Systems Soc., Hosp. Mgmt. Systems Soc., Healthcare Fin. Mgrs. Assn., Mich. Profl. Women's Network. Office: 3601 W 13-Mile Rd Royal Oak MI 48072

WILEY, DEBORAH FRANCES, financial consulting company executive, accountant; b. Toledo, Oct. 17, 1949; d. Bernard Francis and Doris Margaret (Leatherman) W. B.B.A. in Acctg., U. Toledo, 1971, M.B.A. in Health Care Adminstrn., 1978; postgrad. U. Mich., 1977. C.P.A., Ohio Jr. Medicare auditor Blue Cross of Northwest Ohio, 1972-74, sr. Medicare auditor, 1974-76; cost acct. Flower Hosp., Sylvania, Ohio, 1976-78; assoc. exec. dir. 4th Ohio Area Profl. Standards Rev. Orgn., Toledo, 1978-79; mgr. mgmt. services dept. Arthur Young & Co., Toledo, 1979—. Bd. dirs., fin. adviser Northwest Ohio chpt. Sudden Infant Death Syndrome Orgn.; past internat., regional and local officer Cath. Alumni Club. Jr. Achievement scholar, 1967. Mem. Hosp. Fin. Mgmt. Assn. (chmn. chpt. legis. task force), Ohio Soc. C.P.A.s, Am. Coll. Hosp. Adminstrs., Am. Soc. Women Accts. Lodge: Zonta. Office: Arthur Young and Co One SeaGate Toledo OH 43604

WILEY, GEORGE SCHOTT, business executive; b. Cin., May 28, 1935; s. Andrew Foust and Elizabeth (Schott) W.; B.A., Yale U., 1957; postgrad. U. Chgo., 1967-68; m. Sally Pattishall, June 22, 1958; children—Deborah, Michael, Peter. Mgr., Cummins Engine Co., Columbus, Ind., 1957-66; mgr. Standard Oil Co. (Ind.), Chgo., 1966—. Mem. Republican Precinct Com., 1970—, chmn. West Deerfield Twp. Com., 1971-82, mem. Lake County Rep. Exec. Com., 1974-82, alt. del. Rep. Nat. Conv., 1976. Served with U.S. Army, 1958-61. Mem. Conf. Bd. (council on compensation 1985—), Chgo. Compensation Assn. (pres. 1984-85). Presbyterian. Clubs: Exmoor Country, Yale, Sturgeon Bay Yacht. Home: 175 Linden Park Pl Highland Park IL 60035 Office: 200 E Randolph Dr Chicago IL 60601

WILEY, GREGORY ROBERT, sales executive; b. Mpls., Sept. 21, 1951; s. William Joseph and Terese (Kunz) W.; m. Sheila Francis, May 25, 1979; children—Kathleen, Mary Glennon. B.A. in Personnel Adminstrn., U. Kans., 1972-74. Dist. sales mgr. Reader's Digest, St. Louis, 1976-80, regional sales dir., Chgo., 1980-82; nat. sales mgr. retail div. Rand McNally & Co., Chgo., 1982-83, nat. sales mgr. premium and incentive div., 1983—. Mem. Nat. Premium Sales Execs., Promotional Mktg. Assn. Am. Roman Catholic. Avocations: historic restoration, golfing. Home: 2214 Linneman St Glenview IL 60025 Office: Rand McNally & Co 8255 N Central Park Ave Skokie IL 60076

WILEY, JERRY ALDEN, pharmacist; b. Kalkaska, Mich., Nov. 7, 1954; s. Alden Francis and Donna Jane (Carlson) W.; m. Pamela Ann Hentis, July 29, 1978 (div. Mar. 29, 1984); children—Lea Ann, Daniel Alden. B.S. in Pharmacy, U. Iowa, 1979. Registered pharmacist, Iowa. Pharmacist Groves Pharmacy, Manchester, Iowa, 1979-80, Walgreens Pharmacy, Sioux City, Iowa, 1980-82, Hartig's Pharmacy, Dubuque, Iowa, 1984—; CPR instr. ARC, Sioux City, 1981-82. Avocations: golf, racquetball, swimming. Home: 339 W 7th #11 Dubuque IA 52001

WILFONG, GRACE MACLEOD, mortgage company executive; b. Detroit, Sept. 8, 1947; d. James Alexander and Marion Catherine (MacLeod) MacL.; m. Wayne Edward Vicklund, Feb. 15, 1969 (div. Dec. 1980); 1 son, Wayne Kevin; m. Alan Roger Wilfong, July 24, 1982. B.A., Oakland U., 1969. Reservation agt. Holiday Inns of Am., Detroit, 1968; tchr. Warren Consol. Schs. (Mich.), 1969; programmer Detroit Bank & Trust Co., 1969-72; mgr. systems and programming Mfrs. Bank of Southfield (Mich.), 1972-81; sr. systems analyst ACO, Farmington Hills, Mich., 1981; asst. v.p., project mgr. systems and programming Mfrs. Hanover Mortgage Corp., Farmington Hills, 1981—. Singer, Max Davey Singers, Farmington Hills, 1975—; bassoonist Novi and Northville Community Bands (Mich.), 1981—; mem. Birmingham Community Chorus (Mich.), 1969-72, Meadowbrook Festival Chorus, Rochester, Mich., 1971-75. Mem. Am. Inst. Bankers (sec. 1974-75, treas. 1975-76, v.p. 1976-77), Burroughs Users Group (chmn. edn. 1980-81), Detroit Area Trainers Assn. Presbyterian. Home: 24380 Hampton Hill Novi MI 48050 Office: Mfrs Hanover Mortgage Corp 27555 Farmington Rd Farmington Hills MI 48018

WILFONG, LESTER, JR., librarian; b. Perryville, Mo., June 15, 1930; s. Lester B. and Nellie Ann (Ruseller) W.; m. Wanda Lou Hahn, Sept. 9, 1956. Grad. high sch., Patton, Mo. Operator heavy equipment State Hwy., Jefferson City, Mo., 1948-51; carpenter Penzel & Co., Jackson, Mo., 1951-56; audio-visual dir. Riverside Library, Jackson, Mo., 1957—, bookmobile driver regional library, 1957-75, audio-visual dir., 1975—. Served with U.S. Army, 1952-54, Korea. Democrat. Baptist. Lodges: Scottish Rite (pres. 1975-76, worshipful master 1984). Avocations: fishing, horseback riding. Home: Route 5 Hwy 72W Jackson MO 63755 Office: Riverside Regional Library PO Box 389 Jackson MO 63755

WILGARDE, RALPH L., hospital administrator; b. Phila., Jan. 8, 1928; B.A., U. Pa., 1949, M.B.A., 1954; M.Pub. Adminstrn., Cornell U., 1960. Adminstrv. asst. Jefferson Hosp., Phila., 1956-58; asst. adminstr. Frankford Hosp., 1960-64; dir. Irvington (N.J.) Gen. Hosp., 1964-66, Cottage Hosp., Grosse Pointe, Mich., 1966—. Served with AUS, 1950-52. Mem. Am. Hosp. Assn., Am. Coll. Hosp. Adminstrn. Home: 1217 Bishop Rd Grosse Pointe MI 48230 Office: 159 Kercheval Ave Grosse Pointe MI 48236

WILHELM, WILBERT EDWARD, industrial and systems engineering educator; b. Pitts., Oct. 24, 1942; married; 2 children. B.S. in Mech. Engring., W. Va. U., 1964; M.S. in Indsl. Engring., Va. Poly. Inst. and State U., 1970; Ph.D. in Indsl. Engring. and Ops. Research, 1972. Registered profl. engr., Ohio. Facilities engr. lamp glass dept. Gen. Electric Co., Logan, Ohio, 1965, quality control engr. ordinance dept., Pittsfield, Mass., 1966; quality control foreman, Salem, Va., 1966-67, mfg. analyst, 1967, specialist mfg. adminstrn., instr. Va. Poly. Inst., Blacksburg, 1969-72; asst. prof. Ohio State U., Columbus, 1972-78, assoc. prof. dept. indsl. and systems engring., 1978—; cons. Columbus Coated Fabrics, United Airlines, Dorcey Cycle, Gen. Elec. Co., Central Ohio Transit Authority, Ohio State Internat., Ohio Dept. Transp., Def. Constrn. Supply Ctr.; dir. Flexible Mfg. Lab. Contbr. numerous articles to profl. jours. Recipient Ralph Boyer award Ohio State U. Coll. Engring., 1984, research award, 1985; fellow NSF, NASA. Mem. Am. Inst. Indsl. Engrs. (sr., charter mem., pres. 1979-80, bd. dirs. 1980-81, program chmn. 1982-83, chpt. devel. adviser 1983-84, Region Community Affairs award 1980, Chpt. Devel. award 1980), Soc. Mfg. Engrs. (sr.), Ops. Research Soc. Am., Phi Kappa Phi, Alpha Pi Mu. Home: 6745 Merwin Pl Worthington OH 43085 Office: Ohio State U Dept Indsl and Systems Engring 1971 Neil Ave Columbus OH 43210-1271

WILHITE, ROBERT KEITH, educational administrator; b. Alton, Ill., Aug. 9, 1947; s. Bob Lee and Carmen M. (Owens) W.; m. Carol Ann Skupien, Aug. 14, 1976. B.A., So. Ill. U., 1969; M.Ed., Loyola U., Chgo., 1976, Ed.D., 1982. Cert. tchr., sch. supr. and adminstr., Ill. English tchr. Edwardsville (Ill.) Jr. High Sch., 1969-70; lang. arts tchr. Mannheim Jr. High Sch., Melrose Park, Ill., 1972-78; reading specialist Wheaton (Ill.) Pub. Schs. 1978-82; curriculum supr. reading, lang. arts, kindergarten and career edn. Waukegan (Ill.) Pub. Schs. 1982-84, prin. Greenwood Sch., 1984—; chmn. select curriculum com., Wheaton, 1979-82. Served with C.E., U.S. Army, 1970-72. Decorated Army Commendation medal. Mem. Internat. Reading Assn., Nat. Council Tchrs. of English, Assn. Supervision and Curriculum Devel., Ill. Reading Council, Secondary Reading League, Ill. Assn. Sch. Prins., Prins. Roundtable of No. Ill. Author: Techniques of Creative Writing, 1976. Office: Greenwood Sch 1919 North Ave Waukegan IL 60087

WILINKIN, EDWARD MAURICE, optometrist; b. Chgo., Mar. 26, 1923; s. Lee William Wilinkin and Mollie (Pearlman) Wilinkin Seaton; m. Wanda Lee Hall, July 22, 1950. A.S. in Engring., Rose Poly. Tech., 1944; O.D., No. Ill. Coll. Optometry, 1944. Gen. practice optometry, Chgo., 1944—. Served wtih U.S. Army, 1943-46. Fellow Ortokeratology Sect. Nat. Eye Research Found., 1978. Mem. Nat. Eye Research Found., Better Vision Inst., Am. Legion. Lodges: Masons (master 1960-61), Moose. Avocation: music.

WILKE, OWEN CHARLES, optometrist; b. St. Cloud, Minn., June 26, 1920; s. Carl F. and Lillian Eleanor (Knoblaugh) W.; m. Lotty M. James, Dec. 12, 1942; 1 child, Sharon Jean. O.D., Ill. Coll. Optometry, Chgo., 1947. Gen. practice optometry, Marshall, Minn., 1947—. Served to pharmacist 1st class USN, 1942-45; PTO. Fellow Am. Acad. Optometry; mem. Am. Legion, Mo. Valley Optometric Soc. (bd. dirs. 1950's), Minn. Optometric Assn. (pres. 1958-59), Minn. State Bd. Optometry (pres. 1961-72), Am. Optometric Assn., Southwest Minn. Optometric Soc., Tomb and Key, Beta Sigma Kappa, Omega Delta. Lutheran. Lodge: Lions Avocations: biking, dancing. Office: 127 N 3rd St Marshall MN 56758

WILKE, ROBERT NIELSEN, information scientist; b. San Diego, July 7, 1941; s. Kenneth Newell and Dorothy Christine (Gruber) W.; m. Judith Ann Krause, Sept. 29, 1973; children—Amy Marie, Eric Andrew. B.S., San Diego State U., 1964; Ph.D., Case Western Res. U., 1971. Research assoc. Youngstown State U., Ohio, 1971-72; research assoc. U. Chgo., 1972-74; chemist Velsicol Chem. Corp., Chgo., 1974-80; info. scientist Standard Oil Co. (Ind.), Chgo., 1980—; patent task force mem. Am. Petroleum Inst., N.Y.C., 1983—; mem. quality control com. IFI/Pleum Data Corp., Alexandria, Va., 1982—. Patentee in field. Contbr. articles to profl. jours. Mem. Am. Chem. Soc., Royal Soc. Chemistry. Avocations: camping; woodworking; electronics. Office: Standard Oil Co Ind PO Box 400 Naperville IL 60566

WILKEN, PAUL WILLIAM, optometrist; b. Sandusky, Ohio, Nov. 14, 1951; s. Carl Anthony and Mary Ellen (Gentry) W.; m. Linda Irene Nierstheimer, Sept. 1, 1973; children—Jennifer, Carl, Michelle, Benjamin. B.S., Ohio State U., 1973, O.D., 1977. Optometrist, John Wasylik, Sandusky, 1977-79; owner, v.p. John E. Wellman OD, Inc., Celina and St. Marys, Ohio, 1979—, Wellman, Wilken, Fanning & Assocs., Wapakoneta, Ohio, 1983—, Piqua, Ohio, 1984—, Lima, Ohio, 1985—, Van Wert, Ohio, 1985. Author: (newspaper column) Vision Care, 1980-81. Mem. Sch. Curriculum Council, Celina, 1982-84; speaker, cons. Mercer County Council on Aging, Mercer County Diabetic Support Group, Celina, 1980—. Mem. Am. Optometric Assn., Ohio Optometric Assn., N.W. Ohio Optemetric Assn., Ohio State U. Alumni Assn. (life), Epsilon Psi Epsilon (Pledge of Yr. award 1976). Republican. Roman Catholic. Lodge: Rotary (sec. 1979-84, pres. 1985-86). Avocations: flying; motivational speaking. Home: 616 N Main St Celina OH 45822 Office: Wellman Wilken Fanning & Assocs 950 S Main St Celina OH 45822

WILKENS, ROBERT ALLEN, utilities executive, electrical engineer; b. Esmond, S.D., Jan. 3, 1929; s. William J. and Hazel C. (Girch) W.; m. Barbara M. Davis, Apr. 15, 1952; children—Bradley Alan, Beth Ann, Bonnie Sue, William Frank. B.S.E.E., S.D. State U., 1951. Dispatcher, engr. G.O., Northwestern Pub. Service Co., Huron, 1953-55, div. engr., Huron 1955-58, div. elec. supt., 1958-59, div. mgr., 1959-66, asst. to pres., 1966-69, vice pres. ops., G.O., 1969-80, pres., chief operating officer, 1980—, also dir.; v.p. North Central Electric Assn., past dir. Midwest Gas Assn.; dir. Farmers & Mchts. Bank Huron; past adminstrv. chmn. Mid-Continent Area Power Pool. Trustee S.D. Conf. United Methodist Ch., 1969-81; mem. Salvation Army Adv. Bd., 1962; S.D. State R.R. Bd., 1982—; past pres. Huron United Way. Served to capt. USAF, 1951-53. Named Disting. Engr., S.D. State U., 1977. Mem. North Central Elec. Assn., Midwest Gas Assn., S.D. Engring. Soc., Huron C. of C. (pres. 1963). Republican. Methodist. Lodges: Kiwanis, Masons, Shriners. Office: Northwestern Pub Service Co 3d St & Dakota Ave S Huron SD 57350

WILKES, DELANO ANGUS, architect; b. Panama City, Fla., Jan. 25, 1935; s. Burnice Angus and Flora Mae (Scott) W.; m. Dona Jean Murren, June 25, 1960. B.Arch., U. Fla., 1958. Cert. Nat. Council Archtl. Registration Bds. Designer, Perkins & Will Partnership, Chgo., 1960-63; designer, job capt. Harry Weese, Ltd., Chgo., 1963-66; project architect Fitch Larocca Carrington, Chgo., 1967-69; architect Mittelbusher & Tourtelot, Chgo., 1970-71; assoc. Bank Bldg. Corp., Chgo., 1972-75; sr. assoc. Charles Edward Stade & Assocs., Park Ridge, Ill., 1975-77; sr. architect Consoer Morgan Architect, Chgo., 1977-83, mktg. coordinator, 1980-83; design cons. Chamlin & Assocs., Peru and Morris, Ill., 1969-82, dir. architecture, 1983—; mem. coordinating com. Dune Acres Plan Commn. (Ind.), 1983—; building commr. City of Dune Acres, 1984—; cons. Inst. of Crippled and Disabled, N.Y.C., 1978-83; guest lectr., field trip guide Coll. DuPage, Glen Ellyn, Ill., 1968-76; guest architect med. adv. com. to Pres.'s Com. for Handicapped, 1977, 78. Mem. Businessmen for Pub. Interest, Folsom Family Assn. Am. (pres. 1978-82, v.p. 1982—, nominating chmn. 1983, host ann. meeting, Chgo. 1981), SAR, AIA, Chgo AIA (chmn. design awards display com. 1978-79, producer New Mem. Show 1979, chmn. pub. relations com. 1980), Art Inst. Chgo., Chgo. Lyric Opera Guild, Chgo. Assn. Commerce and Industry (display dir. 1979 meeting), Am. Soc. Interior Design (coordinator Info. Fair 1979), N.C. Geneal. Soc., New Eng. Hist. Geneal. Soc., Putnam County Hist. Soc., Soc. Colonial Wars, Gargoyle. Democrat. Unitarian. Author: Colonel Ebenezer Folsom, 1778-1789, North Carolina Patriot and Tory Scourge, 1975; editor Folsom Bull., 1977-80; producer documentary film The Angry Minority, Menninger Found., 1978. Home: 23 Circle Dr Dune Acres IN 46304 Office: 3017 5th St Peru IL 61354

WILKINS, ARTHUR NORMAN, college director; b. Kansas City, Mo., Sept. 24, 1925; s. Arthur Miller and Jean (DeWitt) W.; A.A., Jr. Coll. of Kansas City, 1947; M.A., U. Chgo., 1950; Ph.D., Washington U., 1953. Grad. asst. Washington U., St. Louis, 1950-52; instr. English, La. State U., Baton Rouge, 1953-56; instr. English, Jr. Coll. of Kansas City, 1956-64, chmn. Dept. English, 1961-64; instr. English, Met. Jr. Coll., Kansas City, Mo., 1964-69, chmn. Dept. English, 1964-68, chmn. Div. Humanities, 1968-69; instr. English, Longview Community Coll., Lee's Summit, Mo., 1969-70, chmn. dept. humanities, 1969-70, dean instrn., 1970-84; dir. acad. affairs Met. Community Colls., Kansas City, Mo., 1984—. Mem. Mo. State Library planning com., 1980-83. Served with U.S. Army, 1943-46. Washington U. fellow, 1952-53. Mem. Bookmark Soc., U. Chgo. Library Soc. Author: Mortal Taste, 1965; High Seriousness, 1971; The Leonore Overtures, 1975; Attic Salt, 1984; contbr. articles to profl. jours. Home: 5724 Virginia Ave Kansas City MO 64110 Office: 3200 Broadway Kansas City MO 64111

WILKINS, CHRISTINA L., financial executive; b. Phila., Oct. 20, 1950; d. Harry William and Beverly (Pickering) W. B.A., DePauw U., 1972; M.B.A., Northwestern U., 1974. Comml. banking officer Harris Bank, Chgo., 1974-77, asst. v.p., 1977-80; asst. treas. Hillenbrand Industries, Inc., Batesville, Ind., 1980-83, treas., 1983—. Mem. Nat. Assn. Corp. Treasurers, Nat. Corp. Cash Mgmt. Assn., Cin. Corp. Cash Mgmt. Assn. Avocation: Golf. Office: Hillenbrand Industries Inc Hwy 46 Batesville IN 47006

WILKINSON, MARK EDWARD, optometrist; b. Ottumwa, Iowa, Jan. 16, 1955; s. Edward F. and Margaret A. (McKillip) W.; m. Dana J. Willig, Aug. 5, 1978; 1 child, Lyndsey Jo. Student Iowa State U., 1976; O.D., Ill. Coll. Optometry, 1980. Optometrist in pvt. practice, Bettendorf, Iowa, 1980—; low vision coordinator Iowa Braille and Sight Seeing Sch., Vinton, 1980—, cons., 1980—; low vision clinician U. Iowa Hosp. and Clinics, Iowa City, 1984—; mem. health adv. bd. Head Start, Davenport, Iowa, 1982—. Chmn. Our Lady of Lourdes Bd. Edn., Bettendorf, 1982-84, 85—. Mem. Am. Optometric Assn. (charter mem. low vision sect.), Iowa Optometric Assn., Bettendorf C. of C. (com. mem. 1981—). Roman Catholic. Lodge: Rotary. Avocations: Running; golf; skiing. Home: 1609 Marlo Ave Davenport IA 52803 Office: 3625 Utica Ridge Rd Bettendorf IA 52722

WILKINSON, WILLIAM JAMES, educator, school administrator; b. Findlay, Ohio, Nov. 20, 1937; s. George Wayne and Gerelene Alice (Dick) W.; m. Janice May Krochot, June 11, 1960; children—William Jeffrey, Brant Wayne. B.S. Miami U., Oxford, Ohio, 1959, M.A., 1962, postgrad., 1969; postgrad., Wright State U., 1975—. Cert. secondary teacher, secondary principal, superintendent. Tchr. Versailles Schs., Ohio, 1959-60, Eaton City Schs., Ohio, 1960-63; prin. Eaton City Schs., 1963-70, Oakwood City Schs. Dayton, Ohio, 1970—; lectr. state and regional confs., instr. adult edn. classes computer utilization, chmn. visitation team North Central Assn. Schs. Colls., Sch. Edn. Adv. Com. U. Dayton, 1981—. Author: Educational Management Computer Software, 1983; contbr. articles to profl. jours. Chmn. United Appeals Campaign, Eaton, 1968; Fellow Inst. Devel. Edn. Activities. Mem. Zoning Appeals Bd., Citizens Fiscal Adv. Com., Western Ohio Edn. Assn. (pres. 1968), Ohio Assn. Secondary Sch. Adminstrs., Nat. Assn. Secondary Sch. Prins., Assn. Supervision and Curriculum Devel., Phi Delta Kappa. Democrat. Methodist. Avocations: stained glass art work; sailing; internat. travel. Office: Oakwood Jr High Sch 1200 Far Hills Ave Dayton OH 45419

WILKUS, FRANK JEROME, health care administrator; b. St. Paul, Apr. 20, 1923; s. Anthony and Edna (Johnson) W.; m. Theresa Borsch, May 4, 1946; children—Mary Lynn, Paul, James, Mark, Louann, Annette. B.B.A., Coll. St. Thomas, 1949; postgrad. U. Minn., 1949-51, St. Paul Coll. Law, 1952. Advt. mgr. Water Power Equipment Co., St. Paul, 1948-49; with Emporium Dept. Store, St. Paul, 1949; auditor First Grand Ave. State Bank, 1949-51; examiner Minn. Dept. Taxation, 1952-55, asst. officer mgr., 1952-55, office mgr., 1955-56; adminstr. Olmsted Med. & Surg. Group, P.A., Rochester, Minn., 1956—. Mem. Common Council of Rochester, 1958-64, Park Bd. Rochester, 1970—. Served with USMC, 1941-45. Decorated Purple Heart. Fellow Am. Coll. Med. Group Adminstrs.; mem. So. Minn. Clinic Mgrs. Assn. (sec.), Minn. Med. Group Mgmt. Assn. (pres.). Clubs: Kiwanis, Rochester Growth. Home: 1018 10th Ave NW Rochester MN 55901 Office: 210 9th St SE Rochester MN 55901

WILLE, LOIS JEAN, newspaper editor; b. Chgo., Sept. 19, 1932; d. Walter and Adele S. (Taege) Kroeber; m. Wayne M. Wille, June 6, 1954. B.S., Northwestern U., 1953, M.S., 1954; Litt.D. (hon.), Columbia Coll., Chgo., 1980. Reporter, Chgo. Daily News, 1958-74, nat. corr., 1975-76, assoc. editor charge editorial page, 1977; assoc. editor Chgo. Sun-Times, 1978-83; assoc. editorial page editor Chgo. Tribune, 1984—. Author: Forever Open, Clear and

Free: the Historic Struggle for Chicago's Lakefront, 1972. Recipient Pulitzer prize for pub. service, 1963, William Allen White Found. award for excellence in editorial writing, 1978, numerous awards Chgo. Newspaper Guild, Chgo. Headline Club, Nat. Assn. Edn. Writers, Ill. AP, Ill. UPI. Mem. Chgo. Women's Network (bd. dirs.), Am. Soc. Newspaper Editors. Office: Chgo Tribune Michigan Ave Chicago IL 60611

WILLES, MARK HINCKLEY, food company executive; b. Salt Lake City, July 16, 1941; s. Joseph Simmons and Ruth (Hinckley) W.; A.B., Columbia U., 1963; Ph.D., 1967; m. Laura Fayone, June 7, 1961; children—Wendy Anne, Susan Kay, Keith Mark, Stephen Joseph, Matthew Bryant. Mem. com. staff banking and currency com. Ho. of Reps., Washington, 1966-67; asst. prof. fin. U. Pa., 1967-69; economist Fed. Res. Bank, Phila., 1967, sr. economist, 1967-70, dir. research, 1970-71, v.p., dir. research, 1971, 1st v.p., 1971-77; pres. Fed. Res. Bank of Mpls., 1977-80; exec. v.p., chief fin. officer Gen. Mills, Inc., Mpls., 1980—. Home: 405 Sycamore Ln Plymouth MN 55441 Office: 9200 Wayzata Blvd Minneapolis MN 55426

WILLIAMS, BERNARD T., dentist; b. Mc Leansboro, Ill., Apr. 12, 1943; s. Bernard Taft and Jerry (Dungy) W.; m. Cheryl Susan Foster; 1 son, Ryan Trent. D.D.S., Wash. U., 1969. Practice dentistry specializing in occlusion, reconstructive dentistry, diagnosis and treatment facial pain and dysfunction, Kansas City, Mo., 1971—; mem. staff St. Joseph Hosp., Kansas City, 1980—; cons., lectr. Sch. Dentistry, U. Mo.-Kansas City, 1981—; lectr. in field. Served with U.S. Army, 1969-71. Mem. Mid-Continent Stomatognathic Soc. (founder 1975; pres. 1975-77), Am. Equilibration Soc. (chmn. biology of occlusion 1983), ADA, Am. Coll. Dentists, Acad. Gen. Dentistry, Soc. Occlusal Studies (trustee 1981—, instr. 1978). Author: Therapeutic Exercises for Cranio facial Pain and Dysfunction; Manual for Dentists Diagnosing. and Treating Facial Pain and Dysfunction; contbr. articles to profl. publs. Office: 1010 Carondelet Dr Suite 410 Kansas City MO 64114

WILLIAMS, BRENDA PAULETTE, TV reporter, anchor; b. St. Louis, July 7, 1946; d. Herman and Hattie Williams; B.J., Ohio U., Athens, 1969; postgrad. U. Mo., Columbia. Newscaster, Sta. KATZ, St. Louis, 1969-70; reporter, talk show producer/host Sta. KPLR-TV, St. Louis, 1973-74, Stas. KSD-TV and Radio, St. Louis, 1974-77; weekend anchor-reporter Sta. KMBC-TV, Kansas City, Mo., 1977-81, weekday anchor-reporter, 1981-85. Recipient Cert. of Appreciation St. Louis Urban League-St. Louis Sentinel, 1975; Human Relaions award Nat. Assn. Colored Women's Clubs, 1975; Documentary Reporting award Mo. Radio and TV Assn., 1979; Consumer Reporting award Mo. Dept. Consumer Affairs, 1979; Outstanding Achievement in Journalism award Mo. Black Leadership Assn., 1981; Headliner award, 1982; selected for Am. journalists tour of Israel, Israeli Journalist Assn., 1980; Black Achiever award SCLC, 1981. Mem. Alpha Kappa Alpha (Women of Involvement award 1974), Sigma Delta Chi. Club Zonta Internat.

WILLIAMS, CLYDE E., JR., lawyer; b. Niagara Falls, N.Y., Dec. 17, 1919; s. Clyde E. and Martha (Barlow) W.; m. Ruth Van Aken, Oct. 16, 1948; children—Clyde E. III, Mark Van Aken, Sara. A.B., Denison U., Granville, Ohio, 1942; LL.B., Harvard U., 1945. Bar: Ohio 1945. Practice corp. and real estate law, 1945—; with Spieth, Bell, McCurdy & Newell Co., Cleve., v.p., dir., 1964—; gen. counsel Growth Cos., Inc., Phila., 1950-55; pres., dir. Williams Investment Co., Cleve., 1954—; sec., dir. Williams Internat. Corp., Walled Lake, Mich., 1954—; dir., gen. counsel Techno-Fund, Inc., Columbus, Ohio, 1960-67; pres., dir. C.M.S. Realty Co., Cleve., 1963—; dir. Radio Seaway, Inc.; mem. faculty Fenn Coll. and Cleve. Coll. div. Western Res. U., 1945-50. Vice pres., mem. exec. com., trustee Cleve. Soc. for Blind, 1979-85, pres., 1985—. Mem. ABA, Ohio Bar Assn., Greater Cleve. Bar Assn., Sigma Chi. Clubs: Union, Skating. Office: Spieth Bell McCurdy & Newell Co LPA 2000 Huntington Bldg Cleveland OH 44115

WILLIAMS, CRAIG FOSTER, osteopathic emergency physician; b. Akron, Ohio, July 23, 1949; s. Robert Daniel and Jeanne Marie (Schulte) W.; m. Carol Giglia, May 6, 1978; children—Joy Caroline, Cara Jeanne, Eric James. B.A., Notre Dame U., 1971; D.O., Kansas City Coll. Osteo. Medicine, 1977. Diplomate Am. Bd. Emergency Medicine. Intern, Doctor's Hosp., Columbus, Ohio, 1977-78; resident in emergency medicine Wright State U., Dayton, Ohio, 1978-80, mem. faculty, 1982—, asst. clin. prof. emergency medicine, 1983—; commd. officer USPHS Indian Health Service, Phoenix, 1980-82; staff emergency physician St. Elizabeth Med. Ctr., Dayton, 1982—. Fellow Am. Coll. Emergency Physicians; mem. Univ. Assn. Emergency Medicine, Am. Coll. Osteo. Emergency Physicians, Am. Osteo. Assn., AMA, Notre Dame Alumni Assn. Roman Catholic. Home: 6649 Stamford Pl Dayton OH 45459 Office: Dept Emergency Medicine St Elizabeth Med Center Dayton OH 45408

WILLIAMS, DARRELL KEITH, dentist; b. Detroit, May 27, 1955; s. Troy Lee and Shirley Ann (Jones) W.; m. Yolanda Christina Toran, June 12, 1982; children—Erin Celeste, Ryan Troy. B.A., Albion Coll., 1977; D.D.S., U. Detroit, 1982. Practice dentistry, Inkster, Mich., 1983—; assoc. with Dr. R. Alford, Detroit, 1982—. Mem. Wolverine Dental Assn., Mich. Dental Assn., Delta Sigma Delta. Democrat. Baptist. Office: 27305 Michigan Ave Inkster MI 48141

WILLIAMS, DAVID JAMES, plant science educator; b. Glendora, N.J.; s. David James and Elizabeth Helen (Weber) W.; m. Kathleen Dolores McGough, July 11, 1970; children—David, Christine, Jennifer. B.S., Delaware Valley Coll., 1969; M.S., Rutgers U., 1972, Ph.D., 1974. Research asst. Rutgers U., New Brunswick, N.J., 1969-74; asst. prof. U. Ill., Urbana, 1974-80, assoc. prof., 1980—; contbr. articles to profl. jours. Chmn. Shade Tree Commn., Savoy, Ill., 1980—; pres. Unit 4 Bd. of Edn., Champaign, Ill., 1982-83, sec., 1984—; bd. dirs. Savoy United Meth. Ch., Savoy, 1984. Pesticide Impact Assessment Regulating Office grantee, 1981, 82, IR-4 Regional Office grantee, East Lansing, Mich., 1974—. Mem. Internat. Plant Propagation Soc., Am. Soc. Hort. Sci., Am. Assn. Hort. Sci. (chmn. nursery research, 1979), Weed Sci. Soc. Am. (chmn. ornamentals and turf sect. 1980), Ill. State Nurserymen's Assn. (cons. 1974—). Republican. Episcopalian. Club: Glendora Buck. Lodge: Kiwanis. Avocations: scouting; fishing; hunting. Home: 45 Lange St Savoy IL 61874 Office: U Ill 1107 W Dorner Dr Urbana IL 61801

WILLIAMS, DAVID PRESTON, petroleum geologist, consultant; b. Montrose, Colo., Apr. 23, 1951; s. Norville Preston and Bonnie June (Meyers) W.; m. Connie Rae Richmond, Feb. 2, 1973; children—Robert, Christy, Casey, Michael. B.S., Fort Hays State U., 1974. Jr. field engr. Dresser Atlas-Dresser Industries, Great Bend, Kans., 1973-74; exploration/prodn. geologist Benson Minerals Group, Ind., Denver, 1977-79; ind. cons. petroleum geologist, Great Bend, Kans., 1979—. Mem. Kans. Geol. Soc., Am. Assn. Petroleum Geologists, Soc. Profl. Well-log Analysts, Am. Petroleum Inst. Avocations: pateonlology; paleobotany; record collecting; fishing. Home: 1331 Van Fleet Great Bend KS 67530 Office: PO Box 576 1103 Main Great Bend KS 67530

WILLIAMS, DONALD, SR., vocational center administrator; b. Detroit, July 1, 1936; s. Raymond E. and Martha W.; m. Mary Elizabeth Watson, Dec. 17, 1960; children—Donald, Tanja Marie, Kishna Andrea. B.S., Eastern Mich. U., 1964; M.A., W.Va. U., 1971; A.B.D., Rutgers U., 1981. Psychiat. attendant nurse Northville Hosp., 1956-64; tchr. W.J. Maxey Boys Training Sch., Whitmore Lake, Mich., 1964-67; dir. edn. Charleston Job Corps Ctr., Teledyne, 1967-70; mgr. edn. systems RCA, Cherry Hill, N.J., 1970-73, mgr. ednl. programs, 1976-80; adminstr., faculty Rutgers U., 1973-76; dir. Grand Rapids (Mich.) Job Corps Ctr., 1980—. Bd. govs. Kent Community Action Program, 1980—. Served with U.S. Army, 1959-61. Recipient citations N.J. Ednl. Opportunity Assn., 1976, Adult Assn. N.J., 1977, Nat. Civil Rights Alliance, 1979; Exemplary Mktg. Performance awards, RCA Corp., 1979, 80. Mem. Juvenile Corrections Assn., Nat. Ctr. Dir.'s Workgroup, NAACP, Am. Personnel and Guidance Assn., Kappa Alpha Psi (plaque 1972), Sigma Pi Phi. Office: 110 Hall St SE Grand Rapids MI 49507

WILLIAMS, DUANE ALWIN, chemical engineer; b. Marshfield, Wis., Apr. 6, 1935; s. Alwin W. and Edith L. (Young) W.; m. Judith Carol Bean, Aug. 24, 1957; children—Gary Douglas, Jeffrey Scott. B.S., U. Wis.-Madison, 1956, M.S., 1957, Ph.D. in Chem. Engring 1961. Tech. service engr. Enjay Labs., Linden, N.J., 1957-58; research chem. engr. Kimberly-Clark Corp., Neenah, Wis., 1962-64; with Rockor, Inc., Redmond, Wash., 1964-71; with Kimberly Clark Corp., Neenah, Wis., 1971—, dir. infant care products research and devel., 1983-84, dir. feminine care product devel., 1984—. Author tech. articles. Mem. Am. Inst. Chem. Engrs., Tau Beta Pi, Phi Lambda Upsilon, Theta Tau. Lutheran Home: 632 Kessler Dr Neenah WI 54956

WILLIAMS, EDWARDS J., electronic equipment manufacturing company executive. Chmn., chief operating officer, dir. McGraw-Edison Co., Rolling Meadows, Ill. Office: McGraw-Edison Co 1701 Golf Rd Rolling Meadows IL 60008*

WILLIAMS, FLORA LEONA, economics educator; b. Talahassee, Jan. 21, 1937; d. Noble J. and Dorothy (Rohrer) Rouch; m. Leiw K. Williams, June 26, 1960; children—Chadwick, Lora Lu, Matthew. B.S., Manchester Coll., 1959; M.S., Purdue U., 1964, Ph.D., 1969. Tchr., Mishawaka, Ind., 1959-64, West Lafayette, Ind., 1964-68; research asst. Purdue U., West Lafayette, 1968-69, asst. prof., 1969-75, assoc. prof. home econs., 1975—; vis. prof. U. Calif.-Davis, 1976; cons. in field. Author: The Family Economy, 1973; Guidelines to Financial Counseling, 1980. Contbr. articles to profl. jours. HEW grantee. Mem. Assn. Consumer Research, Am. Econs. Assn., Am. Home Econs. Assn., Am. Council on Consumer Interest, Family and Consumer Research. Home: 3815 Gate Rd Lafayette IN 47905 Office: CSR Dept MTHW Hall Purdue U West Lafayette IN 47907

WILLIAMS, FRANK E., SR., police chief; b. Oak Park, Ill., Apr. 4, 1947; s. Francis E. and Rose M. (Moloney) W.; m. Susan Terris Thompson, May 28, 1968; children—Tiffany, Frank. E. A.A., Harper Coll., 1974; B.A., Aurora Coll., 1978; M.S., Webster U., 1980. Patrolman, Wooddale, Ill., 1971-73, sgt., 1973-76, police chief, 1976—; acting city mgr. City of Wooddale, 1978; adj. prof. Aurora Coll., Ill., 1981-83; cons. Ill. Chiefs of Police Assn., 1982-85; regional dir. U.S. Karate Assn. Police Survival and Defensive Tactics Inst., Pitts., 1984-85; sch. dir. Tzu-Wei Karate Assn., Taipei, 1968-70. Instr., Wooddale Park Dist., 1981; welfare sec. Salvation Army, Wooddale, 1979—. Served with USAF, 1967-71. Recipient Service award Salvation Army, 1984; Mgmt. award Wooddale City Council, 1978. Mem. DuPage Chiefs of Police Assn. (pres. 1982-83; Pres.'s award 1983), Ill. Chiefs of Police Assn. (bd. dirs. 1982-83), N.E. Multi-Regional Tng. Assn. (chmn. tng. com. 1984—), West Suburban Chiefs of Police Assn., Internat. Chiefs of Police Assn., Wooddale C. of C. (bd. dirs. 1979), Ill. Police Assn. Lodges: Lions (pres. 1982-83; Pres.'s award 1983) (Wooddale). Avocation: marathon running. Office: Wooddale Police Dept 404 N Wooddale Rd Wooddale IL 60191

WILLIAMS, G(ERHARD) MENNEN, state supreme court justice; b. Detroit, Feb. 23, 1911; m. Nancy Lace Quirk, June 26, 1937; children—G(erhard) Mennen, Nancy, Wendy. A.B. cum laude, Princeton U., 1933; J.D. cum laude, U. Mich., 1936; hon. degree Wilberforce U., Lawrence Inst. Tech., Mich. State U., U. Liberia, U. Mich., Aquinas Coll., St. Augustine's Coll., Ferris Inst., Western Mich. U., Lincoln U., Morris Brown Coll., World U., P.R., Cleary Coll. Bar: Mich. Various positions State of Mich. and U.S. Govt., 1936-48; ptnr. Griffiths, Williams and Griffiths, from 1948; gov. State of Mich., Lansing, 1949-60; asst. sec. of state for African Affairs, 1961-66; U.S. ambassador to Philippines, 1968-69; justice Mich. Supreme Ct., Detroit, 1971—, chief justice, 1983—. Vestryman, St. Paul's Episcopal Cathedral, Detroit. Served to lt. comdr. USN, 1942-46, PTO. Decorated Legion of Merit with Combat V; grand officer Order of Orange Nassau (Netherlands); grand comdr. Royal Order of Phoenix (Greece); grand officer Nat. Order of Niger; comdr. Nat. Order of Ivory Coast; datu Order of Sikatuna (Philippines); Humane Band of African Redemption (Liberia); Polonia Restituta (Polish Govt. in Exile); Pro Merito (Latvia); recipient numerous awards and recognitions from nat. and Mich. orgns. Mem. AMVETS, Am. Legion, VFW, Res. Officers Assn., SAR, Ahepa, Steuben Soc., various sportsmen's and conservation orgns., Order of Coif, Phi Beta Kappa, Phi Delta Phi, Phi Gamma Delta. Clubs: Navy, University, Edelweiss, Detroit Country. Lodges: Masons (33 degree), Eagles, Elks, Moose, Nat. Grange, Odd Fellows. Author: A Governor's Notes, 1961; (with William Eerdmans) Africa for the Africans, 1969. Office: 1425 Lafayette Bldg Detroit MI 48226 also Law Bldg Lansing MI 48901

WILLIAMS, HARRY JAY, architect; b. Jonesboro, Ark., Mar. 26, 1914; s. John E. and Margaret Edith (Ridgeway) W.; m. Bertha Mae Alexander, Dec. 16, 1963; 1 son, Harry Gene. Student Washington Sch. Art. Carpenter foreman Midwest Engrs., Tulsa, Okla., 1942-46; carpenter subcontractor, 1947-59; architect pub. schs., St. Louis, 1960-79; compliance insp. VA, St. Louis, 1962—. Vice chmn. HUD Rehab. Program, Winfield, Mo. Recipient Oil Painting award St. Charles Artist Guild, 1981. Mem. Am. Arbitration Assn. Home and Office: Route 1 Box 246 Old Monroe MO 63369

WILLIAMS, HOPE DENISE, marketing service company executive, business consultant; b. Chgo., Dec. 24, 1952; d. Welmon and Mary Ann (Brefford) Walker; children—Albert Lee, Ebony Emani Denise. Student Ill. State U., 1971-72; B.A. in Psychology, St. Ambrose Coll., 1975, postgrad. M.B.A. program; postgrad. Harvard U. Grad. Sch. Design, summer 1981. Social service dir. Friendly House, Davenport, Iowa, 1977-78; data collector, cons., 1978; supr. CETA/Summer Youth Employment Program, Davenport, 1978; lead organizer Central and Western Neighborhood Devel. Corp., Davenport, 1978-79; exec. dir. Inner City Devel. Corp., Davenport, 1980-83; owner Midwestern Internat. Mktg. Assocs., San Francisco, 1983—; adminstrv. asst. Parker Ross Assocs., 1984—; bus. cons. Incorporator, sec. bd. dirs. United Neighbors Inc., 1980; bd. dirs. Community Health Care, 1978-80; v.p., treas. Athletes Say More Edn., 1980; treas., exec. com. F&A Community Warehouse, 1982—. Recipient cert. of appreciation Palmer Jr. Coll., Davenport, 1979; cert. of merit Ch. Women United, 1983; NEH grantee, 1979; presdl. grantee Palmer Jr. Coll., 1978. Mem. Quad Cities Career Womens Network (treas., exec. com.), Nat. Assn. Female Execs. Author narrative and final report for oral history project, 1979. Home: PO Box 2741 Davenport IA 52809 Office: 394 5th Ave San Francisco CA 94118

WILLIAMS, HUGH ALEXANDER, JR., mechanical engineer; b. Spencer, N.C., Aug. 18, 1926; s. Hugh Alexander and Mattie Blanche (Megginson) W.; B.S. in Mech. Engring., N.C. State U., 1948, M.S. in Diesel Engring. (Norfolk So. R.R. fellow), 1950; postgrad. Ill. Benedictine Coll. Inst. Mgmt., 1980; m. Ruth Ann Gray, Feb. 21, 1950; children—David Gray, Martha Blanche. Jr. engr.-field service engr. Baldwin-Lima Hamilton Corp., Hamilton, Ohio, 1950-52, project engr., 1953-55; project engr. Electro-Motive div. Gen. Motors Corp., La Grange, Ill., 1955-58, sr. project engr., 1958-63, supr. product devel. engine design sect., 1963—. Trustee Downers Grove (Ill.) San. Dist., 1965—, pres., 1974—; pres. Ill. Assn. San. Dists., 1976-77, bd. dirs., 1977—; mem. statewide policy adv. com. Ill. EPA, 1977-79; ruling elder 1st United Presbyn. Ch., Downers Grove. Served with USAAC, 1945. Registered profl. engr., Ill. Mem. ASME (Diesel and Gas Engine Power Div. Speaker awards 1968, 84, Div. citation 1977, exec. com. internal combustion engine div. 1981-86, chmn. 1985-86), Soc. Automotive Engrs. Republican. Club: Masons (32 deg.). Editor: So. Engr., 1947-48; contbr. articles to profl. jours. Patentee in field. Home: 1119 Blanchard St Downers Grove IL 60516

WILLIAMS, J. D., broadcast executive; b. Detroit, June 21, 1951; s. James Marion and Mabel Glenn (Toliver) W.; m. Deborah Lynn West, June 3, 1978. B.S. in Radio, TV, Film, Murray State U., 1973, M.S. in Communications, 1975. Program dir. Sta. WKMS-FM, Murray, Ky., 1973-75, gen. mgr., 1975; program dir. Sta. WUOL-FM, Louisville, 1976, gen. mgr., 1977; v.p., gen. mgr. Stas. WUME-FM/WKKX-AM, Paoli, Ind. Mem. Nat. Assn. Broadcasters, C. of C. (dir.), Sigma Delta Chi, Alpha Epsilon Rho. Mem. Ch. of Christ. Lodges: Shriners, Masons. Office: PO Box 26 Paoli IN 47454

WILLIAMS, J. MICHAEL, hospital administrator, consultant; b. Springfield, Ohio, Dec. 13, 1947; s. John B. and Mary Alice (Ford) W.; m. Sharon Eileen Cossins, Jan. 1, 1969; children—Jay Michael, Aaron Christopher, Benjamin Micah, Michael Paul. Diploma St. Vincent's Sch. Med. Tech., 1969; B.S., Bowling Green State U., 1969; M.A. in Health Care Adminstrn., Central Mich. U., 1980. Med. technologist St. Vincent's Hosp., Toledo, 1968-69, 70-72; instr. Bapt. Bible Coll., Clark's Summit, Pa., 1969-70; adminstrv. technologist Mercy Med. Ctr., Springfield, 1972-77; med. missionary Assn. Bapts. for World Evangelism, Manila, 1977-78; adminstr. Greenfield Area Med. Ctr., Ohio, 1979-85; chief exec. officer Twin City Hosp. Corp., Dennison, Ohio; mem. adv. com. Edgewood Manor, Greenfield, Ohio, 1980-84; mem. Paint Valley Mental Health Bd., Chillicothe, Ohio, 1983-85; bd. dirs. Tuscarawas County unit Am. Cancer Soc.; cons. to bus.; co-host weekly radio program on health issues and hosps., 1981-84. Co-chmn. parade Greene Countrie Towne Festival, Greenfield, 1980-84; mem. Fayette Christian Sch. Bd., Washington Court House, Ohio, 1983. Mem. Am. Coll. Hosp. Adminstrs., Am. Soc. Clin. Pathologists, Republican. Home: 295 Buckeye Hollow Rd Uhrichsville OH 44683 Office: CEO Twin City Hosp First and Fuhr St Dennison OH 44621

WILLIAMS, JACK RAYMOND, civil engr.; b. Barberton, Ohio, Mar. 14, 1923; s. Charles Baird and Mary (Dean) W.; student Colo. Sch. Mines, 1942-43, Purdue U., 1944-45; B.S., U. Colo., 1946; m. Mary Berneice Jones, Mar. 5, 1947 (dec.); children—Jacqueline Rae, Drew Alan. Gravity and seismograph engr. Carter Oil Co., Western U.S. and Venezuela, 1946-50; with Rock Island R.R., Chgo., 1950-80, structural designer, asst. to engr. bridges, asst. engr. bridges, 1950-63, engr. bridges system, 1963-80; sr. bridge engr. Thomas K. Dyer Inc., 1980-82, Alfred Benesch & Co., 1982—. Served with USMCR, 1943-45. Fellow ASCE; mem. Am. Concrete Inst., Am. Ry. Bridge and Bldg. Assn. (past pres.), Am. Ry. Engring. Assn. Home: 293 Minocqua St Park Forest IL 60466 Office: 233 N Michigan Ave Chicago IL 60604

WILLIAMS, J(AMES) EARL, JR., lawyer, manufacturing company executive; b. Cleve., July 12, 1950; s. James Earl and Lois (Alexander) W.; m. Viveca Lois Gregory, July 28, 1984. B.S., Ohio U., 1972; J.D., Cleve. State U., 1976. Bar: Ohio 1980, U.S. Dist. Ct. (no. dist.) Ohio 1980. Asst. in aviation sales Standard Oil of Ohio, Cleve., 1972-73; law clk. James, Moore, Douglas, L.P.A., Cleve., 1976-78; asst. pub. defender Cuyahoga County Pub. Defender's Office, Cleve., 1978—; exec. v.p. ELSONS, Inc., Cleve., 1981—. Sec. bd. trustees East End Neighborhood House, Cleve., 1980—; mem. exec. com. Cuyahoga County Dem. Party, Cleve., 1982—; mem. allocations panel United Way of Greater Cleve. Served with USAF, 1972. Mem. Bar Assn. Greater Cleve. (exec. com. young lawyers div. 1983—), ABA (com. legal problems elderly 1984—). Mem. United Ch. of Christ. Home: 2475 Belvoir Blvd Cleveland OH 44121 Office: Cuyahoga County Pub Defender 1200 Ontario Ave Cleveland OH 44113

WILLIAMS, JAMES MERRILL, microbiologist; b. Grand Forks, N.D., Aug. 6, 1928; s. Merrill Leroy and Bertha M. (Zintel) W.; B.S., U. N.D., 1950; M.S., N.D. State U., 1952; m. Ruth A. Kirby, June 20, 1954; children—Peter J., Todd K. Bacteriologist, Rocky Mountain Lab., Hamilton, Mont., 1952-54, Mont. State Bd. Health, Helena, 1954-56, Anchor Serum Co., St. Joseph, Mo., 1956-58, St. Mary's Hosp., Rhinelander, Wis., 1958-60, Ancker Hosp., St. Paul, 1960-62; dir. biol. control Philips Roxane, 1962-68; dir. bacteriol. research Boehringer Ingelheim Animal Health, Inc., St. Joseph, 1968-78, dir. biol. research, 1978—; affiliate prof. U. Idaho, 1974—. Served with M.C., AUS, 1946-48. Mem. Am. Soc. Microbiology, U.S. Animal Health Assn., Am. Mgmt. Assn. Republican. Methodist. Clubs: Masons, Shriners. Research on staphylococcal mastitis, vibriosis, reproductive, respiratory disease. Patentee brucella canis vaccine. Office: 2621 N Belt St Saint Joseph MO 64502

WILLIAMS, JEFFREY MICHAEL, biomedical company manager, pharmacologist; b. Ashland, Wis., June 30, 1953; s. Edward Francis and Eleanor Marie (DeBriyn) W.; m. Janet Arlene Harmon, Apr. 8, 1978; 1 dau., Caitlin Marie Harmon. B.S. in Biology and Chemistry, Northland Coll., Ashland, Wis., 1975; M.S. in Pharmacology and Toxicology, Purdue U., 1978. NIH, NSF fellow Purdue U., 1975-78, research assoc., 1977-79; research chemist Great Lakes Chem. Co., Lafayette, Ind., 1979; info. scientist Abbott Labs., North Chicago, Ill., 1979-80, clin. research assoc., 1980-82; mgr. clin. programs, drug adminstrn. devices and systems Medtronic, Inc., Mpls., 1982—. Mem. N.Y. Acad. Scis., AAAS, Parenteral Drug Assn., Am. Inst. Chemists, Sigma Xi. Roman Catholic. Contbr. articles to profl. jours.

WILLIAMS, JIMMIE LEE, criminal justice educator, security consultant; b. Joplin, Mo., July 8, 1943; s. Marion Thad and Lefa Ione (Busse) W.; m. Sharon Irene Kendrick, Aug. 1, 1961 (div. Sept. 1974); children—Christine Diane, Barbara Jean; m. Peggy Sue Callahan, Oct. 1, 1975; children—Jimmie Lee II, Patrick Sean, Jennifer Nicole. A.S. in Law Enforcement, Mo. So. State Coll., 1970, B.S., 1974; M.S. in Criminal Justice Adminstrn., Central Mo. State U., 1976. Juvenile officer Joplin Police Dept., 1967-75, 29th Jud. Dist., Joplin, 1975-76; asst. prof. criminal justice Mo. So. State Coll., Joplin, 1976; owner, mgr. Williams Cons. Co., Seneca, Mo., 1982—. Author: (with others) Transportation Security Personnel Training Manual, 3 vols., 1978. Mem. subcom. Handbook for Law Enforcement Officers (Mo. Criminal Code), 1979. Sec.-treas. Seneca Recreation Bd., 1979-84. Served with U.S. Army, 1965-67, Vietnam. Republican. Mem. Reorganized Ch. of Jesus Christ of Latter Day Saints. Club: Seneca Athletic (pres. 1977-78). Home: Route 2 Box 270 Seneca MO 64865 Office: Mo So State Coll Newman and Duquesne Rds Joplin MO 64801

WILLIAMS, JOHN CARL, educator, researcher; b. Sedalia, Mo., Feb. 19, 1952; s. Frank and Kathleen W. B.A., Columbia (Mo.) Coll., 1979; M.Ed., U. Mo., Columbia, 1981, Ed.S., 1984; postgrad. Northeast Mo. State U., Central Mo. State U., U. Ariz., U. Mo.-Columbia, U. Mo.-St. Louis. Elem. tchr. Jamestown (Mo.) Pub. Schs., 1979-80; tchr. California (Mo.) Pub. Schs., 1980-84, elem. curriculum coordinator, 1982-84; instr. English, faculty officer Camden Mil. Acad., S.C., 1985—; cons. Statewide Testing and Evaluation Service, 1984—. Mem. Assn. Supervision and Curriculum Devel., Mo. State Tchrs. Assn., NEA, Mo. NEA, Pi Lambda Theta, Phi Delta Kappa. Club: Optimists. Lodges: Masons, Order Eastern Star. Contbr. articles to profl. jours. Home: 2123 Bateman Blvd Camden SC 29020 Office: Camden Mil Acad Camden SC 29020

WILLIAMS, JOHN DALE, business and marketing consultant; b. Carrollton, Mo., Oct. 13, 1943; s. Dale C. and Mary (Weinhold) W.; m. Lana L. Elgin, Mar. 22, 1962 (div. 1971); 1 son, Jeffrey D. B.A., U. Mo., 1970, M.A., 1976. Disc jockey, newswriter KAOL Radio, Carrollton, 1959-61; quality assurance engr. Gen. Dynamics/Astronautics, San Diego, 1962-64; prodn. controller solar div. Internat. Harvester Co., San Diego, 1965-67; polit. cons. Mayor Charles B. Wheeler, Kansas City, Mo., 1970-71; clinic dir. Greater Kansas City Mental Health Clinic (Mo.), 1971-81, Kansas City Drug Abuse Program (Mo.), 1981-84; bus. and mktg. cons., 1984—; cons. Jackson County Legislature, Kansas City, Mo., 1981—; dir. Jackson County Mental Health Levy Bd., Kansas City, 1982-83. Bd. dirs. Com. for County Progress, Kansas City, 1982—; mem. Kansas City Jazz Commn., 1982—; pres. Com. of Ind. Young Democrats, 1971-73; v.p. Jackson County Dem. Alliance, 1978-79; Dem. committeeman, Kansas City, 1979-81. Mem. Phi Kappa Phi, Phi Alpha Theta. Office: Kansas City Center Indsl Medicine 917 McGee St Kansas City MO 64106

WILLIAMS, JOHN J., accountant, tax specialist; b. Harrison, Mich., Mar. 7, 1920; s. John Logan and Ethel Beatrice (Erickson) W.; B.A., Ottawa U., 1947; postgrad. John Marshall Law Sch., 1947-49; m. Mary Patricia Howden, Aug. 3, 1968; children—John, Sarah, Robert, Deborah. Acct., Brelsford Gifford & Hardesty, C.P.A.s, 1943-46; acct. Arthur Young & Co., Chgo., 1946-47; income tax specialist Arthur Andersen & Co., 1948-49; owner, mgr. John J. Williams, C.P.A., tax specialist, Arkansas City, Kans., 1949—; lectr. taxation Washburn U. Law Sch., 1946—, spl. lectr. on income taxes, 1949—. Mem. Kans. Turnpike Authority, 1958-61, sec.-treas., 1959-61. C.P.A. Mem. Internat. Accts. Soc. Democrat. Episcopalian. Contbr. articles to profl. jours. Office: 115 E Chestnut St Arkansas City KS 67005

WILLIAMS, JOHN PATTISON, JR., association executive, lawyer; b. Cin., Feb. 14, 1941; s. John P. Williams and Anne (Sawyer) Greene; m. Janie Pepper, Nov. 20, 1971. B.A. in Religion, Princeton U., 1963; J.D., U. Cin., 1966; postgrad. Naval Justice, Newport, R.I., 1967. Bar: Ohio 1966, U.S. Dist. Ct. (so. dist.) Ohio 1966. Assoc., Taft, Stettinius & Hollister, Cin., 1966, 71-77, ptnr., 1977—; pres. Greater Cin. C. of C.; 1984—. dir. Kennedy Mfg. Co., Van Wert, Ohio, Great Trails Broadcasting Corp., Dayton, Ohio, Portman Equipment Co. Trustee Invest in Neighborhoods, Inc., Cin., 1982—, Clovernook Sch. for Blind, Cin., 1983—; mem. President's Council Mt. St. Joseph Coll., Cin., 1983—. Served to capt. USMC, 1966-69; Viet Nam. Mem. ABA, Cin. Bar Assn., Ohio Bar Assn. Republican. Episcopalian. Clubs: Queen City, Cin. Country (Cin.). Avocations: jogging; travel; social golf; canoeing; motorcycles. Home: 3 Resor Pl Cincinnati OH 45220 Office: Cin C of C 120 W Fifth St Cincinnati OH 45202

WILLIAMS, JOHN TROY, librarian, educator; b. Oak Park, Ill., Mar. 11, 1924; s. Michael Daniel and Donna Marie (Shaffer) W.; B.A., Central Mich. U., 1949; M.A. in Library Science, U. Mich., 1951, M.A., 1954; Ph.D., Mich. State U., 1973. Reference librarian U. Mich., Ann Arbor, 1955-59; instr. Bowling Green (Ohio) State U., 1959-60; reference librarian Mich. State U., East Lansing, 1960-62; 1st asst. reference dept. Flint (Mich.) Pub. Library, 1962-65; head reference services, Purdue U., West Lafayette, Ind., 1965-72; head pub. services No. Ill. U., Dekalb, 1972-75; asst. dean, asst. univ. librarian Wright State U., Dayton, Ohio, 1975-80; vis. scholar U. Mich., Ann Arbor, 1980—; cons. in field. Served with U.S. Army, 1943-46. Mich. State fellow, 1963-64; HEW fellow, 1971-72. Mem. Am. Library Assn., Spl. Libraries Assn.,

Genessee County Hist. Soc. (dir.), Am. Soc. for Info. Sciences, Am. Sociol. Assn., AAUP, Council on Fgn. Relations. Contbr. articles to profl. jours. Home: 1473 Wisteria Ann Arbor MI 48104

WILLIAMS, JULIE BELLE, psychiatric social worker; b. Algona, Iowa, July 29, 1950; d. George Howard and Leta Maribelle (Durschmidt) W.; B.A., U. Iowa, 1972, M.S.W., 1973. Social worker Psychopathic Hosp., Iowa City, 1971-72; OEO counselor YOUR, Webster City, Iowa, 1972; social worker Child Devel. Clinic, Iowa City, 1973; therapist Mid-Eastern Iowa Community Mental Health Center, Iowa City, 1973; psychiat. social worker Mental Health Center N. Iowa, Mason City, 1974-79, chief psychiat. social worker, 1979-80; asst. dir. Community Counseling Center, White Bear Lake, Minn., 1980-85, dir., 1985—; lectr., cons. in field. NIMH grantee, 1972-73. Mem. Nat. Assn. Social Workers (pres. local chpt.), NOW, Acad. Cert. Social Workers, Am. Orthopsychiat. Assn., Am. Assn. Sex Educators, Counselors and Therapists, Minn. Women Psychologists, Minn. Lic. Psychologists, Phi Beta Kappa. Democrat. Office: 4820 Cook Ave White Bear Lake MN 55110

WILLIAMS, KEVIN LEE, real estate development executive; b. Anderson, Ind., Dec. 2, 1954; s. Ralph M. and Wanda Lou (Ball) W.; m. Mindy Jo Tudor; 1 child, Lindsi Nicole. B.S., DePauw U., 1977. Legal intern Grant City Prosecutors Office, Marion, Ind., 1974-75, Phila. Dist. Atty.'s Office, 1975-76; ins. adjuster G.A.B. Bus. Service, Indpls., 1977-80; v.p. R.M. Williams & Assocs., Marion, 1981—. Mem. nat. com. Republican Party. Mem. Nat. Assn. Home Builders., Nat. Rifle Assn., Phi Kappa Psi. Mem. Christian Ch. Avocations: golf; hunting; fishing; skiing; trap shooting. Home: 2000 Wilno Dr Marion IN 46952 Office: Ralph M Williams & Assocs 4452 N Wabash Rd Marion IN 46952

WILLIAMS, LARRY E., oil company executive; b. Chickasha, Okla., July 11, 1936; s. J. Emmett and Zella M. (Venrick) W.; m. Xan Z. Hart, Sept. 7, 1957; children—Jesslyn, Jon. B.S. in Mech. Engring., U. N.Mex., 1958, M.S., 1959. With Cities Service Co., various locations, 1959-74, v.p., Tulsa, 1974-83; pres., chief exec. officer Nat. Coop. Refinery Assn., McPherson, Kans., 1983—; dir. McPherson Bank & Trust Co., Jayhawk Pipeline Co., Wichita, Osage Pipeline Co.; pres., dir. Clear Creek, Inc., McPherson, 1983—. Bd. dirs. United Way, McPherson, 1983—. Named Outstanding Sr. Man, U. N.Mex., 1958. Mem. C. of C., Nat. Petroleum Refiners Assn. (bd. dirs.), Am. Petroleum Inst., Am. Ind. Refiners Assn. (bd. dirs., exec. v.p.), Nat. Council Farmer Coops., Coop League U.S.A. Clubs: Country, Petroleum. Office: Nat Coop Refinery Assn 2000 S Main St McPherson KS 67460

WILLIAMS, LINDSEY THEOPOLIS, researcher, educator, institute administrator, museum curator; b. St. Louis, Aug. 13, 1938; s. Lindsey and Lorene (Tillman) W.; 1 child, Lindsey T. B.A., So. Ill. U., 1964; M.A., Webster Coll., 1969; Ph.D., St. Louis U., 1977. Edn. cons. Who Said I Can't Project, Detroit, 1977—; v.p. O'Fallon Community Corp., St. Louis, 1970—; exec. dir. Edn. Service Inst., St. Louis, 1975—; pres., chief exec. officer O'Fallon Redevel. Corp., St. Louis, 1983—; curator, dir. King-Carver-Joplin Mus., St. Louis, 1984—; cons. St. Louis U., 1971—, So. Ill. U., 1971-84. Ward coordinator Jackson for Pres. Campaign, St. Louis, 1984. Recipient NAACP Achievement award, 1975, King Achievement award O'Fallon Community Corp., 1984. Mem. Kappa Alpha Psi. Democrat. Lodges: Kiwanis, Masons. Avocations: tennis; bowling; swimming. Office: Edn Service Inst PO Box 4803 St Louis MO 63108

WILLIAMS, LOUIS CLAIR, JR., public relations agency executive; b. Huntington, Ind., Nov. 7, 1940; s. Louis Clair and Marian Eileen (Bowers) W.; m. Pamela Grace Waller, July 28, 1973 (div.); children—Terri Lynn, L. Bradley, Lisa C. B.A., Eastern Mich. U., 1963. Copywriter, Rochester (N.Y.) Gas and Electric Co., 1963-65, editor RG&E News, 1965-66; employee info. specialist Gen. Ry. Signal Co., Rochester, 1966-67, supr. employment and employee relations, 1967-69; supr. pub. relations Heublein, Inc., Hartford, Conn., 1969-70; dir. corp. communications Jewel Cos., Inc., Chgo., 1970-71; account exec. Ruder & Finn of Mid-Am., Chgo., 1971-73, v.p., 1973-76, sr. v.p., 1976-78; cons. Towers, Perrin, Forster & Crosby, Los Angeles, 1978-79; exec. v.p., gen. mgr. Harshe-Rotman & Druck, Inc., Chgo., 1979, pres. midwest region, 1979-80; v.p. Hill & Knowlton, Inc., Chgo., 1980-81, sr. v.p., 1981-83; pres. Savlin Williams Assocs., Evanston, Ill., 1983—. Recipient Clarion award Women in Communications, 1978, award of Excellence, Internat. Council Indsl. Editors, 1969, Bronze Oscar-of-Ind., Fin. World, 1974. Mem. Internat. Assn. Bus. Communicators (pres. 1979-80), Chgo. Assn. Bus. Communicators (pres.), Publicity Club Chgo., Pub. Relations Soc. Am.

WILLIAMS, LOY ASBURY, psychotherapist, clergyman; b. Dallas, Oct. 19, 1941; s. Carl Woodly and N. Ruth (Gardner) W.; m. Linda Kerry Rich, Aug. 14, 1965; 1 child, Carl Randolph. B.A., So. Meth. U., 1963; Th.M., 1966; M.S.W., U. Iowa, 1972. Ordained to ministry Meth. Ch., 1967. Assoc. minister 1st Meth. Ch., Denton, Tex., 1966-69; student counselor Iowa Wesleyan Coll., Mount Pleasant, 1969-70; dir. family therapy Iowa Tng. Sch., Eldora, 1972-76; exec. dir. Tri City Family Counseling, Geneva, Ill., 1976-81; pvt. practice psychotherapy, St. Charles, Ill., 1981—; parish assoc. Fox Valley Presbyn. Ch., Geneva, 1981—; cons. bus. programs Ecker Ctr. for Mental Health, Elgin, Ill., 1982—; mental health cons. Assn. for Individual Devel., Aurora, Ill., 1981—. Contbr. articles to profl. jours. Cubmaster Two Rivers council Boy Scouts Am., 1983—; pres. Fox Valley Arthritis Action Council, 1978; elder Iowa Ann. Conf. United Meth. Ch. Recipient Social Ethics award B'nai B'rith, Dallas, 1963. Mem. Nat. Assn. Social Workers, Acad. Cert. Social Workers (cert.), St. Charles C. of C. Democrat. Avocations: sailing; skiing. Home: 1016 Fargo Blvd Geneva IL 60134 Office: Loy Williams and Assocs 24 Mosedale St Saint Charles IL 60174

WILLIAMS, LOYAL DEAN, social service agency executive; b. Lamar, Ark., May 14, 1935; s. Lester Lee and Lean Rookh (Overton) W.; m. Beverly Jane Grossman, Dec. 23, 1973; children—Loyal Dean II, Christopher Henry. B.A., Memphis State U., 1958; M.S.W., U. Denver, 1963. Social service dir. Tulsa Boys' Home, 1970-74; dir. social service St. Francis Hosp., Tulsa, 1974-77; exec. dir. Woodland Hills, Duluth, Minn., 1977-81; pres., chief exec. officer Family and Children's Ctr., Mishawaka, Ind., 1981—; bd. dirs. Family Service Council, Indpls., Ind. Coalition. Mem. adv. bd. Child Welfare League Am., N.Y.C., 1984—; bd. dirs. Residential Assn., Indpls., 1983—. Mem. Nat. Assn. Social Workers (Spl. Recognition award 1974, treas. 1984—), Acad. Cert. Social Workers. Democrat. Mem. Ch. of Christ. Lodge: Rotary. Avocations: golf; gardening; camping. Office: Family and Children's Ctr 1411 Lincoln Way W Mishawaka IN 46544

WILLIAMS, MARY G. (TRUDI), insurance executive; b. Columbus, Ohio, May 3, 1946; d. Harold E. and Mary J. (McShane) W.; m. Thomas N. Adolph, Apr. 28, 1969 (div. 1973). Student Ohio State U., 1964-65. Various mktg. and underwriting positions Western Casualty & Surety Co., Columbus, 1966-73; mgr. agy. services Motorists Mut. Ins. Co., Columbus, 1973-75; mktg. rep. Beacon Ins. Co., Columbus, 1975-77; sr. mktg. rep. CG/Aetna Ins. Co., Columbus, 1977-79, mktg. mgr., 1979-82; territorial mgr. INA/Aetna, Cleve., 1982—; mktg. v.p. INA/Aetna-CIGNA, Cleve., 1985—; pres. INA of Ohio, Cleve., 1985—. Mem. Exec. Women's Roundtable (sec. 1985), Cleve. Ins. Mgrs. Assn. Home: 3656 Traynham St Shaker Heights OH 44122 Office: INA/Aetna Ins-CIGNA 14650 Detroit St Lakewood OH 44107

WILLIAMS, P. J., civil engr.; b. Bradley, Ark., Aug. 10, 1938; s. Johnnie and Corene (Davis) W.; B.S., Prairie View A&M U., 1965; m. Wenta Dean O'Hara, Aug. 23, 1971; children—Courtney, Makeba, Charmion. Asst. county supr. Farmers Home Adminstrn., Independence, Kans., 1966-67, civil engr., Topeka, 1967—. Active Topeka Panhellenic Council, 1975—. Recipient Superior Service award Dept. Agr., 1979; Equal Employment Opportunity award Farmers Home Adminstrn., 1979; named Fed. Civil Servant of Yr., 1980. Mem. Am. Water Works Assn., Jack and Jill of Am., Alpha Phi Alpha. Mem. Ch. of Christ. Home: 3601 Randolph St Topeka KS 66611 Office: 444 SE Quincy St Topeka KS 66683

WILLIAMS, PHILIP COPELAIN, physician; b. Vicksburg, Miss., Dec. 9, 1917; s. John Oliver and Eva (Copelain) W.; B.S. magna cum laude, Morehouse Coll., 1937; M.D., U. Ill., 1941; m. Constance Shielda Rhetta, May 29, 1943; children—Philip, Susan Carol, Paul Rhetta. Intern, Cook County Hosp., Chgo., 1942-43, resident in ob-gyn, 1946-48; resident in gynecology U. Ill., 1948-49; practice medicine specializing in ob-gyn, Chgo., 1949—; mem. staff St. Joseph Hosp., Augustana Hosp., Cook County Hosp., McGaw Hosp.; clin. prof. Med. Sch. Northwestern U., Chgo. Bd. dirs. Am. Cancer Soc. Chgo. unit and Ill. div. Served with U.S. Army, 1943-45. Recipient Civic award Loyola U., 1970; Edwin S. Hamilton Interstate Teaching award, 1984; diplomate Am. Bd. Ob-Gyn, Fellow ACS, Internat. Coll. Surgeons; mem. AMA, Chgo., Ill. med. socs., AMA, Chgo. Gynecol. Soc. (treas. 1975-78, pres. 1980-81), Am. Fertility Soc., Inst. Medicine, N.Y. Acad. Scis., AAAS. Presbyn. Clubs: Ill. Athletic, Carleton, Plaza. Contbr. articles to profl. jours. Home: 1040 N Lake Shore Dr Chicago IL 60611 Office: 200 E 75th St Chicago IL 60619

WILLIAMS, PHILLIP LANE, theatre arts educator; b. Memphis, Aug. 24, 1949; s. Percy Henry and Doris Jean (Moss) W. B.A., Tenn. State U., 1970, M.S., 1972. Instr. Kennedy-King Coll., Chgo., 1972-77; resident dir. U. Mich., Ann Arbor, 1977-79; artistic dir. Back Alley Players, Ann Arbor, 1978-79; tng. cons. Goekens Systems, Chgo., 1979-81; dept. chmn. Kennedy-King Coll., Chgo., 1981—, artistic dir. Katherine Dunham Theatre; drama instr. YWCA, Nashville, 1969-70; talk show host WDCN-TV, Nashville, 1970-71; mng. dir. Katherine Dunham Studio, Chgo., 1973-77. Author: Le Stardust Revue, 1982. Named Educator of Yr., Phi Delta Kappa, 1984, Outstanding Black Am., Chgo., 1984. Mem. Nat. Assn. Dramatic and Speech Arts (regional dir. 1974-76, v.p. 1982-85, nat. pres.), Theta Alpha Phi. Democrat. Baptist. Avocations: choreography; forensics; archery. Office: Kennedy-King Coll 6800 S Wentworth St Chicago IL 60621

WILLIAMS, RAYNNA DIANE, educator; b. Detroit, June 29, 1946; d. Miles Edward and Willie Belle (Austin) Mangrum; m. Raymond Williams, Jan. 30, 1971; children—Raynna Nicole, Raymond Kyle. B.S., Eastern Mich. U., 1969; M.A., U. Mich., 1971; Ed.S., Wayne State U., 1980, postgrad., 1980—. Paraprofl., Detroit Pub. Schs., 1966-67, substitute tchr., 1967-68, tchr., 1969-76, guidance counselor Parker Elem. Sch., 1976-79, elem. staff coordinator Herman Elem. Sch., 1979-80, asst. adminstr. Title I dept. Region One Office, 1980-82, coordinator Mastery Learning Ctr., 1982—. Vol., Channel 56 Auction; rep. Local Sch. Community Council; vol. cons. Youth on the Move Program, Boulevard Child Devel. Ctr.; founder parent interest group Boulevard Child Devel. Ctr.; chmn. tutorial program Delta Sigma Theta Lambda area. Recipient Vol. Cert. of Recognition, Community Edn. Program, 1980; named Woman of Yr., Hartford Ave. Bapt. Ch., 1982. Mem. Assn. Supervision and Curriculum Devel., Nat. Alliance Black Sch. Educators, Mich. Assn. State and Fed. Programs, Mich. Personnel Guidance Assn., Mich. Reading Council, Orgn. Sch. Adminstrs. and Suprs., Guidance Assn. Met. Detroit, Cass Tech. Black Alumni Assn. (founding mem., chmn.), Delta Sigma Theta. Baptist.

WILLIAMS, RICHARD JAMES, food service executive; b. Goliad, Tex., Aug. 19, 1942; s. L. D. and Freida Irene (Watkins) W.; m. Shirley Ann Mihalik, July 11, 1967; children—Kenneth F., Dawn L. A.A., Santa Ana Jr. Coll. (Calif.), 1965. Area mgr. Jack in the Box Restaurant, San Diego, 1972-80; v.p. ops. Franchise Dirs., Inc., Bradley, Ill., 1980-81; area supr. Pizza Hut of Am., Inc., Lombard, Ill., 1981-83; regional dir. of food service Montgomery Ward Co., Chgo., 1983-84, v.p. ops. subs. Golden Bear Restaurants, Mt. Prospect, Ill., 1983-84; franchise area dir. Wendy's Internat., Oakbrook Terrace, Ill., 1985—. Author: Anthology of American High School Poetry, 1959. Served with USMC, 1960-72. Decorated Silver Star, Bronze Star. Republican. Mem. Chs. of Christ. Home: 221 Wianno Ln Schaumburg IL 60194 Office: Wendy's Internat 2 Trans Am Plaza Dr Suite 330 Oakbrook Terrace IL 60148

WILLIAMS, ROBERT ARTHUR, II, laboratory executive; b. Chgo., June 20, 1951; s. Robert A. and Rose Dolores (Merritello) W.; m. Cathy S. Chada, Oct. 2, 1976; children—Anne, Julia, Kate. B.B.A., Loyola U., Chgo., 1973, M.S., 1975. With Underwriters Labs., Inc., Northbrook, Ill., 1973—, corp. mgr. adminstrv. services, 1984—.

WILLIAMS, ROBERT JERREL, psychiatrist; b. Lindsay, Okla., Jan. 21, 1932; s. Jesse Willie and Florence Irene (Southern) W.; m. Oleta Jean Williams, Jan. 17, 1975; children—Tannalynn, David, William, Elizabeth, Kathleen, Roberta, Judy, Ellen, Athrienna, Carolyn, Nancy. B.S., Central Okla. State U., 1950; D.O., Univ. of Health Scis., Kansas City, Mo., 1954; postgrad. in psychology, Okla. State U., 1970-71; postgrad. in mental health adminstrn. U. Minn. Sch. Pub. Health, 1983—. Lic. physician, S.D.; diplomate Am. Bd. Psychiatry and Neurology. Intern teaching hosps. Univ. Health Scis., 1954-55; resident in surgery Huntington Hosp., Boston, 1955-58; practice medicine specializing in surgery, Boston, 1958-69; pvt. practice, Marshall, Mo., 1973; with Mo. Div. Mental Health, 1972, 74-80, resident in psychiatry, U. Mo., 1977-80; dir. psychiatry USPHS Regional Inpatient Program, Rapid City, S.D., 1981—; chief psychiat. cons. various mental health services, Indian Health Service in 9 states; clin. instr. psychiatry U. Mo., 1980-81; asst. prof. psychiatry U. S.D., 1982—, also asst. prof. family practice; police surgeon, Boston, 1959-63; frequent panelist radio and TV. Chmn. Rapid City Mayor's Health Com.; mem. Mayor's Indian/White Relations Com., Rapid City Law Enforcement Com., Rapid City Media Com., Am. Civil Def. Served with USAR, 1949-53. Recipient Spl. Service award Mo. Spl. Olympics, 1972; Mayor's Health service award City of Rapid City, 1983. Mem. AMA, Am. Psychiat. Assn., Am. Acad. Family Practice, S.D. Psychiat. Assn., S.D. Med. Assn., Mo. Med. Assn., Met. Med. Assn., Black Hills Med. Assn., S.D. Acad. Family Practice, Corp. for Advancement of Psychiatry, Internat. Psychiat. Assn., Am. Assn. Clin. Psychiatrists, Am. Psychosomatic Assn., Internat. Assn. Med. Specialists, Rapid City C. of C., Atlas Frat., Black Hills Writers Group. Unitarian. Club: Optimists. Contbr. articles profl. jours.; contbg. editor Mother's Manual, 1962-65. Home and Office: 3200 Canyon Lake Dr Rapid City SD 57701

WILLIAMS, ROBERT ODUS, accountant; b. Oakland, Calif., July 1, 1954; s. Robert Wesley and Mary Frances (Pendergrass) W.; Student, Calif. State U., 1972-76, Maharishi Internat. U., 1977-78. Musician with Paul Horn, 1977, Beach Boys, 1977, Charles Lloyd, Santa Barbara, Calif., 1978; profl. acct. Love Songs Prodn., Inc., 1977-79, Western Audio, 1980-81; owner E.B.S. Bookkeeping and Acctg. Service, San Rafael, Calif., also Fairfield, Iowa, 1981—; gen. mgr. Unity Records, Corte Madera, Calif.; cons. advisor to musicians, 1977-82. Mem. Am. Philatelic Soc. Composer various mus. pieces including: Vision, 1976. Home: 2117 Bockman Rd San Lorenzo CA 94580 Office: 501 W Adams St Suite 4 Fairfield IA 52556

WILLIAMS, RONALD EUGENE, manufacturing company executive; b. Sioux City, Iowa, May 7, 1941; s. David E. Williams and Joyce Elizabeth (Williams) Whitaker; m. Judith Ellen Pratt, Dec. 30, 1960 (div. Apr. 1970); children—Stephen Eugene, Katherine Elizabeth; m. Doreen Elizabeth Aeilts, Feb. 26, 1977. B.A., U. S.D., 1965; M.A., U. Wyo., 1966; A.B.D., Ariz. State U., 1970. Instr., Iowa State U., Ames, 1966-69; dredging ops. Hess Oil Co., St. Croix, V.I., 1972; asst. prof. Ferris State Coll., Big Rapids, Mich., 1970-73; services 3M Co., St. Paul, 1973—. Fellow: NDEA, 1969, Alta., 1969; Iowa Merit scholar, 1959. Mem. Standards Engring. Soc. (vice chmn. Minn. sect.). Lutheran. Office: Hardgoods Tech Ctr Bldg 235-1F 3M Center St Paul MN 55144

WILLIAMS, SHARON, interior designer; b. Waukegan, Ill., Aug. 23, 1948; d. John Issac and Ruth (Robertson) Williams; B.S. in Bus. Edn. and Interior Design, Western Ill. U., 1970; postgrad. U. Minn., 1975, 79. Interior designer masterplan sales and interior design studio Dayton's Dept. Store, St. Paul, 1973-77; owner, pres., dir. interior design Sherry Williams-Ricks, Studio of Interior Design, Mpls., 1977—; mem. faculty dept. applied arts U. Wis.-Stout; mfrs. rep. contract and furnishings for instns. Recipient design and sales achievement award Dayton's Dept. Store, 1974. Mem. Am. Soc. Interior Designers, Mpls. Soc. Fine Arts, Mpls. Inst. Arts, Nat. Assn. Women Bus. Owners, Nat. Assn. Female Execs., Minn. Soc. AIA (interiors com.), Greater Mpls. C. of C., North Suburban C. of C. Alpha Omicron Phi. Methodist. Home: 235 Mackubin Saint Paul MN 55102 Office: Sta 19 2001 University Ave SE Minneapolis MN 55414

WILLIAMS, SUSAN JAN, nurse, consultant; b. Flint, Mich., Nov. 29, 1939; d. Arnold Raymond and Dorothy Francis (Howell) Hinterman; m. Frank Earl Williams, Jr., June 23, 1975 (dec.); 1 son, Stephen. R.N., St. Joseph Sch. Nursing, 1961; B.S. in Human Services and Edn., U. Detroit, 1983. Nurse various depts. including pediatrics, emergency room, operating room, intensive care, med. and surg. units, obstetrics St. Joseph Hosp., Flint, Mich., 1961—, infection control coordinator, 1972—; vol. cons. and tchr.; speaker confs. Active Holy Redeemer Catholic Ch.; leader local Boy Scouts Am., 1972-74. Recipient Florence Nightingale Nursing award trophy, St. Joseph Sch. Nursing, 1961. Mem. Mich. Soc. for Infection Control (founding pres. 1972-74, award 1974). Clubs: Golf, Ski. Contbr. article to profl. publ.; planner workshops and confs. hosps. and nursing homes. Home: 1490 Williamsburg Rd Flint MI 48507 Office: 302 Kensington Ave Flint MI 48502

WILLIAMS, WALTER RANDOLPH, insurance executive; b. Cairo, Ill., May 20, 1939; s. Randolph and Catherine (White) W.; student U. Philippines, 1957-59; B.A., Chgo. Tchrs. Coll., 1964; postgrad. Coll. Fin. Planning., 1981—; m. Lisa R., Mar. 31, 1978; children—J. Arthur and Shareeff J. (twins). Counselor, Chgo. Bd. Edn., 1965-68; sales rep. Met. Life, 1967-68; dist. mgr. Nat. Research Cons., Skokie, Ill., 1968-72; dist. mgr. Family Life, Wilmette, Ill., 1972-78; mktg. dir. Multi-Fin. Corp., Chgo., 1982-84, Capitol Life, others; exec. sales dir. Am. Bankers Life, Miami, Fla., 1983-84; regional v.p. Am. Investors Life Ins. Co., Chgo., 1984—; investment instr. Cosmopolitan C. of C., 1979-82; cons. in field Chmn., Ill. House Ins. Com. on Red-Lining-Rate Fixing, 1979. Served with USAF, 1956-59. Recipient Spl. award. Chgo. Jaycees, 1979. Mem. Nat. Assn. Term Life Underwriters, Internat. Life Ins. Assn., Internat. Assn. Fin. Planners. Club: Sno-Gophers Ski. Contbr. articles to profl. jours.; fin. editor Chgo. Mahogany Mag., 1980-81. Office: 1020 S Wabash Ave Chicago IL

WILLIAMSON, EVANGELINE FLOANN, vocational rehabilitation corporate executive; b. Ft. Wayne, Ind., Nov. 29, 1934; d. David Samuel and Anna Florence (Baker) McNelly; m. Clark Murray Williamson, Dec. 20, 1957 (div. 1964); 1 child, Dawn Valerie (dec.). B.A., Transylvania U., 1956. Asst. dir. publs. ABA, Chgo., 1958-66; pres., owner Herringshaw-Smith, Inc., Chgo., 1966-77; internal cons. Monarch Printing Corp., Chgo., 1978-80, Callaghan & Co., Wilmette, Ill., 1980-82; v.p., co-owner Career Evaluation Systems, Inc., Niles, Ill., 1983—. Author: From Typist to Typesetter, 1978. Editor: Transylvania: Tutor to the West, 1975; editor, designer: Silvermiths, Jewelers, Clock and Watchmakers of Kentucky, 1785-1900, 1980. Bd. dirs., treas. West Central Assn., Chgo., 1976-77; bd. dirs. Martha Washington Hosp., Chgo., 1975-76, Mary Thompson Hosp., Chgo., 1977. Mem. Am. Voc. Assn., Nat. Rehab. Assn., Niles C. of C. Republican. Mem. Christian Ch. Avocations: antique clock and furniture collecting; writing. Office: Career Evaluation Systems Inc 7788 Milwaukee Ave Niles IL 60648

WILLIAMSON-STOUTENBURG, JANE SUE, health and safety training executive; b. Davenport, Iowa, Mar. 10, 1949; d. George Baker and Hazel Elaine (Kline) Williamson; m. Noel Wayne Stoutenburg, Aug. 25, 1979; 1 dau., Karen Elaine. Assoc. with honors, Black Hawk Coll., Moline, Ill., 1970; B.A. with honors in Med. Tech., Augustana Coll., Rock Island, Ill., 1973, B.S., 1974; cert. in fire sci., Harper Coll., Palatine, Ill., 1983. Cert. emergency med. technician. Pvt. investigator and security cons., Per Mar Security, Davenport, Iowa, 1975-76; pre-trial release investigator, 7th Judicial Dist., Scott County, Davenport, 1975-76; pharmal. rep. and territory mgr. Bristol Labs. Div., Bristol-Myers, Iowa and Ill., 1976-80; dir. tng. Zee Medical, Addison, Ill., 1981-82; founder and dir. Lake County Rescue, 1982—; asst. EMS coordinator Robbins Fire Dept.; tng. specialist ARC, Chgo., 1983—; chmn. Barrington Area Devel. Council. Recipient Grand award Quint Cities Sci. Fair, 1967; Navy Sci. award, 1967; Future Scientists Am. award Ford Found., 1967; award for Outstanding Sci. Achievement in the Field of Physics, AUS, 1964-67; Nat. Sci. Tchrs. Assn. award, 1964-67; Am. Acad. Scis. award, 1967; Service award ARC. Mem. Am. Soc. Safety Engrs., Am. Soc. Tng. and Devel., Am. Soc. Med. Technologists, Rescue and Emergency Specialists Assn., Am. Acad. Sci., Ill. Acad. Sci., Prehosp. Care Providers Ill. (charter), Illiana Club Traditional Jazz, Ill. Soc. Microbiologists, Phi Theta Kappa, Alpha Phi Omega (life). Republican. Episcopalian. Club: PEO. Author, poetry and profl. articles. Home: 203 S Glendale Barrington IL 60010 Office: PO Box 85 Barrington IL 60010

WILLIS, DONNA LAVERNE, physician; b. Oberlin, Ohio, Nov. 7, 1953; d. Robert Leslie and Bettye LaRue (Palmer) W. Student Oakwood Coll., 1971-74; B.S., M.D., Loma Linda U., 1977. Diplomate Nat. Bd. Examiners. Intern, resident in internal medicine Mayo Grad. Sch. Edn., Rochester, Minn., 1977-80; med. dir. West Dayton Health Ctr., Dayton, Ohio, 1980-82; assoc. program dir. internal medicine residency Kettering Med. Ctr. (Ohio), 1982—; clin. instr. Wright State U. Sch. Medicine, Dayton, 1980—; moderator radio talk show, Dayton, 1984. Author newsletter Caring Family; columnist Ask the Doctor in Caring mag.; med. news editor NBC affiliate Sta. WKEF. Trustee, West Dayton Health Ctr., 1980-82, Kettering Coll. Med. Arts; trustee United Way/United Health Services, 1982—, chairperson nutrition com., 1983—, vice chairperson Health-O-Rama, 1984—, chairperson, 1985. Recipient Appreciation award Nat. Alliance Bus., 1982-83; YWCA Career Women award, 1984. Seventh-Day Adventist. Office: Kettering Med Center 3535 Southern Blvd Kettering OH 45429

WILLMANN, CAMILLA CLAUDIA, tax preparation company executive; b. Greenville, Ill., Jan. 27, 1916; d. Charles Harrison and Dorcas Camilla (Foulon) McLean; m. Frederick E. Willmann, Jan. 27, 1945; children—Charles L., Mary S., William E., Max Louie. Owner, mgr. H & R Block, Greenville. Treas. Bond County Health Improvement; sec. Utlaut Hosp. Aux.; charter mem. Bond County Extension, U. Ill.; mem., Sponsor Illini Midstate Tumblers; sponsor women's slowpitch softball team. Recipient various awards H & R Block. Enrolled agt. IRS, U.S. Treasury Dept. Mem. Greenville C. of C., Bond County Bus. and Profl. Club (charter; treas., chmn. fin. com.), Greenville Retailers Assn. Republican. Roman Catholic. Home: Rt 2 Pocahontas IL 62275 Office: 115 E College Ave Greenville IL 62246

WILLMANN, WENDEL EDGAR, lawyer; b. Greenville, Ohio, Feb. 25, 1935; s. R. Wayne and Twila I. (DeWalt) W.; m. Doris M. Meister, July 1, 1961; children—Diane L., Jeffrey S. Student, U. Mich., 1955-56; B.A., Capital U., 1957; M. Ed., Kent State U., 1964; J.D., Cleve. Marshall Law Sch., 1969. Bar: Ohio, 1969, U.S. Dist. Ct. (no. dist.) Ohio, 1972, U.S. Supreme Ct. 1981, U.S. Ct. Appeals (6th cir.) 1983. Tchr. Parma High Sch., Ohio, 1959-66; salesman Conn. Gen. Life., Cleve., 1966-67; tchr. Fairview High Sch., Ohio, 1968-71; sole practice law, Cleve., 1969—. Vice pres. Parma Sch. Bd., 1980-81; bd. regents Capital U., Columbus, Ohio, 1975; bd. dirs. Luth. Children's Aid Soc., Cleve., 1972-75. Served wih U.S. Army, 1958. Named to Parma Schs. Hall of Fame, 1983. Mem. Fairview Park Tchrs. Assn. (pres. 1971), ABA, Ohio State Bar Assn., Cleve. Bar Assn., Parma Bar Assn., Parma C. of C., Middleburg Heights C. of C., Delta Theta Phi. Lutheran. Lodge: Kiwanis (pres. 1975-76). Avocations: softball; golf; investing. Home: 2118 Oaklawn Dr Parma OH 44134 Office: Sharratt Willmann James & Mille 6837 Pearl Rd Cleveland OH 44130

WILLNER, ROBERT FRANKLIN, b. Cobleskill, N.Y., Aug. 13, 1942; s. Charles Benjamin and Catherine Spencer (McNeil) W.; m. Marie Angela Muchiarone, Apr. 15, 1972; children—Karen Marie, Stephanie Agnes. A.B., Franklin and Marshall Coll., 1964; M.H.A., Med. Coll. Va., 1966; D.Minn., Chgo. Theol. Sem., 1979. Adminstrv. resident Washington (Pa.) Hosp., 1965-66; asst. adminstrv. officer USPHS Hosp., Carville, La., 1966-68; asst. adminstr./acting adminstr. Nat. Orthopedic and Rehab. Hosp., Arlington, Va., 1968-69, adminstr., 1969-72; assoc. adminstr. Cook County Hosp., Chgo., 1972, Oak Forest (Ill.) Hosp., 1973-79; pres. Billings (Mont.) Deaconess Hosp., 1979-82; pres. United Meth. Assn. of Health and Welfare Ministries, Dayton, Ohio, 1983—; vice chmn. South Suburban Adv. Council, Suburban Cook County, Dupage County Health Systems Agy., 1977-79; bd. dirs. South Suburban Council on Aging, 1977-79; community profl. Sch. Health Scis., Governors State U., 1978-79; chmn. Big Sky Hospice, Billings, from 1980; bd. dirs. Dist. 6 Learning Ctr. Mem. health and fitness com. Billings YMCA, 1981-82; mem. exec. com., chmn. Christian Action com. Leighton Ford Billings Crusade, 1982; mem. health and welfare com. Yellowstone Conf., United Methodist Ch.; vice chmn. diaconal minister, W. Ohio Conf., United Meth. Ch.; bd. dirs., chmn. worship for worship planning Grace United Meth. Ch., Billings. Served with USPHS, 1966-68. Recipient spl. appreciation recognition med. staff of Oak Forest Hosp., 1979, cert. and recognition for services rendered in field of rehab., 1979; lic. nursing home adminstr., Ill. Fellow Am. Coll. Hosp. Adminstrs. (regent); mem. Am. Hosp. Assn., United Wesleyan Hosp. Assn. Dist. 6 Hosp. Assn. (vice chmn.), Mont. Hosp. Assn., Am. Protestant Hosp. Assn. (health and religious values council, govt. relations council and fin. com.), Commd. Officers Assn. USPHS, Woman Line (bd. dir.) (Dayton, Ohio). Lodge: Rotary. Office: 601 W Riverview Ave Dayton OH 45406

WILLOUGHBY, DAVID CHARLES, biological photographer; b. Indpls., Nov. 16, 1940; s. Charles C. and Mabelle L. (Haller) W.; student Ind. U., 1958-62, Butler U., 1962-64; m. Victoria LaMarre, Mar. 6, 1971; children—Brian D., Kara L. Med. photographer Ind. U. Sch. Medicine, Indpls., 1962-68; dir. med. media prodns. Meth. Hosp. of Indpls., 1968-85; owner, operator BioMed. Photography, Indpls., 1985—. Registered biol. photographer. Fellow

Biol. Photog. Assn. (dir. 1978-80, exec. sec. bd. of registry 1981-85); mem. Profl. Photographers Am., Hosp. Audiovisual Dirs. Assn., Ind. Ofcls. Assn., Internat. Assn. Approved Basketball Ofcls. Republican. Methodist. Lodges: Masons, Shriners (Indpls.); Order of Eastern Star. Home: 6711 Studebaker Ct Indianapolis IN 46224 Office: 6711 Studebaker Ct Indianapolis IN 46224

WILLS, TOMMY GEORGE, musician, band leader; b. Middletown, Ohio, Aug. 7, 1924; s. Orval C. and Lucille M. (May) W.; m. Verla Jane Bane, Apr. 13, 1970; children—Terry G., Thomas G., Todd A. Student pub. schs., Middletown, Ohio. Owner, musician Town and Country Entertainers, Indpls., 1970—. Served with USMC, 1945. Mem. Am. Legion. Clubs: Moose, Elk. Composer: La Dee Dah, 1963; Sweet Soul, 1965; Tex. Twister, 1965; Walkin' Mr. Sax, 1965; V.J.'s Blues, 1973.

WILMES, MARY JO, pharmacist, educator; b. Omaha, Aug. 18, 1955; d. Joseph Filadelpho and Marion Ann (Cardella) Cimino; m. Robert Mark Wilmes, Dec. 29, 1979. B.S. in Pharmacy, U. Nebr., 1978, Pharm.D., 1979. Registered pharmacist, Nebr. Mgr., pharmacist-in-charge W.A. Piel Drug, Omaha, 1978—; vol. faculty Coll. Pharmacy U. Nebr., Omaha, 1982—; lic. pharmacy preceptor State of Nebr., 1978—; mem. profl. adv. bd. Epilepsy Assn. Nebr., 1984—. Active Assistance League of Omaha. Barbara Osborn Manchester scholar, 1977; recipient Upjohn Achievement award, 1978. Mem. Am. Pharm. Assn., Nebr. Pharm. Assn., Kappa Epsilon, Zeta Tau Alpha. Roman Catholic. Avocations: Needlework and handcrafts; music; aerobic dance; travel. Office: W A Piel Inc 4239 Farnam St Omaha NE 68131

WILSON, C. DANIEL, JR., public library administrator; b. Middletown, Conn., Nov. 8, 1941; s. Clyde Daniel and Dorothy (Neal) W.; m. Edith de Plantay, Sept. 9, 1965; children—Christine, Cindy, Clyde Daniel III, Benjamin. B.A., Elmhurst Coll., Ill., 1967; M.A., Rosary Coll., 1968. Instr., U. Ill.-Urbana, 1968-70; asst. dir. Perrot Meml. Library, Old Greenwich, Conn., 1970-76; dir. Wilton Library, Conn., 1976-79; assoc. dir. Birmingham Pub. Library, Ala., 1979-83; dir. Davenport Pub. Library, Iowa, 1983—. Mem. city council Town of Westport, Conn., 1972-78. Mem. ALA, Am. Soc. Pub. Adminstrn., Davenport C. of C., Pi Gamma Mu. Episcopalian. Lodge: Rotary (Davenport). Office: Davenport Pub Library 321 Main St Davenport IA 52801

WILSON, CHARLES STEPHEN, cardiologist; b. Geneva, Nebr., June 14, 1938; s. Robert Butler and Naoma Luella (Norgren) W.; B.A. cum laude, U. Nebr., 1960; M.D., Northwestern U., 1964; m. Linda Stern Walt, Aug. 21, 1960; children—Michael Scott, Amy Lynn, Cynthia Lee. Intern, Fitzsimons Gen. Hosp., Denver, 1964-65; fellow in internal medicine and cardiology Mayo Grad. Sch. Medicine, Rochester, Minn., 1968-72; practice medicine specializing in cardiology, Lincoln, Nebr., 1972—; attending staff Bryan Meml. Hosp., Lincoln, 1972—, chmn. cardiology, 1976-79; attending staff Lincoln Gen. Hosp., 1978—; assoc. prof. medicine and cardiology U. Nebr. Med. Center, Omaha; mem. Mayor's Council on Emergency Med. Services, Lincoln, 1974-78; founder, chmn. Nebr. State Hypertension Screening Program; med. dir. Lincoln Mobile Heart Team, 1977-80, Lincoln Cardiac Rehab. Program, 1978-79. Trustee U. Nebr. Found., 1983—, Nebr. Coordinating Commn. for Postsecondary Edn., 1984—; mem. Gov.'s Exec. Council, 1983—. Served as maj., M.C., USAR, 1963-68. Diplomate Am. Bd. Internal Medicine subsplty. bd. cardiovascular disease, Nat. Bd. Med. Examiners; Gen. Motors Nat. scholar, 1956-60, Nat. Found. Med. scholar, 1960-64, Mead Johnson scholar ACP, 1968-71. Fellow ACP, Am. Coll. Cardiology, Am. Coll. Chest Physicians, Am. Heart Assn.; mem. Am. Soc. Echocardiography, Mayo Cardiovascular Soc., Nebr. Cardiovascular Soc., Nebr. Heart Assn. (dir. 1973-80, pres. 1976-77), Lincoln Heart Assn. (dir. 1972-75, pres. 1974-75), AMA, Nebr. Med. Assn., Lancaster County Med. Soc., Am. Soc. Internal Medicine, Lincoln Found., Phi Beta Kappa, Sigma Xi, Alpha Omega Alpha, Phi Delta Theta (pres. Nebr. Alpha chpt. 1959-60). Congregationalist. Clubs: U. Nebr. Chancellor's, Lincoln U. (dir. 1981-84). Lodge: Elks. Contbr. articles to profl. jours.; editorial cons. Chest, 1975-76; assoc. editor Nebr. Med. Jour., 1981—. Home: 7430 N Hampton Rd Lincoln NE 68506 Office: 2121 S 56th St Lincoln NE 68506

WILSON, CLAUDE LLEWELLYN, spring manufacturing company executive; b. Lake City, Tenn., Mar. 18, 1906; s. William Llewellyn and Ida F. (Elliott) W.; m. Elizabeth Willa Aldinger, Mar. 7, 1934; 1 dau., Claudia Llewellyn Wilson Opat. Student U. Tenn., 1926-27. With Exxon Co., Memphis, 1928-35, Firestone Tire & Rubber Co., Atlanta, 1935-42, Moog Industries, Inc., St. Louis, 1942-50; with Salina (Kans.) Spring Co., 1950—, chmn. bd., 1974—. Mem. Salina C. of C. Republican. Presbyterian. Club: Mason, Shriner. Contbr. articles on Rolls-Royce to profl. jours. Home: 823 Manor Rd Salina KS 67401

WILSON, DELBERT RAY, newspaper publisher, author; b. Riverdale, Calif., Jan. 16, 1926; s. Elmer Ray and Hanna Marie (Pelto) W.; m. Beatrice Joy Wilson, Oct. 5, 1947; children—Jeri Rae, Vicky Joy, Juli Anne, Margaret Erin. B.S., No. Ill. U., 1980; A.A., A.S., Elgin Community Coll., Ill., 1976; LL.D. (hon.), Judson Coll., Elgin, 1985. Advt. sales rep. Union-Tribune, San Diego, 1959-60, merchandising mgr., 1960-65, gen. advt. mgr., 1965-66; editor-pub. Evening Star-News, Culver City, Calif., Evening Vanguard, Venice, Calif., 1966-70, Daily Jour., Wheaton Ill., 1971—, Daily Courier-News, Elgin, Ill., 1970—; v.p. Copley Press, Inc., La Jolla, Calif., 1970—, mem. sr. mgmt. bd., 1975—; editor, pub. Ill. DAV News, 1978—. Author: The Folks, 1974; Ft. Kearny on the Platte, 1980; Episode on Hill 616, 1981; Nebraska Historical Tour Guide, 1983; Wyoming Historical Tour Guide, 1984. Founding dir., pres. Home of Guiding Hands, Lakeside, Calif., 1961-68; trustee sec. Judson Coll., Elgin, 1971—; bd. mgrs. Sherman Hosp., Elgin, 1971—; founder, chmn. VIP Friendship Council of Ill., Wheaton, 1972, DuPage Heritage Gallery, Wheaton, 1976; pres. Two Rivers council Boy Scouts Am., St. Charles, Ill., 1974-76; bd. govs. State Colls. and Univs. of Ill., Springfield, 1981—; mem. Ill. Vets. Adv. Council, Springfield, 1981—; state comdr. DAV of Ill., Chgo., 1981-82, bd. dirs. DAV Thrift Stores, Chgo., 1978—; bd. dirs. Luth. Social Services of Ill., DesPlaines, 1983—; bd. dirs. Cornerstone Found., Chgo., 1985—; chmn. bd. Christian Coll. of South Africa, Harare, Zimbabwe, 1983—; pres. Elgin Sesquicentennial, Inc., 1984-85. Served with USN, 1943-45, PTO; served to sgt. USAF, 1946-49. Recipient Golden Eagle award Judson Coll., 1972; Silver Beaver award Boy Scouts Am., 1977; Man of Yr. award DAV, 1978. Mem. Am. Newspaper Pubs. Assn., Inland Daily Press Assn., Nebr. Hist. Soc. (life), Am. Legion, DAV, Sigma Delta Chi. Republican. Lutheran. Lodge: Elks. Home: 1507 Laurel Ct Dundee IL 60118 Office: Daily Courier-News 300 Lake St Elgin IL 60120*

WILSON, DORSEY VERNON, transportation executive; b. Bonneville, Ky., July 17, 1920; s. Arthur and Laura Belle (Treadway) W.; m. Yolanda Maria Maccarone, Aug. 25, 1956; 1 dau., Melissa Ann Richards. A.B. in Commerce, Morehead State U., 1947; M.B.A., Fla. State U., 1949. Dept. head Bridgeport High Sch. (Ill.), 1946-47; asst. prof., Fla. State U., Tallahassee, Fla., 1948-49; logistics adminstr. U.S. Navy, 1951-76; pres. Wilson's Truckaway, Chgo., 1981—. Author: Methods of Business Education, 1949. Sr. advisor Stanwyck Corp., Iran, 1978. U.S. Sec. Navy Leadership award, 1965, Achievement award, 1968; named Ky. Col., 1966. Mem. Navy Supply Corps Assn., Defense Transp. Assn., Chgo. Assn. Commerce and Industry, Chgo. Traffic Club. Democrat. Club: Gaslight (Chgo.). Lodge: Masons. Office: Wilson's Truckaway Inc 120 W Madison Suite 14N PO Box A3501 Chicago IL 60690

WILSON, DOUGLAS FREDERICK, professional hockey player; b. Ottawa, Ont., Can., July 5, 1957; s. Douglas and Verna Wilson; m. Katherine Ann Kivisto, July 11, 1981; children—Lacey Anne. Defenseman Chgo. Black Hawks Hockey Team, 1985—; account exec. Coca-Cola, Chgo. Recipient James Norris Meml. Trophy for best NHL defenseman, 1981-82. Avocations: golf; travel. Office: Chicago Black Hawks 1800 Madison St Chicago IL 60612

WILSON, EDWARD CHURCHILL, lawyer; b. Chgo., Oct. 15, 1940; s. Max Elroy and Margaret (Tufts) W.; m. Patricia Daley, Sept. 2, 1961; children—Edward Wallace, David Maxwell. B.S. with honors, Lewis U., 1974, J.D., 1978. Bars: Ill. 1978, U.S. Dist. Ct. (no. dist.) Ill. 1978, U.S. Ct. Appeals (7th cir.) 1978, U.S. Supreme Ct. 1982. Assoc. Conklin and Adler, Chgo., 1978-81; sole practice, LaGrange, Ill., 1981—. Named mem. Barional Order of Magna Charta, 1970. Mem. Chgo. Bar Assn., Ill. State Bar Assn., ABA, Lawyer/Pilots Bar Assn., Internat. Soc. Air Safety Investigators, Aircraft Owners and Pilots Assn. (legis. liaison com. 1980—). Home: 724 N LaGrange Rd LaGrange Park IL 60525 Office: 521 S LaGrange Rd LaGrange IL 60525

WILSON, EDWARD MILLER, lawyer; b. Fort Dodge, Iowa, July 30, 1954; s. Charles Robert and Viola Arvella (Miller) W.; m. Joanna Marie Bohn, Aug. 21, 1976; 1 child, Joanna Lynn. A.B., Princeton U., 1977; J.D., U. Iowa, 1980. Bar: Iowa 1980, U.S. Dist. Ct. (no. dist.) Iowa 1983. Assoc. Birdwell Law Office, Corydon, Iowa, 1980-82; asst. county atty. Wayne County, Iowa, Corydon, 1980-82, Clinton County, Iowa, 1982; county atty., Calhoun County, Iowa, Manson, 1983—; proprietor Wilson Law Office, Manson, 1983—. Mem. ABA, Iowa State Bar Assn., Iowa County Attys. Assn., Calhoun County Bar Assn., Dist. 2 Bar Assn. Republican. Home: 1636 11th St Manson IA 50563 Office: Wilson Law Office 1110 10th Ave Manson IA 50563

WILSON, FLORABELLE, academic librarian; b. Indpls., Jan. 12, 1927; d. James Samuel and Hattie Virginia (Hollis) Williams; m. John A. Wilson, Mar. 28, 1964. B.S.E., Ind. Central U., 1949; M.A. in Library Sci., Ind. U., 1961. Elem. tchr. Indpls. Pub. Schs. 1949-57; asst. librarian Ind. Central U., Indpls., 1957-71, librarian, 1971—; interviewer Sta. WICR, Indpls., 1982—. Mem. Ind. Hist. Soc. Library Bd., Indpls., 1979; mem. Ind. Library and Hist. Bd., 1979—; vice chmn., 1984—. Named Outstanding Black Woman, Nat. Council Negro Women, Indpls., 1983. Mem. Ind. Library Assn. (chmn. Awards Honors Commn. 1982-85), ALA, NAACP (life), Beta Phi Mu. Democrat. Presbyterian. Club: Zonta Internat. (dir. Indpls. 1980-81, chmn. membership com. 1983-85). Contbr. (exhibit and booklet) This Far By Faith, 1982; creator, presentor (Black History Puppets) Lets' Tell the Whole Story, 1981; West African Experience (slides and narration), Invisible Sinew: Black Family. Office: Indiana Central Univ 1400 E Hanna Ave Indianapolis IN 46227

WILSON, GEORGE MCCONNELL, religious organization executive; b. Churchs Ferry, N.D., Oct. 19, 1913; s. Clarence McNair and Mary Belle (McConnell) W.; m. Helen Josephine Bjorck, Sept. 3, 1940; children—Jean Elizabeth (Mrs. Ralph Bertram Greener), Judith (Mrs. Larry Grimes), Janet (Mrs. Steve Hanks.) Student N.D. State Sch. of Sci., 1932-33, U. Minn., 1935, Northwestern Coll., 1933-37; Litt. D. (hon.) Houghton Coll., 1962; LL.D. (hon.) Gordon Coll., 1969. Owner, mgr. Wilson Press & NW Book & Bible House, Mpls., 1940-50; asst. to pres., bus. mgr. Northwestern Coll., Mpls., 1947-50; bus. mgr., sec.-treas. Billy Graham Evangelistic Assn., Mpls., 1950—, exec. v.p., 1962—; pres. World Wide Pubs., Mpls., 1970—; dir. Billy Graham Evangelistic Assn., Eng., Australia, Can., France, Ger., Hong Kong, U.S.; pres., founder Evang. Council for Fin. Accountability, Washington; Sec. Christian Broadcasting Assn., Honolulu, Global Concern, Montrose, Calif.; treas. Blue Ridge Broadcasting Corp., Black Mountain, N.C.; asst. treas. World Wide Pictures, Burbank, Calif.; v.p., bd. dirs. Bank of Mpls. and Trust Co., chmn. bd., 1985—. Author: 20 Years Under God, 1971. Compiler: Words of Wisdom, 1967. Mng. editor Decision mag. Bd. dirs. Children's Heart Fund, Mpls., pres., 1980-83; chmn. bd. Prison Fellowship, Washington; bd. dirs. Mail Users Council, chmn. 1969, bd. dirs. Lauback Literacy Found., 1963-67, Youth for Christ U.S.A., Wheaton, Ill., Mpls. Youth for Christ, Northwestern Coll., Roseville, Minn., Community Coll. Mpls. Named Layman of Yr., Nat. Assn. Evangelicals; recipient Managerial Achievement award Adminstrv. Mgmt. Soc.; award of Distinction, Direct Mail Advertising Assn., 1980; William W. Holes Direct Mail award, 1973; Disting. Service award Greater Mpls. C. of C., 1972; Disting. Service award City of Mpls., 1977; Exec. of Yr. award Mpls. Gopher Chpt. Nat. Secs. Assn., 1979; Good Neighbor award Sta. WCCO, Mpls., 1983; Appreciation award Downtown Council of Mpls. Mem. Mpls. Press Club, Direct Mail Mktg. Assn., Adminstrv. Mgmt. Soc., Nat. Religious Broadcasters, Religious Pub. Relations Council, Nat. Soc. Fund Raisers, Loring-Nicollet Community Council, Citizens League Mpls., Independent-Republicans of Minn. Elephant Club. Baptist. Clubs: Decathlon; Mpls. Athletic; Six O'clock. Lodge: Kiwanis (bd. dirs. Kiwanis Found.). Home: 3113 Humboldt Ave S Minneapolis MN 55408 Office: Billy Graham Evangelistic Assn 1300 Harmon Pl Minneapolis MN 55403

WILSON, HENRY ARTHUR, JR., accounting company executive; b. Detroit, June 12, 1939; s. Henry Arthur and Ruth (Scott) W.; m. Mildred Rendell, June 17, 1961; 1 child, Suzanne. B.S., Mich. Luth. Coll., 1968; M.A., U. Detroit, 1976. Police officer Grosse Pointe Park Police Dept., Mich., 1960-68; v.p. Uniflight, Inc., St. Clare Shore, Mich., 1968-73; coordinator Criminal Justice Inst., Detroit, 1973-76; ptnr. Alexander Grant & Co., Detroit, 1976—. Author: Michigan Harbors/Ports 1985, 1985; Masonic Etiquette and Protocol, 1985. Sponsor Ebenhardt re-election, Detroit, 1984—; usher St. Columba Episcopal Ch., Detroit, 1976—. Served with USAF, 1957-60. Mem. Certified Data Processing Auditors Assn. Republican. Lodge: Masons (grand master Mich. 1984-85). Avocation: boating. Home: 1022 Nottingham St Grosse Pointe Park MI 48230 Office: Alexander Grant & Co 2400 Penobscot Bldg Detroit MI 48226

WILSON, J(ESSE) FRANK, physician, educator; b. Huntsville, Mo., Jan. 10, 1941; s. Carl Franklin and Wilma Pauline (Brogan) W.; m. Vera Noursi, July 3, 1971; children—Julie Pauline, Frank David. A.B. in Zoology, U. Mo., 1961, M.D., 1965. Diplomate Am. Bd. Radiology. Intern, USPHS, New Orleans, 1965-66; resident Penrose Cancer Hosp., Colorado Springs, Colo., 1966-69, assoc. radiotherapist, 1971-74; sr. investigator Nat. Cancer Inst., Bethesda, Md., 1969-71; assoc. prof. radiation oncology Med. Coll. Wis., Milw., 1974—. Author: Brachytherapy, 1978; editor, author: Modern Brachytherapy, 1985; author articles. Bd. dirs. Milw. div. Am. Cancer Soc., 1984—; sec. profl. staff Milwaukee County Med. Complex, 1985. Served to lt. comdr. USPHS, 1965-71. Mem. Am. Coll. Radiology (com. on profl. edn., commn. on radiation therapy), Am. Soc. Radiation Therapy and Oncology, Am. Radium Soc. Avocations: Photography; sports. Office: Med Coll Wis 8700 W Wisconsin Ave Milwaukee WI 53226

WILSON, JOHN GEORGE, manufacturing company executive; b. Toronto, Ont., Can., July 21, 1925; s. Thomas Gibson and Edith (Freshwater) W.; m. Vivian Caroline Harrison, May 24, 1946 (dec.); children—Randy, David, Judy; m. Audrey Doreen Warner, Oct. 25, 1957; 1 dau., Shari Lee. Tool and die maker Pedlar People Ltd., Oshawa, Ont., 1947-53; owner, pres. John G. Wilson Machine Ltd., Cathcart, Ont., 1953—; mfg. cons.; chmn. Brantford Indsl. Tng. Adv. com. Served with Can. Army, 1944-45. Mem. Soc. Mfg. Engrs., Brantford Regional C. of C.

WILSON, LARRY CHARLES, superintendent schools, educator; b. Toledo, May 5, 1938; s. Guy Carl and Velda Mae (Hildabrandt) W.; m. JoAnn Louise Puls, Aug. 13, 1960; children—Paula Jean Gorden, Pamela Sue Lawler. B.E., U. Toledo, 1961; M.A., Eastern Mich. U., 1966; Ph.D., Wayne State U., 1976. Tchr. Whiteford Schools, Ottawa Lake, Mich., 1960-64, Oregon (Ohio) Pub. Schs., 1964-65; prin. Sandusky (Mich.) Community Schs., 1965-79; asst. supt., 1974-76, supt., 1976-79; supt. schs. Blissfield (Mich.) Community Schs., 1979—; asst. prof. Siena Heights Coll., Adrian, Mich., 1979—. Pres. Sandusky (Mich.) Econ. Devel. Commn.; mem. Urban Devel. Commn., Sandusky. Recreation Advisory Council, Sandusky. Recipient George Washington Freedom Found. Middle Sch. award, 1972; NSF fellow, 1981-82. Mem. Am. Assn. Sch. Adminstrs., Mich. Assn. Sch. Adminstrs. (council), Assn. Supervision and Curriculum Devel., Mich. Assn. Sch. Bds., Nat. Assn. Sch. Bds., Phi Delta Kappa (award recipient, 1982). Clubs: Elks (Adrain, Mich.); Rotary (Blissfield); Masons, Scottish Rite (Toledo); Optimist (co-organizer) (Sandusky). Home: 501 Giles Ave Blissfield MI 49228 Office: 630 South Ln Blissfield MI 49228

WILSON, LESLIE JEAN, educator; b. Bedford, Ind., June 26, 1943; d. Don Bernell and Rose E. (Bridwell) Armstrong; m. M. Duane Wilson, June 17, 1965; children—Douglas Troy, Marisa Lynn. B.S., Ind. U., 1965, M.S., 1971; Ed.S., Ind.-Purdue U.-Indpls., 1984. Cert. tchr. and prin., Ind. Elem. tchr. Fontana, Calif., 1965-67, Churubusco, Ind., 1967-69; dir. presch., Goshen, Ind., 1977-85; tchr. Pittsboro Elem. Sch. (Ind.), 1980—. Dir. summer library; sponsor Bible Bowl. Mem. Internat. Reading Assn., Mortar Bd., Enomone, Pleiades, Phi Delta Kappa, Delta Kappa Gamma. Republican. Mem. Christian Ch. (Disciples of Christ). Co-author: Energy Play, 1982, operattas for local schs. Office: N Meridian Pittsboro IN 46167

WILSON, MARC F., museum director, curator; Dir., curator Oriental art Nelson-Atkins Mus. of Art, Kansas City, Mo. Office: Nelson-Atkins Mus of Art 4525 Oak St Kansas City MO 64111*

WILSON, MARTIN JAMES, lawyer; b. Memphis, Jan. 20, 1936; s. Elliott and Elliott (Martin) W.; m. Fannie Clara Stephens, Aug. 17, 1963; 1 son, Stephen Thomas. A.A., Crane Jr. Coll., 1966; B.S., Chgo. State U., 1971; J.D., DePaul U., 1976. Bar: Ill. 1979, U.S. Ct. Appeals (7th cir.) 1979. Sole practice, Chgo., 1979—. Served with USAF, 1956-60. Office: 201 N Wells Suite 1206 Chicago IL 60606

WILSON, MICHAEL JOHN, biologist, educator; b. Iowa City, June 3, 1942; s. James H. and Doris E (Lackender) W.; m. Martha J. Swartzwelter, June 7, 1969; 1 child, Matthew. A.A., Divine Word Coll., 1962; B.A., St. Ambrose Coll., 1964; M.S., U. Iowa, 1967, Ph.D., 1971. Research fellow Harvard Med. Sch., Boston, 1971-73; research assoc. U. Minn., Mpls., 1973-75, asst. prof., 1975-82; research biochemist Mpls. VA Med. Ctr., 1976—; assoc. prof. U. Minn., 1982-85. Contbr. articles to profl. jours. Chmn. spl. edn. council St. Paul Pub. Schs., Minn., 1982-85; bd. dirs. United Cerebral Palsy of Minn. Mem. Endocrine Soc., Am. Soc. Zoologist, Am. Physiol. Soc., Am. Soc. Study Cell Biology. Democrat. Roman Catholic. Home: 2053 Dayton Ave Saint Paul MN 55104 Office: Research Service VA Med Center 54th

WILSON, MYRON FRANK, electronics company executive; b. Cleve., Oct. 18, 1924; s. Maransus Frank and Nettie Mae (Bean) W.; m. Esther June Secor, Aug. 5, 1950; children—M. Frank, Eric L., Joyce A., Rebecca J. B.S. in Mech. Engring., Case Inst. Tech., 1947, B.S.E.E., 1951, B.S. in Engring. Adminstrn., 1951. Registered profl. engr., Iowa, Ohio; cert. mfg. engr., quality engr. Various prodn. and engring. positions Collins Radio Co., Cedar Rapids, Iowa, 1951-73, v.p. mfg., 1973-75; dir. quality assurance Rockwell Internat., Dallas, 1975-77, dir. product assurance, Cedar Rapids, 1977-81, dir. group ops. Avionics Group, 1981—. Served with USN, 1944-46. Fellow Am. Soc. Quality Control (chmn. electronics div. 1983—, bd. dirs. 1970-72); mem. Inst. Indsl. Engrs. (v.p. region 11 1983-85, exec. v.p. chpt. ops. 1985—, trustee 1983—, sr. mem.), IEEE (sr. mem.). Congregationalist. Club: Collins Mgmt. (pres. 1984—). Lodge: Kiwanis (bd. dirs. 1983—). Home: 4221 Trailridge Rd SE Cedar Rapids IA 52403 Office: Rockwell Internat Avionics Group 400 Collins Rd NE Cedar Rapids IA 52498

WILSON, R. V., JR., state educational administrator; b. Omaha, Ark., Mar. 19, 1926; s. R.V. and Dorothy Mae (Varner) W.; m. Leona Cox, July 2, 1945; children—Barbara, Janene, Brenda, Keith, Melody. B.A., Ouachita Bapt. U., Arkadelphia, Ark., 1960; M.Ed., Lincoln U., Jefferson City, Mo., 1970. Cert. elem., secondary prin. and tchr., Mo. Elem. tchr. Jessieville Sch., Ark., 1958-59; secondary tchr. Cole RV Sch., Eugene, Mo., 1960-63, prin., 1964-67, dir. tchr. edn. Mo. State Dept. Edn., Jefferson City, 1967—. Contbr. articles to profl. jours. Retreat guide Central Mo Alcoholics Anonymous, Lake of the Ozarks, 1981, 82, 83; counselor Rawleigh Hills Hosp. Drug Abuse Ctr., Jefferson City, 1983. Served to staff sgt. USAF, 1944-46, ETO. Mem. Mo. State Tchrs. Assn., Mo. Assn. Colls. Tchr. Edn., Am. Assn. Tchr. Educators (Mo. unit Educator of Yr. award 1984). Republican. Baptist. Home: Route 2 Box 127 Holts Summit MO 65043 Office: Mo State Dept Edn 515 East High St PO Box 480 Jefferson City MO 65102

WILSON, ROBERT M., accountant, lawyer; b. St. Louis, Aug. 10, 1952; s. William H. and Mary E. (Sacksteder) W.; m. Joli Schneeberger, Oct. 7, 1978. B.S., Miami U. Oxford, Ohio, 1974; J.D. magna cum laude, Cleve. State U., 1977. Bar: Ohio 1977; C.P.A., Ohio. With Touche Ross & Co., Dayton, Ohio, 1972—, tax ptnr., 1983—; sec., treas. Inst. for Study of Corp. Responsibility. Pres. Friends of Dayton Ballet, Inc.; mem. fin. com. Dayton Ballet Assn.; treas. Downtown Dayton Assn., Leadership Dayton; Montgomery County Rep. Party. Mem. ABA (chmn. com.), Ohio Bar Assn., Dayton Bar Assn., Ohio Soc. C.P.A.s (pres.). Republican. Club: Dayton Racquet. Home: 6 Lookout Dr Dayton OH 45409 Office: Touche Ross & Co 1700 Courthouse Plaza NE Dayton OH 45402

WILSON, RUDOLPH SHAFFNER, educational administrator; b. Indpls., Dec. 21, 1932; s. Mattie Wilson; m. Corrie Wilson, Aug. 26, 1960; 1 child, Rudolph, Jr. B.S. in Edn., Ball State U., 1956, MA. in Edn., 1963; DEd., Ind. U., 1976. Dean of boys, tchr. Indpls. Pub. Schs., 1956-68; doctoral student, grad. asst. Ind. U., Bloomington, 1975-76; secondary prin. Met. Sch. Dist. of Wash. Twp., Indpls., 1969-75, adminstrv. asst. to supt., 1976-80, prin., secondary, 1980—; coll. instr. Butler U., Indpls., 1976-78; ednl. cons., Indpls., 1976—. Chmn. ARC, Indpls., 1962-67; mem. Young Republicans, 1980, Community Improvement Bd., 1982. Recipient Grade Tchrs. scholarship Indpls. Pub. Schs., 1954. Served with U.S. Army, 1977-79. Mem. Nat. Assn. of Secondary Prins., Ind. Assn. of Secondary Prins., Indpls. Jr. C. of C., Epsilon Pi Tau, Phi Delta Kappa, Kappa Alpha Psi (pres. 1953-55). Republican. Baptist. Club: Republican (Indpls.). Avocations: bowling; golf; travel. Home: 6150 Munsee Ln Indianapolis IN 46208 Office: North View Middle Sch 8401 Westfield Blvd Indianapolis IN 46240

WILSON, SHARON KAY, planning consulting company executive; b. Floyd County, Ind., Mar. 4, 1946; d. Heber and Norma A. (Turner) W.; student Ind. U., 1971-75, Ind.U.-Southeast, 1981-83. Public adminstrn. specialist Kentuckiana Regional Planning and Devel. Agy., Louisville, 1975-76; exec. dir. Clark County Regional Planning Bd., Jeffersonville, Ind., 1976-78; pres., chmn. bd. S.K. Wilson Assos., Inc., Sellersburg, Ind., 1976—. Pres., Clark County (Ind.) Parks and Recreation Bd., 1979, bd. dirs., 1976-79; organizer Interlocal San. Sewer Commn., Clark County, 1977; bd. dirs. designee Kentuckiana Regional Planning and Devel. Agy., 1976-79; mgmt. cons. Clark County Regional Planning Bd., 1977-79; public adminstrn. cons. Kentuckiana Regional Planning and Devel. Agy., 1976-77. Recipient Cert. of Appreciation, Clark County Superior Ct., 1970. Mem. Nat. Park and Recreation Assn., Am. Planning Assn., Clark County C. of C. (bd. dirs. 1984-87), Womens Polit. Caucus, Ind. Planning Assn. (bd. dirs. 1975-77), Ind. Park and Recreation Assn. Home: 2307 Allentown Rd Sellersburg IN 47172 Office: 506 E Utica St Sellersburg IN 47172

WILSON, STEPHEN CURTIS, public relations specialist; b. Peoria, Ill., Aug. 10, 1954; s. Eugene Taylor and Mary Elizabeth (Curtis) W. A.A., Ill. Central Coll., 1978-80. Pub. relations dir. Peoria Pub. Library, 1980—; free lance pub. relations Graphic Design Works, Washington, Ill., 1982—; exhibited watercolor, pastels and collage throughout state. Bd. dirs. C. of C. Leadership Council, 1982—. Mem. Pub. Relations Assn. (v.p. 1983-84), Internat. Assn. Bus. Communicators, ALA. Home: 56 U Georgetown Rd Washington IL 61571 Office: Peoria Pub Library 107 NE Monroe St Peoria IL 61602

WILSON, THOMAS ADAMS, writer, consultant; b. Providence, Apr. 22, 1938; s. Arthur Edward and Mabel Blakesley (Peabody) W.; m. Anne Irving, Sept. 10, 1960 (div.); children—John Douglass, Debby, Peter North. Student Coll. Cevenol, France, 1956, Christian Coll., India, 1956; B.A., Earlham Coll., Richmond, Ind., 1961; M.A., Howard U., 1965; Ed.D., Harvard U., 1970. English tchr., Washington pub. schs., 1963-65; asst. prof. edn. research in urban edn. U. Ill., Chgo., 1969-71; founder, pres. Ctr. for New Schs., Chgo., 1971-79; pres. Cambium Inc., Chgo., 1979—; bd. dirs. Ctr. New Schs., Chgo., 1971-79; cons. to sch. systems, Worcester, Mass., Newton, Iowa, Cleveland Heights, Ohio, others, 1970—; planner Metro High Sch., Chgo.; cons. devel. Englewood Learning Ctr., Chgo., 1981—, other agys. writer. Sec. Neighborhood Com Mayor's Transition Task Force, 1983; mem. policy com. Ctr. Neighborhood Tech., 1982—. Cert. fund raiser. Mem. Nat. Soc. Fund Raising Execs. Writer on not for profit agys., pub. schs. research and policy, relation of service agys. to communities, descriptions of not-for-profit human service orgns.; contbr. articles to profl. jours.

WILSON, THOMAS EDWARD, environmental engineer; b. Chgo., Feb. 20, 1942; s. David and Annabelle Pauline (Thompson) W.; m. Cheryl Ann Wegener, June 11, 1966; children—Christopher, Scott. B.S. in Chem. Engring., Northwestern U., 1964, M.S. in Environ. Engring., 1967; Ph.D., Ill. Inst. Tech., 1969. Registered profl. engr., Ill., Ind. diplomate Am. Acad. Environ. Engring. Asst. prof. Rutgers U., New Brunswick, N.J., 1967-70; prin. process engr. Greeley and Hansen, Chgo., 1970—, assoc., 1976—. Contbr. articles to profl. jours. Mem. Water Pollution Control Fedn., Am. Water Works Assn., Internat. Assn. for Water Pollution Research, Am. Inst. Chem. Engrs., ASCE. Episcopalian. Home: 1527 E Fleming Dr S Arlington Heights IL 60004 Office: Greeley and Hansen 222 S Riverside Plaza Chicago IL 60606

WILSON, W. IRA, research chemist, engineer; b. Pickens County, Ala., Jan 6, 1940; s. Ira Lee and Bessie Mae (Wilson) W.; m. Doris Jones; children—Henry, Valeria, Christopher. B.S. Ala. A&M U., 1961; M.S., U. Notre Dame, 1971, Ph.D., 1976; postgrad., N.C. Agrl. & Tech. State U., 1964-65. Tchr. pub. schs., Hale County, Ala., 1961-64, Tuscaloosa County, Ala., 1965-73; research chemist, engr. Argonne Nat. Lab. (Ill.), 1973—; instr. Stillman Coll., Tuscaloosa, 1971-73. Election judge, 1978-82. Mem. Am. Inst. of Chem. Engrs., Nat. Orgn. for the Profl. Advancement of Black Chemists and Chem.

Engrs., N.Y. Acad. Scis., Sigma Xi, Alpha Phi Alpha. A.M.E. Ch. Office: 11 S 336 Seeley Ave Lemont IL

WILSON, WILLIS A., JR., state appraiser; b. Cimarron, Kans., May 1, 1934; s. Willis A. and Iva Irene (Sells) W.; m. Mary Jo Crick, June 6, 1954; children—Terry Dwane, Meredith Sue. B.S., Okla. State U., 1956. Cert. assessor evaluator. Engring. draftsman Douglas Aircraft Tulsa, 1956, Chance Vaught Aircraft, Dallas, 1957; v.p., gen. mgr. Wilson Lumber Co. Inc., Cimarron, Kans., 1957-67; project mgr. Roy C. Houston Appraisal Co., Dodge City, Kans., 1967-69; property appraiser Div. Property Valuation, Kans. Dept. Revenue, Topeka, 1969-72, edn. coordinator, 1977—; supr. Kans. Assessed Public Utilities, 1972-77; treas. Indsl. Problem Solvers, Inc.; pres. Wilson Real Estate Mgmt. Co., Wilson Investment Co., Nat. Appraisal Service. Served with U.S. Army Res., 1955-57. Mem. Am. Soc. Appraisers (sr. mem., state dir., past pres. Topeka chpt.), Kans. County Appraisers Assn. (assoc.), Cert. Kans. Assessors (dir. 1972-77), Internat. Assoc. Assessing Officers, Am. Inst. Real Estate Appraisers (residential mem.). Mem. Christ's Church. Clubs: Rotary; Odd Fellow. Home: 3031 S E Starlite Topeka KS 66605 Office: 526 S State Office Bldg 10th and Topeka Topeka KS 66625

WILSON-KENNEDY, RUTH ANN, marketing and management educator, consultant; b. Delaware, Ohio, Nov. 20, 1944; d. Horace Henry and Fern Jeanette (Dutt) Wilson; 1 dau., Wendi Sue (dec.). B.S. Bowling Green State U., 1966. Sales clk., sec. acct. various firms, 1959-65; distributive edn. coordinator, Newark and Sandusky Pub. Sch. Systems; 1966-69; instr., student activities dir. Marion (Ohio) Tech. Coll., 1971-78, mktg., mgmt. coordinator, acting dir. bus. techs., coop. edn. coordinator, 1971-78; cons. advt., indsl and banking firms, 1975-79; part-time instr. Ownes Tech. Community Coll., Monroe County Community Coll., Toledo U., Marion Tech. Coll., 1978-83; adv. bd. gifted programs Toledo Pub. Sch. System, 1978-79; edn!. adv. Am. Motors Corp. Encore Challenge, 1983; research adv. Ohio Jaycees, 1983. Recipient Innovative Mid-Mgmt. Edn. award Nat. Assn. Mktg.-Mgmt. Educators, 1975. Mem. Nat. Assn. Mktg.-Mgmt Educators (chmn. bd. 1982, v.p. bus. and industry (1983).

WILTSE, DORR NORMAN, insurance executive; b. Caro, Mich., Sept. 20, 1911; s. Norman Anson and Evie Markham (McCartney) W.; student Eastern Mich. U., 1931-33; teaching cert. Central Mich. U., 1933-37; m. Gladys May Garner, Nov. 11, 1932; children—Dorr Norman, Saire Christina. Tchr., Tuscola County (Mich.) Public Schs., 1931-42; br. mgr. Mich. Mut. Ins. Co., Caro, 1942-75; city assessor, Caro, 1964—, also casualty ins. cons., Caro, 1975-79. Vice pres. Caro Devel. Corp., 1975-79, pres., 1983—; adv. bd. DeMolay Found. of Mich., 1965-67; founder, pres. Watrousville-Caro Area Hist. Soc., 1972-75, 78; pres. Caro Hist. Commn., 1975-79; chmn. bd. Caro Community Hosp. Endowment Found., 1982—; chmn. Caro Bicentennial Commn., 1975-76; mem. Com. to Elect Pres. Gerald R. Ford, 1975-76; mem. Indianfields-Caro-Almer Planning Commn., 1972-79. Named Citizen of Yr., Caro C. of C., 1975. Mem. Mich. Assessors Assn., Caro Masonic Bldg. Assn., Inc. (pres. 1974-79), Nat. Trust Hist. Preservation, Nat. Hist. Soc., Hist. Soc. Mich., Huguenot Soc. Mich., Saginaw Geneal. Soc., Mich. Archaeol. Soc. Democrat. Presbyterian (elder). Clubs: Caro Lions (pres. 1946), Mich. Mut. Quarter Century, Masons (past master), Shriners. Author: The First Hundred Years, 1978; The Hidden Years of the Master, 1976; The Wiltse Saga, 1980; A Look in Your Own Backyard, 1983. Home: 708 W Sherman St Box 143 Caro MI 48723 Office: 247 S State St Caro MI 48723

WIMER, CONNIE, publisher; b. Merrill, Iowa, Oct. 28, 1932; d. Horace Allen and Irene (Carey) Horton; m. William Wimer, Nov. 3, 1954; children—Amy, Carey, Annabel. Student Morningside Coll., 1951. Pres. Iowa Title Co., Des Moines, 1976—; pub. Bus. Record, Des Moines, 1981—, Skywalker, Des Moines, 1983—; dir. West Des Moines State Bank; mem. small bus. adv. bd. Fed. Res. Bank, Chgo., 1985. Mem. Tax Study Com. Iowa, Des Moines, 1984; mem. small bus. adv. council Iowa Devel. Commn., Des Moines, 1984—; mem. adv. council Region VII SBA, Des Moines, 1983—; bd. dirs. Conv. Bur., Des Moines, 1981—; bd. dirs., exec. com. YWCA. Named Woman of Achievement, YWCA, 1983, Person of Yr., Beta Sigma, 1982, Media Adviser of Yr., SBA, 1984, Small Bus. Adviser of Yr., 1980; recipient Employers Golden Key award Bus. and Profl. Women, 1984. Mem. Greater Des Moines C. of C. (vice chmn.). Office: 516 3d St Des Moines IA 50309

WIMMER, MYRON JOSEPH, architect; b. Chgo., May 7, 1935; s. Myron Joseph and Estelle Helen (Bielat) W.; m. Louise Helen Peters, Sept. 10, 1960; children—April, Laura, Monica, Celeste, Myron, III, Jonathon. B. Arch., U. Ill., 1963. Lic. architect, Ill., Cole. Archtl. draftsman Tigerman and Koglin, Chgo., 1963; project mgr. Harry Weese, Chgo., 1964-65, C.F. Murphy & Assoc., Chgo., 1966-67, Graham Anderson, Probst & White, Chgo., 1967-72; pres. M.J. Wimmer & Assoc., Ltd., Architects-Planners, Elmhurst, Ill., 1972—; tchr. design Harper Coll., YMCA Jr. Coll., Chgo. Past chmn. Riverside Hist. Commn., 1972-82. Served with USMC, 1956-58. Recipient Koppers Archtl. Design award, 1963; ARA Design award merit, 1982, Lighting award Lighting Inst., 1981, 82. Mem. Am. Registered Architects, AIA. Republican. Roman Catholic. Club: Internat. Lions. Home: 180 Parkview Rd Riverside IL 60546 Office: 100 S York Rd Elmhurst IL 60126

WINDECKER, LOUIS EDWIN, pharmaceutical executive, pharmacist; b. Hackensack, N.J., Nov. 12, 1931; s. William and Louise Anna (Manss) W.; m. Eleanor J. Steed, Mar. 20, 1955; children—Deborah, Cynthia, Louis Jr., Marilyn. A.A. in Humanities, George Washington U., 1952, B.S. in Pharmacy, 1955. Registered pharmacist, Ill., Ind., N.J., Mass. Supr. Warner-Lambert, Morris Plains, N.J., 1955-57; supt. mfg. Revlon, Edison, N.J., 1957-70; dir. ops. Textron-Speidel, Newark, 1970-72; Astra Pharm., Worcester, Mass., 1972-74; asst. v.p. ops. Whitehall Labs., Hammonton, N.J., 1974-82; v.p. ops. Miles Sci. div. Miles Labs., Naperville, Ill., 1982—. Vice-pres. Ridgefield Park Bd. Edn., N.J., 1960-64; commr. pub. works, Ridgefield Park, 1964-68; commr. human relations City Commn. Govt., Elkhart, Ind., 1976-78. Recipient Industry award of Yr., Hammonton C. of C., 1980. Mem. Soc. Cosmetic Chemists, Am. Pharm. Assn. Republican. Episcopalian. Club: John Purdue. Lodges: Optimists (bd. dirs. 1976-78), Lions (sec. 1979-82), Elks. Avocations: college football; horseback riding; gardening; public service. Home: 901 Hidden Lake Rd Naperville IL 60565 Office: Miles Labs 2000 N Aurora Rd Naperville IL 60566

WINDHAM, JAMES HAROLD, army officer; b. Cisco, Tex., Dec. 5, 1950; s. Joe Higdon and Dorothy Marie (Ray) W.; B.A. in Polit. Sci., U. Tex., 1973; M.S. in Logistics Mgmt., Fla. Inst. Tech., 1978. Commd. 2d lt. U.S. Army, 1973; advanced through grades to capt., 1977; service support platoon leader, Ft. Campbell, Ky., 1973-75, co. comdr., personnel mgr., 1975-76; stock and inventory control officer, Camp Darby, Pisa, Italy, 1979-82; systems designer automated worksta. environ., St. Louis, 1982—. Decorated Army Commendation medal, others. Mem. Ch. of Christ. Office: ALMSA 210 Tucker St Saint Louis MO 63188

WINDHORST, TODD EDWARD, aerospace company executive; b. Pitts., June 18, 1950; s. Walter Theodore and Dorothy Agnes (Keating) W.; m. Merrylou Hurt, July 17, 1976; children—Brian Thomas, Mary Kristin. B.B.A., U. Pitts., 1974. Tool and die maker apprentice Westinghouse Electric Corp., East Pittsburg, Pa., 1968-72, tool and die maker, 1972-76; chief inspector Ohio Nuclear, Inc., Solon, 1976-77, buyer mech. parts, 1977-79; sr. buyer tooling Goodyear Aerospace Corp., Akron, Ohio, 1979—, adminstr. socio-econ. program, 1985—. Mem. Nat. Assn. Purchasing Mgmt., Internat. Union Elec. Workers (div. steward 1972-76). Republican. Roman Catholic. Avocations: golf; bowling; running. Home: 274 Dorchester Rd Akron OH 44313 Office: Goodyear Aerospace Corp 1210 Massillon Rd Akron OH 44315

WINDLE, JOHN TAYLOR, museum director; b. West Lafayette, Ind., June 13, 1901; s. Allen Jay and Pearl Binford (Taylor) W.; m. Ann Steinbrecher, Apr. 17, 1937. A.B., U. Ill., 1925; M.A., U. Chgo., 1942; LL.D. (hon.), Hanover Coll., 1976. Reference asst. Newberry Library, Chgo., 1928-29, chief reference librarian, head of research, 1930-48; owner, dir. Shrewsbury House Mus., Madison, Ind., 1948—; founder Hist. Madison, Inc., 1960, pres., 1960-81, emeritus, 1981—; restorer hist. bldgs., Madison, 1948-73; cons. hist. preservation. Mem. exec. bd. Chgo. Civic Music Assn., 1946-48, pres., 1947-48; pres. Madison-Jefferson County Community Council, 1952-54; dir. Madison-Jefferson County Pub. Library, 1955-79. Recipient Community Service award Madison Area C. of C., 1964, citation for archtl. restoration Ind. U., 1975, Don E. Gibson Meml. award Ind. Soc. Architects, 1975, 1st Guardian of Our Heritage award Jefferson County Hist. Soc., 1982; inducted to Ind. Acad., 1978, Sagamore of the Wabash, 1981. Mem. Nat. Trust for Hist. Preservation (bd. advisers Ind. sect. 1973-79; Honor award 1984), Hist. Landmarks Found. Ind. (bd. dirs. 1972-80, adv. council, 1980—), Ind. Hist. Soc. (bd. dirs. 1972-81), Ind. Library Trustees Assn. (bd. dirs. 1955-56, 66-67). Republican. Quaker. Clubs: Caxton, Cliff Dwellers (Chgo.); Indpls. Athletic; Madison Country. Address: Shrewsbury House 301 W 1st St Madison IN 47250

WINE, RAYMOND LISLE, hospital administrator; b. Oelwein, Iowa, Feb. 26, 1925; s. George A. and Gladys E. (Lisle) W.; m. Winnifred L. Anderson, Apr. 14, 1946; children—Pamela Rae, David Allan. B.S. in Acctg., Drake U., 1950. Bus. mgr. Freeport Meml. Hosp., Ill., 1950-55, asst. adminstr., 1955, acting adminstr., 1955-56, chief exec. officer, 1956—; pres. Freeport Health Care Found., 1984—. Served with USN, 1943-46. Recipient Young Man of Yr. award Jr. C. of C., 1959. Mem. Am. Coll. Hosp. Adminstrs., Ill. Hosp. Assn. (council legis. affairs 1984-85, council on nursing 1978, council on human resources 1978-81, council on shared services 1982-83), Freeport C. of C. (past pres., past bd. dirs.), Stephenson County Mental Health Assn. (bd. dirs.). Club: Freeport Country. Lodges: Masons (consistory), Rotary (past pres., past bd. dirs.). Avocations: golf; bowling. Home: 1452 S Demeter Dr Freeport IL 61032 Office: Freeport Meml Hosp 1045 W Stephenson St Freeport IL 61032

WINEMILLER, JAMES D., accountant; b. Sullivan, Ind., July 22, 1944; s. Floyd Maurice and Doris Marie (Lone) W.; A.S., Vincennes U., 1964; B.S., Ind. U., 1966, M.B.A., 1967; m. Nancy Kay Walters, Aug. 10, 1963; 1 dau., Nancy Marie. Accountant, Peat, Marwick, Mitchell & Co., C.P.A.s, Honolulu, 1967-71; with Blue & Co., C.P.A.s, Indpls., 1971—, partner-in-charge, 1974-76, mng. partner, 1977—. Grad. teaching asst. dept. accounting Ind. U., Bloomington, 1966-67; instr. accounting Coll. Gen. Studies, U. Hawaii, Honolulu, 1968-69; dir. Poland State Bank (Ind.), 1974-75. Mem. state adv. com. Vincennes U. Recipient Gold Medal for highest grades in state on C.P.A. examination, State Ind., 1966; Elizah Watt Sells Nat. Honorable Mention award, 1966. C.P.A., Ind., Hawaii; Vincennes U. Found. fellow. Mem. Am. Inst. C.P.A.s, Ind. C.P.A. Soc. (dir. 1980—, treas. 1981-82, exec. com. 1983—, pres.-elect 1984-85, pres. 1985-86), Ind. C.P.A. Ednl. Found. (life), Hawaii Soc. C.P.A.s, Continental Assn. C.P.A. Firms (dir. 1978—, v.p. 1982-83, pres. 1983-84), Nat. Assn. Accountants, Am. Acctg. Assn., Ind. U. Well House Soc., Ind. U. Bus. Sch. Deans Assn. (sr), Ind. U. Alumni Assn. (life), Ind. U. Varsity-Hoosier Hundred, Vincennes U. Alumni Assn. (life). Methodist. Clubs: Rotary (dir. 1973-75, 84—, v.p. 1984-85, pres. 1974-75, Paul Harris fellow), Indpls. Columbia, Indpls. Econ., Hillcrest Country. Home: 9242 Whitehall Ct Indianapolis IN 46256 Office: 6609 E 82d St PO Box 50920 Indianapolis IN 46250

WING, JOHN FISKE, psychologist, educator, researcher, psychotherapist, consultant; b. Detroit, Sept. 10, 1931; s. Forrest Bond and Margaret Williams (Haddock) W.; m. Rachelle Ehrlich, Mar. 29, 1955; children—Amy, Leah, Jesse; m. 2d, Sandra Kay Painter, May 23, 1978; 1 son, John. A.B., Antioch Coll., 1954, M.A., 1961; Ph.D., Ohio State U., 1966. Lic. psychologist, Ohio. Asst. dir. Behavior Research Lab., Antioch Coll., Yellow Springs, Ohio, 1958-61; research psychologist Aerospace Med. Lab., Wright-Patterson Air Force Base, Dayton, Ohio, 1961-66; asst. prof. psychology Wright State U., Dayton, 1966-69; prof. psychology Wittenberg U., Springfield, Ohio, 1969—; research dir. Mental Health Services Clark County, 1971-79; cons. Dow Chem. Co., 1967-69. Served with U.S. Army, 1955-57. Recipient Matthies award Wittenberg U., 1982. Mem. Am. Psychol. Assn. (J.P. Guilford award 1964), AAAS (life), Ohio Acad. Sci. (life), Sigma Xi (life). Contbr. chpts. to books, articles to profl. jours. Office: Wittenberg U PO Box 720 Springfield OH 45501

WINKLE, CHARLES EDWARD, educator; b. Cin., Dec. 19, 1949; s. Gerald N. and Lorena Belle (Carrington) W.; m. Donna Jean Crawford, Dec. 3, 1971; children—Matthew Jared, Mark Edward, Rebecca Mae. B.Sc., Ohio State U., 1971, M.Sc., 1978. Tchr. vocat. agr. Blanchester (Ohio) High Sch., 1971—, agr. edn. coordinator; salesman Donald E. Fender Realtors, Hillsboro, Ohio, 1978-81, Ray Houk Realty, 1981—; cons. agr. mgmt.; mem. del. People to People Citizen Ambassadors of Agr. to China, 1985. Named Outstanding Young Tchr. of Ohio, 1977. Mem. Ohio Vocat. Agr. Tchrs. Assn. (Tchr. of Tchrs. 1984, life mem.), Nat. Vocat. Agr. Tchrs. Assn. (life mem.), Am. Vocat. Assn., Ohio Vocat. Assn., Ohio State U. Alumni Assn., Am. Farm Bur. Fedn., Am. Soybean Assn., Ohio Young Farmers Assn. (advisor), Nat. Future Farmers Assn. Alumni (advisor), Ohio State Tractor Pullers Assn., Nat. Tractor Pullers Assn. Contbr. articles to profl. jours.

WINOKUR, GEORGE, psychiatrist; b. Phila., Feb. 10, 1925; s. Louis and Vera P. W.; A.B., Johns Hopkins U., 1944; M.D., U. Md., 1947; m. Betty Stricklin, Sept. 15, 1951; children—Thomas, Kenneth, Patricia. Intern, Ch. Home and Hosp., Balt., 1947-48; resident Seton Inst., Balt., 1948-50, Barnes Hosp., Washington U. Sch. Medicine, 1950-51, St. Louis, research asso. Washington U., asst. prof. psychiatry, 1955-59, asso. prof., 1959-66, prof., 1966-71; prof., head dept. psychiatry U. Iowa, 1971—. Served as capt. USAF, 1952-54. Recipient 1st prize award Anna Monika Stiftung, 1973; Paul Hoch award, 1981; Gold Medal award Soc. Biol. Psychiatry, 1984; diplomate Am. Bd. Psychiatry and Neurology. Mem. Psychiat. Research Soc., Am. Psychiat. Assn. (Hofheimer prize 1972), Am. Fedn. Clin. Research, Am.Psychopathol. Assn. (pres. 1977, Samuel W. Hamilton award 1977), Am. Soc. Human Genetics, Internat. Group for Study Affective Disorders, Am. Acad. Clin. Psychiatrists, Am. Assn. Chmn. Depts. Psychiatry, Iowa Psychiat. Soc. Author: Manic Depressive Illness, 1969; Determinants of Human Sexual Behavior, 1974; Depression: The Facts, 1981; contbr. numerous articles to profl. jours.; editor Jour. Affective Disorders, 1978—; editorial bd. Archives Gen. Psychiatry, 1975—, Neuropsychobiology, 1975—, Comprehensive Psychiatry, 1977—, Jour. Affective Disorders, 1980—. Office: U Iowa Coll Medicine Dept Psychiatry 500 Newton Rd Iowa City IA 52242

WINSLOW, ALFRED AKERS, retired government official; b. Gary, Ind., June 16, 1923; s. Harry Wendell and Lenora (Allen) W.; A.A., Wilson Jr. Coll., 1964; B.B.A., Northwestern U., 1969; m. Maud Esther Franklin, Jan. 15, 1954. With Chgo. Post Office, 1947-66; with U.S. Postal Service, Chgo. Central Region, 1967-83, dir. Office Employee Relations, 1973-83. Ptnr., Winslow's Apparel Shop, Chgo., 1954-66. Mem. adv. com. on human relations City of Chgo., 1969-73; pres. Cheryl Condominium, Chgo., 1965-67, Evans-Langley Neighborhood Club, Chgo., 1960-64; chmn. Post Office Bd. U.S. Civil Service Examiners Ill., Mich., 1967-71. Served with USCGR, 1943-46. Recipient Outstanding Achievement award, Chgo. Assn. Commerce and Industry, 1969, 70, 68; Great Guy award, Radio Sta. WGRT, 1969. Mem. Northwestern U. Bus. Honor Soc., NAACP bd. dirs. 1968-83), Soc. Personnel Adminstrn., Indsl. Relations Assn. Chgo., Am. Legion, Field Mus. Natural History, Chgo. Art Inst., Lyric Opera, Chgo. Ednl. TV Assn., Northwestern U. Alumni Assn.

WINSTEIN, STEWART ROBERT, lawyer; b. Viola, Ill., May 28, 1924; s. Abram and Esther (Meyer) W.; A.B., Augustana Coll., 1935; J.D., U. Chgo., 1938; m. Dorothy Shock Adams, Nov. 2, 1960; 1 son, Arthur. Bar: Ill. 1939. Sr. ptnr. Winstein, Kavensky, Wallace & Doughty, Rock Island, Ill., 1966—. Fin. officer State of Ill., 1963-70; del. Democratic Nat. Conv., 1968, 72, Mid-Term Conf., 1974, 78; committeeman Dem. State Central Com., 1970—; vice chmn. Ill. Dem. State Central Com., 1973—; public adminstr. Rock Island County, 1974-78; mem. Met. Airport Commn. Trustee, Marycrest Coll. Mem. Rock Island County Bar Assn., Ill. Bar Assn., Am. Bar Assn., Chgo. Bar Assn., Assn. Trial Lawyers Am. Jewish. Club: Elks. Home: 3535 24th St Rock Island IL 61201 Office: PO Box 428 4th Floor Rock Island Bank Bldg Rock Island IL 61201

WINTER, ALISON A., bank investment executive; b. Omaha, June 16, 1946; d. Robert Kenneth and Kathleen Lenore (McCaffrey) Adams; m. Joseph Earl Winter, Apr. 25, 1970; children—Leigh Adams, John Adams. B.A., San Francisco Coll. for Women, 1968; M.B.A., U. Chgo., 1975. Chartered fin. analyst. Investment officer No. Trust Co., Chgo., 1973-77, 2d v.p., 1977-80, v.p., 1980—, div. head, 1982-84, dept. head bank investment mgmt. service, 1984—. Mem. antique show com. Community House, Hinsdale, Ill., 1979-80; bd. dirs. Family Shelter Service, Glen Ellyn, Ill., 1983. Mem. Investment Analysts Soc. Chgo. (v.p. 1983-84, pres. 1984-85). Clubs: Metropolitan, River (Chgo.). Home: 625 W Hickory Hinsdale IL 60521 Office: No Trust Co 50 S LaSalle St Chicago IL 60675

WINTER, JOHN ALEXANDER, realtor, real estate appraiser; b. Cin., July 2, 1935; s. George Edward and Mary Alma (McAuliffe) W. BS., Georgetown U., 1957. Ptnr. Winter & Winter, Cleve., 1957-76; residential salesman Moreland Hills Co., Chagrin Falls, Ohio, 1976-77; residential appraiser Kiebler, Smith & Co., Chardon, Ohio, 1977—; v.p., dir. The Gas Pipe Co., Chagrin Falls, 1973—. Contbr. articles to profl. jours. Pres. New Eng. Soc. of Cleve. and Western Res., 1976-77, 83-84, Shaker Heights Republican Club, 1977-84; v.p., trustee Shaker Hist. Soc., 1985—; founder, pres. Cert. Appraisal Service Co., Shaker Heights, 1985—. Recipient Service award Pres. Ronald Reagan, 1984, New Eng. Heritage award New Eng. Soc., 1984. Mem. Cleve. Independance Day Assn. (v.p., trustee 1957—, Treharne award 1984), Am. Assn. Cert. Appraisers, Ohio Assn. Realtors, Nat. Assn. Realtors (Ben Franklin award 1983), Cathedral Latin Sch. Alumni Assn. (trustee 1965—). Roman Catholic. Clubs: Georgetown (pres. 1966-67); Cleve. of Washington (trustee 1984—). Avocations: tennis; sailing; coin collecting. Home: 19271 Shaker Blvd Shaker Heights OH 44122 Office: Cert Appraisal Service Co 19271 Shaker Blvd Shaker Heights OH 44122

WINTER, MAX, professional football team executive; b. Ostrava, Austria, June 29, 1904; s. Jacob and Bertha (Ruker) W.; came to U.S., 1913, naturalized, 1920; student Hamline U., 1925-26, U. Chgo., 1927; m. Helen Horovitz, Dec. 5, 1939; children—Susan (Mrs. Robert Diamond), Nancy (Mrs. Dennis Ditlove), Diane (Mrs. Richard Cohen). Co-owner, gen. mgr. Mpls. Lakers Basketball Team, 1947-56; originator Minn. Vikings (Nat. Football League), Mpls., 1960, pres., 1960—; chmn. bd., dir. Viking Enterprises; pres. Max Winter Enterprises, Max Winter Enterprises Hawaii; dir. Downtown Bank St. Paul, Bank of Mpls. Mem. County Park Bd., 1959-64; chmn. Muscular Dystrophy, 1961; mem. Gov.'s Bus. Adv. Com., 1965; chmn. Nat. Govs. Conf., 1965. Recipient Hon. Scout award, 1946, 47, 48. Mem. Mpls. C. of C. (v.p.). Jewish. Clubs: Optimists; Minneapolis Athletic; Oak Ridge Country, Waialae Country, Honolulu Internat. Country, Olympic Hills Country, Outrigger (Honolulu); Rotary. Author: Sports Books for Children, 1957. Office: care Minn Vikings 9520 Viking Dr Eden Prairie MN 55344*

WINTER, RICHARD LAWRENCE, financial and health care consulting company executive; b. St. Louis, Dec. 17, 1945; s. Melvin Lawrence and Kathleen Jane (O'Leary) W.; B.S. in Math., St. Louis U., 1967, M.S. in Math. (fellow), 1969; M.B.A., U. Mo., St. Louis, 1976; m. Pauline Alma Pardee, Nov. 10, 1984; children from previous marriage—Leigh Ellen, Jessica Marie. Research analyst Mo. Pacific R.R., St. Louis, 1971-73; dir. fin. relations Linclay Corp., St. Louis, 1973-74; asst. v.p. 1st Nat. Bank in St. Louis (name now Centerre Bank, N.A.), 1974-79; v.p. fin. UDE Corp., St. Louis, 1979-81; pres. Health Care Investments, Ltd., St. Louis, 1981—, Fin. & Investment Cons., Ltd., St. Louis, 1981; lectr. math. U. Mo.-St. Louis, 1972-74, St. Louis U., 1982—. Trustee, Mt. Vernon Hosp.; active various fund raising activities including St. Louis Symphony, Jr. Achievement, United Way St. Louis, Arts and Edn. Fund, St. Louis, 1974-79. Served with U.S. Army, 1969-71. Mem. Pi Mu Epsilon. Roman Catholic. Club: Mo. Athletic (St. Louis). Home: 1321 Green Tree Ln Saint Louis MO 63122 Office: PO Box 11586 Saint Louis MO 63105

WINTER, WINTON ALLEN, JR., lawyer, state senator; b. Ft. Knox, Ky., Apr. 19, 1953; s. Winton A. and Nancy (Morsbach) W.; m. Mary Boyd, July 28, 1978; children—Katie, Molly, Elizabeth. B.A., U. Kans., 1975, J.D., 1978. Bar: Kans. 1978. Ptnr. law firm Stevens, Brand, Lungstrum, Golden & Winter, Lawrence, Kans., 1978—; mem. Kans. Senate, 1982—. Bd. dirs. Lawrence United Fund, Boys Club of Lawrence. Mem. ABA, Am. Judicature Soc., Kans. Bar Assn., Douglas County Bar Assn. Kans. U. Law Soc. Republican. Roman Catholic. Club: Rotary. Note and comment editor Kans. Law Rev., 1977-78. Office: 502 First Nat Bank Tower PO Box 1200 Lawrence KS 66044

WINTERS, STEVEN PAUL, accountant; b. New Castle, Ind., Jan. 10, 1945; s. Paul Henry and Marguerite (Harcourt) W.; cert. in acctg. Ind. U., 1969; B.S., Ball State U., 1972; m. Roberta L. Rahn, 1981; 1 dau., Karen. Audit supr. Coopers & Lybrand, Indpls. and Ft. Wayne, Ind., 1972-77; corp. controller Oxford Devel. Corp., Indpls., 1977-80; real estate tax specialist Kern, Hall, Ford & Co., C.P.A.s, Indpls., 1980-81; founder Steven P. Winters, C.P.A., Inc., 1981—; co-founder Genesis Group, Inc., 1982—; co-developer Indpls. Downtown Heliport, 1985—. C.P.A., Ind. Mem. Am. Inst. C.P.A.s, Ind. C.P.A. Soc., Nat. Council Corvette Clubs. Republican. Mem. The Way Internat. Club: Toastmasters (past corr. sec.). Home: 5875 N Washington Blvd Indianapolis IN 46220 Office: 51 S New Jersey St Indianapolis IN 46204

WINTERS, THOMAS BERNARR, mechanical engineer, campground director; b. Ironton, Ohio, Sept. 18, 1931; s. Raymond Franklin and Adryenne Beryl (Lynd) W.; m. Dolores Jean Leis, Aug. 30, 1953. Student Franklin U. With Westinghouse Electric Co., Columbus, Ohio, 1956-69; with Westreco, Marysville, Ohio, 1969—, design engr., 1969—; owner, mgr. Winters Farm Campground, Raymond, Ohio, 1981—. Patentee icemaker, water delivery, defrost timer, and others. Served with USNR, 1949-59. Methodist. Office: 20267 SR 347 Raymond OH 43067

WINZENBURG, STEPHEN MARK, radio station executive; b. Mankato, Minn., Dec. 18, 1954; s. Frank Edward and Kathryn Helen (Trier) W.; m. Patricia Ann Liffrig, Dec. 20, 1981; children—Kathryn Frances, Mary Collette. B.A., U. S.D.; M.A. in Journalism, U. Minn. News dir. Sta. WCIE, Lakeland, Fla., 1977-80; prof. Fla. So. Coll., Lakeland, 1982-84, Marycrest Coll., Davenport, Iowa, 1984; dir. syndication Second Thoughts, Belleville, Ill., 1984-85; gen. mgr. Sta. KNDR, Bismarck, N.D., 1985—; corr. Internat. Media Service, Washington, 1977-80. Author: The Happy Homemaker Cookbook, 1978. Recipient Commendation award Am. Women in Radio and TV, 1985, Fla. News award AP, 1980, Enterprise award Enterprise Radio Network, 1978; named Citizen of Yr., Women for Responsible Legislation, 1980. Republican. Lodges: Kiwanis, Rotary. Office: Sta KNDR Radio 1400 3d St NE Mandan ND 58554

WIRTH, RICHARD MARVIN, educator; b. Grosse Pointe, Mich., Aug. 26, 1929; s. Marvin Oscar and Marion (Maxfield) W.; B.Sc., Wayne State U., 1950, M.A., 1952; postgrad. U. Wis., Western State Coll. Colo., Ball State Tchrs. Coll. Tchr. drama and debate Warren (Mich.) Consol. Schs., 1951—. Former organist and choir dir. St. John's Evang. United Ch. of Christ, lay minister, 1979; ordained minister of worship, 1982; former kapellmeister St. John-St. Luke United Ch. Christ; former master Co. of Lay Ministries. Mem. scholastic writing awards adv. com. SE Mich. Named Vol. of Week, United Found., 1963; recipient Silver Beaver award Boy Scouts Am., 1962; Disting. Educator award Mich. State Fair, 1964; Disting. Tchr. award Mich. Assn. Classroom Tchrs., 1969. Mem. Mich. (pres. dept. classroom tchrs., Tchr. of Yr. 1962, dir. area 6, parliamentarian 1972—, dir.), Ky. (parliamentarian 1974), Kans., Okla. (parliamentarian 1979—) Warren (editor Harbinger, past pres., sr. trustee) edn. assns., Mich. Student Congress (parliamentarian), Southfield Public Employees, Speech Assn. Am., Nat. Cath. Forensic League (parliamentarian 1979, 82), Nat. Council Tchrs. of English, Mich. League Credit Unions, Mich. League Practical Nurses (parliamentarian), Delta Sigma Rho. Editor of ednl. publs. Contbr. articles to profl. jours. Home: Box 283 Algonac MI 48001 Office: 5460 Arden St Warren MI 48092

WIRTZ, GERALD PAUL, engineering educator, consultant, researcher; b. Wisconsin Rapids, Wis., Dec. 22, 1937; s. Theodore Anton and Grace (Vincent) W.; m. Darlene Yvonne Haupt, June 3, 1961; children—Cynthia, Melissa, Lauralee. B.S., St. Norbert Coll., 1959; B.M.E., Marquette U., 1961; Ph.D. in Materials Sci., Northwestern U., 1966. Materials research scientist Airco Inc., Niagara Falls, N.Y., 1966-68; asst. prof. ceramic engring. U. Ill.-Urbana, 1968-73, asst. dean engring., 1973-74, assoc. prof. ceramic engring., 1973—; cons. Brookhaven Nat. Lab., L.I., N.Y., U.S. Army C.E., Mil. Inst. Engring., Rio de Janeiro. OAS fellow, 1977; Fulbright Hays lectr. U. Aveiro (Portugal), 1980; Fulbright lectr. U. Coimbra (Portugal), 1985. Mem. Am. Ceramic Soc., Keramos, Sigma Xi, Tau Beta Pi, Pi Tau Sigma. Roman Catholic. Patentee; contbr. articles to tech. jours. Home: Rural Route 2 Box 159 Urbana IL 61801 Office: 105 S Goodwin Ave Urbana IL 61801

WIRTZ, WILLIAM WADSWORTH, diversified investor; b. Chgo., Oct. 5, 1929; s. Arthur Michael and Virginia (Wadsworth) W.; A.B., Brown U., 1950; m. Joan Roney, Dec. 15, 1950; children—William R., Gail W., Karen K., Peter R., Alison M. Pres., Chgo. Blackhawk Hockey Team, Inc., 1966—, Chgo. Stadium Corp., 1966—, Consol. Enterprises, Inc., Chgo., 1966—, Forman Realty Corp., Chgo., 1965—, 333 Building Corp., Chgo., 1966—, Wirtz Corp., Chgo., 1964—. Clubs: Saddle and Cycle, Racquet, Mid-America (Chgo.); Sunset Ridge Country (Northbrook, Ill.); Fin and Feather (Elgin, Ill.). Home: Winnetka IL Office: 666 Lake Shore Dr Chicago IL 60611*

WISDOM, GUYRENA KNIGHT, psychologist, educator; b. St. Louis, July 27, 1923; d. Gladys Margaret (Hankins) McCullin; A.B., Stowe Tchrs. Coll.,

1945; A.M., U. Ill., 1951; postgrad. St. Louis U., Washington U., St. Louis, Fontbonne Coll., U. Mo., Harris Tchrs. Coll., U. Chgo., Drury Coll. Tchr. elementary sch. St. Louis Pub. Sch. System, 1945-63, psychol. examiner, 1963-68, sch. psychologist, 1968-74, cons. spl. edn., 1974-77, supr. spl. edn. dept., 1977-79, coordinator staff devel. div., 1979-81, on leave, 1981-83; pvt. tutor, 1971-72; sch. psychologist, 1984-85; free-lance psychologist, St. Louis, 1985—; instr. Harris Tchrs. Coll., St. Louis, 1973-74, Harris-Stowe Coll., 1979. Mem. Nat. Assn. Sch. Psychologists, Mo. Assn. Children with Learning Disabilities, Council for Exceptional Children, United Teaching Profession Orgn., NEA, Mo., St. Louis tchrs. assn., Pi Lambda Theta, Kappa Delta Pi. Roman Catholic. Author, editor works in field. Home: 5046 Wabada St Saint Louis MO 63113

WISE, DAVID GLENN, lawyer; b. Dayton, Ohio, Oct. 3, 1942; s. Glenn David and Mary (Dickey) W.; m. Patricia Klick, Aug. 13, 1966; children—Katherine, James, Amy. B.A., Wittenberg U., 1964; J.D., U. Mich., 1967. Bar: Ohio 1967, Mich. 1967, U.S. Supreme Ct. 1980. Ptnr. Spengler, Nathanson, Heyman, McCarthy & Durfee, Toledo, 1967—; dir. Westhaven Adminstrv. Corp. Mem. Perrysburg Bd. Edn., 1980—, pres., 1983. Mem. ABA, Ohio Bar Assn., Mich. Bar Assn., Toledo Bar Assn., Soc. Advancement of Mgmt., Tau Pi Phi. Republican. Lutheran. Club: Belmont Country. Lodge: Rotary. Avocations: golf; tennis; softball. Home: 924 Bexley Dr Perrysburg OH 43551 Office: Spengler Nathanson Heyman McCarthy & Durfee 1000 Nat Bank Bldg Toledo OH 43604

WISE, LELAND JOHN, JR., educational administrator; b. Geneva, N.Y., Sept. 26, 1944; s. Leland John and Julia Marie (Lancia) W.; m. Helen Wannetta Dahlen, Jan. 6, 1954; children—Shannon Marie, Lee Jackson, Zachary Dahlen. B.A., State Coll. Iowa, 1967; M.A., U. No. Iowa, 1970; Ph.D., U. Iowa, 1978. Cert. tchr., Iowa. Tchr., Decorah (Iowa) Jr. High Sch., 1967-68; tchr. LaSalle High Sch., Cedar Rapids, Iowa, 1968-69; grad. asst. dept. phys. edn. U. No. Iowa, Cedar Falls, 1969-70; instr. Muscatine (Iowa) Community Coll., 1970-71; tchr. Cedar Rapids Community Sch., 1971-75; cons. No. Trails A.E.A., Clear Lake, Iowa, 1975-76; prin. Latimer (Iowa) Elem./Middle Sch., 1976-79; prin. Marion (Iowa) High Sch., 1979-83; supt. Benton Community Schs., Van Horne, Iowa, 1983—; ednl. cons. Actice YMCA. Iowa Dept. Pub. Instrn. Title IV grantee, 1979. Mem. Assn. Supervision and Curriculum Devel., Am. Assn. Sch. Adminstrs., Rural Edn. Assn., Assn. Sch. Bus. Ofcls., Assn. Negotiators and Contract Adminstrs., Iowa Assn. Sch. Adminstrs. Iowa High Sch. Athletic Assn., Phi Delta Kappa. Roman Catholic. Clubs: Lions Internat., Optimists. Author book; contbr. article to profl. jour. Office: Central Adminstrn Bldg Van Horne IA 52346

WISE, WILMA MARK, credit bureau and employment agency executive; b. Frankfort, Ill., Mar. 13, 1926; d. Paul and Louise (Staedke) Mark; m. Perry Kenneth Wise, Sept. 5, 1948; children—Douglas Kent, Dennis Mark. Student, Met. Bus. Coll., 1943-44; grad. exec. devel. program Ind. U. Grad. Sch. Bus., 1975. Owner, ptnr. Naperville Credit Bur. (Ill.), 1958-70; gen. mgr., v.p. First Suburban Services, Naperville, 1970-75; pres., gen. mgr. Wise Suburban Services, Inc., divs. Snelling and Snelling, Wise Credit Bur., Wise Telephone Answering Service, Naperville, Ill., 1975—. Mem., pres. Naperville Dist. No. 203 Career Edn. Adv. Council, 1971—; mem. exec. com. North Central Coll. Community Fund Drive, 1980—, chmn., 1984-85; mem. exec. com. DuPage County Pvt. Industry Council, 1983—; 1st pres. Ill. Bus. Week, 1984. Recipient Woman of Achievement award Women in Mgmt., Oak Brook chpt., 1982; Internat. Key Leadership award Assoc. Credit Burs., 1979; named Boss of Year, Am. Bus. Women's Assn., 1979. Mem. Ill. Assn. Personnel Cons. (dir. 1976-81) Ill. Collector's Assn. (dir. 1982—, v.p. 1983-84, pres. 1985-86), Am. Collector's Assn., Internat. Fellowship Cert. Collectors, Associated Credit Burs. Inc. (award of excellence 1984), Associated Credit Burs. Ill. (dir. 1975—, pres. 1979-80), Women in Mgmt., Naperville C. of C. (dirs.), Downers Grove C. of C. (dirs. 1972-75), Naperville Organ Soc. Lutheran (mem. council 1978-84). Club: Cosmopolitan Dance (Naperville). Home: 7S410 Arbor Dr Naperville IL 60540 Office: 638-40 E Ogden Ave Twin Center Naperville IL 60540

WISHEK, MAX ALBERT, lawyer, banker; b. Ashley, N.D., Aug. 29, 1901; s. John Henry and Nina (Farley) W.; m. Viola Hezel, Apr. 8, 1925; children—Max, Sally Erickson. Student U. N.D., 1919; J.D., U. Mich., 1924. Bar: N.D., 1924. Sole practice, Ashley, 1924; states atty. McIntosh County, Ashley, 1931-38, 39-40; dir. McIntosh County Bank, Ashley, chmn. bd., 1942—; dir. several local corps., Ashley. Del., Republican Nat. Conv., 1948, 64; presdl. elector, N.D., 1968. Served as govt. appeal atty., McIntosh County, World War II. Mem. ABA, N.D. Bar Assn., McIntosh County Bar Assn., McIntosh County Hist. Soc. (charter mem., dir., sec.), Sigma Delta Kappa. Lutheran. Lodges: Lions (charter), Odd Fellows. Address: 314 E Main St Ashley ND 58413

WITCHER, DANIEL DOUGHERTY, pharmaceutical company executive; b. Atlanta, May 17, 1924; s. Julius Gordon and Myrtice Eleanor (Daniel) W.; m. Mary Helen Wilson, Apr. 7, 1946 (div. Oct. 1982); children—Beth, Daniel, J. Wright, Benjamin; m. Betty Lou Middaugh, Oct. 30, 1982. Student Mercer U., 1946-47, Am. Grad. Sch. Internat. Mgmt., Glendale, Ariz., 1949-50. Regional dir. Sterling Drug Co., Rio de Janeiro and Sao Paulo, Brazil, 1950-56; gen. mgr. Mead Johnson Co., Sao Paulo, 1956-60; area mgr. The Upjohn Co., Sao Paulo, 1960-64, div. v.p. Latin Am. and Far East, Kalamazoo, 1964-73, corp. v.p., 1973—; pres., gen. mgr. Upjohn Internat., Inc., 1973-84; corp. v.p. Worldwide Human Health Businesses, 1985—. Trustee Am. Grad. Sch. Internat. Mgmt., Glendale, Ariz., 1981—. Served with USN, 1943-46. Recipient Jonas Mayer Am. Bus. Enlightenment award Am. Grad. Sch. Internat. Mgmt., 1973. Mem. Pharm. Mfrs. Assn. (twice past pres. internat. sect.). Republican. Episcopalian. Office: 7000 Portage Rd Kalamazoo MI 49001

WITHERELL, DENNIS PATRICK, lawyer; b. Toledo, Ohio, Dec. 15, 1951; s. Thomas William and Kathryn Marie (Savage) W.; m. Leslie Buckholtz, Dec. 15, 1979; children—Natalie and Jay. A.B. with highest honors, U. Mich., 1973; J.D. summa cum laude, Ohio State U., 1977. Bar: Ohio, U.S. Dist. Ct. (no. dist.) Ohio, U.S. Ct. Appeals (6th cir.). Law clk. U.S. Ct. Appeals (6th cir.), Cin., 1977-78; assoc. Shumaker, Loop & Kendrick Toledo, 1978-83, ptnr., 1983—. Mem. exec. bd. March of Dimes Birth Defects Found., N.W. Ohio Chpt., Toledo, 1978—, chmn. N.W. Ohio chpt., 1982-84. Mem. Am. Acad. of Hosp. Attys., Nat. Health Lawyers Assn., ABA, Ohio State Bar Assn., Toledo Bar Assn., Ohio Soc. of Hosp. Attys. Roman Catholic. Home: 2644 Meadowwood Dr Toledo OH 43606 Office: Shumaker Loop & Kendrick 1000 Jackson Toledo OH 43624

WITHEROW, JUDITH KAY, educator; b. Marion, Ind., Jan. 17, 1943; d. Ivan Brazilla and Bertha Mae (Comer) Seward; B.S. in Edn., Ball State U., 1965, M.A., 1971, Reading Specialist, 1979; m. William David Witherow, Aug. 23, 1964; children—Stephen William, Terri Lyn, Brian David. Elem. tchr. South Madison Community Sch. Corp., Markleville, Ind., 1967-73; tchr. grade 5 No. Community Schs. Tipton County, Windfall, Ind., 1973-79; reading specialist, 1979-83; reading specialist No. Community Sch. Tipton County, Sharpsville, Ind., 1983—. Leader Methodist Youth Fellowship, Vanlue, Ohio. Recipient Tchr. of Yr. award No. Community Schs., 1980, 81. Mem. Internat. Reading Assn., Mid-Central Reading Council (pres. 1982-83), Assn. Supervision and Curriculum Devel., Am. Fedn. Tchrs. Democrat. Home: Rural Route 1 Box 36 Sharpsville IN 46068 Office: No Community Schs Tipton County Rural Route 2 Sharpsville IN 46068

WITHERSPOON, FREDDA LILLY, educator; b. Houston; d. Fred D. and Vanita E. (Meredith) Lilly; A.B., Bishop Coll.; M.S.W., Washington U., St. Louis, M.A. in Guidance and Counseling, M.A. in Ednl. Psychology, Ph.D., St. Louis U., 1965; m. Robert L. Witherspoon; children—Robert L., Vanita. Social worker, supr. St. Louis City Welfare Office, Homer G. Phillips Hosp.; tchr. English, guidance counselor St. Louis Pub. Schs., 1950-65; prof. student personnel services Forest Park Community Coll., St. Louis, 1965—; cons. Ednl. Testing Service, Princeton, N.J., Head Start program, 1965-68; counseling cons. St. Louis Job Corps Center for Women, 1966-68. Organizer teenage service guild Annie Malone Children's Home, 1964; v.p. St. Louis chpt. NAACP, 1969-83, pres. Mo. Conf., 1973—, also organizer Forest Park young adult council, also bd. dirs.; mem. Challenge of 70's Crime Commn., 1970-75; mem. adv. council Central Inst. for Deaf, 1970-78; mem. exec. bd. Mayor's St. Louis Ambassadors; mem. Mayor's Council Youth, 1970-75; dir. teens fund drive March of Dimes, 1960-72, Lily Day drive for Crippled Children, 1966-72; founder Met. St. Louis chpt. Coalition of 100 Black Women, Inc., 1984; mem. speakers bur. United Way, 1969-82; bd. dirs. children's services City of St. Louis, Mo. Heart Assn.; bd. dirs., also founder Met. St. Louis inter-alumni council United Negro Coll. Fund; bd. dirs. Social Health Assn., Conservatory Assn. Schs. for Arts, St. Louis Heart Assn., Girl Scouts; pres. St. Louis Met. YWCA, 1978-79, bd. dirs.; bd. dirs. St. Louis Urban League, vice chmn., 1977-81; organizer Jr. Annie Malone Service Guild. Named Woman of Year, Greyhound Bus Corp., 1967, St. Louis Argus, 1968, Nat. Outstanding Woman, Iota Phi Lambda, 1970; named Outstanding Woman of Achievement, Globe Dem., 1970, Outstanding Educator of Am., 1971, Nat. Top Lady Distinction, 1974; recipient Negro History award, 1971; George Washington Carver award, 1976; Health and Welfare Council award, 1975; Vol. of Yr. award United Negro Coll. Fund.; Continental Socs. award, 1984. Mem. NAACP (life; Nat. Outstanding Youth Adv. 1977, numerous awards 1977-84), Am. Personnel and Guidance Assn., AAUP (pres. 1975-81), AAUW, Nat. Assn. Women Deans and Counselors, Am. Sch. Counselors Assn., Am. Vocational Guidance Assn., Assn. Measurement and Evaluation in Guidance, Nat. Assn. Jr. Colls., Nat. Faculty Assn. Jr. Colls., LWV, Nat. Council Negro Women (life), Mo. Assn. Social Welfare, Jack and Jill, Mound City (pres. 1946-49), Nat. Assn. Women Lawyers, Nat. Bar Assn., Nat. Barristers Wives (founder), Mound City Bar Aux. (founder, pres. 1946-49), Top Ladies of Distinction (organizer Met. St. Louis chpt.), Continental Socs. (founder Met. St. Louis chpt.), Kappa Delta Pi, Iota Phi Lambda (nat. pres. 1977-81), Sigma Gamma Rho, Phi Delta Kappa. Research on high sch. drop outs with police records, uses of group guidance techniques in jr. colls., community resources for jr. coll. students. Home: 20 Lewis Pl Saint Louis MO 63113

WITHERSPOON, WILLIAM, investment economist; b. St. Louis, Nov. 21, 1909; s. William Conner and Mary Louise (Houston) W.; student Washington U. Evening Sch., 1928-47; m. Margaret Telford Johanson, June 25, 1938; children—James Tomlin, Jane Witherspoon Peltz, Elizabeth Witherspoon Vodra. Research dept. A. G. Edwards & Sons, 1928-31; pres. Witherspoon Investment Co., 1931-34; head research dept. Newhard Cook & Co., 1934-43; chief price analysis St. Louis Ordnance Dist., 1943-45; head research dept. Newhard Cook & Co., 1945-53; owner Witherspoon Investment Counsel, 1953-64; ltd. partner Newhard Cook & Co., economist, investment analyst, 1965-68; v.p. research Stifel, Nicolaus & Co., 1968-81; lectr. on investments Washington U., 1948-67. Mem. Clayton Bd. of Edn., 1955-68, treas., 1956-68, pres., 1966-67; mem. Clayton Park and Recreation Commn., 1959-60; trustee Ednl. TV, KETC, 1963-64; mem. investment com. Gen. Assembly Mission Bd. Presbyterian Ch. U.S., Atlanta, 1976-79, mem. permanent com. ordination exams, 1979-85. Served as civilian Ordnance Dept., AUS, 1943-45. Chartered fin. analyst. Mem. St. Louis Soc. Fin. Analysts (pres. 1949-50). Club: Mo. Athletic (St. Louis). Home: 6401 Ellenwood Clayton MO 63105

WITHROW, J. D., automobile manufacturing company executive. Exec. v.p. Chrysler Corp., Highland Park, Mich. Office: Chrysler Corp 12000 Lynn Townsend Dr Highland Park MI 48288*

WITHROW, MARY ELLEN, state treasurer; b. Marion, Ohio, Oct. 2, 1930; d. Clyde Welsh and Mildred (Stump) Hinamon; m. Norman David Withrow, Sept. 4, 1948; children—Linda Rizzo, Leslie Legge, Norma, Rebecca. Student, pub. schs., Marion, Ohio. With Elgin Bd. Edn., Marion, Ohio, 1969-72; safety problems dir. ARC, Marion, 1969-72; dep. registrar State of Ohio, Marion, 1972-75; dep. county auditor Marion County (Ohio), 1975-77, county treas., 1977-83; treas. State of Ohio, Columbus, 1983—; chmn. Ohio State Bd. Deposits, 1983—. Mem. Democratic Nat. Com., Met. Women's Ctr.; pres. Marion County Dem. Club, 1976. Mem. State Assn. County Treas. (legis. chmn., 1979-83, treas. 1982), Nat. Assn. State Treas. (v.p. 1983—). Club: Bus. and Profl. Women's. Office: State of Ohio 30 E Broad St 9th Floor Columbus OH 43215

WITT, ELDON EARL, agricultural education administrator, educator; b. Bowen, Ill. Oct. 8, 1922; s. Mack and Alta Mae (Stull) W.; m. Mary Lou Strader, Aug. 27, 1950; children—Brian, Lynn. B.S. in Agr., Western Ill. U., 1950; B.S. in Agr., U. Ill., 1952, M.Ed., 1958. Cert. supervisory tchr., Ill. Tchr. pub. high schs., Ill., 1952-70; exec. sec. Ill. Assn. Vocat. Agr. Tchrs., 1970—; exec. sec. Ill. Assn. Future Farmers Am., 1973—; chmn. Ill. Coordinating Council Vocat. Student Orgns. Bd. dirs. Roanoke-Benson High Sch., Roanoke, Ill., 1972-78; pres. Nat. Future Farmers Am. Alumni. Served to sgt. USAAF, 1943-46. Recipient Disting. Service award Ill. Future Farmers Am., 1974, named Hon. State Farmer, 1969, named Hon. Am. Farmer, nat. group, 1974. Mem. Nat. Vocat. Agr. Tchrs. Assn. (outstanding service award 1974), Am. Vocat. Assn., Ill. Vocat. Assn., Am. Legion (Ill. vice comdr. 4th div. 1980), Gamma Sigma Delta, Alpha Tau Alpha. Democrat. Club: Rotary (Roanoke, Ill.) Author numerous ednl. leadership books.

WITT, FRED THEODORE, jeweler; b. Downs, Kans., Jan. 28, 1916; s. Edward Henry and Barbara Elena (Brock) W.; m. Norma Lee Patten, June 6, 1937 (div. Jan. 1985); children—Sharon Lee Witt Dunham, George Clinton, Fred T. Grad. Downs High Sch., 1933. Owner, operator Fred T. Witt Jewelers Inc., Lincoln, Nebr., 1984—. Served with AUS, 1945-46. Mem. Nebr.-S.D. Jewelers Assn., Retail Jewelers Am. Am Legion. Republican. Presbyterian. Club: Nebraska. Lodges: Kiwanis, Masons, Elks. Home: 4110 Fiene St Lincoln NE 68502 Office: Fred T Witt Jewelers Inc 1033 O St Lincoln NE 68508

WITTENBERG, SANDRA KAY, educational administrator; b. Toledo, Jan. 20, 1948; d. Robert Deery and Orpha Irene (Burton) Lloyd; m. Craig Lee Wittenberg, Aug. 28, 1967; children—Claudia Lee, Clark Lloyd. B.A., U. Toledo, 1976, M.Ed., 1980, Ph.D., 1984. Cert. tchr., ednl. adminstr., prin., supt., Ohio. With Toledo Pub. Schs., 1976—, coordinator Alt. Learning Center, 1982-83, supr. occupational work experience program, 1983—; staff devel. cons. adult edn. Mem. Northwestern Ohio Family Health Planning Council, 1972-74; sec. adv. council Adult and Continuing Edn., 1981—; pres. bd. trustees Apple Tree Cooperative Nursery Sch., U. Toledo, 1974-78; ednl. cons. Daedalus Co. Recipient U. Toledo Bd. Trustees Scholarship award, 1979-83; recipient Cert. Significant Profl. Contbn. as Tchr.-Educator, U. Toledo, 1981-82. Mem. Adult Edn. Assn., Assn. Supervision and Curriculum Devel., Phi Delta Kappa, Phi Kappa Phi, Pi Lambda Theta, Delta Kappa Gamma, Beta Sigma Phi. Mem. Ch. of Christ. Contbr. articles to profl. jours. Home: 2458 Sterns Rd Temperance MI 48182 Office: Manhattan and Elm Sts Toledo OH 43608

WITTGREN, JACK ARTHUR, III, steel company administrator; b. Chgo., Sept. 9, 1932; s. Jack Alex and Mary Ann (Eckert) W.; m. Janice Helen Faucett, Jan. 6, 1954; 1 dau., Deborah Lynn Wittgren Cooper. Student, Lawrence Coll., 1949-50, Roosevelt Coll., 1950-51, Ind. U. NW, 1975, MIT, 1982. Rigger, Republic Steel, Chgo., 1955-66, foreman mech. dept., 1966-67, gen. foreman mech. dept., 1968-73, asst. mech. supt., 1973-76, supt. mech. dept., 1976-77, supt. primary mills, 1977-79, gen. supt. ops., 1979—. Mem. Republican Presdl. Task Force, 1982. Served with USCG, 1951-54. Mem. Assn. Iron and Steel Engrs. (chmn. Chgo. sect. 1979-80, nat. bd. dirs. 1981), Am. Inst. Metall. Engrs. Lodge: Masons. Home: 10105 White Oak Dyer IN 46311 Office: 116th Burley Ave Chicago IL 60617

WITTLINGER, TIMOTHY DAVID, lawyer; b. Dayton, Ohio, Oct. 12, 1940; s. Charles Frederick and Dorothy Elizabeth (Golden) W.; m. Diane Cleo Dominy, May 20, 1967; children—Kristine Elizabeth, David Matthew. B.S. in Math., Purdue U., 1962; J.D. with distinction, U. Mich., 1965. Bar: Mich. 1966, U.S. Dist. Ct. (ea. dist.) Mich. 1966, U.S. Ct. Appeals (6th cir.) 1968, U.S. Supreme Ct. 1971. Assoc. Hill, Lewis, Adams, Goodrich & Tait, Detroit, 1965-72, ptnr., 1973—, head litigation dept., 1976—; mem. profl. assistance com. U.S. Dist. Ct. (ea. dist.) Mich., 1981-82. Mem. house of deps. Episcopal Ch., N.Y.C., 1979—; sec. bd. trustees Episcopal Ch., Diocese of Mich., Detroit, 1983—; bd. dirs., sec. Grubb Inst. Behavioral Studies Ltd., Washington. Mem. State Bar Mich., ABA, Engring. Soc. Detroit. Home: 736 N Glenhurst Birmingham MI 48009 Office: Hill Lewis Adams Goodrich & Tait 100 Renaissance Ctr 32 Floor Detroit MI 48243

WITTMAIER, ALVIN, coal company executive; b. Zap, N.D., July 2, 1929; s. Carl and Leah Mathilda (Kiehlbauch) W.; m. June 9, 1951; children—Patty, Jim, Joan. Ed., U. N.D., 1950. Mining engr. Knife River Coal Mining Co., 1950-53; gas engr. MDU, Shelby, Mont., 1953-55; mine engr., Knife River Coal Mining Co., Beulah, Mont., 1955-60, gen. supt., Bismarck, N.D., 1960, then asst. v.p., v.p., pres., chief operating officer, 1979-83, chief exec. officer, 1983—. Served with AUS, 1951-53. Mem. Am. Inst. Mining Engrs., Mont. Coal Council (pres.). Republican. Lutheran. Office: 1915 N Kavaney Dr Bismarck ND 58501

WITTMAN, JAMES SMYTHE, business educator; b. Ft. Bragg, N.C., Mar. 1, 1943; s. James S. and O. Ardelle (Huber) W.; m. W. Sue Thigpen, Jan. 23, 1965 (div.); children—Monica, Natalie, Peter, Lydia. B.A. in Chemistry, La. Coll., 1964; Ph.D. in Biochemistry, Tulane U., 1970; M.B.A. in Indsl. Mgmt., Fairleigh Dickenson U., 1978. Chemist, SRRL of U.S. Dept. Agr., New Orleans, 1962-65, U.S. Customs Lab., 1965-66; scientist Hoffmann-LaRoche, Nutley, N.J., 1968-79; tech. dir. Batter-Lite Foods, Beloit, Wis., 1980-81; bus. educator Rock Valley Coll., Rockford, Ill., 1981—. Patentee (3) chemical food industry; contbr. articles to profl. jours. Mem. Am. Inst. Nutrition, Midwest Bus. Educators Assn. Republican. Avocations: aviation; hand crafts. Home: 1548 Rural St Rockford IL 61107 Office: Rock Valley Coll 3101 N Mulford Rd Rockford IL 61101

WITTSTOCK, LAURA WATERMAN, radio programming executive; b. Cattaraugus, N.Y., Sept. 11, 1937; d. Isaac and Clarinda (Jackson) Waterman; student San Francisco State Coll., 1961, Fla. Jr. Coll., 1964; m. Lloyd Carl Wittstock, Aug. 30, 1970; children by previous marriage—Joe O. Simas III, Tedi Marie Wittstock, Arthur Waterman Simas, James O. Simas, Rose Marie Wittstock. Editor, Legis. Rev., Washington, 1971-73; dir. Project Media, Nat. Indian Edn. Assn., Mpls., 1973-75; exec. dir. Am. Indian Press Assn., Washington, 1975-76; pres., dir. MIGIZI Communications, Mpls., 1976—; ind. cons., 1977-81. Mem. Nat. Commn. Alcoholism and Alcohol Related Problems; participant Internat. Women's Yr., 1975; mem. Seminar on Women and Devel.; mem. Mpls. Community Bus. Employment Alliance; mem. Gov.'s Job Tng. Council; vice chmn. devel. Juel Fairbanks Aftercare Residence, 1979-80; mem. Am. Indian Policy Rev. Commn. Task Force Urban Indian Concerns, 1976; exec. dir. Am. Indian Press Assn., 1975; adminstr. Red Sch. House, 1976-76, Heart of the Earth Sch., Mpls., 1982-85. Mem. Nat. Indian Edn. Assn. Mem. Hondenosaunee, People of the Longhouse. Contbr. to Comparative Perspectives of Third World Women, 1980. Home: 3031 Dakota Ave S Saint Louis Park MN 55416 Office: 2300 Cedar Ave S Minneapolis MN 55404

WIXOM, THEODORE MERSHON, linen rental company official; b. Galesburg, Ill., June 15, 1937; s. Robert Nelson and Doris (Cox) W.; B.S. in Indsl. Mgmt., Miami U., Oxford, Ohio, 1960; children—Elizabeth Kay, Margaret Marie. Plant mgr. F.W. Means & Co., Lexington, Ky., 1964-66, South Bend, Ind., 1966-68; staff plant mgr. Asso. Linen Services, Utica, N.Y., 1968-70, gen. mgr., 1970-74; v.p. ops. Community Linen Rental Services, Los Angeles, 1974-76; v.p., dir. Spalding's Services Ltd., Louisville, 1976-78; gen. mgr. N.Y. area Morgan Services, Inc., Buffalo, 1978-84; dir. health care services Faultless Health Care Services, Inc., Kansas City, Mo., 1984—. Instr. driving course Nat. Safety Council, Utica, 1972-73. Served to lt. (j.g.) USNR, 1960-62. Named Engr. of Yr., Joint Engrs. Council Mohawk Valley, 1971; cert. mfg. engr. Mem. Am. Inst. Indsl. Engrs. (v.p. region 5; sr. mem.; nat. bd. dirs.), Mohawk Valley Joint Engrs. Council (chmn. pub. relations com.), Soc. Mfg. Engrs., Linen Supply Assn. Am. (mem. nat. ops. com.), Alpha Kappa Psi, Theta Chi. Clubs: Masons, Rotary. Contbr. articles to profl. jours. Home: 7438 Beverly Overland Park KS 66204 Office: Faultless Health Care Services 2100 E 19th Terr Kansas City MO 64127

WOBST, FRANK GEORG, See *Who's Who in America,* 43rd edition.

WODLINGER, MARK LOUIS, broadcasting company executive; b. Jacksonville, Fla., July 13, 1922; s. Mark H. and Beatrice May (Boney) W.; B.S., U. Dla., 1943; m. Connie Jean Bates, May 3, 1974; children—Mark, Jacqueline, Steven, Mike, Kevin. Salesman, Sta. WQUA Moline, Ill., 1948; mgr. Sta. WOC AM FM TV, Davenport, Iowa, 1949-58; v.p. Sta. WMBD TV, Peoria, Ill., 1959-61; v.p., gen mgr. Sta. WZZM-TV, Grand Rapids, Mich., 1962-63, Sta. KMBC-TV, Kansas City, Mo., 1963-69; pres. Intermedia, Kans., 1969-73; builder, owner, comml. radio sta., Swaziland, operator Radio Malawai, Blantyre and Marknews TV and Radio News Bur., Nairobi, Kenya, 1971-74; owner, pres. Sta. KBEQ, Kansas City, 1973-77; dir Sta. KCPT TV, Kansas City; chmn., owner Wodlinger Broadcasting KZZC-FM, Kansas City, KCLO-FM, Leavenworth, Kans., 1982; chmn., owner Channel 5, Houston, Miami FM,; Naples FM. Bd. dirs. Kansas City Civic Council, Naples YMCA, Fla. Served to lt. USN, 1941-45. Mem. Nat. Assn. Broadcasters, Mo. Assn. Broadcasters, Broadcast Pioneers. Republican. Episcopalian. Clubs: Kansas City, University, Carriage, Port Royal; Naples Yacht, White Lake Yacht (Mich.). Lodge: Rotary. Home: 800 Galleon Dr Naples FL 33940 Office: 6439 Wenonga Rd Mission Hills KS 66208

WOECKEL, ALLAN JOHN, library administrator; b. LaSalle, Ill., Oct. 3, 1944; s. August and Victoria Harriet (Grochowski) W.; m. Vicki Lynn Flori, Oct. 3, 1964 (div. 1978); children—Renee Lynn, Scott Allan. B.A. in History, No. Ill. U., 1966, Cert. Edn., 1967, M.A. In Library Sci., 1969. Asst. dir. Plum Meml. Library, Lombard, Ill., 1969-71; ref. librarian Coll. of DuPage, Glen Ellyn, Ill., 1970-72; instr. Ill. Valley Community Coll., Oglesby, Ill., 1971-72; dir. Reddick Library, Ottawa, Ill., 1971—. Mem. regional conf. com. Ill. White House Conf. on Library and Info. Services, 1978-79; library automation rev. group Starved Rock Library System, Ottawa, 1983-84, system adv. com., 1971—; program and edn. dir. Parents Without Ptnrs., Inc., 1979-81, LaSalle, Ill., 1978-79, newsletter dir., 1979-80, pres., 1981-82, treas., 1982—. Recipient Disting. Service Award, Ottawa Lions, 1976. Mem. DuPage County Librarians Assn., ALA, Ottawa Area C. of C. and Industry, Ill. Library Assn. Lodges: Lions (pres. 1975-76), Moose. Home: 420 Park Ave Ottawa IL 61350 Office: Reddick Library 1010 Canal St Ottawa IL 61350

WOELFEL, JAMES WARREN, philosophy and religious studies educator; b. Galveston, Tex., Aug. 6, 1937; s. Warren Charles and Mary Frances (Washinka) W.; m. Sarah Chappell Trulove, Nov. 24, 1982; children—Skye, Allegra, Sarah. B.A., U. Okla., 1959; M.Div., Episcopal Divinity Sch., Cambridge, Mass., 1962; M.A., Yale U., 1964; Ph.D., U. St. Andrews, Scotland, 1967. Asst. prof. philosophy and religious studies U. Kans., Lawrence, 1966-70, asst. prof. philosophy, 1970-71, assoc. prof., 1971-75, prof., 1975—, dir. western civilization program, 1985—. Author: Bonhoeffer's Theology, 1970; Borderland Christianity, 1973; Camus: A Theological Perspective, 1975; Augustinian Humanism, 1979. Contbr. articles to profl. jours. Editorial cons., manuscript reader for various pubs., jours. Danforth fellow, 1959-66; Fulbright scholar, 1962-63; NEH grantee, 1973. Mem. Am. Acad. Religion, Soc. Values in Higher Edn., Collegium of Liberal Religious Scholars, Internat. Bonhoeffer Soc., Phi Beta Kappa. Democrat. Mem. United Ch. of Christ. Avocations: piano, walking. Home: 808 Alabama Lawrence KS 66044 Office: Western Civilization Program U Kans 2106 Wescoe Hall Lawrence KS 66045

WOESSNER, MICHAEL EDWARD, engineering company executive; b. St. Louis, Aug. 31, 1954; s. Edward Charles and Stella Mary (Pasco) W.; m. Linda Celeste Cunningham, May 7, 1977; 1 son, Matthew Lee. B.S.C.E., U. Mo.-Rolla, 1976. Registered profl. engr., Mo., Kans. Design engr. BCI Corp., Rolla, 1976-82, v.p. sales and engring., 1982—; owner, broker Investment Realty, Inc., St. James, Mo., 1981—. Mem. ASCE, Mo. Soc. Profl. Engrs., Nat. Soc. Profl. Engrs. Roman Catholic. Lodge: Lions. Author: (with others) Truss Talk, 1978. Home: Route 1 Box 129 W Saint James MO 65559 Office: 1737 N Bishop Rolla MO 65401

WOESSNER, WARREN DEXTER, lawyer, poet, chemist; b. New Brunswick, N.J., May 31, 1944; s. Warren Wendling and Flora Coffin (Dexter) W.; m. Joyce Howe, Apr. 17, 1971 (div. 1978); m. Carol Lipetz, Apr. 30, 1983. B.A., Cornell U., 1966; Ph.D. in Chemistry, U. Wis.-Madison, 1971, J.D. cum laude, 1981. Bar: Wis. 1981, U.S. Patent Office 1981, N.Y. 1982, Minn. 1984. Sr. research scientist Miles Labs., Madison, Wis., 1972-78; assoc. Kenyon & Kenyon, N.Y.C., 1981-84, Merchant, Gould, Smith, Edell, Welter & Schmidt, Mpls., 1984—; sr. editor Abraxas Press, Inc., 1981—, bd. dirs., 1981-84. Contbr. to books, articles to profl. jours. Bd. dirs. Sta. WORT-FM, Madison, 1975-78, Council Small Mag. Editors and Pubs., San Francisco, 1975-77. Nat. Endowment for Arts Individual fellow creative writing, 1974; Wis. Arts. Bd. Individual fellow, 1975, 76; Loft-McKnight fellow, 1985. Mem. Am. Chem. Soc. ABA, Council Small Mag. Editors and Pubs. Home: 1253 W Minnehaha Pkwy Minneapolis MN 55419 Office: Merchant Gould Smith Edell Welter & Schmidt 1600 Midwest Plaza Minneapolis MN 55402

WOFFORD, CLINTON FRIE, clergyman; b. Senath, Mo., May 15, 1933; s. Charles Clinton and Ella Eulalie (Frie) W.; m. Carolyn Lowell Christian, June 11, 1955; children—David Clinton, Cheryl Lynn, Susan Carol. B.S., U. Mo., 1955, Ph.D., 1962; M.Div., St. Paul Sch. Theology, 1972. Ordained to ministry United Methodist Ch., 1970, elder, 1973. Research chemist Phillips Petroleum

Co., Bartlesville, Okla., 1961-67, group leader, 1967-69; pastor South Prospect United Meth. Ch., Kansas City, Mo., 1970-72, New Arlington United Meth. Ch., Kansas City, 1972; assoc. minister Trinity United Meth. Ch., Kansas City, 1973-74; interim pastor, 1974; pastor College Heights United Meth. Ch., Kansas City, 1974-78; dir. ch. relations Central Meth. Coll., Fayette, Mo., 1978-79; pastor Wayland (Mo.) Circuit, United Meth. Ch., 1979-83; pastor United Meth. Ch., Centralia, Mo., 1983—; dir. Nowlin Hall, Kansas City, 1974-78; mem. East Central Bd., Kansas City, 1975-79; mem. Met. Interchurch Agy. Quality Edn. Task Force, Kansas City, 1976-79. Community rep. to Head Start Policy Council N.E. Mo., 1982-83. Served with USNR, 1955-57. McNeil fellow, 1959. Fellow Am. Inst. Chemists; mem. Mo. East Ann. Conf. United Meth. Ch., Sigma Xi. Clubs: Masons, Rotary. Patentee polymer chemistry. Home: 485 Miles Ave Centralia MO 65240 Office: PO Box 108 Centralia MO 65240

WOGAMAN, GEORGE ELSWORTH, insurance executive; b. Mikado, Mich., May 29, 1937; s. Edgar R. and Leah Katherine (McGuire) W.; grad. various ins. courses; m. Sandra Lee Jensen, Apr. 10, 1965; children—Jennifer, Christopher. With Blair Transit Co., Dun & Bradstreet, Chrysler Engring. Co., 1955-61; exec. chef Westward Ho!, 1961-68; owner, mgr. George Wogaman Ins. Agy., Grand Forks, N.D., 1969—; alderman East Grand Forks (Minn.) City Council, 1979—, v.p., 1982-86. Corp. mem. United Hosp., Grand Forks, 1982—; mem. Nat. Republican Congl. Com., Rep. Presdl. Task Force; mem. fin. com. Wesley United Meth. Ch., Grand Forks. Recipient Pub. Service award East Grand Forks City Council, 1979; C.L.U.; chartered fin. cons. Mem. North Valley Life Underwriters Assn., Am. Soc. C.L.U.s. Club: Elks. Home: 1703 20th St NW East Grand Forks MN 56721 Office: 2612 Gateway Dr Grand Forks ND 58201

WOGSLAND, DAN, state senator. Mem. N.D. State Senate from Dist. 23, 1983—. Democrat. Office: Hannaford ND 58448*

WOHL, MARTIN H., chemical engineer; b. N.Y.C., Feb. 12, 1935; s. Rubin and Helen (Brown) W.; m. Suzanne Cassell, June 15, 1957; children—Jeffrey David, Eric Stephen. B.Ch.E., Cornell U., 1957; postgrd. U. Mass., 1960-68. Engr., Monsanto Co., Springfield, Mass., 1957-66, research specialist, 1966-68, group leader, Kenilworth, N.J., 1968-75, tech. mgr., 1975-78, project dir., St. Louis, 1978—. Contbg. author: Reaction Injection Molding, 1985. Contbr. articles to tech. jours. Patentee colored interlayer. Bd. dirs. Head Start, Springfield, 1966-68, Springfield Action Commn., 1966-68; pres. Greater Springfield Mental Health Assn., 1966-67; Democratic precinct capt., 1966-68; scoutmaster Boy Scouts Am., 1959-63; mem. No. N.J. Com. Minorities in Engring., 1977-78. Mem. Am. Inst. Chem. Engrs., Soc. Rheology, Soc. Plastics Engrs., Soc. Automotive Engrs., Phi Kappa Phi. Jewish. Avocations: skiing; tennis; sailing. Office: Monsanto Co 800 N Lindbergh Blvd Saint Louis MO 63167

WOHLERS, NORMA JEAN, publishing clearing agency executive; b. Charleston, W.Va., Dec. 1, 1935; d. Sterling Patrick and Rosalie Pebble (Anderson) Brown; grad. airline sch. TWA, 1954; m. Gerhard Andrew Wohlers, Mar. 5, 1960 (dec. 1977); children—Gerhard Andrew III, Shannon Diane. Sec., Ohio Nat. Bank, Columbus, 1955-57; mgr. Slenderama, Columbus and Cin., 1957-59; mgr. Civic Reading Club, Look mag., Grand Rapids, Mich., 1959-70, gen. mgr., 1972-77, v.p., 1972; pres., owner Am. Guild Circulation Corp., Detroit, 1972—, chmn. bd., 1977—; pres. Am. Guild Corp., Detroit, 1980—; founder, pres. G.N.S. Publs. Sch. Plan, 1982—, Nationwide Mag. Network. Recipient Presdl. Sports award for tennis, 1973. Mem. Audit Bur. Circulations. Republican. Office: Am Guild Circulation Corp 24453 Grand River St Detroit MI 48219

WOITH, TERRY M., financial consultant, dentist; b. Peoria, Ill., Jan. 22, 1948; m. Karen LaBeau Marante; children—Tera, Maymie. B.S., Bradley U., 1970, M.B.A., 1974; D.D.S., So. Ill. U., 1977. Pvt. practice dentistry Jacksonville, Ill., 1977—; pres., chief exec. officer Money & Woith Fin. Cons., Jacksonville, 1984—; lectr. in field. Active community programs Jacksonville; presented dental care programs in schs. Lodges: Moose, Kiwanis, Jaycees.

WOIWODE, JOHN GREGORY, fisheries scientist, research company executive; b. L.I., N.Y., Aug. 16, 1951; s. Louis Henry and Kathryn Madeline (Uht) W. B.S. in Fish and Wildlife Resources U. Idaho, 1973, M.S. in Fisheries Resources, 1980. Vol. Peace Corps, Philippines, 1975-77, fisheries tech. tng. dir., 1977; research asst. U. Idaho and Dept. Energy, Moscow, Idaho and Raft River, Idaho, 1978-80; assoc. fisheries scientist U. Minn., St. Paul, 1980—; pres. AquaMatrix, Inc.; cons. fish culture system design. Mem. AAAS, Am. Fisheries Soc., Wildlife Soc., Nat. Audubon Soc., Sigma Xi. Contbr. articles to profl. publs. Home: 1945 Lakeaires Blvd White Bear lake MN 55110 Office: 219 Hodson U Minn Saint Paul MN 55108

WOJACK, DAVID E., writer, public relations consultant; b. Detroit, Dec. 16, 1946; s. Edward George and Elena Gisella (Diguisto) W.; m. Andrea Eve Pakulski, Apr. 17, 1970. B.A. cum laude, U. Detroit, 1968, 1976; M.A., U. Cin., 1969. M.Ed., Chmn. dept. history, asst. prin. St. Agatha High Sch., Redford, Mich., 1969-75, head publs., 1970-76; chmn. lang. arts dept., head publs. Bishop Foley High Sch., Madison Heights, Mich., 1976-77; head press relations Henry Ford Mus., Greenfield Village, Edison Inst., Dearborn, Mich., 1977-83; founder, prin. Publicreations Services, Detroit, 1983—; cons. Midwest Travel Writers Assn., 1981—, Chacma Inc., N.Y., 1980-83; speaker La. Tourism Assn., 1984; lectr. Detroit Student Press Assn., 1967-71; free-lance writer and photographer, 1974—. Contbg. editor: Marketplace Mag., 1983—. Contbr. articles to profl. jours. Civic Fine Mess award chmn. Detroit Dancing Cuckoos, 1977-83. Mem. Midwest Travel Writers Assn. (assoc. v.p. 1980-83), Detroit Press Club (mem. steak out com. 1979—), Phi Alpha Theta. Clubs: Baker St. Irregulars, Sons of Desert (Detroit and N.Y.C.). Office: 18700 Codding Detroit MI 48219

WOJAN, JAMES LAWRENCE, wire and cable manufacturing company executive; b. Green Bay, Wis., June 4, 1946; s. Richard Clayton and Harriette (Tremel) W.; m. Nancy Jo Miller, Oct. 1, 1982. B.S., Calif. Western U., 1970; M.S., U. Wis.-Milw., 1970. Materials mgr. Electri-Wire Corp., Milw., 1973-74; OEM sales specialist Midwest Electroline, Milw., 1974-75; wire and cable sales and dist. specialist Gen. Electric Corp., Cleve., 1975-82; mgr. sales and mktg. Therm-O-Link Inc., Garrettsville, Ohio, 1982-83; Mid-Atlantic sales mgr. wire and cable Phalo Wire & Cable, Cleve., 1983-84; nat. OEM field mktg. specialist wire and cable dept. Gen. Electric Co., Cleve., 1984—. Mem. Nat. Republican Com., 1976. Republican. Roman Catholic. Author: The Quotation Decision, 1979. Home: 22372 Beech Creek Trail Strongsville OH

WOJNAROWSKI, RICHARD ROBERT, lawyer; b. Chgo., Dec. 25, 1953; s. Edward F. and Sally A. (Szrama) W.; m. Jan Noel Hanski, Aug. 9, 1975; 1 child, Lisa. B.A., St. Xavier Coll., 1975; J.D., DePaul U., 1978. Bar: Ill. 1978. Sole practice, Worth, Ill., 1978—; instr. real estate law St. Xavier Coll., Chgo., 1980—. Mem. ABA, Ill. State Bar Assn., St. Xavier Coll. Alumni Bd. Roman Catholic. Office: 11212 S Harlem Worth IL 60482

WOJTAK, RUTH MARIE, retail company executive; b. Kenosha, Wis., Sept. 25, 1956; d. Richard Stanley and Anne Theresa (Steplyk) W. Assoc. Applied Sci., Gateway Tech. Inst., 1976; B.A., U. Wis.-Parkside, 1980. Transp. aide Kenosha Achievement Ctr. (Wis.), 1977; lifeguard U. Wis.-Parkside, Kenosha, 1980, library clk., 1978-80; asst. mgr. K Mart Corp., Troy, Mich., 1980—. Mem. Distributive Edn. Clubs Am. (parliamentarian 1976), Nat. Assn. Female Execs., U. Wis.-Parkside Alumni Assn., Career Guild. Roman Catholic. Home: 2352C Montezuma Dr Florissant MO 63031 Office: K Mart 3520 7220 N Lindbergh Blvd Hazelwood MO 63042

WOLANIN, SOPHIE MAE, civic worker; b. Alton, Ill., June 11, 1915; d. Stephen and Mary (Fijalka) Wolanin; student Pa. State Coll., 1943-44; certificate secretarial sci. U. S.C., 1946, B.S. in Bus. Adminstrn. cum laude, 1948; Ph.D. honoris causa, Colo. State Christian Coll., 1972. Clk., stenographer, sec. Mercer County (Pa.) Tax Collector's Office, Sharon, 1932-34; receptionist, social sec., nurse-technician to doctor, N.Y.C., 1934-37; coil winder, assembler Westinghouse Electric Corp., Sharon, 1937-39, duplicator operator, typist, stenographer, 1939-44, confidential sec., Pitts., 1949-54; exec. sec., charter mem. Westinghouse Credit Corp., Pitts., 1954-72, hdqrs. sr. sec., 1972-80, reporter WCC News, 1967-68, asst. editor, 1968-71, asso. editor, 1971-74; student office sec. to dean U. S.C. Sch. Commerce, 1944-46, instr. math., bus. adminstrn., secretarial sci., 1946-48. Publicity and pub. relations chmn., corr. sec. South Oakland Rehab. Council, 1967-69; mem. nat. adv. bd. Am. Security Council; mem. Friends Winston Churchill Meml. and Library, Westminster Coll., Fulton, Mo.; charter mem. Presdl. Task Force; Fellow/patron Intercontinental Biog. Assn. (life), Intercontinental Inst. Community Service (life); mem. Allegheny County Scholarship Assn. (life), Allegheny County League Women voters, AAUW (life), Internat. Fedn. U. Women, N.E. Historic Geneal. Soc. (life), U. S.C. Alumni Assn. Ednl. Found. (Pa. state fund chmn. 1967-68, pres. council 1972—, ofcl. del., rep. inauguration Bethany Coll. pres.), Hypatian Lit. Soc. (hon.), Acad. Polit. Sci. (Columbia) (life), Bus. and Profl. Women's Club Pitts. (bd. dirs. 1963-80, editor Bull. 1963-65, treas. 1965-66, historian 1969-70, pub. relations 1971-76, Woman of Year 1972), Named to Nat. Woman's Hall of Fame; recipient numerous prizes Allegheny County Fair, 1952-67; citation Congl. Record, 1969; medal of Merit, Pres. Reagan, 1982; others. Liturgical Conf. N. Am. (life), Westinghouse Vet. Employees Assn., Nat. Soc. Lit. and Arts, Early Am. Soc., Am. Acad. Social and Polit. Sci., Societe Commemorative de Femmes Celebres, Nat. Trust Historic Preservation, Am. Counselors Soc. (life), Am. Mus. Natural History (asso.), Nat. Hist. Soc. (founding mem.), Anglo-Am. Hist. Soc. (charter), Nat. Assn. Exec. Secs., Internat. Platform Assn., Smithsonian Assos., Asso. Nat. Archives, Nat., Pa., Fed. bus. and profl. women's clubs, Mercer County Hist. Soc. (life), Am. Bible Soc., Polish Am. Numismatic Assn., Polonus Philatelic Soc. UN Assn. U.S. Republican. Roman Catholic (mem. Cathedral Altar Soc., patron organ recitals). Clubs: Jonathan Maxcy of U. S.C. (charter); Univ. Catholic of Pitts.; Key of Pa., Fedn. Bus. and Profl. Women (hon.); Coll. (hon.) (Sharon). Contbr. articles to newspapers; Am. corr. Polish radio and TV. Home: 5223 Smith-Stewart Rd SE Girard OH 44420

WOLD, PETER BERTRAM, consulting engineer, engineering educator; b. Hillsboro, N.D., Nov. 19, 1926; s. Peter Bertram and Marie M. (Gadberry) W.; m. Beggy M. Benson, Nov. 20, 1952 (dec. 1954); children—Mary Kate, Peter Benson; m. 2d, Ann, June, 1956 (div. Jan. 1978); children—Jeffrey, Robert L., Nancy A. A.S. in Civil Engring., N.D. State Sch. Forestry, 1948; B.S. in Civil Engring., N.D. State U., Fargo, 1950; M.S., U. N.D., 1957. Registered profl. engr., N.D., Mont., Ala. Engaged in constrn. F.H. McGraw & Co., Hartford, Conn., 1950-51; engr. U.S. Bur. Interior, Velua, N.D. and East Chgo., Ind., 1951-52; prof. engring. N.D. Sch. Forestry, Hungry Horse, Mont., 1952-59; pres. WoldEngring., P.C., Bottineau, N.D., 1956—; mem. Pres.' adv. com. on solar energy, 1982. County chmn. Republican party, N.D., 1964-75, mem. nat. com., 1976-80; hockey coach Bottineau Park Bd.; chmn. Bottineau County ARC; bd. dirs. No. Lights council Boy Scouts Am., Water Users Assn. Served with USN, 1944-46, N.G., 1946-60. Mem. Cons. Engrs. Council, Nat. Soc. Profl. Engrs., DAV, VFW, Am. Legion. Methodist. Clubs: Lions, Elks. Home: 509 Nichol St Bottineau ND 58318 Office: Wold Engring P C 915 E 11th St Bottineau ND 58318

WOLF, ANDREW, food manufacturing company executive; b. Budapest, Hungary, May 20, 1927; came to U.S., 1947, naturalized, 1952; s. Alfred and Magda Farkas. Diploma, Baking Inst. Tech., Budapest, 1942-45; B.S. in Mech. Engring., CCNY, 1955-62; postgrad. Ill. Inst. Tech., Chgo., 1962-64; M.B.A., U. Chgo., 1973. Pres., owner, Mignon Pastry Shops, N.Y.C., 1948-51, 1952-54; dir. new products Arnold Bakers, N.Y. and Conn., 1955-60; dir. new products research and devel. Kitchens of Sara Lee, Deerfield, Ill., 1960-71, v.p. research and devel., 1971—; cons. Hanscom Bakeries, N.Y.C., 1954-55; rep. Consol. Foods Corp., Grocery Mfrs. Am. Tech. Com. for Food Protection, 1975—; spokesman Frozen Food Action Communications Team, Inc., radio and TV, 1982—. Contbr. articles to profl. jours. Patentee bakery equipment and methods. Served with U.S. Army, 1947-48, 1951-52. Recipient Hon. Tex. Citizenship award State of Tex., 1969; Bishop award Tex. Dept. Mental Health, 1972. Mem. White House Conf. on Food and Nutrition, 1959, Pres. Reagan's Task Force on Phys. Fitness and Nutrition, 1983. Mem. Am. Frozen Food Inst. (research and tech. services council, quality maintenance task force council), Am. Bakers Assn. (liaison com. U.S. Dept. Agr.), Inst. Food Technologists, Am. Soc. Bakery Engrs., Tau Beta Pi, Pi Tau Sigma. Home: 2785 Daiquiri Dr Deerfield IL 60015

WOLF, CARL RICHARD, police chief, educator; b. Sedelia, Mo., Dec. 19, 1944; s. Lawerence John and Aetna Charolette (Raiffeisen) W.; m. Mary Kay Schulte, Dec. 21, 1970; children—Kristen, Bryce, Kelly. B.S., So. Ill. U., 1974, M.S., 1979. Patrolman, Ladue Police Dept., Mo., 1970; asst. chief Dupo Police Dept., Ill., 1970-77, chief, 1977-80; instr. Belleville Area Coll., Ill., 1977—, McKendree Coll., Lebanon, Ill., 1983—; chief Highland Police Dept., Ill., 1980—; dir. Law Enforcement Adv. Speaker of House, Springfield, Ill., Atty. Gen., Sec. State. Contbr. articles to profl. jours. Chmn. Am. Cancer Soc., Highland, 1984; bd. dirs. Belleville Area Coll., Police Acad., Belleville, 1984, Crisis Services Madison County, Granit City, Ill., 1984. Served with USN, 1965-69, Vietnam. Mem. Internat. Assn. Chiefs Police, Ill. Assn. Chiefs Police (4th v.p. 1985), So. Ill. Police Chiefs Assn. (pres. 1983), Ill. Police Assn. Roman Catholic. Avocations: golf, swimming. Home: 195 Sunflower Highland IL 62249 Office: 820 Mulberry Highland IL 62249

WOLF, CONSTANCE B., chemical company executive; b. Wilmington, Del., Dec. 10, 1944; d. Arthur A. and Beatrice (Forman) Brace; m. Arnold Alfred Wolf, Oct. 20, 1974. B.S., Pa. State U., 1966. Sr. media buyer Compton Advt., N.Y.C., 1966-68; sr. media planner Grey Advt., 1969-73; account exec. N.C.K. Advt., 1974-78; market mgr. Dow Corning, Midland, Mich., 1978-83, mgr. planning and devel., 1984—. Mem. Am. Soc. Tng. and Devel. Jewish. Avocations: painting; reading; dancing. Home: 1208 Sterling Ct Midland MI 48640 Office: Dow Corning Co PO Box 994 C01134 Midland MI 48640

WOLF, DAVID LAWRENCE, dentist; b. Keokuk, Iowa, Mar. 14, 1932; s. William Waldemar and Margaret May (Stadler) W.; m. Carol Ann Zeman, June 9, 1956; children—Monica Wolf Vernon, Matthew D., Gretchen E., Thomas A., Paul L. D.D.S., U. Iowa, 1957. Sole practice dentistry, Cedar Rapids, Iowa, 1959—; chmn. Iowa Bd. Dental Examiners, 1975-76. Served to capt. USAF, 1957-59. Mem. Am. Dental Assn., Am. Acad. Operative Dentistry. Roman Catholic. Lodge: Rotary. Avocations: bicycling; skiing; jogging. Home: 316 Forest Dr SE Cedar Rapids IA 52403 Office: 119 3d St NE Cedar Rapids IA 52401

WOLF, DAVID LYNN, osteopathic obstetrician, gynecologist; b. Peru, Ind., Feb. 17, 1947; s. Harold Chester and Josephine Marie (Nichols) W.; m. Anita Sue Kingery, July 17, 1971; children—Raquel Diane, Bradley David. B.S., Manchester Coll. (Ind.), 1969; M.S.W., Ind. U.-Indpls., 1971; D.O., Coll. Osteo. Medicine and Surgery, Des Moines, 1974. Intern, Riverside Osteo. Hosp., Trenton, Mich., 1974-75, resident in ob-gyn, 1975-79; practice osteo. medicine specializing in ob-gyn, Trenton, 1980—; mem. staff Riverside Osteo. Hosp. Bd. dirs. Wayne County Cancer Soc., 1977-78. Mem. Am. Osteo. Assn., Mich. Assn. Osteo. Physicians and Surgeons, Wayne County Osteo. Assn., Am. Coll. Osteo. Ob-Gyn. Mem. Ch. of Brethren. Lodge: Rotary. Contbr. articles to profl. jours. Home: 3109 Edison St Trenton MI 48183 Office: 2171 W Jefferson St Trenton MI 48183

WOLF, DIANE LOUISE, lawyer; b. Evansville, Ind., Oct. 21, 1955; d. Thomas Joseph, Sr., and Margaret Gertrude (Horn) Wolf. B.B.A. with highest honors, U. Notre Dame, 1977, J.D. cum laude, 1980. Bar: Ind. 1980; C.P.A., Ill. Assoc., Kahn, Dees, Donovan & Kahn, Evansville, 1980—. Bd. dirs. Vis. Nurse Assn. Southwestern Ind., 1983—, United Way Southwestern Ind., 1984—, Health Skills, Inc., 1984—; chmn. study group steering com. Leadership Evansville, 1983-84. Recipient Ernst & Ernst award U. Notre Dame, 1976. Mem. ABA, Ind. Bar Assn., Evansville Bar Assn., Am. Inst. C.P.A.s, Ill. Soc. C.P.A.s, Beta Gamma Sigma, Beta Alpha Psi. Roman Catholic.

WOLF, DON ALLEN, See *Who's Who in America,* 43rd edition.

WOLF, FRANK LOUIS, mathematics educator; b. St. Louis, Apr. 18, 1924; s. Louis and Helen Dorcas (Below) W.; m. Joy Eleanor Gifford, Aug. 16, 1947; children—Joan, Allison, Barbara, Jon. B.S. in Chem. Engring., Washington U.-St. Louis, 1944, M.A., 1948; Ph.D., U. Minn., 1955. Instr., St. Cloud State Coll., Minn., 1949-51; prof. Carleton Coll., Northfield, Minn., 1952—. Author: Elements of Probability and Statistics, 1962, 74; Number Systems and Their Uses, 1972. Served with U.S. Army, 1944-46. Mem. Math. Assn. Am., Am. Statis. Assn., AAAS. Unitarian. Office: Carleton Coll Northfield MN 55057

WOLF, FREDRIC M., educational psychologist; b. Canton, Ohio, Aug. 7, 1945; s. Wayne S. and Anita (Manheim) W. B.S., U. Wis., 1967; postgrad. Law Sch. Georgetown U., 1967-68; M.Ed., Kent State U., 1977, PH.D., 1980. Instr. math. Cuyahoga Community Coll., Cleve., 1978-79; research assoc. behavioral scis. Northeastern Ohio U. Med. Coll., Rootstown, 1979-80; research assoc. med. edn. Ohio State U. Coll. Medicine, Columbus 1980-82, clin. asst. prof. pediatrics, 1981-82; asst. prof. postgrad. medicine U. Mich. Med. Sch., Ann Arbor, 1982—; assoc. dir. edn. Mich. Diabetes Research and Tng. Ctr., Ann Arbor, 1982—. Contbr. articles to profl. jours. Vol., Peace Corps, Latin Am., 1969-72. Grantee Mich. Dept. Pub. Health, 1984-86, Spencer Found., 1983-84. Mem. AAAS, Am. Diabetes Assn., Am. Psychol. Assn., Am. Statis. Assn., Midwestern Ednl. Research Assn. (v.p. 1984-85), Sigma Xi. Office: Dept Postgrad Medicine U Mich Ann Arbor MI 48109

WOLF, SISTER MARY WILMA, nun, home economics educator; b. Little Cedar, Iowa, Apr. 2, 1918; d. William Michael and Sophia Emma (Miller) W. B.A., State U. Iowa, 1943, M.A., 1944. Joined Sisters of Mercy, Roman Catholic Ch., 1936. Tchr. St. Berchman's Sch., Marion, Iowa, 1937-38, Immaculate Conception Sch., Charles City, Iowa, 1939-40, St. John's Sch., Waterloo, Iowa, 1940-41; asst. prof. home econs. Mount Mercy Coll., Cedar Rapids, Iowa, 1945—. Demonstrator, Gazette Cook-Off, Cedar Rapids, 1984, 85; speaker Mount Mercy Speaker's Bur., 1960-76. Avocations: cooking; sewing; crafts. Home and Office: Mount Mercy Coll 1330 Elmhurst Dr NE Cedar Rapids IA 52402

WOLF, RICHARD EDWARD, physician, medical educator; b. Phila., Jan. 28, 1914; s. Lester and Florence (Leopold) W.; m. Margaret Wertheimer, Dec. 22, 1938; children—Richard E., Jr., Susan W. Kaufman, William L. B.A., Harvard U., 1935; M.D., U. Pa., 1939. Diplomate Am. Bd. Pediatrics. Intern, Phila. Children's Hosp., 1939-41; resident Children's Hosp., 1941-43; fellow pediatric psychiatry Payne Whitney Clinic, 1946-48; prof. pediatrics U. Cin. Coll. Medicine, 1950-84, prof. emeritus, 1984—; dir. pediatric psychiatry Children's Hosp., Cin., 1948-73; med. dir. Babies Milk Fund Assn., 1970-84. Contbr. numerous articles to pediatric jours. Bd. dirs. Radio Reading Services, Cin., 1978—. Mem. Phi Beta Kappa, Sigma Xi. Home: 115 Lafayette Circle Cincinnati OH 45220

WOLF, ROBERT MICHAEL, lawyer; b. Evansville, Ind., June 5, 1953; s. Thomas Joseph and Margaret Gertrude (Horn) W. B.B.A., U. Notre Dame, 1975; J.D., So. Ill. U., 1978; LL.M., Emory U., 1979. Bar: Ill. 1980, U.S. Dist. Ct. (so. dist.) Ill. 1984, U.S. Ct. Appeals (7th cir.) 1985. Pub. defender Saline County, Ill., 1980-84; sole practice, Harrisburg, Ill., 1980—. Mem. ABA, Assn. Trial Lawyers Am., Ill. State Bar Assn., Saline County Bar Assn. Harrisburg Jaycees. Roman Catholic. Home: Route 4 Harrisburg IL 62946

WOLF, TERRI ANN, optometrist; b. Lansing, Mich., Mar. 18, 1954; d. Robert Bruce and Jean (Smith) W.; m. Brian David Onweller, Mar. 15, 1980; 1 child, Shane David. O.D., Ohio State U., 1978. Clin. assoc. Ferris State Coll. Optometry, Big Rapids, Mich., 1978-79; gen. practice optometry, Okemos, Mich., 1979—; bd. dirs. Mich. State Bd. Optometry, Lansing, 1984—. Bd. dirs. Williamston Schs. Found., Mich., 1980—. Mem. Am. Optometric Assn., Mich. Optometric Assn., Central Mich. Optometric Assn. (pres. 1983-84). Club: East Lansing Zonta. Avocations: horses, sports. Office: 1665 Hamilton Okemos MI 48864

WOLF, VIRGINIA LEORA, English educator; b. Caney, Kans., Feb. 12, 1939; d. Harry B. and Strelsa G. (Puckett) Bonham; m. John P. Wolf, June 13, 1966; children—Laura Tiffany, David Scott. B.S., U. Kans., 1961, M.A., 1966, Ph.D., 1980. Lectr., U. Kans., Lawrence, 1970-77; asst. prof. English, U. Wis.-Stout, Menomonie, 1977-82, assoc. prof., 1982-84, prof., 1984—. Mem. Children's Lit. Assn. (treas. 1982-85, v.p., 1985—), Midwest Modern Lang. Assn. (sec., chmn. elect children's lit. sect. 1984—). Avocations: skiing, racquetball, gardening. Home: 2916 State Eau Claire WI 54701 Office: U Wis-Stout English Dept Menomonie WI 54751

WOLFE, ANN, sculptor, educator, lecturer; b. Mlawa, Poland, Nov. 14, 1905, came to U.S., 1911, naturalized, 1927; d. Jacob and Sarah Wolfe; m. Mark A. Graubard, Mar. 5, 1927; children—Jane Strovas, Maya Jones. B.A., Hunter Coll., 1926; pvt. study, Manchester, Eng., Paris, 1931-33. Tchr. sculpture Minnetonka Art Center, Minn., 1971-73, pvt classes, Mpls, 1965-70. One man shows include Worcester Art Mus, Mass, 1939, Grace Horne Gallery, Boston, 1941, Whyte Gallery, Washington, 1946, Hamline U., St. Paul, 1951, Walker Art Center, Mpls., 1955, Mpls. Inst. Arts, 1964, Adele Bednarz Galleries, Los Angeles, 1966, Stewardt-Verde Galleries, San Francisco, 1966, Westlake Gallery, Mpls. 1970; represented in numberous group, national and regional exhibitions in N.Y.C., Chgo., Penn. Acad. Fine Arts, Third Sculpture Internat., 1949. Recipient sculpture awards Allied Artists of Am., N.Y.C., 1936, Soc. Wash. Artists, 1944, 45, Mpls. Inst. Arts, 1951, Soc. Minn. Sculptors, 1955. Mem. Soc. Minn. Sculptors. Home: 2928 Dean Pkwy Minneapolis MN 55416

WOLFE, GOLDIE BRANDELSTEIN, real estate company executive; b. Linz, Austria, Dec. 20, 1945; d. Albert and Regina (Sandman) Brandelstein; student U. Ill., 1963-64; B.S. with honors in Bus. Adminstrn., Roosevelt U., 1967; postgrad. U. Chgo. Grad. Sch. Bus., 1968-69; 1 dau., Alicia Danielle Schuyler. Account research mgr. J. Walter Thompson Advt., Chgo., 1967-71, assoc. account exec., 1971-72; account exec. Needham, Harper & Steers, Advt., Chgo., 1972; real estate broker office leasing dept. Arthur Rubloff & Co., Chgo., 1972—, asst. v.p., 1975-77, v.p. office leasing, 1977-80, sr. v.p., 1980—. Bd. dirs. realty div. Jewish United Fund, 1976-77; bd. dirs. Michael Reese Hosp. Med. Research Inst. Council, 1979—, United Charities, Met. Planning Council; chmn. services group Chgo. Public TV, 1974-75. Named Top Producer of Yr., Authur Rubloff & Co., 1981-84; recipient Disting. Communal Service award B'nai B'rith Internat., 1985. Mem. Chgo. Real Estate Bd. (sales council, Salesman of Yr. award 1981, 82, 83), Chgo. Council Fgn. Relations, Roosevelt U. Alumni Assn. (bd. govs.), Ill. Assn. Realtors, Nat. Assn. Realtors, Young Execs. Club (program v.p. 1980-81), Chgo. Network. Clubs: Chgo. Econ., East Bank. Home: 1332 Sutton Pl Chicago IL 60610 Office: Rubloff Inc 69 W Washington St Chicago IL 60602

WOLFE, HILDA LOUISE, orthopaedic clinic administrator, investment company executive; b. Bay County, Mich., Oct. 31, 1944; d. Albert and Delores Louise (Arturo) Arndt; m. Neil Dexter, Oct. 23, 1963; 1 child, Teri Louise. A.S. in Bus., Ctr. for Degree Studies, Scranton, Pa., 1980. Sec., Dow Corning Corp., Midland, Mich., 1961-63; sec. Dow Chem. Co., Midland, 1963-64; nursing service adminstrv. asst. Midland Hosp. Ctr., Mich., 1971-76, mgr. neuroscis., 1976-80; bus., mgr., adminstr. Bush Orthopaedic Clinic, P.C., Midland, 1980—, Cherokee Investments, Midland, 1980—. Mem. Nat. Assn. Female Execs., Credit Bur. Midland (bd. dirs. 1985—), Mich. Med. Group Mgmt. Assn., Orthopaedic Office Mgrs. Group. Home: 3071 E Shaffer Rd Midland MI 48640 Office: Rush Orthopaedic Clinic PC 1414 E Wackerly Rd Midland MI 48640

WOLFE, JAMES RICHARD, lawyer, business executive; b. Hannibal, Mo., Nov. 7, 1929; s. James Edward and Grace (Kirn) W.; student Georgetown U., 1947-49; B.S., Loyola U., 1951; J.D., DePaul U., 1953; m. Helen Lorraine Rosedale, Dec. 29, 1951; children—Yvonne Bazar, Mary Viano, Theresa Eileen, James E., Michaela Ann, Kathleen Grace, Lorraine Helene. Admitted to Ill. bar, 1953, U.S. Ct. Mil. Appeals bar, 1957, U.S. Supreme Ct. bar, 1961; practiced in Chgo., 1953—; atty. Burlington R.R., Chgo., 1953-55, 58-59; mem. Nat. R.R. Adjustment Bd., Chgo., 1959-63; counsel U.S. R.R.'s, Nat. Labor Cases, 1959-65; gen. atty. Nat. Ry. Labor Conf., 1965-67, gen. counsel, 1967-68; v.p. labor relations Chgo. and Northwestern Transp. Co., 1968-73, v.p. operations, 1973-76, pres., chief exec. officer, 1976—, also chmn., dir., 1985—; dir. Nicor, No. Ill. Gas Co., Nalco Chem. Co., Continental Ill. Holding Corp., C. & N.W. subs. cos. Chmn. bd. trustees DePaul U.; trustee Fenwick High Sch., Rush St. Luke's Med. Ctr. Served as 1st lt. AUS, 1955-58; capt. Res. Mem. Assn. Am. Rys. (dir. 1976—), Western Ry. Assn. (dir.), Nat. Ry. Labor Conf. (dir.). Clubs: Chicago; Commercial; Economic of Chgo.; Butler Nat.; Hinsdale Golf; Sombrero Country; Mid-Am. Lodge: Knights of Malta. Home: 422 S Oak St Hinsdale IL 60521 Office: One Northwestern Center Chicago IL 60606

WOLFE, PATRICIA ROBERTS, educator, curriculum consultant; b. Kings Mt., N.C., July 1, 1942; d. Garland Miller and Pearl (Webb) Roberts; m. Thomas M. Wolfe, Aug. 23, 1963 (div. Jan. 1980); 1 dau., Mary Alice. B.A., U. N.C., 1964; postgrad. U. Philippines, 1965-66, Portland State U., 1969-70; M.Ed., U. Mass., 1972; postgrad. U. Cin., 1980. Cert. tchr., prin., Ohio, Mass. Instr., Clark AFB Edn. Center, Philippines, 1964-67; tchr. Klamath Falls (Oreg.) Schs., 1967-70, Gastonia (N.C.) Schs., 1970-71; reading specialist Chicopee (Mass.) Schs., 1971-74, Greene Joint Vocat. Sch., Xenia, Ohio,

1975—; cons. in curriculum and mgmt. Mem. exec. com. Greene County (Ohio) Democratic Party; exec. treas. Greene County Mental Health Bd. Mem. Am. Vocat. Assn., Ohio Vocat. Assn., NEA, Western Ohio Edn. Assn., Ohio Spl. Needs Assn., DAR, Bus. and Profl. Women, AAUW, Jamestown Grange, Internat. Platform Assn., Phi Delta Kappa. Democrat. Methodist. Author: The You Need to Read Book; contbr. poetry to mag. Home: 6565 US 35 E Jamestown OH 45335 Office: 2960 W Enon Rd Xenia OH 45385

WOLFE, PAUL JAY, geophysics educator, exploration consultant; b. Mansfield, Ohio, Oct. 2, 1938; s. Walter Williamson and Irva Louisa (Fulton) W.; m. Carolyn Jean Mogg, July 9, 1960; children—Bruce L., Craig C. B.S. in Physics, Case Inst. Tech., 1960, M.S. in Physics, 1963, Ph.D. in Physics, 1966. Design engr. Gen. Electric Co., East Cleveland, Ohio, 1960-61; asst. prof. Wright State U., Dayton, Ohio, 1966-70, assoc. prof. geophysics, 1971—, chmn. dept. physics, 1972-75, chmn. dept. geology, 1983-84. NSF fellow U.S. Bur. Mines, Denver, 1979-80. Mem. Soc. Exploration Geophysicists, Am. Assn. Physics Tchrs., Ohio Acad. Sci., Am. Phys. Soc., Sigma Pi Sigma, Tau Beta Pi. Democrat. Lutheran. Home: 1418 Mapleridge Dr Fairborn OH 45324 Office: Wright State U Dept Physics Dayton OH 45435

WOLFE, ROBERT, JR., artist, educator, printmaker; b. Oxford, Ohio, May 15, 1930; s. Robert and Bessie (Lowe) W. B.F.A., Miami U., Oxford, 1952, B.S., 1955; M.F.A., U. Iowa, 1960; pvt. study, Rome, 1961. Tchr. art Cin. Pub. Schs., 1955-57; instr. art Clarion Coll., Pa., 1961-62; prof. art Miami U., Oxford, 1963—; vis. artist Dayton Art Inst., Ohio, 1970, U. Nebr.-Lincoln, 1978, Fed. U. of Parana, Curitiba, Brazil, 1983. Artist-printmaker over 200 competions, 1957—; 16 one man exhbns. prints, paintings, drawings, 1970—; hand-printed, hand-bound book: Voiles Before Regatta, 1984. Bd. dirs. Oxford Neighborhood Assn., 1982—. Served to sgt. U.S. Army, 1952-54. Recipient award for contbr. to arts in Ohio, Ohio Arts Council, 1972; recipient numerous research awards, Miami U., Oxford, 1972, 75, 78, 82-84. Mem. Ohio Parana Com., Phi Kappa Phi, Delta Phi Delta (treas. 1950-52). Democrat. Avocation: horse raising. Home: 418 Bouden Ln Oxford OH 45056 Office: Dept Art Miami U Oxford OH 45056

WOLFE, ROBERT BRIAN, pharmacist; b. Mt. Vernon, Ind., Mar. 1, 1956; s. John Robert and Gladys Fern (Grabert) W. B.S. in Pharmacy, Purdue Univ., 1979. Registered pharmacist, Ind. Pharmacist, Welborn Bapt. Hosp., Evansville, Ind., 1979-80, USPHS, New Orleans, 1980-81, St. Vincent Hosp., Indpls., 1982—. Developer pharmacists role in care of oncology patients (Partner in Quality Care award 1984), 1983. Com. mem. Am. Cancer Soc., Indpls., 1982—, workshop chmn., 1983—, bd. dirs., 1984—. Served to lt. (j.g.) USPHS, 1980-81. Recipient H. George DeKay award Purdue Univ., 1979; Spl. Assignment Ribbon USPHS, 1980; Eagle Scout award Boy Scouts Am., 1973. Mem. Am. Pharm. Assn., Am. Soc. Hosp. Pharmacists (spl. interest group oncology 1981—), Ind. Soc. Hosp. Pharmacists (nominations chmn. 1984-85), Ind. Soc. Hosp. Pharmacists Region I (pres. 1985—), Kappa Psi Pharm. Frat., Purdue Univ. Alumni Assn. Mem. United Ch. Christ. Lodge: Order DeMolay. Avocations: Travel; photography; camping; bicycling; music.

WOLFE, SHEEMON AARON, podiatrist; b. Dayton, Ohio, Oct. 27, 1923; s. Jacob and Fannie (Froug) W.; student U. Dayton, 1942; D.P.M., Ohio Coll. Podiatric Medicine, 1951; m. Rachell Goldrich, Jan. 2, 1960; 1 dau., Andrea Nicole. Med. staff affiliate Good Samaritan Hosp., Dayton, 1955-83, chmn. podiatry sect., 1965-72; podiatric surgeon, courtesy staff, podiatry residency dir. Greene Meml. Hosp., Xenia, Ohio, 1975—; podiatric surgeon assoc. attending staff St. Elizabeth Med. Center, Dayton, 1981—; asst. prof. clin. services Ohio Coll. Podiatric Medicine, 1972-76, adj. clin. instr., 1977; clin. instr. Scholl Sch. Podiatric Medicine, Chgo., 1983—. Served with 217th F.A., 44th Inf. Div., U.S. Army, 1943-46; ETO. Decorated Bronze Star medal. Diplomate Am. Bd. Podiatric Orthopedics lic. gen. class amateur radio operator, pvt. pilot. Mem. Am. Coll. Foot Surgeons (asso.), Ohio Podiatry Assn. (chmn. bd. trustees, 1978-79, pres., 1979-80, Silver Gavel Club 1980), Am. Podiatry Assn., Am. Acad. Podiatry Sports Medicine, Am. Assn. Hosp. Podiatrists, Am. Radio Relay League (life), Dayton Amateur Radio Assn., Quarter Century Wireless Assn., Jewish War Vets. Jewish. Club: Masons. Patentee in field. Home: 180 Burgess Ave Dayton OH 45415 Office: 2422 Salem Ave Dayton OH 45406

WOLFE, WARREN DWIGHT, lawyer; b. Boston, July 30, 1926; s. Louis Julius and Rose (Daniels) W.; B.S. in Journalism, Northwestern U., 1949; M. Internat. Affairs, Columbia U., 1951; J.D. with high honors, U. Toledo, 1959; m. Caroline M. DuMont, Dec. 29, 1973. Reporter, Wilmington (Del.) Record, 1951-52; Sunday editor, asst. news editor Middletown (Ohio) Jour., 1952-55; copy reader, sect. editor Toledo Blade, 1955-60; admitted to Ohio bar, 1959, Mich. bar, 1960; assoc. Bugbee & Conkle, Toledo, 1960-64, partner, 1964—. Pres. Health Planning Assn. Northwest Ohio, 1970-73; mem. Comprehensive Health Planning Adv. Council to Ohio Dept. Health, 1972-75; mem. Ohio Gov.'s Task Force on Health, 1973-74. Trustee Toledo Legal Aid Soc., 1968—, pres., 1973-75; trustee Toledo Animal Shelter Assn., 1962-75; trustee Lucas County unit Am. Cancer Soc., 1964—, v.p., 1976-81, pres., 1981-83; trustee Ohio div., 1969-74, 85—. Served with USNR, 1944-46. Mem. Am., Ohio, Lucas County (pres. 1966), Toledo (exec. com. 1969-75) bar assns., State Bar Mich., Am. Trial Lawyers Assn., Law Alumni Assn. U. Toledo Coll. Law (pres. 1965), Sigma Delta Chi. Mason. Club: Toledo Ski (treas. 1972-75, pres. 1975-76). Home: 4562 Westbourne Toledo OH 43623 Office: 1301 Toledo Trust Bldg Toledo OH 43604

WOLFE, WILLIAM KEITH, educational administrator; b. Potosi, Wis., Dec. 9, 1933; s. Vilas Dawson and Jessie May (Schramm) W.; m. Kathleen Leola Grattan, Oct. 9, 1960; children—Gary, Gretchen, Aaron, Darwyn, Sean. B.S., U. Wis.-Platteville, 1961, M.S., 1966. Tchr., Platteville, Potosi and Cassville, Wis., 1952-61; elem. prin. Platteville Pub. Schs., 1961-68, middle sch. prin., 1968-69; communications instr. Southwest Wis. Vocat. Tech. Inst., Fennimore, 1969-80, div. chmn. gen. edn., 1980—. Author: Articulation of Adult Basic Education with Career Exploration, 1978; Articulation of General Education and Occupational Competenties, 1974; (with others) Vocat.-Tech. Adult Education's Curriculum Guide for Career Development, 1977. Lay moderator Davies Meml. United Ch. of Christ, Potosi, 1965, 81-82; asst. scoutmaster U.S. Grant council Boy Scouts Am., Potosi, 1955-57. Served with U.S. Army, 1957-59. Named Outstanding Young Educator Platteville Jaycees, 1965. Mem. Am. Vocat. Assn., Wis. Assn. for Vocat. Adult Edn. (bd. dirs. 1981-83, Teaching Excellence award 1980), NEA, Upper Midwest Regional Edn. Lab. Assn. Platteville Ed. Assn. (pres. 1964-65), Blackhawk Schs. Edn. Assn. (sec. 1954-55), Silas Shepherd Lodge Research, Phi Delta Kappa. Republican. Avocations: author, acting, choir direction, travel. Home: Route 2 Box 83 Potosi WI 53820 Office: Southwest Wis Vocat Tech Inst Rt 1 Box 500 Fennimore WI 53809

WOLFER, GEORGE KOOBS, osteopathic physician, radiologist; b. Pekin, Ill.; Feb. 9, 1928; s. John Edgar and Minnie (Koobs) W.; m. Natalie Joy, Aug. 19, 1951; children—James, Dean, George Koobs II, William, Lori. B.A., Andrews U., 1952; D.O., Chgo. Coll. Osteopathy, 1958. Intern, Chgo. Osteo. Hosp., 1958-59; resident in radiology Art Centre Hosp., Detroit, 1962-65; practice osteo. medicine specializing in radiology; gen. practice, Howard City, Mich., 1959-62; chief radiologist Belding (Mich.) Osteo. Hosp., Mecosta Meml. Hosp., Stanwood, Mich., Sheridan (Mich.) Osteo. Hosp., 1965—; assoc. plin. prof. Mich. State U., 1978—. Trustee Seaway Community Hosp., Muskegon (Mich.), 1968-70; mem. U.S. Senate Bus. Adv. Bd., 1982-83; mem. Republican Presdl. Task Force, (charter). Mem. Am. Osteo. Coll. Radiology, Am. Osteo. Assn. (cert. radiologist), Mich. Osteo. Assn., Central Mich. Osteo. Assn., Mich. Radiology Soc. (assoc.). Seventh-Day Adventist. Contbr. articles in field to profl. jours. Home: 7817 N Cedar Lake Rd Edmore MI 48820 Office: Route 2 Edmore MI 48829

WOLFF, GEORGE THOMAS, atmospheric scientist, educator; b. Irvington, N.J., Nov. 29, 1947; s. George C. and Margaret M. (Leroy) W.; m. Carol Ann Wirth, Aug. 12, 1972; children—Elaine, Meg. B.S. in Chem. Engring., N.J. Inst. Tech., 1969; M.S., NYU, 1970; Ph.D., Rutgers U., 1974. Assoc. engr. Interstate Sanitation Commn., N.Y.C., 1973-77; sr. staff scientist Gen. Motors Research Labs., Warren, Mich., 1977—; cons. U.S. EPA, Research Triangle Park, N.C., 1975—; cons. EPA Sci. Adv. Bd., Washington, 1984—; adj. prof. atmospheric sci. U. Mich., Ann Arbor, 1984—. Editor: Carbonaceous Particles in the Atmosphere, 1981. Contbr. articles to profl. jours. Chmn. Environ. Commn., Caldwell, N.J., 1974-77. Recipient Environ. Achievement award Gen. Motors Corp., Detroit, 1983; John Campbell award, G.M. Research Labs., Warren, Mich., 1984. Russel fellow, Rutgers U., New Brunswick, N.J., 1972-73. Mem. Air Pollution Control Assn. (tech. chmn. 1984-85), Am. Meteorol. Soc. (atmospheric chemistry chmn. 1972—), Sigma Xi. Roman Catholic. Office: Gen Motors Research Labs Environ Sci Dept Warren MI 48090

WOLFF, JOANNE SLAY, human resource management consultant; b. Detroit, Apr. 2, 1953; d. Lorenzo and Mahala (Rowell) Slay; m. Mervin Gary Wolff, July 22, 1978; 1 dau., Garen S. B.S. in Psychology, Tenn. State U., 1976; M.A. in Library and Info. Sci., U. Toledo, 1979. Drug abuse counselor Comprehensive Neighborhood Health Services Methadone Clinic, Detroit, 1974-75; on-site data collector W.O.M.A.N., Detroit, 1976-77; info. and referral specialist Toledo Mental Health Ctr., 1977; acting dir. Learning Resource Ctr., John Wesley Coll., Owosso, Mich., 1978-79; program specialist sch. and community affairs Mich. Dept. Edn., Lansing, 1980-81; co-owner, founder Wolff-Harris Research and Cons., Detroit, 1980-81; pres., founder J.S. Wolff Co., Detroit, 1981—; founder and developer In-House Workshops, at home, 1984. Recipient Outstanding Service award NCCJ, 1984. Democrat. Baptist. Avocations: tennis; chess. Home and Office: 8051 Third Ave Detroit MI 48202

WOLFF, KENNETH RAY, education educator; b. Liberty Center, Ohio, Apr. 28, 1933; s. Joseph H. and Hazel I. (Mayer) W.; m. Joyce Follin, Aug. 31, 1957; children—Scott, Lori, Karen. B.S. in Edn., Bowling Green State U., 1959, M.Ed., 1964; Ph.D., Ohio U., 1969. Tchr. Holgate Schs., Ohio, 1959, Bryan City Schs., Ohio. 1959-64; prin. Keystone Schs., LaGrange, Ohio, 1964-66; teaching fellow Ohio U., Athens, 1966-68; social studies specialist Supplementary Edn. Ctr., Logan, Ohio, 1968-69; mem. faculty Kent State U., Canton, Ohio, 1969—, now assoc. prof. elem. and secondary edn.; cons. social studies Ginn & Co., Lexington, Mass., 1982—. Served to capt., USAF, 1952-56. Tchr. Devel. grantee State of Ohio, 1978. Mem. Nat. Council Social Studies (mem. exec. com.; bd. dirs.), Ohio Council Social Studies (pres. 1981-82). Avocations: Reading, camping, photography, travel. Home: 408 Middlesworth Blvd North Canton OH 44720 Office: Kent State U 6000 Frank Rd NW Canton OH 44720

WOLFROM, GLEN WALLACE, animal nutritionist, researcher; b Freeport, Ill., Apr. 8, 1947; s. Glen Edward and Wilma Orlean (Trost) W.; m. Rebecca Ann McNeily, Aug. 16, 1969; children—Cynthia Kay, Katie Jo. B.S., with honors, Western Ill. U., 1969; M.S., So. Ill. U., 1972; Ph.D., U. Mo., 1976. Nutritionist, Pet Inc., Greenville, Ill., 1976-78; research nutritionist Internat. Minerals and Chem. Corp., Terre Haute, Ind., 1978—. Contbr. articles to profl. jours. Patentee in field. Ill. State Scholar, 1965-69; William H. Hatch fellow, 1971-73. Mem. Am. Soc. Animal Sci. (Scholarship award 1967, 68), AAAS, Creation Research Soc. (membership sec. 1984—). Baptist. Avocations: fishing; photography. Office: Internat Minerals and Chem Corp 1331 S 1st St Terre Haute IN 47808

WOLK, ALAN MURRAY, lawyer, labor arbitrator; b. Cleve., Mar. 17, 1932; s. Samuel Louis and Jean (Mintz) W.; m. Phyllis Grossberg, Dec. 1, 1957; children—Martin, Jeff, Scott. B.B.A., Cleve. State Coll., 1953; J.D., Ohio State Coll., 1955; postgrad. Case Western Res. Sch. Law, 1959-62; student Ohio State Bar Assn. Coll., 1983-84. Bar: Ohio 1955, U.S. Supreme Ct., 1965. Asst. atty. gen. State of Ohio, 1958-62, 70-81; acting judge Mcpl. Ct., Shaker Heights, Ohio, 1969-77; dir. of law City of University Heights, Ohio, 1980—; seminar chmn. Cuyahoga County Law Dirs., Cleve., 1981—, labor panel mem. Am. Arbitration Assn., Cleve., 1974—, Fed. Mediation and Conciliation Service, Washington, 1979—; mem. panel Ohio State Employment Relations Bd., 1985—. Editor mag. Cuyahoga County Bar Bull., 1958-63. Contbr. articles to profl. jours. Pres. University Heights Democratic Club, Ohio, 1968-74; jud. scanning com. Citizens League Cleve., 1977; bd. dirs. Temple Emanu El, University Heights, 1982-84; trustee Handgun Fedn. Ohio, 1985—. Fellow Cleve. Acad. Trial Lawyers; mem. Cuyahoga County Bar Assn. (sec. 1963-70, pres. 1984—, exec. dir. 1963-70) (Special Merit award 1970), ABA, Ohio Assn. Civil Trial Attys., Ohio State Bar Assn. (ho. of dels. 1974—), Tau Epsilon Rho (chancellor, 1963). Lodges: Masons (master 1974-75), B'nai B'rith (fin. sec. 1958-63). Office: 1525 Leader Bldg Cleveland OH 44114

WOLK, JOHN PAUL, auditor; b. St. Louis, Feb. 13, 1948; s. Albert F. and Patricia R. (Shannon) W.; m. Mary Theresa Lacey, June 5, 1971; children—Christopher, Laura, John, Lisa, B.S. in Bus., U. Mo.-St. Louis, 1970; M.B.A, St. Louis U., 1974. Cons., United Way of St. Louis, 1972-74; asst. to controller Peabody Holding Co., St. Louis, 1975-76, mgr. fin. analysis, 1976-78, asst. controller, 1978-80, controller Ind. div., Evansville, 1981-85, dir. internal auditor, St. Louis, 1985—. Chmn. fin. com. Holy Rosary Parish, Evansville, 1982-85, mem. parish bd., 1982-85. Served to 1st lt. U.S. Army, 1970-72. Republican. Roman Catholic. Avocations: golf; tennis; racquetball. Home: 488 Runnymede Saint Louis MO 63141 Office: Peabody Holding Co 301 N Memorial Dr Saint Louis MO 63102

WOLK, YALE M., health care executive, service company executive; b. Mpls., Apr. 11, 1945; s. Arnold D. and Marcia (Moorvitz) W.; m. Roberta Lynn Goldman, Mar. 4, 1967; children—Sonya, Erin. B.A., Mich. State U., 1966; M.H.A., U. Minn., 1971. Adminstrv. asst. Dekalb Gen. Hosp., Smithville, Tenn., 1971-73; asst. adminstr. Saginaw Osteo. Hosp., Mich., 1973; asst. adminstr. Community Hosp. Ottawa, Ill., 1973-74, chief exec. officer, pres., 1974—, North Central Service Corp., Ottawa, 1984—; dir. Community Hosp. Ottawa, North Central Service Corp.; mem. council on pub. relations Ill. Hosp. Assn., Naperville, 1984—. Advisor: A Guide to Stategic Planning for Hospitals, 1979. Bd. dirs., sec., treas. Camp Fire Council, Ottawa, 1980-83; bd. dirs. LaSalle County Council on Alcoholism, Ottawa, 1982—; task force mem. LaSalle County State Atty., Ottawa, 1984. Served to 1st lt. U.S. Army, 1967-69. Named Outstanding Young Person Ottawa Jaycees, 1979. Mem. Am. Coll. Hosp. Adminstrs., Minn. Program Alumni Assn., C. of C. (bd. dirs. 1984—). Lodge: Rotary. Avocations: handball, racketball, golf, cycling. Office: Community Hosp Ottawa 1100 E Norris Dr Ottawa IL 61350

WOLLENBURG, LEAH RENEE, athletic trainer; b. Wisconsin Rapids, Wis., Sept. 18, 1955; d. Virgil Lee and Lorraine (Suhr) W. B.S., U. N.D., 1977; M.A., Colo. State U., 1978. Cert. athletic trainer. Head trainer women's athletics U. Minn., Mpls., 1978—; athletic trainer Minn. State High Sch. League, Mpls., 1979—; lectr. workshop Cramer Products, Gardner, Kans., 1979—. mem. Nat. Athletic Trainers Assn., Minn. Athletic Trainers Assn. (treas. 1981—), Gt. Lakes Athletic Trainers Assn. (state rep.). Office: U Minn Women's Athletics 169 BFAB 516 15th Ave SE Minneapolis MN 55455

WOLLER, EDWARD ALBERT, lawyer, business law educator; b. Ottawa, Ill., Oct. 20, 1954; s. Fred Allen and Dorothy Ann (Underhill) W.; m. Lynn Marie Rowbottom, May 22, 1976. B.A. magna cum laude, Loras Coll., 1976; J.D., So. Ill. U., 1979. Bar: Ill. 1979, U.S. Dist Ct. (cen. dist.) Ill. 1979. Assoc., Law Office of D.J. McRae, Kewanee, Ill., 1979—; mem. bus. law faculty Black Hawk Coll.-East Campus, Kewanee. Mem. Henry County Bar Assn., Ill. State Bar Assn., ABA, Am. Trial Lawyers Assn., Delta Epsilon Sigma. Democrat. Roman Catholic. Lodges: Kiwanis, Elks. Home: 1041 Rockwell Kewanee IL 61443 Office: Law Office D J McRae 217 W Second Kewanee IL 61443

WOLLER, JACK EMIL, manufacturing company executive; b. Champaign, Ill., Oct. 19, 1925; s. Emil Albert and Melita Marie (Davis) W.; m. Phyllis Carson, Nov. 27, 1947; children—Jack, Jill, Timothy, Kim, Amy. B.S., U. Ill., 1950. Mem. sales staff Internat. Silver Co., Meriden, Conn., 1952-64; with Bissell, Inc., Grand Rapids, Mich., 1964—, now nat. incentive sales mgr. Served with USN, 1943-45, 50-52; PTO. Mem. Nat. Premium Sales Execs. (pres. 1978), Assn. Retail Mkgt. Services (dir.). Republican. Methodist. Office: Bissell Inc 2345 Walker Ave NW Grand Rapids MI 49504

WOLLMAN, ROGER LELAND, federal judge; b. Frankfort, S.D., May 29, 1934; s. Edwin and Katherine Wollman; B.A., Tabor Coll., Hillsboro, Kans., 1957; J.D. magna cum laude, U. S.D., 1962; LL.M., Harvard U., 1964; m. Diane Marie Schroeder, June 21, 1959; children—Steven James, John Mark, Thomas Roger. Admitted to S.D. bar, 1964, practiced in Aberdeen, 1964-71; justice S.D. Supreme Ct., 1971-85, chief justice, 1978-82; judge U.S. Ct. Appeals (8th cir.), 1985—; states atty. Brown County, Aberdeen, 1967-71. Served with AUS, 1957-59. Office: Room 212 Fed Bldg Pierre SD 57501*

WOLLNEY, JOHN LOWELL, orthodontist; b. Portland, Maine, Feb. 4, 1942; s. Arthur Edward and Kathleen Harper (Hudson) W.; children—Kataryn Ann, John Lowell, Elizabeth Giltner. B.A., Tulane U., 1963; D.D.S., Loyola U., New Orleans, 1967; orthodontic cert. Loyola U., Chgo., 1971. Assoc., Milton Braun, Olympia Fields, Ill., 1970-72, John R. Thompson & A. Venezia, Flossmoor, Ill., 1974-76; practice dentistry specializing in orthodontics, Libertyville, Ill., 1976—; asst. prof. Loyola U., Maywood, Ill., 1976—. Patentee dental instrument. Served to capt. U.S. Army, 1967-69. Mem. Ill. Soc. Orthodontists (sec. treas. 1982-83, pres. 1984-85), ADA. Republican. Presbyterian. Home: 55 Milwaukee Ave Vernon Hills IL 60061 Office: 109 W Maple Ave Libertyville IL 60048

WOLNERMAN, ALLEN PHILIP, pharmacist; b. Cleve., Sept. 1, 1953; s. David and Jennie W.; m. Amy Hollander, July 2, 1978; 1 son, Daniel Gary. B.S., Ind. U., 1975; B.S., Drake U., 1980. Registered pharmacist, Iowa, Fla., Tex. Pres., Graw Inc., Des Moines, 1983—; pres. 20/20 Optical, Inc., Des Moines, 1982—; cons., 1980—. Fellow Am. Soc. Cons. Pharmacists; mem. Nat. Assn. Retail Druggists, Am. Pharm. Assn., Iowa Pharmacists Assn., Ind. U. Alumni Assn., Fla. Pharmacists Assn. Jewish. Home: 5792 Linden Ct Des Moines IA 50324 Office: 70th and Douglas Sts Urbandale IA 50322

WOLPE, HOWARD E., congressman; b. Los Angeles, Nov. 2, 1939; s. Leon and Zelda Wolpe; B.A., Reed Coll., 1960; Ph.D., M.I.T., 1967; 1 son, Michael. Asst. prof. polit. sci. Western Mich. U., 1967-69, assoc. prof., 1970-72; cons. Peace Corps, 1966-67, Fgn. Service Inst., U.S. Dept. State, 1967-72; regional rep., state liaison to U.S. Senator Donald Riegle, 1977-78; mem. Mich. Ho. of Reps., 1973-76; city commr. Kalamazoo, 1969-73; mem. 96th-99th Congresses from 3d Dist. Mich., chmn. Fgn. Affairs subcom. on Africa, mem. house budget com.; chmn. N.E.-Midwest Congl. Coalition. Democrat. Jewish. Author: Urban Politics in Nigeria: A Study of Port Harcourt, 1974; (with Robert Melson) Nigeria: Modernization and the Politics of Communalism, 1974. Office: 1527 Longworth House Office Bldg Washington DC 20515

WOLSKI, RICHARD STANLEY, manufacturing company manager; b. Detroit, Nov. 6, 1939; s. Stanley Thomas Harriett (Pillerowski) W.; m. Faith Ann Orlando, Feb. 21, 1967; children—Christopher, Sheryl, Jewel; m. Brenda Joyce Cabeen, June 21, 1980. B.S., U. Md., 1963. Div. mgr. VEMCO Products Co., Piqua, Ohio, 1965-67; gen. mgr. Fastener Assembly Co. div. Key Internat., Southfield, Mich., 1967-72; pres. F&F Industries, Mt. Clemens, Mich., 1972-75; gen. mgr. Cuzco Products Co., Fowlersville, Mich., 1977-79; dir. mfg. Impex Co., div. Keystone Consol. Industries, 1979-81; gen. mgr. Barker Wire Products Inc., Keosauqua, Iowa, 1982—. Candidate for U.S. Ho. of Reps., 1972; nominated for mayor, Warren, Mich., 1977. Served with USAF, 1956-59. Sr. mem. Soc. Mfg. Engrs. Republican. Roman Catholic. Designed and marketed pickup truck safe, 1982; redisigned and marketed rally wheel lugs, 1968.

WOLSKY, ALAN MARTIN, physicist; b. Bklyn., May 17, 1943; s. Lorenz Albert and Roselyn (Casper) W.; m. Mary-Jo Bryan, Dec. 31, 1969; 1 child, Rebecca Jeanette. A.B., Columbia U., 1964; M.S., U. Pa., 1965, Ph.D., 1969. Vis. fellow Courant Inst. Math. Scis., N.Y.C., 1970-71; asst. prof. Temple U., Phila., 1971-75; scientist Argonne Nat. Lab., Ill., 1975—, sect. leader, 1980—; mem. com. on data for sci. and tech. Internat. Council Sci. Unions, 1984—. Contbr. articles to profl. jours.; reviewer Rev. Econs. and Statistics, 1982—, Resources & Energy, 1982—, Internat. Jour. Hydrogen Energy, 1984—, NSF, 1984—. Photographer, exhibited in group shows, 1975, 80. Vice pres. Maple Hill Improvement Assn., Downers Grove, Ill., 1980-81; v.p. Congregation Etz Chaim, Lombard, Ill., 1982-85, pres., 1985—. Post-doctoral fellow NRC-Air Force Office Sci. Research, 1970. Mem. Internat. Assn. Energy Economists, Am. Physics Soc. Avocations: exercise, reading. Home: 5461 Hillcrest Ave Downers Grove IL 60515 Office: Argonne Nat Lab 9700 S Cass Ave Argonne IL 60439

WOLTER, JOHN THOMAS, air force officer; b. Houston, Aug. 8, 1953; s. John Ernst and Doris Linnea (Johnson) W.; m. Marguerite Paty, Oct. 23, 1976; children—Lindsey Malia, David Andrew. B.S., U.S. Air Force Acad., 1975; M.A., Central Mich. U., 1985. Commd. 2d lt. U.S. Air Force, 1975, advanced through grades to capt.; undergrad. pilot trainee 82d Student Squadron, Williams AFB, Ariz., 1975-76; pilot 20th Aeromed. Airlift Squadron, Clark AFB, Philippines, 1977-79, 4th Mil. Airlift Squadron, McChord AFB, Wash., 1979-82; air staff tng. Air Nat. Guard, Pentagon, Washington, 1982-83; pilot 46th Bomb Squadron, Grand Forks AFB, N.D., 1983-85, exec. officer 319th Bomb Wing, 1985—, pres. Base Jr. Officer Council, 1984. Tchr. various Sunday schs., Washington, Wash. state, Grand Forks, 1980-85; vol. Muscular Dystrophy Telethon, Grand Forks, 1984; com. chmn., event dir. N.D. Spl. Olympics, Grand Forks, 1984-85. Mem. Air Force Assn., 15th Air Force Assn., Order of Daedalians. Club: Toastmasters (ednl. v.p. 1982-83). Presbyterian. Avocations: long distance running; racquetball. Office: 319th Bombardment Wing Grand Forks AFB ND 58205

WOLTERS, PHILLIP JOHN, JR., information specialist, consultant; b. Grand Rapids, Mich., Oct. 31, 1943; s. Phillip John Sr. and Emogene (Lynn) W.; m. Mary Ann Grandy, June 4, 1968; children—Phillip John III, Theresa Lynn. B.S. in Bus. Admintrn., Aquinas Coll., 1967. Systems analyst Wolverine World Wide, Rockford, Mich., 1969-72; lead implementation analyst Foremost Ins., Grand Rapids, Mich., 1972-78; sr. systems analyst Interstate Motor Freight, Grand Rapids, 1978-79; systems analyst Rapistan div. Lear Siegler, Grand Rapids, 1979-81; info. specialist Amway Corp., Ada, Mich., 1982-85; sr. systems analyst Foremost Ins. Co., Grand Rapids, 1985—. Mem. West Michigan Water Ski Assn. (high jump champion, 1980), Assn. Systems Mgmt. (treas. 1982-83), Rockford Jaycees (sec.-treas. 1969-72). Club: Chess (Grandville, Mich.) (pres. 1961-62). Lodge: Masons. Avocations: camping; tennis; water and snow skiing. Home: 197 Gaylord Dr Rockford MI 49341 Office: Foremost Service Center 5251 36th St SE Grand Rapids MI 49501

WOLTHUIS, LORETTA MAE, home economics educator; b. Holstein, Iowa, May 26, 1941; d. Lester Peter and Erma Hariett (Thorborg) Clausen; m. Marven Harm Wolthuis, Aug. 5, 1967; 1 child, Karla. B.S., U. No. Iowa, 1963; M.S., Mankato State U., 1972. Home econs. tchr. Humboldt Community Sch., Iowa, 1963-66, Blue Earth Community Sch., Minn., 1966-67, Dist. 77, Mankato, Minn., 1970-72; grad. asst. Mankato State U., 1967-68, 69-70, instr. home econs., 1972—, chmn. dept. home econs., 1980—. Mem. Am. Home Econs. Assn., Assn. Coll. Profs. Textiles and Clothing, Delta Kappa Gamma. Lutheran. Club: HE in Homemaking (chmn. 1976-77). Avocations: Golf, spectator sports, sewing, reading, crewel. Home: 123 Long Mankato MN 56001 Office: Mankato State U Dept Home Econs Box 44 Mankato MN 56001

WOLYNES, PETER GUY, chemistry educator, researcher; b. Chgo., Apr. 21, 1953; s. Peter and Evelyn Eleanor (Etter) W.; m. Jane Lee Fox, Nov. 26, 1976 (div.); m. Kathleen Cull Bucher, Dec. 22, 1984. A.B., Ind. U., 1971; A.M., Harvard U., 1972, Ph.D. in Chem. Physics, 1976. Research assoc. MIT, 1975-76; asst. prof. Harvard U., 1976-79, assoc. prof., 1979-80; assoc. prof. U. Ill., Urbana, 1980-83, prof., 1983—; vis. scientist Max Planck Inst. Biophys. Chemistry, Gottingen, W.Ger., 1977, Inst. Molecular Sci., Okazaki, Japan, 1982. Mem. Ill. Alliance to Prevent Nuclear War. Sloan Found. fellow, 1981-83. Mem. Am. Phys. Soc., Am. Chem. Soc. (award for pure chemistry 1986), AAAS, Sigma Xi. Contbr. articles to profl. jours. Office: 505 S Mathews Sch Chem Scis U Ill Urbana IL 61801

WONG, MARGARET WAI, lawyer; b. Hong Kong, July 27, 1950; d. Mien Lin and Kuan Kuo (Kwan) Hwang; m. Kam M. Chan, Jan. 3, 1983. A.A., Ottumwa Heights Coll. (Iowa), 1971; B.Sc. in Chemistry-Biology, Western Ill. U., 1973; J.D., SUNY-Buffalo, 1976. Bar: Ohio 1977, N.Y. 1977, D.C. 1980, U.S. Dist. Ct. 1980, U.S. Ct. Appeals (6th cir.) 1983. Instr. bus. law SUNY-Fredonia, 1977; mgmt. trainee Central Nat. Bank, Cleve., 1977-78; chief legal and fin. officer Buffalo City Govt., 1979-80; assoc. Berger & Kirchenbaum, Cleve., 1980-81; prin. Margaret W. Wong & Assocs., Cleve., 1981—; co-founder, co-owner Pearl of the Orient Restaurant, Cleve., 1978—, Richmond Apothecary, Cleve., 1983—; spl. counsel State of Ohio, 1985. Contbr. articles to legal jours. Trustee, Women Space, Cleve., 1982—, Fedn. Community Planning, Cleve., 1983—, Women City Club, Cleve., 1983—, Orgn. Chinese Ams., Cleve., 1983—, Cleve. Council Human Relations, 1983—; sec., trustee Chinese Assn. Greater Cleve., 1980—; trustee Women's Law Fund, 1984—, YWCA, 1984—. Named one of Top Ten Outstanding Young Women, Glamour mag., 1983; YWCA Career Woman of Yr., 1984. Mem. Fed. Bar Assn. (sec., trustee chpt. 1983—), ABA, N.Y. State Bar Assn., D.C. Bar Assn., Cuyahoga County Bar Assn., Cleve. Bar Assn. (trustee 1983—), Ohio Bar Assn., Cleve. Trial Lawyers Assn., Am. Assn. Immigration Lawyers. Club: Zonta (trustee 1983-84) (Cleve.). Office: 330 Standard Bldg Cleveland OH 44113

WONG, STEPHEN RYAN, restaurant operator; b. Albert Lea, Minn., Aug. 10, 1948; s. Benjamin C.S. and Mae Sherill (Mah) W. B.A., U. Minn., 1973; B.Laws, U. B.C., 1978. Bar: B.C., 1980. Clerk, assoc. Griffiths & Co., Vancouver, B.C., 1978-80; assoc., lawyer Burnet & Fenton, Vancouver, 1980-81; barrister-at-law Wong & Co., Vancouver, 1981-82; co-owner, ptnr. Wong's Cafe, Rochester, Minn., 1982—. Served to sgt. USMC, 1968-70. Recipient Meritorious Mast Base Material Batalion U.S. Marine Corps, 1970. Mem. Soc. Wine Educators, Am. Inst. Wine and Food, Quill and Scroll. Democrat. Methodist. Avocations: wine collecting; tennis; golf; jazz and swing record collecting; reading. Home: 118-12th Ave SE Rochester MN 55904 Office: Wong's Cafe 4 Third St SW Rochester MN 55902

WOOD, CHERLYE ANN, school board official; b. Princeton, Ill., Oct. 30, 1947; d. Harry Allen and Florence Madeline (Harmon) Carmichael; m. Jerry Lynn Wood, Sept. 11, 1966; children—James W., Angela M., Melissa L. Cert. Hi-Fashion Beauty Coll., Peoria, Ill., 1965—. Tchr., Hi-Fashion Beauty Coll., 1966-71; owner, operator Isle of Beauty Salon, Chillicothe, Ill., 1971-76; mem. Bd. Edn., Sparland, Ill., 1979, pres., 1984—. Mem. Ill. Hairdresser Assn. Democrat. Methodist. Clubs: Sparland Mother's (pres. 1979-81), Sparland Parent Orgn. (pres. 1981-82). Avocations: coaching baseball, swimming, crocheting, reading. Home: Rural Route 1 Box 158 Sparland IL 61565 Office: Sparland Community Unit Sch Dist #3 RR 1 Sparland IL 61565

WOOD, DONALD GENE, architect; b. Castleton, Ind., Feb. 3, 1937; s. Donald and Dora Marie (Sowers) W.; m. Carolyn Sue Wood-Stewart, Sept. 20, 1957; children—Deborah Ann, Donald Gene. B.S. in Arch., U. Cin., 1961. Ptnr., Taylor & Wood Architects, Columbus, Ind., 1961-69; owner Wood & Burd Assocs., Columbus, 1969-74; pres. Wood & Burd, Inc., Columbus, 1974-85; pres. Architect Group, Inc., 1985—; mem. Ind. State Bd. Registration for Architects, 1982—. Served with Ind. N.G., 1954-55, USAR, 1955-61. Mem. AIA, Columbus C. of C., Ind. Soc. Architects, Constrn. Specifications Inst. Clubs: Hoosier Assocs., Harrison Lake Country. Office: PO Box 730 Columbus IN 47202

WOOD, EMMA LOU, real estate mgmt. corp. exec.; b. Jasonville, Ind., Sept. 29, 1935; d. Leo William and Elizabeth (White) Warrick; student Ind. U., 1957-72; m. C.J. Wood, Jan. 31, 1966 (dec.); children—Elizabeth Marie, Charles John. Bookkeeper, Place & Co., South Bend, Ind., 1959-65; pres. C.J. Wood, Inc., South Bend, 1976—. Mem. South Bend C. of C. Clubs: Knollwood Country (Granger, Ind.); Orchard Hills Country (Niles, Mich.). Office: C J Wood Inc 1119 S Franklin St South Bend IN 46624

WOOD, HARLINGTON, JR., judge; b. Springfield, Ill., Apr. 17, 1920; s. Harlington and Marie (Green) W.; A.B., U. Ill., 1942, J.D., 1948. Admitted to Ill. bar, 1948, practiced in Springfield, 1948-69; U.S. atty. So. Dist. Ill., 1958-61; partner firm Wood & Wood, 1961-69; asso. dep. atty. gen. for U.S. attys. U.S. dept. Justice, 1969-70; assoc. dep. atty. gen. Justice Dept., Washington, 1970-72, asst. atty. gen. civil div., 1972-73; U.S. dist. judge So. Dist. Ill., Springfield, 1973-76; judge U.S. Ct. Appeals for 7th Circuit, 1976—. Mem. Am., Ill. bar assns. Address: US Court House Springfield IL 62705

WOOD, JACALYN KAY, educational consultant; b. Columbus, Ohio, May 25, 1949; d. Carleston John and Grace Anna (Schumacher) W. B.A., Georgetown Coll., 1971; M.S., Ohio State U., 1976; Ph.D., Miami U., 1981. Elem. tchr. Bethel-Tate Schs., Ohio, 1971-73, Columbus (Ohio) Christian Sch., 1973-74, Franklin (Ohio) Schs., 1974-79; teaching fellow Miami U., Oxford, Ohio, 1979-81; cons. intermediate grades Erie County Schs., Sandusky, Ohio, 1981— presenter tchr. inservice tng. Mem. council Sta. WVIZ-TV, 1981—; mem. exec. com. Perkins Community Schs., 1981—; mem. community adv. bd. Sandusky Vols. Am., Sandusky Soc. Bank. Mem. Am. Businesswomen's Assn. (local pres. 1985), Assn. Supervision and Curriculum Devel., Internat. Reading Assn., Ohio Sch. Suprs. Assn. (regional pres. 1986), Phi Delta Kappa (local sec. 1985). Lutheran. Home: 4512 7 Venice Heights Blvd Sandusky OH 44870 Office: 2902 Columbus Ave Sandusky OH 44870

WOOD, JAMES NOWELL, See *Who's Who in America,* 43rd edition.

WOOD, JAMES ROBERT, printing company executive; b. Bridgeport, Ill., Apr. 17, 1922; s. George Earl and Fannie Ruth Wood; m. Frances Vivian Fleshman, Sept. 2, 1943; 1 child, David Allan. M.E., Purdue U., 1945. Litho supr. Am. Book-Stratford Press, Saddlebrook, N.J., 1975-76; plant supr. Intercollegiate Press, Kansas City, Kans., 1976-78; plant tech. rep. Hearst Publs., Salem, Ill., 1978-80; sr. project engr. World Color Press, Effingham, Ill., 1980-85; dir. research and engring. St. Dennis Mfg. Co., 1985—. Served to capt. USAF, 1951-53. Mem. Graphic Arts Tech. Found. Republican. Lodge: Rotary (Salem). Avocation: music. Home: 240 Oak Tree Dr Salem IL 62881 Office: St Dennis Mfg Co 1204 W Wabash St Effingham IL 62401

WOOD, JOHN BENSON, mathematics and statistics educator, researcher; b. Ames, Iowa, Oct. 11, 1934; s. Lyman Wench and Alice Mae (Benson) W.; children—Judith L., Elizabeth A., James S. B.S., U. Wis., 1956; M.A., U. Minn., 1962, Ph.D., 1968. Asst. prof. math. Hampton Inst., Va., 1967-70; asst. prof. elem. edn. U. N.D., Grand Forks, 1970-74; elem. tchr., math. specialist New City Sch., St. Louis, 1974-75; research psychologist II, St. Louis State Hosp., 1975-81; adj. asst. prof. Mo. Inst. Psychiatry, St. Louis, 1981-82; asst. prof. U. Wis.-Marathon County Ctr., Wausau, 1982—. Author: (with others) Computers in Mental Health, 1981. Contbr. articles to profl. jours. Mem. Am. Statis. Assn., Nat. Council Tchrs. Math., AAAS. Democrat. Avocations: Design Geometric furniture. Office: U Wis Ctr Marathon County 518 S 7th Ave Wausau WI 54401

WOOD, JOSEPH ROBERTS, music educator, composer; b. Pitts., May 12, 1915; s. Joseph Roberts and Eliza (Bell) W.; Carol Streater, Sept. 4, 1940 (div.); 1 dau., Lynne Roberts Wood Dimopoulos; m. 2d, Wendy Elizabeth Bradley, Nov. 10, 1961 (div.); 1 dau., Lorna Elizabeth. Student Bucknell U., 1932-34, Inst. Musical Art, 1934-36; piano diploma Juilliard Grad. Sch., 1940, B.S., diploma composition, 1949; M.A., Columbia U., 1949, 1950. Composer, Chekhov Theater, 1939-41; free-lance composer/arranger, N.Y., 1941-50; tchr. Oberlin Conservatory, Ohio, 1950-85; resident composer Villa Montalvo, Calif., 1957. musician. Served with U.S. Army, 1943-46. Juilliard fellow, 1936-40; MacDowell Colony fellow, 1953—; Huntington Hartford fellow, 1960; Ditson award Columbia U., 1946; Mem. Am. Composers Alliance, Ohio Tchrs. Composition and Theory (past pres.). Club: Oberlin City. Composer 4 symphonies; 4 string quartets, orchestral, choral, chamberworks; book re-viewer.

WOOD, KENNETH, lawyer; b. East Cleveland, Ohio, Oct. 16, 1947; s. Joseph and Florence Wood; m. JoAnn Mrazek, July 1, 1967. B.A., Cleve. State U., 1971; J.D., Marshall Coll. Law, Cleve., 1974. Bar: Ohio 1974, U.S. Dist. Ct. Ohio 1974, U.S. Supreme Ct. 1979. Assoc., Bremer, Thompson Morhard & Coyne, Cleve., 1974-75; div. legal counsel Scott & Fetzer, Lakewood, Ohio, 1975-76; sole practice law, Twinsburg, Ohio, 1976. Author: Animal Rights and the Law, 1985; Humane Officer's Handbook, 1985. Chmn. bd. dirs. Humane Soc. Greater Akron, Ohio, 1985; mem. Summit County Republican Club, 1971. Roman Catholic. Avocations: animal rights activist. Home: 65 E Streetsboro Hudson Village OH 44236 Office: 10568 Ravenna Rd Twinsburg OH 44087

WOOD, LEONARD CLAIR, history educator, writer; b. Utica, Pa., Jan. 1, 1923; s. John Barnard and Ethel Leota (Boughner) W.; m. Tanya Bogoslovsky, July 19, 1952; children—Stephen (dec.), Anthony, John, Sarah. B.S., Pa. State Coll., 1943; M.A. in History, U. Pa., 1948, Ph.D., 1960; postgrad. U. London. Writer, editor McGraw-Hill, 1951-55; chief social studies editor Henry Holt and Co., N.Y.C., 1955-58; sr. editor Macmillan and Co., N.Y.C., 1958-60; prof. history, dir. coop. edn. Eastern Ill. U., Charleston, 1960-82, prof. history, 1982—; cons. to ednl. pubs. Served with USN, 1943-46. Harrison fellow, 1948-50; Fulbright scholar, 1951-52. Mem. Am. Hist. Assn., Nat. Coop. Edn. Assn. Democrat. Author: The Soviet Army, 1953; The Satellite Armies, 1953; Sir Edmond Monson, 1960; American Civics, 1967, 74; America: Its People and Values, 1971, 75, 79, 83; Land of Promise, 1983. Home: RR 2 PO Box 153 Charleston IL 61920 Office: History Dept Eastern Ill Univ Charleston IL 61920

WOOD, PAUL EUGENE, manufacturing company manager; b. St. Louis, Dec. 21, 1944; s. George Clarence and Maria Anna (Hoffert) W.; m. Janet Susan Leahy, Sept 5, 1970; children—Kent Eugene, Kurt Donald, Christine Elizabeth, Student Flo Valley Coll., 1972-76. Mailboy, Lincoln Co., St. Louis, 1962-64, cost acct., 1964-65, prodn. planner, 1965-75, asst. mgr. prodn. planners, 1976-80, material mgr., 1980—. Mem. Am. Prodn. Inventory Control Soc., Am. Assn. Indsl. Mgmt. Avocations: camping; German Shepherd dogs; photography. Home: 1010 Lakeview Saint Louis MO 63138 Office: Lincoln 1 Lincoln Way Saint Louis MO 63120

WOOD, RICHARD DONALD, pharmaceutical company executive; b. Brazil, Ind., Oct. 22, 1926; s. Howard T. and Dorothy F. (Norfolk) W.; B.S., Purdue U., 1948, LL.D., 1973; M.B.A., U. Pa., 1950; D.Sc., Butler U., 1974; LL.D., DePauw U., 1972, Phila. Coll. Pharmacy and Sci., 1975, Ind. State U., 1978; m. Billie Lou Carpenter, Dec. 29, 1951; children—Catherine Ann Wood Lawson, Marjorie Elizabeth. Gen. mgr. ops. in Argentina, Eli Lilly & Co., 1961, dir. ops., Mex. and Central Am., 1962-70, pres. Eli Lilly Internat. Corp., 1970-72, now dir.; pres. Eli Lilly & Co., Indpls., 1972-73, pres., chmn. bd., chief exec. officer, dir., 1973—, also dir.; dir. Chem. N.Y. Corp., Amoco Corp., Dow Jones & Co. Bd. dirs. Lilly Endowment, Inc., Indpls. Mus. Art; trustee DePauw U., Am. Enterprise Inst. for Public Policy Research, Com. Econ. Devel.; bd. govs. Purdue Found. Mem. Council on Fgn. Relations, Bus. Roundtable, Indsl. Conf. Bd. Presbyterian. Clubs: Links (N.Y.C.); Meridian Hills Country, Woodstock (Indpls.). Office: Lilly Corporate Ctr Indianapolis IN 46285

WOOD, ROBERT EDWIN, lighting manufacturing company executive; b. Paris, Mo., Jan. 29, 1938; s. Charles Robert and Thelma (Capps) W.; m. Judith Nickels, Dec. 31, 1955 (div. 1961); children—Roberta, Melanie; m. Elizabeth Harris, Nov. 24, 1963; 1 child, Jennifer. B.S., NE Mo. U., 1969. Acct. Chesebrough Ponds, Jefferson City, Mo., 1969-70, acct. supr., 1970-76; controller Musco Lighting, Muscatine, Iowa, 1976-77, gen. mgr., 1977-83, v.p., 1983—. Served with USAF, 1956-60. Mem. Nat. Assn. accts. (pres. 1974-75), Jaycees (pres. Paris chpt. 1963). Republican. Presbyterian. Avocations: reading; racquetball. Home: 420 Northwood Dr Muscatine IA 52761 Office: Musco Lighting 2107 Stewart Rd Muscatine IA 52761

WOOD, ROBERT WILLIAM, education educator, educational consultant and speaker; b. Winona, Minn., July 28, 1940; s. William Edward and Harriet Louise (Tust) Green; m. Elizabeth Ann Gunhus, Aug. 20, 1966; 1 child, William Robert. B.S., Winona State U., 1962, M.S., 1963; Ed.D., U. Mont., 1968. Cert. elem. tchr., Minn., Mont. Elem. tchr. Rochester Schs., Minn., 1963-65, Bonner, Schs., Mont., 1967-68; prof. U. S.D., Vermillion, 1968—. Editor, Modernization Process in India, 1975, Indian Society and the Process of Social Change, 1977, Reflections of India from American Educators, 1981, Reflections of Egypt from American Educators, 1985. Recipient Merit Tchr. award Nat. Council for geog. Edn., 1981; Fulbright fellow India, 1974, 77, 80, Egypt, 1983. Mem. Nat. Council for the Social Studies (recipient Outstanding Social Studies Tchr. award 1983), NEA, S.D. Edn. Assn. Avocations: amateur radio; camping; international travel. Home: RR1 Box 166 Vermillion SD 57069

WOOD, RODNEY DAVID, pharmaceutical company executive; b. Lansing, Mich., Aug. 19, 1932; s. Lawrence Earl and Ruth May (Shelton) W.; m. Margaret Grace Kemp, Sept. 2, 1961; children—Lawrence, Thomas, Catherine, Elizabeth. B.E., Yale U., 1954; M.S., Mich. State U., 1959; Ph.D., Northwestern U., 1963. Asst. prof. U. Nebr., 1962-64 research engr. Tex. Instruments, Dallas, 1964-70; sr. engr. Sherwin Williams, Toledo, 1970-73, tech. dir., Coffeyville, Kans., 1973-77; dir. process engring. Mead Johnson, Evansville, Ind., 1977-80, mgr. sterile drugs, 1980—. Recipient Achievement award Ohio Soc. Profl. Engrs., 1972. NSF fellow, 1960. Mem. Am. Chem. Soc., Am. Inst. Chem. Engrs. (presentation award 1964), Parenteral Drug Assn., Am. Soc. Engring. Mgmt., Sigma Xi. Home: 524 Plaza Dr Evansville IN 47715 Office: Mead Johnson & Co Evansville IN 47721

WOODALL, W. DALLAS, lawyer; b. Youngstown, Ohio, June 8, 1937; s. William L. and Roberta (Gibson) W.; m. Velma H. Szakacs, June 7, 1958; children—John M., Laura Love, Christine L. Woodall Scarmuzzi. B.S. in Edn., Youngstown State U., 1964; J.D., Ohio State U., 1967. Bar: Ohio 1967. Sole practice law, Warren, Ohio, 1967-68; assoc. Letson, Letson, Griffith and Kightlinger, Warren, 1968-71; ptnr. Letson, Griffith, Woodall and Lavelle, Warren, 1971—. Vice pres. Western Reserve council Boy Scouts Am., 1978; chmn. bd. trustees First Presbyterian Ch., Warren 1980, 84. Mem. Ohio State Bar Assn., Trumbull County Bar Assn. (pres.-elect 1985-86). Republican. Club: Buckeye (Warren). Lodge: Rotary (bd. dirs. 1982-84). Home: 3204 Crescent Dr NE Warren OH 44483 Office: Letson Griffith Woodall and Lavelle 155 S Park Ave Warren OH 44481

WOODBRIDGE, ANNIE SMITH, emerita librarian, foreign language educator; b. Wingo, Ky., July 7, 1915; d. Ernest Herbert and Flora Susan (Parrish) Smith; B.A., Murray State Coll., 1935; M.A., Peabody Coll., 1936; postgrad. U. Wis., Tex. State Coll. for Women, U. Ky., Sorbonne, Universidad Interamericana; m. Hensley C. Woodbridge, Aug. 28, 1953; 1 dau., Ruby Susan Woodbridge Jung. Tchr. Cadiz High Sch., 1936-37, David Lipscomb Coll., 1937-43, Bethel Coll., 1943-46, Murray State Coll., 1946-54, 59-65; instr. So. Ill. U., Carbondale, 1966-74, researcher Morris Library, 1974-85. Mem. NOW, Midwest Latin Am. Studies Assn., Ellen Glasgow Soc., Soc. Study of Midwestern Lit. Democrat. Mem. Ch. of Christ. Editor: (with others) Collected Short Stories of Mary Johnston; contbr. articles jours. and newsletters. Home: 1804 W Freeman St Carbondale IL 62901 Office: Morris Library Southern Illinois University Carbondale IL 62901

WOODBRIDGE, FREDERICK, lawyer, educator; b. Sidnaw, Mich., Apr. 10, 1904; s. James Randall and Florence Rosina W.; m. Marian Wilson, Sept. 7, 1934; children—Frederick, Ann. A.B., Ohio No. U., 1935; LL.B., U. Cin., 1933; LL.M., Harvard U., 1938; S.J.D., U. Mich., 1940. Bar: Ohio 1933, U.S. Dist. Ct. (so. and no. dists.) Ohio 1936, 54, U.S. Ct. Appeals (6th cir.) 1936, U.S. Supreme Ct. 1944. Instr. law Ohio No. U., Ada, 1933-35, U. Cin., 1935-37, asst. prof. law, 1940-45, faculty editor Law Rev., 1940-43; research fellow Harvard Law Sch., Cambridge, Mass., 1937-38; teaching fellow Law Sch. U. Mich., Ann Arbor, 1938-39, vis. asst. prof. law, 1939-40; legal assoc. Jones, Day, Cockley & Reavis (now Jones, Day, Reavis & Pogue), Cleve., 1943-47, ptnr., then sr. ptnr., 1948-76, ret. 1976; prof. law Case Western Res. U., Cleve., 1944-46; research cons. Household Fin. Corp., Chgo., 1940-41. Author study: Wage Earners' Receiverships, 1939; contbr. articles to legal publs. and travel mag. Trustee Cin. Legal Aid Soc., 1941-43. Mem. ABA (life), Ohio State Bar Assn. (life, various coms.), Order of Coif. Republican. Episcopalian. Club: Bermuda Run Country (N.C.). Lodge: Masons. Avocations: legal research; writing world travel and study. Home: 623 Spyglass Dr Po Box 839 Bermuda Run NC 27006

WOODFILL, ROGER WAYNE, land surveyor, real estate consultant; b. Cin., Oct. 17, 1945; s. Robert Gamaliel and Ella Grace (Stow) W.; m. Helen Jean Kirkpatrick, Aug. 31, 1968; children—Susan, Brian, Molly, Craig. A.S., Purdue Univ., 1967, B.S. in Tech., 1969. Cert. land surveyor. Owner, prin. Dist. 9 Land Survey Co., Lawrenceburg, Ind., 1971—. Sec., Community Activities, Inc., Lawrenceburg, Ind., 1984; candidate Ind. Gen. Assembly, 1980. Mem. Ind. Soc. Profl. Land Surveyors (pres. 1978, Bridge award 1982, dir.), Nat. Soc. Land Surveyors (v.p. 1983), Am. Congress on Surveying and Mapping (Pres.'s citation 1980). Avocations: Remodeling; gardening. Office: District 9 Land Survey Co 202 W High St Lawrenceburg IN 47025

WOODFORD, CHARLES JACKSON, night club management executive, automobile importer; b. Weston, W.Va., Sept. 7, 1950; s. Charles Cletus and Leota (Greenlief) W.; m. Denise E. LeWay, Oct. 18, 1975 (div. 1979); 1 child, Kyla Ann. Student Kent State, 1968-69; student Stark Tech., 1979. Owner, pres. Exec. Limousine, Canton, Ohio, 1973—; pres. Am. Dining Cars, Canton, 1970-75, Valentino's Inc., Canton, 1980—, The Dillinger Corp., Canton, 1983—; chmn. Woodford & Co. Rolls-Royce, Canton, 1981—; pres., cons. Ohio Gay Rights Assn., Canton, 1983-84; v.p. Ohio Importers Assn., Akron, Canton, 1981-83. V.P. Massillen Community Theatre, Ohio, 1975, Palace Theatre Preservation, Canton, 1977. Recipient Mayor's Citation, City of Canton, 1981, Outstanding Achievement award Pro-Football Hall of Fame, 1979-80. Mem. Nat. Assn. Interior Designers, Smithsonian Inst., Nat. Assn. Hist. Preservation, Rolls-Royce Club Am., Rolls-Royce Club Gt. Britian, Army-Navy Union. Republican. Lodge: Moose. Avocation: automobiles. Office: The Dillinger Corp 201-12th St NE Canton OH 44704

WOODFORD, DUANE HUGH, electrical equipment manufacturing company executive, electrical engineer; b. Dunseith, N.D., Jan. 1, 1939; s. Harold George and Edna Evelyn (Lagerquist) W.; m. Grace Carol Vandal, July 18, 1962; children—Robert Kent, Kim Ann. B.S. in Elec. Engring., U. N.D., 1961; student Western Electric grad. engring. tng. program, 1962; Mini M.B.A., Coll. St. Thomas, 1977, postgrad., 1978. Sr. sales engr. Electric Machinery Turbodyne div. Dresser Industries, Inc., Hartford, Conn., 1969-76, product mktg. mgr., Mpls., 1976-79, mgr. parts and service, 1979-80, commercial ops. mgr., 1980-83, gen. mgr., 1983—; power engr. Western Electric, Chgo., 1961-63; application engr. Electric Machinery-Turbodyne div. Dresser Industries, Inc., Mpls., 1963-65, sales engr., N.Y.C., Pitts., 1965-68. Coach, Babe Ruth Baseball, Plymouth, Minn., 1978-80; treas. PTO, Wayzata (Minn.) Sch. Dist. 284, 1978-79. Served with USMC, 1960-66. Mem. ASME (sec. gas turbine div. electric utility com. 1972-74), TAPPI. Republican. Methodist. Home: 1630 Shadyview Ln Plymouth MN 55447 Office: Electric Machinery Turbodyne Div Dresser Industries Inc 800 Central Ave Minneapolis MN 55413

WOODGATE, GERALD HERBERT, sheriff; b. North Platte, Nebr., Aug. 25, 1939; s. Vernon B. and Dorthea G. (Newsome) W.; m. Elvera C. Wennstedt, Nov. 22, 1959; children—Denise Ann Woodgate O'Neel, Gerald Bryan. Grad. high sch., cert. Law Enforcement Tng. Inst., 1983. Patrolmen, Fremont Police Dept., Nebr., 1962-64; conservation officer Nebr. Game and Parks Dept., Lincoln, 1964-74; criminal justice specialist Nebr. Crime Commn., Lincoln, 1974-80; sheriff Valley County, Ord, Nebr., 1980—; dir. county CD, 1980—; cons. Sec.-treas., Nebr. Council Sportsmen, 1978; mem. Ord Vol. Fire Dept., 1978; mem. Valley County Republicans. Recipient Meritorious award City of Fremont, 1964. Mem. Nebr. Sheriffs Assn., Nat. Sheriffs Assn., Nebr. County Ofcls. Assn., Jaycees (pres. Ord 1968). Republican. Club: Krap and Krow (past pres.) (Ord). Lodges: Elks, Masons (past master), Shriners. Avocations: hunting; fishing. Home: PO Box 38 Ord NE 68862 Office: County Courthouse Ord NE 68862

WOODHALL, DENNIS ROBERT, choral music educator, director; b. Los Angeles, June 15, 1951; s. William Rozelle and Elsie Lucille (Fulton) W.; m. Cynthia Loraine Morgan, July 28, 1973; 1 child, William Morgan. B.A., Calif. State U.-Fullerton, 1976, M.A., 1978; D. Mus. Arts, Ariz. State U., 1983. Research assoc. Ariz. State U., Tempe, 1979-81; prof. St. Mary of the Plains Coll., Dodge City, Kans., 1981—. Editor: Kans. Am. Choral Dirs. Assn. Newsletter, 1983—. Madrigal in Ev'ry Place; Help, I Fall. Music Assoc. scholar Calif. State U., 1976. Mem. Music Educators Nat. Conf., Am. Choral Dirs. Assn. (newsletter editor), Kans. Music Educators Assn., Pi Kappa Lambda, Phi Mu Alpha Sinfonia. Avocations: Water color painting; drawing; tennis; racquetball; swimming; cycling. Office: St Mary Plains Coll San Jose Dr Dodge City KS 67801

WOODHALL, JOHN ALEXANDER, JR., construction company executive; b. Peoria, Ill., Oct. 10, 1929; s. John Alexander and Marion Ellen (Solstad) W.; B.B.A., U. Minn., 1952; m. Donna Irene Simmons, Aug. 21, 1948; children—John Alexander, Susan, Cheryl, Douglas, Robert. Project supt. Central States Constrn. Co., Willmar, Minn., 1953-57, v.p., project mgr., 1957-60; v.p., area mgr. Allied Enterprises, Willmar, 1960-69; exec. v.p. Central Allied Enterprises, Inc., Canton, Ohio, 1969-74, chmn., chief exec. officer, 1974—; chmn. bd. Clark Irrigation Co.; dir. Road Info. Program. Vice chmn. Minn. Gov.'s Occupational Safety Health Adv. Council; bd. dirs., chmn. Minn. Safety Council, chmn., 1983; pres. W. Central Safety Council, 1979; bd. dirs. Nat. Safety Council, 1984—; dist. commr. Viking council Boy Scouts Am., 1969-71. Mem. Am. Mgmt. Assn., Vets. of Safety, Am. Arbitration Assn., Associated Gen. Contractors Am. (dir.), Associated Gen. Contractors Minn. (pres. 1977), Pres.'s Assn. Lutheran. Clubs: Kiwanis (Willmar); Masons, Shriners, Mpls. Athletic. Home: 190 Lake Ave E Spicer MN 56288 also 4 Belleview Blvd Apt 404 Belleair FL 33516 Office: PO Box 1317 Willmar MN 56201 also PO Box 1387 Sta C Canton OH 44708

WOODHAM, ROBERT B(ENTLY), optometrist; b. Chgo., Aug. 11, 1950; s. James William and Joy (Boswell) W.; m. Rita M. Frommelt, Feb. 9, 1973; children—Rachael, Rebecca, Matthew, Sarah. O.D., Ill. Coll. Optometry, 1979. Practice optometry, Platteville, Wis., 1979—. Mem. Platteville Vol. Fire Dept., 1980—. Served to sgt. U.S. Army, 1968-72; Vietnam. Decorated Silver Star, Bronze Star with 2 oak leaf clusters, Purple Heart, Army Commendation medal. Mem. Am. Optometric Assn., Wis. Optometric Assn. Roman Catholic. Lodge: Lions (Platteville). Home: 1410 Karla Platteville WI 53818 Office: 125 E Main Platteville WI 53818

WOODIN, KAREN ESTELLE, clinical researcher; b. Kalamazoo, July 3, 1940; d. John Charles and Estelle Anne (Herring) Thompson; m. Norman James Woodin, Nov. 23, 1962; children—Joseph Edward, Jon William. B.S., Western Mich. U., 1962. M.S. in Stats., 1978. Biostatistician, Upjohn Co., Kalamazoo, 1978-84, clin. research assoc., 1984—. Mem. Women in Sci. Adv. Bd., 1982. Recipient Teaching Excellence award dept. math. Western Mich. U., 1978. Mem. Am. Statis. Assn. pres. Southwest Mich. chpt. 1984—), Assocs. Clin. Pharmacology. Office: Upjohn Co Unit 7272-24-3 Kalamazoo MI 49001

WOODKA, CECIL PAUL, electric company executive; b. Scandia, Kans., Mar. 8, 1936; s. Chester Julius and Lottie Maxine (Young) W.; m. LaVonne Fae Wisch, Aug. 9, 1959; children—Dawn Renee, Clay Phillip. Student in human relations U. Nebr., 1978-81, in bus. mgmt., 1981-83; student North East Tech. Coll., 1980-85. With Cuming County Pub. Power Dist., West Point, Nebr., 1954—, meter supt., power use adviser, 1965-73, ops. supt., 1973—. Cubmaster, chmn. West Point council Boy Scouts Am.; Chmn. West Point Park and Recreation Bd., West Point Bd. Edn., 1972-85; elder, treas., chmn. Lutheran Ch. served with USAF, 1957-59. Mem. Internat. Assn. Elec. Inspectors, Illuminating Engring. Soc., Nebr. Assn. Sch. Bds. (pres. 1984-85). Republican. Home: 626 S Monitor St West Point NE 68788 Office: Cuming County Pub Power Dist 500 S Main St West Point NE 68788

WOODMAN, GEORGE BEACH, lawyer; b. Youngstown, Ohio, Nov. 11, 1923; s. Thaddeus A. and Margaret (Beach) W. B.A., Coll. Wooster, 1945; B. Laws, U. Mich., 1947. Bar: Ohio 1947. Sole practice, Youngstown, 1948-60; assoc. Mitchell, Mitchell & Reed, Youngstown, 1960-61, ptnr., 1961—; dir. probate and trust law sec. Ohio State Bar Assn., 1980—. Trustee Mahoning Valley council Boy Scouts Am., Jr. Achievement of Youngstown Area, Mahoning Valley Hist. Soc. Mem. Mahoning County Bar Assn. Republican. Presbyterian. Clubs: Torch (Youngstown) (pres. 1965-66), SAR (Youngstown) (pres. 1981—). Avocations: fishing; canoeing; camping. Office: Mitchell Mitchell & Reed 709 Bank One Bldg Youngstown OH 44503

WOODMAN, GREY MUSGRAVE, psychiatrist; b. Birmingham, Eng., Jan. 26, 1922; came to U.S., 1959, naturalized, 1963; s. Edward Musgrave and Ida (Cullen) W.; children—Sheila, Shonagh. B.A., U. Oxford (Eng.), 1943, M.A., B.M., B.Ch., 1945. Ship's surgeon, 1946-48; intern Whipps Cross Hosp., London, 1948-49, med. registrar, 1951-54, also Newcastle-on-Tyne, Eng., 1951-54; resident in Psychiatry U. Okla., 1959-62; staff psychiatrist Western Mo. Mental Health Ctr., Kansas City, 1962-76; med. dir. Mental Health Ctr. Clinton County, Clinton, Iowa, 1976—; practice medicine specializing in psychiatry, Clinton, 1976—; mem. staff Lincolnshire Clinic, Jane Lamb Health Ctr., Mercy Hosp.; cons. Mufon. Served with Brit. Merc. Marines, 1946-48. Mem. Am. Psychiat. Assn., Brit. Med. Assn., AMA, Royal Soc. Medicine (London), World Fedn. Mental Health, Internat. Assn. Social Psychiatry. Republican. Episcopalian. Home: 1334 7th St NW Clinton IA 52732 Office: 320 Tucker Bldg Clinton IA 52732 also Lincolnshire Clinic 318 Howes Bldg Clinton IA 52732

WOODRING, DEWAYNE STANLEY, association executive; b. Gary, Ind., Nov. 10, 1931; s. J. Stanley and Vera Luella (Brown) W.; B.S. with distinction, Northwestern U., 1954, postgrad.; M.Div., Garrett Theol. Sem., 1957; L.H.D., Mt. Union Coll., 1967; D.D., Salem Coll., 1970; m. Donna Jean Wishart, June 15, 1957; children—Judith Lynn (Mrs. Richard Bigelow), Beth Ellen. YMCA Youth dept. staff, Gary, 1946-50, asso. youth dir., 1950-55; staff mem. radio services dept. Second Assembly, World Council of Chs., Evanston, Ill., 1954; minister edn. Griffith Meth. Ch., Ind., 1955-57; minister adminstrn. and program 1st Meth. Ch., Eugene, Oreg., 1957-59; dir. pub. relations Dakotas Area Meth. Ch., 1959-60, Ohio Area, 1960-64; adminstrv. exec. to bishop, Ohio E. Area, 1964-77; asst. gen. sec. Council on Fin. and Adminstrn., United Meth. Ch., Evanston, Ill., 1977-79, asso. gen. sec., 1979-84; exec. dir. Religious Conf. Mgmt. Assn., Indpls., 1982—; chmn. bd. mgrs. United Meth. Bldg., Evanston, 1977-84. Exec. sec. Ohio Meth. TV, Radio and Film Commn., 1960-72; del. World Meth. Conf., London, Eng., 1966, Dublin, Ireland, 1976, Honolulu, 1981; mem. mass communications com. Meth. N. Central Jurisdiction, 1964-68; chmn. commn. on communications Ohio Council Chs., 1961-65; mem. div. interpretation United Meth. Ch., 1969-72, mem. commn. on gen. conf., 1972—, bus. mgr., exec. dir., 1976—, mem. program com. N. Central Jurisdictional Conf., 1968-76, chmn., 1972-76, mem. council on ministries,

1972-76; exec. com. Assn. United Meth. Founds., 1968-72; participant U.S. Dept. Def. Joint Civilian Orientation Conf., 1970; lectr., cons. on fgn. travel. Trustee, Ohio East Area United Meth. Found, 1967-78, v.p., 1967-76; pres. Guild Assocs. 1971—; trustee, v.p. Copeland Oaks Retirement Center Sebring, Ohio, 1969-76. Mem. Am. Soc. Assn. Execs., Conv. Liaison Council (bd. dirs., exec. com.), Nat. Assn. Exposition Mgrs., Meeting Planners Internat., Cert. Meeting Profls. (exec. bd.), Def. Orientation Conf. Assn. (dir.). Home: 7224 Chablis Ct Indianapolis IN 46278 Office: 1 Hoosier Dome Suite 120 Indianapolis IN 46225

WOODS, CHARLES HARRISON, chemist; b. Kirwan Heights, Pa., Dec. 10, 1934; s. Leroy Homer and Julia (Voinovich) W.; student Carnegie Inst. Tech., 1952, Muskingum Coll., 1957, Muskingum Area Tech. Coll., 1979-80; m. Ruth Ann Gildea, Oct. 20, 1956; children—Tamara Sue Woods Border, Charles K., Crystal, David. Chief chemist John M. Sherry Labs., Muncie, Ind., 1961-64; chief spectroscopist Vanadium Corp. Am., Cambridge, Ohio, 1965-68; analytical chemist, lab. supr. Foote Mineral Co., Exton, Pa., 1968-70; corp. dir. analytical chemistry Ohio Ferro-Alloys Corp., Philo, Ohio, 1970—, mgr. quality control, 1982—. Mem. citizens adv. com. Ohio EPA Muskingum River Basin; mem. data processing tech. adv. com. Muskingum Area Tech. Coll., 1979-84; loaned exec. United Way, 1978, 79; judge sci. fairs, high sch. Mem. Am. Chem. Soc., Am. Soc. Metals, Nat. Mgmt. Assn. (pres. Zanesville area 1982-83). Democrat. Lutheran. Home: 3655 Sunset Circle Zanesville OH 43701 Office: PO Box 158 Philo OH 43771

WOODS, HARRIETT RUTH, state official; b. Cleve., June 2, 1927; d. Armin and Ruth (Wise) Friedman; student U. Chgo., 1945; B.A., U. Mich., 1949; m. James B. Woods, Jan. 2, 1953; children—Christopher, Peter, Andrew. Reporter, Chgo. Herald-Am., 1948, St. Louis Globe-Democrat, 1949-51; producer Star. KPLR-TV, St. Louis, 1964-74; moderator, writer Sta. KETC-TV, St. Louis, 1962-64; council mem. University City, Mo., 1967-74; mem. Mo. Hwy. Commn., 1974, Mo. Transp. Commn., 1974-76; mem. Mo. Senate, 1976-84, lt. gov. State of Mo., 1985—. Bd. dirs. LWV of Mo., 1963; Democratic nominee for U.S. Senate, 1982. Recipient Democracy in Action award Am. Jewish Congress, 1980; Maryville Coll. Civic Service award 1980. Mem. Crusade Against Crime, Orgn. Women Legislators. Jewish. Office: State Capitol Jefferson City MO 65101

WOODS, MARY JOAN, pediatric nurse practitioner; b. Vincennes, Ind., July 11, 1928; d. John Arthur and Maud Claribel (Davidson) Caniff; m. John Thomas Woods, Sept. 17, 1949; children—John Thomas, William Patrick, Richard, Michael, Elizabeth, Stephen, Jennifer, Cynthia. Diploma, Deaconess Hosp., 1949; cert. Sch. Nurse Practitioner, U. Evansville, 1974; cert. Pediatric Nurse Practitioner, Ind. U., 1976. Supr., Well Baby Clinic, Pub. Health Nursing Assn., Evansville, Ind., 1972; supr. Sweetser Clinic, Evansville, 1973; pediatric nurse practitioner, Evansville-Vanderburgh Health Dept., Evansville, Ind., 1973—; tchr. parenting class Welborn Clinic, Evansville State Hosp., Prevention Crisis Nursery, Friendship Ministries; instr. parenting class and CPR, ARC; lectr. U. Evansville, also Deaconess Hosp. Tchr. St. James Ch.; taskforce mem. Latchkey Program. Fellow Nat. Assn. Pediatric Nurse Assocs. and Practitioners; mem. Ind. State Nurses Assn. (former state officer), DAR (vice regent Mary Anthony McGary chpt.). Republican. Roman Catholic. Home: Rural Route 6 Baseline Rd Box 339 Evansville IN 47711 Office: Civic Center Complex Health Dept Nursing Div Evansville IN 47708

WOODS, RUTH FORTUNE, forester, soil scientist; b. Detroit, Oct. 29, 1935; d. Bill D. Woods, Aug. 11, 1954 (div. 1964); children—Billie Ruth Woods McLaghlin, Steve, Lucy Woods Gasperich, Walter. B.S. in Bus. Adminstrn., Ferris State Coll., 1966; B.S. in Forestry, Mich. Tech. U., 1977; M.S. in Forest Biology, Colo. State U., 1980; Ph.D. in Forestry/Soils, Mich. State U., 1984. Tchr. public schs., Mich., 1966-75; greenhouse mgr. Mich. Tech. U.-Houghton, 1975-77; forester, silviculturist Mich. Dept. Natural Resources, Escanaba, 1977-78; grad. research asst. Colo. State U., Ft. Collins, 1978-80, Mich. State U., East Lansing, 1980-81; research soil scientist, U.S. Dept. Energy Research grantee, prin. investigator Packaging Corp. Am. subs. Tenneco Oil, Manistee, Mich., 1981-84; prin. Ruth F. Woods, cons. forestry and soils research, Okemos, Mich., 1983—. Victor Spathelf Presdl. scholar Ferris State Coll., 1962-66. Mem. Soc. Am. Foresters, Soil Sci. Soc. Am., Agronomy Soc., Soil Conservation Soc. Am., Soc. Range Mgmt., AAAS. Republican. Club: Bus. and Profl. Women's. Author: Tree Planter's Notes, 1981; contbr. Jour. Range Mgmt., Jour. Forestry. Office: Dept Forestry Mich State U East Lansing MI 48824

WOODSON, RILEY DONALD, thoracic and cardiovascular surgeon, lawyer; b. Winfield, Kans., Dec. 24, 1931; s. Riley Delma and Ruth Philena (Benedict) W.; B.A., U. Kans., 1953, M.D., 1956; J.D., U. Toledo, 1984; children—Riley David, Wade Clinton. Intern, Parkland Meml. Hosp., Dallas, 1956-57, resident in surgery U. Minn. Hosp., Mpls., 1957-63; fellow in cardio-thoracic surgery U. Oreg. Hosp., Portland, 1965-67; mem. staff U. Ill. Hosp., Chgo., 1967-68; asst. prof. surgery U. Ill., Chgo., 1967-68; asso. prof. surgery Med. Coll. Ohio, Toledo, 1969-78, clin. assoc. prof. surgery, 1978—; pvt. practice cardiothoracic and vascular surgery, 1978—; mng. partner DJB Enterprises, 1976—. Sec. bd. trustees, med. dir. Regional Emergency Med. Services of N.W. Ohio, 1975-81. Served to capt., M.C., USNR, 1963—. Diplomate Am. Bd. Surgery, Am. Bd. Cardio-Thoracic Surgery. Fellow A.C.S., Am. Coll. Cardiology, Am. Coll. Chest Physicians, Am. Coll. Legal Medicine; mem. AMA, Pan Am. Med. Assn., ABA, Assn. Trial Lawyers Am., Undersea Med. Soc., Soc. Thoracic Surgeons, Am. Thoracic Soc., Internat. Cardiovascular Soc., Soc. Vascular Surgery, Am. Assn. Surgery of Trauma, Am. Trauma Soc., Assn. Mil. Surgeons, Profl. Assn. Diving Instrs., N.W. Ohio Heart Assn. (exec. com., chmn. emergency cardiac care 1975-81), Mensa, Beta Theta Pi, Omicron Delta Kappa, Phi Kappa Phi. Contbr. articles on thoracic and cardiovascular surgery, cardiopulmonary physiology, diving physiology, legal medicine to books and profl. jours. Office: 6005 Monclova Rd Maumee OH 43537

WOODWARD, DAVID ALFRED, geography educator; b. Leamington, Eng., Aug. 29, 1942, came to U.S., 1964; s. Max Wakerley and Kathleen May (Beaty) W.; m. Rosalind Lenice Bailey, July 27, 1966; children—Jennifer, Rachel, Justin. B.A. with honors, U. Wales, 1964; M.A. in Geography, U. Wis., 1967, Ph.D. in Geography, 1970. Cartographer, Directorate of Overseas Surveys, Tolworth, Eng., 1961; compiler, editor Reader's Digest Assn., London, 1966; project asst. U. Wis. Cartographic Lab., Madison, 1964-67, teaching asst. in cartography, 1967-68, research asst., 1968-69, assoc. prof. geography, 1980-81, prof., 1981—, dir. Univ. Cartographic Lab., 1983—; cartographic specialist Newberry Library, 1970-71, dir. Hermon Dunlap Smith Ctr. for History of Cartography, 1972-80; lectr., map designer. Am. Council Learned Socs. travel grantee, 1971, 73, 75, 79, 83; Clark Library research fellow, 1973; Brit. Acad. exchange fellow, 1973; John Simon Guggenheim Meml. fellow, 1977-78; research and travel grants U. Wis. Mem. Royal Geog. Soc., Brit. Cartographic Soc., Am. Congress Surveying and Mapping (dir. cartography div. 1980-82), Am. Cartographic Assn., Can. Cartographic Assn., Assn. Am. Geographers, N.Am. Cartographic Info. Soc., Internat. Soc. History of Cartography (dir.), Am. Printing History Assn., Printing Hist. Soc. London, Soc. History of Discoveries, Chgo. Map Soc., Hakluyt Soc. Author: Five Centuries of Map Printing, 1975; The All-American Map, 1977; Art and Cartography: Six Historical Essays, 1987; History of Cartography, Vol. I, 1987; gen. editor Studies in the History of Discoveries, 1971-76; assoc. editor Am. Cartographer, 1982-85; mem. editorial bd. Cartographica, 1971-78; contbr. articles to profl. jours. Office: 443 Science Hall Madison WI 53706

WOODWARD, JACK CARLTON, pottery co. exec.; b. Roseville, Ohio, July 26, 1923; s. Floyd Harris and Clara Marie (Ungemach) W.; B.B.A., lMeredith Coll., 1942; m. Janice Colleen Harper, Nov. 8, 1962: children—Jon, Jo Ellen, Sharon, Vickie, Jane. With Robinson Ransbottom Pottery Co., Roseville, 1937—, treas., 1970-72, exec. v.p., 1972-78, pres., gen mgr., 1978—, also dir. Mem. Republican Central Com., Zanesville, 1949-53. Served with U.S. Army, 1943-46. Mem. Pottery, China and Glass Assn., Southeastern Ohio Ceramic Assn., U.S. C. of C., Ohio C. of C., Zanesville Area C. of C. (dir. 1976). Presbyterian. Clubs: Elks, Masons (32 deg.), Eagles. Office: Roseville OH 43777

WOODWARD, PAMELA ROSE, nurse administrator, school administrator, nurse; b. Canton, Ohio, Sept. 18, 1943; d. Wallace Ralph and Ruth Lucille (Hershberger) Hutchison; children—Angela Kay, Alison Rae. Grad. Aultman Hosp. Sch. Nursing, 1965; B.S. in Edn., Kent State U., 1973; M.S. in Edn., U. Akron, 1978. R.N., cert. tchr., Ohio. Staff nurse Aultman Hosp., Canton, 1965-66; mem. faculty, supr. Aultman Hosp. and Aultman Hosp. Sch. Nursing, 1966-70, mem. faculty sch. nursing, 1970-79, adminstrv. coordinator research, 1979-81, asst. dir. curriculum, 1981-84, dir. nursing quality assurance and nursing research, 1984—; instr. CPR. Mem. Am. Nursing Assn., Ohio Nursing Assn., Am. Assn. Critical Care Nurses, Emergency Dept. Nurses Assn., Assn. Supervision and Curriculum Devel., Aultman Hosp. Nurses Alumni Assn., Minerva Area Nurses Assn., Sigma Theta Tau. Presbyterian. Home: 901 Lynnwood Dr Minerva OH 44657 Office: 2614 6th St SW Canton OH 44710

WOODWARD, ROBERT SIMPSON, IV, economics educator; b. Easton, Pa., May 7, 1943; s. Robert Simpson and Esther Evans (Thomas) W.; B.A., Haverford Coll., 1965; Ph.D., Washington U., St. Louis, 1972; m. Mary P. Hutton, Feb. 15, 1969; children—Christopher Thomas, Rebecca Marie. Brookings Econ. Policy fellow Dept. HEW, Washington, 1975-76; asst. prof. U. Western Ont. (Can.), London, 1972-77; asst. prof. Sch. Medicine, Washington U., St. Louis, 1978—. Mem. adv. council Mo. Kidney Program, 1980—, vice-chmn., 1983, chmn. 1984-85; coop. mem. Haverford Coll., 1968—. NDEA fellow, 1968-71; Kellogg Nat. fellow, 1981-84. Mem. Am. Econs. Assn., Am. Statis. Assn. Contbr. articles to profl. jours. Home: 7050 Westmoreland St University City MO 63130 Office: 4547 Clayton Ave Saint Louis MO 63110

WOOLSEY, WILLIAM STOVER, printing company executive; b. Chgo., Dec. 22, 1917; s. William Robert and Grace (Peck) W.; B.S. in Mech. Engring., U. Mich., 1939, M.S., 1940; m. Doris Marie Neely, Jan. 5, 1946; children—Robert, Mary Woolsey Porter, Carolyn. Engr., Commonwealth Edison Co., Chgo., 1940-55; exec. Neely Printing Co., Chgo., 1955-60, pres., dir., 1960—; pres., dir. Dayanite Corp., Chgo., 1957—, Franklin Offset Litho Co., Chgo., 1960—, N.B.L. Corp., Chgo., 1960—, 917 Bldg. Corp., Chgo., 1960—. Trustee Pressman Sch. Fund; chmn. Lithographer Health and Welfare Fund. Served to lt. col. USAAF, 1940-45. Decorated Bronze Star. Mem. Western Soc. Engrs., Printing Industry of Ill. (dir.), Union Employers Assn. (exec. bd.), Chgo. Lithographers Bd. (dir.), Franklin Assn. (dir.), Printing Industry Am. (exec. bd. union employers sect., chmn. budget com., mem. Ash Kahn Gew). Club: Westmoreland Country. Home: 1500 Sheridan Rd Wilmette IL 60091 Office: 871 N Franklin St Chicago IL 60610

WOOTEN, BILLY MACK, health care centers adminstr.; b. San Angelo, Tex., Feb. 25, 1947; s. Billy S. and Maxine C. (Watson) W.; B.A. in Psychology, N.Mex. State U., 1969, M.A., 1976; B.A. in Social Work, St. Cloud (Minn.) State U., 1974; M.S. in Mental Retardation, Mankato (Minn.) State U., 1980; Ph.D. in Psychology, Columbia Pacific U., 1981; m. Linda Ruth Lundgren, Apr. 7, 1973; children—Joshua S., Joseph A. Mental health counselor Southwest Mental Health Center, Alamogordo, N.Mex., 1972-73; exec. dir. REM, Inc., Marshall, Minn., 1975—; pres. Prairie Systems, Inc., 1983—; adj. prof. spl. edn., Mankato State U.; chmn. Services Industries, Inc.; cons. REM Cons. & Services, Inc., Mpls. Served with USAF, 1969-73; pvt. practice Behavior Analysts, 1978—. Served with USAF, 1969-73. Mem. Am. Assn. Mental Deficiency (vice chairperson psychology 1977-79, editor Region VIII Newsletter 1979—, Minn. sec.-treas.), Assn. Advancement of Behavior Therapy, Assn. Behavior Analysis, Minn. Assn. Behavior Analysis (membership chmn., pres. 1982-83). Democrat. Unitarian. Club: Kiwanis. Author: (with David C. Pfriem) An Introduction to Behavioral Techniques, 1979; A Rational Approach to Counseling the Mentally Retarded, 1981; contbr. articles to profl. jours. Home: 305 E Lyon St Marshall MN 56258 Office: 1005 N 4th St Marshall MN 56258

WOOTTEN, GEORGE SIMMONS, JR., data processing and communications profl.; b. Evanston, Ill.; s. George Simmons and Mildred (Knispel) W.; B.S. in Bus. Adminstrn., Northwestern U.; children—George III, Stephanie Lynn. With Union Tank Car Co., Chgo., 1951-60; mgmt. cons. William Kordsiemon & Assos., Chgo., 1960-63; dir. data processing and communications Marquette Cement Co., Chgo., 1966-74; sr. partner Wootten & Assos., Glenview, Ill., 1974—; mgr. info. systems Kinkead Industries, Downers Grove, Ill., 1976-80; v.p., dir. Comprehensive Acctg. Co., Aurora, Ill., 1957-60, data processing cons., 1960—; dir. info. systems A. Finkl & Sons, Chgo., 1980—; v.p., dir. Waterloo Ideas Co. (Iowa), 1963-66. Served with USN, 1948-50. Mem. Assn. Computer Machinery, Internat. Communication Assn., Armed Forces Communications and Electronic Assn., Assn. Systems Mgmt. Mason. Club: Executives (Chgo.). Home: 4200 W Lake Ave Glenview IL 60025

WOOTTON, ROBERT JAMES, architect; b. Muskegon, Mich., Oct. 10, 1938; s. Frank W. and Leona M. (Hack) W.; m. Barbara Gean Archambeau, June 23, 1966; children—Brian, Bobby. B.Archtl. Engring., Chgo. Tech. Coll., 1967; B.S., Ill. Inst. Tech., 1975; postgrad. Morton Coll., 1980-83. Registered architect, Ill. Draftsman Magnuson and Sumner, Muskegon, Mich., 1960-62; archtl. engr. Clearing Indsl. Dist., Chgo., 1967-70, Hansen Nakawatase, Ruthkowski and Wyns, Chgo., 1970-80; architect Leobl, Schlossman and Hackl, Chgo., 1980—. Dist. commr. asst. scoutmaster, post adviser Boy Scouts Am. Served with Ill. N.G., 1960-66. Mem. AIA (Chgo. chpt.), Nat. Council Archtl. Registration Bds. Roman Catholic. Office: Loebl Schlossman & Hackl 845 N Michigan Ave Chicago IL 60611

WORK, JAMES HOWARD, JR., tng. and communications co. exec.; b. Hartford, Conn., July 7, 1949; s. James Howard and Florence Harriet (Gilde) W.; B.A., U. N.C., 1971. Mgmt. cons. Wheeler Asso., Nashua, N.H., 1971-72; dealer devel. specialist John Williamson Assos., Birmingham, Ala., 1972-75; account supr. Sandy Corp., Southfield, Mich., 1975-78, account dir. product and service systems, 1978-79, dir. Can. ops., 1980-83, v.p., 1983—; dir. Bill Sandy Orgn. Ltd., Toronto, Ont., Can., GM Truck and Bus. Ops., Sandy Corp. Mem. Am. Mgmt. Assn. Club: Sports Car Am. Home: 30038 W 12 Mile Rd Farmington Hills MI 48018 Office: Sandy Corp 1500 W Big Beaver Rd Troy MI 48084

WORKMAN, GEORGE HENRY, engineering consultant; b. Muskegon, Mich., Sept. 18, 1939; s. Harvey Merton and Bettie Jane (Meyers) W.; Asso. Sci., Muskegon Community Coll., 1960; B.S.E., U. Mich., 1966, M.S.E., 1966, Ph.D., 1969; m. Vicki Sue Hanish, June 17, 1967; children—Mark, Larry. Prin. engr. Battelle Meml. Inst., Columbus, Ohio, 1969-76; pres. Applied Mechanics Inc., Columbus, 1976—; instr. dept. civil engring. Ohio State U., 1973, 82. Served with USN, 1961-64. Named Outstanding Undergrad. Student, Engring. Mechanics dept. U. Mich., 1965-66, Outstanding Grad. Student, Civil Engring. dept., 1968-69. Registered profl. engr., Ohio. Mem. Am. Acad. of Mechanics, ASME, ASCE, Nat. Soc. Profl. Engrs., Sigma Xi, Chi Epsilon, Phi Kappa Phi, Phi Theta Kappa. Congregationalist. Contbr. tech. papers to nat. and internat. confs. Home and Office: 4690 Bayford Ct Columbus OH 43220

WORLEY, MARVIN GEORGE, JR., architect; b. Oak Park, Ill., Oct. 10, 1934; s. Marvin George and Marie Hyancinth (Donahue) W.; B.Arch., U. Ill., 1958; m. Maryalice Ryan, July 11, 1959; children—Michael Craig, Carrie Ann, Alissa Maria. Project engr. St. Louis area Nike missile bases U.S. Army C.E., Granite City, Ill., 1958-59, architect N.Central div. U.S. Army C.E., Chgo., 1960; architect Yerkes & Grunsfeld, architects, Chgo., 1961-65, asso., 1965; asso. Grunsfeld & Assos., architects, Chgo., 1966—. Dist. architect Oak Park Elementary Schs. Dist. 97, 1973-80. Mem. Oak Park Community Improvement Commn., 1973-75; mem. exec. bd. Oak Park Council PTA, 1970-73, pres., 1971-72. Served with AUS, 1959. Mem. AIA (corporate), Chgo. Assn. Commerce and Industry. Home: 811 N Ridgeland Ave Oak Park IL 60302 Office: 520 N Michigan Ave Chicago IL 60611

WORMAN, RICHARD W., insurance company executive, state senator; b. Noble County, Ind., July 3, 1933; s. William D. and Leah M. W.; m. Marna Jo Neuhouser, Sept. 29, 1951; children—Terry Jo, Renny, Denny, Rex, Tammy. Buyer, Neuhouser Poultry, Leo, Ind., 1951-53; salesman Allen Dairy, Ft. Wayne, Ind., 1953-57; with Nationwide Ins. Co., Columbus, Ohio, 1951—, dist. sales mgr.; mem. Ind. Ho. of Reps., 1972-76, Ind. Senate, 1978—; trustee, assessor County of Allen, Ind., 1970-72. C.L.U. Mem. Life Underwriters Assn., Republican. Methodist. Clubs: Lions (past pres.), Mason (past master), Shriner. Office: 3737 Lake Ave Fort Wayne IN 46805

WORMINGTON, BARRY LEE, medical supply company marketing executive; b. Denver, Aug. 5, 1942; s. Everett Glendon Wormington and Berniece Lucille (Foster) Van Scoy; m. Regina Louise Rollo, Jan. 10, 1964; children—Christine, Aric, Amanda. B.A. in Bus. Adminstrn., U. Colo., 1971; ops. mgr. McKesson & Robbins, Denver, 1967-70; ops. mgr. Foremost-McKesson, Portland, Oreg., 1970-74, div. mgr., 1974-76; div. mgr. Gentec Hosp. Supply Co., Milw., 1976-79; regional v.p. Gentec Health Care, Milw., 1979-81; v.p. mktg. R & J Med. Supply Co., Milw., 1981—. Served with USN, 1960-63. Republican. Roman Catholic. Lodge: Rotary (bd. dirs. West Allis, Wis. 1981). Home: 8421 Kenyon Ave Wauwatosa WI 53226 Office: R & J Med Supply Inc 1647 S 101st St Milwaukee WI 53214

WORRELL, EVERETT ELDON, educational administrator; b. DeKalb, Ill., July 15, 1932; s. Arthur Elmer and Norma Gerhardine (Westphal) W.; m. Virginia Ann Brown, Sept. 8, 1951; children—Elizabeth Ann, David Arthur. B.S. in Edn., No. Ill. U., 1956, M.S. in Edn., 1960. Adminstrv. cert. in edn., Ill. Tchr. indsl. edn. North Boone High Sch., Poplar Grove, Ill., 1956-60; tchr. indsl. arts Jefferson Jr. High Sch., Rockford, Ill., 1960-74, chmn. dept., 1966-74; asst. prin. Rockford Area Vocat. Center, 1974-80, dir., 1980-83. Dir. Boy Scout Camp, summers 1965-66; mem. exec. bd. Blackhawk Area council Boy Scouts Am. Served with USN, 1951-55. Mem. Ill. Indsl. Edn. Assn. (past pres., editor newsletter 1972-82), Ill. Vocat. Assn. (past dir., editor newsletter 1974-78), Full Gospel Business Men's Fellowship, Phi Delta Kappa (sec. No. Ill. chpt., Service Key 1976). Presbyterian (deacon, elder). Contbr. articles to profl. jours.

WORTHAM, JAMES CALVIN, educator; b. Oconee County, Ga., Sept. 12, 1928; s. James Notley and Effie (Cross) W.; B.A., U. Akron, 1957; M.A. (NSF Scholar), Ohio State U., 1969; m. Mary Helena Shelley, Dec. 23, 1953; children—Sharon Elaine, Marilyn Kay, Deborah Louise, James Donald. Tchr. high sch. Akron Pub. Schs., 1956-62, tchr. sr. high sch., 1962-66; math. curriculum specialist Akron (Ohio) Pub. Schs., 1966—; instr. math. U. Akron, 1966—. Served with USAF, 1951-55. Mem. NEA, Ohio Edn. Assn., Math. Assn. Am., Nat., Ohio councils tchrs. of math., Nat. Council Supvrs. of Math., Greater Akron Math. Educators Soc. (pres. 1984-86), Pi Mu Epsilon. Republican. Mem. Ch. of Nazarene. Home: 1665 Wiltshire Rd Akron OH 44313 Office: 70 N Broadway Akron OH 44308

WORTHINGTON, MARC STEPHEN, banker, educator; b. Coshocton, Ohio, Oct. 1, 1947; s. Robert Marc and Sophia Ellen (Clark) W.; m. Julia Frances Funderburk, Oct. 1, 1978; children—Craig Alan, Marc Stephen, David Andrew. B.S. in Bus. Adminstrn., Franklin U., 1973. Mgmt./coll. trainee Ohio Nat. Bank, Columbus, 1969; staff auditor BancOhio Corp., Columbus, 1970; asst. mgr. Henderson Rd. Office Ohio Nat. Bank, Columbus, 1971-76; mgr. Port Columbus Internat. Airport Office Ohio Nat. Bank, Columbus, 1976-78, staff officer bus. devel. dept., credit analysis, 1978-79; v.p., sr. lender comml. lending div. mgr. BancOhio Nat. Bank, Washington Court House, Ohio, 1979-83, v.p., mgr. bus. and profl. loan dept., Cin., 1983—. Mem. Am. Inst. Banking, Washington Court House C. of C. (dir. 1981-83). Republican. Methodist. Lodge: Rotary. Office: 300 W Loveland Ave Loveland OH 45140

WORTINGER, KEITH WAYNE, educational administrator; b. French Lick, Ind., Dec. 2, 1947; s. Arthur Herbert and Edna Orean (Condra) W.; m. Joanne Matheson, Aug. 24, 1968; children—Brian, Heather. B.S., Union Coll., 1969; M.A., Western Mich. U., 1976; postgrad. Ball State U., 1981-83. Cert. prin., Ind. Tchr. South Haven Pub. Schs., Mich., 1969-79; asst. prin. Tippacanoe Valley High Sch., Mantons, Ind., 1979-83; prin. Dubois Middle Sch., Northeast Dubois County Sch., Ind., 1983—. Mem. Ruritan Internat., Ind. Secondary Sch. Adminstrs., Nat. Assn. Secondary Sch. Adminstrs. Home: PO Box 91 Dubois IN 47527 Office: Dubois Middle Sch PO Box 187 Dubois IN 47527

WORTMAN, GLORIA CLARA, food service executive; b. St. Louis, June 22, 1925; d. John Adolph and Mary Louise (Kulage) Pfeiffer; m. James Bernard Wortman, June 14, 1947; children—Mary, Sarah, Susan, Martha. B.S. in Home Econs., Fontbonne Coll., St. Louis, 1947. Cert. home economist. Mgr., Luncheon is Served, St. Louis, 1948-52; owner Glo-Jon Foods, St. Louis, 1971-74; home economist-sales J & R Custom Food, St. Louis, 1974-77, United Instl. Sale, St. Louis, 1977-82, Food Service Enterprises, St. Louis, 1982—. Pres., Ladies of Lourdes, St. Louis, 1969; leader St. Louis council Girl Scouts U.S.A., 1964-69; v.p. Rosati Kain PTA, St. Louis, 1977-79, pres., 1979-80. Mem. Sch. Food Service Assn., Home Economists in Bus. (pres. 1978-79), Am. Home Econs. Assn. Republican. Roman Catholic. Home: 7014 Lindell St University City MO 63130 Office: Food Service Enterprises 11200 Natural Bridge Bridgeton MO 63044

WOZNAK, GEORGE BRIAN, management consultant information systems; b. Cleve., Dec. 13, 1949; s. Walter George and Eva (Popick) W.; m. Diana Victoria Lesniak, Nov. 18, 1978; 1 child, Jonathan George. B.S. in Bus. Adminstrn., Ohio State U., 1971; M.B.A., Baldwin Wallace Coll., 1977; cert. Case Western Res. U., 1984. Cert. industry cons., AT&T. Dir. mktg. Jury Verdict Research, Inc., Cleve., 1975-77, exec. dir., 1977-80; industry cons. Ohio Bell Telephone Co., Cleve., 1980-82; mktg. mgr. AT&T Info. Systems, Cleve., 1983-84; mgmt. cons. Price Waterhouse, 1984—; cons. various orgns. and corps. Developer and leader seminar: Control of Operating 1981 Expenses in Mfg. Facility: A Corporate Focus for the 1980's. Mem. Pres.'s Club Ohio Bell Telephone Co., 1982, Regional Leaders' Club, AT&T Info Systems, 1983. Mem. Am. Mktg. Assn., Soc. Telecommunications Profls., Greater Cleve. Growth Assn. Club: Univ. (Cleve.). Home: 3122 Helen Dr North Royalton OH 44133 Office: Price Waterhouse 1900 Central Nat Bank Bldg Cleveland OH 44114

WRAY, BRUCE ROBERT, marketing executive; b. Camden, N.J., Jan. 10, 1952; s. Robert Donald and Dolores (Graden) W.; m. Cheryl Ann Fogelberg, Aug. 17, 1974; children—Jennifer Ann, Mark Robert. B.A., Bethel Coll., 1974; M.B.A., Coll. St. Thomas, 1981. Mktg. coordinator Interior Wood Products, St. Paul, 1975-80; mktg. mgr. Computype, Inc., St. Paul, 1980-84, dir. mktg., 1984—; co. del. Automatic Identification Mfrs., Pitts., 1982—. Contbr. articles to profl. jours. Mem. Am. Product and Inventory Control Soc., Assn. M.B.A. Execs., Am. Mktg. Assn. Republican. Presbyterian. Avocations: music, bicycling, hiking, tennis. Office: Computype Inc 2285 W County Rd C St Paul MN 55113

WRAY, DONN HAYES, lawyer; b. Gary, Ind., May 12, 1955; s. Donald Robert and Violet (Hayes) W. Student Ind. U., 1975-76; B.A., Valparaiso U., 1977, J.D., 1980. Bar: Ind. 1980, Ill. 1980, U.S. Dist. Ct. (so. dist.) Ind. 1980. Law clk. Ind. Ct. Appeals, 1980-82; assoc. Stewart, Irwin, Gilliom, Meyer & Guthrie, Indpls., 1982—. Mem. ABA, Ind. State Bar Assn., Ill. State Bar Assn., Indpls. Bar Assn. Republican. Club: Columbia (Indpls.). Home: 5707 Brockton Dr #108 Indianapolis IN 46220 Office: Stewart Irwin Gilliom Meyer & Guthrie 300 Merchants Bank Bldg Indianapolis IN 46204

WREN, CHRISTOPHER GOVE, lawyer; b. Rochester, N.Y., Jan. 9, 1950; s. Carl Ulmer and Barbara Jean (Nichols) W.; m. Jill Darline Robinson, June 12, 1976. Student Brown U., 1968-69; B.A., George Washington U., 1976; J.D., Harvard U., 1979. Bar: Mass. 1979, U.S. Ct. Mil. Appeals 1979, Wis. 1980, U.S. Dist. Ct. Mass. 1980, U.S. Dist. Ct. (we. and ea. dists.) Wis. 1980, U.S. Ct. Appeals (1st and 7th cirs.) 1980. Research assoc. Atty. Douglas Danner, Boston, 1979-80; law clk. U.S. Dist. Ct. (we. dist.) Wis., Madison, 1980-81; assoc. Michael, Best & Friedrich, Madison, 1981-84; asst. atty. gen. Wis. Dept. Justice, Madison, 1984—, dir. Statewide Prosecutor and Edn. Tng. Program, 1985—. Co-Author: The Legal Research Manual: A Game Plan for Legal Research and Analysis, 1983. Mem. Dane County Democratic Exec. Bd., Madison, 1981—; mem. Wis. Dem. Platform Com., Madison, 1982—. Served with U.S. Army, 1969-71. Mem. ABA, State Bar Wis., Dane County Bar Assn., Assn. Trial Lawyers Am., Wis. Acad. Trial Lawyers, Soc. Profl. Journalists (Nat. Mark of Excellence award 1974). Home: 702 Emerson St Madison WI 53715 Office: Wis Dept Justice PO Box 7857 Madison WI 53707

WREN, LINNEA HOLMER, art history educator, consultant; b. Mpls., Nov. 12, 1948; d. Paul LeRoy and Phyllis June (Schulberg) Holmer; m. David John Wren, Oct. 18, 1970; 1 dau., Nayla Kristin. B.A., Radcliffe Coll., 1970; M.A., Harvard U., 1972; Ph.D., U. Minn., 1978. Asst. prof. art St. Cloud (Minn.) U., 1974; instr. art history Gustavus Adolphus Coll., St. Peter, Minn., 1977-79, asst. prof., 1979-83, assoc. prof., 1983—; cons. on Maya art Sci. Mus. Minn. NEH fellow, 1980-81; Bunting Inst. fellow, 1980-81. Mem. Coll. Art Assn., Soc. for Am. Archaeology, Phi Beta Kappa, Phi Kappa Phi. Democrat. Lutheran. Home: 675 Tyrol Ln Shakopee MN 55379 Office: Gustavus Adolphus Coll Saint Peter MN 56082

WRIGHT, ANNA BEEBE, nurse; b. Burlington, Iowa, Sept. 8, 1925; d. Charles Howard and Ruth Ernestine (Bovell) Beebe; m. Donald Carlyle Wright, July 28, 1946; children—Jacalyn Gale, Bradley Carlyle. Student Burlington Jr. Coll. (Iowa), 1943-44; R.N., U. Iowa, 1947. Staff nurse University Hosp., Iowa City, 1947-49; staff nurse Stormont-Vail Hosp.,

Topeka, Kans., 1949-51, clin. instr., staff nurse, 1951-53, 53-58; staff nurse University Hosp., Iowa City, 1958-60; head nurse, staff nurse Meml. Hosp., Topeka, Kans., 1964-71, charge nurse, 1971—; clinic vol. Am. Heart Assn., 1979, 82. Mem. Am. Assn. Critical Care Nurses. Republican. Methodist. Home: 3719 Munson St Topeka KS 66604 Office: Memorial Hosp 600 Madison St Topeka KS 66607

WRIGHT, BARBARA ANNE, county official; b. Cedar Rapids, Iowa, Dec. 11, 1941; d. Daniel Dean and Shirley Ann (O'Rourke) Lemon; m. Kenneth E. Wright; children—Kip, Kevin, Anne. B.S., Mt. Mercy Coll., 1966. Mem. Maquoketa (Iowa) City Council, 1972-76; mayor pro-tem, Maquoketa, 1974-76; mem. Jackson County (Iowa) Bd. Adjustment, 1976-82; Jackson County supr., 1982—. Mem. Sacred Heart Sch. Bd., Maquoketa. Democrat. Roman Catholic. Club: Univ. Women. Office: Court House Maquoketa IA 52060

WRIGHT, CREIGHTON BOLTER, cardiovascular surgeon, educator; b. Washington, Jan. 29, 1939; s. Benjamin Washington and Catherine Adele (Bolter) W.; m. Carolyn Eleanor Craver, Jan. 29, 1966; children—Creighton Bolter, Benson, Kathryn, Elizabeth. B.A., Duke U., 1961, M.D., 1965. Diplomate Am. Bd. Thoracic Surgery, Am. Bd. Surgery, subbd. Gen. Vascular Surgery. Intern, Duke U., Durham, N.C., 1965-66; resident in surgery U. Va., Charlottesville, 1966-71; from asst. prof. to assoc. prof. George Washington U., 1974-76; assoc. prof., then prof. surgery U. Iowa, 1976-81; prof. clin. surgery U. Cin., also clin. prof. surgery Uniformed Services U., 1981—. Served to col. USAR, 1966-83. Decorated Meritorious Service medal; recipient Kindred Resident Teaching award, 1967, Golden Apple Teaching award, 1975. Mem. Assn. Acad. Surgery (pres. 1980), Central Surg. Assn., Soc. Univ. Surgeons, Soc. Vascular Surgery, Internat. Soc. Cardiovascular Surgery, Am. Assn. Thoracic Surgery, Soc. Thoracic Surgery, So. Thoracic Surg. Assn., Midwestern Vascular Surg. Soc., Alpha Omega Alpha, Sigma Chi. Editor: Vascular Grafting, 1983; (with others) Venous Trauma, 1983; contbr. articles to profl. jours., chpts. to books. Home: 1242 Edwards Rd Cincinnati OH 45208 Office: 2139 Auburn Ave Cincinnati OH 45219

WRIGHT, DOROTHY MARIE, educational administrator; b. Kansas City, Mo., Mar. 9, 1926; s. Everett and Gertrude (Kerr) W. A.A., Kansas City Jr. Coll., 1946; B.S. in Edn., Central Mo. State Coll., Warrensburg, 1948; M.A., U. Iowa, 1951; Pd.D., Nova U., Fort Lauderdale, Fla., 1976. Cert. tchr., Mo., Kans. Tchr., Lyndon Pub. Sch., Kans., 1948-51, Winfield Pub. Sch., Kans., 1951-55; tchr., counselor Penn Valley Community Coll., Kansas City, Mo., 1955-64, registrar, dir. admissions, 1965-70, dean instrn., 1970-79, 80-84, interim pres., 1979-80, asst. to pres., 1984—, mem. speakers' bur., 1980—; evaluator North Central Assn., Chgo., 1975—; test evaluator Stevens Thorow, Chgo., 1965—. Author: (corres. manual) Guide For Writing, 1970. Contbr. articles, poems to profl. publs. Mem. Women's C. of C., Am. Vocat. Assn., Mo. Vocat. Assn., Am. Assn. Women in Community and Jr. Colls., Nat. Assn. Acad. Deans (pres. 1980), Mo. Assn. Community and Jr. Colls., Nat. Assn. Acad. Deans (pres. 1980), Mo. Assn. Community and Jr. Colls., Nat. Assn. Community Colls, Alpha Delta Kappa, Sweet adelines (sec., vice regent, regent). Republican. Presbyterian. Club: Women's City (Kansas City, Mo.). Avocations: Singing barbershiр harmony, teaching knitting, stained glass, reading, writing poetry. Home: 13942 Falkirk Circle 3201 Southwest Trafficway Kansas City MO 64111

WRIGHT, DOUGLAS SCOTT, mayor, lawyer; b. Kansas City, Mo., Nov. 10, 1948; s. Charles Wesley and Alice Clare (Brownfield) W.; m. Susan Lydia Kennedy, June 3, 1971; children—Sara, Adam. B.A., Washburn U., 1970, J.D., 1973. Bar: Kans. 1973. Dep. city atty. City of Topeka, Kans., 1973-83, mayor, 1983—. Mem. bd. regents Washburn U., Topeka, 1983—; mem. exec. bd. Jayhawk Area council Boy Scouts Am., Topeka, 1983—. Republican. Office: City of Topeka 215 E 7th St Topeka KS 66603

WRIGHT, HELEN KENNEDY, editor; b. Indpls., Sept. 23, 1927; d. William Henry and Ida Louise (Crosby) Kennedy; B.A., Butler U., 1945, M.S., 1950; M.S., Columbia U., 1952; m. Samuel A. Wright, Sept. 5, 1970; 1 son, Carl F. Prince II. Reference librarian N.Y. Pub. Library, N.Y.C., 1952-53, Bklyn. Pub. Library, 1953-54; cataloger U. Utah, 1954-57; librarian Chgo. Pub. Library; asst. dir. pub. dept. ALA, Chgo., 1958-62, editor Reference Books Bull., 1962-85; asst. dir. for new product planning, pub. services, 1985—. Mem. Phi Kappa Phi, Kappa Delta Pi, Sigma Gamma Rho. Roman Catholic. Contbr. to Ency. of Careers, Ency. of Library and Info. Sci. Home: 1138 W 111th St Chicago IL 60643 Office: 50 E Huron Chicago IL 60611

WRIGHT, JAMES LYNN, savs. and loan co. exec.; b. Springfield, Ill., Sept. 22, 1940; s. Glenn LaRue and Freida Pearl (Bloomfield) W.; B.S., Ill. Coll., 1963; M. Accounting Sci., U. Ill., 1965, postgrad., 1969-71; m. Karen Ann Barber, Nov. 24, 1976; children—Jeffrey Michael, Timothy Lynn. Staff auditor Arthur Young & Co., Chgo., 1965-66, 68-69; teaching asst. accounting U. Ill., Urbana, 1969-70; instr. accounting Ill. State U., Normal, 1970-71; accountant Bloomington (Ill.) Fed. Savs. & Loan Assn., 1972, asst. treas., 1972-73, dir. data processing, 1974-76, v.p., 1976-78, comptroller, 1976-78, v.p., treas., 1978-81, sr. v.p., treas., 1981—; treas., dir. Midwest Travel Bur., Inc., Bloomington; dir. MARC Ctr., Bloomington. Served with U.S. Army, 1966-68. Club: Univ. (Chgo.). Home: 308 Vista Dr Bloomington IL 61701 Office: 115 E Washington St Bloomington IL 61701

WRIGHT, JAMES RUSSELL, veterinarian; b. Pontiac, Mich., Aug. 13, 1946; s. Alvin and Alice (Forbes) W.; m. Janice Mae Bales, Sept. 8, 1967. B.S., Mich. State U., 1968; D.V.M., 1969. Staff orthopedic and neurosurgeon Gasow Vet. Hosp., Birmingham, Mich., 1969—. Evans Scholars scholar 1966-68. Contbr. numerous articles to various publs. Mem. Southeastern Vet. Med. Assn. (pres. 1981-82), Veterinary Orthopedic Soc. (bd. dirs. 1981-83), Am. Vet. Med. Assn., Mich. Vet. Med. Assn., Southeastern Mich. Vet. Med. Assn. (Outstanding Contbn. to Clin. Practice award 1984), Oakland County Vet. Med. Assn., Mich. State U. Alumni Assn., Evans Scholars Alumni Assn. Republican. Lutheran. Home: 2540 Yorkshire St Birmingham MI 48008 Office: 1521 N Woodward Birmingham MI 48008

WRIGHT, JOHN BALDWIN, medical advertising, publishing company; b. Hartford, Conn., Nov. 27, 1933; s. John Baldwin and Lillian Harriet (Piller) W.; m. Caryl Brainard Moore, Dec. 29, 1951; children—Hilary, Jocelyn. Diplome Superieure, U. Sorbonne, Paris, 1954; B.A., Wesleyan U., 1955; M.B.A., NYU, 1962. Advt. mgr. Merck Sharp & Dohme Internat., N.Y.C., 1958-62; account exec. L.W. Frohlich, N.Y.C., 1962-64; v.p., account supr. Needham, Harper & Steers, N.Y.C., 1964-66; pres. Robert E. Wilson, Inc., N.Y.C., 1966-72; exec. v.p. Corbett div. Butten, Barton, Durstine, Osborne, N.Y.C., 1973-75; v.p., account supr. Sieber & McIntyre, Chgo., 1975-79; pres. Lifetime Learning, Inc., Chgo., 1979—; bd. cons. Osteoporosis Found., Chgo., 1984—. Served as cpl. U.S. Army, 1956-58. Mem. Midwest Pharm. Advt. Council, Med. Mktg. Assn. Republican. Episcopalian. Club: Chgo. Farmers. Avocation: farming. Home: 1350 N State Pkwy Chicago IL 60610 Office: Lifetime Learning Inc 612 N Michigan Ave Chicago IL 60611

WRIGHT, JOSEPH MALCOLM, university dean; b. Toomsboro, Ga., Sept. 27, 1944; s. Ed and May O. (Dixon) W.; m. Sheilah Broome, Aug. 10, 1967; children—Joseph Oliver, Tiffany Michele, Jennifer Nicole. B.S., Eastern Mich. U., 1969; J.D., Wayne State U., 1974; diploma ednl. mgmt. Harvard U., 1983. Bar: Fla. 1977, U.S. Ct. Appeals 1978, US. Tax Ct. 1982. Data processing clk. Gen. Motors Corp., Flint, Mich., 1965-67, mem. fin. staff, Ypsilanti, Mich., 1967-69; supr. payroll and budgets U. Mich., Ann Arbor, 1969-71; adminstrv. mgr., U. Mich.-Dearborn, 1971-73, dean student affairs, 1973—; chmn. bd. United Motors Corp., Pontiac, Mich., dir. Pink Ltd., Allen Park, Mich. Author: The U.S. Department of Housing and Urban Development Program for Urban Renewal, 1972. Contbr. articles to profl. jours. Chmn. Western Wayne/Oakland County Community Housing Resource Bd., 1978—, Assn. for Legal Edn., Detroit, 1977—; mem. Oak Park Urban Renewal Council, Flint, 1969-75; bd. dirs. Inner City Bus. Improvement Forum, Detroit, 1984—. Served with USAFR, 1966-69. Mem. Fla. Bar Assn., ABA, (chmn. family law taxation com. 1978), Wolverine Bar Assn., Nat. Assn. Student Personnel Adminstrs., Washtenaw County Black Contractors Assn. (bd. dirs.). Office: U Mich 4901 Evergreen St Dearborn MI 48128

WRIGHT, KATHERYN THORNE, civic worker; b. Ravenswood, Ill., Sept. 19, 1895; d. Albert H. and Sarah (Chapman) Wright; A.B., Mather Coll. (now Western Res. Coll.), 1917, A.M., Case Western Res. U., 1927. Substitute tchr. Cleve. Public Schs., 1917-18; sec. First Meth. Ch., Cleve., 1920; sec. clk.'s office Cleveland Heights (Ohio) Bd. of Edn., 1921-22; sec. Squire, Sanders & Dempsey, Cleve., 1924-62, ret.; also freelance writer, 1962—. Vol., ARC, Am. Cancer Soc.; tutorial program Episcopal Ch. Recipient Cleve. Vol. of Yr. award, 1969; Vol. award Am. Cancer Soc., 1977. Mem. Cleve. Coll. Writers Club, Profl. Secs. Internat. (charter mem. Forest City chpt.), Greater Cleve. Orchid Soc., DAR (Western Res. chpt.), Women's Assn. for Continuing Edn. Episcopalian (lay reader 1973—). Clubs: Quota (charter mem.), College. Home: 2543 Derbyshire Rd Cleveland OH 44106

WRIGHT, MICHAEL WILLIAM, food wholesaling executive; b. Mpls., June 13, 1938; s. Thomas W. and Winifred M. W.; m. Susan Marie Guzy. B.A. in Liberal Arts, U. Minn., 1961; LL.B., 1963. Ptnr. Dorsey & Whitney, Mpls., 1966-77; sr. v.p. Super Valu Stores, Inc., Mpls., 1977-78, pres., chief operating officer, 1978—, pres., chief exec. officer, 1981—, chmn., 1982—; dir. Deluxe Check Printers, Mpls., Control Data Corp., Mpls.; dir., dep. chmn. Fed. Res. Bank of Mpls.; chmn. Uniform Product Code Council, Dayton, Ohio. Served as 1st lt. U.S. Army, 1964-66. Mem. Nat. Am. Wholesale Grocers Assn. (chmn.), Food Mktg. Inst. Washington (bd. dirs.), Mpls. C. of C. (bd. dirs.). Office: Super Valu Stores Inc PO Box 990 Minneapolis MN 55440 also 11840 Valley View Rd Eden Prairie MN 55344

WRIGHT, PAUL NATHAN, health care facility administrator; b. Greenville, Mich., Dec. 16, 1950; s. Roger Johnson and Mildred Ruth (Cottrell) W. A.S., Davenport Coll., Grand Rapids, Mich., 1971; hon. degree nursing home adminstrn. George Washington U., 1974. Custodian, Belding Christian Nursing Home, (Mich.), 1966-73, asst. adminstr., 1973, adminstr., 1973-76; adminstr. Maccabee Gardens, Saginaw, Mich., 1976-78, Beverly Manor, Grand Blanc, Mich., 1978-80; adminstr., chief exec. officer Grand Blanc Convalescent Center, 1980—. Author health care regional position paper, 1981. Charter mem. Republican Presdl. Task Force; mem. Rep. Nat. Com., U.S. Senatorial Club; mem. Holy Redeemer Choir. Mem. Health Care Assn. of Mich. (regional dir., legal services com., nominations com. 1985-86), Genesee, Lapeer, Shiawasee Adminstrs. Council, Am. Coll. Health Care Adminstrs. (treas., fin. com.), Flint Area Health Found. (edn. com.), Social Work Discharge Planning Com. (nursing home rep., ECF grant adv. com.), Internat. Platform Assn., Am. Security Council (nat. adv. bd.). Roman Catholic. Lodge: Rotary (Grand Blanc). Home: 6042 Westknoll Dr A550 Grand Blanc MI 48439 Office: Grand Blanc Convalescent Center 8481 Holly Rd Grand Blanc MI 48439

WRIGHT, RONALD A., college dean, veterinarian; b. Terre Haute, Ind., Apr. 6, 1932; s. Hugh Edgar and Alma (Ainsworth) W.; m. Jackie Stark, July 27, 1952; children—Ronald Gregory, Kim Denise, Kurt Allen. B.S. in Agr., Purdue U., 1954; D.V.M., 1961, M.S., 1964. Life scientist Battelle Inst., Columbus, Ohio, 1966-68, assoc. dir. life sci., 1968-70; devel. officer Ohio State U. Research Found., Columbus, 1970-72, dir. program devel., 1972-78, assoc. dean Coll. Vet. Medicine, 1978-80, dean, 1980—. Co-author: University Connected Research Founds., 1977; Soviet Aerospace Biology, 1969. Trustee Columbus Zoo, 1982, Internat. Ctr. Preservation Wild Animals, Columbus, 1984. Served to capt. USAF, 1954-57. Grantee Org. Research Founds., NSF, 1975, AEC, 1967. Mem. AVMA, Ohio Vet. Med. Assn., AAAS, Aircraft Owners and Pilots Assn., Quiet Birdmen. Republican. Lodge: Rotary. Avocation: piloting. Office: Ohio State Coll Vet Medicine 1900 Coffey Rd Columbus OH 43210

WRIGHT, RONALD WAYNE, manufacturing company executive, consultant; b. Tacoma, Wash., May 9, 1943; s. Wayne C. and Betty M. (Foreman) W.; m. Susan M. Nowak, Oct. 23, 1982; children—Gregory L., Timothy A. Student Central Washington U., 1961-62; Highline Community Coll., 1964-66; cert. Boeing Sch. Management, 1964-68. Sr. supr. The Boeing Co., Seattle, 1962-71; prodn. control mgr. Western Gear Corp., Jamestown, N.D., 1971-77, mgr. mgmt. info. systems, 1977-79, mfg. systems cons., 1979, ops. mgr., 1984—; gen. mgr. Western Cedar corp., Everett, Wash., 1977; mfg. mgr. Brownline Brooks & Perkins, Torrance, Calif., 1979-84. Mem. Soc. Mfg. Engrs., Am. Prodn. and Inventory Control Soc. Roman Catholic. Avocations: Pilot; general aviation; hunting. Office: Western Gear Corp Box 629 Jamestown ND 58402-0629

WRIGHT, ROY DEAN, sociologist, educator, association executive; b. Stroud, Okla., Sept. 12, 1938; s. Leland and Ella (Murray) W.; m. Susan E. Walker; 1 child, Ehren Dean. B.S., Pitts. State U., 1960, M.S., 1961; Ph.D., U. Mo., 1970. Asst. prof. Va. Poly. Inst., Blacksburg, 1968-71; vis. prof. Meml. U. Nfld., St. John's, 1971; prof. Drake U., Des Moines, 1971—, chmn. dept. sociology, 1978-81. Author: Marginality and Identity, 1973; Alternatives to Prison. Issues and Options, 1979. Contbr. articles to profl. jours. Chmn., Adult Instnl. Commn., State of Iowa, 1980-81, Iowa Criminal and Juvenile Justice Council, 1982-86; active Community-Based Corrections Council, State of Iowa, 1983-84, Classification Com., State of Iowa, 1984—. Served to capt. U.S. Army, 1954-66. Fulbright grantee, 1963-64; NSF grantee, 1967; Univ. House fellow U. Iowa, 1979. Mem. Midwest Sociology Soc. (bd. dirs. 1980—, co-editor Newsletter). Home: 920 45th St W Des Moines IA 50265 Office: Dept Sociology Drake U Des Moines IA 50265

WRIGHT, STEPHANIE JEANNE, hospital administrator; b. N.Y.C., Sept. 18, 1952; d. Charles Howard and Louise Powell (Lovett) W.; m. William Martin Griggs, May 22, 1982. B.A., Am. U., 1974; M.H.A., George Washington U., 1980. Adminstrv. resident Loyola Med. Ctr., Maywood, Ill., 1980; asst. adminstr. Mt. Sinai Hosp. Med. Ctr., Chgo., 1981-82, asst. v.p. patient care services, 1982—. Bd. dirs. Mus. African Am. History, Detroit, Mid Am. chpt. ARC, Bus. and Profl. People for Pub. Interest; trustee Dusable Mus. African-Am. History, Chgo.; mem. Chgo. Dist. Child Life Network Adv. Bd. ITT fellow to Venezuela, 1974-75. Mem. Nat. Assn. Health Service Execs., NAACP (life). Home: 4200 N Marine Dr Apt 604 Chicago IL 60613 Office: Mount Sinai Hosp Med Ctr California Ave and 15th St Chicago IL 60608

WRIGHT, WAYNE MITCHELL, physicist; b. Sanford, Maine, July 12, 1934; s. Carl Roberts and Edith (Mitchell) W.; m. Mary Urbanowicz, Oct. 18, 1959; children—Catherine, Peter, Laura, Daniel. A.B., Bowdoin Coll., 1956; M.S., Harvard U., 1957, Ph.D., 1961. Postdoctoral fellow, dep. dir. Acoustics Research Lab., Harvard U., 1961-62; asst. prof. to prof. physics Kalamazoo Coll., 1962—, chmn. dept., 1975—; cons. in acoustics U. Calif.-San Diego, 1964; vis. prof. U. Rochester, 1967, Naval Postgrad. Sch., 1969-70, U. Colo., 1976, U. Mich., 1979-80; acoustical cons. industry and local govt. Fellow Acoustical Soc. Am.; mem. Am. Assn. Physics Tchrs. (pres. Mich. sect. 1981-82), Phi Beta Kappa, Sigma Xi. Episcopalian. Contbr. articles to profl. jours. Home: 2267 Benjamin Ave Kalamazoo MI 49008 Office: Kalamazoo Coll Kalamazoo MI 49007

WRIGHT, WAYNE PAUL, music educator, researcher; b. Dowagiac, Mich., Oct. 4, 1936; s. Leslie and Florence (Johnson) W. B.A. in Music, Western Mich. U., 1959, M.A., 1961; Ph.D., Columbia Pacific U., 1982. Cert. tchr. fine arts. Educator Edn. Facility, Superior, Wis., 1961-63, Decatur, Mich., 1963-64; asst. prof. Wheaton Coll., Ill., 1964-70; educator, peformer Charlotte Symphony, N.C., 1970-72; educator, pedagogue stringed instruments, Louisville Ky., 1972—; staff testing, assessment dept. Jefferson Schs., Louisville, 1972—; music cons. Wheaton, 1964-70. Author: Violin Techniques to Develop Competent Performance Standards on Selected Compositions, 1982. Recipient Grad. awards U. Ala., U. Ill., Mich. State U., 1959-64, Spl. Tchr. Recognition award Ky. Edn. Assn., 1976; Western Mich. U. scholar, 1955-59. Mem. NEA, Mich. Edn. Assn., Ky. Edn. Assn., Am. String Tchrs., Internat. Platform Assn. Avocations: theology, horticulture.

WRIGHT, WILLIAM RONALD, university administrator; b. Joliet, Ill., Nov. 4, 1936; m. Roselyn A. Wise, June 13, 1959; children—Stephen, David. Diploma Joliet Jr. Coll., 1956; B.S. in Edn., Ill. State U., 1958; M.Ed., U. Ill., 1961; Ph.D., Purdue U., 1969. Tchr., Carl Sandburg High Sch., Orland Park, Ill., 1959-63; prin. Grant Park High Sch., Ill., 1963-65; adult edn. specialist Office Edn., Washington, 1966-67; asst. dir. Wabash Valley Edn. Ctr., West Lafayette, Ind., 1967-70; dir. continuing edn. Purdue U.-Calumet, Hammond, Ind., 1970—, chmn., dir. Ind. Council Continuing Edn., Indpls., 1985. Vice chmn. panel III Lake Area United Way, Griffith, Ind., 1975-78; mem. Gifted Talented Planning Orgn., Gary, Ind., 1981—. U.S. Office Edn. fellow, 1966; grantee Purdue U., 1967, U.S. Office Edn., 1968. Mem. Nat. Univ. Continuing Edn. Assn., Ind. Council for Continuing Edn. (sec. 1981, 83), East Chicago C. of C. (edn. com. 1975—), Hammond C. of C. (edn. com. 1981—). Avocations: reading; travel; horticulture. Office: Purdue U-Calumet 2233 171st St Hammond IN 46323

WRIGLEY, WILLIAM, corp. exec.; b. Chgo., Jan. 21, 1933; s. Philip Knight and Helen (Atwater) W.; B.A., Yale U., 1954; m. Alison Hunter, June 1, 1957 (div.); children—Alison, Philip, William; m. Julie Burns, Nov. 28, 1981. With Wm. Wrigley Jr. Co., Chgo., 1956—, dir., 1960—, pres., chief exec. officer, 1961—; dir. Wrigley Co. S.A. (Spain), The Wrigley Co. Ltd. (U.K.), The Wrigley Co. Pty. Ltd. (Australia), The Wrigley Co. (N.Z.) Ltd., New Zealand, Wrigley Philippines, Inc., Wrigley Co. (H.K.) Ltd. (Hong Kong), Wrigley & Co. Ltd., Japan, Wrigley Co. (East Africa) Ltd. (Kenya), Wrigley N.V. (Netherlands); dir., mem. compensation com. Nat. Blvd. Bank; dir., mem. audit com., com. non-mgmt. dirs., exec. com., chmn. nominating com. Texaco, Inc.; dir., mem. audit com. Am. Home Products Corp.; dir., pres., chief exec. officer, mem. exec. com. Santa Catalina Island Co.; dir. Grocery Mfrs. Am., Inc. Bd. dirs., pres. Wrigley Meml. Garden Found.; bd. dirs. Northwestern Meml. Hosp. Mgmt. Corp.; trustee Chgo. Latin Sch. Found., 1975—; bd. dirs. Geneva Lake Water Safety Com., 1966—, mem. exec. com., 1968—; mem. adv. bd. Center for Sports Medicine, Northwestern U. Med. Sch., 1976—, mem. exec. com. Baccalaureate Degree Program in Nursing; bd. dirs. Cowboy Artists Am. Mus. Served from ensign to lt. (j.g.) USNR, 1954-56, lt. comdr. Res. ret. Mem. Chgo. Hist. Soc., Art Inst. Chgo., Field Mus. Natural History, Navy League U.S., Wolf's Head Soc., Santa Catalina Island Conservancy (benefactor mem.), USC Oceanographic Assocs., Catalina Island Mus. Soc., Delta Kappa Epsilon. Clubs: Chicago Yacht, Racquet, Saddle and Cycle, Tavern, Commercial (Chgo.); Lake Geneva (Wis.) Country, Lake Geneva Yacht; Brook (N.Y.C.); California, Tuna of Santa Catalina Island (hon.), Catalina Island Yacht (Calif.); Los Angeles Yacht. Office: 410 N Michigan Ave Chicago IL 60611

WRISTON, NAOMI FAYE, osteopathic physician, teacher; b. Mossy, W. Va., Dec. 15, 1944; d. Leonard Orville and Lessie Faye (Coleman) Wriston. B.S., W. Va. U., 1967; M.Sc. Edn., U. Md.-Coll. Park, 1970; D.O., W. Va. Sch. Osteo. Medicine, 1978. Diplomate Nat. Bd. Osteo. Physicians and Surgeons Tchr., Sligo Jr. High, Silver Spring, Md., 1967-70, Collins High Sch., Oak Hill, W. Va., 1970-74; intern Riverside Hosp., Trenton, Mich., 1978-79; gen. practice Osteo. medicine Physicians for Gen. Practice, Inc., Columbus, Ohio, 1979—; clin. preceptor Ohio State U. Sch. Medicine, Columbus, 1981—; vol. faculty Ohio U., Athens, 1980—; mem. credentials com. Drs. Hosp., Columbus, 1985—; chmn. pharmacy com. United Health Plan, Inc., Columbus, 1984—. Lectr. Columbus Sr. Citizen Ctrs., 1983—. Grantee NSF, 1970, 71, 73, 74. Fellow Am. Soc. Colposcopy and Cervical Pathology; mem. Am. Coll. Gen. Practitioners, Am. Osteo. Assn., Ohio Osteo. Assn., Columbus Acad. Osteo. Medicine. Methodist. Avocations: traveling; swimming; sailing. Office: Physicians for Gen Practice Inc 4337 Cleveland Ave Columbus OH 43224

WROBLOWA, HALINA STEFANIA, electrochemist; b. Gdansk, Poland, July 5, 1925; came to U.S., 1960, naturalized, 1970; M.Sc., U. Lodz (Poland), 1949; Ph.D., Warsaw Inst. Tech., 1958; 1 dau., Krystyna Wrobel-Knight. Chmn. dept. prep. studies U. Lodz, 1950-53; adj. Inst. for Phys. Chemistry, Acad. Scis., Warsaw, Poland, 1958-60; dep. dir. electrochemistry lab. Energy Inst., U. Pa., Phila., 1960-67, dir. electrochemistry lab., 1968-75; prin. research scientist Ford Motor Co., Dearborn, Mich., 1978—. Served with Polish Underground Army, 1943-45. Decorated Silver Cross of Merit with Swords. Mem. Electrochem. Soc., Internat. Electrochem. Soc., Mensa, Sigma Xi. Contbr. chpts. to books, articles to profl. jours., patent lit. Office: Ford Motor Co SRL S-2079 PO Box 2053 Dearborn MI 48121

WRONKOSKI, RICHARD EDWARD, food and feed ingredients manufacturing executive; b. Los Angeles, Mar. 2, 1947; s. Edward Joseph and Ann Louise (Dougherty) W.; m. Roberta Woodin, June 12, 1977 (div. Jan. 1979); m. Barbara Mann, Feb. 8, 1985. B.S. in Chemistry, Le Moyne Coll., 1969. Instrumental analyst Bendix Corp., Elmira Heights, N.Y., 1971-72; tchr. sci. and math. Glen Springs Acad., Lakemont, N.Y., 1973-74; quality engr. Internat. Salt Co., Retsof, N.Y., 1974-75, quality control mgr., Avery Island, La., 1975-77; quality control mgr. Hardy Salt Co., Manistee, Mich., 1977—. Treas., Manistee Civic Players, 1981—; co-organizer Manistee Trail Pro-Rally, 1984; advisor Jr. Achievement, Manistee, 1981. Roman Catholic. Club: Manistee Golf and Country. Home: 514 Ramsdell St Manistee MI 49660 Office: Hardy Salt Co 1501 Main St Manistee MI 49660

WRONSKI, STEPHANIE, educator; b. Oak Park, Ill., Oct. 9, 1916; d. Romuald August and Lillian (Romanowicz) Wronski. B.S. in Edn., Clarke Coll., 1957; Th. B., St. Joseph's Coll., 1966. Cert. tchr., Iowa, Ill. Joined Sisters of Charity, Roman Catholic Ch., 1935; tchr. Mary Queen of Heaven, Cicero, Ill., 1937-38, Holy Cross Sch., Chgo., 1938-53, 57-58, St. Anthony, Davenport, Iowa, 1953-57, St. Tarcissus, Chgo., 1958—, past coordinator for reading, sci., audio-visual dept.; local coordinator Cath. TV Network of Chgo.; past mem. math. com. Archdiocese of Chgo.; past mem. TV com. Chgo. Area Schs. Archdiocese of Chgo. grantee, 1967, 69, 82, 83. Mem. Nat. Cath. Edn. Assn. Developer Math. Progress Record Chart.

WU, ANNA FANG, physician, medical administrator; b. Chengtu, China, Mar. 25, 1940; d. Tsun Chun and Chi Chu Fang; m. Tai Te Wu, 1966; children—Richard Gee-Fang. B.A., Cornell U., 1962; Ph.D., MIT, 1967; M.D., U. Chgo., 1974. Diplomate Am. Bd. Internal Medicine. Research assoc. Muscle Inst., N.Y.C., 1967-68, Coll. Physicians and Surgeons Columbia U., N.Y.C., 1968-70; resident in internal medicine Northwestern U. Med. Sc., Chgo., 1974-77, instr., 1977-80, asst. prof. medicine, 1980—; med. dir. employee health service Northwestern Meml. Hosp., Chgo., 1979—. Mem. ACP, Am. Occupational Medicine Assn. Club: Med. Dirs. (Chgo.). Avocation: travel. Office: Northwestern Meml Hosp 303 E Superior St Chicago IL 60611

WU, CHING-HSONG, research scientist; b. Taipei, Taiwan, Republic of China, Apr. 22, 1939; came to U.S., 1963, naturalized, 1977; s. Bing H. and Hsiu Y. (Lai) W.; m. Su-Mei Lin, Sept. 5, 1967; children—Elaine, Yolanda. B.S., Nat. Taiwan U., Taipei, 1962; M.S., N.Mex. Highlands U., Las Vegas, 1965; Ph.D., U. Calif.-Berkeley, 1969. Prin. research sci. assoc. Ford Motor Co., Dearborn, Mich., 1969—. Contbr. articles to. profl. jours. Patentee low cost thermally stable TWC, 1984. Sec., Chinese Sch. Greater Detroit, Birmingham, Mich., 1985. Mem. Am. Chem. Soc., Detroit Chinese Engrs. Assn. (bd. dirs. 1985). Avocations: travel, sports, music. Home: 30691 Turtle Creek Farmington Hills MI 48018 Office: Ford Motor Co Dearborn MI 48018

WU, HARRY PAO-TUNG, librarian; b. Chinan, Shantung, China, May 1, 1932; s. James Ching-Mei and Elizabeth Hsiao (Lu) W.; B.A., Nat. Taiwan U., Taipei, 1959; student Ohio State U., 1962; M.L.S., Kent State U., 1966; m. Irene I-Len Sun, June 23, 1961; children—Eva Pei-Chen, Walter Pei-Liang. Came to U.S., 1960. Archive and library asst. Taiwan Handicraft Promotion Center, Taipei, 1959-60; student asst. Kent State U. Library, 1960-61; reference librarian Massillon (Ohio) Pub. Library, 1964-65, acting asst. dir., 1965, asst. dir., head adult services, 1966; dir. Flesh Pub. Library, Piqua, Ohio, 1966-68; dir. St. Clair County Library System, Port Huron, Mich., 1968—; founder and dir. Blue Water Library Fedn., Port Huron, 1974—; pres. Mich. Library Film Circuit, Lansing, 1977-79; bd. dirs. Mich. Waterways council Girl Scouts U.S.A., Port Huron, 1985-86. Mem. Am., Mich. (chmn. library systems roundtable 1974-75) library assns., Am. Mgmt. Assn., Assn. Ednl. Communications and Tech., Detroit Suburban Librarians Roundtable. Clubs: Port Huron Internat., Rotary (dir. 1972-74). Home: 1518 Holland Ave Port Huron MI 48060 Office: 210 McMorran Blvd Port Huron MI 48060

WU, JAMES BI-CHENG, metallurgical engineer, researcher; b. Chendu, China, Nov. 29, 1943; came to U.S., 1968, naturalized, 1980; s. Cheng-Bi and Yen-Yu (Zhou) W.; m. Lee Nan Jan, June 19, 1971; 1 child, Eva. B.S., Cheng Kung U., Taiwan, 1965; M.S., Stevens Inst. Tech., 1970; Ph.D., U. Rochester, 1975. Postdoctoral fellow U. Pa., Phila., 1975-76; research metallurgist Republic Steel Corp. Research Ctr., Independence, Ohio, 1976-81; research engr. tech. dept. cabot Corp., Kokomo, Ind., 1981-83, group leader corrosion, 1983—; mem. tech. adv. com. Materials Tech. Inst., Columbus, Ohio, 1983—. Contbr. (with others) articles to profl. jours. Fellow Am. Electroplaters Soc.; mem. Am. Soc. Metals, Nat. Assn. Corrosion Engrs. (v. chmn. T 5K com. 1984—), AIME. Unitarian, Avocations: Golf; tennis; fishing; photography. Office: Cabot Corp 1020 West Park Ave Kokomo IN 46901

WU, KUANG-MING, philosophy educator; b. Tainan, Taiwan, China, July 24, 1933; came to U.S. 1960, naturalized, 1972; s. Yung-show and Sing (Tsai) Wu; m. Wen-yen Tsai, Jan. 2, 1960; children—John Y., Mary A., Mark L., Peter K. B.D., Yale U., 1962, S.T.M., 1963, Ph.D., 1965. Instr., Yale U., New Haven, Conn., 1965; prof. U. Wis.-Oshkosh, 1968—; vis. prof. U. Tex. El Paso, 1981-82; keynote speaker Symposium on Comparative Philosophy SUNY-Stony Brook, 1980, U. Tex-El Paso, 1979. Author: Chuang Tzu-World

Philosopher at Play, 1982. Contbr. articles to profl. jours. Pres. Our Saviour's Luth. Ch., Oshkosh, 1972-74. Mem. Internat. Soc. Chinese Philosophy (sec. treas. 1983-86), Am. Philos. Soc. Office: Dept Philosophy U Wis Oshkosh WI 54901

WU, TIEN HSING, civil engineering educator, consulting engineer; b. Shanghai, China, Mar. 2, 1923; came to U.S., 1947, naturalized, 1957; s. Chong-Yung and Ying Mei (Pih) Woo; m. Peihsing Lin, Aug. 14, 1952; children—Mei, Anne. B.S., St. John's U., Shanghai, 1947; M.S., U. Ill., 1948, Ph.D., 1951. Registered profl. engr., Ohio, Mich. Civil engr. DeLeuw Cather & Co., Chgo., 1951-52, Ill. Div. Hwys., Springfield, 1952-53; from asst. prof. to prof. Mich. State U., East Lansing, 1953-65; prof. civil engring. Ohio State U., Columbus, 1965—; vis. prof. Norwegian Geotech. Inst., Oslo, 1959, 70, 76, Nat. U. Mexico, Mexico City, 1964, Royal Inst. Tech., Stockholm, 1980; UN cons. Punjab Agrl. U., Ludhiana, India, 1981. Author: Soil Mechanics, 2d. rev. edit., 1976; Soil Dynamics, 1970; also papers, numerous articles. Recipient Lichtenstein award Ohio State U., 1973, research award Ohio State U., 1984. Fellow ASCE; mem. Transp. Research Bd., ASTM, Sigma Xi. Home: 160 Brookside Oval E Worthington OH 43085 Office: Ohio State U Dept Civil Engring 2070 Neil Ave Columbus OH 43210

WU, TING-SHU, mechanical engineer, engineering educator; b. Hsinchang, Chekiang, China; s. Pen-I and Yuan-Whan (Vane) W.; m. Rita Hsu; children—Sinclair, Christina, Sandra. B.S., Nat. Taiwan U.; M.S., U. Minn.; Sc.D., Columbia U. Registered profl. engr., Ill. Assoc. prof. Ohio State U., Columbus; prof. U. Singapore; engr. Argonne Nat. Lab., Ill.; prof. Midwest Coll. Engring., Lombard, Ill., World Open U., Rapid City, S.D.; cons. BTA Engring., Inc., Westmont, Ill. Contbr. articles to profl. jours. Pres., The Coop. Chinese Lang. Sch., Woodridge, Ill. Mem. ASME. Home: 721 81st St Downers Grove IL 60516 Office: Argonne Nat Lab 9700 S Cass Ave Argonne IL 60439

WUBBELS, GENE GERALD, chemistry educator; b. Preston, Minn., Sept. 21, 1942; s. Victor and Genevieve M. (Sikkink) W.; m. Joyce Ruth Honebrink, Aug. 26, 1967; children—Kristen, Benjamin, John. B.S., Hamline U., 1964; Ph.D., Northwestern U., 1968; asst. prof. Grinnell Coll., Iowa, 1968-73, assoc. prof., 1973-79, prof. chemistry, 1979—. Editor: Survey of Progress in Chemistry, vol. 10, 1983. Moderator United Ch. of Christ Congl., Grinnell, 1980-82, 83-84. Grantee NSF, 1971-84; recipient Science Faculty Prof. Devel. award NSF, 1981-82. Fellow Iowa Acad. Sci.; mem. Am. Chem. Soc. (research grantee 1970-85, editor adv. bd. Accounts Chem. Research 1977-83). Republican. Club: Fortnightly (Grinnell). Avocation: music. Home: 1403 Summer St Grinnell IA 50112 Office: Grinnell Coll Grinnell IA 50112

WUERTH, RICHARD OSBORN, lawyer; b. Cleve., Nov. 12, 1946; s. H. Louis and Suzanne (Wilkinson) W.; m. Margaret Ann Pyle, Aug. 23, 1968; children—Jay Richard, Miriam Elise, Anna Christine. B.A. in History, Wittenberg U., 1968; J.D., Washington U., St. Louis, 1973. Bar: Ohio 1973. Ptnr., Lane, Alton & Horst, Columbus, Ohio, 1973—. Mem. Ohio Bar Assn., ABA. Democrat. Club: Athletic. Avocations: Running, bicycling, cross-country skiing. Home: 774 Vernon Rd Columbus OH 43209 Office: Lane Alton & Horst 155 E Broad St Columbus OH 43215

WUESCHNER, SILVANO ALFONS, management consultant, educator; b. Fischbach, W. Ger., Sept. 2, 1950; s. Alfons and Caroline (Weber) W.; B.A., Pepperdine U., 1977, M.A. in Human Resource Mgmt., 1979; m. F. Eleanor Mahaffey, Sept. 3, 1971; children—Edward Andrew, Erika Gretchen. Came to U.S., 1961, naturalized, 1966. Instr. psychology, mgmt. Los Angeles Met. Coll., 1979-80; instr. mgmt. devel. Rockwell Internat., Cedar Rapids, Iowa, 1981; mgmt. cons. S.E. Iowa Mgmt. Consultants, Ottumwa, 1981—; mgmt. cons. Ivano Shokai, Ltd., Okinawa, Japan, 1980; cons. Inst. Comparative Medicine, Columbia U., N.Y.C., 1981-82; faculty Inst. Continuing Edn., Iowa Wesleyan Coll., 1980-83; guest lectr. philosophy dept. U. Ryukus, Okinawa, 1980; behavioral cons. Tamaki Mental Hosp., Ginowan City, Okinawa, Japan, 1980. Served with USMC, 1971-80. Mem. Am. Mgmt. Assn. Home: Rural Route 2 Box 258 Ottumwa IA 52501 Office: SE Iowa Mgmt Consultants Rural Route 2 Ottumwa IA 52501

WULF, ROBERT WILLIAM, manufacturing company executive; b. Chgo., Sept. 17, 1937; s. Arthur Frederick and Annabelle Edna (Peters) W.; A.A., Wilson Jr. Coll., 1955-57; postgrad. U. Ill., 1959-60, Roosevelt U., 1962-63; m. Elizabeth Connolly; children—Robert, Brian, Barbara, Jennifer, Julianne. Cost analyst ITT Kellog, Chgo., 1959-64, Globe Industries, Chgo., 1964-65, Advance Transformer, Chgo., 1965-67; plant controller Joslyn Mfg. and Supply Co., Chgo., 1967-74, sect. acctg. mgr., 1974-75, div. controller, 1975-80; controller Camcraft, Inc., Franklin Park, Ill., 1981—. Fin. chmn. Parish Council, 1969-70; treas. Bolingbrook (Ill.) Park Bd. Commn., 1978—; area rep. Am. Cancer Soc., 1978-80; bldg. chmn. SW Asso. Block Clubs, 1970. Served with U.S. Army, 1960-62. Recipient Public Service award Bolingbrook, 1979. Republican. Roman Catholic. Home: 7 Westchester Ct Bolingbrook IL 60439 Office: 9867 Pacific Ave Franklin Park IL 60131

WULFECK, JAMES ANDREW, JR., educational administrator; b. Covington, Ky., Nov. 8, 1946; s. James Andrew and Della Mae (Testerman) W.; B.E.S., Thomas More Coll., 1975; postgrad. Xavier U., 1976-77; m. Kathleen Kordenbrock, Oct. 16, 1971; children—Christopher, Daniel. Sales promotion and tng. mgr. Merrell-Nat. Labs., Cin., 1973-76; coporate tng. officer Richardson-Merrell, Inc., Wilton, Conn., 1976-77; exec. v.p. Instructional Techniques Ltd., Manhasset, N.Y., 1977-78; pres. GMP Inst., Cin., 1979—; dir. Rocket Supply, Cin., Jet Machine & Mfg. Co., Inc. Coll. and high sch. basketball and football referee. Served with U.S. Army, 1970-71. Mem. Nat. Assn. Sports Ofcls., Am. Soc. Tng. and Devel., Am. Soc. Quality Control. Republican. Roman Catholic. Office: 3823 Pacific Ave Cincinnati OH 45212

WUNDER, GENE CARROLL, marketing educator, business consultant; b. Waterloo, Iowa, Feb. 11, 1939; s. Lloyd Carl and Alice Marie (Reed) W.; B.B.A., U. Iowa, 1969; postgrad. U. Mo. Sch. Law, 1968-70; M.B.A., U. Mo., 1971; postgrad. U. Mo., 1972-75; grad. assoc. in Econs., U. Ark., 1977-78, Ph.D., U. Ark.; m. Judy Kay Stone, Dec. 16, 1966; children—Lara Anne, Sara Elizabeth. Underwriter Security Mut. Life, 1964-69, State Farm Mut. Ins., 1969-71; instr. bus. adminstrn. N.E. Mo. State U., Kirksville, 1972-75, asst. prof. bus. adminstrn., 1976-82; asst. prof. mktg. Ball State U., Muncie, Ind., 1982—; cons. in field. Chmn. supervisory com. N.E. Mo. Credit Union, 1976-82. Recipient Alpha Kappa Psi Outstanding Alumni award, 1968. Mem. S.W. Fin. Assn., Midwest Fin. Assn., Am. Mktg. Assn., Am. Risk Mgmt. Assn., So. Regional Bus. Law Assn., So. Mktg. Assn., S.W. Mktg. Assn., Midwest Mktg. Assn., AAUP, Alpha Kappa Psi, Phi Alpha Delta, Phi Delta Kappa, Gamma Iota Sigma. Republican. Methodist. Clubs: Masons (32 deg.), Shriners, Kiwanis, Pachyderms, Elks Country. Contbr. articles to profl. jours. Home: 9 Redbud Ln Muncie IN 47302 Office: Coll Bus Ball State U Muncie IN 47306

WUNDERLICH, KEITH DAVID, educator; b. Detroit, Oct. 6, 1956; s. Robert Edwin and Jean Dorothy (Holmes) W. B.A. in Spl. Edn., Mich. State U., 1978; M.A., U. Mich., 1982. Spl. edn. tchr. Lutz Sch., Mt. Clemens, Mich., 1978—; pres. Detroit Sampler Co., Detroit, 1982—. Mem. Detroit Visitors and Conv. Bur., 1983—, Cityscape, 1985—. Mem. Am. Assn. Mental Deficiency, Mich. Occupational Edn. Assn., Greater Detroit C. of C. Presbyterian. Avocations: water skiing; cross country skiing; racquetball. Office: Detroit Sampler Co 11849 E Seven Mile Detroit MI 48205

WUNDERLICH, PAUL HAROLD, hosp. adminstr.; b. Winfield, Kans., Jan. 5, 1941; s. Lorenz and Mildred (Heger) W.; B.A., Valparaiso U., 1962; M.H.A., Washington U., St. Louis, 1967; m. Sharon Marion Dragschutz, Dec. 29, 1962; children—Jeffrey, Todd. Adminstrv. asst. St. Louis Lutheran Hosp., 1967-69, dir. profl. services, 1969-73; asso. adminstr. St. Lukes Hosp., St. Louis, 1973-74, pres., chief exec. officer, 1974—. Mem. St. Matthews Luth. Ch. Sch. Bd., 1967-69; mem. adv. bd. and corp. assembly St. Louis Blue Cross, 1975—. Served to capt. USMC, 1962-65. Fellow Am. Coll. Hosp. Adminstrs.; mem. Am. Hosp. Assn., Mo. Hosp. Assn. (dir.), Hosp. Assn. Met. St. Louis (dir., mem. bd. exec. com.), Greater St. Louis Health Systems Agy., Am. Legion. Clubs: University, Forest Hills Country (St. Louis). Home: 227 Pennington Ln Chesterfield MO 63017 Office: 5535 Delmar Blvd Saint Louis MO 63112 also 232 S Woods Mill Rd Chesterfield MO 63017

WUNDERMAN, LORNA ELLEN, medical association administrator, biostatistician; b. Hollywood, Calif., Mar. 23, 1954; d. Irwin and Gilda Shirley (Margulies) Wunderman; m. Scott Howard Robbins, Sept. 24, 1978. A.A., Foothill Coll., 1972; B.S., U. Calif.-Berkeley, 1976, M.P.H., 1978. Cert. Community Coll. tchr., Calif. Research asst. AMA, Chgo., 1978-79, research assoc., 1979-81, dir. dept., 1981—; researcher, cons. Am. Med. Polit. Action Com., Washington, 1984—. Editor: Characteristics of Physicians, 1979, Contbr. articles to med. jours. Grantee Dept. Health and Human Services, Washington, 1979-80, 82, scholar Washington, 1976-78. Mem. Am. Soc. Assn. Execs. (com. mem. 1982—), Am. Statis. Assn., Am. Mktg. Assn., Am. Pub. Health Assn. Avocations: Tennis; swimming; traveling. Home: 719 Thatcher River Forest IL 60304 Office: AMA 535 N Dearborn Chicago IL 60610

WURDEMAN, LEW EDWARD, data processing corporation consultant; b. Colorado Springs, Colo., Oct. 31, 1949; s. Robert Martin and Shirley Gladys (Reetz) W. Student U. Tex.-El Paso, 1967-69, U. Minn., 1969-72. Adminstr. Control Data Corp., Bloomington, Minn., 1969-81, product specialist, 1981-83, systems mgr., 1983-84, cons., 1984—. Republican. Lutheran. Club: German Shepherd Dog of Mpls., German Shepherd Dog of Am. Avocations: dog breeding; training. Home: 13204 Ferris Ave Apple Valley MN 55124 Office: Control Data Corp PO Box 0 Minneapolis MN 55440

WURST, THOMAS WILLIAM, architect, planner; b. Dayton, Ohio, May 1, 1950; s. Wilbur William and Mildred Mary (Miller) W.; m. Celine Joyce Skurka, May 17, 1980. A.A., Miami U., 1974, B.Arch., 1973. Cert. Nat. Council Archtl. Registration Bds., 1979. Designer, W.W. Wurst, Architect, Dayton, 1968-72, Lecklider & Jay, Inc., Dayton, 1973-75; project architect Schrieber & Little & Assocs., Springfield, Ohio, 1975-77; project architect Lorenz & Williams, Inc., Dayton, 1977-79; architect, constrn. mgr. Sutherly Mgmt. Group, Springfield, 1979-80; propr. Thomas W. Wurst & Assocs., Dayton, 1980—, Design & Constrn. Team, 1981—. Mem. AIA, Architects Soc. Ohio. Office: 4699 Salem Ave Dayton OH 45416

WURSTER, DALE ERWIN, university professor, dean emeritus; b. Sparta, Wis., Apr. 10, 1918; s. Edward Emil and Emma Sophia (Steingraeber) W.; m. June Margaret Peterson, June 16, 1944; children—Dale Eric, Susan Gay. B.S., U. Wis., 1942, Ph.D., 1947. With faculty U. Wis. Sch. Pharmacy, 1947-71, prof., 1958-71; prof., dean N.D. State U. Coll. Pharmacy, 1971-72, U. Iowa Coll. Pharmacy, Iowa City, 1972-84, prof., 1972—, dean emeritus, 1984—; George B. Kaufman Meml. lectr. Ohio State U., 1968; cons. in field; phys. sci. adminstr. U.S. Navy, 1960-63; sci. adv. Wis. Alumni Research Found., 1968-72; mem. revision com. U.S. Pharmacopoeia, 1961-70, pharmacy rev. com. USPHS, 1966-72; Contbr. articles to profl. jours., chpts. to books. Patentee in field. Served as officer USNR, 1944-46. Recipient Superior Achievement citation Navy Dept., 1964, merit citation U. Wis., 1976; named Hancher Finkbine Medallion Prof. U. Iowa, 1984; recipient Disting. Alumni award U. Wis. Sch. Pharmacy, 1984. Mem. Am. Assn. Colls. Pharmacy (exec. com. 1964-66, chmn. conf. tchrs. 1960-61, vis. scientist 1963-70, recipient Disting. Educator award 1983), Acad. Pharm. Scis. (exec. com. 1967-70, chmn. basic pharmaceutics sect. 1965-67, pres. 1975, Indsl. Pharm. Tech. award 1980), Am. Pharm. Assn. (chmn. sci. sect. 1964-65, Research Achievement award 1965), Wis. (Disting. Service award 1971), Iowa pharm. assns., Wis. Acad. Scis., Arts and Letters, Soc. Investigative Dermatology, Rumanian Soc. Med. Sci. (hon.), Sigma Xi, Kappa Psi (past officer), Rho Chi, Phi Lambda Upsilon, Phi Sigma. Home: Rural Route 6 16 Brickwood Knoll River Heights Iowa City IA 52240

WURSTER, THELMA PAULINE, nurse; b. Celina, Ohio, June 9, 1932; d. Francis Q. and Mary Lee (Kindel) Wade; R.N., Miami Valley Hosp., Dayton, Ohio, 1953; B.S. in Nursing, Marquette U., Milw., 1961; M.Ed. in Profl. Devel., U. Wis., Whitewater, 1982; postgrad. Coll. St. Joseph, Joliet, Ill.; m. Charles Wayne Wurster, Aug. 18, 1952. Staff and head nurse hosps. in Ohio and Wis., 1953-80; dir. operating rm. Milw. Children's Hosp., 1966-78, asst. dir. nursing, 1979-80; supr. operating room Eye Inst., Milw. County Med. Complex, Wauwatosa, Wis., 1980—. R.N., Ohio, Wis. Mem. Assn. Operating Room Nurses, AAUW, Phi Delta Kappa. Republican. Club: Kettle Moraine Curling (Hartland, Wis.). Contbr. articles to profl. jours. Home: 1932 Moraine End Delafield WI 53018 Office: 8700 W Wisconsin Ave Wauwatosa WI 53226

WUTSCHKE, LYNN KAY, psychotherapist; b. Northfield, Minn., Dec. 18, 1951; d. Kenneth Earl and Patricia Ruth (Bailey) Wutschke; B.A. magna cum laude, U. Minn., 1973, M.S.W., 1977; m. Scott S. Quiggle, July 28, 1973 (div.). Psychiat. social worker No. Community Mental Health Center, Ashland, Wis., 1977-79; psychotherapist Human Devel. Center, Duluth, Minn., 1980-83; psycho therapist Luth. Social Services, Wis. Indianhead Tech. Inst., 1983—; lectr. on family and individual dynamics, condr. workshops and seminars on personal growth, stress mgmt. Mem. Northwoods Women (co-founder), NOW. Home: PO Box 102 Madeline Island La Pointe WI 54850 Office: 12 E 3d St Washburn WI 54891

WYANT, JOSEPH ANDREW, cablevision company executive, photographer; b. Weston, W.Va., Jan. 23, 1949; s. John Frederick and Evelyn Isabel (Mount) W.; m. Deborah Ann De Ring, Jan. 28, 1978; 3 children. B.A. in Geography, W.Va. U., 1971; postgrad. Ohio State U., 1975—. CCTV prodn. coordinator Columbus State Inst. (Ohio), 1972-77; mgr. Ponderosa System, Inc., Lancaster, Ohio, 1978; media specialist Cleveland Heights-University Heights Bd. Edn. (Ohio), 1979-81; dir. programming Viacom Cablevision, Cleve., 1981-84, dir. mktg. Viacom Cablevision, Dayton, Ohio, 1984—; freelance photographer, Cleve., 1979—; speaker. Mem. dist. communications com. United Methodist Ch., Cleve., 1982-83; cons. lay pub. relations adv. com. Cleveland Heights-University Heights Bd. Edn., 1983; mem. citizens adv. com. Kettering Bd. Edn., 1985. Recipient Cert. of Honor, Radio-TV Council Greater Cleve., Inc., 1982. Mem. Ohio Cable TV Assn. (cablecasting com. 1982-84), Nat. Fedn. Local Cable Programmers, Cable TV Adminstrn. and Mktg. Soc. Author: Viacom Is..., 1983; contbr. photog. studies to profl. publs. Office: PO Box 213 North Dayton Station Dayton OH 45404

WYATT, GLENN THOMAS, chemical company executive; b. Springfield, Ill., Jan. 31, 1939; s. Glenn Eason and Elsie May (Crouse) W.; m. Barbara Kay Miller, Mar. 18, 1960; children—Diane Michelle, Cheryl Lynn. B.S. in Acctg., Bradley U., 1960. C.P.A., Ill., Ohio. Supr. audit Ernst & Whinney, Chgo., 1960-66; mgr. audit Price Waterhouse & Co., Peoria, Ill., 1966-72; fin. analyst Borden, Inc., Columbus, Ohio, 1972-74, group controller, 1974-77, controller foods div., 1977-79; v.p. fin. and treas. Sherex Chem. Co., Inc., Dublin, Ohio, 1979—. Trustee, Knolls Civic Assn., Columbus, 1977-82. Mem. Am. Inst. C.P.A.s, Ohio Soc. C.P.A.s, Fin. Execs. Inst., Columbus C. of C., Treasurers Club (dir. 1982—). Office: Sherex Chem Co Inc 5777 Frantz Rd Dublin OH 43017

WYATT, ROSE MARIE, psychiatric and medical social worker; b. San Angelo, Tex., Feb. 16; d. James Odis and Annie LaVernia (Lott) W.; B.A. (Ford Found. scholar, 1953-57), Fisk U., 1957; M.S., U. So. Calif., 1963; M.A., M.S.W. (univ. scholar 1970-72, United Charities scholar 1970-72), U. Chgo., 1972; postgrad. in indsl. psychology Ill. Inst. Tech., 1976—. Elem. tchr. Chgo. Bd. Edn., 1959-63, clin. social worker, 1979—; adult program dir. Chgo. YWCA, 1963-64; youth counselor Chgo. Commn. on Youth Welfare, 1964-66; supervising social worker for Head Start, Chgo. Com. on Urban Opportunity, 1966; social worker Chgo. Commn. on Youth Welfare, 1966-68, Jewish Vocat. Service, 1968; social worker Sch. Community Relations, Detroit Public Schs., 1968-70; social worker United Charities, 1972-74; clin. social worker Rosman-Wyatt and Assos., Chgo., 1980—, pres., 1981—; instr. dept. corrections Chgo. State U., 1972—. Adv. bd. United Charities, Calumet Area, program com. chmn., 1974-80; vol. Assn. of Community Agts. 1968-70, Southside Sr. Citizens Coalition, Chgo., 1963-66, Roseland Health Planning Com., 1974-76, Teen Pregnancy Caucus, 1978-82; mem. social work adv. council Chgo. Bd. Edn., 1976. Recipient Outstanding Employee award for med.-social work services Maternal and Child Health Services div. HEW; 1971. Mem. Nat. Assn. Social Workers, Acad. Cert. Social Workers, Ill. Cert. Social Workers, Chgo. Psychol. Club, Ill Acad. Criminology, NEA, Ill. Assn. Sch. Social Workers, Am. Assn. Mental Deficiency, Qualified Mental Retardation Profls., Fisk U. Alumni Assn., Alpha Kappa Alpha. Roman Catholic. Clubs: Am. Bridge Assn., Civenos Bridge.

WYDRA, RALPH EDWARD, offset printing executive; b. Chgo., Dec. 4, 1939; s. Edward J. and Bernice A. (Darge) W.; m. Helen Margaret Bartu, July 7, 1962 (div. Feb. 1974); children—Paul Edward, Steven Peter; m. 2d, Maureen Ann Neenan, June 15, 1974; children—Laura Lynn, Jennifer Ann, Michael Patrick. B.B.A., Northwestern U., 1972. Asst. controller I.S. Berlin Press, Chgo., 1959-75; controller Collins, Miller & Hutchings, Chgo., 1975-85; controller, v.p. fin., corp. sec. Tempo Graphics Inc., Carol Stream, Ill., 1983—; cons. to various printing corps., 1975—. Mgmt. advisor Jr. Achievement, Chgo., 1970-75. Mem. Pres.s Honor Club, Beatrice Foods Co., 1982. Mem. Alpha Sigma Phi (pres. 1962-63). Roman Catholic. Home: 500 N Rohlwing Rd Palatine IL 60067 Office: Tempo Graphics Inc 455 E North Ave Carol Stream IL 60188

WYDRZYNSKI, THOMAS JOHN, research scientist; b. St. Louis, July 8, 1947; s. Stanly John and Eva (Kedro) W. A.B. in Biology, U. Mo., 1969; Ph.D. in Biology, U. Ill., Urbana, 1977. Teaching asst. dept. botany U. Ill., Urbana, 1972-74, research asst. dept. botany and physiology and biophysics, 1974-75; guest scientist Laboratoire de Photosynthese, Centre Nat. de la Research Scientifique, Gif-sur-Yvette, France, 1977, Lab. Chem. Biodynamics, Lawrence Berkeley Lab., Berkeley, Calif., 1977-79; vis. research assoc. dept. chemistry U. Ill., Urbana, 1979-80; research chemist corp. research Standard Oil Co. (Ind.), Naperville, Ill., 1980—; adj. research assoc. Plant Research Lab., Mich. State U., 1983-84; guest scientist Solar Energy Research Group, Rikagaku Kenkyusho Inst. for Phys. and Chem. Research, Wako-Shi, Saitama, Japan, 1983, Service Biophysique, Commissariat a l'Energie Atomique, CEN-Saclay, Gif-sur-Yvette, France, 1983, Schwerpunk Biophysik, Universitat Osnabruck, W.Ger., 1983. NSF fellow, 1977-78; USPHS Nat. Research Service grantee, 1975-77; NSF recipient NATO Travel award, 1978. Mem. Am. Soc. Plant Physiology, Biophys. Soc., Am. Soc. Photobiology, Am. Chem. Soc., Sigma Xi. Lutheran. Author tech. papers; contbr. articles to profl. jours. Home: 414 W Benton Ave Naperville IL 60540 Office: Amoco Research Ctr PO Box 400 Naperville IL 60566

WYKOFF, JOHN ROBERT, lawyer; b. Erie, Pa., Sept. 17, 1951; s. Robert George and Dorothy Jean (Conrad) W.; m. Jean Marie Vincent, Aug. 17, 1973; children—Bradford Conrad, Julie Marie. Student in bus. Ohio U., 1970-73; B.B.A. cum laude, U. Cin., 1974; J.D. cum laude, U. Dayton, 1979. Bar: Ohio 1979, U.S. Dist. ct. (so. dist.) Ohio 1979. Assoc. Brannon & Cox, Dayton, 1979-80, Lang, Horenstein & Dunlevey, Dayton, 1980-84, White, Getgey & Meyer, Cin., 1984—; law dir. Village of New Lebanon, Ohio, 1982—; legal adviser KDI, Inc., handicapped workshop, Dayton, 1983-84; legal counsel, trustee Miami Valley Golf Club, Dayton, 1984. Mem. central com., mem. jud. screening com. Montgomery County Republican Party, Dayton, 1983-84; bd. dirs. Montgomery County unit Am. Cancer Soc., 1983-84, Daybreak, Inc., Dayton, 1984. Mem. ABA, Ohio State Bar Assn. (aviation law com.), Cin. Bar Assn., Dayton Bar Assn., Assn. Trial Lawyers Am., Ohio Assn. Trial Lawyers. Roman Catholic. Clubs: Miami Valley Golf (trustee); Terrace Park Country. Office: White Getgey & Meyer Co LPA 2021 Auburn Ave Cincinnati OH 45219

WYLIE, CHALMERS PANGBURN, congressman; b. Norwich, Ohio, Nov. 23, 1920; s. Chalmer C. and Margaret (Pangburn) W.; student Otterbein Coll., 1939-40, LL.D. (hon.), 1983; student Ohio State U., 1940-43; LL.B., Harvard, 1948; m. Marjorie Ann Siebold, Sept. 19, 1964; children—Jacquelyn, Bradley. Admitted to Ohio bar, 1948; city atty., Columbus, Ohio, 1953-57; adminstr. Ohio Bur. Workmen's Compensation, 1957; 1st asst. to gov. Ohio, 1957-58; formerly partner firm Gingher & Christensen, Columbus; mem. Ohio Ho. of Reps., 1961-67; mem. 90th-98th congresses from 15th Ohio Dist. Past trustee Blue Cross Central Ohio, Inc. Served from pvt. to 1st lt. AUS, World War II. Decorated Silver Star, Bronze Star, Purple Heart, Croix de Guerre (France), Belgian Fouragier. Named One of 10 Men of Year, Columbus Citizen Jour., One of 5 Outstanding Young Men of Ohio, Nat. Jr. C. of C.; recipient Disting. Service award Columbus Jr. C. of C., 1955, Man of Year award Columbus C. of C., 1983. Mem. Ohio, Columbus bar assns., Am. Legion. Republican. Methodist (past trustee). Mason (33 deg.), Kiwanian. Home: 1019 Spring Grove Ln Columbus OH 43085 Office: 2310 Rayburn House Office Bldg Washington DC 20515

WYNDEWICKE, KIONNE ANNETTE, educator; b. Preston, Miss.; d. Clifton Thomas and Missouria (Jackson) Johnson; student Columbia Coll., Chgo., 1972; B.S., Ill. State Normal U., 1961; postgrad. Williams Coll., Williamstown, Mass., 1972; M.Ed., Nat. Coll. Edn., 1982; m. Eugene C. Moorer, Sept. 23, 1961 (div.). Social worker Cook County Dept. Pub. Aid, 1961; tchr. reading Chgo. Bd. Edn., 1961—; asst. to news dir. WCIU-TV, 1972-74; asst. women's editor Chgo. Defender, 1970-72; social sec. Dr. William R. Clarke, 1972—; part-time photog. model, fashion commentator, pub. relations cons., pub. speaker. Co-chmn. installation Profl. Womens Aux., Provident Hosp., 1961, corr. sec., 1969, publicity chmn., 1969-72, 74-77. Selected one of 13 persons in U.S. to attend Innovative Tchr. Tng. Seminar, funded by Henry Luce Found. at Williams Coll., 1972; one of 25 Black women of Chgo. to receive Kizzy award, 1977; recipient Outstanding Community Service award Beatrice Caffrey Youth Service, Inc., 1978, 83, 85. Mem. Ill. Speech and Theatre Assn., WTTW Channel 11 Ednl. TV, Mus. Contemporary Art, Speech Communication Assn. Am., YWCA. Lutheran. Contbr. articles to local newspapers. Office: 707 E 37th St Chicago IL 60653

WYNN, CLINTON SLYVESTER, hotel executive; b. Brunswick, Ga., Dec. 3, 1944; s. Hilton P. and Relma (Lang) W.; m. Juanita Julia Franco, June 22, 1975; children—Desiree Juanita, Clint Pedro. B.A., Coll. Md., 1966; Ph.D. (hon.), Golden State U., 1979; M.A. (hon.), Southeastern State U., Dixon, Mo., 1980; degree Ctr. for Studies, Scranton, Pa., 1984. Wing rep. WANA Prodn., Kansas City, Kans., 1970-74; sales mgr., Kansas City, Mo., 1974-79; acct. exec. Health Maintenance Orgn., Kansas City, Mo., 1979-82; loan mgr. World Savs., Shawnee, Kans., 1982-83; dir. sales Nat. Hotel, Kansas City, Mo., 1983—; moderator, pub. dir. Wynn Report, Inc., Kansas City, Kans., 1978—. Contbr. articles to profl. jours. Bd. dirs. Wyd Mental Health, 1979-80, Wyd Assn. Child Care, 1981-82, Bethel Glen, 1979—, Vis. Nurses Assn., 1982; pub. relations dir. Salvation Army, Kansas City, Kans., 1978-82; regional campaign mgr. Democratic presdl. candidate, Kansas City, Kans., 1982; v.p. Kansas City Crime Commn., Mo., 1980. Served with USAF, 1966-70. Recipient Top Salesman award Bus. Systems, Inc., Hartford, Conn., 1974, Regional Salesman of Yr. award Am. Coll., Chgo., 1980, Zone Salesman of Yr. award Royal Office Equipment, Kansas City, Mo., 1978. Mem. Am. Mgmt. Assn., Broadcasters Assn. Mem. Nazarene Ch. Avocations: public speaking; bowling; woodcraft; art; painting. Home: 5736 Miami Ave Kansas City KS 66106 Office: WANA Prodn Co Inc Box 12053 Kansas City KS 66112

WYSE, LAMAR LARAY, hospital administrator, musician; b. Manistee, Mich., Oct. 21, 1946; s. Lester A. and Miriam (Johns) W.; m. Karon Eve Swanson, Nov. 2, 1968; children—Adam Christopher, Jason LaMar. B.A., Malone Coll., 1968; M.H.A., Ohio State U., 1980. Chief technician respiratory therapy Ind. U. Med. Ctr., Indpls., 1968-71; dir. cardio-pulmonary dept. Riverview Hosp., Noblesville, Ind., 1971-74; dir. cardio-pulmonary dept. Mary Rutan Hosp., Bellefontaine, Ohio, 1974-76, adminstrv. asst., 1976-80, assoc. adminstr., 1980-81; adminstr. Bluffton Community Hosp., Ohio, 1981-85, Hardin Meml. Hosp., Kenton, Ohio, 1985—; pres. Western Ohio Hosp. Council, Lima, 1983-85; vice-chmn. New Century Health Alliance, Findlay, Ohio, 1983-85. Composer, arranger instrumental and choral music. Bd. dirs. Adriel Sch., West Liberty, Ohio, 1980-85, Mennonite Meml. Home, Bluffton, 1985—; mem. awards com. Ohio Lung Assn., Columbus, 1978—; pres. United Way of Bluffton Richland Twp., 1984; mem. ch. council First Mennonite Ch., Bluffton, 1984-85. USPHS traineeship grantee, 1978, 79. Mem. Am. Coll. Hosp. Adminstrs., Am. Acad. Med. Adminstrs., Mennonite Health Assn., Ohio Hosp. Assn. (mem. various coms. 1982—). Avocations: music (choral conducting, organ), carpentry, running, gardening, travel. Home: 10 Clover Ln Kenton OH 43326 Office: Hardin Meml Hosp 921 E Franklin St Kenton OH 43326

WYSLOTSKYI, IHOR, engineering company executive; b. Kralovane, Czechoslovakia, Dec. 22, 1930; s. Ivan and Nadia (Alexiew) W.; came to U.S., 1958, naturalized, 1961; M.E., Sch. Aeros., Buenos Aires, Argentina, 1955; m. Marta Farion, Sept. 21, 1983; children—Katria W., Bohdan W., Roman F., Alexander F. Design engr. Kaiser Industries, Buenos Aires, 1955-58; cons. design engr., Newark, 1959-64; chief engr. Universal Tool Co., Chgo., 1964-69; pres. CBC Devel Co., Inc., Chgo., 1969-74; pres. TEC, Inc., Chgo., 1972-83; pres. Redex, Inc., 1983—. engring. adviser to bd. Biosystems Assos., Inc., La Jolla, Calif. Chmn. Ukrainian studies com. U. Ill. Mem. Packaging Inst. U.S., Modern Plastics Inst. (mgmt. adv. panel), Am.-Israeli C. of C. (v.p.), Brit. Engring. Assn. Plate River, Soc. Mfg. Engrs. Patentee in field. Home: 6133 Forest Glen Chicago IL 60646 Office: 835 N Wood St Chicago IL 60622

WYSZYNSKI, VALENTINE ADAM, sound designer, producer, graphics consultant; b. Chgo., Dec. 24, 1941; s. Anthony Marion and Genevieve Ann

(Stabosz) W.; m. Joy Anne Halverson, Oct. 5, 1966 (div.); children—April Suzanne, Brian Matthew, Charlotte Lillian. Student U.S. Air Force Inst., 1965-68, Nat. Tech Schs., 1968-70; B.I.S.E.E., N.Mex. State U., 1980-81. With U.S. Post Office, Lyons, Ill., 1959-64, Circle News, Joliet, Ill., 1971-73, Combined Ins. Co. of Am., So. N.Mex., 1973-76; lead guitarist, mgr. "Majestics," Chgo., 1959-64, "The 1st Nat. Bank," Chgo., 1968-73; faculty drama dept., N.Mex. State U., Las Cruces, 1977-81; graphics, audio-visual engrng. con., Las Cruces, 1984—; owner, pres. Tierra-com Systems, audio-visual-lighting TVRO cons., installations, 1978-84; owner Heartline Prodns., Cicero, Ill., 1984—. Contbr. articles to profl. jours. Served with USAF, 1964-70. Mem. Soc. Broadcast Engrs., Electronic Music Engrs., U.S. Inst. Theatre Tech. Home: 4420 Prescott Lyons IL 60534 Office: Heartline Prodns PO Box 508163 Cicero IL 60650

XAGAS, STEVE GEORGE JAMES, executive search firm executive, consultant, researcher; b. St. Charles, Ill., May 9, 1951; s. Gus and Carolyn Ann (Schneider) X.; m. Yvonne Schafer, Oct. 19, 1985. B.S. in Psychology, Guilford Coll., 1974; postgrad. George Williams Coll., 1975. Homebound detention supr., sr. counselor 16th Judicial Ct. Dist., Geneva, Ill., 1974-77; project coordinator, family counselor Tri City Family Project and Kane County Sch. Office, Geneva, 1977-80; exec. recruiter Search Dynamics, Chgo., 1980-82, CPS, Inc., Westchester, 1982-83; owner, pres. Xagas & Assocs., Geneva, Ill., 1983—; employment cons., met. area Chgo., 1980—. Fundraiser Cancer Soc., Kane County, Ill., 1975—, Heart Assn., Kane County, 1982—; community vol. numerous mental health orgns., Kane County, 1974—. Recipient Community Service Recognition, Tri City Family Project, Geneva, 1980; Exemplary status Law Enforcement Assistance Adminstrn., 1980. Cert. personnel cons. Mem. Am. Soc. Quality Control, Intercity Personnel Assocs. (cert.), Ill. Mgmt. and Exec. Search Cons. Employment Mgmt. Assn. (affiliate), Soc. Mfg. Engrs. (sr.). Lutheran. Office: Xagas & Assocs 701 E State St Suite 1 Geneva IL 60134

YACKTMAN, DONALD ARTHUR, financial executive, investment counselor; b. Chgo., Sept. 12, 1941; s. Victor and Matilda (Chamberlain) Y.; m. Carolyn I. Zuppann, June 15, 1965; children—Donald, Stephen, Jennifer, Melissa, Brian, Robert. B.S., U. Utah, 1965; M.B.A., Harvard U., 1967. Chartered investment counselor. Trainee, Continental Bank, Chgo., 1967-68; ptnr. Stein Roe & Farnham, Chgo., 1968-82; pres. Selected Am. Shares; sr. v.p. Prescott Asset Mgmt., Prescott Ball & Turben, Chgo., 1982—; v.p. Domestic Utility Services Co., Glenview, Ill. Dist. chmn. Northwest Suburban council Boy Scouts Am., 1984—. Mem. Fin. Analysts Soc. Mormon. Office: Selected Am Shares 230 W Monroe St Suite 2800 Chicago IL 60606

YAGER, JOHN WARREN, lawyer, financial executive; b. Toledo, Ohio, Sept. 16, 1920; s. Joseph Arthur and Edna Gertrude (Pratt) Y.; m. Dorothy W. Merki, July 25, 1942; children—Julia M., John M. A.B., U. Mich., 1942, J.D., 1948. Practice law, Toledo, 1948-64; trust officer Toledo Trust Co., 1964-69; v.p., trust officer, sec. First Nat. Bank Toledo, 1969—; sec. First Ohio Bankshares, Inc., 1980—. Pres. Toledo Met. Park Dist., 1971—, Toledo Council Chs., 1962-63, Toledo Legal Aid Soc., 1964-65, Toledo Mcpl. League, 1965-66; councilman City of Toledo, 1955-57, 60-61, mayor 1958-59. Served to maj. USMC, 1942-46, 50-52, South Pacific, Korea. Decorated Bronze Star. Mem. Ohio State Bar Assn., Toledo Bar Assn., Toledo Estate Planning Council. Clubs: Belmont (Perrysburg, Ohio); Toledo. Home: 4117 Sheraton Rd Toledo OH 43606 Office: First Nat Bank Toledo 606 Madison Ave Toledo OH 43604

YAGODA, ANDREA RENEE, lawyer; b. Bklyn., Apr. 25, 1953; d. Bernard and Ruth (Katz) Y. B.A. in Psychology and Philosophy, SUNY-Buffalo, 1974; J.D., Capital U., 1977. Bar: Ohio 1977, U.S. Dist. Ct. (so. dist.) Ohio 1979. Law clk. Franklin County Pub. Defender, Columbus, Ohio, 1976-77; law clk. Weiner, Lippe & Cromley, L.P.A., Columbus, 1976-78, assoc., 1978-80; sole practice, Columbus, 1980—. Mem. Ohio State Bar Assn., Columbus Bar Assn., Federated Democratic Women's Orgn., Columbus Women's Caucus, Westside Dem. Club. Jewish. Office: 336 S High St Columbus OH 43215

YAKIN, PAUL MAURICE, psychologist; b. Mexico City, Mex., Oct. 12, 1928; came to U.S., 1958; s. Abraham and Victoria (Ballas) Y.; m. Mary Eileen Brennan, Nov. 2, 1970; children—Audrey Jane, Jeanne Anne. B.S. in Psychology, U. Wis., 1953; M.A. in Clin. Psychology, Ind. U., 1955; M.A. in Personality and Psychopathology, U. Chgo., 1970. Registered psychologist, Ill. Grad. asst., animal lab. Ind. U., Bloomington, 1954-55; instr. dept. psychology Mich. State U., East Lansing, 1955-56; psychologist Lansing (Mich.) Bd. Edn., 1957-58; intern Hawthorn Center, Northville, Mich., 1958-59; asst. to hypnosis U. Chgo., 1963; prin. psychologist Chgo. Alcoholic Treatment Center, 1959-64; chief psychologist, asst. chief gen. psychiat. services Kankakee (Ill.) State Hosp., 1964-74; psychologist rep. Kankakee (Ill.) State Hosp., 1964-74; pvt. practice psychotherapy, Chgo., 1974-77; team leader Tinley Park (Ill.) Mental Health Center, 1977-79, dir. psychotherapy program, 1980—; exec. dir. Bridgeport Mental Health Center, Chgo., 1981—. George Davis Bivin fellow, 1959-61. Mem. Am. Psychol. Assn., AAAS, Nat. Geog. Soc., Psi Chi. Club: Internat. (U. Chgo.). Home: 4800 S Lake Shore Dr Apt 1302 S Chicago IL 60615 Office: 2959 S Wallace St Chicago IL 60616

YALE, BENJAMIN F., lawyer; b. Lima, Ohio, Sept. 4, 1951; s. E. Benjamin and Edith Martha (Dancy) Y.; m. Bonnie Krista Gay, Apr. 14, 1973; children—David Benjamin, Jennifer Lynne. B.A., Yale U., 1973; J.D., Ohio No. U., 1980. Bar: Ohio 1980, U.S. Dist. Ct. (no. dist.) Ohio 1981. Asst. gen. counsel Nat. Farmers Orgn., Minster, Ohio, 1980—; sole practice, Waynesfield and Celina, Ohio, 1980—. Chmn. Auglaize Bd. Mental Retardation and Developmentally Disabled, New Bremen, Ohio, 1983-84. Mem. Ohio Bar Assn., ABA, Auglaize County Bar Assn., Assn. Trial Lawyers Am., Agrl. Law Assn. Republican. Baptist. Office: 102 W Wapakoneta St Waynesfield OH 45896

YAMIN, JOSEPH FRANCIS, lawyer, counselor; b. Detroit, Mar. 12, 1956; s. Raymond Samuel and Sadie Ann (John) Y. B.A., Oakland U., 1975; B.A., U. Mich., 1978; J.D., London Sch. Econs., 1981; J.D., Detroit Coll. Law, 1982. Bar: U.S. Ct. Appeals (6th cir.) 1982, U.S. Dist. Ct. (ea. dist.) Mich. 1982. Assoc. Alan R. Miller, P.C., Birmingham, Mich., 1981—; dir., Am. Wash Systems, Birmingham, 1979—; instr. Detroit Coll. Law, 1984—. Contbr. to publs., book. Campaign chmn. Republican Party, Royal Oak, Mich., 1976. Recipient Am. Jurisprudence Book award Am. Jurisprudence Soc., 1981. Mem. Oakland County Bar Assn., State of Mich. Bar Assn., ABA, Chi Phi. Roman Catholic. Office: Alan R Miller PC 300 E Maple Suite 200 Birmingham MI 48011

YAMMINE, RIAD NASSIF, oil company executive; b. Hammana, Lebanon, Apr. 12, 1934; s. Nassib Nassif and Emilie (Daou) Y.; came to U.S., 1952, naturalized, 1963; B.S. in Petroleum Engring., Pa. State U., 1956; postgrad. Advanced Mgmt. Program, Harvard U., 1977; m. Beverly Ann Hosack, Sept. 14, 1954; children—Kathleen Yammine Griffiths, Cynthia Yammine Rotman, Michael. Engr., Trans-Arabian Pipe Line Co., Saudi Arabia, 1956-61; with Marathon Pipe Line Co., 1961-75, mgr. Western div., Casper, Wyo., 1971-74, mgr. Eastern div., Martinsville, Ill., 1974-75; mktg. ops. div. mgr. Marathon Oil Co., 1975-83; pres. Marathon Pipeline Co., 1983-84; v.p. supply and transp., dir. Marathon Petroleum Co., 1984—; also officer, dir. various subs. Mem. ch. council, chmn. finance com. First Luth. Ch., Findlay. Past trustee, Fisk U. Registered profl. engr., Ohio. Mem. ASME, Am. Petroleum Inst. Republican. Club: Findlay Country. Patentee in field. Home: 624 Winterhaven St Findlay OH 45840 Office: 539 S Main St Findlay OH 45840

YAMOOR, MOHAMMED YOUNIS, animal nutritionist; b. Mosul, Iraq, July 7, 1941; s. Younis Yousif and Sabiha Ziyada (Husein) Y.; m. Catherine Marie Hagen, Sept. 11, 1965; children—Nadia Marie, Omar Wayne. B.S., U. Baghdad, 1962; M.S., U. Minn., 1967, Ph.D., 1971. Prof., head dept. animal prodn. U. Tripoli, Libya, 1972-78; expert FAO, Rome, 1978-79; Mid-East cons. agrl. devel. projects, 1979-83; expert animal prodn. FAO, Rome, Saudi Arabia, 1983—; lectr., cons. agrl. devel. specialist. Mem. U. Minn. Alumni Assn., Sigma Chi.

YANEY, WILLIAM ALLEN, music industry executive, music educator, concert organist; b. Decatur, Ala., Mar. 27, 1945; s. Wayne Allen and Jessie Louise (Holben) Y.; m. Monica Lynne Haydu, Sept. 10, 1982. Student U. Toledo, 1963-65. Sales mgr. Brenner Music Co., Toledo, Ohio, 1965-68; v.p. Howards Organs and Pianos, Inc., Toledo, 1968-81; cons., product specialist, tchr. Gt. Lakes Pianos and Organs, Toledo, 1981—; profl. performer radio and TV, concert artist, 1959—. Mem. Am. Fedn. Musicians, Am. Theater Organ Soc., Toledo Area Theater Organ Soc., Detroit Theater Organ Club. Home: 6537 Abbey Run Sylvania OH 43560 Office: 5212 Monroe St Toledo OH 43623

YANG, HENRY KELL, ophthalmologist; b. Phila., Oct. 27, 1951; s. Stephen Y.H. and Stella (Koo) Y. B.A., U. Pa., 1972; M.D., N.Y. Med. Coll., 1975. Diplomate Am. Bd. Ophthalmology. Intern Hosp. U. Pa., Phila., 1975-76; resident in ophthalmology U. Md., Balt., 1976-79; fellow Oram R. Kline, Jr., Woodbury, N.J., 1979-80; asst. prof. ophthalmology U. Mo., Columbia, 1980-82; courtesy med. staff Wills Eye Hosp., Phila., 1980—; active staff Boone Hosp. Ctr., Columbia, 1982—. Author: (with others) Posterior Chamber Implant Surgery, 1983. Contbr. articles to profl. jours. Vice-pres. Mus. Assocs. Mus. Art and Archaeology, U. Mo., Columbia, 1983-84. Fellow Am. Acad. Ophthalmology. Republican. Avocations: tennis; art history. Home: Cedar Grove Blvd Columbia MO 65201 Office: Doctors Park 203 W Broadway Columbia MO 65203

YANG, WEN-JEI, engineering educator; b. Kaohsiung, China, Oct. 14, 1931; came to U.S., 1955, naturalized, 1971; s. Shui-Lai and Chin-Tsa (Lin) Y.; m. Shu-Yuan Lin, May 31, 1960; children—Ling-Hsiang, Mimi Ling-Ing, Paul Po-Tsang. B.S. in Mech. Engring., Nat. Taiwan U., 1954; M.S., U. Mich., 1956, Ph.D., 1960. Research engr. Ford Motor Co., Dearborn, Mich., 1956-57, Mitsui Shipbldg. Co., Tomano, Japan, 1960-61; lectr. mech. engring. U. Mich., Ann Arbor, 1961-62, asst. prof., 1962-65, assoc. prof., 1965-70, prof., 1970—. Author, editor numerous books. Contbr. articles to profl. jours. Fellow ASME (Heat Transfer Meml award 1984); mem. AAAS, Japan Soc. Flow Visualization, Chinese Soc. Theoretical and Applied Mechanics (hon.), Italian Acad. Medicine and Surgery (corr.), Sigma Xi, Tau Beta Pi. Presbyterian. Avocations: music; swimming. Home: 3925 Waldenwood Dr Ann Arbor MI 48105 Office: U Mich 2150 GG Brown Ann Arbor MI 48109

YANG, WILOX, physicist; b. Canton, China, May 25, 1922; s. Shaw Hong and Ah Han (Lee) Y.; m. Constance Lee Bycofski, Jan. 20, 1960 (dec. June 1964); m. Janet D. Smith, Mar. 23, 1966; children—Eleanor, Lisa, Lori. B.Sc., Huachung U., Wuchang, China, 1947; M.Sc., Poly. Inst. N.Y., 1963, Ph.D., 1974. Mem. staff Princeton-Penn Accelerator, Princeton (N.J.) U., 1962-69; mem. staff high energy physics research U. Pa., Phila., 1969-75; engring. physicist Fermilab, Batavia, Ill., 1975—. Mem. Am. Phys. Soc., N.Y. Acad. Sci., Sigma Xi. Democrat. Club: Sigma Xi. Contbr. articles to profl. jours. Home: 30 W 113 Lindenwood Ct Warrenville IL 60555 Office: Fermi Nat Accelerator Lab PO Box 500 Batavia IL 60510

YANICKE, GEORGIA ANN, educational administrator; b. Milw., July 10, 1945; d. George Elmer and Lucille Sylvia (Schroeder) Y. Student Goethe Inst., Murnau,-W.Ger., 1966, U. Innsbruck (Austria), 1966; B.A., Cornell Coll., 1967; M.S., U. Wis. Milw., 1970; Ph.D., U. Wis., Madison, 1975. Cert. spl. edn. supr., tchr., Wis. Tchr. mentally retarded McKinley Sch., West Allis, Wis., 1967-69; lectr. U. Wis.-Milw., 1970-74, 77-79; practicum supr. U. Wis.-Madison, 1974-75; asst. prof. Creighton U., Omaha, 1975-77; supr. programs for emotionally disturbed and generic early childhood Milw. Pub. Schs., 1977—; cons. Sitters for Handicapped Children Project, Milw. area Girl Scouts U.S., 1973-74, Milw. Pub. Schs., 1976, Creighton U. Inst. for Bus., Law and Social Research, 1976-77; inservice coordinator for Blessed Sacrament St. Richards and St. Philip Neri Catholic Schs., Omaha, Nebr., 1975-76; developer, adminstr. pre-kindergarten screening instrument, 1976-77; mem. child care adv. com. Milw. Area Tech. Coll., 1979-80; mem. edn. study group Wis. Dept. Pub. Instrn., Madison, 1981; condr. workshops in field; speaker profl. meetings. Active Greater Milw. Girl Scouts U.S., 1961-77, bd. dirs., 1971-75; mem. ad hoc study com. Children's Day Services, Planning Council for Mental Health and Social Services, Inc., Milw., 1981-82; mem. ad hoc early childhood aquatics Greater Milw. chpt. ARC, mem. adaptive aquatics com., 1983-85; mem. vol. day care com. for ednl. programming, Milw. County Zoo, 1984. U.S. Office Edn. fellow, 1969-70; U. Wis.-Madison Grad. Sch. fellow, 1974. Mem. Council for Exceptional Children (div. children with learning disabilities state and province com. 1976-77), Am. Assn. on Mental Deficiency, Internat. Reading Assn., Nat. Soc. for Autistic Children (bd. dirs. Milw. Assn. 1983—), Nat. Council Tchrs. of English, Wis. Assn. for Children with Behavior Disorders (adv. bd. 1977-82, 84—, pres. 1983-84), Wis. Assn. Infant/Toddler Devel. (sec. 1982—), Phi Delta Kappa, Pi Lambda Theta, Delta Kappa Gamma (sec. 1985—). Home: 9085 N 85th St Milwaukee WI 53224 Office: Elem Zone Milw Pub Schs 3620 N 18th St Milwaukee WI 53206

YANITY, JOSEPH BLAIR, JR., lawyer; b. Homer City, Pa., Nov. 11, 1925; s. Joseph Blair and Perina Maria (Carcelli) Y.; m. Joyce Ann Gilham, Jan. 9, 1954; children—Joseph B., John M., Jennifer A. A.B. with honors, Eastern Ky. U., 1949; J.D., Washington and Lee U., 1952. Bar: Ohio 1953, U.S. Dist. Ct. (so. dist.) Ohio 1966. Ptnr., Lavelle & Yanity, Athens, Ohio, 1953-78, Yanity & De Vean, Athens, 1978—; pros. atty. County of Athens, 1958-61; dir. Bank One of Athens; gen. counsel O'Bleness Meml. Hosp., Athens, 1970—. Mem. Vets. Commn. Athens County, 1961—; v.p., trustee Ohio Valley Health Services Found., Athens, 1965—; pres., trustee Auto Club of Southeastern Ohio, Portsmouth, 1970—. Served to 1st lt. U.S. Army, 1943-53, ETO. Recipient Outstanding Alumnus prize Eastern Ky. U., 1976 E.E. Davis award Ohio Valley Health Services Found., 1981. Mem. Athens County Bar Assn. (pres. 1971), Ohio State Bar Assn., ABA, Am. Legion. Republican. Roman Catholic. Club: Synposiarchs (pres. 1979). Lodges: K.C. (grand Knight 1965), Elks (exalted ruler 1961). Avocation: football officiating. Home: 42 Utah Pl Athens OH 45701 Office: Yanity & DeVean PO Drawer 748 Athens OH 45701

YANTIS, JOHN THOMAS, university administrator; b. Winfield, Kans., Nov. 13, 1936; s. Norval K. and Ethel May (Beaty) Y.; m. Lois Jane Kirk, June 27, 1959; children—Cynthia, Deborah. B.S., Pittsburg State U., 1959, M.S., 1963; Ed.D., U. Wyo., 1968. Prin., Winfield Sch. Dist., Kans., 1963-67; assoc. prof. edn. adminstrn. Central Mich. U., Mt. Pleasant, 1968-72, dir. Inst. for Personal U. Career Devel., 1972-81, dean Sch. Extended Learning, 1981—; speaker on edn., 1972—; cons. in edn., Mt. Pleasant, 1968—. Contbr. numerous articles to profl. jours. Mem. Nat. Continuing Edn. Assn., N.Am. Assn. Summer Schs., Phi Delta Kappa (pres. Central Mich. U. chpt. 1971-74), Kappa Delta Pi, Sigma Iota Epsilon (hon.). Presbyterian. Lodge: Mt. Pleasant Rotary (v.p. 1985). Avocations: skiing; guitar playing; reading. Home: 1010 Glen St Mount Pleasant MI 48858 Office: Sch Extended Learning Central Michigan U Mount Pleasant MI 48858

YAO, ALBERT REN-FENG, mechanical engineer; b. Taiwan, Nov. 11, 1947; s. Wen-Chin W. and Shang-Ju C. Yao; m. Judy Y. Hsiao, Nov. 21, 1949; children—Alice Y., Lisa Y. B.S., Chunhsing U., Taiwan, 1970; M.S., U. Iowa, 1974, Ph.D. in Mech. Engring., 1976. Cert. mfg. technologist. Teaching asst. Chunghsing U., Taiwan, 1971-72; researcher asst. U. Iowa, 1972-76; mfg. engr. Internat. Harvester Co., Rock Island, Ill., 1976-83; mech. engr. for computer application Rock Island Arsenal, 1983—. Mem. Computer and Automated Systems Assn., Soc. Mfg. Engrs., ASME, Sigma Xi. Home: 3885 Tanglefoot Ct Bettendorf IA 52722 Office: SMCRI-ENE 110 Rock Island Arsenal Rock Island IL 61299

YAO, JOSEPH HUNG, physical therapist; b. Hangchu, China, Jan. 8, 1935; s. Stephen C. and Pei-Hsing (Shen) Y.; came to U.S., 1958, naturalized, 1969; B.A., Tamkang Coll., Republic of China, 1955; postgrad. U. Madrid (Spain), 1955-56, U. Barcelona (Spain), 1956-58; B.A., Loras Coll., 1961; certificate phys. therapy U. Iowa Sch. Medicine, 1963; certificate acupuncture China Med. Coll., Republic of China, 1973; m. Jessie Lee Collingsworth, Dec. 26, 1964; children—Dana, David, E. Stephen. Staff phys. therapist Univ. Hosps., Iowa City, 1963-64; chief phys. therapist St. Mary's Hosp., Streator, Ill., 1964-66; dir. phys. therapy dept. St. Therese Hosp., Waukegan, Ill., 1966-70; staff phys. therapy dept. VA Med. Center, North Chicago, Ill., 1970-74, dir. phys. therapy dept., 1974-82; owner, dir. Gurnee Phys. Therapy Clinic (Ill.), 1979—; dir. No. Ill. Phys. Therapy Services, 1984—; clin. instr. Northwestern U. Med. Sch., 1975—, Chgo. Med. Coll., 1975—; lectr. on acupuncture to univs., various civic groups; Mem. Am. Phys. Therapy Assn. (ednl. coordinator clin. studies on acupuncture in Peoples Republic of China 1981-83), Nat. Soc. Crippled Children and Adults, Am. Center Chinese Med. Scis., Acupuncture Research Inst., Am. Acupuncture Assn. Author: The Selected Acupuncture Points, 1972; Acupuncture and TENS Techniques, 1978; Acutherapy, Acupuncture, TENS, and Acupressure, 1984. Home: 808 Paddock Ln Libertyville IL 60048 Office: Gurnee Phys Therapy Clinic Gurnee Med Profl Ctr 1170 Route 41 Gurnee IL 60031

YAO, TITO GO, physician; b. Manila, May 30, 1943; came to U.S., 1970, naturalized, 1984; s. Vicente and Sin Keng (Go) Y.; M.D., Far Eastern U., Manila, 1969; m. Lilia Ytem, July 3, 1976; children—Robert James, Richard. Diplomate Am. Bd. Pediatrics, Am. Bd. Quality Assurance. Intern, Evang. Deaconess Hosp., Milw., 1970-71; resident in pediatrics T.C. Thompson Children's Hosp., Chattanooga, 1971-72, Methodist Hosp., Bklyn., 1972-73; fellow St. Christopher Hosp. Children, Phila., 1973-74, Cook County Children's Hosp., Chgo., 1974-75; dir. GSK Med. Center, Chgo., 1976—, RJ Med. Center, Chgo.; mem. staff St. Anne's Loretto and Walther Meml. hosps. Fellow Am. Acad. Pediatrics, Am. Coll. Utilization Rev. Physicians; mem. AMA (Physician Recognition award 1973—), Assn. Philippine Physicians Practicing in Am., Ill. Med. Assn., Am. Assn. Individual Investors, Chgo. Med. Soc., Chgo. Pediatric Soc. Office: 5140 W Chicago Ave Chicago IL 60651

YAP, CHONG-BUN, neurologist; b. Amoy, Fukien, China, Apr. 2, 1930; s. Chin-Chay and Ben-Chu (Chua) Y.; came to U.S., 1959, naturalized, 1973; M.D. cum laude, U. Santo Tomas, 1958; m. Le-Kheng Chua; children—Renee Mei, Eric Wei. Intern, Santo Tomas U. Hosp., Manila, Pilippines, 1957-58; resident in neurology U. Louisville Hosp., 1959-62; neurology fellow, Montreal (Que., Can.) Neurol. Inst., 1962-64; instr., Louisville U., 1964-65; asst. prof., Northwestern U., Chgo., 1965-75; chmn. dept. medicine, Henrotin Hosp., 1976-77, pres. med. staff, 1978; dir. EEG dept. Swedish Covenant, Bethesda Hosps. Diplomate Am. Bd. Neurology. Certified Am. Bd. of Qualification in Electroencephalography, Inc. Fellow Am. Acad. Neurology; mem. AMA, Am. Assn. Electromyography and Electrodiagnosis, Am. Epilepsy Soc. Contbr. articles to med. jours. Home: 245 Sheridan Rd Kenilworth IL 60043 Office: 44 Green Bay Rd Winnetka IL 60093

YARGER, ORVAL J., bookseller, transportation executive; b. Milw., Feb. 6, 1943; s. Orval F. and Rosie (Rassmussen) Y.; m. Maureen Anne O'Grady, May 16, 1981; children—Kevin M., Daniel J. B.S., Ill. State U., 1977. Ptnr., The Alamo II, bookstore, Normal, Ill., 1969—; pres. Bloomington Avionics, Inc., Ill., 1979—; owner Twin City Transports, Normal, 1979—; pilot AmbuAir and Clark Aviation, Bloomington, 1982—. Served with USAF, 1965-68. Office: The Alamo II 319 North St Normal IL 61761

YAROS, ALMA PROFFITT, lawyer; b. Cin., Jan. 29, 1949; d. Travers C. and Regina M. (Osborne) Proffitt; m. G. David Yaros, May 15, 1977. B.A. magna cum laude, Mt. St. Joseph Coll., 1971; J.D., Chase Law Sch., 1976. Bar: Ohio 1977, U.S. Dist. Ct. (so. dist.) Ohio 1977. Ptnr. Yaros, Yaros & Latter, Cin., 1979-82, Yaros & Yaros Legal Counsel, Cin., 1982-83; in-house counsel UAW Legal Services Plan, Cin., 1983—. Assoc. Kibbutz Evron, Israel, 1967. Mem. Cin. Bar Assn. (chmn. delivery of legal services to handicapped 1980, mem. exec. com. 1980). Office: UAW-Gen Motors Legal Services Plan Carousel Tower Suite 200 8075 Reading Rd Cincinnati OH 45237

YASKANICH, JOHN STEVEN, pharmacist; b. Steubenville, Ohio, Oct. 17, 1952; s. John Stephen and Mildred V. Yaskanich; children—John Steven, Robert Jason. B.S. in Pharmacy, Ohio No. U., 1976. Registered pharmacist. Mgr. Cunningham Drug Stores, Cleve., 1976-78, staff pharmacist, Sheffield Lake, Ohio, 1978-81; asst. mgr. Discount Drugmart, Inc., Lorain, Ohio, 1981—. Mem. Lorain County Pharm. Assn. Democrat. Roman Catholic. Avocation: woodworking. Home: 874 Kenilworth Ave Sheffield Lake OH 44054 Office: 4253 Colorado Ave Lorain OH 44052

YASKO, CARYL ANNE, painter, sculptor, educator; b. Racine, Wis., Mar. 11, 1941; d. Walter Nikolai and Josephine Angeline Nelson; m. Richard A. Yasko, June 29, 1963; children—Guy Thomas, James Walter, Nikolai Karel, Lyudmila Jane. B.A., Dominican Coll., Racine, 1963. Co-founder Art Tillers, Chgo., 1970-73; dir. Chgo. Mural Group Workshop, Chgo., 1973-76; instr. Sch. Art Inst. Chgo., 1976; pub. sponsored muralist, 1970—; artist-in-residence Wis. Arts Bd., 1978—; art lectr. U. Mich., Ann Arbor, 1978, Morton Grove Community Coll., Ill., 1977; mem. visual arts panel Wis. Arts Bd., Madison, 1979-80. Executed numerous murals. Mem. Community Devel. Com., Whitewater, Wis., 1980-83, Whitewater Plan Commn., 1984—; insp., clk. Whitewater Election Bd., 1983-85. Recipient Chgo. Beautiful award, 1975, 76; Nat. Endowment Arts grantee, 1972-76; named hon. citizen City of Lemont (Ill.), 1975; film premier in honor for work in schs. Gov. Wis., 1978. Mem. Chgo. Mural Group (pub. art award 1977), Chgo. Artist Coalition, Wis. Mural Works. Avocations: preservation and study of native American plants, especially midwest wildflowers. Home: 136 Whiton St Whitewater WI 53190

YASSIN, ROBERT ALAN, art museum director; b. Malden, Mass., May 22, 1941; s. Harold Benjamin and Florence Gertrude (Hoffman) Y.; B.A., Dartmouth Coll., 1962; M.A., U. Mich., 1964; postgrad. Yale U., U. Mich.; m. Marilyn Kramer, June 9, 1963; children—Frederic Giles, Aaron David. Asst. to dir. U. Mich. Mus. Art, 1964-65, asst. dir., 1971-73, asso. and acting dir., 1973; Ford fellow Yale U. Art Gallery, 1966-68; instr. art history U. Mich., 1970-73; chief curator Indpls. Mus. Art, 1973-75, acting dir., 1975, dir., 1975—; adj. prof. Herron Sch. Art, Ind. U., 1976—. Bd. dirs. Indpls. Consortium for Urban Edn., 1976—, Indpls. Cultural Consortium, 1984—, Indpls. Econ. Devel. Com., 1984—, Intermuseum Conservation Assn., Oberlin. Samuel H. Kress Found. fellow, 1968-70. Mem. Am. Assn. Museums, Assn. Art Mus. Dirs., Am. Assn. State and Local History, Midwest Mus. Assn., Am., Midwest coll. art assns., Nat. Trust Historic Preservation. Club: Rotary (Indpls.). Editor Yale U. Art Gallery Bull., 1966-68, U. Mich. Mus. Art Bull., 1970-73; editor: Durer's Cities, Nuremberg and Venice, 1971; Art and the Excited Spirit, 1972; Painting and Sculpture Today, 1976, 78, 80, 82, 84; Ind. Artists Show, 1977, 79, 81, 83, 85; George Carlson, 1979, others. Office: 1200 W 38th St Indianapolis IN 46208*

YASSO, JOSEPH MICHAEL, osteopathic physician; b. Kansas City, Mo., Feb. 26, 1949; s. Joseph Mario and Dorothy Louise (Aitkens) Y.; m. Virginia Christine Marx, June 21, 1975; children—Joseph Timothy, Michael Anthony, Nicholas Andrew. A.A., Wentworth Mil. Acad., 1969; B.A., Park Coll., 1972; D.O., U. Health Scis., 1977. Diplomate Nat. Bd. Osteo. Physicians and Surgeons. Intern, Lakeside Hosp., Kansas City, Mo., 1977-78; gen. practice osteo. medicine Independence (Mo.) Family Medicine, Inc., 1980—; plant physician Kansas City Assembly Plant, Ford Motor Co., 1980—. Mem. Gov.'s Adv. Council Maternal and Child Health. Served to capt. M.C., U.S. Army, 1978-80. Mem. Jackson County Osteo. Assn. (bd. govs., v.p. 1984-85), Mo. Assn. Osteo. Physicians and Surgeons (budget com.), Am. Osteo. Assn., Southwest Clin. Soc., Assn. U.S. Army. Roman Catholic. Home: 216 Country Ln Ct Lee's Summit MO 64063 Office: Joseph Yasso DO 620 W 23d St Independence MO 64055

YATES, SIDNEY R(ICHARD), congressman, lawyer; b. Chgo., Aug. 27, 1909; s. Louis and Ida (Siegel) Y.; Ph.B., U. Chgo., 1931; J.D., 1933; m. Adeline Holleb, June 24, 1935; 1 son, Stephen R. Admitted to Ill. bar, 1933; asst. atty. for Ill. State Bank Receiver, 1935-37; asst. atty. gen. attached to Ill. Commerce Commn. as traction atty., 1937-40; mem. 81st to 87th, 89th to 99th Congresses from 9th Ill. Dist. U.S. del. UN Trusteeship Council with rank of ambassador, 1963-64. Served to lt. USNR, 1944-46. Mem. Am., Ill., Chgo. bar assns., Decalogue Soc. Laws. Democrat. Jewish. Clubs: City, Bryn Mawr Country. Office: 2234 Rayburn House Office Bldg Washington DC 20515

YAZEL, EUGENE ALLEN, lawyer; b. Marion, Ohio, Oct. 20, 1924; s. William M. and Dorothy Gay (Jones) Y.; m. Joan Regina Smith, Mar. 22, 1958; children—Jennifer Jill, Kathryn Kay, Laura Lynn. B.S. in Civil Engring., Case Inst. Tech., 1949; LL.B., Ohio State U., 1953; postgrad. U. Tenn., 1950. Bar: Ohio 1953. Atty. City of Marion, 1962-65, mayor, 1966-71; sole practice law, 1972-81, 83—; judge Common Pleas Ct., 1980, 81; part time asst. judge Mcpl. Ct., 1972-81. Served with USAAF, 1943-45. Mem. Ohio Bar Assn., Marion County Bar Assn. Republican. Avocation: golf. Office: Eugene A Yazel 202 E Center St Marion OH 43302

YEAGER, ANSON ANDERS, columnist, former newspaper editor; b. Salt Lake City, June 5, 1919; s. Charles Franklin and Elise Marie (Thingelstad) Y.; m. Ada May Bidwell, Sept. 10, 1944; children—Karen Ann, Anson Anders, Harry H., Terry Douglas, Ellen Elise. B.S., S.D. State U.-Brookings, 1946; LL.D., Dakota State Coll., Madison, S.D., 1972. Printer's devil, linotype operator Faith Ind. and Gazette (S.D.), 1935-38; printer S.D. State U., 1940-41; staff writer Argus Leader, Sioux Falls, S.D., 1947-55, Sunday editor, 1955-60, exec. editor, 1961-77, assoc. editor, 1978-84, editor editorial page, 1961-84, columnist, 1984—, author editorials and column of commentary; lectr. dept. journalism U. S.D., 1953-55. Contbr. World Book Ency., 1966—. Bd. dirs. Sioux Falls Devel. Found., 1967; dir. Sioux council Boy Scouts Am., Sioux Falls, 1967-72, v.p., 1970-72; bd. dirs. Boys' Club of Sioux Falls, 1966-68. Served to capt. U.S. Army, 1942-46, 50-52; lt. col. Res. (ret.). Decorated Army

Commendation medal; recipient Editorial Excellence award William Allen White Found., 1976; Disting. Alumni award S.D. State U., 1980; Ralph D. Casey Minn. award for Disting. Service in Journalism U. Minn., 1981, Eminent Service award East River Elec. Power Coop., 1984, Mass Communications award S.D. State U., 1985. Mem. Sioux Falls Area C. of C. (dir. 1967-70), Am. Soc. Newspaper Editors, S.D. AP Mng. Editors (Newsman of Yr. award 1978, Les Helgeland Community Service award 1985), Sigma Delta Chi. Republican. Methodist. Lodge: Rotary.

YEAGLEY, MICHAEL DAVID, architect; b. Port Clinton, Ohio, Mar. 3, 1943; s. Daun Albert and Katherine Louisa (Koch) Y.; m. Cynthia Susan Leedy, Sep. 4, 1965; children—David Michael, Jennifer Susan. B.Arch., Kent State U., 1969. Registered architect, Ohio. Assoc. architect Dansizen Architects, North Canton, Ohio, 1969-73; design supr. Ohio Power Co., Canton, 1973—; archtl. cons., Louisville, 1973—. Cons., Louisville School System, Canton Area YMCA; chmn. bd. mgrs. Louisville YMCA, 1985; bd. dirs. Stark County Blood Donor Program; mem. Louisville Planning Commn., Louisville Zoning Bd. Appeals, 1984—. Rotary Internat. Found. grantee for Group Study Exchange to Austria, 1972. Mem. AIA (corp. mem.), Architects Soc. Ohio, Constrn. Specification Inst., Nat. Council Archtl. Registration Bds. Clubs: Rotary of Louisville (past pres.), Canton YMCA Athletic, North Canton YMCA Health. Mem. United Ch. of Christ. Home: 234 Dogwood Ave Louisville OH 44641 Office: 301 Cleveland Ave Canton OH 44702

YEAMANS, GEORGE THOMAS, library science educator, consultant; b. Richmond, Va., Nov. 7, 1929; s. James Norman and Dolphine Sophia (Manhart) Y.; m. Mary Ann Seng, Feb. 1, 1958; children—Debra, Susan, Julia. A.B., U. Va., 1950; M.S.L.S., U. Ky., 1955; Ed.D., Ind. U., 1965. Asst. audio-visual dir. Ind. State U., Terre Haute, 1957-58; asst. film librarian Ball State U., Muncie, Ind., 1958-61, film librarian, 1961-69, assoc. prof. library sci., 1969-72, prof., 1972—; cons. Pendleton (Ind.) Sch. Corp., 1962, 67, Captioned Films for the Deaf Workshop, Muncie, Ind., 1963, 64, 65, Decatur (Ind.) Sch. System, 1978; adjudicator Ind. Media Fair, 1979-85. Author: Projectionists' Programmed Primer, 1969, rev. edit., 1982; Mounting and Preserving Pictorial Materials, 1976; Tape Recording, 1978; Transparency Making, 1977; Photographic Principles, 1981; Computer Literacy—A Programmed Primer, 1985; contbr. articles to profl. jours. Campaign worker Wilson for Mayor, Muncie, Ind., 1979. Served with USMC, 1950-52. Recipient Citations of Achievement, Internat. Biog. Assn., Cambridge, Eng., 1973, Am. Biog. Assn., 1976. Mem. NEA (del. assembly dept. audiovisual instrn. 1967), Am. Film Inst., ALA, Audio-Visual Instrn. Dirs. Ind. (exec. bd. 1962-68, pres. 1966-67), Ind. Assn. Ednl. Communications and Tech. (dist. dir. 1972-75), Assn. Ind. Media Educators (chmn. auditing com. 1979-81), Internat. TV Assn., Am. Film Inst., Phi Delta Kappa. Republican. Unitarian. Club: Catalina (Muncie). Home: 4507 W Burton Dr Muncie IN 47304 Office: Ball State U Muncie IN 47306

YEARLING, JOSEPH HUSTON, lawyer; b. Columbus, Ohio, July 27, 1931; s. Joseph Howard and Dorothy (Huston) Y.; m. Constance Hazzard, Sept. 21, 1956 (dec. 1961); m. Janet Schellenger, June 26, 1965; children—Michael Joseph, Kelly Ann. B.S., Northwestern U., 1953; J.D., Ohio State U., 1956. Atty. Legal Aid and Pub. Defender Office, Columbus, Ohio, 1960; pvt. practice various firms, Columbus, 1960—; mem. firm Morrison, Bodycombe, Yearling & Fais, Columbus, 1970—; city prosecutor City of Upper Arlington, Ohio, 1961—. Scoutmaster Central Ohio council Boy Scouts Am., 1972; trustee N.W. Counseling Services, Inc., Columbus, 1984; pres. Big Bros./Big Sisters Assn., Columbus, 1962—; pres. Big Bros./Big Sisters Found., Columbus, 1976-85; chmn. governing bd. First Community Ch., Columbus, 1982. Served to lt. USAF, 1957-60. Mem. Ohio State Bar Assn., Columbus Bar Assn., Franklin County Trial Lawyers Assn. (pres. 1982-83), Barrister's Club (past pres.). Republican. Club: Hickory Hills Golf (Columbus, Ohio). Avocations: golf; hiking; gardening; reading. Home: 2276 Abington Rd Columbus OH 43221 Office: Morrison Bodycombe Yearling & Fais 1350 W 5th Ave Columbus OH 43212

YEAROUS, LOIS MARLENE, registered nurse, psychotherapist; b. Linden, Wis., Aug. 29, 1935; d. John and Blanche (Reger) Womack; m. Richard Henry Anderson, Sept. 27, 1951 (div. 1957); children—LeRoy, Mark, Karen; m. 2d, Loren Francis Yearous, Jan. 30, 1960; 1 son, Loren. B.S. in Nursing with honors, 1973, M.S. in Psychiat. Mental Health Nursing, 1978. R.N., Wis. Nurse, William S. Middleton VA Hosp., Madison, Wis., 1973—; psychotherapist in pvt. practice, Madison, 1981—; speaker, trainer in field of psychotherapy. Recipient Outstanding sr. award U. Wis. Nurses Alumni. Mem. Madison Dist. Nurses Assn. (mem. legis. com.), Wis. Nurses Assn., Phi Kappa Phi, Sigma Theta Tau. Methodist. Home: 818 Woodlawn Dr Madison WI 53716

YEAWORTH, ROSALEE COCKERILL, nursing education administrator, educator; b. Greenfield, Ohio, June 24, 1929; d. Robert Craig and Bernice (Miller) Cockerill; m. James Thomas Yeaworth, Dec. 29, 1951; children—James Thomas, Robert Shortness, Susan Elaine. B.S. in Nursing, U. Cin., 1951, M.S. in Nursing, 1966, Ph.D., 1970. Lic. R.N., Ohio, Nebr. Asst. instr. U. Cin., 1951-52; asst. head nurse Cin. Gen. Hosp., 1952-53; part time instr. Sch. Nursing Christ Hosp., Cin., 1954-64; faculty, asst. dean, acting dean U. Cin., 1969-79; dean and prof. Coll. Nursing, Med. Ctr. U. Nebr., Omaha, 1979—; mem. adv. council Nurse Faculty Research Devel. Project, U. Ill., Chgo., 1978-79, Midwest Data Base Project, U. Ill., Chgo., 1978-79; mem. task force for nurse practitioner legislation Nebr. Legis. Commn., Lincoln, 1980-84. Author, co-author book chpts., jour. articles. Mem. Triangle Club YMCA Wives, Cin., 1951-79, Dundee Presbyn. Ch., Omaha, 1979—. NIMH trainee, 1964-70, grad. nurse tng. grantee, 1976-79; spl. project grantee Div. Nursing USPHS, 1975-78. Fellow Am. Acad. Nursing; mem. Am. Nurses Assn. (chmn. edn. cabinet Nebr. 1983—), Nat. League for Nursing, Midwest Nursing Research Soc. (bd. dirs. 1982-84), Am. Assn. Colls. of Nursing (rep.), Sigma Theta Tau. Republican. Avocations: golf; fishing; bridge; travel. Office: Coll Nursing U Nebr Med Ctr 42d and Dewey Sts Omaha NE 68105

YEH, YANG-CHU JAMES, engineering consultant, executive; b. Taipei, Taiwan, June 11, 1948; came to U.S., 1971; s. Yuan Ping and Hsueh Ming (Yang) Y.; m. Wu-Pei Patricia Lay, Aug. 4, 1973; children—Yun-Feng Steven, Yun-Hao Kevin, Yun-Hsin Jamie. B.S. in Mech. Engring., Nat. Taiwan U., 1970; M.S. in Mech. Engring., Bucknell U., 1972; M.B.A., SUNY-Albany, 1973. Registered profl. engr. Republic of China and Mo. Systems engr. IBM, Albany, 1974-75; sr. v.p. William Tao & Assocs., St. Louis, 1975—. Editor company newsletter, 1976. Pres. Chinese Cultural Ctr., St. Louis, 1984. Recipient Solar Energy Demonstration award Dept. Energy, 1977. Mem. Nat. Soc. Profl. Engrs., ASME, ASHRAE, Assn. M.B.A. Execs. Club: Jaycees (pres. Jaycees Internat., St. Louis 1976). Home: 310 Jamboree Dr Manchester MO 63021 Office: William Tao & Assocs Inc 2357 59th St Saint Louis MO 63110

YELLIN, ABSALOM MOSES, psychophysiologist, educator, research administrator, clinical psychologist; b. Israel, July 25, 1936; s. Isaac Naphtali Yellin and Ann Trachtenberg; m. Judith Ann Himell, Aug. 29, 1965; children—Elana, Talia. B.A., U. Del., 1965, M.A., 1968, Ph.D., 1970. Lic. cons. psychologist, Minn. Postdoctoral scholar Neuropsychiat. Inst., UCLA, 1969-71; asst. prof. U. Calif.-Davis, 1972-74; asst. prof. psychiatry U. Minn., Mpls., 1974-80, assoc. prof., 1980—, dir. research div. child/adolescent psychiatry, 1983—, dir. lab. neuroscis., 1983—. Contbr. numerous articles to profl. jours., chpts. to sci. texts. Fellow Internat. Orgn. Psychophysiology; mem. Am. Psychol. Assn., Soc. Psychophysiol. Research, N.Y. Acad. Scis., Psychonomic Soc., Internat. Soc. Developmental Psychobiology. Avocations: Hebrew studies; gardening. Office: U Minn Dept Psychiatry Box 95 Mayo Bldg Minneapolis MN 55455

YELVINGTON, DANA JONES, college administrator, typography educator, editor; b. Libertyville, Ill., Apr. 3, 1952; d. Ralph William and Martha Jane (Rinehart) Jones; 1 son, Timothy Jones. B.S., U. Ill., 1974; postgrad. Webster U., 1985. Typesetter, proofreader Sarasota Jour., Fla., 1974-75; asst. news editor, feature editor Colo. Springs Sun, Colo., 1975-77; legis. reporter S.E. Alaska Empire, Juneau, 1977-78; mag. editor News Gazette, Champaign, Ill., 1979; dir. pub. info. Belleville Area Coll., Ill., 1981—. Contbr. articles to newspapers. Organizer, exhibitor numerous art shows. Leader Girl Scouts Am., Alaska, Colo.; various positions United Methodist Ch., Colo., Alaska, Ill.; friend St. Louis Art Mus.; mem. Homemakers, YMCA, St. Louis Zoo, Channel 9. Mem. Nat. Council on Community Relations (dist. dir. 1984-86), Ill. Coll. Relations Council, Am. Assn. Community and Jr. Colls. (pub. relations com. 1985-86). Democrat. Avocations: sewing; hand crafts; fine art-drawing and painting; canoeing; swimming. Office: Belleville Area Coll 2500 Carlyle Rd Belleville IL 62221

YEN, ANDREW, biophysicist, biomedical researcher; b. N.Y.C., Mar. 4, 1948; s. Andrew and Josephine Y.; m. Kathleen Betit, Feb. 1, 1975; children—Jennifer, Christopher. B.A., Haverford Coll., 1969; M.S., U. Wash., 1970; Ph.D., Cornell U., 1976. Research fellow Farber Cancer Inst. Harvard, Boston, 1976-78; staff mem. Sloan-Kettering Inst., N.Y.C., 1978-81; dir. flow cytometry facility U. Iowa, Iowa City, 1981—. Contbr. articles to profl. jours. Fellow Woodrow Wilson Found., Leukemia Soc. Am. Mem. Am. Assn. for Cancer Research, Biophys. Soc., Am. Physiol. Soc., Haverford Coll. Corp. Office: Univ Iowa SE313GH Dept Medicine Iowa City IA 52242

YEN, TERENCE TSINTSU, research scientist; b. Shanghai, China, May 2, 1937; came to U.S., 1961; s. Chia Chang and Chung Ying (Yeh) Y.; m. Margaret Shih, May 30, 1964; children—Lisa, Grace, Tina. B.S. in Agrl. Chemistry, Nat. Taiwan U., 1958; Ph.D. in Biochemistry, U. N.C.-Chapel Hill, 1966. Sr. scientist Lilly Research Labs., Indpls., 1965-70, research scientist, 1971—. Mem. Am. Soc. Biol. Chemists, Am. Chem. Soc., AAAS, N.Am. Assn. Study of Obesity, Sigma Xi. Office: Lilly Research Labs Lilly Corp Ctr Indianapolis IN 46285

YENER, MUZAFFER, educator, consultant, researcher; b. Iskenderun, Turkey, June 30, 1947; s. Celal and Rahmiye (Koraltan) Y.; m. Barbara Ann Valovage, Dec. 14, 1980; 1 son, Devren Adem. B.S. in Civil Engring., NYU, 1969, M.S., 1971; Ph.D., Cornell U., 1979. Design engr. Herbert Fleisher Assocs., N.Y.C., 1970; teaching asst., research assoc. Cornell U., Ithaca, N.Y., 1974-80; design engr. Turkish Army Engring. Corps., 1976; supervising engr. Dalsar Corp., Turkey, 1977; asst. prof. Purdue U., West Lafayette Ind., 1980—; cons. Served with Turkish Army, 1976. Recipient govt. grants for coll. edn., 1966-72. Mem. ASCE, Am. Concrete Inst., Sigma Xi, Chi Epsilon. Author: Dynamics of Bridge Structures, 1984; contbr. articles to profl. jours. Office: Civil Engring Bldg Purdue U West Lafayette IN 47907

YENKIN, FRED, paint manufacturing company executive; b. U.S., June 20, 1911; s. Jacob and Mary (Maggied) Y.; children—Judith Yenkin Brachman, Cynthia Yenkin Levinson. B.C.E., Ohio State U., 1932, M.Ch.E., 1934. With Frey-Yenkin Paint Co., Columbus, Ohio, 1934-55, tchr. dir., 1937-55; R&D, tech. sales of polymers and chem. coatings staffs Yenkin-Majestic Paint Corp., Columbus, Ohio, 1955-77, chmn. bd., 1977—. Bd. dirs. Planned Parenthood Assn., Columbus TB Soc.; pres. Columbus Jewish Fedn., 1955-56; pres. Zionist Orgn., 1948-51, Columbus Hebrew Sch., 1948-52; officer Columbus Jewish Center. Mem. Fedn. Soc. Coatings Tech. (officer), Nat. Coatings Assn., NAACP, Anti-Defamation League, Am. Chem. Soc., Inst. Chem. Engrs., Nat. Soc. Profl. Engrs. Clubs: Columbus Athletic, Winding Hollow Country. Capital; President Country (Palm Beach, Fla.). Home: 3300 S Ocean Blvd Palm Beach FL Office: 1920 Leonard Ave Columbus OH 43219

YENTIS, JAY MARTIN, economist; b. Bklyn., Dec. 21, 1948; s. Jacob and Muriel (Hindin) Y. B.A. in Econs., Hofstra U., 1970; M.A. in Econs., Mich. State U., 1972, M.B.A. in Fin., 1973. Instr. Lansing Community Coll., Mich., 1972-74; pricing analyst Foremost Ins., Grand Rapids, Mich., 1974-77; planning coordinator GTE of Ind., Fort Wayne, 1977-82; forecasting adminstr. Midwestern Telephone Ops. Westfield, Ind., 1982-83; pricing/econ. mgr. N.Am. Van Lines, Fort Wayne, 1983-85; mgr. market research Lincoln Nat. Pension, Fort Wayne, 1985—; instr. project bus. Jr. Achievement, Fort Wayne, 1979-80; v.p. Gen. Telephone Employees Credit U., Fort Wayne, 1979, pres., 1980. Capt. for N.Am. Van Lines, U.S. Savs. Bond Drive, Fort Wayne, 1984. Mem. Nat. Assn. Bus. Economists, Inst. Mgmt. Accts., Pi Gamma Mu, Omicron Delta Epsilon. Jewish. Avocations: camping; world travel; theatre; tennis; softball. Home: 1309 Clarion Dr Fort Wayne IN 46825 Office: Lincoln Nat Pension 1300 S Clinton St PO Box 1110 Fort Wayne IN 46801

YEOH, JOSEPHINE WHITE, medical librarian; b. Moscow, USSR, July 22, 1938; d. John Edward and Helen Marie (Magnuson) W.; m. Vincent Yeoh, July 14, 1962 (div. Feb. 1975); children—Stacy, Jeffrey and Jennifer (twins). B.S., Cornell U., 1960; M.S.L.S., Case Western Res. U., 1972. Info. specialist John Hopkins Med. Inst., Balt., 1972-73; med. library dir. Riverside Meth. Hosp., Columbus, Ohio, 1973—; cons. in field. Bd. dirs. local PTA, 1976-80. Mem. Med. Library Assn., Central Ohio Hosp. Library Consortium, Ohio Health Info. Orgn., ALA, NOW, SANE, Beta Phi Mu. Democrat. Quaker. Contbr. articles to profl. jours. Office: Med Library Riverside Meth Hosp Columbus OH 43214

YERIAN, MICHAEL ALEXANDER, dentist; b. Springfield, Ohio, Feb. 18, 1949; s. Marcus Dale and Mary Katherine (Kotsanos) Y. B.S. in Biology, Ohio State U., 1971, D.D.S., 1974. Dental officer U.S. Naval Dental Corp., 1974-77; dental intern, La. State Med. Ctr., New Orleans, 1978-80; dentist USPHS, State of Ohio, 1980-81; gen. practice dentistry, Springfield, Ohio, 1981—; mem. med. staff Community Hosp., 1981-85. assoc. dir. clin. services Loncon Correctional Inst., Ohio Bur. Corrections, 1984—. Mem. Am. Security Council, Washington, 1980-84, Republican Nat. Com., Washington, 1980-84. Health Professions scholar, 1973-74. Mem. ADA, Ohio Dental Assn. Republican. Lutheran. Clubs: Gen. Dentistry Study, Springfield Racquet. Home: 2024 Providence Ave Springfield OH 45503

YETKA, LAWRENCE ROBERT, state supreme court justice; b. Cloquet, Minn., Oct. 1, 1924; s. Frank and Martha (Norkowski) Y.; B.S., U. Minn., 1947, J.D., 1948; m. Ellen Marie Fuller, Nov. 11, 1950; children—Frank Barry, Lawrence George, Christopher Hubert. Admitted to Minn. bar, 1949; founder, partner firm Yetka & Newby, Cloquet, 1949-73; spl. mcpl. judge, 1960-66; city atty., Cloquet, 1964-73; atty. Duluth Port Authority, 1957-60; atty. Western Lake Superior San. Dist., 1970-73; asso. justice Minn. Supreme Ct., St. Paul, 1973—; atty., dir. Carlton County Fed. Savs. & Loan Assn., 1958-73; chmn. State Jud. Council, 1974-79, Select Com. on State Jud. System, 1974-77, State Jud. Planning Agy., 1976-84. Del., 12 state Dem. convs., 1948-72, Dem. Nat. Conv., 1956, 64, 68; chmn. Students for Humphrey for Mayor, 1947; Democratic Farmer Labor county officer, 1948-72, 8th Dist., 1962-66; state Dem. vice chmn., 1966-70; mem. Minn. Ho. of Reps., 1951-61, chmn. Ho. Jud. Com., 1955-61, asst. majority leader, 1959-61. Grad., Appellate Judges Seminar sponsored by Inst. Jud. Adminstrn. at N.Y. U. Law Sch., 1976. Mem. Am., Minn., Carlton County (pres. 1963-73) bar assns., Am. Judicature Soc., Inst. Jud. Adminstrn. Lutheran. Office: Supreme Ct Minn 230 State Capitol Saint Paul MN 55155*

YIAMOUYIANNIS, JOHN ANDREW, health consultant; b. Hartford, Conn., Sept. 25, 1942; s. Andrew John and Caroline (Hofstetter) Y.; m. Natalie Brinkman, Oct. 6, 1962; children—Carmen, Zeus, Athena, Lurleen, Portia, Apollo. B.S. in Biochemistry, U. Chgo., 1963; Ph.D. in Biochemistry, U. R.I., 1967. Postdoctoral fellow Western Res. U., Cleve., 1967-68; biochem. editor Chem. Abstracts Service, Columbus, Ohio, 1968-72; sci. dir. Nat. Health Fedn., Monrovia, Calif., 1974-80; pres. Safe Water Found., Delaware, Ohio, 1979-84; dir. Ctr. Health Action, Delaware, 1984—; cons. Scottish Legal Soc., Edinburgh, 1980-82. Author: Fluoride: The Aging Factor, 1983. Contbr. articles to profl. publs. Mem. Am. Chem. Soc. Home: 6439 Taggart Rd Delaware OH 43015

YIM, B(URGESS) CASEY, lawyer; b. Honolulu, Sept. 10, 1948; s. Albert S.U. and Ruth N. (Burgess) Y. A.B., San Diego State U., 1971; J.D. cum laude, Cleve. State U., 1975. Bar: Ohio 1975, Calif. 1982. profl. assoc. Squire, Sanders & Dempsey, Cleve., 1975-83; profl. assoc. Lewis, D'Amato, Brisbois & Bisgaard, Los Angeles, 1983, ptnr. 1985—; ann. seminar lectr. Assoc. Industries of Cleve., 1979-82; Editor-in-chief Cleve. State U. Law Rev., 1974-75. Recipient Am. Jurisprudence Book award Lawyers Coop. Pub. Co., 1974; Corpus Juris Secundum award, 1973. Mem. ABA (litigation sect.), Ohio State Bar Assn., Cleve. Bar Assn., Los Angeles County Bar Assn., Calif. State Bar Assn., Assn. Bus. Trial Lawyers. Office: Lewis D'Amato Brisbois & Bisgaard 261 S Figueroa St Suite 300 Los Angeles CA 90012

YINGST, DOUGLAS ROY, physiologist; b. Chgo., Nov. 1, 1946; s. Kenneth Harry and Sylvia LaVonne (Vannorsdel) Y.; children—Rebecca Ann, Stuart Michael. A.B., McPherson Coll., 1969; Ph.D., U. So. Calif., 1976. Postdoctoral fellow Yale U., 1976-78, postdoctoral assoc., 1979; asst. prof. dept. physiology Sch. Medicine, Wayne State U., 1980-85, assoc. prof., 1985—. NIH research service awardee, 1976-78; NIH research career devel. award, 1984-89. Mem. Am. Heart Assn., Mich. Heart Assn., N.Y. Acad. Scis., Detroit Physiol. Soc., Soc. Gen. Physiologists, Biophys. Soc., Sierra Club, Sigma Xi. Mem. Ch. Brethren. Contbr. articles to sci. jours. Home: 18295 Birchcrest Dr Detroit MI 48221 Office: Dept Physiology Wayne State U 540 E Canfield Ave Detroit MI 48201

YLVISAKER, WILLIAM TOWNEND, manufacturing executive; b. St. Paul, Feb. 25, 1924; s. Lauritz S. and Winifred Jean (Townend) Y.; grad. Lawrenceville Sch., 1943; B.S., Yale U., 1948; m. Jane Penelope Mitchell, May 11, 1972; 1 son, Jon Alastair; children by previous marriage—Laurie Ellen, Elizabeth Maren, Amy Townend. Security analyst Bank of N.Y., 1948-49; gen. mgr. Lake Forest Motor Sales (Ill.), 1949-52; v.p., gen. mgr. Pheoll Mfg. Co., Chgo., 1952-58; pres. Parker-Kalon div. Gen. Am. Transp. Corp., Clifton, N.J., 1958-61, group v.p., dir. Gen. Am. Transp. Corp., Chgo., 1961-67; chmn. bd., chief exec. officer Gould Inc., 1967—; dir. Penske Corp., Piscataway, N.J., Compagnie Francaise D'Electro Chimie, France, Accumuladores Tudor, S.A., Mexico. Bd. dirs. NCCJ, Nat. Found. on Youth and Drugs, Bus. Com. for Arts; trustee Lawrenceville (N.J.) Sch., Rush-Presbyn.-St. Luke's Med. Sch., Solomon R. Guggenheim Found., Orchestral Assn. Chgo. Symphony; mem. citizens bd. U. Chgo. Served as ensign USNR, 1943-45. Mem. Chgo. Assn. Commerce and Industry (dir.), Nat. Alliance Businessmen (dir.), U.S. Polo Assn., Northwestern U. Assos. Clubs: Univ., Racquet and Tennis, Links (N.Y.C.); Barrington Hills Country; Oak Brook (Ill.) Polo (gov.); Racquet, Chicago, Yale, Economic (Chgo.); Palm Beach Polo and Country (West Palm Beach, Fla.); Meadow (Rolling Meadows, Ill.). Office: Gould Inc 10 Gould Center Rolling Meadows IL 60008

YOAKAM, LARRY E., insurance company executive; b. Columbus, Ohio, Jan. 20, 1928; s. Lawrnece R. and Helen M. (Fitzsimmons) Y.; m. Margaret N. Tibbs, July 3, 1950. B.B.A., Washington U., 1954. Dir. underwriting and pricing Grange Mut. Cos., Columbus, 1955—. Vice pres. St. Ann's Hosp Community Service, Columbus, 1981—; pres. Northland Community Council, Columbus, 1981-83; councilman Village of Minerva Park, Ohio. Served to sgt. USAF, 1946-51. Recipient Commendation, Ohio Ho. of Reps., 1983, 84, Columbus City Council, 1983. Village of Minerva Park, 1982. Mem. Air Force Assn. Republican. Lodges: Shriners, Masons. Avocation: Country/western singing. Home: 2681 Maplewood Dr Minerva Park Columbus OH 43229

YOCHUM, YORK FOX, acquisition executive; b. Pitts., Sept. 21, 1941; s. Edward and Genevieve (Fox) Y.; m. Mary Nina Whitaker, Dec. 26, 1970. B.A., Washington and Jefferson Coll., 1974; M.B.A., U. Pa., 1966. Mktg. analyst Rockwell Internat., Pitts., 1967-69, supr. mktg. projects, 1969-71, mgr. mktg. research, Detroit, 1971-73, mgr. market devel., 1973-74, sales mgr., Norristown, Pa., 1974; v.p. mktg. Hayes-Albion Corp., Norristown, 1974-77; dir. product planning Hoover Universal, Inc., Saline, Mich., 1977-80, dir. mktg. and planning services, 1980-81, dir. planning, 1982; v.p., gen. mgr. J.P.I. Plumbing Products Co., Ann Arbor, Mich., 1982; dir. acquisitions J.P. Industries, Inc., Ann Arbor, 1983-84; sr. v.p. Mgmt. Collaborative Group, Ann Arbor, 1984—. Del. Republican State Conv., 1980. Mem. Assn. for Corp. Growth, Planning Forum (bd. dirs. 1985-86), Am. Mktg. Assn. Washington and Jefferson Coll. Alumni Club (chmn. 1984). Episcopalian. Club: Wharton of Mich. Avocations: biking, racquetball, travel, reading. Home: 2029 Delaware Dr Ann Arbor MI 48103 Office: Mgmt Collaborative Group 2029 Delaware Dr Ann Arbor MI 48103

YOCK, JOSEPH P(OWELL), JR., paper company manager, plant manager; b. Battle Creek, Mich., July 5, 1946; s. Joseph P. and Agnes K. (Miller) Y.; m. Joyce S. Rogosz, June 20, 1970; children—Angela, Kristopher, Gregory. Student, Kellogg Community Coll., 1964-66; B.S., Western Mich. U., 1969, M.B.A., 1976. Tech. asst. printing Gen. Foods Corp., Battle Creek, 1968-70, gravure inks supr., 1970-72, graphic arts and engraving mgr., 1972-77; ops. tech. mgr. Am. Can Co., Neenah, Wis., 1977-79, plant supt., 1979-82; plant mgr. James River Corp., Neenah, 1982—; instr. Lakeland Coll., Sheboygan, Wis., 1981—, Fox Valley Tech. Inst., Appleton, Wis., 1977—, Kellogg Community Coll., Battle Creek, 1976-77. Served with USAR, 1969-75. Kalamazoo Valley Craftsman Club scholar, 1965-69. Mem. Gravure Tech. Assn. (chmn. 1969—), Appleton C. of C. (bd. 1983—). Republican. Roman Catholic. Club: Rotary (bd. Neenah 1981-83). Home: 760 Manchester Rd Neenah WI 54956 Office: PO Box 899 160 Washington St Neenah WI 54956

YOCUM, CHARLES FREDRICK, biology educator; b. Storm Lake, Iowa, Oct. 31, 1941; s. Vincent Cary and Olive Lucille (Cammack) Y.; m. Patricia Joan Bury, Jan. 1, 1981; 1 son, Erik Charles. B.S., Iowa State U., 1963; M.S., Ill. Inst. Tech., 1968; Ph.D., Ind. U., 1971. Research biochemist Ill. Inst. Tech. Research Inst., Chgo., 1963-68; grad. fellow Ind. U., Bloomington, 1968-71; postdoctoral fellow Cornell U., Ithaca, N.Y., 1971-73; asst. prof. U. Mich., Ann Arbor, 1973-77, assoc. prof., 1978-82, prof. biol. scis. and chemistry, 1983—; vis. prof. Mich. State U., East Lansing, 1980-81; cons. NSF, Washington, 1982—. Contbr. articles to various publs. Recipient Henry Russel award U. Mich., 1977; Research grantee NSF, 1978—, USDA, 1978—. Mem. AAAS, Am. Chem. Soc., Am. Soc. Plant Pyysiologists, Am. Soc. Biol. Chemists, Am. Soc. Photobiology. Advocations: Classical music, travel. Office: Div Biol Scis U Mich Ann Arbor MI 48109

YODER, ALFRED LOYD, college dean, educator; b. Drexel, Mo., Apr. 7, 1928; s. Alfred L. and Zella (Slayden) Y.; m. V. Irene Hershberger, Aug. 10, 1952; 1 dau., Melody June. B.S. in Elem. Edn., Central Mo. State U., 1960; M.A. in Elem. Adminstrn., U. No. Colo., 1967; postgrad., cert. spl. edn. of gifted Kans. State U., 1978. Cert. spl. edn. tchr., Mo., Kans., adminstr., Kans., Colo. Tchr. elem. schs. Mo., Colo., after 1948; asst. prin. Jefferson County Pub. Sch., Lakewood, Colo.; elem. curruculum cons., prin. Aurora (Colo.) Pub. Schs., 1972-73; instr. Univ. Lab. Sch. U. Wyo., 1972-74; prin. elem. sch., Hesston, Kans., 1975-78; instr. Hesston Coll., Tabor Coll., 1978-80; curriculum coordinator, tchr. Dist. 460, Hesston, Kans., 1978-80; now assoc. dean, instr. Hesston Coll. Mem. bd. of elders Hesston Mennonite Ch. Mem. Nat. Assn. Sch. Curriculum Devel., Phi Delta Kappa. Mennonite-Ana-Baptist. Author: Learning Center Handbook, 1974. Home: 125 S College Dr Box 933 Hesston KS 67062 Office: Hesston Coll Hesston KS 67062

YODER, EILEEN RHUDE, nutrition and health management executive, consultant; b. Evergreen Park, Ill., Aug. 20, 1946; d. Howard Vernon and Diana Joan (Lemon) Rhude; m. Bernard J. Yoder, Oct. 9, 1965 (div. July 1985); children—Laura Joyce, Patricia Carolyn. Lic. nurse Triton Coll., 1966; lic. health facility adminstr. Ball State U., 1979; B.A., Govs. State U., Park Forest, Ill., 1981. Dir. E. Yoder & Assocs., Goshen, Ind., 1966-79; exec. dir. Healthful Living, N.Y.C., 1979-83; pres. Med. Diet Systems, Palos Park, Ill., 1983—; cons. and writer for various orgns. Author: Allergy-Free Cooking, 1982; Milk, Egg, and Wheat Free Cooking, 1984; Maintaining Patient Compliance, 1985; also articles. Mem. Asthma and Allergy Found. (bd. dirs.), AAAS, Am. Heart Assn. (bd. dirs.), Am. Home Econs. Assn. (bd. dirs.). Office: Med Diet Systems Inc 11701 S 82 Ct Palos Park IL 60464

YODER, JAMES THOMAS, manufacturing executive; b. Columbus, Ohio, May 28, 1928; s. James G. and Mary E. (Elder) Y.; m. Camille Lorine Clark, June 3, 1950; children—Karen Ann Yoder Siemers, James J., Gary M. B.S., U. Kans., 1949. Pres., Air Reps., Overland Park, Kans., 1960—, Air Plastics, Overland Park, 1968—; v.p. Shawnee Producers, Overland Park, 1979—; dir. Artex Internat., Highland, Ill., SOR Inc., Olathe, Kans. Served with U.S. Army, 1945-47. Republican. Roman Catholic. Home: 11207 Rosewood Leawood KS 66211 Office: PO Box 12328 Overland Park KS 66212

YODER, LEVON LEE, physics educator; b. Middlebury, Ind., June 22, 1936; s. Leonard C. and Cleo (Pletcher) Y.; m. Anita R. Hoffman, Aug. 21, 1960; 1 dau., Teryl Lyn. B.A., Goshen Coll., 1958; M.A., U. Mich., Ann Arbor, 1961, Ph.D., 1963. Asst. prof. physics Millikin U., 1963-65; assoc. prof. physics Adrian Coll., 1965-69, prof., 1969—, chmn. dept., 1965-75, 78—; researcher high energy particle interactions, musical acoustics. Mem. Am. Assn. Physics Tchrs., AAAS. Home: 2499 Sword Hwy Adrian MI 49221 Office: Adrian Coll Dept Physics Adrian MI 49221

YODER, ROBERT LEE, banker; b. Auburn, Ala., Oct. 23, 1935; s. Ora Mae Yoder; m. Susan E. Yoder; m. Victoria Frances Gordon-Johnson, May 21, 1983; children—Cynthia Ann, Elizabeth Marie. B.A., Coll. of Wooster, 1957; M.B.A., U. Pa., 1959. Sr. v.p. No. Trust Co., Chgo., 1960-81; exec. v.p., chief fin. officer AmeriTrust Co. Nat. Assn., Cleve., 1981—. Sect. leader Prochnow Grad. Sch., Madison, Wis.; bd. dirs., exec. com. ARC. Served to 1st lt. USAR. Mem. Res. City Bankers, Am. Bankers Assn. (bd. dirs.). Home: 12000

Edgewater Dr Lakewood OH 44107 Office: AmeriTrust Co Nat Assn 900 Euclid Ave Cleveland OH 44101

YODER, VANCE A., college dean, educator; b. McPherson, Kans., Jan. 21, 1942; s. Wilbur and Una (Ring) Y.; m. Marilyn J. Taylor, Aug. 20, 1966; children—Philip, Michael, Daniel. B.S., Manchester Coll., 1964; M.M., Ind. U., 1967; Ph.D., Ohio State U., 1970. Tchr. music Twin Valley Schs., Lewisburg, Ohio, 1964-65; prof. Bluffton Coll., Ohio, 1969-70; prof. music and acad. dean Grace Coll., Winona Lake, Ind., 1970—; cons., evaluator and commr. North Central Assn. Colls. and Schs., 1978—. Contbr. articles to profl. jours. Bd. dirs. Lakeland Christian Acad., Winona Lake, 1981—. Paul Harris fellow, 1980. Mem. Am. Assn. Higher Edn., Music Educators Nat. Conf., Lakeland Community Concert Assn. (pres. 1973-74), Phi Delta Kappa. Republican. Lodge: Rotary (Warsaw, Ind.). Avocations: travel; swimming. Home: Rural Route 8 Box 265 Warsaw IN 46580 Office: Grace Coll 200 Seminary Dr Winona Lake IN 46590

YOERGER, ROGER RAYMOND, engineering educator, agricultural engineer; b. Le Mars, Iowa, Feb. 17, 1929; s. Raymond Herman and Crystal Victoria (Ward) Y.; m. Barbara Mary Ellison, Feb. 14, 1953 (div. 1971); 1 child, Karen; m. Laura Maxine Kelsey, Dec. 23, 1971; step-children—Daniel Summitt, Linda Canull, Anita Smith. B.S., Iowa State U., 1949, M.S., 1951, Ph.D., 1957. Registered profl. engr., Ill., Pa., Iowa. Asst. prof. Iowa State U., Ames, 1949-56; assoc. prof. Pa. State U., University Park, 1956-58; prof. U. Ill., Urbana, 1959—, prof., head agrl. engring., 1978—. Patentee in field. Recipient Honorary Am. Farmer degree Future Farmers Am., 1983. Fellow Am. Soc. Agrl. Engrs. (Tech. Paper awards, 1967, 68, 70, 75, 76); mem. Am. Soc. Engring. Edn., Sigma Xi, Gamma Sigma Delta, Alpha Epsilon, Phi Kappa Phi (dir. fellowships, 1972-83, pres. elect 1983-86). Roman Catholic. Lodge: Rotary. Avocations: travel, real estate investment. Home: 107 W Holmes St Urbana IL 61801 Office: U Ill U-C 1304 West Pennsylvania Ave Urbana IL 61801

YOEST, DONALD DEANE, real estate and insurance executive; b. California, Mo., Jan. 17, 1941; s. Andrew John and Agnes Elizabeth (Hartman) Y.; B.S., U. Mo., 1965; m. Marilyn Kay Null, Sept. 18, 1965; children—Scott, Kent, Joel, Neal. Field editor Rural Electric Missourian, Jefferson City, Mo., 1965-68, asso. editor, 1968-69, mng. editor, 1969-72, editor, 1972-77; br. mgr. Strout Realty, Inc., Tipton, Mo., 1977-85; broker/owner Don Yoest Realty & Ins. Agy., 1985—. Mem. Mid-Mo. Comprehensive Health Care Com., 1972-74. Recipient George W. Haggard Meml. Journalism award Nat. Rural Elec. Co-op Assn., 1972; various sales awards, 1979, 80, 81, 82, 83, 84. Mem. Nat. Electric Co-op. Editorial Assn. (pres. 1974-75), Co-op. Editorial Assn. (pres. 1973-74). Home: Route 2 Tipton MO 65081 Office: Don Yoest Realty & Ins Agy PO Box 154 Hwy 5 S Tipton MO 65081

YOGGERST, JAMES PAUL, educator, journalist, public relations consultant; b. Springfield, Ill., Oct. 9, 1924; s. Paul Anthony and Helen (Ford) Yoggerst; m. Norma Jean White, Nov. 25, 1948 (dec. Aug. 1976); children—Maureen, Karen, Dianne, Patricia, Paul, Steven. B.S. in Journalism, U. Ill., 1949, M.A. in English, 1950, postgrad. Reporter, Ill. State Register, Springfield, 1950-51; asst. editor Austin News, Chgo., 1951-55; tchr. journalism and English, Waukegan East High Sch., 1956-85; part-time lectr. Roosevelt U., Chgo., 1971-85; instr. Coll. of Lake County, Grayslake, 1965-72; part-time reporter News-Sun, Waukegan, Ill., 1956-70; contbg. editor La Montage Mag., Lake Bluff, Ill., 1977; dir. J. P. Yoggerst and Assoc., Pub. Relations and Writing Cons., Waukegan; lectr. in field, leader seminars; writing cons. Cherry Electric Co., Waukegan, 1971-72; pub. relations dir. Lake County Contractors Assn., Waukegan, 1973-74; pub. affairs cons. Social Security Adminstrn., Chgo., 1973-74. Author weekly column —Our Prairie State—, Waukegan News-Sun, 1977-79; contbr. articles and short stories to newspapers and mags. Pub. relations dir. Ray Bradbury Soc., Waukegan, 1978, Stonebridge Priory, Servite Fathers, Lake Bluff, Ill., 1971; mem. adv. bd. of Checagov, DuSable Fort Dearborn Hist. Commn., Chgo., 1985—. Served with AUS, 1943-46; PTO. Democrat. Roman Catholic. Home: 2528 N Jackson St Waukegan IL 60087 Office: J P Yoggerst and Assocs 19 N Genesee St Waukegan IL 60085

YOH, JOHN, physicist; b. Shanghai, China, Oct. 9, 1944; came to U.S., 1957, naturalized, 1963; s. Joseph and Esther (Way) Y.; m. Hua Zheng, June 23, 1983. B.A., Cornell U., 1964; M.S., Calif. Inst. Tech., 1966, Ph.D., 1970. NATO postdoctoral fellow CERN, Geneva, 1970-71, vis. scientist, 1971-73; research assoc. Columbia U., N.Y.C., 1973-77, asst. prof., 1977-80; scientist Fermilab, Batavia, Ill., 1980—. Co-discoverer Upsilon, 1977, 10 other mems. of Upsilon and Bottomquark families, 1980-82. Avocations: playing viola; singing. Office: Fermilab MS 223 PO Box 500 Batavia IL 60510

YOHN, RICHARD VAN, clergyman; b. Lancaster, Pa., Apr. 16, 1937; s. Henry Martin and Ada (Dommel) Y.; m. Linda Harriet Anderson, June 18, 1960; children—Richard Van, Steven Eric. Student Franklin and Marshall Coll., 1956; B.S., Phila. Coll. Bible, 1960; Th.M., Dallas Theol. Sem., 1964; D.Min., Talbot Theol. Sem., 1980. Ordained to ministry Evangelical Free Ch., 1971; dir. Christian edn. Oliver Presbyn. Ch., Mpls., 1964-67; pastor Windsor Park Evang. Free Ch., Winnipeg, Man., Can. 1967-71, Evang. Free Ch. Fresno, Calif., 1971-84, Grace Ch., Edina, Minn., 1984—; orginator radio program Living Word, 1980; pres. Contact Ministries Inc., 1980—; mem. faculty Winnipeg Bible Coll., 1969-70. Recipient Mark of Excellence award Campus Life Mag., 1975. Mem. Nat. Assn. Evangelicals. Author: Discover Your Spiritual Gift and Use It, 1974; Now That I'm A Disciple, 1976; What Every Christian Should Know About God, 1976; God's Answers to Life's Problems, 1976; God's Holy Spirit for Christian Living, 1977; Getting Control of Your Life, 1978; God's Answer to Financial Problems, 1978; Getting Control of Your Inner Self, 1981; What Every Christian Should Know About Bible Prophecy, 1982; First-hand Joy, 1982; Finding Time, 1984; Overcoming, 1985; Living Securely in an Unstable World, 1985. Home: 6612 Hillside Ln Edina MN 55435 Office: 5300 France Ave S Edina MN 55410

YOHO, EARL RAY, JR., construction company executive, adhesives and sealers manufacturing company executive; b. Hammond, Ind., Sept. 24, 1935; s. Earl Ray and Laura Ida (Hoeckelberg) Y.; m. Elaine Margie Hatfield, Oct. 13, 1956; children—Sharon Kay, Linda Jean, Donna Lynn, Janice Sue, Brenda Ann. Grad., Ind. Mil. Acad., Indpls., 1961, U.S. Army Engr. Sch., Ft. Belvoir, Va., 1966, U.S. Army Comd. and Gen. Staff Coll., Kans., 1972, U.S. Army Mil. Police Sch., Ark., 1976; cert. metallurgy Purdue U., 1962. Cert. Profl. Mgr., 1976. Mgr. quality control Youngstown Steel, East Chicago, Ind., 1959-61, gen. foreman ops., 1961-70, asst. supt. ops., 1970-75; mgr. ops. Nat. Steel, Houston, 1975-76; pres. Concrete Maintenance Engring. Inc., Highland, Ind., 1978—; pres. Specialty Compounds, Inc., Merrillville, Ind., 1976—. Patentee thickness gage pipe threading. Served with AUS, 1961-64. Mem. Soc. Am. Mil. Engrs., Calumet Purchasing Assn., Ind. Sheriff's Assn., Am. Concrete Inst., Midwest Coke Plant Blast Furnace Assn., Engr. Officers Assn. (pres. 1966-67), Am. Legion, Nat. Rifle Assn. Club: Smetlake Tennis. Lodge: Masons, Shriners. Home: 3630 44th St Highland IN 46322 Office: Specialty Compounds Inc 3300 E 84th Pl Merrillville IN 46410

YOON, BONG-HYUN, physician, educator; b. Chonnam, S.D., Apr. 11, 1939; s. Joe Jin and Jum Hyo (Lim) Y.; m. Chung-Ja Suh, May 8, 1968; children—Richard, Janet. B.A., Choman U., Korea, 1960; M.D., Chonnam Nat. Med. Sch., 1964. Diplomate Am. Bd. Radiology. Resident Sacred Heart Hosp., Allentown, Pa., 1971-74; assoc. prof. U. Health Scis. and Chgo. Med. Sch., North Chicago, 1980—; chief vascular radiology Chgo. Med. Sch., 1978—. Mem. Korean Med. Assn. (pres. 1979, v.p. 1980, editor jour. 1982), AMA, Am. Coll. Radiology, Roentgen Soc. N.Am., Assn. Univ. Radiologist, Soc. Ultra Sound. Home: 812 Whitman Ct Libertyville IL 60048 Office: VA Hosp Buckly Rd North Chicago IL 60064

YOON, JONG SIK, geneticist, educator; b. Suwon, Korea, Jan. 25, 1937; came to U.S., 1962, naturalized, 1976; s. Ki and Pil (Kang) Y.; m. Kyung-Soon Ahn, Sept. 10, 1962; children—Edward, Mimi, Sunny. B.S., Yonsei U., Seoul, Korea, 1961; M.A., U. Tex.-Austin, 1964, Ph.D., 1965. Research scientist U. Tex.-Austin also Houston, 1965-68; asst. prof. Yonsei U., 1968-71; research scientist U. Tex.-Austin, 1971-78; assoc. prof. Bowling Green State U., 1978-83, prof. genetics, 1983—, dir. Nat. Drosophila Species Resource Ctr., 1982—. Presbyterian. Contbr. articles to profl. jours. Home: 4 Picardie Ct Bowling Green OH 43402 Office: Dept Biol Scis Bowling Green State U Bowling Green OH 43403

YORDE, BETTY SMITH, counselor; b. Cleve., Feb. 22, 1925; d. Chester Arthur and Mary Emeline (Rockey) Smith; B.S. in Edn., Ohio U., 1969, M.A., 1974, Ph.D., 1977; m. Richard Eugene Yorde Sr., May 9, 1947; children—Richard Eugene, William Myron. Various secretarial positions, Cleve. and Columbus, Ohio, 1943-59; sec. Dunbar, Kienzle & Murphey, law firm, Columbus, 1959-61; tchr. Nelsonville-York High Sch., Nelsonville, Ohio, 1969-73; instr. oral interpretation, group dynamics, biofeedback Ohio U., Athens, 1973-77; coll. counselor Rio Grande Coll./Community Coll., Rio Grande, Ohio, 1977-78; individual practice counseling, Nelsonville, Ohio; affiliate staff Drs. Hosp.; cons., lectr. in stress mgmt. Ohio U. Coll. Osteo. Medicine. Trustee Ohio U. Coll. Edn. Soc. Alumni and Friends, Southeastern Ohio Hearing and Speech Center, Inc. Mem. Biofeedback Soc. Am., Am. Psychol. Assn., Am. Acad. Psychosomatic Medicine, Internat. Soc. Hypnosis, Ohio Psychol. Assn., Soc. Clin. and Exptl. Hypnosis, Am., Ohio (pres.) biofeedback socs., Phi Delta Kappa, Phi Kappa Phi, Order Eastern Star. Home: PO Box 29 Nelsonville OH 45764

YORK, DONALD HAROLD, physiology educator, neurosurgery and neurology educator; b. Moose Jaw, Sask., Can., Jan. 30, 1944; came to U.S., 1975; s. Henry Harold and Dorothy Marguerite (Sparrow) Y.; m. Catherine Louise Robbie, Oct. 1, 1966; children—Andrew, Deborah, Jamie. B.S. with honors, U. B.C., 1965, M.S., 1966; Ph.D., Monash U., Australia, 1969. Asst. prof. Queen's U., Kingston, Ont., Can., 1968-73, assoc. prof., 1973-75; assoc. prof. U. Mo., Columbia, 1975-82, prof. dept. physiology, 1982—; vis. fellow John Curtin Sch. Med. Research, Australia, 1983-84; cons. Assn. Am. Med. Colls., 1977-83, VA, Washington, 1977—; external reviewer NSF, 1975—. Author book chpts., jour. articles. Coach Columbia Soccer Assn., 1978-83; asst. scoutmaster Gt. Rivers council Boy Scouts Am., Columbia, 1981-83. Med. Research Council Can. scholar, 1970-75. Mem. Soc. for Neurosci. (pres. Mo. chpt. 1979-80), Am. Physiol. Soc., IEEE, Can. Physiol. Soc., Sigma Xi. Avocations: wood carving; graphic arts. Office: Dept Physiology MA415 Med Sci U Mo Columbia MO 65212

YORK, JOSEPH RUSSELL, media production technician; b. Royal Center, Ind., Oct. 19, 1940; s. William Russell and Naomi (Wellman) Y.; Student Olivet Nazarene Coll., until 1965; B.S., Ball State U. student, 1980, M.S., 1982; m. Teresa Luanne Ping, June 15, 1963; children—Sherra JoAnn, Kerra SuzAnn, Darren Joseph, Terra LeAnn. Photojournalist, Danville (Ill.) Comml. News, 1961-62, Kankakee (Ill.) Daily Jour., 1963; motion picture dir.-editor Calvin Prodns., Inc., Kansas City, Mo., 1965-71, Communico, Inc., St. Louis, 1971-73; editing supr. Premier Film & Rec. Co., Inc., St. Louis, 1973—; producer, dir. TV programming Kans. Fish and Game Commn., 1983—; owner, operator Trinity Prodns., St. Louis, 1963-83. Pastor, Ch. of the Nazarene, Selma, Ind. Recipient 1st Pl. award U.S. Indsl. Film Festival, 1972; 2d Pl. award Festival of Ams.-V.I., 1977. Mem. Profl. Photographers Am., Golden Key Nat. Honor Soc. Home: 506 Stout St Pratt KS 67124 Office: Route 2 PO Box 54A Pratt KS 67124

YORTY, ROLLIN DALE, bookstore executive; b. Lebanon, Pa., Feb. 12, 1924; s. Clayton Amos and Helen Louise (Wealand) Y.; m. Ethel Belle Yorty, Sept. 15, 1948; children—Bonnie, Heather, Tami, Melodie. B.S., Central Mich. U., 1951, M.A., 1962. Tchr. Gerrish-Higgins Schs., Roscommon, Mich., 1951-59, Saginaw Twp. Schs., Mich., 1959-60, Merritt Pub. Schs., Mich., 1960-62, Grayling Pub. Schs., Mich., 1962-66, Gerrish-Higgins Schs., Roscommon, 1966-83; owner Yorty's Antiques & Books, 1951—. Served with USAAF, 1943-46. Republican. Avocations: stamps; photography; swimming. Home and Office: 103 Yorty Dr Roscommon MI 48653

YOST, LYLE EDGAR, farm equipment manufacturing company executive; b. Hesston, Kans., Mar. 5, 1913; s. Joseph and Alma (Hensley) Y.; B.S., B.A., Goshen Coll., 1937; postgrad. U. Ind., 1940; m. Erma Martin, July 31, 1938; children—Byron, Winston, Susan, Cameron. With St. Joseph Valley Bank, Elkhart, Ind., 1938-41; tchr. Wakarusa (Ind.) High Sch., 1942-45; founder Hesston Corp. (Kans.), 1947, pres., 1949—, now chmn.; dir. 4th Nat. Bank, Wichita, Hesston State Bank. Bd. dirs., past pres. Farm and Indsl. Equipment Inst.; mem. Kans. Gov.'s Com. for Partners for Progress Kans.-Paraquay; chmn. com. establishing creamery in Uruguay, 1967; mem. State Dept. cultural del. to USSR, 1967. Bd. dirs. Mennonite Econ. Devel. Assos.; chmn. Prince of Peace Chapel, Aspen Colo. Named Farmarketing Man of Year, Nat. Agrl. Advt. and Marketing Assn., 1969; Kansan of Achievement in Bus., 1972, Kansan of Year, 1974. Mem. Alpha Kappa Psi. Home: 1200 Ridge Rd Hesston KS 67062 Office: 420 W Lincoln Blvd Hesston KS 67062

YOST, WILLIAM ALBERT, psychology research director, educator, consultant; b. Dallas, Sept. 21, 1944; s. William Jacque and Gladys Funk Y.; m. Lee Prater, June 15, 1969; children—Kelley Ann, Alyson Leigh. B.A., Colo. Coll., 1966; Ph.D., Ind. U., 1970. Assoc. prof. psychology U. Fla., Gainesville, 1971-75; prof. psychology Loyola U., Chgo., 1977—; dir. Parmly Hearing Inst., Chgo., 1977—; dir. sensory physiology and perception program NSF, Washington, 1982-83, ad hoc reviewer, 1972—. Assoc. editor Jour. Acoustical Soc. Am., 1983—. Cons. editor Random House Coll. Div., 1980—. Author: (with D. Nielsen) Fundamentals of Hearing, 1977, 84. Editor (with G. Gourevitch) Directional Hearing, 1984. Contbr. articles to profl. jours. and chpts. to books. Grantee NSF, NIH. Mem. Assn. Research in Otolaryngology (sec., treas. 1984—), N.Y. Acad. Sci., Nat. Acad. Scis. (mem. exec. com. on hearing, bioacoustics, biomechanics, 1981—); fellow Acoustical Soc. Am. (chmn. standards com. on bioacoustics 1978-84). Club: Evanston Tennis Assn. (pres. 1984). Office: Parmly Hearing Inst Loyola U Chicago 6525 N Sheridan Rd Chicago IL 60626

YOUNG, CAROL SCHELLINGER, environmental consultant, microbiologist; b. Council Bluffs, Iowa, Mar. 8, 1937; d. Ralph and Thelma (Paulson) Schellinger; m. Richard A. Young, June 28, 1958; children—Steven, Karen, Christopher. B.A., U. Iowa, 1958; postgrad. IIT, 1962-65; med. tech. Michael Reese Hosp. Sch. Med. Tech., Chgo., 1962. Asst. Micro Lab. dir. Michael Reese Hosp., Chgo., 1962-66; pres. Young Environ. Services, Glenview, Ill., 1972—. Contbr. articles to profl. jours. Bd. dirs. Glenview Caucus, Ill. Mem. Am. Soc. Med. Tech., Am. Soc. Clin. Pathologists. Office: Young Environ Services Inc 1253 Roosevelt Ave Glenview IL 60025

YOUNG, CHARLES STEPHEN, marketing executive, metallurgist; b. Pitts., July 9, 1947; s. Charles Sylvester and Marion Joan (Bakowski) Y.; m. Denise Mary Gerhart, Apr. 4, 1970; children—Keith Edward and Andrew Charles. B.S. in Metall. and Materials Sci., Carnegie-Mellon U., 1969, M.S. in Metall. and Materials Sci., 1971. Tech. service engr. St. Joseph Minerals Corp., Monaca, Pa., 1971-74; mgr. zinc tech. devel. St. Joseph Minerals, Monaca, 1974-80; mgr. galvinized steel Zinc Inst., N.Y.C., 1980-81; mgr. metall. devel. Titanium Inc., Fairfield, N.J., 1981-83; product mgr., new products Astro Metall., Wooster, Ohio, 1983—. Contbr. articles to prof. jours. Mem. bd. dirs. Wayne County Performing Arts Council, Wooster, 1984—. Served to capt., USAR, 1971-79. Mem. Nat. Assn. Corrosion Engrs., ASTM (mem. B-10 exec. com.), Am. Soc. for Metals, AIME. Republican. Avocations: golfing; tennis. Office: PO Drawer 520 3225 Lincoln Way West Wooster OH 44691

YOUNG, COLEMAN ALEXANDER, mayor; b. Tuscaloosa, Ala., May 24, 1918; s. Coleman and Ida Reese (Jones) Y.; LL.D., Eastern Mich. U., U. Mich., U. Detroit, Wayne State U.; Ph.D., Stillman Coll., Central State U. Del., Mich. Constl. Conv., 1961-62; mem. Mich. Senate, 1964-73, also Democratic floor leader; mayor of Detroit, 1974—. Del., Dem. Nat. Conv., 1968, 72, 76, 80, 84; Dem. nat. committeeman from Mich.; bd. dirs. Ferndale Coop. Credit Union, Kirwood Hosp., Detroit; vice chmn. Dem. Nat. Com., 1977-81. Served to 2d lt. USAAF, World War II. Recipient Springarn medal NAACP. Mem. U.S. Conf. Mayors (pres. 1982-83), NAACP, Brooker T. Washington Bus. Men's Assn., Trade Union Leadership Council, Assn. for Study Negro Life and History, AFL-CIO Council (spl. rep.). Baptist. Office: Office of Mayor 2 Woodward Ave Detroit MI 48226

YOUNG, DIANA ROSE, electronics company executive; b. Kokomo, Ind., July 12, 1942; d. Marian Thomas and Verna Inajean (Davison) Herren; student Ind. U.; B.S. in Bus. Adminstrn., St. Mary of the Woods, Terre Haute, Ind., 1981; children—Raymond, Steven, Jared. Cert. profl. mgr. Prodn. worker Delco Electronics Co. div. Gen. Motors Corp., Kokomo, 1967-72, prodn. supr., 1972-79, gen. supr. mfg., Milw., 1979-83, sr. labor relations rep., plant communication mgr., 1983—. Coordinating supt. Kokomo chpt. Ind. Research Assn. for Dyslexia, 1976-77, supr. tutorial program, Indpls., 1974-75, bd. dirs., 1977—. Recipient Mem. Nat. Mgmt. Assn. (charter mem.; bd. dirs.; cert. achievement 1977, cert. outstanding service 1978), Himalayan Breeders Soc., Kokomo Art Assn. Mem. United Brethren Ch. Home: Route 2 84S 24695 W Pheasant Hill Mukwonago WI 53149 Office: 7929 S Howell Oak Creek WI 53154

YOUNG, EUGENE SAMUEL, educational administrator, photographer; b. N.Y.C., Oct. 6, 1941; s. Martin and Fannie (Bogorad) Y.; m. Barbara Whyne, June 16, 1962; children—David, Paul. B.A., CCNY, 1962; M. in Music, Ind. U., 1966; Ed.D., Columbia U., 1973. Chmn. music and drama dept. Garden Sch., Jackson Heights, N.Y., 1965-71; researcher, cons. Columbia U., N.Y.C., 1971-73; prin. Chippewa Jr. High Sch. Mounds View Pub. Schs., St. Paul, 1973—; adj. prof. Coll. of St. Thomas, St. Paul, 1976-77; organizer, cons. com. to create a high sch. for the arts in Minn., St. Paul, 1977—. Author: Kurt Weill: The Man and His Music, 1966. Photographer nature, landscapes and cityscapes. Fed. govt. scholar Tchrs. Coll., N.Y.C., 1971-73, N.Y. State scholar CCNY, 1959-62; research grantee Kurt Weill Found. for Music, N.Y.C., 1966. Mem. Nat. Assn. Secondary Sch. Prins., Nat. Assn. Supervision and Curriculum Devel., Minn. Assn. Supervision and Curriculum Devel. (exec. bd. 1980—). Avocations: music; theatre; travel; antique collecting; Home: 5317 84th Ave N Brooklyn Park MN 55443 Office: Chippewa Jr High Sch Mounds View Pub Schs 5000 Hodgson Rd Saint Paul MN 55112

YOUNG, FRANK NELSON, JR., biology educator, entomologist; b. Oneonta, Ala., Nov. 2, 1915; s. Frank N. and Mary (Loe) Y.; m. Frances Norman Young, July 2, 1943; children—Elizabeth Von Herrmann, Frank N. III. B.S., U. Fla., 1938, M.S., 1940, Ph.D., 1942. Asst. prof. biology U. Fla., Gainesville, 1946-49; asst. prof. biology Ind. U., Bloomington, 1949-51, assoc. prof., 1951-62, prof., 1963—. Served to capt. U.S. Army, 1942-46. Recipient Phi Sigma medal, 1940; Guggenheim fellow, 1960-61; La. State U. fellow, 1963. Fellow Ind. Acad. Sci., Royal Entomol. Soc.; mem. AAAS, Am. Inst. Biol. Scis. Baptist. Author: Water Beetles of Florida, 1954; contbr. articles on aquatic insects to profl. jours. Home: 405 S Mitchell St Bloomington IN 47401 Office: 201 Morrison Hall Ind U Bloomington IN 47405

YOUNG, GLENN MACARTHUR, food distributor executive; b. Petersburg, Ind., June 27, 1942; s. Arnold and Elma (Whitman) Y.; m. Sue Ellen Young, Mar. 19, 1968; 1 child, Vanessa. Cert. U.S. Army. Owner, operator Sure Fine Foods Inc., Evansville, Ind. Avocations: world travel; raquetball; flying. Office: Sure-Fine Foods Inc 4014 E Eichel Evansville IN 47715

YOUNG, JACK ALLISON, financial executive; b. Aurora, Ill., Dec. 31, 1931; s. Neal A. and Gladys W. Young; m. Virginia Dawson, Jan. 24, 1959; children—Amy D., Andrew A. B.S. in Journalism, U. Ill., 1954. C.L.U.; registered security rep. Advt. writer Caterpillar Tractor Co., 1956-58; ins. agent Equitable Life Assurance Soc., St. Charles, Ill., 1958—, ins. broker, 1972—; pres. Jack A. Young and Assocs., 1978—, Tax Sav Inc., St. Charles, 1983—; pres. Creative Brokerage, Inc., 1982—; pres., gen. securities prin. Chartered Planning, Ltd., 1985—; v.p. Old Mill Leasing Co., 1985—; past trustee Equitable CLU Assn.; past chmn. Equitable Nat. Agents Forum. Bd. dirs. Tri-City Family Services, 1975-83, pres., 1979-81; trustee Delnor Community Hosp. Systems, 1985—. Served to lt. (j.g.), USN, 1954-56. Named to Equitable Hall of Fame, 1978. Mem. Million Dollar Round Table (life), Am. Soc. C.L.U.s, Am. Coll. C.L.U. Golden Key Soc., Fox Valley Estate Planning Council, Internat. Assn. for Fin. Planning, Inc., Aurora Assn. Life Underwriters (past pres., nat. committeeman), Nat. Assn. Securities Dealers (registered prin.). Club: Geneva Golf. Home: 18 Campbell St Geneva IL 60134 Office: 28 N Bennett St Geneva IL 60134

YOUNG, JAMES ALLEN, lawyer; b. Dayton, Ohio, Apr. 24, 1932; s. J. Otis and Gladys (Riffle) Y.; m. Sally Kimmel, Oct. 23, 1954; children—James A., Jr., Jeffrey, Karen, Gregory. B.A., Ohio Wesleyan U., 1954; M.A. in Fgn. Affairs, George Washington U., 1958; J.D., Case Western Res. U., 1960. Bar: Ohio 1960. Assoc., Hahn, Loeser, Freedheim, Dean & Wellman, Cleve., 1960-67, ptnr., 1967—; dir. Garco Machinery, Inc., Cleve. Editor-in-chief Case Western Res. Law Rev., 1959-60. Trustee, sec. Goodwill Industries, Cleve., 1974—; pres. Nat. Jr. Tennis League, Inc., N.Y.C., 1975-79; founder, chmn. bd. Nat. Jr. Tennis League of Cleve., 1973—, vice chmn. com., 1985—; trustee Ohio Wesleyan U., 1972—, vice chmn. bd., 1984—; founding trustee, bd. dirs. Shaker Schs. Found., Cleve., 1982—; trustee Ch. of the Saviour, Cleve., 1973-83, 85—. Served with U.S. Army, 1954-56. Recipient Alumni award Ohio Wesleyan U., 1964; Applause award Cleve. Jaycees-Jr. League, 1976; Wolcott fellow George Washington U., 1958. Mem. Cleve. Bar Assn. (past chmn. young lawyers sect.), Ohio Bar Assn., ABA, Ohio Wesleyan U. Alumni Assn. (nat. pres. 1970-73), Order of Coif, Omicron Delta Kappa. Republican. Methodist. Clubs: Mid Day, Play House, Cleve. City University (Cleve.); Millcreek. Lodge: Masons. Avocations: tennis, reading, coaching youth sports. Home: 3308 Warrington Rd Shaker Heights OH 44120 Office: Hahn Loeser Freedheim Dean & Wellman 800 Nat City E 6th Bldg Cleveland OH 44114

YOUNG, JAMES EDWARD, lawyer; b. Painesville, Ohio, Apr. 20, 1946; s. James M. and Isabel P. (Rogers) Y. B.B.A., Ohio U., 1968; J.D., Ohio State U., 1972. Bar: Ohio 1972; Law clk. to chief judge U.S. Ct. Appeals, Nashville, 1972-73; chief counsel City of Cleve., 1980-81, law dir., 1981-82; assoc. Jones, Day, Reavis & Pogue, 1973-79, ptnr., 1983—. Office: Jones Day Reavis & Pogue 1700 Huntington Bldg Cleveland OH 44115

YOUNG, JEROME M., psychiatrist, educator; b. N.Y.C., Jan. 5, 1941; s. Henry and Sylvia (Adler) Y.; m. Deborah Miller, June 26, 1980. B.A., Lafayette Coll., Pa., 1962; M.D., U. Louisville, 1966. Diplomate Am. Bd. Psychiatry, 1977. Intern, Montefiore Hosp., Bronx, N.Y., 1966-67; resident NYU-Bellevue Hosp., 1967-70, staff/instr., 1970-73; staff Dayton VA Med. Ctr., Ohio, 1977-78, chief of psychiatry, 1978—; assoc. prof. Wright State U. Med. Sch., Dayton, 1982—; cons. USAF Med. Ctr., Dayton, 1978—. Served to lt. col. USAF, 1973-77. Fellow Acad. Psychosomatic Medicine; mem. Dayton Psychiat. Soc. (program chair 1984), Am. Psychiat. Assn., Ohio Med. Assn., Am. Soc. Clin. Hypnosis. Republican. Avocations: reading; swimming; walking. Home: 4617 Merrick Dr Dayton OH 45415 Office: 4100 W 3d St Dayton OH 45428

YOUNG, JERRY WAYNE, minister, science educator; b. Memphis, Oct. 2, 1946; s. Elmer Louis and Hazel Marie (Shell) Y.; m. Sandra Lee Henning, Mar. 6, 1971; children—Tara, Tasha, Tory. B.S., Memphis State U., 1969; M.Ed., Drury Coll., 1974; D.Min., Luther Rice Sem., 1979. Ordained to ministry, 1975. Cert. tchr. Chmn. sci. dept. Gainesville High Sch., Mo., 1969-79; prin. Temple Christian Sch., Dallas, 1979-81; prof., dean of students Bapt. Bible Coll., Springfield, Mo., 1981—; pastor Calvary Bapt. Ch., Gainesville, 1974-79; minister of edn. Pleasant Grove Bapt. Ch., Dallas, 1979-81; evangelist Cherry St. Bapt. Ch., Springfield, 1984—. Author: Creation and Evolution: A Serious Analysis, 1979. Contbr. articles to profl. jours. Republican. Avocations: fishing; gardening; art. Office: Bapt Bible Coll 628 E Kearney Springfield MO 65803

YOUNG, LAURENS DOLAN, psychiatrist; b. Chgo., Dec. 15, 1942; s. John Laurens and Viola Ann (Dolan) Y.; m. Joanne Mary Trimble, June 22, 1968; children—Jennifer, Elisabeth, Christina. A.B., Harvard U., 1965; M.D., U. Chgo., 1969. Diplomate Am. Bd. Psychiatry and Neurology. Intern, U. Ill.-Chgo., 1969-70; resident in psychiatry U. Wis.-Madison, 1970-74; asst. prof. Med. U. S.C., Charleston, 1974-76; asst. prof. Med. Coll. Wis., Milw., 1976-80, assoc. prof., 1980—; practice medicine specializing in psychiatry, Milw., Milw., 1982—; dir. dept. psychiatry Milw. County Med. Ctr., 1982—; head Div. Gen. Hosp. Psychiatry, Milw., 1982—. Contbr. articles to profl. jours. Fellow NSF, 1960, NIMH, 1967; recipient Research award in Alcoholism, Sumner Found., 1975. Mem. Wis. Psychiat. Assn. (councillor 1984, pres. elect Milw. chpt. 1985—). Clubs: Milw. Athletic; Union League (Chgo.). Avocations: squash; tennis; fishing; photography. Office: Milw County Med Complex PO Box 175 8700 W Wisconsin Ave Wauwatosa WI 53226

YOUNG, LESTER FRANK, agricultural engineer; b. Iola, Kans., Aug. 7, 1953; s. Kenneth Leroy and Eva Faye (Hunt) Y.; m. Sharon Kay Douglas, June 5, 1976; children—Sara Marie, Janice Elizabeth, Audrey Elaine. B.S. in Agrl. Engring., Kans. State U., 1975, M.S. in Agrl. Engring., 1977. Registered profl. engr., Kans., Mo. Research asst. Kans. State U., Manhattan, 1975-77, instr., 1977; cons. engr. Agrl. Engring. Assocs., Uniontown, Kans., 1977—. Mem. Am. Soc. Agrl. Engrs., Am. Congress Surveying and Mapping, U.S. Com. Irrigation and Drainage, Soil Conservation Soc. Am. Baptist. Home: Route 2 Erie KS 66733 Office: Agrl Engring Assocs Route 1 Uniontown KS 66779

YOUNG, MAXINE KATHERINE, accountant; b. Grand Rapids, Mich., Aug. 11, 1934; d. Peter and Gladys (Saltness) Vander Veen; m. Gerald Young, July 3, 1954; children—Kathleen Jo, Derk Alan, Daryl Evan. B.S. in Acctg., Ind. U., 1975. C.P.A., Ind. Data processor Grand Rapids Wholesale Grocers, 1951-54; staff acct. Deloitte, Haskins & Sells, C.P.A.s, Ft. Wayne, Ind., 1975-76; ptrn. Young & Co., CPAs, Ft. Wayne, 1976—. Democratic precinct vice-committeeman, 1971-72; treas. Carol Angel campaign, 1978; mem. audit rev. com. and ad hoc audit subcom. Ft. Wayne United Way, 1980. Recipient Dir.'s award SBA, 1977. Mem. Am. Inst. C.P.A.s, Ind. Soc. C.P.A.s, Am. Women's Soc. C.P.A.s, Am. Soc. Women Accts., Nat. Assn. Accts. (pres. Ft. Wayne chpt. 1984-85), Nat. Conf. C.P.A. Practitioners (dir.). Lutheran. Home: 8026 Manor Dr Fort Wayne IN 46825 Office: 202 W Berry St Fort Wayne IN 46802

YOUNG, MICHAEL ROBERT, pharmacist; b. Springfield, Mo., Apr. 18, 1956; s. Robert Floyd and Martha (Schmideskamp) Y. B.S. in Pharmacy, U. Okla., 1981; B.S. in Chemistry, So. Mo. State U., 1985. Registered pharmacist, Mo. Researcher, Drug Analysis Lab., Oklahoma City, 1979-80; student pharmacist Windham Pharmacy, Springfield, Mo., summer 1980, Bethany Gen. Hosp., Okla., 1980-81, Choctaw Pharmacy, Okla., 1980-81; pharmacy mgr. Wal-Mart Stores, Springfield, Mo., 1981-82; pharmacist St. John's Hosp., Springfield, 1982—; pharmacy cons. Mercy Villa Nursing Home, Springfield, 1983—. Recipient Music award Regional Music Contest, 1972; Logic Probability award So. Mo. State U., 1974. Mem. Ozark Soc. Hosp. Pharmacists, Am. Pharm. Assn., Mo. Pharm. Assn. (polit. action com. 1982—). Democrat. Methodist. Avocations: flying; photography; tennis; woodworking; fishing. Home: Route 2 Box 61 Strafford MO 65757

YOUNG, PAUL F., real estate executive; b. Shelbyville, Ind., Sept. 18, 1946; s. S. Maurice and Pauline (Clouse) Y.; m. Sandra M. Tracy, Feb. 12, 1977; children—Carolyn Christine, Alexandra Marie, Victoria Ann. A.B. in Econs., Muhlenberg Coll., 1971; M.B.A. in Fin., Pa. State U., 1973. Asst. regional dir. Mass. Mut. Life Ins. Co., Chgo., 1972-78; v.p. fin., Am. Invsco Corp., Chgo., 1978-79; exec. v.p. Kafka, Inc., Downers Grove, Ill., 1979-81; v.p. William G. Ceas & Co., Rolling Meadows, Ill., 1981-82; pres. Prime Realty, Inc., Chgo., 1983-84; pres. Focus Real Estate Securities Corp., Chgo., 1984—. Bd. dirs. United Way of Glen Ellyn, 1982—. Served to sgt. USMC, 1966-72. Mem. Mortgage Bankers Assn. Am., Real Estate Securities and Syndication Inst., Chgo. Real Estate Bd., Young Mortgage Bankers Chgo. (vice chmn. 1975-78). Office: Focus Real Estate Securities Corp 200 W Madison St Suite 3000 Chicago IL 60606

YOUNG, PEGGY SANBORN, psychologist, consultant; b. Painesville, Ohio, Aug. 25, 1926; d. Philip Harold and Josephine Diana (Masters) Sanborn; m. Philip Percy Young, Nov. 14, 1947 (div.); children—Philip Harold, Timothy Mark, Don Sanborn. B.S. in Edn., Baldwin Wallace Coll., 1956; M.A., Case Western Res. U., 1963; Ph.D., Kent State U., 1977. Cert. sch. adminstr., tchr., Ohio; lic. sch. psychologist, Ohio. Sch. psychologist, Mentor, Ohio, 1963-65, Tuslaw and Fairless Schs., Stork County, Ohio, 1965-67; vocat. psychologist Salvation Army Hosp., Cleve., 1961-62; chief psychologist, adminstr., Mentor Exempted Village Schs., 1967-75, coordinator spl. edn. and related services, 1975—; cons. psychologist. Mem. children's service bd. Lake County Welfare Dept.; mem. adv. bd. Comprehensive Regional Program for Hearing Impaired; psychologist, mem. adv. bd. Spl. Edn. Regional Resource Ctr. Mem. Am. Psychol. Assn., Nat. Assn. Sch. Psychologists, Ohio Psychol. Assn., Ohio Assn. Sch. Psychologists, Cleve. Area Sch. Psychologists. Republican. Episcopalian. Home: 9956 Johnnycake Ridge Apt C-5 Painesville OH 44077 Office: 6451 Center St Mentor OH 44060

YOUNG, RANDY MAURICE, psychologist, educator; b. Maryville, Mo., Aug. 6, 1952; s. Jack Maurice and Twyla Lee (Wolverton) Y.; m. Marjorie Louise Lasley, Aug. 22, 1975; children—James Allen, Timothy Lee. A.A., Iowa Western Community Coll., 1975; B.A., N.W. Mo. State U., 1977, M.S. in Counseling Psychology, 1979. Mental health worker Clarinda (Iowa) Treatment Complex, 1973-77, social work assoc., 1977-78, social worker, 1978-80, psychologist, 1980—, adminstrv. dir. alcohol and drug treatment unit, 1979—, also pres. clin. staff orgn.; instr. Iowa Western Community Coll.; outpatient therapist Waubonsie Mental Health Service, 1982-83. Bd. dirs. S.W. Iowa Family Systems Project, 1978-80. Mem. Am. Psychol. Assn. (assoc.). Baptist. Home: 609 W Nishna Clarinda IA 51632 Office: Clarinda Treatment Complex PO Box 338 Clarinda IA 51632

YOUNG, ROBERT ANTON, congressman; b. St. Louis, Nov. 27, 1923; s. Melvin A. and Margaret (Degnan) Y.; student pub. schs., St. Louis; m. Irene Slawson, Nov. 27, 1947; children—Anne Young Lewis, Robert A., Margaret Mary. Mem. 95th-99th Congresses from 2d Mo. Dist., mem. Pub. Works and Transp. Com., Sci. and Tech. Com.; Democratic committeeman Airport Twp., St. Louis County, 1952-77; mem. Mo. Ho. of Reps., 1956-62; mem. Mo. Senate, 1962-76. Mem. Pipefitters Union, Am. Legion, VFW (post comdr.), Amvets (life). Club: St. Ann Lions. Recipient awards for meritorious service St. Louis Globe Democrat, 1972, 74, 76. Office: 4150 Cypress Rd Saint Ann MO 63074 also 2430 Rayburn Bldg Washington DC 20515

YOUNG, ROBERT BRUCE, lawyer, real estate broker; b. Chgo., June 23, 1936; s. James T. and Julia A. (Frey) Y.; m. Janice C. Crowhurst, Aug. 12, 1961; children—Robert W., William J., Leslie B. B.S. in Engring., Millikin U., 1959; J.D., John Marshall Law Sch., 1978. Bar: Ill. 1978, U.S. Dist. Ct. (no. dist.) Ill. 1978. Assoc., Gifford, Detuno & Gifford, Ltd., Chgo., 1978—. Served with U.S. Army, 1959-61. Mem. ABA, Ill. Bar Assn., Workers Compensation Lawyers Assn. Home: 4056 Ellington St Western Springs IL 60558 Office: Gifford Detuno & Gifford 221 N LaSalle St Chicago IL 60601

YOUNG, ROBERT LAWRENCE, ophthalmologist, educator; b. Harlem, Mont., Oct. 25, 1918; s. Morris David and Esther Rae (Urkov) Yampolsky; B.S., U. Ill., 1940, M.D., 1943; m. Roberta Sternberg, Oct. 10, 1943; children—Fredric, Barbara, James, Michael. Intern, Michael Reese Hosp., Chgo., 1944, resident, 1949-50; resident U. Ill. Hosp., 1948-49, Aspinwall VA Hosp., Pitts., 1950; practice medicine specializing in ophthalmology, Gary, Ind., 1951-74, Munster, Ind., 1974—; mem. staff, pres. St. Mary of Mercy Hosp., Gary; sr. staff Meth. Hosp., Ind. U. Hosp., both Gary, Community Hosp., Munster, Ind.; mem. adv. com. Ind. U. N.W. br. Med. Sch.; asst. prof. ophthalmology Ind. U. Bd. dirs. Munster Community Hosp. Served to capt. M.C., AUS, 1946-48. Diplomate Am. Bd. Ophthalmology. Fellow Internat. Coll. Surgeons; mem. AMA, Assn. Research in Ophthalmology, World Med. Assn., Am. Acad. Ophthalmology, Ind., N.W. Ind., Chgo. ophthalmology socs., AAAS, Ind., Munster chambers commerce, Tau Delta Phi, Phi Delta Epsilon. Democrat. Jewish (temple mens' club). Clubs: B'nai B'rith. Home: 8809 Crestwood Munster IN 46321 Office: 1646 45th Ave Munster IN 46321

YOUNG, ROBERT MANNING, educational administrator; b. Butler County, Pa., June 2, 1928; s. Jesse Hamilton and Margaret Blanche (Pounds) Y.; m. Opal Roberta Newton, July 16, 1948; 1 dau., Roberta Lynn. B.S., Indiana State Coll., Pa., 1958; M.S., U. Mich., 1962; Ed.D., Wayne State U., 1972. Cert. secondary sch. adminstr., Mich. Tchr. Dearborn Schs., Mich., 1958-66, asst. prin. sr. high sch., 1966-72, prin. Bryant Jr. High Sch., 1972—; instr. bus. Henry Ford Community Coll., Dearborn, 1977—. Contbr. articles to profl. jours. Chmn. bd. Fairlane Family YMCA, Dearborn, 1976-77; mem. long-range planning com. Met. Detroit YMCA, 1979—. Mem. Nat. Assn. Secondary Sch. Prins., Dearborn Sch. Adminstrs. Assn. (pres. 1971-72, negotiator 1978—), Dearborn Fedn. Tchrs. (treas. 1964-65), Phi Delta Kappa, Delta Phi Epsilon. Presbyterian. Lodges: Masons, Elks, Rotary (pres. 1980-81, pres. found. 1984—, Paul Harris fellow 1981, bd. dirs. 1975-82). Avocations: water skiing, gardening. Home: 1510 Belmont Dr Dearborn MI 48128 Office: Bryant Jr High Sch 460 N Vernon St Dearborn MI 48128

YOUNG, SHELDON MIKE, lawyer, author; b. Cleve., Aug. 27, 1926; s. Jack and Rae (Goldenberg) Y.; m. Margery Ann Polster, Dec. 25, 1948; children—Jeffrey, Martin, Janet. B.A., Ohio State U., 1948, LL.B., 1951; LL.M., Case Western Res. U., 1962. Bar: Ohio 1951, U.S. Dist. Ct. (no. dist.) Ohio. Gen. counsel Eugene M. Klein & Assocs., Actuaries, Cleve., 1952-72; assoc. Shapiro, Persky & Marken, Cleve., 1972-74; counsel pension tech. services dept. CNA Ins., Chgo., 1974-76; ptnr. Weiss & Young, Cleve., 1976; of counsel Arter & Hadden, Cleve., 1977-85, Squire, Sanders & Dempsey, Cleve., 1985—; instr. Case Western Res. U. Law Sch., 1962-82, U. Akron Law Sch., 1984—. Author: Pension and Profit Sharing Plans, 5 vols.; contbr. articles to profl. jours. Served with USN, World War II. Recipient award Nathan Burkan Meml. Copyright Competition, 1951. Mem. ABA, Cleve. Bar Assn., Ohio Bar Assn. Democrat. Jewish. Lodge: Mason. Office: Suite 1800 Huntington Bldg Cleveland OH 44115

YOUNG, STEPHEN BONSAL, law school dean, educator; b. Washington, Nov. 2, 1945; s. Kenneth Todd and Patricia (Morris) Y.; m. Hoa Thi Pham, Mar. 22, 1970; children—Ian, Warren, Antonia. A.B., Harvard U., 1967, J.D., 1974. Bar: N.Y. Chief village devel. AID, Saigon, Vietnam, 1968-71; assoc. Simpson, Thatcher & Bartlett, N.Y.C., 1974-78; asst. dean Harvard U. Law Sch., Cambridge, Mass., 1978-80, research assoc., 1978-81; dean Hamline U. Law Sch., St. Paul, 1981—. Author: Virtue and Law: Human Rights in Traditional China and Vietnam; Understanding Vietnam. Contbr. articles to profl. jours. Mem., Citizens Commn. for Indochinese Refugees, N.Y.C., 1978—; mem. Jud. Planning Commn., Minn., 1982—; dir. Hmong Farming Coop., Minn., 1983—, Resources for Child Caring, Minn., 1984—. Mem. Council on Fgn. Relations, ABA, Minn. State Bar Assn. (bd. govs. 1981—). Clubs: University, Minnesota (St. Paul). Advocation: archaeologic discovery. Office: Hamline U Law Sch 1536 Hewitt Ave Saint Paul MN 55104

YOUNG, THOMAS EARL, English educator; b. Baldwin, Mich., Dec. 22, 1948; s. Sidney Earl and Edith Irene (Andersen) Y.; m. Soon Hyo-Sun Pak, Aug. 28, 1973; children—Stephanie Lynn, Steven Thomas. B.A., Grand Valley State Coll., Allendale, Mich., 1971; M.A., Mich. State U., 1974, Ph.D., 1980. Instr. English, Tri-State U., Angola, Ind., 1974-75, 77-79, asst. prof., 1979-83, assoc. prof., 1983—, chmn. dept. English, 1983—; grad. asst. Mich. State U., East Lansing, 1976-77. Mem. Ind. Tchrs. Writing, Ind. Coll. English Assn., Angola Community Theatre, Coll. English Assn. Avocation: music. Home: 800 Pine Run Dr Angola IN 46703 Office: Tri-State U 200 S Darling Angola IN 46703

YOUNG, THOMAS LEE, lawyer; b. Los Angeles, Feb. 21, 1944; s. J. Donald and Nancy M. Young; m. Kathleen Grace Jacob, Sept. 10, 1967; children—Barbara, Deborah, Amy. Student Marquette U., 1963; B.A., St. John's Coll., 1966; J.D., Notre Dame U., 1972; postgrad. Harvard U., 1984-85. Bar: Ohio. Assoc. Fuller, Henry, Hodge & Snyder, Toledo, 1972-75; assoc. counsel Scott Paper Co., Phila., 1975-76; asst. gen counsel Owens-Ill., Inc., Toledo, 1976—; dir. Prudent Supply, Inc., Mpls., Health Group, Inc., Nashville, Cajas Corrugadas de Mex., Mexico City. Asst. sec. Greater Toledo Corp. Served to 1st lt. U.S. Army, 1966-69, Vietnam. Mem. ABA, Ohio State Bar Assn., Toledo Bar Assn. Roman Catholic. Avocations: tennis. Office: Owens-Illinois Inc One SeaGate Toledo OH 43666

YOUNG, VERNON LEWIS, lawyer; b. Seaman, Ohio, Oct. 13, 1919; s. Ezra S. and Anna (Bloom) Y.; m. Eileen Humble, Sept. 20, 1941; children—Robert, Loretta, Bettie Jo., Jon W., Denise L. Student Alfred Holbrook Coll., 1938-39; J.D., Ohio No. U., 1942. Bar: Ohio 1942. Sole practice, West Union, Ohio, 1942-50, 78-81; ptnr. Young & Young, West Union, 1959-78, Young & Caldwell, West Union, 1981—; spl. councel Office of Atty. Gen., State of Ohio, West Union, solicitor Cities of Jamestown, Seaman, Winchester, Manchester, Ohio; pros. atty. Adams County, Ohio, 1952-56, acting county judge, 1968-79. Mayor City of Seaman, 1944-46; mem. Adams County Health Bd., West Union, 1968-75; chmn. membership com. Eastern Shore Inst. Lifelong Learning, Fairhope, Ala., 1983-84; mem. Republican Presdl. Task Force, 1980—. Mem. Ohio State Bar Assn., Adams County Bar Assn. (former pres.), Sigma Delta Kappa (chancellor 1940). Lodges: Masons, Lions (pres. 1950-51, dist. gov. 1951-52). Avocations: fishing; hunting; gardening. Home: 10 Hickory Dr Seaman OH 45679

YOUNG, VIRGINIA GARTON, lecturer, author; b. Mountain View, Mo., Jan. 16, 1919; d. Charles Clinton and Mattie Belle (Cartwright) Garton; m. Raymond Arthur Young, June 18, 1940; 1 son, David Bruce. A.B., So. Mo. State U., 1939; M.L.S., U. Okla., 1940; H.H.D. (hon.) Tarkio Coll., 1978, U. Mo., 1982. Mem., past pres. Mo. State Library Commn., 1956-66, Columbia (Mo.) Pub. Library Bd., 1953—; mem. adv. com. to U.S. Commr. of Edn., Library Services br. HEW, 1960-65; mem. exec. bd. Nat. Book Com., 1967-74; trustee Am. Library in Paris, 1968-73; mem., past. chmn. Mo. Coordinating Bd. for Higher Edn., 1974-82; mem. adv. com. for White House Conf. on Library and Info. Services, 1975-79; mentor Assn. Governing Bds. (higher edn.), 1977; mem. Carnegie Found. adv. panel on governance, 1980-82; cons., workshop dir. Library Trustees and Library Systems; guest lectr. Library Schs. Columbia U., La. State U., U. Mo.; past pres., bd. mem. Friends of U. Mo. Library, 1960—; del. Internat. Fedn. Library Assns., 1965—; trustee Mo. Council on Econ. Edn., 1983—. Editor: The Trustee of a Small Public Library, 1962, rev. edit., 1977, Japanese edit., 1970; The Library Trustee: A Practical Guidebook, 1964, rev. edit., 1969, Spanish edit., 1974. Contbr. numerous articles to library periodicals. Pres. Columbia LWV; hon. commr. Mo. Am. Revolution Bicentennial Commn.; active mem. Def. Adv. Com. of Women in the Services, U.S. Dept. Def., 1963-65; vice chmn. Citizens Adv. Com. on Legis. Modernization, 1973-75; sec. Mo. Press-Bar Commn., 1974—. Mem. ALA (trustee citation of merit 1962), Am. Library Trustee Assn. (pres. 1959-61), Mo. Library Assn. (pres. 1967-68, meritorious achievement award 1956). Home: 10 E Parkway Dr Columbia MO 65203

YOUNG, WILLIAM CHARLES, food equipment company executive; b. Manitowoc, Wis., Oct. 9, 1940; s. Raymond Charles and Ida Caroline (Wernecke) Y.; m. Bonnie Lue, July 13, 1968. B.S., U. Wis., 1963. Sales mgmt. trainee Firestone Tire Co., Akron, Ohio, 1963-65; dist. mgr. Chrysler Corp., Los Angeles, 1965-69; sales mgr. Container Devel. Corp., Watertown, Wis., 1969-77, Stoelting, Inc., Kiel, Wis., 1977-85; gen. sales mgr. Manitowoc Equipment Works, Wis., 1985—. Elder Good Shepherd Lutheran Ch., Plymouth, Wis., 1979—. Mem. United Soft Service Assn. (bd. dirs. 1979-85), Nat. Assn. Food Equipment Mfrs. Republican. Avocations: restoring old cars; photography. Home: Route 3 Burkshire Ln Plymouth WI 53073 Office: Manitowoc Equipment Works 2110 S 26th St Manitowoc WI 54220

YOUNGER, KENNETH WAYNE, human resources and management consultant; b. Jacksonville, Fla., Oct. 26, 1951; s. Ralph B., Jr. and Henrietta (Wingate) Y.; m. Nancy Lynn Ford, June 5, 1971; children—Kenan, Lynden. B.A., Carson-Newman Coll., 1972; M.S., Okla. State U., 1974, Ph.D., 1975. Asst. prof. psychology and computer sci. Calumet Coll., Whiting, Ind., 1975-76; asst. prof. psychology Carson-Newman Coll., Jefferson City, Tenn., 1976-79; project mgr. mgmt. devel. Arthur Andersen & Co., Chgo., 1979-80; v.p. Drake Beam Morin Inc., Chgo., 1980-82; mng. ptnr. Savard Younger Cons. Group, Chgo., 1982—. Adj. prof.; guest lectr. Recipient Outstanding Sci. Achievement award U.S. Navy, 1969; Meritorious Research award Okla. Psychol. Assn., 1973; Outstanding Faculty Service award Carson-Newman Student Found., 1977; NSF scholar, 1967; Regents scholar State of Fla., 1969. Mem. Greater O'Hare Assn. Industry and Commerce, U.S. Jaycees (Outstanding Young Am. 1981), Tenn. Squires, Phi Kappa Phi. Baptist. Office: 8600 W Bryn Mawr Ave Suite 200 N Chicago IL 60631

YOUNGMAN, OWEN RALPH, newspaper editor; b. Chgo., Apr. 24, 1953; s. Ralph Elmer and Charlotte Earldine (Ottoson) Y.; m. Linda Ann Erlandson, Aug. 24, 1975. B.A., North Park Coll., 1975. Sportswriter Ashtabula Star-Beacon, Ohio, 1969-71; office clerk Chgo. Tribune, 1971-73, transcriber, 1973-75, copy editor, slotman, 1976-79, copy chief, news editor, 1979-83, dep. sports editor, 1984—. Mem. Evangelical Covenant Ch. Club: President's Club of North Park Coll. Avocations: philately; personal computing. Home: 2309-E W Greenleaf Ave Chicago IL 60645 Office: Chicago Tribune 435 N Michigan Ave Chicago IL 60611

YOUNGS, JOHN OMER, III, office products manufacturing executive; b. Chgo., Feb. 11, 1953; s. John Omer and Mary Elizabeth (Wienke) Y.; m. Susan Kay Kaspar, May 26, 1974; children—Jacqueline Kay, Kelly Anne. B.S.B.A., No. Ill. U., 1974; mgmt. cert. U. Minn., 1983. Sales rep. Philip Morris U.S.A., Chgo., 1974-75, div. mgr., 1975-79, dir. nat. accounts, 1979-80; Midwest regional mgr. Jostens, Inc., Mpls., 1980, nat. sales mgr., 1980-82, dir. sales and mktg., 1982-83, v.p./gen. mgr., 1983—. Mem. Nat. Office Products Assn., Young Execs. Forum. Patentee data binder slide design. Office: 939 W 35th St Chicago IL 60609

YOUNGSTEADT, NORMAN STANLEY, agricultural products marketing executive; b. Chattanooga, Oct. 23, 1926; s. Ralph Wilhelm and Edith Margaret (Simpson) Y.; m. Mary Lillian Young, Nov. 14, 1944 (dec. July 1966); children—Norman S., Barbara Ann, Denise Gayle; m. Noubhar Mohammed Abdul Nabi, May 6, 1972. B.A., U. N.C., 1948; postgrad. Art Inst., Chgo., 1948-50. Assoc. mng. editor Progressive Farmer, Birmingham, Ala., 1955-60; agrl. info. advisor U.S. AID, Dept. State, Khartoum, Sudan, 1960-64; editor So. Living, Birmingham, 1964-65; mng. editor Progressive Farmer, Birmingham, 1965-66; agrl. info. advisor U.S. AID, State Dept., Addis Ababa, Ethiopia, 1966-69; dir. internat. mktg. programs Internat. Minerals & Chem. Corp., Mundelein, Ill., 1969—; mem. adv. bd. Internat. Devel. Inst., Washington, 1982—; dir., organizer IMC World Food Prodn. Confs., 1970—. Served with USN, 1944-46. Mem. Nat. Fertilizer Solutions Assn. (com. mem. 1983—), Fertilizer Inst., Internat. Fertilizer Assn., Chgo. Council on Fgn. Relations. Republican. Episcopalian. Home: 213 Atlantic Dr Vernon Hills IL 60061 Office: Internat Minerals and Chem Corp 421 E Hawley St Mundelein IL 60060

YOUNT, KATHY CHRISTINE, educator; b. Poplar Bluff, Mo., Oct. 6, 1947; d. Chris F. and Kathryn Elizabeth (Short) Scheihing; m. Michael Ray Yount, June 1, 1968; children—Michelle Renee, Melody Rae, Mark Richard. B.S. in Edn., U. Mo.-Columbia, 1979. Cert. tchr., Mo. Office clerk Black River Cooperative, Fredericktown, Mo., 1967-68; typist U. Mo.-Rolla Library, 1968-70; sec. Calvary Baptist Ch., Jefferson City, Mo., 1971-72; bus. instr. Mexico (Mo.) Area Vocat. Sch., 1979—. Mem. Am. Vocat. Assn., Mo. Vocat. Assn., Mo. Bus. Edn. Assn., PTA. Baptist. Home: 1514 Webster Dr Mexico MO 65265 Office: 905 N Wade Mexico MO 65265

YOURZAK, ROBERT JOSEPH, management consultant, educator; b. Mpls., Aug. 27, 1947; s. Ruth Phyllis Sorenson. B.C.E., U. Minn., 1969; M.S.C.E., U. Wash., 1971, M.B.A., 1975. Surveyor N.C. Hoium & Assocs., Mpls., 1965-68, Lot Surveys Co., Mpls., 1968-69; site layout engr. Sheehy Constrn. Co., St. Paul, 1968; structural engring. aide Dunham Assocs., Mpls., 1969; aircraft and aerospace structural engr., program rep. Boeing Co., Seattle, 1969-75; engr., estimator Howard S. Wright Constrn. Co., Seattle, 1976-77; dir. project devel. and adminstrn. DeLeuw Cather & Co., Seattle, 1977-78; sr. mgmt. cons. Alexander Grant & Co., Mpls., 1978-79; mgr. project systems dept., project mgr. Henningson, Durham & Richardson, Mpls., 1979-80; dir. project mgmt., regional offices Ellerbe Assocs., Inc., Mpls., 1980-81; pres. Robert Yourzak & Assocs., Mpls., 1981—; lectr. engring. mgmt. U. Wash., 1977-78; adj. asst. prof. dept. civil and mineral engring. and mech./indsl. engring. Inst. Tech., mgmt. scis. dept. Sch. Mgmt., U. Minn., 1979—; founding mem., mem. membership com., mem. univ./industry programs com. U. Minn., 1983—; mem. Minn. High Tech. Council, 1983—. Chmn. regional art group experience Seattle Art Mus., 1975-78; mem. Pacific N.W. Arts Council, 1977-78, ex-officio adviser Mus. Week, 1976; bd. dirs. Friends of the Rep. Seattle Repertory Theatre, 1973-77; mem. Symphonics Seattle Symphony Orch., 1975-78. Scholar Boeing Co., 1967-68, Sheehy Constrn. Co., summer 1967. Named An Outstanding Young Man of Am., U.S. Jaycees, 1978. Registered profl. engr., Wash., Minn. Mem. Am. Soc. Tng. and Devel., Project Mgmt. Inst. (founding pres. 1985, program com. chmn. and organizing com. mem. Minn. chpt. 1984, project mgr. nat. mktg. program 1985—), Am. Cons. Engrs. Council, Assn. Systems Mgmt., Data Processing Mgmt. Assn., Minn. Surveyors and Engrs. Soc., ASCE (chmn. continuing edn. subcom. Seattle chpt. 1976-79, chmn. program com. 1978, mem. transp. and urban planning tech. group 1978, Edmund Friedman Young Engr. award for profl. achievement 1979, chmn. continuing edn. subcom. 1979-80, chmn. energy com. Minn. chpt. 1980-81, sec. bd. dirs. 1981-83, v.p. profl. services 1983-84, v.p. info. services 1984-85, pres.-elect 1985-86), Inst. Indsl. Engrs. (pres. Twin Cities chpt. 1985-86), Cons. Engrs. Council Minn. (chmn. pub. relations com. 1983-85), Mpls. Soc. Fine Arts, Chi Epsilon (life). Clubs: Rainier (co-chmn. Oktoberfest), Sierra, Chowder Soc., Mountaineers. Author: Project Management and Motivating and Managing the Project Team, 1984. Office: 7320 Gallagher Dr 325 Minneapolis MN 55435

YU, ANNE RAMONA WING-MUI, psychologist; b. Hong Kong, Apr. 9, 1948; came to U.S., 1968, naturalized, 1974; d. Hing-wan and Sin-wah (Yau) Yu; B.A. with honors in Psychology, Ohio U., 1971; M.A., So. Ill. U., 1975. Psychol. examiner Delta Counseling and Guidance Center, Monticello, Ark., 1975-76; psychologist Mid-Nebr. Community Mental Health Center, Grand Island, Nebr., 1977—; supr. satellite clinic Loup Valley Mental Health Center, Loup City, Nebr., 1978-79; project dir. Protection from Domestic Abuse, 1978-79; pres. Taskforce on Domestic Violence and Sexual Assault, Grand Island, 1980-82. Mem. mem. Mental Health Bd. Hall County, 1979; mem. fellows Menninger Found., 1983-84; bd. dirs. YWCA, 1984—. Ohio U. Psi Chi scholar, 1968-71. Mem. Nebr. Assn. Profl. Psychologists (membership chmn. 1977-78), Am. Psychol. Assn., Nebr. Assn. for Marriage and Family Therapy (v.p. 1981-84, pres. elect 1984-85, pres. 1985-87), Am. Assn. Sex Educators, Counselors, and Therapists, AAUW (pres. Grand Island chpt. 1984-86), Internat. Platform Assn., Asian-Am. Psychol. Assn. Home: Apt 97 1524 Coventry Ln Grand Island NE 68801 Office: Mid-Nebr Community Mental Health Center 914 Baumann Dr Grand Island NE 68801

YU, JOHN K(UO-AN), hydrologist, consultant; b. Tsingtao, China, July 10, 1944; came to U.S., 1971, naturalized, 1982; s. Wen Hao and Ming Yueh (Sun) Y.; m. Gloria C. Tsui-Tao Chang, Oct. 10, 1971; children—Muhan Samuel, Muchueh Ann. B.S., Taiwan Provincial Chung Hsing U., Taichung, 1968; M.S., U. Ariz., 1974, Ph.D., 1977. Irrigation engr. Taiwan Sugar Corp., 1969-71; research assoc. U. Ariz., 1971-73, grad. research assoc., 1973-77, grad. research asst., 1977-78; sr. hydrologist VTN Consol., Irvine, Calif., 1978-80; sr. geohydrologist Tera Corp., Berkeley, Calif., 1980-81, Morrison-Knudsen, Boise, Idaho, 1981-82; project mgr., hydrogeologist Soil Exploration Co., St. Paul, 1982—; cons. in field. Served to 2d lt. inf. Chinese Nat. Army, 1968-69. Mem. Am. Water Resources Assn., Am. Geophys. Union, Nat. Water Well Assn., Soil Sci. Soc. Am., Minn. Ground Water Assn. Home: 1168 W Roselawn Ave Roseville MN 55113 Office: 662 Cromwell Ave Saint Paul MN 55114

YU, RONALD KER-WEI, engineer, real estate investor; b. Penang, Malaysia, July 23, 1958; came to U.S., 1962; s. Frank Chung-Tien and Helen (Goh). B.S. in Mech. Engring., Rensselaer Poly. Inst., 1979; M.B.A., U. Mich., 1981. Research asst. Hwy. Safety Research Inst., Ann Arbor, 1979-80; assoc. Hunan Restaurant, N.Y.C., 1974; banking asst. Bank Am., N.Y.C., 1975-77; engr. Colt Crucible Steel Co., Syracuse, 1978; investment analyst Beneficial Capital Corp., N.Y.C., 1979; systems engr. IBM, Southfield, Mich., 1980—; cons. IBM, 1980—; photographer, Garden City, Mich., 1978—. Editor: Transit, 1979. Lang. instr. United Meth. Ch., Jackson Heights, N.Y., 1980. Mem. Soc. Automotive Engrs. (assoc.), Am. Mgmt. Assn., Assn. M.B.A.s, Pi Tau Sigma. Republican. Methodist. Clubs: Rensselaer Poly. Inst. Alumni Assn. (treas. Detroit 1983—), Photo Techniques Guild, IBM Club (dir. 1983—). Home: 501 Henry Ruff Rd Garden City MI 48135 Office: IBM 18000 W 9 Mile Rd Southfield MI 48037

YU, SHIU YEH, chemistry educator, consultant; b. ChanHwa, China, June 1, 1926; came to U.S., 1952, naturalized, 1965; s. Cheh and Eng (Su) Y.; m. Noriko Murata, Feb. 28, 1958; 1 child, Kiyoshi M. B.S., Taiwan Provincial Coll., 1951; M.S., Okla. State U., 1955; Ph.D., St. Louis U., 1963. Chemist, Taiwan Indsl. Research Inst., Taipei, China, 1951-52; research assoc. Inst. Exptl. Pathology, Jewish Hosp., St. Louis, 1955-62; clin. lab. cons. St. Louis Hosp. and Sch. for Mental Retarded Children, 1968-69; cons. clin. chemistry, 1966-68; research asst. prof. dept. internal medicine Washington U., St. Louis, 1972-78, clin. asst. prof., dept. pathology, 1978-83, research assoc. prof. dept. medicine, 1983—; cons. TOA Electronics, Tokyo, 62-72. Contbr. articles for profl. jours. Recipient NIH grantee, 1958-65, 72-78, 83—. Mem. Biochem. Soc. of London, Am. Assn. of Pathologists, Council of Atherosclerosis, Am. Heart Assn., Soc. of Exptl. Biology and Medicine, Sigma Xi. Buddhist. Avocations: horse riding; mountain climbing. Office: VA Hosp Jefferson Barracks Saint Louis MO 63125

YUILL, THOMAS MACKAY, university administrator, microbiology educator; b. Berkeley, Calif., June 14, 1937; s. Joseph Stuart and Louise (Dunlop) Y.; m. Ann Warnes, Aug. 24, 1960; children—Eileen, Gwen. B.S., Utah State U., 1959; M.S., U. Wis., 1962, Ph.D., 1964. Lab. officer Walter Reed Army Inst. Research, Washington, 1964-66; med. biologist SEATO Med. Research Lab., Bangkok, Thailand, 1966-68; asst. prof. U. Wis.-Madison, 1968-72, assoc. prof., 1972-76, prof., 1976—, dept. chmn., 1979-82, assoc. dean., 1982; cons. NIH, Bethesda, 1976—; chmn. Viral Diseases Panel, U.S.-Japan Biomed. Scis. Program, 1979—, Am. Com. Arbovirology, 1982—. Contbr. chpts. to books, articles to profl. jours. Served to capt. U.S. Army, 1964-66. Recipient grants state and fed. govts., 1968—. Mem. Orgn. Tropical Studies (pres. 1979-85), Wildlife Disease Assn. (treas. 1980-85, pres. 1985—), Am. Soc. Tropical Medicine and Hygiene (editorial bd. 1984—), Royal Soc. Tropical Medicine and Hygiene, Am. Soc. Microbiology, Am. Soc. Virology, Wildlife Soc., Council Agrl. Sci. and Tech., Sigma Xi. Avocations: flying; cross-country skiing; music. Office: U Wis Sch Vet Medicine 2015 Linden Dr W Madison WI 53706

YUNG, CHEUK WO, dermatologist; b. Hong Kong, Jan. 17, 1949; came to U.S., 1969, naturalized, 1974; s. Hau S. and Bun C. (Mui) Y.; m. Betsy K. Poon, May 30, 1977; children—Sophia, Steve. B.S., Columbia U., 1972; M.D., NYU, 1977. Diplomate Am. Bd. Dermatology. Intern Maimonides Med. Ctr., Bklyn., 1977-78; resident Cin. Med. Ctr., 1978-79; resident U. Chgo. Med. Ctr., 1979-80; chief resident, 1980-81, instr., 1981-82; practice medicine specializing in dermatology, Orland Park, Ill., 1982—; cons. Oak Forest Hosp., Ill., Palos Community Hosp., Holy Cross Hosp., Chgo. Contbr. articles to profl. jours. Bd. dirs. Chinatown Planning Council, N.Y.C., 1971. Fellow Am. Bd. Dermatology, Am. Acad. Dermatology; mem. AMA, Chgo. Med. Soc., Ill. Med Soc. Home: 13629 Idlewild Dr Orland Park IL 60462 Office: 64 Orland Square Dr Orland Park IL 60462

YUZON, FLORENCIO ESTAVILLO, physician; b. Ilocos Norte, Philippines, Oct. 23, 1941; came to U.S., 1965; s. Florencio A. and Julia (Estavillo) Y.; M.D., U. Santo Tomas, Philippines, 1964. Intern, St. Mary Hosp., Hoboken, N.J., 1965-66; med. resident Grasslands Hosp., Valhalla, N.Y., 1966-68; fellow Martland Hosp., Newark, N.J., 1968-70, chief med. resident, 1970-71; practice medicine specializing in internal medicine, Lorain, Ohio, 1974—; instr. dept. medicine N.J. Coll. Medicine, Newark, 1968-72, asst. prof., 1973-74; attending gastroenterologist Martland Hosp., 1971-74, full attending physician, 1972-74; chief staff, bd. dirs., mem. exec. com. Lorain Community Hosp., chief med. staff, 1979-80, 81-82; mem. staff Amherst (Ohio) Hosp., St. Joseph Hosp., Lorain; pres. HCM Lab., Physicians Med. Care Ctr., Inc., Urgent Care Ctr. Trustee Lake Ridge Acad. Diplomate Am. Bd. Internal Medicine; named One of Outstanding Faculty Members, N.J. Med. Sch., 1970-71. Mem. Am. Soc. Gastroenterology, AMA. Roman Catholic. Office: 3885 Oberlin Ave Lorain OH 44053

ZABECKI, DAVID TADEUSZ, quality engr.; b. Springfield, Mass., Aug. 8, 1947; s. Julian Tadeusz and Virginia Charlotte (Luthgren) Z.; B.A., Xavier U., 1972, M.A., 1973; M.S., Fla. Inst. Tech., 1976; 1 son, Konrad Josef. Patrolman, Xavier U. Campus Police, Cin., 1972-74; quality assurance specialist Rock Island (Ill.) Aresenal, 1974-77; quality engr. Deere & Co., Moline, Ill., 1977—; adj. instr. Fla. Inst. Tech., 1977-79; lectr. in field. Served with U.S. Army, 1966-69; capt. Ill. N.G. Decorated Combat Infantryman's Badge, Bronze Star, Army Commendation medal, others. Mem. Am. Soc. Quality Control (sr. mem., cert. quality and reliability engr.), Res. Officers Assn., Am., German philatelic socs., V.F.W., Co. Mil. Historians, Royal Arty. Assn., Nat. Eagle Scouts Assn., Alpha Sigma Nu. Author: Karl Doenitz: A Defense, 1972; Field Artillery in the 1980's, 1983; also articles; developer contbn. differential concept of quality cost analysis. Home: 29 Oak Ln Davenport IA 52803 Office: John Deere Harvester Works East Moline IL 61244

ZABEL, HARTMUT, educator, research physicist; b. Radolfzell, Germany, Mar. 21, 1946; came to U.S., 1978; s. Gerhard and Klara (Hirling) Z.; m. Rosemarie Havers, Dec. 12, 1973; children—Cordula Daphne, Astrid Mirijam, Julia Elisabeth. Vordiplom, U. Bonn, 1969; diploma Technische U. Munich, 1973; Ph.D., U. Munich, 1978. Research assoc. U. Houston, 1978-79; asst. prof. U. Ill., Urbana, 1979-83, assoc. prof., 1983—. Author sci. publs. Mem. Deutsche Physik Gesellschaft, Am. Phys. Soc., Materials Research Soc. Office: U Ill 1110 W Green St Urbana IL 61801

ZABEL, JERRY, manufacturing company executive; b. Feldafing, Fed. Republic Germany, Jan. 5, 1947, came to U.S., 1949, naturalized, 1955; s. Sam and Sara (Turetz) Z.; m. Diane L. Silverman, Feb. 16, 1969; children—Steven, Rachel, Brian, Tracy. B.B.A., Roosevelt U., 1974, M.B.A., 1978. Factory mgr. Hart Schaffner & Marx, Chgo., 1969-74; planner Abbott Labs., North Chicago, Ill., 1974-79; mgr. Addressograph Multigraph, Mt. Prospect, Ill., 1979-80; dir. Internat. Jensen, Schiller Park, Ill., 1980—; instr. Webster Coll., Fort Sheridan, Ill., 1981, Columbia Coll., Fort Sheridan, 1978-81. Served with U.S. Army, 1965-68, Vietnam. Decorated. Mem. Am. Prodn. and Inventory Control Soc., Internat. Material Mgmt. Soc., Cosmopolitan C. of C. (Cert. of Appreciation 1974). Home: 1203 Devonshire Buffalo Grove IL 60090

ZABRANSKY, RONALD JOSEPH, microbiologist; b. Little Ferry, N.J., Mar. 18, 1935; s. Joseph and Anna (Engleberger) Z.; m. Suzanne Elizabeth Tolson, Aug. 16, 1958; children—Gwenn Elizabeth, Neal Joseph, Mark William. B.S. in Biology, Rutgers State U., 1956; M.S. in Microbiology, Ohio State U., 1961; Ph.D. in Microbiology, 1963. Diplomate Am. Bd. Med. Microbiology. Prin. bacteriologist Battelle Meml. Inst., Columbus, Ohio, 1959-61; research asst. Ohio State U., Columbus, 1961-63; cons. in microbiology Mayo Clinic, Rochester, Minn., 1963-69; dir. microbiology Mt. Sinai Med. Ctr., Milw., 1969-84; prof. pathology and lab. medicine U. Wis. Sch. Medicine, Milw., 1984—; cons. in field; dir. postdoctoral microbiology edn. program Mt. Sinai Med. Ctr., Milw., 1978—; clin. prof. allied health U. Wis.-Milw., 1983—; adj. prof. microbiology Med. Coll. Wis., Milw., 1983—. Contbr. articles to profl. jours. Mem. Bd. Health, Mequon, Wis., 1980—, Sea Scout Com., Mequon, 1983—. Served to 1st lt. U.S. Army, 1956-58. Fellow Am. Acad. Microbiology; mem. Am. Soc. Microbiology, Henrici Soc. Microbiology, Am. Pub. Health Assn., Nat. Com. Clin. Lab. Scis., Sigma Xi. Lutheran. Avocations: sailing, cross country skiing. Home: 1916 W Donges Bay Road Mequon WI 53092 Office: Mt Sinai Med Center Box 342 Milwaukee WI 53201

ZACHAR, KAREL ALOIS, international trade executive; b. Pardubice, June 2, 1926; s. Jan and Karolina (Slavikova) Zachar; m. Dagmar Urbankova, June 15, 1955; children—Charles K., Lenka. Comml. Engr., Coll. Fgn. Trade, U. Charles IV, 1950. Second comml. attaché The Caribbean, 1961-65, dir. Far East div., 1965-67, comml. attaché Permanent Trade Mission, Quito, Ecuador, 1967-70; export mgr. Nat. Oats Co., Inc., Cedar Rapids, Iowa, 1971-77, dir. export ops., 1977-78, v.p. internat. div., 1978—, dir., 1980—. Contbr. articles to profl. jours. Mem. Internat. Trade Bur., Am. Mgmt. Assn., Am. Soc. Internat. Execs. Roman Catholic. Lodge: Lions. Avocations: chess; volleyball; tennis; oil painting. Home: 4103 Falbrook Dr NE Cedar Rapids IA 52402 Office: National Oats Co Inc 1515 H Ave NE Cedar Rapids IA 52402

ZACHARY, ANDREA ANNE, geneticist; b. Cleve., Sept. 25, 1946; d. Anthony A. and Audrey J. (Klaus) Z. B.S., Ohio State U., 1967, M.S., 1969; Ph.D., Case Western Res. U., 1982. Research asst. Ohio State U., Columbus, 1969-70; technologist Cleve. Clinic Found., 1970-74, supr. lab., 1974-81, project scientist, 1981-82, staff, 82-84, assoc. lab. dir., 1984—. Co-editor: AACHT Laboratory Manual, 1981. Author audio-visual program on immunogenetics, 1983. Contbr. articles to profl. jours. and chpts. to scholarly tests. Grantee Kidney Found. of Ohio, 1984, Cleve. Clinic Found., 1985. Mem. Am. Soc. for Histocompatibility and Immunogenetics (councillor 1977-78, 83—, edn. program faculty 1971-83, 85), Am. Soc. Human Genetics, Transplant Soc. of Northeast Ohio, Audobon Soc., Nat. Wildlife Fedn. Avocations: nature photography, cross-country skiing, music, leather carving. Office: Cleve Clinic Found 9500 Euclid Ave Cleveland OH 44106

ZACHER, ALLAN NORMAN, JR., clergyman, psychologist, lawyer; b. Decatur, Ill., May 23, 1928; s. Allan Norman and Eleanor (Shaw) Z.; student Washington U. Sch. Bus. and Pub. Adminstrn., St. Louis, 1946, 48-50; J.D., Washington U., 1952, Ph.D., 1971; M.Div., Va. Theol. Sem., 1955; S.T.M., Eden Theol. Sem., 1966; m. Estelle Medalie, July 19, 1952 (dec. Mar. 1982); children—Allan Norman III, Mark, John. Admitted to Mo. bar, 1952; asso. firm Fred B. Whalen, St. Louis, 1950-52; ordained to ministry Episcopal Ch., 1955; asst. rector Truro Episcopal Ch., Fairfax, Va., 1955-58; canon counselor Christ Ch. Cathedral, St. Louis, 1958-64; dir. Pastoral Counseling Inst., St. Louis, 1958—; vicar Grace Episcopal Ch., St. Louis, 1958-63; vis. lectr. Eden Sem., St. Louis, Washington U. Sch. Law; chmn. dept. Christian social relations Diocese of Mo., 1959-63, mem. council, 1969-63; cons. to family life, asso. joint family life com. Nat. Council Episcopal Ch., 1962-65; labor arbitrator Fed. Mediation and Conciliation Service, 1959—. Pres. mem. steering com. St. Louis Group Psychotherapy Forum, 1962-65; mem. St. Louis Bd. Edn., 1963-69; pres. Northside Neighborhood Council, St. Louis, 1959-61; treas. Mo. Council Family Relations. Chmn. psychodrama and religion round table, 1st Internat. Congress of Psychodrama, Milan, Italy, 1964, 2d Internat. Congress, Barcelona, Spain, 1966. Bd. dirs. Grace Hill House, St. Louis, chaplain, 1958-63. Served with AUS, 1946-48, Kent fellow, 1968; Community Mental Health Research fellow, 1968; cert. trainer and practitioner in psychodrama and group psychotherapy Am. Bd. Examiners; lic. clin. psychologist, Mo., Ill.; mem. Nat. Register Health Service Providers in Psychology. Fellow Am. Acad. Matrimonial lawyers; mem. St. Louis (family law com.), Am. (family law com. on marriage and family counseling conciliation), Mo. (family law com.), Fed. bar, assns., Am. Soc. Group Psychotherapy and Psychodrama, Episcopal Soc. for Racial Unity (nat. bd.), Am. Assn. Pastoral Counselors (diplomate; mem. funding bd. 1963-65), Am. Assn. Marriage Counselors, Mo. Psychol. Assn., Soc. St. Louis Psychologists (past pres.), Assn. for Clin. Pastoral Edn., Soc. for Religion in Higher Edn. Contbr. articles to religious, psychol. and legal publs. Home: 16 Hortense Pl Saint Louis MO 63108 Office: 8420 Delmar Blvd Saint Louis MO 63124

ZACKAROFF, PETER TIMOTHY, lawyer, educator; b. Yonkers, N.Y., Aug. 23, 1955; s. Alexander George and Bernadette Ann (Gateley) Z.; m. Ilene Gay Cohen, July 31, 1982; 1 child, Scott Andrew. B.A., Fairleigh Dickinson U., 1977; J.D., U. Akron, 1980; student Coll. Fin. Planning, Denver, 1984—. Bar: Ohio 1980, U.S. Dist. Ct. (no. dist.) Ohio 1980, D.C. 1982. Assoc. Schwab, Grosenbaugh, Fort & Seamon Co., L.P.A., Akron, Ohio, 1980-83, ptnr. Schwab, Grosenbaugh, Fort, Seamon & Zackaroff, 1984—; instr. Ohio Paralegal, Cleve., 1980-83, Career Studies Inst., Canton, Ohio, 1983—. Panel atty. Vol. Legal Services Project, Akron, 1984; bd. dirs. Big Bros. & Sisters Greater Akron. Mem. ABA, Ohio State Bar Assn. (bd. govs. young lawyer div.), Akron Bar Assn., D.C. Bar Assn., Ohio Bar Coll., Assn. Trial Lawyers Am., Ohio Acad. Trial Lawyers, Akron Jaycees (legal counsel 1980—, Jaycee of Month 1983, 84, Silver Key award 1983, 84, Presdl. award of Honor 1983-84). Republican. Roman Catholic. Home: 249 Sand Run Rd Akron OH 44313 Office: Schwab Grosenbaugh Fort Seamon & Zackaroff Co LPA 40 E Mill St Akron OH 44308

ZACKHEIM, MARC ALLEN, child psychologist, editor; b. N.Y.C., Oct. 12, 1950; s. Seymour David and Blanche (Kalt) Z.; m. Elisa Freiden, Mar. 14, 1978 (div.). A.A., U. Fla., 1970, B.A. with high honors, 1972; M.S., Fla. State U., 1974, Ph.D., 1977. Lic. psychologist, Fla., Ill. Intern, Duke U. Med. Ctr., Durham, N.C., 1976; postdoctoral fellow in psychology Fla. State U., 1978; resident in psychology Rush-Presbyn. St. Luke's Med. Ctr., Chgo., 1979; attending child psychologist Assocs. in Adolescent Psychiatry, Chgo., 1979—, dir. tng., 1981—; faculty Auburn (Ala.) U.; attending child psychologist Riveredge Hosp., Forest Park, Ill., 1979—; cons. editor Ednl. and Psychol. Research. USPHS fellow, 1973-76. Mem. Am. Psychol. Assn., Ill. Psychol. Assn., Midwest Psychol. Assn., Fla. Psychol. Assn., S.E. Psychol. Assn., Chgo. Assn. for Psychoanalytic Psychology, Acad. Psychosomatic Medicine. Democrat. Jewish. Contbr. articles to profl. jours. Home: 1322 W Chase Ave Chicago IL 60626 Office: Riveredge Hospital 8311 W Roosevelt Rd Forest Park IL 60130

ZADROZNY, MITCHELL GEORGE, geography educator; b. Chgo., Dec. 23, 1923; s. John and Jeanette (Ulick) Z. B.S., Ill. State U., 1947; S.M., U. Chgo., 1949, Ph.D., 1956. Geog. analyst Dept. Army, Tokyo, 1950-52; lectr. geography U. Chgo., 1953-55, dir. research Cambodia Laos project, 1954-55; vis. assoc. prof. econ. geography NYU, 1958; research assoc. Mississippi Valley Investigations, So. Ill. U., Carbondale, 1955-61; tchr. geography Wright City Coll., Chgo., 1955-63, asst. prof., 1963-66, assoc. prof., 1963-69, prof., 1969—; prof. geography Chgo. WTTW-TV Coll., 1961. Bd. dirs. Uptown Chgo. Com., 1963-73; comptroller Nat. Republican Heritage Groups Council, 1970-74; treas. Ill. State Republican Nationalities Council, 1974—; treas. Great Lakes Naval Mus., Chgo., 1980—; dir. Pres. Water Pollution Adv. Bd., 1970-74. Served to lt. USAAF, 1942-45. Mem. Assn. Am. Geographers, Chgo. Geog. Soc., Ill. Geog. Soc., Ill. Edn. Assn., Soc. des Etudes Indochinoise, Royal Asiatic Soc. Japan, Hist. Naval Ships N.Am., Explorers Club. Republican. Roman Catholic. Club: Capital Hill (Washington). Author: Cambodia Handbook, 1955; Laos Handbook, 1956; Water Utilization in the Middle Mississippi Valley, 1956; World Geography TV Handbook and Map Supplement, 1961. Home: 4158 N McVicker Ave Chicago IL 60634 Office: 3400 N Austin Ave Chicago IL 60634

ZAHN, JOHN JOSEPH, research engineer; b. Beaver Dam, Wis., May 8, 1932; s. George Anton and Veronica (Neihoff) Z.; m. Nancy Josephine Turgeson, Nov. 9, 1955 (div.); children—Margaret Emily, Elizabeth Ann, Rebecca Marie; m. 2d, Carol Marie Walsh, Oct. 9, 1978. B.S. in Mech. Engring. (Morse Meml. scholar), U. Wis., 1954, M.S. in Mech. Engring. (fellow), 1959, Ph.D. in Mech. Engring., 1964. Instr. mechanics U. Wis.-Madison, 1958-64, lectr. in forest products, 1964—; research engr. Forest Products Lab. U.S. Dept. Agr., Madison, 1964—. Contbr. tech. articles in field to profl. jours. Served with S.C., U.S. Army, 1954-56. Mem. Am. Soc. Civil ENgrs., Forest Products Research Soc. (recipient L. V. Markwardt award 1978), Am. Acad. Mechanics, Fedn. Am. Scientists, Sigma Xi, Tau Beta Pi. Democrat. Unitarian. Home: 2648 Van Hise Ave Madison WI 53705 Office: Forest Products Lab 1 Gifford Pinchot Dr Madison WI 53705

ZAHNOW, MELVIN JOHN, foundation executive; b. Saginaw, Mich., Sept. 21, 1911; s. August Christian and Caroline Wilhemena (Kuble) Z.; m. Lillian Ruth O'Brien, Sept. 29, 1935; children—Ruth Ann, Beth Jean. B.A. in Bus. Adminstrn., Albion Coll., 1934; LL.D., Saginaw Valley State Coll., 1982. Sec., dir. Wickes Boiler Co. and Wickes Bros., Saginaw, 1940-47; sec., treas., dir. Wickes Corp., Saginaw, 1947-54; v.p. fin., dir, 1954-64, sr. v.p., dir., 1964-67; pres., trustee Wickes Found., Saginaw, 1967-84, chmn., trustee, 1985—. Trustee Albion Coll., Mich., 1967-71, Saginaw Gen. Hosp., 1975-79, Citizens Research Council Mich., Detroit, 1977; trustee, treas. Delta Coll., University Center, Mich., 1961-64; incorporator Saginaw Valley State Coll., 1963, trustee, treas., 1963-82; trustee, vice chmn. St. Luke's Hosp., Saginaw, 1956-83; trustee, chmn. Saginaw Med. Ctr., 1977-80; bd. dirs., pres. Neighborhood House community ctr., Saginaw, 1943-50. Recreation Bldg. at Neighborhood House named in his honor, 1976, also Library at Saginaw Valley State Coll., 1985; recipient Community Service award Saginaw C. of C., 1985. Republican. Lutheran. Clubs: Saginaw, Germania (Saginaw). Avocations: Abraham Lincoln history. Office: Harvey Randall Wickes Found 4800 Fashion Square Blvd Saginaw MI 48604

ZAHORCHAK, MICHAEL JOSEPH, clergyman, theology and philosophy educator; b. East Pittsburgh, Pa., Apr. 6, 1928; s. Michael Joseph and Erma (Bakara) Z. J.C.B., Cath. U. of Am., 1957, J.C.L., 1958; M.A. in philosophy, U. Detroit, 1975. Ordained priest Roman Cath. Ch., 1956. With Marriage Tribunal Diocese, Steubenville, Ohio, 1958-64; tchr. Latin and philosophy Steubenville and Detroit High Schs., 1964-80; chaplain, prof. theology and philosophy Calumet Coll., Whiting, Ind., 1980-83, dean of students, 1983—; condr. religious seminars. Contbr. Shavings weekly coll. newspaper, 1981—. Mem. Hammond Centennial Council, Ind., 1984; pub. Relations dir. Calumet Region Clergy Council, 1983—. Mem. Ind. Officer Campus Ministry, Ind. Cath. Campus Ministry (exec. council 1984—). Lodges: K.C., Kiwanis. Avocations: golf; racquetball; theater; reading. Office: Avila Coll 11901 Wornall Rd Kansas City MO 64145

ZAIS, EDITH MOREIN, college administrator; b. Providence, Apr. 8, 1931; d. Samuel Joshua and Sona Morein; A.B., Brown U., 1952; M.A. in Teaching, R.I. Coll., 1964; 6th year diploma edn. U. Conn., 1968; m. Robert S. Zais, Sept. 14, 1952; children—Louis Scott, Roberta Susan. Tchr. English, E. Providence (R.I.) Sr. High Sch., 1964-66; staff writer Willimantic (Conn.) Chronicle, 1966-67; tchr. reading Crestwood Schs., Mantua, Ohio, 1969-70; coordinator learning devel. program Kent (Ohio) State U., 1970—, instr. Exptl. Coll., 1973—; mem. admissions com. Northeastern Ohio Univs. Coll. Medicine, 1979-81; project co-dir. spl. services disadvantaged students Dept. Edn., 1978—. Mem. Nat. Assn. Women Deans, Adminstrs. and Counselors, Internat. Reading Assn., Assn. Children and Adults with Learning Disabilities, Mid-Am. Assn. Ednl. Opportunity Program Personnel, LWV (chmn. edn. com. Kent chpt. 1976-78), Omicron Delta Kappa. Home: 431 Wilson Ave Kent OH 44240 Office: Kent State U Kent OH 44242

ZAJICEK, BARBARA JEANNE (ZEE), health care company executive; b. Peoria, Ill., Jan. 12, 1932; d. Gale Edward and Thelma Beatrice (Drury) Allen; m. Allen H. Hahn, Apr. 28, 1951 (div. 1970); children—Gregg, Lisa Hahn Jeffries, Dana; m. Albert Frank Zajicek, July 5, 1973. Student pub. schs. Office supr., then exec. asst. to pres. Larry Smith & Co., Northfield, Ill., 1970-74, 76-77; asst. to pres., leasing agt. Devel. Control Corp., Northfield, 1974-76; bus. mgr. EMSCO, Ltd., Des Plaines, Ill., 1978-85; dir., v.p., asst. sec.-treas. Midwest Med. Mgmt., Inc., 1981-85; mng. dir. Emergency Medicine Mgmt. Assn., 1985—; exec. dir. Fla. chpt. Am. Coll. Emergency Physicians, 1985—. Mem. Emergency Medicine Mgmt. Assn. (past pres.), Internat. Platform Assn., Nat. Assn. Freestanding Ambulatory Care Ctrs. Republican. Lutheran. Home: 619 Hillside Rd Glenview IL 60025 Office: 600 Courtland St Orlando FL 32804

ZAK, BENNIE, pathology educator; b. Detroit, Sept. 29, 1919; s. Morris and Lena (Snyder) Z.; m. Doris Kitty Selby; children—Steven Dennis, Deborah Lise Zak Tataranowicz, Marsha Gale. B.S., Wayne State U., 1948, Ph.D., 1952. Jr. assoc. pathology Detroit Receiving Hosp., 1951-59; asst. prof. clin. chemistry in pathology Wayne State U., Detroit, 1957, from asst. prof. to assoc. prof. pathology, 1961-63, prof., 1965—; cons. in field. Contbr. articles to profl. jours. Served to 1st lt. USAF, 1941-45. Recipient Faculty Research award Wayne State U., 1973, Disting. Service award, 1983; Benedetti-Pichler award Am. Microchem. Soc., 1984. Fellow Nat. Acad. Clin. Biochemists; mem. Am. Chem. Soc., Am. Assn. Clin. Chemistry (Ames award 1974, Gen. Diagnostics lectr. 1981). Avocation: writing. Home: 25435 Southwood Dr Southfield MI 48075 Office: Wayne State U Sch Medicine 540 E Canfield Detroit MN 48201

ZAKIN, JACQUES LOUIS, chemical engineering; b. N.Y.C., Jan. 28, 1927; s. Mordecai and Ada Davies (Fishbein) Z.; m. Laura Peinkny, June 11, 1950; children—Richard J., David F., Barbara E., Emily A., Susan B. B. Chem. Engring., Cornell U., Ithaca, N.Y., 1949; M.S. in Chem. Engring., Columbia U., 1950; D. Engring. Sci. in Chem. Engring., NYU, 1959. Registered profl. engr., Ohio. Adj. asst. prof. engring. Hofstra Coll., 1959-60, 62; assoc. prof. chem. engring. U. Mo.-Rolla, 1962-65, prof. 1965-77; prof., chmn. dept. chem. engring. Ohio State U., 1977—; research assoc. U. So. Calif., 1963; vis. prof. chem. engring. Technion-Israel Inst. Tech., Haifa, 1968-69; vis. scientist Naval Research Lab., Washington, 1975-76; researcher Socony Mobil Oil Co., Bklyn., 1951-56, 58-62; with Flintkote Co. Research Labs., Whippany, N.J., 1950-51; mem. bd. judges Kirkpatrick award Chem. Engring. Mag., N.Y.C., 1981, 83, 85; chmn. sci. manpower and resources com. Council Chem. Research, Bethlehem, Pa., 1984, 85. Editor jour. Polymer Engring. and Sci., 1980. Contbr. articles to profl. publs. Patentee in field. Bd. dirs., v.p. Rolla Community Concert Assn. (Mo.), 1966-77; bd. dirs. Ozark Mental Health Assn., Rolla, 1976-77, Congregation Beth Tikvah, Worthington, Ohio, 1983-85; bd. dirs., treas. Ohio State Hillel Found., Columbus, Ohio, 1981—. Served with USNR, 1945-46. McMullen War scholar, 1944; fellow Socony Mobil Employee Incentive, 1956-58, Am. Chem. Soc., 1968-69; Outstanding Research award U.Mo.-Rolla, 1970. Fellow Am. Inst. Chem. Engrs.; mem. Am. Chem. Soc., Soc. Rheology, Am. Soc. Engring. Edn. Avocations: tennis; jogging; Jewish history. Office: Ohio State U Dept Chem Engring 140 W 19th Ave Columbus OH 43210

ZALD, MAYER NATHAN, sociology educator; b. Detroit, June 17, 1931; s. Harold and Ann (Levitt) Z.; m. Joan Kadri, June 15, 1958; children—Ann Karen, David Harold, Harold S.J. B.A., U. Mich., 1953, Ph.D., 1961; M.A., U. Hawaii, 1955. Asst. prof. U. Chgo., 1960-64; assoc. prof. Vanderbilt U., Nashville, 1964-68, prof., 1968-77, chmn., 1971-75; prof. U. Mich., Ann Arbor, 1977—, chmn., 1981—; mem. sociology panel NSF, Washington, 1980-81; behavioral sci. panel NIMH, 1973-76; mem. editorial bd. Adminstrn. and Soc., Blacksburg, Va., 1977—. Author: Organizational Change; The Political Economy of the YMCA, 1970; The Political Economy of Public Organizations, 1973. Editor: The Dynamics of Social Movements, 1979; Social Welfare Society, 1981; The American Welfare State, Trends and Prospects, 1985. Contbr. articles to profl. jours. Founding mem. ACLU of Tenn., chmn. Nashville chpt., 1974. Served with U.S. Army, 1955-56, Germany. Recipient NIH Career Devel. award, 1967-72. Mem. Am. Sociol. Assn. (council mem. 1980-82, pres. sect. occupation and orgn. 1985-86, pres. sect. collective behavior and social movements 1982-83), So. Sociol. Soc. Avocations: tennis; reading; bird watching; music. Office: Dept Sociology U Mich Ann Arbor MI 48109

ZALESKI, JANET LORRAINE, graphic designer; b. Evanston, Ill., July 20, 1954; d. Mitchell Joseph and Susanne Elsie (Meinert) Z. B.F.A, Drake U., 1976. Art dept. supr. E.R. Moore, Niles, Ill., 1976-78; graphic designer Assocs. Printing Service, Glenview, Ill., 1979-80, Emphasis Communications, Chgo., 1980-83; v.p., sr. design cons., account mgr. new bus. devel. Din & Pangrazio, Chgo., 1983—. Mem. Chi Omega aux. Children's Home and Aid Soc. of Ill. Mem. Chgo. Ad Club, STA Profl. Communication Design Orgn. (bd. dirs.), Chi Omega. Republican. Lutheran. Office: Din & Pangrazio 415 N Dearborn St Chicago IL 60610

ZALETEL, JOSEPH HENRY, JR., librarian; b. Ames, Iowa, Apr. 8, 1947; s. Joseph Henry and Myrtle Douglas (Bunch) Z.; m. Linda Rane Ford, Aug. 12, 1972; children—Anne Betny, Elizabeth Ford. B.A., Drake U., 1973; M.L.S., Rosary Coll., 1976. Librarian Northwest Hosp., Chgo., 1976-77, Iowa Dept. Transp., Ames, 1978—; chmn. Pub. Library Bd., Colo, Iowa, 1985. Active Story County Conservation Bd., Iowa, 1982—. Served with U.S. Army, 1967-69, Vietnam. Mem. Iowa State Agy. Library Assn. (chmn. 1982-83), Iowa Ornithologist Union (treas. 1981—), Ames Audubon Soc. (v.p. 1981-83). Democrat. Roman Catholic. Avocations: tennis; birdwatching. Home: 715 West St Colo IA 50056 Office: Iowa Dept Transp Library 800 Lincoln Way Ames IA 50010

ZALEWSKI, WITOLD THEODORE, energy engineering executive; b. Poznan, Poland, Oct. 22, 1949; came to U.S., 1965; s. Witold Adolf and Cecylia (Kozera) Z.; m. Darlene Fimiano, Nov. 3, 1977 (div. May 1978); m. 2d, Penelope Wiley, Dec. 29, 1981. Assoc. Engr., Sch. Energetics, Poznan, 1965; diploma engr. Poly. Inst. (W. Ger.), 1971; M.S., U. Wis.-Milw., 1972. Registered profl. engr., Wis. Mfrs. rep. Contract Design Assocs., Denver, 1973-75, D. H. Baldwin, Cin., 1975-77; zone mgr. Memorex Corp., Santa Clara, Calif., 1977-80; pres. Intex, Mequon, Wis., 1980—; cons. Wis. Vocat. Colls., Madison, 1982—, Wis. Electric Co., Milw., 1981—, Kenosha Pub. Schs. (Wis.), 1981—. Patentee in field. Named Memorex Zone Mgr. of Yr., 1979. Mem. ASHRAE, Assn. Energy Engrs. Roman Catholic. Office: 11563 N Spring Ave -65W Mequon WI 53092

ZALK, MORTON L., chemical company executive. Pres., chief operating officer, dir. Gelco Corp., Eden Prairie, Minn. Office: Gelco Corp One Gelco Dr Eden Prairie MN 55344*

ZALMAN, MARVIN, criminal justice educator; b. Bronx, N.Y., Jan. 9, 1942; s. Harry and Violet (Bar David) Z.; m. Greta Ann Durst, July 28, 1966; children—Amy, Ruth, Seth Philip. B.A., Cornell U., 1963; J.D., Bklyn. Law Sch., 1966; M.A., SUNY-Albany, 1971, Ph.D., 1977. Bar: N.Y., 1966. Lectr. law, Peace Corps Vol. Almadu Bello U., Zaria, Nigeria, 1967-69; assoc. prof. Mich. State U., East Lansing, 1971-80; project leader Mich. Felony Sentencing project, State Ct. Adminstrv. Office, Lansing, 1978-79; chmn. dept. criminal justice Wayne State U., Detroit, 1980—; exec. dir. N.Y. State Com. on sentencing Guidelines, Albany, 1984; mem. Mich. state bar prison and corrections com., 1976-84. Contbr. articles to legal jours. Mem. Pub. Safety and Justice Com., New Detroit, Inc., 1981-84. Mem. Am. Soc. Criminology, Acad. Criminal Justice Scis. (chmn. awards com. 1983-84), Law and Soc. Assn., Mich. Council Crime and Delinquency, Nat. Council Crime and Delinquency. Jewish. Home: 1074 Wakefield Dr Birmingham MI 48009 Office: Dept Criminal Justice Wayne State U Detroit MI 48202

ZAMBORSKY, JOHN VALENTINE, accountant; b. Trenton, N.J., Feb. 12, 1953; s. Joseph Coloman and Carolyn (Moore) Hemple Z. B. Indsl. Adminstrn., Motors Inst., 1976; M.B.A., Riutgers U., 1980; m. Amy Sara Feinstein Aug. 4, 1973; children—Jessica Lynn, Noah Alexander, Trevor Joseph. Tech. prodn. supr. Fisher Body div. Gen. Motors Corp., Trenton, N.J., 1976-80, sr. cost analyst, 1980-82, supr. gen. acctg. Columbus Regional Acctg. Ctr., 1982—; project bus. cons. Jr. Achievement Columbus. Coach, Ewing Twp. Little League, 1970-79. Mem. Am. Mgmt. Assn., Gen. Motors Inst. Alumni Assn., Delta Tau Delta. Roman Catholic. Republican. Office: 200 Georgesville Rd Columbus OH 43228

ZAMIR, JAN ROSHAN, educator; b. Caspian Sea area, Persia, Nov. 13, 1941; came to U.S., 1961, naturalized, 1974; s. Hedayat Roshan and Mohtram (Naji) Z.; m. Sonia LuAnn Nelson, Aug. 8, 1964; children—Brett, Nicole. B.A., Huron Coll., 1966; M.A. Northeastern Ill. U., 1972; A.M., U. Ill., 1979, Ph.D., 1981. Dept. chmn. fgn. lang. St. George High Sch., Evanston, Ill., 1966-69; instr. German and Spanish, John Hersey High Sch., Arlington Heights, Ill., 1969—. Contbr. articles to profl. jours. Mem. Linguistic Soc. Am., Am. Assn. Tchrs. German, Am. Assn. Tchrs. Spanish, Phi Kappa Phi. Home: 1402 Lama Lane Mount Prospect IL 60056 Office: John Hersey High Sch 1900 E Thomas Arlington Heights IL 60004

ZAMORE, JOSEPH DAVID, lawyer, consultant; b. Bklyn., May 20, 1944; s. Harry and Eleanor (Shientag) Z.; m. Frances S. Zelikow, Nov. 24, 1968; children—Michael Seth, Rachel Anne, Judith Gail. A.B. with high honors, Brown U., 1966; J.D., Columbia U., 1969. Bar: N.Y. 1969; R.I. 1971; U.S. Dist. Ct. R.I. 1971; U.S. Dist. Ct. (so., ea. and no. dists.) N.Y. 1970, Ohio 1971; U.S. Dist. Ct. (no. dist.) Ohio 1971, Fla. 1977; U.S. Dist. Ct. (so. dist.) Fla. 1977, U.S. Ct. Appeals (6th cir.) 1979. Law clk. to U.S. Chief Dist. Judge R.I.,

1970-71; assoc. Guren, Merritt, Sogg & Cohen, Cleve., 1971-77; ptnr. Guren, Merritt, Feibel, Sogg & Cohen, Cleve., 1977-82; prin. Joseph D. Zamore Co., L.P.A., Shaker Heights, Ohio, 1982—; mem. adj. faculty Cleve. State U. Sch. Law, 1983—; pres. Telewave Systems, Inc., computer systems and cons., Cleve., 1980-84. Bd. dirs. Am. ORT Fedn., 1983—; pres. Cleve. Men's ORT, 1985—; mem. Shaker Hts. Recreation Bd., 1985—. Mem. ABA (chmn. com. bus. torts litigation Litigation Sect. 1979-81, vice-chmn. com. on computers in small law office Gen. Practice Sect. 1982-83, vice chmn. corp., banking and bus. law com. Gen. Practice sect. 1985—), Computer Law Assn., Fla. Bar Assn. (chmn. out-of-state lawyers com. 1981-82), Cuyahoga County Bar Assn. (chmn. corp. law com. 1982-83), Greater Cleve. Bar Assn. (council Sect. on Securities Law 1980—, chmn. sect. liaison and long-range planning com. 1982-83). Clubs: Oakwood, Masons (Cleve.). Contbr. articles to profl. jours. Office: 3645 Warrensville Ctr Suite 206 Shaker Heights OH 44122

ZAMPARO, ROGER, JR., lawyer; b. Hobokan, N.J., July 20, 1950; s. Roger Sr. and Teresa Emma (Terminiello) Z.; m. Katherine Schneider, Aug. 11, 1984. B.S. in Journalism, Ohio U., 1971; J.D., John Marshall Law Sch., 1978. Bars: Ill. 1979, U.S. Dist. Ct. (no. dist.) Ill. 1979. Advt. media planner Young & Rubican, N.Y.C., 1971-73; advt. media supr. Post Keyes Gardner, Chgo., 1973-74; advt. acct. exec. Biddle Advt., Chgo., 1974-77, J. Walter Thompson Corp., Chgo., 1977-79; ptnr. Zamparo, Frejlich, Russell & Kolb, Chgo., 1979-82, Salinger, Gignilliat, Hymen & Zamparo, P.C., Chgo., 1982—. Vol. atty. Five Hosp. Homebound Elderly Program, Chgo., 1979—. Mem. Chgo. Bar Assn., ABA, Ill. State Bar Assn., Assn. Trial Lawyers Am. Roman Catholic. Club: Western Advt. Golf Assn. Office: Salinger Gignilliat Hymen & Zamparo PC 135 S LaSalle St Chicago IL 60603

ZAPP, WILLIAM ANDREW, lawyer; b. Columbus, Ohio, Nov. 4, 1947; s. Robert Louis and Harriet Evelyn (Miller) Z.; m. Susan Lee Armstrong, Apr. 11, 1981: 1 child, Andrew Michael. B.A., Ohio State U., 1969; J.D., Capitol U., 1972. Bar: Ohio 1972. Adminstrv. law judge Ohio Bur. Motor Vehicles, Columbus, 1973-74, Ohio Bd. Tax Appeals; judge Ohio Bd. Tax Appeals, Columbus, 1974-79; sole practice, Columbus, 1979—. Bd. dirs. Big Brothers Big Sisters Assn., Columbus, 1982-84; chmn. Camp Oty-Okwa council Big Bros./Big Sisters Assn. of Columbus, 1985; candidate for judge Franklin County Mcpl. Ct., Columbus, 1979. Mem. Columbus Bar Assn. (taxation com. 1975—), Southside Columbus Jaycees. Democrat. Roman Catholic. Office: 326 S High St Suite 200 Columbus OH 43215

ZAREMBA, THOMAS EDMUND MICHAEL BARRY, educator; b. Detroit, May 6; s. Edmund Julius Thiel and Ethel Grace (Barry) Z. Ed. Oakland U., Rochester, Mich., U. Detroit, Wayne State U. Tchr., Center Line (Mich.) Public Schs., Livonia (Mich.) Public Schs.; instr. biol. scis. Wayne State U., Detroit. Mem. AAAS, Mich. Eye Bank, Nat., Mich. funeral dirs. assns., Am. Film Inst. (sponsor), Met. Opera Guild, Friends of Detroit Symphony Orch., Founders Soc., Detroit Inst. Arts, Internat. Platform Assn., Detroit Sci. Ctr., Friends for Orch. Hall, Wayne State U. Alumni Assn., Oakland U. Alumni Assn., Detroit Grand Opera Assn. Roman Catholic. Club: Scarab (life), Players (Detroit). Office: 217 Farnsworth St Detroit MI 48202 also 5980 Cass Ave Detroit MI 48202

ZARLENGA, RINALDO ANGELICO, artist, educator; b. Pietrabbondante, Italy, Apr. 25, 1919; came to U.S., 1949, naturalized, 1957; s. Angelomaria Luigi and Giovannina (Di Benedetto) Z. B.A., Pontifical U. of St. Thomas Aquinas, Rome, 1940, M.A., 1942, Ph.D. in Theology, 1944; M.F.A., Art Istituto B. Angelico, Rome, 1947; postgrad. Nat. Acad. St. Luca, Rome, 1946-47. Ordained priest Order of Dominicans, Roman Catholic Ch., 1941. Assoc. editor SS. Sacramento, 1942-43; librarian Biblioteca B. Angelico, Rome, 1944-49; dir. higher art course Istituto B. Angelico, 1946-48, prof. philosophy and theology St. Therese Coll., Winona, Minn., 1952-53, St. Xavier Coll., Chgo., 1953-54, DePaul U., Chgo., 1954-57; dir. Studio Angelico, Oak Park, Ill., 1957-72, River Forest, Ill., 1972—; one man shows: Rome, 1949, 64, 67, Cin., 1950, Chgo., 1950-52; represented in permanent collections chs., hosps., restaurants, Rome, Chgo., Oak Park, River Forest Alsip, Harvey, Norridge and Kankakee, Detroit, New Orleans, Cin., Pitts., Can., Australia, Italy. Bd. dirs. Istituto B. Angelico, Rome, 1944-49; mem. Mcpl. Art League Chgo., 1970-72; mem. commn. on arts Dominican Central Province. Mem. Unione Cattolica Artisti Italiani, Internat. Soc. Thomas Aquinas. Address: 7200 W Division St River Forest IL 60305

ZARSE, LEIGH BRYANT, architect, architectural engineer; b. Wauwatosa, Wis., Sept. 26, 1930; s. Alfred Henry and Cecile (Moreau) Z.; student U. Wis., Milw., 1948-50, Ohio State U., 1950-52; B. Archtl. Engring., U. Ill., 1954; m. Hannelore Schilling, June 30, 1973. Partner, Zarse & Zarse, Inc., Milw., 1957-84, pres., 1967-84; structural project engr. Milw. Met. Sewerage Dist., 1984—; mem. municipal planning com. City Club of Milw., 1965—, sec. bd. dirs., 1971. Served to maj. USAFR, 1954-57. Registered architect and profl. engr., Wis.; certified multi-disaster design protection specialist CD Preparedness Agy. Mem. AIA (Top Honor award 1963), ASCE, Am. Concrete Inst., Engrs. and Scientists of Milw., Aircraft Owners Pilots Assn., Alpha Rho Chi, Sigma Delta Omega (pres. local chpt. 1949-50). Designer numerous local, state and fed. govt. bldgs., including: 1500 seat amphitheater for Gen. McCormack, Lackland AFB, San Antonio, 1954, 40 schs. in S.E. Wis., 1957—, Kenosha (Wis. City Hall, 1971, St. Francis (Wis.) City Hall, 1963, Hales Corners (Wis.) City Hall, 1968, FAA and Weather Bur. Bldg. at Gen. Billy Mitchell Field, Milw., 1970. Home: 1812 Mountain Ave Wauwatosa WI 53213 Office: 436 W Wisconsin Ave Milwaukee WI 53203

ZARVELL, RAYMOND KENNETH, university administrator; b. Kewanee, Ill., May 12, 1938; s. Raymond William and Lillian (Odey) Z.; m. Georgia Lu Watkins, Sept. 30, 1972; children—Douglas Lee, Paul Eric. B.S., Bradley U., 1962, M.A., 1968; L.H.D. (hon.), Inst. Tech., Morrison, Ill., 1980. Cert. tchr., Ill., nat. cert. counselor. Tchr. Williamsfield Sch. Dist., Ill., 1962-67, Limestone High Sch., Bartonville, Ill., 1968-69; counselor Bradley U., Peoria, Ill., 1969-72, dir. orientation, advisement and retention, 1972-81, unit dir. ednl. devel., 1981—; cons. in field. Author: (manual) Taxonomic Key for Academic Exploration Students, 1984; co-author: A Sequential, Narrative Guide for Acad. Advisors, 1985. Coach Christian Ctr., Peoria, 1978; bd. dirs. YMCA, Peoria, 1978. Recipient Tchr. of Yr. award State of Ill., 1968; named hon. mayor City of Peoria, 1983. Mem. Nat. Orientation Dirs. Assn. (editor, publs. coordinator 1984), Am. Assn. Counseling and Devel., Am. Coll. Personnel Assn., Nat. Acad. Advising Assn., Nat. Peer Counselor Assn., Little John Conservation Club (editor 1977—) Ill. Guidance Personnel Assn., Phi Delta Kappa (advisor 1979-81). Avocations: photography; music; conservation projects; botany. Home: 5506 N Graceland Dr Peoria IL 61614 Office: Bradley U 1501 Bradley Ave Peoria IL 61625

ZATZMAN, MARVIN LEON, physiologist, educator; b. Phila., Aug. 6, 1927; s. Morris Bernard and Clara (Fuhrman) Z.; m. Barbara Clair Mishkin, Sept. 9, 1951; children—Allen, Robin. B.S., CCNY, 1950; M.S., Ohio State U., 1952, Ph.D., 1955. Asst. prof. Ohio State U., Columbus, 1955-56; asst. prof. U. Mo., Columbia, 1956-61, assoc. prof., 1961-73, prof., 1973—; cons. NSF, 1980-81, NIH, 1978-82. Author jour. articles. Served with U.S. Army, 1945-47, Italy. Mem. Am. Physiol. Soc., Soc. for Cryobiology (program com. 1983—), Biophysics Soc., Internat. Soc. Nephrology, Am. Soc. Nephrology. Jewish. Lodge: Spinoza (pres. 1958-59). Avocations: Crafts. Home: 2409 Braemore Rd Columbia MO 65203 Office: Univ Mo Health Sci Ctr Dept Physiology Columbia MO 65212

ZAVELSON, LESTER SANFORD, business management consultant; b. Cleve., July 10, 1915; s. Abraham Phillip and Sophia (Miller) Z.; m. Maxine Lois Abrams, Dec. 26, 1938; children—Thomas M., Daniel Lee. B.B.A., Ohio State U., 1937. Exec. v.p. Ind. Towel Supply Co., Mansfield, Ohio, 1938-78; pres., chmn. bd. Reed Road, Inc., Mansfield, 1978—; ptnr. Mansfield Assocs., 1960—; columnist Laundry Digest, Chgo., 1980—. Bd. dirs. Hospice, Score, ARC, Mansfield Cancer Found.; mem. Richland County Recreation Bd.; mem. local Democratic exec. com., 1960-83; v.p. Temple Emanuel, 1980-83. Recipient Ty award Mktg. Club, 1976. Mem. Mktg. Club N. Central Ohio (past pres., dir.), Ohio State U. Alumni Assn. (past pres.), Clubs: Exchange (past pres., dir.), University, International Trade of Ohio. Lodges: Shriners, Masons, Elks. Home: 666 W Andover Rd Mansfield OH 44907 Office: PO Box 1562 210 W Longview Ave Mansfield OH 44901

ZAVISLAK, HENRY CRAIG, county law enforcement official, educator; b. Detroit, Sept. 26, 1948; s. Henry Eugene and Irene M. (Polchowski) Z.; m. Nancy Carol Griffiths, Oct. 2, 1971; children—Jonathon, Adam. B.S. in Police Adminstrn., Wayne State U., 1970, M.P.A., 1976. Officer pub. safety, investigator Wayne State U., Detroit, 1969-73; asst. adminstr. Jackson City Police Dept., Mich., 1973-76; dir. criminal justice program Jackson Community Coll., Mich., 1978-80; adj. faculty, 1981-84; sheriff Jackson County Sheriff's Dept., Mich., 1980—; v.p. Police Mgmt. Assn., Inc., Saginaw, Mich., 1973-76; presenter U.S. Dept. Justice Community Relations Forum, Dallas, 1979; chmn. administrv. bd. Jackson Emergency Dispatch, 1983; apptd. by Gov. to Mich. Law Enforcement Officers Tng. Council, Lansing, 1983, chmn., 1985; vice chmn. Region II Criminal Justice Planning Commn., Jackson, 1984; chmn. Substance Abuse Commn. Criminal Justice Task Force, Jackson, 1984. Bd. dirs. Council for Prevention of Child Abuse and Neglect, Jackson, 1984; div. chmn. United Way of Jackson, 1981; bd. dirs. Jackson Unit, Am. Heart Assn., 1982; mem. Jackson County Republic Party, 1981; chmn. Redeemer Lutheran Ch. Council, Jackson, 1978. Recipient County Achievement award Nat. Assn. of Counties, 1983, 84. Recipient numerous grants for criminal justice and hwy. safety planning. Mem. Nat. Sheriffs Assn., Mich. Sheriffs Assn. (chmn. corrections com. 1984), Internat. Assn. Chiefs of Police, Mich. Criminal Justice Educators Assn. (pres. 1979, 1980), Am. Correctional Assn. Lodge: Lions. Office: Jackson County Sheriff's Dept 212 W Wesley St Jackson MI 49201

ZAWADA, EDWARD THADDEUS, JR., physician, educator; b. Chgo., Oct. 3, 1947; s. Edward Thaddeus and Evelyn Mary (Kovarek) Z.; m. Nancy Ann Stephen, Mar. 26, 1977; children—Elizabeth, Nicholas. B.S. summa cum laude, Loyola U., Chgo., 1969; M.D. summa cum laude, Loyola-Stritch Sch. Medicine, 1973. Diplomate Am. Bd. Internal Medicine, Am. Bd. Nephrology. Intern UCLA Hosp., 1973, resident, 1974-76; asst. prof. medicine UCLA, 1978-79, U. Utah, Salt Lake City, 1979-81; assoc. prof. medicine Med. Coll. Va., Richmond, 1981-83; assoc. prof. medicine, physiology, pharmacology U. S.D. Sch. Medicine, Sioux Falls, 1983—, also chief div. nephrology and hypertension, 1981—; chief renal sect. Salt Lake VA Med. Ctr., 1980-81; asst. chief med. service McGuire VA Med. Ctr., Richmond, 1981-83. Contbr. articles to profl. publs. Editor: Geriatric Nephrology and Urology, 1984. Pres. Minnehaha div. Am. Heart Assn., 1984—. VA Hosp System grantee, 1981-85, 85—. Fellow ACP, Am. Coll. Chest Physicians, Am. Coll. Nutrition; mem. Internat. Soc. Nephrology, Am. Soc. Nephrology, Am. Soc. Pharmacology and Exptl. Therapeutics. Democrat. Roman Catholic. Club: Westward Ho Country (Sioux Falls). Avocations: golf; tennis; skiing; cinema; music. Home: 1608 Cedar Lane Sioux Falls SD 57103 Office: U SD Sch Medicine 2501 W 22d St Sioux Falls SD 57105

ZBOROWSKI, BEVERLY JEAN, school district administrator, educator; b. Gary, Ind., Apr. 23, 1948; d. Stephen Joseph and Mary Helen (Petrovich) Soohey; m. Joseph Richard Zborowski, Aug. 10, 1968; children—Annemarie Nicole, Natalie Joelle, Nicholas Joseph. B.S., Ind. U., Gary, 1970; M.S., Purdue U., 1975. Life lic. elem. edn. Elem. tchr. Portage Twp. Sch. Corp., Portage, Ind., 1970-73, pres. Portage Twp. Sch. Corp. Bd. Edn., Hebron, Ind., sec. Porter County Vocat. Edn. Com., Valparaiso, Ind., 1984-85. Pres. Porter County Extension Homemakers, 1981-83; mem. Assn. County Neighbors Group, Hebron. Mem. Sigma Beta (chpt. sec. 1982-84). Republican. Roman Catholic. Avocations: gourmet cooking; creative needlework; photography; reading. Office: Porter Twp Sch Corp 208 S 725 W Hebron IN 46341

ZECK, RICHARD MICHAEL, computer company executive, educator; b. Chgo., Apr. 13, 1955; s. Richard Charles and Gloria Eileen (DiMuzio) Z.; m. Jane Ann Budilovsky, Sept. 23, 1979; children—Richard John, Rebecca Ann. B.S. in Computer Sci., Ill. Inst. Tech., 1977, M.S., 1979. Instr., Sperry-UNIVAC, Chgo., 1978-81; owner, mgr. Profl. Computing, Lombard, Ill., 1978—; research engring. programmer Rockwell Graphic Systems, 1979-81; cons. Analysts Internat. Corp., Schaumburg, Ill., 1981-82; asst. prof. computer sci. DeVry Inst. Tech., Lombard, 1983—; part-time instr. Ill. Inst. Tech. Mem. IEEE, AAAS, Assn. Computing Machinery, (mem. various spl. interest groups). Libertarian. Roman Catholic. Author: High-Level Language for Process Control, 1980; Use of Outside Data Processing Consultants, 1981; Meta-Game Theory in Design Engineering, 1981; Computer Programming for Human Beings, 1983. Home: 405 E Maple St Lombard IL 60148 Office: 2000 Finley Rd Lombard IL 60148

ZEE-CHENG, ROBERT K.-Y., organic chemist; b. Kashan, Chekiang, China, Sept. 2, 1925; came to U.S., 1956; s. Kan-Yi and Fu-Chen Zee-Cheng; m. Yu-Lan Lan Yu Oct. 10, 1949; children—Chi-Lui, Chi-Sung, Chi-Feng, Chi-Wa. B.S. in Ch. E., China Tech. Inst., Shanghai, 1945; M.S. in Organic Phys. Chemistry, N.M. Highland U.-Las Vegas, 1957; Ph.D. in Organic Chemistry, U. Tex.-Austin, 1963. Teaching asst. U. Tex.-Austin, 1957-59; sr. chemist Celanese Chem. Co. Tech. Ctr., Corpus Christi, Tex., 1962-65; prin. chemist Midwest Research Inst., Kansas City, Mo., 1965-78; asst. research prof. St. Louis U., 1978-80; prin. chemist U. Kans. Med. Ctr., Kansas City, 1980-82, research prof. pharmacology, 1982—; medicinal chemist U. Kans. Cancer Ctr., 1980—; assoc. dir. Drug Devel. Lab., 1980—. Contbr. numerous articles to sci. jours. Patentee anticancer agts, anticancer methods, antileukemic compounds, antineoplastic compounds. Recipient Council Prin. Scientists Sci. award, 1973. Mem. Am. Chem. Soc., Sci. Research Soc. North Am., AAAS. Club: Chinese. Home: 9570A W 86th St Overland Park KS 66212 Office: U Kans Med Ctr Rainbow Blvd & 39th St Kansas City KS 66103

ZEGIOB-DEVEREAUX, LESLIE ELAINE, clinical psychologist; b. Cleve., Oct. 17, 1948; d. Charles G. and Elinore Lois (Jones) Zegiob; m. James Michael Devereaux, July 11, 1981. Student Allegheny Coll., 1966-68; B.A., Am. U., 1971; M.S., U. Ga., 1976, Ph.D., 1976. Lic. psychologist, Ariz., Ind. Asst. prof. dept. psychology Ariz. State U., Tempe, 1976-78, dir. psychology clinic, 1977-78; dir. childrens services Dogwood Village, Memphis, 1978; adj. prof. dept. psychology Notre Dame (Ind.) U., 1979-80; clin. psychologist dept. psychology and psychiatry The Med. Group, Michigan City, Ind., 1978—; cons. Headstart program Michigan City schs.; mem. adv. bd. Headstart, 1979—. Ariz. State U. faculty grantee, 1978. Mem. Am. Psychol. Assn., Assn. for Advancement Behavior Therapy, Southeastern Psychol. Assn., Sierra Club, Animal Protection Inst., Wilderness Soc., Ind. Cat Soc. Phi Kappa Phi, Phi Beta Kappa. Democrat. Contbr. articles to profl. jours. Office: 1225 E Coolspring Ave Michigan City IN 46360

ZEHNDER, JOHN WILLIAM, restaurant executive, chef; b. Bay City, Mich., Oct. 12, 1947; s. Herman Frederick and Lenore Ruth (Eckert) Z.; m. Janet Sue Lockhart, Aug. 23, 1968; children—John Michael, Robert Matthew. B.A., Mich. State U., 1969. Food service mgr. Saga Food Service, Bloomington, Ill. and Alma, Mich., 1969-71, Catering Mgmt. Inc., Anderson, Ind. and Hiram, Ohio, 1971-73; exec. chef Zehnders of Frankenmuth, Mich., 1973—; lectr. Mich. Restaurant Assn. Mem. Round Table com., Lake Huron council Boy Scouts Am., 1980, Webelos leader, 1981-82. Recipient 1st prize Pillsbury Recipe Contest, 1972, Kraft Creative Foods Contest, 1978, 1st prize Dessert of Yr. award, Nat. Frozen Food Assn., 1978, grand prize Nat. Frozen Food Assn., 1980, Procter and Gamble Cooking with Whirl, 1984, others. Mem. Saginaw Valley Restaurant Assn., Nat. Restaurant Assn., Les Amin Du Vin. Democrat. Lutheran. Avocation: Tae Kwon Do. Home: 515 Heine St Frankenmuth MI 48734 Office: Zehnder's of Frankenmuth 730 S Main St Frankenmuth MI 48734

ZEIDLER, ROBERT BERNARD, physiological educator; b. Wheeling, W.V., Jan. 3, 1943; m. Sharon Conley, Dec. 27, 1982. B.S., West Liberty State U., 1969; Ph.D., W.V. U., 1973. Postdoctoral researcher U. Ill., Urbana, 1973-75, U. Ariz., Tucson, 1975-78; asst. prof. U. Rhodesia, Salisbury, 1978-79; research asst., prof. U. Ala., Birmingham, 1980-82, U. Mo., Columbia, 1982—. Contbr. articles to profl. jours. Grantee NIH, 1976, U. Rhodesia, 1978, Ala. Lung Assn., 1981, Nat. Lung Assn., 1984. Mem. Am. Physiol. Soc., Biophys. Soc., Red Cell Club. Home: 2809 Lynnwood Dr Columbia MO 65203 Office: Dept Pharmacology School Medicine Univ Missouri Columbia MO 65212

ZEIDMAN, BENJAMIN, nuclear physicist; b. N.Y.C., Oct. 6, 1931; s. Samuel and Eve (Ellmann) Z.; m. Ruth Leona Goldstein, Dec. 25, 1956 (dec. July 1970); 1 son, Michael; m. Anne Macfarland, June 3, 1972. B.S., CCNY, 1952; postgrad. George Washington U., Washington, 1952-54; Ph.D., Washington U., St. Louis, 1957. Assoc. physicist Argonne Nat. Lab., Ill., 1957-59; Ford fellow Niels Bohr Inst., Copenhagen, 1963-64; mem. staff, cons. Los Alamos Nat. Lab., N.Mex., 1968—; mem. vis. staff Brookhaven Nat. Lab., Upton, L.I., N.Y., 1972; vis. prof. SUNY-Stonybrook, 1972; Humboldt awardee Max Planck Institute für Kernphysik, Heidelberg, Germany, 1975-76; physicist Argonne Nat. Lab., Ill., 1959-79, sr. physicist, 1979—. Contbr. articles on nuclear physics to profl. jours. Recipient Humboldt award Av Humboldt Found., Bonn, W.Ger., 1975; Ford fellow, Copenhagen, 1963. Fellow Am. Phys. Soc., AAAS, Sigma Xi. Republican. Avocations: woodworking; sports. Home: 354 Cumnor Ave Glen Ellyn IL 60137 Office: Argonne Nat Lab 203-PHY Argonne IL 60439

ZEIMER, RAN CLAUDE, physicist, consultant; b. Paris, France, Aug. 11, 1945; emmigrated to Israel, 1960; came to U.S., 1978, naturalized 1983; s. Harry and Moussia Zeimer; divorced; children—Ilan, Nadav; m. Lisa Smukler, Oct. 20, 1984. M.S., Hebrew U., Jerusalem, Israel, 1972, Ph.D., 1978. Research asst. Hebrew U., 1973-78; research assoc. Eye and Ear Infirmary, U. Ill.-Chgo., 1979-80, asst. prof., 1980-83, assoc. prof. applied physics, 1984—; vis. scholar U. Chgo., 1979-80; adj. asst. prof. Northwestern U., Evanston, Ill., 1980-84, adj. assoc. prof., 1984; cons. Galil Co., Israel, 1981, Coherent, Palo Alto, Calif., 1981—; prin. investigator research grants NIH, 1980, 81—, mem. study group, 1984. Inventor, patentee in field. Contbr. publs. and abstracts in referenced jours. Mem. Midwest Biolaser Inst. (bd. dirs. 1981—), Internat. Soc. Ocular Fluorophotometry (sci. com. 1982—), Am. Inst. Physics, Am. Optical Soc., Assoc. Research in Vision and Ophthalmology, AAAS. Avocations: painting, hiking, photography, family. Office: U Ill Lions of Ill Eye Research Inst Room L149 1905 W Taylor St Chicago IL 60612

ZEIMET, EDWARD JOSEPH, educator; b. Madison, Wis., Jan. 16, 1925; s. Anthony Joseph and Stella Mary (Orlowicz) Z.; B.A., U. Wis., 1948, M.S., 1950, Ph.D., 1970; m. Frances Ann Ward, May 29, 1954; children—Edward, Stephanie, Ann, Thomas, Symantha. Biology tchr. Ft. Atkinson (Wis.) High Sch., 1948-49; biologist Holtzman-Rolfsmeyer Co., Madison, 1949-52; salesman Oscar Mayer Co., Madison, 1952-54; project asst. endocrine research U. Wis. at Madison, 1954-61, zoology specialist, 1964-70; tech. rep. Spinco div. Beckman Industries, Palo Alto, Calif., 1961-64; prof. ednl. media dept. U. Wis. at LaCrosse, 1970—, dir. ednl. media program, 1975-80; chmn. Western Wis. Media Conf., 1979; community care orgn. cons. Mem. budget rev. bd. United Way, LaCrosse, 1974; campus coordinator Gene McCarthy for Pres., 1972, state alternate del., 1972; campus coordinator Alvin Baldus for U.S. Congress, 1974, 76; mem. candidate selection com. Mil. Acad.; mem. Nat. Telemedia Council; mem. adv. com. for library and info. sci. U. Wis. Extension; Served with AUS, 1943-46; PTO. Mem. Assn. Ednl. Communication Tech., Wis. Audio Visual Assn., Internat. Visual Literacy Assn., Am. Council for Better Broadcast, Wis. Acad. Sci., Arts and Letters, Phi Sigma. Democrat. Author: College Biology II, 1969; The Microslide Viewer, 1969; College Biology I, 1970; Trigger Tapes: A Tool for Teacher Education, 1975; Children's Television: Rough Stuff on Saturday; asst. editor Wis. Audiovisual Dispatch, 1975-76. Home: 445 S 19th St LaCrosse WI 54601

ZEIS, JAMES FRANCIS, manufacturing engineer, pollution control company executive; b. Tiffin, Ohio, July 6, 1942; s. James Francis and Evelyn Mae (Mason) Z.; m. Betty Jean Sams, July 18, 1970; children—Alicia, Michael, Michelle, James Francis. Student, U. Toledo, 1960-63, Ohio State U., 1964-65. B.S. in Mech. Engring. Purdue U., 1966. Registered profl. engr., Ohio. Sr. process engr. Whirlpool Corp., Clyde, Ohio, 1972-78; mgr. engring. Nordson Corp., Amherst, Ohio, 1978-81; dist. mgr. Donaldson Corp., Cleve., 1981—. Patentee powder coating booth. Mem. Soc. Mfg. Engrs. Lodge: Masons. Avocation: firearms. Home: 1321 Caldwell Rd Bradner OH 43406 Office: Donaldson Corp 5474 Omega Ave Bedford Heights OH 44146

ZEISS, DONALD VERNON, educational administrator; b. Lincoln, Nebr., Sept. 16, 1942; s. Donald Vernon and Genevieve Katherine (Knippel) Z.; m. Janice Marie Steiner, Feb. 16, 1961; children—Jeffery Jay, Jill Marie, Jess D. B.S. in Edn., U. Nebr.-Lincoln, 1964, M.Ed., 1969, Ed.S., 1972, Ed.D., 1978. Tchr., coach Adams Pub. Schs., Nebr., 1965-66, Wilber Pub. Sch., Nebr., 1966-70; prin. Weeping Water Sch., Nebr., 1970-72, Tecumseh Sch., Nebr., 1972-74, Wayne Pub. Sch., Nebr., 1974—; mem. NCA Rev. Com., Chgo., 1974—; mem. Wayne State Coll. Community Relations Com., 1980. Contbr. articles to profl. jours. Bd. dirs. Wayne Community Chest; mem. Wayne State Coll. Second Guessers. Mem. Northeast Council Sch. Adminstrs., North Central Assn. Rev. Com., Phi Delta Kappa, Phi Epsilon Kappa. Democrat. Lutheran. Avocations: golf; weight-lifting; skiing; swimming. Home: 906 Sherman St Wayne NE 68787 Office: Wayne Pub Schs 611 W 7th St Wayne NE 68787

ZELICKSON, SUE, newspaper and cookbook editor, television reporter and host, food consultant; b. Mpls., Sept. 13, 1934; d. Harry M. and Bernice (Gross) Zipperman; m. Alvin S. Zelickson, Aug. 21, 1956; children—Barry M., Brian D. B.S. in Edn., U. Minn., 1956. Cert. elem. tchr., S.C., Minn. Tchr. various schs. Mpls., S.C., Golden Valley, Minn., 1956-79; writer, editor, columnist Mpls.-St. Paul Mag., 1980—, Buylines, Mpls., 1984—; TV-radio reporter Sta. WCCO-KSTP, Mpls, 1980—; restaurant developer, cons. Mpls., 1978—; v.p. Passage Tours, Mpls., 1984—. Coordinator, editor: Much Ado About Food, 1978; Minnesota Heritage Cookbook, 1979; Lee Ann Chin's Chinese Cuisine, 1981; Collins Back Room Cooking Secrets, 1981; The Governor's Table Cookbook, 1981; Chocolate Days & Chocolate Nights, 1982; Food for Show, Food on the Go, 1983; Wild Rice Star of The North, 1985; Look What's Cooking Now, 1985. Contbr. articles to Sun Newspaper, Post Publs., Mpls., Tribune. Public relations, promoter, fundraiser Mpls. Boys & Girls Club, Mpls. Inst. Arts, Hennepin County Med. Soc. Aux., Ronald McDonald House, Bonaventure Mall, Women's Assn. Minn. Symphony Orchestra, Council Jewish Women, Mt. Sinai Hosp., Brandeis U. Women, Minn. Opera Assn., Guthrie Theatre, Sholom Home, Am. Cancer Soc; bd. dirs. U. Minn. Alumni Bd., Golden Valley State Bank. Recipient Outstanding Achievement award Am. Cancer Soc., Duluth, Minn., 1984; Outstanding Achievement award Boys & Girls Club Minn., 1984. Mem. Nat. Council Jewish Women, Women's Assn. Minn. Orch., numerous others. Avocations: reading, travel; writing; painting. Home and Office: 101 Ardmore Dr Minneapolis MN 55422

ZELLER, FRANCIS JOSEPH, college dean; b. Chgo., July 31, 1943; s. Charles Joseph Paul and Erma (Kile) Z.; m. Frances Joan McGrath, Aug. 3, 1968; children—Patrick, Brian. B.A. in English, Lewis U., 1967; M.A., No. Ill. U., 1970, Ed.D., 1983. Tchr., chmn. English dept. Schaumburg Dist. 54, Ill., 1967-70; asst. bus. mgr. Park Ridge Sch. Dist. 64, Ill., 1970-71; bus. mgr. Barrington Sch. Dist. 224, Ill., 1971-73; dean bus. services Ill. Valley Community Coll., Oglesby, 1973—. Exec. mem. Boy Scouts of Am., Peoria, Ill., 1983—; mem. Peoria Diocesan Pastoral Council, 1983—. Mem. Internat. Assn. Sch. Bus. Ofcls., Ill. Assn. Sch. Bus. Ofcls., Ill. Assn. Community Coll. Bus. Adminstrs. (dir. 1984—), NEA, Delta Sigma Pi. Roman Catholic. Lodge: Rotary. Avocations: cross country skiing; tennis; hunting; distance bicycling. Office: Ill Valley Community Coll 2578 E 350th Rd Oglesby IL 61348

ZELLER, LYLE DEAN, management consultant, architect; b. Highland, Ill., Feb. 17, 1956; s. A. Gene and Mary Thelma (Willeford) Z.; m. Carla Sue Wilson, No. 6, 1976; 1 dau., Lauren Anne. A.A.S. (with honors), So. Ill. U., 1976, B.S. (with honors), 1979; M.B.A., Wash. U., St. Louis, 1983. Registered architect, Ill., Mo. Sr. archtl. technician Fischer-Stein Assocs., Carbondale, Ill., 1976-79; project architect Ralph Korte Inc., Highland, 1980-82; mgmt. cons. Peat Marwick Mitchell & Co., St. Louis, 1983-84, sr. cons., 1984—. Recipient Certs. Scholastic Achievement So. Ill. U., 1976, 79. Mem. AIA (St. Louis chpt.). Office: 1010 Market St Saint Louis MO 63101

ZELLING, DANIEL AMUNA, physician, hypnoanalyst; b. Flagy, France, Mar. 1, 1936; came to U.S., 1962, naturalized, 1968; s. Anton and Leonie Anne-Marie (Lowositz) Z.; m. Kathleen Dawn Murphy, Aug. 11, 1969; children—Martin Rudolph, Inge Sophia, Michael Patrick, Megan Anne-Marie. H.B.S.-B., Lyceum Noctua, 1956; M.D., Ryks U., Leiden, Netherlands, 1961. Intern, Ch. Homes Hosp., Balt., 1962-63; resident Barberton (Ohio) Citizens Hosp., 1963-64; gen. practice medicine, Akron, Ohio, 1964-76; exec. dir. Ohio Inst. Med. Hypnosis, Inc., Akron, 1976—; lectr. med. hypnosis Northeastern Ohio U., Rootstown, 1980—. Fellow Am. Acad. Family Physicians; mem. Soc. Med. Hypnoanalyst (pres. 1982—), Am. Soc. Clin. Hypnosis, Internat. Soc. Hypnosis, AMA, Summit County Med. Soc., Ohio Med. Soc. Republican. Home: 255 Harmony Hills Dr Akron OH 44321 Office: 80 N Miller Rd Akron OH 44313

ZELLNER, ARNOLD, economics educator; b. Bklyn., Jan. 2, 1927; s. Israel and Doris (Kleiman) Z.; m. Agnes Marie Summares, June 20, 1953; children—David, Philip, Samuel, Daniel, Michael. B.A., Harvard U., 1949; Ph.D., U. Calif.-Berkeley, 1957. Asst., then assoc. prof. econs. U. Wash., Seattle, 1955-60; assoc. prof., then prof. econs. U. Wis., Madison, 1961-66; H.G.B. Alexander prof. econs. and stats. Grad. Sch. Bus., U. Chgo., 1966—; Fulbright prof., Netherlands, 1960-61; vis. prof. U. Chgo., 1964-65, U.

Calif.-Stanford U., Berkeley, 1970, 1980-81; bd. dirs. Nat. Bur. Econ. Research, 1982—; dir. H.G.B. Alexander Research Found., U. Chgo., 1972—. Served with U.S. Army, 1951-53. NSF grantee, 1964—. Fellow Am. Statis. Assn. (Outstanding Statistician of Yr., Chgo. chpt. 1982), Econometric Soc., AAAS, Am. Acad. Arts and Scis.; mem. Am. Econs. Assn., Am. Statis. Assn. (editor Jour. Bus. and Econ. Stats. 1982—). Club: Quadrangle. Author: (with others) Systems Simulation for Regional Analysis, 1969; Estimating the Markov Probability Model, 1970; Bayesian Inference in Econometrics, 1971; Basic Issues in Econometrics, 1984. Editor: Seasonal Analysis of Economic Time Series, 1978. Contbr. articles to profl. jours. Office: 1101 E 58th St U Chicago Grad Sch Bus Chicago IL 60637

ZEMEL, DAVID MICHAEL, charitable organization administrator, human services educator; b. St. Louis, Feb. 16, 1949; s. Jack and Delores Mae (Aubuchon) Z.; m. Jane Mary Sandler, Jan. 14, 1973; 1 child, Abby Sandler. B.S. in Edn., U. Mo., 1971; M. in Social Work, Washington U., St. Louis, 1975. Tchr. Title I, St. James Schs., Mo., 1971-72; social worker II Boys Town Mo., St. James, 1972-75; program dir. St. Louis County Juvenile Court, 1975-79; dir. devel. Providence Program, Inc., St. Louis, 1979-80; devel. officer United Way Greater St. Louis, 1980-82, v.p., 1982—; assoc. prof. human services St. Louis Community Coll., 1975—; cons. in field. Author tng. manuals on fundraising. Mem. com. alternative edn. University City Schs., 1979—; trainer United Way Mgmt. Assistance Ctr., St. Louis, 1980—; bd. dirs. Confluence St. Louis, 1983-84, Boys Town Mo., St. Louis, 1977-79. Mem. Nat. Soc. Fund Raising Execs. (chmn. legis. 1982-83), Washington U. Alumni Assn. (ann. program com.). Jewish. Home: 7015 Lindell Blvd University City MO 63130 Office: United Way Greater Saint Louis 915 Olive St Saint Louis MO 63101

ZENDER, ANGELINA ELIZABETH, social services executive; b. Brighton, Mass., Apr. 19, 1933; d. Sabatino and Giovanina (Beninati) Fantasia; A.S., U. Wis., Madison, 1973, B.S., 1980; m. Frederick Robert Zender, Dec. 30, 1949; children—Richard, Kathryn, James, Nancy, Debra. Waitress, 1955-66; founder Ricky Zender Meml. Home, Inc., Wausau, Wis., 1973, adminstr., daily living coordinator, 1973—; mem. Wis. State Service for Oral Exams, 1974-75. Bd. dirs. Halfway House Fedn. Wis., 1980—. Recipient presdl. citation for community service Apogee, 1975. Mem. Assn. Retarded Citizens (state dir.), Marathon County Assn. Retarded Citizens (treas. 1971, pres. 1973-82), Nat. Assn. Pvt. Residential Facilities for Mentally Retarded (dir. 1976-85), Nat. Soc. Autistic Children, United Comml. Travelers Aux., United Cerebral Palsy Assn., Wis. Assn. Community Human Services Programs, Am. Assn. Mental Deficiency, Wis. Assn. Residential Facilities (sec. 1982), Wis. Epilepsy Assn., Wis. Assn. Devel. Disabilities (v.p. 1981), Wausau C. of C. (Personnel Club, chmn. interclub coordinating council), Assn. for Retarded Citizens (Hall of Fame 1980), Community Living Alliance for Mentally Retarded, Milw. Italian Community Ctr. Clubs: Toastmaster, Toastmistress (pres.). Author: (with others) Quality of Life, 1977; mem. rev. com. Guidelines to Community Living Systems for the Developmentally Disabled, 1975. Home: 110 E Moonlite Ave Wausau WI 54401 Office: PO Box 354 Wausau WI 54401

ZENERE, RENO P., marketing executive; b. Chgo., Oct. 31, 1929; s. John and Margarita Trevisan Z.; m. Dorothy Ann Cromwell, Dec. 7, 1952; children—Mark Alan, Cheryl Ann, Marie Antoinette. Laborer, Acme Steel Corp. (now Interlake, Inc.), Chgo., after 1947, apprentice electrician, to 1955, project technician, 1956, engr., 1959, sales rep., 1963, mktg. specialist, 1969, product mgr., 1974, gen. mgr. mktg., 1977, v.p. mktg., 1982—. Past chmn. bd. dirs. Pullman Civic Orgn.; bd. dirs. Met. Chgo. Coalition for Aged. Served to 1st lt. Ill. N.G. Democrat. Roman Catholic. Clubs: Olympia Fields Country (Olympia Fields, Ill.); KC (San Salvador).

ZENIAN, SHAHE LEVON, clinical psychologist; b. Beirut, Lebanon, Oct. 12, 1931; s. Levon Nazareth and Araxie (Bodourian) Z.; m. Jan Cooper, July 1, 1982; Student Westminster Coll., 1949-52, Washington State Coll., 1952; B.A., U. Mich., 1958; M.A., U. Mo., 1962. Asst. clin. psychologist Student Health Service, U. Mo., Columbia, 1960-63; clin. psychologist Fulton State Hosp. (Mo.), 1963-65; supr. psychol. services Maximum Security Unit, State Hosp. No. 1, Fulton, 1965-69, chief psychologist, 1969-75; chief clin. psychologist St. Francis Community Mental Health Ctr., Cape Girardeau, Mo., 1974-76; clin. psychologist Broadlawns Med. Ctr., Des Moines, Iowa, 1976—. Served with USAF, 1952-56. Mem. Fellow Am. Orthopsychiat. Assn.; mem. Am. Psychol. Assn., Iowa Psychol. Assn., Am. Personnel and Guidance Assn., Am. Assn. Correctional Psychologists, Am. Psychology-Law Soc., Law and Society Assn., Am. Correctional Assn., Iowa Corrections Assn., Nat. Jail Assn., Am. Assn. Correctional Officers. Home: PO Box 7123 Grand Station Des Moines IA 50309 Office: Broadlawns Medical Ctr 18th & Hickman Rd Des Moines IA 50314

ZENK, GEORGE EDWARD, elec. engr.; b. Erie, Pa., June 8, 1923; s. Otto John and Charlotte (Shafer) Z.; B.A., Westminster Coll., 1949; B.Sc., Carnegie Inst. Tech., 1949, M.Sc., 1950, Ph.D., 1953; m. Irma Rose Haberman, June 13, 1953. Mem. tech. staff Bell Tel. Labs., Whippany, N.J., 1953-61; sr. engr. Honeywell Aero Co., Mpls., 1962-63; cons. Control Data Corp., Mpls., 1964—. Vice pres Found. for Living, Abbott-Northwestern Hosp., Mpls., 1977-78. Served with AUS, 1943-46. NRC fellow, 1950-51; Buhl Found. fellow, 1951-52. Mem. IEEE, Sigma Xi, Tau Beta Pi, Eta Kappa Nu, Phi Kappa Phi. Patentee computer man-machine interface, spacecraft nav. system, electronic filters. Home: 6905 10th Ave S Richfield MN 55423 Office: 2300 E 88th St Bloomington MN 55420

ZERBI, PAUL GENOESE, thoracic and cardiovascular surgeon; b. Italy, Aug. 2, 1933; s. Domenico Genoese and Rose (Contestabile) Z.; came to U.S., 1962, naturalized, 1972; M.D., U. Modena (Italy), 1960; m. Mary Martha Berring, Jan. 11, 1964; children—Paula, Jayne, Dominic. Intern U. Hosp., U. Modena, 1960; physician with U.S. Army, Germany, 1961; resident in surgery Aultman Hosp., Canton, Ohio, 1962-63, Mercy Hosp., Canton, 1963-65, Columbus Hosp., N.Y.C., 1965-66; resident in thoracic and cardiovascular surgery Emory U. Hosps., Atlanta, 1966-68; chief surgery Central State Hosp., Milledgeville, Ga., 1968-70; practice medicine specializing in thoracic and cardiovascular surgery, Warren, Ohio, 1970—; active staff Trumbull Meml. Hosp., 1973—. Diplomate Am. Bd. Surgery, Am. Bd. Thoracic Surgery. Fellow A.C.S., Am. Coll. Chest Physicians; mem. Am., Ohio State med. assns., Trumbull County Med. Soc., Cleve. Surg. Soc., Soc. Thoracic Surgeons, Am. Heart Assn. Roman Catholic. Home: 9710 King Graves Rd Warren OH 44484 Office: 3893 E Market St Warren OH 44484

ZERKLE, JAMES KARL, lawyer; b. Macomb, Ill., Sept. 6, 1954; s. Robert W. and Mary L. (Myatt) Z.; m. Carol M. Tvrdy, July 1, 1979; children—Adam James, John Robert. B.A., Western Ill. U., 1976; J.D., Chgo.-Kent Coll. Law, 1979. Bar: Ill. 1979, U.S. Dist. Ct. (cen. dist.) Ill. 1980. Asst. appellate defender Office State Appellate Defender, Springfield, Ill., 1979-81; asst. corp. counsel City of Springfield, Ill., 1981-82; atty. Midwest div. Roadway Express, Inc., Chicago Heights, Ill., 1982—. Mem. Ill. Bd. Higher Edn., Springfield, 1975-76; mem. Ill. Ednl. TV Commn., Springfield, 1976-78; trustee Lincoln Land Coll., Springfield, 1973-74. Ill. Gov.'s Fellowship program fellow, 1976. Mem. Ill. Bar Assn., Blue Key. Office: Roadway Express Inc 2000 Lincoln Hwy Chicago Heights IL 60411

ZERNER, RICHARD EGON, lawyer; b. Toledo, Aug. 27, 1947; s. Carl Egon and Erma K. (Klein) Z.; m. Nancy L. Goodman, Apr. 6, 1972; children—Loryn Brooke, Robert Egon. B.A., Hillsdale Coll., 1969; J.D., U. Toledo, 1972. Bar: Ohio 1973. Sole practice law, Toledo, 1973—; assoc. Associated Legal Group, Toledo, 1982—; legal counsel Northwestern Ohio Gasoline Dealers Assn. Mem. pres.'s council Toledo Mus. Art; past trustee Maumee Valley Country Day Sch. Mem. ABA, Ohio Bar Assn., Toledo Bar Assn., Jewish Community Ctr., Maumee Valley Country Day Sch. Alumni Assn. (past pres.). Clubs: Belmont Country, Carranor Hunt & Polo, Toledo Tennis, Masons. Home: 5045 Cartagena Dr Toledo OH 43623 Office: 3223 Sylvania Ave Toledo OH 43613

ZETTELMAIER, JOHN L., physician; b. Chgo., Dec. 17, 1937; s. John C. and Eleanor L. Zettelmaier; m. Mary Ann DeSantis; children—Michael, Martha, Joseph, Jacob. A.B., Western Mich. U., 1960; M.S., Mich. State U., 1962; M.D., U. Mich., 1965. Diplomate Am. Bd. Family Practice. Intern, Borgess Hosp., Kalamazoo, 1965-66; gen. practice medicine, Almena Twp., Mich., and Kalamazoo, Mich., 1965-85; mem. staff Borgess Hosp., Bronson Hosp., Lakeview Hosp., Gen. Practice Med. Group., Chesterton, Ind., St. Anthony Hosp., Michigan City, Ind.; assoc. clin. prof. family medicine Mich. State U.; adj. clin. instr. Western Mich. U. Charter mem. Republican Presdl. Task Force, 1981; mem. Gobles Sch. Bd.; mem. Mich. Rep. State Issues Com.; chmn. Issues Com. 4th Dist. Reps.; mem. Van Buren County (Mich.) Exec. Com. Reps.; mem. U.S. Senatorial Bus. Adv. Bd. Served to capt. USAR. Mem. AMA, Mich. State Med. Soc., Gobles Alumni Assn., Western Mich. U. Alumni Assn., Am. Acad. Polit. Sci., Mich. State U. Alumni Assn., U. Mich. Alumni Assn., C. of C. Chesterton, Beta Beta Beta, Kappa Rho Sigma. Roman Catholic. Lodges: Lions, Rotary. Author: Enuf Already, 1983. Home: 501 Honeyshade Dr Chesterton IN 46304

ZETTLE, PAULA RUTH, nurse; b. Youngstown, Ohio, Aug. 9, 1938; d. Paul Vincent and Doris Esther (Snively) Webb; R.N., St. Luke's Hosp. Sch. Nursing, 1959; postgrad. Cuyahoga Community Coll., 1969, St. Joseph's Coll., 1984; m. Donald Richard Zettle; children—Peter, Lisa, Jonathan, James. Nurse, Lakewood (Ohio) Hosp., 1960-61; employee health service nurse Mt. Sinai Hosp., Hillcrest Hosp., Cleve., 1972-78; day supr., patient care coordinator Shaker Med. Center, Cleve., 1978-80; asst. dir. nursing Americana Healthcare, Mayfield Heights, Ohio, 1981; utilization rev. coordinator Kaiser Found., East Side Hosps., Cleve., 1982-84, regional utilization auditor, quality assurance coordinator, 1984—; mem. adv. bd. Upjohn Healthcare Services, also mem. clin. rev. com.; instr. CPR; cons. Leader, Girl Scouts U.S.A., 1968-73; den mother, trainer Boy Scouts Am., 1967-69; active ARC. Mem. St. Luke's Hosp. and Greater Cleve. Gen. Alumni Assn., Nat. Assn. Quality Assurance Profls. Presbyterian. Home: 993 Professor Rd Lyndhurst OH 44124 Office: 36100 Euclid Ave Willoughby OH 44094

ZICHEK, MELVIN EDDIE, retired clergyman, educator; b. Lincoln, Nebr., May 5, 1918; s. Eddie and Agnes (Varga) Z.; A.B., Nebr. Central Coll., 1942; M.A., U. Nebr., 1953; D.Litt., McKinley-Roosevelt Ednl. Inst., 1955; m. Dorothy Virginia Patrick, May 28, 1942; 1 dau., Shannon Elaine. Ordained to ministry Christian Ch., 1942; minister Christian chs., Brock, Nebr., 1941, Ulysses, Nebr., 1942-43, Elmwood, Nebr., 1943-47, Central City, Nebr., 1947-83, ret., 1983; rural tchr., Merrick County, Nebr., 1937-40; prin. Alvo (Nebr.) Consol. High Sch., 1943-47; supt. Archer (Nebr.) Pub. Schs., 1948-57; head dept. English and speech Central City (Nebr.) High Sch., 1957-63; supt. Marquette (Nebr.) Consol. Schs., 1963-79. Served as chaplain's asst. AUS, 1942. Mem. Internat. Platform Assn., Disciples of Christ Hist. Soc., Nat. Sch. Adminstrs. Assn. Club: Buffy. Home: 2730 North Rd Grand Island NE 68803

ZICK, BERNARD HALE, real estate consultant; b. Ft. Worth, July 18, 1944; s. James Mercer and Alice Viola (Hale) Z.; B.S., U. Mo., 1968; M.B.A., Northwestern U., 1969; m. Carol Jean Demuth, Nov. 12, 1977. Portfolio mgr. Stein Roe & Farnham, N.Y.C., 1969-70; cons.; lectr. Real Estate Investors Tng., Inc. Mem. Mayor's Corp. of Progress; mem. adv. bd. Metro Pollution, 1974; mem. Citizens Environ. Council, 1970-75. Cert. comml. investment. Mem. Nat. Assn. Realtors (CCIM award). Kans. Assn. Realtors, Kansas City Bd. Realtors, Acad. of Real Estate (ACE award), Interex (Cert. Exchangor award), Nat. Speaker Assn. Club: Kansas City. Author: Money Making Formulas In Creative Real Estate, 1978; Creative Real Estate Financing, Vol. I, 1979, Vol. II, 1981; Creative Formulas Workbook, 1982; How To Become a Paper Millionaire, 1983. Home: 1049 Cerro Verde Dr Solana Beach CA 92075 Office: 7180 W 107th St Overland Park KS 66212 also Box 630 Solana Beach CA 92075

ZIDEK, BERNICE LOUISE (MRS. STEPHEN P. ZIDEK), wire mfg. exec.; b. Chgo., Oct. 10, 1906; d. Albert and Bessie (Kaberna) Vonder; diploma Englewood (Ill.) Secretarial Coll., 1923; m. Stephen Paul Zidek, July 22, 1925; children—Louise Ann Zidek Pavlin, Charles Edward. Asst. to asst. mgr. Emerson Drug Co., Chgo., 1923-24; office mgr. Van Dyke Industries, Chgo., 1936-38; partner Midland Metal Products Co., Chgo., 1941—. Troop leader to leader trainer Lone Tree Area council Girl Scouts U.S.A., 1938-68; mem. Insight for the Blind, Inc., Ft. Lauderdale Oral Sch. Aux., Holy Cross Hosp. Aux. MacNeal Meml. Hosp. Recipient Thank You award Girl Scouts U.S.A., 1957. Mem. Nat., Fla. assns. parliamentarians, Am. Inst. Parliamentarians, Am. Guild Flower Arrangers, Fla. Fedn. Garden Clubs (life), Nat. Council State Garden Clubs (life), Nat. Council Flower Show Judges (master judge), Freedoms Found. at Valley Forge, Moraine Valley Parliamentary Unit (Ill.), Oriental Study Club South Fla. Republican. Roman Catholic. Clubs: Bauhinia Garden Circle (pres. 1965-67), Federated Garden Circles of Ft. Lauderdale (pres. 1974-75), Coral Springs Garden, Women's Civic, Coral Ridge Yacht (Ft. Lauderdale); Country of Coral Springs; Riverside (Ill.) Golf. Home: 250 N Delaplaine Rd Riverside IL 60546 also 2791 NW 112th Ave Coral Springs FL 33065

ZIEGLER, ELAINE EDYTHE, personnel executive; b. Phila., Oct. 7, 1944; d. Louis Henry and Ada M. (Hoffmeister) Leypoldt. B.A. cum laude, Lenoir-Rhyne Coll., Hickory, N.C., 1966; M.Ed. with honors, Rutgers U., New Brunswick, N.J., 1979. Tchr. South Brunswick (N.J.) Bd. Edn., 1966-69, 71-80, Amherst (Mass.) Bd. Edn., 1969-71; dir. human resource devel. Am. Collectors Assn., Edina, Minn., 1981—. Mem. Wayzata Planning Commn., 1982—, Wayzata Charter Commn., 1982—; del. UN Yr. of Child, 1979. Mem. Twin Cities Personnel Assn., Am. Soc. Personnel Adminstrn., Wayzata C. of C., AAUW (past dir.), Kappa Delta Pi, Delta Theta. Lutheran. Office: 4040 W 70th St Edina MN 55435

ZIEGLER, PAUL WILLIAM, lawyer; b. Cleve., Mar. 19, 1946; A.B., Georgetown U., 1968, J.D., 1971. Bar: Ohio 1971, D.C. 1982. Ptnr. McNeal, Schick, Archibald & Biro, Cleve., 1971—. Mem. ABA, Cleve. Bar Assn., Ohio State Bar Assn., Cuyahoga County Bar Assn., D.C. Bar Assn. Club: Cleve. Athletic. Avocations: golf, sailing, skiing, handball. Office: McNeal Schick Archibald & Biro 55 Public Sq 10 Floor Cleveland OH 44113

ZIEGMAN, RONALD ALLEN, electrical engineer; b. Garfield Heights, Ohio, May 28, 1951; s. Gerald Andrew and Blanche Eva (Chrulski) Z. B.S.E. cum laude, Cleve. State U., 1974, M.S.E., 1976; postgrad. Case Western Res. U., 1977-79. Registered profl. engr., Ohio. Research technologist LTV Steel Co., Independence, Ohio, 1976-83, sr. research engr., 1983—. Mem. IEEE, Assn. Iron and Steel Engrs. (com. mem.), Tau Beta Pi (chpt. pres. 1973-74), Eta Kappa Nu (chpt. treas. 1973-74). Office: LTV Steel Research Ctr 6801 Brecksville Rd Independence OH 44131

ZIELASKO, GUS WILLIAM, judge; b. Canton, Ohio, June 15, 1915; s. Gustav A. and Marie (Gross) Z.; m. Helen M. Trenary, Dec. 24, 1946 (div. Dec. 1954); m. Marilyn A. Jenkins, Oct. 21, 1956; children—Douglas E., Becky J., Tracy J. B.A., Coll. of Wooster, 1938; M.A., U. Mich., 1939; postgrad. Ohio State U., 1939-40; LL.B., William McKinley Sch. of Law, 1950. Bar: Ohio 1950. Instr., coach U. N. Mex., Albuquerque, 1941-42, 46-47; mem. firm Eberly, Lesh & Miller, Canton, 1950-81; judge Canton Mcpl. Ct., 1981—. Bd. dirs. N.C. Student Loan Found. Served to 2d lt. U.S. Army, 1942-46, ETO. Mem. Stark County Bar Assn. (pres. 1975-76), Ohio State Bar Assn., Ohio Mcpl. Judges Assn. Republican. Methodist. Avocations: photography, golf. Office: Canton Mcpl Ct City Hall Canton OH 44702

ZIENTY, FERDINAND BENJAMIN, chemical company executive, research executive, consultant; b. Chgo., Mar. 21, 1915; s. Albert Frank and Rose Cecelia (Przypyszny) Z.; B.S., U. Ill., 1935; M.S., U. Mich., 1936, Ph.D., 1938; m. Claylain Lorraine Cawiezell, Apr. 14, 1945; children—Jane Zienty Wheeler, Donald Ferd. Research chemist organic chems. div. Monsanto Co., St. Louis, 1938-40, research group leader, 1940-47, asst. dir. research, 1947-50, asso. dir. research, 1950-56, dir. research, 1956-60, dir. advanced organic chems. research, 1960-64, mgr. research and devel., 1964-79, dir. chemistry bio med program, 1979-83, dir. research Health Care div., 1983, cons., 1983—, v.p. research George Lueders & Co. subs. Monsanto Co., St. Louis, 1968-70. Recipient Hodel, Saltiel, Hodel prize for scholarship, 1935, Sesquicentennial award U. Mich., 1967; Disting. Alumnus award U. Mich. Coll. Pharmacy, 1981. Fairchild scholar, 1935, Frederick Stearns fellow, 1936-37. Fellow AAAS, N.Y. Acad. Scis.; mem. Am. Chem. Soc., Am. Inst. Chem. Engrs., Am. Pharm. Assn., Inst. Food Technologists, Mo. Acad. Sci., Soc. Chem. Industry (London). Clubs: Triple A Country, Normandie Golf. Contbr. articles to profl. jours. Patentee in field. Home: 850 Rampart Dr Warson Woods MO 63122 Office: 850 Rampart Dr Warson Woods MO 63122

ZIETH, RANDALL LEE, optometrist; b. Kenosha, Wis., June 16, 1952; s. Raymond and Jayne (Johansen) Z.; m. Gwyenda Teleane Vincent, June 8, 1979; one child, Caroline Reynolds Zieth. Student U. Wis.-Parkside, 1971-72; O.D., Ill. Coll. Optometry, 1972. Lic. optometrist. Resident Gesell Inst. Child Devel., New Haven, 1976-77; assoc. in pvt. practice of optometry, Watertown, Wis., Kenosha, 1978-79; gen. practice optometry, Ripon, Wis., 1979—. Chmn. United Way, Ripon, 1980. E.B. Alexander fellow Optometry Extension, Yale, U., 1977; recipient Vision Therapy Splty. award Ill. Coll. Optometry, 1976; Key Man award Ripon Jaycees, 1982. Mem. Optometric Extension Program (bd. dirs.), Wis. Optometric Assn., Am. Optometric Assn., Better Vision Inst. Lutheran. Lodges: Lions (dir. Ripon club 1983), Rotary. Avocations: karate; tennis; hunting; fishing. Home: 117 Howard St Ripon WI 54971

ZIKMUND, DOUGLAS BRUCE, pharmacist, farm owner; b. Astoria, Oreg., Apr. 10, 1945; s. Lloyd Donald and Patricia Ruth (Strong) Z.; m. Carol Joan Leininger, May 28, 1967. Student Kearney State Coll., 1964-66, U. Nebr., 1973-76, B.S. in Pharmacy, 1978. Registered pharmacist. Pharmacy intern Bradfield Drug, Lincoln, Nebr., 1974-76; pharmacist Alexander's Pharmacy, Norfolk, Nebr., 1978-79; pharmacist, owner Blevin's Drive-in Pharmacy, Columbus, Nebr., 1979—; vice chmn. Nebr. Pharmacists Polit. Action Com., Lincoln, 1981—. Served with USN, 1966-73, with USNR, 1973—. Mem. Nebr. Pharmacists Assn. (bd. dirs. 1981-85, pres. 1983-84), Nat. Assn. Retail Druggists, U. Nebr. Alumni Assn., VFW, Am. Legion. Democrat. Methodist. Lodges: Eagles, Elks. Avocations: hunting; fishing; water skiing; farming. Home: 107 S Calle Colombo Columbus NE 68601 Office: Blevins Drive-in Pharmacy 1461 28th Ave Columbus NE 68601

ZIMANY, ROLAND DANIEL, theology educator; b. East Orange, N.J., Aug. 5, 1936; s. Daniel and Margaret (Zigo) Z.; m. Barbara Bowen, May 15, 1976. A.B., Princeton U., 1958; M.B.A., NYU, 1965; M.Div., Union Theol. Sem., 1974; Ph.D., Duke U., 1980; postgrad. U. Tübingen, W. Germany, 1976-77. Mgmt. analyst, personnel rep. Port Authority N.Y. and N.J., N.Y.C., 1958-69; mgmt. cons. Mgmt. Practice Cons. Ptnrs., N.Y.C., 1969-70; mgr. mgmt. systems Nat. Urban League, N.Y.C., 1970-72; teaching asst. theology Duke Div. Sch., Durham, N.C., 1975,77; asst. prof. philosophy, religion Blackburn Coll., Carlinville, Ill., 1980—; project dir. directory Ednl. Opportunities in Pub. Admin., 1968. Contbr. articles to profl. jours. Served with U.S. Army, 1958-59. Duke U. grad. scholar, 1975,77; alt. travelling fellow Union Theol. Sem., 1974; recipient Duke U. travel award, 1976. Mem. Am. Acad. Religion. Democrat. Lutheran. Home: 413 Morgan St Carlinville IL 62626 Office: Blackburn Coll Carlinville IL 62626

ZIMELIS, JANIS (JOHN), educator; b. Rezekne, Latvia, May 21, 1936; came to U.S., 1949, naturalized, 1954; s. Jezups and Bronislava (Papins) Z.; m. Mary Juanita Corby, Jan. 28, 1961; children—Renee, Janis, John, William. B.S., Aquinas Coll., 1961; M.S., Mich. State U., 1966. Cert. tchr., Mich. Lab. technician Dow Chem. Co., Midland, Mich., 1957-59; tchr. Grand Rapids (Mich.) Bd. Edn., 1961-66; tchr. East Grand Rapids (Mich.) Bd. Edn., 1966—, asst. prin., 1970-73; prin. Kent Intermediate Sch., Grand Rapids, summer 1971-73. Served with USNG, 1954-61. Mem. Nat. Sci. Tchrs. Assn., Mich. Sci. Tchrs. Assn., Phi Delta Kappa. Roman Catholic. Home: 1164 Forest Hill St SE Grand Rapids MI 49506 Office: East Grand Rapids Bd Ed 2211 Lake Dr SE East Grand Rapids MI 49506

ZIMMER, JOHN HERMAN, lawyer; b. Sioux Falls, S.D., Dec. 30, 1922; s. John Francis and Veronica (Berke) Z.; student Augustana Coll., Sioux Falls, 1941-42, Mont. State Coll., 1943; LL.B., U. S.D., 1948; m. Deanna Langner, 1976; children by previous marriage—June, Mary Zimmer Levine, Robert Joseph, Judith Maureen Zimmer Rose. Admitted to S.D. bar, 1948; practice law, Turner County, S.D., 1948—; partner firm Zimmer, Richter, Duncan & Neiles, Parker, S.D.; states atty. Turner County, 1955-58, 62-64; asst. prof. med. jurisprudence; minority counsel S.D. Senate Armed Services Com. on Strategic and Critical Materials Investigation, 1962-63; chmn. Southeastern Council Govts., 1973-75; mem. U. S.D. Law Sch. adv. council, 1973-74. Chmn. Turner County Republican Com., 1955-56; mem. S.D. Rep. adv. com., 1959-60; alt. del. Rep. Nat. Conv., 1968. Served with AUS, 1943-46; PTO. Decorated Bronze Star, Philippine Liberation ribbon. Mem. Am., Fed., S.D. (commr. 1954-57) bar assns., Am. Trial Lawyers Assn., S.D. Trial Lawyers Assn. (pres. 1967-68), VFW, Am. Legion, Phi Delta Phi. Clubs: Elks, Shriners. Home: Parker SD 57053 Office: Law Bldg Parker SD 57053

ZIMMERMAN, DANIEL RAY, educator; b. Chgo., Nov. 22, 1948; s. Raymond Zimmerman and Kathleen (Benton) Dickie. A.A., Triton Coll., 1968; B.S. in Edn., No. Ill. U., 1970; Ph.D., Universal Life U., 1982, D.D. (hon.), 1978; postgrad. Inst. for Advanced Study of Human Sexuality, 1984—. Cert. tchr., Ill., Iowa. Tchr. Cedar Rapids Schs., Iowa, 1970—, now spl. edn. tchr.; minister Universal Life Ch., Cedar Rapids, 1976—, adminstr., Modestor, Calif., 1980—, supr., 1982—, at law witness, 1982—; assoc. prof. religion Universal Life U., Modesto, 1983—, counselor sexual minorities, 1984—; presenter seminars in field. Author: Universal Life Church Principles and Practices, 1983. Foster parent Linn County Human Services, Cedar Rapids, 1976-83; activist Civil Rights Advocates, Washington, 1985. Recipient Tchr. Incentive award Dept. Edn. State of Iowa, 1974. Mem. Am. Humanist Assn., Am. Fedn. Tchrs., NEA. Democrat. Avocations: group presentations; networking and network information.

ZIMMERMAN, DEAN ROLAND, animal nutrition educator; b. Compton, Ill., July 2, 1932; s. Arthur George and Freda Anna Maria (Kutter) Z.; m. Wendy Gretchen, Aug. 16, 1953; children—Dale, Dee. B.S., Iowa State U., 1954, Ph.D., 1960. Research assoc. Notre Dame U., South Bend, Ind., 1960-62; asst. prof. Wartburg Coll., Waverly, Iowa, 1962-65; assoc. prof. animal nutrition Purdue U., Lafayette, Ind., 1965-67; prof., Iowa State U., Ames, 1967—. Mem. Am. Soc. Animal Sci., Sigma Xi. Republican. Lutheran. Lodge: Kiwanis. Avocations: jogging; skiing; fishing. Home: 2918 Northwood Dr Ames IA 50010 Office: Iowa State U Dept Animal Sci Ames IA 50011

ZIMMERMAN, DELANO ELMER, physician; b. Fond du Lac, Wis., Mar. 21, 1933; s. Elmer Herbert and Agatha Angeline (Freund) Z.; B.S., U. Wis., 1961, M.D., 1965; m. Nancy Margaret Garry, Aug. 13, 1966; children—Kate, Joseph, Nick. Intern, Hennepin County Hosp., Mpls., 1965; physician, surgeon Winnebago (Wis.) State Hosp., 1966-67; gen. practice medicine, Neenah, Wis., 1967-73; emergency room physician Community Emergency Services, Appleton, 1973-77, Meml. Med. Center, Springfield, Ill., 1977—; faculty So. Ill. U. Sch. Medicine, Springfield, 1977—. Served with USN, 1951-56. Mem. AMA, Am. Coll. Emergency Physicians, Sangamon County Med. Soc., Soc. Tchrs. Emergency Medicine. Roman Catholic. Home: 1404 S Park Ave Springfield IL 62704 Office: Meml Med Center 800 N Rutledge Springfield IL 62781

ZIMMERMAN, FRANCES ADDIE HOWELL, government official; b. Kansas City, Mo., Oct. 10; d. Dewey J. and Louise Frances (Wydick) Howell; Asso. Degree, Park Coll., Parkville, Mo., 1944; student Rockhurst Coll., 1970, U. Mo., Kansas City, 1972, U. Mich., 1976, 77, U. Houston, 1977, U. Kans., 1979; m. Eugene R. Zimmerman, Aug. 10, 1945 (dec. Nov. 1982); children—Donald, Nancy Zimmerman Giller, Robert J., Laura. Dir. public relations program, county organizer Am. Cancer Soc., Kansas City, Mo., 1959-60; public relations Mo. Employment Service, 1962-75; instr., art dir. Regional Tng. Center, U.S. Dept. Labor, Overland Park, Kans., 1975-80, public relations and employer com. coordinator, Kansas, Mo., 1980—; instr. Mo. Div. Employment Security, 1983—; cons. in field. Pres., Scarritt Sch. PTA, 1950; bd. dirs. Shawnee Mission (Kans.) High Sch., 1960; v.p. Jefferson City Women's Polit. Caucus, 1983; mem. Mo. Commn. on Status of Women, 1983. Mem. Internat. Assn. Personnel (v.p. Mo. 1975, exec. bd. internat. award of merit Mo. 1975), Am. Soc. Trainers and Developers (charter mem. orgnl. devel. media div., program com.), Nat. Assn. Female Execs., Nelson Gallery Art, Kansas City C. of C., Urban League Greater Kansas City, Personal Dynamics Assn., Mid Am. Soc. Assn. Execs., Park Coll. Alumni Assn. Art Dirs. Club Kansas City, Nelson Gallery Art Soc. Baptist. Clubs: Kansas City Art Dirs., Overland Park Lioness. Home: 10568 Century Ln Overland Park KS 66215 Office: 1411 Main Kansas City MO 64105

ZIMMERMAN, FRANK RAYWORTH, telecommunications products and services company executive; b. Ypsilanti, Mich., Aug. 22, 1931; s. Frank B. and Hazel (Rayworth) Z.; Barbara Faye Marie Kellogg, June 30, 1951; children—Deborah, Paul, Judith, John. B.S., Eastern Mich. U., 1955. Mgr. traffic Mich. Bell, Detroit, 1955-74, gen. mgr. operator services, 1974-75, asst. v.p. revenues, 1976-78, v.p. pub. relations/revenues, 1978-83, exec. v.p., chief operating officer, 1983; sr. v.p. corp. affairs Ameritech, Chgo., 1983—; dir. Ind. Bell Telephone Co., Indpls. Bd. dirs. Eastern Mich. U. Coll. Bus. Devel., Ypsilanti, 1983—, pub. utilities exec. program adv. com. U. Mich., Ann Arbor, 1983—, Midwest Bus. Group on Health, Chgo., 1985—, Jr. Achievement S.E. Mich., 1977-83, Greater Mich. Found., Detroit, 1978-83, United Found. Adv. Bd., Detroit, 1982-83. Recipient Bronze award Jr. Achievement, Detroit, 1982,

Silver award, 1983. Republican. Methodist. Avocations: swimming; boating. Office: Ameritech 30 S Wacker Dr Floor 38 Chicago IL 60606

ZIMMERMAN, JILL SARAH, clinical social worker; b. Chgo., Feb. 12, 1951; d. Robert Edward and Jane Frances (Hefter) Zimmerman; m. Robert Eugene Rutledge, May 30, 1981; 1 son, Daniel Ernest; 1 stepson, Jonathan Lee. B.A. in Sociology, U. Colo., 1973; M.S.W., U. Ill., 1976; postgrad. Northwestern U., 1981, Loyola Stritch Sch. Medicine, 1976. Lic. social worker, Ill. Clin. social worker Chgo. Osteo. Hosp., 1977-78; clin. social worker, supr. N.W. Mental Health Center, Arlington Heights, Ill., 1978-81, staff cons., supr. for family treatment, 1981-84; pvt. practice psychotherapy, specializing in eating disorders and div./remarried families, Evanston, Ill., 1981—; facilitator Nat. Orgn. Anorexia Nervosa and Assoc. Disorders, Support Group, Evanston, 1982—; cons. in field; instr. Ctr. Family Studies, Family Inst. Chgo., Northwestern U., Chgo. Bd. dirs. YWCA, Evanston, 1983—. Mem. Nat. Assn. Social Workers, Ill. Soc. Clin. Social Workers, Acad. Cert. Social Workers, Alumni Assn. of Ctr. for Family Studies/Family Inst. Chgo. (alumni bd. 1984—). Contbr. articles to profl. jours. Address: 636 Church St Evanston IL 60202

ZIMMERMAN, JOHN WALLACE, SR., corporate strategy formulation consultant; b. Milw., Apr. 25, 1929; s. Wallace R. and Gladys P. (Parker) Z.; m. Charlotte McCallen, Aug. 28, 1951; children—John W., Paul E., Mark W., James P. Student Carroll Coll., Waukesha, Wis., 1947-49; B.S., U. Tenn.-Knoxville, 1951; M.B.A., U. Wis.-Madison, 1952, postgrad., 1953; postgrad., U. Minn., 1959-60. Indsl. engr. Oscar Mayer Co., Madison, Wis., 1951-53; prodn. supr., indsl. engr. Pillsbury Co., Springfield, Ill., 1953-55, assoc. tng. mgr., Mpls., 1955-57, tng. mgr., 1957-61, assoc. Kepner-Tregoe, Inc., Princeton, N.J., 1961-69, sr. v.p., 1969—, dir., 1973—, mgmt. cons. affiliated with Kepner-Tregoe, Inc., 1984—. Author: (with Tregoe) Top Management Strategy, 1980. Contbr. numerous articles to profl. jours. Guest lectr. Internat. Mgmt. Inst., Geneva, 1972—. Mem. Am. Soc. Tng. and Devel. (pres. So. Minn. chpt. 1959-60, pres. mid-N.J. chpt. 1976-77, nat. dir., 1979-81, Torch Award, 1978). Republican. Avocations: travel; reading; writing.

ZIMMERMAN, LOIS RUTH, physician; b. Tiffin, Ohio, Feb. 12, 1931; s. Russell and Ruth Beatrice (Baum) Z.; B.A., Bowling Green State U., 1951; M.D., Ohio State U., 1955. Diplomate Tropical Medicine and Hygiene, London U., 1959. Intern, Youngstown City Hosp., Ohio, 1955-56; gen. resident, Lafayette, La., 1958-59; resident in surgery Hartford Hosp., Conn., 1956-57, Youngstown City Hosp., 1962-63; med. missionary Meth. Ch., Ganta, Liberia, 1959-65; gen. practice medicine, Arcadia, Wis., 1965-67, Bellaire Med. Found., Ohio, 1967-76, Barnesville Med. Group, Ohio, 1976-79; pvt. practice, St. Clairsville, Ohio, 1979—. Mem. Am. Acad. Family Practice (cert.), AMA (vol. physician Vietnam Project 1967, pres. local chpt. 1977-78), Am. Med. Women's Assn. Republican. Presbyterian. Home: Route 3 Country Club Rd Saint Clairsville OH 43950 Office: St Clair Med Park Route 1 Saint Clairsville OH 43950

ZIMMERMAN, RAYMOND DALE, mechanical engineer, business executive; b. East Cleveland, Ohio, June 24, 1949; s. Julius Eugene and Shirley Ione (Carter) Z.; student math. Case Inst. Tech., 1966; B.S. cum laude in Mech. Engring. (scholar), U. Cin., 1972, M.S., 1978, postgrad., 1978-81. Engring. trainee Arthur G. McKee & Co., Independence, Ohio, 1968-71; project engr. Structural Dynamics Research Corp., Milford, Ohio, 1972-73, mem. tech. staff, 1973-76; research asst. U. Cin., 1976-81; exec. v.p. Quixote Measurement Dynamics, Inc., Cin., 1981-82, chmn. bd., 1981—, pres., 1982—; cons. engr., 1976—; lectr. modal analysis U. Cin., 1977—. Active Big Bros. Am., 1979-82. Structural Dynamics Research Corp. study grantee, 1976-77; Foundry Ednl. Found. grantee, 1969-71. Mem. ASME (tech. reviewer div. dynamic systems and control 1980—), Soc. Exptl. Mechanics, Sigma Xi. Contbr. articles to profl. publs. Office: PO Box 19299 Cincinnati OH 45219

ZIMMERMAN, RICHARD MICHAEL, SR., police chief; b. Columbus, Ohio, Oct. 21, 1947; s. Richard Henry and Pamela Rita (Coon) Z.; m. Wanda D. Pelfrey, May 30, 1970; children—Richrd Michael Jr., James L., Angela D. A.S. in Police Adminstrn., St. Petersburg Jr. Coll., 1979. Chief dep. Vinton County sheriff, McArthur, Ohio, 1973; LEADS control officer Ohio Hwy. Patrol, Columbus, 1973-75; dep. sheriff Pinellas County Sheriff Dept., Largo, Fla., 1975-80; chief of police Cadiz Police Dept., Ohio, 1981—; intoxilyzer technician, Ohio and Fla.; radar instr.; police firearms instr. Pinellas Police Acad. Served with U.S. Army, 1966-72. Decorated Bronze star, Air medal with 30 Oak Leaf clusters, Purple Heart; recipient Citation U.S. Coast Guard, 1980, Citation, Office of the Ohio Atty. Gen., 1982, Cert. of Appreciation award Medic Alert Found. Internat., 1984. Republican. Roman Catholic. Avocations: flying, competitive marksmanship, tennis, bowling. Home: 364 Grant St Cadiz OH 43907 Office: Cadiz Police Dept 128 Court St Cadiz OH

ZIMMERMAN, ROBERT RAYMOND, management consultant; b. N.Y.C., Jan. 24, 1919; s. Isador and Nettie (Shulman) Z.; m. Helen Eugenie Sperry, Oct. 8, 1949; children—Laurence Irving, Marc Sperry. B.A. in Econs. and Indsl. Psychology, U. Minn., 1941; M.B.A. with honors in Indsl. Relations, U. Chgo., 1947. Indsl. relations mgr. Continental Can Co., Chgo., 1948-54; personnel and orgn. planning cons. to sr. assoc. Booz, Allen & Hamilton, Chgo., 1954-65; personnel v.p. Sanger Harris Dept. Store, Dallas, 1965-66; operating v.p. orgn. and key manpower planning Federated Dept. Stores, Cin., 1966-79; sr. v.p. human resources Central Bancorp., Cin., 1979-84; pres. Zimmerman Cons., Inc., also sr. v.p. Schonberg Assocs., Inc., 1984—; former lectr. mgmt. and orgn. planning Indsl. Relations Ctr. of U. Chgo.; lectr., forum leader Am. Mgmt. Assn., Conf. Bd.; mem. Orgn. Planning Council, Conf. Bd., 1975-79. Bd. dirs. South Suburban Mental Health and Family Counseling Service, Ill., 1960-65. Served to capt. Adj. Gen. Dept., U.S. Army, 1941-46. Mem. Beta Gamma Sigma. Club: Indian Hill (Ohio). Author: Auditing the Organization Structure, 1965. Office: Zimmerman Cons Inc 6340 Miami Rd Cincinnati OH 45253 also Schonberg Assocs Inc 1527 Madison Rd Cincinnati OH 45206

ZIMMERMAN, STEPHEN HARLEY, manufacturing company executive; b. Decatur, Ind., Oct. 17, 1941; s. Gerald Vincent and Mary Elizabeth (Pierson) Z.; m. Susan Jane Boyle, Oct. 16, 1965; children—Andrea Diane, Christopher David, Scott Nichols. Student, Purdue U., 1960-64; B.S. in Indsl. Mgmt., Ind. U., 1975. Mfg. systems staff Internat. Harvester, Fort Wayne, Ind., 1965-70; data processing mgr. Allen County, Fort Wayne, 1970-75; mgr. info. systems Zollner Corp., Fort Wayne, 1975-80, prodn. mgr., 1980-83; mgr. prodn. ops., 1983—; educator-cons. Warner Gear, Auburn, Ind., 1983. Designer plantwide mfg. systems. Mem. Fort Wayne Jaycees (bd. dirs. 1970-71, service award 1971), Common Computer Users Group (pres. 1975-77), Assn. Systems Mgmt. (pres. 1978-79, merit award 1983), Am. Prodn. and Inventory Control Soc. (pres. 1979-80), Soc. Automotive Engrs. Republican. Roman Catholic. Home: 8205 Cha Capeta Pass Fort Wayne IN 46825 Office: Zollner Corp 2425 Coliseum Blvd S Fort Wayne IN 46803

ZIMMERMAN, SUSAN WILSON, educational administrator; b. Albany, N.Y., Sept. 17, 1948; d. James T. and Lillian F. (O'Brien) Wilson. B.A. cum laude, SUNY-Cortland, 1971; M.A.T., Ind. U., 1973, Ed.S., 1977, Ed.D., 1984, postgrad. Law Sch., 1983—. Cert. Spanish and math. tchr.; adminstr., Ind., N.Y. Assoc. instr. Ind. U., Bloomington, 1971-73; math. and Spanish tchr. Pike Twp. Schs., Indpls., 1973-77, Carmel/Clay Schs., Carmel, Ind., 1977-80; audit/program cons. Ind. Dept. Edn., Indpls., 1980-82, state math. cons., div. curriculum, 1982-84, coordinator sci., math., social studies and tech. edn., 1984—; grant writer; speaker. Author articles in field. Mem. Proud Hoosiers, 1980—, Meridian-Kessler Neighborhood Assn., Indpls., 1982—. N.Y. State Regents scholar, 1966-70; Jenkins Meml. Found. scholar, 1966-70; SUNY-Cortland Presdl. scholar, 1969, 70. Mem. Am. Council Teaching of Fgn. Langs., Nat. Council Tchrs. of Math., Ind. Reading Assn., Hoosier Assn. Sci. Tchrs., Am. Assn. Tchrs. of Spanish and Portuguese, Assn. Supervision and Curriculum Devel., Assn. State Suprs. Math., Ind. Assn. Pub. Sch. Supts., Sigma Gamma Phi (treas. 1968-69, pres. 1969-70), Kappa Delta Pi, Phi Delta Kappa. Republican. Avocations: swimming; hiking; raising roses; cooking; Renaissance art history. Home: 5531 N Carrollton Ave Indianapolis IN 46220 Office: 7523 Mooresville Rd West Newton IN 46183

ZIMMERMAN, THOMAS FLETCHER, clergyman; b. Indpls., Mar. 26, 1912; s. Thomas Fletcher and Carrie D. (Kenagy) Z.; student U. Ind., 1929; D.D., N.W. Coll.; m. Elizabeth H. Price, June 17, 1933; children—Betty Zimmerman Tinlin, Thomas Fletcher III, David. Ordained to ministry Assemblies of God, 1936; asst. pastor, Indpls., 1928-32; pastor, Kokomo, Ind., 1933-34, Harrodsburg, Ind., 1934-35, South Bend, Ind., 1935-39, Granite City, Ill., 1939-42, Springfield, Mo., 1943-47, Cleve., 1951-52; asst. supt. Ill. dist. Assemblies of God, 1941-43; asst. supt. So. Mo. Assemblies of God, 1944-47, sec.-treas., 1949-51; asst. gen. supt. Assemblies of God, 1952-59, gen. supt., 1960—; first dir. Assemblies of God Radio Broadcast, 1945-49; exec. com. Nat. Religious Broadcasters; mem. exec. bd. Nat. Assn. Evangs., 1957—; chmn. advisory com. Pentecostal World Confs., 1970, 73, 76, 79, 82, 85; mem. exec. com. Lausanne Com. World Evangelization, 1975—; pres. Assemblies of God Grad. Sch., Springfield, 1973—; Protestant chmn. Yr. of the Bible; mem. exec. com. Convocation on Evangelizing Ethnic Am. Bd. dirs. Central Bible Coll., Springfield, 1953—, chmn. bd., 1959—; bd. dirs. Evangel. Coll., Springfield, Cox Med. Center, Springfield, Jr. Achievement, Springfield, United Way of Springfield and Greene County; chmn. bd. Maranatha Village Retirement Complex, Springfield; mem. religious relationships com. Boy Scouts Am. Recipient Silver Beaver award Boy Scouts Am., 1969. Mem. Springfield C. of C. (Springfieldian of Yr. award 1974), Am. Bible Soc. (bd. mgrs. 1967—). Club: Rotary. Co-author: Operation Sunday School, 1958. Home: 2551 W Norton Rd Springfield MO 65803 Office: 1445 Boonville Ave Springfield MO 65802

ZINNEL, ALICE MARIE, controller; b. Washington, Iowa, Feb. 8, 1951; d. Frank Burdette and Martha Ellen (Caldwell) Moore; m. Stan A. Zinnel, May 25, 1974; children—Lynne Ann, Eric Alan. B.S., Westmar Coll., 1973. Staff acct. McGladrey & Co., Mason City, Iowa, 1973-75; controller Snyder-Pappajohn & Assocs., Inc., Mason City, 1975—. Mem. Nat. Assn. Future Women (treas. 1983—), Am. Guild Organists (treas. 1976-79). Republican. Presbyterian. Home: 1203 E State St Mason City IA 50401 Office: Synder-Pappajohn & Assocs Inc 202 1st St NW Mason City IA 50401

ZIRKLE, KENNETH EDWARD, college president; b. Meadville, Pa., July 28, 1940; s. Dorman and Mary Elizabeth (Dougherty) Z.; married; children—Laura, Andrea, Brianne, Dara, Lindsay. B.S. Edinboro State Coll., 1962; M.Ed., Rutgers U., 1965; D.Ed., Pa. State U., 1973. Residence Hall coordinator Pa. State U., 1970-73; dean student affairs Elizabethtown Coll., Pa., 1973-78; v.p. student affairs SUNY, Cortland, 1978-83; pres. Findlay Coll., Ohio, 1983—. Contbr. articles to profl. jours. Bd. dirs. Findlay Area Arts Council, 1984, Family Services of Hancock County, Findlay, 1984. Lodge: Rotary. Avocation: racquetball. Home: 1115 N Main St Findlay OH 45840 Office: Findlay College 1000 N Main St Findlay OH 45840

ZISLA, HAROLD, fine arts educator; b. Clev., June 28, 1925; s. Barney and Rebecca (Weinberg) Z.; m. Doreen G. Edelman, Aug. 13, 1946; children—Beverly and Paul. B.S., Case-Western Res. U., 1950, M.A., 1951. Designer, Uniroyal, Mishawaka, Ind., 1952-57; dir. South Bend Art Ctr. (Ind.), 1957-66, trustee, 1967—; prof. Ind. U.-South Bend, 1966—. Served with USN, 1943-46. Recipient Disting. Teaching Award Ind. Univ., 1978, First Annual Eldon Lundquist Faculty Fellowship award Ind. U., 1985. Avocation: golf. Home: 1230 Dennis Dr South Bend IN 46614 Office: Ind Univ South Bend 1700 Mishawaka Ave South Bend IN 46615

ZITNIK, RALPH STERLE, cardiologist, internist; b. Chgo., June 24, 1931; s. Charles and Marjorie (Allen) Z.; B.S., Georgetown U., 1953; M.D., Loyola U., Chgo., 1957; m. Ethel Margaret Ladd, June 15, 1957; children—Ralph J., John C. (dec.), Steven J. Intern, Little Company of Mary Hosp., Evergreen Park, Ill., 1957-58, dir. dept. cardiology, 1972—, sr. attending staff, 1972—; fellow in internal medicine Mayo Grad. Sch. Medicine, Rochester, Minn., 1958-62, asst. prof. internal medicine, 1969-72, dir. heart sta. and cardiac clinics, 1969-72, chmn. cardiac and cardiovascular facilities com., 1971-72; asst. in internal medicine Peter Bent Brigham Hosp., 1962-63; research asst. Harvard Med. Sch., 1962-63; mem. attending staff VA Research Hosp., 1963-65; mem. adj. staff Passavant Meml. Hosp., 1963-65; asst. attending staff Chgo. Wesley Meml. Hosp., 1963-65, asst. dir. heart sta., 1963-65; asso. internal medicine Northwestern U., 1962-63, dir. Cardiac Clinics, 1962-63; asso. clin. prof. medicine U. Chgo., 1972-73; pres. Chgo. Med. Computers, Inc., 1972—; asso. prof. medicine Rush U., Chgo., 1974—; asso. attending staff Rush-Presbyn.-St. Luke's Hosp., Chgo., 1974—; mem. courtesy attending staff Hinsdale (Ill.) Sanitarium and Hosp., 1974—; cons. cardiology Palos Community Hosp., Palos Heights, Ill. Bd. dirs. Chgo. Architecture Found. Aux., 1984—. Diplomate Am. Bd. Internal Medicine, also sub-bd. Cardiovascular Disease. Fellow Am. Coll. Chest Physicians, Am. Coll. Cardiology, ACP, Inst. Medicine Chgo., Am. Heart Assn. Council on Clin. Cardiology; mem. Am. Fedn. Clin. Research, Central Soc. Clin. Research, Assn. Advancement Med. Instrumentation, AAAS, Am. Inst. Ultrasound in Medicine, AMA, Ill. State Med. Soc., Chgo. Med. Soc., South Suburban Heart Assn. (dir. 1974-79, pres. 1975) Chgo. Heart Assn. (dir. 1975—, pres. 1980). Roman Catholic. Clubs: Butterfield Country, Beverly Country, Mid-America. Contbr. articles to profl. jours. Office: 2800 W 95th St Evergreen Park IL 60642

ZITZ, JON THEODORE, food broker, retired coffee company executive; b. Hammond, Ind., Sept. 5, 1914; s. John Theodore and Veronica (Nowicki) Z.; m. Mary Virginia Kubicek, Aug. 17, 1939 (dec. 1976); children—Jay, Diane Zitz Scaletta; m. 2d, Geraldine Weber, May 17, 1978; children—Margaret Duffy, Janet Dionne, Sue Duffy. B.A. cum laude, Yankton Coll., 1937; postgrad. Northwestern U., 1938-39. Sports editor Yankton Press & Dakotan (S.D.), 1935-38; asst. sales mgr. Nat. Stamping & Electric Works, Chgo., 1939-41; with Hill Shaw Co., Chgo., 1941-84, now v.p. Mem. Nat. Coffee Assn., Nat. Assn. Food Equipment Mfrs. Republican. Roman Catholic. Club: Park Ridge Country. Contbr. articles to industry related trade papers. Home: 914 S Chester Ave Park Ridge IL 60068 Office: 914 S Chester Ave Park Ridge IL 60068

ZIV, FEDERIC WILLIAM, telecommunications educator, writer; b. Cin., Aug. 17, 1905; s. William and Rose (Silverglade) Z. J.D., U. Mich., 1928; Litt.D., Coll. Mt. St. Joseph, 1979. D. Performing Arts (hon.), U. Cin., 1985. Founder, producer Ziv Radio and TV Co. (sold to United Artists 1961), Cin., 1930-65; programs include: Bold Venture, 1951, Favorite Story, 1947; TV shows include: Cisco Kid, 1950, Highway Patrol, 1955, Sea Hunt, 1958, Bat Masterson, 1958; chmn. bd., 1960-65; disting. prof. telecommunications U. Cin., 1967—. Author: The Valiant Muse, 1935; The Business of Writing, 1930. Home: 2330 Victory Pkwy Cincinnati OH 45206 Office: U Cin Coll Conservatory Music Clifton Ave Cincinnati OH 45221

ZOBEL, MILTON MILFORD, contracting executive; b. Ida Grove, Iowa, Jan. 22, 1922; s. Louis G. and Anna (Schwenk) Z.; m. Frieda Reuscher, May 20, 1947; 1 dau., Carol Ann. Pres., United Builders, Inc., Ida Grove, 1962—. Chmn. Ida County Land Use Commn., 1982—. Served USAAF, 1942-46. Mem. Master Builders Iowa (pres. 1973), C. of C., Am. Legion. Republican. Lutheran. Clubs: Kiwanis (pres. 1977-78), Med. Arts-Rec. (dir. 1977—). Home: Valley View Dr Ida Grove IA 51445 Office: 200 2d St Ida Grove IA 51445

ZOBRIST, BENEDICT KARL, library director; b. Moline, Ill., Aug. 21, 1921; s. Benedict and Lila Agnas (Colson) Z.; A.B., Augustana Coll., Rock Island, Ill., 1946; postgrad. Stanford, 1946-47; M.A., Northwestern U., 1948, Ph.D., 1953; postgrad. U. Ill., 1961, Tunghai U., Taiwan, 1962, Columbia, 1962-63, Fed. Exec. Inst., Charlottesville, Va., 1974, Hebrew U. (Israel), 1978; m. Donna Mae Anderson, Oct. 23, 1948; children—Benedict Karl II, Markham Lee, Erik Christian. Manuscript specialist in recent Am. history Library of Congress, Washington, 1952-53; asst. reference librarian Newberry Library, Chgo., 1953-54; command historian Ordnance Weapons Command, Rock Island Arsenal, 1954-60; prof. history Augustana Coll., 1960-69, asst. dean faculty, 1964-69, asso. dean, dir. grad. studies, 1969; asst. dir. Harry S. Truman Library, Independence, Mo., 1969-71, dir., 1971—. Sec. Harry S. Truman Library Inst., Independence, 1971—; mem. steering com. Harry S. Truman Statue Com., Independence, 1973-76; mem. adv. bd. Harry S. Truman Good Neighbor Award Found., 1974—; mem. Independence Truman Award Commn., 1975—; mem. Mo. Hist. Records Adv. Bd., 1978—; adj. prof. history U. Mo.-Kansas City, 1975—. Served with AUS, 1942-46. Recipient Outstanding Alumni Achievement award Augustana Coll., 1975; Ky. Col. Mem. Am., Jackson County (Mo.) (v.p. 1972-83) hist. socs., Orgn. Am. Historians, Assn. Asian Studies, Am. Assn. State, Local History, Soc. Am. Archivists, A.A.U.P. Club: Mo. Yacht. Contbr. articles, revs. to profl. jours. Office: Harry S Truman Library Independence MO 64050

ZOERKLER, RAYMOND NORBERT, geologist, consultant; b. Cin., Aug. 7, 1926; s. Louis Wendell and Lisa Othelia (Weisheit) Z.; m. Phyllis Lorraine Goble, July 16, 1949; children—Cynthia Rae Zoerkler Miller, Jennifer Louise. B.S. in Geology, U. Cin., 1954. Geologist, Stanolind Oil Co., New Orleans, 1954-56, Hanley and Bird, Bradford, Pa., 1956-63, Pennzoil Co., Bradford, 1963-69; cons. petroleum cos., Marietta, Ohio, 1969—. Bd. dirs. U. Pitts., 1963—. Served with USAF, 1945-47, ETO. Mem. Am. Inst. Profl. Geologists (cert.), Am. Assn. Petroleum Geologists, Soc. Petroleum Engrs., Soc. Well Log Analysts, Delta Phi Alpha. Republican. Roman Catholic. Lodges: Rotary, Elks. Home and Office: 133 Hillcrest Dr Marietta OH 45750

ZOLD, ROBERT KENNETH, educational administrator; b. Racine, Wis., Sept. 16, 1933; s. Joseph and Pearl Julian (Despins) Z.; m. Margaret Jean Oman, June 30, 1978; children—Kenneth, Kevin. B.S., U. Wis.-La Crosse, 1955; M.A., U. Iowa, 1961; Ph.D., U. Wis.-Madison, 1972. Tchr. Roosevelt Jr. High Sch., Cedar Rapids, Iowa, 1957-62; tchr., asst. prin. McKinley Jr. High Sch., 1962-66; prin. McKinley Middle Sch., Racine, 1966-84; asst. supt. pupil personnel services Racine Unified Schs., 1984—. Served with U.S. Army, 1955-57. Named Citizen of Yr., McKinley PTA Council, 1981, 82; named Prin. of Yr., Racine Unified Sch. Dist., 1982, 83. Mem. Assn. Wis. Sch. Adminstrs. (pres. 1984—), Nat. Assn. Secondary Sch. Prins., Racine Adminstrs. Assn. (pres. 1980-82), Lodge: Kiwanis. Avocations: Fishing, traveling. Office: Racine Unified Sch Dist 2220 Northwestern Ave Racine WI 53404

ZOLLER, RICHARD ROY, chemist, consultant; b. Geneva, Ohio, Aug. 16, 1953; s. Donald Kent and Elizabeth (Pepoy) Z.; m. Karen Ann Klodor, Jan. 31, 1981. B. Natural Sci., Case-Western Res. U., 1975; postgrad. Cleve. State U., 1983. Asst. chemist Macco Adhesives, Wickliffe, Ohio, 1975-76; chemist Gen. Tire, Akron, Ohio, 1976-78; quality control mgr. Lamotite Products, Cleve., 1978-81; quality control mgr. Uniroyal Chem., Painesville, Ohio, 1981-83, chief chemist, spl. coordinator 1983—; cons. Lamashield, Cleve., 1982-84. Recipient Bausch & Lomb sci. award, 1971. Mem. Am. Soc. Quality Control, Internat. Mgmt. Club.

ZONA, LOUIS ALBERT, museum director, educator; b. New Castle, Pa., June 28, 1944; s. Louis A. and Katherine (Rozzi) Z. B.S. in Art Edn. magna cum laude, Youngstown State U., 1966; M.S. in Art Edn., U. Pitts., 1969; Ph.D., Carnegie-Mellon U., 1973; postgrad. Wagner Coll., 1973, Westminster Coll., 1974. Tchr. Sharon City Schs. (Pa.), 1966, New Castle pub. schs., 1967-70; prof. art/museology Youngstown State U. (Ohio), 1970—, chmn. dept. art, 1978-81; asst. to dir. Butler Inst. Am. Art, Youngstown, 1980-81, exec. dir., 1981—. Bd. dirs. Ohio Museum Assn., Trumbull Art Guild, Youngstown Area Arts Council, Ohio Found for Arts. Recipient Disting. Prof. award Youngstown State U., 1978; Outstanding Young Educator award Lawrence County (Pa.) Jaycees, 1970; Spl. Recognition award Youngstown State U. Alumni Assn.; Disting. Profl. Service award Steel Valley Tchrs. Assn., 1982. Contbr. essays to art catalogues, articles to profl. jours. Home: 625 Rich Dr New Castle PA 16101 Office: 524 Wick Ave Youngstown OH 44502

ZONDERVAN, PETER JOHN, book publisher, distributor; b. Paterson, N.J., Apr. 2, 1909; s. Louis and Nellie (Eerdmans) Z.; m. Mary Swier, May 21, 1934; children—Robert Lee, Patricia Lucille, William J., Mary Beth. Student pub. and parochial schs., Grand Rapids, Mich.; D.Litt. (hon.), John Brown U., 1969, D.Litt.D. (hon.), Lee Coll., 1973 L.L.D. (hon.), Campbellsville Coll., 1985. Co-founder, chmn. bd. emeritus Zondervan Corp., Grand Rapids, Mich., 1931—; mem. Gideons Internat., Grand Rapids, 1938— trustee, 1950-52, v.p., 1952-55, pres., 1956-59, treas., 1972-75, chaplain, 1975-78; bd. dirs. Bibletown Bible Conf., Boca Raton, Fla., Winona Lake, (Ind.) Christian Assembly; speaker rep. ministry of Gideons, originated Taiwan, Hong Kong, Australia, New Zealand, re-established in Philippines, Rhodesia, South Africa, Germany. Pres. Bibletown Community Ch., Boca Raton. Recipient Award of Honor, Wisdom Mag., 1964; Gold Medallion Achievement award Evang. Christian Pubs. Assn., 1981; Key Man award Christian Booksellers Assn., 1981; elected to Profl. Hall of Fame, Internat. Gutenberg Soc. of Mainz, Germany; hon. fellow Shenandoah Soc., recipient award Disting. Outstanding Service. Mem. Calvin Christian Reformed Ch.

ZONKA, CONSTANCE ZIPPRODT, public relations executive; b Evanston, Ill., May 23, 1937; d. Herbert Edward and Agnes Irene (Turpin) Zipprodt; m. Leif B. Sorensen, June 29, 1959 (div. Mar. 1964); 1 child, Heidi Liselotte; m. Robert F. Zonka, Aug. 5, 1970 (div. June 1982) 1 son, Milo Matthew. B.A., U. Fla., 1958; student Smith Coll., 1955-56; postgrad U. Chgo., 1958-59. Dir. publicity WIND Radio, Chgo., 1962-64; Midwest asst. pub. relations dir. Time Inc., Chgo., 1964-66; account exec. D.J. Edelman, Inc., Chgo., 1966-69; pres. Connie Zonka & Assocs., Chgo., 1970—; dir. Facets Multimedia, Chgo., 1983—; mem. adv. com. Passage Theatre, Chgo., 1982—; coordinator Chgo. Communications, 1974—. Bd. dirs. Victory Gardens Theatre, Chgo., 1971-74; mem. benefit com. Midwest Women's Ctr., Chgo., 1983, 84. Mem. NOW, Nat. Assn. Female Execs., Nat. Assn Women Bus. Owners., Chgo. Press Club, Publicity Club Chgo. (Golden Trumpet award 1980, Merit award 1982). Democrat. Clubs: Arts, East Bank (Chgo.). Home: 666 N Lake Shore Dr #923 Chicago IL 60611 Office: Connie Zonka & Assocs 666 N Lake Shore Dr Chicago IL 60611

ZONNEVILLE, ROBERT E., trucking company executive; b. Williamson, N.Y., Jan. 23, 1925; s. Adrian J. and Matie L. Z.; student U. Buffalo, 1949-52; m. Carol A. Alliger, June 7, 1947; children—Bethann, Robin, Kim, David. Dock worker Associated Transport, Buffalo, 1952-53, terminal mgr., 1960-66; terminal mgr. Spector Redball, Cleve., 1966-68, regional mgr., Wis., Minn. and Ill., 1968-71, v.p. central area, Northfield, Ohio, 1971—. Pres. local Presbyn. Ch., Home Owners Assn.; mem. golf com. City of Euclid, Ohio, 1975, com. to elect mayor of Euclid, 1979. Served with U.S. Army, 1943-45. Decorated Purple Heart with oak leaf cluster, Bronze Star. Recipient awards for community activities, K.C., 1979. Mem. Western Res. Traffic Club. Clubs: Elks, Masons, Scottish Rite, Shriners. Home: 7627 Buchanan Ct Mentor OH 44060 Office: 21877 Euclid Ave Room 218 Euclid OH 44117

ZORINSKY, EDWARD, U.S. senator; b. Omaha, Nov. 11, 1928; B.S. in Chemistry and Zoology, U. Nebr., 1949; postgrad. Harvard U., 1966; m. Cece Rottman, 1950; children—Barry, Jeffrey, Susan. Engaged in wholesale tobacco and candy bus.; mayor, Omaha, 1973-77; mem. U.S. Senate, 1977—; mem. Agr., Nutrition and Forestry Com., Fgn. Relations Com.; mem. Omaha Pub. Power Dist. Bd., 1968-73, Nebr. Jud. Qualifications Commn., 1968, 71; mem. urban econ. policy com. U.S. Conf. Mayors, 1973-76. Served to capt. M.P., U.S. Army. Recipient Bicentennial Agr. award Triumph of Agr. Expn., Omaha; cited by Nat. Telephone Coop Assn., Nebr. Rural Electric Assn., Fed. Farm Credit Bd., other groups. Mem. Omaha Press Club, Res. Officers Assn. Clubs: Downtown Optimists, Eagles, Elks. Office: SR 443 Russell Senate Office Bldg Washington DC 20510

ZORN, ROBERT LYNN, ednl. adminstr.; b. Youngstown, Ohio, Mar. 22, 1938; s. Robert S. and Frances L. Zorn; B.S. Ed., Kent State U., 1959; M.Ed., Westminster Coll., 1964; Ph.D., U. Pitts., 1970; m. Joan M. Wilkos, Apr. 26, 1957; children—Deborah Lynn, Patricia Lynn. Tchr., West Branch (Ohio) Schs., 1961-62; elem. prin. Poland (Ohio) Schs., 1962-67, supt. schs., 1976—; high sch. unit prin. Boardman (Ohio) Schs., 1967-70; dir. adminstrv. services Mahoning County (Ohio) Schs., 1970-73, asst. supt., 1973-76; adj. prof. edn. Youngstown State U., 1970—; chmn. Ohi Adv. Com. to State Dept. Edn.; chmn. McGuffey Hist. Soc. Nat. Educator's Hall of Fame. Chmn. Mahoning County chpt. Am. Cancer Soc.; pres. bd. trustees Poland Methodist Ch.; trustee Mahoning County chpt. Am. Heart Assn. Served to lt. USAF, 1959-61. Mem. Doctoral Assn. Educators (life), Am. Assn. Sch. Adminstrs., Ohio PTA (life; Educator of Yr. 1980-81), Phi Delta Kappa. Republican. Clubs: Fonderlac County, Rotary, Protestant Men's. Author books, the most recent being: Speed Reading, 1980; contbr. articles to profl. jours. Home: 7386 N Lima Rd Poland OH 44514 Office: 53 College St Poland OH 44514

ZORNOW, WILLIAM FRANK, educator; b. Cleve., Aug. 13, 1920; s. William Frederick Emil and Viola (Schulz) Z.; A.B., Western Res. U., 1942, A.M., 1944, Ph.D., 1952. Vice pres., treas. Glenville Coal & Supply Co., Real Value Coal Corp., Zornow Coal Corp., 1941-45; dep. clk. Probate Ct., Cuyahoga County, Ohio, 1941-43; prodn. planning engr. Hickok Elec. Instrument Co., Cleve., 1943-46; teaching asst. Western Res. U., 1944-47; instr. U. Akron, 1946-47, Case Inst. Tech., 1947-50, Washburn U., 1950-51; lectr. Cleve. Coll., 1948-49; asst. prof. Kans. State U., 1951-58; asst. prof. Kent (Ohio) State U., 1958-61, asso. prof., 1961-66, prof. history, 1966—; collection corr. for Berkshire Loan & Fin. Co., Painesville, Ohio, Security Credit Acceptance Corp., Mentor, Ohio, 1951-60; cons. Karl E. Mundt Library Dakota State Coll., Madison, S.D. Mem. Am. Acad. Polit. and Social Sci., Am. Assn. State and Local History (award of merit 1958), Am. Hist. Assn., Orgn. Am. Historians, Ohio Acad. History (chmn. awards com.), Ohio Hist. Soc.

(library adv. com. 1969—), Ohio Soc. N.Y., Center for Study of Presidency, Acad. Polit. Sci., Sierra Club, Delta Tau Delta, Pi Gamma Mu, Phi Alpha Theta, Phi Delta Kappa. Author: Lincoln and the Party Divided, 1954, 72; Kansas: A History of the Jayhawk State, 1957; America at Mid-Century, 1959; contbr. to Abraham Lincoln: A New Portrait, 1959, Kansas: The First Century, 1956; also articles to encys., profl. jours.; editor: Shawnee County (Kans.) Hist. Bull., 1950-51; abstracter: Am. History and Life, Hist. Abstracts, 1964—. Home: 7893 Middlesex Rd Mentor OH 44060 Office: 305 Bowman Hall Kent State U Kent OH 44242

ZUBLER, EDWARD GEORGE, physical chemistry research advisor, researcher; b. Lackawanna, N.Y., Mar. 12, 1925; s. Arthur George and Merriam Ann (Donnelly) Z.; m. Marybelle Browning, Jan. 30, 1950; children—Karen, Kurt, Rena. B.S. in Chemistry, Canisius Coll., 1949; Ph.D. in Physical Chemistry, U. Notre Dame, 1953. Research chemist Gen. Electric Co., Cleve., 1953-64, tech. leader, 1964-72, research adv., 1972—; chemistry lectr. Fenn Coll., Cleve., 1960-65, Cleve. State U., 1965-66. Editor Proc. Symposium on Sci. and Tech. of High Temperature Light Sources, 1985. Contbr. articles to profl. jours. Patentee in field. Served as sgt. U.S. Army, 1943-46, ETO. Decorated Bronze Star with cluster; recipient Steinmetz award Gen. Electric Co., Elenbaas award N.V. Philips; named to Hall of Lamp Pioneers Toshiba Sci. Inst. (Japan). Mem. Am. Chem. Soc., Electrochem. Soc. (mem.-at-large exec. com. of high temperature materials div. 1984—), Sigma Xi. Avocations: sailing; gardening; personal computers. Home: 28430 Hidden Valley Dr Chagrin Falls OH 44022 Office: General Electric Co Nela Park Room 1312 Cleveland OH 44112

ZUBROFF, LEONARD SAUL, surgeon; b. Minersville, Pa., Mar. 27, 1925; s. Abe and Fannie (Freedline) Z.; B.A., Wayne State U., 1945, M.D., 1949. Intern Garfield Hosp., Washington, 1949-50, resident in surgery, 1951-55, chief resident surgery, 1954-55; practice medicine specializing in surgery, 1958-76; med. dir. Chevrolet Gear and Axle Plant, Chevrolet Forge Plant, Gen. Motors Corp., Detroit, 1977-78, divisional med. dir. Detroit Diesel Allison div., 1978—; mem. staff Hutzel Hosp., Detroit Meml. Hosp. Served with USAF, 1956-58. Diplomate Am. Bd. Surgery. Fellow A.C.S.; mem. AMA, Mich. State, Wayne County med. socs., Acad. Surgery Detroit, Am. Occupational Med. Assn., Mich. Occupational Med. Assn., Detroit Occupational Physicians Assn., NAACP, Phi Lambda Kappa. Lodge: Masons (33 deg.). Home: 16233 Nine Mile Rd Apt 201 Southfield MI 48075 Office: 13400 W Outer Dr Detroit MI 48239

ZUCKER, ROBERT A(LPERT), psychologist; b. N.Y.C., Dec. 9, 1935; s. Morris and Sophie (Alpert) Z.; m. Martine Latil, July 9, 1960; children—Lisa, Alex, Eleanor; m. Kristine Ellen Freeark, Mar. 10, 1979. B.C.E., CCNY, 1956; postgrad. UCLA, 1956-58; Ph.D., Harvard U., 1966. Lic. psychologist, Mich. Instr., then asst. prof. psychology Rutgers U., 1963-68; asst. prof. Mich. State U., East Lansing, 1968-70, assoc. prof., 1970-75, prof., 1975—, dir. Psychol. Clinic, 1970-74. Vis. prof. U. Tex.-Austin, 1975; vis. scholar Nat. Inst. Alcohol Abuse and Alcoholism, 1980, co-dir. clin. tng., 1982—; cons. Bd. dirs. Nat. Council Alcoholism (Mich.). Mich. State U. scholar, 1979. Fellow Am. Psychol. Assn.; mem. Midwestern Psychol. Assn., Southwestern Psychol. Assn., Eastern Psychol. Assn., Soc. Life History Research in Psychopathology. Contbr. articles to profl. jours., chpts. to books; editor: (with Rabin, Barclay and Aronoff) Further Explorations in Personality, 1981; (with Aronoff and Rabin) Personality and the Prediction of Behavior, 1984. Office: Dept Psychology Mich State U East Lansing MI 48824

ZUIDWEG, DONALD RICHARD, pharmaceutical chemical company official; b. Kalamazoo, Oct. 2, 1936; s. Adrian and Lucille Edna (Mulder) Z.; B.B.A. cum laude, Western Mich. U., 1958; M.B.A., Ind. U., 1960; m. Jean Ann Skidmore, July 21, 1956; children—Scot Richard, Alan Adrian, Lauri Marie. Various mktg., distbn. and fin. positions Upjohn Co., Kalamazoo, 1958-67, v.p. ops. lab. div., controller, 1967-73, regional distgn. mgr., 1976, corp. acctg. and fin./group mgr., 1976-79, group mgr. corp. acct'g. systems, cost acctg. and mehods and records, 1979-81, group mgr. corp. telecommunications, office automation, methods and records, 1981-83, dir. info. and telecommunication services, 1983—; cons. small bus. Active various sch. and ch. orgns. Served to capt. Fin. Corps, U.S. Army, 1960-66. Mem. Kalamazoo Accountants Assn. (pres. 1975), Ind. U. Sch. Bus. Alumni Assn. (life), Assn. M.B.A. Execs., Western Mich. U. Alumni Assn. (life). Office: 7000 Portage Rd Kalamazoo MI 49001

ZUKERMAN, PINCHAS, concert violinist; b. Tel Aviv, Israel, July 16, 1948; came to U.S., 1962, naturalized, 1976; s. Jehuda and Miriam (Lieberman) Z.; m. Eugenia Rich, May 26, 1968; 2 daus. Am.-Israel Cultural Found. scholar, Helena Rubinstein scholar, Juilliard Sch. Music, 1965-68. With impressario, Sol Hurok, 1967-76; concert and recital tours in maj. cities world-wide, 1968—; condr., soloist, English Chamber Orch., 1974, Mostly Mozart Festival, N.Y.C., 1975; guest condr., soloist, Los Angeles Philharm, Boston Symphony, Phila. Orch., N.Y. Philharm.; music dir., South Bank Festival, London, 1978-80, St. Paul Chamber Orch., 1980—; tour with, Isaac Stern; mem. trio with, Daniel Barenboim and Jacqueline du Pre; recorded with, CBS, EMI, recs. Winner Internat. Levintritt Competition, 1967. Office: St Paul Chamber Orch Landmark Ctr 75 W 5th St Saint Paul MN 55102

ZULAUF, LARRY DOUGLAS, job search company executive; b. St. Louis, Dec. 29, 1945; s. Gene Donald and Velda Evelyn (Dinkela) Z.; m. Candace Martha DeAngelo, Dec. 3, 1983. Student Fla. State U., 1967-68; B.S. cum laude Lincoln U., 1973, M.A., 1975. Mgmt. analyst Mo. Dept. Revenue, Jefferson City, 1975-77; research analyst Mo. Dept. Social Services, Jefferson City, 1977-78, project dir., 1978-81; pres., chief exec. officer Job Search Assistance, Jefferson City, 1981—; cons. U.S. Dept. Labor, Washington, 1981-83. Presentor, Nat. Gov. Assn., Washington, 1982; moderator U.S. Conf. Mayors, 1983; testified U.S. Senate Subcom. on Welfare Reform, Washington, 1983. Mem. Phi Alpha Theta. Methodist. Lodge: Elks. (chmn. house com. 1982-83). Avocations: sport fishing; boating; fast pitch softball. Home: 1101 Cimarron Jefferson City MO 65101 Office: Job Search Assistance Inc 204A Metro Dr Jefferson City MO 65101

ZULLO, PETER FRANK, lawyer; b. Chgo., Aug. 2, 1953; m. Monica Ann Murphy, Feb. 26, 1983; children—Kyla Marie, Peter Frank. Student St. Olaf Coll., 1971-73; B.A. in Sociology, U. Ill., 1975; J.D., John Marshall Law Sch., 1979. Bar: Ill. 1979, U.S. Dist. Ct. (no. dist.) Ill. 1982. Atty. City of Chgo., 1979—. Mem. Justinian Soc. Roman Catholic. Office: City of Chgo 121 N LaSalle St Chicago IL 60602

ZUNG, THOMAS TSE-KWAI, architect; b. Shanghai, China, Feb. 8, 1933; s. Bate and Rose Yu-Sun (Fong) Z.; came to U.S., 1937, naturalized, 1954; student Drew U., 1950-51, (Rose scholar) Va. Poly. Inst., 1951-53, Columbia U., 1955-57; B.Arch., U. Mich., 1960; M.S. in Design Sci. (student R. Buckminster Fuller), Internat. Coll., 1982; m. Carol Ann Williams, Dec. 28, 1963; 1 son, Thomas Ba-Tse. Project architect Edward Durell Stone, architect, N.Y.C., 1958, 60-65; architect, Cleve., 1967—; pres. Buckminster Fuller, Sadao and Zung, architects, 1979—; prin. archtl. works include City Cleve. Pub. Utilities Bldg., Cleve. State U. Sports Center Dome, Mayfran, Inc., Sawmill Creek Lodge, U. Akron Guzzetta Hall, music, speech and theater arts center, Alumni Center Bowling Green State U., U. Akron Master Plan-West, City of East Cleveland, Superior Euclid beautification plan, student recreation center at Bowling Green State U., Glenville Public Library, campus bldg. Tex. Wesleyan Coll., recreation, health and phys. edn. bdg. Wittenberg U., Medina Res. Park Office, arena, health, phys. edn. complex U. Akron, Dyke Coll., Lima State Prison, Cleve. Children's Christian Home, numerous others. Task force chmn. Greater Cleve. Growth Assn., 1970; mem. Council Human Relations, 1972, Leadership Cleve. Class '77; cubmaster local Boy Scouts Am., 1977-79; trustee Pace Assn., 1970-73, Karamu House, 1974-80, Cleve. Inst. Music, 1979—, Ohio Arts Council, 1982-84, Chinese Cultural Assn., 1980-84. Served with Signal Corps, U.S. Army, 1953-55. Decorated 4 medals; recipient Design award Cleve. chpt. AIA, 1972, Korean Inst. Constrn. Tech., 1984; Anicka Design award U. Mich., 1959, Sr. design prize, 1960; Public Works award State of Ohio, 1971, others. Mem. AIA (dir. Cleve. chpt. 1980), Am. Soc. Planning Ofcls., English Speaking Union (trustee 1972-75), Ohio Soc. Architects, Ohio Assn. Minority Architects and Engrs. (trustee 1982-84); vestryman St. Christopher-by-River, 1980-83. Clubs: Hermit, City (dir. 1972-74, v.p. 1974) (Cleve.). Lodge: Rotary. Patentee in field. Home: Echo Glen Gates Mills OH 44040 Office: 1303 Prospect Ave Cleveland OH 44115

ZNIGA, MARIA LUISA, nurse educator; b. Santiago, Chile, Nov. 11, 1935; d. Manuel M. and Luisa J. (Gutierrez) Arriagada; came to U.S., 1964, naturalized, 1973; m. Robert Zniga, Mar. 20, 1965; children—Maria Luisa, Roberto Manuel. B.S. in Nursing, Catholic U. Santiago, 1957; postgrad. U. Chile Sch. Pub. Health, 1964; postgrad. (W.K. Kellogg Found. fellow), UCLA, 1964; M.A. with honors, Western Mich. U., 1977, cert. in gerontology, 1982. Nursing supr. employee's clinic Internat. Petroleum Co. Barrancabermeja, Colombia, 1958-60; instr. med.-surg. Cath. U. Santiago, 1960-64; instr. orthopedics Borgess Hosp. Sch. Nursing, Kalamazoo, 1968-69; instr. community health nursing Nazareth (Mich.) Coll., 1969-76, asst. prof. fundamentals of nursing, 1977-82, assoc. prof., 1982—; guest lectr. Borgess Med. Ctr., Nazareth Coll.; mem. adv. bd. on gerontology Western Mich. U.; apptd. mem. Kalamazoo County Commn. on Aging, mem. South Central Mich. Commn. on Aging. Named Exchange Student Am. Nurses Assn., 1960. Mem. Nat. League for Nursing, Mich. League for Nursing, Am. Pub. Health Assn., Mich. Soc. of Gerontology, Delta Kappa Gamma Soc., Alpha Iota, Alpha Psi Chpt. (Kalamazoo). Roman Catholic.

ZUNKER, WILLIAM FREDERICK, III, insurance agency executive, consultant; b. Milw., Aug. 15, 1945; s. William F. and June M. (Henke) Z.; m. Pam Scherer, Apr. 26, 1969 (div. May 1972); m. Denise M. Zunker, Apr. 2, 1977. B.S., U. Wis.-Milw., 1968. Group rep. Equitable Life Ins. Co., Chgo., 1969-78; ind. ins. broker, Chgo., 1978-80; v.p. Kehe, Foy & Snelten, Arlington Heights, Ill., 1980-83; pres. Kaddatz, Zunker, Snelten & Assocs., Arlington Heights, 1983—. Republican. Home: 1914 E Avon Ln Arlington Heights IL 60004

ZVEITEL, JAMIE L., lawyer; b. Cheyenne, Wyo., July 24, 1957; d. Irving and Sylvia (Bensky) Z. B.S. in Mktg. with distinction, Ind. U., 1978; J.D., U. Colo., 1981. Bar: Colo. 1982, U.S. Dist. Ct. (ea. dist.) Colo. 1983, Mo. 1983. Office clk. Home Life Ins. Co., Clayton, Mo., 1973, Merc. Mortgage Co., Clayton, 1973-74; accounts payable clk. Broadmoor Apts., Clayton, 1974-75; girl Friday, Clayton C. of C., 1975-76; classified ads salesperson Ind. Daily Student newspaper, Bloomington, 1978; assoc. Isaacson, Rosenbaum & Friedman, P.C., Denver, 1981-83, Suelthaus, Kaplan, Cunningham, Yates, Fitzsimmons & Wright, P.C., Clayton, 1983—; cons. employee benefits, Denver, 1983. Mem. ABA (tax div.), Met. Bar Assn. St. Louis, St. Louis County Bar Assn., Colo. Bar, Mo. Bar. Office: Suelthaus Kaplan et al 8000 Maryland Ave 9th Floor Clayton MO 63105

ZWERG, CHARLES ALVIN, machine tool manufacturing executive; b. Appleton, Wis., Nov. 13, 1936; s. Alvin William and Mary Ruth (Gregory) Z.; m. Lynn Louise Harrmann, June 22, 1956; children—Charles Alvin, Carl, Lisa. B.S., U. Wis., 1959, M.S. in Indsl. Relations, 1961. Mgr. Wis. Telephone Co., Milw., 1961-64; supr. A.O. Smith, Milw., 1964-65; mgr. Giddings & Lewis, Fond du Lac, Wis., 1965-74, v.p., 1974—; chmn. Nat. Machine Tool Builders Indsl. Relations Commn., 1978-80. Dir. St. Agnes Hosp., Fond du Lac, 1983—; commr. Police and Fire Depts., City of Fond du Lac, 1968-76; pres. Fond du Lac United Way, 1969, Fond du Lac Safety Council, 1970-71, Giddings & Lewis Staff Club, 1970-71. Recipient Disting. Service award Jaycees, Fond du Lac, 1971. Mem. Nat. Assn. Mgmt. (v.p., pres. 1969—), Nat. Mfrs. Assn., Area Metal Trades. Republican. Mem. United Ch. of Christ. Avocations: Golf; fishing; sailing; boating. Home: 2438 Deadwood Point Beach Rd RR 4 Fond du Lac WI 54935 Office: Giddings & Lewis 142 Doty St Fond du Lac WI 54935

ZWICK, ROSEMARY G., artist; b. Chgo., July 13, 1925; d. Ida K. Pearce; m. Sidney B. Zwick, Dec. 26, 1948; children—Somara, Marissa, Andrew, Stephan. B.F.A., Iowa State U., 1945; postgrad. Art Inst. Chgo., 1946-47, DePaul U., 1947. Staff artist, art editor Jr. Arts and Activities Mag., Chgo., 1946-48; assoc. dir. 4 Arts Gallery, Evanston, Ill., 1962-83; free-lance artist, Evanston, 1983—; 2d v.p. Evanston Art Ctr., 1978-79, program chmn., 1980-82, exhbn. com., 1983—. Prin. sculptures include Wonderland Shopping Ctr., Livonia, Mich., Bedford Pub. Library, Ill., Blue Island Pub. Library, Ill., others; one woman shows include Indpls. Mus. Art, 1982, Evanston Pub. Library, 1981, First Fed. Savs. Bank, Chgo., 1972, Arnold Hendler Assocs., Houston, 1970, Nat. Coll. Edn., Evanston, 1970, Bloomington, Art Assn., Ill., 1970, others; exhibited in group shows at Chgo. Hist. Soc., 1979, Toledo Mus. Art, Roswell Mus., N.Mex., Union League Club, Chgo., 1974, others. Mem. Chgo. Soc. Artists, Chgo. Artists Coalition, Renaissance Soc. U. Chgo., World Print Council. Unitarian.

ZWIEBEL, JOHN WILLIAM, entrepreneurship educator, researcher; b. Ainsworth, Nebr., Apr. 14, 1921; s. William J. and Metha L. (Bohl) Z.; m. Virginia Ann Ortlip, June 30, 1950; children—John M., Carol Jean, Mary Louise, James Alan, Robert T., Zandra Ann. B.S., U. Minn., 1950, M.A., 1958. Cert. mgmt. edn., Minn. Farm mgmt. educator, New Bichland, Minn., 1951-53, Owatonna, Minn., 1953—. Served with USAAF, 1940-45. Recipient Minn. Outstanding Vocat. Educator, 1979; award of appreciation Minn. Jaycees, 19—. Mem. Council Agr. Service and Tech., Internat. Platform Assn., Minn. Edn. Assn., NEA, Am.-Minn. Vocat. Agr. Instrs. Assn., Minn. Vocat. Assn. (dir.), Nat. Vocat. Agr. Tchrs. Assn., Minn. Vocat. Agr. Instrs. Assn. (dir.), Minn. Vocat. Educators Minn. Edn. Assn. (dir.). Republican. Lutheran. Clubs: Toastmasters Internat., Jaycees, Owatonna Exchange. Contbr. articles to profl. jours. Home: 619 Truman Owatonna MN 55060 Office: 333 E School Owatonna MN 55060

ZWIKKER, KEES, graphics company executive; b. Eindhoven, Netherlands, Apr. 29, 1927; s. Cornelius and Johanna Dorothea (Theinert) Z.; M.B.A. with honors, U. Utrecht (Netherlands), 1950; m. Marie Jean Aylward, Dec. 20, 1952 (dec.); children—Robert Kees, Jacqueline Margaret; m. Donna Jeane Kohler, June 11, 1982; stepchildren—Charles Brian, Edward Martin Testa. Advt. prodn. mgr. Lee Donneley Advt. Agy., Cleve., 1952-56; dist. sales mgr. Standard Pub. Co., Cin., 1956-62; advt. mgr. Hess & Clark div. Vick Chem. Corp., Ashland, Ohio, 1962-66; v.p. Topper Assos. Advt. Agy., Ashland, 1966-71; account exec. Cross Assos. Advt., Chagrin Falls, Ohio, 1971-72; mgr. communications mgr. Norton Co., Akron, Ohio, 1972-81; global mktg. mgr. Meistergram, Inc., Cleve., 1981-83; mktg. services specialist Gen. Electric Co., Cleve., 1984—; chmn. bd. Ashland Graphic Art Co., 1963—. Mem. Aurora (Ohio) City Council, 1977-81; sec. Aurora Planning and Zoning Commn., 1974-77. Served to capt. Dutch Army, 1947-51. Mem. Nat. Advt. Assn. (cert. bus. communicator), Internat. Trade Show Exhibit Assn. (dir. 1978-83), Indsl. Marketers of Cleve., Bus. and Profl. Advt. Assn., Internat. Advt. Assn. (v.p. Cleve. chpt.), Internat. Mktg. Club (v.p. 1984, pres. 1985—). Republican. Roman Catholic. Club: Boating of Aurora Shores. Contbr. articles to profl. jours. Home: 3674 Nautilus Trail Aurora OH 44202 Office: Nela Park Cleveland OH 44112

ZYDLO, STANLEY MATHEW, physician; b. Chgo., Dec. 15, 1933; s. Stanley Mathew and Estelle Helen (Tubilewicz) Z.; B.A., Westminster Coll., 1956; M.D., Loyola U., Chgo., 1960; m. Joyce M. Reid, Aug. 29, 1976; children—Kristi, Sheryl, Scott, Mark, Josh, Matt, Brad. Intern, St. Francis Hosp., Evanston, Ill., 1960-61; gen. practice medicine, Wabash, Ind., 1963-69; emergency physician, past pres. Med. Emergency Service Assos., Chgo., now chmn. bd.; founder, co-owner Vernon Manor, home for retarded children, Wabash, 1968—; dir. mobile intensive care unit system N.W. Community Hosp., Arlington Heights, Ill.; med. cons. Nat. Registry Emergency Med. Technicians, 1975-78; del. AMA Commn. Emergency Med. Services, 1975-77. Served with USAF, 1961-63. Mem. Am. Coll. Emergency Physicians (chmn. bd. dirs. Ill. 1971—, past chmn. emergency med. systems com.), Am., Ind., Ill., Chgo. med. assns., Wabash County, Chgo. med. socs., Aerospace Med. Assn., AIAA, Air Force Assn., Soc. Flight Surgeons, Am. Profl. Practice Assn., Am. Assn. Physicians and Surgeons, Ill. Project Med. Dirs. Assn. (chmn. 1982—), Isaac Walton League, Frat. Order Police. Clubs: Elks, Optimists (charter). Developer, dir. 1st multicommunity mobile intensive care emergency system in 17 N.W. Chgo. suburbs with paramedic level emergency aid. Home: 1745 Clover Dr Palatine IL 60067 Office: 800 W Central Rd Arlington Heights IL 60005